Standard & Poor's SmallCap 600 Guide

1999 Edition

Standard & Poor's

McGraw-Hill

New York   San Francisco   Washington, D.C.   Auckland   Bogotá
Caracas   Lisbon   London   Madrid   Mexico City   Milan
Montreal   New Delhi   San Juan   Singapore
Sydney   Tokyo   Toronto

FOR STANDARD & POOR'S
Vice President, Index Products & Services: Elliott Shurgin
Managing Editor: Joseph Spiers
Associate Publisher: Frank LoVaglio

McGraw-Hill

A Division of The McGraw-Hill Companies

1 2 3 4 5 6 7 8 9 0   AGM/AGM   9 0 3 2 1 0 9 8

ISBN 0-07-052763-6

*The sponsoring editor for this book was Susan Barry and the
production supervisor was Clare Stanley. The front matter
and introduction were set by North Market Street
Graphics.*

Printed and bound by Quebecor / Martinsburg.

This book is printed on acid-free paper.

The companies contained in this handbook represented the
components of the S&P SmallCap 600 Index as of October 3,
1998. Additions to and deletions from the Index will cause its
composition to change over time. Company additions and company deletions from the Standard & Poor's equity indexes do
not in any way reflect an opinion on the investment merits of
the company.

ABOUT THE AUTHOR

Standard & Poor's, a division of The McGraw-Hill Companies, Inc., is the nation's leading securities information company. It provides a broad range of financial services, including the respected Standard & Poor's ratings and stock rankings, advisory services, data guides, and the most closely watched and widely reported gauges of stock market activity—the S&P 500, S&P MidCap 400, S&P SmallCap 600, and the S&P Super Composite 1500 stock price indexes. Standard & Poor's products are marketed around the world and used extensively by financial professionals and individual investors.

ABOUT THE AUTHOR

Standard & Poor's, a division of The McGraw-Hill Companies, Inc., is the nation's leading securities information company. It provides a broad range of financial services, including the respected Standard & Poor's ratings and stock rankings, advisory services, data guides, and the most closely watched and widely reported gauges of stock market activity—the S&P 500, S&P MidCap 400, S&P SmallCap 600, and the S&P Super Composite 1500 stock price indexes. Standard & Poor's products are marketed around the world and used extensively by financial professionals and individual investors.

Introduction

by James M. Nevler, C.F.A.

If you open any copy of *The Wall Street Journal* you will find numerous stock market indexes listed for your reading pleasure and investment research. On January 3, 1995, that list got a new addition, the Standard & Poor's SmallCap 600 Index. You will find it with its older siblings, the S&P 500 and S&P MidCap 400 Stock Indexes, and the S&P Super Composite 1500 Index, which was introduced in May 1995.

The S&P SmallCap 600 is a list of 600 companies which, on average, are considerably smaller than those in the S&P 500 or in the S&P Mid-Cap 400 Index. Since there already were plenty of other stock indexes to follow, it would be logical to ask why the world needed another one. The answer: because institutional investors—the people who manage the funds in corporate retirement plans and mutual funds—asked Standard & Poor's to develop a better way of monitoring the small-company sector of the stock market, as well as provide an index that could be used to build an investment portfolio of small but easily tradable companies.

Few individual investors can afford to build a personal portfolio of 600 common stocks. However, investors who do their own stock picking and understand why all stock portfolios should be diversified will find the SmallCap 600 to be a valuable tool. Research has shown that, over long investment horizons, stocks of smaller companies, as an investment class, will outperform stocks of larger companies. It was not that long ago that Microsoft, Wal-Mart, and COMPAQ Computer were all small companies. It only takes a reasonable number of such winners to turn a well-balanced portfolio of small-company stocks into a highly profitable investment.

However, those same studies of investment results have also shown that, over shorter time horizons, small companies can be much riskier to own than the far larger companies in the S&P 500. Many small companies—whether they are restaurant chains or technology firms—fail every year. Many others mature into solid companies that prosper for decades serving niche markets or loyal local customers. There are many such consistently profitable companies that provide hundreds of well-paying jobs and reliable dividends year in and year out. Yet their common stock prices may languish for years because they are in industries that are out of favor, because Wall Street analysts do not follow them, or because they may have once had financial problems. There is a crucial difference between a great company and a great stock; unfortunately, there is no sure-fire way to determine which is which. With literally thousands of small companies to choose from, the odds that any one of them, selected at random, will become the next Home Depot or Intel are about as long as the odds that any college basketball player, also chosen at random, will become the next Larry Bird or Michael Jordan.

If indeed the next Home Depot and Intel are hidden somewhere in the S&P SmallCap 600, it is not because Standard & Poor's expects them to be superstars. On the contrary, as with all of the Standard & Poor's Indexes, the stocks in the SmallCap 600 are there because they are expected to produce an index whose performance would be *typical* of the market segment from which they were selected. Standard & Poor's mission is not to beat the market, but to define it. Unlike the children in Lake Wobegon, all of the stocks in the S&P SmallCap 600 cannot be above average. As is the case in the S&P 500 and the MidCap 400, some stocks will beat their Index by a wide margin, others will be spectacularly worse, and most will perform somewhere in the middle of the pack. Ironically, however, over the long-term, the average performance of large, medium, and small capitalization stocks, as measured by their respective Standard & Poor's Indices, has proven to be more than good enough to outperform most investment professionals.

Using the Standard & Poor's Indexes to Measure the Market

While each day's trading on the stock market is often described in terms of bulls and bears, most individual common stocks could be described as members in a school of fish. That is because, more often than not, they tend to swim in the same direction as the overall market. Many studies of securities prices, including the theories for which Harry Markowitz and William Sharpe shared the 1990 Nobel Prize in Economic Science, have shown that one of the most important factors in the price performance of virtually any common stock is the overall performance of the stock market—the investment pool from which the school that the stock swims in is drawn.

Of course, some stocks move faster than others and lead the market—whether up or down—while most swim along unnoticed in the middle of the school. Others lag the market, both when prices head upstream and when they head for the bottom of the sea, and some stocks always go their own way. These volatility relationships to the overall market tend to be stable over relatively long periods of time and are measured with a statistic called beta. Betas are derived by running a statistical test called a regression on the performance of a stock against the performance of the overall stock market. However, before you can begin the test, you must first define the "market." The best way to do that is through a stock index. Thanks in large part to the work of Markowitz, Sharpe and their many disciples, the index universally used for that purpose is the Standard and Poor's 500 Index.

By definition, the S&P 500 has a beta of 1.0. A stock that moved in perfect correlation with the S&P 500 also would have a beta of 1.0. A stock with a beta of 1.5 would be expected to gain 1.5% for every 1% gain in the S&P 500, but would lose 1.5% for every 1% drop in the Index. However, as Markowitz pointed out, the performance of a properly diversified collection of smaller, more volatile stocks will not be much more risky than the overall market. Stocks with high betas in that portfolio will be canceled out by the performance of stocks with betas below 1.0 that lag the market, or by stocks with extremely low betas that have almost no response to the market. A stock with a negative beta, if you could find one, would move in the opposite direction to the S&P 500.

Using the Standard & Poor's Indexes for Investment Management

One of the most important purposes of a stock index is to tell investors, in a way, where the fish are and which way the fish are running.

When the S&P 500 was introduced in 1957, all of the fish in its pool were listed on the New York Stock Exchange. The S&P 500 was designed as a sample drawn from that pool to represent the market performance of the leading companies in the leading industries in the U.S.

As both the U.S. economy and the equity markets grew, Standard & Poor's expanded the selection pool for the S&P 500 to include stocks traded on the American Stock Exchange and over the counter on the Nasdaq quotation system. The S&P 500 remains broadly based, containing stocks in approximately 104 different industry groups ranging from aerospace/defense to trucking.

Because of the Index's mandate to select leading stocks in leading industries, the S&P 500 has evolved into a measure of large-capitalization stocks with a distinct, but modest, bias toward growth stocks. The average market capitalization of the companies in the S&P 500 at the end of 1998's third quarter was $16.3 billion, and the median valuation, the point at which the 500 stocks could be split into pools of the 250 largest and 250 smallest companies, was $6.8 billion.

The S&P MidCap 400 Index was created in 1991 to monitor the investment performance of midsized companies. When the MidCap 400 was created, it was drawn from a pool of companies not already in the S&P 500 Index with market capitalizations of between $5.2 billion and $300 million. The average market capitalization of a MidCap 400 stock at the end of the third quarter of 1998 was $2.1 billion.

Together, the S&P 500 and MidCap 400 account for 85% of the stock market's capitalization. However, they still do not track the performance of more than 6,000 other common stocks. That is the objective of the S&P SmallCap 600.

SmallCap Stocks

The first question to answer is the obvious one: What exactly is a small-cap stock? There is no obvious answer. Almost every expert has a unique definition. Some well-respected academic studies, for example, included stocks with market values of up to $2 billion. However, the consensus market value range at the end of 1993 appeared to run from $600 million down to $80 million, or from approximately the 50th percentile in market value down to about the 83rd percentile. This percentile range not only was used in developing and testing the Small-Cap 600 Index, but it will also be used in screening future candidates for the Index. As overall market capitalizations rise or fall, so will the SmallCap's selection parameters.

As was noted above, potential investment performance is not one of the criteria for membership in any Standard & Poor's equity index. Inclusion in any Standard & Poor's Index—and this also goes for the decision not to select a stock—is not based on the investment merits of the company in question. A good company may pass all of our screens for inclusion but be passed over when a vacancy appears because its industry is already overrepresented in the appropriate index for that stock. Some of the screens are computer-generated, but unlike the Russell 1000 and Russell 2000 indexes, our mechanical market-capitalization screen is only the start of the selection process. The approximately 1,850 common stocks that met the SmallCap's capitalization parameters at the end of 1993 were subjected to the following additional requirements:

1. The company must be listed on either the New York Stock Exchange, American Stock Exchange, or Nasdaq Stock Market.

2. The company must have been trading for at least six months in order to be considered, whether it was an initial public offering or a spin-off by an established company.

3. Stocks that did not trade on any three business days during a 12-month period or, in the case of new issues, over the time period they have been public companies, are not considered.

4. Companies with stock prices below $1 are not considered.

5. The annualized share turnover rate must exceed 20% of the common shares outstanding. Standard & Poor's defines share turnover as the trading volume over the previous 12 months divided by the average number of common shares outstanding during that time period.

6. Corporate ownership is reviewed. If 50% or more of the total common shares of a company are owned by another corporation, that company is not eligible because it is considered to be controlled by the other company. Companies in which 60% or more of the common shares are held by insiders, or by insiders in conjunction with another corporation's holdings, also are not eligible.

7. Companies in bankruptcy or in extreme financial distress are not selected for inclusion in the index. Except in rare instances, a filing for bankruptcy by a company in any Standard & Poor's Index will result in its immediate removal. However, as long as it appears to be viable, a company is not removed from an Index just because it is in financial trouble.

8. Finally, the companies that survive the other screens are checked for their bid-ask spreads. The spread is calculated as the average of the percentage of the last sale for 30 consecutive trading days. Only those companies with spreads of 5% or less are considered. For example, if a stock has an average closing price of $5 a share, its closing spread can be no wider than 25 cents (5 bid—5 ¼ ask). Many Nasdaq stocks have spreads of more than 10%, and 20% to 25% is not unheard of.

The stocks in the candidate pool for the S&P SmallCap 600 are classified into the same economic sectors used in the other Standard & Poor's Indexes. There now are 11 sectors, of which eight are Industrials: Basic Materials, Capital Goods, Communications Services, Consumer Cyclicals, Consumer Staples, Energy, Health Care, and Technology. The other three economic sectors are: Utilities, Transportation, and Financials. As is the case in the S&P 500 and S&P MidCap 400 Indexes, stocks are selected from each sector so that the total S&P SmallCap 600 Index reflects the economic balance of the stocks in the Standard & Poor's internal database. That diversity results in an Index that has a strong family resemblance to its big brothers. As the following table shows, each of Standard & Poor's major industry sectors is well-represented within each Index and across all three Indexes.

Industry Group Representation as of 9/30/98

	S&P 500 Index	S&P MidCap 400 Index	S&P SmallCap 600
	Cos.	Cos.	Cos
Industrials	376 cos. 75.2%	311 cos. 77.7%	495 cos. 82.4%
Utilities	37 cos. 7.4%	44 cos. 11.0%	28 cos. 4.7%
Financials	77 cos. 15.4%	34 cos. 8.5%	58 cos. 9.7%
Transportation	10 cos. 2.0%	11 cos. 2.8%	19 cos. 3.2%

Because the stocks in the SmallCap 600 are selected using the same general principles applied to the other Standard & Poor's

Indexes, they form a coherent package. In fact, Standard & Poor's has developed a super-composite index that reflects the market-value-weighted performance of all 1,500 stocks in the three Indexes. The S&P Super Composite 1500 Index was introduced in May 1995. It consists of a market-value-weighted position in every stock in the S&P 500, S&P MidCap 400, and S&P SmallCap 600 Indexes. Yet, despite their strong family resemblances, the MidCap 400 and Small-Cap 600 Indexes are not—like standard and toy poodles—simply scaled-down versions of the S&P 500 Index.

Using the SmallCap 600 for Investment Research

The total market value of the 600 companies in the SmallCap Index at the end of the third quarter of 1998 was nearly $294 billion. That equaled about 3% of the market value of all the stocks in the Standard & Poor's equity database, or about $236 billion less than the $530 billion combined capitalization of the two largest companies in the S&P 500, General Electric and Microsoft. However, while they are dwarfed by the larger companies in the S&P 500, many of the stocks in the SmallCap 600 Index are large fish in their own small ponds. The Index includes such famous brand names as Chiquita Brands International and Toro Co., as well as companies such as Chemed Corp. (which wholly owns Roto-Rooter) and the Swiss Army Brands (the importer of Swiss Army knives and watches) whose products are household names. Many others have strong positions in important niche markets.

The average market value of a SmallCap company is about $581 million, less than 5% of the average in the S&P 500 and about 28% of the average market value in the MidCap 400. This difference was due both to a smaller number of shares outstanding at most SmallCap companies and to much lower per-share prices. The median share price of an S&P SmallCap stock was $24.50, compared with $33.312 for a MidCap stock and $46.375 for a company in the S&P 500.

The smaller number of shares outstanding and the lower prices at which many SmallCap 600 shares trade are two of the reasons why the stocks in the SmallCap tend to be more volatile than those in the S&P 500 or the MidCap 400. Another, as reflected in the Index's September 1997 average P/E ratio of 33.5, is their earnings patterns. High P/E ratios (calculated by dividing a company's per share price by its earnings per share) can be generated in two different ways, either by the market paying up for anticipated growth, or by a company's earnings falling short of expectations. Dividend yield is another significant difference between the average SmallCap stock and those in the MidCap 400 or S&P 500. Because many of the industrial companies in the SmallCap are in their expansion phase, they retain earnings to fund their growth and pay no dividends. As a result, the September 1998

dividend yield on the SmallCap 600 was 0.94%, compared with 1.60% on the S&P 500 and 1.38% on the MidCap 400.

Given their increased risk relative to the S&P 500 and the MidCap 400, why should investors own SmallCap stocks? Because, given a long-term time horizon, the SmallCap should outperform both of its larger siblings by a margin that will more than compensate for its higher short-term risks.

It is also possible for an individual investor to construct a well-diversified portfolio of small-cap stocks that will outperform the larger-cap indexes. Many of the 6,000 or more small companies to choose from are followed by very few brokerage firm analysts. There are hidden gems out there, not just neglected value stocks, but also classic growth stocks that have yet to develop a following. The problem is finding them, finding out enough about them, and finding their shares trading at a fair bid/ask spread.

Those three problems are minimized if the search begins with the stocks in the SmallCap 600. The stocks have been screened for liquidity, and each is covered by an unbiased Stock Report prepared by an analyst in the Standard & Poor's Equity Research department. Those reports, which make up the remainder of this book, are an excellent place to begin researching a potential investment. Organize your search by first reading the names and the business summaries of each of the 600 companies, making a list as you go along of those that catch your fancy. Next, return to the reports, study those you've selected, and—using the information provided in the reports—pick the ones that you feel deserve serious additional investigation.

We have already prescreened the 600 companies in this book for several of the stock characteristics in which investors generally are most interested, including companies with consistently strong earnings growth, superior dividend payment histories, and those under-followed issues which could include some interesting "hidden values" for those investors willing to accept some degree of incremental risk. At the end of this introduction you will find charts listing companies which score highest on the basis of these criteria. So if you, like most investors, find these characteristics important in potential investments, you might want to turn first to the companies on these lists in your search for attractive investments.

Other Uses of this Book

Given this vast array of data, how might a business person seeking to find out about her competition, a marketing manager looking for clients, or a job seeker use it to best serve their respective purposes?

If you fall into one of these categories—a business person seeking to find out information about her competition, a marketing manager looking for clients, or a job seeker—your task will be arduous to be sure, but this book will provide you with an excellent starting point and your payoff can make it all worthwhile. You will have to go through this book page by page, looking for those companies that are in the industries in which you are interested, that are of the size and financial strength that appeal to you, that are located geographically in your territory or where you're willing to relocate, that have been profitable and growing, and so forth. And then you will have to read about just what's going on at those companies by referring to the appropriate "Business Summary" comments in these reports. But the companies you end up with can be those high-growth entities with the greatest potential.

Of course, this book won't do it all for you. It is, after all, just a starting point, not a conclusive summary of everything you might need to know. It is designed to educate, not to render advice or provide recommendations. But it will get you pointed in the right direction.

How to Read the Reports on the SmallCap 600

In the pages that follow, you will find a wealth of information on each of the 600 companies which comprise the S&P SmallCap 600 Index, information which will allow you to make reasoned investment, business, and personal judgments regarding these companies. But to get the most value from this book, you should take a few moments to familiarize yourself with just what you'll find on these pages.

Following is a glossary of terms and definitions used throughout this book. Please refer to this section as you encounter terms which need further clarification.

Stock Report Terms

Quantitative Evaluations

Standard & Poor's Opinion—Buy, hold or sell recommendations are provided using Standard & Poor's unique STARS (Stock Appreciation Ranking System), which measures short-term (six- to 12-month) appreciation potential of stocks. STARS performance is measured against the performance of the S&P 500 Index.

STARS Rankings are as follows:

***** Buy—Expected to be among the best performers over the next 12 months.

**** Accumulate—Expected to be an above-average performer.

*** Hold—Expected to be an average performer.

** Avoid—Likely to be a below-average performer.

* Sell—Expected to be a well-below-average performer and fall in price.

Outlook—Using Standard & Poor's exclusive proprietary quantitative model, stocks are ranked in one of five Outlook Groups—ranging from Group 5, listing the most undervalued stocks, to Group 1, the most overvalued issues. Group 5 stocks are expected to generally outperform all others. To identify a stock that is in a strengthening or weakening position, a positive (+) or negative (–) Timing Index is placed next to the Outlook ranking. Using these rankings, here's what action should be taken:

5+ = Buy	2+ = Hold if in portfolio
5 = Hold if in portfolio	2– = Sell
4+ = Hold if in portfolio	1+ = Hold if in portfolio
4– = Sell	1– = Sell
3+ = Hold if in portfolio	
3– = Sell	

The Timing Index helps identify the right time to buy stocks, but its most important function is to indicate when it is time to sell. Because Group 5 stocks have historically produced the best results, Standard & Poor's recommends buying only Group 5 stocks with a positive Timing Index. Then, hold onto each one for as long as it remains in a positive trend (positive Timing Index), even if the ranking falls as the stock appreciates toward overvalued status. This will reduce transaction costs and substantially raise your chances of outperforming the market in the long run. It will also raise the number of transactions which qualify as long-term capital gains for tax purposes.

Fair Value—The price at which a stock should sell today as calculated by Standard & Poor's computers using our quantitative model based on the company's earnings, growth potential, return on equity relative to the S&P 500 and its industry group, price to book ratio history, current yield relative to the S&P 500, and other factors. The current fair price is shown given today's S&P 500 level.

Risk—Rates the volatility of the stock's price over the past year.

Technical Evaluation—In researching the past market history of prices and trading volume for each company, Standard & Poor's computer models apply special technical methods and formulas to identify and project price trends for the stock. They analyze how the price of the stock is moving and evaluate the interrelationships between the moving averages to ultimately determine buy or sell signals—and to decide whether they're bullish, neutral or bearish for the stock. The date the signals were initiated is also provided so you can take advantage of a recent or ongoing uptrend in price, or see how a stock has performed over time since our last technical signal was generated.

Relative Strength Rank—Shows, on a scale of 1 to 99, how the stock has performed compared with all other companies in Standard & Poor's universe of companies on a rolling 13-week basis.

Insider Activity—Gives an insight as to insider sentiment by showing whether directors, officers and key employees—who may have proprietary information not available to the general public—are buying or selling the company's stock during the most recent six months.

Key Stock Statistics

Avg. Daily Vol.—The average daily trading volume of the stock for the past 20 days on a rolling basis, shown in millions.

Market Cap.—The price of the stock multiplied by the number of shares outstanding, shown in billions.

Insider Holdings—The percentage of outstanding shares held by directors, officers and key employees of the company, and others who hold a minimum of 10% of the outstanding shares.

Value of $10,000 Invested 5 years ago—The value today of a $10,000 investment in the stock made five years ago, assuming year-end reinvestment of dividends.

Standard & Poor's Ranking

The investment process involves assessment of various factors—such as products and industry position, company resources and financial policy—with results that make some common stocks more highly esteemed than others. In this assessment, Standard & Poor's believes that earnings and dividend performance is the end result of the interplay of these factors and that, over the long run, the record of this performance has a considerable bearing on relative quality. The rankings, however, do not reflect all of the factors that may bear on stock quality.

Growth and stability of earnings and dividends are the key elements in Standard & Poor's earnings and dividend rankings for common stocks, which are designed to capsulize the nature of this record in a single symbol. It should be noted, however, that the process also takes into consideration certain adjustments and modifications deemed desirable in establishing such rankings.

These rankings are derived by means of a computerized scoring system based on per share earnings and dividend records of the most recent ten years. If a company does not have a ten-year public track record, Standard & Poor's does not rank it. The lack of a Standard & Poor's ranking in no way reflects upon the investment merits of a company. Basic scores are computed for earnings and dividends and then adjusted by a set of predetermined modifiers for growth, stability, and cyclicality. Adjusted scores for earnings and dividends are then combined to yield a final score.

The ranking system also makes allowance for the fact that, in general, corporate size imparts certain recognized advantages from an investment standpoint. Minimum size limits (in terms of corporate sales) are set for the various rankings, but exceptions may be made where a score reflects an outstanding earnings-dividend record.

The final score is then translated into one of the following rankings:

A+   Highest

A   High

A−   Above Average

B+   Average

B   Below Average

B−   Lower

C   Lowest

D   In Reorganization

NR   No Ranking

In some instances, rankings may be modified by special considerations, such as natural disasters, massive strikes, or nonrecurring accounting adjustments.

It is important to note that a ranking is not a forecast of future market price performance, but is basically an appraisal of past performance of earnings and dividends and relative current standing. Consequently, rankings should not be used as market recommendations: a high-score stock may at times be so overpriced as to justify its sale while a low-score stock may be attractively priced for purchase. Rankings based upon earnings and dividend records are no substitute for complete analysis. They cannot take into account the potential effects of management changes, internal company policies not yet fully reflected in the earnings and dividend record, public relations standings, recent competitive shifts, and a host of other factors that may be relevant in investment decision making.

Beta

The beta coefficient is a measure of the volatility of a stock's price relative to the S&P 500 Index, which, as we have seen, is the proxy for the overall market. Because calculating a beta requires 60 months of performance data, Standard & Poor's does not calculate betas of stocks that have been trading for less than five years.

Per Share Data ($) Tables

Tangible Book Value; Book Value (See also: "Common Equity" under Industrial)—Indicates the theoretical dollar amount per common share one might expect to receive from a company's tangible "book" assets should liquidation take place. Generally, book value is determined by adding the stated value of the common stock, paid-in capital and retained earnings and then subtracting intangible assets (excess cost over equity of acquired companies, goodwill, and patents), preferred stock at liquidating value and unamortized debt discount. Divide that amount by the outstanding shares to get book value per common share.

Cash Flow—Net income plus depreciation, depletion, and amortization, divided by shares used to calculate earnings per common share. (Also see: "Cash Flow" for Industrial Companies.)

Earnings—The amount a company reports as having been earned for the year on its common stock based on generally accepted accounting standards. Earnings per share are presented on a *"Diluted"* basis pursuant to FASB 128, which became effective December 15, 1997, and are generally reported from continuing operations, before extraordinary items. This reflects a change from previously reported *Primary* earnings per share. INSURANCE companies report *operating earnings* before gains/losses on security transactions and *earnings* after such transactions.

Dividends—Generally total cash payments per share based on the ex-dividend dates over a twelve-month period. May also be reported on a declared basis where this has been established to be a company's payout policy.

Payout Ratio—Indicates the percentage of earnings paid out in dividends. It is calculated by dividing the annual dividend by the earnings. For INSURANCE companies *earnings* after gains/losses on security transactions are used.

Prices High/Low—Shows the calendar year high and low of a stock's market price.

P/E Ratio High/Low—The ratio of market price to earnings—essentially indicates the valuation investors place on a company's earnings. Obtained by dividing the annual earnings into the high and low market price for the year. For INSURANCE companies *operating earnings* before gains/losses on security transactions are used.

Net Asset Value—Appears on investment company reports and reflects the market value of stocks, bonds, and net cash divided by outstanding shares. The % DIFFERENCE indicates the percentage premium or discount of the market price over the net asset value.

Portfolio Turnover—Appears on investment company reports and indicates percentage of total security purchases and sales for the year to overall investment assets. Primarily mirrors trading aggressiveness.

Income/Balance Sheet Data Tables

Banks

Net Interest Income—Interest and dividend income, minus interest expense.

Loan Loss Provision—Amount charged to operating expenses to provide an adequate reserve to cover anticipated losses in the loan portfolio.

Taxable Equivalent Adjustment—Increase to render income from tax-exempt loans and securities comparable to fully taxed income.

Noninterest Income—Service fees, trading and other income, excluding gains/losses on securities transactions.

% Expenses/Op. Revenues—Noninterest expense as a percentage of taxable equivalent net interest income plus noninterest income (before securities gains/losses). A measure of cost control.

Commercial Loans—Commercial, industrial, financial, agricultural loans and leases, gross.

Other Loans—Gross consumer, real estate and foreign loans.

% Loan Loss Reserve—Contra-account to loan assets, built through provisions for loan losses, which serves as a cushion for possible future loan charge-offs.

% Loans/Deposits—Proportion of loans funded by deposits. A measure of liquidity and an indication of bank's ability to write more loans.

Earning Assets—Assets on which interest is earned.

Money Market Assets—Interest-bearing interbank deposits, federal funds sold, trading account securities.

Investment Securities—Federal, state, and local government bonds and other securities.

Gains/Losses on Securities Transactions—Realized losses on sales of securities, usually bonds.

Net Before Taxes—Amount remaining after operating expenses are deducted from income, including gains or losses on security transactions.

Effective Tax Rate—Actual income tax expense divided by net before taxes.

Net Income—The final profit before dividends (common/preferred) from all sources after deduction of expenses, taxes, and fixed charges, but before any discontinued operations or extraordinary items.

Net Interest Margin—A percentage computed by dividing net interest income, on a taxable equivalent basis, by average earning assets. Used as an analytical tool to measure profit margins from providing credit services.

% Return on Revenues—Net income divided by gross revenues.

% Return on Assets—Net income divided by average total assets. An analytical measure of asset-use efficiency and industry comparison.

% Return on Equity—Net income (minus preferred dividend requirements) divided by average common equity. Generally used to measure performance.

Total Assets—Includes interest-earning financial instruments—principally commercial, real estate, consumer loans and leases; investment securities/trading accounts; cash/money market investments; other owned assets.

Cash—Mainly vault cash, interest-bearing deposits placed with banks, reserves required by the Federal Reserve and items in the process of collection—generally referred to as float.

Government Securities—Includes United States Treasury securities and securities of other U.S. government agencies at book or carrying value. A bank's major "liquid asset."

State and Municipal Securities—State and municipal securities owned at book value.

Loans—All domestic and foreign loans (excluding leases), less unearned discount and reserve for possible losses. Generally considered a bank's principal asset.

Deposits—Primarily classified as either *demand* (payable at any time upon demand of depositor) or *time* (not payable within thirty days).

Deposits/Capital Funds—Average deposits divided by average capital funds. Capital funds include capital notes/debentures, other long-term debt, capital stock, surplus, and undivided profits. May be used as a "leverage" measure.

Long-Term Debt—Total borrowings for terms beyond one year including notes payable, mortgages, debentures, term loans, and capitalized lease obligations.

Common Equity—Includes common/capital surplus, undivided profits, reserve for contingencies and other capital reserves.

% Equity to Assets—Average common equity divided by average total assets. Used as a measure of capital adequacy.

% Equity to Loans—Average common equity divided by average loans. Reflects the degree of equity coverage to loans outstanding.

Industrial Companies

Following data is based on Form 10K Annual Report data as filed with SEC.

Revenues—Net sales and other operating revenues. Includes franchise/leased department income for retailers, and royalties for publishers and oil and mining companies. Excludes excise taxes for tobacco, liquor, and oil companies.

Operating Income—Net sales and operating revenues less cost of goods sold and operating expenses (including research and development, profit sharing, exploration and bad debt, but excluding depreciation and amortization).

% Operating Income of Revenues—Net sales and operating revenues divided into operating income. Used as a measure of operating profitability.

Capital Expenditures—The sum of additions at cost to property, plant and equipment and leaseholds, generally excluding amounts arising from acquisitions.

Depreciation—Includes noncash charges for obsolescence, wear on property, current portion of capitalized expenses (intangibles), and depletion charges.

Interest Expense—Includes all interest expense on short/long-term debt, amortization of debt discount/premium and deferred expenses (e.g., financing costs).

Net Before Taxes—Includes operating and nonoperating revenues (including extraordinary items not net of taxes), less all operating and nonoperating expenses, except income taxes and minority interest, but including equity in nonconsolidated subsidiaries.

Effective Tax Rate—Actual income tax charges divided by net before taxes.

Net Income—Profits derived from all sources after deduction of expenses, taxes, and fixed charges, but before any discontinued operations, extraordinary items, and dividends (preferred/common).

% Net Income of Revenues—Net income divided by sales/operating revenues.

Cash Flow—Net income (before extraordinary items and discontinued operations, and after preferred dividends) plus depreciation, depletion, and amortization.

Cash—Includes all cash and government and other marketable securities.

Current Assets—Those assets expected to be realized in cash or used up in the production of revenue within one year.

Current Liabilities—Generally includes all debts/obligations falling due within one year.

Current Ratio—Current assets divided by current liabilities. A measure of liquidity.

Total Assets—Current assets plus net plant and other noncurrent assets (intangibles and deferred items).

% Return on Assets—Net income divided by average total assets on a per common share basis. Used in industry analysis and as a measure of asset-use efficiency.

Long-Term Debt—Debts/obligations due after one year. Includes bonds, notes payable, mortgages, lease obligations, and industrial revenue bonds. Other Long-Term Debt, when reported as a separate account, is excluded. This account generally includes pension and retirement benefits.

Common Equity (See also: "Book Value" under Per Share Data Table)—Common stock plus capital surplus and retained earnings, less any difference between the carrying value and liquidating value of preferred stock.

Total Invested Capital—The sum of stockholders' equity plus long-term debt, capital lease obligations, deferred income taxes, investment credits, and minority interest.

% Long-Term Debt of Invested Capital—Long-term debt divided by total invested capital. Indicates how highly "leveraged" a business might be.

% Return on Equity—Net income less preferred dividend requirements divided by average common shareholders' equity on a per common share basis. Generally used to measure performance and industry comparisons.

Utilities

Operating Revenues—Represents the amount billed to customers by the utility.

Depreciation—Amounts charged to income to compensate for the decline in useful value of plant and equipment.

Maintenance—Amounts spent to keep plants in good operating condition.

Operating Ratio—Ratio of operating costs to operating revenues or the proportion of revenues absorbed by expenses. Obtained by dividing operating expenses including depreciation, maintenance, and taxes by revenues.

Fixed Charges Coverage—The number of times income before interest charges (operating income plus other income) after taxes covers total interest charges and preferred dividend requirements.

Construction Credits—Credits for interest charged to the cost of constructing new plant. A combination of allowance for equity funds used during construction and allowance for borrowed funds used during construction—credit.

Effective Tax Rate—Actual income tax expense divided by the total of net income and actual income tax expense.

Net Income—Amount of earnings for the year which is available for preferred and common dividend payments.

% Return on Revenues—Obtained by dividing net income for the year by revenues.

% Return on Invested Capital—Percentage obtained by dividing income available for fixed charges by average total invested capital.

% Return on Common Equity—Percentage obtained by dividing income available for common stock (net income less preferred dividend requirements) by average common equity.

Gross Property—Includes utility plant at cost, plant work in progress, and nuclear fuel.

Capital Expenditures—Represents the amounts spent on capital improvements to plant and funds for construction programs.

Net Property—Includes items in gross property less provision for depreciation.

% Earned on Net Property—Percentage obtained by dividing operating income by average net property for the year. A measure of plant efficiency.

Total Invested Capital—Sum of total capitalization (common-preferred-debt), accumulated deferred income taxes, accumulated investment tax credits, minority interest, contingency reserves, and contributions in aid of construction.

Total Capitalization—Combined sum of total common equity, preferred stock, and long-term debt.

Long-Term Debt—Debt obligations due beyond one year from balance sheet date.

Capitalization Ratios—Reflect the percentage of each type of debt/equity issues outstanding to total capitalization. % DEBT is obtained by dividing total debt by the sum of debt, preferred, common, paid-in capital and retained earnings. % PREFERRED is obtained by dividing the preferred stocks outstanding by total capitalization. % COMMON, divide the sum of common stocks, paid-in capital and retained earnings by total capitalization.

Finally, at the very bottom of the right-hand page, you'll find general information about the company: its address and telephone number, the names of its senior executive officers and directors (usually including the name of the investor contact), the transfer agent and registrar for the stock, and the state in which the company is incorporated.

HIGH PROJECTED GROWTH AND TRADING BELOW $20

All the issues below meet the following criteria: a projected five-year growth rate of at least 20%; at least a 20% increase in 1998 and 1999 estimated earnings; a share price of less than $20; and a P/E ratio of less than 15 based on projected 1999 earnings. The list is sorted by the five-year projected growth rate.

Company (Ticker)	Business	1998— High	1998— Low	Recent Price	Fiscal Year End	Earnings Per Share $ 1997 Actual	Earnings Per Share $ 1998 Est.	Earnings Per Share $ 1999 Est.	5-Year Proj. Growth Rate (%)	P/E on 1999 Est.
Orthodontic Centers of Am (OCA)	Manage orthodontic centers	24.06	11.75	13.00	Dec	0.50	0.70	0.95	34	13.7
Brightpoint Inc (CELL)	Wholesale cellular phones	21.62	5.00	5.94	Dec	0.53	0.76	1.03	32	5.8
NBTY Inc (NBTY)	Mfr vitamins,food supplem'ts	24.37	5.62	6.53	Sep	0.29	0.62	0.87	32	7.5
Insituform Technol'A' (INSUA)	Mkts sewer/PL repair process	15.75	7.75	10.38	Dec	0.36	0.63	0.80	31	13.0
Just For Feet (FEET)	Athletic/outdoor footwear	29.12	11.12	12.13	Jan	0.70	1.02	1.40	31	8.7
Inter-Tel Inc (INTL)	Mfr electronic telecommun eqp	28.50	9.50	10.50	Dec	0.57	0.81	1.14	28	9.2
Amer Oncology Res (AORI)	Provides managed oncology svcs	17.62	7.81	9.38	Dec	0.48	0.61	0.76	27	12.3
Ashworth Inc (ASHW)	Design/mkt golf apparel	18.37	5.43	5.69	Oct	0.37	0.50	0.69	27	8.2
BE Aerospace (BEAV)	Airline audio/video ctrl sys	35.75	13.00	16.13	Feb	1.30	2.29	3.38	26	4.8
Standard Pacific (SPF)	Single family home builder	21.00	9.12	9.75	Dec	0.92	1.49	1.90	26	5.1
Billing Concepts (BILL)	Bill'g clearinghse/telecom svc	30.00	7.62	10.63	Sep	0.11	0.81	1.00	25	10.6
Bio-Technology Genl (BTGC)	Health prod thru biotechn'y	13.81	4.18	6.00	Dec	0.28	0.35	0.46	25	13.0
Halter Marine Group (HLX)	Ship, barge building U.S.	29.00	6.68	7.19	Mar	0.78	1.14	1.50	25	4.8
Paxar Corp (PXR)	Mfr/mkts product ID systems	15.50	7.81	8.50	Dec	0.49	0.72	0.86	25	9.9
Watsco, Inc (WSO)	Dstrb air cond/heat'g pd	24.45	11.75	14.44	Dec	0.68	0.89	1.11	25	13.0
Michaels Stores (MIKE)	Specialty retail stores	39.92	16.75	18.13	Jan	1.05	1.41	1.81	24	10.0
AmeriCredit Corp (ACF)	Provides used-car financing	18.65	6.62	9.31	Jun	0.63	*0.93	1.17	23	8.0
Eagle Hardware & Garden (EAGL)	Oper home improvement ctrs	26.25	15.93	18.44	Jan	0.98	1.13	1.35	22	13.7
Interim Services (IS)	Temporary help services	34.25	13.25	14.25	Dec	1.05	1.27	1.58	22	9.0
Premier Bancshares (PMB)	General banking, Georgia	30.00	15.25	17.00	Dec	0.73	0.98	1.20	22	14.2
Stride Rite (SRR)	Mfr/retail children's shoes	15.75	6.62	7.81	Nov	0.40	0.55	0.77	22	10.1
CEC Entertainment (CEC)	Family restr/enter'nt ctrs	41.18	17.62	19.25	Dec	1.34	1.79	2.15	21	9.0
Checkpoint Sys (CKP)	Electronic detection sys	22.18	7.06	7.69	Dec	0.23	0.51	0.73	21	10.5

*Actual 1998 EPS.

Chart based on October 9, 1998 prices and data.

Note: All earnings estimates are Wall Street consensus projections.

STOCKS OF COMPANIES WITH CONSISTENTLY STRONG EPS GROWTH

These issues have been selected for superior earnings growth. Each company has actual and estimated annual compounded earnings growth rates of 15% or higher. The list is sorted by estimated 1999 P/E.

Company (Ticker)	Business	Fiscal Year End	Earnings Per Share $			5-Year Proj. Growth Rate (%)	Recent Price	P/E on 1999 Est.
			1997 Actual	1998 Est.	1999 Est.			
Brightpoint Inc (CELL)	Wholesale cellular phones	Dec	0.53	0.76	1.03	32	5.94	5.8
Goody's Family Clothing (GDYS)	Sells Moder'tly-priced apparel	Jan	0.99	1.28	1.49	19	8.75	5.9
Interface Inc'A' (IFSIA)	Mfr carpet/tile	Dec	0.76	0.99	1.18	16	8.38	7.1
Wolverine World Wide (WWW)	Mfr branded footwear	Dec	0.96	1.13	1.32	19	9.38	7.1
CMAC Investment (CMT)	Private mortgage insurance	Dec	3.06	3.67	4.30	16	35.19	8.2
Enhance Financial Svcs Grp (EFS)	Muni/asset-backed debt reinsr	Dec	1.78	2.11	2.48	16	21.00	8.5
Hughes Supply (HUG)	Fla distr elect, plumb'g:mfg	Jan	2.30	2.65	3.05	16	26.06	8.5
Just For Feet (FEET)	Athletic/outdoor footwear	Jan	0.70	1.02	1.40	31	12.13	8.7
Roper Industries (ROP)	Mfr fluid handl'g/ctrl prd	Oct	1.16	1.41	1.64	17	14.19	8.7
Nautica Enterprises (NAUT)	Mfr men's robes,sportswear	Feb	1.35	1.63	1.92	20	17.25	9.0
Applebee's Int'l (APPB)	Franchised restau't operator	Dec	1.43	1.71	1.97	17	18.13	9.2
SPS Technologies (ST)	Ind'l fasteners:mtls hldg	Dec	2.54	3.37	3.97	20	39.00	9.8
Pre-Paid Legal Svcs (PPD)	Sells legal svc contracts	Dec	0.83	1.19	1.53	40	16.88	11.0
AAR Corp (AIR)	Mkts aviation parts/service	May	0.91	*1.27	1.54	15	18.44	12.0
Amer Oncology Res (AORI)	Provides managed oncology svcs	Dec	0.48	0.61	0.76	27	9.38	12.3
Valassis Communications (VCI)	Prints consumer promotion prd	Dec	1.69	2.20	2.58	15	32.38	12.6
Watsco, Inc (WSO)	Dstrb air cond/heat'g pd	Dec	0.68	0.89	1.11	25	14.44	13.0
Expeditors Int'l,Wash (EXPD)	Int'l air freight forward'g	Dec	1.46	1.80	2.11	21	28.88	13.7
Orthodontic Centers of Amer (OCA)	Manage orthodontic centers	Dec	0.50	0.70	0.95	34	13.00	13.7
Premier Bancshares (PMB)	General banking, Georgia	Dec	0.73	0.98	1.20	22	17.00	14.2
Univl Health Svs Cl'B' (UHS)	Acute care hospitals	Dec	2.03	2.40	2.88	18	42.75	14.8

*Actual 1998 EPS.

Chart based on October 9, 1998 prices and data.

Note: All earnings estimates are Wall Street consensus projections.

S&P SMALLCAP 600 STOCK SCREENS

SMALLCAP 600 LOW-P/E ISSUES

SMALLCAP 600 - LOW 1999 P/E, HIGH PROJECTED GROWTH RATE

These issues are all members of the Standard & Poor's SmallCap 600 stock price index. Each is expected to show a 20% increase in its 1998 and 1999 earnings. All have a five-year projected earnings growth rate of at least 20% and are currently selling at less than 20% estimated 1999 earnings. The list is sorted by their 1999 estimated price–to–earnings ratio.

| Company (Ticker) | Business | Fiscal Year End | Earnings Per Share $ | | | | 5-Year Proj. Growth Rate (%) | Recent Price | P/E on 1999 Est. |
			1996 Actual	1997 Actual	1998 Est.	1999 Est.			
BE Aerospace (BEAV)	Airline audio/video ctrl sys	Feb	0.72	1.30	2.29	3.38	26	16.13	4.8
Halter Marine Group (HLX)	Ship, barge building U.S.	Mar	0.59	0.78	1.14	1.50	25	7.19	4.8
Standard Pacific (SPF)	Single family home builder	Dec	0.28	0.92	1.49	1.90	26	9.75	5.1
Brightpoint Inc (CELL)	Wholesale cellular phones	Dec	0.30	0.53	0.76	1.03	32	5.94	5.8
Mentor Corp (MNTR)	Medical devices/hlth care pr	Mar	1.06	0.91	1.25	1.52	20	11.00	7.2
NBTY Inc (NBTY)	Mfr vitamins,food supplem'ts	Sep	0.22	0.29	0.62	0.87	32	6.53	7.5
AmeriCredit Corp (ACF)	Provides used-car financing	Jun	0.35	0.63	*0.93	1.17	23	9.31	8.0
Ashworth Inc (ASHW)	Design/mkt golf apparel	Oct	0.12	0.37	0.50	0.69	27	5.69	8.2
Just For Feet (FEET)	Athletic/outdoor footwear	Jan	0.55	0.70	1.02	1.40	31	12.13	8.7
CEC Entertainment (CEC)	Family restr/enter'nt ctrs	Dec	0.70	1.34	1.79	2.15	21	19.25	9.0
Interim Services (IS)	Temporary help services	Dec	0.69	1.05	1.27	1.58	22	14.25	9.0
Inter-Tel Inc (INTL)	Mfr electronic telecommun eqp	Dec	0.34	0.57	0.81	1.14	28	10.50	9.2
Michaels Stores (MIKE)	Specialty retail stores	Jan	-1.35	1.05	1.41	1.81	24	18.13	10.0
Stride Rite (SRR)	Mfr/retail children's shoes	Nov	0.05	0.40	0.55	0.77	22	7.81	10.1
Checkpoint Sys (CKP)	Electronic detection sys	Dec	0.60	0.23	0.51	0.73	21	7.69	10.5
Billing Concepts (BILL)	Bill'g clearinghse/telecom svc	Sep	0.58	0.11	0.81	1.00	25	10.63	10.6
CKE Restaurants (CKR)	Fast svc restaurant chain	Jan	0.36	1.07	1.76	2.18	30	23.00	10.6
Consolidated Graphics (CGX)	Commercial printing services	Mar	0.81	1.40	2.13	2.83	25	33.00	11.7
Amer Oncology Res (AORI)	Provides managed oncology svcs	Dec	0.37	0.48	0.61	0.76	27	9.38	12.3
Kronos Inc (KRON)	Mfr data collection systems	Sep	1.37	1.34	1.71	2.11	21	27.00	12.8
Bio-Technology Genl (BTGC)	Health prod thru biotechn'y	Dec	0.47	0.28	0.35	0.46	25	6.00	13.0
Insituform Technol'A' (INSUA)	Mkts sewer/PL repair process	Dec	0.17	0.36	0.63	0.80	31	10.38	13.0
Watsco, Inc (WSO)	Distrb air cond/heat'g pd	Dec	0.60	0.68	0.89	1.11	25	14.44	13.0

*Actual 1998 EPS.

Chart based on October 9, 1998 prices and data.

Note: All earnings estimates are Wall Street consensus projections.

DIVIDEND ARISTOCRATS

COMPANIES THAT HAVE STEADILY INCREASED THEIR DIVIDENDS OVER THE PAST FIVE YEARS

Each of the companies below carries a 5-year compound annual dividend growth rate of at least 10%, has increased its cash payment each year for at least 5 years, has at least a 10% five-year projected earnings growth rate and has a current indicated dividend rate greater than its actual 1997 payment. All of those listed, moreover, are expected to post 10% earnings increases in 1998 and 1999, have a dividend coverage ratio (1999 earnings estimate divided by dividends) of 1.4 or better, and have a 1999 estimated P/E of less than 20. The list is sorted by 5-year dividend growth rate.

Company (Ticker)	Fiscal Year End	Earnings Per Share $ 1997 Actual	1998 Est.	1999 Est.	5-Year Dividend Growth Rate (%)	Recent Price	Indicated Dividend Rate ($)	Yield (%)	P/E on 1999 Est.	5-Year Proj. Growth Rate (%)
Roper Industries (ROP)	Oct	1.16	1.41	1.64	40.0	14.19	0.24	1.7	8.7	17
Hughes Supply (HUG)	Jan	2.30	2.65	3.05	29.4	26.06	0.34	1.3	8.5	16
Wolverine World Wide (WWW)	Dec	0.96	1.13	1.32	26.9	9.38	0.11	1.2	7.1	19
Life Re (LRE)	Dec	3.48	3.97	4.68	26.3	91.31	0.60	0.7	19.5	14
Analysts Intl (ANLY)	Jun	0.73	*0.99	1.26	21.2	22.25	0.40	1.8	17.7	23
AptarGroup Inc (ATR)	Dec	1.27	1.46	1.65	21.1	20.63	0.16	0.8	12.5	15
Mutual Risk Management (MM)	Dec	1.16	1.42	1.71	20.4	27.50	0.20	0.7	16.1	19
Baldor Electric (BEZ)	Dec	1.09	1.23	1.39	19.7	19.69	0.40	2.0	14.2	12
Commerce Bancorp (CBH)	Dec	1.80	2.08	2.38	18.2	35.88	0.78	2.2	15.1	13
Werner Enterprises (WERN)	Dec	1.00	1.19	1.35	16.9	13.31	0.10	0.8	9.9	15
Myers Indus (MYE)	Dec	1.21	1.58	1.80	16.2	23.81	0.24	1.0	13.2	12
Wabash National (WNC)	Dec	0.74	1.58	2.02	16.1	10.56	0.14	1.3	5.2	18
ABM Industries Inc (ABM)	Oct	1.22	1.44	1.67	14.5	26.81	0.48	1.8	16.1	17
Blount Intl Cl'A' (BLT.A)	Dec	1.53	1.72	1.93	14.4	22.31	0.29	1.3	11.6	13
First Midwest Bancorp (FMBI)	Dec	1.92	2.33	2.59	14.3	36.31	0.90	2.5	14.0	11
Rollins Truck Leasing (RLC)	Sep	0.67	0.84	0.94	14.0	10.50	0.16	1.5	11.2	12
Eaton Vance (EV)	Oct	1.04	1.27	1.50	13.6	20.44	0.24	1.2	13.6	13
Casey's Genl Stores (CASY)	Apr	0.51	*0.63	0.76	12.2	14.88	0.06	0.4	19.6	20
FirstMerit Corp (FMER)	Dec	1.36	1.53	1.74	12.1	21.84	0.64	2.9	12.6	11
Frontier Insurance Gr (FTR)	Dec	0.92	1.67	1.97	12.1	13.06	0.28	2.1	6.6	17
Centura Banks (CBC)	Dec	3.15	3.61	4.02	11.6	62.06	1.16	1.9	15.4	12
Enhance Financial Svcs Grp (EFS)	Dec	1.78	2.11	2.48	11.3	21.00	0.24	1.1	8.5	16
CCB Financial (CCB)	Dec	2.27	2.91	3.24	10.9	45.50	1.04	2.3	14.0	10

*Actual 1998 EPS.

Chart based on October 9, 1998 prices and data.

Note: All earnings estimates are Wall Street consensus projections.

S&P SMALLCAP 600 STOCK SCREENS

LOW ANALYTICAL COVERAGE, HIGH GROWTH RATE

The companies listed below are covered by three or fewer analysts out of the approximately 2,300 analysts that contribute earnings estimates to S&P. While broader coverage might result in stronger agreement on earnings projections, relative neglect by the financial community often gives purchasers of the stock an advantage. These issues are all expected to have at least a 15% increase in earnings in 1998 and again in 1999. Additionally, their five-year projected growth rate is at least 15%. They are sorted by their five-year projected growth rate.

Company (Ticker)	Business	Fiscal Year End	–1998– High	Low	Recent Price	Earnings Per Share $ 1997 Actual	1998 Est.	1999 Est.	5-Yr. Proj. Growth Rate (%)	P/E on 1999 Est.
Instuform Technol'A'(INSUA)	Mkts sewer/PL repair process	Dec	15.75	7.75	10.38	0.36	0.63	0.80	31	13.0
Zebra Technologies'A'(ZBRA)	Mfr bar code labeling sys	Dec	44.62	25.50	29.00	1.65	1.92	2.25	29	12.9
Paxar Corp(PXR)	Mfr/mkts product ID systems	Dec	15.50	7.81	8.50	0.49	0.72	0.86	25	9.9
VISX Inc(VISX)	Mfr vision correct'n sys	Dec	71.00	19.50	53.38	0.89	2.10	2.61	24	20.5
Premier Bancshares(PMB)	General banking, Georgia	Dec	30.00	15.25	17.00	0.73	0.98	1.20	22	14.2
Lillian Vernon(LVC)	Direct mail catalog sales	Feb	18.62	13.12	13.00	0.93	1.11	1.54	20	8.4
TCBY Enterprises(TBY)	Franchises frozen yogurt strs	Nov	10.25	5.12	5.56	0.37	0.43	0.53	20	10.5
Baker(J.J.) Inc(JBAK)	Self-svc footwear retailer	Jan	13.62	3.43	3.88	0.27	0.65	0.87	19	4.5
Natl Computer Sys(NLCS)	Optical mark/read process eq	Jan	30.25	15.50	27.75	0.80	0.98	1.15	19	24.1
Timberland Co Cl'A'(TBL)	Mfrs men/women footwear	Dec	87.75	28.81	30.75	4.03	5.13	6.08	19	5.1
Boole & Babbage(BOOL)	Mfr IBM-compatible software	Sep	26.00	16.00	18.38	0.45	1.15	1.33	18	13.8
CTS Corp(CTS)	Electronic components/subsys	Dec	38.00	23.62	24.75	1.43	2.51	2.94	18	8.4
Diagnostic Products(DP)	Medical immunodiagnostic kits	Dec	32.87	20.87	21.31	1.32	1.55	1.90	18	11.2
ABM Industries Inc(ABM)	Janitorial & building maint	Oct	37.00	25.00	26.81	1.22	1.44	1.67	17	16.1
Insurance Auto Auctions(IAAI)	Sells insur recovered vehicles	Dec	14.75	8.37	11.38	0.40	0.62	0.89	17	12.8
Primark Corp(PMK)	Fin'l info/hlth care svcs	Dec	44.50	23.37	25.06	0.78	1.01	1.40	16	17.9
Analogic Corp(ALOG)	Data conversion products	Jul	48.00	31.12	33.00	1.58	*1.87	2.17	15	15.2
Astec Industries(ASTE)	Asphalt mix plants,pav'g eqp	Dec	45.00	15.12	39.13	1.42	2.10	2.44	15	16.0
Southern Energy Homes(SEHI)	Producer of manufactured homes	Dec	13.37	6.00	6.59	0.75	0.90	1.05	15	6.3

*Actual 1998 EPS.

Chart based on October 9, 1998 prices and data.

Note: All earnings estimates are Wall Street consensus projections.

Stock Reports

In using the Stock Reports in this handbook, please pay particular attention to the dates attached to each evaluation, recommendation, or analysis section. Opinions rendered are as of that date and may change often. It is strongly suggested that before investing in any security you should obtain the current analysis on that issue.

To order the latest Standard & Poor's Stock Report on a company, for as little as $3.00 per report, please call:

S&P Reports On-Demand at 1-800-292-0808.

03-OCT-98

Industry:
Aerospace/Defense

Summary: AIR is a leading supplier of products and services for the commercial and military aviation aftermarkets; it also makes containerization products and materials-handling equipment.

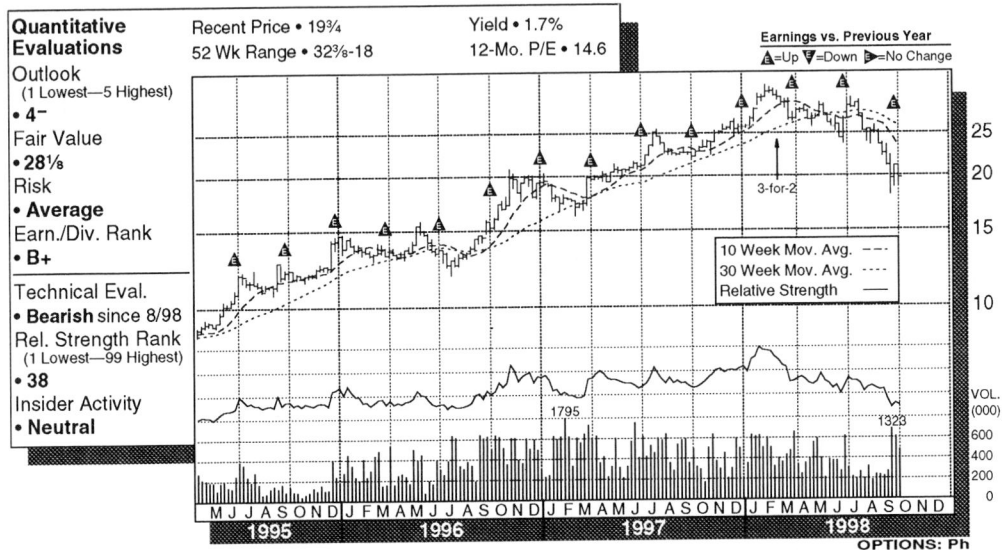

Quantitative Evaluations

Recent Price • 19¾
52 Wk Range • 32⅜-18

Yield • 1.7%
12-Mo. P/E • 14.6

Earnings vs. Previous Year
▲=Up ▼=Down ▶=No Change

Outlook
(1 Lowest—5 Highest)
• **4⁻**

Fair Value
• **28⅛**

Risk
• **Average**

Earn./Div. Rank
• **B+**

Technical Eval.
• **Bearish** since 8/98

Rel. Strength Rank
(1 Lowest—99 Highest)
• **38**

Insider Activity
• **Neutral**

3-for-2

10 Week Mov. Avg. - - -
30 Week Mov. Avg. · · · · ·
Relative Strength —

1795

1323

VOL. (000)
600
400
200
0

M J J A S O N D J F M A M J J A S O N D J F M A M J J A S O N D J F M A M J J A S O N D
1995   1996   1997   1998

OPTIONS: Ph

Business Profile - 02-JUL-98

AAR continues to win long-term contracts, and grow through both acquisitions and internal development. In November 1997, the company signed a three-year parts agreement with Delta Air Lines. At the end of 1997, AAR acquired AVSCO Aviation Service Corp. ($80 million in sales), a new parts distributor. The company has increased the scope of technical services and manufactured products through additional investment in upgraded facilities, tooling and systems. AAR completed a significant expansion of its FAA-licensed Oklahoma airframe maintenance facility in May 1998, providing 20% additional capacity. It also plans to expand its engine component repair shop in Connecticut in early FY 99 (May). A three-for-two stock split along with a 6% dividend hike was effected in February 1998.

Operational Review - 02-JUL-98

Based on a preliminary report, net sales in the fiscal year ended May 31, 1998, advanced 33% from those of the preceding year, reflecting increased engine, airframe and large component part sales. Margins widened on the increased volume, an improved mix of inventories sold in certain aircraft and engine businesses, and well controlled operating costs and expenses; net income rose 55%, to $35,657,000 ($1.27 a diluted share, on 11% more shares), from $23,025,000 ($0.91, as adjusted for the 3-for-2 stock split).

Stock Performance - 02-OCT-98

In the past 30 trading days, AIR's shares have declined 21%, compared to a 7% fall in the S&P 500. Average trading volume for the past five days was 96,480 shares, compared with the 40-day moving average of 92,638 shares.

Key Stock Statistics

Dividend Rate/Share	0.34	Shareholders	9,500
Shs. outstg. (M)	27.7	Market cap. (B)	$0.547
Avg. daily vol. (M)	0.138	Inst. holdings	86%
Tang. Bk. Value/Share	9.90		
Beta	0.55		

Value of $10,000 invested 5 years ago: $ 28,721

Fiscal Year Ending May 31

	1999	1998	1997	1996	1995	1994
Revenues (Million $)						
1Q	215.9	170.9	136.0	109.6	97.19	98.30
2Q	—	180.2	135.7	121.3	99.4	93.19
3Q	—	208.5	154.1	136.1	125.2	96.20
4Q	—	222.6	163.5	138.1	129.6	120.1
Yr.	—	782.1	589.3	505.0	451.4	407.8
Earnings Per Share ($)						
1Q	0.34	0.27	0.20	0.13	0.09	0.11
2Q	—	0.31	0.21	0.15	0.09	0.10
3Q	—	**0.33**	0.24	0.17	0.12	0.09
4Q	—	**0.37**	0.26	0.21	0.15	0.10
Yr.	—	**1.27**	0.92	0.67	0.44	0.40

Next earnings report expected: mid December

Dividend Data (Dividends have been paid since 1973.)

Amount ($)	Date Decl.	Ex-Div. Date	Stock of Record	Payment Date
3-for-2	Jan. 13	Feb. 24	Feb. 02	Feb. 23 '98
0.085	Jan. 13	Feb. 26	Mar. 02	Mar. 24 '98
0.085	Apr. 15	Apr. 30	May. 04	Jun. 03 '98
0.085	Jul. 14	Jul. 30	Aug. 03	Sep. 03 '98

A Division of The McGraw·Hill Companies

STANDARD
&POOR'S

STOCK REPORTS

AAR Corp.

4

03-OCT-98

Business Summary - 02-JUL-98

This leading provider of aftermarket aviation-related products and services has not been left on the runway during the recent resurgence in the aerospace/aviation industry. Rebounding from the gloomy days of the early 1990s, airlines have continued to experience increased fleet utilization, higher revenue passenger, and improved operating earnings. AIR has mirrored this trend, as its revenues grew 33% and 17%, in FY 98 (May) and FY 97, respectively, while earnings increased 55% and 44%.

The rising equipment needs of airlines -- particularly start-up airlines, and air cargo and small-package carriers -- have boosted demand for AIR's trading activities (59% of net sales in FY 97). Trading activities comprise the sale and lease of aviation products (mainly engines and engine parts, airframes and avionics) that have been purchased new, used, or overhauled. AIR also sells, leases and finances new and used jet aircraft.

Investments in AIR's overhaul business (25% of net sales in FY 97) have resulted in expanded technical capabilities, especially for the newer generations of sophisticated fuel and electric systems and advanced avionics. This business primarily overhauls, repairs, and modifies components for both commercial and military aircraft.

Over the last few years, the web of U.S. military bases located both domestically and overseas has been reduced, due to budget cuts and downsizing. With fewer bases, the need for rapid deployment support products for moving supplies to various hot spots around the world in times of crisis has increased. In response, AIR has stepped up its development and design efforts for these types of products. The U.S. government accounted for 13.9% of AIR's net sales in FY 97, down from 18.3% in FY 96. In addition to making products for rapid deployment forces, AIR's manufacturing segment (16% of sales in FY 97) makes and installs cargo handling systems, pallets and containers for airframe manufacturers, commercial airlines and others. Export sales in FY 97 were 35% of total net sales. The company's backlog at May 31, 1997, totaled $84.8 million, down from $86.1 million a year earlier.

In September 1997, AAR agreed to purchase British Airways-owned fleet of 14 Boeing aircraft. In June 1997, AIR acquired Cooper Aviation Industries, Inc. ($45 million), a distributor of factory-new aircraft parts, expanding the company's presence in the general and regional/commuter markets.

Per Share Data ($)

(Year Ended May 31)	1998	1997	1996	1995	1994	1993	1992	1991	1990	1989
Tangible Bk. Val.	9.90	9.65	8.29	7.98	7.68	7.66	7.96	7.83	7.55	6.82
Cash Flow	1.81	1.41	1.09	0.87	0.70	0.47	0.91	0.97	1.37	1.31
Earnings	1.27	0.92	0.67	0.44	0.40	0.01	0.42	0.62	1.07	1.04
Dividends	0.32	0.32	0.32	0.32	0.32	0.32	0.32	0.32	0.31	0.28
Payout Ratio	25%	35%	48%	73%	80%	NM	76%	52%	29%	27%
Cal. Yrs.	1997	1996	1995	1994	1993	1992	1991	1990	1989	1988
Prices - High	27	20⅞	14⅝	11⅝	10	10⅝	11¼	24⅝	25	18⅝
- Low	16⅛	11⅞	8⅛	7⅞	7⅝	7⅛	6⅛	6⅛	16	11⅛
P/E Ratio - High	21	23	22	26	25	NM	27	40	23	18
- Low	13	13	12	18	19	NM	15	10	15	11

Income Statement Analysis (Million $)

	1998	1997	1996	1995	1994	1993	1992	1991	1990	1989
Revs.	782	589	505	451	408	383	423	467	445	406
Oper. Inc.	79.0	55.2	42.6	34.8	29.1	27.2	38.2	42.0	54.0	51.1
Depr.	14.3	12.3	10.1	10.3	7.3	10.9	11.6	8.3	7.2	6.4
Int. Exp.	14.5	10.8	10.6	10.9	9.6	8.1	8.4	10.1	10.0	7.8
Pretax Inc.	51.2	33.0	22.8	14.7	13.7	-1.9	13.6	21.4	38.2	37.0
Eff. Tax Rate	30%	30%	30%	29%	31%	NM	26%	31%	33%	33%
Net Inc.	35.7	23.0	16.0	10.5	9.5	0.3	10.0	14.8	25.7	24.8

Balance Sheet & Other Fin. Data (Million $)

	1998	1997	1996	1995	1994	1993	1992	1991	1990	1989
Cash	17.2	51.7	33.6	22.5	18.1	2.3	2.3	1.6	4.0	4.6
Curr. Assets	468	414	338	322	308	265	290	268	276	257
Total Assets	671	530	438	426	418	365	395	380	389	356
Curr. Liab.	149	100	79.4	73.0	68.0	72.0	92.0	79.0	91.0	128
LT Debt	178	117	118	120	116	66.3	67.3	69.0	72.3	25.7
Common Eqty.	301	269	205	197	189	189	197	194	190	172
Total Cap.	516	419	354	348	344	294	303	301	298	228
Cap. Exp.	17.5	30.3	7.5	9.1	6.4	8.9	8.2	8.9	10.4	11.0
Cash Flow	49.9	35.3	26.1	20.8	16.8	11.2	21.6	23.1	32.8	31.3
Curr. Ratio	3.1	4.1	4.3	4.4	4.5	3.7	3.1	3.4	3.0	2.0
% LT Debt of Cap.	34.4	27.9	33.3	34.5	33.6	22.6	22.2	22.9	24.3	11.3
% Net Inc.of Revs.	4.6	3.9	3.9	2.4	2.3	0.1	2.4	3.2	5.8	6.1
% Ret. on Assets	5.9	4.8	3.7	2.5	2.4	0.1	2.6	3.9	6.9	7.7
% Ret. on Equity	12.5	9.8	8.0	5.5	5.0	0.1	5.1	7.8	14.2	15.3

Data as orig. reptd.; bef. results of disc. opers. and/or spec. items. Per share data adj. for stk. divs. as of ex-div. date. Bold denotes diluted EPS (FASB 128). E-Estimated. NA-Not Available. NM-Not Meaningful. NR-Not Ranked.

Office—One AAR Place, 1100 N. Wood Dale Rd., Wood Dale, IL 60191. **Tel**—(630) 227-2000. **Website**—http://www.aarcorp.com **Chrmn**—J. A. Eichner. **Pres & CEO**—D. P. Storch. **VP-Treas & CFO**—T. J. Romenesko. **VP-Secy**—H. A. Pulsifer. **VP-Investor Contact**—Ann T. Baldwin. **Dirs**—A. R. Abboud, H. B. Bernick, I. A. Eichner, E. D. Jannotta, R. D. Judson, E. E. Schulze, J. D. Spungin, L. B. Stern, D. P. Storch, R. D. Tabery. **Transfer Agents & Registrars**—First National Bank of Chicago; First Chicago Trust Co. of New York, Jersey City, N.J. **Incorporated**—in Delaware in 1966. **Empl**— 2,100. **S&P Analyst:** Stewart Scharf

ABM Industries 4G

NYSE Symbol **ABM**

In S&P SmallCap 600

03-OCT-98

Industry:
Services (Facilities & Environmental)

Summary: The largest facility services contractor on the NYSE, this company provides janitorial, air-conditioning, elevator, engineering, lighting, parking and security services.

Quantitative Evaluations		
Outlook (1 Lowest—5 Highest)	Recent Price • 27½	Yield • 1.7%
• **3⁻**	52 Wk Range • 37-25	12-Mo. P/E • 20.4

Recent Price • 27½   52 Wk Range • 37-25

Yield • 1.7%   12-Mo. P/E • 20.4

Quantitative Evaluations

Outlook (1 Lowest—5 Highest)
• **3⁻**

Fair Value
• **34**

Risk
• **Average**

Earn./Div. Rank
• **A**

Technical Eval.
• **NA**

Rel. Strength Rank (1 Lowest—99 Highest)
• **75**

Insider Activity
• **Neutral**

Earnings vs. Previous Year
▲=Up ▼=Down ▶=No Change

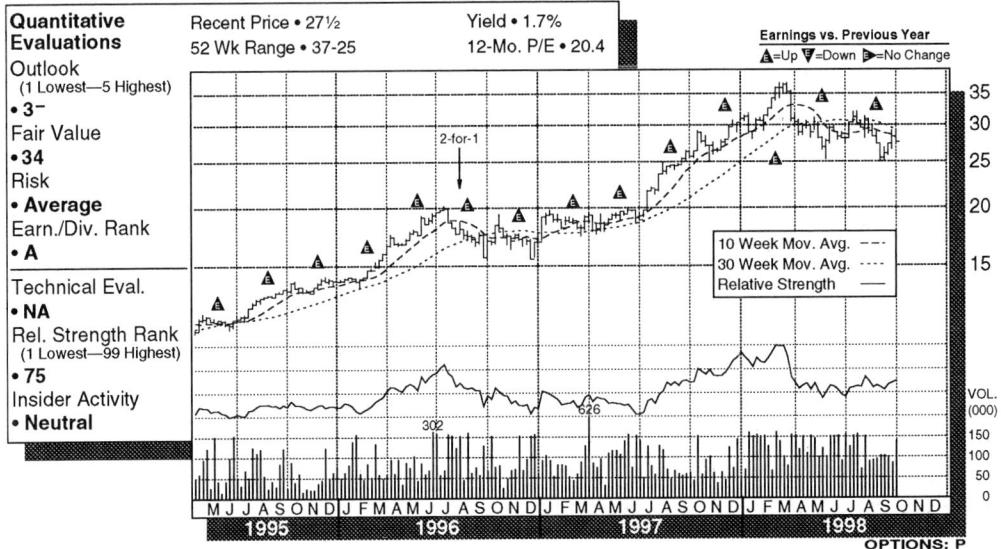

10 Week Mov. Avg. - - -
30 Week Mov. Avg. ·····
Relative Strength —

2-for-1

VOL. (000)

M J J A S O N D | J F M A M J J A S O N D | J F M A M J J A S O N D | J F M A M J J A S O N D
1995 | 1996 | 1997 | 1998

OPTIONS: P

Business Profile - 12-AUG-98

ABM achieved double-digit increases in revenues, net income and earnings per share in FY 97 (Oct.), reflecting rising multi-service sales, inter-company sales referrals and national account sales, as well as recent acquisitions and the accelerated pace of outsourcing and privatization. After reporting the record results, the company increased its quarterly dividend 20% with the February 1998 payment. In June 1998 ABM acquired the ongoing business of Lighting Maintenance, Inc. (LMI) and Fecht Electric Co. Both LMI and Fecht are based in Chicago and perform lighting, sign and electrical maintenance and repair.

Operational Review - 12-AUG-98

Revenues and other income in the six months ended April 30, 1998, rose 24%, year to year, primarily reflecting acquisitions during 1997, as well as new business and price increases. Gross margins narrowed, chiefly on higher labor and related costs. SG&A expenses were well controlled, and pretax income was up 19%. After taxes at 41.5%, versus 42.0%, net income advanced 20%, to $12,840,000 ($0.55 a share, on 7.2% more shares), from $10,689,000 ($0.48).

Stock Performance - 02-OCT-98

In the past 30 trading days, ABM's shares have declined 3%, compared to a 7% fall in the S&P 500. Average trading volume for the past five days was 27,680 shares, compared with the 40-day moving average of 20,549 shares.

Key Stock Statistics

Dividend Rate/Share	0.48	Shareholders	4,900
Shs. outstg. (M)	21.4	Market cap. (B)	$0.588
Avg. daily vol. (M)	0.022	Inst. holdings	61%
Tang. Bk. Value/Share	5.39		
Beta	0.60		

Value of $10,000 invested 5 years ago: $ 31,004

Fiscal Year Ending Oct. 31

	1998	1997	1996	1995	1994	1993
Revenues (Million $)						
1Q	358.8	291.6	254.4	232.1	210.8	187.2
2Q	369.0	294.3	262.1	234.4	215.9	188.7
3Q	381.0	308.5	281.9	245.8	225.0	192.2
4Q	—	358.5	288.6	253.1	233.0	205.2
Yr.	—	1,252	1,087	965.4	884.6	773.3
Earnings Per Share ($)						
1Q	**0.25**	0.22	0.20	0.17	0.15	0.14
2Q	**0.30**	0.26	0.23	0.20	0.18	0.15
3Q	**0.40**	0.34	0.29	0.26	0.23	0.20
4Q	—	0.40	0.33	0.29	0.27	0.23
Yr.	—	1.22	1.05	0.92	0.82	0.72

Next earnings report expected: mid December

Dividend Data (Dividends have been paid since 1965.)

Amount ($)	Date Decl.	Ex-Div. Date	Stock of Record	Payment Date
0.120	Dec. 16	Jan. 13	Jan. 15	Feb. 05 '98
0.120	Mar. 17	Apr. 13	Apr. 15	May. 05 '98
0.120	Jun. 12	Jul. 13	Jul. 15	Aug. 05 '98
0.120	Sep. 15	Oct. 13	Oct. 15	Nov. 05 '98

A Division of The **McGraw·Hill** *Companies*

Business Summary - 12-AUG-98

Not only is ABM Industries the largest U.S.-based facility services contractor listed on the New York Stock Exchange, but it also cleans some of the country's biggest buildings. Some of its clients include the 107-story twin towers of the World Trade Center in New York City, the 76-story Columbia Seafirst Center in Seattle, the 57-story Key Tower in Cleveland and the tallest building in the Western Hemisphere, the 100-story Sears Tower in Chicago. Services provided to these skyscrapers as well as thousands of commercial, industrial and institutional customers across the U.S. and Canada include air-conditioning, elevator, engineering, janitorial, lighting, parking and security.

Janitorial cleaning services as well as janitorial supplies and equipment are provided by ABM's janitorial division (which includes American Building Maintenance and Easterday Janitorial Supply); it has accounted for roughly 55% of revenues over the past few fiscal years. In FY 97 (Oct.), significant gains in many geographic regions bolstered revenues of American Building Maintenance. A larger customer base and additional sales generated by outside brokers led to higher revenues from Easterday Janitorial Supply.

Parking lot and garage operations and commercial security and investigative services are offered by the Public Service Divisions segment (which contributed about 20% of revenues in recent years); it recorded continued revenue growth in FY 97, with the addition of new customers and acquisitions benefiting American Commercial Security Services; Ampco System Parking revenues were bolstered by greater business at airport operations and new parking locations in the Northwest region.

The Technical Divisions (which offer various elevator, engineering, heating, ventilation and air-conditioning and lighting services) accounted for about 25% of revenues in recent years and recorded strong earnings growth in FY 97, primarily due to the absence of losses reported in FY 96 by its Mexican subsidiary, which was sold in May 1996.

Acquisitions have played a major role in ABM's revenue and earnings growth in recent years. Companies acquired in the three fiscal years through FY 97 contributed about $123 million to FY 97 revenues. ABM's latest deals included the June 1998 acquisition of the ongoing business of Lighting Maintenance, Inc. (LMI) and Fecht Electric Co. Both LMI and Fecht are based in Chicago and perform lighting, sign and electrical maintenance and repair.

Per Share Data ($)

(Year Ended Oct. 31)	1997	1996	1995	1994	1993	1992	1991	1990	1989	1988
Tangible Bk. Val.	4.45	4.51	3.87	3.48	2.98	4.01	3.56	2.95	2.56	2.42
Cash Flow	1.96	1.72	1.52	1.34	1.14	1.11	1.11	1.06	1.00	0.94
Earnings	1.22	1.05	0.93	0.82	0.72	0.71	0.68	0.62	0.56	0.47
Dividends	0.40	0.35	0.30	0.26	0.25	0.24	0.24	0.23	0.23	0.23
Payout Ratio	33%	33%	33%	32%	34%	34%	35%	38%	42%	49%
Prices - High	31½	20¼	14¼	12	10⅞	10¼	8⅞	10⅜	10	7⅛
- Low	17⅜	13½	10½	8⅝	7¼	7⅞	6⅛	6¼	6⅞	4½
P/E Ratio - High	26	19	15	14	15	14	13	17	18	15
- Low	14	13	11	10	10	11	9	10	12	10

Income Statement Analysis (Million $)

	1997	1996	1995	1994	1993	1992	1991	1990	1989	1988
Revs.	1,252	1,087	965	885	773	758	739	679	638	582
Oper. Inc.	65.8	55.4	46.6	37.8	29.6	26.7	21.4	19.9	23.6	21.2
Depr.	16.1	13.7	11.5	9.3	7.2	6.6	7.0	7.0	6.8	7.3
Int. Exp.	2.7	3.6	3.7	3.5	2.2	2.1	3.1	2.7	2.2	1.2
Pretax Inc.	46.9	38.1	31.4	25.1	20.2	20.4	18.6	10.5	14.6	12.7
Eff. Tax Rate	42%	43%	42%	40%	38%	41%	40%	6.60%	40%	44%
Net Inc.	27.2	21.7	18.2	15.2	12.6	12.0	11.1	9.8	8.7	7.1

Balance Sheet & Other Fin. Data (Million $)

	1997	1996	1995	1994	1993	1992	1991	1990	1989	1988
Cash	1.8	1.6	1.8	7.4	1.7	2.4	2.5	1.6	2.5	3.5
Curr. Assets	294	234	210	189	167	154	142	132	122	111
Total Assets	467	380	335	299	268	226	212	202	190	172
Curr. Liab.	157	114	114	99	90.3	78.5	80.1	66.5	63.6	66.1
LT Debt	38.4	33.7	22.6	25.3	20.9	15.4	9.5	20.0	20.0	14.0
Common Eqty.	198	164	142	124	110	101	90.0	79.6	69.4	61.9
Total Cap.	236	204	171	156	138	116	99	100	89.4	76.0
Cap. Exp.	13.3	10.8	10.2	8.5	6.2	5.2	5.7	6.1	6.0	5.5
Cash Flow	42.8	34.9	29.2	24.0	19.7	18.6	18.1	16.9	15.5	14.4
Curr. Ratio	1.9	2.1	1.8	1.9	1.8	2.0	1.8	2.0	1.9	1.7
% LT Debt of Cap.	16.3	16.5	13.2	16.2	15.2	13.3	9.6	20.1	22.4	18.5
% Net Inc.of Revs.	2.2	2.0	1.9	1.7	1.6	1.6	1.5	1.4	1.4	1.2
% Ret. on Assets	6.4	6.1	5.7	5.3	5.0	5.4	5.3	5.0	4.8	4.4
% Ret. on Equity	15.0	13.9	13.3	12.3	11.7	12.4	13.0	13.1	13.1	10.7

Data as orig. reptd.; bef. results of disc. opers. and/or spec. items. Per share data adj. for stk. divs. as of ex-div. date. Bold denotes diluted EPS (FASB 128). E-Estimated. NA-Not Available. NM-Not Meaningful. NR-Not Ranked.

Office—160 Pacific Ave., Suite 222, San Francisco, CA 94111.**Tel**—(415) 733-4000.**Website**—http://www.abm.com **Chrmn**—M. H. Mandles.**Pres & CEO**—W. W. Steele. **VP & Secy**—H. H. Kahn. **VP & CFO**—D. H. Hebble. **Dirs**—M. B. Cattâni, L. Chavez, L. Helms, J. F. Egan, C. T. Horngren, H. L. Kotkins, M. H. Mandles, T. Rosenberg, W. W. Steele, W. E. Walsh.**Transfer Agent & Registrar**—ChaseMellon Shareholder Services, San Francisco. **Incorporated**—in California in 1955; reincorporated in Delaware in 1985. **Empl**— 52,000. **S&P Analyst:** M.I.

03-OCT-98

Industry: Health Care (Specialized Services)

Summary: This company is the leading provider of membership-based personal health management services.

Quantitative Evaluations	
Outlook (1 Lowest—5 Highest) • **5**	
Fair Value • **49**	
Risk • **High**	
Earn./Div. Rank • **NR**	
Technical Eval. • **Bearish** since 5/98	
Rel. Strength Rank (1 Lowest—99 Highest) • **98**	
Insider Activity • **NA**	

Recent Price • 37⅞
52 Wk Range • 40¾-20⅝

Yield • Nil
12-Mo. P/E • 63.9

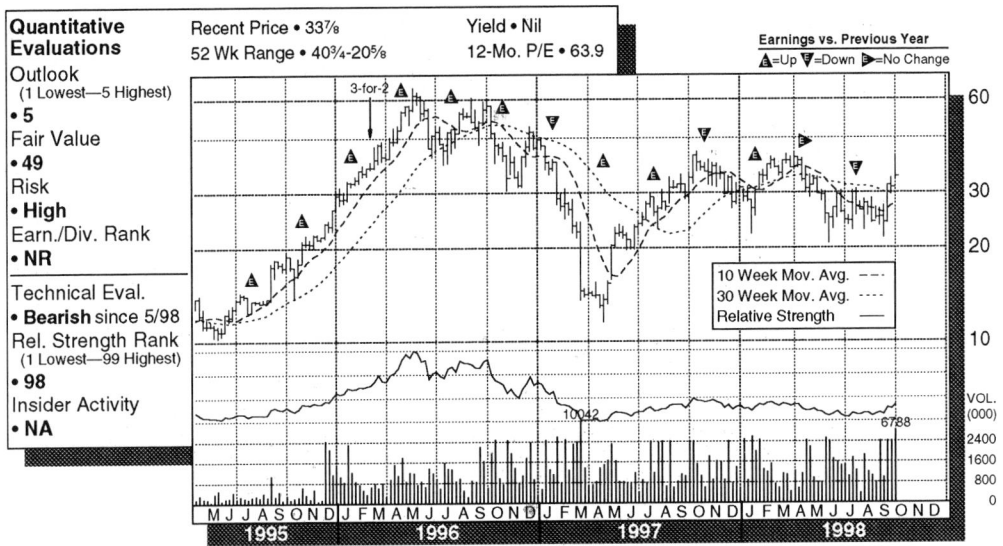

Earnings vs. Previous Year
▲=Up ▼=Down ▶=No Change

10 Week Mov. Avg. -- -
30 Week Mov. Avg. ....
Relative Strength —

VOL. (000)

Business Profile - 15-SEP-98

In June 1998, the company acquired InterQual, Inc., a leading provider of clinical decision support criteria and systems to health care insurers, plans and providers, for 4.5 million common shares. The company anticipates that the acquisition of InterQual will extend Access Health's care management capabilities to assist providers and plans in making appropriate care selection decisions. Access Health assists managed healthcare providers to lower their medical expenses by educating and empowering consumers to make more informed healthcare decisions, thereby reducing inappropriate use of the healthcare system.

Operational Review - 15-SEP-98

Revenues in the nine months ended June 30, 1998, advanced 25%, year to year, primarily due to a 23% increase in care management service enrollment. Gross profit margins narrowed to 44.8% from 48.2%, largely reflecting costs associated with the downward price adjustments on existing contracts. However, operating margins widened due to well controlled expenses, and a $4.3 million decline in transaction, integration and restructuring costs, from the year-earlier level. After taxes at 38.0%, versus 26.2%, net income more than doubled to $12,750,000 ($0.52 a share, based on 4.9% more shares), from $5,377,000 ($0.23). Results for the 1997 period were restated for the acquisition of InterQual, Inc., on a pooling-of-interest basis.

Stock Performance - 02-OCT-98

In the past 30 trading days, ACCS's shares have increased 40%, compared to a 7% fall in the S&P 500. Average trading volume for the past five days was 1,357,560 shares, compared with the 40-day moving average of 471,474 shares.

Key Stock Statistics

Dividend Rate/Share	Nil	Shareholders	700
Shs. outstg. (M)	23.6	Market cap. (B)	$0.799
Avg. daily vol. (M)	0.644	Inst. holdings	64%
Tang. Bk. Value/Share	5.05		
Beta	1.00		

Value of $10,000 invested 5 years ago: $ 84,687

Fiscal Year Ending Sep. 30

	1998	1997	1996	1995	1994	1993
Revenues (Million $)						
1Q	29.05	24.64	12.01	4.94	5.47	3.70
2Q	31.22	25.10	15.06	7.29	5.20	4.20
3Q	38.57	26.49	17.04	8.73	3.86	3.96
4Q	—	28.10	17.98	10.60	4.12	6.53
Yr.	—	104.3	62.07	31.55	18.63	18.48
Earnings Per Share ($)						
1Q	**0.27**	-0.34	0.11	-0.04	0.02	0.03
2Q	**0.29**	0.29	0.14	0.02	-0.02	0.04
3Q	**0.05**	0.29	0.17	0.05	-0.17	0.04
4Q	—	-0.02	0.18	0.09	-0.07	0.02
Yr.	—	0.24	0.61	0.14	-0.24	0.13

Next earnings report expected: early November

Dividend Data

No cash dividends have been paid. Access Health intends to retain earnings for use in its business, and does not expect to pay cash dividends in the foreseeable future.

A Division of The McGraw-Hill Companies

Business Summary - 15-SEP-98

With over 27.5 million members, Access Health is the leading provider of care management products and services to the healthcare industry. The company's products are designed to reduce unnecessary healthcare service utilization, improve health plan member satisfaction, lower healthcare costs and improve the quality of care. In 1997, managed care services membership increased 39%, year to year, reflecting expanded and new relationships with HMOs, PPOs, Blue Cross/Blue Shield plans and other managed care providers.

The flagship product, Personal Health Advisor (PHA), features a core set of care management products and services that provide members with consistent clinical assessment and guidance about the use of healthcare services for both chronic and acute conditions and to help guide these individuals to the most appropriate point of care within a managed care network. PHA products are used by managed care organizations as the primary "gateway" to a plan network, as an emergency room pre-certification tool, as a healthcare management tool for persons with chronic conditions or solely as a healthcare information service for members.

The company's 24-hour-a-day telephone triage service is based on First Help, a clinically-advanced, proprietary process for assessing a caller's symptoms, integrating provider recommendations and offering consistent care advice. This product helps health plans and providers lower emergency room and physician office visits for conditions which can be safely treated in less intensive settings. First Help consists of over 550 risk-sorting clinical algorithms, including modules for pediatrics, adults, women, seniors and mental health. By utilizing a predetermined set of questions in a set order, nurses can effectively guide callers to the most appropriate level of care, and this advice is believed to mimic that of the patient's own doctor over 90% of the time.

Other acute care products include ER Access, designed to reduce unnecessary emergency room utilization; Open Access, which offers health plans an alternative to the primary care "gatekeeper" referral process by allowing nurses to match patients with appropriate providers based on health plan rules; and Provider Profile, a PC-based software tool designed to collect data about a provider's background and current practice for use in patient-provider matching.

Disease and condition management programs are offered to proactively assist patients with the management of certain conditions in accordance with physician prescribed regimens. These programs currently extend to asthma, diabetes, congestive heart failure, maternity, hypertension and depression.

Acquisitions are an integral part of the company's growth strategy. Most recently, in June 1998, ACCS acquired InterQual Inc., a provider of clinical decision-making support criteria and systems to healthcare insurers, plans and providers, for 4.3 million common shares.

Per Share Data ($)

(Year Ended Sep. 30)	1997	1996	1995	1994	1993	1992	1991	1990	1989	1988
Tangible Bk. Val.	4.24	4.84	1.76	1.48	1.75	1.49	1.35	NA	NA	NA
Cash Flow	0.56	0.88	0.31	-0.09	0.25	0.25	0.27	0.06	0.15	NA
Earnings	0.24	0.61	0.14	-0.24	0.13	0.16	0.14	-0.03	0.07	NA
Dividends	Nil	Nil	Nil	Nil	Nil	Nil	Nil	Nil	Nil	Nil
Payout Ratio	Nil	Nil	Nil	Nil	Nil	Nil	Nil	Nil	Nil	Nil
Prices - High	45¼	65½	30⅜	14⅞	8⅛	5	NA	NA	NA	NA
- Low	11½	27½	9½	5	3⅛	1¹⁵⁄₁₆	NA	NA	NA	NA
P/E Ratio - High	NM	NM	NM	NM	60	31	NA	NA	NA	NA
- Low	NM	NM	NM	NM	24	12	NA	NA	NA	NA

Income Statement Analysis (Million $)

	1997	1996	1995	1994	1993	1992	1991	1990	1989	1988
Revs.	104	62.1	31.6	18.6	18.5	12.4	10.1	5.8	3.9	2.2
Oper. Inc.	32.7	15.7	3.9	-2.7	2.8	2.9	2.5	1.2	1.0	NA
Depr.	6.3	3.6	1.9	1.4	1.1	0.9	0.9	0.5	0.4	NA
Int. Exp.	0.3	0.0	0.1	0.1	0.2	0.3	0.3	0.2	0.1	NA
Pretax Inc.	2.3	13.5	2.6	-3.6	2.0	2.3	1.7	-0.3	0.6	0.2
Eff. Tax Rate	NM	40%	41%	NM	36%	40%	41%	NM	40%	40%
Net Inc.	4.6	8.1	1.5	-2.3	1.3	1.4	1.0	-0.2	0.3	0.1

Balance Sheet & Other Fin. Data (Million $)

	1997	1996	1995	1994	1993	1992	1991	1990	1989	1988
Cash	16.0	39.8	11.7	8.2	9.9	11.5	2.9	2.1	NA	NA
Curr. Assets	82.2	55.3	18.9	16.4	17.1	16.0	7.9	5.7	NA	NA
Total Assets	103	78.8	31.1	25.9	24.2	20.8	12.1	10.8	4.8	1.6
Curr. Liab.	21.6	14.4	8.7	5.7	5.5	4.2	5.3	4.3	NA	NA
LT Debt	0.2	Nil	0.4	0.7	1.0	0.9	1.2	1.5	0.7	NA
Common Eqty.	80.3	64.4	22.0	19.5	17.7	15.7	5.6	4.7	1.6	NA
Total Cap.	80.5	64.4	22.4	20.2	18.7	16.6	6.8	6.4	2.2	NA
Cap. Exp.	NA	10.9	4.6	1.1	2.0	0.7	0.1	0.6	1.0	NA
Cash Flow	10.9	11.7	3.4	-0.9	2.4	2.1	1.9	0.3	0.7	NA
Curr. Ratio	3.8	3.8	2.2	2.9	3.1	3.8	1.3	1.3	NA	NA
% LT Debt of Cap.	0.1	Nil	1.7	3.4	5.6	5.3	17.8	23.8	29.4	NA
% Net Inc.of Revs.	4.4	13.1	4.8	NM	6.9	11.0	10.0	NM	8.9	4.4
% Ret. on Assets	5.1	14.8	5.4	NM	5.6	3.4	8.9	NM	10.7	7.8
% Ret. on Equity	6.4	18.8	7.4	NM	7.6	13.6	19.7	NM	NA	NA

Data as orig. reptd.; bef. results of disc. opers. and/or spec. items. Per share data adj. for stk. divs. as of ex-div. date. Bold denotes diluted EPS (FASB 128). E-Estimated. NA-Not Available. NM-Not Meaningful. NR-Not Ranked.

Office—310 Interlocken Parkway, Broomfield, CO 80021. **Tel**—(303) 466-9500. **Website**—http://www.access-health.com **Chrmn**—F. Washington. **Pres & CEO**—J. P. Tallman. **SVP & CFO**—T. H. Connor. **SVP & Treas.**—J. V. Crisan. **SVP & Secy**—J. A. Brooks**Investor Contact**—Matt Plavan (916-851-4102). **Dirs**—J. R. Durant, K. L. Johnson, A. H. Lusk, R. C. Miller, K. B. Plumlee, E. K. Rygiel, J. P. Tallman, F. Washington. **Transfer Agent & Registrar**—First Chicago Trust Co. of New York. **Incorporated**—in California in 1987; reincorporated in Delaware in 1992. **Empl**—692. **S&P Analyst**: John J. Arege

STANDARD &POOR'S
STOCK REPORTS

Acxiom Corp.
NASDAQ Symbol **ACXM**

3015N

In S&P SmallCap 600

03-OCT-98

Industry:
Services (Advertising & Marketing)

Summary: This company provides data products, data integration services and mailing list processing services, as well as data warehousing and decision support services.

Quantitative Evaluations

Recent Price • 23⅜
52 Wk Range • 28¼-14⅛

Yield • Nil
12-Mo. P/E • 37.1

Outlook
(1 Lowest—5 Highest)
• **4⁻**

Fair Value
• **36⅛**

Risk
• **Average**

Earn./Div. Rank
• **B+**

Technical Eval.
• **Bullish** since 2/98

Rel. Strength Rank
(1 Lowest—99 Highest)
• **84**

Insider Activity
• **NA**

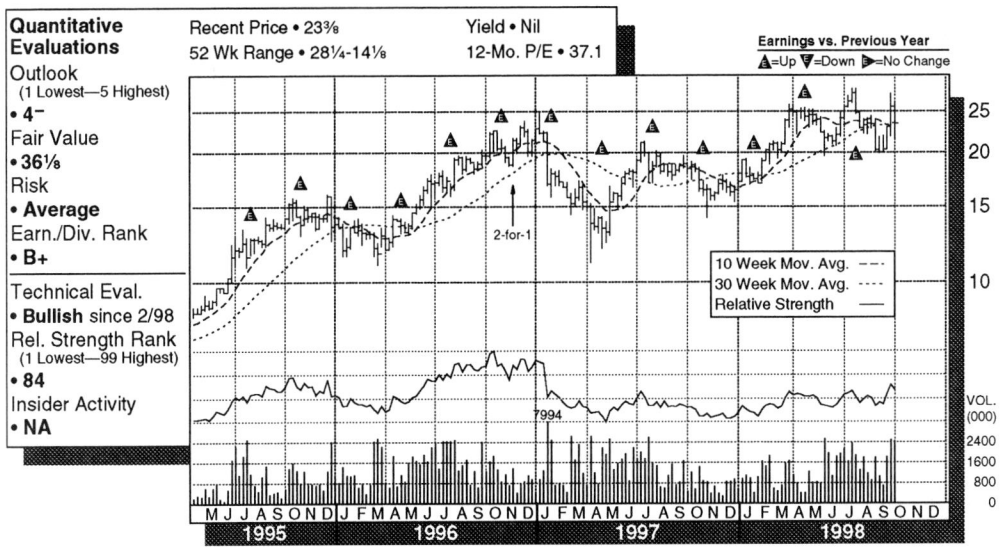

Earnings vs. Previous Year
▲=Up ▼=Down ▶=No Change

- 10 Week Mov. Avg. — — -
- 30 Week Mov. Avg. - - - -
- Relative Strength —

2-for-1

VOL.
(000)

Business Profile - 20-AUG-98

This provider of data products, data integration services, and mailing list processing services, as well as data warehousing and decision support services, primarily to direct marketing organizations, is increasingly supporting the marketing departments of large corporations in the U.S. and the U.K. Acquisitions are a key component of its growth strategy. In the FY 98 (Mar.) third quarter, ACXM acquired, for about $14.2 million, Buckley Demont, an Illinois-based provider of list management services. In May 1998, the company agreed to acquire May & Speh Inc. (NASDAQ: SPEH), a leading provider of technology-based information management services. The transaction, expected to close shortly, would create the world's leading database marketing services company, with revenues of nearly $700 million.

Operational Review - 20-AUG-98

Revenues in the first quarter of FY 99 rose 28%, year to year, driven by strong gains in all operating divisions. Margins widened, aided by well controlled equipment and data costs, partly offset by higher payroll and other expenditures; operating income climbed 34%. With 34% higher depreciation and amortization charges, and a 12% increase in net other expense, pretax income advanced 36%. After taxes at 37.0%, versus 37.5%, net income soared 37%, to $7,291,000 ($0.12 a share, on more shares), from $5,313,000 ($0.09).

Stock Performance - 02-OCT-98

In the past 30 trading days, ACXM's shares have increased 0.27%, compared to a 7% fall in the S&P 500. Average trading volume for the past five days was 573,320 shares, compared with the 40-day moving average of 346,085 shares.

Key Stock Statistics

Dividend Rate/Share	Nil	Shareholders	1,500
Shs. outstg. (M)	73.4	Market cap. (B)	$ 1.7
Avg. daily vol. (M)	0.438	Inst. holdings	43%
Tang. Bk. Value/Share	2.90		
Beta	1.13		

Value of $10,000 invested 5 years ago: $ 51,232

Fiscal Year Ending Mar. 31

	1999	1998	1997	1996	1995	1994
Revenues (Million $)						
1Q	128.6	100.3	93.95	59.18	46.88	31.77
2Q	—	110.0	97.55	62.38	47.85	36.66
3Q	—	120.7	104.5	71.32	52.74	41.43
4Q	—	134.1	106.0	77.03	54.97	41.81
Yr.	—	465.1	402.0	269.9	202.4	151.7
Earnings Per Share ($)						
1Q	0.12	0.09	0.08	0.06	0.04	0.03
2Q	—	0.14	0.10	0.08	0.06	0.05
3Q	—	0.19	0.15	0.11	0.09	0.06
4Q	—	0.18	0.14	0.10	0.09	0.06
Yr.	—	0.60	0.47	0.35	0.27	0.19

Next earnings report expected: mid October

Dividend Data

No cash dividends have been paid. A shareholder rights plan was adopted in February 1998.

Business Summary - 20-AUG-98

Acxiom Corp. (ACXM) is a provider of a wide range of data products, data integration services, and mailing list processing services, as well as data warehousing and decision support services. Its customers are direct marketing organizations and the marketing departments of large corporations in the U.S. and the U.K.

The company is now organized into four operating divisions. Management believes that this divisional structure can support Acxiom's expected future growth. The four divisions include three in the U.S. and one international division.

The Acxiom Alliances division achieved a 14% gain in revenues in FY 98 (Mar.), to $147 million, and the company intends to expand its existing strategic corporate relationships, which include Trans Union, Polk, ADP, and M/A/R/C, and to find opportunities to build new alliances.

The Acxiom Services division includes most of ACXM's traditional computer processing services customers, including Allstate, Citibank, IBM, and insurance, telecommunications, publishing, retail, high tech and utilities industry customers. This division contributed revenues of $153 million in FY 98, up 18% from the level of FY 97.

The Data Products division contributed $132 million in revenues in FY 98, representing a 15% advance from its revenues in FY 97. Its long-term goal is to be a leading provider of both consumer and business data.

The Acxiom International division, based in London, England, recorded a 19% gain in revenues, to $34 million, in FY 98. The division intends to expand both through acquisitions and through internal growth in Europe, the Asia Pacific region, and other areas of the world. In addition to major facilities in England, the division maintains small offices in the Netherlands and Malaysia.

With recent acquisitions, the company has added real property data, marketing lists and telephone reference data, strengthening its position as a data provider. Two acquisitions were completed in FY 98, preceded by two in FY 97.

In May 1998, ACXM agreed to acquire May & Speh, Inc. (NASDAQ: SPEH), a leading provider of information management services. The company believes that the combined entity will be the world's leading database marketing services concern, bringing together ACXM's data and data products with May & Speh's modeling and analytics to provide the most comprehensive marketing and customer information management solutions available.

Per Share Data ($)

(Year Ended Mar. 31)	1998	1997	1996	1995	1994	1993	1992	1991	1990	1989
Tangible Bk. Val.	2.79	2.28	2.29	1.96	1.46	1.24	1.13	NA	NA	NA
Cash Flow	1.28	1.03	0.77	0.69	0.64	0.54	0.29	NA	NA	NA
Earnings	0.60	0.47	0.35	0.27	0.19	0.15	0.06	NA	NA	NA
Dividends	Nil	Nil	Nil	Nil	Nil	Nil	Nil	Nil	Nil	Nil
Payout Ratio	Nil	Nil	Nil	Nil	Nil	Nil	Nil	Nil	Nil	Nil
Cal. Yrs.	1997	1996	1995	1994	1993	1992	1991	1990	1989	1988
Prices - High	24	25	16$\frac{1}{8}$	7$\frac{1}{2}$	6$\frac{1}{8}$	4$\frac{7}{8}$	2$\frac{3}{4}$	NA	NA	NA
- Low	11$\frac{1}{8}$	11	6$\frac{7}{8}$	4$\frac{5}{8}$	3$\frac{1}{8}$	1$\frac{3}{4}$	1$\frac{1}{4}$	NA	NA	NA
P/E Ratio - High	40	53	46	28	32	32	50	NA	NA	NA
- Low	19	23	19	17	16	12	23	NA	NA	NA

Income Statement Analysis (Million $)

	1998	1997	1996	1995	1994	1993	1992	1991	1990	1989
Revs.	465	402	270	202	152	116	91.0	NA	NA	NA
Oper. Inc.	100	84.9	53.3	42.6	34.7	27.8	15.2	NA	NA	NA
Depr.	40.7	33.2	21.6	19.6	19.4	16.1	9.1	NA	NA	NA
Int. Exp.	6.0	3.9	1.9	2.4	2.3	2.4	2.2	NA	NA	NA
Pretax Inc.	56.5	44.0	29.4	20.1	13.4	10.2	3.2	NA	NA	NA
Eff. Tax Rate	37%	38%	38%	38%	38%	39%	34%	NA	NA	NA
Net Inc.	35.6	27.5	18.2	12.4	8.4	6.2	2.1	NA	NA	NA

Balance Sheet & Other Fin. Data (Million $)

	1998	1997	1996	1995	1994	1993	1992	1991	1990	1989
Cash	5.7	2.7	3.5	3.1	0.5	NA	NA	NA	NA	NA
Curr. Assets	115	84.5	54.0	43.5	35.9	36.0	29.9	NA	NA	NA
Total Assets	394	300	194	148	123	113	87.0	NA	NA	NA
Curr. Liab.	68.3	36.1	31.2	25.0	12.9	14.9	12.5	NA	NA	NA
LT Debt	100	87.1	26.9	18.2	35.0	33.2	23.0	NA	NA	NA
Common Eqty.	200	156	123	97.2	61.9	52.2	47.4	NA	NA	NA
Total Cap.	326	261	161	123	110	93.0	70.0	NA	NA	NA
Cap. Exp.	55.8	59.8	39.0	24.4	27.3	28.8	NA	NA	NA	NA
Cash Flow	76.3	60.7	39.8	32.0	27.8	22.3	11.3	NA	NA	NA
Curr. Ratio	1.7	2.3	1.7	1.7	2.8	2.4	2.4	NA	NA	NA
% LT Debt of Cap.	30.6	33.4	16.7	14.9	31.8	35.7	32.7	NA	NA	NA
% Net Inc.of Revs.	7.7	6.8	6.8	6.1	5.5	5.4	2.4	NA	NA	NA
% Ret. on Assets	10.3	11.1	10.6	9.1	7.1	6.2	2.4	NA	NA	NA
% Ret. on Equity	20.0	19.7	16.6	15.6	14.7	12.5	4.7	NA	NA	NA

Data as orig. reptd.; bef. results of disc. opers. and/or spec. items. Per share data adj. for stk. divs. as of ex-div. date. Bold denotes diluted EPS (FASB 128). E-Estimated. NA-Not Available. NM-Not Meaningful. NR-Not Ranked.

Office—301 Industrial Blvd., Conway, AR 72032-7103. **Tel**—(501) 336-1000. **Website**—http://www.acxiom.com **Chrmn, Pres & CEO**—C. D. Morgan Jr. **EVP, Treas & COO**—R. S. Kline. **CFO & Investor Contact**—Robert S. Bloom. **Dirs**—A. H. Die, W. T. Dillard II, H. C. Gambill, R. S. Kline, C. D. Morgan, R. A. Pritzker, W. V. Smiley, J. T. Womble. **Transfer Agent & Registrar**—First National Bank of Chicago. **Incorporated** —in Delaware in 1983. **Empl**— 3,600. **S&P Analyst**: S.A.H.

ADAC Laboratories   3007
NASDAQ Symbol **ADAC**
In S&P SmallCap 600

03-OCT-98

Industry:
Health Care (Medical Products & Supplies)

Summary: This company designs, makes, markets and services medical imaging and information management products worldwide.

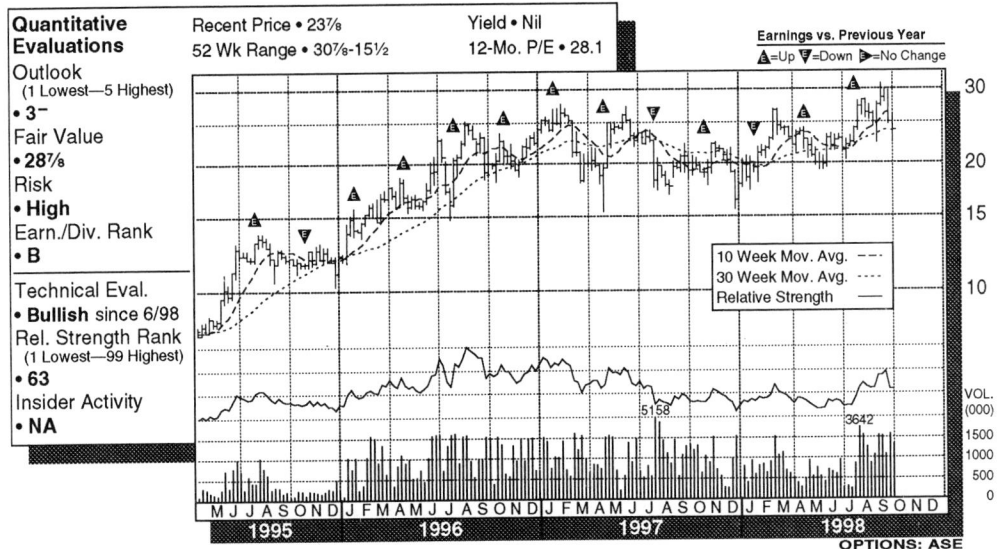

Quantitative Evaluations	
Outlook (1 Lowest—5 Highest)	• **3⁻**
Fair Value	• **28⅞**
Risk	• **High**
Earn./Div. Rank	• **B**
Technical Eval.	• **Bullish** since 6/98
Rel. Strength Rank (1 Lowest—99 Highest)	• **63**
Insider Activity	• **NA**

Recent Price • 23⅞   Yield • Nil
52 Wk Range • 30⅞-15½   12-Mo. P/E • 28.1

Earnings vs. Previous Year
▲=Up ▼=Down ▶=No Change

10 Week Mov. Avg. – – –
30 Week Mov. Avg. ·····
Relative Strength ——

OPTIONS: ASE

Business Profile - 14-SEP-98

In July 1998, ADAC signed a contract to supply China's first Molecular Coincidence Detection camera. In February 1998, the company discontinued its Healthcare Information Systems product, LabStat, recording $12.9 million in charges. In the FY 98 first half (Sep.), ADAC solidified its refurbished nuclear equipment and service line by acquiring O.N.E.S. Medical Services, Inc., CT Solutions, Inc., Southern CAT, Inc. and Photon Diagnostic Technologies. ADAC also expanded other product and services lines by acquiring Cortet, Inc., a designer of cardiac catheterization laboratory computer systems.

Operational Review - 14-SEP-98

Revenues in the nine months ended June 28, 1998, advanced 13%, year to year, on higher product and service revenue. Costs and expenses rose sharply as a result of first quarter charges for discontinued products and writeoffs totaling $16.4 million. Excluding the first quarter discontinued operations charge, operating margins improved as a result of greater volume and effective cost controls. Net income was up slightly, to $10,806,000 ($0.54 per share on 3.7% more shares) from $10,751,000 ($0.55).

Stock Performance - 02-OCT-98

In the past 30 trading days, ADAC's shares have declined 8%, compared to a 7% fall in the S&P 500. Average trading volume for the past five days was 265,680 shares, compared with the 40-day moving average of 298,562 shares.

Key Stock Statistics

Dividend Rate/Share	Nil	Shareholders	2,800
Shs. outstg. (M)	20.0	Market cap. (B)	$0.479
Avg. daily vol. (M)	0.344	Inst. holdings	65%
Tang. Bk. Value/Share	6.48		
Beta	0.93		

Value of $10,000 invested 5 years ago: $ 18,555

Fiscal Year Ending Sep. 30

	1998	1997	1996	1995	1994	1993
Revenues (Million $)						
1Q	75.52	68.37	54.99	44.23	46.55	36.30
2Q	77.38	69.98	58.44	44.73	47.30	37.60
3Q	83.52	71.51	62.43	45.62	40.08	39.72
4Q	—	72.48	64.93	50.23	42.36	43.34
Yr.	—	282.3	240.8	184.8	176.3	156.9
Earnings Per Share ($)						
1Q	-0.19	0.27	0.20	0.15	0.32	0.25
2Q	0.35	0.29	0.22	0.17	0.33	0.27
3Q	0.37	0.01	0.24	0.18	0.02	0.28
4Q	—	0.31	0.26	0.16	0.39	0.30
Yr.	—	0.86	0.90	0.65	1.06	1.10

Next earnings report expected: early November

Dividend Data

Dividends, suspended in 1990, were resumed in 1992 and omitted in late 1996.

A Division of The McGraw·Hill Companies

Business Summary - 14-SEP-98

ADAC Laboratories is a leading worldwide supplier of nuclear medicine products (with over a 50% share of the U.S. market alone), and has a major presence in radiology and laboratory information systems. Its medical imaging and information systems are used in hospitals and clinics in nuclear medicine, cardiology, radiology and oncology.

ADAC's medical systems (88% of FY 97 revenues) include nuclear medicine and radiation therapy planning systems, as well as ADAC Medical Technologies, the company's medical imaging equipment refurbishing business. ADAC also provides customer support and field service for its products.

Nuclear medicine is a diagnostic imaging procedure in which the patient is administered a radiotracer compound, which flows to organs under examination. The patient is then scanned with a gamma camera that detects radiotracer emissions from the organs. The company designs, manufactures and sells a broad line of nuclear medicine cameras and related computer systems, which consist of gamma cameras, computer workstations and clinical software that permits the physician to process the resulting data. In FY 97, nuclear medicine products represented about 76% of total product revenues.

Radiation therapy planning systems assist hospital radiation oncology departments and cancer treatment centers in planning patient treatments. In FY 97, these products represented 6% of ADAC's total product revenues. In 1996, the company acquired Geometrics Corp., which develops software used in planning radiation therapy treatments, for about $3.9 million. Geometrics operates as the product development unit of this division.

ADAC's healthcare information systems (12% of FY 97 revenues) includes a computer-based patient record system, used by radiology departments and hospitals, and a radiology information systems, used in patient record-keeping functions, as well as cardiology and laboratory information systems.

In FY 97, the company enhanced its presence in the nuclear medicine market by acquiring Southern Cats, Inc., a provider of refurbished diagnostic imaging equipment, Cortet, Inc., a maker of integrated computer systems for use in cardiac catheterization laboratories, and Photon Diagnostic Technologies, Inc., a leader in nuclear medicine imaging systems remanufacturing, service and support.

In July 1998, ADAC signed a contract to supply China's first Molecular Coincidence Detection camera. In June 1998, ADAC also became the exclusive distributor of UGM Medical Systems' leading PET systems worldwide.

In February 1998, the company discontinued its Healthcare Information Systems (HCIS) product, Lab-Stat, recording $12.9 million in charges in the first quarter of FY 98. However, it retained the HCIS laboratory support and maintenance business.

Per Share Data ($)

(Year Ended Sep. 30)	1997	1996	1995	1994	1993	1992	1991	1990	1989	1988
Tangible Bk. Val.	6.19	4.98	4.20	4.65	3.60	2.76	2.58	2.55	2.52	1.59
Cash Flow	1.42	1.43	1.02	1.41	1.40	0.99	0.27	0.39	1.26	0.93
Earnings	0.86	0.90	0.65	1.06	1.10	0.81	0.06	0.24	1.17	0.81
Dividends	Nil	0.48	0.60	0.48	0.40	0.36	Nil	0.24	0.36	Nil
Payout Ratio	Nil	53%	92%	45%	40%	41%	Nil	102%	30%	Nil
Prices - High	27³⁄₄	25¹⁄₄	13³⁄₄	14¹⁄₈	16⁷⁄₈	15³⁄₄	7⁷⁄₈	18³⁄₄	18³⁄₄	15
- Low	15³⁄₈	11⁵⁄₈	7¹⁄₄	6¹⁄₈	9¹⁄₄	5¹⁄₈	3	2¹⁄₁₆	12	5¹⁄₄
P/E Ratio - High	32	28	21	13	15	19	NM	78	16	19
- Low	18	13	11	6	8	6	NM	9	10	6

Income Statement Analysis (Million $)

	1997	1996	1995	1994	1993	1992	1991	1990	1989	1988
Revs.	282	241	185	176	157	121	101	76.0	98.0	80.0
Oper. Inc.	51.4	39.1	24.8	25.9	24.8	16.4	7.9	5.4	19.4	14.7
Depr.	11.0	9.8	6.4	5.8	5.0	3.0	3.1	2.4	1.5	1.9
Int. Exp.	NA	NA	NA	NA	NA	NA	NA	0.1	0.3	1.4
Pretax Inc.	29.6	25.9	1.7	11.2	19.5	14.2	1.0	3.5	18.1	11.7
Eff. Tax Rate	43%	36%	35%	NM	7.50%	9.40%	11%	3.30%	5.20%	2.70%
Net Inc.	16.8	16.6	11.1	17.5	18.1	12.9	0.9	3.3	17.1	11.4

Balance Sheet & Other Fin. Data (Million $)

	1997	1996	1995	1994	1993	1992	1991	1990	1989	1988
Cash	5.1	3.1	7.6	7.2	6.7	11.9	5.7	10.6	7.6	4.1
Curr. Assets	142	135	107	92.1	69.5	54.2	47.7	48.2	52.3	39.6
Total Assets	207	187	158	122	95.1	77.2	60.1	59.0	60.4	46.1
Curr. Liab.	65.8	80.5	71.3	43.6	39.2	31.8	22.8	21.9	23.9	23.7
LT Debt	Nil	Nil	Nil	Nil	Nil	Nil	Nil	Nil	0.2	0.5
Common Eqty.	126	100	82.8	74.7	54.7	43.3	37.0	36.5	35.4	19.2
Total Cap.	137	102	82.8	74.7	54.7	43.3	37.0	36.5	35.6	21.2
Cap. Exp.	6.2	2.8	2.6	4.4	3.0	2.4	2.5	2.0	1.1	1.4
Cash Flow	27.8	26.5	17.5	23.3	23.1	15.9	4.0	5.8	18.6	13.3
Curr. Ratio	2.2	1.7	1.5	2.1	1.8	1.7	2.1	2.2	2.2	1.7
% LT Debt of Cap.	Nil	Nil	Nil	Nil	Nil	Nil	Nil	Nil	0.5	2.2
% Net Inc.of Revs.	5.9	6.9	6.0	9.9	11.5	10.6	0.9	4.4	17.4	14.2
% Ret. on Assets	8.5	9.7	8.0	15.8	20.6	18.5	1.5	5.6	29.9	23.2
% Ret. on Equity	14.8	18.3	14.1	26.5	36.3	31.6	2.4	9.2	59.0	NM

Data as orig. reptd.; bef. results of disc. opers. and/or spec. items. Per share data adj. for stk. divs. as of ex-div. date. Bold denotes diluted EPS (FASB 128). E-Estimated. NA-Not Available. NM-Not Meaningful. NR-Not Ranked.

Office—540 Alder Dr., Milpitas, CA 95035. **Tel**—(408) 321-9100. **Website**—http://www.adaclabs.com **Chrmn**—D. L. Lowe. **Pres, COO & CEO**—R. A. Eckert. **VP-Fin, CFO & Treas**—P. A. Simone. **Investor Contact**—Andre Simone. **Secy**—K.L. Masterson.**Dirs**—S. D. Czerwinski, R. A. Eckert, G. O. King, D. L. Lowe, F. D. Rollo, E. H. Shea Jr. **Transfer Agent & Registrar**—Chase Trust Co. of California, SF. **Incorporated**—in California in 1970. **Empl**— 880. **S&P Analyst:** John J. Arege

STANDARD &POOR'S
STOCK REPORTS

Advanced Tissue Sciences   3028D

NASDAQ Symbol **ATIS**

In S&P SmallCap 600

03-OCT-98

Industry: Biotechnology

Summary: This company is engaged in the development and manufacture of living human tissue products for therapeutic applications.

Quantitative Evaluations	Recent Price • 3⅜	Yield • Nil
	52 Wk Range • 18⅜-1¾	12-Mo. P/E • NM

Outlook (1 Lowest—5 Highest)
• **NA**

Fair Value
• **NA**

Risk
• **High**

Earn./Div. Rank
• **C**

Technical Eval.
• **NA**

Rel. Strength Rank (1 Lowest—99 Highest)
• **71**

Insider Activity
• **Neutral**

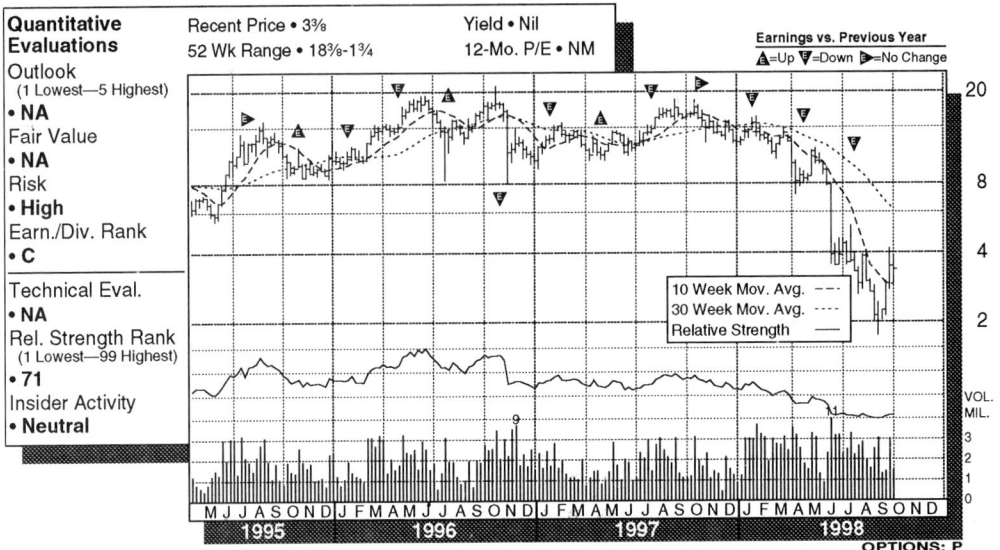

Earnings vs. Previous Year
▲=Up ▼=Down ▶=No Change

10 Week Mov. Avg. ---
30 Week Mov. Avg. ....
Relative Strength ——

OPTIONS: P

Business Profile - 11-SEP-98

ATIS is engaged in the worldwide commercialization of skin, cartilage and cardiovascular products. The two leading products are Dermagraft-TC, a temporary covering for severe and partial-thickness burns; and Dermagraft(R), a dermal replacement for diabetic foot ulcers. In January 1998, an FDA advisory Panel recommended FDA pre-market approval of Dermagraft(R). The product was launched in Canada and the U.K. during 1997. ATIS recently expanded its Dermagraft joint venture with Smith & Nephew PLC to include Dermagraft-TC (to be renamed TransCyte) for the treatment of burns in the U.S. As a result, the venture now has worldwide rights to market the product for all wound care applications.

Operational Review - 11-SEP-98

Revenues in the six months ended June 30, 1998, surged 55%, year to year, as higher product sales to the Dermagraft joint venture outweighed reduced amounts of contract fees recognized for R&D and clinical activities performed on behalf of several products. Sales in the 1998 period were also restricted by a voluntary recall of certain product lots of Dermagraft and Dermagraft-TC. Costs and expenses were well-controlled but continued to exceed revenues. After greater equity in losses of joint ventures and higher interest expense, the net loss widened to $22.9 million ($0.59 a share) from $15.6 million ($0.42).

Stock Performance - 02-OCT-98

In the past 30 trading days, ATIS's shares have increased 26%, compared to a 7% fall in the S&P 500. Average trading volume for the past five days was 289,040 shares, compared with the 40-day moving average of 428,728 shares.

Key Stock Statistics

Dividend Rate/Share	Nil	Shareholders	1,300
Shs. outstg. (M)	39.3	Market cap. (B)	$0.133
Avg. daily vol. (M)	0.378	Inst. holdings	21%
Tang. Bk. Value/Share	0.28		
Beta	0.97		

Value of $10,000 invested 5 years ago: $ 2,410

Fiscal Year Ending Dec. 31

	1998	1997	1996	1995	1994	1993
Revenues (Million $)						
1Q	5.31	2.65	1.23	1.11	0.66	2.72
2Q	4.43	3.62	11.86	1.10	0.61	1.37
3Q	—	3.27	2.10	1.24	0.98	1.28
4Q	—	3.61	1.77	1.30	0.97	0.50
Yr.	—	13.15	16.96	4.75	3.22	5.87
Earnings Per Share ($)						
1Q	-0.28	-0.20	-0.21	-0.18	-0.19	-0.10
2Q	-0.30	-0.22	0.05	-0.19	-0.19	-0.15
3Q	—	-0.24	-0.24	-0.16	-0.20	-0.19
4Q	—	-0.30	-0.21	-0.19	-0.17	-0.23
Yr.	—	-0.96	-0.61	-0.72	-0.75	-0.67

Next earnings report expected: mid November

Dividend Data

No cash dividends have been paid.

A Division of The McGraw-Hill Companies

Advanced Tissue Sciences, Inc.

Business Summary - 11-SEP-98

Advanced Tissue Sciences, Inc. is engaged in the development of living human tissue products for therapeutic applications. The company has a number of therapeutic tissue products in various stages of clinical trials, preclinical studies and research. Its primary product focus is currently directed toward skin (for burns and ulcers), orthopedic cartilage and cardiovascular products. Using principles of cell biology, biochemistry and polymer science, ATIS has developed and is applying its patented core technology that permits living human cells to be cultured ex vivo in a manner that allows the cells to develop and assemble into a functioning three-dimensional tissue.

These therapeutic skin products, designed as a temporary or permanent replacement for human dermis, were developed to treat conditions where the dermis (the inner skin layer) has been injured or destroyed. Their two lead products are Dermagraft-TC, a temporary covering for severe and partial-thickness burns; and Dermagraft(R), a dermal replacement for diabetic foot ulcers. In January 1998, an FDA advisory Panel recommended FDA pre-market approval of Dermagraft(R). In March 1998, the FDA issued a warning letter concerning the manufacturing and quality assurance processes for these products. ATIS continues to manufacture the products but implemented a voluntary recall of certain lots. In August 1997, the company received approval to market Dermagraft in Canada. In October 1997, Dermagraft(R) was launched in the U.K. through a 50/50 joint venture with Smith & Nephew.

ATIS has successfully replicated cartilage tissue ex vivo using its proprietary three-dimensional culture system. Through a joint venture with Smith & Nephew plc, it is developing several orthopedic applications of tissue engineered cartilage. The joint venture is currently in a pivotal preclinical trial for articular resurfacing.

As part of their joint venture, Smith & Nephew paid ATIS an initial fee of $10 million in 1996 and purchased $20 million of ATIS common stock. The company will receive an additional $15 million upon the earlier of FDA approval for the marketing of Dermagraft in the treatment of diabetic foot ulcers, or January 4, 1999. It could also receive, subject to the achievement of certain milestones, further payments of up to $136 million. The companies share equally in the expenses and revenues of the Joint Venture. In January 1998, the agreement was expanded to include venous ulcers, pressure sores, burns and other skin tissue wounds. Subsequently, in August 1998, the agreement was further expanded to include exclusive rights to Dermgraft-TC for full and partial-thickness burns in the U.S.

ATIS is also developing tissue engineered blood vessels that will grow and repair normally. This product is aimed toward minimizing or eliminating the potential for clotting or thrombogenesis.

Per Share Data ($)

(Year Ended Dec. 31)	1997	1996	1995	1994	1993	1992	1991	1990	1989	1988
Tangible Bk. Val.	0.33	1.26	0.73	0.90	0.89	1.57	NA	NA	NA	NA
Cash Flow	-0.90	-0.56	-0.67	-0.72	NA	NA	NA	NA	NA	NA
Earnings	-0.96	-0.61	-0.72	-0.75	-0.67	-1.40	NA	NA	NA	NA
Dividends	Nil	Nil	Nil	Nil	Nil	Nil	Nil	Nil	Nil	Nil
Payout Ratio	Nil	Nil	Nil	Nil	Nil	Nil	Nil	Nil	Nil	Nil
Prices - High	18½	21¼	15	9½	14	19¼	NA	NA	NA	NA
- Low	9⅞	8	5½	4¼	6½	7⅜	NA	NA	NA	NA
P/E Ratio - High	NM	NM	NM	NM	NM	NM	NM	NM	NM	NM
- Low	NM	NM	NM	NM	NM	NM	NM	NM	NM	NM

Income Statement Analysis (Million $)

	1997	1996	1995	1994	1993	1992	1991	1990	1989	1988
Revs.	13.2	14.6	3.6	2.0	4.9	0.8	NA	NA	NA	NA
Oper. Inc.	-21.1	-22.9	-22.9	-24.0	-18.5	-11.9	NA	NA	NA	NA
Depr.	2.1	1.8	1.4	1.1	0.9	0.6	NA	NA	NA	NA
Int. Exp.	0.9	0.0	0.0	0.0	NM	0.2	NA	NA	NA	NA
Pretax Inc.	-36.1	-22.4	-23.1	-22.8	-17.7	-32.0	NA	NA	NA	NA
Eff. Tax Rate	NM	NM	Nil	Nil	Nil	Nil	Nil	Nil	Nil	Nil
Net Inc.	-36.1	-22.4	-23.1	-22.8	-17.7	-32.0	NA	NA	NA	NA

Balance Sheet & Other Fin. Data (Million $)

	1997	1996	1995	1994	1993	1992	1991	1990	1989	1988
Cash	15.1	40.2	18.9	22.0	21.7	NA	NA	NA	NA	NA
Curr. Assets	23.1	44.0	21.0	24.1	23.0	NA	NA	NA	NA	NA
Total Assets	50.5	56.5	31.1	33.4	30.4	NA	NA	NA	NA	NA
Curr. Liab.	9.9	8.0	5.2	5.0	5.5	NA	NA	NA	NA	NA
LT Debt	26.2	0.1	0.0	0.0	0.1	NA	NA	NA	NA	NA
Common Eqty.	14.0	43.4	25.9	28.4	24.9	NA	NA	NA	NA	NA
Total Cap.	40.4	43.4	25.9	28.4	24.9	NA	NA	NA	NA	NA
Cap. Exp.	15.6	3.1	1.5	3.1	4.3	0.8	NA	NA	NA	NA
Cash Flow	-34.0	-20.6	-21.7	-21.7	16.8	-31.4	NA	NA	NA	NA
Curr. Ratio	2.3	5.5	4.0	4.8	4.2	NA	NA	NA	NA	NA
% LT Debt of Cap.	64.8	Nil	0.1	0.1	0.2	NA	NA	NA	NA	NA
% Net Inc.of Revs.	NM	NM	NM	NM	NM	NM	NM	NM	NM	NM
% Ret. on Assets	NM	NM	NM	NM	NM	NM	NM	NM	NM	NM
% Ret. on Equity	NM	NM	NM	NM	NM	NM	NM	NM	NM	NM

Data as orig. reptd.; bef. results of disc. opers. and/or spec. items. Per share data adj. for stk. divs. as of ex-div. date. Revs. in Income Statement tbl. do not incl. int. inc. E-Estimated. NA-Not Available. NM-Not Meaningful. NR-Not Ranked.

Office—10933 N. Torrey Pines Rd., La Jolla, CA 92037. **Tel**—(619) 450-5730. **Website**—http://www.advancedtissue.com **Chrmn & CEO**—A. J. Benvenuto. **Pres & COO**—G. K. Naughton. **VP-Fin & CFO**—M. V. Swanson. **Dirs**—A. J. Benvenuto, J. E. Groopman, J. L. Heckel, G. K. Naughton, R. L. Nelson, D. Ogden, D. S. Tappan, W. B. Walsh, G. R. Wilensky. **Transfer Agent**—ChaseMellon Shareholder Services, Ridgefield Park, NJ. **Incorporated**—in Delaware in 1987. **Empl**— 196. **S&P Analyst:** R.M.G.

03-OCT-98

Industry:
Services (Advertising & Marketing)

Summary: ADVO is the largest direct-mail marketing company in the U.S. It offers programs that pool advertisers and significantly reduce their postage costs.

Quantitative Evaluations

Outlook
(1 Lowest—5 Highest)
• **5+**

Fair Value
• **36¼**

Risk
• **High**

Earn./Div. Rank
• **B**

Technical Eval.
• **Bullish** since 3/98

Rel. Strength Rank
(1 Lowest—99 Highest)
• **46**

Insider Activity
• **Neutral**

Recent Price • 23⅝
52 Wk Range • 33⅝-18

Yield • Nil
12-Mo. P/E • 16.1

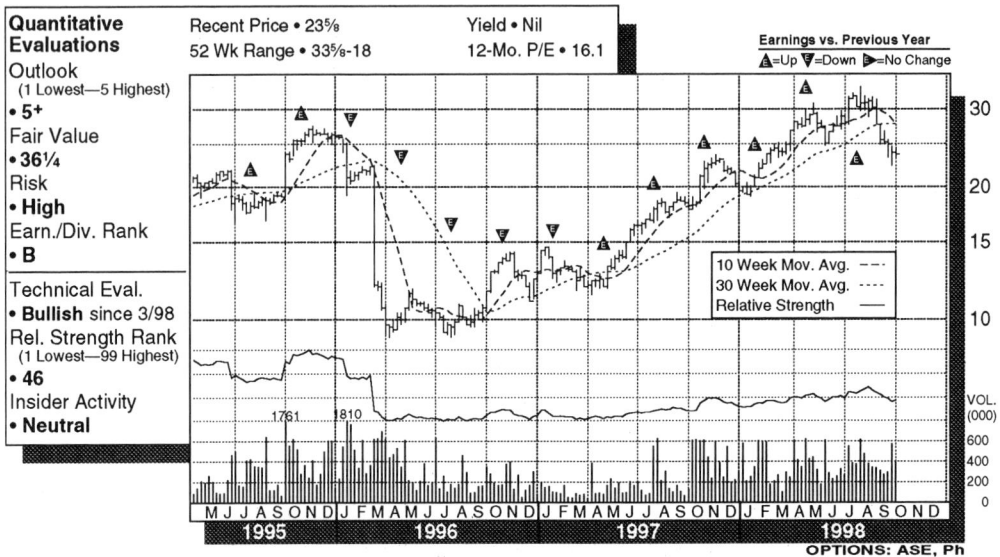

Earnings vs. Previous Year
▲=Up ▼=Down ▶=No Change

10 Week Mov. Avg. — — —
30 Week Mov. Avg. ·····
Relative Strength ——

VOL. (000)

OPTIONS: ASE, Ph

Business Profile - 31-AUG-98

AD shares have risen sharply since March 1997, reflecting strong earnings growth. Despite lackluster top-line growth in recent quarters, operating performance showed great improvement, driven by strict cost control efforts. One goal of the firm is to improve operating profit margin as a percentage of revenues. Based on AD's revenue per piece growth, management believes that results will remain strong for the rest of this year. The company expects that FY 98 (Sept.) full year results will be in line with current estimates. Effective in January 1999, the CEO of ADVO will step aside to succeeded by the company's current President and COO. As part of the senior management succession plan, the retiring CEO will remain with the company as Chairman.

Operational Review - 31-AUG-98

Revenues in the nine months ended June 27, 1998, rose 3.8%, year to year, due to an increase in revenue per piece, an improved product mix, and added sales resulting from the acquisition of MailHouse, Inc. Operating margins expanded through postage savings and strict cost controls that lowered both the cost of sales and SG&A as a percentage of revenue. Profitability was also enhanced by a reduced provision for bad debts and a decline in net interest expense and net income surged 42%, to $25,956,000 ($1.12 a share, on 6.3% fewer shares), from $18,225,000 ($0.74).

Stock Performance - 02-OCT-98

In the past 30 trading days, AD's shares have declined 22%, compared to a 7% fall in the S&P 500. Average trading volume for the past five days was 78,180 shares, compared with the 40-day moving average of 74,082 shares.

Key Stock Statistics

Dividend Rate/Share	Nil	Shareholders	900
Shs. outstg. (M)	22.4	Market cap. (B)	$0.529
Avg. daily vol. (M)	0.078	Inst. holdings	80%
Tang. Bk. Value/Share	NM		
Beta	0.95		

Value of $10,000 invested 5 years ago: $ 19,551

Fiscal Year Ending Sep. 30

	1998	1997	1996	1995	1994	1993
Revenues (Million $)						
1Q	262.1	255.1	256.5	248.1	246.8	228.0
2Q	253.2	242.5	232.0	239.6	229.7	212.8
3Q	269.0	258.2	245.7	256.7	256.1	235.4
4Q	—	260.6	251.9	267.5	242.9	234.6
Yr.	—	1,016	986.2	1,012	975.5	910.8
Earnings Per Share ($)						
1Q	**0.36**	**0.25**	0.29	0.44	0.29	—
2Q	**0.24**	0.11	-0.32	0.12	0.10	—
3Q	**0.52**	0.38	0.18	0.39	0.38	0.74
4Q	—	0.35	0.29	0.33	0.28	-0.53
Yr.	—	1.09	0.47	1.33	1.05	0.21

Next earnings report expected: NA

Dividend Data

A special cash dividend of $10 a share was paid in March 1996.

A Division of The **McGraw·Hill** *Companies*

Business Summary - 31-AUG-98

Established in 1929, this direct mail marketer is the U.S. Post Office's largest customer. ADVO, Inc. (AD) delivers more than 27 billion pieces of advertising annually to over 61 million households.

As a result of a difficult FY 96 (Sep.), AD underwent a major transformation, replacing its old geographic structure with one built around core processes such as sales, operations and finance. In addition, a new compensation plan for sales people, based upon profitability, rather than gross revenues, was instituted. As a way of enhancing shareholder value, AD effected a major recapitalization by issuing debt and paying out a special $10 a share dividend to its shareholders.

Fiscal 1997 proved to be successful year for ADVO, in respect to both operating performance and stock appreciation. Operating income surged 59%, on a 3% revenue increase, driven by a decrease in cost of sales. AD's shares followed suit, rising over 70% since March 1997.

Advo's Mailbox Values and Marriage Mail branded shared mail programs are currently distributed in 120 markets to over 61 million households weekly. In early FY 97, the company formed a new network, called A.N.N.E. (ADVO National Network Extension), which combines regional shared mail companies to provide its clients with extended coverage outside existing markets. The Mailbox Values and Marriage Mail programs combine the advertisements of several different customers in a single mail package, targeted by ZIP code. AD pays the total postage expense and charges advertisers a fee based upon the weight of their promotional pieces. Economies of scale allow AD to charge its customers one-third of the solo mail rate.

To serve its clients nationwide, AD employs approximately 2,700 production employees and operates 19 mail processing facilities and 65 sales offices. The company maintains a proprietary mailing list of over 114 million residential addresses, organized by ZIP code in letter carrier walk-sequence order. In addition, this list contains updated demographic, psychographic and consumer behavioral data to assist in the development of direct marketing solutions for its clients. Management believes this list is particularly valuable and that replication of it by competitors would be challenging and expensive.

For companies that wish to maintain an exclusive image and complete control over the timing and targeting of their mailings, AD provides solo mailing services including addressing and processing brochures and circulars for distribution through the U.S. Post Office. AD also rents its mailing list to organizations interested in distributing their own solo mailings.

Per Share Data ($) (Year Ended Sep. 30)	1997	1996	1995	1994	1993	1992	1991	1990	1989	1988
Tangible Bk. Val.	NM	NM	6.26	4.60	4.72	5.13	4.64	3.56	2.59	2.21
Cash Flow	1.82	1.10	1.89	1.51	0.57	1.21	1.18	1.05	0.52	0.04
Earnings	1.09	0.47	1.33	1.05	0.21	0.89	0.85	0.76	0.27	-0.31
Dividends	Nil	10.03	0.13	0.10	0.06	Nil	Nil	Nil	Nil	Nil
Payout Ratio	Nil	NM	9%	9%	29%	Nil	Nil	Nil	Nil	Nil
Prices - High	$23\frac{5}{8}$	$26\frac{1}{8}$	$27\frac{1}{2}$	20	$24\frac{3}{4}$	$22\frac{1}{4}$	$18\frac{7}{8}$	10	$8\frac{7}{8}$	$5\frac{1}{2}$
- Low	$11\frac{3}{8}$	$9\frac{1}{8}$	$16\frac{1}{2}$	15	$14\frac{1}{4}$	$12\frac{3}{8}$	9	$6\frac{3}{4}$	$3\frac{3}{4}$	3
P/E Ratio - High	22	56	21	19	118	25	22	13	33	NM
- Low	10	19	12	14	68	14	11	9	14	NM
Income Statement Analysis (Million $)										
Revs.	1,016	986	1,012	975	911	788	697	655	618	589
Oper. Inc.	76.8	52.0	59.2	51.6	41.8	36.2	33.0	28.7	12.7	-1.3
Depr.	18.2	15.2	13.0	11.0	9.2	7.6	7.3	6.2	5.9	5.1
Int. Exp.	14.8	9.7	NA	NA	0.2	Nil	Nil	Nil	Nil	0.0
Pretax Inc.	43.7	18.5	50.5	41.3	8.1	30.1	28.3	24.8	7.7	-5.8
Eff. Tax Rate	39%	40%	39%	39%	34%	32%	32%	34%	31%	NM
Net Inc.	26.8	11.3	30.9	25.2	5.4	20.5	19.3	16.4	5.3	-4.1
Balance Sheet & Other Fin. Data (Million $)										
Cash	26.0	13.3	54.5	71.1	71.4	65.7	52.6	41.6	22.2	7.6
Curr. Assets	116	104	156	151	151	129	104	88.0	62.0	52.0
Total Assets	209	209	234	226	227	190	156	133	108	99
Curr. Liab.	116	102	97.0	104	91.3	72.7	56.6	55.7	49.2	46.3
LT Debt	141	161	Nil	Nil	Nil	Nil	Nil	Nil	Nil	Nil
Common Eqty.	-59.9	-85.2	130	108	118	95.7	78.1	56.3	40.5	34.2
Total Cap.	90.3	82.5	136	112	118	116	98.0	76.0	59.0	50.0
Cap. Exp.	28.6	17.8	20.3	13.3	14.2	11.2	7.8	6.8	5.3	10.8
Cash Flow	45.0	26.5	43.9	36.1	14.6	28.1	26.6	22.5	11.2	0.5
Curr. Ratio	1.0	1.0	1.6	1.4	1.7	1.8	1.8	1.6	1.3	1.1
% LT Debt of Cap.	155.7	195.0	Nil	Nil	Nil	Nil	Nil	Nil	Nil	Nil
% Net Inc.of Revs.	2.6	1.1	3.0	2.6	0.6	2.6	2.8	2.5	0.9	NM
% Ret. on Assets	13.6	5.4	13.4	11.5	2.2	11.7	13.1	13.5	5.1	NM
% Ret. on Equity	NM	0.5	25.9	23.0	4.4	23.3	28.3	33.6	12.7	NM

Data as orig. reptd.; bef. results of disc. opers. and/or spec. items. Per share data adj. for stk. divs. as of ex-div. date. Divs. for fiscal 1996 incl. $10 spec. div. EPS for 3Q 1993 represent 9 mos. results. E-Estimated. NA-Not Available. NM-Not Meaningful. NR-Not Ranked.

Office—One Univac Lane, Windsor, CT 06095. **Tel**—(860) 285-6100. **Website**—http://www.advo.com **Chrmn & CEO**—R. Kamerschen. **Pres & COO**—G. M. Mulloy. **SVP, CFO & Investor Contact**—Donald McCombs (860-285-6391). **Dirs**—B. Crawford, D. F. Dyer, J. Eskridge, J. W. Fritz, R. Kamerschen, G. M. Mulloy, H. H. Newman, J. R. Rockwell, J. L. Vogelstein. **Transfer Agent & Registrar**—ChaseMellon Shareholder Services, East Hartford, CT. **Incorporated**—in Delaware in 1971. **Empl**— 4,700. **S&P Analyst:** Jordan Horoschak

03-OCT-98

Industry:
Air Freight

Summary: This company provides air and ocean freight forwarding and customs brokerage services. Foreign markets contribute a majority of revenues.

S&P Opinion: Accumulate (★★★★)	Recent Price • 15⅛	Yield • 1.6%
	52 Wk Range • 36¼-14¼	12-Mo. P/E • 10.4

Quantitative Evaluations

Outlook (1 Lowest—5 Highest)
• **4**

Fair Value
• **22⅞**

Risk
• **Low**

Earn./Div. Rank
• **B+**

Technical Eval.
• **Bearish** since 10/97

Rel. Strength Rank (1 Lowest—99 Highest)
• **22**

Insider Activity
• **Neutral**

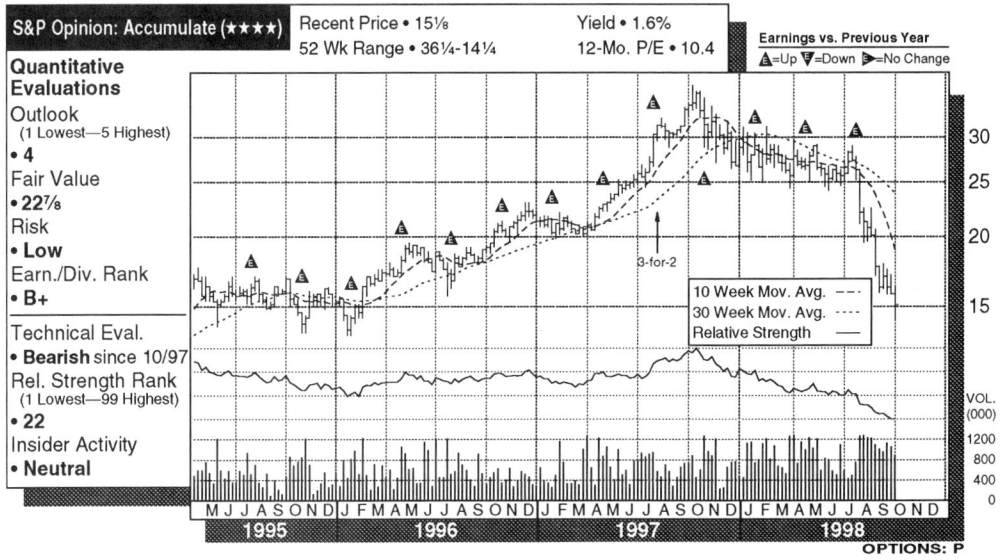

Earnings vs. Previous Year
▲=Up ▼=Down ▶=No Change

10 Week Mov. Avg. — — —
30 Week Mov. Avg. ....
Relative Strength ——

3-for-2

OPTIONS: P

Overview - 27-JUL-98

Air freight forwarding volume is projected to grow at a 10% pace in 1998, versus 14% in 1997. The fastest growth is anticipated on the international side, as domestic markets are hurt by a slowdown in the high-tech sector. Tightening its control over its international agents through equity investment should let the company's service levels improve, helping AEIC to expand its share of air forwarding business. Weak consumer demand in Asian countries will be offset by increased exports from those nations that have suffered sharp currency depreciation. AEIC will also benefit from expansion of its relationship with Caterpillar. Good growth is anticipated for ocean forwarding. Customs brokerage activity will slow. Terminal costs will rise less rapidly than revenues, and administrative costs will be held in check. However, acceleration in purchased transportation costs will limit improvement. Air freight rates will be stable in most markets. Net interest costs will ease. Comparisons will be restricted by the absence of a gain on the sale of a foreign affiliate.

Valuation - 27-JUL-98

The shares of this forwarder have fallen sharply since October 1997. Investors have been spooked by troubles in Asia. However, as demonstrated in first quarter results, faster exports from Asia have compensated for reduced import activity. Consequently, AEIC's overall growth rate is likely to be maintained. The shares also corrected because their P/E multiple far exceeded the company's expected growth rate. While a 1,000,000 stock repurchase plan was authorized in November 1997, no shares have yet been bought, as AEIC now anticipates deploying its cash for acquisitions. We think that valuations are now attractive but believe the shares may remain locked in a trading range until the situation in Asia begins to improve.

Key Stock Statistics

S&P EPS Est. 1998	1.60	Tang. Bk. Value/Share	6.08
P/E on S&P Est. 1998	9.5	Beta	1.15
S&P EPS Est. 1999	1.85	Shareholders	900
Dividend Rate/Share	0.24	Market cap. (B)	$0.524
Shs. outstg. (M)	34.6	Inst. holdings	72%
Avg. daily vol. (M)	0.213		

Value of $10,000 invested 5 years ago: $ 13,199

Fiscal Year Ending Dec. 31

	1998	1997	1996	1995	1994	1993
Revenues (Million $)						
1Q	372.4	351.2	294.8	280.0	204.8	153.0
2Q	378.5	386.6	320.7	299.4	238.0	168.5
3Q	—	395.4	340.9	314.3	258.1	192.1
4Q	—	412.6	379.1	328.6	296.4	211.8
Yr.	—	1,546	1,335	1,222	997.4	725.7
Earnings Per Share ($)						
1Q	**0.28**	**0.25**	0.22	0.19	0.13	0.13
2Q	**0.39**	**0.37**	0.33	0.28	0.24	0.20
3Q	—	**0.38**	0.32	0.26	0.24	0.14
4Q	—	**0.41**	0.35	0.32	0.25	0.18
Yr.	**E1.60**	**1.41**	1.21	1.05	0.85	0.66

Next earnings report expected: early November

Dividend Data (Dividends have been paid since 1991.)

Amount ($)	Date Decl.	Ex-Div. Date	Stock of Record	Payment Date
0.050	Nov. 14	Jan. 07	Jan. 09	Jan. 30 '98
0.050	Apr. 16	Apr. 17	Apr. 03	Apr. 24 '98
0.060	Jun. 18	Jul. 08	Jul. 10	Jul. 31 '98
0.060	Sep. 11	Oct. 07	Oct. 09	Oct. 30 '98

Business Summary - 27-JUL-98

Air Express International is a transportation intermediary; it buys transportation services in bulk from air and ocean carriers at wholesale rates, and makes a spread by offering at retail rates transportation consolidation services (or forwarding). Because freight forwarders face less competition from integrated air carriers in international markets, AEIC has focused on foreign markets (60% of 1997 total revenues). Growth in recent years was aided by acquisitions. Segment contributions to net revenues in recent years were:

	1997	1996
Air freight	64%	63%
Ocean freight	12%	12%
Customs brokerage & other	24%	25%

An air freight forwarder obtains shipments from or for its customers, consolidates those bound for common destinations, and delivers them in bulk to air carriers for transportation to various distribution points. Company employees or agents receive the shipments and distribute individual parcels to their final destinations. As a forwarder, AEIC neither owns nor operates aircraft, but is fully liable for lost or damaged shipments.

AEIC provides air freight services to 3,000 cities in more than 200 nations through a network of 711 offices. It owns and operates 44% of these facilities. In recent years, AEIC has sought greater control over its agents by making equity investments or full purchase. It believes that such tighter control, coupled with integration of operating systems, lets it deliver a higher and more consistent level of service. Accordingly, in December 1997, AEIC agreed to buy a 37% stake in Corporacion Cormar, its Costa Rican agent. In May 1997, it bought a 50% stake in its Korean agent.

AEIC's niche is the movement of heavy international cargo. In 1997 AEIC moved 2,097,000 shipments with an average weight of 554 lbs; in 1996 AEIC handled 1,839,000 shipments averaging 535 lbs.

As an ocean forwarder, AEIC provides consolidation services similar to those of its air operation, buying bulk space on container ships. In 1997, AEIC handled 122,000 container loads of freight, versus 95,000 in 1996.

An integral part of AEIC's service is to provide customs clearance. A customs broker prepares and assembles the required documents needed to move cargo through international gateways. AEIC also pays customs duties, arranges for transportation after clearance has been obtained, may place surety bonds on behalf of clients, recover excess duty payments and arrange for bonded warehouse services. The customs brokerage segment has been AEIC's fastest growing in recent years, aided by acquisitions. In 1996, AEIC acquired Radix Ventures, a U.S. broker, and John V. Carr & Sons, which operates in the U.S. and Canada.

Per Share Data ($)

(Year Ended Dec. 31)	1997	1996	1995	1994	1993	1992	1991	1990	1989	1988
Tangible Bk. Val.	6.04	4.90	2.47	1.81	1.57	1.54	1.46	0.91	0.35	-0.07
Cash Flow	1.86	1.60	1.41	1.15	0.90	0.99	0.75	0.66	0.50	0.52
Earnings	1.41	1.21	1.05	0.85	0.66	0.72	0.53	0.44	0.34	0.32
Dividends	0.19	0.19	0.09	0.12	0.08	0.05	0.02	Nil	Nil	Nil
Payout Ratio	13%	15%	9%	14%	11%	8%	4%	Nil	Nil	Nil
Prices - High	37⅛	23	17⅝	13⅜	13⅛	12¼	6⅜	3¾	3⅞	4¼
- Low	19⅞	13⅜	12⅜	8⅛	8	5⅞	2⅞	2⅛	2¾	2¼
P/E Ratio - High	26	19	17	16	20	17	12	8	11	13
- Low	14	11	12	10	12	8	5	5	8	7

Income Statement Analysis (Million $)

	1997	1996	1995	1994	1993	1992	1991	1990	1989	1988
Revs.	1,546	1,335	1,222	997	726	672	602	568	514	526
Oper. Inc.	86.8	71.4	59.3	45.9	37.7	39.0	30.2	27.6	21.2	21.5
Depr.	15.8	12.7	9.8	7.6	6.3	7.0	5.5	5.3	4.2	5.0
Int. Exp.	1.0	1.3	3.3	3.2	3.7	2.2	2.6	3.8	5.3	5.5
Pretax Inc.	79.1	62.1	47.6	36.8	28.0	29.9	23.0	19.2	14.9	13.5
Eff. Tax Rate	38%	38%	39%	39%	38%	38%	40%	42%	43%	39%
Net Inc.	49.5	38.5	29.0	22.6	17.3	18.6	13.8	11.1	8.5	8.2

Balance Sheet & Other Fin. Data (Million $)

	1997	1996	1995	1994	1993	1992	1991	1990	1989	1988
Cash	67.6	46.5	54.5	44.2	65.2	14.1	27.9	19.9	14.1	12.8
Curr. Assets	442	399	328	253	219	147	151	138	128	130
Total Assets	638	581	487	381	296	208	208	193	180	187
Curr. Liab.	307	299	251	194	139	136	118	112	107	117
LT Debt	31.0	16.6	82.8	84.0	78.5	7.1	24.9	28.4	32.3	36.2
Common Eqty.	292	259	148	99	78.1	65.4	65.3	52.4	40.5	33.4
Total Cap.	323	276	230	185	158	72.5	90.2	80.9	72.8	69.6
Cap. Exp.	18.7	13.8	20.4	12.1	4.9	15.2	6.8	6.4	3.0	4.5
Cash Flow	65.3	51.2	38.8	30.3	23.6	25.7	19.3	16.3	12.7	13.2
Curr. Ratio	1.4	1.3	1.3	1.3	1.6	1.1	1.3	1.2	1.2	1.1
% LT Debt of Cap.	9.6	6.0	36.0	45.4	49.8	9.8	27.6	35.2	44.4	52.0
% Net Inc.of Revs.	3.2	2.9	2.4	2.3	2.4	2.8	2.3	1.9	1.7	1.6
% Ret. on Assets	8.1	7.2	6.7	6.7	6.9	8.8	6.9	5.9	4.6	4.2
% Ret. on Equity	18.0	18.9	23.6	25.4	24.2	28.2	23.3	23.5	22.8	27.9

Data as orig. reptd.; bef. results of disc. opers. and/or spec. items. Per share data adj. for stk. divs. as of ex-div. date. E-Estimated. NA-Not Available. NM-Not Meaningful. NR-Not Ranked.

Registrar & Transfer Agent—Chemical Mellon Shareholder Services, NYC. **Office**—120 Tokeneke Rd., Darien, CT 06820. **Tel**—(203) 655-7900. **Website**—http://www.aeilogistics.com **Chrmn**—H. J. Hartong Jr. **Pres & CEO**—G. Rohrmann. **VP, CFO & Investor Contact**—Dennis M. Dolan (203-655-5713). **VP & Secy**—D. J. McCauley. **Dirs**—J. M. Fowler, H. J. Hartong Jr., D. J. Keller, A. L. Lewis IV, R. T. Niner, J. Radziwill, G. Rohrmann, N. E. Vargas. **Transfer Agent & Registrar**—ChaseMellon Shareholder Services, NYC. **Incorporated**—in Illinois in 1946; reincorporated in Delaware in 1982. **Empl**—7,419. **S&P Analyst:** Stephen R. Klein

Allen Telecom   60

NYSE Symbol **ALN**

In S&P SmallCap 600

03-OCT-98

Industry:
Communications
Equipment

Summary: This company (formerly Allen Group) primarily supplies equipment and services to the two-way wireless communications marketplace.

Quantitative Evaluations

Recent Price • 6⅜   Yield • Nil
52 Wk Range • 28⅜-6⅛   12-Mo. P/E • 33.6

Outlook
(1 Lowest—5 Highest)
• **5**
Fair Value
• **15¼**
Risk
• **High**
Earn./Div. Rank
• **B**

Technical Eval.
• **Bullish** since 9/98
Rel. Strength Rank
(1 Lowest—99 Highest)
• **20**
Insider Activity
• **Neutral**

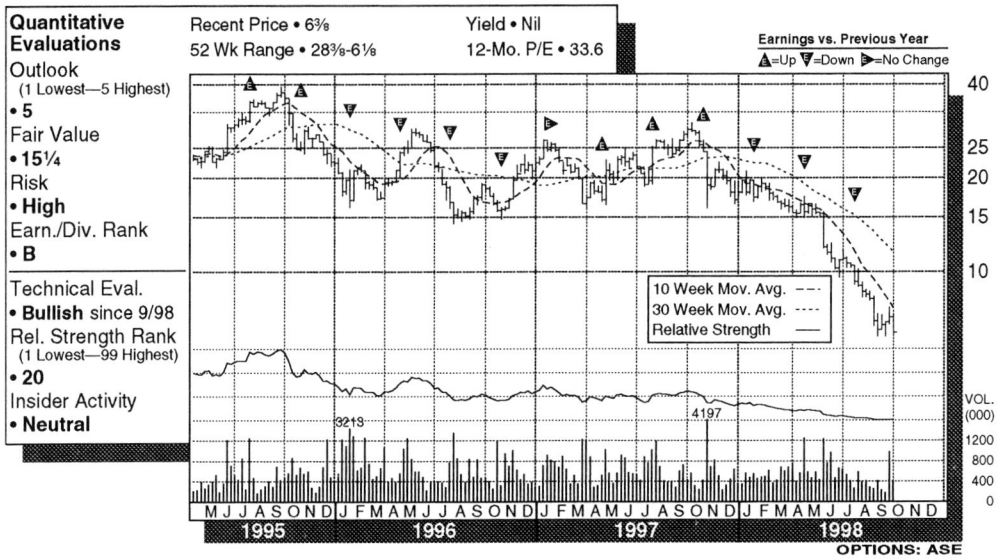

Earnings vs. Previous Year
▲=Up ▼=Down ►=No Change

10 Week Mov. Avg. - - -
30 Week Mov. Avg. ·····
Relative Strength —

OPTIONS: ASE

Business Profile - 08-SEP-98

In response to disappointing results in the second quarter of 1998, ALN took a $15.8 million special charge to reduce its workforce by 175 employees, or 7% of the total workforce, consolidate two manufacturing operations and discontinue development of the SmartCell wireless loop product, which did not gain adequate market acceptance. A short-term reduction in orders for site management components, as well as a decline in orders for system products, led to a revenue shortfall in the second quarter. ALN expects sales to improve in the second half of the year.

Operational Review - 08-SEP-98

Sales in the first half of 1998 were flat, year to year, as softness in the second quarter in both Asian and domestic markets coupled with the need for certain OEMs to reduce inventories offset strong growth in the first quarter. Gross margins narrowed, and results were hurt by increased operating costs, a $15.8 million special charge and the recognition of a $10.4 million loss reserve related to two telecom investments, which more than offset an $11.5 million pretax gain on the sale of ALN's investment in RF Micro Devices. A net loss of $4,796,000 ($0.18 a share) compared unfavorably with net income of $13,760,000 ($0.51).

Stock Performance - 02-OCT-98

In the past 30 trading days, ALN's shares have declined 22%, compared to a 7% fall in the S&P 500. Average trading volume for the past five days was 75,640 shares, compared with the 40-day moving average of 79,156 shares.

Key Stock Statistics

Dividend Rate/Share	Nil	Shareholders	1,900
Shs. outstg. (M)	27.4	Market cap. (B)	$0.175
Avg. daily vol. (M)	0.089	Inst. holdings	69%
Tang. Bk. Value/Share	4.49		
Beta	2.14		

Value of $10,000 invested 5 years ago: NA

Fiscal Year Ending Dec. 31

	1998	1997	1996	1995	1994	1993
Revenues (Million $)						
1Q	113.4	102.5	84.47	59.27	76.94	66.00
2Q	98.01	108.9	88.46	83.88	81.77	69.41
3Q	—	111.4	95.01	88.30	84.48	65.60
4Q	—	109.8	101.6	83.93	88.16	79.00
Yr.	—	432.5	369.5	315.4	331.4	280.0
Earnings Per Share ($)						
1Q	**0.23**	**0.26**	0.18	0.27	0.21	0.28
2Q	**-0.41**	**0.25**	0.21	0.35	0.25	0.29
3Q	—	**0.29**	0.13	0.35	0.33	0.30
4Q	—	**0.08**	0.25	0.25	0.33	0.32
Yr.	—	**0.88**	0.76	1.22	1.12	1.19

Next earnings report expected: late October

Dividend Data

Dividends, omitted in 1987 and resumed in 1991, were omitted again in September 1996. A "poison pill" stock purchase rights plan was adopted in 1988.

A Division of The McGraw-Hill Companies

Business Summary - 08-SEP-98

Allen Telecom changed its name from The Allen Group Inc. in February 1997, in order to emphasize its shift away from the automotive business and toward wireless communications products. A leading supplier of equipment and services to the worldwide two-way wireless communications market, the company intends to use the Allen Telecom name as a unifying entity under which it can present a broad range of products with strong brand names. In September 1995, ALN completed the spinoff of its entire truck products segment into a new entity, TransPro. In 1996, the company decided to exit the automotive emissions testing business, and now accounts for that business as a discontinued operation.

Products sold by Allen include system expansion, site management, and mobile and base station antennas for the worldwide wireless communications market. Demand for the company's equipment is a function of the development of wireless communications systems around the world, along with ALN's ability to develop new products and technologies related to system coverage and capacity and components for other manufacturers' wireless systems. In 1995, the company introduced its Smartcell microcell, which can enhance

geographic coverage, and can also serve as a platform for wireless PBX systems. Other recent product introductions included new wireless test and measurement products that have applications in cellular, PCS, trunking and paging systems.

The Comsearch division provides frequency planning and coordinating services, as well as system design and field engineering services and software products for the wireless markets and PCS market. Through its expertise in spectrum sharing, microwave interconnectivity, microwave migration and system design, the subsidiary has been able to obtain orders from most major PCS carriers.

International sales have increased steadily over the years, and totaled 60% of sales in 1997. ALN continues to see significant growth in international markets in the future as existing cellular systems are expanded and new cellular licenses are granted, and as other parts of the world begin to install advanced wireless systems. Export sales from the U.S. are primarily to major wireless telephone companies. European sales are primarily to major European original equipment manufacturers and cellular or PCS operators. Four major telecommunications equipment companies together accounted for about 22% of sales in 1997.

Per Share Data ($)

(Year Ended Dec. 31)	1997	1996	1995	1994	1993	1992	1991	1990	1989	1988
Tangible Bk. Val.	4.91	5.60	5.35	6.30	7.52	1.97	4.46	3.77	4.04	3.22
Cash Flow	1.47	1.28	1.63	1.47	1.56	1.19	1.01	0.08	0.82	0.51
Earnings	0.88	0.76	1.22	1.12	1.19	0.81	0.68	-0.28	0.34	-0.04
Dividends	Nil	Nil	0.20	0.17	0.22	0.10	0.05	Nil	Nil	Nil
Payout Ratio	Nil	Nil	16%	15%	18%	13%	7%	Nil	Nil	NM
Prices - High	30	28⁷/₈	39³/₈	25⁵/₈	29¹/₄	15	10¹/₈	9¹/₈	7⁵/₈	6³/₈
- Low	16	14¹/₄	21¹/₄	13¹/₂	13	9¹/₂	4¹/₂	4¹/₂	4¹/₈	3⁵/₈
P/E Ratio - High	34	38	32	23	25	19	15	NM	23	NM
- Low	18	19	17	12	11	12	7	NM	12	NM

Income Statement Analysis (Million $)

	1997	1996	1995	1994	1993	1992	1991	1990	1989	1988
Revs.	433	369	315	331	280	296	262	352	362	344
Oper. Inc.	66.0	66.1	60.7	56.8	44.1	41.5	33.0	38.7	34.1	27.9
Depr.	16.2	14.1	11.1	9.2	8.3	7.4	6.3	6.7	8.7	9.7
Int. Exp.	4.5	3.8	3.2	4.4	3.2	6.8	7.0	11.2	10.4	11.2
Pretax Inc.	46.7	46.5	47.8	46.9	33.0	23.7	18.4	3.0	15.0	7.0
Eff. Tax Rate	38%	42%	40%	38%	11%	16%	9.40%	142%	32%	52%
Net Inc.	24.0	20.6	32.6	29.2	29.5	19.9	16.6	-1.3	10.2	3.4

Balance Sheet & Other Fin. Data (Million $)

	1997	1996	1995	1994	1993	1992	1991	1990	1989	1988
Cash	30.8	23.9	15.7	55.2	11.2	4.4	7.5	0.8	22.7	14.4
Curr. Assets	242	199	178	178	131	164	159	179	186	208
Total Assets	514	411	364	358	325	388	308	330	318	328
Curr. Liab.	131	105	84.4	70.0	59.0	NA	NA	70.0	73.0	135
LT Debt	97.9	50.0	47.0	45.0	52.0	131	93.0	114	101	66.0
Common Eqty.	261	226	210	224	195	102	84.0	71.0	74.0	58.0
Total Cap.	366	295	257	271	247	291	236	242	233	182
Cap. Exp.	22.2	17.5	16.8	8.9	11.4	6.7	5.0	6.6	7.4	10.5
Cash Flow	40.2	34.7	43.7	38.4	35.7	23.3	18.9	1.4	14.9	9.1
Curr. Ratio	1.8	1.9	2.1	2.5	2.2	NA	NA	2.5	2.6	1.5
% LT Debt of Cap.	26.8	16.9	18.3	16.6	21.0	45.1	39.5	47.1	43.2	36.4
% Net Inc.of Revs.	5.5	5.6	10.4	8.8	10.5	6.7	6.3	NM	2.8	1.0
% Ret. on Assets	5.2	5.3	9.1	8.5	7.1	5.6	5.2	NM	3.1	1.1
% Ret. on Equity	9.9	9.4	15.1	13.9	16.7	16.6	16.2	NM	9.2	NM

Data as orig. reptd.; bef. results of disc. opers. and/or spec. items. Per share data adj. for stk. divs. as of ex-div. date. Bold denotes diluted EPS (FASB 128). E-Estimated. NA-Not Available. NM-Not Meaningful. NR-Not Ranked.

Office—25101 Chagrin Blvd., Suite 350, Beachwood, OH 44122. **Tel**—(216) 765-5818. **Website**—http://www.allentelecom.com **Chrmn**—P. W. Colburn. **Pres & CEO**—R. G. Paul.**EVP & CFO**—R. A. Youdelman. **VP, Treas & Contr**—J. L. LePorte, III.**VP & Secy**—M. P. Folan III. **Investor Contact**—Dianne B. McCormick.**Dirs**—P. W. Colburn, J. K. Conway, A. H. Gordon, W. O. Hunt, J. C. Lyons, J. F. McNiff, R. G. Paul, C. W. Robinson, M. F. Roetter, W. M. Weaver Jr. **Transfer Agent & Registrar**—Harris Trust Co. of New York, Cleveland.**Incorporated**—in Michigan in 1928; reincorporated in Delaware in 1969. **Empl**— 3,300. **S&P Analyst:** Jim Corridore

03-OCT-98

Industry:
Health Care (Drugs - Generic & Other)

Summary: This biotechnology firm is developing drugs based on its perfluorochemical technology, including a blood substitute and an intrapulmonary oxygen carrier.

Quantitative Evaluations	
Outlook (1 Lowest—5 Highest) • **NA**	
Fair Value • **NA**	
Risk • **High**	
Earn./Div. Rank • **C**	

Technical Eval.
• **Bullish** since 3/98

Rel. Strength Rank
(1 Lowest—99 Highest)
• **30**

Insider Activity
• **Favorable**

Recent Price • 3¼
52 Wk Range • 12⅞-2⅜

Yield • Nil
12-Mo. P/E • NM

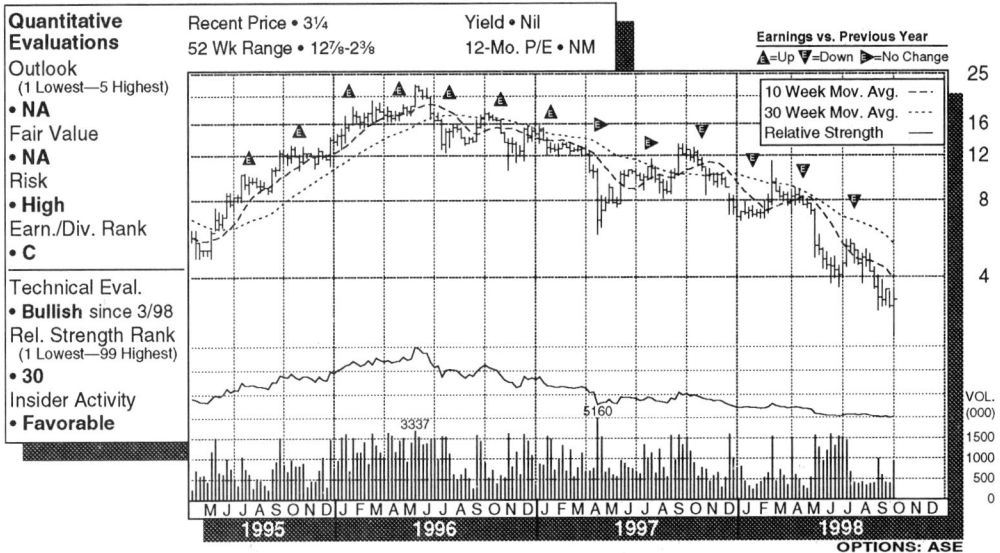

Earnings vs. Previous Year
▲=Up ▼=Down ▶=No Change

10 Week Mov. Avg. — - —
30 Week Mov. Avg. - - - -
Relative Strength ——

OPTIONS: ASE

Business Profile - 28-SEP-98

ALLP has been unprofitable since inception, and expects to continue to spend substantial amounts on R&D, preclinical and clinical testing, regulatory activities, and commercial start-up. The company has three products in or nearing late stage clinical (human) testing; Imagent (Phase III), Oxygent and LiquiVent (both in Phase II). In May 1998, ALLP restructured its collaboration with Johnson & Johnson (J&J). ALLP is now solely responsible for the costs and further development of Oxygent, as it approaches Phase III; J&J retained exclusive marketing rights to the product. In August 1998, the firm sold 100,000 shares of convertible preferred stock for $6 million, and in September, ALLP filed to issue 1,750,000 additional common shares, which may be issued to holders of the new preferred shares.

Operational Review - 28-SEP-98

Revenues for FY 98 (Jun.) fell 52%, year to year, reflecting decreased milestone payments, and the termination of a license agreement with Hoechst Marion Roussel. Despite a 16% rise in R&D expenditures related to higher product development costs, operating expenses declined 17%, due to the absence of a $16,450,000 charge from the acquisition of MDV Technologies, Inc. Following lower other income, the net loss widened to $33,003,000 ($1.04 a share, on 5% more shares), from $19,016,000 ($0.63). Cash and short-term investments totaled $50 million at the end of FY 98.

Stock Performance - 02-OCT-98

In the past 30 trading days, ALLP's shares have declined 22%, compared to a 7% fall in the S&P 500. Average trading volume for the past five days was 186,380 shares, compared with the 40-day moving average of 112,941 shares.

Key Stock Statistics

Dividend Rate/Share	Nil	Shareholders	1,700
Shs. outstg. (M)	32.0	Market cap. (B)	$0.104
Avg. daily vol. (M)	0.124	Inst. holdings	36%
Tang. Bk. Value/Share	2.07		
Beta	1.44		

Value of $10,000 invested 5 years ago: $ 2,826

Fiscal Year Ending Jun. 30

	1998	1997	1996	1995	1994	1993
Revenues (Million $)						
1Q	6.54	5.75	2.15	5.18	0.15	0.76
2Q	5.27	22.13	2.04	2.03	0.10	0.48
3Q	4.33	6.84	7.23	2.48	0.12	0.58
4Q	5.07	9.87	5.91	2.13	0.04	0.55
Yr.	21.21	44.58	17.32	11.82	0.41	2.37
Earnings Per Share ($)						
1Q	**-0.20**	-0.15	-0.31	-0.38	-0.41	-0.26
2Q	**-0.24**	-0.18	-0.29	-0.34	-0.52	-0.37
3Q	**-0.32**	-0.15	-0.15	-0.31	-0.38	-0.37
4Q	**-0.28**	-0.16	-0.16	-0.40	-0.52	-0.39
Yr.	**-1.04**	-0.63	-0.91	-1.35	-1.83	-1.39

Next earnings report expected: mid November

Dividend Data

No cash has been paid.

 A Division of The McGraw-Hill Companies

Alliance Pharmaceutical Corp.

3063E
03-OCT-98

Business Summary - 28-SEP-98

Alliance Pharmaceutical Corp. (ALLP) develops medical therapeutic products based on perfluorochemical and emulsion technologies. The company focuses on licensing its scientific discoveries to multinational pharmaceutical companies in exchange for fixed payments and royalties. To date, ALLP has three products in or entering late stage human clinical trials.

Oxygent (perflubron emulsion) is a temporary intravascular oxygen carrier, or "blood substitute," for use in combination with autologous blood conservation methods to maintain tissue oxygenation during moderate to high-blood-loss surgeries. Data from two Phase II clinical trials using Oxygent as a temporary blood substitute during surgery demonstrated that it enhanced oxygenation status and reversed transfusion triggers more frequently and for longer duration than fresh blood. ALLP received a $15 million milestone payment from its collaborating partner, Johnson & Johnson (J&J), in December 1996. In May 1998, ALLP restructured its agreement with J&J and is now solely responsible for the costs and further development of Oxygent, as it approaches Phase III; J&J retained exclusive marketing rights to the product.

LiquiVent (sterile perflubron) is being developed as an intrapulmonary oxygen carrier to reduce a patient's exposure to the harmful effects of mechanical ventilation. ALLP has temporarily suspended its Phase III studies with pediatric patients for protocol review. The company intends to initiate a Phase II/III clinical study for Li-

quiVent before the end of calender 1998. The FDA has granted LiquiVent Subpart E ("fast track") status due to the life threatening nature of the condition it treats.

In December 1997, Hoechst Marion Roussel, Inc. (HMRI) terminated its agreement with ALLP, in which it had agreed to pay most of the marketing and development costs for LiquiVent and make various milestone payments to ALLP in exchange for worldwide manufacturing rights. The company has not been reimbursed for LiquiVent development expenses since July 1, 1997, and will now be responsible for these expenses. As a result the company expects a continued decrease in 1998 revenues and milestone payments.

Alliance is also conducting Phase II and III studies with Imagent, an intravenous contrast agent for the enhancement of ultrasound images. Imagent is being developed jointly by ALLP and Germany's Schering AG to aid in the assessment of cardiac function and myocardial perfusion, and to improve the detection of blood flow abnormalities, and organ lesions in the breast, prostate, liver, and kidneys.

In November 1996, Alliance acquired MDV Technologies Inc., and its thermo-reversible gel product, FloGel, a potential anti-adhesion treatment for persons undergoing abdominal or pelvic surgeries. ALLP is preparing the FloGel formulation to begin clinical trials in the U.S.

In August 1998, the company sold 100,000 shares of convertible preferred stock for $6 million, and in September, filed to issue 1,750,000 common shares, which may be issued to holders of the new preferred shares.

Per Share Data ($)

(Year Ended Jun. 30)	1998	1997	1996	1995	1994	1993	1992	1991	1990	1989
Tangible Bk. Val.	2.07	2.93	3.38	1.32	2.33	2.68	3.99	0.91	1.93	1.30
Cash Flow	-0.88	-0.50	-0.79	-1.22	-1.67	-1.24	-1.09	-1.02	-0.82	-4.04
Earnings	-1.04	-0.63	-0.91	-1.35	-1.83	-1.39	-1.25	-1.24	-0.94	-4.12
Dividends	Nil	Nil	Nil	Nil	Nil	Nil	Nil	Nil	Nil	Nil
Payout Ratio	Nil	Nil	Nil	Nil	Nil	Nil	Nil	Nil	Nil	Nil
Prices - High	11³/₈	15³/₄	22⁷/₈	14¹/₄	12¹/₄	15	44	32¹/₄	12¹/₂	14¹/₂
- Low	2⁷/₈	5⁷/₈	10¹/₂	4¹/₄	5⁵/₈	7¹/₄	8¹/₄	9	5¹/₄	7⁷/₈
P/E Ratio - High	NM	NM	NM	NM	NM	NM	NM	NM	NM	NM
- Low	NM	NM	NM	NM	NM	NM	NM	NM	NM	NM

Income Statement Analysis (Million $)

	1998	1997	1996	1995	1994	1993	1992	1991	1990	1989
Revs.	21.2	44.6	17.3	11.8	0.4	2.4	1.8	1.6	1.7	2.3
Oper. Inc.	-31.7	2.6	-20.5	-27.5	-35.4	-25.8	-19.8	-15.4	-12.8	-4.3
Depr.	5.1	4.0	3.1	2.9	3.1	3.0	2.8	3.1	1.6	0.6
Int. Exp.	Nil	Nil	Nil	NM	NM	0.0	0.3	0.9	0.9	0.1
Pretax Inc.	-33.0	-19.0	-22.2	-29.1	-36.9	26.4	-21.8	-17.7	-12.5	-30.8
Eff. Tax Rate	NM	NM	NM	NM	NM	NM	Nil	Nil	Nil	Nil
Net Inc.	-33.0	-19.0	-22.2	-29.1	-36.9	-26.4	-21.8	-17.7	-12.5	-31.3

Balance Sheet & Other Fin. Data (Million $)

	1998	1997	1996	1995	1994	1993	1992	1991	1990	1989
Cash	11.8	71.6	71.4	23.4	21.1	39.5	66.4	16.8	30.6	20.9
Curr. Assets	57.4	80.0	79.0	27.5	22.4	42.7	68.2	17.7	32.0	21.8
Total Assets	93.7	112	108	56.0	53.1	72.5	98.0	44.8	59.5	48.1
Curr. Liab.	8.7	17.8	5.7	5.1	3.0	3.0	2.7	2.0	2.1	1.9
LT Debt	8.9	2.7	0.9	Nil	Nil	Nil	0.2	8.3	8.5	8.6
Common Eqty.	76.1	91.3	101	50.1	49.8	69.1	94.6	33.9	48.8	37.5
Total Cap.	85.0	94.1	102	50.1	49.8	69.1	94.8	42.2	57.3	46.2
Cap. Exp.	10.1	6.8	4.0	1.3	1.9	2.5	3.6	1.3	3.0	0.9
Cash Flow	-27.9	-15.0	-20.1	-26.9	-33.9	-23.4	-19.0	-14.6	-10.9	-30.7
Curr. Ratio	6.6	4.5	13.8	5.4	7.6	14.5	25.6	8.7	15.0	11.3
% LT Debt of Cap.	10.5	2.9	1.0	Nil	Nil	Nil	0.2	19.8	14.8	18.7
% Net Inc.of Revs.	NM	NM	NM	NM	NM	NM	NM	NM	NM	NM
% Ret. on Assets	NM	NM	NM	NM	NM	NM	NM	NM	NM	NM
% Ret. on Equity	NM	NM	NM	NM	NM	NM	NM	NM	NM	NM

Data as orig. reptd.; bef. results of disc. opers. and/or spec. items. Per share data adj. for stk. divs. as of ex-div. date. Bold denotes diluted EPS (FASB 128). E-Estimated. NA-Not Available. NM-Not Meaningful. NR-Not Ranked.

Office—3040 Science Park Rd., San Diego, CA 92121. **Tel**—(619) 558-4300. **Website**—http://www.allp.com **Chrmn & CEO**—D. J. Roth. **Pres & COO**—T. D. Roth. **CFO & Treas.**—T. T. Hart. **Dirs**—P. Cuatrecasas, C. O. Johnson, S. M. McGrath, D. E. O'Neill, H. M. Ranney, J. G. Riess, D. J. Roth, T. D. Roth, T. F. Zuck. **Transfer Agent & Registrar**—American Stock Transfer Co., NYC. **Incorporated**—in New York in 1983. **Empl**— 284.
S&P Analyst: David Moskowitz

Alliant Techsystems   64D

NYSE Symbol **ATK**

In S&P SmallCap 600

03-OCT-98

Industry: Aerospace/Defense

Summary: This aerospace and defense company has munitions, space and strategic propulsion, defense systems, and emerging business operations, and an integration program.

Quantitative Evaluations

Outlook (1 Lowest—5 Highest)
- **4+**

Fair Value
- **85¼**

Risk
- **Low**

Earn./Div. Rank
- **NR**

Technical Eval.
- **Bearish** since 7/98

Rel. Strength Rank (1 Lowest—99 Highest)
- **91**

Insider Activity
- **NA**

Recent Price • 68
52 Wk Range • 68⅞-53¾
Yield • Nil
12-Mo. P/E • 13.1

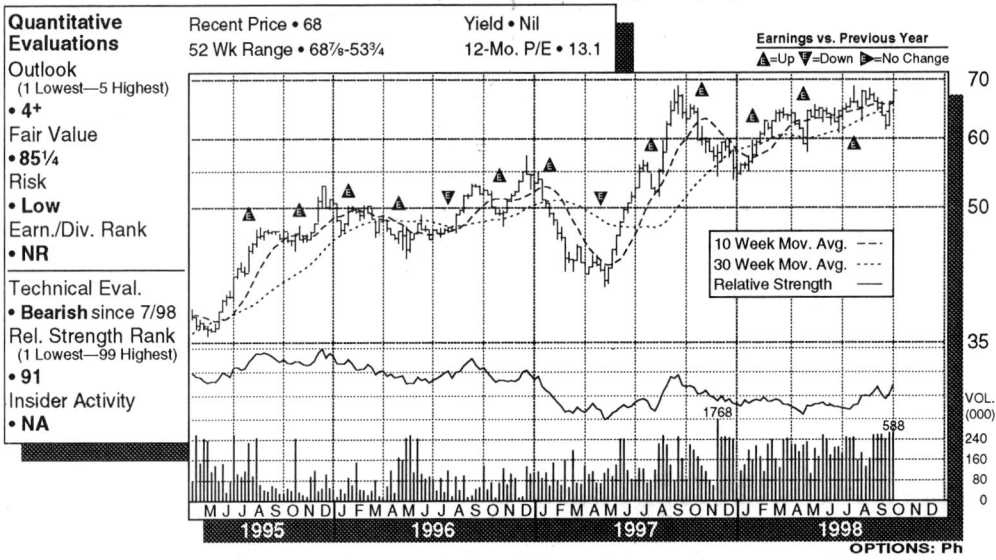

Earnings vs. Previous Year
▲=Up ▼=Down ▶=No Change

10 Week Mov. Avg. ---
30 Week Mov. Avg. ·····
Relative Strength —

OPTIONS: Ph

Business Profile - 31-AUG-98

ATK has been enhancing its international operations, developing commercial applications, and pursuing several defense programs. It has also consolidated operations. In FY 98 (Mar.) and again in FY 99, it reorganized its operations. ATK recorded an after tax gain of $1.32 a share in FY 97, from the sale of the Marine Systems Group. In October 1997, Hercules, Inc. (NYSE: HPC) agreed to sell its 30% stake in ATK, and subsequently sold 21.8 million shares in a public offering. Thus far in 1998, ATK has repurchased 813,000 shares from HPC, and will buy back 271,000 more later in the year. The company has repurchased more than 12% of its shares since April 1995. In August 1998, ATK began a cash tender offer for its $150 million of 11.75% senior subordinated notes.

Operational Review - 31-AUG-98

Sales in the three months ended June 30, 1998, edged up 1.9%, year to year, as lower defense systems volume outweighed increased space and strategic systems sales, and slightly higher conventional munitions volume. Results benefited from well controlled operating costs, improved operating efficiencies, and lower interest expense; net income was up 7.8%, to $15,801,000 ($1.21 a share, diluted), from $14,657,000 ($1.10). ATK continues to aim for 15% average EPS growth, through wider margins and the effective use of its strong cash flow. Backlog at June 28, 1998, reached $2.4 billion. ATK projects sales for FY 99 at $1.1 billion.

Stock Performance - 02-OCT-98

In the past 30 trading days, ATK's shares have increased 1%, compared to a 7% fall in the S&P 500. Average trading volume for the past five days was 117,660 shares, compared with the 40-day moving average of 77,782 shares.

Key Stock Statistics

Dividend Rate/Share	Nil	Shareholders	13,000
Shs. outstg. (M)	12.7	Market cap. (B)	$0.862
Avg. daily vol. (M)	0.094	Inst. holdings	74%
Tang. Bk. Value/Share	7.53		
Beta	NA		

Value of $10,000 invested 5 years ago: $ 23,777

Fiscal Year Ending Mar. 31

	1999	1998	1997	1996	1995	1994
Revenues (Million $)						
1Q	256.3	251.6	230.2	292.9	168.9	168.5
2Q	—	266.9	247.7	267.6	137.2	137.9
3Q	—	269.2	300.8	298.2	173.2	169.7
4Q	—	287.7	310.8	335.0	309.7	299.3
Yr.	—	1,076	1,089	1,194	789.1	775.3
Earnings Per Share ($)						
1Q	1.21	1.10	0.57	0.78	0.68	0.83
2Q	—	1.18	0.85	0.86	-1.44	0.82
3Q	—	1.33	1.20	1.10	0.37	0.84
4Q	—	1.45	0.11	1.69	-6.45	0.71
Yr.	—	5.08	2.73	4.43	-7.22	3.21

Next earnings report expected: NA

Dividend Data

No cash dividends have been paid on the common stock since its distribution in October 1990. Poison pill stock purchase rights were distributed with the common stock.

A Division of The McGraw-Hill Companies

STANDARD
&POOR'S
STOCK REPORTS

Alliant Techsystems Inc.

64D

03-OCT-98

Business Summary - 31-AUG-98

Alliant Techsystems (ATK) continues to focus on improving its core businesses and strengthening its market leadership through mergers and acquisitions. The sale of the marine systems unit during FY 97 (Mar.) improved the company's financial position and increased its strategic flexibility.

In early FY 98, ATK reorganized its operations into four business groups: conventional munitions, space and strategic systems, defense systems, and emerging business. In April 1998, the company again reorganized, eliminating its emerging business. The reorganization will allow management to focus more on the conventional and smart weapons market.

The Conventional Munitions Group supplies and develops medium caliber ammunition, tank ammunition, munitions propellants, commercial gun powders, solid rocket propulsion systems, flares, warheads, and composite structures for the U.S. and allied governments, as well as for commercial applications.

The Space and Strategic Systems group produces solid propulsion systems for space launch vehicles and strategic missile systems, and provides reinforced composite structures and components for aircraft, space-

craft and space launch vehicles, and provides safety management services. In August 1998, it opened a new 110,000 sq. ft. plant, which will be used for the manufacture of composite structures for the new Boeing Delta IV family of space launch vehicles. ATK estimates its long-term contract with Boeing to be worth $1 billion.

The Defense Systems business is engaged in development and production of smart munitions, electronic systems and unmanned vehicles.

In January 1998, ATK received a $91 million contract to produce tank ammunition training rounds for the U.S. Army.

Backlog at the end of FY 98 was $1.7 billion. Orders increased to $1.4 billion from $822 million a year earlier. The debt to capital ratio dropped to 43% in FY 98, from 55% in FY 97 and 72% in FY 96. In FY 98, 82% of sales were derived from contracts with the U.S. government.

Chairman and CEO Richard Schwartz retired on September 1, 1998, but will remain a director and chairman until January 1, 1999, at which time he will become a consultant to the company. President and COO Peter A. Buckowick will serve as acting CEO until a permanent successor is found.

Per Share Data ($)

(Year Ended Mar. 31)	1998	1997	1996	1995	1994	1993	1992	1991	1990	1989
Tangible Bk. Val.	6.92	7.11	NM	5.51	6.44	5.21	16.92	NA	13.06	NA
Cash Flow	8.63	6.67	9.08	-4.74	5.23	-2.03	7.50	NA	6.08	5.78
Earnings	5.08	2.73	4.43	-7.22	3.21	-4.68	4.57	NA	2.55	2.81
Dividends	Nil	Nil	Nil	Nil	Nil	Nil	Nil	Nil	Nil	NA
Payout Ratio	Nil	Nil	Nil	Nil	Nil	Nil	Nil	Nil	Nil	NA
Cal. Yrs.	1997	1996	1995	1994	1993	1992	1991	1990	1989	1988
Prices - High	69	57³/₈	53	40⁵/₈	31	28⁵/₈	29¹/₄	15¹/₄	NA	NA
- Low	40¹/₂	43³/₄	34⁷/₈	21³/₄	22	19¹/₈	13	8⁵/₈	NA	NA
P/E Ratio - High	14	21	12	NM	10	NM	6	6	NA	NA
- Low	8	16	8	NM	7	NM	3	3	NA	NA

Income Statement Analysis (Million $)

	1998	1997	1996	1995	1994	1993	1992	1991	1990	1989
Revs.	1,076	1,089	1,194	789	775	1,005	1,187	NA	1,248	1,259
Oper. Inc.	140	123	177	42.6	60.0	86.0	120	NA	118	115
Depr.	47.5	52.7	62.4	25.0	20.5	26.9	29.2	NA	33.7	31.6
Int. Exp.	27.6	35.1	45.1	11.4	8.2	22.7	16.2	NA	10.8	13.5
Pretax Inc.	67.9	36.7	76.4	-72.6	32.5	-70.3	74.2	NA	33.6	57.6
Eff. Tax Rate	NM	NM	22%	NM	Nil	NM	38%	NA	27%	37%
Net Inc.	67.9	36.7	59.6	-72.6	32.5	-45.2	45.7	NA	24.4	42.3

Balance Sheet & Other Fin. Data (Million $)

	1998	1997	1996	1995	1994	1993	1992	1991	1990	1989
Cash	69.0	123	45.4	26.5	50.9	81.3	74.5	NA	13.9	2.4
Curr. Assets	373	425	425	464	287	350	345	NA	344	316
Total Assets	932	1,010	1,017	1,052	438	457	522	NA	507	479
Curr. Liab.	277	331	367	336	255	229	209	NA	225	204
LT Debt	181	237	350	395	Nil	65.0	108	NA	136	111
Common Eqty.	221	219	157	140	92.0	66.0	178	NA	132	NA
Total Cap.	402	456	507	539	109	141	298	NA	271	NA
Cap. Exp.	20.4	28.5	28.0	19.3	20.7	11.3	19.5	NA	31.6	36.6
Cash Flow	115	89.4	122	-47.6	53.0	-18.3	74.9	NA	58.1	73.9
Curr. Ratio	1.3	1.3	1.2	1.4	1.1	1.5	1.7	NA	1.5	1.6
% LT Debt of Cap.	45.0	52.0	69.0	73.3	Nil	46.5	36.0	NA	50.4	NA
% Net Inc.of Revs.	6.3	3.4	5.0	NM	4.2	NM	3.9	NA	2.0	3.4
% Ret. on Assets	7.0	3.6	5.8	NM	7.2	NM	8.8	NA	NA	NA
% Ret. on Equity	30.9	19.5	40.0	NM	41.1	NM	29.2	NA	NA	NA

Data as orig. reptd.; bef. results of disc. opers. and/or spec. items. Per share data adj. for stk. divs. as of ex-div. date. Prior to 1992, yr. ended Dec. 31. Results in FY 95, FY 93 include substantial restructuring charges. Bold denotes diluted EPS (FASB 128). E-Estimated. NA-Not Available. NM-Not Meaningful. NR-Not Ranked.

Office—600 Second St., N.E., Hopkins, MN 55343-8384. **Tel**—(612) 931-6000. **E-mail**—R_Jowett@atk.com **Website**—http://www.atk.com **Chrmn**—R. Schwartz. **Pres, COO & Acting CEO**—P. A. Bukowick. **Secy**—C. H. Gauck. **VP & CFO**—S. S. Meyers. **VP & Investor Contact**—Richard N. Jowett (612-931-6080). **Dirs**—P. A. Bukowick, G. F. Decker, T. L. Gossage, J. M. Greenblatt, J. G. Guss, D. E. Jeremiah, G. N. Kelley, J. F. Mazzella, D. L. Nlr, R. Schwartz, M.T. Smith. **Transfer Agent & Registrar**—ChaseMellon Shareholder Services, NYC. **Incorporated**—in Delaware in 1990. **Empl**— 6,600. **S&P Analyst:** Stewart Scharf

03-OCT-98

Industry:
Health Care (Drugs - Generic & Other)

Summary: This company develops, makes and markets specialty generic and proprietary human pharmaceuticals and animal health products.

Quantitative Evaluations		
Recent Price • 25⅞		Yield • 0.7%
52 Wk Range • 26¼-18⅞		12-Mo. P/E • 32.3

Outlook
(1 Lowest—5 Highest)
• **3⁻**

Fair Value
• **28¾**

Risk
• **High**

Earn./Div. Rank
• **B-**

Technical Eval.
• **Bullish** since 1/98

Rel. Strength Rank
(1 Lowest—99 Highest)
• **94**

Insider Activity
• **Neutral**

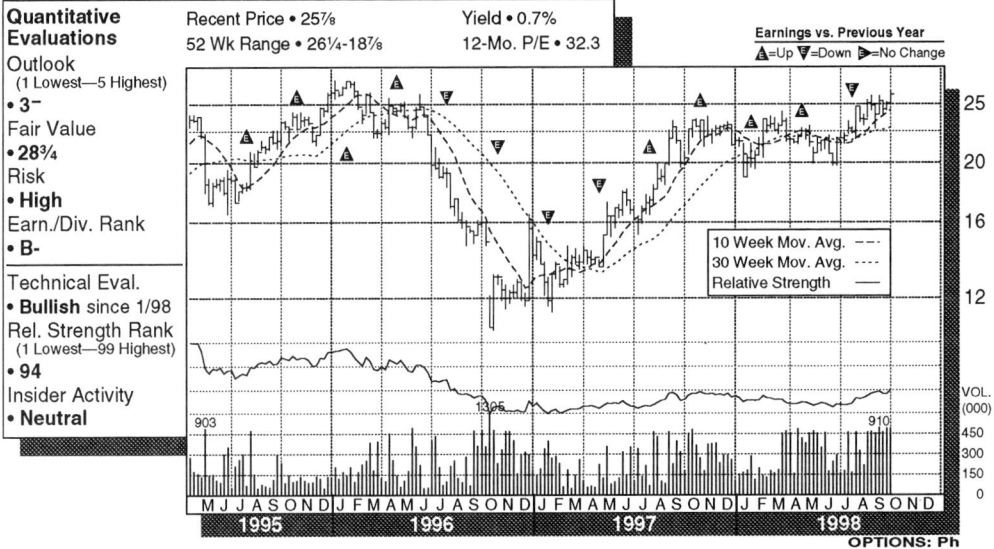

Earnings vs. Previous Year
▲=Up ▼=Down ▶=No Change

10 Week Mov. Avg. - - -
30 Week Mov. Avg. - - - -
Relative Strength —

OPTIONS: Ph

Business Profile - 28-SEP-98

A leader in the competitive generic drug industry, ALO continues to pursue worldwide product approvals to maintain market leadership positions, expand geographically, and establish brand identity. During the second quarter of 1998, ALO received about 25 new product approvals worldwide. As of August 1998, the company had over 30 bacitracin methylene disalicylate (BMD) combination products, and 76 other products utilized in the poultry industry. The firm's BMD products continue to be the most widely used combination drug products in the U.S. poultry market. In August 1998, ALO reported that it may exchange all of its outstanding warrants for Class A Common Stock at the difference between the exercise price ($20.69) and the market price plus a premium of $1.00 a share.

Operational Review - 28-SEP-98

Total revenues in the first half of 1998, increased 11%, year to year, as higher sales in the Human Pharmaceuticals and Animal Health Segments offset unfavorable foreign currency translations. Gross profit margins widened, as a result of higher sales prices and increased volume. With SG&A rising only 8.8%, operating income increased 24%. After taxes at 44.8%, versus 38.5%, and an after-tax charge of $3.1 million from the Cox Pharmaceuticals acquisition, net income rose to $7,707,000 ($0.30 a share, on 18% more shares), from $5,730,000 ($0.26 per share). Cash and equivalents totaled $18.2 million on June 30, 1998.

Stock Performance - 02-OCT-98

In the past 30 trading days, ALO's shares have increased 3%, compared to a 7% fall in the S&P 500. Average trading volume for the past five days was 178,640 shares, compared with the 40-day moving average of 132,700 shares.

Key Stock Statistics

Dividend Rate/Share	0.18	Shareholders	1,000
Shs. outstg. (M)	25.4	Market cap. (B)	$0.412
Avg. daily vol. (M)	0.165	Inst. holdings	61%
Tang. Bk. Value/Share	NM		
Beta	0.11		

Value of $10,000 invested 5 years ago: $ 10,593

Fiscal Year Ending Dec. 31

	1998	1997	1996	1995	1994	1993
Revenues (Million $)						
1Q	126.6	121.4	127.8	126.1	107.4	77.79
2Q	139.5	119.0	121.2	123.8	111.0	81.75
3Q	—	125.2	122.4	132.4	117.4	83.02
4Q	—	134.6	114.7	138.6	133.5	95.67
Yr.	—	500.3	486.2	520.9	469.3	338.2
Earnings Per Share ($)						
1Q	**0.21**	**0.10**	0.21	0.18	0.16	0.18
2Q	**0.09**	**0.16**	-0.20	0.14	0.13	0.12
3Q	—	**0.22**	Nil	0.29	0.19	0.03
4Q	—	**0.26**	-0.54	0.26	-0.56	0.07
Yr.	—	**0.76**	-0.53	0.86	-0.08	0.40

Next earnings report expected: early November

Dividend Data (Dividends have been paid since 1984.)

Amount ($)	Date Decl.	Ex-Div. Date	Stock of Record	Payment Date
0.045	Dec. 12	Jan. 07	Jan. 09	Jan. 23 '98
0.045	Mar. 25	Apr. 07	Apr. 10	Apr. 24 '98
0.045	Jun. 01	Jul. 08	Jul. 10	Jul. 24 '98
0.045	Sep. 11	Oct. 07	Oct. 09	Oct. 23 '98

A Division of The McGraw·Hill Companies

Business Summary - 28-SEP-98

ALPHARMA is a multinational pharmaceutical company that has distinguished itself in the generic drug industry and is the largest manufacturer of generic liquid and topical pharmaceuticals in the U.S. and one of the world's largest producers of specialty antibiotics. ALO also develops, makes and sells proprietary branded pharmaceuticals and animal health products.

ALO was originally organized as a wholly owned subsidiary of the Norwegian company A.L. Industrier AS. In 1994, ALO acquired the pharmaceutical and animal health businesses of its parent company and reorganized into two segments: (human pharmaceuticals 65% and animal health products 35% of 1997 revenues) .

Generic pharmaceutical sales have increased in recent years, due to managed care cost containment, increased acceptance of generic drugs, and patent expirations on branded drugs. ALO received FDA approvals to manufacture and sell Minoxidil Topical Solution, the generic equivalent of Rogaine, in 1996, and for Phenytoin Oral Suspension, a generic equivalent to Dilantin for control of seizures, in 1997.

ALO's U.S. Pharmaceuticals Division makes and markets over 170 generic products under the Alpharma, Barre or NMC labels and private labels. Products include liquid pharmaceuticals for colds, coughs and the flu; cream and ointment products (mostly prescription) and suppositories. ALO also distributes over 1,600 generic prescription and over-the-counter pharmaceuticals mainly to U.S. independent retail pharmacies.

The International Pharmaceutical Division makes and sells more than 170 products including branded generic and specialty dosage-form tablets, ointments, liquid and injectable preparations, oral adhesive bandages and surgical tapes in Europe, the Middle East and the Asia Pacific region. The Fine Chemicals Division makes and sells bulk antibiotics to the pharmaceutical industry.

ALO's Animal Health Division is a leading worldwide supplier of antibiotics, growth promoters, and nutritional additives to poultry and swine producers, feed manufacturers and veterinarians. The Aquatic Animal Health Division makes vaccines for farmed fish and cattle.

ALO's 1997 revenue increased 2.9% to $500 million. ALO had a net income of $17.4 million versUs a net loss of $11.5 million the previous year, mainly attributable to new product introduction in the human pharmaceuticals business, new offices in Latin America, Europe and the Far East, strategic acquisitions and reduction in manufacturing costs through consolidation.

ALO sees continued growth in generics worldwide driven by health care cost containment and views upcoming patent expirations as market opportunity for new products. The animal health business is benefiting from trends in healthier eating.

In May 1998, the company acquired Arthur H. Cox and Co. for about $200 million in cash. Cox manufactures and markets generic pharmaceuticals with revenues of $88 million in 1997, which represents a 20% share of the U.K. market.

Per Share Data ($)

(Year Ended Dec. 31)	1997	1996	1995	1994	1993	1992	1991	1990	1989	1988
Tangible Bk. Val.	3.50	3.04	3.55	2.43	3.22	4.07	1.49	2.26	1.63	0.86
Cash Flow	2.12	0.92	2.29	0.77	0.93	1.16	0.85	1.33	1.09	0.95
Earnings	0.76	-0.53	0.86	-0.08	0.40	0.62	0.30	0.84	0.71	0.58
Dividends	0.18	0.18	0.18	0.18	0.18	0.17	0.16	0.11	0.09	0.08
Payout Ratio	24%	NM	21%	NM	45%	34%	54%	13%	12%	14%
Prices - High	23⅞	27⅜	26⅜	20⅝	29⅜	28½	24¾	17	12¼	10½
- Low	11⅜	10⅝	16½	12⅝	12¾	18	14⅜	11¼	8⅝	5⅛
P/E Ratio - High	31	NM	31	NM	73	46	83	20	17	18
- Low	15	NM	19	NM	32	29	48	13	12	9

Income Statement Analysis (Million $)

	1997	1996	1995	1994	1993	1992	1991	1990	1989	1988
Revs.	500	486	521	469	338	295	291	275	266	236
Oper. Inc.	77.8	35.4	83.5	34.3	32.4	38.3	24.3	41.9	37.5	33.9
Depr.	30.9	31.5	31.0	18.3	11.5	9.8	9.2	8.3	6.4	5.7
Int. Exp.	18.6	20.0	22.0	16.1	6.9	10.3	12.3	11.9	11.7	11.7
Pretax Inc.	27.8	-16.3	30.2	1.7	14.8	17.6	7.7	22.7	20.5	17.5
Eff. Tax Rate	37%	NM	38%	198%	42%	35%	34%	38%	42%	50%
Net Inc.	17.4	-11.5	18.8	-1.7	8.6	11.4	5.1	14.1	11.8	8.8

Balance Sheet & Other Fin. Data (Million $)

	1997	1996	1995	1994	1993	1992	1991	1990	1989	1988
Cash	11.0	15.9	18.4	15.5	8.4	5.6	4.2	8.5	2.8	6.0
Curr. Assets	274	275	283	250	176	155	160	148	126	114
Total Assets	632	613	635	592	423	372	359	328	290	267
Curr. Liab.	134	156	169	155	125	87.0	106	96.0	78.0	77.0
LT Debt	224	234	220	220	82.0	74.0	119	101	102	94.0
Common Eqty.	238	186	205	181	185	184	114	111	93.0	82.0
Total Cap.	489	450	456	429	290	281	250	230	210	189
Cap. Exp.	27.8	30.9	24.8	44.3	20.6	16.9	10.5	13.2	18.0	19.8
Cash Flow	48.3	20.0	49.8	16.6	20.1	21.1	14.3	22.4	18.2	14.4
Curr. Ratio	2.0	1.8	1.7	1.6	1.4	1.8	1.5	1.5	1.6	1.5
% LT Debt of Cap.	45.8	52.0	48.2	51.3	28.2	26.2	47.8	44.1	48.3	49.8
% Net Inc.of Revs.	3.5	NM	3.6	NM	2.5	3.9	1.7	5.1	4.4	3.7
% Ret. on Assets	2.8	NM	5.7	NM	2.2	2.8	1.5	4.6	4.3	3.0
% Ret. on Equity	8.2	NM	9.7	NM	4.7	6.9	4.5	13.8	13.5	11.7

Data as orig. reptd.; bef. results of disc. opers. and/or spec. items. Per share data adj. for stk. divs. as of ex-div. date. Bold denotes diluted EPS (FASB 128). E-Estimated. NA-Not Available. NM-Not Meaningful. NR-Not Ranked.

Office—One Executive Drive, Fort Lee, NJ 07024. **Reincorporated**—in Delaware in 1983. **Tel**—(201) 947-7774. **Chrmn & CEO**—E. W. Sissener. **Pres & COO**—G. W. Munthe. **VP-Fin & CFO**—J. E. Smith. **Secy**—B. P. Hecht. **Treas**—A. N. Marchio, II. **VP & Investor Contact**—Diane M. Cady. **Dirs**—I. R. Cohen, T. G. Gibian, G. E. Hess, G.W. Munthe, E. W. Sissener, E. G. Tandberg, P. G. Tombros. **Transfer Agent & Registrar**—First National Bank of Boston. **Empl**— 2,550. **S&P Analyst:** David Moskowitz

Amcast Industrial

79M

NYSE Symbol **AIZ**

In S&P SmallCap 600

03-OCT-98

Industry: Manufacturing (Diversified)

Summary: Amcast manufactures metal products, including flow control products and engineered components for OEMs.

Quantitative Evaluations

Recent Price • 14¾
52 Wk Range • 25¾-14½

Yield • 3.8%
12-Mo. P/E • 7.8

Outlook (1 Lowest—5 Highest)
• **3⁻**

Fair Value
• **16¼**

Risk
• **Average**

Earn./Div. Rank
• **B**

Technical Eval.
• **Bearish** since 12/97

Rel. Strength Rank (1 Lowest—99 Highest)
• **43**

Insider Activity
• **Favorable**

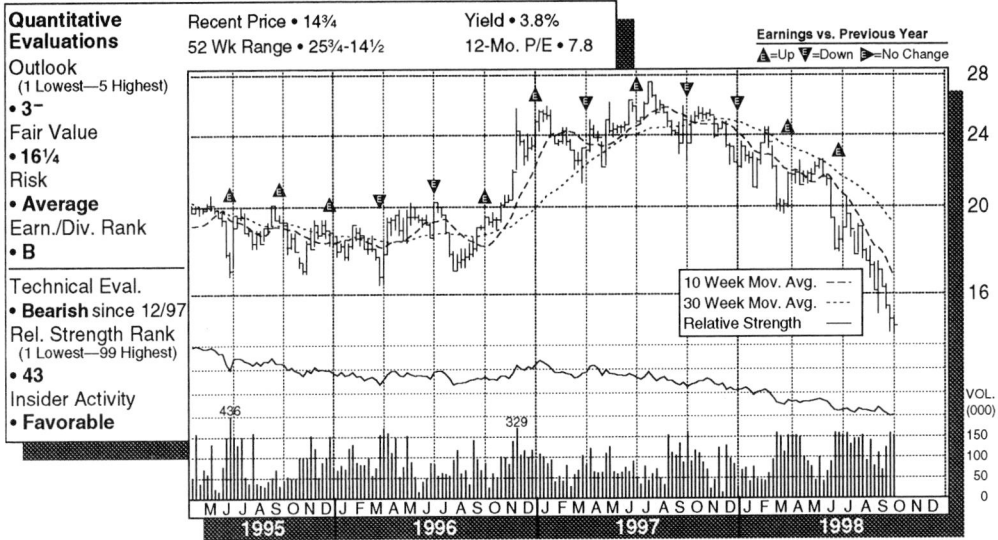

Earnings vs. Previous Year
▲=Up ▼=Down ▶=No Change

10 Week Mov. Avg. ---
30 Week Mov. Avg. ----
Relative Strength ——

Business Profile - 24-JUL-98

In July 1998, due to the General Motors strike, Amcast curtailed production at its North American automotive facilities and laid off 1,000 workers (22% of its staff). AIZ ceased production at some locations and reduced production to levels from 20-80% at others. GM accounted for 37% of AIZ's 1997 revenues. Amcast's European operations are unaffected by the GM strike. In April 1998, the company acquired Lee Brass Company, a brass products manufacturer, for some $15.3 million. AIZ plans to consolidate its brass operations with Lee Brass by January 1999. In March 1998, AIZ sold its only aerospace industry operation for $25.4 million.

Operational Review - 24-JUL-98

Net sales for 1998's first nine months increased 52%, year-to-year, due primarily to AIZ's recent acquisition of Speedline S.p.A. and Lee Brass, and strong North American aluminum wheel demand. Net sales for Flow Control Products rose 8%, and Engineered Components 83%. Gross profit increased 34%, but gross profit percentage was lower than that of previous years, reflecting a change in AIZ's sales mix to a higher percentage of lower margin Engineered Components sales and operating inefficiencies at one plant. SG&A expenses rose 38%, and after a $9.8 million restructuring charge related to its brass operations and a $12 million gain on the sale of its aerospace business, net income rose 40%, to $10,513,000 ($1.59 per share), from $14,715,000 ($1.21).

Stock Performance - 02-OCT-98

In the past 30 trading days, AIZ's shares have declined 14%, compared to a 7% fall in the S&P 500. Average trading volume for the past five days was 36,220 shares, compared with the 40-day moving average of 26,387 shares.

Key Stock Statistics

Dividend Rate/Share	0.56	Shareholders	6,100
Shs. outstg. (M)	9.2	Market cap. (B)	$0.136
Avg. daily vol. (M)	0.031	Inst. holdings	51%
Tang. Bk. Value/Share	11.99		
Beta	0.51		

Value of $10,000 invested 5 years ago: $ 10,876

Fiscal Year Ending Aug. 31

	1998	1997	1996	1995	1994	1993
Revenues (Million $)						
1Q	141.0	90.79	86.47	77.00	60.33	53.10
2Q	137.0	91.33	81.80	81.76	67.70	56.41
3Q	159.3	106.2	87.57	86.40	70.90	55.77
4Q	—	98.71	88.11	83.08	72.93	57.39
Yr.	—	387.1	343.9	328.2	271.9	222.6
Earnings Per Share ($)						
1Q	0.44	0.48	0.47	0.43	0.32	0.30
2Q	**0.57**	0.24	0.46	0.50	0.42	0.35
3Q	**0.58**	0.50	0.34	0.55	0.51	0.41
4Q	—	0.28	0.58	0.54	0.47	0.38
Yr.	—	1.50	1.85	2.02	1.72	1.44

Next earnings report expected: mid October

Dividend Data (Dividends have been paid since 1936.)

Amount ($)	Date Decl.	Ex-Div. Date	Stock of Record	Payment Date
0.140	Oct. 17	Nov. 28	Dec. 02	Dec. 20 '97
0.140	Feb. 24	Mar. 09	Mar. 11	Mar. 26 '98
0.140	May. 27	Jun. 09	Jun. 11	Jun. 26 '98
0.140	Aug. 27	Sep. 09	Sep. 11	Sep. 28 '98

A Division of The **McGraw·Hill** Companies

Business Summary - 24-JUL-98

Amcast is a leading manufacturer of technology-intensive metal products. It has two balanced business segments: brand name Flow Control Products, consisting of plumbing fittings, specialty valves and related controls distributed through national channels; Engineered Components, including light-alloy wheels, aluminum castings and tubular products used by automotive equipment manufacturers.

The August 1997 and April 1998 acquisitions of Speedline s.P.a. and Lee Brass Company have significantly contributed to AIZ's sales and earnings. Sales from the two companies increased total company sales some 53% for the third quarter and 45% for the first three quarters of fiscal 1998. The company's acquisition of Speedline significantly broadened AIZ's line of aluminum wheel products and established a European launching pad for its aluminum automotive underbody components. Speedline, which had sales of $193 million in 1996, makes light-alloy wheels for Audi, Fiat, Mercedes-Benz, Rolls-Royce and other European automakers.

When acquired, Lee Brass was a privately-owned, major manufacturer of cast brass products for residential, commercial and industrial plumbing systems, with 1997 sales of $39 million. The acquisition of Lee Brass enhances AIZ's product offerings and builds on its strong plumbing distribution franchise. After the acquisition, AIZ announced a plan to consolidate its two previous brass operations, consisting of selling or closing one facility and terminating 95 employees. AIZ expects the consolidation of its brass activities to have long-term benefits for its industrial, plumbing and marine customers.

In the third quarter of 1998, the company's pre-tax share of losses from Casting Technology Company, AIZ's joint venture with Izumi Industries, was $200,000 compared to a $300,000 loss in the year- ago period. For the first nine months of fiscal 1998, AIZ's pre-tax share of losses from CTC was $200,000, versus a loss of $2.6 million for the first nine months of 1997. The launch of several new automotive products at CTC in fiscal 1997 resulted in significant inefficiencies and high launch-related costs associated with meeting required volumes.

In July 1998, due to the GM strike, AIZ curtailed production at its North American automotive facilities and laid off 1,000 workers (22% of its staff). GM accounted for 37% of AIZ's 1997 revenues. AIZ's Chairman and CEO was quoted as saying, "When the work stoppage ends, we expect heavy demand from GM and will respond accordingly to satisfy customer requirements."

Per Share Data ($)

(Year Ended Aug. 31)	1997	1996	1995	1994	1993	1992	1991	1990	1989	1988
Tangible Bk. Val.	13.23	15.80	14.52	12.70	11.46	11.01	10.33	8.93	10.88	10.59
Cash Flow	3.86	3.88	3.71	3.24	2.88	3.55	2.90	-0.20	2.58	2.80
Earnings	1.50	1.85	2.02	1.72	1.44	1.66	1.04	-1.97	1.12	1.30
Dividends	0.42	0.56	0.54	0.49	0.48	0.48	0.48	0.48	0.47	0.44
Payout Ratio	28%	30%	27%	28%	33%	29%	46%	NM	42%	34%
Prices - High	27½	25¾	22¼	25⅞	22½	25	21¾	12½	13⅝	15¼
- Low	21¼	16⅜	16¾	19⅜	15½	11⅝	6	6¼	10⅞	8¼
P/E Ratio - High	18	14	11	15	16	15	21	NM	12	12
- Low	14	9	8	11	11	7	6	NM	10	6

Income Statement Analysis (Million $)

	1997	1996	1995	1994	1993	1992	1991	1990	1989	1988
Revs.	387	344	328	272	223	237	271	274	329	312
Oper. Inc.	47.7	44.8	41.4	36.0	30.9	34.9	27.2	22.0	30.4	30.7
Depr.	20.5	17.4	14.4	12.8	12.0	13.6	12.1	12.0	10.5	10.8
Int. Exp.	5.1	2.4	1.4	1.6	2.1	3.3	4.7	4.7	5.1	5.5
Pretax Inc.	20.0	24.7	26.1	22.1	18.8	18.7	10.9	-19.8	12.4	14.8
Eff. Tax Rate	35%	36%	34%	35%	36%	36%	38%	NM	35%	37%
Net Inc.	13.0	15.9	17.2	14.5	12.1	12.0	6.7	-13.4	8.0	9.3

Balance Sheet & Other Fin. Data (Million $)

	1997	1996	1995	1994	1993	1992	1991	1990	1989	1988
Cash	9.6	5.4	1.3	15.4	2.3	3.1	1.6	1.7	1.0	0.5
Curr. Assets	203	109	103	97.0	75.0	74.0	91.0	94.0	101	95.0
Total Assets	509	509	229	194	177	174	179	185	195	191
Curr. Liab.	177	425	55.2	48.8	38.8	41.2	46.4	53.1	54.2	50.7
LT Debt	145	58.8	29.7	13.9	17.9	22.3	40.4	41.2	33.0	39.0
Common Eqty.	158	136	124	110	99	94.4	69.3	67.4	90.0	88.7
Total Cap.	303	207	161	128	119	117	116	113	134	133
Cap. Exp.	40.3	48.6	41.7	15.6	14.0	23.8	9.9	16.7	17.6	10.5
Cash Flow	33.4	33.4	31.6	27.3	24.1	25.6	18.8	-1.4	18.6	20.1
Curr. Ratio	1.1	2.1	1.9	2.0	1.9	1.8	2.0	1.8	1.9	1.9
% LT Debt of Cap.	47.8	28.4	18.4	10.9	15.1	19.0	34.9	36.5	24.7	29.2
% Net Inc.of Revs.	3.4	4.6	5.2	5.3	5.4	5.1	2.5	NM	2.4	3.0
% Ret. on Assets	3.3	6.4	8.1	7.8	6.9	5.9	3.8	NM	4.2	5.0
% Ret. on Equity	8.8	12.2	14.7	13.8	12.4	13.0	10.0	NM	9.0	10.9

Data as orig. reptd.; bef. results of disc. opers. and/or spec. items. Per share data adj. for stk. divs. as of ex-div. date. Bold denotes diluted EPS (FASB 128). E-Estimated. NA-Not Available. NM-Not Meaningful. NR-Not Ranked.

Office—7887 Washington Village Dr., Dayton, OH 45459. **Tel**—(937) 291-7000. **Website**—http://www.amcast.com.**Chrmn, Pres & CEO**—J. H. Shuey. **VP-Fin**—D. D. Watts. **VP-Secy**—D. G. Daly. **Investor Contact**—Michael Higgins (937) 291-7015. **Dirs**—J. K. Baker, W. E. Blankley, P. H. Forster, I. W. Gorr, L. W. Ladehoff, E. T. O'Loughlin, W. G. Roth, J. H. Shuey, R. W. Van Sant. **Transfer Agent & Registrar**—First Chicago Trust Co.**Incorporated**—in Ohio in 1869. **Empl**—4,630. **S&P Analyst:** Scott H. Kessler.

03-OCT-98

Industry:
Manufacturing (Diversified)

Summary: This leading producer of bentonite and bentonite specialty blends for industrial applications also makes superabsorbent polymers and has its own transportation operations.

Quantitative Evaluations

Outlook (1 Lowest—5 Highest)
- **NA**

Fair Value
- **NA**

Risk
- **Average**

Earn./Div. Rank
- **A-**

Technical Eval.
- **NA**

Rel. Strength Rank (1 Lowest—99 Highest)
- **35**

Insider Activity
- **Neutral**

Recent Price • 10⅛   Yield • 2.4%
52 Wk Range • 17¼-9⅜   12-Mo. P/E • 13.0

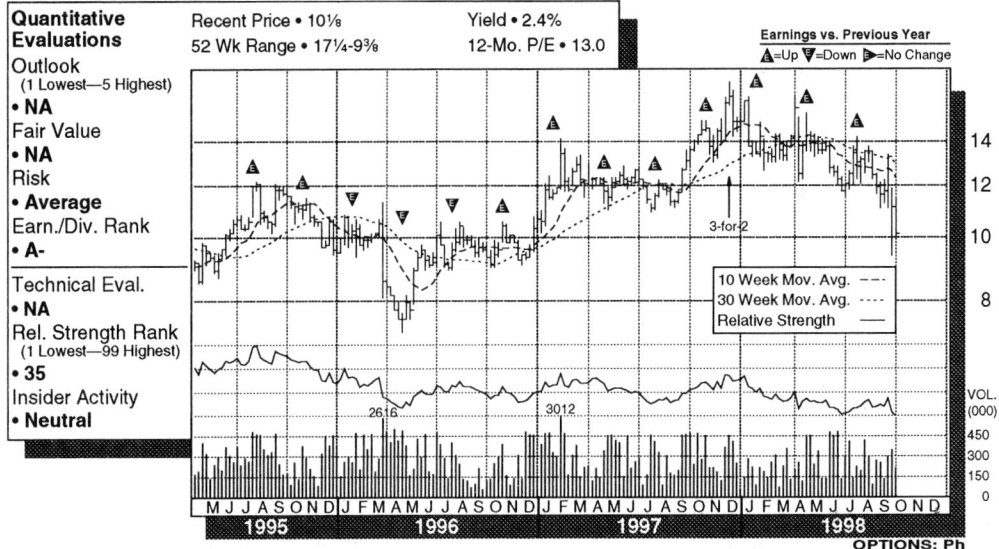

Earnings vs. Previous Year
▲=Up ▼=Down ▶=No Change

10 Week Mov. Avg. -- --
30 Week Mov. Avg. - - - -
Relative Strength ——

3-for-2

OPTIONS: Ph

Business Profile - 24-SEP-98

The change in the company's name from American Colloid Co. to AMCOL International reflected not only its international presence, but also a transition from its traditional concentration on highly cyclical industrial markets to growing diversification into consumable markets. After growing largely through acquisitions in 1994 and 1995, the company successfully integrated the acquisitions in 1996 and achieved strong gains in sales and operating earnings through internal growth. Having largely achieved critical mass in its core segments and with increased global presence, AMCOL believes it is well positioned for continued growth, especially in its cat litter business. In February 1998, the company noted that the Far East has been targeted for the expansion of each of its primary segments. AMCOL's shares began trading on the NYSE under the symbol ACO in September 1998.

Operational Review - 24-SEP-98

Revenues in the first half of 1998 rose 12%, year to year, reflecting increases in all segments, paced by an 18% gain in absorbent polymers. Gross margins narrowed, reflecting less profitable absorbent polymer acquisitions, and weaker results from the environmental and transportation segments. Following controlled SG&A expenses and lower net other expense, pretax income was up 22%. After taxes at 36.0%, versus 37.0%, net income climbed 24%, to $9,216,000 ($0.32 a share), from $7,455,000 ($0.26).

Stock Performance - 02-OCT-98

In the past 30 trading days, ACO's shares have declined 19%, compared to a 7% fall in the S&P 500. Average trading volume for the past five days was 42,220 shares, compared with the 40-day moving average of 48,685 shares.

Key Stock Statistics

Dividend Rate/Share	0.24	Shareholders	2,100
Shs. outstg. (M)	27.9	Market cap. (B)	$0.283
Avg. daily vol. (M)	0.050	Inst. holdings	40%
Tang. Bk. Value/Share	5.59		
Beta	0.76		

Value of $10,000 invested 5 years ago: $ 18,367

Fiscal Year Ending Dec. 31

	1998	1997	1996	1995	1994	1993
Revenues (Million $)						
1Q	121.6	107.9	85.54	78.75	57.85	48.90
2Q	125.6	113.5	96.76	83.66	64.01	55.25
3Q	—	126.1	109.5	92.98	71.98	56.97
4Q	—	129.5	113.5	92.30	71.61	57.99
Yr.	—	477.1	405.4	347.7	265.4	219.2
Earnings Per Share ($)						
1Q	**0.12**	**0.11**	0.04	0.13	0.09	0.09
2Q	**0.20**	**0.15**	0.10	0.16	0.11	0.11
3Q	—	**0.24**	0.20	0.17	0.15	0.15
4Q	—	**0.23**	0.18	0.15	0.17	0.15
Yr.	—	**0.72**	0.52	0.60	0.52	0.51

Next earnings report expected: NA

Dividend Data (Dividends have been paid since 1937.)

Amount ($)	Date Decl.	Ex-Div. Date	Stock of Record	Payment Date
0.055	Nov. 07	Dec. 04	Dec. 08	Jan. 03 '98
0.055	Feb. 20	Feb. 24	Mar. 26	Mar. 10 '98
0.055	May. 12	May. 20	May. 25	Jun. 05 '98
0.060	Aug. 11	Aug. 26	Aug. 28	Sep. 08 '98

A Division of The McGraw-Hill Companies

Business Summary - 24-SEP-98

Bentonite, a nonmetallic clay composed of a mineral called montmorillonite, is at the very core of AMCOL International Corp.'s past, present and future business. Bentonite's unique chemical structure gives it a diverse range of capabilities, enabling it to act as "glue" for foundry sand molds, a lubricating agent for well drilling, a binder for medical tables, an additive in body lotion, a clumping material in scoopable cat litter, and a moisture barrier in commercial construction and landfills. The largest customers for bentonite are the metalcasting industry and the cat litter market.

ACO, a company whose history as a bentonite mining and manufacturing concern dates back to the 1920s, produces and markets a wide range of specialty minerals and chemicals used for industrial, environmental and consumer-related applications. ACO's operations are generally divided into three segments: minerals (34% of sales and 22% of profits in 1997), whose operations include the mining of bentonite; absorbent polymers (41% and 55%), which are used in most baby diapers and other disposable hygienic products; and environmental (19% and 20%), where its products serve the wastewater treatment, groundwater monitoring and heavy construction industries. The company

also operates a transportation business (6% and 3%) mainly for delivery of its own products. ACO's proven reserves of sodium bentonite and calcium bentonite are estimated to be adequate for more than 30 years and 20 years, respectively.

Nanocor, a business formed in 1995, could become a significant part of ACO as it develops opportunities to enhance the performance of plastics through technologies that use bentonite clay. These nanocomposites have many potential commercial applications, such as their use in engineered plastics for automobile parts and computer hardware housing, and as additives to plastic food wrap and drink bottles to extend shelf life.

In November 1997, ACO expanded its European presence by acquiring absorbent polymer assets and a cat litter business in England, and two environmental distribution companies in France.

In April 1998, AMCOL sold its fuller's earth business (with customers primarily in cat litter and agrochemical businesses) to Oil-Dri Corporation of America. The company noted that it exited the fuller's earth business, which was a marginal contributor to the overall business mix, to concentrate on increasing the market share of bentonite based products. The company also believes that the transaction will not affect its share of the scoopable cat litter business.

Per Share Data ($)

(Year Ended Dec. 31)	1997	1996	1995	1994	1993	1992	1991	1990	1989	1988
Tangible Bk. Val.	5.53	5.13	4.69	4.47	4.31	2.13	2.09	1.96	1.85	1.73
Cash Flow	1.82	1.47	1.32	0.99	0.91	0.74	0.55	0.49	0.55	0.50
Earnings	0.72	0.52	0.60	0.52	0.51	0.34	0.17	0.10	0.21	0.19
Dividends	0.21	0.19	0.17	0.16	0.13	0.11	0.10	0.10	0.10	0.09
Payout Ratio	29%	36%	29%	31%	26%	30%	57%	97%	45%	48%
Prices - High	17¼	11⅜	12⅛	16⅞	22	6¼	2⅞	3	3½	3¾
- Low	10⅛	7⅛	7⅞	7	6	2⅝	1⅝	1¹⁵⁄₁₆	2⅛	1¾
P/E Ratio - High	24	22	20	32	43	19	17	29	16	20
- Low	14	14	13	13	12	8	10	19	10	9

Income Statement Analysis (Million $)

	1997	1996	1995	1994	1993	1992	1991	1990	1989	1988
Revs.	477	405	348	265	219	183	149	132	125	111
Oper. Inc.	73.4	60.2	53.7	37.6	31.6	26.3	18.8	17.3	18.7	16.4
Depr.	31.9	27.9	21.3	13.6	10.5	9.8	9.2	9.1	8.1	7.0
Int. Exp.	8.6	8.4	6.7	3.0	3.0	3.5	4.4	4.8	4.5	2.9
Pretax Inc.	32.4	23.2	26.9	22.2	18.8	12.7	5.5	3.3	7.1	6.8
Eff. Tax Rate	35%	34%	34%	31%	30%	32%	26%	28%	29%	32%
Net Inc.	21.0	15.2	17.8	15.3	13.1	8.5	4.0	2.4	5.0	4.6

Balance Sheet & Other Fin. Data (Million $)

	1997	1996	1995	1994	1993	1992	1991	1990	1989	1988
Cash	3.1	3.0	1.9	10.4	20.5	3.5	2.9	2.9	2.4	2.8
Curr. Assets	150	148	126	106	93.0	60.2	60.1	54.2	51.5	49.0
Total Assets	351	351	322	261	181	127	127	125	121	114
Curr. Liab.	67.2	51.9	35.9	36.6	27.4	21.1	20.8	14.2	16.0	16.3
LT Debt	94.4	119	117	71.5	16.7	38.3	43.8	47.8	43.7	40.9
Common Eqty.	176	167	155	141	125	55.6	54.4	52.7	51.2	48.5
Total Cap.	277	293	279	218	147	99	100	103	98.0	92.0
Cap. Exp.	32.7	34.3	62.8	81.0	32.1	11.3	7.9	8.5	14.4	13.6
Cash Flow	53.0	43.1	39.1	28.9	23.7	18.3	13.2	11.4	13.2	12.0
Curr. Ratio	2.2	2.9	3.5	2.9	3.4	2.9	2.9	3.8	3.2	3.0
% LT Debt of Cap.	34.1	40.6	41.9	32.8	11.3	38.6	43.9	46.4	44.7	44.7
% Net Inc.of Revs.	4.4	3.8	5.1	5.8	6.0	4.7	2.7	1.8	4.0	4.2
% Ret. on Assets	6.0	4.5	6.1	6.9	7.9	6.7	3.2	1.9	4.3	4.3
% Ret. on Equity	12.3	9.4	11.9	11.4	13.7	15.4	7.5	4.5	10.1	9.7

Data as orig. reptd.; bef. results of disc. opers. and/or spec. items. Per share data adj. for stk. divs. as of ex-div. date. Bold denotes diluted EPS (FASB 128). E-Estimated. NA-Not Available. NM-Not Meaningful. NR-Not Ranked.

Office—One North Arlington, 1500 W. Shure Dr., Suite 500, Arlington Heights, IL 60004-7803. **Tel**—(847) 394-8730. **Website**—http://www.amcol.com **Chrmn**—C. E. Ray. **Pres & CEO**—J. Hughes. **SVP & CFO**—P. G. Shelton. **Secy**—C. O. Redman. **Investor Contact**—Jodi Warner. **Dirs**—A. Brown, R. E. Driscoll III, R. A. Foos, J. Hughes, J. A. McClung, J. D. Propps, C. E. Ray, C. O. Redman, P. G. Shelton, D. E. Stahl, L. E. Washow, A. L.Weaver, P. C. Weaver. **Transfer Agent**—Harris Trust & Savings Bank, Chicago. **Incorporated**—in Delaware in 1959. **Empl**—1,546. **S&P Analyst:** E. Hunter

03-OCT-98   Industry: Insurance (Multi-Line)   **Summary:** In March 1998, this specialty insurer agreed to be acquired by Cendant Corp. for $67 a share.

Quantitative Evaluations	
Outlook (1 Lowest—5 Highest)	• **1⁻**
Fair Value	• **39½**
Risk	• **Low**
Earn./Div. Rank	• **A+**
Technical Eval.	• **NA**
Rel. Strength Rank (1 Lowest—99 Highest)	• **19**
Insider Activity	• **NA**

Recent Price • 40⅜   Yield • 1.1%
52 Wk Range • 66-35⅞   12-Mo. P/E • 44.9

Earnings vs. Previous Year
▲=Up ▼=Down ▶=No Change

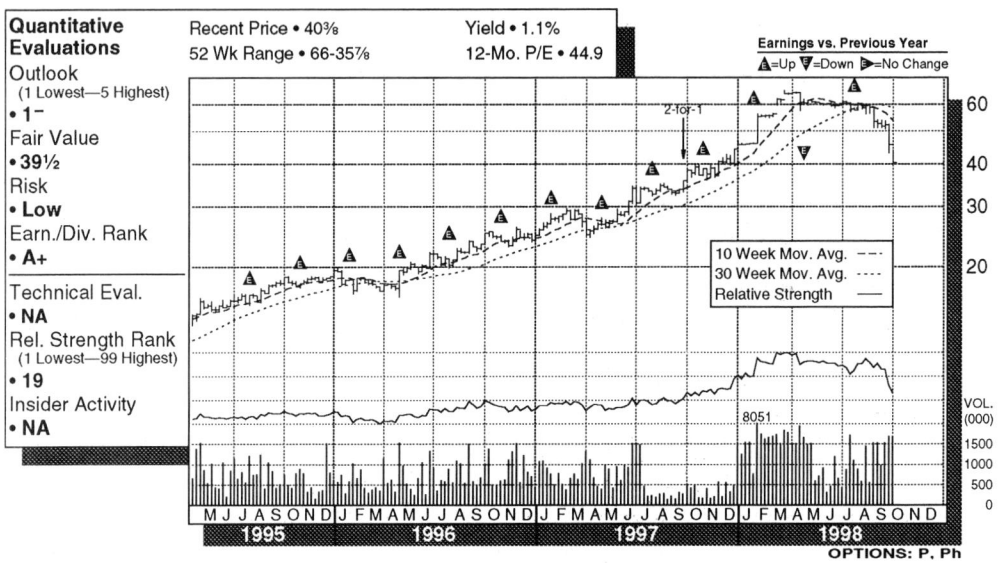

10 Week Mov. Avg. ---
30 Week Mov. Avg. ····
Relative Strength —

2-for-1

8051

VOL. (000)

OPTIONS: P, Ph

Business Profile - 22-MAY-98

After a well publicized corporate battle, ABI finally entered into an agreement to merge with Cendant Corp (CD), for a revised tender offer of $67 per ABI share. Consequently, the company has terminated its pending merger agreement with American International Group (AIG). Under the terms of the termination, AIG waived certain provisions of the merger, for a fee of $100 million from ABI and $5 million from CD. Separately, in May 1998, American Bankers announced an agreement to buy MS Diversified Corp., an insurance group specializing in the extended service contract market in the southeastern U.S. Recent earnings continued to be buoyed by strong growth in investment income. ABI has raised its dividend in each of the past six years.

Operational Review - 22-MAY-98

Gross collected premiums advanced about 10% in the first quarter of 1998, year to year, while net investment income rose 10% as well. Margins widened slightly, as net operating income increased 11% on favorable underwriting results, to 28.0 million ($0.60 per share), from $25.2 million ($0.54). However, following a $109.3 million pretax merger termination fee paid to American International Group, the company posted a net loss of $44.1 million (anti-dilutive), compared with net income of $25.2 million. Results exclude net realized investment gains of of $0.03 a share in both periods.

Stock Performance - 02-OCT-98

In the past 30 trading days, ABI's shares have declined 31%, compared to a 7% fall in the S&P 500. Average trading volume for the past five days was 740,200 shares, compared with the 40-day moving average of 406,941 shares.

Key Stock Statistics

Dividend Rate/Share	0.44	Shareholders	1,500
Shs. outstg. (M)	43.1	Market cap. (B)	$ 1.7
Avg. daily vol. (M)	0.522	Inst. holdings	45%
Tang. Bk. Value/Share	16.61		
Beta	0.88		

Value of $10,000 invested 5 years ago: $ 37,621

Fiscal Year Ending Dec. 31

	1998	1997	1996	1995	1994	1993
Revenues (Million $)						
1Q	400.2	404.9	375.7	309.8	284.3	204.6
2Q	414.0	406.0	386.0	326.2	298.1	220.8
3Q	—	408.2	399.6	357.3	302.4	262.4
4Q	—	402.3	367.7	367.6	302.1	—
Yr.	—	1,621	1,529	1,361	1,187	973.3
Earnings Per Share ($)						
1Q	-1.06	0.56	0.49	0.36	0.23	0.34
2Q	0.64	0.64	0.59	0.39	0.34	0.32
3Q	—	0.66	0.51	0.45	0.30	0.28
4Q	—	0.64	0.58	0.55	0.50	0.48
Yr.	—	2.45	2.19	1.74	1.37	1.43

Next earnings report expected: late October

Dividend Data (Dividends have been paid since 1950.)

Amount ($)	Date Decl.	Ex-Div. Date	Stock of Record	Payment Date
0.110	Nov. 14	Nov. 25	Nov. 28	Dec. 12 '97
0.110	Feb. 20	Feb. 26	Mar. 02	Mar. 13 '98
0.110	May. 14	May. 29	Jun. 02	Jun. 15 '98
0.110	Aug. 14	Aug. 31	Sep. 02	Sep. 15 '98

STANDARD
&POOR'S
STOCK REPORTS

American Bankers Insurance Group, Inc.

86G

03-OCT-98

Business Summary · 22-MAY-98

In 1947, Kirk A. Landon, founder of American Bankers Insurance Group, Inc. (ABI), sought out innovative distribution channels for his casualty insurance products. The first were banks. By 1952, it was clear that other insurance products could be marketed the same way. ABI then entered the market with life and accident and health products. Since then, ABI has evolved into an international wholesaler and marketer of insurance products, services and programs. ABI concentrates on marketing through financial institutions, retailers and other entities that provide consumer financing as a regular part of their business.

ABI differs from most insurance companies in that a substantial portion of its property and casualty segment is credit property and unemployment versus traditional property. Operations now fan out from the U.S. to Canada, the Caribbean, Latin America and the United Kingdom. ABI's business mix of net premiums earned approximates 72% property and casualty (credit unemployment, credit property, extended service contracts, mobile home physical damage) and 28% life (credit life, credit accident and health, group life, mortgage acci-

dent and health, and group accident and health). Distribution channels include retailers, financial institutions, manufactured housing, travel trailer and equipment manufacturers, dealers and lenders, and independent agents.

In 1997, net premiums earned totaled $1.45 billion--up 5.5% from 1996's $1.38 billion--and were divided among the following product lines: unemployment 16%, credit accident and health (A&H) 14%, credit property 14%, credit life 12%, mobile home physical damage 7%, extended service contracts 10%, homeowners 6%, mortgage A&H 4%, group A&H 3% and other 14%. Benefiting from favorable loss experience and lower interest expense, net income in 1997 jumped 22%, to $114.9 million, from $94.5 million the year before. Results in 1997 were also aided by a reduction in operating losses in the United Kingdom insurance subsidiary.

ABI's future business focus includes: the continuing development of new and proven profitable products, such as developing products for the utility industry or mortality coverage on purebred and thoroughbred animals; new distribution channels; and key acquisitions, such as its acquisition of BIG, a wholly owned subsidiary in the United Kingdom, in 1997.

Per Share Data ($)

(Year Ended Dec. 31)	1997	1996	1995	1994	1993	1992	1991	1990	1989	1988
Tangible Bk. Val.	16.83	14.56	12.67	10.07	9.94	8.19	7.25	6.16	5.46	4.95
Oper. Earnings	NA	NA	NA	NA	NA	NA	1.27	0.96	0.61	0.66
Earnings	2.45	2.19	1.74	1.37	1.43	1.28	1.27	0.96	0.61	0.66
Dividends	0.42	0.40	0.38	0.35	0.34	0.30	0.30	0.25	0.25	0.25
Relative Payout	17%	18%	22%	26%	24%	23%	24%	26%	41%	38%
Prices - High	46⅛	26¼	19¾	13⅜	15⅜	12	10⅜	6⅛	6⅝	6½
- Low	24⅜	16¼	11¾	9½	11⅝	7	4¼	2⅞	5⅛	4¼
P/E Ratio - High	19	12	11	10	11	9	8	6	11	10
- Low	10	7	7	7	8	5	3	3	8	6

Income Statement Analysis (Million $)

	1997	1996	1995	1994	1993	1992	1991	1990	1989	1988
Life Ins. In Force	53,694	48,704	42,708	32,129	30,848	27,878	29,168	31,098	31,710	30,949
Prem. Inc.: Life A & H	406	384	377	360	305	260	235	233	216	252
Prem. Inc.: Cas./Prop.	1,048	995	864	734	577	473	456	428	367	373
Net Invest. Inc.	134	121	99	74.4	70.4	67.5	68.1	72.3	63.3	65.0
Oth. Revs.	23.1	21.5	20.7	18.0	21.0	11.7	9.0	11.4	10.7	41.0
Total Revs.	1,621	1,529	1,361	1,187	973	812	768	746	657	731
Pretax Inc.	160	136	104	79.8	75.7	59.4	52.2	40.0	27.6	42.8
Net Oper. Inc.	NA	NA	30.6	NA	NA	NA	37.4	27.8	17.6	16.8
Net Inc.	115	94.5	72.3	56.5	53.3	42.3	37.4	27.8	17.6	16.8

Balance Sheet & Other Fin. Data (Million $)

	1997	1996	1995	1994	1993	1992	1991	1990	1989	1988
Cash & Equiv.	23.3	30.4	23.3	89.5	53.6	23.8	25.7	42.3	26.3	28.3
Premiums Due	144	129	131	106	133	96.1	92.5	104	101	72.4
Invest. Assets: Bonds	1,810	1,665	1,384	1,044	1,015	899	833	810	775	747
Invest. Assets: Stocks	141	113	113	65.4	73.5	59.6	53.4	24.4	15.7	15.2
Invest. Assets: Loans	18.6	18.5	19.6	20.6	22.3	23.5	26.6	32.6	41.8	46.8
Invest. Assets: Total	1,171	1,968	1,688	1,265	1,111	982	913	867	832	812
Deferred Policy Costs	458	388	311	230	199	175	156	172	170	172
Total Assets	3,782	3,470	2,988	2,432	2,160	1,404	1,277	1,260	1,197	1,145
Debt	243	222	236	198	159	140	177	197	148	136
Common Eqty.	699	710	513	406	399	268	216	178	158	143
Comb. Loss-Exp. Ratio	NA	97.0	95.0	96.0	94.1	95.3	100.1	101.8	98.1	107.5
% Return On Revs.	7.7	6.2	5.3	4.8	5.5	5.2	4.9	3.7	3.1	2.3
% Ret. on Equity	17.8	15.4	15.7	16.0	15.7	17.4	19.0	16.6	13.5	12.7
% Invest. Yield	7.7	6.6	6.7	6.2	6.7	7.1	7.6	8.5	8.8	7.6

Data as orig. reptd.; bef. results of disc. opers. and/or spec. items. Per share data adj. for stk. divs. as of ex-div. date. Bold denotes diluted EPS (FASB 128). E-Estimate. NA-Not Available. NM-Not Meaningful. NR-Not Ranked.

Office—11222 Quail Roost Dr., Miami, FL 33157-6596. **Tel**—(305) 253-2244. **Chrmn**—R. K. Landon. **Vice Chrmn, CEO & Pres**—G. N. Gaston. **VP & Treas**—L. F. Garcia. **EVP & Secy**—A. W. Heggen. **Investor Contact**—P. Bruce Camacho (305-252-7060). **Dirs**—W. H. Allen Jr., N. A. Buoniconti, A. M. Codina, P. Dolora, G. N. Gaston, D. L. Jones, J. F. Jorden, J. F. Kemp, R. K. Landon, M. G. MacNeill, E. M. Matalene Jr., A. H. Nahmad, N. J. St. George, R. C. Strauss, G. E. Williamson II. **Transfer Agent & Registrar**—Chase Bank, NYC. **Incorporated**—in Florida in 1978. **Empl**— 2,874. **S&P Analyst:** L. A. Olive

American Freightways   3091

Nasdaq Symbol **AFWY**

In S&P SmallCap 600

03-OCT-98

Industry: Truckers

Summary: This non-union LTL motor carrier provides regional and interregional less-than-truckload service in 28 states, Canada and Mexico.

S&P Opinion: Accumulate (★★★★)	Recent Price • 7⅛	Yield • Nil
	52 Wk Range • 20-6½	12-Mo. P/E • 11.3

Quantitative Evaluations

Outlook
(1 Lowest—5 Highest)
• **5**

Fair Value
• **15⅞**

Risk
• **High**

Earn./Div. Rank
• **B**

Technical Eval.
• **Bearish** since 1/98

Rel. Strength Rank
(1 Lowest—99 Highest)
• **34**

Insider Activity
• **Favorable**

Earnings vs. Previous Year
▲=Up ▼=Down ▷=No Change

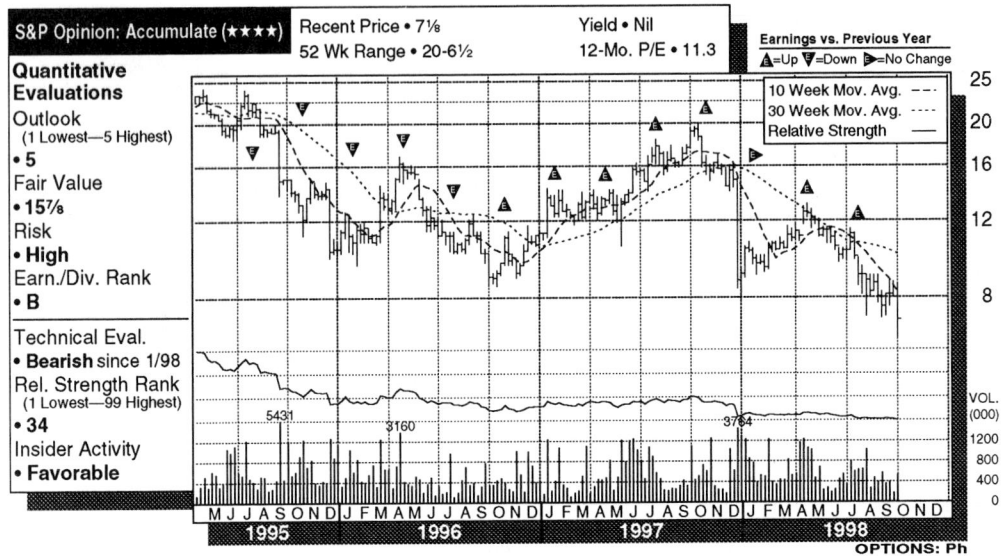

10 Week Mov. Avg. — —
30 Week Mov. Avg. - - - -
Relative Strength —

OPTIONS: Ph

Overview - 28-JUL-98

AFWY's traffic growth will slow somewhat in 1998 as it benefited in 1997 from the UPS strike and the exit of two leading competitors. AFWY's growth rate will exceed that of its peers as it gains market share within established territories, enjoys a full year of service to New Mexico and obtains business from the initiation of all-point service to Michigan in January 1998. AFWY also added full coverage to Alaska and Hawaii in April 1998 via arrangements with freight forwarders. Margins will increase slightly. AFWY's educational program should help it achieve improved pick-up and delivery density and load factors. AFWY also will enjoy lower fuel prices, stable depreciation and insurance costs and the absence of start-up costs for Michigan service. Offsetting will be higher labor costs, maintenance expense and purchased transportation costs. Revenue per LTL ton is seen increasing about 2%-3%, versus the 5.7% improvement in 1997. Interest expense will be lower in 1998.

Valuation - 28-JUL-98

The shares of this regional LTL carrier re-tested their late 1997 low in mid-1998. Though profits have resumed their uptrend, and AFWY continues to gain share from its peers, investors have bailed out as they appear to be anticipating an economic slowdown. AFWY has fallen more than other truckers because of its spotty profit performance of late, which was related to its Michigan expansion, lane imbalances and training costs. AFWY is expected to sport faster growth than its peers over the next few years as it expands its system to all 48 contiguous states. We believe investors should take advantage of the current price weakness to accumulate AFWY.

Key Stock Statistics

S&P EPS Est. 1998	0.80	Tang. Bk. Value/Share	7.55
P/E on S&P Est. 1998	8.9	Beta	0.54
S&P EPS Est. 1999	1.00	Shareholders	3,300
Dividend Rate/Share	Nil	Market cap. (B)	$0.225
Shs. outstg. (M)	31.6	Inst. holdings	28%
Avg. daily vol. (M)	0.073		

Value of $10,000 invested 5 years ago: $ 6,129

Fiscal Year Ending Dec. 31

	1998	1997	1996	1995	1994	1993
Revenues (Million $)						
1Q	230.7	193.1	166.2	132.5	99.3	72.55
2Q	246.4	219.1	181.1	142.0	123.7	80.94
3Q	—	233.8	192.5	149.4	124.1	87.60
4Q	—	224.4	189.3	148.2	118.5	87.37
Yr.	—	870.3	729.0	572.1	465.6	328.5
Earnings Per Share ($)						
1Q	**0.10**	0.05	0.02	0.20	0.14	0.12
2Q	**0.24**	0.22	0.09	0.26	0.32	0.16
3Q	**E0.30**	0.25	0.10	0.08	0.25	0.19
4Q	**E0.16**	0.05	0.04	-0.12	0.19	0.12
Yr.	**E0.80**	0.56	0.25	0.42	0.89	0.59

Next earnings report expected: early October

Dividend Data

The company has not paid cash dividends in the past and does not intend to pay any in the foreseeable future.

A Division of The **McGraw·Hill** *Companies*

STANDARD
&POOR'S
STOCK REPORTS

American Freightways Corporation

3091

03-OCT-98

Business Summary - 28-JUL-98

American Freightways has been one of the fastest growing truckers serving the less-than-truckload (LTL) segment. The company has deliberately slowed its pace of expansion in recent years to get its profits back on track. Aiding AFWY's growth has been its unique blend of full coverage to all points in the states it serves and the maintenance of consistent scheduled service.

AFWY, formed in 1982 initially to serve shippers in Arkansas, is one of the few successful LTL carriers launched in the post-deregulation environment. As of April 1998, the company offered service to 28 states located primarily in the Midwest, South, Mid-Atlantic and parts of the Southwest. Service to Canada is provided via an alliance with Day & Ross and to most of Mexico through a partnership with Autolineas Mexicanas. In 1997, AFWY began service to Puerto Rico and, in April 1998, launched service to Alaska, Hawaii and Guam through alliances with freight forwarders.

After bringing its service to five states in 1996, AFWY added only one state (New Mexico) in 1997 (August); service was launched in January 1998 in Michigan. AFWY is deliberately limiting near-term growth to gain better control over costs and boost the bottom line. In 1997, AFWY's operating ratio (expenses divided by revenues) improved to 94.8% from 89.3% in 1994.

One way AFWY holds down costs is to operate all of its equipment with uniform specifications. This simplifies mechanic and driver training and improves control over

spare parts. Another strategy designed to improve returns was the restructuring of its linehaul process in 1996. The restructuring cut the amount of freight sent from satellite terminals to central consolidation facilities from 35% to 20%. Instead, freight moves directly from the originating service center to the destination terminal. Thus, more freight can be upgraded to next day service. Costs are cut as less handling means less potential damage and fewer dock workers; some 950 dock positions were eliminated in 1996.

The restructuring of AFWY's linehaul system will help the company gain a larger share of short-haul regional LTL freight. Currently, some 45% of the firm's shipments are next day (regional) LTL while 40% is second-day and 15% is third day. The company's goal is to derive 50% of its shipments from regional LTL, which is the industry's fastest growing market.

AFWY differentiates itself from other carriers by offering total coverage to all points in the states in which it operates. Additionally, the company provides regularly scheduled runs and prides itself on a high on-time delivery performance. To provide shippers with shipment tracing services, AFWY has installed equipment at its service centers that can scan in freight information as the shipment is handled. Information about shipment location is fed into AFWY's network via mobile communications equipment and accessed by shippers through the firm's website.

At March 6, 1998, some 38% of AFWY's common shares were owned by members of the Garrison family.

Per Share Data ($)

(Year Ended Dec. 31)	1997	1996	1995	1994	1993	1992	1991	1990	1989	1988
Tangible Bk. Val.	7.20	6.60	6.32	5.81	3.91	3.24	2.80	NA	NA	NA
Cash Flow	2.22	1.75	1.62	1.81	1.34	1.10	0.81	NA	NA	NA
Earnings	0.56	0.25	0.42	0.89	0.59	0.50	0.31	NA	NA	NA
Dividends	Nil	Nil	Nil	Nil	Nil	Nil	Nil	Nil	Nil	Nil
Payout Ratio	Nil	Nil	Nil	Nil	Nil	Nil	Nil	Nil	Nil	Nil
Prices - High	20	16⅞	24¼	24⅞	20½	12	9¾	NA	NA	NA
- Low	7⅞	8½	9⅞	15½	11⅜	6¾	4¾	NA	NA	NA
P/E Ratio - High	36	67	58	28	35	24	32	NA	NA	NA
- Low	14	34	24	17	19	14	16	NA	NA	NA

Income Statement Analysis (Million $)

	1997	1996	1995	1994	1993	1992	1991	1990	1989	1988
Revs.	870	729	572	466	328	262	198	NA	NA	NA
Oper. Inc.	97.9	74.0	69.1	77.6	52.4	43.4	30.4	NA	NA	NA
Depr.	52.6	46.9	37.6	27.9	21.5	17.1	14.5	NA	NA	NA
Int. Exp.	16.3	14.7	10.2	7.8	5.8	5.4	5.1	NA	NA	NA
Pretax Inc.	29.3	12.8	21.3	43.6	27.0	22.0	12.6	NA	NA	NA
Eff. Tax Rate	39%	39%	39%	38%	38%	37%	36%	NA	NA	NA
Net Inc.	17.8	7.9	13.1	27.0	16.8	13.9	8.0	NA	NA	NA

Balance Sheet & Other Fin. Data (Million $)

	1997	1996	1995	1994	1993	1992	1991	1990	1989	1988
Cash	1.8	4.4	2.6	4.0	0.2	NA	NA	NA	NA	NA
Curr. Assets	105	92.0	77.2	54.2	37.7	NA	NA	NA	NA	NA
Total Assets	576	550	478	355	251	NA	NA	NA	NA	NA
Curr. Liab.	78.5	66.2	52.5	44.4	35.1	NA	NA	NA	NA	NA
LT Debt	210	227	189	105	89.0	NA	NA	NA	NA	NA
Common Eqty.	227	206	195	177	109	NA	NA	NA	NA	NA
Total Cap.	497	484	425	311	216	NA	NA	NA	NA	NA
Cap. Exp.	67.9	107	138	116	95.0	49.0	35.0	NA	NA	NA
Cash Flow	70.4	54.8	50.7	54.9	38.3	31.0	22.6	NA	NA	NA
Curr. Ratio	1.3	1.4	1.5	1.2	1.1	NA	NA	NA	NA	NA
% LT Debt of Cap.	42.3	46.9	44.5	33.7	41.2	NA	NA	NA	NA	NA
% Net Inc.of Revs.	2.0	10.8	2.3	5.7	5.1	5.3	4.1	NA	NA	NA
% Ret. on Assets	3.2	1.5	3.2	8.9	7.9	NA	NA	NA	NA	NA
% Ret. on Equity	8.2	3.9	3.6	18.9	16.8	NA	NA	NA	NA	NA

Data as orig. reptd.; bef. results of disc. opers. and/or spec. items. Per share data adj. for stk. divs. as of ex-div. date. Bold denotes diluted EPS (FASB 128). E-Estimated. NA-Not Available. NM-Not Meaningful. NR-Not Ranked.

Office— 2200 Forward Drive, Harrison, AR 72601.**Tel**—(870) 741-9000. **Website**—http://www.arfw.com **Chrmn & CEO**—F. S. Garrison. **Pres**—T. Garrison. **VP, Secy & Treas**—W. Garrison. **VP, CFO & Investor Contact**—Frank Conner. **Dirs**—F. Conner, B. A. Garrison, F. S. Garrison, T. Garrison, W. Garrison, J. P. Hammerschmidt, T. J. Jones, K. Reeves, D. Z. Williams. **Transfer Agent**—Wachovia Bank of North Carolina, N.A. **Incorporated**—in Arkansas in 1985. **Empl**— 12,900. **S&P Analyst:** Stephen R. Klein

03-OCT-98

Industry:
Computer (Software & Services)

Summary: This company offers business and information technology consulting and systems integration services for U.S. and multinational organizations.

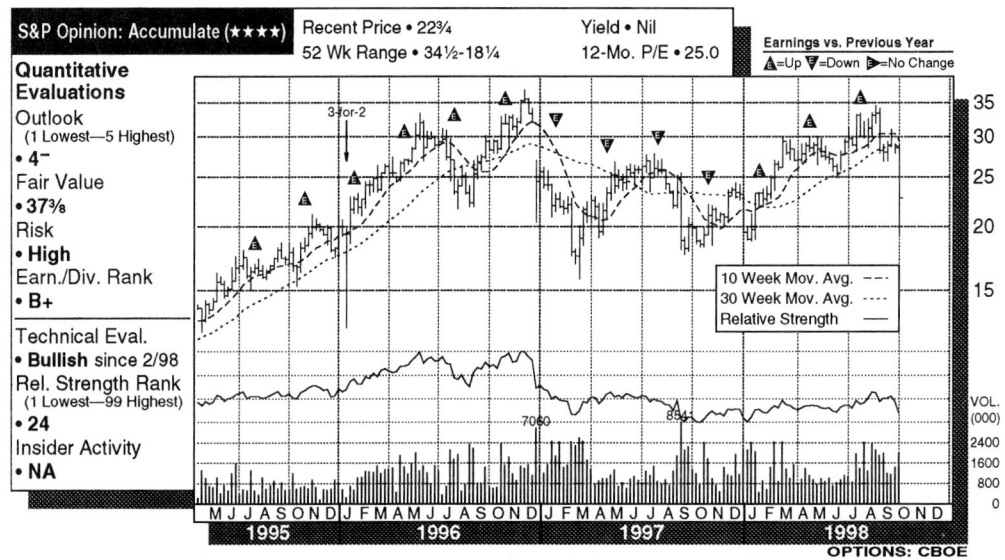

S&P Opinion: Accumulate (★★★★)

Recent Price • 22¾	Yield • Nil
52 Wk Range • 34½-18¼	12-Mo. P/E • 25.0

Earnings vs. Previous Year
▲=Up ▼=Down ▶=No Change

Quantitative Evaluations

Outlook
(1 Lowest—5 Highest)
• **4⁻**

Fair Value
• **37⅜**

Risk
• **High**

Earn./Div. Rank
• **B+**

Technical Eval.
• **Bullish** since 2/98

Rel. Strength Rank
(1 Lowest—99 Highest)
• **24**

Insider Activity
• **NA**

10 Week Mov. Avg. – – –
30 Week Mov. Avg. .....
Relative Strength —

OPTIONS: CBOE

Overview - 22-JUL-98

Revenues should increase about 15% in 1998, on continued strong demand for most of the company's information technology services. Telecommunications revenues should be flat, due to a reorganization, as a result of the cancellation of a major contract. However, growth across all other segments should remain strong. Financial services should rise 20%; state and local government could increase 25%-30%; federal government should grow 20%. International growth declined in 1997, especially in Europe, but should rebound in 1998. Margins should expand somewhat in 1998, aided by the restructured telecom unit and other cost cutting measures, although the company will face a higher tax rate. Earnings in the third quarter of 1997 were lower than expected due to the canceled telecom contract. However, earnings in 1998 should benefit from the strong revenue growth and higher margins.

Valuation - 22-JUL-98

The shares of this leading provider of consulting, systems integration and customized software fell in early September 1997 after the company announced the cancellation of a major contract. However, the shares have rebounded strongly in 1998, as revenues across all other business segments remain strong. We do not believe the loss of the contract is symptomatic of any larger problems. Revenues from the telecom unit should grow in the second half of 1998. We expect the company to build on its historical record of growth. Much of this success can be attributed to AMSY's repeat business, which accounts for between 85% and 90% of revenues. With a high rate of recurring revenues, the shares deserve their market premium. We recommend accumulating the shares.

Key Stock Statistics

S&P EPS Est. 1998	1.12	Tang. Bk. Value/Share	6.17
P/E on S&P Est. 1998	20.3	Beta	0.72
S&P EPS Est. 1999	1.40	Shareholders	1,000
Dividend Rate/Share	Nil	Market cap. (B)	$0.966
Shs. outstg. (M)	42.5	Inst. holdings	59%
Avg. daily vol. (M)	0.303		

Value of $10,000 invested 5 years ago: $ 23,005

Fiscal Year Ending Dec. 31

	1998	1997	1996	1995	1994	1993
Revenues (Million $)						
1Q	223.0	196.3	181.4	135.8	100.3	86.30
2Q	250.7	220.9	188.8	157.5	109.8	91.80
3Q	—	225.5	217.5	162.7	119.1	88.98
4Q	—	229.6	224.5	176.5	130.7	96.97
Yr.	—	872.3	812.2	632.4	459.9	364.0
Earnings Per Share ($)						
1Q	0.21	0.14	0.16	0.12	0.12	0.10
2Q	0.28	0.18	0.20	0.16	0.15	0.12
3Q	E0.29	0.11	0.25	0.19	0.15	0.08
4Q	E0.33	0.31	-0.24	0.25	0.18	0.16
Yr.	E1.12	0.74	0.37	0.72	0.60	0.46

Next earnings report expected: mid October

Dividend Data

No cash dividends have been paid. Three-for-two stock splits were effected five times since 1985.

Business Summary - 22-JUL-98

The long term goal of this international business and information technology consulting firm is to grow its earnings 20% per year. Recently, the company has focused more on improving profit margins than growing rapidly. American Management Systems attempts to partner with clients to achieve breakthrough performance through the intelligent use of information technology.

Through 55 offices worldwide, AMSY helps clients use information technology to improve the performance of their organizations, targeting businesses and governmental units in selected markets where the potential benefits of a technology-based solution are greatest. The company develops and integrates information systems for clients, and it develops and licenses proprietary software products.

Target markets include telecommunications (30% of 1997 services and products revenues, down from 40% in 1996), financial services (25%, 23%), state and local governments and education (20%, 18%) and the federal government (22%, 15%). The company's telecom revenues declined in 1997 due to the cancellation of a major Swiss contract.

AMSY assists telecommunications clients with order processing, billing and collections, and it helps financial institutions develop systems for risk management, credit collections and loan originations. In its government and education markets, AMSY provides services and software products for financial and revenue management and other functions.

AMSY considers its long-term relationships with clients and its development of specialized areas of expertise to be among its greatest strengths. Each year, approximately 85%-90% of the company's business comes from clients with which AMSY had worked the year before. AMSY believes it has established a leadership position in the state and local government market by performing successfully under contracts with state taxation departments that link its own compensation with enhanced revenue collections for the state. The company's areas of specialization are not necessarily home-grown: AMSY's capabilities in comprehensive risk management for large financial institutions, for example, were developed largely in Europe.

International business accounted for 28% of total revenues in 1997, down from 34% in 1996, due to the canceled Swiss telecom contract.

Per Share Data ($)

(Year Ended Dec. 31)	1997	1996	1995	1994	1993	1992	1991	1990	1989	1988
Tangible Bk. Val.	5.60	4.81	4.21	3.33	2.65	2.35	1.96	1.54	1.32	1.20
Cash Flow	1.56	1.31	1.46	1.13	0.69	0.67	0.53	0.48	0.32	0.34
Earnings	0.74	0.37	0.72	0.60	0.46	0.45	0.33	0.31	0.16	0.21
Dividends	Nil	Nil	Nil	Nil	Nil	Nil	Nil	Nil	Nil	Nil
Payout Ratio	Nil	Nil	Nil	Nil	Nil	Nil	Nil	Nil	Nil	Nil
Prices - High	27¾	37⅛	21⅛	12⅞	10½	10½	8½	5⅞	5½	5½
- Low	15¾	18¼	11	8	6⅝	5⅜	4⅞	3⅛	3⅛	3½
P/E Ratio - High	37	46	29	21	23	23	25	19	33	26
- Low	21	23	15	13	14	12	15	10	19	17

Income Statement Analysis (Million $)

	1997	1996	1995	1994	1993	1992	1991	1990	1989	1988
Revs.	872	812	632	460	364	333	285	262	225	213
Oper. Inc.	89.0	66.9	80.9	61.0	39.0	37.1	28.0	25.2	14.8	18.8
Depr.	34.7	39.3	30.2	20.7	8.3	7.7	7.1	6.0	5.4	4.6
Int. Exp.	5.8	3.2	2.3	1.4	0.7	1.0	1.5	1.7	2.2	1.3
Pretax Inc.	51.4	26.2	49.8	39.5	30.7	29.4	21.0	19.2	9.5	10.5
Eff. Tax Rate	39%	41%	41%	41%	42%	41%	38%	38%	34%	30%
Net Inc.	31.2	15.5	29.2	23.4	17.8	17.5	13.1	12.0	6.2	7.4

Balance Sheet & Other Fin. Data (Million $)

	1997	1996	1995	1994	1993	1992	1991	1990	1989	1988
Cash	49.6	62.8	35.8	34.2	15.6	32.5	28.4	25.4	19.0	2.5
Curr. Assets	299	324	251	182	125	123	104	95.0	91.0	71.0
Total Assets	421	424	338	252	185	166	146	134	124	103
Curr. Liab.	130	199	135	92.5	57.9	50.3	47.9	47.3	41.6	41.5
LT Debt	27.9	13.7	20.4	12.9	11.0	4.4	10.0	12.3	14.0	11.1
Common Eqty.	239	203	176	138	99	85.5	68.9	53.5	47.5	43.8
Total Cap.	282	224	202	159	126	115	97.0	85.0	81.0	59.0
Cap. Exp.	15.9	27.5	22.5	17.0	13.3	7.6	9.4	6.8	7.4	6.8
Cash Flow	65.9	54.8	59.4	43.8	25.2	23.7	18.6	16.5	11.2	12.0
Curr. Ratio	2.3	1.6	1.9	2.0	2.2	2.4	2.2	2.0	2.2	1.7
% LT Debt of Cap.	9.9	6.1	10.1	8.1	8.7	3.8	10.3	14.5	17.4	18.9
% Net Inc.of Revs.	3.6	1.9	4.6	5.1	4.9	5.3	4.6	4.6	2.8	3.5
% Ret. on Assets	7.4	4.1	9.9	10.3	10.0	11.0	9.2	9.4	5.5	7.9
% Ret. on Equity	14.1	8.2	18.6	18.8	18.2	20.2	18.7	20.9	12.6	18.7

Data as orig. reptd.; bef. results of disc. opers. and/or spec. items. Per share data adj. for stk. divs. as of ex-div. date. Bold denotes diluted EPS (FASB 128). E-Estimated. NA-Not Available. NM-Not Meaningful. NR-Not Ranked.

Office—4050 Legato Rd., Fairfax, VA 22033. **Tel**—(703) 267-8000. **Website**—http://www.amsinc.com **Chrmn**—C. O. Rossotti. **Vice Chrmn & CEO**—P. A. Brands. **Vice Chrmn**—P. W. Gross. **Pres**—P. M. Giuntini. **EVP, Treas & Secy**—F. A. Nicolai. **Dirs**—D. J. Altobello, P. A. Brands, J. J. Forese, P. M. Giuntini, P. W. Gross, D. Leonard, W. W. Lewis, F. L. Malek, F. A. Nicolai, C. O. Rossotti, A. G. Spoon. **Transfer Agent & Registrar**—Mellon Securities Trust Co., NYC. **Incorporated**—in Delaware in 1970. **Empl**— 7,100. **S&P Analyst:** Brian Goodstadt

American Oncology Resources 3107M

NASDAQ Symbol **AORI**

In S&P SmallCap 600

03-OCT-98

Industry: Health Care (Managed Care)

Summary: This national physician practice management company focuses on oncology.

Quantitative Evaluations

Recent Price • 9⅞
52 Wk Range • 19-7¾

Yield • Nil
12-Mo. P/E • 18.0

Outlook
(1 Lowest—5 Highest)
• **NA**

Fair Value
• **NA**

Risk
• **High**

Earn./Div. Rank
• **NR**

Technical Eval.
• **Bullish** since 1/98

Rel. Strength Rank
(1 Lowest—99 Highest)
• **59**

Insider Activity
• **Neutral**

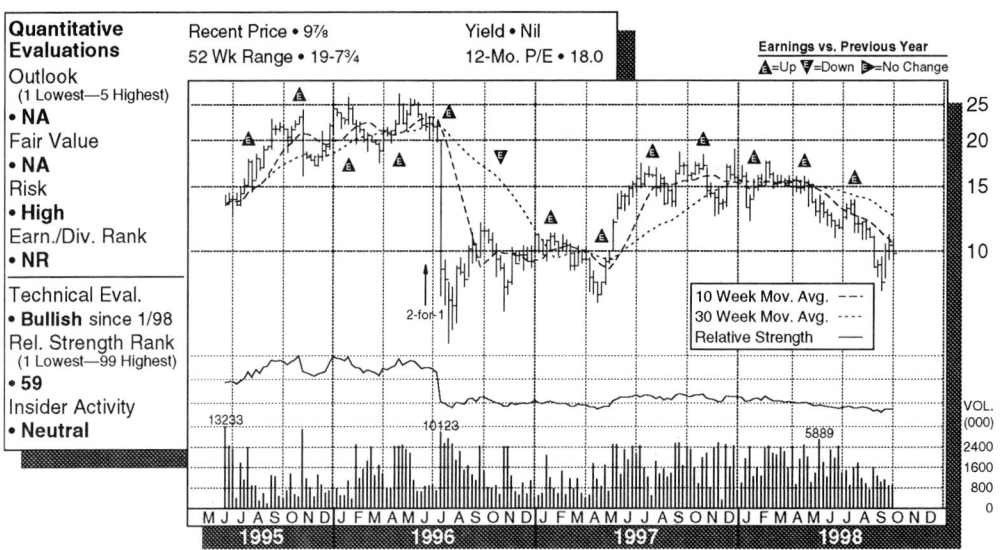

Earnings vs. Previous Year
▲=Up ▼=Down ▶=No Change

10 Week Mov. Avg. ---
30 Week Mov. Avg. ····
Relative Strength —

2-for-1

13233   10123   5889

VOL. (000)
2400
1600
800
0

M J J A S O N D J F M A M J J A S O N D J F M A M J J A S O N D J F M A M J J A S O N D
1995   1996   1997   1998

Business Profile - 13-AUG-98

The company currently provides comprehensive management services, including practice operations, practice development, marketing, facility development, managed care contracting and information systems, to 339 physicians practicing in 18 states. AORI is continuing to expand its strategic relationships with the pharmaceutical and biotechnology industry, strengthening its ability to control resource costs while enhancing its clinical research initiatives. The company plans to open five new cancer centers by October 1998. An additional seven centers are also under development.

Operational Review - 13-AUG-98

Revenues in the six months ended June 30, 1998, advanced 42%, year to year, aided by acquisitions as well as recruitment of new physicians. Margins were well controlled and operating income was also up 42%. After a 47% jump in depreciation and amortization charges, and a 55% rise in interest expense, pretax income climbed only 36%. Following taxes of 38.0%, versus 38.5%, net income increased 37%, to $14,763,000 ($0.30 a share), from $10,791,000 ($0.23).

Stock Performance - 02-OCT-98

In the past 30 trading days, AORI's shares have declined 10%, compared to a 7% fall in the S&P 500. Average trading volume for the past five days was 178,540 shares, compared with the 40-day moving average of 215,433 shares.

Key Stock Statistics

Dividend Rate/Share	Nil	Shareholders	600
Shs. outstg. (M)	32.6	Market cap. (B)	$0.322
Avg. daily vol. (M)	0.209	Inst. holdings	67%
Tang. Bk. Value/Share	8.90		
Beta	NA		

Value of $10,000 invested 5 years ago: NA

Fiscal Year Ending Dec. 31

	1998	1997	1996	1995	1994	1993
Revenues (Million $)						
1Q	101.0	70.40	40.75	14.60	2.35	—
2Q	111.6	79.53	47.37	24.64	4.15	—
3Q	—	82.29	53.70	25.50	5.94	—
4Q	—	89.63	63.64	34.43	7.97	—
Yr.	—	321.8	205.5	99.2	20.41	—
Earnings Per Share ($)						
1Q	**0.14**	**0.11**	0.10	0.03	-0.01	—
2Q	**0.16**	**0.12**	0.09	0.06	0.01	—
3Q	—	**0.12**	0.09	0.10	0.02	—
4Q	—	**0.13**	0.10	0.09	0.03	—
Yr.	—	**0.48**	0.37	0.29	0.04	-0.01

Next earnings report expected: late October

Dividend Data

No cash dividends have been paid.

A Division of The McGraw-Hill Companies

Business Summary - 13-AUG-98

In recent years, there has been a trend among oncologists (cancer specialists) to form larger group practices that provide a broad range of services to cancer patients in outpatient settings, rather than in hospitals or other inpatient settings. American Oncology Resources Inc. (AORI) believes that the coordinated delivery of comprehensive cancer care in an outpatient setting offers high quality care that is more cost-effective than traditional approaches, and that is increasingly preferred by patients, payors and physicians. The company believes that many larger oncology practices recognize the need for outside managerial, financial and business expertise to more efficiently manage the increasingly complex, burdensome and time-consuming nonmedical aspects of their practices, and feels that such practices will increasingly elect to enter into management relationships with entities such as AORI.

AORI enters into management agreements with, and purchases the nonmedical assets of, medical and radiation oncology practices. Under the terms of the management agreements, the company provides comprehensive management services to its affiliated oncology practices, including operational and administrative services, and furnishes personnel, facilities, supplies and equipment. These practices provide a broad range of medical services to cancer patients, integrating the specialties of medical oncology, hematology and radiation

oncology. AORI's revenue consists of management fees, and includes all medical practice operating costs for which the company is contractually responsible. Since its incorporation in October 1992, AORI has grown rapidly, from managing six affiliated physicians in one state, to 339 affiliated physicians in 18 states as of July 27, 1998.

The company's objective is to be the leading national physician practice management company providing comprehensive services to an integrated network of affiliated oncology practices. It intends to achieve this objective by (i) focusing exclusively on oncology, (ii) affiliating with leading oncology practices throughout the U.S., (iii) expanding each affiliated oncology group's presence in its market, (iv) assisting affiliated oncology practices in offering coordinated, comprehensive cancer care, (v) negotiating and expanding managed care relationships and (vi) expanding the clinical research operations of the affiliated physician groups. Based on AORI's success in expanding its business to date, it believes that it has effective strategies for achieving its objective of becoming the leading national oncology practice management company.

In 1997, the payor mix of the affiliated physician groups' medical practice revenue, expressed as a percentage, was 33% for Medicare and Medicaid, 47% for managed care and 20% for private insurance and other payors.

Per Share Data ($)

(Year Ended Dec. 31)	1997	1996	1995	1994	1993	1992	1991	1990	1989	1988
Tangible Bk. Val.	8.88	8.11	6.96	2.03	NA	NA	NA	NA	NA	NA
Cash Flow	0.77	0.57	0.81	0.07	NM	-0.04	NA	NA	NA	NA
Earnings	0.48	0.37	0.29	0.04	-0.01	-0.05	-0.01	NA	NA	NA
Dividends	Nil	Nil	Nil	Nil	Nil	Nil	Nil	Nil	Nil	Nil
Payout Ratio	Nil	Nil	Nil	Nil	Nil	Nil	Nil	Nil	Nil	Nil
Prices - High	19	26$7/8$	24$3/4$	NA	NA	NA	NA	NA	NA	NA
- Low	7$1/4$	5$5/8$	10$1/2$	NA	NA	NA	NA	NA	NA	NA
P/E Ratio - High	40	72	85	NA	NA	NA	NA	NA	NA	NA
- Low	15	15	36	NA	NA	NA	NA	NA	NA	NA

Income Statement Analysis (Million $)

Revs.	322	205	99	20.4	7.2	4.4	NA	NA	NA	NA
Oper. Inc.	59.4	41.3	22.2	2.2	-0.1	-0.4	NA	NA	NA	NA
Depr.	14.2	9.3	4.7	0.8	0.2	0.0	NA	NA	NA	NA
Int. Exp.	8.7	4.3	3.7	0.2	0.1	0.1	NA	NA	NA	NA
Pretax Inc.	36.8	28.7	17.5	1.4	-0.3	-1.1	NA	NA	NA	NA
Eff. Tax Rate	38%	39%	33%	9.20%	NM	NM	NM	NM	NM	NM
Net Inc.	22.9	17.6	11.6	1.2	-0.3	-1.1	NA	NA	NA	NA

Balance Sheet & Other Fin. Data (Million $)

Cash	5.0	3.4	14.8	4.2	NA	NA	NA	NA	NA	NA
Curr. Assets	115	75.7	95.8	12.5	NA	NA	NA	NA	NA	NA
Total Assets	484	339	272	55.7	5.4	3.4	NA	NA	NA	NA
Curr. Liab.	71.2	32.8	36.1	5.8	NA	NA	NA	NA	NA	NA
LT Debt	140	81.8	44.2	18.7	0.1	1.0	NA	NA	NA	NA
Common Eqty.	264	222	191	31.0	1.3	0.4	NA	NA	NA	NA
Total Cap.	413	307	236	49.9	NA	NA	NA	NA	NA	NA
Cap. Exp.	22.5	10.0	3.7	1.0	0.5	NA	NA	NA	NA	NA
Cash Flow	37.0	27.0	16.3	2.0	-0.1	-1.1	NA	NA	NA	NA
Curr. Ratio	1.6	2.3	2.7	2.1	NA	NA	NA	NA	NA	NA
% LT Debt of Cap.	33.9	26.6	18.7	37.5	NA	NA	NA	NA	NA	NA
% Net Inc.of Revs.	7.1	8.6	11.7	6.1	NM	NM	NM	NM	NM	NM
% Ret. on Assets	5.6	5.8	7.1	4.1	NM	NM	NM	NM	NM	NM
% Ret. on Equity	9.4	8.5	10.5	7.7	NM	NM	NM	NM	NM	NM

Data as orig. reptd.; bef. results of disc. opers. and/or spec. items. Per share data adj. for stk. divs. as of ex-div. date. Bold denotes diluted EPS (FASB 128). E-Estimated. NA-Not Available. NM-Not Meaningful. NR-Not Ranked.

Office—16825 Northchase Drive, Suite 1300, Houston, TX 77060. **Tel**— (281) 873-2674. **Website**—http://www.aori.com **Chrmn & CEO**—R. D. Ross. **Pres**—L. K. Everson. **VP & CFO**—L. F. Pounds. **Secy**—L. E. Sands. **Dirs**—R. L. Carson, J. E. Dalton, Jr., L. K. Everson, K. M. Fink, S. M. Marks, R. B. Mayor, M. S. Murali, R. A. Ortenzio, E. E. Rogoff, R. D. Ross. **Transfer Agent & Registrar**—American Stock Transfer & Trust Co., NYC. **Incorporated**—in Delaware in 1992. **Empl**— 1,162. **S&P Analyst:** M.J.C.

American States Water   2065

NYSE Symbol **AWR**

In S&P SmallCap 600

03-OCT-98   Industry:
Water Utilities

Summary: This water supply company serves customers in areas of Southern, Northern and Coastal California, and provides electric service to a small section of San Bernardino County.

Quantitative Evaluations

Recent Price • 26¼   Yield • 4.8%
52 Wk Range • 27⅛-21⅛   12-Mo. P/E • 14.7

Outlook
(1 Lowest—5 Highest)
• **2**

Fair Value
• **23¾**

Risk
• **Low**

Earn./Div. Rank
• **B+**

Technical Eval.
• **NA**

Rel. Strength Rank
(1 Lowest—99 Highest)
• **94**

Insider Activity
• **Neutral**

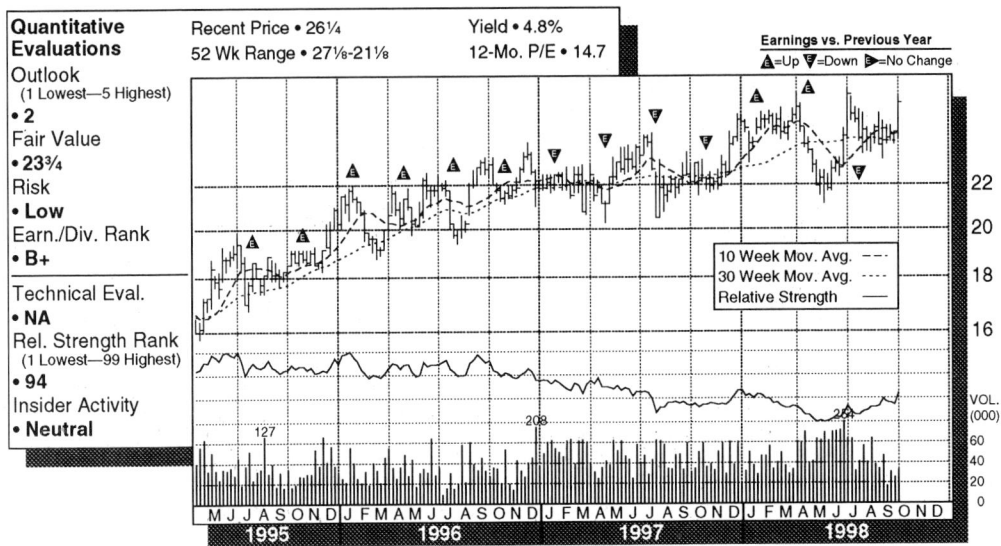

Earnings vs. Previous Year
▲=Up ▼=Down ▷=No Change

10 Week Mov. Avg. - - -
30 Week Mov. Avg. · · · ·
Relative Strength —

Business Profile - 21-JUL-98

As of February 1998, AWR (formerly South California Water Co.) was providing water service to one out of every 30 California residents, located in 75 communities throughout 10 counties, and was also providing electricity to about 20,000 customers in the Big Bear recreational area. The company saw a slight improvement in earnings in 1997, which management attributed to the effects of a shift, experienced primarily during the first half of the year, in water supply mix from pumped sources to purchased sources, due in part to water quality issues. On July 1, 1998, Southern California Water adopted a holding company format, and became a subsidiary of American States Water Co. (AWR).

Operational Review - 21-JUL-98

Operating revenues in the first quarter of 1998 declined 7.0%, year to year, primarily reflecting wet weather conditions, which led to lower water usage, and heavier winter snows, which led to lower electricity sales. Margins widened, reflecting a 33% decline in water purchased expenses, and recovery of previously under-collected supply costs; operating income was up 17%. With greater other income, partly offset by higher interest charges, net income surged 40%, to $1,843,000 ($0.20 a share, after preferred dividends), from $1,312,000 ($0.14).

Stock Performance - 02-OCT-98

In the past 30 trading days, AWR's shares have increased 6%, compared to a 7% fall in the S&P 500. Average trading volume for the past five days was 6,400 shares, compared with the 40-day moving average of 8,356 shares.

Key Stock Statistics

Dividend Rate/Share	1.26	Shareholders	4,100
Shs. outstg. (M)	9.0	Market cap. (B)	$0.235
Avg. daily vol. (M)	0.005	Inst. holdings	24%
Tang. Bk. Value/Share	20.04		
Beta	0.52		

Value of $10,000 invested 5 years ago: $ 17,993

Fiscal Year Ending Dec. 31

	1998	1997	1996	1995	1994	1993
Revenues (Million $)						
1Q	29.96	32.21	30.40	24.95	24.18	22.20
2Q	35.00	39.34	39.89	32.37	30.49	28.61
3Q	—	45.70	45.22	39.53	38.69	31.73
4Q	—	36.51	36.02	32.93	29.31	25.99
Yr.	—	153.8	151.5	129.8	122.7	108.5
Earnings Per Share ($)						
1Q	**0.20**	**0.14**	0.27	0.14	0.15	0.23
2Q	**0.31**	**0.34**	0.52	0.38	0.29	0.44
3Q	—	**0.67**	0.68	0.67	0.66	0.57
4Q	—	**0.40**	0.22	0.34	0.33	0.42
Yr.	—	**1.56**	1.69	1.54	1.43	1.66

Next earnings report expected: NA

Dividend Data (Dividends have been paid since 1931.)

Amount ($)	Date Decl.	Ex-Div. Date	Stock of Record	Payment Date
0.315	Oct. 28	Nov. 13	Nov. 17	Dec. 01 '97
0.315	Jan. 26	Feb. 05	Feb. 09	Mar. 01 '98
0.315	Apr. 27	May. 07	May. 11	Jun. 01 '98
0.315	Aug. 03	Aug. 12	Aug. 14	Sep. 01 '98

A Division of The McGraw-Hill Companies

Business Summary - 21-JUL-98

Unlike their fellow utilities in the electric, gas and telecommunications fields, water companies are expected to retain, at least for the near term, their monopoly status, and to remain for the most part under traditional cost-of-service regulation. Nevertheless, water utilities are not entirely immune to the currents of change that have already injected competition into the business mix of other public utility sectors. American States Water Co. (AWR) sees opportunities on the horizon, as change gradually comes to the water industry. AWR is a holding company, formed in July 1998, for Southern California Water Co., which serves customers in 10 counties throughout California,

AWR buys, produces, distributes and sells water (92% of revenues in 1997) to 241,581 customers in 21 separate customer service areas. About 73% of its water customers are located in the greater metropolitan areas of Los Angeles and Orange counties. In 1997, the company produced 55% of its water needs from its own wells, and purchased the balance from others, principally member agencies of the Metropolitan Water District of Southern California. In addition to providing water service, the company also distributes electricity (8% of revenues) to 20,698 customers in one California community.

The company believes that the need to ensure future source development and treatment, effective system management and adequate financing will drive smaller water companies into the acquiring arms of larger ones, such AWR. Private ownership or management of publicly owned utility systems presents additional opportunities. Such alternative arrangements arise out of the financial needs of local governments or their realization that they may not be the lowest-cost provider of utility services. In 1996, the company formed a joint venture, Golden State Water Co. LLC, to pursue opportunities involving the long-term lease or operation and maintenance of municipally owned water and wastewater systems.

In addition to potential acquisitions of economically viable operating properties, initiatives designed to improve growth prospects include the continuing pursuit of efficiencies in water and electric operations, and selective participation in non-regulated activities.

Per Share Data ($)

(Year Ended Dec. 31)	1997	1996	1995	1994	1993	1992	1991	1990	1989	1988
Tangible Bk. Val.	20.04	19.69	19.03	18.42	14.92	13.28	12.59	11.31	10.96	10.61
Earnings	1.56	1.69	1.54	1.43	1.66	1.81	2.34	1.41	1.38	0.97
Dividends	1.25	1.23	1.21	1.20	1.19	1.15	1.10	1.08	1.03	1.01
Payout Ratio	80%	72%	78%	84%	125%	63%	47%	77%	75%	104%
Prices - High	25⅝	24⅛	21	22	24⅜	20⅝	17⅞	15¾	15⅜	14⅝
- Low	20¼	18¾	15¾	15¼	19⅝	16	13⅝	12⅝	12⅛	11½
P/E Ratio - High	16	14	14	15	15	11	8	11	11	15
- Low	13	11	10	11	12	9	6	9	9	12

Income Statement Analysis (Million $)

	1997	1996	1995	1994	1993	1992	1991	1990	1989	1988
Revs.	154	152	130	123	109	101	90.7	90.4	85.6	80.2
Depr.	11.0	10.1	8.5	8.1	7.4	6.5	6.0	5.2	4.7	4.4
Maint.	7.3	7.8	5.8	6.9	6.5	5.1	5.2	5.0	4.6	5.0
Fxd. Chgs. Cov.	3.9	3.2	3.2	3.5	3.0	3.5	3.0	2.4	2.1	1.9
Constr. Credits	Nil	Nil	Nil	Nil	Nil	Nil	Nil	Nil	Nil	Nil
Eff. Tax Rate	42%	43%	42%	45%	24%	41%	36%	42%	38%	39%
Net Inc.	14.1	13.5	12.2	11.3	12.0	12.1	15.4	8.9	8.7	6.1

Balance Sheet & Other Fin. Data (Million $)

	1997	1996	1995	1994	1993	1992	1991	1990	1989	1988
Gross Prop.	510	472	438	408	380	355	331	300	275	274
Cap. Exp.	34.7	32.0	25.8	30.9	28.1	28.2	32.5	27.1	25.7	24.0
Net Prop.	385	358	335	315	295	278	259	236	214	214
Capitalization:										
LT Debt	115	107	107	92.9	84.3	84.2	82.6	67.3	67.8	73.5
% LT Debt	43	42	47	43	42	48	49	48	49	52
Pfd.	2.0	2.1	2.1	2.2	2.2	2.2	2.3	2.3	2.4	2.4
% Pfd.	0.80	0.80	0.90	1.00	1.10	1.30	1.40	1.60	1.70	1.70
Common	151	147	122	119	117	88.2	83.2	71.1	68.6	66.1
% Common	56	57	53	56	57	51	50	51	50	47
Total Cap.	NA	327	300	279	267	214	206	171	170	172
% Oper. Ratio	85.0	84.5	83.5	84.6	81.5	81.0	81.4	83.7	82.7	84.8
% Earn. on Net Prop.	6.3	6.8	6.6	6.2	7.0	7.1	6.8	6.5	6.9	6.0
% Return On Revs.	9.1	8.9	9.4	9.2	11.1	12.1	16.9	9.9	10.2	7.6
% Return On Invest. Capital	10.3	7.6	10.5	7.0	8.5	9.5	12.2	9.0	9.6	7.5
% Return On Com. Equity	9.4	9.7	10.0	9.5	11.7	14.1	19.9	12.6	12.8	9.1

Data as orig. reptd.; bef. results of disc. opers. and/or spec. items. Per share data adj. for stk. divs. as of ex-div. date. Bold denotes diluted EPS (FASB 128). E-Estimated. NA-Not Available. NM-Not Meaningful. NR-Not Ranked.

Office—630 East Foothill Blvd., San Dimas, CA 91773. **Tel**—(909) 394-3600. **Website**—http://www.scwater.com **Chrmn**—W. V. Caveney. **Pres & CEO**—F. E. Wicks. **VP-Fin, CFO, Treas, Secy & Investor Contact**—McClellan Harris III.**Dirs**—J. L. Anderson, J. E. Auer, W. V. Caveney, N. P. Dodge Jr., R. F. Kathol, L. E. Ross, F. E. Wicks. **Transfer Agent & Registrar**—ChaseMellon Shareholder Services, LA. **Incorporated**—in California in 1998. **Empl**— 467. **S&P Analyst:** J. Robert Cho

03-OCT-98 **Industry:** Consumer Finance

Summary: This consumer finance company specializes in financing automobile sales contracts and also purchases and sells home equity loans.

S&P Opinion: Accumulate (★★★★)	Recent Price • 10¾	Yield • Nil
	52 Wk Range • 18⅝-9⅞	12-Mo. P/E • 11.6

Earnings vs. Previous Year
▲=Up ▼=Down ▶=No Change

Quantitative Evaluations

Outlook (1 Lowest—5 Highest)
• **4⁻**

Fair Value
• **18¼**

Risk
• **Average**

Earn./Div. Rank
• **B-**

Technical Eval.
• **Bearish** since 9/98

Rel. Strength Rank (1 Lowest—99 Highest)
• **19**

Insider Activity
• **Neutral**

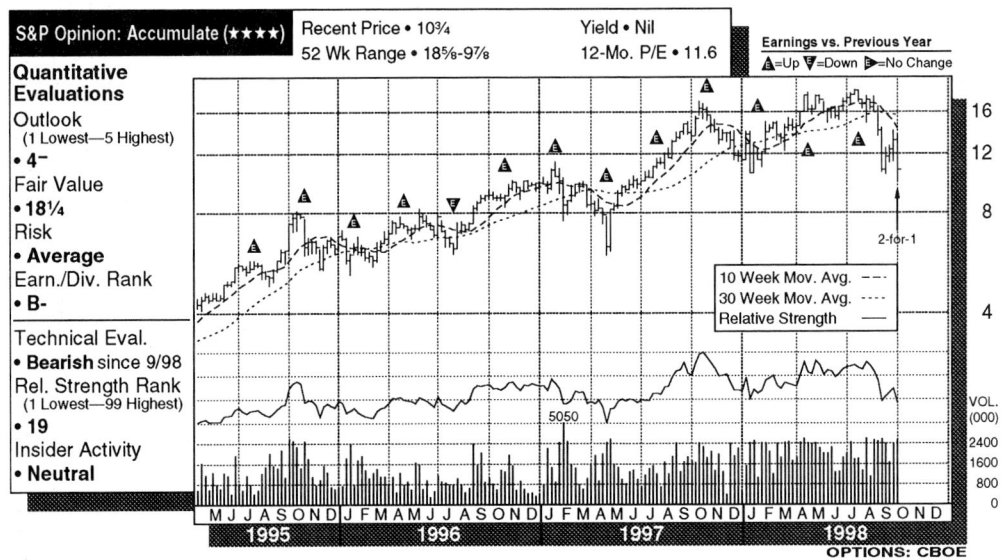

10 Week Mov. Avg. — - —
30 Week Mov. Avg. - - - -
Relative Strength —

2-for-1

VOL. (000)
2400
1600
800
0

1995 1996 1997 1998

OPTIONS: CBOE

Overview - 14-AUG-98

We are maintaining our accumulate rating on this consumer auto finance company, as growth in total managed receivables more than doubled in FY 98 (Jun), on loan volume from new branches and increased market share at mature offices. We believe Americredit's proprietary credit scoring model, using static auto loan pool data from 1992 to the present, enables the company to more accurately set pricing and predict delinquencies. As a result, chargeoffs have fallen to 5.1% of average managed receivables at FY 98 year-end, from 5.5% a year earlier. Revenues surged 66% during FY 98, largely on gains from the sale of loans and greater servicing income, as ACF sold more than $1.6 billion in loans during FY 98, with servicing retained. Expenses continue to fall as a percentage of total managed receivables, despite the addition of 44 branches during the year. Net income jumped 57%, to $60.7 million (1.86 a share, on 5.9% more shares), from $38.7 million ($1.26). ACF had a total of 129 offices in 36 states at June 30, 1998.

Valuation - 14-AUG-98

Investor's have shown confidence in ACF's strategy of statistical based lending and low-cost operation. Securitizations have fueled the growth in ACF's business, as gains from these sales provide current income and capital for future loan purchases. Continuing the cycle, loan servicing income has surged in line with the expanding portfolio. We believe that ACF will succeed in this difficult, consolidating industry, as it continues to capitalize on selective lending opportunities. Although growth may slow as the portfolio base expands, we project annual long-term earnings growth of around 25%. ACF remains attractive, at a recent level of about 15X our revised FY 99 EPS estimate of $2.35.

Key Stock Statistics

S&P EPS Est. 1998	NA	Tang. Bk. Value/Share	4.43
P/E on S&P Est. 1998	NA	Beta	1.27
S&P EPS Est. 1999	1.13	Shareholders	400
Dividend Rate/Share	Nil	Market cap. (B)	$0.657
Shs. outstg. (M)	61.1	Inst. holdings	83%
Avg. daily vol. (M)	0.575		

Value of $10,000 invested 5 years ago: $ 53,750

Fiscal Year Ending Jun. 30

	1998	1997	1996	1995	1994	1993
Revenues (Million $)						
1Q	49.29	27.80	13.92	4.83	3.70	10.30
2Q	52.94	31.88	20.26	6.78	3.98	7.02
3Q	58.43	36.73	22.35	8.97	3.91	3.88
4Q	67.29	41.35	24.45	11.68	4.29	3.67
Yr.	227.9	137.8	80.98	33.08	15.88	24.88
Earnings Per Share ($)						
1Q	0.20	0.14	0.04	0.03	0.02	-0.01
2Q	**0.22**	0.15	0.09	0.04	0.02	-0.36
3Q	**0.24**	0.17	0.10	0.05	0.02	0.02
4Q	**0.27**	0.18	0.12	0.36	0.03	0.02
Yr.	**0.93**	0.63	0.35	0.47	0.08	-0.33

Next earnings report expected: **NA**

Dividend Data

Amount ($)	Date Decl.	Ex-Div. Date	Stock of Record	Payment Date
2-for-1	Aug. 18	Oct. 01	Sep. 11	Sep. 30 '98

A Division of The McGraw-Hill Companies

AmeriCredit Corp.

Business Summary - 14-AUG-98

AmeriCredit Corp. is a consumer finance company that specializes in financing automobile sales contracts. As of June 1997, it had 85 branch offices in 30 states.

Total revenues in recent fiscal years (Jun.) were derived as follows:

	FY 97	FY 96	FY 95
Finance charge income	33%	64%	91%
Investment income	2%	1%	4%
Gain on sale of receivables	49%	28%	---
Servicing fee income	15%	5%	---
Other	1%	2%	5%

Through its AmeriCredit Financial Services (AFS) branch network, ACF purchases loans, acting as a funding source for franchised and independent dealers to finance customer purchases, primarily of used cars. Target customers typically are unable to obtain financing from traditional sources. They may have had financial difficulties and are attempting to re-establish credit or may not have sufficient credit history. Consumer finance loans made to such customers typically range from $9,000 to $15,000, with repayment terms generally from 42 to 60 months.

At June 30, 1997, the portfolio of net finance receivables (after allowance for losses of $12.9 million) totaled $266.6 million. Finance charge income in FY 97 came almost entirely from indirect consumer lending, as was the case in FY 96 as well.

The most cost effective source of funds for continued loan purchases has been through securitization. The company uses net proceeds from the sale of these loans to pay down borrowings, thus increasing availability for future purchases. Revenue is recognized as a gain on the sale of receivables, which represents net proceeds (minus the carrying value of the receivables), plus an estimate of the present value of all future excess cash flows above those obligated to investors. Unfortunately, any future losses or prepayments that exceed the company's estimates would be charged against earnings. Through June 30, 1997, ACF had securitized about $1.3 billion in loans, with no such charges having been made.

In November 1996, ACF acquired Rancho Vista Mortgage Corp. (now operating under the name AmeriCredit Mortgage Services), which originates and sells home equity loans. The purchase price of $7,100,000 consisted of 400,000 ACF common shares. Receivables originated in this business are generally packaged and sold to investors for cash on a servicing released, whole-loan basis. While this business does not currently represent a material portion of revenues or assets, management intends to devote substantial resources to pursue growth in home equity origination to sub-prime borrowers.

Per Share Data ($)

(Year Ended Jun. 30)	1998	1997	1996	1995	1994	1993	1992	1991	1990	1989
Tangible Bk. Val.	NA	3.57	2.86	2.56	2.08	2.11	2.35	2.74	3.31	0.69
Earnings	0.93	0.63	0.35	0.47	0.08	-0.33	-0.39	-0.57	0.34	0.10
Dividends	Nil	Nil	Nil	Nil	Nil	Nil	Nil	Nil	Nil	Nil
Payout Ratio	Nil	Nil	Nil	Nil	Nil	Nil	Nil	Nil	Nil	Nil
Prices - High	18⅝	17¼	10	5¾	4⅛	2⅜	2⅜	2⅞	11½	5¾
- Low	10½	6	5¼	2⅝	2⅝	1¹/₁₆	1¹/₁₆	1¹/₁₆	1¹¹/₁₆	3¾
P/E Ratio - High	20	27	28	12	51	NM	NM	NM	34	59
- Low	11	9	15	6	32	NM	NM	NM	5	38

Income Statement Analysis (Million $)

	1998	1997	1996	1995	1994	1993	1992	1991	1990	1989
Total Revs.	NA	138	81.0	33.1	15.9	24.9	74.2	190	164	41.2
Int. Exp.	NA	16.3	13.1	4.0	0.2	0.2	0.3	2.5	2.0	0.8
Exp./Op. Revs.	NA	54%	58%	70%	68%	178%	131%	125%	85%	89%
Pretax Inc.	NA	62.9	34.3	10.0	5.1	-19.4	-23.3	-47.2	24.1	4.5
Eff. Tax Rate	NA	39%	37%	NM	Nil	Nil	NM	NM	34%	36%
Net Inc.	NA	38.7	21.6	28.9	5.1	-19.4	-24.2	-36.2	15.8	2.9

Balance Sheet & Other Fin. Data (Million $)

	1998	1997	1996	1995	1994	1993	1992	1991	1990	1989
Cash & Secs.	NA	80.4	24.0	33.6	42.3	68.4	39.3	14.3	71.9	3.2
Loans	NA	267	251	222	72.2	43.9	69.5	115	112	26.3
Total Assets	NA	493	330	286	122	131	154	181	223	46.0
ST Debt	NA	16.6	30.4	70.5	0.2	0.4	0.5	1.6	0.4	NA
Capitalization:										
Debt	NA	132	37.8	64.7	0.2	0.9	1.3	1.3	2.4	15.9
Equity	NA	217	163	147	120	123	147	172	208	22.0
Total	NA	349	201	212	120	124	149	173	211	38.0
Price Times Bk. Val.: High	NA	4.2	3.5	2.2	2.0	1.1	1.0	1.0	3.5	8.2
Price Times Bk. Val.: Low	NA	1.7	1.8	1.0	1.2	0.5	0.5	0.4	0.5	5.3
% Return On Revs.	NA	28.1	26.7	87.3	31.9	NM	NM	NM	9.6	7.0
% Ret. on Assets	NA	9.4	7.0	14.2	4.0	NM	NM	NM	11.7	10.7
% Ret. on Equity	NA	20.4	13.9	21.7	4.2	NM	NM	NM	13.7	25.1
Loans/Equity	NA	136.2	152.2	110.2	47.9	42.0	57.9	59.9	60.1	NM

Data as orig. reptd.; bef. results of disc opers. and/or spec. items. Per share data adj. for stk. divs. as of ex-div. date. Bold denotes diluted EPS (FASB 128). E-Estimated. NA-Not Available. NM-Not Meaningful. NR-Not Ranked.

Office—200 Bailey Ave., Fort Worth, TX 76107. **Tel**—(817) 332-7000. **Chrmn & CEO**—C. H. Morris Jr. **Pres & COO**—M. R. Barrington. **CFO**—D. E. Berce. **SVP & Secy**—C. A. Choate. **Investor Contact**—Kim Welch. **Dirs**—M. R. Barrington, D. E. Berce, E. H. Esstman, J. H. Greer, G. W. Haddock, D. K. Higgins, K. H. Jones Jr., C. H. Morris Jr. **Transfer Agent & Registrar**—Chasemellon Shareholder Services, Dallas. **Incorporated**—in Texas in 1988. **Empl**—900. **S&P Analyst:** L. A. Olive

AMRESCO, INC.
3125H

NASDAQ Symbol **AMMB**

In S&P SmallCap 600

03-OCT-98   **Industry:** Financial (Diversified)

Summary: This diversified financial services company specializes in commercial and residential real estate lending, asset management workout services and commercial finance.

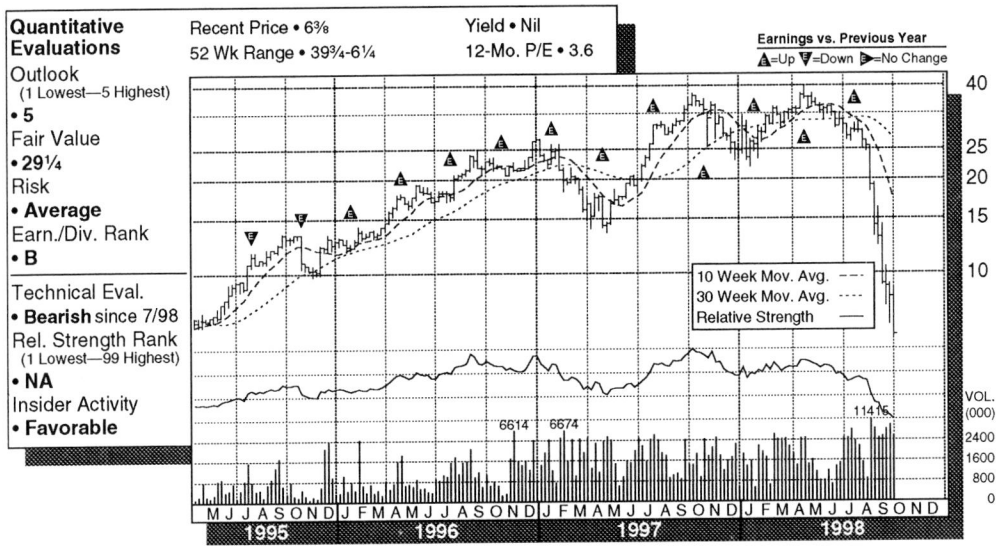

Quantitative Evaluations

Recent Price • 6⅜
52 Wk Range • 39¾-6¼

Yield • Nil
12-Mo. P/E • 3.6

Earnings vs. Previous Year
▲=Up ▼=Down ▶=No Change

Outlook (1 Lowest—5 Highest)
• **5**

Fair Value
• 29¼

Risk
• **Average**

Earn./Div. Rank
• **B**

Technical Eval.
• **Bearish** since 7/98

Rel. Strength Rank (1 Lowest—99 Highest)
• **NA**

Insider Activity
• **Favorable**

10 Week Mov. Avg. — - -
30 Week Mov. Avg. - - - -
Relative Strength ——

Business Profile - 18-AUG-98

In 1994, AMMB implemented a growth strategy designed to expand its businesses in markets that capitalize on the company's strengths. Some of the key elements of the company's business strategy include growing its participation in the origination, acquisition and securitization of residential mortgage sub-prime loans, expanding its presence in the commercial banking mortgage market, and investing for its own account in asset portfolios. In August 1998, AMMB continued its growth and diversification efforts with the acquisition of privately held Mortgage Investors Corp. (MIC). MIC is a specialized producer of VA streamlined re-financed loans, also known as IRRRLs. MIC will become AMMB's fifth line of business, identified as Residential Mortgage Banking. AMMB's existing residential business will be renamed Home Equity Lending.

Operational Review - 18-AUG-98

Revenues in the first six months of 1998 rose 80%, year to year, powered by large increases in interest and other investment income, gains on the sale of loans, and higher mortgage banking and servicing fees. Total expenses advanced 84%, led by sharply higher interest and personnel costs; pretax income rose 61%. After taxes at 38.9%, versus 38.6%, net income increased 60%, to $33,709,000 ($0.80 a share, based on 18% more shares), from $21,047,000 ($0.59).

Stock Performance - 02-OCT-98

In the past 30 trading days, AMMB's shares have declined 67%, compared to a 7% fall in the S&P 500. Average trading volume for the past five days was 856,880 shares, compared with the 40-day moving average of 1,218,564 shares.

Key Stock Statistics

Dividend Rate/Share	Nil	Shareholders	2,800
Shs. outstg. (M)	44.3	Market cap. (B)	$0.281
Avg. daily vol. (M)	1.243	Inst. holdings	76%
Tang. Bk. Value/Share	10.87		
Beta	1.88		

Value of $10,000 invested 5 years ago: $ 17,079

Fiscal Year Ending Dec. 31

	1998	1997	1996	1995	1994	1993
Revenues (Million $)						
1Q	143.1	74.84	36.90	20.18	40.56	51.61
2Q	177.9	103.9	46.81	23.48	40.46	38.00
3Q	—	112.8	45.49	25.42	46.78	42.86
4Q	—	132.3	70.87	41.41	29.38	44.05
Yr.	—	423.8	200.1	110.5	157.2	176.5

Earnings Per Share ($)						
1Q	0.35	0.25	0.18	0.13	0.23	0.61
2Q	0.45	0.34	0.27	0.17	0.23	0.58
3Q	—	0.41	0.31	0.21	0.37	0.63
4Q	—	0.53	0.36	0.25	0.05	0.33
Yr.	—	1.53	1.12	0.76	0.88	2.15

Next earnings report expected: late October

Dividend Data

Dividends, which were omitted in 1989 and reinstated in 1993, were again omitted in 1995. A stockholder rights plan was adopted in May 1997.

A Division of The **McGraw·Hill** *Companies*

Business Summary - 18-AUG-98

In 1994, 85% of Dallas-based AMRESCO, INC.'s revenue was derived from a single line of business, asset management. Since that time, management has expanded the company's reach; with the August 1998 acquisition of Mortgage Investors Corporation (MIC), AMMB now operates five lines of business. In just a few years, AMMB has transformed itself into a diversified financial services company that provides financing and value-added services to commercial and consumer borrowers and institutional investors.

The company's residential mortgage banking business (now called Home Equity Lending following the August 1998 acquisition of MIC) comprised 39% of revenues in 1997 (28% in 1996). This business unit originates, acquires, warehouses and securitizes residential mortgage loans. Loan production increased to $3.6 billion in 1997 from $1.9 billion a year earlier. Management attributes the growth in this market to a number of factors, including a large number of borrowers seeking to consolidate their revolving credit debt and auto loans for a lower rate and payment, and slow growth in real estate appreciation causing an increase in the number of borrowers seeking to make home improvements.

Asset management accounted for 26% of AMMB's total revenues in 1997 (42% the year before). The company's asset management business resolves loans and provides accounting services for portfolios that generally include secured loans. While the need for this service by government agencies has declined in recent years, management sees an active market for this service emerging in the private sector.

AMMB believes the commercial mortgage banking market offers great growth opportunities due to the estimated $150 billion in refinancings done each year, in addition to mortgage financing for new construction. The company, which performs a wide range of commercial mortgage banking services (23% of 1997 revenues and 27% of 1996 revenues), expects to improve its position as a nationwide mortgage banker through internal development and acquisitions.

In 1996, AMMB organized the Commercial Finance Group to provide financing to commercial borrowers in various targeted markets. This business unit focuses on loans to franchisees of nationally recognized restaurant, hospitality and automotive organizations, structured finance activities, with an emphasis on the real estate and communications industries, and single family residential construction lending. Loans originated by the franchise lending operation are sold to third parties, principally through securitization, while the real estate, communications and single family residential construction loans are retained for AMMB's own portfolio. After contributing just over 1% of revenues in 1996, this segment accounted for 12% of revenues in 1997.

Per Share Data ($)

(Year Ended Dec. 31)	1997	1996	1995	1994	1993	1992	1991	1990	1989	1988
Tangible Bk. Val.	8.07	6.35	4.09	4.81	3.65	2.41	3.05	3.10	2.24	3.58
Earnings	1.53	1.12	0.76	0.88	2.15	0.50	0.33	0.20	-0.75	0.22
Dividends	Nil	Nil	0.10	0.20	0.15	Nil	Nil	Nil	0.18	0.24
Payout Ratio	Nil	Nil	13%	23%	7%	Nil	Nil	Nil	NM	105%
Prices - High	37⁷/₈	27³/₈	13¹/₂	9¹/₄	7¹/₂	4¹/₂	5	3³/₈	5¹/₂	7¹/₂
- Low	13¹/₂	11³/₄	5⁷/₈	5¹/₂	3³/₄	2³/₈	2¹/₂	2	2¹/₈	4¹/₈
P/E Ratio - High	25	24	18	11	3	9	15	17	NM	34
- Low	9	10	8	6	2	5	8	10	NM	19

Income Statement Analysis (Million $)

	1997	1996	1995	1994	1993	1992	1991	1990	1989	1988
Premium Inc.	Nil	Nil	Nil	NA	NA	NA	NA	NA	NA	NA
Invest. Inc.	204	104	40.1	13.1	2.6	NA	NA	NA	NA	NA
Oth. Revs.	220	96.5	70.4	NA	NA	NA	NA	NA	NA	NA
Total Revs.	424	200	111	157	177	47.2	40.7	37.5	25.4	41.5
Int. Exp.	102	36.8	6.9	1.8	0.8	0.1	0.2	0.8	1.3	0.8
Exp./Op. Revs.	79%	75%	73%	77%	77%	NA	NA	NA	NA	NA
Pretax Inc.	92.1	50.5	30.3	35.7	40.2	5.4	3.6	2.2	-7.0	3.6
Eff. Tax Rate	39%	38%	38%	41%	40%	21%	6.20%	13%	NM	45%
Net Inc.	56.2	31.3	18.7	20.9	24.2	5.3	3.3	1.9	-7.0	2.0

Balance Sheet & Other Fin. Data (Million $)

	1997	1996	1995	1994	1993	1992	1991	1990	1989	1988
Receivables	19.2	12.2	20.2	20.7	39.4	NA	NA	NA	NA	NA
Cash & Invest.	25.9	63.2	38.0	20.4	43.4	3.5	2.0	1.0	1.2	8.8
Loans	1,979	417	299	30.9	33.8	NA	NA	NA	NA	NA
Total Assets	2,634	1,076	522	172	164	44.3	50.6	49.6	57.7	52.3
Capitalization:										
Debt	839	375	173	16.5	28.1	0.3	0.2	1.6	9.2	0.6
Equity	409	302	161	114	91.7	35.7	43.8	38.5	33.5	38.5
Total	1,248	677	334	130	120	36.0	45.1	40.1	42.7	39.2
Price Times Bk. Val.: High	4.7	4.3	3.3	1.9	2.1	1.9	1.6	1.1	2.5	2.1
Price Times Bk. Val.: Low	1.7	1.9	1.4	1.1	1.0	1.0	0.8	0.6	0.9	1.2
% Return On Revs.	13.3	15.6	16.9	13.3	13.7	11.2	8.2	5.2	NM	4.9
% Ret. on Assets	3.0	3.9	5.4	12.5	23.3	13.0	6.7	3.6	NM	4.1
% Ret. on Equity	18.8	13.5	13.5	20.4	43.4	16.3	8.1	5.4	NM	5.3
Loans/Equity	372.4	138.1	217.9	31.5	30.6	NA	NA	NA	NA	NA

Data as orig. reptd.; bef. results of disc. opers. and/or spec. items. Per share data adj. for stk. divs. as of ex-div. date. Bold denotes diluted EPS (FASB 128). E-Estimated. NA-Not Available. NM-Not Meaningful. NR-Not Ranked.

Office—700 N. Pearl St., Suite 2400, LB 342, Dallas, TX 75201 Tel—(214) 953-7700. Website—http://www.amresco.com Chrmn & CEO—R. H. Lutz Jr. Pres & COO—R. L. Adair III. EVP & CFO—B. L. Edwards. Secy—L. K. Blackwell. VP, Treas & Investor Contact—Thomas J. Andrus. Dirs—R. L. Adair III, J. P. Cotton Jr., R. L. Cravey, G. E. Eickhoff, S. E. Harris, A. J. Jorgensen, R. H. Lutz Jr., B. W. Schnitzer, E.A. Wahlen Jr. Transfer Agent & Registrar—Trust Company Bank, Atlanta. Incorporated—in Delaware in 1977. Empl— 1,650. S&P Analyst: Michael Schneider

03-OCT-98

Industry: Electronics (Instrumentation)

Summary: ALOG designs and makes high-technology, high-precision analog/digital signal processing equipment for the worldwide medical, industrial and scientific industries.

Quantitative Evaluations

Recent Price • 40
52 Wk Range • 48-31⅛

Yield • 0.6%
12-Mo. P/E • 22.1

Outlook (1 Lowest—5 Highest)
• 4

Fair Value
• 40%

Risk
• Average

Earn./Div. Rank
• B

Technical Eval.
• Bullish since 9/98

Rel. Strength Rank (1 Lowest—99 Highest)
• 94

Insider Activity
• NA

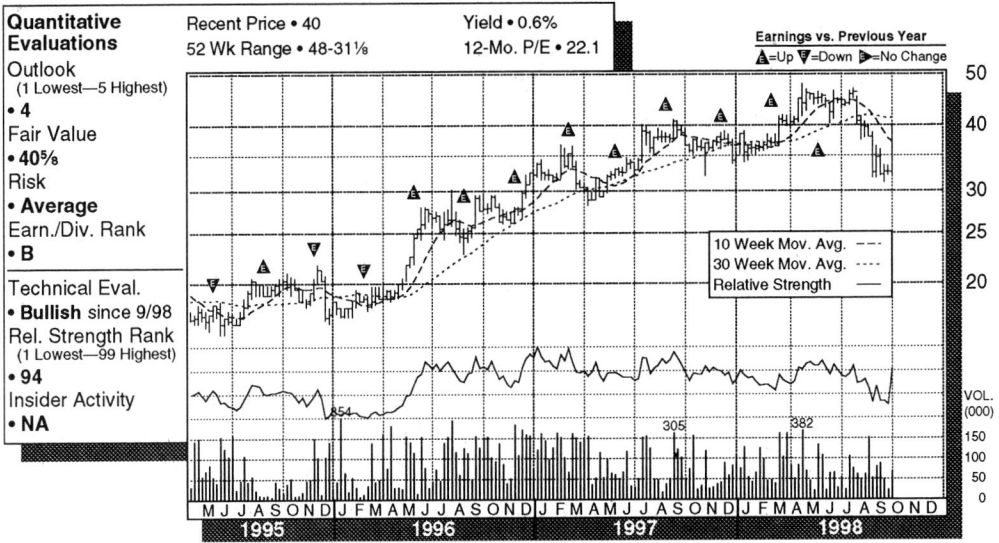

Earnings vs. Previous Year
▲=Up ▼=Down ▶=No Change

10 Week Mov. Avg. — - —
30 Week Mov. Avg. ....
Relative Strength ——

Business Profile - 20-AUG-98

Although results were consistently profitable during the decade through FY 97 (Jul.), earnings have been somewhat erratic. In June 1997, ALOG, L-3 Communications Corp. and Europ Scan submitted a proposal to the French Directorate General in response to its upcoming order for Computer Tomography airport security systems. The proposed systems would be installed at major airports in France and its overseas departments. Europ Scan will be responsible for the integration, installation and system support of the installed units. The company and L-3 Communications are jointly developing the system for the FAA. In February 1998, ALOG raised its dividend 20%. Capital expenditures totaled about $9.7 million during the nine months ended Apr. 30, 1998.

Operational Review - 20-AUG-98

Total revenues in the nine months ended April 30, 1998, advanced 15%, year to year, reflecting increased sales of medical technology, signal processing and industrial technology products. Gross margins narrowed, restricted by higher than anticipated costs on engineering projects. SG&A and R&D costs were well controlled and results also benefited from a gain on sale of marketable securities, partly offset by an impairment on investment. After taxes at 33.8%, versus 29.9%, and minority interest, net income was up 22%, to $16,678,000 ($1.31 a share), from $13,720,000 ($1.08).

Stock Performance - 02-OCT-98

In the past 30 trading days, ALOG's shares have increased 5%, compared to a 7% fall in the S&P 500. Average trading volume for the past five days was 13,400 shares, compared with the 40-day moving average of 14,928 shares.

Key Stock Statistics

Dividend Rate/Share	0.24	Shareholders	900
Shs. outstg. (M)	12.6	Market cap. (B)	$0.505
Avg. daily vol. (M)	0.012	Inst. holdings	45%
Tang. Bk. Value/Share	18.15		
Beta	0.55		

Value of $10,000 invested 5 years ago: $ 28,690

Fiscal Year Ending Jul. 31

	1998	1997	1996	1995	1994	1993
Revenues (Million $)						
1Q	63.93	59.47	46.48	50.93	46.11	41.00
2Q	71.65	61.73	53.15	52.54	49.59	42.98
3Q	77.38	64.17	60.49	49.10	47.13	46.84
4Q	—	71.36	70.35	56.25	50.93	47.04
Yr.	—	256.7	230.5	208.8	193.8	177.9
Earnings Per Share ($)						
1Q	0.36	0.31	0.11	0.28	0.26	0.23
2Q	**0.45**	0.36	0.16	0.25	0.30	0.24
3Q	**0.50**	0.41	0.30	0.15	0.29	0.26
4Q	—	0.50	0.47	0.34	0.33	0.28
Yr.	—	1.58	1.04	1.02	1.18	1.01

Next earnings report expected: early October

Dividend Data (Dividends have been paid since 1995.)

Amount ($)	Date Decl.	Ex-Div. Date	Stock of Record	Payment Date
0.050	Oct. 09	Oct. 21	Oct. 23	Nov. 06 '97
0.060	Jan. 23	Feb. 04	Feb. 06	Feb. 20 '98
0.060	Mar. 12	Mar. 25	Mar. 27	Apr. 10 '98
0.060	Jun. 11	Jun. 24	Jun. 26	Jul. 10 '98

A Division of The McGraw-Hill Companies

Business Summary - 20-AUG-98

Analogic Corporation designs, makes and sells standard and customized high-precision data acquisition, conversion and signal processing equipment, which is primarily incorporated by OEMs into systems used in medical, industrial and scientific applications. Revenues by product group in recent fiscal years (Jul.) were:

	1997	1996
Medical Technology	73%	71%
Signal Processing Technology	20%	20%
Industrial Technology	7%	9%

Product, service, engineering and licensing export revenue from foreign companies accounted for 34% of sales in FY 97, and 36% in FY 95.

Medical Technology products, primarily medical imaging data acquisition systems, are used in advanced X-ray equipment known as computer-assisted tomography (CAT) scanners. Analogic also makes CAT scanners using proprietary technology, electronic equipment for diagnostic image printers, ultrasound imaging equipment and systems, magnetic resonance imaging equipment, and fetal monitoring products. Camtronics Ltd. (68% owned) designs and makes medical image processing equipment.

Signal Processing Technology products consist of analog-to-digital (A/D) and digital-to-analog (D/A) converters and supporting modules. A/D devices convert continuously varying analog signals into the numerical digital form required by computers, while D/A converters transform computer output in digital form into analog signals required by process control equipment. The group also produces interconnecting and supporting modules for the A/D and D/A converters, high-speed digital signal processors, such as Array Processors, and image processing equipment.

Industrial Technology products include digital panel instruments, which measure analog inputs and display the results in numerical (digital) form. They are incorporated in precision thermometers, blood analyzers and automatic test equipment. The group also produces industrial data acquisition and conversion systems, test and measurement devices and automation systems.

Analogic is designing a computed tomography scanner to be incorporated into Lockheed Martin Corp.'s eXaminer 3DX 6000 system, which is designed to scan checked luggage at airports. The effort is being jointly funded by the company and an FAA grant.

The three largest customers in FY 97, Phillips, General Electric and Siemens, accounted for 17%, 8% and 8% of total revenues, respectively.

Per Share Data ($)

(Year Ended Jul. 31)	1997	1996	1995	1994	1993	1992	1991	1990	1989	1988
Tangible Bk. Val.	18.15	17.03	16.22	14.97	13.53	12.76	11.97	10.86	9.99	8.88
Cash Flow	2.00	1.54	1.51	1.69	1.67	1.47	1.49	1.38	1.44	0.52
Earnings	1.58	1.04	1.02	1.18	1.01	0.78	0.91	0.85	0.97	0.07
Dividends	0.20	0.18	0.08	Nil	Nil	Nil	Nil	Nil	Nil	Nil
Payout Ratio	13%	17%	8%	Nil	Nil	Nil	Nil	Nil	Nil	Nil
Prices - High	41	33½	21¾	20	16¾	13⅛	14¾	10⅛	11⅛	8¾
- Low	28⅛	17¼	16	14⅝	12¾	10¼	8	8	8⅜	5½
P/E Ratio - High	26	32	21	17	17	17	16	12	11	NM
- Low	18	17	16	12	13	13	9	9	9	NM

Income Statement Analysis (Million $)

	1997	1996	1995	1994	1993	1992	1991	1990	1989	1988
Revs.	251	224	204	189	174	145	137	138	133	120
Oper. Inc.	31.4	17.1	17.7	21.1	22.8	14.1	21.0	20.1	16.0	-2.1
Depr.	5.4	6.2	6.5	6.4	8.1	8.8	7.8	7.8	7.0	7.3
Int. Exp.	0.6	0.8	0.8	1.3	1.1	1.6	1.0	1.0	1.1	1.4
Pretax Inc.	28.0	16.2	16.9	19.6	18.6	13.3	17.0	17.9	21.3	1.6
Eff. Tax Rate	24%	26%	22%	16%	30%	19%	24%	26%	32%	53%
Net Inc.	20.1	13.1	12.7	14.7	12.4	9.9	12.2	12.4	14.5	1.2

Balance Sheet & Other Fin. Data (Million $)

	1997	1996	1995	1994	1993	1992	1991	1990	1989	1988
Cash	114	101	100	94.4	87.8	72.4	82.2	77.2	65.5	53.1
Curr. Assets	222	202	196	177	165	138	145	142	132	126
Total Assets	282	265	260	240	223	197	190	185	181	176
Curr. Liab.	35.5	33.5	30.6	26.2	25.6	19.1	16.5	17.4	18.2	20.2
LT Debt	8.6	9.5	10.2	11.0	13.2	16.5	13.0	11.2	11.6	12.1
Common Eqty.	228	212	201	184	169	156	157	154	147	139
Total Cap.	246	230	228	212	196	178	174	168	162	155
Cap. Exp.	6.3	6.2	8.2	7.3	4.4	4.5	7.7	5.7	4.4	7.9
Cash Flow	25.5	19.3	18.9	21.1	20.5	18.7	20.1	20.3	21.5	8.5
Curr. Ratio	6.3	6.0	6.4	6.8	6.4	7.2	8.8	8.1	7.3	6.2
% LT Debt of Cap.	3.5	4.1	4.4	5.2	6.7	9.3	7.5	6.7	7.1	7.8
% Net Inc.of Revs.	8.0	5.8	6.2	7.8	7.2	6.8	8.9	9.0	10.9	1.0
% Ret. on Assets	7.3	5.0	5.0	6.2	5.9	5.3	6.7	6.9	8.4	0.7
% Ret. on Equity	9.2	6.4	6.5	8.3	7.6	6.6	8.2	8.5	10.5	0.8

Data as orig. reptd.; bef. results of disc. opers. and/or spec. items. Per share data adj. for stk. divs. as of ex-div. date. Quarterly revenues table includes interest and dividend income. E-Estimated. NA-Not Available. NM-Not Meaningful. NR-Not Ranked.

Office—8 Centennial Drive, Peabody, MA 01960. **Tel**—(978) 977-3000. **Website**—http://www.analogic.com **Chrmn & CEO**—B. M. Gordon. **Pres & COO**—B. R. Rusch. **Sr VP, Treas & Investor Contact**—John A. Tarello. **Dirs**—M. R. Brown, B. M. Gordon, B. R. Rusch, B. W. Steinhauer, J. A. Tarello, E. F. Voboril, G. L. Wilson. **Transfer Agent**—Boston EquiServe, L.P. **Incorporated**—in Massachusetts in 1967. **Empl**— 1,500. **S&P Analyst:** M.I.

03-OCT-98

Industry:
Services (Computer Systems)

Summary: This company provides contract programming and related software services through its branch and field offices to users and manufacturers of computers.

Quantitative Evaluations		
Recent Price • 23⅛	Yield • 1.7%	
52 Wk Range • 36½-20	12-Mo. P/E • 23.4	

Outlook
(1 Lowest—5 Highest)
• **4**

Fair Value
• **37⅝**

Risk
• **Average**

Earn./Div. Rank
• **A**

Technical Eval.
• **Bearish** since 7/98

Rel. Strength Rank
(1 Lowest—99 Highest)
• **44**

Insider Activity
• **Favorable**

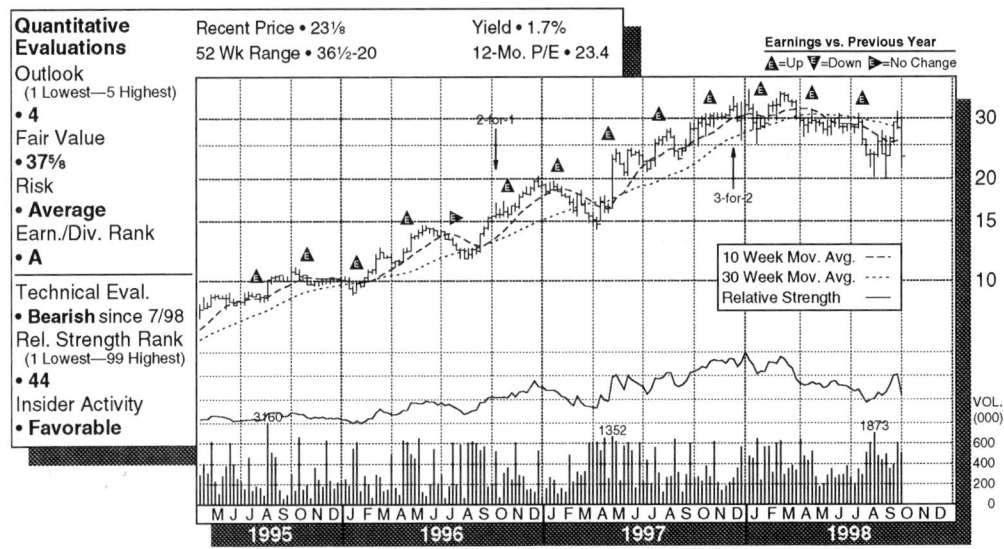

Earnings vs. Previous Year
▲=Up ▼=Down ►=No Change

10 Week Mov. Avg. ---
30 Week Mov. Avg. ····
Relative Strength —

Business Profile - 09-SEP-98

The dramatic proliferation of computers and networking, together with the need for specialized technical expertise for certain projects, and the trend of businesses to eliminate non-essential computer support staff by outsourcing, led to record revenue and income levels in FY 95 (Jun.), FY 96 and FY 97. Recent revenue growth has been enhanced by assisting customers with the preparation of computer systems for the Year 2000 date conversion. ANLY has offices in more than 40 cities in the United States, Canada, and the United Kingdom, and serves more than 900 corporate and governmental clients. In August 1998, the company's board voted to increase the regular quarterly dividend to $0.10 per share, up 25% from $0.08 per share.

Operational Review - 09-SEP-98

Based on a preliminary report, revenues in FY 98 (Jun.) rose 34% from those of the prior year, reflecting strong demand for information technology services, particularly with regard to Year 2000 conversions. While the company added a significant number of employees, total expenses grew at a slightly slower rate than sales; operating profit was up 39%. With a 24% increase in non-operating income, and after taxes at 40.0%, versus 39.8%, net income was up 38%, to $22,610,000 ($0.99 a share, diluted), from $16,381,000 ($0.73).

Stock Performance - 02-OCT-98

In the past 30 trading days, ANLY's shares have declined 10%, compared to a 7% fall in the S&P 500. Average trading volume for the past five days was 100,620 shares, compared with the 40-day moving average of 133,054 shares.

Key Stock Statistics

Dividend Rate/Share	0.40	Shareholders	500
Shs. outstg. (M)	22.4	Market cap. (B)	$0.520
Avg. daily vol. (M)	0.097	Inst. holdings	60%
Tang. Bk. Value/Share	3.54		
Beta	1.17		

Value of $10,000 invested 5 years ago: $ 45,554

Fiscal Year Ending Jun. 30

	1998	1997	1996	1995	1994	1993
Revenues (Million $)						
1Q	135.2	98.02	73.07	48.40	41.74	37.00
2Q	141.3	101.8	78.79	50.72	42.86	40.17
3Q	150.0	113.7	85.98	55.22	45.05	41.55
4Q	161.0	126.0	91.71	64.09	46.33	40.98
Yr.	587.4	439.6	329.5	218.4	176.0	159.7
Earnings Per Share ($)						
1Q	0.23	0.17	0.13	0.11	0.09	0.08
2Q	**0.22**	0.17	0.13	0.12	0.09	0.10
3Q	**0.24**	0.19	0.15	0.13	0.08	0.09
4Q	**0.29**	0.19	0.15	0.15	0.10	0.11
Yr.	**0.99**	0.73	0.56	0.51	0.37	0.38

Next earnings report expected: mid October

Dividend Data (Dividends have been paid since 1988.)

Amount ($)	Date Decl.	Ex-Div. Date	Stock of Record	Payment Date
0.080	Dec. 18	Jan. 28	Jan. 30	Feb. 13 '98
0.080	Feb. 19	Apr. 28	Apr. 30	May. 15 '98
0.080	Jun. 18	Jul. 29	Jul. 31	Aug. 14 '98
0.100	Aug. 20	Oct. 28	Oct. 30	Nov. 13 '98

A Division of The McGraw-Hill Companies

STANDARD
&POOR'S
STOCK REPORTS

Analysts International Corporation

3129

03-OCT-98

Business Summary - 09-SEP-98

Analysts International Corporation (ANLY) seeks to win multiple service contracts through the technical expertise of its personnel. The company also seeks to capitalize on the immediate need for Year 2000 software conversions. ANLY offers a wide range of services, including custom programming, project management, systems analysis and design, software-related consulting and specialized software-related educational courses for computer programmers and analysts. The company provides its services to a variety of industry segments, ranging from manufacturing to food. In FY 97 (Jun.), customers in the telecommunications, electronics, services and manufacturing sectors provided 28%, 24%, 10% and 10% of total revenues, respectively.

Two of ANLY's customers, U S WEST and IBM, provide a relatively large percentage of total revenues. ANLY's TechWest division supplies technical personnel who serve U S WEST's information technology and software engineering needs. Revenues from U S WEST accounted for 22% of total revenues during FY 97 and FY 96. U S WEST's three-year contract with ANLY expires on May 31, 1998, and the company believes it is likely that the contract will be renewed for an additional two years. ANLY provides technical services to IBM and its customers. Revenues from IBM accounted for about 20% of total revenues during the last three fiscal years.

In December 1997, the company renewed its contract with IBM for three more years.

ANLY provided services to approximately 900 clients and was engaged in about 6,500 customer projects during FY 97. Major projects during the year included: the enhancement and support of two operations systems for Lucent Technologies, assisting the Goodyear Tire and Rubber Company in its move into an advanced computer-assisted design environment, and assisting Brooklyn Union in the determination of the scope and complexity of its Year 2000 exposure.

Out of the company's 4,650 employees at June 30, 1997, approximately 4,000 were systems analysts, computer programmers and other technical personnel whose services are billable to clients on an hourly rate. Several years of programming experience is generally a prerequisite to employment with ANLY.

In August 1996, the company announced the formation of a business unit to assist companies in solving the Year 2000 problem. The unit consists of a team of consultants with expertise in the problem that acts as a central resource to other consultants in the field. During FY 97, the company assisted over 50 clients with Year 2000 software conversions. As of October 1997, ANLY was working on 75 additional conversion projects.

In April 1997, ANLY formed a strategic alliance with Viasoft Inc., under which the company is licensed to use Viasoft's Year 2000 technology and services in helping its clients manage the century date change.

Per Share Data ($)

(Year Ended Jun. 30)	1998	1997	1996	1995	1994	1993	1992	1991	1990	1989
Tangible Bk. Val.	NA	2.79	2.44	2.07	1.71	1.50	1.23	1.09	0.95	0.76
Cash Flow	NA	0.85	0.66	0.60	0.44	0.45	0.31	0.30	0.31	0.26
Earnings	0.99	0.73	0.56	0.52	0.37	0.38	0.25	0.26	0.29	0.24
Dividends	0.36	0.29	0.24	0.17	0.15	0.13	0.12	0.12	0.11	0.11
Payout Ratio	36%	40%	43%	33%	41%	29%	49%	45%	31%	46%
Prices - High	36	28	20³/₈	11	6⁷/₈	8	5³/₄	4	5¹/₄	4¹/₂
- Low	20¹/₈	36¹/₂	9¹/₈	6⁵/₈	4⁷/₈	5	3¹/₂	2⁵/₈	2¹/₄	1¹⁵/₁₆
P/E Ratio - High	36	50	26	21	19	21	23	15	18	19
- Low	20	19	16	13	13	13	14	10	8	8

Income Statement Analysis (Million $)

	NA	1997	1996	1995	1994	1993	1992	1991	1990	1989
Revs.	NA	440	330	218	176	160	130	117	108	90.0
Oper. Inc.	NA	29.0	21.9	19.6	14.2	14.4	9.3	9.0	9.7	8.3
Depr.	NA	2.8	2.2	1.8	1.7	1.4	1.1	0.7	0.5	0.4
Int. Exp.	NA	Nil	Nil	Nil	Nil	Nil	Nil	Nil	Nil	Nil
Pretax Inc.	Nil	27.2	20.7	18.5	12.8	13.5	8.7	8.9	9.9	8.4
Eff. Tax Rate	NA	40%	40%	39%	38%	39%	38%	38%	39%	41%
Net Inc.	NA	16.4	12.4	11.3	8.0	8.3	5.4	5.6	6.0	5.0

Balance Sheet & Other Fin. Data (Million $)

	1998	1997	1996	1995	1994	1993	1992	1991	1990	1989
Cash	NA	17.9	17.0	12.6	10.7	9.9	7.4	7.0	5.3	6.6
Curr. Assets	NA	87.8	69.0	56.8	41.3	35.0	29.1	23.8	23.1	20.7
Total Assets	NA	105	81.4	67.5	51.2	44.9	38.1	32.1	29.3	25.3
Curr. Liab.	NA	32.8	22.0	17.0	9.8	8.9	8.6	6.8	7.4	8.3
LT Debt	NA	Nil	Nil	Nil	Nil	Nil	Nil	Nil	Nil	Nil
Common Eqty.	Nil	72.5	53.7	45.1	36.6	31.7	25.8	22.7	19.6	15.3
Total Cap.	NA	66.1	53.7	45.1	36.6	31.7	25.8	22.7	19.6	15.3
Cap. Exp.	NA	3.0	2.9	1.9	1.3	1.6	2.2	2.1	1.6	0.6
Cash Flow	NA	19.2	14.6	13.0	9.6	9.7	6.5	6.3	6.5	5.4
Curr. Ratio	NA	2.7	3.1	3.3	4.2	3.9	3.4	3.5	3.1	2.5
% LT Debt of Cap.	NA	Nil	Nil	Nil	Nil	Nil	Nil	Nil	Nil	Nil
% Net Inc.of Revs.	Nil	3.7	3.8	5.1	4.5	5.2	4.1	4.8	5.6	5.5
% Ret. on Assets	NA	17.5	16.7	18.9	16.5	19.8	15.2	18.1	21.7	20.9
% Ret. on Equity	NA	24.8	25.1	27.5	23.2	28.6	22.1	26.3	34.0	35.5

Data as orig. reptd.; bef. results of disc. opers. and/or spec. items. Per share data adj. for stk. divs. as of ex-div. date. Bold denotes diluted EPS (FASB 128). E-Estimated. NA-Not Available. NM-Not Meaningful. NR-Not Ranked.

Office—7615 Metro Blvd., Minneapolis, MN 55439-3050. **Tel**—(612) 835-5900. **Website**—http://www.analysts.com **Chrmn & CEO**—F. W. Lang. **Pres & COO**—V. C. Benda. **VP-Fin, Treas & Investor Contact**—Gerald M. McGrath. **Secy**—T. R. Mahler. **Dirs**—W. K. Drake, F. W. Lang, M. A. Loftus, E. M. Mahoney, R. L. Prince. **Transfer Agent**—State Street Bank & Trust Co., Boston. **Incorporated**—in Minnesota in 1966. **Empl**—5,050.
S&P Analyst: Mark Cavallone

Anchor BanCorp Wisconsin   3130C
NASDAQ Symbol **ABCW**
In S&P SmallCap 600

03-OCT-98

Industry:
Savings & Loan Companies

Summary: This company's main subsidiary is AnchorBank, a savings and loan with 35 offices located mainly in southern and western Wisconsin.

Quantitative Evaluations

Outlook
(1 Lowest—5 Highest)
- **1+**

Fair Value
- **20¾**

Risk
- **Low**

Earn./Div. Rank
- **NR**

Technical Eval.
- **Bullish** since 6/95

Rel. Strength Rank
(1 Lowest—99 Highest)
- **69**

Insider Activity
- **Neutral**

Recent Price • 20⅞
52 Wk Range • 24-14

Yield • 1.0%
12-Mo. P/E • 18.3

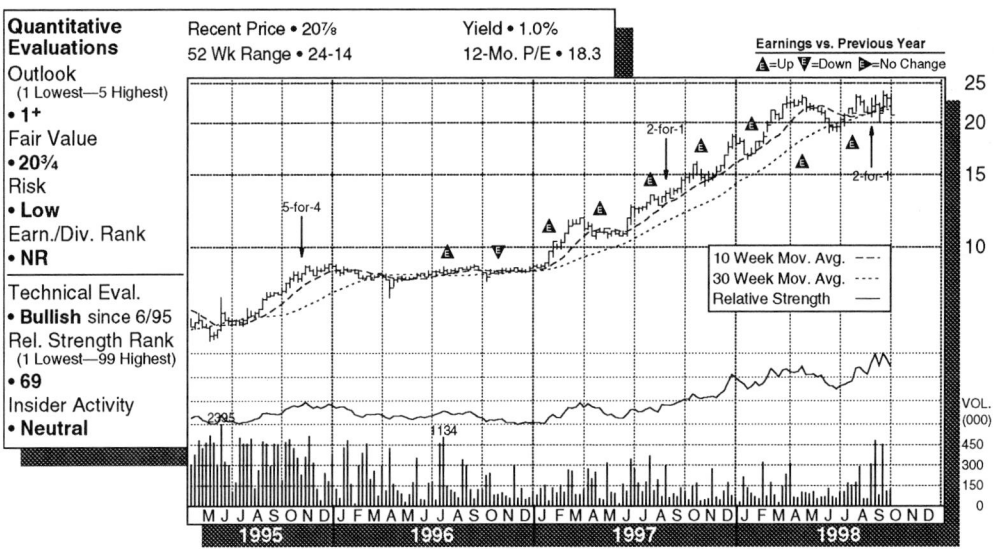

Earnings vs. Previous Year
▲=Up ▼=Down ▶=No Change

10 Week Mov. Avg. ---
30 Week Mov. Avg. ·····
Relative Strength ——

Business Profile - 22-SEP-98

This company focuses its lending efforts on residential mortgage loans, mostly single-family loans secured by properties located in Wisconsin. In line with its conservative lending portfolio, non-accrual loans accounted for only 0.24% of total loans at June 30, 1998, while net chargeoffs were equal to only 0.05% of average loans in the first quarter of FY 99 (Mar.). The economy of the company's principal Dane County, WI, market area is characterized by diversified industries, major medical facilities, state, federal and university government bodies, and an agricultural base.

Operational Review - 22-SEP-98

Net interest income in the three months ended June 30, 1998, advanced 10%, year to year, reflecting growth in loan originations and a wider net interest margin. The provision for loan losses was $125,000, versus none in the 1997 period. Noninterest income climbed 53%, aided by sharply higher gains on the sale of loans, and with 5.2% greater noninterest expense, pretax income gained 32%. After taxes at 38.1%, versus 38.4%, net income was also up 32%, to $6,119,000 ($0.33 a share, as adjusted), from $4,621,000 ($0.24).

Stock Performance - 02-OCT-98

In the past 30 trading days, ABCW's shares have declined 1%, compared to a 7% fall in the S&P 500. Average trading volume for the past five days was 24,120 shares, compared with the 40-day moving average of 51,615 shares.

Key Stock Statistics

Dividend Rate/Share	0.20	Shareholders	2,000
Shs. outstg. (M)	17.8	Market cap. (B)	$0.371
Avg. daily vol. (M)	0.045	Inst. holdings	30%
Tang. Bk. Value/Share	7.33		
Beta	0.38		

Value of $10,000 invested 5 years ago: $ 62,058

Fiscal Year Ending Mar. 31

	1999	1998	1997	1996	1995	1994
Revenues (Million $)						
1Q	42.93	39.05	38.26	30.78	—	26.27
2Q	—	39.86	40.35	34.10	—	27.57
3Q	—	41.34	40.64	34.69	—	29.01
4Q	—	40.93	—	35.41	26.40	—
Yr.	—	161.2	157.8	135.0	112.4	108.3
Earnings Per Share ($)						
1Q	0.33	0.24	0.23	0.17	—	—
2Q	—	0.26	0.00	0.16	—	—
3Q	—	0.29	0.24	0.16	—	—
4Q	—	0.27	0.24	0.18	—	—
Yr.	—	1.06	0.71	0.68	0.67	0.58

Next earnings report expected: late October

Dividend Data (Dividends have been paid since 1993.)

Amount ($)	Date Decl.	Ex-Div. Date	Stock of Record	Payment Date
0.080	Jan. 19	Jan. 28	Jan. 31	Feb. 15 '98
0.090	Apr. 22	Apr. 29	May. 01	May. 15 '98
0.100	Jul. 15	Jul. 29	Aug. 01	Aug. 15 '98
2-for-1	Jul. 28	Aug. 25	Aug. 10	Aug. 24 '98

A Division of The McGraw-Hill Companies

Business Summary - 22-SEP-98

With its main subsidiary, AnchorBank, first organized in 1919, Anchor BanCorp Wisconsin operates a savings and loan business mainly in the metropolitan area of Madison, WI, the suburban communities of Dane County, WI, and southern Wisconsin, as well as contiguous counties in Iowa and Illinois. In addition to its main office in Madison, the bank operates 35 full-service offices and two loan origination offices.

Lending efforts are focused on the origination of single-family residential loans secured by properties located mainly in Wisconsin. Total loans of $1.68 billion at March 31, 1998, versus $1.54 billion a year earlier, were divided as follows:

	1998	1997
Mortgage loans		
Single-family residential	49%	47%
Multi-family residential	10%	11%
Commercial real estate	11%	11%
Other	8%	8%
Consumer loans	20%	21%
Commercial loans	2%	2%

At March 31, 1998, the allowance for loan losses, set aside for possible loan defaults, was $21.8 million (1.30% of total loans), down from $22.8 million (1.48%) a year earlier. Net chargeoffs, which are written off as uncollectible, were $1.2 million (0.08% of average loans) in FY 98 (Mar.), up from $557,000 (0.04%) in FY 97. Nonperforming assets, which included non-accrual loans, real estate held for development or sale, and foreclosed properties, totaled $12.8 million (0.64% of total assets) at March 31, 1998, down from $13.8 million (0.73%).

Interest income on loans provided 80% of total income in FY 98, interest on securities 12%, loan servicing income 2%, services charges on deposits 2%, and other noninterest income 4%.

Total deposits of $1.38 billion at the end of FY 98 were divided: NOW accounts 12%, money market accounts 14%, passbook accounts 7% and certificates of deposit 67%.

Average interest-earning assets, from which interest income is derived, were $1.86 billion in FY 98. The average yield on interest-earning assets was 7.99% in FY 98 (7.91% in FY 97), while the average rate paid on interest-bearing liabilities was 4.99% (4.96%), for a net spread of 3.00% (2.95%).

Per Share Data ($)

(Year Ended Mar. 31)	1998	1997	1996	1995	1994	1993	1992	1991	1990	1989
Tangible Bk. Val.	6.91	6.43	6.00	5.49	4.87	4.29	NA	NA	NA	NA
Earnings	1.06	0.71	0.68	0.66	0.58	NA	NA	NA	NA	NA
Dividends	0.23	0.14	0.10	0.08	0.05	0.05	NA	NA	NA	NA
Payout Ratio	22%	0%	0%	11%	9%	NA	NA	NA	NA	NA
Cal. Yrs.	1997	1996	1995	1994	1993	1992	1991	1990	1989	1988
Prices - High	18³/₄	9¹/₈	9¹/₈	6³/₈	5¹/₄	3⁵/₈	NA	NA	NA	NA
- Low	8⁷/₈	7¹/₂	5⁷/₈	4³/₈	3³/₈	2³/₈	NA	NA	NA	NA
P/E Ratio - High	18	12	13	9	9	8	NA	NA	NA	NA
- Low	8	10	8	6	5	5	NA	NA	NA	NA

Income Statement Analysis (Million $)

	1998	1997	1996	1995	1994	1993	1992	1991	1990	1989
Net Int. Inc.	59.4	55.5	50.7	50.6	47.8	47.9	37.4	NA	NA	NA
Loan Loss Prov.	0.3	0.5	0.5	1.6	4.3	7.4	7.8	NA	NA	NA
Non Int. Inc.	12.2	17.2	9.0	7.6	11.0	11.6	8.9	NA	NA	NA
Non Int. Exp.	38.3	47.4	37.1	33.0	32.8	NA	NA	NA	NA	NA
Pretax Inc.	33.0	21.5	22.5	23.5	21.7	17.8	8.9	NA	NA	NA
Eff. Tax Rate	38%	35%	35%	39%	38%	39%	35%	NA	NA	NA
Net Inc.	20.5	13.9	14.5	14.4	13.5	10.9	5.8	NA	NA	NA
% Net Int. Marg.	3.18	3.14	3.18	NA	NA	NA	NA	NA	NA	NA

Balance Sheet & Other Fin. Data (Million $)

	1998	1997	1996	1995	1994	1993	1992	1991	1990	1989
Total Assets	1,999	1,885	1,755	1,511	1,380	1,297	1,265	NA	NA	NA
Loans	1,804	1,627	1,486	1,358	1,220	NA	NA	NA	NA	NA
Deposits	1,392	1,312	1,241	1,098	1,066	NA	NA	NA	NA	NA
Capitalization:										
Debt	412	392	317	275	187	NA	NA	NA	NA	NA
Equity	128	118	118	111	105	NA	NA	NA	NA	NA
Total	540	510	435	386	292	NA	NA	NA	NA	NA
% Ret. on Assets	NA	0.8	0.9	1.0	1.0	0.8	NA	NA	NA	NA
% Ret. on Equity	NA	11.8	12.6	13.3	13.0	14.1	NA	NA	NA	NA
% Loan Loss Resv.	1.2	1.5	1.6	1.8	2.0	1.9	1.6	NA	NA	NA
% Risk Based Capital	10.2	10.7	NA	NA	NA	NA	NA	NA	NA	NA
Price Times Book Value:										
Hi	2.7	1.4	1.5	1.2	1.1	0.9	NA	NA	NA	NA
Low	1.3	1.2	1.0	0.8	0.7	0.6	NA	NA	NA	NA

Data as orig. reptd.; bef. results of disc opers. and/or spec. items. Per share data adj. for stk. divs. as of ex-div. date. Bold denotes diluted EPS (FASB 128). E-Estimated. NA-Not Available. NM-Not Meaningful. NR-Not Ranked.

Office—25 West Main St., Madison, WI 53703. Tel—(608) 252-8700. Website—http://www.anchorbank.com Chrmn, Pres & CEO—D. J. Timmerman. CFO & Treas—M. W. Helser. Dirs—H. C. Berkenstadt, R. C. Buehner, R. D Kropidlowski, G. M. Larson, A. M. Mucks, Jr., P Richter, B. A. Robertson, D. J. Timmerman. Transfer Agent & Registrar—Firstar Trust, Milwaukee. Incorporated—in Wisconsin in 1992. Empl— 663. S&P Analyst: Stephen R.Biggar

STANDARD &POOR'S
STOCK REPORTS

Angelica Corp.

201

NYSE Symbol **AGL**

In S&P SmallCap 600

03-OCT-98

Industry:
Services (Commercial & Consumer)

Summary: AGL provides textile rental and laundry services to health care institutions, manufactures uniforms, and operates a national chain of specialty retail stores.

Quantitative Evaluations

Recent Price • 14¾
52 Wk Range • 24½-14⅛

Yield • 6.5%
12-Mo. P/E • NM

Outlook
(1 Lowest—5 Highest)
• **2⁻**

Fair Value
• **17⅜**

Risk
• **Average**

Earn./Div. Rank
• **B-**

Technical Eval.
• **Bullish** since 5/98

Rel. Strength Rank
(1 Lowest—99 Highest)
• **23**

Insider Activity
• **Favorable**

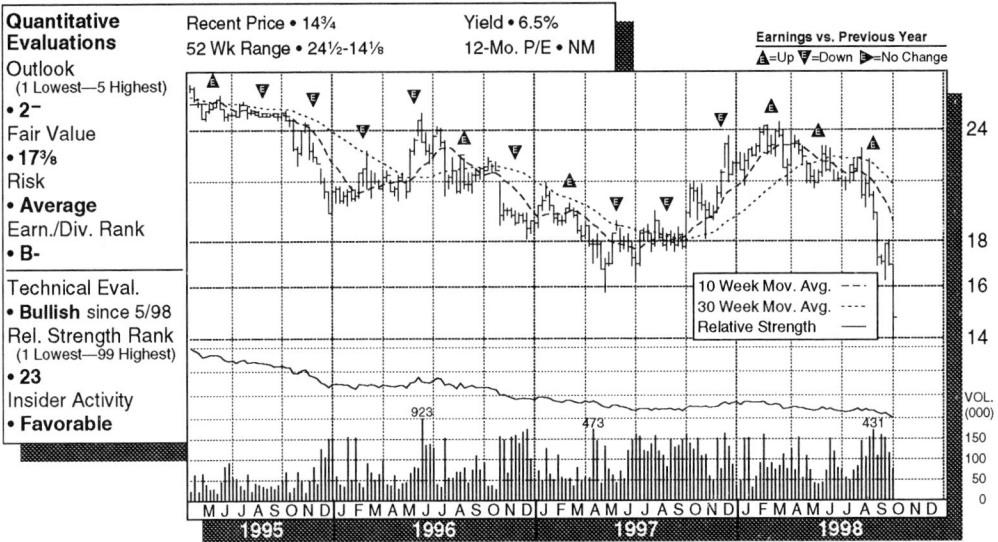

Earnings vs. Previous Year
▲=Up ▼=Down ▶=No Change

10 Week Mov. Avg. - - -
30 Week Mov. Avg. ·······
Relative Strength ——

Business Profile - 30-SEP-98

Following several years of disappointing financial performance, this provider of textile rental and laundry services re-evaluated its strategy and operations. As a result, Angelica eliminated certain underperforming facilities, leading to a pretax restructuring charge of $23.2 million in the third quarter of FY 98 (Jan.). The company expects the restructuring to produce annual pretax cost savings of $1 million to $1.5 million. In June 1998, AGL said it plans to make acquisitions for its retail segment and textile services divisions. The company's goals are to increase customer retention and generate more profitable business at its textile services operations; raise same-store-sales growth at Life Uniform and Shoe Shops; and improve gross margins at the manufacturing and marketing operations.

Operational Review - 30-SEP-98

Total revenues in the six months ended August 1, 1998, declined 1.8%, year to year, as a 9.7% decrease in textile service revenues outweighed an 8.2% increase in manufacturing and marketing and retail sales, reflecting the sale of the Las Vegas casino laundry business. Gross margins widened, largely on improvement at the textile services business, resulting from the sale of the laundry business. with a 1.4% rise in SG&A expenses, and after taxes at 38.0% in each period, net income climbed 29%, to $4,228,000 ($0.46 a share), from $3,276,000 ($0.36).

Stock Performance - 02-OCT-98

In the past 30 trading days, AGL's shares have declined 27%, compared to a 7% fall in the S&P 500. Average trading volume for the past five days was 14,860 shares, compared with the 40-day moving average of 36,977 shares.

Key Stock Statistics

Dividend Rate/Share	0.96	Shareholders	1,600
Shs. outstg. (M)	9.2	Market cap. (B)	$0.136
Avg. daily vol. (M)	0.031	Inst. holdings	70%
Tang. Bk. Value/Share	18.14		
Beta	0.57		

Value of $10,000 invested 5 years ago: $ 7,534

Fiscal Year Ending Jan. 31

	1999	1998	1997	1996	1995	1994
Revenues (Million $)						
1Q	128.7	127.4	121.6	123.8	117.0	104.1
2Q	123.2	129.2	122.6	121.9	118.2	104.0
3Q	—	132.8	124.3	123.6	120.1	110.5
4Q	—	137.2	120.7	117.7	117.5	108.5
Yr.	—	526.5	489.2	487.0	472.8	427.1
Earnings Per Share ($)						
1Q	**0.26**	**0.22**	0.33	0.38	0.35	0.28
2Q	**0.20**	**0.14**	0.30	0.29	0.35	0.26
3Q	—	**-1.29**	0.20	0.31	0.46	0.43
4Q	—	**0.18**	0.05	-0.85	0.28	0.26
Yr.	—	**-0.75**	0.88	0.13	1.44	1.23

Next earnings report expected: mid November

Dividend Data (Dividends have been paid since 1954.)

Amount ($)	Date Decl.	Ex-Div. Date	Stock of Record	Payment Date
0.240	Nov. 25	Dec. 11	Dec. 15	Jan. 01 '98
0.240	Feb. 25	Mar. 12	Mar. 16	Apr. 01 '98
0.240	May. 27	Jun. 11	Jun. 15	Jul. 01 '98
0.240	Aug. 26	Sep. 11	Sep. 15	Oct. 01 '98

A Division of The McGraw·Hill Companies

STANDARD
&POOR'S
STOCK REPORTS

Angelica Corporation

201

03-OCT-98

Business Summary - 30-SEP-98

Since 1878, Angelica Corporation has provided products and services to a variety of institutions and individuals in health services, hospitality and other service industries. The company believes that it is the leading U.S. provider of textile rental and laundry services; it also says it is the leading U.S. operator of specialty retail stores primarily for nurses and other health care professionals. Sales in recent fiscal years (Jan.) were derived as follows:

	FY 98	FY 97
Textile Services	52%	51%
Manufacturing and Marketing	33%	34%
Life Retail Stores	15%	15%

The textiles services division has laundry plants that are located in or near major metropolitan areas in the U.S. AGL offers textile rental and laundry services for health care institutions. At the end of FY 98, the company served approximately 1,000 institutions, with approximately 161,000 beds. General linen services are also offered to hotels, motels and restaurants.

AGL's manufacturing and marketing division is operated under the Angelica Image Apparel name. The company manufactures and sells uniforms and business career apparel for a wide range of institutions and businesses. The majority of the division's business is located in the U.S., with smaller operations in Canada and the U.K. To make its apparel lines, AGL purchases raw materials, including textile piece goods, thread and trimmings such as buttons, zippers and labels. Most goods are bought from U. S. manufacturers of textile products.

Retail stores are operated through a nationwide chain called Life Uniform and Shoe Shops. These stores are typically located in malls and strip shopping centers, and offer uniforms and shoes primarily for nurses and other health care professionals.

In June 1998, AGL said it was in the process of evaluating each of its businesses. It plans to reduce inventories in its manufacturing and marketing segment; certain facilities were closed, and will be converted to cash later in the year; and a new performance measure has been implemented to use as a basis of compensation plans. The company also plans to make acquisitions for its retail stores and for the textile services segments. No acquisitions are planned for the manufacturing and marketing segment. AGL expects improvement in its business in FY 99.

Per Share Data ($)

(Year Ended Jan. 31)	1998	1997	1996	1995	1994	1993	1992	1991	1990	1989
Tangible Bk. Val.	18.15	19.86	19.82	20.77	20.49	20.87	20.43	18.92	17.01	15.73
Cash Flow	0.75	2.34	1.63	2.90	2.64	2.86	3.68	3.47	3.08	2.70
Earnings	-0.75	0.88	0.13	1.44	1.23	1.50	2.43	2.37	2.06	1.79
Dividends	0.96	0.96	0.95	0.94	0.93	0.92	0.89	0.84	0.77	0.73
Payout Ratio	NM	109%	NM	65%	76%	60%	37%	35%	37%	41%
Cal. Yrs.	1997	1996	1995	1994	1993	1992	1991	1990	1989	1988
Prices - High	23⅝	25⅛	27½	29½	28⅜	40	40¼	33⅞	30⅜	27⅜
- Low	15¾	18⅛	19⅜	24½	22½	22¼	29⅝	27	22	19⅝
P/E Ratio - High	NM	29	NM	20	23	27	17	14	15	15
- Low	NM	21	NM	17	18	15	12	11	11	11

Income Statement Analysis (Million $)

	1998	1997	1996	1995	1994	1993	1992	1991	1990	1989
Revs.	527	489	487	473	427	431	434	414	369	328
Oper. Inc.	30.8	38.5	42.0	45.5	41.9	45.0	57.2	53.4	45.6	37.9
Depr.	13.7	13.4	13.8	13.3	12.9	12.6	11.7	10.3	9.4	8.5
Int. Exp.	10.7	9.6	9.1	7.9	7.4	7.5	7.0	6.3	5.1	2.8
Pretax Inc.	-11.1	12.9	1.9	21.3	18.1	22.3	36.5	35.9	31.2	27.1
Eff. Tax Rate	NM	38%	39%	39%	38%	38%	38%	39%	39%	39%
Net Inc.	-6.9	8.0	1.1	13.1	11.2	13.8	22.7	22.1	19.2	16.6

Balance Sheet & Other Fin. Data (Million $)

	1998	1997	1996	1995	1994	1993	1992	1991	1990	1989
Cash	2.8	2.1	11.0	2.2	2.0	2.7	6.1	2.0	6.9	2.5
Curr. Assets	229	232	227	220	210	205	211	205	184	156
Total Assets	379	374	353	354	333	327	335	316	279	233
Curr. Liab.	87.4	69.4	69.4	69.2	53.1	43.7	50.4	70.4	53.7	51.8
LT Debt	96.7	97.4	100	69.7	72.3	78.2	80.5	57.8	50.6	19.0
Common Eqty.	174	189	190	197	192	189	190	176	161	150
Total Cap.	276	291	293	270	269	273	275	238	218	175
Cap. Exp.	21.3	23.6	8.8	11.5	12.2	11.8	13.3	14.1	13.6	7.5
Cash Flow	6.8	21.4	14.9	26.4	24.0	26.4	34.4	32.4	28.6	25.2
Curr. Ratio	2.6	3.3	5.0	3.2	4.0	4.7	4.2	2.9	3.4	3.0
% LT Debt of Cap.	35.0	33.5	34.2	25.8	26.9	28.7	29.3	24.3	23.2	10.9
% Net Inc.of Revs.	NM	1.7	NM	2.8	2.6	3.2	5.2	5.3	5.2	5.1
% Ret. on Assets	NM	2.2	NM	3.8	3.4	4.2	6.9	7.4	7.5	7.4
% Ret. on Equity	NM	4.3	NM	6.7	5.8	7.4	12.4	13.1	12.4	11.5

Data as orig. reptd.; bef. results of disc. opers. and/or spec. items. Per share data adj. for stk. divs. as of ex-div. date. Bold denotes diluted EPS (FASB 128). E-Estimated. NA-Not Available. NM-Not Meaningful. NR-Not Ranked.

Office—424 S. Woods Mill Rd., Chesterfield, MO 63017-3406. **Tel**—(314) 854-3800. **Chrmn, Pres & CEO**—D. W. Hubble. **SVP-Fin, CFO & Investor Contact**—Theodore M. Armstrong. **Treas**—T. M. Degnan. **VP & Secy**—J. Witter. **Dirs**—D. A. Abrahamson, S. S. Elliot, E. H. Harbison Jr., D. H. Hubble, L. F. Loewe, C. W. Mueller, W. A. Peck, W. P. Stiritz, H. E. Trusheim. **Transfer Agent & Registrar**—Boatmen's Trust Co., St. Louis. **Incorporated**—in Missouri in 1904; reincorporated in Missouri in 1968. **Empl**— 9,700. **S&P Analyst:** Kathleen J. Fraser

STANDARD &POOR'S
STOCK REPORTS

Anixter International

201E

NYSE Symbol **AXE**

In S&P SmallCap 600

03-OCT-98

Industry:
Communications
Equipment

Summary: This company (formerly Itel Corp.) distributes wiring systems and networking products for voice, data, video and electrical power applications.

Quantitative Evaluations

Recent Price • 15¾	Yield • Nil
52 Wk Range • 22¾-13¾	12-Mo. P/E • 10.2

Outlook
(1 Lowest—5 Highest)
• **4+**

Fair Value
• **22½**

Risk
• **Average**

Earn./Div. Rank
• **B**

Technical Eval.
• **Bearish** since 9/98

Rel. Strength Rank
(1 Lowest—99 Highest)
• **58**

Insider Activity
• **Neutral**

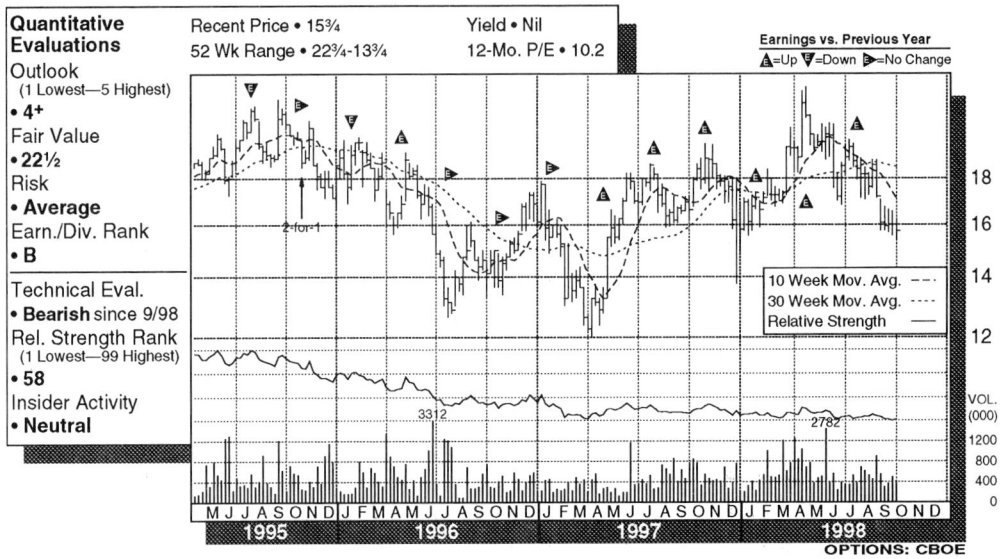

Earnings vs. Previous Year
▲=Up ▼=Down ▶=No Change

10 Week Mov. Avg. ---
30 Week Mov. Avg. ·····
Relative Strength —

OPTIONS: CBOE

Business Profile - 19-FEB-98

This leading distributor of wiring systems and networking products has been enjoying increased revenues as a result of continued growth of the North American communications and electrical wire and cable businesses. During 1997, sales growth was driven by improved demand and pricing across all product sets and in particular for structured wiring products in North America. AXE continued to see revenue growth slowed by the stronger dollar in Europe and by a sharp fall in several Southeast Asian currencies. Improvements in operating margins in the fourth quarter reflected continuing productivity improvements in the network services business in North America.

Operational Review - 19-FEB-98

Total revenues in 1997 rose 13%, reflecting continued demand for communication products in North America, partially offset by slower growth in Europe as a result of a stronger dollar, and by weakness in several Southeast Asian currencies. Gross margins narrowed slightly, but operating income climbed 24%, on lower operating expenses. After a nonrecurring gain of $2.2 million related to the merger of ANTEC with TSX Corp., versus a $4.1 million equity gain in ANTEC, and taxes at 43.0%, versus 44.2%, net income was up 25%, to $45.3 million ($0.95 a share, on 4.4% fewer shares), from $36.1 million ($0.73).

Stock Performance - 02-OCT-98

In the past 30 trading days, AXE's shares have declined 15%, compared to a 7% fall in the S&P 500. Average trading volume for the past five days was 80,840 shares, compared with the 40-day moving average of 101,626 shares.

Key Stock Statistics

Dividend Rate/Share	Nil	Shareholders	5,700
Shs. outstg. (M)	44.6	Market cap. (B)	$0.703
Avg. daily vol. (M)	0.082	Inst. holdings	59%
Tang. Bk. Value/Share	4.99		
Beta	0.90		

Value of $10,000 invested 5 years ago: $ 13,770

Fiscal Year Ending Dec. 31

	1998	1997	1996	1995	1994	1993
Revenues (Million $)						
1Q	748.5	658.7	567.4	502.9	362.8	431.5
2Q	783.4	682.6	611.8	542.0	423.0	476.5
3Q	—	726.5	631.5	571.1	456.3	492.7
4Q	—	737.4	664.6	578.8	490.6	508.5
Yr.	—	2,805	2,475	2,195	1,733	1,909
Earnings Per Share ($)						
1Q	0.35	0.23	0.20	0.19	0.04	-0.10
2Q	0.46	0.22	0.16	0.16	0.26	-0.08
3Q	—	0.24	0.18	0.17	0.17	0.62
4Q	—	0.26	0.19	0.19	0.26	-0.27
Yr.	—	0.95	0.73	0.71	0.72	0.21

Next earnings report expected: late October

Dividend Data

Common dividends were last paid in 1979. A two-for-one stock split was effected in 1995.

A Division of The McGraw-Hill Companies

Business Summary - 19-FEB-98

Anixter International is a leading supplier of wiring systems, networking and internetworking products for voice, data and video networks and electrical power applications. Some 80,000 products are distributed to more than 80,000 active accounts through 86 facilities in the U.S., 20 in Canada, and 82 locations in the U.K., Continental Europe, Latin America, Asia and Australia. The company distributes products used to connect PCs, peripheral equipment, mainframe equipment and various networks to each other. Products include an assortment of transmission media (copper and fiber optic cable) and components, as well as active data components for networking applications. AXE's products are incorporated in local area networks (LANs) and the internetworking of LANs to form wide area networks (WANs). Products also include electrical wiring systems used to transmit electrical energy and control or monitor industrial processes.

ANTEC Corp. (now 19% owned) is a communications technology company that specializes in the design and engineering of hybrid fiber/coax (HFC) broadband networks and the manufacturing, materials management and distribution of products for these networks.

In 1995, the company largely completed its strategy of selling its non-core businesses and investments, including the sale of its 9% holding of Santa Fe Energy Resources common stock. In July 1994, AXE sold its railcar leasing unit to private investors for $204.5 million in cash and notes. Its lease fleet consisted of about 73,000 railcars.

In 1996, Anixter reorganized its sales force into two distinct entities: one serving cabling infrastructure customers and suppliers, and the other specializing in products and services required by networking customers and suppliers.

In October 1997, Anixter introduced a new Internet access and firewall solution that integrates Bay Networks' Instant Internet Access Server, provisioned by Anixter, with discounts on AT&T's WorldNet Managed Internet Service(MIS). This bundled offering gives businesses Internet gateway hardware, built-in firewall security, up to 10% off their monthly WorldNet MIS Internet access charges, free domain name services, and free remote installation support via phone.

Per Share Data ($)

(Year Ended Dec. 31)	1997	1996	1995	1994	1993	1992	1991	1990	1989	1988
Tangible Bk. Val.	10.09	5.26	5.07	6.05	-0.20	-2.74	2.02	2.49	4.21	3.65
Cash Flow	1.62	1.27	1.10	0.97	1.57	0.17	-0.20	0.53	1.62	1.97
Earnings	0.95	0.73	0.71	0.72	0.21	-1.13	-1.21	-0.41	0.23	0.22
Dividends	Nil	Nil	Nil	Nil	Nil	Nil	Nil	Nil	Nil	Nil
Payout Ratio	Nil	Nil	Nil	Nil	Nil	Nil	Nil	Nil	Nil	Nil
Prices - High	19⅝	20	22⅛	18⅛	16⅞	12¼	10⅛	12	14½	10⅞
- Low	12	12⅝	16⅝	11⅜	10⅛	8	4⅞	3⅞	9	7¾
P/E Ratio - High	21	27	31	25	78	NM	NM	NM	61	49
- Low	13	17	23	16	47	NM	NM	NM	38	35

Income Statement Analysis (Million $)

	1997	1996	1995	1994	1993	1992	1991	1990	1989	1988
Revs.	2,805	2,475	2,195	1,733	1,909	1,682	1,689	1,977	2,121	1,644
Oper. Inc.	143	115	121	86.0	240	234	253	286	491	371
Depr.	31.9	26.9	21.7	16.0	82.0	76.0	69.0	89.0	139	115
Int. Exp.	33.5	29.9	24.8	NA	NA	190	207	236	299	201
Pretax Inc.	79.6	64.8	74.4	70.0	45.8	-79.8	-83.6	-39.7	71.1	52.3
Eff. Tax Rate	43%	44%	48%	34%	65%	NM	NM	NM	58%	53%
Net Inc.	45.3	36.1	39.1	46.2	16.1	-59.8	-77.0	-32.8	29.9	24.8

Balance Sheet & Other Fin. Data (Million $)

	1997	1996	1995	1994	1993	1992	1991	1990	1989	1988
Cash	10.6	18.2	10.5	14.0	53.0	45.0	29.0	56.0	28.0	50.0
Curr. Assets	1,014	869	781	621	681	564	607	742	681	648
Total Assets	1,441	1,261	1,185	1,111	2,494	2,641	2,752	3,443	4,126	4,001
Curr. Liab.	448	314	332	267	365	412	617	498	520	514
LT Debt	469	468	334	281	1,514	1,738	1,568	2,142	2,717	2,571
Common Eqty.	477	436	449	544	405	284	431	541	749	702
Total Cap.	979	934	818	833	2,117	2,190	2,081	2,766	3,563	3,368
Cap. Exp.	27.8	32.9	31.3	17.0	13.0	17.0	81.0	82.0	296	1,098
Cash Flow	77.2	63.0	60.8	62.0	95.0	10.0	-14.0	50.0	163	129
Curr. Ratio	2.3	2.8	2.4	2.3	1.9	1.4	1.0	1.5	1.3	1.3
% LT Debt of Cap.	47.9	50.2	40.9	33.7	71.5	79.4	75.3	77.4	76.3	76.3
% Net Inc.of Revs.	1.6	1.5	1.8	2.7	0.8	NM	NM	NM	1.4	1.5
% Ret. on Assets	3.4	2.9	3.4	2.8	0.6	NM	NM	NM	0.7	0.7
% Ret. on Equity	9.9	8.2	7.9	10.2	3.5	NM	NM	NM	3.3	2.4

Data as orig. reptd.; bef. results of disc. opers. and/or spec. items. Per share data adj. for stk. divs. as of ex-div. date. Bold denotes diluted EPS (FASB 128). E-Estimated. NA-Not Available. NM-Not Meaningful. NR-Not Ranked.

Office—Two North Riverside Plaza, Chicago, IL 60606. **Tel**—(312) 902-1515. **Website**—www.anixter.com **Chrmn**—S. Zell. **Pres & CEO**—R. F. Dammeyer. **SVP-Fin & CFO**—D. J. Letham. **SVP & Secy**—J. E. Knox. **SVP & Investor Contact**—Kirk E. Brewer (312-466-4042). **Dirs**—Sir James Blyth, R. F. Dammeyer, R. E. Fowler Jr., R. W. Grubbs Jr., F. P. Handy, M. N. Klein, J. R. Petty, S. Z. Rosenberg, S. M. Sloan, T. C. Theobald, S. Zell. **Transfer Agent & Registrar**—ChaseMellon Shareholder Services, Ridgefield Park, NJ.**Incorporated**— in Delaware in 1967.**Empl**— 5,600.
S&P Analyst: Aydin Tuncer

STANDARD &POOR'S
STOCK REPORTS

AnnTaylor Stores

201H

NYSE Symbol **ANN**

In S&P SmallCap 600

03-OCT-98

Industry:
Retail (Special-ty-Apparel)

Summary: This leading specialty retailer of women's better-quality apparel, shoes and accessories operates more than 330 stores in 41 states and the District of Columbia.

Quantitative Evaluations	
Outlook (1 Lowest—5 Highest)	**4**
Fair Value	**32**
Risk	**High**
Earn./Div. Rank	**NR**
Technical Eval.	**NA**
Rel. Strength Rank (1 Lowest—99 Highest)	**31**
Insider Activity	**Unfavorable**

Recent Price • 19⅞
52 Wk Range • 30⅛-11¼

Yield • Nil
12-Mo. P/E • 28.5

Earnings vs. Previous Year
▲=Up ▼=Down ▶=No Change

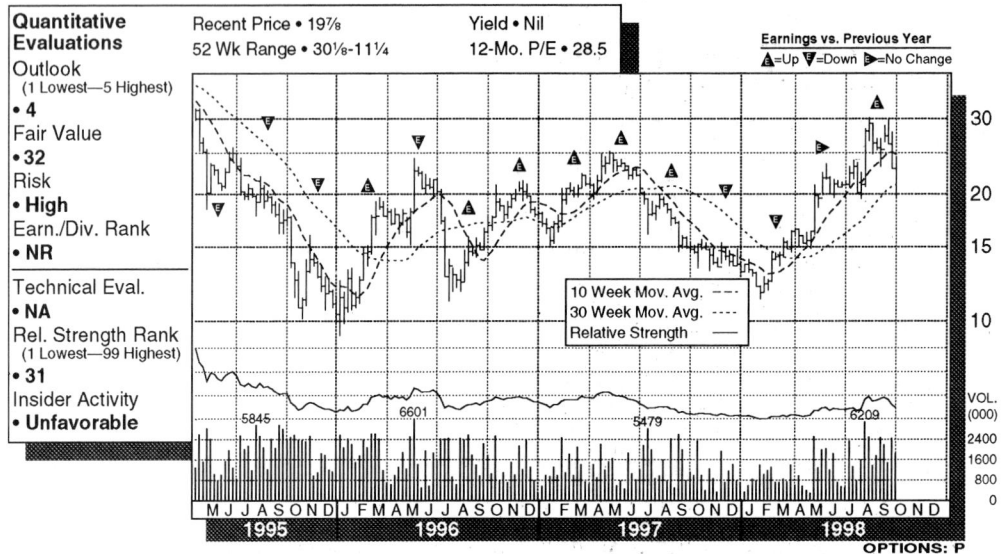

10 Week Mov. Avg. - - - -
30 Week Mov. Avg. - - -
Relative Strength ——

OPTIONS: P

Business Profile - 17-JUL-98

Same-store sales at AnnTaylor rebounded in May and June 1998, to 2.8% and 9.0% gains, following comparable-store sales declines of 5.5% for both the first quarter of FY 99 (Jan.) and the full fiscal year 1998. The recent turnaround is attributed to strong consumer acceptance of a new merchandise mix, particularly its well-suited and tops categories. Beginning in the second half of FY 98, ANN returned to a less promotional strategy in an effort to restore its upscale image. Initial sales following this plan were lackluster but consumer response in recent months turned positive.

Operational Review - 17-JUL-98

Revenues for the quarter ended May 2, 1998, edged up 0.6%, year to year, reflecting the opening of new stores and expansion of existing stores. Comparable store sales dropped 5.5%. Margins narrowed, due to decreased leverage on fixed expenses resulting from lower same-store sales and increased investments in marketing; operating income was down 8.2%. Following taxes at 48.8%, versus 51.8%, net income decreased slightly to $6,419,000 ($0.25 a share) from $6,475,000 ($0.25).

Stock Performance - 02-OCT-98

In the past 30 trading days, ANN's shares have declined 24%, compared to a 7% fall in the S&P 500. Average trading volume for the past five days was 369,020 shares, compared with the 40-day moving average of 451,685 shares.

Key Stock Statistics

Dividend Rate/Share	Nil	Shareholders	800
Shs. outstg. (M)	25.7	Market cap. (B)	$0.512
Avg. daily vol. (M)	0.437	Inst. holdings	0%
Tang. Bk. Value/Share	2.83		
Beta	0.22		

Value of $10,000 invested 5 years ago: $ 9,725

Fiscal Year Ending Jan. 31

	1999	1998	1997	1996	1995	1994
Revenues (Million $)						
1Q	198.2	197.1	184.5	168.3	145.0	120.2
2Q	223.4	185.0	187.9	183.7	159.9	124.8
3Q	—	187.2	212.7	212.7	164.6	122.0
4Q	—	211.8	213.1	200.6	188.9	134.6
Yr.	—	781.0	798.1	731.1	658.8	501.6
Earnings Per Share ($)						
1Q	**0.25**	0.25	0.08	0.15	0.36	0.15
2Q	**0.27**	0.04	0.03	-0.13	0.34	0.16
3Q	—	0.08	0.13	0.03	0.35	0.20
4Q	—	**0.09**	0.12	-0.05	-1.05	0.14
Yr.	—	**0.47**	0.36	-0.04	1.40	0.66

Next earnings report expected: mid November

Dividend Data

No dividends have been paid.

A Division of The McGraw·Hill Companies

Business Summary - 17-JUL-98

Long known as a leading specialty retailer of women's better-quality apparel, shoes and accessories, AnnTaylor Stores offers its customers a distinct fashion point of view. The company believes that its customer base is made up primarily of relatively affluent, fashion-conscious women who prefer classic styles, updated to reflect current fashion trends. ANN stores offer a collection of ready-to-wear sportswear, dresses and suits, consisting primarily of private-label fashions complemented by a selection of designer and brandname goods. As of May 2, 1998, the company operated 339 stores in 41 states and the District of Columbia.

The company emphasizes a total wardrobing strategy, whereby it trains its sales associates to assist customers in coordinating their wardrobe, helping them to achieve the Ann Taylor look, while reflecting each customer's personal style. Stores offer a variety of coordinated apparel and an assortment of shoes and accessories to enable customers to assemble complete outfits. The company has also been introducing product line extensions, such as its own line of denim jeans and petite sizes, fragrances and personal care products.

New moderate-priced stores are also being operated under the name AnnTaylor Loft.

AnnTaylor stores are located primarily in malls and up-scale specialty retail centers, with the balance located in downtown and village locations. There are also 27 AnnTaylor Loft stores, all located in factory outlet centers, as well as 14 stores in factory outlet centers operated under the name Ann Taylor Factory Store.

In September 1996, ANN acquired Cygne Designs, Inc., which had been its primary source of merchandise purchases. ANN believes that the acquisition gave it greater control over pre-production and production processes, providing operational efficiencies and quality improvements. The division is now known as Ann Taylor Global Sourcing.

In FY 95 (Jan.), ANN introduced Ann Taylor Studio Shoe stores, offering a broad assortment of shoes and accessories. In the fourth quarter of FY 97, the company decided that these stores, which had not been profitable, were not consistent with its total wardrobe strategy. ANN recorded a pretax charge of $3.6 million associated with the closing of all nine of these stores.

Total sales for June 1998 were $85.3 million, up 19.4% from the year ago period. Same-store sales rose 9.0%.

Per Share Data ($)

(Year Ended Jan. 31)	1998	1997	1996	1995	1994	1993	1992	1991	1990	1989
Tangible Bk. Val.	2.03	1.02	0.36	0.13	-3.42	-4.69	-6.24	-21.14	-21.91	NA
Cash Flow	1.98	1.82	1.18	2.32	1.47	1.08	0.87	1.08	0.26	NA
Earnings	0.47	0.36	-0.04	1.40	0.66	0.28	0.05	0.08	-0.91	NA
Dividends	Nil	Nil	Nil	Nil	Nil	Nil	Nil	Nil	Nil	Nil
Payout Ratio	Nil	Nil	Nil	Nil	Nil	Nil	Nil	Nil	Nil	Nil
Cal. Yrs.	1997	1996	1995	1994	1993	1992	1991	1990	1989	1988
Prices - High	25¼	24¼	38	44⅞	30	25	36½	NA	NA	NA
- Low	13	9¼	9⅞	20½	17½	14½	12	NA	NA	NA
P/E Ratio - High	54	67	NM	32	45	89	NM	NA	NA	NA
- Low	28	26	NM	15	27	52	NA	NA	NA	NA

Income Statement Analysis (Million $)

Revs.	781	798	731	666	508	474	444	411	354	274
Oper. Inc.	88.8	89.9	53.6	99	69.0	59.5	58.9	72.2	60.0	44.3
Depr.	38.8	36.3	28.3	21.3	18.0	17.0	15.7	14.2	14.7	11.1
Int. Exp.	20.0	24.4	21.0	14.2	17.7	21.3	34.0	50.1	55.9	Nil
Pretax Inc.	29.5	21.6	4.3	62.9	31.5	17.1	8.7	7.8	-10.6	32.9
Eff. Tax Rate	59%	60%	1.21%	48%	55%	65%	88%	86%	NM	48%
Net Inc.	12.0	8.7	-0.9	32.6	14.3	5.9	1.0	1.1	-11.2	17.0

Balance Sheet & Other Fin. Data (Million $)

Cash	31.4	7.0	1.3	1.6	0.3	0.2	0.2	0.1	0.1	NA
Curr. Assets	210	197	199	168	121	108	99	104	82.0	NA
Total Assets	684	688	679	598	513	488	492	511	493	NA
Curr. Liab.	87.9	78.0	112	65.9	68.1	78.5	72.4	61.9	58.3	NA
LT Debt	105	131	232	200	180	158	186	367	356	NA
Common Eqty.	384	371	326	326	259	245	229	58.0	58.0	NA
Total Cap.	489	598	559	526	440	404	415	446	433	NA
Cap. Exp.	22.9	16.1	78.4	61.3	25.1	4.3	10.0	11.8	6.1	6.1
Cash Flow	50.8	45.0	27.4	53.9	32.3	22.9	16.7	15.2	3.5	28.1
Curr. Ratio	2.4	2.5	1.8	2.6	1.8	1.4	1.4	1.7	1.4	NA
% LT Debt of Cap.	21.5	21.9	41.5	38.0	41.0	39.2	44.8	82.4	82.1	NA
% Net Inc.of Revs.	1.5	1.1	NM	4.9	2.8	1.2	0.2	0.3	NM	6.2
% Ret. on Assets	1.7	1.3	NM	5.7	2.8	1.2	0.1	0.2	NM	NM
% Ret. on Equity	3.2	2.5	NM	10.8	5.6	2.4	0.6	2.1	NM	NM

Data as orig. reptd.; bef. results of disc. opers. and/or spec. items. Per share data adj. for stk. divs. as of ex-div. date. Bold denotes diluted EPS (FASB 128). E-Estimated. NA-Not Available. NM-Not Meaningful. NR-Not Ranked.

Office—142 W. 57th St., New York, NY 10019.**Tel**—(212) 541-3300. **Chrmn & CEO**—J. P. Spainhour. **Pres & COO**—P. DeRosa. **SVP, CFO & Treas**—W. J. Parks. **SVP & Secy**—Jocelyn F. L. Barandiaran. **Dirs**—G. S. Armstrong, J. J. Burke Jr., P. DeRosa, R. C. Grayson, R. B. Lazarus, H. M. Merriman, J. P. Spainhour. **Transfer Agent & Registrar**—Continental Stock Transfer & Trust Co., NYC. **Incorporated**—in Delaware in 1988. **Empl**— 6,300. **S&P Analyst:** Ray Lam, CFA

03-OCT-98

Industry:
Building Materials

Summary: This leading supplier of window and glass products and services derives the majority of its revenues from the automobile and construction industries.

Quantitative Evaluations

Outlook
(1 Lowest—5 Highest)
• **1**

Fair Value
• **6⅛**

Risk
• **Average**

Earn./Div. Rank
• **B-**

Technical Eval.
• **Bullish** since 5/97

Rel. Strength Rank
(1 Lowest—99 Highest)
• **45**

Insider Activity
• **Neutral**

Recent Price • 10¼

52 Wk Range • 25¼-8⅛

Yield • 2.0%

12-Mo. P/E • NM

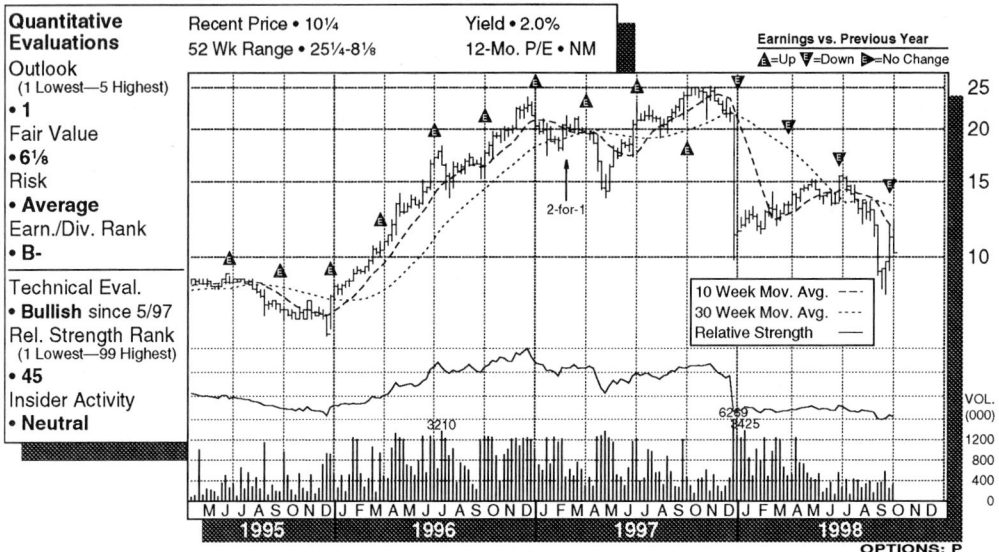

Earnings vs. Previous Year
△=Up ▽=Down ▷=No Change

10 Week Mov. Avg. — — —
30 Week Mov. Avg. · · · · ·
Relative Strength ————

2-for-1

VOL. (000)

OPTIONS: P

Business Profile - 14-AUG-98

APOG realigned into three business segments during 1996 to reflect its emphasis on its Glass Technologies and Automotive Glass businesses. The company recorded a $16 million after-tax charge in the FY 98 (Feb.) third quarter to restructure its New Construction curtainwall unit and focus on its core U.S. and U.K. operations. The charge primarily covered expenses related to exiting Asian operations. Following the restructuring, APOG expects the unit to be profitable and account for less than 12% of revenues. In March 1998, APOG said it would invest $35 million over the next two or three years in a new glass fabricating plant in Statesboro, GA.

Operational Review - 14-AUG-98

Net sales in the three months ended May 30, 1998, fell 4.1%, year to year, as higher glass technologies and auto glass sales were partially offset by slightly lower building products and services sales. Profitability was hurt by a weak glass technologies segment due to the suspension of its Optium CRT coating line, and lower building products and services results; net income declined 43%, to $3,878,000 ($0.14 a share), from $6,774,000 ($0.24). Backlog at May 30, 1998, totaled $312 million. Although APOG sees lower comparisons for the FY 99 (Feb.) second quarter, it expects improvement in the second half and projects full year earnings to be on par with the $0.93 a diluted share reported in FY 97.

Stock Performance - 02-OCT-98

In the past 30 trading days, APOG's shares have declined 21%, compared to a 7% fall in the S&P 500. Average trading volume for the past five days was 62,020 shares, compared with the 40-day moving average of 69,536 shares.

Key Stock Statistics

Dividend Rate/Share	0.20	Shareholders	1,900
Shs. outstg. (M)	27.6	Market cap. (B)	$0.282
Avg. daily vol. (M)	0.077	Inst. holdings	51%
Tang. Bk. Value/Share	2.04		
Beta	0.69		

Value of $10,000 invested 5 years ago: $ 20,484

Fiscal Year Ending Feb. 28

	1999	1998	1997	1996	1995	1994
Revenues (Million $)						
1Q	233.1	223.9	228.6	219.0	179.0	148.8
2Q	250.9	246.0	253.2	222.2	186.0	175.6
3Q	—	235.0	228.8	215.5	186.3	184.5
4Q	—	208.0	240.2	214.4	205.4	179.4
Yr.	—	912.8	950.8	871.1	756.5	688.2
Earnings Per Share ($)						
1Q	**0.14**	0.24	0.18	0.13	0.10	0.04
2Q	**0.33**	0.34	0.28	0.20	0.16	0.09
3Q	—	-0.37	0.27	0.19	0.14	-0.11
4Q	—	**-2.06**	0.20	0.13	0.09	-0.11
Yr.	—	**-1.84**	0.93	0.65	0.48	0.13

Next earnings report expected: mid December

Dividend Data (Dividends have been paid since 1974.)

Amount ($)	Date Decl.	Ex-Div. Date	Stock of Record	Payment Date
0.050	Oct. 14	Oct. 24	Oct. 28	Nov. 12 '97
0.050	Jan. 12	Jan. 23	Jan. 27	Feb. 11 '98
0.050	Apr. 21	May. 01	May. 08	May. 20 '98
0.050	Jul. 24	Aug. 07	Aug. 11	Aug. 26 '98

A Division of The **McGraw·Hill** *Companies*

Business Summary - 14-AUG-98

Apogee Enterprises, Inc. (APOG) makes custom aluminum window systems for nonresidential buildings, fabricates glass for architectural and automotive markets, and installs these products in buildings and automobiles. At the end of FY 96 (Feb.), the company reorganized into three business segments, from two. APOG has been taking steps to improve its profitability in the buildings products and services, and the auto glass segments. Revenues and operating profits (in 000s) in FY 98 were:

	Revenues	Profits
Building products & services	38%	-$96,433
Glass technologies	24%	27,330
Automotive glass	38%	15,046

The building products and services segment's operating units consist of nonresidential construction and architectural metals. The division's new construction unit, Harmon Ltd., is one of the largest designers and installers of curtainwall and window systems for nonresidential construction in the U.S. In FY 98, APOG decided to exit its European and Asian international curtainwall operations. The architectural products unit operates under the name Wausau Metals, which fabricates high-quality aluminum window and curtainwall systems. Operations also include Linetec, which operates two metal coating plants. Approximately 60% of APOG's revenues are generated from the architectural and nonresidential construction markets, with the other 40% derived from operations serving the auto glass market.

The glass technologies unit consists of Viracon and Tru Vue, which were moved from the buildings products and services segment, and the Viratec Thin Films joint venture (spun out of the former glass fabrication division). The unit produces flat laminated safety glass, architectural glass, coated glass for computer anti-glare screens, and picture framing glass. A new Optium facility for the cathode ray tubes (CaRT) business is expected to be operating by the end of calendar 1998. A new Viracon facility in Statesboro, GA, together with the planned expansion at the Owatonna facility, are expected to add 80% of production capacity over the next few years.

The automotive glass segment is engaged in the replacement and repair business through its Harmon Glass service centers (retail), Glass Depot distribution centers (wholesale) and Curvlite fabrication center. In January 1997, Harmon acquired Portland Glass, a regional auto glass retailer in the Northeast with 46 auto glass shops in five states. As of June 1998, the segment had 73 wholesale locations, 346 retail service centers and eight Midas Muffler franchises.

Per Share Data ($)

(Year Ended Feb. 28)	1998	1997	1996	1995	1994	1993	1992	1991	1990	1989
Tangible Bk. Val.	2.15	4.29	4.75	4.33	4.21	4.08	4.02	3.86	3.36	2.90
Cash Flow	-0.97	1.66	1.26	1.04	0.71	0.74	0.92	1.11	0.96	0.83
Earnings	-1.84	0.93	0.66	0.48	0.13	0.17	0.32	0.63	0.52	0.50
Dividends	0.19	0.35	0.17	0.16	0.15	0.14	0.13	0.12	0.10	0.08
Payout Ratio	NM	38%	26%	34%	121%	84%	41%	19%	19%	16%
Cal. Yrs.	1997	1996	1995	1994	1993	1992	1991	1990	1989	1988
Prices - High	25¼	23¾	9⅛	9¼	8⅞	7	9	10⅛	9⅜	7⅛
- Low	9¾	8⅛	6½	5¾	4⅞	4⅛	4¾	6⅞	6	4½
P/E Ratio - High	NM	26	14	19	71	41	29	16	18	14
- Low	NM	9	10	12	39	24	15	11	11	9

Income Statement Analysis (Million $)

	1998	1997	1996	1995	1994	1993	1992	1991	1990	1989
Revs.	913	951	871	757	688	572	596	600	590	434
Oper. Inc.	64.9	67.0	49.0	39.5	28.0	21.5	41.4	46.6	44.2	33.1
Depr.	24.0	20.5	16.5	15.2	15.7	15.1	16.3	13.3	12.1	9.0
Int. Exp.	9.4	8.1	7.0	5.0	3.6	3.0	2.9	3.8	6.2	3.6
Pretax Inc.	-63.5	40.0	27.1	20.9	6.6	6.5	15.8	28.8	23.4	21.6
Eff. Tax Rate	NM	35%	36%	39%	40%	30%	46%	41%	40%	38%
Net Inc.	-51.1	26.2	17.8	13.1	3.3	4.5	8.5	17.0	14.1	13.4

Balance Sheet & Other Fin. Data (Million $)

	1998	1997	1996	1995	1994	1993	1992	1991	1990	1989
Cash	7.9	4.1	7.4	2.9	10.8	8.9	18.7	20.5	12.2	3.0
Curr. Assets	262	305	259	257	221	169	166	163	155	127
Total Assets	464	501	386	362	306	251	250	250	244	208
Curr. Liab.	178	177	142	136	141	100	101	102	95.0	72.0
LT Debt	152	128	79.1	80.6	35.7	28.4	25.3	29.4	41.4	46.3
Common Eqty.	110	172	139	125	114	112	114	109	96.0	84.0
Total Cap.	262	300	219	207	151	141	141	142	144	136
Cap. Exp.	38.2	35.6	22.6	25.0	15.2	9.3	15.9	17.2	18.1	29.1
Cash Flow	-27.1	46.7	34.4	28.2	19.0	19.6	24.8	30.3	26.2	22.4
Curr. Ratio	1.5	1.7	1.8	1.9	1.6	1.7	1.6	1.6	1.6	1.8
% LT Debt of Cap.	58.1	42.6	36.0	39.0	23.6	20.2	17.9	20.7	28.8	34.0
% Net Inc.of Revs.	NM	2.8	2.0	1.7	0.5	0.8	1.4	2.8	2.4	3.1
% Ret. on Assets	NM	6.0	4.8	3.9	1.2	1.8	3.4	6.9	6.2	7.6
% Ret. on Equity	NM	16.9	13.5	10.9	2.9	4.0	7.6	16.6	15.7	17.2

Data as orig. reptd.; bef. results of disc. opers. and/or spec. items. Per share data adj. for stk. divs. as of ex-div. date. Bold denotes diluted EPS (FASB 128). E-Estimated. NA-Not Available. NM-Not Meaningful. NR-Not Ranked.

Office—7900 Xerxes Ave. South, Minneapolis, MN 55431. **Tel**—(612) 835-1874. **Chrmn**—D. W. Goldfus. **Pres & CEO**—R. Huffer. **EVP**—J. L. Martineau. **VP-Fin, CFO & Investor Contact**—R. G. Barbieri. **Treas**—M. A. Bevilacqua. **Secy**—M. L. Richards. **Dirs**—J. B. Cohen, D. W. Goldfus, B. B. Grogan, H. A. Hammerly, R. Huffer, J. L. Martineau, S. C. Mitchell, L. J. Niederhofer, D. E. Nugent, M. E. Shannon. **Transfer Agent & Registrar**—American Stock Transfer & Trust Co., NYC. **Incorporated**—in Minnesota in 1949. **Empl**— 6,672. **S&P Analyst:** Stewart Scharf

03-OCT-98 Industry: Restaurants

Summary: This company develops, franchises and operates a growing chain of more than 1,000 full-service Applebee's restaurants and 62 restaurants in the Rio Bravo group.

| S&P Opinion: Accumulate (★★★★) | Recent Price • 20 | Yield • 0.3% |
| | 52 Wk Range • 26-16⅛ | 12-Mo. P/E • 13.1 |

Quantitative Evaluations

Outlook
(1 Lowest—5 Highest)
• **5+**

Fair Value
• **32⅞**

Risk
• **Average**

Earn./Div. Rank
• **A-**

Technical Eval.
• **Bearish** since 8/98

Rel. Strength Rank
(1 Lowest—99 Highest)
• **67**

Insider Activity
• **Unfavorable**

Earnings vs. Previous Year
▲=Up ▼=Down ▶=No Change

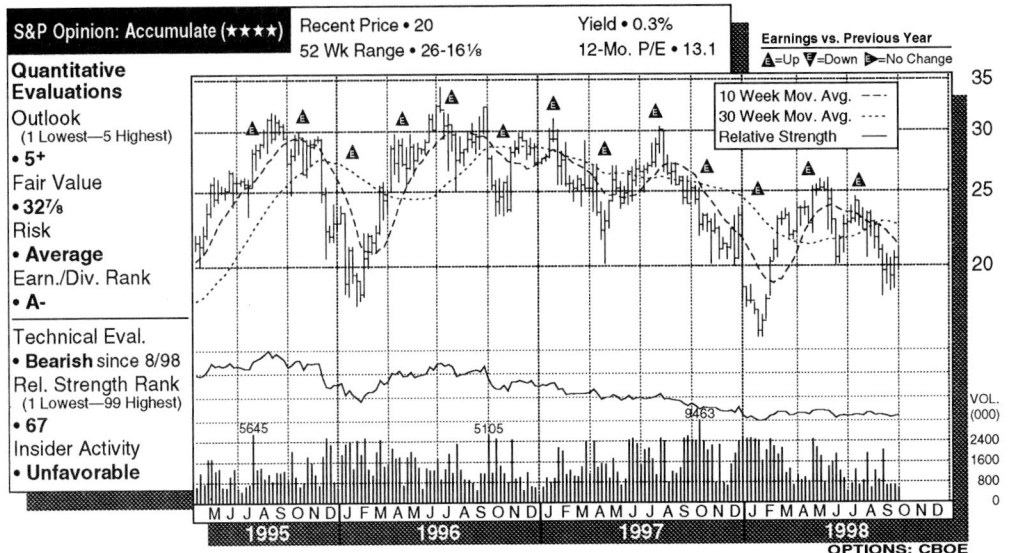

OPTIONS: CBOE

Overview - 11-AUG-98

Overall company restaurant sales should increase about 28% to 30% in 1998, primarily as a result of new openings of 32 Applebee's restaurants and 10 Rio Bravo Cantina restaurants. Comparable-unit sales at Applebee's are projected to increase only modestly, as many restaurants already operate near sales capacity, and many markets continue to experience competitive pressures. Cost of sales should increase slightly as a percentage of company restaurant sales, mainly due to higher occupancy costs and higher labor costs. Modest menu price increases instituted at the end of the third quarter of 1997 should partially offset increased costs. General and administrative costs should decline as a percentage of sales, on the larger revenue base. Interest expense should remain about level with that of 1997. APPB has purchased 33 restaurants from its largest franchisee, AppleSouth (APSO), for $93.4 million; APSO is divesting itself of all Applebee's units. APPB expects these restaurants to be accretive to earnings in 1998. EPS should increase about 20% in each of the next few years.

Valuation - 11-AUG-98

The shares have dropped back from their May 1998 high as same-unit sales have weakened, decreasing 1.2% in the second quarter. Earnings per share were on track in the second quarter, up 13% from a year earlier. Higher labor costs will continue to hurt expense ratios in 1998, but we still anticipate operating earnings gains of at least 20% in 1998. Earnings per share will be boosted by a share repurchase program, offset by the higher interest expense from the increased debt used to fund the repurchase. APPB has repurchased $31.6 million in shares out of a $50 million program. The company believes there is ample room for 1,500 Applebee's units in the U.S.

Key Stock Statistics

S&P EPS Est. 1998	1.70	Tang. Bk. Value/Share	6.05
P/E on S&P Est. 1998	11.8	Beta	1.28
S&P EPS Est. 1999	2.00	Shareholders	1,200
Dividend Rate/Share	0.07	Market cap. (B)	$0.606
Shs. outstg. (M)	30.3	Inst. holdings	58%
Avg. daily vol. (M)	0.138		

Value of $10,000 invested 5 years ago: $ 22,171

Fiscal Year Ending Dec. 31

	1998	1997	1996	1995	1994	1993
Revenues (Million $)						
1Q	146.6	116.3	95.04	75.44	45.63	21.98
2Q	166.4	130.7	104.6	83.80	49.70	28.43
3Q	—	133.9	107.1	88.08	54.88	32.75
4Q	—	135.0	106.4	96.24	58.32	33.92
Yr.	—	515.8	413.1	343.6	208.5	117.1
Earnings Per Share ($)						
1Q	**0.39**	**0.34**	0.27	0.15	0.11	0.09
2Q	**0.44**	**0.39**	0.31	0.24	0.14	0.10
3Q	**E0.43**	**0.39**	0.35	0.28	0.19	0.13
4Q	**E0.44**	**0.31**	0.29	0.26	0.18	0.13
Yr.	**E1.70**	**1.43**	1.22	0.94	0.62	0.44

Next earnings report expected: late October

Dividend Data (Dividends have been paid since 1991.)

Amount ($)	Date Decl.	Ex-Div. Date	Stock of Record	Payment Date
0.070	Oct. 10	Dec. 18	Dec. 22	Jan. 26 '98

A Division of The **McGraw·Hill** Companies

Business Summary - 11-AUG-98

Applebee's restaurants are a fixture in suburban shopping districts and shopping malls across the U.S. Applebee's International, Inc. is one of the fastest growing U.S. restaurant companies. It is the second largest company (in terms of revenues) in the dinnerhouse segment of the restaurant industry. As of December 31, 1997, there were 960 Applebee's Neighborhood Grill & Bar restaurants, of which 770 were operated by franchisees and 190 by the company, with the greatest concentration in the Southeast. In addition, it operates more than 50 specialty restaurants as part of the Rio Bravo group.

The company opend its first restaurant in 1986 and initially developed and operated six restaurants as a franchisee of the Applebee's Neighborhood Grill & Bar division of Creative Food 'N Fun Co., an indirect subsidiary of W. R. Grace & Co. In March 1988, substantially all assets of the Applebee's division were purchased for about $21 million. At that time, the division operated 13 restaurants (excluding one not acquired), and there were 41 franchised units (including the company's six restaurants).

Each Applebee's restaurant offers an extensive selection of moderately priced high-quality food and beverage items appealing both to families and adults. Systemwide sales totaled $1.82 billion in 1997, an increase of 18% from 1996. Systemwide sales include franchisee sales and company-owned and operated sales.

Weighted average weekly sales at company-owned restaurants increased 0.1% in 1997, to about $40,770. The anemic sales increase reflected the fact that many Applebee's company-owned restaurants operate near sales capacity, and various markets continue to experience competitive pressures. Although market share increases with the opening of multiple restaurants within a market, decreases in same-unit sales may result.

Growth of the Applebee's chain since March 1988 has reflected active franchising efforts. APPB has also begun pursuing international franchising of the Applebee's concept, initially focusing on Canada, the Caribbean and Europe. At the end of 1997, the company operated six restaurants in Canada, three in Germany, four in the Netherlands and one each in Curacao, Greece and Sweden.

The company's second restaurant concept, the Tex-Mex chain of Rio Bravo Cantinas, acquired in 1995, is an entry into the fast-growing ethnic food category. The atmosphere recreates the look of a bordertown cantina. The company ended 1997 with 55 restaurants, up from 30 a year earlier. Capital expenditures in 1997 were about $120 million.

Per Share Data ($)

(Year Ended Dec. 31)	1997	1996	1995	1994	1993	1992	1991	1990	1989	1988
Tangible Bk. Val.	7.55	6.93	5.56	2.82	2.38	2.42	1.00	0.73	0.57	0.03
Cash Flow	2.19	1.72	1.42	1.01	0.67	0.41	0.39	0.29	0.19	0.01
Earnings	1.43	1.22	0.94	0.62	0.44	0.27	0.22	0.13	Nil	-0.10
Dividends	0.07	0.07	0.06	0.05	0.04	0.03	0.02	0.01	Nil	Nil
Payout Ratio	5%	6%	6%	8%	9%	12%	9%	10%	Nil	Nil
Prices - High	31$\frac{1}{8}$	34$\frac{1}{4}$	31$\frac{3}{4}$	25$\frac{1}{4}$	22$\frac{1}{2}$	9$\frac{5}{8}$	5$\frac{1}{8}$	7$\frac{1}{4}$	5$\frac{3}{8}$	NA
- Low	17$\frac{3}{4}$	17$\frac{3}{4}$	13$\frac{3}{8}$	11	7$\frac{3}{8}$	4$\frac{3}{4}$	2$\frac{5}{16}$	2	4$\frac{1}{4}$	NA
P/E Ratio - High	22	28	34	41	51	35	23	57	NM	NA
- Low	12	15	14	18	17	17	10	16	NM	NA

Income Statement Analysis (Million $)

	1997	1996	1995	1994	1993	1992	1991	1990	1989	1988
Revs.	516	413	344	209	117	56.5	45.1	38.2	29.9	24.2
Oper. Inc.	96.6	80.1	62.6	36.0	19.0	9.4	6.3	5.0	3.7	2.4
Depr.	24.1	15.7	14.3	8.7	5.1	2.6	2.4	2.3	2.2	1.2
Int. Exp.	1.7	1.6	2.5	1.2	0.2	Nil	Nil	Nil	1.7	2.1
Pretax Inc.	71.8	60.7	47.8	25.6	15.4	8.3	5.0	2.9	-0.1	-0.9
Eff. Tax Rate	37%	37%	37%	34%	39%	39%	39%	39%	Nil	Nil
Net Inc.	45.1	38.0	27.4	16.9	9.5	5.1	3.1	1.8	-0.1	-0.9

Balance Sheet & Other Fin. Data (Million $)

	1997	1996	1995	1994	1993	1992	1991	1990	1989	1988
Cash	8.9	57.4	52.0	17.2	16.2	22.8	9.7	2.4	2.2	1.0
Curr. Assets	44.0	84.0	74.6	31.6	24.4	28.2	12.1	5.0	4.3	2.7
Total Assets	377	314	271	152	104	68.1	30.0	26.2	22.6	21.8
Curr. Liab.	62.5	42.0	38.4	27.9	19.2	8.0	6.2	5.4	2.8	7.2
LT Debt	22.6	24.6	25.8	23.7	2.2	0.1	Nil	Nil	Nil	12.1
Common Eqty.	290	245	204	96.7	79.2	58.6	23.2	20.4	19.3	1.9
Total Cap.	313	270	230	122	82.5	59.1	23.2	20.4	19.3	14.6
Cap. Exp.	90.5	65.7	51.8	40.4	37.8	9.2	1.3	4.7	1.6	5.1
Cash Flow	69.2	53.7	41.8	25.6	14.6	7.8	5.4	4.1	1.9	0.1
Curr. Ratio	0.7	2.0	1.9	1.1	1.3	3.5	1.9	0.9	1.5	0.4
% LT Debt of Cap.	7.2	9.1	12.6	19.4	2.6	0.1	Nil	Nil	Nil	83.2
% Net Inc.of Revs.	8.7	9.2	8.0	8.1	8.1	9.1	6.8	4.7	NM	NM
% Ret. on Assets	13.0	13.0	12.2	12.4	10.7	9.1	11.0	7.4	NM	NM
% Ret. on Equity	16.8	16.9	17.5	18.0	13.3	11.1	14.2	9.1	NM	NM

Data as orig. reptd.; bef. results of disc. opers. and/or spec. items. Per share data adj. for stk. divs. as of ex-div. date. Bold denotes diluted EPS (FASB 128). E-Estimated. NA-Not Available. NM-Not Meaningful. NR-Not Ranked.

Office—4551 W. 107th Street, Suite 100, Overland Park, KS 66207. **Tel**—(913) 967-4000. **Chrmn & Co-CEO**—A. J. Gustin Jr. **Pres, Co-CEO & COO**—L. L. Hill. **EVP, CFO & Treas**—G. D. Shadid. **VP & Secy**—R. T. Steinkamp. **Dirs**—D. P. Curran, A. J. Gustin Jr., E. Hansen, J. P. Helms, K. D. Hill, L. L. Hill, R. A. Martin, B. Sack. **Transfer Agent & Registrar**—American Stock Transfer & Trust Co., NYC. **Incorporated**—in Delaware in 1988. **Empl**— 16,300. **S&P Analyst:** Karen J. Sack, CFA

03-OCT-98

Industry:
Auto Parts & Equipment

Summary: This company distributes bearings, mechanical and electrical drive systems, industrial rubber products, fluid power components and specialty maintenance and repair products.

Quantitative Evaluations

Outlook
(1 Lowest—5 Highest)
• **4⁻**

Fair Value
• **23½**

Risk
• **Low**

Earn./Div. Rank
• **B**

Technical Eval.
• **NA**

Rel. Strength Rank
(1 Lowest—99 Highest)
• **30**

Insider Activity
• **NA**

Recent Price • 15⅛   Yield • 3.2%
52 Wk Range • 34-15⅛   12-Mo. P/E • 11.0

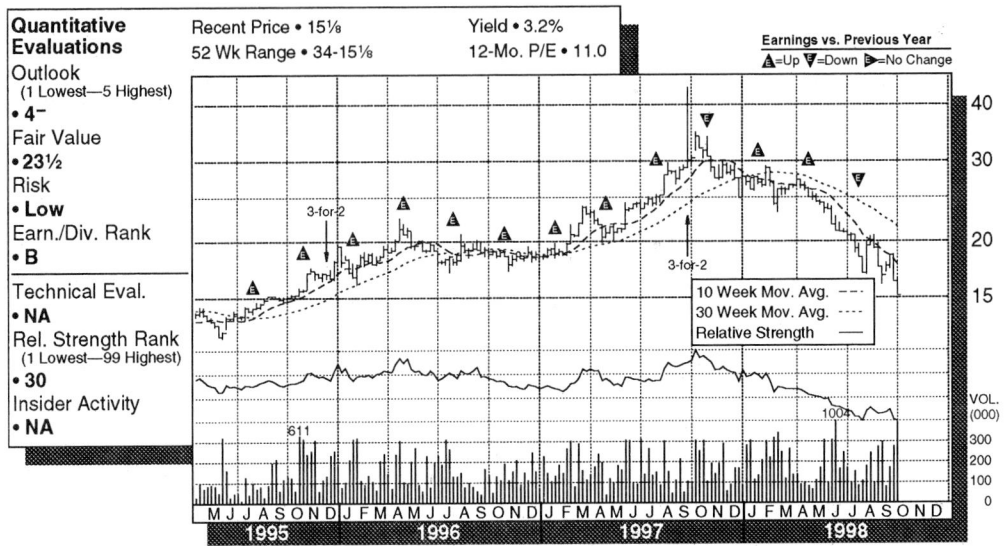

Earnings vs. Previous Year
▲=Up ▼=Down ▶=No Change

10 Week Mov. Avg. – – –
30 Week Mov. Avg. · · · ·
Relative Strength ——

1995   1996   1997   1998

Business Profile - 10-JUL-98

The company's name change from Bearings, Inc., effective January 1, 1997, underscored its shift in emphasis toward non-bearing, high-growth technologies and toward providing total system solutions, rather than only distribution. As part of that change of focus, the company entered into a number of business combinations to improve its market position in non-bearing products. In July 1997, APZ purchased Invetech Co., a privately held distributor of industrial components based in Detroit for $94 million in cash and stock. The company is optimistic about the success of its key strategies in the marketplace and the impact on internal growth with new and existing customers, but is cautious about the near-term direction of the U.S. industrial economy as lower commodity prices, a decline in demand for U.S. products in Asia, and tightening labor markets weaken some customer segments.

Operational Review - 10-JUL-98

Net sales in the first nine months of FY 98 (Jun.) advanced 30%, year to year, primarily reflecting the acquisition of Invetech in July 1997. Gross margins narrowed modestly on higher freight costs, lower purchase allowances and a less favorable product mix, and operating income increased 19%. With 50% higher interest expense, pretax income climbed 14%. After taxes at 38.9%, versus 40.9%, net income was up 17%, to $21,326,000 ($0.98 a share) from $18,163,000 ($0.97).

Stock Performance - 02-OCT-98

In the past 30 trading days, APZ's shares have declined 22%, compared to a 7% fall in the S&P 500. Average trading volume for the past five days was 192,460 shares, compared with the 40-day moving average of 61,351 shares.

Key Stock Statistics

Dividend Rate/Share	0.48	Shareholders	1,400
Shs. outstg. (M)	22.1	Market cap. (B)	$0.334
Avg. daily vol. (M)	0.076	Inst. holdings	53%
Tang. Bk. Value/Share	10.92		
Beta	0.04		

Value of $10,000 invested 5 years ago: $ 17,078

Fiscal Year Ending Jun. 30

	1998	1997	1996	1995	1994	1993
Revenues (Million $)						
1Q	344.7	282.3	277.1	247.6	222.7	204.0
2Q	368.6	275.0	275.1	249.9	226.3	199.0
3Q	393.9	297.2	296.1	277.0	239.7	210.8
4Q	384.2	305.8	295.5	280.3	247.5	217.9
Yr.	1,491	1,160	1,144	1,055	936.3	831.4
Earnings Per Share ($)						
1Q	0.22	0.29	0.25	0.18	0.14	0.09
2Q	**0.35**	0.32	0.28	0.20	0.14	0.11
3Q	**0.41**	0.37	0.33	0.25	0.17	0.15
4Q	**0.40**	0.48	0.41	0.36	0.30	0.20
Yr.	**1.38**	1.46	1.27	0.98	0.75	0.55

Next earnings report expected: mid October

Dividend Data (Dividends have been paid since 1957.)

Amount ($)	Date Decl.	Ex-Div. Date	Stock of Record	Payment Date
0.120	Jan. 15	Feb. 11	Feb. 13	Feb. 27 '98
0.120	Apr. 16	May. 13	May. 15	May. 29 '98
0.120	Jul. 16	Aug. 12	Aug. 14	Aug. 31 '98
0.120	Jul. 16	Aug. 12	Aug. 14	Aug. 31 '98

A Division of The **McGraw·Hill** Companies

Business Summary - 10-JUL-98

Sometimes a name can be overbearing. In January 1997, Bearings, Inc. changed its name to Applied Industrial Technologies, Inc. (APZ), in order to more accurately reflect the total scope of the company's businesses as well as its future strategy. That strategy emphasizes higher growth technologies and total system solutions, rather than just the distribution of bearings.

APZ distributes bearings, mechanical and electrical drive systems, industrial rubber products, fluid power components and specialty maintenance and repair products through 9 distribution centers, 32 mechanical, rubber and power shops and more than 380 branches in 45 states. Sales contributions by product category in recent fiscal years (Jun.) were:

	1997	1996	1995
Bearings	41%	43%	45%
Drive system products	31%	30%	30%
Specialty/other items	28%	26%	25%

Products distributed include ball, roller, thrust and linear bearings, mechanical and electrical drive systems, industrial rubber products, fluid power transmission components and related specialty items such as seals, lubricants, locking devices, sealing compounds, adhesives and tools. APZ is one of the leading independent U.S. distributors of replacement bearings, power transmission components and related items.

Distribution is conducted on a nonexclusive basis for many manufacturers. Although APZ does not generally manufacture products sold, it does assemble filter carts and fluid power units. It also rebuilds precision machine spindles, assembles speed reducers, pumps, valves, cylinders and hydraulic motors, provides custom machining, assembles fluid power systems, operates rubber shops that modify conveyor belts and provides hose assemblies. Products are purchased from more than 100 major suppliers, and resold to a wide range of industrial and commercial customers and government agencies.

In July 1997, APZ completed the largest acquisition in its history. The company acquired Invetech Co., a distributor of industrial components based in Detroit, MI, for a combination of $22.9 million in cash and 2.1 million shares of Applied's common stock. The company anticipates that the acquisition will lead to a 25% increase in revenues for FY 98 (Jun.).

In February 1996, the company acquired Engineered Sales, Inc., an applied technology distributor. In August 1996, it signed an agreement to become the primary supplier for Electronic Data Systems Corp.'s new integrated supply service. Also in August, 1996, the company sold its aircraft bearings business.

Per Share Data ($)

(Year Ended Jun. 30)	1998	1997	1996	1995	1994	1993	1992	1991	1990	1989
Tangible Bk. Val.	NA	10.87	9.91	9.44	8.86	7.83	7.64	8.00	8.32	8.12
Cash Flow	NA	2.13	1.95	1.73	1.55	1.33	0.68	0.97	1.26	1.61
Earnings	1.38	1.46	1.27	0.98	0.75	0.55	-0.11	0.27	0.76	1.09
Dividends	0.47	0.41	0.36	0.31	0.28	0.28	0.28	0.28	0.28	0.25
Payout Ratio	34%	28%	28%	32%	38%	52%	105%	37%	23%	
Prices - High	29¼	43⅝	22½	19¾	16⅝	13⅞	10⅜	10½	12⅝	14⅝
- Low	16¾	18¼	16	12¼	12⅜	9⅛	7½	7	6	10⅝
P/E Ratio - High	21	30	18	20	22	25	NM	39	17	13
- Low	12	12	13	12	17	17	NM	26	8	10

Income Statement Analysis (Million $)

	1998	1997	1996	1995	1994	1993	1992	1991	1990	1989
Revs.	NA	1,160	1,144	1,055	936	831	818	814	651	630
Oper. Inc.	NA	64.2	62.8	50.2	41.4	33.3	25.1	28.3	37.4	42.2
Depr.	NA	13.6	13.5	13.3	13.6	12.8	12.6	11.1	8.2	8.8
Int. Exp.	NA	6.5	9.0	7.7	6.4	5.5	7.0	10.3	5.4	4.4
Pretax Inc.	NA	45.1	40.8	29.7	21.7	15.5	-1.9	7.5	20.3	29.4
Eff. Tax Rate	NA	40%	43%	43%	41%	42%	NM	43%	40%	38%
Net Inc.	NA	27.1	23.3	16.9	12.7	8.9	-1.7	4.3	12.2	18.3

Balance Sheet & Other Fin. Data (Million $)

	1998	1997	1996	1995	1994	1993	1992	1991	1990	1989
Cash	NA	22.4	9.2	4.8	10.9	4.6	9.3	8.4	5.7	7.1
Curr. Assets	NA	285	295	265	249	221	234	235	300	187
Total Assets	NA	394	404	359	344	316	331	328	380	251
Curr. Liab.	NA	121	143	112	105	90.0	192	181	236	112
LT Debt	NA	51.4	62.9	74.0	80.0	80.0	Nil	Nil	Nil	Nil
Common Eqty.	Nil	208	189	165	150	135	129	134	135	135
Total Cap.	NA	259	252	241	234	221	134	139	140	139
Cap. Exp.	NA	21.6	23.5	15.1	16.6	13.6	20.4	21.1	17.5	20.1
Cash Flow	NA	40.7	36.8	30.2	26.3	21.7	10.9	15.4	20.4	27.1
Curr. Ratio	NA	2.4	2.1	2.4	2.4	2.4	1.2	1.3	1.3	1.7
% LT Debt of Cap.	NA	19.9	24.9	30.9	34.2	36.3	Nil	Nil	Nil	Nil
% Net Inc.of Revs.	Nil	2.3	2.0	1.6	1.4	1.1	NM	0.5	1.9	2.9
% Ret. on Assets	NA	6.8	6.1	4.7	3.8	2.7	NM	1.2	3.9	7.9
% Ret. on Equity	NA	13.7	13.2	10.7	8.9	6.7	NM	3.2	9.2	14.2

Data as orig. reptd.; bef. results of disc. opers. and/or spec. items. Per share data adj. for stk. divs. as of ex-div. date. E-Estimated. NA-Not Available. NM-Not Meaningful. NR-Not Ranked.

Office—One Applied Plaza, Cleveland, OH 44115. **Tel**—(216) 426-4000. **Fax**—(216) 426-4845. **Website**—http://appliedindustrial.com **Chrmn, Pres & CEO**—J. C. Dannemiller. **Vice Chrmn**—J. C. Robinson. **CFO, Treas & Investor Contact**—John R. Whitten. **VP-Secy**—R. C. Stinson. **Dirs**—W. G. Bares, R.D. Blackwell, W. E. Butler, J. C. Dannemiller, R. B. Every, R. R. Gifford, L. T. Hiltz, J. J. Kahl, J. M. Moore, J. C. Robinson, J. S. Thornton. **Transfer Agent & Registrar**—Harris Trust and Savings Bank, Chicago. **Incorporated**—in Delaware in 1928; reincorporated in Ohio in 1988. **Empl**—4,101. **S&P Analyst:** S.R.B.

03-OCT-98

Industry: Computers (Peripherals)

Summary: This company makes recording heads for rigid disk drives.

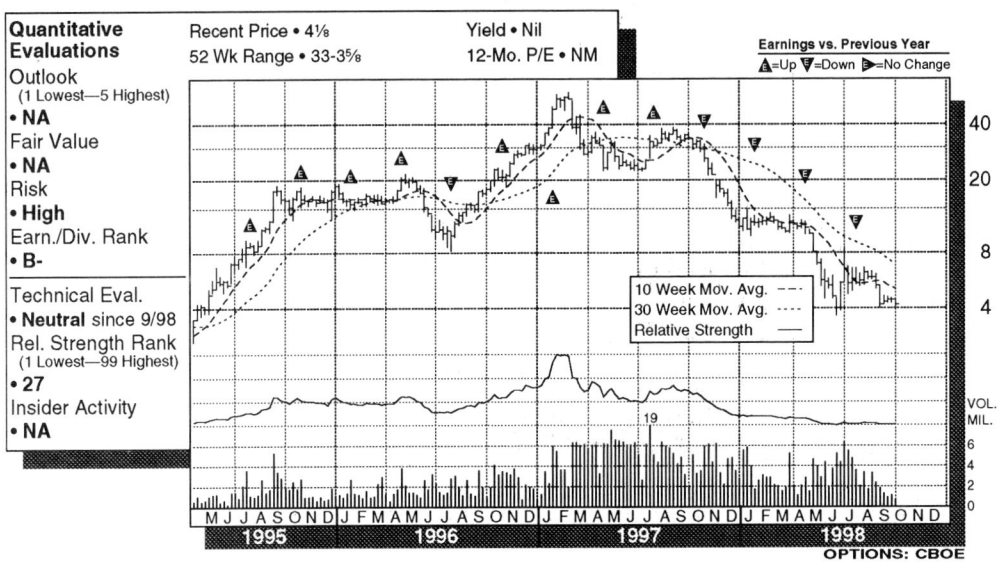

Quantitative Evaluations

Outlook (1 Lowest—5 Highest)
• **NA**

Fair Value
• **NA**

Risk
• **High**

Earn./Div. Rank
• **B-**

Technical Eval.
• **Neutral** since 9/98

Rel. Strength Rank (1 Lowest—99 Highest)
• **27**

Insider Activity
• **NA**

Recent Price • 4⅛
52 Wk Range • 33-3⅝

Yield • Nil
12-Mo. P/E • NM

Earnings vs. Previous Year
▲=Up ▼=Down ▶=No Change

10 Week Mov. Avg. ---
30 Week Mov. Avg. ·····
Relative Strength —

OPTIONS: CBOE

Business Profile - 24-JUL-98

Revenue decline from primary product sales carried over into the second quarter of FY 98 (Sep). Management indicated that the continuing decline in demand for disk drives based on inductive thin-film technology caused the drop in both price and sales volume of APM's disk heads and that future operating results will be dependent on the successful qualification and timely production ramp up of new magnetoresistive (MR) and advanced inductive thin-film products. The company continued to experience process and production delays for new MR products and anticipates that revenue may decline more than 25% next quarter, then increase during the fourth quarter of FY 98 as MR head shipments become a significant source of revenue.

Operational Review - 24-JUL-98

Net sales in the first six months of FY 98 fell 46% year to year reflecting lower shipments to a large customer and an industry-wide shift to the newer MR technology. Cost of sales declined 11%, leading to a negative gross profit, compared with a gross profit of $95 million. Although SG&A expenses declined 18%, a $35 million increase in R&D expenditures caused by the shift to MR technology, and an $8.4 million restructuring charge gave rise to a net loss of $71,680,000 ($3.00 a share, diluted), compared with net income of $62,963,000 ($2.03, diluted).

Stock Performance - 02-OCT-98

In the past 30 trading days, APM's shares have declined 29%, compared to a 7% fall in the S&P 500. Average trading volume for the past five days was 122,680 shares, compared with the 40-day moving average of 336,449 shares.

Key Stock Statistics

Dividend Rate/Share	Nil	Shareholders	1,700
Shs. outstg. (M)	24.1	Market cap. (B)	$0.101
Avg. daily vol. (M)	0.212	Inst. holdings	25%
Tang. Bk. Value/Share	5.58		
Beta	2.15		

Value of $10,000 invested 5 years ago: $ 3,987

Fiscal Year Ending Sep. 30

	1998	1997	1996	1995	1994	1993
Revenues (Million $)						
1Q	74.41	121.6	94.71	55.37	71.24	74.60
2Q	58.84	126.3	86.71	64.92	69.83	86.87
3Q	33.58	124.1	74.04	79.86	70.29	97.35
4Q	—	122.8	89.30	92.45	64.56	77.12
Yr.	—	494.8	344.8	292.6	275.9	335.9
Earnings Per Share ($)						
1Q	**-1.67**	1.30	0.38	-0.53	-0.28	0.13
2Q	**-1.33**	1.24	0.36	-0.12	-0.42	0.18
3Q	**-1.50**	0.85	0.10	0.30	-0.75	0.33
4Q	—	0.49	0.51	0.40	-0.93	-2.57
Yr.	—	3.88	1.35	0.08	-2.39	-2.17

Next earnings report expected: late October

Dividend Data

No cash dividends have ever been paid.

A Division of The McGraw·Hill Companies

Applied Magnetics Corporation

Business Summary - 24-JUL-98

Increasing demand for greater data storage capacity and performance in smaller form factor disk drives have kept disk drive manufacturers busy developing newer generations of products to match these needs. Reflecting this trend, Applied Magnetics (APM), as a key supplier of magnetic recording heads to disk drive makers, has focused its long range strategy on its magnetoresistive (MR) and giant magnetoresistive (GMR) disk head technologies. It believes that GMR disk heads, which afford performance advantages over thin-film or MR heads, represent the next important magnetic recording head technology.

Multimedia personal computers and high-end computer applications such as network servers (Internet and intranet), workstations and mainframes, are driving the demand for greater data storage capacity and performance. In addition, the market growth of notebook and sub-notebook computers has increased demand for smaller form factor disk drives. Due to these trends, customer demand began to shift from inductive thin-film product technology to MR technology. By the end of FY 97 (Sep.), some customers had discontinued development of new products based on thin-film disk head technology. MR disk heads, which generally permit greater storage capacities per disk and provide higher data transfer rates than thin film disk heads, now represent the fastest growing segment of the recording head industry.

Late in the first quarter of FY 98, the disk drive industry entered into a general slowdown accelerating the transition to newer magnetoresistive (MR) disk drive head technology. In the first quarter of FY 98, APM recorded an $8.4 million pretax charge primarily related to costs associated with a plan to shut down its Ireland production facility and write down production assets related to thin-film inductive technology. Operating losses in the first six months of FY 98 were primarily due to a significant decrease in shipments to APM's largest customer causing a sharp reduction in production schedules and increased pricing pressure. APM has taken several measures to reduce expenditures, including a reduction in SG&A expenses and capital spending in order to realign costs with the current level of business.

The company stated at the end of the second quarter of FY 98 that it had continued to experience process and production delays in qualifying for new MR programs, resulting in the inability to participate in MR programs currently in production by disk drive manufacturers. APM was continuing its R&D program toward MR and other advanced technologies and anticipated that revenue could decline more than 25% in the third quarter of FY 98, then increase during the fourth quarter of FY 98 as MR head shipments became a significant source of revenue.

Per Share Data ($) (Year Ended Sep. 30)	1997	1996	1995	1994	1993	1992	1991	1990	1989	1988
Tangible Bk. Val.	10.10	6.04	4.60	4.46	6.84	7.60	8.49	9.62	10.14	10.38
Cash Flow	5.43	2.56	1.31	-1.31	-0.69	1.57	0.69	0.95	1.21	2.47
Earnings	4.05	1.35	0.08	-2.39	-2.17	0.02	-1.12	-0.62	0.07	1.47
Dividends	Nil	Nil	Nil	Nil	Nil	Nil	Nil	Nil	Nil	Nil
Payout Ratio	Nil	Nil	Nil	Nil	Nil	Nil	Nil	Nil	Nil	Nil
Prices - High	60½	31⅞	19	7½	14½	11⅞	13	15	14¾	16⅝
- Low	10⅝	8¼	2½	2⅛	4⅞	5	4⅜	6⅜	8¼	10½
P/E Ratio - High	16	24	NM	NM	NM	NM	NM	NM	NM	11
- Low	3	6	NM	NM	NM	NM	NM	NM	NM	7
Income Statement Analysis (Million $)										
Revs.	495	345	293	276	336	298	455	368	314	293
Oper. Inc.	145	64.7	26.4	-24.4	42.1	32.7	35.7	34.5	23.6	42.6
Depr.	38.5	28.9	27.6	23.6	29.9	25.7	29.5	25.2	18.5	16.3
Int. Exp.	12.3	9.1	4.8	4.2	6.6	6.9	7.3	7.0	7.1	1.4
Pretax Inc.	98.2	33.1	2.3	-51.6	-40.9	0.1	-17.6	-11.2	1.5	27.3
Eff. Tax Rate	2.16%	2.60%	25%	NM	NM	64%	NM	NM	23%	13%
Net Inc.	96.1	32.2	1.8	-52.7	-43.7	0.3	-18.3	-10.0	1.2	23.7
Balance Sheet & Other Fin. Data (Million $)										
Cash	162	127	48.2	20.8	49.4	11.5	3.9	3.1	8.1	11.6
Curr. Assets	278	217	128	78.0	142	119	123	152	135	134
Total Assets	478	359	247	221	279	263	300	327	296	273
Curr. Liab.	117	99	134	114	108	100	105	80.0	46.0	52.0
LT Debt	116	116	3.3	0.7	11.6	27.2	33.3	69.4	64.7	41.0
Common Eqty.	241	140	104	98.0	151	124	150	167	174	168
Total Cap.	357	256	107	99	163	152	184	237	241	210
Cap. Exp.	96.1	69.9	23.4	31.5	56.7	29.8	35.7	39.9	38.8	58.7
Cash Flow	135	61.1	29.3	-29.0	-13.9	26.0	11.2	15.2	19.7	40.0
Curr. Ratio	2.4	2.2	1.0	0.7	1.3	1.2	1.2	1.9	3.0	2.6
% LT Debt of Cap.	32.5	45.4	3.0	0.7	7.1	18.0	18.1	29.3	26.9	19.5
% Net Inc.of Revs.	19.4	9.3	0.6	NM	NM	0.1	NM	NM	0.4	8.1
% Ret. on Assets	23.0	10.6	0.7	NM	NM	0.1	NM	NM	0.4	10.2
% Ret. on Equity	50.5	26.5	1.7	NM	NM	0.2	NM	NM	0.7	15.0

Data as orig. reptd.; bef. results of disc. opers. and/or spec. items. Per share data adj. for stk. divs. as of ex-div. date. Bold denotes diluted EPS (FASB 128). E-Estimated. NA-Not Available. NM-Not Meaningful. NR-Not Ranked.

Office—75 Robin Hill Rd., Goleta, CA 93117. **Tel**—(805) 683-5353. **Website**—http://www.appmag.com **Chrmn, CEO, CFO & Investor Contact**—Craig D. Crisman. **Contr & Secy**—P. T. Altavilla. **Dirs**—C. D. Crisman, H. M. Dwight Jr., H. R. Frank, J. E. Goldress, R. C. Mercure Jr. **Transfer Agent & Registrar**—ChaseMellon Shareholder Services, Ridgefield Park, NJ. **Incorporated**—in California in 1957; reincorporated in Delaware in 1987. **Empl**— 8,500. **S&P Analyst:** D. Moskowitz

Applied Power

205C

NYSE Symbol **APW**

In S&P SmallCap 600

03-OCT-98

Industry: Machinery (Diversified)

Summary: This diversified manufacturer makes hydraulic tools, hydraulic components and technical office furniture.

Quantitative Evaluations	
Outlook (1 Lowest—5 Highest)	• 3⁻
Fair Value	• 34¼
Risk	• **Low**
Earn./Div. Rank	• **B+**

Recent Price • 23⅞
52 Wk Range • 40⅛-23⅛

Yield • 0.3%
12-Mo. P/E • 13.7

Technical Eval.
• **Bearish** since 2/97

Rel. Strength Rank (1 Lowest—99 Highest)
• **30**

Insider Activity
• **Neutral**

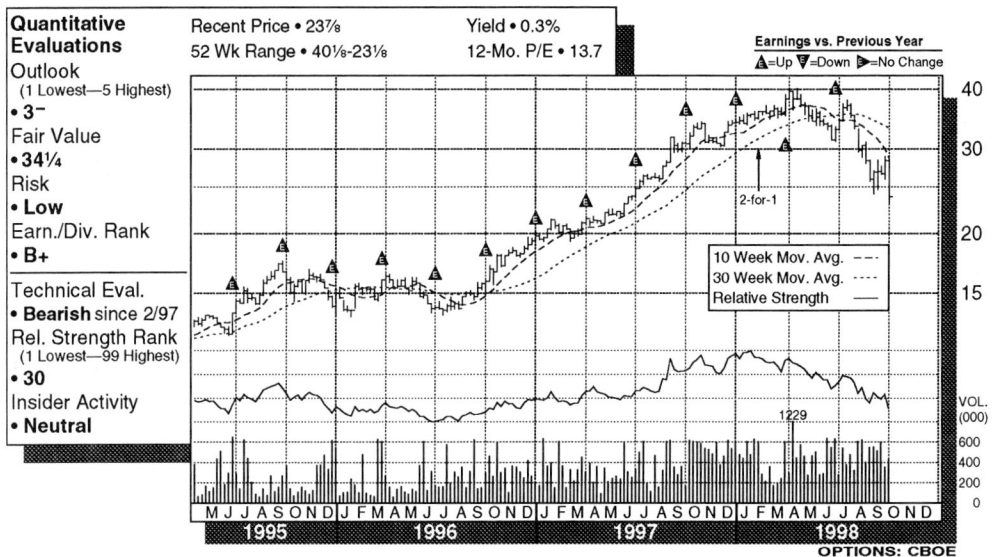

Earnings vs. Previous Year
▲=Up ▼=Down ▶=No Change

10 Week Mov. Avg. ---
30 Week Mov. Avg. ····
Relative Strength —

2-for-1

1229

VOL. (000)

OPTIONS: CBOE

Business Profile - 01-OCT-98

Applied Power believes that the information age is just getting started, and that the electronic enclosure systems market will have above-average growth for many years to come. Thus, over the last three years, the company has been pursuing the electronic enclosure systems market. APW has projected sales for FY 99 (Aug.) at approximately $1.6 billion, including the ZERO Corp. and VERO Group acquisitions, which it expects to be accretive in 1999. The company expects Technical Environments & Enclosures' (TEE) segment sales to reach $750 million in 1999. APW will continue to make bolt-on acquisitions within the TEE unit to expand its geographic and product capabilities in electronic enclosure systems.

Operational Review - 01-OCT-98

Revenues in the first nine months of FY 98 (Aug.) advanced 38%, year to year, led by acquisitions, the success of new products in the Engineered Solutions unit and expansion of the Technical Environments & Enclosures' (TEE) sales force. Margins widened, and operating income rose 42%. Following sharply higher depreciation and amortization expense and net financing costs, net income rose 30%, to $39.1 million ($1.33 a share), from $30.1 million ($1.05, adjusted). At May 31, 1998, working capital stood at $80 million, down 22% from $102 million at February 28, 1998.

Stock Performance - 02-OCT-98

In the past 30 trading days, APW's shares have declined 16%, compared to a 7% fall in the S&P 500. Average trading volume for the past five days was 86,020 shares, compared with the 40-day moving average of 109,503 shares.

Key Stock Statistics

Dividend Rate/Share	0.06	Shareholders	500
Shs. outstg. (M)	38.5	Market cap. (B)	$0.919
Avg. daily vol. (M)	0.099	Inst. holdings	56%
Tang. Bk. Value/Share	NM		
Beta	0.51		

Value of $10,000 invested 5 years ago: $ 31,013

Fiscal Year Ending Aug. 31

	1998	1997	1996	1995	1994	1993
Revenues (Million $)						
1Q	208.7	153.1	139.3	125.8	103.6	91.70
2Q	217.2	157.2	137.1	124.5	101.9	86.41
3Q	241.7	173.8	147.6	139.3	111.3	92.58
4Q	—	188.2	147.3	137.4	116.8	89.78
Yr.	—	672.3	571.2	527.1	433.6	360.5
Earnings Per Share ($)						
1Q	0.41	0.34	0.28	0.20	0.11	0.13
2Q	**0.40**	0.33	0.28	0.17	0.13	0.10
3Q	**0.51**	0.39	0.33	0.27	0.20	0.15
4Q	—	0.41	0.33	0.28	0.20	-0.24
Yr.	—	1.46	1.21	0.91	0.64	0.33

Next earnings report expected: early October

Dividend Data (Dividends have been paid since 1987.)

Amount ($)	Date Decl.	Ex-Div. Date	Stock of Record	Payment Date
2-for-1	Jan. 09	Feb. 04	Jan. 22	Feb. 03 '98
0.015	Jan. 09	Feb. 06	Feb. 10	Feb. 27 '98
0.015	May. 05	May. 18	May. 20	Jun. 01 '98
0.015	Aug. 06	Aug. 14	Aug. 18	Aug. 31 '98

A Division of The McGraw-Hill Companies

STANDARD
&POOR'S
STOCK REPORTS

Applied Power Inc.

205C
03-OCT-98

Business Summary - 01-OCT-98

This diversified company derives over 40% of revenues from sales of hydraulic tools to the general industrial and construction markets, 30% from sales of hydraulics to truck and auto makers, and 30% from sales of technical office workstations and cabinets. Gross profit margins by segment in recent fiscal years (Aug.) were:

	FY 97	FY 96	FY 95
Tools & Supplies	38%	40%	42%
Engineered Solutions	33%	31%	29%
Technical Environments & Enclosures	43%	50%	49%

The company has a fairly large international exposure; it obtains about 24%, 8% and 2% of total revenues from sales to Europe, Asia and Latin America, respectively.

The Tools & Supplies segment (formerly Distributed Products) primarily makes hydraulic tools for industrial and construction customers. T&S sells its products through 2,500 independent distributors worldwide. This segment also makes electrical products for electrical contractors and the do-it-yourself market. It sells its products to about 4,000 wholesale distributors, as well as to retail home centers such as Home Depot, Ace Hardware and Sears.

The Engineered Solutions Group (ESG) makes hydraulics for retractable truck cabs, truck suspensions and automobile convertible tops. ESG also produces hydraulics for medical equipment manufacturers. In addition, the group makes devices that reduce vibration, shock and noise. ESG primarily sells its vibration reduction devices to aircraft manufacturers, airlines and medical instrument makers.

APW's higher-margin Technical Environments & Enclosures (TEE) group makes a broad line of cabinets and related enclosures for various electronic and other technical equipment. TEE also makes workstations for computer-oriented offices. The company has targeted what it believes are the fast-growing local area network (LAN) office, media production, telecom and laboratory markets. APW has been augmenting TEE's growth by purchasing other technical office furniture manufacturers.

The company's businesses face competition to varying degrees in each of APW's markets. Each product line generally competes with a small group of different competitors. No one company competes directly in all of APW's businesses. Management believes that the company's technical skills, global presence, good customer relationships, and patents bolster its competitive position.

In July 1998, APW acquired ZERO Corp. for 11.2 million shares (valued at $386 million). ZERO's primary business is protecting electronics; its system packaging, thermal management and engineered cases serve the telecommunications, instrumentation and data-processing markets.

Per Share Data ($)

(Year Ended Aug. 31)	1997	1996	1995	1994	1993	1992	1991	1990	1989	1988
Tangible Bk. Val.	4.65	2.81	2.38	1.48	0.79	0.99	0.70	0.44	-0.14	1.74
Cash Flow	4.57	1.96	1.58	1.36	0.94	0.93	1.06	1.49	1.08	0.75
Earnings	1.46	1.21	0.91	0.64	0.33	0.36	0.30	0.74	0.76	0.56
Dividends	0.06	0.06	0.06	0.06	0.06	0.06	0.06	0.06	0.06	0.05
Payout Ratio	4%	5%	7%	9%	18%	16%	20%	8%	7%	9%
Prices - High	35⅛	20	17⅝	12⅝	9¼	10	10	13⅝	12⅞	9⅞
- Low	19¼	13⅜	11⅜	8⅛	7¼	6¾	5¼	6¼	8	3⅞
P/E Ratio - High	24	17	19	20	28	27	33	18	17	16
- Low	13	11	12	13	22	18	18	8	11	8

Income Statement Analysis (Million $)

	1997	1996	1995	1994	1993	1992	1991	1990	1989	1988
Revs.	672	571	527	433	360	357	434	445	246	177
Oper. Inc.	96.5	78.5	67.3	61.6	46.6	50.7	62.7	75.0	43.2	30.1
Depr.	23.7	21.1	18.5	19.4	15.8	14.8	19.9	19.9	8.7	4.9
Int. Exp.	12.0	8.5	10.3	11.4	11.7	14.6	19.8	20.4	7.9	3.7
Pretax Inc.	62.7	49.2	29.5	25.3	13.4	15.9	16.9	34.4	33.0	22.9
Eff. Tax Rate	33%	32%	32%	33%	35%	40%	54%	43%	40%	37%
Net Inc.	42.0	34.0	25.0	16.9	8.7	9.5	7.8	19.6	19.8	14.5

Balance Sheet & Other Fin. Data (Million $)

	1997	1996	1995	1994	1993	1992	1991	1990	1989	1988
Cash	5.8	1.0	0.9	1.9	0.9	3.0	3.6	6.5	19.9	2.3
Curr. Assets	226	207	190	175	162	156	144	191	193	81.0
Total Assets	464	381	333	317	291	289	326	394	371	150
Curr. Liab.	128	108	97.4	102	93.0	79.0	86.0	127	110	49.0
LT Debt	102	76.5	74.2	78.0	87.0	105	114	142	87.0	70.0
Common Eqty.	204	168	132	107	88.0	97.0	117	115	87.0	70.0
Total Cap.	320	260	222	185	175	202	231	257	256	96.0
Cap. Exp.	22.7	23.0	16.0	12.7	11.5	9.3	12.6	16.8	9.3	8.6
Cash Flow	65.7	54.8	43.5	36.3	24.5	24.3	27.8	39.5	28.5	19.5
Curr. Ratio	1.8	1.9	2.0	1.7	1.7	2.0	1.7	1.5	1.8	1.7
% LT Debt of Cap.	31.7	29.4	33.3	42.2	49.6	52.1	49.5	55.1	66.1	27.1
% Net Inc.of Revs.	6.3	5.9	4.7	3.9	2.4	2.7	1.8	4.4	8.1	8.2
% Ret. on Assets	10.0	9.5	6.7	5.6	3.0	3.1	2.2	5.1	7.6	11.5
% Ret. on Equity	22.6	22.5	2.1	17.3	9.4	8.9	6.7	19.3	25.2	22.8

Data as orig. reptd.; bef. results of disc. opers. and/or spec. items. Per share data adj. for stk. divs. as of ex-div. date. Bold denotes diluted EPS (FASB 128). E-Estimated. NA-Not Available. NM-Not Meaningful. NR-Not Ranked.

Office—13000 W. Silver Spring Dr., Butler, WI 53007. **Tel**—(414) 781-6600. **Fax**—(414) 781-0629. **Chrmn, Pres & CEO**—R. G. Sim. **VP & CFO**—R. C. Arzbaecher. **Treas**—D. R. Dorszynski. **Secy**—A. W. Asmuth III. **Dirs**—H. R. Crowther, J. L. Heckel, R. A. Kashnow, L. D. Kozlowski, J. J. McDonough, R. G. Sim. **Transfer Agent & Registrar**—Firstar Trust Co., Milwaukee. **Incorporated**—in Wisconsin in 1910. **Empl**—4,235. **S&P Analyst:** John A. Massey

AptarGroup, Inc.

205G

NYSE Symbol **ATR**

In S&P SmallCap 600

03-OCT-98

Industry: Manufacturing (Specialized)

Summary: This company is a leading manufacturer of pumps, aerosol valves and dispensing closures for fragrance/cosmetic, personal care, pharmaceutical, household and food products.

Quantitative Evaluations	
Outlook (1 Lowest—5 Highest)	• 3
Fair Value	• 28⅜
Risk	• Average
Earn./Div. Rank	• NR
Technical Eval.	• Bearish since 8/98
Rel. Strength Rank (1 Lowest—99 Highest)	• 25
Insider Activity	• Unfavorable

Recent Price • 22
52 Wk Range • 33½-20½

Yield • 0.7%
12-Mo. P/E • 16.1

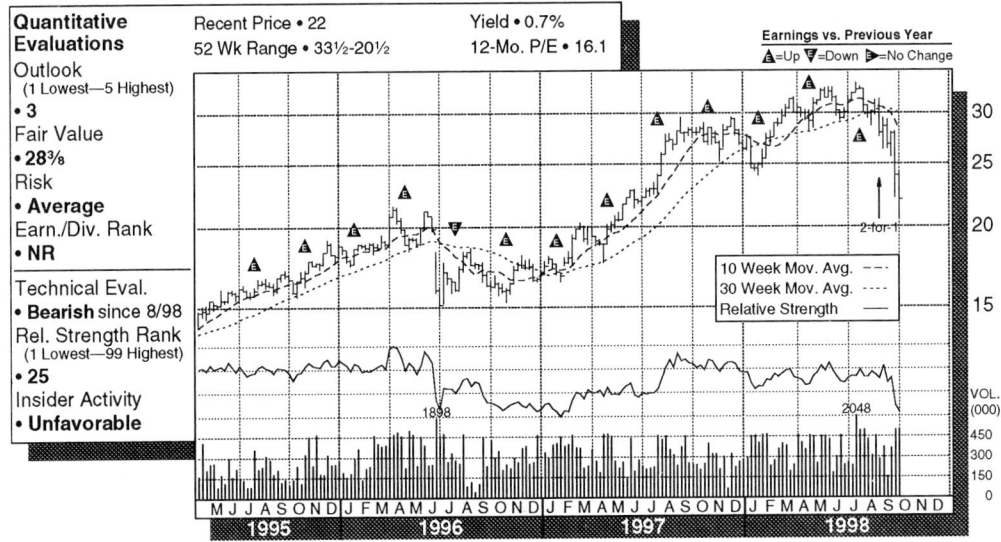

Earnings vs. Previous Year
▲=Up ▼=Down ▶=No Change

10 Week Mov. Avg. – – –
30 Week Mov. Avg. ⋯⋯⋯
Relative Strength ——

2-for-1

VOL. (000)

Business Profile - 19-MAR-98

Although revenues rose 6.4% in 1997, the company said sales would have risen 15% if the U.S. dollar had remained constant. Historically, exchange rate fluctuations have affected results, as a significant portion of ATR's operations are located outside the U.S. In the fourth quarter of 1997, the French government increased the tax rate by 5%, retroactive to the beginning of the year; this increased income tax expense for the year by $1.8 million. The company believes that revenues have benefited from customer desire to differentiate packaging. In addition, during 1997, the use of dispensing systems expanded to a wider variety of products, leading the company to view future trends and profitability with optimism. The dividend was boosted 14% with the August 1997 payment.

Operational Review - 19-MAR-98

Based on a preliminary report, net sales in 1997 rose 6.4%, reflecting continued strong demand for the company's major product lines. Margins widened, and operating income increased 15%. Following lower interest income and increased equity in income of affiliates, pretax income advanced 31%. After taxes at 40.8%, versus 37.6%, net income rose 24%, to $46,529,000 ($2.55 a diluted share) from $37,548,000 ($2.05).

Stock Performance - 02-OCT-98

In the past 30 trading days, ATR's shares have declined 27%, compared to a 7% fall in the S&P 500. Average trading volume for the past five days was 210,680 shares, compared with the 40-day moving average of 103,679 shares.

Key Stock Statistics

Dividend Rate/Share	0.16	Shareholders	900
Shs. outstg. (M)	36.0	Market cap. (B)	$0.793
Avg. daily vol. (M)	0.132	Inst. holdings	68%
Tang. Bk. Value/Share	8.94		
Beta	0.35		

Value of $10,000 invested 5 years ago: NA

Fiscal Year Ending Dec. 31

	1998	1997	1996	1995	1994	1993
Revenues (Million $)						
1Q	170.9	158.3	152.9	135.6	117.2	95.20
2Q	181.8	171.8	151.1	142.4	118.2	107.9
3Q	—	163.5	155.9	140.6	120.0	105.0
4Q	—	161.8	155.9	138.8	118.9	103.4
Yr.	—	655.4	615.8	557.5	474.3	411.5
Earnings Per Share ($)						
1Q	0.36	0.32	0.30	0.27	0.23	—
2Q	0.39	0.33	0.24	0.28	0.23	0.38
3Q	—	0.34	0.25	0.23	0.20	0.16
4Q	—	0.29	0.25	0.21	0.17	0.14
Yr.	—	1.27	1.04	0.99	0.82	0.67

Next earnings report expected: late October

Dividend Data (Dividends have been paid since 1993.)

Amount ($)	Date Decl.	Ex-Div. Date	Stock of Record	Payment Date
0.080	Jan. 22	Feb. 02	Feb. 04	Feb. 26 '98
0.080	Apr. 23	May. 04	May. 06	May. 27 '98
0.080	Jul. 23	Jul. 31	Aug. 04	Aug. 25 '98
2-for-1	Jul. 23	Aug. 26	Aug. 04	Aug. 25 '98

A Division of The **McGraw·Hill** Companies

Business Summary - 19-MAR-98

Its client list reads like a Who's Who of leading companies and brands in the fragrance/cosmetics and personal care industries -- L'Oreal, Estee Lauder, Calvin Klein, Mary Kay, Avon, Ivory, Crest. AptarGroup, Inc. (ATR), which makes dispensing systems for a variety of consumer products, derived 63% of its sales from these markets in 1996. ATR also supplies the pharmaceutical, household and food products industries with its broad offering of pumps, closures and aerosol valves, adding value to its customers' products by making them easier for consumers to use.

The company's pumps (63% of sales in 1996) are finger-driven dispensing systems which disperse a spray or lotion from non-pressurized containers. The style of pump depends on the product being dispensed, with smaller, fine mist pumps used for perfumes, for instance, and less dainty high-output trigger pumps employed to squirt out household cleaners. Dispensing closures (18%) are plastic caps used mainly for squeezable containers which allow a product to be dispensed without removing the cap. ATR sees future growth opportunities as consumer marketers continue to convert non-dispensing closures (such as twist-off caps for shampoo bottles) to dispensing closures.

Aerosol valves (17%) are mechanisms that dispense products from pressurized containers. The company's continuous spray valves are often used with hair spray, spray paint, and certain household and automotive products. A second type of valve, the metered aerosol valve, is sold mainly to the pharmaceutical market for lung and heart medications that need to be dispensed in precise amounts.

A significant portion of the company's operations are located in Europe, and sales there accounted for 58% of ATR's total in 1996. A new plant in China began making aerosol valves in early 1997, with output of closures and pumps to be added later in the year.

The company's sales rose 10% in 1996, largely as a result of volume increases to the pharmaceutical and personal care markets. ATR expects sales to the pharmaceutical market to continue to expand, and in 1996 it worked with several pharmaceutical customers to develop pumps and aerosol valves for a variety of new prescription drugs. Improvements in volume during the year, however, were partially offset by price decreases and softness of pump sales to customers in the European fragrance/cosmetics market. ATR experienced reduced demand from its fragrance/cosmetics customers -- the company's largest market -- throughout 1996.

In 1997, revenues improved 6.4%, despite adverse exchange rate fluctuations.

Per Share Data ($)

(Year Ended Dec. 31)	1997	1996	1995	1994	1993	1992	1991	1990	1989	1988
Tangible Bk. Val.	16.75	8.05	7.37	7.55	5.92	4.39	NA	NA	NA	NA
Cash Flow	5.28	2.38	2.21	1.99	1.61	1.69	NA	NA	NA	NA
Earnings	1.27	1.04	0.99	0.82	0.67	0.59	NA	NA	NA	NA
Dividends	0.15	0.14	0.13	0.12	0.05	NA	NA	NA	NA	NA
Payout Ratio	12%	13%	13%	14%	8%	NA	NA	NA	NA	NA
Prices - High	29⅝	21⅝	19⅛	14½	11	NA	NA	NA	NA	NA
- Low	16⅜	14½	12⅜	10⅛	8	NA	NA	NA	NA	NA
P/E Ratio - High	23	21	19	18	17	NA	NA	NA	NA	NA
- Low	13	14	12	12	12	NA	NA	NA	NA	NA

Income Statement Analysis (Million $)

	1997	1996	1995	1994	1993	1992	1991	1990	1989	1988
Revs.	655	616	557	474	412	445	NA	NA	NA	NA
Oper. Inc.	129	112	103	87.0	71.3	72.8	NA	NA	NA	NA
Depr.	49.9	47.9	43.5	38.4	30.3	35.3	NA	NA	NA	NA
Int. Exp.	5.3	6.3	5.9	8.2	10.2	14.7	NA	NA	NA	NA
Pretax Inc.	78.9	60.5	57.6	43.2	35.5	29.2	NA	NA	NA	NA
Eff. Tax Rate	41%	37%	38%	37%	37%	35%	NA	NA	NA	NA
Net Inc.	46.5	37.5	35.7	27.3	21.6	19.0	NA	NA	NA	NA

Balance Sheet & Other Fin. Data (Million $)

	1997	1996	1995	1994	1993	1992	1991	1990	1989	1988
Cash	17.7	16.4	17.3	20.1	16.4	12.2	NA	NA	NA	NA
Curr. Assets	256	237	224	184	158	167	NA	NA	NA	NA
Total Assets	585	576	559	465	408	420	NA	NA	NA	NA
Curr. Liab.	125	116	123	106	153	160	NA	NA	NA	NA
LT Debt	70.7	76.6	80.7	53.8	41.3	47.6	NA	NA	NA	NA
Common Eqty.	342	336	312	271	190	180	NA	NA	NA	NA
Total Cap.	439	440	416	345	247	246	NA	NA	NA	NA
Cap. Exp.	71.2	62.8	55.5	42.0	112	45.6	NA	NA	NA	NA
Cash Flow	96.4	85.4	79.2	65.6	51.8	54.3	NA	NA	NA	NA
Curr. Ratio	2.0	2.0	1.8	1.7	1.0	1.0	NA	NA	NA	NA
% LT Debt of Cap.	16.1	17.4	19.4	15.6	16.7	19.3	NA	NA	NA	NA
% Net Inc.of Revs.	7.1	6.1	6.4	5.7	5.2	4.3	NA	NA	NA	NA
% Ret. on Assets	8.0	6.6	7.0	5.9	NM	NA	NA	NA	NA	NA
% Ret. on Equity	13.7	11.6	12.3	11.3	NM	NA	NA	NA	NA	NA

Data as orig. reptd.; bef. results of disc. opers. and/or spec. items. Per share data adj. for stk. divs. as of ex-div. date. Bold denotes diluted EPS (FASB 128). E-Estimated. NA-Not Available. NM-Not Meaningful. NR-Not Ranked.

Office—475 West Terra Cotta Ave., Suite E, Crystal Lake, IL 60014. **Tel**—(815) 477-0424. **Chrmn**—King Harris. **Pres & CEO**—C. A. Siebel. **EVP, CFO, Secy & Treas**—Stephen J. Hagge. **Dirs**—E. L. Barnett, R. Gruska, L. A. Guthart, K. Harris, W. W. Harris, E. J. LeCoque, A. Pilz, P. Pfeiffer, C. A. Siebel. **Transfer Agent & Registrar**—ChaseMellon Shareholder Services, Ridgefield Park, NJ. **Incorporated**—in Delaware in 1992. **Empl**—3,900. **S&P Analyst:** B.G.

STANDARD &POOR'S

STOCK REPORTS

Aquarion Co.

205M

NYSE Symbol **WTR**

In S&P SmallCap 600

03-OCT-98

Industry:
Water Utilities

Summary: This holding company provides water service to 30 Connecticut and Long Island towns, and operates a utility consulting service.

Quantitative Evaluations

Recent Price • 34¼
52 Wk Range • 36⅞-26⅛

Yield • 4.8%
12-Mo. P/E • 15.7

Outlook
(1 Lowest—5 Highest)
• **2−**

Fair Value
• **35⅛**

Risk
• **Low**

Earn./Div. Rank
• **B+**

Technical Eval.
• **Bearish** since 5/98

Rel. Strength Rank
(1 Lowest—99 Highest)
• **83**

Insider Activity
• **NA**

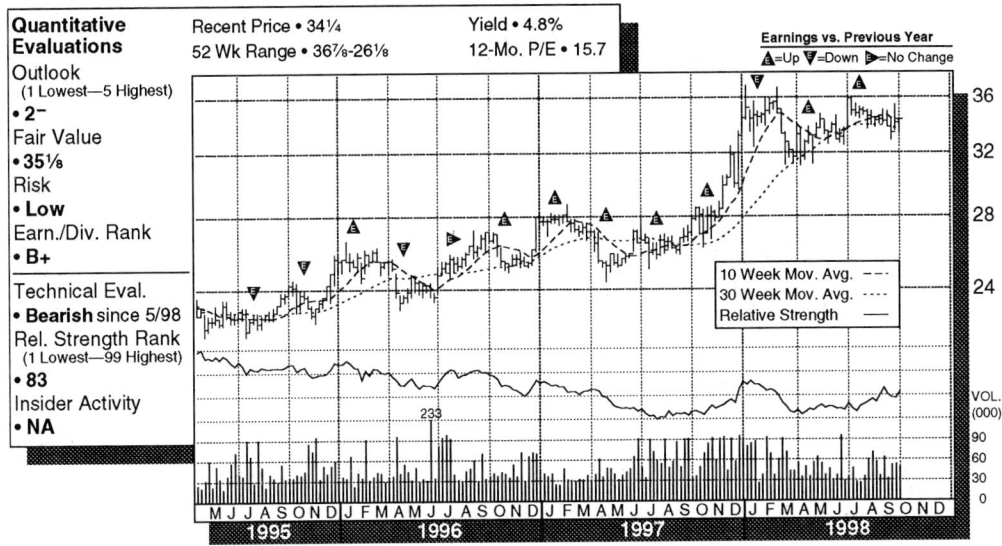

Earnings vs. Previous Year
▲=Up ▼=Down ▶=No Change

10 Week Mov. Avg. ---
30 Week Mov. Avg. ·····
Relative Strength —

Business Profile - 11-MAY-98

Through its two subsidiaries, WTR operates one of the 10 largest investor-owned water companies in the U.S., providing water service to 30 Connecticut and Long Island, NY, towns. Non-regulated segments include utility consulting services, forest products and a small real estate operation. Following the January 1997 merger of the company's Connecticut subsidiaries with the Bridgewater Hydraulic unit, in March 1997, WTR sold the operations of Industrial and Environmental Analysts, Inc., its environmental testing laboratory business, for about $10 million. Reflecting improved operating results, the company raised its quarterly dividend 1.2% with the October 1997 payment.

Operational Review - 11-MAY-98

Operating revenues in the first quarter of 1998 advanced 9.0%, year to year, reflecting surplus land sales and an increase in BHC's Eastern division water rates, which became effective August 1, 1997. Margins widened, primarily on the higher sales; operating income climbed 18%. After lower interest expense, and taxes at 43.4%, versus 44.3%, net income gained 27%, to $3,035,000 ($0.40 a share, on 5.8% more shares), from $2,388,000 ($0.33). The net after tax gain from the sale of BHC's surplus, off-watershed land was $0.03 a share for the first quarter of 1998; BHC did not sell any surplus land in the 1997 period.

Stock Performance - 02-OCT-98

In the past 30 trading days, WTR's shares have increased 0.18%, compared to a 7% fall in the S&P 500. Average trading volume for the past five days was 9,820 shares, compared with the 40-day moving average of 10,551 shares.

Key Stock Statistics

Dividend Rate/Share	1.66	Shareholders	8,000
Shs. outstg. (M)	7.4	Market cap. (B)	$0.256
Avg. daily vol. (M)	0.010	Inst. holdings	25%
Tang. Bk. Value/Share	22.71		
Beta	0.03		

Value of $10,000 invested 5 years ago: $ 19,137

Fiscal Year Ending Dec. 31

	1998	1997	1996	1995	1994	1993
Revenues (Million $)						
1Q	25.38	23.39	20.99	25.60	25.85	24.69
2Q	26.83	26.52	23.01	28.41	29.62	26.19
3Q	—	29.23	25.50	30.00	29.65	28.91
4Q	—	27.97	25.30	34.19	36.86	27.57
Yr.	—	107.1	94.80	118.2	122.0	107.4
Earnings Per Share ($)						
1Q	**0.40**	0.34	0.30	0.35	0.40	0.36
2Q	**0.53**	0.50	0.46	0.46	0.55	0.44
3Q	—	0.80	0.60	0.48	0.52	0.58
4Q	—	0.46	0.64	0.61	0.40	0.36
Yr.	—	**2.08**	1.98	1.90	1.87	1.76

Next earnings report expected: late October

Dividend Data (Dividends have been paid since 1890.)

Amount ($)	Date Decl.	Ex-Div. Date	Stock of Record	Payment Date
0.410	Dec. 16	Jan. 07	Jan. 09	Jan. 30 '98
0.410	Mar. 24	Apr. 07	Apr. 09	Apr. 30 '98
0.410	Jun. 23	Jul. 08	Jul. 10	Jul. 30 '98
0.415	Sep. 22	Oct. 07	Oct. 09	Oct. 30 '98

A Division of The **McGraw·Hill** Companies

Business Summary - 11-MAY-98

The water supply business may not appear to be a growth industry, but Aquarion Co. (NYSE: WTR), a water utility holding company, is seeking to expand its water business, and believes that industry conditions will support such growth. The company believes that a major industry consolidation is on the horizon, based on several factors. First, there is an increasing number of water quality laws and a need to replace aging infrastructure that will require large capital expenditures that will drive some players out of the industry. In addition, municipalities are increasingly looking to outsource their water supply operations, providing opportunities for private suppliers. Finally, the industry is highly fragmented, with more than 57,000 operating water systems in the U.S., 95% of which serve populations of fewer than 10,000. As the industry consolidates, Aquarion hopes to grow by entering new markets and by acquiring other water system operators.

Aquarion's utility subsidiaries, BHC Co. (BHC) and Sea Cliff Water Co. (SCWC) collect, treat and distribute water to residential, commercial and industrial customers, to other utilities for resale, and for private and municipal fire protection. The utilities provide water to customers in 30 communities with a population of approximately 500,000 people, serving approximately

139,000 customer accounts, in Connecticut and in Long Island, NY. These communities include those served by other utilities to which water is made available by WTR's utilities on a wholesale basis for back-up supply or peak demand purposes.

In 1997, the utilities derived 62% of their operating revenues from residential customers, 16% from commercial customers, 14% from fire protection customers, 4% from industrial customers, and 4% from other sources. In 1997, 88% of the utilities' water supply was provided by reservoirs, 11% by producing wells and 1% by purchases. At the end of 1997, the utilities had an aggregate safe daily yield of 113 million gallons. The average daily demand for water from the utilities in 1997 was 68 million gallons/day, leaving the utilities with ample excess water supply needed to increase its customer base.

Aquarion is also engaged in various non-utility activities. The company owns Timco, Inc., a timber processing company based in New Hampshire. WTR is also engaged in the utility management service business through Aquarion Management Services, Inc., and owns Main Street South Corp., a small real estate subsidiary originally formed to assist the utilities in marketing surplus land. In March 1997, the company sold its environmental testing laboratory subsidiary, Industrial and Environmental Analysts, Inc., for about $10 million.

Per Share Data ($)

(Year Ended Dec. 31)	1997	1996	1995	1994	1993	1992	1991	1990	1989	1988
Tangible Bk. Val.	22.48	20.85	19.72	19.14	18.64	17.71	16.87	17.34	22.29	21.12
Earnings	2.08	2.00	1.90	1.87	1.76	1.51	-1.75	1.48	2.10	2.04
Dividends	1.63	1.62	1.22	2.02	1.62	1.62	1.61	1.60	1.58	1.52
Payout Ratio	78%	81%	64%	108%	92%	107%	NM	108%	75%	75%
Prices - High	36⁷/₈	28¹/₄	26	28	29¹/₄	25¹/₂	27¹/₄	25⁷/₈	29⁵/₈	36
- Low	24³/₈	23	21⁵/₈	21¹/₂	24⁵/₈	20¹/₈	19⁷/₈	19	24³/₈	25¹/₈
P/E Ratio - High	18	14	14	15	17	17	NM	17	14	18
- Low	12	11	11	11	14	13	NM	13	12	12

Income Statement Analysis (Million $)

	1997	1996	1995	1994	1993	1992	1991	1990	1989	1988
Revs.	107	94.8	118	122	107	104	100	77.8	78.3	67.6
Depr.	13.4	13.8	13.0	11.6	10.6	9.5	8.9	7.6	6.8	6.3
Maint.	NA	NA	NA	NA	NA	NA	NA	NA	NA	NA
Fxd. Chgs. Cov.	3.3	3.4	3.4	3.7	2.8	2.5	0.4	2.2	3.4	3.6
Constr. Credits	0.8	1.1	0.9	0.6	0.6	0.7	0.4	0.8	0.5	0.5
Eff. Tax Rate	44%	40%	44%	46%	38%	40%	NM	22%	43%	38%
Net Inc.	15.0	13.8	12.9	12.2	11.0	8.6	-8.5	7.1	10.0	9.7

Balance Sheet & Other Fin. Data (Million $)

	1997	1996	1995	1994	1993	1992	1991	1990	1989	1988
Gross Prop.	482	455	432	379	368	352	327	311	289	269
Cap. Exp.	28.7	38.6	41.6	19.8	17.9	25.4	17.9	19.1	20.1	17.9
Net Prop.	340	323	296	256	250	243	227	219	206	193
Capitalization:										
LT Debt	151	148	132	115	116	106	95.3	100	68.2	69.5
% LT Debt	53	55	52	51	51	52	55	52	42	43
Pfd.	Nil	Nil	0.3	0.3	0.4	0.4	2.2	2.5	3.2	4.0
% Pfd.	Nil	Nil	0.10	0.20	0.20	0.20	1.20	1.30	2.00	2.40
Common	134	123	122	112	111	97.2	75.5	90.5	90.3	86.5
% Common	47	45	48	49	49	48	44	47	56	54
Total Cap.	356	344	325	319	317	285	212	229	195	188
% Oper. Ratio	76.2	76.8	82.0	83.6	81.7	83.2	84.1	81.1	78.0	76.7
% Earn. on Net Prop.	15.3	14.6	7.7	7.9	8.0	7.4	7.1	6.9	8.6	8.4
% Return On Revs.	14.0	14.6	10.9	10.0	10.2	8.3	NM	9.1	12.7	14.3
% Return On Invest. Capital	10.7	9.4	7.1	6.3	5.9	7.3	0.6	6.9	9.0	8.4
% Return On Com. Equity	11.7	11.3	10.9	10.8	10.6	9.1	NM	7.8	11.3	11.3

Data as orig. reptd.; bef. results of disc opers. and/or spec. items. Per share data adj. for stk. divs. as of ex-div. date. Bold denotes diluted EPS (FASB 128). E-Estimated. NA-Not Available. NM-Not Meaningful. NR-Not Ranked.

Office—835 Main St., Bridgeport, CT 06604. **Tel**—(203) 335-2333. **Chrmn**—G.W. Edwards. **Pres & CEO**—R. K. Schmidt. **EVP, CFO & Treas**—Janet M. Hansen. **VP, Secy & Investor Contact**—Larry L. Bingaman (203-336-7626). **Dirs**—G. W. Edwards Jr., G. Etherington, J. D. Greenwood, D. M. Halsted, Jr., E. G. Hotard, J. E. McGregor, G. J. Ratcliffe, R. K. Schmidt, J. A. Urquhart. **Transfer Agent & Registrar**—ChaseMellon Securities Trust Co., Ridgefield Park, NJ. **Incorporated**—in Connecticut in 1857; reincorporated in Delaware in 1968. **Empl**—399. **S&P Analyst:** J. Robert Cho

Arctic Cat Inc.

3145N

NASDAQ Symbol **ACAT**

In S&P SmallCap 600

03-OCT-98

Industry: Leisure Time (Products)

Summary: This company designs, makes and markets snowmobiles, personal watercraft, all-terrain vehicles, and related parts and accessories.

Quantitative Evaluations

Outlook (1 Lowest—5 Highest)
• **4+**

Fair Value
• **11⅜**

Risk
• **Average**

Earn./Div. Rank
• **B+**

Technical Eval.
• **Bearish** since 12/97

Rel. Strength Rank (1 Lowest—99 Highest)
• **79**

Insider Activity
• **Neutral**

Recent Price • 9
52 Wk Range • 12½-8

Yield • 2.7%
12-Mo. P/E • 10.0

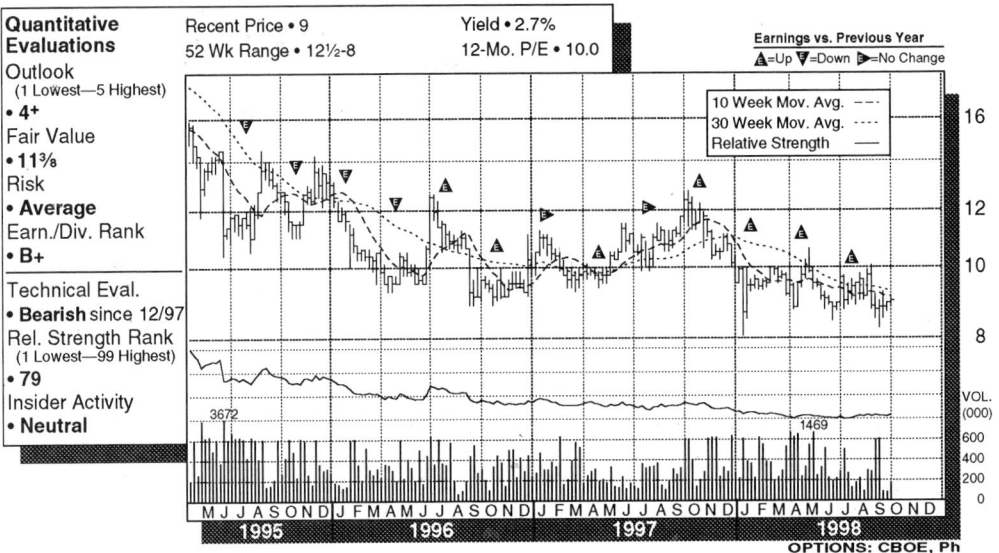

Earnings vs. Previous Year
▲=Up ▼=Down ▶=No Change

10 Week Mov. Avg. ---
30 Week Mov. Avg. ....
Relative Strength —

OPTIONS: CBOE, Ph

Business Profile - 26-AUG-98

ACAT is one of only a few major companies that produce snowmobiles, personal watercraft and all-terrain vehicles. It expects to be a significant beneficiary of continued growth in these related industries. In FY 98 (Mar.) ACAT posted its 15th consecutive year of increased retail sales, and boosted its North American snowmobile market share. However, based on dealer orders, revenues are expected be moderately lower in FY 99; the company is identifying expense and cost reductions to soften the impact on earnings. Suzuki Motor Co., which owns all of the Class B common shares, is the largest stockholder.

Operational Review - 26-AUG-98

Net sales in the three months ended June 30, 1998, advanced 3.6%, year to year, as increased shipments of full-sized snowmobiles and greater garment and accessory sales outweighed lower all-terrain and personal watercraft unit volume, primarily reflecting order and shipment timing differences. Gross margins narrowed, but with a 1.9% reduction in SG&A expense, operating profit climbed 94%. After taxes at 35.5% in each period, net income was up 75%, to $1,529,000 ($0.05 a share, on 3.3% fewer shares), from $872,000 ($0.03).

Stock Performance - 02-OCT-98

In the past 30 trading days, ACAT's shares have declined 8%, compared to a 7% fall in the S&P 500. Average trading volume for the past five days was 32,860 shares, compared with the 40-day moving average of 57,372 shares.

Key Stock Statistics

Dividend Rate/Share	0.24	Shareholders	800
Shs. outstg. (M)	27.9	Market cap. (B)	$0.183
Avg. daily vol. (M)	0.070	Inst. holdings	39%
Tang. Bk. Value/Share	6.16		
Beta	0.26		

Value of $10,000 invested 5 years ago: $ 11,995

Fiscal Year Ending Mar. 31

	1999	1998	1997	1996	1995	1994
Revenues (Million $)						
1Q	88.65	85.47	89.13	61.70	56.00	37.40
2Q	—	196.8	177.9	166.1	149.2	106.9
3Q	—	139.8	133.9	123.6	112.8	88.20
4Q	—	82.09	67.66	53.56	49.10	35.60
Yr.	—	504.2	468.6	404.9	367.1	268.1
Earnings Per Share ($)						
1Q	0.05	0.03	0.03	-0.14	0.12	0.09
2Q	—	0.68	0.63	0.60	0.64	0.48
3Q	—	0.21	0.20	0.20	0.36	0.33
4Q	—	-0.05	-0.08	-0.10	Nil	0.04
Yr.	—	0.88	0.78	0.56	1.13	0.94

Next earnings report expected: late October

Dividend Data (Dividends have been paid since 1992.)

Amount ($)	Date Decl.	Ex-Div. Date	Stock of Record	Payment Date
0.060	Oct. 30	Nov. 13	Nov. 17	Dec. 02 '97
0.060	Jan. 30	Feb. 12	Feb. 17	Mar. 03 '98
0.060	May. 12	May. 13	May. 15	Jun. 02 '98
0.060	Jul. 28	Aug. 13	Aug. 17	Sep. 01 '98

A Division of The McGraw-Hill Companies

Business Summary - 26-AUG-98

Arctic Cat Inc. (formerly Arctco, Inc.) designs, engineers, makes and markets full lines of snowmobiles and all-terrain vehicles (ATVs) under the Arctic Cat name, personal watercraft under the Tigershark name, and related parts, garments and accessories.

The company produces a full line of snowmobiles, which accounted for 59% of total net sales in FY 98 (Mar.). There were 34 basic models at the end of FY 98, all marketed under the Arctic Cat brand name. Snowmobiles, with suggested retail prices ranging from $3,399 to $9,799 (except for a children's model with a suggested price of $1,299), are sold in the U.S., Canada, Scandinavia, and other international markets. ACAT is one of only four major participants in the North American market. In FY 98, over 85% of the company's snowmobile sales were from models or model variations not available three years earlier.

ACAT began shipping all-terrain vehicles (18% of total net sales), also marketed under the Arctic Cat name, in December 1995, with the Bearcat 454 4x4. Since then, the company's ATV line has grown to include seven models (ranging in price from $4,399 to $6,449), all of which are designed for the utility, farming/ranching, and hunting/fishing markets. ACAT believes that a sharp increase in its ATV sales in FY 98 reflected favorable dealer and consumer reception of the Arctic Cat product, expansion of the company's model line, and growth in the ATV market.

The company's personal watercraft (7%), sold under the Tigershark brand name, combine performance, durability and style. The seven models offered are sold at prices ranging from $4,799 to $7,899. The company attributed a 49% decline in personal watercraft unit sales volume in FY 98 to an industry-wide softening in consumer demand.

Parts, garments and accessories accounted for 16% of net sales in FY 98.

ACAT sells its products through an extensive network of independent dealers located throughout the contiguous U.S. and Canada, and through distributors representing dealers in Alaska, Europe, the Middle East, Asia, and other international markets.

Through July 24, 1998, the company spent $19.9 million to purchase 2,045,000 common shares, under a stock repurchase program initiated in FY 96, covering up to 3 million shares.

Per Share Data ($)

(Year Ended Mar. 31)	1998	1997	1996	1995	1994	1993	1992	1991	1990	1989
Tangible Bk. Val.	6.25	5.73	5.27	4.96	4.02	3.23	2.73	2.41	NA	NA
Cash Flow	1.34	0.83	0.82	1.32	1.10	0.74	NA	NA	NA	NA
Earnings	0.88	0.78	0.56	1.13	0.94	0.62	0.46	0.49	NA	NA
Dividends	0.24	0.24	0.24	0.21	0.15	0.12	0.03	Nil	Nil	Nil
Payout Ratio	27%	31%	43%	19%	16%	19%	7%	Nil	Nil	Nil
Cal. Yrs.	1997	1996	1995	1994	1993	1992	1991	1990	1989	1988
Prices - High	12¾	13⅛	19½	21¾	18⅛	9⅛	NA	NA	NA	NA
- Low	9¼	8⅞	10⅜	13⅜	8⅛	4½	NA	NA	NA	NA
P/E Ratio - High	14	17	35	19	19	15	NA	NA	NA	NA
- Low	11	11	19	12	9	7	NA	NA	NA	NA

Income Statement Analysis (Million $)

	1998	1997	1996	1995	1994	1993	1992	1991	1990	1989
Revs.	504	469	405	367	268	185	148	152	NA	NA
Oper. Inc.	51.0	45.4	31.2	54.4	44.8	29.2	NA	NA	NA	NA
Depr.	13.4	11.4	7.7	5.5	4.6	3.6	NA	NA	NA	NA
Int. Exp.	0.1	0.1	Nil	0.0	0.1	0.2	0.3	0.6	NA	NA
Pretax Inc.	39.5	35.8	25.8	51.4	41.7	26.9	19.6	20.3	NA	NA
Eff. Tax Rate	36%	36%	36%	35%	34%	33%	33%	34%	NA	NA
Net Inc.	25.4	23.0	16.6	33.4	27.5	18.0	13.2	13.4	NA	NA

Balance Sheet & Other Fin. Data (Million $)

	1998	1997	1996	1995	1994	1993	1992	1991	1990	1989
Cash	24.8	50.7	44.0	65.2	59.9	54.8	59.6	42.9	NA	NA
Curr. Assets	190	178	178	164	140	NA	NA	NA	NA	NA
Total Assets	230	218	208	184	155	122	104	91.0	NA	NA
Curr. Liab.	47.6	46.9	48.3	35.1	35.2	NA	NA	NA	NA	NA
LT Debt	Nil	Nil	Nil	Nil	Nil	0.6	1.3	2.1	NA	NA
Common Eqty.	178	167	156	147	118	94.0	79.0	66.0	NA	NA
Total Cap.	182	171	160	149	120	94.9	80.7	68.5	NA	NA
Cap. Exp.	13.7	21.2	17.2	10.7	6.7	5.8	NA	NA	NA	NA
Cash Flow	38.8	34.4	24.3	38.8	32.1	21.6	NA	NA	NA	NA
Curr. Ratio	4.0	3.8	3.7	4.7	4.0	NA	NA	NA	NA	NA
% LT Debt of Cap.	Nil	Nil	Nil	Nil	Nil	0.6	1.7	3.0	NA	NA
% Net Inc.of Revs.	5.0	4.9	4.1	9.1	10.3	0.7	8.9	8.9	NA	NA
% Ret. on Assets	11.4	10.8	8.5	19.7	19.9	15.9	13.7	18.3	NA	NA
% Ret. on Equity	14.8	14.2	10.9	25.2	25.9	20.7	18.4	26.5	NA	NA

Data as orig. reptd.; bef. results of disc. opers. and/or spec. items. Per share data adj. for stk. divs. as of ex-div. date. Bold denotes diluted EPS (FASB 128). E-Estimated. NA-Not Available. NM-Not Meaningful. NR-Not Ranked.

Office—601 Brooks Ave. South, Thief River Falls, MN 56701. **Tel**—(218) 681-8558. **Website**—http://www.arctic-cat.com **Chrmn**—W. G. Ness. **Pres & CEO**—C. A. Twomey. **CFO & Secy**—T. C. Delmore. **Dirs**—R. J. Dondelinger, W. I. Hagen, T. Natori, W. G. Ness, G. A. Ostrander, K.J. Roering, L. T. Swenson, C. A. Twomey. **Transfer Agent & Registrar**—Norwest Bank Minnesota, South St. Paul. **Incorporated**—in Minnesota in 1982. **Empl**— 1,808. **S&P Analyst**: S.A.H.

Arkansas Best

3147M

NASDAQ Symbol **ABFS**

In S&P SmallCap 600

03-OCT-98 **Industry:** Truckers

Summary: ABFS is engaged mainly in motor carrier and freight forwarding operations, as well as truck tire retreading and sales.

Quantitative Evaluations		
Outlook (1 Lowest—5 Highest) • **4**	Recent Price • 5¼ 52 Wk Range • 12½-4⅜	Yield • Nil 12-Mo. P/E • 6.0

Earnings vs. Previous Year
▲=Up ▼=Down ▶=No Change

Fair Value
• **8¼**

Risk
• **High**

Earn./Div. Rank
• **NR**

Technical Eval.
• **Bullish** since 6/98

Rel. Strength Rank
(1 Lowest—99 Highest)
• **15**

Insider Activity
• **NA**

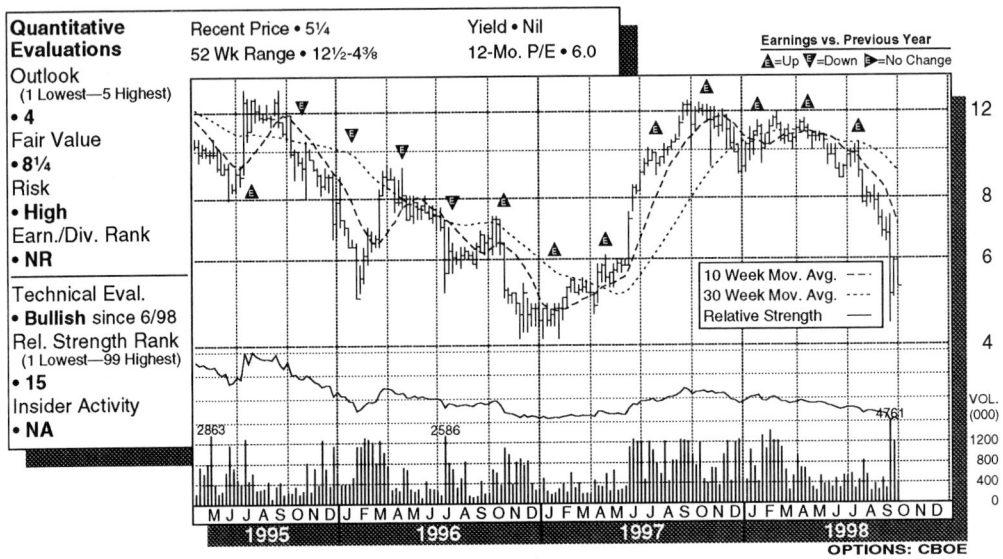

10 Week Mov. Avg. ----
30 Week Mov. Avg. ·····
Relative Strength —

OPTIONS: CBOE

Business Profile - 22-JUN-98

The company incurred losses in 1995 and 1996, and omitted its dividend in May 1996. In an effort to return to profitability, ABFS cut costs, improved efficiency, sold non-essential assets, and reduced debt. In July 1997, the Cardinal Freight Carriers unit was sold for $38 million, with proceeds used to reduce bank debt; an after tax gain of $2.5 million on the transaction was recorded in the 1997 third quarter. In August 1997, the company sold its Complete Logistics Co. subsidiary for about $2.5 million; in November 1997, it exited the logistics business with the sale of Integrated Distribution (IDI). Profitability was restored in 1997.

Operational Review - 22-JUN-98

Operating revenues in the three months ended March 31, 1998, fell 1.7%, year to year, reflecting the July 1997 sale of the truckload motor carrier operations. Operating expenses declined more rapidly than sales, and operating income increased. With a net gain on sales of property, versus a net loss, and lower interest expense, despite taxes at 42.0%, versus tax credits of $143,000, income surged to $3,618,000 ($0.13 a share), from $580,000 (a loss of $0.03, after preferred dividends). Results exclude a loss of $0.04 a share from discontinued operations in the 1997 period.

Stock Performance - 02-OCT-98

In the past 30 trading days, ABFS's shares have declined 33%, compared to a 7% fall in the S&P 500. Average trading volume for the past five days was 78,920 shares, compared with the 40-day moving average of 205,282 shares.

Key Stock Statistics

Dividend Rate/Share	Nil	Shareholders	800
Shs. outstg. (M)	19.6	Market cap. (B)	$0.103
Avg. daily vol. (M)	0.337	Inst. holdings	54%
Tang. Bk. Value/Share	1.52		
Beta	0.82		

Value of $10,000 invested 5 years ago: $ 3,733

Fiscal Year Ending Dec. 31

	1998	1997	1996	1995	1994	1993
Revenues (Million $)						
1Q	387.9	406.8	401.4	311.2	265.0	229.2
2Q	416.9	435.8	414.5	312.1	210.8	244.6
3Q	—	425.3	428.5	398.6	294.3	267.1
4Q	—	400.1	414.8	415.4	328.4	269.0
Yr.	—	1,644	1,659	1,437	1,098	1,010
Earnings Per Share ($)						
1Q	**0.13**	-0.07	-0.54	0.21	0.23	0.08
2Q	**0.31**	0.20	-0.51	0.03	-0.23	0.18
3Q	—	0.41	-0.49	-0.73	0.42	0.38
4Q	—	**0.19**	-0.56	-1.41	0.32	0.24
Yr.	—	**0.84**	-2.10	-1.90	0.74	0.89

Next earnings report expected: mid October

Dividend Data

The quarterly cash dividend was omitted in May 1996.

 A Division of The **McGraw·Hill** *Companies*

Business Summary - 22-JUN-98

From a humble beginning as Arkansas Motor Freight with 10 employees over 60 years ago, Arkansas Best Corp. (ABFS) has grown into a multi-industry holding company, with interests in international freight transportation and forwarding, truck tire retreading and sales, warehousing, and computer information services. Acquisitions played an important role in revenue growth in recent years. After two years of losses, the company returned to profitability in 1997.

The company operates in three business segments: motor carrier, which includes less-than-truckload (LTL) operations; intermodal operations; and tire operations.

The largest subsidiary, ABF Freight System, Inc. (ABF), is the fourth largest U.S. LTL motor carrier; ABF accounted for 69% of ABFS's 1997 revenue, and 91% of LTL revenue. ABF provides direct service to over 98.5% of the cities in the U.S. having a population of 25,000 or more. It concentrates on long-haul transportation of general commodities freight, involving mainly LTL shipments. General commodities include food, textiles, apparel, furniture, appliances, chemicals, rubber, plastics, metal and other. Operations were expanded significantly through the August 1995 acquisition of WorldWay

Corp. for about $76 million; WorldWay's principal subsidiaries included Carolina Freight Carriers Inc. and Red Arrow Freight Lines, Inc., which were merged into ABF in September 1995.

The G.I. Trucking subsidiary (6% of total revenues in 1997; 8% of LTL operations revenues) provides one to three-day regional transportation services and coverage throughout 15 western states, including Alaska and Hawaii.

The Clipper Group subsidiary conducts international freight services, utilizing a variety of transportation modes including over-the-road, rail, ocean and air.

The Treadco subsidiary (46% owned) is the largest independent U.S. tire retreader for the trucking industry and the fourth largest commercial truck tire dealer. Retreading tires is significantly less expensive for trucking companies than buying new tires. Revenues in this segment accounted for 10% of total consolidated revenues in 1997.

In July 1997, the Cardinal Freight Carriers unit was sold for $38 million.

In August 1997, the Complete Logistics Co. subsidiary was sold to a private company, for about $2.5 million. The sale resulted in a pretax loss of about $1.3 million.

Per Share Data ($)

(Year Ended Dec. 31)	1997	1996	1995	1994	1993	1992	1991	1990	1989	1988
Tangible Bk. Val.	0.93	NM	1.68	3.31	5.00	NA	NA	NA	NA	NA
Cash Flow	3.52	1.25	0.97	2.60	2.73	2.95	2.66	NA	NA	NA
Earnings	0.84	-2.10	-1.90	0.74	0.89	0.99	0.61	NA	NA	NA
Dividends	Nil	0.01	0.04	0.04	0.04	0.02	Nil	Nil	Nil	Nil
Payout Ratio	Nil	NM	NM	5%	4%	2%	Nil	Nil	Nil	Nil
Prices - High	12⅝	9⅜	13⅜	15¾	17	17⅛	NA	NA	NA	NA
- Low	4⅛	4⅛	6⅝	10⅛	8⅛	8⅞	NA	NA	NA	NA
P/E Ratio - High	15	NM	NM	21	19	17	NA	NA	NA	NA
- Low	5	NM	NM	14	9	9	NA	NA	NA	NA

Income Statement Analysis (Million $)

	1997	1996	1995	1994	1993	1992	1991	1990	1989	1988
Revs.	1,644	1,659	1,437	1,098	1,010	960	884	NA	NA	NA
Oper. Inc.	112	38.7	28.3	79.7	82.7	94.8	85.9	NA	NA	NA
Depr.	48.9	61.0	51.8	31.6	31.3	37.5	42.8	NA	NA	NA
Int. Exp.	23.9	31.9	17.3	7.6	7.2	17.3	34.4	NA	NA	NA
Pretax Inc.	40.4	-58.5	-47.0	36.6	40.3	35.6	15.5	NA	NA	NA
Eff. Tax Rate	48%	NM	NM	49%	48%	47%	50%	NA	NA	NA
Net Inc.	20.9	-36.6	-32.8	18.7	21.0	18.8	7.8	NA	NA	NA

Balance Sheet & Other Fin. Data (Million $)

	1997	1996	1995	1994	1993	1992	1991	1990	1989	1988
Cash	7.2	1.8	16.9	3.5	7.0	NA	NA	NA	NA	NA
Curr. Assets	237	259	322	186	151	NA	NA	NA	NA	NA
Total Assets	698	843	986	569	448	NA	NA	NA	NA	NA
Curr. Liab.	268	301	303	223	140	NA	NA	NA	NA	NA
LT Debt	203	327	399	59.3	43.7	NA	NA	NA	NA	NA
Common Eqty.	149	137	178	217	202	NA	NA	NA	NA	NA
Total Cap.	408	498	564	340	304	NA	NA	NA	NA	NA
Cap. Exp.	11.6	27.7	49.7	47.3	13.7	21.1	19.4	NA	NA	NA
Cash Flow	69.8	24.4	19.0	50.3	52.3	56.3	50.6	NA	NA	NA
Curr. Ratio	0.9	0.9	1.1	0.8	1.1	NA	NA	NA	NA	NA
% LT Debt of Cap.	49.6	65.6	70.8	17.5	14.4	NA	NA	NA	NA	NA
% Net Inc.of Revs.	12.7	NM	NM	1.7	2.1	2.0	0.9	NA	NA	NA
% Ret. on Assets	2.7	NM	NM	3.7	4.8	NA	NA	NA	NA	NA
% Ret. on Equity	14.6	NM	NM	8.9	12.5	NA	NA	NA	NA	NA

Data as orig. reptd.; bef. results of disc. opers. and/or spec. items. Per share data adj. for stk. divs. as of ex-div. date. Bold denotes diluted EPS (FASB 128). E-Estimated. NA-Not Available. NM-Not Meaningful. NR-Not Ranked.

Office—3801 Old Greenwood Rd., Fort Smith, AR 72903. **Tel**—(501) 785-6000. **Website**—http://www.arkbest.com/ **Chrmn**—W. A. Marquard. **Pres & CEO**—R. A. Young III. **VP-CFO & Treas**—D. E. Loeffler. **Investor Contact**—David Humphrey (501) 785-6200. **Dirs**—F. Edelstein, A. J. Fritz, W. A. Marquard, J. H. Morris, R. A. Young III, A. J. Zakon. **Transfer Agent & Registrar**—Harris Trust & Savings Bank, Chicago. **Incorporated**—in Delaware in 1988. **Empl**— 14,757. **S&P Analyst**: B.G.

03-OCT-98

Industry:
Textiles (Apparel)

Summary: This company designs and manufactures Ashworth golf apparel and footwear and Ashworth Harry Logan men's sportswear.

Quantitative Evaluations	
Outlook (1 Lowest—5 Highest) • **5**	
Fair Value • **13⅜**	
Risk • **Average**	
Earn./Div. Rank • **B**	
Technical Eval. • **Bearish** since 10/96	
Rel. Strength Rank (1 Lowest—99 Highest) • **33**	
Insider Activity • **Neutral**	

Recent Price • 6½
52 Wk Range • 18⅜-5⅜

Yield • Nil
12-Mo. P/E • 14.3

Earnings vs. Previous Year
▲=Up ▼=Down ▶=No Change

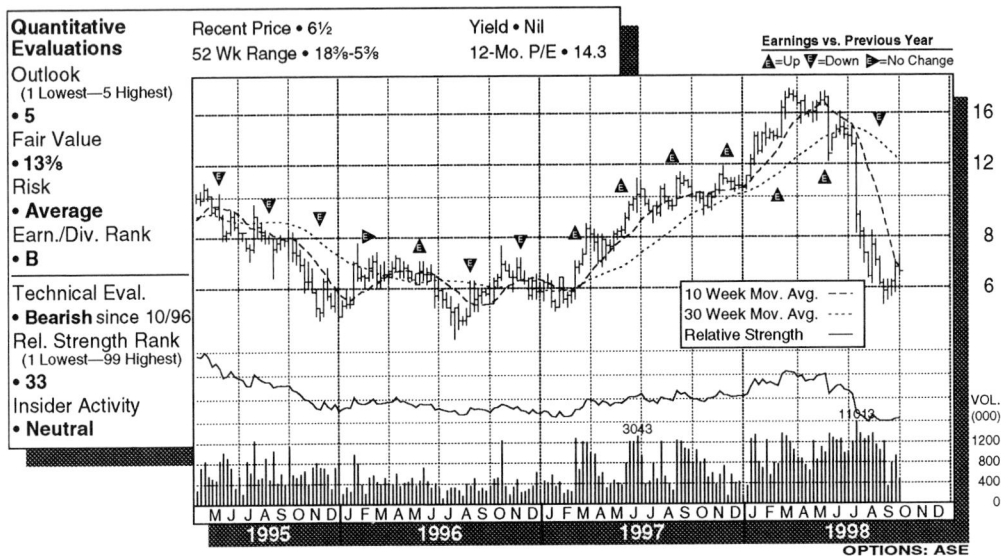

10 Week Mov. Avg. -- --
30 Week Mov. Avg. ·······
Relative Strength —

OPTIONS: ASE

Business Profile - 30-SEP-98

This manufacturer and marketer of golf related apparel attributed its improved overall operating performance in the first nine months of FY 98 (Oct.) to strong domestic and European sales that reflect the strong demand for the Ashworth brand. During the third quarter, ASHW added 142 new in-store Golfman locations, increasing the total to 475. By the end of FY 98, ASHW expected to have a total of approximately 525 in-store shops. In May 1998, ASHW said it had formed Ashworth Canada, a new subsidiary, to sell directly into the Canadian market, improve gross margins and provide more competitive pricing in Canada.

Operational Review - 30-SEP-98

Sales in the nine months ended July 31, 1998, increased 22%, year to year, reflecting a 28% gain in domestic sales (to $72.1 million), which outweighed a 2.1% decline in foreign sales, due to a 78% decline to sales to Asia. European sales rose 31%. Gross margins widened significantly on international sourcing, reduced production related expenses and increased domestic business. Income from operations surged 42%. Profitability also benefited from a decline in net interest expense, an increase in interest income and lower other expense. After taxes at 38.7% in both periods, net income was up 48%, to $7,161,000 ($0.48 a share, diluted and on 22% more shares), from $4,823,000 ($0.39).

Stock Performance - 02-OCT-98

In the past 30 trading days, ASHW's shares have declined 6%, compared to a 7% fall in the S&P 500. Average trading volume for the past five days was 93,940 shares, compared with the 40-day moving average of 260,697 shares.

Key Stock Statistics

Dividend Rate/Share	Nil	Shareholders	9,000
Shs. outstg. (M)	14.1	Market cap. (B)	$0.092
Avg. daily vol. (M)	0.133	Inst. holdings	82%
Tang. Bk. Value/Share	5.02		
Beta	1.36		

Value of $10,000 invested 5 years ago: $ 8,749

Fiscal Year Ending Oct. 31

	1998	1997	1996	1995	1994	1993
Revenues (Million $)						
1Q	24.03	19.84	17.07	14.59	11.04	7.40
2Q	38.06	30.62	26.36	26.44	21.27	16.69
3Q	25.60	21.70	17.88	20.38	16.96	12.81
4Q	—	16.99	14.10	13.11	11.57	8.93
Yr.	—	89.15	75.41	74.52	60.84	45.82
Earnings Per Share ($)						
1Q	**0.13**	0.10	0.07	0.07	0.06	0.04
2Q	**0.30**	0.23	0.21	0.15	0.20	0.15
3Q	**0.05**	0.06	0.02	0.07	0.13	0.10
4Q	—	Nil	-0.18	-0.17	0.01	0.05
Yr.	—	0.37	0.12	0.12	0.40	0.34

Next earnings report expected: mid December

Dividend Data

No cash dividends have been paid.

A Division of The **McGraw-Hill** Companies

Business Summary - 30-SEP-98

Over the past decade, a new look has emerged on the golf course, with classically styled, natural fiber golfwear with a loose, relaxed fit. Ashworth Inc. has been credited with developing this new industry standard. The company designs and markets golfwear under the Ashworth brand name. It sells its apparel to the younger active male consumer in the middle/upper middle income range at prices in the middle to upper middle price range for golf apparel.

Ashworth designs eight product lines each year, with each line consisting of 30 to 40 styles. Through the fall of 1996, the company designed two labels, Ashworth and Ashworth Harry Logan. Following the holiday season of 1996, product labels carry only the Ashworth brand name. The product line includes knit and woven shirts, pullovers, sweaters, vests, pants, shorts, hats, shoes and accessories.

In 1996, Ashworth teed off its new Weather Systems collection, which are produced for a variety of weather conditions, including cold and rainy, and hot and humid. The company has also placed stronger emphasis on its casual and golf training shoes rather than spiked golf shoes. It is also considering licensing its shoe production and sales operations.

ASHW also introduced a new Basics line consisting of shirts, pants and shorts during 1996. This line accounted for approximately 25% of revenues in 1997. The company also designed a line of apparel for the younger golfer for the 1997 fall season. Ashworth is the national apparel sponsor of American Junior Golf Association, and provides team uniforms to many college golf teams.

The company distributes and sells its products through four channels of distribution. Golf pro shops located at golf courses make up Ashworth's core business. The company is the leading golf apparel company in golf pro shops in the U.S., with a 10% market share and distribution in all 50 states. ASHW also sells its products to selected department and specialty stores; as of March 1998, the company was in 245 upscale department stores, an increase of 30% from the prior year. In addition, products are sold in Europe through a wholly owned subsidiary, and in Asia through distributors. The company has recently launched men's sportswear and accessories.

At the end of the third quarter of FY 98, ASHW had 475 locations for its in-store Golfman shops, and planned to open an additional 50 shops in the fourth quarter of FY 98, for a total of approximately 525 by the end of FY 98.

Per Share Data ($)

(Year Ended Oct. 31)	1997	1996	1995	1994	1993	1992	1991	1990	1989	1988
Tangible Bk. Val.	3.95	3.20	3.06	2.84	2.31	1.87	0.73	0.50	0.03	0.04
Cash Flow	0.53	0.31	0.32	0.55	0.42	0.24	0.16	0.05	0.01	-0.11
Earnings	0.37	0.12	0.12	0.40	0.34	0.19	0.13	0.04	-0.01	-0.11
Dividends	Nil	Nil	Nil	Nil	Nil	Nil	Nil	Nil	Nil	Nil
Payout Ratio	Nil	Nil	Nil	Nil	Nil	Nil	Nil	Nil	Nil	Nil
Prices - High	11$7/8$	7$3/4$	10$7/8$	13$1/4$	12	9	7$1/4$	4$1/8$	NA	NA
- Low	5$1/4$	4$1/2$	5	7$3/8$	6$1/4$	4$3/8$	2$3/16$	1	NA	NA
P/E Ratio - High	32	65	91	33	35	47	56	NM	NA	NA
- Low	14	37	42	18	18	23	17	NM	NA	NA

Income Statement Analysis (Million $)

	1997	1996	1995	1994	1993	1992	1991	1990	1989	1988
Revs.	89.1	75.4	74.5	60.8	45.8	28.6	17.0	7.5	2.1	0.4
Oper. Inc.	11.0	5.6	6.0	10.2	7.7	4.1	2.6	0.7	0.1	-0.2
Depr.	2.1	2.3	2.5	1.9	1.1	0.6	0.3	0.1	0.1	0.0
Int. Exp.	0.6	1.1	1.1	0.6	0.3	0.3	0.2	0.1	0.1	0.0
Pretax Inc.	7.9	2.4	2.4	8.1	6.5	3.4	2.1	0.5	0.0	-0.3
Eff. Tax Rate	39%	41%	42%	40%	40%	40%	42%	45%	NM	NM
Net Inc.	4.8	1.4	1.4	4.9	4.0	2.0	1.2	0.3	0.0	-0.3

Balance Sheet & Other Fin. Data (Million $)

	1997	1996	1995	1994	1993	1992	1991	1990	1989	1988
Cash	3.8	1.9	1.6	5.3	7.7	5.8	0.6	1.4	0.0	0.0
Curr. Assets	55.0	41.7	45.2	34.6	26.5	21.2	8.4	4.9	1.3	0.3
Total Assets	68.8	54.9	58.1	47.3	33.5	25.7	10.1	5.4	1.6	0.5
Curr. Liab.	10.1	10.2	16.0	8.6	4.6	3.8	3.0	1.4	0.8	0.3
LT Debt	4.3	5.3	5.2	5.8	2.9	1.7	0.7	0.3	0.6	0.1
Common Eqty.	53.0	38.9	36.4	32.9	26.1	20.2	6.4	3.8	0.1	0.1
Total Cap.	58.0	44.8	42.1	38.7	28.9	21.9	7.2	4.1	0.7	0.2
Cap. Exp.	2.0	2.5	2.1	6.8	2.7	1.6	0.4	0.2	0.1	0.1
Cash Flow	7.0	3.7	3.9	6.7	5.0	2.6	1.5	0.4	0.0	-0.3
Curr. Ratio	5.4	4.1	2.8	4.0	5.8	5.6	2.8	3.6	1.5	1.2
% LT Debt of Cap.	7.5	11.9	12.4	14.9	10.0	7.8	10.4	6.8	86.2	35.0
% Net Inc.of Revs.	5.4	1.9	1.9	8.0	8.6	7.1	7.3	3.4	NM	NM
% Ret. on Assets	7.8	2.5	2.6	11.9	13.1	10.6	15.1	5.9	NM	NM
% Ret. on Equity	10.5	3.7	4.0	16.3	16.7	14.4	22.9	12.8	NM	NM

Data as orig. reptd.; bef. results of disc. opers. and/or spec. items. Per share data adj. for stk. divs. as of ex-div. date. Bold denotes diluted EPS (FASB 128). E-Estimated. NA-Not Available. NM-Not Meaningful. NR-Not Ranked.

Office—2791 Loker Avenue West, Carlsbad, CA 92008. **Tel**—(720) 438-6610. **Chrmn**—G. W. Montiel. **Pres & CEO**—R. L. Herrel. **VP-Fin, CFO & Treas**—A. J. Newman. **Secy**—Monica M. McKenzie. **Dirs**—S. Bartolin, Jr., A. P. Gambucci, J. M. Hanson, R. L. Herrel Sr., G. W. Montiel, J. Nantz. **Transfer Agent & Registrar**—American Securities Transfer, Inc., Denver. **Incorporated**—in Delaware in 1987. **Empl**— 420. **S&P Analyst:** Kathleen J. Fraser

Aspect Telecommunications   3167

Nasdaq Symbol **ASPT**

In S&P SmallCap 600

03-OCT-98

Industry:
Communications
Equipment

Summary: This company is a global provider of comprehensive business solutions for mission-critical call centers that exist to generate revenue, service customers, and handle inquiries.

S&P Opinion: Accumulate (★★★★)	Recent Price • 22⅝ Yield • Nil
	52 Wk Range • 37⅛-18¼ 12-Mo. P/E • NM

Earnings vs. Previous Year
▲=Up ▼=Down ▶=No Change

Quantitative Evaluations

Outlook
(1 Lowest—5 Highest)
• **5**

Fair Value
• **44¼**

Risk
• **High**

Earn./Div. Rank
• **B**

Technical Eval.
• **Bearish** since 8/98

Rel. Strength Rank
(1 Lowest—99 Highest)
• **33**

Insider Activity
• **Unfavorable**

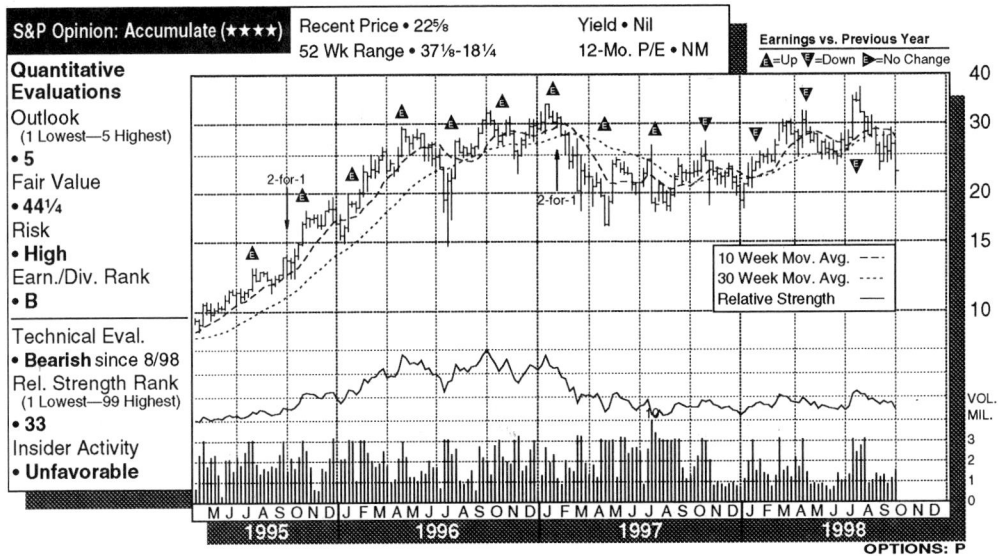

10 Week Mov. Avg. ---
30 Week Mov. Avg. ····
Relative Strength —

MJJASOND|JFMAMJJASOND|JFMAMJJASOND|JFMAMJJASOND|JFMAMJJASOND
1995 | 1996 | 1997 | 1998

OPTIONS: P

Overview - 23-JUL-98

We expect revenues to grow 34% in 1998. Aspect's flagship CallCenter system has gained widespread acceptance, as companies realize the need for mission-critical call center products to give them a competitive edge. Aspect added 15 new customers to its impressive list of ACD clients, including Dell Computer and TCI. Results should also benefit from the steady release of enhancement add-ons for CallCenter, including World Wide Web integration for Agility, the company's interactive voice response system. The acquisitions of Envoy Holdings and Prospect Software provide entry into the promising computer-telephony integration market. In April 1998, ASPT acquired privately held Voicetek Corp., a provider of software platforms and application solutions for interactive voice response, for approximately $72 million in cash.

Valuation - 23-JUL-98

The shares have advanced steadily since we raised our opinion to accumulate, from hold, in October 1997, due to the settlement of a product litigation suit with Lucent Technologies and to validation of the company's stated 30% plus long-term growth rate. Revenues in the 1998 second quarter were up 11% sequentially, and gross margins were stable. Steady average selling prices for the company's CallCenter system give positive visibility for gross margins in coming periods. Great potential for growth in international markets exists, as evidenced by strong sales of Automated Call Distributors in Europe. Given the company's estimated 35% long-term growth rate, ASPT shares are attractive at a recent level of 20X our $1.48 1999 EPS estimate. Second quarter 1998 EPS included a charge of $1.34 a share, related to acquisitions.

Key Stock Statistics

S&P EPS Est. 1998	1.08	Tang. Bk. Value/Share	3.73
P/E on S&P Est. 1998	20.9	Beta	0.88
S&P EPS Est. 1999	1.48	Shareholders	700
Dividend Rate/Share	Nil	Market cap. (B)	$ 1.1
Shs. outstg. (M)	50.8	Inst. holdings	74%
Avg. daily vol. (M)	0.253		

Value of $10,000 invested 5 years ago: $ 61,880

Fiscal Year Ending Dec. 31

	1998	1997	1996	1995	1994	1993
Revenues (Million $)						
1Q	113.5	91.62	67.30	42.73	32.89	21.80
2Q	126.1	93.54	72.91	46.23	35.12	23.15
3Q	—	99.2	80.22	49.30	38.17	27.94
4Q	—	106.3	88.55	60.72	41.06	33.55
Yr.	—	390.6	308.7	199.0	147.2	106.5
Earnings Per Share ($)						
1Q	**-1.10**	0.21	0.18	0.12	0.09	0.05
2Q	**-1.10**	0.24	0.20	0.14	0.10	0.05
3Q	—	0.13	0.20	0.14	0.10	0.08
4Q	—	**0.08**	0.20	0.15	0.11	0.10
Yr.	—	**0.67**	**0.75**	0.55	0.41	0.27

Next earnings report expected: mid October

Dividend Data

No cash dividends have been paid.

A Division of The McGraw-Hill Companies

Business Summary - 23-JUL-98

When you dial the customer service number of a company, such as a bank or a utility, you are actually contacting something known as a call center. A call center allows companies to effectively handle large volumes of calls from existing and potential customers. Aspect Telecommunications Corp. is a global provider of comprehensive business solutions for call centers. The company offers solutions for call transaction processing, call center automation, interactive voice response and call center networking, as well as tools and applications for collecting and sharing management information. It also provides services necessary to call center environments, including business applications consulting, training and call center integration services. Aspect's customers operate in a variety of industries, including financial services, insurance, technology, utilities, hotels and travel, and government.

Revenues in recent years were derived as follows:

	1997	1996
Product sales	70%	75%
Customer support	30%	25%

The company's primary product, the Aspect CallCenter System, is an automatic call distributor (ACD) designed specifically for call transaction processing applications. The CallCenter system, which integrates call processing, voice processing and data processing technologies, is designed to provide benefits in four key areas: intelligent call management, staff productivity, management information and system availability. The system offers several features, including the ability to dynamically change the routing of calls, the summary and detailed views of calling volumes, call handling efficiencies, trends, and other information about each business application, and the ability to control redundancy, which reduces the risk of downtime due to component failure. In addition, Aspect's optional Application Bridge allows the CallCenter to communicate directly with a company's data processing systems.

Agility allows companies to expand the ways in which they interact with customers through call centers. Agility automates call center transactions and processes by complementing call centers with software agent technology.

In May 1998, Aspect announced the acquisition of privately held Voicetek Corp., a provider of software platforms and application solutions for interactive voice response (IVR) and network-deployed enhanced services solutions. Voicetek's products and partnerships will complement and enhance Aspect's set of integrated call center solutions. The purchase price consisted of approximately $72 million in cash for all Voicetek common and preferred shares outstanding; in addition, all outstanding Voicetek options were converted into approximately 450,000 Aspect options, and Aspect assumed certain operating assets and liabilities of Voicetek.

Per Share Data ($)

(Year Ended Dec. 31)	1997	1996	1995	1994	1993	1992	1991	1990	1989	1988
Tangible Bk. Val.	4.50	3.90	1.94	1.99	1.58	1.26	1.13	1.17	-1.27	0.17
Cash Flow	1.00	1.02	0.75	0.58	0.38	0.19	0.06	0.17	0.08	-0.10
Earnings	0.67	0.79	0.55	0.41	0.27	0.10	-0.04	0.09	0.03	-0.15
Dividends	Nil	Nil	Nil	Nil	Nil	Nil	Nil	Nil	Nil	Nil
Payout Ratio	Nil	Nil	Nil	Nil	Nil	Nil	NM	Nil	Nil	Nil
Prices - High	33⅝	32¾	19⅝	11½	10⅞	3¾	2¾	6	NA	NA
- Low	16½	14⅝	7¾	6	3½	1¾	1⁷⁄₁₆	1½	NA	NA
P/E Ratio - High	50	41	36	28	40	38	NM	64	NA	NA
- Low	25	19	14	15	13	17	NM	16	NA	NA

Income Statement Analysis (Million $)

	1997	1996	1995	1994	1993	1992	1991	1990	1989	1988
Revs.	391	309	199	147	106	71.0	44.2	47.9	30.6	11.3
Oper. Inc.	69.8	74.0	44.3	35.2	22.6	8.8	0.5	6.8	3.3	-2.9
Depr.	17.2	16.3	8.7	7.1	4.5	3.5	3.9	2.8	1.4	1.3
Int. Exp.	0.3	2.8	3.2	3.2	0.9	0.2	0.3	0.4	0.3	0.3
Pretax Inc.	60.3	59.8	38.1	28.3	18.8	6.6	-1.7	5.7	2.3	-4.1
Eff. Tax Rate	42%	37%	37%	38%	39%	38%	Nil	39%	55%	Nil
Net Inc.	35.2	37.6	24.0	17.6	11.5	4.1	-1.7	3.5	1.0	-4.1

Balance Sheet & Other Fin. Data (Million $)

	1997	1996	1995	1994	1993	1992	1991	1990	1989	1988
Cash	106	116	93.6	103	93.1	36.2	32.8	32.3	8.7	3.1
Curr. Assets	266	199	153	143	123	55.5	48.2	44.9	15.7	7.3
Total Assets	370	283	216	166	138	64.6	57.0	54.5	20.8	9.8
Curr. Liab.	96.0	59.1	44.0	30.2	18.9	14.2	10.6	6.1	6.8	4.4
LT Debt	6.5	4.5	59.5	55.0	55.0	0.1	0.7	1.5	1.2	0.5
Common Eqty.	268	219	112	80.8	64.3	50.2	45.6	46.7	12.6	4.7
Total Cap.	274	224	172	136	119	50.2	46.3	48.2	13.8	5.2
Cap. Exp.	24.9	33.2	16.6	13.1	8.8	4.5	3.0	5.6	2.9	1.1
Cash Flow	52.4	53.9	32.7	24.6	16.0	7.6	2.2	6.3	2.5	-2.8
Curr. Ratio	2.8	3.4	3.5	4.7	6.5	3.9	4.6	7.3	2.3	1.7
% LT Debt of Cap.	2.4	2.0	34.6	40.5	46.1	0.1	1.5	3.0	8.8	10.0
% Net Inc.of Revs.	9.0	12.2	12.1	11.9	10.8	5.8	NM	7.2	3.3	NM
% Ret. on Assets	10.8	15.1	12.6	11.5	11.2	6.8	NM	4.3	6.6	NM
% Ret. on Equity	14.4	22.7	24.8	24.2	19.9	8.6	NM	NM	11.8	NM

Data as orig. reptd.; bef. results of disc. opers. and/or spec. items. Per share data adj. for stk. divs. as of ex-div. date. Bold denotes diluted EPS (FASB 128). E-Estimated. NA-Not Available. NM-Not Meaningful. NR-Not Ranked.

Office—1730 Fox Dr., San Jose, CA 95131-2312. **Tel**—(408) 325-2200. **Website**—http://www.aspect.com **Chrmn & CEO**—J. R. Carreker. **Pres & COO**—D. L. Haar. **VP-Fin & CFO**—E. J. Keller. **Secy**—C. W. Johnson. **Dirs**—J. R. Carreker, D. J. Engel, N. A. Fogelsong, J. L. Patterson, J. W. Peth.**Transfer Agent & Registrar**—First National Bank of Boston. **Incorporated**—in California in 1985. **Empl**— 1,610. **S&P Analyst:** Aydin Tuncer

Astec Industries   3171C
NASDAQ Symbol ASTE
In S&P SmallCap 600

03-OCT-98

Industry:
Manufacturing (Specialized)

Summary: This company designs, engineers, manufactures and markets equipment and components used in the production and application of hot-mix asphalt and other construction aggregates.

Quantitative Evaluations	
Outlook (1 Lowest—5 Highest) • **1⁻**	
Fair Value • **36⅜**	
Risk • **Low**	
Earn./Div. Rank • **B-**	
Technical Eval. • **Bullish** since 3/97	
Rel. Strength Rank (1 Lowest—99 Highest) • **98**	
Insider Activity • **Neutral**	

Recent Price • 43¼
52 Wk Range • 44½-15⅛

Yield • Nil
12-Mo. P/E • 22.3

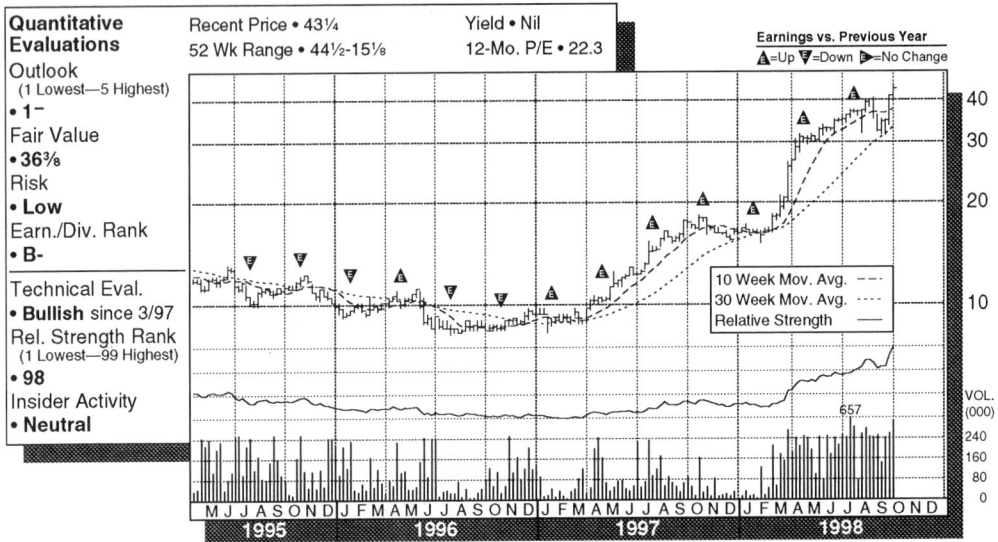

Earnings vs. Previous Year
▲=Up ▼=Down ►=No Change

10 Week Mov. Avg. – – –
30 Week Mov. Avg. ·······
Relative Strength ———

Business Profile - 29-SEP-98

This company has undertaken a major expansion and modernization of its facilities, which should greatly enhance operating efficiencies. In December 1997, ASTE acquired the construction equipment division of Portec, Inc. of South Dakota, now known as the Kolberg-Pioneer subsidiary. The acquisition included several lines of aggregate processing equipment, and was expected to add about $35 million to $40 million to 1998 sales. In June 1995, Astec sold Germany-based Wibau-Astec, and in February 1996, it announced that it would discontinue its unprofitable Astec-Europa manufacturing operations in Germany. The company will continue European marketing, either on a direct basis or through a licensee to manufacture its product line. International sales accounted for 22% of net sales in 1997. Chairman and president J. Don Brock owns about 14% of the shares.

Operational Review - 29-SEP-98

Revenues in the first half of 1998 rose 44%, year to year, reflecting the acquisition of Kolberg-Pioneer and strong demand for asphalt mixing plants and aggregate crushing equipment. Margins widened, reflecting well controlled SG&A expenses; pretax income climbed 59%. After taxes at 39.8% in both periods, net income was also up 59%, to $12,948,000 ($1.34 a share, on 2.8% fewer shares), from $8,150,000 ($0.82).

Stock Performance - 02-OCT-98

In the past 30 trading days, ASTE's shares have increased 8%, compared to a 7% fall in the S&P 500. Average trading volume for the past five days was 123,840 shares, compared with the 40-day moving average of 74,800 shares.

Key Stock Statistics

Dividend Rate/Share	Nil	Shareholders	700
Shs. outstg. (M)	9.4	Market cap. (B)	$0.407
Avg. daily vol. (M)	0.076	Inst. holdings	41%
Tang. Bk. Value/Share	12.65		
Beta	0.44		

Value of $10,000 invested 5 years ago: $ 42,716

Fiscal Year Ending Dec. 31

	1998	1997	1996	1995	1994	1993
Revenues (Million $)						
1Q	88.16	62.98	59.57	57.54	46.23	43.40
2Q	108.1	73.16	63.21	70.37	62.69	52.44
3Q	—	65.04	47.18	65.02	49.02	38.84
4Q	—	64.19	51.45	49.67	55.87	38.13
Yr.	—	265.4	221.4	242.6	213.8	172.8
Earnings Per Share ($)						
1Q	0.58	0.35	0.28	0.25	0.29	0.21
2Q	0.76	0.48	0.22	0.47	0.53	0.45
3Q	—	0.30	0.10	0.27	0.32	0.22
4Q	—	0.30	-0.17	-0.54	1.23	0.22
Yr.	—	1.42	0.43	0.45	2.38	1.07

Next earnings report expected: mid October

Dividend Data

No cash dividends have been paid. A two-for-one stock split was effected in 1993. A shareholder rights plan was adopted in 1995.

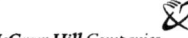

A Division of The *McGraw-Hill* Companies

Business Summary - 29-SEP-98

It's a long way from the stone quarry to the superhighway, but Astec Industries, Inc. (ASTE) makes the journey every day with a range of products used in all phases of road construction: rock crushers, hot-mix asphalt plants, milling machines that remove old asphalt, asphalt pavers that apply fresh asphalt to the road surface. ASTE's equipment is used in other construction activities as well, and the company also serves the mining industry and environmental markets.

The company believes that it is an industry leader in technological innovation. It brought portability to hot-mix asphalt plants in 1979, and, in 1996, it developed an improved version of its portable "Six Pack" plant (named for its six components), which is more portable and self-erecting than earlier models. The enhanced version is especially useful in less populated areas where plants must be moved from job to job. The company also produces the "Shuttle Buggy," a mobile, self-propelled material transfer vehicle that permits continuous paving for a smoother road surface.

In 1996, ASTE acquired Production Engineered Products, Inc. (PEP), which makes screening units for sand and gravel and asphalt operations. The company regarded PEP as good fit with its Telsmith subsidiary, a producer of portable crushing plants, and expected the high-production capacity of the PEP screens to enhance sales of Telsmith's product line. In December 1997, ASTE acquired the Construction Equipment division of Portec, Inc., now known as the Kolberg-Pioneer subsidiary, whose jaw crushers and other products would complement the lines of aggregate processing equipment ASTE already offers through Telsmith and PEP.

ASTE produces the heating and storage equipment used in its asphalt mixing plants, and it makes industrial heaters for a wide range of applications. The company's mammoth trenching machines (weights up to 400,000 pounds) can cut trenches 30 ft. deep, and its "Roadminers" have applications in mining and aggregates processing in addition to road construction.

International sales in 1997 rebounded to 22% of total sales, from 17% in 1996. With the 1995 disposal of its German operations, ASTE no longer conducts manufacturing operations overseas. Its Astec-Europa subsidiary produced $10 million in pretax losses in 1995, including a large loss on the unit's abandonment. Net sales for the company as a whole in 1996 fell 9%, to $221 million, as domestic gains could not offset lower sales abroad. However, sales in 1997 were up 20%, reflecting increased demand for ASTE's products in recent periods.

Per Share Data ($)

(Year Ended Dec. 31)	1997	1996	1995	1994	1993	1992	1991	1990	1989	1988
Tangible Bk. Val.	10.45	9.38	9.10	8.20	6.34	3.54	2.70	2.19	4.41	5.15
Cash Flow	2.17	1.01	1.02	2.78	1.43	1.28	0.53	-1.29	-0.04	1.20
Earnings	1.42	0.43	0.45	2.38	1.07	0.82	0.08	-1.86	-0.55	0.80
Dividends	Nil	Nil	Nil	Nil	Nil	Nil	Nil	Nil	Nil	Nil
Payout Ratio	Nil	Nil	Nil	Nil	Nil	Nil	Nil	Nil	Nil	Nil
Prices - High	18³⁄₈	11¹⁄₈	14¹⁄₄	20¹⁄₈	15³⁄₄	10¹⁄₄	3⁵⁄₈	5¹⁄₄	8³⁄₄	9⁵⁄₈
- Low	8¹⁄₄	8¹⁄₈	9³⁄₄	11⁵⁄₈	8¹⁄₂	2³⁄₄	1⁹⁄₁₆	¹⁵⁄₁₆	4¹⁄₈	7¹⁄₂
P/E Ratio - High	13	26	32	8	15	13	48	NM	NM	12
- Low	6	19	22	5	8	3	21	NM	NM	9

Income Statement Analysis (Million $)

	1997	1996	1995	1994	1993	1992	1991	1990	1989	1988
Revs.	265	221	243	214	173	149	135	135	189	177
Oper. Inc.	31.6	14.1	16.0	17.7	13.5	11.1	9.6	4.2	3.6	11.1
Depr.	6.9	5.8	5.7	3.9	3.1	3.5	3.3	4.1	3.8	3.0
Int. Exp.	2.4	1.7	2.1	0.7	1.8	3.2	4.6	6.3	6.8	4.2
Pretax Inc.	23.0	7.0	6.1	25.7	9.8	6.4	0.6	-13.1	-4.3	6.6
Eff. Tax Rate	40%	39%	26%	8.90%	4.40%	6.60%	10%	NM	NM	7.60%
Net Inc.	13.8	4.3	4.6	23.4	9.3	6.0	0.5	-13.5	-4.0	6.1

Balance Sheet & Other Fin. Data (Million $)

	1997	1996	1995	1994	1993	1992	1991	1990	1989	1988
Cash	2.9	3.4	3.1	10.5	15.8	13.8	13.7	8.6	0.8	1.0
Curr. Assets	119	104	96.6	102	76.5	67.8	68.0	90.3	96.2	91.1
Total Assets	192	168	154	156	103	88.0	91.0	112	128	121
Curr. Liab.	47.2	34.4	38.6	49.1	35.7	34.1	36.8	40.5	36.0	38.4
LT Debt	35.2	36.5	17.1	16.2	Nil	22.7	29.4	50.3	53.6	40.4
Common Eqty.	106	99	95.9	90.4	64.1	27.6	21.3	17.2	33.4	37.4
Total Cap.	144	133	113	107	64.1	50.3	50.7	67.5	87.0	78.1
Cap. Exp.	25.3	8.7	15.1	21.9	8.8	2.5	2.1	1.8	6.1	8.3
Cash Flow	20.8	10.2	10.2	27.4	12.4	9.5	3.8	-9.3	-0.3	9.1
Curr. Ratio	2.5	3.0	2.5	2.1	2.1	2.0	1.8	2.2	2.7	2.4
% LT Debt of Cap.	24.4	23.0	15.1	15.2	Nil	45.1	58.0	74.5	61.5	51.7
% Net Inc.of Revs.	5.2	2.0	1.9	11.0	5.4	4.0	0.4	NM	NM	3.4
% Ret. on Assets	7.7	4.8	2.9	18.0	8.5	6.7	0.5	NM	NM	5.5
% Ret. on Equity	13.5	4.5	0.8	30.1	18.5	24.4	2.7	NM	NM	17.6

Data as orig. reptd.; bef. results of disc. opers. and/or spec. items. Per share data adj. for stk. divs. as of ex-div. date. Bold denotes diluted EPS (FASB 128). E-Estimated. NA-Not Available. NM-Not Meaningful. NR-Not Ranked.

Office—4101 Jerome Ave. (P.O. Box 72787), Chattanooga, TN 37407. **Tel**—(423) 867-4210. **Fax**—(423) 867-4127. **Chrmn & Pres**—J. D. Brock. **VP, Secy**—R. W. Bethea, Jr. **VP & CFO**—F. M. Hall **Dirs**—J. D. Brock, G. C. Dillon, R. Dressler, R. W. Dunmire, D. K. Frierson, A. E. Guth, G. W. Jones, W. B. Sansom, E. D. Sloan Jr., W. N. Smith, R. G. Stafford. **Transfer Agent**—ChaseMellon Shareholder Services, Ridgefield Park, NJ. **Incorporated**—in Tennessee in 1972. **Empl**—1,925. **S&P Analyst:** E. Hunter

03-OCT-98

Industry:
Savings & Loan Companies

Summary: ASFC is the holding company for a savings bank with over $11 billion in assets, operating in the New York City metropolitan area and in upstate New York.

Quantitative Evaluations

Outlook
(1 Lowest—5 Highest)
- **2⁻**

Fair Value
- **40⅞**

Risk
- **Low**

Earn./Div. Rank
- **NR**

Technical Eval.
- **Bearish** since 5/98

Rel. Strength Rank
(1 Lowest—99 Highest)
- **51**

Insider Activity
- **Neutral**

Recent Price • 40⅜
52 Wk Range • 63⅜-34

Yield • 2.0%
12-Mo. P/E • 12.6

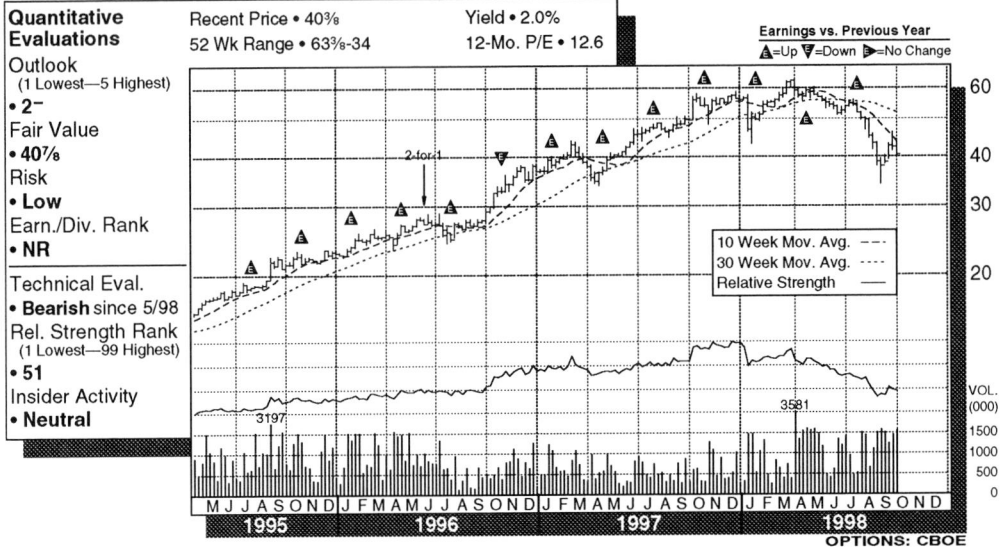

Earnings vs. Previous Year
△=Up ▽=Down ▷=No Change

10 Week Mov. Avg. ----
30 Week Mov. Avg. ·······
Relative Strength ———

OPTIONS: CBOE

Business Profile - 08-SEP-98

In April 1998, the company announced a definitive agreement to acquire Long Island Bancorp (Nasdaq: LISB). The $1.8 billion transaction, expected to close at the end of the 1998 third quarter, would make ASFC the sixth largest U.S. thrift, with about $16.6 billion in assets, up from $10.5 billion at year-end 1997. The acquisition of LISB would add 35 branches in the Long Island area, and 22 loan production offices in seven states, for a total of 96 branches (88 in New York City and Long Island, three in Westchester County, and five in the upstate counties of Otsego and Chenango). Earlier, in October 1997, ASFC acquired The Greater New York Savings Bank. In January 1998, the dividend was boosted 33%.

Operational Review - 08-SEP-98

In the first half of 1998, net interest income climbed 42%, year to year, reflecting growth in the mortgage loan portfolio, partly offset by a slightly narrower net interest margin (2.68%, versus 2.70%). The provision for loan losses was $614,000, down from $1,914,000. Non-interest income climbed 101%, led by greater gains on sales of securities and loans; non-interest expense increased 44%, as goodwill amortization increased to $9.7 million, from $4.2 million, as a result of the acquisition of The Greater New York Savings Bank. After taxes at 43.1%, versus 41.7%, net income advanced 50%, to $45,932,000 ($1.65 a share, on 26% more shares), from $30,641,000 ($1.48).

Stock Performance - 02-OCT-98

In the past 30 trading days, ASFC's shares have declined 7%, compared to a 7% fall in the S&P 500. Average trading volume for the past five days was 411,000 shares, compared with the 40-day moving average of 310,705 shares.

Key Stock Statistics

Dividend Rate/Share	0.80	Shareholders	2,800
Shs. outstg. (M)	54.4	Market cap. (B)	$ 2.2
Avg. daily vol. (M)	0.332	Inst. holdings	33%
Tang. Bk. Value/Share	25.91		
Beta	NA		

Value of $10,000 invested 5 years ago: NA

Fiscal Year Ending Dec. 31

	1998	1997	1996	1995	1994	1993
Revenues (Million $)						
1Q	192.3	132.5	119.4	99.9	71.96	—
2Q	200.8	140.1	124.7	110.5	76.55	—
3Q	—	143.7	130.1	115.7	78.60	—
4Q	—	185.3	130.7	118.4	80.50	—
Yr.	—	601.7	504.9	444.4	307.6	—
Earnings Per Share ($)						
1Q	**0.80**	**0.74**	0.68	0.53	0.46	--
2Q	**0.85**	**0.74**	0.56	0.50	0.45	--
3Q	--	**0.83**	-0.17	0.52	0.47	--
4Q	--	**0.74**	0.64	0.53	0.47	--
Yr.	--	**3.04**	1.79	2.07	1.85	0.18

Next earnings report expected: late October

Dividend Data (Dividends have been paid since 1995.)

Amount ($)	Date Decl.	Ex-Div. Date	Stock of Record	Payment Date
0.150	Oct. 15	Nov. 13	Nov. 17	Dec. 01 '97
0.200	Jan. 22	Feb. 11	Feb. 13	Mar. 02 '98
0.200	Apr. 15	May. 13	May. 15	Jun. 01 '98
0.200	Jul. 16	Aug. 12	Aug. 14	Sep. 01 '98

A Division of The McGraw·Hill Companies

Business Summary - 08-SEP-98

Astoria Financial Corp. (ASFC), parent of New York's third largest thrift, grew to $10.5 billion in assets at year-end 1997, including $2.4 billion in assets added in October 1997, when the Astoria Federal Savings and Loan Association unit acquired The Greater New York Savings Bank. The addition of The Greater's 14 banking offices boosted Astoria Federal's already sizeable presence in Queens, Nassau and Suffolk counties, moved it into neighboring Brooklyn, and increased its operations to 61 banking offices, including 56 in the New York metropolitan area and five in the central New York counties of Otsego and Chenango.

In April 1998, AFSC announced plans to acquire Long Island Bancorp (Nasdaq: LISB), Melville, NY, the parent of The Long Island Savings Bank, a federally chartered thrift institution with assets of $6.1 billion and deposits of $3.7 billion at December 31, 1997. The $1.8 billion transaction, through an exchange of common stock, is expected to close at the end of the 1998 third quarter, and would add 35 banking offices in Queens, Nassau and Suffolk counties, and 22 loan production offices in seven states. The combined company would have assets of $16.6 billion, a market capitalization of $3.25 billion, and would be the sixth largest U.S. thrift. ASFC expects to incur a $75 million after tax charge in the 1998 fourth quarter, for costs associated with the

merger; the acquisition is expected to be accretive to earnings in 1999.

ASFC offers a wide variety of loan products and other retail financial services. The company views its financial strength and customer service as competitive advantages in attracting customers. At year-end 1997, it served 375,000 customers, up from 170,000 in 1993, when AFSC adopted a strategy of growth through acquisitions. The company believes its retail operation to be an efficient one; the ratio of general and administrative costs to average assets improved to 1.25% in 1997, from 1.37% in 1996. The efficiency ratio improved to 45.20%, from 48.37%.

The loan portfolio rose to $4.3 billion at year-end 1997, from $2.6 billion a year earlier. At December 31, 1997, $3.6 billion (82%) of the total loan portfolio was in one-to-four-family residential loans, including $2.2 billion of adjustable rate loans. The remainder of the portfolio was in multi-family mortgage loans (8%), commercial real estate mortgages (9%), and consumer and other loans (1%).

At December 31, 1997, non-performing assets totaled $59.1 million, up 30% from $45.6 million a year earlier. The 1997 total includes $11.8 million of nonperforming assets from The Greater New York Savings acquisition that ASFC intends to sell. In late 1997, ASFC completed a bulk sale of $216.5 million of nonperforming assets received from The Greater.

Per Share Data ($)

(Year Ended Dec. 31)	1997	1996	1995	1994	1993	1992	1991	1990	1989	1988
Tangible Bk. Val.	24.40	22.75	21.30	22.65	20.13	NA	NA	NA	NA	NA
Earnings	3.04	1.77	2.07	1.85	0.18	NA	NA	NA	NA	NA
Dividends	0.56	0.43	0.20	Nil	Nil	Nil	Nil	Nil	Nil	Nil
Payout Ratio	18%	24%	10%	Nil	Nil	Nil	Nil	Nil	Nil	Nil
Prices - High	58⅞	38⅜	23⅜	17⅜	15	NA	NA	NA	NA	NA
- Low	33¾	22¼	13	12⅝	12½	NA	NA	NA	NA	NA
P/E Ratio - High	19	22	11	10	79	NA	NA	NA	NA	NA
- Low	11	13	6	7	66	NA	NA	NA	NA	NA

Income Statement Analysis (Million $)

	1997	1996	1995	1994	1993	1992	1991	1990	1989	1988
Net Int. Inc.	215	187	169	151	127	110	NA	NA	NA	NA
Loan Loss Prov.	3.1	4.0	2.0	3.1	7.0	5.9	NA	NA	NA	NA
Non Int. Inc.	22.7	12.7	9.5	6.2	6.4	5.8	NA	NA	NA	NA
Non Int. Exp.	116	133	95.6	79.4	82.0	73.9	NA	NA	NA	NA
Pretax Inc.	118	67.5	81.2	74.6	44.0	36.5	NA	NA	NA	NA
Eff. Tax Rate	42%	45%	44%	41%	43%	48%	NA	NA	NA	NA
Net Inc.	68.5	36.9	45.4	43.7	25.3	19.0	NA	NA	NA	NA
% Net Int. Marg.	2.71	2.74	2.77	2.85	3.53	3.60	3.53	NA	NA	NA

Balance Sheet & Other Fin. Data (Million $)

	1997	1996	1995	1994	1993	1992	1991	1990	1989	1988
Total Assets	10,528	10,528	6,620	4,643	4,121	NA	NA	NA	NA	NA
Loans	4,305	2,637	3,391	3,917	3,318	NA	NA	NA	NA	NA
Deposits	6,221	4,513	4,263	3,281	2,898	NA	NA	NA	NA	NA
Capitalization:										
Debt	3,273	2,112	1,705	767	653	NA	NA	NA	NA	NA
Equity	897	589	591	551	537	NA	NA	NA	NA	NA
Total	4,170	2,701	2,296	1,317	1,190	NA	NA	NA	NA	NA
% Ret. on Assets	0.8	0.5	0.8	1.0	0.7	0.6	NA	NA	NA	NA
% Ret. on Equity	9.0	6.2	8.0	8.0	8.4	8.1	NA	NA	NA	NA
% Loan Loss Resv.	0.9	0.5	0.7	0.6	0.8	NA	NA	NA	NA	NA
% Risk Based Capital	Nil	Nil	Nil	22.6	NA	NA	NA	NA	NA	NA
Price Times Book Value:										
Hi	2.4	1.7	1.1	0.8	0.7	NA	NA	NA	NA	NA
Low	1.4	1.0	0.6	0.6	0.6	NA	NA	NA	NA	NA

Data as orig. reptd.; bef. results of disc opers. and/or spec. items. Per share data adj. for stk. divs. as of ex-div. date. Bold denotes diluted EPS (FASB 128). E-Estimated. NA-Not Available. NM-Not Meaningful. NR-Not Ranked.

Office—One Astoria Federal Plaza, Lake Success, NY 11042-1085. **Tel**—(516) 327-3000. **Chrmn, Pres & CEO**—G. L. Engelke, Jr. **EVP & CFO**—M. N. Redman. **VP & Investor Contact**—Peter J. Cunningham. **Dirs**—R. G. Bolton, A. M. Burger, D. J. Connors, T. J. Donahue, G. L. Engelke, Jr. W. J. Fendt, P. C. Haeffner, G. C. Keegan, R. F. Palleschi, T. V. Powderly. **Transfer Agent & Registrar**—ChaseMellon Shareholder Services, Ridgefield Park, NJ. **Incorporated**—in Delaware in 1993. **Empl**— 1,241. **S&P Analyst:** Thomas W. Smith, CFA

Atmos Energy

246M
NYSE Symbol **ATO**

In S&P SmallCap 600

03-OCT-98

Industry: Natural Gas

Summary: This company, following its recent acquisition of United Cities Gas Co., distributes natural gas to more than one million customers in 13 states.

Quantitative Evaluations

Outlook (1 Lowest—5 Highest)
• **2⁻**

Fair Value
• **27¼**

Risk
• **Average**

Earn./Div. Rank
• **B+**

Technical Eval.
• **Bearish** since 9/98

Rel. Strength Rank (1 Lowest—99 Highest)
• **87**

Insider Activity
• **NA**

Recent Price • 29⅛
52 Wk Range • 31⅛-24¼
Yield • 3.6%
12-Mo. P/E • 23.5

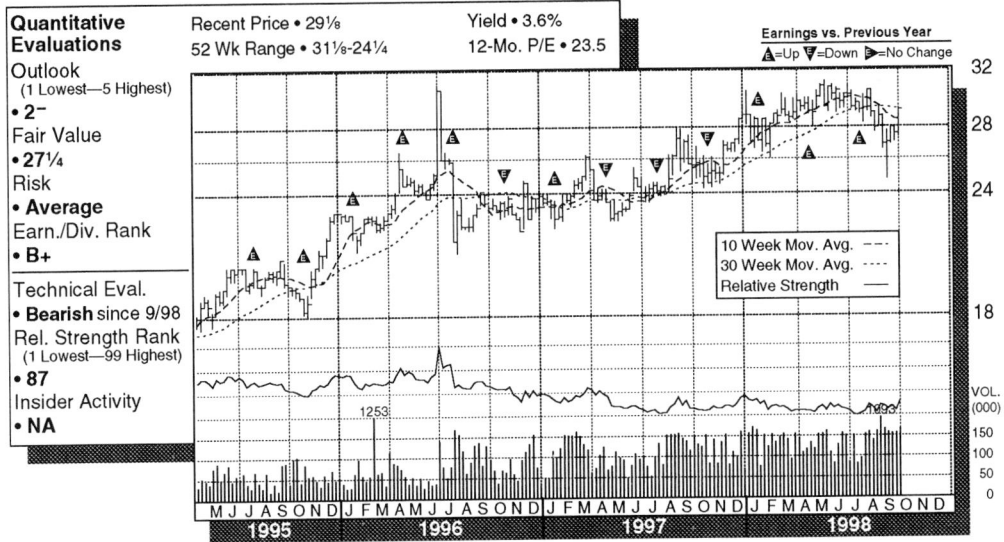

Earnings vs. Previous Year
▲=Up ▼=Down ▶=No Change

10 Week Mov. Avg.
30 Week Mov. Avg.
Relative Strength

Business Profile - 22-MAY-98

Following its recent acquisition of United Cities Gas (UCG), Atmos Energy became one of the largest natural gas distribution companies in the country. ATO is greatly affected by weather patterns throughout the states in which it operates; natural gas is used to operate irrigation pumps and heating devices, which are tied to rainfall and temperature, respectively. Therefore, Atmos' financial performance is highly seasonal. The company is also affected by regulatory agencies and competition in each state in which it operates. Atmos has made several major acquisitions during the past decades, and plans to continue in this direction. By acquiring other firms, the company diversifies its exposure to particular weather, economic, and regulatory conditions in different states.

Operational Review - 22-MAY-98

Operating revenues during the six month period ending March 31, 1998, decreased 9% to $584 million from $643 million during the comparable six month period ending March 31, 1997. The decrease was attributable to lower gas prices. Operating expenses during the six month period decreased 10.5%, as the company realized cost efficiencies with the United Cities acquisition. Net income during the six month period increased 18% to $57.5 million ($1.95 a share, diluted) from $48.8 million ($1.66), primarily due to the decreased operating expenses and increased gross profit.

Stock Performance - 02-OCT-98

In the past 30 trading days, ATO's shares have increased 4%, compared to a 7% fall in the S&P 500. Average trading volume for the past five days was 72,660 shares, compared with the 40-day moving average of 73,785 shares.

Key Stock Statistics

Dividend Rate/Share	1.06	Shareholders	29,900
Shs. outstg. (M)	30.3	Market cap. (B)	$0.881
Avg. daily vol. (M)	0.054	Inst. holdings	31%
Tang. Bk. Value/Share	12.51		
Beta	0.17		

Value of $10,000 invested 5 years ago: $ 23,544

Fiscal Year Ending Sep. 30

	1998	1997	1996	1995	1994	1993
Revenues (Million $)						
1Q	295.3	280.6	130.5	117.8	145.5	112.4
2Q	288.6	362.6	191.1	157.3	186.9	136.2
3Q	137.3	143.7	93.57	84.69	90.01	77.18
4Q	—	119.9	68.60	75.99	77.35	62.75
Yr.	—	906.8	483.7	435.8	499.8	388.5
Earnings Per Share ($)						
1Q	**0.68**	0.62	0.59	0.42	0.47	0.55
2Q	**1.25**	1.04	1.15	0.91	0.87	1.02
3Q	**0.06**	-0.10	0.02	0.01	-0.08	0.11
4Q	—	-0.74	-0.25	-0.11	-0.29	-0.21
Yr.	—	0.81	1.51	1.22	0.97	1.45

Next earnings report expected: mid November

Dividend Data (Dividends have been paid since 1984.)

Amount ($)	Date Decl.	Ex-Div. Date	Stock of Record	Payment Date
0.265	Nov. 12	Nov. 21	Nov. 25	Dec. 10 '97
0.265	Feb. 10	Feb. 23	Feb. 25	Mar. 10 '98
0.265	May. 13	May. 21	May. 26	Jun. 10 '98
0.265	Aug. 12	Aug. 21	Aug. 25	Sep. 10 '98

A Division of The McGraw·Hill Companies

Business Summary - 22-MAY-98

Atmos Energy Corp.'s plan for success in the newly competitive world of natural gas distribution has been to expand geographically through acquisitions. Atmos believes that geographic expansion will allow it to diversify its exposure to weather patterns, economic conditions and regulatory climates.

The company distributes and sells natural gas and propane to approximately 1.02 million residential, commercial, industrial, agricultural, and other customers. It sells natural gas to about 985,000 customers in 802 cities, towns and communities located in Texas, Louisiana, Kentucky, Colorado, Kansas, Illinois, Tennessee, Iowa, Virginia, Georgia, South Carolina, and Missouri. ATO also transports gas for others through parts of its distribution system. ATO's utility divisions consist of Energas, Greeley Gas, Trans Louisiana, United Cities and Western Kentucky.

ATO also operates certain non-utility businesses through wholly owned subsidiaries. UCG Storage provides natural gas storage services, and owns natural gas storage fields in Kentucky and Kansas. UCG Energy Corp. leases appliances, real estate and equipment, owns a small interest in a partnership engaged in exploration and production, and has a 45% interest in a gas marketing business. Atmos Propane sells and transports propane to both wholesale and retail customers.

The natural gas and propane distribution industries are subject to a number of factors, including the ongoing need to obtain adequate and timely rate relief from regulatory authorities, the inherent seasonality of the business, competition with alternate fuels, competition with other gas sources for industrial customers, and possible volatility in the supply and price of natural gas and propane. About 89% of revenues in FY 97 (Sep.) came from sales at rates set by or subject to approval by local or state authorities.

In FY 97, ATO sold 164 million Mcf of gas, at an average price of $5.11 per Mcf and an average cost of $3.51 per Mcf, and transported 49 million Mcf of gas. This compared with 178 million Mcf sold in FY 96, at an average price of $4.51 per Mcf and an average cost of $3.15 per Mcf, and 44 million Mcf of gas transported. Heating degree days (a measure of the relative coldness of weather, and the equivalent to each degree that the average of the high and low temperatures for a day is below 65 degrees) totaled 3,909, which is 98% of normal, compared to 4,043 days, which is 101% of normal.

Per Share Data ($)

(Year Ended Sep. 30)	1997	1996	1995	1994	1993	1992	1991	1990	1989	1988
Tangible Bk. Val.	11.04	10.75	10.20	9.78	10.39	9.17	8.88	8.71	8.51	8.37
Earnings	0.81	1.51	1.22	0.97	1.45	0.97	0.80	0.98	0.89	1.52
Dividends	1.01	0.96	0.92	0.88	0.85	0.83	0.80	0.77	0.75	0.67
Payout Ratio	125%	64%	75%	91%	59%	85%	100%	79%	84%	44%
Prices - High	27⅞	31	23	20¼	21⅛	15⅞	15⅜	12½	12	11½
- Low	22⅛	20⅞	16⅛	15⅞	15⅛	12⅝	10½	10⅜	9¾	8⅛
P/E Ratio - High	34	21	19	21	15	16	19	13	14	8
- Low	27	14	13	16	10	13	13	11	11	5

Income Statement Analysis (Million $)

	1997	1996	1995	1994	1993	1992	1991	1990	1989	1988
Revs.	907	484	436	500	388	340	336	352	342	323
Depr.	45.3	20.8	20.7	18.8	13.6	13.6	12.6	13.5	12.7	11.0
Maint.	12.0	4.2	4.3	5.9	3.8	3.3	3.9	4.3	5.8	5.0
Fxd. Chgs. Cov.	2.1	3.5	3.1	2.9	3.5	2.4	2.1	2.2	2.2	2.6
Constr. Credits	NA	NA	NA	NA	NA	NA	NA	NA	NA	NA
Eff. Tax Rate	37%	36%	34%	36%	37%	33%	28%	32%	31%	38%
Net Inc.	23.8	23.9	18.9	14.7	15.7	10.0	7.9	9.0	8.1	10.6

Balance Sheet & Other Fin. Data (Million $)

	1997	1996	1995	1994	1993	1992	1991	1990	1989	1988
Gross Prop.	1,333	666	595	544	399	364	333	307	300	277
Cap. Exp.	122	77.6	62.9	50.4	38.4	33.3	30.2	25.3	21.6	19.9
Net Prop.	849	414	363	327	241	219	206	195	195	189
Capitalization:										
LT Debt	303	122	131	138	85.3	91.3	95.6	81.8	91.9	80.6
% LT Debt	48	42	45	48	42	49	51	51	54	51
Pfd.	Nil	Nil	Nil	Nil	Nil	Nil	Nil	Nil	Nil	Nil
% Pfd.	Nil	Nil	Nil	Nil	Nil	Nil	Nil	Nil	Nil	Nil
Common	327	172	158	150	118	96.0	90.3	79.8	77.7	76.3
% Common	52	59	55	52	58	51	49	49	46	49
Total Cap.	718	334	323	318	232	214	212	189	195	181
% Oper. Ratio	94.2	91.9	92.5	94.7	93.3	94.0	94.6	94.5	94.9	93.7
% Earn. on Net Prop.	8.3	10.0	9.3	8.4	11.3	9.6	9.0	9.9	9.1	13.3
% Return On Revs.	2.6	5.0	4.3	2.9	4.0	2.9	2.4	2.5	2.4	3.3
% Return On Invest. Capital	8.2	11.8	10.1	9.1	11.6	9.7	9.0	10.4	9.6	14.9
% Return On Com. Equity	9.5	14.5	12.2	10.2	14.7	10.8	9.3	11.4	10.5	17.8

Data as orig. reptd.; bef. results of disc opers. and/or spec. items. Per share data adj. for stk. divs. as of ex-div. date. Bold denotes diluted EPS (FASB 128). E-Estimated. NA-Not Available. NM-Not Meaningful. NR-Not Ranked.

Office—1800 Three Lincoln Centre, 5430 LBJ Freeway, Dallas, TX 75240. **Tel**—(972) 934-9227. **Chrmn, Pres & CEO**—R. W. Best. **EVP & CFO**—L. J. Dagley. **Secy**—G. A. Blanscet. **VP & Investor Contact**—Lynn Hord (972-788-3729). **Dirs**—T. W. Bain II, R. W. Best, D. Busbee, R.W. Cardin, T. J. Garland, G. C. Koonce, V. J. Lewis, T. C. Meredith, P. E. Nichol, C. S. Quinn, L. Schlessman. **Transfer Agent & Registrar**—First National Bank of Boston. **Organized**—in Texas in 1983. **Empl**— 2,679. **S&P Analyst:** Ephraim Juskowicz

Au Bon Pain

3175D

NASDAQ Symbol **ABPCA**

In S&P SmallCap 600

03-OCT-98

Industry:
Restaurants

Summary: This company recently agreed to sell its Au Bon Pain operations in order to concentrate on its Saint Louis Bread bakery cafes business.

Quantitative Evaluations

Recent Price • 5¾
52 Wk Range • 11⅝-5¼

Yield • Nil
12-Mo. P/E • NM

Earnings vs. Previous Year
▲=Up ▼=Down ▶=No Change

Outlook
(1 Lowest—5 Highest)
• **NA**

Fair Value
• **NA**

Risk
• **Average**

Earn./Div. Rank
• **B-**

Technical Eval.
• **Bearish** since 9/98

Rel. Strength Rank
(1 Lowest—99 Highest)
• **28**

Insider Activity
• **Favorable**

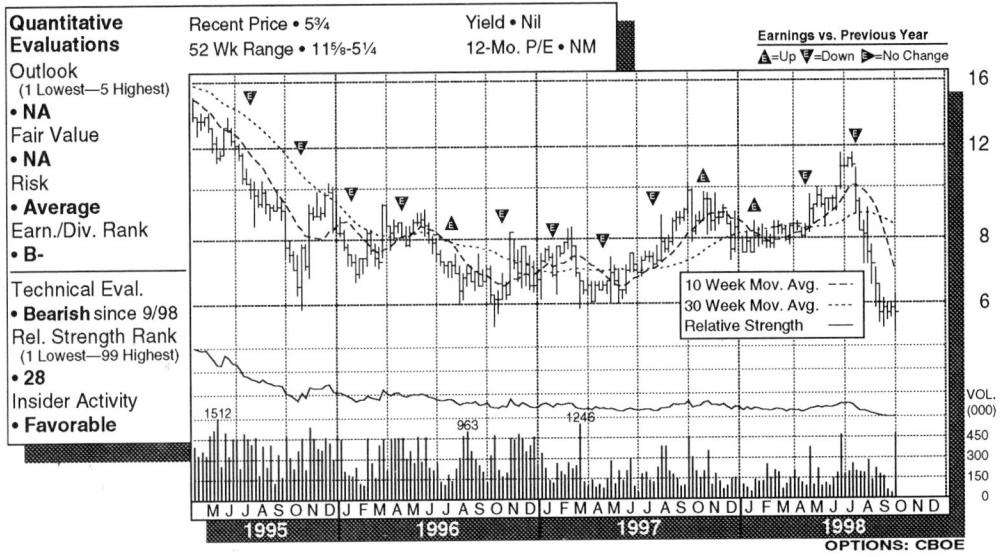

10 Week Mov. Avg. ---
30 Week Mov. Avg. ····
Relative Strength —

OPTIONS: CBOE

Business Profile - 09-SEP-98

In August 1998, the company agreed to sell its Au Bon Pain business unit to a company controlled by Bruckman, Rosser, Sherrill & Co., Inc., for about $78 million. This unit includes all 152 company-owned bakery cafes as well as the franchise business which encompasses 69 domestic locations and 42 International cafes. Following the sale, ABPCA will concentrate on its Saint Louis Bread Co. business, which currently operates 65 company-owned bakery cafes and 32 franchised units. By year-end, the company expects to have about 129 total bakery cafes in 16 states. In March 1998, the company completed the sale of its Mexico, Missouri Frozen Dough Production Facility and wholesale business to Bunge Foods Corp. for about $13 million in cash.

Operational Review - 09-SEP-98

Revenues in the first half of 1998 rose 1.4%, year to year, reflecting a 1.5% rise in restaurant sales and flat franchise sales and other revenues. Results were hurt by increases in food costs, particularly butter and previously contracted for coffee, as well as a weakening in comparable restaurant sales growth. In addition, sales from franchised cafes were lower than expected. Following a $1.2 million nonrecurring charge, the net loss widened to $2,729,183 ($0.23 a share) from $153,682 ($0.01).

Stock Performance - 02-OCT-98

In the past 30 trading days, ABPCA's shares have declined 19%, compared to a 7% fall in the S&P 500. Average trading volume for the past five days was 136,820 shares, compared with the 40-day moving average of 44,872 shares.

Key Stock Statistics

Dividend Rate/Share	Nil	Shareholders	1,600
Shs. outstg. (M)	12.0	Market cap. (B)	$0.060
Avg. daily vol. (M)	0.047	Inst. holdings	50%
Tang. Bk. Value/Share	5.01		
Beta	1.17		

Value of $10,000 invested 5 years ago: $ 2,169

Fiscal Year Ending Dec. 31

	1998	1997	1996	1995	1994	1993
Revenues (Million $)						
1Q	74.96	71.51	69.44	62.99	46.73	33.62
2Q	57.25	58.82	54.43	51.49	40.88	27.86
3Q	—	60.17	54.97	54.92	44.11	29.77
4Q	—	60.39	58.09	57.07	51.16	31.66
Yr.	—	250.9	236.9	226.5	182.9	122.9
Earnings Per Share ($)						
1Q	-0.16	Nil	0.07	0.14	0.16	0.14
2Q	-0.07	-0.01	0.05	0.03	0.14	0.13
3Q	—	0.12	-0.51	-0.39	0.18	0.16
4Q	—	0.04	0.02	0.09	0.20	0.18
Yr.	—	0.15	-0.37	-0.14	0.67	0.60

Next earnings report expected: mid November

Dividend Data

The company has never paid dividends on its capital stock and has no intention of paying cash dividends in the foreseeable future.

A Division of The **McGraw·Hill** Companies

STANDARD
&POOR'S
STOCK REPORTS

Au Bon Pain Co., Inc.

3175D
03-OCT-98

Business Summary - 09-SEP-98

Au Bon Pain (ABPCA) has made a lot of dough (and other good-tasting stuff) since its formation with three Boston area bakeries and one cookie store in 1981. In August 1998, the company agreed to sell its Au Bon Pain business in order to concentrate on its Saint Louis Bread Co. concept.

As of December 28, 1997, ABPCA had 220 company-operated and 115 franchised bakery cafes operating under two concepts: Au Bon Pain, with 160 company-operated and 96 franchise-operated bakery cafes, and Saint Louis Bread Co. (SLB), with 60 company-operated and 19 franchise-operated bakery cafes. Both concepts specialize in high-quality food for breakfast and lunch, including fresh baked goods, made-to-order sandwiches on freshly baked breads, soups, salads, custom-roasted coffees and other cafe beverages.

The company's Au Bon Pain bakery cafes are located principally in Boston, other New England cities, New York City, Connecticut, Washington, D.C., Chicago, Maryland, New Hampshire, New Jersey, California, Philadelphia, Pittsburgh, Rhode Island, Texas, Santiago, Chile, The Philippines, Indonesia, Sao Paulo, Brazil, Bangkok, Thailand and London, England. The Saint Louis Bread bakery cafes are primarily located in St. Louis, Atlanta, Kansas, Detroit and Chicago.

Target customers of Au Bon Pain and SLB include urban office employees, suburban dwellers, shoppers, travelers, students and other adults who are time sensitive, yet desire a higher-quality breakfast and lunch experience than is typically found at quick-service restaurants. The company's menu is focused on foods in the following categories: fresh baked goods, made-to-order sandwiches on freshly baked breads, soups, salads, custom roasted coffees, and cafe beverages. The company's strategy is to create distinctive food offerings at reasonable prices within these categories that are fresher, of higher quality and of greater variety than those offered by its competitors. In addition, the company believes its operational excellence, speed of service and convenient locations further differentiate it from its competitors. Average revenue per company-operated bakery cafe open for all of 1997 was approximately $1,014,211 for the Au Bon Pain concept and approximately $1,200,257 for the Saint Louis Bread concept.

The average customer purchase is about $3.09 at Au Bon Pain and $4.92 at SLB. Breakfast and lunch checks average $2.12 and $4.23, respectively at Au Bon Pain and $3.51 and $5.84, respectively, at SLB.

Per Share Data ($)

(Year Ended Dec. 31)	1997	1996	1995	1994	1993	1992	1991	1990	1989	1988
Tangible Bk. Val.	5.06	4.78	4.95	4.92	4.24	5.70	4.06	NA	NA	NA
Cash Flow	1.57	1.01	1.14	1.70	1.30	1.08	0.88	NA	NA	NA
Earnings	0.15	-0.37	-0.14	0.67	0.60	0.48	0.30	NA	NA	NA
Dividends	Nil	Nil	Nil	Nil	Nil	Nil	Nil	Nil	Nil	Nil
Payout Ratio	Nil	Nil	Nil	Nil	Nil	Nil	Nil	Nil	Nil	Nil
Prices - High	10¼	9⅜	17¼	26½	28¼	29	17	NA	NA	NA
- Low	5⅞	5⅜	5⅞	14⅜	18	13½	9	NA	NA	NA
P/E Ratio - High	68	NM	NM	40	47	60	57	NA	NA	NA
- Low	39	NM	NM	21	30	28	30	NA	NA	NA

Income Statement Analysis (Million $)

	1997	1996	1995	1994	1993	1992	1991	1990	1989	1988
Revs.	251	237	226	183	123	97.0	68.0	NA	NA	NA
Oper. Inc.	24.6	21.0	24.2	27.1	19.8	15.4	11.1	NA	NA	NA
Depr.	16.9	16.2	14.9	11.9	8.0	6.6	5.2	NA	NA	NA
Int. Exp.	7.2	5.1	3.4	1.7	0.1	0.2	1.0	NA	NA	NA
Pretax Inc.	0.3	-7.3	-4.4	13.3	11.7	8.9	4.3	NA	NA	NA
Eff. Tax Rate	NM	NM	NM	41%	42%	41%	40%	NA	NA	NA
Net Inc.	1.8	-4.4	-1.6	7.8	6.8	5.3	2.6	NA	NA	NA

Balance Sheet & Other Fin. Data (Million $)

	1997	1996	1995	1994	1993	1992	1991	1990	1989	1988
Cash	0.9	2.6	6.4	1.0	4.9	4.7	NA	NA	NA	NA
Curr. Assets	21.4	27.9	27.1	17.4	17.6	13.4	NA	NA	NA	NA
Total Assets	187	196	193	166	120	77.0	NA	NA	NA	NA
Curr. Liab.	21.4	25.2	26.3	20.9	12.4	6.7	NA	NA	NA	NA
LT Debt	72.5	79.7	72.5	49.1	30.2	0.3	NA	NA	NA	NA
Common Eqty.	92.3	90.1	93.2	94.2	68.3	NA	NA	NA	NA	NA
Total Cap.	165	170	167	145	108	70.0	NA	NA	NA	NA
Cap. Exp.	14.7	17.0	38.7	39.4	19.1	20.4	NA	NA	NA	NA
Cash Flow	18.7	11.8	13.3	19.7	14.8	11.9	7.8	NA	NA	NA
Curr. Ratio	1.0	1.1	1.0	0.8	1.4	2.0	NA	NA	NA	NA
% LT Debt of Cap.	44.0	46.8	43.5	33.5	28.0	1.0	NA	NA	NA	NA
% Net Inc.of Revs.	0.7	NM	NM	4.3	5.5	5.4	3.8	NA	NA	NA
% Ret. on Assets	0.9	NM	NM	5.5	6.8	7.0	NA	NA	NA	NA
% Ret. on Equity	2.0	NM	NM	9.2	9.4	8.0	NA	NA	NA	NA

Data as orig. reptd.; bef. results of disc. opers. and/or spec. items. Per share data adj. for stk. divs. as of ex-div. date. Bold denotes diluted EPS (FASB 128). E-Estimated. NA-Not Available. NM-Not Meaningful. NR-Not Ranked.

Office—19 Fid Kennedy Ave., Boston, MA 02210.**Tel**—(617) 423-2100. **Co-Chrmn**—L. I. Kane. **Co-Chrmn & CEO**—R. M. Shaich. **SVP, Treas, CFO & Investor Contact**—Anthony J. Carroll. **Dirs**—F. W. Hatch, G. E. Kane, L. I. Kane, J. R. McManus, H. J. Nasella, J. P. Shaich, R. M. Shaich. **Transfer Agent & Registrar**—Boston Financial Data Services, Quincy, MA.**Incorporated**—in Delaware in 1988. **Empl**— 1,378. **S&P Analyst:** J.C.

STANDARD &POOR'S
STOCK REPORTS

Auspex Systems

3175H

NASDAQ Symbol **ASPX**

In S&P SmallCap 600

03-OCT-98 Industry: Computers (Hardware)

Summary: ASPX manufactures client/server computer systems.

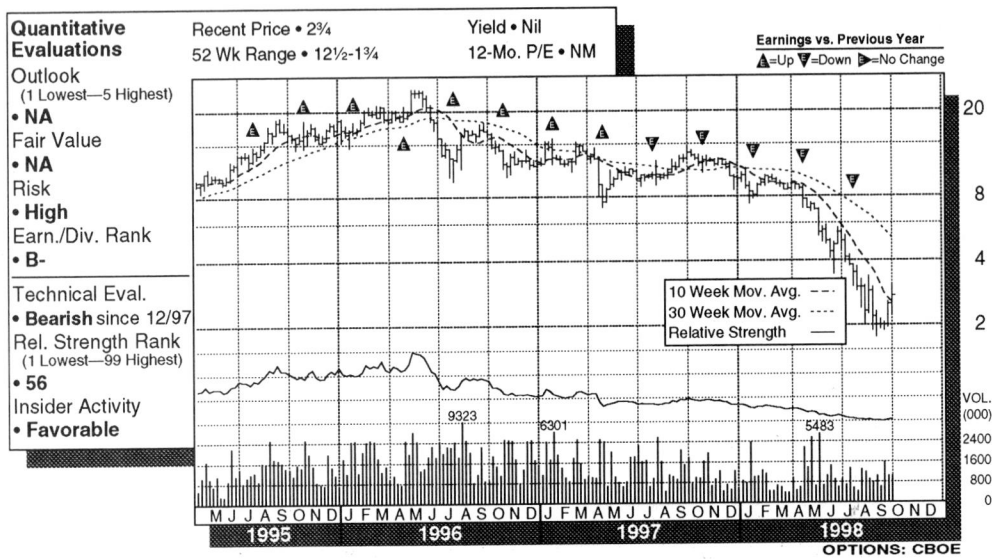

Quantitative Evaluations	
Outlook (1 Lowest—5 Highest)	• **NA**
Fair Value	• **NA**
Risk	• **High**
Earn./Div. Rank	• **B-**
Technical Eval.	• **Bearish** since 12/97
Rel. Strength Rank (1 Lowest—99 Highest)	• **56**
Insider Activity	• **Favorable**

Recent Price • 2¾
52 Wk Range • 12½-1¾
Yield • Nil
12-Mo. P/E • NM

Earnings vs. Previous Year
▲=Up ▼=Down ▶=No Change

10 Week Mov. Avg. – – –
30 Week Mov. Avg. - - - -
Relative Strength ——

OPTIONS: CBOE

Business Profile - 27-AUG-98

Auspex characterized FY 98 (Jun.) as a challenging year in which it took several steps to better align its organization to execute on the company's strategic objectives, including a recently completed restructuring that has enabled it to improve time-to-market. Although it has taken pricing action to make its products more competitive, the company does not expect improved business volumes until the introduction of its next-generation products later in FY 99. Auspex plans to re-establish momentum in the second half of FY 99.

Operational Review - 27-AUG-98

Based on a preliminary report, total revenues in FY 98 (Jun.) fell 17% from those of the prior year. The company attributed the decline to the Asian economic crisis and weak demand from the semiconductor segment. Gross margins narrowed, hurt by pricing pressures, and with 20% higher operating expenses, a pretax loss contrasted with pretax income. After a tax benefit of $9,334,000, versus taxes at 44.9%, a net loss of $17,334,000 ($0.69 a share) compared to net income of $13,420,000 ($0.52).

Stock Performance - 02-OCT-98

In the past 30 trading days, ASPX's shares have declined 5%, compared to a 7% fall in the S&P 500. Average trading volume for the past five days was 207,040 shares, compared with the 40-day moving average of 207,510 shares.

Key Stock Statistics

Dividend Rate/Share	Nil	Shareholders	700
Shs. outstg. (M)	25.5	Market cap. (B)	$0.070
Avg. daily vol. (M)	0.214	Inst. holdings	58%
Tang. Bk. Value/Share	5.13		
Beta	1.54		

Value of $10,000 invested 5 years ago: NA

Fiscal Year Ending Jun. 30

	1998	1997	1996	1995	1994	1993
Revenues (Million $)						
1Q	48.59	43.01	33.54	23.87	20.40	15.70
2Q	43.44	49.08	38.00	26.44	20.38	16.40
3Q	40.39	55.61	43.33	30.03	21.44	19.70
4Q	36.50	54.79	47.77	35.28	21.09	21.80
Yr.	168.9	202.5	162.6	115.6	83.28	73.50
Earnings Per Share ($)						
1Q	0.07	0.17	0.14	0.09	0.10	0.08
2Q	**-0.30**	0.19	0.18	0.11	0.09	0.09
3Q	**-0.09**	0.25	0.21	0.14	0.09	0.10
4Q	**-0.36**	-0.09	0.24	0.18	0.07	0.09
Yr.	**-0.69**	0.52	0.77	0.51	0.34	0.36

Next earnings report expected: late October

Dividend Data

No cash dividends have been paid. A "poison pill" stock purchase rights plan was adopted in 1995.

Business Summary - 27-AUG-98

As the data explosion continues, companies are making more information available to a growing and diverse constituency of employees, vendors, customers and shareholders, and it must be available 24 hours a day, seven days a week. Auspex Systems has responded to this daunting challenge with a unique family of high-performance, network data-serving solutions, including a full line of network data servers, high-availability software products and data storage management solutions, each designed to meet businesses' need for fast, reliable and continuously available access to information.

The traditional approach to moving data, using multiple general purpose servers that are designed to perform "compute" tasks such as transaction processing and applications, typically results in degraded performance when the amount of network traffic increases. Auspex's unique family of high-performance network data-serving solutions offers a fundamentally different approach to delivering immediate and secure access to information. The company's NetServer is based on a patented system to "serve" large amounts of data quickly and reliably to the desktop.

The company's core business ranges from the semiconductor industry, where huge files containing design

information on the latest generation of microprocessors are under development, to software companies where a terabyte of source code files and libraries are shared among hundreds of developers in concurrent engineering environments.

As more companies struggle to manage their growing data requirements, Auspex has found an opportunity to provide solutions to segments with similar data management challenges, such as mechanical computer-aided design (MCAD) environments in the automotive and aerospace industries, seismic data analysis by engineers for oil and gas exploration, as well as Internet service and on-line providers.

In 1995, Auspex began shipping its first software product, DataGuard, which allows users to continually access their data in the event of a disruption associated with the UNIX host operating system. In March 1996, it introduced its second software product, ServerGuard, which provides a local and wide area network-based fail-over and disaster recovery system.

During FY 97 (Jun.), ASPX decided to expand its services beyond its current capabilities, to provide customers with comprehensive network data management solutions. In June 1997, in an effort to reach this goal, the company acquired Alphatronix, Inc., a software company that provides a graphical user interface library.

Per Share Data ($)

(Year Ended Jun. 30)	1998	1997	1996	1995	1994	1993	1992	1991	1990	1989
Tangible Bk. Val.	NA	5.13	4.51	3.46	2.91	2.66	4.20	NA	NA	NA
Cash Flow	NA	1.01	1.12	0.84	0.64	0.59	0.38	NA	NA	NA
Earnings	-0.69	0.52	0.77	0.51	0.34	0.36	0.25	NA	NA	NA
Dividends	Nil	Nil	Nil	Nil	Nil	Nil	Nil	Nil	Nil	Nil
Payout Ratio	Nil	Nil	Nil	Nil	Nil	Nil	Nil	Nil	Nil	Nil
Prices - High	10³/₄	14⁷/₈	25¹/₂	18³/₄	10	15¹/₂	NA	NA	NA	NA
- Low	2⁷/₈	7¹/₈	9³/₈	6¹/₂	3⁷/₈	7¹/₂	NA	NA	NA	NA
P/E Ratio - High	NM	29	33	37	29	43	NA	NA	NA	NA
- Low	NM	14	12	13	11	22	NA	NA	NA	NA

Income Statement Analysis (Million $)

	1998	1997	1996	1995	1994	1993	1992	1991	1990	1989
Revs.	NA	202	163	116	83.3	73.5	51.5	NA	NA	NA
Oper. Inc.	NA	41.7	36.6	21.9	15.8	14.5	8.0	NA	NA	NA
Depr.	NA	12.4	8.9	8.0	7.5	5.0	2.6	NA	NA	NA
Int. Exp.	NA	0.0	0.1	0.1	0.1	0.1	0.1	NA	NA	NA
Pretax Inc.	NA	24.4	29.6	15.9	9.8	10.0	5.6	NA	NA	NA
Eff. Tax Rate	NA	45%	33%	22%	15%	19%	12%	NA	NA	NA
Net Inc.	NA	13.4	19.8	12.4	8.3	8.1	4.9	NA	NA	NA

Balance Sheet & Other Fin. Data (Million $)

	1998	1997	1996	1995	1994	1993	1992	1991	1990	1989
Cash	NA	25.1	50.5	44.6	42.1	49.8	16.3	NA	NA	NA
Curr. Assets	NA	134	117	93.6	75.8	68.2	27.4	NA	NA	NA
Total Assets	NA	157	136	107	85.4	76.7	33.0	NA	NA	NA
Curr. Liab.	NA	28.8	26.0	25.7	18.3	14.4	9.8	NA	NA	NA
LT Debt	NA	0.0	0.0	0.2	0.4	0.8	0.7	NA	NA	NA
Common Eqty.	NA	128	110	80.7	66.6	61.6	21.0	NA	NA	NA
Total Cap.	NA	128	110	80.9	67.0	62.4	21.7	NA	NA	NA
Cap. Exp.	NA	16.4	15.4	8.1	7.9	7.0	5.1	NA	NA	NA
Cash Flow	NA	25.9	28.7	20.4	15.8	13.1	7.5	NA	NA	NA
Curr. Ratio	NA	4.7	4.5	3.6	4.1	4.7	2.8	NA	NA	NA
% LT Debt of Cap.	NA	NM	NM	0.2	0.6	1.3	3.1	NA	NA	NA
% Net Inc.of Revs.	NA	6.6	12.2	10.7	10.0	11.1	9.5	NA	NA	NA
% Ret. on Assets	NA	9.2	16.3	12.9	10.3	7.1	22.2	NA	NA	NA
% Ret. on Equity	NA	11.3	20.8	16.8	13.0	10.2	39.8	NA	NA	NA

Data as orig. reptd.; bef. results of disc. opers. and/or spec. items. Per share data adj. for stk. divs. as of ex-div. date. Bold denotes diluted EPS (FASB 128). E-Estimated. NA-Not Available. NM-Not Meaningful. NR-Not Ranked.

Office—2300 Central Expy., Santa Clara, CA 95050.**Tel**—(408) 566-2000. **Website**—http://www.auspex.com **Pres & CEO**—B. N. Moore. **VP- Fin & CFO**—R. M. Case.**Investor Contact**—Sharon Travers (408) 566-2213.**Dirs**—R. S. Cheheyl, W. F. King, D. F. Marquardt, B. N. Moore. **Transfer Agent & Registrar**—Boston EquiServe, L.P. **Incorporated**—in California in 1987; reincorporated in Delaware in 1991. **Empl**— 600. **S&P Analyst:** SRB

Authentic Fitness

255M

NYSE Symbol **ASM**

In S&P SmallCap 600

03-OCT-98

Industry: Textiles (Apparel)

Summary: This company designs, manufactures and sells swimwear, swimwear accessories and active fitness apparel.

Quantitative Evaluations	
Outlook (1 Lowest—5 Highest)	**5**
Fair Value	**23¾**
Risk	**Average**
Earn./Div. Rank	**NR**
Technical Eval.	**Neutral** since 8/98
Rel. Strength Rank (1 Lowest—99 Highest)	**91**
Insider Activity	**NA**

Recent Price • 14¼
52 Wk Range • 21¼-10½

Yield • 0.4%
12-Mo. P/E • 14.1

Earnings vs. Previous Year
▲=Up ▼=Down ▶=No Change

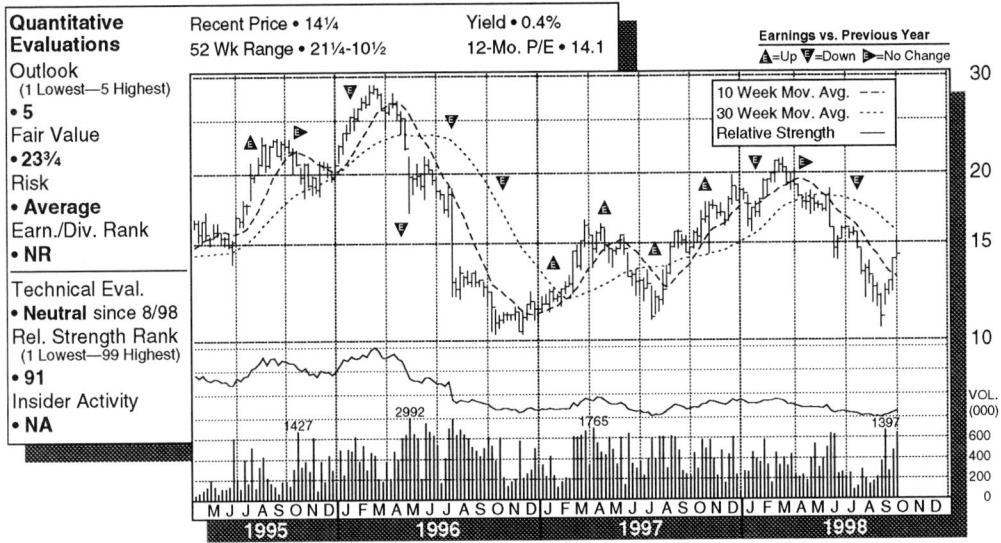

10 Week Mov. Avg. – – –
30 Week Mov. Avg. ‑‑‑‑‑
Relative Strength —

Business Profile - 28-MAY-98

ASM seeks to leverage its leading brand names by expanding its distribution channels and extending its product lines. Key elements of its strategy include opening new Speedo Authentic Fitness retail stores, expanding product offerings through mass merchandising, and entering international markets. In line with this strategy ASM has opened about 140 company-owned Speedo Authentic Fitness retail stores during the last four years.

Operational Review - 28-MAY-98

Net revenues for the nine months ended April 4, 1998, advanced 11%, year to year, reflecting 18.8% sales growth at the designer swimwear division and 19.1% sales increase at Authentic Fitness retail stores, partly offset by the discontinued skiwear business. Margins widened, due to favorable manufacturing variances, improved Speedo sales mix and higher retail sales; operating income rose 40.6%. After a nonrecurring pretax charge of $1.4 million related the closing of the company's Bally's Fitness Center stores and the consolidation of manufacturing facilities and taxes at 36.1% versus 36.4%, net income leaped 54%, to $10,800,000 ($0.48 a share), from $7,000,000 ($0.31).

Stock Performance - 02-OCT-98

In the past 30 trading days, ASM's shares have increased 15%, compared to a 7% fall in the S&P 500. Average trading volume for the past five days was 223,200 shares, compared with the 40-day moving average of 106,274 shares.

Key Stock Statistics

Dividend Rate/Share	0.05	Shareholders	100
Shs. outstg. (M)	22.5	Market cap. (B)	$0.321
Avg. daily vol. (M)	0.169	Inst. holdings	34%
Tang. Bk. Value/Share	2.84		
Beta	-0.07		

Value of $10,000 invested 5 years ago: $ 13,401

Fiscal Year Ending Jun. 30

	1998	1997	1996	1995	1994	1993
Revenues (Million $)						
1Q	36.97	38.67	42.91	37.60	28.61	23.90
2Q	72.65	70.44	77.30	56.32	36.82	29.00
3Q	127.9	105.0	98.86	74.85	53.30	36.67
4Q	129.9	109.0	90.54	97.37	59.83	43.36
Yr.	367.5	323.1	309.6	266.1	178.6	132.9
Earnings Per Share ($)						
1Q	-0.31	-0.52	0.10	0.10	0.10	0.09
2Q	**0.16**	0.21	-0.06	0.21	-0.04	0.15
3Q	**0.62**	0.62	-0.27	0.28	0.20	0.17
4Q	**0.53**	0.54	-1.78	0.32	0.20	0.14
Yr.	**1.01**	0.85	-2.00	0.90	0.49	0.56

Next earnings report expected: early November

Dividend Data (Dividends have been paid since 1995.)

Amount ($)	Date Decl.	Ex-Div. Date	Stock of Record	Payment Date
0.013	Nov. 21	Dec. 03	Dec. 05	Jan. 06 '98
0.013	Feb. 24	Mar. 10	Mar. 12	Apr. 09 '98
0.013	May. 11	Jun. 03	Jun. 05	Jul. 07 '98
0.013	Aug. 20	Sep. 01	Sep. 03	Oct. 06 '98

A Division of The McGraw-Hill Companies

Business Summary - 28-MAY-98

Authentic Fitness designs, manufactures and markets swimwear, swim accessories, and active fitness apparel under the Speedo, Speedo Authentic Fitness, Catalina, Anne Cole, Cole of California, Sunset Beach, Sandcastle, Sporting Life and Oscar de la Renta brand names; and activewear and swimwear under the White Stag brand name. ASM also operates Authentic Fitness retail stores, which sell active fitness apparel under the Speedo and Speedo Authentic Fitness names. In FY 97 (Jun.), 53% of revenues were derived from the Speedo division, 28% from the Designer Swimwear division, 15% from the Retail division, and 4% from the White Stag divisions. Consistent with its intention to focus on core Speedo businesses, ASM exited the skiwear and outlet store businesses in May 1996.

The Speedo division's product lines consist of women's and men's competition swimwear and swimwear accessories, men's swimwear and coordinating T-shirts, women's fitness swimwear and Speedo Authentic Fitness activewear and children's swimwear. The Speedo brand name is prominent in the competition swimwear market, and is the dominant brand in that market in the U.S. and Canada (over 60% market share in 1997). The majority of its sales are to repeat customers in a fairly constant core group of basic body styles. Speedo accessories include swim goggles, swimming caps, nose clips, masks, snorkels, ear plugs, kickboards, floatation devices, and aquatic exercise gear.

At May 19, 1998, ASM was operating a total of 139 Authentic Fitness retail stores, which offer a complete line of Speedo and Speedo Authentic Fitness products and average approximately 1,100 sq. ft. in size. In FY 97, the company opened 52 new stores and plans to open about 20 additional stores per year over the next several years. New stores require about $200,000 in capital expenditures and each store employs about five full and part-time employees.

The Designer Swimwear division markets women's swimwear under the brandnames Catalina, Anne Cole, Cole of California, Oscar de la Renta, Sandcastle, Sunset Beach, White Stag and Sporting Life. Anne Cole and Oscar de la Renta are designer brands, Cole of California, Sandcastle and Sporting Life are missy brands, and Sunset is a junior brand. The Catalina and White Stag brands are targeted to the mass merchandise market. During the 1997 selling season, three of ASM's designer brands were among the top 10 sellers at retail. Anne Cole was the fourth best selling missy brand, Cole of California was the eighth best selling missy brand, and Sunset Beach was the third best selling junior brand.

In May 1997, directors authorized the repurchase of up to $10 million of the company's common stock, subsequently increased to $20 million. As of May 15, 1998, ASM had repurchased 385,700 shares at an average price of about $16 per share.

Per Share Data ($) (Year Ended Jun. 30)	1998	1997	1996	1995	1994	1993	1992	1991	1990	1989
Tangible Bk. Val.	NA	2.58	2.11	3.45	2.63	0.64	-0.14	-0.30	NA	NA
Cash Flow	NA	1.28	-1.22	1.20	0.70	0.72	0.58	0.39	NA	NA
Earnings	1.01	0.85	-2.00	0.90	0.49	0.56	0.42	0.23	NA	NA
Dividends	0.05	0.05	0.05	Nil	Nil	Nil	Nil	NA	NA	NA
Payout Ratio	5%	6%	NM	Nil	Nil	Nil	Nil	NA	NA	NA
Prices - High	21¼	19¾	29	23⅜	16	16	11⅞	NA	NA	NA
- Low	11⅝	10⅞	10⅜	11⅞	10⅞	8½	6⅛	NA	NA	NA
P/E Ratio - High	21	19	NM	26	33	29	28	NA	NA	NA
- Low	12	13	NM	13	22	15	14	NA	NA	NA
Income Statement Analysis (Million $)										
Revs.	NA	323	310	266	179	133	101	86.0	NA	NA
Oper. Inc.	NA	55.8	-16.3	45.1	30.8	22.3	19.9	14.0	NA	NA
Depr.	NA	9.8	15.5	6.5	4.3	2.8	2.7	2.8	NA	NA
Int. Exp.	NA	13.6	11.5	7.0	4.4	4.3	3.8	5.0	NA	NA
Pretax Inc.	NA	29.1	-57.0	31.6	16.4	15.2	13.3	6.2	NA	NA
Eff. Tax Rate	NA	35%	NM	38%	42%	36%	44%	36%	NA	NA
Net Inc.	NA	19.0	-39.4	19.5	9.6	9.8	7.4	4.0	NA	NA
Balance Sheet & Other Fin. Data (Million $)										
Cash	NA	1.2	1.5	0.8	1.1	0.1	0.4	0.1	NA	NA
Curr. Assets	NA	194	165	163	104	65.2	44.9	55.8	NA	NA
Total Assets	NA	322	281	278	198	118	98.0	109	NA	NA
Curr. Liab.	NA	140	112	96.5	49.8	37.9	24.2	35.5	NA	NA
LT Debt	NA	42.7	51.9	32.4	19.2	21.5	26.0	27.6	NA	NA
Common Eqty.	NA	134	117	142	122	57.0	47.8	44.2	NA	NA
Total Cap.	NA	181	169	182	148	80.2	73.8	73.7	NA	NA
Cap. Exp.	NA	16.9	12.7	19.3	13.9	1.8	0.8	NA	NA	NA
Cash Flow	NA	28.9	-23.9	26.0	13.9	12.6	10.2	6.8	NA	NA
Curr. Ratio	NA	1.4	1.5	1.7	2.1	1.7	1.9	1.6	NA	NA
% LT Debt of Cap.	NA	23.5	30.7	17.8	12.9	26.8	35.2	37.4	NA	NA
% Net Inc.of Revs.	NA	5.9	NM	7.3	5.3	7.4	6.3	4.6	NA	NA
% Ret. on Assets	NA	6.3	NM	8.2	6.0	7.5	NA	NA	NA	NA
% Ret. on Equity	NA	15.2	NM	14.8	10.7	18.4	NA	NA	NA	NA

Data as orig. reptd.; bef. results of disc. opers. and/or spec. items. Per share data adj. for stk. divs. as of ex-div. date. Bold denotes diluted EPS (FASB 128). E-Estimated. NA-Not Available. NM-Not Meaningful. NR-Not Ranked.

Office—6040 Bandini Blvd., Commerce, CA 90040. **Tel**—(213) 726-1262. **Chrmn & CEO**—L. J. Wachner. **Pres & COO**—C. G. Staff. **SVP & CFO**—W. H. Brooks. **VP-Fin & Secy**—W. W. Chan. **Dirs**—S. S. Arkin, S. D. Buchalter, J. A. Califano Jr., W. S. Finkelstein, L. J. Wachner, R. D. Walter. **Transfer Agent**—Bank of New York, NYC.**Incorporated**—in Delaware in 1990. **Empl**— 1,211. **S&P Analyst:** Ray Lam , CFA

Avid Technology

3184M

NASDAQ Symbol **AVID**

In S&P SmallCap 600

03-OCT-98

Industry: Computer (Software & Services)

Summary: This company develops, markets, sells and supports a wide range of disk-based systems for capturing, editing and distributing digital media.

Quantitative Evaluations

Outlook
(1 Lowest—5 Highest)
• 5

Fair Value
• 37¼

Risk
• Average

Earn./Div. Rank
• NR

Technical Eval.
• **Bullish** since 7/98

Rel. Strength Rank
(1 Lowest—99 Highest)
• 24

Insider Activity
• Neutral

Recent Price • 23
52 Wk Range • 47¾-18⅝

Yield • Nil
12-Mo. P/E • 16.3

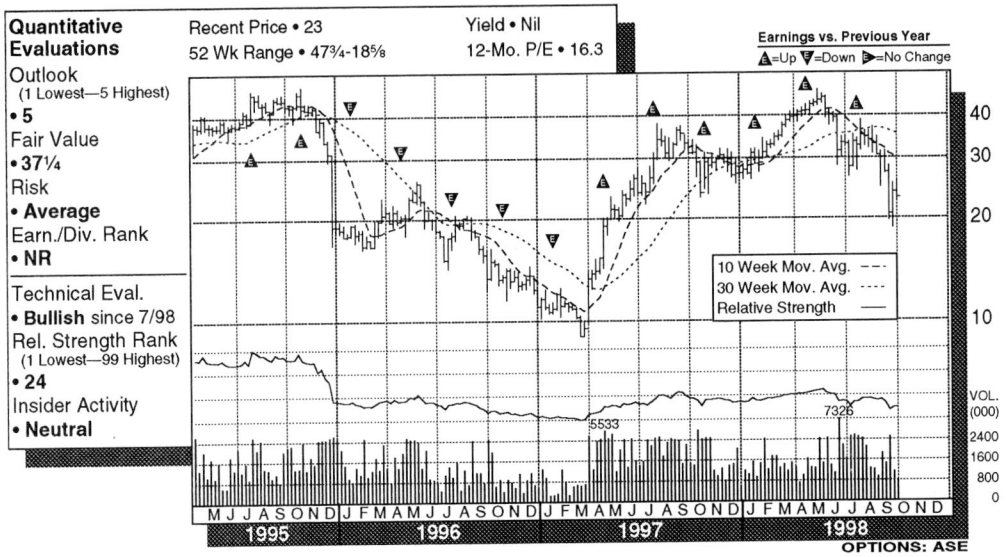

10 Week Mov. Avg. — — —
30 Week Mov. Avg. ·······
Relative Strength ——

OPTIONS: ASE

Business Profile - 14-MAY-98

Avid Technology's editing and effects systems continue to gain wide acceptance by the film industry. In the blockbuster movie "Titanic," Avid's Film Composer system was used extensively to pre-visualize many of the film's effects shots. Also, nine of the 16 feature films premiering at the 1998 Sundance Film Festival were edited on either Avid's Film Composer or Media Composer systems. The company believes that as digital effects in films increase, demand for Avid's products will grow. In February 1998, directors authorized the repurchase of up to 1.5 million company common shares, after completing a 1 million share buyback program in 1997's fourth quarter.

Operational Review - 14-MAY-98

Net revenues in the three months ended March 31, 1998, edged up 0.5%, year to year, reflecting lower revenue in the Asia Pacific region. Margins widened significantly, due to lower material costs, improved service margins and manufacturing efficiency; operating income jumped 472%. Following a 105% increase in other income and taxes at 31.0%, versus 35.0%, net income rose 331% to $7,705,000 ($0.31 a share, based on 13% more shares) from $1,786,000 ($0.08).

Stock Performance - 02-OCT-98

In the past 30 trading days, AVID's shares have declined 30%, compared to a 7% fall in the S&P 500. Average trading volume for the past five days was 154,220 shares, compared with the 40-day moving average of 308,413 shares.

Key Stock Statistics

Dividend Rate/Share	Nil	Shareholders	600
Shs. outstg. (M)	25.0	Market cap. (B)	$0.574
Avg. daily vol. (M)	0.344	Inst. holdings	78%
Tang. Bk. Value/Share	10.33		
Beta	1.34		

Value of $10,000 invested 5 years ago: NA

Fiscal Year Ending Dec. 31

	1998	1997	1996	1995	1994	1993
Revenues (Million $)						
1Q	108.7	108.2	92.04	83.89	37.50	19.80
2Q	112.8	122.9	109.1	98.45	45.10	26.30
3Q	—	116.5	114.7	114.4	54.00	31.00
4Q	—	123.7	113.2	109.9	67.00	35.80
Yr.	—	471.3	429.0	406.6	203.7	112.9
Earnings Per Share ($)						
1Q	0.31	0.08	-1.08	-0.05	0.11	-0.53
2Q	0.37	0.27	-0.17	0.31	0.26	0.09
3Q	—	0.34	-0.32	0.43	0.33	0.18
4Q	—	0.37	-0.23	0.07	0.40	0.27
Yr.	—	1.08	-1.80	0.77	1.10	0.38

Next earnings report expected: NA

Dividend Data

No cash dividends have been paid. The company intends to retain earnings for use in the operation of its business and does not expect to pay cash dividends in the foreseeable future. A shareholder rights plan was adopted in 1996.

A Division of The **McGraw·Hill** Companies

Business Summary - 14-MAY-98

Avid Technology develops, markets, sells and supports a wide range of disk-based systems for creating and manipulating digital media content. Its digital, non-linear video and film editing systems are designed to improve the productivity of video and film editors by permitting them to edit moving pictures and sound in a faster, easier, more creative and more cost-effective manner than traditional analog systems.

Products are divided into the following categories: editing, audio, digital news gathering, newsroom computer systems, graphics and special effects products, and storage systems. Editing products include the Media Composer, a nonlinear editing system designed for professional film and video editors; the Film Composer, a 24-frames-per-second editing system for projects that originate and finish on film; Avid Cinema, a desktop editing product for people with no previous editing experience; and MCXpress, a video editing system for CD-ROM and Internet distribution. Over 75% of 1997 prime time shows, including "ER" and "Home Improvement," were edited on Avid's industry leading Media Composer and Film Composer systems.

Audio products consist of two audio workstations for professional use: Pro Tools, for the radio and music markets, and AudioVision, for post-production work with film and video.

Digital news gathering includes NewsCutter, which en-

ables broadcast news editors to quickly edit hard news, features and news series; AirPlay MP, which allows television broadcasters and cable operators to transmit short-form video to air directly from disks; MediaServer, a workgroup video production server; AvidNet, a local area network configuration providing high-speed communications between news production and playback systems; and CamCutter, which enables users to capture, edit and play digital media.

Graphics and special effects products include Media Illusion, a digital compositioning, layering and special effects software solution; Matador, a two-dimensional post-production paint software system; Elastic Reality, which provides animation, warping and morphing of shapes and images; and Jester, a cartoon ink and paint package designed to accelerate cartoon production.

Storage systems are offered for all of Avid's systems and are used to add media editing or playback capacity, improve image quality, support media sharing and protect media from loss due to hardware failure.

Sales outside of North America accounted for 49% of net revenues in 1997 (40% in 1996).

In March 1997, Avid entered into a strategic alliance with Intel to offer video and audio editing products on Intel platforms. Intel acquired a 6.8% interest in the company for about $14.75 million.

In February 1998, directors authorized the repurchase of up to 1.5 million company common shares.

Per Share Data ($)

(Year Ended Dec. 31)	1997	1996	1995	1994	1993	1992	1991	1990	1989	1988
Tangible Bk. Val.	10.42	10.00	11.84	9.90	7.89	7.11	NA	NA	NA	NA
Cash Flow	2.13	-0.40	1.73	1.97	0.88	0.41	NA	NA	NA	NA
Earnings	1.08	-1.80	0.77	1.10	0.38	0.29	-0.27	-0.84	NA	NA
Dividends	Nil	Nil	Nil	Nil	Nil	Nil	Nil	Nil	Nil	Nil
Payout Ratio	Nil	Nil	Nil	Nil	Nil	Nil	Nil	Nil	Nil	Nil
Prices - High	38	26	49¼	43¾	27½	NA	NA	NA	NA	NA
- Low	9	10⅛	16¾	20½	16	NA	NA	NA	NA	NA
P/E Ratio - High	35	NM	64	40	72	NA	NA	NA	NA	NA
- Low	8	NM	22	19	42	NA	NA	NA	NA	NA

Income Statement Analysis (Million $)

	1997	1996	1995	1994	1993	1992	1991	1990	1989	1988
Revs.	471	429	407	204	113	52.0	NA	NA	NA	NA
Oper. Inc.	55.5	-0.8	47.6	27.2	7.9	5.2	NA	NA	NA	NA
Depr.	25.4	29.6	19.5	10.4	4.9	1.6	NA	NA	NA	NA
Int. Exp.	0.2	0.4	0.8	0.1	0.1	0.1	NA	NA	NA	NA
Pretax Inc.	38.2	-55.9	24.0	17.7	4.6	3.5	NA	NA	NA	NA
Eff. Tax Rate	31%	NM	36%	27%	19%	54%	NA	NA	NA	NA
Net Inc.	26.4	-38.0	15.4	13.0	3.7	2.3	NA	NA	NA	NA

Balance Sheet & Other Fin. Data (Million $)

	1997	1996	1995	1994	1993	1992	1991	1990	1989	1988
Cash	108	93.0	32.8	28.3	38.9	NA	NA	NA	NA	NA
Curr. Assets	301	232	243	121	91.0	NA	NA	NA	NA	NA
Total Assets	357	301	332	148	105	NA	NA	NA	NA	NA
Curr. Liab.	115	86.3	81.0	48.4	23.3	NA	NA	NA	NA	NA
LT Debt	0.4	1.2	3.0	2.4	0.6	NA	NA	NA	NA	NA
Common Eqty.	242	213	248	97.8	81.5	NA	NA	NA	NA	NA
Total Cap.	242	215	251	100	82.0	NA	NA	NA	NA	NA
Cap. Exp.	15.7	28.2	42.4	22.5	11.9	6.4	NA	NA	NA	NA
Cash Flow	51.8	-8.4	35.0	23.4	8.6	3.1	NA	NA	NA	NA
Curr. Ratio	2.6	2.7	3.0	2.5	3.9	NA	NA	NA	NA	NA
% LT Debt of Cap.	0.0	0.6	1.8	2.4	0.7	NA	NA	NA	NA	NA
% Net Inc.of Revs.	5.6	NM	3.8	6.4	3.3	4.5	NA	NA	NA	NA
% Ret. on Assets	8.0	NM	6.0	10.3	5.3	NA	NA	NA	NA	NA
% Ret. on Equity	11.6	NM	8.2	14.5	9.7	NA	NA	NA	NA	NA

Data as orig. reptd.; bef. results of disc. opers. and/or spec. items. Per share data adj. for stk. divs. as of ex-div. date. Bold denotes diluted EPS (FASB 128). E-Estimated. NA-Not Available. NM-Not Meaningful. NR-Not Ranked.

Office—One Park West, Tewksbury, MA 01876. **Tel**—(978) 640-6789. **Website**—http://www.avid.com **Chrmn, Pres & CEO**—W. J. Miller. **SVP-Fin & CFO**—W. L. Flaherty. **Investor Contact**—Cheryl Reault (978) 640-3563.**Dirs**—C. T. Brumback, W. E. Foster, P. C. Gotcher, R. M. Halperin, N. Hawthorne, R. J. Heinen Jr., D. Langlois, W. J. Miller, L. S. Salhany, W. J. Warner. **Transfer Agent & Registrar**—Boston EquiServe, L.P., Canton, MA. **Incorporated**—in Delaware in 1987. **Empl**— 1,599. **S&P Analyst:** Ray Lam, CFA

STANDARD &POOR'S
STOCK REPORTS

Aztar Corp.

262R
NYSE Symbol **AZR**

In S&P SmallCap 600

03-OCT-98 **Industry:** Gaming, Lottery & Pari-mutuel Cos.

Summary: Aztar operates casino/hotels in Atlantic City and Nevada, as well as casino boats in Evansville, IN, and Caruthersville, MO.

Quantitative Evaluations

Outlook
(1 Lowest—5 Highest)
• **3**

Fair Value
• **4⅝**

Risk
• **Average**

Earn./Div. Rank
• **B-**

Technical Eval.
• **Bullish** since 6/98

Rel. Strength Rank
(1 Lowest—99 Highest)
• **21**

Insider Activity
• **NA**

Recent Price • 3¾
52 Wk Range • 9⅞-3⅝

Yield • Nil
12-Mo. P/E • 76.2

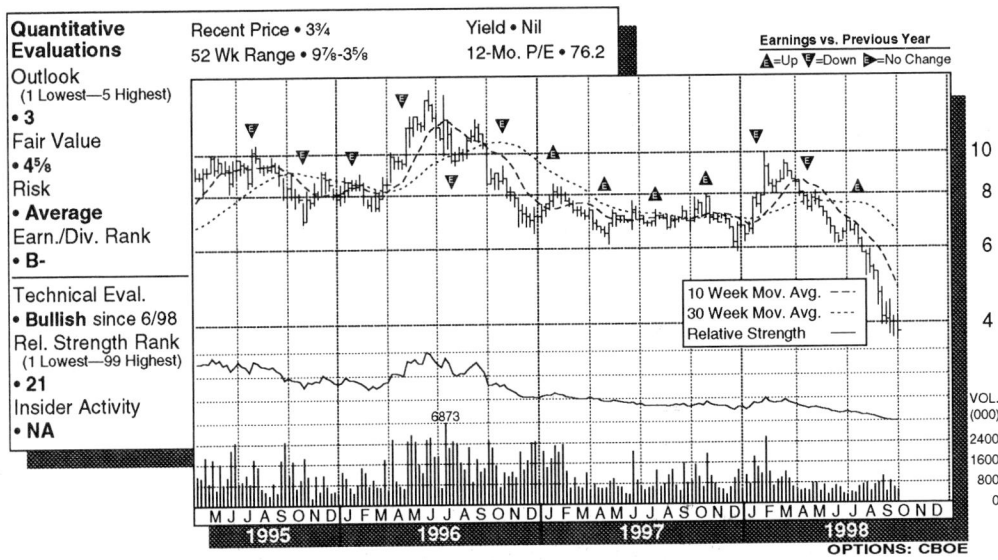

OPTIONS: CBOE

Business Profile - 04-AUG-98

In February 1998, this gaming company said it had obtained an option to buy out its partner in the Tropicana casino/hotel in Las Vegas, and had engaged Goldman, Sachs & Co. to explore alternatives for a major development of that property. AZR signed an 18-month option that would allow it to acquire its partner's 50% interest for $120 million. The Las Vegas Tropicana has a potentially strong location, but posted an operating loss in 1997. In June 1998, AZR said it had completed a financing package that included both the refinancing of previous bank borrowings and the availability of an additional $175 million. In 1998, AZR's earnings are expected to be generated mostly by the Tropicana casino/hotel in Atlantic City, and by a casino boat project in Evansville, IN., where AZR opened a 250-room hotel in late 1996. Aztar operates casino/hotels in Atlantic City and Nevada, as well as casino boats in Evansville, IN, and Caruthersville, MO.

Operational Review - 04-AUG-98

Revenues in the six months ended July 2, 1998, increased 2.5%, year to year. Operating profit was down slightly, but with lower interest expense and smaller equity in loss of affiliates, pretax income gained 20%. In the absence of a tax credit of $2.3 million (about $0.05 a share), net income fell 29%, to $4.3 million ($0.09 a share), from $6.1 million ($0.12).

Stock Performance - 02-OCT-98

In the past 30 trading days, AZR's shares have declined 27%, compared to a 7% fall in the S&P 500. Average trading volume for the past five days was 92,960 shares, compared with the 40-day moving average of 133,838 shares.

Key Stock Statistics

Dividend Rate/Share	Nil	Shareholders	10,600
Shs. outstg. (M)	45.2	Market cap. (B)	$0.172
Avg. daily vol. (M)	0.123	Inst. holdings	43%
Tang. Bk. Value/Share	9.88		
Beta	0.90		

Value of $10,000 invested 5 years ago: $ 5,257

Fiscal Year Ending Dec. 31

	1998	1997	1996	1995	1994	1993
Revenues (Million $)						
1Q	196.8	189.8	180.2	135.6	130.6	122.3
2Q	203.2	200.4	189.5	145.4	135.8	130.8
3Q	—	201.9	204.3	154.9	146.8	144.0
4Q	—	190.3	203.5	137.0	128.3	121.6
Yr.	—	782.4	777.5	572.9	541.4	518.8
Earnings Per Share ($)						
1Q	0.01	0.05	0.02	0.05	0.11	0.04
2Q	0.08	0.07	Nil	0.01	0.17	0.10
3Q	—	0.07	Nil	0.11	0.19	0.13
4Q	—	-0.11	0.43	-0.31	-0.05	0.01
Yr.	—	0.08	0.47	-0.14	0.42	0.28

Next earnings report expected: late October

Dividend Data

Initiation of common share dividends is not expected.

A Division of The McGraw-Hill Companies

Business Summary - 04-AUG-98

Although it operates five casinos in four states, this gaming company is sometimes overshadowed by its larger competitors. Aztar's earnings record is lackluster, but the company is sometimes seen as a candidate to be acquired in a consolidating industry. In addition, AZR's Las Vegas casino/hotel site may be redeveloped.

In total, the five gaming projects operated by AZR include about 285,000 sq. ft. of casino space, 8,900 slot machines, 375 table games, and approximately 5,250 hotel rooms.

Like many other gaming companies, AZR has looked to newly legalized casino markets for expansion opportunities. In Indiana, an AZR casino boat that opened in December 1995 has been generating more than 30% of AZR's operating profit. However, a competing casino boat, closer to potential customers in the Louisville, KY, area, may open in the next year or two. Since AZR's casino debut in Evansville, AZR has opened other facilities there, including a 250-room hotel and a parking garage. In Caruthersville, MO, Aztar opened a smaller-scale casino boat in April 1995. This casino's relatively remote location, plus the existence of loss limits ($500 per customer) in Missouri, have contributed to lackluster results.

Much of Aztar's operating profit is generated by its largest casino/hotel, the renamed Tropicana in Atlantic City. Following a 1996 expansion, the Tropicana is one of Atlantic City's biggest casino/hotels, with 1,624 hotel rooms and about 124,000 sq. ft. of casino space. However, most of the visitors to Atlantic City are daytrippers, whose per capita spending is relatively small. Atlantic City has 12 casino/hotels, and has yet to approach Las Vegas as an overnight destination market.

In the glitter of Las Vegas, Aztar's Tropicana casino/hotel is at the southern end of the famous Strip. The age and island motif of the Tropicana may pale alongside such neighbors as the castle-themed Excalibur or the recently opened New York, New York casino/hotel, but Aztar is considering a major redevelopment at its increasingly prime Las Vegas location. The Tropicana site and facility are leased by AZR from an unconsolidated partnership in which AZR has a 50% interest. AZR has an option to acquire the other 50% interest. In recent times, the Las Vegas Tropicana, which has 1,875 hotel rooms and about 63,000 sq. ft. of casino space, has been providing AZR with no more than a modest profit.

In Laughlin, NV, which is about 85 miles south of Las Vegas, AZR operates the Ramada Express, which has a Victorian-era railroad theme, including a train that runs on the property. The facility includes about 1,500 guest rooms and a 50,000 sq. ft. casino.

Per Share Data ($)

(Year Ended Dec. 31)	1997	1996	1995	1994	1993	1992	1991	1990	1989	1988
Tangible Bk. Val.	NM	3.46	9.40	9.52	9.13	8.84	8.21	8.05	8.28	NA
Cash Flow	1.18	1.64	0.88	1.39	1.10	1.14	0.76	0.24	0.05	NA
Earnings	0.08	0.47	-0.14	0.42	0.28	0.41	0.05	-0.42	-1.18	-0.04
Dividends	Nil	Nil	Nil	Nil	Nil	Nil	Nil	Nil	Nil	NM
Payout Ratio	Nil	Nil	Nil	Nil	Nil	Nil	Nil	Nil	Nil	NM
Prices - High	8½	14⅛	10½	7⅞	10⅛	7⅝	7⅝	8¼	9	NM
- Low	5⅞	6½	5⅝	5⅜	6	4⅝	2¾	2⅜	6½	NM
P/E Ratio - High	NM	30	NM	19	36	19	NM	NM	NM	NM
- Low	NM	14	NM	13	21	11	NM	NM	NM	NM

Income Statement Analysis (Million $)

Revs.	782	777	573	541	519	512	481	508	522	456
Oper. Inc.	119	111	82.0	106	66.2	54.7	35.6	45.1	1.4	35.7
Depr.	51.5	49.4	39.5	37.0	31.6	27.6	27.0	26.5	34.2	24.7
Int. Exp.	62.5	63.1	56.3	52.4	48.9	32.2	32.4	33.4	43.7	24.8
Pretax Inc.	2.3	-2.1	-10.2	18.7	12.4	26.0	2.8	-14.0	-62.2	-1.8
Eff. Tax Rate	NM	NM	NM	10%	8.30%	37%	2.20%	NM	NM	NM
Net Inc.	4.4	20.6	-5.0	16.8	11.4	16.4	2.7	-15.9	-47.7	-1.8

Balance Sheet & Other Fin. Data (Million $)

Cash	46.1	44.1	26.5	52.0	40.0	100	82.2	74.1	99	23.9
Curr. Assets	119	113	73.0	94.0	82.0	158	121	116	149	75.0
Total Assets	1,091	1,120	1,013	915	877	850	638	642	678	705
Curr. Liab.	125	120	102	73.0	74.0	77.0	93.0	94.0	106	100
LT Debt	492	527	496	430	404	378	177	180	181	276
Common Eqty.	444	439	360	357	341	327	311	304	339	296
Total Cap.	943	972	880	821	781	749	520	521	545	581
Cap. Exp.	25.1	120	136	54.0	78.0	24.0	22.0	24.0	116	129
Cash Flow	55.3	69.3	34.5	53.2	42.3	43.4	28.9	9.7	2.1	NA
Curr. Ratio	1.0	0.9	0.7	1.3	1.1	2.0	1.3	1.2	1.4	0.7
% LT Debt of Cap.	52.2	54.2	56.4	52.4	51.7	50.5	34.0	34.6	33.2	47.5
% Net Inc.of Revs.	0.6	2.7	NM	3.1	2.2	3.2	0.6	NM	NM	NM
% Ret. on Assets	0.4	1.9	NM	1.9	1.3	2.2	0.4	NM	NM	NM
% Ret. on Equity	0.9	5.2	NM	4.6	3.2	5.0	0.6	NM	NM	NM

Data as orig. reptd.; bef. results of disc. opers. and/or spec. items. Per share data adj. for stk. divs. as of ex-div. date. Bold denotes diluted EPS (FASB 128). E-Estimated. NA-Not Available. NM-Not Meaningful. NR-Not Ranked.

Office—2390 E. Camelback Rd., Suite 400, Phoenix, AZ 85016-3452. **Tel**—(602) 381-4100. **Chrmn, Pres & CEO**—P. E. Rubeli. **EVP & CFO**—R. M. Haddock. **Treas**—N. A. Ciarfalia. **VP & Secy**—N. W. Armstrong Jr. **VP & Investor Contact**—Joe C. Cole. **Dirs**—J. B. Bohle, E. M. Carson, L. C. Faiss, R. M. Haddock, J. R. Norton III, R. S. Rosow, P. E. Rubeli, R. Snell, V. V. Temen, T. W. Thomas. **Transfer Agent & Registrar**—ChaseMellon Shareholder Services, LA. **Incorporated**—in Delaware in 1989. **Empl**— 10,800. **S&P Analyst:** Tom Graves, CFA

BISYS Group

3280G

NASDAQ Symbol **BSYS**

In S&P SmallCap 600

03-OCT-98

Industry:
Services (Data Processing)

Summary: This company is a leading U.S. third-party provider of data processing and related services to financial institutions.

Quantitative Evaluations

Outlook
(1 Lowest—5 Highest)
• **4⁻**

Fair Value
• **61¾**

Risk
• **Average**

Earn./Div. Rank
• **NR**

Technical Eval.
• **Bearish** since 9/98

Rel. Strength Rank
(1 Lowest—99 Highest)
• **80**

Insider Activity
• **NA**

Recent Price • 41¼
52 Wk Range • 45⅝-29¼

Yield • Nil
12-Mo. P/E • 28.3

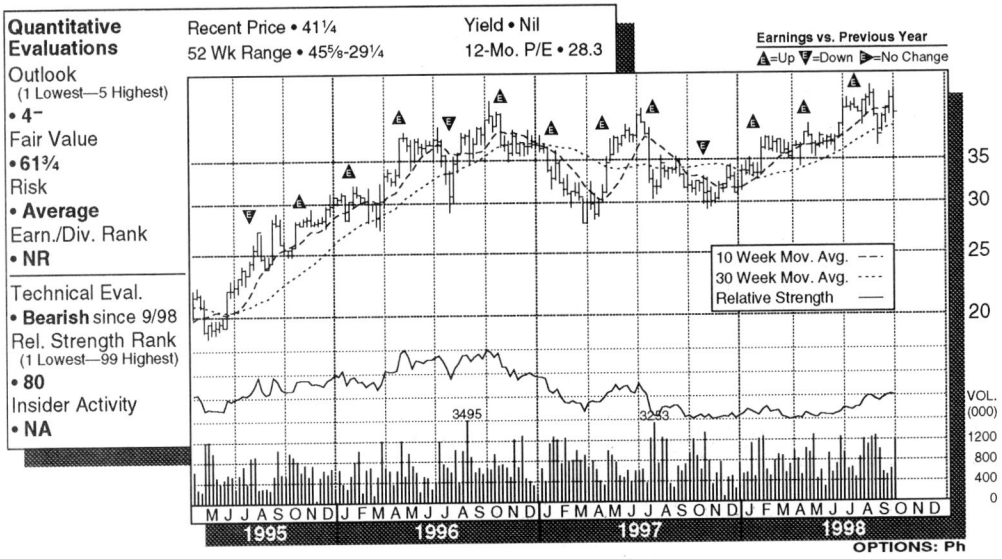

Earnings vs. Previous Year
▲=Up ▼=Down ▶=No Change

10 Week Mov. Avg. — — —
30 Week Mov. Avg. ‑ ‑ ‑ ‑
Relative Strength —

OPTIONS: Ph

Business Profile - 14-SEP-98

Strong demand for outsourcing, internal growth, and acquisitions have helped BISYS become the largest bank mutual fund administrator and distributor, and the largest and fastest growing service partner for small- and mid-sized company retirement plans. The company supports more than 6,000 financial institutions and corporate clients through its strategic business units. In September 1997, a contract with Pacific Horizon Funds for mutual fund administration and distribution services was terminated, which had a negative impact on earnings growth in FY 98 (Jun.). In the first quarter of FY 98, BISYS recorded a $12 million charge related to three recent acquisitions. In August 1998, the company expanded its stock buy-back program to $100 million from $30 million.

Operational Review - 14-SEP-98

Based on a preliminary report, revenues advanced 21% in FY 98 (Jun.) from the previous year. Margins narrowed, and results were penalized by an acquisition charge of $12 million, versus a charge of $1.5 million in the prior year; income from operations fell 5.7%. After a 119% rise in interest income, and taxes at 40.0% in both years, the drop in net income was held to 1.8%, to $40,024,000 ($1.46 a diluted share), from $40,751,000 ($1.55). Excluding the unusual charges, net income would have been $47,250,000 ($1.73), compared with $41,651,000 ($1.58).

Stock Performance - 02-OCT-98

In the past 30 trading days, BSYS's shares have declined 7%, compared to a 7% fall in the S&P 500. Average trading volume for the past five days was 245,120 shares, compared with the 40-day moving average of 222,015 shares.

Key Stock Statistics

Dividend Rate/Share	Nil	Shareholders	3,700
Shs. outstg. (M)	26.6	Market cap. (B)	$ 1.1
Avg. daily vol. (M)	0.149	Inst. holdings	87%
Tang. Bk. Value/Share	5.57		
Beta	0.45		

Value of $10,000 invested 5 years ago: $ 37,078

Fiscal Year Ending Jun. 30

	1998	1997	1996	1995	1994	1993
Revenues (Million $)						
1Q	91.46	72.40	52.27	37.46	25.21	20.20
2Q	91.43	74.80	55.94	39.59	35.33	20.80
3Q	98.95	83.96	65.92	49.06	36.72	23.27
4Q	104.5	87.84	72.92	54.70	39.40	24.01
Yr.	386.3	319.0	247.1	200.5	136.7	88.28
Earnings Per Share ($)						
1Q	0.06	0.29	0.22	0.17	0.16	0.13
2Q	**0.37**	**0.34**	0.28	0.17	0.21	0.15
3Q	**0.49**	0.42	0.38	-0.62	0.25	-0.25
4Q	**0.55**	0.50	-0.50	0.03	0.25	0.21
Yr.	**1.46**	1.55	0.72	-0.27	0.86	0.23

Next earnings report expected: NA

Dividend Data

No cash dividends have been paid on the common shares. The company does not intend to pay cash dividends in the foreseeable future.

A Division of The **McGraw·Hill** *Companies*

Business Summary - 14-SEP-98

An outsourcing pioneer, The BISYS Group, Inc. (BISYS) performs many functions for its financial services clients that could be handled in-house. The company supports over 6,000 financial institutions and corporate clients. It provides image and data processing outsourcing to more than 650 banks nationwide; designs, administers and distributes over 60 families of proprietary mutual funds consisting of over 700 portfolios; provides 401(k) marketing support, administration and recordkeeping services to over 5,000 companies in partnership with 30 of the nation's leading bank and investment management companies; provides growth enabling loan-by-phone solutions, product pricing research and marketing services; and provides outsourcing services for the distribution of insurance products.

The company's operating philosophy is to be a single source of outsourcing solutions to meet client hardware, software, marketing and sales needs. Services are offered through two major business units: Information Services and Investment Outsourcing Services. The Information Service Group provides a full range of computing services using its single product family, TOTALPLUS.

TOTALPLUS provides bank-wide automation which enables community banks to compete with super regionals, and non-bank competitors. All TOTALPLUS host computer functions and client data reside on IBM mainframe (or compatible) computers located at two major data processing centers. TOTALPLUS supports virtually all aspects of a banking institution's automation requirements related to its operation, customer management and product distribution functions, proprietary central site and client site computing solutions. Capabilities include deposit and loan requirements and general financial management of the institution, transaction and data management, electronic banking and customer information management.

Through its Investment Outsourcing Services unit, BISYS integrates its banking and mutual fund expertise to provide a wide array of specialized services. The group takes a consultative approach to its client relationships, offering innovative fee generated solutions. In addition, the group offers 401(k) marketing support, administration and record keeping through financial business partners to client companies.

During the first quarter of FY 97 (Jun.), the company made three separate acquisitions: an enterprise-wide network service company, an outsourcer of group health care and life insurance services, and an outsourcer of long-term health care insurance services. In connection with these transactions, BISYS recorded a $12 million charge in the first quarter of FY 98.

Per Share Data ($)

(Year Ended Jun. 30)	1998	1997	1996	1995	1994	1993	1992	1991	1990	1989
Tangible Bk. Val.	NA	4.61	2.52	1.30	-0.30	3.99	1.09	-0.24	NA	NA
Cash Flow	NA	1.99	1.12	0.21	1.28	0.53	-0.33	0.74	0.26	NA
Earnings	1.46	1.55	0.72	-0.27	0.86	0.23	-2.64	-3.01	-4.32	NA
Dividends	Nil	Nil	Nil	Nil	Nil	Nil	Nil	Nil	Nil	Nil
Payout Ratio	Nil	Nil	Nil	Nil	Nil	Nil	Nil	Nil	Nil	Nil
Prices - High	45⅝	42⅛	43⅜	31⅛	22⅜	24½	20	NA	NA	NA
- Low	32½	27⅞	27¼	17½	17	16½	9⅞	NA	NA	NA
P/E Ratio - High	31	27	60	NM	26	NM	NM	NM	NM	NM
- Low	22	18	38	NM	20	NM	NM	NM	NM	NM

Income Statement Analysis (Million $)

	1998	1997	1996	1995	1994	1993	1992	1991	1990	1989
Revs.	NM	319	247	201	137	88.3	74.5	62.9	54.7	NA
Oper. Inc.	NA	79.0	62.1	16.0	26.0	20.2	12.4	13.1	10.2	NA
Depr.	NA	11.8	10.0	11.0	6.6	4.4	20.2	23.4	22.6	NA
Int. Exp.	NA	Nil	Nil	0.7	1.0	0.3	4.8	7.0	7.4	NA
Pretax Inc.	NA	67.9	30.3	-4.0	18.4	7.4	-21.9	-17.3	-19.7	NA
Eff. Tax Rate	NA	40%	41%	NM	25%	54%	Nil	Nil	Nil	Nil
Net Inc.	Nil	40.8	18.0	-6.4	13.8	3.4	-21.9	-17.3	-19.7	NA

Balance Sheet & Other Fin. Data (Million $)

	1998	1997	1996	1995	1994	1993	1992	1991	1990	1989
Cash	NA	80.0	39.3	7.2	5.9	40.2	6.4	0.2	Nil	Nil
Curr. Assets	Nil	152	104	54.9	28.8	55.3	17.7	11.6	9.3	NA
Total Assets	NA	265	215	165	139	85.1	37.3	56.8	74.1	NA
Curr. Liab.	NA	64.4	64.0	50.0	25.0	13.1	14.0	14.3	10.7	NA
LT Debt	NA	1.6	1.7	Nil	27.4	0.1	6.2	50.6	54.4	NA
Common Eqty.	NA	192	143	115	84.8	70.1	13.6	-28.7	-9.9	NA
Total Cap.	NA	200	150	115	112	70.3	19.8	42.0	63.1	NA
Cap. Exp.	NA	16.0	12.7	9.2	6.8	4.3	1.5	2.7	1.9	NA
Cash Flow	NA	52.5	28.0	5.0	20.4	7.8	-2.9	4.6	1.3	NA
Curr. Ratio	NA	2.4	1.6	0.9	1.2	4.2	1.3	0.8	0.9	NA
% LT Debt of Cap.	NA	0.8	1.2	Nil	24.4	0.2	31.3	120.4	86.1	NA
% Net Inc.of Revs.	NA	12.8	7.3	NM	10.1	3.8	NM	NM	NM	NM
% Ret. on Assets	NM	17.0	9.5	NM	12.2	5.2	NM	NM	NM	NM
% Ret. on Equity	NM	24.3	14.0	NM	17.7	7.8	NM	NM	NM	NM

Data as orig. reptd.; bef. results of disc. opers. and/or spec. items. Per share data adj. for stk. divs. as of ex-div. date. Bold denotes diluted EPS (FASB 128). E-Estimated. NA-Not Available. NM-Not Meaningful. NR-Not Ranked.

Office—150 Clove Rd., Little Falls, NJ 07424. **Tel**—(973) 812-8600. **Website**—http://www.bisys.com**Chrmn & CEO**—L. J. Mangum. **Pres & COO**—P. H. Bourke. **EVP & CFO**—D. R. Sheehan. **Dirs**—R. J. Casale, T. A. Cooper, J. W. DeDapper, J. J. Lyons, L. J. Mangum, N. P. Marcous, T. E. McInerney. **Transfer Agent & Registrar**—Bank of New York, NYC. **Incorporated**—in Delaware in 1989. **Empl**— 2,100. **S&P Analyst:** Mark Cavallone

03-OCT-98

Industry:
Manufacturing (Specialized)

Summary: One of the world's largest makers of aperture masks for color TV tubes and computer monitors, BMC is also a leading producer of polycarbonate, glass and plastic eyewear lenses.

Quantitative Evaluations

Outlook
(1 Lowest—5 Highest)
• **5+**

Fair Value
• **12⅝**

Risk
• **Average**

Earn./Div. Rank
• **B-**

Technical Eval.
• **Bearish** since 11/97

Rel. Strength Rank
(1 Lowest—99 Highest)
• **20**

Insider Activity
• **Favorable**

Recent Price • 5¼
52 Wk Range • 33¼-3¾

Yield • 1.1%
12-Mo. P/E • NM

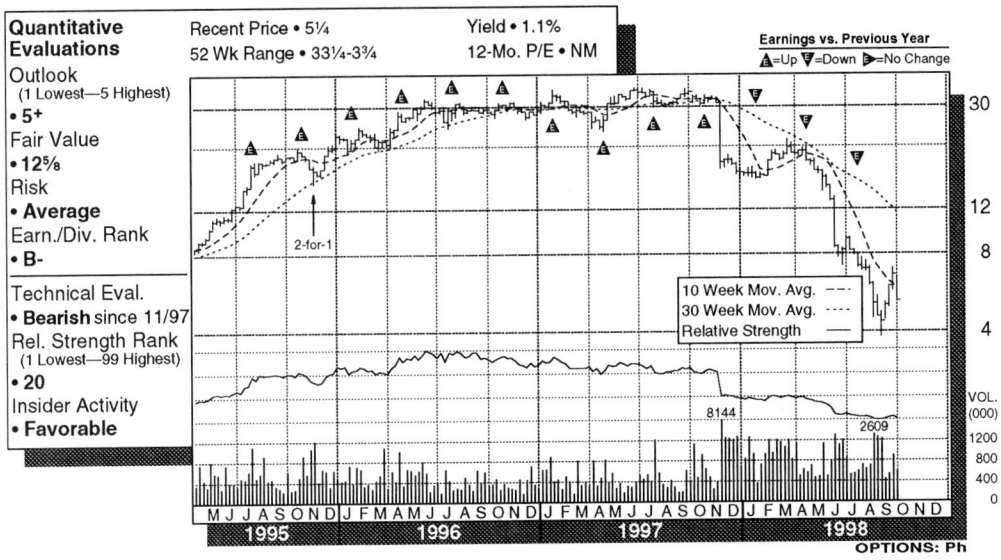

Earnings vs. Previous Year
▲=Up ▼=Down ▶=No Change

10 Week Mov. Avg. - - - -
30 Week Mov. Avg. - - - -
Relative Strength ——

OPTIONS: Ph

Business Profile - 09-JUN-98

This company is one of the world's largest manufacturers of aperture masks for color television tubes and computer monitors. It also manufactures polycarbonate, glass and plastic eyeglass lenses and precision-etched metal and glass products. BMC's strategy is based on continuous process improvement and the expansion of operations through capacity upgrades. In June 1998, BMC said that it expected earnings from operations to fall short of analysts' expectations for the second quarter of 1998 and the full year, reflecting soft market considerations being experienced by the mask operations division. It expected EPS from operations in 1998's second quarter of $0.08 - $0.13 and full year EPS of $0.50 - $0.60.

Operational Review - 09-JUN-98

Revenues in the three months ended March 31, 1998, advanced 3.8%, year to year, as sales of computer monitor masks rose 145% and revenues from high end optical products climbed 25%. Gross margins narrowed on high start-up costs for BMC's new computer monitor mask production line. and with operating expenses increasing at a more rapid pace than revenues, operating income was down 19%. After higher net interest expense, and taxes at 30.9% versus 33.0%, net income dropped 52%, to $3,809,000 ($0.14 a share), from $7,883,000 ($0.28).

Stock Performance - 02-OCT-98

In the past 30 trading days, BMC's shares have increased 2%, compared to a 7% fall in the S&P 500. Average trading volume for the past five days was 116,220 shares, compared with the 40-day moving average of 235,526 shares.

Key Stock Statistics

Dividend Rate/Share	0.06	Shareholders	1,000
Shs. outstg. (M)	26.9	Market cap. (B)	$0.141
Avg. daily vol. (M)	0.133	Inst. holdings	60%
Tang. Bk. Value/Share	2.30		
Beta	0.94		

Value of $10,000 invested 5 years ago: $ 19,456

Fiscal Year Ending Dec. 31

	1998	1997	1996	1995	1994	1993
Revenues (Million $)						
1Q	80.08	77.13	68.30	61.33	52.41	46.02
2Q	84.94	80.26	68.17	69.65	57.31	49.28
3Q	—	79.09	68.16	59.20	53.98	45.21
4Q	—	76.07	75.86	65.17	56.28	54.93
Yr.	—	312.5	280.5	255.4	220.0	195.4
Earnings Per Share ($)						
1Q	**0.14**	**0.28**	0.22	0.17	0.10	0.06
2Q	**-1.42**	**0.42**	0.35	0.27	0.17	0.15
3Q	—	**0.31**	0.25	0.16	0.08	0.06
4Q	—	**0.24**	0.42	0.28	0.19	0.14
Yr.	—	**1.25**	1.24	0.87	0.55	0.42

Next earnings report expected: late October

Dividend Data (Dividends have been paid since 1994.)

Amount ($)	Date Decl.	Ex-Div. Date	Stock of Record	Payment Date
0.015	Dec. 12	Dec. 19	Dec. 23	Jan. 05 '98
0.015	Mar. 18	Mar. 26	Mar. 30	Apr. 13 '98
0.015	Jun. 04	Jun. 15	Jun. 17	Jul. 01 '98
0.015	Sep. 18	Sep. 28	Sep. 30	Oct. 14 '98

A Division of The McGraw·Hill Companies

Business Summary - 09-JUN-98

BMC Industries (BMC), which dates back to 1907, consists of two product groups: Precision Imaged Products and Optical Products. Precision Imaged Products is comprised of two units: mask operations, producing aperture masks, an integral component of every color television and computer monitor picture tube; and Buckbee-Mears St. Paul, a leading domestic producer of precision photo-etched parts. The Optical Products group makes and markets polycarbonate, glass and hard-resin plastic ophthalmic lenses

The principal business of the Precision Imaged Products group is the manufacture of aperture masks, which accounted for 61% of BMC's 1997 revenues. BMC is the sole independent manufacturer of aperture masks outside of Asia. As such, the company is a principal supplier to virtually every non-Japanese picture tube manufacturer. BMC is also engaged in ongoing efforts to develop the manufacturing and technical expertise necessary to produce masks for high-definition television (HDTV). As a result, the company has delivered limited quantities of prototype HDTV masks to customers engaged in HDTV research and development. During 1997, BMC began implementing a strategy for growth through joint research and product development with large end-product manufacturers. BMC was successful in reaching co-development agreements with several leading suppliers to the automotive, healthcare and other industries.

The Optical Products group, which operates under the Vision-Ease Lens trade name, is a leading designer and manufacturer of polycarbonate, glass and hard-resin plastic ophthalmic lenses. Vision-Ease supplies lenses to ophthalmic laboratories and retail dispensers throughout the world, offering a full line of lenses in each material. Bifocal and other multifocal lenses account for the majority of Vision-Ease's sales. With double-digit worldwide market growth, polycarbonate lenses continue to be an area of growth and strategic focus for Vision-Ease. Polycarbonate lenses are lighter in weight and can be made thinner, and thus more cosmetically appealing, than glass and traditional hard-resin plastic lenses. Moreover, polycarbonate lenses absorb harmful ultraviolet rays and are the most shatterproof lenses available.

In May 1998, BMC acquired the Monsanto Co.'s Orcolite operations, based in Azusa, CA, for $100 million. Orcolite, a producer of polycarbonate and hard-resin plastic ophthalmic lenses, will be managed as part of BMC's Vision-Ease Lens subsidiary.

BMC repurchased 1,000,000 shares of its common stock in the open market between January 6, 1998, and January 13, 1998, at an average price of $16.59 per share. On January 23, 1998, BMC's directors authorized the repurchase of up to an additional 1,000,000 common shares.

Per Share Data ($) (Year Ended Dec. 31)	1997	1996	1995	1994	1993	1992	1991	1990	1989	1988
Tangible Bk. Val.	6.43	5.26	4.01	3.06	2.57	1.70	1.42	1.02	0.82	0.64
Cash Flow	1.72	1.60	1.16	0.85	0.73	0.65	0.71	0.40	0.49	0.44
Earnings	1.25	1.24	0.87	0.55	0.42	0.30	0.37	0.09	0.24	0.23
Dividends	0.06	0.05	0.07	0.02	Nil	Nil	Nil	Nil	Nil	Nil
Payout Ratio	5%	4%	8%	4%	Nil	Nil	Nil	Nil	Nil	Nil
Prices - High	35 5/8	32 3/8	23 5/8	8 3/8	5 3/8	3	2 3/8	2 7/8	2 5/8	2 1/8
- Low	15 3/4	19 3/4	7 3/4	4 7/8	2 5/16	1 5/8	13/16	13/16	1 11/16	1 1/4
P/E Ratio - High	28	26	27	15	13	10	6	33	11	9
- Low	13	16	9	9	6	5	2	9	7	5
Income Statement Analysis (Million $)										
Revs.	313	280	255	220	195	181	203	175	164	160
Oper. Inc.	65.4	62.6	46.9	35.0	27.7	21.5	26.5	18.5	19.0	19.3
Depr.	13.3	10.2	8.3	8.3	7.8	8.0	7.6	6.9	5.6	4.5
Int. Exp.	1.3	0.5	0.6	3.1	5.1	6.7	8.2	7.8	7.5	7.3
Pretax Inc.	51.2	52.4	38.9	24.3	15.2	7.7	10.0	3.9	6.6	7.3
Eff. Tax Rate	30%	33%	37%	38%	32%	9.20%	18%	53%	18%	33%
Net Inc.	35.7	35.1	24.5	15.0	10.4	7.0	8.2	1.9	5.4	4.9
Balance Sheet & Other Fin. Data (Million $)										
Cash	2.4	2.5	15.9	14.3	10.9	9.4	12.2	1.9	10.9	17.1
Curr. Assets	122	91.7	83.4	78.8	72.0	68.0	70.0	74.0	68.0	69.0
Total Assets	319	233	182	139	130	119	125	128	116	114
Curr. Liab.	46.9	50.3	50.6	40.0	37.0	33.0	35.0	39.0	29.0	26.0
LT Debt	73.4	16.6	Nil	Nil	18.3	35.4	46.4	56.4	61.7	66.3
Common Eqty.	179	144	108	81.8	58.9	37.5	30.9	22.4	17.9	13.6
Total Cap.	255	163	110	82.8	78.0	74.0	79.0	81.0	81.0	81.0
Cap. Exp.	75.1	54.7	39.2	13.5	7.9	6.8	6.3	10.1	15.6	12.9
Cash Flow	49.1	45.3	32.8	23.3	18.2	15.1	15.8	8.7	11.0	9.4
Curr. Ratio	2.6	1.8	1.6	2.0	1.9	2.1	2.0	1.9	2.4	2.6
% LT Debt of Cap.	28.7	10.2	Nil	0.1	23.5	47.8	58.8	70.0	76.2	81.9
% Net Inc.of Revs.	11.4	12.5	9.6	6.8	5.3	3.9	4.1	1.1	3.3	3.0
% Ret. on Assets	12.9	16.9	15.3	10.3	8.2	5.7	6.5	1.5	4.7	4.5
% Ret. on Equity	22.1	27.9	25.8	19.8	21.2	20.4	30.8	9.1	34.5	43.2

Data as orig. reptd.; bef. results of disc. opers. and/or spec. items. Per share data adj. for stk. divs. as of ex-div. date. Bold denotes diluted EPS (FASB 128). E-Estimated. NA-Not Available. NM-Not Meaningful. NR-Not Ranked.

Office—One Meridian Crossings, Suite 850, Minneapolis, MN 55423. **Tel**—(612) 851-6000. **Fax**—(612) 851-6050. **Website**—http://www.bmcind.com.**Chrmn, Pres & CEO**—P. B. Burke. **VP-Fin, CFO, Secy & Investor Contact**—Michael P. Hawks. **Dirs**—L. D. Altman, P. B. Burke, J. W. Castro, H. T. Davis, J. E. Davis, H. A. Hammerly, J. Ramich.**Transfer Agent & Registrar**—Norwest Bank Minnesota, South St. Paul. **Incorporated**—in Minnesota in 1907. **Empl**— 2,597. **S&P Analyst:** M.I.

Baker (J.) Inc.

3196

NASDAQ Symbol **JBAK**

In S&P SmallCap 600

03-OCT-98

Industry: Retail (Specialty)

Summary: Following the sale of its Parade of Shoes and Shoe Corp. of America divisions, J. Baker operates specialty apparel store chains and licensed discount footwear departments.

Quantitative Evaluations	
Outlook (1 Lowest—5 Highest)	• 4
Fair Value	• 9⅛
Risk	• High
Earn./Div. Rank	• B
Technical Eval.	• Bearish since 6/98
Rel. Strength Rank (1 Lowest—99 Highest)	• 2
Insider Activity	• Neutral

Recent Price • 4
52 Wk Range • 13⅝-3⅞

Yield • 1.5%
12-Mo. P/E • 12.1

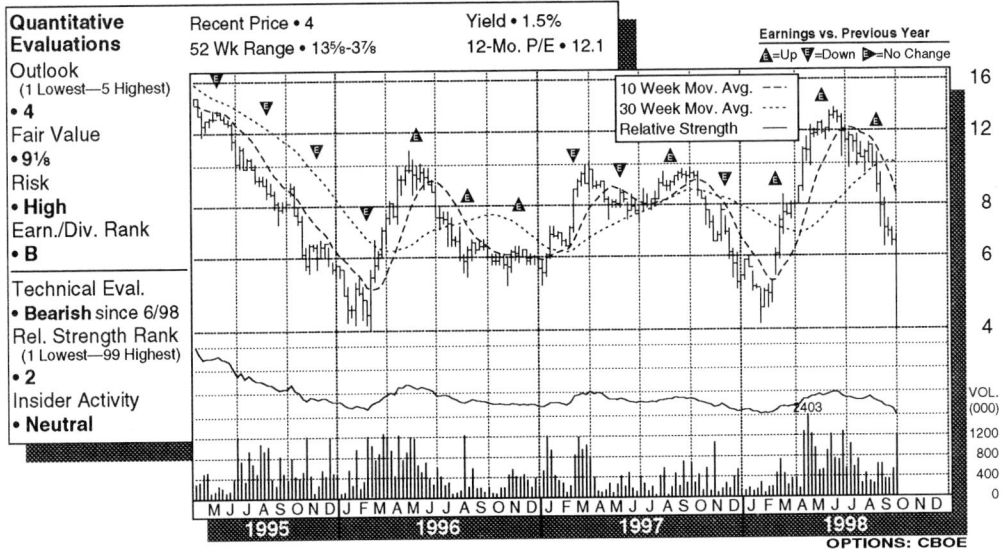

Earnings vs. Previous Year
▲=Up ▼=Down ▷=No Change

10 Week Mov. Avg. ---
30 Week Mov. Avg. ····
Relative Strength —

OPTIONS: CBOE

Business Profile - 11-SEP-98

This specialty retailer specializes in niche markets including big and tall men's apparel and shoes, workwear and various uniforms, and health care apparel. The company also operates discount shoe departments within department stores. BAK recently launched a new Casual Male store model, which enhances merchandise displays and creates a more inviting shopping environment. The new stores have more branded apparel and categorizes its merchandise by product classification. Management intends to open 10 new Casual Male stores and 28 licensed footwear departments during FY 99 (Jan.).

Operational Review - 11-SEP-98

Net sales in the six months ended August 1, 1998, slipped 2.9%, year to year, as the absence of revenues from the divested Shoe Corp. of America and Parade of Shoes divisions was only partially offset by increased apparel sales and expanding demand in the remaining footwear operations. Same-store sales rose 2.6%. Gross profit margins widened to 45.8% from 44.7%, and results were further aided by a 3.2% decline in SG&A costs. Despite higher depreciation and amortization charges and increased interest expense, net income surged 43%, to $3,110,508 ($0.22 a share) from $2,173,119 ($0.16).

Stock Performance - 02-OCT-98

In the past 30 trading days, JBAK's shares have declined 60%, compared to a 7% fall in the S&P 500. Average trading volume for the past five days was 270,900 shares, compared with the 40-day moving average of 112,054 shares.

Key Stock Statistics

Dividend Rate/Share	0.06	Shareholders	500
Shs. outstg. (M)	14.1	Market cap. (B)	$0.056
Avg. daily vol. (M)	0.129	Inst. holdings	76%
Tang. Bk. Value/Share	5.65		
Beta	1.14		

Value of $10,000 invested 5 years ago: $ 2,138

Fiscal Year Ending Jan. 31

	1999	1998	1997	1996	1995	1994
Revenues (Million $)						
1Q	126.6	137.3	195.5	231.4	221.0	193.0
2Q	146.5	143.9	231.8	272.5	256.3	232.5
3Q	—	139.2	222.8	245.3	262.0	224.4
4Q	—	171.7	247.4	271.3	303.3	268.5
Yr.	—	592.1	897.5	1,020	1,043	918.9
Earnings Per Share ($)						
1Q	0.04	0.02	0.06	0.05	0.23	0.18
2Q	0.18	0.14	0.11	0.10	0.52	0.47
3Q	—	-0.10	0.10	-2.98	0.47	0.48
4Q	—	0.22	-8.29	0.05	0.49	0.57
Yr.	—	0.27	-8.02	-2.79	1.71	1.70

Next earnings report expected: late November

Dividend Data (Dividends have been paid since 1987.)

Amount ($)	Date Decl.	Ex-Div. Date	Stock of Record	Payment Date
0.015	Dec. 09	Jan. 15	Jan. 20	Jan. 30 '98
0.015	Mar. 25	Apr. 17	Apr. 21	May. 01 '98
0.015	Jun. 10	Jul. 17	Jul. 21	Jul. 31 '98
0.015	Sep. 15	Oct. 16	Oct. 20	Oct. 30 '98

A Division of The McGraw-Hill Companies

Business Summary - 11-SEP-98

J. Baker, Inc. is a specialty retailer focused on apparel and footwear sales in three niche markets: big and tall men's apparel and shoes; workwear and uniforms for industry and services businesses; and health care apparel. On a proforma basis to exclude sales generated by the divested Shoe Corporation of America and Parade of Shoes businesses, sales contributions and the number of stores by business segment in FY 98 (Jan.) were:

	% Sales	Stores
Casual Male Big & Tall	45%	459
Work 'n Gear	9%	66
Licensed Shoe Depts.	46%	859

Casual Male Big & Tall is the company's chain of big and tall apparel stores providing fashion, casual and dress clothing and footwear for the big and tall man. The chain specializes in a wide range of high quality apparel and accessories for men with waist sizes between 40" and 66" and who are 6'2" or taller. These stores offer private label and some brand name casual sportswear and dress wear such as sport coats, dress pants, dress shirts, a wide variety of casual clothing, and shoes. The stores target the middle income male, and limits the amount of high-fashion-oriented and low-turnover tailored clothing offered, and focuses on

basic items and classic fashion sportswear, therby minimizing fashion risk and markdowns.

The Work 'n Gear division is focused entirely on utility workwear, uniforms, health care apparel and footwear. The chain carries a wide variety of workwear products, including rugged specialty outerwear, work shirts and pants, cold weather accessories, as well as a complete line of health care apparel and uniforms for industry and service businesses. Work 'n Gear stores are generally located in strip shopping centers or are free standing.

The licensed discount shoe division enters into licensing agreements to exclusively operate shoe departments for mass merchandising department stores. Under these agreements, J. Baker operates under the store name and pays a licensing fee based on a percentage of sales. This division sells a wide variety of family footwear, including men's, women's and children's dress, casual and athletic footwear, along with work shoes, boots and slippers. Most of its licensed footwear departments are operated on a self-service basis.

In March 1997, the company sold its Parade of Shoes division to Payless ShoeSource, Inc. for net cash proceeds of about $20 million, and completed the sale of its Shoe Corp. of America division for about $40 million. Proceeds were used to reduce bank debt. During the fourth quarter of FY 96, JBAK disposed of its Fayva shoe chain.

Per Share Data ($)

(Year Ended Jan. 31)	1998	1997	1996	1995	1994	1993	1992	1991	1990	1989
Tangible Bk. Val.	5.41	5.05	12.36	16.13	14.51	12.81	9.88	9.05	8.40	4.57
Cash Flow	1.35	-5.87	-0.45	3.08	2.74	2.13	1.63	1.45	2.00	1.34
Earnings	0.27	-8.02	-2.79	1.71	1.70	1.25	0.78	0.73	1.46	1.00
Dividends	0.06	0.06	0.06	0.06	0.06	0.06	0.06	0.06	0.06	0.06
Payout Ratio	22%	NM	NM	4%	4%	6%	8%	8%	5%	6%
Cal. Yrs.	1997	1996	1995	1994	1993	1992	1991	1990	1989	1988
Prices - High	10⅛	10⅞	15⅞	23⅜	25⅞	21¼	14⅛	22⅛	22⅜	13¾
- Low	5	4	5⅜	14½	15⅜	9⅛	3	3¼	9⅞	6¾
P/E Ratio - High	37	NM	NM	13	15	17	18	30	15	14
- Low	19	NM	NM	8	9	7	4	4	7	7

Income Statement Analysis (Million $)

Revs.	592	898	1,020	1,043	919	532	494	421	399	250
Oper. Inc.	38.2	7.3	47.8	65.0	58.0	38.6	32.0	29.0	33.7	19.0
Depr.	15.1	29.4	32.4	19.0	14.2	9.4	8.8	7.4	4.9	2.8
Int. Exp.	13.5	13.1	11.0	9.7	8.1	8.2	10.4	10.4	8.9	3.3
Pretax Inc.	6.3	-157	-64.2	36.9	36.4	21.1	12.9	12.9	20.1	12.9
Eff. Tax Rate	39%	NM	NM	36%	36%	37%	38%	35%	35%	37%
Net Inc.	3.8	-110	-38.6	23.6	23.3	13.3	8.0	7.4	13.1	8.1

Balance Sheet & Other Fin. Data (Million $)

Cash	4.0	4.0	3.3	4.9	3.6	6.4	2.5	4.5	4.5	1.1
Curr. Assets	192	272	337	374	322	279	198	191	161	89.0
Total Assets	335	382	526	579	502	432	297	283	237	111
Curr. Liab.	69.3	90.2	132	138	135	140	99	81.0	88.0	52.0
LT Debt	186	214	207	205	155	95.9	79.5	97.5	58.4	19.7
Common Eqty.	75.3	72.0	184	223	200	173	105	92.0	85.0	37.0
Total Cap.	261	286	391	434	355	271	193	196	149	58.0
Cap. Exp.	8.8	16.4	28.1	44.5	24.1	11.2	5.5	15.0	16.9	6.6
Cash Flow	18.9	-81.6	-6.2	42.6	37.5	22.6	16.8	14.8	18.1	11.0
Curr. Ratio	2.8	3.0	2.5	2.7	2.4	2.0	2.0	2.4	1.8	1.7
% LT Debt of Cap.	71.2	74.8	5.3	47.1	43.6	35.4	41.1	49.7	39.3	33.9
% Net Inc.of Revs.	0.6	NM	NM	2.3	2.5	2.5	1.6	1.8	3.3	3.3
% Ret. on Assets	1.1	NM	NM	4.4	4.9	3.3	2.7	2.8	7.0	8.0
% Ret. on Equity	5.2	NM	NM	11.1	12.4	8.7	8.0	8.3	20.0	24.2

Data as orig. reptd.; bef. results of disc. opers. and/or spec. items. Per share data adj. for stk. divs. as of ex-div. date. Bold denotes diluted EPS (FASB 128). E-Estimated. NA-Not Available. NM-Not Meaningful. NR-Not Ranked.

Office—555 Turnpike St., Canton, MA 02021. **Tel**—(617) 828-9300. **Chrmn**—S. N. Baker. **Pres & CEO**—A. I. Weinstein. **EVP, CFO & Treas**—P. G. Rosenberg. **Dirs**—S. N. Baker, J. C. Clifford, E. D. Cruce, D. Kahn, H. Leppo, D. Pulver, M. M. Rosenblatt, N. Ryan, A. I. Weinstein. **Transfer Agent & Registrar**—Fleet National Bank, Providence, RI. **Incorporated**—in Massachusetts in 1985. **Empl**—6,630. **S&P Analyst**: R.M.G.

STANDARD &POOR'S
STOCK REPORTS

Baldor Electric

269

NYSE Symbol **BEZ**

In S&P SmallCap 600

03-OCT-98

Industry:
Electrical Equipment

Summary: Baldor designs, makes and sells a diverse line of industrial electric motors and variable-speed drives.

Quantitative Evaluations		
Outlook (1 Lowest—5 Highest) • **1⁻**	Recent Price • 20⅝	Yield • 1.9%
Fair Value • **20¼**	52 Wk Range • 27⅛-19⅝	12-Mo. P/E • 17.8

Risk • **Low**

Earn./Div. Rank • **A**

Technical Eval. • **Bearish** since 8/98

Rel. Strength Rank (1 Lowest—99 Highest) • **65**

Insider Activity • **Favorable**

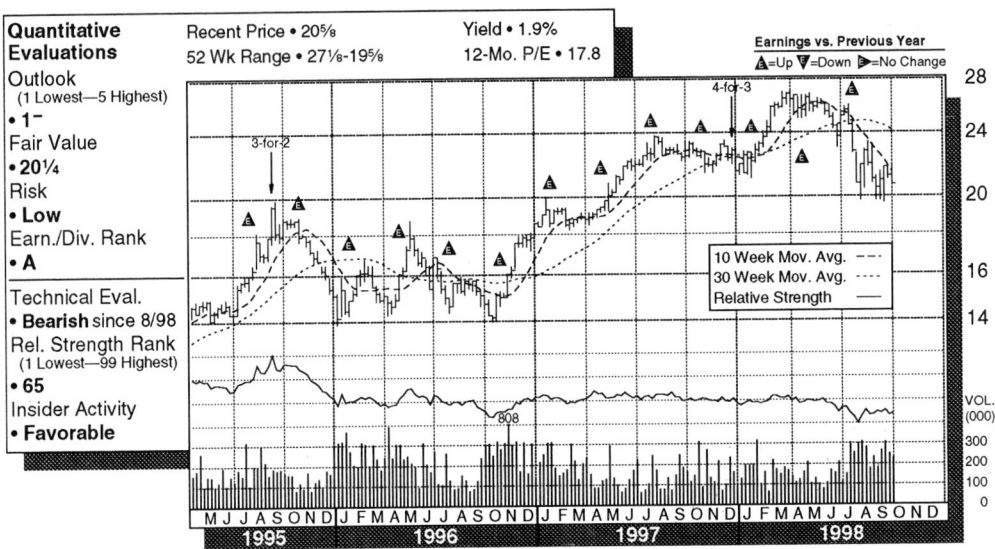

Business Profile - 26-MAR-98

This leading manufacturer of industrial electric motors and drives for a wide variety of markets has experienced six consecutive years of rising sales and earnings through 1997. Contributing to Baldor's strong performance were improved productivity, reduced manufacturing costs and successful new product introductions. The company's solid financial position has enabled it to increase the cash dividend, most recently by 11% in conjunction with a four-for-three stock split. Baldor also authorized a 1.3 million-share (adjusted) stock repurchase program during the fourth quarter of 1996.

Operational Review - 26-MAR-98

Based on a preliminary report, sales increased 11% in 1997 (53 weeks), reflecting broad growth across many product lines, industries and geographic regions. After taxes at 38.5% in both years, net income rose 15%, to $40,365,000 ($1.09 a diluted share, as adjusted for the four-for-three stock split in December 1997), from $35,173,000 ($0.97).

Stock Performance - 02-OCT-98

In the past 30 trading days, BEZ's shares have declined 6%, compared to a 7% fall in the S&P 500. Average trading volume for the past five days was 45,280 shares, compared with the 40-day moving average of 50,708 shares.

Key Stock Statistics

Dividend Rate/Share	0.40	Shareholders	4,900
Shs. outstg. (M)	37.2	Market cap. (B)	$0.770
Avg. daily vol. (M)	0.056	Inst. holdings	32%
Tang. Bk. Value/Share	7.05		
Beta	0.62		

Value of $10,000 invested 5 years ago: $ 24,809

Fiscal Year Ending Dec. 31

	1998	1997	1996	1995	1994	1993
Revenues (Million $)						
1Q	154.2	129.9	121.5	114.6	97.48	86.55
2Q	152.1	141.9	129.9	121.8	104.8	90.67
3Q	—	142.5	125.1	120.0	105.4	90.70
4Q	—	143.6	126.3	116.6	110.4	88.67
Yr.	—	557.9	502.9	473.1	418.1	356.6
Earnings Per Share ($)						
1Q	**0.31**	**0.26**	0.23	0.20	0.15	0.13
2Q	**0.30**	**0.28**	0.25	0.21	0.17	0.14
3Q	—	**0.27**	0.24	0.22	0.18	0.13
4Q	—	**0.28**	0.26	0.21	0.19	0.13
Yr.	—	**1.09**	0.97	0.84	0.70	0.52

Next earnings report expected: early October

Dividend Data (Dividends have been paid since 1938.)

Amount ($)	Date Decl.	Ex-Div. Date	Stock of Record	Payment Date
0.100	Nov. 13	Dec. 24	Dec. 29	Jan. 12 '98
0.100	Feb. 09	Mar. 06	Mar. 10	Mar. 31 '98
0.100	May. 04	Jun. 05	Jun. 09	Jun. 30 '98
0.100	Aug. 10	Sep. 04	Sep. 09	Sep. 30 '98

A Division of The McGraw·Hill Companies

Business Summary - 26-MAR-98

Baldor Electric designs, manufactures and markets electric motors and drives. Additional products include speed reducers, industrial grinders, buffers, polishing lathes, stampings and repair parts. The company has made several small acquisitions; however, the majority of its growth has come internally from broadening its markets and product lines. New products introduced in the past five years accounted for 30% of total sales in 1996. Sales distribution in recent years was:

	1996	1995	1994
Industrial electric motors	76%	78%	80%
Industrial controls (drives)	22%	20%	18%
Other	2%	2%	2%

The AC (alternating current) motor product line ranges in size from 1/50th through 800 horsepower and the DC (direct current) motor product line ranges from 1/50th through 700 horsepower. Industrial control products include servo products, brushless DC and SCR controls, and inverter and vector drives. The combination of these products allows Baldor's customers to purchase electronic controls (drives) from one manufacturer.

Motors and drives are manufactured for general-purpose uses (stock products) and for individual customer requirements and specifications (custom prod-

ucts). Stock product sales represent approximately 63% of the company's business, with most going to customers who place orders for immediate shipment.

Marketing of products is conducted throughout the U.S. and in more than 55 other countries. The field sales organization consists of more than 50 independent manufacturers' representative groups, including 25 in the U.S., with the remainder in Canada, Europe, Latin America, Australia and the Far East. Export and international sales represented 15% of total 1996 revenues, up from 14% in 1995.

Custom products are sold directly to original equipment manufacturers (OEMs). Stock products are sold to independent distributors for resale, often as replacement components in industrial machinery that is being modernized or upgraded for improved performance.

Many of the components used in the company's products are manufactured by Baldor itself, including laminations, motor hardware and aluminum die castings. Manufacturing its own components permits the company to achieve a high degree of control over cost, quality and availability. Baldor's motor manufacturing operations also include machining, stamping, welding, winding, assembly and finishing operations.

In April 1997, the company acquired Optimised Control Ltd. for a combination of cash and Baldor common stock.

Per Share Data ($) (Year Ended Dec. 31)	1997	1996	1995	1994	1993	1992	1991	1990	1989	1988
Tangible Bk. Val.	6.76	5.73	5.69	5.03	4.47	4.08	3.80	3.57	3.29	3.03
Cash Flow	1.61	1.45	1.25	1.04	0.81	0.71	0.64	0.72	0.64	0.57
Earnings	1.09	0.97	0.84	0.69	0.52	0.42	0.33	0.40	0.38	0.31
Dividends	0.36	0.30	0.25	0.21	0.16	0.14	0.13	0.13	0.12	0.10
Payout Ratio	33%	31%	29%	30%	31%	34%	39%	33%	31%	31%
Prices - High	$23^{7}/_{8}$	$18^{3}/_{4}$	$19^{7}/_{8}$	$13^{3}/_{4}$	$12^{3}/_{8}$	$9^{3}/_{8}$	7	$6^{1}/_{8}$	$6^{3}/_{4}$	5
- Low	$18^{1}/_{4}$	$13^{7}/_{8}$	13	$10^{5}/_{8}$	$8^{1}/_{8}$	$6^{1}/_{8}$	$4^{3}/_{8}$	$4^{1}/_{2}$	$4^{1}/_{4}$	$3^{7}/_{8}$
P/E Ratio - High	22	19	24	20	24	23	21	15	18	16
- Low	17	14	15	15	16	15	13	11	11	13

Income Statement Analysis (Million $)

	1997	1996	1995	1994	1993	1992	1991	1990	1989	1988
Revs.	558	503	473	418	357	319	286	294	281	243
Oper. Inc.	85.3	74.6	67.2	55.9	42.6	35.9	30.9	34.1	31.5	26.6
Depr.	19.3	17.3	15.5	13.1	10.7	10.8	10.9	10.4	9.3	9.1
Int. Exp.	2.1	2.7	1.3	1.3	1.0	0.9	1.3	1.2	1.4	0.9
Pretax Inc.	65.6	57.2	52.9	43.2	32.4	25.0	19.4	23.2	21.5	17.5
Eff. Tax Rate	39%	39%	39%	39%	40%	39%	39%	39%	39%	39%
Net Inc.	40.4	35.2	32.3	26.4	19.4	15.3	11.9	14.1	13.1	10.6

Balance Sheet & Other Fin. Data (Million $)

	1997	1996	1995	1994	1993	1992	1991	1990	1989	1988
Cash	9.6	25.8	34.8	34.8	30.2	22.7	12.0	7.7	6.8	6.1
Curr. Assets	219	218	212	181	152	129	117	113	104	103
Total Assets	356	325	313	283	238	212	203	201	186	167
Curr. Liab.	78.2	71.2	67.0	62.6	43.4	32.0	32.4	38.0	33.9	35.5
LT Debt	27.9	45.0	25.2	26.3	22.5	23.2	24.4	25.3	22.5	14.1
Common Eqty.	243	200	211	184	161	145	134	124	115	104
Total Cap.	278	254	246	221	195	180	171	163	152	131
Cap. Exp.	26.9	23.2	23.1	22.1	15.0	11.6	9.8	13.7	14.9	16.8
Cash Flow	59.7	52.5	47.9	39.5	30.1	26.0	22.8	24.6	22.4	19.7
Curr. Ratio	2.8	3.1	3.2	2.9	3.5	4.0	3.6	3.0	3.1	2.9
% LT Debt of Cap.	10.0	17.7	10.2	11.9	11.6	12.9	14.3	15.5	14.8	10.8
% Net Inc.of Revs.	7.2	7.0	6.8	6.3	5.4	4.8	4.2	4.8	4.7	4.4
% Ret. on Assets	11.8	11.0	10.8	10.0	8.6	7.3	5.9	7.3	7.4	6.9
% Ret. on Equity	18.2	17.1	16.3	15.2	12.6	10.9	9.2	11.8	11.9	10.6

Data as orig. reptd.; bef. results of disc. opers. and/or spec. items. Per share data adj. for stk. divs. as of ex-div. date. Bold denotes diluted EPS (FASB 128). E-Estimated. NA-Not Available. NM-Not Meaningful. NR-Not Ranked.

Office—5711 R.S. Boreham Jr. St., Fort Smith, AR 72908. **Tel**—(501) 646-4711. **Website**—http://www.baldor.com.**Chrmn**—R. S. Boreham Jr. **Vice Chrmn**—R. L. Qualls. **Pres & Investor Contact**—John A. McFarland.**Exec VP-Fin, CFO, Secy, Treas**—L. G. Davis.**Dirs**—J. W. Asher Jr., F. C. Ballman, O. A. Baumann, R. S. Boreham Jr., J. A. McFarland, R. J. Messey, R. L. Proost, R. L. Qualls, W. J. Wheat. **Transfer Agent & Registrar**—Wachovia Bank of North Carolina, Boston, MA. **Incorporated**—in Missouri in 1920. **Empl**— 4,000. **S&P Analyst:** M.I.

STANDARD &POOR'S
STOCK REPORTS

Ballard Medical Products 272E

NYSE Symbol **BMP**

In S&P SmallCap 600

03-OCT-98

Industry:
Health Care (Medical Products & Supplies)

Summary: This company manufactures specialized disposable products designed to protect healthcare workers and reduce cost to patients and hospitals.

Quantitative Evaluations	
Outlook (1 Lowest—5 Highest)	• **4⁻**
Fair Value	• **24⁷⁄₈**
Risk	• **Low**
Earn./Div. Rank	• **B+**
Technical Eval.	• **Bearish** since 5/98
Rel. Strength Rank (1 Lowest—99 Highest)	• **73**
Insider Activity	• **Neutral**

Recent Price • 19¼
52 Wk Range • 27⁵⁄₈-17⅛

Yield • 0.5%
12-Mo. P/E • NM

Earnings vs. Previous Year
▲=Up ▼=Down ▶=No Change

10 Week Mov. Avg. – – –
30 Week Mov. Avg. · · · ·
Relative Strength —

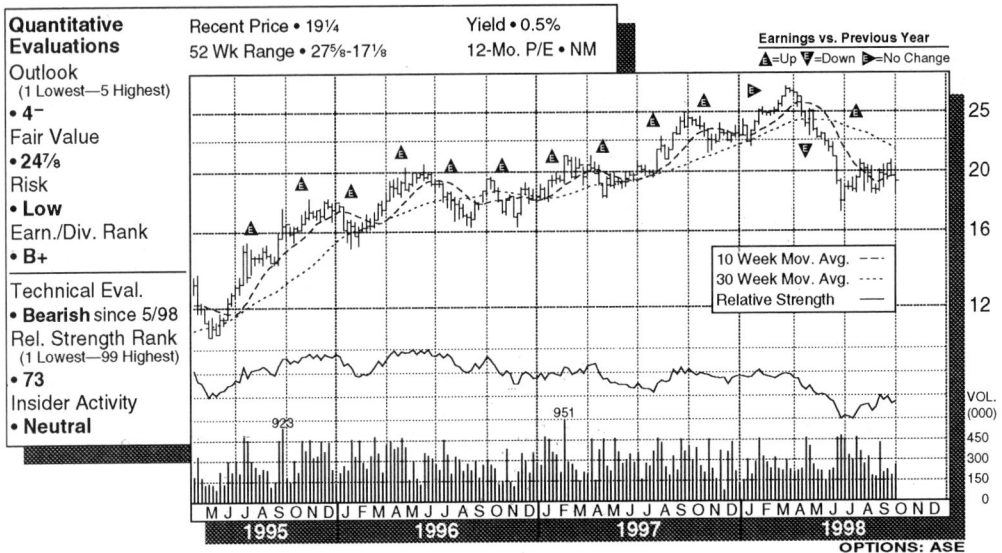

OPTIONS: ASE

Business Profile - 18-SEP-98

This company provides medical products for specialized critical care, operating room and alternate care sites, which it believes will be least affected by changes in the healthcare industry. In response to pressures from hospitals and group purchasing organizations, BMP reduced product prices during the first nine months of FY 98 (Sep.), negatively affecting profitability. In February 1998, the company acquired, for approximately $26 million of BMP common stock, Tri-Med Specialties Inc., a manufacturer of medical diagnostic products. BMP believed that the acquisition would allow it to further penetrate foreign markets.

Operational Review - 18-SEP-98

Net sales in the nine months ended June 30, 1998, increased 15%, year to year, aided by higher sales of existing products, acquisitions, and expansion in international markets. Margins widened, but results were penalized by $2 million of non-recurring charges. After taxes at 39.1%, versus 35.7%, net income slid 1.0%, to $22,899,826 ($0.74 a share, on 2.4% more shares), from $22,688,625 ($0.75).

Stock Performance - 02-OCT-98

In the past 30 trading days, BMP's shares have increased 3%, compared to a 7% fall in the S&P 500. Average trading volume for the past five days was 51,820 shares, compared with the 40-day moving average of 50,438 shares.

Key Stock Statistics

Dividend Rate/Share	0.10	Shareholders	1,300
Shs. outstg. (M)	30.5	Market cap. (B)	$0.586
Avg. daily vol. (M)	0.045	Inst. holdings	61%
Tang. Bk. Value/Share	5.45		
Beta	0.52		

Value of $10,000 invested 5 years ago: $ 8,610

Fiscal Year Ending Sep. 30

	1998	1997	1996	1995	1994	1993
Revenues (Million $)						
1Q	34.15	28.46	23.67	18.51	16.04	14.69
2Q	36.14	30.81	25.81	20.03	18.05	16.29
3Q	38.25	32.22	26.85	21.35	18.45	16.68
4Q	—	33.82	27.20	21.87	12.54	17.08
Yr.	—	125.3	103.5	81.76	65.06	64.80
Earnings Per Share ($)						
1Q	**0.28**	**0.28**	0.20	0.17	0.16	0.15
2Q	**0.18**	0.26	0.22	0.18	0.18	0.17
3Q	**0.29**	0.27	0.23	0.19	0.16	0.18
4Q	—	0.28	0.24	0.20	0.05	0.18
Yr.	—	1.04	0.90	0.73	0.55	0.68

Next earnings report expected: late October

Dividend Data (Dividends have been paid since 1996.)

Amount ($)	Date Decl.	Ex-Div. Date	Stock of Record	Payment Date
0.050	Dec. 02	Dec. 12	Dec. 16	Jan. 05 '98
0.050	Jun. 05	Jun. 12	Jun. 16	Jul. 03 '98

A Division of The McGraw·Hill Companies

Business Summary - 18-SEP-98

This maker and marketer of specialized, niche medical products has grown steadily, from $9.6 million in sales and $800,000 in net income in FY 87 (Sep.) to $125 million in sales and $30 million in net income in FY 97, reflecting a successful strategy emphasizing acquisitions, research and development, and product development.

BMP's is continuing to focus on the specialized critical care, operating room and alternative care sites. Products are sold to more than 16,000 hospitals and other medical care facilities in 47 countries. Sales are generated for hospital use in areas that include intensive-care units, emergency services, anestesiology departments, onocology departments, pain clinics, gastrointestinal and radiology procedure rooms, burn units, respiratory therapy, bone marrow transplant units, general nursing floors and post-anesthesia care units, as well as main hospital operating rooms and outpatient/satellite surgical centers. Sales are also generated for the alternative care market; these sales continue to improve as patients are moved into these locations at an increasing rate.

The company's flagship product in intensive care/critical care is Trach Care, a closed endotracheal suctioning catheter system that lets patients with endotracheal tubes, on ventilators, have their airways suctioned clean while maintaining ventilator support, thus improving patient care. Trach Care is available in sizes from adult to neonatal.

Other BMP products include Easi-Lav (closed gastric lavage system), Char Flo (a charcoal delivery system designed for use in overdose patients) and BAL CATH (catheter designed to obtain samples from smaller airways for use in the lungs for use in the diagnosis of respiratory infections without using a bronchoscope). Foam Care foamers and solutions are designed for use throughout the hospital, but are the company's principal product in the operating room.

The principal products of Medical Innovations Corp. (MIC; acquired in 1993) include the MIC Gastrostomy Tube (which has a unique design that eliminates inadvertent tube displacement and controls gastric leakage), the MIC-KEY Skin Level Gastrostomy Feeding Kit (a device with an intra-stomach balloon, thus allowing for easy replacement) and the MIC Transgastric Jejunal Tube (which allows for simultaneous gastric decompression and jejunal feeding).

Sales growth in recent years has reflected the company's ability to maintain and expand its market share through long-term alliances with group purchasing organizations and distributors, as well as through acquisitions. In February 1998, BMP acquired, for approximately $26 million of common stock, Tri-Med Specialties Inc., a manufacturer of medical diagnostic products.

Per Share Data ($)

(Year Ended Sep. 30)	1997	1996	1995	1994	1993	1992	1991	1990	1989	1988
Tangible Bk. Val.	4.93	4.16	3.51	2.98	2.33	2.09	1.27	0.84	0.59	0.39
Cash Flow	1.28	1.03	0.85	0.64	0.74	0.72	0.79	0.83	0.82	0.81
Earnings	1.04	0.90	0.73	0.55	0.68	0.49	0.36	0.24	0.17	0.12
Dividends	0.10	0.08	Nil	0.06	0.05	0.06	0.02	0.04	Nil	Nil
Payout Ratio	0%	0%	Nil	0%	0%	0%	6%	9%	Nil	Nil
Prices - High	25	20⅝	18⅛	15¼	22⅞	26½	23¼	7⅞	4⅝	3⅛
- Low	17⅞	15	10⅛	8½	11¼	14⅛	6⅞	4⅜	3	1¾
P/E Ratio - High	24	22	24	27	33	52	66	31	28	28
- Low	17	16	13	15	16	28	19	17	17	15

Income Statement Analysis (Million $)

	1997	1996	1995	1994	1993	1992	1991	1990	1989	1988
Revs.	125	104	81.8	65.1	64.8	49.8	38.0	29.1	20.6	15.1
Oper. Inc.	49.5	39.0	30.6	22.2	26.9	20.2	14.4	8.4	6.2	4.1
Depr.	6.9	3.9	3.1	2.5	1.8	1.2	1.0	0.8	0.4	0.4
Int. Exp.	Nil	Nil	Nil	Nil	Nil	Nil	Nil	0.0	0.0	0.0
Pretax Inc.	48.2	40.4	31.7	23.2	28.8	21.5	14.8	9.5	6.3	4.0
Eff. Tax Rate	37%	37%	36%	36%	36%	37%	37%	37%	37%	32%
Net Inc.	30.4	25.6	20.4	14.8	18.5	13.5	9.3	6.0	4.0	2.7

Balance Sheet & Other Fin. Data (Million $)

	1997	1996	1995	1994	1993	1992	1991	1990	1989	1988
Cash	21.1	14.2	45.7	31.4	23.2	5.5	4.0	2.6	0.2	0.3
Curr. Assets	99	81.1	75.0	59.8	52.2	45.5	28.0	21.0	14.2	10.1
Total Assets	186	142	113	92.6	80.3	58.8	36.7	24.9	15.9	11.6
Curr. Liab.	6.8	5.4	4.2	2.2	7.5	4.3	4.4	4.3	2.2	2.6
LT Debt	Nil	Nil	Nil	Nil	Nil	Nil	Nil	Nil	Nil	Nil
Common Eqty.	180	136	109	90.4	72.5	54.2	31.9	20.4	13.6	8.9
Total Cap.	180	137	109	90.4	72.8	54.5	32.4	20.5	13.8	9.0
Cap. Exp.	14.4	15.3	2.8	6.3	4.0	5.3	5.5	2.6	0.7	0.6
Cash Flow	37.3	29.5	23.5	17.3	20.3	14.7	10.3	6.8	4.4	3.1
Curr. Ratio	14.7	14.9	17.8	27.1	7.0	10.6	6.4	4.8	6.5	3.9
% LT Debt of Cap.	Nil	Nil	Nil	Nil	Nil	Nil	Nil	Nil	Nil	Nil
% Net Inc.of Revs.	24.3	24.7	25.0	22.7	28.6	27.0	24.4	20.7	19.3	18.1
% Ret. on Assets	18.5	20.0	19.9	17.1	26.7	28.2	30.1	29.6	28.9	28.8
% Ret. on Equity	19.3	20.9	20.5	18.1	29.3	31.2	35.4	35.4	35.3	37.3

Data as orig. reptd.; bef. results of disc. opers. and/or spec. items. Per share data adj. for stk. divs. as of ex-div. date. EPS and estimates in bold or bold/italic follow FASB 128 definition of Diluted EPS; all other EPS and estimates generally follow earlier use of Primary EPS. E-Estimated. NA-Not Available. NM-Not Meaningful. NR-Not Ranked.

Office—12050 Lone Peak Parkway, Draper, UT 84020. **Tel**—(801) 572-6800. **Chrmn, CEO & Pres**—D. H. Ballard. **VP & Secy**—E. M. Chamberlain. **CFO, Treas & Investor Contact**—Kenneth R. Sorenson. **Dirs**—D. H. Ballard, D. H. Ballard Jr., J. I. Bloomberg, E. M. Chamberlain, P. W. Hess, R. B. Petersen, J. D. VanWagoner.**Transfer Agent**—First Security Bank of Utah, Salt Lake City. **Incorporated**—in Utah in 1978.**Empl**—1,145. **S&P Analyst:** John J. Arege

STANDARD &POOR'S
STOCK REPORTS

BancTec, Inc.

278

NYSE Symbol **BTC**

In S&P SmallCap 600

03-OCT-98

Industry:
Services (Computer Systems)

Summary: BTC provides integrated financial transaction processing systems, workflow and imaging products, application software, and professional services.

Quantitative Evaluations	
Outlook (1 Lowest—5 Highest) • **4+**	Recent Price • 14
Fair Value • **18¾**	52 Wk Range • 28¾-12½
Risk • **Average**	Yield • Nil
Earn./Div. Rank • **B**	12-Mo. P/E • 7.8
Technical Eval. • **NA**	
Rel. Strength Rank (1 Lowest—99 Highest) • **53**	
Insider Activity • **Favorable**	

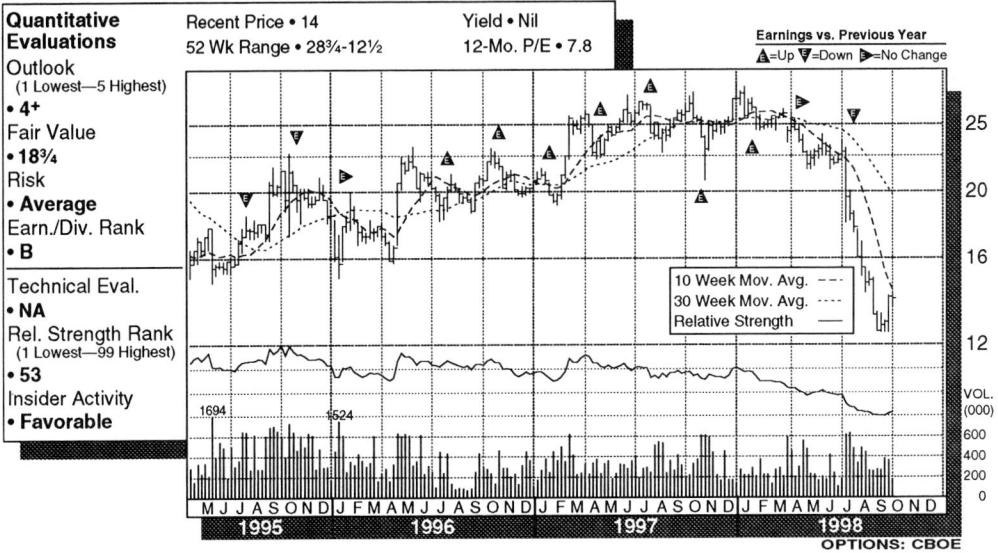

Earnings vs. Previous Year
▲=Up ▼=Down ▷=No Change

10 Week Mov. Avg. ---
30 Week Mov. Avg. ·····
Relative Strength —

VOL. (000)

OPTIONS: CBOE

Business Profile - 20-SEP-98

Banctec attributes slower orders for its transaction processing systems and software through the second quarter of FY 98, to Year 2000 spending commitments, bank mergers and consolidations, and competitive pressures. In early 1998, Banctec said that it planned to shift focus to single-product solutions, from customized development, to improve margins in the systems integration area. The company is aggressively pursuing strategic alliances to leverage its services infrastructure, and build on its excellent service reputation. Banctec recently completed the repurchase of 2.0 million shares under the repurchase program authorized in October 1997.

Operational Review - 20-SEP-98

Revenues for the six months ended June 30, 1998, dropped 1.8%, as a decline in large-scale financial processing system sales, outweighed gains from maintenance and other services. While cost of sales for equipment and software decreased 10%, on the lower volume, cost for maintenance and other services grew 12%, following an increase in network services. Operating expenses increased, as higher SG&A expenses offset a decline in product development charges. After net interest expense, and taxes at 36% in both periods, net income fell 15%, to $17.6 million ($0.82 a share), from $20.6 million ($0.94).

Stock Performance - 02-OCT-98

In the past 30 trading days, BTC's shares have declined 6%, compared to a 7% fall in the S&P 500. Average trading volume for the past five days was 35,320 shares, compared with the 40-day moving average of 61,921 shares.

Key Stock Statistics

Dividend Rate/Share	Nil	Shareholders	2,900
Shs. outstg. (M)	20.9	Market cap. (B)	$0.292
Avg. daily vol. (M)	0.062	Inst. holdings	76%
Tang. Bk. Value/Share	8.09		
Beta	0.40		

Value of $10,000 invested 5 years ago: $ 7,241

Fiscal Year Ending Dec. 31

	1998	1997	1996	1995	1994	1993
Revenues (Million $)						
1Q	142.4	142.3	140.1	—	69.47	54.88
2Q	145.9	151.3	134.0	124.7	73.23	53.34
3Q	—	150.5	136.4	134.3	77.80	59.54
4Q	—	159.3	143.5	125.0	77.10	79.80
Yr.	—	603.5	554.0	384.0	297.5	247.5
Earnings Per Share ($)						
1Q	0.46	0.46	0.42	—	0.33	0.30
2Q	0.36	0.48	0.45	0.18	0.36	0.30
3Q	—	0.48	0.45	0.23	0.40	0.38
4Q	—	0.50	0.47	-3.02	-3.02	0.48
Yr.	—	1.92	1.76	-2.63	1.12	1.45

Next earnings report expected: late October

Dividend Data

No cash has been paid. The company intends to continue a policy of retaining earnings for operations and planned expansion of its business or to repurchase its common stock. A three-for-two stock split was effected in March 1993.

A Division of The McGraw-Hill Companies

Business Summary - 20-SEP-98

BancTec (BTC) started out in 1972 by developing and manufacturing check sorting and other banking-related systems for the banking industry. Fast-forward to the high-tech world of 1998: BancTec is now a provider of complete financial transaction processing solutions for customers such as the Federal Reserve, GTE, NatWest, NationsBank and Citicorp. As an example of the technological leadership it has developed in its field, in April 1997, BTC introduced its release of the fastest document scanner available in the market, with a processing speed of 220 documents per minute.

BTC produces systems solutions, software products and equipment, offers network management services and equipment maintenance, and operates service bureau facilities. BancTec has three main divisions: U.S. Banking and Commercial Systems (including Plexus), North American Service and Manufacturing, and Support Products.

In the U.S. Banking and Commercial division, BTC focuses on financial document processing systems (sold to banks, phone companies, utilities, and retailers); image archival and retrieval systems (serving high-volume document processors); system solutions and products for banks; software products for electronic funds transfer (EFT) and point of sale (for retailers, groceries, and financial institutions), and outsourcing document and electronic financial transactions and data processing.

The company's TRACE products, can process documents in excess of 2,000 a minute. The ImageFIRST OpenArchive allows companies to archive tons of financial documents and transactions extremely quickly. BancTec provides BANKER-II, ACCESS, and PODExpress products to banks (POD means proof of deposit). Banks also use the company's CheckMender, which automatically applies HeatStrip material to damaged checks.

BancTec provides large companies with LAN (Local Area Network) and PC hardware support and services in the areas of systems integration, asset management, help desk, and installation coordination.

In April 1997, Plexus announced that, with the addition of its Object/Storage Management Suite (for storage and retrieval of documents) software, the entire Plexus program is now available on Microsoft Windows. Plexus also integrated its Document Image Processing (DIP), Computer Output to Laser Disc (COLD), and Document Management technologies into a single environment called ImageFIRST Office software. Plexus is also working with Meta Software Corp. to link its workflow products to Meta's popular graphical business process reengineering tools.

In May 1997, the company sold $150 million of 7.5% Senior Notes, due June 1, 2008, in a Rule 144A private offering. Proceeds from the offering were used to retire a $105 million bank debt, with the remaining proceeds to be used for other requirements.

Per Share Data ($) (Year Ended Dec. 31)	1997	1996	1995	1994	1993	1992	1991	1990	1989	1988
Tangible Bk. Val.	7.93	5.35	3.17	4.65	3.41	6.41	5.42	8.57	7.45	3.37
Cash Flow	3.56	3.62	-0.14	3.29	3.14	2.65	2.49	2.01	2.09	1.43
Earnings	1.92	1.79	-2.63	1.12	1.45	1.32	1.18	1.08	1.06	0.83
Dividends	Nil	Nil	Nil	Nil	Nil	Nil	Nil	Nil	Nil	Nil
Payout Ratio	Nil	Nil	Nil	Nil	Nil	Nil	Nil	Nil	Nil	Nil
Prices - High	$28\frac{3}{4}$	$23\frac{1}{4}$	$22\frac{3}{4}$	$27\frac{1}{4}$	$24\frac{1}{4}$	$19\frac{7}{8}$	$11\frac{3}{8}$	16	$13\frac{1}{8}$	$7\frac{3}{4}$
- Low	$19\frac{1}{8}$	15	$14\frac{3}{4}$	$18\frac{1}{4}$	$15\frac{1}{2}$	$11\frac{1}{8}$	5	$6\frac{1}{2}$	$6\frac{3}{4}$	$4\frac{1}{4}$
P/E Ratio - High	15	13	NM	24	17	15	10	15	12	9
- Low	10	8	NM	16	11	8	4	6	6	5
Income Statement Analysis (Million $)										
Revs.	604	554	384	298	248	234	191	184	186	124
Oper. Inc.	114	102	-13.3	52.1	44.3	40.6	35.6	27.9	28.2	14.4
Depr.	40.0	37.9	50.6	24.2	18.8	14.5	13.0	9.2	10.1	5.7
Int. Exp.	7.7	7.9	7.3	5.7	1.9	2.2	3.7	4.8	6.3	1.8
Pretax Inc.	66.6	58.0	-70.7	19.8	22.9	21.1	18.7	14.6	12.2	8.6
Eff. Tax Rate	36%	36%	NM	43%	40%	40%	38%	27%	14%	11%
Net Inc.	42.6	37.1	-53.5	12.5	16.3	14.4	11.7	10.7	10.5	7.7
Balance Sheet & Other Fin. Data (Million $)										
Cash	21.7	27.1	26.8	11.1	12.6	25.3	7.8	6.3	16.7	11.7
Curr. Assets	291	275	236	156	137	117	97.5	87.0	91.8	96.3
Total Assets	502	467	440	307	276	195	173	153	157	149
Curr. Liab.	224	187	189	124	90.6	66.9	54.4	45.2	49.9	44.8
LT Debt	11.9	65.9	83.0	42.5	50.6	12.2	19.6	27.4	34.4	44.2
Common Eqty.	261	205	156	137	128	110	92.3	78.9	70.0	58.1
Total Cap.	272	271	239	180	180	126	117	106	104	102
Cap. Exp.	60.6	40.0	29.9	26.7	24.8	15.2	16.1	13.7	10.9	5.9
Cash Flow	82.6	75.0	-2.9	36.7	35.2	28.8	24.7	19.9	20.6	13.4
Curr. Ratio	1.3	1.5	1.2	1.3	1.5	1.7	1.8	1.9	1.8	2.1
% LT Debt of Cap.	4.3	24.3	34.6	23.6	28.1	9.7	16.8	25.8	33.0	43.2
% Net Inc.of Revs.	7.1	6.7	NM	4.2	6.6	6.1	6.1	5.8	5.6	6.2
% Ret. on Assets	8.8	8.2	NM	4.3	6.9	7.5	7.1	7.0	6.7	6.8
% Ret. on Equity	18.3	20.6	NM	9.5	13.5	13.6	13.5	14.5	16.1	14.1

Data as orig. reptd.; bef. results of disc. opers. and/or spec. items. Per share data adj. for stk. divs. as of ex-div. date. Nine mos. in 1995. Yrs. ended Mar. 31 of the foll. cal. yr. prior to 1995. Bold denotes diluted EPS (FASB 128). E-Estimated. NA-Not Available. NM-Not Meaningful. NR-Not Ranked.

Reincorporated— in Delaware in 1987. **Office**—4851 LBJ Freeway, Dallas, TX 75244. **Tel**—(972) 450-7700. **Website**—http://www.banctec.com **Chrmn & CEO**—G. N. Clark, Jr. **EVP**—W. E. Bassett. **VP, CFO, Treas & Investor Contact**—Raj Rajaji. **SVP & Secy**—T. V. Mongan. **Dirs**—G. N. Clark, Jr., M. E. Faherty, P. J. Ferri, R. Fulgham, T. G. Kamp, A. A. Meitz, M. A. Stone, N. A. Stuart, Jr. **Transfer Agent & Registrar**—ChaseMellon Shareholder Services, NYC. **Empl**— 3,800. **S&P Analyst:** A. Bensinger

03-OCT-98 Industry:
Electric Companies

Summary: This company, Maine's second largest electric utility, serves about 105,000 customers in the eastern and east coastal parts of the state.

Quantitative Evaluations

Outlook
(1 Lowest—5 Highest)
- **NA**

Fair Value
- **NA**

Risk
- **Low**

Earn./Div. Rank
- **B**

Technical Eval.
- **Bullish** since 1/98

Rel. Strength Rank
(1 Lowest—99 Highest)
- **95**

Insider Activity
- **Neutral**

Recent Price • 9¾   Yield • Nil
52 Wk Range • 10⅞-5   12-Mo. P/E • 21.8

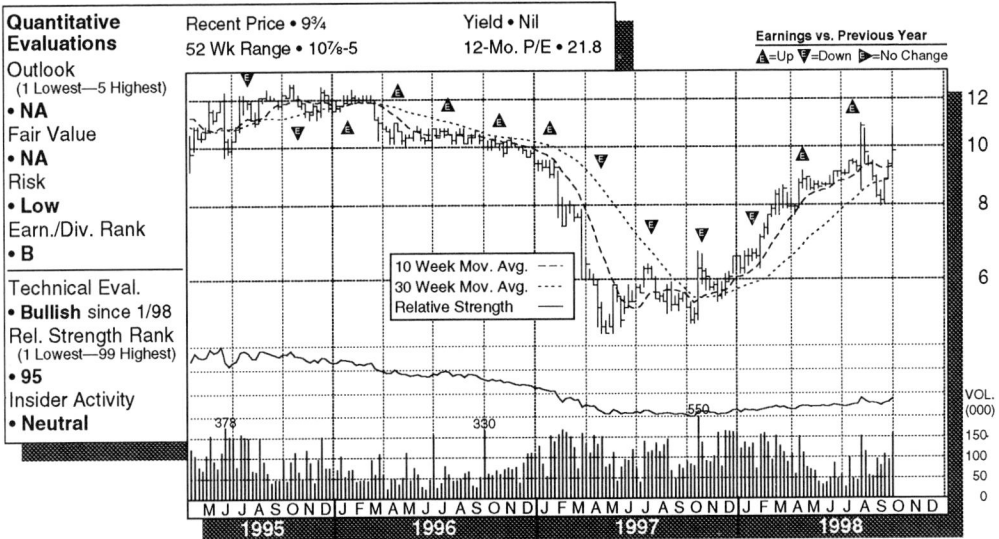

Earnings vs. Previous Year
▲=Up ▼=Down ▶=No Change

10 Week Mov. Avg. – – –
30 Week Mov. Avg. · · · ·
Relative Strength ——

Business Profile - 09-APR-98

The company has recorded very little growth in energy sales in recent periods, as the economy in its service area remains sluggish. Efforts to increase revenues include innovative pricing and marketing, as well as various diversification initiatives. The major factor affecting the company's financial results in 1997 was the experience at Maine Yankee, a nuclear power plant in which the company owns a 7% interest, which historically provided low-cost energy to the company and its New England utility owners. Beginning in late 1995, Maine Yankee was plagued by regulatory and operational difficulties, causing significant increases in costs and causing its owners to incur significantly higher costs for replacement power during periods that the plant did not operate. Maine Yankee did not operate at all in 1997, and in August its owners decided to permanently close the plant.

Operational Review - 09-APR-98

Revenues were virtually unchanged in 1997. The company reported a loss of $0.24 per common share for the year, versus earnings of $1.33 in 1996, reflecting significantly higher costs for replacement power during periods that the Maine Yankee plant did not operate. In addition, in the fourth quarter, the company recorded a one-time charge of $1.8 million (about $0.15 per common share, after taxes) related to certain Maine Yankee costs.

Stock Performance - 02-OCT-98

In the past 30 trading days, BGR's shares have increased 5%, compared to a 7% fall in the S&P 500. Average trading volume for the past five days was 48,300 shares, compared with the 40-day moving average of 21,367 shares.

Key Stock Statistics

Dividend Rate/Share	Nil	Shareholders	7,700
Shs. outstg. (M)	7.4	Market cap. (B)	$0.072
Avg. daily vol. (M)	0.026	Inst. holdings	20%
Tang. Bk. Value/Share	15.35		
Beta	0.57		

Value of $10,000 invested 5 years ago: $ 7,202

Fiscal Year Ending Dec. 31

	1998	1997	1996	1995	1994	1993
Revenues (Million $)						
1Q	49.10	48.18	48.16	48.30	46.40	49.70
2Q	46.60	42.24	43.15	43.70	39.70	40.50
3Q	—	47.56	47.35	46.02	42.60	43.50
4Q	—	49.36	48.71	46.93	45.50	45.00
Yr.	—	187.3	187.4	184.9	174.1	178.0
Earnings Per Share ($)						
1Q	0.28	0.05	0.51	0.40	0.11	0.46
2Q	0.27	-0.19	0.32	-0.29	0.22	0.42
3Q	—	-0.07	0.26	0.05	0.37	0.46
4Q	—	-0.03	0.24	0.20	0.12	-0.71
Yr.	—	-0.24	1.33	0.36	0.84	0.63

Next earnings report expected: mid October

Dividend Data (Dividends have been paid since 1925.)
No dividends have been paid since 1996.

A Division of The **McGraw·Hill** *Companies*

STANDARD
&POOR'S
STOCK REPORTS

Bangor Hydro-Electric Company

279

03-OCT-98

Business Summary - 09-APR-98

Despite its name, this electric utility company (the second largest in Maine) obtained only 13% of its electric generation in 1997 from hydroelectric sources. More than half of its power requirements are purchased from the New England Power Pool and others. About 19% of its power in 1996 was supplied by the Maine Yankee nuclear power plant, in which it has a 7% ownership interest. Maine Yankee has been shut down because of safety and other concerns since December 1996; the only thing it is generating right now is static for BGR and the other co-owners.

BGR serves some 105,000 customers in a 5,275 sq. mi. area in eastern and east coastal Maine. Counties served include Penobscot, Hancock, Washington, Waldo, Piscataquis and Aroostook. BGR also sells energy to other utilities for resale.

In 1997, 31% of the company's kilowatt hour (kwh) sales were to residential customers, 30% to commercial customers, and 39% to industrial customers. The maximum peak electric demand experienced during the 1997-98 winter was about 277.1 megawatts (mw), on December 15, 1997. At that time, the company had about 338 mw of generating capacity and firm purchased power, comprised of 104 mw from company-owned generating units, 9.6 mw from Hydro Quebec, 55 mw from nonutility power producers and 170 mw from short-term economy purchases.

Following a year-long shutdown for repairs to the steam generators in 1995, Maine Yankee came under intense regulatory scrutiny in a series of events beginning in December 1995 with an anonymous letter about an allegedly faulty computer program. The events led to a number of investigations by Maine Yankee's primary licensing authority, the U.S. Nuclear Regulatory Commission, and by Maine Yankee itself. Civil enforcement penalties have been initiated by the NRC to impose monetary penalties on Maine Yankee for alleged violations of regulations. The NRC has also referred certain issues to the U.S. Department of Justice for further investigation, which could result in further civil or criminal penalties. In August 1997, Maine Yankee's directors decided to permanently close the plant. The planned closing relieved BGR of certain costs it otherwise would have incurred in 1997; however, the company's need to purchase replacement power will continue.

Bangor Gas, a joint venture with Energy Pacific, is building a natural gas distribution system to serve the greater Bangor area.

Per Share Data ($)

(Year Ended Dec. 31)	1997	1996	1995	1994	1993	1992	1991	1990	1989	1988
Tangible Bk. Val.	14.34	14.71	14.13	14.50	15.09	15.17	14.86	15.16	14.89	14.21
Earnings	-0.24	1.33	0.36	0.84	0.63	1.60	1.33	1.52	1.91	1.69
Dividends	Nil	0.72	0.87	1.32	1.32	1.32	1.29	1.25	1.18	1.10
Payout Ratio	Nil	54%	NM	163%	223%	83%	105%	82%	62%	65%
Prices - High	9½	12½	12⅞	19	24⅛	20¼	18⅛	16¾	16¾	15¾
- Low	4⅞	9¼	9⅛	9⅜	17⅞	16¾	14¼	13⅞	13½	12½
P/E Ratio - High	NM	9	36	23	38	13	14	11	9	9
- Low	NM	7	25	11	28	10	11	9	7	7

Income Statement Analysis (Million $)

	1997	1996	1995	1994	1993	1992	1991	1990	1989	1988
Revs.	187	187	185	174	178	177	147	134	121	114
Depr.	11.9	7.4	6.5	5.4	4.8	4.1	3.8	4.2	4.3	4.4
Maint.	32.5	32.4	35.7	33.5	29.5	27.0	25.3	23.9	22.4	20.2
Fxd. Chgs. Cov.	0.9	1.5	1.2	1.7	1.4	2.3	NA	NA	NA	NA
Constr. Credits	0.8	1.1	1.3	2.6	5.3	2.4	NA	NA	NA	NA
Eff. Tax Rate	NM	30%	29%	33%	28%	37%	32%	36%	36%	37%
Net Inc.	-0.4	11.3	4.3	7.5	5.3	10.3	8.2	8.4	8.8	7.8

Balance Sheet & Other Fin. Data (Million $)

	1997	1996	1995	1994	1993	1992	1991	1990	1989	1988
Gross Prop.	353	342	324	304	282	256	232	210	188	NA
Cap. Exp.	17.5	18.8	19.5	21.5	37.6	24.3	NA	NA	NA	NA
Net Prop.	256	254	242	228	210	188	166	146	127	NA
Capitalization:										
LT Debt	222	274	288	116	119	101	82.0	99	67.0	61.0
% LT Debt	65	69	71	48	51	50	44	53	44	NA
Pfd.	13.9	15.4	16.8	18.5	19.9	19.8	19.8	19.8	19.7	NA
% Pfd.	4.00	3.90	4.20	7.70	8.60	9.80	11	11	13	NA
Common	107	108	103	106	94.0	82.0	80.0	68.0	66.0	63.0
% Common	31	27	25	44	40	40	44	36	43	NA
Total Cap.	414	472	480	311	301	245	225	216	187	158
% Oper. Ratio	75.3	80.7	87.2	90.1	90.6	89.5	NA	NA	NA	NA
% Earn. on Net Prop.	9.4	14.7	10.1	7.9	8.4	10.5	NA	NA	NA	NA
% Return On Revs.	NM	6.1	2.4	4.3	3.0	5.8	5.6	6.2	7.3	6.8
% Return On Invest. Capital	5.1	9.1	7.6	6.1	5.2	8.6	NA	NA	NA	NA
% Return On Com. Equity	NM	9.1	2.5	5.5	3.9	10.6	8.2	10.1	13.1	12.1

Data as orig. reptd.; bef. results of disc opers. and/or spec. items. Per share data adj. for stk. divs. as of ex-div. date. Bold denotes diluted EPS (FASB 128). E-Estimated. NA-Not Available. NM-Not Meaningful. NR-Not Ranked.

Office—33 State St. (P.O. Box 932), Bangor, ME 04402-0932. **Tel**—(207) 945-5621. **Fax**—(207) 990-6954. **Pres & CEO**—R. S. Briggs. **SVP & COO**—C. R. Lee. **VP-Fin, Treas & Investor Contact**—Frederick S. Samp. **Secy**—A. Landry. **Dirs**—R. S. Briggs, W. C. Bullock Jr., J. J. Bush, D. M. Carlisle, A. E. Cianchette, G. C. Eames, M. M. Kane, N. A. Ledwin, R. Lee. **Transfer Agent & Registrar**—ChaseMellon Shareholder Services, Ridgefield Park, NJ. **Incorporated**—in Maine in 1924. **Empl**— 421. **S&P Analyst:** C.F.B.

Banknorth Group

3218J

NASDAQ Symbol **BKNG**

In S&P SmallCap 600

03-OCT-98

Industry:
Banks (Regional)

Summary: This New England-based multibank holding company, with total assets of $3 billion, owns seven community banks, a mortgage company, and an investment management firm.

Quantitative Evaluations	
Outlook (1 Lowest—5 Highest)	**• 3+**
Fair Value	**• 31⅛**
Risk	**• Low**
Earn./Div. Rank	**• B**
Technical Eval.	**• Bullish** since 9/98
Rel. Strength Rank (1 Lowest—99 Highest)	**• 53**
Insider Activity	**• NA**

Recent Price • 28¼
52 Wk Range • 42¾-26

Yield • 2.3%
12-Mo. P/E • 14.1

Earnings vs. Previous Year
▲=Up ▼=Down ▶=No Change

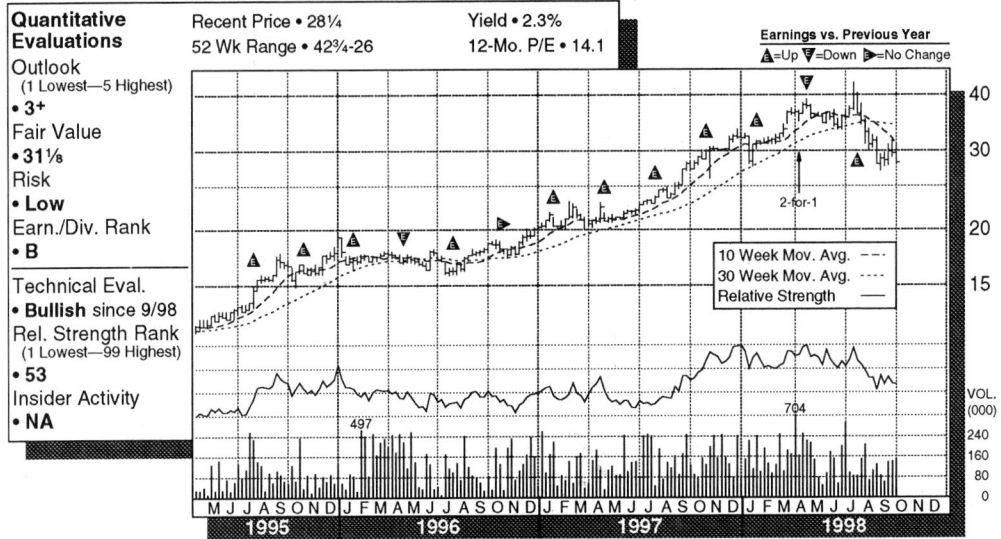

10 Week Mov. Avg. ---
30 Week Mov. Avg. ·····
Relative Strength ——

2-for-1

VOL. (000)

Business Profile - 27-MAY-98

BKNG, the largest bank holding company in Vermont, operates through seven community banks with 60 branch offices throughout Vermont, New Hampshire and Massachusetts. Banknorth also owns the First Massachusetts bank, a denovo bank formed from Shawmut branch acquisitions; and the Stratevest Group, a limited purpose trust bank with about $1.6 billion under management. The bank has recently seen record loan production in its mortgage subsidiary, due to current low interest rates. During the first quarter of 1998, BKNG repurchased 160,000 of its common shares under an October 1997 authorization to buy up to 5% of its stock.

Operational Review - 27-MAY-98

Net interest income in the first quarter of 1998 advanced 3.7%, year to year, as growth in earning assets outweighed a narrowing of the net interest margin to 4.43%, from 4.73%. The loan loss provision rose 5.4%, to $1.8 million, although nonperforming assets declined to 0.55% of total assets, from 0.76%. Noninterest operating income increased 8.4%, on higher trust and investment management income and service charges. Total noninterest expenses and charges grew 9.0%, mainly on expenses related to compensation and the issuance of capital securities. After taxes at 29.9%, versus 32.5%, net income slid 1.8%, to $6.9 million ($0.44 a share, diluted), from $7.1 million ($0.45).

Stock Performance - 02-OCT-98

In the past 30 trading days, BKNG's shares have declined 10%, compared to a 7% fall in the S&P 500. Average trading volume for the past five days was 30,340 shares, compared with the 40-day moving average of 22,403 shares.

Key Stock Statistics

Dividend Rate/Share	0.64	Shareholders	4,200
Shs. outstg. (M)	15.2	Market cap. (B)	$0.431
Avg. daily vol. (M)	0.025	Inst. holdings	51%
Tang. Bk. Value/Share	13.41		
Beta	0.94		

Value of $10,000 invested 5 years ago: $ 47,632

Fiscal Year Ending Dec. 31

	1998	1997	1996	1995	1994	1993
Revenues (Million $)						
1Q	63.18	57.61	49.02	41.84	32.75	34.19
2Q	65.53	60.89	53.91	43.26	34.41	33.95
3Q	—	64.32	55.63	44.37	36.62	35.30
4Q	—	67.01	56.75	44.06	40.61	32.75
Yr.	—	249.8	215.3	173.5	144.4	137.9
Earnings Per Share ($)						
1Q	**0.44**	0.45	0.33	0.39	0.17	0.20
2Q	**0.53**	0.45	0.43	0.40	0.25	0.22
3Q	—	0.48	0.43	0.43	0.33	0.20
4Q	—	**0.55**	0.45	0.43	0.42	0.22
Yr.	—	**1.93**	**1.64**	1.65	1.17	0.84

Next earnings report expected: mid October

Dividend Data (Dividends have been paid since 1993.)

Amount ($)	Date Decl.	Ex-Div. Date	Stock of Record	Payment Date
0.320	Jan. 27	Feb. 18	Feb. 20	Mar. 06 '98
2-for-1	Feb. 24	Apr. 07	Mar. 20	Apr. 06 '98
0.160	Apr. 28	May. 20	May. 22	Jun. 05 '98
0.160	Jul. 28	Aug. 19	Aug. 21	Sep. 04 '98

Business Summary - 27-MAY-98

Banknorth Group is well on its way toward achieving its principal goal of financial performance in the top 25% of its peers nationwide. Through internal growth and acquisitions, BKNG has become the largest multibank holding company in Vermont, operating 60 branch offices through seven community banks in northern and central New England. In addition, the bank offers mortgage banking services and investment and asset management.

Interest on loans contributes the majority of revenue to the bank. Loans outstanding totaled $1.93 billion at December 31, 1997. Loans at the end of recent years were divided as follows:

	1997	1996	1995
Real estate:			
Residential	39%	40%	35%
Commercial	29%	29%	30%
Construction/Land	2%	2%	1%
Commercial, financial & agricultural	17%	16%	17%
Instalment	13%	14%	17%

Unfortunately, banks must regularly reserve against potential losses. Banknorth's allowance for possible loan losses represented 1.31% of total loans at 1997 year-end, up from 1.27% a year earlier. Asset quality has improved over the past several years, as nonperforming assets declined to 0.56% of total assets in 1997, from 1.95% in 1993, and net chargeoffs declined to 0.29% of average total loans, from 0.50%, over the same period.

Deposits represent the main (and most cost effective) source of funds to the bank. During 1997, core deposits averaged $2.0 billion, and were apportioned: noninterest bearing demand 14%, NOW accounts and money market savings 41%, regular savings 10%, time deposits under $100,000 35%.

Lending profitability, commonly measured by the yield on a bank's average earning assets, or the net interest margin, is affected by changes in the mix and volume of assets and liabilities, as well as changes in interest rates. During 1997, Banknorth saw a narrowing of its net interest margin, to 4.57%, from 4.86% in 1996, as lower yields on loans combined with an unfavorable shift in the mix and rates paid on deposits.

During 1997, BKNG formed a marketing alliance with a merchant processor, providing for increased customer services, continued fee opportunities for Banknorth, and the elimination of future merchant processing expense.

Per Share Data ($)

(Year Ended Dec. 31)	1997	1996	1995	1994	1993	1992	1991	1990	1989	1988
Tangible Bk. Val.	12.84	10.90	10.88	9.04	9.73	9.36	9.21	9.46	9.47	8.65
Earnings	1.93	1.65	1.65	1.17	0.84	0.16	-0.27	0.55	1.31	1.22
Dividends	0.58	0.50	0.46	0.30	0.20	Nil	Nil	0.54	0.49	0.45
Payout Ratio	30%	30%	28%	26%	24%	Nil	Nil	99%	37%	37%
Prices - High	33¹/₂	20³/₄	19³/₄	13	10³/₄	7³/₄	5³/₄	9⁵/₈	12	NA
- Low	20	15³/₄	10⁷/₈	8⁷/₈	6⁷/₈	4¹/₈	2⁵/₈	4¹/₈	7³/₄	NA
P/E Ratio - High	17	13	12	11	13	48	NM	18	9	NA
- Low	10	10	7	8	8	25	NM	8	6	NA

Income Statement Analysis (Million $)

	1997	1996	1995	1994	1993	1992	1991	1990	1989	1988
Net Int. Inc.	119	109	84.6	74.8	68.5	65.1	70.3	70.0	72.4	64.9
Tax Equiv. Adj.	0.6	0.6	0.7	0.5	0.6	0.9	1.3	2.0	2.3	2.8
Non Int. Inc.	31.1	25.3	21.3	22.2	23.6	23.6	19.5	23.8	21.4	17.7
Loan Loss Prov.	7.7	5.6	4.4	3.1	4.0	13.1	29.3	20.2	7.2	5.0
Exp./Op. Revs.	65%	68%	66%	72%	78%	82%	76%	67%	64%	65%
Pretax Inc.	45.3	37.4	30.6	21.6	16.7	2.3	-8.8	9.4	25.8	22.5
Eff. Tax Rate	33%	32%	27%	27%	31%	7.00%	NM	21%	31%	27%
Net Inc.	30.5	25.4	22.4	15.9	11.5	2.2	-3.7	7.4	17.8	16.5
% Net Int. Marg.	4.57	4.86	4.79	4.65	4.68	4.52	4.73	4.75	4.81	4.81

Balance Sheet & Other Fin. Data (Million $)

	1997	1996	1995	1994	1993	1992	1991	1990	1989	1988
Earning Assets:										
Money Mkt	85.8	92.0	90.0	86.0	70.0	108	85.0	108	115	107
Inv. Securities	734	565	409	436	403	292	337	266	235	234
Com'l Loans	332	301	628	588	553	543	554	653	635	619
Other Loans	1,628	1,547	723	708	566	538	613	581	639	582
Total Assets	2,923	2,601	1,910	1,874	1,662	1,562	1,660	1,654	1,627	1,533
Demand Deposits	324	288	402	428	363	381	741	715	709	787
Time Deposits	1,876	1,778	1,159	1,015	900	957	684	746	710	629
LT Debt	16.5	26.0	56.0	122	96.8	17.6	14.0	NM	0.5	1.6
Common Eqty.	230	207	160	136	132	127	125	129	124	112
% Ret. on Assets	1.1	1.1	1.2	0.9	0.7	0.1	NM	0.5	1.1	1.1
% Ret. on Equity	14.0	13.8	15.1	12.1	8.9	1.7	NM	5.7	14.3	14.7
% Loan Loss Resv.	1.3	1.3	1.6	1.7	1.9	2.0	1.9	2.0	1.2	1.0
% Loans/Deposits	88.4	89.4	86.6	89.7	88.6	80.8	80.4	82.7	87.3	83.8
% Equity to Assets	7.9	8.2	7.8	7.6	8.1	7.8	7.8	7.8	7.6	7.3

Data as orig. reptd.; bef. results of disc opers. and/or spec. items. Per share data adj. for stk. divs. as of ex-div. date. Bold denotes diluted EPS (FASB 128). E-Estimated. NA-Not Available. NM-Not Meaningful. NR-Not Ranked.

Office—300 Financial Plaza, P.O. Box 5420, Burlington, VT 05401. **Tel**—(802) 658-9959. **Chrmn**—A. P. Pizzagalli. **Pres & CEO**—W. H. Chadwick. **EVP, CFO & Investor Contact**—Thomas J. Pruitt (802-860-5558). **Treas**—N. E. Robinson. **Dirs**—T. J. Amidon, J. Arthur, R. A. Carrara, S. C. Crampton, W. H. Chadwick, L. F. Hackett, K. Hoisington, D. G. Hyde, R. M. Narkewicz, R. A. Paul, A. P. Pizzagalli, J. B. Packard, T. P. Salmon, P. Welch. **Transfer Agent & Registrar**—Registrar and Transfer Co., Cranford, NJ. **Incorporated**—in Delaware in 1989. **Empl**— 1,153. **S&P Analyst:** L. A. Olive

STANDARD &POOR'S
STOCK REPORTS

Barnes Group

288T

NYSE Symbol **B**

In S&P SmallCap 600

03-OCT-98

Industry:
Manufacturing (Diversified)

Summary: Barnes is a leading manufacturer of precision springs and complex aerospace components, and a major direct-to-user distributor of industrial maintenance and repair products.

Quantitative Evaluations

Outlook
(1 Lowest—5 Highest)
• **NA**

Fair Value
• **NA**

Risk
• **Low**

Earn./Div. Rank
• **B+**

Technical Eval.
• **Bearish** since 8/98

Rel. Strength Rank
(1 Lowest—99 Highest)
• **90**

Insider Activity
• **Neutral**

Recent Price • 28½
52 Wk Range • 34-21¼

Yield • 2.5%
12-Mo. P/E • 16.2

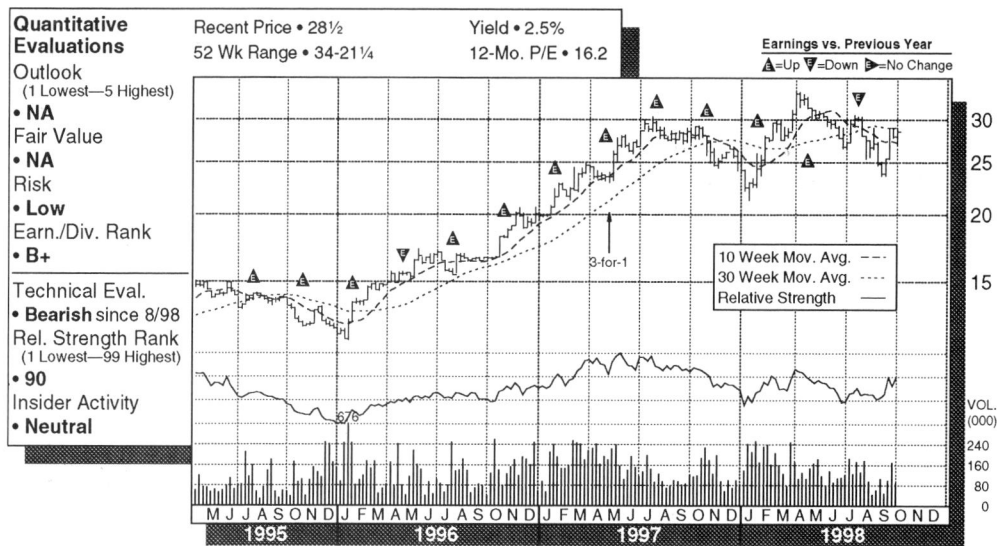

Earnings vs. Previous Year
▲=Up ▼=Down ▶=No Change

10 Week Mov. Avg. – – –
30 Week Mov. Avg. · · · ·
Relative Strength —

Business Profile - 23-SEP-98

In July 1998, the company said that the economic crisis in Asia and the GM strike had a negative effect on 1998 second quarter results. However, Barnes Aerospace continued to maintain its momentum, reporting strong sales and profit gains. Continuing to capitalize on the strong commercial aviation market for engines and airframes, two of Barnes Aerospace's divisions, Windsor Manufacturing and Windsor Airmotive, posted significant sales and earnings improvement for the second quarter. The dividend was boosted 7.8% with the September 1998 payment. The company's chairman, president and CEO, Theodore E. Martin, plans to retire by year-end.

Operational Review - 23-SEP-98

Net sales in the six months ended June 30, 1998, advanced 4.8%, year to year, reflecting growth in the Associated Spring and Barnes Aerospace businesses. Gross margins were flat, and with a 17% rise in selling and administrative expenses, operating income fell 16%. Results were penalized by a one-time charge of $12.9 million related to an early retirement package for the company's chairman. After taxes at 37.5% in each period, net income dropped 21%, to $16,487,000 ($0.81 a share), from $20,832,000 ($1.01).

Stock Performance - 02-OCT-98

In the past 30 trading days, B's shares have increased 5%, compared to a 7% fall in the S&P 500. Average trading volume for the past five days was 17,760 shares, compared with the 40-day moving average of 18,159 shares.

Key Stock Statistics

Dividend Rate/Share	0.72	Shareholders	3,700
Shs. outstg. (M)	20.1	Market cap. (B)	$0.573
Avg. daily vol. (M)	0.022	Inst. holdings	44%
Tang. Bk. Value/Share	8.31		
Beta	0.79		

Value of $10,000 invested 5 years ago: $ 34,253

Fiscal Year Ending Dec. 31

	1998	1997	1996	1995	1994	1993
Revenues (Million $)						
1Q	168.9	158.1	150.1	158.6	142.1	127.0
2Q	169.2	165.9	152.6	151.0	143.2	127.5
3Q	—	158.5	147.1	141.7	140.3	123.1
4Q	—	160.1	145.2	141.2	143.7	124.7
Yr.	—	642.7	595.0	592.5	569.2	502.3
Earnings Per Share ($)						
1Q	**0.58**	**0.49**	0.34	0.43	0.26	0.02
2Q	**0.23**	**0.52**	0.43	0.37	0.29	0.16
3Q	—	**0.49**	0.44	0.32	0.28	0.15
4Q	—	**0.46**	0.43	0.28	0.24	-0.09
Yr.	—	**1.96**	1.63	1.40	1.07	0.23

Next earnings report expected: mid October

Dividend Data (Dividends have been paid since 1934.)

Amount ($)	Date Decl.	Ex-Div. Date	Stock of Record	Payment Date
0.167	Oct. 17	Nov. 26	Dec. 01	Dec. 10 '97
0.167	Feb. 20	Feb. 25	Feb. 27	Mar. 10 '98
0.167	May. 15	May. 28	Jun. 01	Jun. 10 '98
0.180	Jul. 17	Aug. 28	Sep. 01	Sep. 10 '98

*A Division of The **McGraw·Hill** Companies*

Business Summary - 23-SEP-98

Barnes Group Inc. is a diversified international manufacturer and distributor, serving a range of industrial and transportation markets with precision metal parts and industrial supplies. The company, which is headquartered in Bristol, CT, where it was founded in 1857, currently consists of three separate businesses, with total annual sales of about $650 million.

Associated Spring produces and distributes custom-made springs and other close-tolerance engineered metal components. Bowman Distribution distributes consumable repair and replacement products for industrial, heavy equipment and transportation markets. Barnes Aerospace produces precision machined and fabricated assemblies for the aircraft and aerospace industries and refurbishes jet engine components. Business segment contributions (operating income in millions) in 1997 were:

	Sales	Operating Income
Associated Spring	45%	$43.0
Bowman Distribution	34%	26.7
Barnes Aerospace	21%	14.4

International operations accounted for 21% of sales and 15% of operating income in 1997.

Associated Spring makes and distributes precision springs and a wide range of custom metal parts for mechanical purposes. It is equipped to produce nearly every type of spring requiring precision engineering, as well as an extensive line of precision metal components and assemblies. The automotive and automotive parts industries constitute Associated's largest single custom metal parts market.

Bowman Distribution markets a variety of replacement parts and other products, including fasteners and special-purpose hardware, automotive parts, automotive specialties and accessories, electric and gas welding supplies, industrial maintenance supplies and industrial aerosols such as adhesives, lubricants and sealants.

Barnes Aerospace is engaged in the advanced fabrication and precision machining of components for jet engines and airframes, the repair and overhaul of jet engine components, the manufacture of machined and fabricated parts and assemblies, the refurbishing of jet engine components and the hot forming and fabrication of titanium and other high-temperature alloys for use in precision details and assemblies for aircraft engine and airframe applications.

The company's goal is to continue its global expansion in Europe, Asia, South America, and Central America; and to focus on building profitable sales, improving productivity, and reducing cost in all three of its businesses. Barnes believes that it is on track to becoming one of the leading companies in distribution and manufacturing worldwide.

Per Share Data ($)

(Year Ended Dec. 31)	1997	1996	1995	1994	1993	1992	1991	1990	1989	1988
Tangible Bk. Val.	8.04	6.89	5.53	4.49	3.74	3.85	6.21	5.58	4.83	5.28
Cash Flow	3.39	2.97	2.76	2.31	1.47	1.59	1.94	1.88	1.61	1.97
Earnings	2.00	1.63	1.40	1.07	0.23	0.31	0.87	0.92	0.65	1.02
Dividends	0.65	0.60	0.53	0.48	0.47	0.47	0.47	0.47	0.47	0.40
Payout Ratio	33%	37%	38%	45%	NM	149%	54%	51%	76%	40%
Prices - High	30⅜	20⅝	15¼	13¼	11	12	12⅝	10½	12⅞	12⅜
- Low	19¾	11⅝	12	9⅞	10	9⅜	8⅝	8	9⅝	10
P/E Ratio - High	15	13	11	12	47	38	15	11	20	12
- Low	10	7	9	9	43	30	10	9	15	10

Income Statement Analysis (Million $)

	1997	1996	1995	1994	1993	1992	1991	1990	1989	1988
Revs.	643	595	593	569	502	529	536	546	511	496
Oper. Inc.	93.9	81.9	75.6	60.4	40.5	48.8	57.8	58.7	57.1	59.4
Depr.	28.1	26.6	26.8	23.7	23.1	23.7	19.8	17.5	16.6	15.7
Int. Exp.	4.9	5.0	5.3	5.1	5.2	6.6	8.9	10.2	10.2	8.7
Pretax Inc.	64.5	52.3	45.5	33.9	8.4	7.7	28.8	30.0	23.1	33.2
Eff. Tax Rate	37%	38%	39%	40%	48%	24%	45%	44%	47%	43%
Net Inc.	40.4	32.6	27.5	20.3	4.4	5.8	15.9	16.8	12.4	18.8

Balance Sheet & Other Fin. Data (Million $)

	1997	1996	1995	1994	1993	1992	1991	1990	1989	1988
Cash	32.5	24.0	17.7	22.0	24.1	39.1	21.4	17.0	18.0	18.1
Curr. Assets	203	190	173	176	169	186	191	193	189	182
Total Assets	408	390	362	352	333	348	342	342	328	312
Curr. Liab.	89.9	80.1	77.5	87.0	82.0	93.0	88.0	102	100	80.0
LT Debt	62.0	75.0	77.5	79.8	82.0	84.0	94.3	96.3	98.3	79.3
Common Eqty.	181	157	129	107	92.0	94.0	139	126	113	113
Total Cap.	243	232	206	190	177	180	246	233	219	220
Cap. Exp.	33.3	33.9	35.9	31.8	22.2	10.2	19.1	21.6	18.2	21.4
Cash Flow	68.5	59.2	54.2	44.0	27.5	29.6	39.1	34.3	27.7	32.4
Curr. Ratio	2.3	2.4	2.2	2.0	2.1	2.0	2.2	1.9	1.9	2.3
% LT Debt of Cap.	25.5	32.3	37.6	42.1	46.4	46.6	38.4	41.3	44.8	36.0
% Net Inc.of Revs.	6.3	5.5	4.6	3.6	0.9	1.1	3.0	3.1	2.4	3.8
% Ret. on Assets	10.1	8.7	7.7	5.9	1.3	1.7	4.6	5.0	3.7	6.1
% Ret. on Equity	23.9	22.8	23.2	20.2	4.7	5.0	11.9	14.0	9.4	15.8

Data as orig. reptd.; bef. results of disc. opers. and/or spec. items. Per share data adj. for stk. divs. as of ex-div. date. Bold denotes diluted EPS (FASB 128). E-Estimated. NA-Not Available. NM-Not Meaningful. NR-Not Ranked.

Office—123 Main St., Bristol, CT 06011-0489. **Tel**—(860) 583-7070. **Website**—http://www.barnesgroupinc.com **Chrmn**—T. O. Barnes. **Pres & CEO**—T. E. Martin. **VP & Treas**—J. J. Locher. **VP & Secy**—W. V. Grickis Jr. **Investor Contact**—Robert D. LiPira. **Dirs**—T. O. Barnes, G. G. Benanav, W. S. Bristow Jr., R. J. Callander, G. T. Carpenter, D. R. Ecton, R. W. Fiondella, F. E. Grzelecki, M. P. Joseph, T. E. Martin. **Transfer Agent & Registrar**—ChaseMellon Shareholder Services, Ridgefield Park, NJ. **Incorporated**—in Delaware in 1925. **Empl**— 3,900. **S&P Analyst**: M.I.

Barrett Resources 289E

NYSE Symbol **BRR**

In S&P SmallCap 600

03-OCT-98

Industry:
Oil & Gas (Exploration & Production)

Summary: This independent natural gas and oil exploration and production company is also involved in gas gathering, marketing and trading activities.

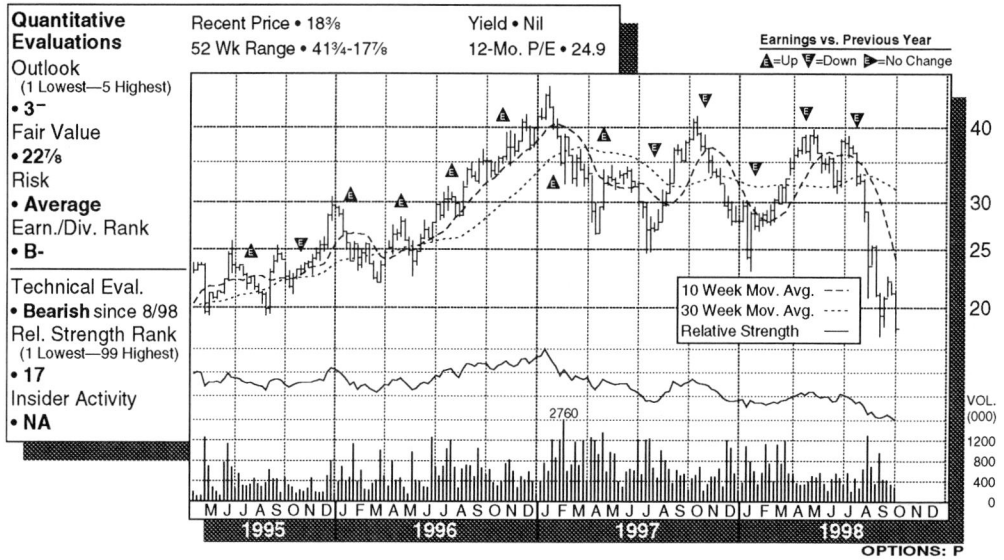

Quantitative Evaluations

Outlook
(1 Lowest—5 Highest)
- **3⁻**

Fair Value
- **22⅞**

Risk
- **Average**

Earn./Div. Rank
- **B-**

Technical Eval.
- **Bearish** since 8/98

Rel. Strength Rank
(1 Lowest—99 Highest)
- **17**

Insider Activity
- **NA**

Recent Price • 18⅜
52 Wk Range • 41¾-17⅞

Yield • Nil
12-Mo. P/E • 24.9

Earnings vs. Previous Year
▲=Up ▼=Down ▶=No Change

10 Week Mov. Avg. ---
30 Week Mov. Avg. ·····
Relative Strength —

OPTIONS: P

Business Profile - 04-AUG-98

On July 20, 1998, Barret Resources completed the second of three test wells in Peru; BRR has a 70% working interest in this prospect. If successful, Peru will be added to the company's existing core areas which include the Rocky Mountain Region, the Mid-Continent Region, and the Gulf of Mexico Region. The company has various other test wells and exploratory projects in process in the Wind River and Anadarko Basins, and in the Gulf of Mexico. However, the company's 1998 capital expenditure budget was dramatically reduced in response to low oil prices, from $334 million of actual spending in 1997 to $190 million. In December 1997, Barrett abandoned its efforts to divest the Uinta Basin, Utah properties.

Operational Review - 04-AUG-98

Revenues during the quarter ended March 31, 1998, advanced 72%, year to year, primarily reflecting increased trading revenue, which more than tripled; production revenue was up 2.2%. However, operating expenses doubled due to trading costs which rose more than three-fold, 72% greater depreciation, depletion an amortization charges and a significant jump in interest expense. With total costs outpacing revenues, net income declined 37% to $6.2 million ($0.20 per share) from $9.9 million ($0.31).

Stock Performance - 02-OCT-98

In the past 30 trading days, BRR's shares have declined 27%, compared to a 7% fall in the S&P 500. Average trading volume for the past five days was 57,520 shares, compared with the 40-day moving average of 150,277 shares.

Key Stock Statistics

Dividend Rate/Share	Nil	Shareholders	4,100
Shs. outstg. (M)	31.9	Market cap. (B)	$0.588
Avg. daily vol. (M)	0.100	Inst. holdings	75%
Tang. Bk. Value/Share	13.62		
Beta	0.72		

Value of $10,000 invested 5 years ago: $ 17,352

Fiscal Year Ending Dec. 31

	1998	1997	1996	1995	1994	1993
Revenues (Million $)						
1Q	131.7	76.55	41.98	33.06	9.37	13.04
2Q	131.9	71.22	46.91	31.28	9.72	9.67
3Q	—	89.17	46.06	27.22	11.61	7.51
4Q	—	145.7	66.30	35.07	14.88	9.58
Yr.	—	382.6	201.3	126.6	--	--
Earnings Per Share ($)						
1Q	0.19	0.31	0.14	0.11	0.14	0.14
2Q	0.08	0.14	0.25	0.13	0.07	0.09
3Q	—	0.14	0.22	-0.47	0.07	0.16
4Q	—	0.32	0.41	0.14	0.02	0.09
Yr.	—	0.92	1.02	-0.09	--	--

Next earnings report expected: **NA**

Dividend Data

No cash dividends have been paid. Barrett anticipates that all earnings will be retained for the development of its business and that no cash dividends will be declared for the foreseeable future.

A Division of The McGraw-Hill Companies

Business Summary - 04-AUG-98

Denver-based Barrett Resources Corp. (BRR) is an independent oil and natural gas exploration and production company whose significant producing regions include: the Rocky Mountain Region of Colorado, Wyoming and Utah; the Mid-Continent Region of Kansas, Oklahoma, New Mexico and Texas; and the Gulf of Mexico region of offshore Texas and Louisiana. However, the company is also developing international properties; on July 20, 1998, BRR announced the completion of the second of three exploratory wells in Peru. The company's initial interest in the region was brought about by geological similarities between Peru and the Rockies.

Net interests in producing natural gas and oil properties, drilling activity (exploratory and development), total productive wells in which the company had an interest, and number of wells operated in recent years:

	1997	1996
Oil production (MMBbls)	2.2	1.9
Gas production (Bcf)	76.6	60.9
Average daily production (MMcfe)	247	198
Wells drilled (gross/net)	299/163.7	171/93.5
Wells productive (gross/net)	2541/1380	2106/1153
Wells operated	1368	1310

Total proved reserves as of December 31, 1997, were 851.2 Bcf of natural gas and 18.7 MMBbls. of crude oil and condensate, which equals 963.2 Bcf of gas

equivalent (Bcfe), comprised of 88% and 12% natural gas and oil, respectively. Total proved reserves as of December 31, 1996, were 674.9 Bcf of natural gas, and 23.2 MMBbls. of crude oil and condensate, or 814.3 Bcf of gas equivalent (Bcfe), comprised of 83% and 17% natural gas and oil, respectively. Proved developed reserves represented 64% and 74% of total reserves at the end of 1997 and 1996, respectively. The company replaced 265% of total 1997 production - 73% through the drill bit and 27% through acquisitions. Most of the acquisitions are located in the Rocky Mountain region, primarily the Piceance and the Powder river basins. Estimated pretax future net revenues, discounted by 10%, amounted to $745,000,000 at December 31, 1997, versus $1,121,000,000 million at December 31, 1996. The lower figure reflects decreased prices for oil and gas, respectively $15.52 per bbl. and $2.19 per Mcf, versus $24.12 per bbl. and $3.46 per Mcf. The average sales price for gas and oil in 1997 were $2.18 and $17.69, respectively, versus $1.88 and $19.51 in 1996.

BRR utilizes its own exploration staff to develop a geologic concept into an exploration prospect, which is drilled either solely by the company or with partners. Oil and gas leases are acquired primarily in strategic core areas of interest. Typically, Barrett retains an interest and serves as operator of a joint-venture exploration program on the prospect acreage. The company also acquires interests in exploration and development programs operated by other companies through acquisition or farm-ins.

Per Share Data ($)

(Year Ended Dec. 31)	1997	1996	1995	1994	1993	1992	1991	1990	1989	1988
Tangible Bk. Val.	13.13	12.06	7.64	6.15	5.82	4.49	4.25	4.09	2.89	2.70
Cash Flow	3.18	2.61	1.25	0.95	1.08	0.43	0.42	0.43	0.43	0.37
Earnings	0.92	1.02	-0.09	0.37	0.53	0.09	0.17	0.19	0.14	0.15
Dividends	Nil	Nil	Nil	Nil	Nil	Nil	Nil	Nil	Nil	Nil
Payout Ratio	Nil	Nil	Nil	Nil	Nil	Nil	Nil	Nil	Nil	Nil
Prices - High	46⅞	43	30⅝	22¾	16	10¾	6½	8¾	7	3½
- Low	24⅝	22	16⅞	10⅜	8⅜	3⅛	3¼	5⅛	2⅞	2
P/E Ratio - High	51	42	NM	61	30	NM	38	46	50	23
- Low	27	22	NM	28	16	NM	19	27	21	13

Income Statement Analysis (Million $)

	1997	1996	1995	1994	1993	1992	1991	1990	1989	1988
Revs.	378	201	127	40.3	41.6	23.6	13.9	7.5	6.0	5.1
Oper. Inc.	130	92.6	51.1	10.4	10.9	3.6	3.0	2.8	2.5	1.9
Depr. Depl. & Amort.	72.4	45.8	33.5	6.9	6.1	3.3	2.4	1.9	1.7	137
Int. Exp.	13.2	3.7	5.0	0.0	0.0	0.0	0.0	0.1	0.0	0.1
Pretax Inc.	47.2	44.5	-0.4	4.5	5.9	0.9	1.9	1.8	1.2	1.4
Eff. Tax Rate	38%	34%	NM	1.50%	2.60%	1.90%	7.80%	18%	24%	34%
Net Inc.	29.3	29.5	-2.2	4.4	5.8	0.9	1.7	1.5	0.9	0.9

Balance Sheet & Other Fin. Data (Million $)

	1997	1996	1995	1994	1993	1992	1991	1990	1989	1988
Cash	14.5	14.5	7.5	9.7	35.2	11.3	18.9	19.9	5.3	3.3
Curr. Assets	122	89.7	39.7	28.8	53.3	19.9	24.4	28.6	8.6	6.0
Total Assets	873	577	340	106	91.0	57.0	55.0	51.0	26.0	22.0
Curr. Liab.	125	78.3	36.1	33.0	22.5	13.3	12.9	10.9	8.1	5.1
LT Debt	266	70.0	89.0	Nil	Nil	Nil	Nil	Nil	0.1	0.1
Common Eqty.	412	378	192	72.9	68.2	43.3	42.0	40.4	17.6	16.6
Total Cap.	748	499	304	72.9	68.2	43.3	42.6	40.4	17.7	16.6
Cap. Exp.	341	203	82.8	47.8	21.4	9.9	10.9	8.1	4.6	4.0
Cash Flow	102	75.3	31.2	11.3	11.8	4.2	4.1	3.4	2.6	2.3
Curr. Ratio	1.0	1.1	1.1	0.9	2.4	1.5	1.9	2.6	1.1	1.2
% LT Debt of Cap.	35.7	14.0	29.2	Nil	Nil	Nil	Nil	Nil	0.5	0.5
% Ret. on Assets	4.0	6.4	NM	4.5	7.2	1.7	3.2	3.1	3.7	4.2
% Ret. on Equity	7.4	10.4	NM	6.3	9.5	2.2	4.2	4.3	5.2	5.7

Data as orig. reptd.; bef. results of disc. opers. and/or spec. items. Per share data adj. for stk. divs. as of ex-div. date. Prior to 1995, year ended Sep. 30. E-Estimated. NA-Not Available. NM-Not Meaningful. NR-Not Ranked.

Office—1515 Arapahoe St., Tower 3, Suite 1000, Denver, CO 80202. **Tel**—(303) 572-3900. **Website**—http://www.brr.com **Chrmn & CEO**—W. J. Barrett. **Pres & COO**—A. R. Reed. **Sr VP-Fin & Treas**—R. W. Howard. **CFO & Exec VP**—J. Frank Keller. **VP & Investor Contact**—Larry Bufnardo. **Dirs**—W. J. Barrett, C. R. Buford, D. Cody, J. M. Fitzgibbons, W. W. Grant, J. F. Keller, P. M. Rady, A. R. Reed, J. T. Rodgers, P. S. E. Schreiber, H. S. Welch. **Transfer Agent & Registrar**—First National Bank of Boston. **Incorporated**—in Delaware in 1987. **Empl**— 207. **S&P Analyst:** Ephraim Juskowicz.

Bassett Furniture Industries   3234

NASDAQ Symbol **BSET**

In S&P SmallCap 600

03-OCT-98

Industry: Household Furnishings & Appliances

Summary: Bassett is a leading producer of wood furniture for bedroom, dining room, living room and nursery use, as well as upholstered furniture and other related products.

Quantitative Evaluations

Outlook (1 Lowest—5 Highest)
• **2**

Fair Value
• **28⅝**

Risk
• **Low**

Earn./Div. Rank
• **B-**

Technical Eval.
• **Bullish** since 9/98

Rel. Strength Rank (1 Lowest—99 Highest)
• **70**

Insider Activity
• **Neutral**

Recent Price • 26½   Yield • 3.0%
52 Wk Range • 34-22   12-Mo. P/E • NM

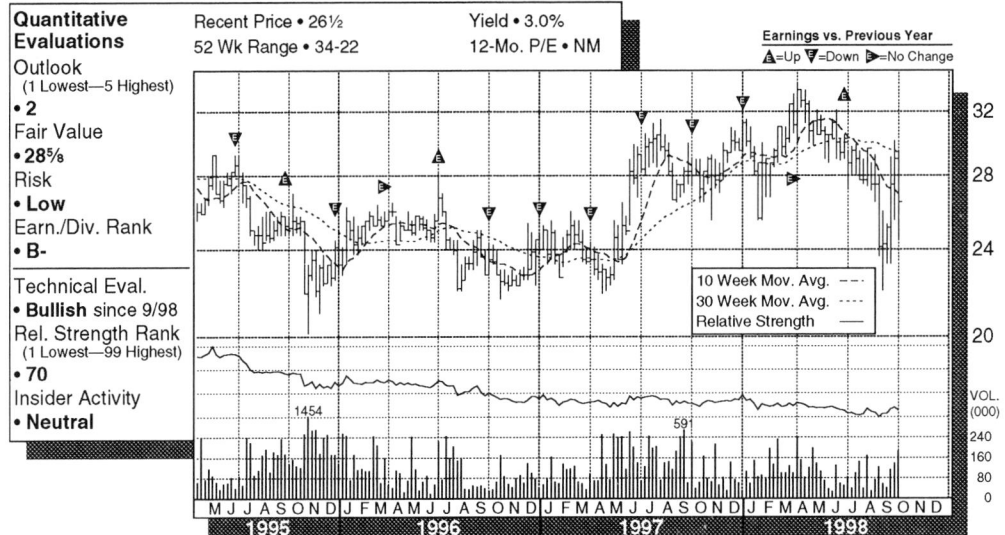

Earnings vs. Previous Year
▲=Up ▼=Down ▶=No Change

10 Week Mov. Avg. – –
30 Week Mov. Avg. ····
Relative Strength —

Business Profile - 17-JUL-98

Results in FY 97 (Nov.) were hurt by several nonrecurring charges. In the fourth quarter, charges totaling $13.7 million were recorded, primarily related to closing three plants. In July 1997, one of the company's major customers filed for Chapter 11 bankruptcy protection; as a result, BSET recorded an after-tax charge of $3.7 million ($0.28 a share). In May 1997, the company recorded an $18.9 million net charge ($1.45) related to the elimination of certain product lines, as well as the closing and integration of certain plants. Sales in the second quarter of FY 98 fell 13%, year to year, as a result of closing certain divisions. BSET expects additional charges of $10.5 million related to plant inefficiencies and idle facilities in FY 98. Recently, the company announced a $40 million share repurchase program.

Operational Review - 17-JUL-98

Net sales in the six months ended May 31, 1998, declined 12%, year to year, as a decrease in sales for the upholstery and mattress divisions outweighed an increase in the wood division. Gross margins widened and SG&A expenses fell; an operating profit contrasted with an operating loss. In the absence of a $13,929,000 restructuring charge, net income was $7,394,000 ($0.56 a share), against a loss of $9,301,000 ($0.81).

Stock Performance - 02-OCT-98

In the past 30 trading days, BSET's shares have declined 4%, compared to a 7% fall in the S&P 500. Average trading volume for the past five days was 36,980 shares, compared with the 40-day moving average of 19,374 shares.

Key Stock Statistics

Dividend Rate/Share	0.80	Shareholders	2,100
Shs. outstg. (M)	13.1	Market cap. (B)	$0.347
Avg. daily vol. (M)	0.024	Inst. holdings	45%
Tang. Bk. Value/Share	20.35		
Beta	0.85		

Value of $10,000 invested 5 years ago: $ 8,932

Fiscal Year Ending Nov. 30

	1998	1997	1996	1995	1994	1993
Revenues (Million $)						
1Q	98.33	109.8	112.0	123.5	121.7	120.3
2Q	98.34	113.2	111.3	119.0	134.6	128.9
3Q	—	110.3	109.0	119.2	125.0	121.2
4Q	—	113.6	118.5	129.1	129.3	133.4
Yr.	—	446.9	450.7	490.8	510.6	503.8
Earnings Per Share ($)						
1Q	**0.26**	0.26	0.35	0.35	0.33	0.43
2Q	**0.30**	-1.07	0.37	0.35	0.53	0.53
3Q	—	-0.39	0.36	0.41	0.32	0.32
4Q	—	-0.30	0.31	0.52	0.57	0.55
Yr.	—	-1.50	1.39	1.63	1.75	1.79

Next earnings report expected: mid October

Dividend Data (Dividends have been paid since 1935.)

Amount ($)	Date Decl.	Ex-Div. Date	Stock of Record	Payment Date
0.200	Nov. 07	Nov. 13	Nov. 17	Dec. 01 '97
0.200	Jan. 13	Feb. 11	Feb. 16	Mar. 02 '98
0.200	May. 10	May. 13	May. 15	Jun. 01 '98
0.200	Jun. 23	Aug. 13	Aug. 17	Sep. 01 '98

A Division of The McGraw-Hill Companies

STANDARD
&POOR'S
STOCK REPORTS

Bassett Furniture Industries, Incorporated

3234

03-OCT-98

Business Summary - 17-JUL-98

Bassett Furniture Industries, one of the largest furniture manufacturers in the U.S., was hurt by a number of problems within the past 15 months. In May 1997, the company said it would record pretax charges related to a strategy to focus on its core business marketed under the Bassett brand name (Wood Products, Upholstery and Bedding) and initiatives, including dropping product lines and closing plants, to rationalize its manufacturing capacity by retaining and utilizing its most efficient facilities. In addition, a leading furniture retailing customer of BSET filed for bankruptcy protection in July 1997, prompting the company to record a charge of $6.0 million. This charge and others related to environmental matters and the Mattress Division totaled $12.5 million. After tax benefits, these charges reduced FY 97 (Nov.) earnings by $0.56 a share. In FY 97, restructuring and impaired asset charges were $20.6 million and additional nonrecurring charges were $31.7 million. After these charges and a tax benefit of $20.4 million, net income was reduced by $2.34 a share. BSET expects additional charges of $10.5 million related to plant inefficiencies and idle facilities in FY 98.

Virginia-based Bassett manufactures and sells a full line of furniture including bedroom and dining suites and accent pieces, occasional tables, wall and entertainment units, home office systems and computer workstations, upholstered sofas, love seats, and chairs (both motion and stationary), recliners, and mattresses and box springs. The three main product lines are made of wood (which accounted for 46% of sales in FY 97), upholstery (29%), and bedding (12%). Almost all of the company's sourcing is done domestically.

Products are distributed through a large number of retailers, including mass merchandisers, department stores, independent furniture stores, chain furniture stores, decorator showrooms, warehouse showrooms, specialty stores and rent-to-own stores. Other distribution channels include proprietary retail outlets known as Bassett Furniture Direct, and the Bassett Gallery stores and warehouse stores called Bassett Direct Plus. Sales to J.C. Penney Co. accounted for 14% of revenues in FY 97, versus 15% in FY 96.

Although the furniture industry is highly competitive, BSET believes it has been one of the largest domestic furniture retailers for a number of reasons. The company believes it offers its customers a product with superior quality and styling at attractive prices. BSET also feels that its prompt delivery and courteous service have been significant factors as well.

Per Share Data ($)

(Year Ended Nov. 30)	1997	1996	1995	1994	1993	1992	1991	1990	1989	1988
Tangible Bk. Val.	20.01	22.29	21.88	20.95	19.99	18.99	17.72	16.89	17.29	17.16
Cash Flow	-1.03	1.85	2.24	2.36	2.41	2.50	1.92	0.88	1.76	1.72
Earnings	-1.50	1.39	1.63	1.75	1.79	1.90	1.37	0.34	1.22	1.18
Dividends	0.80	0.80	1.00	0.80	0.78	0.64	0.53	0.67	1.07	0.69
Payout Ratio	NM	58%	61%	46%	44%	33%	39%	187%	85%	59%
Prices - High	31½	28¼	30¼	37¼	44	35¼	21¼	20¼	21¼	23½
- Low	21⅞	21⅝	20⅛	25¼	27½	19½	16⅞	15⅛	18½	16
P/E Ratio - High	NM	20	19	21	25	18	15	58	17	20
- Low	NM	16	12	14	15	10	12	43	15	14

Income Statement Analysis (Million $)

	1997	1996	1995	1994	1993	1992	1991	1990	1989	1988
Revs.	447	451	491	511	504	473	402	436	460	466
Oper. Inc.	-28.5	13.6	25.7	33.9	36.2	36.7	22.7	23.5	25.5	29.7
Depr.	6.2	6.3	8.6	8.8	9.0	8.5	7.9	7.9	8.3	8.5
Int. Exp.	Nil	Nil	Nil	Nil	Nil	Nil	Nil	Nil	Nil	Nil
Pretax Inc.	-42.0	22.3	30.1	34.8	36.5	39.3	26.9	6.9	26.7	27.0
Eff. Tax Rate	NM	17%	24%	28%	29%	30%	26%	25%	29%	32%
Net Inc.	-19.6	18.5	22.9	25.0	25.9	27.5	19.8	5.1	19.0	18.3

Balance Sheet & Other Fin. Data (Million $)

	1997	1996	1995	1994	1993	1992	1991	1990	1989	1988
Cash	29.6	57.3	51.3	42.3	53.0	50.2	74.0	57.6	76.4	69.0
Curr. Assets	200	195	205	199	202	193	202	183	212	212
Total Assets	320	335	347	340	331	319	291	271	305	301
Curr. Liab.	47.9	30.3	35.4	35.0	33.2	36.9	29.0	20.1	42.2	33.5
LT Debt	Nil	Nil	Nil	Nil	Nil	Nil	Nil	Nil	Nil	Nil
Common Eqty.	261	291	299	295	289	274	255	244	263	268
Total Cap.	261	294	301	296	289	274	255	244	263	268
Cap. Exp.	10.8	9.6	7.2	10.0	6.2	9.9	7.9	9.1	8.2	8.9
Cash Flow	-13.4	24.8	31.5	33.8	34.9	36.0	27.7	13.0	27.3	26.8
Curr. Ratio	4.2	6.4	5.8	5.7	6.1	5.2	7.0	9.1	5.0	6.3
% LT Debt of Cap.	Nil	Nil	0.7	Nil	Nil	Nil	Nil	Nil	Nil	Nil
% Net Inc.of Revs.	NM	4.1	4.7	4.9	5.1	5.8	4.9	1.2	4.1	3.9
% Ret. on Assets	NM	5.4	6.7	7.5	8.0	9.0	7.1	1.8	6.2	6.2
% Ret. on Equity	NM	6.3	7.7	8.7	9.2	10.4	8.0	2.1	7.2	6.9

Data as orig. reptd.; bef. results of disc. opers. and/or spec. items. Per share data adj. for stk. divs. as of ex-div. date. Bold denotes diluted EPS (FASB 128). E-Estimated. NA-Not Available. NM-Not Meaningful. NR-Not Ranked.

Office—P.O. Box 626, Bassett, VA 24055. **Tel**—(540) 629-6000. **Chrmn & CEO**—P. Fulton.**Pres & COO**—G. A. Hunsucker. **EVP-Fin, Treas & Investor Contact**—B. M. Brammer. **VP & Secy**—J. S. Payne. **Dirs**—A. W. Brinkley, P. W. Brown, T. E. Capps, W. D. Davis, A. T. Dickson, P. Fulton, W. H. Goodwin Jr., H. H. Haworth, J. W. McGlothlin, T. W. Moss, Jr., M. E. Murphy, A. F. Sloan, R. H. Spilman, Jr.**Transfer Agent & Registrar**—Co.'s office. **Incorporated**—in Virginia in 1930. **Empl**— 5,700. **S&P Analyst:** Kathleen J. Fraser

BE Aerospace

NASDAQ Symbol **BEAV**

3188E

In S&P SmallCap 600

03-OCT-98

Industry: Aerospace/Defense

Summary: BEAV makes cabin interior products for commercial aircraft, including seating, passenger entertainment and service systems, and galley structures and inserts.

Quantitative Evaluations

Outlook (1 Lowest—5 Highest)
- **4−**

Fair Value
- **29⅝**

Risk
- **High**

Earn./Div. Rank
- **NR**

Technical Eval.
- **NA**

Rel. Strength Rank (1 Lowest—99 Highest)
- **13**

Insider Activity
- **NA**

Recent Price • 18⅛
52 Wk Range • 36⅝-17⅝

Yield • Nil
12-Mo. P/E • NM

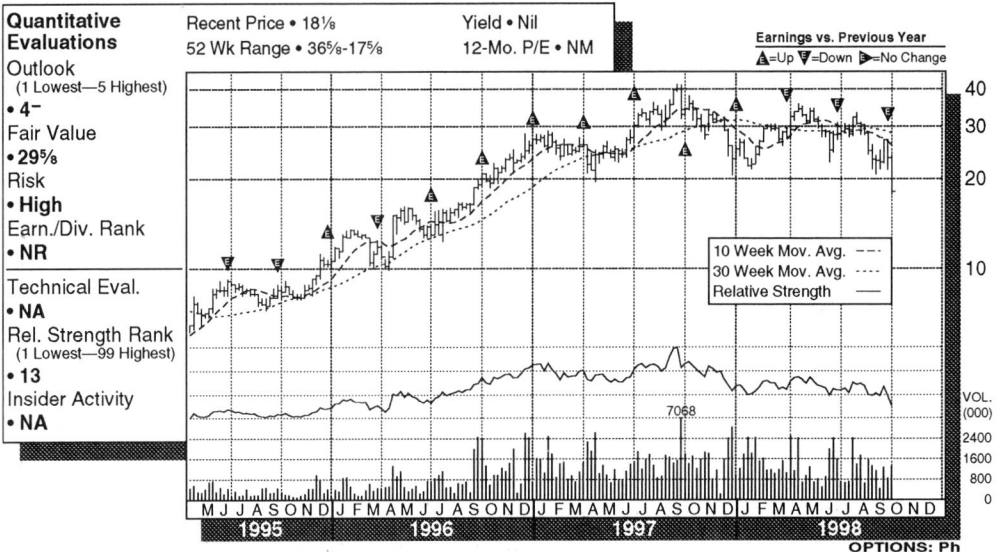

Earnings vs. Previous Year
▲=Up ▼=Down ▶=No Change

10 Week Mov. Avg. – – –
30 Week Mov. Avg. ·······
Relative Strength ——

7068

VOL. (000)

OPTIONS: Ph

Business Profile - 14-AUG-98

BE Aerospace, which expects to benefit from the continued recovery in the airline industry, has been growing both internally and through acquisitions. In August 1998, BEAV acquired Aerospace Lighting Corp, a maker of interior cabin lighting. Separately, it acquired SMR Aerospace, Inc., a provider of cabin services, for $142 million. In April 1998, BEAV acquired Puritan-Bennett Aero Systems, a maker of aircraft oxygen delivery systems, for $70 million, and Aircraft Modular Products, a maker of cabin interior products, for $118 million. BEAV also increased its credit facility to $200 million. At February 28, 1998, backlog totaled $560 million, reflecting new orders for seating and in-flight entertainment products.

Operational Review - 14-AUG-98

Net sales in the three months ended May 30, 1998, advanced 23%, year to year, reflecting strong aftermarket sales. Gross margins widened on the expanded sales volume and an improved product mix. However, with higher SG&A expenses, and a nonrecurring charge of $98 million for in-process R&D and acquisition costs, a net loss of $89,383,000 ($3.87 a diluted share) contrasted with net income of $6,943,000 ($0.30). Excluding the charge, per share earnings rose 23%, to $0.37. BEAV noted that it has exceeded consensus earnings estimates for nine consecutive quarters, and it expects a strong second half.

Stock Performance - 02-OCT-98

In the past 30 trading days, BEAV's shares have declined 27%, compared to a 7% fall in the S&P 500. Average trading volume for the past five days was 260,920 shares, compared with the 40-day moving average of 217,290 shares.

Key Stock Statistics

Dividend Rate/Share	Nil	Shareholders	300
Shs. outstg. (M)	28.3	Market cap. (B)	$0.513
Avg. daily vol. (M)	0.202	Inst. holdings	64%
Tang. Bk. Value/Share	NM		
Beta	1.57		

Value of $10,000 invested 5 years ago: $ 15,104

Fiscal Year Ending Feb. 28

	1999	1998	1997	1996	1995	1994
Revenues (Million $)						
1Q	140.0	113.8	97.30	55.59	57.57	47.80
2Q	156.3	119.8	103.0	57.45	55.20	45.10
3Q	—	129.0	107.8	55.19	57.28	50.70
4Q	—	125.3	104.2	64.35	59.30	59.76
Yr.	—	488.0	412.4	232.6	229.3	203.4
Earnings Per Share ($)						
1Q	-3.87	0.30	0.08	Nil	0.07	0.11
2Q	-2.37	0.35	0.11	-0.02	0.06	0.11
3Q	—	0.40	0.23	-0.21	-0.90	0.03
4Q	—	0.26	0.29	-1.92	0.03	0.10
Yr.	—	1.30	0.72	-3.71	-0.75	0.35

Next earnings report expected: mid December

Dividend Data

The company has not paid cash dividends, and it does not intend to pay any in the immediate future.

A Division of The **McGraw·Hill** Companies

Business Summary - 14-AUG-98

BE Aerospace, Inc. (formerly BE Avionics) is the world's largest manufacturer of commercial aircraft cabin interior products, serving virtually all major airlines. It also offers upgrade, maintenance and repair services. Having achieved leading global market share in each of its major product categories, BEAV's strategy is to maintain its leadership position through various initiatives, including new product development and acquisitions. In the first quarter of FY 99 (Feb.), BEAV acquired Puritan-Bennett Aero Systems and Aircraft Modular Products, expanding its product offerings in commercial aircraft cabin interiors.

Revenues come mainly from refurbishment or upgrade programs for airlines' existing aircraft fleet and new aircraft deliveries. BEAV believes that its large installed base of products gives it significant advantage over competitors in obtaining orders for refurbishment programs, since airlines typically purchase equipment from original suppliers.

Major product lines include first, business, tourist class and commuter seats; a broad range of galley products such as coffee and beverage makers, ovens, liquid containers, refrigeration equipment and galley structures; and in-flight entertainment products including an interactive video system.

In FY 98 (Feb.), seating products accounted for 52%

of revenues, interior systems 26%, entertainment systems 16% and services 6%. Approximately 67% of BEAV's revenues are derived from refurbishment, retrofit, spares and service revenues. The company expects this percentage for aftermarket revenues to increase over the next several years as arilines complete the retrofits of the cabin interiors in their fleets.

Tourist-class seats include top-mounted passenger control units, foot rests and improved oxygen systems. First-class seats and some business-class seats are equipped with an articulating bottom cushion suspension system, hydraulic leg-rests, and large tables. BEAV has also developed two types of seats that can be converted from tourist-class, triple-row seats to business-class, double-row seats.

BEAV has a leading share of the market for passenger control units as well as related wiring and harness assemblies. It also makes an individual interactive seat video system, MDDS (multimedia digital distribution system), with features such as video games, pay-per-view and shopping, advanced multiplexer systems, hard-wired distribution systems (also sold to rail and bus lines) and other passenger entertainment and service products.

In February 1998, the company sold $250 million of subordinated notes and, in March, it redeemed its $125 million 9 3/4% senior notes.

Per Share Data ($)

(Year Ended Feb. 28)	1998	1997	1996	1995	1994	1993	1992	1991	1990	1989
Tangible Bk. Val.	8.60	7.57	2.69	7.79	8.38	7.39	5.42	3.18	2.36	0.62
Cash Flow	2.33	1.98	-2.60	0.25	1.20	1.70	0.24	0.88	0.78	NM
Earnings	1.30	0.72	-3.71	-0.75	0.35	1.03	-0.18	0.65	0.43	-0.13
Dividends	Nil	Nil	Nil	Nil	Nil	Nil	Nil	Nil	Nil	Nil
Payout Ratio	Nil	Nil	Nil	Nil	Nil	Nil	Nil	Nil	Nil	Nil
Cal. Yrs.	1997	1996	1995	1994	1993	1992	1991	1990	1989	1988
Prices - High	41½	28⅜	11¼	11¾	15¼	15¾	16¾	10¾	NA	NA
- Low	19½	9⅞	5¼	7	8¾	9⅞	7½	4¾	NA	NA
P/E Ratio - High	32	39	NM	NM	44	15	NM	17	NA	NA
- Low	15	14	NM	NM	25	10	NM	7	NA	NA

Income Statement Analysis (Million $)

	1998	1997	1996	1995	1994	1993	1992	1991	1990	1989
Revs.	488	412	233	229	203	198	12.0	24.0	23.0	4.0
Oper. Inc.	82.8	66.5	-23.0	36.0	34.5	30.8	0.7	8.7	6.8	0.4
Depr.	24.2	24.1	18.4	16.1	13.1	8.0	4.0	1.7	1.9	0.7
Int. Exp.	22.8	27.1	18.6	15.0	14.1	4.0	NM	0.1	1.6	0.3
Pretax Inc.	35.9	15.2	-60.0	-18.9	8.8	18.8	-2.6	7.2	3.3	-0.6
Eff. Tax Rate	15%	10%	NM	NM	39%	36%	NM	35%	30%	NM
Net Inc.	30.5	13.7	-60.0	-12.1	5.4	12.2	-1.7	4.7	2.3	-0.6

Balance Sheet & Other Fin. Data (Million $)

	1998	1997	1996	1995	1994	1993	1992	1991	1990	1989
Cash	165	44.1	15.4	8.3	13.7	14.3	7.2	6.3	3.5	0.2
Curr. Assets	382	213	150	143	136	205	57.0	17.0	11.0	3.0
Total Assets	682	491	434	380	375	314	135	26.0	21.0	6.0
Curr. Liab.	120	91.1	108	66.0	59.5	71.0	30.0	3.4	3.5	1.1
LT Debt	350	225	273	173	159	128	41.0	Nil	2.0	2.0
Common Eqty.	197	166	44.2	125	134	108	57.0	22.0	16.0	2.0
Total Cap.	548	391	319	309	311	239	100	23.0	18.0	5.0
Cap. Exp.	28.9	14.4	13.7	12.2	11.0	7.3	1.1	0.4	0.4	0.2
Cash Flow	54.7	37.8	-41.6	4.1	18.5	20.1	2.3	6.4	4.2	NM
Curr. Ratio	3.2	2.3	1.4	2.2	2.3	2.9	1.9	5.0	3.1	2.4
% LT Debt of Cap.	63.8	57.5	85.7	55.8	51.2	53.6	40.6	Nil	9.1	49.8
% Net Inc.of Revs.	6.3	3.3	NM	NM	2.6	6.1	NM	19.4	10.1	NM
% Ret. on Assets	5.2	2.9	NM	NM	1.5	6.6	NM	19.6	14.4	NA
% Ret. on Equity	16.8	13.0	NM	NM	4.2	15.7	NM	24.0	22.6	NA

Data as orig. reptd.; bef. results of disc. opers. and/or spec. items. Per share data adj. for stk. divs. as of ex-div. date. Bold denotes diluted EPS (FASB 128). E-Estimated. NA-Not Available. NM-Not Meaningful. NR-Not Ranked.

Office—1400 Corporate Center Way, Wellington, FL 33414. **Tel**—(561) 791-5000. **Fax**—(561) 791-7900. **Chrmn**—A. J. Khoury. **Vice Chrmn & CEO**—R. J. Khoury. **Pres & COO**—P. E. Fulchino. **SVP & CFO**—T. P. McCaffrey. **Treas**—J. P. Holtzman. **Secy**—E. J. Moriarty. **Investor Contact**—Jay Jacobson (914-722-2737). **Dirs**—J. C. Cowart, P. E. Fulchino, R. G. Hamermesh, A. J. Khoury, R. J. Khoury, B. H. Rowe, H. Wyss. **Transfer Agent & Registrar**—BankBoston, N.A., Boston, MA. **Incorporated**—in Delaware in 1987. **Empl**—3,500. **S&P Analyst:** Stewart Scharf

STANDARD &POOR'S
STOCK REPORTS

Belden Inc.

304A

NYSE Symbol **BWC**

In S&P SmallCap 600

03-OCT-98

Industry: Electrical Equipment

Summary: Belden manufactures wire, cable and cord products for the electronics and electrical markets.

Quantitative Evaluations

Outlook (1 Lowest—5 Highest)
- **5+**

Fair Value
- **24⅜**

Risk
- **Average**

Earn./Div. Rank
- **NR**

Technical Eval.
- **Bearish** since 2/98

Rel. Strength Rank (1 Lowest—99 Highest)
- **7**

Insider Activity
- **Favorable**

Recent Price • 13	Yield • 1.5%
52 Wk Range • 43⅞-12¾	12-Mo. P/E • 5.5

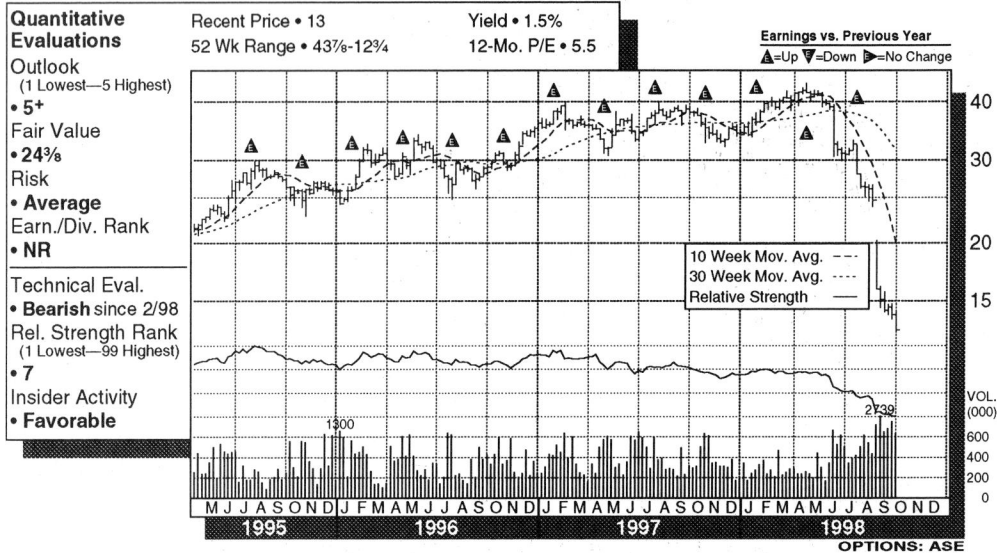

Earnings vs. Previous Year
▲=Up ▼=Down ▶=No Change

10 Week Mov. Avg. – – –
30 Week Mov. Avg. ·······
Relative Strength ——

OPTIONS: ASE

Business Profile - 13-AUG-98

While market conditions remain healthy in the U.S., the company recently indicated that it is experiencing weakness in many of its international markets, especially in the Asia/Pacific region. BWC said, however, that it remains committed to these markets as it considers their current weakness to be temporary. In July 1998, the company increased its stock buyback authorization to purchase up to a total of two million shares. BWC has spent $12.3 million to purchase 392,000 shares to date under this program.

Operational Review - 13-AUG-98

Revenues rose 4.9%, year to year, in the the six months ended June 30, 1998, primarily reflecting strong growth in demand for computer networking and telecommunication cable. Revenues from industrial wire and cable were up slightly despite lower pricing due to the pass-through of copper costs, which are down approximately 30% this year. These gains were partially offset by declines in revenues for audio/video and electrical products. Net income increased 8.1%, to $30.6 million ($1.16 a share, diluted), from $28.3 million ($1.08).

Stock Performance - 02-OCT-98

In the past 30 trading days, BWC's shares have declined 47%, compared to a 7% fall in the S&P 500. Average trading volume for the past five days was 192,080 shares, compared with the 40-day moving average of 293,144 shares.

Key Stock Statistics

Dividend Rate/Share	0.20	Shareholders	1,000
Shs. outstg. (M)	25.8	Market cap. (B)	$0.336
Avg. daily vol. (M)	0.336	Inst. holdings	76%
Tang. Bk. Value/Share	6.21		
Beta	1.27		

Value of $10,000 invested 5 years ago: NA

Fiscal Year Ending Dec. 31

	1998	1997	1996	1995	1994	1993
Revenues (Million $)						
1Q	190.4	176.0	169.3	114.1	99.9	--
2Q	196.3	192.6	167.7	160.0	103.4	188.0
3Q	—	183.7	159.0	156.7	110.0	92.80
4Q	—	194.9	171.4	177.8	126.4	102.9
Yr.	—	747.2	667.4	608.6	439.7	383.7
Earnings Per Share ($)						
1Q	**0.59**	**0.53**	0.48	0.37	0.31	--
2Q	**0.58**	**0.55**	0.51	0.41	0.33	0.53
3Q	—	**0.55**	0.51	0.43	0.37	0.30
4Q	—	**0.68**	0.61	0.55	0.46	0.38
Yr.	—	**2.30**	2.11	1.76	1.46	1.21

Next earnings report expected: late October

Dividend Data (Dividends have been paid since 1994.)

Amount ($)	Date Decl.	Ex-Div. Date	Stock of Record	Payment Date
0.050	Nov. 13	Dec. 02	Dec. 04	Jan. 02 '98
0.050	Feb. 26	Mar. 10	Mar. 12	Apr. 03 '98
0.050	May. 08	May. 26	May. 28	Jul. 02 '98
0.050	Aug. 20	Sep. 08	Sep. 10	Oct. 02 '98

Business Summary - 13-AUG-98

Belden Inc. is a leader in the design, manufacture and marketing of specialty wire, cable and cord products. It serves many major growing and competitive markets, such as computer networking and computer equipment; broadcast, entertainment and cable TV; industrial instrumentation and control; and electrical equipment, including power tools, floor care equipment, home appliances and motor and test apparatus. Belden's products are positioned at the upper end of the value-added range used for electrical signal transmission in broadcast, data and industrial automation applications.

Sales contributions by market in 1997, and change from 1996:

	Revs.	% Change
Computer	37%	29%
Audio/visual	22%	-8%
Industrial	20%	26%
Electrical	21%	1%

Sales to several business units of Anixter International Inc. accounted for 16% of the total in 1997, versus 17% in 1996 and 18% in 1995. Sales in Europe accounted for 10% of the total in 1997, Canada 6%, and export (largely to the Pacific Rim) 10%.

Belden meets the demands of its markets with various product configurations, which include, for the electronic markets, multiconductor products, coaxial cable, fiber optic cables, heat-shrinkable tubing and wire management products; and for the electrical markets, cords and lead, hook-up and other wire.

A multiconductor cable consists of two or more insulated conductors that are cabled together. Major end-uses for multiconductor cable include computer networking and computer equipment, as well as various applications within the industrial signal, instrumentation and control market.

Coaxial cable consists of a central inner conductor surrounded by a concentric outer conductor. Primary applications are in audio/video markets, such as broadcast and entertainment (which use broadcast cables to distribute audio and video signals for the TV, music and other entertainment industries) and cable TV.

Fiber optic cables are used to transmit light signals through glass or plastic fibers. The principal application is premises data distribution systems using multimode fiber.

A cord is a two- or three-conductor cable with a molded plug on one or both ends. Most cords are sold directly to OEMs for incorporation in portable electric power tools, floor care equipment and home appliances. Cord products are marketed through distributors and appliance wholesalers. Lead, hook-up and other wire consists of single-conductor wire that is used for electrical leads in motors, internal wiring and test equipment.

Per Share Data ($)

(Year Ended Dec. 31)	1997	1996	1995	1994	1993	1992	1991	1990	1989	1988
Tangible Bk. Val.	5.49	5.79	4.44	3.15	1.85	1.27	NA	NA	NA	NA
Cash Flow	3.06	2.78	2.39	1.92	1.72	1.55	NA	NA	NA	NA
Earnings	2.30	2.11	1.76	1.46	1.21	1.05	NA	NA	NA	NA
Dividends	0.20	0.20	0.20	0.20	Nil	NA	NA	NA	NA	NA
Payout Ratio	9%	9%	11%	14%	Nil	NA	NA	NA	NA	NA
Prices - High	39⁷/₈	37	29⁷/₈	22¹/₂	18⁵/₈	NA	NA	NA	NA	NA
- Low	30⁵/₈	24¹/₈	19³/₄	16¹/₈	14¹/₄	NA	NA	NA	NA	NA
P/E Ratio - High	17	18	17	15	15	NA	NA	NA	NA	NA
- Low	13	11	11	11	12	NA	NA	NA	NA	NA

Income Statement Analysis (Million $)

	1997	1996	1995	1994	1993	1992	1991	1990	1989	1988
Revs.	747	667	609	440	384	366	NA	NA	NA	NA
Oper. Inc.	127	112	95.5	77.3	68.7	62.2	NA	NA	NA	NA
Depr.	19.8	17.6	15.9	12.0	12.0	13.0	NA	NA	NA	NA
Int. Exp.	7.0	3.5	3.9	2.6	2.7	3.2	NA	NA	NA	NA
Pretax Inc.	99	90.8	75.7	62.7	53.9	44.2	NA	NA	NA	NA
Eff. Tax Rate	39%	39%	39%	39%	39%	38%	NA	NA	NA	NA
Net Inc.	60.7	55.2	46.2	38.1	32.7	27.2	NA	NA	NA	NA

Balance Sheet & Other Fin. Data (Million $)

	1997	1996	1995	1994	1993	1992	1991	1990	1989	1988
Cash	0.9	1.8	0.8	4.7	2.4	0.2	NA	NA	NA	NA
Curr. Assets	237	191	173	110	102	100	NA	NA	NA	NA
Total Assets	475	372	333	204	197	192	NA	NA	NA	NA
Curr. Liab.	83.1	82.7	83.2	45.7	40.6	40.7	NA	NA	NA	NA
LT Debt	124	71.6	81.5	37.3	68.0	78.4	NA	NA	NA	NA
Common Eqty.	229	180	132	93.6	60.5	45.2	NA	NA	NA	NA
Total Cap.	366	262	221	138	136	130	NA	NA	NA	NA
Cap. Exp.	28.7	26.1	21.8	13.3	16.6	NA	NA	NA	NA	NA
Cash Flow	80.5	72.8	62.1	50.1	44.8	40.2	NA	NA	NA	NA
Curr. Ratio	2.9	2.3	2.1	2.4	2.5	2.5	NA	NA	NA	NA
% LT Debt of Cap.	33.9	27.4	36.8	26.9	50.1	60.1	NA	NA	NA	NA
% Net Inc.of Revs.	8.1	8.3	7.6	8.7	8.5	7.4	NA	NA	NA	NA
% Ret. on Assets	14.3	15.7	17.2	19.0	NM	NA	NA	NA	NA	NA
% Ret. on Equity	29.7	35.5	40.9	49.4	NA	NA	NA	NA	NA	NA

Data as orig. reptd.; bef. results of disc. opers. and/or spec. items. Per share data adj. for stk. divs. as of ex-div. date. Bold denotes diluted EPS (FASB 128). E-Estimated. NA-Not Available. NM-Not Meaningful. NR-Not Ranked.

Office—7701 Forsyth Blvd., Suite 800, St. Louis, MO 63105. **Tel**—(314) 854-8000. **Fax**—(314) 854-8001. **Website**—http://www.belden.com **Chrmn, CEO & Pres**—C. B. Cunningham. **VP, CFO, Treas & Investor Contact**—Richard K. Reece. **VP & Secy**—K. L. Bloomfield. **Dirs**—L. D. Bain, C. I. Byrnes, J. R. Coppola, C. B. Cunningham, J. R. Dallepezze, A. E. Riedel, B. G. Rethore. **Transfer Agent & Registrar**—Boatmen's Trust Co., St. Louis. **Incorporated**—in Delaware in 1993. **Empl**— 4,500. **S&P Analyst:** C.F.B.

Bell Industries

STANDARD &POOR'S
STOCK REPORTS

313

NYSE Symbol **BI**

In S&P SmallCap 600

03-OCT-98

Industry:
Electronics (Component Distributors)

Summary: Bell Industries distributes products for the electronics, computer, graphics and other industrial markets.

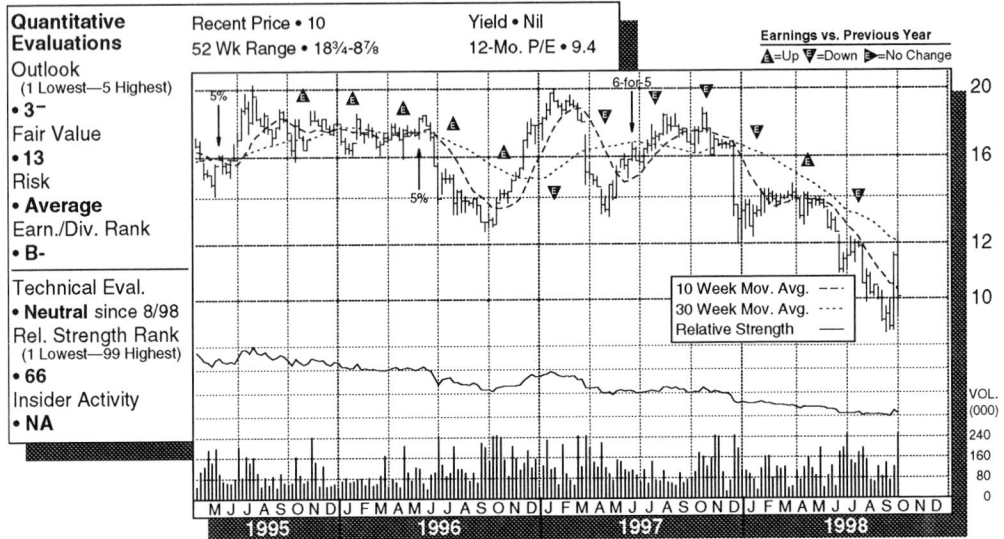

Quantitative Evaluations	
Outlook (1 Lowest—5 Highest)	**3⁻**
Fair Value	**13**
Risk	**Average**
Earn./Div. Rank	**B-**
Technical Eval.	**Neutral** since 8/98
Rel. Strength Rank (1 Lowest—99 Highest)	**66**
Insider Activity	**NA**

Recent Price • 10
52 Wk Range • 18¾-8⅞

Yield • Nil
12-Mo. P/E • 9.4

Earnings vs. Previous Year
▲=Up ▼=Down ▶=No Change

10 Week Mov. Avg. ---
30 Week Mov. Avg. ----
Relative Strength —

Business Profile - 08-JUL-98

In January 1997, the company acquired Milgray Electronics, Inc., another distributor of electronic components, for about $100 million in cash. In July 1997, the company reported that its integration of Milgray was proceeding ahead of schedule, with BI beginning to realize synergies and economies of scale. BI recently consolidated three distribution facilities at its new distribution center in California. Earnings in the past two quarters have been restricted by market weakness in two of the company's three business segments.

Operational Review - 08-JUL-98

Net sales in the three months ended March 31, 1998, declined 2.3%, year to year, primarily reflecting market softness in the electronics and graphics/imaging groups. Gross margins narrowed slightly, but SG&A expenses fell more rapidly than sales. In the absence of a $4.1 million integration charge, pretax income tripled. Following taxes at 46.6%, versus 45.7%, income recovered to $2,441,000 ($0.26 a share) from $829,000 ($0.09). Results for the 1997 period exclude a $0.07 loss on early retirement of debt.

Stock Performance - 02-OCT-98

In the past 30 trading days, BI's shares have declined 4%, compared to a 7% fall in the S&P 500. Average trading volume for the past five days was 71,820 shares, compared with the 40-day moving average of 26,054 shares.

Key Stock Statistics

Dividend Rate/Share	Nil	Shareholders	1,500
Shs. outstg. (M)	9.4	Market cap. (B)	$0.095
Avg. daily vol. (M)	0.035	Inst. holdings	55%
Tang. Bk. Value/Share	9.06		
Beta	0.76		

Value of $10,000 invested 5 years ago: $ 12,573

Fiscal Year Ending Dec. 31

	1998	1997	1996	1995	1994	1993
Revenues (Million $)						
1Q	213.4	218.5	143.1	126.9	--	106.7
2Q	210.3	233.8	156.7	141.6	--	102.2
3Q	—	225.4	164.3	148.6	127.1	113.5
4Q	—	213.0	159.1	147.2	128.3	128.7
Yr.	—	890.7	623.2	564.3	255.4	451.2
Earnings Per Share ($)						
1Q	**0.26**	**0.09**	0.36	0.29	--	0.29
2Q	**0.20**	**0.37**	0.50	0.48	--	0.16
3Q	—	**0.40**	0.48	0.48	0.33	0.23
4Q	—	**0.21**	0.41	0.44	0.28	0.41
Yr.	—	**1.07**	1.75	1.68	0.60	1.04

Next earnings report expected: mid October

Dividend Data

No cash dividends have been paid in recent years.

Business Summary - 08-JUL-98

Bell Industries is primarily a distributor of electronic components. It also distributes graphics and electronic imaging and recreational-related products. Business segment contributions in recent years were:

	1997	1996
Electronics	77%	74%
Graphics & electronic imaging	18%	19%
Recreational products	5%	7%

Electronic components distribution involves the sale of semiconductors, passive components, connectors, power supplies, board-level products, and microcomputers and related products from more than 30 sales facilities located nationwide. Major lines include Samsung Semiconductor, Analog Devices, SGS-Thomson, IBM Microelectronics, Microchip, Maxim, Aromat, Kemet, Berg and Power-One. These products are sold to more than 20,000 customers nationwide.

In January 1997, Bell acquired Milgray Electronics, a distributor of electronic components, for about $100 million. Milgray's fiscal 1996 revenues were $272 million.

Although Bell and Milgray operate in many of the same markets, management believes that the two companies have different customer bases and, in some cases, complementary, rather than competitive, product lines. In addition, Bell gained access to Milgray's established markets in New York, Kansas City and Canada.

The graphics and electronic imaging group distributes graphic and electronic imaging supplies and equipment, including film, plates, chemicals and printing supplies from Agfa, DuPont, Eastman Kodak and 3M, as well as prepress and related electronic imaging equipment from Agfa, Apple, Howtek, Intergraph and Screen to the advertising and printing industries. The group operates distribution facilities in Arizona, California, Colorado, Oregon, Washington and Texas.

Recreational products include marine equipment and motorcycle helmets and replacement parts for the motorcycle, mobile home, snowmobile and marine industries. The group supplies over 9,000 recreational vehicle-related products, as well as more than 9,500 marine items, 10,000 motorcycle items and 7,000 snowmobile items. Major product lines include Bieffe Helmets, Dunlop, Nordyne, NGK and Whirlpool. Sales are made from facilities in St. Paul, MN and Milwaukee, WI.

Per Share Data ($)

(Year Ended Dec. 31)	1997	1996	1995	1994	1993	1992	1991	1990	1989	1988
Tangible Bk. Val.	8.43	14.38	12.81	11.09	10.40	9.48	9.90	10.04	10.17	12.20
Cash Flow	2.13	13.45	2.34	0.93	1.69	1.12	0.53	0.64	1.53	1.13
Earnings	1.07	1.75	1.67	0.60	1.04	0.58	0.05	0.08	0.97	0.52
Dividends	Nil	Nil	Nil	Nil	Nil	0.28	0.28	1.66	1.62	0.19
Payout Ratio	Nil	Nil	Nil	Nil	Nil	48%	NM	NM	165%	36%
Prices - High	20	18$\frac{1}{2}$	20$\frac{3}{8}$	17$\frac{1}{4}$	14$\frac{1}{4}$	13$\frac{1}{2}$	9$\frac{1}{8}$	9$\frac{3}{8}$	13	12$\frac{1}{4}$
- Low	12	12$\frac{1}{2}$	14$\frac{1}{8}$	10	10$\frac{1}{2}$	6$\frac{3}{8}$	6$\frac{5}{8}$	6$\frac{1}{4}$	8$\frac{3}{8}$	10$\frac{1}{8}$
P/E Ratio - High	19	11	12	NM	14	23	NM	NM	13	24
- Low	11	7	8	NM	10	11	NM	NM	9	20

Income Statement Analysis (Million $)

	1997	1996	1995	1994	1993	1992	1991	1990	1989	1988
Revs.	891	623	564	255	451	365	414	399	396	418
Oper. Inc.	45.2	37.4	35.0	13.9	25.8	18.8	14.9	14.7	21.4	16.6
Depr.	10.0	6.2	5.9	2.9	5.6	4.6	4.1	4.8	4.7	5.4
Int. Exp.	12.3	3.7	3.6	1.9	4.5	5.5	5.4	4.5	2.4	2.9
Pretax Inc.	18.8	27.5	25.8	9.2	15.7	8.7	1.0	1.8	14.2	7.3
Eff. Tax Rate	46%	42%	42%	42%	42%	42%	58%	62%	42%	38%
Net Inc.	10.1	15.9	15.0	5.3	9.1	5.0	0.4	0.7	8.2	4.6

Balance Sheet & Other Fin. Data (Million $)

	1997	1996	1995	1994	1993	1992	1991	1990	1989	1988
Cash	5.4	12.1	4.8	3.6	4.4	10.7	14.6	6.1	3.3	7.0
Curr. Assets	309	205	209	174	157	139	161	157	142	149
Total Assets	431	241	234	200	185	175	192	189	176	181
Curr. Liab.	101	72.3	73.0	57.7	49.2	41.4	46.6	38.0	51.5	41.9
LT Debt	172	24.6	37.4	36.3	36.1	44.4	49.6	53.3	24.0	20.1
Common Eqty.	158	139	118	102	96.0	86.0	92.0	94.0	95.0	112
Total Cap.	324	165	155	138	132	131	142	148	121	134
Cap. Exp.	16.2	9.6	5.0	1.4	2.6	5.7	8.7	5.7	5.4	4.0
Cash Flow	20.1	22.2	20.9	8.2	14.6	9.6	4.5	5.5	12.9	10.0
Curr. Ratio	3.1	2.8	2.9	3.0	3.2	3.4	3.5	4.1	2.8	3.6
% LT Debt of Cap.	53.1	15.1	24.2	26.3	27.4	34.0	34.9	36.0	19.9	15.0
% Net Inc.of Revs.	1.1	2.6	2.7	2.1	2.0	1.4	0.1	0.2	2.1	1.1
% Ret. on Assets	3.0	6.7	6.9	NM	5.0	2.7	0.2	0.4	4.6	2.5
% Ret. on Equity	6.8	12.5	13.7	NM	10.0	5.6	0.4	0.7	7.9	4.1

Data as orig. reptd.; bef. results of disc. opers. and/or spec. items. Per share data adj. for stk. divs. as of ex-div. date. Yrs. ended Jun. 30 of fol. cal. yr. prior to 1994. Data for 1994 is for six mos. ended Jun. 30. Bold denotes diluted EPS (FASB 128). E-Estimated. NA-Not Available. NM-Not Meaningful. NR-Not Ranked.

Office—2201 E. El Segundo Blvd., El Segundo, CA 90245-4608**Tel**—(310) 563-2355. **Website**—http://www.bellind.com **Chrmn**—T. Williams. **Pres & CEO**—G. M. Graham. **VP, CFO & Investor Contact**—Tracy A. Edwards. **Secy**—J. J. Cost. **Dirs**—J. J. Cost, A. L. Craig, H. S. Davidson G. M. Graham, M. Rosenberg, C. S. Troy, T. Williams. **Transfer Agent & Registrar**—Harris Trust Co., Los Angeles. **Incorporated**—in California in 1959; reincorporated in Delaware in 1979; reincorporated in California in 1995. **Empl**— 1,900. **S&P Analyst:** B.G.

03-OCT-98

Industry:
Electrical Equipment

Summary: BHE provides contract manufacturing and engineering services to original equipment manufacturers in various industries.

Quantitative Evaluations	
Outlook (1 Lowest—5 Highest)	• **4**
Fair Value	• **33¼**
Risk	• **Average**
Earn./Div. Rank	• **B+**
Technical Eval.	• **Bearish** since 4/98
Rel. Strength Rank (1 Lowest—99 Highest)	• **94**
Insider Activity	• **Neutral**

Recent Price • 22⅝
52 Wk Range • 30½-17⅝

Yield • Nil
12-Mo. P/E • 17.5

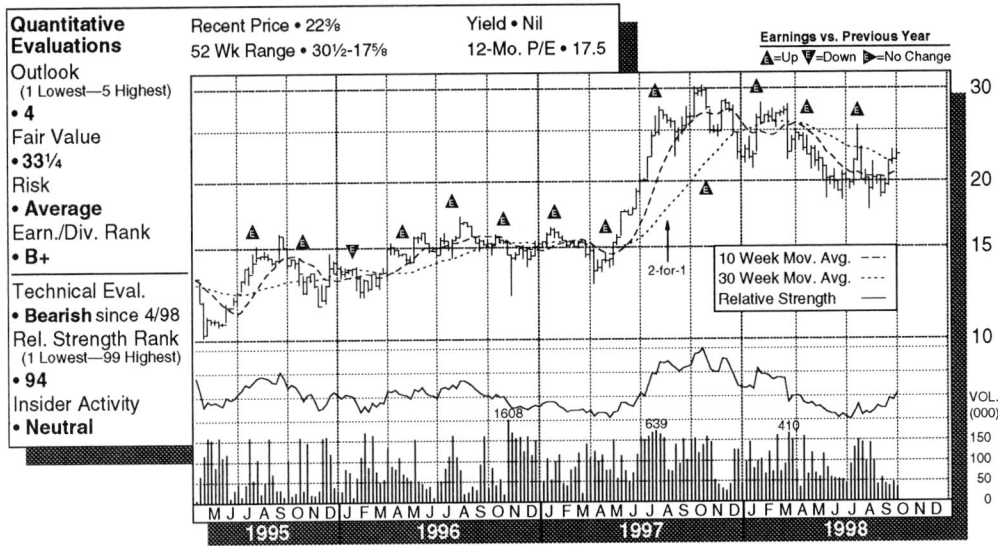

Earnings vs. Previous Year
▲=Up ▼=Down ▶=No Change

10 Week Mov. Avg. – – –
30 Week Mov. Avg. ·····
Relative Strength —

2-for-1

Business Profile - 28-SEP-98

BHE seeks growth by acquiring additional facilities or businesses, and by achieving additional operating efficiencies in its existing operations. In February 1998, the company acquired Lockheed Martin's commercial electronics unit, LCEC, for $70 million in cash. With the addition of LCEC, one of New England's largest electronics manufacturing services companies, Benchmark expanded the scope of its operations considerably. In the first half of 1998, BHE's three largest customers accounted for 53% of sales. The company continues to seek ways to reduce its dependence on any one customer or industry. In May 1997, trading in the shares moved to the New York Stock Exchange, from the American Stock Exchange.

Operational Review - 28-SEP-98

Sales in the six months ended June 30, 1998, advanced 56%, year to year, reflecting increased sales volume from existing customers, the addition of new customers, and the LCEC acquisition. Gross margins narrowed, on lower margins on LCEC programs, changes in the product mix, costs to start new programs and underutilization at the Hudson facility. SG&A expenses rose less rapidly, but with higher interest expense and amortization costs, the gain in pretax income was held to 11%. After taxes at 38.7%, versus 37.9%, net income was up 9.2%, to $7,478,000 ($0.61 a share, on 3.1% more shares), from $6,848,000 ($0.58, adjusted).

Stock Performance - 02-OCT-98

In the past 30 trading days, BHE's shares have increased 11%, compared to a 7% fall in the S&P 500. Average trading volume for the past five days was 6,340 shares, compared with the 40-day moving average of 12,533 shares.

Key Stock Statistics

Dividend Rate/Share	Nil	Shareholders	100
Shs. outstg. (M)	11.6	Market cap. (B)	$0.260
Avg. daily vol. (M)	0.008	Inst. holdings	66%
Tang. Bk. Value/Share	6.70		
Beta	0.64		

Value of $10,000 invested 5 years ago: $ 27,403

Fiscal Year Ending Dec. 31

	1998	1997	1996	1995	1994	1993
Revenues (Million $)						
1Q	108.0	75.72	30.38	23.12	24.28	15.20
2Q	132.6	78.16	33.50	23.65	25.05	17.06
3Q	—	83.18	62.30	24.39	25.10	19.57
4Q	—	88.17	75.11	26.20	23.75	24.03
Yr.	—	325.2	201.3	97.35	98.17	75.86
Earnings Per Share ($)						
1Q	0.31	0.28	0.23	0.19	0.17	0.10
2Q	0.31	0.30	0.24	0.20	0.17	0.13
3Q	—	0.33	0.26	0.19	0.18	0.15
4Q	—	0.35	0.24	0.17	0.20	0.17
Yr.	—	1.25	0.96	0.75	0.70	0.55

Next earnings report expected: mid October

Dividend Data

The company has never paid a cash dividend. A 2-for-1 stock split was effected in August 1997.

A Division of The **McGraw·Hill** *Companies*

Business Summary - 28-SEP-98

Benchmark Electronics, Inc. (BHE) manufactures complex printed circuit boards (CBPs) for companies that make medical devices, telecommunications equipment, test and instrumentation, high-end computers, and industrial controls. The company was founded in 1979, and went public in 1990.

In 1996, the company acquired EMD Technologies, Inc. The acquisition moved BHE into the top tier of electronic manufacturing services industry (EMSI) providers. During 1996, the company improved its ability to offer current design-through-delivery solutions to its customers. With the acquisition of EMD, BHE is now able to offer product software and circuit design, bare printed circuit board layout (PCB), mechanical product design, and test fixture/software development all under one roof. In February 1998, BHE acquired Lockheed Commercial Electronics Co. (LCEC) from Lockheed Martin, for $70 million in cash. LCEC is one of New England's largest electronics manufacturing services companies. It provides a broad range of services, including printed circuit board assembly and test, system assembly and test, prototyping, depot repair and engineering support services.

BHE offers the most advanced manufacturing processes: ball grid arrays (BGA), chip on board (COB), and multi chip modules (MCM) technologies. It also provides production experience for new generations of products. The company believes that these technologies allow increases in electronic packaging density and circuit performance as compared to surface mount (SMT) or thru-hole interconnects. EMD's added capabilities included world class process analysis equipment (like scanning electron microscopes), and provided initial process development, ongoing failure analysis, and corrective action capabilities.

Despite the EMD acquisition, BHE says that it has not changed its overall business strategy, which includes strengthening customer service, emphasizing continuing development of management, and retaining a conservative financial philosophy. The company states that its mission is to maintain a leadership position in the medium-volume, high technology EMSI. BHE plans to accomplish this through customer satisfaction, as measured by customer expectations for world class quality, flexible manufacturing, product delivery, leading edge technology, financial strength, and managerial integrity.

In May 1997, trading in the shares moved from the American Stock Exchange to the New York Stock Exchange.

Per Share Data ($)

(Year Ended Dec. 31)	1997	1996	1995	1994	1993	1992	1991	1990	1989	1988
Tangible Bk. Val.	8.48	7.03	5.80	5.00	4.29	3.71	2.55	2.22	0.84	0.57
Cash Flow	2.09	1.66	1.00	0.94	0.72	0.57	0.46	0.46	0.36	NA
Earnings	1.25	0.96	0.75	0.70	0.55	0.41	0.33	0.38	0.33	0.17
Dividends	Nil	Nil	Nil	Nil	Nil	Nil	Nil	Nil	Nil	Nil
Payout Ratio	Nil	Nil	Nil	Nil	Nil	Nil	Nil	Nil	Nil	Nil
Prices - High	$30\frac{1}{2}$	$17\frac{1}{4}$	16	14	12	$8\frac{7}{8}$	$6\frac{1}{8}$	$4\frac{3}{8}$	NA	NA
- Low	$12\frac{3}{4}$	$12\frac{1}{8}$	$10\frac{1}{8}$	$11\frac{1}{4}$	$7\frac{1}{2}$	$5\frac{1}{4}$	$2\frac{5}{16}$	$1\frac{13}{16}$	NA	NA
P/E Ratio - High	24	18	21	20	22	21	19	12	NA	NA
- Low	10	13	13	16	14	13	7	5	NA	NA

Income Statement Analysis (Million $)

	1997	1996	1995	1994	1993	1992	1991	1990	1989	1988
Revs.	325	201	97.4	98.2	75.9	50.6	33.3	21.3	18.1	8.1
Oper. Inc.	35.3	21.8	11.3	10.7	8.0	5.4	3.8	3.0	2.0	0.8
Depr.	10.2	6.4	2.1	1.9	1.4	1.1	0.8	0.4	0.2	0.0
Int. Exp.	2.5	1.4	Nil	Nil	Nil	Nil	Nil	0.1	0.1	0.0
Pretax Inc.	24.0	14.4	9.5	9.0	6.9	4.8	3.3	3.1	1.9	0.8
Eff. Tax Rate	37%	39%	36%	36%	36%	34%	36%	35%	29%	14%
Net Inc.	15.1	8.9	6.2	5.8	4.5	3.1	2.1	2.0	1.4	0.7

Balance Sheet & Other Fin. Data (Million $)

	1997	1996	1995	1994	1993	1992	1991	1990	1989	1988
Cash	21.0	13.8	2.8	8.4	10.1	13.3	3.1	7.1	0.1	0.1
Curr. Assets	125	103	47.0	38.5	42.0	30.3	15.6	15.7	5.1	3.5
Total Assets	190	168	57.0	48.2	47.4	34.4	20.0	17.4	6.6	3.9
Curr. Liab.	37.3	30.7	9.7	7.6	12.9	4.5	3.3	2.8	2.3	1.4
LT Debt	30.3	30.4	Nil	Nil	Nil	Nil	Nil	Nil	0.1	0.1
Common Eqty.	121	105	46.6	40.1	34.2	29.6	16.3	14.2	3.5	1.9
Total Cap.	153	137	47.4	40.7	34.6	29.8	16.5	14.3	3.7	2.0
Cap. Exp.	10.4	8.7	2.3	6.3	2.8	0.9	7.2	0.5	1.3	0.3
Cash Flow	25.2	15.2	8.2	7.7	5.9	4.3	2.9	2.4	1.5	NA
Curr. Ratio	3.4	3.4	4.9	5.1	3.3	6.8	4.7	5.6	2.2	2.6
% LT Debt of Cap.	19.8	22.2	Nil	Nil	Nil	Nil	Nil	Nil	2.4	5.2
% Net Inc.of Revs.	4.6	4.4	6.4	5.9	5.9	6.2	6.3	9.4	7.6	8.8
% Ret. on Assets	8.4	7.9	11.7	12.0	10.9	10.6	11.3	14.6	26.1	22.5
% Ret. on Equity	13.4	11.7	14.2	15.5	14.0	12.5	13.8	20.6	50.3	59.9

Data as orig. reptd.; bef. results of disc. opers. and/or spec. items. Per share data adj. for stk. divs. as of ex-div. date. E-Estimated. NA-Not Available. NM-Not Meaningful. NR-Not Ranked.

Office—3000 Technology Dr., Angleton, TX 77515. **Tel**—(409) 849-6550. **Fax**—(409) 848-5271 **Website**—http://www.bench.com **Chrmn**—J. C. Custer. **Pres & CEO**—D. E. Nigbor. **EVP**—Cary T. Fu. **Secy**—L. A. Gurton. **Dirs**—D. H. Arnold, S. A. Barton, G. W. Bodzy, J. C. Custer, P. G. Dorflinger, C. T. Fu, D. E. Nigbor. **Transfer Agent & Registrar**—Harris Trust & Savings Bank, c/o Harris Trust Co. of New York, NYC. **Incorporated**—in Texas in 1981. **Empl**—1,644. **S&P Analyst:** S.A.H.

Benton Oil & Gas   320P
NYSE Symbol **BNO**

In S&P SmallCap 600

03-OCT-98

Industry: Oil & Gas (Exploration & Production)

Summary: This independent oil and gas exploration and production company has operations mainly in western Siberia (Russia) and eastern Venezuela.

Quantitative Evaluations

Recent Price • 5¼	Yield • Nil
52 Wk Range • 21⅞-4⅝	12-Mo. P/E • NM

Outlook (1 Lowest—5 Highest)
• **NA**

Fair Value
• **NA**

Risk
• **High**

Earn./Div. Rank
• **NR**

Technical Eval.
• **NA**

Rel. Strength Rank (1 Lowest—99 Highest)
• **14**

Insider Activity
• **NA**

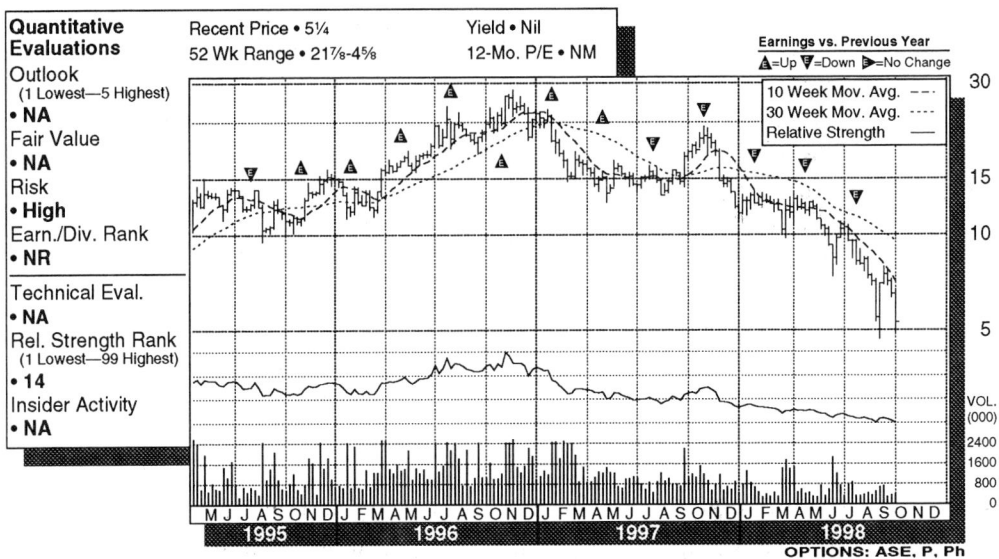

OPTIONS: ASE, P, Ph

Business Profile - 22-APR-98

Benton, which currently derives most of its revenues from an 80% interest in a Venezuelan subsidiary, also owns a 34% equity stake in the North Gubkinskoye Field in western Siberia. In April 1998, it reached an agreement to earn a 40% equity interest in the Russian Open Joint Stock Company Severneftegaz. Benton's capital commitment will be in the form of a $100 million loan to the project, estimated to be disbursed over the initial two-year development phase. Benton and Severneftegaz anticipate gas and condensate production and sales in the second half of 1999, to be followed by oil production in subsequent years.

Operational Review - 22-APR-98

Revenues rose 8.4% in 1997, reflecting the growth of Benton Vinccler in Venezuela, partly offset by lower crude oil prices. Results were restricted by higher water handling, gas handling, workover, transportation and chemical costs, and by greater interest expense resulting from the issuance of notes in 1996 and 1997. In the absence of a gain on the sale of properties, and after taxes and minority interest, income fell 53%, to $18,049,000 ($0.59 a share), from $38,357,000 ($1.29). Results in 1996 exclude a charge of $0.34 a share related to the retirement of debt.

Stock Performance - 02-OCT-98

In the past 30 trading days, BNO's shares have declined 25%, compared to a 7% fall in the S&P 500. Average trading volume for the past five days was 77,560 shares, compared with the 40-day moving average of 93,572 shares.

Key Stock Statistics

Dividend Rate/Share	Nil	Shareholders	1,100
Shs. outstg. (M)	29.6	Market cap. (B)	$0.157
Avg. daily vol. (M)	0.094	Inst. holdings	51%
Tang. Bk. Value/Share	4.31		
Beta	0.81		

Value of $10,000 invested 5 years ago: $ 9,041

Fiscal Year Ending Dec. 31

	1998	1997	1996	1995	1994	1993
Revenues (Million $)						
1Q	33.26	46.30	32.94	12.66	3.76	1.74
2Q	28.21	40.98	41.89	13.21	8.48	1.63
3Q	—	45.19	40.90	18.29	9.57	1.36
4Q	—	46.56	49.34	20.91	12.90	3.08
Yr.	—	179.0	165.1	65.07	34.70	7.81
Earnings Per Share ($)						
1Q	-0.71	0.28	0.23	0.08	-0.05	-0.04
2Q	-1.69	0.15	0.47	0.04	0.05	-0.04
3Q	—	0.09	0.29	0.11	0.07	-0.07
4Q	—	0.07	0.30	0.17	0.05	-0.10
Yr.	—	0.59	1.30	0.40	0.12	-0.26

Next earnings report expected: mid November

Dividend Data

No cash dividends have been paid. A poison pill stockholder rights plan was adopted in 1995. Two-for-one stock splits were effected in 1990 and 1991.

 A Division of The McGraw-Hill Companies

Business Summary - 22-APR-98

Originally active only in the U.S., this independent energy company, which began operations in 1989, has developed significant interests in oil and gas properties in Venezuela and Russia, and has recently acquired certain interests in China, Jordan, Senegal, and the U.S. Operations of Benton Oil & Gas (BNO) are currently conducted mainly through its 80%-owned Venezuelan subsidiary, Benton-Vinncler, C.A., which operates the South Monagas Unit in Venezuela, and its 34%-owned Russian joint venture, GEOILBENT, which operates the North Gubkinskoye Field in West Siberia, Russia.

BNO has recently expanded into projects that involve exploration components, in Venezuela through its participation in the Delta Centro exploration block, in Santa Barbara County, CA, through the acquisition of a participation interest in three state offshore oil and gas leases, and in China through a farmout agreement with Shell Exploration (China) Ltd.

During the four years through 1997, the company expanded its reserves and production. Estimated proved reserves increased from 42,785,000 bbl. of oil

equivalent (BOE) to 120,784 MBOE in 1996, and net production rose from 519 MBOE to 16,275 MBOE.

BNO's business strategy is to identify and exploit new oil and gas reserves in underdeveloped areas, while seeking to minimize the associated risk of those activities. BNO attempts to minimize risk by using several strategies: seek new reserves in areas of low geologic risk; use proven advanced technology in both exploration and development to maximize recovery; establish a local presence through joint-venture partners and the use of local personnel; commit capital in a phased manner to limit total commitments at any one time; and reduce foreign exchange risks through receipt of revenues in U.S. currency.

The company has used its experience to seek and develop new reserves in countries where perceived potential political and operating difficulties have sometimes discouraged other energy companies from competing. As a result, it has established operations in Venezuela and Russia with significant reserves that have been acquired and developed at relatively low costs. BNO is seeking similar opportunities in other countries and areas that it believes have high potential.

Per Share Data ($)

(Year Ended Dec. 31)	1997	1996	1995	1994	1993	1992	1991	1990	1989	1988
Tangible Bk. Val.	6.71	6.05	4.06	3.54	3.40	2.89	1.96	1.17	0.57	-0.04
Cash Flow	2.13	2.46	1.05	0.53	-0.12	0.01	0.28	0.12	-0.10	NA
Earnings	0.59	1.30	0.40	0.12	-0.26	-0.22	0.03	0.01	-0.13	NA
Dividends	Nil	Nil	Nil	Nil	Nil	Nil	Nil	Nil	Nil	Nil
Payout Ratio	Nil	Nil	Nil	Nil	NM	NM	Nil	Nil	Nil	Nil
Prices - High	24¾	28⅝	16⅛	9⅛	10¼	11⅛	18¾	8⅜	2⅝	NA
- Low	11¼	11¼	8⅝	4¼	3⅞	5	6⅛	2	1¼	NA
P/E Ratio - High	42	22	40	76	NM	NM	NM	NM	NM	NA
- Low	19	9	22	35	NM	NM	NM	NM	NM	NM

Income Statement Analysis (Million $)

	1997	1996	1995	1994	1993	1992	1991	1990	1989	1988
Revs.	164	148	62.2	32.1	7.4	8.4	11.2	4.4	0.3	NA
Oper. Inc.	99	104	42.0	17.3	-0.5	1.7	4.9	1.0	-0.4	NA
Depr. Depl. & Amort.	47.6	34.5	17.4	10.3	2.6	3.0	3.0	0.8	0.1	NA
Int. Exp.	24.2	16.1	7.5	3.9	2.0	1.8	1.7	0.3	0.1	NA
Pretax Inc.	41.9	68.8	18.4	5.8	-4.8	-2.9	0.5	0.2	-0.5	NA
Eff. Tax Rate	42%	30%	14%	12%	NM	NM	34%	26%	NM	NM
Net Inc.	18.0	38.4	10.6	3.0	-4.8	-2.9	0.3	0.1	-0.5	NA

Balance Sheet & Other Fin. Data (Million $)

	1997	1996	1995	1994	1993	1992	1991	1990	1989	1988
Cash	86.3	88.9	26.5	33.7	36.3	13.7	3.7	5.1	1.5	0.4
Curr. Assets	224	151	51.6	62.4	39.5	14.8	7.0	8.1	2.2	0.6
Total Assets	584	436	215	163	109	68.2	49.4	27.3	4.5	0.8
Curr. Liab.	58.4	52.1	54.5	40.6	12.8	4.3	21.8	9.9	1.5	0.9
LT Debt	280	175	49.5	31.9	11.8	11.3	7.4	7.3	0.4	Nil
Common Eqty.	198	175	104	88.3	84.0	50.5	20.2	10.1	2.6	-0.1
Total Cap.	526	384	160	122	95.8	63.9	27.6	17.3	3.0	-0.1
Cap. Exp.	110	95.5	68.3	38.4	26.1	17.0	25.4	22.6	4.8	NA
Cash Flow	65.6	72.8	28.0	13.3	-2.2	0.1	3.4	1.0	-0.4	NA
Curr. Ratio	3.8	2.9	0.9	1.5	3.1	3.4	0.3	0.8	1.5	0.7
% LT Debt of Cap.	53.2	45.6	30.9	26.2	12.3	17.7	26.9	41.9	13.9	NM
% Ret. on Assets	3.5	12.0	5.6	2.2	NM	NM	0.8	0.7	NM	NA
% Ret. on Equity	9.7	27.5	11.0	3.4	NM	NM	2.1	1.6	NM	NA

Data as orig. reptd.; bef. results of disc opers. and/or spec. items. Per share data adj. for stk. divs. as of ex-div. date. Bold denotes diluted EPS (FASB 128). E-Estimated. NA-Not Available. NM-Not Meaningful. NR-Not Ranked.

Office—1145 Eugenia Place, Suite 200, Carpinteria, CA 93013. **Tel**—(805) 566-5600. **Chrmn, CEO & COO**—A. E. Benton. **SVP & CFO**—J. M. Whipkey. **VP & Contr**—C. C. Hickok. **Dirs**—A. E. Benton, R. W. Fetzner, G. A. Garrettson, W. H. Gumma, B. M. McIntyre, M. B. Wray. **Transfer Agent & Registrar**—ChaseMellon Shareholder Services, LA. **Incorporated**—in Delaware in 1988. **Empl**— 246. **S&P Analyst:** C.F.B.

STANDARD &POOR'S
STOCK REPORTS

Billing Concepts
3270

NASDAQ Symbol **BILL**

In S&P SmallCap 600

03-OCT-98

Industry:
Services (Data Processing)

Summary: This company is a third-party billing clearinghouse and information management services provider to the telecommunications industry.

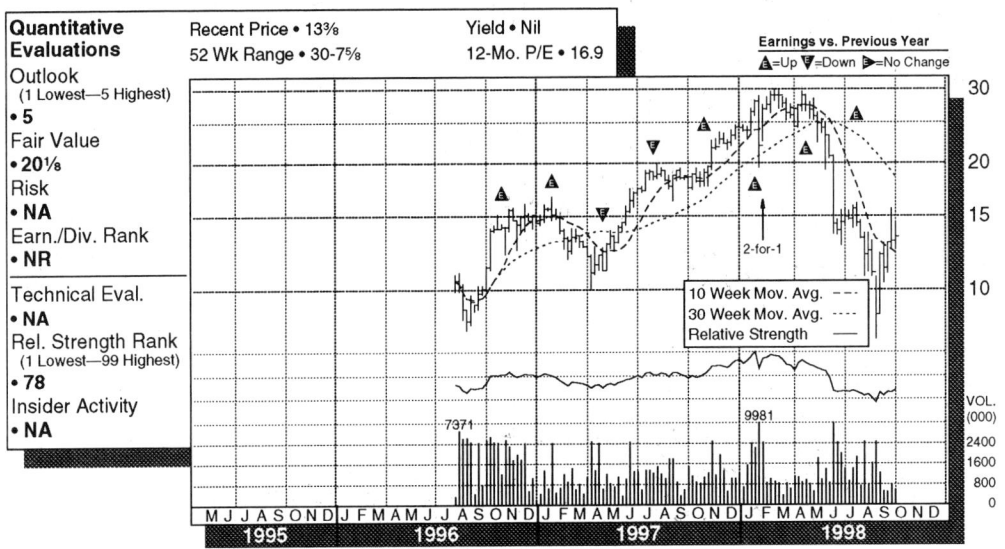

Quantitative Evaluations	Recent Price • 13⅜	Yield • Nil
	52 Wk Range • 30-7⅝	12-Mo. P/E • 16.9

Outlook
(1 Lowest—5 Highest)
• **5**

Fair Value
• **20⅛**

Risk
• **NA**

Earn./Div. Rank
• **NR**

Technical Eval.
• **NA**

Rel. Strength Rank
(1 Lowest—99 Highest)
• **78**

Insider Activity
• **NA**

Earnings vs. Previous Year
▲=Up ▼=Down ▶=No Change

2-for-1

10 Week Mov. Avg. - - -
30 Week Mov. Avg. ·····
Relative Strength ——

7371 9981

VOL. (000)

Business Profile - 09-SEP-98

In August 1998, the company agreed to acquire, for $10 million, 22% of the capital stock of Princeton TeleCom Corporation (PTC). PTC is a New Jersey-based privately held company specializing in electronic bill publishing over the Internet and advanced payment solutions. In connection with the deal, BILL expects to take a one-time charge in the fourth quarter of FY 98 (Sep.) for in-process R&D. A two-for-one stock split was effected in February 1998.

Operational Review - 09-SEP-98

Operating revenues in the nine months ended June 30, 1997, rose 37%, year to year, mainly reflecting a 27% gain in billing services revenues, stemming from an increase in the number of telephone call records processed and billed on behalf of direct dial long distance customers. Margins narrowed, reflecting larger increases in SG&A and R&D expenditures; operating income grew 33%. With a jump in net interest income and in the absence of $21,252,000 of special charges incurred in 1997, and after taxes of $13,222,000, versus $6,465,000, net income amounted to $21,122,000 ($0.60 a share), in contrast to a loss of $2,554,000 ($0.08).

Stock Performance - 02-OCT-98

In the past 30 trading days, BILL's shares have increased 22%, compared to a 7% fall in the S&P 500. Average trading volume for the past five days was 113,560 shares, compared with the 40-day moving average of 225,531 shares.

Key Stock Statistics

Dividend Rate/Share	Nil	Shareholders	500
Shs. outstg. (M)	33.9	Market cap. (B)	$0.453
Avg. daily vol. (M)	0.119	Inst. holdings	70%
Tang. Bk. Value/Share	2.50		
Beta	NA		

Value of $10,000 invested 5 years ago: NA

Fiscal Year Ending Sep. 30

	1998	1997	1996	1995	1994	1993
Revenues (Million $)						
1Q	38.25	27.82	23.35	17.01	—	—
2Q	41.01	27.38	26.95	17.93	—	—
3Q	40.41	31.89	25.73	21.37	—	—
4Q	—	35.74	27.85	24.54	—	—
Yr.	—	122.8	103.9	80.85	57.75	46.45
Earnings Per Share ($)						
1Q	0.20	0.15	0.14	0.10	—	—
2Q	0.21	0.16	0.17	0.10	—	—
3Q	0.20	-0.41	0.14	0.14	—	—
4Q	—	0.18	0.14	0.14	—	—
Yr.	—	0.12	0.58	0.48	0.30	—

Next earnings report expected: late November

Dividend Data

Amount ($)	Date Decl.	Ex-Div. Date	Stock of Record	Payment Date
2-for-1	Jan. 09	Feb. 02	Jan. 20	Jan. 30 '98

Business Summary - 09-SEP-98

Spun off by U.S. Long Distance Corp. to its shareholders in August 1996, Billing Concepts Corp. (formerly Billing Information Concepts Corp.) is one of the largest U.S. third-party providers of billing clearinghouse and information services to the telecommunications industry. In addition to processing call records, BILL also provides customer service, data processing, tax filings, accounting services and an advance funding program.

As markets for its services continue to develop and its target market continues to demand increasingly sophisticated billing clearinghouse and information management services, BILL believes that significant opportunities exist to continue the expansion of its business base as new and existing customers seek to outsource these services to the company.

The company's customers include direct dial long distance telephone companies, operator services providers, information providers, telecommunications equipment suppliers and other telecommunication services providers. BILL maintains contractual billing arrangements with more than 1,200 local telephone companies that provide access lines to, and collect for services from, end-users of telecommunication services.

As part of its business strategy, the company intends to expand its customer base. It believes that its reputation for high quality services will make it an important

resource for providers of services and products, such as 900 pay-per-call transactions, cellular services, paging services, voice mail services, Internet services, personal communications services, caller ID and other telecommunications equipment.

BILL believes that certain new or enhanced services it is developing present significant opportunities. It plans to enhance its systems and billing and collection agreements with the local telephone companies to include an "invoice ready" billing option for its customers. An invoice ready billing platform will enable it to offer a customized bill page for inclusion in the local telephone company bill. The invoice ready product began generating revenue in the first quarter of FY 98 (Sep.).

The company expects the Telecommunications Act to create new opportunities for third-party clearinghouses. The Telecommunications Act requires that the Regional Bell Operating Companies use separate subsidiaries to provide services not related to their existing regulated local services. BILL is negotiating with several Regional Bell Operating Companies to provide both in-territory and out-of-territory billing for their long distance services.

Management has said that the June 1997 acquisition of Computer Resources Management, Inc. for about $8.5 million in cash and 325,000 common shares gives it the ability to offer a much broader range of billing solutions to virtually any size company.

Per Share Data ($)

(Year Ended Sep. 30)	1997	1996	1995	1994	1993	1992	1991	1990	1989	1988
Tangible Bk. Val.	3.01	0.75	NA	NA	NA	NA	NA	NA	NA	NA
Cash Flow	0.46	NA	NA	NA	NA	NA	NA	NA	NA	NA
Earnings	0.12	0.58	0.48	0.30	NA	NA	NA	NA	NA	NA
Dividends	Nil	Nil	Nil	Nil	Nil	Nil	Nil	Nil	Nil	Nil
Payout Ratio	Nil	Nil	Nil	Nil	Nil	Nil	Nil	Nil	Nil	Nil
Prices - High	23¾	16⅛	NA	NA	NA	NA	NA	NA	NA	NA
- Low	10	8	NA	NA	NA	NA	NA	NA	NA	NA
P/E Ratio - High	NM	28	NA	NA	NA	NA	NA	NA	NA	NA
- Low	NM	14	NA	NA	NA	NA	NA	NA	NA	NA

Income Statement Analysis (Million $)

	1997	1996	1995	1994	1993	1992	1991	1990	1989	1988
Revs.	123	104	80.8	57.7	46.5	33.2	NA	NA	NA	NA
Oper. Inc.	38.5	30.8	23.5	14.3	NA	NA	NA	NA	NA	NA
Depr.	3.8	2.1	1.2	0.9	NA	NA	NA	NA	NA	NA
Int. Exp.	0.5	0.3	0.2	0.1	NA	NA	NA	NA	NA	NA
Pretax Inc.	14.0	28.8	22.8	13.6	NA	NA	NA	NA	NA	NA
Eff. Tax Rate	74%	38%	38%	37%	NA	NA	NA	NA	NA	NA
Net Inc.	3.7	17.9	14.1	8.6	6.4	5.8	NA	NA	NA	NA

Balance Sheet & Other Fin. Data (Million $)

	1997	1996	1995	1994	1993	1992	1991	1990	1989	1988
Cash	41.4	34.1	26.8	NA	NA	NA	NA	NA	NA	NA
Curr. Assets	141	124	101	NA	NA	NA	NA	NA	NA	NA
Total Assets	167	138	107	89.7	74.7	63.6	NA	NA	NA	NA
Curr. Liab.	113	110	83.4	NA	NA	NA	NA	NA	NA	NA
LT Debt	2.6	5.0	2.2	0.8	0.4	0.3	NA	NA	NA	NA
Common Eqty.	48.7	22.6	Nil	NA	NA	NA	NA	NA	NA	NA
Total Cap.	53.3	27.7	23.4	NA	NA	NA	NA	NA	NA	NA
Cap. Exp.	17.6	15.7	1.9	6.1	NA	NA	NA	NA	NA	NA
Cash Flow	7.5	20.0	15.3	9.5	NA	NA	NA	NA	NA	NA
Curr. Ratio	1.2	1.1	1.2	NA	NA	NA	NA	NA	NA	NA
% LT Debt of Cap.	4.9	18.1	9.4	NA	NA	NA	NA	NA	NA	NA
% Net Inc.of Revs.	3.0	17.2	17.5	14.8	13.9	17.5	NA	NA	NA	NA
% Ret. on Assets	2.4	14.6	14.3	10.4	9.3	NA	NA	NA	NA	NA
% Ret. on Equity	10.4	NA	NA	NA	NA	NA	NA	NA	NA	NA

Data as orig. reptd.; bef. results of disc. opers. and/or spec. items. Per share data adj. for stk. divs. as of ex-div. date. Bold denotes diluted EPS (FASB 128). E-Estimated. NA-Not Available. NM-Not Meaningful. NR-Not Ranked.

Office—7411 John Smith Drive, San Antonio, TX 78229. **Tel**—(210) 949-7000.**Chrmn & CEO**—P. H. Holmes Jr.**Pres & COO**—A. W. Saltzman.**SVP, CFO & Secy**—K. E. Simmons.**Dirs**—L. Cooke, P. H. Holmes Jr., T. G. Loeffler, A. W. Saltzman, J. E. Sowell.**Transfer Agent & Registrar**—Montreal Trust Co., Montreal. **Incorporated**—Delaware in 1996.**Empl**— 530. **S&P Analyst:** Stephen J. Tekirian

Bindley Western Industries   328

NYSE Symbol **BDY**

In S&P SmallCap 600

03-OCT-98

Industry:
Distributors (Food & Health)

Summary: This company is one of the largest U.S. drug wholesalers, specializing in the distribution of ethical pharmaceuticals and related products.

Quantitative Evaluations		
Outlook (1 Lowest—5 Highest) • **2⁻**	Recent Price • 31⅜	Yield • 0.3%
Fair Value • **32**	52 Wk Range • 34¾-19¼	12-Mo. P/E • 23.9

Outlook
(1 Lowest—5 Highest)
• **2⁻**

Fair Value
• **32**

Risk
• **Low**

Earn./Div. Rank
• **A-**

Technical Eval.
• **Bearish** since 1/97

Rel. Strength Rank
(1 Lowest—99 Highest)
• **87**

Insider Activity
• **Neutral**

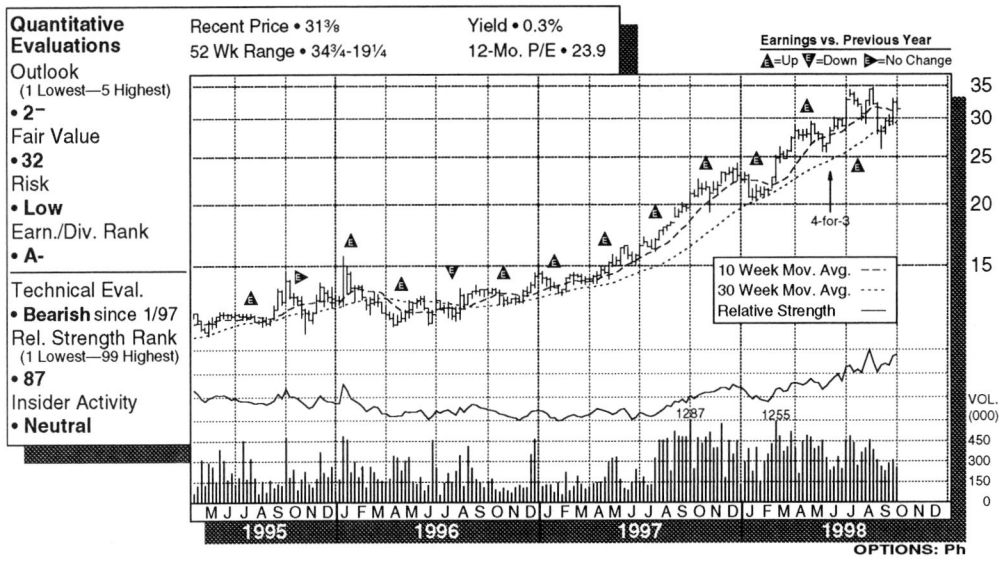

Earnings vs. Previous Year
▲=Up ▼=Down ▶=No Change

10 Week Mov. Avg. ---
30 Week Mov. Avg. ····
Relative Strength —

VOL. (000)

OPTIONS: Ph

Business Profile - 30-MAR-98

In September 1997, nearly all the company's $67.35 million of 6.5% subordinated debentures due 2002 were converted into 3.4 million common shares. In August, BDY's Priority Healthcare Corp. (PHC) subsidiary sold publicly two million Class B common shares. Following the offering, BDY owned 83.6% of the PHC Class B shares and retained 93.9% of the voting power. In July 1997, the company acquired Tennessee Wholesale Drug Company, Inc., a drug wholesaler with annual sales of $308 million. Also in July, BDY signed a supply contract with NCS pharmacies, expected to generate over $600 million in revenues over three years. In the 1997 third quarter, TWD contributed about 10% of the increase in total sales and 29% of the increase in gross profit.

Operational Review - 30-MAR-98

Revenues in 1997 (preliminary) climbed 37% from those of the prior year, reflecting a 43% increase in brokerage sales and a 30% gain in stock sales. Gross margins narrowed, but SG&A expenses were well controlled, and after taxes at 39.7%, versus 41.7%, net income was up 32%, to $23,746,000 ($1.59 a share, on 5.6% more shares) from $18,006,000 ($1.36).

Stock Performance - 02-OCT-98

In the past 30 trading days, BDY's shares have declined 2%, compared to a 7% fall in the S&P 500. Average trading volume for the past five days was 50,420 shares, compared with the 40-day moving average of 65,459 shares.

Key Stock Statistics

Dividend Rate/Share	0.08	Shareholders	1,000
Shs. outstg. (M)	22.0	Market cap. (B)	$0.691
Avg. daily vol. (M)	0.055	Inst. holdings	60%
Tang. Bk. Value/Share	15.12		
Beta	1.01		

Value of $10,000 invested 5 years ago: $ 33,945

Fiscal Year Ending Dec. 31

	1998	1997	1996	1995	1994	1993
Revenues (Million $)						
1Q	1,962	1,635	1,189	1,114	917.0	--
2Q	1,848	1,811	1,218	1,126	987.0	--
3Q	--	1,813	1,336	1,122	1,013	--
4Q	--	2,053	1,576	1,309	1,118	--
Yr.	--	7,312	5,319	4,670	4,034	3,426
Earnings Per Share ($)						
1Q	0.34	0.30	0.29	0.28	0.25	--
2Q	0.36	0.29	0.26	0.28	0.26	--
3Q	--	0.28	0.26	0.23	0.23	--
4Q	--	0.32	0.33	0.28	0.27	--
Yr.	--	1.19	1.14	1.06	1.00	0.66

Next earnings report expected: late October

Dividend Data (Dividends have been paid since 1990.)

Amount ($)	Date Decl.	Ex-Div. Date	Stock of Record	Payment Date
0.020	Mar. 03	Mar. 11	Mar. 13	Mar. 24 '98
4-for-3	Apr. 15	Jun. 04	May. 21	Jun. 03 '98
0.020	May. 27	Jun. 10	Jun. 12	Jun. 26 '98
0.020	Sep. 17	Sep. 18	Sep. 22	Sep. 30 '98

A Division of The McGraw-Hill Companies

Business Summary - 30-MAR-98

Bindley Western Industries (BDY) is the fifth largest wholesale distributor of pharmaceuticals and related healthcare products in the U.S. The number of individuals in the U.S. older than 65 has grown 23%, from about 26 million in 1980 to 32 million in 1990, and is projected to increase an additional 9%, to more than 35 million, by 2000. This age group suffers from a greater incidence of chronic illnesses and disabilities than the rest of the population, and it is estimated that it will account for about two-thirds of total healthcare expenditures by the end of the decade, boding well for continued growth at BDY. With wholesale drug industry sales having grown from $25 billion in 1989 to approximately $58 billion in 1995, a compound annual growth rate of 15%, BDY's growth potential looks bright.

BDY's sales of $5.32 billion for 1996 marked the 28th consecutive year of record sales, with a compound growth rate of 20% since inception in 1968, even higher than the recent industrywide growth rate. This growth was the result of market share gains in existing markets, expansion into new markets, and overall growth in the healthcare delivery industry.

BDY's product lines include ethical pharmaceuticals (prescription drugs), dialysis supplies, health and beauty products and home healthcare merchandise. Since 1987, BDY has focused its marketing efforts on direct store delivery customers, increasing sales to these customers from $171 million in 1987 to $1.859 billion in 1996. To further its growth, the company purchased J.E. Goold in 1992 and Kendall Drug in 1994, to strengthen its position in the Northeast and Southeast, respectively.

The company's markets are highly competitive. Not only does BDY compete with national and regional full-line, full-service wholesale drug distributors, some of which are larger and have substantially greater financial resources, but additional competition is provided by direct selling manufacturers and specialty distributors. While competition is primarily price oriented, it can also be affected by delivery requirements, credit terms, depth of product line, and other customer service requirements. In recent years, there has been a trend toward consolidation in the wholesale drug industry, as evidenced by the purchase of a number of distributors by national wholesalers. BDY estimates that there are currently 50 wholesale drug distributors in the U.S.

In July 1997, the company acquired Tennessee Wholesale Drug Company, Inc., a Nashville-based drug wholesaler with annual sales of $308 million. Separately, BDY signed a supply contract with NCS Health-Care pharmacies, expected to generate over $600 million in revenues over the three-year term of the contract.

Per Share Data ($)

(Year Ended Dec. 31)	1997	1996	1995	1994	1993	1992	1991	1990	1989	1988
Tangible Bk. Val.	19.71	12.04	11.46	10.57	9.67	9.27	8.92	7.89	NA	NA
Cash Flow	1.93	1.56	1.48	1.40	1.05	1.11	1.12	1.13	NA	NA
Earnings	1.19	1.14	1.06	1.00	0.66	0.77	1.21	0.75	NA	NA
Dividends	0.06	0.06	0.06	0.06	0.05	0.05	0.05	0.02	NA	NA
Payout Ratio	5%	5%	6%	6%	8%	6%	4%	3%	NA	NA
Prices - High	24³/₈	15³/₄	14⁵/₈	11³/₄	10⁷/₈	15⁵/₈	13³/₄	10³/₄	NA	NA
- Low	13	11¹/₄	10¹/₄	8³/₈	7¹/₈	8³/₄	8¹/₂	6¹/₂	NA	NA
P/E Ratio - High	20	14	14	12	16	20	11	14	NA	NA
- Low	11	10	10	8	11	11	7	9	NA	NA

Income Statement Analysis (Million $)

	1997	1996	1995	1994	1993	1992	1991	1990	1989	1988
Revs.	7,310	5,318	4,670	4,034	3,426	2,911	2,393	2,042	NA	NA
Oper. Inc.	61.6	49.9	41.8	38.7	32.7	30.2	30.7	21.8	NA	NA
Depr.	7.4	6.7	6.3	5.8	5.7	4.7	3.8	3.3	NA	NA
Int. Exp.	15.9	13.0	10.1	11.2	8.1	8.4	13.4	13.1	NA	NA
Pretax Inc.	39.8	30.9	28.0	25.0	16.4	16.0	17.7	10.3	NA	NA
Eff. Tax Rate	40%	42%	41%	41%	42%	35%	36%	36%	NA	NA
Net Inc.	23.7	18.0	16.4	14.7	9.6	10.4	11.4	6.7	NA	NA

Balance Sheet & Other Fin. Data (Million $)

	1997	1996	1995	1994	1993	1992	1991	1990	1989	1988
Cash	42.9	63.7	34.8	40.9	38.3	NA	NA	NA	NA	NA
Curr. Assets	1,185	851	773	736	665	NA	NA	NA	NA	NA
Total Assets	1,291	941	844	803	732	680	NA	NA	NA	NA
Curr. Liab.	898	616	569	547	490	NA	NA	NA	NA	NA
LT Debt	32.1	100	69.5	69.5	69.7	70.2	NA	NA	NA	NA
Common Eqty.	346	222	201	180	166	157	NA	NA	NA	NA
Total Cap.	393	325	275	256	242	230	NA	NA	NA	NA
Cap. Exp.	22.6	15.6	7.9	3.6	5.7	22.1	NA	NA	NA	NA
Cash Flow	31.2	24.7	22.7	20.6	15.2	15.1	15.1	9.9	NA	NA
Curr. Ratio	1.3	1.4	1.4	1.3	1.4	NA	NA	NA	NA	NA
% LT Debt of Cap.	8.1	30.8	25.3	27.1	28.8	30.5	NA	NA	NA	NA
% Net Inc.of Revs.	0.3	0.3	0.0	0.4	0.3	0.4	0.5	0.3	NA	NA
% Ret. on Assets	2.1	2.0	2.0	1.9	1.4	NA	NA	NA	NA	NA
% Ret. on Equity	8.4	8.5	8.6	8.5	5.9	8.5	NA	NA	NA	NA

Data as orig. reptd.; bef. results of disc. opers. and/or spec. items. Per share data adj. for stk. divs. as of ex-div. date. Bold denotes diluted EPS (FASB 128). E-Estimated. NA-Not Available. NM-Not Meaningful. NR-Not Ranked.

Office— 10333 N. Meridian St., Suite 300, Indianapolis, IN 46290. **Tel**—(317) 298-9900.**Chrmn, Pres & CEO**—W. E. Bindley.**EVP & Secy**—M. D. McCormick.**EVP, CFO & Investor Contact**—T. J. Salentine.**Treas**—M. L. Shinn.**Dirs**—W. E. Bindley, W. F. Bindley II, K. W. Burks, S. B. Harris, R. L. Koch II, M. D. McCormick, J. T. McGinley, J. K. Risk III, T. J. Salentine, K. C. Smith, C. Woo. **Transfer Agent & Registrar**—Bank One, Indianapolis.**Incorporated**—in Indiana in 1983.**Empl**— 909. **S&P Analyst:** C.C.P.

Bio-Technology General   3277K

NASDAQ Symbol **BTGC**

In S&P SmallCap 600

03-OCT-98

Industry: Biotechnology

Summary: This company develops, manufactures and markets pharmaceuticals and biotechnology products for human health care, with a focus on treatments for growth and weight disorders.

Quantitative Evaluations

Outlook
(1 Lowest—5 Highest)
- **NA**

Fair Value
- **NA**

Risk
- **High**

Earn./Div. Rank
- **B-**

Technical Eval.
- **Bearish** since 11/97

Rel. Strength Rank
(1 Lowest—99 Highest)
- **94**

Insider Activity
- **NA**

Recent Price • 6⅞   Yield • Nil
52 Wk Range • 15⅛-4⅛   12-Mo. P/E • 23.1

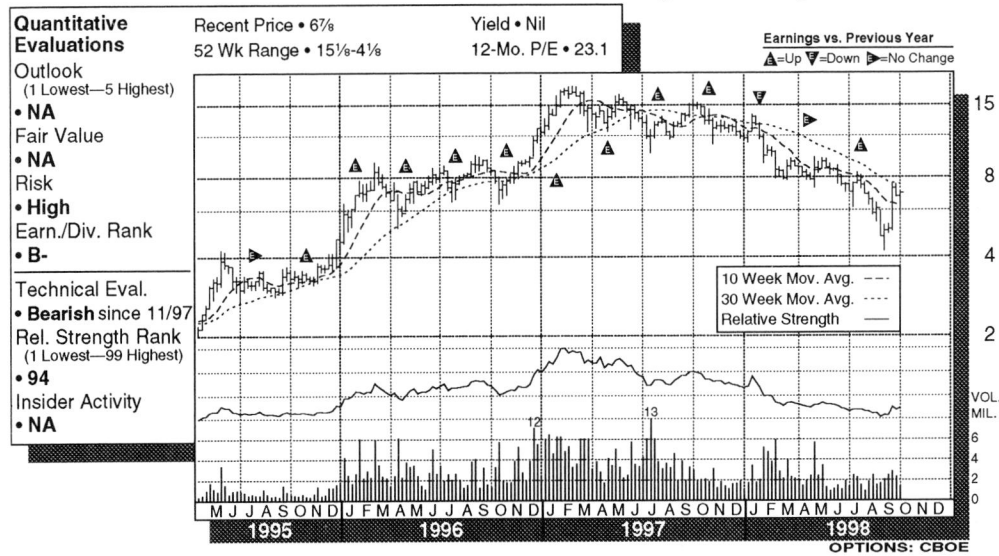

Earnings vs. Previous Year
▲=Up ▼=Down ▶=No Change

10 Week Mov. Avg. ---
30 Week Mov. Avg. ····
Relative Strength —

OPTIONS: CBOE

Business Profile - 28-SEP-98

This biopharmaceutical drug developer currently has five products that have received regulatory approval, four of which are presently being marketed for involuntary weight loss, growth hormone deficiency in children, hypogonadism, and to protect the corneal endothelium during ophthalmic surgery. Future revenue and earnings growth prospects are bolstered by several products awaiting regulatory approval or in advanced clinical development. In April 1998, the FDA approved Mircette, an oral contraceptive using BTGC's proprietary dosing regimen, to be marketed by an affiliate of Organon, Inc. later this year. In July 1998, the FDA approved BioLon, BTGC's opthalmic surgical aid, which will be marketed in the U.S. by Akorn, Inc.

Operational Review - 28-SEP-98

Total revenues in the six months ended June 30, 1998, rose 18%, year to year, reflecting higher product sales of Oxandrin and a sharp gain in contract fees, generated from the licensing of BioLon and other products, partly offset by lower human growth hormone sales. Research and development spending grew 23% on clinical Phase III and post-clinical (Phase IV) activities related to Oxandrin. After increased marketing and sales costs, and taxes at 30.6% versus 27.1%, net income increased fractionally to $7,908,000 ($0.16 a share, on 2.3% fewer shares) from $7,309,000 ($0.14). Cash, equivalents, and short term investments totaled $48.3 million on June 30, 1998.

Stock Performance - 02-OCT-98

In the past 30 trading days, BTGC's shares have increased 14%, compared to a 7% fall in the S&P 500. Average trading volume for the past five days was 271,140 shares, compared with the 40-day moving average of 425,559 shares.

Key Stock Statistics

Dividend Rate/Share	Nil	Shareholders	1,600
Shs. outstg. (M)	48.3	Market cap. (B)	$0.335
Avg. daily vol. (M)	0.458	Inst. holdings	14%
Tang. Bk. Value/Share	1.93		
Beta	1.51		

Value of $10,000 invested 5 years ago: $ 11,807

Fiscal Year Ending Dec. 31

	1998	1997	1996	1995	1994	1993
Revenues (Million $)						
1Q	17.44	14.77	10.71	5.75	5.68	1.23
2Q	18.65	15.69	12.19	7.29	7.76	3.00
3Q	—	17.92	12.13	5.06	1.90	4.35
4Q	—	15.24	12.67	9.86	2.10	5.29
Yr.	—	63.62	47.74	27.96	17.44	13.87
Earnings Per Share ($)						
1Q	**0.07**	0.07	0.02	0.01	-0.02	-0.10
2Q	**0.09**	0.08	0.06	0.01	0.01	-0.07
3Q	—	0.09	0.07	-0.02	-0.12	-0.09
4Q	—	**0.05**	0.32	0.08	-0.10	-0.38
Yr.	—	**0.28**	0.47	0.08	-0.23	-0.63

Next earnings report expected: late October

Dividend Data

The company has never paid a cash dividend.

STANDARD
&POOR'S
STOCK REPORTS

Bio-Technology General Corporation

3277K
03-OCT-98

Business Summary - 28-SEP-98

With strong demand for its human growth hormone and weight gain products bulking up its bottom line, Bio-Technology General (BTGC), incorporated in 1980, is one of only a handful of profitable biotechnology concerns. BTGC's genetically engineered products address conditions such as endocrinology and metabolic disorders, cardio/pulmonary diseases, and ophthalmic and skin disorders.

The company's biggest seller, Oxandrin, was launched in late 1995 for the treatment of involuntary weight loss. Oxandrin is an oral anabolic agent used to promote weight gain after weight loss following extensive surgery, chronic infections and severe trauma. The company is currently conducting Phase IV (post approval) clinical studies to further support the role of Oxandrin in the treatment of many of these conditions. BTGC is also pursuing expanded use of Oxandrin in severe AIDS wasting patients and alcoholic hepatitis through Phase III studies. The drug accounted for 52% of 1997 product sales, up from 37% in 1996.

Bio-Technology's other lead drug, Bio-Tropin, an authentic human growth hormone (hGh), is used in the treatment of short stature and growth disorders. Bio-Tropin is marketed in Western Europe through licensee Ferring Group and in Japan through JCR Pharmaceuticals. After receiving U.S. FDA approval to market Bio-Tropin, the company was issued a preliminary injunction prohibiting sale of the drug in the U.S. The action resulted from a motion filed by Genentech claiming patent infringement on one of its own growth hormone drugs. Bio-Tropin accounted for 31% of product revenues in 1997, down from 45% in 1996.

The company also markets BioLon (sodium hyaluronate) for the protection of the corneal endothelium during intraocular surgery. In 1997, this product provided 13% of revenues. Other products include Bio-Hep-B, a vaccine against the hepatitis B virus; Silkis, a vitamin D derivative for the topical treatment of recalcitrant psoriasis, contact dermatitis and other skin disorders; and porcine growth hormone.

The research pipeline includes OxSODrol (recombinant superoxide dismutase), which entered a Phase III clinical trial in January 1997 for the prevention of bronchopulmonary dysplasia (BPD), a chronic lung disease that develops in premature infants. The trial is currently on hold pending a report on the drug's efficacy by an independent Data Safety and Monitoring Committee.

In January 1998, the FDA found that information submitted for the company's sublingual testosterone product for the treatment of hypogonadism, Androtest-SL, was inadequate for approval. BTGC is working with the FDA to develop additional clinical data needed to more fully establish the safety and efficacy of the product.

Per Share Data ($)

(Year Ended Dec. 31)	1997	1996	1995	1994	1993	1992	1991	1990	1989	1988
Tangible Bk. Val.	1.69	1.31	0.47	0.41	0.38	0.65	1.05	0.42	-0.01	-1.17
Cash Flow	0.33	0.53	0.14	-0.16	-0.53	-0.30	-0.30	-0.30	-0.93	-0.97
Earnings	0.28	0.47	0.08	-0.23	-0.63	-0.38	-0.38	-0.40	-1.17	-1.17
Dividends	Nil	Nil	Nil	Nil	Nil	Nil	Nil	Nil	Nil	Nil
Payout Ratio	Nil	Nil	Nil	Nil	Nil	Nil	Nil	Nil	Nil	Nil
Prices - High	17¾	13¼	5	5⅞	6¾	11⅝	10½	4⅜	3	7⅛
- Low	9⅞	4½	2	1½	4½	4⅜	1⁵⁄₁₆	1	1	2¼
P/E Ratio - High	63	28	62	NM	NM	NM	NM	NM	NM	NM
- Low	35	10	25	NM	NM	NM	NM	NM	NM	NM

Income Statement Analysis (Million $)

	1997	1996	1995	1994	1993	1992	1991	1990	1989	1988
Revs.	63.6	46.6	27.2	16.9	13.3	4.9	4.7	2.6	3.2	4.6
Oper. Inc.	22.4	14.1	6.2	-6.3	-7.8	-8.4	-6.6	-6.4	-5.2	-4.7
Depr.	2.6	2.8	2.6	2.9	3.6	2.0	1.6	1.6	1.6	1.2
Int. Exp.	0.3	0.2	0.2	0.3	0.4	0.5	0.2	0.1	2.0	2.8
Pretax Inc.	21.2	10.9	3.4	-8.9	22.8	-9.8	-7.9	-6.2	-8.0	-6.8
Eff. Tax Rate	32%	NM	NM	NM	NM	NM	Nil	Nil	Nil	Nil
Net Inc.	14.5	22.9	3.4	-8.9	-22.8	-9.8	-7.9	-6.2	-8.0	-6.8

Balance Sheet & Other Fin. Data (Million $)

	1997	1996	1995	1994	1993	1992	1991	1990	1989	1988
Cash	9.3	19.8	6.9	16.9	16.1	18.4	24.0	8.1	5.2	11.6
Curr. Assets	76.9	49.7	20.6	21.4	19.6	20.4	26.2	9.4	6.2	13.2
Total Assets	95.4	73.6	31.7	32.3	31.1	32.9	36.1	16.7	14.6	26.3
Curr. Liab.	8.6	9.1	5.4	7.8	7.4	2.9	2.1	1.5	1.7	2.6
LT Debt	Nil	0.3	0.7	1.3	3.5	5.8	3.6	4.8	8.1	30.2
Common Eqty.	82.9	60.6	25.7	23.2	20.1	24.1	29.9	8.2	0.3	-6.4
Total Cap.	82.9	60.8	26.4	24.5	23.6	29.8	33.5	13.0	8.4	23.7
Cap. Exp.	3.1	3.0	1.6	1.8	1.6	1.5	0.6	0.3	0.3	4.3
Cash Flow	17.1	25.7	6.0	-6.1	-19.2	-7.7	-6.3	-4.6	-6.4	-5.6
Curr. Ratio	9.0	5.5	3.8	2.8	2.7	7.0	12.4	6.4	3.6	5.1
% LT Debt of Cap.	Nil	0.5	2.5	5.2	14.8	19.4	10.8	37.1	96.1	127.2
% Net Inc.of Revs.	22.8	49.1	12.2	NM	NM	NM	NM	NM	NM	NM
% Ret. on Assets	17.1	42.7	10.7	NM	NM	NM	NM	NM	NM	NM
% Ret. on Equity	20.2	53.1	14.0	NM	NM	NM	NM	NM	NM	NM

Data as orig. reptd.; bef. results of disc. opers. and/or spec. items. Per share data adj. for stk. divs. as of ex-div. date. Bold denotes diluted EPS (FASB 128). E-Estimated. NA-Not Available. NM-Not Meaningful. NR-Not Ranked.

Office—70 Wood Ave. South, Iselin, NJ 08830. **Tel**—(908) 632-8800. **Chrmn, Pres, CEO & Treas**—S. Fass. **SVP & COO**—D. Haselkorn. **VP-Fin & CFO**—Y. Sternlicht. **Dirs**—H. J. Conrad, S. Fass, M. Marx, A. Rosenfield, D. Tendler, V. Thompson, D. Tolkowsky, F. Wattleton, H. Weissbach. **Transfer Agent & Registrar**—American Stock Transfer & Trust Co., NYC. **Incorporated**—in Delaware in 1980. **Empl**— 247. **S&P Analyst:** David Moskowitz

STANDARD &POOR'S
STOCK REPORTS

Birmingham Steel

329F

NYSE Symbol **BIR**

In S&P SmallCap 600

03-OCT-98

Industry: Iron & Steel

Summary: This company operates mini-mills that produce rebar and merchant products. It also specializes in making high-quality rod and wire at its American Steel & Wire subsidiary.

S&P Opinion: Avoid (★★)	

Recent Price • 7⅛
52 Wk Range • 18-6⅜

Yield • 5.6%
12-Mo. P/E • NM

Earnings vs. Previous Year
▲=Up ▼=Down ▶=No Change

Quantitative Evaluations

Outlook
(1 Lowest—5 Highest)
• **5**

Fair Value
• **12⅛**

Risk
• **Low**

Earn./Div. Rank
• **B-**

Technical Eval.
• **Bullish** since 4/98

Rel. Strength Rank
(1 Lowest—99 Highest)
• **28**

Insider Activity
• **NA**

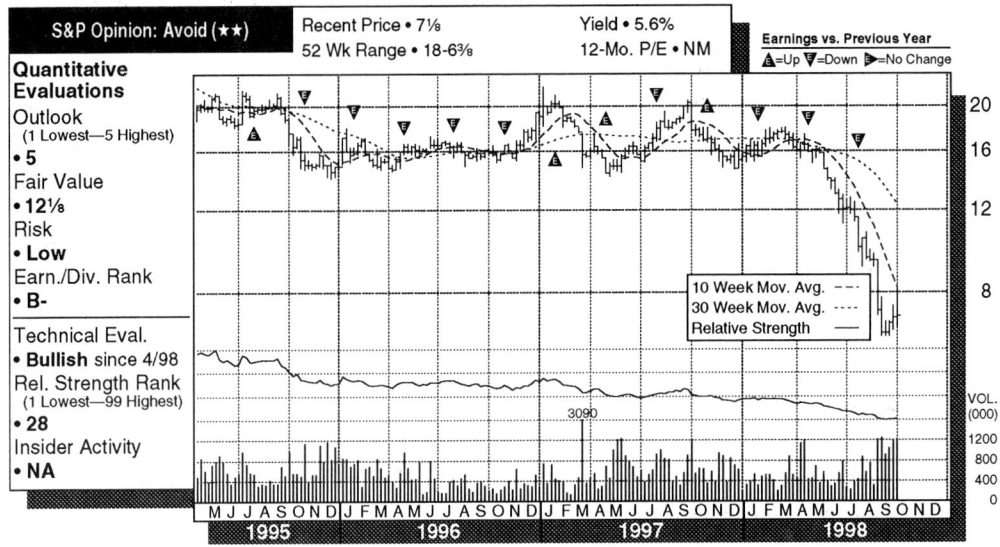

10 Week Mov. Avg. - - -
30 Week Mov. Avg. - - -
Relative Strength —

VOL. (000)

Overview - 14-AUG-98

We project sales growth of 10% in FY 99 (Jun.), reflecting an improved product mix and a 7.0% gain in shipment volume. Increased shipments of merchant and bar products relative to rebar will lead to a more lucrative business mix and partially offset lower prices in the aggregate. Overall margins should improve over FY 98 as much lower start-up costs along with a substantial decrease in raw material costs offset continued high levels of depreciation charges and interest expense. Accordingly, BIR should post a large gain in FY 99.

Valuation - 14-AUG-98

On July 30, 1998 we downgraded BIR to avoid from hold after the company announced a writedown on its Laclede Steel investment. The Laclede writedown was the latest in a series of disappointments and setbacks that has plagued BIR over the past several years. Following fourth quarter results and a company meeting on August 12, we are maintaining our avoid rating. As a result of sharply higher imports and our fears that the start-up costs from the Memphis plant will continue to hurt EPS, we cut our FY 99 estimate to $0.90 from $1.10. Rising imports will depress prices and offset some of the benefits of higher volume in FY 99. The adverse impact of imports partly accounted for the lower per ton revenue in FY 98's fourth quarter relative to FY 98's third quarter and FY 97's fourth quarter. Additionally, the continuing operational problems at Memphis and Cartersville confirm our fears that management is stretched too thin and that more negative surprises may be in store for FY 99. Despite substantially increasing its debt to capitalization to finance an aggressive capital spending program, BIR has precious little to show except EPS shortfalls and losses. Thus, we think the stock remains vulnerable to further disappointment.

Key Stock Statistics

S&P EPS Est. 1998	NA	Tang. Bk. Value/Share	13.97
P/E on S&P Est. 1998	NA	Beta	0.98
S&P EPS Est. 1999	0.90	Shareholders	1,800
Dividend Rate/Share	0.40	Market cap. (B)	$0.211
Shs. outstg. (M)	29.6	Inst. holdings	59%
Avg. daily vol. (M)	0.237		

Value of $10,000 invested 5 years ago: $ 3,207

Fiscal Year Ending Jun. 30

	1998	1997	1996	1995	1994	1993
Revenues (Million $)						
1Q	287.6	233.4	207.3	220.6	127.6	112.0
2Q	267.4	210.1	197.4	203.2	146.8	98.10
3Q	298.2	257.9	197.1	236.9	204.2	115.1
4Q	282.8	277.5	230.8	224.8	224.3	117.2
Yr.	1,136	979.0	832.5	885.5	702.9	442.3
Earnings Per Share ($)						
1Q	0.24	0.22	0.29	0.42	0.15	0.31
2Q	0.09	0.21	0.02	0.42	0.17	0.16
3Q	-0.14	0.02	-0.51	0.45	0.20	0.02
4Q	-0.14	0.05	0.12	0.45	0.31	0.11
Yr.	0.05	0.50	-0.08	1.74	0.86	0.60

Next earnings report expected: mid October

Dividend Data (Dividends have been paid since 1988.)

Amount ($)	Date Decl.	Ex-Div. Date	Stock of Record	Payment Date
0.100	Oct. 14	Oct. 22	Oct. 24	Nov. 04 '97
0.100	Jan. 13	Jan. 21	Jan. 23	Feb. 03 '98
0.100	Apr. 14	Apr. 22	Apr. 24	May. 05 '98
0.100	Aug. 04	Aug. 12	Aug. 14	Aug. 25 '98

A Division of The McGraw·Hill Companies

STANDARD
&POOR'S
STOCK REPORTS

Birmingham Steel Corporation

329F

03-OCT-98

Business Summary - 14-AUG-98

The growth strategy of the second largest U.S. mini-mill steel company entails efforts to increase its market share of higher-margin steel products, expand its production capacity and develop alternative sources of raw materials to reduce production costs. Birmingham Steel (BIR) has embarked on a large multi-year capital spending program devoted mostly to construction of new facilities to accomplish its goals.

BIR's main products are steel reinforcing bar (rebar) used in the construction industry, and merchant steel products sold to distributors and to fabricators and OEMs for conversion into finished goods. Through American Steel & Wire (ASW), it makes steel rod and wire primarily for the automotive, fastener, welding, appliance and aerospace industries.

In May 1996, BIR began the startup of its $115 million high-quality bar mill in Cleveland. The addition of this mill nearly doubled ASW's annual rolling capacity, to 1.1 million tons, and will let ASW make larger, higher-margin bar products. The mill will help achieve BIR's long-term goal of improving the product mix by increasing shipments of rod/bar relative to rebar.

In August 1996, BIR began construction of a $200 million Memphis melt shop. The shop will supply one million tons of high-quality billets (pieces of semi-finished steel) annually to the Cleveland bar mill and end the current practice of purchasing high-cost billets from outside vendors. The melt shop began start-up in November 1997.

Besides reducing its dependence on outside sources of billets, BIR formed a joint venture with GS Industries to build a direct reduced iron (DRI) plant to cut scrap costs. DRI is a scrap substitute manufactured from virgin iron ore. The use of DRI in its electric arc furnaces will enable the company to substantially reduce its dependence on expensive low-residual scrap. BIR and GS will each receive half of the plant's minimum annual production of 1.2 million metric tons of DRI. Startup commenced in January 1998. In FY 97 (Jun.), scrap costs accounted for 53% of total manufacturing costs at its mini-mills, versus 56% in FY 96.

BIR shipped 3,329,000 tons in FY 98, versus 2,835,731 tons in FY 97 and 2,402,697 tons in FY 96, Of total tonnage shipped in FY 98, 43% (46% in FY 97) was rebar, 28% (25%) merchant products, 20% (23%) rod/bar, and 9% (6%) was semi-finished billet. Upon completion of its capital program in late 1999, BIR's shipment capacity will be about 4.0 million tons annually.

In calendar 1996, BIR shipped 21.2% of the rebar and 5.0% of the merchant products consumed that year in the U.S.

BIR's main competitors in rebar and merchant steel are Bayou Steel, Chaparral Steel, Co-Steel Inc., Commercial Metals Co. and Nucor Corp.

Per Share Data ($)

(Year Ended Jun. 30)	1998	1997	1996	1995	1994	1993	1992	1991	1990	1989
Tangible Bk. Val.	14.07	14.20	14.06	15.00	14.21	10.36	10.03	7.80	8.13	7.69
Cash Flow	1.92	2.07	1.14	2.85	1.99	1.41	2.04	0.83	1.62	2.72
Earnings	0.05	0.50	-0.08	1.74	0.86	0.60	1.11	NM	0.89	2.11
Dividends	0.40	0.40	0.40	0.40	0.75	0.37	0.33	0.33	0.33	0.27
Payout Ratio	NM	80%	NM	23%	29%	61%	35%	NM	37%	13%
Prices - High	18	22	19³/₈	22³/₄	32⁵/₈	20³/₄	25³/₄	15⁵/₈	18³/₄	20
- Low	9	14¹/₈	14¹/₂	14	18³/₄	15³/₄	13⁵/₈	8³/₈	7	13⁷/₈
P/E Ratio - High	NM	44	NM	13	38	46	23	NM	21	9
- Low	NM	28	NM	8	22	30	12	NM	8	7

Income Statement Analysis (Million $)

	1998	1997	1996	1995	1994	1993	1992	1991	1990	1989
Revs.	1,136	979	832	885	703	442	418	408	443	443
Oper. Inc.	124	95.4	64.3	119	69.9	42.7	55.0	36.5	57.6	82.4
Depr.	58.3	45.8	34.7	32.3	27.7	17.3	16.8	14.0	13.4	11.4
Int. Exp.	35.5	29.0	18.5	8.8	11.1	8.7	9.9	9.1	9.7	10.3
Pretax Inc.	4.4	22.4	-2.4	86.0	35.8	21.3	32.2	1.0	26.4	62.6
Eff. Tax Rate	26%	46%	NM	41%	41%	40%	38%	98%	38%	38%
Net Inc.	1.6	14.4	-2.2	50.6	21.2	12.8	19.9	NM	16.3	39.1

Balance Sheet & Other Fin. Data (Million $)

	1998	1997	1996	1995	1994	1993	1992	1991	1990	1989
Cash	0.9	1.0	6.7	4.3	28.9	0.3	0.5	0.5	0.1	1.0
Curr. Assets	394	367	328	303	276	147	128	127	136	141
Total Assets	1,245	1,211	928	757	690	456	388	345	314	301
Curr. Liab.	156	138	116	96.0	62.7	114	54.0	92.0	114	108
LT Debt	559	526	307	143	143	90.1	93.7	98.4	27.2	31.0
Common Eqty.	461	472	448	460	439	223	215	134	151	145
Total Cap.	1,081	1,067	806	513	623	339	331	250	197	191
Cap. Exp.	147	197	172	76.1	40.4	76.0	56.1	69.8	35.4	24.8
Cash Flow	56.9	603	32.5	82.9	48.9	30.1	36.7	14.5	29.7	50.5
Curr. Ratio	2.5	2.7	2.7	3.1	4.4	1.3	2.4	1.4	1.2	1.3
% LT Debt of Cap.	51.7	49.3	38.2	27.9	22.9	26.6	28.3	39.3	13.8	16.2
% Net Inc.of Revs.	0.1	1.5	NM	5.7	3.0	2.9	4.8	NM	3.7	8.8
% Ret. on Assets	0.1	1.3	NM	17.4	3.7	3.0	4.8	NM	5.3	14.0
% Ret. on Equity	0.3	3.1	NM	11.2	6.4	5.8	10.4	NM	11.1	30.7

Data as orig. reptd.; bef. results of disc. opers. and/or spec. items. Per share data adj. for stk. divs. as of ex-div. date. Bold denotes diluted EPS (FASB 128). E-Estimated. NA-Not Available. NM-Not Meaningful. NR-Not Ranked.

Office—1000 Urban Center Parkway, Suite 300, Birmingham, AL 35242-2516. **Tel**—(205) 970-1200. **Website**—http://www.birsteel.com **Chrmn & CEO**—R. A. Garvey. **EVP & CFO**—K. E. Walsh. **VP & Investor Contact**—J. Daniel Garrett. **Secy**—C. W. Pecher. **Dirs**—W. J. Cabaniss Jr., C. S. Clegg, E. M. de Windt, R. A. Garvey, H. Holiday Jr., E. B. Jones, R. H. Jones, R. D. Kennedy, R. de J. Osborne, G. A. Stinson, T. E. Wyckoff. **Transfer Agent & Registrar**—First Union National Bank, Charlotte, NC. **Incorporated**—in Delaware in 1983. **Empl**—1,789. **S&P Analyst:** Leo Larkin

10-OCT-98

Industry: Manufacturing (Diversified)

Summary: This company manufactures and markets products in three areas: outdoor products; industrial and power equipment; and sporting equipment.

Quantitative Evaluations		
Outlook (1 Lowest—5 Highest) • **NA**	Recent Price • 22¼	Yield • 1.3%
	52 Wk Range • 34⅜-19⅞	12-Mo. P/E • 14.0

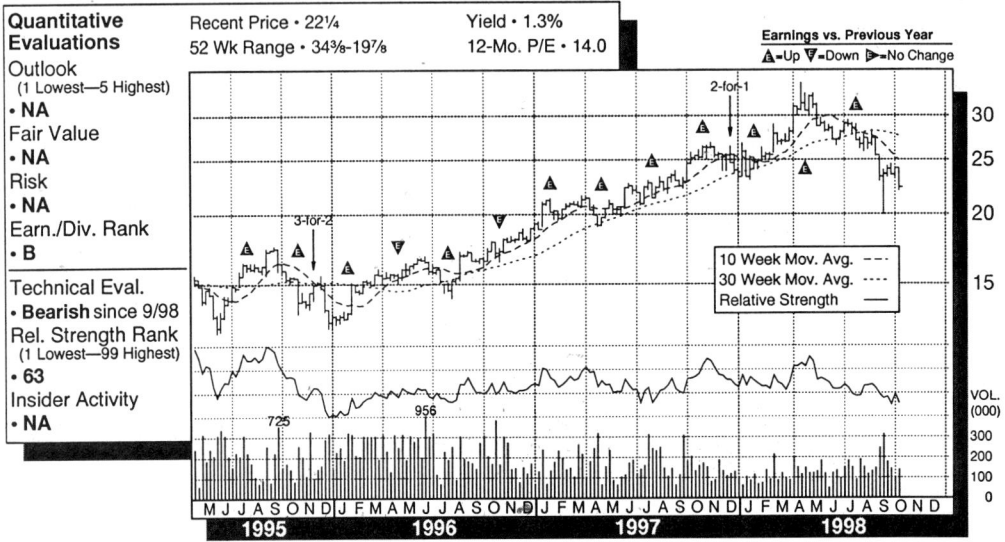

Earnings vs. Previous Year
▲=Up ▼=Down ▶=No Change

Fair Value • **NA**

Risk • **NA**

Earn./Div. Rank • **B**

Technical Eval. • **Bearish** since 9/98

Rel. Strength Rank (1 Lowest—99 Highest) • **63**

Insider Activity • **NA**

- 10 Week Mov. Avg. – – –
- 30 Week Mov. Avg. · · · ·
- Relative Strength —

Business Profile - 01-APR-98

In November 1997, Blount acquired Federal Cartridge Co., a rifle and pistol ammunition manufacturer, in an all-cash transaction for about $112 million. With Federal's sales of about $140 million in 1997, the acquisition boosted annual sales of the Sporting Equipment Group to over $300 million. In January 1997, Blount acquired the Frederick and Orbex Companies, suppliers of lawn mowers and sporting goods. This acquisition resulted in synergies in international distribution and increased Blount's sales by some $24 million annually. The Class A common dividend was increased nearly 13% in conjunction with a two-for-one stock split late in 1997.

Operational Review - 01-APR-98

Sales in 1997 rose 10% from those of 1996 on sales increases from each operating segment. Gross margins narrowed, and income from operations was up 7.6%. Results were hurt by higher forestry equipment product and warranty costs and lower operating income from the sporting equipment segment, offset partially by an improved performance by the outdoor products segment. With increased other income (net) and taxes at 36.9%, versus 37.0%, net income was up 9.9%, to $59.1 million $1.53 a diluted share), from $53.8 million ($1.38). Earnings in 1996 exclude income of $0.03 a share from discontinued operations.

Stock Performance - 09-OCT-98

In the past 30 trading days, BLT.A's shares have declined 12%, compared to a 4% fall in the S&P 500. Average trading volume for the past five days was 27,200 shares, compared with the 40-day moving average of 38,756 shares.

Key Stock Statistics

Dividend Rate/Share	0.29	Shareholders	9,300
Shs. outstg. (M)	37.6	Market cap. (B)	$0.578
Avg. daily vol. (M)	0.028	Inst. holdings	28%
Tang. Bk. Value/Share	5.93		
Beta	0.42		

Value of $10,000 invested 5 years ago: $ 51,504

Fiscal Year Ending Dec. 31

	1998	1997	1996	1995	1994	1993
Revenues (Million $)						
1Q	199.7	170.1	173.3	164.2	146.0	117.4
2Q	205.1	160.5	142.0	147.2	138.8	118.4
3Q	—	182.1	160.0	158.0	157.5	127.6
4Q	—	204.3	174.1	175.0	146.5	124.0
Yr.	—	716.9	649.3	644.3	588.4	487.3
Earnings Per Share ($)						
1Q	0.36	0.35	0.34	0.35	0.23	0.13
2Q	0.35	0.30	0.27	0.27	0.25	0.17
3Q	—	0.41	0.35	0.43	0.32	0.22
4Q	—	0.47	0.41	0.32	0.23	0.12
Yr.	—	1.53	1.38	1.38	1.03	0.64

Next earnings report expected: mid October

Dividend Data (Dividends have been paid since 1983.)

Amount ($)	Date Decl.	Ex-Div. Date	Stock of Record	Payment Date
0.071	Nov. 10	Dec. 11	Dec. 15	Jan. 02 '98
0.071	Mar. 02	Mar. 12	Mar. 16	Apr. 01 '98
0.071	May. 18	Jun. 11	Jun. 15	Jul. 01 '98
0.071	Aug. 24	Sep. 10	Sep. 14	Oct. 01 '98

A Division of The McGraw-Hill Companies

STANDARD
&POOR'S
STOCK REPORTS

Blount International, Inc.

337M

10-OCT-98

Business Summary - 01-APR-98

Tim Allen would love this company. Blount International, Inc. (formerly Blount, Inc.) numbers among its products equipment for chain saws; home and garden tools; lawn mowers; concrete cutters; and industrial and power equipment. Other Blount products include small arms ammunition and gun care products.

Blount, based in Montgomery, AL, started out just after World War II building fish ponds, roads and bridges. Blount grew into a major construction company, concentrating its efforts on complex and unique projects such as the nation's first atomic energy plant, an indoor ocean for the Navy and a university campus built for the Kingdom of Saudi Arabia. After diversifying by acquiring a number of manufacturing companies in the 1970s, Blount left the construction business in 1994 to concentrate exclusively on manufacturing.

Blount's Outdoor Products Group (45% of sales in 1997) consists of Oregon saw chain, bars, sprockets and accessories for use on portable gasoline and electric chain saws; timber harvesting equipment; industrial concrete cutters; lawn mower blades and accessories; home and garden products such as pruning tools; and Dixon ZTR (zero turning radius) lawn mowers.

The Industrial and Power Products Group (33% of sales in 1997) sells timber harvesting and log loading equipment, industrial tractors and loaders, rotation bearings and mechanical power transmission components. Major markets are timber harvesting, land reclamation companies, contractors and scrap yard operators.

The company's Sporting Equipment Group (22% of sales in 1997) manufactures ammunition for hunters, sportsmen and law enforcement and military personnel; reloading equipment; Outers gun care and trap-shooting products; primers; Polar Cap scope covers; Weaver shooting mounts and scopes; and Simmons binoculars, scopes and telescopes. The November 1997 acquisition of Federal Cartridge Co. added shotgun shells to Blount's product line and significantly expanded the company's share of centerfire rifle ammunition market. Based on Federal's sales of $140 million in 1997, the acquisition placed Blount among the leading U.S. manufacturers of ammunition products.

Total backlog at December 31, 1997, was $117.9 million, up from $74.2 million a year earlier, due to gains at each operating segment. Blount expects that difficult conditions in certain international markets, and a stronger U.S. dollar, will restrict operations in 1998, but anticipates continued sales and income growth with the help of the Federal acquisition.

Per Share Data ($)

(Year Ended Dec. 31)	1997	1996	1995	1994	1993	1992	1991	1990	1989	1988
Tangible Bk. Val.	5.33	5.44	4.37	3.56	2.86	2.54	2.43	2.71	2.97	2.47
Cash Flow	2.18	1.98	1.95	1.62	1.22	0.83	0.48	0.53	0.95	-1.51
Earnings	1.53	1.38	1.38	1.03	0.64	0.20	-0.15	0.03	0.50	-2.01
Dividends	0.25	0.23	0.27	0.17	0.15	0.15	0.15	0.15	0.32	0.32
Payout Ratio	16%	17%	20%	17%	24%	75%	NM	517%	63%	NM
Prices - High	26⅞	19½	17⅝	16	9⅝	4¾	4⅞	4½	4⅝	5⅞
- Low	18⅞	12¾	12¼	8¾	4	2³⁄₁₆	1¹⁵⁄₁₆	2¼	3⅛	3¼
P/E Ratio - High	18	14	13	15	15	24	NM	151	9	NM
- Low	12	9	9	9	6	11	NM	75	6	NM

Income Statement Analysis (Million $)

	1997	1996	1995	1994	1993	1992	1991	1990	1989	1988
Revs.	717	649	644	588	487	691	637	673	684	1,137
Oper. Inc.	124	116	113	100	73.0	45.3	27.6	28.8	35.5	-77.1
Depr.	25.0	23.6	22.3	22.9	22.4	23.1	22.6	18.2	16.2	18.1
Int. Exp.	9.5	9.9	10.8	11.2	11.1	11.0	16.1	14.8	13.4	12.1
Pretax Inc.	93.7	85.4	83.7	66.0	36.0	11.0	-8.0	2.0	19.0	-115
Eff. Tax Rate	37%	37%	36%	39%	33%	34%	NM	43%	4.70%	NM
Net Inc.	59.1	53.8	53.6	40.1	24.3	7.4	-5.3	1.0	18.0	-72.5

Balance Sheet & Other Fin. Data (Million $)

	1997	1996	1995	1994	1993	1992	1991	1990	1989	1988
Cash	4.8	58.7	14.6	43.0	52.0	18.0	7.0	22.0	78.0	122
Curr. Assets	301	281	285	292	277	218	222	253	296	417
Total Assets	638	534	546	518	493	447	466	496	518	665
Curr. Liab.	130	115	149	169	173	160	159	166	221	366
LT Debt	139	84.6	95.9	100	108	82.0	106	124	100	105
Common Eqty.	316	291	255	203	167	155	151	155	158	143
Total Cap.	470	391	371	322	288	250	278	308	290	286
Cap. Exp.	17.8	21.2	18.5	9.8	14.7	18.0	15.5	21.3	19.0	13.2
Cash Flow	84.1	77.4	75.8	63.0	46.7	30.5	17.3	19.2	34.2	-54.4
Curr. Ratio	2.3	2.4	1.9	1.7	1.6	1.4	1.4	1.5	1.3	1.1
% LT Debt of Cap.	29.5	21.6	25.8	31.0	37.4	32.8	38.0	40.3	34.6	36.6
% Net Inc.of Revs.	8.2	8.3	8.3	6.8	5.0	1.1	NM	0.2	2.6	NM
% Ret. on Assets	10.1	10.2	10.0	7.9	5.1	1.6	NM	0.2	3.1	NM
% Ret. on Equity	19.5	20.1	23.1	21.6	15.0	4.8	NM	0.7	12.0	NM

Data as orig. reptd.; bef. results of disc. opers. and/or spec. items. Per share data adj. for stk. divs. as of ex-div. date. Prior to 1996, yrs. ended Feb. 28 of the foll. cal. yr. E-Estimated. NA-Not Available. NM-Not Meaningful. NR-Not Ranked.

Office—4520 Executive Park Dr., Montgomery, AL 36116-1602. **Tel**—(334) 244-4000. **Website**—http://www.blount.com **Chrmn**—W. M. Blount. **Pres & CEO**—J. M. Panettiere. **Exec VP-CFO**—H. E. Layman. **Exec VP-Secy**—D. J. McInnes. **VP-Treas**—J. D. Marshall. **Dirs**—H. Barbour, W. H. Blount, W. M. Blount, S. R. Blount, R. E. Cartledge, C. T. Conover, H. C. Day, E. M. Folmar, M. D. Nelson, J. M. Panettiere, A. P. Ronan, A. A. Sorensen. **Transfer Agent & Registrar**—First National Bank of Boston. **Incorporated**—in Delaware in 1979. **Empl**—5,700. **S&P Analyst:** S.A.H.

03-OCT-98

Industry:
Retail (Specialty)

Summary: This specialty retailer markets traditionally styled furniture, prints and accessories through a chain of more than 400 Bombay Company stores in the U.S. and Canada.

Quantitative Evaluations

Outlook
(1 Lowest—5 Highest)
• **3**

Fair Value
• 6⅜

Risk
• **High**

Earn./Div. Rank
• **B-**

Technical Eval.
• **Bullish** since 7/98

Rel. Strength Rank
(1 Lowest—99 Highest)
• **75**

Insider Activity
• **NA**

Recent Price • 5⅛
52 Wk Range • 8⅛-3¾

Yield • Nil
12-Mo. P/E • 32.4

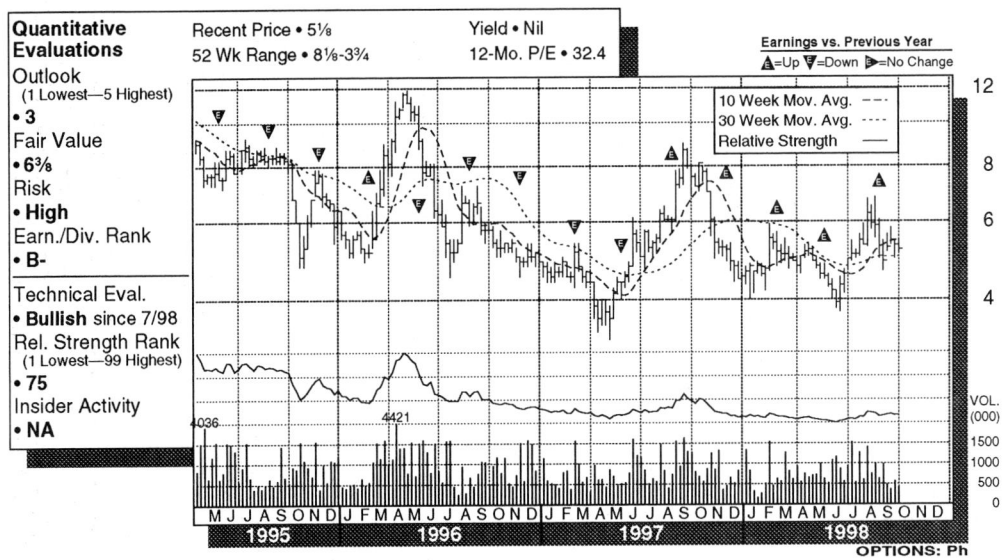

OPTIONS: Ph

Business Profile - 10-JUN-98

In FY 99 (Jan.), Bombay's primary focus will be on increasing sales. The company believes that it needs to reach the critical mass that would enable it to leverage its infrastructure. BBA will refresh its product assortment, particularly the non-furniture segment of its business, in an effort to attract more impulse buying. The company plans to open 15 to 20 new stores, and to convert 20 regular stores to large-format stores in FY 99. In addition, some existing stores will be updated with new designs. Through the first four months of FY 99, total sales grew 5.5%, and same-store sales rose 6%.

Operational Review - 10-JUN-98

Net sales in the three months ended May 2, 1998, edged up 1.7%, year to year, reflecting 3% same-store sales growth. Gross margins narrowed, but SG&A expenses were lower, due to stringent cost controls. With lower interest expense, the pretax loss narrowed to $6,412,000, from $7,645,000. After tax credits of $2,531,000, versus $3,020,000, the net loss decreased to $3,881,000 ($0.10 a share), from $4,625,000 ($0.12).

Stock Performance - 02-OCT-98

In the past 30 trading days, BBA's shares have declined 12%, compared to a 7% fall in the S&P 500. Average trading volume for the past five days was 78,640 shares, compared with the 40-day moving average of 130,446 shares.

Key Stock Statistics

Dividend Rate/Share	Nil	Shareholders	2,700
Shs. outstg. (M)	37.9	Market cap. (B)	$0.196
Avg. daily vol. (M)	0.093	Inst. holdings	50%
Tang. Bk. Value/Share	4.01		
Beta	0.92		

Value of $10,000 invested 5 years ago: $ 3,197

Fiscal Year Ending Jan. 31

	1999	1998	1997	1996	1995	1994
Revenues (Million $)						
1Q	68.34	67.23	68.08	77.94	64.34	49.08
2Q	82.01	68.74	71.20	69.67	78.20	63.00
3Q	—	71.33	72.82	70.42	77.47	62.85
4Q	—	126.3	124.2	127.4	142.9	115.7
Yr.	—	332.6	336.3	345.4	362.9	290.7
Earnings Per Share ($)						
1Q	-0.10	-0.12	-0.08	0.05	0.06	-0.18
2Q	-0.01	-0.03	-0.06	0.01	0.06	0.09
3Q	—	-0.05	-0.16	-0.04	0.01	0.07
4Q	—	0.31	0.23	0.32	-0.38	0.38
Yr.	—	0.12	-0.07	0.33	-0.25	0.36

Next earnings report expected: mid November

Dividend Data

A three-for-two stock split was effected in December 1993, following similar splits in July 1993, December 1992, March 1992 and October 1987. The most recent cash payment was in 1983. Tandy Brands Accessories Inc. was spun off in December 1990.

A Division of The **McGraw·Hill** Companies

Business Summary - 10-JUN-98

The Bombay Company is a leading specialty retailer that markets traditional and classic furniture. As of May 21, 1998, it was operating 408 Bombay stores throughout the U.S. and Canada. In FY 98 (Jan.), the company had an assortment of about 3,000 stock keeping units (SKUs), of which 1,200 were introduced in FY 98, up from 1,000 SKU introductions in FY 97. The geographic breakdown of sales in recent fiscal years was as follows:

	FY 98	FY 97
U.S.	88%	89%
Canada	12%	11%

Bombay Company stores sell 18th and 19th century English-style reproduction furniture, prints and accessories, with more than 90% of the stores located in upscale malls. The stores formerly averaged 1,700 sq. ft. in size, but in 1992, the company began to convert to a larger format of between 2,500 sq. ft. and 3,500 sq. ft. In February 1993, BBA said it would convert nearly all existing stores to the larger format over a five-year period. As of January 31, 1998, a total of 228

larger-format stores were in operation, including 139 stores that were converted to the large format from the regular format. The sales mix in FY 98 consisted of: 49% furniture, 26% wood and metal accessories, 17% wall decor (principally prints, mirrors and sconces) and, 8% lamps and other categories.

In FY 99, Bombay plans to accelerate the growth of its non-furniture business, which currently accounts for about 50% of total sales. Since its stores are located in many of North America's premier malls, the company believes that they are the ideal venue for impulse purchases. Among the categories that BBA will expand are home fragrances, candles and textiles.

Merchandise is manufactured to company specifications through a network of manufacturers located principally in Asia and North America. Internally designed or styled products account for about 95% of Bombay's products. Approximately 60% of production needs is satisfied through overseas sources, and about 75% of the company's merchandise requirements are provided from 35 contractors in eight countries.

Net sales in the four weeks ended May 30, 1998, were up 19%, year to year. Comparable-store sales rose 18%.

Per Share Data ($)

(Year Ended Jan. 31)	1998	1997	1996	1995	1994	1993	1992	1991	1990	1989
Tangible Bk. Val.	4.14	4.04	4.07	3.66	4.02	3.21	1.81	1.48	1.69	1.28
Cash Flow	0.38	0.22	0.65	-0.21	0.83	0.42	0.46	0.35	0.33	0.37
Earnings	0.12	-0.07	0.33	-0.39	0.60	0.23	0.29	0.18	0.21	0.24
Dividends	Nil	Nil	Nil	Nil	Nil	Nil	Nil	Nil	Nil	Nil
Payout Ratio	Nil	Nil	Nil	Nil	Nil	Nil	Nil	Nil	Nil	Nil
Cal. Yrs.	1997	1996	1995	1994	1993	1992	1991	1990	1989	1988
Prices - High	9	11$7/8$	11	32$3/4$	32$7/8$	16$1/4$	5$1/4$	5$1/2$	5$1/2$	2$3/16$
- Low	3$1/4$	4$1/2$	4$3/4$	8$3/4$	12$5/8$	4$1/2$	1$15/16$	1$7/8$	2$3/16$	1$3/8$
P/E Ratio - High	75	NM	33	55	NM	56	29	27	22	18
- Low	27	NM	14	15	NM	15	10	9	9	11

Income Statement Analysis (Million $)

	1998	1997	1996	1995	1994	1993	1992	1991	1990	1989
Revs.	333	336	345	241	317	232	176	139	112	109
Oper. Inc.	14.8	6.2	25.5	23.7	45.7	32.7	21.5	15.2	13.5	12.7
Depr.	9.9	11.2	11.9	6.8	8.9	6.7	5.7	5.2	3.6	2.9
Int. Exp.	Nil	Nil	0.1	0.4	0.1	0.2	0.5	0.6	0.9	1.7
Pretax Inc.	7.3	-4.4	20.4	-24.3	37.6	13.4	15.7	9.8	9.5	8.9
Eff. Tax Rate	39%	NM	39%	NM	39%	39%	39%	41%	38%	39%
Net Inc.	4.5	-2.8	12.4	-14.7	22.9	8.2	9.6	5.9	5.9	5.4

Balance Sheet & Other Fin. Data (Million $)

	1998	1997	1996	1995	1994	1993	1992	1991	1990	1989
Cash	56.1	63.1	24.1	30.7	20.4	42.8	10.1	1.0	3.3	8.2
Curr. Assets	149	145	133	128	119	111	45.0	34.2	27.7	36.5
Total Assets	195	195	191	190	181	143	79.2	66.2	69.2	59.7
Curr. Liab.	30.4	35.1	31.7	50.1	29.3	24.1	17.4	14.5	11.8	12.4
LT Debt	Nil	Nil	Nil	Nil	Nil	Nil	Nil	2.5	2.5	10.9
Common Eqty.	158	154	152	135	147	116	59.1	47.3	53.6	35.0
Total Cap.	158	154	152	135	147	116	59.1	49.7	56.1	45.9
Cap. Exp.	4.0	4.4	5.9	22.1	35.3	15.0	7.5	8.9	11.6	7.0
Cash Flow	14.3	8.3	24.3	-7.9	31.8	14.9	15.3	11.0	9.5	8.3
Curr. Ratio	4.9	4.1	4.2	2.5	4.1	4.6	2.6	2.4	2.4	2.9
% LT Debt of Cap.	Nil	Nil	Nil	Nil	Nil	Nil	Nil	5.0	4.4	23.7
% Net Inc.of Revs.	1.3	NM	3.6	NM	7.2	3.5	5.5	4.2	5.3	5.0
% Ret. on Assets	2.3	NM	6.6	NM	14.0	7.1	13.1	8.6	8.1	9.7
% Ret. on Equity	2.9	NM	8.7	NM	17.3	9.0	17.9	11.6	12.0	20.4

Data as orig. reptd.; bef. results of disc. opers. and/or spec. items. Per share data adj. for stk. divs. as of ex-div. date. Yrs. ended Jun. 30 prior to 1995; data for FY 95 in Per Share Data & Income Statement tbls. for seven mos. ended Jan. E-Estimated. NA-Not Available. NM-Not Meaningful. NR-Not Ranked.

Office—550 Bailey Ave., Fort Worth, TX 76107. **Tel**—(817) 347-8200. **Website**—http://www.bombayco.com **Chrmn**—C. E. Niles. **CEO**—R. S. Jackson. **Pres & COO**—C. Mehrlander. **VP & Secy**—M. J. Veitenheimer. **VP-Fin & Treas**—E. D. Crowley. **Dirs**—B. Bass, E. H. Damon, G. E. Hemmerle, R. S. Jackson, A. R. Megarry, C. Mehrlander, C. E. Niles, R. E. Runice, C. R. Thompson. **Transfer Agent & Registrar**—Boston EquiServe, Canton, MA. **Incorporated**—in Delaware in 1975. **Empl**— 5,000. **S&P Analyst:** Ray Lam, CFA

Books-A-Million   3299K

NASDAQ Symbol **BAMM**

In S&P SmallCap 600

03-OCT-98

Industry:
Retail (Specialty)

Summary: This leading book retailer operates 166 stores in 17 states (mainly in the Southeast), selling books, magazines, newspapers, collectibles, greeting cards and gifts.

Quantitative Evaluations		
Recent Price • 2⅝	Yield • Nil	
52 Wk Range • 7½-2¼	12-Mo. P/E • 8.4	

Outlook
(1 Lowest—5 Highest)
• **5**

Fair Value
• 9¼

Risk
• **High**

Earn./Div. Rank
• **B+**

Technical Eval.
• **Bearish** since 3/98

Rel. Strength Rank
(1 Lowest—99 Highest)
• **15**

Insider Activity
• **NA**

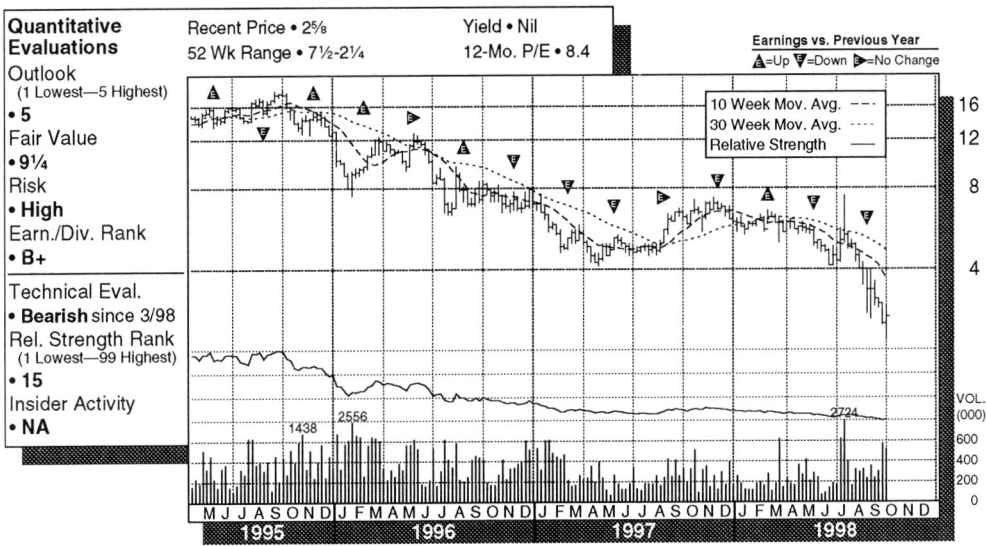

Earnings vs. Previous Year
▲=Up ▼=Down ▶=No Change

10 Week Mov. Avg. ‒ ‒ ‒
30 Week Mov. Avg. · · · · ·
Relative Strength ——

Business Profile - 02-SEP-98

Books-A-Million is one of the dominant book retailers in the Southeast. Its strategy has been to take advantage of the environment of each particular area by opening bookstores in three different formats. The company opened 21 new stores in FY 98 (Jan.), including 16 superstores, and opened an additional five superstores during the first half of FY 99. As of August 1, 1997, superstore sales accounted for about 90% of total retail sales. BAMM has emphasized its goal of building customer loyalty by offering its customers the best value, selection and service.

Operational Review - 02-SEP-98

Net sales in the 26 weeks ended August 1, 1998, advanced 8.8%, year to year; comparable-store sales were down 3.9%. Earnings before interest, depreciation and taxes were down 14%. A net loss of $504 million ($0.03 a share) contrasted with net income of $896,000 ($0.05).

Stock Performance - 02-OCT-98

In the past 30 trading days, BAMM's shares have declined 33%, compared to a 7% fall in the S&P 500. Average trading volume for the past five days was 103,700 shares, compared with the 40-day moving average of 72,249 shares.

Key Stock Statistics

Dividend Rate/Share	Nil	Shareholders	7,800
Shs. outstg. (M)	17.4	Market cap. (B)	$0.047
Avg. daily vol. (M)	0.085	Inst. holdings	24%
Tang. Bk. Value/Share	5.82		
Beta	0.68		

Value of $10,000 invested 5 years ago: $ 3,838

Fiscal Year Ending Jan. 31

	1999	1998	1997	1996	1995	1994
Revenues (Million $)						
1Q	74.47	68.24	56.59	44.01	30.94	23.48
2Q	77.96	71.87	60.46	52.03	37.28	26.26
3Q	—	71.61	64.51	48.77	37.19	27.43
4Q	—	113.0	97.06	84.99	66.96	46.10
Yr.	—	324.8	278.6	229.8	172.4	123.3
Earnings Per Share ($)						
1Q	Nil	0.02	0.06	0.06	0.05	0.04
2Q	-0.03	0.03	0.03	-0.02	0.07	0.05
3Q	—	-0.02	Nil	0.04	0.03	0.02
4Q	—	**0.37**	0.25	0.35	0.32	0.23
Yr.	—	**0.40**	0.33	0.43	0.47	0.37

Next earnings report expected: late November

Dividend Data

No cash dividends have been paid.

Business Summary - 02-SEP-98

From its humble beginnings in 1917 as a single store made out of old piano crates by the company's founder, Clyde W. Anderson, Books-A-Million has grown to 166 stores in 17 southeastern states. With FY 98 (Jan.) net sales of about $325 million, BAMM was one of the three leading U.S. retail bookstore chains. The company's current growth strategy is focused on opening superstores and combination stores in new and existing market areas. It also continuing to review profitability trends and prospects of existing stores and closing or relocating underperforming stores or converting stores to different formats.

In 1988, BAMM was taken in a new direction by Clyde B. Anderson, the founder's grandson and the company's current president; BAMM opened its first superstore. Since then, more than 110 superstores have been opened. As of August 1998, the stores, which are operate under the name Books-A-Million, accounted for 90% of the company's retail store sales. The stores, which average about 25,000 sq. ft., sell books, magazines, newspapers, collectibles, cards and gifts. Most stores feature Joe Muggs bars, which sell coffee, espresso and other refreshments. Each store also has a special section, called Kids-A-Million, that offers children's books, educational resources and gifts. Many

promotional events are held, with authors from Newt Gingrich and Hillary Clinton to Charlton Heston appearing to sign books. The stores seek to differentiate themselves from competitors by offering a broad selection, discounted prices, convenient hours (stores are open from 9 a.m. to 11 p.m., seven days a week), knowledgeable salespersons, and excellent service.

In addition to the superstore format, BAMM operates two other types of stores. It currently operates 27 traditional Bookland stores. These mall-based stores average 3,500 sq. ft. and sell books, magazines and newspapers. In smaller areas of the Southeast, BAMM operates 31 Bookland combination stores. These stores sell books, magazines, newspapers and greeting cards. The combined greeting card and bookstore format generates increased customer traffic, allowing the stores to be successful in small areas where a bookstore or greeting card store alone would not be. BAMM is also a wholesaler of hardcover, paperback and bargain books.

In recent fiscal years, BAMM has closed traditional and combination stores that no longer meet profit objectives, mainly as a result of the opening of a nearby Books-A-Million superstore. In FY 96, the company recorded a $2.9 million charge to close 24 such stores. As of the end of FY 98, all 24 stores closings had been completed.

Per Share Data ($)

(Year Ended Jan. 31)	1998	1997	1996	1995	1994	1993	1992	1991	1990	1989
Tangible Bk. Val.	5.85	5.45	5.11	4.66	4.29	2.61	NA	NA	NA	NA
Cash Flow	1.06	0.88	0.82	0.71	0.56	0.55	0.40	0.29	NA	NA
Earnings	0.40	0.33	0.43	0.47	0.37	0.32	0.21	0.13	NA	NA
Dividends	Nil	Nil	Nil	Nil	Nil	Nil	Nil	Nil	Nil	Nil
Payout Ratio	Nil	Nil	Nil	Nil	Nil	Nil	Nil	Nil	Nil	Nil
Cal. Yrs.	1997	1996	1995	1994	1993	1992	1991	1990	1989	1988
Prices - High	7⅝	12⅞	18⅝	17¾	12⅞	9⅛	NA	NA	NA	NA
- Low	4⅛	6⅜	12⅜	9¼	5⅞	6½	NA	NA	NA	NA
P/E Ratio - High	19	39	43	28	35	28	NA	NA	NA	NA
- Low	10	19	29	20	16	20	NA	NA	NA	NA

Income Statement Analysis (Million $)

	1998	1997	1996	1995	1994	1993	1992	1991	1990	1989
Revs.	325	279	230	172	123	95.0	73.0	65.0	NA	NA
Oper. Inc.	27.2	21.7	22.1	16.7	11.7	8.4	6.1	5.0	NA	NA
Depr.	11.6	9.5	6.8	4.3	3.0	2.4	1.7	1.5	NA	NA
Int. Exp.	4.3	2.8	0.7	0.0	Nil	0.7	1.3	1.6	NA	NA
Pretax Inc.	11.2	9.3	11.9	13.0	9.1	5.4	3.0	1.9	NA	NA
Eff. Tax Rate	38%	38%	37%	38%	38%	38%	37%	37%	NA	NA
Net Inc.	7.0	5.8	7.5	8.1	5.6	3.3	1.9	1.2	NA	NA

Balance Sheet & Other Fin. Data (Million $)

	1998	1997	1996	1995	1994	1993	1992	1991	1990	1989
Cash	3.9	4.8	1.9	21.5	35.4	NA	NA	NA	NA	NA
Curr. Assets	178	169	140	120	99	NA	NA	NA	NA	NA
Total Assets	246	234	191	158	115	68.0	41.0	NA	NA	NA
Curr. Liab.	95.7	98.1	85.3	70.3	40.2	NA	NA	NA	NA	NA
LT Debt	45.2	37.6	14.1	4.6	Nil	Nil	3.8	NA	NA	NA
Common Eqty.	103	96.4	90.5	82.4	74.2	37.7	8.1	NA	NA	NA
Total Cap.	150	135	106	87.8	74.8	37.7	11.9	NA	NA	NA
Cap. Exp.	14.4	23.7	23.9	24.4	8.3	6.7	NA	NA	NA	NA
Cash Flow	18.6	15.3	14.3	12.3	8.6	5.7	3.7	2.7	NA	NA
Curr. Ratio	1.9	1.7	1.6	1.7	2.5	1.6	NA	NA	NA	NA
% LT Debt of Cap.	30.1	27.8	13.3	5.2	Nil	Nil	31.6	NA	NA	NA
% Net Inc.of Revs.	2.1	2.1	3.3	4.7	4.6	3.5	2.6	1.8	NA	NA
% Ret. on Assets	2.9	2.7	4.2	5.9	6.2	6.2	5.0	NA	NA	NA
% Ret. on Equity	7.0	6.2	8.6	10.3	10.1	14.6	26.8	NA	NA	NA

Data as orig. reptd.; bef. results of disc. opers. and/or spec. items. Per share data adj. for stk. divs. as of ex-div. date. Bold denotes diluted EPS (FASB 128). E-Estimated. NA-Not Available. NM-Not Meaningful. NR-Not Ranked.

Office—402 Industrial Lane, Birmingham AL 35211.**Tel**—(205) 942-3737. **Chrmn**—C. C. Anderson.**Pres & CEO**—C. B. Anderson. **EVP & COO**—R. L. Burdette. **EVP, CFO & Investor Contact**—Sandra B. Cochran. **Dirs**—C. B. Anderson, C. C. Anderson, T. C. Anderson, R. G. Bruno, J. B. Mason, J. E. Southwood.**Transfer Agent & Registrar**—AmSouth Bank, Birmingham. **Incorporated**—in Alabama in 1964; reincorporated in Delaware in 1992. **Empl**— 4,300. **S&P Analyst:** S.A.H.

Boole & Babbage
3299L
NASDAQ Symbol **BOOL**
In S&P SmallCap 600

03-OCT-98

Industry: Computer (Software & Services)

Summary: This company provides enterprise automation software designed to help large corporations worldwide organize and manage complex computer systems.

Quantitative Evaluations

Outlook (1 Lowest—5 Highest)
• **4-**

Fair Value
• **32%**

Risk
• **Average**

Earn./Div. Rank
• **B**

Technical Eval.
• **Bearish** since 3/98

Rel. Strength Rank (1 Lowest—99 Highest)
• **83**

Insider Activity
• **NA**

Recent Price • 23
52 Wk Range • 26-17

Yield • Nil
12-Mo. P/E • 20.9

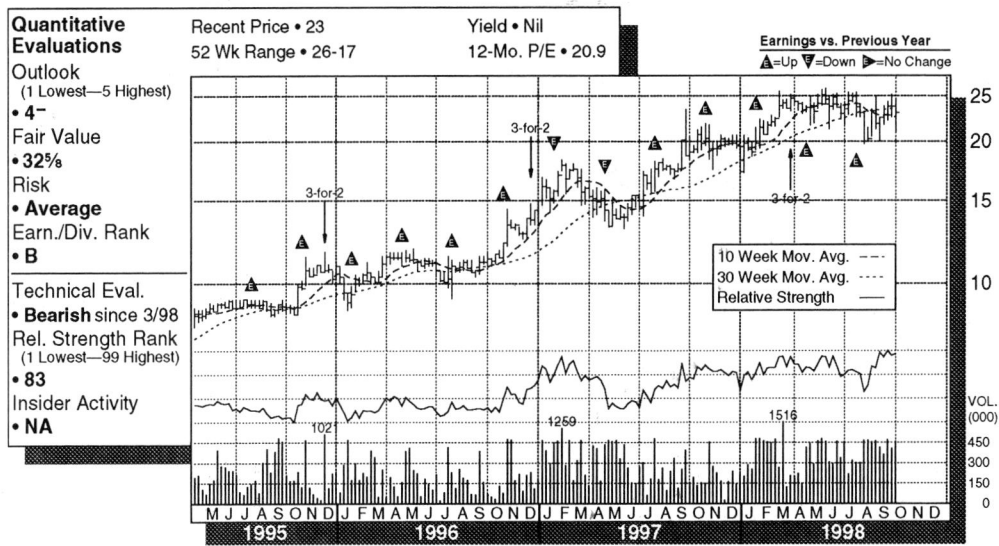

Earnings vs. Previous Year
▲=Up ▼=Down ▶=No Change

10 Week Mov. Avg. ---
30 Week Mov. Avg. ·····
Relative Strength —

Business Profile - 29-JUL-98

This company is the recognized market leader in tactical, end-to-end availability management. BOOL's COMMAND/POST enterprise service management solution is utilized to manage customers' mainframe, mid-range and client/server environments running mission-critical applications. The company's products enable worldwide organizations to reduce operational costs and improve service delivery. BOOL recently posted record third quarter results, driven by growth in its client/server revenues, despite the negative impact of currency rates. The company also completed the rollout of several new products during the most recent quarter, including a new release of COMMAND/POST.

Operational Review - 29-JUL-98

Total revenues in the first nine months of FY 98 (Sep.) advanced 11%, year to year, reflecting 48% growth in client/server revenues. Margins widened, as general and administrative expenses fell. In the absence of $11.3 million of acquisition and other costs, operating profit grew to $25.24 million from $4.85 million. With 74% greater net interest and other income, and after taxes at 28.0%, versus 45.7%, net income surged to $26,394,000 ($0.86 a share) from $6,206,000 ($0.21, as adjusted).

Stock Performance - 02-OCT-98

In the past 30 trading days, BOOL's shares have declined 0.81%, compared to a 7% fall in the S&P 500. Average trading volume for the past five days was 102,820 shares, compared with the 40-day moving average of 102,900 shares.

Key Stock Statistics

Dividend Rate/Share	Nil	Shareholders	500
Shs. outstg. (M)	28.2	Market cap. (B)	$0.649
Avg. daily vol. (M)	0.099	Inst. holdings	69%
Tang. Bk. Value/Share	5.00		
Beta	0.38		

Value of $10,000 invested 5 years ago: $ 52,926

Fiscal Year Ending Sep. 30

	1998	1997	1996	1995	1994	1993
Revenues (Million $)						
1Q	52.93	49.76	40.12	38.57	31.12	29.47
2Q	53.59	46.45	40.67	37.25	32.02	28.48
3Q	53.68	48.76	40.92	37.37	33.03	28.90
4Q	—	52.13	45.48	41.17	35.63	31.40
Yr.	—	197.1	167.2	154.4	131.8	118.3
Earnings Per Share ($)						
1Q	**0.27**	0.07	0.16	0.13	0.10	0.09
2Q	**0.31**	-0.09	0.16	0.14	0.11	0.10
3Q	**0.28**	-0.07	0.15	0.12	0.01	0.08
4Q	—	0.24	0.20	0.15	0.07	0.09
Yr.	—	0.45	0.67	0.54	0.32	0.38

Next earnings report expected: mid November

Dividend Data

Amount ($)	Date Decl.	Ex-Div. Date	Stock of Record	Payment Date
3-for-2	Feb. 19	Mar. 26	Mar. 06	Mar. 25 '98

A Division of The McGraw-Hill Companies

Business Summary - 29-JUL-98

Boole & Babbage, Inc.'s software products are used by information systems (IS) professionals in many large corporations worldwide that depend on the performance of their computing resources to conduct business. BOOL is a major developer and marketer of enterprise automation software products for managing distributed computer systems in multivendor, multiplatform computing environments. The company is committed to supporting open systems and the growing client/server market to help IS organizations augment systems availability and lower costs. The majority of BOOL's customers are large corporate and government organizations including industrial companies, commercial banks, insurance companies, communications companies, retailers, utilities and federal, state and local governments. No customer accounted for more than 10% of the company's revenues in FY 97 (Sep.), 96, or 95.

BOOL sells its products domestically through its own distribution division and internationally through several subsidiaries in Europe, Japan and Australia. In FY 97, revenues from non-North American operations accounted for 60% of total revenues and 81% of operating profits. Fluctuations in currency exchange rates adversely affected revenue growth in recent years.

The company derives its revenues mainly from the li-

censing of computer software programs, consulting and education services (together accounting for about 55% of revenues in FY 97) and from the sales of software maintenance services (45%).

With over 50% of BOOL's license revenue derived from transactions that close in the last month of a quarter (as is common in the industry), quarterly revenues are difficult to predict. Moreover, the inability to attain projected revenues could hurt operating results, as operating expenses are relatively fixed.

The company provides both client/server and mainframe products for its corporate customers. management expects that the client/server group of products will show higher growth rates in FY 98. The success of the client/server product area is dependent on the new Explorer family of Windows NT and Web-base products. The mainframe product area includes plex products which enable customers to handle large groups of computer processors, especially the parallel processing machines by IBM.

Maintenance revenue stems from services BOOL provides, including technical support, product enhancements, system updates and user documentation.

In January 1997, BOOL acquired privately held MAXM Systems Corp. for about 1.1 million common shares. MAXM incurred a net loss of $6.6 million on revenues of $15.5 million in FY 96 (Sep.).

Per Share Data ($)

(Year Ended Sep. 30)	1997	1996	1995	1994	1993	1992	1991	1990	1989	1988
Tangible Bk. Val.	4.19	3.66	2.86	2.03	1.43	1.18	NA	NA	NA	NA
Cash Flow	0.77	0.99	0.91	0.82	0.73	NA	NA	NA	NA	NA
Earnings	0.45	0.67	0.54	0.33	0.37	0.25	NA	NA	NA	NA
Dividends	Nil	Nil	Nil	Nil	Nil	Nil	Nil	Nil	Nil	Nil
Payout Ratio	Nil	Nil	Nil	Nil	Nil	Nil	Nil	Nil	Nil	Nil
Prices - High	23½	16⅝	11¾	7⅞	5⅝	5	NA	NA	NA	NA
- Low	13⅛	8¾	7⅝	4⅜	4⅛	2⅝	NA	NA	NA	NA
P/E Ratio - High	53	25	33	24	15	20	NA	NA	NA	NA
- Low	29	13	21	14	11	14	NA	NA	NA	NA

Income Statement Analysis (Million $)

	1997	1996	1995	1994	1993	1992	1991	1990	1989	1988
Revs.	197	167	154	132	118	111	NA	NA	NA	NA
Oper. Inc.	32.8	28.0	25.7	24.7	18.2	13.7	NA	NA	NA	NA
Depr.	9.7	8.9	9.7	11.9	8.6	NA	NA	NA	NA	NA
Int. Exp.	Nil	0.5	1.1	1.5	NA	NA	NA	NA	NA	NA
Pretax Inc.	21.0	25.1	19.9	11.5	11.2	7.7	NA	NA	NA	NA
Eff. Tax Rate	36%	28%	30%	31%	31%	28%	NA	NA	NA	NA
Net Inc.	13.5	18.0	13.9	7.9	9.2	5.6	NA	NA	NA	NA

Balance Sheet & Other Fin. Data (Million $)

	1997	1996	1995	1994	1993	1992	1991	1990	1989	1988
Cash	33.9	60.1	38.1	34.0	23.7	16.1	NA	NA	NA	NA
Curr. Assets	160	136	104	83.6	NA	NA	NA	NA	NA	NA
Total Assets	260	207	164	132	101	88.0	NA	NA	NA	NA
Curr. Liab.	102	84.1	74.3	67.6	NA	NA	NA	NA	NA	NA
LT Debt	1.9	2.5	1.4	3.1	5.2	5.2	NA	NA	NA	NA
Common Eqty.	119	93.0	70.2	48.2	34.5	29.0	NA	NA	NA	NA
Total Cap.	120	95.5	71.5	51.2	39.7	34.2	NA	NA	NA	NA
Cap. Exp.	3.8	3.5	3.3	2.9	2.8	NA	NA	NA	NA	NA
Cash Flow	23.1	26.9	23.6	19.9	17.8	NA	NA	NA	NA	NA
Curr. Ratio	1.6	1.6	1.4	1.2	NA	NA	NA	NA	NA	NA
% LT Debt of Cap.	1.6	2.6	1.6	6.0	13.0	15.2	NA	NA	NA	NA
% Net Inc.of Revs.	6.8	10.8	9.1	6.0	7.8	5.0	NA	NA	NA	NA
% Ret. on Assets	5.8	9.8	9.4	6.8	8.1	7.0	NA	NA	NA	NA
% Ret. on Equity	12.7	22.1	23.6	18.9	24.2	21.0	NA	NA	NA	NA

Data as orig. reptd.; bef. results of disc. opers. and/or spec. items. Per share data adj. for stk. divs. as of ex-div. date. Bold denotes diluted EPS (FASB 128). E-Estimated. NA-Not Available. NM-Not Meaningful. NR-Not Ranked.

Office—3131 Zanker Road, San Jose, CA 95134-1933. **Tel**—(408) 526-3000. **Fax**—(408) 526-3055. **Website**—http://www.boole.com **E-mail**—aknapp@boole.com **Chrmn**—F. P. Johnson Jr. **Pres & CEO**—P. E. Newton. **SVP, CFO & Secy**—A. F. Knapp Jr. **Dirs**—J. S. Bruggeling, R. E. Cairns, F. P. Johnson Jr., T. R. McGowan, P. E. Newton, C. H. Reynolds. **Transfer Agent & Registrar**—First National Bank of Boston. **Incorporated**—in Delaware in 1986. **Empl**— 880. **S&P Analyst:** Mark Cavallone

Bowne & Co.

7348

ASE Symbol **BNE**

In S&P SmallCap 600

03-OCT-98

Industry: Specialty Printing

Summary: This company specializes in financial documentation and communications services for corporate compliance and public financing worldwide.

Quantitative Evaluations

Outlook
(1 Lowest—5 Highest)
• **5**

Fair Value
• **30⅜**

Risk
• **Average**

Earn./Div. Rank
• **A-**

Technical Eval.
• **Bullish** since 9/98

Rel. Strength Rank
(1 Lowest—99 Highest)
• **43**

Insider Activity
• **Neutral**

Recent Price • 16⅜

52 Wk Range • 23⅞-15⅜

Yield • 1.3%

12-Mo. P/E • 11.9

Earnings vs. Previous Year
▲=Up ▼=Down ▷=No Change

10 Week Mov. Avg. – – –
30 Week Mov. Avg. ·····
Relative Strength ——

2-for-1

Business Profile - 14-SEP-98

This company mainly provides printing and other related services, with revenues from its transactional financial printing business affected by the cyclical conditions of the capital markets. Over the past year, the company has expanded its service offerings to include information management, global document creation and dissemination and Internet services. The company's goal is to become the empowerer of information to global companies, and it is spending heavily to build its resources outside the U.S.

Operational Review - 14-SEP-98

Net sales in the first half of 1998 advanced 19%, year to year, aided by higher demand for transactional printing, growth in non-transactional printing services and, to a lesser extent, acquisitions. Gross margin widened on a more favorable product mix, but following substantially higher selling and administrative expenses related to acquired businesses and the absence of a $35.3 million gain on the sale of a subsidiary, pretax income fell 39%. After taxes at 41.8%, versus 42.7%, net income was down 38%, to $28,405,000 ($0.75 a share, as adjusted for a two-for-one stock split in August 1998) from $45,937,000 ($1.24).

Stock Performance - 02-OCT-98

In the past 30 trading days, BNE's shares have declined 15%, compared to a 7% fall in the S&P 500. Average trading volume for the past five days was 47,740 shares, compared with the 40-day moving average of 71,490 shares.

Key Stock Statistics

Dividend Rate/Share	0.22	Shareholders	1,400
Shs. outstg. (M)	36.8	Market cap. (B)	$0.605
Avg. daily vol. (M)	0.058	Inst. holdings	72%
Tang. Bk. Value/Share	8.13		
Beta	1.35		

Value of $10,000 invested 5 years ago: $ 21,785

Fiscal Year Ending Dec. 31

	1998	1997	1996	1995	1994	1993
Revenues (Million $)						
1Q	194.3	153.7	90.73	76.81	82.08	61.00
2Q	219.3	193.8	136.4	102.5	119.2	89.60
3Q	—	177.7	134.2	103.1	95.59	82.48
4Q	—	191.5	140.1	110.3	83.80	100.1
Yr.	—	716.6	501.4	392.7	380.6	333.3
Earnings Per Share ($)						
1Q	**0.34**	**0.83**	0.10	0.06	0.19	0.12
2Q	**0.41**	**0.41**	0.35	0.17	0.43	0.34
3Q	—	**0.28**	0.38	0.20	0.17	0.21
4Q	—	**0.34**	0.38	0.24	0.10	0.36
Yr.	—	**1.99**	1.21	0.67	0.90	1.02

Next earnings report expected: mid December

Dividend Data (Dividends have been paid since 1941.)

Amount ($)	Date Decl.	Ex-Div. Date	Stock of Record	Payment Date
0.090	Nov. 20	Dec. 23	Dec. 26	Jan. 14 '98
0.090	Apr. 29	May. 13	May. 15	May. 27 '98
0.110	Jun. 25	Aug. 12	Aug. 14	Aug. 26 '98
2-for-1	Jun. 25	Aug. 27	Aug. 14	Aug. 26 '98

A Division of The McGraw-Hill Companies

Business Summary - 14-SEP-98

If you've ever received a printed 10-K or an IPO prospectus, there's a good chance the document was produced by Bowne & Co. Bowne is an information technology company and the world's largest financial printer. The company is also a leading provider of software and Web-site localization services for the global marketplace, and the market leader in electronic (EDGAR) filing services for U.S. corporations, law firms, investment banks, and mutual fund groups. Established in 1775 in New York, Bowne provides document-building solutions and Internet and custom print services, in multiple languages and in print and electronic formats. BNE serves the international market from offices in Canada, Mexico, Europe, and Asia.

The company is in the midst of a major re-focusing of its business, one that will take a number of years to accomplish. Its business is being re-directed on "Empowering Information," a term used to define the management, repurposing and distribution of a client's information to any audience, through any medium, in any language, anywhere in the world. The company manages and repurposes the information for distribution by digital, Internet or paper media. It manages documents on the clients' site or at its own facilities, and provides business services and solutions for transactional financial, corporate reporting and mutual fund printing, digital data management, Internet services, localization, trans-

lation and document management outsourcing, among others.

Management believes this transition will allow it to leverage the document management and information management technologies it has traditionally employed into a variety of new business solutions for customers worldwide. Newer services complement the company's older business, as well as one another. The company views its business as providing solutions that empower its clients' information on any medium.

The transactional financial printing market consists primarily of transactional financial, corporate reporting, and mutual fund printing. Transactional financial printing includes registration statements, tax-exempt offering circulars, prospectuses, loan agreements, special proxy statements, tender offer materials and other documents related to corporate financings, acquisitions and mergers.

One of the company's newer solution offerings, digital data management, assists customers by providing their individual clients with high-speed, customized periodic statements or other on demand printing. Such customers include mutual funds, stock brokers, investment banks, retail banks and other financial institutions that manage multi-option client portfolios, healthcare providers, insurance companies and others that manage 401(k) and other retirement plans.

In July 1998, Bowne acquired Donnelley Enterprise Solutions, which provides document services, desktop publishing and imaging services, for $105 million.

Per Share Data ($)

(Year Ended Dec. 31)	1997	1996	1995	1994	1993	1992	1991	1990	1989	1988
Tangible Bk. Val.	8.06	7.54	6.53	6.41	5.68	4.86	4.23	3.90	3.29	3.28
Cash Flow	2.67	1.81	1.19	1.33	1.35	1.15	0.74	0.56	0.52	0.58
Earnings	1.99	1.21	0.67	0.90	1.02	0.82	0.42	0.24	0.23	0.35
Dividends	0.18	0.18	0.18	0.16	0.15	0.13	0.13	0.13	0.13	0.13
Payout Ratio	9%	15%	27%	18%	12%	16%	30%	51%	53%	36%
Prices - High	$20^3/_8$	13	$10^1/_2$	$14^1/_4$	$10^7/_8$	$9^1/_4$	$8^1/_4$	$7^1/_2$	$7^1/_4$	$7^5/_8$
- Low	$10^7/_8$	$8^5/_8$	$7^3/_4$	$7^3/_4$	$7^3/_8$	$6^5/_8$	$4^7/_8$	4	$5^1/_4$	$4^3/_4$
P/E Ratio - High	10	11	16	16	11	11	20	31	32	22
- Low	5	7	11	9	7	8	11	16	23	14

Income Statement Analysis (Million $)

	1997	1996	1995	1994	1993	1992	1991	1990	1989	1988
Revs.	717	501	393	381	333	282	236	201	190	188
Oper. Inc.	114	92.0	56.8	65.3	68.4	57.0	35.7	24.7	23.0	29.2
Depr.	29.7	21.2	17.9	15.2	11.4	10.9	10.8	10.8	10.2	8.3
Int. Exp.	1.6	0.7	0.9	1.1	2.3	2.9	3.5	3.4	3.5	3.5
Pretax Inc.	121	75.0	41.8	54.2	59.0	47.0	25.1	14.5	15.9	22.1
Eff. Tax Rate	42%	43%	44%	42%	40%	40%	43%	42%	50%	42%
Net Inc.	69.5	42.5	23.3	31.2	35.3	28.3	14.3	8.4	8.2	12.8

Balance Sheet & Other Fin. Data (Million $)

	1997	1996	1995	1994	1993	1992	1991	1990	1989	1988
Cash	40.6	36.5	36.6	38.5	33.1	55.7	30.8	29.7	37.8	55.0
Curr. Assets	286	235	184	158	153	131	113	93.0	100	109
Total Assets	501	386	326	292	284	244	226	204	205	214
Curr. Liab.	121	87.5	107	51.3	64.7	42.7	38.7	26.6	28.5	30.4
LT Debt	2.5	2.5	2.8	3.2	8.8	22.3	30.8	34.2	34.4	34.8
Common Eqty.	377	281	242	223	197	167	144	132	131	138
Total Cap.	361	284	244	226	206	189	175	167	166	174
Cap. Exp.	35.2	44.5	20.0	27.2	24.5	17.5	9.3	13.8	12.0	16.8
Cash Flow	99	63.8	41.2	46.4	46.7	39.2	25.1	19.2	18.3	21.1
Curr. Ratio	2.4	2.7	2.7	3.1	2.4	3.1	2.9	3.5	3.5	3.6
% LT Debt of Cap.	0.7	0.9	1.1	1.4	4.3	11.8	17.6	20.6	20.7	20.0
% Net Inc.of Revs.	9.7	8.5	5.9	8.2	10.6	10.0	6.1	4.2	4.3	6.8
% Ret. on Assets	15.7	11.9	7.6	10.8	13.3	12.0	6.6	4.1	4.0	6.1
% Ret. on Equity	20.7	16.3	10.0	14.9	19.4	18.1	10.3	6.4	6.2	9.6

Data as orig. reptd.; bef. results of disc. opers. and/or spec. items. Per share data adj. for stk. divs. as of ex-div. date. Prior to 1998, yrs. ended Oct. 31. E-Estimated. NA-Not Available. NM-Not Meaningful. NR-Not Ranked.

Office—345 Hudson St., New York, NY 10014. **Tel**—(212) 924-5500. **Website**—http://www.bowne.com **Chrmn & CEO**—R. M. Johnson.**Pres & COO**—J. P. O'Neil.**VP-Fin & CFO**—D. K. Fletcher.**VP-Secy**—D. F. Bauer. **Investor Contact**—D. L. Rosenstein. **Dirs**—R. M. Conway, R. M. Johnson, E. H. Meyer, J. P. O'Neil, H. M. Schwarz, J. Shapiro, W. M. Smith, T. O. Stanley, V. Tese, R. R. West. **Transfer Agent & Registrar**—Bank of New York, NYC. **Incorporated**—in New York in 1968. **Empl**—4,975. **S&P Analyst:** SRB

03-OCT-98

Industry: Manufacturing (Specialized)

Summary: This company (formerly W.H. Brady Co.) is an international manufacturer and marketer of coated films and industrial identification products.

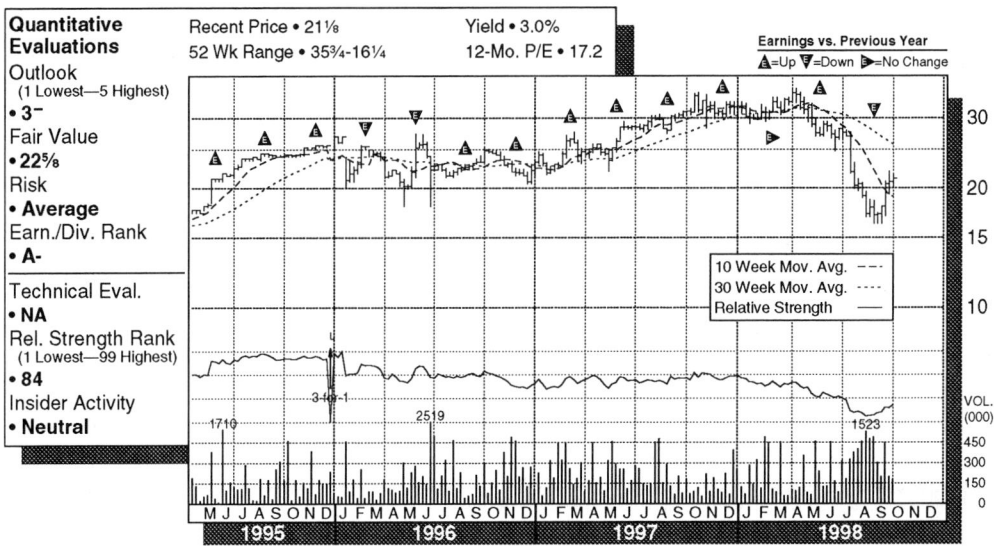

Quantitative Evaluations	
Outlook (1 Lowest—5 Highest)	• **3⁻**
Fair Value	• **22⅝**
Risk	• **Average**
Earn./Div. Rank	• **A-**
Technical Eval.	• **NA**
Rel. Strength Rank (1 Lowest—99 Highest)	• **84**
Insider Activity	• **Neutral**

Recent Price • 21⅛ 52 Wk Range • 35¾-16¼ Yield • 3.0% 12-Mo. P/E • 17.2

Earnings vs. Previous Year
▲=Up ▼=Down ▷=No Change

10 Week Mov. Avg. – – –
30 Week Mov. Avg. ·····
Relative Strength —

Business Profile - 20-MAR-98

This company, which specializes in coatings and adhesives, continues to focus on global expansion (largely through acquisitions and joint ventures) and on the development of new products. Its latest deal was the March 1998 acquisition of a French software developer specializing in barcode labeling software. International sales growth was strong in FY 97 (Jul.), reflecting increased penetration in existing markets, and startups in Malaysia, Taiwan, Korea and Brazil. Latin America and the Pacific Rim are two of the key target areas for future growth. The company adopted its present corporate title in August 1998.

Operational Review - 20-MAR-98

Net sales in the first half of FY 98 advanced 7.4%, year to year, reflecting strong international growth, particularly in Europe and the Asia/Pacific region. Operating margins narrowed, as increased research and development expenditures outweighed the effects of a favorable product mix, and well controlled SG&A expenses; the gain in operating income was held to 6.6%. With higher investment income, pretax income climbed 15%. After taxes at 39.5% in both periods, net income also increased 15%, to $15,379,000 ($0.68 a share), from $13,372,000 ($0.60).

Stock Performance - 02-OCT-98

In the past 30 trading days, BRCOA's shares have increased 19%, compared to a 7% fall in the S&P 500. Average trading volume for the past five days was 35,560 shares, compared with the 40-day moving average of 117,310 shares.

Key Stock Statistics

Dividend Rate/Share	0.64	Shareholders	500
Shs. outstg. (M)	22.5	Market cap. (B)	$0.439
Avg. daily vol. (M)	0.053	Inst. holdings	52%
Tang. Bk. Value/Share	7.38		
Beta	0.69		

Value of $10,000 invested 5 years ago: $ 19,039

Fiscal Year Ending Jul. 31

	1998	1997	1996	1995	1994	1993
Revenues (Million $)						
1Q	115.3	97.22	79.22	69.04	59.64	57.70
2Q	107.2	109.9	87.82	78.86	64.11	61.58
3Q	118.8	108.3	94.65	83.32	65.89	62.74
4Q	113.9	110.7	97.85	83.14	66.21	60.96
Yr.	455.1	426.1	359.5	314.4	255.8	243.0
Earnings Per Share ($)						
1Q	0.37	0.30	0.30	0.23	0.20	0.16
2Q	**0.31**	0.31	0.26	0.28	0.18	0.16
3Q	**0.44**	0.43	0.36	0.43	0.25	0.19
4Q	**0.11**	0.40	0.36	0.33	0.22	0.27
Yr.	**1.23**	1.44	1.27	1.28	0.85	0.78

Next earnings report expected: mid November

Dividend Data (Dividends have been paid since 1984.)

Amount ($)	Date Decl.	Ex-Div. Date	Stock of Record	Payment Date
0.150	Nov. 21	Jan. 07	Jan. 09	Jan. 31 '98
0.150	Feb. 25	Apr. 07	Apr. 10	Apr. 30 '98
0.150	May. 12	Jul. 08	Jul. 10	Jul. 31 '98
0.160	Sep. 15	Oct. 07	Oct. 09	Oct. 31 '98

A Division of The McGraw·Hill Companies

Business Summary - 20-MAR-98

This international manufacturer produces identification, safety and graphics products that help customers create safer work environments for their employees and keep better track of their non-human assets. Brady Corp. (formerly W.H. Brady Co.), which operates in 18 countries around the world, makes over 30,000 stock and custom items as well as complete identification systems for a broad range of industrial, commercial, utility and other markets.

Brady's industrial and facility identification products include self-adhesive and mechanically applied pipe markers and plastic and metal valve tags that give information about the contents, direction of flow and special hazardous properties of materials contained in piping systems. Brady also offers markets that identify wires and cables and specify their origination or destination. Other identification products are used to identify facilities, bins and shelving in factories and warehouses. Computer-printable labels, as well as printing systems and software, are also sold.

The company's safety products include a wide variety of signs that warn of hazardous or toxic materials, point the way out of a building or call attention to fire equipment. Brady also offers traffic control devices, such as barriers and cones, and "lockout/tagout" products that

"lock out" energy sources while machinery is being serviced or maintained. Many of these safety products are purchased by customers to meet standards or regulations imposed by industry groups or government agencies, such as OSHA.

Brady also makes specialty tapes that employ high-performance adhesives, reinforcing rings for floppy discs and precision die-cut tapes used in the assembly of electronic and other equipment, die cut components for cell phones and pagers, and wide format digital color inkjet printing systems.

The company places great emphasis on the development of new products, and over 100 of its employees were engaged in research and development activities in FY 97 (Jul.) The company strives to obtain about 25% of its sales from products introduced in the past three years, and it has made new product development its number one growth strategy for FY 98.

Also important to Brady's growth has been its increasing presence overseas. Sales from international operations accounted for 43% of sales in FY 97, and Brady believes that foreign markets will continue to present significant opportunities for growth. It plans to focus geographic expansion in FY 98 on Mexico, the Philippines and China; however, less than 10% of current sales are derived from the Asia Pacific region.

Per Share Data ($)

(Year Ended Jul. 31)	1998	1997	1996	1995	1994	1993	1992	1991	1990	1989
Tangible Bk. Val.	NA	7.63	6.95	7.69	6.54	5.78	5.42	5.22	4.69	4.03
Cash Flow	NA	2.08	1.77	1.70	1.27	1.23	0.77	1.04	0.98	0.71
Earnings	1.23	1.44	1.27	1.28	0.85	0.78	0.38	0.71	0.70	0.44
Dividends	0.60	0.52	0.40	0.32	0.23	0.20	0.19	0.16	0.13	0.09
Payout Ratio	49%	36%	31%	25%	27%	26%	49%	23%	19%	21%
Prices - High	35³/₄	35	27¹/₂	24¹/₂	16³/₈	14³/₈	12¹/₂	14	12¹/₈	10³/₈
- Low	16¹/₄	21⁵/₈	18	15⁵/₈	14¹/₈	11³/₈	10	8¹/₂	6¹/₂	6⁷/₈
P/E Ratio - High	29	24	22	19	19	16	33	20	18	24
- Low	13	15	14	12	17	15	27	12	9	16

Income Statement Analysis (Million $)

	1998	1997	1996	1995	1994	1993	1992	1991	1990	1989
Revs.	NA	426	360	314	256	243	236	211	191	174
Oper. Inc.	NA	64.5	51.7	49.7	38.8	33.9	30.4	27.4	28.5	27.4
Depr.	NA	14.2	10.6	9.2	9.3	9.8	8.4	7.2	6.3	6.2
Int. Exp.	NA	0.3	0.3	0.6	0.4	0.1	0.2	0.6	0.7	0.4
Pretax Inc.	NA	51.3	45.4	44.6	29.9	25.8	15.4	22.5	25.6	16.7
Eff. Tax Rate	NA	38%	38%	38%	38%	35%	45%	31%	41%	41%
Net Inc.	NA	31.7	28.0	27.9	18.5	16.9	8.4	15.4	15.0	9.9

Balance Sheet & Other Fin. Data (Million $)

	1998	1997	1996	1995	1994	1993	1992	1991	1990	1989
Cash	NA	65.3	49.2	89.1	66.1	42.4	28.5	36.0	38.4	27.5
Curr. Assets	NA	188	156	164	132	188	94.6	96.1	94.0	77.1
Total Assets	NA	292	262	230	203	180	173	157	147	130
Curr. Liab.	NA	57.2	46.4	34.5	31.7	27.7	28.5	25.2	26.2	24.0
LT Debt	NA	3.9	1.8	1.9	1.9	2.0	2.5	2.0	3.3	3.6
Common Eqty.	NA	204	186	168	142	125	117	112	101	86.0
Total Cap.	NA	211	190	173	147	130	122	117	107	93.0
Cap. Exp.	NA	6.7	10.4	8.1	6.5	12.3	24.1	15.1	13.4	10.8
Cash Flow	NA	45.6	38.6	37.1	27.6	26.4	16.6	22.4	21.0	15.8
Curr. Ratio	NA	3.3	3.4	4.8	4.2	3.8	3.3	3.8	3.6	3.2
% LT Debt of Cap.	NA	1.8	0.9	1.1	1.3	1.5	2.1	1.7	3.1	3.9
% Net Inc.of Revs.	NA	7.4	7.8	8.9	7.2	6.9	3.6	7.3	7.9	5.7
% Ret. on Assets	NA	11.5	11.4	12.9	9.7	9.5	5.1	10.1	10.8	8.2
% Ret. on Equity	NA	16.1	15.8	17.8	13.7	13.7	7.1	14.2	15.8	11.7

Data as orig. reptd.; bef. results of disc. opers. and/or spec. items. Per share data adj. for stk. divs. as of ex-div. date. Bold denotes diluted EPS (FASB 128). E-Estimated. NA-Not Available. NM-Not Meaningful. NR-Not Ranked.

Office—6555 West Good Hope Road, Milwaukee, WI 53223. **Tel**—(414) 358-6600. **Pres & CEO**—K. M. Hudson. **VP & CFO**—F. M. Jaehnert. **Secy**—P. J. Lettenberger. **Investor Contact**—Laurie Bernardy (414) 438-6880. **Dirs**—R. A. Bemis, R. C. Buchanan, F. W. Harris, K. M. Hudson, P. J. Lettenberger, G. E. Nei, R. D. Peirce. **Transfer Agent**—Firstar Trust Co., Milwaukee. **Incorporated**—in 1939. **Empl**- 2,600. **S&P Analyst:** E. Hunter

Breed Technologies 360V

NYSE Symbol **BDT**

In S&P SmallCap 600

03-OCT-98

Industry: Auto Parts & Equipment

Summary: Breed Technologies designs and manufactures steering wheels, automotive crash sensors and complete airbag systems.

S&P Opinion: Hold (★★★)	Recent Price • 6⅜	Yield • Nil
	52 Wk Range • 25⅜-4¾	12-Mo. P/E • NM

Earnings vs. Previous Year
▲=Up ▼=Down ▶=No Change

Quantitative Evaluations

Outlook
(1 Lowest—5 Highest)
• **1⁻**

Fair Value
• **3½**

Risk
• **Average**

Earn./Div. Rank
• **B-**

Technical Eval.
• **Bearish** since 5/98

Rel. Strength Rank
(1 Lowest—99 Highest)
• **6**

Insider Activity
• **NA**

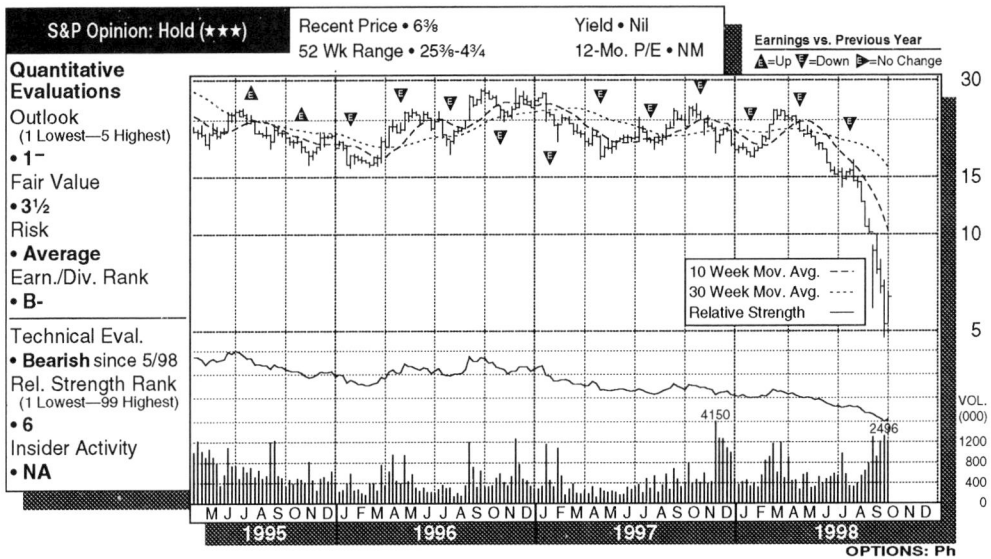

10 Week Mov. Avg. ---
30 Week Mov. Avg. ····
Relative Strength —

4150   2496

VOL.
(000)

OPTIONS: Ph

Overview - 02-OCT-98

Sales in FY 99 (Jun.), should continue to benefit from the November 1997 acquisition of AlliedSignal's safety restraint systems (SRS) business ($850 million in annual sales). Although BDT is a leader in mechanical crash sensors, its position in the airbag industry has been threatened by the development of competing systems that use electronic sensors for future models. In response, it has acquired several companies capable of producing key components for electronic models. It has also broadened its product line to include complete airbag systems and steering wheels. Competitors such as TRW and Autoliv have already established large market positions in complete airbag systems, and have displayed variable deployment systems, which BDT is only now beginning to develop. The company recently announced a restructuring program to lower costs and realize the synergies of the SRS merger. As part of the plan, BDT will reduce worldwide headcount; consolidate manufacturing, engineering and sales facilities; and write down goodwill, equipment, tooling and certain other assets associated with acquisitions. It also incurred a charge for in-process research and development at SRS.

Valuation - 02-OCT-98

We recently upgraded the shares to hold, from avoid, on news of a settlement with the SEC regarding the company's handling of certain restructuring charges, resulting in only minor restatements of financial results. The company also recently announced $1.35 billion of new contract wins through 2006. Despite expected long-term benefits from restructuring, including estimated cash savings in excess of $850 million over five years, and enhanced earnings power, given that BDT is highly leveraged, we remain cautious about adding to positions.

Key Stock Statistics

S&P EPS Est. 1998	NA	Tang. Bk. Value/Share	NM
P/E on S&P Est. 1998	NA	Beta	1.37
Dividend Rate/Share	Nil	Shareholders	1,200
Shs. outstg. (M)	36.8	Market cap. (B)	$0.235
Avg. daily vol. (M)	0.338	Inst. holdings	35%

Value of $10,000 invested 5 years ago: $ 3,925

Fiscal Year Ending Jun. 30

	1998	1997	1996	1995	1994	1993
Revenues (Million $)						
1Q	195.2	158.7	92.60	87.36	46.83	29.60
2Q	340.7	182.6	105.7	99.0	69.52	38.19
3Q	431.7	209.4	103.9	109.9	75.57	38.85
4Q	417.7	244.2	129.5	104.7	85.77	46.84
Yr.	1,385	794.9	431.7	401.0	277.7	153.5
Earnings Per Share ($)						
1Q	-0.13	0.25	0.40	0.36	0.15	0.10
2Q	-10.07	0.10	0.57	0.58	0.34	0.13
3Q	-0.07	0.05	0.47	0.70	0.49	0.16
4Q	-0.50	0.07	0.56	0.66	0.57	0.19
Yr.	-10.73	0.47	2.00	2.30	1.56	0.59

Next earnings report expected: mid November

Dividend Data (Dividends have been paid since 1994.)

Amount ($)	Date Decl.	Ex-Div. Date	Stock of Record	Payment Date
0.070	Sep. 02	Oct. 29	Oct. 31	Nov. 04 '97

A Division of The **McGraw·Hill** Companies

STANDARD
&POOR'S
STOCK REPORTS

Breed Technologies, Inc.

360V
03-OCT-98

Business Summary - 02-OCT-98

Breed Technologies designs and manufactures automotive crash sensors and airbag systems in 57 facilities worldwide. Its products are used in more than 290 models of vehicles produced by 51 automakers. In November 1997, the company doubled its revenues by acquiring AlliedSignal's safety restraint systems business ($850 million in annual revenues).

The company offers a complete range of airbag products, including electronic, electromechanical and all-mechanical crash sensors; sodium-azide, environmentally friendly non-sodium-azide and stored-gas inflators; airbag modules; and complete driver-side, passenger-side and side-impact airbag systems. BDT has started to develop occupant-sensing and intelligent airbag systems with variable deployment based on crash conditions and occupant size and position.

Having studied thousands of automobile crashes since 1968, BDT has accumulated an extensive library of crash data, which it uses to develop airbag restraint systems. The company has extensive sensor and occupant motion simulation capability, which shortens the development process.

The company acquired Hamlin and Vaisala Technologies (since renamed VTI Hamlin Oy) in FY 95 (Jun.). Hamlin produces reed switches, which are used in electronic crash sensing systems and non-automotive shock

sensing applications such as security systems, copy machines, modems, cellular phones, process controls and exercise machines. VTI Hamlin is a leader in micromachined silicon sensors, including accelerometers used in automotive electronic crash sensing.

The Fiat Group accounted for 32% of FY 97 sales, Ford 25%, and GM's Delco-GM unit for 13%. In the past, BDT was a Tier 2 supplier to GM. However, in April 1997, GM awarded it a steering wheel contract as a Tier 1 supplier, recognizing BDT's increased global presence. Long-term contracts with Ford expire in 1998.

Sales outside of North America accounted for 52% of BDT's total revenues in FY 97. Customers included Fiat, Toyota, Mercedes-Benz, Jaguar, Mazda, Nissan, Chrysler, Peugeot, Audi, Renault, Volvo, Aston-Martin, Rover, Sungwoo and Proton. In May 1997, the company announced new supply agreements with Korean, Chinese and Japanese customers.

In March 1997, BDT acquired BTI Investments, Inc., a holding company that owns Custom Trim Group ($108 million in sales). Custom Trim supplies leather-wrapped steering wheels, shift knobs and other components. The purchase, combined with BDT's October 1996 acquisition of United Technologies Automotive, solidified the company's position as the world's largest manufacturer of steering wheels, expanded its global customer base, and added new patented technologies.

Per Share Data ($)

(Year Ended Jun. 30)	1997	1996	1995	1994	1993	1992	1991	1990	1989	1988
Tangible Bk. Val.	1.44	7.27	6.65	4.85	3.25	0.56	NA	NA	NA	NA
Cash Flow	2.00	2.64	2.74	1.83	0.80	0.32	0.26	0.72	NA	NA
Earnings	0.47	2.00	2.30	1.56	0.59	0.13	0.08	0.58	-0.31	0.05
Dividends	0.35	0.22	0.20	Nil	Nil	NA	NA	NA	NA	NA
Payout Ratio	74%	11%	9%	Nil	Nil	NA	NA	NA	NA	NA
Prices - High	27½	28⅜	29	44	19½	21¾	NA	NA	NA	NA
- Low	17	16	16⅜	15¼	10¾	16	NA	NA	NA	NA
P/E Ratio - High	59	14	13	28	33	NM	NA	NA	NA	NA
- Low	36	8	7	10	18	NM	NM	NM	NM	NM

Income Statement Analysis (Million $)

Revs.	795	432	401	278	156	93.0	78.2	112	27.0	7.8
Oper. Inc.	99	113	119	80.2	32.0	14.4	8.5	28.9	NA	NA
Depr.	48.5	20.1	13.9	8.2	6.0	4.9	4.6	3.5	NA	NA
Int. Exp.	24.5	2.7	0.8	0.2	1.2	2.2	2.9	2.7	1.0	0.1
Pretax Inc.	29.6	98.3	110	75.3	25.8	5.0	3.2	22.7	-8.1	2.0
Eff. Tax Rate	50%	36%	34%	37%	35%	31%	33%	34%	NM	30%
Net Inc.	14.8	63.0	72.3	47.4	16.8	3.5	2.1	15.1	-8.1	1.4

Balance Sheet & Other Fin. Data (Million $)

Cash	18.7	95.8	36.9	54.9	42.2	1.5	NA	NA	NA	NA
Curr. Assets	316	267	132	119	78.2	25.6	NA	NA	NA	NA
Total Assets	877	504	279	181	124	62.0	NA	NA	NA	NA
Curr. Liab.	363	176	56.5	32.6	25.5	20.0	NA	NA	NA	NA
LT Debt	232	42.1	1.9	Nil	Nil	27.1	NA	NA	NA	NA
Common Eqty.	266	275	219	148	99	14.6	NA	NA	NA	NA
Total Cap.	498	317	221	148	99	42.0	NA	NA	NA	NA
Cap. Exp.	75.9	45.4	69.3	22.4	15.8	8.0	6.5	7.5	NA	NA
Cash Flow	63.4	83.1	86.2	55.5	22.8	8.4	6.8	18.6	NA	NA
Curr. Ratio	0.9	1.5	2.3	3.6	3.1	1.3	NA	NA	NA	NA
% LT Debt of Cap.	46.5	13.3	0.8	Nil	Nil	64.5	NA	NA	NA	NA
% Net Inc.of Revs.	1.9	14.6	18.0	17.1	10.8	3.8	2.7	13.5	NM	17.6
% Ret. on Assets	2.2	16.2	29.8	31.1	17.1	NA	NA	NA	NA	NA
% Ret. on Equity	5.5	25.6	39.1	38.4	29.0	NA	NA	NA	NA	NA

Data as orig. reptd.; bef. results of disc. opers. and/or spec. items. Per share data adj. for stk. divs. as of ex-div. date. Bold denotes diluted EPS (FASB 128). E-Estimated. NA-Not Available. NM-Not Meaningful. NR-Not Ranked.

Office—P.O. Box 33050, Lakeland, FL 33807.Tel—(941) 668-6000.Fax—(941) 668-6007.Website—http://www.breedtech.com Chrmn & CEO—J. C. Breed. Vice Chrmn—C. J. Speranzella Jr. EVP, CFO & Investor Contact—F. J. Gnisci. Secy—Lizanne Guptill. Dirs—A. K. Breed, J. C. Breed, P. A. Lewis, L. W. McCurdy, F. J. Musone, C. J. Speranzella Jr.Transfer Agent & Registrar—Bank of New York, NYC.Incorporated—in Delaware in 1986.Empl— 11,100. S&P Analyst: Efraim Levy

STANDARD &POOR'S
STOCK REPORTS

Brightpoint, Inc.　3329

NASDAQ Symbol **CELL**

In S&P SmallCap 600

03-OCT-98

Industry:
Communications
Equipment

Summary: A leading worldwide distributor of wireless communications products, this company also provides logistics services such as inventory management and packaging.

Quantitative Evaluations	
Outlook (1 Lowest—5 Highest)	• **5**
Fair Value	• **17⅝**
Risk	• **High**
Earn./Div. Rank	• **NR**
Technical Eval.	• **Bearish** since 6/98
Rel. Strength Rank (1 Lowest—99 Highest)	• **10**
Insider Activity	• **NA**

Recent Price • 7½
52 Wk Range • 24¼-6½
Yield • Nil
12-Mo. P/E • 11.7

Earnings vs. Previous Year
▲=Up ▼=Down ▶=No Change

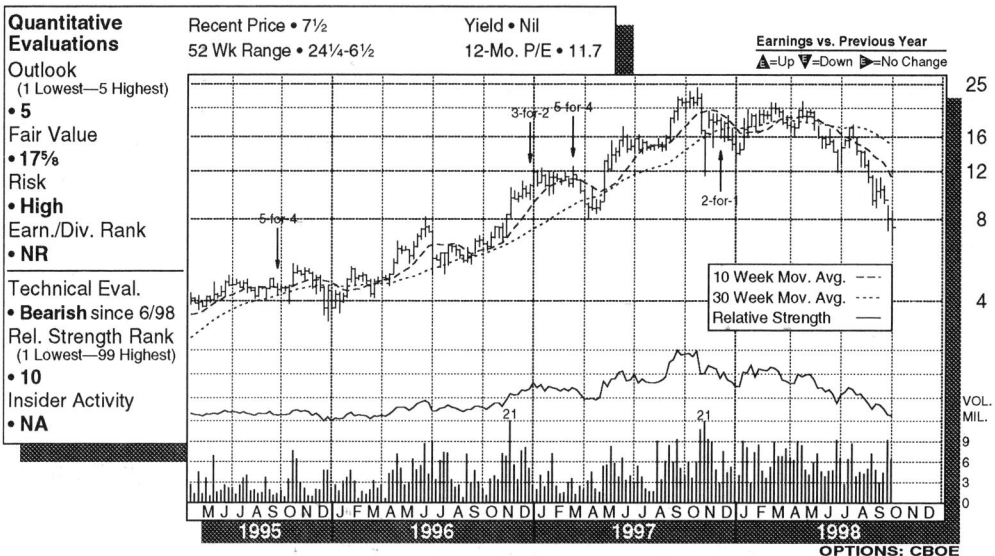

10 Week Mov. Avg. ---
30 Week Mov. Avg. ····
Relative Strength ——

OPTIONS: CBOE

Business Profile - 14-SEP-98

Brightpoint facilitates the effective and efficient distribution of wireless handsets and related accessories from leading manufacturers to network operators, agents, resellers, dealers and retailers. The company also provides value-added logistics services to its handset suppliers. In November 1997, Brightpoint extended its alliance with Ericsson, a Swedish wireless phone manufacturer, to provide logistics services and to develop new customers and markets in the U.S. In January 1998, CELL completed an agreement with Nokia, a Finnish handset producer, to become Nokia's sole authorized distributor of wireless phones in the U.S. During the first six months of 1998, the company completed nine acquistions, primarily in international markets.

Operational Review - 14-SEP-98

Net sales in the first six months of 1998 advanced 61%, year to year, due to continued penetration of the Asia-Pacific (APAC) and Europe, Middle East & Africa (EMA) regions. Gross margins improved primarily due to the continued increase in the amount of higher-margin logistics services sales; operating income grew 92%. Following a $572,000 net investment gain, versus a $1.4 million gain, and higher interest expenses, net income was up 74%, to $17,901,000 ($0.33 a share, on 16% more diluted shares), from $10,283,000 ($0.22).

Stock Performance - 02-OCT-98

In the past 30 trading days, CELL's shares have declined 34%, compared to a 7% fall in the S&P 500. Average trading volume for the past five days was 1,266,780 shares, compared with the 40-day moving average of 1,175,205 shares.

Key Stock Statistics

Dividend Rate/Share	Nil	Shareholders	100
Shs. outstg. (M)	52.1	Market cap. (B)	$0.390
Avg. daily vol. (M)	1.272	Inst. holdings	69%
Tang. Bk. Value/Share	3.15		
Beta	NA		

Value of $10,000 invested 5 years ago: NA

Fiscal Year Ending Dec. 31

	1998	1997	1996	1995	1994	1993
Revenues (Million $)						
1Q	343.3	199.2	113.0	—	—	—
2Q	329.8	220.0	119.9	—	—	—
3Q	—	243.2	145.3	—	—	—
4Q	—	373.2	211.6	—	—	—
Yr.	—	1,036	589.7	419.0	309.0	—
Earnings Per Share ($)						
1Q	0.17	0.12	0.06	—	—	—
2Q	0.17	0.10	0.01	—	—	—
3Q	—	0.12	0.08	—	—	—
4Q	—	0.18	0.10	—	—	—
Yr.	—	0.53	0.24	0.21	0.16	—

Next earnings report expected: late October

Dividend Data

Amount ($)	Date Decl.	Ex-Div. Date	Stock of Record	Payment Date
2-for-1	Oct. 22	Nov. 24	Nov. 06	Nov. 21 '97

A Division of The **McGraw·Hill** Companies

Business Summary - 14-SEP-98

The market for wireless products and services has grown substantially and continues to expand. The number of wireless subscribers in the United States has increased from approximately 300,000 in 1985 to more than 59 million in 1998, growing by more than 10 million in 1997 alone. On a worldwide basis, wireless subscribers increased by 60 million, or 40%, to 200 million total subscribers in 1998. Brightpoint is a leading worldwide distributor of wireless communications products and provider of value-added logistics services such as inventory management, fulfillment, packaging and programming. Revenues in recent years were derived as follows:

	1997	1996
Wireless telephones	88%	88%
Accessories	6%	11%
Value-added logistics	6%	1%

The company offers products from manufacturers under brand names such as Nokia, Ericsson, Motorola, Siemens, Philips and Samsung, and has developed a global customer base of more than 10,000 carriers, agents, resellers, dealers and retailers.

Brightpoint's primary strategies include: being the most efficient market channel for its vendors and the low cost/high service provider to its customers, meeting the growing outsourcing demands of manufacturers and wireless service providers with value-added logistics services, and increasing its worldwide presence and benefiting from the development of new technologies that allow it to offer new products and services.

Brightpoint offers a selection of wireless communications products purchased from various manufacturers designed to work on all operating platforms (AMPS, GSM, TDMA and CDMA) and/or specific frequencies. In addition, the company distributes wireless accessory products, such as batteries, battery eliminators and chargers, cases, antennas and "hands-free" kits.

CELL also provides distribution and value-added logistics services. Such distribution services include purchasing, packaging, warehousing, shipping and "just-in-time" delivery. Value-added logistics services consist of end-user product fulfillment, private labeling, product branding, product warranty, and repair services.

In 1997, the company's three largest suppliers -- Nokia, Ericsson and Siemens -- accounted for approximately 28%, 28% and 9%, respectively, of product purchases. In April 1998, CELL signed an agreement with Sprint PCS to provide distribution and logistics services, including accessory procurement, inventory maintenance, and Sprint packaging.

International sales as a percentage of net sales increased from 51% in 1996 to 76% in 1997.

Per Share Data ($)

(Year Ended Dec. 31)	1997	1996	1995	1994	1993	1992	1991	1990	1989	1988
Tangible Bk. Val.	3.34	2.19	1.63	NA	NA	NA	NA	NA	NA	NA
Cash Flow	0.61	0.27	0.21	0.17	NA	NA	NA	NA	NA	NA
Earnings	0.53	0.24	0.21	0.16	NA	NA	NA	NA	NA	NA
Dividends	Nil	Nil	Nil	Nil	Nil	Nil	Nil	Nil	Nil	Nil
Payout Ratio	Nil	Nil	Nil	Nil	Nil	Nil	Nil	Nil	Nil	Nil
Prices - High	24¼	12⅛	5½	3½	NA	NA	NA	NA	NA	NA
- Low	8	3⅝	2⅞	1¼	NA	NA	NA	NA	NA	NA
P/E Ratio - High	46	49	26	22	NA	NA	NA	NA	NA	NA
- Low	15	15	14	8	NA	NA	NA	NA	NA	NA

Income Statement Analysis (Million $)

	1997	1996	1995	1994	1993	1992	1991	1990	1989	1988
Revs.	1,036	590	419	309	NA	NA	NA	NA	NA	NA
Oper. Inc.	45.9	26.1	13.6	7.8	NA	NA	NA	NA	NA	NA
Depr.	4.0	1.1	0.2	0.1	NA	NA	NA	NA	NA	NA
Int. Exp.	6.4	2.1	1.4	0.2	NA	NA	NA	NA	NA	NA
Pretax Inc.	12.0	20.1	12.0	7.5	NA	NA	NA	NA	NA	NA
Eff. Tax Rate	32%	39%	39%	39%	NA	NA	NA	NA	NA	NA
Net Inc.	25.5	10.6	7.3	4.6	NA	NA	NA	NA	NA	NA

Balance Sheet & Other Fin. Data (Million $)

	1997	1996	1995	1994	1993	1992	1991	1990	1989	1988
Cash	6.4	32.3	0.7	NA	NA	NA	NA	NA	NA	NA
Curr. Assets	392	267	117	NA	NA	NA	NA	NA	NA	NA
Total Assets	457	299	120	NA	NA	NA	NA	NA	NA	NA
Curr. Liab.	110	123	54.3	NA	NA	NA	NA	NA	NA	NA
LT Debt	147	79.6	0.6	NA	NA	NA	NA	NA	NA	NA
Common Eqty.	199	95.0	64.9	NA	NA	NA	NA	NA	NA	NA
Total Cap.	347	176	65.5	NA	NA	NA	NA	NA	NA	NA
Cap. Exp.	18.1	6.0	2.5	4.5	NA	NA	NA	NA	NA	NA
Cash Flow	29.5	11.7	7.5	4.7	NA	NA	NA	NA	NA	NA
Curr. Ratio	3.4	2.2	2.2	NA	NA	NA	NA	NA	NA	NA
% LT Debt of Cap.	42.3	45.2	0.8	NA	NA	NA	NA	NA	NA	NA
% Net Inc.of Revs.	2.5	1.8	1.7	NA	NA	NA	NA	NA	NA	NA
% Ret. on Assets	6.8	5.1	NA	NA	NA	NA	NA	NA	NA	NA
% Ret. on Equity	17.3	13.3	NA	NA	NA	NA	NA	NA	NA	NA

Data as orig. reptd.; bef. results of disc. opers. and/or spec. items. Per share data adj. for stk. divs. as of ex-div. date. Bold denotes diluted EPS (FASB 128). E-Estimated. NA-Not Available. NM-Not Meaningful. NR-Not Ranked.

Office—6402 Corporate Dr., Indianapolis, IN 46278. **Tel**—(317) 297-6100. **Website**—http://www.brightpoint.com **Chrmn & CEO**—R. J. Laikin. **Pres**—J. M. Howell. **EVP & COO**—T. Kapostasy. **EVP-Fin, CFO & Treas**—P. A. Bounsall. **EVP & Secy**—S. E. Fivel. **Dirs**—J. W. Adams, R. M. Dick, T. S. Housefield, J. M. Howell, R. J. Laikin, S. B. Sands, S. H. Simon, T. H. Stuart, R. F. Wagner. **Transfer Agent & Registrar**—Continental Stock Transfer & Trust Co. NYC. **Incorporated**—in Delaware in 1994; previously incorporated in Indiana in 1989. **Empl**— 675. **S&P Analyst:** Mark Cavallone

BroadBand Technologies 3338

NASDAQ Symbol **BBTK**

In S&P SmallCap 600

03-OCT-98

Industry:
Communications
Equipment

Summary: This company designs, manufactures, markets and supports a sophisticated electronics and software platform for the telecommunications industry.

Quantitative Evaluations		
Outlook (1 Lowest—5 Highest) • **NA**	Recent Price • 2⅝	Yield • Nil
Fair Value • **NA**	52 Wk Range • 9⅛-2⅛	12-Mo. P/E • NM

Risk
• **High**

Earn./Div. Rank
• **NR**

Technical Eval.
• **Bearish** since 9/98

Rel. Strength Rank
(1 Lowest—99 Highest)
• **15**

Insider Activity
• **NA**

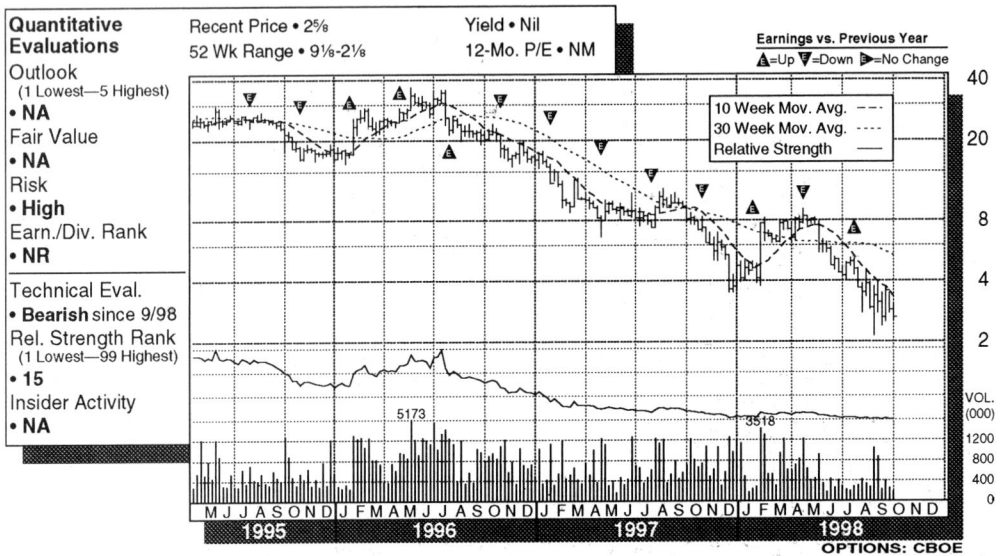

Earnings vs. Previous Year
▲=Up ▼=Down ▶=No Change

10 Week Mov. Avg. ---
30 Week Mov. Avg. ----
Relative Strength —

OPTIONS: CBOE

Business Profile - 16-SEP-98

Sales of the company's FLX-2500 product in the U.S. are substantially dependent on sales of Lucent's Switched Digital Broadband Access System. As part of a recently announced business strategy, the company is developing a new digital loop carrier product that should decrease its reliance on Lucent for U.S. sales upon the product's completion, which is expected in late 1999 to early 2000. In light of declines in the market price of the company's stock, NASDAQ has notified the company that it intends to review eligibility for continued listing. Helped by cost reduction and reallocation, Broadband expects to show a reduction in net losses in the third quarter of 1998 and beyond.

Operational Review - 16-SEP-98

Total revenues in the first half of 1998 advanced 112%, year to year, as lower product sales were offset by $12 million of initial technology transfer and license agreement fees resulting from a new alliance with Bosch and a $5 million settlement of patent litigation. Margins widened significantly, and despite $2.6 million of restructuring charges related the company's new business strategy, the net loss narrowed to $3,669,310 ($0.27 a share, on 13.4 million shares) from $17,256,932 ($1.30, on 3.3 million shares).

Stock Performance - 02-OCT-98

In the past 30 trading days, BBTK's shares have declined 11%, compared to a 7% fall in the S&P 500. Average trading volume for the past five days was 34,720 shares, compared with the 40-day moving average of 90,705 shares.

Key Stock Statistics

Dividend Rate/Share	Nil	Shareholders	9,000
Shs. outstg. (M)	13.4	Market cap. (B)	$0.035
Avg. daily vol. (M)	0.054	Inst. holdings	8%
Tang. Bk. Value/Share	NM		
Beta	1.05		

Value of $10,000 invested 5 years ago: NA

Fiscal Year Ending Dec. 31

	1998	1997	1996	1995	1994	1993
Revenues (Million $)						
1Q	2.51	5.31	4.00	3.22	8.78	0.73
2Q	19.81	5.23	5.51	5.46	8.46	2.45
3Q	—	2.13	5.71	7.07	5.13	3.83
4Q	—	2.34	7.93	6.97	4.64	8.12
Yr.	—	15.01	23.14	22.71	27.01	15.14
Earnings Per Share ($)						
1Q	-0.83	-0.64	-0.57	-0.61	-0.39	-0.54
2Q	0.55	-0.66	-0.49	-0.50	-0.43	-0.64
3Q	—	-1.25	-0.64	-0.49	-0.45	-0.43
4Q	—	-0.45	-0.64	-0.53	-0.58	-0.37
Yr.	—	-3.00	-2.35	-2.13	-1.85	-1.89

Next earnings report expected: late October

Dividend Data

No cash dividends have been paid. A "poison pill" shareholder rights plan was adopted in 1996.

A Division of The McGraw·Hill Companies

Business Summary - 16-SEP-98

BroadBand Technologies, Inc. (BBTK) was founded in 1988 with a mission to help telephone companies transform the local network from providing voice-telephony using low-speed copper wire to a switched digital broadband network using fiber optic cable to deliver high-speed data, video and telephony services.

BBTK designs and manufactures a sophisticated electronics and software platform for the telecommunications industry, focusing primarily on operators of local exchange telephone networks in the U.S. The company's platform provides operators of fiber-based distribution networks with the capability to transmit voice, video and data in a wide array of advanced, interactive entertainment, information, communications, transaction and other services to residential and business subscribers. During 1994 and 1995, the company expanded its marketing efforts in Canada, Europe and the Asia/Pacific markets.

The company's first-generation product, the Fiber Loop Access (FLX-1100) System, consists of software and multiple electronic modules installed at different points in a fiber-to-the-curb (FTTC) local distribution network, which includes switched digital video and telephony features. The FLX System allows fiber optic cables to be used to extend the public telecommunications network from the local telephone company's central office switch to the individual home or business (the "Local Loop"). The FLX System consists of a Host Digital Terminal, an Optical Network Unit, a Video Headend and sophisticated software programs.

Introduced in 1995, the FLX-2500 is BBTK's second-generation product. The single, integrated full-service system allows customers to build FTTC local distribution networks that combine the improved switched digital features of the telephone company with the telephony and analog video features of established telecommunications systems suppliers.

BBTK's FLX System was deployed for initial service in the third quarter at Bell Atlantic and has been in trials at most domestic and international telephone companies. During the third quarter, SBC Communications more than doubled the number of customers in its Richardson, TX, field trial. In February 1998, BBT signed agreements with Lucent Technologies in excess of $50 million over three years for an OEM agreement, an intellectual property license, and a contract manufacturing agreement.

Per Share Data ($)

(Year Ended Dec. 31)	1997	1996	1995	1994	1993	1992	1991	1990	1989	1988
Tangible Bk. Val.	NM	1.93	4.48	6.07	7.94	NA	NA	NA	NA	NA
Cash Flow	-2.60	-1.90	-1.82	-1.61	-1.74	-1.44	NA	NA	NA	NA
Earnings	-3.00	-2.35	-2.13	-1.85	-1.89	-1.54	-1.55	NA	NA	NA
Dividends	Nil	Nil	Nil	Nil	Nil	Nil	Nil	Nil	Nil	Nil
Payout Ratio	Nil	Nil	Nil	Nil	Nil	Nil	Nil	Nil	Nil	Nil
Prices - High	17³/₄	37	31³/₄	33¹/₂	52¹/₄	NA	NA	NA	NA	NA
- Low	3¹/₂	14¹/₂	15³/₄	11	18	NA	NA	NA	NA	NA
P/E Ratio - High	NM	NM	NM	NM	NM	NA	NA	NA	NA	NA
- Low	NM	NM	NM	NM	NM	NM	NM	NM	NM	NM

Income Statement Analysis (Million $)

	1997	1996	1995	1994	1993	1992	1991	1990	1989	1988
Revs.	15.0	23.1	22.7	27.0	15.1	5.3	2.6	NA	NA	NA
Oper. Inc.	-35.7	-27.1	-28.3	-24.4	-18.6	-10.6	NA	NA	NA	NA
Depr.	5.2	6.0	4.0	3.2	1.6	0.9	NA	NA	NA	NA
Int. Exp.	6.5	4.1	0.1	0.1	0.3	0.4	NA	NA	NA	NA
Pretax Inc.	-39.8	-31.0	-27.9	-24.2	-19.0	-11.8	-8.4	NA	NA	NA
Eff. Tax Rate	NM	NM	Nil	Nil	Nil	Nil	Nil	Nil	Nil	Nil
Net Inc.	-39.8	-31.0	-27.9	-24.2	-19.0	-11.8	-8.4	NA	NA	NA

Balance Sheet & Other Fin. Data (Million $)

	1997	1996	1995	1994	1993	1992	1991	1990	1989	1988
Cash	60.5	108	65.4	80.0	107	17.0	NA	NA	NA	NA
Curr. Assets	99	139	72.4	88.0	119	NA	NA	NA	NA	NA
Total Assets	136	171	85.9	96.0	125	22.0	NA	NA	NA	NA
Curr. Liab.	17.8	24.4	27.0	16.7	21.2	NA	NA	NA	NA	NA
LT Debt	115	115	0.0	0.3	0.8	6.2	NA	NA	NA	NA
Common Eqty.	-10.5	28.9	58.9	79.0	103	12.0	NA	NA	NA	NA
Total Cap.	105	144	59.0	80.0	104	18.0	NA	NA	NA	NA
Cap. Exp.	3.9	4.4	9.6	4.6	5.2	1.6	NA	NA	NA	NA
Cash Flow	-34.6	-25.1	-23.9	-21.0	-17.4	-10.8	NA	NA	NA	NA
Curr. Ratio	5.6	5.7	2.7	5.3	5.7	NA	NA	NA	NA	NA
% LT Debt of Cap.	110.0	79.9	0.1	0.4	0.8	34.6	NA	NA	NA	NA
% Net Inc.of Revs.	NM	NM	NM	NM	NM	NM	NM	NM	NM	NM
% Ret. on Assets	NM	NM	NM	NM	NM	NM	NM	NM	NM	NM
% Ret. on Equity	NM	NM	NM	NM	NM	NM	NM	NM	NM	NM

Data as orig. reptd.; bef. results of disc. opers. and/or spec. items. Per share data adj. for stk. divs. as of ex-div. date. Bold denotes diluted EPS (FASB 128). E-Estimated. NA-Not Available. NM-Not Meaningful. NR-Not Ranked.

Office—4024 Stirrup Creek Dr.,Durham, NC 27703. **Tel**—(919) 544-0015. **Website**—http://www.bbt.com **Chrmn**—J.R. Hutchins III. **Pres & CEO**—D. E. Orr. **Dirs**—F. R. Boswell, R. P. Clark, J. R. Hutchins III, J. R. Jones, C. T. Lee, L. A. McLemon, A. E. Negrin, D. E. Orr. **Incorporated**—in Delaware in 1988. **Empl**— 333. **S&P Analyst:** SRB

03-OCT-98

Industry: Footwear

Summary: This company manufactures, imports and retails a wide variety of women's, men's and children's shoes.

Quantitative Evaluations

Recent Price • 14⅛
52 Wk Range • 20-12⅜
Yield • 2.8%
12-Mo. P/E • NM

Outlook (1 Lowest—5 Highest)
• **4**

Fair Value
• **22⅜**

Risk
• **Average**

Earn./Div. Rank
• **B-**

Technical Eval.
• **Bearish** since 7/98

Rel. Strength Rank (1 Lowest—99 Highest)
• **44**

Insider Activity
• **NA**

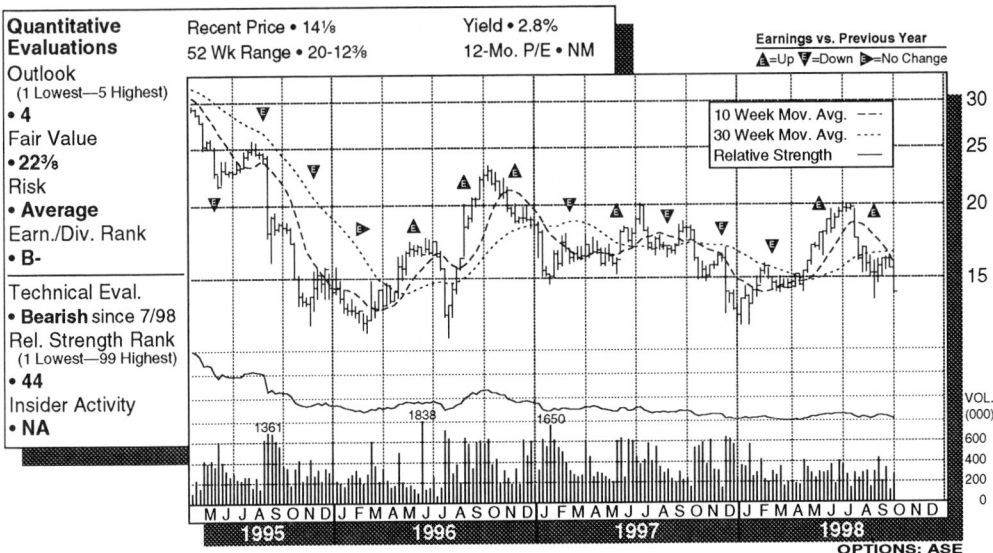

Earnings vs. Previous Year
▲=Up ▼=Down ▶=No Change

10 Week Mov. Avg. - - -
30 Week Mov. Avg. ·····
Relative Strength —

OPTIONS: ASE

Business Profile - 01-OCT-98

Brown Group took a number of restructuring charges in FY 98 (Jan.), totaling $31 million after taxes. Although the company believes it has improved its core operations, it has noted that the costs for its Pagoda International division were a disappointment. In the first half of FY 99, operating losses and additional charges for Pagoda International were $5.5 million; total losses for FY 99 are expected to be between $7 and $8 million. During the first half of FY 99, same store sales at Famous Footwear were up 2.1% and Naturalizer's retail division same store sales increased 4.9%. The company said that results in the first half of FY 99 benefited from record sales and operating earnings at Famous Footwear and an earnings gain in its Canadian operations. These gains outweighed lower than expected results at the Brown Shoe Company in the second quarter. Directors cut the quarterly dividend 60%, to $0.10 a share from $0.25 with the January 1998 payment.

Operational Review - 01-OCT-98

Net sales in the 26 weeks ended August 1, 1998, advanced 2.0%, year to year, reflecting higher sales at Famous Footwear and Naturalizer stores, which outweighed a decline in wholesale sales. Gross margins widened on higher margins at Famous Footwear. With only a modest rise in SG&A expenses and lower interest expense, pretax income surged 77%. After taxes at 44.5%, versus 38.7%, net income climbed 61% to $8,166,000 ($0.46 a share), from $5,072,000 ($0.29).

Stock Performance - 02-OCT-98

In the past 30 trading days, BG's shares have declined 7%, compared to a 7% fall in the S&P 500. Average trading volume for the past five days was 52,920 shares, compared with the 40-day moving average of 53,274 shares.

Key Stock Statistics

Dividend Rate/Share	0.40	Shareholders	5,500
Shs. outstg. (M)	18.0	Market cap. (B)	$0.255
Avg. daily vol. (M)	0.047	Inst. holdings	56%
Tang. Bk. Value/Share	11.25		
Beta	0.65		

Value of $10,000 invested 5 years ago: $ 7,059

Fiscal Year Ending Jan. 31

	1999	1998	1997	1996	1995	1994
Revenues (Million $)						
1Q	402.3	391.8	355.8	357.4	369.5	389.1
2Q	383.6	378.8	390.0	342.9	353.0	381.0
3Q	—	433.9	420.4	406.9	406.9	445.8
4Q	—	362.7	358.9	348.7	322.2	381.9
Yr.	—	1,567	1,525	1,456	1,462	1,598
Earnings Per Share ($)						
1Q	**0.22**	0.09	0.03	-0.25	0.42	0.24
2Q	**0.24**	0.20	0.31	-0.48	0.43	0.32
3Q	—	.0.75	0.73	0.55	0.85	0.81
4Q	—	**-0.72**	0.08	0.21	0.21	-1.76
Yr.	—	**-1.19**	1.15	0.04	1.91	-0.39

Next earnings report expected: early December

Dividend Data (Dividends have been paid since 1923.)

Amount ($)	Date Decl.	Ex-Div. Date	Stock of Record	Payment Date
0.100	Dec. 04	Dec. 11	Dec. 15	Jan. 02 '98
0.100	Mar. 05	Mar. 12	Mar. 16	Apr. 01 '98
0.100	May. 28	Jun. 04	Jun. 08	Jul. 01 '98
0.100	Sep. 17	Sep. 24	Sep. 28	Oct. 01 '98

 A Division of The McGraw·Hill Companies

STANDARD
&POOR'S
STOCK REPORTS

Brown Group, Inc.

379

03-OCT-98

Business Summary - 01-OCT-98

Brown Group, founded in 1878, operates in the highly fragmented footwear business. The company's wholesale operation distributes shoes to about 5,000 retailers, including department stores, mass merchandisers and independent retailers. Retail operations include 1,279 shoe stores in the U.S. and Canada, under the names, Famous Footwear, Naturalizer and F.X. LaSalle. In FY 98 (Jan.), about 66% of footwear sales were made at retail, up from 63% in FY 97. During 1997, the composition of footwear sales was: 60% women's; 24% men's; and 16% children's.

Famous Footwear is America's largest retailer of branded footwear for the entire family. Founded over 30 years ago, Famous Footwear was purchased in 1981 as a 32 store chain and has grown to 815 stores in the U.S. at the end of FY 98. Naturalizer stores are showcases for the company's flagship brand of women's shoes. BG also operates 341 Naturalizer stores in the U.S. and Canada. The target customer is between 40 and 60 year of age. The typical store product is priced between $50 and $85 per pair. At the end of FY 98, the Canadian retailing division operated 16 F. X. LaSalle stores, and 107 Naturalizer retail stores. Better grade men's and women's footwear in the $100 to $250 range are available.

Footwear is distributed by the company's Branded Marketing, Pagoda and Brown Shoe Sourcing divisions to retailers in the U.S., Europe, South America, the Far East and to affiliates. In Canada, footwear is distributed through the company's Canadian Wholesale division. The Branded Marketing division designs and markets many of the company's brands, including Naturalizer, Life Stride, LS Studio and Night Life brands. These shoes are sold to nearly all major U.S. department stores. Each brand is targeted to a specific customer segment. The Pagoda division sources and markets private brand footwear for many of the nation's retailers, including Dillard's, Edison Brothers, Famous Footwear, Kmart, Mercantile, Payless Shoe Source, Sears, Target and Wal-Mart. It provided wholesale customers with 43 million pairs of shoes in 1997, down from 49 million in 1996. The Brown Shoe Sourcing division (formerly known as Pagoda Trading) sources substantially all of the footwear globally. In 1997, this division sourced 72 million pairs of shoes, with over half from China.

Losses and nonrecurring charges at Pagoda exceeded $45 million in FY 98. BG has implemented measures to improve operations at Pagoda and plans to reduce inventories and complete a restructuring by the end of 1998. In February 1998, BG sold Pagoda's Brazilian inventory to Calcados Dilly Ltda.

Per Share Data ($)

(Year Ended Jan. 31)	1998	1997	1996	1995	1994	1993	1992	1991	1990	1989
Tangible Bk. Val.	11.04	13.19	12.92	13.90	13.27	16.69	18.10	19.47	19.39	19.10
Cash Flow	0.33	2.61	1.39	3.17	3.17	1.93	2.68	3.52	3.39	3.26
Earnings	-1.19	1.15	0.04	1.91	-0.39	0.27	0.92	1.85	1.78	1.74
Dividends	0.85	1.00	1.30	1.60	1.60	1.60	1.60	1.60	1.60	1.56
Payout Ratio	NM	87%	NM	84%	NM	594%	176%	87%	91%	90%
Cal. Yrs.	1997	1996	1995	1994	1993	1992	1991	1990	1989	1988
Prices - High	20⅛	23⅜	33⅜	38⅞	35⅞	29	28⅜	30	35½	38½
- Low	12⅜	11⅞	12½	30⅝	28⅜	21	21⅝	19¾	26¾	31
P/E Ratio - High	NM	20	NM	20	NM	NM	31	16	20	22
- Low	NM	10	NM	16	NM	NM	24	11	15	18

Income Statement Analysis (Million $)

	1998	1997	1996	1995	1994	1993	1992	1991	1990	1989
Revs.	1,567	1,525	1,456	1,465	1,598	1,791	1,728	1,764	1,821	1,707
Oper. Inc.	45.8	71.1	37.0	89.0	74.0	59.0	65.0	91.0	91.0	89.0
Depr.	26.7	25.9	23.8	22.1	22.8	28.4	30.1	28.6	28.0	26.5
Int. Exp.	21.8	19.3	16.0	15.8	17.6	16.8	16.0	18.2	20.7	17.0
Pretax Inc.	-2.2	27.2	-5.0	60.0	-11.8	5.0	22.0	49.0	47.0	48.0
Eff. Tax Rate	NM	25%	NM	44%	NM	8.50%	30%	35%	34%	38%
Net Inc.	-20.9	20.3	0.7	33.6	-6.7	4.7	15.7	31.8	30.8	30.1

Balance Sheet & Other Fin. Data (Million $)

	1998	1997	1996	1995	1994	1993	1992	1991	1990	1989
Cash	50.1	38.7	35.1	18.9	16.9	21.6	18.7	16.3	22.3	12.0
Curr. Assets	539	565	505	479	612	580	514	536	531	527
Total Assets	695	722	661	637	772	760	705	737	713	728
Curr. Liab.	278	264	296	220	371	318	217	250	225	244
LT Debt	197	197	105	133	135	123	145	129	132	136
Common Eqty.	199	237	232	250	234	289	313	336	339	333
Total Cap.	403	443	348	396	376	419	468	483	485	481
Cap. Exp.	21.7	21.0	26.9	32.5	30.2	24.3	24.7	32.6	31.3	42.0
Cash Flow	5.8	46.2	24.5	55.7	16.1	33.1	45.8	60.4	58.8	56.6
Curr. Ratio	1.9	2.1	1.7	2.2	1.6	1.8	2.4	2.1	2.4	2.2
% LT Debt of Cap.	48.9	44.5	30.2	33.7	36.0	29.4	30.9	26.6	27.3	28.3
% Net Inc.of Revs.	NM	1.3	0.1	2.3	NM	0.3	0.9	1.8	1.7	1.8
% Ret. on Assets	NM	2.9	0.1	4.7	NM	0.6	2.2	4.4	4.3	4.3
% Ret. on Equity	NM	8.7	0.3	13.8	NM	1.5	4.8	9.5	9.2	8.8

Data as orig. reptd.; bef. results of disc. opers. and/or spec. items. Per share data adj. for stk. divs. as of ex-div. date. Bold denotes diluted EPS (FASB 128). E-Estimated. NA-Not Available. NM-Not Meaningful. NR-Not Ranked.

Office—8300 Maryland Ave., St. Louis, MO 63105. **Tel**—(314) 854-4000. **Website**—http://www.browngroup.com **Chrmn, Pres & CEO**—B. A. Bridgewater, Jr. **EVP, CFO & Investor Contact**—H. E. Rich. **VP & Secy**—R. D. Pickle. **Dirs**—J. L. Bower, B. A. Bridgewater, Jr., J. C. Esrey, R. A. Liddy, J. P. MacCarthy, J. D. Macomber, W. E. Maritz,E. C. Meyer, H. E. Rich, J. E. Ritter.**Transfer Agent & Registrar**— Boatmen's Trust Co., St. Louis. **Incorporated**—in New York in 1913. **Empl**— 11,500. **S&P Analyst:** Kathleen J. Fraser

Brush Wellman

384

NYSE Symbol **BW**

In S&P SmallCap 600

03-OCT-98

Industry:
Metal Fabricators

Summary: Shs company is a worldwide supplier of beryllium alloy and specialty engineered products.

Quantitative Evaluations	
Outlook (1 Lowest—5 Highest)	• 3
Fair Value	• 17½
Risk	• Low
Earn./Div. Rank	• B
Technical Eval.	• **Bearish** since 5/98
Rel. Strength Rank (1 Lowest—99 Highest)	• 31
Insider Activity	• **Favorable**

Recent Price • 13¾
52 Wk Range • 30-12⅜

Yield • 3.5%
12-Mo. P/E • 49.3

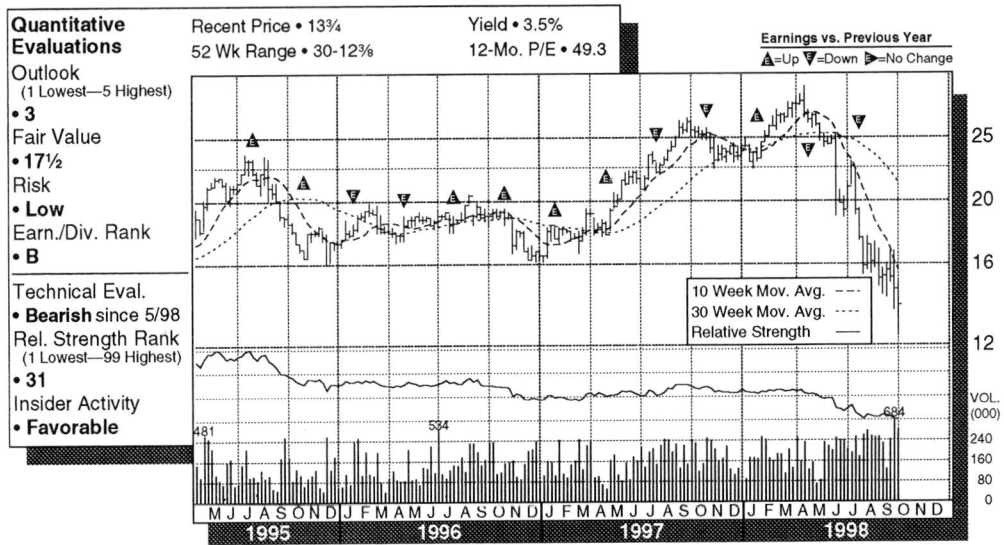

Earnings vs. Previous Year
▲=Up ▼=Down ▶=No Change

10 Week Mov. Avg. – – –
30 Week Mov. Avg. · · · ·
Relative Strength ——

Business Profile - 24-SEP-98

Brush Wellman expects to begin to see some of the benefits of its $120 million, three-year capital investment program in 1998, and also reports that demand is at an all-time high and growing. The new Brush Engineered Bronze facility began operating in the fourth quarter of 1997, and new capacity at the Elmore alloy production facility is scheduled to come on stream in the fourth quarter of 1998. BW is continuing to develop new applications for beryllium alloys in automotive electronics, appliances, telecommunications and commercial aircraft markets.

Operational Review - 24-SEP-98

Net sales in the first half of 1998 rose 1.9%, year to year, as increased revenue from metal systems outweighed lower sales from the microelectronics group. Gross margins narrowed, reflecting greater than expected start-up costs and related manufacturing issues, higher fixed costs, and adverse currency effects. Following $18.7 million in net other expense (primarily reflecting writedowns of fixed assets and intangibles to their fair market value), a net loss of $6,922,000 ($0.42 a share) contrasted net income of $13,979,000 ($0.86).

Stock Performance - 02-OCT-98

In the past 30 trading days, BW's shares have declined 14%, compared to a 7% fall in the S&P 500. Average trading volume for the past five days was 107,980 shares, compared with the 40-day moving average of 77,318 shares.

Key Stock Statistics

Dividend Rate/Share	0.48	Shareholders	2,500
Shs. outstg. (M)	16.4	Market cap. (B)	$0.226
Avg. daily vol. (M)	0.082	Inst. holdings	69%
Tang. Bk. Value/Share	13.76		
Beta	0.69		

Value of $10,000 invested 5 years ago: $ 10,208

Fiscal Year Ending Dec. 31

	1998	1997	1996	1995	1994	1993
Revenues (Million $)						
1Q	114.2	99.7	93.80	98.91	84.79	69.38
2Q	103.0	113.4	104.3	97.28	86.56	70.85
3Q	—	109.1	88.31	89.36	86.73	76.82
4Q	—	111.7	89.82	84.06	87.79	78.43
Yr.	—	433.8	376.3	369.6	345.9	295.5
Earnings Per Share ($)						
1Q	0.37	0.40	0.32	0.42	0.35	0.07
2Q	-0.80	0.46	0.51	0.40	0.00	0.01
3Q	—	0.24	0.28	0.20	0.15	0.10
4Q	—	0.46	0.41	0.24	0.28	0.22
Yr.	—	1.56	1.53	1.26	1.14	0.40

Next earnings report expected: late October

Dividend Data (Dividends have been paid since 1972.)

Amount ($)	Date Decl.	Ex-Div. Date	Stock of Record	Payment Date
0.120	Dec. 02	Dec. 17	Dec. 19	Jan. 02 '98
0.120	Mar. 03	Mar. 18	Mar. 20	Mar. 31 '98
0.120	Jun. 02	Jun. 17	Jun. 19	Jun. 30 '98
0.120	Sep. 08	Sep. 17	Sep. 21	Sep. 30 '98

A Division of The McGraw-Hill Companies

Business Summary - 24-SEP-98

With over two-thirds of its sales coming from defense, aerospace and mainframe computer applications at the start of the decade, this leading producer of beryllium-based materials was handed a major challenge when the Cold War ended and significant changes in mainframe computer design occurred in the early 1990s. Facing sharply reduced demand from its traditional markets, Brush Wellman Inc. (BW) developed new applications for its products, targeting markets as diverse as automotive electronics, personal computers, appliances, telecommunications, commercial aerospace, plastic molds and high-performance sporting goods. Net sales grew 64% from 1992 to 1997, when they reached a record $434 million, and 1997 net income of $25.6 million represented a 144% improvement over 1992 net income of $10.5 million. Now BW is implementing a three-part strategic plan it hopes will boost returns to its shareholders by delivering faster and more consistent growth in the future.

BW is the world's only fully integrated supplier of beryllium, beryllium-containing alloys (principally copper beryllium) and beryllia ceramic. BW removes beryllium-bearing bertrandite ore from its mines in central Utah and at a nearby plant extracts the element beryllium from this ore as well as from imported beryl ore. In addition to beryllium-containing products, which accounted for 66% of 1997 sales, the company also supplies specialty metal systems and precious metal products.

The company's beryllium materials can simultaneously provide light weight and strength, and they can withstand high temperatures, readily conduct electricity and resist stress and fatigue. BW believes that continuing trends in product manufacturing toward miniaturization, weight reduction and increased electronic content will enable its materials to increase their share of the worldwide specialty materials market.

BW's strategic "blueprint for growth" calls for an improvement in the company's base business, the expansion of its alloy capabilities and a more effective presence in microelectronics markets, which already account for one-fifth of the company's sales. In mid-1996, BW broke ground on a $110 million expansion and upgrading of alloy strip capabilities at its Elmore, OH facility. BW hopes the project will enable it to compete for a wider assortment of applications by reducing costs and permitting the production of strip in much larger coils; the facility is expected to be operational by the fourth quarter of 1998. The company's growth strategy in non-ferrous alloys also calls for the introduction of new alloys, including non-beryllium-containing alloys, and by the end of 1997 BW had added its Brush Engineered Bronze family of specialty alloys to its product line.

Per Share Data ($)

(Year Ended Dec. 31)	1997	1996	1995	1994	1993	1992	1991	1990	1989	1988
Tangible Bk. Val.	14.45	13.46	12.46	11.59	10.70	10.49	10.10	13.43	13.10	13.49
Cash Flow	2.70	2.67	2.36	2.35	1.75	1.90	-0.30	2.58	2.35	2.94
Earnings	1.56	1.52	1.26	1.14	0.40	0.65	-1.72	1.09	1.10	1.79
Dividends	0.46	0.42	0.36	0.26	0.20	0.26	0.59	0.71	0.67	0.63
Payout Ratio	29%	28%	29%	23%	50%	40%	NM	65%	58%	33%
Prices - High	26³/₄	20¹/₂	23⁵/₈	18⁵/₈	17¹/₂	19	20	25¹/₄	30¹/₄	31
- Low	16¹/₈	16¹/₈	14¹/₂	13³/₈	11	12¹/₄	9¹/₂	11¹/₂	20¹/₄	22¹/₂
P/E Ratio - High	17	13	19	16	44	29	NM	23	28	17
- Low	10	11	12	12	28	19	NM	11	18	13

Income Statement Analysis (Million $)

	1997	1996	1995	1994	1993	1992	1991	1990	1989	1988
Revs.	434	376	370	346	295	265	267	297	318	346
Oper. Inc.	55.0	53.8	48.4	47.3	34.6	38.4	44.8	52.9	61.1	76.5
Depr.	18.7	18.5	18.0	19.6	21.7	20.2	34.9	23.2	23.2	21.0
Int. Exp.	0.6	1.1	1.6	2.4	3.2	3.8	4.4	3.9	3.6	3.6
Pretax Inc.	35.5	33.2	27.4	23.0	7.7	13.7	-36.2	24.8	26.3	51.9
Eff. Tax Rate	28%	26%	25%	19%	16%	24%	NM	29%	30%	37%
Net Inc.	25.6	24.5	20.7	18.6	6.5	10.5	-27.5	17.6	18.5	32.5

Balance Sheet & Other Fin. Data (Million $)

	1997	1996	1995	1994	1993	1992	1991	1990	1989	1988
Cash	7.2	31.7	29.6	20.4	7.7	4.2	1.7	1.9	5.2	5.4
Curr. Assets	179	197	192	181	156	148	145	152	150	156
Total Assets	384	356	332	317	293	310	307	339	338	358
Curr. Liab.	78.3	69.1	66.6	65.9	51.0	59.9	64.7	62.8	71.6	63.9
LT Debt	17.9	18.9	17.0	18.5	24.0	33.8	34.9	26.7	21.1	29.9
Common Eqty.	237	219	200	187	172	169	162	216	212	233
Total Cap.	255	239	220	209	202	210	205	267	258	284
Cap. Exp.	53.1	26.8	25.0	17.8	12.7	14.5	20.0	21.9	20.1	27.0
Cash Flow	44.3	43.0	38.7	38.2	28.2	30.7	-4.8	41.6	39.7	53.6
Curr. Ratio	2.3	2.9	2.9	2.7	3.1	2.5	2.2	2.4	2.1	2.4
% LT Debt of Cap.	7.0	7.9	7.8	8.9	11.9	16.1	17.1	10.0	8.2	10.5
% Net Inc.of Revs.	5.9	6.6	5.6	5.4	2.2	4.0	NM	5.9	5.8	9.4
% Ret. on Assets	6.9	7.2	6.4	6.1	2.1	3.4	NM	5.2	5.5	9.3
% Ret. on Equity	11.2	11.7	10.7	10.3	3.8	6.3	NM	8.2	8.6	14.1

Data as orig. reptd.; bef. results of disc. opers. and/or spec. items. Per share data adj. for stk. divs. as of ex-div. date. Bold denotes diluted EPS (FASB 128). E-Estimated. NA-Not Available. NM-Not Meaningful. NR-Not Ranked.

Office—17876 St. Clair Ave., Cleveland, OH 44110.**Tel**—(216) 486-4200. **Fax**—(216) 383-4091. **Chrmn, Pres, & CEO**—G. D. Harnett. **VP & CFO**—C. Cramer. **VP-Investor Contact**—Timothy J. Reid.**Dirs**—A. C. Bersticker, C. F. Brush III, D. L. Burner, G. D. Harnett, J. P. Keithley, W. P. Madar, R. M. McInnes, W. R. Robertson, J. Sherwin, Jr. **Transfer Agent & Registrar**—KeyCorp Shareholder Service, Inc. **Incorporated**—in Ohio in 1931. **Empl**— 2,160. **S&P Analyst:** E. Hunter

Buckeye Technologies 393D

NYSE Symbol **BKI**

In S&P SmallCap 600

03-OCT-98

Industry:
Paper & Forest Products

Summary: Buckeye is a leading manufacturer and worldwide marketer of specialty cellulose pulps.

Quantitative Evaluations

Outlook
(1 Lowest—5 Highest)
- **NA**

Fair Value
- **NA**

Risk
- **Low**

Earn./Div. Rank
- **NR**

Technical Eval.
- **NA**

Rel. Strength Rank
(1 Lowest—99 Highest)
- **51**

Insider Activity
- **NA**

Recent Price • 17⅜
52 Wk Range • 25⅜-14

Yield • Nil
12-Mo. P/E • 12.0

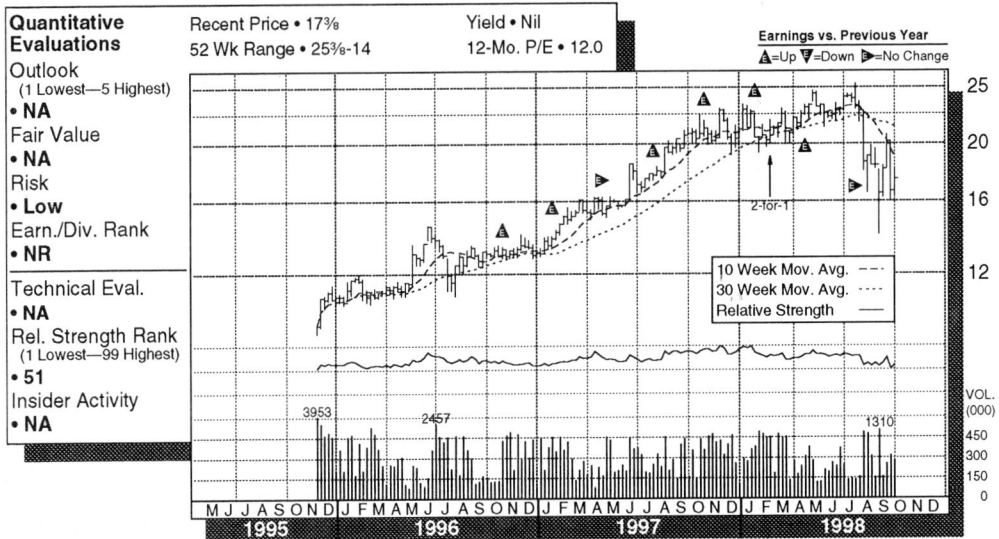

Earnings vs. Previous Year
▲=Up ▼=Down ▶=No Change

10 Week Mov. Avg. — — —
30 Week Mov. Avg. · · · · ·
Relative Strength ————

Business Profile - 04-MAR-98

In May 1997, BKI completed a tender offer for Merfin International, Inc., a Canadian maker of air-laid materials; 97.5% of the shares were tendered at C$7.50 a share (a total of about U.S.$200 million). The company believes that Merfin adds a new dimension to its efforts to build a major business covering the full range of absorbent products. BKI began operations in 1993 by acquiring the production, research and administrative facilities of Procter & Gamble Cellulose Co. Procter & Gamble, the world's largest maker of diapers, remains the company's largest individual customer, accounting for 32% of sales in FY 97 (Jun.). In February 1998, BKI split its shares two-for-one and authorized the repurchase of over 5% of the company's shares outstanding.

Operational Review - 04-MAR-98

Based on a brief report, net sales in the first half of FY 98 (Jun.) advanced 14%, year to year. Gross margins widened and despite higher selling, general, and administrative costs, operating profit grew 19%. Sharply higher net interest expense cut the gain in pretax income to 9%. After taxes at 35.9%, versus 34.9%, net income advanced 7.2%, to $22,499,000 ($0.69 a diluted share, as adjusted, on 1.5% fewer shares), from $24,699,000 ($0.64).

Stock Performance - 02-OCT-98

In the past 30 trading days, BKI's shares have declined 5%, compared to a 7% fall in the S&P 500. Average trading volume for the past five days was 54,960 shares, compared with the 40-day moving average of 89,600 shares.

Key Stock Statistics

Dividend Rate/Share	Nil	Shareholders	5,200
Shs. outstg. (M)	36.8	Market cap. (B)	$0.642
Avg. daily vol. (M)	0.059	Inst. holdings	35%
Tang. Bk. Value/Share	0.24		
Beta	NA		

Value of $10,000 invested 5 years ago: NA

Fiscal Year Ending Jun. 30

	1998	1997	1996	1995	1994	1993
Revenues (Million $)						
1Q	153.3	126.5	108.6	--	--	--
2Q	153.6	143.0	117.0	--	--	--
3Q	162.5	139.5	113.3	--	--	--
4Q	160.8	149.9	132.2	--	--	--
Yr.	630.2	558.9	471.0	464.2	--	--
Earnings Per Share ($)						
1Q	0.34	0.31	0.18	**	--	--
2Q	0.34	0.33	0.23	--	--	--
3Q	0.37	0.37	0.36	--	--	--
4Q	0.38	0.39	0.34	--	--	--
Yr.	1.45	1.40	1.11	0.83	—	—

Next earnings report expected: late October

Dividend Data

Amount ($)	Date Decl.	Ex-Div. Date	Stock of Record	Payment Date
2-for-1	Jan. 22	Feb. 18	Feb. 10	Feb. 17 '98

A Division of The McGraw·Hill Companies

Business Summary - 04-MAR-98

Following its May 1997 acquisition of Merfin International Inc., Buckeye Technologies (formerly Buckeye Cellulose Corp.) reorganized into two divisions: the Specialty Cellulose division, supplying the chemical, textile fibers and specialty paper industries; and the Absorbent Products division, supplying consumer product companies that market absorbent and hygienic brands. BKI is a leading manufacturer and worldwide marketer of high-quality, value-added specialty cellulose pulps and, through Merfin, is a leading manufacturer of air-laid fabrics used in feminine hygiene and adult incontinence products. The company believes that it is the world's only manufacturer of both wood-based and cotton linter-based specialty cellulose pulps and, as such, produces the broadest range of specialty pulps in the industry.

The cellulose pulp market can be divided into two categories: commodity pulps and specialty cellulose pulps. BKI participates exclusively in the estimated $7 billion annual specialty cellulose pulp market, which accounts for about 3% of the total cellulose pulp market. Specialty cellulose pulps are used to impart unique chemical or physical characteristics to a broad and diverse range of specialty end-products. Specialty pulps generally command higher prices and tend to be less cyclical than commodity pulps. The more demanding performance requirements for specialty pulps limit customer ability to substitute other products.

The company's specialty pulps can be broadly grouped into three categories: chemical cellulose pulps, which accounted for 45% of FY 96 (Jun.) gross sales; absorbent pulps (37%); and customized paper pulps (18%).

About 30% of BKI's FY 97 sales were derived from the U.S., 41% from Europe, 19% from Asia, and 10% from other regions. Procter & Gamble, the world's largest diaper manufacturer, is the company's largest single customer, accounting for 32% of FY 97 net sales. Under a long-term agreement, Procter & Gamble is required to purchase a specified tonnage of the company's fluff pulp through 2002.

On May 27, 1997, the company completed a tender offer for Merfin International Inc.; 27,280,541 Merfin common shares (97.5%) were tendered at C$7.50 a share. The acquisition cost was about U.S.$200 million, including assumed debt, and was funded with borrowings from a $275 million credit facility. Merfin is a leading manufacturer of air-laid fabrics used as ultra-thin absorbent cores in feminine hygiene and adult incontinence products, as well as in hot towels, baby wipes, table top products and a variety of industrial wipes. Merfin manufactures, converts and distributes paper products for commercial, industrial and institutional markets in North and South America, Europe and the Pacific Rim countries of Japan, Korea, Taiwan, Hong Kong and Singapore.

Per Share Data ($)

(Year Ended Jun. 30)	1998	1997	1996	1995	1994	1993	1992	1991	1990	1989
Tangible Bk. Val.	NA	NM	3.13	1.85	NA	NA	NA	NA	NA	NA
Cash Flow	NA	2.35	1.75	NA	NA	NA	NA	NA	NA	NA
Earnings	1.45	1.40	1.11	0.83	NA	NA	NA	NA	NA	NA
Dividends	Nil	Nil	Nil	NA	NA	NA	NA	NA	NA	NA
Payout Ratio	Nil	Nil	Nil	NA	NA	NA	NA	NA	NA	NA
Prices - High	25⅜	23⅜	14⅝	11½	NA	NA	NA	NA	NA	NA
- Low	16½	12⅞	10⅝	9¼	NA	NA	NA	NA	NA	NA
P/E Ratio - High	17	17	13	14	NA	NA	NA	NA	NA	NA
- Low	11	9	10	11	NA	NA	NA	NA	NA	NA

Income Statement Analysis (Million $)

	1998	1997	1996	1995	1994	1993	1992	1991	1990	1989
Revs.	NA	559	471	464	NA	NA	NA	NA	NA	NA
Oper. Inc.	NA	145	135	NA	NA	NA	NA	NA	NA	NA
Depr.	NA	36.1	26.7	NA	NA	NA	NA	NA	NA	NA
Int. Exp.	NA	28.7	18.1	22.3	NA	NA	NA	NA	NA	NA
Pretax Inc.	NA	80.2	72.5	56.5	NA	NA	NA	NA	NA	NA
Eff. Tax Rate	NA	34%	35%	37%	NA	NA	NA	NA	NA	NA
Net Inc.	NA	53.3	47.0	35.6	NA	NA	NA	NA	NA	NA

Balance Sheet & Other Fin. Data (Million $)

	1998	1997	1996	1995	1994	1993	1992	1991	1990	1989
Cash	NA	8.1	2.9	3.7	NA	NA	NA	NA	NA	NA
Curr. Assets	NA	201	179	142	NA	NA	NA	NA	NA	NA
Total Assets	NA	737	453	413	NA	NA	NA	NA	NA	NA
Curr. Liab.	NA	83.0	61.4	43.3	NA	NA	NA	NA	NA	NA
LT Debt	NA	475	218	242	NA	NA	NA	NA	NA	NA
Common Eqty.	NA	128	141	99	NA	NA	NA	NA	NA	NA
Total Cap.	NA	633	374	353	NA	NA	NA	NA	NA	NA
Cap. Exp.	NA	42.8	34.8	NA	NA	NA	NA	NA	NA	NA
Cash Flow	NA	89.4	73.7	NA	NA	NA	NA	NA	NA	NA
Curr. Ratio	NA	2.4	2.9	3.3	NA	NA	NA	NA	NA	NA
% LT Debt of Cap.	NA	75.0	58.3	68.7	NA	NA	NA	NA	NA	NA
% Net Inc.of Revs.	NA	9.5	10.0	7.7	NA	NA	NA	NA	NA	NA
% Ret. on Assets	NA	9.0	11.3	NA	NA	NA	NA	NA	NA	NA
% Ret. on Equity	NA	39.6	41.7	NA	NA	NA	NA	NA	NA	NA

Data as orig. reptd.; bef. results of disc. opers. and/or spec. items. Per share data adj. for stk. divs. as of ex-div. date. Bold denotes diluted EPS (FASB 128). E-Estimated. NA-Not Available. NM-Not Meaningful. NR-Not Ranked.

Office—1001 Tillman St., Memphis, TN 38112. **Tel**—(901) 320-8100. **Chrmn & CEO**—R. E. Cannon. **Pres & COO**—D. B. Ferraro. **Investor Contact**—Frank A. McGrew IV (901) 320-8100.**Dirs**—R. E. Cannon, R. H. Cannon, R. Cavaney, D. B. Ferraro, H. F. Frigon, S. M. Mencoff, H. J. Phillips Sr. **Transfer Agent & Registrar**—Union Planters National Bank. **Incorporated**—in Delaware in 1992.**Empl**— 1,725. **S&P Analyst:** A.O.T.

Building Materials Holding Corp. 3365E

NASDAQ Symbol **BMHC**

In S&P SmallCap 600

03-OCT-98

Industry: Retail (Building Supplies)

Summary: BMHC is the holding company for BMC West Corp, a regional distributor and retailer of building materials, operating 55 centers in 18 distinct regional markets in 10 western states.

Quantitative Evaluations	
Outlook (1 Lowest—5 Highest)	• **4⁻**
Fair Value	• **17½**
Risk	• **Average**
Earn./Div. Rank	• **NR**
Technical Eval.	• **NA**
Rel. Strength Rank (1 Lowest—99 Highest)	• **61**
Insider Activity	• **Neutral**

Recent Price • 11½
52 Wk Range • 15-10
Yield • Nil
12-Mo. P/E • 12.8

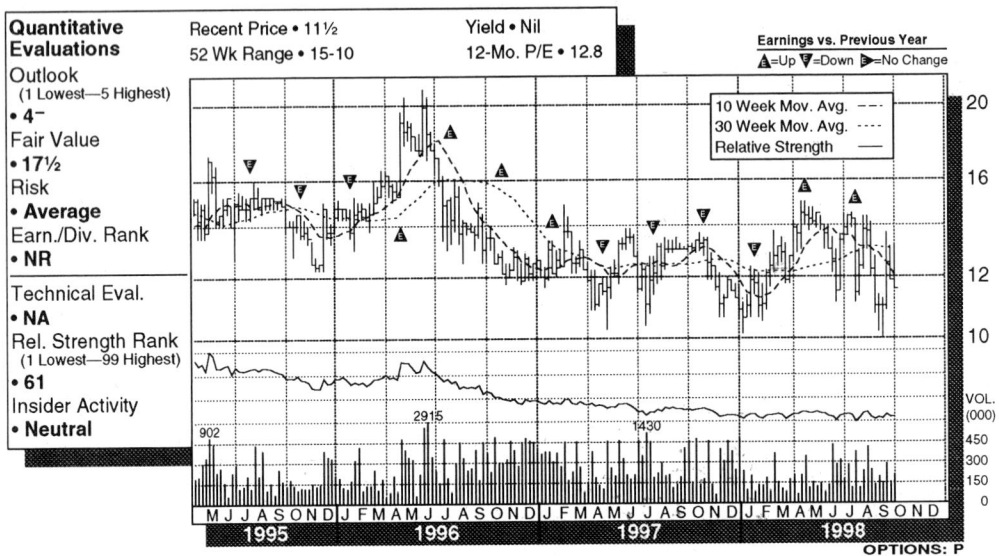

Earnings vs. Previous Year
▲=Up ▼=Down ▶=No Change

10 Week Mov. Avg. – – –
30 Week Mov. Avg. ·····
Relative Strength ——

OPTIONS: P

Business Profile - 12-MAY-98

In 1998, Building Materials plans to focus on growing same-store sales at all locations, particularly with value-added products, improving efficiency and productivity at underperforming stores, and growing through strategic acquisitions. In March 1998, BMHC reorganized into three major operating divisions to enable management to be closer to customers and employees. Each operating division will be responsible stores within a particular region of the U.S. Under this plan, local management would have more responsibility for day-to-day operations and the introduction of new products or services for its markets.

Operational Review - 12-MAY-98

Net sales for the three months ended March 31, 1998, advanced 25%, reflecting good weather in many markets and robust building permit activity, partly offset by wood product price deflation. Same-store sales grew 13%. Margins widened, due to a larger percentage of higher margin, value-added products in the sales mix; operating income leaped 49%. Following lower interest expense as a percentage of sales, net income jumped 87% to 850,000 ($0.07 a share) from $456,000 ($0.04).

Stock Performance - 02-OCT-98

In the past 30 trading days, BMHC's shares have declined 6%, compared to a 7% fall in the S&P 500. Average trading volume for the past five days was 41,760 shares, compared with the 40-day moving average of 45,741 shares.

Key Stock Statistics

Dividend Rate/Share	Nil	Shareholders	200
Shs. outstg. (M)	12.6	Market cap. (B)	$0.146
Avg. daily vol. (M)	0.044	Inst. holdings	70%
Tang. Bk. Value/Share	10.38		
Beta	0.76		

Value of $10,000 invested 5 years ago: $ 18,749

Fiscal Year Ending Dec. 31

	1998	1997	1996	1995	1994	1993
Revenues (Million $)						
1Q	183.6	146.8	147.6	120.5	112.1	73.90
2Q	226.0	190.6	193.0	166.2	141.8	103.3
3Q	—	201.9	206.5	178.5	157.8	110.2
4Q	—	188.7	170.9	165.0	135.3	112.2
Yr.	—	728.1	718.0	630.2	547.1	399.6
Earnings Per Share ($)						
1Q	**0.07**	0.04	0.00	0.00	0.00	0.00
2Q	**0.38**	0.29	0.38	0.25	0.54	0.37
3Q	—	0.35	0.38	0.35	0.55	0.43
4Q	—	0.11	0.16	0.14	0.27	0.28
Yr.	—	**0.78**	1.00	0.79	1.62	1.13

Next earnings report expected: late October

Dividend Data

No cash dividends have been paid on the common stock. A three-for-two stock split was effected March 4, 1994. A shareholder rights plan was adopted in July 1993.

A Division of The McGraw·Hill Companies

Business Summary - 12-MAY-98

Building Materials Holding Corp. is a holding corporation for BMC West Corp., a leading distributor and retailer of building materials in the western U.S. Products are sold primarily to professional contractors, as well as to advanced, service-oriented consumers. In addition to distributing products, the company conducts value-added conversion activities that include fabricating roof trusses, pre-hanging doors, pre-assembling windows and pre-cutting lumber to meet customer specifications.

As of March 12, 1998, the company was operating 55 building materials centers in 10 states. Building Materials groups its stores by location into three operating divisions: Intermountain (Arizona, Colorado, Idaho, Montana, Nevada, Utah and Eastern Washington), Pacific Northwest (California, Oregon and Western Washington) and South Central (Texas). BMHC believes that most of these centers hold first or second place in local market share and that it has the largest sales volume in each region of any distributor and retailer of building materials serving the professional contractor. Retail floor space varies from store to store, ranging from approximately 1,000 sq. ft. to in excess of 49,000 sq. ft.

The company's products are used primarily for new residential construction, light commercial construction and repair and remodeling projects, and include lumber,

oriented strand board, plywood, roofing materials, wallboard, pre-hung doors, roof trusses, pre-assembled windows, cabinets, hardware, paint and tools. Each BMHC store carries about 15,000 stock-keeping units (SKUs). Although product mix varies by location, a core group of about 9,000 SKUs is typically stocked in each center. Wood products accounted for 47% of 1997 sales.

In 1997, professional contractors accounted for 78% of net sales (77% in 1996), advanced, service-oriented consumers 21% (22%) and wholesale customers 2% (1%). No one customer accounted for over 1% of 1997 net sales. About 89% of BMHC's sales in 1997 were to customers to whom the company had extended credit. The remaining 11% consisted of cash purchases and purchases made with third-party credit cards and the company's private label credit card.

In the fourth quarter of 1997, the company acquired Logan Lumber Company, a leading supplier of building materials in Reno, NV, and Lone Star Plywood & Door Corp, an operator of pre-hung door plants, for a total of $40 million in cash and common stock. The two companies have combined annual sales of $83 million.

In September 1997, BMHC reorganized to form a holding company structure that would allow the company to more effectively participate in the consolidation of the contractor focused building materials distribution business.

Per Share Data ($)

(Year Ended Dec. 31)	1997	1996	1995	1994	1993	1992	1991	1990	1989	1988
Tangible Bk. Val.	9.85	10.48	7.92	9.43	6.17	4.57	3.71	2.81	1.93	NA
Cash Flow	1.69	1.93	1.83	2.25	1.53	1.09	0.78	1.62	1.09	0.58
Earnings	0.78	1.00	0.79	1.62	1.13	0.62	0.21	0.82	0.39	-0.01
Dividends	Nil	Nil	Nil	Nil	Nil	Nil	Nil	Nil	Nil	Nil
Payout Ratio	Nil	Nil	Nil	Nil	Nil	Nil	Nil	Nil	Nil	Nil
Prices - High	14⁷/₈	21	17¹/₄	30¹/₂	21¹/₂	7¹/₂	6⁷/₈	NA	NA	NA
- Low	10¹/₈	11³/₄	11¹/₄	12	5⁷/₈	5³/₈	3⁷/₈	NA	NA	NA
P/E Ratio - High	19	21	22	19	19	12	33	NA	NA	NA
- Low	13	12	14	7	5	9	19	NA	NA	NA

Income Statement Analysis (Million $)

	1997	1996	1995	1994	1993	1992	1991	1990	1989	1988
Revs.	728	718	630	547	400	291	219	224	196	164
Oper. Inc.	33.5	37.5	31.0	33.5	21.3	12.1	7.5	9.5	6.6	5.4
Depr.	11.0	10.3	9.2	5.5	3.0	2.6	2.2	2.4	2.1	1.8
Int. Exp.	8.7	10.4	10.7	6.5	4.5	5.0	5.3	5.8	5.3	4.1
Pretax Inc.	15.7	17.9	12.7	23.0	14.7	4.9	0.9	2.6	1.2	0.0
Eff. Tax Rate	40%	39%	39%	38%	40%	27%	12%	4.90%	Nil	Nil
Net Inc.	9.5	11.0	7.8	14.3	8.8	3.6	0.8	2.5	1.2	0.0

Balance Sheet & Other Fin. Data (Million $)

	1997	1996	1995	1994	1993	1992	1991	1990	1989	1988
Cash	8.2	7.1	6.0	5.2	1.6	0.7	0.6	0.4	0.8	NA
Curr. Assets	177	157	141	128	94.0	59.8	46.1	43.8	40.1	NA
Total Assets	340	288	265	222	142	92.0	73.5	68.1	57.8	54.8
Curr. Liab.	58.2	46.8	41.0	51.4	33.7	20.9	16.2	15.0	14.1	NA
LT Debt	113	90.2	121	76.4	53.3	32.3	32.9	40.2	33.2	NA
Common Eqty.	161	145	96.0	85.9	48.4	33.8	19.4	8.2	5.7	4.6
Total Cap.	279	235	220	170	108	71.1	57.3	53.2	43.7	41.5
Cap. Exp.	13.3	14.4	16.9	15.1	15.5	7.6	4.8	6.3	1.9	2.1
Cash Flow	20.5	21.3	17.0	19.8	11.8	6.2	3.0	4.9	3.3	1.8
Curr. Ratio	3.0	3.4	3.4	2.5	2.8	2.9	2.8	2.9	2.8	NA
% LT Debt of Cap.	40.7	38.4	55.0	45.0	49.5	45.5	57.4	75.6	76.0	NA
% Net Inc.of Revs.	1.3	1.5	1.2	2.6	2.2	1.2	0.4	1.1	0.6	NM
% Ret. on Assets	3.0	7.4	3.2	7.4	7.3	3.7	0.8	4.0	2.2	NM
% Ret. on Equity	6.2	9.1	8.5	20.0	20.8	11.6	4.7	35.5	22.9	NM

Data as orig. reptd.; bef. results of disc. opers. and/or spec. items. Per share data adj. for stk. divs. as of ex-div. date. Bold denotes diluted EPS (FASB 128). E-Estimated. NA-Not Available. NM-Not Meaningful. NR-Not Ranked.

Office—One Market Plaza, Steuart Tower, Ste. 2650, San Francisco, CA 94105. **Tel**—(415) 227-1650. **Chrmn**—G. E. McCown. **Pres & CEO**—R. E. Mellor. **SVP, Treas & Investor Contact**—Ellis C. Goebel. **Dirs**—A. F. Beck, H. J. Brown, W. J. Fix, R. V. Hansberger, D. S. Hendrickson, G. O. Mabry, G. E. McCown, R. E. Mellor, P. S. O'Neill. **Transfer Agent & Registrar**—American Stock Transfer & Trust Co., NYC. **Incorporated**—in Delaware in 1987. **Empl**— 3,500. **S&P Analyst:** Ray Lam, CFA

STANDARD &POOR'S
STOCK REPORTS

Burr-Brown Corp.   3373E

NASDAQ Symbol **BBRC**

In S&P SmallCap 600

03-OCT-98

Industry:
Electronics (Semiconductors)

Summary: This company makes high-performance analog and mixed-signal integrated circuits used in the processing of electronic signals.

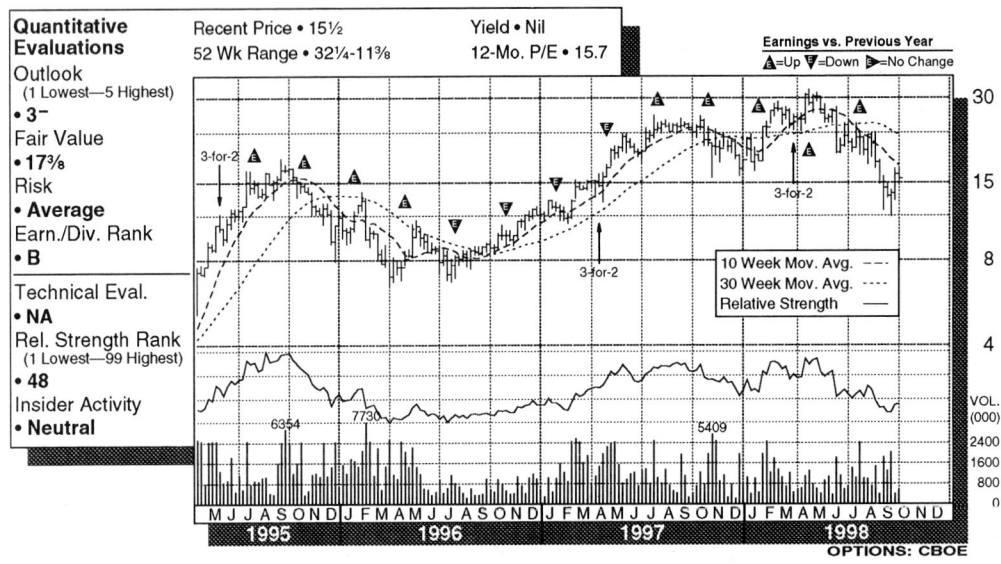

Quantitative Evaluations

Recent Price • 15½
52 Wk Range • 32¼-11⅜

Yield • Nil
12-Mo. P/E • 15.7

Earnings vs. Previous Year
▲=Up ▼=Down ▶=No Change

Outlook (1 Lowest—5 Highest)
• **3⁻**

Fair Value
• **17⅜**

Risk
• **Average**

Earn./Div. Rank
• **B**

Technical Eval.
• **NA**

Rel. Strength Rank (1 Lowest—99 Highest)
• **48**

Insider Activity
• **Neutral**

10 Week Mov. Avg. — ▪ —
30 Week Mov. Avg. ▪ ▪ ▪ ▪
Relative Strength ——

OPTIONS: CBOE

Business Profile - 28-JUL-98

In 1994, Burr-Brown reorganized to emphasize the company's core analog and mixed-signal processing product lines. As part of this same strategy to focus on its core operations, the company sold its Power Convertibles subsidiary in early 1996, resulting in a $5.35 million after-tax gain. In 1997, BBRC posted record profits and also introduced a record number of new products. The company expects to maintain an annual revenue growth rate between 15% and 20% for the foreseeable future. BBRC believes that its second half financial results will be better than its first half.

Operational Review - 28-JUL-98

For the six months ended July 4, 1998, net revenues rose 15%, year to year, with most of the gain in the first quarter. Gross margins widened slightly, and operating expenses were well controlled; operating profit gained 37%. After taxes at 28.5%, versus 30.0%, net income rose 37%, to $19,600,000 ($0.51 a share), from $14,319,000 ($0.38, as adjusted for a 3-for-2 stock split in March 1998).

Stock Performance - 02-OCT-98

In the past 30 trading days, BBRC's shares have declined 12%, compared to a 7% fall in the S&P 500. Average trading volume for the past five days was 105,500 shares, compared with the 40-day moving average of 221,415 shares.

Key Stock Statistics

Dividend Rate/Share	Nil	Shareholders	5,500
Shs. outstg. (M)	36.7	Market cap. (B)	$0.571
Avg. daily vol. (M)	0.236	Inst. holdings	61%
Tang. Bk. Value/Share	7.00		
Beta	1.90		

Value of $10,000 invested 5 years ago: $ 72,443

Fiscal Year Ending Dec. 31

	1998	1997	1996	1995	1994	1993
Revenues (Million $)						
1Q	68.69	54.77	61.17	59.55	47.36	42.28
2Q	66.52	62.51	58.18	69.59	47.61	42.49
3Q	—	65.93	50.11	70.22	49.22	42.94
4Q	—	68.90	50.53	69.80	50.02	40.88
Yr.	—	252.1	220.0	269.2	194.2	168.6
Earnings Per Share ($)						
1Q	**0.27**	0.17	0.31	0.14	0.05	0.02
2Q	**0.25**	**0.20**	0.18	0.20	0.06	0.02
3Q	—	0.22	0.16	0.24	0.05	0.02
4Q	—	0.26	0.16	0.24	0.03	0.03
Yr.	—	0.86	0.79	0.83	0.20	0.09

Next earnings report expected: early October

Dividend Data

Amount ($)	Date Decl.	Ex-Div. Date	Stock of Record	Payment Date
3-for-2	Feb. 23	Mar. 23	Mar. 06	Mar. 20 '98

Business Summary - 28-JUL-98

Traditionally a well diversified manufacturer of high-performance analog and mixed-signal integrated circuits (ICs), Burr-Brown Corp (BBRC) has been increasingly penetrating the fast growing communications market. During 1997, revenue contributions from communications applications grew to 20% of total revenues, up from 6% in 1994. Including communications, BBRC has targeted five key markets in 1998. The other areas are industrial and product control, test and instrumentation, digital video and audio, and computing and multimedia. The company's traditional industrial and product control and test and instrumentation markets accounted for nearly half of revenues in 1997.

The company's product strategy has been to concentrate on proprietary high-precision or high-performance products. Burr-Brown identifies specific high-volume markets in which its enhanced high-performance products are required. It then develops and supplies as complete a function as possible, often becoming a customer's sole source for particular components. Its strategy has generally enabled the company to avoid direct competition with major semiconductor manufacturers, which typically focus on low-cost, high-volume products.

Analog signal-processing ICs are used to process and transmit analog data signals prior to their conversion to digital signals. Burr-Brown's analog circuits include operational amplifiers, instrumentation amplifiers, programmable gain amplifiers, isolation amplifiers, current transmitters, and other analog signal-processing components.

Data conversion components are IC devices used to convert analog signals to digital form (A/D converters) and vice versa (D/A converters). Such conversion is necessary in virtually all applications in which digital computers or processors measure and control the analog signals from a physical condition.

Through majority-owned Intelligent Instrumentation Inc., the company also manufactures and markets a line of data acquisition products, including plug-in boards, portable data acquisition systems, microterminals, and supporting software for IBM-compatible PCs, as well as signal conditioning accessories for such systems, and signal processing software and hardware products designed to run on IBM-compatible PCs.

In January 1998, BBRC announced Hotwire, a system that transforms regular copper telephone wiring and in-house wiring into high-speed access to the Internet. The system was the result of a collaboration between BBRC and Paradyne Corporation.

Per Share Data ($)

(Year Ended Dec. 31)	1997	1996	1995	1994	1993	1992	1991	1990	1989	1988
Tangible Bk. Val.	6.47	8.37	4.89	2.71	2.47	2.48	2.50	2.81	2.62	2.37
Cash Flow	1.23	1.14	1.19	0.52	0.40	0.37	0.09	0.49	0.61	0.78
Earnings	0.86	0.79	0.83	0.20	0.09	0.03	-0.30	0.13	0.27	0.35
Dividends	Nil	Nil	Nil	Nil	Nil	Nil	Nil	Nil	Nil	Nil
Payout Ratio	Nil	Nil	Nil	Nil	Nil	Nil	Nil	Nil	Nil	Nil
Prices - High	26^1/$_8$	14	18^3/$_8$	4^5/$_8$	2^7/$_8$	2^1/$_2$	3	3^3/$_8$	4^1/$_4$	5^3/$_8$
- Low	10^3/$_4$	6^1/$_2$	3	1^{11}/$_{16}$	1^7/$_{16}$	1^1/$_4$	1^9/$_{16}$	1^{11}/$_{16}$	2^1/$_{16}$	2^5/$_{16}$
P/E Ratio - High	30	18	22	23	34	85	NM	26	16	15
- Low	13	8	4	9	16	41	NM	13	8	7

Income Statement Analysis (Million $)

	1997	1996	1995	1994	1993	1992	1991	1990	1989	1988
Revs.	252	220	269	194	169	163	179	177	169	177
Oper. Inc.	57.4	43.4	53.2	21.1	17.9	18.0	24.1	22.6	30.7	36.2
Depr.	13.8	13.3	12.7	10.6	10.1	11.0	12.8	11.7	11.1	14.1
Int. Exp.	0.4	0.7	1.1	1.7	2.3	3.8	4.3	3.6	4.6	2.7
Pretax Inc.	46.7	39.8	40.0	8.3	4.5	1.7	-9.4	7.8	15.4	20.3
Eff. Tax Rate	30%	26%	27%	22%	38%	42%	NM	45%	44%	43%
Net Inc.	32.7	29.7	29.2	6.5	2.8	1.0	-9.7	4.3	8.7	11.5

Balance Sheet & Other Fin. Data (Million $)

	1997	1996	1995	1994	1993	1992	1991	1990	1989	1988
Cash	54.3	52.8	86.2	9.9	13.1	9.5	3.3	3.1	2.4	2.6
Curr. Assets	173	154	196	92.0	95.0	90.0	101	93.0	89.0	78.0
Total Assets	299	262	252	143	142	141	163	164	161	133
Curr. Liab.	58.5	55.6	66.0	46.5	44.5	37.1	43.1	40.1	46.0	38.4
LT Debt	1.5	1.8	1.8	1.8	8.8	11.7	33.7	27.5	24.4	13.0
Common Eqty.	235	199	179	87.6	79.6	80.0	80.8	90.4	84.4	76.4
Total Cap.	240	203	181	91.0	90.0	95.0	118	122	114	93.0
Cap. Exp.	25.6	31.9	17.6	12.1	7.1	5.6	11.9	14.1	28.0	21.3
Cash Flow	46.5	43.0	41.9	17.1	12.9	12.0	3.1	16.0	19.8	25.6
Curr. Ratio	2.9	2.8	3.0	2.0	2.1	2.4	2.4	2.3	1.9	2.0
% LT Debt of Cap.	0.6	0.9	1.0	2.0	9.8	12.3	28.5	22.5	21.5	13.9
% Net Inc.of Revs.	13.0	13.5	10.9	3.3	1.7	0.6	NM	2.4	5.1	6.5
% Ret. on Assets	11.6	11.6	14.8	4.5	2.0	0.7	NM	2.6	5.9	9.1
% Ret. on Equity	15.0	15.7	21.9	7.7	3.5	1.2	NM	4.9	10.8	16.2

Data as orig. reptd.; bef. results of disc. opers. and/or spec. items. Per share data adj. for stk. divs. as of ex-div. date. Bold denotes diluted EPS (FASB 128). E-Estimated. NA-Not Available. NM-Not Meaningful. NR-Not Ranked.

Office—6730 S. Tucson Blvd., Tucson, AZ 85706. **Tel**—(520) 746-1111. **Website**—http://www.burr-brown.com **Pres, Chrmn & CEO**—S. P. Madavi. **CFO**—J. S. Blouin. **Dirs**—F. J. Aguilar, J. S. Anderegg Jr., T. R. Brown Jr., M. A. Gumucio, S. P. Madavi. **Transfer Agent & Registrar**—Harris Trust & Savings Bank, Chicago. **Incorporated**—in Arizona in 1956; reincorporated in Delaware in 1983. **Empl**— 1,311. **S&P Analyst:** Mark Cavallone

Butler Manufacturing 402E

NYSE Symbol **BBR**

In S&P SmallCap 600

03-OCT-98

Industry:
Engineering & Construction

Summary: This company is a leading supplier of pre-fab buildings and related products, and construction services for the commercial construction market.

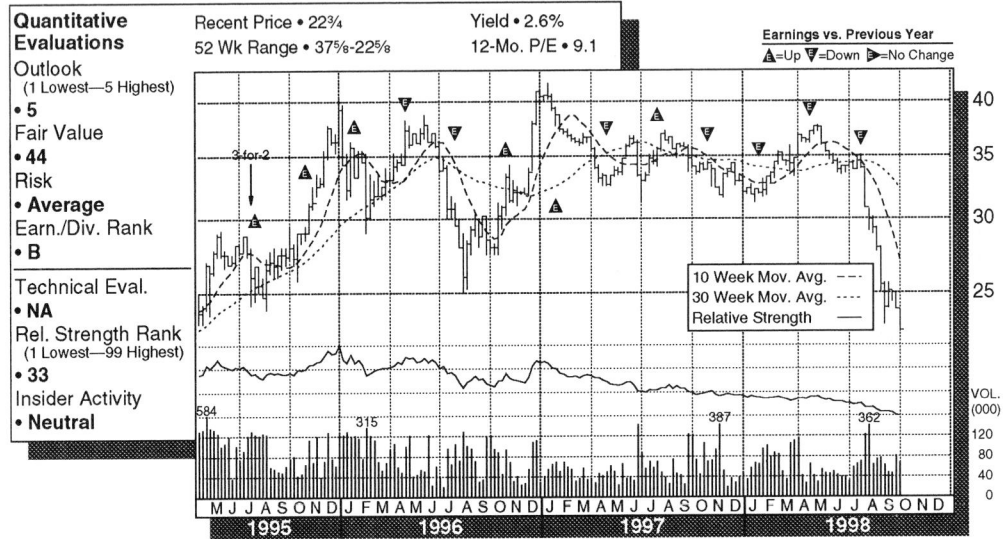

Quantitative Evaluations	Recent Price • 22¾	Yield • 2.6%
	52 Wk Range • 37⅝-22⅝	12-Mo. P/E • 9.1

Quantitative Evaluations

Outlook
(1 Lowest—5 Highest)
• **5**

Fair Value
• **44**

Risk
• **Average**

Earn./Div. Rank
• **B**

Technical Eval.
• **NA**

Rel. Strength Rank
(1 Lowest—99 Highest)
• **33**

Insider Activity
• **Neutral**

Earnings vs. Previous Year
▲=Up ▼=Down ▶=No Change

10 Week Mov. Avg. – – –
30 Week Mov. Avg. ·····
Relative Strength ——

Business Profile - 22-SEP-98

In August, Butler said that the outlook for the construction market was currently mixed. A recent survey of 200 construction executives concluded that while the construction market remained strong, a mild deceleration in growth rates could be taking shape. Although there are several reasons for the company to be cautious, its prospect, proposal and order activity remain strong. BBR intends to improve the results of its international buildings businesses. In Brazil, the company is taking aggressive actions to contain near-term losses, and to address longer term challenges and opportunities. The dividend was recently boosted 7.1%.

Operational Review - 22-SEP-98

Revenues in the first half of 1998 rose fractionally, year to year, as increased sales in the Architectural Products segment offset lost revenue resulting from the sale of the Grain Systems division in June 1997. Operating margins narrowed, reflecting higher selling, general and administrative expenses as a percentage of sales. Income declined 20%, to $6.1 million ($0.79 a share), from $7.6 million ($0.99, before a gain on the sale of the Grain Systems division). At June 30, 1998, backlog totaled $341 million, up 13% from the level a year earlier.

Stock Performance - 02-OCT-98

In the past 30 trading days, BBR's shares have declined 18%, compared to a 7% fall in the S&P 500. Average trading volume for the past five days was 13,400 shares, compared with the 40-day moving average of 13,254 shares.

Key Stock Statistics

Dividend Rate/Share	0.60	Shareholders	2,300
Shs. outstg. (M)	7.7	Market cap. (B)	$0.175
Avg. daily vol. (M)	0.012	Inst. holdings	47%
Tang. Bk. Value/Share	21.00		
Beta	0.64		

Value of $10,000 invested 5 years ago: $ 26,963

Fiscal Year Ending Dec. 31

	1998	1997	1996	1995	1994	1993
Revenues (Million $)						
1Q	193.8	188.1	175.7	194.8	117.0	111.0
2Q	238.5	241.1	193.4	206.8	175.0	145.0
3Q	—	241.0	229.0	206.6	190.0	164.0
4Q	—	254.4	272.0	218.3	210.0	156.0
Yr.	—	924.6	870.2	826.5	692.0	576.0
Earnings Per Share ($)						
1Q	0.15	0.25	0.42	0.48	-0.19	-0.18
2Q	0.64	2.46	0.76	0.91	0.69	0.24
3Q	—	0.86	1.14	1.00	0.89	0.58
4Q	—	0.86	1.04	0.78	0.67	1.75
Yr.	—	4.43	3.35	3.07	2.09	2.56

Next earnings report expected: mid October

Dividend Data (Dividends have been paid since 1994.)

Amount ($)	Date Decl.	Ex-Div. Date	Stock of Record	Payment Date
0.140	Dec. 16	Dec. 23	Dec. 26	Jan. 13 '98
0.140	Jan. 20	Mar. 20	Mar. 24	Apr. 07 '98
0.140	Jun. 16	Jun. 24	Jun. 26	Jul. 10 '98
0.150	Sep. 15	Sep. 29	Oct. 01	Oct. 15 '98

A Division of The McGraw-Hill Companies

STANDARD
&POOR'S
STOCK REPORTS

Butler Manufacturing Company

402E
03-OCT-98

Business Summary - 22-SEP-98

Butler believes that it is the largest U.S. maker of pre-fab steel buildings and the second largest maker of wood frame buildings. In recent years, the company has been focusing on expanding its overseas presence, and it now has wholly owned subsidiaries in the U.K., France, Germany, China, and Brazil, as well as a 90%-owned joint venture in Hungary, and 30%-owned joint venture in Saudi Arabia.

Butler Manufacturing is comprised of three related businesses: Building Systems - designs, produces and markets custom designed pre-fabricated commercial buildings; Construction Services - construction management; and Architectural Products - curtain wall and window systems.

Two target growth areas consist of structural sections produced in Shanghai, China, and a software development project aimed at significantly enhancing systems for engineering design, pricing and ordering of virtually any building configuration.

The building systems segment consists primarily of one- to five-story steel and one- to two-story wood framed buildings for use as office buildings, manufacturing, facilities, warehouses, schools, shopping centers, livestock and farm buildings.

The Vistawall group, curtain wall/window systems segment, makes aluminum curtain wall systems for low-rise retail and commercial markets. In early 1997, the company acquired Rebco West, a west coast producer of entrance doors, and in June 1997, purchased Modu-Line Windows. In mid-1997, the company sold the segment's Grain Systems division, in order to focus on core building products businesses.

Segment revenue contributions and pretax profit margins in recent years were:

	1997	1996	1995
REVENUES			
Building systems	72.6%	64%	69%
Other building products	14.4%	18%	17%
Construction services	13.1%	18%	14%
PRETAX PROFIT MARGINS			
Building systems	5.7%	7.2%	6.9%
Other building products	Nil	Nil	1.1%
Construction services	1.3%	10.0%	9.6%

The construction services segment, through BUCON, Inc., provides a full range of construction management services to major purchasers of construction. Revenues are derived primarily from general contracting.

Per Share Data ($)

(Year Ended Dec. 31)	1997	1996	1995	1994	1993	1992	1991	1990	1989	1988
Tangible Bk. Val.	20.50	16.46	13.54	10.47	8.28	5.76	5.46	7.15	6.06	17.77
Cash Flow	6.04	4.61	4.19	2.99	3.65	1.39	-0.29	2.77	3.02	3.95
Earnings	4.43	3.35	3.07	2.09	2.56	0.17	-1.74	1.21	1.43	2.27
Dividends	0.52	0.44	0.37	0.13	Nil	Nil	Nil	Nil	13.80	0.91
Payout Ratio	12%	13%	12%	6%	Nil	Nil	Nil	Nil	NM	40%
Prices - High	41⅞	41	40½	23⅝	21	10⅛	13½	12½	30⅞	23⅞
- Low	31¼	25	19⅞	14⅜	9	7	6⅛	8⅛	11⅛	17⅞
P/E Ratio - High	9	12	13	11	8	59	NM	10	22	10
- Low	7	7	6	7	4	40	NM	7	8	8

Income Statement Analysis (Million $)

	1997	1996	1995	1994	1993	1992	1991	1990	1989	1988
Revs.	925	870	827	692	576	500	461	564	580	646
Oper. Inc.	54.2	59.2	56.6	40.1	23.6	18.8	10.6	38.5	35.7	35.1
Depr.	12.5	9.7	8.9	6.7	7.7	8.4	4.9	10.7	15.4	11.4
Int. Exp.	5.1	4.3	4.1	3.9	4.6	6.0	9.9	10.6	8.0	4.8
Pretax Inc.	59.8	46.0	42.3	28.7	29.8	2.4	-13.7	16.0	19.2	24.7
Eff. Tax Rate	43%	44%	45%	46%	39%	53%	NM	49%	49%	38%
Net Inc.	34.4	25.8	23.4	15.1	18.1	1.1	-11.9	8.2	9.8	15.3

Balance Sheet & Other Fin. Data (Million $)

	1997	1996	1995	1994	1993	1992	1991	1990	1989	1988
Cash	5.5	2.0	7.3	5.3	14.9	7.7	6.2	10.5	2.2	9.1
Curr. Assets	233	222	187	189	128	120	115	132	145	170
Total Assets	375	337	283	271	205	200	203	226	241	266
Curr. Liab.	165	161	126	136	98.0	73.0	85.0	88.0	77.0	93.0
LT Debt	33.9	38.4	43.0	40.0	30.0	67.0	68.0	71.0	105	28.0
Common Eqty.	157	124	102	79.0	62.0	42.0	39.0	50.0	42.0	124
Total Cap.	194	167	148	124	97.0	116	114	130	158	165
Cap. Exp.	30.2	22.7	22.7	13.7	6.5	5.0	5.7	8.0	9.1	9.9
Cash Flow	46.9	35.5	32.0	22.0	25.8	9.5	-2.0	18.9	20.7	26.7
Curr. Ratio	1.4	1.4	1.5	1.4	1.3	1.6	1.3	1.5	1.9	1.8
% LT Debt of Cap.	17.5	23.0	28.9	32.5	31.4	58.0	59.4	54.5	66.6	17.2
% Net Inc.of Revs.	3.7	3.0	2.8	2.2	3.1	0.2	NM	1.4	1.7	2.4
% Ret. on Assets	9.7	8.3	8.4	6.4	8.8	0.6	NM	3.5	3.9	5.7
% Ret. on Equity	24.5	22.7	25.9	21.5	34.4	2.8	NM	17.7	11.8	12.9

Data as orig. reptd.; bef. results of disc. opers. and/or spec. items. Per share data adj. for stk. divs. as of ex-div. date. Bold denotes diluted EPS (FASB 128). E-Estimated. NA-Not Available. NM-Not Meaningful. NR-Not Ranked.

Office—BMA Tower - Penn Valley Park, P.O. Box 419917-0917, Kansas City, MO 64141-0917. **Reincorporated**—in Delaware in 1969. **Tel**—(816) 968-3000. **Chrmn & CEO**—R. H. West. **Pres**—D. H. Pratt. **VP & Secy**—R. O. Ballentine. **VP-Fin & CFO**—L. C. Miller. **EVP & Investor Contact**—John J. Holland. **Dirs**—H. G. Bernthal, A. M. Hallene, C. L. W. Haw, R. J. Novello, G. E. Powell Jr., D. H. Pratt, R. J. Reintjes, J. A. Rogala, G. L. Tapella, R. H. West. **Transfer Agent & Registrar**—UMB Bank, Kansas City. **Incorporated**— in Missouri in 1902; reincorporated in Delaware in 1969. **Empl**— 5,177. **S&P Analyst:** John A. Massey

03-OCT-98

Industry: Banks (Regional)

Summary: Through subsidiaries, CCB operates some 200 offices throughout the Carolinas.

Quantitative Evaluations	
Outlook (1 Lowest—5 Highest) • **1+**	
Fair Value • **46**	
Risk • **Low**	
Earn./Div. Rank • **A**	
Technical Eval. • **Bearish** since 9/98	
Rel. Strength Rank (1 Lowest—99 Highest) • **66**	
Insider Activity • **Favorable**	

Recent Price • 48⅞
52 Wk Range • 58½-43⅛

Yield • 2.1%
12-Mo. P/E • 20.0

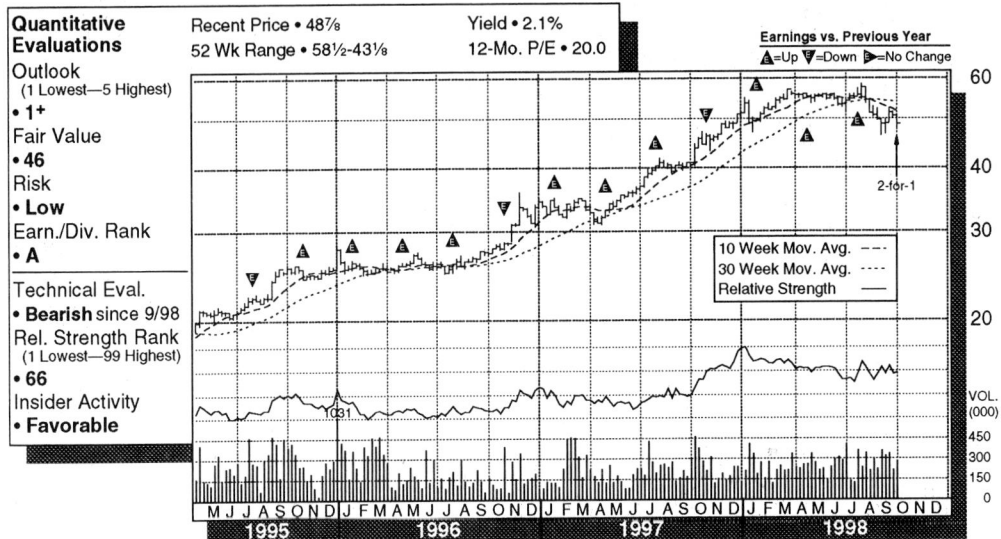

Earnings vs. Previous Year
▲=Up ▼=Down ▶=No Change

2-for-1

10 Week Mov. Avg. – – –
30 Week Mov. Avg. · · · · ·
Relative Strength ———

VOL. (000)

1995 1996 1997 1998

Business Profile - 18-MAY-98

CCB has increased its dividend for 33 consecutive years, a record unmatched by any other banking institution. During 1997, the bank acquired Salem Trust Bank and American Federal Bank, for about $325.1 million in stock. The consolidated bank, with approximately $7.3 billion in assets, is currently the sixth largest in the Carolinas, operating about 200 offices and 215 ATMs in a market area that spans 40 counties. Asset quality remains stellar, with net chargeoffs falling to 0.18% of average total loans in the first quarter of 1998, from 0.22% a year earlier.

Operational Review - 18-MAY-98

Net interest income advanced 9.1%, year to year, in the first quarter of 1998, reflecting a 4.4% increase in average earning assets, coupled with a wider net interest margin (4.79% versus 4.59%). The loan loss provision grew 18%, to $3.1 million, despite solid asset quality and a strong reserve. Noninterest income rose 13%, primarily on increased service charges and greater sales and insurance commissions. After only 4.0% higher noninterest expenses, aided by the absence of a $1.0 million merger-related charge in the 1997 quarter, and taxes at 36.6%, versus 36.8%, net income climbed 18%, to $29.3 million ($1.39 a share, diluted), from $24.9 million ($1.19).

Stock Performance - 02-OCT-98

In the past 30 trading days, CCB's shares have declined 4%, compared to a 7% fall in the S&P 500. Average trading volume for the past five days was 56,080 shares, compared with the 40-day moving average of 57,600 shares.

Key Stock Statistics

Dividend Rate/Share	1.04	Shareholders	9,200
Shs. outstg. (M)	40.6	Market cap. (B)	$ 2.0
Avg. daily vol. (M)	0.060	Inst. holdings	33%
Tang. Bk. Value/Share	16.27		
Beta	0.79		

Value of $10,000 invested 5 years ago: $ 32,064

Fiscal Year Ending Dec. 31

	1998	1997	1996	1995	1994	1993
Revenues (Million $)						
1Q	166.4	155.0	111.2	105.2	64.21	48.39
2Q	174.1	161.2	113.0	109.6	68.51	53.34
3Q	—	162.0	116.5	109.1	71.93	60.11
4Q	—	165.7	119.7	111.9	77.62	67.91
Yr.	—	643.9	459.8	435.8	282.3	229.8
Earnings Per Share ($)						
1Q	**0.69**	**0.59**	0.59	0.49	0.45	0.41
2Q	**0.72**	**0.66**	0.61	0.31	0.51	0.41
3Q	—	0.36	0.50	0.56	0.54	0.41
4Q	—	0.66	0.64	0.57	0.54	0.52
Yr.	—	**2.27**	2.08	1.94	2.03	1.75

Next earnings report expected: late October

Dividend Data (Dividends have been paid since 1934.)

Amount ($)	Date Decl.	Ex-Div. Date	Stock of Record	Payment Date
0.470	Jan. 20	Mar. 12	Mar. 16	Apr. 01 '98
0.470	Apr. 21	Jun. 11	Jun. 15	Jul. 01 '98
0.260	Jul. 21	Sep. 11	Sep. 15	Oct. 01 '98
2-for-1	Jul. 21	Oct. 02	Sep. 15	Oct. 01 '98

A Division of The McGraw·Hill Companies

Business Summary - 18-MAY-98

The second "C" in CCB Financial Corp. (CCB) stands for Carolina, and, in mid-1997, CCB, the holding company for Central Carolina Bank & Trust Co. of Durham, NC, became an establishment of both Carolinas by acquiring American Federal Bank, FSB, and extending its franchise further down the Interstate 85 corridor into northwest South Carolina. Acquisition of the Greenville, SC-based bank, which involved the issuance of 4.9 million common shares, led to the formation of the sixth largest financial institution in the Carolinas, with $7.1 billion in assets and $6.0 billion in deposits.

Before the transaction, which added 40 banking offices to CCB's existing branch network, the company counted among its strengths the high concentration of its assets in larger, faster-growing urban areas of North Carolina, such as Raleigh-Durham, Greensboro-Winston Salem and Charlotte. The acquisition of American Federal provided CCB with a new metropolitan area, Greenville-Spartanburg, in a new state.

CCB has enhanced the availability of its services in recent years by venturing into the realm of alternative delivery, including an experiment with seven-day-a-week CCB7 offices in Harris Teeter supermarkets, the opening of a telebanking center, and the launch of a computer banking service. CCB offers commercial and retail banking, savings and trust services through 209 offices (including the CCB7s) and 207 ATMs, in addition to the telebanking and on-line options.

In 1997, internally generated loan growth and a focus on boosting noninterest income while controlling noninterest expense resulted in a 10% increase in net income to $95 million. CCB ended the year with loan and lease balances of $5.1 billion, 7.3% higher than at the end of 1996, with increases in CCB's consumer, commercial and construction portfolios leading loan growth for the year.

In 1997, average earning assets, from which interest income is derived, amounted to $6.6 billion and consisted mainly of loans and lease financing (74%) and U.S. treasury and other U.S. government securities (20%). Average sources of funds, on which the company generally pays interest expense, included savings and time deposits (83%), demand deposits (11%), and debt and other (6%). At year-end 1997, nonperforming assets and past-due loans represented 0.25% of total assets, down from 0.28% a year earlier.

Per Share Data ($)

(Year Ended Dec. 31)	1997	1996	1995	1994	1993	1992	1991	1990	1989	1988
Tangible Bk. Val.	16.40	15.86	14.49	13.80	13.19	12.20	11.12	10.19	9.34	8.43
Earnings	2.27	2.33	1.94	2.03	1.75	1.65	1.41	1.35	1.39	1.31
Dividends	0.89	0.80	0.72	0.66	0.62	0.57	0.52	0.49	0.47	0.43
Payout Ratio	39%	34%	37%	33%	35%	35%	37%	37%	34%	33%
Prices - High	55	35$^7/_8$	28$^1/_4$	22$^1/_4$	21$^1/_4$	18$^1/_8$	15	13$^1/_2$	14$^5/_8$	12
- Low	31	24$^5/_8$	17	16$^3/_8$	16$^1/_4$	11$^1/_8$	8$^3/_8$	8$^1/_8$	11$^1/_8$	10$^3/_4$
P/E Ratio - High	24	15	15	11	12	11	11	10	10	9
- Low	14	11	9	8	9	7	6	6	8	8

Income Statement Analysis (Million $)

	1997	1996	1995	1994	1993	1992	1991	1990	1989	1988
Net Int. Inc.	300	216	204	145	117	99	92.1	86.1	79.5	73.2
Tax Equiv. Adj.	9.2	8.2	8.6	5.2	4.7	4.4	5.0	4.8	4.7	3.8
Non Int. Inc.	92.9	62.0	53.3	39.7	36.4	30.6	32.6	29.7	27.3	25.5
Loan Loss Prov.	16.4	12.8	8.2	892	6.5	6.0	7.4	6.3	4.9	3.5
Exp./Op. Revs.	58%	56%	60%	63%	67%	66%	67%	66%	65%	NA
Pretax Inc.	151	105	88.0	57.4	43.9	37.2	30.3	30.0	30.4	29.4
Eff. Tax Rate	37%	33%	34%	33%	33%	32%	29%	32%	31%	33%
Net Inc.	95.4	70.3	57.9	38.5	29.2	25.3	21.5	20.5	21.0	19.7
% Net Int. Marg.	4.70	4.70	4.70	4.90	4.90	5.20	5.10	5.00	5.00	5.10

Balance Sheet & Other Fin. Data (Million $)

	1997	1996	1995	1994	1993	1992	1991	1990	1989	1988
Earning Assets:										
Money Mkt	42.0	297	380	174	205	106	NA	117	NA	NA
Inv. Securities	1,464	979	1,040	592	617	498	419	394	371	308
Com'l Loans	731	429	531	544	411	346	373	313	296	263
Other Loans	4,368	3,347	2,820	1,964	1,751	1,179	1,077	1,072	1,012	945
Total Assets	7,139	5,384	5,090	3,548	3,258	2,312	2,158	2,102	1,984	1,795
Demand Deposits	740	594	538	430	421	344	298	298	305	280
Time Deposits	5,245	3,995	3,759	2,602	2,395	1,684	1,587	1,547	1,431	1,278
LT Debt	101	57.8	79.0	77.0	78.0	27.7	25.6	25.7	29.3	30.0
Common Eqty.	681	478	434	251	251	190	170	155	142	127
% Ret. on Assets	1.5	1.3	1.2	1.2	1.1	1.2	1.0	1.0	1.1	1.2
% Ret. on Equity	16.5	12.4	14.6	14.9	13.9	14.3	13.3	14.0	15.8	16.6
% Loan Loss Resv.	1.3	1.3	1.3	1.3	1.3	1.3	1.2	1.2	1.1	1.1
% Loans/Deposits	85.1	82.2	77.8	82.7	76.7	75.0	76.6	74.8	75.1	77.1
% Equity to Assets	9.3	8.7	8.2	7.8	7.8	8.1	7.8	7.3	7.2	7.1

Data as orig. reptd.; bef. results of disc opers. and/or spec. items. Per share data adj. for stk. divs. as of ex-div. date. Bold denotes diluted EPS (FASB 128). E-Estimated. NA-Not Available. NM-Not Meaningful. NR-Not Ranked.

Office—111 Corcoran St., P.O. Box 931, Durham, NC 27702. **Tel**—(919) 683-7777. **Website**—http://www.ccbonline.com **Chrmn, Pres & CEO**—E. C. Roessler. **SVP & CFO**—R. L. Savage Jr.**Investor Contact**—Jenny R. Kobin (919) 683-7646.**Dirs**—W. L. Abercrombie Jr., J. M. Barnhardt, J. H. Beall III, J. B. Brame Jr., T. B. Burnett, W. L. Burns Jr., B. P. Garrett Jr., E. S. Holmes, B. McElveen-Hunter, D. B. Jordan, C. D. Joyner, O. G. Kenan, E. J. McDonald, H. W. McKay Jr., G. J. Morrow, E. B. Munson, E. C. Roessler, D. E. Shi, M. J. Smith Jr., J. K. Stegall, H. A. Tate Jr.,—J. L. Williamson, P. Wynn Jr.**Transfer Agent**—Registrar & Transfer Co., Cranford, NJ**Incorporated**—in North Carolina in 1903.**Empl**— 2,643. **S&P Analyst:** L. A. Olive

C-COR Electronics   3379R

NASDAQ Symbol CCBL

In S&P SmallCap 600

03-OCT-98

Industry:
Electrical Equipment

Summary: C-COR designs and manufactures electronic equipment used in a variety of communication networks worldwide.

Quantitative Evaluations

Recent Price • 11⅞
52 Wk Range • 20-10⅞

Yield • Nil
12-Mo. P/E • 13.5

Outlook
(1 Lowest—5 Highest)
• **5**

Fair Value
• **22⅜**

Risk
• **High**

Earn./Div. Rank
• **B-**

Technical Eval.
• **Neutral** since 9/98

Rel. Strength Rank
(1 Lowest—99 Highest)
• **45**

Insider Activity
• **Neutral**

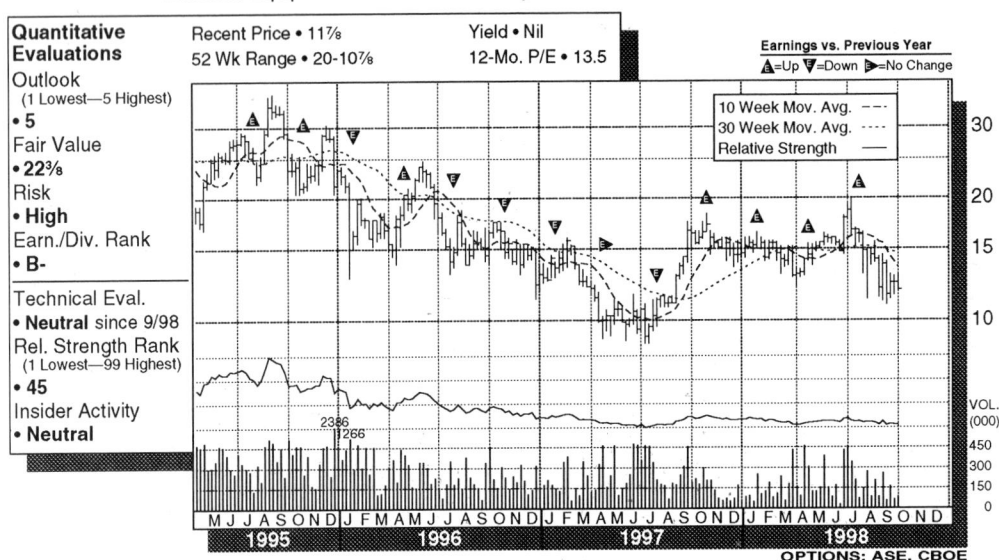

Earnings vs. Previous Year
▲=Up ▼=Down ►=No Change

10 Week Mov. Avg. – – –
30 Week Mov. Avg. ·····
Relative Strength ——

OPTIONS: ASE, CBOE

Business Profile - 20-APR-98

Following several quarters of poor earnings performance, the company implemented a restructuring plan aimed at increasing gross margins and improving operating efficiencies. In July 1997, CCBL said it was discontinuing its digital fiber optic business, located in Fremont, CA. In addition, during the summer of 1997, the company completed the transfer of certain manufacturing operations to Mexico. Results improved in the first three quarters of FY 98 (Jun.), with a 20% rise in sales and a 55% jump in income from continuing operations. The book-to-bill ratio for the third quarter was 0.76, and backlog at the end of the quarter period was $27.2 million. The company attributes these lower order rates to weakness in international markets.

Operational Review - 20-APR-98

Net sales in the nine months ended March 27, 1998, rose 20%, year to year, driven by strong growth of domestic operations. Margins widened, reflecting a more favorable product mix, increased volumes, cost-reduction efforts, and a supplier discount program; operating profit soared 111%. Following a substantial increase in other expense, pretax income rose 95%. After taxes at 33.9%, versus 17.0%, income from continuing operations advanced 55%, to $5,344,000 ($0.57 a share, on 3.7% fewer shares), from $3,442,000 ($0.35). Results in the respective periods exclude a $0.04 gain on the disposal of a business segment and a loss of $0.22 a share from discontinued operations.

Stock Performance - 02-OCT-98

In the past 30 trading days, CCBL's shares have declined 16%, compared to a 7% fall in the S&P 500. Average trading volume for the past five days was 17,060 shares, compared with the 40-day moving average of 25,531 shares.

Key Stock Statistics

Dividend Rate/Share	Nil	Shareholders	700
Shs. outstg. (M)	9.7	Market cap. (B)	$0.115
Avg. daily vol. (M)	0.023	Inst. holdings	43%
Tang. Bk. Value/Share	5.34		
Beta	0.70		

Value of $10,000 invested 5 years ago: $ 16,964

Fiscal Year Ending Jun. 30

	1998	1997	1996	1995	1994	1993
Revenues (Million $)						
1Q	37.07	31.84	39.64	27.55	15.72	13.69
2Q	37.19	30.70	35.66	29.73	15.60	13.17
3Q	40.25	32.80	36.90	29.99	17.83	14.47
4Q	37.65	36.60	36.70	50.17	25.90	14.66
Yr.	152.1	131.9	148.9	137.4	75.05	55.99
Earnings Per Share ($)						
1Q	**0.20**	0.16	0.27	0.23	0.13	0.11
2Q	**0.17**	0.06	0.07	0.20	0.10	0.08
3Q	**0.20**	0.14	0.14	0.07	0.05	0.09
4Q	**0.21**	0.09	0.12	0.35	0.15	0.00
Yr.	**0.78**	0.45	0.60	0.84	0.43	0.37

Next earnings report expected: mid October

Dividend Data

No cash dividends have been paid. A two-for-one stock split was effected in 1994.

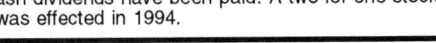

A Division of The McGraw-Hill Companies

Business Summary - 20-APR-98

For more than 40 years, this company has designed and manufactured electronic equipment used in a variety of communications networks which affect our everyday lives. C-Cor's radio frequency (RF) and fiber-optic products and services support and maintain the transmission of voice, video and data communications in such common activities as watching cable television and making a telephone call. The company is a global player, with 19% of FY 97 (Jun.) net sales generated from international operations, primarily in Canada, Asia, Europe and Latin America. Time-Warner Cable accounted for 36% of net sales in FY 97.

The company recently implemented a restructuring plan, aimed at increasing gross margins and improving operating efficiencies. In July 1997, C-Cor said it was discontinuing its digital fiber optic business, located in Fremont, CA. In addition, during FY 97, the company transferred certain manufacturing operations to Mexico, reconfigured its worldwide sales territories, and consolidated its sales force.

C-Cor's RF amplifiers, under the FlexNet series name, allow for the delivery of both analog and digital channels. Product additions in FY 97 included I-Flex, a specially designed fiber-intensive architecture. The company's AM fiber optic series includes FlexNode, developed to operate within two-way network architec-

tures. The company is also developing System 4000, which can serve cable television networks, link studios to satellites and connect schools which are geographically separated.

C-Cor's manufacturing facilities have been approved for ISO 9001 registration, a comprehensive series of requirements that include quality assurance in design, development, production, installation and servicing. This designation, it is believed, will benefit the company's strategy of competing on the basis of premium quality.

C-Cor's ability to compete successfully depends heavily on whether it can adapt to rapid changes in technology. Consequently, the company invests significantly in research and development. In FY 97 and FY 96, R&D expenditures were roughly $5.7 million and $4.9 million, respectively, primarily aimed at developing fiber optic technology, new RF products and network management capabilities.

In 1996, Congress passed the Telecommunications Act, designed to enhance competition in the industry. C-Cor believed that it would benefit from this legislation, because of its position as a supplier of key equipment to the telecommunications field.

In September 1997, directors approved the repurchase up to 500,000 common shares, following the completion in May 1997 of a December 1996 program to buy 500,000 shares.

Per Share Data ($)

(Year Ended Jun. 30)	1998	1997	1996	1995	1994	1993	1992	1991	1990	1989
Tangible Bk. Val.	5.34	4.56	5.47	4.63	3.54	3.00	2.54	2.25	2.95	2.32
Cash Flow	1.43	0.96	1.08	1.24	0.68	0.58	0.44	-0.20	0.73	0.69
Earnings	0.78	0.45	0.60	0.84	0.43	0.37	0.25	-0.39	0.64	0.60
Dividends	Nil	Nil	Nil	Nil	Nil	Nil	Nil	Nil	Nil	Nil
Payout Ratio	Nil	Nil	Nil	Nil	Nil	Nil	Nil	Nil	Nil	Nil
Prices - High	20	18³/₈	24³/₄	36¹/₂	36¹/₂	10	7³/₄	5¹/₈	7¹/₂	8³/₄
- Low	11¹/₄	8³/₄	11¹/₄	16³/₄	6³/₄	5³/₈	4¹/₄	1¹¹/₁₆	1⁵/₈	4⁷/₈
P/E Ratio - High	26	41	41	43	85	27	31	NM	12	14
- Low	14	19	19	20	16	15	17	NM	3	8

Income Statement Analysis (Million $)

	1998	1997	1996	1995	1994	1993	1992	1991	1990	1989
Revs.	152	132	149	137	75.0	56.0	52.2	32.7	60.3	53.8
Oper. Inc.	18.2	10.7	14.0	16.7	8.1	7.0	5.2	-4.5	8.9	8.3
Depr.	6.1	4.9	4.7	3.9	2.4	1.9	1.8	1.6	0.9	0.7
Int. Exp.	0.3	0.3	1.0	0.7	0.0	0.0	0.1	0.2	0.1	0.3
Pretax Inc.	10.8	5.7	8.7	12.4	6.0	5.0	3.4	-5.8	8.9	8.0
Eff. Tax Rate	32%	25%	32%	33%	33%	33%	33%	NM	38%	35%
Net Inc.	7.3	4.3	5.9	8.3	4.0	3.4	2.3	-3.5	5.5	5.2

Balance Sheet & Other Fin. Data (Million $)

	1998	1997	1996	1995	1994	1993	1992	1991	1990	1989
Cash	2.3	0.8	1.8	1.9	5.1	9.7	4.6	4.3	3.6	2.2
Curr. Assets	44.7	43.8	51.5	64.1	39.2	28.9	25.8	21.4	27.8	23.9
Total Assets	75.5	71.1	78.4	87.7	49.5	37.3	33.9	30.2	32.6	27.2
Curr. Liab.	17.4	21.0	16.0	39.7	14.2	6.8	6.9	5.8	6.8	7.7
LT Debt	5.5	6.4	7.2	2.0	0.4	0.5	0.7	0.8	0.4	0.5
Common Eqty.	50.2	41.7	53.3	44.7	34.1	29.5	25.7	23.4	25.4	19.1
Total Cap.	57.1	49.4	61.9	47.6	35.0	30.1	26.7	24.3	25.8	19.6
Cap. Exp.	8.8	5.9	8.0	15.4	4.1	1.9	0.6	1.9	1.9	1.0
Cash Flow	13.4	9.2	10.6	12.2	6.4	5.3	4.0	-1.8	6.4	5.9
Curr. Ratio	2.6	2.1	3.2	1.6	2.8	4.2	3.7	3.7	4.1	3.1
% LT Debt of Cap.	9.7	12.9	11.6	4.3	1.3	1.7	2.7	3.3	1.6	2.6
% Net Inc.of Revs.	4.8	3.2	4.0	6.0	5.4	6.1	4.4	NM	9.2	9.7
% Ret. on Assets	10.0	5.7	7.1	12.0	9.3	9.5	7.1	NM	18.1	20.2
% Ret. on Equity	15.9	9.0	12.0	20.8	12.6	12.2	9.3	NM	24.3	31.6

Data as orig. reptd.; bef. results of disc. opers. and/or spec. items. Per share data adj. for stk. divs. as of ex-div. date. Bold denotes diluted EPS (FASB 128). E-Estimated. NA-Not Available. NM-Not Meaningful. NR-Not Ranked.

Office—60 Decibel Rd., State College, PA 16801. **Tel**—(814) 238-2461. **Chrmn & Interim CEO**—R. E. Perry. **VP-Fin, Treas & Secy**—C. A. Miller. **Investor Contact**—Sally O. Thiel. **Dirs**—D. M. Cook Jr., I. N. R. Harper Jr., J. K. Hassan, A. P. Jones, J. J. Omlor, R. E. Perry, F. Rusinko Jr., J. J. Tietjen, P. L. Walker Jr. **Transfer Agent & Registrar**—American Stock Transfer & Trust Co., NYC. **Incorporated**—in Pennsylvania in 1953. **Empl**—1,200. **S&P Analyst:** Stephen J. Tekirian

C-Cube Microsystems   3380

NASDAQ Symbol **CUBE**

In S&P SmallCap 600

03-OCT-98

Industry:
Communications
Equipment

Summary: C-Cube is a leading provider of integrated circuits and software that implement international standards for the compression of digital images and video.

Quantitative Evaluations	
Outlook (1 Lowest—5 Highest) • 5	
Fair Value • 43	
Risk • **High**	
Earn./Div. Rank • **NR**	
Technical Eval. • **Bearish** since 6/98	
Rel. Strength Rank (1 Lowest—99 Highest) • 87	
Insider Activity • **Neutral**	

Recent Price • 17½
52 Wk Range • 35-14¼

Yield • Nil
12-Mo. P/E • 15.9

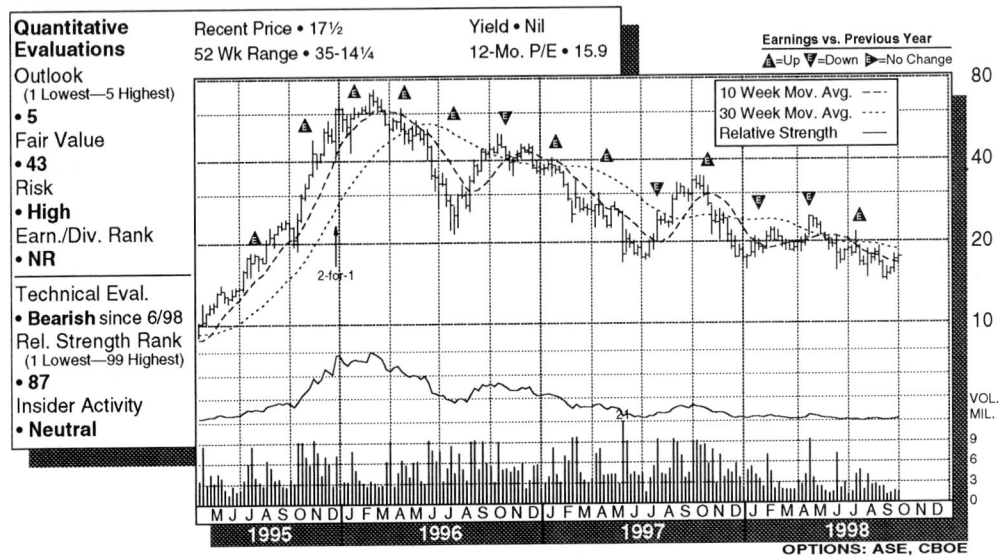

OPTIONS: ASE, CBOE

Business Profile - 24-JUL-98

Recent research and development efforts of this market leader in the digital video field, which offers highly integrated, standards-based digital video compression solutions, have been geared toward the development of chips for use in Digital Video Disk (DVD) systems, which incorporate a new format for recording data onto a compact disk. Results in 1997 were affected by the Asian economic crisis, as the Asian consumer electronic market accounted for about 55% of total sales. The majority of CUBE's 1998 second quarter revenues came from its communications business. Management believes that the communications and consumer recordable digital video markets provide the best growth opportunities for the company.

Operational Review - 24-JUL-98

Net revenues in the six months ended June 30, 1998, rose 2.8%, year to year. Margins narrowed, as operating expenses rose 11%; operating profit fell 26%. With other income, versus other expense, and after taxes at 30.0%, versus 34.1%, income was down 9.7%, to $20,847,000 ($0.52 a share), from $23,079,000 ($0.60). Results in the 1998 period exclude an extraordinary gain of $0.03 a share.

Stock Performance - 02-OCT-98

In the past 30 trading days, CUBE's shares have declined 3%, compared to a 7% fall in the S&P 500. Average trading volume for the past five days was 267,220 shares, compared with the 40-day moving average of 371,838 shares.

Key Stock Statistics

Dividend Rate/Share	Nil	Shareholders	900
Shs. outstg. (M)	37.4	Market cap. (B)	$0.654
Avg. daily vol. (M)	0.264	Inst. holdings	27%
Tang. Bk. Value/Share	5.43		
Beta	NA		

Value of $10,000 invested 5 years ago: NA

Fiscal Year Ending Dec. 31

	1998	1997	1996	1995	1994	1993
Revenues (Million $)						
1Q	87.32	94.13	68.10	17.11	8.50	5.00
2Q	82.52	71.10	72.96	21.61	10.00	5.10
3Q	—	81.72	83.18	35.32	12.31	5.70
4Q	—	90.07	95.22	50.55	14.15	7.90
Yr.	—	337.0	319.8	124.6	45.02	23.70
Earnings Per Share ($)						
1Q	**0.27**	0.41	0.38	0.10	0.02	-0.03
2Q	**0.25**	0.20	0.00	0.12	0.02	-0.01
3Q	—	0.25	-3.46	0.24	0.04	0.01
4Q	—	**0.30**	0.45	0.26	0.06	0.01
Yr.	—	**1.15**	-2.15	0.72	0.16	-0.02

Next earnings report expected: mid October

Dividend Data

No cash dividends have been paid. The company intends to retain earnings to finance its business and does not expect to pay cash dividends in the foreseeable future.

A Division of The McGraw-Hill Companies

Business Summary - 24-JUL-98

C-Cube Microsystems Inc. seeks to benefit from a continuing transition from analog to digital video formats, through use of its digital compression technology. Digital video offers a number of fundamental advantages over analog video, including the ability to be compressed in order to gain efficiencies in transmission and storage, transmitted and reproduced without perceptible image degradation, as well as random accessing and nonlinear editing capabilities. Digital video compressions has enabled the development of a significant number of applications in the consumer electronics field, including video compact disc and digital video (DVD) players.

The most significant barrier to the widespread acceptance of digital video has been the huge amount of data required to represent images and video in a digital format, making storage or transmission economically impractical. CUBE's video compression technology uses complicated mathematical algorithms operating at high speeds to detect and eliminate a substantial number of redundancies inherent in video data, thereby significantly reducing the overall amount of data needed to be retained without affecting perceived image quality.

The company has focused on providing highly integrated, standards-based, programmable compression solutions that are cost-effective and deliver high image quality for a broad range of mass-market applications. It offers a complete range of video compression solutions, including encoders, decoders and codecs and development systems that are fully compatible.

CUBE is a world leader in the supply of MPEG-1 decoders which are used in VideoCD products. The company also produces MPEG-1 and MPEG-2 encoders, which allow for data compression, and are used to provide content for the VideoCD market. CUBE's products are also used for a variety of other applications, including digital camcorders, video conferencing equipment, color laser printers, direct broadcast satellite receivers and telephone distribution systems.

The company believes that the introduction of new products in target markets is essential to its growth. R&D spending in 1997 totaled $64.2 million (19% of sales), up from $44.2 million (14%) in 1996.

In August 1996, CUBE acquired DiviCom Inc., in exchange for $65.7 million in cash and about 2.3 million common shares. A related $131 million charge for acquired in-process technology was recorded in 1996. In August 1997, the company unveiled its DVx digital video architecture, providing a cost-effective platform for use in PC and consumer electronic applications.

Per Share Data ($)

(Year Ended Dec. 31)	1997	1996	1995	1994	1993	1992	1991	1990	1989	1988
Tangible Bk. Val.	4.02	1.96	2.55	1.67	1.52	NA	NA	NA	NA	NA
Cash Flow	1.48	-1.93	0.81	0.23	0.04	NA	NA	NA	NA	NA
Earnings	1.15	-2.15	0.72	0.16	-0.02	NA	NA	NA	NA	NA
Dividends	Nil	Nil	Nil	Nil	Nil	Nil	Nil	Nil	Nil	Nil
Payout Ratio	Nil	Nil	Nil	Nil	Nil	Nil	Nil	Nil	Nil	Nil
Prices - High	41	73½	65	12⅜	NA	NA	NA	NA	NA	NA
- Low	15¾	21½	7½	7½	NA	NA	NA	NA	NA	NA
P/E Ratio - High	36	NM	90	77	NM	NM	NM	NM	NM	NM
- Low	14	NM	10	47	NM	NM	NM	NM	NM	NM

Income Statement Analysis (Million $)

	1997	1996	1995	1994	1993	1992	1991	1990	1989	1988
Revs.	337	320	125	45.0	23.7	NA	NA	NA	NA	NA
Oper. Inc.	86.1	32.0	31.0	6.5	1.3	NA	NA	NA	NA	NA
Depr.	17.4	7.7	3.1	2.1	1.4	NA	NA	NA	NA	NA
Int. Exp.	6.0	6.0	1.6	NA	0.6	NA	NA	NA	NA	NA
Pretax Inc.	67.0	-39.8	29.8	5.1	-0.4	NA	NA	NA	NA	NA
Eff. Tax Rate	34%	NM	16%	1.40%	NM	NM	NM	NM	NM	NM
Net Inc.	44.3	-73.0	24.9	5.0	-0.5	NA	NA	NA	NA	NA

Balance Sheet & Other Fin. Data (Million $)

	1997	1996	1995	1994	1993	1992	1991	1990	1989	1988
Cash	145	82.0	144	43.8	39.2	NA	NA	NA	NA	NA
Curr. Assets	248	193	186	61.0	NA	NA	NA	NA	NA	NA
Total Assets	304	280	204	67.9	56.6	NA	NA	NA	NA	NA
Curr. Liab.	40.0	68.2	27.6	12.3	NA	NA	NA	NA	NA	NA
LT Debt	87.5	87.7	88.0	2.1	2.6	NA	NA	NA	NA	NA
Common Eqty.	175	119	87.5	53.5	43.1	NA	NA	NA	NA	NA
Total Cap.	264	211	176	55.6	45.7	NA	NA	NA	NA	NA
Cap. Exp.	13.6	17.1	5.4	1.5	1.5	NA	NA	NA	NA	NA
Cash Flow	61.7	-65.3	27.9	7.1	1.0	NA	NA	NA	NA	NA
Curr. Ratio	6.2	2.8	14.8	5.0	NA	NA	NA	NA	NA	NA
% LT Debt of Cap.	33.2	41.6	50.0	3.7	5.7	NA	NA	NA	NA	NA
% Net Inc.of Revs.	13.2	NM	19.9	11.1	NM	NM	NM	NM	NM	NM
% Ret. on Assets	15.2	NM	18.3	10.1	NM	NM	NM	NM	NM	NM
% Ret. on Equity	30.2	NM	17.6	14.9	NM	NM	NM	NM	NM	NM

Data as orig. reptd.; bef. results of disc. opers. and/or spec. items. Per share data adj. for stk. divs. as of ex-div. date. Bold denotes diluted EPS (FASB 128). E-Estimated. NA-Not Available. NM-Not Meaningful. NR-Not Ranked.

Office—1778 McCarthy Blvd., Milpitas, CA 95035. **Tel**—(408) 944-6300. **Website**—http://www.c-cube.com **Chrmn**—D. T. Valentine. **Pres & CEO**—A. A. Balkanski. **VP-Fin, CFO, Secy & Investor Contact**—W. Walczykowski. **Dirs**—A. A. Balkanski, B. S. Futa, D. McKinney, G. Reyes, T. J. Rodgers, D. T. Valentine. **Transfer Agent & Registrar**—First National Bank of Boston. **Incorporated**—in California in 1988; reincorporated in Delaware in 1994. **Empl**— 750. **S&P Analyst:** Mark Cavallone

STANDARD &POOR'S
STOCK REPORTS

CDI Corp.

409

NYSE Symbol **CDI**

In S&P SmallCap 600

03-OCT-98 **Industry:** Services (Employment)

Summary: CDI provides technical and engineering services and temporary office support and executive recruitment services.

Quantitative Evaluations

Outlook
(1 Lowest—5 Highest)
• **5**

Fair Value
• **39⅛**

Risk
• **Average**

Earn./Div. Rank
• **B**

Technical Eval.
• **Bullish** since 5/98

Rel. Strength Rank
(1 Lowest—99 Highest)
• **48**

Insider Activity
• **Neutral**

Recent Price • 22½
52 Wk Range • 47⅞-21⅞

Yield • Nil
12-Mo. P/E • 12.8

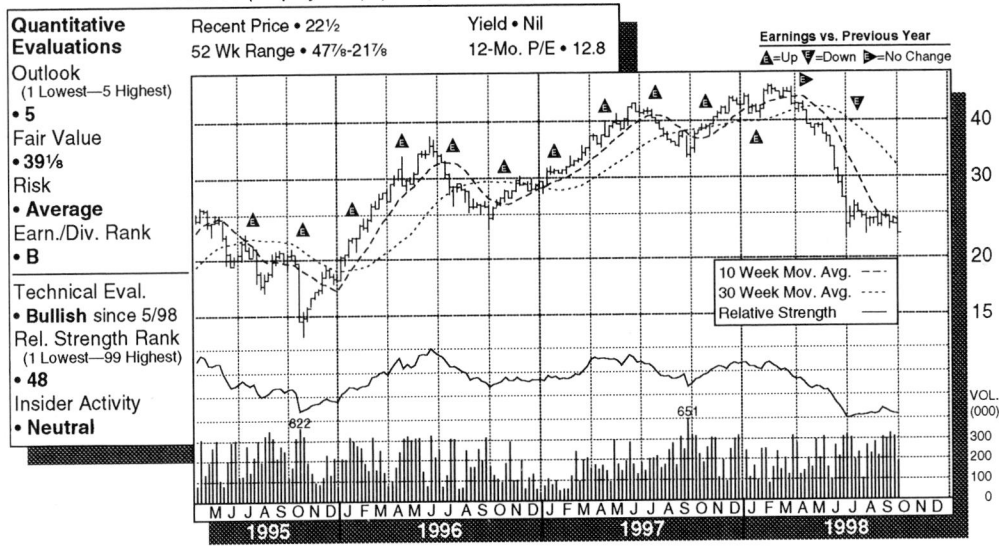

Earnings vs. Previous Year
▲=Up ▼=Down ▶=No Change

10 Week Mov. Avg. ---
30 Week Mov. Avg. ....
Relative Strength ——

Business Profile - 28-SEP-98

Earnings growth in recent years has been aided by a trend toward outsourcing. In response, CDI has broadened its services to include managed staffing and information systems staffing services. As part of a plan to position itself for sustainable growth, the company is designing an incentive program to accelerate cross-selling of its services across business lines, and is implementing strategic initiatives at its management recruiting and temporary services units. CDI is also restructuring its technical services business, in order to generate long-term growth from a broader customer base served by more strategically focused business unit. In late 1997, CDI sold its aircraft maintenance staffing business to a group of private investors. A stock buyback plan for up to 5% of the shares outstanding was recently authorized.

Operational Review - 28-SEP-98

Revenues from continuing operations in the first half of 1998 rose 3.9%, year to year, as higher revenues in information technology, temporary services and management recruiters outweighed lower technical services revenues. Gross margins narrowed, on increased cost of services. Restructuring charges related to the technical services operation offset lower interest expense; pretax income declined 13%. After taxes at 39.0%, versus 40.1%, income from continuing operations was down 11%, to $20,078,000 ($1.01 a share), from $22,656,000 ($1.14). Results include nonrecurring charges of $0.07 a share in the 1998 period.

Stock Performance - 02-OCT-98

In the past 30 trading days, CDI's shares have declined 7%, compared to a 7% fall in the S&P 500. Average trading volume for the past five days was 36,480 shares, compared with the 40-day moving average of 65,546 shares.

Key Stock Statistics

Dividend Rate/Share	Nil	Shareholders	600
Shs. outstg. (M)	19.9	Market cap. (B)	$0.448
Avg. daily vol. (M)	0.076	Inst. holdings	39%
Tang. Bk. Value/Share	9.97		
Beta	0.62		

Value of $10,000 invested 5 years ago: $ 26,865

Fiscal Year Ending Dec. 31

	1998	1997	1996	1995	1994	1993
Revenues (Million $)						
1Q	379.0	360.5	330.8	292.4	249.2	217.5
2Q	388.9	378.1	338.9	312.5	264.9	233.5
3Q	—	383.1	353.8	331.5	288.7	232.7
4Q	—	375.1	351.4	334.0	294.8	237.6
Yr.	—	1,497	1,375	1,270	1,098	921.3
Earnings Per Share ($)						
1Q	0.54	0.54	0.44	0.32	0.20	0.05
2Q	0.47	0.60	0.53	0.40	0.23	0.08
3Q	—	0.69	0.65	0.45	0.34	0.15
4Q	—	0.53	0.52	0.38	0.37	0.12
Yr.	—	2.30	2.14	1.56	1.13	0.40

Next earnings report expected: late October

Dividend Data

No cash dividends have been paid since 1970.

A Division of The McGraw-Hill Companies

STANDARD
&POOR'S
STOCK REPORTS

CDI Corp.

409

03-OCT-98

Business Summary - 28-SEP-98

CDI Corporation (CDI) is a leading provider of technical and temporary personnel and is a top management recruiter. The Technical Services division accounted for 62% of revenues in 1997; Information Technology 19%; Temporary Services (Todays Temporary) 13%; and Management Recruitment 6%. During 1997, CDI completed the divestiture of two automotive-related divisions.

Technical Services, believed to be the largest operation of its kind in the U.S., provides staffing, outsourcing, and consulting services in the fields of engineering, technical and other fields. Customers use CDI for expansion programs, to staff special projects, and to meet peak period personnel needs. Services include project planning and feasibility studies, conceptual engineering, detail engineering and design, procurement and project management. The division serves about 3,000 customers, mainly in the aircraft, aerospace, automotive, chemicals, construction, electronics, industrial equipment, marine, power/energy, and telecommunications fields.

The Information Technology Services segment, formerly part of the the technical services segment, provides staffing and outsourcing services in the information technology field. In staffing, the division manages a customer's entire information technology contract staffing needs. In outsourcing, it focuses on application de-velopment and maintenance, distributed systems management, and help desk services. In 1997, one company provided 30% of the division's revenues.

The Temporary Services segment offers clerical, secretarial, office support, legal, financial staffing, and other temporary personnel; the division, with about 11,000 customers, operates through a network of 120 offices in the U.S. and Canada. In September 1998, CDI acquired five affiliated Todays franchise offices in the Tampa Bay area.

Management Recruiters searches for and recruits management, technical, sales, clerical, and other personnel for permanent employment positions in numerous fields including accounting, finance, administrative, information technology, managerial, personnel, production, research and development, sales, supervision, and technical. Management Recruiters has 677 franchised offices and 45 company-owned offices throughout North America, providing services to both large and small employers.

Under a plan implemented in 1997, growth strategies include designing an incentive program to accelerate cross-selling CDI's services across its core businesses; implementing several initiatives at Management Recruiters International and Todays Temporary to position these businesses for increased revenues and profitability; winning new contracts with existing customers; and expanding into the financial and banking markets with a recent agreement with the Bank of Boston.

Per Share Data ($)

(Year Ended Dec. 31)	1997	1996	1995	1994	1993	1992	1991	1990	1989	1988
Tangible Bk. Val.	10.02	8.14	6.50	5.93	4.70	4.17	4.08	4.85	4.38	3.79
Cash Flow	2.96	2.70	2.17	1.85	1.17	0.95	0.45	1.36	1.66	1.37
Earnings	2.36	2.14	1.55	1.13	0.40	0.17	-0.39	0.61	1.05	0.84
Dividends	Nil	Nil	Nil	Nil	Nil	Nil	Nil	Nil	Nil	Nil
Payout Ratio	Nil	Nil	Nil	Nil	Nil	Nil	Nil	Nil	Nil	Nil
Prices - High	45³/₄	37¹/₄	26⁵/₈	19⁷/₈	13¹/₈	10³/₈	9³/₄	15⁵/₈	18¹/₂	10¹/₄
- Low	27³/₄	18	13¹/₂	10¹/₄	6⁷/₈	6	5³/₄	5⁵/₈	9⁷/₈	5¹/₄
P/E Ratio - High	19	17	17	18	33	61	NM	26	18	12
- Low	12	8	9	9	17	35	NM	9	9	6

Income Statement Analysis (Million $)

	1997	1996	1995	1994	1993	1992	1991	1990	1989	1988
Revs.	1,497	1,375	1,270	1,098	921	855	768	921	887	734
Oper. Inc.	91.3	84.7	68.3	55.1	31.7	25.2	16.6	42.8	52.9	40.3
Depr.	12.1	11.2	12.4	14.2	15.3	15.2	16.6	14.7	12.0	10.1
Int. Exp.	2.3	3.5	4.5	4.1	3.7	4.1	4.7	7.7	6.7	4.3
Pretax Inc.	76.8	70.2	51.4	36.8	12.6	5.9	-9.2	20.3	34.1	25.8
Eff. Tax Rate	37%	39%	40%	39%	38%	43%	NM	40%	41%	38%
Net Inc.	46.9	42.5	30.7	22.4	7.8	3.4	-7.6	12.0	20.7	16.0

Balance Sheet & Other Fin. Data (Million $)

	1997	1996	1995	1994	1993	1992	1991	1990	1989	1988
Cash	7.0	6.1	4.5	5.2	20.4	2.5	3.3	4.3	4.0	2.6
Curr. Assets	290	288	272	224	193	172	157	174	195	151
Total Assets	349	340	329	298	267	244	228	255	274	203
Curr. Liab.	121	107	110	96.2	85.1	56.8	49.5	73.0	71.7	58.9
LT Debt	Nil	48.9	67.9	58.8	62.0	72.2	67.1	61.2	90.9	50.5
Common Eqty.	226	17.0	145	139	117	109	105	113	102	82.0
Total Cap.	217	226	213	198	179	185	176	179	199	141
Cap. Exp.	11.9	13.5	16.7	14.0	11.2	8.8	4.1	17.3	24.6	12.1
Cash Flow	59.1	53.7	43.1	36.5	23.2	18.7	8.9	26.8	32.7	26.2
Curr. Ratio	2.4	2.7	2.5	2.3	2.3	3.0	3.2	2.4	2.7	2.6
% LT Debt of Cap.	NM	21.6	31.8	29.7	34.7	39.0	38.1	34.1	45.6	35.7
% Net Inc.of Revs.	3.1	3.1	2.4	2.0	0.8	0.4	NM	1.3	2.3	2.2
% Ret. on Assets	13.6	12.8	10.0	7.9	3.1	1.5	NM	4.6	8.7	8.3
% Ret. on Equity	22.9	26.5	21.6	17.5	7.0	3.2	NM	11.2	22.5	22.3

Data as orig. reptd.; bef. results of disc. opers. and/or spec. items. Per share data adj. for stk. divs. as of ex-div. date. Bold denotes diluted EPS (FASB 128). E-Estimated. NA-Not Available. NM-Not Meaningful. NR-Not Ranked.

Office—1717 Arch St., 35th Fl., Philadelphia, PA 19103-2768. **Tel**—(215) 569-2200. **Fax**—(215) 496-0799. **Website**—www.cdicorp.com **Pres & CEO**—M. Wienick. **EVP & CFO**—J. D. Sanford. **EVP & COO**—R. J. Mannarino. **SVP & Secy**—J. R. Seiders. **Dirs**—W. E. Blankley, J. M. Coleman, W. R. Garrison, K. H. Harrell, L. C. Karlson, A. M. Levantin, A. B. Miller, M. Wienick, B. J. Winokur. **Transfer Agent & Registrar**—ChaseMellon Shareholder Services, Ridgefield Park, NJ. **Incorporated**—in Pennsylvania in 1950. **Empl**—2,000. **S&P Analyst**: S.S.

03-OCT-98   Industry:
Restaurants

Summary: This family restaurant/entertainment center company operates or franchises over 300 Chuck E. Cheese's restaurants in 44 states.

Quantitative Evaluations	
Outlook (1 Lowest—5 Highest)	• **4**
Fair Value	• **27½**
Risk	• **Average**
Earn./Div. Rank	• **B-**
Technical Eval.	• **NA**
Rel. Strength Rank (1 Lowest—99 Highest)	• **30**
Insider Activity	• **Neutral**

Recent Price • 20¼   Yield • Nil
52 Wk Range • 41⅛-17⅜   12-Mo. P/E • 12.5

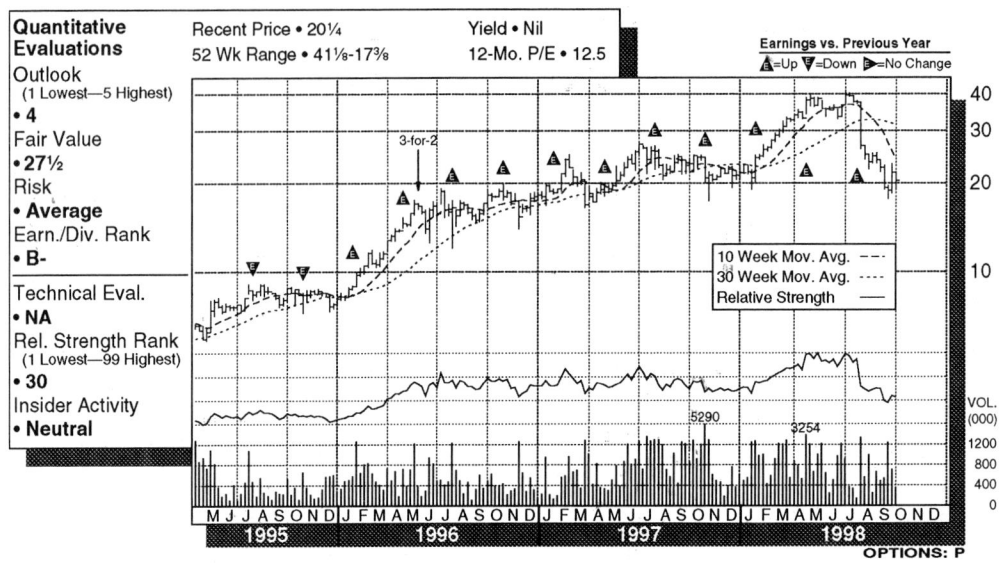

Earnings vs. Previous Year
▲=Up ▼=Down ▶=No Change

10 Week Mov. Avg. — —
30 Week Mov. Avg. - - -
Relative Strength —

3-for-2

5290   3254

VOL. (000)

OPTIONS: P

Business Profile - 24-AUG-98

In July 1998, the company changed its name from ShowBiz Pizza Time (SHBZ) to CEC Entertainment, and began trading on the NYSE with the ticker symbol CEC. The company has completed upgrades of 107 restaurants, with another 100 to 115 locations scheduled for upgrade in 1998. In addition, CEC expects to increase the number of company-owned restaurants by 18 to 22 restaurants during 1998. In July 1998, directors authorized the repurchase of up to $15 million of CEC common stock. Under a previous buyback plan, the company purchased shares at a total cost of $20 million.

Operational Review - 24-AUG-98

Revenues in the six months ended July 5, 1998, rose 10%, year to year, aided by a 5.1% increase in same-store sales. Margins widened, reflecting well-controlled direct costs and SG&A expenditures; operating income grew 14%. Following a decline in interest expense, pretax income was up 33%. After taxes at 38.7%, versus 40.5%, net income advanced 37%, to $19,024,000 ($1.01 a share), from $13,838,000 ($0.72).

Stock Performance - 02-OCT-98

In the past 30 trading days, CEC's shares have declined 18%, compared to a 7% fall in the S&P 500. Average trading volume for the past five days was 67,880 shares, compared with the 40-day moving average of 143,328 shares.

Key Stock Statistics

Dividend Rate/Share	Nil	Shareholders	4,200
Shs. outstg. (M)	18.4	Market cap. (B)	$0.373
Avg. daily vol. (M)	0.165	Inst. holdings	85%
Tang. Bk. Value/Share	9.79		
Beta	1.10		

Value of $10,000 invested 5 years ago: $ 9,094

Fiscal Year Ending Dec. 31

	1998	1997	1996	1995	1994	1993
Revenues (Million $)						
1Q	105.0	91.59	78.45	72.75	76.37	73.38
2Q	88.90	84.03	69.85	62.64	64.02	64.67
3Q	—	85.60	74.78	66.98	68.29	71.64
4Q	—	89.04	70.91	61.41	59.15	62.31
Yr.	—	350.3	292.9	263.8	267.8	272.0
Earnings Per Share ($)						
1Q	0.63	0.42	0.20	0.14	0.10	0.32
2Q	0.39	0.31	0.12	-0.07	0.07	0.09
3Q	—	0.32	0.19	Nil	0.05	0.19
4Q	—	0.30	0.12	-0.08	-0.28	-0.03
Yr.	—	1.34	0.70	-0.01	0.02	0.57

Next earnings report expected: mid October

Dividend Data

No cash dividends have been paid. A shareholder rights plan was adopted in 1997. A three-for-two common stock split was effected in May 1996.

A Division of The McGraw-Hill Companies

STANDARD
&POOR'S
STOCK REPORTS

CEC Entertainment, Inc.

5214W

03-OCT-98

Business Summary - 24-AUG-98

Mention the name Chuck E. Cheese to kids just about anywhere in the U.S. and they'll jump up and down and beg to be taken there for food and fun. The popular restaurant chain is operated by CEC Entertainment (formerly ShowBiz Pizza Time), which owns or franchises approximately 313 Chuck E. Cheese restaurants in 44 states. In addition to pizza, salads, sandwiches and desserts, the combo restaurant/entertainment centers offer family-oriented games, rides, arcade activities, computer-controlled robots, and musical and comic entertainment. The restaurants, which cater to children ages two to 12, are especially popular for birthday parties.

The company opened its first Chuck E. Cheese Restaurant in March 1980. The restaurants, typically located in shopping centers or in free-standing buildings nearby, are big, ranging in size from 8,000 to 14,000 sq. ft.; 40% of the space is devoted to the family-oriented playroom. The fun room includes coin and token operated attractions, arcade-style games, kiddie rides, video games, skill oriented games, and other attractions such as "Sky Tubes" suspended from or reaching to the ceiling.

CEC reported record revenues and earnings for 1997. Revenues grew 19%, to $350.3 million, aided by a 10.7% increase in comparable store sales, the acquisi-

tion of new restaurants and higher average annual sales per store. With Increased menu prices and lower cheese costs, margins improved significantly, and net income climbed 93%, to $25.5 million ($1.37 a share), from $13.2 million ($0.71).

Strategies outlined by the company for 1998 include a number of key components, such as expansions of the customer areas at 15 to 20 restaurants by an average 1,000 to 4,000 sq. ft. per store, and the upgrade of as many as 120 locations under a Phase II remodeling program featuring an enhanced game package. An overall increase in the number of locations has begun, with the acquisition by the company of 19 restaurants from its largest franchisee in late 1996, the opening of two new restaurants in 1997, and the opening or acquisition of another 8 Chuck E. Cheese restaurants in the first quarter of 1998. CEC anticipated adding 18 to 22 stores in total in 1998 through acquisitions or new store openings.

Beyond these plans, CEC is looking forward to further improvement of the entertainment value of its playrooms, potential development of a smaller market prototype, and international expansion with quality franchise partners. In September 1997, directors authorized the repurchase of up to $20 million of common stock. In July 1998, an additional $15 million in common stock was authorized for repurchase.

Per Share Data ($)

(Year Ended Dec. 31)	1997	1996	1995	1994	1993	1992	1991	1990	1989	1988
Tangible Bk. Val.	8.62	7.68	6.90	6.82	6.88	6.47	5.62	5.01	NA	NA
Cash Flow	2.70	2.06	1.28	1.45	1.72	1.69	1.10	0.87	NA	NA
Earnings	1.34	0.70	-0.01	0.02	0.57	0.74	0.85	0.41	NA	NA
Dividends	Nil	Nil	Nil	Nil	Nil	Nil	Nil	Nil	Nil	Nil
Payout Ratio	Nil	Nil	Nil	Nil	Nil	Nil	Nil	Nil	Nil	Nil
Prices - High	27³/₈	20	9¹/₈	10¹/₄	23⁵/₈	23¹/₈	17	11⁵/₈	NA	NA
- Low	16¹/₂	8	4⁷/₈	4⁷/₈	8¹/₄	13¹/₄	6³/₈	3¹/₂	NA	NA
P/E Ratio - High	20	29	NM	NM	41	31	31	20	NA	NA
- Low	12	11	NM	NM	14	18	12	9	NA	NA

Income Statement Analysis (Million $)

	1997	1996	1995	1994	1993	1992	1991	1990	1989	1988
Revs.	349	293	263	268	272	253	208	182	NA	NA
Oper. Inc.	69.9	50.0	25.9	27.7	42.4	46.4	37.3	30.4	NA	NA
Depr.	25.5	25.1	23.2	26.0	23.1	19.2	16.1	13.1	NA	NA
Int. Exp.	2.9	3.5	3.1	1.9	0.8	NA	NA	NA	NA	NA
Pretax Inc.	42.7	22.2	0.4	3.1	18.2	25.2	19.0	13.9	NA	NA
Eff. Tax Rate	40%	41%	83%	78%	35%	39%	5.50%	4.90%	NA	NA
Net Inc.	25.5	13.2	0.1	0.7	11.9	15.5	17.9	13.2	NA	NA

Balance Sheet & Other Fin. Data (Million $)

	1997	1996	1995	1994	1993	1992	1991	1990	1989	1988
Cash	7.3	3.4	5.6	2.4	4.5	NA	NA	NA	NA	NA
Curr. Assets	25.3	27.6	20.0	15.9	20.4	NA	NA	NA	NA	NA
Total Assets	226	217	199	188	194	173	158	NA	NA	NA
Curr. Liab.	39.0	33.6	29.9	36.6	24.8	NA	NA	NA	NA	NA
LT Debt	23.8	34.7	35.8	19.9	26.8	27.7	21.4	NA	NA	NA
Common Eqty.	156	141	128	126	137	132	116	NA	NA	NA
Total Cap.	182	178	167	148	166	150	137	NA	NA	NA
Cap. Exp.	48.5	51.7	28.3	29.4	44.6	33.9	25.1	21.5	NA	NA
Cash Flow	50.8	38.1	23.0	26.5	34.7	34.5	34.0	26.3	NA	NA
Curr. Ratio	0.6	0.8	0.7	0.4	0.8	NA	NA	NA	NA	NA
% LT Debt of Cap.	13.1	19.5	21.4	13.4	16.2	11.8	15.6	NA	NA	NA
% Net Inc.of Revs.	7.3	4.5	NM	0.3	4.4	6.1	8.6	7.2	NA	NA
% Ret. on Assets	11.5	6.4	NM	0.4	6.1	8.4	7.6	NA	NA	NA
% Ret. on Equity	17.0	9.8	NM	0.3	8.5	12.3	10.5	NA	NA	NA

Data as orig. reptd.; bef. results of disc. opers. and/or spec. items. Per share data adj. for stk. divs. as of ex-div. date. Bold denotes diluted EPS (FASB 128). E-Estimated. NA-Not Available. NM-Not Meaningful. NR-Not Ranked.

Office—4441 West Airport Freeway, P. O. Box 152077, Irving, TX 75015. **Tel**—(214) 258-8507. **Website**—http://www.chuckecheese.com **Chrmn & CEO**—R. M. Frank. **Pres**—M. H. Magusiak. **EVP, CFO & Treas**—L. Page. **Dirs**—R. M. Frank, M. H. Magusiak, L. P. Neeb, C. I. Pharr. **Transfer Agent & Registrar**—First National Bank of Boston, Canton, MA. **Incorporated**—in Kansas in 1980. **Empl**— 13,600. **S&P Analyst:** Stephen J. Tekirian

CKE Restaurants   410T

NYSE Symbol **CKR**

In S&P SmallCap 600

03-OCT-98

Industry: Restaurants

Summary: This restaurant company owns, franchises or licenses more than 700 Carl's Jr. fast-service units, more than 2,900 Hardee's, and more than 200 restaurants under other brands.

Quantitative Evaluations

Outlook
(1 Lowest—5 Highest)
• **5**

Fair Value
• **49¾**

Risk
• **Average**

Earn./Div. Rank
• **B**

Technical Eval.
• **Bearish** since 8/98

Rel. Strength Rank
(1 Lowest—99 Highest)
• **29**

Insider Activity
• **Neutral**

Recent Price • 27

52 Wk Range • 46¼-26

Yield • 0.3%

12-Mo. P/E • 18.4

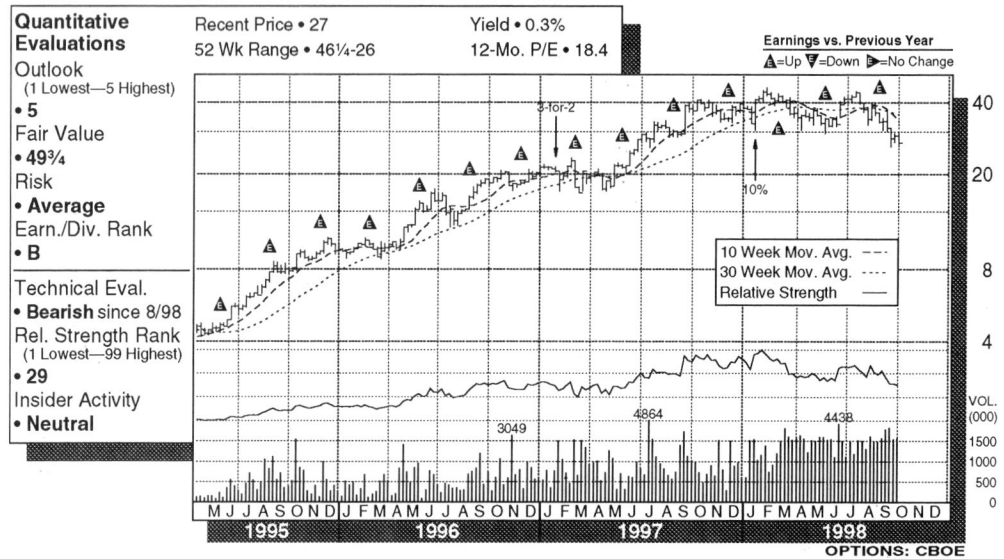

Earnings vs. Previous Year
▲=Up ▼=Down ▶=No Change

10 Week Mov. Avg. ─ ─
30 Week Mov. Avg. ┈┈┈
Relative Strength ──

OPTIONS: CBOE

Business Profile - 17-JUN-98

First quarter FY 99 (Jan.) results benefited from the April 1998 acquisition of 557 Hardee's restaurants from Advantica Restaurant Group, Inc. for $380.8 million and the assumption of $45.6 million in capital lease obligations. With ownership of just under 50% of the restaurants in the Hardee's system, CKR believes that it is in a better position to promote a consistent image and increase customer satisfaction. In order to boost sales, the company recently launched a new advertising program urging fast food consumers to "go all out" when deciding where to eat.

Operational Review - 17-JUN-98

Total revenues in the 16 weeks ended May 18, 1998, advanced 124%, year to year, reflecting the inclusion of Hardee's restaurants acquired from Advantica Restaurant Group, Inc. and Hardee's Food Systems, Inc. Margins benefited from lower relative occupancy and other operating expenses, and a smaller increase in franchise expenses than the rise in franchise revenues; operating profit climbed 148%. After a significant jump in interest expense, pretax income was up 114%. After taxes at 39.9%, versus 40.1%, net income climbed 115%, to $22,732,000 ($0.47 a share, on 34% more shares), from $10,586,000 ($0.28, as adjusted).

Stock Performance - 02-OCT-98

In the past 30 trading days, CKR's shares have declined 25%, compared to a 7% fall in the S&P 500. Average trading volume for the past five days was 449,160 shares, compared with the 40-day moving average of 511,710 shares.

Key Stock Statistics

Dividend Rate/Share	0.08	Shareholders	1,800
Shs. outstg. (M)	47.1	Market cap. (B)	$ 1.3
Avg. daily vol. (M)	0.600	Inst. holdings	82%
Tang. Bk. Value/Share	7.58		
Beta	1.21		

Value of $10,000 invested 5 years ago: $ 54,224

Fiscal Year Ending Jan. 31

	1999	1998	1997	1996	1995	1994
Revenues (Million $)						
1Q	528.2	235.4	152.9	137.6	135.0	139.9
2Q	474.8	242.1	128.1	108.0	105.3	108.2
3Q	—	347.5	162.3	113.1	103.8	106.4
4Q	—	324.8	170.7	106.7	99.6	105.8
Yr.	—	1,150	614.1	465.4	443.8	460.4
Earnings Per Share ($)						
1Q	**0.47**	**0.28**	0.17	0.07	0.02	0.03
2Q	**0.46**	**0.25**	0.16	0.09	0.03	0.08
3Q	—	**0.27**	0.17	0.10	0.01	0.05
4Q	—	**0.26**	0.16	0.10	-0.02	-0.01
Yr.	—	**1.07**	0.66	0.35	0.04	0.15

Next earnings report expected: early December

Dividend Data (Dividends have been paid since 1988.)

Amount ($)	Date Decl.	Ex-Div. Date	Stock of Record	Payment Date
0.040	Sep. 16	Oct. 01	Oct. 03	Oct. 31 '97
10%	Jan. 08	Jan. 15	Jan. 20	Feb. 04 '98
0.040	Apr. 02	Apr. 13	Apr. 15	Apr. 30 '98
0.040	Sep. 23	Oct. 02	Oct. 06	Oct. 30 '98

A Division of The McGraw-Hill Companies

CKE Restaurants, Inc.

Business Summary - 17-JUN-98

CKE Restaurants, Inc is a leading U.S. owner, operator and franchisor of quick-service restaurants. As of mid-June 1998, the company operated 732 Carl's Jr. quick-service restaurants, including 137 Carl's Jr./Green Burrito dual-brand locations, primarily located in California, Nevada, Oregon, Arizona and Mexico; 2,927 Hardee's quick-service restaurants in 39 states and 10 foreign countries, including 99 Carl's Jr./Hardee's dual-brand locations; 110 Taco Bueno quick-service restaurants in Texas and Oklahoma; 28 Rally's quick-service restaurants in California and Arizona; 82 JB's restaurants; and six Galaxy Diners.

Carl's Jr. was founded in 1956. Based on domestic system-wide sales, it is the seventh largest U.S. quick-service hamburger restaurant chain. Restaurants are primarily located on the West Coast, with a leading market presence in California. The chain's menu features several charbroiled hamburgers, chicken sandwiches, steak sandwiches, and other items. CKE believes that Carl's Jr. maintains a strong price-value image with its customers because its menu items are generally made-to-order, meet exacting quality standards, offer generous portions, and have a strong reputation for quality and taste.

Hardee's, founded in 1961, was acquired by the company in July 1997; based on domestic system-wide sales, it is the fourth largest U.S. quick-service hamburger chain. The restaurants have a leading market presence in the Southeast and Midwest. Generating 30% of overall sales, the chain's strength is its breakfast menu which features made-from-scratch biscuits, biscuit breakfast sandwiches and other items such as hash browns and breakfast platters. The lunch and dinner menu consists of hamburgers and fried chicken. To improve the Hardee's menu, CKE has streamlined its product offerings, and is in the process of adding Carl's Jr. lunch and dinner menu items in selected markets to complement the strong Hardee's breakfast offerings.

The Taco Bueno concept is a quick-service chain of Mexican restaurants located in Texas and Oklahoma. The chain seeks to differentiate itself from its main competitors by offering a diverse menu that features generous portions of freshly prepared, high quality food items. Together with its signature menu items such as MexiDips & Chips and Bueno Chilada Platter, the chain also offers typical Mexican quick-service items such as burritos, tacos, tostadas, and combination meals.

Per Share Data ($) (Year Ended Jan. 31)	1998	1997	1996	1995	1994	1993	1992	1991	1990	1989
Tangible Bk. Val.	8.66	5.88	3.31	2.94	2.99	2.84	3.03	2.65	2.25	2.10
Cash Flow	2.13	1.47	1.05	0.78	0.90	0.75	1.32	1.28	0.90	1.13
Earnings	1.07	0.66	0.36	0.04	0.15	-0.10	0.44	0.44	0.18	0.59
Dividends	0.07	0.05	0.05	0.05	0.05	0.05	0.05	0.05	0.05	0.04
Payout Ratio	7%	7%	14%	114%	33%	NM	11%	11%	26%	6%
Cal. Yrs.	1997	1996	1995	1994	1993	1992	1991	1990	1989	1988
Prices - High	41 1/4	22	10 7/8	8 3/4	6 1/2	6 3/4	6	7 3/4	10 3/4	7 7/8
- Low	16 3/4	8 3/4	3 7/8	4	4 1/8	4 1/8	3 3/8	3 3/8	6 7/8	4
P/E Ratio - High	39	33	31	NM	44	NM	14	18	59	13
- Low	16	13	11	NM	28	NM	8	8	37	7
Income Statement Analysis (Million $)										
Revs.	1,150	614	465	444	460	503	532	520	510	444
Oper. Inc.	133	69.1	47.1	31.4	38.0	29.0	44.5	55.8	53.3	52.4
Depr.	46.4	73.6	21.4	22.8	22.8	25.2	26.6	25.3	22.3	19.2
Int. Exp.	16.9	9.9	10.0	9.2	10.4	13.7	16.9	18.7	19.3	15.7
Pretax Inc.	76.6	36.7	18.0	2.4	6.3	-7.3	18.9	18.8	7.5	32.0
Eff. Tax Rate	39%	39%	39%	47%	29%	NM	31%	31%	26%	35%
Net Inc.	46.8	22.3	11.0	1.3	4.4	-3.1	13.0	13.0	5.6	20.8
Balance Sheet & Other Fin. Data (Million $)										
Cash	30.4	39.8	25.9	18.2	32.9	44.4	36.7	31.6	34.6	34.7
Curr. Assets	92.2	72.9	57.0	57.0	69.0	91.0	84.0	81.0	82.0	72.0
Total Assets	957	401	247	244	242	269	293	305	307	265
Curr. Liab.	176	83.9	61.0	72.0	67.0	91.0	92.0	105	110	95.0
LT Debt	196	81.9	71.0	70.0	63.0	80.0	102	117	125	109
Common Eqty.	499	215	101	88.0	92.0	85.0	90.0	79.0	67.0	61.0
Total Cap.	695	297	172	158	155	165	192	196	192	171
Cap. Exp.	89.2	47.9	27.0	40.0	22.0	12.9	31.6	34.1	45.4	49.5
Cash Flow	93.2	49.4	32.0	24.0	27.3	22.1	39.6	38.3	27.8	39.9
Curr. Ratio	0.5	0.9	0.9	0.8	1.0	1.0	0.9	0.8	0.7	0.8
% LT Debt of Cap.	28.2	27.6	41.3	44.1	40.7	48.6	53.2	59.8	65.3	64.1
% Net Inc.of Revs.	4.1	3.7	2.4	0.3	1.0	NM	2.5	2.5	1.1	4.7
% Ret. on Assets	6.9	6.9	4.5	0.5	1.7	NM	4.4	4.2	1.9	8.7
% Ret. on Equity	13.1	14.2	11.6	1.4	4.9	NM	15.5	17.9	8.6	28.6

Data as orig. reptd.; bef. results of disc. opers. and/or spec. items. Per share data adj. for stk. divs. as of ex-div. date. Bold denotes diluted EPS (FASB 128). E-Estimated. NA-Not Available. NM-Not Meaningful. NR-Not Ranked.

Office—1200 North Harbor Blvd., Anaheim, CA 92801. **Organized**—in California in 1966. **Tel**—(714) 774-5796. **Website**—http://www.ckr.com **Chrmn & CEO**—W. P. Foley II. **Vice Chrmn**—D. D. Lane. **Pres & COO**—C. T. Thompson. **EVP & CFO**—C. A. Strunk. **SVP, Treas & Investor Contact**—Loren C. Pannier. **SVP & Secy**—A. F. Puzder. **Dirs**—B. Allumbaugh, P. Churm, W. P. Foley II, C. L. Karcher, C. N. Karcher, D. D. Lane, W. H. Lester, F. P. Willey. **Transfer Agent & Registrar**—ChaseMellon Shareholder Services, LA. **Incorporated**—Delaware. **Empl**— 46,500. **S&P Analyst:** Robert J. Izmirlian

STANDARD & POOR'S
STOCK REPORTS

CMAC Investment

411M

NYSE Symbol **CMT**

In S&P SmallCap 600

03-OCT-98

Industry:
Insurance (Property-Casualty)

Summary: This company provides private mortgage insurance to residential mortgage lenders, including mortgage bankers, mortgage brokers, commercial banks and savings institutions.

| **S&P Opinion: Accumulate (★★★★)** | Recent Price • 41⅛ | Yield • 0.3% |
| | 52 Wk Range • 70-36½ | 12-Mo. P/E • 12.3 |

Quantitative Evaluations

Outlook
(1 Lowest—5 Highest)
• **3**

Fair Value
• **47⅞**

Risk
• **Low**

Earn./Div. Rank
• **B+**

Technical Eval.
• **Bearish** since 8/98

Rel. Strength Rank
(1 Lowest—99 Highest)
• **43**

Insider Activity
• **Neutral**

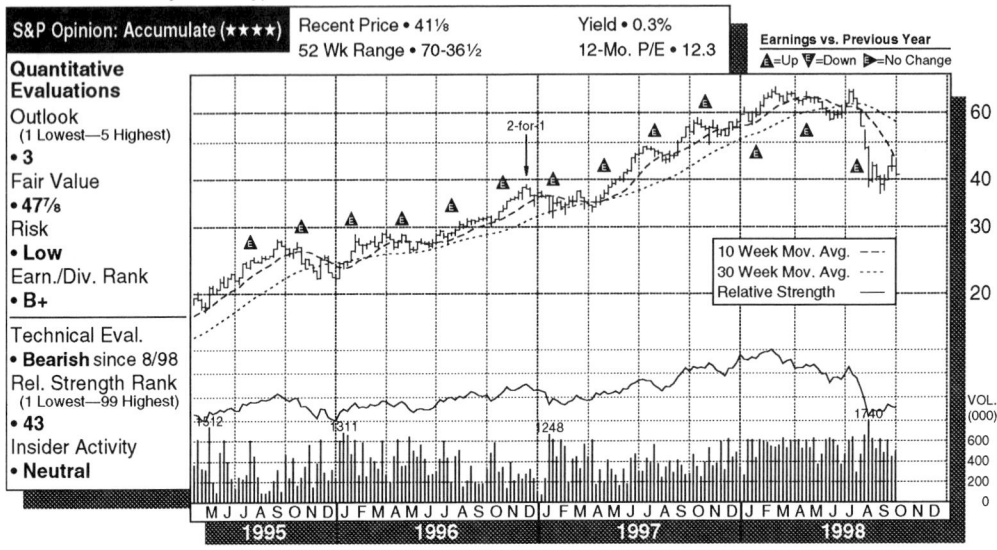

Earnings vs. Previous Year
▲=Up ▼=Down ▶=No Change

10 Week Mov. Avg. ---
30 Week Mov. Avg. ····
Relative Strength —

1995   1996   1997   1998

Overview - 20-JUL-98

Earnings per share increased 20%, year to year, in 1998's second quarter, as an 80% increase in new insurance written (NIW) and 15% higher direct primary insurance in force drove earned premiums up 20%. In addition, deeper coverage requirements (more mortgage insurance protection for a given low down payment loan) by Fannie Mae and Freddie Mac continue to boost growth. Persistency rates were down sharply in the quarter, due to the record level of refinancing activity, but record levels of new business offset this runoff. Over the next few quarters, we expect persistency rates to trend back up, as refinancing activity slows. Growth in new business should continue to be robust, reflecting low interest rate levels and low unemployment rates. Management continued to add to loss reserves in the quarter, boosting its level of reserves to $173.5 million, from $125.2 million a year ago. The percentage of loans in default was 2.31%, compared to 2.32% at year end 1997. In addition, CMT's California book of business continues to improve.

Valuation - 20-JUL-98

CMAC's shares have underperformed the broader market this year, rising 6% against a more than 20% rise in the S&P 500. Nevertheless, we feel the shares warrant an accumulate recommendation. CMT should be able to deliver high-teen EPS growth going forward, given the favorable macroeconomic backdrop and the positive factors underlying the private mortgage industry. We feel that the shares of this quality growth company are undervalued at roughly 15X our 1999 EPS estimate of $4.30. Given the positive outlook for the private mortgage insurance industry, CMT's ability to achieve high-teen EPS growth going forward, and the company's compelling valuation, we are recommending accumulation of CMT shares for capital appreciation.

Key Stock Statistics

S&P EPS Est. 1998	3.65	Tang. Bk. Value/Share	20.99
P/E on S&P Est. 1998	11.3	Beta	1.35
S&P EPS Est. 1999	4.30	Shareholders	4,500
Dividend Rate/Share	0.12	Market cap. (B)	$0.933
Shs. outstg. (M)	22.7	Inst. holdings	85%
Avg. daily vol. (M)	0.111		

Value of $10,000 invested 5 years ago: $ 32,147

Fiscal Year Ending Dec. 31

	1998	1997	1996	1995	1994	1993
Revenues (Million $)						
1Q	79.04	63.60	50.53	36.93	30.10	23.83
2Q	81.30	67.70	54.48	39.69	32.33	27.94
3Q	—	71.36	57.22	43.04	33.24	27.94
4Q	—	74.66	60.36	45.98	34.87	30.18
Yr.	—	277.3	222.6	165.6	130.5	107.2
Earnings Per Share ($)						
1Q	**0.86**	**0.71**	0.59	0.47	0.38	0.28
2Q	**0.91**	**0.76**	0.03	0.52	0.42	0.00
3Q	**E0.93**	**0.78**	0.65	0.54	0.44	0.37
4Q	**E0.95**	**0.81**	0.68	0.57	0.47	0.41
Yr.	**E3.65**	**3.06**	2.55	2.09	1.71	1.39

Next earnings report expected: mid October

Dividend Data (Dividends have been paid since 1993.)

Amount ($)	Date Decl.	Ex-Div. Date	Stock of Record	Payment Date
0.030	Oct. 14	Nov. 05	Nov. 07	Dec. 02 '97
0.030	Jan. 20	Jan. 30	Feb. 03	Mar. 03 '98
0.030	Apr. 14	May. 01	May. 05	Jun. 02 '98
0.030	Jul. 14	Aug. 03	Aug. 05	Sep. 03 '98

A Division of The **McGraw·Hill** Companies

Business Summary - 20-JUL-98

If you have ever tried to purchase a house with less than the normal 20% down payment, then you probably have a very good understanding of what CMAC Investment Corp. does. CMAC is the parent company of Commonwealth Mortgage Assurance Company, which provides private mortgage insurance to residential mortgage lenders, including mortgage bankers, mortgage brokers, commercial banks and savings institutions. Private mortgage insurance (also called mortgage guarantee insurance) protects lenders from default-related losses on residential first mortgage loans made to home buyers who make down payments of less than 20% of a home's purchase price.

By enabling would-be homeowners to purchase homes with low down payments, CMT greatly increases the homeownership opportunities of many first-time homebuyers such as low and middle income families, minorities, and immigrants. Private mortgage insurance also facilitates the sale of mortgage loans in the secondary mortgage market.

Management believes the private mortgage insurance market continues to offer promising growth opportunities. This is partly due to macroeconomic forces driving increases in homeownership rates. However, CMT feels affordable housing initiatives and revolutionary work in assessing, managing and pricing risk have also led to the industry boom. Advances in risk modeling have led to risk-based pricing practices, which CMT believes gives the company a competitive advantage.

In the near term, the current interest rate environment is expected to prompt a wave of refinancings. Refinancings will tend to lower CMT's persistency ratio (74.8% for the 12 months ended June 30, 1998, versus 87.9% the year before), but increase the volume of loans that are underwritten and require mortgage insurance. Primary new insurance written was $5.7 billion in 1998's second quarter, up 80%, year to year.

Over the long term, the industry will continue to be influenced by two primary factors. The first is the financial industry's push to continually increase operating efficiency and reduce costs. The second is the unabated consolidation of mortgage lenders (banks, etc.). CMAC's plan for dealing with these long-term trends include strengthening the company's risk-modeling capabilities, developing new ways of doing business with both national and local lenders, and implementing innovative services, systems and technologies for customers.

Per Share Data ($)

(Year Ended Dec. 31)	1997	1996	1995	1994	1993	1992	1991	1990	1989	1988
Tangible Bk. Val.	19.08	15.91	13.42	10.91	9.71	8.25	7.76	NA	NA	NA
Oper. Earnings	NA	NA	NA	NA	NA	NA	NA	NA	NA	NA
Earnings	3.06	2.55	2.09	1.71	1.39	1.40	0.91	0.65	-0.16	-0.17
Dividends	0.12	0.11	0.10	0.10	0.10	Nil	NA	NA	NA	NA
Payout Ratio	4%	4%	5%	6%	7%	Nil	NA	NA	NA	NA
Prices - High	61⁷/₈	38³/₄	27⁷/₈	15¹/₂	17⁵/₈	13¹/₄	NA	NA	NA	NA
- Low	31⁵/₈	22	14³/₈	11⁵/₈	11¹/₂	9	NA	NA	NA	NA
P/E Ratio - High	20	15	13	9	13	9	NA	NA	NA	NA
- Low	10	9	7	7	8	6	NA	NA	NA	NA

Income Statement Analysis (Million $)

	1997	1996	1995	1994	1993	1992	1991	1990	1989	1988
Premium Inc.	238	188	137	106	81.6	67.1	61.7	53.2	54.7	52.8
Net Invest. Inc.	33.8	30.0	25.9	22.6	20.9	13.9	12.3	12.0	11.9	12.1
Oth. Revs.	5.8	4.7	2.6	1.8	4.6	2.5	-2.6	0.2	0.2	0.9
Total Revs.	277	223	166	131	107	83.5	71.4	65.4	66.8	65.8
Pretax Inc.	102	82.6	68.2	56.4	48.2	32.4	17.8	14.4	1.4	-3.2
Net Oper. Inc.	NA	NA	NA	NA	NA	20.8	13.9	9.5	-0.1	2.1
Net Inc.	75.0	62.2	50.8	41.1	34.1	21.8	12.7	9.1	-2.2	-2.5

Balance Sheet & Other Fin. Data (Million $)

	1997	1996	1995	1994	1993	1992	1991	1990	1989	1988
Cash & Equiv.	2.4	3.2	3.6	3.9	7.6	2.3	NA	NA	NA	NA
Premiums Due	NA	NA	NA	NA	NA	NA	NA	NA	NA	NA
Invest. Assets: Bonds	586	508	433	359	327	304	NA	NA	NA	NA
Invest. Assets: Stocks	Nil	Nil	Nil	Nil	Nil	Nil	NA	NA	NA	NA
Invest. Assets: Loans	Nil	Nil	Nil	Nil	Nil	Nil	Nil	Nil	Nil	Nil
Invest. Assets: Total	597	513	438	359	327	304	NA	NA	NA	NA
Deferred Policy Costs	25.0	23.9	21.4	16.9	16.2	NA	NA	NA	NA	NA
Total Assets	705	593	499	410	375	335	NA	NA	NA	NA
Debt	Nil	Nil	Nil	Nil	Nil	Nil	Nil	Nil	Nil	Nil
Common Eqty.	430	356	299	240	213	181	170	NA	NA	NA
Prop. & Cas. Loss Ratio	50.6	50.6	44.3	37.7	38.6	47.0	59.8	65.3	NA	NA
Prop. & Cas. Expense Ratio	21.2	23.2	28.5	27.6	27.6	27.6	30.6	32.8	NA	NA
Prop. & Cas. Combined Ratio	71.8	73.8	72.8	65.3	66.2	74.6	90.4	98.1	NA	NA
% Return On Revs.	27.0	27.9	30.6	31.5	31.8	26.0	17.8	14.0	NM	NM
% Ret. on Equity	19.1	18.9	18.9	18.2	15.7	15.9	NM	NM	NM	NM

Data as orig. reptd.; bef. results of disc. opers. and/or spec. items. Per share data adj. for stk. divs. as of ex-div. date. Bold denotes diluted EPS (FASB 128). E-Estimated. NA-Not Available. NM-Not Meaningful. NR-Not Ranked.

Office—1601 Market St., Philadelphia, PA 19103.**Tel**—(215) 564-6600. **Chrmn**—H. Wender. **Pres & CEO**—F. P. Filipps. **SVP & Secy**—H. S. Yaruss. **SVP & CFO**—C. R. Quint. **Dirs**—D. C. Carney, C. M. Fagin, F. P. Filipps, J. W. Jennings, J. C. Miller, R. W. Moore, R. W. Richards, A. W. Schweiger, H. Wender. **Transfer Agent & Registrar**—Bank of New York, NYC. **Incorporated**—in Delaware in 1991. **Empl**— 607. **S&P Analyst:** Michael Schneider

03-OCT-98

Industry:
Services (Commercial & Consumer)

Summary: This company operates photographic studios as a licensee of Sears, and also operates a chain of print, poster and framing stores.

Quantitative Evaluations

Outlook
(1 Lowest—5 Highest)
• **NA**

Fair Value
• **NA**

Risk
• **Average**

Earn./Div. Rank
• **B**

Technical Eval.
• **Bullish** since 12/97

Rel. Strength Rank
(1 Lowest—99 Highest)
• **78**

Insider Activity
• **NA**

Recent Price • 22¾
52 Wk Range • 28-17¼

Yield • 2.5%
12-Mo. P/E • 18.2

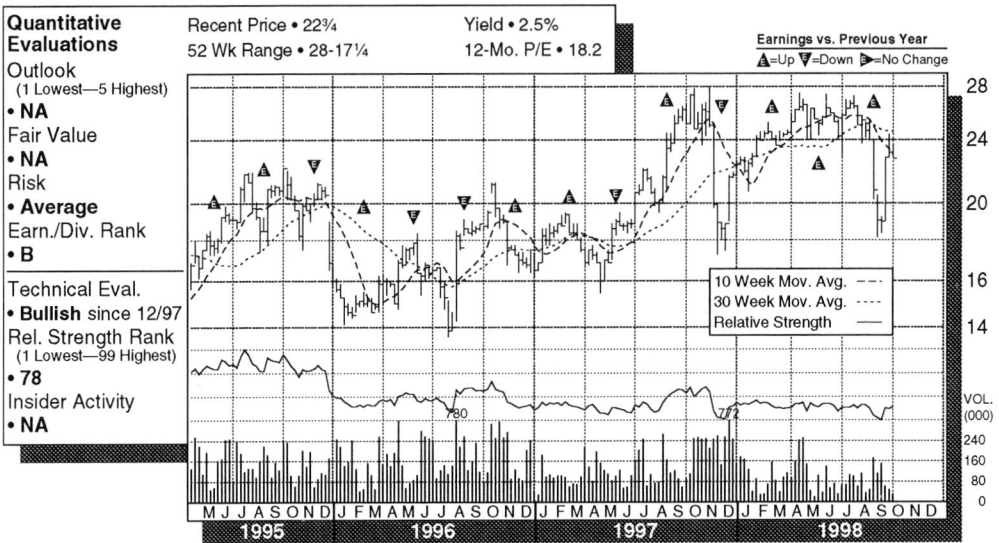

Business Profile - 07-JUL-98

This company derives most of its income from the operation of portrait photography studios as a licensee of Sears, Roebuck and Co. In October 1997, CPI sold its remaining 49% interest in Fox Photo, Inc., a one-hour photofinishing business, to Eastman Kodak Co., for a $44 million note due January 1999. In February 1998, as a result of a Dutch auction self tender offer, the company repurchased about 2 million of its common shares at or below $23 a share. Results in the first quarter of FY 98 (Jan.) were negatively affected by continued operating losses at Prints Plus, CPI's wall decor division, despite an increase in sales.

Operational Review - 07-JUL-98

Net sales in the 12 weeks ended May 2, 1998, rose 4.5%, reflecting 3.6% higher sales for portrait studios and a 9.2% increase in wall decor sales. Margins narrowed, on an 8.0% rise in SG&A expenses; operating income fell 2.9%. With lower net interest expense, higher other income, and in the absence of a loss in a joint venture, after tax benefits in each period, the seasonal net loss narrowed to $506,000 ($0.05 a share, on 15% fewer shares), from $2,411,000 ($0.21).

Stock Performance - 02-OCT-98

In the past 30 trading days, CPY's shares have declined 5%, compared to a 7% fall in the S&P 500. Average trading volume for the past five days was 5,700 shares, compared with the 40-day moving average of 16,626 shares.

Key Stock Statistics

Dividend Rate/Share	0.56	Shareholders	2,100
Shs. outstg. (M)	10.0	Market cap. (B)	$0.228
Avg. daily vol. (M)	0.015	Inst. holdings	71%
Tang. Bk. Value/Share	10.11		
Beta	0.50		

Value of $10,000 invested 5 years ago: $ 13,957

Fiscal Year Ending Jan. 31

	1999	1998	1997	1996	1995	1994
Revenues (Million $)						
1Q	73.35	70.17	104.7	103.4	100.1	88.79
2Q	71.00	68.49	105.4	107.1	104.7	95.39
3Q	—	108.2	145.4	166.2	175.4	145.3
4Q	—	119.9	111.5	150.0	153.0	146.0
Yr.	—	366.7	467.0	526.6	533.1	475.5
Earnings Per Share ($)						
1Q	-0.05	-0.20	-0.15	-0.03	-0.17	-0.17
2Q	0.13	0.12	-0.06	0.18	0.11	0.14
3Q	—	-0.06	0.36	0.24	0.28	0.23
4Q	—	1.22	0.91	0.88	0.86	0.56
Yr.	—	1.07	1.06	1.26	1.05	0.76

Next earnings report expected: early December

Dividend Data (Dividends have been paid since 1985.)

Amount ($)	Date Decl.	Ex-Div. Date	Stock of Record	Payment Date
0.140	Nov. 06	Nov. 13	Nov. 17	Nov. 24 '97
0.140	Feb. 05	Feb. 12	Feb. 17	Feb. 23 '98
0.140	May. 07	May. 14	May. 18	May. 26 '98
0.140	Aug. 06	Aug. 13	Aug. 17	Aug. 24 '98

A Division of The **McGraw·Hill** *Companies*

Business Summary - 07-JUL-98

CPI Corp. derives most of its earnings from photographic studios that it operates in Sears, Roebuck and Co. department stores. It also operates the Prints Plus chain of print, poster and framing stores. Until October 1997, the company was also engaged in the one-hour photofinishing business. Contributions to sales and operating profits (millions) in FY 98 (Jan.) were:

	Sales	Profits
Portrait studios	83%	$44.6
Wall decor	17%	-1.0

As of June 1998, the company operated 1,027 portrait studios in the U.S., Puerto Rico and Canada as a licensee of Sears. Under the license agreement, CPI pays a fee of 15% of net sales per fixed location studio, and 7.5% of sales for freestanding studios in retail malls that operate under the Sears name. CPI also provides all studio furniture, equipment and fixtures and conducts advertising at its expense. In addition, CPI operates 154 Prints Plus wall decor stores in malls throughout the U.S.

In October 1996, the company entered into a joint-venture agreement with Eastman Kodak Co., which agreed to acquire a 51% stake in CPI's retail photofinishing business for $56.1 million in cash. This business segment had been operated by the company's Fox Photo and Proex Photo Systems, Inc. CPI recognized a gain of $3.9 million ($0.29 a share) on the transaction.

In October 1997, CPI sold its remaining 49% interest in Fox to Kodak for a $43.9 million noninterest-bearing promissory note due in January 1999. Due to the noninterest-bearing nature of the note, a discount of $3.9 million was established, and will be amortized into income until the note matures. Simultaneously, the company entered into a non-competition agreement with Fox. In return, CPI received $10 million in cash, which will be amortized into income over the two-year period of the agreement. As a result of the sale, the effect of the non-compete agreement and the discount on the note, CPI recorded a loss of about $2.6 million ($0.21 a share) in the third quarter of FY 98.

In June 1997, CPI prepaid the balance of its existing senior notes and placed privately $60 million in new senior notes. The company incurred $591,000 in related issuance costs, which are being amortized over the 10-year life of the notes. In February 1998, CPI completed a Dutch auction self tender offer, purchasing about 2 million of its common shares at or below $23 a share.

Per Share Data ($) (Year Ended Jan. 31)	1998	1997	1996	1995	1994	1993	1992	1991	1990	1989
Tangible Bk. Val.	10.26	11.90	8.88	7.93	7.84	7.33	7.09	9.66	8.17	7.68
Cash Flow	3.60	3.86	4.19	3.63	2.95	3.42	3.46	3.66	3.32	2.95
Earnings	1.07	1.06	1.26	1.05	0.76	1.54	1.80	2.19	1.97	1.81
Dividends	0.56	0.56	0.56	0.56	0.56	0.56	0.56	0.50	0.42	0.25
Payout Ratio	52%	53%	44%	53%	74%	36%	30%	22%	21%	14%
Cal. Yrs.	1997	1996	1995	1994	1993	1992	1991	1990	1989	1988
Prices - High	28	21 1/4	22 1/8	21 7/8	20 7/8	27 1/8	34 3/4	34 3/8	33 7/8	22 1/4
- Low	15 3/8	13 5/8	13 3/4	14	13 3/4	14 7/8	21 3/4	23 1/2	19 3/4	16 3/4
P/E Ratio - High	26	20	18	21	27	18	19	16	17	12
- Low	14	13	11	13	18	10	12	11	10	9
Income Statement Analysis (Million $)										
Revs.	367	467	527	533	476	449	415	374	351	328
Oper. Inc.	58.2	58.3	72.7	63.8	50.9	62.4	64.4	69.6	66.8	63.5
Depr.	30.0	37.9	41.0	36.4	32.1	27.5	26.5	22.6	21.3	19.1
Int. Exp.	4.5	5.1	5.1	5.3	2.0	0.2	0.1	0.1	0.1	0.1
Pretax Inc.	20.9	22.8	27.6	23.5	18.5	36.5	43.3	53.5	48.3	50.1
Eff. Tax Rate	39%	37%	36%	37%	40%	38%	37%	37%	36%	40%
Net Inc.	12.7	14.3	17.7	14.8	11.1	22.6	27.1	33.6	30.9	30.3
Balance Sheet & Other Fin. Data (Million $)										
Cash	1.2	21.9	8.3	14.4	66.4	21.0	31.2	88.3	70.0	65.5
Curr. Assets	94.4	63.7	72.8	82.0	128	73.0	84.0	130	106	104
Total Assets	229	247	300	300	306	238	239	219	196	197
Curr. Liab.	47.4	50.8	64.0	69.8	65.2	56.8	67.1	51.4	47.8	47.3
LT Debt	59.5	44.9	54.8	59.7	59.8	0.3	0.6	0.5	0.3	0.5
Common Eqty.	102	140	174	166	176	172	160	152	133	137
Total Cap.	164	191	231	226	236	175	165	159	141	145
Cap. Exp.	21.7	35.0	48.8	77.1	45.4	13.3	40.6	20.3	25.6	29.7
Cash Flow	42.7	52.2	58.7	51.2	43.3	50.1	53.6	56.2	52.2	49.4
Curr. Ratio	2.0	1.3	1.1	1.2	2.0	1.3	1.2	2.5	2.2	2.2
% LT Debt of Cap.	36.3	23.5	23.7	26.4	25.4	0.2	0.3	0.3	0.2	0.3
% Net Inc.of Revs.	3.5	3.1	3.4	2.8	2.3	5.0	6.5	9.0	8.8	9.2
% Ret. on Assets	5.3	5.2	5.9	5.0	4.1	9.5	12.0	16.4	16.2	16.7
% Ret. on Equity	10.5	9.1	10.4	8.9	6.4	13.6	17.6	23.8	23.6	24.1

Data as orig. reptd.; bef. results of disc. opers. and/or spec. items. Per share data adj. for stk. divs. as of ex-div. date. Bold denotes diluted EPS (FASB 128). E-Estimated. NA-Not Available. NM-Not Meaningful. NR-Not Ranked.

Office—1706 Washington Ave., St. Louis, MO 63103-1790. **Tel**—(314) 231-1575. **Website**—www.cpicorp.com **Chrmn & CEO**—A. V. Essman. **Pres**—R. Isaak. **EVP, CFO & Treas**—B. Arthur.**Secy**—J. E. Nelson. **Dirs**—M. Bohm, A. V. Essman, R. Isaak, M. A. Krey, L. M. Liberman, P. J. Morris, N. L. Reding, M. Sneider, R. L. Virgil. **Transfer Agent & Registrar**—Boatman's Trust Co, St. Louis. **Incorporated**—in Delaware in 1982. **Empl**— 7,911. **S&P Analyst:** Kathleen J. Fraser

03-OCT-98

Industry:
Manufacturing (Specialized)

Summary: CTS makes electronic components and subsystems primarily for OEMs in the defense/aerospace, communications, automotive, data processing and instruments and controls industries.

Quantitative Evaluations	
Outlook (1 Lowest—5 Highest)	• 2+
Fair Value	• 31⅛
Risk	• Low
Earn./Div. Rank	• B+
Technical Eval.	• Bearish since 10/96
Rel. Strength Rank (1 Lowest—99 Highest)	• 69
Insider Activity	• Neutral

Recent Price • 28¼
52 Wk Range • 38-26⅜

Yield • 0.8%
12-Mo. P/E • 16.9

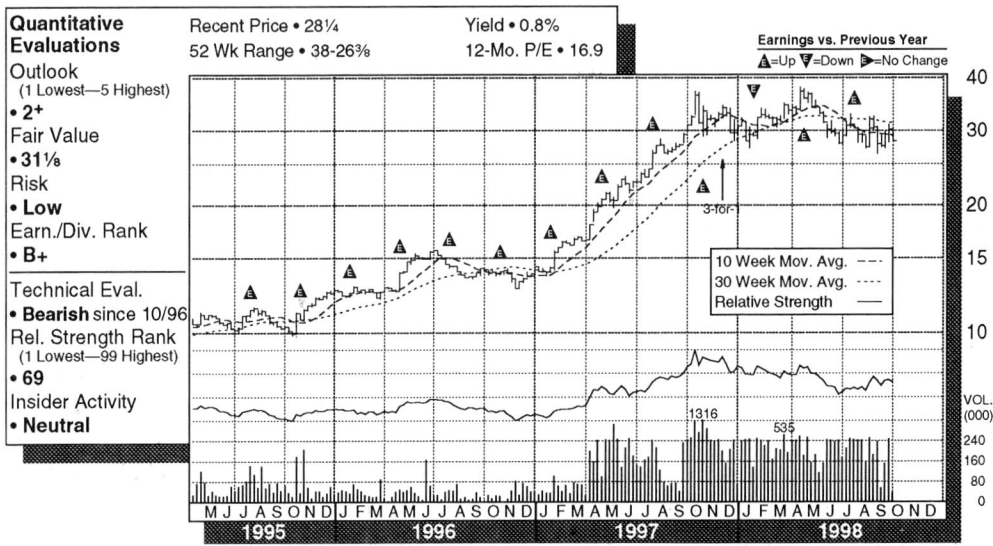

Earnings vs. Previous Year
▲=Up ▼=Down ▶=No Change

10 Week Mov. Avg. ---
30 Week Mov. Avg. ....
Relative Strength —

Business Profile - 04-MAY-98

CTS in October 1997 completed its acquisition of the remaining interest in Dynamics Corp. of America it did not already own, in a transaction whereby each common share of Dynamics not held by the company was converted into either $58 in cash or 0.88 of a CTS common share. As of late March 1998, CTS had integrated certain of Dynamics' businesses into its electronics manufacturing operations and had established a task force to study the repositioning or possible divestiture of Dynamics' remaining businesses (small appliances, power and controlled environmental systems, and fabricated metal products and equipment, having combined net sales of $100 million), with the objective of selling, closing or integrating them by 1998 year end.

Operational Review - 04-MAY-98

Based on a brief report, net sales in the three months ended March 31, 1998, advanced 38%, year to year, reflecting the October 1997 acquisition of Dynamics Corp. and continued strength in the company's core businesses. Gross margins narrowed; despite well controlled SG&A and R&D expenses, operating earnings were up 25%. Following sharply higher interest expense, but taxes at 35.0%, versus 37.0%, net income also rose 25%, to $8,712,000 ($0.56 a share), from $6,954,000 ($0.44).

Stock Performance - 02-OCT-98

In the past 30 trading days, CTS's shares have declined 7%, compared to a 7% fall in the S&P 500. Average trading volume for the past five days was 6,940 shares, compared with the 40-day moving average of 38,479 shares.

Key Stock Statistics

Dividend Rate/Share	0.24	Shareholders	1,400
Shs. outstg. (M)	13.7	Market cap. (B)	$0.387
Avg. daily vol. (M)	0.028	Inst. holdings	52%
Tang. Bk. Value/Share	8.17		
Beta	0.72		

Value of $10,000 invested 5 years ago: $ 52,649

Fiscal Year Ending Dec. 31

	1998	1997	1996	1995	1994	1993
Revenues (Million $)						
1Q	126.0	91.27	80.19	75.98	64.36	60.44
2Q	124.5	107.5	83.82	76.41	70.62	62.61
3Q	—	89.98	76.46	73.89	65.95	58.11
4Q	—	126.4	80.83	73.88	67.78	55.82
Yr.	—	415.1	321.3	300.2	268.7	237.0
Earnings Per Share ($)						
1Q	**0.56**	**0.44**	0.28	0.21	0.16	0.11
2Q	**0.66**	**0.53**	0.34	0.30	0.25	0.12
3Q	—	**0.48**	0.32	0.27	0.20	0.07
4Q	—	**-0.02**	0.40	0.32	0.29	0.12
Yr.	—	**1.43**	1.34	1.10	0.90	0.42

Next earnings report expected: mid October

Dividend Data (Dividends have been paid since 1930.)

Amount ($)	Date Decl.	Ex-Div. Date	Stock of Record	Payment Date
0.060	Oct. 31	Dec. 29	Dec. 31	Jan. 30 '98
0.060	Feb. 12	Mar. 27	Mar. 31	Apr. 30 '98
0.060	Apr. 24	Jun. 26	Jun. 30	Jul. 31 '98
0.060	Aug. 28	Sep. 28	Sep. 30	Oct. 30 '98

A Division of The McGraw-Hill Companies

Business Summary - 04-MAY-98

This designer of a broad line of electronic products for original equipment manufacturers completed the acquisition in October 1997 of Dynamics Corp. of America, a diversified manufacturer of commerical and industrial products, which prior to the acquisition owned about 44% of CTS common shares. Post-acquisition results of Dynamics added $33 million in revenues and earnings of about $0.06 per share to the company's full-year 1997 results.

During the past several years, two product classes -- electronic components and electronic component assemblies -- each accounted for more than 10% of CTS revenues. Contributions to revenues in recent years were:

	1997	1996
Electronic components	57%	67%
Electronic component assemblies	36%	32
Other	7%	1%

Sales by market segment in 1997 were: automotive 29%, computer equipment 28%, communications equipment 17%, and other 26%. In 1997, sales to a major automotive manufacturer accounted for 12% of sales. Two other customers within the computer equipment industry individually contributed 12% and 10% of sales. International sales in 1997 were about 40% of net sales to unaffiliated customers.

Automotive products include throttle position sensors, exhaust gas recirculation subsystems, other automotive application sensors, resistor networks, variable resistors, and loudspeakers for automotive entertainment systems.

Products for the computer equipment market include flex cable assemblies, backpanels, resistor networks, switches, frequency control devices, fiber-optic transceivers and heat dissipators. Products are principally used in computers and computer peripheral equipment.

Communications equipment includes backpanels, frequency control devices, hybrid microcircuits, switches, fiber-optic transceivers, insulated metal circuits and resistor networks. These products are mainly used in telephones and telephone switching systems.

With the addition of Dynamics, CTS gained a line of electronic components, as well as other product lines which included electronic appliances, power and controlled environmental systems and fabricated metal products. CTS is evaluating various strategic alternatives with respect to the non-electronic component lines. CTS estimates that cost savings and synergies from the acquisition will well exceed the $2.0 million it originally targeted. In addition, it expects that planned option and share repurchase transactions in connection with the Dynamics acquisition and as part of its authorized stock repurchase program will be accretive to 1998 share earnings.

Per Share Data ($)

(Year Ended Dec. 31)	1997	1996	1995	1994	1993	1992	1991	1990	1989	1988
Tangible Bk. Val.	9.72	10.35	9.05	8.15	7.34	7.29	7.48	7.43	7.09	6.47
Cash Flow	2.49	2.13	1.85	1.62	1.21	0.88	1.13	1.32	1.69	1.45
Earnings	1.43	1.34	1.10	0.90	0.42	0.12	0.27	0.47	0.87	-0.13
Dividends	0.24	0.23	0.20	0.15	0.13	0.22	0.25	0.25	0.21	0.17
Payout Ratio	17%	17%	18%	17%	31%	180%	91%	52%	24%	NM
Prices - High	37¹/₄	15⁵/₈	12⁵/₈	10³/₈	7³/₈	8¹/₈	8	7⁷/₈	8¹/₂	9¹/₈
- Low	13⁵/₈	12	9¹/₈	6¹/₂	5⁵/₈	5⁵/₈	5¹/₂	5³/₈	7³/₈	5⁷/₈
P/E Ratio - High	26	12	11	11	17	66	29	17	10	NM
- Low	10	9	8	7	13	46	20	11	9	NM

Income Statement Analysis (Million $)

	1997	1996	1995	1994	1993	1992	1991	1990	1989	1988
Revs.	415	321	300	269	237	227	230	251	262	276
Oper. Inc.	68.3	45.9	39.2	31.9	23.2	14.9	17.5	23.9	29.4	43.2
Depr.	17.0	12.5	11.7	11.2	12.1	11.7	13.1	13.1	13.4	26.4
Int. Exp.	2.9	1.4	1.8	0.7	1.0	1.3	1.3	1.4	1.6	2.8
Pretax Inc.	35.1	33.6	27.7	21.5	10.3	3.8	6.2	9.5	17.4	0.8
Eff. Tax Rate	35%	37%	38%	35%	36%	50%	33%	23%	18%	NM
Net Inc.	22.8	21.2	17.2	14.0	6.6	1.9	4.2	7.3	14.3	-2.2

Balance Sheet & Other Fin. Data (Million $)

	1997	1996	1995	1994	1993	1992	1991	1990	1989	1988
Cash	39.8	45.0	37.3	2.9	23.5	18.5	18.1	13.4	13.3	23.4
Curr. Assets	186	138	126	111	97.0	87.0	91.0	91.0	95.0	106
Total Assets	330	249	227	207	185	171	176	173	177	188
Curr. Liab.	92.4	51.4	51.0	44.8	49.9	37.3	39.6	39.1	37.9	47.4
LT Debt	63.5	11.2	13.7	15.6	4.8	9.7	9.3	6.0	8.3	17.7
Common Eqty.	147	166	146	132	119	119	122	122	125	116
Total Cap.	233	194	172	157	129	132	135	131	135	136
Cap. Exp.	22.4	17.2	11.0	10.0	11.7	8.8	16.0	11.8	10.8	10.0
Cash Flow	39.8	33.7	28.8	25.2	18.7	13.6	17.3	20.4	27.6	24.2
Curr. Ratio	2.0	2.7	2.5	2.5	1.9	2.3	2.3	2.3	2.5	2.2
% LT Debt of Cap.	27.3	5.8	8.0	10.0	3.7	7.4	6.9	4.6	6.1	13.0
% Net Inc.of Revs.	5.5	6.6	5.7	5.2	2.8	0.8	1.8	2.9	5.4	NM
% Ret. on Assets	7.9	8.9	7.9	7.1	3.7	1.1	2.4	4.3	7.8	NM
% Ret. on Equity	14.5	13.5	12.3	11.1	5.5	1.6	3.4	6.1	11.9	NM

Data as orig. reptd.; bef. results of disc. opers. and/or spec. items. Per share data adj. for stk. divs. as of ex-div. date. Bold denotes diluted EPS (FASB 128). E-Estimated. NA-Not Available. NM-Not Meaningful. NR-Not Ranked.

Office—905 West Blvd. North, Elkhart, IN 46514. **Tel**—(219) 293-7511. **Fax**—(219) 293-6146. **Chrmn, Pres & CEO**—J. P. Walker. **VP & Secy**—Jeannine M. Davis. **Investor Contact**—Gary N. Hoipkemier.**Dirs**—L. J. Ciancia, G. H. Frieling Jr., A. Lozyniak, R. A. Profusek, J. P. Walker. **Transfer Agent & Registrar**—State Street Bank, Quincy, MA. **Incorporated**—in Indiana in 1929. **Empl**— 5,044. **S&P Analyst:** S.A.H.

Cable Design Technologies 417V

NYSE Symbol **CDT**

In S&P SmallCap 600

03-OCT-98

Industry:
Communications
Equipment

Summary: This company designs and manufactures technologically advanced electronic data transmission cables for various applications.

Quantitative Evaluations

Outlook
(1 Lowest—5 Highest)
• **5**

Fair Value
• **23⅞**

Risk
• **High**

Earn./Div. Rank
• **NR**

Technical Eval.
• **NA**

Rel. Strength Rank
(1 Lowest—99 Highest)
• **16**

Insider Activity
• **NA**

Recent Price • 12¼
52 Wk Range • 32¼-11⅞

Yield • Nil
12-Mo. P/E • 9.5

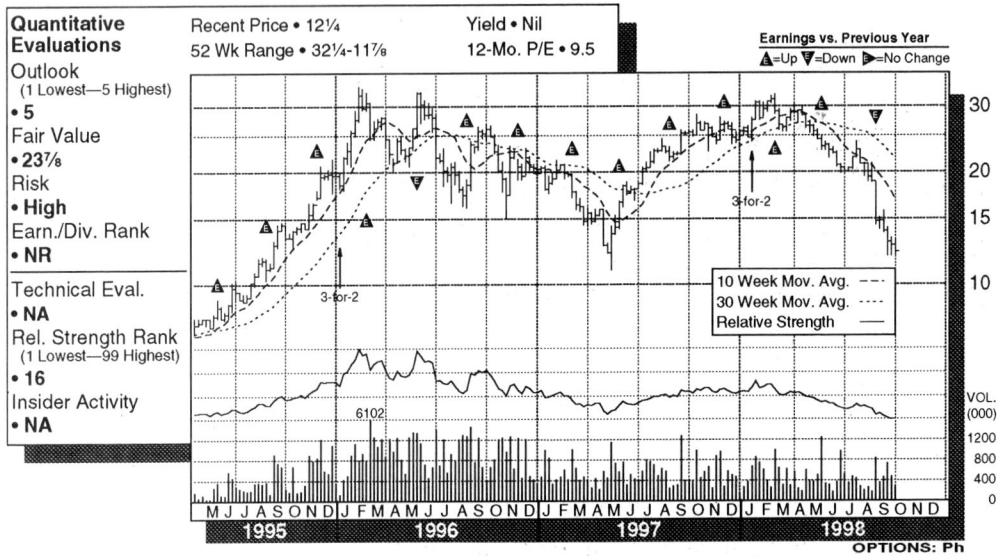

Earnings vs. Previous Year
▲=Up ▼=Down ▶=No Change

10 Week Mov. Avg. − − −
30 Week Mov. Avg. · · · ·
Relative Strength ——

OPTIONS: Ph

Business Profile - 01-APR-98

In February 1998, management said demand for its communications cable remained strong and that it expects to increase manufacturing capacity by 10% to 15% by summer 1998. Acquisitions have played an important role in the company's development. In September 1997, CDT acquired all the outstanding stock of Barcel, a manufacturer of high performance specialty cable for commercial and military aviation applications. CDT recently announced a number of new products, including a complete line of products that will support emerging high-speed applications, such as the Ethernet, and new enhanced cabling systems that are optimized for gigabit networking environments over unshielded twisted-pair cabling. A three-for-two stock split was effected in early 1998.

Operational Review - 01-APR-98

Net sales in the six months ended January 31, 1998, advanced 38%, year to year, reflecting increased sales in all business groups, aided by acquisitions. Gross margins narrowed on a less favorable product mix, and operating income was up 34%. Following sharply higher Interest expense, other income of $1.1 million, against other expense of $140,000, and after taxes at 37.9%, versus 36.9%, net income advanced 33%, to $21,376,000 ($0.68 a share) from $16,078,000 ($0.52, as adjusted for the January 1998 3-for-2 stock split).

Stock Performance - 02-OCT-98

In the past 30 trading days, CDT's shares have declined 35%, compared to a 7% fall in the S&P 500. Average trading volume for the past five days was 58,100 shares, compared with the 40-day moving average of 90,951 shares.

Key Stock Statistics

Dividend Rate/Share	Nil	Shareholders	200
Shs. outstg. (M)	30.1	Market cap. (B)	$0.369
Avg. daily vol. (M)	0.098	Inst. holdings	65%
Tang. Bk. Value/Share	5.41		
Beta	NA		

Value of $10,000 invested 5 years ago: NA

Fiscal Year Ending Jul. 31

	1998	1997	1996	1995	1994	1993
Revenues (Million $)						
1Q	162.1	116.0	65.05	44.92	34.65	—
2Q	155.6	114.0	67.24	44.39	33.30	—
3Q	167.7	130.0	112.2	47.94	38.12	—
4Q	166.2	157.1	112.8	51.70	39.32	—
Yr.	651.7	517.0	357.4	188.9	145.4	126.7
Earnings Per Share ($)						
1Q	0.37	0.27	0.22	0.13	0.12	—
2Q	0.32	0.26	0.21	0.12	0.10	—
3Q	0.34	0.30	-0.13	0.15	0.10	—
4Q	0.27	0.35	0.27	0.18	0.12	—
Yr.	1.29	1.17	0.57	0.57	0.44	0.30

Next earnings report expected: late November

Dividend Data

Amount ($)	Date Decl.	Ex-Div. Date	Stock of Record	Payment Date
3-for-2	Dec. 10	Jan. 12	Dec. 30	Jan. 09 '98

A Division of The McGraw-Hill Companies

Business Summary - 01-APR-98

CDT Design Technologies Corp. designs and manufactures specialty electronic data transmission cables and network structured wiring systems. The company's products include high performance copper, fiber optic and composite cable constructions, connectors and component assemblies that are used in network, communications, computer interconnect, wireless, commercial aviation, automotive, automation, sound & safety and other applications.

Sales contributions by product group in recent fiscal years (Jul.) were:

	FY 97	FY 96
Network structured wiring	49%	52%
Automation, sound & safety	14%	19%
Computer interconnect	4%	5%
Communications	18%	14%
Other	15%	10%

CDT serves markets that are primarily involved in specialty cables and network structured wiring components for computer local area networks (LANS) and wide area networks (WANS), communications, computer interconnect, wireless, commercial aviation, automotive, automation, sound & safety, and other applications.

The network structured wiring product group includes the cables, connectors, racks, panels, outlets and interconnecting hardware to complete the end-to-end network system requirements of LANS and WANS. The company has greatly increased its capacity in this product area over the past three years through capital expenditures and acquisitions.

The automation, sound and safety product group encompasses three distinct applications for data and signal transmission cables. Automation applications include climate control and sophisticated security and signal systems involving motion detection, electronic card and video surveillance technologies. Sound includes voice activation, evacuation and other similar systems, and safety refers to certain attributes of data transmission cable that improve the safety and performance of such cable under hazardous conditions.

The computer interconnect product group includes data transmission cables used to internally connect components of computers, telecommunication switching and related electronic equipment, and to externally connect computers to peripheral devices.

Through the NORDX/CDT acquisition in FY 96, CDT entered the market for outside communications, switchboard and equipment cable. CDT also manufactures products for various other electronic wire and cable applications and markets.

Per Share Data ($)

(Year Ended Jul. 31)	1998	1997	1996	1995	1994	1993	1992	1991	1990	1989
Tangible Bk. Val.	NA	5.41	5.33	0.83	0.12	0.55	NM	NM	NM	NM
Cash Flow	NM	1.49	0.79	0.72	0.58	0.46	0.37	NA	NA	NA
Earnings	1.29	1.17	0.57	0.57	0.43	0.30	0.23	NA	NA	NA
Dividends	Nil	Nil	Nil	Nil	Nil	Nil	Nil	Nil	Nil	Nil
Payout Ratio	Nil	Nil	Nil	Nil	Nil	Nil	Nil	Nil	Nil	Nil
Prices - High	32¼	28½	34	21⅝	8¾	5	5	NA	NA	NA
- Low	13¾	10⅞	14¾	6⅜	4⅜	4⅜	4⅜	NA	NA	NA
P/E Ratio - High	25	24	60	38	20	17	21	NA	NA	NA
- Low	11	9	32	11	10	14	19	NA	NA	NA

Income Statement Analysis (Million $)

	1998	1997	1996	1995	1994	1993	1992	1991	1990	1989
Revs.	NA	517	357	189	145	127	127	NA	NA	NA
Oper. Inc.	NA	72.7	54.2	33.4	25.2	22.5	20.5	NA	NA	NA
Depr.	NA	10.1	6.0	3.8	3.4	3.1	2.8	NA	NA	NA
Int. Exp.	NA	5.3	5.4	5.1	5.3	8.4	10.4	NA	NA	NA
Pretax Inc.	NA	57.3	25.9	24.5	16.9	10.5	8.0	NA	NA	NA
Eff. Tax Rate	NA	37%	39%	40%	40%	43%	42%	NA	NA	NA
Net Inc.	NA	36.0	15.3	14.7	10.1	6.0	4.7	NA	NA	NA

Balance Sheet & Other Fin. Data (Million $)

	1998	1997	1996	1995	1994	1993	1992	1991	1990	1989
Cash	NA	9.0	16.1	2.2	2.2	0.3	NA	NA	NA	NA
Curr. Assets	NA	248	208	74.3	60.6	46.9	NA	NA	NA	NA
Total Assets	NA	429	320	119	103	83.7	NA	NA	NA	NA
Curr. Liab.	NA	85.5	72.7	30.9	21.4	21.7	NA	NA	NA	NA
LT Debt	NA	127	73.1	52.7	63.8	77.5	NA	NA	NA	NA
Common Eqty.	NA	205	165	31.9	16.2	-16.3	-21.4	NA	NA	NA
Total Cap.	NA	338	243	88.1	81.4	62.1	NA	NA	NA	NA
Cap. Exp.	NA	26.7	15.9	5.7	4.0	2.5	1.6	NA	NA	NA
Cash Flow	NA	46.1	21.9	18.5	13.5	9.1	7.4	NA	NA	NA
Curr. Ratio	NA	2.9	2.9	2.4	2.8	2.2	NA	NA	NA	NA
% LT Debt of Cap.	NA	37.4	30.1	59.8	78.4	124.8	NA	NA	NA	NA
% Net Inc.of Revs.	NA	7.0	4.3	7.8	7.0	4.7	3.9	NA	NA	NA
% Ret. on Assets	NA	9.6	7.0	13.2	10.9	8.0	NA	NA	NA	NA
% Ret. on Equity	NA	19.4	15.5	61.0	NM	NM	NM	NM	NM	NM

Data as orig. reptd.; bef. results of disc. opers. and/or spec. items. Per share data adj. for stk. divs. as of ex-div. date. Bold denotes diluted EPS (FASB 128). E-Estimated. NA-Not Available. NM-Not Meaningful. NR-Not Ranked.

Office—Foster Plaza 7, 661 Andersen Drive, Pittsburgh, PA 15220.**Tel**—(412) 937-2300. **Fax**—(412) 937-9690. **Website**—http://www.cdtc.com **Pres & CEO**—P. M. Olson. **VP, CFO & Secy**—K. O. Hale. **Dirs**—B. J. Bannan, B. C. Cressey, M. S. Gelbach Jr., M. F. O. Harris, G. Kalnasy, P. M. Olson, R. C. Tuttle. **Transfer Agent & Registrar**—Bank of Boston. **Incorporated**—in Delaware in 1988. **Empl**— 2,900. **S&P Analyst:** C.C.P.

Cabot Oil & Gas

418E

NYSE Symbol **COG**

In S&P SmallCap 600

03-OCT-98

Industry:
Oil & Gas (Exploration & Production)

Summary: This company explores for, produces, purchases and markets natural gas and, to a lesser extent, produces and sells crude oil.

Quantitative Evaluations

Recent Price • 16

52 Wk Range • 25⅛-12⅝

Yield • 1.0%

12-Mo. P/E • 23.2

Outlook
(1 Lowest—5 Highest)
• **3**-

Fair Value
• **17¼**

Risk
• **Average**

Earn./Div. Rank
• **NR**

Technical Eval.
• **Neutral** since 6/98

Rel. Strength Rank
(1 Lowest—99 Highest)
• **77**

Insider Activity
• **Favorable**

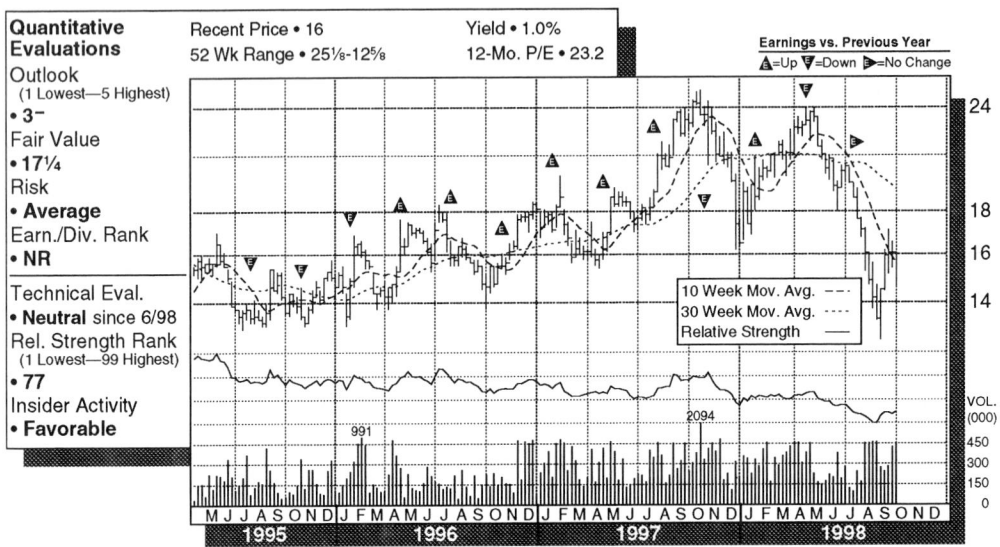

Earnings vs. Previous Year
▲=Up ▼=Down ▷=No Change

10 Week Mov. Avg. ---
30 Week Mov. Avg. ....
Relative Strength —

Business Profile - 10-MAR-98

The company benefited in 1997 from higher oil and gas prices and greater production. As part of its effort to enhance shareholder value and to succeed in the current industry environment, Cabot has implemented an aggressive drilling program to boost production while maintaining reserves. COG is also focusing on improving cash flows by increasing production and reducing costs. In October 1997, COG converted all of its $3.125 convertible preferred stock into approximately 1.65 million common shares. Also in October, Cabot received a commitment from six insurance companies for a $100 million private placement of senior notes.

Operational Review - 10-MAR-98

Revenues in 1997 (preliminary) advanced 13.5%, due to improved drilling success, a 8.6% increase in natural gas production (to 63.9 Bcf), and a 10.4% rise in crude oil production (to 574,000 barrels), further aided by 8.1% higher natural gas prices. These gains outweighed lower brokered natural gas and a drop in other revenue. Results benefited from the greater volume and well controlled expenses; operating income rose 16%. Following lower depreciation charges, and flat interest expense, pretax income climbed 46%. After taxes at 38.2%, versus 33.6%, net income was up 36%, to $28,334,000 ($1.00 a share, after preferred dividends, on 2% more shares), from $15,258,000 ($0.67).

Stock Performance - 02-OCT-98

In the past 30 trading days, COG's shares have increased 13%, compared to a 7% fall in the S&P 500. Average trading volume for the past five days was 92,480 shares, compared with the 40-day moving average of 84,862 shares.

Key Stock Statistics

Dividend Rate/Share	0.16	Shareholders	1,500
Shs. outstg. (M)	24.9	Market cap. (B)	$0.398
Avg. daily vol. (M)	0.072	Inst. holdings	70%
Tang. Bk. Value/Share	7.67		
Beta	0.99		

Value of $10,000 invested 5 years ago: $ 9,451

Fiscal Year Ending Dec. 31

	1998	1997	1996	1995	1994	1993
Revenues (Million $)						
1Q	40.79	52.79	41.20	58.12	65.84	43.48
2Q	41.67	39.41	37.35	51.35	56.45	38.38
3Q	—	40.77	35.50	47.98	55.76	33.50
4Q	—	52.16	49.02	56.47	59.02	48.96
Yr.	—	185.1	163.1	213.9	237.1	164.3
Earnings Per Share ($)						
1Q	0.12	0.42	0.23	-0.36	0.23	0.19
2Q	0.09	0.09	0.04	-0.23	-0.11	0.04
3Q	—	0.10	0.13	-3.22	-0.20	-0.16
4Q	—	0.38	0.27	-0.24	-0.14	0.04
Yr.	—	0.97	0.67	-4.05	-0.25	0.10

Next earnings report expected: late October

Dividend Data (Dividends have been paid since 1990.)

Amount ($)	Date Decl.	Ex-Div. Date	Stock of Record	Payment Date
0.040	Oct. 23	Nov. 12	Nov. 14	Nov. 28 '97
0.040	Feb. 03	Feb. 11	Feb. 13	Feb. 27 '98
0.040	May. 12	May. 20	May. 22	May. 29 '98
0.040	Aug. 05	Aug. 12	Aug. 14	Aug. 28 '98

A Division of The McGraw-Hill Companies

Business Summary - 10-MAR-98

This company was formed in 1990 through the initial public offering of about 18% of the outstanding common shares of the oil and gas business of Cabot Corp., which was started in 1891. The remaining common shares of the company were distributed to the shareholders of Cabot Corp. in 1991.

Cabot Oil & Gas (COG) explores for, develops, produces, stores, transports, purchases and markets natural gas and, to a lesser extent, produces and sells crude oil. The company's core areas are concentrated in two regions: the Appalachian Region of West Virginia and Pennsylvania, and the Western Region, with operations in the Anadarko area of Kansas, Oklahoma and onshore the Gulf Coast of Texas. At December 31, 1996, estimated proved reserves aggregated 946,600,000 Mcf, of which 95% was natural gas.

COG is one of the largest producers of natural gas in the Appalachian basin, where it has conducted operations for more than a century. The company acquired its operations in the Rocky Mountains and the Gulf Coast through the 1994 merger with Washington Energy Resources. Cabot has maintained its reserve base (84% developed and 16% undeveloped in 1996) through low-risk development drilling and strategic acquisitions. The company continues to focus its operations in the Appalachian and Western Regions through development of undeveloped reserves and acreage, ac-

quisition of oil and gas producing properties and, to a lesser extent, exploration.

Through marketing activities, the company provides a wide array of services that includes gas supply and transportation management, short- and long-term supply contracts, capacity brokering and risk management alternatives. Marketing of natural gas has changed significantly since the Federal Energy Regulatory Commission issued Order 636 in 1992, which required pipelines to unbundle their gas sales, storage and transportation services. In recent years, as a result of Order 636, Cabot has had the opportunity to serve broader markets, but has experienced increased competition, which has placed pressure on its margins.

In October 1997, COG completed the sale of its Meadville properties in Northwest PA for $92.5 million to Lomak Petroleum, Inc. The company also completed its $44 million purchase of the Green River basin assets in Wyoming of Equitable Resources Energy Co., which included 74 Bcfe of reserves, 65 wells, and 70 additional drilling locations. In November 1996, COG acquired 18 wells and associated acreage, 9.9 Bcfe of reserves and 2.5 Mmcf equivalent of daily production in the Moxa Arch of the Green River basin, for $3.5 million.

In 1997, Cabot replaced 294% of its production through its ongoing drilling and acquisition efforts. From the drill bit, Cabot replaced 168% of production, adding 114.0 Bcfe, while acquisitions replaced 114%, or 77.4 Bcfe. Year-end reserves were 939 Bcfe, less than 1% below the comparable year-ago number.

Per Share Data ($)

(Year Ended Dec. 31)	1997	1996	1995	1994	1993	1992	1991	1990	1989	1988
Tangible Bk. Val.	7.46	7.03	6.48	10.67	5.61	5.78	5.83	5.62	4.67	NA
Cash Flow	2.74	2.54	-1.73	2.23	1.78	1.65	1.34	1.84	1.82	NA
Earnings	1.00	0.67	-4.05	-0.25	0.10	0.11	0.01	0.57	0.02	NA
Dividends	0.16	0.16	0.16	0.16	0.16	0.16	0.16	0.12	NA	NA
Payout Ratio	16%	24%	NM	NM	160%	147%	430%	21%	NA	NA
Prices - High	25⅛	18½	17	23¾	27	20	18⅛	18½	NA	NA
- Low	15⅜	13⅛	12⅜	13⅜	15⅜	10¼	11¼	14	NA	NA
P/E Ratio - High	25	28	NM	NM	NM	NM	NM	32	NA	NA
- Low	15	20	NM	NM	NM	NM	NM	25	NA	NA

Income Statement Analysis (Million $)

	1997	1996	1995	1994	1993	1992	1991	1990	1989	1988
Revs.	185	163	214	237	164	148	140	128	132	NA
Oper. Inc.	63.8	47.0	-115	69.5	54.0	48.9	44.8	38.8	42.9	NA
Depr. Depl. & Amort.	40.6	42.7	47.2	54.6	34.5	31.5	27.2	23.1	36.0	NA
Int. Exp.	18.0	17.4	24.9	16.7	10.3	9.8	9.4	5.4	9.3	NA
Pretax Inc.	45.9	31.4	-141	-1.6	9.7	8.2	6.1	22.6	-2.2	NA
Eff. Tax Rate	38%	34%	NM	NM	64%	73%	79%	36%	NM	NM
Net Inc.	28.3	20.8	-86.6	-1.0	3.5	2.2	1.3	14.6	0.4	NA

Balance Sheet & Other Fin. Data (Million $)

	1997	1996	1995	1994	1993	1992	1991	1990	1989	1988
Cash	1.8	1.4	3.0	3.8	2.9	1.1	2.2	2.0	0.6	NA
Curr. Assets	70.5	79.6	52.3	52.0	44.6	41.7	32.9	25.2	25.3	NA
Total Assets	542	561	528	688	445	349	334	302	289	NA
Curr. Liab.	85.9	72.6	60.9	53.7	37.3	32.8	35.9	33.6	38.5	NA
LT Debt	183	248	249	268	169	120	105	80.0	92.0	NA
Common Eqty.	184	161	148	243	115	118	119	115	93.0	NA
Total Cap.	447	478	460	629	401	310	296	260	247	NA
Cap. Exp.	73.5	60.7	25.7	73.0	129	37.0	46.1	39.5	NA	NA
Cash Flow	63.8	57.9	-39.4	49.2	36.5	33.8	27.4	37.7	36.4	NA
Curr. Ratio	0.8	1.1	0.9	1.0	1.2	1.3	0.9	0.8	0.7	NA
% LT Debt of Cap.	40.9	51.9	54.2	42.6	42.1	38.7	35.5	30.8	37.1	NA
% Ret. on Assets	5.1	3.8	NM	NM	0.9	0.7	0.4	4.9	NA	NA
% Ret. on Equity	13.5	9.9	NM	NM	1.8	1.9	0.2	9.7	NA	NA

Data as orig. reptd.; bef. results of disc opers. and/or spec. items. Per share data adj. for stk. divs. as of ex-div. date. Bold denotes diluted EPS (FASB 128). E-Estimated. NA-Not Available. NM-Not Meaningful. NR-Not Ranked.

Office—15375 Memorial Dr., Houston, TX 77079. **Tel**—(281) 589-4600. **Website**—http://www.cabotog.com **Chrmn**—C. P. Siess Jr. **Pres & CEO**—R. R. Seegmiller. **Secy**—Lisa A. Machesney. **Dirs**—R. F. Bailey, S. W. Bodman, H. O. Boswell, J. G. L. Cabot, W. E. Esler, W. H. Knoell, C. W. Nance, R. R. Seegmiller, C. P. Siess Jr., W. P. Vititoe. **Transfer Agent & Registrar**—Boston EquiServe, L.,P.**Incorporated**—in Delaware in 1989. **Empl**— 360. **S&P Analyst:** A.O.T.

California Microwave 3394

NASDAQ Symbol **CMIC**

In S&P SmallCap 600

03-OCT-98

Industry:
Communications
Equipment

Summary: This company is the leading U.S. supplier of telecommunications satellite earth stations and microwave radios used in wireless communications.

Quantitative Evaluations

Outlook
(1 Lowest—5 Highest)
• **1+**

Fair Value
• **5¼**

Risk
• **Average**

Earn./Div. Rank
• **B**

Technical Eval.
• **Bearish** since 6/98

Rel. Strength Rank
(1 Lowest—99 Highest)
• **14**

Insider Activity
• **Favorable**

Recent Price • 9¼
52 Wk Range • 24¼-7

Yield • Nil
12-Mo. P/E • NM

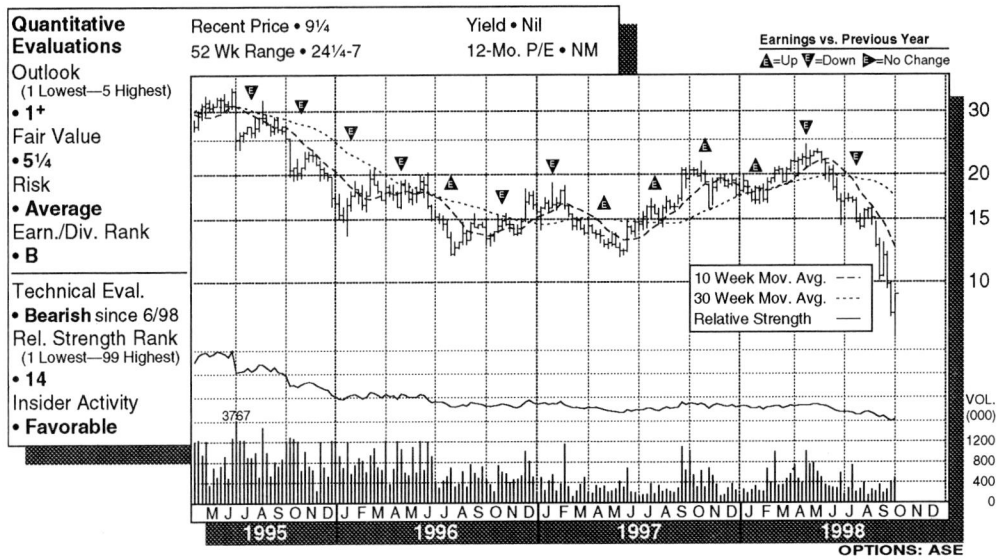

Earnings vs. Previous Year
▲=Up ▼=Down ▶=No Change

10 Week Mov. Avg. — -
30 Week Mov. Avg. - - - -
Relative Strength ——

OPTIONS: ASE

Business Profile - 27-FEB-98

This leading provider of terrestrial radio and communication satellite earth station systems and products operates facilities in nine U.S. states and the U.K., and sells to 110 countries. In 1996, a restructuring program begun in 1995 was expanded to include merging the operations of TTS with Microwave Networks (MN) and certain operations of the Microwave Radio Communications division into a new unit, Microwave Network Systems (MNS). In June 1997, CMIC said it would divest MNS and Satellite Transmission Systems (STS). In January 1998, CMIC agreed to sell the STS business for $27 million in cash.

Operational Review - 27-FEB-98

Based on a brief report, revenues from continuing operations in the first half of FY 98 advanced 5%. Following improving gross margins and lower operating expenses, operating income replaced an operating loss. Following a $1.9 million loss in a litigation settlement, the absence of $2.7 million gain on the sale of a subsidiary, and taxes at 36.0%, versus $907,000 in tax benefits, income from continuing operations was $4,184,000 ($0.25 a share, on 3.7% more shares), contrasted with a loss from continuing operations of $1,838,000 ($0.11). Results for the FY 97 period exclude $1.58 a share of losses from discontinued operations.

Stock Performance - 02-OCT-98

In the past 30 trading days, CMIC's shares have declined 39%, compared to a 7% fall in the S&P 500. Average trading volume for the past five days was 96,940 shares, compared with the 40-day moving average of 58,546 shares.

Key Stock Statistics

Dividend Rate/Share	Nil	Shareholders	2,000
Shs. outstg. (M)	16.2	Market cap. (B)	$0.150
Avg. daily vol. (M)	0.069	Inst. holdings	49%
Tang. Bk. Value/Share	4.62		
Beta	1.14		

Value of $10,000 invested 5 years ago: $ 5,648

Fiscal Year Ending Jun. 30

	1998	1997	1996	1995	1994	1993
Revenues (Million $)						
1Q	64.43	61.78	115.8	115.1	62.52	60.10
2Q	66.55	62.75	116.3	119.1	82.60	62.70
3Q	66.63	58.56	100.1	121.9	104.7	72.10
4Q	71.58	71.07	128.5	111.8	119.2	72.27
Yr.	269.2	254.2	460.6	467.9	369.0	267.2
Earnings Per Share ($)						
1Q	0.14	0.06	0.31	0.32	0.27	0.23
2Q	**0.11**	-0.18	0.23	0.37	0.28	0.24
3Q	**0.19**	1.86	0.08	0.37	0.30	0.25
4Q	Nil	0.16	0.10	-1.60	0.35	0.26
Yr.	**0.44**	0.16	0.72	-0.51	1.20	0.98

Next earnings report expected: mid October

Dividend Data

No cash dividends have been paid. A poison pill stock purchase rights plan was adopted in 1989.

A Division of The McGraw-Hill Companies

Business Summary - 27-FEB-98

California Microwave (CMIC) could have continued in its existing business, which was domestically oriented and heavily reliant on U.S. government sales. However, as management noted, this would in time have meant saturated or diminished markets, slow growth, and mediocre profitability. Instead, in 1992, the company chose wireless communications as its avenue of growth. CMIC's multi-year transition from niche player to a leading global manufacturer of systems and products used in satellite and wireless communications for voice, data, facsimile and video transmission continues to be an arduous one.

In December 1996, directors decided to focus on maintaining and expanding product areas where the company had leading market share positions and high profitability. To that end, CMIC announced its latest restructuring move in June 1997: the planned divestiture of both its Microwave Networks and Satellite Transmission Systems businesses. Now classified as discontinued operations, the units produced combined losses (after tax) of $59.3 million in FY 97 (Jun.), including after tax charges of $8.3 million and $26.6 million related to the divestiture and the restructuring, respectively.

Following the divestiture of MN and STS, the company is now a leading U.S. supplier of satellite earth station and microwave radio infrastructure products, installed in more than 110 countries. The retained businesses are grouped as satellite communications and up-link services (EFData and Services divisions), terrestrial video and data radio (Microwave Radio Communications and Microwave Data Systems divisions), and information collection and communications systems (Airborne Systems Integration and Government Electronics divisions). These six remaining divisions all participate in point-to-point and point-to-multipoint data transmission markets. The company indicated that an important consideration in its decision was to focus on maintaining and expanding its leading market positions in its remaining businesses.

Satellite communications accounted for 34% of FY 97 sales, information collection and communications for 36%, and radio products 30%. The markets for these products were made up of the U.S. government (41% of sales), U.S. commercial (30%), and international (29%).

In December 1997, CMIC entered into an agreement with L-3 Communications Corporation to sell its Satellite Transmission Systems (STS) division to L-3 for $27 million in cash. It is expected that no gain or loss will be reported on the divestiture. The sale is part of CMIC's plans to focus its resources on maintaining and expanding its leading market positions in satellite, terrestrial data radio and other wireless product businesses.

Per Share Data ($)

(Year Ended Jun. 30)	1998	1997	1996	1995	1994	1993	1992	1991	1990	1989
Tangible Bk. Val.	NA	5.40	7.49	6.47	6.34	7.26	4.57	6.79	5.84	4.93
Cash Flow	NA	0.74	1.69	0.41	1.96	1.65	0.97	1.32	1.26	1.02
Earnings	0.44	0.16	0.72	-0.51	1.20	0.98	0.56	0.93	0.80	0.63
Dividends	Nil	Nil	Nil	Nil	Nil	Nil	Nil	Nil	Nil	Nil
Payout Ratio	Nil	Nil	Nil	Nil	Nil	Nil	Nil	Nil	Nil	Nil
Prices - High	24¼	21¾	20¾	39¾	38¼	31¼	19½	25	10	10⅝
- Low	14	11¾	11⅞	16¼	16½	12¾	8¾	6⅜	5⅝	7⅜
P/E Ratio - High	55	NM	29	NM	32	32	35	27	13	17
- Low	32	NM	16	NM	14	13	16	7	7	12

Income Statement Analysis (Million $)

	1998	1997	1996	1995	1994	1993	1992	1991	1990	1989
Revs.	NA	254	461	468	369	267	199	177	146	125
Oper. Inc.	NA	16.5	38.0	31.9	35.8	24.7	13.9	17.1	16.1	11.5
Depr.	NA	9.5	15.7	14.2	9.6	6.7	3.8	3.4	4.0	3.2
Int. Exp.	NA	5.9	4.3	4.8	2.8	2.3	0.9	1.1	1.8	0.7
Pretax Inc.	NA	3.8	18.2	-11.3	23.9	15.9	8.0	12.7	10.5	7.9
Eff. Tax Rate	NA	33%	36%	NM	37%	37%	36%	37%	37%	35%
Net Inc.	NA	2.6	11.6	-7.9	15.1	10.0	5.1	8.0	6.6	5.1

Balance Sheet & Other Fin. Data (Million $)

	1998	1997	1996	1995	1994	1993	1992	1991	1990	1989
Cash	NA	5.0	6.1	2.6	13.7	5.4	4.7	4.2	1.7	1.3
Curr. Assets	NA	184	230	223	193	108	88.3	74.7	67.4	62.6
Total Assets	NA	266	338	327	294	170	147	98.0	90.0	85.0
Curr. Liab.	NA	72.1	89.2	97.2	81.3	45.1	31.6	28.8	29.0	30.6
LT Debt	NA	72.3	78.8	67.8	70.1	5.3	40.3	2.2	5.2	6.2
Common Eqty.	NA	118	170	154	141	119	75.3	67.5	55.7	48.2
Total Cap.	NA	190	249	222	211	124	116	70.0	61.0	54.0
Cap. Exp.	NA	7.1	27.7	26.8	16.4	10.8	9.6	3.6	3.9	6.3
Cash Flow	NA	12.0	27.3	6.3	24.7	16.7	8.9	11.4	10.6	8.3
Curr. Ratio	NA	2.5	2.6	2.3	2.4	2.4	2.8	2.6	2.3	2.0
% LT Debt of Cap.	NA	38.1	31.6	30.5	33.2	4.2	34.9	3.2	8.6	11.5
% Net Inc.of Revs.	NA	1.0	2.5	NM	4.1	3.7	2.6	4.5	4.6	4.1
% Ret. on Assets	NA	0.9	3.5	NM	6.4	5.5	4.1	8.3	7.5	6.9
% Ret. on Equity	NA	1.8	7.3	NM	11.4	9.2	7.0	12.7	12.7	11.2

Data as orig. reptd.; bef. results of disc. opers. and/or spec. items. Per share data adj. for stk. divs. as of ex-div. date. Bold denotes diluted EPS (FASB 128). E-Estimated. NA-Not Available. NM-Not Meaningful. NR-Not Ranked.

Office—1143 Borregas Avenue, Sunnyvale, CA 94089. **Tel**—(650) 596-9000. **Website**—http://www.calmike.com **Chrmn, Pres & CEO**—F. D. Lawrence. **COO**—L F. Blachowicz. **EVP & CFO**—D. S. Birks. **VP & Investor Contact**—Stephanie M. Day. **Dirs**—A. M. Gray, A. H. Hausman, F. D. Lawrence, W. B Marx, T. W. Ward, F. W. Whitridge, Jr.. **Transfer Agent & Registrar**—First National Bank of Boston. **Incorporated**—in California in 1968; reincorporated in Delaware in 1987. **Empl**— 1,412. **S&P Analyst:** Aydin Tuncer

STANDARD &POOR'S
STOCK REPORTS

Cambrex Corp.

422R

NYSE Symbol **CBM**

In S&P SmallCap 600

03-OCT-98

Industry:
Chemicals (Specialty)

Summary: This company is an international manufacturer of a wide range of specialty chemicals, fine chemicals and commodity chemical intermediates.

Quantitative Evaluations

Recent Price • 22⅞

52 Wk Range • 29¾-20⅝

Yield • 0.5%

12-Mo. P/E • 27.3

Outlook
(1 Lowest—5 Highest)
• **1⁻**

Fair Value
• **22¾**

Risk
• **Low**

Earn./Div. Rank
• **B**

Technical Eval.
• **Bearish** since 8/98

Rel. Strength Rank
(1 Lowest—99 Highest)
• **60**

Insider Activity
• **Favorable**

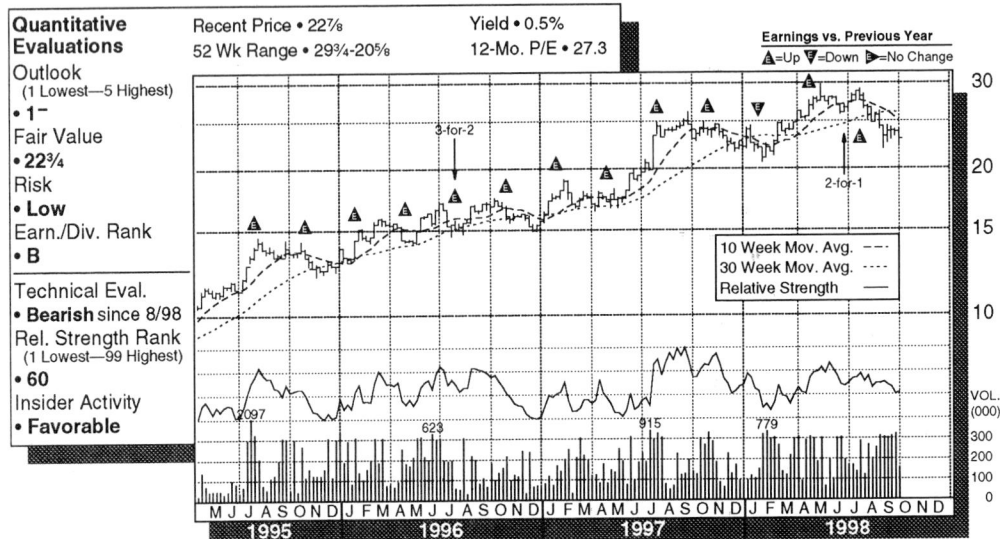

Earnings vs. Previous Year
▲=Up ▼=Down ▶=No Change

10 Week Mov. Avg. ‒ ‒ ‒
30 Week Mov. Avg. ‒ ‒ ‒
Relative Strength ——

Business Profile - 09-JUL-98

CBM recently acquired the chiral intermediates business of Celgene Corp., following the September 1997 acquisition of BioWhittaker, Inc. Results in 1997 benefited from strength in active pharmaceutical ingredients and pharmaceutical intermediates. Further expansion is expected to come from internal growth and through strategic acquisitions in selective niche markets. The company's shares began trading on the New York Stock Exchange on March 5, 1998. The ticker symbol CBM, which it used on the American Stock Exchange since 1991, was retained.

Operational Review - 09-JUL-98

Revenues in the first quarter of 1998 advanced 24%, year to year, reflecting the inclusion of BioWhittaker sales, and increased sales from each of the company's six product categories. Gross margins widened, as improved results from pharmaceutical and organic intermediates outweighed decreased profitability from polymer systems. Following higher interest expense, pretax income was up 30%. After taxes at 36.0%, versus 32.0%, net income rose 23%, to $9,143,000 ($0.36 a share, on 4.4% more shares outstanding), from $7,448,000 ($0.31). Per-share figures for both periods are adjusted for the June 1998 2-for-1 stock split.

Stock Performance - 02-OCT-98

In the past 30 trading days, CBM's shares have declined 11%, compared to a 7% fall in the S&P 500. Average trading volume for the past five days was 31,120 shares, compared with the 40-day moving average of 69,628 shares.

Key Stock Statistics

Dividend Rate/Share	0.12	Shareholders	1,600
Shs. outstg. (M)	24.3	Market cap. (B)	$0.557
Avg. daily vol. (M)	0.073	Inst. holdings	65%
Tang. Bk. Value/Share	4.98		
Beta	0.82		

Value of $10,000 invested 5 years ago: $ 41,932

Fiscal Year Ending Dec. 31

	1998	1997	1996	1995	1994	1993
Revenues (Million $)						
1Q	113.6	91.89	93.93	93.39	51.05	47.65
2Q	123.5	98.26	90.27	88.22	58.22	52.78
3Q	—	80.71	86.05	87.39	57.61	48.07
4Q	—	101.5	89.15	88.19	74.76	48.70
Yr.	—	371.3	359.4	357.2	241.6	197.2
Earnings Per Share ($)						
1Q	**0.36**	**0.31**	0.26	0.25	0.13	0.12
2Q	**0.43**	**0.37**	0.32	0.29	0.20	0.10
3Q	—	0.30	0.26	0.23	0.14	0.14
4Q	—	-0.26	0.35	0.22	0.18	0.13
Yr.	—	0.73	1.19	0.95	0.65	0.55

Next earnings report expected: late October

Dividend Data (Dividends have been paid since 1989.)

Amount ($)	Date Decl.	Ex-Div. Date	Stock of Record	Payment Date
0.050	Jan. 22	Feb. 04	Feb. 06	Feb. 20 '98
0.050	Apr. 23	May. 06	May. 08	May. 22 '98
2-for-1	May. 28	Jun. 25	Jun. 10	Jun. 24 '98
0.030	Jul. 23	Aug. 05	Aug. 07	Aug. 21 '98

A Division of The **McGraw·Hill** Companies

Business Summary - 09-JUL-98

This producer of specialty and fine chemicals for pharmaceutical and other markets achieved a 13% increase in income from operations in 1997 (excluding a $14 million nonrecurring charge related to the BioWhittaker acquisition), on 3% growth in revenues. In September 1997, CBM completed the acquisition of BioWhittaker, Inc. through a cash tender offer valued at approximately $135 million. In January 1998, CBM acquired the chiral intermediate business of Celgene Corp. (NASDAQ: CELG) for $7.5 million plus a royalty on future sales of up to $7.5 million. The company expects new facilities which started up in 1997, and alliances forged with outside product development companies, to advance its strategy to expand in pharmaceutical markets by offering support to the industry during all stages of drug development.

The company operates in two segments, biotechnology (4% of 1997 gross sales) and pharmaceutical specialty and fine chemicals, which fall into five product categories: active pharmaceutical ingredients (27%), pharmaceutical intermediates (20%), organic intermediates (19%), performance enhancers (18%) and polymer systems (12%). Active pharmaceutical ingredients are the chemical ingredients responsible for the therapeutic benefits of pharmaceutical preparations. Although over 80% of current business is with generic companies, CBM believes that sales to "innovator"

companies with patented products will lead growth in this product category over the next few years. In late 1997, it began commercial production of the bulk active for Tolterodine, a treatment for incontinence, at a new production unit in Sweden.

CBM's pharmaceutical intermediates are used in the production of drug, health, food and cosmetics products. Intermediates for the production of vitamins and other health care products accounted for 28% of sales in this product category in 1996. Late in the year, the company began producing an advanced intermediate for a protease inhibitor used in the treatment of AIDS.

Organic intermediates are used in animal feed additives, crop protection chemicals and pigments. Shipments returned to normal levels in 1997 after increased competition in feedgrade Vitamin B-3 markets in 1996 resulted in lower prices and thinner margins for Vitamin B-3 and its intermediates.

CBM's performance enhancers include catalysts for pharmaceutical manufacturing and other applications and chemicals used in photographic products.

Sales of polymer systems declined 11% in 1997, reflecting declines in each of the four major product lines, telecommunications, coatings, engineering plastics, and biomedical.

The biotechnology segment, which was formed with the acquisition of BioWhittaker, produces and sells cell culture and endtoxin detection products used in the production of biopharmaceutical products.

Per Share Data ($)

(Year Ended Dec. 31)	1997	1996	1995	1994	1993	1992	1991	1990	1989	1988
Tangible Bk. Val.	4.13	7.66	6.14	6.39	5.62	5.21	4.88	4.97	5.19	5.08
Cash Flow	2.00	2.38	2.22	1.48	1.22	1.06	0.49	0.10	0.49	0.68
Earnings	0.73	1.19	0.98	0.65	0.55	0.42	0.00	-0.35	0.18	0.42
Dividends	0.10	0.08	0.07	0.07	0.07	0.07	0.07	0.07	0.02	Nil
Payout Ratio	14%	7%	7%	10%	12%	15%	NM	NM	9%	Nil
Prices - High	26¼	17½	14½	9⅛	7⅛	6⅛	3⅜	4⅜	5¾	6⅜
- Low	16	12⅞	8⅞	6⅝	5⅝	2¾	1⁵/₁₆	1⅜	4⅛	3¾
P/E Ratio - High	36	15	15	14	13	14	NM	NM	31	15
- Low	22	11	9	10	10	7	NM	NM	22	9

Income Statement Analysis (Million $)

	1997	1996	1995	1994	1993	1992	1991	1990	1989	1988
Revs.	374	359	357	242	197	179	145	134	131	120
Oper. Inc.	81.8	74.8	69.5	35.0	28.4	24.9	7.2	12.3	13.4	18.6
Depr.	31.1	28.4	25.0	14.0	10.7	9.3	6.9	6.5	6.8	6.0
Int. Exp.	5.6	6.2	11.1	4.7	2.8	2.5	2.7	2.2	1.4	0.8
Pretax Inc.	32.6	40.7	31.2	16.9	13.4	10.3	0.1	-4.3	5.1	11.6
Eff. Tax Rate	45%	31%	37%	34%	36%	40%	40%	NM	40%	40%
Net Inc.	17.8	28.2	19.7	11.1	8.6	6.2	0.0	-5.1	3.1	7.0

Balance Sheet & Other Fin. Data (Million $)

	1997	1996	1995	1994	1993	1992	1991	1990	1989	1988
Cash	21.5	7.3	4.8	9.1	0.2	0.6	0.1	2.2	0.8	15.0
Curr. Assets	185	137	144	131	66.8	59.4	48.2	54.3	59.7	60.8
Total Assets	552	404	403	360	167	148	112	110	129	112
Curr. Liab.	67.9	73.9	74.3	111	28.3	23.5	16.9	14.9	12.9	16.4
LT Debt	194	60.1	100	116	36.3	39.8	19.0	18.5	22.2	6.0
Common Eqty.	226	229	189	102	87.6	75.2	68.7	69.2	87.0	83.8
Total Cap.	464	311	309	232	130	118	91.0	91.0	116	95.0
Cap. Exp.	35.9	32.3	46.4	20.8	15.8	9.1	16.1	6.3	7.7	7.6
Cash Flow	48.9	56.7	44.6	25.1	19.4	15.6	6.9	1.4	9.9	13.0
Curr. Ratio	2.7	1.9	1.9	1.2	2.4	2.5	2.9	3.6	4.6	3.7
% LT Debt of Cap.	41.8	19.3	32.2	49.9	27.9	33.7	20.9	20.2	19.2	6.3
% Net Inc.of Revs.	4.8	7.8	5.5	4.6	4.4	3.5	NM	NM	2.3	5.8
% Ret. on Assets	3.7	7.0	5.2	4.2	5.3	4.7	NM	NM	2.5	6.6
% Ret. on Equity	7.8	13.5	13.5	11.6	10.2	8.6	NM	NM	3.6	8.8

Data as orig. reptd.; bef. results of disc. opers. and/or spec. items. Per share data adj. for stk. divs. as of ex-div. date. Bk. Val. figs. in Per Share Data incl. intangibles. Bold denotes diluted EPS (FASB 128). E-Estimated. NA-Not Available. NM-Not Meaningful. NR-Not Ranked.

Office—One Meadowlands Plaza, East Rutherford, NJ 07073. **Tel**—(201) 804-3000. **Fax**—(201) 804-9852. **Website**—http://www.cambrex.com **Chrmn**—C. C. Baldwin Jr. **Pres & CEO**—J. A. Mack. **EVP & Investor Contact**—Peter Tracey. **VP & CFO**—D. H. MacMillan. **VP & Secy**—P. E. Thauer. **Dirs**—C. C. Baldwin Jr., R. B. Dixon, F. X. Dwyer, G. J. W. Goodman, K. R. Harrigan, L. J. Hendrix, I. Kaufthal, R. LeBuhn, J. A. Mack, D. P. Phypers. **Transfer Agent & Registrar**—American Stock Transfer & Trust Co., NYC. **Incorporated**—in Delaware in 1983. **Empl**— 1,790. **S&P Analyst:** E. Hunter

Canandaigua Brands 3426M

Nasdaq Symbol **CBRNA**

In S&P SmallCap 600

06-OCT-98

Industry:
Beverages (Alcoholic)

Summary: Formerly Canandaigua Wine Co., this leading U.S. producer and marketer of alcoholic beverages has grown rapidly over the past few years, primarily through acquisitions.

S&P Opinion: Buy (★★★★★)

| Recent Price • 42⅞ | Yield • Nil |
| 52 Wk Range • 59¾-35¼ | 12-Mo. P/E • 14.4 |

Earnings vs. Previous Year
▲=Up ▼=Down ▶=No Change

Quantitative Evaluations

Outlook (1 Lowest—5 Highest)
• 5

Fair Value
• 61¾

Risk
• Average

Earn./Div. Rank
• B

Technical Eval.
• NA

Rel. Strength Rank (1 Lowest—99 Highest)
• 78

Insider Activity
• NA

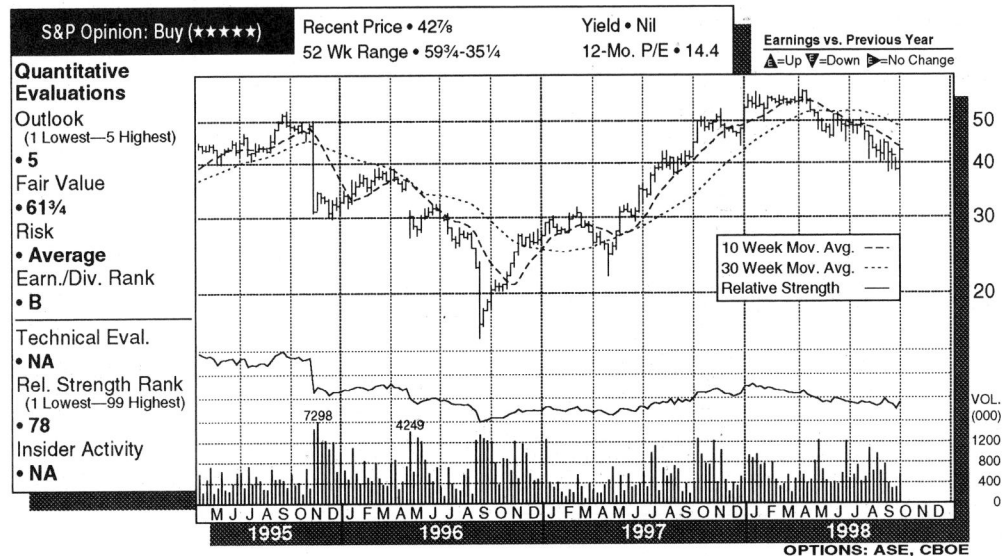

10 Week Mov. Avg. ---
30 Week Mov. Avg. ....
Relative Strength —

7298   4249

VOL. (000)

OPTIONS: ASE, CBOE

Overview - 06-OCT-98

Net sales (after excise taxes) are projected to rise at an approximate 10% annual pace through FY 99 (Feb.), led by continued unit volume growth for imported beers and, to a lesser extent, by higher wine selling prices and unit volume growth in other product segments. Profit margins should widen, aided by these factors, and by cost structure improvements and increasing emphasis on more profitable varietal wines. The abundant 1997 California grape harvest should ease grape costs in coming quarters and add further support to profitability in the near term. Assuming a relatively steady level of net interest expense and a 5% to 6% reduction in the number of shares outstanding, EPS are seen climbing to $3.18 in FY 99, from FY 98's $2.62. For FY 00, $3.60 is possible.

Valuation - 06-OCT-98

We recently upgraded the shares to a Buy, from Hold, due to improving market trends for the company's beer and wine products. Volume shipments of import beers are likely to remain strong, while wine volumes should continue to improve on new product introductions. Improved operating earnings may be offset somewhat by higher advertising expenditures associated with newly-introduced wine products, and increased promotional spending targeted at increasing market shares for beer and wine. Results going forward should also benefit from cost reduction efforts, lower grape prices and aggressive share repurchases. Finances are sound, with a healthy 2.0 current ratio (at August 31, 1998), and reliable cash generation ability. These defensive shares are attractive for purchase at a recent 12x our estimated FY 00 EPS, a sharp discount to the S&P 500, CBRNA's peers and its EPS growth rate.

Key Stock Statistics

S&P EPS Est. 1999	3.18	Tang. Bk. Value/Share	22.74
P/E on S&P Est. 1999	13.5	Beta	0.86
S&P EPS Est. 2000	3.60	Shareholders	1,700
Dividend Rate/Share	Nil	Market cap. (B)	$0.636
Shs. outstg. (M)	17.9	Inst. holdings	57%
Avg. daily vol. (M)	0.079		

Value of $10,000 invested 5 years ago: $ 25,202

Fiscal Year Ending Feb. 28

	1999	1998	1997	1996	1995	1994
Revenues (Million $)						
1Q	312.9	306.0	276.5	—	243.5	154.5
2Q	349.4	301.5	279.2	—	210.9	140.0
3Q	—	322.7	317.7	—	222.8	154.2
4Q	—	282.6	261.6	—	229.3	180.8
Yr.	—	1,213	1,135	535.0	906.5	629.6
Earnings Per Share ($)						
1Q	**0.70**	**0.53**	0.43	—	0.61	0.40
2Q	**0.83**	**0.65**	0.25	—	0.50	0.35
3Q	**E1.00**	**0.92**	0.42	—	0.53	0.41
4Q	**E0.65**	**0.53**	0.31	—	0.50	-0.39
Yr.	**E3.18**	**2.62**	1.41	0.17	2.14	0.74

Next earnings report expected: late December

Dividend Data

No cash dividends have been paid. The Class A and Class B shares were split three for two in 1991 and 1992.

A Division of The **McGraw-Hill** *Companies*

Business Summary - 06-OCT-98

Through an aggressive acquisition policy over the past few years, Canandaigua Brands, Inc. (formerly Canandaigua Wine Co.) is today the second largest supplier of wines, the second largest importer of beers and the fourth largest supplier of distilled spirits in the U.S. Net sales contributions by segment in recent fiscal years were:

	1998	1997
Wine	44.0%	45.2%
Beer	31.0%	26.3%
Spirits	16.5%	16.2%
Other	8.5%	12.3%

Canandaigua develops and manages a portfolio of well-recognized national and regional brands of popular- to medium-priced wines that include more than 130 brands covering all classifications. The company's principal branded products include Inglenook, Almaden, Paul Masson, Taylor California Cellars, Cribari, Manischewitz, Taylor, Marcus James, Deer Valley and

Dunnwood table wines; Cook's, J. Roget, Great Western and Taylor sparkling wines; Richards Wild Irish Rose, Cisco and Taylor dessert wines; Corona, St. Pauli Girl, Modelo Especial and Tsingtao imported beers; and Fleischmann's, Barton, Mr. Boston, Canadian LTD, Ten High, Montezuma, Inver House and Monte Alban distilled spirits.

As a related part of its wine business, the company produces grape juice concentrate, which is sold to the food and wine industries as raw material for the production of juice-based products, no-sugar-added foods and beverages. The company is one of the leading grape juice concentrate producers in the United States.

The company's business strategy is to manage its existing portfolio of brands and businesses in order to maximize profit and return on investment and to reposition its portfolio of brands to benefit from growth trends in the alcoholic beverage industry. To achieve these goals, the company intends to adjust the price/volume relationships of certain brands; develop new brands and introduce line extensions; expand geographic distribution; and acquire businesses that meet its strategic and financial objectives.

Per Share Data ($)

(Year Ended Feb. 28)	1998	1997	1996	1995	1994	1993	1992	1991	1990	1989
Tangible Bk. Val.	9.29	19.32	18.17	17.97	12.76	9.92	8.21	5.76	4.90	4.44
Cash Flow	4.36	3.03	0.86	3.22	1.41	1.92	1.66	1.38	0.98	0.72
Earnings	2.62	1.41	0.17	2.14	0.74	1.30	1.08	0.84	0.46	0.23
Dividends	Nil	Nil	Nil	Nil	Nil	Nil	Nil	Nil	Nil	Nil
Payout Ratio	Nil	Nil	Nil	Nil	Nil	Nil	Nil	Nil	Nil	Nil
Cal. Yrs.	1997	1996	1995	1994	1993	1992	1991	1990	1989	1988
Prices - High	57⅝	39½	53	53	38½	32	17	12	6¼	5⅝
- Low	21⅞	15¾	29¾	29¾	20¼	13½	10½	5¼	4⅛	3⅜
P/E Ratio - High	22	28	NM	25	52	25	16	14	14	24
- Low	8	11	NM	14	27	10	10	6	9	14

Income Statement Analysis (Million $)

	1998	1997	1996	1995	1994	1993	1992	1991	1990	1989
Revs.	1,213	1,135	535	907	630	306	245	177	180	164
Oper. Inc.	150	113	40.4	114	71.5	38.8	30.1	20.3	15.2	12.5
Depr.	33.2	31.9	14.0	20.7	10.5	7.4	6.1	5.0	5.0	4.9
Int. Exp.	32.2	34.1	17.4	25.1	18.4	6.3	6.5	4.6	4.6	4.9
Pretax Inc.	84.9	47.8	6.7	66.7	18.9	25.3	17.9	11.7	6.4	3.2
Eff. Tax Rate	41%	42%	50%	39%	38%	38%	37%	34%	31%	27%
Net Inc.	50.1	27.8	3.3	41.0	11.7	15.6	11.4	7.7	4.4	2.4

Balance Sheet & Other Fin. Data (Million $)

	1998	1997	1996	1995	1994	1993	1992	1991	1990	1989
Cash	1.2	10.0	3.3	4.2	1.5	3.7	2.2	28.6	26.3	20.0
Curr. Assets	564	501	518	402	454	244	134	98.0	91.0	88.0
Total Assets	1,073	1,020	1,055	786	827	355	218	147	143	139
Curr. Liab.	283	247	300	175	238	96.8	52.2	24.6	23.8	25.5
LT Debt	309	339	328	199	289	108	61.9	62.3	63.1	63.0
Common Eqty.	415	365	357	352	204	126	95.5	52.0	47.2	42.8
Total Cap.	783	765	742	600	537	255	165	122	118	1,113
Cap. Exp.	31.2	31.6	16.1	37.0	141	20.3	38.1	4.4	4.1	4.0
Cash Flow	83.2	59.7	17.3	61.7	22.3	23.0	17.4	12.7	9.4	7.3
Curr. Ratio	2.0	2.0	1.7	2.3	1.9	2.5	2.4	4.0	3.8	3.4
% LT Debt of Cap.	39.5	44.3	44.2	33.2	53.8	42.5	37.5	51.0	53.3	55.7
% Net Inc.of Revs.	4.1	2.4	0.6	4.6	1.9	5.1	4.6	4.4	2.5	1.4
% Ret. on Assets	4.8	2.7	NA	5.1	1.8	5.3	5.6	5.5	3.1	1.8
% Ret. on Equity	12.8	7.7	NA	14.8	6.5	13.5	14.0	16.0	9.9	5.7

Data as orig. reptd.; bef. results of disc. opers. and/or spec. items. Per share data adj. for stk. divs. as of ex-div. date. E-Estimated. NA-Not Available. NM-Not Meaningful. NR-Not Ranked. Yrs. ended Aug. 31 prior to 1996; FY 96 revs., EPS and inc. data are for six mos.

Office—235 N. Bloomfield Rd., Canandaigua, NY 14424. **Tel**—(716) 393-4130. **Fax**—(716) 394-6017. **Chrmn**—Marvin Sands. **Pres & CEO**—Richard Sands. **EVP & Secy**—Robert Sands. **SVP & CFO**—T. Summer. **VP & Investor Contact**—Kristen Jenks. **Dirs**—G. Bresler, J. A. Locke, T. C. McDermott, M. Sands, Richard Sands, Robert Sands, B. Silk, P. L. Smith. **Transfer Agent & Registrar**—Bank of Boston. **Incorporated**—in Delaware in 1972. **Empl**— 2,500. **S&P Analyst:** Richard Joy

Capital Re

443K

NYSE Symbol **KRE**

In S&P SmallCap 600

03-OCT-98

Industry: Insurance (Property-Casualty)

Summary: KRE provides specialty reinsurance, particularly financial guaranty for investment-grade municipal bonds, mortgage guaranty, credit and title reinsurance.

Quantitative Evaluations

Outlook
(1 Lowest—5 Highest)
- **2**

Fair Value
- **29¼**

Risk
- **Average**

Earn./Div. Rank
- **NR**

Technical Eval.
- **Bullish** since 9/98

Rel. Strength Rank
(1 Lowest—99 Highest)
- **35**

Insider Activity
- **Neutral**

Recent Price • 25⅜
52 Wk Range • 38¾-24¼
Yield • 0.6%
12-Mo. P/E • 10.9

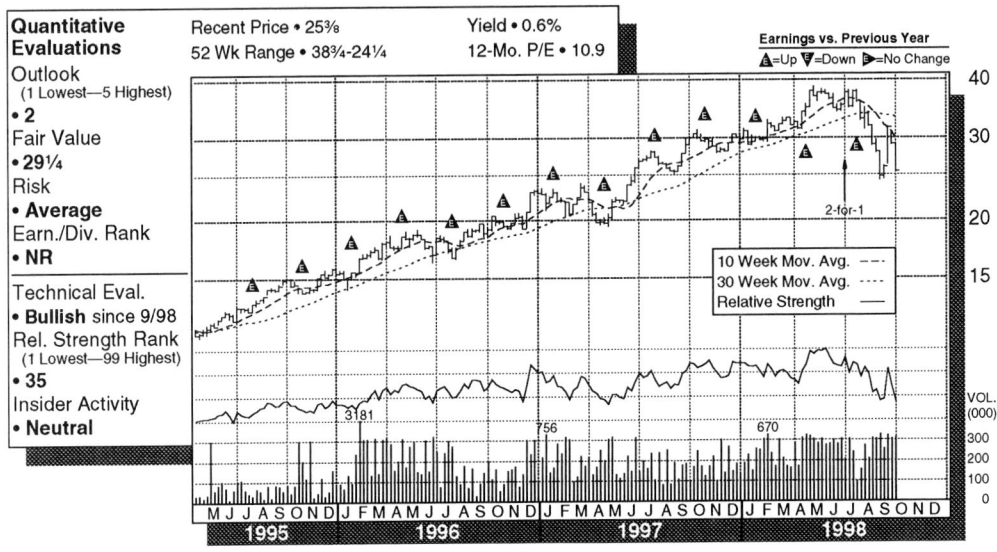

Earnings vs. Previous Year
▲=Up ▼=Down ▷=No Change

10 Week Mov. Avg. ---
30 Week Mov. Avg. ·····
Relative Strength —

Business Profile - 21-AUG-98

Capital Re continues to diversify through product development in its core financial reinsurance lines, expansion into complementary financial and credit-based areas of insurance and reinsurance, and the provision of related financial products and services. In 1997, directors adopted a strategic investment policy, the objective of which is to create a portfolio of investments in businesses related to KRE's core financial lines reinsurance business. The policy permits aggregate expenditures of up to $50 million in connection with such investments and establishes a maximum ownership interest in any one entity of 50%, with a target ownership of 10% to 20%. The policy establishes expected after-tax return targets of 15% on the overall strategic investment portfolio. After reporting seven consecutive years of share earnings gains through 1997, KRE said, in April 1998, that it expected a mid-teen percentage increase for 1998. The shares were split 2-for-1 in June 1998.

Operational Review - 21-AUG-98

Total revenues for the first half of 1998 advanced 49%, year to year, led by 68% growth in net premiums earned. However, expenses rose 80%, and the gain in pretax income was 18%. After taxes at 27.8%, against 29.2%, net income was up 20%, to $39,981,000 ($1.21 a share, split-adjusted), from $33,244,000 ($1.03).

Stock Performance - 02-OCT-98

In the past 30 trading days, KRE's shares have declined 12%, compared to a 7% fall in the S&P 500. Average trading volume for the past five days was 83,860 shares, compared with the 40-day moving average of 82,182 shares.

Key Stock Statistics

Dividend Rate/Share	0.16	Shareholders	NA
Shs. outstg. (M)	31.9	Market cap. (B)	$0.810
Avg. daily vol. (M)	0.085	Inst. holdings	48%
Tang. Bk. Value/Share	18.98		
Beta	0.63		

Value of $10,000 invested 5 years ago: $ 24,732

Fiscal Year Ending Dec. 31

	1998	1997	1996	1995	1994	1993
Revenues (Million $)						
1Q	70.73	—	32.54	25.57	27.46	16.67
2Q	70.49	—	35.34	28.10	27.00	18.80
3Q	—	—	34.81	24.90	23.02	25.60
4Q	—	—	41.93	28.51	23.97	18.41
Yr.	—	201.7	146.4	107.1	101.5	79.48
Earnings Per Share ($)						
1Q	0.60	0.53	0.42	0.38	0.35	0.30
2Q	0.61	0.49	0.42	0.38	0.35	0.30
3Q	—	0.56	0.44	0.39	0.33	0.32
4Q	—	0.57	0.52	0.40	0.32	0.29
Yr.	—	2.15	1.77	1.54	1.34	1.22

Next earnings report expected: late October

Dividend Data (Dividends have been paid since 1992.)

Amount ($)	Date Decl.	Ex-Div. Date	Stock of Record	Payment Date
0.080	Dec. 11	Dec. 18	Dec. 22	Dec. 29 '97
0.080	Feb. 25	Mar. 17	Mar. 19	Mar. 26 '98
0.080	May. 20	Jun. 11	Jun. 15	Jun. 26 '98
2-for-1	May. 20	Jul. 01	Jun. 15	Jun. 30 '98

Business Summary - 21-AUG-98

Capital Re Corp. is an insurance holding company for companies that provide reinsurance to insurers in four principal areas of specialization: financial guaranty insurance, mortgage guaranty insurance, trade credit insurance and title insurance. Gross premiums written by business line in recent years:

	1997	1996
Mortgage	32%	41%
Municipal	24%	37%
Lloyds	23%	Nil
Credit	10%	12%
Non-municipal	8%	8%
Title and financial lines	3%	1%

In all of its principal areas of specialization, KRE seeks to provide innovative reinsurance solutions to satisfy the diverse risk and financial management demands of its primary clients. These solutions often take the form of complex reinsurance arrangements that provide value other than pure risk management, such as financial statement benefit, regulatory relief, and rating agency qualified capital.

As of year-end 1997, Capital Re was providing its reinsurance products through five subsidiaries: Capital Reinsurance Co., Capital Mortgage Reinsurance Co., KRE Reinsurance Ltd., Capital Credit Reinsurance Co. Ltd., and Capital Title Reinsurance Co.

Capital Reinsurance is engaged in the business of financial guaranty reinsurance, primarily the reinsurance of municipal and non-municipal bond insurance obligations. Capital Mortgage Reinsurance reinsures only residential mortgage guaranty insurance obligations.

KRE Reinsurance Ltd. (formerly Capital Mortgage Reinsurance Co.) reinsures financial guaranty, mortgage guaranty, financial insurance, trade credit and other specialty lines of insurance, both as a direct reinsurer of third party primary insurers and as a retrocessionaire of Capital Reinsurance, Capital Mortgage Reinsurance, Capital Credit Reinsurance, and Capital Title Reinsurance.

Capital Credit Reinsurance reinsures trade credit, political risk, and other specialty insurance lines concentrated in Western Europe and the U.S. and is a retrocessionaire of Capital Reinsurance and Capital Mortgage. Capital Title Reinsurance reinsures title insurance policies.

In November 1997, KRE acquired C.I. de Rougement Group (CIDER), a syndicate agency that manages two syndicates operating in the Lloyd's of London insurance market. In October 1997, KRE acquired 50% of newly-formed Lenders Mortgage Alliance Co. LLC, which provides marketing and consulting services to mortgage lenders.

Per Share Data ($)

(Year Ended Dec. 31)	1997	1996	1995	1994	1993	1992	1991	1990	1989	1988
Tangible Bk. Val.	17.71	15.18	14.09	11.01	10.83	9.36	8.19	7.11	NA	NA
Oper. Earnings	NA	NA	NA	1.30	1.20	0.95	1.00	NA	NA	NA
Earnings	2.15	1.80	1.54	1.34	1.22	1.08	1.07	0.97	NA	NA
Dividends	0.14	0.13	0.10	0.10	0.10	0.08	NA	NA	NA	NA
Payout Ratio	7%	7%	7%	8%	8%	7%	NA	NA	NA	NA
Prices - High	31½	23⅜	15⅞	13¾	14½	12⅛	NA	NA	NA	NA
- Low	19⅜	14¼	11	9¼	10¼	8⅝	NA	NA	NA	NA
P/E Ratio - High	15	13	10	10	12	11	NA	NA	NA	NA
- Low	9	8	7	7	8	8	NA	NA	NA	NA

Income Statement Analysis (Million $)

	1997	1996	1995	1994	1993	1992	1991	1990	1989	1988
Premium Inc.	134	92.4	60.1	58.9	44.9	27.8	19.7	13.8	10.3	5.8
Net Invest. Inc.	56.6	51.6	46.7	40.1	32.1	23.8	16.5	15.5	14.6	9.2
Oth. Revs.	11.4	2.4	2.0	2.5	2.4	6.9	5.0	1.8	1.3	0.9
Total Revs.	202	146	107	102	79.5	58.4	41.3	31.0	26.2	15.9
Pretax Inc.	102	77.2	60.1	53.1	49.9	39.6	28.6	22.7	20.0	12.3
Net Oper. Inc.	NA	NA	NA	38.7	35.8	26.6	20.7	16.4	12.7	8.0
Net Inc.	70.1	56.5	45.5	39.8	36.4	30.2	22.2	16.9	13.5	8.1

Balance Sheet & Other Fin. Data (Million $)

	1997	1996	1995	1994	1993	1992	1991	1990	1989	1988
Cash & Equiv.	18.9	27.6	14.0	13.5	10.0	8.3	5.5	4.3	6.0	NA
Premiums Due	27.6	5.8	17.9	4.0	3.1	13.2	9.8	9.6	4.3	NA
Invest. Assets: Bonds	1,011	901	772	574	514	416	238	180	NA	NA
Invest. Assets: Stocks	Nil	Nil	Nil	Nil	Nil	Nil	Nil	Nil	NA	NA
Invest. Assets: Loans	Nil	Nil	Nil	Nil	Nil	Nil	Nil	Nil	NA	NA
Invest. Assets: Total	101	901	772	637	552	444	273	203	181	148
Deferred Policy Costs	135	111	102	90.6	75.5	53.9	40.9	28.2	19.7	NA
Total Assets	1,388	1,156	982	810	712	538	339	254	212	176
Debt	175	100	90.7	90.7	90.7	74.6	2.3	Nil	NA	NA
Common Eqty.	569	489	412	326	324	280	190	145	122	108
Prop. & Cas. Loss Ratio	NA	NA	NA	NA	NA	NA	NA	NA	NA	NA
Prop. & Cas. Expense Ratio	NA	NA	NA	NA	NA	NA	NA	NA	NA	NA
Prop. & Cas. Combined Ratio	NA	NA	NA	NA	NA	NA	NA	NA	NA	NA
% Return On Revs.	48.6	38.6	42.6	39.2	45.7	51.6	53.6	54.4	51.7	51.0
% Ret. on Equity	13.2	12.5	5.1	12.2	12.3	12.8	14.3	12.7	11.7	8.2

Data as orig. reptd.; bef. results of disc. opers. and/or spec. items. Per share data adj. for stk. divs. as of ex-div. date. Bold denotes diluted EPS (FASB 128). E-Estimated. NA-Not Available. NM-Not Meaningful. NR-Not Ranked.

Office—1325 Ave. of the Americas, 18th Fl., New York, NY 10019.**Tel**—(212) 974-0100. **Chrmn & Pres**—M. E. Satz. **EVP-CFO**—D. A. Buzen. **SVP-Secy**—A. S. Roseman. **Investor Contact**—Cathy C. Bailey. **Dirs**—H. W. Conrad Jr., R. L. Huber, S. D. Kesler, P. H. Robinson, E. L. Russell, M. E. Satz, D. R. Skowronski, B. D. Stewart, J. F. Stuermer. **Transfer Agent & Registrar**—Registrar & Transfer Co., Cranford, NJ. **Incorporated**—in Delaware in 1991. **Empl**— 150. **S&P Analyst:** T. W. Smith, CFA

03-OCT-98

Industry:
Paper & Forest Products

Summary: This major manufacturer of recycled paperboard and converted paperboard products operates 51 converting facilities and 25 recycling and waste collection facilities.

Quantitative Evaluations

Recent Price • 23⅝
52 Wk Range • 38⅛-20½

Yield • 2.7%
12-Mo. P/E • 11.3

Outlook
(1 Lowest—5 Highest)
• **3-**

Fair Value
• **23⅜**

Risk
• **Average**

Earn./Div. Rank
• **A-**

Technical Eval.
• **Bullish** since 1/98

Rel. Strength Rank
(1 Lowest—99 Highest)
• **67**

Insider Activity
• **NA**

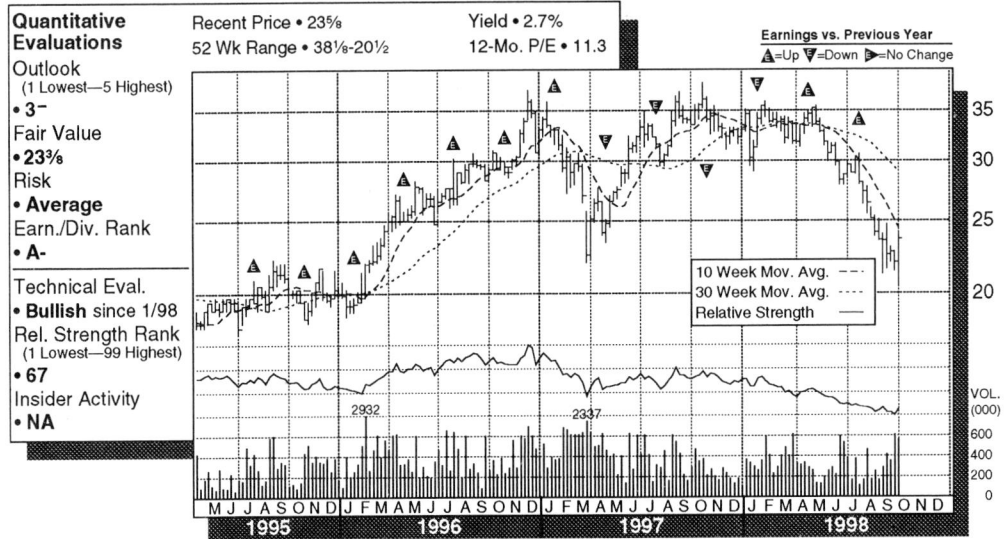

Earnings vs. Previous Year
▲=Up ▼=Down ▶=No Change

10 Week Mov. Avg. – – –
30 Week Mov. Avg. ·····
Relative Strength ——

Business Profile - 19-AUG-98

CSAR expects to spend about $45 million annually through 2000, following expenditures of nearly $53 million in 1997, to continue to upgrade and expand paperboard production and converting capacity. In June 1998, CSAR acquired Tenneco Packaging's 20% stake in the CPI joint venture for $27 million. In March 1998, CSAR acquired Chesapeake Paperboard Co. ($42 million in revenues) for $21 million (including assumption of $8.2 million of debt), expanding its annual recycled paperboard capacity to over 1,050,000 tons. CSAR has purchased 2,258,000 of its common shares since January 1996, and an additional 1,742,000 shares are authorized for repurchase. The dividend was raised 14% with the January 1998 payment.

Operational Review - 19-AUG-98

Net sales in the first half of 1998 advanced 15%, year to year, reflecting contributions from acquisitions. Gross margins narrowed as acquired companies have lower margins than other operations, and with lower margins at the converting operations. Despite well controlled SG&A expenses, operating income rose only 6.1%. Net income was up 7.7%, to $26,508,000 ($1.04 a diluted share), from $24,560,000 ($0.98). CSAR said that with improved operating efficiencies and contributions from acquisitions, it expects better year-to-year comparisons for the second half of 1998.

Stock Performance - 02-OCT-98

In the past 30 trading days, CSAR's shares have declined 2%, compared to a 7% fall in the S&P 500. Average trading volume for the past five days was 112,180 shares, compared with the 40-day moving average of 73,823 shares.

Key Stock Statistics

Dividend Rate/Share	0.64	Shareholders	600
Shs. outstg. (M)	25.4	Market cap. (B)	$0.601
Avg. daily vol. (M)	0.102	Inst. holdings	53%
Tang. Bk. Value/Share	4.67		
Beta	0.38		

Value of $10,000 invested 5 years ago: $ 17,634

Fiscal Year Ending Dec. 31

	1998	1997	1996	1995	1994	1993
Revenues (Million $)						
1Q	176.9	157.6	144.5	130.4	97.00	80.40
2Q	189.7	160.8	140.4	139.7	102.7	84.20
3Q	—	173.7	158.2	138.0	112.4	85.30
4Q	—	176.0	159.6	136.6	119.1	92.50
Yr.	—	668.1	602.7	544.6	431.2	342.4
Earnings Per Share ($)						
1Q	0.52	0.47	0.53	0.35	0.29	0.26
2Q	0.52	0.51	0.61	0.40	0.31	0.28
3Q	—	0.50	0.58	0.40	0.36	0.29
4Q	—	0.55	0.56	0.51	0.42	0.25
Yr.	—	2.03	2.28	1.66	1.38	1.08

Next earnings report expected: mid October

Dividend Data (Dividends have been paid since 1993.)

Amount ($)	Date Decl.	Ex-Div. Date	Stock of Record	Payment Date
0.160	Oct. 24	Dec. 16	Dec. 18	Jan. 08 '98
0.160	Mar. 02	Mar. 18	Mar. 20	Apr. 07 '98
0.160	Apr. 21	Jun. 17	Jun. 19	Jul. 07 '98
0.160	Jul. 21	Sep. 10	Sep. 14	Oct. 06 '98

A Division of The **McGraw-Hill** *Companies*

Business Summary - 19-AUG-98

Caraustar Industries, Inc. (CSAR) continues to grow by acquiring companies that can aid its principal operations and closing those that are not a strategic fit. The company manufactures recycled paperboard and converted paperboard products through 82 facilities in the U.S., Mexico and the U.K. It makes its products primarily from recycled wastepaper. CSAR also operates 25 recycling and waste collection facilities.

In August 1997, the company acquired Oak Tree Packaging Corp. ($44 million in annual revenues; three folding carton facilities) for $16.9 million in equity and the assumption of $17 million in debt and preferred stock; the acqusition increased CSAR's folding carton and contract packaging sales by more than 40%. In April 1997, the company acquired General Packaging Service, Inc., a New Jersey-based packager of pharmaceutical, medical and personal care products, for 416,000 common shares. Also in 1997, CSAR formed a joint venture with Paccess, a packaging materials company, to manufacture paperboard tubes and cores. During 1996, the company formed a joint venture with Tenneco Packaging, a unit of Tenneco, Inc., to operate clay coated recycled paperboard mills in Ohio and Iowa, and also sold a 50% stake in its Standard Gypsum Corp. unit, a producer of gypsum wallboard, for $11 million.

The company's primary manufacturing activity is the production of uncoated recycled paperboard. In this process, wastepaper is reduced to pulp, cleaned and refined and then processed into various grades of paperboard for internal consumption or sale in four principal markets: tubes, cores and composite containers; folding cartons; gypsum wallboard facing paper; and other specialty and converted products. CSAR is the only major producer of recycled paperboard products operating in all four of these markets. The company operates 15 recycled paperboard mills in 12 states. In 1997, 32% of the recycled paperboard sold by its paperboard mills was consumed internally by CSAR converting facilities; the remaining 68% was sold to manufacturers in various industries. External sales of unconverted paperboard accounted for 38% of 1997 net sales.

CSAR derived 33% of net sales in 1997 from sales of tubes, cores and composite containers, together with sales of unconverted paperboard to independent manufacturers of tubes, cores and composite containers, and 32% from folding cartons and related products, together with external sales of boxboard grades of unconverted paperboard.

The company's tube and core converting plants obtain most of their recycled paperboard from its paperboard mills. Because of the relatively high cost of shipping tubes and cores, facilities generally serve customers within a relatively small geographic area.

Per Share Data ($)

(Year Ended Dec. 31)	1997	1996	1995	1994	1993	1992	1991	1990	1989	1988
Tangible Bk. Val.	4.32	3.57	4.73	3.76	2.86	1.93	-3.89	NA	NA	NA
Cash Flow	3.37	3.31	2.34	1.95	1.57	1.74	1.68	NA	NA	NA
Earnings	2.03	2.28	1.66	1.38	1.08	1.26	1.19	NA	NA	NA
Dividends	0.58	0.50	0.43	0.38	0.33	0.08	Nil	Nil	Nil	Nil
Payout Ratio	29%	22%	26%	27%	30%	8%	Nil	Nil	Nil	Nil
Prices - High	38⅛	37¼	23	22½	20¼	20¼	NA	NA	NA	NA
- Low	22	18⅝	15¾	15	13¼	14⅞	NA	NA	NA	NA
P/E Ratio - High	19	16	14	16	19	16	NA	NA	NA	NA
- Low	11	8	9	11	12	12	NA	NA	NA	NA

Income Statement Analysis (Million $)

	1997	1996	1995	1994	1993	1992	1991	1990	1989	1988
Revs.	668	603	545	456	365	309	276	NA	NA	NA
Oper. Inc.	130	125	93.0	78.9	61.0	61.7	59.1	NA	NA	NA
Depr.	34.0	26.3	17.7	14.5	12.5	9.5	8.5	NA	NA	NA
Int. Exp.	14.0	10.6	7.0	6.9	6.8	12.3	16.4	NA	NA	NA
Pretax Inc.	81.7	95.2	69.1	57.6	42.5	39.9	34.2	NA	NA	NA
Eff. Tax Rate	38%	38%	38%	38%	36%	38%	38%	NA	NA	NA
Net Inc.	51.1	57.9	43.0	35.5	27.3	24.9	21.2	NA	NA	NA

Balance Sheet & Other Fin. Data (Million $)

	1997	1996	1995	1994	1993	1992	1991	1990	1989	1988
Cash	1.4	11.9	8.8	12.5	14.4	23.7	3.1	NA	NA	NA
Curr. Assets	141	127	114	101	82.6	75.1	48.8	NA	NA	NA
Total Assets	550	476	322	267	221	184	134	NA	NA	NA
Curr. Liab.	69.3	74.7	67.1	52.3	39.6	28.6	47.4	NA	NA	NA
LT Debt	83.1	83.2	83.4	83.0	84.0	83.0	126	NA	NA	NA
Common Eqty.	214	171	139	102	74.4	47.6	-68.7	NA	NA	NA
Total Cap.	343	292	245	204	171	146	71.0	NA	NA	NA
Cap. Exp.	36.2	32.0	28.0	29.3	21.3	16.6	10.6	NA	NA	NA
Cash Flow	85.1	84.2	60.7	50.0	39.8	34.4	29.8	NA	NA	NA
Curr. Ratio	2.0	1.7	1.7	1.9	2.1	2.6	1.0	NA	NA	NA
% LT Debt of Cap.	24.2	28.4	34.0	41.0	48.9	57.3	176.7	NA	NA	NA
% Net Inc.of Revs.	7.6	9.6	7.9	7.8	7.5	8.1	7.7	NA	NA	NA
% Ret. on Assets	9.9	14.5	14.6	14.5	13.4	13.5	NA	NA	NA	NA
% Ret. on Equity	26.5	37.3	35.7	39.9	44.6	NM	NA	NA	NA	NA

Data as orig. reptd.; bef. results of disc. opers. and/or spec. items. Per share data adj. for stk. divs. as of ex-div. date. Bold denotes diluted EPS (FASB 128). E-Estimated. NA-Not Available. NM-Not Meaningful. NR-Not Ranked.

Office—3100 Washington St., Austell, GA 30001. **Tel**—(770) 948-3101. **Chrmn**—R. M. Robinson II. **Pres & CEO**—T. V. Brown. **VP, CFO & Investor Contact**—H. Lee Thrash III. **Secy**—Marinan R. Mays. **Dirs**—T. V. Brown, M. F. Forrest, J. H. Hance Jr., R. M. Holt, Jr., J. D. Munford, B. M. Prillaman, R. M. Robinson II, J. E. Rogers, H. L. Thrash III. **Transfer Agent & Registrar**—First Union National Bank of North Carolina, Charlotte. **Incorporated**—in North Carolina in 1980. **Empl**— 4,701. **S&P Analyst:** Stewart Scharf

Carmike Cinemas 447R

NYSE Symbol **CKE**

In S&P SmallCap 600

03-OCT-98 **Industry:** Entertainment

Summary: This company is the largest U.S. motion picture exhibitor in terms of total theatres and screens operated.

Quantitative Evaluations

Outlook (1 Lowest—5 Highest)
• **4**

Fair Value
• **26⅝**

Risk
• **Average**

Earn./Div. Rank
• **B-**

Technical Eval.
• **Bearish** since 5/98

Rel. Strength Rank (1 Lowest—99 Highest)
• **34**

Insider Activity
• **NA**

Recent Price • 18¼
52 Wk Range • 33⅞-17⅜

Yield • Nil
12-Mo. P/E • 14.4

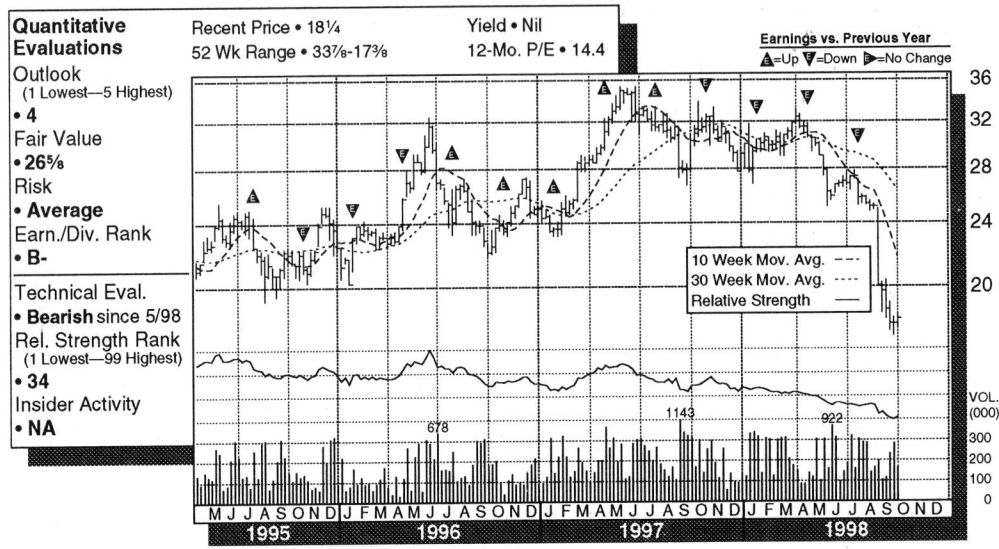

Earnings vs. Previous Year
▲=Up ▼=Down ▶=No Change

10 Week Mov. Avg. — - —
30 Week Mov. Avg. - - - -
Relative Strength ———

Business Profile - 29-APR-98

In 1997, Carmike opened 156 screens in new complexes, added 30 screens to existing locations, and acquired 104 screens from First International Theatres. In the future, the company intends to focus on building, rather than acquiring, screens. In 1998, CKE plans to build 350 new screens, most of which will feature stadium seating and Lucasfilm's THX digital sound surround. The company's long-term goal is to operate 5,000 screens, up from a recent total of 2,700. CKE expects an increase in film releases from about 140 in 1997 to approximately 200 in 1998, as a result of increased competition in the motion picture industry to produce more and better quality films.

Operational Review - 29-APR-98

Total revenues in the three months ended climbed 8.0%, reflecting record breaking sales generated by the movie Titanic as well as a 17% increase in concession sales. Margins widened, due to well controlled film exhibition other theater costs; operating income was up 11%. Following much higher interest and depreciation charges, and taxes at 38.0% in both periods, net income slipped 4.3%, to $3,794,000 ($0.33 a share), from $3,965,000 ($0.35).

Stock Performance - 02-OCT-98

In the past 30 trading days, CKE's shares have declined 27%, compared to a 7% fall in the S&P 500. Average trading volume for the past five days was 32,520 shares, compared with the 40-day moving average of 35,792 shares.

Key Stock Statistics

Dividend Rate/Share	Nil	Shareholders	800
Shs. outstg. (M)	11.4	Market cap. (B)	$0.181
Avg. daily vol. (M)	0.040	Inst. holdings	66%
Tang. Bk. Value/Share	12.34		
Beta	0.66		

Value of $10,000 invested 5 years ago: $ 12,807

Fiscal Year Ending Dec. 31

	1998	1997	1996	1995	1994	1993
Revenues (Million $)						
1Q	117.1	108.5	92.16	63.90	67.43	43.00
2Q	110.7	110.1	104.7	91.23	68.09	50.98
3Q	—	128.7	121.1	112.4	109.0	82.40
4Q	—	111.3	108.8	97.20	83.10	65.40
Yr.	—	458.6	426.7	364.8	327.6	241.8
Earnings Per Share ($)						
1Q	**0.33**	0.35	-2.30	-0.18	0.20	0.11
2Q	**0.03**	0.50	0.40	0.07	0.00	0.04
3Q	—	0.72	0.85	0.70	1.25	0.90
4Q	—	0.18	0.37	0.28	0.36	0.22
Yr.	—	1.78	-0.65	1.16	2.00	1.50

Next earnings report expected: late October

Dividend Data

No dividends have been paid since the company's initial public stock offering. Carmike's loan agreement prohibits the payment of cash dividends.

A Division of The McGraw-Hill Companies

Business Summary - 29-APR-98

Carmike is the largest U.S. motion picture exhibitor in terms of the number of theatres and screens operated. It did not earn that distinction by chance. The company's strategy for growth includes acquiring theatre chains and building its own theatres and screens in markets with little or no competition.

As of April 23, 1998, the company was operating 2,721 screens in 36 states. Theatres are principally in smaller communities, with populations of 40,000 to 200,000, where Carmike is the sole or leading exhibitor.

Total revenues in recent years were derived as follows:

	1997	1996	1995	1994
Admissions	70%	70%	70%	71%
Concessions & other	30%	30%	30%	29%

Of 519 theatres operated at December 31, 1997, nearly all were multi-screen. Of the screens owned by Carmike, nearly all were located in multi-screen theatres, with more than 93% in theatres with three or more screens. The company plans to increase its average number of screens per theatre, from the current 5.2, by building multiplex theatres with 10 to 16 screens each. More screens per theatre increases profit margins, as infrastructure, such as the box office and concession stands, are leveraged over more movie selections and seats. Most of the theatres principally exhibit first-run films, but the company also converts marginally profitable theatres to Discount Theatres that exhibit films that were formerly shown on a first-run basis. At the end of 1997, there were 132 Discount Theatres (441 screens).

During 1997, the company acquired 104 (79 in 1996) screens and had grand openings of 156 (101) screens. The total number of screens in operation at year-end 1997 was 2,720 (2,519). Plans call for the construction of 350 additional screens in 1998. The company may also pursue acquisition candidates.

In addition to the number of screens in operation, profitability is dependent upon the success of first run movie releases.

Via an equally owned joint venture with Wal-Mart Stores, Inc., Carmike is developing entertainment centers, which will include multi-screen theatres, indoor roller skating rinks, themed putting golf courses, bumper car attractions, state-of-the-art games arcades, restaurants and laser tag arenas. The first center opened in May 1997.

Per Share Data ($)

(Year Ended Dec. 31)	1997	1996	1995	1994	1993	1992	1991	1990	1989	1988
Tangible Bk. Val.	11.88	10.32	11.27	11.54	7.94	8.51	8.63	7.85	5.60	4.28
Cash Flow	4.72	1.89	3.58	4.66	3.55	2.25	1.95	1.83	2.23	1.74
Earnings	1.78	-0.65	1.16	2.00	1.50	0.80	0.75	0.84	1.22	0.66
Dividends	Nil	Nil	Nil	Nil	Nil	Nil	Nil	Nil	Nil	Nil
Payout Ratio	Nil	Nil	Nil	Nil	Nil	Nil	Nil	Nil	Nil	Nil
Prices - High	35³/₈	32¹/₂	25¹/₂	24³/₈	20³/₄	17	17¹/₄	16³/₈	13⁷/₈	8¹/₂
- Low	23¹/₈	20¹/₄	18³/₄	16³/₈	12⁷/₈	10¹/₂	9	7¹/₄	7³/₄	5³/₄
P/E Ratio - High	20	NM	22	12	14	21	23	19	11	13
- Low	13	NM	16	8	9	13	12	9	6	9

Income Statement Analysis (Million $)

	1997	1996	1995	1994	1993	1992	1991	1990	1989	1988
Revs.	459	427	365	328	242	172	146	127	99	84.0
Oper. Inc.	89.1	82.4	65.0	67.8	50.3	32.9	28.8	26.0	22.6	17.2
Depr.	33.4	28.4	27.2	22.5	16.3	11.1	9.2	7.4	5.2	5.5
Int. Exp.	23.1	21.4	16.8	17.4	14.8	11.8	10.2	8.3	7.4	6.8
Pretax Inc.	32.6	-11.7	21.7	28.2	19.8	10.1	9.6	10.5	10.5	5.4
Eff. Tax Rate	38%	NM	40%	40%	40%	40%	41%	40%	41%	38%
Net Inc.	20.2	-7.3	13.1	17.0	11.9	6.1	5.7	6.3	6.2	3.3

Balance Sheet & Other Fin. Data (Million $)

	1997	1996	1995	1994	1993	1992	1991	1990	1989	1988
Cash	16.5	12.3	18.8	22.7	32.7	32.1	24.0	30.4	15.2	17.6
Curr. Assets	31.0	26.1	39.6	33.5	42.2	39.0	32.7	40.2	20.1	21.3
Total Assets	620	489	478	378	327	230	184	179	135	112
Curr. Liab.	63.0	53.7	56.2	44.2	37.2	27.3	17.0	15.8	12.5	10.8
LT Debt	342	253	218	144	181	120	91.6	94.0	85.1	71.1
Common Eqty.	203	178	185	172	93.9	75.7	69.2	63.3	32.8	26.0
Total Cap.	557	436	422	333	290	203	167	163	122	101
Cap. Exp.	126	71.0	58.0	29.1	33.5	13.3	22.7	34.1	31.0	16.7
Cash Flow	53.6	21.1	40.3	39.5	28.1	17.2	14.9	13.7	11.4	8.8
Curr. Ratio	0.5	0.5	0.7	0.8	1.1	1.4	1.9	2.5	1.6	2.0
% LT Debt of Cap.	61.4	58.1	51.8	43.2	62.3	59.2	54.8	57.7	69.5	70.4
% Net Inc.of Revs.	4.4	NM	3.6	5.2	4.9	3.6	3.9	4.9	6.3	3.9
% Ret. on Assets	3.6	NM	3.1	4.1	4.2	2.9	3.1	3.3	5.0	3.0
% Ret. on Equity	10.6	NM	7.3	11.2	13.6	8.4	8.6	11.3	21.2	13.6

Data as orig. reptd.; bef. results of disc. opers. and/or spec. items. Per share data adj. for stk. divs. as of ex-div. date. Bold denotes diluted EPS (FASB 128). E-Estimated. NA-Not Available. NM-Not Meaningful. NR-Not Ranked.

Office—1301 First Ave., Columbus, GA 31901. **Tel**—(706) 576-3400. **Chrmn**—C. L. Patrick. **Pres & CEO**—M. W. Patrick. **SVP-Fin, Treas, CFO & Investor Contact**—Phil Smitley (706) 576-2836.**VP & Secy**—F. L. Champion, III. **Dirs**—J. W. Jordan II, C. L. Patrick, C. L. Patrick, Jr., M. W. Patrick, C. E. Sanders, D. W. Zalaznick. **Transfer Agent & Registrar**—Synovus Trust Co., Columbus, GA. **Incorporated**— in Delaware in 1982. **Empl**— 10,500. **S&P Analyst:** Robert J. Izmirlian

Carolina First 3446W

NASDAQ Symbol **CAFC**

In S&P SmallCap 600

03-OCT-98

Industry: Banks (Regional)

Summary: This bank holding company owns Carolina First Bank, the largest South Carolina-based commercial bank, with about 65 branch offices and $2.3 billion in assets.

Quantitative Evaluations

Recent Price • 21¼
52 Wk Range • 30⅝-18½

Yield • 1.5%
12-Mo. P/E • 17.6

Outlook (1 Lowest—5 Highest)
• **NA**

Fair Value
• **NA**

Risk
• **Average**

Earn./Div. Rank
• **B+**

Technical Eval.
• **Bearish** since 3/98

Rel. Strength Rank (1 Lowest—99 Highest)
• **61**

Insider Activity
• **NA**

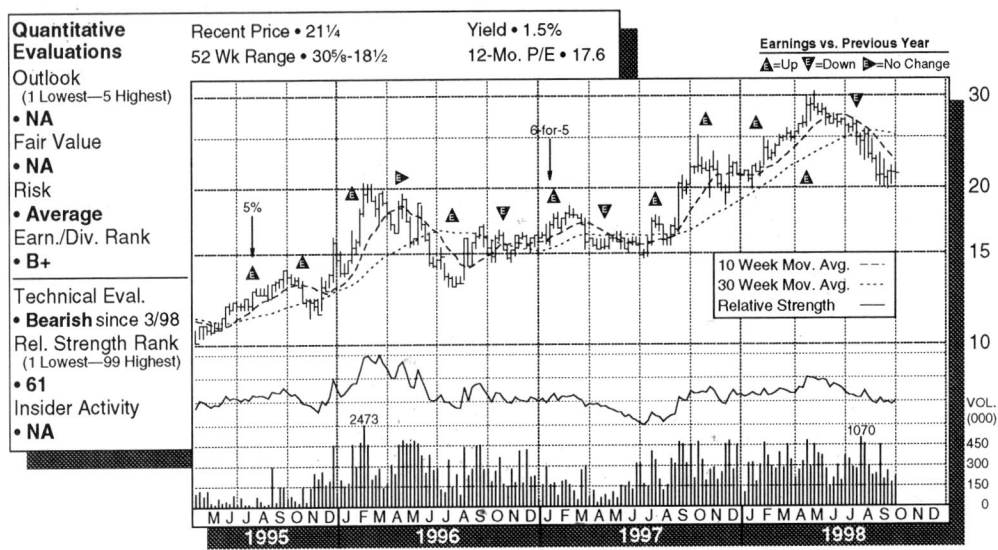

Earnings vs. Previous Year
▲=Up ▼=Down ▶=No Change

10 Week Mov. Avg. – – –
30 Week Mov. Avg. · · · ·
Relative Strength —

Business Profile - 14-SEP-98

Through a series of acquisitions since its founding a decade ago, CAFC has become the largest South Carolina-based commercial bank and the second-largest mortgage loan servicer in the state, establishing itself in South Carolina's largest markets. In the second quarter of 1998, CAFC agreed to acquire two South Carolina banks: Poinsett Financial Corp. ($88.3 million in assets) for $15.6 million in stock and Colonial Bank of South Carolina ($59.8 million in assets) for $12.8 million in stock. This follows the 1997 acquisitions of Lowcountry Savings Bank, with five offices in the Charleston area, and First Southeast Financial Corp., with branches throughout strategic Anderson County.

Operational Review - 14-SEP-98

Net interest income climbed 32% year to year in the first six months of 1998, as growth in average earning assets outweighed a narrower net interest margin (4.22% versus 4.45%). The provision for loan losses fell 6.7%, to $5.6 million from $6.0 million. Noninterest income of $9.7 million was unchanged from the year earlier period. Despite an acquisition-related 17% increase in noninterest expenses, net income climbed 60%, to $10.2 million ($0.59 a share, diluted, on about 60% more shares), from $6.4 million ($0.56).

Stock Performance - 02-OCT-98

In the past 30 trading days, CAFC's shares have declined 6%, compared to a 7% fall in the S&P 500. Average trading volume for the past five days was 42,840 shares, compared with the 40-day moving average of 53,018 shares.

Key Stock Statistics

Dividend Rate/Share	0.32	Shareholders	3,200
Shs. outstg. (M)	18.2	Market cap. (B)	$0.386
Avg. daily vol. (M)	0.043	Inst. holdings	14%
Tang. Bk. Value/Share	11.01		
Beta	0.96		

Value of $10,000 invested 5 years ago: $ 24,784

Fiscal Year Ending Dec. 31

	1998	1997	1996	1995	1994	1993
Revenues (Million $)						
1Q	46.74	33.48	32.39	28.07	15.69	11.04
2Q	—	38.55	32.15	27.64	18.84	13.90
3Q	—	40.45	38.68	30.24	21.40	14.64
4Q	—	42.85	35.00	33.12	23.51	15.36
Yr.	—	155.3	138.2	119.1	79.46	54.94
Earnings Per Share ($)						
1Q	0.28	0.15	0.23	0.20	0.21	0.17
2Q	0.31	0.41	0.23	0.20	0.20	0.13
3Q	—	0.30	0.21	0.23	0.22	0.19
4Q	—	0.32	0.28	0.23	-1.37	0.23
Yr.	—	1.18	0.96	0.87	-0.75	0.71

Next earnings report expected: mid October

Dividend Data (Dividends have been paid since 1994.)

Amount ($)	Date Decl.	Ex-Div. Date	Stock of Record	Payment Date
0.080	Dec. 17	Jan. 13	Jan. 15	Feb. 01 '98
0.080	Feb. 18	Apr. 13	Apr. 15	May. 01 '98
0.080	May. 20	Jul. 13	Jul. 15	Aug. 01 '98
0.080	Sep. 16	Oct. 13	Oct. 15	Nov. 01 '98

STANDARD
&POOR'S
STOCK REPORTS

Carolina First Corporation

3446W
03-OCT-98

Business Summary - 14-SEP-98

Since its inception in 1986, Carolina First Corporation has grown its assets, loans and deposits at a compound annual rate in excess of 20%, and is now the largest independent bank holding company in South Carolina. Through its 65 banking offices statewide, the company strives to be a "super community bank," serving individuals and small-to-midsize companies. Subsidiaries also include Carolina First Mortgage Co., Blue Ridge Finance Co. (an automobile finance company), and CF Investment Co.

Interest on loans provides the majority of revenue. Totaling $1.6 billion at year-end 1997, net loans broke down as follows in recent years:

	1997	1996	1995
Commercial/industrial	14%	17%	18%
Mortgage	55%	55%	42%
Consumer/credit cards	12%	16%	22%
Other	19%	12%	18%

Banks must regularly provision against possible losses. CAFC's allowance for loan losses covered nonperforming loans by over 6.6 times at year-end 1997, up from around 3.9 times a year earlier. Concurrently, asset quality improved during the year, as nonperforming assets fell to only 0.23% of total loans,

from 0.52%, substantially below the 1.04% and 1.20% of CAFC's peers.

Deposits are the largest (and most cost effective) source of funds to the bank. At December 31, 1997, deposits totaled approximately $1.75 billion, and were apportioned 12% non interest-bearing demand, 18% interest-bearing demand, 10% money market, 4% savings, and 55% time.

Lending profitability, commonly measured by the yield on a bank's average earning assets, or net interest margin, is affected by changes in the volume and mix of assets and liabilities, as well as changes in interest rates. During 1997, Carolina First's net interest margin remained virtually unchanged at 4.36%, from 4.35%, as an unfavorable shift in the mix of earning assets offset a higher rate paid on funds.

As of June 30, 1998, CAFC owned 2.5 million common shares and warrants to purchase another 3.5 million shares (a 17% ownership stake) in Affinity Technology Group, a Columbia, SC, enterprise that is developing a new generation of bank machines. It has also invested in Atlanta Internet Bank, FSB (NET.B@nk, Inc.), a de novo banking operation formed to provide banking services on the Internet, introduced in October 1996. Following the initial public offering of Net.B@nk, Inc. stock in July 1997, CAFC now owns an 18% stake in the operation.

Per Share Data ($)

(Year Ended Dec. 31)	1997	1996	1995	1994	1993	1992	1991	1990	1989	1988
Tangible Bk. Val.	9.75	7.79	5.27	6.81	5.17	6.60	6.79	7.33	7.08	6.94
Earnings	1.18	0.96	0.87	-0.75	0.72	0.45	0.41	0.26	0.23	0.32
Dividends	0.28	0.23	0.19	0.16	Nil	Nil	Nil	Nil	Nil	Nil
Payout Ratio	24%	24%	22%	NM	Nil	Nil	Nil	Nil	Nil	Nil
Prices - High	25¼	20½	16⅛	12½	11⅛	9½	6¾	9⅝	9⅝	NA
- Low	14⅝	12⅞	10⅛	9⅛	8¼	5⅝	5¼	6	7⅛	NA
P/E Ratio - High	21	21	19	NM	16	21	16	38	43	NA
- Low	12	13	12	NM	11	13	13	23	32	NA

Income Statement Analysis (Million $)

	1997	1996	1995	1994	1993	1992	1991	1990	1989	1988
Net Int. Inc.	66.7	57.1	50.8	41.6	26.9	17.8	12.9	10.2	8.0	7.0
Loan Loss Prov.	11.6	10.3	6.8	0.9	0.9	1.4	1.4	0.8	0.9	0.6
Non Int. Inc.	16.6	21.3	17.3	7.9	6.3	3.1	1.6	1.1	1.0	0.6
Non Int. Exp.	52.2	51.7	46.9	50.5	25.2	16.1	11.6	8.9	NA	NA
Pretax Inc.	22.4	16.4	14.4	-1.9	7.1	3.7	2.1	1.6	NA	NA
Eff. Tax Rate	36%	36%	35%	NM	31%	32%	21%	36%	NA	NA
Net Inc.	14.3	10.5	9.4	-1.9	4.9	2.5	1.7	1.1	0.9	1.3
% Net Int. Marg.	4.36	4.35	4.54	4.89	4.31	4.06	3.63	3.37	3.00	3.36

Balance Sheet & Other Fin. Data (Million $)

	1997	1996	1995	1994	1993	1992	1991	1990	1989	1988
Total Assets	2,156	1,574	1,415	1,120	816	529	447	346	326	264
Loans	1,351	1,113	1,054	795	559	392	335	273	231	191
Deposits	1,747	1,281	1,095	925	725	476	407	300	288	221
Capitalization:										
Debt	39.1	26.4	26.3	1.2	1.2	1.3	1.3	NA	NA	NA
Equity	202	104	62.0	42.0	47.2	33.9	31.9	30.2	28.8	27.9
Total	241	131	121	80.2	64.1	45.5	33.2	NA	NA	NA
% Ret. on Assets	0.8	0.7	0.7	NM	0.7	0.5	0.4	0.3	0.3	0.6
% Ret. on Equity	9.4	12.7	11.9	NM	8.5	6.3	5.4	3.5	3.3	4.9
% Loan Loss Resv.	1.2	1.0	0.8	0.6	1.0	1.1	1.1	0.9	0.9	0.8
% Risk Based Capital	11.2	10.4	10.2	8.4	9.4	11.6	NA	NA	NA	NA
Price Times Book Value:										
Hi	2.6	2.6	3.1	1.8	2.2	1.4	1.0	NA	NA	NA
Low	1.5	1.7	1.9	1.3	1.6	0.9	0.8	NA	NA	NA

Data as orig. reptd.; bef. results of disc. opers. and/or spec. items. Per share data adj. for stk. divs. as of ex-div. date. Bold denotes diluted EPS (FASB 128). E-Estimated. NA-Not Available. NM-Not Meaningful. NR-Not Ranked.

Office—102 S. Main St., Greenville, SC 29601. **Tel**—(864) 255-7900. **Website**—www.carolinafirst.com **Chrmn**—W. R. Timmons Jr. **Pres & CEO**—M. I. Whittle Jr. **EVP, CFO, Secy & Investor Contact**—William S. Hummers III. **Dirs**—J. B. Farr, C. C. Grimes Jr., M. D. Hagy, W. S. Hummers III, V. E. Merchant, Jr., W. R. Phillips, H. E. Russell, Jr., C. B. Schooler, E. P. Stall, E. E. Stone IV, W. R. Timmons Jr., D. C. Wakefield III, M. I. Whittle Jr. **Transfer Agent & Registrar**—Reliance Trust Co., Atlanta. **Incorporated**—in South Carolina in 1986. **Empl**—622. **S&P Analyst:** C. A. S.

03-OCT-98

Industry: Natural Gas

Summary: This natural gas distributor serves more than 90 communities in Washington and Oregon.

Quantitative Evaluations

Recent Price • 16⅝

52 Wk Range • 19-14⅝

Yield • 5.8%

12-Mo. P/E • 21.9

Outlook
(1 Lowest—5 Highest)
• **1**

Fair Value
• **11¾**

Risk
• **Low**

Earn./Div. Rank
• **B+**

Technical Eval.
• **Bullish** since 3/98

Rel. Strength Rank
(1 Lowest—99 Highest)
• **93**

Insider Activity
• **NA**

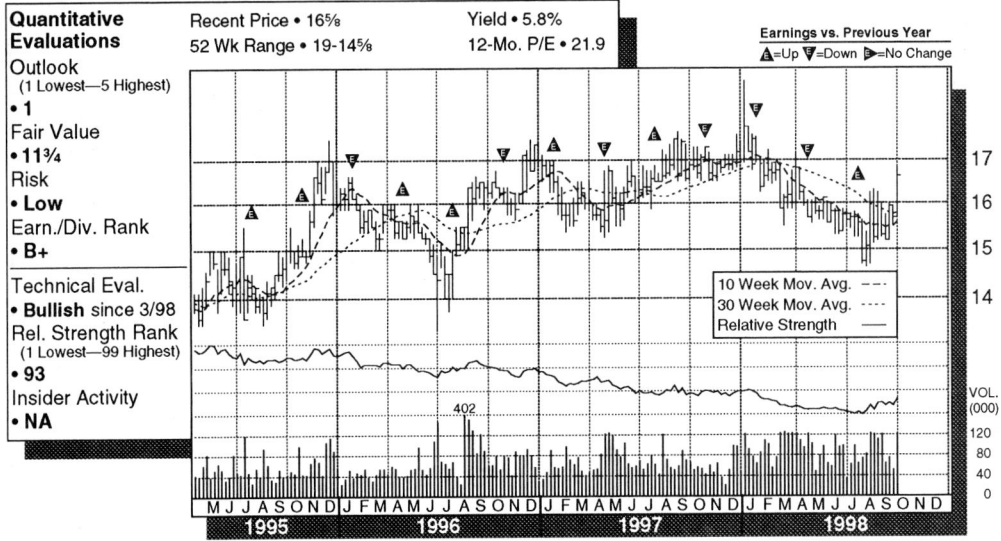

Earnings vs. Previous Year
▲=Up ▼=Down ▶=No Change

10 Week Mov. Avg. – – –
30 Week Mov. Avg. · · · ·
Relative Strength ——

Business Profile - 13-MAR-98

Customer growth contributed to higher earnings in FY 97 (Sep.), and management believes there are still significant opportunities for profitable customer expansion, with forecasters expecting population and economic growth in Washington and Oregon to continue at rates far above national averages. The company anticipates robust levels of new construction continuing to supplement its market for converting existing homes and businesses to natural gas from other fuels. Moreover, the company has signed contracts to serve several new or expanded large volume loads, including food processors, a lumber mill and a diatomaceous earth plant in FY 98 and a new state prison in 1999.

Operational Review - 13-MAR-98

Revenues in the first three months of FY 98 (Sep.) declined 6.1%, year to year. Operating margins were down slightly, as lower residential and commercial margins, due to warmer weather, were offset by improved margins from industrial and other customers. Following a 5.6% increase in operating costs and 6.6% higher net interest and other deductions, pretax income fell 9.5%. After taxes at 37.5%, versus 35.8%, net income was down 12%, to $5,682,000 ($0.51 a share, after preferred dividends), from $6,448,000 ($0.59).

Stock Performance - 02-OCT-98

In the past 30 trading days, CGC's shares have increased 9%, compared to a 7% fall in the S&P 500. Average trading volume for the past five days was 26,780 shares, compared with the 40-day moving average of 21,462 shares.

Key Stock Statistics

Dividend Rate/Share	0.96	Shareholders	10,000
Shs. outstg. (M)	11.0	Market cap. (B)	$0.184
Avg. daily vol. (M)	0.016	Inst. holdings	30%
Tang. Bk. Value/Share	10.51		
Beta	0.07		

Value of $10,000 invested 5 years ago: $ 14,826

Fiscal Year Ending Sep. 30

	1998	1997	1996	1995	1994	1993
Revenues (Million $)						
1Q	60.98	64.97	56.91	64.61	64.75	61.73
2Q	65.55	71.17	67.62	34.71	36.26	37.14
3Q	37.00	33.73	33.46	26.51	28.87	29.44
4Q	—	25.91	26.58	56.91	62.53	59.15
Yr.	—	195.8	184.6	182.7	192.4	187.4
Earnings Per Share ($)						
1Q	**0.51**	0.59	0.56	0.63	0.54	0.84
2Q	**0.57**	0.69	0.72	-0.11	-0.16	-0.13
3Q	**-0.07**	-0.10	-0.20	-0.27	-0.28	-0.25
4Q	—	-0.23	-0.22	0.56	0.50	0.59
Yr.	—	0.93	0.84	0.80	0.60	1.05

Next earnings report expected: early November

Dividend Data (Dividends have been paid since 1964.)

Amount ($)	Date Decl.	Ex-Div. Date	Stock of Record	Payment Date
0.240	Dec. 15	Jan. 13	Jan. 15	Feb. 13 '98
0.240	Mar. 18	Apr. 13	Apr. 15	May. 15 '98
0.240	Jun. 16	Jul. 13	Jul. 15	Aug. 14 '98
0.240	Sep. 18	Oct. 13	Oct. 15	Nov. 13 '98

A Division of The McGraw-Hill Companies

Business Summary - 13-MAR-98

With a 5.3% increase in customers during FY 97 (Sep.), Cascade Natural Gas Corp. (CGC) continues to be one of the fastest growing gas distribution companies in the U.S. Forecasters project population and job growth within CGC's core markets (Washington and Oregon) to be well above the national averages far into the next decade. Thus, CGC intends to maintain its strategic focus on natural gas distribution.

Anchored in Seattle, WA, CGC's service territory fans out to some 90 communities in Washington and Oregon, where it distributes natural gas to a population of 744,000. Washington accounts for about 84% of its business. As of September 30, 1997, CGC had about 160,000 core customers and 162 non-core customers.

Core customers are principally residential and small customers who take traditional "bundled" natural gas service which includes supply, peaking service and upstream interstate pipeline transportation. Sales to its core customers account for about 22% of gas deliveries and 68% of operating margin.

Non-core customers are generally large industrial and institutional customers who have chosen "unbundled"

service, meaning that they select from among several supply and upstream pipeline transportation options, independent of CGC's distribution service. CGC's margin from non-core customers is derived only from this distribution service. The principal activities of its customers include the processing of forest products, production of chemicals, refining of crude oil, production of aluminum, generation of electricity, and processing of food.

Share earnings in FY 97 were 10.7% higher than in the prior year, with results affected primarily by operating margins. In FY 97, earnings were reduced $0.06 per share by gas cost increases in Oregon. Additionally, in FY 96 earnings were $0.10 per share lower due to a charge against income for unrecovered gas costs and valuation adjustments to non-utility assets.

The majority of CGC's natural gas supply is transported through Northwest Pipeline Corp. Baseload supply is provided by six major long-term gas supply contracts. About 93% of the gas supplied under the contracts is from Canadian sources. The remainder is domestic. In FY 97, CGC purchased 79% of its total gas supplies under firm gas supply contracts and 21% on the spot market.

Per Share Data ($)

(Year Ended Sep. 30)	1997	1996	1995	1994	1993	1992	1991	1990	1989	1988
Tangible Bk. Val.	10.18	10.12	9.79	9.84	10.00	9.05	8.59	8.33	7.91	7.45
Earnings	0.93	0.84	0.80	0.60	1.05	0.63	1.14	1.26	1.29	0.84
Dividends	0.96	0.96	0.96	0.96	0.94	0.93	0.90	0.87	0.85	0.85
Payout Ratio	103%	114%	120%	160%	90%	146%	79%	69%	66%	102%
Prices - High	19	17½	17½	18⅛	19½	17	16⅞	12⅝	13¾	10⅞
- Low	15¼	13⅜	13	12¾	15½	13⅝	11⅛	10⅛	9⅜	9⅛
P/E Ratio - High	20	21	22	30	18	27	15	10	11	13
- Low	16	16	16	21	14	21	10	8	7	11

Income Statement Analysis (Million $)

	1997	1996	1995	1994	1993	1992	1991	1990	1989	1988
Revs.	196	185	183	192	187	152	154	161	174	158
Depr.	13.4	12.4	11.7	10.1	9.2	8.4	7.7	7.3	6.8	6.5
Maint.	NA	NA	NA	NA	NA	NA	NA	NA	NA	NA
Fxd. Chgs. Cov.	2.5	1.8	2.0	2.0	2.5	1.9	2.4	2.5	2.6	1.9
Constr. Credits	0.5	0.6	0.4	0.2	0.3	0.2	0.2	0.1	0.1	0.1
Eff. Tax Rate	37%	34%	37%	35%	37%	37%	36%	35%	38%	34%
Net Inc.	10.6	8.2	7.7	5.8	8.9	4.8	7.7	8.4	8.5	5.6

Balance Sheet & Other Fin. Data (Million $)

	1997	1996	1995	1994	1993	1992	1991	1990	1989	1988
Gross Prop.	426	403	378	342	315	284	249	231	217	205
Cap. Exp.	29.2	41.1	37.6	27.0	33.0	35.3	19.7	16.4	12.9	10.4
Net Prop.	265	256	239	214	197	175	148	137	129	124
Capitalization:										
LT Debt	121	102	102	100	87.0	74.7	57.1	60.8	60.1	64.6
% LT Debt	51	47	51	45	48	49	47	51	52	56
Pfd.	6.6	6.8	6.8	7.2	7.5	8.0	8.3	2.4	2.9	3.2
% Pfd.	2.80	3.20	3.50	3.70	4.20	5.20	6.70	2.10	2.50	2.70
Common	112	109	89.5	87.7	85.7	69.2	57.2	54.9	51.7	48.2
% Common	47	50	45	45	48	46	47	47	45	42
Total Cap.	256	237	218	214	198	168	137	132	129	130
% Oper. Ratio	90.0	90.2	90.5	92.6	91.4	92.0	90.8	89.8	90.2	91.3
% Earn. on Net Prop.	7.6	7.3	9.6	7.0	8.7	7.5	9.9	12.2	13.5	11.2
% Return On Revs.	5.4	4.4	4.2	3.0	4.7	3.2	5.0	5.2	4.9	3.5
% Return On Invest. Capital	8.1	8.0	10.4	6.9	8.8	8.2	11.6	13.0	13.0	11.1
% Return On Com. Equity	9.2	7.7	8.1	6.0	11.0	6.7	13.4	15.4	16.6	11.2

Data as orig. reptd.; bef. results of disc. opers. and/or spec. items. Per share data adj. for stk. divs. as of ex-div. date. Yrs. ended Dec. 31 prior to 1996. Bold denotes diluted EPS (FASB 128). E-Estimated. NA-Not Available. NM-Not Meaningful. NR-Not Ranked.

Office—222 Fairview Ave. North, Seattle, WA 98109. **Tel**—(206) 624-3900. **Chrmn & CEO**—W. B. Matsuyama. **Pres & COO**—R. E. Boyd. **VP-Fin, CFO & Investor Contact**—J. D. Wessling. **Contr**—J. E. Haug. **Dirs**— C. Burnham, Jr., M. C. Clapp, T.E. Cronin, D. A. Ederer, H. L. Hubbard, W. B. Matsuyama, L. L. Pinnt, B. G. Ragen, M. A. Williams. **Transfer Agent & Registrar**—Bank of New York, NYC. **Incorporated**—in Washington in 1953. **Empl**— 484. **S&P Analyst:** C.C.P.

STANDARD &POOR'S
STOCK REPORTS

Casey's General Stores　**3450**

NASDAQ Symbol **CASY**

In S&P SmallCap 600

03-OCT-98　**Industry:** Retail (Specialty)

Summary: This company operates 1,100 convenience stores in nine midwestern states, selling a broad selection of food, beverage, health and automotive products.

Quantitative Evaluations

Outlook (1 Lowest—5 Highest)
• **4**

Fair Value
• **18¾**

Risk
• **Average**

Earn./Div. Rank
• **A**

Technical Eval.
• **Bearish** since 9/98

Rel. Strength Rank (1 Lowest—99 Highest)
• **94**

Insider Activity
• **NA**

Recent Price • 15½
52 Wk Range • 18¼-11½

Yield • 0.4%
12-Mo. P/E • 23.1

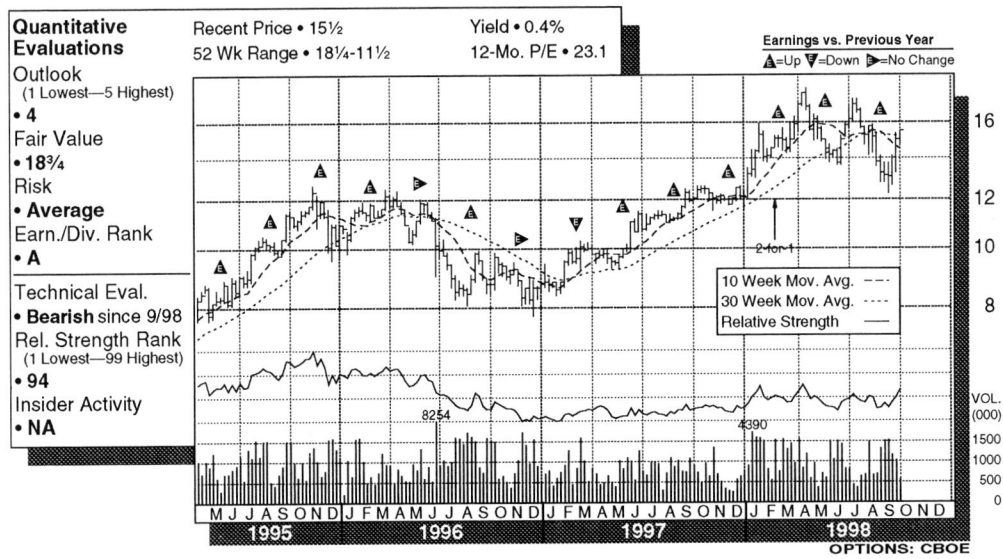

Earnings vs. Previous Year
▲=Up ▼=Down ▶=No Change

10 Week Mov. Avg. — — —
30 Week Mov. Avg. · · · · ·
Relative Strength ——

OPTIONS: CBOE

Business Profile - 11-SEP-98

Results in recent periods benefited from an aggressive store opening program, strict cost controls, higher gasoline volumes, and continued emphasis on marketing prepared foods, which carry higher profit margins than general staple items. The company expects to open 80 stores in FY 99 (Apr.). Casey's sold a record 176 million gallons of gasoline in the first quarter, reflecting retail prices that average 15.6 cents a gallon less than a year ago. Gasoline sales account for over 50% of retail sales, but a much smaller portion of profits. As a result of the company's reliance on the wholesale price of gasoline, profit margins can be difficult to predict on a quarterly basis.

Operational Review - 11-SEP-98

Net sales in the three months ended July 31, 1998, advanced 3.7%, year to year, reflecting 68 more stores in operation. Gross margins widened on better merchandise margins on gasoline sales and grocery sales; operating income was up 17%. Despite a sharp rise in interest expense, pretax income climbed 19%. After taxes at 37.5% in both periods, net income also advanced 19%, to $12,497,000 ($0.24 a share), from $10,541,000 ($0.20).

Stock Performance - 02-OCT-98

In the past 30 trading days, CASY's shares have increased 12%, compared to a 7% fall in the S&P 500. Average trading volume for the past five days was 110,540 shares, compared with the 40-day moving average of 222,513 shares.

Key Stock Statistics

Dividend Rate/Share	0.06	Shareholders	2,700
Shs. outstg. (M)	52.6	Market cap. (B)	$0.816
Avg. daily vol. (M)	0.232	Inst. holdings	65%
Tang. Bk. Value/Share	5.23		
Beta	0.60		

Value of $10,000 invested 5 years ago: $ 38,077

Fiscal Year Ending Apr. 30

	1999	1998	1997	1996	1995	1994
Revenues (Million $)						
1Q	332.4	320.6	286.9	253.0	221.3	193.7
2Q	—	317.4	286.3	244.6	223.7	187.0
3Q	—	276.9	273.3	221.6	199.4	172.6
4Q	—	271.0	262.5	236.9	204.5	177.9
Yr.	—	1,187	1,109	954.8	848.8	731.2
Earnings Per Share ($)						
1Q	0.24	0.20	0.17	0.15	0.13	0.11
2Q	—	0.20	0.17	0.17	0.14	0.12
3Q	—	0.14	0.10	0.13	0.11	0.09
4Q	—	0.09	0.07	0.06	0.06	0.05
Yr.	—	0.63	0.52	0.51	0.44	0.36

Next earnings report expected: **early December**

Dividend Data (Dividends have been paid since 1990.)

Amount ($)	Date Decl.	Ex-Div. Date	Stock of Record	Payment Date
2-for-1	—	Feb. 17	Feb. 02	Feb. 16 '98
0.015	Mar. 03	Apr. 29	May. 01	May. 15 '98
0.015	Jun. 12	Jul. 30	Aug. 03	Aug. 17 '98
0.015	Aug. 25	Oct. 29	Nov. 02	Nov. 16 '98

A Division of The McGraw-Hill Companies

Business Summary - 11-SEP-98

One company has found a way to make a big business out of small towns. Casey's General Stores, Inc. (CASY) has left the city behind and caters to the needs of many of the small towns in the Midwest. Casey's, through its company stores and franchises, operates 1,109 convenience stores that serve gasoline and freshly prepared food. Approximately 70% of all Casey's General Stores are located in areas with populations of fewer than 5,000 persons.

Casey's revenue is derived from the sale of food, and beverages and non-food products such as health and beauty aids, tobacco products, automotive products and gasoline by company stores and from the wholesale sale of merchandise items and gasoline to franchised stores. The company also generates revenues from continuing monthly royalties based on sales by franchised stores.

Casey's, headquartered in Ankeny, Iowa, was incorporated in 1967 and began marketing made-from-scratch pizza, its most popular prepared food product, in 1984, offering it to 93% of its stores by 1997. The company tries to define the space between the convenience store

and the traditional small town general store. It experiments with additions to the company's product line and each Casey's General Store typically carries approximately 1,800 food and non-food items. Each store also sells gasoline or gasohol and may sell hardware, ammunition and pet supplies.

The company makes substantial capital investments in its stores. During the first three months of FY 99 (Apr.), it spent $25,535,000 for property and equipment, primarily for the construction and remodeling of company stores, compared with $22,163,966 in the same period in the prior year. In FY 98, capital expenditures totaled over $85 million.

Including company stores and franchises, Casey's as of April 1998 was operating 317 stores in Iowa, 283 in Illinois, 238 in Missouri, 95 in Kansas, 67 in Minnesota, 54 in Nebraska, 20 in South Dakota, 19 in Indiana, and 16 in Wisconsin. The company intends to continue to increase the number of the profitable company stores. Casey's derives approximately 95% of its gross profits from retail sales by company-owned stores. For the near term, Casey's will limit its expansion to small communities in its current market before pursuing expansion in other territories.

Per Share Data ($)

(Year Ended Apr. 30)	1998	1997	1996	1995	1994	1993	1992	1991	1990	1989
Tangible Bk. Val.	5.01	4.42	3.93	3.46	3.06	2.44	2.16	1.93	1.74	1.55
Cash Flow	1.21	1.02	0.98	0.86	0.77	0.65	0.56	0.47	0.40	0.34
Earnings	0.63	0.52	0.51	0.44	0.36	0.30	0.26	0.20	0.18	0.15
Dividends	0.10	0.05	0.05	0.05	0.04	0.03	0.03	0.03	Nil	Nil
Payout Ratio	17%	10%	10%	11%	10%	10%	12%	12%	Nil	Nil
Cal. Yrs.	1997	1996	1995	1994	1993	1992	1991	1990	1989	1988
Prices - High	12⁷/₈	12¹/₂	12³/₄	7³/₄	6¹/₄	4⁷/₈	4¹/₄	2⁷/₈	3⁵/₈	4
- Low	8³/₈	7³/₄	7¹/₄	5¹/₄	3³/₄	3¹/₈	1⁵/₁₆	1¹/₄	1¹⁵/₁₆	2⁷/₈
P/E Ratio - High	20	24	25	17	17	16	16	14	20	26
- Low	13	15	14	12	10	11	6	6	11	19

Income Statement Analysis (Million $)

	1998	1997	1996	1995	1994	1993	1992	1991	1990	1989
Revs.	1,192	1,114	960	854	615	578	525	519	456	386
Oper. Inc.	89.8	76.1	73.4	65.2	51.9	42.2	36.6	31.3	27.4	22.4
Depr.	30.4	26.9	24.7	22.2	18.4	15.5	13.3	12.2	10.1	8.3
Int. Exp.	6.6	7.9	7.2	6.4	8.0	6.2	5.4	5.4	5.4	4.2
Pretax Inc.	53.5	43.2	43.0	37.4	27.0	21.5	18.5	14.4	13.3	11.2
Eff. Tax Rate	38%	38%	38%	39%	39%	38%	38%	37%	37%	37%
Net Inc.	33.5	27.0	26.8	22.9	16.6	13.3	11.5	9.0	8.4	7.0

Balance Sheet & Other Fin. Data (Million $)

	1998	1997	1996	1995	1994	1993	1992	1991	1990	1989
Cash	4.0	10.0	26.6	6.8	11.9	18.1	8.8	8.9	7.7	7.0
Curr. Assets	52.5	54.8	70.0	43.2	41.4	46.5	33.0	31.6	30.5	31.1
Total Assets	480	427	405	345	318	281	219	198	185	162
Curr. Liab.	90.0	73.8	83.0	77.0	75.5	55.5	46.6	35.8	29.9	29.1
LT Debt	79.1	79.7	81.0	60.0	61.4	99	61.4	63.8	64.5	52.4
Common Eqty.	266	232	206	180	158	108	95.9	84.8	79.5	71.1
Total Cap.	387	352	320	267	242	224	172	161	155	132
Cap. Exp.	85.3	66.7	40.5	52.6	67.1	51.4	35.4	22.7	35.2	41.2
Cash Flow	63.8	53.9	51.4	45.1	35.0	28.8	24.8	21.3	18.5	15.3
Curr. Ratio	0.6	0.7	0.8	0.5	0.5	0.8	0.7	0.9	1.0	1.1
% LT Debt of Cap.	20.4	22.6	25.4	22.5	25.4	44.1	35.7	39.5	41.6	39.7
% Net Inc.of Revs.	2.8	2.4	2.8	2.7	2.7	2.3	2.2	1.7	1.8	1.8
% Ret. on Assets	7.4	6.5	7.2	6.9	5.1	5.3	5.5	4.8	4.8	4.7
% Ret. on Equity	13.4	12.3	13.9	13.5	11.6	13.1	12.7	11.2	11.1	10.5

Data as orig. reptd.; bef. results of disc. opers. and/or spec. items. Per share data adj. for stk. divs. as of ex-div. date. Bold denotes diluted EPS (FASB 128). E-Estimated. NA-Not Available. NM-Not Meaningful. NR-Not Ranked.

Office—One Convenience Blvd., Ankeny, IA 50021. Tel—(515) 965-6100. Chrmn & CEO—D. F. Lamberti. Pres & COO—R. M. Lamb. Secy—J. G. Harmon. CFO, Treas & Investor Contact—Douglas K. Shull. Dirs—J. R. Fitzgibbon, J. G. Harmon, K. H. Haynie, R. M. Lamb, D. F. Lamberti, P. C. Sullivan, J. P. Taylor. Transfer Agent & Registrar—United Missouri Bank of Kansas City. Incorporated—in Iowa in 1967.Empl— 10,366. S&P Analyst: M. S.

Cash America International   458M
NYSE Symbol **PWN**
In S&P SmallCap 600

03-OCT-98

Industry: Consumer Finance

Summary: Cash America International operates the largest chain of pawn shops in the world, with over 450 locations in the U.S., the U.K. and Sweden.

Quantitative Evaluations		
Recent Price • 11	Yield • 0.5%	
52 Wk Range • 20⅞-10⅜	12-Mo. P/E • 17.6	

Outlook (1 Lowest—5 Highest)
• **2⁻**

Fair Value
• **10¾**

Risk
• **Average**

Earn./Div. Rank
• **A-**

Technical Eval.
• **Bearish** since 7/98

Rel. Strength Rank (1 Lowest—99 Highest)
• **34**

Insider Activity
• **Neutral**

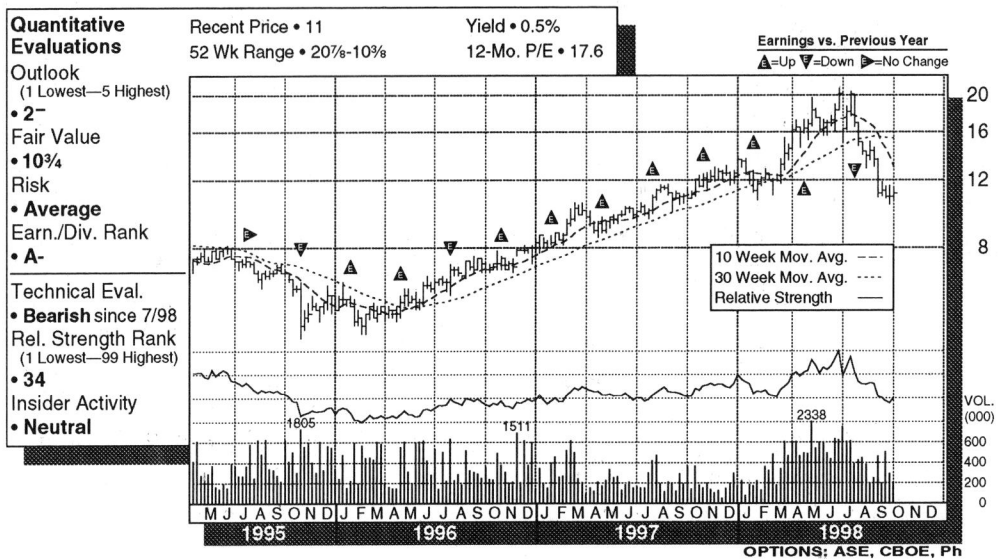

Earnings vs. Previous Year
▲=Up ▼=Down ▶=No Change

10 Week Mov. Avg. - - -
30 Week Mov. Avg. ····
Relative Strength —

OPTIONS: ASE, CBOE, Ph

Business Profile - 27-JUL-98

In addition to its core pawn shop operations, PWN owns Mr. Payroll Corp., a Texas-based check cashing company, and Express Rent A Tire, Ltd., which offers new automobile and truck tires and wheels on a rent-to-own basis. In May 1998, PWN acquired privately owned Doc Holliday's Pawhbrokers & Jewellers, Inc. The acquisition added 40 pawnshops to PWN's existing franchise, boosting its total number of locations to 455. In 1998's second quarter, Mr. Payroll announced a joint venture with Wells Fargo & Company (NYSE: WFC) to develop and distribute a new generation of financial services vending machines targeting the gaming industry. In the third quarter, Mr. Payroll formed an alliance with Circle K to install Mr. Payroll Check Cashing Machines in Circle K convenience stores.

Operational Review - 27-JUL-98

Based on a brief report, total revenues in the first six months of 1998 rose 11%, year to year. Total operating expenses advanced 14%, and income from operations fell 1.4%. After 13% higher interest expense, net income declined 9.3%, to $6,168,000 ($0.24 a share, based on 4.6% more shares), from $6,801,000 ($0.27). Results in the 1998 period were negatively impacted by $2.8 million in net losses generated by PWN's Mr. Payroll Corporation subsidiary.

Stock Performance - 02-OCT-98

In the past 30 trading days, PWN's shares have declined 23%, compared to a 7% fall in the S&P 500. Average trading volume for the past five days was 41,260 shares, compared with the 40-day moving average of 63,567 shares.

Key Stock Statistics

Dividend Rate/Share	0.05	Shareholders	1,100
Shs. outstg. (M)	25.1	Market cap. (B)	$0.277
Avg. daily vol. (M)	0.061	Inst. holdings	74%
Tang. Bk. Value/Share	3.72		
Beta	0.73		

Value of $10,000 invested 5 years ago: $ 10,553

Fiscal Year Ending Dec. 31

	1998	1997	1996	1995	1994	1993
Revenues (Million $)						
1Q	84.19	76.52	68.54	60.27	55.31	52.10
2Q	78.25	69.42	65.93	60.10	57.20	52.45
3Q	—	70.31	64.67	57.64	63.26	55.08
4Q	—	87.12	81.83	75.58	86.33	65.34
Yr.	—	303.4	281.0	253.6	262.1	225.0
Earnings Per Share ($)						
1Q	**0.18**	0.15	0.11	0.09	0.10	0.10
2Q	**0.06**	0.12	0.10	0.11	0.11	0.09
3Q	—	0.14	0.12	0.06	0.15	0.13
4Q	—	**0.25**	0.21	0.19	0.18	0.17
Yr.	—	**0.66**	0.54	0.45	0.54	0.48

Next earnings report expected: late October

Dividend Data (Dividends have been paid since 1988.)

Amount ($)	Date Decl.	Ex-Div. Date	Stock of Record	Payment Date
0.013	Oct. 22	Oct. 31	Nov. 04	Nov. 18 '97
0.013	Jan. 21	Jan. 30	Feb. 03	Feb. 17 '98
0.013	Apr. 22	May. 01	May. 05	May. 19 '98
0.013	Jul. 22	Jul. 31	Aug. 04	Aug. 18 '98

A Division of The McGraw-Hill Companies

Business Summary - 27-JUL-98

Cash America International is a market leader in providing secured, non-recourse loans to individuals, commonly referred to as pawn loans. The company caters to a small but growing niche of consumers who are either unable or unwilling to transact with traditional financial institutions. At year-end 1997, Cash America operated through 352 domestic shops and 49 foreign locations.

Pawn lending, the most basic form of consumer financing, is a centuries-old mechanism for allocating capital among borrowers and lenders. Borrowers pledge collateral, often liquid items such as jewelry or other personal property, and receive small dollar, short-term financing. At December 31, 1997, PWN had roughly 1,137,000 outstanding loans totaling $112,240,000, for an average of $99 a loan. Approximately 70% of these loans are repaid; if loans are not repaid, the pledged collateral becomes the property of Cash America and is available for sale on the open market. Collateral forfeited in the U.K. and Sweden is sold through public auctions.

In 1997, pawn service charges accounted for 59% of net revenues, and profits on the sale of forfeited collateral accounted for the remaining 41%. Effective January 1, 1995, PWN changed its method of accounting for pawn loan income. Under the new method, the company only recognizes revenue based on cash collection activities, such as the sale of unredeemed collateral or the collection of pawn service charges. The company accrues pawn service charges only for loans it deems collectible based on historical redemption statistics.

Cash America employs a proprietary loan and inventory tracking system that links its domestic locations and efficiently manages loans and inventory. The company believes this system effectively processes unredeemed collateral and quickens the pace of inventory turnover, an important measure of performance in the pawn industry.

In addition to its pawnshop operations, PWN provides check cashing services through its wholly-owned subsidiary Mr. Payroll Corporation. At December 31, 1997, Mr. Payroll's system of manned check cashing centers consisted of 145 units operated by independent franchisees in 21 states. Mr. Payroll earns franchise fees from the sale of the check cashing franchises and royalties from franchisees based on a percentage of the gross revenue from a franchisee's check cashing business. Mr. Payroll has developed an automated check cashing system and deployed its first check cashing machine in June 1997. At year end 1997, it had deployed 21 check cashing machines which Mr. Payroll markets and sells to a variety of end users, including financial institutions and retailers.

Per Share Data ($)

(Year Ended Dec. 31)	1997	1996	1995	1994	1993	1992	1991	1990	1989	1988
Tangible Bk. Val.	4.23	3.63	3.92	4.17	3.77	3.58	2.74	2.50	2.22	2.19
Cash Flow	1.29	1.10	0.97	0.34	0.71	0.70	0.63	0.52	0.42	0.34
Earnings	0.66	0.54	0.45	0.54	0.48	0.45	0.43	0.37	0.30	0.23
Dividends	0.05	0.05	0.05	0.05	0.05	0.05	0.04	0.03	0.02	0.02
Payout Ratio	8%	9%	11%	9%	10%	10%	9%	7%	7%	10%
Prices - High	13¾	8½	9¾	10⅛	11	12⅞	9¾	10¼	7⅝	6
- Low	8	4¾	4⅝	7½	6⅜	7¼	6	5¾	3¼	3¼
P/E Ratio - High	21	16	22	19	23	29	23	28	26	27
- Low	12	9	10	14	13	16	14	16	11	15

Income Statement Analysis (Million $)

	1997	1996	1995	1994	1993	1992	1991	1990	1989	1988
Revs.	303	281	254	262	225	186	138	116	87.0	67.0
Oper. Inc.	54.2	51.4	46.8	40.2	31.9	28.7	22.0	19.1	14.2	10.7
Depr.	15.9	16.1	15.3	8.8	6.7	7.0	4.7	3.9	3.1	2.6
Int. Exp.	11.6	9.4	10.4	6.3	3.8	1.6	1.8	1.5	0.5	0.7
Pretax Inc.	26.2	25.1	20.6	25.0	21.8	20.3	17.5	13.7	11.1	8.0
Eff. Tax Rate	37%	38%	38%	38%	36%	36%	40%	37%	37%	36%
Net Inc.	16.6	15.7	12.8	15.5	13.8	13.0	10.5	8.7	7.0	5.1

Balance Sheet & Other Fin. Data (Million $)

	1997	1996	1995	1994	1993	1992	1991	1990	1989	1988
Cash	1.1	1.3	3.4	4.8	2.2	4.2	1.4	3.0	3.8	18.2
Curr. Assets	202	190	178	189	132	122	77.8	66.5	53.0	51.1
Total Assets	341	325	315	324	245	216	138	117	98.0	90.0
Curr. Liab.	26.8	25.0	16.0	21.0	14.2	12.5	7.1	6.9	6.7	5.0
LT Debt	146	146	123	120	64.0	50.0	30.5	20.1	9.6	2.7
Common Eqty.	168	154	176	183	167	154	100	89.9	81.6	82.5
Total Cap.	314	300	299	303	231	204	131	110	91.0	85.0
Cap. Exp.	16.4	7.2	13.5	22.8	16.7	19.6	7.7	5.8	5.2	3.0
Cash Flow	32.5	31.8	28.1	24.3	20.5	20.0	15.3	12.6	10.1	7.7
Curr. Ratio	7.5	7.6	11.1	9.0	9.3	9.8	11.0	9.6	7.9	10.2
% LT Debt of Cap.	46.5	48.7	41.2	39.5	27.7	24.5	23.4	18.2	10.5	3.2
% Net Inc.of Revs.	5.5	5.6	5.1	5.9	6.2	7.0	7.6	7.5	8.0	7.6
% Ret. on Assets	5.0	4.9	4.0	5.4	6.0	6.8	8.3	8.0	7.7	5.9
% Ret. on Equity	10.3	9.5	7.1	8.8	8.6	9.5	11.1	10.1	8.9	6.8

Data as orig. reptd.; bef. results of disc. opers. and/or spec. items. Per share data adj. for stk. divs. as of ex-div. date. Bold denotes diluted EPS (FASB 128). E-Estimated. NA-Not Available. NM-Not Meaningful. NR-Not Ranked.

Office—1600 W. 7th St., Fort Worth, TX 76102-2599. **Tel**—(817) 335-1100. **Chrmn & CEO**—J. R. Daugherty. **Pres & COO**—D. R. Feehan. **SVP & CFO**—T. A. Bessant, Jr.**Dirs**—J. R. Daugherty, A. R. Dike, D. R. Feehan, J. H. Graves, B. D. Hunter, T. J. McKibben, A. M. Micallef, C. H. Morris Jr., C. P. Motheral, S. W. Rizzo, R. Rogers. **Transfer Agent & Registrar**—First Interstate Bank of Texas.**Incorporated**—in Texas in 1984. **Empl**—2,787. **S&P Analyst:** Michael Schneider

STANDARD &POOR'S
STOCK REPORTS

Castle (A.M.)

7460

ASE Symbol **CAS**

In S&P SmallCap 600

03-OCT-98 **Industry:** Metal Fabricators

Summary: This independent metals service center company provides a complete range of inventories and preprocessing services; it also distributes a broad range of industrial plastics.

Quantitative Evaluations

Recent Price • 14⅜
52 Wk Range • 26½-14

Yield • 5.4%
12-Mo. P/E • 8.1

Outlook (1 Lowest—5 Highest)
• 4

Fair Value
• 20½

Risk
• **Average**

Earn./Div. Rank
• **B**

Technical Eval.
• **Bearish** since 4/98

Rel. Strength Rank (1 Lowest—99 Highest)
• 21

Insider Activity
• **NA**

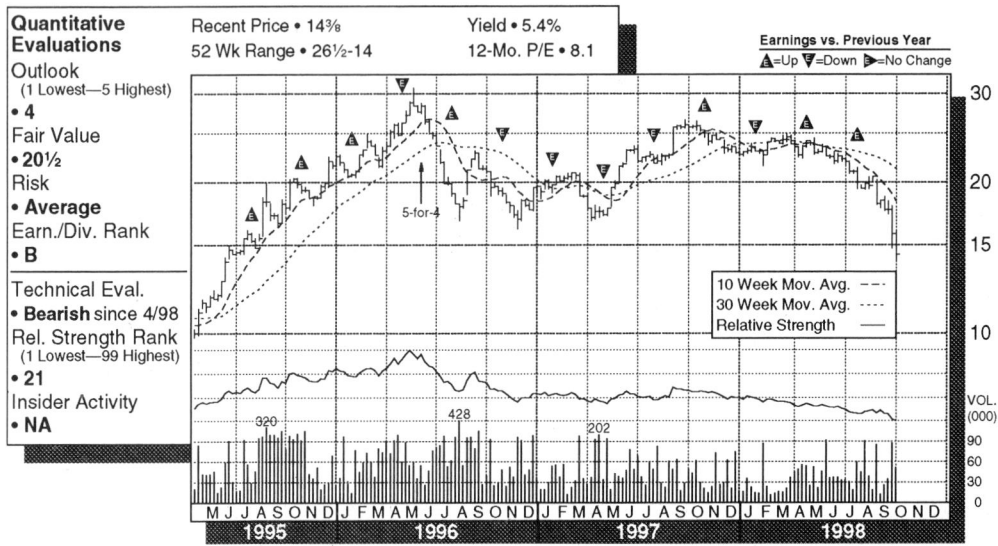

Business Profile - 27-AUG-98

Aided by its strong cash position, the company continues to make acquisitions in an effort to leverage its core competencies in materials management and industrial distribution. In August 1998, CAS acquired Twinsburg, OH-based Oliver Steel Plate Corp., a privately held metals service center and processor. This was the company's third acquisition in 1998, and the 13th since early 1996. CAS anticipates building a presence in the plastics distribution business, increasing its range of value-added services, and providing worldwide sourcing abilities. CAS believes that internal and external growth initiatives will allow it to become a $1.5 billion company within 5 years.

Operational Review - 27-AUG-98

Net sales in the six months ended June 30, 1998, advanced 14%, year to year, reflecting increased core business volume and contributions from acquisitions. Gross margins widened, on well controlled costs of material sold and expansion of valued added services. However, operating expenses rose 16%, primarily in the areas of payroll, transportation, operating supplies and outside services. With significantly higher net interest expense, the gain in pretax income was held to 8.4%. After taxes at 39.8%, versus 40.2%, net income rose 9.2%, to $13,452,000 ($0.96 a share), from $12,318,000 ($0.88).

Stock Performance - 02-OCT-98

In the past 30 trading days, CAS's shares have declined 30%, compared to a 7% fall in the S&P 500. Average trading volume for the past five days was 10,220 shares, compared with the 40-day moving average of 8,979 shares.

Key Stock Statistics

Dividend Rate/Share	0.78	Shareholders	1,600
Shs. outstg. (M)	14.0	Market cap. (B)	$0.202
Avg. daily vol. (M)	0.010	Inst. holdings	54%
Tang. Bk. Value/Share	10.33		
Beta	0.52		

Value of $10,000 invested 5 years ago: $ 27,243

Fiscal Year Ending Dec. 31

	1998	1997	1996	1995	1994	1993
Revenues (Million $)						
1Q	211.7	177.3	175.1	169.1	133.8	119.9
2Q	205.1	188.0	174.8	163.1	131.8	121.0
3Q	—	192.7	162.3	149.0	132.2	117.1
4Q	—	196.8	160.4	146.7	138.7	116.1
Yr.	—	754.9	672.6	627.8	536.6	474.1
Earnings Per Share ($)						
1Q	0.51	0.44	0.54	0.59	0.27	0.13
2Q	0.45	0.44	0.50	0.50	0.24	0.12
3Q	—	0.41	0.38	0.38	0.27	0.11
4Q	—	0.41	0.44	0.46	0.34	0.15
Yr.	—	1.69	1.86	1.93	1.12	0.50

Next earnings report expected: mid October

Dividend Data (Dividends have been paid since 1934.)

Amount ($)	Date Decl.	Ex-Div. Date	Stock of Record	Payment Date
0.170	Oct. 23	Nov. 05	Nov. 07	Nov. 14 '97
0.170	Jan. 22	Jan. 28	Jan. 30	Feb. 11 '98
0.195	Apr. 23	May. 06	May. 08	May. 18 '98
0.195	Jul. 23	Aug. 05	Aug. 07	Aug. 14 '98

Business Summary - 27-AUG-98

During the 1970s and much of the 1980s, America's industrial companies were thought to be on life support. Today, however, they are widely to have becoene global leaders in building the capital equipment that drives the world economy. A.M. Castle & Co. (CAS), one of America's largest specialty metal distributors, has benefited in the past few years from the rejuvenated producer durable equipment sector of the U.S. economy, posting record sales again in 1997.

The company , founded in 1890, provides highly engineered materials and value-added processing services to a wide range of industrial companies in the $600 billion producer durable equipment sector. CAS's customer base includes many Fortune 500 companies, as well as thousands of medium and smaller-sized ones spread across the entire spectrum of metal-using industries. The company feels that one of its strengths lies in its market diversification, with no single industry accounting for more than 6% of its total business and no one customer more than 2%.

CAS serves a broad range of industries: aerospace (with nickel alloys, aluminum and titanium), bearings (alloy bars), specialized machinery (heavy processed plate, carbon and alloy bar), oil patch (alloy bar and plate), chemicals (corrosion resistant nickels and stainless steels), hand tools (alloy bar), defense (beveled plate, aerospace nickel, stainless and aluminum), machine tools (heavy plate and alloy bar), healthcare (tltanium), transportation (cold finished and alloy bar), and recreation (alloy bar). Metals offered are inventoried in many forms including round, hexagon, square and flat bars; plates; tubing; shapes; and sheet and coil. CAS also distributes a wide variety of industrial plastics.

Fueled by strong contributions from acquisitions, net sales increased 12% in 1997, to $755 million; net income fell 9%, to $23.8 million, primarily reflecting higher operating expenses. In 1997, carbon and stainless metals accounted for 73% of sales (74% in 1996), and non-ferrous 27% (26%).

CAS operates 41 metal distribution centers throughout North America, with the largest anchored in Franklin Park, IL, serving metropolitan Chicago and a nine-state area. The Chicago, Los Angeles and Cleveland centers together account for about 50% of sales. CAS's coast-to-coast network of metals service centers provides next-day delivery to over 90% of the markets it services, and two-day delivery to virtually all of the rest.

In 1997, the company acquired Keystone Honing Corp., a processor and distributor of mechanical tubing and chrome plated bars. In May 1998, CAS acquired a 50% stake in Energy Alloys, Inc., a specialty metals distributer to oil field equipment manufacturing companies.

Per Share Data ($)

(Year Ended Dec. 31)	1997	1996	1995	1994	1993	1992	1991	1990	1989	1988
Tangible Bk. Val.	10.36	9.30	7.81	5.88	5.04	4.74	4.67	4.94	5.15	4.86
Cash Flow	2.14	2.22	2.25	1.45	0.86	0.60	0.40	0.61	0.97	1.31
Earnings	1.70	1.86	1.93	1.12	0.51	0.25	0.02	0.23	0.64	1.01
Dividends	0.66	0.57	0.43	0.26	0.21	0.21	0.29	0.36	0.34	0.26
Payout Ratio	39%	31%	22%	24%	42%	86%	955%	158%	54%	25%
Prices - High	26⁵/₈	30⁷/₈	22⁵/₈	13¹/₈	9¹/₄	6⁷/₈	7⁵/₈	7¹/₂	8⁷/₈	9¹/₄
- Low	16³/₄	16¹/₈	9³/₄	8⁷/₈	6	5⁵/₈	5¹/₄	5¹/₈	6⁵/₈	4⁵/₈
P/E Ratio - High	16	17	12	12	18	28	NM	33	14	9
- Low	10	9	5	8	12	22	NM	22	10	5

Income Statement Analysis (Million $)

	1997	1996	1995	1994	1993	1992	1991	1990	1989	1988
Revs.	755	673	628	537	474	424	436	479	501	499
Oper. Inc.	49.9	51.0	51.7	33.1	20.2	15.3	12.5	17.8	23.8	31.6
Depr.	6.2	5.0	4.5	4.6	4.8	4.9	5.3	5.2	4.4	3.9
Int. Exp.	4.4	3.2	3.0	3.3	3.9	4.4	7.0	6.9	5.3	5.3
Pretax Inc.	39.5	43.1	44.3	25.3	11.6	6.1	0.4	5.8	14.3	22.6
Eff. Tax Rate	40%	40%	40%	39%	41%	44%	47%	46%	39%	40%
Net Inc.	23.8	26.1	26.8	15.4	6.9	3.4	0.2	3.1	8.7	13.7

Balance Sheet & Other Fin. Data (Million $)

	1997	1996	1995	1994	1993	1992	1991	1990	1989	1988
Cash	2.8	1.8	0.7	1.0	1.5	0.7	0.3	0.3	1.8	1.6
Curr. Assets	243	164	162	158	152	142	133	163	149	167
Total Assets	366	261	223	213	204	195	190	227	202	212
Curr. Liab.	124	84.0	77.5	82.1	66.1	66.7	53.5	73.3	73.4	77.6
LT Debt	90.7	40.9	28.0	38.5	58.0	53.0	63.3	76.7	51.0	61.0
Common Eqty.	137	122	103	82.2	69.5	65.5	64.7	68.3	69.7	65.5
Total Cap.	240	174	142	128	136	126	137	153	129	134
Cap. Exp.	16.2	22.5	11.8	7.9	4.6	1.8	3.3	13.4	10.4	7.8
Cash Flow	30.1	31.1	31.3	20.0	11.7	8.3	5.5	8.3	13.0	17.6
Curr. Ratio	2.0	2.0	2.1	1.9	2.3	2.1	2.5	2.2	2.0	2.1
% LT Debt of Cap.	37.8	23.5	19.7	30.0	42.8	42.0	46.2	50.0	39.6	45.5
% Net Inc.of Revs.	3.2	3.9	4.3	2.9	1.5	0.8	NM	0.7	1.7	2.7
% Ret. on Assets	7.6	10.8	12.3	7.3	3.5	1.8	0.1	1.5	4.2	7.3
% Ret. on Equity	18.4	23.2	28.9	20.2	10.2	5.2	0.3	4.5	12.8	22.5

Data as orig. reptd.; bef. results of disc. opers. and/or spec. items. Per share data adj. for stk. divs. as of ex-div. date. Bold denotes diluted EPS (FASB 128). E-Estimated. NA-Not Available. NM-Not Meaningful. NR-Not Ranked.

Office—3400 N. Wolf Rd., Franklin Park, IL 60131. **Reincorporated**—in Delaware in 1967. **Tel**—(847) 455-7111. **Fax**—(847) 455-7136. **Chrmn**—M. Simpson. **Pres & CEO**—R. G. Mork. **VP & CFO**—E. F. Culliton. **Treas & Contr**—J. A. Podojil. **Secy**—J. M. Aufox. **Investor Contact**—Debra Davis (312 266-7800). **Dirs**—D. T. Carroll, E. F. Culliton, W. K. Hall, R. S. Hamada, J. P. Herbert III, J. P. Keller, J. W. McCarter, Jr., W. J. McDermott, R. G. Mork, J.W. Puth, M. Simpson, R. A. Virzi. **Transfer Agent & Registrar**—American Stock Transfer & Trust Co., NYC. **Empl**— 1,850. **S&P Analyst:** D.R.J.

03-OCT-98

Industry:
Services (Advertising & Marketing)

Summary: Catalina is a leader in point-of-scan electronic marketing, delivering customized checkout coupons for manufacturers' products to targeted customers based on their purchases.

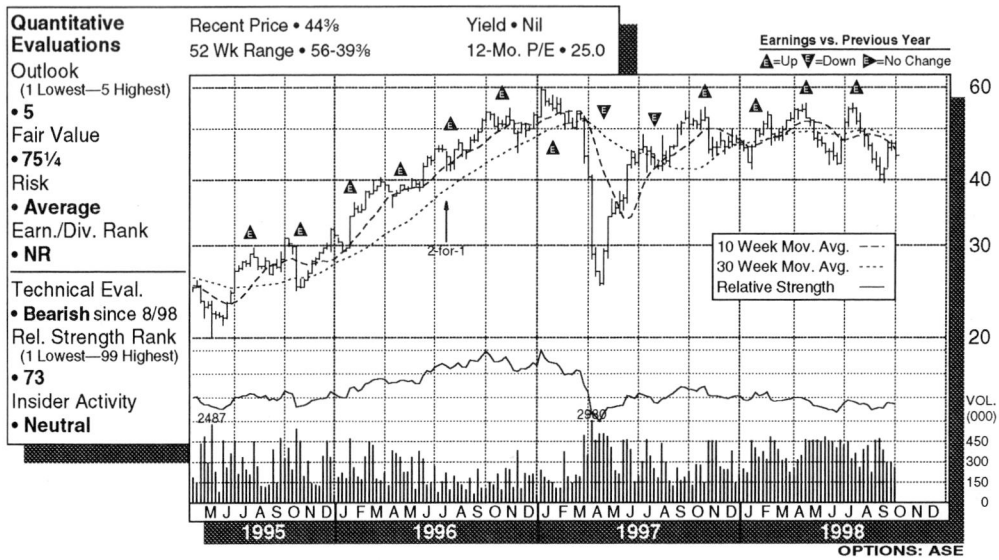

Quantitative Evaluations	
Recent Price • 44⅜	Yield • Nil
52 Wk Range • 56-39⅜	12-Mo. P/E • 25.0

Outlook (1 Lowest—5 Highest)
• **5**

Fair Value
• **75¼**

Risk
• **Average**

Earn./Div. Rank
• **NR**

Technical Eval.
• **Bearish** since 8/98

Rel. Strength Rank (1 Lowest—99 Highest)
• **73**

Insider Activity
• **Neutral**

Earnings vs. Previous Year
▲=Up ▼=Down ▶=No Change

10 Week Mov. Avg. – – –
30 Week Mov. Avg. · · · ·
Relative Strength ——

OPTIONS: ASE

Business Profile - 25-AUG-98

During the first quarter of FY 98 (Mar.), Catalina Marketing increased their domestic and international installed base by 352 stores, highlighting expansion in U.K. and France. Growth in existing operations drove incremental profit for the period and resulted in an average revenue per store increase of 11%. Core domestic business increased 17% over year-ago levels. In mid-January 1998, management said it expects FY 99 revenues and earnings to advance at a 20% to 25% rate, driven by continued strength of domestic operations, as well as growth in international business and new venture initiatives. In July 1998, the company announced it had acquired Market Logic, a marketing firm specializing in direct marketing for retailers.

Operational Review - 25-AUG-98

Revenues for the three months ended June 30, 1998, rose 22%, primarily due to growth in core domestic business and improved international operations. Profitability was restricted by higher direct operating expenses, stemming from an increase in loyalty marketing programs which have a higher percentage of direct costs to revenue than POS's other base business products. After taxes at 41.6% in both periods, net income advanced 20%, to $6,738,000 ($0.35 per share), versus $5,637,000 ($0.30).

Stock Performance - 02-OCT-98

In the past 30 trading days, POS's shares have increased 2%, compared to a 7% fall in the S&P 500. Average trading volume for the past five days was 51,280 shares, compared with the 40-day moving average of 79,851 shares.

Key Stock Statistics

Dividend Rate/Share	Nil	Shareholders	600
Shs. outstg. (M)	18.5	Market cap. (B)	$0.822
Avg. daily vol. (M)	0.070	Inst. holdings	79%
Tang. Bk. Value/Share	4.25		
Beta	0.94		

Value of $10,000 invested 5 years ago: $ 23,235

Fiscal Year Ending Mar. 31

	1999	1998	1997	1996	1995	1994
Revenues (Million $)						
1Q	56.83	46.66	38.13	30.61	27.45	18.08
2Q	—	52.73	41.62	30.94	24.75	21.23
3Q	—	63.70	46.34	36.55	30.27	25.19
4Q	—	54.06	46.05	36.05	30.78	26.96
Yr.	—	217.2	172.1	134.2	113.3	91.45
Earnings Per Share ($)						
1Q	0.35	0.30	0.31	0.26	0.23	0.13
2Q	—	0.43	0.35	0.27	0.21	0.10
3Q	—	0.57	0.40	0.30	0.23	0.17
4Q	—	0.43	0.27	0.28	0.18	0.14
Yr.	—	1.73	1.33	1.10	0.85	0.62

Next earnings report expected: mid October

Dividend Data

Catalina does not expect to pay cash dividends in the forseeable future.

A Division of The McGraw-Hill Companies

STANDARD
&POOR'S
STOCK REPORTS

Catalina Marketing Corporation

459

03-OCT-98

Business Summary - 25-AUG-98

Catalina Marketing Corporation provides manufacturers of consumer and pharmaceutical products and retailers with a cost-effective method of delivering advertising messages and promotional incentives directly to targeted customers based on their purchasing behavior. The company helps manufacturers and retailers implement long-term marketing strategies to develop customer loyalty, promote products and improve brand awareness and sales.

Catalina developed an electronic network designed to utilize the Universal Product Code (UPC) labeling standard and its widespread use in retail stores. The company's system links POS's software, personal computers, databases and specially designed printers to point of scan controllers. When a shopper makes a purchase, the system evaluates the product's UPC data, matches it with manufacturer or retailer programmed promotions, and directs the printer, which is located near the register, to print the appropriate message or coupon. Printing takes place throughout the checkout process and the coupons are handed directly to the customer at the conclusion of the transaction. Catalina's U.S. Checkout Coupon programs generated roughly 83% and 89% of total revenues in FY 98 (Mar.) and FY 97, respectively.

Catalina offers manufacturers 13 four-week cycles annually for more than 500 product categories. These categories are typically based on standard industry classifications of household and consumer products sold in supermarkets, such as coffee, baby foods and frozen dinners.

POS's revenues are a function of the total number of coupons distributed based on a per-coupon fee, as well as a minimum category fee paid to Catalina prior to the beginning of the purchased cycle.

At March 31, 1998, the company's network was installed in 11,164 stores in the U.S., reaching about 143 million shoppers weekly. Outside the U.S., the network was installed in 1,372 stores, reaching approximately 20 million shoppers each week.

In August 1997, the company announced the signing of an installation agreement with Rite-Aid, a 4,000 store chain of pharmacies. The program was rolled out on the West Coast and includes condition-specific information on patients' medication, compliance messages and advertising for related products.

In July, 1998, the company announced the acquisition of Market Logic, a full service targeted marketing organization that specializes in the development and fulfillment of direct marketing programs for retailers. Management feels that the acquisition strengthens Catalina's targeted direct mail capabilities.

Per Share Data ($)

(Year Ended Mar. 31)	1998	1997	1996	1995	1994	1993	1992	1991	1990	1989
Tangible Bk. Val.	3.86	3.99	3.65	2.83	2.27	1.54	1.02	0.93	NA	NA
Cash Flow	2.97	2.21	1.82	1.60	1.18	0.86	0.67	0.34	NA	NA
Earnings	1.73	1.33	1.10	0.85	0.62	0.41	0.26	0.08	NA	NA
Dividends	Nil	Nil	Nil	Nil	Nil	Nil	Nil	NA	NA	NA
Payout Ratio	Nil	Nil	Nil	Nil	Nil	Nil	Nil	NA	NA	NA
Cal. Yrs.	1997	1996	1995	1994	1993	1992	1991	1990	1989	1988
Prices - High	60	55½	32½	28⅛	25⅛	19⅝	NA	NA	NA	NA
- Low	25⅛	29¼	20	20⅝	14¼	10	NA	NA	NA	NA
P/E Ratio - High	35	42	29	33	41	49	NA	NA	NA	NA
- Low	15	22	18	24	23	25	NA	NA	NA	NA

Income Statement Analysis (Million $)

	1998	1997	1996	1995	1994	1993	1992	1991	1990	1989
Revs.	217	172	134	113	91.4	71.9	51.7	33.1	24.6	15.8
Oper. Inc.	76.6	61.3	49.1	42.9	29.8	25.5	14.1	5.8	2.7	-0.1
Depr.	23.7	17.9	14.5	15.1	11.4	9.3	7.8	4.9	2.4	1.4
Int. Exp.	Nil	Nil	Nil	Nil	Nil	0.1	0.3	0.3	0.3	0.4
Pretax Inc.	51.9	45.1	36.2	27.9	19.2	13.3	6.7	1.8	0.7	-1.1
Eff. Tax Rate	37%	40%	41%	40%	40%	38%	29%	20%	15%	NM
Net Inc.	32.9	27.2	22.0	17.2	12.7	8.2	4.8	1.4	0.6	-1.1

Balance Sheet & Other Fin. Data (Million $)

	1998	1997	1996	1995	1994	1993	1992	1991	1990	1989
Cash	18.4	13.7	25.8	30.7	26.9	25.6	6.5	4.2	NA	NA
Curr. Assets	63.6	61.7	65.3	60.2	51.2	39.9	25.8	12.5	NA	NA
Total Assets	157	155	114	99	85.5	61.2	44.5	31.1	NA	NA
Curr. Liab.	61.5	53.5	40.5	42.7	40.2	31.9	23.3	18.1	NA	NA
LT Debt	0.4	0.9	Nil	Nil	Nil	Nil	2.4	2.5	NA	NA
Common Eqty.	90.0	96.9	71.2	55.5	44.9	29.3	18.8	10.5	NA	NA
Total Cap.	95.5	97.8	73.7	56.6	45.3	29.3	21.2	13.0	NA	NA
Cap. Exp.	24.2	34.7	23.6	20.3	25.2	12.2	11.6	9.8	3.7	2.7
Cash Flow	56.6	45.2	36.4	32.3	24.1	17.5	12.6	6.3	3.0	0.2
Curr. Ratio	1.0	1.2	1.6	1.4	1.3	1.3	1.1	0.7	NA	NA
% LT Debt of Cap.	0.5	1.0	Nil	Nil	Nil	Nil	11.2	19.3	NA	NA
% Net Inc.of Revs.	15.1	15.9	16.4	15.2	13.9	11.4	9.2	4.3	2.3	NM
% Ret. on Assets	21.1	20.3	20.9	18.7	17.0	15.4	13.2	NA	NA	NA
% Ret. on Equity	35.2	32.4	34.8	34.4	33.7	33.8	36.9	NA	NA	NA

Data as orig. reptd.; bef. results of disc. opers. and/or spec. items. Per share data adj. for stk. divs. as of ex-div. date. E-Estimated. NA-Not Available. NM-Not Meaningful. NR-Not Ranked.

Office—11300 Ninth St. North, St. Petersburg, FL 33716-2329. **Tel**—(813) 579-5000. **Website**—http://www.catalinamktg.com **Chrmn**—G. W. Off. **Pres, CEO**—D. D. Granger. **SVP & CFO**—P.B. Livingston. **Dirs**—F. H. Barker, F. W. Beinecke, P. W. Collins, S. I. D'Agostino, D. D. Granger, T. D. Greer, H. Monat, G. W. Off, T. W. Smith, M. B. Wilson. **Transfer Agent & Registrar**—ChaseMellon Shareholder Services, Los Angeles. **Incorporated**—in Delaware in 1992. **Empl**— 751. **S&P Analyst:** Jordan Horoschak

03-OCT-98

Industry:
Retail (Special-
ty-Apparel)

Summary: This long-established retailer operates more than 690 stores in 21 states, offering women's popular-priced apparel for fashion-conscious junior, missy and large-size customers.

Quantitative Evaluations

Outlook
(1 Lowest—5 Highest)
• **3⁻**

Fair Value
• **12¾**

Risk
• **Average**

Earn./Div. Rank
• **B-**

Technical Eval.
• **Bearish** since 7/98

Rel. Strength Rank
(1 Lowest—99 Highest)
• **19**

Insider Activity
• **NA**

Recent Price • 9½
52 Wk Range • 19⅛-7

Yield • 2.1%
12-Mo. P/E • 11.9

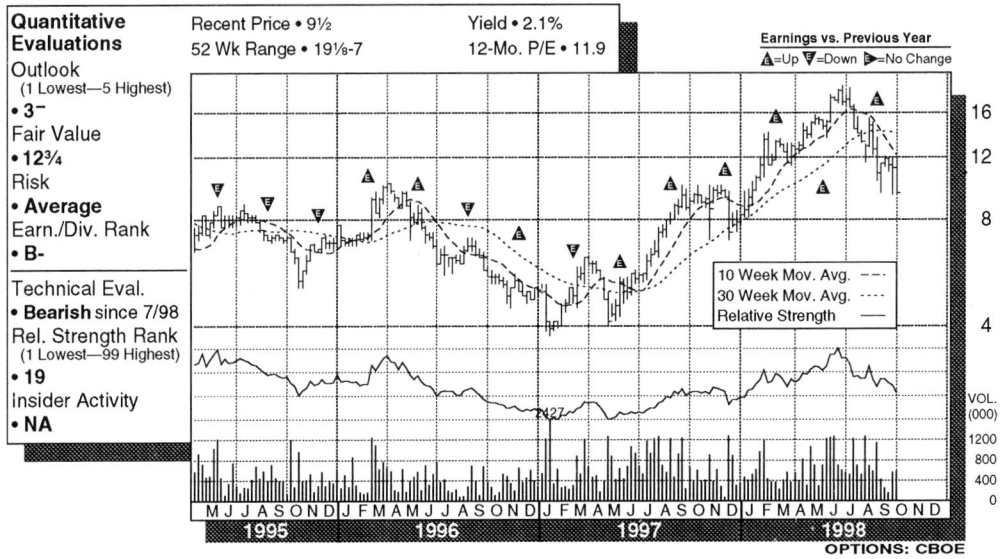

Earnings vs. Previous Year
▲=Up ▼=Down ►=No Change

10 Week Mov. Avg. - - -
30 Week Mov. Avg. ......
Relative Strength ——

VOL.
(000)

OPTIONS: CBOE

Business Profile - 20-MAR-98

In FY 99 (Jan.), Cato plans to open 65 new stores, close 15 and relocate 20, for a net increase in selling square footage of about 5%. After closing 40 stores in January 1997, the company opened 55 new stores, closed 17 and relocated 16 in FY 98, for a 3% rise in selling square footage. CACOA believes it can continue to improve results in the current fiscal year by focusing on better execution, tightly controlling expenses and identifying additional initiatives to enhance profitable growth. Cato began FY 99 on a positive note, posting 9% total sales growth and 5% same-store sales gains in February.

Operational Review - 20-MAR-98

Based on a preliminary report, total revenues rose 4.3% in FY 98 (Jan.), reflecting 4% same-store sales growth and an advance of 7.6% in other income from greater finance charge income on the company's credit card accounts. Gross margins widened as the company adopted lower everyday competitive pricing, improved merchandise offerings, and eliminated unprofitable promotions and events; operating income soared 34%. Following lower depreciation charges and taxes at 31.5%, versus 35.5%, net income increased 148%, to $17,401,000 ($0.62 a share), from $7,029,000 ($0.25).

Stock Performance - 02-OCT-98

In the past 30 trading days, CACOA's shares have declined 25%, compared to a 7% fall in the S&P 500. Average trading volume for the past five days was 113,500 shares, compared with the 40-day moving average of 111,708 shares.

Key Stock Statistics

Dividend Rate/Share	0.20	Shareholders	4,700
Shs. outstg. (M)	27.5	Market cap. (B)	$0.211
Avg. daily vol. (M)	0.078	Inst. holdings	51%
Tang. Bk. Value/Share	6.28		
Beta	0.56		

Value of $10,000 invested 5 years ago: $ 6,770

Fiscal Year Ending Jan. 31

	1999	1998	1997	1996	1995	1994
Revenues (Million $)						
1Q	141.0	127.5	123.5	117.8	113.1	96.71
2Q	132.6	124.5	116.0	117.8	113.3	98.36
3Q	—	113.7	111.5	109.3	112.2	97.52
4Q	—	146.8	140.5	145.1	137.6	127.3
Yr.	—	512.5	491.5	490.0	476.2	419.9
Earnings Per Share ($)						
1Q	**0.39**	**0.28**	0.27	0.26	0.28	0.32
2Q	**0.20**	**0.13**	0.08	0.10	0.15	0.20
3Q	—	**0.05**	-0.03	-0.05	0.10	0.15
4Q	—	**0.15**	-0.07	0.11	0.10	0.17
Yr.	—	**0.62**	0.25	0.42	0.62	0.84

Next earnings report expected: mid November

Dividend Data (Dividends have been paid since 1992.)

Amount ($)	Date Decl.	Ex-Div. Date	Stock of Record	Payment Date
0.040	Dec. 04	Dec. 18	Dec. 22	Jan. 05 '98
0.045	Mar. 05	Mar. 12	Mar. 16	Mar. 30 '98
0.045	May. 21	May. 28	Jun. 01	Jun. 15 '98
0.050	Aug. 27	Sep. 10	Sep. 14	Sep. 28 '98

A Division of The **McGraw-Hill** *Companies*

Business Summary - 20-MAR-98

When the specialty apparel market perks up, Cato Corporation plans to be ready. Cato (CACOA) sells apparel to women in the lower- and middle-income brackets. Its 692 stores are operated as Cato, Cato Plus or It's Fashion! stores in 21 states throughout the South and Midwest. More than 50 years old, CACOA is headquartered in Charlotte, NC.

The number of stores, average sales per store and average sales per sq. ft. of selling space at the end of recent fiscal years (Jan.) were:

	FY 97	FY 96	FY 95
Stores open	655	671	646
Avg. sales per store	$710,000	$721,000	$749,000
Avg. sales per sq. ft.	$153	$158	$172

Cato and Cato Plus stores are generally between 4,000 and 6,000 square feet, while the more-than-100 It's Fashion! off-price stores are between 3,000 and 4,000 square feet. Both kinds of stores are located in non-metropolitan area strip shopping centers that are anchored by a large department store or grocery store.

The target customer for Cato is the fashion-oriented woman, between 18 and 50, in the middle- or lower-income range. Its merchandising strategy is to provide quality, affordably priced head-to-toe apparel and accessories for the fashion-conscious junior, missy or large-size customer. Its current overall strategy is to wait out the market and conservatively build on its core business while it recovers from the stiff competition and dropping prices that have described the specialty apparel retail market in the past two years. The company plans to open about 65 new stores, close 15 and relocate 20 stores in FY 99.

The It's Fashion division achieved a record year in FY 98 despite posting disappointing fourth quarter results. Divisional plans provide for another record year in FY 99.

For the four-week period ended February 28, 1998, same-store sales were up 5% from the same period last year and overall sales reached $41.0 million, compared with $37.5 million for the same period in FY 98.

In September 1997, directors authorized the repurchase of 1,000,000 Class A common shares.

Per Share Data ($)

(Year Ended Jan. 31)	1998	1997	1996	1995	1994	1993	1992	1991	1990	1989
Tangible Bk. Val.	5.75	5.34	5.27	4.98	4.50	2.94	1.37	0.91	1.37	1.67
Cash Flow	0.89	0.54	0.69	0.86	1.02	0.89	0.63	-0.23	-0.04	0.01
Earnings	0.62	0.25	0.42	0.62	0.84	0.74	0.43	-0.45	-0.24	-0.18
Dividends	0.16	0.16	0.16	0.14	0.09	0.04	Nil	0.01	0.05	0.05
Payout Ratio	26%	64%	38%	23%	10%	5%	Nil	Nil	NM	NM
Cal. Yrs.	1997	1996	1995	1994	1993	1992	1991	1990	1989	1988
Prices - High	10	10⅛	8⅞	21½	24¾	16⅝	10⅛	2⁷/₁₆	3½	3⅛
- Low	3¾	4½	5	5½	14¾	7⅛	⅜	⅜	2³/₁₆	1¹³/₁₆
P/E Ratio - High	16	40	21	35	29	23	23	NM	NM	NM
- Low	6	18	12	9	18	10	1	NM	NM	NM

Income Statement Analysis (Million $)

	1998	1997	1996	1995	1994	1993	1992	1991	1990	1989
Revs.	497	492	490	476	420	341	274	238	257	233
Oper. Inc.	17.8	10.5	12.8	35.7	44.0	35.1	22.7	7.5	7.6	4.4
Depr.	7.7	8.3	7.8	6.8	5.5	4.2	4.3	4.9	4.5	4.4
Int. Exp.	0.3	0.3	0.3	0.4	0.3	1.2	3.3	3.4	3.6	2.9
Pretax Inc.	25.4	10.9	18.0	28.5	38.3	29.7	15.1	-15.0	-10.4	-7.3
Eff. Tax Rate	32%	36%	34%	37%	35%	36%	37%	NM	NM	NM
Net Inc.	17.4	7.0	12.0	18.1	24.8	19.1	9.5	-10.0	-5.3	-4.0

Balance Sheet & Other Fin. Data (Million $)

	1998	1997	1996	1995	1994	1993	1992	1991	1990	1989
Cash	41.6	16.6	26.1	46.2	42.6	29.7	16.6	3.0	5.1	4.1
Curr. Assets	186	161	150	143	139	94.2	69.5	55.3	60.2	66.0
Total Assets	241	218	210	201	179	122	95.0	83.0	97.0	104
Curr. Liab.	72.2	56.1	48.2	48.9	47.2	40.4	36.3	29.9	26.6	29.4
LT Debt	Nil	Nil	Nil	Nil	Nil	Nil	24.9	29.4	34.0	30.2
Common Eqty.	158	152	150	142	128	78.2	30.5	20.0	30.3	36.8
Total Cap.	163	156	154	146	131	80.9	56.2	49.4	69.3	73.7
Cap. Exp.	7.4	8.4	9.4	25.5	17.2	7.6	1.7	1.8	4.3	8.2
Cash Flow	25.1	15.4	19.8	24.9	30.3	23.3	13.9	-5.1	-0.9	0.4
Curr. Ratio	2.6	2.9	3.1	2.9	2.9	2.3	1.9	1.8	2.3	2.2
% LT Debt of Cap.	Nil	Nil	Nil	Nil	Nil	Nil	44.3	59.6	49.0	41.0
% Net Inc.of Revs.	3.5	1.4	2.4	3.8	5.9	5.6	3.5	NM	NM	NM
% Ret. on Assets	7.6	3.3	5.8	9.5	16.1	16.2	10.6	NM	NM	NM
% Ret. on Equity	11.2	4.7	8.2	13.4	23.5	33.3	37.6	NM	NM	NM

Data as orig. reptd.; bef. results of disc. opers. and/or spec. items. Per share data adj. for stk. divs. as of ex-div. date. Bold denotes diluted EPS (FASB 128). E-Estimated. NA-Not Available. NM-Not Meaningful. NR-Not Ranked.

Office—8100 Denmark Rd., Charlotte, NC 28273-5975. **Tel**—(704) 554-8510. **Chrmn & CEO**—W. H. Cato Jr. **Vice Chrmn, Pres & COO**—J. D. D. Cato.**Sr EVP, CFO, Secy & Investor Contact**—Alan E. Wiley. **Dirs**—R. W. Bradshaw Jr., E. T. Cato, J. P. D. Cato, T. E. Cato, W. H. Cato Jr., G. S. Currin, P. Fulton, C. Cato Goodyear, G. Hamrick, L. McFarland Jenkins, H. A. Severson, J. H. Shaw, A. F. Sloan, A. E. Wiley. **Transfer Agent & Registrar**—First Union National Bank, Charlotte, NC. **Incorporated**—in Delaware in 1946. **Empl**— 6,800. **S&P Analyst:** Ray Lam, CFA

Centigram Communications   3457C
NASDAQ Symbol **CGRM**
In S&P SmallCap 600

03-OCT-98

Industry:
Services (Computer Systems)

Summary: This company develops and markets voice, data and fax communications server products for telephones and personal computers.

Quantitative Evaluations

Outlook
(1 Lowest—5 Highest)
• **1⁻**

Fair Value
• **6⅝**

Risk
• **Average**

Earn./Div. Rank
• **C**

Technical Eval.
• **Bearish** since 1/98

Rel. Strength Rank
(1 Lowest—99 Highest)
• **27**

Insider Activity
• **NA**

Recent Price • 7¾
52 Wk Range • 21⅞-7¼

Yield • Nil
12-Mo. P/E • NM

Earnings vs. Previous Year
▲=Up ▼=Down ▶=No Change

10 Week Mov. Avg. – –
30 Week Mov. Avg. · · · ·
Relative Strength —

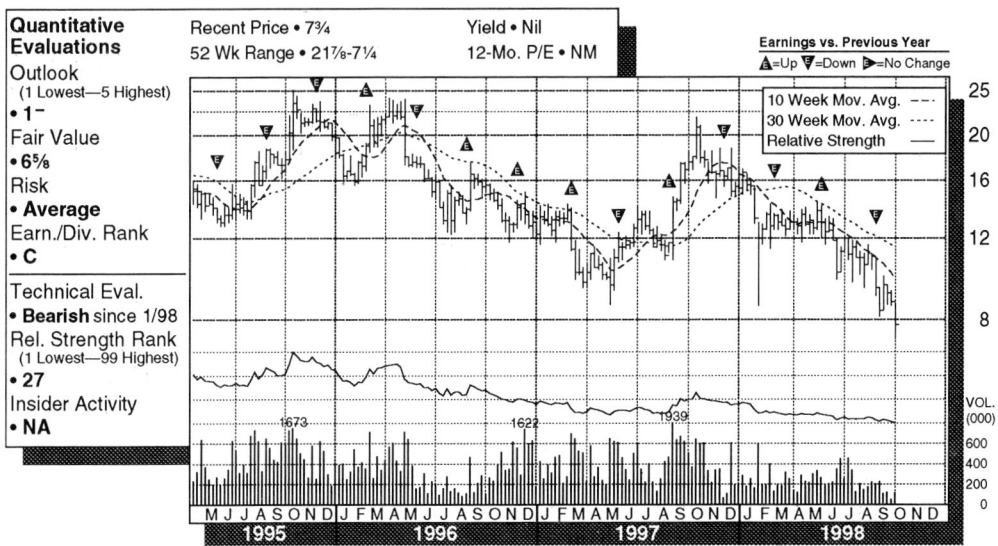

Business Profile - 08-JUL-98

Centigram offers its corporate customers a variety of communication technologies, including voice messaging, facisimile, and call management. The company enables users to access these technologies in an integrated environment, using either the telephone or the PC as a communications workstation. Centigram's current strategy is to focus on the development of new applications for its product platform and its MESA architecture. The company recently sold its CPE unit to Mitel Corp., in order to focus on its worldwide Service Provider market.

Operational Review - 08-JUL-98

Net revenues in the six months ended May 2, 1998, fell 25%, year to year, reflecting lower sales of both large system and small system products. Gross margins narrowed; although operating expenses declined, the operating loss widened, to $7,637,000, from $1,937,000. Despite higher net other income, after taxes of $140,000, versus $76,000, the net loss widened to $10,584,000 ($1.51 a share), from $5,624,000 ($0.81).

Stock Performance - 02-OCT-98

In the past 30 trading days, CGRM's shares have declined 29%, compared to a 7% fall in the S&P 500. Average trading volume for the past five days was 23,080 shares, compared with the 40-day moving average of 31,062 shares.

Key Stock Statistics

Dividend Rate/Share	Nil	Shareholders	400
Shs. outstg. (M)	7.2	Market cap. (B)	$0.056
Avg. daily vol. (M)	0.021	Inst. holdings	64%
Tang. Bk. Value/Share	8.43		
Beta	0.73		

Value of $10,000 invested 5 years ago: $ 6,127

Fiscal Year Ending Oct. 31

	1998	1997	1996	1995	1994	1993
Revenues (Million $)						
1Q	18.16	27.91	24.01	14.91	17.00	13.01
2Q	21.20	24.90	24.53	16.45	17.92	14.38
3Q	18.14	27.01	26.50	17.57	19.50	15.38
4Q	—	29.01	29.28	20.44	21.61	17.24
Yr.	—	108.8	104.3	69.37	79.20	60.00
Earnings Per Share ($)						
1Q	-0.85	0.10	0.07	-0.12	0.15	0.20
2Q	**-0.66**	-0.90	-0.19	-0.05	0.11	0.22
3Q	**-0.45**	0.45	0.10	-0.26	0.11	0.26
4Q	—	0.11	0.16	-0.21	0.46	0.32
Yr.	—	-0.24	0.14	-0.63	1.18	1.00

Next earnings report expected: early December

Dividend Data

No cash dividends have been paid. Terms of a credit facility restrict payments.

 *A Division of The McGraw·Hill Companies*

Business Summary - 08-JUL-98

Centigram is a leading global provider of advanced wireless and wireline messaging and communications solutions to network operators in the telecom service provider market. Headquartered in San Jose, CA, CGRM has sales and support offices in North America, Asia, Europe, Latin America and Australia; for more than 10 years, it has served customers in more than 45 countries on six continents. The company delivers integrated systems that provide competitive, revenue-generating enhanced services.

Centigram's applications operate on a common software platform, the company's implementation of its Modular Expandable System Architecture (MESA). The MESA architecture allows CGRM's systems to be upgraded in continual, cost-effective increments. Systems are available in configurations ranging from four ports, supporting 50 to 100 users, to multiple 240 port clusters, supporting up to one million users. The systems can be integrated with central office systems, most telephone PBX systems, and mobile switch and paging terminal systems. CGRM's products can also connect with a broad range of host and local area network (LAN)-based computer systems. Systems are sold at prices ranging from under $10,000 to more than several hundred thousand dollars.

CGRM's Series 6 platform, introduced in the first quarter of FY 96 (Oct.), was designed to extend across the company's entire product line. Series 6 includes a complex message storage system, with voice boards for speech recognition and text-to-speech (converts text stored in computer databases into synthesized speech) applications.

Centigram's family of communications products includes: VoiceMemo, which provides voice messaging and call processing capabilities; Telephone Answering, which automatically answers a busy telephone and records a voice message; and Automated Attendant, which answers incoming calls and allows callers to direct calls to extensions without the aid of a human operator.

In the FY 97 third quarter, the company sold its text-to-speech software, TruVoice, and related business to Lernout and Hauspie (L&H) Speech Products N.V. In connection with the transaction, L&H agreed to license its automatic speech recognition, text-to-speech, and speech coding technologies to Centigram on mutually acceptable terms.

In recent periods, CGRM has been increasing its focus on international sales, particularly direct sales to international service providers. The company currently has sales offices in Europe, China, Australia and Latin America. Exports sales accounted for 44%, 30% and 23% of net revenue in FY 97, FY 96 and FY 95, respectively.

Per Share Data ($)

(Year Ended Oct. 31)	1997	1996	1995	1994	1993	1992	1991	1990	1989	1988
Tangible Bk. Val.	11.60	11.78	11.59	12.82	NA	NA	NA	NA	NA	NA
Cash Flow	1.02	1.24	0.20	1.72	1.48	NA	NA	NA	NA	NA
Earnings	-0.24	0.14	-0.63	1.18	1.00	0.49	0.67	NA	NA	NA
Dividends	Nil	Nil	Nil	Nil	Nil	Nil	Nil	Nil	Nil	Nil
Payout Ratio	Nil	Nil	Nil	Nil	Nil	Nil	Nil	Nil	Nil	Nil
Prices - High	21⅞	24⅛	25⅛	43	39¾	14¼	NA	NA	NA	NA
- Low	8⅝	11⅝	12¼	10	11¼	3¾	NA	NA	NA	NA
P/E Ratio - High	NM	NM	NM	36	40	NA	NA	NA	NA	NA
- Low	NM	NM	NM	8	11	NA	NA	NA	NA	NA

Income Statement Analysis (Million $)

	1997	1996	1995	1994	1993	1992	1991	1990	1989	1988
Revs.	109	104	69.4	79.2	60.0	44.7	36.0	NA	NA	NA
Oper. Inc.	5.0	6.5	-0.3	12.7	9.5	NA	NA	NA	NA	NA
Depr.	8.7	7.7	5.4	3.5	2.5	NA	NA	NA	NA	NA
Int. Exp.	0.1	0.1	0.1	0.2	0.4	NA	NA	NA	NA	NA
Pretax Inc.	-0.8	1.1	-4.1	10.8	7.3	NA	NA	NA	NA	NA
Eff. Tax Rate	NM	0.06%	NM	28%	29%	NA	NA	NA	NA	NA
Net Inc.	-1.7	1.0	-4.1	7.7	5.2	2.3	2.3	NA	NA	NA

Balance Sheet & Other Fin. Data (Million $)

	1997	1996	1995	1994	1993	1992	1991	1990	1989	1988
Cash	19.8	42.1	55.7	60.4	NA	NA	NA	NA	NA	NA
Curr. Assets	85.1	85.6	83.5	91.1	NA	NA	NA	NA	NA	NA
Total Assets	100	104	99	102	48.0	34.0	21.0	NA	NA	NA
Curr. Liab.	18.3	20.6	19.0	18.7	NA	NA	NA	NA	NA	NA
LT Debt	Nil	0.1	0.2	0.4	0.8	1.1	1.6	NA	NA	NA
Common Eqty.	81.6	83.4	79.8	83.2	32.0	24.0	11.0	NA	NA	NA
Total Cap.	81.6	83.5	80.0	83.6	32.8	25.1	12.6	NA	NA	NA
Cap. Exp.	6.2	10.6	8.0	7.2	3.2	NA	NA	NA	NA	NA
Cash Flow	7.1	8.7	1.3	11.3	7.7	NA	NA	NA	NA	NA
Curr. Ratio	4.7	4.2	4.4	4.9	NA	NA	NA	NA	NA	NA
% LT Debt of Cap.	Nil	0.1	0.3	0.5	2.5	4.4	12.4	NA	NA	NA
% Net Inc.of Revs.	NM	1.0	NM	9.8	8.7	NA	NA	NA	NA	NA
% Ret. on Assets	NM	1.0	NM	10.3	12.8	8.4	NA	NA	NA	NA
% Ret. on Equity	NM	1.2	NM	13.4	18.5	13.1	NA	NA	NA	NA

Data as orig. reptd.; yr. ended Sep. prior to 1995; bef. results of disc. opers. and/or spec. items. Per share data adj. for stk. divs. as of ex-div. date. E-Estimated. NA-Not Available. NM-Not Meaningful. NR-Not Ranked.

Office—91 E. Tasman Dr., San Jose, CA 95134. **Tel**—(408) 944-0250. **Fax**—(408) 428-3732. **Website**—http://www.centigram.com **Email**—dan.spalding@centigram.com **Pres & CEO**—R. L. Puette. **SVP & CFO**—D. P. Wolf. **VP & Contr**—T. E. Brunton. **Secy**—L. W. Sonsini. **Investor Contact**—Dan Spalding (408-428-3559). **Dirs**—J. H. Boyle, D. Chance, J. F. Gibbons, D. S. Lee, D. O. Morton. **Transfer Agent & Registrar**—First National Bank of Boston. **Incorporated**—in California in 1980; reincorporated in Delaware in 1991. **Empl**—418. **S&P Analyst:** M.J.C.

03-OCT-98

Industry:
Electric Companies

Summary: This medium-sized utility provides electric and, to a lesser extent, gas service to a large area of New York's mid-Hudson River Valley.

Quantitative Evaluations		
Recent Price • 42⅜	Yield • 5.1%	
52 Wk Range • 47-34⅝	12-Mo. P/E • 14.9	

Outlook (1 Lowest—5 Highest)
• **1+**

Fair Value
• **40⅜**

Risk
• **Low**

Earn./Div. Rank
• **B+**

Technical Eval.
• **Bullish** since 5/96

Rel. Strength Rank (1 Lowest—99 Highest)
• **78**

Insider Activity
• **NA**

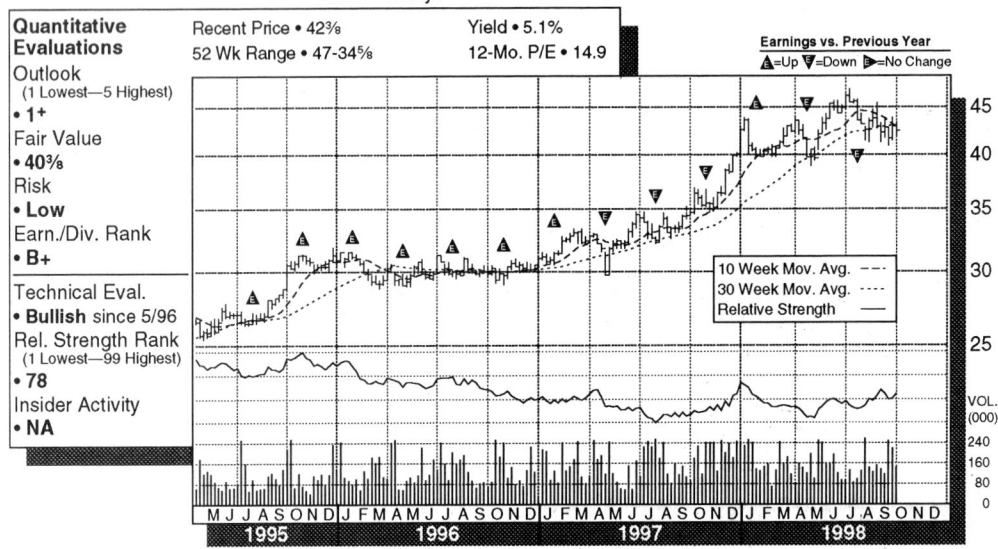

Earnings vs. Previous Year
▲=Up ▼=Down ▷=No Change

10 Week Mov. Avg. - - -
30 Week Mov. Avg. ·····
Relative Strength ——

Business Profile - 04-MAY-98

CNH's Hudson River Valley territory in New York reflects a diversified economy, but one that has been adversely affected by the downsizing of its largest electricity customer, IBM. Electric power is mainly supplied by coal and, to a lesser extent, nuclear (about 14%), oil, gas and hydro facilities, and through purchases. The company's construction program, aimed at improving generating facilities and expanding distribution capabilities, will require total cash expenditures of about $110 million in 1998 and 1999. In February 1998, the New York Department of Public Service approved a revised settlement agreement with CNH regarding the competitive opportunities proceeding being conducted to open the state's electric industry to competitive forces.

Operational Review - 04-MAY-98

Operating revenues in the first quarter of 1998 fell 5.3%, year to year, reflecting a decline in amounts collected from customers for gas cost adjustments, as well as decreased revenues from electric and gas residential, commercial and industrial customers due to milder winter weather. The decreases were partly offset by greater revenues from electric sales to other utilities. Fuel and purchased electric and gas costs fell 8.2%. However, with higher interest costs and depreciation and amortization charges, and reduced other income and deductions, net income was down 11%, to $19,167,000 ($1.06 a share, after preferred dividends), from $21,485,000 ($1.18).

Stock Performance - 02-OCT-98

In the past 30 trading days, CNH's shares have declined 3%, compared to a 7% fall in the S&P 500. Average trading volume for the past five days was 28,720 shares, compared with the 40-day moving average of 35,018 shares.

Key Stock Statistics

Dividend Rate/Share	2.16	Shareholders	24,200
Shs. outstg. (M)	17.0	Market cap. (B)	$0.721
Avg. daily vol. (M)	0.042	Inst. holdings	36%
Tang. Bk. Value/Share	27.38		
Beta	0.25		

Value of $10,000 invested 5 years ago: $ 19,765

Fiscal Year Ending Dec. 31

	1998	1997	1996	1995	1994	1993
Revenues (Million $)						
1Q	143.9	151.9	153.8	144.7	162.8	153.4
2Q	112.1	118.6	117.0	118.6	117.2	117.7
3Q	—	123.5	117.7	127.5	116.1	120.1
4Q	—	126.3	125.5	121.4	119.5	126.2
Yr.	—	520.3	514.0	512.2	515.7	517.4
Earnings Per Share ($)						
1Q	1.06	1.18	1.20	1.06	1.22	1.15
2Q	0.54	0.55	0.58	0.55	0.45	0.59
3Q	—	0.72	0.73	0.70	0.65	0.55
4Q	—	0.52	0.48	0.43	0.36	0.41
Yr.	—	2.97	2.99	2.74	2.68	2.68

Next earnings report expected: mid October

Dividend Data (Dividends have been paid since 1903.)

Amount ($)	Date Decl.	Ex-Div. Date	Stock of Record	Payment Date
0.535	Dec. 19	Jan. 07	Jan. 09	Feb. 02 '98
0.535	Mar. 27	Apr. 07	Apr. 10	May. 01 '98
0.540	Jun. 26	Jul. 08	Jul. 10	Aug. 01 '98
0.540	Sep. 25	Oct. 07	Oct. 09	Nov. 02 '98

A Division of The McGraw-Hill Companies

Business Summary - 04-MAY-98

In recent years, Central Hudson Gas & Electric Corp. (CNH) has prepared for the advent of deregulation in the electric power industry by cutting fuel costs, boosting purchases of electric power and strengthening its balance sheet; all with an eye toward improving its competitive position.

CNH supplies electricity to 266,000 customers and gas to 61,000 customers in a 2,600 square-mile service area that begins 25 miles north of New York City and extends along the Hudson River almost as far as Albany, taking in parts of eight counties. Electric sales to CHN's customers in 1997 declined 3%, and "firm" natural gas sales fell 5%, largely as a result of unseasonal weather conditions. Billing heating degree days were 8% lower than in 1996, while cooling degree days down 16%. Earnings were down slightly in 1997, as the impact of the unusual weather was mostly offset by tax credits, other non-recurring items, and increases in other income. Electric sales accounted for 80% of revenues and 85% of operating earnings in 1997.

In anticipation of a more competitive marketplace, CNH has launched an aggressive cost management program. Increasingly, it is turning to purchased electricity for its power requirements when the cost of buying power is less than the cost of producing it. In 1997, the company purchased 34% of its electric energy requirements from outside providers. In addition, CNH has cut the cost of coal by negotiating new contracts, including one that will satisfy half of its coal requirements with coal from South America. Coal was used to produce 39% of energy generated or purchased in 1997, far exceeding the contribution of oil (about 7%) or nuclear power (14%). By reducing its debt ratio (total debt divided by total capitalization) to under 42% and refinancing debt at lower rates, CNH has also benefited from declining interest charges over the last several years.

Under a settlement with the staff of New York's Public Service Commission approved in February 1998, the company agreed to freeze electric rates through June 2001, reduce rates for its largest industrial customers, and phase in customer choice. The agreement will serve as a blueprint for introducing competition to CNH and its customers.

The customer mix in 1997 (based on electric revenues) was 43% residential, 31% commercial, 17 % industrial, and 9% other. IBM, CNH's largest customer, accounted for 9% of total electric revenues in 1997. Sales to IBM stabilized in 1996, after declining sharply as a result of corporate downsizing.

Per Share Data ($)

(Year Ended Dec. 31)	1997	1996	1995	1994	1993	1992	1991	1990	1989	1988
Tangible Bk. Val.	27.29	26.48	24.82	22.46	21.91	22.69	21.96	21.76	21.11	20.59
Earnings	2.97	2.99	2.74	2.68	2.68	2.65	2.40	2.38	2.28	2.63
Dividends	2.13	2.11	2.10	2.07	2.03	1.96	1.88	1.80	1.76	1.72
Payout Ratio	72%	71%	77%	77%	77%	74%	78%	76%	77%	65%
Prices - High	43$^7/_8$	31$^1/_2$	31$^7/_8$	30$^3/_8$	35$^3/_4$	31$^1/_4$	29	24$^7/_8$	24$^1/_8$	21$^7/_8$
- Low	29$^3/_4$	28$^3/_4$	25$^3/_8$	22$^7/_8$	28$^3/_8$	25$^7/_8$	22$^5/_8$	20	20$^3/_8$	16$^7/_8$
P/E Ratio - High	15	11	12	11	13	12	12	10	11	8
- Low	10	10	9	9	11	10	9	8	9	6

Income Statement Analysis (Million $)

	1997	1996	1995	1994	1993	1992	1991	1990	1989	1988
Revs.	520	514	512	516	517	524	495	504	470	438
Depr.	43.9	42.6	41.5	40.4	39.7	39.6	37.2	36.1	35.3	31.9
Maint.	27.6	28.9	29.4	32.7	34.5	34.2	31.5	30.4	23.9	23.8
Fxd. Chgs. Cov.	3.6	3.7	3.2	3.6	3.4	2.7	2.4	2.2	2.1	2.3
Constr. Credits	0.7	1.0	1.5	1.4	1.5	1.5	2.2	1.7	0.9	1.0
Eff. Tax Rate	32%	36%	35%	35%	35%	34%	33%	33%	33%	33%
Net Inc.	55.1	56.1	52.7	50.9	50.4	47.7	42.9	41.0	39.1	43.8

Balance Sheet & Other Fin. Data (Million $)

	1997	1996	1995	1994	1993	1992	1991	1990	1989	1988
Gross Prop.	1,474	1,442	1,405	1,359	1,329	1,302	1,272	1,212	1,173	1,131
Cap. Exp.	43.9	49.9	50.3	58.0	54.0	62.0	71.0	51.0	42.0	53.0
Net Prop.	971	940	937	931	915	905	885	855	848	845
Capitalization:										
LT Debt	362	362	389	389	392	441	416	408	447	449
% LT Debt	40	41	43	43	44	49	49	50	53	54
Pfd.	56.0	56.0	56.0	81.0	81.0	80.2	81.0	81.0	81.0	81.0
% Pfd.	6.30	6.30	6.20	8.90	7.20	8.90	9.50	9.90	9.50	9.70
Common	477	472	454	437	418	378	360	334	321	309
% Common	53	53	51	48	37	42	42	41	38	37
Total Cap.	1,100	1,087	1,089	1,146	1,122	1,012	962	913	931	908
% Oper. Ratio	86.5	85.2	86.2	85.8	85.6	85.8	84.7	84.5	83.7	81.6
% Earn. on Net Prop.	7.5	8.1	7.6	7.9	8.2	8.3	8.7	9.1	9.0	9.6
% Return On Revs.	10.6	10.9	10.3	9.9	9.7	9.1	8.7	8.1	8.3	10.0
% Return On Invest. Capital	7.4	7.7	7.5	7.2	7.5	8.1	8.4	8.9	8.8	9.6
% Return On Com. Equity	10.9	11.3	10.7	10.7	11.3	10.8	10.6	10.8	10.1	12.4

Data as orig. reptd.; bef. results of disc opers. and/or spec. items. Per share data adj. for stk. divs. as of ex-div. date. Bold denotes diluted EPS (FASB 128). E-Estimated. NA-Not Available. NM-Not Meaningful. NR-Not Ranked.

Office—284 South Ave, Poughkeepsie, NY 12601-4879. **Tel**—(914) 452-2000. **Chrmn & CEO**—J. E. Mack III. **Pres & COO**—P. J. Ganci. **Contr**—D. S. Doyle. **Treas & Investor Contact**—Steven V. Lant .(914-486-5254). **Dirs**—J. Effron, F. D. Fergusson, H. K. Fridrich, E. F. X. Gallagher, P. J. Ganci, C. LaForge, J. E. Mack III, E. P. Swyer. **Transfer Agent & Registrar**—First Chicago Trust Co. of New York, Jersey City, NJ. **Incorporated**—in New York in 1926. **Empl**— 1,196. **S&P Analyst:** S.A.H.

Central Parking

480T

NYSE Symbol **CPC**

In S&P SmallCap 600

10-OCT-98

Industry:
Services (Commercial & Consumer)

Summary: PK is a leading provider of parking services in the U.S.

Quantitative Evaluations	
Outlook (1 Lowest—5 Highest)	
• **NA**	
Fair Value	
• **NA**	
Risk	
• **Average**	
Earn./Div. Rank	
• **NR**	
Technical Eval.	
• **NA**	
Rel. Strength Rank (1 Lowest—99 Highest)	
• **35**	
Insider Activity	
• **Neutral**	

Recent Price • 35⅝   Yield • 0.2%
52 Wk Range • 53⅜–33⅞   12-Mo. P/E • 36.7

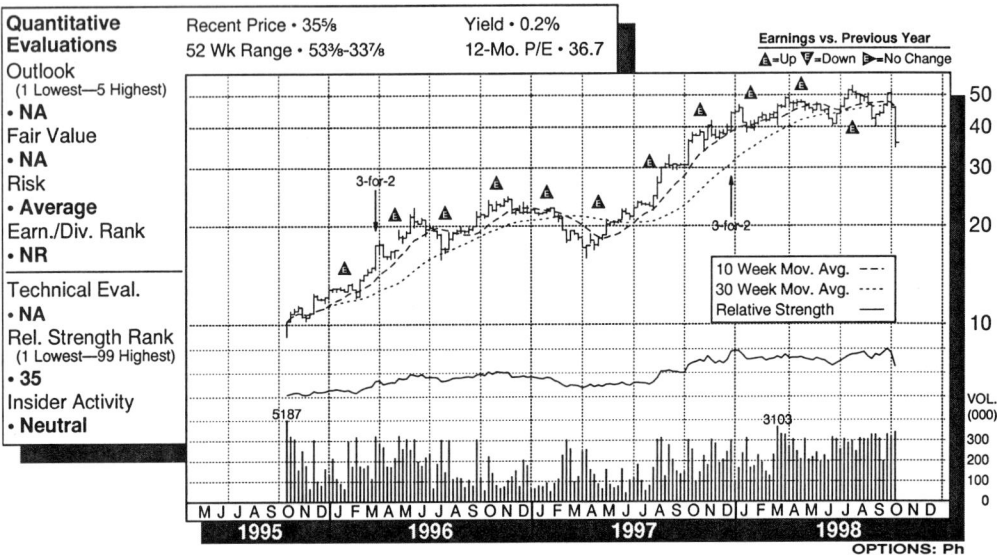

Earnings vs. Previous Year
▲=Up ▼=Down ▷=No Change

10 Week Mov. Avg. ‐ ‐ ‐
30 Week Mov. Avg. ‐ ‐ ‐ ‐
Relative Strength ——

OPTIONS: Ph

Business Profile - 02-APR-98

As of February 1998, PK operated more than 2,200 parking facilities with more than 925,000 spaces, at locations in 34 states and overseas. The total size of PK's system was expanded 23% by the February 1998 acquisition of Kinney System Holding Corp., one of the largest private operators of parking facilities in the Northeast, in a transaction valued at about $225 million, including cash, common shares and assumption of certain liabilities. In March 1998, PK sold publicly 2,625,000 common shares at $44 a share; net proceeds were used to repay indebtedness. In September 1997, the company acquired Diplomat Parking Corp., one of the largest private providers of parking services in the Mid-Atlantic area.

Operational Review - 02-APR-98

Total revenues for the three months ended December 31, 1997, advanced 72%, year to year, on an 84% gain in parking revenues and 30% higher management contract revenues. The higher revenues stemmed from acquisitions, the addition of leased and owned locations, and rate increases and higher utilization of parking spaces at existing facilities. Profitability was restricted by $1.4 million of interest expense (versus none a year earlier). Pretax income was up 52%. After taxes at 38.0%, versus 35.0%, net income rose 45%, to $5,642,000 ($0.21 a share, diluted) from $3,899,000 ($0.15).

Stock Performance - 09-OCT-98

In the past 30 trading days, CPC's shares have declined 16%, compared to a 4% fall in the S&P 500. Average trading volume for the past five days was 275,080 shares, compared with the 40-day moving average of 120,187 shares.

Key Stock Statistics

Dividend Rate/Share	0.06	Shareholders	7,000
Shs. outstg. (M)	29.6	Market cap. (B)	$ 1.1
Avg. daily vol. (M)	0.138	Inst. holdings	25%
Tang. Bk. Value/Share	2.93		
Beta	NA		

Value of $10,000 invested 5 years ago: NA

Fiscal Year Ending Sep. 30

	1998	1997	1996	1995	1994	1993
Revenues (Million $)						
1Q	71.19	41.42	33.30	29.90	26.70	—
2Q	91.22	55.92	35.68	31.20	27.20	—
3Q	112.2	60.03	37.50	32.40	29.80	—
4Q	—	65.60	36.88	32.70	28.50	—
Yr.	—	223.0	143.3	126.2	112.2	95.42

	1998	1997	1996	1995	1994	1993
Earnings Per Share ($)						
1Q	**0.21**	0.15	0.13	0.11	0.08	—
2Q	**0.23**	0.17	0.13	0.10	0.07	—
3Q	**0.27**	0.20	0.14	0.11	0.10	—
4Q	—	0.25	0.13	0.10	0.07	—
Yr.	—	0.77	0.53	0.43	0.37	—

Next earnings report expected: NA

Dividend Data (Dividends have been paid since 1996.)

Amount ($)	Date Decl.	Ex-Div. Date	Stock of Record	Payment Date
0.015	Nov. 24	Dec. 18	Dec. 22	Jan. 02 '98
0.015	Mar. 09	Mar. 27	Mar. 31	Apr. 13 '98
0.015	Jun. 12	Jun. 26	Jun. 30	Jul. 10 '98
0.015	Sep. 11	Sep. 28	Sep. 30	Oct. 09 '98

A Division of The McGraw-Hill Companies

STANDARD
&POOR'S
STOCK REPORTS

Central Parking Corporation

480T

10-OCT-98

Business Summary - 02-APR-98

A leading provider of parking services in the United States, Central Parking Corp. (PK) expanded the total size of its system by about 23% via the February 1998 acquisition of Kinney System Holding Corp., the largest operator of parking facilities in the New York City metropolitan area and one of the largest parking companies in the Northeast. The transaction was valued at $225 million at closing, including cash, common shares and assumption of certain liabilities. Management expects the acquisition to contribute favorably to earnings, beginning in FY 98 (Sep.).

Including the Kinney System operations, Central Parking operates 2,237 parking facilities containing more than 925,000 spaces at locations in 34 states, the District of Columbia, Canada, Puerto Rico, the United Kingdom, Mexico, Germany, Malaysia, and Spain.

PK operates facilities under management contracts, leases, or as an owner. The company's responsibilities under a management contract include hiring, training and staffing parking personnel and providing collection, accounting, marketing and other services. PK generally receives a base monthly fee for managing the facilities plus additional fees for ancillary services, and it receives a percentage of facility revenues above a base amount. The typical management contract is for a term of one to three years.

Lease arrangements are typically for three to ten

years, and provide for a contractually established payment to the facility owner regardless of the operating earnings of the parking facility. PK's rent can be a flat annual amount, a percentage of gross revenues, or a combination of both. Leased facilities require a longer commitment and a larger capital investment by the company but provide a more stable source of revenue and greater opportunity for long-term revenue growth.

Ownership of parking facilities, either independently or through joint ventures, typically requires a larger capital investment than managed or leased facilities but provides maximum control over operations, and all growth in revenues flows directly to the company. Of PK's 1,644 facilities at the end of FY 97, 877 were operated under management contracts, 709 were leased and the rest were owned.

PK complements internal growth achieved through ongoing marketing activities with an aggressive acquisition strategy, and it has added hundreds of facilities (in addition to the Kinney System) since the beginning of FY 97 (Sep.). In January 1997, PK acquired Square Industries, Inc., adding 116 facilities and 61,000 spaces. The acquisition of Diplomat Parking Corp., effective October 1, 1997, brought 37,000 spaces in the Mid-Atlantic. Marketing efforts at the local level are designed to boost market share. PK also targets developers and asset managers with a national presence and high-use facilities that combine commuter demand with off-hour use.

Per Share Data ($)

(Year Ended Sep. 30)	1997	1996	1995	1994	1993	1992	1991	1990	1989	1988
Tangible Bk. Val.	2.28	2.71	1.51	1.98	NA	NA	NA	NA	NA	NA
Cash Flow	0.95	0.57	0.52	0.49	0.31	0.29	NA	NA	NA	NA
Earnings	0.77	0.53	0.43	0.37	0.21	0.22	0.11	NA	NA	NA
Dividends	0.06	0.05	NA	NA	NA	NA	NA	NA	NA	NA
Payout Ratio	8%	10%	NA	NA	NA	NA	NA	NA	NA	NA
Prices - High	46¾	24⅝	13⅛	NA	NA	NA	NA	NA	NA	NA
- Low	15⅞	12	8	NA	NA	NA	NA	NA	NA	NA
P/E Ratio - High	61	47	30	NA	NA	NA	NA	NA	NA	NA
- Low	21	23	18	NA	NA	NA	NA	NA	NA	NA

Income Statement Analysis (Million $)

	1997	1996	1995	1994	1993	1992	1991	1990	1989	1988
Revs.	223	143	126	112	95.0	46.0	31.0	NA	NA	NA
Oper. Inc.	32.8	19.4	16.5	13.8	10.1	7.6	5.2	NA	NA	NA
Depr.	5.0	2.5	2.9	2.6	2.3	1.4	1.1	NA	NA	NA
Int. Exp.	4.6	Nil	Nil	0.0	0.2	0.2	NA	NA	NA	NA
Pretax Inc.	32.4	21.7	15.5	14.1	8.7	8.4	4.2	NA	NA	NA
Eff. Tax Rate	38%	33%	36%	37%	40%	36%	36%	NA	NA	NA
Net Inc.	20.2	13.7	9.9	9.0	5.2	5.4	2.7	NA	NA	NA

Balance Sheet & Other Fin. Data (Million $)

	1997	1996	1995	1994	1993	1992	1991	1990	1989	1988
Cash	10.0	28.6	10.2	NA	NA	NA	NA	NA	NA	NA
Curr. Assets	39.6	45.2	26.5	NA	NA	NA	NA	NA	NA	NA
Total Assets	234	107	70.4	NA	NA	NA	NA	NA	NA	NA
Curr. Liab.	48.8	25.7	23.8	NA	NA	NA	NA	NA	NA	NA
LT Debt	73.3	Nil	Nil	Nil	Nil	Nil	Nil	Nil	Nil	Nil
Common Eqty.	100	76.8	41.3	57.3	NA	NA	NA	NA	NA	NA
Total Cap.	177	78.4	41.9	NA	NA	NA	NA	NA	NA	NA
Cap. Exp.	6.3	16.7	5.4	4.3	2.6	6.7	NA	NA	NA	NA
Cash Flow	25.2	15.2	12.0	11.3	7.3	6.5	NA	NA	NA	NA
Curr. Ratio	0.8	1.8	1.1	NA	NA	NA	NA	NA	NA	NA
% LT Debt of Cap.	41.4	Nil	Nil	NA	NA	NA	NA	NA	NA	NA
% Net Inc.of Revs.	9.1	9.5	7.9	8.0	5.5	11.7	8.8	NA	NA	NA
% Ret. on Assets	11.8	15.4	15.2	NA	NA	NA	NA	NA	NA	NA
% Ret. on Equity	22.5	23.2	25.9	NA	NA	NA	NA	NA	NA	NA

Data as orig. reptd.; bef. results of disc. opers. and/or spec. items. Per share data adj. for stk. divs. as of ex-div. date. Bold denotes diluted EPS (FASB 128). E-Estimated. NA-Not Available. NM-Not Meaningful. NR-Not Ranked.

Office—2401 21st Ave. South, Suite 200, Nashville, TN 37212. **Tel**—(615) 297-4255. **Chrmn & CEO**—M. J. Carell, Jr. **Pres & COO**—J. H. Bond. **CFO**—S. A. Tisdell. **VP & Secy**—H. J. Abbott. **Dirs**—J. H. Bond, M. J. Carell, Jr., C. Conlee, J. Eakin, L. Harwood, E. Nelson, W. O'Neil, P. E. Sadler. **Transfer Agent & Registrar**—SunTrust Bank of Atlanta. **Incorporated**—in Tennessee in 1968. **Empl**— 9,300. **S&P Analyst:** J.J.S.

03-OCT-98

Industry: Electric Companies

Summary: This small electric utility serves a large portion of Vermont and parts of New Hampshire.

Quantitative Evaluations	
Recent Price • 10¾	Yield • 8.1%
52 Wk Range • 15⅜-9¾	12-Mo. P/E • 18.6

Outlook
(1 Lowest—5 Highest)
• **NA**

Fair Value
• **NA**

Risk
• **Low**

Earn./Div. Rank
• **B**

Technical Eval.
• **Bearish** since 7/98

Rel. Strength Rank
(1 Lowest—99 Highest)
• **56**

Insider Activity
• **Unfavorable**

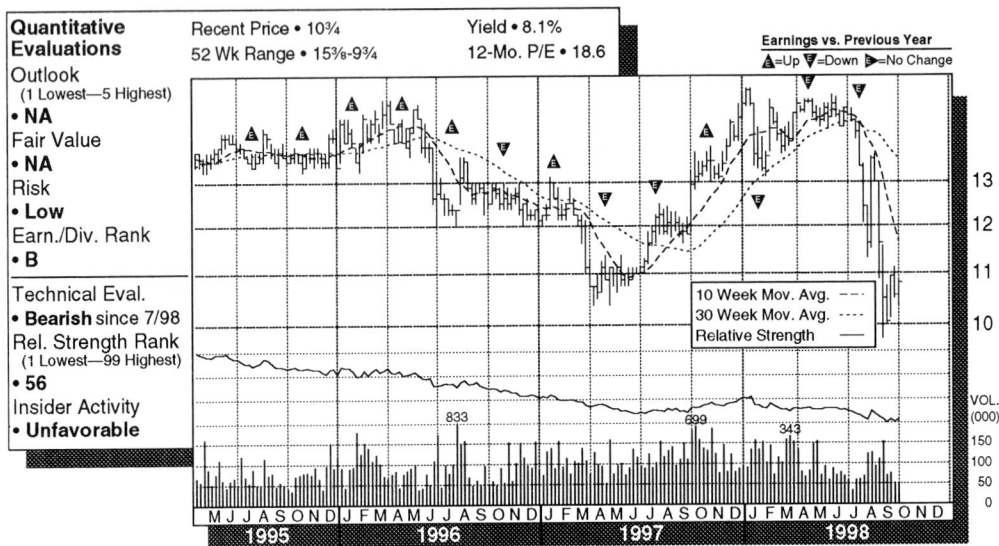

Earnings vs. Previous Year
▲=Up ▼=Down ▶=No Change

10 Week Mov. Avg. — —
30 Week Mov. Avg. - - - -
Relative Strength ——

833   699   343

VOL. (000)

Business Profile - 23-MAR-98

This Vermont electric utility company has announced specific organizational plans to create five new business units: distribution, generation, retail sales, unregulated generation development, and service companies. CV also presented early retirement and voluntary separation offers designed to reduce employee counts by 97 people, or about 15% of current staff. The company believed that these moves were essential for it to be highly competitive in the expected deregulation of its main business. Catamount Energy, an unregulated subsidiary, will continue in the small-scale generation business, and will expand its focus in Western Europe. CV recently filed for a 6.6% rate hike to be effective in June 1998 and elimination of the current winter-summer differential.

Operational Review - 23-MAR-98

Revenues in 1997 (preliminary) advanced 4.8% from 1996, as strong industrial sales and a modest rise in retail sales outweighed a decline in wholesale sales. Results were impacted by increased power costs and non-recurring charges of $3,575,000, or $0.31 a share (after-tax) in the 1997 fourth quarter relating to regulatory and court actions requiring the Connecticut Valley Electric Co. subsidiary to terminate its contract with CV and seek power at available market prices. Net income declined 12%, to $17,151,000 ($1.32 a share, after preferred dividends), from $19,442,000 ($1.51). Results in 1997 exclude a $0.07-a-share extraordinary charge.

Stock Performance - 02-OCT-98

In the past 30 trading days, CV's shares have declined 17%, compared to a 7% fall in the S&P 500. Average trading volume for the past five days was 9,280 shares, compared with the 40-day moving average of 19,149 shares.

Key Stock Statistics

Dividend Rate/Share	0.88	Shareholders	14,700
Shs. outstg. (M)	11.4	Market cap. (B)	$0.124
Avg. daily vol. (M)	0.014	Inst. holdings	34%
Tang. Bk. Value/Share	16.27		
Beta	0.91		

Value of $10,000 invested 5 years ago: $ 6,559

Fiscal Year Ending Dec. 31

	1998	1997	1996	1995	1994	1993
Revenues (Million $)						
1Q	83.96	88.49	84.25	86.86	83.89	85.32
2Q	66.41	65.44	61.39	62.85	57.68	57.00
3Q	—	67.99	63.83	60.31	59.03	60.99
4Q	—	82.81	81.33	78.25	76.56	76.10
Yr.	—	304.7	290.8	288.3	277.2	279.4
Earnings Per Share ($)						
1Q	**0.78**	1.20	1.23	1.13	1.04	1.26
2Q	**-0.52**	-0.21	-0.08	-0.13	-0.22	-0.14
3Q	—	0.14	-0.11	0.11	-0.11	-0.09
4Q	—	**0.19**	0.47	0.42	0.38	0.61
Yr.	—	**1.32**	1.51	1.53	1.08	1.64

Next earnings report expected: NA

Dividend Data (Dividends have been paid since 1944.)

Amount ($)	Date Decl.	Ex-Div. Date	Stock of Record	Payment Date
0.220	Oct. 06	Oct. 29	Oct. 31	Nov. 14 '97
0.220	Dec. 02	Jan. 28	Jan. 30	Feb. 13 '98
0.220	Apr. 06	Apr. 28	Apr. 30	May. 15 '98
0.220	Jun. 01	Jul. 29	Jul. 31	Aug. 14 '98

STANDARD
&POOR'S
STOCK REPORTS

Central Vermont Public Service Corporation

486F

03-OCT-98

Business Summary - 23-MAR-98

Central Vermont Public Service and its Connecticut Valley Electric unit supply electricity to customers in nearly three-quarters of Vermont's towns, villages and cities and to parts of New Hampshire bordering the Connecticut River. About half of Vermont's residents receive service from the company, as do 10,000 customers in 13 New Hampshire towns. Contributions to revenues by customer class in recent years were:

	1996	1995	1994
Residential	45%	45%	45%
Commercial	41%	41%	40%
Industrial	13%	13%	14%
Other	1%	1%	1%

Power sources in 1996 were 36% nuclear, 8% coal, 6% company-owned hydro; 2% jointly owned units; 6% small power producers; 12% other; 30% of the power supply was imported from Canada. Peak load in 1996 was 409.9 mw, and system capability at time of peak was 635.9 mw, for a reserve margin of 36%.

CV's nuclear power is derived primarily from its 31.3% (156-mw entitlement) interest in the Vermont Yankee plant. The company also has interests in the Maine Yankee nuclear plant (2.0%, 16.9 mw), Connecticut Yankee (2.0%, 11.6 mw) and Yankee Atomic (3.5%). In early 1992, Yankee Atomic decided to permanently discontinue operation of its plant. CV's share of the remaining shutdown cost is about $6.1 million, which it believes will be recovered through the regulatory process.

In October 1995, the company filed for a rate increase of $31 million (14.6%). In February 1996, the Vermont Public Service Board and CV reached an agreement under which rates increased 5.5% in June 1996, and another 2% in January 1997. The rate increase would raise the company's return on equity to 11%, from 10%. The company recently filed to end the winter-summer rate differential and add a 6.6% rate hike in June 1998; it is also seeking to remove a 0.75% ROE penalty imposed in 1994.

Wholly owned Catamount Energy Corp. invests in non-regulated energy-related projects. It currently has interests in five operating independent power projects, following the recent sale of its interest in its Williams Lake facility. CV's nonutility subsidiary, SmartEnergy Services, Inc., provides reliable energy-efficient products and services, including the rental of electric water heaters. In August 1996, Catamount purchased a 10% interest in a biomass power generating station in Thetford, England, from Fibrowatt Ltd. The company's interest in the $107 million plant will increase to 44% when it becomes operational in September 1998.

Per Share Data ($)

(Year Ended Dec. 31)	1997	1996	1995	1994	1993	1992	1991	1990	1989	1988
Tangible Bk. Val.	16.38	16.19	15.51	14.56	15.03	14.21	14.03	13.68	13.36	12.92
Earnings	1.32	1.51	1.53	1.08	1.64	1.71	1.65	1.62	1.73	1.72
Dividends	0.88	0.84	0.80	1.42	1.42	1.39	1.39	1.37	1.34	1.29
Payout Ratio	67%	56%	52%	131%	87%	81%	84%	85%	78%	75%
Prices - High	15⅜	15⅛	14⅜	22	25¾	25	22⅞	19⅝	19⅜	17⅜
- Low	10⅜	12	13¼	12⅛	20⅛	19½	17	14⅝	14¾	14⅛
P/E Ratio - High	12	10	9	20	16	15	14	12	11	10
- Low	8	8	9	11	12	11	10	9	9	8

Income Statement Analysis (Million $)

	1997	1996	1995	1994	1993	1992	1991	1990	1989	1988
Revs.	305	291	288	277	279	275	233	232	227	219
Depr.	16.9	18.0	17.3	16.5	15.4	14.4	12.4	11.2	10.2	9.1
Maint.	15.3	14.9	12.9	12.2	11.7	11.9	11.2	12.6	10.8	12.2
Fxd. Chgs. Cov.	2.8	3.0	3.0	3.6	3.7	3.0	2.6	2.6	3.1	3.0
Constr. Credits	0.1	0.5	3.5	0.4	0.1	0.4	0.7	0.1	0.9	0.3
Eff. Tax Rate	35%	34%	36%	45%	38%	37%	25%	31%	40%	40%
Net Inc.	17.2	19.4	19.9	14.8	21.3	21.4	18.6	17.5	18.2	19.2

Balance Sheet & Other Fin. Data (Million $)

	1997	1996	1995	1994	1993	1992	1991	1990	1989	1988
Gross Prop.	507	471	463	450	432	419	401	386	339	317
Cap. Exp.	14.0	19.0	21.3	22.6	20.5	20.5	19.0	21.2	28.0	24.9
Net Prop.	355	325	327	325	319	316	312	306	268	252
Capitalization:										
LT Debt	110	136	139	141	144	131	154	154	115	107
% LT Debt	34	39	40	41	41	40	45	50	43	43
Pfd.	27.1	28.1	28.0	28.1	35.1	35.1	35.1	15.1	15.1	15.1
% Pfd.	8.40	8.00	8.10	8.30	9.90	11	10	4.90	5.70	6.00
Common	187	186	180	171	174	159	152	142	135	129
% Common	58	53	52	50	49	49	45	46	51	51
Total Cap.	385	415	412	401	414	361	374	346	301	289
% Oper. Ratio	89.4	92.0	91.6	92.4	90.7	89.5	88.4	88.9	87.7	87.3
% Earn. on Net Prop.	5.2	7.1	7.4	6.6	8.2	9.2	8.8	8.9	10.7	11.5
% Return On Revs.	5.6	6.7	6.9	5.3	7.6	7.8	8.0	7.6	8.0	8.8
% Return On Invest. Capital	5.9	4.7	7.4	6.1	7.8	9.3	8.8	9.7	10.6	10.6
% Return On Com. Equity	8.1	9.5	10.2	7.2	11.0	11.8	11.8	12.0	13.0	13.1

Data as orig. reptd.; bef. results of disc. opers. and/or spec. items. Per share data adj. for stk. divs. as of ex-div. date. Bold denotes diluted EPS (FASB 128). E-Estimated. NA-Not Available. NM-Not Meaningful. NR-Not Ranked.

Office—77 Grove St., Rutland, VT 05701. **Tel**—(802) 773-2711. **Chrmn**—F. H. Bertrand. **Pres & CEO**—R. H. Young Jr. **VP & CFO**—F. J. Boyle. **Secy**—J. M. Kraus. **Treas & Investor Contact**—Jonathan W. Booraem (802-747-5223). **Dirs**—R.L. Barnett, F. H. Bertrand, R. L. Brooks, R. G. Clarke, L. F. Hackett, F. R. Keyser Jr., P. J. Martin, M. A. McKenzie, P. L. Smith, R. H. Young. **Transfer Agents & Registrars**—Co.'s office; First National Bank of Boston. **Incorporated**—in Vermont in 1929. **Empl**— 637. **S&P Analyst:** S.A.H.

STANDARD &POOR'S
STOCK REPORTS

Centura Banks

487J

NYSE Symbol **CBC**

In S&P SmallCap 600

03-OCT-98

Industry: Banks (Regional)

Summary: This bank holding company provides banking, investment, insurance and trust services to individuals and businesses throughout North Carolina and the Hampton Roads area of Virginia.

Quantitative Evaluations

Recent Price • 63¼
52 Wk Range • 76-54¾

Yield • 1.8%
12-Mo. P/E • 18.3

Outlook (1 Lowest—5 Highest)
• **1⁻**

Fair Value
• **58⅝**

Risk
• **Low**

Earn./Div. Rank
• **A**

Technical Eval.
• **Bearish** since 8/98

Rel. Strength Rank (1 Lowest—99 Highest)
• **80**

Insider Activity
• **Neutral**

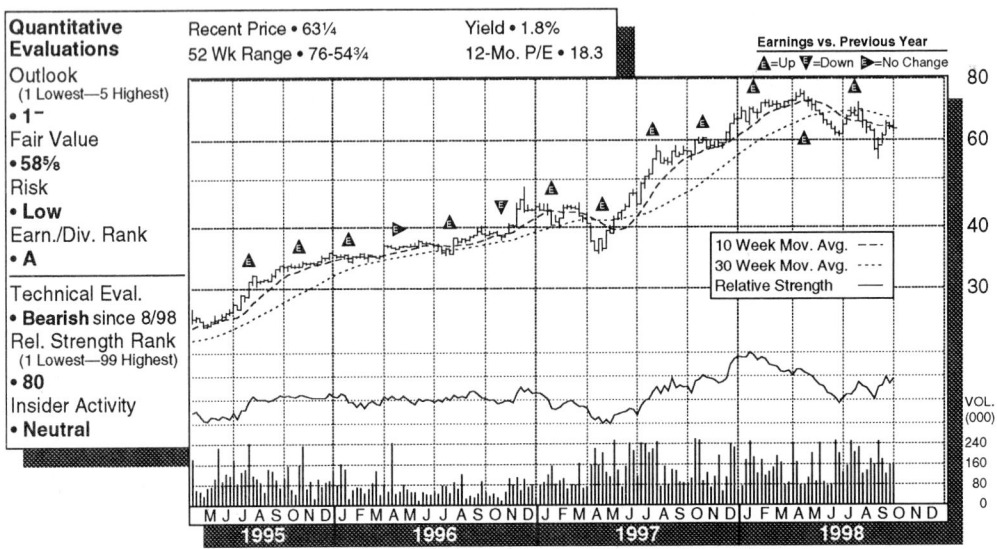

Earnings vs. Previous Year
▲=Up ▼=Down ▶=No Change

10 Week Mov. Avg. ---
30 Week Mov. Avg. ·····
Relative Strength —

VOL. (000)

1995   1996   1997   1998

Business Profile - 08-JUL-98

CBC provides its services through over 200 financial centers (including 30 supermarkets) and more than 300 automated transaction machines (ATMs) mainly in North Carolina. In the face of increasing competition from traditional and non-traditional providers of financial services, CBC has set out to become the primary provider of all financial services to each of its customers. CBC's total assets at June 30, 1998, were approximately $7.6 billion, up 14% from a year earlier, reflecting an active acquisition campaign. During 1998's first quarter, Centura completed the acquisition of Pee Dee State Bank. In the second quarter, CBC opened five financial offices in Hannaford supermarkets and agreed to purchase four in-store financial offices in Kroger supermarkets in Winston-Salem and Kernersville.

Operational Review - 08-JUL-98

Net interest income in the first six months of 1998 rose 12%, year to year, as a 15% increase in average earning assets offset a narrower net interest margin (4.43% versus 4.55%). The provision for loan losses advanced 16%, to $7,028,000 from $6,083,000. Total noninterest income rose 32% and noninterest expense advanced 16%. After taxes at 33.8%, versus 35.2%, net income was up 23%, to $46,531,000 ($1.74 a share), from $37,854,000 ($1.44).

Stock Performance - 02-OCT-98

In the past 30 trading days, CBC's shares have increased 1%, compared to a 7% fall in the S&P 500. Average trading volume for the past five days was 32,280 shares, compared with the 40-day moving average of 36,885 shares.

Key Stock Statistics

Dividend Rate/Share	1.16	Shareholders	13,500
Shs. outstg. (M)	26.5	Market cap. (B)	$ 1.7
Avg. daily vol. (M)	0.034	Inst. holdings	23%
Tang. Bk. Value/Share	22.21		
Beta	0.93		

Value of $10,000 invested 5 years ago: $ 35,866

Fiscal Year Ending Dec. 31

	1998	1997	1996	1995	1994	1993
Revenues (Million $)						
1Q	168.3	145.8	137.9	96.25	80.34	69.61
2Q	177.5	153.5	138.2	105.9	82.52	73.29
3Q	—	161.8	144.1	116.8	87.79	77.83
4Q	—	171.3	150.4	120.6	91.06	83.14
Yr.	—	632.3	570.6	439.6	341.7	303.9
Earnings Per Share ($)						
1Q	0.85	0.68	0.67	0.67	0.50	0.47
2Q	0.89	0.76	0.67	0.63	0.57	0.51
3Q	—	0.82	0.57	0.66	0.63	0.59
4Q	—	0.89	0.70	0.68	0.65	0.57
Yr.	—	3.15	2.60	2.64	2.35	2.14

Next earnings report expected: **early October**

Dividend Data (Dividends have been paid since 1990.)

Amount ($)	Date Decl.	Ex-Div. Date	Stock of Record	Payment Date
0.270	Oct. 02	Nov. 25	Nov. 28	Dec. 15 '97
0.270	Dec. 17	Feb. 25	Feb. 27	Mar. 13 '98
0.290	Apr. 15	May. 27	May. 29	Jun. 15 '98
0.290	Aug. 14	Aug. 27	Aug. 31	Sep. 15 '98

A Division of The McGraw-Hill Companies

Centura Banks, Inc.

Business Summary - 08-JUL-98

Centura, a $7.6 billion asset Rocky Mount, NC-based bank, is transforming itself into a full line retailer of financial services to face what it deems to be the future of the banking industry. In the process, Centura hopes to become the primary provider of all of its customers' financial services, including investments, insurance, and traditional banking.

Centura was formed in 1990 through the merger of two North Carolina banks, Peoples Bancorp. and Planters Corp. Since then, the bank has adopted an aggressive growth strategy, formed around its stated mission to become the primary financial services provider to its customers. To that end, Centura made four acquisitions in 1997 with assets totaling $416 million.

An additional component to CBC's customer driven strategy is investment in technology, which it hopes will improve its delivery channels without the added costs of constructing additional offices. Centura was the first bank in North Carolina to offer an electronic payment service via telephone and PC. Centura Highway, CBC's direct banking center, allows customers to open accounts, apply for loans, and transfer money between accounts.

Through the use of a customer database and sales tracking system that combines financial, demographic, behavioral and psychographic data, CBC is able to gain in-depth knowledge about its customers. This information supports decision-making about services offered, delivery channels, locations, staffing and marketing. Management anticipates it will continue to refine Centura's product and service offerings and related delivery systems and technologies in order to reach its goal of becoming its customers' primary financial services provider.

CBC adheres to the Economic Value Added (EVA) management system, focusing on revenue growth, increased capital efficiency and capital structure as drivers of shareholder value. In keeping with its focus on becoming a retailer of a broad base of financial services, Centura is diversifying its revenue sources and generating a larger portion of its income from noninterest revenues. In addition, the company believes its push into supermarket banking and its use of asset securitizations to fund loan growth will add to shareholder value by improving capital efficiency. Like many other banks, Centura is also repurchasing its stock as a means of returning capital to shareholders.

Per Share Data ($)

(Year Ended Dec. 31)	1997	1996	1995	1994	1993	1992	1991	1990	1989	1988
Tangible Bk. Val.	20.82	18.51	18.13	15.79	14.98	13.36	12.29	12.45	11.78	10.64
Earnings	3.15	2.60	2.64	2.35	2.14	1.70	0.62	1.27	1.70	1.51
Dividends	1.06	1.00	0.85	0.74	0.69	0.63	0.60	0.15	NA	NA
Payout Ratio	34%	38%	32%	31%	32%	37%	98%	NM	NA	NA
Prices - High	69	48¼	35½	25¼	24⅝	20½	16	13¾	NA	NA
- Low	35¼	33¾	22½	18	19¼	12½	11⅝	12⅜	NA	NA
P/E Ratio - High	22	18	13	11	12	12	26	11	NA	NA
- Low	11	13	9	8	9	7	19	10	NA	NA

Income Statement Analysis (Million $)

	1997	1996	1995	1994	1993	1992	1991	1990	1989	1988
Net Int. Inc.	268	250	204	182	153	125	105	108	102	94.0
Tax Equiv. Adj.	7.7	6.0	5.2	5.7	6.1	6.1	6.7	6.1	NA	NA
Non Int. Inc.	28.5	99	59.8	48.6	51.1	36.3	29.1	37.8	28.1	28.2
Loan Loss Prov.	13.4	9.6	7.4	6.7	8.5	15.1	20.8	10.0	6.1	5.3
Exp./Op. Revs.	113%	66%	62%	62%	64%	65%	72%	72%	69%	72%
Pretax Inc.	125	107	90.0	77.4	62.2	39.9	11.5	26.2	34.2	29.2
Eff. Tax Rate	34%	37%	36%	36%	34%	33%	24%	32%	31%	29%
Net Inc.	83.1	68.2	58.0	49.6	41.1	26.9	8.8	17.7	23.7	20.8
% Net Int. Marg.	4.56	4.66	4.76	4.96	4.81	4.87	4.80	4.80	NA	NA

Balance Sheet & Other Fin. Data (Million $)

	1997	1996	1995	1994	1993	1992	1991	1990	1989	1988
Earning Assets:										
Money Mkt	44.0	33.0	40.0	376	521	63.1	28.2	20.2	38.0	NA
Inv. Securities	1,829	1,578	1,259	539	668	566	530	504	465	NA
Com'l Loans	846	743	3,018	2,950	2,579	441	413	636	1,684	1,556
Other Loans	3,741	3,366	30.2	NA	NA	1,675	1,386	1,168	NA	NA
Total Assets	7,125	6,294	5,326	4,240	4,139	3,029	2,612	2,605	2,434	2,260
Demand Deposits	816	721	607	536	507	397	324	344	361	NA
Time Deposits	4,549	2,945	2,475	2,934	3,103	2,259	1,993	1,960	1,766	NA
LT Debt	382	311	227	109	44.9	45.9	16.4	22.4	17.4	18.0
Common Eqty.	538	475	391	324	311	211	182	174	164	148
% Ret. on Assets	1.2	1.1	1.2	1.2	1.1	0.9	0.3	0.7	1.0	1.0
% Ret. on Equity	16.4	14.8	16.2	15.6	15.6	13.3	5.0	10.5	15.2	14.9
% Loan Loss Resv.	1.4	1.4	1.4	1.5	1.6	1.5	1.5	1.1	1.1	NA
% Loans/Deposits	85.5	86.1	86.5	85.0	71.5	79.7	77.6	78.3	79.2	78.5
% Equity to Assets	7.6	7.6	7.5	7.8	7.3	7.0	7.0	6.7	6.7	6.6

Data as orig. reptd.; bef. results of disc. opers. and/or spec. items. Per share data adj. for stk. divs. as of ex-div. date. Bold denotes diluted EPS (FASB 128). E-Estimated. NA-Not Available. NM-Not Meaningful. NR-Not Ranked.

Office—134 North Church St., Rocky Mount, NC 27804. **Tel**—(919) 977-4400. **Website**—http://www.centura.com **Chrmn & CEO**—C.W. Sewell. **CFO**—S.J. Goldstein. **Investor Contact**—Frank Pattillo (252) 454-8341.**Dirs**—R. H. Barnhardt, C. W. Beasley, T. A. Betts Jr., E.L. Evans, J. R. Futrell Jr., J. H. High, M.K. Hooker, W.D. Hoover, R. L. Hubbard, W. H. Kincheloe, H.K. Landis III, C. T. Lane, R. R. Mauldin, —J.A. Moody, J.H. Nelson, D.E. Painter, D.E. Pardue, O.T. Parks III F.L. Pattillo, H.T. Powers, W.H. Redding, Jr., C.M. Reeves III, C.W. Sewell, G.T. Stronach III, A.P. Thorpe III, J.L. Wallace, Jr., W.H. Wilkerson. C.P. Wilkins. **Transfer Agent & Registrar**—Registrar & Transfer Co., Cranford, NJ. **Incorporated**—in North Carolina in 1990. **Empl**— 2,675. **S&P Analyst:** Michael Schneider

STANDARD
&POOR'S

STOCK REPORTS

Cephalon, Inc.

3482

NASDAQ Symbol **CEPH**

In S&P SmallCap 600

03-OCT-98

Industry:
Health Care (Drugs - Generic & Other)

Summary: This neuroscience company is developing therapeutic products to treat neurodegenerative diseases, such as ALS (Lou Gehrig's disease), Alzheimer's, and head and spinal injuries.

Quantitative Evaluations

Recent Price • 6⅞
52 Wk Range • 16⅛-3⅞

Yield • Nil
12-Mo. P/E • NM

Outlook
(1 Lowest—5 Highest)
• **NA**
Fair Value
• **NA**
Risk
• **High**
Earn./Div. Rank
• **NR**

Technical Eval.
• **Bullish** since 7/98
Rel. Strength Rank
(1 Lowest—99 Highest)
• **79**
Insider Activity
• **NA**

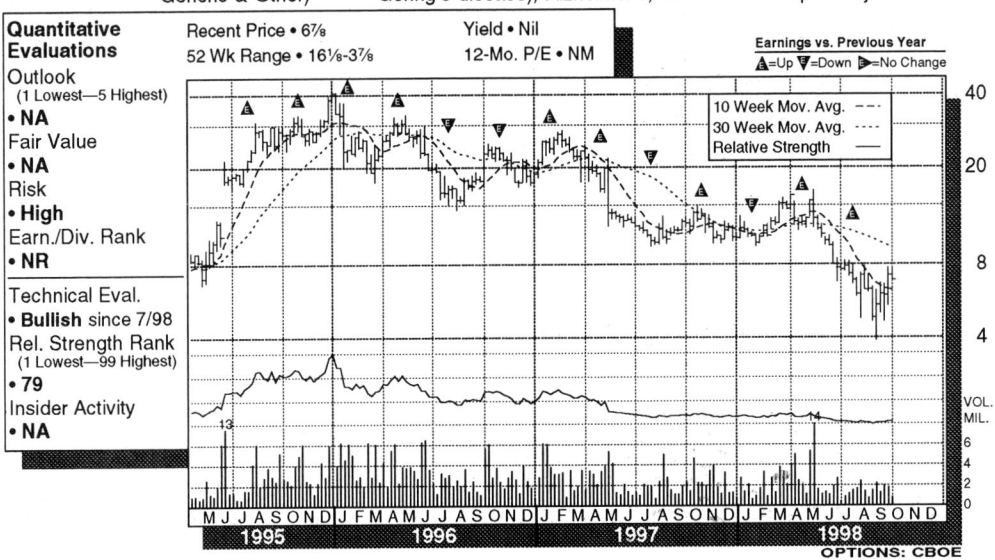

Earnings vs. Previous Year
▲=Up ▼=Down ▶=No Change

10 Week Mov. Avg. – – –
30 Week Mov. Avg. ‧‧‧‧
Relative Strength —

OPTIONS: CBOE

Business Profile - 14-SEP-98

Cephalon plans to submit additional clinical data on its Myotropin drug to the FDA in an attempt to obtain marketing approval for this new treatment for ALS. In May, the FDA said the company's Myotropin application was potentially approvable, contingent upon the submission of additional data. In December 1997, the FDA indicated that the company's application to market its narcolepsy drug Provigil was approvable pending a request for clarification and/or confirmation of certain information. CEPH submitted a response to this request, and the FDA set a target date of December 31, 1998 for a decision on Provigil. Provigil was recently approved in Ireland and is currently being marketed in the U.K. Major collaborative arrangements include those with Chiron, TAP Pharmaceuticals, Medtronic Inc., and Bristol-Myers Squibb.

Operational Review - 14-SEP-98

Revenues in the six months ended June 30, 1998, fell 27%, year to year, as increased revenue from co-promotion agreements were outweighed by lower payments from Chiron and the absence of funding from SmithKline Beecham and Schering-Plough. Results benefited from sharply lower R&D expenditures and SG&A costs, and the net loss narrowed to $27,274,000 ($0.97 a share, on 13% more shares), from $34,202,000 ($1.37). Cash, equivalents and investments totaled $91.7 million at the end of the second quarter.

Stock Performance - 02-OCT-98

In the past 30 trading days, CEPH's shares have increased 9%, compared to a 7% fall in the S&P 500. Average trading volume for the past five days was 159,340 shares, compared with the 40-day moving average of 297,815 shares.

Key Stock Statistics

Dividend Rate/Share	Nil	Shareholders	500
Shs. outstg. (M)	28.6	Market cap. (B)	$0.197
Avg. daily vol. (M)	0.315	Inst. holdings	36%
Tang. Bk. Value/Share	2.95		
Beta	1.40		

Value of $10,000 invested 5 years ago: $ 6,111

Fiscal Year Ending Dec. 31

	1998	1997	1996	1995	1994	1993
Revenues (Million $)						
1Q	3.57	5.63	3.73	2.63	3.14	1.98
2Q	3.41	3.89	4.06	14.91	7.41	6.91
3Q	—	4.60	3.62	19.17	5.21	4.40
4Q	—	9.02	9.96	10.29	5.92	3.64
Yr.	—	23.14	21.37	47.00	21.68	16.92
Earnings Per Share ($)						
1Q	**-0.53**	-0.61	-0.62	-0.69	-0.81	-0.64
2Q	**-0.44**	-0.76	-0.70	-0.22	-0.39	-0.18
3Q	—	-0.47	-0.08	-0.22	-0.42	-0.44
4Q	—	-0.52	-0.20	-0.51	-0.54	-0.53
Yr.	—	**-2.36**	-2.19	-1.63	-2.13	-1.77

Next earnings report expected: NA

Dividend Data

Cash dividends have never been paid. Cephalon intends to retain any earnings to finance growth. A "poison pill" stock purchase rights plan was adopted in 1993.

A Division of The McGraw-Hill Companies

STANDARD
&POOR'S
STOCK REPORTS

Cephalon, Inc.

3482

03-OCT-98

Business Summary - 14-SEP-98

Since its inception in 1987, Cephalon, Inc. has engaged primarily in research and development related to the discovery of therapeutic drugs for neurodegenerative disorders, including ALS, Alzheimer's disease, head and spinal injuries, stroke and other diseases of the nervous system.

The company's research strategy has focused on exploiting the potential of neurotrophic recombinant proteins, or trophic factors, for treating certain neurologic disorders. The company believes that its technology may allow for medicinal chemical approaches toward creating novel small synthetic molecules which would cross the blood-brain barrier and mimic the action of proteins by intervening in the progression of neurodegenerative disorders. Cephalon's broad-based research program currently focuses on neurotrophic factors, protease inhibition, signal transduction modulation and regulation of gene transcription.

Cephalon is developing Myotrophin to treat ALS (Lou Gehrig's disease), which affects an estimated 25,000 persons in the U.S. Phase III trial results were mixed, with a North American trial showing statistically significant, dose-related success in slowing the progression of the disease. However, a European clinical trial failed to confirm the results of the North American trial. Cephalon filed for marketing approval in the United

States in February 1997, and in Europe in May 1997. The FDA designated Myotrophin an orphan drug for the treatment of ALS in 1991.

The company has a collaboration with Chiron Corp. for the global (excluding Japan) development and commercialization of Myotrophin and certain other technologies in the neurological field. In the area of peripheral neuropathy, the company plans to focus on development of Myotrophin for chemotherapy-induced neuropathies, post-polio syndrome, and diabetic neuropathy, disorders believed to affect about a million persons in the U.S.

Cephalon's other lead drug, Provigil (formerly Modafinil), for the treatment of patients with narcolepsy (excessive daytime sleepiness), is currently being reviewed for marketing clearance by the FDA. Narcolepsy is a chronic, lifelong sleep disorder affecting approximately 125,000 people in the U.S. The FDA designated Provigil an orphan drug in March 1993 for the treatment of narcolepsy. CEPH received an approvable letter for Provigil from the FDA in December 1997. Provigil is the first new chemical entity to treat narcolepsy in over 20 years.

The company has established a specialty sales force that co-promotes, to neurologists in the United States, Bristol-Myers Squibb's Stadol NS and Serzone, and a product of Medtronic, Inc. Cephalon also has a collaborative agreement with TAP Pharmaceuticals Inc. to develop compounds for the treatment of prostate disease.

Per Share Data ($)

(Year Ended Dec. 31)	1997	1996	1995	1994	1993	1992	1991	1990	1989	1988
Tangible Bk. Val.	3.66	5.58	7.56	6.17	5.28	6.25	6.91	1.90	1.12	NA
Cash Flow	-2.27	-2.02	-1.34	-1.74	-1.28	-0.55	-0.18	-0.54	-0.35	-0.27
Earnings	-2.36	-2.19	-1.63	-2.13	-1.77	-0.80	-0.26	-0.59	-0.39	-0.27
Dividends	Nil	Nil	Nil	Nil	Nil	Nil	Nil	Nil	Nil	Nil
Payout Ratio	Nil	Nil	Nil	Nil	Nil	Nil	Nil	Nil	Nil	Nil
Prices - High	28½	40⅞	41½	19½	18¾	16¾	19½	NA	NA	NA
- Low	9½	13⅜	5¾	7½	8½	7	11	NA	NA	NA
P/E Ratio - High	NM	NM	NM	NM	NM	NM	NM	NM	NM	NM
- Low	NM	NM	NM	NM	NM	NM	NM	NM	NM	NM

Income Statement Analysis (Million $)

	1997	1996	1995	1994	1993	1992	1991	1990	1989	1988
Revs.	23.1	21.4	47.0	21.7	16.9	9.1	5.0	0.1	0.1	Nil
Oper. Inc.	-62.9	-65.1	-36.9	-28.3	-14.6	-8.0	-4.0	-3.0	-1.8	-0.5
Depr.	2.2	4.2	5.8	6.7	5.3	2.2	0.6	0.3	0.1	0.0
Int. Exp.	3.2	2.3	3.1	1.4	0.8	0.2	0.0	0.0	0.0	NM
Pretax Inc.	-60.4	-53.3	-33.0	-36.1	-19.2	-7.2	-2.0	-3.0	-1.6	-0.4
Eff. Tax Rate	NM	NM	NM	NM	NM	NM	Nil	Nil	Nil	Nil
Net Inc.	-60.4	-53.3	-33.0	-36.1	-19.2	-7.2	-2.0	-3.0	-1.6	-0.4

Balance Sheet & Other Fin. Data (Million $)

	1997	1996	1995	1994	1993	1992	1991	1990	1989	1988
Cash	10.3	147	178	105	49.4	33.8	24.4	9.7	4.7	4.5
Curr. Assets	127	155	188	113	51.7	37.3	25.0	10.0	4.9	NA
Total Assets	151	178	221	140	78.1	71.1	61.7	10.9	5.6	5.1
Curr. Liab.	20.5	21.6	18.4	10.8	3.4	2.3	0.8	0.7	0.4	NA
LT Debt	27.6	17.0	21.7	16.1	11.6	12.0	Nil	0.4	0.4	0.1
Common Eqty.	100	137	180	113	63.1	56.7	60.9	9.7	4.8	4.7
Total Cap.	128	154	202	129	74.7	68.7	60.9	10.2	5.2	4.7
Cap. Exp.	0.8	2.1	17.5	10.5	6.8	4.7	1.2	0.1	0.1	0.4
Cash Flow	-58.2	-49.1	-27.2	-29.4	-13.9	-4.9	-1.4	-2.8	-1.5	-0.4
Curr. Ratio	6.2	3.8	10.2	10.4	15.1	16.1	30.0	14.2	12.4	NA
% LT Debt of Cap.	21.6	11.0	10.7	12.5	15.5	17.5	Nil	4.3	7.8	1.2
% Net Inc.of Revs.	NM	NM	NM	NM	NM	NM	NM	NM	NM	NM
% Ret. on Assets	NM	NM	NM	NM	NM	NM	NM	NM	NM	NM
% Ret. on Equity	NM	NM	NM	NM	NM	NM	NM	NM	NM	NM

Data as orig. reptd.; bef. results of disc. opers. and/or spec. items. Per share data adj. for stk. divs. as of ex-div. date. Bold denotes diluted EPS (FASB 128). E-Estimated. NA-Not Available. NM-Not Meaningful. NR-Not Ranked.

Office—145 Brandywine Pkwy., West Chester, PA 19380. **Tel**—(610) 344-0200. **Pres & CEO**—F. Baldino Jr. **EVP & COO**—B. A. Peacock. **SVP-Fin & CFO**—J. K. Buchi. **SVP & Secy**—B. S. Schilberg. **Dirs**—F. Baldino Jr., W. P. Egan, R. J. Feeney, M. D. Greenacre, K. E. Moley, B. A. Peacock, H. Witzel. **Transfer Agent & Registrar**—American Stock Transfer & Trust Co., NYC. **Incorporated**—In Delaware in 1987. **Empl**— 282. **S&P Analyst:** Herman Saftlas

03-OCT-98

Industry:
Services (Commercial & Consumer)

Summary: CERN provides health care organizations with health information systems that allow information to be shared among clinical disciplines and across multiple facilities.

Quantitative Evaluations

Recent Price • 22⅝
52 Wk Range • 31⅞-18½

Yield • Nil
12-Mo. P/E • 48.1

Outlook
(1 Lowest—5 Highest)
• **5**

Fair Value
• **47¾**

Risk
• **High**

Earn./Div. Rank
• **B**

Technical Eval.
• **Bullish** since 4/98

Rel. Strength Rank
(1 Lowest—99 Highest)
• **36**

Insider Activity
• **NA**

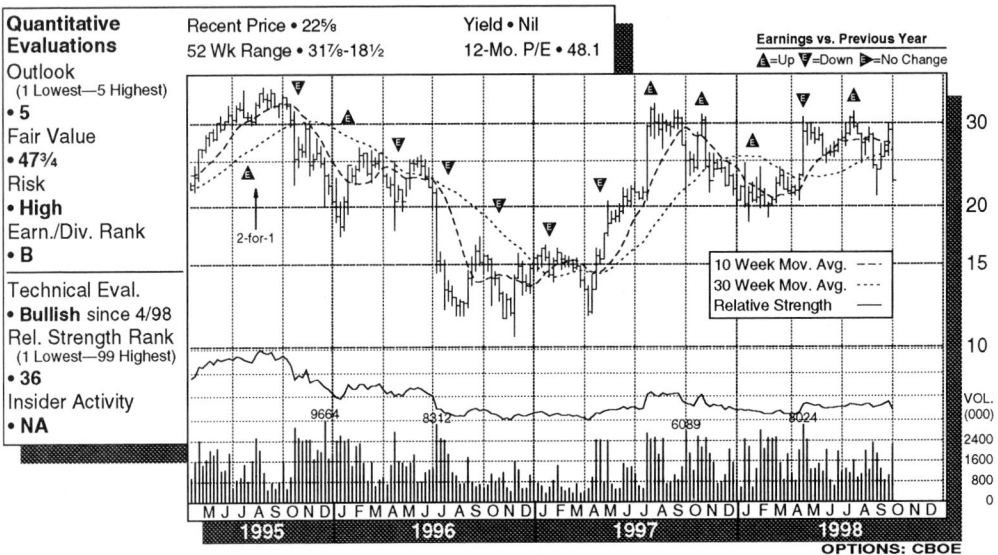

Earnings vs. Previous Year
▲=Up ▼=Down ▶=No Change

10 Week Mov. Avg. ---
30 Week Mov. Avg. ·····
Relative Strength ——

OPTIONS: CBOE

Business Profile - 11-AUG-98

This company is a developer of clinical and management information systems that support the health services industry. CERN's systems are designed around a single Health Network Architecture (HNA), and are interrelated to share patient information. Elements of the company's strategy include the expansion of its core business and products and services, and a commitment to a unified architecture. In July 1998, management said it expects to deliver strong results through 1999, driven by additional business from existing and new clients, and improved operating margins reflecting a shift toward more profitable fee-based services.

Operational Review - 11-AUG-98

Based on a brief report, revenues in the six months ended July 4, 1998, rose 34%, year to year, due to the continuation of new business bookings, attributed to the successful introduction of CERN's fifth generation client/server application platform. Before non-recurring charges, gross profit grew 41% and operating income surged 99%. After taxes at 38.8%, versus 38.5%, income advanced 74%, to $9,138,000 ($0.27 a share), from $5,260,000 ($0.16). Results in 1998 exclude non-recurring acquisition charges of $0.09 a share.

Stock Performance - 02-OCT-98

In the past 30 trading days, CERN's shares have declined 20%, compared to a 7% fall in the S&P 500. Average trading volume for the past five days was 440,680 shares, compared with the 40-day moving average of 324,974 shares.

Key Stock Statistics

Dividend Rate/Share	Nil	Shareholders	1,400
Shs. outstg. (M)	32.8	Market cap. (B)	$0.741
Avg. daily vol. (M)	0.273	Inst. holdings	51%
Tang. Bk. Value/Share	7.09		
Beta	1.84		

Value of $10,000 invested 5 years ago: $ 16,380

Fiscal Year Ending Dec. 31

	1998	1997	1996	1995	1994	1993
Revenues (Million $)						
1Q	73.67	51.12	52.58	43.20	30.50	24.10
2Q	79.15	63.32	46.71	49.00	39.80	29.80
3Q	—	60.78	43.40	41.72	40.90	32.30
4Q	—	69.38	46.42	53.02	44.70	34.30
Yr.	—	245.1	189.1	186.9	155.9	120.6
Earnings Per Share ($)						
1Q	0.02	0.08	0.13	0.15	0.10	0.09
2Q	0.16	0.10	0.05	0.21	0.17	0.12
3Q	—	0.13	0.02	0.11	0.17	0.14
4Q	—	0.16	0.05	0.25	0.22	0.16
Yr.	—	0.45	0.25	0.72	0.66	0.50

Next earnings report expected: mid October

Dividend Data

No cash dividends have been paid. The company intends to retain its earnings for use in its business and does not anticipate paying cash dividends in the foreseeable future. The common stock was split two for one in May 1992, March 1993 and August 1995.

A Division of The **McGraw·Hill** Companies

STANDARD
&POOR'S
STOCK REPORTS

Cerner Corporation

3487

03-OCT-98

Business Summary - 11-AUG-98

As the health care industry becomes more and more consolidated and interconnected, there is a need for information systems that link all parties. Cerner Corp. (CERN) provides clinical and management information systems for all points in the health care process. The company's interrelated systems are designed to automate the health care process by accumulating data on care provided to members/patients, maintaining such data in a database repository and providing access to this data for users of clinical information across a health care system.

CERN's systems are designed around its Health Network Architecture (HNA), a single unified system. HNA allows each participating facility within an integrated health care enterprise to access an individual's clinical record at the point of care, to organize it for specific needs of the physician, nurse, laboratory technician or other care provider on a real-time basis, and to use the information in management decisions. HNA Millennium, the company's fifth generation of HNA, uses a three-tier client/server technology and features Windows 95 and Windows NT graphical desktops that can be personalized for specific needs, scaleability, point-of-care interfaces, and data analysis capabilities.

CERN's process-based systems automate the clinical, management and business information processes throughout and between entities. The company provides systems for acute or institutional settings, emergency departments, physician offices or clinics, home health organizations, medical records departments and others.

The company believes that a new center of health care is emerging: the Integrated Health Organization (IHO), a combination of payers, physicians and institutional providers affiliated to service a community or defined member population. The focus of the IHO is to be accountable for the health status of a defined population, with substantial financial incentives to manage health on a preventative or wellness basis and reduce costs. Cerner expects that many large IHOs will emerge in the U.S. in the next decade. These IHOs will need to implement information systems that manage the delivery of care across an entire community while simultaneously managing the business side of health management.

Key elements of CERN's business strategy include the penetration of the integrated health care market; penetration of the physician market as physicians combine to form organizations such as independent practice associations and preferred provider organizations; and expansion of its core businesses such as its clinical domain systems.

Total revenue backlog was $411.1 million ($266.8 million in contract backlog and $144.4 million in support backlog) at the end of the second quarter of 1998, up 49% from a year earlier.

Per Share Data ($)

(Year Ended Dec. 31)	1997	1996	1995	1994	1993	1992	1991	1990	1989	1988
Tangible Bk. Val.	6.97	6.90	6.68	2.84	2.05	1.51	1.09	0.96	0.97	0.85
Cash Flow	0.99	0.71	1.10	0.86	0.63	0.44	0.25	0.12	0.17	0.15
Earnings	0.45	0.25	0.72	0.66	0.50	0.35	0.18	0.06	0.12	0.12
Dividends	Nil	Nil	Nil	Nil	Nil	Nil	Nil	Nil	Nil	Nil
Payout Ratio	Nil	Nil	Nil	Nil	Nil	Nil	Nil	Nil	Nil	Nil
Prices - High	33$^1/_8$	26$^3/_4$	36	24$^3/_4$	22$^7/_8$	14$^1/_8$	3$^1/_4$	1$^3/_4$	2	3$^1/_4$
- Low	11$^5/_8$	10$^1/_2$	20	11$^3/_4$	7$^7/_8$	2$^7/_8$	1$^1/_8$	$^5/_8$	1$^3/_{16}$	1$^9/_{16}$
P/E Ratio - High	74	107	50	38	46	41	18	31	17	29
- Low	26	42	28	18	16	8	7	14	10	14

Income Statement Analysis (Million $)

	1997	1996	1995	1994	1993	1992	1991	1990	1989	1988
Revs.	245	189	187	156	121	101	77.0	51.0	57.0	41.0
Oper. Inc.	40.2	26.1	49.5	39.9	28.1	19.3	10.0	4.2	7.2	6.5
Depr.	18.1	15.5	12.2	6.1	3.8	2.8	1.9	1.6	1.5	1.1
Int. Exp.	2.4	2.5	2.4	1.9	0.7	0.7	0.9	0.7	0.6	0.7
Pretax Inc.	24.5	10.6	37.2	32.5	24.1	16.3	7.6	2.5	5.6	5.2
Eff. Tax Rate	38%	36%	40%	40%	40%	39%	38%	37%	36%	34%
Net Inc.	15.1	8.3	22.5	19.5	14.6	9.9	4.7	1.6	3.6	3.4

Balance Sheet & Other Fin. Data (Million $)

	1997	1996	1995	1994	1993	1992	1991	1990	1989	1988
Cash	7.5	111	112	15.3	16.8	13.7	8.7	7.1	7.4	7.3
Curr. Assets	208	212	217	83.7	67.2	45.9	39.7	38.6	45.2	38.7
Total Assets	332	315	304	156	105	67.0	56.0	52.0	55.0	47.0
Curr. Liab.	51.5	41.2	42.8	31.3	24.6	15.4	17.1	17.8	23.3	19.5
LT Debt	30.0	30.0	30.1	30.2	10.4	8.3	8.0	7.7	1.6	1.4
Common Eqty.	234	231	221	85.8	64.2	38.6	27.5	24.1	28.1	24.2
Total Cap.	280	274	261	125	80.0	51.0	39.0	35.0	32.0	27.0
Cap. Exp.	14.8	15.3	18.9	32.2	7.1	4.7	1.8	3.2	1.3	2.7
Cash Flow	33.2	23.8	34.7	25.6	18.3	12.7	6.6	3.2	5.0	4.5
Curr. Ratio	4.0	5.1	5.1	2.7	2.7	3.0	2.3	2.2	1.9	2.0
% LT Debt of Cap.	10.7	11.0	11.5	24.2	12.9	16.2	20.5	22.4	5.1	5.1
% Net Inc.of Revs.	6.2	4.4	12.0	12.5	12.1	9.8	6.1	3.0	6.3	8.4
% Ret. on Assets	4.7	2.7	13.6	14.8	16.6	16.1	8.6	3.1	7.0	7.9
% Ret. on Equity	6.5	3.7	14.7	25.7	27.7	29.8	18.1	6.4	13.6	15.2

Data as orig. reptd.; bef. results of disc. opers. and/or spec. items. Per share data adj. for stk. divs. as of ex-div. date. Bold denotes diluted EPS (FASB 128). E-Estimated. NA-Not Available. NM-Not Meaningful. NR-Not Ranked.

Office—2800 Rockcreek Pky., Suite 601, Kansas City, MO 64117. **Tel**—(816) 221-1024. **Website**—http://www.cerner.com **Chrmn & CEO**—N. L. Patterson. **Pres & COO**—C. W. Illig. **VP & CFO**—M. G. Naughton. **Dirs**—G. E. Bisbee, Jr., J. C. Danforth, M. E. Herman, C. W. Illig, T. A. McDonnell, N. L. Patterson, III, T. C. Tinstman. **Transfer Agent & Registrar**—Securities Transfer Division, UMB Bank, Kansas City, MO. **Incorporated**—in Missouri in 1980. **Empl**—2,049. **S&P Analyst**: Stephen J. Tekirian

Champion Enterprises 489T

NYSE Symbol **CHB**

In S&P SmallCap 600

03-OCT-98 **Industry:** Homebuilding

Summary: CHB produces manufactured homes.

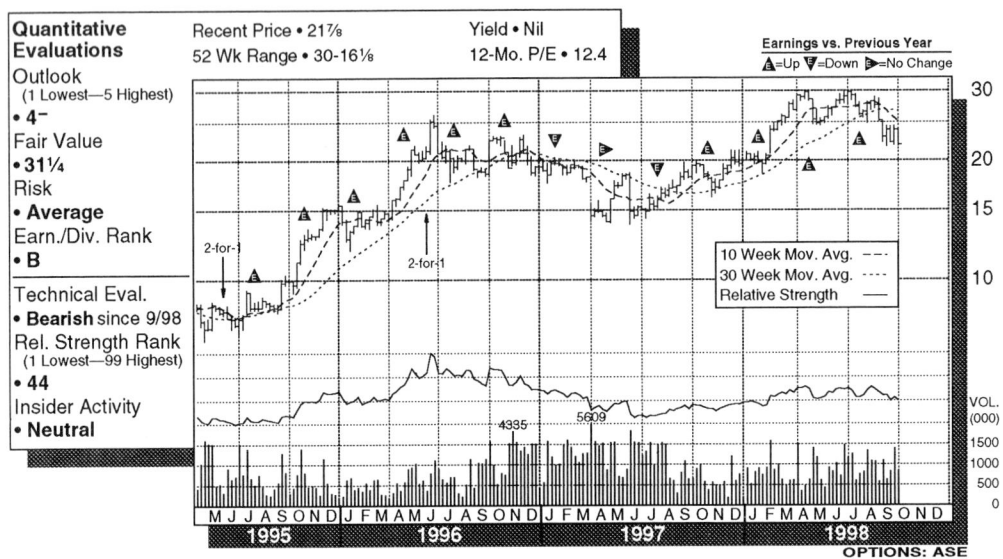

Quantitative Evaluations

Recent Price • 21⅞
52 Wk Range • 30-16⅛

Yield • Nil
12-Mo. P/E • 12.4

Outlook
(1 Lowest—5 Highest)
• **4⁻**

Fair Value
• **31¼**

Risk
• **Average**

Earn./Div. Rank
• **B**

Technical Eval.
• **Bearish** since 9/98

Rel. Strength Rank
(1 Lowest—99 Highest)
• **44**

Insider Activity
• **Neutral**

Business Profile - 03-SEP-98

CHB, which recently acquired eight manufacturing retailers, expects retail revenues to reach $1 billion by 2000. The company has said that retail acquisitions should be accretive to earnings within 12 months, and should add materially to 1999 results. CHB expects 1998 earnings to reflect startup costs for staffing and support systems, and a non-cash accounting adjustment related to its retail acquisitions. The company also anticipates improved manufacturing productivity, and has set a long-term goal of at least 15% compound annual EPS growth. CHB has opened two new facilities in North Carolina in 1998, with two more planned for Texas and Idaho. As of June 1998, the company had repurchased 2.25 million common shares under a four million share buyback plan.

Operational Review - 03-SEP-98

Revenues in the first half of 1998 advanced 30%, year to year, reflecting higher wholesale manufacturing volume and retail acquisitions. Gross margins widened, on the greater volume, improved manufacturing margins, and expanded retail operations. Although SG&A expense increased, due to acquisition related costs, and net interest expense contrasted with interest income, income from continuing operations was up 37%, to $43,447,000 ($0.88 a share, diluted), from $31,761,000 ($0.64). Results exclude income from discontinued operations of $0.01 a share in the 1997 period.

Stock Performance - 02-OCT-98

In the past 30 trading days, CHB's shares have declined 21%, compared to a 7% fall in the S&P 500. Average trading volume for the past five days was 169,200 shares, compared with the 40-day moving average of 192,110 shares.

Key Stock Statistics

Dividend Rate/Share	Nil	Shareholders	24,000
Shs. outstg. (M)	48.0	Market cap. (B)	$ 1.1
Avg. daily vol. (M)	0.192	Inst. holdings	76%
Tang. Bk. Value/Share	NM		
Beta	1.29		

Value of $10,000 invested 5 years ago: $ 83,333

Fiscal Year Ending Dec. 31

	1998	1997	1996	1995	1994	1993
Revenues (Million $)						
1Q	463.0	378.9	342.8	170.3	125.0	75.00
2Q	582.5	456.0	428.6	206.6	157.1	84.71
3Q	—	455.1	447.1	215.1	168.8	91.99
4Q	—	429.7	425.6	205.8	164.8	90.26
Yr.	—	1,675	1,644	797.9	615.7	341.9
Earnings Per Share ($)						
1Q	**0.36**	0.28	0.28	0.18	0.16	0.07
2Q	**0.52**	0.37	0.39	0.28	0.26	0.10
0Q		0.42	0.41	0.30	0.20	0.13
4Q	—	**0.39**	0.01	0.24	0.14	0.08
Yr.	—	**1.45**	1.09	1.01	0.81	0.39

Next earnings report expected: mid October

Dividend Data

No cash dividends have been paid since July 1974.

A Division of The **McGraw-Hill** Companies

Business Summary - 03-SEP-98

Champion Enterprises (CHB) is the holding company for Champion Home Builders, which has the new leader in mobile and modular (manufactured) home sales in the U.S. CHB homes include Champion, Chandeleur, Crest Ridge, Dutch Housing, Grand Manor, Homes of Legend, Lamplighter, Moduline International, Redman, Western Homes, and Moduline Industries (Canada).

During the past four years, CHB has significantly expanded its manufactured housing operations through acquisitions, internal growth and, in October 1996, a pooling-of-interests merger with Redman Industries, then the third largest manufactured home producer, based in Dallas, TX.

The company's strategy is twofold: to expand current operations to take advantage of the growing market, and to continue to seek acquisitions that provide further growth and strong returns. In early 1998, CHB acquired four manufacturing housing retailers with combined sales of $200 million. In July 1998, CHB acquired ICA Group, an operator of 23 housing retail locations. In April 1998, CHB acquired Homes America Group ($65 million in sales; 25 retail housing sales centers) and four manufacturing housing sales in Louisiana. As of August 1998, CHB was operating 188 retail home centers in 22 states. The company had 57 home building facilities in 33 locations. CHB continues to expand it

manufacturing operations with 1998 capital expenditures expected at close to $58 million for internal expansions and the construction of new facilities. By the end of 1998, CHB expects to have opened 40 new stores through internal expansions during the year and be operating 220 home centers.

The company has 3,500 home dealerships strategically located in the U.S. and Canada. It maintains a regional focus with the ability to respond quickly to local changes in customer demands and expectations. A June 1996 survey revealed that customers have an average income of $35,000, are typically 40 years old, with a household of three or more.

In February 1998, CHB sold its Champion Motor Coach commercial vehicles business to Thor Industries, Inc. (THO; NYSE), for $11 million. The unit ($60 million in 1997 sales) produced mid-size buses under the brand names Challenger, CTS, Centurion, Champ, Crusader Commodore, Contender, Solo and Commander.

With CHB's recent rapid growth, larger size, and lower than anticipated inflation, the company reduced its targeted compound annual growth rate to 15%, from 20%. In 1997, CHB sold 102,468 homes, up from 96,839 homes in 1996. CHB's share of the U.S. market in 1997 (based on homes sold) was 17.7%, up from 16.5% in 1996. The company has 56 housing production facilities in 33 locations.

Per Share Data ($)

(Year Ended Dec. 31)	1997	1996	1995	1994	1993	1992	1991	1990	1989	1988
Tangible Bk. Val.	3.45	2.14	1.02	1.40	1.59	1.22	1.16	0.89	0.88	1.36
Cash Flow	1.80	1.39	1.21	0.94	0.46	0.23	0.06	0.10	-0.41	-0.16
Earnings	1.45	1.09	1.01	0.81	0.39	0.17	-0.02	0.01	-0.49	-0.25
Dividends	Nil	Nil	Nil	Nil	Nil	Nil	Nil	Nil	Nil	Nil
Payout Ratio	Nil	Nil	Nil	Nil	Nil	Nil	Nil	Nil	Nil	Nil
Prices - High	21¼	26⅛	15½	10⅛	5	2¾	1½	1	1¼	1⁹/₁₆
- Low	13¾	11⅞	6¾	4⅜	2⁵/₁₆	¾	⅝	½	⁹/₁₆	¹³/₁₆
P/E Ratio - High	15	24	15	12	13	16	NM	80	NM	NM
- Low	9	11	7	5	6	4	NM	38	NM	NM

Income Statement Analysis (Million $)

	1997	1996	1995	1994	1993	1992	1991	1990	1989	1988
Revs.	1,675	1,644	798	616	342	235	270	288	313	364
Oper. Inc.	134	131	61.1	40.6	13.8	7.2	1.4	4.7	-8.8	-2.0
Depr.	17.1	14.9	6.2	3.9	2.2	1.6	2.2	2.3	2.4	2.7
Int. Exp.	1.2	2.3	2.3	0.8	0.5	0.7	1.1	1.4	1.8	2.5
Pretax Inc.	117	94.2	53.5	34.1	12.6	6.0	0.1	1.4	-13.1	-6.6
Eff. Tax Rate	40%	43%	40%	26%	11%	19%	NM	75%	NM	NM
Net Inc.	70.8	53.6	32.3	25.2	11.2	4.8	-0.6	0.3	-13.9	-7.2

Balance Sheet & Other Fin. Data (Million $)

	1997	1996	1995	1994	1993	1992	1991	1990	1989	1988
Cash	60.3	19.0	15.0	73.0	34.4	20.7	15.1	10.9	7.8	3.5
Curr. Assets	230	217	108	97.8	74.4	58.5	56.7	48.0	51.9	76.6
Total Assets	501	501	236	171	98.0	81.0	81.0	77.0	83.0	118
Curr. Liab.	183	195	104	79.1	42.5	36.6	39.2	40.5	45.1	60.6
LT Debt	1.8	1.2	Nil	Nil	2.8	3.8	4.5	5.4	6.5	14.7
Common Eqty.	280	227	113	79.3	45.9	34.0	31.4	24.1	23.3	39.1
Total Cap.	282	228	113	79.3	48.7	37.8	35.8	29.5	30.0	54.1
Cap. Exp.	38.3	50.7	9.0	10.6	6.6	2.8	2.3	1.7	5.1	3.2
Cash Flow	87.9	68.5	38.4	29.1	13.4	6.5	1.5	2.6	-11.5	-4.5
Curr. Ratio	1.3	1.1	1.0	1.2	1.8	1.6	1.4	1.2	1.2	1.3
% LT Debt of Cap.	0.7	0.5	Nil	Nil	5.8	10.1	12.5	18.4	21.8	27.2
% Net Inc.of Revs.	4.2	3.2	4.0	4.1	3.3	2.0	NM	0.1	NM	NM
% Ret. on Assets	14.5	12.6	15.8	18.4	12.3	5.9	NM	0.4	NM	NM
% Ret. on Equity	27.9	26.6	33.5	39.5	27.6	14.5	NM	1.4	NM	NM

Data as orig. reptd.; bef. results of disc. opers. and/or spec. items. Per share data adj. for stk. divs. as of ex-div. date. Bold denotes diluted EPS (FASB 128). Prior to 1992 yrs. ended Feb. of fol. cal. yr. E-Estimated. NA-Not Available. NM-Not Meaningful. NR-Not Ranked.

Office—2701 University Dr., Suite 320, Auburn Hills, MI 48326. **Tel**—(810) 340-9090. **Chrmn & Pres**—W. R. Young, Jr. **EVP & CFO**—A. Jacqueline Dout. **VP & Secy**—L. M. Balius. **Dirs**—R. W. Anestis, F. J. Feraco, S. Isakow, G. R. Mrkonic, J. S. Savary, R. L. Stark, C. S. Valdiserri, W. R. Young, Jr. **Transfer Agent & Registrar**—Harris Trust and Savings Bank, Chicago. **Incorporated**—in Michigan in 1953. Reincorporated in Delaware in 1987. **Empl**— 11,300. **S&P Analyst:** Stewart Scharf

Checkpoint Systems   502M

NYSE Symbol **CKP**

In S&P SmallCap 600

03-OCT-98 **Industry:** Electrical Equipment

Summary: Checkpoint makes electronic article merchandising systems, used by retailers to prevent theft, and electronic access control systems, which restrict access to areas or buildings.

Quantitative Evaluations

Recent Price • 8⅜
52 Wk Range • 22⅛-7⅝

Yield • Nil
12-Mo. P/E • 52.3

Outlook
(1 Lowest—5 Highest)
• **5+**

Fair Value
• **16⅛**

Risk
• **High**

Earn./Div. Rank
• **B**

Technical Eval.
• **Bearish** since 6/98

Rel. Strength Rank
(1 Lowest—99 Highest)
• **27**

Insider Activity
• **NA**

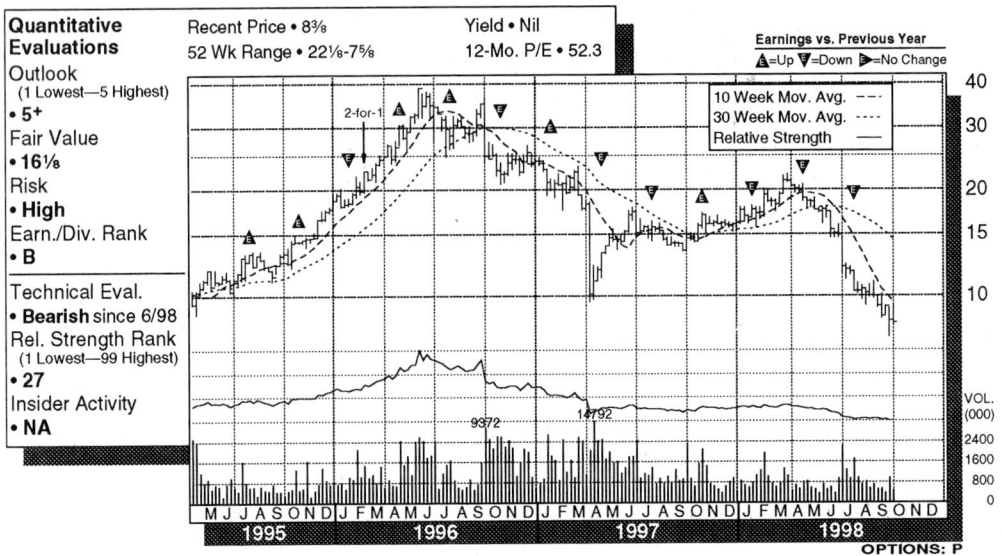

Earnings vs. Previous Year
▲=Up ▼=Down ▶=No Change

10 Week Mov. Avg. – – –
30 Week Mov. Avg. · · · ·
Relative Strength —

OPTIONS: P

Business Profile - 15-MAY-98

More than 330,000 Checkpoint electronic article surveillance (EAS) systems are installed worldwide. The company has achieved substantial growth in the past five years through both internal expansion and acquisitions. CKP is expanding its presence in the supermarket industry as part of its efforts to further penetrate the worldwide security market. The company took $17.1 million in restructuring and one-time charges in the fourth quarter of 1997 related to severance, lease terminations, expansion of manufacturing facilities, termination of master reseller agreements, consolidation of R&D facilities and marketing investments.

Operational Review - 15-MAY-98

In the first quarter of 1998, revenues advanced 17%, year to year, reflecting new chain-wide roll-outs of the company's EAS systems, as well as growth in the CCTV and fire alarm businesses. Gross margins narrowed, but SG&A expenses were well controlled (35.9% of sales, down from 39.2%); operating profit was up 118%. However, after net interest expense versus net interest income, and following sharply lower other income, net income declined 48%, to $1,273,000 ($0.04 a share) from $2,435,000 ($0.07).

Stock Performance - 02-OCT-98

In the past 30 trading days, CKP's shares have declined 16%, compared to a 7% fall in the S&P 500. Average trading volume for the past five days was 92,900 shares, compared with the 40-day moving average of 125,190 shares.

Key Stock Statistics

Dividend Rate/Share	Nil	Shareholders	1,800
Shs. outstg. (M)	32.4	Market cap. (B)	$0.271
Avg. daily vol. (M)	0.117	Inst. holdings	64%
Tang. Bk. Value/Share	5.93		
Beta	0.37		

Value of $10,000 invested 5 years ago: $ 10,002

Fiscal Year Ending Dec. 31

	1998	1997	1996	1995	1994	1993
Revenues (Million $)						
1Q	79.86	68.18	66.99	37.36	26.22	20.02
2Q	90.58	81.04	74.79	49.74	28.66	18.03
3Q	—	87.96	73.77	52.80	33.93	26.60
4Q	—	98.79	76.22	64.84	39.52	28.39
Yr.	—	336.0	291.8	204.7	128.3	93.03
Earnings Per Share ($)						
1Q	**0.04**	**0.07**	0.10	0.01	0.03	0.03
2Q	**0.11**	**0.14**	0.19	0.13	0.05	0.05
3Q	—	**0.17**	0.15	0.16	0.10	0.01
4Q	—	**-0.15**	0.16	0.11	0.12	0.01
Yr.	—	**0.23**	0.60	0.42	0.29	0.08

Next earnings report expected: late October

Dividend Data

No regular cash dividends have been paid.

A Division of The **McGraw·Hill** Companies

Business Summary - 15-MAY-98

Checkpoint Systems designs and manufactures integrated electronic security systems aimed primarily at helping retailers prevent the theft of merchandise. The company's systems include electronic article surveillance (EAS), closed-circuit television (CCTV), point-of-sale (POS) monitoring and electronic access control systems. Contributions to revenues in recent years were:

	1997	1996	1995	1994
EAS tags	32%	32%	35%	41%
EAS sensors	26%	27%	23%	27%
CCTV/POS monitoring	16%	13%	16	---
Deactivation units	12%	13%	12%	12%
Access control	3%	3%	3%	5%
Service & other	11%	12%	11%	15%

EAS systems generally consist of three components: circuits embedded in tags or labels, called tags, which can be detected and be placed in the items to be protected; sensors that detect the tags when they enter a detection area, such as the doorway of a store; and deactivation equipment, which disarms the tag when items are properly paid for. CKP's principal products are the components of its EAS system, which includes various sensors and a variety of patented targets. De-

pending on their product mix, customers can choose from a wide variety of targets, including disposable paper tags and reusable hard plastic tags (used primarily in the apparel market).

Electronic access controls utilize an electronic key, such as a card with a magnetic strip, and a card reader to restrict access to certain areas to authorized individuals. The most advanced EAC systems use plastic cards containing an encoded digital integrated circuit that can be coded with specific information, such as cardholder identity and security clearance/access level, and can record that information along with time of entry and exit.

CCTV systems and monitoring services include a full line of camera, monitoring, perimeter protection and fire/intrusion alarm equipment, as well as POS monitoring systems that record and store on videotape every transaction at each check-out -- both visual and individual transaction data.

To position itself for future growth, CKP took non-recurring restructuring and special charges totaling $17.1 million in the fourth quarter of 1997. These charges were principally related to severance, lease terminations, expansion of manufacturing facilities, termination of master reseller agreements, consolidation of R&D facilities and marketing investments. The charges resulted in a net loss of $5.1 million in the fourth quarter ($0.15 a share).

Per Share Data ($)

(Year Ended Dec. 31)	1997	1996	1995	1994	1993	1992	1991	1990	1989	1988
Tangible Bk. Val.	5.77	6.18	2.16	2.92	2.64	2.55	1.99	2.03	1.59	1.24
Cash Flow	0.90	1.14	0.86	0.66	0.34	0.41	0.18	0.47	0.40	0.14
Earnings	0.23	0.60	0.42	0.29	0.08	0.23	0.03	0.36	0.30	0.06
Dividends	Nil	Nil	Nil	Nil	Nil	Nil	Nil	Nil	Nil	Nil
Payout Ratio	Nil	Nil	Nil	Nil	Nil	Nil	Nil	Nil	Nil	Nil
Prices - High	24¾	39	19½	10¾	10⅛	9⅛	5⅞	8	6¼	5
- Low	9⅝	17⅞	8	5⅜	4⅛	4	3⅜	3⅛	3¼	3⅜
P/E Ratio - High	NM	65	48	37	NM	40	NM	22	20	83
- Low	NM	30	19	19	NM	18	NM	9	10	55

Income Statement Analysis (Million $)

Revs.	336	292	205	128	93.0	72.2	52.9	56.7	50.8	44.4
Oper. Inc.	43.2	48.4	31.2	19.8	4.9	8.9	3.8	9.4	8.3	2.5
Depr.	23.5	18.3	12.2	8.0	5.5	3.8	3.0	2.2	1.8	1.6
Int. Exp.	9.6	9.6	4.6	3.1	0.9	0.4	0.3	0.2	0.2	0.3
Pretax Inc.	13.6	29.9	16.6	8.4	2.1	4.9	0.6	6.7	6.9	1.3
Eff. Tax Rate	40%	32%	31%	25%	22%	9.50%	20%	NM	19%	18%
Net Inc.	8.2	20.4	11.4	6.3	1.6	4.4	0.5	6.9	5.6	1.1

Balance Sheet & Other Fin. Data (Million $)

Cash	64.1	186	77.5	0.9	Nil	2.3	1.3	3.0	4.5	8.1
Curr. Assets	298	348	215	69.2	54.9	39.7	29.1	29.7	29.3	26.6
Total Assets	516	522	362	128	105	74.3	57.7	53.1	44.4	37.2
Curr. Liab.	86.1	62.4	66.6	29.8	26.9	14.0	14.8	11.8	10.6	9.6
LT Debt	151	153	156	35.6	24.3	9.3	0.8	Nil	1.2	2.1
Common Eqty.	278	301	138	61.3	53.8	51.1	42.1	41.3	32.6	25.6
Total Cap.	430	459	296	98.1	78.1	60.4	42.9	41.3	33.8	27.7
Cap. Exp.	26.7	10.5	9.4	4.5	12.0	7.7	6.9	10.0	6.7	1.6
Cash Flow	31.8	38.7	23.6	14.3	7.1	8.2	3.5	9.1	7.4	2.6
Curr. Ratio	3.5	5.6	3.2	2.3	2.0	2.8	2.0	2.5	2.8	2.8
% LT Debt of Cap.	35.1	33.3	52.7	36.2	31.1	15.4	1.8	Nil	3.5	7.6
% Net Inc.of Revs.	2.4	7.0	5.6	4.9	1.7	6.1	1.0	12.2	11.0	2.4
% Ret. on Assets	1.6	4.6	4.7	5.3	1.8	6.5	0.9	14.1	13.6	3.0
% Ret. on Equity	2.8	9.2	11.5	10.8	3.1	9.3	1.2	18.6	19.0	4.3

Data as orig. reptd.; bef. results of disc. opers. and/or spec. items. Per share data adj. for stk. divs. as of ex-div. date. Bold denotes diluted EPS (FASB 128). E-Estimated. NA-Not Available. NM-Not Meaningful. NR-Not Ranked.

Office—101 Wolf Dr., P.O. Box 188, Thorofare, NJ 08086. **Tel**—1 800 257-5540.**Website**—www.checkpointsystems.com **Chrmn**—A. E. Wolf. **Pres & CEO**—K. P. Dowd. **EVP-COO**—Steven G. Selfridge.**VP & CFO**—J. A. Reinhold. **VP & Secy**—N. D. Austin. **Investor Relations**—1-800 257-5540.**Dirs**—R. O. Aders, R. D. Blackwell, R. J. Censits, D. W. Clark Jr., K. P. Dowd, A. S. Kalish, E. Margaona, J. B. Porter, A. Soffa, A. E. Wolf. **Transfer Agent**—American Stock Transfer & Trust Co., NYC. **Incorporated**—in Pennsylvania in 1969. **Empl**—3,605. **S&P Analyst**: Jim Corridore

Cheesecake Factory   3501M

NASDAQ Symbol **CAKE**

In S&P SmallCap 600

03-OCT-98 **Industry:** Restaurants

Summary: This company operates 24 upscale, moderately priced, casual dining restaurants under The Cheesecake Factory name with an extensive menu offering over 200 items.

Quantitative Evaluations	
Outlook (1 Lowest—5 Highest)	**5**
Fair Value	**30⅞**
Risk	**Average**
Earn./Div. Rank	**NR**
Technical Eval.	**Bearish** since 5/98
Rel. Strength Rank (1 Lowest—99 Highest)	**34**
Insider Activity	**Neutral**

Recent Price • 15¼
52 Wk Range • 27-14¼
Yield • Nil
12-Mo. P/E • 23.1

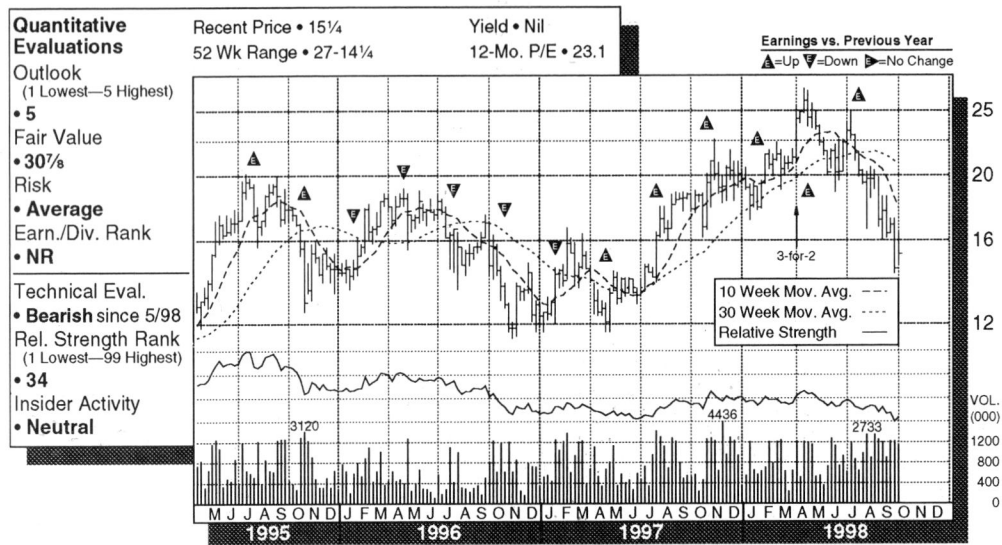

Earnings vs. Previous Year
▲=Up ▼=Down ►=No Change

10 Week Mov. Avg. - - - -
30 Week Mov. Avg. ·····
Relative Strength ——

3-for-2

Business Profile - 16-SEP-98

In July 1998, the company said its goal is to increase its total restaurant operating weeks and productive square feet by 25% or more during 1998. CAKE opened its 24th restaurant at Aventura Mall in the Miami, FL, market on June 9, 1998 with stronger-than-expected sales. The company also said it has five additional restaurant locations currently under construction or in design for potential 1998 openings, and already has three signed leases in hand for potential 1999 openings. In 1997, CAKE opened six new restaurants, with another six or seven restaurants expected to open in 1998. The company has also developed a bakery cafe concept and opened its first four bakery cafes during 1997, with one additional bakery cafe to open in 1998. The common stock was split 3-for-2 in April 1998.

Operational Review - 16-SEP-98

Total revenues in the 26 weeks ended June 30, 1998, rose 29%, year to year, primarily reflecting the openings of new restaurants, as well as a 3.7% increase in comparable restaurant sales. Gross margins narrowed slightly, mainly due to new restaurant openings. Following a significant increase in net interest income, and taxes at 34.4%, versus 34.5%, net income increased 66%, to $6,861,000 ($0.33 a share, based on 24% more shares) from $4,128,000 ($0.25).

Stock Performance - 02-OCT-98

In the past 30 trading days, CAKE's shares have declined 24%, compared to a 7% fall in the S&P 500. Average trading volume for the past five days was 229,620 shares, compared with the 40-day moving average of 291,787 shares.

Key Stock Statistics

Dividend Rate/Share	Nil	Shareholders	600
Shs. outstg. (M)	20.1	Market cap. (B)	$0.306
Avg. daily vol. (M)	0.242	Inst. holdings	74%
Tang. Bk. Value/Share	9.22		
Beta	1.49		

Value of $10,000 invested 5 years ago: $ 14,005

Fiscal Year Ending Dec. 31

	1998	1997	1996	1995	1994	1993
Revenues (Million $)						
1Q	59.50	45.23	35.38	24.97	18.75	13.84
2Q	59.84	51.00	39.21	28.50	20.43	17.39
3Q	—	53.55	42.20	29.37	22.20	17.41
4Q	—	58.81	43.52	34.33	24.21	18.39
Yr.	—	208.6	160.3	117.2	85.59	67.03
Earnings Per Share ($)						
1Q	**0.15**	0.11	0.10	0.11	0.09	0.07
2Q	**0.19**	0.15	0.13	0.15	0.12	0.10
3Q	—	0.17	0.10	0.15	0.13	0.09
4Q	—	0.16	0.03	0.13	0.13	0.09
Yr.	—	0.58	0.35	0.52	0.46	0.34

Next earnings report expected: late October

Dividend Data

Amount ($)	Date Decl.	Ex-Div. Date	Stock of Record	Payment Date
3-for-2	Feb. 26	Apr. 02	Mar. 12	Apr. 01 '98

A Division of The **McGraw-Hill** *Companies*

Business Summary - 16-SEP-98

The Cheesecake Factory (CAKE) has given new meaning to the word diversification; it makes and sells about 40 varieties of cheesecake including chocolate chip cookie dough, double-chocolate upside-down Jack Daniel's, Adam's peanut butter cup fudge ripple, pumpkin, and white chocolate raspberry truffle. The company sells the creamy confections, as well as a variety of other food items, through a chain of Cheesecake Factory restaurants throughout the U.S. The company also sells its bakery products to grocery stores, other restaurants and chains, food-service facilities, and through mail order.

Founded in 1972 as a retail and wholesale bakery, CAKE opened its first restaurant in Beverly Hills in 1978. After opening six new restaurants in 1997, CAKE now operates 24 restaurants in 12 states. The company expects to open six or seven new restaurants in 1998, and several more in 1999.

Cheesecake Factory Restaurants have an upscale decor combined with moderate prices (average check per person was $14.18 in 1997), and offer over 200 items including hamburgers, chicken, omelets, pasta, pizza, salads, sandwiches, seafood, steaks, and desserts.

The company has created a new restaurant concept, a bakery cafe under The Cheesecake Factory brand name. The cafes are designed to emphasize the company's distinctive desserts, accompanied by beverages, sandwiches, and salads in a self-service format. The first bakery cafe opened in July 1997. As of March 1998, the company was operating four bakery cafes which range in size from from 250 to 1,640 square feet. One additional bakery cafe is expected to open in 1998.

At its bakery production facility in Calabasas Hills, CA, the company produces approximately 50 varieties of cheesecake and other bakes desserts based on proprietary recipes. CAKE markets its cheesecakes on a wholesale basis to grocery and retail outlets, other restaurant operators and foodservice distributors.

In October 1997, the company agreed to be the exclusive foodservice operator for The Walt Disney Co.'s new DisneyQuest concept, which is planned to be launched in the summer of 1998. Previously, in June 1997, CAKE agreed to develop and operate a casual dining concept in the Venetian casino and resort complex scheduled to open in Las Vegas in 1999. The restaurant will be called The Grand Lux Cafe.

In 1997, restaurant sales contributed about 90% of total revenues, up from 87% in 1996, and 85% in 1995. Bakery sales attributed for the remaining revenues.

Per Share Data ($)

(Year Ended Dec. 31)	1997	1996	1995	1994	1993	1992	1991	1990	1989	1988
Tangible Bk. Val.	11.40	5.09	4.68	4.04	2.05	NA	NA	NA	NA	NA
Cash Flow	2.04	0.35	1.12	0.69	0.50	NA	NA	NA	NA	NA
Earnings	0.58	0.35	0.52	0.46	0.34	NA	NA	NA	NA	NA
Dividends	Nil	Nil	Nil	Nil	Nil	Nil	Nil	Nil	Nil	Nil
Payout Ratio	Nil	Nil	Nil	Nil	Nil	Nil	Nil	Nil	Nil	Nil
Prices - High	22⁵/₈	19¹/₈	20¹/₈	16¹/₂	15⁷/₈	NA	NA	NA	NA	NA
- Low	11⁵/₈	11³/₈	9¹/₈	9	9¹/₄	NA	NA	NA	NA	NA
P/E Ratio - High	39	54	39	36	47	NA	NA	NA	NA	NA
- Low	20	32	18	20	27	NA	NA	NA	NA	NA

Income Statement Analysis (Million $)

	1997	1996	1995	1994	1993	1992	1991	1990	1989	1988
Revs.	209	160	117	86.0	67.0	52.0	NA	NA	NA	NA
Oper. Inc.	27.6	19.5	16.2	12.6	9.1	5.7	NA	NA	NA	NA
Depr.	13.3	10.7	5.8	3.6	2.3	1.4	NA	NA	NA	NA
Int. Exp.	NA	Nil	Nil	0.0	0.0	0.3	NA	NA	NA	NA
Pretax Inc.	15.2	8.9	11.7	10.7	7.6	4.2	NA	NA	NA	NA
Eff. Tax Rate	34%	34%	26%	32%	37%	NM	NM	NM	NM	NM
Net Inc.	9.9	5.9	8.6	7.3	4.8	4.2	NA	NA	NA	NA

Balance Sheet & Other Fin. Data (Million $)

	1997	1996	1995	1994	1993	1992	1991	1990	1989	1988
Cash	43.5	10.3	14.2	9.5	NA	NA	NA	NA	NA	NA
Curr. Assets	78.0	27.4	29.6	21.0	NA	NA	NA	NA	NA	NA
Total Assets	180	108	91.8	73.2	34.7	27.5	NA	NA	NA	NA
Curr. Liab.	27.4	18.6	15.7	8.9	NA	NA	NA	NA	NA	NA
LT Debt	Nil	6.0	Nil	Nil	0.3	4.5	NA	NA	NA	NA
Common Eqty.	153	83.5	76.2	64.3	23.1	3.0	NA	NA	NA	NA
Total Cap.	153	89.5	76.2	64.3	23.5	7.5	NA	NA	NA	NA
Cap. Exp.	21.7	23.2	29.5	13.1	7.5	NA	NA	NA	NA	NA
Cash Flow	23.3	16.6	14.5	10.9	7.0	5.6	NA	NA	NA	NA
Curr. Ratio	2.8	1.5	1.9	2.4	NA	NA	NA	NA	NA	NA
% LT Debt of Cap.	Nil	6.7	Nil	Nil	1.4	60.1	NA	NA	NA	NA
% Net Inc.of Revs.	4.8	3.7	7.4	8.4	7.1	8.1	NA	NA	NA	NA
% Ret. on Assets	6.9	5.9	10.4	13.3	15.5	NA	NA	NA	NA	NA
% Ret. on Equity	8.4	7.4	12.3	15.5	18.6	NA	NA	NA	NA	NA

Data as orig. reptd.; bef. results of disc. opers. and/or spec. items. Per share data adj. for stk. divs. as of ex-div. date. Bold denotes diluted EPS (FASB 128). E-Estimated. NA-Not Available. NM-Not Meaningful. NR-Not Ranked.

Office—26950 Agoura Rd., Calabasas Hills, CA 91301. **Tel**—(818) 871-3000. **Website**—http://www.thecheesecakefactory.com **Chrmn, Pres & CEO**—D. Overton. **EVP-CFO**—G. W. Deitchle. **EVP-COO**—M. A. Nahkunst. **Dirs**—T. L. Gregory, J. I. Kransdorf, D. Overton, W. H. White. **Transfer Agent & Registrar**—U. S. Stock Transfer Co., Glendale, CA. **Incorporated**—in Delaware in 1992. **Empl**—5,002. **S&P Analyst:** W.P.A.

STANDARD &POOR'S
STOCK REPORTS

Chemed Corp.

503D

NYSE Symbol **CHE**

In S&P SmallCap 600

03-OCT-98

Industry:
Services (Commercial & Consumer)

Summary: CHE provides the following services: plumbing and drain cleaning; home health care; and residential appliance and air-conditioning repair.

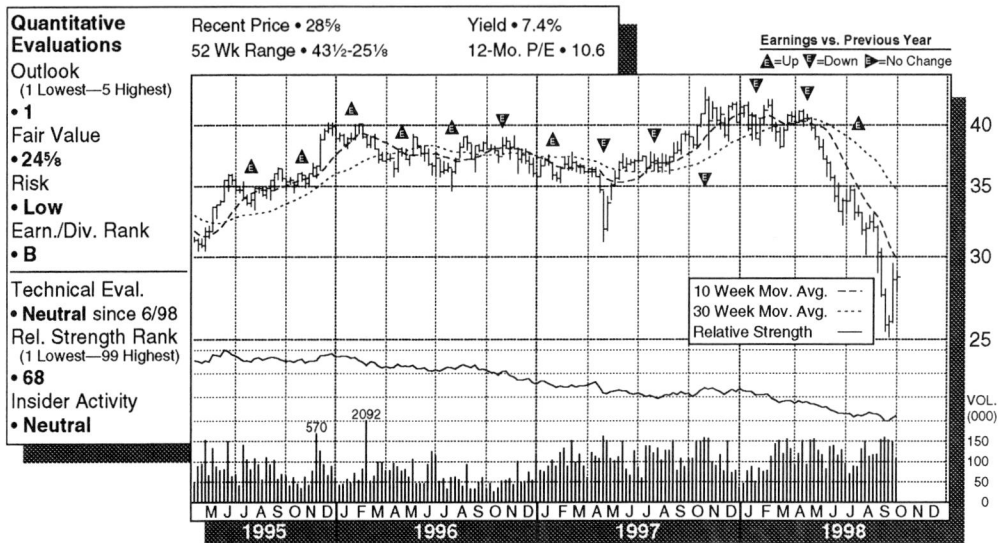

Quantitative Evaluations	
Outlook (1 Lowest—5 Highest)	• **1**
Fair Value	• **24⅝**
Risk	• **Low**
Earn./Div. Rank	• **B**
Technical Eval.	• **Neutral** since 6/98
Rel. Strength Rank (1 Lowest—99 Highest)	• **68**
Insider Activity	• **Neutral**

Recent Price • 28⅝
52 Wk Range • 43½-25⅛
Yield • 7.4%
12-Mo. P/E • 10.6

Earnings vs. Previous Year
▲=Up ▼=Down ▶=No Change

10 Week Mov. Avg. ----
30 Week Mov. Avg. ....
Relative Strength ——

Business Profile - 23-SEP-98

During 1997, Chemed sold its Omnia Group medical products and National Sanitary Supply Co. businesses, enabling it to place greater focus on remaining core service operations. In addition, these divestitures generated about $150 million in cash that strengthened CHE's balance sheet and provided the company with a source of funds for potential acquisitions. During the first half of 1998 and into the third quarter, CHE made a series of small acquisitions to expand its core operations. It is also open to acquisitions that can operate as stand-alone businesses. The company believes that its portfolio continues to offer capital gains opportunities to augment core earnings. Chemed's various employee stock ownership plans own about 14% of CHE common shares outstanding.

Operational Review - 23-SEP-98

Revenues from continuing operations for the first half of 1998 advanced 12%, year to year, reflecting internal growth and acquisitions. However, larger increases for selling & marketing expenses and depreciation cut the gain in operating profit to 1.8%. After 35% lower interest expenses and taxes at 38.9% versus 37.6%, net income rose 4.4%, to $11.8 million ($1.17 a share), from $11.3 million ($1.13, before $0.35 earnings from discontinued operations).

Stock Performance - 02-OCT-98

In the past 30 trading days, CHE's shares have declined 10%, compared to a 7% fall in the S&P 500. Average trading volume for the past five days was 21,500 shares, compared with the 40-day moving average of 32,259 shares.

Key Stock Statistics

Dividend Rate/Share	2.12	Shareholders	5,400
Shs. outstg. (M)	10.0	Market cap. (B)	$0.286
Avg. daily vol. (M)	0.037	Inst. holdings	38%
Tang. Bk. Value/Share	7.22		
Beta	0.24		

Value of $10,000 invested 5 years ago: $ 14,692

Fiscal Year Ending Dec. 31

	1998	1997	1996	1995	1994	1993
Revenues (Million $)						
1Q	88.41	77.66	167.5	169.9	152.1	120.5
2Q	94.94	86.02	170.5	177.3	161.4	127.2
3Q	—	87.43	173.7	177.6	166.1	139.8
4Q	—	90.62	172.2	174.4	165.5	137.5
Yr.	—	341.7	683.8	699.2	645.0	525.1
Earnings Per Share ($)						
1Q	**0.63**	0.74	1.24	0.55	0.33	0.42
2Q	**0.55**	0.39	0.58	0.54	0.45	0.50
3Q	—	0.21	0.39	0.58	0.33	0.43
4Q	—	**0.36**	1.01	0.41	0.37	0.41
Yr.	—	**1.71**	3.23	2.07	1.47	1.75

Next earnings report expected: mid October

Dividend Data (Dividends have been paid since 1971.)

Amount ($)	Date Decl.	Ex-Div. Date	Stock of Record	Payment Date
0.530	Nov. 06	Nov. 19	Nov. 21	Dec. 10 '97
0.530	Feb. 05	Feb. 18	Feb. 20	Mar. 10 '98
0.530	May. 18	May. 29	Jun. 02	Jun. 16 '98
0.530	Aug. 05	Aug. 19	Aug. 21	Sep. 10 '98

A Division of The McGraw-Hill Companies

STANDARD
&POOR'S
STOCK REPORTS

Chemed Corporation

503D

03-OCT-98

Business Summary - 23-SEP-98

Chemed Corp. provides the following services: plumbing and drain cleaning (Roto-Rooter); home health care (Patient Care); and residential appliance and air-conditioning repair (Service America).

Business segment contributions from continuing operations in 1997:

	Sales	Profits
Roto-Rooter	45%	66%
Patient Care	35%	21%
Service America	20%	13%

The Roto-Rooter segment consists of the combined operations of the Roto-Rooter Group, a group of wholly owned businesses that provide repair and maintenance services to residential and commercial accounts. Services consist primarily of sewer, drain, and pipe cleaning, plumbing and HVAC (heating, ventilating, and air conditioning) services. These services are delivered through both company-owned and franchised locations. Roto-Rooter also manufactures and sells certain products and equipment used to provide such services.

The Patient Care segment consists of the consolidated operations of the wholly owned businesses comprising the company's Patient Care Group. This group offers complete, professional home-healthcare services primarily in the New York-New Jersey-Connecticut area. Services provided to patients at home consist primarily of skilled nursing; home health aid; physical, speech, respiratory, and occupational therapies; medical social work; and nutrition.

Management closely monitors accounts receivable balances and has established policies regarding extension of credit and compliance therewith. CHE stated that its Patient Care segment historically has experienced a relatively low level of losses on the collection of its receivables. About 37% of Patient Care's net revenues in 1997 were derived from services provided to patients with coverage under various Medicare programs.

The Service America segment consists of the consolidated operations of the wholly owned businesses comprising the company's Service America Systems Group. This group provides HVAC and appliance repair and maintenance services primarily to residential customers through service contracts and retail sales. In addition, Service America sells air conditioning equipment and duct cleaning services.

During 1997, the company made 12 acquisitions within the Patient Care and Roto-Rooter segments for a total cost of $12.7 million in cash. The Patient Care acquisition is a home healthcare provider. The Roto-Rooter acquisitions are primarily in the business of providing plumbing repair, HVAC, and drain cleaning services.

Per Share Data ($)

(Year Ended Dec. 31)	1997	1996	1995	1994	1993	1992	1991	1990	1989	1988
Tangible Bk. Val.	7.09	1.37	7.21	5.24	2.05	5.65	7.58	11.04	11.77	11.86
Cash Flow	3.22	5.14	3.92	3.08	3.10	2.40	1.90	3.82	4.77	4.31
Earnings	1.71	3.23	2.07	1.47	1.75	1.45	1.10	1.60	2.61	2.23
Dividends	2.09	2.08	2.06	2.04	2.01	2.00	1.97	1.96	1.84	1.72
Payout Ratio	122%	64%	100%	139%	115%	137%	177%	121%	72%	78%
Prices - High	43½	40⅛	40¼	36⅛	32¾	32⅜	28¼	36¾	38¾	38½
- Low	31	34⅝	30⅜	30¼	25½	24¼	17¼	18	32½	29½
P/E Ratio - High	25	12	19	25	19	22	26	23	15	17
- Low	18	11	15	21	15	17	16	11	12	13

Income Statement Analysis (Million $)

	1997	1996	1995	1994	1993	1992	1991	1990	1989	1988
Revs.	342	684	699	645	525	401	352	599	592	501
Oper. Inc.	34.6	50.2	51.2	44.9	36.3	24.3	18.6	57.7	71.2	62.7
Depr.	15.2	18.8	18.2	15.8	13.1	9.2	8.1	23.1	21.7	19.3
Int. Exp.	10.6	9.0	8.5	8.8	8.9	5.7	5.7	7.6	8.9	8.2
Pretax Inc.	27.9	57.4	41.0	29.8	30.2	23.9	19.2	29.7	44.3	37.1
Eff. Tax Rate	39%	38%	38%	37%	31%	27%	28%	35%	34%	37%
Net Inc.	17.1	31.7	20.4	14.5	17.1	14.3	11.0	16.6	26.2	20.6

Balance Sheet & Other Fin. Data (Million $)

	1997	1996	1995	1994	1993	1992	1991	1990	1989	1988
Cash	71.0	11.9	19.2	24.2	15.8	47.7	83.0	1.4	6.5	4.4
Curr. Assets	177	192	219	183	145	162	163	144	150	143
Total Assets	449	559	532	505	430	405	364	328	335	323
Curr. Liab.	94.4	125	145	143	128	104	85.0	94.0	88.0	83.0
LT Debt	83.7	158	85.4	92.0	98.0	104	78.0	82.0	86.0	90.0
Common Eqty.	228	218	209	186	137	134	139	113	121	111
Total Cap.	312	387	310	322	267	266	245	227	242	235
Cap. Exp.	20.1	19.0	15.4	18.4	13.9	8.2	11.4	13.0	14.1	14.6
Cash Flow	32.2	50.6	38.6	30.3	30.3	23.4	19.1	39.6	47.9	39.9
Curr. Ratio	1.9	1.5	1.5	1.3	1.1	1.6	1.9	1.5	1.7	1.7
% LT Debt of Cap.	26.8	40.9	27.5	28.6	36.7	39.0	31.8	36.2	35.5	38.5
% Net Inc.of Revs.	5.0	4.6	2.9	2.3	3.3	3.6	3.1	2.8	4.4	4.1
% Ret. on Assets	3.4	5.8	3.9	3.1	4.1	3.7	3.5	5.0	7.6	6.8
% Ret. on Equity	7.7	14.9	10.3	9.0	12.6	10.5	9.0	14.2	21.6	17.8

Data as orig. reptd.; bef. results of disc. opers. and/or spec. items. Per share data adj. for stk. divs. as of ex-div. date. Bold denotes diluted EPS (FASB 128). E-Estimated. NA-Not Available. NM-Not Meaningful. NR-Not Ranked.

Office—2600 Chemed Center, 255 E. Fifth St, Cincinnati, OH 45202.**Tel**—(513) 762-6900. **Website**—http://www.chemed.com **Chrmn & CEO**—E. L. Hutton. **Pres**—K. J. McNamara. **EVP, Treas & Investor Contact**—Timothy S. O'Toole. **VP & Secy**—Naomi C. Dallob. **Dirs**—J. H. Devlin, C. H. Erhart Jr., J. F. Gemunder, L. J. Gillis, P. P. Grace, E. L. Hutton, T. C. Hutton, W. L. Krebs, S. E. Laney, K. J. McNamara, J. M. Mount, T. S. O'Toole, D. W. Robbins Jr., D. E. Saunders, P. C. Voet, G. J. Walsh, III. **Transfer Agent & Registrar**—ChaseMellon Shareholder Services, Ridgefield Park, NJ. **Incorporated**—in Delaware in 1970. **Empl**— 6,849. **S&P Analyst:** N.J. DeVita

STANDARD &POOR'S
STOCK REPORTS

ChemFirst

503G
NYSE Symbol **CEM**

In S&P SmallCap 600

03-OCT-98 | **Industry:** Chemicals

Summary: This company consists of the former chemicals and other technology businesses of First Mississippi Corp.

S&P Opinion: Hold (★★★)	Recent Price • 17¼	Yield • 2.3%
	52 Wk Range • 28⅝-15⅞	12-Mo. P/E • 9.7

Quantitative Evaluations

Outlook (1 Lowest—5 Highest)
• **4+**

Fair Value
• **22⅛**

Risk
• **NA**

Earn./Div. Rank
• **NR**

Technical Eval.
• **NA**

Rel. Strength Rank (1 Lowest—99 Highest)
• **53**

Insider Activity
• **Neutral**

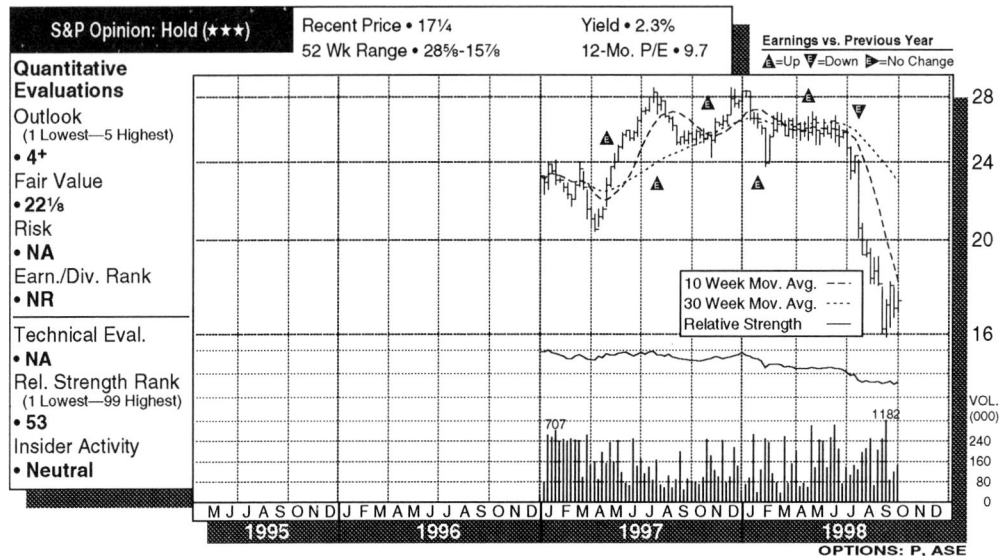

Earnings vs. Previous Year ▲=Up ▼=Down ▶=No Change

10 Week Mov. Avg. – – –
30 Week Mov. Avg. ·····
Relative Strength ——

OPTIONS: P, ASE

Overview - 10-AUG-98

After lower 1998 first half operating EPS, we now see a modest decline in full year operating performance from 1997's $1.30 from ongoing operations. The First Chemicals unit should recover in the 1998 second half, on increased aniline production as a result of routine production at the Pascagoula plant, which had an usual amount of maintenance downtime in the first half, and higher output rates at the new Baytown plant. CEM started up its new facility in March 1998, thereby doubling its aniline capacity. Electronic chemicals will be adversely affected in the second half by the slowdown in the semiconductor industry. Earnings will also be limited by dilution from an acquisition in electronic chemicals at the end of 1997. While sales and profits in 1998 for custom manufacturing will decline, due to the completion in 1997 of a major project, potential new projects enhance the outlook for 1999. The engineered products business should stay in the black, on a high quality backlog of orders. CEM realized a gain of $0.25 a share from the first quarter sale of its 50% interest in a joint venture; cash proceeds were $10.5 million. Fourth quarter 1997 EPS included a $0.43 gain from the sale of a 23% interest in Melamine Chemicals; proceeds were $16.6 million. CEM is seeking to sell its steel melting business.

Valuation - 10-AUG-98

As a means of increasing shareholder value, ChemFirst was formed in December 1996, following the spinoff of the chemicals and technology businesses of First Mississippi Corp. CEM intends to expand its chemicals businesses through internal development and complementary acquisitions. With comparable chemicals stocks trading at similar P/E multiples, we view the stock as fairly valued.

Key Stock Statistics

S&P EPS Est. 1998	1.05	Tang. Bk. Value/Share	14.77
P/E on S&P Est. 1998	16.5	Beta	0.97
S&P EPS Est. 1999	1.30	Shareholders	5,500
Dividend Rate/Share	0.40	Market cap. (B)	$0.329
Shs. outstg. (M)	19.0	Inst. holdings	49%
Avg. daily vol. (M)	0.078		

Value of $10,000 invested 5 years ago: NA

Fiscal Year Ending Dec. 31

	1998	1997	1996	1995	1994	1993
Revenues (Million $)						
1Q	111.4	113.1	97.14	—	—	—
2Q	117.0	111.2	98.07	—	—	—
3Q	—	106.1	95.43	—	—	—
4Q	—	117.8	93.00	—	—	—
Yr.	—	445.8	383.6	353.0	—	—
Earnings Per Share ($)						
1Q	0.48	0.39	0.11	—	—	—
2Q	0.20	0.38	-0.51	—	—	—
3Q	—	0.33	0.20	—	—	—
4Q	—	0.78	-0.30	—	—	—
Yr.	—	1.86	-0.11	0.09	—	—

Next earnings report expected: late October

Dividend Data (Dividends have been paid since 1997.)

Amount ($)	Date Decl.	Ex-Div. Date	Stock of Record	Payment Date
0.100	Nov. 26	Dec. 09	Dec. 11	Dec. 29 '97
0.100	Feb. 24	Mar. 09	Mar. 11	Mar. 26 '98
0.100	May. 27	Jun. 09	Jun. 11	Jun. 26 '98
0.100	Aug. 26	Sep. 08	Sep. 10	Sep. 25 '98

A Division of The McGraw-Hill Companies

Business Summary - 10-AUG-98

ChemFirst was formed in December 1996, through the spinoff of the chemicals and technology businesses of First Mississippi Corp., which than merged its remaining business, fertilizers, with Mississippi Chemical Group. CEM began life as an independent company with virtually no debt and is focused on its chemicals and combustion and thermal plasma businesses. CEM's healthy balance sheet has come in handy, because it is expanding its chemicals businesses through capacity expansions and acquisitions. CEM is completing a $200 million capital spending program begun in 1996 that will boost capacities of major product lines by up to 100% by 1999. Contributions by business segment in 1997 were:

	Sales	Profits
Chemicals	67%	$51.7
Engineered products	16%	2.9
Steel	17%	-1.0

The company's chemicals operations are conducted through four divisions. First Chemicals is a major producer of intermediates (aniline, nitrotoluenes) and specialty derivatives for use in polyurethane foam, plastics, polymer additives and herbicides with facilities in Pascagoula, MS and Baytown, TX. Specialty chemical

batch capacity at Pascagoula was increased by 25% in July 1997. CEM completed in March 1998 a worldscale aniline facility at Bayer Corp.'s Baytown, TX, complex. The project doubled CEM's aniline capacity. Quality Chemicals is a custom maker of fine chemicals for chemical, agricultural and pharmaceutical applications at two sites in the U.S. Custom manufacturing capacity was increased by 30% at one facility at the end of 1996, with further expansions planned. EKC Technology is a world leader in photoresist removers and cleaning solutions for use during the manufacture of semiconductors. EKC recently acquired chemical mechanical planarization (CMP) assets for semiconductor production. TriQuest (87.5%-owned, acquired December 1997) produces acylation derivatives used for photoresists and polymer additives.

The engineered products and services business consists of Callidus Technologies, which produces industrial burners, flares, and incinerators, and thermal plasma energy systems and equipment for waste treatment and steel production. CEM is seeking to sell FirstMiss Steel, which operates a steel melting and casting facility.

CEM repurchased 776,976 of its common shares in 1997, essentially completing a $20 million buyback authorization announced in January 1997. An additional 1.1 million shares were acquired in the first half of 1998, for $28 million, under a new $40 million program announced in November 1997.

Per Share Data ($)

(Year Ended Dec. 31)	1997	1996	1995	1994	1993	1992	1991	1990	1989	1988
Tangible Bk. Val.	15.15	14.42	NA	NA	NA	NA	NA	NA	NA	NA
Cash Flow	2.85	0.37	NA	NA	NA	NA	NA	NA	NA	NA
Earnings	1.86	-0.11	0.09	NA	NA	NA	NA	NA	NA	NA
Dividends	0.40	Nil	Nil	Nil	Nil	Nil	Nil	Nil	Nil	Nil
Payout Ratio	22%	Nil	Nil	Nil	Nil	Nil	Nil	Nil	Nil	Nil
Prices - High	28⅝	23¼	NA	NA	NA	NA	NA	NA	NA	NA
- Low	20⅜	22¼	NA	NA	NA	NA	NA	NA	NA	NA
P/E Ratio - High	15	NM	NM	NM	NM	NM	NM	NM	NM	NM
- Low	11	NM	NM	NM	NM	NM	NM	NM	NM	NM

Income Statement Analysis (Million $)

	1997	1996	1995	1994	1993	1992	1991	1990	1989	1988
Revs.	446	384	353	NA	NA	NA	NA	NA	NA	NA
Oper. Inc.	59.0	NA	NA	NA	NA	NA	NA	NA	NA	NA
Depr.	20.6	NA	NA	NA	NA	NA	NA	NA	NA	NA
Int. Exp.	0.4	NA	NA	NA	NA	NA	NA	NA	NA	NA
Pretax Inc.	62.7	NA	NA	NA	NA	NA	NA	NA	NA	NA
Eff. Tax Rate	38%	NM	NA	NA	NA	NA	NA	NA	NA	NA
Net Inc.	38.9	-10.4	9.5	NA	NA	NA	NA	NA	NA	NA

Balance Sheet & Other Fin. Data (Million $)

	1997	1996	1995	1994	1993	1992	1991	1990	1989	1988
Cash	7.8	NA	NA	NA	NA	NA	NA	NA	NA	NA
Curr. Assets	173	NA	NA	NA	NA	NA	NA	NA	NA	NA
Total Assets	459	NA	NA	NA	NA	NA	NA	NA	NA	NA
Curr. Liab.	95.4	NA	NA	NA	NA	NA	NA	NA	NA	NA
LT Debt	4.9	NA	NA	NA	NA	NA	NA	NA	NA	NA
Common Eqty.	322	NA	NA	NA	NA	NA	NA	NA	NA	NA
Total Cap.	345	NA	NA	NA	NA	NA	NA	NA	NA	NA
Cap. Exp.	95.6	NA	NA	NA	NA	NA	NA	NA	NA	NA
Cash Flow	59.5	NA	NA	NA	NA	NA	NA	NA	NA	NA
Curr. Ratio	1.8	NA	NA	NA	NA	NA	NA	NA	NA	NA
% LT Debt of Cap.	1.4	NA	NA	NA	NA	NA	NA	NA	NA	NA
% Net Inc.of Revs.	8.7	NM	NA	NA	NA	NA	NA	NA	NA	NA
% Ret. on Assets	8.9	NM	NA	NA	NA	NA	NA	NA	NA	NA
% Ret. on Equity	14.1	NM	NA	NA	NA	NA	NA	NA	NA	NA

Data as orig. reptd.; pro forma; bef. results of disc. opers. and/or spec. items. Per share data adj. for stk. divs. as of ex-div. date. Prior to 1997, fiscal year ended June 30. E-Estimated. NA-Not Available. NM-Not Meaningful. NR-Not Ranked.

Office—700 North St., P.O. Box 1249, Jackson, MS 39215-1249. **Registrars**—Bank of New York, NYC; Deposit Guaranty National Bank, Jackson, MS. **Tel**—(601) 948-7550. **Fax**—(601) 949-0228. **Website**—http://www.chemfirst.com **Chrmn & CEO**—J. K. Williams. **Pres**—T. G. Tepas. **VP & CFO**—R. M. Summerford. **Secy & Investor Contact**—James L. McArthur. **Dirs**—R. P. Anderson, P. A. Becker, J. W. Crook, M. J. Ferris, J. E. Fligg, R. P. Guyton, P. W. Murrill, W. A. Percy II, D. F. Smith, L. R. Speed, R. G. Turner, J. K. Williams. **Transfer Agents**—Bank of New York, NYC; Co.'s office. **Incorporated**—in Mississippi in 1957. **Empl**—1,175. **S&P Analyst:** Richard O'Reilly, CFA

03-OCT-98 | **Industry:** Foods | **Summary:** This company is a leading producer, processor and distributor of fresh fruits and vegetables and prepared food products marketed under the Chiquita and other brand names.

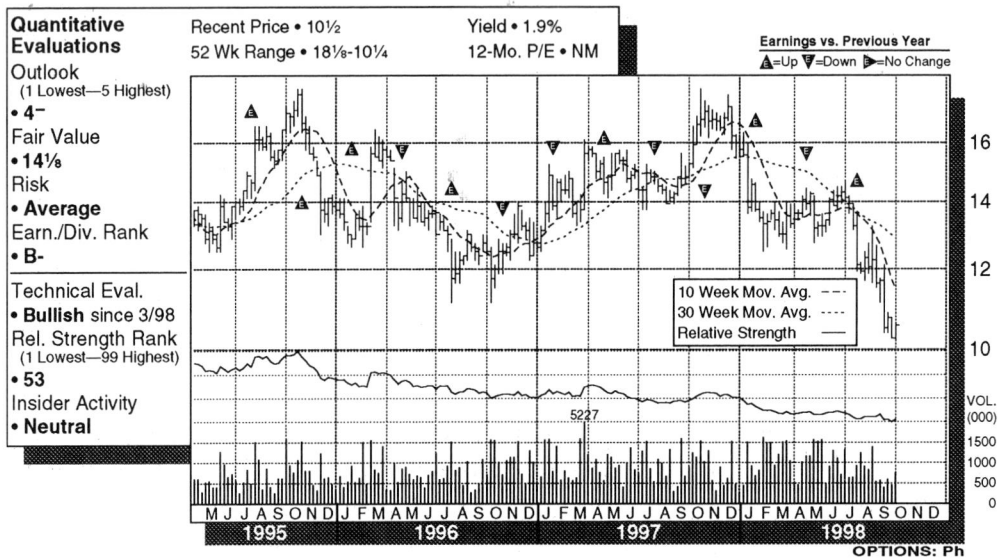

Quantitative Evaluations

Outlook (1 Lowest—5 Highest)
- **4⁻**

Fair Value
- **14⅛**

Risk
- **Average**

Earn./Div. Rank
- **B-**

Technical Eval.
- **Bullish** since 3/98

Rel. Strength Rank (1 Lowest—99 Highest)
- **53**

Insider Activity
- **Neutral**

Recent Price • 10½   Yield • 1.9%
52 Wk Range • 18⅛-10¼   12-Mo. P/E • NM

Earnings vs. Previous Year
▲=Up ▼=Down ▶=No Change

10 Week Mov. Avg. ---
30 Week Mov. Avg. ----
Relative Strength ——

OPTIONS: Ph

Business Profile - 24-APR-98

The company has said that the primary cause of losses and reduced profitability in recent years was an increasingly restrictive and discriminatory trade policy imposed by the European Union (EU) on the Latin American banana industry. CQB would benefit significantly if non-EU banana prices recovered from depressed levels. To Chiquita's relief, the World Trade Organization (WTO) Appellate Body recently issued a ruling that repudiated the EU's banana trade policy. The EU will now be required by law to allow Chiquita open, non-discriminatory and fair market access. Previously, over 50% of Chiquita's EU market share was taken from them, due to previous EU policy.

Operational Review - 24-APR-98

Net sales in the first quarter of 1998 climbed 14%, year to year, as higher volumes outweighed lower prices in North America. Margins were flat, due to lower gross margins, offset by volume increases and some SG&A leverage. With higher interest expense and depreciation charges, pretax income fell 5.3%. After taxes at 8.9%, versus 9.0%, net income was down 5.1%, to $41,100,000 ($0.52 a share, on 10% more shares), from $43,300,000 ($0.60).

Stock Performance - 02-OCT-98

In the past 30 trading days, CQB's shares have declined 14%, compared to a 7% fall in the S&P 500. Average trading volume for the past five days was 148,100 shares, compared with the 40-day moving average of 140,903 shares.

Key Stock Statistics

Dividend Rate/Share	0.20	Shareholders	6,500
Shs. outstg. (M)	65.4	Market cap. (B)	$0.690
Avg. daily vol. (M)	0.113	Inst. holdings	73%
Tang. Bk. Value/Share	6.32		
Beta	0.41		

Value of $10,000 invested 5 years ago: $ 6,824

Fiscal Year Ending Dec. 31

	1998	1997	1996	1995	1994	1993
Revenues (Million $)						
1Q	717.0	631.4	624.8	674.3	1,056	674.2
2Q	744.2	646.2	713.7	727.5	1,007	727.5
3Q	—	556.3	541.6	569.0	900.9	569.0
4Q	—	599.8	555.2	595.2	997.4	567.1
Yr.	—	2,434	2,435	2,566	3,962	2,533
Earnings Per Share ($)						
1Q	**0.52**	**0.60**	0.10	0.55	0.62	0.50
2Q	**0.66**	**0.57**	0.73	0.52	0.51	0.15
3Q	—	**-0.57**	-0.20	-0.19	-1.59	-0.50
4Q	—	**-1.01**	-1.65	-0.58	-0.70	-1.17
Yr.	—	**-0.29**	-0.72	0.37	-1.07	-0.99

Next earnings report expected: late October

Dividend Data (Dividends have been paid since 1985.)

Amount ($)	Date Decl.	Ex-Div. Date	Stock of Record	Payment Date
0.050	Oct. 21	Nov. 19	Nov. 21	Dec. 07 '97
0.050	Feb. 13	Feb. 18	Feb. 21	Mar. 07 '98
0.050	Apr. 22	May. 19	May. 21	Jun. 07 '98
0.050	Jul. 22	Aug. 19	Aug. 21	Sep. 07 '98

A Division of The **McGraw-Hill** Companies

Business Summary - 24-APR-98

Chiquita Brands International is a leading producer, processor and distributor of bananas and other fresh and prepared food products marketed under the Chiquita and other brand names. Principal production and processing operations are conducted in the U.S. and Central and South America. Geographic sales contributions in recent years was:

	1997	1996
North America	55%	53%
Europe & Other	43%	44%
Central & South America	2%	3%

The fresh foods segment features a full line of fresh fruits and vegetables, including bananas (the company's principal product). In recent years, the product base has been widened to include additional fresh fruits sold under the Chiquita name (including avocados, citrus, grapes, kiwi, nectarines and mangos), and apples, apricots, peaches, grapes, strawberries, cherries, pears, tomatoes and plums sold under other brand names. Fresh vegetables include lettuce, celery, onions, broccoli, carrots, beans, potatoes and asparagus. As a result of the more diverse product line, banana sales accounted for 60% of total sales in the last three years, down from 72% in 1990. Bananas are grown by subsidiaries or purchased from suppliers in areas that include Colombia, Panama, Costa Rica, Ecuador, Guatemala and Honduras.

Prepared foods include fruit- and vegetable-based juices sold primarily in the U.S.; processed fruit and vegetables, including processed bananas, sold worldwide under the Chiquita, Friday and other brand names; fresh-cut and ready-to-eat salads sold under the Club Chef brand; and other consumer foods (primarily edible oils) sold in Honduras under the Numar and other brand names.

In February 1996, Ecuador, the world's largest exporter of bananas, joined the U.S. and several Latin American governments in an international trade challenge to the EU, using procedures of the World Trade Organization (WTO), in an attempt to resolve the dispute with the EU over EU restrictions on banana imports from Latin America. In March 1997, in a preliminary ruling, the WTO said that the EU's banana import policy violates world trade rules. After the EU appealed the WTO panel report in June 1997, in January 1998, a WTO arbitrator ruled that the EU must implement banana policies consistent with the WTO report findings no later than January 1, 1999.

Per Share Data ($)

(Year Ended Dec. 31)	1997	1996	1995	1994	1993	1992	1991	1990	1989	1988
Tangible Bk. Val.	5.75	5.25	6.38	5.63	7.77	9.01	15.38	11.53	8.84	7.21
Cash Flow	1.31	1.03	2.33	1.07	0.92	-2.73	3.87	3.43	2.81	2.34
Earnings	-0.29	-0.72	0.37	-1.07	-0.99	-4.28	2.55	2.23	1.70	1.47
Dividends	0.20	0.20	0.20	0.20	0.44	0.66	0.55	0.35	0.20	0.20
Payout Ratio	NM	NM	54%	NM	NM	NM	21%	17%	11%	13%
Prices - High	18⅛	16½	18⅛	19⅜	17¾	40⅛	50¾	32⅛	17⅝	19⅞
- Low	12⅝	11⅛	12⅛	11¼	10	15¼	29⅜	16	12⅞	13¾
P/E Ratio - High	NM	NM	49	NM	NM	NM	20	14	10	14
- Low	NM	NM	33	NM	NM	NM	12	7	8	9

Income Statement Analysis (Million $)

	1997	1996	1995	1994	1993	1992	1991	1990	1989	1988
Revs.	2,434	2,435	2,566	3,962	2,533	2,723	4,627	4,273	3,823	3,503
Oper. Inc.	192	181	280	283	206	45.1	293	224	190	183
Depr.	91.6	96.5	105	116	103	80.4	66.7	50.4	44.0	35.7
Int. Exp.	109	130	164	174	178	176	117	71.0	62.0	46.0
Pretax Inc.	8.5	-16.7	41.9	-35.0	-39.0	-216	183	152	111	110
Eff. Tax Rate	96%	NM	33%	NM	NM	NM	30%	38%	39%	45%
Net Inc.	0.3	-27.7	28.0	-49.0	-51.0	-221	128	94.0	68.0	60.0

Balance Sheet & Other Fin. Data (Million $)

	1997	1996	1995	1994	1993	1992	1991	1990	1989	1988
Cash	126	286	271	179	151	413	830	349	289	193
Curr. Assets	783	844	877	918	770	1,071	1,682	1,136	918	782
Total Assets	2,402	2,467	2,624	2,902	2,741	2,881	3,143	2,174	1,613	1,436
Curr. Liab.	483	464	510	651	504	588	698	698	499	395
LT Debt	962	1,079	1,242	1,365	1,438	1,411	1,227	522	417	402
Common Eqty.	527	460	528	443	544	617	968	688	464	401
Total Cap.	1,742	1,804	1,914	2,010	2,040	2,086	2,195	1,210	881	803
Cap. Exp.	76.2	74.6	64.6	149	197	410	411	323	131	78.0
Cash Flow	75.0	56.8	124	56.0	47.0	-140	195	144	112	96.0
Curr. Ratio	1.6	1.8	1.7	1.4	1.5	1.8	2.4	1.6	1.8	2.0
% LT Debt of Cap.	55.2	59.8	64.9	67.9	70.5	67.7	55.9	43.1	47.3	50.1
% Net Inc.of Revs.	0.0	NM	1.1	NM	NM	NM	2.8	2.2	1.8	1.7
% Ret. on Assets	0.0	NM	0.6	NM	NM	NM	4.6	4.6	4.4	5.0
% Ret. on Equity	NM	NM	4.0	NM	NM	NM	14.9	15.3	15.6	15.6

Data as orig. reptd.; bef. results of disc. opers. and/or spec. items. Per share data adj. for stk. divs. as of ex-div. date. Bold denotes diluted EPS (FASB 128). E-Estimated. NA-Not Available. NM-Not Meaningful. NR-Not Ranked.

Office—250 East Fifth St., Cincinnati, OH 45202. **Tel**—(513) 784-8000. **Website**—http://www.chiquita.com **Chrmn & CEO**—C. H. Lindner. **Vice Chrmn**—K. E. Lindner. **Pres & COO**—S. G. Warshaw. **SVP & CFO**—W. J. Ligan. **VP & Secy**—R. W. Olson. **Investor Contact**—Joseph W. Hagin. **Dirs**—C. H. Lindner, K. E. Lindner, F. J. Runk, J. H. Sisco, W. W. Verity, O. W. Waddell, R. F. Walker, S. G. Warshaw. **Transfer Agent & Registrar**—Securities Transfer Co., Cincinnati. **Incorporated**—in New Jersey in 1899 as United Fruit Co. **Empl**— 40,000. **S&P Analyst:** Robert J. Izmirlian

STANDARD &POOR'S
STOCK REPORTS

CIBER, Inc.

532R

NYSE Symbol **CBR**

In S&P SmallCap 600

03-OCT-98 | **Industry:** Services (Computer Systems)

Summary: CBR provides information technology consulting services.

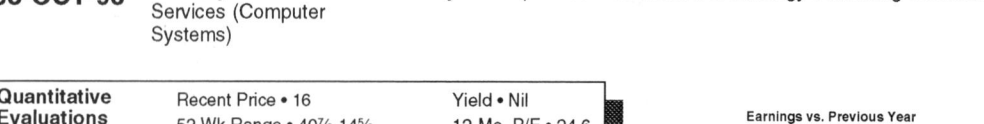

Quantitative Evaluations

Outlook (1 Lowest—5 Highest)
- **5**

Fair Value
- **53¾**

Risk
- **High**

Earn./Div. Rank
- **B+**

Technical Eval.
- **NA**

Rel. Strength Rank (1 Lowest—99 Highest)
- **3**

Insider Activity
- **Neutral**

Recent Price • 16
52 Wk Range • 40⅞-14⅝

Yield • Nil
12-Mo. P/E • 24.6

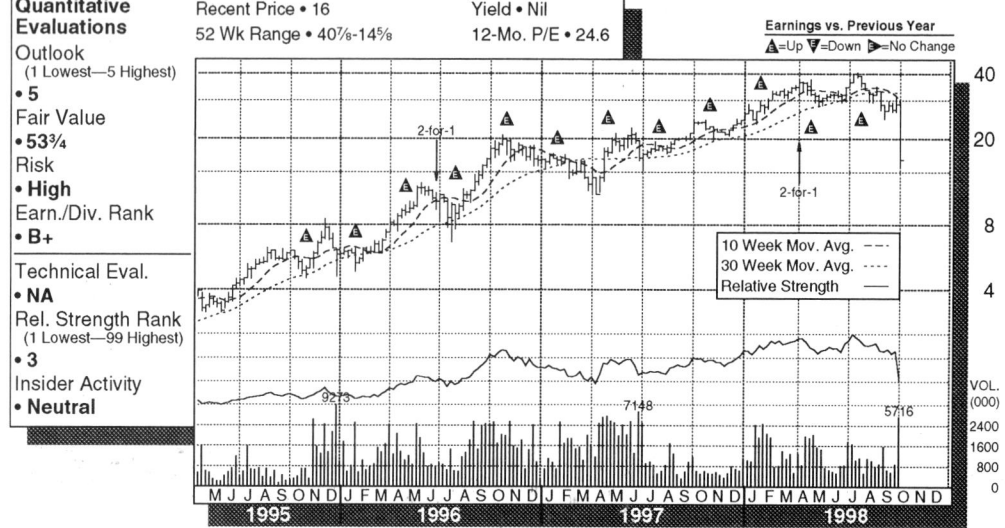

10 Week Mov. Avg. ---
30 Week Mov. Avg. ····
Relative Strength —

Earnings vs. Previous Year
▲=Up ▼=Down ▶=No Change

Business Profile - 14-SEP-98

Thus far in 1998, the company has continued its aggressive acquisition activity. In recent months, CBR has completed mergers with EJR Computer Associates, a New Jersey-based provider of data processing consulting and project management services, and The Cushing Group, which offers distributed object technology consulting services. The two companies have combined annualized revenues of $36 million. In May 1998, the company acquired The Summit Group, Inc., a privately held leading provider of enterprise resource solutions (ERS) with annual revenues exceeding $60 million.

Operational Review - 14-SEP-98

Based on a preliminary report, revenues in the fiscal year ended June 30, 1998, rose 41%, as restated for pooling acquisitions, led by a 46% jump in consulting service revenues. Margins widened, reflecting well-controlled direct costs; operating income surged 81%. After taxes at 38.4%, versus 38.0%, net income was up 76%, to $36,510,000, from $20,696,000. Pro forma net income (after income tax adjustment) was up 72% to $34.3 million ($0.65 a share, based on 6.5% more shares outstanding), from $19.9 million ($0.40).

Stock Performance - 02-OCT-98

In the past 30 trading days, CBR's shares have declined 52%, compared to a 7% fall in the S&P 500. Average trading volume for the past five days was 1,143,120 shares, compared with the 40-day moving average of 308,374 shares.

Key Stock Statistics

Dividend Rate/Share	Nil	Shareholders	1,000
Shs. outstg. (M)	51.1	Market cap. (B)	$0.817
Avg. daily vol. (M)	0.411	Inst. holdings	50%
Tang. Bk. Value/Share	2.54		
Beta	NA		

Value of $10,000 invested 5 years ago: NA

Fiscal Year Ending Jun. 30

	1998	1997	1996	1995	1994	1993
Revenues (Million $)						
1Q	123.2	54.03	31.55	26.66	—	—
2Q	135.3	59.72	32.40	27.91	—	—
3Q	141.6	69.65	36.70	31.82	—	—
4Q	150.2	78.87	45.26	33.76	—	—
Yr.	550.4	262.3	156.9	120.2	79.80	37.49
Earnings Per Share ($)						
1Q	0.12	0.07	0.06	0.04	—	—
2Q	0.13	0.07	0.05	0.03	—	—
3Q	0.20	0.12	0.07	0.05	—	—
4Q	0.20	0.14	0.07	0.03	—	—
Yr.	0.65	0.39	0.24	0.14	0.09	0.06

Next earnings report expected: mid October

Dividend Data

Amount ($)	Date Decl.	Ex-Div. Date	Stock of Record	Payment Date
2-for-1	Feb. 06	Apr. 01	Mar. 18	Mar. 31 '98

A Division of The McGraw·Hill Companies

Business Summary - 14-SEP-98

Founded in 1974 and public since 1994, CIBER, Inc. is a provider of information technology consulting services, consisting primarily of: application software staff supplementation; management consulting solutions for business/IT problems; package software implementation services; system life-cycle project responsibility; millennium date conversion services; and networking procurement and engineering services.

Revenues are generated from two areas: the CIBER Information Services (CIS) division; and CIBER Solutions. Revenue breakdown in recent fiscal years (ended June):

	1997	1996
CIS	71%	77%
Solutions	29%	23%

The CIS division provides application software development and maintenance services and, through its CIBR2000 division, millennium date change solutions. CIBER Solutions is comprised of the following wholly owned subsidiaries: Spectrum Technology Group (Spectrum), Business Information Technology (BIT), The Summit Group (acquired in 1998) and CIBER Network Services (CNSI).

Spectrum provides information technology consulting solutions to business problems, specifically in the areas of data warehousing, data modeling and enterprise architecture, as well as project management and systems integration services. BIT specializes in the implementation and integration of human resource and financial software application products, plus workflow automation and manufacturing/distribution software systems, primarily for client/server networks. A substantial portion of BIT's revenues is derived from assisting clients implementing PeopleSoft, Inc. software. Summit is a leading provider of enterprise resource solutions (ERS). CNSI provides a wide range of local-area and wide-area network solutions, from design and procurement to installation and maintenance with services including Internet and intranet connectivity.

With a network of over 80 offices in more than 20 states and abroad, CBR has numerous long-term clients, including American Express, AT&T, Fidelity Investments, Ford Motor, GTE, IBM, MCI Telecommunications, Monsanto, U S West Communications and Xerox.

In July 1997, CBR acquired privately held KCM Computer Consulting, Inc. for 430,850 common shares. KCM, a provider of information technology services, generates annual revenues of $15 million to $20 million.

In August 1997, CBR acquired privately held Reliant Integration Services, Inc. for 591,638 common shares. RIS provides network integration services and generates annual revenues of about $30 million.

Per Share Data ($)

(Year Ended Jun. 30)	1998	1997	1996	1995	1994	1993	1992	1991	1990	1989
Tangible Bk. Val.	2.54	1.72	1.25	0.40	0.30	0.62	NA	NA	NA	NA
Cash Flow	0.90	0.47	0.32	0.19	NA	NA	NA	NA	NA	NA
Earnings	0.65	0.39	0.24	0.14	0.09	0.06	0.04	NA	NA	NA
Dividends	Nil	Nil	Nil	Nil	Nil	Nil	Nil	Nil	Nil	Nil
Payout Ratio	Nil	Nil	Nil	Nil	Nil	Nil	Nil	Nil	Nil	Nil
Prices - High	40$7/8$	29	20$7/8$	8$1/2$	2$3/4$	NA	NA	NA	NA	NA
- Low	23$3/8$	11	4$3/4$	2$1/4$	1$15/16$	NA	NA	NA	NA	NA
P/E Ratio - High	63	74	85	63	33	NA	NA	NA	NA	NA
- Low	36	28	20	17	23	NA	NA	NA	NA	NA

Income Statement Analysis (Million $)

	1998	1997	1996	1995	1994	1993	1992	1991	1990	1989
Revs.	550	262	157	120	79.8	63.1	51.3	NA	NA	NA
Oper. Inc.	71.7	31.5	16.8	10.3	NA	NA	NA	NA	NA	NA
Depr.	9.4	4.5	2.5	1.9	NA	NA	NA	NA	NA	NA
Int. Exp.	0.2	Nil	0.2	0.3	NA	NA	NA	NA	NA	NA
Pretax Inc.	59.3	26.7	13.8	7.2	NA	NA	NA	NA	NA	NA
Eff. Tax Rate	38%	45%	44%	44%	36%	NA	NA	NA	NA	NA
Net Inc.	36.5	14.6	8.5	4.3	2.3	1.4	1.0	NA	NA	NA

Balance Sheet & Other Fin. Data (Million $)

	1998	1997	1996	1995	1994	1993	1992	1991	1990	1989
Cash	37.4	23.0	16.6	2.1	NA	NA	NA	NA	NA	NA
Curr. Assets	161	80.8	48.4	26.1	NA	NA	NA	NA	NA	NA
Total Assets	216	123	64.6	40.8	30.8	15.7	12.7	NA	NA	NA
Curr. Liab.	53.1	20.1	9.2	16.4	NA	NA	NA	NA	NA	NA
LT Debt	Nil	Nil	0.2	0.3	NA	NA	NA	NA	NA	NA
Common Eqty.	163	103	55.2	24.0	19.1	5.4	3.9	NA	NA	NA
Total Cap.	163	103	55.4	24.3	NA	NA	NA	NA	NA	NA
Cap. Exp.	11.6	3.1	1.5	0.8	NA	NA	NA	NA	NA	NA
Cash Flow	46.0	19.2	11.0	6.1	NA	NA	NA	NA	NA	NA
Curr. Ratio	3.0	4.0	5.3	1.6	NA	NA	NA	NA	NA	NA
% LT Debt of Cap.	Nil	Nil	0.1	0.1	NA	NA	NA	NA	NA	NA
% Net Inc.of Revs.	6.6	5.6	5.4	3.6	NA	NA	NA	NA	NA	NA
% Ret. on Assets	NA	15.0	16.2	11.9	9.6	9.6	NA	NA	NA	NA
% Ret. on Equity	NA	18.1	21.5	20.0	18.8	30.9	NA	NA	NA	NA

Data as orig. reptd.; bef. results of disc. opers. and/or spec. items. Per share data adj. for stk. divs. as of ex-div. date. Bold denotes diluted EPS (FASB 128). E-Estimated. NA-Not Available. NM-Not Meaningful. NR-Not Ranked.

Office—5251 DTC Parkway, Suite 1400, Englewood, CO 80111. **Tel**—(303) 220-0100. **Website**—http://www.ciber.com **Chrmn, CEO & Secy**—B. G. Stevenson. **Pres & Treas**—M. J. Slingerlend. **VP-CFO**—Kara Kennedy. **Dirs**—R. L. Burger, A. McGill, R. A. Montoni, J. A. Rutherford, M. J. Slingerlend, J. C. Spira, B. G. Stevenson. **Transfer Agent & Registrar**—American Securities Transfer, Inc., Denver. **Incorporated**—in Delaware in 1994. **Empl**— 5,000. **S&P Analyst**: C.F.B.

STANDARD &POOR'S
STOCK REPORTS

CILCORP Inc.

532W

NYSE Symbol **CER**

In S&P SmallCap 600

03-OCT-98 | **Industry:** Electric Companies | **Summary:** CILCORP is the holding company for Central Illinois Light Co., which supplies electricity and gas to central and east central Illinois.

Quantitative Evaluations

Outlook (1 Lowest—5 Highest)
- **2**

Fair Value
- **52¼**

Risk
- **Low**

Earn./Div. Rank
- **B**

Technical Eval.
- **Bullish** since 6/98

Rel. Strength Rank (1 Lowest—99 Highest)
- **95**

Insider Activity
- **NA**

Recent Price • 53⅝
52 Wk Range • 54⅛-40½

Yield • 4.6%
12-Mo. P/E • NM

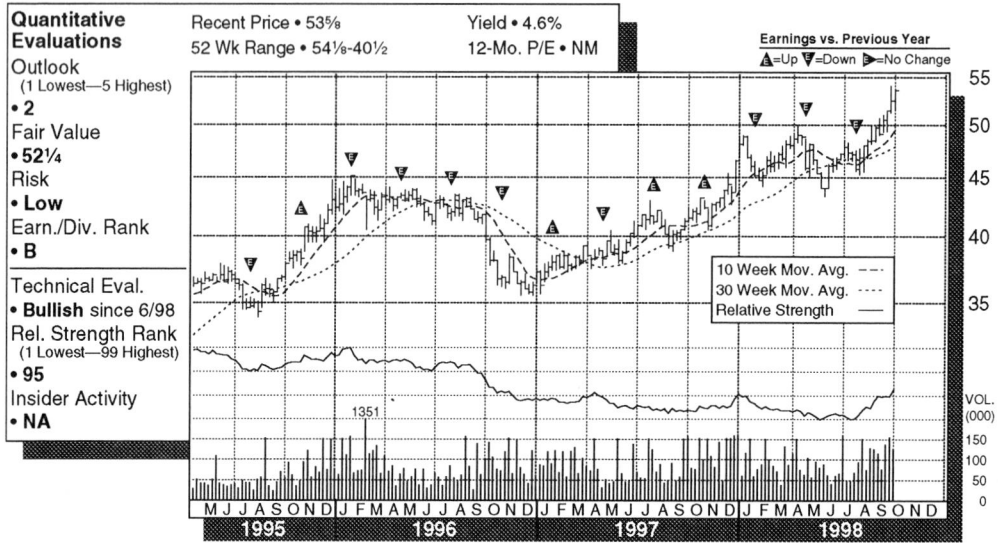

Earnings vs. Previous Year
▲=Up ▼=Down ▶=No Change

10 Week Mov. Avg. — — —
30 Week Mov. Avg. · · · · ·
Relative Strength ———

Business Profile - 13-APR-98

Earnings have been restricted recently by sharply higher purchased gas costs. CER is incurring transition costs to prepare for customer choice in retail energy markets. These include outlays for the development of new product offerings, customer data systems and employee training and recruitment. The company has set up pilot programs under which certain of its electric and gas customers may use other suppliers for all or part of their power requirements. In 1995, CER formed QST Energy, Inc. to provide non-regulated energy and related services. The May 1997 acquisition of Trebor Energy, a natural gas marketing and trading company, will facilitate QST's mission of delivering a comprehensive package of energy products and services to customers.

Operational Review - 13-APR-98

Revenues in 1997 rose 59% from those of the prior year, as higher gas and electric sales and contributions from the new QST operations outweighed lower environmental and engineering revenues. Operating expenses rose 71%, due primarily to much higher purchased gas costs and losses at QST. After taxes at 61.0%, versus 34.2%, income from continuing operations fell 66%, to $9,637,000 ($0.71 a share), from $28,139,000 ($2.08). Results in 1997 exclude an extraordinary gain of $0.30 a share and income from discontinued operations of $0.19 a share; results in 1996 exclude a loss of $0.01 a share from discontinued operations.

Stock Performance - 02-OCT-98

In the past 30 trading days, CER's shares have increased 11%, compared to a 7% fall in the S&P 500. Average trading volume for the past five days was 25,420 shares, compared with the 40-day moving average of 25,182 shares.

Key Stock Statistics

Dividend Rate/Share	2.46	Shareholders	12,500
Shs. outstg. (M)	13.6	Market cap. (B)	$0.730
Avg. daily vol. (M)	0.028	Inst. holdings	27%
Tang. Bk. Value/Share	25.19		
Beta	0.25		

Value of $10,000 invested 5 years ago: $ 19,045

Fiscal Year Ending Dec. 31

	1998	1997	1996	1995	1994	1993
Revenues (Million $)						
1Q	376.1	192.2	178.0	170.6	177.0	165.0
2Q	265.0	173.1	129.7	132.5	137.0	126.0
3Q	—	228.5	138.6	157.6	146.0	142.0
4Q	—	382.7	182.1	154.1	144.7	152.0
Yr.	—	976.5	628.4	614.7	605.1	585.0
Earnings Per Share ($)						
1Q	0.56	0.72	0.78	0.88	0.75	0.72
2Q	-0.04	0.41	0.19	0.43	0.53	0.31
3Q	—	0.95	0.92	1.47	0.73	0.98
4Q	—	-1.37	0.18	0.15	0.49	0.59
Yr.	—	0.71	2.07	2.93	2.50	2.60

Next earnings report expected: late October

Dividend Data (Dividends have been paid since 1921.)

Amount ($)	Date Decl.	Ex-Div. Date	Stock of Record	Payment Date
0.615	Oct. 28	Nov. 19	Nov. 21	Dec. 19 '97
0.615	Jan. 27	Feb. 18	Feb. 20	Mar. 20 '98
0.615	Apr. 28	May. 20	May. 22	Jun. 19 '98
0.615	Jul. 28	Aug. 19	Aug. 21	Sep. 18 '98

A Division of The **McGraw·Hill** Companies

Business Summary - 13-APR-98

CILCORP (CER) is the holding company for Central Illinois Light Co. (CILCO), which provides electric service to about 193,000 customers and natural gas service to about 202,000 customers in central and east central Illinois. In 1997, the sale of electricity contributed about 35% of CER's revenues and the sale of gas 21%. In 1995, the company formed QST Enterprises, Inc. (QST) to facilitate the company's expansion into non-regulated energy and related service businesses. In 1997, revenues from QST accounted for 35% of the CER's total revenues.

Electric sales in 1997 totaled 6,171,970 kilowatt-hours (kwh), with 37% made to residential, 31% to commercial, 24% to industrial and 8% to other customers. The company uses coal for nearly 100% of its electrical generation. Existing coal contracts with suppliers in central Illinois were expected to supply all of the company's 1998 requirements.

CILCO provides gas service in 128 Illinois communities. In 1997, 38% of CILCO's total operating revenues were derived from the sale and transportation of natural gas. About 60% of gas revenue resulted from residential sales, 24% from commercial sales, 4% from industrial sales, 3% from transportation and 9% from other sales.

In anticipation of the movement toward increased customer choice in the electric and natural gas industries, in 1996 CILCO began Power Quest, which consists of two electric pilot programs and one natural gas pilot retail program, under which certain customers are able to secure part or all of their power requirements from other suppliers.

In 1995, CER formed QST, which provides a portfolio of non-regulated, energy related products and services including wholesale and retail sales of electricity and natural gas in markets that are open to competition. QST also provides fiber optic telecommunication services in Central Illinois. The initial focus of QST was to compete against energy suppliers who participate in the Power Quest programs.

Wholly owned QST Environmental, Inc., which became a subsidiary of QST in October 1996, is an environmental consulting and engineering firm. Its services are intended to address the concern over the quality of the environment, the numerous complex federal, state and local regulations and enforcement efforts in support of environmental laws. Revenues from QST Environmental accounted for about 7% of CER's total revenues in 1997.

Per Share Data ($)

(Year Ended Dec. 31)	1997	1996	1995	1994	1993	1992	1991	1990	1989	1988
Tangible Bk. Val.	25.85	25.30	25.30	24.50	24.41	24.22	24.19	23.23	25.77	24.65
Earnings	0.90	2.07	2.93	2.50	2.60	2.48	3.14	2.69	3.58	3.31
Dividends	2.46	2.46	2.46	2.46	2.46	2.46	2.46	2.46	2.46	2.40
Payout Ratio	273%	119%	84%	98%	95%	99%	80%	90%	69%	72%
Prices - High	49	45¹/₈	44³/₄	37¹/₂	43³/₄	40⁵/₈	38¹/₄	38⁵/₈	39¹/₄	34⁵/₈
- Low	35⁵/₈	35¹/₂	31⁷/₈	28³/₄	35³/₄	33⁵/₈	31	29³/₄	31⁵/₈	29³/₈
P/E Ratio - High	54	22	15	15	17	16	12	14	11	10
- Low	40	17	11	12	14	14	10	11	9	9

Income Statement Analysis (Million $)

	1997	1996	1995	1994	1993	1992	1991	1990	1989	1988
Revs.	976	628	615	605	585	581	590	537	459	471
Depr.	66.7	65.7	63.3	61.1	60.0	57.7	55.4	52.9	48.3	47.3
Maint.	NA	NA	NA	NA	25.6	24.3	25.3	23.8	22.2	21.0
Fxd. Chgs. Cov.	2.8	2.6	3.2	2.8	2.5	2.6	2.6	2.7	2.8	2.8
Constr. Credits	0.1	0.1	-0.5	1.0	0.2	0.3	0.5	0.3	0.2	0.2
Eff. Tax Rate	61%	34%	38%	36%	35%	39%	42%	40%	36%	36%
Net Inc.	9.6	27.9	38.6	32.6	37.6	36.5	44.9	40.8	52.8	49.3

Balance Sheet & Other Fin. Data (Million $)

	1997	1996	1995	1994	1993	1992	1991	1990	1989	1988
Gross Prop.	1,659	1,579	1,523	1,448	1,417	1,370	1,329	1,287	1,250	1,244
Cap. Exp.	61.2	46.7	74.0	95.8	78.3	69.1	63.7	84.7	52.0	45.1
Net Prop.	889	855	840	794	798	778	770	764	750	740
Capitalization:										
LT Debt	299	321	344	327	326	308	325	298	301	326
% LT Debt	42	43	45	44	44	43	44	44	42	45
Pfd.	66.1	66.1	66.1	66.1	66.1	64.6	64.6	64.6	64.6	64.6
% Pfd.	9.20	8.70	8.60	9.00	9.00	9.10	9.00	9.50	9.10	9.00
Common	353	368	362	345	342	339	341	320	348	333
% Common	49	49	47	47	47	48	47	47	49	46
Total Cap.	979	1,013	1,038	1,010	991	1,034	1,053	1,043	1,037	1,025
% Oper. Ratio	93.4	88.0	84.5	86.8	88.9	88.6	89.4	87.1	83.6	84.0
% Earn. on Net Prop.	6.4	8.9	19.6	7.7	7.6	7.5	7.9	8.0	8.1	82.0
% Return On Revs.	1.0	4.4	6.3	5.4	6.4	6.3	7.6	7.6	11.5	10.5
% Return On Invest. Capital	1.2	7.3	9.2	6.1	8.1	8.0	9.6	9.4	10.4	10.0
% Return On Com. Equity	2.7	7.7	10.9	9.5	10.0	9.5	11.8	10.7	14.2	13.7

Data as orig. reptd.; bef. results of disc opers. and/or spec. items. Per share data adj. for stk. divs. as of ex-div. date. Bold denotes diluted EPS (FASB 128). E-Estimated. NA-Not Available. NM-Not Meaningful. NR-Not Ranked.

Office—300 Hamilton Blvd., Suite 300, Peoria, IL 61602. **Registrars**—First of America Trust Co., Peoria; Continental Stock Transfer & Trust Co., NYC. **Tel**—(309) 675-8810. **Fax**—(309) 675-8800. **Pres & CEO**—R. O. Viets. **Exec VP**—W. M. Shay.**VP & Secy**—J. G. Sahn. **Treas**—M. P. Austin. **Dirs**—M. Alexis, J. R. Brazil, W. Bunn III, J. D. Caulder, H. J. Holland, H. S. Peacock, K. E. Smith, R. N. Ullman, R. O. Viets, M. M. Yeomans. **Transfer Agents**—Continental Stock Transfer & Trust Co., NYC; Co.'s office. **Incorporated**—in Illinois in 1913. **Empl**— 1,953. **S&P Analyst:** C.C.P.

Circon Corp. 3534P

NASDAQ Symbol **CCON**

In S&P SmallCap 600

03-OCT-98

Industry:
Health Care (Medical Products & Supplies)

Summary: This company manufactures and markets medical endo-scope and electrosurgery systems for diagnosis and minimally invasive surgery.

Quantitative Evaluations

Outlook
(1 Lowest—5 Highest)
• **NA**

Fair Value
• **NA**

Risk
• **High**

Earn./Div. Rank
• **B-**

Technical Eval.
• **Bearish** since 5/98

Rel. Strength Rank
(1 Lowest—99 Highest)
• **15**

Insider Activity
• **NA**

Recent Price • 9⅜
52 Wk Range • 19⅛-8⅜

Yield • Nil
12-Mo. P/E • 18.9

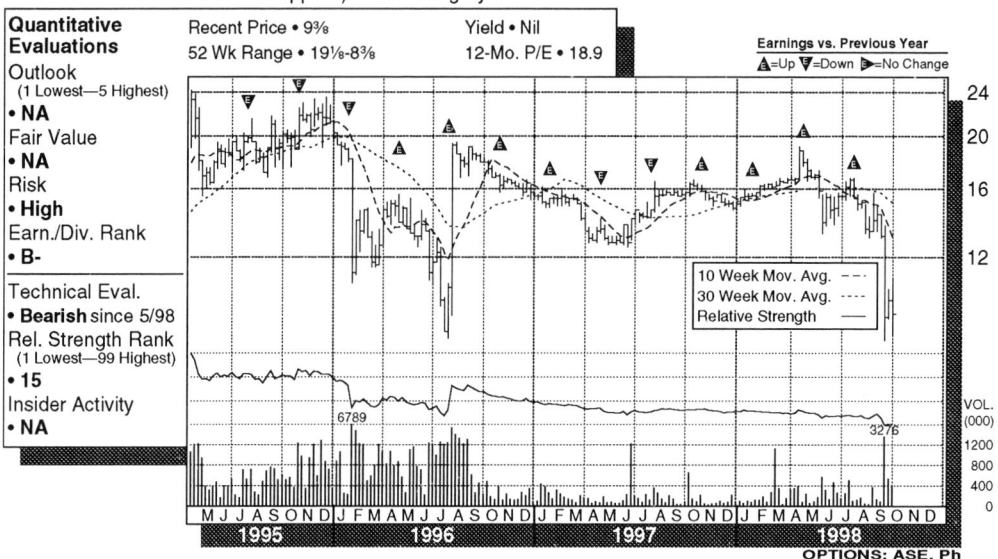

Earnings vs. Previous Year
▲=Up ▼=Down ▶=No Change

10 Week Mov. Avg. – – –
30 Week Mov. Avg. ·······
Relative Strength ——

VOL. (000)

OPTIONS: ASE, Ph

Business Profile - 24-AUG-98

In August 1996, U.S. Surgical (USS) made a hostile tender offer for all of CCON's outstanding common stock for $18 a share. The offer, (currently $16.50 per share), has been extended until September 15, 1998. As of July 1998, 3.8 million CCON shares (29% of outstanding shares) had been tendered to USS. At Circon's 1997 shareholder meeting, nearly 70% of all shareholders supported a sale of Circon to the highest bidder. In connection with a pending lawsuit commenced by USS arising out of the tender offer, Circon has agreed to hold its 1998 annual meeting on or before November 24, 1998, at which time two nominees proposed by USS are up for election. USS currently holds two seats on CCON's seven-member board.

Operational Review - 24-AUG-98

Net sales for the six months ended June 30, 1998, fell 6.7%, year to year. U.S. sales were down 2.6% due to higher than normal sales force turnover, and international sales were 29% lower primarily as a result of a strong U.S. dollar and reduced health care expenditures in the Pacific Rim. Profitability benefited from wider gross margins due to sales mix, improved manufacturing efficiencies and reduced manufacturing overhead, and from lower operating expenses as a result of cost-cutting programs instituted in August 1997. After taxes at 35.0%, in both periods, net income surged 139%, to $2,944,000 ($0.22 per share), from $1,231,000 ($0.09).

Stock Performance - 02-OCT-98

In the past 30 trading days, CCON's shares have declined 29%, compared to a 7% fall in the S&P 500. Average trading volume for the past five days was 75,260 shares, compared with the 40-day moving average of 124,095 shares.

Key Stock Statistics

Dividend Rate/Share	Nil	Shareholders	900
Shs. outstg. (M)	13.4	Market cap. (B)	$0.126
Avg. daily vol. (M)	0.215	Inst. holdings	29%
Tang. Bk. Value/Share	8.06		
Beta	0.82		

Value of $10,000 invested 5 years ago: $ 4,289

Fiscal Year Ending Dec. 31

	1998	1997	1996	1995	1994	1993
Revenues (Million $)						
1Q	36.30	38.40	39.96	37.92	20.83	21.70
2Q	37.25	40.46	37.06	41.83	21.93	20.93
3Q	—	41.30	38.37	42.11	22.47	22.45
4Q	—	40.07	38.39	38.58	23.71	22.30
Yr.	—	159.9	153.8	160.4	88.94	87.30
Earnings Per Share ($)						
1Q	0.09	0.06	0.13	0.05	0.10	0.18
2Q	0.13	0.03	0.05	0.03	0.11	0.02
3Q	—	0.09	-0.11	-0.56	0.14	0.12
4Q	—	0.19	0.09	0.08	0.12	-0.07
Yr.	—	0.37	0.16	-0.41	0.47	0.25

Next earnings report expected: mid October

Dividend Data

No cash has been paid, and Circon's intention is to continue to retain all of its earnings for use in the business.

A Division of The McGraw-Hill Companies

Business Summary - 13-APR-98

CILCORP (CER) is the holding company for Central Illinois Light Co. (CILCO), which provides electric service to about 193,000 customers and natural gas service to about 202,000 customers in central and east central Illinois. In 1997, the sale of electricity contributed about 35% of CER's revenues and the sale of gas 21%. In 1995, the company formed QST Enterprises, Inc. (QST) to facilitate the company's expansion into non-regulated energy and related service businesses. In 1997, revenues from QST accounted for 35% of the CER's total revenues.

Electric sales in 1997 totaled 6,171,970 kilowatt-hours (kwh), with 37% made to residential, 31% to commercial, 24% to industrial and 8% to other customers. The company uses coal for nearly 100% of its electrical generation. Existing coal contracts with suppliers in central Illinois were expected to supply all of the company's 1998 requirements.

CILCO provides gas service in 128 Illinois communities. In 1997, 38% of CILCO's total operating revenues were derived from the sale and transportation of natural gas. About 60% of gas revenue resulted from residential sales, 24% from commercial sales, 4% from industrial sales, 3% from transportation and 9% from other sales.

In anticipation of the movement toward increased customer choice in the electric and natural gas industries, in 1996 CILCO began Power Quest, which consists of two electric pilot programs and one natural gas pilot retail program, under which certain customers are able to secure part or all of their power requirements from other suppliers.

In 1995, CER formed QST, which provides a portfolio of non-regulated, energy related products and services including wholesale and retail sales of electricity and natural gas in markets that are open to competition. QST also provides fiber optic telecommunication services in Central Illinois. The initial focus of QST was to compete against energy suppliers who participate in the Power Quest programs.

Wholly owned QST Environmental, Inc., which became a subsidiary of QST in October 1996, is an environmental consulting and engineering firm. Its services are intended to address the concern over the quality of the environment, the numerous complex federal, state and local regulations and enforcement efforts in support of environmental laws. Revenues from QST Environmental accounted for about 7% of CER's total revenues in 1997.

Per Share Data ($)

(Year Ended Dec. 31)	1997	1996	1995	1994	1993	1992	1991	1990	1989	1988
Tangible Bk. Val.	25.85	25.30	25.30	24.50	24.41	24.22	24.19	23.23	25.77	24.65
Earnings	0.90	2.07	2.93	2.50	2.60	2.48	3.14	2.69	3.58	3.31
Dividends	2.46	2.46	2.46	2.46	2.46	2.46	2.46	2.46	2.46	2.40
Payout Ratio	273%	119%	84%	98%	95%	99%	80%	90%	69%	72%
Prices - High	49	45$^1/_8$	44$^3/_4$	37$^1/_2$	43$^3/_4$	40$^5/_8$	38$^1/_4$	38$^5/_8$	39$^1/_4$	34$^5/_8$
- Low	35$^5/_8$	35$^1/_2$	31$^7/_8$	28$^3/_4$	35$^3/_4$	33$^5/_8$	31	29$^3/_4$	31$^5/_8$	29$^3/_8$
P/E Ratio - High	54	22	15	15	17	16	12	14	11	10
- Low	40	17	11	12	14	14	10	11	9	9

Income Statement Analysis (Million $)

	1997	1996	1995	1994	1993	1992	1991	1990	1989	1988
Revs.	976	628	615	605	585	581	590	537	459	471
Depr.	66.7	65.7	63.3	61.1	60.0	57.7	55.4	52.9	48.3	47.3
Maint.	NA	NA	NA	NA	25.6	24.3	25.3	23.8	22.2	21.0
Fxd. Chgs. Cov.	2.8	2.6	3.2	2.8	2.5	2.6	2.6	2.7	2.8	2.8
Constr. Credits	0.1	0.1	-0.5	1.0	0.2	0.3	0.5	0.3	0.2	0.2
Eff. Tax Rate	61%	34%	38%	36%	35%	39%	42%	40%	36%	36%
Net Inc.	9.6	27.9	38.6	32.6	37.6	36.5	44.9	40.8	52.8	49.3

Balance Sheet & Other Fin. Data (Million $)

	1997	1996	1995	1994	1993	1992	1991	1990	1989	1988
Gross Prop.	1,659	1,579	1,523	1,448	1,417	1,370	1,329	1,287	1,250	1,244
Cap. Exp.	61.2	46.7	74.0	95.8	78.3	69.1	63.7	84.7	52.0	45.1
Net Prop.	889	855	840	794	798	778	770	764	750	740
Capitalization:										
LT Debt	299	321	344	327	326	308	325	298	301	326
% LT Debt	42	43	45	44	44	43	44	44	42	45
Pfd.	66.1	66.1	66.1	66.1	66.1	64.6	64.6	64.6	64.6	64.6
% Pfd.	9.20	8.70	8.60	9.00	9.00	9.10	9.00	9.50	9.10	9.00
Common	353	368	362	345	342	339	341	320	348	333
% Common	49	49	47	47	47	48	47	47	49	46
Total Cap.	979	1,013	1,038	1,010	991	1,034	1,053	1,043	1,037	1,025
% Oper. Ratio	93.4	88.0	84.5	86.8	88.9	88.6	89.4	87.1	83.6	84.0
% Earn. on Net Prop.	6.4	8.9	19.6	7.7	7.6	7.5	7.9	8.0	8.1	82.0
% Return On Revs.	1.0	4.4	6.3	5.4	6.4	6.3	7.6	7.6	11.5	10.5
% Return On Invest. Capital	1.2	7.3	9.2	6.1	8.1	8.0	9.6	9.4	10.4	10.0
% Return On Com. Equity	2.7	7.7	10.9	9.5	10.0	9.5	11.8	10.7	14.2	13.7

Data as orig. reptd.; bef. results of disc opers. and/or spec. items. Per share data adj. for stk. divs. as of ex-div. date. Bold denotes diluted EPS (FASB 128). E-Estimated. NA-Not Available. NM-Not Meaningful. NR-Not Ranked.

Office—300 Hamilton Blvd., Suite 300, Peoria, IL 61602. **Registrars**—First of America Trust Co., Peoria; Continental Stock Transfer & Trust Co., NYC. **Tel**—(309) 675-8810. **Fax**—(309) 675-8800. **Pres & CEO**—R. O. Viets. **Exec VP**—W. M. Shay. **VP & Secy**—J. G. Sahn. **Treas**—M. P. Austin. **Dirs**—M. Alexis, J. R. Brazil, W. Bunn III, J. D. Caulder, H. J. Holland, H. S. Peacock, K. E. Smith, R. N. Ullman, R. O. Viets, M. M. Yeomans. **Transfer Agents**—Continental Stock Transfer & Trust Co., NYC; Co.'s office. **Incorporated**—in Illinois in 1913. **Empl**— 1,953. **S&P Analyst:** C.C.P.

STANDARD &POOR'S
STOCK REPORTS

Circon Corp.

3534P

NASDAQ Symbol **CCON**

In S&P SmallCap 600

03-OCT-98

Industry:
Health Care (Medical Products & Supplies)

Summary: This company manufactures and markets medical endoscope and electrosurgery systems for diagnosis and minimally invasive surgery.

Quantitative Evaluations		
Recent Price • 9⅜	Yield • Nil	
52 Wk Range • 19⅛-8⅜	12-Mo. P/E • 18.9	

Outlook
(1 Lowest—5 Highest)
• **NA**

Fair Value
• **NA**

Risk
• **High**

Earn./Div. Rank
• **B-**

Technical Eval.
• **Bearish** since 5/98

Rel. Strength Rank
(1 Lowest—99 Highest)
• **15**

Insider Activity
• **NA**

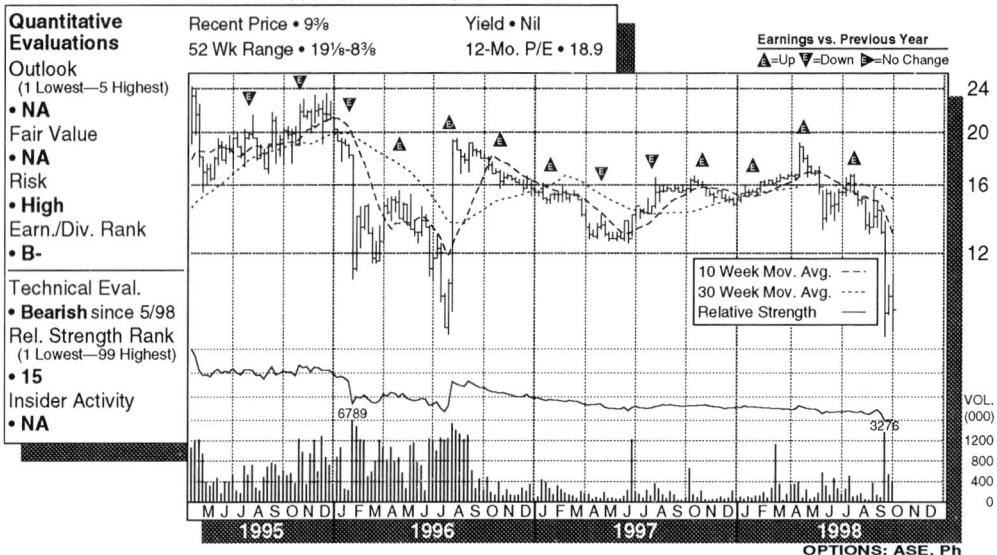

Earnings vs. Previous Year
▲=Up ▼=Down ▷=No Change

10 Week Mov. Avg. - - -
30 Week Mov. Avg. ·····
Relative Strength ——

OPTIONS: ASE, Ph

Business Profile - 24-AUG-98

In August 1996, U.S. Surgical (USS) made a hostile tender offer for all of CCON's outstanding common stock for $18 a share. The offer, (currently $16.50 per share), has been extended until September 15, 1998. As of July 1998, 3.8 million CCON shares (29% of outstanding shares) had been tendered to USS. At Circon's 1997 shareholder meeting, nearly 70% of all shareholders supported a sale of Circon to the highest bidder. In connection with a pending lawsuit commenced by USS arising out of the tender offer, Circon has agreed to hold its 1998 annual meeting on or before November 24, 1998, at which time two nominees proposed by USS are up for election. USS currently holds two seats on CCON's seven-member board.

Operational Review - 24-AUG-98

Net sales for the six months ended June 30, 1998, fell 6.7%, year to year. U.S. sales were down 2.6% due to higher than normal sales force turnover, and international sales were 29% lower primarily as a result of a strong U.S. dollar and reduced health care expenditures in the Pacific Rim. Profitability benefited from wider gross margins due to sales mix, improved manufacturing efficiencies and reduced manufacturing overhead, and from lower operating expenses as a result of cost-cutting programs instituted in August 1997. After taxes at 35.0%, in both periods, net income surged 139%, to $2,944,000 ($0.22 per share), from $1,231,000 ($0.09).

Stock Performance - 02-OCT-98

In the past 30 trading days, CCON's shares have declined 29%, compared to a 7% fall in the S&P 500. Average trading volume for the past five days was 75,260 shares, compared with the 40-day moving average of 124,095 shares.

Key Stock Statistics

Dividend Rate/Share	Nil	Shareholders	900
Shs. outstg. (M)	13.4	Market cap. (B)	$0.126
Avg. daily vol. (M)	0.215	Inst. holdings	29%
Tang. Bk. Value/Share	8.06		
Beta	0.82		

Value of $10,000 invested 5 years ago: $ 4,289

Fiscal Year Ending Dec. 31

	1998	1997	1996	1995	1994	1993
Revenues (Million $)						
1Q	36.30	38.40	39.96	37.92	20.83	21.70
2Q	37.25	40.46	37.06	41.83	21.93	20.93
3Q	—	41.30	38.37	42.11	22.47	22.45
4Q	—	40.07	38.39	38.58	23.71	22.30
Yr.	—	159.9	153.8	160.4	88.94	87.30
Earnings Per Share ($)						
1Q	**0.09**	0.06	0.13	0.05	0.10	0.18
2Q	**0.13**	0.03	0.05	0.03	0.11	0.02
3Q	—	0.09	-0.11	-0.56	0.14	0.12
4Q	—	0.19	0.09	0.08	0.12	-0.07
Yr.	—	0.37	0.16	-0.41	0.47	0.25

Next earnings report expected: mid October

Dividend Data

No cash has been paid, and Circon's intention is to continue to retain all of its earnings for use in the business.

A Division of The McGraw·Hill Companies

STANDARD
&POOR'S
STOCK REPORTS

Circon Corporation

3534P
03-OCT-98

Business Summary - 24-AUG-98

Circon Corporation (CCON) manufactures, markets and services medical endoscope and electrosurgery systems for diagnosis and minimally invasive surgery. The company also designs, assembles and markets miniature color video systems used in endoscope systems. In August 1995, Circon acquired Cabot Medical Corp., a producer and seller of ureteral stents, urological diagnostic equipment and other medical devices, for about 4.3 million shares.

Minimally invasive surgery refers to surgical procedures that can be accomplished without a major incision or other traumatization of the patient. One of the most important minimally invasive surgical techniques is endoscopy, a procedure that utilizes optical instruments inserted into the body either through a natural orifice or through a small incision. In addition to decreasing patient trauma and frequently avoiding general anesthesia, endoscopy can reduce or eliminate postoperative hospitalization. Resulting cost savings and patient benefits have caused government reimbursement programs, as well as private insurance and prepaid health plans, to encourage the use of endoscopic procedures over traditional open surgery.

Circon offers the complete optical-video chain, which combines the use of a medical endoscope system with a medical video system and consists of an endoscope, a miniature color video camera, adapter optics, a high-intensity light source, a fiber-optic light cable, one or more video monitors and a videocassette recorder. The system allows the surgeon to perform procedures viewing a magnified image of the subject organ or tissue on a video monitor, rather than directly through the endoscope eyepiece, thereby reducing surgeon fatigue by alleviating eye and back strain caused by prolonged viewing through the eyepiece of the endoscope and increasing operating room coordination, staff efficiency and motivation by allowing the entire operating room to view the medical procedure.

Circon also offers customers all the separate components constituting the optical-video chain. Other systems and products sold include electrosurgery systems, ureteral stents, and urinary diagnostic, gynecological diagnostic, cryosurgery, tubal ligation and vacuum curettage products. To simplify purchasing decisions, Circon now provides complete packages of products and accessories needed to diagnose and treat patients.

The company's products are sold through 129 direct sales personnel in the U.S. and through 70 local dealers worldwide. International sales accounted for 23% of the total in 1997 and 1996.

In August 1996, Circon's directors rejected U.S. Surgical's initial unsolicited cash tender offer of $18 a share. The offer, currently priced at $16.50 per share, has been extended and expires on September 15, 1998. As of July 1998, U.S. Surgical held about 29% of the outstanding common shares of Circon.

Per Share Data ($) (Year Ended Dec. 31)	1997	1996	1995	1994	1993	1992	1991	1990	1989	1988
Tangible Bk. Val.	5.77	5.19	6.94	9.58	9.11	8.94	8.05	2.90	2.55	2.28
Cash Flow	0.95	0.80	0.22	0.73	0.52	1.00	0.71	0.34	0.25	-0.16
Earnings	0.37	0.16	-0.41	0.47	0.25	0.77	0.45	0.06	-0.02	-0.46
Dividends	Nil	Nil	Nil	Nil	Nil	Nil	Nil	Nil	Nil	Nil
Payout Ratio	Nil	Nil	Nil	Nil	Nil	Nil	Nil	Nil	Nil	Nil
Prices - High	16⅝	20¼	24¼	14¼	22¾	50	33½	11¼	6⅝	5¼
- Low	12½	8½	11	8½	9¾	15¾	10½	4⅜	3½	2⅝
P/E Ratio - High	45	NM	NM	30	91	65	74	NM	NM	NM
- Low	34	NM	NM	18	39	20	23	NM	NM	NM

Income Statement Analysis (Million $)

	1997	1996	1995	1994	1993	1992	1991	1990	1989	1988
Revs.	160	154	160	88.9	87.3	83.5	68.9	54.7	49.5	41.4
Oper. Inc.	18.7	18.0	20.5	7.7	7.2	10.4	7.4	4.3	3.8	0.3
Depr.	7.9	8.6	8.3	2.1	2.1	1.9	1.7	1.6	1.5	1.6
Int. Exp.	4.1	4.2	5.9	0.3	0.0	Nil	0.8	1.7	1.7	1.6
Pretax Inc.	6.5	Nil	-6.4	5.9	3.0	9.3	4.9	1.1	0.4	-2.5
Eff. Tax Rate	22%	NM	NM	35%	32%	32%	38%	72%	NM	NM
Net Inc.	5.1	2.1	-5.4	3.8	2.0	6.3	3.0	0.3	-0.1	-2.4

Balance Sheet & Other Fin. Data (Million $)

	1997	1996	1995	1994	1993	1992	1991	1990	1989	1988
Cash	3.7	7.3	24.1	20.8	22.3	24.0	25.5	0.3	0.1	0.1
Curr. Assets	84.9	80.9	90.8	59.4	58.4	61.4	56.2	24.8	22.9	21.2
Total Assets	169	168	181	95.0	87.5	83.5	75.0	41.9	39.8	38.5
Curr. Liab.	16.6	19.7	35.5	10.8	8.5	8.7	9.1	7.8	10.8	9.4
LT Debt	48.8	50.6	56.4	0.1	Nil	0.3	Nil	14.8	11.7	12.2
Common Eqty.	104	99	87.0	78.6	74.6	72.2	65.2	19.3	17.2	16.8
Total Cap.	153	150	146	84.0	78.4	74.7	66.0	34.1	28.9	29.0
Cap. Exp.	4.9	6.3	12.8	8.3	8.3	5.1	3.1	1.9	1.1	0.8
Cash Flow	13.0	10.7	2.9	5.9	4.2	8.2	4.7	1.9	1.4	-0.9
Curr. Ratio	5.1	4.1	2.6	5.5	6.8	7.1	6.2	3.2	2.1	2.3
% LT Debt of Cap.	31.9	33.8	38.7	0.2	Nil	0.4	Nil	43.5	40.6	42.2
% Net Inc.of Revs.	3.2	1.3	NM	4.3	2.4	7.6	4.4	0.6	NM	NM
% Ret. on Assets	3.0	1.2	NM	4.1	2.4	8.0	4.5	0.8	NM	NM
% Ret. on Equity	5.0	2.2	NM	4.9	2.8	9.2	6.5	1.8	NM	NM

Data as orig. reptd.; bef. results of disc. opers. and/or spec. items. Per share data adj. for stk. divs. as of ex-div. date. Bold denotes diluted EPS (FASB 128). E-Estimated. NA-Not Available. NM-Not Meaningful. NR-Not Ranked.

Office—6500 Hollister Ave., Santa Barbara, CA 93117-3019. **Tel**—(805) 685-5100. **Website**—http//www.Circoncorp.com.**Chrmn, Pres & CEO**—R. A. Auhll. **Exec VP, CFO & Investor Contact**—R. Bruce Thompson. **VP & Secy**—A.D. Simons. **Dirs**—R. Auhill, J. F. Blokker, G. Cloutier, C. M. Elson, H. R. Frank, V. H. Krulak, R. B. Thompson. **Transfer Agent & Registrar**—First Interstate Bank, Los Angeles. **Incorporated**—in California in 1977; reincorporated in Delaware in 1987. **Empl**— 1,204. **S&P Analyst:** John J. Arege

03-OCT-98

Industry: Manufacturing (Diversified)

Summary: This company produces filters and also makes containers and packaging used primarily for consumer products.

Quantitative Evaluations

Outlook (1 Lowest—5 Highest)
- **1**

Fair Value
- **14⅞**

Risk
- **Low**

Earn./Div. Rank
- **B+**

Technical Eval.
- **Bearish** since 3/98

Rel. Strength Rank (1 Lowest—99 Highest)
- **53**

Insider Activity
- **NA**

Recent Price • 15½   Yield • 2.9%
52 Wk Range • 24⅝-14½   12-Mo. P/E • 12.4

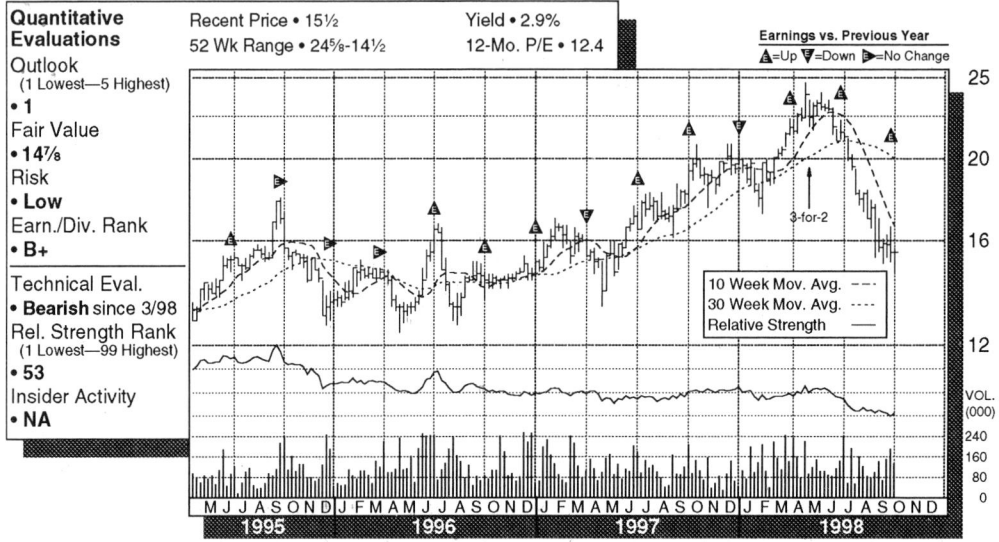

Earnings vs. Previous Year
▲=Up ▼=Down ▶=No Change

10 Week Mov. Avg. ---
30 Week Mov. Avg. .....
Relative Strength —

3-for-2

Business Profile - 20-JUL-98

CLC seeks growth through acquisitions and internal expansion, with emphasis on entry into new markets and product development. Earnings have been in an uptrend since bottoming in FY 92 (Nov.). Earnings edged up in FY 97, on higher sales and operating profit at each of the company's three business segments; however, results were restricted by after tax merger-related charges of $0.15 a share. The dividend rate was increased in FY 97, for the 14th consecutive year. In December 1997, directors authorized the repurchase of up to 1,500,000 (adjusted) common shares. A three-for-two stock split was effected in April 1998.

Operational Review - 20-JUL-98

Net sales in the six months ended May 30, 1998, advanced 12%, year to year, reflecting a 23% gain in the industrial/environmental filtration segment, and a 9.7% rise in engine/mobile filtration sales. Gross margins widened on the increased volume, and although selling and administrative expenses were up, in the absence of merger-related expenses of $3.0 million, net income rose 34%, to $13,367,000 ($0.54 a diluted share), from $10,065,000 ($0.41, adjusted). Although management anticipates improved results for FY 98 overall, plans are in place to curtail certain discretionary spending in the event the recent softening in export sales to Europe and Asia continues.

Stock Performance - 02-OCT-98

In the past 30 trading days, CLC's shares have declined 11%, compared to a 7% fall in the S&P 500. Average trading volume for the past five days was 26,540 shares, compared with the 40-day moving average of 23,954 shares.

Key Stock Statistics

Dividend Rate/Share	0.45	Shareholders	1,800
Shs. outstg. (M)	24.4	Market cap. (B)	$0.379
Avg. daily vol. (M)	0.027	Inst. holdings	53%
Tang. Bk. Value/Share	6.62		
Beta	0.78		

Value of $10,000 invested 5 years ago: $ 14,265

Fiscal Year Ending Nov. 30

	1998	1997	1996	1995	1994	1993
Revenues (Million $)						
1Q	97.79	86.96	72.08	62.14	55.89	41.91
2Q	107.3	96.68	81.57	70.48	65.13	49.73
3Q	110.1	104.6	88.93	71.83	67.72	64.63
4Q	—	106.0	90.81	85.75	81.38	69.04
Yr.	—	394.3	333.4	290.2	270.1	225.3
Earnings Per Share ($)						
1Q	**0.21**	0.13	0.18	0.18	0.15	0.14
2Q	**0.33**	0.29	0.26	0.22	0.19	0.13
3Q	**0.35**	0.33	0.29	0.27	0.27	0.23
4Q	—	0.36	0.39	0.32	0.32	0.28
Yr.	—	1.11	1.12	0.99	0.93	0.77

Next earnings report expected: late January

Dividend Data (Dividends have been paid since 1921.)

Amount ($)	Date Decl.	Ex-Div. Date	Stock of Record	Payment Date
0.165	Mar. 24	Apr. 07	Apr. 10	Apr. 24 '98
3-for-2	Mar. 24	Apr. 27	Apr. 10	Apr. 24 '98
0.110	Jun. 22	Jul. 15	Jul. 17	Jul. 31 '98
0.113	Sep. 23	Oct. 14	Oct. 16	Oct. 30 '98

A Division of The **McGraw·Hill** *Companies*

STANDARD
&POOR'S
STOCK REPORTS

CLARCOR Inc.

547

03-OCT-98

Business Summary - 20-JUL-98

This diversified maker of filtration and packaging products is seeking a better balance in its filtration business, which accounts for over 80% of its revenues. The filtration unit's business is currently dominated by engine-related products, but CLARCOR Inc. (CLC) wants to diversify its product mix by pursuing opportunities in industrial and environmental air filtration, the company's fastest growing area. The February 1997 acquisition of United Air Specialists, Inc., a maker of commercial and industrial air cleaners with 1996 sales of $41 million, was a step in that direction, and also meshed with other key strategies.

CLC operates in three segments: Engine/Mobile Filtration, Industrial/Environmental Filtration; and Consumer Packaging. Through the first half of FY 98 (Nov.), the engine division accounted for 53% of revenues, while 31% came from the industrial segment and 15% from consumer packaging.

United Air Specialists (UAS) complements the business of CLC's Airguard Industries subsidiary, whose air filter cartridges are used in dust collectors made by UAS. The company can now provide customers a full product offering, from installation of a complete air cleaning system to aftermarket filter replacements. Other synergistic benefits hoped for include additional engineering muscle to design and build gas turbine filtration systems (a new area for the company), and fresh expertise in telemarketing, which can be applied elsewhere in the organization. The UAS acquisition also presents the company with opportunities to grow sales in Europe, where UAS has operations, and other foreign markets, where CLC's existing capabilities could help UAS.

Encouraged by the size and growth of its overseas markets, the company hopes to increase international sales to 25% of total sales by the year 2000.

Filtration products (81% of FY 97 sales) include filters for oil, air, fuel, coolants and hydraulic fluids used in trucks, automobiles, construction and industrial equipment, locomotives and other engine/mobile applications; and air and antimicrobial treated filters for industrial or environmental applications such as commercial and residential buildings, factories, paint spray booths, gas turbine systems and dust collector systems.

CLC's other business is packaging products (19%), which include lithographed metal containers, engineered plastic containers and closures and collapsible metal tubes.

In February 1998, CLC acquired Air Technologies, Inc., a Kansas manufacturer of air filtration products, for an undisclosed amount of cash.

Per Share Data ($)

(Year Ended Nov. 30)	1997	1996	1995	1994	1993	1992	1991	1990	1989	1988
Tangible Bk. Val.	6.41	5.87	5.21	4.62	4.00	3.86	3.35	2.75	2.22	3.65
Cash Flow	1.60	1.56	1.36	1.25	1.06	0.97	1.16	1.27	0.59	1.03
Earnings	1.11	1.12	0.99	0.93	0.77	0.73	0.83	0.91	0.31	0.77
Dividends	0.43	0.43	0.42	0.41	0.41	0.40	0.37	0.35	0.32	0.30
Payout Ratio	39%	38%	43%	45%	52%	55%	44%	38%	91%	39%
Prices - High	20$7/8$	16$3/4$	18	14$7/8$	14$1/8$	15	15$1/8$	11$7/8$	12$5/8$	9$3/4$
- Low	13$3/8$	12$3/8$	12$3/8$	10$5/8$	10$5/8$	10	9$3/8$	7$7/8$	7$1/8$	7$1/2$
P/E Ratio - High	19	15	18	16	18	20	18	13	40	13
- Low	12	11	13	11	14	14	11	9	25	10

Income Statement Analysis (Million $)

Revs.	394	333	290	270	225	180	180	215	204	202
Oper. Inc.	59.0	50.3	43.6	39.7	35.4	32.0	38.2	41.6	35.8	38.8
Depr.	11.6	9.8	8.2	7.3	6.3	5.4	7.3	7.8	7.1	7.0
Int. Exp.	2.8	3.2	2.7	2.8	3.5	3.8	3.7	3.7	1.4	0.2
Pretax Inc.	44.2	40.0	34.1	32.6	27.1	25.3	28.5	32.6	19.0	33.1
Eff. Tax Rate	39%	37%	36%	37%	36%	35%	35%	37%	58%	38%
Net Inc.	26.9	25.0	22.0	20.6	17.3	16.5	18.5	20.4	7.9	20.6

Balance Sheet & Other Fin. Data (Million $)

Cash	30.3	17.4	18.8	19.6	13.8	15.1	9.6	14.8	4.8	20.9
Curr. Assets	161	125	118	99	86.2	93.6	75.2	72.6	58.0	70.0
Total Assets	283	244	223	188	170	161	158	144	131	144
Curr. Liab.	54.2	45.0	42.5	39.5	23.3	25.3	20.6	20.8	21.4	14.2
LT Debt	37.7	35.5	34.4	17.0	24.6	29.3	35.8	35.8	32.6	1.1
Common Eqty.	171	146	131	117	105	100	96.0	83.0	73.0	125
Total Cap.	219	191	171	140	133	132	137	123	110	130
Cap. Exp.	11.3	21.7	13.9	11.4	17.9	6.6	8.1	8.6	8.3	6.1
Cash Flow	38.5	34.8	30.2	27.9	23.5	21.9	25.8	28.2	15.1	27.6
Curr. Ratio	3.0	2.8	2.8	2.5	2.6	3.7	3.7	3.5	2.7	4.9
% LT Debt of Cap.	17.2	18.7	20.1	12.1	18.4	22.1	26.1	29.0	29.8	0.9
% Net Inc.of Revs.	6.8	7.5	7.6	7.6	7.7	8.8	10.3	9.5	3.9	10.2
% Ret. on Assets	10.2	10.7	10.7	11.5	10.5	10.3	12.2	14.9	6.3	14.9
% Ret. on Equity	17.0	18.0	17.7	18.6	17.0	16.9	20.7	26.4	8.9	17.3

Data as orig. reptd.; bef. results of disc. opers. and/or spec. items. Per share data adj. for stk. divs. as of ex-div. date. Bold denotes diluted EPS (FASB 128). E-Estimated. NA-Not Available. NM-Not Meaningful. NR-Not Ranked.

Office—2323 Sixth St., P.O. Box 7007, Rockford, IL 61125. **Tel**—(815) 962-8867. **Chrmn, CEO & Investor Contact**—Lawrence E. Gloyd. **Pres & COO**—N. E. Johnson. **VP-Fin & CFO**—B. A. Klein. **VP & Treas**—W. F. Knese. **VP & Secy**—M. S. Blaylock. **Dirs**—J. M. Adam, M. R. Brown, C. J. Dargene, L. E. Gloyd, D. J. Godfrey Jr., N. E. Johnson, J. L. Packard, S. K. Smith Jr., D. A. Wolf. **Transfer Agent & Registrar**—First Chicago Trust Co. of New York, Jersey City, NJ. **Incorporated**—in Delaware in 1969. **Empl**—2,872. **S&P Analyst**: S.S.

Coca-Cola Bottling Co. Consol. 3553K
NASDAQ Symbol **COKE**
In S&P SmallCap 600

03-OCT-98

Industry:
Beverages
(Non-Alcoholic)

Summary: This company is engaged in bottling, canning and marketing carbonated soft drinks, primarily products of The Coca-Cola Co., in the Southeast.

Quantitative Evaluations

Recent Price • 58¼
52 Wk Range • 75¾-56

Yield • 1.7%
12-Mo. P/E • 38.1

Outlook
(1 Lowest—5 Highest)
• **1**

Fair Value
• **50¼**

Risk
• **Low**

Earn./Div. Rank
• **B**

Technical Eval.
• **Bearish** since 9/98

Rel. Strength Rank
(1 Lowest—99 Highest)
• **59**

Insider Activity
• **NA**

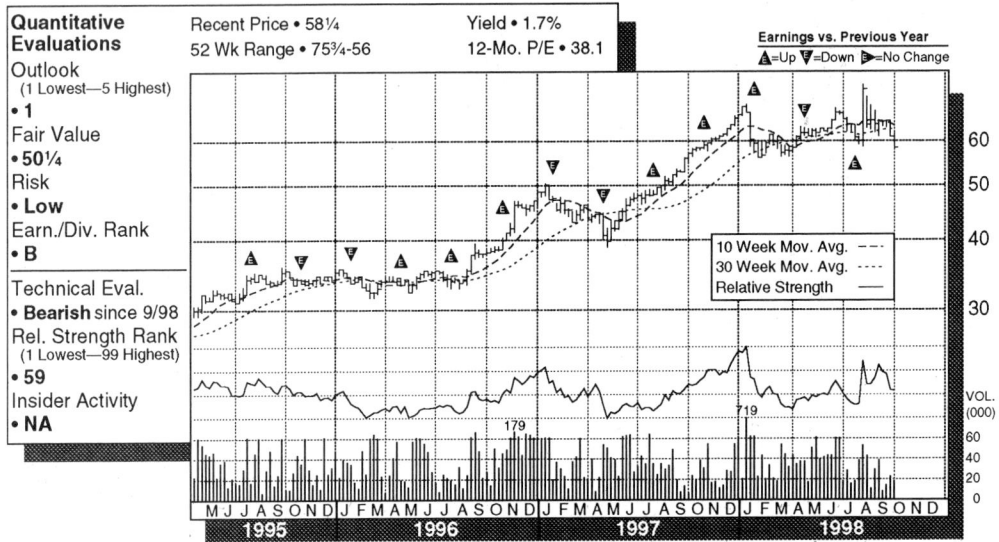

Earnings vs. Previous Year
△=Up ▽=Down ▶=No Change

10 Week Mov. Avg. — — —
30 Week Mov. Avg. - - - -
Relative Strength ——

Business Profile - 10-SEP-98

Over the past decade, COKE has experienced dramatic sales growth, posting volume gains of more than 250%. This growth was fueled by acquisitions as well as stronger per capita consumption of its products in relation to the industry. As a result, current annualized revenues exceed $900 million, up from $328 million in 1988, and sales volume has vaulted from 78 million equivalent cases to 200 million cases. In continuing with its acquisition strategy, the company acquired St. Paul Coca-Cola Bottling Company (in Virginia) and Coca-Cola Bottling Company Southeast (in Alabama and Tennessee) in the first half of 1998.

Operational Review - 10-SEP-98

Net sales in the first half of 1998 rose 15%, year to year, reflecting a 13% increase in franchise volume and an 18% advance in fountain volume, partially offset by a 1.0% decline in net prices. Margins narrowed, impacted by the lower prices, higher selling expenses and greater employment costs to support expansion; operating income fell 0.9%. Following higher depreciation and amortization charges, and after taxes at 37.1%, versus 37.0%, net income fell 25%, to $6,927,000 ($0.82 a share), from $9,245,000 ($1.08).

Stock Performance - 02-OCT-98

In the past 30 trading days, COKE's shares have declined 11%, compared to a 7% fall in the S&P 500. Average trading volume for the past five days was 3,580 shares, compared with the 40-day moving average of 4,695 shares.

Key Stock Statistics

Dividend Rate/Share	1.00	Shareholders	2,400
Shs. outstg. (M)	8.4	Market cap. (B)	$0.410
Avg. daily vol. (M)	0.003	Inst. holdings	28%
Tang. Bk. Value/Share	NM		
Beta	0.32		

Value of $10,000 invested 5 years ago: $ 36,586

Fiscal Year Ending Dec. 31

	1998	1997	1996	1995	1994	1993
Revenues (Million $)						
1Q	203.3	178.4	172.0	171.0	163.8	154.3
2Q	241.4	208.2	213.6	207.9	200.7	194.5
3Q	—	219.1	204.6	203.6	188.4	182.2
4Q	—	196.5	183.6	179.5	171.0	156.0
Yr.	—	802.1	773.8	761.9	723.9	687.0
Earnings Per Share ($)						
1Q	-0.29	0.01	0.10	0.21	0.16	0.15
2Q	1.11	1.08	1.03	0.87	0.72	0.65
3Q	—	0.78	0.70	0.50	0.53	0.62
4Q	—	-0.07	-0.09	0.09	0.11	0.18
Yr.	—	1.79	1.74	1.67	1.52	1.60

Next earnings report expected: late October

Dividend Data (Dividends have been paid since 1967.)

Amount ($)	Date Decl.	Ex-Div. Date	Stock of Record	Payment Date
0.250	Nov. 04	Nov. 19	Nov. 21	Dec. 05 '97
0.250	Feb. 03	Feb. 18	Feb. 20	Mar. 06 '98
0.250	May. 05	May. 20	May. 22	Jun. 05 '98
0.250	Aug. 04	Aug. 19	Aug. 21	Sep. 04 '98

A Division of The McGraw-Hill Companies

Business Summary - 10-SEP-98

Coca-Cola Bottling Co. Consolidated holds franchises under which it bottles, cans and markets carbonated soft drinks, primarily products of The Coca-Cola Co. Prior to 1984, the company's business was concentrated in North Carolina, but, through a major expansion program, its operating territory has been extended to an 11-state area in the Southeast, covering a franchise territory of approximately 12.3 million people. Major markets include North Carolina, South Alabama, South Georgia, middle Tennessee, Western Virginia, and West Virginia. In addition, South Carolina is covered through a joint venture.

COKE's franchises from The Coca-Cola Company allow it to produce and market Coca-Cola Co. soft drinks in bottles, cans and five gallon, pressurized, pre-mix containers. Products under franchise from The Coca-Cola Company include Coca-Cola classic, caffeine free Coca-Cola classic, diet Coke, caffeine free diet Coke, Cherry Coke, TAB, Sprite, diet Sprite, Surge, Mello Yellow, diet Mello Yellow, Mr. PiBB, Barq's Root Beer, Fresca, Minute Maid orange and diet Minute Maid orange sodas. In addition, the company also distributes and markets POWERaDE, Cool from Nestea, Fruitopia, Minute Maid Juices To Go and LeBlue water in certain of its markets. Also, in most of its regions, the company produces and markets Dr Pepper.

In 1997, products of The Coca-Cola Co. accounted for 90% of soft drink sales. A majority of total sales are through the "take-home market" (supermarkets, convenience stores and other retail outlets); the remaining sales were made in the "cold drink market" (primarily vending machines).

Piedmont Coca-Cola Bottling Partnership (formed in July 1993) is an equally owned joint venture with Coca-Cola Co. It produces and markets soft drink products in certain North and South Carolina bottling territories. COKE provides a majority of the soft drink products to Piedmont and receives a fee for managing the business.

During the past several years, COKE has attempted to concentrate its soft drink production into fewer facilities for efficiency and to meet changing market conditions. At the end of 1997, COKE had four production facilities and 55 distribution centers.

Per Share Data ($)

(Year Ended Dec. 31)	1997	1996	1995	1994	1993	1992	1991	1990	1989	1988
Tangible Bk. Val.	NA	NM	NM	-31.61	-33.39	-56.60	-40.28	-12.94	-10.26	-10.19
Cash Flow	7.20	6.13	5.87	5.45	5.71	4.19	3.47	3.19	2.70	2.85
Earnings	1.79	1.74	1.67	1.52	1.60	-0.23	0.24	-0.02	-0.32	-0.23
Dividends	1.00	1.00	1.00	1.00	0.88	0.88	0.88	0.88	0.88	0.88
Payout Ratio	56%	57%	60%	66%	55%	NM	366%	NM	NM	NM
Prices - High	69	48³/₄	35⁷/₈	37¹/₄	41¹/₂	20³/₄	26¹/₂	25	32¹/₂	34
- Low	38³/₄	31¹/₂	26	24	17	15¹/₄	16¹/₄	15	22	20¹/₄
P/E Ratio - High	39	28	21	25	26	NM	NM	NM	NM	NM
- Low	22	18	16	16	11	NM	NM	NM	NM	NM

Income Statement Analysis (Million $)

	1997	1996	1995	1994	1993	1992	1991	1990	1989	1988
Revs.	802	774	762	724	687	656	465	431	384	328
Oper. Inc.	109	101	101	92.2	95.3	84.4	56.6	59.3	51.3	49.3
Depr.	46.0	40.8	39.0	36.5	38.1	40.5	29.7	29.5	27.5	25.0
Int. Exp.	37.5	30.4	33.1	31.4	31.0	36.9	21.6	24.1	24.7	23.5
Pretax Inc.	24.3	26.0	25.2	24.4	24.0	4.9	3.0	2.2	-2.5	-1.0
Eff. Tax Rate	37%	37%	38%	42%	38%	57%	0.70%	90%	NM	NM
Net Inc.	15.3	16.2	15.5	14.1	14.8	2.1	2.9	0.2	-2.9	-1.8

Balance Sheet & Other Fin. Data (Million $)

	1997	1996	1995	1994	1993	1992	1991	1990	1989	1988
Cash	4.4	2.9	2.4	1.8	1.3	1.4	1.0	3.2	3.4	1.7
Curr. Assets	127	111	70.3	59.6	58.4	49.2	59.5	35.5	36.9	49.6
Total Assets	778	702	677	664	648	786	785	468	449	400
Curr. Liab.	107	76.7	89.6	78.2	81.9	66.1	72.6	46.8	39.6	35.0
LT Debt	494	439	420	433	434	555	479	238	230	217
Common Eqty.	9.3	22.3	39.0	34.0	30.0	26.0	155	161	167	137
Total Cap.	615	570	556	556	544	691	696	409	400	357
Cap. Exp.	100	30.0	37.0	49.0	29.0	33.0	24.0	16.0	26.0	17.0
Cash Flow	61.3	56.9	54.5	50.6	52.9	38.4	31.9	29.3	24.6	23.2
Curr. Ratio	1.2	1.4	0.9	0.8	0.7	0.7	0.8	0.8	0.9	1.4
% LT Debt of Cap.	80.3	77.1	75.5	77.8	79.8	80.4	68.9	58.0	57.5	60.7
% Net Inc.of Revs.	1.9	2.1	2.0	2.0	2.2	0.3	0.6	0.1	NM	NM
% Ret. on Assets	2.1	2.3	2.3	2.2	2.1	0.3	0.5	0.1	NM	NM
% Ret. on Equity	96.8	52.8	42.7	44.5	53.2	NM	1.4	NM	NM	NM

Data as orig. reptd.; bef. results of disc. opers. and/or spec. items. Per share data adj. for stk. divs. as of ex-div. date. Bold denotes diluted EPS (FASB 128). E-Estimated. NA-Not Available. NM-Not Meaningful. NR-Not Ranked.

Reincorporated—in Delaware in 1980. **Office**—1900 Rexford Rd., Charlotte, NC 28211. **Tel**—(704) 551-4400. **Chrmn & CEO**—J. F. Harrison III. **Vice-Chrmn**—R. M. Henson. **Pres & COO**—J. L. Moore, Jr. **VP-CFO & Investor Contact**—D. V. Singer. **VP & Treas**—W. B. Elmore. **Secy**—J. F. Henry, Jr. **Dirs**—J. M. Belk, J. F. Harrison III, R. M. Henson, E. Holyfield, H. R. Jones, Jr., H. W. McKay Belk, N. McWherter, J. L. Moore, J. W. Murrey III, C. L. Wallace. **Transfer Agent**—First Union National Bank, Charlotte. **Empl**— 5,500. **S&P Analyst:** R.J.I.

Coeur d'Alene Mines   564

NYSE Symbol **CDE**

In S&P SmallCap 600

03-OCT-98

Industry:
Gold & Precious Metals
Mining

Summary: Based in Coeur d'Alene, Idaho, this company is a leading producer of silver and gold, with controlling interests in mines in Nevada, Chile and New Zealand.

S&P Opinion: Accumulate (★★★★)	Recent Price • 7⅛	Yield • Nil
	52 Wk Range • 16-4	12-Mo. P/E • NM

Quantitative Evaluations

Outlook
(1 Lowest—5 Highest)
• **NA**

Fair Value
• **NA**

Risk
• **Average**

Earn./Div. Rank
• **C**

Technical Eval.
• **NA**

Rel. Strength Rank
(1 Lowest—99 Highest)
• **96**

Insider Activity
• **NA**

Earnings vs. Previous Year
▲=Up ▼=Down ▶=No Change

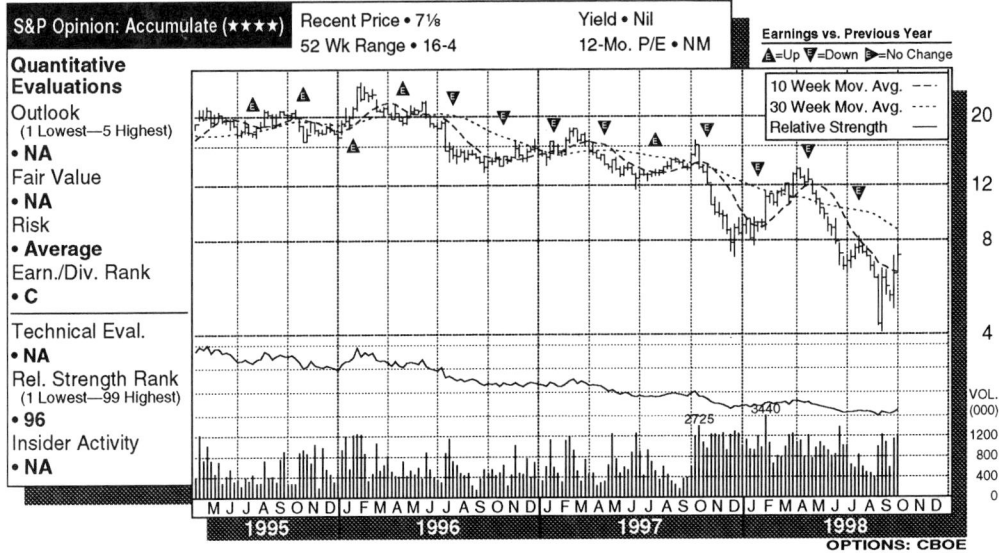

10 Week Mov. Avg. – – –
30 Week Mov. Avg. ·····
Relative Strength ——

OPTIONS: CBOE

Overview - 19-AUG-98

The second quarter loss exceeded the consensus estimate of $0.13 due to a decline in both silver and gold production and higher costs. The decline in output resulted from previously announced mine closures, lower production at the Rochester mine due to heavy rainfall and a special project at Fachinal. Gold production will drop substantially in 1998 due to sharply lower production from Golden Cross and suspension of operations at El Bronce. Silver output should approximate 1997's 11.0 million oz.

Valuation - 19-AUG-98

Despite disappointing results so far in 1998, we still rate CDE accumulate because of attractive silver market fundamentals. We view CDE as a proxy for the metal. CDE has higher costs than its two main silver competitors, partly reflecting operations at two gold mines. Also, investors remain deeply skeptical about the viability of the Kensington project. But CDE is the nation's leading primary silver producer and we believe investor interest in silver stocks will ultimately outweigh concerns over CDE's cost position and the outcome of Kensington. CDE will benefit from stronger silver market fundamentals. Notwithstanding the immense volatility thus far in 1998, we believe the trend in silver prices is higher. According to The Silver Institute, silver consumption in 1997 exceeded supply from mine production and recycled scrap by 198 million oz. Thus, for the ninth consecutive year, above ground silver stocks were liquidated in 1997 to help bridge the chronic gap between primary and secondary supplies and fabrication demand. We believe this liquidation has continued in 1998, albeit at a slower rate. As of mid-August 1998, silver supplies on the Comex stood at 78.9 million oz., versus 203.5 million oz. at 1996 year end and 110.7 million oz. at the end of 1997.

Key Stock Statistics

S&P EPS Est. 1998	-3.50	Tang. Bk. Value/Share	11.27
P/E on S&P Est. 1998	NM	Beta	1.51
S&P EPS Est. 1999	-0.50	Shareholders	7,900
Dividend Rate/Share	Nil	Market cap. (B)	$0.157
Shs. outstg. (M)	21.9	Inst. holdings	43%
Avg. daily vol. (M)	0.231		

Value of $10,000 invested 5 years ago: $ 6,400

Fiscal Year Ending Dec. 31

	1998	1997	1996	1995	1994	1993
Revenues (Million $)						
1Q	21.17	24.67	22.61	17.89	22.90	11.98
2Q	32.26	33.66	18.75	23.62	22.29	18.66
3Q	—	38.63	21.56	24.80	23.53	22.60
4Q	—	42.28	29.81	22.93	22.31	26.56
Yr.	—	139.0	92.73	89.24	91.02	83.72
Earnings Per Share ($)						
1Q	-2.77	-0.20	-0.02	-0.21	-0.17	-0.13
2Q	-0.36	-0.13	-2.75	0.08	-0.09	-0.07
3Q	E-0.20	-0.41	-0.03	0.13	0.11	-0.68
4Q	E-0.17	-0.39	-0.11	-0.08	-0.11	0.01
Yr.	E-3.50	-1.12	-2.93	-0.08	-0.26	-0.87

Next earnings report expected: mid November

Dividend Data

Cash dividends, initiated in 1988 and paid annually, were omitted in March 1997. A "poison pill" stock purchase rights plan was adopted in 1989.

A Division of The **McGraw·Hill** Companies

Business Summary - 19-AUG-98

Coeur d'Alene, the largest primary silver producer in the U.S., also mines and explores for gold. CDE's main strategy for achieving reserve and production growth is to seek exploration and acquisition opportunities in politically stable countries having mining traditions. Because of its strong confidence in the long-term fundamentals for gold and silver, CDE engages in only a limited amount of hedging or forward sales of production.

The Kensington gold project, located in Juneau, AK, is CDE's principal development project. The company estimates Kensington has gold reserves of 1,896,000 oz. and will produce at a rate of about 200,000 oz. a year. In April 1998 CDE received the necessary permits for construction of the mine. Construction and commercialization of the mine is subject to the results of an optimization study currently being undertaken to reduce costs and improve the economic viability of the mine.

The following table presents significant operating and reserve data for recent years (reserves at year end.)

	1997	1996	1995
Gold production	290,962	214,130	167,985
Gold reserves	3,100,000	3,400,000	3,500,000
Silver production	11,024,225	9,520,009	7,200,000
Silver reserves	99,000,000	109,000,000	124,400,000

CDE's 100%-owned Rochester silver-gold mine in Nevada is one of North America's largest and lowest cost silver producing mines. Silver production totaled 6.69

million oz. in 1997, versus 6.25 million oz. in 1006 and 6.48 million oz. in 1995; gold production was 90,019 oz. in 1997, versus 74,293 oz. in 1996. At year-end 1997, Rochester's proven and probable reserves stood at 74.2 million oz. of silver and 603,000 oz. of gold, versus 80.5 million oz. of silver and 696,000 oz. of gold at 1996's year end,

CDE's 80%-owned Golden Cross mine (New Zealand) produced 83,110 oz. of gold in 1997 and 217,776 oz. of silver, versus 64,365 oz. of gold and 205,070 oz. of silver in 1996. There will be small residual production in 1998 as mining operations will cease.

In January 1995, CDE, ASARCO Inc. and Callahan Mining formed Silver Valley Resources by combining their interests in the Galena and Coeur mines. Operations began at the Coeur mine in May 1996 and output totaled 833,267 oz. of silver at a $3.18/oz. cash cost. Production totaled 1,717,357 oz. in 1997 at a cash cost of $3.74/oz.

CDE's Fachinal mine (Chile) became operational in November 1995. Fachinal mined 30,601 oz. of gold in 1997 and 2,243,761 oz. of silver, versus 25,064 oz. of gold in 1996 and 2,154,347 oz. of silver.

In 1998's third quarter, CDE repurchased some $3.8 million of its 6% convertible debentures due 2002 and some $23 million of the 7.25% convertible debentures due 2005. As a result, interest expense will decline by some $1.9 million annually and CDE will realize an extraordinary net gain of some $6.3 million in 1998's third quarter.

Per Share Data ($)

(Year Ended Dec. 31)	1997	1996	1995	1994	1993	1992	1991	1990	1989	1988
Tangible Bk. Val.	13.99	15.31	11.49	10.29	11.14	11.81	12.01	13.86	12.04	11.26
Cash Flow	0.50	-2.31	0.98	0.90	-0.03	0.30	-0.48	0.50	1.94	2.12
Earnings	-1.12	-2.93	-0.08	-0.26	-0.87	-0.05	-0.94	-0.17	0.94	1.45
Dividends	Nil	0.15	0.15	0.15	0.15	0.15	0.15	0.15	0.15	0.10
Payout Ratio	Nil	NM	NM	NM	NM	NM	NM	NM	16%	7%
Prices - High	18³/₈	25³/₄	21⁵/₈	23¹/₂	24⁵/₈	18³/₈	23	31	24¹/₈	22¹/₈
- Low	7	13¹/₄	14¹/₂	14³/₈	9⁷/₈	10⁷/₈	13³/₈	13³/₈	15¹/₂	15
P/E Ratio - High	NM	NM	NM	NM	NM	NM	NM	NM	26	15
- Low	NM	NM	NM	NM	NM	NM	NM	NM	16	10

Income Statement Analysis (Million $)

	1997	1996	1995	1994	1993	1992	1991	1990	1989	1988
Revs.	139	93.0	89.0	91.0	78.2	51.5	59.2	52.1	69.3	78.2
Oper. Inc.	10.7	2.5	16.1	13.5	5.4	-2.9	-1.3	5.6	15.9	26.5
Depr.	35.6	13.4	16.9	17.8	12.9	5.4	7.0	7.0	10.0	9.5
Int. Exp.	10.3	3.6	9.7	15.6	9.3	4.1	3.9	4.0	4.3	4.6
Pretax Inc.	-14.3	-55.8	-1.1	-3.7	-16.7	-4.5	-15.0	-2.7	10.7	20.2
Eff. Tax Rate	NM	NM	NM	NM	NM	NM	NM	NM	12%	24%
Net Inc.	-14.1	-54.6	-1.3	-3.9	-13.3	-0.8	-14.4	-1.7	9.4	15.4

Balance Sheet & Other Fin. Data (Million $)

	1997	1996	1995	1994	1993	1992	1991	1990	1989	1988
Cash	114	168	81.8	143	85.0	156	111	105	80.0	80.0
Curr. Assets	260	211	127	192	129	192	145	138	102	96.0
Total Assets	661	580	446	413	326	325	262	239	196	191
Curr. Liab.	38.5	32.0	21.0	18.5	21.6	9.8	14.2	9.9	9.5	9.5
LT Debt	290	190	174	227	129	131	58.0	60.0	61.0	63.0
Common Eqty.	315	339	240	160	171	181	184	166	120	112
Total Cap.	615	406	415	389	302	315	246	229	186	180
Cap. Exp.	2.9	4.8	44.9	33.3	68.6	21.5	16.7	17.9	12.7	36.7
Cash Flow	11.0	-49.6	15.6	13.9	-0.4	4.7	-7.4	5.2	19.4	24.9
Curr. Ratio	6.8	6.6	6.0	10.4	6.0	19.5	10.3	13.9	10.8	10.1
% LT Debt of Cap.	47.2	46.8	42.0	58.4	42.8	41.6	23.5	26.0	33.0	34.9
% Net Inc.of Revs.	NM	NM	NM	NM	NM	NM	NM	NM	13.6	19.7
% Ret. on Assets	NM	NM	NM	NM	NM	NM	NM	NM	4.9	8.4
% Ret. on Equity	NM	NM	NM	NM	NM	NM	NM	NM	8.1	15.0

Data as orig. reptd.; bef. results of disc. opers. and/or spec. items. Per share data adj. for stk. divs. as of ex-div. date. Bold denotes diluted EPS (FASB 128). E-Estimated. NA-Not Available. NM-Not Meaningful. NR-Not Ranked.

Office—P.O. Box I, Coeur d'Alene, ID 83816-0316. **Tel**—(208) 667-3511. **Fax**—(208) 667-2213. **Website**—http://www.coeur.com **Chrmn, Pres & CEO**—D. E. Wheeler. **SVP & COO**—M. L. Clark. **VP, CFO & Treas**—K. L. Packard. **Secy**—R. Gardner. **VP & Investor Contact**—Jack Kucera. **Dirs**—C. D. Andrus, J. C. Bennett, J. J. Curran, D. B. Hagadone, J. A. McClure, J. H. Robinson, D. E. Wheeler. **Transfer Agent & Registrar**—ChaseMellon Shareholder Services, L.L.C., Ridgefield Park, NJ. **Incorporated**—in Idaho in 1928. **Empl**— 949. **S&P Analyst:** Leo J. Larkin

Cognex Corp.
3557C
Nasdaq Symbol CGNX
In S&P SmallCap 600

03-OCT-98

Industry: Manufacturing (Specialized)

Summary: This company designs, develops, manufactures and markets a family of machine vision systems used to gauge, guide, inspect and identify products in manufacturing operations.

S&P Opinion: Hold (★★★)	Recent Price • 11⅜	Yield • Nil
	52 Wk Range • 36-9	12-Mo. P/E • 12.1

Earnings vs. Previous Year
▲=Up ▼=Down ▶=No Change

Quantitative Evaluations

Outlook (1 Lowest—5 Highest)
• **5+**

Fair Value
• **19¼**

Risk
• **High**

Earn./Div. Rank
• **B+**

Technical Eval.
• **Bearish** since 11/97

Rel. Strength Rank (1 Lowest—99 Highest)
• **18**

Insider Activity
• **NA**

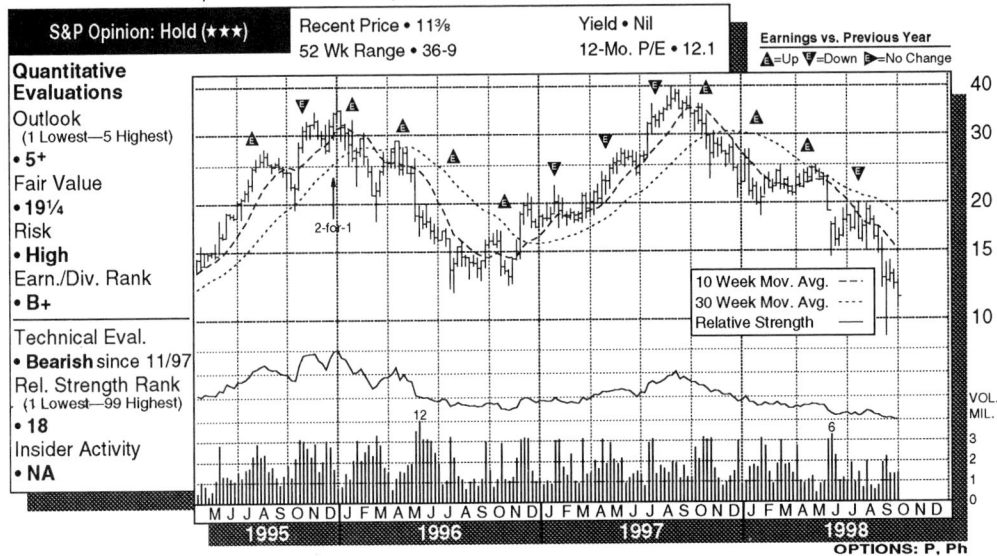

Overview - 14-SEP-98

The core markets for CGNX's machine vision systems in the semiconductor and electronics industries have continued to deteriorate since early 1998, with the decline accelerating in late summer. This does not bode well for the remainder of the year. We expect revenues in the second half of the year to be down 40%-50% from the 1997 period. Revenues from the acquisition of the Allen-Bradley machine vision business from Rockwell Automation are expected to be at the low end of a $5-$15 million range for sales in the first 12 months after the purchase. CGNX has implemented strict cost controls including a hiring freeze, and will have a mandatory two-week shutdown at the end of December, which should enable it to report marginal profitability in the second half. We have cut our already downward revised EPS estimate for 1998 from $0.69 to $0.46. The outlook for 1999 is very unsettled at this point, as recovery in recessionary foreign economies still seems distant. We have cut our 1999 earnings outlook in half from $0.92, and see flat EPS at $0.45. Operations should remain cash flow positive during this period, and with the company's $160 million cash arsenal, it will consider an aggressive stock buyback on top of a $20 million repurchase program already conducted this year.

Valuation - 14-SEP-98

We see the shares, rated as a hold, remaining in a trading range, and expect CGNX to be only an average market performer for the time being. As we advised when we earlier downgraded the shares from a positive to neutral view, the impact on the U.S. economy of the global economic slowdown that began in Asia has yet to become fully apparent, and we would not add to long positions in the stock until greater clarity on the global situation is apparent.

Key Stock Statistics

S&P EPS Est. 1998	0.46	Tang. Bk. Value/Share	5.63
P/E on S&P Est. 1998	24.7	Beta	1.69
S&P EPS Est. 1999	0.45	Shareholders	300
Dividend Rate/Share	Nil	Market cap. (B)	$0.465
Shs. outstg. (M)	40.9	Inst. holdings	63%
Avg. daily vol. (M)	0.342		

Value of $10,000 invested 5 years ago: $ 23,037

Fiscal Year Ending Dec. 31

	1998	1997	1996	1995	1994	1993
Revenues (Million $)						
1Q	40.06	28.14	34.89	19.40	12.80	8.80
2Q	32.04	36.27	34.95	23.70	15.00	10.40
3Q	—	43.94	26.54	29.78	16.60	11.80
4Q	—	46.99	26.47	31.60	18.10	12.30
Yr.	—	155.3	122.8	104.5	62.50	43.40
Earnings Per Share ($)						
1Q	**0.24**	**0.15**	0.25	0.14	0.09	0.06
2Q	**0.15**	**0.21**	0.22	0.18	0.10	0.07
3Q	**E0.03**	**0.24**	0.08	-0.02	0.12	0.09
4Q	**E0.04**	**0.31**	0.14	0.25	0.13	0.10
Yr.	**E0.46**	**0.91**	**0.69**	0.55	0.43	0.32

Next earnings report expected: mid October

Dividend Data

No cash dividends have been paid. The company intends to retain its earnings to finance the development and expansion of its business and does not anticipate paying cash dividends in the foreseeable future.

A Division of The **McGraw·Hill** Companies

STANDARD
&POOR'S
STOCK REPORTS

Cognex Corporation

3557C
03-OCT-98

Business Summary - 14-SEP-98

Cognex Corp. designs, develops, manufactures and markets a family of machine vision systems used to replace human vision in a wide range of manufacturing processes. Such systems capture an image of an object in the manufacturing process and use sophisticated image analysis software to extract information. The company's strategy is to expand its position as a leading worldwide supplier of machine vision systems for factory automation. Cognex believes that this market offers the greatest opportunity for selling high value-added, products in high volume.

The company's machine vision systems consist of hardware and software designed to give customers the flexibility to easily configure complete vision solutions without requiring extensive in-house expertise in image processing or analysis. Cognex offers a library of vision software tools and a family of board-level vision hardware that ranges in performance and platform. The typical machine vision solution ranges from $7,500 to $20,000, though the company's Web Inspection Systems range from $250,000 to $2,000,000. Cognex estimates that it had sold about 70,000 machine vision systems as of December 31, 1997.

The machine vision systems sold by the company are defined as either general-purpose or application-specific products. General-purpose machine vision products enable customers to solve a wide range of problems. Customers select the tools necessary to solve their vision problem from the company's vision software library and configure their solution by either writing a C-language program or utilizing a graphical user interface. Application-specific machine vision products are "packaged" combinations of software and hardware that are designed to solve targeted problems without any customization by the company or its customers.

Machine vision systems are used in a variety of industries such as the electronics and semiconductor industries in which human vision is inadequate due to fatigue, visual acuity or speed, or in cases where substantial cost savings are obtained through the reduction of direct labor and improved product quality. Principal customers are original equipment manufacturers in the electronics and semiconductor industries; system integrators that create complete, automated inspection systems for end users on the factory floor; and the end users themselves -- companies that manufacture products such as radios, phones and ball-point pens. International sales, mostly to Japan and Europe, accounted for 62% of total revenues in 1997 (55% in 1996).

In August 1997, the company announced that it had purchased the assets of Mayan Automation, Inc., a privately-held manufacturer of machine vision systems, for approximately $5 million in cash.

Per Share Data ($)

(Year Ended Dec. 31)	1997	1996	1995	1994	1993	1992	1991	1990	1989	1988
Tangible Bk. Val.	5.66	4.47	3.85	2.77	1.62	1.24	1.08	0.73	0.47	NA
Cash Flow	1.04	0.81	0.63	0.48	0.35	0.20	0.29	0.20	0.14	NA
Earnings	0.91	0.69	0.55	0.43	0.32	0.17	0.27	0.19	0.13	NA
Dividends	Nil	Nil	Nil	Nil	Nil	Nil	Nil	Nil	Nil	Nil
Payout Ratio	Nil	Nil	Nil	Nil	Nil	Nil	Nil	Nil	Nil	Nil
Prices - High	39⅞	35	38½	14	8⅞	7½	8¼	4¼	2⅝	NA
- Low	17¼	11¾	10½	5⅞	4⅝	2⅜	3¼	1¹¹/₁₆	1¼	NA
P/E Ratio - High	44	51	70	32	28	43	31	22	22	NA
- Low	19	17	19	14	15	14	12	9	10	NA

Income Statement Analysis (Million $)

	1997	1996	1995	1994	1993	1992	1991	1990	1989	1988
Revs.	155	123	105	62.5	43.4	28.6	31.5	23.6	15.9	NA
Oper. Inc.	60.6	43.4	48.0	23.6	16.0	8.2	13.3	9.2	5.0	NA
Depr.	5.8	5.1	3.2	1.8	1.3	0.9	0.7	0.5	0.4	NA
Int. Exp.	Nil	Nil	Nil	Nil	Nil	Nil	Nil	Nil	Nil	Nil
Pretax Inc.	58.3	43.7	37.6	23.3	16.0	8.4	14.0	10.0	5.2	NA
Eff. Tax Rate	31%	31%	39%	31%	30%	28%	32%	35%	28%	NA
Net Inc.	40.5	30.4	23.0	16.1	11.1	6.1	9.5	6.5	3.7	NA

Balance Sheet & Other Fin. Data (Million $)

	1997	1996	1995	1994	1993	1992	1991	1990	1989	1988
Cash	178	134	90.6	81.5	44.6	37.5	33.5	20.7	14.1	NA
Curr. Assets	224	169	136	97.7	57.4	45.0	39.4	25.2	16.9	NA
Total Assets	262	201	162	113	61.0	48.0	42.0	28.0	18.0	NA
Curr. Liab.	24.4	17.0	16.4	9.2	5.8	6.9	5.3	3.9	3.8	NA
LT Debt	Nil	Nil	Nil	Nil	Nil	Nil	Nil	Nil	Nil	Nil
Common Eqty.	236	183	144	104	55.0	41.0	36.0	24.0	14.0	NA
Total Cap.	236	183	144	104	55.0	41.0	36.0	24.0	14.0	NA
Cap. Exp.	10.9	10.2	10.5	13.1	1.8	1.5	1.1	1.1	1.0	NA
Cash Flow	46.3	35.5	26.2	17.8	12.4	7.0	10.2	7.0	4.1	NA
Curr. Ratio	9.2	9.9	8.3	10.6	10.0	6.5	7.5	6.5	4.5	NA
% LT Debt of Cap.	Nil	Nil	Nil	NM	NM	NM	NM	NM	NM	NM
% Net Inc.of Revs.	26.1	24.7	22.0	25.7	25.7	21.3	30.1	27.7	23.4	NA
% Ret. on Assets	17.5	16.7	16.7	17.9	20.3	13.7	26.9	27.6	NA	NA
% Ret. on Equity	19.3	18.6	18.6	19.6	23.0	15.8	31.1	33.3	NA	NA

Data as orig. reptd.; bef. results of disc. opers. and/or spec. items. Per share data adj. for stk. divs. as of ex-div. date. Bold denotes diluted EPS (FASB 128). E-Estimated. NA-Not Available. NM-Not Meaningful. NR-Not Ranked.

Office—One Vision Dr., Natick, MA 01760-2059. **Tel**—(508) 650-3000. **Website**—http://www.cognex.com **Chrmn, Pres & CEO**—R. J. Shillman. **EVP, CFO & Treas**—J. J. Rogers, Jr. **Dirs**—J.G. Fishman, W. A. Krivsky, R. J. Shillman, A. Sun, R. Wasserman. **Transfer Agent**—Bank Boston, N.A. **Incorporated**—in Massachusetts in 1981. **Empl**— 529. **S&P Analyst:** Mark Basham

03-OCT-98

Industry: Electronics (Instrumentation)

Summary: This company is a leading manufacturer of products based on laser, optics and microelectronic technologies for medical, scientific and telecommunications markets.

S&P Opinion: Hold (★★★)	Recent Price • 9⅛	Yield • Nil	Earnings vs. Previous Year
	52 Wk Range • 29¼-8½	12-Mo. P/E • 11.3	▲=Up ▼=Down ▶=No Change

Quantitative Evaluations

Outlook
(1 Lowest—5 Highest)
• **NA**

Fair Value
• **NA**

Risk
• **Average**

Earn./Div. Rank
• **B**

Technical Eval.
• **Bearish** since 6/98

Rel. Strength Rank
(1 Lowest—99 Highest)
• **24**

Insider Activity
• **Favorable**

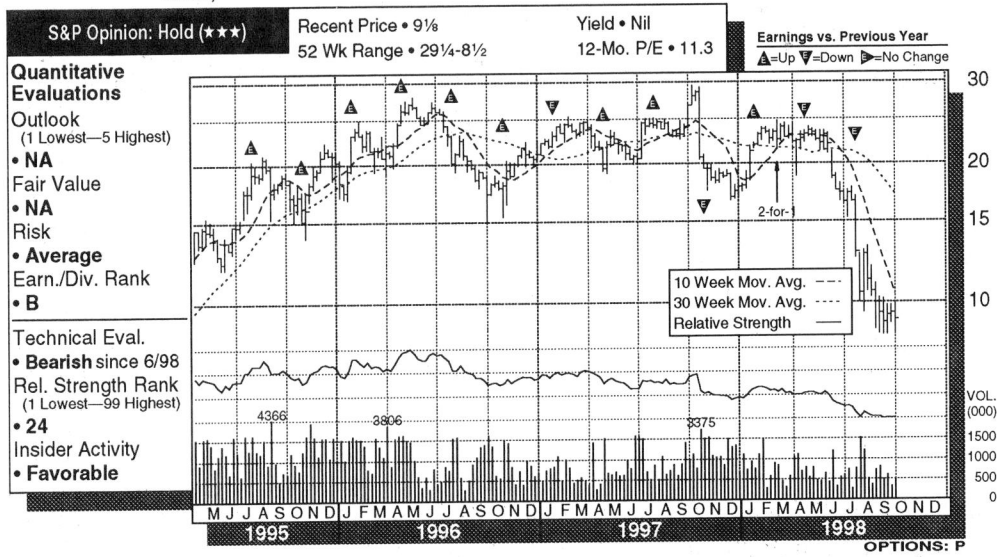

10 Week Mov. Avg. - - -
30 Week Mov. Avg. ......
Relative Strength —

2-for-1

OPTIONS: P

Overview - 28-JUL-98

In the past, revenue growth had been spurred by strategic acquisitions in faster-growing, technologically advanced niche markets and strong demand in both the semiconductor and medical equipment markets. However, we expect revenues to decline over the next few quarters, reflecting the negative impact of an increase in medical product returns, the unfavorable effects of a plunging Japanese yen, and pricing pressure. Margins should narrow substantially, as necessary investments in research and development will be spread over a smaller revenue base. In addition, a less favorable product mix and manufacturing inefficiencies will limit profitability. We have revised our estimates downward and now see FY 98 (Sep.) EPS falling to $0.66, but expect FY 99 EPS to rebound 8%, to $0.72. Results in FY 97 include a one-time charge for the acquisition of in-process technology.

Valuation - 28-JUL-98

In June 1998, the company warned the investment community that its FY 98 (Sep.) third quarter results would fall below analysts' expectations. Actual results were worse than our revised forecast, as revenues fell nearly 4%, on a 27% decline in medical sales. The poor performance was attributed to manufacturing inefficiencies, medical product returns and negative currency translations. Consequently, we have reduced our earnings forecast for the second time in as many months and have downgraded the shares to hold, from accumulate. Following the release of third quarter earnings, the shares fell sharply, and are currently trading at 27 times our calendar 1998 EPS estimate of $0.47 a share (16X our 1999 estimate of $0.82). Despite an unfavorable near-term outlook, the shares should be supported by an attractive price to book value ratio and a balance sheet with little long-term debt.

Key Stock Statistics

S&P EPS Est. 1998	0.66	Tang. Bk. Value/Share	10.21
P/E on S&P Est. 1998	13.9	Beta	1.50
S&P EPS Est. 1999	0.72	Shareholders	2,000
Dividend Rate/Share	Nil	Market cap. (B)	$0.218
Shs. outstg. (M)	23.7	Inst. holdings	66%
Avg. daily vol. (M)	0.099		

Value of $10,000 invested 5 years ago: $ 16,332

Fiscal Year Ending Sep. 30

	1998	1997	1996	1995	1994	1993
Revenues (Million $)						
1Q	101.4	93.89	83.68	58.58	47.03	46.75
2Q	105.9	90.99	90.55	66.46	55.22	51.33
3Q	98.55	102.3	89.33	76.25	55.26	47.21
4Q	—	103.8	100.9	84.21	57.87	51.59
Yr.	—	391.0	364.4	285.5	215.4	196.9
Earnings Per Share ($)						
1Q	0.32	-0.03	0.28	0.17	0.07	0.13
2Q	0.29	0.38	0.32	0.20	0.14	0.14
3Q	-0.07	0.48	0.34	0.23	0.14	0.09
4Q	E0.12	0.28	0.37	0.28	0.14	0.11
Yr.	E0.66	1.12	1.31	0.88	0.50	0.47

Next earnings report expected: late October

Dividend Data

Amount ($)	Date Decl.	Ex-Div. Date	Stock of Record	Payment Date
2-for-1	Feb. 03	Mar. 02	Feb. 17	Mar. 01 '98

A Division of The McGraw-Hill Companies

STANDARD
&POOR'S
STOCK REPORTS

Coherent, Inc.

3558
03-OCT-98

Business Summary - 28-JUL-98

Coherent (COHR), the leading maker of electro-optical systems and medical instruments utilizing laser, precision optic and microelectronic technologies, is focused on laser product innovations. Over the past several years, the company has committed from 10% to 11% of annual revenues to R&D efforts, and today has about 189 U.S. patents in force. During FY 97 (Sep.), more than half of the growth in COHR's annual sales came from products introduced in the last three years. Growth is also being driven by increasing penetration of global markets; international sales accounted for 55% of FY 97 (Sep.) total sales, up from 51% in FY 95.

Founded in 1966, COHR operates through two key product segments: electro-optical products and medical products. Electro-optical products (59% of revenues and 57% of profits in FY 97) include lasers and laser systems for scientific, medical research, micromachining, commercial applications, precision optics and related accessories. These lasers have a broad range of power and operate in the visible (V), ultraviolet (UV) and infrared (IR) portions of the electromagnetic spectrum. Coherent's optics and optical products include special-purpose lenses, mirrors and advanced optical coatings.

Medical products (42% of revenues and 43% of profits in FY 97) consist of a broad line of surgical laser systems used in ophthalmology, gynecology, urology, dermatology, plastic surgery, aesthetic surgery, orthopedic surgery and many other medical specialties. These lasers are designed to improve the quality of patient care, frequently decreasing overall treatment costs compared with conventional procedures. Most of the products also make it possible to perform treatments in a doctor's office, surgery centers or outpatient centers in hospitals, instead of requiring inpatient hospitalization.

In FY 97, COHR entered the telecommunications market and expanded its semiconductor laser capabilities with the acquisition of Micracor, Inc. and the purchase of an 80% interest in Tutcore, OY, Ltd. It expanded its precision optics capability and enhanced its product line with the acquisition of Ealing Electro-Optics. It also entered the laser hair removal market through a partnering agreement with Palomar Medical Technologies.

In addition to the two families of laser instruments launched in FY 96, COHR introduced a new laser that can be used for the removal of tattoos and treatment of both vascular and pigmented lesions, such as birthmarks, the unsightly veins of the legs and face, and lesions containing larger vessels that often do not respond to conventional lasers. This new laser technology allows physicians to achieve the capabilities offered by a single laser that would usually take up to four separate laser systems.

Per Share Data ($)

(Year Ended Sep. 30)	1997	1996	1995	1994	1993	1992	1991	1990	1989	1988
Tangible Bk. Val.	9.51	8.34	6.95	6.21	5.66	5.11	4.95	5.00	4.86	4.29
Cash Flow	1.75	1.94	1.28	0.88	0.82	0.55	0.45	0.40	0.87	0.34
Earnings	1.12	1.31	0.88	0.50	0.47	0.14	0.01	-0.03	0.47	-0.08
Dividends	Nil	Nil	Nil	Nil	Nil	Nil	Nil	Nil	Nil	Nil
Payout Ratio	Nil	Nil	Nil	Nil	Nil	Nil	Nil	Nil	Nil	Nil
Prices - High	29½	28	22¼	8¾	8⅛	8¼	8¾	7½	9⅞	7
- Low	16⅝	15⅛	8¼	5¾	5⅛	3⅞	4¼	3⅝	4⅞	4⅜
P/E Ratio - High	26	21	25	18	17	59	NM	NM	21	NM
- Low	15	11	9	11	11	28	NM	NM	10	NM

Income Statement Analysis (Million $)

	1997	1996	1995	1994	1993	1992	1991	1990	1989	1988
Revs.	391	364	285	215	197	215	208	191	202	188
Oper. Inc.	56.9	57.1	38.9	24.2	21.2	13.3	10.2	10.7	19.7	8.4
Depr.	14.6	12.4	9.0	7.9	7.3	7.9	8.2	7.7	7.3	7.0
Int. Exp.	1.2	Nil	1.1	1.9	2.0	1.8	1.3	1.2	1.4	1.0
Pretax Inc.	48.1	50.1	32.1	16.9	13.9	5.9	3.5	4.6	18.4	3.2
Eff. Tax Rate	43%	39%	39%	38%	35%	47%	82%	91%	48%	NM
Net Inc.	26.3	30.3	19.3	10.3	9.3	2.6	0.2	-0.4	8.6	-1.3

Balance Sheet & Other Fin. Data (Million $)

	1997	1996	1995	1994	1993	1992	1991	1990	1989	1988
Cash	21.5	34.6	44.7	43.8	37.1	29.7	16.3	24.2	21.6	13.9
Curr. Assets	255	218	185	156	144	141	130	123	121	109
Total Assets	362	231	256	212	194	188	169	164	162	154
Curr. Liab.	102	94.9	78.2	58.6	56.0	62.9	55.5	52.3	51.9	58.9
LT Debt	9.7	3.9	5.1	8.9	14.1	15.6	6.6	7.0	6.3	3.5
Common Eqty.	231	198	161	133	117	103	97.0	96.0	95.0	83.0
Total Cap.	249	202	173	148	136	125	112	110	108	92.0
Cap. Exp.	24.9	24.9	8.4	10.7	12.7	15.7	7.0	6.9	6.1	9.1
Cash Flow	40.9	42.7	28.3	18.2	16.6	10.6	8.4	7.2	15.8	5.7
Curr. Ratio	2.5	2.3	2.4	2.7	2.6	2.2	2.3	2.3	2.3	1.9
% LT Debt of Cap.	3.9	2.0	3.0	6.0	10.3	12.4	5.9	6.3	5.8	3.8
% Net Inc.of Revs.	6.7	8.3	6.8	4.8	4.7	1.2	0.1	NM	4.2	NM
% Ret. on Assets	7.8	10.7	8.3	5.1	4.8	1.5	0.1	NM	5.3	NM
% Ret. on Equity	12.3	16.9	13.1	8.1	8.3	2.6	0.2	NM	9.4	NM

Data as orig. reptd.; bef. results of disc. opers. and/or spec. items. Per share data adj. for stk. divs. as of ex-div. date. Bold denotes diluted EPS (FASB 128). E-Estimated. NA-Not Available. NM-Not Meaningful. NR-Not Ranked.

Office—5100 Patrick Henry Dr., Santa Clara, CA 95054. **Tel**—(408) 764-4000. **Fax**—(408) 764-4800. **Website**—http://www.cohr.com **Chrmn**—H. E. Gauthier. **Pres & CEO**—B. J. Couillaud. **EVP-CFO**—Robert J. Quillinan. **Treas**—D. C. Bucek. **Secy**—L. W. Sonsini. **Investor Contact**—Peter Schuman (408-764-4174).**Dirs**—C. W. Cantoni, F. Carrubba, B. J. Couillaud, H. E. Gauthier, T. S. Nelsen, J. E. Robertson. **Transfer Agent & Registrar**—First National Bank of Boston. **Incorporated**—in California in 1966; reincorporated in Delaware in 1990. **Empl**— 2,131. **S&P Analyst:** Stephen J. Tekirian

Comair Holdings 3568K
Nasdaq Symbol COMR
In S&P SmallCap 600

03-OCT-98

Industry: Airlines

Summary: This regional airline and Delta Connection carrier serves 79 cities in the U.S., Canada and the Bahamas, primarily flying Canadair jet aircraft.

S&P Opinion: Hold (★★★)	Recent Price • 27½	Yield • 0.6%
	52 Wk Range • 35¼-17⅞	12-Mo. P/E • 16.7

Earnings vs. Previous Year
▲=Up ▼=Down ▶=No Change

Quantitative Evaluations

Outlook (1 Lowest—5 Highest)
• 3

Fair Value
• 36¾

Risk
• High

Earn./Div. Rank
• A

Technical Eval.
• Bearish since 8/98

Rel. Strength Rank (1 Lowest—99 Highest)
• 64

Insider Activity
• NA

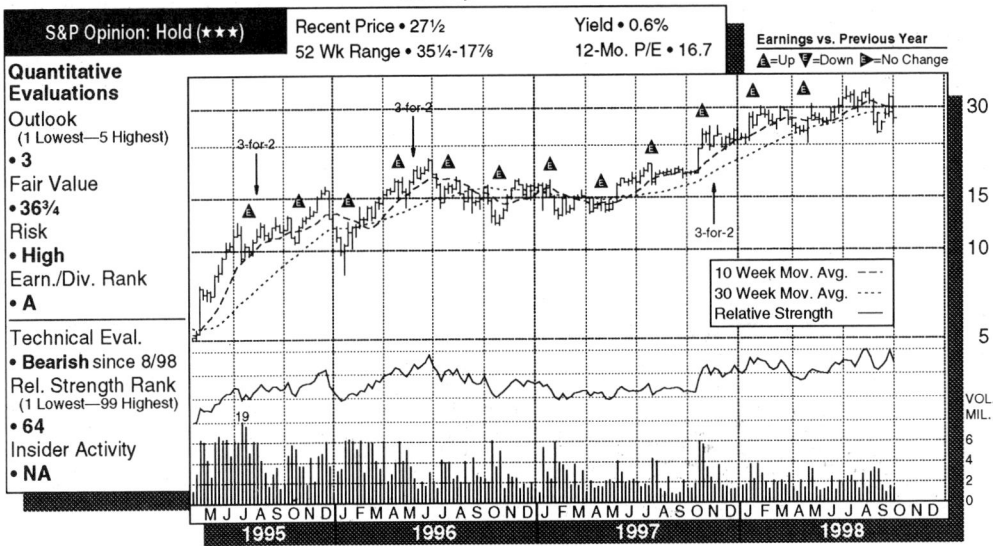

10 Week Mov. Avg. − − −
30 Week Mov. Avg. - - - -
Relative Strength ——

VOL. MIL.

1995 1996 1997 1998

Overview - 15-JUN-98

Traffic growth in FY 99 (Mar.) is expected to slow to a still healthy 10% to 12% pace, from a 13.4% increase in FY 98. COMR's new, faster and quieter jets will continue to attract additional business and leisure travelers for point-to-point as well as short hub connection flights. Increased traffic will be obtained by expanding flight frequencies through the company's Cincinnati hub to new locations such as Houston. In June 1998, COMR launched service between New York and Dayton. COMR's Florida service will benefit from a code-share arrangement with AirTran Airways, and from reduced service by competing airlines. Margins will widen, reflecting increased load factors, lower fuel costs, savings from commission cuts, and flat aircraft rentals. Offsetting will be increased labor costs, maintenance spending (as new jets come off their warranty coverage), and costs to phase out turboprop aircraft. Landing fees and airport facility rentals will be stable. Yields will be flat or decline slightly, as softness in leisure markets outweighs a mix improvement with increased premium business travelers. Depreciation charges will increase, as COMR purchases additional regional jets. Interest income should exceed interest expense.

Valuation - 15-JUN-98

COMR's shares broke out of a trading range in October 1997, and have continued climbing ever since. COMR's outlook is favorable. It leads the industry in use of regional jet aircraft, which it has applied to grab a larger share of the market. Despite the ramp-up in capital spending, COMR remains cash rich. However, very little of its hoard is being used to buy back its shares. During FY 98, COMR bought just 435,000 shares, for $11.6 million. The shares, which were split three for two in November 1997, are rated a hold, because of their premium P/E multiple.

Key Stock Statistics

S&P EPS Est. 1999	1.75	Tang. Bk. Value/Share	5.86
P/E on S&P Est. 1999	15.7	Beta	0.77
S&P EPS Est. 2000	2.05	Shareholders	2,300
Dividend Rate/Share	0.16	Market cap. (B)	$ 1.8
Shs. outstg. (M)	66.4	Inst. holdings	50%
Avg. daily vol. (M)	0.296		

Value of $10,000 invested 5 years ago: $ 61,266

Fiscal Year Ending Mar. 31

	1998	1997	1996	1995	1994	1993
Revenues (Million $)						
1Q	187.9	139.0	115.4	87.87	70.50	55.90
2Q	162.9	137.5	111.3	89.98	72.71	57.60
3Q	163.2	138.3	112.7	90.06	76.17	66.10
4Q	166.1	149.0	124.0	92.80	77.26	68.60
Yr.	651.2	563.8	463.3	360.7	296.6	248.2
Earnings Per Share ($)						
1Q	0.51	0.33	0.25	0.13	0.11	0.04
2Q	0.37	0.28	0.21	0.12	0.09	0.04
3Q	0.36	0.23	0.19	0.10	0.11	0.10
4Q	0.42	0.29	0.25	0.08	0.08	0.12
Yr.	1.51	1.13	0.91	0.43	0.39	0.31

Next earnings report expected: mid October

Dividend Data (Dividends have been paid since 1987.)

Amount ($)	Date Decl.	Ex-Div. Date	Stock of Record	Payment Date
3-for-2	Oct. 23	Nov. 14	Nov. 03	Nov. 13 '97
0.040	Jan. 20	Jan. 29	Feb. 02	Feb. 12 '98
0.040	Apr. 21	Apr. 30	May. 04	May. 14 '98
0.040	Jul. 21	Jul. 30	Aug. 03	Aug. 13 '98

A Division of The McGraw-Hill Companies

STANDARD
&POOR'S
STOCK REPORTS

Comair Holdings, Inc.

3568K
03-OCT-98

Business Summary - 15-JUN-98

The principal subsidiary of Comair Holdings, Inc. is COMAIR, Inc., a Cincinnati-based regional air carrier. COMAIR derives a substantial portion of its traffic from participating in the Delta Connection program. (Delta Air Lines owns 21% of COMR.) COMR, as the largest operator of regional jet aircraft, enjoys a competitive edge in the market for business travel.

Operating data (passenger and seat miles in millions) in recent fiscal years (Mar.):

	FY 98	FY 97	FY 96
Revenue passenger miles	1,824	1,551	1,281
Available seat miles	3,002	2,775	2,366
Load factor	60.7%	55.9%	54.1%
Breakeven load factor	46.3%	44.9%	42.9%
Revenue per RPM (cents)	34.0	34.7	34.7
Cost per ASM (cents)	15.7	15.5	15.0

About 45% of the company's business in FY 97 was derived through interlining flights with Delta Air Lines under the Delta Connection program. COMR has served as a Delta Connection carrier since 1984; its current marketing arrangement with Delta expires in 1999. As a Delta Connection carrier, COMAIR generally performs the short-haul portions of a longer

multi-carrier trip. COMAIR participates in Delta's frequent flyer program and has reservations, passenger and aircraft handling provided (for a fee) by Delta.

The majority of COMR passengers travel for business purposes. While fares paid by business travelers tend to be higher than leisure travelers, business travel has not grown as rapidly as leisure travel in recent years. To increase its share of the business market and attract more leisure fliers, COMR pioneered the substitution of regional jet aircraft for turboprops. Since FY 93, COMR has acquired 54 Canadair Regional Jets (CRJ), represents 80% of the company's capacity. These jets have a longer range and greater seating capacity than the turboprop aircraft they replaced. Consequently, COMR has been able to introduce longer-haul routes that appeal to leisure travelers. The faster, quieter jets are also preferred by business travelers. In January 1998, COMR said it would take delivery of 17 more CRJs in FY 99, and would have 80 jets by the end of calendar 1999.

Some 35% of COMAIR's work force is represented by labor unions. Contracts covering pilots and maintenance employees become amendable in June 1998 and June 1999, respectively. In FY 97, a representation election for COMR's flight attendants was held on behalf of the Teamsters. Results of that election are currently the subject of litigation.

Per Share Data ($)

(Year Ended Mar. 31)	1998	1997	1996	1995	1994	1993	1992	1991	1990	1989
Tangible Bk. Val.	5.43	4.19	3.19	2.38	2.33	2.00	1.28	1.13	0.97	0.81
Cash Flow	1.95	1.51	1.22	0.87	0.73	0.63	0.54	0.52	0.44	0.30
Earnings	1.51	1.13	0.91	0.43	0.39	0.31	0.20	0.21	0.21	0.11
Dividends	0.16	0.14	0.11	0.10	0.07	0.06	0.05	0.05	0.04	0.04
Payout Ratio	11%	13%	12%	24%	18%	21%	27%	25%	21%	37%
Cal. Yrs.	1997	1996	1995	1994	1993	1992	1991	1990	1989	1988
Prices - High	26⅛	20⅜	16½	8⅛	10¼	4⅞	3⅛	2⅝	1¹⁵/₁₆	1³/₁₆
- Low	12⅝	8¼	4⅜	4⅛	4⅜	2¼	1⅝	1⁷/₁₆	1⅛	¹³/₁₆
P/E Ratio - High	17	18	18	19	26	16	16	13	9	11
- Low	8	7	5	9	11	7	8	7	5	8

Income Statement Analysis (Million $)

	1998	1997	1996	1995	1994	1993	1992	1991	1990	1989
Revs.	651	564	463	361	297	248	217	202	158	118
Oper. Inc.	191	141	116	77.0	71.4	53.0	41.9	40.7	34.3	22.9
Depr.	29.8	24.9	21.0	30.0	24.1	20.7	20.7	19.0	14.2	12.1
Int. Exp.	7.8	6.1	6.1	3.8	2.8	3.5	3.7	3.0	2.0	1.6
Pretax Inc.	165	120	96.8	47.7	49.2	32.1	20.7	21.8	21.6	11.5
Eff. Tax Rate	38%	37%	38%	39%	42%	40%	40%	40%	40%	39%
Net Inc.	102	75.4	60.0	29.3	28.5	19.3	12.4	13.1	13.0	7.0

Balance Sheet & Other Fin. Data (Million $)

	1998	1997	1996	1995	1994	1993	1992	1991	1990	1989
Cash	156	177	152	84.0	111	110	45.7	38.7	32.2	29.3
Curr. Assets	308	241	197	120	141	130	59.8	58.3	46.8	39.1
Total Assets	670	589	429	347	285	256	181	167	128	84.0
Curr. Liab.	120	121	105	78.8	63.9	60.2	45.1	37.8	27.0	14.8
LT Debt	114	128	70.7	79.9	27.1	34.6	41.6	48.7	33.0	14.2
Common Eqty.	362	280	213	157	169	145	79.5	69.4	60.0	50.0
Total Cap.	540	460	320	265	218	192	133	128	101	68.0
Cap. Exp.	49.8	147	38.0	112	40.4	27.9	44.7	54.8	53.4	19.0
Cash Flow	132	100	81.0	59.3	52.7	40.0	33.1	32.0	27.2	19.1
Curr. Ratio	2.6	2.0	1.9	1.5	2.2	2.2	1.3	1.5	1.7	2.6
% LT Debt of Cap.	21.1	27.8	22.2	30.2	12.4	18.0	31.4	38.0	32.8	20.8
% Net Inc.of Revs.	15.7	13.3	13.0	8.1	9.6	7.8	5.7	6.5	8.3	5.9
% Ret. on Assets	16.2	14.8	15.5	9.7	10.5	8.3	7.1	8.9	12.3	8.8
% Ret. on Equity	31.8	30.5	32.5	18.9	18.1	16.2	16.6	20.2	23.7	14.4

Data as orig. reptd.; bef. results of disc. opers. and/or spec. items. Per share data adj. for stk. divs. as of ex-div. date. Bold denotes diluted EPS (FASB 128). E-Estimated. NA-Not Available. NM-Not Meaningful. NR-Not Ranked.

Office—P.O. Box 75021, Cincinnati/Northern Kentucky International Airport, Cincinnati, OH 45275. **Tel**—(606) 767-2550. **Website**—http://fly-comair.com **Chrmn & CEO**—D. R. Mueller. **Pres & COO**—D. A. Siebenburgen. **SVP, CFO & Investor Contact**—Randy D. Rademacher. **Secy**—R. D. Siegel. **Dirs**—R. H. Castellini, P. H. Forster, J. A. Haas, D. R. Mueller, R. A. Mueller, C. J. Murphy III, D. A. Siebenburgen, G. L. Wolken, M. W. Worth. **Transfer Agent & Registrar**—ChaseMellon Shareholder Services, Ridgefield Park, NJ. **Incorporated**—in Ohio in 1981. **Empl**—2,897. **S&P Analyst:** Stephen R. Klein

Commerce Bancorp (N.J.) 591H

NYSE Symbol **CBH**

In S&P SmallCap 600

03-OCT-98

Industry: Banks (Regional)

Summary: This multibank holding company operates a network of branch offices serving New Jersey and metropolitan Philadelphia.

Quantitative Evaluations

Outlook (1 Lowest—5 Highest)
- **NA**

Fair Value
- **NA**

Risk
- **Average**

Earn./Div. Rank
- **A-**

Technical Eval.
- **NA**

Rel. Strength Rank (1 Lowest—99 Highest)
- **61**

Insider Activity
- **Neutral**

Recent Price • 37⅞

52 Wk Range • 49¼-27⅜

Yield • 2.1%

12-Mo. P/E • 21.4

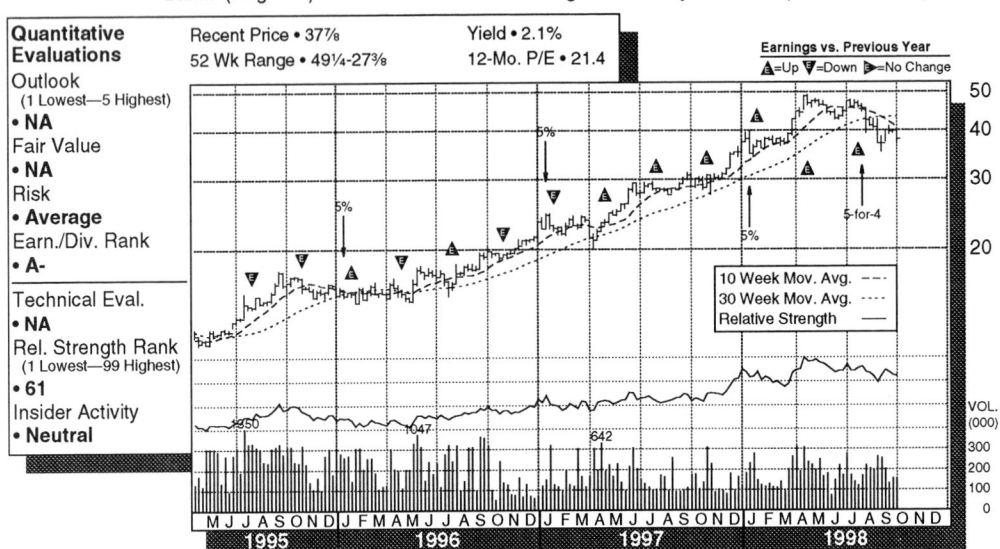

Earnings vs. Previous Year ▲=Up ▼=Down ▶=No Change

10 Week Mov. Avg. - - - -
30 Week Mov. Avg. ·····
Relative Strength ——

Business Profile - 20-JUL-98

Commerce Bancorp's long-term prospects are enhanced by the continuing expansion of the branch network and diversification into noninterest revenue sources. CBH plans to add 15 to 20 additional branch offices in 1998, on its way to a goal of 175 branches and $8 billion in assets by the end of 2002. Recently, the bank announced the acquisition of J. A. Montgomery, Inc., the largest insurance brokerage firm in Delaware. Separately, the bank completed the purchase of A. H. Williams, the largest public investment firm in the Philadelphia region, whose expanding presence in the bank's traditional markets is expected to further enhance earnings.

Operational Review - 20-JUL-98

Net interest income advanced 17%, year to year, in the first six months of 1998, mainly attributable to a 22% increase in net loans, to $1.64 billion. The provision for loan losses fell 5.9%, to $2.8 million, as non-performing assets declined to 0.30% of total assets at June 30, 1998, from 0.41% three months earlier. Noninterest income surged 53% in the first half, primarily reflecting revenue from service charges on deposits and trading account profits. Following a 31% rise in noninterest expense, due partly to the addition of branch offices in the first quarter, net income climbed 21%, to $23.59 million ($1.25 per share, diluted, after preferred dividends, on 6.2% more shares), from $19.47 million ($1.09).

Stock Performance - 02-OCT-98

In the past 30 trading days, CBH's shares have declined 7%, compared to a 7% fall in the S&P 500. Average trading volume for the past five days was 31,060 shares, compared with the 40-day moving average of 39,754 shares.

Key Stock Statistics

Dividend Rate/Share	0.78	Shareholders	15,000
Shs. outstg. (M)	22.6	Market cap. (B)	$0.856
Avg. daily vol. (M)	0.034	Inst. holdings	29%
Tang. Bk. Value/Share	12.52		
Beta	0.97		

Value of $10,000 invested 5 years ago: $ 48,388

Fiscal Year Ending Dec. 31

	1998	1997	1996	1995	1994	1993
Revenues (Million $)						
1Q	87.78	68.29	48.33	45.01	38.74	28.37
2Q	—	72.72	50.08	46.41	40.78	31.84
3Q	—	79.69	52.79	47.04	43.33	34.29
4Q	—	80.85	58.18	48.55	42.68	36.84
Yr.	—	301.6	209.4	187.0	165.5	131.3
Earnings Per Share ($)						
1Q	0.49	0.42	0.38	0.36	0.37	0.26
2Q	0.51	0.45	0.40	0.36	0.42	0.30
3Q		0.46	0.26	0.22	0.42	0.21
4Q	—	0.46	0.45	0.38	0.36	0.33
Yr.	—	1.80	1.43	1.47	1.57	1.20

Next earnings report expected: mid October

Dividend Data (Dividends have been paid since 1984.)

Amount ($)	Date Decl.	Ex-Div. Date	Stock of Record	Payment Date
.25 Spl.	Jun. 29	Jul. 09	Jul. 13	Jul. 24 '98
0.240	Jun. 16	Jul. 09	Jul. 13	Jul. 24 '98
25%	Jun. 29	Jul. 27	Jul. 13	Jul. 24 '98
0.195	Sep. 15	Oct. 02	Oct. 06	Oct. 20 '98

Business Summary - 20-JUL-98

Through acquisitions and internal growth, this $3.9 billion New Jersey-based bank holding company continues toward its goal of 175 offices and $8.0 billion in assets by 2002. At year-end 1997, Commerce Bancorp operated 76 offices through four banking subsidiaries: Commerce NJ ($2.7 billion in assets, 40 offices), Commerce Shore ($399 million, 10 offices), Commerce PA ($476 million, 16 offices) and Commerce North ($467 million, 10 offices). Additionally, the company provides regional insurance brokerage through Commerce Insurance and securities dealer services through Commerce Capital Markets.

Traditionally, banks derive the majority of their revenue from interest on loans. CBH's loan portfolio, totaling $1.41 billion at year-end 1997, was divided in recent years:

	1997	1996	1995
Real estate:			
Commercial	40%	40%	43%
Residential	12%	12%	13%
Commercial loans	18%	19%	19%
Consumer loans	30%	28%	25%

Unfortunately, banks must regularly reserve against possible loan losses. At year-end 1997, Commerce's allowance for loan losses represented 1.51% of loans outstanding, up from 1.42% a year earlier. A portion of this increase is a result of an improvement in asset quality, as net chargeoffs fell to only 0.10% of average loans in 1997, versus 0.25% a year earlier.

Recent performance has been aided by strong growth in deposits, which are the main (and most cost effective) source of funds to the bank. Averaging $3.2 billion during 1997 ($2.7 billion in 1996), total deposits were apportioned: interest-bearing demand 31%, noninterest-bearing demand 21%, savings 21% and time 27%.

Lending profitability, commonly measured by the yield on a bank's average earning assets, or the net interest margin, is affected by changes in the volume and mix of assets and liabilities, as well as changes in interest rates. CBH's net interest margin narrowed to 4.51% in 1997, from 4.68% a year earlier, as a drop in lending yields combined with a rise in the cost of funds.

During 1997, Commerce continued to grow through acquisitions, adding Independence Bancorp in northern New Jersey and announcing an agreement to acquire A. H. Williams & Co., a Philadelphia-based public finance company (completed in 1998).

Per Share Data ($) (Year Ended Dec. 31)	1997	1996	1995	1994	1993	1992	1991	1990	1989	1988
Tangible Bk. Val.	11.87	10.35	9.74	7.60	6.62	7.20	6.93	7.44	7.67	7.37
Earnings	1.80	1.58	1.47	1.58	1.20	0.93	0.61	0.39	0.90	0.86
Dividends	0.64	0.50	0.45	0.41	0.31	0.27	0.25	0.48	0.43	0.36
Payout Ratio	34%	32%	30%	26%	26%	29%	41%	123%	47%	42%
Prices - High	39 5/8	24 1/8	17 3/4	15 5/8	11 7/8	9 1/4	6	7 3/8	9	9 1/2
- Low	19 7/8	14 5/8	10 3/4	9 3/4	9	5 1/4	3	3 1/2	6	7 3/8
P/E Ratio - High	21	15	12	10	10	10	10	19	10	11
- Low	11	9	7	6	7	6	5	9	7	9
Income Statement Analysis (Million $)										
Net Int. Inc.	147	109	95.3	90.5	69.7	51.5	38.4	36.0	32.3	23.2
Tax Equiv. Adj.	1.4	0.9	0.4	0.4	0.5	0.6	0.8	1.2	1.6	1.6
Non Int. Inc.	55.1	30.0	21.4	16.9	14.4	12.1	10.0	8.7	6.5	4.2
Loan Loss Prov.	4.7	3.0	2.2	4.2	6.0	6.3	5.5	5.1	1.4	1.1
Exp./Op. Revs.	68%	70%	66%	67%	68%	67%	79%	76%	75%	67%
Pretax Inc.	61.9	41.5	36.9	32.0	23.2	14.4	8.0	5.3	7.8	6.9
Eff. Tax Rate	35%	36%	36%	36%	37%	31%	25%	19%	17%	22%
Net Inc.	40.3	26.6	23.5	20.4	14.6	10.0	6.0	4.3	6.5	5.4
% Net Int. Marg.	4.55	4.63	4.49	4.40	4.40	4.50	4.40	5.10	5.30	5.40
Balance Sheet & Other Fin. Data (Million $)										
Earning Assets:										
Money Mkt	168	173	177	129	106	137	88.0	147	86.0	NA
Inv. Securities	2,197	1,449	1,203	1,264	1,091	603	343	187	140	148
Com'l Loans	254	661	572	514	469	419	391	333	304	NA
Other Loans	1,157	435	336	288	232	202	188	221	212	NA
Total Assets	3,939	2,862	2,416	2,291	2,033	1,426	1,058	934	786	691
Demand Deposits	763	1,303	1,097	878	763	550	451	420	343	NA
Time Deposits	2,607	1,271	1,128	957	982	786	536	447	381	NA
LT Debt	23.0	26.3	27.4	28.4	29.0	6.5	7.3	8.2	0.7	5.0
Common Eqty.	248	181	162	104	78.2	81.9	58.2	54.3	55.9	40.1
% Ret. on Assets	1.2	1.0	1.0	0.9	0.8	0.8	0.6	0.5	0.9	1.1
% Ret. on Equity	18.6	15.5	16.7	19.4	16.5	14.4	11.0	7.7	15.2	17.4
% Loan Loss Resv.	1.5	1.4	1.5	1.5	1.4	1.4	1.5	1.2	0.7	NA
% Loans/Deposits	39.9	42.1	40.8	42.0	40.2	46.5	58.6	63.9	71.3	NA
% Equity to Assets	6.3	6.5	5.8	4.9	4.0	5.6	5.5	6.7	5.9	NA

Data as orig. reptd.; bef. results of disc. opers. and/or spec. items. Per share data adj. for stk. divs. as of ex-div. date. Bold denotes diluted EPS (FASB 128). E-Estimated. NA-Not Available. NM-Not Meaningful. NR-Not Ranked.

Office—Commerce Atrium, 1701 Route 70 East, Cherry Hill, NJ 08034-5400. **Tel**—(609) 751-9000. **Chrmn & Pres**—V. W. Hill II. **EVP, CFO & Investor Contact**—C. Edward Jordan, Jr. **Secy**—R. C. Beck. **Dirs**—D. Baird IV, R. C. Beck, J. R. Bershad, J. Buckelew, V. W. Hill II, C. E. Jordan, Jr., M. N. Kerr, S. M. Lewis, D. J. Ragone, W. A. Schwartz, Jr., J. T. Tarquini, Jr., F. C. Videon, Sr. **Transfer Agent & Registrar**—ChaseMellon Shareholder Services, Ridgefield Park, NJ. **Incorporated**—in New Jersey in 1982. **Empl**— 2,160. **S&P Analyst:** L. A. Olive

Commercial Federal

591K

NYSE Symbol **CFB**

In S&P SmallCap 600

03-OCT-98   **Industry:** Banks (Regional)

Summary: Through its principal subsidiary, Commercial Federal Bank, this company conducts banking operations primarily in Iowa, Kansas, Nebraska and Colorado.

Quantitative Evaluations

Outlook (1 Lowest—5 Highest)
- **2-**

Fair Value
- **23¼**

Risk
- **Low**

Earn./Div. Rank
- **B-**

Technical Eval.
- **Bearish** since 5/98

Rel. Strength Rank (1 Lowest—99 Highest)
- **48**

Insider Activity
- **Neutral**

Recent Price • 23⅛

52 Wk Range • 39-21⅝

Yield • 1.0%

12-Mo. P/E • 14.1

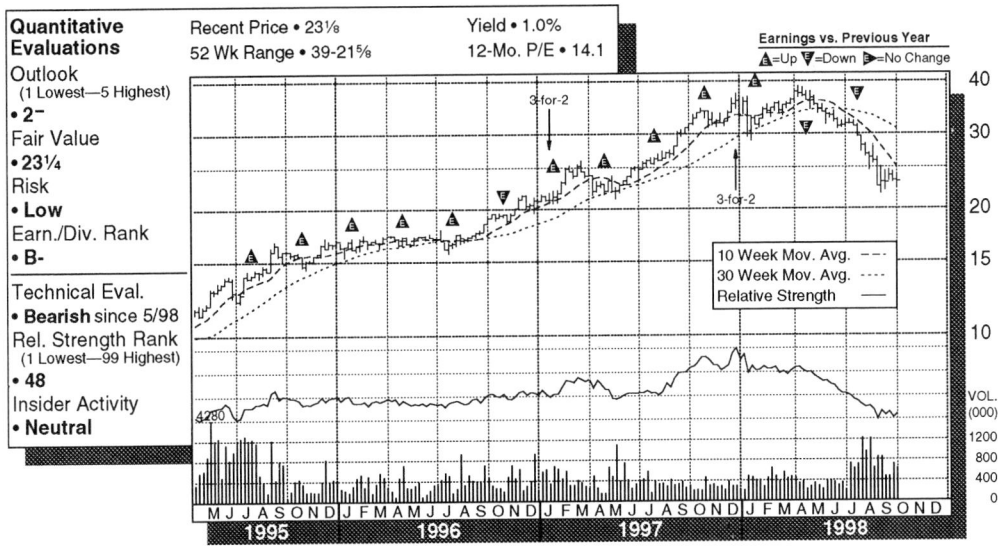

Business Profile - 18-MAY-98

Commercial Federal continues its robust expansion into nearby states through acquisitions. Since December 31, 1997, the bank has acquired First National Bank Shares, with seven branches in Kansas and $155 million in assets; Liberty Financial Corp., with 38 branches in Iowa and Arizona and $670 million in assets; AmerUs Bank, with 48 branches and about $201 million in assets; and First Colorado, with 27 locations. Most recently, the company announced an agreement to purchase Perpetual Midwest Financial, an Iowa-based bank with five offices and $402 million in assets.

Operational Review - 18-MAY-98

Net interest income, after provision for loan losses, in the first nine months of FY 98 (Jun.) rose 7.7%, year to year, on growth in interest earning assets resulting from recent acquisitions as well as internal growth. Margins widened, as operating earnings grew 16%, to $63.3 million. Following merger-related and other nonrecurring charges totaling $0.40 a share in FY 98 and $0.51 in FY 97, reported net income advanced 38%, to $47.5 million ($1.19 a share, diluted), from $34.5 million ($0.88).

Stock Performance - 02-OCT-98

In the past 30 trading days, CFB's shares have declined 11%, compared to a 7% fall in the S&P 500. Average trading volume for the past five days was 125,540 shares, compared with the 40-day moving average of 154,418 shares.

Key Stock Statistics

Dividend Rate/Share	0.22	Shareholders	2,300
Shs. outstg. (M)	58.6	Market cap. (B)	$ 1.4
Avg. daily vol. (M)	0.118	Inst. holdings	42%
Tang. Bk. Value/Share	12.79		
Beta	1.25		

Value of $10,000 invested 5 years ago: $ 30,504

Fiscal Year Ending Jun. 30

	1998	1997	1996	1995	1994	1993
Revenues (Million $)						
1Q	148.5	136.4	120.6	106.1	97.36	99.4
2Q	151.3	142.5	134.3	111.4	90.47	99.8
3Q	174.2	148.5	135.6	113.7	99.2	99.5
4Q	—	144.4	150.2	118.3	93.53	97.32
Yr.	—	563.5	540.7	449.5	397.8	396.1
Earnings Per Share ($)						
1Q	0.52	-0.12	0.34	0.02	0.25	0.21
2Q	0.54	0.47	0.36	0.04	0.31	0.26
3Q	0.20	0.49	0.48	0.46	0.33	0.29
4Q	0.43	0.52	0.46	0.42	-1.13	0.32
Yr.	1.60	1.36	1.66	0.94	-0.20	1.08

Next earnings report expected: late October

Dividend Data (Dividends have been paid since 1995.)

Amount ($)	Date Decl.	Ex-Div. Date	Stock of Record	Payment Date
0.055	Nov. 18	Dec. 29	Dec. 31	Jan. 14 '98
0.055	Feb. 11	Mar. 26	Mar. 30	Apr. 14 '98
0.055	Jun. 10	Jun. 24	Jun. 26	Jul. 14 '98
0.055	Sep. 02	Sep. 25	Sep. 29	Oct. 14 '98

A Division of The **McGraw·Hill** Companies

Commercial Federal Corporation

Business Summary - 18-MAY-98

Having gone nearly a year since closing its last significant acquisition, Commercial Federal Corp. (CFB) began a fresh round in August 1997, announcing that it would acquire via an exchange of stock transaction Iowa-based Liberty Financial Corp. The acquisition, completed in February 1998, greatly expanded the company's presence in Iowa, and took it into Arizona. Liberty Financial had $533 million in deposits, and added 42 branch locations to CFB's existing network. In December, in separate announcements, CFB said it would acquire two Kansas banks with combined deposits of nearly $400 million. In October 1996, CFB added six branch offices in Iowa by acquiring Heritage Financial, Ltd., parent of Hawkeye Federal Savings Bank. A small acquisition added $26 million in deposits in May 1997.

Rapid growth, fueled primarily by acquisitions, is nothing new to CFB. Before implementation of its strategic acquisitions and expansion program in the fall of 1993, CFB's retail franchise consisted of 49 branch offices in four states, primarily Nebraska and Colorado. The intervening years, marked by eight acquisitions, have seen CFB double the size of its franchise, while maintaining and strengthening its midwestern character. As of September 1997 (before completion of the Liberty Financial and the Kansas acquisitions), the company, operating through wholly owned Commercial Federal Bank, had 107 branches, in Nebraska (34), Colorado (20), Oklahoma (19), Kansas (27) and Iowa (7).

CFB views its growth strategy as a way to expand its customer base, permitting the company to sell new products and services to a greater number of prospects. Although the anticipated merger of Liberty Financial's banking subsidiaries into Commercial Federal Bank launches CFB's movement into commercial banking, Commercial Federal will remain a consumer-oriented financial institution that emphasizes single-family residential real estate lending, consumer lending, retail deposit activities, including demand deposit accounts, and mortgage banking. In addition to its branch office network, CFB conducts loan origination activities through the offices of its mortgage banking subsidiary and through a correspondent network consisting of hundreds of mortgage loan originators.

Net income of $44.1 million in FY 97 (Jun.) reflected an after tax charge of $17.3 million, representing the company's share of a one-time, industry-wide assessment to recapitalize the Savings Association Insurance Fund. CFB reported net income of $55.3 million in FY 96. In FY 97, average earning assets, from which interest income is derived, amounted to $6.5 billion and consisted of loans (77%), mortgage-backed securities (17%) and investments (6%).

Per Share Data ($)

(Year Ended Jun. 30)	1998	1997	1996	1995	1994	1993	1992	1991	1990	1989
Tangible Bk. Val.	NA	12.67	10.97	9.49	7.38	6.68	5.73	3.45	1.22	-0.84
Earnings	1.60	1.36	1.66	0.94	-0.20	1.08	2.24	0.53	-2.05	0.02
Dividends	0.21	0.19	0.18	Nil	Nil	Nil	Nil	Nil	Nil	Nil
Payout Ratio	13%	14%	11%	Nil	Nil	Nil	Nil	Nil	Nil	Nil
Prices - High	39	37½	21½	17	12⅜	12⅝	8⅛	2¾	1¾	3⅞
- Low	26½	20⅝	15⅜	9	7¾	7¼	2¼	1	¾	1½
P/E Ratio - High	24	28	13	18	NM	12	4	5	NM	NM
- Low	17	15	9	10	NM	7	1	2	NM	NM

Income Statement Analysis (Million $)

	1998	1997	1996	1995	1994	1993	1992	1991	1990	1989
Net Int. Inc.	NM	168	163	134	126	116	85.0	55.1	61.0	89.1
Loan Loss Prov.	NA	8.1	6.1	6.0	6.0	5.7	7.4	9.1	27.6	9.8
Non Int. Inc.	NA	58.5	49.6	37.6	32.3	23.3	68.5	52.8	20.2	43.9
Non Int. Exp.	NA	150	124	117	143	83.2	78.8	74.4	83.2	119
Pretax Inc.	NA	68.5	82.3	48.3	8.6	50.6	67.4	24.4	-29.6	4.1
Eff. Tax Rate	NA	35%	33%	43%	166%	39%	37%	63%	NM	93%
Net Inc.	NA	44.7	55.3	27.5	-5.6	30.8	42.3	9.1	-31.9	0.3
% Net Int. Marg.	NA	2.60	2.60	2.40	2.30	2.53	1.98	1.42	1.50	1.52

Balance Sheet & Other Fin. Data (Million $)

	1998	1997	1996	1995	1994	1993	1992	1991	1990	1989
Total Assets	NA	7,097	6,608	5,954	5,521	4,871	4,641	5,078	5,619	6,064
Loans	NA	5,190	4,724	5,323	4,898	4,231	3,860	4,074	4,630	5,153
Deposits	NA	4,379	4,305	3,591	3,356	2,391	2,301	2,249	2,405	2,852
Capitalization:										
Debt	NA	2,184	1,790	1,712	1,584	1,924	1,509	1,414	1,317	1,430
Equity	NA	426	413	310	279	278	237	166	141	130
Total	NA	2,610	2,203	2,022	1,863	2,202	1,746	1,580	1,457	1,560
% Ret. on Assets	NA	0.7	0.8	0.4	NM	0.7	0.9	0.2	NM	NM
% Ret. on Equity	NM	11.0	14.7	9.3	NM	12.0	21.0	6.0	NM	0.2
% Loan Loss Resv.	NA	0.9	1.0	0.9	1.2	1.3	1.2	1.3	0.5	0.6
% Risk Based Capital	NA	13.8	13.6	13.5	13.1	12.8	8.9	6.6	6.3	NA
Price Times Book Value:										
Hi	NA	2.2	1.6	1.8	1.7	1.9	1.2	0.8	1.4	0.5
Low	NA	1.6	1.1	1.0	1.1	1.1	0.4	0.3	0.6	0.3

Data as orig. reptd.; bef. results of disc. opers. and/or spec. items. Per share data adj. for stk. divs. as of ex-div. date. Bold denotes diluted EPS (FASB 128). E-Estimated. NA-Not Available. NM-Not Meaningful. NR-Not Ranked.

Organized—in Nebraska in 1887. Office—2120 S. 72nd St., Omaha, NE 68124. Tel—(402) 554-9200. Chrmn & CEO—W. A. Fitzgerald. Pres & COO—J. A. Laphen. EVP & Secy—G. L. Matter. Fin VP & Investor Contact—Larry R. Goddard (402-390-6553). Dirs—T. A. Anderson, W. A. Fitzgerald, M. P. Glinsky, W. A. Krause, R. F. Krohn, C. G. Mammel, R. S. Milligan, J. P. O'Donnell, R. D. Taylor, A. J. Tesi. Transfer Agent—Harris Trust & Savings Bank, Chicago. Empl— 2,310. S&P Analyst: L. A. Olive

STANDARD
&POOR'S
STOCK REPORTS

Commercial Metals 592

NYSE Symbol **CMC**

In S&P SmallCap 600

03-OCT-98

Industry:
Metal Fabricators

Summary: This company manufactures, recycles and markets steel, metal products and other materials, and provides related services.

S&P Opinion: Hold (★★★)	Recent Price • 22⅞	Yield • 2.3%
	52 Wk Range • 36-21⅞	12-Mo. P/E • 8.6

Quantitative Evaluations

Outlook
(1 Lowest—5 Highest)
• **4+**

Fair Value
• **32⅞**

Risk
• **Low**

Earn./Div. Rank
• **B+**

Technical Eval.
• **Bearish** since 6/97

Rel. Strength Rank
(1 Lowest—99 Highest)
• **46**

Insider Activity
• **Neutral**

Earnings vs. Previous Year
▲=Up ▼=Down ▶=No Change

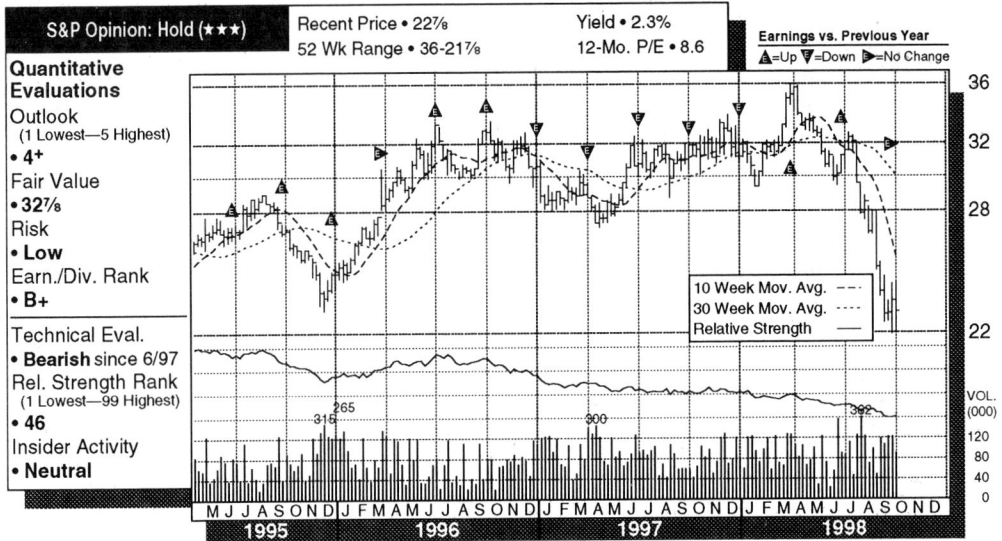

10 Week Mov. Avg. – – –
30 Week Mov. Avg. · · · ·
Relative Strength ——

Overview - 26-JUN-98

We anticipate 7.0% sales growth in FY 99 (Aug.) on continued strong gains in steel manufacturing and marketing/trading and a smaller decline in recycling. Increased prices and volume for rebar, merchant and fabricated products will lift sales in the manufacturing unit. More stable business conditions in Asia will lead to an improvement in marketing/trading, while low scrap prices will continue to depress recycling. However, gains in steel manufacturing and marketing/trading should again offset weakness in recycling and permit higher EPS in FY 99.

Valuation - 26-JUN-98

Although CMC beat consensus estimates for both the second and third quarters of FY 98 (Aug.), its shares are virtually unchanged for the year through late June, versus a gain of 16.7% for the S&P 500. Sharply higher profits in steel manufacturing and surprising strength in marketing/trading offset weakness in recycling in both quarters. However, market psychology toward cyclicals remains negative due to deteriorating business conditions in Asia, and this may account for CMC's underperformance despite better than expected EPS. Currently, CMC is trading at about 10X our estimated earnings for FY 99, which is a discount to its five year EPS growth rate. Because CMC's businesses and EPS are highly cyclical, we see no reason why the market is going to give CMC a higher multiple on FY 99 EPS given the very extended length of the current business cycle. Thus, we don't view the stock as an accumulate or buy even though the shares are undervalued. Additionally, CMC's diversified business mix makes it difficult to place a multiple on its EPS. There are no other companies that can be readily compared to CMC so deriving an appropriate valuation is problematic.

Key Stock Statistics

S&P EPS Est. 1998	2.65	Tang. Bk. Value/Share		25.44
P/E on S&P Est. 1998	8.7	Beta		0.64
S&P EPS Est. 1999	2.95	Shareholders		2,700
Dividend Rate/Share	0.52	Market cap. (B)		$0.344
Shs. outstg. (M)	15.0	Inst. holdings		45%
Avg. daily vol. (M)	0.028			

Value of $10,000 invested 5 years ago: $ 12,763

Fiscal Year Ending Aug. 31

	1998	1997	1996	1995	1994	1993
Revenues (Million $)						
1Q	550.5	531.0	590.2	413.7	380.0	324.4
2Q	568.2	525.8	518.2	533.0	389.9	411.7
3Q	606.0	589.6	639.1	574.2	440.6	438.0
4Q	—	612.0	574.8	595.9	447.2	387.2
Yr.	—	2,258	2,322	2,117	1,658	1,558
Earnings Per Share ($)						
1Q	0.54	0.00	0.70	0.44	0.00	0.00
2Q	**0.56**	0.47	0.67	0.67	0.28	0.33
3Q	**0.75**	0.63	0.79	0.73	0.48	0.43
4Q	**E0.85**	0.85	0.86	0.66	0.63	0.49
Yr.	**E2.65**	2.53	3.01	2.52	1.75	1.46

Next earnings report expected: mid October

Dividend Data (Dividends have been paid since 1964.)

Amount ($)	Date Decl.	Ex-Div. Date	Stock of Record	Payment Date
0.130	Dec. 05	Jan. 07	Jan. 09	Jan. 22 '98
0.130	Mar. 16	Apr. 07	Apr. 10	Apr. 24 '98
0.130	Jun. 24	Jul. 08	Jul. 10	Jul. 24 '98
0.130	Sep. 14	Oct. 07	Oct. 09	Oct. 23 '98

A Division of The McGraw-Hill Companies

Business Summary - 26-JUN-98

Commercial Metals engages in raw material and industrial product-related activities, including worldwide marketing and trading, manufacturing and fabrication of steel, copper tube production, and metals recycling. Segment contributions in FY 97 (Aug.) were:

	Sales	Profits
Manufacturing	48%	68%
Marketing and trading	32%	22%
Recycling	20%	10%

International sales accounted for 33% of total revenues in FY 97, versus 39% in FY 96 and 35% in FY 95.

The manufacturing group includes the CMC Steel Group, Howell Metal Company and a railroad salvage company. CMC Steel is engaged in minimill steel production, steel fabricating, steel joist manufacturing, fence post manufacturing and railcar rebuilding. The steel minimills manufacture reinforcing bar, angles, rounds, channels, flats and special sections used in highways, concrete structures and general manufacturing. Minimill shipments totaled 1,926,000 tons in FY 97, versus 1,730,000 tons in FY 96. Steel processing entails fabrication of reinforcing and structural steel used primarily in construction of commercial and non-commercial businesses.

CMC's principal competitors in the minimill industry are Bayou Steel, Birmingham Steel, Co-Steel and Nucor Corp.

Howell Metal manufactures copper water, air conditioning and refrigeration tubing for use in commercial, industrial and residential construction.

The railroad salvage company dismantles and recovers steel rail, track components and other materials from obsolete or abandoned railroads.

Through a network of 17 trading offices around the world, CMC markets and trades primary and secondary metals, steel, ores and concentrates, industrial minerals, ferroalloys, chemicals, and other materials used by a variety of industries. The marketing and trading segment also provides services including market and technical information, financing, transportation and shipping, storage, insurance and hedging.

The recycling segment processes ferrous and nonferrous scrap metals for further recycling into new metal products at 33 plants. The new metal products are sold to steel mills and foundries, aluminum sheet and ingot manufacturers, specialty steel mills and other industrial manufacturers. Shipments for this segment totaled 1,367,000 tons in FY 97, with ferrous metals accounting for 1,155,000 tons and nonferrous metals 212,000 tons. Ferrous scrap is the primary raw material for minimills such as those operated by CMC and its competitors.

Per Share Data ($) (Year Ended Aug. 31)	1997	1996	1995	1994	1993	1992	1991	1990	1989	1988
Tangible Bk. Val.	24.04	22.20	19.72	17.01	15.96	14.92	14.43	13.97	12.69	11.12
Cash Flow	5.41	5.73	5.04	3.77	3.31	2.64	2.49	3.16	3.15	2.83
Earnings	2.53	3.01	2.52	1.75	1.46	0.87	0.84	1.70	1.84	1.60
Dividends	0.52	0.48	0.48	0.46	0.39	0.39	0.39	0.38	0.31	0.21
Payout Ratio	21%	16%	19%	26%	27%	44%	46%	21%	17%	13%
Prices - High	33 7/8	33 1/2	29	29 1/8	30	20 1/8	16 3/4	16 3/4	17 7/8	17 3/4
- Low	27 1/8	24 3/8	23	21	19 3/8	14 1/8	12 1/4	12 1/8	14 7/8	10 3/8
P/E Ratio - High	13	11	12	17	21	23	20	10	10	11
- Low	11	8	9	12	13	16	15	7	8	6
Income Statement Analysis (Million $)										
Revs.	2,248	2,310	2,107	1,666	1,569	1,166	1,161	1,137	1,309	1,129
Oper. Inc.	109	118	109	80.3	71.8	55.9	50.5	70.6	73.8	53.3
Depr.	43.7	41.6	38.1	30.1	27.4	25.6	23.6	22.2	20.2	19.0
Int. Exp.	14.6	16.1	15.4	10.4	9.8	10.1	9.6	8.8	10.8	4.5
Pretax Inc.	61.0	72.9	58.0	40.9	35.1	20.3	18.3	39.8	43.4	37.8
Eff. Tax Rate	37%	37%	34%	36%	38%	38%	35%	35%	34%	34%
Net Inc.	38.6	46.0	38.2	26.2	21.7	12.5	12.0	25.9	28.5	24.4
Balance Sheet & Other Fin. Data (Million $)										
Cash	33.0	24.3	21.0	38.3	47.4	47.4	33.2	38.6	65.6	25.8
Curr. Assets	585	539	534	446	398	378	319	289	315	230
Total Assets	839	767	748	605	542	516	461	416	419	337
Curr. Liab.	278	264	268	271	215	204	199	149	155	125
LT Debt	185	147	158	72.1	76.7	87.2	45.5	54.4	60.5	30.8
Common Eqty.	355	335	303	243	235	212	204	200	191	168
Total Cap.	561	503	480	334	327	312	262	267	264	212
Cap. Exp.	71.0	48.0	39.3	48.2	37.6	24.5	42.7	43.7	26.4	24.4
Cash Flow	82.3	87.6	76.3	56.3	49.0	38.1	35.6	48.1	48.6	43.8
Curr. Ratio	2.1	2.0	2.0	1.6	1.9	1.9	1.6	1.9	2.0	1.8
% LT Debt of Cap.	33.1	29.2	32.9	21.6	23.5	28.0	17.4	20.4	23.0	14.5
% Net Inc.of Revs.	1.7	2.0	1.8	1.6	1.4	1.1	1.0	2.3	2.2	2.2
% Ret. on Assets	4.8	6.1	5.6	4.6	4.0	2.6	2.8	6.4	7.5	8.0
% Ret. on Equity	11.2	14.5	14.0	11.1	9.5	6.0	6.0	13.6	15.9	15.8

Data as orig. reptd.; bef. results of disc. opers. and/or spec. items. Per share data adj. for stk. divs. as of ex-div. date. Revs. in quarterly table incl. other inc. Bold denotes diluted EPS (FASB 128). E-Estimated. NA-Not Available. NM-Not Meaningful. NR-Not Ranked.

Office—7800 Stemmons Freeway, P.O. Box 1046, Dallas, TX 75221. **Tel**—(214) 689-4300. **Website**—http://www.commercialmetals.com **Pres & CEO**—S. A. Rabin. **VP & Secy**—D. M. Sudbury. **VP, Treas & CFO**—L. A. Engels. **Investor Contact**—Debbie Okle - (214) 689-4354. **Dirs**—A. A. Eisenstat, M. Feldman, L. E. Hirsch, A. L. Howell, W. F. Kammann, R. E. Loewenberg, D. G. Owen, C. B. Peterson, S. A. Rabin, M. Selig. **Transfer Agent & Registrar**—ChaseMellon Shareholder Services, Ridgefield Park, NJ. **Incorporated**—in Delaware in 1946. **Empl**— 7,100. **S&P Analyst:** Leo J. Larkin

Commonwealth Energy System 594F

NYSE Symbol **CES**

In S&P SmallCap 600

03-OCT-98

Industry: Electric Companies

Summary: This Massachusetts public utility holding company offers energy supply and delivery services, including natural gas, electricity, liquefied natural gas and steam.

Quantitative Evaluations

Outlook
(1 Lowest—5 Highest)
• **1**

Fair Value
• **29⅜**

Risk
• **Average**

Earn./Div. Rank
• **B+**

Technical Eval.
• **Bearish** since 9/98

Rel. Strength Rank
(1 Lowest—99 Highest)
• **93**

Insider Activity
• **NA**

Recent Price • 35½
52 Wk Range • 41-25¼

Yield • 4.6%
12-Mo. P/E • 15.2

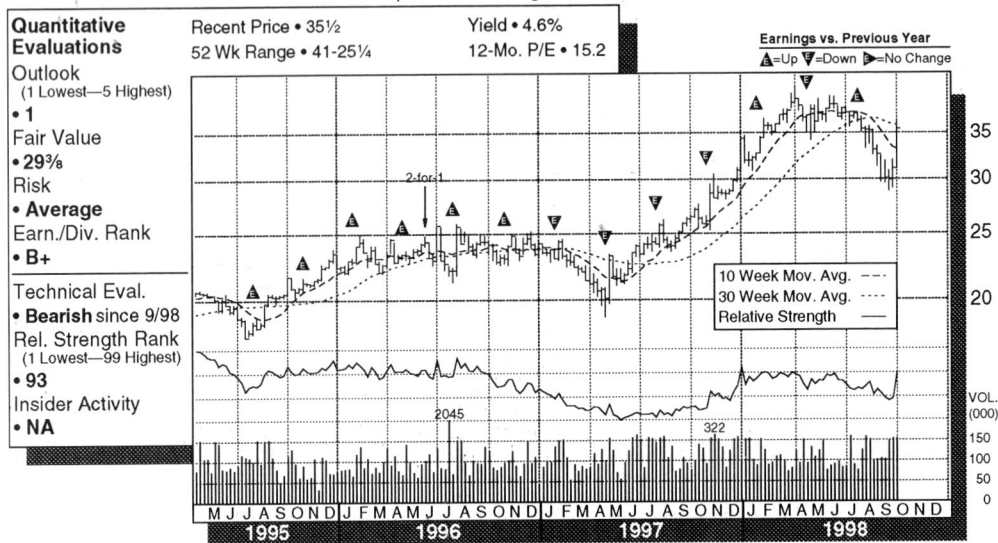

Business Profile - 15-APR-98

Due to the dramatically changing nature of the electric and gas industries, CES announced the consolidation of management personnel of Commonwealth Electric, Commonwealth Gas and COM/Energy Services Co. in February 1997. In addition, CES initiated a voluntary personnel reduction program during the second quarter of 1997 which reduced the total number of regular employees by approximately 13%. Through this and prior work force reductions and attrition, CES has reduced its full-time work force approximately 33% since 1990. CES has yet to be significantly impacted by the increase in competition and believes that its current business strategy and entrance into unregulated markets will have a positive impact in the near-term.

Operational Review - 15-APR-98

Revenues increased 3.1% in 1997, reflecting a greater level of wholesale electric sales, partially offset by a drop in gas firm unit sales to all customer segments due to warmer weather in 1997. Results were hurt by the absence of a 1996 refund associated with a power contract settlement agreement, costs associated with new business development, the absence of a 1996 reversal of a reserve for Canal Electric Company's postretirement benefits costs that were subsequently recovered in wholesale rates and a lower investment base on generation assets. Net income fell 16%, to $49,901,000 ($2.27 a share, after preferred dividends) from $59,175,000 ($2.70).

Stock Performance - 02-OCT-98

In the past 30 trading days, CES's shares have increased 7%, compared to a 7% fall in the S&P 500. Average trading volume for the past five days was 37,820 shares, compared with the 40-day moving average of 27,700 shares.

Key Stock Statistics

Dividend Rate/Share	1.62	Shareholders	13,700
Shs. outstg. (M)	21.5	Market cap. (B)	$0.764
Avg. daily vol. (M)	0.032	Inst. holdings	32%
Tang. Bk. Value/Share	20.41		
Beta	0.81		

Value of $10,000 invested 5 years ago: $ 23,837

Fiscal Year Ending Dec. 31

	1998	1997	1996	1995	1994	1993
Revenues (Million $)						
1Q	276.6	316.2	298.6	265.6	312.9	276.9
2Q	204.3	221.9	222.7	209.3	213.6	203.3
3Q	—	222.1	176.6	208.1	223.3	217.9
4Q	—	281.9	263.1	248.3	228.7	262.7
Yr.	—	1,042	1,011	931.4	978.6	940.7
Earnings Per Share ($)						
1Q	**1.18**	1.21	1.28	0.97	1.34	1.17
2Q	**0.03**	-0.07	0.43	0.29	0.16	0.09
3Q	—	0.32	0.37	0.32	0.28	0.26
4Q	—	**0.81**	0.62	0.78	0.51	0.67
Yr.	—	**2.27**	2.70	2.36	2.29	2.19

Next earnings report expected: late October

Dividend Data (Dividends have been paid since 1947.)

Amount ($)	Date Decl.	Ex-Div. Date	Stock of Record	Payment Date
0.395	Dec. 18	Jan. 12	Jan. 14	Feb. 01 '98
0.405	Mar. 26	Apr. 08	Apr. 13	May. 01 '98
0.405	Jun. 25	Jul. 09	Jul. 13	Aug. 01 '98
0.405	Sep. 24	Oct. 08	Oct. 13	Nov. 01 '98

A Division of The **McGraw·Hill** *Companies*

Business Summary - 15-APR-98

A holding company for four public utilities, Commonwealth Energy System (CES) provides electricity to about 367,000 customers, and gas to some 237,000 customers in central, eastern and southeastern Massachusetts, including the town of Cambridge, and Cape Cod and Martha's Vineyard. It counts Harvard University among its electric customers. CES produces and distributes steam and holds real estate, through other subsidiaries, and also owns a small interest in the Seabrook 1 nuclear power plant.

Business segment contributions in 1997 were:

	Revs.	Profits
Electric	66%	71%
Gas	32%	30%
Steam & other	2%	(1%)

In 1997, electric sales totaled 8,713,086 mwh, up from 7,404,628 mwh in 1996 and gas sales totaled 49,826 billion British thermal units (BBTU), down from 51,214 BBTU in 1996. Included in electric sales was 3,916,974 mwh of wholesale sales, up from 2,721,623 in 1996, reflecting the availability of a generating unit which had been out of service for maintenance and repair for several months in 1995.

In November 1997, the Governor of Massachusetts signed into law the Electric Industry Restructuring Act. Provisions of this legislation include, among other things, a 10% discount on standard offer service and retail choice of energy supplier effective March 1, 1998, with a subsequent increase in the discount on standard offer service of up to 15% upon completion of divestiture of non-nuclear generating assets and securitization of net non-mitigable stranded costs (which, for the system, are primarily the result of above-market purchased power contracts with non-utility generators) and, recovery of stranded costs subject to review and an audit process. In February, 1998, the Massachusets Department of Telecommunications and Energy (DTE) approved the system's restructuring plan stating that the plan complies with the act.

In July 1997, the DTE directed the ten Massachusetts gas utilities, including Commonwealth Gas, to initiate a collaborative process that will establish guiding principles and specific procedures for unbundling rates and services for all customers. The DTE has ordered Commonwealth Gas to submit, no later than April 15, 1998, a consensus-based settlement, or partial settlement, of unbundled rate tariffs.

Per Share Data ($)

(Year Ended Dec. 31)	1997	1996	1995	1994	1993	1992	1991	1990	1989	1988
Tangible Bk. Val.	20.00	19.27	18.11	17.20	16.37	15.54	15.03	15.56	15.94	15.26
Earnings	2.27	2.70	2.36	2.29	2.19	1.92	0.91	1.08	2.07	1.75
Dividends	1.57	2.29	1.50	1.49	1.46	1.46	1.46	1.45	1.40	1.40
Payout Ratio	69%	85%	64%	65%	67%	76%	160%	134%	68%	80%
Prices - High	34⅝	25⅞	23⅞	23	25¼	21⅝	20	19½	19¼	16½
- Low	18⅞	21¼	17¾	17¾	20⅛	17½	15	14⅝	14⅞	13¼
P/E Ratio - High	15	10	10	10	12	11	22	18	9	9
- Low	8	8	7	8	9	9	16	13	7	8

Income Statement Analysis (Million $)

	1997	1996	1995	1994	1993	1992	1991	1990	1989	1988
Revs.	1,042	1,011	931	979	941	906	850	813	806	689
Depr.	53.4	51.8	54.1	50.1	48.5	50.9	42.0	34.6	29.8	28.3
Maint.	36.8	40.9	38.4	36.5	40.6	39.8	44.3	53.8	48.1	42.8
Fxd. Chgs. Cov.	3.0	3.2	2.6	3.3	3.2	3.0	2.2	2.1	3.2	3.2
Constr. Credits	0.4	0.3	0.9	0.1	0.2	4.1	0.8	6.5	12.9	19.2
Eff. Tax Rate	38%	38%	31%	53%	54%	53%	49%	30%	32%	26%
Net Inc.	49.9	59.2	51.4	49.0	45.8	39.9	19.5	22.6	41.6	35.0

Balance Sheet & Other Fin. Data (Million $)

	1997	1996	1995	1994	1993	1992	1991	1990	1989	1988
Gross Prop.	1,628	1,582	1,516	1,460	1,410	1,385	1,336	1,304	1,232	1,134
Cap. Exp.	57.6	52.9	81.0	58.0	54.0	51.0	61.0	87.0	106	117
Net Prop.	1,050	1,046	1,028	999	985	979	963	966	916	838
Capitalization:										
LT Debt	376	355	390	432	463	377	384	430	348	229
% LT Debt	46	45	49	53	57	53	55	57	51	42
Pfd.	12.2	13.0	14.0	14.7	15.5	16.3	17.1	17.9	18.8	19.6
% Pfd.	1.50	1.70	1.80	1.80	1.90	2.30	2.40	2.40	2.80	3.60
Common	431	416	391	363	337	315	301	307	311	294
% Common	53	53	49	45	41	45	43	41	46	54
Total Cap.	1,020	998	993	1,094	1,090	967	931	971	884	715
% Oper. Ratio	91.6	90.4	89.6	90.5	90.9	91.2	90.6	92.2	91.2	93.0
% Earn. on Net Prop.	8.4	9.3	9.5	9.4	8.8	8.2	8.2	6.7	8.1	6.1
% Return On Revs.	4.8	5.9	5.5	5.0	4.9	4.4	2.3	2.8	5.2	5.1
% Return On Invest. Capital	8.9	10.2	9.6	8.5	8.8	8.6	6.9	7.1	9.4	7.8
% Return On Com. Equity	11.6	14.4	13.3	13.7	13.7	12.5	6.0	6.9	13.3	11.6

Data as orig. reptd.; bef. results of disc opers. and/or spec. items. Per share data adj. for stk. divs. as of ex-div. date. Bold denotes diluted EPS (FASB 128). F-Estimated. NA-Not Available. NM-Not Meaningful. NR-Not Ranked.

Office—One Main St., P.O. Box 9150, Cambridge, MA 02142-9150. **Organized**—in Massachusets in 1926. **Tel**—(617) 225-4000. **Website**—http://www.comenergy.com **Chrmn**—S. A. Buckler. **Pres & CEO**—W. G. Poist. **VP-Secy**—M. P. Sullivan. **VP-Fin, Treas & Investor Contact**—James D. Rappoli. **Trustees**—K. C. Bryant, S. A. Buckler, P. H. Cressy, B. L. Francis, F. M. Hundley, W. J. O'Brien, W. G. Poist, M. C. Ruettgers, G. L. Wilson. **Transfer Agent & Registrar**—First National Bank of Boston. **Empl**— 1,727. **S&P Analyst:** M.I.

03-OCT-98

Industry: Aluminum

Summary: CMIN is a leading manufacturer of aluminum sheet for the transportation, construction and consumer durables markets.

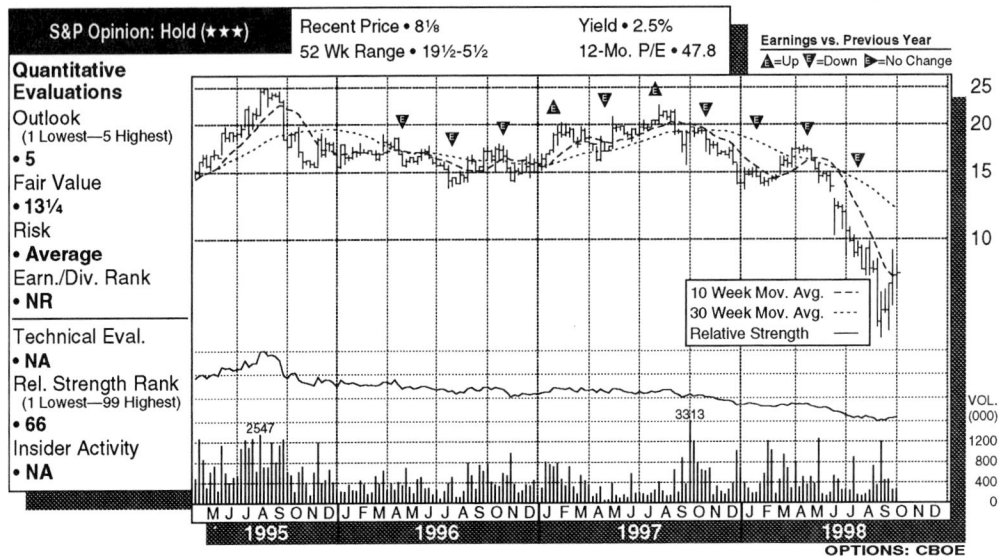

S&P Opinion: Hold (★★★)	Recent Price • 8⅛	Yield • 2.5%	Earnings vs. Previous Year
	52 Wk Range • 19½-5½	12-Mo. P/E • 47.8	▲=Up ▼=Down ▶=No Change

Quantitative Evaluations

Outlook (1 Lowest—5 Highest)
• 5

Fair Value
• 13¼

Risk
• Average

Earn./Div. Rank
• NR

Technical Eval.
• NA

Rel. Strength Rank (1 Lowest—99 Highest)
• 66

Insider Activity
• NA

10 Week Mov. Avg. ---
30 Week Mov. Avg. ·····
Relative Strength —

OPTIONS: CBOE

Overview - 25-SEP-98

We project a 10% sales decline in 1998, reflecting both reduced volume and lower prices in the company's aluminum business. Part of the decline in volume will be the result of a deliberate effort by CMIN to upgrade its product mix by turning down lower margin commodity products. Other contributing factors will be lower production from the Lewisport plant, and generally weak pricing. Penalized further by lower volume and margin pressure in wire products, we expect CMIN to report a drop in operating income and EPS in 1998.

Valuation - 25-SEP-98

Following discussions with the company we upgraded CMIN to hold from avoid on September 22, 1998 based on a more positive EPS outlook for 1998. After concluding a new labor pact, operations at the Lewisport plant are improving. Previously, production shortfalls at that plant led to losses in 1998's second quarter and depressed first quarter EPS. As best we can tell, the worst of the facility's problems appear to be over and the negative impact on EPS will cease. Another positive factor is that the company's order book is strong. The combination of a more efficiently run plant along with firm demand has prompted us to increase our estimate for 1998 to $0.45 from $0.20 previously. However, for the time being, we are keeping our $0.90 estimate for 1999. CMIN has good turnaround potential but we remain concerned that the consensus estimate of $1.30 for 1999 is too aggressive and may lead to investor disappointment down the road. Consequently, we prefer to take a wait and see approach to determine weather or not CMIN warrants a more aggressive recommendation. At the same time, with the shares off 41% so far in 1998 and a better short term EPS outlook, the stock is no longer an avoid.

Key Stock Statistics

S&P EPS Est. 1998	0.45	Tang. Bk. Value/Share		9.91
P/E on S&P Est. 1998	18.1	Beta		NA
S&P EPS Est. 1999	0.90	Shareholders		4,800
Dividend Rate/Share	0.20	Market cap. (B)		$0.130
Shs. outstg. (M)	15.9	Inst. holdings		86%
Avg. daily vol. (M)	0.077			

Value of $10,000 invested 5 years ago: NA

Fiscal Year Ending Dec. 31

	1998	1997	1996	1995	1994	1993
Revenues (Million $)						
1Q	248.9	272.2	167.5	173.9	104.2	—
2Q	258.4	287.2	159.7	192.2	121.4	—
3Q	—	271.2	170.1	160.3	137.0	—
4Q	—	260.2	241.9	145.1	134.0	—
Yr.	—	1,091	739.2	671.5	496.5	—
Earnings Per Share ($)						
1Q	0.10	0.01	0.22	0.95	—	—
2Q	-0.17	0.41	0.21	1.27	—	—
3Q	E0.19	0.15	0.45	0.75	—	—
4Q	E0.25	0.08	0.55	0.45	—	—
Yr.	E0.45	0.78	1.44	3.32	—	—

Next earnings report expected: mid October

Dividend Data (Dividends have been paid since 1995.)

Amount ($)	Date Decl.	Ex-Div. Date	Stock of Record	Payment Date
0.050	Oct. 14	Oct. 23	Oct. 27	Nov. 10 '97
0.050	Dec. 16	Feb. 05	Feb. 09	Feb. 23 '98
0.050	Feb. 10	Apr. 30	May. 04	May. 18 '98
0.050	Jul. 16	Jul. 23	Jul. 27	Aug. 10 '98

A Division of The McGraw·Hill Companies

Business Summary - 25-SEP-98

Commonwealth Industries Inc., (formerly Commonwealth Aluminum) is a leading manufacturer of aluminum sheet for the transportation, construction and consumer durables end-use markets. The company owns and operates at Lewisport, KY, one of the largest multi-purpose aluminum rolling mills in North America.

Following its acquisition of CasTech Aluminum Group Inc. in September 1996, CMIN's shipment capability increased to over 1.0 billion lbs. of aluminum sheet. In addition, the acquisition provided 476 million ft. of electrical wiring products. CasTech, with 1995 sales of $418 million, is a leading manufacturer of continuous cast aluminum sheet, manufacturing from recycled aluminum utilizing low cost, scrap-based mini-mill production technology, and is also a leading manufacturer of electrical flexible conduit and prewired armored cable. The addition of CasTech will create new market opportunities domestically and internationally.

The aluminum sheet products manufactured by the company are generally referred to as common alloy products. They are sold to distributors and end-users, principally for use in transportation equipment such as truck trailers and bodies and automotive parts; building and construction products such as roofing, siding, windows and gutters; beverage cans and consumer durables such as cookware and appliances.

Unlike integrated aluminum producers, CMIN relies on scrap and purchased aluminum ingot as its basic raw material. It melts scrap or ingot in a furnace, and transforms the molten metal into a finished aluminum sheet product. The company does not own or mine bauxite or make alumina. CMIN's capital costs are substantially less than those of its integrated rivals, because it doesn't require mining, material handling, smelters and other equipment needed to transform bauxite into ingot and finished aluminum products. Consequently, CMIN's operating leverage and earnings are less volatile vis a vis the integrated companies.

However, the scrap based method used by CMIN and other aluminum minimills is incapable of producing a high quality product that can compete with the top of the line sheet produced via the integrated process that uses bauxite and alumina as raw materials.

CMIN's principal integrated rivals are Alcoa, Alcan, Alumax Inc., Kaiser Aluminum, Pechiney and Reynolds Metals. The company's minimill rivals are Quanex Corp.'s Nichols Homeshield subsidiary and Century Aluminum.

CMIN's shipments by market in 1997 were: building and construction, 37%; can stock, 8%; consumer durables and other, 14%; distribution, 30%; and transportation, 11%. Aluminum shipments totaled 990.2 million lbs. in 1997, up from 712.5 million lbs. in 1996. Shipments of electrical wiring products totaled 521.7 million sq. ft., versus 137 million sq. ft. in 1996.

Per Share Data ($)

(Year Ended Dec. 31)	1997	1996	1995	1994	1993	1992	1991	1990	1989	1988
Tangible Bk. Val.	9.84	5.11	20.90	17.86	NA	NA	NA	NA	NA	NA
Cash Flow	3.74	3.65	5.14	NA	NA	NA	NA	NA	NA	NA
Earnings	0.78	1.44	3.32	NA	NA	NA	NA	NA	NA	NA
Dividends	0.20	0.20	0.15	Nil	Nil	Nil	Nil	Nil	Nil	Nil
Payout Ratio	26%	14%	5%	Nil	Nil	Nil	Nil	Nil	Nil	Nil
Prices - High	22½	18⅞	24⅞	NA	NA	NA	NA	NA	NA	NA
- Low	13½	13⅝	14	NA	NA	NA	NA	NA	NA	NA
P/E Ratio - High	29	13	7	NA	NA	NA	NA	NA	NA	NA
- Low	17	9	4	NA	NA	NA	NA	NA	NA	NA

Income Statement Analysis (Million $)

Revs.	1,091	739	672	497	NA	NA	NA	NA	NA	NA
Oper. Inc.	76.3	41.7	60.8	37.7	NA	NA	NA	NA	NA	NA
Depr.	34.7	22.5	18.6	17.4	NA	NA	NA	NA	NA	NA
Int. Exp.	30.5	9.9	3.5	0.1	NA	NA	NA	NA	NA	NA
Pretax Inc.	11.5	9.5	43.1	22.8	NA	NA	NA	NA	NA	NA
Eff. Tax Rate	21%	NM	22%	3.10%	NA	NA	NA	NA	NA	NA
Net Inc.	9.1	14.8	33.8	22.1	NA	NA	NA	NA	NA	NA

Balance Sheet & Other Fin. Data (Million $)

Cash	Nil	1.9	2.7	Nil	Nil	Nil	Nil	Nil	Nil	Nil
Curr. Assets	217	332	227	236	NA	NA	NA	NA	NA	NA
Total Assets	667	795	421	439	NA	NA	NA	NA	NA	NA
Curr. Liab.	104	125	73.9	102	NA	NA	NA	NA	NA	NA
LT Debt	126	336	37.4	6.5	NA	NA	NA	NA	NA	NA
Common Eqty.	330	227	213	243	NA	NA	NA	NA	NA	NA
Total Cap.	456	563	250	250	NA	NA	NA	NA	NA	NA
Cap. Exp.	21.7	14.8	15.2	19.7	NA	NA	NA	NA	NA	NA
Cash Flow	43.8	37.2	52.4	39.5	NA	NA	NA	NA	NA	NA
Curr. Ratio	2.1	2.7	3.1	2.3	NA	NA	NA	NA	NA	NA
% LT Debt of Cap.	27.6	59.7	15.0	2.6	NA	NA	NA	NA	NA	NA
% Net Inc.of Revs.	0.8	2.0	5.0	4.4	NA	NA	NA	NA	NA	NA
% Ret. on Assets	1.2	2.4	7.9	NA	NA	NA	NA	NA	NA	NA
% Ret. on Equity	3.5	6.7	14.8	NA	NA	NA	NA	NA	NA	NA

Data as orig. reptd.; bef. results of disc. opers. and/or spec. items. Per share data adj. for stk. divs. as of ex-div. date. Bold denotes diluted EPS (FASB 128). E-Estimated. NA-Not Available. NM-Not Meaningful. NR-Not Ranked.

Office—500 West Jefferson St., 19th floor, Louisville, KY 40202-2823. **Tel**—(502) 589-8100. **Fax**—(502) 589-8158. **Website**—http://www.cacky.com **Chrmn**—P. E. Lego. **Pres & CEO**—M. V. Kaminski. **Secy**—D. L. Marsh, Jr. **Investor Contact**—William G. Toler (502-589-8138). **Dirs**—C. G. Burke, C. F. Fetterholf, M. V. Kaminski, P. E. Lego, J. E. Merow, V. Torasso. **Transfer Agent**—National City Bank, Cleveland. **Incorporated**—in Delaware in 1984. **Empl**— 2,015. **S&P Analyst:** Leo J. Larkin

STANDARD
&POOR'S
STOCK REPORTS

Commscope, Inc.

600P

NYSE Symbol **CTV**

In S&P SmallCap 600

03-OCT-98

Industry:
Communications
Equipment

Summary: CommScope is the world's largest manufacturer of coaxial cable and is a leading supplier of high-performance cables for LAN and other applications.

Quantitative Evaluations		
Recent Price • 11	Yield • Nil	
52 Wk Range • 20¾-9⅜	12-Mo. P/E • 22.0	

Outlook
(1 Lowest—5 Highest)
• **NA**

Fair Value
• **NA**

Risk
• **NA**

Earn./Div. Rank
• **NR**

Technical Eval.
• **NA**

Rel. Strength Rank
(1 Lowest—99 Highest)
• **25**

Insider Activity
• **NA**

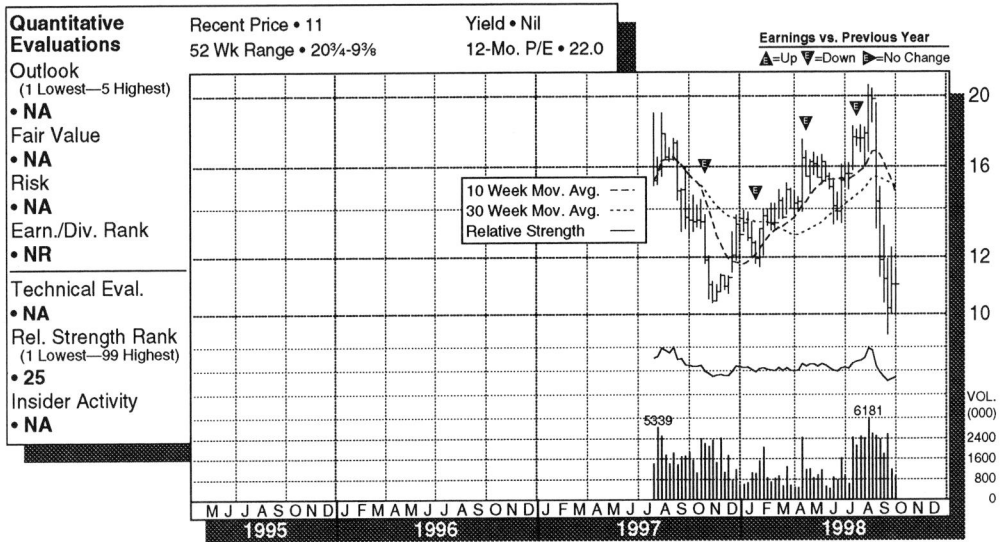

Earnings vs. Previous Year
▲=Up ▼=Down ▶=No Change

10 Week Mov. Avg. – – –
30 Week Mov. Avg. ·····
Relative Strength —

5339   6181

Business Profile - 13-AUG-98

CommScope was spun off by General Instrument (now known as General Semiconductor) in July 1997. The company expects the surging growth in Internet access, primarily through 2-way hybrid fiber coaxial (HFC) cable modems, to be a fundamental driver of future growth for its core business. While CommScope is optimistic about its longer-term outlook, the competitive pricing environment and weak international sales have affected recent performance.

Operational Review - 13-AUG-98

Sales fell 10% year to year in the first half of 1998, primarily reflecting a significant reduction in international sales due to the economic turmoil in key overseas markets. Profitability deteriorated on the lower volume, and net income plunged 40%, to $14,831,000 ($0.30 a share), from $24,661,000 ($0.50) on a pro forma basis. Second quarter results improved sequentially, with a 17% increase in international sales, and gross margin expansion as a result of engineered cost savings, manufacturing efficiencies and improving sales volumes.

Stock Performance - 02-OCT-98

In the past 30 trading days, CTV's shares have declined 44%, compared to a 7% fall in the S&P 500. Average trading volume for the past five days was 179,940 shares, compared with the 40-day moving average of 637,892 shares.

Key Stock Statistics

Dividend Rate/Share	Nil	Shareholders	NA
Shs. outstg. (M)	49.2	Market cap. (B)	$0.541
Avg. daily vol. (M)	0.432	Inst. holdings	67%
Tang. Bk. Value/Share	NM		
Beta	NA		

Value of $10,000 invested 5 years ago: NA

Fiscal Year Ending Dec. 31

	1998	1997	1996	1995	1994	1993
Revenues (Million $)						
1Q	133.6	147.9	130.9	—	—	—
2Q	141.9	159.3	142.0	—	—	—
3Q	—	147.3	148.6	—	—	—
4Q	—	144.8	150.7	—	—	—
Yr.	—	599.2	572.2	—	—	—
Earnings Per Share ($)						
1Q	0.13	0.26	0.23	—	—	—
2Q	0.17	0.24	0.24	—	—	—
3Q	—	0.14	0.29	—	—	—
4Q	—	0.06	0.30	—	—	—
Yr.	—	0.70	1.12	—	—	—

Next earnings report expected: late October

Dividend Data

No dividends have been paid.

A Division of The McGraw·Hill Companies

Business Summary - 13-AUG-98

In July 1997, General Instrument (now known as General Semiconductor -- SEM; NYSE) transferred all the assets and liabilities relating to the manufacture and sale of broadband communications products used in the cable television, satellite and telecommunications industries to its wholly owned subsidiary NextLevel Systems, Inc., and all the assets and liabilities relating to the manufacture and sale of coaxial, fiber optic and other electronic cable used in the cable television, satellite and other industries to CommScope, Inc. (then a wholly owned subsidiary of General Instrument). It then distributed all of the outstanding shares of capital stock of NextLevel Systems and CommScope to its stockholders.

As cable television, telephone, Internet access and other communications services converge, broadband communication systems are increasingly being configured in a hybrid design that includes both fiber optic and coaxial cables. Commscope is the largest manufacturer and supplier of coaxial cable for cable television applications in the U.S. in terms of sales volume, with more than a 50% market share in 1997, and is a leading supplier of coaxialcable for satellite television applications. It also supplies thedeveloping market for high-bandwidth coaxial cables used in hybrid fiber coaxial (HFC) networks that provide local access to a combination of services that can include cable television, telephone and Internet access. International sales accounted for about a third of the total in 1997.

The company has recently expanded into additional markets through internal development of new products and by acquisition. Cell Reach is an internally developed coaxial cable product designed to be installed on antenna towers for cellular telephone, personal communication services (PCS) and other wireless or cellular communication applications. Commscope has recently started marketing its Cell Reach cables and accessories to cellular network operators located in the U.S. and certain international markets.

In February 1998, CommScope sold its high-temperature aerospace and industrial cable business to Alcatel Cable for approximately $13 million, resulting in a gain of $2 million ($0.03 a share). Sales from CommScope's high-temperature business, located in Elm City, NC, totaled approximately $16 million in 1997. The Elm City facility, which was included in the sale, occupies approximately 250,000 square feet and employs 200. CommScope and Alcatel also announced that they have fully resolved the patent issues between the two companies. This resolution enables CommScope to enhance its portfolio of fiber-cable products for the Hybrid-Fiber Coax (HFC) market while resolving patent issues with Alcatel in Europe.

Per Share Data ($)

(Year Ended Dec. 31)	1997	1996	1995	1994	1993	1992	1991	1990	1989	1988
Tangible Bk. Val.	NM	NM	NM	NM	NM	NM	NM	NM	NM	NM
Cash Flow	1.20	NA	NA	NA	NA	NA	NA	NA	NA	NA
Earnings	0.70	1.12	NA	NA	NA	NA	NA	NA	NA	NA
Dividends	Nil	Nil	Nil	Nil	Nil	Nil	Nil	Nil	Nil	Nil
Payout Ratio	Nil	Nil	Nil	Nil	Nil	Nil	Nil	Nil	Nil	Nil
Prices - High	19	NA	NA	NA	NA	NA	NA	NA	NA	NA
- Low	10³/₈	NA	NA	NA	NA	NA	NA	NA	NA	NA
P/E Ratio - High	27	NA	NA	NA	NA	NA	NA	NA	NA	NA
- Low	15	NA	NA	NA	NA	NA	NA	NA	NA	NA

Income Statement Analysis (Million $)

	1997	1996	1995	1994	1993	1992	1991	1990	1989	1988
Revs.	599	572	NA	NA	NA	NA	NA	NA	NA	NA
Oper. Inc.	101	NA	NA	NA	NA	NA	NA	NA	NA	NA
Depr.	21.7	NA	NA	NA	NA	NA	NA	NA	NA	NA
Int. Exp.	13.7	NA	NA	NA	NA	NA	NA	NA	NA	NA
Pretax Inc.	61.5	84.4	NA	NA	NA	NA	NA	NA	NA	NA
Eff. Tax Rate	39%	38%	NA	NA	NA	NA	NA	NA	NA	NA
Net Inc.	37.5	52.4	NA	NA	NA	NA	NA	NA	NA	NA

Balance Sheet & Other Fin. Data (Million $)

	1997	1996	1995	1994	1993	1992	1991	1990	1989	1988
Cash	3.3	NA	NA	NA	NA	NA	NA	NA	NA	NA
Curr. Assets	156	171	NA	NA	NA	NA	NA	NA	NA	NA
Total Assets	484	493	NA	NA	NA	NA	NA	NA	NA	NA
Curr. Liab.	43.0	58.0	NA	NA	NA	NA	NA	NA	NA	NA
LT Debt	266	275	NA	NA	NA	NA	NA	NA	NA	NA
Common Eqty.	150	135	NA	NA	NA	NA	NA	NA	NA	NA
Total Cap.	431	426	NA	NA	NA	NA	NA	NA	NA	NA
Cap. Exp.	29.9	NA	NA	NA	NA	NA	NA	NA	NA	NA
Cash Flow	59.1	NA	NA	NA	NA	NA	NA	NA	NA	NA
Curr. Ratio	3.6	2.9	NA	NA	NA	NA	NA	NA	NA	NA
% LT Debt of Cap.	61.7	64.6	NA	NA	NA	NA	NA	NA	NA	NA
% Net Inc.of Revs.	6.3	9.2	NA	NA	NA	NA	NA	NA	NA	NA
% Ret. on Assets	7.8	NA	NA	NA	NA	NA	NA	NA	NA	NA
% Ret. on Equity	13.8	NA	NA	NA	NA	NA	NA	NA	NA	NA

Data as orig. reptd. (pro forma in 1996; bal. sheet as of Mar. 31, 1997); bef. results of disc. opers. and/or spec. items. Per share data adj. for stk. divs. as of ex-div. date. Bold denotes diluted EPS (FASB 128). E-Estimated. NA-Not Available. NM-Not Meaningful. NR-Not Ranked.

Office—1375 Lenoir Rhyne Blvd., P.O. Box 1729, Hickory, NC 28603. **Tel**—(704) 324-2200. **Website**—www.commscope.com **Chrmn & CEO**—F. M. Drendel. **Pres & COO**—B. D. Garrett. **EVP & CFO**—J. L. Leonhardt. **VP & Secy**—F. B. Wyatt II. **Investor Contact**—Phil Armstrong (828-323-4848).**Dirs**—E. D. Breen, F. M. Drendel, N. C. Forstmann, B. L. George, G. N. Hutton Jr., J. N. Whitson. **Transfer Agent & Registrar**—ChaseMellon Shareholder Services, Ridgefield Park, NJ. **Incorporated**—in Delaware in 1997. **Empl**— 2,700. **S&P Analyst:** C.F.B.

STANDARD &POOR'S
STOCK REPORTS

CompDent Corp.
3587N

Nasdaq Symbol **CPDN**

In S&P SmallCap 600

03-OCT-98

Industry:
Health Care (Managed Care)

Summary: This dental management company has reached a definitive agreement to merge with a privately owned firm, with shareholders, other than management, to receive $18 a share in cash.

S&P Opinion: Hold (★★★)	Recent Price • 14 — Yield • Nil
	52 Wk Range • 27¾-9 — 12-Mo. P/E • NM

Quantitative Evaluations

Outlook
(1 Lowest—5 Highest)
• **NA**

Fair Value
• **NA**

Risk
• **Average**

Earn./Div. Rank
• **NR**

Technical Eval.
• **Bearish** since 10/97

Rel. Strength Rank
(1 Lowest—99 Highest)
• **67**

Insider Activity
• **NA**

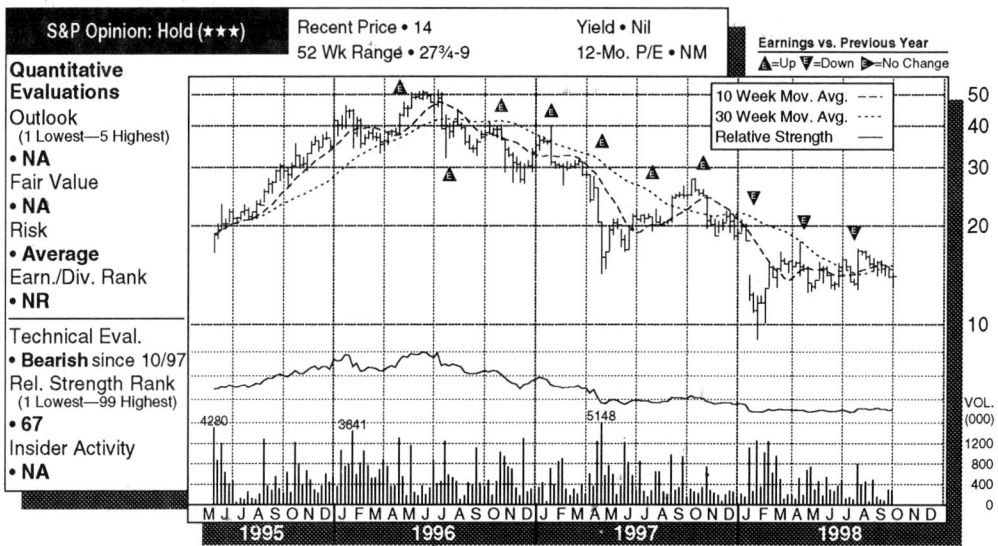

Earnings vs. Previous Year
▲=Up ▼=Down ►=No Change

10 Week Mov. Avg. — · —
30 Week Mov. Avg. - - - -
Relative Strength ——

Overview - 05-AUG-98

On July 28, 1998, CompDent announced that its directors approved a definitive merger agreement with a new, privately held company formed by Golder, Thoma, Cressey, Rauner, Inc., TA Associates, Inc., and NMS Capital Partners. Under the agreement, each outstanding CPDN common share, other than shares held by management, will be converted into the right to receive $18 in cash. Shares held by management will be converted into shares of the surviving company. The transaction is subject to regulatory and shareholder approval and is expected to be completed in four to six months. Since inception in 1978, this leading provider of managed dental products to employers in the Midwest and Southeast has expanded from a single state to over 2.1 million members in more than 23 states. In July 1997, CPDN jump started its recently formed dental practice management subsidiary, Dental Health Management, by acquiring 21 dental facilities located in central and southern Illinois. Currently, CompDent manages 48 dental facilities in seven states.

Valuation - 05-AUG-98

The shares have surged on news of the merger agreement, and the stock is currently trading near the cash buy-out figure of $18 per share. The company has indicated that the deal has been approved by directors and the financing is in place. Subject to regulatory and shareholder approval, the merger should be completed by the end of the year. With the shares trading slightly below the $18 acquisition price, we recommended that investors hold the shares until the transaction is completed.

Key Stock Statistics

S&P EPS Est. 1998	1.10	Tang. Bk. Value/Share	NM
P/E on S&P Est. 1998	12.7	Beta	NA
S&P EPS Est. 1999	1.25	Shareholders	1,600
Dividend Rate/Share	Nil	Market cap. (B)	$0.142
Shs. outstg. (M)	10.1	Inst. holdings	75%
Avg. daily vol. (M)	0.038		

Value of $10,000 invested 5 years ago: NA

Fiscal Year Ending Dec. 31

	1998	1997	1996	1995	1994	1993
Revenues (Million $)						
1Q	42.44	37.84	31.39	23.03	13.17	—
2Q	43.56	38.20	34.76	23.48	13.58	—
3Q	—	41.13	37.15	31.87	13.95	—
4Q	—	41.56	37.78	28.28	14.94	—
Yr.	—	158.7	141.1	106.7	55.19	—
Earnings Per Share ($)						
1Q	**0.25**	0.28	0.22	0.12	—	—
2Q	**0.26**	0.28	0.24	0.15	—	—
3Q	**E0.28**	0.29	0.26	0.18	—	—
4Q	**E0.31**	-6.17	0.26	0.25	—	—
Yr.	**E1.10**	-5.32	0.97	0.68	0.30	—

Next earnings report expected: late October

Dividend Data

No cash dividends have been paid on the common stock, and the company does not intend to pay cash dividends in the foreseeable future. A shareholder rights plan was adopted in 1996.

STANDARD
&POOR'S
STOCK REPORTS

CompDent Corporation

3587N
03-OCT-98

Business Summary - 05-AUG-98

A dental management company, CompDent Corp. (CPDN) announced in July 1998 that it had approved a definitive merger agreement with a new privately held company formed by Golder, Thoma, Cressey, Rauner, Inc., TA Associates, Inc., and NMS Capital Partners. Under the agreement, each outstanding share of common stock, other than shares held by management, will be converted into $18 in cash. Shares held by management will be converted into shares of the surviving company. The transaction is subject to various conditions and approvals and is expected to be completed by the end of 1998.

CompDent provides a broad array of managed dental benefit plans, including dental HMO, dual choice, discount fee-for-service, network rental, ASO (Administrative Services Organization), specialty benefit plans and dental facilities management. CompDent's provider network includes over 9,000 dentist spread across all of its markets, predominantly in Florida, Illinois, Texas, Georgia, Kentucky and Ohio.

As a result of internal growth and acquisitions, CPDN has grown to providing dental coverage for more than 2.1 million plan members in more than 23 states.

Through its Dental Health Management Inc. (DHM) subsidiary, (formed in March 1997), CPDN provides management services to dental practices. DHM also acquires existing dental practices and funds new practices through its minority (less than 20%) interest in Dental Health Development (the remaining equity is supplied by venture capitalists and other third-party investors). DHM manages 48 dental facilities in seven states.

Members of managed dental HMO plans (about 85% of revenues) obtain certain basic dental procedures, such as exams, X-rays, cleanings, and certain fillings, at no charge beyond a nominal co-payment per visit.

Dual choice dental plans offer members the choice of receiving dental benefits through a dental HMO plan or through an indemnity plan. With dual choice, the company can provide dental benefits to employers with employees within and outside of the area served by CPDN's panel dentists.

Discount fee-for-service products are marketed principally under the brand name CompSave. Members receive dental care from participating dentists who offer discounts from their usual and customary fees.

Network rental plans allow members of the HMO to receive certain dental services from network providers at discounted rates as part of their overall HMO benefit package. The company has contracted to provide a discount dental benefit plan to members of several HMOs.

ASO services, which are provided to employers and other groups offering self insured dental plans, include administrative services such as billing and collection, claims processing and payments, member eligibility processing and customer service. The specialty benefit plans allow members to receive covered dental services from participating specialty dentists in exchange for a premium and co-payment.

Per Share Data ($)

(Year Ended Dec. 31)	1997	1996	1995	1994	1993	1992	1991	1990	1989	1988
Tangible Bk. Val.	NM	NM	2.95	NM	NM	NM	NM	NM	NM	NM
Cash Flow	-4.75	1.49	1.07	0.87	NA	NA	NA	NA	NA	NA
Earnings	-5.32	0.97	0.68	0.30	NA	NA	NA	NA	NA	NA
Dividends	Nil	Nil	Nil	Nil	Nil	Nil	Nil	Nil	Nil	Nil
Payout Ratio	Nil	Nil	Nil	Nil	Nil	Nil	Nil	Nil	Nil	Nil
Prices - High	40	51¾	42¾	NA	NA	NA	NA	NA	NA	NA
- Low	14¼	26¾	14½	NA	NA	NA	NA	NA	NA	NA
P/E Ratio - High	NM	53	63	NA	NA	NA	NA	NA	NA	NA
- Low	NM	28	21	NA	NA	NA	NA	NA	NA	NA

Income Statement Analysis (Million $)

	1997	1996	1995	1994	1993	1992	1991	1990	1989	1988
Revs.	159	141	107	55.0	NA	NA	NA	NA	NA	NA
Oper. Inc.	118	24.1	13.0	7.5	NA	NA	NA	NA	NA	NA
Depr.	5.7	5.3	2.9	2.4	NA	NA	NA	NA	NA	NA
Int. Exp.	3.2	1.9	2.0	2.5	NA	NA	NA	NA	NA	NA
Pretax Inc.	-48.8	17.8	9.0	2.3	NA	NA	NA	NA	NA	NA
Eff. Tax Rate	NM	44%	42%	48%	NA	NA	NA	NA	NA	NA
Net Inc.	-53.7	9.9	5.2	1.4	NA	NA	NA	NA	NA	NA

Balance Sheet & Other Fin. Data (Million $)

	1997	1996	1995	1994	1993	1992	1991	1990	1989	1988
Cash	24.3	27.0	40.4	9.7	NA	NA	NA	NA	NA	NA
Curr. Assets	37.3	34.1	46.3	14.5	NA	NA	NA	NA	NA	NA
Total Assets	151	151	129	63.0	NA	NA	NA	NA	NA	NA
Curr. Liab.	26.1	24.3	21.0	16.6	NA	NA	NA	NA	NA	NA
LT Debt	56.6	41.7	Nil	29.9	NA	NA	NA	NA	NA	NA
Common Eqty.	60.6	112	102	4.2	NA	NA	NA	NA	NA	NA
Total Cap.	117	154	102	39.3	NA	NA	NA	NA	NA	NA
Cap. Exp.	4.0	2.4	1.1	0.3	NA	NA	NA	NA	NA	NA
Cash Flow	-48.0	15.1	7.8	3.7	NA	NA	NA	NA	NA	NA
Curr. Ratio	1.4	1.4	2.2	0.9	NA	NA	NA	NA	NA	NA
% LT Debt of Cap.	48.3	27.1	Nil	76.1	NA	NA	NA	NA	NA	NA
% Net Inc.of Revs.	NM	7.0	4.9	2.5	NA	NA	NA	NA	NA	NA
% Ret. on Assets	NM	6.3	5.8	28.1	NA	NA	NA	NA	NA	NA
% Ret. on Equity	NM	9.2	9.4	42.5	NA	NA	NA	NA	NA	NA

Data as orig. reptd.; bef. results of disc. opers. and/or spec. items. Per share data adj. for stk. divs. as of ex-div. date. Bold denotes diluted EPS (FASB 128). E-Estimated. NA-Not Available. NM-Not Meaningful. NR-Not Ranked.

Office—100 Mansell Court, Roswell, GA 30076. **Registrar & Transfer Agent**—State Street Bank & Trust Co., Boston.**Tel**—(770) 998-8936. **Fax**—(770) 992-4349. **Website**—http://www.compdent.com**Chrmn & CEO**—D. R. Klock.**Pres**—P. A. Klock.**SVP-Fin**—W. Jens, Jr.**EVP, Secy & Interim CFO**—B. A. Mitchell. **Dirs**—J. A. Ciffolillo, P. Hertik, D. R. Klock, D. F. Scott Jr., J. E. Stephenson. **Transfer Agent & Registrar**—State Street Bank & Trust Co., Boston. **Incorporated**—in Delaware in 1993. **Empl**—460. **S&P Analyst:** John J. Arege

03-OCT-98

Industry: Services (Computer Systems)

Summary: TSK provides information technology services and solutions to the Fortune 500 and other companies through strategic partnerships.

Quantitative Evaluations

Outlook (1 Lowest—5 Highest)
- **5**

Fair Value
- **52¼**

Risk
- **Average**

Earn./Div. Rank
- **B+**

Technical Eval.
- **Bearish** since 5/98

Rel. Strength Rank (1 Lowest—99 Highest)
- **62**

Insider Activity
- **Neutral**

Recent Price • 27¾   Yield • 0.2%
52 Wk Range • 45-23   12-Mo. P/E • 23.3

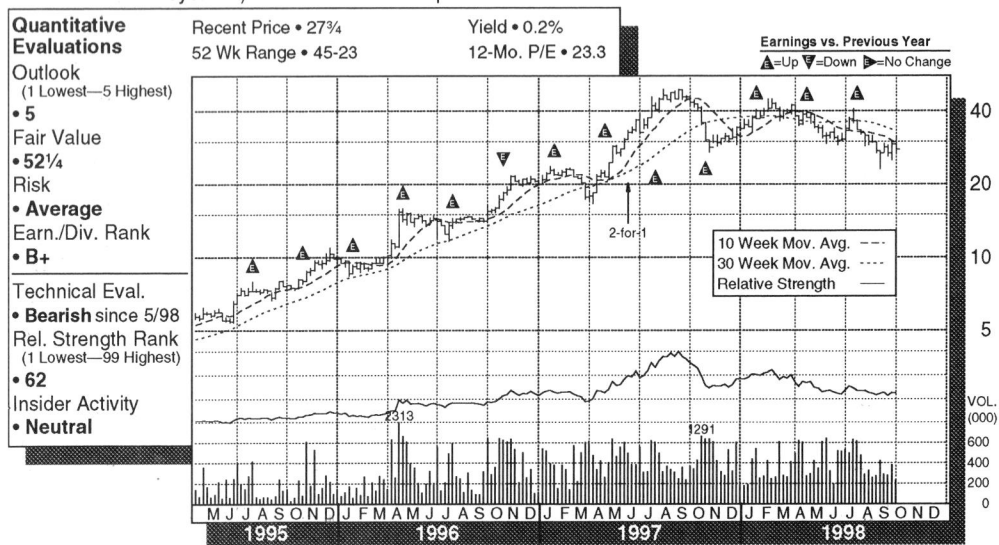

Earnings vs. Previous Year
▲=Up ▼=Down ▶=No Change

2-for-1

10 Week Mov. Avg. — · —
30 Week Mov. Avg. · · · ·
Relative Strength —

Business Profile - 15-MAY-98

The company is focusing on attracting and retaining the best information technology professionals. Initiatives in the areas of career development, training and benefits have been implemented toward that end. TSK attributes its strong recent growth to its ability to deliver value-added services to key clients and strategic partners. In addition, the company has made significant investments aimed at strengthening its global sales and recruiting approaches. IBM remains TSK's largest customer. The company's financial condition is strong, with a current ratio of 2.1, and no long term debt as of March 1998. Through the end of March 1998, TSK had repurchased 2.5 million of its common shares, and was authorized to repurchase an additional 0.9 million shares.

Operational Review - 15-MAY-98

Revenues in the three months ended March 31, 1998, advanced 16%, year to year, paced by strength in Europe (up 36%), despite the strength of the U.S. dollar. Results benefited from the continued implementation of the company's key client strategy, which focuses on building its core business around certain strategic companies, as well as a trend toward higher value-added services, increased billing rates, and ongoing efforts to reduce overhead costs as a percentage of revenue. Net income was up 38%, to $5,077,000 ($0.30 a share, diluted, on fewer shares), from $3,669,000 ($0.21, as adjusted).

Stock Performance - 02-OCT-98

In the past 30 trading days, TSK's shares have declined 7%, compared to a 7% fall in the S&P 500. Average trading volume for the past five days was 45,900 shares, compared with the 40-day moving average of 62,831 shares.

Key Stock Statistics

Dividend Rate/Share	0.05	Shareholders	3,500
Shs. outstg. (M)	20.8	Market cap. (B)	$0.576
Avg. daily vol. (M)	0.062	Inst. holdings	58%
Tang. Bk. Value/Share	3.11		
Beta	1.72		

Value of $10,000 invested 5 years ago: $ 68,695

Fiscal Year Ending Dec. 31

	1998	1997	1996	1995	1994	1993
Revenues (Million $)						
1Q	109.7	94.94	90.01	82.23	77.01	77.89
2Q	117.7	100.1	91.32	84.61	77.95	73.96
3Q	—	101.1	89.41	85.61	69.00	71.20
4Q	—	111.4	94.34	86.96	77.61	72.40
Yr.	—	407.6	365.1	339.4	301.6	295.5
Earnings Per Share ($)						
1Q	**0.30**	**0.21**	0.13	0.10	0.06	0.03
2Q	**0.34**	**0.26**	0.15	0.11	0.07	Nil
3Q	Nil	**0.26**	0.17	0.29	0.07	0.03
4Q	—	**0.29**	0.18	0.12	0.08	-1.35
Yr.	—	**1.01**	0.62	0.61	0.26	-1.31

Next earnings report expected: mid October

Dividend Data (Dividends have been paid since 1976.)

Amount ($)	Date Decl.	Ex-Div. Date	Stock of Record	Payment Date
0.050	Apr. 29	May. 07	May. 11	May. 29 '98

A Division of The McGraw·Hill Companies

Computer Task Group, Incorporated

Business Summary - 15-MAY-98

Computer Task Group is one of the largest U.S. providers of computer-related professional services to commercial clients. Through a network of 55 offices in North America and Europe, the company provides clients, primarily large industrial and service companies, with professional services in the areas of software development, consulting and systems engineering. IBM accounted for 35% of revenues in 1997, up from 29% in 1996. In December 1997, the company renewed a contract with IBM for three additional years; TSK is one of IBM's national technical service providers for the U.S. Contributions by geographic area in 1997 were:

	Revs.	Profits
North America	89%	82%
Europe	11%	18%

TSK's business strategy is based on being cost competitive while also being responsive in supplying qualified staff to work on client engagements. Services are sold and delivered on a local level through its network of teams of sales managers, resource managers and business consultants. The company has developed a professional staff resource database, CTG-Smartsource, which is used to screen and qualify individuals who are available to work on client information technology needs. The database has more than 170,000 candidates available for assignments.

The company works with customers to develop effective business solutions through information systems and technology. TSK's professional staff may support a customer's software development team on a specific application or project or may manage the project entirely for the customer. The range of services extends from flexible staffing provided on a per diem basis to managing multimillion-dollar technology projects. Approximately 56% of the company's services are provided to customers in the services industry, followedby 18% in the manufacturing industry, 8% in the banking andfinance industries, and 18% in other industries. Most of TSK's servicesare provided on-site at the customer's facilities. TSK's network of offices provides wide geographical coverage with the capability of servicing large companies with multiple locations.

TSK's strategy is to build the core of its business around its key clients: companies that offer it the greatest opportunity to add value to their business as a strategic partner.

Per Share Data ($)

(Year Ended Dec. 31)	1997	1996	1995	1994	1993	1992	1991	1990	1989	1988
Tangible Bk. Val.	2.33	6.48	2.71	2.54	3.33	3.07	2.77	5.47	5.05	4.27
Cash Flow	1.32	2.11	0.97	0.57	-0.94	0.63	0.35	0.63	-0.20	0.64
Earnings	1.01	0.63	0.61	0.26	-1.31	0.28	0.05	0.39	-0.44	0.40
Dividends	0.05	0.05	0.05	0.05	0.05	0.03	0.03	0.03	0.03	0.03
Payout Ratio	5%	8%	8%	19%	NM	8%	50%	6%	NM	6%
Prices - High	49³/₈	21³/₄	11	5¹/₄	4¹/₂	5	5⁵/₈	6¹/₈	7⁷/₈	8⁵/₈
- Low	16⁵/₈	8³/₈	4¹/₈	3³/₈	3	3¹/₂	3¹/₂	3³/₈	4¹/₄	4³/₄
P/E Ratio - High	49	35	18	20	NM	18	NM	16	NM	22
- Low	16	13	7	13	NM	13	NM	9	NM	12

Income Statement Analysis (Million $)

	1997	1996	1995	1994	1993	1992	1991	1990	1989	1988
Revs.	408	365	339	302	295	303	285	244	233	219
Oper. Inc.	34.4	26.2	18.9	6.2	12.7	17.6	8.8	15.9	7.7	14.0
Depr.	5.4	7.7	6.2	5.9	7.9	7.0	5.7	4.6	4.3	3.8
Int. Exp.	0.8	0.8	1.3	1.2	1.1	1.4	2.0	0.7	2.0	2.1
Pretax Inc.	30.3	18.5	12.0	8.1	-30.7	10.1	1.6	12.6	-11.6	10.8
Eff. Tax Rate	41%	40%	11%	41%	NM	45%	43%	43%	NM	41%
Net Inc.	17.9	11.1	10.8	4.8	-27.7	5.6	0.9	7.2	-7.8	6.4

Balance Sheet & Other Fin. Data (Million $)

	1997	1996	1995	1994	1993	1992	1991	1990	1989	1988
Cash	25.0	41.5	16.5	5.1	11.8	13.3	10.6	14.6	19.6	19.6
Curr. Assets	88.9	101	78.8	68.2	78.8	75.8	71.1	68.5	67.1	68.4
Total Assets	108	121	105	95.0	109	138	139	134	107	111
Curr. Liab.	41.8	39.7	29.3	29.3	27.5	28.1	30.3	33.0	15.7	26.3
LT Debt	Nil	Nil	3.6	6.1	8.4	10.5	13.8	11.6	1.4	12.1
Common Eqty.	65.1	71.5	61.5	50.7	62.5	92.6	87.2	83.3	83.6	67.0
Total Cap.	55.3	71.5	65.1	57.0	71.0	105	103	97.0	87.0	82.0
Cap. Exp.	4.8	3.6	5.4	4.2	5.4	4.3	7.6	5.8	3.2	5.6
Cash Flow	23.3	18.7	16.9	10.7	-19.9	12.5	6.5	11.8	-3.5	10.2
Curr. Ratio	2.1	2.5	2.7	2.3	2.9	2.7	2.3	2.1	4.3	2.6
% LT Debt of Cap.	Nil	Nil	5.6	10.8	11.9	10.1	13.4	12.0	1.6	14.9
% Net Inc.of Revs.	4.4	3.1	3.2	1.6	NM	1.9	0.3	3.0	NM	2.9
% Ret. on Assets	15.6	9.8	10.8	4.5	NM	3.9	0.6	6.2	NM	6.7
% Ret. on Equity	24.6	16.7	19.3	8.1	NM	5.9	0.9	8.9	NM	9.9

Data as orig. reptd.; bef. results of disc. opers. and/or spec. items. Per share data adj. for stk. divs. as of ex-div. date. Bold denotes diluted EPS (FASB 128). E-Estimated. NA-Not Available. NM-Not Meaningful. NR-Not Ranked.

Office—800 Delaware Ave., Buffalo, NY 14209. Tel—(716) 882-8000. Fax—(716) 887-7456. Website—http://www.ctg.com Chrmn & CEO—Gale S. Fitzgerald. VP & Secy—J. G. Makowski. VP-Fin, CFO & Investor Contact—James R. Boldt. Dirs—G. B. Beitzel, R. L. Crandall, R. K. Elliott, G. S. Fitzgerald, R. A. Marks, B. Z. Shattuck. Transfer Agent & Registrar—First National Bank of Boston. Incorporated—in New York in 1966. Empl—5,800. S&P Analyst: C.F.B.

STANDARD
&POOR'S
STOCK REPORTS

Cone Mills　　**603**

NYSE Symbol **COE**

In S&P SmallCap 600

03-OCT-98　　Industry:　　**Summary:** The world's largest producer of denim fabrics, Cone also
　　　　　　　　Textiles (Specialty)　　makes a variety of other apparel fabrics and sells decorative fabrics
　　　　　　　　　　　　　　　　　　to home furnishings markets.

Quantitative Evaluations	
Outlook (1 Lowest—5 Highest)	• 3
Fair Value	• 7¼
Risk	• Low
Earn./Div. Rank	• NR
Technical Eval.	• Bullish since 1/98
Rel. Strength Rank (1 Lowest—99 Highest)	• 13
Insider Activity	• Neutral

Recent Price • 4⅞
52 Wk Range • 10¼-4¾

Yield • Nil
12-Mo. P/E • NM

Earnings vs. Previous Year
▲=Up ▼=Down ▶=No Change

10 Week Mov. Avg. ‒ ‒ ‒
30 Week Mov. Avg. ‒ ‒ ‒ ‒
Relative Strength ———

Business Profile - 28-JUL-98

After several quarters of losses, Cone Mills reported its
second consecutive period of profitability in the second
quarter of 1998. In early 1997, COE implemented a
plan to refocus on its core businesses (denim, sportswear fabrics and home furnishings fabrics) and to dispose of several non-core businesses. COE's plans included the sale of Greeff Fabrics, part of the Cone
Decorative Fabrics group; the sale of the synthetic
fabric business; the sale of Cornwallis Development
Co., its real estate subsidiary; and the closing of the
Granite Finishing Plant in Haw River, NC. As a result,
the company recorded $3.1 million in pretax charges
during the first three quarters of 1997, versus $4.5 mil-
lion in gains for the comparable 1996 period.

Operational Review - 28-JUL-98

Net sales in the 26 weeks ended June 28, 1998, rose
7.5%, year to year, as higher sales of denim products,
finishing services and jacquard fabrics outweighed
lower sales of specialty sportswear. Gross margins widened, and operating profit rose sharply. After a modest
decline in interest expense, pretax income contrasted
with a pretax loss. With taxes at 33.0%, versus a tax
benefit, and equity in income of an affiliate versus a
loss, net income of $4,595,000 ($0.12 a share) contrasted with a net loss of $3,066,000 ($0.17). Results
in the 1997 period include a pretax charge of
$1,809,000.

Stock Performance - 02-OCT-98

In the past 30 trading days, COE's shares have declined 38%, compared to a 7% fall in the S&P 500.
Average trading volume for the past five days was
49,860 shares, compared with the 40-day moving average of 44,928 shares.

Key Stock Statistics

Dividend Rate/Share	Nil	Shareholders	500
Shs. outstg. (M)	26.2	Market cap. (B)	$0.128
Avg. daily vol. (M)	0.047	Inst. holdings	51%
Tang. Bk. Value/Share	6.10		
Beta	0.34		

Value of $10,000 invested 5 years ago: $ 3,421

Fiscal Year Ending Dec. 31

	1998	1997	1996	1995	1994	1993
Revenues (Million $)						
1Q	190.2	174.7	199.3	226.2	195.9	195.0
2Q	197.3	185.8	208.1	232.9	201.7	202.5
3Q	—	185.5	180.8	231.7	203.5	192.6
4Q	—	170.8	157.7	219.4	205.1	179.0
Yr.	—	716.9	745.9	910.2	806.2	769.2
Earnings Per Share ($)						
1Q	0.03	-0.10	0.24	0.11	0.34	0.42
2Q	0.09	-0.07	0.11	-0.06	0.33	0.47
3Q	—	-0.08	-0.11	0.19	0.28	0.40
4Q	—	-0.22	-0.44	-0.46	0.24	0.39
Yr.	—	-0.47	-0.19	-0.22	1.19	1.68

Next earnings report expected: late October

Dividend Data

No cash has been paid.

A Division of The **McGraw·Hill** Companies

Business Summary - 28-JUL-98

Cone Mills is the largest producer of denim fabrics in the world and the largest commission printer of home furnishings fabrics in North America. Industry segment sales contributions in recent years were:

	1997	1996
Apparel fabrics	85%	84%
Home furnishings fabrics	15%	16%

The company manufactures a variety of denim apparel fabrics and believes that it produces a broader range of fashion denim than any of its competitors. Denim sales accounted for more than 80% of apparel fabric sales in 1997. It is the largest supplier to Levi Strauss and the sole supplier of denims for Levi's 501 jeans. In 1997, Levi Strauss accounted for 37% of COE's revenues (49% in 1996).

Cone is also a producer of specialty sportswear fabrics, including plaid flannel and solid shade, and chamois flannel shirting fabrics. The company also also offers piece-dyed fabrics based on dye, finishing and yarn formation technologies and provides fabrics such as fade resistant Deepdown fabric and the wrinkle resistant fabric Prospin.

The company serves the home furnishings market through three divisions: Cone Finishing, which provides custom printing services to leading home furnishings stylists and distributors through it Carlisle and Raytex plants; Cone Decorative Fabrics, a leading designer of printed and solid woven fabrics for use in upholstery, draperies and bedspreads; and Cone Jacquard (which began in 1995), a provider of jacquard woven fabrics to furniture, drapery and other markets.

The company's sales and marketing activities are conducted through a worldwide distribution network. About 35% of Cone's current denim production was exported in 1997 and total international sales represented nearly 25% of sales in 1997.

In early 1997, the company decided to refocus on its core businesses: the casualwear fabrics (denim and specialty sportswear) and home furnishings fabrics and commission finishing used in the drapery, bedding and furniture markets. COE's plans called for the sale of Greeff Fabrics, a fabric distributor that was part of the Cone Decorative Fabrics group; the sale of Cornwallis Development Co., its real estate subsidiary; and the closing of the Granite Finishing Plant in Haw River, NC.

In February 1998, COE stated that it was dedicated to continuing the operations of John Wolf Decorative Fabrics. A restructuring program for the division has been designed and includes marketing and merchandising efforts. Additionally, a cost reduction plan has been implemented in order to return the division to profitability.

Per Share Data ($)

(Year Ended Dec. 31)	1997	1996	1995	1994	1993	1992	1991	1990	1989	1988
Tangible Bk. Val.	4.82	5.22	5.28	5.84	6.19	4.52	3.35	NA	NA	NA
Cash Flow	0.52	0.80	0.91	2.02	2.43	2.50	1.07	NA	NA	NA
Earnings	-0.47	-0.19	-0.22	1.19	1.68	1.67	0.29	NA	NA	NA
Dividends	Nil	Nil	Nil	Nil	Nil	Nil	NA	NA	NA	NA
Payout Ratio	Nil	Nil	Nil	Nil	Nil	Nil	NA	NA	NA	NA
Prices - High	9³/₈	12³/₈	14³/₈	17¹/₄	19⁵/₈	16	NA	NA	NA	NA
- Low	7	7¹/₄	10⁵/₈	11¹/₈	13³/₈	10	NA	NA	NA	NA
P/E Ratio - High	NM	NM	NM	14	12	10	NA	NA	NA	NA
- Low	NM	NM	NM	9	8	6	NA	NA	NA	NA

Income Statement Analysis (Million $)

	1997	1996	1995	1994	1993	1992	1991	1990	1989	1988
Revs.	717	746	910	806	769	705	633	NA	NA	NA
Oper. Inc.	22.8	44.9	63.7	86.0	107	98.0	56.0	NA	NA	NA
Depr.	25.9	26.9	28.3	23.3	21.0	20.0	20.4	NA	NA	NA
Int. Exp.	14.2	15.5	15.1	7.9	7.0	10.9	19.0	NA	NA	NA
Pretax Inc.	-17.4	-4.5	20.9	55.5	79.5	70.2	19.8	NA	NA	NA
Eff. Tax Rate	NM	NM	35%	36%	38%	35%	38%	NA	NA	NA
Net Inc.	-9.4	-2.2	-3.3	35.8	49.6	45.4	12.2	NA	NA	NA

Balance Sheet & Other Fin. Data (Million $)

	1997	1996	1995	1994	1993	1992	1991	1990	1989	1988
Cash	0.9	1.0	0.3	1.2	0.5	7.3	6.4	NA	NA	NA
Curr. Assets	180	204	234	213	202	216	259	NA	NA	NA
Total Assets	507	530	584	524	432	402	443	NA	NA	NA
Curr. Liab.	121	120	151	118	104	121	127	NA	NA	NA
LT Debt	140	150	162	126	77.0	77.0	138	NA	NA	NA
Common Eqty.	158	210	184	198	172	125	135	NA	NA	NA
Total Cap.	336	400	425	400	324	277	312	NA	NA	NA
Cap. Exp.	36.2	36.2	61.7	37.5	38.7	25.4	NA	NA	NA	NA
Cash Flow	13.7	21.7	25.0	56.3	67.8	60.8	28.0	NA	NA	NA
Curr. Ratio	1.5	1.7	1.6	1.8	1.9	1.8	2.0	NA	NA	NA
% LT Debt of Cap.	41.7	37.5	38.1	31.5	23.8	27.6	44.1	NA	NA	NA
% Net Inc.of Revs.	NM	NM	NM	4.4	6.4	6.4	1.9	NA	NA	NA
% Ret. on Assets	NM	NM	NM	7.5	11.9	6.3	NA	NA	NA	NA
% Ret. on Equity	NM	NM	NM	18.0	31.5	49.3	NA	NA	NA	NA

Data as orig. reptd.; bef. results of disc. opers. and/or spec. items. Per share data adj. for stk. divs. as of ex-div. date. Bold denotes diluted EPS (FASB 128). E-Estimated. NA-Not Available. NM-Not Meaningful. NR-Not Ranked.

Office—3101 N. Elm St., Greensboro, NC 27408. **Tel**—(336) 379-6220.**Chrmn**—D. L. Trogdon. **Pres & CEO**—J. P. Danahy. **VP & COO**—J. L. Bakane. **VP-CFO**—Anthony L. Furr.**Treas & Investor Contact**—David E. Bray. **VP & Secy**—T. L. Weatherford. **Dirs**—J. L. Bakane, D. R. Bray, J. P. Danahy, J. C. Kimmel, C. M. Reid, J. W. Rosenblum, N. Shreiber, D. L. Trogdon, C. C. Wilson. **Transfer Agent & Registrar**—First Union National Bank of North Carolina, Charlotte. **Incorporated**—in North Carolina. **Empl**— 6,100. **S&P Analyst:** Kathleen J. Fraser

03-OCT-98

Industry: Natural Gas

Summary: CNE is a holding company whose principal subsidiary, Southern Connecticut Gas Co., provides natural gas to over 157,000 customers in Fairfield, New Haven and Middlesex counties.

Quantitative Evaluations	
Recent Price • 27	Yield • 5.0%
52 Wk Range • 32¼-22¾	12-Mo. P/E • 15.9

Outlook (1 Lowest—5 Highest)
• **1⁻**

Fair Value
• **25**

Risk
• **Low**

Earn./Div. Rank
• **A-**

Technical Eval.
• **Bearish** since 7/98

Rel. Strength Rank (1 Lowest—99 Highest)
• **77**

Insider Activity
• **NA**

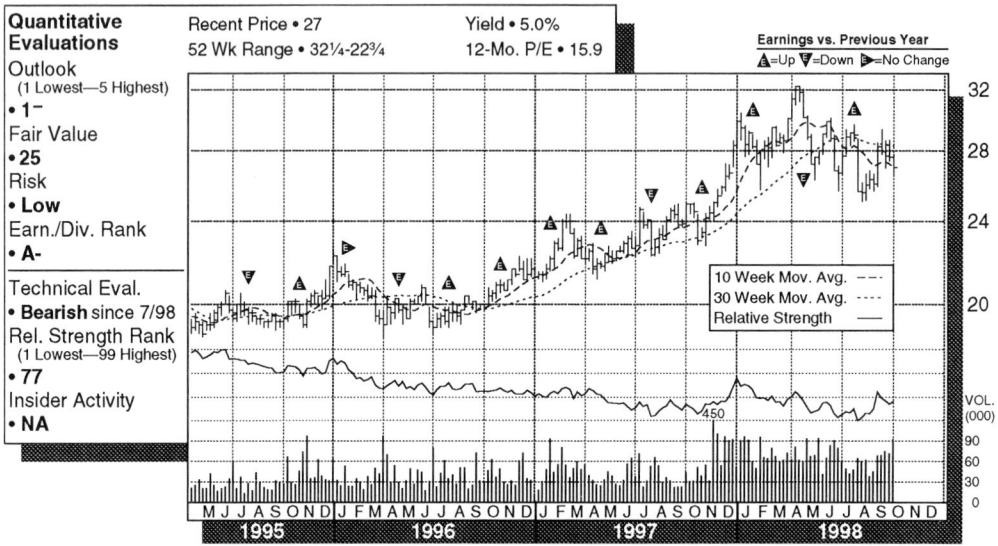

Earnings vs. Previous Year
▲=Up ▼=Down ▶=No Change

10 Week Mov. Avg. - - -
30 Week Mov. Avg. ·······
Relative Strength ——

Business Profile - 27-AUG-98

Although Connecticut Energy expects to continue to focus on expanding its utility customer base as the deregulation of the gas utility industry continues, it anticipates that an increasing portion of earnings will come from unregulated operations. The latter consist of marketing energy commodities and services to commercial and industrial customers throughout New England and New York, bulk purchases and storage of natural gas, and investing in energy-related technology innovations. CNE expects gas utility operations to experience higher volumes of throughput in coming years, with the addition of two new major projects in 1998: a firm sales contract to supply gas to Yale University's new 13.5 mw cogeneration plant; and the transportation of natural gas to a new 520 mw electric generating plant built at Bridgeport Harbor by Duke Energy Trading and Marketing LLC.

Operational Review - 27-AUG-98

Revenues in the first nine months of FY 98 (Sep.) fell 4.7%, year to year. Firm customer margins for the company's principal subsidiary, Southern Connecticut Gas Co., grew by over 1%, but this growth was offset by reduced interruptible margins compared to FY 97 levels, as a result of the continued lower cost of competitive fuels throughout the year. Interest expense was 4.3% lower; net income was up 5.1%, to $20,397,000 ($2.03 a share, diluted), from $19,415,000 ($2.14).

Stock Performance - 02-OCT-98

In the past 30 trading days, CNE's shares have increased 3%, compared to a 7% fall in the S&P 500. Average trading volume for the past five days was 22,260 shares, compared with the 40-day moving average of 13,785 shares.

Key Stock Statistics

Dividend Rate/Share	1.34	Shareholders	10,400
Shs. outstg. (M)	10.3	Market cap. (B)	$0.277
Avg. daily vol. (M)	0.017	Inst. holdings	34%
Tang. Bk. Value/Share	17.60		
Beta	0.25		

Value of $10,000 invested 5 years ago: $ 16,014

Fiscal Year Ending Sep. 30

	1998	1997	1996	1995	1994	1993
Revenues (Million $)						
1Q	76.51	74.87	69.78	65.52	66.71	64.20
2Q	100.8	106.9	120.2	103.3	111.8	91.61
3Q	38.00	44.03	43.95	39.76	36.84	33.78
4Q	—	26.24	27.18	23.53	25.49	23.21
Yr.	—	252.0	261.1	232.1	240.9	212.8
Earnings Per Share ($)						
1Q	**0.64**	0.60	0.57	0.57	0.67	0.80
2Q	**1.49**	1.67	1.64	1.79	1.77	1.59
3Q	**0.10**	0.10	-0.08	-0.23	-0.16	-0.31
4Q	—	-0.32	-0.42	-0.52	-0.53	-0.57
Yr.	—	1.81	1.70	1.60	1.58	1.50

Next earnings report expected: early November

Dividend Data (Dividends have been paid since 1850.)

Amount ($)	Date Decl.	Ex-Div. Date	Stock of Record	Payment Date
0.330	Nov. 25	Dec. 04	Dec. 08	Dec. 31 '97
0.330	Jan. 27	Mar. 18	Mar. 20	Mar. 31 '98
0.335	May. 26	Jun. 17	Jun. 19	Jun. 30 '98
0.335	Jul. 29	Sep. 16	Sep. 18	Sep. 30 '98

A Division of The McGraw-Hill Companies

STANDARD
&POOR'S
STOCK REPORTS

Connecticut Energy Corporation

605

03-OCT-98

Business Summary - 27-AUG-98

Connecticut Energy Corp. is a utility holding company that, through its predecessor companies, has compiled the longest consecutive dividend payment record of any nonfinancial company listed on the New York Stock Exchange. Cash dividends have been paid on the common stock since 1850.

Through wholly owned Southern Connecticut Gas Co. (Southern), CNE delivers natural gas in 22 Connecticut communities to more than 157,000 customers. The service area consists of towns along the southern Connecticut coast from Westport to Old Saybrook; the service area also includes the urban communities of Bridgeport and New Haven.

Southern provides three types of gas service: firm sales, firm transportation, and interruptible.

Firm service is provided to residential, commercial and industrial customers who require a continuous gas supply throughout the year. Southern serves about 181,000 firm residential units. Firm transportation is available to commercial and industrial customers who have secured their own gas supply and require that Southern transport this supply on its distribution system. Interruptible service is available to those commercial and industrial customers and multifamily residential dwellings that have dual fuel capabilities, allowing them to alternate between natural gas and another fuel source.

From FY 92 (Sep.) to FY 97, the average number of on-system customers served by Southern grew from about 152,100 to 156,600, with residential accounting for 57.9% of customers at the end of FY 97, commercial firm for 19.5%, industrial firm 4.3% and interruptible and other 18.3%.

Southern concentrates on customer additions that are the most cost-effective to achieve. Over the past several years, Southern has focused on adding load along its existing mains, which generally requires a lower capital outlay. About 59% of the residences along Southern's mains heat with natural gas. The conversion of these homes from an alternative fuel to natural gas heat has been a major factor in increased load growth.

In an effort to capture new markets, CNE has been expanding its two unregulated subsidiaries, CNE Energy Services Group and CNE Development, both formed in FY 95. It has also developed a third unregulated subsidiary, CNE Venture-Tech. Energy Services provides various energy products and services to commercial and industrial customers throughout New England, from installation and maintenance of equipment to procuring the most cost-effective energy commodity. CNE Development participates in a natural gas purchasing cooperative. Venture-Tech seeks investment opportunities in information technology related to utility operations.

Per Share Data ($)

(Year Ended Sep. 30)	1997	1996	1995	1994	1993	1992	1991	1990	1989	1988
Tangible Bk. Val.	15.10	15.31	14.15	13.72	12.47	11.91	12.36	11.74	11.98	11.90
Earnings	1.81	1.70	1.60	1.58	1.50	1.43	1.38	1.12	1.28	1.49
Dividends	1.32	1.31	1.30	1.29	1.28	1.26	1.24	1.23	1.20	1.17
Payout Ratio	73%	77%	81%	82%	85%	88%	90%	110%	94%	79%
Prices - High	30³/₈	22¹/₄	22³/₈	25	26¹/₂	24³/₄	20³/₈	18	18⁷/₈	15¹/₄
- Low	21	18⁵/₈	18¹/₂	18⁵/₈	22¹/₂	18⁷/₈	14¹/₄	14¹/₂	14	13¹/₂
P/E Ratio - High	17	13	14	16	18	17	15	16	15	10
- Low	12	11	12	12	15	13	10	13	11	9

Income Statement Analysis (Million $)

	1997	1996	1995	1994	1993	1992	1991	1990	1989	1988
Revs.	252	261	232	241	213	203	179	174	171	157
Depr.	15.8	14.8	14.1	13.0	12.1	11.3	10.5	10.7	10.3	8.5
Maint.	3.6	3.8	3.7	4.0	3.7	3.6	3.6	4.0	3.9	4.2
Fxd. Chgs. Cov.	2.9	2.8	2.8	2.6	2.3	2.2	2.4	2.2	2.4	2.7
Constr. Credits	Nil	Nil	Nil	Nil	Nil	Nil	Nil	Nil	Nil	Nil
Eff. Tax Rate	35%	33%	35%	30%	26%	24%	39%	41%	43%	43%
Net Inc.	16.4	15.2	14.1	12.8	11.1	10.2	9.0	6.9	7.8	8.7

Balance Sheet & Other Fin. Data (Million $)

	1997	1996	1995	1994	1993	1992	1991	1990	1989	1988
Gross Prop.	403	376	355	332	314	294	274	255	242	222
Cap. Exp.	28.5	25.3	27.6	26.7	26.1	22.8	20.4	23.4	23.7	20.1
Net Prop.	272	258	248	234	222	210	199	189	181	167
Capitalization:										
LT Debt	134	139	119	120	121	94.1	87.4	91.5	79.7	69.1
% LT Debt	48	50	48	49	55	50	49	55	51	46
Pfd.	NA	NA	NA	NA	0.6	0.7	0.7	0.8	0.8	6.4
% Pfd.	NA	NA	NA	NA	0.30	0.40	0.40	0.50	0.60	4.30
Common	145	138	136	126	100	92.6	88.6	74.4	75.0	73.3
% Common	52	50	52	51	45	49	50	45	48	49
Total Cap.	279	277	251	301	239	205	194	182	170	163
% Oper. Ratio	88.5	89.1	88.4	89.6	89.1	89.0	88.9	90.3	80.8	88.7
% Earn. on Net Prop.	10.8	11.4	11.2	11.0	10.7	10.9	10.2	9.1	9.9	11.0
% Return On Revs.	6.5	5.8	6.1	5.3	5.2	5.0	5.0	4.0	4.6	5.5
% Return On Invest. Capital	4.8	8.7	8.6	9.1	10.2	10.9	10.4	9.7	10.1	11.1
% Return On Com. Equity	11.6	11.9	10.9	11.4	11.5	11.3	11.0	9.3	10.6	12.9

Data as orig. reptd.; bef. results of disc. opers. and/or spec. items. Per share data adj. for stk. divs. as of ex-div. date. Bold denotes diluted EPS (FASB 128). E-Estimated. NA-Not Available. NM-Not Meaningful. NR-Not Ranked.

Office—855 Main St., Bridgeport, CT 06604. Tel—(800) 760-7776. Website—www.connenergy.com Chrmn & Pres—J. R. Crespo. VP, CFO & Treas—C. A. Forest. VP & Secy—S. W. Bowlby. Investor Contact—Judith E. Falango (203-382-8156).Dirs—H. Chauncey Jr., J. P. Comer, J. R. Crespo, R. F. Freeman, R. M. Hoyt, P. H. Johnson, N. M. Marsilius III, S. M. Sugden, C. D. Turner, H. B. Wasserman. Transfer Agent & Registrar—Boston EquiServe. Incorporated—in Connecticut in 1967; reincorporated in Connecticut in 1979. Empl— 501. S&P Analyst: C.F.B.

03-OCT-98

Industry:
Specialty Printing

Summary: This company provides general commercial printing services through 25 printing companies in 20 U.S. markets.

Quantitative Evaluations	
Outlook (1 Lowest—5 Highest)	• **NA**
Fair Value	• **NA**
Risk	• **Average**
Earn./Div. Rank	• **NR**
Technical Eval.	• **NA**
Rel. Strength Rank (1 Lowest—99 Highest)	• **18**
Insider Activity	• **Unfavorable**

Recent Price • 37½   Yield • Nil
52 Wk Range • 67⅛-35   12-Mo. P/E • 23.8

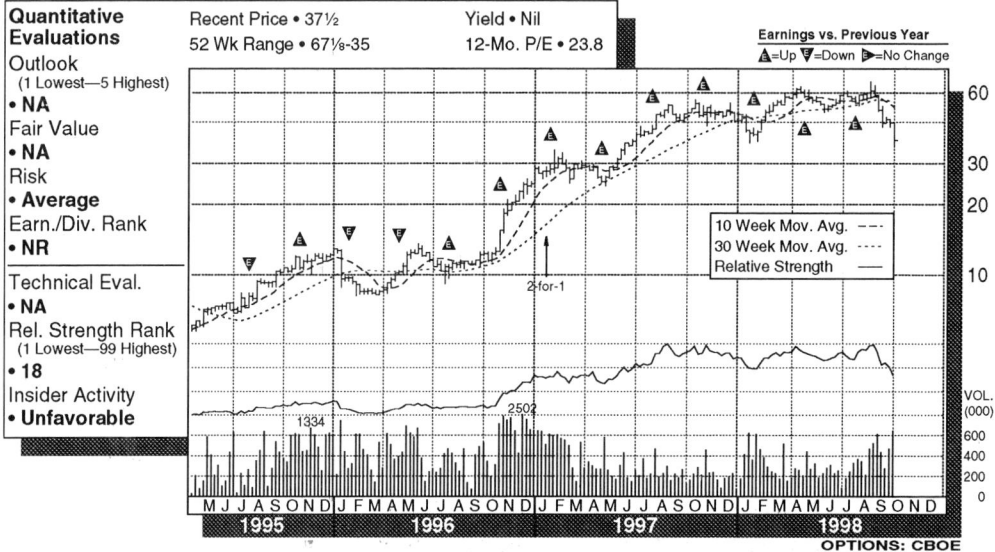

Earnings vs. Previous Year
▲=Up ▼=Down ▶=No Change

10 Week Mov. Avg. – – –
30 Week Mov. Avg. ·······
Relative Strength ——

OPTIONS: CBOE

Business Profile - 04-MAY-98

Consolidated Graphics seeks to continue its rapid growth in the highly fragmented printing services industry by increasing its market share through internal growth and acquisitions. The company's strategy is to add value to its acquisitions through managerial and operational expertise, financial strength and economies of scale. Since February 1998, the company has agreed to acquire printing companies in five new markets: Philadelphia, Milwaukee, Boston, Wichita and San Francisco. Upon completion of pending transactions, Consolidated Graphics will have 37 companies with annualized revenues in excess of $370 million.

Operational Review - 04-MAY-98

Based on a preliminary report, sales soared 61% in FY 98 (Mar.), reflecting sales from acquired companies, as well as internal growth. Margins widened, aided by operating efficiencies gained through economies of scale, and benefits resulting from investments in technology and equipment; pretax income surged 85%. After taxes at 38.0%, versus 37.0%, net income was up 82%, to $18,390,000 ($1.40 a share, on 5.6% more shares), from $10,100,000 ($0.81, as adjusted).

Stock Performance - 02-OCT-98

In the past 30 trading days, CGX's shares have declined 39%, compared to a 7% fall in the S&P 500. Average trading volume for the past five days was 33,680 shares, compared with the 40-day moving average of 44,867 shares.

Key Stock Statistics

Dividend Rate/Share	Nil	Shareholders	100
Shs. outstg. (M)	13.3	Market cap. (B)	$0.499
Avg. daily vol. (M)	0.118	Inst. holdings	71%
Tang. Bk. Value/Share	6.21		
Beta	NA		

Value of $10,000 invested 5 years ago: NA

Fiscal Year Ending Mar. 31

	1999	1998	1997	1996	1995	1994
Revenues (Million $)						
1Q	85.10	50.68	28.26	19.48	11.53	—
2Q	—	53.36	34.45	19.31	10.79	—
3Q	—	60.98	38.19	22.26	16.33	—
4Q	—	66.27	43.19	24.09	18.52	—
Yr.	—	231.3	144.1	85.13	57.17	48.64
Earnings Per Share ($)						
1Q	0.48	0.30	0.14	0.10	0.15	—
2Q	—	0.33	0.20	0.13	0.10	—
3Q	—	0.37	0.22	0.03	0.09	—
4Q	—	0.41	0.25	0.10	0.13	—
Yr.	—	1.40	0.81	0.36	0.46	0.53

Next earnings report expected: NA

Dividend Data

No cash dividends have been paid. A two-for-one split was effected in 1997.

A Division of The McGraw-Hill Companies

Business Summary 04-MAY-98

As a result of an ongoing acquisition program, this provider of general commercial printing services in the U.S. has expanded its network of printing companies to more than 20 operating in 16 markets from just nine companies in early 1996. Upon completion of all pending acquisitions, CGX will have 37 companies with annualized revenues of more than $370 million.

Management believes that an abundance of acquisition opportunities exist, because of the fragmented nature of the U.S. general commercial printing industry. The commercial printing business is composed of a large number of locally oriented, family-owned businesses, many of which tend to be viable acquisition targets. The owners are eager to expand by becoming part of a larger organization and, in some instances, wish to retire from the business. Because there are relatively few buyers with adequate financing and management expertise attempting to acquire these local printing companies, CGX has been and expects to continue to be able to implement its acquisition strategy at attractive prices.

CGX's strategy is to grow through acquisitions of smaller, locally oriented printing companies (generally having $2 million to $20 million in annual sales), to enhance the acquired company's competitiveness and profitability, and develop a group of companies in individual geographic markets.

Each of the company's operations provides general commercial printing services relating to the production of annual reports, training manuals, product and capability brochures, direct mail pieces, catalogs and other promotional material, all of which tend to be recurring in nature. One of its printing companies also provides transaction-oriented financial printing services, including the printing of registration and information statements filed with the SEC.

CGX's commercial printing focuses on the production of promotional, investor relations and other sales materials for various customers including corporations, mutual fund companies, advertising agencies, graphic design firms and direct mail and catalog retailers. The company's customer list includes major corporations headquartered in the markets in which the company operates. It believes it is one of the leading general commercial printers in the Houston and Denver markets.

Since February 1998, Consolidated Graphics has agreed to acquire printing companies in five new markets: Philadelphia, Milwaukee, Boston, Wichita and San Francisco, and increased its presence in San Diego.

Per Share Data ($)

(Year Ended Mar. 31)	1998	1997	1996	1995	1994	1993	1992	1991	1990	1989
Tangible Bk. Val.	5.95	4.85	3.78	3.49	1.61	1.06	NA	NA	NA	NA
Cash Flow	2.17	1.28	0.70	0.88	0.82	0.48	0.23	0.24	NA	NA
Earnings	1.40	0.81	0.36	0.46	0.53	0.37	0.14	0.17	NA	NA
Dividends	Nil	Nil	Nil	Nil	Nil	Nil	Nil	Nil	Nil	Nil
Payout Ratio	Nil	Nil	Nil	Nil	Nil	Nil	Nil	Nil	Nil	Nil
Cal. Yrs.	1997	1996	1995	1994	1993	1992	1991	1990	1989	1988
Prices - High	56⅛	29	13⅛	11¼	NA	NA	NA	NA	NA	NA
- Low	23⅞	8⅛	4¾	4⅞	NA	NA	NA	NA	NA	NA
P/E Ratio - High	40	36	36	24	NA	NA	NA	NA	NA	NA
- Low	17	10	13	11	NA	NA	NA	NA	NA	NA

Income Statement Analysis (Million $)

	1998	1997	1996	1995	1994	1993	1992	1991	1990	1989
Revs.	231	144	85.1	57.2	48.6	28.9	20.5	14.9	NA	NA
Oper. Inc.	43.4	24.1	12.3	11.4	7.9	4.7	2.9	1.9	NA	NA
Depr.	10.0	5.8	3.8	4.1	1.6	0.6	0.5	0.4	NA	NA
Int. Exp.	3.8	2.3	0.9	0.4	1.1	0.7	0.6	0.5	NA	NA
Pretax Inc.	29.7	16.0	6.1	6.9	5.3	3.3	1.8	1.5	NA	NA
Eff. Tax Rate	38%	37%	35%	35%	34%	37%	38%	34%	NA	NA
Net Inc.	18.4	10.1	4.0	4.5	3.5	2.1	0.8	0.9	NA	NA

Balance Sheet & Other Fin. Data (Million $)

	1998	1997	1996	1995	1994	1993	1992	1991	1990	1989
Cash	5.3	3.6	3.1	1.7	2.1	NA	NA	NA	NA	NA
Curr. Assets	71.7	43.1	31.5	24.3	16.6	NA	NA	NA	NA	NA
Total Assets	238	136	87.8	60.3	36.8	34.7	13.6	12.4	NA	NA
Curr. Liab.	43.6	21.0	12.6	10.5	8.7	NA	NA	NA	NA	NA
LT Debt	73.0	39.3	20.1	8.8	13.5	13.8	4.1	4.0	NA	NA
Common Eqty.	105	66.4	49.9	38.2	9.0	6.0	3.6	2.8	NA	NA
Total Cap.	194	115	75.2	49.8	25.8	22.9	7.7	6.9	NA	NA
Cap. Exp.	10.6	10.2	6.0	2.4	3.4	NA	NA	NA	NA	NA
Cash Flow	28.4	15.9	7.8	8.5	4.5	2.7	1.3	1.3	NA	NA
Curr. Ratio	1.6	2.0	2.5	2.3	1.9	NA	NA	NA	NA	NA
% LT Debt of Cap.	37.6	34.2	26.7	17.7	52.2	60.3	53.0	58.9	NA	NA
% Net Inc.of Revs.	8.0	7.1	4.7	7.8	7.2	7.3	3.8	6.3	NA	NA
% Ret. on Assets	9.9	9.1	5.4	9.2	9.8	8.7	6.0	7.4	NA	NA
% Ret. on Equity	21.4	17.4	9.1	18.8	39.4	42.8	24.4	32.8	NA	NA

Data as orig. reptd.; bef. results of disc. opers. and/or spec. items. Per share data adj. for stk. divs. as of ex-div. date. Bold denotes diluted EPS (FASB 128). E-Estimated. NA-Not Available. NM-Not Meaningful. NR-Not Ranked.

Office—2210 W. Dallas St., Houston, TX 77019. **Tel**—(713) 529-4200. **Pres & CEO**—J. R. Davis. **VP & CFO**—G. C. Colville. **VP, Treas & Investor Contact**—Ronald E. Hale Jr. **Dirs**—L. J. Alexander, B. F. Carruth, C. C. Comer, J. R. Davis, G. L. Forbes, W. D. Hawkins, J. H. Limmer, T. E. Smith, H. N. West. **Transfer Agent & Registrar**—American Stock Transfer & Trust Co., NYC. **Incorporated**—in Texas in 1985. **Empl**— 1,417. **S&P Analyst:** Ray Lam, CFA

03-OCT-98 Industry: Restaurants

Summary: This growing restaurant operator has more than 260 units in the Midwest and Southeast, operating mainly under the Steak n Shake name.

S&P Opinion: Buy (★★★★)	Recent Price • 17¼	Yield • Nil
	52 Wk Range • 21⅝-14⅝	12-Mo. P/E • 19.2

Earnings vs. Previous Year
▲=Up ▼=Down ▶=No Change

Quantitative Evaluations

Outlook
(1 Lowest—5 Highest)
• 4-

Fair Value
• 24⅞

Risk
• Average

Earn./Div. Rank
• NR

Technical Eval.
• NA

Rel. Strength Rank
(1 Lowest—99 Highest)
• 71

Insider Activity
• Neutral

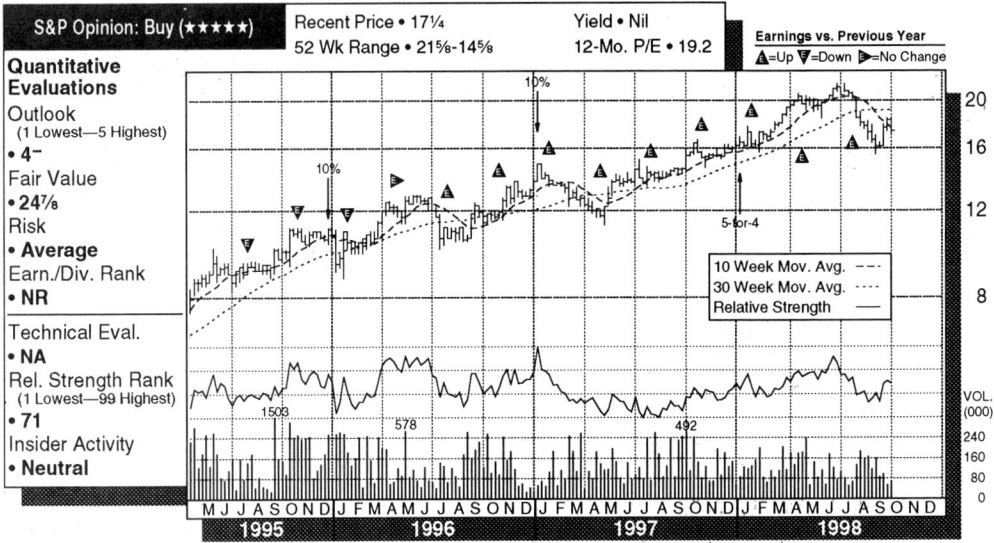

10 Week Mov. Avg. ---
30 Week Mov. Avg. ·····
Relative Strength —

5-for-4

Overview - 04-AUG-98

Sales of this growing restaurant operator should rise about 16% in FY 98 (Sep.), reflecting continued aggressive expansion of the Steak 'n' Shake chain. The company plans to open 18 company-operated units in the fourth quarter of FY 98, followed by 13 new restaurants in the first quarter of FY 99. COP's long-term growth plan calls for 20% annual increases in the number of company-owned units thorough fiscal 2002. In addition, near-term performance will be aided by 1%-2% gains in same-store sales. Margins are expected to remain steady, as favorable food prices will offset wage pressures, which are the result of a tight domestic labor market. Yearly comparisons will be aided by a reduction in interest expense, but will be limited by an increase in the number of shares outstanding. We forecast FY 98 EPS of $0.91 and see earnings rising nearly 20%, to $1.09 in FY 99.

Valuation - 04-AUG-98

Shares of COP have moved higher with the overall market in 1998 and are currently selling at 10 times our calendar 1998 EPS estimate of $0.96 (16X our calendar 1999 estimate of $1.14), which represents a discount to the broader market. As a result, we continue to recommend investors buy the shares. We believe the company will benefit from a variety of factors, including an aggressive expansion program and favorable economic conditions. While same-store sales are unlikely rise more than a few percentage points, top-line growth will be driven by 20% annual increases in the number of restaurants. Furthermore, current economic conditions bode well for COP, as a healthy domestic economy has allowed many people the luxury of dining out. In addition, as more families consist of two breadwinners, time has become a scarce resource, limiting the time available for in-home meal preparation.

Key Stock Statistics

S&P EPS Est. 1998	0.91	Tang. Bk. Value/Share	5.20
P/E on S&P Est. 1998	19.0	Beta	0.82
S&P EPS Est. 1999	1.09	Shareholders	4,700
Dividend Rate/Share	Nil	Market cap. (B)	$0.363
Shs. outstg. (M)	21.0	Inst. holdings	39%
Avg. daily vol. (M)	0.016		

Value of $10,000 invested 5 years ago: $ 36,209

Fiscal Year Ending Sep. 30

	1998	1997	1996	1995	1994	1993
Revenues (Million $)						
1Q	63.42	54.34	47.01	39.63	33.66	29.30
2Q	91.14	78.24	65.02	54.71	45.69	38.04
3Q	72.53	65.73	56.44	45.39	38.86	31.44
4Q	—	67.07	56.92	47.01	40.43	33.73
Yr.	—	262.7	224.2	186.7	158.6	132.5
Earnings Per Share ($)						
1Q	**0.19**	0.17	0.15	0.16	0.13	0.11
2Q	**0.23**	0.19	0.15	0.13	0.11	0.07
3Q	**0.25**	0.23	0.19	0.15	0.17	0.12
4Q	**E0.24**	0.22	0.19	0.17	0.17	0.14
Yr.	**E0.91**	0.82	0.67	0.62	0.58	0.45

Next earnings report expected: mid November

Dividend Data

Amount ($)	Date Decl.	Ex-Div. Date	Stock of Record	Payment Date
5-for-4	Dec. 03	Dec. 29	Dec. 15	Dec. 26 '97

A Division of The McGraw·Hill Companies

Business Summary - 04-AUG-98

Despite an increasingly competitive restaurant environment over the past few years, revenues and earnings have sizzled at this operator of Steak n Shake restaurants, which has been aggressively expanding its restaurant base. Founded in 1934, Consolidated Products (formerly Steak n Shake, Inc.) primarily operates and franchises 261 (211 company-owned and 50 franchised units) Steak n Shake restaurants in 12 states in the Midwest and Southeast. It also operates 11 specialty restaurants in Indiana and Illinois, primarily under the Colorado Steakhouse name.

After opening 33 company-owned and 8 franchised units in FY 97 (Sep.), Consolidated plans to open 40 company-owned units in FY 98 and has no plans to slow down after that. COP's five-year expansion plan calls for an annual increase of at least 20% in company-operated Steak n Shake units. This growth is expected to be funded by cash flow from operations, capital raised through sale and leaseback transactions, bank borrowings, and the issuance of debt and equity securities.

The 249 Steak n Shake restaurants at September 24, 1997, were in Missouri (53), Indiana (52 units), Illinois (49), Florida (39), Georgia (18), Ohio (12), Kentucky and Michigan (seven each), Tennessee (five), Arkansas and Iowa (two each), and North Carolina, Kansas and Mississippi (one each).

Steak n Shake caters to a distinct niche in the mid-scale, casual dining segment of the restaurant industry by offering counter, dining room, drive-through and carry-out service. The units feature steakburgers, french fries and hand-dipped milk shakes, as well as grilled chicken breast sandwiches, beef or chicken taco salads, homestyle soups and a variety of salads. The restaurants serve a complete breakfast, and most operate 24 hours a day.

Most Steak n Shake restaurants are freestanding units with adequate parking. Unlike fast-food restaurants, Steak n Shake's food is freshly prepared, cooked in view of the customer and served by a friendly staff. In FY 97, the average customer check was $5.00 per person; however, the average check during peak lunch and dinner hours was approximately $5.50 and $5.75, respectively.

The 11 specialty restaurants, in Indiana and Illinois, consisted primarily of Colorado Steakhouse units with a western theme reminiscent of a Colorado log cabin. The menu features steak and prime rib with limited non-beef choices such as salmon, chicken and pork. Average check at the specialty restaurants generally approximates $15.

Per Share Data ($)

(Year Ended Sep. 30)	1997	1996	1995	1994	1993	1992	1991	1990	1989	1988
Tangible Bk. Val.	3.58	3.31	2.52	1.64	0.97	0.18	-0.46	2.40	1.93	1.52
Cash Flow	1.08	1.11	1.17	1.06	0.93	0.91	0.84	1.01	0.91	0.87
Earnings	0.82	0.67	0.63	0.58	0.45	0.40	0.33	0.53	0.47	0.39
Dividends	Nil	Nil	Nil	Nil	Nil	Nil	1.92	0.09	0.06	0.04
Payout Ratio	Nil	Nil	Nil	Nil	Nil	Nil	NM	16%	14%	11%
Prices - High	16⁷/₈	14¹/₈	11¹/₈	7	5⁷/₈	4³/₄	2⁵/₈	5⁷/₈	5¹/₈	3³/₈
- Low	11¹/₄	8³/₄	6	5¹/₈	3⁷/₈	2³/₈	1³/₈	¹⁵/₁₆	3³/₈	2
P/E Ratio - High	21	21	18	12	13	12	8	11	11	9
- Low	14	13	10	9	9	6	4	2	7	5

Income Statement Analysis (Million $)

	1997	1996	1995	1994	1993	1992	1991	1990	1989	1988
Revs.	263	224	187	160	133	127	116	106	99	93.0
Oper. Inc.	34.3	27.4	23.0	20.5	18.2	17.1	14.7	13.7	12.3	11.0
Depr.	10.7	8.6	7.0	5.9	5.6	5.3	4.9	4.5	4.1	4.4
Int. Exp.	3.6	3.8	3.8	4.6	5.1	5.6	5.5	1.9	2.1	2.4
Pretax Inc.	25.6	20.9	16.1	11.3	8.4	7.0	5.4	8.3	7.2	5.1
Eff. Tax Rate	37%	38%	38%	37%	38%	41%	40%	40%	40%	32%
Net Inc.	16.1	13.0	10.0	7.2	5.2	4.2	3.3	5.0	4.3	3.5

Balance Sheet & Other Fin. Data (Million $)

	1997	1996	1995	1994	1993	1992	1991	1990	1989	1988
Cash	2.7	0.6	1.4	10.3	8.8	12.6	8.3	0.6	2.8	3.3
Curr. Assets	20.0	15.1	14.5	19.4	16.3	19.4	13.1	5.7	7.6	6.9
Total Assets	167	131	100	80.3	70.6	67.1	64.1	55.8	50.0	46.8
Curr. Liab.	38.5	37.3	28.9	24.5	18.5	19.5	17.2	17.2	13.7	11.0
LT Debt	34.6	32.0	28.3	36.1	41.0	45.7	51.2	16.0	18.1	21.4
Common Eqty.	93.0	57.8	42.6	19.7	11.0	1.8	-4.4	22.5	18.0	13.8
Total Cap.	129	90.1	70.9	55.8	52.1	47.5	46.9	38.6	36.3	35.9
Cap. Exp.	52.2	46.2	42.9	20.6	15.2	6.8	8.1	13.8	10.3	4.3
Cash Flow	26.8	21.6	17.0	13.1	10.8	9.4	8.2	9.4	8.4	7.8
Curr. Ratio	0.5	0.4	0.5	0.8	0.9	1.0	0.8	0.3	0.6	0.6
% LT Debt of Cap.	26.9	35.5	39.9	64.7	78.7	96.3	109.2	41.4	49.8	59.8
% Net Inc.of Revs.	6.1	5.8	5.4	4.5	3.9	3.3	2.8	4.7	4.4	3.7
% Ret. on Assets	10.8	11.3	11.2	9.3	7.0	6.3	5.4	9.3	8.8	7.1
% Ret. on Equity	21.4	25.7	32.2	45.8	78.9	NM	NM	24.4	26.8	25.7

Data as orig. reptd.; bef. results of disc. opers. and/or spec. items. Per share data adj. for stk. divs. as of ex-div. date. Bold denotes diluted EPS (FASB 128). E-Estimated. NA-Not Available. NM-Not Meaningful. NR-Not Ranked.

Office—500 Century Bldg., 36 S. Pennsylvania St., Indianapolis, IN 46204. **Tel**—(317) 633-4100. **Chrmn**—E. W. Kelley. **Vice Chrmn & Secy**—S. S. Aramian. **Pres & CEO**—A. B. Gilman. **SVP, Treas & Investor Contact**—James W. Bear. **VP & Secy**—C. J. Wendling. **Dirs**—S. S. Aramian, A. T. Bonda, N. Gilliatt, A. B. Gilman, E. W. Kelley, C. E. Lanham, J. F. Risk, J. Williamson Jr. **Transfer Agent & Registrar**—Harris Trust & Savings Bank, Chicago. **Incorporated**—in Delaware in 1951; reincorporated in Indiana in 1977. **Empl**— 10,500. **S&P Analyst:** Stephen J. Tekirian

Consumers Water 3612

NASDAQ Symbol **CONW**

In S&P SmallCap 600

03-OCT-98

Industry:
Water Utilities

Summary: This water utility holding company has agreed to be acquired by Philadelphia Suburban Corp. for about $270 million in common stock.

Quantitative Evaluations

Outlook
(1 Lowest—5 Highest)
- **1⁻**

Fair Value
- **26⅝**

Risk
- **Low**

Earn./Div. Rank
- **B**

Technical Eval.
- **Neutral** since 7/98

Rel. Strength Rank
(1 Lowest—99 Highest)
- **89**

Insider Activity
- **NA**

Recent Price • 28⅜
52 Wk Range • 29-17

Yield • 4.4%
12-Mo. P/E • 15.9

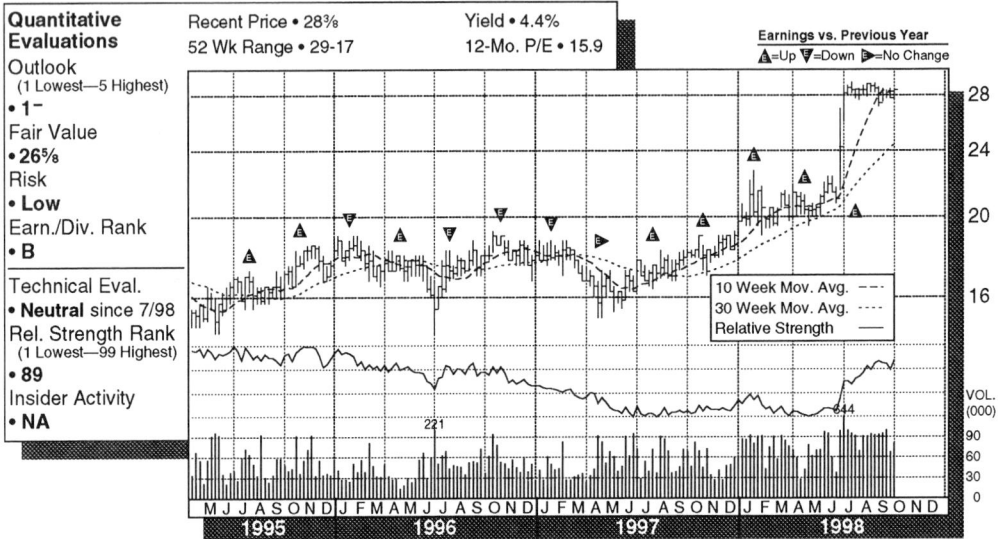

Earnings vs. Previous Year
▲=Up ▼=Down ▶=No Change

10 Week Mov. Avg. - - - -
30 Week Mov. Avg. ·······
Relative Strength ——

Business Profile - 10-SEP-98

In June 1998, the company entered into a definitive agreement to be acquired by Philadelphia Suburban Corp. (PSC) for approximately $270 million in common stock. Terms call for each Consumers common share to be exchanged for 1.459 PSC common shares; the transaction, which is subject to various conditions and approvals, will be accounted for as a pooling-of-interests. The acquisition will create the second largest investor-owned water utility in the U.S., serving over 1.6 million residents in Pennsylvania, Ohio, Illinois, New Jersey and Maine. CONW has acquired a number of water systems in recent years and intends to continue its acquisition program. The company has three rate cases pending in which $3.5 million of revenues is sought. In April 1998, CONW sold its New Hampshire Water unit for nearly $35 million.

Operational Review - 10-SEP-98

Revenues in the first half of 1998 edged up 0.9%, year to year, reflecting rate increases. Operating expenses were well controlled, and aided by gains from sales of properties, pretax earnings more than doubled, to $15,244,000, from $7,072,000. After taxes at 39.0%, versus 36.1%, income from continuing operations also more than doubled, to $9,301,000 ($1.03 per share), from $4,520,000 ($0.51). Results exclude losses from discontinued technical services operations of $0.21 a share in the 1997 period.

Stock Performance - 02-OCT-98

In the past 30 trading days, CONW's shares have declined 1%, compared to a 7% fall in the S&P 500. Average trading volume for the past five days was 15,980 shares, compared with the 40-day moving average of 24,800 shares.

Key Stock Statistics

Dividend Rate/Share	1.24	Shareholders	6,300
Shs. outstg. (M)	9.0	Market cap. (B)	$0.256
Avg. daily vol. (M)	0.026	Inst. holdings	14%
Tang. Bk. Value/Share	20.92		
Beta	0.18		

Value of $10,000 invested 5 years ago: $ 22,842

Fiscal Year Ending Dec. 31

	1998	1997	1996	1995	1994	1993
Revenues (Million $)						
1Q	23.41	22.93	25.06	22.53	20.82	20.94
2Q	24.16	24.22	26.68	25.52	23.45	22.50
3Q	—	27.23	29.35	28.48	25.17	24.50
4Q	—	23.96	26.30	25.25	23.90	21.12
Yr.	—	98.34	107.4	101.8	93.34	89.08
Earnings Per Share ($)						
1Q	**0.24**	**0.21**	0.21	0.19	0.14	0.29
2Q	**0.79**	**0.30**	0.19	0.35	0.31	0.24
3Q	—	**0.53**	0.42	0.53	0.40	0.50
4Q	—	**0.32**	-0.10	0.28	0.37	0.60
Yr.	—	**1.36**	0.72	1.34	1.22	1.63

Next earnings report expected: NA

Dividend Data (Dividends have been paid since 1951.)

Amount ($)	Date Decl.	Ex-Div. Date	Stock of Record	Payment Date
0.305	Dec. 10	Feb. 06	Feb. 10	Feb. 25 '98
0.305	Feb. 04	May. 07	May. 11	May. 26 '98
0.305	Jun. 03	Aug. 06	Aug. 10	Aug. 25 '98
0.310	Sep. 15	Nov. 06	Nov. 10	Nov. 25 '98

Business Summary - 10-SEP-98

Ohio, Illinois, New Jersey, Pennsylvania and Maine all have something in common: units of Consumers Water Co. (CONW) supply water in each of these states. Founded in 1926, CONW, a holding company, operates through seven small to medium sized water utilities which provide water and sewer services from 27 separate systems to a total of more than 223,000 customers in these five states. The technical services unit was substantially shut down in 1997, and the New Hampshire Water unit was sold in 1998.

CONW supplies water for public use to residential customers (65% of 1997 water revenues); commercial users (13%); industrial accounts (8%); and for private and municipal fire protection purposes and miscellaneous uses (14%). The water utility business is seasonal, with the demand for water during the warmer months generally greater than during the cooler months.

CONW owned 3,428 miles of mains at year-end 1997. The company owns directly or indirectly at least 90% of the voting stock of its five water companies, the largest of which, Consumers Ohio Water Co., accounted for 32% of water utility revenues in 1997.

Of CONW's 27 primary water systems, 14 have surface supplies (lakes, ponds and streams) as their source of supply; 12 obtain water principally or entirely from wells; and two obtain their water supplies from adjacent systems. Less than 5% of the subsidiaries' water usage is purchased from other systems. In general, the company considers the surface and well supplies at its subsidiaries to be adequate for anticipating average daily demand and normal peak demand.

In April 1998, the company sold its Consumers New Hampshire Water Co. utility assets to the town of Hudson, N.H. for $34.5 million. The sale generated an after-tax gain of $3.9 million, or $0.43 a share, and was recorded in the second quarter of 1998.

CONW expects capital expenditures for 1998 through 2000 to be $72 million, net of contributions and advances. The capital construction budget is down from $103 million for the 1995-1997 planning period due to the completion of many improvements required by the Safe Drinking Water Act, the Clean Water Act, and other regulations. The company is engaged in a project that will replace a major plant at Consumers Pennsylvania Water Co. -- Shenango Valley division. The cost of the project is estimated at $32 million.

Per Share Data ($)

(Year Ended Dec. 31)	1997	1996	1995	1994	1993	1992	1991	1990	1989	1988
Tangible Bk. Val.	20.74	20.52	20.42	19.67	12.05	11.82	11.62	10.56	11.95	11.81
Earnings	1.36	0.72	1.34	1.22	1.63	1.14	1.46	1.21	1.15	1.59
Dividends	1.21	1.20	1.19	1.17	1.15	1.13	1.11	1.09	1.05	0.98
Payout Ratio	89%	167%	88%	96%	70%	99%	76%	90%	91%	62%
Prices - High	20¾	19¼	19	18¾	21½	19¾	18½	18¼	20½	21¼
- Low	15⅛	14½	14½	15¼	17	14¼	13¾	10	14¾	15¾
P/E Ratio - High	15	27	14	15	13	17	13	15	18	13
- Low	11	20	11	12	10	13	9	6	13	10

Income Statement Analysis (Million $)

	1997	1996	1995	1994	1993	1992	1991	1990	1989	1988
Revs.	98.3	107	102	93.3	89.1	89.6	85.2	81.6	87.1	87.9
Depr.	11.3	12.1	10.5	9.0	8.0	7.7	6.4	6.0	6.0	5.8
Maint.	NA	NA	NA	NA	NA	5.3	5.7	5.3	5.4	NA
Fxd. Chgs. Cov.	2.2	1.7	2.1	2.1	2.0	1.7	1.5	1.5	1.5	1.9
Constr. Credits	Nil	Nil	1.0	1.4	0.8	0.4	1.1	0.3	0.8	1.4
Eff. Tax Rate	35%	38%	36%	34%	33%	34%	34%	32%	32%	30%
Net Inc.	12.1	6.3	11.3	10.0	12.0	8.0	9.4	7.3	6.9	9.4

Balance Sheet & Other Fin. Data (Million $)

	1997	1996	1995	1994	1993	1992	1991	1990	1989	1988
Gross Prop.	511	475	436	396	360	349	313	303	287	263
Cap. Exp.	27.6	35.2	40.5	39.3	34.7	26.3	30.7	24.3	26.1	30.3
Net Prop.	418	392	362	327	297	289	258	251	237	217
Capitalization:										
LT Debt	172	173	162	130	124	120	101	105	100	89.0
% LT Debt	61	61	60	56	55	58	55	61	57	55
Pfd.	2.6	3.3	3.4	3.3	3.3	3.3	3.3	3.4	3.4	3.5
% Pfd.	1.00	1.20	1.30	1.40	1.50	1.60	1.80	1.90	1.90	2.20
Common	109	106	106	101	96.9	84.2	80.1	64.0	71.5	69.8
% Common	39	38	39	43	43	41	43	37	41	43
Total Cap.	315	312	366	322	303	276	244	228	226	212
% Oper. Ratio	67.5	77.2	77.6	78.8	79.0	78.8	79.5	78.9	79.4	80.5
% Earn. on Net Prop.	10.5	9.3	6.6	6.3	6.4	6.9	6.9	7.0	7.9	8.3
% Return On Revs.	12.3	5.8	11.1	10.7	13.5	9.0	11.1	9.0	7.9	10.7
% Return On Invest. Capital	10.8	8.0	7.1	7.1	6.7	7.6	8.0	8.8	8.7	9.5
% Return On Com. Equity	11.2	5.8	10.9	10.1	13.2	9.8	13.1	10.8	9.7	14.0

Data as orig. reptd.; bef. results of disc. opers. and/or spec. items. Per share data adj. for stk. divs. as of ex-div. date. Bold denotes diluted EPS (FASB 128). E-Estimated. NA-Not Available. NM-Not Meaningful. NR-Not Ranked.

Office—Three Canal Plaza, Portland, ME 04101. **Tel**—(207) 773-6438. **Fax**—(207) 761-7903. **Website**—http://www.consumerswater.com **Pres & CEO**—P. L. Haynes. **VP & Secy**—B. R. Mullany. **SVP-CFO**—J. F. Isacke. **VP & Treas**—R. E. Ervin. **Dirs**—M. Avenas, P. L. Haynes, J. S. Ketchum, J. E. Menario, J. E. Newman, J. E. Palmer Jr., W. B. Russell, J. H. Schiavi, R. O. Viets. **Transfer Agent**—Continental Stock Transfer & Trust Co., NYC. **Incorporated**—in Maine in 1926. **Empl**— 448. **S&P Analyst:** K.S.

03-OCT-98

Industry:
Health Care (Medical Products & Supplies)

Summary: COO develops, manufactures and markets proprietary specialty health care products for eye care and gynecology, and operates psychiatric facilities.

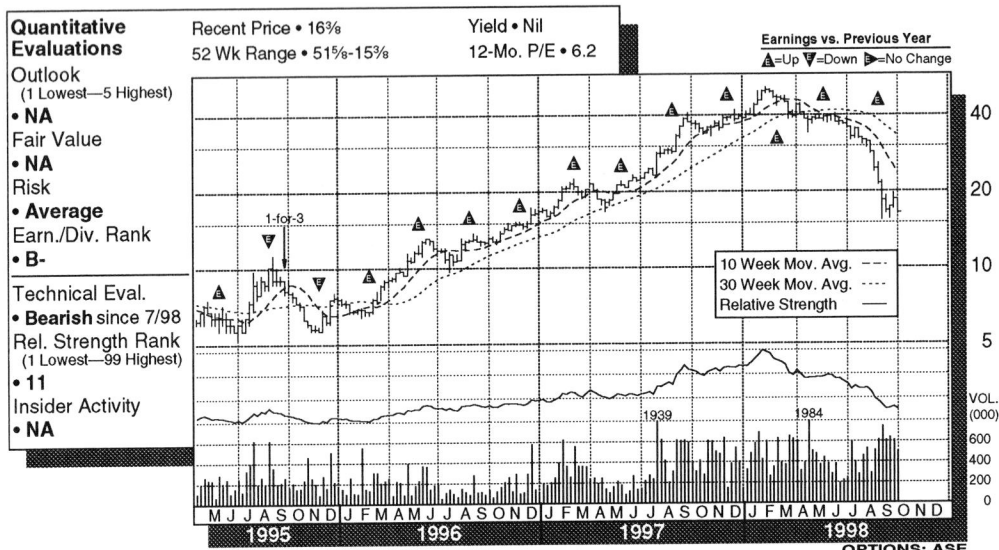

Quantitative Evaluations	
Outlook (1 Lowest—5 Highest)	• **NA**
Fair Value	• **NA**
Risk	• **Average**
Earn./Div. Rank	• **B-**
Technical Eval.	• **Bearish** since 7/98
Rel. Strength Rank (1 Lowest—99 Highest)	• **11**
Insider Activity	• **NA**

Recent Price • 16⅜
52 Wk Range • 51⅝-15⅜

Yield • Nil
12-Mo. P/E • 6.2

Earnings vs. Previous Year
▲=Up ▼=Down ▶=No Change

10 Week Mov. Avg. — · —
30 Week Mov. Avg. - - - -
Relative Strength ———

OPTIONS: ASE

Business Profile - 26-SEP-98

During 1998, COO has introduced Hydrasoft Toric Options and Frequency 55 disposable contact lenses, two new women's health care product lines and the Cooper-Surgical Infrared Coagulator for the removal of lesions. In December 1997, the company acquired Aspect Vision Care, an England-based manufacturer of contact lenses, for about $51 million. Cooper's goal is to increase market penetration in the U.S. and overseas with its existing products and services, as well as to accelerate its business development efforts. In September 1998, the company's directors authorized the repurchase of up to one million shares of COO's common stock.

Operational Review - 26-SEP-98

Net operating revenues for the nine months ended July 31, 1998, rose 47%, year to year, primarily due to a 70% increase in product sales reflecting sales from the Aspect Vision Care acquisition and increased sales of existing product lines. Gross margins narrowed due to a change in product mix. SG&A expenses rose 48%, largely as a result of the Aspect acquisition, and higher sales and promotional costs relating to COO's contact lens business. After a tax benefit of $1,787,000, versus $1,870,000, net income rose 55%, to $24,650,000 ($1.60 per share, based on 24% more shares), from $15,869,000 ($1.28).

Stock Performance - 02-OCT-98

In the past 30 trading days, COO's shares have declined 33%, compared to a 7% fall in the S&P 500. Average trading volume for the past five days was 100,220 shares, compared with the 40-day moving average of 157,431 shares.

Key Stock Statistics

Dividend Rate/Share	Nil	Shareholders	2,800
Shs. outstg. (M)	14.9	Market cap. (B)	$0.245
Avg. daily vol. (M)	0.156	Inst. holdings	61%
Tang. Bk. Value/Share	3.23		
Beta	0.77		

Value of $10,000 invested 5 years ago: $ 43,827

Fiscal Year Ending Oct. 31

	1998	1997	1996	1995	1994	1993
Revenues (Million $)						
1Q	42.84	28.38	22.25	23.21	22.91	22.36
2Q	51.76	33.66	26.78	23.79	24.46	23.66
3Q	54.18	38.95	28.87	25.25	23.90	24.50
4Q	—	40.49	31.24	24.84	24.38	22.14
Yr.	—	141.5	109.1	97.09	95.65	92.65
Earnings Per Share ($)						
1Q	**0.39**	0.28	0.06	0.03	-0.51	-0.27
2Q	**0.55**	0.44	0.24	0.06	-0.39	-0.66
3Q	**0.66**	0.55	0.40	0.24	0.27	-1.38
4Q	—	2.14	0.72	-0.31	0.12	-1.14
Yr.	—	3.70	1.41	0.01	-0.45	-3.39

Next earnings report expected: mid December

Dividend Data

Cash dividends were omitted in 1988, after having been paid since 1983. A one-for-three reverse stock split was effected in 1995. A "poison pill" stock purchase rights plan was adopted in 1987.

A Division of The **McGraw-Hill** *Companies*

STANDARD
&POOR'S
STOCK REPORTS

The Cooper Companies, Inc.

659M

03-OCT-98

Business Summary - 26-SEP-98

The Cooper Companies, Inc. provides under-served niches in the health care market with proprietary products and services, such as specialty contact lenses, diagnostic and surgical instruments for women's health care, and treatment for a variety of mental illnesses. Its operations comprise three main subsidiaries: CooperVision, Inc., CooperSurgical, Inc., and Hospital Group of America, Inc.

CooperVision (CVI; 45 % of FY 97 revenues) produces contact lenses that correct visual defects. It specializes in soft toric lenses that correct astigmatism, an irregularity in the shape of the cornea. Rather than compete in the lower-margin market for lenses used to correct more common cases of nearsightedness, CVI focuses on higher-margin, more technologically advanced specialty lenses for patients whose vision is more difficult to correct. Some of its major brand names include Hydrasoft, Preference, Vantage, Permaflex and Cooper Clear.

In February 1998, Cooper introduced Frequency 55 disposable replacement sphere contact lenses in the United States. The replacement spherical lenses make up the largest contact lens market segment in the U.S.

In May 1998, COO introduced two new toric products: Hydrasoft Toric Options, a custom replacement lens for astigmatic patients with complex correction requirements and Frequency 55 Toric, a replacement lens for replacement at two-week or monthly intervals.

CooperSurgical (CSI; 17.5% of FY 97 revenues) supplies products related to women's health care, including proprietary gynecological and surgical instruments, accessories and related devices. In May 1998, CSI introduced the Cerveillance Scope, which uses digital imaging and proprietary software to provide enhanced visualization and documentation in cervix examinations. COO also introduced the FemExam'r' pH and Amines TestCard 'tm' designed for use in physicians' offices to rapidly and economically screen and diagnose common vaginal infections.

The company's subsidiary, Hospital Group of America (HGA; 37.7% of FY 97 revenues) owns and operates three psychiatric facilities that provide intensive and structured treatment for patients suffering from a variety of mental illnesses and/or chemical dependencies. HGA plans to focus on growing market share in each geographic region through referral and ancillary programs. The company also plans to expand its behavioral health consultation and management services business.

Per Share Data ($) (Year Ended Oct. 31)	1997	1996	1995	1994	1993	1992	1991	1990	1989	1988
Tangible Bk. Val.	5.06	-0.53	NM	-1.68	-1.59	2.10	0.39	3.12	-0.93	-15.66
Cash Flow	4.06	1.63	0.26	-0.09	-3.06	-1.71	-2.91	-0.60	-3.39	-16.50
Earnings	3.70	1.41	0.01	-0.45	-3.39	-1.92	-3.15	-0.78	-3.66	-21.03
Dividends	Nil	Nil	Nil	Nil	Nil	Nil	Nil	Nil	Nil	0.30
Payout Ratio	Nil	Nil	Nil	Nil	Nil	Nil	Nil	Nil	Nil	NM
Prices - High	42	17	11¼	10½	3¾	13⅛	18⅜	14⅝	16⅛	45
- Low	15⅞	6⅜	5¼	1⁵⁄₁₆	¹³⁄₁₆	2⅝	9	7½	6⅜	14¼
P/E Ratio - High	11	12	NM	NM	NM	NM	NM	NM	NM	NM
- Low	4	5	NM	NM	NM	NM	NM	NM	NM	NM

Income Statement Analysis (Million $)	1997	1996	1995	1994	1993	1992	1991	1990	1989	1988
Revs.	142	109	97.0	96.0	93.0	63.1	36.0	48.0	53.0	611
Oper. Inc.	30.5	20.7	13.0	4.1	17.6	-63.3	-28.3	-11.9	-16.9	48.1
Depr.	4.7	2.6	2.7	3.7	3.4	2.3	2.0	1.4	2.1	35.2
Int. Exp.	4.2	5.3	4.7	4.5	6.1	6.7	7.1	9.0	22.4	65.7
Pretax Inc.	21.8	12.1	0.2	-9.0	-34.0	-16.0	-25.0	-4.0	-18.0	-140
Eff. Tax Rate	NM	NM	50%	NM	NM	NM	NM	NM	NM	NM
Net Inc.	48.4	16.6	0.1	-5.0	-34.0	-0.2	-25.0	-1.0	-16.0	-151

Balance Sheet & Other Fin. Data (Million $)	1997	1996	1995	1994	1993	1992	1991	1990	1989	1988
Cash	18.2	6.8	11.2	10.0	17.0	75.0	144	173	230	55.0
Curr. Assets	68.6	42.4	41.2	44.0	52.0	120	174	197	277	787
Total Assets	175	103	92.0	95.0	110	174	188	217	288	1,138
Curr. Liab.	33.6	33.3	39.6	42.0	38.0	54.0	52.0	45.0	64.0	637
LT Debt	9.1	47.9	43.5	46.0	48.0	59.0	49.0	71.0	103	337
Common Eqty.	112	15.3	-1.7	-4.0	Nil	31.0	12.0	33.0	-7.0	29.0
Total Cap.	142	69.6	52.4	43.0	49.0	120	136	172	224	463
Cap. Exp.	7.7	3.2	3.0	0.9	1.8	3.7	1.5	0.5	20.9	39.2
Cash Flow	53.1	19.2	2.8	-1.0	-31.0	-16.0	-25.0	-5.0	-26.0	-127
Curr. Ratio	2.0	1.3	1.0	1.0	1.4	2.2	3.4	4.4	4.3	1.2
% LT Debt of Cap.	6.4	68.8	83.0	108.6	99.1	48.8	35.8	41.1	46.0	72.9
% Net Inc.of Revs.	34.1	15.2	NM	NM	NM	NM	NM	NM	NM	NM
% Ret. on Assets	34.8	16.9	NM	NM	NM	NM	NM	NM	NM	NM
% Ret. on Equity	76.3	1.2	NM	NM	NM	NM	NM	NM	NM	NM

Data as orig. reptd.; bef. results of disc. opers. and/or spec. items. Per share data adj. for stk. divs. as of ex-div. date. Bold denotes diluted EPS (FASB 128). E-Estimated. NA-Not Available. NM-Not Meaningful. NR-Not Ranked.

Office—6140 Stoneridge Mall Rd., Suite 590, Pleasanton, CA 94588. **Tel**—(510) 460-3600. **Website**—http://www.coopercos.com **Chrmn**—A. E. Rubenstein. **Pres & CEO**—A. T. Bender. **EVP-CFO & Treas**—R. S. Weiss. **Investor Contact**—Norris Battin (888-822-2660). **Dirs**—A. T. Bender, M. H. Kalkstein, M. Marx, D. Press, S. Rosenberg, A. E. Rubenstein, R. S. Weiss, S. Zinberg. **Transfer Agent & Registrar**—American Stock Transfer & Trust Co., NYC. **Incorporated**—in Delaware in 1980. **Empl**—1,100. **S&P Analyst:** John J. Arege

COR Therapeutics   3622C

NASDAQ Symbol **CORR**

In S&P SmallCap 600

03-OCT-98

Industry: Biotechnology

Summary: This company is engaged in the discovery, development and commercialization of biopharmaceutical products to treat and prevent severe cardiovascular diseases.

Quantitative Evaluations

Recent Price • 7½
52 Wk Range • 26⅛-6¾

Yield • Nil
12-Mo. P/E • NM

Outlook
(1 Lowest—5 Highest)
• **NA**

Fair Value
• **NA**

Risk
• **High**

Earn./Div. Rank
• **NR**

Technical Eval.
• **Bearish** since 3/98

Rel. Strength Rank
(1 Lowest—99 Highest)
• **9**

Insider Activity
• **NA**

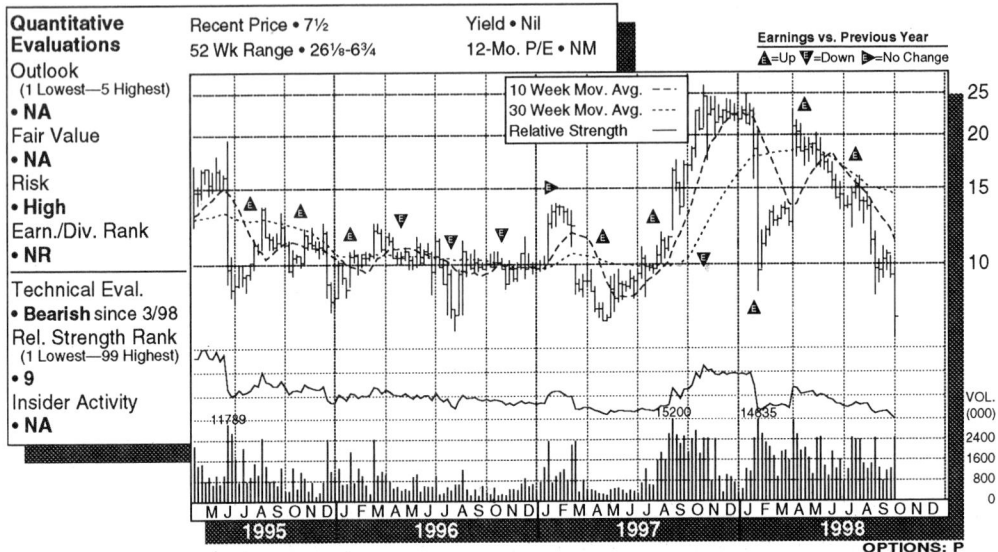

Earnings vs. Previous Year
▲=Up ▼=Down ▶=No Change

10 Week Mov. Avg. ---
30 Week Mov. Avg. ----
Relative Strength —

OPTIONS: P

Business Profile - 10-SEP-98

In May 1998, CORR received marketing approval from the U.S. Food and Drug Administration for Integrilin for the treatment of patients with acute coronary syndromes and to prevent abrupt closure following angioplasty. The company received a $24 million milestone payment during the second quarter from marketing partner Schering-Plough in connection with the regulatory approval of Integrilin. In the first quarter, the company received an $8 million milestone payment from marketing partner Schering-Plough in connection with Integrilin's acceptance for review by European regulatory authorities. Product development efforts include an oral formulation of Integrilin for the prevention of acute ischemic coronary syndromes and stroke.

Operational Review - 10-SEP-98

Revenues in the six months ended June 30, 1998, gained 155%, year to year, due to a higher level of contract milestone payments from Schering-Plough. Research and development spending decreased 27%, to $18.8 million, reflecting the timing of clinical trial activities for Integrilin. Marketing, general and administrative expenses increased 158%, primarily reflecting precommercial activities associated with Integrilin. With interest income of $2,221,000, versus $1,248,000, net income of $3,953,000 ($0.16 a share, on 27% more shares) contrasted with a net loss of $16,637,000 ($0.83). Cash, equivalents and short-term investments totaled $84.5 million at the end of the second quarter.

Stock Performance - 02-OCT-98

In the past 30 trading days, CORR's shares have declined 34%, compared to a 7% fall in the S&P 500. Average trading volume for the past five days was 612,240 shares, compared with the 40-day moving average of 330,349 shares.

Key Stock Statistics

Dividend Rate/Share	Nil	Shareholders	300
Shs. outstg. (M)	24.1	Market cap. (B)	$0.181
Avg. daily vol. (M)	0.313	Inst. holdings	60%
Tang. Bk. Value/Share	3.50		
Beta	1.14		

Value of $10,000 invested 5 years ago: $ 5,000

Fiscal Year Ending Dec. 31

	1998	1997	1996	1995	1994	1993
Revenues (Million $)						
1Q	8.41	6.33	2.53	0.00	0.02	0.50
2Q	24.51	6.58	4.79	21.05	Nil	0.59
3Q	—	2.91	6.54	7.85	Nil	0.10
4Q	—	6.37	4.89	2.95	0.50	1.36
Yr.	—	22.19	18.76	31.85	0.52	2.55
Earnings Per Share ($)						
1Q	-0.22	-0.38	-0.59	-0.45	-0.28	-0.23
2Q	0.36	-0.45	-0.48	0.57	-0.57	-0.29
3Q	—	-0.54	-0.30	-0.05	-0.68	-0.36
4Q	—	-0.26	-0.49	-0.49	-0.53	-0.38
Yr.	—	-1.60	-1.86	-0.39	-2.07	-1.27

Next earnings report expected: late October

Dividend Data

No cash dividends have been paid. In 1995, the company adopted a shareholder rights plan.

A Division of The McGraw-Hill Companies

STANDARD
&POOR'S
STOCK REPORTS

COR Therapeutics, Inc.

3622C
03-OCT-98

Business Summary - 10-SEP-98

Each year about one million people in the U.S. die as a result of heart attacks, strokes and related cardiovascular diseases. COR Therapeutics (CORR) focuses on the discovery, development and commercialization of pharmaceutical products to prevent and treat severe cardiovascular diseases.

CORR is concentrating on the development of inhibitors for the treatment of arterial thrombosis (a blockage occurring in the artery); venous thrombosis; and restenosis (a renarrowing of blood vessels following angioplasty). The company's first product candidate, Integrilin, is being developed for treatment of arterial thrombosis, including complications following angioplasty, acute myocardial infarction, unstable angina and stroke.

In May 1995, Integrilin completed Phase III clinical trials for prevention of abrupt closure following coronary angioplasty. The results were positive, but not strong enough to convince the Food and Drug Administration (FDA) to approve the product on the basis of a single Phase III trial. CORR went on to complete a second Phase III trial of Integrilin. In August 1997, the company announced that the results of a 10,948-patient study demonstrated that Integrilin significantly reduced the occurrence of death or heart attack in patients with unstable angina and non-Q-wave myocardial infarction. In May 1998, the company finally received marketing approval from the FDA for Integrilin for the treatment of

patients with acute coronary syndromes and as an adjunct to PTCA.

CORR's strategy is to combine its expertise in molecular and cellular biology of cardiovascular diseases with advanced drug discovery techniques to create new products where current therapies are inadequate. The company has entered into a number of strategic alliances with pharmaceutical and biotechnology companies to complement and expand its efforts.

In April 1995, the company signed a worldwide collaboration agreement with Schering-Plough to develop and commercialize Integrilin. Schering paid CORR a $20 million licensing fee, and agreed to additional milestone payments (up to $100 million) upon reaching certain performance goals. An $8 million payment was made in the 1998 first quarter, after Integrilin was accepted for review by European regulatory authorities, and a $24 million payment was made in the second quarter of 1998, after Integrilin received marketing approval in the United States.

In October 1996, CORR extended an agreement with Ortho Pharmaceutical for collaborative research with the R.W. Johnson Pharmaceutical Research Institute, a subsidiary of Johnson & Johnson.

The company expects its cash requirements will increase in future periods, due to costs related to continuation and expansion of research and development, including clinical trials, and increased marketing, sales, general and administrative activities.

Per Share Data ($)

(Year Ended Dec. 31)	1997	1996	1995	1994	1993	1992	1991	1990	1989	1988
Tangible Bk. Val.	3.30	2.52	4.23	4.51	6.44	4.09	4.99	-9.10	NM	NM
Cash Flow	-1.43	-1.68	-0.21	-1.96	-1.16	-0.79	-0.52	-0.81	-0.45	-0.28
Earnings	-1.60	-1.86	-0.39	-2.07	-1.27	-0.86	-0.62	-0.93	-0.51	-0.30
Dividends	Nil	Nil	Nil	Nil	Nil	Nil	Nil	Nil	Nil	Nil
Payout Ratio	Nil	Nil	Nil	Nil	Nil	Nil	Nil	Nil	Nil	Nil
Prices - High	26⅛	12½	19½	17¼	19¼	18	22	NA	NA	NA
- Low	7⅜	7	7¾	9	8½	9	7½	NA	NA	NA
P/E Ratio - High	NM	NM	NM	NM	NM	NM	NM	NM	NM	NM
- Low	NM	NM	NM	NM	NM	NM	NM	NM	NM	NM

Income Statement Analysis (Million $)

	1997	1996	1995	1994	1993	1992	1991	1990	1989	1988
Revs.	22.2	18.8	31.9	0.5	2.5	1.7	2.4	0.5	0.4	0.0
Oper. Inc.	-32.2	-35.7	-8.0	-42.1	-21.2	-11.6	-5.0	-5.0	-2.7	-1.0
Depr.	3.5	3.6	3.5	2.1	1.7	0.9	0.9	0.8	0.3	0.1
Int. Exp.	0.6	0.8	0.8	0.2	0.3	0.2	0.3	0.3	0.2	0.0
Pretax Inc.	-33.5	-36.5	-7.5	-39.5	-19.7	-10.2	-5.1	-5.8	-2.7	-1.0
Eff. Tax Rate	NM	NM	NM	NM	NM	NM	Nil	Nil	Nil	Nil
Net Inc.	-33.5	-36.5	-7.5	-39.5	-19.7	-10.2	-5.1	-5.8	-2.7	-1.0

Balance Sheet & Other Fin. Data (Million $)

	1997	1996	1995	1994	1993	1992	1991	1990	1989	1988
Cash	22.2	53.1	84.8	94.0	122	49.1	58.7	4.3	5.6	NA
Curr. Assets	90.0	64.2	92.8	97.0	124	50.1	59.2	4.4	6.1	NA
Total Assets	95.4	71.2	101	106	130	53.8	61.0	6.7	8.2	NA
Curr. Liab.	14.2	17.4	14.1	15.0	8.1	4.4	1.7	0.9	0.8	NA
LT Debt	2.8	3.4	4.6	4.7	3.1	0.8	0.8	1.3	1.1	NA
Common Eqty.	78.4	50.4	82.2	87.0	119	48.6	58.4	-9.4	-3.7	NA
Total Cap.	81.2	53.2	86.8	91.0	122	49.4	59.2	5.7	7.5	NA
Cap. Exp.	1.9	2.6	2.7	6.7	4.4	2.8	0.3	0.9	1.4	0.2
Cash Flow	-29.9	-33.0	-4.0	-37.4	-18.0	-9.3	-4.3	-5.0	-2.4	-0.9
Curr. Ratio	6.3	3.7	6.6	6.5	15.3	11.3	34.4	4.7	7.8	NA
% LT Debt of Cap.	3.5	6.3	5.3	5.1	2.5	1.7	1.4	23.0	15.3	NA
% Net Inc.of Revs.	NM	NM	NM	NM	NM	NM	NM	NM	NM	NM
% Ret. on Assets	NM	NM	NM	NM	NM	NM	NM	NM	NM	NM
% Ret. on Equity	NM	NM	NM	NM	NM	NM	NM	NM	NM	NM

Data as orig. reptd.; bef. results of disc. opers. and/or spec. items. Per share data adj. for stk. divs. as of ex-div. date. Bold denotes diluted EPS (FASB 128). E-Estimated. NA-Not Available. NM-Not Meaningful. NR-Not Ranked.

Office—256 E. Grand Ave., South San Francisco, CA 94080.**Tel**—(415) 244-6800. **Fax**—(415) 244-9208. **Pres & CEO**—V. M. Kailian. **SVP-Fin & CFO**—Laura A. Brege. **VP & Secy**—R. L. Douglas Jr. **Dirs**—S. R. Coughlin, J. T. Doluisio, C. J. Homcy, J. T. Jackson, V. M. Kailian, E. Mario, R. R. Momsen, L. H. Smith Jr.**Transfer Agent & Registrar**—ChaseMellon Shareholder Services, SF. **Incorporated**—in Delaware in 1988. **Empl**— 182.
S&P Analyst: Richard Joy

Corn Products International 670G

NYSE Symbol **CPO**

In S&P SmallCap 600

03-OCT-98

Industry: Agricultural Products

Summary: This company, which was spun off by Bestfoods in late 1997, is one of the world's largest corn refiners.

S&P Opinion: Accumulate (★★★★)	Recent Price • 23¾	Yield • Nil	Earnings vs. Previous Year
	52 Wk Range • 39½-21¾	12-Mo. P/E • 45.7	▲=Up ▼=Down ▶=No Change

Quantitative Evaluations

Outlook
(1 Lowest—5 Highest)
• **NA**

Fair Value
• **NA**

Risk
• **NA**

Earn./Div. Rank
• **NR**

Technical Eval.
• **NA**

Rel. Strength Rank
(1 Lowest—99 Highest)
• **44**

Insider Activity
• **Neutral**

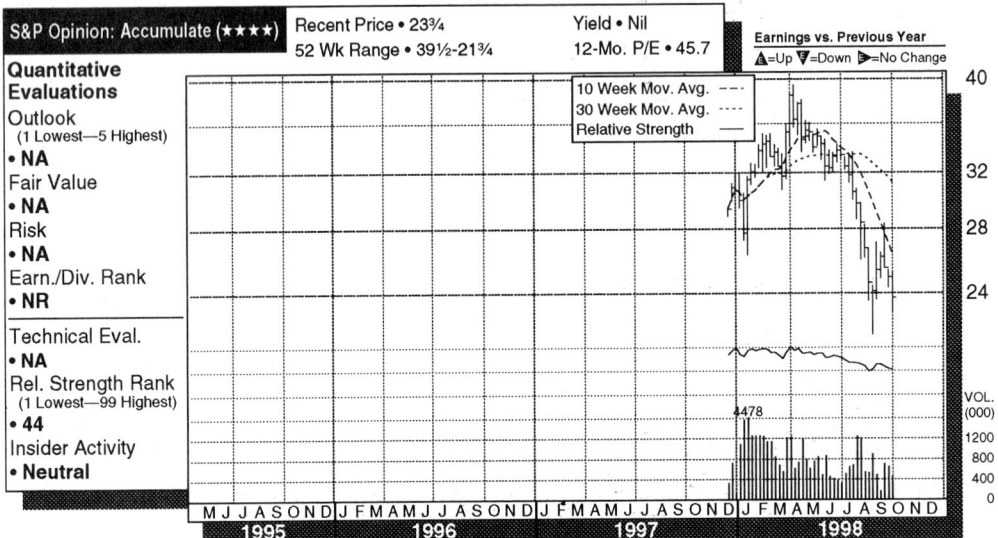

Overview - 27-JUL-98

CPO, which was spun off from Bestfoods in December 1997, is a leading corn refiner, producing sweeteners, starches and co-products; it has a 13% domestic market share. We view international operations as the key to the company's future success; CPO is the largest corn refiner in Latin America, with market leading positions in Chile, Brazil and Colombia. Results in the past few years were hampered by increased high fructose corn syrup capacity in the industry. More recently, this has abated, as demand has picked up, although the industry still suffers from overcapacity. Given slow growth in domestic demand, it is likely that it will take a few more years for demand to catch up to current industry capacity. In 1998, sales growth will be modest, restricted somewhat by negative currency comparisons. Margins should benefit from recent increases in high fructose corn syrup prices, and could potentially expand further in 1999, as an expected increase in the corn crop should result in lower raw material prices.

Valuation - 27-JUL-98

We recently upgraded the shares to accumulate, based on an improved earnings outlook. Profitability is likely to increase in 1999, reflecting the refinancing of the company's joint venture in Mexico, and margin expansion resulting from lower raw material prices and stronger high fructose corn syrup prices. In addition, if the company's recently underperforming dextrose business improves, it is likely that margins could experience greater improvement than anticipated. Although we are maintaining our 1998 EPS estimate at $1.35, we are increasing our 1999 estimate by $0.25, to $1.80. Based on our expectation of earnings acceleration, the shares could appreciate to about $45 in the next 12 months.

Key Stock Statistics

S&P EPS Est. 1998	1.35	Tang. Bk. Value/Share	27.92
P/E on S&P Est. 1998	17.6	Beta	NA
S&P EPS Est. 1999	1.80	Shareholders	NA
Dividend Rate/Share	Nil	Market cap. (B)	$0.846
Shs. outstg. (M)	35.6	Inst. holdings	69%
Avg. daily vol. (M)	0.106		

Value of $10,000 invested 5 years ago: NA

Fiscal Year Ending Dec. 31

	1998	1997	1996	1995	1994	1993
Revenues (Million $)						
1Q	339.0	—	—	—	—	—
2Q	366.8	—	—	—	—	—
3Q	—	—	—	—	—	—
4Q	—	—	—	—	—	—
Yr.	—	1,418	1,524	—	—	—
Earnings Per Share ($)						
1Q	0.21	—	—	—	—	—
2Q	0.30	—	—	—	—	—
3Q	E0.42	—	—	—	—	—
4Q	E0.41	—	—	—	—	—
Yr.	E1.35	-2.02	0.72	3.79	—	—

Next earnings report expected: NA

Dividend Data (Dividends have been paid since 1998.)

Amount ($)	Date Decl.	Ex-Div. Date	Stock of Record	Payment Date
0.080	Sep. 16	Sep. 28	Sep. 30	Oct. 23 '98

A Division of The McGraw·Hill Companies

Business Summary - 27-JUL-98

Corn Products International, Inc., spun off from CPC International (renamed Bestfoods) in late 1997, is one of the word's largest corn refiners. It produces a large variety of food ingredients and industrial products derived from the wet milling of corn and other farinaceous materials for use in more than 60 industries. After seeing profits decline markedly in 1996 and 1997 due to an expansion of high fructose corn syrup capacity that led to a supply/demand imbalance and falling prices, the company plans in 1998 to focus on improving prices, volume, profit margins and efficiencies by striving for optimal product selection and production capacity usage, and cost reductions in purchasing and manufacturing.

The corn refining business supplies customers with value-added products processed from starch and commodity products. The company's most important customers are in the food and beverage, pharmaceuticals, paper products, corrugated and laminated paper, textiles and brewing industries and in the animal feed markets. Corn refining involves the wet milling and processing of corn. During front end grind, corn is steeped in water and separated into starch and co-products such as animal feed and germ. The starch is then either dried for sale or further modified or refined through various processes to make products designed to serve the particular needs of various industries. The germ is refined to produce corn oil.

Products are largely divided into sweeteners (55% of net sales in 1996), starch (22%) and co-products (23%). Sweeteners include high fructose corn syrup used in soft drinks and other beverages and foods; glucose corn syrups used throughout the food industry; high maltose corn syrups with a unique carbohydrate profile; maltodextrin used in applications including dry mixes, sports drinks, baked products and confection; and dextrose, both monohydrate and anhydrous, used in the food industry.

Starch products include mainly corn starch used as a component in the production of paper, corrugated containers, construction materials and textiles, as well as numerous food applications as a thickener and binder. Co-products include corn oil used as cooking oil and in the production of margarine, salad dressings, shortening, mayonnaise and other foods, and corn gluten feed sold as animal feed and corn gluten meal sold as a feed protein, primarily to the poultry industry.

Products are sold directly to manufacturers and distributors by the company's own sales personnel. The company operates in more than 20 countries directly, and through affiliates in nine countries, with 19 plants, and indirectly through joint ventures and technical licensing agreements elsewhere in Latin America, Asia, Africa, Australia and New Zealand. About 68% of net sales are generated in North America, 27% in Latin America, and 5% in other geographic regions.

Per Share Data ($)

(Year Ended Dec. 31)	1997	1996	1995	1994	1993	1992	1991	1990	1989	1988
Tangible Bk. Val.	27.70	NA	NA	NA	NA	NA	NA	NA	NA	NA
Cash Flow	0.87	3.16	NA	NA	NA	NA	NA	NA	NA	NA
Earnings	-2.02	0.72	NA	NA	NA	NA	NA	NA	NA	NA
Dividends	Nil	Nil	Nil	Nil	Nil	Nil	Nil	Nil	Nil	Nil
Payout Ratio	Nil	Nil	Nil	Nil	Nil	Nil	Nil	Nil	Nil	Nil
Prices - High	32	NA	NA	NA	NA	NA	NA	NA	NA	NA
- Low	28⁷/₈	NA	NA	NA	NA	NA	NA	NA	NA	NA
P/E Ratio - High	NM	NM	NM	NM	NM	NM	NM	NM	NM	NM
- Low	NM	NM	NM	NM	NM	NM	NM	NM	NM	NM

Income Statement Analysis (Million $)

	1997	1996	1995	1994	1993	1992	1991	1990	1989	1988
Revs.	1,418	1,524	NA	NA	NA	NA	NA	NA	NA	NA
Oper. Inc.	151	143	NA	NA	NA	NA	NA	NA	NA	NA
Depr.	103	88.0	NA	NA	NA	NA	NA	NA	NA	NA
Int. Exp.	28.0	28.0	NA	NA	NA	NA	NA	NA	NA	NA
Pretax Inc.	-89.0	37.0	NA	NA	NA	NA	NA	NA	NA	NA
Eff. Tax Rate	NM	32%	NA	NA	NA	NA	NA	NA	NA	NA
Net Inc.	-72.0	23.0	NA	NA	NA	NA	NA	NA	NA	NA

Balance Sheet & Other Fin. Data (Million $)

	1997	1996	1995	1994	1993	1992	1991	1990	1989	1988
Cash	85.0	32.0	NA	NA	NA	NA	NA	NA	NA	NA
Curr. Assets	423	434	NA	NA	NA	NA	NA	NA	NA	NA
Total Assets	1,666	1,663	NA	NA	NA	NA	NA	NA	NA	NA
Curr. Liab.	496	287	NA	NA	NA	NA	NA	NA	NA	NA
LT Debt	13.0	350	NA	NA	NA	NA	NA	NA	NA	NA
Common Eqty.	986	1,025	NA	NA	NA	NA	NA	NA	NA	NA
Total Cap.	1,133	1,439	NA	NA	NA	NA	NA	NA	NA	NA
Cap. Exp.	116	NA	NA	NA	NA	NA	NA	NA	NA	NA
Cash Flow	31.0	111	NA	NA	NA	NA	NA	NA	NA	NA
Curr. Ratio	0.9	1.5	NA	NA	NA	NA	NA	NA	NA	NA
% LT Debt of Cap.	1.1	24.3	NA	NA	NA	NA	NA	NA	NA	NA
% Net Inc.of Revs.	NM	1.5	NA	NA	NA	NA	NA	NA	NA	NA
% Ret. on Assets	NM	NA	NA	NA	NA	NA	NA	NA	NA	NA
% Ret. on Equity	NM	NA	NA	NA	NA	NA	NA	NA	NA	NA

Data as orig. reptd.; bef. results of disc. opers. and/or spec. items. Pro forma in 1996, balance sheet as of Jun. 30, 1997. Per share data adj. for stk. divs. as of ex-div. date. Bold denotes diluted EPS (FASB 128). E-Estimated. NA-Not Available. NM-Not Meaningful. NR-Not Ranked.

Office—6500 South Archer Rd., Bedford Park, IL 60501. **Tel**—(708) 563-2400. **Chrmn & CEO**—K. Schlatter. **Pres**—S. C. Scott. **VP & Secy**—M. E. Doane. **VP-Fin & CFO**—J. W. Ripley. **Dirs**—I. Aranguren-Castiello, A. C. DeCrane, Jr., W. C. Ferguson, R. G. Holder, B. H. Kastory, W. S. Norman, K. Schlatter, S. C. Scott, C. B. Storms. **Transfer Agent & Registrar**—First Chicago Trust Co. of New York, Jersey City, NJ. **Incorporated**—in Delaware in 1997. **Empl**— 4,300. **S&P Analyst:** Robert J. Izmirlian

03-OCT-98

Industry:
Health Care (Managed Care)

Summary: This company provides a wide range of managed health care benefits and services to over 1.5 million members in 14 states.

S&P Opinion: Hold (★★★)	Recent Price • 5¾
	52 Wk Range • 19¼-3⅞

Yield • Nil
12-Mo. P/E • NM

Quantitative Evaluations

Outlook
(1 Lowest—5 Highest)
• 5

Fair Value
• 13½

Risk
• Average

Earn./Div. Rank
• C

Technical Eval.
• Bearish since 6/97

Rel. Strength Rank
(1 Lowest—99 Highest)
• 18

Insider Activity
• Favorable

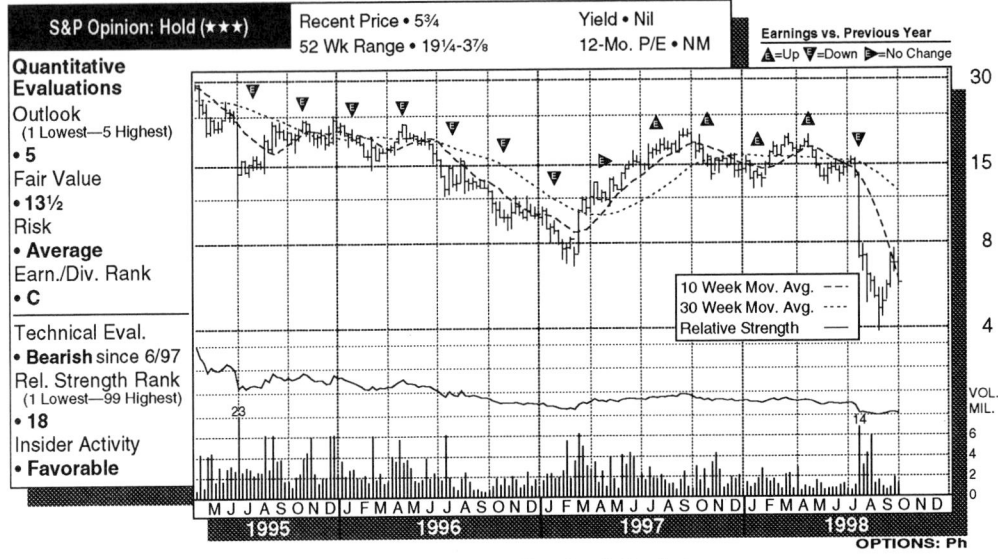

Earnings vs. Previous Year
▲=Up ▼=Down ▶=No Change

10 Week Mov. Avg. – – –
30 Week Mov. Avg. · · · ·
Relative Strength ——

OPTIONS: Ph

Overview - 26-AUG-98

Coventry faces some significant challenges following the Chapter 11 bankruptcy filing of one of its largest health care providers, Allegheny Health, Education & Research Foundation (AHERF). As a result of the bankruptcy, CVTY no longer has capitated arrangements with about 200,000 members in Pennsylvania, and it must assume the risks associated with caring for these individuals until new provider arrangements can be negotiated. On a pro forma basis to include the operations of The Principal Financial Group's health care unit for the full year, we expect 1998 revenues of about $2.5 billion. However, the medical loss ratio will be hurt by the AHERF bankruptcy filing, and earnings visibility has been significantly hampered by the company's heightened exposure to rising medical costs. We cautiously look for 1998 EPS of $0.43 (before charges) and see 1999 EPS of $0.80.

Valuation - 26-AUG-98

The company's operational turnaround was dealt a potentially crippling blow by the AHERF bankruptcy, as much of the earnings recovery hinged on management's ability to re-negotiate its provider contracts on a globally capitated basis. The absence of the AHERF arrangement alone creates significant earnings uncertainties, while an added risk relates to the ongoing integration of the Principal operations. As a result of second quarter charges related to the Principal merger ($7.8 million) and costs associated with the AHERF bankruptcy ($55 million), Coventry was in technical default of its bank debt covenants. However, lenders granted the company a waiver and we do not anticipate a liquidity squeeze in the near future. Given the unfavorable developments and increasingly poor risk/reward profile of the stock, however, we would not add to holdings.

Key Stock Statistics

S&P EPS Est. 1998	-0.19	Tang. Bk. Value/Share	0.89
P/E on S&P Est. 1998	NM	Beta	1.23
S&P EPS Est. 1999	0.80	Shareholders	600
Dividend Rate/Share	Nil	Market cap. (B)	$0.337
Shs. outstg. (M)	58.6	Inst. holdings	38%
Avg. daily vol. (M)	0.239		

Value of $10,000 invested 5 years ago: $ 5,082

Fiscal Year Ending Dec. 31

	1998	1997	1996	1995	1994	1993
Revenues (Million $)						
1Q	330.2	299.4	236.9	209.7	184.8	139.0
2Q	583.8	301.1	257.7	208.9	185.8	141.8
3Q	—	306.7	272.9	211.1	188.8	149.3
4Q	—	321.2	289.6	222.7	187.9	152.8
Yr.	—	1,228	1,057	852.4	747.3	583.0
Earnings Per Share ($)						
1Q	0.13	-0.03	-0.03	0.30	0.24	0.18
2Q	-0.47	0.20	-0.26	0.07	0.27	0.20
3Q	E0.07	0.08	0.01	0.05	0.27	0.20
4Q	E0.08	0.11	-1.58	-0.42	0.20	0.21
Yr.	E-0.19	0.36	-1.86	Nil	0.96	0.80

Next earnings report expected: late October

Dividend Data

No cash dividends have been paid.

A Division of The **McGraw·Hill** *Companies*

Business Summary - 26-AUG-98

Following the April 1998 merger between Coventry Corp. and the health care unit of The Principal Financial Group, Coventry Health Care Inc. stands among the largest managed health care providers in the U.S. It provides a full range of managed care products including health maintenance organization (HMO), preferred provider organization (PPO), point-of-service (POS), Medicare Risk and Medicaid plans to 1,571,518 individuals in 14 states. Geographically, the primary emphasis is on Pennsylvania, Missouri and Florida, where about 55% of the at-risk members are located. On a pro forma basis, Coventry Health Care had 1997 managed care premiums of $2.1 billion.

Health care services provided by the company's HMOs include ambulatory and inpatient physician care, hospitalization, pharmacy, dental, optical, mental health, ancillary diagnostic and therapeutic services. In general, a fixed monthly enrollment fee covers all HMO services, although some plans require co-payments or deductibles in addition to the basic premium. A primary care physician assumes overall responsibility for member care, including preventative and routine medical care and specialist or consulting physician referrals.

Coventry also offers fully insured flexible products, including PPO and POS plans, which permit enrollees to join an HMO but allow them to utilize non network providers in return for higher levels of deductibles and co-payments.

The company offers a Medicare risk product, under which it receives a fixed premium per member which is set annually by the Health Care Financing Administration (HCFA). Coventry also offers a Medicare cost product which allows for reimbursement by HCFA only for the cost of services rendered, including services provided at the health plan's medical offices and a portion of administrative expenses. Under a Medicare supplement product, members enroll individually and pay a monthly premium for health services not covered under Medicare.

CVTY also offers health care coverage to Medicaid recipients, where it receives a monthly premium, set by individual state regulators, based on the age and sex of the recipients enrolled in its health plans.

The company's health plans offer an administrative services only (ASO, or non-risk) product to large employers who are self-insured. Under ASO contracts, employers who fund their own health plans receive the benefit of provider pricing arrangements from the health plan, and the health plan also provides a variety of administrative services such as claims processing, utilization review and quality assurance for the employers. Coventry receives a fee for such services.

Per Share Data ($)

(Year Ended Dec. 31)	1997	1996	1995	1994	1993	1992	1991	1990	1989	1988
Tangible Bk. Val.	0.28	NM	1.30	0.60	0.53	-0.17	-0.78	-1.39	NA	NA
Cash Flow	0.72	-0.56	0.46	1.28	1.07	0.78	0.65	0.96	0.94	0.71
Earnings	0.36	-1.86	Nil	0.96	0.80	0.56	0.40	0.59	0.58	0.41
Dividends	Nil	Nil	Nil	Nil	Nil	Nil	Nil	Nil	Nil	Nil
Payout Ratio	Nil	Nil	Nil	Nil	Nil	Nil	Nil	Nil	Nil	Nil
Prices - High	20¹/₈	21³/₈	31	26³/₄	22¹/₈	12³/₈	9¹/₂	NA	NA	NA
- Low	6⁵/₈	8⁷/₈	11	15³/₄	8³/₄	5¹/₄	3¹/₂	NA	NA	NA
P/E Ratio - High	56	NM	NM	28	28	22	24	NA	NA	NA
- Low	18	NM	NM	16	11	9	9	NA	NA	NA

Income Statement Analysis (Million $)

	1997	1996	1995	1994	1993	1992	1991	1990	1989	1988
Revs.	1,228	1,057	852	747	583	430	340	394	218	84.0
Oper. Inc.	18.5	-38.7	16.0	66.5	48.2	33.5	24.1	28.0	21.1	11.8
Depr.	12.7	42.9	14.7	9.2	7.1	5.3	5.7	6.3	3.6	1.5
Int. Exp.	10.3	6.3	4.9	2.7	2.7	3.7	5.6	9.9	7.6	4.3
Pretax Inc.	20.3	-84.2	1.5	56.0	40.3	25.9	16.0	15.9	13.7	7.5
Eff. Tax Rate	41%	NM	99%	44%	40%	41%	38%	37%	33%	27%
Net Inc.	11.9	-61.3	Nil	28.1	20.3	13.8	8.7	10.0	9.1	5.5

Balance Sheet & Other Fin. Data (Million $)

	1997	1996	1995	1994	1993	1992	1991	1990	1989	1988
Cash	154	98.0	85.8	75.4	71.3	55.3	23.3	43.5	31.6	NA
Curr. Assets	237	208	143	114	100	78.2	43.4	90.0	56.3	NA
Total Assets	469	449	386	332	243	193	164	269	180	NA
Curr. Liab.	261	282	156	132	107	75.9	53.6	97.5	51.0	NA
LT Debt	85.7	57.3	65.6	65.1	37.3	47.4	54.2	80.0	60.5	NA
Common Eqty.	118	100	154	131	87.9	62.4	47.3	64.4	51.5	NA
Total Cap.	204	158	222	196	134	114	105	157	119	NA
Cap. Exp.	7.2	12.7	16.3	21.3	12.8	4.4	3.1	4.0	3.3	0.4
Cash Flow	24.6	-18.4	14.7	37.3	27.4	19.1	14.4	16.3	12.7	7.0
Curr. Ratio	0.9	0.7	0.9	0.9	0.9	1.0	0.8	0.9	1.1	NA
% LT Debt of Cap.	42.1	36.3	29.6	33.2	27.9	41.5	51.8	51.1	51.0	NA
% Net Inc.of Revs.	1.0	NM	NM	3.8	3.5	3.2	2.6	2.5	4.2	6.5
% Ret. on Assets	2.6	NM	NM	9.4	9.1	7.8	0.8	4.5	5.0	NA
% Ret. on Equity	10.9	NM	NM	24.5	26.6	25.2	3.4	17.3	21.6	NA

Data as orig. reptd.; bef. results of disc. opers. and/or spec. items. Per share data adj. for stk. divs. as of ex-div. date. Bold denotes diluted EPS (FASB 128). E-Estimated. NA-Not Available. NM-Not Meaningful. NR-Not Ranked.

Office—53 Century Blvd., Suite 250, Nashville, TN 37214. **Tel**—(615) 391-2440. **Chrmn**—J. H. Austin.**Pres & CEO**—A. F. Wise. **SVP, Treas & CFO**—D. B. Wolf. **EVP & COO**—T. P. McDonough. **VP & Secy**—S. R. Smith. **Dirs**—J. H. Austin, P. N. Bredesen, L. DeFrance, E. D. Farley Jr., P. T. Hackett, R. H. Jones, L. Kugelman, R. W. Moorhead III, A. F. Wise. **Transfer Agent**—ChaseMellon Shareholder Services, Pittsburgh. **Incorporated**—in Delaware in 1986. **Empl**— 2,100. **S&P Analyst:** Robert M. Gold

Cross (A.T.) Co.

7627K

ASE Symbol **ATX.A**

In S&P SmallCap 600

03-OCT-98

Industry: Consumer (Jewelry, Novelties & Gifts)

Summary: This leading maker of fine writing instruments recently entered the personal digital products market.

Quantitative Evaluations

Outlook
(1 Lowest—5 Highest)
- **NA**

Fair Value
- **NA**

Risk
- **NA**

Earn./Div. Rank
- **B-**

Technical Eval.
- **Bearish** since 7/98

Rel. Strength Rank
(1 Lowest—99 Highest)
- **19**

Insider Activity
- **Neutral**

Recent Price • 6¾
52 Wk Range • 14⅞-6⅝

Yield • 4.7%
12-Mo. P/E • NM

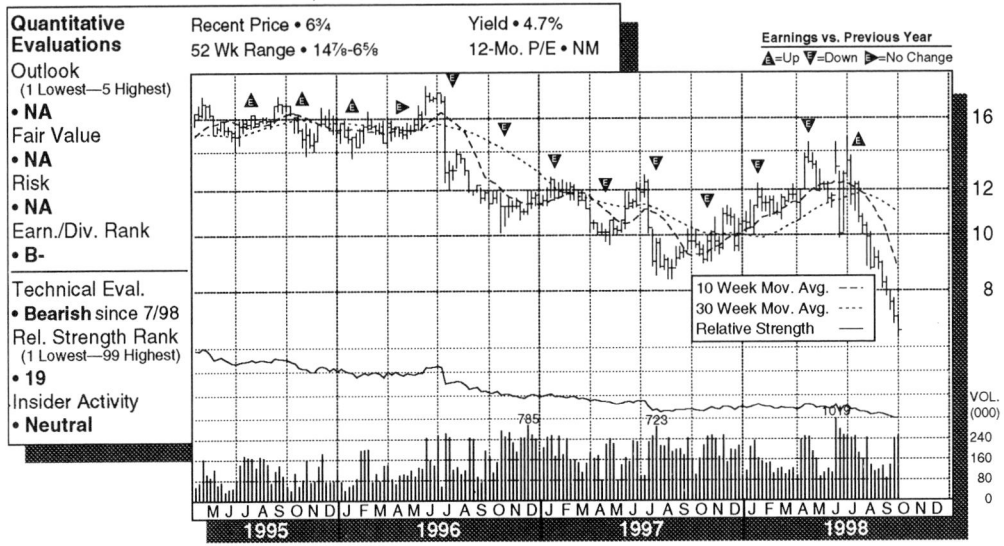

Earnings vs. Previous Year
▲=Up ▼=Down ▶=No Change

10 Week Mov. Avg. ---
30 Week Mov. Avg. ·····
Relative Strength —

Business Profile - 27-AUG-98

One of the highlights for the second quarter of 1998 was the launch of CrossPad, which enables users to write in ink on standard paper and transfer their handwriting directly to a PC. The CrossPad comes from the company's recently created Pen Computing Group (PCG) division, which generated almost 29% of all domestic revenue in the second quarter. Writing instrument sales continue to be soft domestically as well as internationally. The company believes that flat U.S. demand as well as the economic crisis in Asia are affecting revenues. In reaction to the difficult environment, Cross is launching 31 new writing instrument products in the second half of 1998.

Operational Review - 27-AUG-98

Net sales for the six months ended June 30, 1998, rose 2.2%, as the first full quarter of sales in the Pen Computing Group more than offset declines in domestic and international writing instrument revenues. Results benefited from cost reduction programs, which resulted in improved writing instrument profitability, and from well controlled SG&A expenses; the operating loss narrowed. Following 60% higher interest and other income and tax benefits of $620,000 versus $987,000, the loss from continuing operations was $1,316,000 ($0.08 per share), compared with $1,833,000 ($0.11). Results exclude income from discontinued operations of $0.10 in the 1998 period and a loss of $0.14 a share from discontinued operations in the 1997 period.

Stock Performance - 02-OCT-98

In the past 30 trading days, ATX.A's shares have declined 25%, compared to a 7% fall in the S&P 500. Average trading volume for the past five days was 71,280 shares, compared with the 40-day moving average of 34,028 shares.

Key Stock Statistics

Dividend Rate/Share	0.32	Shareholders	1,900
Shs. outstg. (M)	16.5	Market cap. (B)	$0.100
Avg. daily vol. (M)	0.042	Inst. holdings	36%
Tang. Bk. Value/Share	6.84		
Beta	0.64		

Value of $10,000 invested 5 years ago: $ 4,698

Fiscal Year Ending Dec. 31

	1998	1997	1996	1995	1994	1993
Revenues (Million $)						
1Q	31.53	36.80	36.05	35.41	35.19	39.10
2Q	34.69	31.12	41.52	44.88	40.62	37.29
3Q	—	36.63	43.05	44.86	45.93	40.10
4Q	—	53.28	58.57	65.94	55.40	50.74
Yr.	—	154.7	179.2	191.1	177.1	164.6
Earnings Per Share ($)						
1Q	-0.08	0.05	0.10	0.09	0.08	0.01
2Q	Nil	-0.16	0.05	0.10	0.04	-0.35
3Q	—	-0.04	0.10	0.17	0.16	0.14
4Q	—	-0.11	0.15	0.45	0.34	0.24
Yr.	—	-0.26	0.40	0.81	0.62	0.03

Next earnings report expected: late October

Dividend Data (Dividends have been paid since 1952.)

Amount ($)	Date Decl.	Ex-Div. Date	Stock of Record	Payment Date
0.080	Oct. 22	Oct. 31	Nov. 04	Nov. 18 '97
0.080	Dec. 09	Jan. 15	Jan. 20	Feb. 03 '98
0.080	Apr. 23	May. 01	May. 05	May. 19 '98
0.080	Jul. 13	Jul. 31	Aug. 04	Aug. 18 '98

A Division of The McGraw-Hill Companies

A.T. Cross Company

Business Summary - 27-AUG-98

In 1877, Alonzo Cross was granted his first patent for a stylographic pen with an ink reservoir and a pencil-like tip -- a design that would prove to be extremely popular in the years to come. The ball point pen that is synonymous with the name A.T. Cross was first introduced by the company in 1952. The new ball point pen and matching mechanical pencil were successfully marketed to businesses over the next two decades. In 1971, A.T. Cross tapped the equity markets through an initial public offering and used the proceeds to launch a global expansion. Today Cross is a major international manufacturer of fine writing instruments. Foreign sales accounted for 49% of total revenues in 1997.

The company has experienced disappointing sales and earnings in recent quarters, reflecting lower gross profit margins, primarily due to its product mix and the negative effects of currency translations. Its stock price has fallen more than 70% from the all-time high of 41 in 1989. According to market research, fewer than 20% of consumers who purchase quality writing instruments realize that Cross offers a variety of products. As a result, the company plans to change this perception through advertising, point-of-sale materials, displays and promotions that focus on Cross's full line of products. To stimulate revenue growth, Cross is broadening its product

line with the addition of watches for men and women. Additionally, the company is working with high technology firms to develop products that would be complementary to personal electronics. In November 1997, Cross unveiled the CrossPad, which enables users to write in ink on standard paper and transfer their handwriting directly to a PC. Once in the PC, the handwriting can be filed, edited, faxed, e-mailed, printed out in handwritten form or converted to ASCII text.

The company's writing instruments include ball point pens, mechanical pencils, rolling/porous-point pens and fountain pens. Cross offers a variety of styles including the traditional, narrow girth Century line. The company believes it is the leading U.S. provider of fine writing instruments priced from $10 to $50. The company recently entered the premium end of the market ($55 to $250) with its release of the wider girth Townsend line in 1993 and the Pinnacle line in 1997. Solo and Solo Classic, the company's first resin-based products, were introduced in 1994. Cross's business is seasonal, with a significant portion of its earnings occurring in the fourth quarter.

Following the non-renewal of its distribution contract with Fendi Diffusione in June 1997, the company decided to cease its distribution of leather goods and discontinue the operations of its Manetti-Farrow subsidiary.

Per Share Data ($)

(Year Ended Dec. 31)	1997	1996	1995	1994	1993	1992	1991	1990	1989	1988
Tangible Bk. Val.	6.84	7.69	7.96	7.79	7.72	8.64	9.33	9.60	9.20	7.65
Cash Flow	0.23	0.85	1.23	1.00	0.40	0.98	1.58	1.93	2.64	2.48
Earnings	-0.26	0.40	0.81	0.62	0.03	0.64	1.26	1.62	2.15	2.13
Dividends	0.48	0.64	0.64	0.64	0.96	1.28	1.28	1.25	1.18	1.06
Payout Ratio	NM	160%	79%	103%	NM	200%	102%	77%	55%	50%
Prices - High	12¾	18¼	17½	17⅝	20¼	27⅝	28⅛	36	41	37½
- Low	8⅜	10⅛	12⅞	12½	12⅜	17	21½	20	32	26⅜
P/E Ratio - High	NM	46	22	28	NM	43	22	22	19	18
- Low	NM	25	16	20	NM	27	17	12	15	12

Income Statement Analysis (Million $)

	1997	1996	1995	1994	1993	1992	1991	1990	1989	1988
Revs.	155	179	191	177	165	200	217	223	247	228
Oper. Inc.	-0.4	14.8	23.6	21.4	16.3	20.7	29.9	38.5	53.7	54.2
Depr.	8.2	7.5	7.0	6.3	6.2	5.7	5.5	5.2	5.2	5.8
Int. Exp.	Nil	Nil	Nil	Nil	Nil	Nil	Nil	Nil	Nil	0.4
Pretax Inc.	-6.7	9.4	20.0	19.0	1.6	16.0	29.6	38.4	53.7	52.1
Eff. Tax Rate	NM	30%	34%	45%	68%	32%	29%	29%	33%	32%
Net Inc.	-4.4	6.6	13.4	10.5	0.5	10.8	21.2	27.2	36.0	35.4

Balance Sheet & Other Fin. Data (Million $)

	1997	1996	1995	1994	1993	1992	1991	1990	1989	1988
Cash	25.8	43.5	54.0	72.0	71.1	65.2	65.9	70.4	64.5	64.9
Curr. Assets	110	119	135	131	130	144	157	158	149	134
Total Assets	158	175	189	180	179	194	208	207	196	176
Curr. Liab.	39.3	42.9	52.4	46.8	40.2	39.8	42.7	41.5	38.4	36.2
LT Debt	Nil	Nil	Nil	Nil	Nil	Nil	Nil	Nil	Nil	Nil
Common Eqty.	113	127	132	129	134	151	162	162	154	136
Total Cap.	113	127	132	129	134	151	162	162	154	136
Cap. Exp.	7.5	9.1	10.8	7.7	8.5	5.4	8.4	5.9	9.8	12.8
Cash Flow	3.9	14.1	20.4	16.9	6.7	16.6	26.7	32.4	41.2	41.2
Curr. Ratio	2.8	2.8	2.6	2.8	3.2	3.6	3.7	3.8	3.9	3.7
% LT Debt of Cap.	Nil	Nil	Nil	Nil	Nil	Nil	Nil	Nil	Nil	Nil
% Net Inc.of Revs.	NM	3.7	7.0	5.9	0.3	5.4	9.8	12.2	14.6	15.6
% Ret. on Assets	NM	3.6	7.3	5.9	0.3	5.4	10.2	13.5	19.3	21.3
% Ret. on Equity	NM	5.1	10.3	8.1	0.4	6.9	13.1	17.2	24.7	27.8

Data as orig. reptd.; bef. results of disc. opers. and/or spec. items. Per share data adj. for stk. divs. as of ex-div. date. Bold denotes diluted EPS (FASB 128). E-Estimated. NA-Not Available. NM-Not Meaningful. NR-Not Ranked.

Office—One Albion Rd., Lincoln. RI 02865. Registrar—Citizens Trust Co., Providence. Tel—(401) 333-1200. Website—http://www.crossusa.com Chrmn—B. R. Boss. Pres & CEO—R. A. Boss. EVP & COO—J. E. Buckley. SVP, Treas & CFO—J. T. Ruggieri. VP & Secy—T. C. Benik. Dirs—B. R. Boss, R. A. Boss, J. E. Buckley, B. V. Buonanno, Jr., H. F. Krimendahl II, T. Murray, J. C. Tappan, E. G. Torrance, A. Van Dam. Transfer Agent & Registrar—Fleet National Bank of Rhode Island, Providence. Incorporated—in Rhode Island in 1916. Empl— 1,100. S&P Analyst: Jordan Horoschak

STANDARD &POOR'S
STOCK REPORTS

Cross Timbers Oil

687D

NYSE Symbol **XTO**

In S&P SmallCap 600

03-OCT-98

Industry:
Oil & Gas (Exploration & Production)

Summary: This oil and gas production and transportation company has properties in Oklahoma, Texas, New Mexico, Kansas and Wyoming.

Quantitative Evaluations

Outlook
(1 Lowest—5 Highest)
• **1**–

Fair Value
• **14⅛**

Risk
• **Average**

Earn./Div. Rank
• **NR**

Technical Eval.
• **Bearish** since 6/97

Rel. Strength Rank
(1 Lowest—99 Highest)
• **90**

Insider Activity
• **Neutral**

Recent Price • 16
52 Wk Range • 21⅛-11⅜

Yield • 1.0%
12-Mo. P/E • 66.7

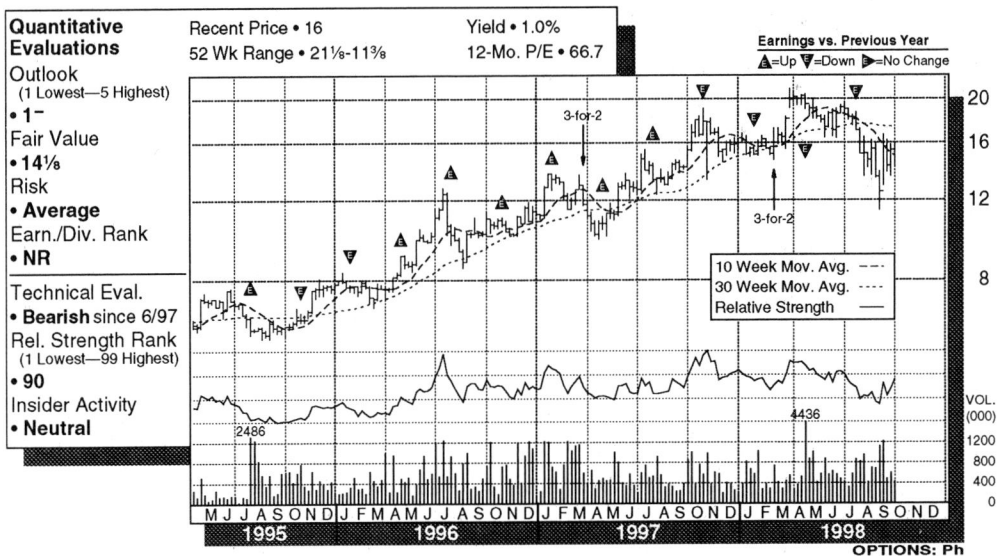

Earnings vs. Previous Year
▲=Up ▼=Down ►=No Change

10 Week Mov. Avg. ---
30 Week Mov. Avg. ····
Relative Strength —

OPTIONS: Ph

Business Profile - 14-APR-98

This company is engaged in acquiring, exploiting and developing oil and gas properties. In November 1997, XTO acquired producing properties in the San Juan Basin of northwestern New Mexico for $252 million and warrants to purchase 625,000 shares. The acquisition added an estimated 258.6 Bcf of natural gas, 16.4 bbl of natural gas liquids and 1.5 bbl of oil equivalent. Management has said that its strategic goals for 1998 and 1999 include a 50% increase in cash flow and proved reserves per share, which would duplicate a like gain in the 1996-97 period. The company also expects to make strategic acquisitions totaling $260 to $280 million by the end of 1999, and spend between $70 million and $90 million annually on exploration and development.

Operational Review - 14-APR-98

Revenues in 1997, advanced 24% from those of the prior year, reflecting a 50% jump in gas revenues, resulting from higher prices and increased volumes, and relatively flat oil revenues. Results for the period also included a $4.2 million gain on the sale of producing properties and equities and $1.3 million in proceeds from a lawsuit settlement. After taxes at 34.5%, versus 34.4%, net income climbed 26%, to $25,684,000 ($0.59 a diluted share, after preferred dividends, as adjusted), from $20,304,000 ($0.48 a share).

Stock Performance - 02-OCT-98

In the past 30 trading days, XTO's shares have increased 3%, compared to a 7% fall in the S&P 500. Average trading volume for the past five days was 84,880 shares, compared with the 40-day moving average of 148,903 shares.

Key Stock Statistics

Dividend Rate/Share	0.16	Shareholders	100
Shs. outstg. (M)	44.9	Market cap. (B)	$0.719
Avg. daily vol. (M)	0.159	Inst. holdings	66%
Tang. Bk. Value/Share	9.59		
Beta	1.09		

Value of $10,000 invested 5 years ago: NA

Fiscal Year Ending Dec. 31

	1998	1997	1996	1995	1994	1993
Revenues (Million $)						
1Q	50.62	53.49	36.08	24.22	22.61	15.47
2Q	67.53	45.97	36.74	27.94	24.02	19.09
3Q	—	44.09	39.20	28.07	25.29	22.47
4Q	—	57.12	49.37	32.68	24.36	21.15
Yr.	—	200.7	161.4	112.9	96.28	78.18
Earnings Per Share ($)						
1Q	Nil	0.26	0.11	0.04	-0.01	Nil
2Q	0.02	0.00	0.04	0.02	0.02	-0.02
3Q	—	0.07	0.12	0.03	0.04	0.00
4Q	—	0.17	0.23	-0.36	0.04	0.02
Yr.	—	0.59	0.49	-0.29	0.08	-0.01

Next earnings report expected: mid October

Dividend Data (Dividends have been paid since 1993.)

Amount ($)	Date Decl.	Ex-Div. Date	Stock of Record	Payment Date
0.040	Jan. 30	Mar. 27	Mar. 31	Apr. 15 '98
3-for-2	Jan. 30	Feb. 25	Feb. 12	Feb. 24 '98
0.040	May. 19	Jun. 26	Jun. 30	Jul. 15 '98
0.040	Aug. 25	Sep. 28	Sep. 30	Oct. 15 '98

A Division of The **McGraw·Hill** Companies

Business Summary - 14-APR-98

This oil and gas company combines an aggressive capital structure with a relatively low-risk operating strategy to grow reserves and earnings. With several acquisitions of gas production properties in recent years, Cross Timbers Oil Co. (XTO) has effected a shift toward natural gas production. Earnings and reserves have increased rapidly, and XTO has set ambitious growth targets through the end of the decade.

The company ended 1997 with proved oil reserves of 48 million barrels, up 13% over 19965, and proved reserves of natural gas of 816 billion cubic feet, 51% higher than the year before. Growth in proved reserves mainly resulted from acquisition of gas-producing properties, as well as development and exploitation activities. Daily oil and gas production in 1997 averaged 10,905 Bbls and 135,855 Mcf. Oil and gas accounted for 37% and 55%, respectively, of revenues in 1997. XTO also has gas gathering, processing and marketing operations, which accounted for 5% of revenues.

During 1997, the company received sales prices of $18.90 per bbl of oil ($21.38 in 1996) and $2.20 per Mcf of natural gas ($1.97). It also drilled 206 gross (142.5 net) development wells and three gross (0.7 net) exploratory wells. The company has generated a substantial inventory of about 950 potential development drilling locations within its existing properties to support future net reserve additions.

XTO has grown mainly through acquisitions of proved reserves, followed by development and strategic acquisitions of additional interests. It has not historically engaged in significant exploratory activities, but for 1998 has allocated 10% to 15% of its budget, or up to $13.5 million, for exploration.

The company's proved reserves are mainly located in relatively long-lived fields with well-established production histories concentrated in western Oklahoma, the Permian Basin of West Texas and New Mexico, the Hugoton Field of Oklahoma and Kansas, the San Juan Basin of northwestern New Mexico (acquired in December 1997) and the Green River Basin of Wyoming.

In May 1997, the company laid out strategic goals for the 1998-1999 period, including 50% increases in cash flow and proved reserves per share. It also plans to make strategic acquisitions totaling $260 to $280 million from May 1997 to the end of 1999.

In February 1998, the company entered into a definitive agreement with EEX Corp. to acquire producing properties and undeveloped acreage in East Texas for about $245 million. Reserves are estimated at 250 Bcf and 1.6 million Bbls. The transaction is expected to be completed in late April 1998.

Per Share Data ($)

(Year Ended Dec. 31)	1997	1996	1995	1994	1993	1992	1991	1990	1989	1988
Tangible Bk. Val.	3.59	2.97	3.16	3.16	3.21	3.25	NA	NA	NA	NA
Cash Flow	1.78	1.45	0.68	0.97	0.63	0.85	NA	NA	NA	NA
Earnings	0.59	0.49	-0.29	0.08	-0.12	0.20	NA	NA	NA	NA
Dividends	0.15	0.13	0.13	0.13	0.10	NA	NA	NA	NA	NA
Payout Ratio	25%	27%	NM	158%	NM	NA	NA	NA	NA	NA
Prices - High	19$^1/_8$	12$^3/_4$	8	7$^3/_8$	8$^3/_8$	NA	NA	NA	NA	NA
- Low	9$^7/_8$	7	5$^7/_8$	5$^1/_2$	5$^3/_4$	NA	NA	NA	NA	NA
P/E Ratio - High	32	26	NM	87	NM	NA	NA	NA	NA	NA
- Low	17	14	NM	66	NM	NA	NA	NA	NA	NA

Income Statement Analysis (Million $)

	1997	1996	1995	1994	1993	1992	1991	1990	1989	1988
Revs.	201	161	113	96.0	78.1	107	NA	NA	NA	NA
Oper. Inc.	114	85.9	52.7	44.2	29.7	39.4	NA	NA	NA	NA
Depr. Depl. & Amort.	47.7	37.9	36.9	31.7	24.6	23.7	NA	NA	NA	NA
Int. Exp.	26.7	17.2	12.9	8.3	5.6	4.7	NA	NA	NA	NA
Pretax Inc.	39.2	31.0	-0.2	4.8	-0.4	11.0	NA	NA	NA	NA
Eff. Tax Rate	34%	34%	NM	36%	NM	34%	NA	NA	NA	NA
Net Inc.	25.7	20.3	-11.2	3.0	-4.0	7.2	NA	NA	NA	NA

Balance Sheet & Other Fin. Data (Million $)

	1997	1996	1995	1994	1993	1992	1991	1990	1989	1988
Cash	3.8	3.9	2.2	7.8	2.1	4.3	NA	NA	NA	NA
Curr. Assets	52.2	51.8	32.7	26.9	22.8	21.8	NA	NA	NA	NA
Total Assets	788	523	403	292	258	220	NA	NA	NA	NA
Curr. Liab.	54.9	52.0	31.1	28.5	25.3	15.9	NA	NA	NA	NA
LT Debt	539	315	238	143	112	79.9	NA	NA	NA	NA
Common Eqty.	142	114	131	113	115	120	NA	NA	NA	NA
Total Cap.	730	468	372	264	233	204	NA	NA	NA	NA
Cap. Exp.	257	114	171	30.0	105	NA	NA	NA	NA	NA
Cash Flow	71.6	57.6	25.7	34.8	20.6	31.0	NA	NA	NA	NA
Curr. Ratio	1.0	1.0	1.1	0.9	0.9	1.4	NA	NA	NA	NA
% LT Debt of Cap.	73.8	67.3	64.0	54.1	48.1	39.1	NA	NA	NA	NA
% Ret. on Assets	3.9	4.4	NM	1.1	NM	NA	NA	NA	NA	NA
% Ret. on Equity	18.7	16.2	NM	2.7	NM	NA	NA	NA	NA	NA

Data as orig. reptd.; bef. results of disc opers. and/or spec. items. Per share data adj. for stk. divs. as of ex-div. date. Bold denotes diluted EPS (FASB 128). E-Estimated. NA-Not Available. NM-Not Meaningful. NR-Not Ranked.

Office—810 Houston St., Suite 2000, Fort Worth, TX 76102. **Organized**—in Delaware in 1990. **Tel**—(817) 870-2800. **Chrmn & CEO**—B. R. Simpson. **Vice Chrmn & Pres**—S. E. Palko.**Sr VP, CFO & Investor Contact**—Louis G. Baldwin. **Dirs**—J. L. King Jr., S. E. Palko, J. P. Randall, S. G. Sherman, B. R. Simpson. **Transfer Agent & Registrar**—ChaseMellon Shareholder Services, Dallas. **Incorporated**—in Delaware in 1990. **Empl**— 349. **S&P Analyst:** SRB

Cullen/Frost Bankers 700G

NYSE Symbol **CFR**

In S&P SmallCap 600

03-OCT-98

Industry: Banks (Regional)

Summary: The largest multibank holding company headquartered in Texas, Cullen/Frost owns two subsidiary banks with 60 offices in six markets in the state.

Quantitative Evaluations

Recent Price • 48
52 Wk Range • 62¾-40⅞

Yield • 2.5%
12-Mo. P/E • 18.5

Outlook
(1 Lowest—5 Highest)
• 1⁻

Fair Value
• 43¼

Risk
• **Low**

Earn./Div. Rank
• **B**

Technical Eval.
• **NA**

Rel. Strength Rank
(1 Lowest—99 Highest)
• **77**

Insider Activity
• **NA**

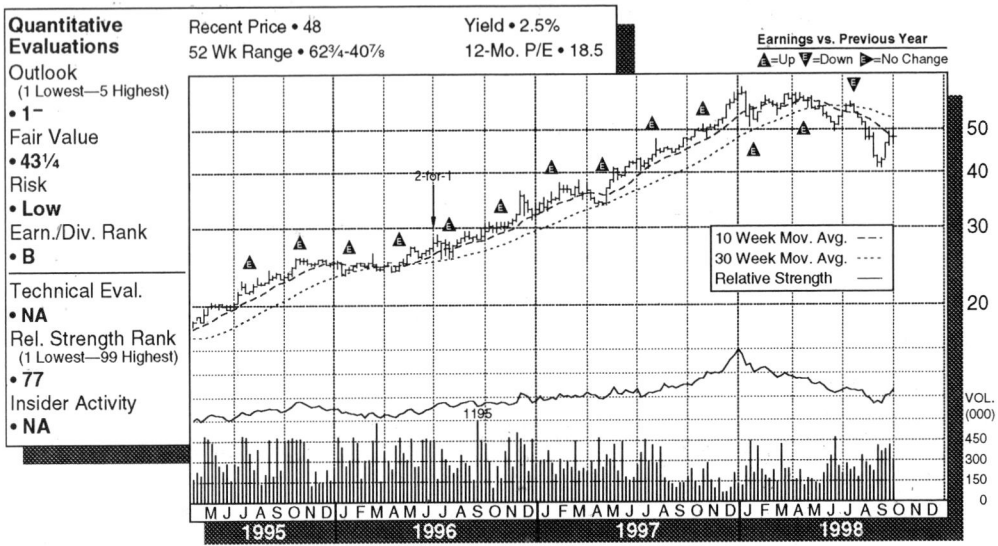

Earnings vs. Previous Year
▲=Up ▼=Down ▶=No Change

10 Week Mov. Avg. ---
30 Week Mov. Avg. ·····
Relative Strength —

Business Profile - 14-MAY-98

This multibank holding company, with about $5.5 billion in assets and $4.8 in deposits, continues to expand through acquisitions, focusing on five major markets in southern Texas: San Antonio, Austin, Houston/Galveston, Corpus Christi, and McAllen (on the Texas-Mexico border). During the first quarter of 1998, Cullen/Frost acquired Harrisburg Bancshares, with $265 million in assets and three branches in the Houston area. Recent results have been aided by growth in noninterest income, which continues to account for over 35% of net revenue.

Operational Review - 14-MAY-98

Net interest income advanced 15% in the first quarter of 1998, year to year, as total loans grew 22%, to $2.8 billion, aided by acquisitions, as well as internal growth. The provision for possible loan losses and real estate valuations rose 38%, mainly on the increase in loans; net chargeoffs were only 0.32% of average loans. Noninterest income increased 18%, largely on strong growth in trust income and certain service charges. Noninterest expenses rose 17%. After taxes at 36.1%, versus 35.9%, net income climbed 11%, to $16,745,000 ($0.73 a share, diluted), from $15,063,000 ($0.65).

Stock Performance - 02-OCT-98

In the past 30 trading days, CFR's shares were unchanged, compared to a 7% fall in the S&P 500. Average trading volume for the past five days was 60,660 shares, compared with the 40-day moving average of 67,459 shares.

Key Stock Statistics

Dividend Rate/Share	1.20	Shareholders	2,400
Shs. outstg. (M)	22.3	Market cap. (B)	$ 1.1
Avg. daily vol. (M)	0.077	Inst. holdings	65%
Tang. Bk. Value/Share	18.77		
Beta	0.96		

Value of $10,000 invested 5 years ago: $ 37,852

Fiscal Year Ending Dec. 31

	1998	1997	1996	1995	1994	1993
Revenues (Million $)						
1Q	117.8	101.8	92.99	79.41	67.08	63.84
2Q	141.2	109.4	96.77	86.66	68.99	67.81
3Q	—	110.3	96.42	87.48	74.12	65.94
4Q	—	112.6	98.87	88.80	72.14	68.26
Yr.	—	434.0	385.1	343.8	282.3	265.9
Earnings Per Share ($)						
1Q	0.73	0.65	0.57	0.47	0.41	0.35
2Q	0.41	0.60	0.50	0.40	0.41	0.40
3Q	—	0.70	0.61	0.53	0.42	0.54
4Q	—	0.72	0.63	0.55	0.42	0.37
Yr.	—	2.75	2.40	2.04	1.67	1.74

Next earnings report expected: mid October

Dividend Data (Dividends have been paid since 1993.)

Amount ($)	Date Decl.	Ex-Div. Date	Stock of Record	Payment Date
0.250	Oct. 28	Nov. 25	Nov. 28	Dec. 15 '97
0.250	Jan. 28	Feb. 25	Feb. 27	Mar. 13 '98
0.300	Apr. 28	May. 27	May. 29	Jun. 15 '98
0.300	Aug. 10	Aug. 28	Sep. 01	Sep. 15 '98

A Division of The McGraw-Hill Companies

Business Summary - 14-MAY-98

This Texas bank holding company, with $5.2 billion in assets (primarily loans and investments) at year-end 1997, is one of the few companies that can boast of providing financial services for 130 years under one name. Cullen/Frost Bankers operates a total of 60 offices in six Texas banking markets: San Antonio, Houston/Galveston, Austin, Corpus Christi, San Marcos and McAllen. CFR has grown its asset base significantly through several acquisitions in recent years. It targets markets where it already has a presence, and typically pays cash for an acquisition, as opposed to stock. CFR is the largest bank headquartered in San Antonio and South Texas.

CFR derives the majority of its income from lending activities, which have benefited from the strong regional economies in its Texas markets. Loans at December 31, 1997, totaled $2.64 billion (up 17% from $2.25 billion at the end of 1996) and were divided in recent years:

	1997	1996	1995
Real estate	43%	46%	46%
Commercial & industrial	30%	29%	28%
Consumer	23%	22%	22%
International (mostly Mexican)	3%	2%	2%

Other	1%	2%	2%

Cullen/Frost also has strong fee-based revenue, which is not dependent on demand for loans. Accounting for about 36% of overall net revenue in 1997, noninterest income growth was largely driven by trust income (CFR ranks among the 60 largest trust banks in the U.S.) and service charges on deposit accounts.

The net interest margin (the amount of interest income earned in loans less what the bank pays to acquire those funds, as a percent of average earning assets) for 1997 was 4.74%, virtually unchanged from the 4.76% in 1996, as the bank's cost of funds rose slightly.

Although CFR continues to have high asset quality, it has been deteriorating in recent years. The ratio of nonperforming assets (loans where principal and interest payments are not being received as per original terms) to total assets at the end of 1997 was 0.33%, up from 0.25% a year earlier. Additionally, the level of net chargeoffs (amount of loans written off as bad debt expense, less any recoveries) represented 0.23% of average net loans, up sharply from the year-earlier level of 0.12%, but still very good compared with the industry average of about 0.63%.

International deposits, principally from Mexico, averaged $608 million, or 14% of average total deposits.

Per Share Data ($)

(Year Ended Dec. 31)	1997	1996	1995	1994	1993	1992	1991	1990	1989	1988
Tangible Bk. Val.	18.34	16.86	15.24	13.28	12.43	9.90	8.78	8.89	9.46	9.40
Earnings	2.75	2.40	2.04	1.67	1.74	0.83	0.01	-0.42	0.14	0.13
Dividends	0.96	0.81	0.57	0.34	0.08	Nil	Nil	Nil	Nil	Nil
Payout Ratio	35%	34%	28%	20%	4%	Nil	Nil	Nil	Nil	Nil
Prices - High	62¾	36½	25¾	19⅝	20⅛	14⅜	7	5⅜	8⅜	6
- Low	32⅝	23⅜	14⅞	14¼	13⅜	6⅛	2⅞	2⅜	4⅝	3¼
P/E Ratio - High	23	15	13	12	12	17	NM	NM	59	47
- Low	12	10	7	9	8	7	NM	NM	33	25

Income Statement Analysis (Million $)

	1997	1996	1995	1994	1993	1992	1991	1990	1989	1988
Net Int. Inc.	197	179	152	136	128	117	109	110	107	98.0
Tax Equiv. Adj.	1.1	1.0	0.9	0.6	0.9	1.1	2.1	2.9	3.6	3.8
Non Int. Inc.	109	95.5	89.1	80.9	74.8	62.1	55.5	50.5	50.0	52.6
Loan Loss Prov.	7.9	7.3	6.3	Nil	-6.1	NM	10.0	32.0	28.9	27.2
Exp./Op. Revs.	65%	66%	67%	71%	85%	85%	93%	84%	78%	79%
Pretax Inc.	99	85.7	71.3	57.6	38.1	25.8	0.8	-8.0	2.9	2.6
Eff. Tax Rate	36%	36%	35%	35%	NM	32%	76%	NM	7.00%	7.70%
Net Inc.	63.5	55.0	46.3	37.4	38.8	17.6	0.2	-8.2	2.7	2.4
% Net Int. Marg.	4.74	4.76	4.56	4.40	4.29	4.47	4.13	3.93	3.60	3.45

Balance Sheet & Other Fin. Data (Million $)

	1997	1996	1995	1994	1993	1992	1991	1990	1989	1988
Earning Assets:										
Money Mkt	190	53.0	101	168	250	283	99	276	449	502
Inv. Securities	1,492	1,476	1,537	1,594	1,612	1,414	1,439	1,237	1,257	958
Com'l Loans	804	650	509	383	312	268	301	377	462	592
Other Loans	1,842	1,602	1,309	1,099	944	756	787	908	922	985
Total Assets	5,231	4,888	4,200	3,794	3,639	3,151	3,079	3,255	3,505	3,386
Demand Deposits	1,339	1,331	992	832	881	766	669	656	647	539
Time Deposits	3,145	2,911	2,654	2,256	2,268	2,003	2,097	2,222	2,333	2,312
LT Debt	98.4	Nil	Nil	Nil	Nil	13.4	14.7	16.3	17.5	18.6
Common Eqty.	408	379	341	293	274	206	176	173	179	175
% Ret. on Assets	1.3	1.2	1.2	1.0	1.1	0.6	0.0	NM	0.1	0.1
% Ret. on Equity	16.1	15.3	14.3	13.0	15.6	9.2	0.1	NM	1.5	1.4
% Loan Loss Resv.	1.6	1.6	1.7	1.7	2.1	3.1	4.0	3.6	3.1	2.6
% Loans/Deposits	NA	53.1	49.8	47.7	39.6	36.5	38.8	44.1	46.0	54.9
% Equity to Assets	7.8	7.9	8.0	7.8	7.1	6.3	5.7	5.4	5.1	5.3

Data as orig. reptd.; bef. results of disc opers. and/or spec. items. Per share data adj. for stk. divs. as of ex-div. date. Bold denotes diluted EPS (FASB 128). E-Estimated. NA-Not Available. NM-Not Meaningful. NR-Not Ranked.

Office—P.O. Box 1600, 100 W. Houston St., San Antonio, TX 78205.**Organized**—in 1966.**Tei**—(210) 220-4011. **Sr Chrmn**—T. C. Frost.**Chrmn & CEO**—R. W. Evans Jr.**Pres**—H. S. McClane.**EVP & CFO**—P. D. Green.**Secy**—Diane M. Jack.**Investor Contact** Bart R. Vincent (210-220-4878).**Dirs**—I. Arnold Jr., R. S. Caldwell. R. R. Cardenas, H. E. Catto, H. H. Cullen, R. H. Cullen, R. W. Evans Jr., W. N. Finnegan III, T. C. Frost, J. W. Gorman Jr., J. L. Hayne Jr., R. M. Kleberg III, R. S. McClane Jr., W. B. Osborn Jr., R. G. Pope,— H. J. Richter, C. Vaughan Jr. **Transfer Agent & Registrar**—Frost National Bank, San Antonio. **Empl**— 2,306. **S&P Analyst:** L. A. Olive

Curative Health Services   3651Y

NASDAQ Symbol **CURE**

In S&P SmallCap 600

03-OCT-98

Industry:
Health Care (Specialized Services)

Summary: This company manages a nationwide network of wound care centers that offer patients comprehensive, multidisciplinary wound treatment programs.

Quantitative Evaluations

Outlook
(1 Lowest—5 Highest)
• **4**-

Fair Value
• **41¼**

Risk
• **High**

Earn./Div. Rank
• **B-**

Technical Eval.
• **Bearish** since 5/98

Rel. Strength Rank
(1 Lowest—99 Highest)
• **83**

Insider Activity
• **NA**

Recent Price • 28½
52 Wk Range • 39¼-20½

Yield • Nil
12-Mo. P/E • 22.1

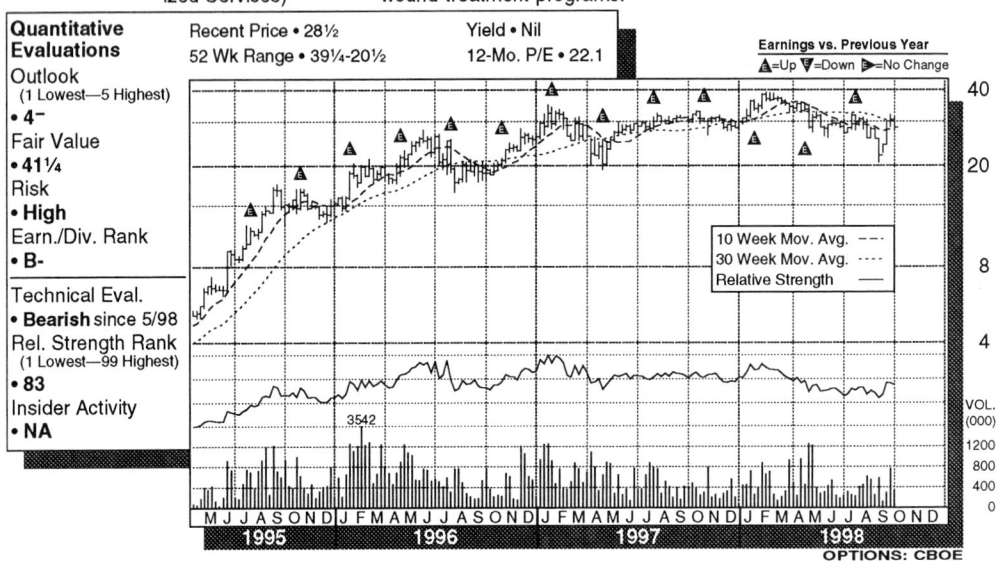

Earnings vs. Previous Year
▲=Up ▼=Down ▶=No Change

10 Week Mov. Avg. - - -
30 Week Mov. Avg. · · · ·
Relative Strength ——

OPTIONS: CBOE

Business Profile - 24-SEP-98

As of September 1998, the company had more than 150 outpatient wound care facilities in 33 states, offering comprehensive patient evaluation for the development of complete individualized treatment programs. CURE is expanding its market by developing new types of specialty servicing for sub-acute care facilities and other market niches. After a costly restructuring in 1994 that refocused efforts on the company's wound care business, CURE has succeeded in achieving EPS growth sequentially over the past 16 quarters. In June 1998, CURE partnered with Accordant Health Services, Inc., to develop and market a wound care disease management program targeted toward managed care providers. CURE agreed to invest $4 million in Accordant, and will own about 11% of its outstanding equity.

Operational Review - 24-SEP-98

Revenues in the six months ended June 30, 1998, advanced 22%, year to year, reflecting more wound care centers in operation and higher patient volumes at existing centers. Gross margins widened, reflecting the leveraging of overhead costs over a growing revenue base, and with well contained SG&A expenses, operating income rose 53%. After taxes at 37.4% versus 15.7%, reflecting the full utilization of operating loss carryforwards in 1997, net income increased 6.6%, to $8,073,000 ($0.61 a share, on 1.5% more shares), from $7,577,000 ($0.59). Cash, equivalents and marketable securities totaled $63,161,000 on June 30, 1998.

Stock Performance - 02-OCT-98

In the past 30 trading days, CURE's shares have increased 2%, compared to a 7% fall in the S&P 500. Average trading volume for the past five days was 65,880 shares, compared with the 40-day moving average of 89,005 shares.

Key Stock Statistics

Dividend Rate/Share	Nil	Shareholders	300
Shs. outstg. (M)	12.7	Market cap. (B)	$0.363
Avg. daily vol. (M)	0.076	Inst. holdings	76%
Tang. Bk. Value/Share	6.46		
Beta	1.87		

Value of $10,000 invested 5 years ago: $ 40,000

Fiscal Year Ending Dec. 31

	1998	1997	1996	1995	1994	1993
Revenues (Million $)						
1Q	24.51	19.65	14.92	12.01	8.89	6.70
2Q	26.04	21.69	16.39	12.92	9.57	7.35
3Q	—	22.71	17.46	13.32	10.54	8.17
4Q	—	23.86	18.63	14.19	11.58	9.05
Yr.	—	87.91	67.40	52.44	40.57	31.27
Earnings Per Share ($)						
1Q	**0.29**	0.28	0.17	0.05	-0.09	-0.14
2Q	**0.32**	0.30	0.21	0.08	-0.23	-0.14
3Q	—	0.33	0.24	0.12	0.02	-0.08
4Q	—	**0.35**	0.28	0.14	0.03	-0.08
Yr.	—	**1.27**	0.90	0.39	-0.27	-0.44

Next earnings report expected: late October

Dividend Data

No cash dividends have been paid. The company intends to retain earnings for use in the development of its business and does not expect to pay cash dividends in the foreseeable future.

A Division of The **McGraw·Hill** Companies

Business Summary - 24-SEP-98

Curative Health Services (CURE) is a leading disease management company in the chronic wound care market. The company manages, on behalf of hospital clients, a nationwide network of wound care centers that offer a comprehensive range of services which enable the company to provide customized wound care.

Chronic wounds are common in patients with diabetes and venous stasis disease, as well as in patients who are immobilized and afflicted with pressure sores. It is estimated that the wound care segment of the U.S. health care industry generated more than $2 billion in expenditures in 1994. The company anticipates that the wound care market will continue to grow due to the aging population and increasing incidence of health disorders, such as diabetes, which may lead to chronic wounds.

The company's wound management program consists of diagnostic and therapeutic treatment regimens designed to meet each patient's specific wound care needs on a cost effective basis. The company's wound care center network consists of over 150 outpatient clinics generally located on or near campuses of acute care hospitals in 33 states.

The company's first product, Procuren (introduced in 1988), is a naturally occurring complex mixture of growth factors that promotes the growth of human skin, soft tissue and blood vessels. Procuren is produced by stimulating the release of growth factors from platelets contained in the patient's own blood. As part of a comprehensive treatment program, it has been used to treat over 45,000 patients, and a company sponsored study of patients with diabetic ulcers found that the average charges for a conventional treatment program were $19,000 as compared to $14,000 for a specialized wound program that included the use of Procuren.

The company believes that the high degree of specialization and expertise offered by its wound care centers provides many benefits: to patients through superior wound care, enhancing quality of life and, in many cases, allowing them to avoid amputation; to affiliated hospitals by enabling them to differentiate themselves from competitors, through better wound care treatment outcomes, and reduce costs by decreasing inpatient lengths of stay; to affiliated physicians by providing greater access to patients; and to insurers and managed care providers by offering a cost effective alternative to traditional wound care.

Virtually all of the company's revenues are generated under its contracts with acute care hospitals for the management of chronic wound care programs and the production of Procuren. The company is expanding its wound care operations into new health care delivery settings, including inpatient facilities and freestanding wound care centers owned and operated by the company. Although these new models accounted for only about 4% of the company's revenues in 1997, the company expects this percentage to increase as the company expands its services across the continuum of care fo r wound management.

Per Share Data ($)

(Year Ended Dec. 31)	1997	1996	1995	1994	1993	1992	1991	1990	1989	1988
Tangible Bk. Val.	5.72	4.05	1.42	0.85	1.70	2.17	2.54	-10.43	NA	NA
Cash Flow	1.43	0.99	0.48	-0.17	-0.36	-0.31	-0.13	-0.62	NA	NA
Earnings	1.27	0.90	0.39	-0.27	-0.44	-0.37	-0.20	-0.67	NA	NA
Dividends	Nil	Nil	Nil	Nil	Nil	Nil	Nil	Nil	Nil	Nil
Payout Ratio	Nil	Nil	Nil	Nil	Nil	Nil	Nil	Nil	Nil	Nil
Prices - High	35	28¼	17	6½	8	21½	23	NA	NA	NA
- Low	19¼	13¼	3⅜	1⅝	3⅞	4½	7½	NA	NA	NA
P/E Ratio - High	28	31	44	NM	NM	NM	NM	NA	NA	NA
- Low	15	15	9	NM	NM	NM	NM	NM	NA	NM

Income Statement Analysis (Million $)

	1997	1996	1995	1994	1993	1992	1991	1990	1989	1988
Revs.	87.9	67.4	52.4	40.6	31.3	26.8	19.5	10.2	NA	NA
Oper. Inc.	19.1	11.5	4.9	-0.5	-4.5	-4.2	-2.1	-4.2	NA	NA
Depr.	2.0	1.2	1.0	1.0	0.8	0.6	0.5	0.3	NA	NA
Int. Exp.	NA	Nil	Nil	Nil	NA	0.1	0.1	0.1	NA	NA
Pretax Inc.	19.8	11.7	4.4	-3.0	-4.7	-3.8	-1.9	-4.2	NA	NA
Eff. Tax Rate	17%	8.60%	4.90%	NM	NM	NM	NM	NM	NM	NM
Net Inc.	16.5	10.7	4.2	-2.7	-4.4	-3.6	-1.6	-4.2	NA	NA

Balance Sheet & Other Fin. Data (Million $)

	1997	1996	1995	1994	1993	1992	1991	1990	1989	1988
Cash	39.7	43.1	12.2	7.3	9.5	18.5	24.9	1.9	NA	NA
Curr. Assets	74.9	56.4	20.8	14.8	19.4	25.5	30.2	5.0	NA	NA
Total Assets	84.9	84.9	25.0	18.6	25.3	29.1	32.5	7.4	NA	NA
Curr. Liab.	12.3	10.6	8.2	7.6	7.7	6.4	5.8	3.2	NA	NA
LT Debt	0.0	1.0	1.2	1.3	0.5	0.2	0.3	0.4	NA	NA
Common Eqty.	72.6	50.3	15.6	9.8	16.8	21.4	25.1	-16.6	NA	NA
Total Cap.	72.6	51.3	16.8	11.0	17.6	22.2	26.2	4.3	NA	NA
Cap. Exp.	6.5	2.5	2.0	0.6	0.9	1.6	0.9	0.1	NA	NA
Cash Flow	18.5	11.9	5.2	-1.7	-3.6	-3.1	-1.1	-3.9	NA	NA
Curr. Ratio	6.1	5.3	2.5	2.0	2.5	4.0	5.2	1.6	NA	NA
% LT Debt of Cap.	NM	2.0	7.1	11.4	2.9	0.9	1.3	10.2	NA	NA
% Net Inc.of Revs.	18.7	15.9	8.0	NM	NM	NM	NM	NM	NM	NM
% Ret. on Assets	22.4	24.6	19.3	NM	NM	NM	NM	NM	NM	NM
% Ret. on Equity	26.8	32.4	33.2	NM	NM	NM	NM	NM	NM	NM

Data as orig. reptd.; bef. results of disc. opers. and/or spec. items. Per share data adj. for stk. divs. as of ex-div. date. Bold denotes diluted EPS (FASB 128). E-Estimated. NA-Not Available. NM-Not Meaningful. NR-Not Ranked.

Office—150 Motor Parkway, Hauppauge, NY 11788-5108. **Tel**—(516) 232-7000. **Website**—http://www.curative.com **Chrmn**—L. J. Stuesser. **Pres & CEO**—J. Vakoutis. **VP-Fin, CFO & Secy**—J. C. Prior. **Dirs**—G. Canet, D. A. Gregorie, L. Hoff, T. I. Mauldin, G. Moufflet, L. J. Stuesser, J. Vakoutis. **Transfer Agent**—Norwest Bank Minnesota, South St. Paul. **Incorporated**—in Minnesota in 1984. **Empl**— 671. **S&P Analyst:** David Moskowitz

CustomTracks Corp. 3125K

NASDAQ Symbol **CUST**

In S&P SmallCap 600

03-OCT-98

Industry:
Electrical Equipment

Summary: This company recently changed its business focus and now plans to concentrate on internet-related businesses, including the marketing of custom digital data products.

Quantitative Evaluations

Recent Price • 4¾
52 Wk Range • 7-3¼

Yield • Nil
12-Mo. P/E • NM

Outlook
(1 Lowest—5 Highest)
• **NA**

Fair Value
• **NA**

Risk
• **High**

Earn./Div. Rank
• **C**

Technical Eval.
• **NA**

Rel. Strength Rank
(1 Lowest—99 Highest)
• **51**

Insider Activity
• **NA**

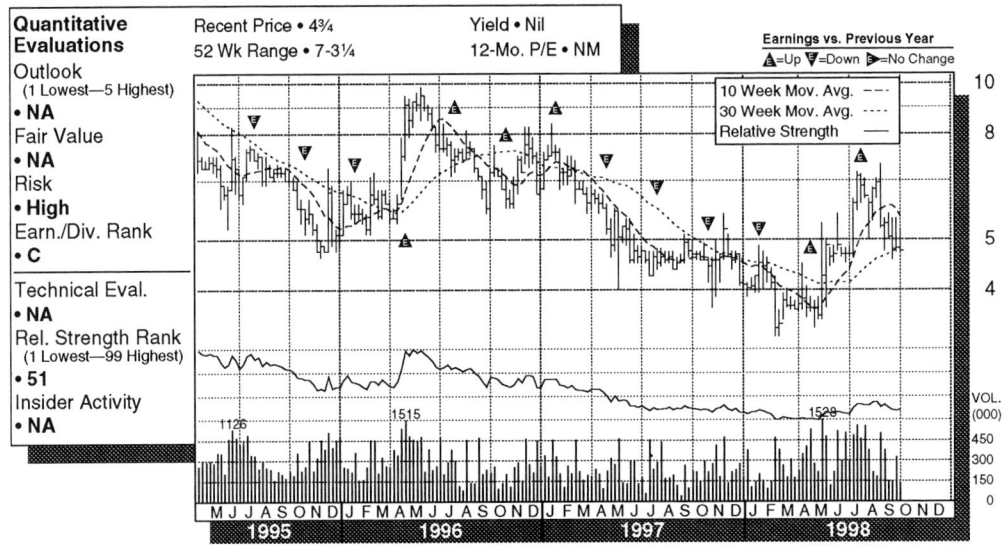

Earnings vs. Previous Year
▲=Up ▼=Down ▶=No Change

10 Week Mov. Avg. – – –
30 Week Mov. Avg. ....
Relative Strength ——

Business Profile - 15-SEP-98

In line with a recent name change to CustomTracks, this company's plan to enter the digital data distribution business has been refined to focus initially on music content. It is in discussions with various parties regarding the acquisition of certain music content rights pertaining to the manufacturing and distribution of customized static-media products, such as CDs or DVDs. The company recently sold its Transportation Systems and Cotag International units, recording a $1.6 million loss in the second quarter of 1998.

Operational Review - 15-SEP-98

Sales in the first half of 1998 advanced 13%, year to year, led by higher sales in the electronic security group unit. Gross margins widened, aided by the higher volume, and results benefited further from lower operating expenses on the disposition of certain business units. Despite a $1.6 million loss on the sale of businesses, pretax income contrasted with a pretax loss. After taxes at 25.8%, versus taxes of $2,676,000, net income of $586,000 ($0.03 a share) replaced a net loss of $10,019,000 ($0.68).

Stock Performance - 02-OCT-98

In the past 30 trading days, CUST's shares have declined 26%, compared to a 7% fall in the S&P 500. Average trading volume for the past five days was 27,380 shares, compared with the 40-day moving average of 64,023 shares.

Key Stock Statistics

Dividend Rate/Share	Nil	Shareholders	800
Shs. outstg. (M)	14.9	Market cap. (B)	$0.071
Avg. daily vol. (M)	0.043	Inst. holdings	24%
Tang. Bk. Value/Share	3.39		
Beta	NA		

Value of $10,000 invested 5 years ago: $ 2,410

Fiscal Year Ending Dec. 31

	1998	1997	1996	1995	1994	1993
Revenues (Million $)						
1Q	31.01	24.15	28.28	13.94	18.96	11.69
2Q	29.08	28.88	29.87	13.00	18.51	13.28
3Q	—	30.19	27.97	24.53	12.21	15.66
4Q	—	34.49	30.39	28.61	11.77	18.81
Yr.	—	117.7	116.5	80.07	61.46	59.42
Earnings Per Share ($)						
1Q	0.02	-0.22	0.02	-0.02	0.25	0.11
2Q	0.01	-0.46	Nil	-0.09	0.23	0.16
3Q	—	-0.11	Nil	-0.03	0.03	0.18
4Q	—	-0.37	-0.06	-0.15	0.01	0.24
Yr.	—	-1.17	-0.04	-0.28	0.52	0.70

Next earnings report expected: mid November

Dividend Data

Quarterly cash dividends, initiated in June 1993, were suspended in May 1995. A five-for-four stock split was effected in 1993, and a three-for-two split in 1992.

A Division of The McGraw-Hill Companies

Business Summary 15-SEP-98

CustomTracks Corp. (formerly Amtech Corp.) is changing its operations from radio frequency identification and related business to new lines of business. It plans to focus on internet-related businesses, including the marketing of custom digital data products under the CustomTracks brand name. The company also owns and operates Cardkey Systems, a leading provider of systems and services to the access control and electronic security markets.

The Electronic Security Group (55% of revenues in 1997) consists of Cardkey Systems. Cardkey is a leading supplier of electronic access control and integrated security management solutions. In July 1998, the company sold its Cotag International unit to Metric Gruppen AB for about $4.4 million. Cotag specialized in advanced hands-free proximity cards, tags and readers and has developed systems using these products for electronic access control.

In June 1998, the company sold its Transportation Systems Group (43% of 1997 revenues) to UNOVA, Inc. for about $33.5 million. Included in the purchase were manufacturing and technology facilities, radio frequency identification technologies and other intellectual properties, the brand name Amtech, and all operations related to the transportation business. Transportation Systems marketed high-frequency RFID technology, which permits remote identification of, and communication with, objects such as automobiles and railcars at higher speeds, at longer distances and in more difficult outdoor and industrial environments than technologies based on optical, magnetic or other techniques.

In May 1998, the company acquired Petabyte Corp., a startup enterprise founded by CEO David P. Cook. Petabyte currently has no operations, but owns certain intellectual property. Petabyte will target scaleable systems that will enable the manufacture and distribution of customized digital data products. The company has agreed to make five annual payments of $200,000 to Mr. Cook for Petabyte.

Per Share Data ($)

(Year Ended Dec. 31)	1997	1996	1995	1994	1993	1992	1991	1990	1989	1988
Tangible Bk. Val.	3.36	4.32	4.36	5.16	4.59	3.40	1.26	1.56	2.12	0.92
Cash Flow	-0.84	0.27	0.28	0.72	0.84	0.63	-0.28	-0.48	-0.74	-0.90
Earnings	-1.17	-0.04	-0.28	0.52	0.70	0.51	-0.40	-0.57	-0.82	-0.97
Dividends	Nil	Nil	0.02	0.08	0.06	Nil	Nil	Nil	Nil	Nil
Payout Ratio	Nil	Nil	NM	15%	9%	Nil	Nil	Nil	Nil	Nil
Prices - High	8³/₈	9⁷/₈	10⁵/₈	33³/₄	32	23³/₄	15⁵/₈	11¹/₄	8	NA
- Low	3⁵/₈	5¹/₈	4⁵/₈	7⁵/₈	18¹/₄	11¹/₄	4³/₄	4¹/₈	6	NA
P/E Ratio - High	NM	NM	NM	65	46	46	NM	NM	NM	NA
- Low	NM	NM	NM	15	26	22	NM	NM	NM	NA

Income Statement Analysis (Million $)

	1997	1996	1995	1994	1993	1992	1991	1990	1989	1988
Revs.	118	117	80.0	61.5	59.4	39.9	18.7	14.8	6.0	1.4
Oper. Inc.	-10.8	1.5	-2.4	12.9	14.5	7.8	-3.9	-7.7	-7.0	-6.3
Depr.	5.0	4.6	3.6	3.0	2.1	1.7	1.5	1.1	0.7	0.4
Int. Exp.	0.1	0.3	0.2	Nil	Nil	Nil	Nil	Nil	Nil	Nil
Pretax Inc.	-14.7	-0.4	-3.9	12.1	14.1	7.4	-5.0	-7.0	-7.3	-6.5
Eff. Tax Rate	NM	NM	NM	57%	27%	1.80%	Nil	Nil	Nil	Nil
Net Inc.	-17.6	-0.6	-4.1	7.7	10.4	7.3	-5.0	-7.0	-7.3	-6.5

Balance Sheet & Other Fin. Data (Million $)

	1997	1996	1995	1994	1993	1992	1991	1990	1989	1988
Cash	15.2	17.1	27.8	49.9	36.8	31.2	12.0	7.5	19.2	3.3
Curr. Assets	60.3	62.3	68.0	67.0	54.8	42.8	17.9	16.9	22.8	5.2
Total Assets	85.5	91.0	93.3	80.6	76.7	57.4	23.0	22.3	27.2	7.5
Curr. Liab.	21.8	19.3	18.2	3.5	7.1	4.7	4.3	3.3	1.7	1.2
LT Debt	Nil	Nil	2.6	Nil	Nil	Nil	Nil	Nil	Nil	Nil
Common Eqty.	63.7	71.8	72.5	75.3	66.8	48.8	16.0	18.9	25.5	6.3
Total Cap.	63.7	71.8	75.0	75.3	66.8	48.8	16.0	18.9	25.5	6.3
Cap. Exp.	2.2	4.2	3.3	2.3	7.3	1.1	1.1	1.9	2.5	1.4
Cash Flow	-12.6	4.0	-0.5	10.6	12.5	8.9	-3.5	-5.8	-6.6	-6.1
Curr. Ratio	2.8	3.2	3.7	19.3	7.7	9.0	4.1	5.1	13.7	4.3
% LT Debt of Cap.	Nil	Nil	13.5	Nil	Nil	Nil	Nil	Nil	Nil	Nil
% Net Inc.of Revs.	NM	NM	NM	12.5	17.4	18.2	NM	NM	NM	NM
% Ret. on Assets	NM	NM	NM	9.7	15.4	17.4	NM	NM	NM	NM
% Ret. on Equity	NM	NM	NM	10.8	17.8	21.7	NM	NM	NM	NM

Data as orig. reptd.; bef. results of disc. opers. and/or spec. items. Per share data adj. for stk. divs. as of ex-div. date. Bold denotes diluted EPS (FASB 128). E-Estimated. NA-Not Available. NM-Not Meaningful. NR-Not Ranked.

Office—One Galleria Tower, 13355 Noel Rd., Suite 1555, Dasllas, TX 75240-6604. **Tel**—972) 702-7057. **Chrmn, Pres & CEO**—D. P. Cook. **SVP, CFO & Treas**—S. M. York. **Secy**—R. A. Woessner. **Investor Contact**—Beverly V. Fuortes. **Dirs**—D. P. Cook, S. M. Evans, M. E. Keane, J. A. Landt, J. S. Marston, A. R. Sanchez Jr. **Transfer Agent**—Society National Bank, Dallas. **Incorporated**—in Texas in 1988. **Empl**— 860. **S&P Analyst**: SRB

STANDARD &POOR'S
STOCK REPORTS

Cygnus, Inc.

3654G

NASDAQ Symbol **CYGN**

In S&P SmallCap 600

03-OCT-98

Industry:
Health Care (Drugs - Generic & Other)

Summary: This company is focused primarily on developing a painless, continuous glucose monitoring device, transdermal drug delivery systems and mucosal drug delivery systems.

Quantitative Evaluations	
Outlook (1 Lowest—5 Highest)	**• NA**
Fair Value	**• NA**
Risk	**• High**
Earn./Div. Rank	**• C**
Technical Eval.	**• NA**
Rel. Strength Rank (1 Lowest—99 Highest)	**• 8**
Insider Activity	**• Neutral**

Recent Price • 3⅜
52 Wk Range • 25-2¾

Yield • Nil
12-Mo. P/E • NM

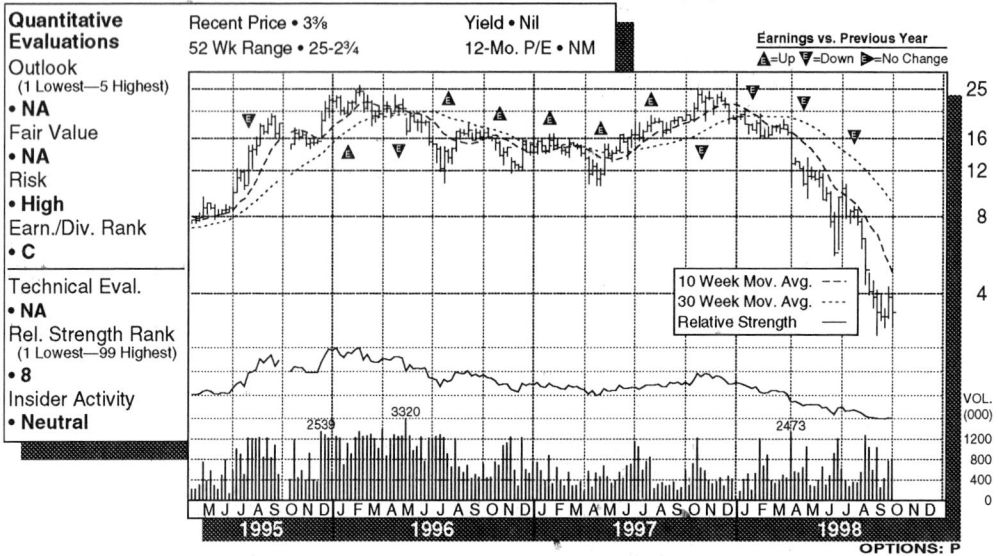

Earnings vs. Previous Year
▲=Up ▼=Down ▶=No Change

10 Week Mov. Avg. ---
30 Week Mov. Avg. ····
Relative Strength —

VOL. (000)

OPTIONS: P

Business Profile - 22-JUL-98

CYGN's strategy is to apply and expand its proprietary technologies, develop a broad portfolio of differentiated products, address large market opportunities, control manufacturing and collaborate with market leaders in each of its target markets. Operations to date have consumed substantial amounts of cash, mostly for research and development, and future capital requirements will depend on product development programs, the time required to file regulatory approvals, the ability to obtain licensing arrangements and the demand for products. CYGN has incurred losses in each year since its inception in 1990. In the 1997 third quarter, the company launched its second commercial product, the FemPatch, a low-dose estrogen replacement patch for the treatment of menopausal symptoms. Proceeds from two recent public offerings, aggregating $56.8 million, will be used for general corporate purposes and expenditures related to commercializing its glucose monitor.

Operational Review - 22-JUL-98

Total revenues for the three months ended March 31, 1998, fell 63%, year to year, primarily due to a 95% drop in royalty and other revenues stemming from the absence of previously deferred royalty payments recognized in the 1997 interim which were related to the 1996 launch of the Nicotrol product in the U.S. Product revenues and contract revenues also declined. The net loss widened to $5.5 million ($0.28 per share, based on 5.9% more shares), from $363,000 ($0.02).

Stock Performance - 02-OCT-98

In the past 30 trading days, CYGN's shares have declined 17%, compared to a 7% fall in the S&P 500. Average trading volume for the past five days was 160,740 shares, compared with the 40-day moving average of 176,726 shares.

Key Stock Statistics

Dividend Rate/Share	Nil	Shareholders	600
Shs. outstg. (M)	20.2	Market cap. (B)	$0.068
Avg. daily vol. (M)	0.119	Inst. holdings	45%
Tang. Bk. Value/Share	NM		
Beta	1.62		

Value of $10,000 invested 5 years ago: $ 2,812

Fiscal Year Ending Dec. 31

	1998	1997	1996	1995	1994	1993
Revenues (Million $)						
1Q	3.46	9.29	3.76	5.40	5.53	12.64
2Q	2.88	8.24	8.99	4.77	5.41	5.15
3Q	—	5.44	10.81	3.87	4.73	4.12
4Q	—	6.53	12.64	4.97	5.59	4.47
Yr.	—	29.50	36.20	19.01	21.27	17.48
Earnings Per Share ($)						
1Q	**-0.28**	-0.02	-0.23	-0.18	-0.07	-0.19
2Q	**-0.48**	-0.02	-0.17	-0.19	-0.13	-0.16
3Q	—	-2.00	-0.15	-0.28	-0.24	-0.21
4Q	—	-0.27	-0.05	-0.15	-0.79	-0.21
Yr.	—	-2.67	-0.60	-0.79	-1.24	-0.77

Next earnings report expected: mid October

Dividend Data

No cash dividends have been paid. The company does not expect to pay cash dividends in the foreseeable future.

Business Summary - 22-JUL-98

Best known for its Nicotrol transdermal patch, which helps people quit smoking, Cygnus is involved in the development of diagnostic and drug delivery systems. It is currently focused on a painless, continuous glucose monitoring device, transdermal drug delivery systems and mucosal drug delivery systems.

CYGN has developed a painless, continuous glucose monitoring device called the GlucoWatch, which is worn like a wristwatch and designed to extract and measure glucose levels automatically and frequently through intact skin and to display and store blood glucose levels and trends. The extracted glucose is collected in the GlucoPad, a transdermal patch that is changed daily.

The company has conducted early-stage clinical studies using an initial GlucoWatch prototype and believes that the results of such studies support the technical feasibility of the product by indicating a level of accuracy and reproducibility comparable to finger stab blood glucose measurement devices commercially available. Current efforts are focused on optimizing, miniaturizing and integrating certain components of the GlucoWatch. In February 1996, Cygnus entered into an agreement with Becton Dickinson giving BD exclusive worldwide marketing and distribution rights for the GlucoWatch, except in Japan and Korea. In July 1996, CYGN signed an agreement with Yamanouchi Pharmaceutical for the marketing and distribution rights in Japan and Korea.

Transdermal delivery systems provide for the controlled release of drugs directly into the bloodstream through intact skin by means of a small adhesive patch. By delivering a steady flow of drugs over an extended period of time, transdermal systems can enable more controlled, effective treatment. CYGN's transdermal product line is currently focused on smoking cessation, hormone replacement therapy and contraception. Its two most commercially advanced products are the currently marketed Nicotrol nicotine patch (licensed in the U.S. by Johnson & Johnson and worldwide by Pharmacia & Upjohn) and the FemPatch estrogen replacement patch, approved by the FDA in December 1996.

In September 1997, the company and Sanofi agreed to a $14 million cash arbitration settlement. Sanofi originally filed to recover excess of $60 million from CYGN for damages attributable to the alleged breach of its existing contract with Sanofi by entering into a product development agreement with another company.

In May 1997, CYGN began arbitration proceedings against Pharmacia & Upjohn (NYSE: PNU) relating to Nicotrol. In March, PNU had exercised its option to purchase the U.S. manufacturing rights for Nicotrol. The agreement provided that PNU pay CYGN for existing inventory costs and certain purchase order commitments. CYGN has been unable to reach an agreement with PNU on these matters. CYGN said its results could be adversely affected if its claims are disallowed.

Per Share Data ($)

(Year Ended Dec. 31)	1997	1996	1995	1994	1993	1992	1991	1990	1989	1988
Tangible Bk. Val.	NA	1.67	2.10	1.16	1.89	2.64	NA	NA	NA	NA
Cash Flow	-2.52	-0.44	-0.62	-1.08	-0.61	-1.21	NA	NA	NA	NA
Earnings	-2.67	-0.60	-0.79	-1.24	-0.77	-1.36	-0.64	-0.43	NA	NA
Dividends	Nil	Nil	Nil	Nil	Nil	Nil	Nil	Nil	Nil	Nil
Payout Ratio	Nil	Nil	Nil	Nil	Nil	Nil	Nil	Nil	Nil	Nil
Prices - High	25	25$7/8$	23$5/8$	12$7/8$	12$1/2$	32$1/4$	NA	NA	NA	NA
- Low	10$1/2$	10$3/4$	5$5/8$	5$1/2$	5$1/2$	8	NA	NA	NA	NA
P/E Ratio - High	NM	NM	NM	NM	NM	NM	NA	NA	NA	NA
- Low	NM	NM	NM	NM	NM	NM	NA	NA	NA	NA

Income Statement Analysis (Million $)

	1997	1996	1995	1994	1993	1992	1991	1990	1989	1988
Revs.	29.5	36.2	19.0	21.3	17.5	25.6	5.1	5.9	NA	NA
Oper. Inc.	-9.2	-10.1	-10.5	-15.7	-9.4	-16.7	NA	NA	NA	NA
Depr.	2.7	2.8	2.7	2.4	2.2	2.0	NA	NA	NA	NA
Int. Exp.	1.8	1.0	0.8	0.3	0.5	0.3	NA	NA	NA	NA
Pretax Inc.	-50.5	-11.1	-12.8	-17.4	-10.6	-17.5	-7.1	-3.4	NA	NA
Eff. Tax Rate	NM	NM	NM	Nil	Nil	Nil	Nil	Nil	Nil	Nil
Net Inc.	-50.5	-11.1	-12.8	-17.4	-10.6	-17.5	-7.1	NA	NA	NA

Balance Sheet & Other Fin. Data (Million $)

	1997	1996	1995	1994	1993	1992	1991	1990	1989	1988
Cash	20.7	49.4	46.5	28.1	28.2	NA	NA	NA	NA	NA
Curr. Assets	39.8	60.5	49.8	30.6	38.2	NA	NA	NA	NA	NA
Total Assets	49.3	68.8	57.9	38.6	46.9	52.7	32.2	9.7	NA	NA
Curr. Liab.	29.8	24.1	11.3	12.6	14.1	NA	NA	NA	NA	NA
LT Debt	27.2	7.5	2.7	2.8	2.6	NA	NA	NA	NA	NA
Common Eqty.	-13.8	31.2	38.3	18.1	26.2	36.2	27.3	5.9	NA	NA
Total Cap.	13.4	38.7	40.2	20.9	28.8	NA	NA	NA	NA	NA
Cap. Exp.	3.1	1.5	2.4	2.7	1.4	4.5	NA	NA	NA	NA
Cash Flow	-47.7	-8.3	-10.2	-15.0	-8.4	15.5	NA	NA	NA	NA
Curr. Ratio	1.3	2.5	4.4	2.4	2.7	NA	NA	NA	NA	NA
% LT Debt of Cap.	203.0	19.4	6.7	13.6	9.0	NA	NA	NA	NA	NA
% Net Inc.of Revs.	NM	NM	NM	NM	NM	NM	NM	NM	NM	NM
% Ret. on Assets	NM	NM	NM	NM	NM	NM	NM	NM	NM	NM
% Ret. on Equity	NM	NM	NM	NM	NM	NM	NM	NM	NM	NM

Data as orig. reptd.; bef. results of disc. opers. and/or spec. items. Per share data adj. for stk. divs. as of ex-div. date. Bold denotes diluted EPS (FASB 128). E-Estimated. NA-Not Available. NM-Not Meaningful. NR-Not Ranked.

Office—400 Penobscot Dr., Redwood City, CA 94063-4719. **Tel**—(415) 369-4300. **Website**—http://www.cygn.com **Chrmn**—G. W. Cleary. **Pres & CEO**—G.B. Lawless. **VP-Fin & CFO**—J. C. Hodgman. **VP & Secy**—J. Grady. **Dirs**—F. T. Cary, G. W. Cleary, G. B. Lawless, A. F. Marion, R. G. Rogers, W. B. Wriston. **Transfer Agent & Registrar**—ChaseMellon Shareholder Services, San Francisco. **Incorporated**—in California in 1985; reincorporated in Delaware in 1995. **Empl**— 157. **S&P Analyst**: John J. Arege

Cyrk, Inc.

3654M

NASDAQ Symbol **CYRK**

In S&P SmallCap 600

03-OCT-98

Industry:
Consumer (Jewelry, Novelties & Gifts)

Summary: This company designs, develops, manufactures, sources and distributes high-quality products for promotional programs and custom-designed sports apparel and accessories.

Quantitative Evaluations

Outlook
(1 Lowest—5 Highest)
• **NA**

Fair Value
• **NA**

Risk
• **High**

Earn./Div. Rank
• **NR**

Technical Eval.
• **Neutral** since 6/98

Rel. Strength Rank
(1 Lowest—99 Highest)
• **73**

Insider Activity
• **NA**

Recent Price • 9½
52 Wk Range • 20⅜-6¾

Yield • Nil
12-Mo. P/E • NM

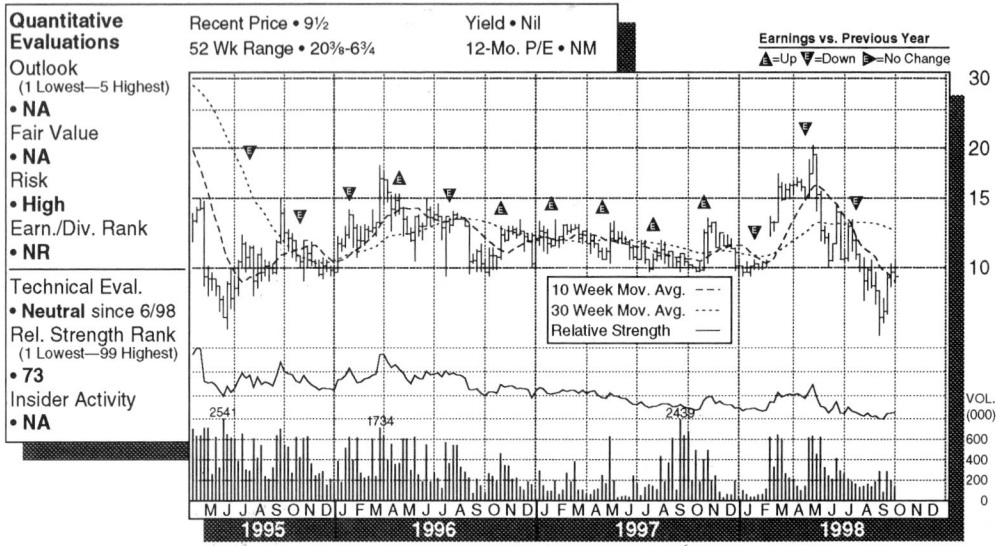

Earnings vs. Previous Year
▲=Up ▼=Down ▶=No Change

10 Week Mov. Avg. - - -
30 Week Mov. Avg. ·······
Relative Strength

Business Profile - 11-SEP-98

In February 1998, the company announced a plan to restructure its worldwide operations in order to focus on its core business in the promotional marketing industry. CYRK will consolidate certain operating facilities, discontinue certain divisions of its apparel business and eliminate about 28% of its worldwide workforce, mainly from the screen printing and embroidery business in Gloucester, MA. As a result, CYRK recorded a charge of $15.5 million in the first quarter of 1998 for asset write-downs, employee termination costs, lease cancellations and other related exit costs associated with the restructuring. The restructuring is expected to be completed during 1998 and once completed, should yield annualized cost savings of between $9 million and $12 million. The company reported further positive developments in its new client relationships including its brand-building partnership with Ty Inc., provider of the enormously popular Beanie Baby line.

Operational Review - 11-SEP-98

Net sales for the six months ended June 30, 1998, advanced 87%, year to year. Gross margins narrowed despite the higher volume, however, and SG&A expenses more than doubled. Following a $15.5 million restructuring charge in 1998, a pretax loss contrasted with pretax income. Despite a $7.1 million tax benefit, against taxes at 60.0%, the net loss was $10,266,000 ($0.70 a share, on 25% more shares), against net income of $2,867,000 ($0.25).

Stock Performance - 02-OCT-98

In the past 30 trading days, CYRK's shares have increased 6%, compared to a 7% fall in the S&P 500. Average trading volume for the past five days was 26,120 shares, compared with the 40-day moving average of 37,008 shares.

Key Stock Statistics

Dividend Rate/Share	Nil	Shareholders	100
Shs. outstg. (M)	15.0	Market cap. (B)	$0.143
Avg. daily vol. (M)	0.036	Inst. holdings	36%
Tang. Bk. Value/Share	5.63		
Beta	0.50		

Value of $10,000 invested 5 years ago: NA

Fiscal Year Ending Dec. 31

	1998	1997	1996	1995	1994	1993
Revenues (Million $)						
1Q	169.1	97.19	65.10	44.00	76.00	31.00
2Q	212.6	106.6	44.14	34.00	142.0	28.00
3Q	—	170.8	55.56	26.00	114.0	36.00
4Q	—	184.1	86.10	31.00	70.00	71.00
Yr.	—	558.6	250.9	136.0	402.0	166.0
Earnings Per Share ($)						
1Q	**-0.69**	0.21	0.15	0.05	0.65	0.34
2Q	**-0.03**	0.05	-0.09	0.01	1.18	0.22
3Q	—	0.01	-0.05	-0.14	0.88	0.19
4Q	—	0.02	0.03	-0.14	0.47	0.43
Yr.	—	**0.25**	0.04	-0.22	3.20	1.18

Next earnings report expected: mid November

Dividend Data

No cash dividends have been paid. The company intends to retain earnings to finance growth and does not expect to pay cash dividends in the foreseeable future.

A Division of The **McGraw·Hill** Companies

Business Summary - 11-SEP-98

Cyrk, Inc. (CYRK) is not interested in promoting itself - only its clients. Gloucester, MA-based CYRK designs, develops, manufactures and distributes products for promotional programs such as McDonald's "Happy Meal" and Pepsi-Cola Company's "Pepsi Stuff". CYRK focuses its sales efforts on large consumer products and services companies seeking to promote their brand names and corporate identities and build brand loyalty.

Many of the company's large-scale consumer promotions include custom product that is conceived, designed and produced by the company's Custom Product and Licensing group. This group has custom designed and developed proprietary products including toys, apparel and accessories for McDonald's and other consumer promotional programs including the Marlboro Gear and Pepsi Stuff promotions. The company expects to expand its licensing activities in 1998, and has entered into licensing agreements with customers such as Ty, Inc. and Mars, Inc.

As part of its continuing plan to diversify its customer base and broaden its capability, the company made two key acquisitions in 1997, including the April 1997 acquisition of Tonkin, Inc., a provider of custom promotional programs and licensed promotional products, and the June 1997 acquisition of Simon Marketing, Inc., a global promotion agency. Simon's business is heavily concentrated with McDonald's Corporation, the latter

accounting for 36% of CYRK's net sales in 1997 and 58% of net sales in the first quarter of 1998.

Historically, the company's business has been heavily concentrated with two customers, Philip Morris, Inc. and Pepsi-Cola, which together accounted for 37% of net sales in 1997. CYRK has been making an effort to reduce its dependence on promotional products of Philip Morris (a business affected by new FDA regulations of tobacco products). Additionally, CYRK's agreements with Pepsi were terminated in December 1997 and the company expects sales to Pepsi to be minimal in 1998. For the first quarter of 1998, sales to Pepsi accounted for just 3% of total net sales, while sales to Philip Morris accounted for only 11%. While it has been seeking new customers to replace the 1997 Pepsi revenues of $117 million, the company believes it is unlikely new customers will materially reduce the revenue shortfall, and therefore expects operating losses for the balance of 1998.

CYRK also sells private-label custom-designed sports apparel and accessories that are incorporated into the product lines of its customers; and designs, manufactures and sells a limited line of CYRK brand sports apparel through retailers such as TJX and Bob's Stores. As part of its restructuring plan announced in February 1998, the company will focus on its core promotional marketing business. As a result, net sales related to the company's private label and Cyrk business fell 46%, year to year, in the first quarter of 1998, contributing only 3.4% of total sales.

Per Share Data ($)

(Year Ended Dec. 31)	1997	1996	1995	1994	1993	1992	1991	1990	1989	1988
Tangible Bk. Val.	6.03	11.52	11.54	11.74	3.34	NA	NA	NA	NA	NA
Cash Flow	0.74	0.30	-0.04	3.28	NA	NA	NA	NA	NA	NA
Earnings	0.25	0.04	-0.22	3.20	1.18	0.44	NA	NA	NA	NA
Dividends	Nil	Nil	Nil	Nil	Nil	Nil	Nil	Nil	Nil	Nil
Payout Ratio	Nil	Nil	Nil	Nil	Nil	Nil	Nil	Nil	Nil	Nil
Prices - High	13⅜	18⅛	41¼	44¾	23	NA	NA	NA	NA	NA
- Low	9½	9½	7	20½	10	NA	NA	NA	NA	NA
P/E Ratio - High	53	NM	NM	14	19	NA	NA	NA	NA	NA
- Low	38	NM	NM	6	8	NA	NA	NA	NA	NA

Income Statement Analysis (Million $)

	1997	1996	1995	1994	1993	1992	1991	1990	1989	1988
Revs.	559	251	136	402	166	53.0	NA	NA	NA	NA
Oper. Inc.	15.6	2.8	-4.3	53.8	15.9	5.6	NA	NA	NA	NA
Depr.	6.4	2.9	2.0	0.8	0.4	0.2	NA	NA	NA	NA
Int. Exp.	2.1	Nil	Nil	1.2	0.7	0.6	NA	NA	NA	NA
Pretax Inc.	8.1	1.3	-3.5	51.7	14.7	4.8	NA	NA	NA	NA
Eff. Tax Rate	60%	65%	NM	41%	41%	40%	NA	NA	NA	NA
Net Inc.	3.2	0.4	-2.3	30.4	8.7	2.9	NA	NA	NA	NA

Balance Sheet & Other Fin. Data (Million $)

	1997	1996	1995	1994	1993	1992	1991	1990	1989	1988
Cash	42.5	46.6	62.2	33.9	10.4	NA	NA	NA	NA	NA
Curr. Assets	205	167	120	137	65.0	NA	NA	NA	NA	NA
Total Assets	314	190	138	147	67.0	NA	NA	NA	NA	NA
Curr. Liab.	144	65.1	13.4	20.8	39.5	NA	NA	NA	NA	NA
LT Debt	9.6	Nil	Nil	0.0	0.1	NA	NA	NA	NA	NA
Common Eqty.	160	124	124	126	28.0	NA	NA	NA	NA	NA
Total Cap.	170	125	124	126	28.0	NA	NA	NA	NA	NA
Cap. Exp.	6.0	3.4	3.9	5.8	2.0	0.4	NA	NA	NA	NA
Cash Flow	9.7	3.3	-0.4	31.2	9.1	12.2	NA	NA	NA	NA
Curr. Ratio	1.4	2.6	8.9	6.6	1.6	NA	NA	NA	NA	NA
% LT Debt of Cap.	5.6	Nil	Nil	NM	0.2	NA	NA	NA	NA	NA
% Net Inc.of Revs.	0.6	0.2	NM	7.6	5.5	5.2	NA	NA	NA	NA
% Ret. on Assets	1.3	0.2	NM	28.4	NM	NM	NM	NM	NM	NM
% Ret. on Equity	2.3	0.3	NM	39.5	NM	NM	NM	NM	NM	NM

Data as orig. reptd.; bef. results of disc. opers. and/or spec. items. Per share data adj. for stk. divs. as of ex-div. date. Data for 1993 and 1992 pro forma. E-Estimated. NA-Not Available. NM-Not Meaningful. NR-Not Ranked.

Office—3 Pond Rd., Gloucester, MA 01930. Tel—(508) 283-5800. Chrmn & CEO—G. P. Shlopak. Pres & COO—P. D. Brady. VP, CFO & Investor Contact—Dominic F. Mammola. Dirs—J. W. Bartlett, P. D. Brady, J. A. Kouba, L. Marx Jr., G. P. Shlopak. Transfer Agent & Registrar—First National Bank of Boston. Incorporated—in Delaware in 1990.Empl—1,425. S&P Analyst: K.J.G.

STANDARD &POOR'S
STOCK REPORTS

D. R. Horton

710W
NYSE Symbol **DHI**

In S&P SmallCap 600

03-OCT-98

Industry: Homebuilding

Summary: This company primarily builds and sells single-family homes in most regions of the U.S.

Quantitative Evaluations

Recent Price • 14⅜
52 Wk Range • 24⅞-14¼

Yield • 0.6%
12-Mo. P/E • NM

Outlook (1 Lowest—5 Highest)
• **4⁻**

Fair Value
• **21½**

Risk
• **Average**

Earn./Div. Rank
• **NR**

Technical Eval.
• **NA**

Rel. Strength Rank (1 Lowest—99 Highest)
• **22**

Insider Activity
• **Unfavorable**

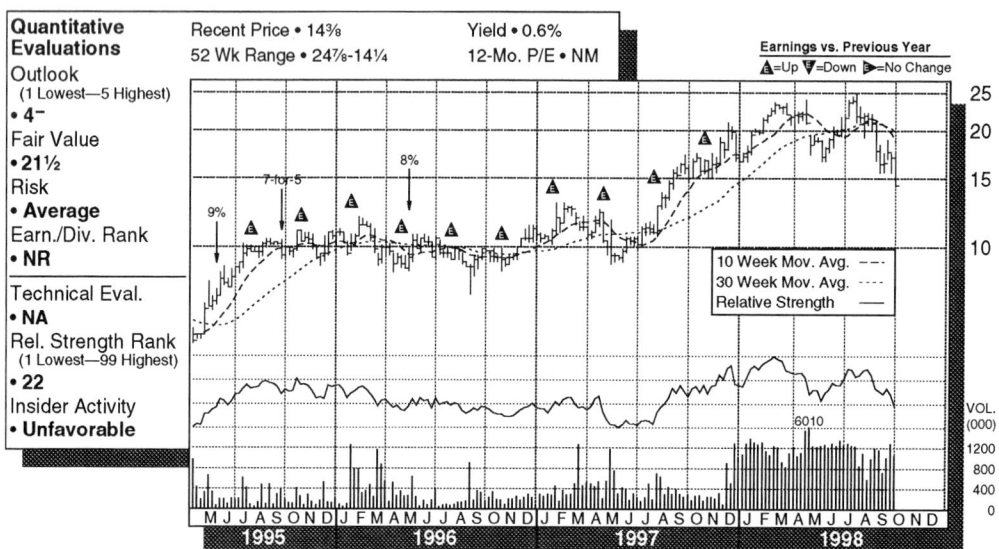

Earnings vs. Previous Year
▲=Up ▼=Down ▶=No Change

10 Week Mov. Avg. ---
30 Week Mov. Avg. ......
Relative Strength —

Business Profile - 31-AUG-98

Horton, one of the most geographically diversified homebuilders in the U.S., positions itself between large-volume and local custom homebuilders and sells its single-family homes to the entry-level and move-up market segments. Management's strategy is to continue entering new markets, primarily through acquisitions of existing homebuilders, as exemplified by DHI's April 1998 acquisition of Continental Homes. The company believes existing homebuilders possess benefits not found in start-up operations, such as brand name recognition, proven product acceptance and local industry relationships. DHI attempts to reduce risk by acquiring approved building lots through options. It will typically refrain from making material investments in land, homes and overhead until its targeted markets demonstrate significant growth potential.

Operational Review - 31-AUG-98

Revenues in the first nine months of FY 98 (Sep.) rose 35%, year to year, with results in both periods restated to include Continental Homes on a pooling-of-interests basis. The higher revenues reflected strong housing demand, several recent acquisitions and the company's entrance into new markets. Operating margins widened on the larger revenue base and well controlled construction costs. Despite $11.9 million of one-time charges related to the Continental acquisition, net income rose 41%, to $60.9 million ($1.02 a share, on 6.3% more shares), from $43.2 million ($0.78), restated.

Stock Performance - 02-OCT-98

In the past 30 trading days, DHI's shares have declined 31%, compared to a 7% fall in the S&P 500. Average trading volume for the past five days was 210,240 shares, compared with the 40-day moving average of 226,759 shares.

Key Stock Statistics

Dividend Rate/Share	0.09	Shareholders	200
Shs. outstg. (M)	55.6	Market cap. (B)	$0.803
Avg. daily vol. (M)	0.252	Inst. holdings	63%
Tang. Bk. Value/Share	8.15		
Beta	1.12		

Value of $10,000 invested 5 years ago: $ 26,768

Fiscal Year Ending Sep. 30

	1998	1997	1996	1995	1994	1993
Revenues (Million $)						
1Q	—	144.4	121.1	168.9	78.90	—
2Q	—	159.6	114.0	87.08	82.61	—
3Q	608.3	250.1	143.3	120.5	107.8	—
4Q	—	283.2	168.9	132.8	124.0	—
Yr.	—	837.3	547.3	437.4	393.3	190.0
Earnings Per Share ($)						
1Q	—	**0.21**	0.19	0.14	0.13	—
2Q	—	0.20	0.16	0.15	0.13	—
3Q	0.30	0.26	0.20	0.22	0.17	—
4Q	—	0.34	0.29	0.24	0.21	—
Yr.	—	1.01	0.87	0.74	0.64	0.32

Next earnings report expected: early November

Dividend Data (Dividends have been paid since 1997.)

Amount ($)	Date Decl.	Ex-Div. Date	Stock of Record	Payment Date
0.023	Jan. 13	Jan. 20	Jan. 22	Feb. 06 '98
0.023	Apr. 16	Apr. 27	Apr. 29	May. 15 '98
0.023	Jul. 22	Jul. 30	Aug. 03	Aug. 14 '98
0.023	Oct. 01	Oct. 14	Oct. 16	Oct. 23 '98

A Division of The McGraw·Hill Companies

Business Summary - 31-AUG-98

With operating divisions in 21 states and 36 markets, D. R. Horton is one of the most geographically diversified homebuilders in the U.S. The company positions itself between large-volume and local custom homebuilders and sells its single-family homes to the entry-level and move-up market segments. DHI believes that it is able to offer a broader selection of homes than high-volume homebuilders and at lower prices than local homebuilders. The revenue breakdown (restated for the April 1998 acquisition of Continental Homes) by geographic region in recent fiscal years (Sep.) was:

	FY 97	FY 96	FY 95
Mid-Atlantic	12%	10%	13%
Midwest	6%	8%	8%
Southeast	16%	10%	8%
Southwest	44%	55%	26%
West	22%	17%	45%

In April 1998, Horton acquired Continental Homes for about 15.5 million shares. Continental is a diversified homebuilder focused on the Southwest market with FY 97 (May) sales of $726 million. Similar to DHI, Continental targets entry-level and first-time move-up homebuyers. Management believes this acquisition will help secure a leading share of important homebuilding markets and increase its financial strength.

Although management believes that there are significant growth opportunities in DHI's existing markets, the company intends to continue entering new markets, primarily through acquisitions of existing homebuilders. DHI believes that its diversification strategy reduces its exposure to market volatility. Management seeks to purchase existing operations that possess established land positions, as well as pre-existing relationships with land owners, developers, subcontractors and suppliers. The company will typically refrain from making material investments in land, homes and overhead until its targeted markets demonstrate significant growth potential. Management attempts to reduce risk by acquiring approved building lots through options.

DHI residences generally range in size from 1,000 to 5,000 sq. ft. and in price from $80,000 to $600,000. The company generally offers between five and 10 home designs per subdivision, but is prepared to customize its designs to the homebuyer's individual taste. DHI primarily uses model and speculative homes to market its units and typically sells homes through commissioned employees and independent real estate brokers.

DHI's activities are conducted through 42 decentralized operation divisions. Management believes its decentralized structure gives more operating flexibility to its local managers. Each operating division is responsible for site selections, contract negotiations and property development.

Per Share Data ($)

(Year Ended Sep. 30)	1997	1996	1995	1994	1993	1992	1991	1990	1989	1988
Tangible Bk. Val.	6.28	5.36	3.75	3.03	2.43	2.09	0.85	NA	NA	NA
Cash Flow	1.13	0.95	0.81	0.68	0.33	0.39	0.41	NA	NA	NA
Earnings	1.01	0.87	0.74	0.64	0.32	0.38	0.40	NA	NA	NA
Dividends	0.06	Nil	Nil	Nil	Nil	Nil	Nil	Nil	Nil	Nil
Payout Ratio	6%	Nil	Nil	Nil	Nil	Nil	Nil	Nil	Nil	Nil
Prices - High	21	11⅞	11	11¼	10¼	6½	NA	NA	NA	NA
- Low	9	7½	5¼	5⅜	5½	4	NA	NA	NA	NA
P/E Ratio - High	21	14	15	18	32	17	NA	NA	NA	NA
- Low	9	9	7	8	17	10	NA	NA	NA	NA

Income Statement Analysis (Million $)

	1997	1996	1995	1994	1993	1992	1991	1990	1989	1988
Revs.	837	547	437	393	190	183	124	NA	NA	NA
Oper. Inc.	66.9	47.0	35.1	29.3	14.1	14.6	10.9	NA	NA	NA
Depr.	4.4	2.6	2.0	1.2	0.4	0.3	0.2	NA	NA	NA
Int. Exp.	5.2	14.8	13.5	7.3	2.5	2.0	2.9	NA	NA	NA
Pretax Inc.	59.9	44.4	32.6	28.6	13.9	14.2	8.0	NA	NA	NA
Eff. Tax Rate	40%	38%	37%	38%	36%	35%	Nil	Nil	Nil	Nil
Net Inc.	36.2	36.2	20.5	17.7	8.8	9.2	8.0	NA	NA	NA

Balance Sheet & Other Fin. Data (Million $)

	1997	1996	1995	1994	1993	1992	1991	1990	1989	1988
Cash	44.0	32.5	16.7	11.2	19.9	8.5	14.4	NA	NA	NA
Curr. Assets	NA	NA	NA	NA	NA	NA	NA	NA	NA	NA
Total Assets	720	403	319	231	159	104	60.0	NA	NA	NA
Curr. Liab.	NA	NA	NA	NA	NA	NA	NA	NA	NA	NA
LT Debt	355	159	135	8.2	13.1	4.0	0.1	NA	NA	NA
Common Eqty.	263	159	106	84.6	65.9	55.9	16.5	NA	NA	NA
Total Cap.	618	336	241	92.7	78.9	59.9	16.5	NA	NA	NA
Cap. Exp.	5.3	2.7	2.4	2.6	1.5	1.4	0.6	NA	NA	NA
Cash Flow	40.6	30.0	22.6	18.9	9.2	9.5	8.2	NA	NA	NA
Curr. Ratio	NA	NA	NA	NA	NA	NA	NA	NA	NA	NA
% LT Debt of Cap.	57.5	47.2	55.9	8.8	16.5	6.6	0.4	NA	NA	NA
% Net Inc.of Revs.	4.3	5.0	4.7	4.5	4.7	5.0	6.5	NA	NA	NA
% Ret. on Assets	6.4	7.6	7.5	9.0	6.7	9.8	NA	NA	NA	NA
% Ret. on Equity	16.4	19.0	21.5	23.4	14.5	23.4	NA	NA	NA	NA

Data as orig. reptd.; bef. results of disc. opers. and/or spec. items. Per share data adj. for stk. divs. as of ex-div. date. Bold denotes diluted EPS (FASB 128). F-Estimated. NA-Not Available. NM-Not Meaningful. NR-Not Ranked.

Office—1901 Ascension Blvd., Suite 100, Arlington, TX 76006. **Tel**—(817) 856-8200. **Chrmn, Pres & CEO**—D. R. Horton. **Exec VP**—R. Beckwitt. **Exec VP, CFO, Treas & Investor Contact**—David J. Keller. **Dirs**—R. Beckwitt, R. I. Galland, T. C. Golden, D. R. Horton, R. L. Horton, T. J. Horton, D. J. Keller, F. I. Neff, S. J. Stone. **Transfer Agent & Registrar**—KeyCorp Shareholder Services, Cleveland. **Incorporated**—in Delaware in 1991. **Empl**— 1,160. **S&P Analyst:** John A. Massey

Dain Rauscher

1237D
NYSE Symbol **DRC**

In S&P SmallCap 600

03-OCT-98

Industry:
Investment Banking/
Brokerage

Summary: This holding company, through Dain Bosworth Inc. and Rauscher Pierce Refsnes, Inc., is one of the largest U.S. regional full-service brokers and investment bankers.

Quantitative Evaluations	
Outlook (1 Lowest—5 Highest) • **3**	
Fair Value • **34¾**	
Risk • **Average**	
Earn./Div. Rank • **B**	
Technical Eval. • **NA**	
Rel. Strength Rank (1 Lowest—99 Highest) • **12**	
Insider Activity • **Neutral**	

Recent Price • 30⅛
52 Wk Range • 70¼-29¾

Yield • 2.9%
12-Mo. P/E • 12.3

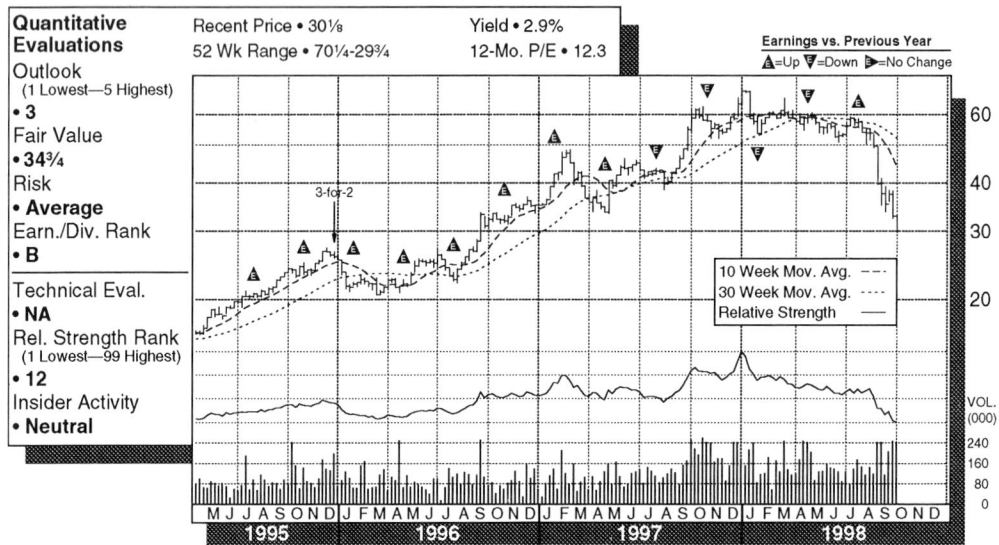

Earnings vs. Previous Year
▲=Up ▼=Down ▶=No Change

10 Week Mov. Avg. - - -
30 Week Mov. Avg. ....
Relative Strength ——

Business Profile - 15-MAY-98

In January 1998, the company completed the combination of its subsidiaries, Dain Bosworth of Minneapolis, MN, and Rauscher Pierce Refsnes of Dallas, TX, into one broker-dealer. As a result, the company changed its name to Dain Rauscher, now the largest regional broker in the western U.S., with about 1,270 registered investment executives. Most recently, DRC announced the acquisition of Wessels, Arnold & Henderson, a Minneapolis-based investment banking and institutional brokerage firm. Wessels will be integrated into the Equity Capital Markets Group.

Operational Review - 15-MAY-98

Net revenues were up 3.9%, year to year, in the first quarter of 1998, primarily as strong results from the Private Client group were partly offset by weakness in Equity Capital Markets productivity due to the recent Wessels acquisition. Operating margins narrowed, as total expenses grew 9.9%; operating earnings fell 31%. Following a $20.0 million pretax merger charge related to the combination of Dain Bosworth and Rauscher Pierce into one broker-dealer and taxes at 36.0%, versus 35.4%, a net loss of $2.02 million ($0.16 a share, diluted) contrasted with net income of $15.8 million ($1.22).

Stock Performance - 02-OCT-98

In the past 30 trading days, DRC's shares have declined 39%, compared to a 7% fall in the S&P 500. Average trading volume for the past five days was 50,940 shares, compared with the 40-day moving average of 42,985 shares.

Key Stock Statistics

Dividend Rate/Share	0.88	Shareholders	5,700
Shs. outstg. (M)	12.4	Market cap. (B)	$0.375
Avg. daily vol. (M)	0.045	Inst. holdings	36%
Tang. Bk. Value/Share	17.16		
Beta	1.81		

Value of $10,000 invested 5 years ago: $ 27,914

Fiscal Year Ending Dec. 31

	1998	1997	1996	1995	1994	1993
Revenues (Million $)						
1Q	188.0	180.1	170.8	134.0	131.1	118.8
2Q	208.5	168.5	167.6	147.2	117.6	122.5
3Q	—	196.6	165.5	160.2	118.2	136.0
4Q	—	205.5	179.5	165.3	129.4	134.3
Yr.	—	750.7	683.3	606.8	496.3	511.6
Earnings Per Share ($)						
1Q	-0.16	1.22	1.20	0.45	0.80	0.81
2Q	0.90	0.86	1.03	0.69	0.47	0.82
3Q	—	0.54	1.02	0.86	0.47	1.15
4Q	—	1.16	1.21	0.86	0.29	1.01
Yr.	—	3.77	4.46	2.86	2.03	3.78

Next earnings report expected: late October

Dividend Data (Dividends have been paid since 1992.)

Amount ($)	Date Decl.	Ex-Div. Date	Stock of Record	Payment Date
0.180	Oct. 21	Oct. 31	Nov. 04	Nov. 18 '97
0.220	Feb. 05	Feb. 27	Mar. 03	Mar. 17 '98
0.220	May. 06	May. 22	May. 27	Jun. 10 '98
0.220	Aug. 06	Aug. 18	Aug. 20	Sep. 03 '98

A Division of The **McGraw·Hill** *Companies*

STANDARD
&POOR'S
STOCK REPORTS

Dain Rauscher Inc.

1237D

03-OCT-98

Business Summary - 15-MAY-98

With roots firmly planted in the North and the Southwest, Dain Rauscher Inc. (formerly Interra Financial Inc.) is one of the largest U.S. regional brokerage and investment banking companies. Through Minneapolis-based Dain Bosworth Inc. and Dallas-based Rauscher Pierce Refsnes, Inc., the company offers securities broker-dealer and investment banking services to individual, institutional, corporate and governmental clients, mainly in the western half of the U.S.

Both Dain Bosworth and Rauscher Pierce Refsnes are dealers in corporate, tax-exempt and government fixed-income securities and corporate equity securities, act as agents in the purchase and sale of securities, options, commodities and futures contracts, help clients raise capital, and act as principals in the purchase and sale to their customers of various types of securities.

In 1997, an 11% increase in net revenues, to $692 million, was led by growth in DRC's Equity Capital Markets and Private Client businesses, which contributed 14% and 63%, respectively, of 1997 operating revenues. DRC invests in higher-margin business units such as Equity Capital Markets to boost overall mar-

gins, and is strengthening this group by adding more research analysts, investment bankers, equity traders and institutional salespeople. Nevertheless, this building process hurt the group's profitability in 1997. Equity Capital Markets includes investment banking (other than municipal finance), mergers and acquisitions, institutional equity sales and trading activities.

The Private Client business collects retail commissions and fees for managing assets in individual accounts. DRC attempts to cushion its overall business against the impact of market cycles by building assets under administration; as of December 31, 1997, such assets totaled $48 billion. DRC is also becoming more fee-oriented and less dependent on commissions in another effort to offset the impact of market cycles. Because they are based on a percentage of assets under management, fees are less volatile than commissions, which fluctuate with changes in trading volumes.

DRC's group structure allows its broker-dealers to leverage fixed costs and share support services through the company's Interra Clearing Services and Interra Advisory Services units. Interra Clearing also provides securities clearing and trade settlement services to numerous correspondent firms.

Per Share Data ($)

(Year Ended Dec. 31)	1997	1996	1995	1994	1993	1992	1991	1990	1989	1988
Tangible Bk. Val.	26.00	22.66	18.44	16.20	14.57	10.89	8.37	6.13	5.01	4.70
Cash Flow	4.67	NA	NA	NA	NA	NA	NA	NA	NA	NA
Earnings	3.77	4.46	2.86	2.03	3.78	2.69	1.67	0.11	0.23	-0.71
Dividends	0.72	0.56	0.43	0.37	0.19	0.08	Nil	Nil	Nil	Nil
Payout Ratio	19%	13%	15%	18%	5%	3%	Nil	Nil	Nil	Nil
Prices - High	70¼	36⅞	27⅛	21¾	22⅝	13	11⅞	5⅝	7⅛	8
- Low	33⅜	20½	14⅞	13⅜	11⅞	8¾	3⅜	3¼	4⅝	4⅞
P/E Ratio - High	19	8	9	11	6	5	7	53	31	NM
- Low	9	5	5	7	3	3	2	30	21	NM

Income Statement Analysis (Million $)

	1997	1996	1995	1994	1993	1992	1991	1990	1989	1988
Commissions	275	223	176	131	139	119	98.0	81.0	82.0	64.0
Int. Inc.	122	111	109	75.2	54.9	55.5	74.7	88.4	95.6	57.8
Total Revs.	751	683	607	496	512	438	378	313	320	255
Int. Exp.	58.6	57.6	64.8	38.9	28.7	32.4	55.7	73.2	83.4	51.7
Pretax Inc.	76.8	87.4	56.3	39.8	77.4	53.7	33.0	1.6	3.9	-7.7
Eff. Tax Rate	36%	35%	36%	36%	38%	36%	36%	18%	26%	Nil
Net Inc.	49.3	56.8	35.9	25.5	47.6	34.5	21.1	1.3	2.9	-7.7

Balance Sheet & Other Fin. Data (Million $)

	1997	1996	1995	1994	1993	1992	1991	1990	1989	1988
Total Assets	2,304	1,827	2,022	1,953	1,786	1,271	1,461	1,368	1,520	1,148
Cash Items	35.9	49.4	437	361	595	536	625	649	724	452
Receivables	1,480	1,238	1,022	917	710	479	502	304	363	282
Secs. Owned	542	289	323	319	271	141	214	204	218	100
Sec. Borrowed	179	25.0	97.0	150	124	19.0	62.0	96.0	117	68.0
Due Brokers & Cust.	1,400	1,169	1,287	1,117	1,149	923	1,047	883	997	643
Other Liabs.	226	330	374	444	314	181	221	268	282	313
Capitalization:										
Debt	366	27.3	41.0	47.0	22.0	16.0	27.0	45.0	62.0	69.0
Equity	319	276	222	195	178	132	103	74.0	59.0	53.0
Total	335	303	263	242	200	148	131	121	124	125
% Return On Revs.	6.6	8.3	5.9	5.1	9.3	7.9	5.6	0.4	0.9	NM
% Ret. on Assets	2.4	3.0	1.8	1.3	3.1	2.5	1.5	0.1	0.2	NM
% Ret. on Equity	16.6	19.3	17.2	13.6	30.7	29.4	23.7	1.7	4.9	NM

Data as orig. reptd.; bef. results of disc. opers. and/or spec. items. Per share data adj. for stk. divs. as of ex-div. date. Bold denotes diluted EPS (FASB 128). E-Estimated. NA-Not Available. NM-Not Meaningful. NR-Not Ranked.

Office—Dain Bosworth Plaza, 60 S. Sixth St., Minneapolis, MN 55402-4422. **Tel**—(612) 371-7750. **Website**—http://www.Dainrauscher.comChrmn, **Pres & CEO**—I. Weiser. **Vice Chrmn & CFO**—J. C. Appel. **SVP & Secy**—Carla J. Smith. **SVP & CIO**—D. J. Strachan. **Investor Contact**—Neal St. Anthony (612-371-2934). **Dirs**—J. C. Appel, J. E. Attwell, S. S. Boren, F. G. Fitz-Gerald, W. F. Mondale, C. A. Rundell Jr., R. L. Ryan, A. R. Schulze Jr., I. Weiser. **Transfer Agent & Registrar**—Norwest Bank Minnesota, Minneapolis. **Incorporated**—in Delaware in 1973. **Empl**—3,600. **S&P Analyst:** L. A. Olive

03-OCT-98 | **Industry:** Electronics (Semiconductors)

Summary: Dallas Semiconductor makes high-performance CMOS integrated circuits and semiconductor-based systems for numerous specialized applications.

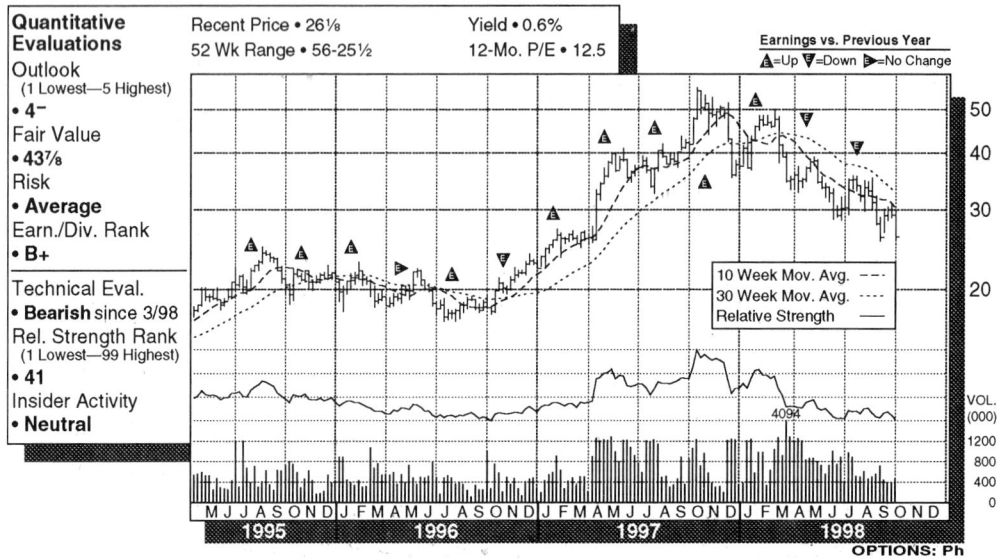

Quantitative Evaluations	Recent Price • 26⅛	Yield • 0.6%
	52 Wk Range • 56-25½	12-Mo. P/E • 12.5

Outlook (1 Lowest—5 Highest)
• **4⁻**

Fair Value
• **43⅞**

Risk
• **Average**

Earn./Div. Rank
• **B+**

Technical Eval.
• **Bearish** since 3/98

Rel. Strength Rank (1 Lowest—99 Highest)
• **41**

Insider Activity
• **Neutral**

Earnings vs. Previous Year
▲=Up ▼=Down ▶=No Change

10 Week Mov. Avg. – – –
30 Week Mov. Avg. ·······
Relative Strength ——

OPTIONS: Ph

Business Profile - 11-AUG-98

In the first half of 1998, revenues fell almost 3%, reflecting a severe downturn in the semiconductor market, which has been plagued by oversupply, pricing pressure and the effects of the Asian flu. In 1997, 23% of DS's sales were generated in Far East markets. Given limited visibility in Dallas's business, the company is focusing on capacity management and cost control measures. Despite a challenging operating environment, DS continues to invest in product development initiatives, in hopes that the company will benefit upon improvement in market conditions.

Operational Review - 11-AUG-98

Net sales in the six months ended June 28, 1998, fell 2.9%, year to year, as a result of industrywide softness in the semiconductor market. Despite a larger decline in direct costs, margins narrowed, reflecting increases in R&D and SG&A expenditures; operating income was down 9.0%. Results benefited from a 19% jump in interest income. After taxes at 32.0%, versus 32.3%, net income decreased 7.3%, to $27,527,000 ($0.92 a share, based on 2.8% more shares), from $29,696,000 ($1.02).

Stock Performance - 02-OCT-98

In the past 30 trading days, DS's shares have declined 16%, compared to a 7% fall in the S&P 500. Average trading volume for the past five days was 94,460 shares, compared with the 40-day moving average of 100,018 shares.

Key Stock Statistics

Dividend Rate/Share	0.16	Shareholders	600
Shs. outstg. (M)	28.0	Market cap. (B)	$0.733
Avg. daily vol. (M)	0.088	Inst. holdings	73%
Tang. Bk. Value/Share	13.78		
Beta	0.70		

Value of $10,000 invested 5 years ago: $ 19,934

Fiscal Year Ending Dec. 31

	1998	1997	1996	1995	1994	1993
Revenues (Million $)						
1Q	87.45	88.70	65.58	52.04	43.18	35.50
2Q	87.03	91.04	70.36	57.04	45.04	38.35
3Q	—	93.07	72.02	60.51	45.20	41.00
4Q	—	95.40	80.39	63.69	48.01	42.00
Yr.	—	368.2	288.4	233.3	181.4	156.9
Earnings Per Share ($)						
1Q	**0.45**	**0.50**	0.36	0.30	0.27	0.21
2Q	**0.47**	**0.52**	0.36	0.32	0.27	0.23
3Q	—	**0.57**	0.28	0.34	0.27	0.25
4Q	—	**0.60**	0.37	0.36	0.28	0.26
Yr.	—	**2.19**	1.37	1.32	1.09	0.95

Next earnings report expected: early October

Dividend Data (Dividends have been paid since 1995.)

Amount ($)	Date Decl.	Ex-Div. Date	Stock of Record	Payment Date
0.035	Oct. 23	Nov. 12	Nov. 14	Dec. 01 '97
0.040	Jan. 22	Feb. 11	Feb. 13	Mar. 02 '98
0.040	Apr. 22	May. 13	May. 15	Jun. 01 '98
0.040	Jul. 21	Aug. 12	Aug. 14	Sep. 01 '98

A Division of The McGraw-Hill Companies

Business Summary - 11-AUG-98

Dallas Semiconductor, which designs, manufactures and markets electronic chips and chip-based subsystems, uses customer problems as an entry point to develop products with widespread applications. Founded in 1984, the company has developed 292 proprietary base products with over 2,000 variations and remains committed to new product development as a means to increase future revenues and diversify markets, product offerings and customers.

The company uses advanced technologies to gain a competitive edge over traditional approaches to semiconductors. Combining lithium power cells with low-power CMOS chips can power the chips for the useful life of the equipment in which they are used. Products are organized around categories sharing common technologies, markets or applications.

Communications products are offered for high capacity voice, data and video transmission and address the requirements of high capacity digital link protocols. DS's transmission line terminators quiet transmission lines between computers and peripherals such as disk drives, permitting high speed, high integrity data transmission.

DS's system extension business provides complete solutions to common problems facing many systems designers, such as managing thermal problems resulting

from the continuous process of putting more power into smaller chips. For example, the system monitors the power supply voltages in a system and issues a warning if any fall below a critical value.

Computer Timekeeping devices offer hardware solutions that correctly address Year 2000 problems in personal computers and embedded systems. Commercial Timekeeping products provide advanced features including clock-calendar display, talk-time, re-dial timing and power management for digital cellular phones, and are used in data communications network routers, hubs and bridges to monitor communications traffic and store network configuration data.

The company has combined its circuitry and understanding of ultra low-power CMOS static random access memory (SRAM) chips with improvements in long-life lithium power sources to develop a family of SRAM products which are able to retain data even in the absence of system power.

Microcontroller products combine a central processing unit, data memory, program memory and input-output devices on a single chip in order to control a wide variety of electronic systems. Automation Information chips, which identify an object and hold relevant information, can facilitate automation by tracking a work piece as it travels along an assembly line or can be used to identify people for access to secure areas.

Per Share Data ($)

(Year Ended Dec. 31)	1997	1996	1995	1994	1993	1992	1991	1990	1989	1988
Tangible Bk. Val.	12.74	10.25	8.92	7.66	6.53	5.47	4.69	4.08	3.53	3.08
Cash Flow	3.41	2.39	1.10	1.65	1.47	1.21	1.08	0.99	0.79	0.52
Earnings	2.19	1.37	1.32	1.09	0.95	0.71	0.58	0.56	0.45	0.30
Dividends	0.14	0.12	0.10	Nil	Nil	Nil	Nil	Nil	Nil	Nil
Payout Ratio	6%	9%	8%	Nil	Nil	Nil	Nil	Nil	Nil	Nil
Prices - High	56	24	24⁷⁄₈	20¹⁄₈	19	14¹⁄₂	12³⁄₈	9⁵⁄₈	8⁵⁄₈	9
- Low	22³⁄₈	17	15	13³⁄₈	11³⁄₄	7	5³⁄₈	4¹⁄₈	5³⁄₄	5⁵⁄₈
P/E Ratio - High	26	18	19	18	20	20	21	17	19	30
- Low	10	12	11	12	12	10	9	7	13	19

Income Statement Analysis (Million $)

	1997	1996	1995	1994	1993	1992	1991	1990	1989	1988
Revs.	368	288	233	181	157	120	104	100	82.0	58.0
Oper. Inc.	126	83.0	66.0	57.2	50.8	39.5	33.4	29.0	21.0	15.0
Depr.	35.8	28.4	14.0	15.3	13.9	13.1	12.9	10.9	8.5	5.6
Int. Exp.	Nil	NA	NA	0.0	0.1	0.3	0.9	1.3	1.4	1.5
Pretax Inc.	94.5	57.1	54.9	45.1	39.7	29.0	23.0	20.4	14.8	11.3
Eff. Tax Rate	32%	33%	33%	34%	36%	36%	36%	32%	25%	35%
Net Inc.	64.6	38.4	36.7	29.7	25.6	18.6	14.7	13.8	11.1	7.3

Balance Sheet & Other Fin. Data (Million $)

	1997	1996	1995	1994	1993	1992	1991	1990	1989	1988
Cash	115	70.3	69.3	17.5	32.3	21.8	45.8	45.9	38.8	40.9
Curr. Assets	250	170	162	92.6	91.2	68.0	80.4	78.8	69.3	63.5
Total Assets	417	314	272	221	187	156	129	120	106	92.0
Curr. Liab.	66.1	41.1	37.0	26.5	21.0	20.6	11.5	15.2	14.0	10.9
LT Debt	Nil	Nil	Nil	Nil	Nil	Nil	4.3	7.7	8.8	9.5
Common Eqty.	351	273	235	195	166	136	113	97.0	83.0	71.0
Total Cap.	351	273	235	195	166	136	118	105	92.0	81.0
Cap. Exp.	58.6	60.5	49.3	44.7	21.1	15.8	13.1	15.7	16.9	12.9
Cash Flow	100	66.8	29.8	45.0	39.5	31.7	27.6	24.8	19.6	12.9
Curr. Ratio	3.8	4.1	4.4	3.5	4.3	3.3	7.0	5.2	4.9	5.9
% LT Debt of Cap.	Nil	Nil	Nil	Nil	Nil	Nil	3.6	7.3	9.6	11.7
% Net Inc.of Revs.	17.5	13.3	15.8	16.4	16.3	15.4	14.2	13.8	13.5	12.5
% Ret. on Assets	17.7	13.1	14.9	14.6	14.8	12.8	11.7	12.2	11.2	8.5
% Ret. on Equity	20.6	15.1	17.1	16.5	16.8	14.7	13.9	15.3	14.3	11.0

Data as orig. reptd.; bef. results of disc. opers. and/or spec. items. Per share data adj. for stk. divs. as of ex-div. date. Bold denotes diluted EPS (FASB 128). E-Estimated. NA-Not Available. NM-Not Meaningful. NR-Not Ranked.

Office—4401 S. Beltwood Parkway, Dallas, TX 75244-3292. **Tel**—(972) 371-4000. **Website**—http://www.dalsemi.com.**Chrmn, CEO & Pres**—C. V. Prothro. **VP-Fin & Investor Contact**—Alan P. Hale. **Secy**—M. K. McLaughlin. **Dirs**—M. L. Bolan, R. L. King, C. C. Mai, C. V. Prothro, M. D. Sampels, C. J. Santoro, E. R. Zumwalt Jr. **Transfer Agent & Registrar**—ChaseMellon Shareholder Services, Ridgefield Park, NJ. **Incorporated**—in Delaware in 1984. **Empl**— 1,497. **S&P Analyst:** Stephen J. Tekirian

DAMARK International **3658B**
NASDAQ Symbol **DMRK**
In S&P SmallCap 600

03-OCT-98

Industry:
Retail (Home Shopping)

Summary: DAMARK is a membership-driven, information-based national direct marketer of brand name and other quality merchandise and services.

Quantitative Evaluations

Recent Price • 6⅞
52 Wk Range • 15-5⅛

Yield • Nil
12-Mo. P/E • NM

Outlook
(1 Lowest—5 Highest)
• **NA**

Fair Value
• **NA**

Risk
• **High**

Earn./Div. Rank
• **B-**

Technical Eval.
• **Bearish** since 7/98

Rel. Strength Rank
(1 Lowest—99 Highest)
• **64**

Insider Activity
• **NA**

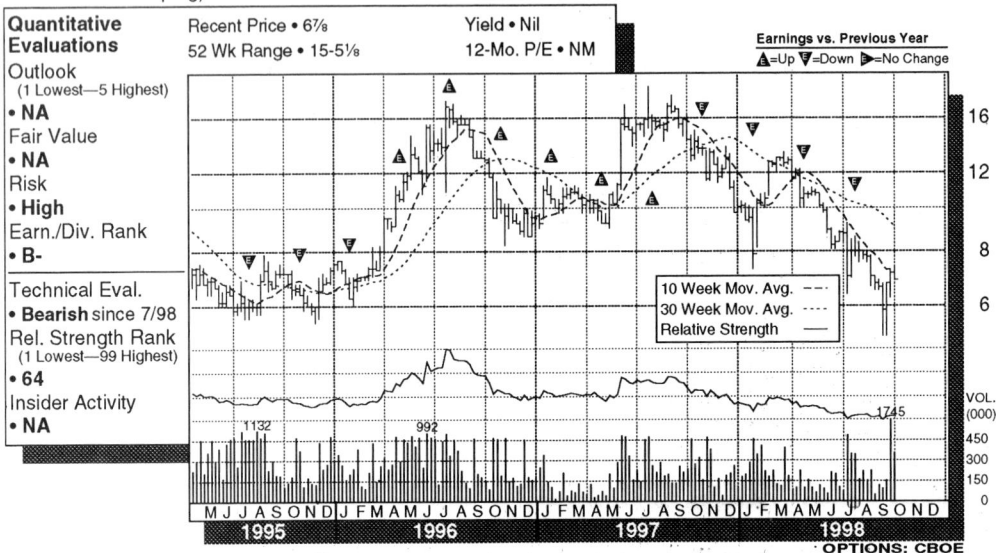

Earnings vs. Previous Year
▲=Up ▼=Down ▶=No Change

10 Week Mov. Avg. — - -
30 Week Mov. Avg. ....
Relative Strength ——

OPTIONS: CBOE

Business Profile - 03-SEP-98

Total membership climbed 30% in 1997, to nearly 1.4 million, as membership renewal rates reached the highest level in the company's history. Membership continued to grow through the first half of 1998, aided by renewals, increased usage of outbound telemarketing, and an expanded suite of membership products. Despite success in increasing membership through the direct-to-consumer channel, DMRK's long-term strategic growth vehicle is the client services channel in which the company markets its membership programs on behalf of large customer list-owning clients, mainly credit card issuers such as financial institutions. An increasing number of new members are being added through this channel.

Operational Review - 03-SEP-98

Net revenues in the first half of 1998 declined 9.2%, year to year, as reduced catalog circulation and lower sales per catalog, and the closing of a call center for a 10-day period during May 1998, outweighed significant membership expansion. Gross margins widened, as a result of a shift to higher-margin membership sales. However, with 16% higher marketing and administrative expenses associated with membership expansion initiatives, an operating loss contrasted with operating income. With increased other expense, despite a tax benefit of $2.3 million, versus taxes at 34.0%, a net loss of $4,471,000 ($0.58 a share) contrasted with net income of $2,540,000 ($0.30).

Stock Performance - 02-OCT-98

In the past 30 trading days, DMRK's shares have declined 2%, compared to a 7% fall in the S&P 500. Average trading volume for the past five days was 71,480 shares, compared with the 40-day moving average of 74,087 shares.

Key Stock Statistics

Dividend Rate/Share	Nil	Shareholders	400
Shs. outstg. (M)	7.3	Market cap. (B)	$0.050
Avg. daily vol. (M)	0.118	Inst. holdings	65%
Tang. Bk. Value/Share	7.82		
Beta	0.98		

Value of $10,000 invested 5 years ago: $ 5,238

Fiscal Year Ending Dec. 31

	1998	1997	1996	1995	1994	1993
Revenues (Million $)						
1Q	135.1	128.6	116.9	128.3	114.0	82.51
2Q	115.7	147.5	124.1	111.7	93.75	69.07
3Q	—	134.8	112.2	112.1	102.3	73.22
4Q	—	183.7	160.5	148.0	167.3	139.5
Yr.	—	594.6	513.7	500.0	477.4	364.3
Earnings Per Share ($)						
1Q	0.02	0.05	-0.02	-0.12	0.14	0.08
2Q	-0.62	0.25	0.17	-0.30	-0.09	0.11
3Q	—	0.09	0.18	0.02	0.12	0.14
4Q	—	0.35	0.37	0.20	0.42	0.34
Yr.	—	0.74	0.70	-0.20	0.59	0.67

Next earnings report expected: mid October

Dividend Data

The company has never paid a cash dividend on its common stock. DAMARK intends to retain earnings for use in the operation and expansion of its business and does not expect to pay any cash dividends in the foreseeable future. In addition, a bank credit agreement restricts the payment of dividends.

A Division of The McGraw-Hill Companies

Business Summary - 03-SEP-98

Damark International (DMRK) is a direct marketer of brand name and other merchandise at value oriented prices. The company's driving force is its membership strategy, the linchpin of which is DMRK's preferred Buyers' Club (PBC). At June 27, 1998, total membership of all clubs exceeded 1.4 million.

The company's products and services are offered through mail order catalogs and a variety of membership clubs which provide members discounts on travel, hospitality and entertainment as well as retail, health and fitness, and other convenience needs. In addition, brand-name, value-priced merchandise is sold through catalogs in six broad categories, which contributed to 1997 sales as follows:

	1997	1996
Computers	31%	30%
Consumer electronics	18%	18%
Home office	15%	16%
Home decor	14%	14%
Home improvements	16%	15%
Sporting goods/fitness	6%	7%

During 1997, DMRK mailed 24 front-end catalog editions and 35 nonclub catalog editions, with aggregate circulation of approximately 12,900,000 to prospective new customers; and mailed 36 catalog editions, with an aggregate circulation of approximately 37,000,000, to club members. At December 31, 1997, the company's proprietary customer list consisted of more than 12,000,000 names. About one million new names were added during 1997 (675,000 in 1996). In the first half of 1998, 750,000 new members were added to the rolls, while 499,000 renewals were realized.

Since 1987, the company has been marketing the PBC. Members of PBC receive a 10% discount on all DMRK purchases, exclusive members-only catalogs and enhanced shopping benefits, along with discounts from many additional third-party marketing partners. Additional membership clubs have been introduced in recent years, including the Vacation Passport travel club (launched in September 1996); the Insiders membership club (November 1996), designed to appeal to customers who shop frequently and desire premium membership benefits; the Great Deal Pack club (October 1997), which focuses on coupon discounts on company merchandise and entertainment theme offers; and the Essential for Home club (December 1997), providing members with discounts on home furnishing products from DMRK and certain third parties.

Until recently, the company marketed its membership clubs solely through direct-to-customer channels, primarily using catalog mailings and outbound telemarketing. During 1997, it began test marketing through the client services channel in which it has targeted large list-owning clients in the financial services industry. As of mid-1998, DMRK had secured client relationships with several nationally recognized financial institutions, including Wachovia Bank and Capital One Bank.

Per Share Data ($)

(Year Ended Dec. 31)	1997	1996	1995	1994	1993	1992	1991	1990	1989	1988
Tangible Bk. Val.	8.56	7.77	7.30	6.82	6.78	3.80	NA	NA	NA	NA
Cash Flow	1.77	1.48	0.35	0.95	0.93	0.54	NA	NA	NA	NA
Earnings	0.74	0.70	-0.20	0.59	0.67	0.21	NA	NA	NA	NA
Dividends	Nil	Nil	Nil	Nil	Nil	Nil	Nil	Nil	Nil	Nil
Payout Ratio	Nil	Nil	Nil	Nil	Nil	Nil	Nil	Nil	Nil	Nil
Prices - High	18⅞	17½	9	31	23¾	14¼	NA	NA	NA	NA
- Low	9	6	5½	5¾	4¾	3¾	NA	NA	NA	NA
P/E Ratio - High	26	25	NM	53	35	68	NA	NA	NA	NA
- Low	12	9	NM	10	7	18	NA	NA	NA	NA

Income Statement Analysis (Million $)

	1997	1996	1995	1994	1993	1992	1991	1990	1989	1988
Revs.	595	514	500	477	364	270	NA	NA	NA	NA
Oper. Inc.	20.1	16.1	3.2	12.9	11.7	6.7	NA	NA	NA	NA
Depr.	8.7	6.9	5.1	3.6	2.2	2.4	NA	NA	NA	NA
Int. Exp.	1.8	0.1	0.2	0.2	0.2	1.6	NA	NA	NA	NA
Pretax Inc.	9.6	9.1	-2.8	8.3	8.8	2.4	NA	NA	NA	NA
Eff. Tax Rate	34%	34%	NM	29%	34%	35%	NA	NA	NA	NA
Net Inc.	6.3	6.1	-1.9	5.9	5.8	1.6	NA	NA	NA	NA

Balance Sheet & Other Fin. Data (Million $)

	1997	1996	1995	1994	1993	1992	1991	1990	1989	1988
Cash	0.5	NM	8.7	7.2	24.7	NA	NA	NA	NA	NA
Curr. Assets	160	98.4	100	117	123	NA	NA	NA	NA	NA
Total Assets	206	143	142	156	147	74.0	NA	NA	NA	NA
Curr. Liab.	136	78.8	75.4	81.5	79.7	NA	NA	NA	NA	NA
LT Debt	Nil	Nil	Nil	0.3	0.5	NA	NA	NA	NA	NA
Common Eqty.	68.7	62.5	64.9	72.0	64.3	29.5	NA	NA	NA	NA
Total Cap.	70.2	63.9	66.3	74.0	67.0	NA	NA	NA	NA	NA
Cap. Exp.	10.0	8.6	NA	19.1	6.1	3.0	NA	NA	NA	NA
Cash Flow	15.0	12.9	3.2	9.5	8.0	4.0	NA	NA	NA	NA
Curr. Ratio	1.2	1.3	1.3	1.4	1.5	NA	NA	NA	NA	NA
% LT Debt of Cap.	Nil	Nil	Nil	0.3	0.7	NA	NA	NA	NA	NA
% Net Inc.of Revs.	1.1	1.2	NM	1.2	1.6	0.6	NA	NA	NA	NA
% Ret. on Assets	3.6	4.3	NM	3.9	5.2	2.3	NA	NA	NA	NA
% Ret. on Equity	9.6	9.5	NM	8.6	12.3	7.7	NA	NA	NA	NA

Data as orig. reptd.; bef. results of disc. opers. and/or spec. items. Per share data adj. for stk. divs. as of ex-div. date. Bold denotes diluted EPS (FASB 128). E-Estimated. NA-Not Available. NM-Not Meaningful. NR-Not Ranked.

Office—7101 Winnetka Ave. North, Minneapolis, MN 55428. **Tel**—(612) 531-0066. **E-mail**—investor.relations@.damark.com **Website**—http:// www.damark.com **Chrmn & CEO**—M. A. Cohn. **Dirs**—M. A. Cohn, T. A. Cusick, J. W. Eugster, S. J. Hemsley, H. Roitenberg, R. Strangis, J. N. Waller. **Transfer Agent & Registrar**—Norwest Bank Minnesota, Minneapolis. **Incorporated**—in Minnesota in 1986. **Empl**— 1,950. **S&P Analyst:** S.A.H.

Dames & Moore
712M
NYSE Symbol **DM**

In S&P SmallCap 600

03-OCT-98

Industry: Services (Facilities & Environmental)

Summary: DM provides environmental, engineering and construction management services worldwide.

Quantitative Evaluations	
Outlook (1 Lowest—5 Highest)	**• 5**
Fair Value	**• 16⅜**
Risk	**• Average**
Earn./Div. Rank	**• NR**
Technical Eval.	**• Bullish** since 9/98
Rel. Strength Rank (1 Lowest—99 Highest)	**• 38**
Insider Activity	**• NA**

Recent Price • 10⅛
52 Wk Range • 14⅜-10⅛
Yield • 1.2%
12-Mo. P/E • 9.5

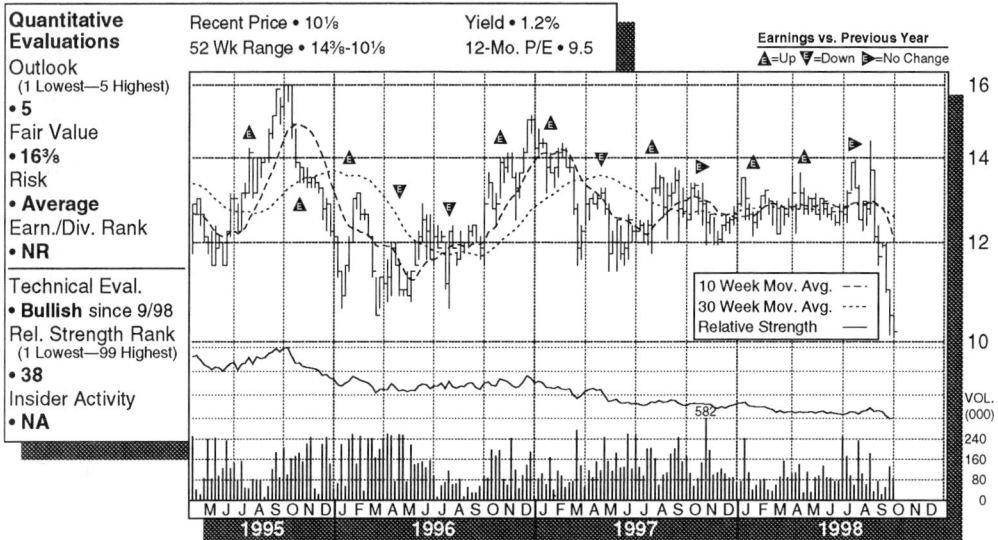

Earnings vs. Previous Year
▲=Up ▼=Down ▶=No Change

10 Week Mov. Avg. - - -
30 Week Mov. Avg. ....
Relative Strength ——

Business Profile - 25-SEP-98

Dames & Moore Group expanded its operations significantly when it acquired Radian International LLC from the Dow Chemical Company for $117 million in July 1998. Radian, with annualized revenues of $300 million, is a multinational engineering, consulting, and construction firm, offering services in the areas of process engineering, detailed design, construction management, pollution monitoring, information management, and remediation. The acquisition raised DM's annualized gross revenues to about $1 billion. By integrating the capabilities of Radian, DM believes it is now able to pursue broader business opportunities and achieve meaningful administrative cost savings. DM expected the acquisition to modestly increase earnings in FY 99 (Mar.) and significantly boost profits in FY 00. In the first quarter of FY 99, DM acquired Signet Testing Laboratories, Inc., a materials engineering and testing firm.

Operational Review - 25-SEP-98

Net revenues for the first quarter of FY 99 (Mar.) advanced 7.5%, year to year, reflecting acquisitions. Profitability was restricted by a 13% increase in general expenses, and the gain in earnings from operations was held to 4.8%. After 9.7% larger other expenses and taxes at 43.2%, versus 41.3%, net income rose only nominally to $4,687,000 ($0.26 a share), from $4,685,000 ($0.26).

Stock Performance - 02-OCT-98

In the past 30 trading days, DM's shares have declined 26%, compared to a 7% fall in the S&P 500. Average trading volume for the past five days was 17,020 shares, compared with the 40-day moving average of 16,195 shares.

Key Stock Statistics

Dividend Rate/Share	0.12	Shareholders	400
Shs. outstg. (M)	18.4	Market cap. (B)	$0.187
Avg. daily vol. (M)	0.014	Inst. holdings	54%
Tang. Bk. Value/Share	1.84		
Beta	0.41		

Value of $10,000 invested 5 years ago: $ 4,999

Fiscal Year Ending Mar. 31

	1999	1998	1997	1996	1995	1994
Revenues (Million $)						
1Q	128.8	120.1	108.1	100.7	70.19	64.97
2Q	—	123.4	115.4	100.5	64.66	63.84
3Q	—	119.2	114.7	97.84	66.25	65.18
4Q	—	119.8	117.1	98.70	67.87	59.83
Yr.	—	482.5	455.3	397.7	269.0	253.8
Earnings Per Share ($)						
1Q	0.26	0.26	0.23	0.25	0.23	0.27
2Q	—	0.28	0.28	0.26	0.25	0.28
3Q	—	0.29	0.28	0.24	0.22	0.29
4Q	—	0.24	0.11	0.11	0.13	0.13
Yr.	—	1.07	0.91	0.98	0.83	0.97

Next earnings report expected: late October

Dividend Data (Dividends have been paid since 1992.)

Amount ($)	Date Decl.	Ex-Div. Date	Stock of Record	Payment Date
0.030	Nov. 07	Dec. 18	Dec. 22	Jan. 05 '98
0.030	Feb. 26	Mar. 19	Mar. 23	Apr. 06 '98
0.030	Jun. 01	Jun. 18	Jun. 22	Jul. 06 '98
0.030	Aug. 13	Sep. 17	Sep. 21	Oct. 06 '98

A Division of The **McGraw·Hill** *Companies*

Business Summary - 25-SEP-98

Dames & Moore Group (formerly Dames & Moore, Inc. is a worldwide provider of comprehensive engineering, consulting, and construction management services, serving a broad range of clients in both the private and public sectors. The July 1998, acquisition of Radian International LLC expanded operations significantly. With annualized revenues of $300 million, Radian is a multinational engineering, consulting, and construction firm, offering services in process engineering, detailed design, construction management, pollution monitoring, information management, and remediation.

As year-end FY 98 (mar.), DM was providing services in the following areas: General Engineering and Consulting; Process and Chemical Engineering; Transportation; Construction and Program Management; and Specialty Engineering and Consulting.

General Engineering and Consulting involves architecture, civil and structural engineering, geotechnical engineering, seismic risk management and earthquake engineering, mining engineering, radiological engineering, offshore engineering, electrical and instrumentation engineering, mechanical engineering, power systems engineering, water and wastewater engineering, agricultural policy and strategy, strategic environmental management, air quality and atmospheric services, environmental health and toxicology, project financial analysis, permitting and licensing, regulatory compliance, remediation, and contaminated property rehabilitation.

Process and Chemical Engineering involves process selection and optimization, conceptual designs, process engineering and design of advanced process controls, facility start-up, process safety management, pollution prevention system design, and economic feasibility studies.

Transportation involves transportation planning, traffic engineering, roadway/highway design, bridge design, transit design, intelligent transportation systems, intermodal facilities, pedestrian facilities/urban design, railroads, airports and ports and harbors.

Construction and Program Management involves program and project management, construction management, value engineering, design-build, general contracting, demolition, estimating, cost and schedule control, contract administration, quality assurance/control, dispute resolution and litigation support, and community relations.

Specialty Engineering and Consulting is provided in the areas of: clinical laboratory services, including contract research, analysis and management services; and communications and information services, including strategic communications, information management and technology, expert witness support, litigation support, and presentation graphics.

Per Share Data ($)

(Year Ended Mar. 31)	1998	1997	1996	1995	1994	1993	1992	1991	1990	1989
Tangible Bk. Val.	1.76	1.22	3.88	4.72	5.79	5.57	4.65	3.64	2.68	2.26
Cash Flow	1.84	1.54	1.41	1.10	1.23	1.30	1.25	1.08	0.82	0.57
Earnings	1.07	0.91	0.98	0.83	0.97	1.03	0.97	0.87	0.67	0.46
Dividends	0.12	0.12	0.12	0.15	0.12	0.12	Nil	Nil	Nil	Nil
Payout Ratio	11%	13%	12%	18%	12%	12%	Nil	Nil	Nil	Nil
Cal. Yrs.	1997	1996	1995	1994	1993	1992	1991	1990	1989	1988
Prices - High	14³/₄	15¹/₈	16	21¹/₄	19⁵/₈	22³/₄	NA	NA	NA	NA
- Low	11³/₈	10¹/₂	11¹/₈	12¹/₂	14¹/₈	14	NA	NA	NA	NA
P/E Ratio - High	14	17	16	26	20	22	NA	NA	NA	NA
- Low	11	12	11	15	15	14	NA	NA	NA	NA

Income Statement Analysis (Million $)

	1998	1997	1996	1995	1994	1993	1992	1991	1990	1989
Revs.	483	455	398	269	254	252	260	236	179	123
Oper. Inc.	56.6	52.5	46.7	38.2	39.9	42.5	36.4	29.4	26.0	17.7
Depr.	13.8	12.9	9.7	6.2	6.0	6.0	5.8	4.2	3.0	2.2
Int. Exp.	10.3	7.4	2.8	0.1	0.1	0.4	1.3	1.6	1.9	0.7
Pretax Inc.	33.5	31.5	37.3	31.8	36.0	37.9	32.4	24.4	22.4	15.3
Eff. Tax Rate	42%	41%	41%	41%	39%	39%	40%	40%	40%	40%
Net Inc.	19.3	18.5	22.1	18.7	21.9	23.1	19.4	14.6	13.4	9.2

Balance Sheet & Other Fin. Data (Million $)

	1998	1997	1996	1995	1994	1993	1992	1991	1990	1989
Cash	9.5	18.7	70.3	25.3	59.2	55.1	47.7	21.4	14.0	NA
Curr. Assets	228	208	216	155	155	146	126	102	90.0	NA
Total Assets	386	358	317	225	180	161	143	116	102	74.0
Curr. Liab.	99	92.9	70.4	59.1	35.5	35.7	37.6	43.2	48.8	NA
LT Debt	132	129	75.0	2.3	Nil	Nil	Nil	Nil	Nil	Nil
Common Eqty.	150	132	168	162	145	125	105	72.9	53.7	45.1
Total Cap.	282	261	243	164	145	126	105	72.9	53.7	45.1
Cap. Exp.	11.9	9.5	7.3	5.0	3.7	4.3	6.0	6.0	4.0	4.3
Cash Flow	33.1	31.5	31.8	24.9	27.8	29.2	25.2	18.7	16.5	11.4
Curr. Ratio	2.3	2.2	3.1	2.6	4.4	4.1	3.4	2.4	1.8	NA
% LT Debt of Cap.	46.8	49.5	30.9	1.4	Nil	Nil	Nil	Nil	Nil	Nil
% Net Inc.of Revs.	4.0	4.1	5.6	6.9	8.6	9.2	7.5	6.2	7.5	7.5
% Ret. on Assets	5.2	5.5	8.2	9.2	12.8	15.2	NA	16.0	15.3	14.2
% Ret. on Equity	13.7	12.4	13.4	12.2	16.2	20.1	NA	27.6	27.2	22.5

Data as orig. reptd.; bef. results of disc. opers. and/or spec. items. Per share data adj. for stk. divs. as of ex-div. date. Bold denotes diluted EPS (FASB 128). E-Estimated. NA-Not Available. NM-Not Meaningful. NR-Not Ranked.

Office—911 Wilshire Blvd., Suite 700, Los Angeles, CA 90017. **Tel**—(213) 996-2200. **Fax**—(213) 996-2290. **Website**—http://www.dames.com **Chrmn, Pres & CEO**—A. C. Darrow. **EVP, CFO & Investor Contact**—Mark A. Snell. **Dirs**—U. M. Burns, R. F. Clarke, A. C. Darrow, G. R. Krieger, G. D. Leal, A. E. Macdonald, A. R. Moore, M. R. Peevey, H. Peipers, A. E. Williams. **Transfer Agent & Registrar**—ChaseMellon Shareholder Services, Los Angeles. **Incorporated**—in Delaware in 1992. **Empl**— 7,500. **S&P Analyst**: N.J.DeVita

Daniel Industries 714R

NYSE Symbol **DAN**

In S&P SmallCap 600

03-OCT-98

Industry:
Manufacturing (Diversified)

Summary: DAN makes fluid measurement, flow control, actuation and analytical products for natural gas and oil producers, transporters and refiners.

Quantitative Evaluations

Recent Price • 13⅛	Yield • 1.4%
52 Wk Range • 22¼-10⅞	12-Mo. P/E • 15.0

Outlook
(1 Lowest—5 Highest)
• **3⁻**

Fair Value
• **16½**

Risk
• **Low**

Earn./Div. Rank
• **B-**

Technical Eval.
• **Bullish** since 9/98

Rel. Strength Rank
(1 Lowest—99 Highest)
• **52**

Insider Activity
• **Neutral**

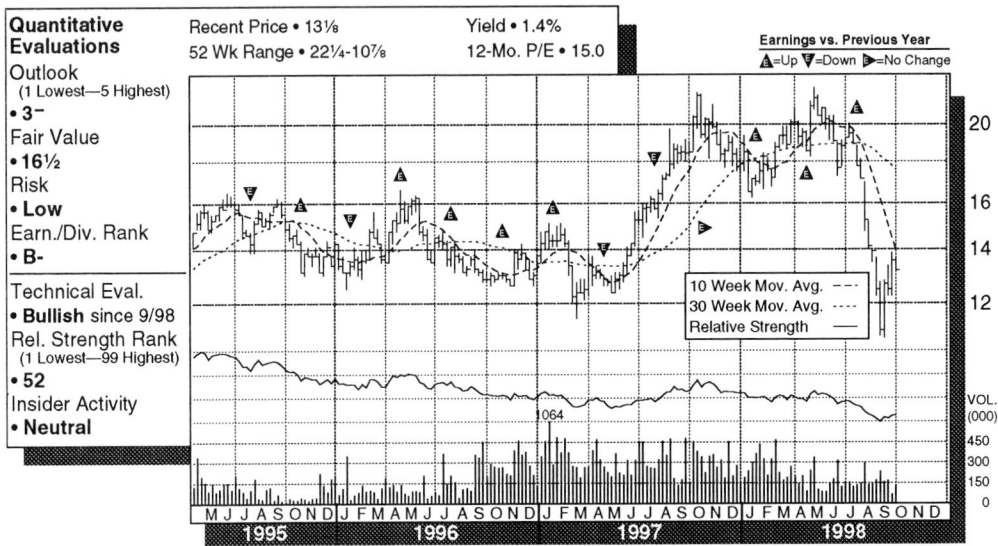

Earnings vs. Previous Year
▲=Up ▼=Down ▶=No Change

10 Week Mov. Avg. – – –
30 Week Mov. Avg. ----
Relative Strength —

VOL. (000)

Business Profile - 22-SEP-98

This company has utilized both internal growth and acquisitions to post revenue and earnings gains in 1997. Bettis Corp., the company's valve actuator business, has grown substantially in recent years, largely due to acquisitions. Three acquisitions in mid-1996 contributed over half of Bettis' 31% sales growth in 1997. Management believes that results in 1998 will improve over 1997, following the complete integration of the three most recent acquisitions and the reorganization of the metering business. Although the valve product division posted lower sales overall in 1997 than in 1996, reflecting a lower number of major oil pipeline projects relative to the prior year, sales in the first half of 1998 increased, year to year.

Operational Review - 22-SEP-98

Revenues for the six months ended June 30, 1998, advanced 15%, year to year, primarily reflecting market strength from the actuator business in Canada and valve business in Latin America. With improved gross margins from the valve and actuator businesses, and well controlled selling, engineering and administrative expenses, income from operations was up 115%. Following a 6.5% increase in interest and other expenses, and after taxes at 37.5% versus 41.6%, net income climbed 155%, to $8,135,000 ($0.45 a share) from $3,195,000 ($0.18).

Stock Performance - 02-OCT-98

In the past 30 trading days, DAN's shares have declined 5%, compared to a 7% fall in the S&P 500. Average trading volume for the past five days was 25,440 shares, compared with the 40-day moving average of 30,500 shares.

Key Stock Statistics

Dividend Rate/Share	0.18	Shareholders	1,200
Shs. outstg. (M)	17.5	Market cap. (B)	$0.231
Avg. daily vol. (M)	0.030	Inst. holdings	65%
Tang. Bk. Value/Share	6.40		
Beta	0.73		

Value of $10,000 invested 5 years ago: $ 12,055

Fiscal Year Ending Dec. 31

	1998	1997	1996	1995	1994	1993
Revenues (Million $)						
1Q	67.21	58.91	39.45	42.30	40.58	35.90
2Q	77.30	67.23	41.00	38.74	48.63	43.11
3Q	—	71.33	39.84	42.03	56.24	50.01
4Q	—	71.39	47.18	45.50	58.32	51.26
Yr.	—	268.9	167.5	168.6	203.8	180.3
Earnings Per Share ($)						
1Q	0.21	0.04	0.18	0.06	0.07	0.00
2Q	0.24	0.15	0.23	-0.81	0.01	0.10
3Q	—	0.21	0.21	0.11	0.04	0.15
4Q	—	0.21	0.19	-0.41	0.13	0.20
Yr.	—	0.61	0.81	-1.06	0.11	0.42

Next earnings report expected: NA

Dividend Data (Dividends have been paid since 1948.)

Amount ($)	Date Decl.	Ex-Div. Date	Stock of Record	Payment Date
0.045	Nov. 18	Nov. 26	Dec. 01	Dec. 15 '97
0.045	Mar. 04	Mar. 12	Mar. 16	Mar. 30 '98
0.045	May. 15	Jun. 11	Jun. 15	Jun. 29 '98
0.045	Aug. 05	Sep. 10	Sep. 14	Sep. 28 '98

 A Division of The McGraw-Hill Companies

STANDARD
&POOR'S
STOCK REPORTS

Daniel Industries, Inc.

714R
03-OCT-98

Business Summary - 22-SEP-98

Daniel Industries, Inc. (DAN), which provides fluid measurement, flow control, actuation and analytical products for oil and gas producers, transporters, and refiners, sold certain non-core assets, including its energy fabrication and fastener subsidiaries as part of restructuring efforts in 1995 and 1996. DAN's operations were significantly expanded through the December 1996 acquisition of Bettis Corp., a producer of valve actuators and control systems, for 4.9 million common shares.

Since 1930, DAN has manufactured products that employ "differential orifice management" to measure fluids, mainly natural gas. These orifice measurement products cause a decline in pressure as fluid flows through the device, with the decline in pressure measured and used to determine rates of flow and accumulated volumes.

Flow measurement and control products (53% of revenues from core operations in 1997) include orifice measurement devices and other types of flow measurement devices made by the company that use turbines or oval gear meters to determine flow and accumulated volumes of fluid, primarily of crude oil. To support these products, DAN also makes electronic instruments that instantaneously compute and display the rate of flow and accumulated volumes of fluid.

The company also makes valve actuators and controls used to remotely and automatically open or close quarter-turn or linear valves. These products are used by any industry that utilizes pipes to transport liquids or gases in supply, manufacture and distribution operations. The company believes that remote automatic operation of valves enhances environmental safety, reduces personnel requirements and provides an accurate, efficient and measurable means of controlling valve positioning in any application. In 1997, worldwide sales of valve actuators contributed 35% of revenues from core operations.

The remainder of the company's revenues from core operations come from the manufacture and sale of gate valves and the repair of pipeline valves. The company offers both slab and expanding gate valves with primary applications as pipeline block valves and for on/off service in liquid and gas systems. In addition, the company makes surge relief and flow control valves for liquid and gas pipeline applications.

The company continues to participate in a broad range of oil and gas industry markets, and, to a lesser extent, other industrial markets such as pulp and paper, water and wastewater treatment, and power generation. Management believes this diversification provides the company with a measure of stability that many oilfield service and equipment companies lack.

DAN sees continued growth in its key markets, noting its growing backlog, which stood at $72.5 million as of December 31, 1997. Although oil prices have fallen to prices not seen since the late 1980s, it believes the longer term prospects look promising, given increasing worldwide demand for hydrocarbons.

Per Share Data ($)

(Year Ended Dec. 31)	1997	1996	1995	1994	1993	1992	1991	1990	1989	1988
Tangible Bk. Val.	6.40	8.78	9.05	10.13	9.67	9.86	9.31	8.64	7.81	7.39
Cash Flow	1.16	1.35	-0.44	0.70	0.93	1.22	0.35	1.31	1.22	0.32
Earnings	0.61	0.81	-1.06	0.11	0.42	0.70	-0.18	0.78	0.60	-0.33
Dividends	0.18	0.18	0.23	0.18	0.18	0.18	0.18	0.18	0.18	0.18
Payout Ratio	30%	22%	NM	164%	43%	26%	NM	23%	30%	NM
Prices - High	21⅞	16⅝	16½	13¾	15⅞	15⅞	24½	17¾	16½	9⅞
- Low	11½	12½	12⅝	9⅞	10¾	10½	9⅛	13⅜	8⅝	6⅜
P/E Ratio - High	36	21	NM	NM	38	23	NM	23	28	NM
- Low	19	15	NM	NM	26	15	NM	17	14	NM

Income Statement Analysis (Million $)

	1997	1996	1995	1994	1993	1992	1991	1990	1989	1988
Revs.	269	167	169	204	180	210	202	171	170	147
Oper. Inc.	30.1	21.0	15.3	11.2	14.8	21.6	23.4	20.7	19.1	9.3
Depr.	9.7	6.6	7.5	7.1	6.1	6.3	5.8	5.5	6.4	6.6
Int. Exp.	3.0	2.0	2.0	1.9	2.1	2.4	2.8	3.0	3.1	2.4
Pretax Inc.	17.5	15.7	-18.5	2.1	8.1	13.0	-2.8	12.3	9.6	-5.4
Eff. Tax Rate	39%	38%	NM	38%	38%	35%	NM	34%	36%	NM
Net Inc.	10.6	9.9	-12.8	1.3	5.0	8.4	-2.0	8.1	6.2	-3.4

Balance Sheet & Other Fin. Data (Million $)

	1997	1996	1995	1994	1993	1992	1991	1990	1989	1988
Cash	7.6	7.0	3.9	2.5	23.2	29.2	31.2	12.7	10.8	2.0
Curr. Assets	135	98.0	109	112	105	112	132	98.0	89.0	81.0
Total Assets	234	234	164	187	178	177	192	156	144	139
Curr. Liab.	58.4	43.0	43.4	45.7	38.0	34.1	53.1	34.0	28.3	37.3
LT Debt	37.2	5.7	8.6	11.4	14.3	17.1	20.0	23.6	26.4	19.7
Common Eqty.	130	116	109	122	121	120	113	94.0	85.0	79.0
Total Cap.	176	128	121	142	140	143	139	122	115	101
Cap. Exp.	11.6	5.0	4.8	13.6	11.8	8.8	11.5	9.5	3.6	3.7
Cash Flow	20.3	16.4	-5.3	8.5	11.1	14.6	3.8	13.6	12.5	3.3
Curr. Ratio	2.3	2.3	2.5	2.4	2.8	3.3	2.5	2.9	3.1	2.2
% LT Debt of Cap.	21.1	4.5	7.1	8.1	10.2	12.0	14.4	19.4	22.9	19.4
% Net Inc.of Revs.	3.9	5.9	NM	0.6	2.8	4.0	NM	4.8	3.6	NM
% Ret. on Assets	5.2	5.8	NM	0.7	2.8	4.5	NM	5.4	4.3	NM
% Ret. on Equity	8.6	8.7	NM	1.1	4.2	7.1	NM	9.1	7.5	NM

Data as orig. reptd.; bef. results of disc. opers. and/or spec. items. Per share data adj. for stk. divs. as of ex-div. date. Yrs. ended Sep. 30 prior to 1997. E-Estimated. NA-Not Available. NM-Not Meaningful. NR-Not Ranked.

Office—9753 Pine Lake Dr., Houston, TX 77055. **Tel**—(713) 467-6000. **Website**—http://www.danielind.com **Chrmn & CEO**—R. C. Lassiter. **Pres & COO**—A. Newton. **Investor Contact**—J. M. Tidwell. **Dirs**—N. M. Avery, M. M. Carroll, R. F. Cox, G. Gayle Jr., W. A. Griffin, T. J. Keefe, R. C. Lassiter, L. E. Linbeck Jr., B. E. O'Neill. **Transfer Agent & Registrar**—Wachovia Bank of North Carolina. **Incorporated**—in Texas in 1965; reincorporated in Delaware in 1988. **Empl**— 1,800. **S&P Analyst:** C.C.P.

03-OCT-98

Industry:
Health Care (Medical Products & Supplies)

Summary: This company makes products for clinical health care markets in interventional cardiology, critical care and cardiovascular and vascular surgery.

Quantitative Evaluations

Recent Price • 20⅝
52 Wk Range • 30½-18¾

Yield • Nil
12-Mo. P/E • 15.6

Outlook
(1 Lowest—5 Highest)
• **4+**

Fair Value
• 27⅞

Risk
• **Average**

Earn./Div. Rank
• **B**

Technical Eval.
• **Bearish** since 7/98

Rel. Strength Rank
(1 Lowest—99 Highest)
• 57

Insider Activity
• **NA**

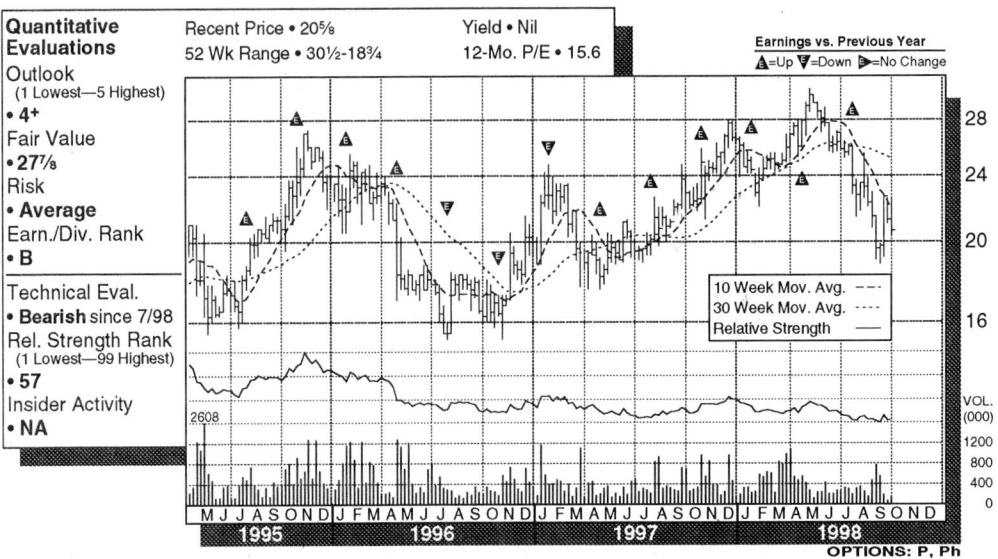

Earnings vs. Previous Year
▲=Up ▼=Down ▶=No Change

10 Week Mov. Avg. – – –
30 Week Mov. Avg. - - - -
Relative Strength ——

OPTIONS: P, Ph

Business Profile - 10-SEP-98

In August 1998, the company received CE mark approval for its second generation arterial puncture sealing device, VasoSeal ES, allowing sale throughout the European Union. VasoSeal VHD was clinically accepted and introduced in the U.S. in November 1995. In June 1998, the company reached an agreement with Fisher Scientific to distribute Datascope's new Genisphere life science research products in the U.S. and Puerto Rico. During the fourth quarter of FY 98 (Jun.), Datascope introduced the new Profile 8Fr. balloon catheter. During the first quarter of FY 99, the company expects to introduce a new balloon pump, the System 98. In August 1998, Datascope's directors announced a plan to repurchase up to $20 million of its common stock over an undefined period of time.

Operational Review - 10-SEP-98

Based on a preliminary report, net sales advanced 7.4% in the fiscal year ended June 30, 1998, due to continued growth in sales of patient monitoring products and increased sales of VasoSeal and InterVascular, Inc., products. Sales of cardiac assist products were flat. Year to year comparisons benefited from $5.1 million ($0.31 per share) in litigation settlement expenses incurred in the year earlier period, and net income rose 53%, to $21.6 million ($1.32 per share) from $14.1 million ($0.86). Excluding litigation expenses, net income increased 13%.

Stock Performance - 02-OCT-98

In the past 30 trading days, DSCP's shares have declined 7%, compared to a 7% fall in the S&P 500. Average trading volume for the past five days was 30,100 shares, compared with the 40-day moving average of 65,651 shares.

Key Stock Statistics

Dividend Rate/Share	Nil	Shareholders	900
Shs. outstg. (M)	15.6	Market cap. (B)	$0.321
Avg. daily vol. (M)	0.049	Inst. holdings	60%
Tang. Bk. Value/Share	12.39		
Beta	0.74		

Value of $10,000 invested 5 years ago: $ 8,088

Fiscal Year Ending Jun. 30

	1998	1997	1996	1995	1994	1993
Revenues (Million $)						
1Q	54.30	47.60	45.90	41.60	38.10	36.00
2Q	62.70	57.60	52.30	48.40	45.20	166.0
3Q	60.30	57.90	54.60	50.50	47.30	41.90
4Q	65.10	62.50	58.50	55.20	52.20	45.40
Yr.	242.0	225.6	211.3	195.7	182.8	166.0
Earnings Per Share ($)						
1Q	**0.16**	-0.20	0.19	0.17	0.15	0.13
2Q	**0.34**	0.31	0.76	0.27	0.24	0.21
3Q	**0.38**	0.35	0.33	0.28	0.26	0.20
4Q	**0.44**	0.40	-0.05	0.35	0.32	0.43
Yr.	**1.32**	0.86	1.24	1.07	0.97	0.97

Next earnings report expected: NA

Dividend Data

No cash has been paid.

Business Summary - 10-SEP-98

Competitive pressures in its core cardiac assist business and delayed access to the U.S. market for its line of vascular grafts and surgical patches slowed sales growth for medical product maker Datascope Corp. (DSCP) in FY 97 (Jun.).

DSCP manufactures products for clinical health care markets in cardiology, anesthesiology, cardiovascular and vascular surgery and for use in emergency medicine and critical care.

Intra-aortic balloon pumping (IABP) systems produced by DSCP's cardiac assist business (46% of sales in FY 97) increase the supply of oxygen-rich blood to the heart while reducing its demand for oxygen. As a pioneer in IABP systems, Datascope introduced the first balloon catheter capable of percutaneous insertion (by arterial puncture through the skin), an innovation which eliminated the need for surgical insertion and expanded the market for IABP products from cardiac surgery to the interventional cardiology market. The company continues to refine its IABP technology.

DSCP's patient monitoring products (39% of FY 97 sales) measure a broad range of physiological data designed to provide for patient safety and management of patient care. The company's monitors are capable of continuous and simultaneous measurement of multiple parameters, and are used in operating rooms, emergency rooms, critical care units, post-anesthesia care units and recover rooms, intensive care units, and labor and delivery rooms. The PASSPORT monitor is a portable, battery-powered, patient monitor that offers the features of a traditional bedside monitor in a transportable unit that can move with the patient to different settings in the hospital.

DSCP's Collagen Products division (8% of FY 97 sales, up from 4% of sales in FY 96) makes the VasoSeal Hemostasis Device, a product used to rapidly seal femoral artery punctures after catheterization procedures. In April 1997, DSCP received FDA approval to market its VasoSeal product for use following stent implantation. Stents are often implanted to support the arterial wall in conjunction with coronary and peripheral balloon angioplasty procedures. In August 1998, DSCP received CE market approval, for its second generation VasoSeal, ES. DSCP believes that it further enhanced VasoSeal's market penetration with the September 1997 FDA approval to allow deployment of its VasoSeal Hemostasis Device by health care professionals other than physicians.

DSCP's InterVascular, Inc. subsidiary makes a line of collagen-coated vascular grafts (7% of FY 97 sales) that are implanted surgically to replace diseased arteries. A government-imposed price reduction in France, InterVascular's single largest market, hurt sales through much of FY 97. The company expected sales growth to resume in FY 98, now that the InterGard collagen-coated grafts have received marketing clearance in Japan and the U.S.

Per Share Data ($)

(Year Ended Jun. 30)	1998	1997	1996	1995	1994	1993	1992	1991	1990	1989
Tangible Bk. Val.	NA	11.84	11.15	10.16	8.98	7.97	7.01	6.46	5.99	5.36
Cash Flow	NA	1.45	1.76	1.57	1.36	1.31	0.76	0.82	0.98	0.95
Earnings	1.32	0.86	1.24	1.07	0.97	0.97	0.47	0.55	0.60	0.69
Dividends	Nil	Nil	Nil	Nil	Nil	Nil	Nil	Nil	Nil	Nil
Payout Ratio	Nil	Nil	Nil	Nil	Nil	Nil	Nil	Nil	Nil	Nil
Prices - High	30$^1/_2$	28	25$^1/_2$	27$^1/_4$	19$^3/_4$	26$^1/_2$	41$^3/_4$	39$^1/_8$	11$^1/_4$	12$^1/_2$
- Low	21$^3/_8$	17$^1/_2$	15$^1/_4$	15$^1/_2$	12	11$^3/_4$	17$^3/_4$	9$^1/_2$	6$^1/_4$	8$^1/_2$
P/E Ratio - High	23	33	21	25	20	27	89	71	19	18
- Low	16	20	12	14	12	12	38	17	10	12

Income Statement Analysis (Million $)

	1998	1997	1996	1995	1994	1993	1992	1991	1990	1989
Revs.	NA	226	211	196	183	166	157	135	120	113
Oper. Inc.	NA	31.6	21.4	30.7	27.1	23.6	20.9	13.6	12.4	18.8
Depr.	NA	9.6	8.6	8.2	6.3	5.5	4.8	4.3	5.9	3.8
Int. Exp.	NA	0.0	0.1	0.1	0.0	0.0	0.2	0.2	0.2	0.1
Pretax Inc.	NA	17.8	26.8	25.0	22.1	22.1	10.6	12.5	14.1	16.0
Eff. Tax Rate	NA	21%	24%	30%	29%	29%	28%	31%	34%	35%
Net Inc.	NA	14.1	20.4	17.3	15.7	15.7	7.7	8.6	9.3	10.5

Balance Sheet & Other Fin. Data (Million $)

	1998	1997	1996	1995	1994	1993	1992	1991	1990	1989
Cash	NA	59.9	67.4	56.2	45.4	45.2	32.1	28.7	19.3	13.1
Curr. Assets	NA	156	163	144	138	122	110	98.0	92.0	79.0
Total Assets	NA	238	234	207	185	158	141	128	124	104
Curr. Liab.	NA	32.5	42.0	33.4	33.3	23.2	25.5	23.9	27.0	17.7
LT Debt	NA	Nil	Nil	Nil	Nil	Nil	Nil	Nil	0.1	0.4
Common Eqty.	NA	192	182	163	144	128	110	100	92.0	82.0
Total Cap.	NA	192	182	163	144	128	110	100	93.0	83.0
Cap. Exp.	NA	5.3	13.0	15.3	19.0	11.2	5.3	4.2	9.3	8.5
Cash Flow	NA	23.7	29.0	25.5	21.9	21.3	12.5	12.9	15.2	14.3
Curr. Ratio	NA	4.8	3.9	4.3	4.2	5.2	4.3	4.1	3.4	4.5
% LT Debt of Cap.	NA	Nil	Nil	Nil	Nil	Nil	Nil	Nil	0.1	0.5
% Net Inc.of Revs.	NA	6.3	9.7	8.8	8.6	9.5	4.9	6.4	7.7	9.3
% Ret. on Assets	NA	6.0	9.3	8.8	9.1	10.4	5.7	6.8	8.2	9.7
% Ret. on Equity	NA	7.5	11.8	11.3	11.5	13.1	7.3	8.9	10.7	14.6

Data as orig. reptd.; bef. results of disc. opers. and/or spec. items. Per share data adj. for stk. divs. as of ex-div. date. Bold denotes diluted FPS (FASB 128). E-Estimated. NA-Not Available. NM-Not Meaningful. NR-Not Ranked.

Office—14 Philips Pkwy., Montvale, NJ 07645-9998. **Tel**—(201) 391-8100. **Fax**—(201) 307-5400. **Chrmn, Pres & CEO**—L. Saper. **SVP, Secy & Investor Contact**—Murray Pitkowsky (201-307-5504). **VP, CFO & Treas**—S. E. Wasserman. **Dirs**—A. Abramson, D. Altschiller, W. L. Asmundson, J. Grayzel, G. Heller, A. Nash, L. Saper. **Transfer Agent**—Continental Stock Transfer & Trust Co., NYC. **Incorporated**—in New York in 1964. **Empl**— 1,200. **S&P Analyst:** John J. Arege

DEKALB Genetics

729

NYSE Symbol **DKB**

In S&P SmallCap 600

03-OCT-98

Industry: Agricultural Products

Summary: This producer of genetically enhanced seeds has agreed to be acquired by Monsanto for $100 per share in cash.

Quantitative Evaluations

Recent Price • 91

52 Wk Range • 98-23

Yield • 0.2%

12-Mo. P/E • NM

Outlook
(1 Lowest—5 Highest)
• **1**

Fair Value
• **61⅞**

Risk
• **Average**

Earn./Div. Rank
• **B+**

Technical Eval.
• **NA**

Rel. Strength Rank
(1 Lowest—99 Highest)
• **82**

Insider Activity
• **NA**

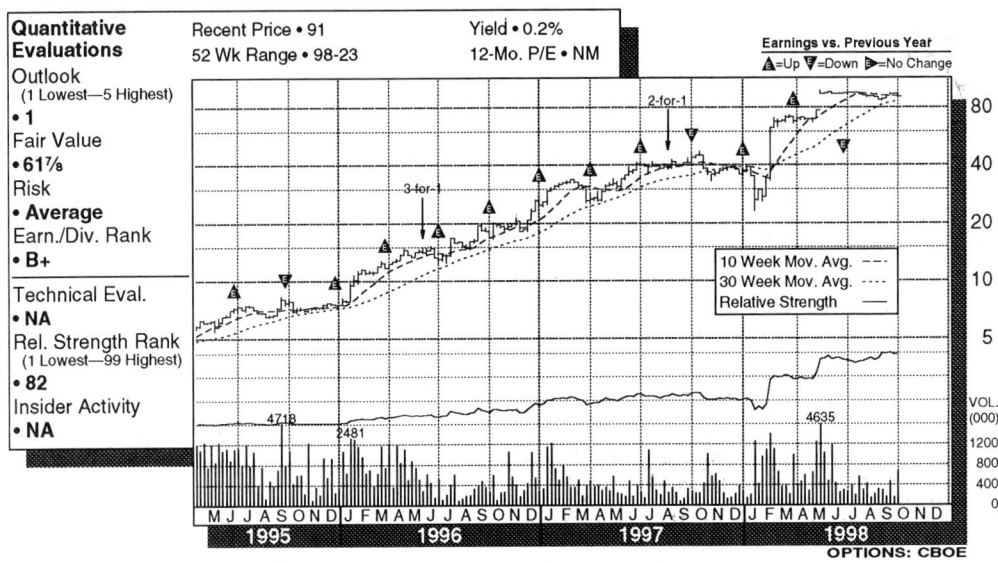

Earnings vs. Previous Year
▲=Up ▼=Down ▶=No Change

10 Week Mov. Avg. – – –
30 Week Mov. Avg. ⋯⋯
Relative Strength —

OPTIONS: CBOE

Business Profile - 17-JUL-98

In May 1998, DKB agreed to be acquired by Monsanto Company (NYSE: MTC), which currently owns 40% of the company's shares, for cash consideration of $100 per common share. The Roberts family, which owns 56% of the Class A voting shares, has agreed to tender its shares. The combination of the two companies will create one of the leading seed germplasm and technology companies in the world. A tender offer for the shares, which was to expire July 10, has been extended to August 7.

Operational Review - 17-JUL-98

Revenues in the nine months ended May 31, 1998, rose 13%, primarily reflecting the company's launch of Roundup Ready corn and the expansion of DKB's Bt corn hybrids line. Margins narrowed as profitability was hurt by significantly higher corn production costs; operating income fell 19%. Following higher net interest and depreciation charges, pretax income slid 30%. After taxes at 31.9%, versus 39.0%, net income decreased 21%, to $24.8 million ($0.68 a share), from $31.5 million ($0.88).

Stock Performance - 02-OCT-98

In the past 30 trading days, DKB's shares have increased 0.90%, compared to a 7% fall in the S&P 500. Average trading volume for the past five days was 133,060 shares, compared with the 40-day moving average of 62,049 shares.

Key Stock Statistics

Dividend Rate/Share	0.14	Shareholders	600
Shs. outstg. (M)	34.9	Market cap. (B)	$ 2.8
Avg. daily vol. (M)	0.076	Inst. holdings	29%
Tang. Bk. Value/Share	5.35		
Beta	1.64		

Value of $10,000 invested 5 years ago: $ 211,584

Fiscal Year Ending Aug. 31

	1998	1997	1996	1995	1994	1993
Revenues (Million $)						
1Q	62.80	67.10	50.10	49.20	40.80	47.20
2Q	213.8	192.3	180.3	148.4	143.0	129.2
3Q	219.9	178.6	137.0	104.9	107.3	92.40
4Q	—	13.40	20.10	25.10	28.90	22.70
Yr.	—	451.4	387.5	319.4	320.0	291.5
Earnings Per Share ($)						
1Q	0.08	0.06	0.00	-0.04	0.04	0.03
2Q	**0.53**	0.46	0.30	0.25	0.20	0.22
3Q	**0.08**	0.36	0.26	0.11	0.07	-0.06
4Q	—	-0.07	-0.04	-0.04	0.04	-0.10
Yr.	—	0.80	0.51	0.30	0.35	0.10

Next earnings report expected: mid October

Dividend Data (Dividends have been paid since 1989.)

Amount ($)	Date Decl.	Ex-Div. Date	Stock of Record	Payment Date
0.035	Nov. 14	Nov. 25	Nov. 28	Dec. 12 '97
0.035	Feb. 13	Feb. 25	Feb. 27	Mar. 13 '98
0.035	May. 15	May. 27	May. 29	Jun. 12 '98
0.035	Aug. 14	Aug. 26	Aug. 28	Sep. 11 '98

A Division of The McGraw-Hill Companies

Business Summary - 17-JUL-98

The worldwide economy is growing, and expanding per capita income in the developing nations of Asia and Latin America is creating increased demand for healthier diets. This is creating increased demand for American farmers' crops and DEKALB Genetics Corporation's products. DEKALB is engaged in the development and continual improvement of products of major importance to two segments of modern agriculture: seed (primarily corn, soybeans, sorghum and sunflower) and hybrid swine breeding stock.

As farmers look for a competitive advantage, such as increased yields from their agricultural inputs, they look to companies like DEKALB to develop genetically enhanced products such as hybrid seeds and swine breeding stock.

Seed operations include the research of hybrid corn, hybrid sorghum, sorghum-sudangrass, hybrid sunflower and varietal soybean seeds. The company contracts with growers to produce the seeds of such plants, and markets them under the DEKALB name. It also markets varietal alfalfa and other forage mixtures. Sales of hybrid corn accounted for about 69% of worldwide seed revenues in FY 97. The international division operates

in most areas of the world where corn, sorghum, soybean, alfalfa and sunflower seed are grown.

DEKALB Swine Breeders Inc. is involved in the research and development of hybrid swine breeding stock, and sells hybrid breeding swine and related services to hog producers in domestic and international markets. The company believes it is the largest such producer in the U.S. Research and development expenditures were $7.1 million and $6.7 million in FY 97 and FY 96, respectively.

Contributions in FY 97 (Aug.) were:

	Revs.	Profit
North American seed	65%	64%
International seed	22%	33%
Swine	13%	3%

Larger companies want to participate in the growing biotechnology for agriculture market; in March 1996, Monsanto invested approximately $157 million in DEKALB Genetics as part of a long-term research and development collaboration. Following the transaction, Monsanto owned 10% of the Class A voting shares and 43% of the Class B nonvoting stock.

Per Share Data ($)

(Year Ended Aug. 31)	1997	1996	1995	1994	1993	1992	1991	1990	1989	1988
Tangible Bk. Val.	4.53	3.73	2.77	2.59	2.31	2.36	2.10	2.17	3.13	2.79
Cash Flow	1.19	0.85	0.65	0.72	0.46	0.66	0.76	0.72	0.61	0.50
Earnings	0.80	0.52	0.30	0.35	0.10	0.32	0.47	0.45	0.36	0.25
Dividends	0.14	0.14	0.14	0.13	0.13	0.13	0.13	0.12	0.05	Nil
Payout Ratio	18%	27%	44%	38%	133%	40%	26%	26%	14%	Nil
Prices - High	$47^{1}/_{8}$	$26^{5}/_{8}$	$8^{3}/_{8}$	6	$5^{5}/_{8}$	$5^{3}/_{4}$	$7^{1}/_{4}$	$7^{1}/_{2}$	$6^{7}/_{8}$	$4^{1}/_{4}$
- Low	$24^{3}/_{4}$	$7^{1}/_{2}$	$4^{1}/_{4}$	$4^{1}/_{8}$	$3^{3}/_{4}$	$3^{7}/_{8}$	$4^{1}/_{2}$	5	$4^{1}/_{8}$	2
P/E Ratio - High	59	52	27	17	58	18	15	16	19	17
- Low	31	15	14	12	38	12	9	11	11	8

Income Statement Analysis (Million $)

	1997	1996	1995	1994	1993	1992	1991	1990	1989	1988
Revs.	451	388	319	320	292	300	276	274	255	230
Oper. Inc.	61.1	44.1	36.7	32.5	16.6	22.7	32.1	47.5	39.8	29.7
Depr.	13.8	11.3	11.1	11.5	11.3	10.4	9.5	9.2	8.6	8.7
Int. Exp.	7.5	8.3	9.6	8.2	8.7	8.0	7.2	9.1	1.8	3.1
Pretax Inc.	46.4	28.1	15.1	14.9	0.6	14.4	24.0	25.2	29.1	19.3
Eff. Tax Rate	38%	40%	27%	26%	NM	31%	35%	39%	24%	33%
Net Inc.	28.8	17.0	9.5	11.0	3.1	10.0	15.7	15.4	12.1	8.3

Balance Sheet & Other Fin. Data (Million $)

	1997	1996	1995	1994	1993	1992	1991	1990	1989	1988
Cash	5.2	23.3	3.0	6.2	3.5	9.4	1.3	0.8	17.8	19.8
Curr. Assets	227	190	175	164	167	156	126	103	112	123
Total Assets	450	363	323	319	316	303	264	238	199	203
Curr. Liab.	134	87.3	95.0	95.0	100	72.4	49.7	47.9	35.9	39.7
LT Debt	90.0	85.0	85.0	85.0	85.2	90.1	84.1	56.4	0.5	6.6
Common Eqty.	196	169	126	121	114	116	107	116	105	94.0
Total Cap.	306	269	223	219	211	223	208	185	159	161
Cap. Exp.	59.4	30.7	15.4	18.2	15.9	21.3	15.5	15.7	15.4	7.2
Cash Flow	42.6	28.3	20.6	22.5	14.4	20.4	25.2	24.6	20.7	17.0
Curr. Ratio	1.7	2.2	1.8	1.7	1.7	2.2	2.5	2.2	3.1	3.1
% LT Debt of Cap.	45.9	31.6	38.1	38.9	40.5	40.3	40.5	30.4	0.3	4.1
% Net Inc.of Revs.	6.4	4.4	3.0	3.4	1.1	3.3	5.7	5.6	4.7	3.6
% Ret. on Assets	7.1	5.0	3.0	3.5	1.0	3.5	6.5	7.0	6.0	4.2
% Ret. on Equity	15.8	11.6	7.7	9.3	2.7	9.0	14.7	13.9	12.2	8.5

Data as orig. reptd.; bef. results of disc. opers. and/or spec. items. Per share data adj. for stk. divs. as of ex-div. date. Bold denotes diluted EPS (FASB 128). E-Estimated. NA-Not Available. NM-Not Meaningful. NR-Not Ranked.

Office—3100 Sycamore Rd., DeKalb, IL 60115-9600.**Tel**—(815) 758-3461. **Fax**—(815) 758-3711. **Website**—http://www.dekalb.com **Chrmn & CEO**—B. P. Bickner. **Pres & COO**—R. O. Ryan. **VP-Fin & CFO**—T. R. Rauman.**SVP & Secy**—J. H. Witmer Jr. **Dirs**—C. J. Arntzen, A. Aves, B. P. Bickner, R. T. Fraley. T. R. Hamachek, P. H. Hatfield, V. R. Holt, D. C. Roberts, J. T. Roberts, R. O. Ryan, H. B. White, W. Ziegler. **Transfer Agent**—American Stock Transfer & Trust Co., NYC.**Incorporated**—in Delaware in 1988. **Empl**— 2,000. **S&P Analyst:** Robert J. Izmirlian

03-OCT-98

Industry:
Insurance (Life & Health)

Summary: Through subsidiaries, Delphi provides a diverse portfolio of life, long-term disability and personal accident insurance to the employee benefits market.

Quantitative Evaluations		
Outlook (1 Lowest—5 Highest)	• **NA**	
Fair Value	• **NA**	
Risk	• **Low**	
Earn./Div. Rank	• **B**	
Technical Eval.	• **NA**	
Rel. Strength Rank (1 Lowest—99 Highest)	• **28**	
Insider Activity	• **NA**	

Recent Price • 39¼
52 Wk Range • 63-35¾

Yield • Nil
12-Mo. P/E • 8.1

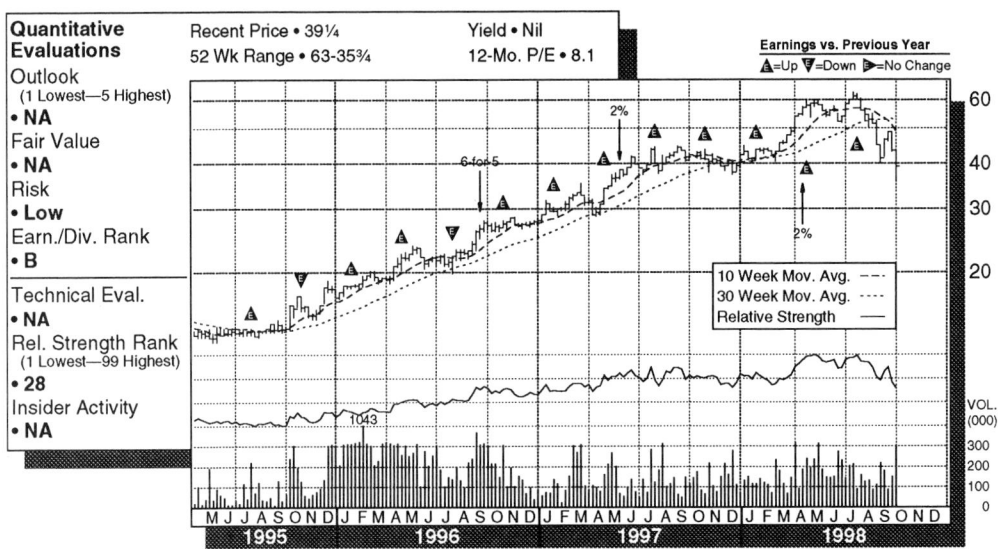

Earnings vs. Previous Year
▲=Up ▼=Down ▶=No Change

10 Week Mov. Avg. ---
30 Week Mov. Avg. ·····
Relative Strength —

Business Profile - 04-AUG-98

This insurance holding company provides group employee benefits, including life, excess workers' compensation, long-term disability and special accident insurance. It also provides asset accumulation products, primarily annuities, to individuals and groups. In addition to its focus on the employee benefits market, DFG has emphasized the acquisition of blocks of insurance business and other financial services companies, and the active management of its investment portfolio. In June 1998, DFG acquired Matrix Absence Management, a leading provider of integrated disability services to the employee benefits market, for $35 million, consisting of 386,000 common shares and the balance in cash and notes.

Operational Review - 04-AUG-98

Total revenues in the first six months of 1998 rose 21%, year to year, reflecting increased insurance premiums and policy holder fees, greater investment income and sharply higher realized investment gains. Following a 9.6% increase in benefits and expenses, essentially flat interest expense and taxes at 33.2% in both periods, net income soared 66%, to $63,009,000 ($2.93 a share, after dividends on Capital Securities), from $37,945,000 ($1.81).

Stock Performance - 02-OCT-98

In the past 30 trading days, DFG's shares have declined 24%, compared to a 7% fall in the S&P 500. Average trading volume for the past five days was 64,660 shares, compared with the 40-day moving average of 32,797 shares.

Key Stock Statistics

Dividend Rate/Share	Nil	Shareholders	1,700
Shs. outstg. (M)	19.9	Market cap. (B)	$0.557
Avg. daily vol. (M)	0.040	Inst. holdings	38%
Tang. Bk. Value/Share	29.74		
Beta	0.82		

Value of $10,000 invested 5 years ago: $ 33,795

Fiscal Year Ending Dec. 31

	1998	1997	1996	1995	1994	1993
Revenues (Million $)						
1Q	171.2	139.1	102.2	86.95	88.77	99.1
2Q	152.4	127.6	120.7	96.80	93.23	104.4
3Q	—	135.5	128.7	92.66	93.30	107.2
4Q	—	133.4	136.0	103.4	90.00	115.6
Yr.	—	535.6	487.3	379.8	365.3	426.3
Earnings Per Share ($)						
1Q	**1.87**	1.01	0.59	0.23	0.33	0.82
2Q	**1.06**	0.79	0.64	0.65	0.42	1.00
3Q	—	0.99	0.71	0.55	0.69	0.92
4Q	—	0.93	0.78	0.58	0.27	0.76
Yr.	—	3.73	2.77	2.02	1.71	3.49

Next earnings report expected: late October

Dividend Data

Amount ($)	Date Decl.	Ex-Div. Date	Stock of Record	Payment Date
2%	Apr. 02	Apr. 16	Apr. 20	May. 04 '98

A Division of The McGraw-Hill Companies

Business Summary   04 AUG-98

Delphi Financial Group, Inc., is the parent company of Reliance Standard Life Insurance Co., and Safety National Casualty Corp. DFG provides group employee benefits including life, short-term and long-term disability, excess workers' compensation, special accident and dental insurance. Premiums generated from group employee benefit products totaled $355.9 million in 1997 ($331.4 million a year earlier). The company's asset accumulation business, which consists mostly of annuity products, benefits from an investment portfolio intensively managed to reduce risk. Asset accumulation premiums totaled $3.1 million in 1997 ($2.1 million in 1996).

DFG's operating strategy is to offer financial products and services that have the potential for significant growth or that require expertise to meet the specialized needs of customers. The successful implementation of this strategy over the past decade has led to impressive financial results. Over the past ten years, net income has grown from $5.0 million to $75 million, a compound annual growth rate of over 30%.

DFG has posted these results by positioning itself in the fast-growing niches of a fast growing industry. It sells employee benefit policies to smaller companies. It is from these companies that nearly all of the employment growth in the U.S. economy has occurred over the past decade. The average size of DFG's insured groups ranges from 100 to 300 employees. The fact that DFG's clients are small companies is significant because these clients allow DFG to retain pricing integrity. This means that none of them is large enough to force insurance suppliers, like Delphi, to accept wafer-thin margins.

Delphi's investment portfolio is an important component of its profitability. Net investment income accounted for 30% of total revenue in 1997. The company manages the portfolio with an emphasis on liquidity and yield, while minimizing risks associated with interest rate fluctuations and credit quality. The weighted average annual yield on DFG's investment portfolio was 7.8% in 1997, compared with 8.5% in 1996.

Per Share Data ($)

(Year Ended Dec. 31)	1997	1996	1995	1994	1993	1992	1991	1990	1989	1988
Tangible Bk. Val.	21.45	14.48	8.72	3.86	6.20	10.72	9.59	8.19	NA	NA
Oper. Earnings	NA	NA	NA	NA	NA	NA	NA	NA	NA	NA
Earnings	3.73	2.77	2.02	1.71	3.49	1.91	1.14	1.31	1.71	1.02
Dividends	Nil	Nil	Nil	Nil	Nil	Nil	Nil	Nil	Nil	Nil
Payout Ratio	Nil	Nil	Nil	Nil	Nil	Nil	Nil	Nil	Nil	Nil
Prices - High	44³/₄	28¹/₂	19	20¹/₄	20⁵/₈	12	8	13	NA	NA
- Low	28¹/₄	16⁷/₈	12⁷/₈	13¹/₄	11	4⁵/₈	5	6³/₈	NA	NA
P/E Ratio - High	12	10	9	12	6	6	7	10	NA	NA
- Low	8	6	6	8	3	2	4	5	NA	NA

Income Statement Analysis (Million $)

	1997	1996	1995	1994	1993	1992	1991	1990	1989	1988
Life Ins. In Force	56,955	51,625	43,468	45,559	39,744	33,148	25,994	20,609	13,739	NA
Prem. Inc.: Life	146	147	129	129	126	107	88.0	75.0	73.0	62.0
Prem. Inc.: A & H	161	187	130	118	103	92.7	83.9	77.7	81.7	70.4
Prem. Inc.: Other	48.4	61.3	2.1	1.7	6.3	3.1	8.0	10.0	6.0	0.9
Net Invest. Inc.	160	155	117	107	177	134	133	149	136	84.0
Total Revs.	536	487	380	365	426	356	333	304	296	217
Pretax Inc.	113	81.3	47.4	37.4	72.9	37.2	24.0	24.4	28.0	14.5
Net Oper. Inc.	NA	NA	NA	NA	NA	NA	NA	NA	NA	NA
Net Inc.	75.0	53.8	30.5	25.8	46.8	24.6	16.8	18.8	20.2	12.4

Balance Sheet & Other Fin. Data (Million $)

	1997	1996	1995	1994	1993	1992	1991	1990	1989	1988
Cash & Equiv.	50.6	89.7	16.7	1.0	94.0	107	76.0	123	NA	NA
Premiums Due	235	215	183	181	39.0	Nil	Nil	Nil	Nil	Nil
Invest. Assets: Bonds	2,165	1,892	1,554	1,671	1,483	1,369	1,319	1,333	NA	NA
Invest. Assets: Stocks	Nil	74.0	127	156	225	167	218	164	NA	NA
Invest. Assets: Loans	Nil	Nil	Nil	Nil	Nil	Nil	Nil	Nil	Nil	Nil
Invest. Assets: Total	2,430	2,295	1,775	1,964	1,948	1,775	1,711	1,898	1,386	1,217
Deferred Policy Costs	NA	94.5	94.4	114	112	Nil	Nil	Nil	Nil	Nil
Total Assets	3,204	2,858	2,327	2,474	2,344	2,184	2,005	2,197	1,541	1,367
Debt	480	950	336	360	310	164	173	187	205	230
Common Eqty.	509	367	223	170	201	129	114	98.0	51.0	31.0
% Return On Revs.	14.0	11.0	8.0	7.1	11.0	6.9	5.0	6.2	6.8	5.7
% Ret. on Assets	2.5	2.1	1.3	1.1	2.1	1.2	0.8	1.0	1.4	1.2
% Ret. on Equity	17.1	18.2	15.5	13.9	28.3	20.2	15.8	25.2	49.3	30.1
% Invest. Yield	6.7	7.6	6.6	5.4	9.5	7.7	8.1	10.6	11.2	11.6

Data as orig. reptd.; bef. results of disc. opers. and/or spec. items. Per share data adj. for stk. divs. as of ex-div. date. Bold denotes diluted EPS (FASB 128). E-Estimated. NA-Not Available. NM-Not Meaningful. NR-Not Ranked.

Office—1105 N. Market St., Suite 1230, Wilmington, DE 19899.**Tel**—(302) 478-5142.**Chrmn, Pres & CEO**—R. Rosenkranz. **Secy**—L. Eike. **VP**—C. W. Coulter. **Dirs**—E. A. Fox, C. P. O'Brien, L. S. Ranieri, R. Rosenkranz, T. L. Rhodes, R. M. Smith Jr., B. K. Werner. **Transfer Agent**—State Street Bank & Trust Co., Boston. **Incorporated**—in Delaware in 1987. **Empl**— 534. **S&P Analyst:** Michael Schneider

STANDARD &POOR'S
STOCK REPORTS

Delta and Pine Land

734C

NYSE Symbol **DLP**

In S&P SmallCap 600

03-OCT-98 **Industry:**
Agricultural Products

Summary: In May 1998 DLP, the largest commercial breeder, producer and marketer of cotton planting seed in the U.S., agreed to be acquired by Monsanto Co.

Quantitative Evaluations

Recent Price • 40⅞
52 Wk Range • 54-23½

Yield • 0.3%
12-Mo. P/E • NM

Outlook
(1 Lowest—5 Highest)
• **1⁻**

Fair Value
• **35⅞**

Risk
• **NA**

Earn./Div. Rank
• **B+**

Technical Eval.
• **NA**

Rel. Strength Rank
(1 Lowest—99 Highest)
• **54**

Insider Activity
• **Unfavorable**

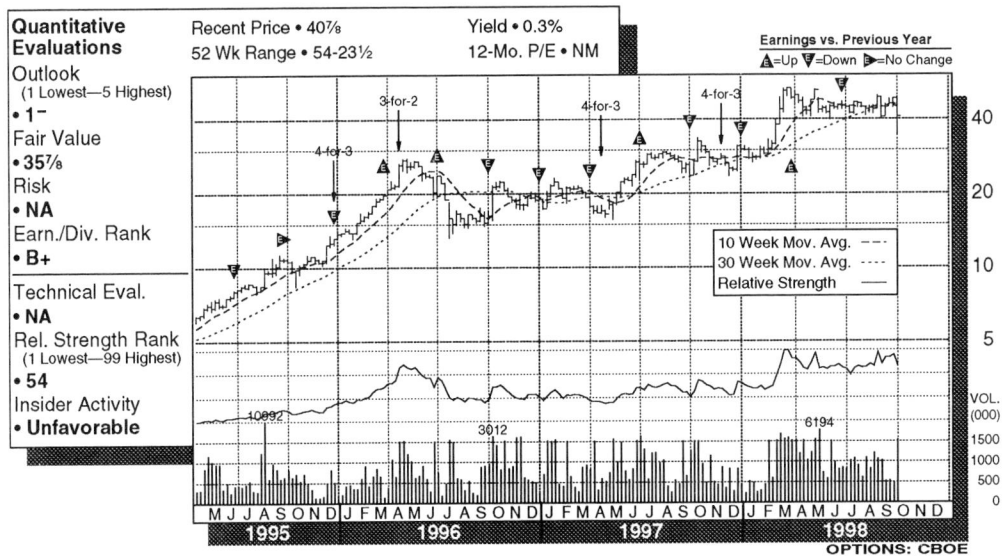

Business Profile - 12-AUG-98

In May 1998, the company entered into a merger agreement with Monsanto Company (NYSE: MTC), under which each DLP shareholder will receive .8625 shares of MTC stock. Subsequent to this agreement, MTC agreed to merge with American Home Products (NYSE: AHP). If the Monsanto/AHP merger closes before Delta's agreement with MTC, each DLP shareholder will receive .991875 shares of Monsanto common stock. Monsanto is a life sciences company, focused on crop protection, biotechnology, nutrition and pharmaceuticals.

Operational Review - 12-AUG-98

Net sales and licensing fees in the nine months ended May 31, 1998, rose 10%, year to year, driven by increased sales of Roundup Ready cotton seed. Margins narrowed, reflecting product development and promotional costs, research costs and the commencement of operations in China; operating income fell 9.4%. Following a substantial increase in acquisition-related expenses, pretax income fell 21%. After taxes at 39.1%, versus 35.6%, net income declined 25%, to $19,105,000 ($0.47 a diluted share, after preferred dividends), from $25,507,000 ($0.64).

Stock Performance - 02-OCT-98

In the past 30 trading days, DLP's shares have declined 7%, compared to a 7% fall in the S&P 500. Average trading volume for the past five days was 386,580 shares, compared with the 40-day moving average of 195,344 shares.

Key Stock Statistics

Dividend Rate/Share	0.12	Shareholders	400
Shs. outstg. (M)	38.3	Market cap. (B)	$ 1.6
Avg. daily vol. (M)	0.179	Inst. holdings	55%
Tang. Bk. Value/Share	1.71		
Beta	1.23		

Value of $10,000 invested 5 years ago: NA

Fiscal Year Ending Aug. 31

	1998	1997	1996	1995	1994	1993
Revenues (Million $)						
1Q	5.34	6.32	5.33	1.50	0.70	2.10
2Q	77.25	66.43	63.40	40.40	30.00	32.90
3Q	126.0	116.4	82.65	36.00	36.70	28.00
4Q	—	—	1.89	0.70	0.10	3.10
Yr.	—	183.3	153.3	78.70	67.50	66.10
Earnings Per Share ($)						
1Q	-0.12	-0.12	--	-0.07	-0.06	--
2Q	0.24	0.24	--	0.23	0.11	--
3Q	0.34	0.53	0.52	0.20	0.24	--
4Q	--	-0.49	-0.13	-0.06	-0.06	--
Yr.	--	0.17	0.40	0.29	0.23	0.26

Next earnings report expected: mid October

Dividend Data (Dividends have been paid since 1993.)

Amount ($)	Date Decl.	Ex-Div. Date	Stock of Record	Payment Date
0.030	Oct. 29	Nov. 26	Dec. 01	Dec. 15 '97
0.030	Feb. 09	Feb. 25	Mar. 01	Mar. 16 '98
0.030	Apr. 17	May. 28	Jun. 01	Jun. 12 '98
0.030	Jun. 26	Aug. 27	Aug. 31	Sep. 11 '98

A Division of The McGraw-Hill Companies

Business Summary - 12-AUG-98

Since 1915, Mississippi-based Delta and Pine Land Co. has been breeding, producing and marketing cotton planting seed for varieties of the crop that are grown primarily east of Texas and in Arizona. DLP may hark back to the waning days of the "Old South", but its business approach is thoroughly modern. In May 1998, the company entered into a merger agreement with Monsanto Company (NYSE: MTC), under which each DLP shareholder will receive .8625 shares of MTC stock. Subsequent to this agreement, MTC agreed to merge with American Home Products (NYSE: AHP). If the Monsanto/AHP merger closes before Delta's agreement with MTC, each DLP shareholder will receive .991875 shares of Monsanto common stock.

DLP is now the largest commercial breeder, producer and marketer of cotton planting seed in the U.S. It has used its extensive classical plant breeding programs to develop a gene pool necessary for producing cotton varieties with improved agronomic traits important to farmers, such as crop yield, and to textile manufacturers, such as enhanced fiber characteristics. Its cotton varieties are produced under the brand names Deltapine, Paymaster, Sure Grow and Supima. In 1980, DLP added soybean seed and in 1988 hybrid sorghum seed to its product line. In connection with its seed operations, DLP farms about 2,000 acres primarily for production of cotton and soybean foundation seed.

The company has annual agreements with various growers to produce seed for cotton and soybeans. The growers plant seed purchased from DLP, and if the seed meets the company's standards upon harvest, DLP is obligated to purchase specified minimum quantities of seed at prices equal to the commodity market price of the seed plus a grower premium. The company then conditions the seed for sale.

The company has a collaborative licensing agreement with Monsanto Co. that provides for the commercialization of Monsanto's Bollgard technology in the company's NuCOTN cotton varieties. Bollgard is toxic to certain lepidopteran larvae, the principal cotton pests in many cotton growing areas. Net of plowdowns and replants, approximately 2,421,000 acres of Bollgard cotton seed and 812,000 acres of Roundup Ready cotton seed (a variety specially bred for use with Monsanto's popular herbicide) were planted in FY 97; according to the USDA, DLP's transgenic products accounted for around 23% of the cotton acres planted in 1997.

Domestically, DLP promotes its cottonseed directly to farmers and sells cottonseed through distributors and dealers. As part of its long-term growth strategy, the company began to focus on the international marketing of its products, mainly cottonseed. A joint venture cotton seed conditioning and storage facility in China began operations in December 1997.

Per Share Data ($)

(Year Ended Aug. 31)	1997	1996	1995	1994	1993	1992	1991	1990	1989	1988
Tangible Bk. Val.	1.71	1.63	1.13	0.81	0.81	NA	NA	NA	NA	NA
Cash Flow	0.31	0.50	0.37	0.29	0.33	NA	NA	NA	NA	NA
Earnings	0.17	0.39	0.29	0.23	0.26	0.25	NA	NA	NA	NA
Dividends	0.08	0.06	0.05	0.05	0.02	NA	NA	NA	NA	NA
Payout Ratio	47%	16%	16%	20%	4%	NA	NA	NA	NA	NA
Prices - High	33⅝	27⅞	14	5⅜	5⅛	NA	NA	NA	NA	NA
- Low	15⅝	13⅛	4¾	3½	3⅜	NA	NA	NA	NA	NA
P/E Ratio - High	NM	71	48	24	20	NA	NA	NA	NA	NA
- Low	NM	33	17	15	13	NA	NA	NA	NA	NA

Income Statement Analysis (Million $)

	1997	1996	1995	1994	1993	1992	1991	1990	1989	1988
Revs.	183	153	78.7	67.5	66.1	68.4	63.2	NA	NA	NA
Oper. Inc.	37.2	31.2	20.1	14.9	17.1	NA	NA	NA	NA	NA
Depr.	5.1	4.0	2.7	2.2	2.0	NA	NA	NA	NA	NA
Int. Exp.	2.2	2.4	1.8	1.2	2.1	NA	NA	NA	NA	NA
Pretax Inc.	9.7	23.7	16.0	12.0	13.4	12.5	9.6	NA	NA	NA
Eff. Tax Rate	29%	36%	37%	36%	38%	NA	NA	NA	NA	NA
Net Inc.	6.9	15.3	10.1	7.7	8.3	7.9	6.1	NA	NA	NA

Balance Sheet & Other Fin. Data (Million $)

	1997	1996	1995	1994	1993	1992	1991	1990	1989	1988
Cash	1.9	0.6	5.6	1.1	NA	NA	NA	NA	NA	NA
Curr. Assets	145	112	29.8	24.8	20.9	24.1	16.7	NA	NA	NA
Total Assets	221	180	75.8	63.6	43.9	43.6	35.2	NA	NA	NA
Curr. Liab.	113	76.0	19.3	15.8	15.2	20.2	15.2	NA	NA	NA
LT Debt	30.5	31.5	11.3	12.0	Nil	13.8	3.6	NA	NA	NA
Common Eqty.	72.5	69.3	43.4	34.4	28.1	11.2	16.1	NA	NA	NA
Total Cap.	103	104	56.5	47.8	NA	NA	NA	NA	NA	NA
Cap. Exp.	17.1	16.0	8.8	3.2	2.3	NA	NA	NA	NA	NA
Cash Flow	11.9	19.3	12.8	9.9	10.3	NA	NA	NA	NA	NA
Curr. Ratio	1.3	1.5	1.5	1.6	1.4	1.2	1.1	NA	NA	NA
% LT Debt of Cap.	29.6	30.4	20.0	25.1	NA	NA	NA	NA	NA	NA
% Net Inc.of Revs.	3.8	10.0	12.8	11.4	12.6	11.5	9.7	NA	NA	NA
% Ret. on Assets	3.5	11.4	14.5	14.3	19.0	20.0	NA	NA	NA	NA
% Ret. on Equity	9.7	26.0	26.0	24.6	42.2	57.9	NA	NA	NA	NA

Data as orig. reptd.; bef. results of disc. opers. and/or spec. items. Per share data adj. for stk. divs. as of ex-div. date. Bold denotes diluted EPS (FASB 128). E-Estimated. NA-Not Available. NM-Not Meaningful. NR-Not Ranked.

Office—One Cotton Row, Scott, MI 38772. **Tel**—(601) 742-3351. **Chrmn & CEO**—R. D. Malkin. **Pres & COO**—F. M. Robinson. **VP-Fin & Treas**—W. T. Jagodinski. **Dirs**—N. Chua, J. E. M. Jacoby, R. Malkin, J. M. Murphy, S. P. Roth, R. E. Scheidt. **Transfer Agent & Registrar**—Harris Trust and Savings Bank, Chicago. **Incorporated**—in Delaware in 1978.**Empl**—580. **S&P Analyst:** Stephen J. Tekirian

03-OCT-98

Industry: Textiles (Specialty)

Summary: This company manufactures woven fabrics for apparel and home furnishings, sells T-shirts, fleece goods and sportswear, and casual apparel under the brand "Duck Head."

Quantitative Evaluations

Outlook (1 Lowest—5 Highest)
• **4**

Fair Value
• 5⅛

Risk
• **Average**

Earn./Div. Rank
• **C**

Technical Eval.
• **Bearish** since 6/98

Rel. Strength Rank (1 Lowest—99 Highest)
• **57**

Insider Activity
• **Favorable**

Recent Price • 4⅛

52 Wk Range • 6½-3⅛

Yield • 2.4%

12-Mo. P/E • NM

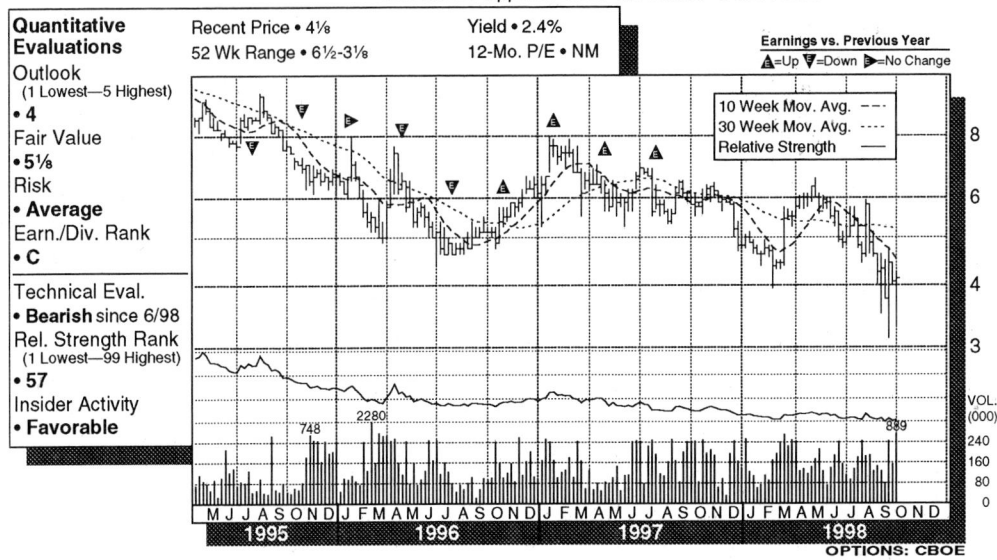

Earnings vs. Previous Year
▲=Up ▼=Down ▶=No Change

- 10 Week Mov. Avg. – – –
- 30 Week Mov. Avg. · · · ·
- Relative Strength ——

OPTIONS: CBOE

Business Profile - 26-MAY-98

This company produces textile fabrics and apparel, a business that has improved in FY 97 (Jun.) after a period of weak demand for textiles. In March 1998, DLW decided to close its Stevecoknit Fabrics division and sell its Nautilus International division. Currently, Stevecoknit's assets are being sold and DLW has retained a firm to sell Nautilus. The company believes these businesses should be disposed by the end of 1998. Results in the first nine months of FY 98 were hurt by a $7.5 million pretax restructuring charge related to the impairment of goodwill at Delta Apparel; and Duck Head recorded a $1.4 million pretax charge primarily related to the closing of certain retail stores.

Operational Review - 26-MAY-98

Net sales from continuing operations for the nine months ended March 28, 1998, rose fractionally, year to year, reflecting 10% higher sales at Duck Head and a 3% increase at Delta Mills Marketing which outweighed a 10% decline at Delta Apparel. Gross margins narrowed due to higher cost inventory being shipped in the last six months and lower unit billing prices at the Delta Apparel division. Results were further penalized by an $8,895,000 restructuring charge, higher SG&A expenses, and a rise in interest expense. Income from continuing operations fell 93%, to $846,000 ($0.03 a share), from $11,280,000 ($0.46). Results exclude losses from discontinued operations of $1.89 and $0.18 a share, respectively.

Stock Performance - 02-OCT-98

In the past 30 trading days, DLW's shares have declined 11%, compared to a 7% fall in the S&P 500. Average trading volume for the past five days was 177,780 shares, compared with the 40-day moving average of 50,582 shares.

Key Stock Statistics

Dividend Rate/Share	0.10	Shareholders	2,000
Shs. outstg. (M)	24.6	Market cap. (B)	$0.101
Avg. daily vol. (M)	0.070	Inst. holdings	41%
Tang. Bk. Value/Share	8.16		
Beta	0.42		

Value of $10,000 invested 5 years ago: $ 2,968

Fiscal Year Ending Jun. 30

	1998	1997	1996	1995	1994	1993
Revenues (Million $)						
1Q	—	144.5	141.0	141.3	146.4	153.0
2Q	—	162.7	150.6	142.5	149.3	163.0
3Q	121.5	163.9	143.3	150.9	155.2	176.4
4Q	149.9	180.8	165.3	162.8	162.8	194.2
Yr.	535.5	651.8	600.2	597.5	613.8	686.2
Earnings Per Share ($)						
1Q	—	0.08	0.05	0.17	0.07	0.28
2Q	—	0.09	0.02	0.02	-1.31	0.23
3Q	-0.17	0.11	0.05	0.01	0.07	0.00
4Q	0.07	0.03	-2.28	0.19	0.26	0.21
Yr.	-0.11	0.30	-2.56	0.42	-0.70	1.07

Next earnings report expected: mid October

Dividend Data (Dividends have been paid since 1988.)

Amount ($)	Date Decl.	Ex-Div. Date	Stock of Record	Payment Date
0.025	Nov. 06	Nov. 19	Nov. 21	Dec. 05 '97
0.025	Feb. 05	Feb. 18	Feb. 20	Mar. 06 '98
0.025	May. 07	May. 20	May. 22	Jun. 05 '98
0.025	Aug. 25	Sep. 02	Sep. 04	Sep. 19 '98

A Division of The **McGraw·Hill** Companies

Business Summary - 26-MAY-98

After posting a $63 million net loss in FY 96 (Jun.) due to high raw material costs and one time charges, operating results in FY 97 improved significantly for Delta Woodside Industries (DLW), a manufacturer of fabrics, apparel and physical equipment (Nautilus) machines. Contributions to revenues and operating income (in 000's) in FY 97 for each of the company's businesses:

	Revs.	Operating profits
Textiles	67%	$65,170
Apparel	30%	-3,960
Fitness equipment & other	3%	6,449

DLW's textile business was the primary driver behind the improved operating performance in FY 97. The textile segment includes the operations of Delta Mills Marketing Co., which sells finished woven fabrics ($336 million FY 97 sales), and Stevcoknit ($128 million), which produces and markets knitted fabrics for use in knit apparel. Although Stevcoknit improved its operating results in FY 97, in March 1998, DLW decided to put this division up for sale. Beginning in FY 92, both Delta Mills Marketing and Stevcoknit underwent consolidations and/or process improvements which, by the end of FY 97, had resulted in large reductions in manufacturing space and employees. At Stevcoknit, this was achieved without a material decline in total capacity. At the end of the first quarter of FY 98, the factories of both divisions were running near full capacity.

Driven by a turnaround at the company's Duck Head branded apparel business ($90 million), the operating loss in the apparel segment narrowed significantly during FY 97. Duck Head sells men's and boys' casual wear in major department stores, mostly in the southeastern U.S., and through 31 Duck Head outlet stores located in 10 states. At the end of FY 97, there were over 200 men's and 150 boys' Duck Head shops in department stores.

At Delta Apparel, the company's knit apparel business ($112 million) that produces knitted T-shirts, sweatshirts and polo-type shirts, results suffered. T-shirt price deterioration, and unseasonably cool Spring 1997 weather, which reduced demand for T-shirts during the typically strongest months of the year, contributed to the decline. The latter caused the company to run its Delta Apparel manufacturing facilities at lower production levels, which resulted in less overhead cost absorption and disappointing earnings for the fourth quarter of FY 97. Approximately one half of the yarn used by Delta Apparel is produced by Stevcoknit.

Nautilus manufactures exercise equipment for commercial club, institutional facility and personal home use. Sales in FY 97 dropped 25%, and its plants were running at 75% of capacity at the end of the first quarter of FY 98. In March 1998, DLW decided to sell Nautilus.

Per Share Data ($)

(Year Ended Jun. 30)	1998	1997	1996	1995	1994	1993	1992	1991	1990	1989
Tangible Bk. Val.	NA	8.16	7.80	10.64	11.75	12.72	12.08	8.17	6.76	6.82
Cash Flow	NA	1.54	-1.35	1.43	0.16	1.71	2.18	1.99	0.97	2.12
Earnings	-0.11	0.30	-2.56	0.42	-0.70	1.07	1.62	1.27	0.32	1.65
Dividends	0.10	Nil	0.30	0.40	0.40	0.40	0.35	0.30	0.30	0.20
Payout Ratio	NM	Nil	NM	95%	NM	37%	23%	26%	95%	12%
Prices - High	6½	8	8	11⅜	12½	16¼	22	25¼	11½	18
- Low	3⅞	4⅝	4⅜	7½	9¾	10¼	11½	5	3⅝	10¼
P/E Ratio - High	NM	27	NM	27	NM	15	14	20	36	11
- Low	NM	15	NM	18	NM	10	7	4	11	6

Income Statement Analysis (Million $)

	1998	1997	1996	1995	1994	1993	1992	1991	1990	1989
Revs.	NA	652	600	598	614	686	705	590	501	569
Oper. Inc.	NA	60.3	-24.4	46.0	38.1	65.6	90.7	72.6	44.1	73.6
Depr.	NA	30.3	29.5	24.6	21.3	17.1	13.7	13.6	12.3	8.6
Int. Exp.	NA	23.7	19.0	13.6	8.6	8.0	11.8	22.2	25.8	22.4
Pretax Inc.	NA	9.4	-83.6	17.8	-25.9	45.2	65.8	37.6	8.0	45.9
Eff. Tax Rate	NA	21%	NM	43%	NM	38%	39%	36%	25%	34%
Net Inc.	NA	7.4	-62.6	10.1	-17.3	28.2	40.0	24.0	6.0	30.3

Balance Sheet & Other Fin. Data (Million $)

	1998	1997	1996	1995	1994	1993	1992	1991	1990	1989
Cash	NA	2.7	6.3	0.7	2.1	3.7	0.8	0.4	1.6	1.9
Curr. Assets	NA	312	280	363	337	346	344	282	258	183
Total Assets	NA	558	538	610	567	574	525	434	414	331
Curr. Liab.	NA	82.4	312	76.2	95.0	84.0	78.0	176	191	109
LT Debt	NA	228	0.3	219	162	130	110	71.2	85.7	88.8
Common Eqty.	NA	225	217	286	285	336	319	173	127	127
Total Cap.	NA	467	218	527	466	484	443	255	222	221
Cap. Exp.	NA	23.2	67.4	32.2	29.9	55.7	42.9	15.9	21.7	60.3
Cash Flow	NA	37.7	-33.1	34.7	4.0	45.3	53.7	37.5	18.2	38.8
Curr. Ratio	NA	3.8	0.9	4.8	3.5	4.1	4.4	1.6	1.4	1.7
% LT Debt of Cap.	NA	48.8	Nil	41.6	34.8	26.9	24.9	27.9	38.6	40.2
% Net Inc.of Revs.	NA	1.1	NM	1.7	NM	4.1	5.7	4.1	1.2	5.3
% Ret. on Assets	NA	1.3	NM	1.7	NM	5.1	7.5	5.3	1.6	11.6
% Ret. on Equity	NA	3.3	NM	3.5	NM	8.6	15.0	15.2	4.7	27.6

Data as orig. reptd.; bef. results of disc. opers. and/or spec. items. Per share data adj. for stk. divs. as of ex-div. date. Bold denotes diluted EPS (FASB 128). E-Estimated. NA-Not Available. NM-Not Meaningful. NR-Not Ranked.

Office—233 North Main St., Hammond Square, Suite 200, Greenville, SC 29601. **Tel**—(864) 232-8301. **Pres & CEO**—E. E. Maddrey II. **EVP, Treas & CFO**—B. C. Rainsford. **VP, Secy & Investor Contact**—Jane H. Greer. **Dirs**—C. C. Guy, J. F. Kane, M. Lennon, E. E. Maddrey II, B. Mickel, B. A. Mickel, B. C. Rainsford. **Transfer Agent**—First Union National Bank of North Carolina, Charlotte. **Incorporated**—in South Carolina in 1972. **Empl**—7,400. **S&P Analyst:** Kathleen J. Connelly

Devon Energy

7689

ASE Symbol **DVN**

In S&P SmallCap 600

03-OCT-98

Industry:
Oil & Gas (Exploration & Production)

Summary: This independent oil and gas exploration, production and development company has grown rapidly through acquisitions in recent years.

Quantitative Evaluations

Outlook
(1 Lowest—5 Highest)
• **3**

Fair Value
• **35⅝**

Risk
• **Average**

Earn./Div. Rank
• **B**

Technical Eval.
• **Bearish** since 3/98

Rel. Strength Rank
(1 Lowest—99 Highest)
• **83**

Insider Activity
• **NA**

Recent Price • 32

52 Wk Range • 49⅛-26⅛

Yield • 0.6%

12-Mo. P/E • 20.4

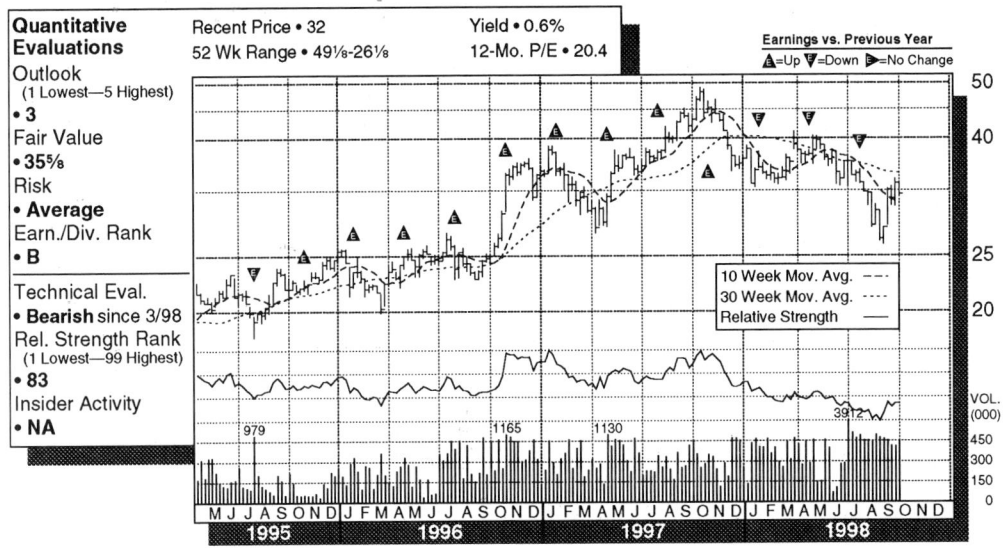

Earnings vs. Previous Year
▲=Up ▼=Down ▶=No Change

10 Week Mov. Avg. -----
30 Week Mov. Avg. ·······
Relative Strength ——

Business Profile - 16-SEP-98

In June 1998, the company said it planned to acquire Canada-based Northstar Energy (TSE: NEN) in exchange for 15.4 million common shares. Following the transaction, DVN would continue to have an equal oil and gas mix, with reserves of 1.2 Tcf of gas and 117 million bbl. of oil, and would rank among the top 15 independent U.S. exploration and production companies. If approved by shareholders, the acquisition was expected to be completed late in the third quarter or early in the fourth quarter. A cash tender offer for the units of beneficial interest of Burlington Resources Coal Seam Gas Royalty Trust expired in March. In September, DVN announced a joint venture to build a 126 mile gas gathering system in the Powder River basin of northeast Wyoming. Devon acquired Kerr-McGee's North American onshore oil and gas exploration and production business in late 1996.

Operational Review - 16 SEP 98

Revenues in the six months ended June 30, 1998, fell 19%, year to year, as a 3% production increase was outweighed by a 22% decline in commodity prices. With significantly higher lease operating expenses, production taxes, and depreciation, depletion and amortization charges, net income plunged 56%, to $17.8 million ($0.55 a share, diluted), from $40.1 million ($1.15).

Stock Performance - 02-OCT-98

In the past 30 trading days, DVN's shares have increased 7%, compared to a 7% fall in the S&P 500. Average trading volume for the past five days was 90,400 shares, compared with the 40-day moving average of 121,118 shares.

Key Stock Statistics

Dividend Rate/Share	0.20	Shareholders	900
Shs. outstg. (M)	32.3	Market cap. (B)	$ 1.0
Avg. daily vol. (M)	0.096	Inst. holdings	60%
Tang. Bk. Value/Share	17.22		
Beta	0.83		

Value of $10,000 invested 5 years ago: $ 21,971

Fiscal Year Ending Dec. 31

	1998	1997	1996	1995	1994	1993
Revenues (Million $)						
1Q	64.88	87.90	34.05	23.76	26.14	23.88
2Q	62.55	69.65	37.30	25.65	25.52	24.87
3Q	—	72.86	39.47	33.77	25.30	23.53
4Q	—	82.73	53.20	30.12	23.81	26.48
Yr.	—	313.1	164.0	113.3	100.8	98.76
Earnings Per Share ($)						
1Q	0.31	0.71	0.25	0.06	0.20	0.10
2Q	0.24	0.44	0.31	0.11	0.19	0.25
3Q	—	0.47	0.35	0.30	0.14	0.18
4Q	—	0.54	0.66	0.20	0.08	0.30
Yr.	—	2.17	1.52	0.66	0.64	0.92

Next earnings report expected: late October

Dividend Data (Dividends have been paid since 1993.)

Amount ($)	Date Decl.	Ex-Div. Date	Stock of Record	Payment Date
0.050	Dec. 02	Dec. 11	Dec. 15	Dec. 31 '97
0.050	Mar. 02	Mar. 12	Mar. 16	Mar. 31 '98
0.050	Jun. 01	Jun. 11	Jun. 15	Jun. 30 '98
0.050	Sep. 02	Sep. 11	Sep. 15	Sep. 30 '98

A Division of The **McGraw·Hill** Companies

Business Summary - 16-SEP-98

Devon Energy Corp. (DVN) is primarily engaged in the exploration, development, production and acquisition of oil and gas properties. The company currently owns interests in 1,700 oil and gas properties concentrated in five regions: the Permian Basin in southeastern New Mexico and West Texas; the San Juan Basin in northwestern New Mexico; the Rocky Mountain region in Wyoming; the Mid-continent region in Oklahoma and the Texas Panhandle; and the Western Canada Sedimentary Basin in Alberta.

Devon's strategy to build production, cash flow and earnings, entails acquiring properties, exploring for new reserves, and optimizing production from current properties. The company stresses its objective to boost value on a per-share basis, measured by BOE per share, rather than increasing the total value of reserves.

In June 1998, the company said it planned to acquire Canada-based Northstar Energy Corp. (TSE: NEN) in exchange for 15.4 million common shares, plus the assumption of $312 million of Northstar's debt. The transaction would create a $2 billion company, and propel Devon to rank among the top 15 independent U.S. exploration and production companies in terms of market capitalization and reserves. Devon would continue to

have a balanced oil and gas mix, with total reserves of 1.2 Tcf of gas and 117 million bbl. of oil. At Dember 31, 1997, reserves were 81.3 million bbl. of oil and 616 Bcf of gas, with an estimated pretax discounted value of $913 million.

Total production in 1997 amounted to 7.0 million bbl. of oil, 1.6 million bbl. of NGLs, and 69.3 Bcf of gas, or 20.2 million bbl. of oil equivalent (BOE), up 88% from the 1996 level. Average oil, NGL and gas prices were $19.05 per bbl., $13.38 per bbl. and $2.17 per Mcf, respectively, essentially unchanged from 1996 levels, on a BOE basis. Total production and operating expenses per BOE rose 5%, to $4.14. In 1997, DVN drilled 277 gross development wells (124.1 net), of which 268 (119.2) were productive, and 18 gross exploratory wells (7.6 net), of which 16 (1.5) were productive. At year-end 1997, the company had 1,760,465 gross developed acres (557,233 net) and 1,399,922 gross undeveloped acres (494,045 net).

In October 1996, Devon acquired Kerr-McGee's North American onshore exploration and production business, in exchange for nearly 10 million shares. The acquisition added 62 million BOE to 1996 reserves, and 370,000 net undeveloped acres. A cash tender for the units of beneficial interest of Burlington Resources Coal Seam Gas Royalty Trust expired in March 1998.

Per Share Data ($)

(Year Ended Dec. 31)	1997	1996	1995	1994	1993	1992	1991	1990	1989	1988
Tangible Bk. Val.	16.82	14.70	9.91	9.36	8.30	7.39	5.96	8.02	8.01	4.84
Cash Flow	4.99	3.53	2.38	2.20	2.28	2.38	1.79	0.95	0.86	0.99
Earnings	2.17	1.57	0.66	0.64	0.92	0.94	-1.99	0.03	0.01	-0.08
Dividends	0.20	0.14	0.12	0.12	0.09	Nil	Nil	Nil	Nil	Nil
Payout Ratio	9%	9%	18%	19%	10%	Nil	Nil	Nil	Nil	Nil
Prices - High	49¹/₈	37	26	26¹/₂	27¹/₄	16	12¹/₂	15¹/₄	14³/₄	6¹/₈
- Low	27³/₈	19⁷/₈	16³/₄	16	14³/₈	7⁵/₈	8⁵/₈	9³/₄	4⁵/₈	3⁵/₈
P/E Ratio - High	23	24	39	41	30	17	NM	NM	NM	NM
- Low	13	13	25	25	16	8	NM	NM	NM	NM

Income Statement Analysis (Million $)

	1997	1996	1995	1994	1993	1992	1991	1990	1989	1988
Revs.	306	163	112	101	99	70.6	29.6	30.7	27.7	21.3
Oper. Inc.	209	111	69.9	60.5	57.6	41.0	-11.8	13.8	10.9	8.9
Depr. Depl. & Amort.	85.3	43.4	38.1	33.7	28.2	19.9	7.8	8.0	7.3	7.4
Int. Exp.	0.3	5.3	7.0	5.4	3.4	2.6	2.2	2.2	2.2	2.2
Pretax Inc.	121	59.3	25.6	21.4	26.0	19.5	-21.1	4.1	1.4	-0.7
Eff. Tax Rate	38%	41%	43%	36%	26%	25%	NM	37%	37%	NM
Net Inc.	75.3	34.8	14.5	13.7	19.2	14.6	-15.0	2.6	0.9	-0.6

Balance Sheet & Other Fin. Data (Million $)

	1997	1996	1995	1994	1993	1992	1991	1990	1989	1988
Cash	42.1	9.4	8.9	8.3	19.6	5.6	7.7	7.3	4.6	1.8
Curr. Assets	93.2	43.4	24.9	25.3	36.4	24.1	17.2	18.1	11.1	6.6
Total Assets	846	746	422	351	286	226	102	124	98.0	89.0
Curr. Liab.	30.8	23.6	15.6	17.0	21.3	11.5	13.0	13.8	7.3	5.7
LT Debt	Nil	8.0	143	98.0	80.0	54.5	32.0	28.0	9.5	30.0
Common Eqty.	544	472	219	206	173	153	51.8	69.6	69.0	41.6
Total Cap.	795	711	396	332	262	212	86.0	106	86.0	77.0
Cap. Exp.	130	99	118	36.0	87.0	135	14.1	31.3	15.4	38.3
Cash Flow	161	78.2	52.6	47.5	47.4	32.8	15.6	8.2	7.4	6.9
Curr. Ratio	3.0	1.8	1.6	1.5	1.7	2.1	1.3	1.3	1.5	1.1
% LT Debt of Cap.	Nil	1.2	36.1	29.5	30.6	25.7	37.2	26.5	11.1	38.9
% Ret. on Assets	9.5	6.0	3.8	4.2	7.5	6.2	NM	2.3	0.9	NM
% Ret. on Equity	14.8	10.1	6.8	7.1	11.7	9.3	NM	0.3	0.1	NM

Data as orig. reptd.; bef. results of disc. opers. and/or spec. items. Per share data adj. for stk. divs. as of ex-div. date. Bold denotes diluted EPS (FASB 128). E-Estimated. NA-Not Available. NM-Not Meaningful. NR-Not Ranked.

Office—20 N. Broadway, Suite 1500, Oklahoma City, OK 73102-8260. **Organized**—in Oklahoma in 1971. **Tel**—(405) 235-3611. **Website**—http:// www.devonenergy.com. **Chrmn**—John . W. Nichols. **Pres & CEO**—J. Larry Nichols. **VP-Fin**—W. T. Vaughn.**Secy**—M. J. Moon. **Treas**—G. L. McGee. **Investor Contact**—Vince White (405-552-4505). **Dirs**—L. R. Corbett, T. F. Ferguson, D. M. Gavrin, M. E. Gellert, T. J. McDaniel, J. L. Nichols, J. W. Nichols, H. R. Sanders Jr., L. H. Towell.**Transfer Agent & Registrar**—Boston EquiServe. **Empl**— 383. **S&P Analyst:** Ephraim Juskowicz

STANDARD &POOR'S
STOCK REPORTS

DeVry Inc.

745N

NYSE Symbol **DV**

In S&P SmallCap 600

06-OCT-98

Industry: Services (Commercial & Consumer)

Summary: DeVry owns and operates the DeVry Institutes, the Keller Graduate School of Management, Corporate Educational Services and Becker CPA Review.

Quantitative Evaluations

Recent Price • 21
52 Wk Range • 26¾-12½

Yield • Nil
12-Mo. P/E • 47.7

Outlook (1 Lowest—5 Highest)
• **3⁻**

Fair Value
• **26⅞**

Risk
• **Average**

Earn./Div. Rank
• **B**

Technical Eval.
• **NA**

Rel. Strength Rank (1 Lowest—99 Highest)
• **76**

Insider Activity
• **Favorable**

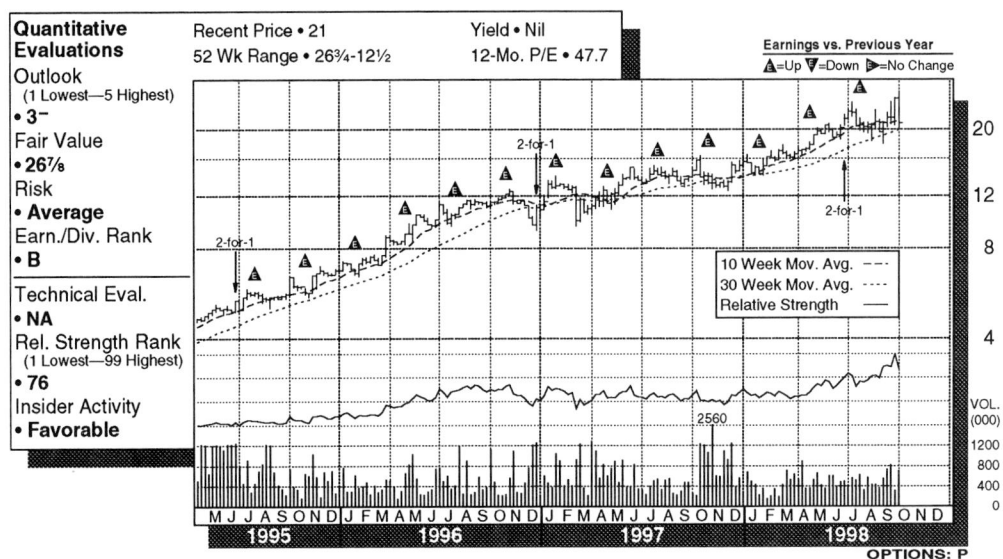

Earnings vs. Previous Year
▲=Up ▼=Down ►=No Change

10 Week Mov. Avg. ---
30 Week Mov. Avg. ·····
Relative Strength —

OPTIONS: P

Business Profile - 06-OCT-98

DV is attempting to grow the strength of its national education brands, which include DeVry Institutes, Keller Graduate School of Management and Becker CPA Review. Cumulative enrollment for the three semesters during FY 98 (Jun.) increased 9.4% over FY 97, reflecting the opening of new institutes in Georgia, California, Indiana and Missouri. Additional sites will open in theFall of 1998 in New York City, NY, and Tampa, FL. Increased marketing and new student recruiting costs were also attributed with generating higher student enrollments during the year. The DeVry Institutes had an increase of 12% in student enrollment for the summer term, whose revenue is included in FY 99.

Operational Review - 06-OCT-98

Total revenues for the fiscal year ended June 30, 1998, rose 15%, year to year, due to increases in student enrollment and a rise in tuition rates. Despite higher marketing costs and implementation of a new financial system, profitability improved on well-controlled wages and cost of facilities; operating income advanced 21%. Aided by sharply lower interest expense, and after taxes at 39.1% versus 39.3%, net income climbed 27%, to $30,724,000 ($0.11 per share), from $24,186,000 ($0.35, adjusted).

Stock Performance - 02-OCT-98

In the past 30 trading days, DV's shares have declined 0.88%, compared to a 7% fall in the S&P 500. Average trading volume for the past five days was 138,300 shares, compared with the 40-day moving average of 110,538 shares.

Key Stock Statistics

Dividend Rate/Share	Nil	Shareholders	500
Shs. outstg. (M)	69.3	Market cap. (B)	$ 1.4
Avg. daily vol. (M)	0.143	Inst. holdings	68%
Tang. Bk. Value/Share	1.42		
Beta	0.94		

Value of $10,000 invested 5 years ago: $ 83,478

Fiscal Year Ending Jun. 30

	1998	1997	1996	1995	1994	1993
Revenues (Million $)						
1Q	80.42	69.25	59.84	51.96	49.75	44.30
2Q	90.34	81.26	66.94	59.30	55.00	49.30
3Q	92.85	81.13	68.41	59.74	55.13	50.10
4Q	89.85	76.68	64.82	57.60	51.55	48.19
Yr.	353.5	308.3	260.0	228.6	211.4	191.9
Earnings Per Share ($)						
1Q	**0.09**	0.07	0.06	0.05	0.04	0.02
2Q	**0.12**	0.10	0.08	0.07	0.06	0.04
3Q	**0.12**	0.10	0.08	0.06	0.05	0.04
4Q	**0.11**	0.09	0.07	0.05	0.04	0.04
Yr.	**0.44**	0.35	0.28	0.22	0.18	0.14

Next earnings report expected: NA

Dividend Data

Amount ($)	Date Decl.	Ex-Div. Date	Stock of Record	Payment Date
2-for-1	May. 06	Jun. 22	Jun. 01	Jun. 19 '98

A Division of The **McGraw·Hill** Companies

Business Summary - 06-OCT-98

DeVry Inc. is capitalizing on a continuing rise in the number of people seeking higher education. The company, one of the leading private-sector higher education providers through its DeVry Institutes and Keller Graduate School of Management, has benefited from a number of trends, including a widely held belief that a high school education is no longer sufficient preparation for the modern job market. Today's student population is older, and has a unique set of needs, including increased scheduling convenience, affordability, and the availability of more career-oriented courses.

A key element of DV's strategy is providing much sought after technology-based training. Over the past two decades, corporate America has been restructuring work to improve quality, productivity and profitability by investing heavily in new computer, network and telecommunications technologies. DV believes that each year of formal schooling after high school can add from 5% to 25% to annual earnings. Moreover, holders of technology-oriented degrees, such as engineering and computer science degrees, can earn some of the highest salaries.

The company expects changing demographics to continue to benefit the DeVry Institutes' future enrollment. After a period of nearly two decades during which the number of graduating high school seniors declined by 25% to 2.4 million, 1995 marked the beginning of a rise in the number of high school graduates. The National Center for Education Statistics forecasts that we will reach 3.1 million graduates by 2005, rivaling the previous peak of 3.1 million in the late 1970's. DV believes that these statistics translate into an increase in potential DeVry Institute students.

Founded in 1931, DeVry Institutes operates 12 campuses in the U.S. and three in Canada. For the 1998 summer semester, enrollment totaled more than 33,088 full and part-time students, up 12.1%, year to year. DeVry Institutes offer associate and bachelors degree programs in electronics, engineering, computer information systems, telecommunications, accounting, business administration and technical management. The DeVry Institutes' operations accounted for approximately 87% of company revenues in FY 98 (Jun.).

The Keller Graduate School of Management offers graduate degrees in business administration and project and human resource management. More than 3,857 students registered for the summer 1998 semester, up 23% from the 1997 level.

In 1996, DV acquired Becker CPA Review, the leading international training firm preparing students to take the Certified Public Accountant exam. More than one-third of all students passing the CPA exam are Becker students at one of the 190 class locations worldwide. Becker CPA Review alumni now number over 200,000 since the course was founded in 1957.

Per Share Data ($)

(Year Ended Jun. 30)	1998	1997	1996	1995	1994	1993	1992	1991	1990	1989
Tangible Bk. Val.	1.42	0.98	0.29	0.54	0.32	0.13	-0.02	-0.44	-7.20	-7.64
Cash Flow	0.64	0.52	0.40	0.32	0.29	0.24	0.20	0.52	1.45	1.39
Earnings	0.44	0.35	0.28	0.22	0.18	0.14	0.09	-0.35	-0.64	-2.33
Dividends	Nil	Nil	Nil	Nil	Nil	Nil	Nil	Nil	NA	NA
Payout Ratio	Nil	Nil	Nil	Nil	Nil	Nil	Nil	Nil	NA	NA
Prices - High	24⅝	16½	12¾	7	4¼	3¾	2¾	2¹/₁₆	NA	NA
- Low	14	9½	6½	3⅞	3	2⁷/₁₆	1¹¹/₁₆	1⅛	NA	NA
P/E Ratio - High	56	46	44	32	23	26	29	NM	NA	NA
- Low	32	27	23	17	16	17	18	NM	NA	NA

Income Statement Analysis (Million $)

	1998	1997	1996	1995	1994	1993	1992	1991	1990	1989
Revs.	352	307	259	227	211	192	179	162	156	152
Oper. Inc.	63.8	53.0	40.3	33.8	32.1	28.8	28.3	25.9	27.7	24.8
Depr.	14.0	11.3	7.6	6.2	7.1	6.7	7.1	8.6	19.2	34.1
Int. Exp.	0.9	2.9	1.1	3.1	4.6	6.8	9.7	13.8	16.0	18.0
Pretax Inc.	50.5	39.9	32.7	25.8	21.0	15.6	9.9	-3.7	-6.3	-22.1
Eff. Tax Rate	39%	39%	41%	42%	42%	40%	40%	NM	NM	NM
Net Inc.	30.7	24.2	19.2	14.9	12.2	9.4	5.9	-3.5	-5.9	-21.4

Balance Sheet & Other Fin. Data (Million $)

	1998	1997	1996	1995	1994	1993	1992	1991	1990	1989
Cash	48.8	51.0	46.5	46.4	33.8	22.9	25.4	20.5	18.4	22.1
Curr. Assets	69.7	70.5	61.6	58.0	48.9	37.7	42.9	32.3	30.8	33.5
Total Assets	224	207	178	127	107	99	112	96.0	109	132
Curr. Liab.	66.0	58.3	52.5	48.9	40.2	44.4	41.6	34.5	37.0	44.5
LT Debt	10.0	33.0	61.5	33.0	40.0	42.0	67.0	83.0	112	118
Common Eqty.	136	105	57.3	38.0	23.0	11.0	1.3	-23.1	-53.0	-43.9
Total Cap.	150	141	121	71.0	62.9	53.5	70.2	60.7	71.6	86.7
Cap. Exp.	31.8	28.8	18.4	14.6	6.3	5.1	3.9	2.1	2.3	2.2
Cash Flow	44.7	35.4	26.8	21.1	19.3	16.2	13.0	5.1	13.3	12.7
Curr. Ratio	1.1	1.2	1.2	1.2	1.2	0.8	1.0	0.9	0.8	0.8
% LT Debt of Cap.	NA	23.3	50.8	46.5	63.1	79.4	95.8	137.3	156.9	136.2
% Net Inc.of Revs.	6.7	7.9	7.4	6.6	5.8	4.9	3.3	NM	NM	NM
% Ret. on Assets	14.3	12.6	12.6	11.8	11.9	8.8	5.4	NM	NM	NA
% Ret. on Equity	25.4	29.8	40.4	48.9	71.9	152.5	NM	NM	NM	NA

Data as orig. reptd.; bef. results of disc. opers. and/or spec. items. Per share data adj. for stk. divs. as of ex-div. date. Bold denotes diluted EPS (FASB 128). E-Estimated. NA-Not Available. NM-Not Meaningful. NR-Not Ranked.

Office—One Tower Lane,Suite 1000, Oakbrook Terrace, IL 60181-4624. **Tel**—(630) 571-7700. **Website**—http://www.devry.com **Chrmn & CEO**—D. J. Keller. **Pres & COO**—R. L. Taylor. **VP-Fin, CFO & Contr**—N. M. Levine. **SVP & Secy**—M. J. Cason. **Investor Contact**—Diane Salucci (630) 574-1931. **Dirs**—E. M. Akin, C. A. Bowsher, D. S. Brown, A. I. Gannon, D. J. Keller, R. E. King, F.A. Krehbiel, T. E. Manning, R. C. McCormack, J. A. McGee, H. J. Melvoin, R. L. Taylor. **Transfer Agent**—Harris Trust & Savings Bank, Chicago. **Incorporated**—in Delaware in 1987. **Empl**— 2,850. **S&P Analyst:** Jordan Horoschak

03-OCT-98

Industry:
Health Care (Medical Products & Supplies)

Summary: This company is the world's leading independent producer of immunodiagnostic test kits and related instrumentation.

Quantitative Evaluations	
Recent Price • 25	Yield • 1.9%
52 Wk Range • 32⅞-24⅜	12-Mo. P/E • 19.2

Outlook (1 Lowest—5 Highest)
• **4⁻**

Fair Value
• **35⅝**

Risk
• **Average**

Earn./Div. Rank
• **B+**

Technical Eval.
• **NA**

Rel. Strength Rank (1 Lowest—99 Highest)
• **60**

Insider Activity
• **Neutral**

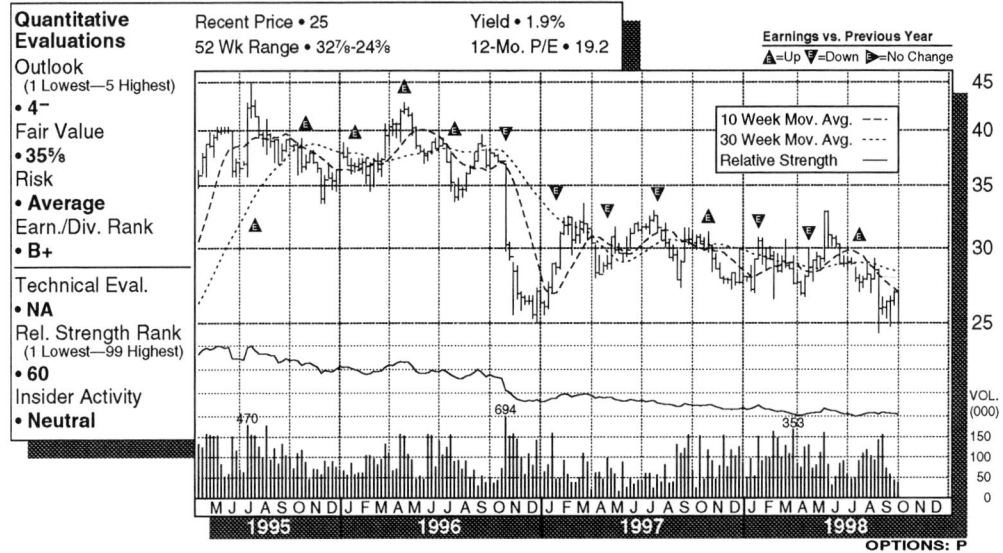

Earnings vs. Previous Year
▲=Up ▼=Down ▷=No Change

10 Week Mov. Avg. - - -
30 Week Mov. Avg. - - - -
Relative Strength —

OPTIONS: P

Business Profile - 29-JUL-98

Key elements of the company's growth strategy include maintaining strong IMMULITE systems placement, introducing new assays, and managing the decline of its mature RIA business through penetration of new markets. DP expects IMMULITE to continue to be its fastest growing line for the foreseeable future, as laboratories seek easy-to-use technologies and improved productivity. Because it derives about 80% of its sales from international markets, DP anticipates that a stronger dollar will continue to put pressure on profits. However, the company has said it continues to experience solid growth in IMMULITE reagent sales, has significant new assays released and in the pipeline, and sees strong shipments of IMMULITE systems. In February 1998, DP acquired its primary Norwegian distributor, which had 1997 sales of about $3 million.

Operational Review - 29-JUL-98

Sales for the six months ended June 20, 1998, rose 4.6%, year to year, reflecting increased sales of the IMMULITE system, as well as sales of the IMMULITE test kits, partly offset by weakness in the mature RIA product line and the negative impact on international sales due to a strong dollar. Gross margins were 56%, unchanged from a year ago. Following an 18% increase in R&D expenses, pretax income was up 1.2%. After taxes at 29.6%, versus 26.8%, net income fell 2.7%, to $9,298,000 ($0.67 per share), from $9,555,000 ($0.69).

Stock Performance - 02-OCT-98

In the past 30 trading days, DP's shares have declined 12%, compared to a 7% fall in the S&P 500. Average trading volume for the past five days was 7,460 shares, compared with the 40-day moving average of 19,054 shares.

Key Stock Statistics

Dividend Rate/Share	0.48	Shareholders	500
Shs. outstg. (M)	13.8	Market cap. (B)	$0.345
Avg. daily vol. (M)	0.011	Inst. holdings	30%
Tang. Bk. Value/Share	12.96		
Beta	0.45		

Value of $10,000 invested 5 years ago: $ 9,276

Fiscal Year Ending Dec. 31

	1998	1997	1996	1995	1994	1993
Revenues (Million $)						
1Q	46.10	44.40	43.25	39.20	27.77	27.03
2Q	49.28	46.76	43.37	38.53	30.13	26.40
3Q	—	46.40	43.36	40.53	30.64	26.59
4Q	—	48.70	46.86	41.38	37.91	26.77
Yr.	—	186.3	176.8	159.7	126.5	106.8
Earnings Per Share ($)						
1Q	**0.30**	0.34	0.47	0.42	0.26	0.30
2Q	**0.37**	0.35	0.47	0.44	0.29	0.33
3Q	—	0.37	0.31	0.43	0.32	0.19
4Q	—	0.26	0.40	0.46	0.37	0.22
Yr.	—	1.32	1.65	1.75	1.24	1.04

Next earnings report expected: late October

Dividend Data (Dividends have been paid since 1988.)

Amount ($)	Date Decl.	Ex-Div. Date	Stock of Record	Payment Date
0.120	Jan. 05	Feb. 02	Feb. 04	Feb. 18 '98
0.120	Apr. 01	May. 04	May. 06	May. 20 '98
0.120	Jul. 01	Aug. 03	Aug. 05	Aug. 19 '98
0.120	Oct. 01	Nov. 02	Nov. 04	Nov. 18 '98

A Division of The McGraw·Hill Companies

STANDARD
&POOR'S
STOCK REPORTS

Diagnostic Products Corporation

750

03-OCT-98

Business Summary - 29-JUL-98

Since its founding in 1971, Diagnostic Products (DP) has become the world's leading developer, producer and seller of medical immunodiagnostic test kits and related instrumentation that use state-of-the-art technology derived from immunology and molecular biology.

DP's kits are used by hospitals, clinical, veterinary, research and forensic laboratories, and doctors' offices to obtain precise and rapid identification and measurement of hormones, drugs, viruses, bacteria and other substances present in body fluids and tissues at infinitesimal concentrations.

The principal clinical applications of the company's more than 300 assays relate to diagnosis of thyroid conditions and anemia; testing for pregnancy, fertility and fetal well-being; management of diabetes and certain types of cancer; drug abuse testing; rapid diagnosis of infectious diseases (including sexually transmitted diseases); allergy testing; and diagnosis of disorders due to hormone and steroid imbalances. DP believes it is the market leader in fertility testing, with the most comprehensive line of kits currently available. Its kits are used for in-vitro (outside the body) testing, typically in a test tube.

With the May 1992 acquisition of Cirrus Diagnostics Inc., DP entered the market for fully automated, non-isotopic diagnostic instrumentation systems, the fastest growing segment of the immunoassay market. The IMMULITE system, developed by Cirrus, is a fully automated, random-access instrument that performs immunoassays utilizing chemiluminescent technology, and can process up to 120 samples per hour.

As of December 31, 1997, DP had 81 IMMULITE assays available in the international markets, of which 51 had been approved by the FDA for marketing in the U.S. DP has focused on offering the most complete panel of tests for specific disease states, including thyroid, fertility and cancer testing. Since its introduction in 1992, DP has manufactured 3,120 IMMULITE systems, 720 of which were shipped in 1997.

Prior to 1992, DP had concentrated on radioimmunoassay (RIA), which utilizes radioisotopes to achieve high levels of test specificity and sensitivity. RIA tests are labor intensive and must be performed by skilled technicians. In the 1980s, the immunodiagnostic market began to shift away from RIA, reflecting concerns regarding the disposal of radioactive materials used in RIA tests and demand for labor-saving, automated immunodiagnostic systems that utilize nonisotopic tests. As a result, sales of RIA products have decreased, from more than 50% of sales in 1995, to approximately 30% in 1997.

In the first quarter of 1998, DP began shipping the IMMULITE 2000, a high speed continuous random access analyzer with a throughput of up to 200 tests per hour. IMMULITE 2000 also includes advanced features, such as primary tube sampling and proprietary auto-dilution capability.

Per Share Data ($)

(Year Ended Dec. 31)	1997	1996	1995	1994	1993	1992	1991	1990	1989	1988
Tangible Bk. Val.	12.56	12.32	10.87	9.36	8.30	7.92	7.38	6.51	5.40	4.60
Cash Flow	2.42	2.69	1.49	1.67	1.35	1.60	1.79	1.64	1.42	1.14
Earnings	1.32	1.65	1.75	1.24	1.04	1.26	1.49	1.35	1.20	1.00
Dividends	0.48	0.48	0.46	0.40	0.30	0.32	0.32	0.24	0.20	0.12
Payout Ratio	36%	29%	26%	32%	29%	24%	20%	17%	16%	11%
Prices - High	33½	42⅞	44⅞	26⅝	30¾	44	53¾	44	38	22¾
- Low	25½	25	24¼	17¾	17⅛	20⅛	28¼	22¼	19¼	14
P/E Ratio - High	25	26	26	21	30	35	36	33	32	23
- Low	19	15	14	14	16	16	19	16	16	14

Income Statement Analysis (Million $)

	1997	1996	1995	1994	1993	1992	1991	1990	1989	1988
Revs.	186	177	160	126	107	103	90.1	75.9	60.3	47.0
Oper. Inc.	39.0	43.1	35.0	26.3	22.3	26.6	26.2	23.1	20.1	15.2
Depr.	15.3	14.4	6.1	5.9	4.2	4.7	4.0	3.8	2.7	1.8
Int. Exp.	NA	NM	NM	Nil	Nil	Nil	Nil	Nil	Nil	Nil
Pretax Inc.	25.7	31.7	19.9	22.6	19.9	23.7	27.9	24.5	22.1	17.9
Eff. Tax Rate	29%	28%	29%	26%	29%	27%	31%	30%	31%	31%
Net Inc.	18.2	22.9	14.2	16.7	14.2	17.3	19.3	17.3	15.2	12.4

Balance Sheet & Other Fin. Data (Million $)

	1997	1996	1995	1994	1993	1992	1991	1990	1989	1988
Cash	20.4	13.8	16.5	14.8	12.9	22.7	30.2	24.3	20.3	20.8
Curr. Assets	119	106	96.6	78.3	68.9	70.3	76.3	64.3	53.4	44.3
Total Assets	222	207	189	153	137	134	131	102	84.0	65.0
Curr. Liab.	35.9	24.7	26.1	17.6	13.9	14.8	23.9	15.4	12.4	7.6
LT Debt	Nil	NM	NM	Nil	Nil	Nil	Nil	Nil	Nil	Nil
Common Eqty.	186	182	163	135	123	120	107	87.0	71.2	57.6
Total Cap.	186	182	163	135	123	120	107	87.0	71.2	57.6
Cap. Exp.	10.5	8.0	7.6	8.5	7.7	15.1	9.5	6.0	6.0	4.8
Cash Flow	33.5	37.4	20.3	22.6	18.4	22.0	23.3	21.1	17.9	14.2
Curr. Ratio	3.3	4.3	3.7	4.4	5.0	4.8	3.2	4.2	4.3	5.8
% LT Debt of Cap.	Nil	NM	NM	Nil	Nil	Nil	Nil	Nil	Nil	Nil
% Net Inc.of Revs.	9.8	13.0	8.9	13.2	13.3	16.7	21.5	22.8	25.2	26.4
% Ret. on Assets	8.5	12.3	8.3	11.6	10.5	12.6	16.5	18.5	20.3	21.6
% Ret. on Equity	9.9	13.3	9.5	13.0	11.7	14.8	19.8	21.7	23.5	23.8

Data as orig. reptd.; bef. results of disc. opers. and/or spec. items. Per share data adj. for stk. divs. as of ex-div. date. Bold denotes diluted EPS (FASB 128). E-Estimated. NA-Not Available. NM-Not Meaningful. NR-Not Ranked.

Office—5700 W. 96th St., Los Angeles, CA 90045-5597. **Tel**—(213) 776-0180. **Website**—http://www.dpcweb.com **Chrmn, CEO & Investor Contact**—S. Ziering. **Pres & COO**—Michael Ziering. **VP-Fin**—J. R. Bockserman. **Secy**—Marilyn Ziering. **Dirs**—S. A. Aroesty, F. Frank, M. H. Salter, J. D. Watson, Michael Ziering, S. Ziering. **Transfer Agent & Registrar**—First Interstate Bank of California, Los Angeles. **Incorporated**—in California in 1971. **Empl**— 1,325. **S&P Analyst:** John J. Arege

STANDARD &POOR'S
STOCK REPORTS

Dialogic Corp. 3685G

NASDAQ Symbol **DLGC**

In S&P SmallCap 600

03-OCT-98

Industry:
Communications
Equipment

Summary: Dialogic is the leading manufacturer of high performance, standards-based computer telephony systems.

Quantitative Evaluations

Recent Price • 26⅝

52 Wk Range • 52⅛-24½

Yield • Nil

12-Mo. P/E • 12.3

Outlook
(1 Lowest—5 Highest)
• **5**

Fair Value
• **55¾**

Risk
• **High**

Earn./Div. Rank
• **NR**

Technical Eval.
• **Bullish** since 3/98

Rel. Strength Rank
(1 Lowest—99 Highest)
• **49**

Insider Activity
• **Unfavorable**

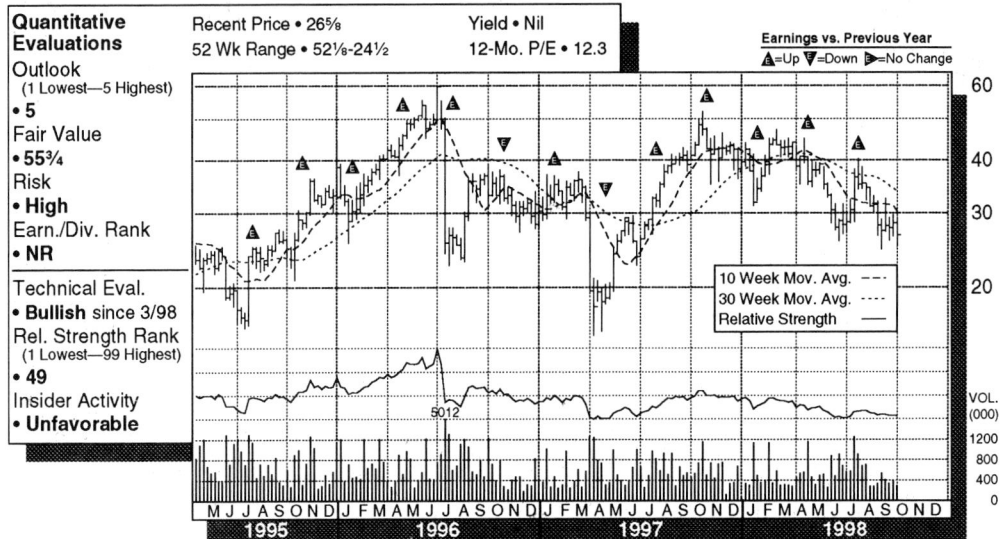

Earnings vs. Previous Year
▲=Up ▼=Down ▶=No Change

10 Week Mov. Avg. ---
30 Week Mov. Avg. ····
Relative Strength —

Business Profile - 02-SEP-98

Computer telephony systems built with Dialogic products manage more than one-third of all telephone, facsimile and multimedia calls answered by computers over wireline and wireless networks worldwide. The company's growth in recent years has reflected its strategy of promoting industry standards, pursuing collaborative customer relationships and strategic partnerships, expanding globally, and developing or acquiring new capabilities. The shares dropped sharply following a report of disappointing domestic revenues in the 1997 first quarter, but recovered on improvement in the past five quarters. In February 1998, the company sold Spectron Microsystems to Texas Instruments, for $26 million.

Operational Review - 02-SEP-98

Revenues in the first half of 1998 advanced 16%, year to year, as 19% higher North American revenues, coupled with increased European and Latin American growth, outweighed a 34% decline in Asia/Pacific markets. Margins widened, aided by cost reduction efforts and a more favorable product mix; operating income increased 39%. Aided by a $23.4 million gain on the sale of the Spectron Microsystems subsidiary, despite a $5.3 million asset impairment charge, net income surged 182%, to $22,607,000 ($1.41 a share, on 1.7% more shares), from $8,006,000 ($0.49).

Stock Performance - 02-OCT-98

In the past 30 trading days, DLGC's shares have declined 15%, compared to a 7% fall in the S&P 500. Average trading volume for the past five days was 57,700 shares, compared with the 40-day moving average of 72,328 shares.

Key Stock Statistics

Dividend Rate/Share	Nil	Shareholders	300
Shs. outstg. (M)	16.0	Market cap. (B)	$0.426
Avg. daily vol. (M)	0.072	Inst. holdings	47%
Tang. Bk. Value/Share	10.31		
Beta	NA		

Value of $10,000 invested 5 years ago: NA

Fiscal Year Ending Dec. 31

	1998	1997	1996	1995	1994	1993
Revenues (Million $)						
1Q	66.39	57.09	48.73	35.81	28.60	—
2Q	73.13	63.20	50.05	40.63	30.65	—
3Q	—	68.76	55.43	44.03	32.24	—
4Q	—	72.27	59.39	48.19	35.75	—
Yr.	—	261.3	213.6	168.7	127.2	95.61
Earnings Per Share ($)						
1Q	0.93	0.20	0.65	0.13	0.20	—
2Q	0.42	0.29	0.28	0.25	0.23	—
3Q	—	0.30	0.29	0.31	0.25	—
4Q	—	0.44	0.34	0.33	0.25	—
Yr.	—	1.31	1.56	1.02	0.94	—

Next earnings report expected: mid October

Dividend Data

No dividends have been paid.

A Division of The McGraw·Hill Companies

Business Summary - 02-SEP-98

At the crossroads of the Internet, the telephone system, and the corporate LAN (local area network), a new world is developing, where a pager, phone or fax can be used to gain access to information on the Web, and voice, e-mail or fax messages can be retrieved from a single universal inbox, without regard to origin. The technologies that allow the computer to add its intelligence to the functions of the telephone come together in the field of computer telephony (CT), which Dialogic Corp. (DLGC) serves by producing components for CT systems. CT systems built with company products manage telephone, facsimile and multi-media calls answered by computers throughout the world. Voice, fax, data, voice recognition, speech synthesis and call center management are among the technologies and applications embraced by DLGC's range of CT products.

DLGC's products typically include a network interface and signal processing resources that digitize, compress or otherwise process telephony and data signals. In the call center, the products are used in large-scale switching systems that can intelligently route calls and link them with customer-specific information in a database. DLGC's Global DPD software brings sophisticated CT services to areas of the world where touchtone service is not universally available.

The company has focused much of its development effort on such emerging, high-growth areas as the Internet, intelligent peripherals and unified messaging. Intelligent peripherals built with DLGC's components allow telecommunications carriers to offer voice-activated dialing and other enhanced services. Unified messaging is enhancing the delivery and retrieval of messages for office workers who had relied on simple voice messaging. The company is also developing components for use in Internet gateway applications in which voice and fax messages can be sent over the Internet.

DLGC has benefited from growing acceptance of open, non-proprietary CT systems that use standards-based components such as the company's. In January 1997, it introduced its DM3 mediastream resource architecture, which will govern the design of DLGC's next generation of products. The company recently began shipping the first products based on its DM3 technology, an Internet Protocol technology server development system.

In 1997, the company spent $51.5 million (20% of 1997 revenues) on research and development, including efforts related to the DM3 initiative, up from $40.7 million in 1996 (19% of revenues). International sales accounted for 24% of total revenues in 1997, up from 23% in 1996.

Per Share Data ($) (Year Ended Dec. 31)	1997	1996	1995	1994	1993	1992	1991	1990	1989	1988
Tangible Bk. Val.	8.81	7.63	5.99	4.54	3.19	NA	NA	NA	NA	NA
Cash Flow	1.88	1.93	1.22	1.08	0.83	NA	NA	NA	NA	NA
Earnings	1.31	1.56	1.02	0.94	0.69	NA	NA	NA	NA	NA
Dividends	Nil	Nil	Nil	Nil	NA	NA	NA	NA	NA	NA
Payout Ratio	Nil	Nil	Nil	Nil	NA	NA	NA	NA	NA	NA
Prices - High	52⅛	60	44¼	23½	NA	NA	NA	NA	NA	NA
- Low	15⅜	22½	16	10¾	NA	NA	NA	NA	NA	NA
P/E Ratio - High	40	38	43	25	NA	NA	NA	NA	NA	NA
- Low	12	14	16	11	NA	NA	NA	NA	NA	NA

Income Statement Analysis (Million $)

	1997	1996	1995	1994	1993	1992	1991	1990	1989	1988
Revs.	261	214	169	127	96.0	65.0	50.0	47.0	NA	NA
Oper. Inc.	41.8	34.2	28.3	22.1	15.0	9.0	NA	NA	NA	NA
Depr.	9.5	6.1	3.2	2.0	1.7	1.5	NA	NA	NA	NA
Int. Exp.	0.2	0.1	0.0	0.1	0.1	0.1	NA	NA	NA	NA
Pretax Inc.	34.0	39.7	26.2	21.3	13.4	7.5	6.3	7.5	NA	NA
Eff. Tax Rate	36%	36%	38%	36%	37%	40%	34%	37%	NA	NA
Net Inc.	21.8	25.5	16.3	13.6	8.5	4.5	4.2	4.7	NA	NA

Balance Sheet & Other Fin. Data (Million $)

	1997	1996	1995	1994	1993	1992	1991	1990	1989	1988
Cash	18.8	38.3	30.7	30.0	1.9	NA	NA	NA	NA	NA
Curr. Assets	152	121	99	68.7	31.4	NA	NA	NA	NA	NA
Total Assets	182	148	117	81.9	38.6	24.5	20.6	20.7	NA	NA
Curr. Liab.	32.3	20.5	22.3	12.6	16.5	NA	NA	NA	NA	NA
LT Debt	2.5	2.9	2.3	2.5	0.6	0.3	0.2	0.2	NA	NA
Common Eqty.	145	125	92.8	66.8	21.4	17.3	15.2	13.8	NA	NA
Total Cap.	150	128	95.1	69.3	22.0	17.6	15.4	14.0	NA	NA
Cap. Exp.	10.7	10.7	7.6	7.2	2.6	1.9	NA	NA	NA	NA
Cash Flow	31.2	31.7	19.5	15.6	10.2	6.0	NA	NA	NA	NA
Curr. Ratio	4.7	5.9	4.5	5.5	1.9	NA	NA	NA	NA	NA
% LT Debt of Cap.	1.7	2.3	2.4	3.6	2.9	1.9	1.4	1.2	NA	NA
% Net Inc.of Revs.	8.3	12.0	9.7	10.7	8.9	6.9	8.4	10.0	NA	NA
% Ret. on Assets	13.2	19.2	16.4	22.6	27.0	20.0	20.3	NA	NA	NA
% Ret. on Equity	16.1	23.5	20.4	22.6	43.9	27.7	29.0	NA	NA	NA

Data as orig. reptd.; bef. results of disc. opers. and/or spec. items. Per share data adj. for stk. divs. as of ex-div. date. Bold denotes diluted EPS (FASB 128). E-Estimated. NA-Not Available. NM-Not Meaningful. NR-Not Ranked.

Office—1515 Route 10, Parsippany, NJ 07054. **Tel**—(973) 993-3000. **Fax**—(973) 993-3060. **Website**—http://www.dialogic.com **E-mail**—IR@dialogic.com **Chrmn**—N. Zwick. **Pres & CEO**—H. G. Bubb. **VP, CFO & Treas**—T. G. Amato. **VP & Secy**—T. M. Weitz. **Dirs**—H. G. Bubb, K. J. Burkhardt Jr., M. Konomi, J. N. Lemasters, F. G. Rodgers, J. J. Shinn, N. Zwick. **Transfer Agent & Registrar**—First Union National Bank, Charlotte, NC. **Incorporated**—in New Jersey in 1983. **Empl**— 994. **S&P Analyst:** Jim Corridore

03-OCT-98

Industry:
Computers (Networking)

Summary: Digi is a leading producer of data communications hardware and software products that permit microcomputers to function as multiuser and networked computer systems.

Quantitative Evaluations	
Outlook (1 Lowest—5 Highest)	• **4-**
Fair Value	• **16¼**
Risk	• **High**
Earn./Div. Rank	• **B**
Technical Eval.	• **Bearish** since 8/98
Rel. Strength Rank (1 Lowest—99 Highest)	• **25**
Insider Activity	• **NA**

Recent Price • 12½
52 Wk Range • 29½-9⅝

Yield • Nil
12-Mo. P/E • 16.4

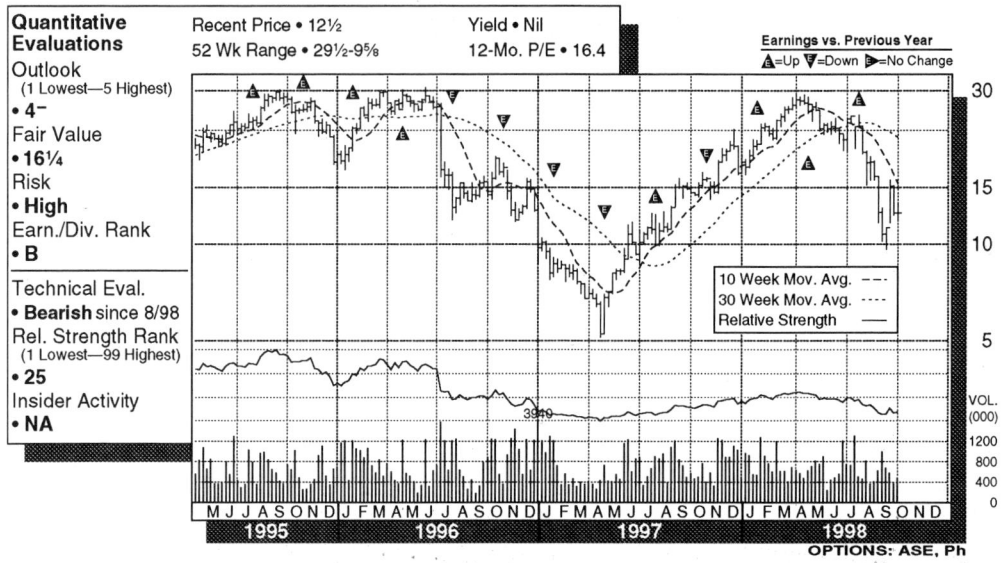

Earnings vs. Previous Year
▲=Up ▼=Down ▶=No Change

10 Week Mov. Avg. ---
30 Week Mov. Avg. ·····
Relative Strength —

VOL. (000)

OPTIONS: ASE, Ph

Business Profile - 13-AUG-98

The completion of efforts to reduce inventories in the channels led to improved revenue growth in the past two quarters of FY 98 (Sep.). Profitability has benefited from improved gross margins and lower operating expenses, reflecting the results of a restructuring program. In July 1998, Digi acquired Central Data Corp. and ITK International, providers of remote access communications. Fourth quarter FY 98 earnings will be reduced by a restructuring charge of one to two million dollars related to these acquisitions. In the fourth quarter of FY 97, the company wrote off its remaining investment of $2.4 million in AetherWorks.

Operational Review - 13-AUG-98

Revenues in the first nine months of FY 98 (Sep.) advanced 8.6%, year to year, reflecting the completion of efforts to reduce inventories in the first quarter of FY 98. Gross margins widened, and with lower SG&A expenses and R&D costs due to a restructuring program initiated in February 1997, operating income compared with an operating loss. In the absence of a $10.5 million restructuring charge, and after a $1.4 million gain associated with the company's AetherWorks investment (which was written off in September 1997) versus a $4.6 million loss, net income of $14,918,582 ($1.05 a share, on 6.3% more shares) contrasted with a net loss of $11,910,948 ($0.89).

Stock Performance - 02-OCT-98

In the past 30 trading days, DGII's shares have declined 23%, compared to a 7% fall in the S&P 500. Average trading volume for the past five days was 94,960 shares, compared with the 40-day moving average of 114,854 shares.

Key Stock Statistics

Dividend Rate/Share	Nil	Shareholders	400
Shs. outstg. (M)	13.9	Market cap. (B)	$0.174
Avg. daily vol. (M)	0.114	Inst. holdings	58%
Tang. Bk. Value/Share	7.81		
Beta	1.58		

Value of $10,000 invested 5 years ago: $ 5,291

Fiscal Year Ending Sep. 30

	1998	1997	1996	1995	1994	1993
Revenues (Million $)						
1Q	42.59	42.24	43.87	37.88	25.99	22.63
2Q	45.06	40.39	48.50	40.08	31.65	22.74
3Q	46.45	40.84	50.32	41.18	35.19	23.56
4Q	—	42.13	53.15	45.84	38.12	24.45
Yr.	—	165.6	195.8	165.0	130.9	93.39
Earnings Per Share ($)						
1Q	**0.27**	-0.19	0.33	0.32	0.28	0.28
2Q	**0.33**	0.70	0.04	0.33	0.28	0.28
3Q	**0.45**	0.01	Nil	0.35	0.29	0.26
4Q	—	-0.29	0.02	0.38	0.31	0.23
Yr.	—	-1.18	0.69	1.38	1.15	1.02

Next earnings report expected: mid November

Dividend Data

No cash dividends have been paid. A two-for-one stock split was effected in 1991 and a three-for-two stock split was effected in 1992.

A Division of The **McGraw·Hill** Companies

Business Summary - 13-AUG-98

Formed in 1985, Digi International Inc. (DGII) is a leading producer of data communications hardware and software products that deliver connectivity solutions for multiuser environments, remote access markets (LAN and WAN) and the LAN connect market. Minnesota-based DGII believes it is the market leader in the multiuser segment of the computer industry and in the server centric portion of the remote access market.

DGII's communications interface cards (76% of FY 97 sales) are used for multiuser and remote access environments. The core multiport access products connect terminals, PCs running on terminal emulation software and other serial devices to a PC-based host. These products can be used for point-of-sale applications, on-line transaction processing, factory automation, dial-in/dial-out connections and data dissemination. In addition, DGII's server-based remote access products address the need for high-performance, dial-in/dial-out connections for wide area networking, including accessing the internet. These products connect telecommuters, mobile workers and branch offices to corporate LANs, or branch offices to other branches, and are also used to make connections to the internet.

DGII entered the LAN connect market with the 1993 acquisition of MiLAN Technology Corp. DGII's LAN connect group (24% of FY 97 sales) provides Ethernet, Fast Ethernet and Token Ring networking products.

Digi markets its products to a broad range of customers, including major domestic and international distributors, system integrators, value-added resellers, and original equipment manufacturers (OEMs). Products are sold through a network of more than 201 distributors in the U.S., Canada and 70 countries worldwide, as well as through OEM contracts. International customers, mainly in Europe, accounted for 20% of net sales in FY 97 (Sep.) and FY 96. In FY 97, Ingram Micro and Tech Data accounted for 15.1% and 10.5% of net sales, respectively.

In February 1997, DGII announced a restructuring that included work force reductions, business and asset writedowns .and other cost saving actions. A related $10.5 million charge was recorded in the FY 97 second quarter. Specific actions included more emphasis on server-based communications, and the consolidation of some research and development and manufacturing operations. Subsequent to these actions, additional headcount reductions and R&D facility consolidations were made.

In July 1998, the company acquired two companies engaged in providing server-based, remote access communications services: Central Data Corp., with annual revenues of about $15 million; and ITK International, with annual revenues of approximately $30 million. Central Data was acquired for 220,000 common shares valued at about $4.5 million and $13.5 million in cash; and ITK was acquired for 615,000 common shares valued at about $12.5 million and $12.5 million in cash.

Per Share Data ($)

(Year Ended Sep. 30)	1997	1996	1995	1994	1993	1992	1991	1990	1989	1988
Tangible Bk. Val.	6.58	7.43	6.96	6.64	5.68	4.62	3.77	1.72	0.70	0.36
Cash Flow	-0.68	1.16	1.62	1.25	1.14	0.94	0.75	0.44	0.33	0.19
Earnings	-1.18	0.69	1.38	1.15	1.02	0.82	0.65	0.41	0.31	0.17
Dividends	Nil	Nil	Nil	Nil	Nil	Nil	Nil	Nil	Nil	Nil
Payout Ratio	Nil	Nil	Nil	Nil	Nil	Nil	Nil	Nil	Nil	Nil
Prices - High	22¾	30¾	30¼	22½	26¼	24¼	20½	7⅜	3⅞	NA
- Low	5⅛	8⅝	17⅛	11¼	16	11	5⅞	2⅞	3	NA
P/E Ratio - High	NM	45	22	20	26	30	32	18	13	NA
- Low	NM	12	12	10	16	13	9	7	9	NA

Income Statement Analysis (Million $)

	1997	1996	1995	1994	1993	1992	1991	1990	1989	1988
Revs.	166	196	165	131	93.4	57.8	40.8	23.2	14.6	8.4
Oper. Inc.	12.8	26.4	30.8	25.8	23.1	16.7	12.3	6.8	4.2	2.3
Depr.	6.7	6.4	3.4	1.5	1.9	1.7	1.3	0.4	0.2	0.2
Int. Exp.	Nil	Nil	Nil	Nil	Nil	Nil	Nil	Nil	Nil	Nil
Pretax Inc.	-15.7	16.8	29.4	25.4	22.5	16.6	11.9	7.4	4.2	2.2
Eff. Tax Rate	NM	45%	34%	34%	34%	31%	33%	32%	32%	33%
Net Inc.	-15.8	9.3	19.3	16.7	14.8	11.4	8.0	5.0	2.8	1.5

Balance Sheet & Other Fin. Data (Million $)

	1997	1996	1995	1994	1993	1992	1991	1990	1989	1988
Cash	31.3	8.9	28.0	37.3	51.5	40.3	34.6	12.7	2.5	1.5
Curr. Assets	84.8	89.7	94.3	84.3	78.0	59.4	45.9	18.9	6.5	4.1
Total Assets	118	130	126	103	88.9	66.5	53.2	21.4	7.5	4.4
Curr. Liab.	22.8	20.0	20.2	11.6	8.4	4.0	2.4	1.0	1.6	1.4
LT Debt	Nil	Nil	Nil	Nil	Nil	Nil	Nil	Nil	Nil	Nil
Common Eqty.	95.5	110	106	91.1	80.5	62.5	50.9	20.4	5.8	3.0
Total Cap.	95.5	110	106	91.1	80.5	62.5	50.9	20.4	5.8	3.0
Cap. Exp.	8.8	12.9	9.6	3.9	2.4	1.2	2.2	0.7	0.5	0.3
Cash Flow	-9.1	15.6	22.8	18.2	16.6	13.2	9.3	5.4	3.0	1.7
Curr. Ratio	3.7	4.5	4.7	7.2	9.3	15.0	19.5	18.5	4.0	2.8
% LT Debt of Cap.	Nil	Nil	Nil	Nil	Nil	Nil	Nil	Nil	Nil	Nil
% Net Inc.of Revs.	NM	4.7	11.7	12.8	15.8	19.8	19.5	21.7	19.3	17.6
% Ret. on Assets	NM	7.3	16.9	17.7	18.7	19.1	20.6	31.5	47.6	43.4
% Ret. on Equity	NM	8.6	19.6	19.8	20.3	20.2	21.5	35.2	64.5	67.5

Data as orig. reptd.; bef. results of disc. opers. and/or spec. items. Per share data adj. for stk. divs. as of ex-div. date. Bold denotes diluted EPS (FASB 128). E-Estimated. NA-Not Available. NM-Not Meaningful. NR-Not Ranked.

Office—11001 Bren Rd. East, Minnetonka, MN 55344. **Tel**—(612) 912-3444. **Website**—http://www.dgii.com **Chrmn**—J. P. Schinas. **Pres & CEO**—J. A. Dusa. **SVP, CFO, Treas & Investor Contact**—Jonathon E. Killmer. **Secy**—J. E. Nicholson. **Dirs**—W. K. Drake, J. A. Dusa, R. E. Eichhorn, R. S. Moe, M. Moroz, J. P. Schinas, D. Stanley. **Transfer Agent & Registrar**—Norwest Bank Minnesota, South St. Paul. **Incorporated**—in Delaware in 1989. **Empl**— 490. **S&P Analyst:** Jim Corridore

STANDARD &POOR'S
STOCK REPORTS

Digital Microwave
3691M

NASDAQ Symbol **DMIC**

In S&P SmallCap 600

10-OCT-98

Industry:
Communications
Equipment

Summary: DMIC makes advanced, high-performance, short-haul digital microwave radio communication products.

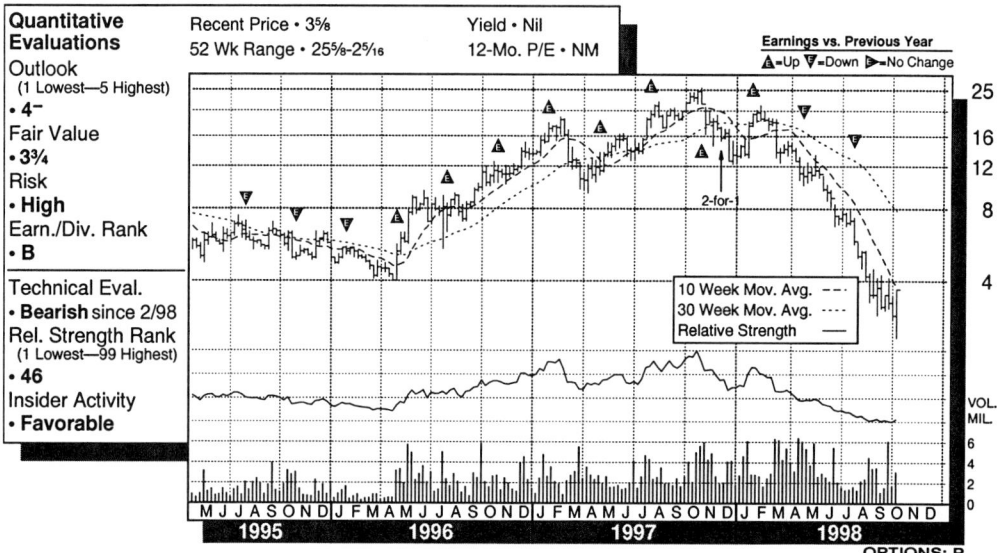

Quantitative Evaluations	
Outlook (1 Lowest—5 Highest)	• **4⁻**
Fair Value	• **3¾**
Risk	• **High**
Earn./Div. Rank	• **B**
Technical Eval.	• **Bearish** since 2/98
Rel. Strength Rank (1 Lowest—99 Highest)	• **46**
Insider Activity	• **Favorable**

Recent Price • 3⅝
52 Wk Range • 25⅝-2⁵⁄₁₆

Yield • Nil
12-Mo. P/E • NM

Earnings vs. Previous Year
▲=Up ▼=Down ▶=No Change

10 Week Mov. Avg. - - -
30 Week Mov. Avg. ·····
Relative Strength —

2-for-1

VOL. MIL.

OPTIONS: P

Business Profile - 01-SEP-98

In July 1998, the company agreed to acquire Innova Corporation (Nasdaq: INVA), a provider of wireless products and services, for about 18.5 million shares of its common stock. Separately, the company said it would reduce its workforce by 15%, as a result of a slowdown in demand for wireless telecommunications equipment.

Operational Review - 01-SEP-98

Net sales in the three months ended June 30, 1998, fell 18%, year to year, as restated, due to a slowdown in demand from Asian customers. Margins narrowed significantly, reflecting capacity underutilization, pricing pressure, higher inventory provisions, greater R&D spending and a jump in SG&A expenditures; the operating loss was $4,339,000, in contrast with operating income of $8,209,000. Results were adversely affected by restructuring costs of $7.2 million. After taxes of $27,000, versus $682,000, the net loss was $13,962,000 ($0.30 a share, based on 4.3% more shares), compared to net income of $5,810,000 ($0.13).

Stock Performance - 09-OCT-98

In the past 30 trading days, DMIC's shares have increased 5%, compared to a 4% fall in the S&P 500. Average trading volume for the past five days was 609,540 shares, compared with the 40-day moving average of 638,551 shares.

Key Stock Statistics

Dividend Rate/Share	Nil	Shareholders	200
Shs. outstg. (M)	46.7	Market cap. (B)	$0.172
Avg. daily vol. (M)	0.631	Inst. holdings	64%
Tang. Bk. Value/Share	3.48		
Beta	2.49		

Value of $10,000 invested 5 years ago: $ 13,407

Fiscal Year Ending Mar. 31

	1999	1998	1997	1996	1995	1994
Revenues (Million $)						
1Q	53.00	56.73	36.81	39.69	34.28	23.52
2Q	—	67.11	41.53	41.79	37.09	30.31
3Q	—	71.95	47.76	32.70	48.92	30.64
4Q	—	81.87	52.25	36.24	33.36	31.54
Yr.	—	310.5	178.3	150.4	153.7	116.0
Earnings Per Share ($)						
1Q	-0.30	0.15	0.04	0.01	0.07	0.01
2Q	—	0.18	0.07	0.01	0.00	0.05
3Q	—	0.22	0.12	-0.21	0.10	-1.01
4Q	—	-0.13	0.13	0.01	-0.18	0.06
Yr.	—	0.42	0.34	-0.20	0.07	-0.91

Next earnings report expected: mid October

Dividend Data

Amount ($)	Date Decl.	Ex-Div. Date	Stock of Record	Payment Date
2-for-1	Aug. 28	Nov. 25	Nov. 06	Nov. 24 '97

A Division of The McGraw·Hill Companies

Business Summary - 01-SEP-98

Digital Microwave (DMIC) designs, manufactures and markets advanced wireless solutions for worldwide telephone network interconnection and access. Products are designed to meet the requirements of mobile communications networks and fixed access networks. In July 1998, the company agreed to acquire Innova Corporation (Nasdaq: INVA), a provider of wireless products and services. Under the agreement, DMIC will exchange 1.05 shares of Digital Microwave common stock for each INVA common share. DMIC is expected to issue 18.5 million shares of common stock to Innova shareholders.

The company believes itself well positioned to address the worldwide market for wireless infrastructure suppliers, and its current strategy calls for building on the strength of its current products, which offer point-to-point solutions, and its strong global sales, service and support organization to become a leading worldwide supplier of wireless network connectivity products. In particular, it believes that there are substantial telecommunications infrastructures being built for the first time in many Asian countries, infrastructures being expanded in Europe, while personal communications services (PCS) interconnect networks are being constructed in the U.S.

DMIC offers a broad line of products, operating using a variety of transmission frequencies (0.3 to 38 GigaHertz) and transmission capacities (64 Kilobits to 45 Megabits per second), allowing it to market and sell its products to service providers in many locations worldwide with varying interconnection and access requirements.

Principal products families include the SPECTRUM II, FIBRENEX and DMC Net. The company intends to focus significant resources on product development to maintain competitiveness and support entry into new wireless opportunities including wireless local loop, wireless data transport and alternative local telephone facilities access.

Products are marketed directly to service providers, which incorporate products into their telecommunications networks to deliver services directly to consumers, and through relationships with original equipment manufacturers, such as Motorola, Siemens and Northern Telecom, which provide and install integrated systems to service providers. The company has developed a global sales, service and support organization, with offices in North America, South America, Europe, the Middle East, Asia, Africa, New Zealand and Australia.

In a March 1997 public offering, 2.2 million common shares were sold, with the net proceeds of about $51.3 million available for general corporate purposes, including working capital, the development and marketing of new products, and for acquisitions of complementary technologies, businesses or products.

Per Share Data ($)

(Year Ended Mar. 31)	1998	1997	1996	1995	1994	1993	1992	1991	1990	1989
Tangible Bk. Val.	3.58	3.17	1.57	1.28	1.11	1.91	2.21	3.04	2.85	2.24
Cash Flow	0.69	0.52	0.02	0.30	-0.65	0.04	-0.52	0.39	0.66	0.56
Earnings	0.42	0.34	-0.20	0.07	-0.91	-0.28	-0.82	0.15	0.54	0.47
Dividends	Nil	Nil	Nil	Nil	Nil	Nil	Nil	Nil	Nil	Nil
Payout Ratio	Nil	Nil	Nil	Nil	Nil	Nil	Nil	Nil	Nil	Nil
Cal. Yrs.	1997	1996	1995	1994	1993	1992	1991	1990	1989	1988
Prices - High	25⅝	15⅛	10⅜	14¾	15	6¼	10⅛	17¼	17⅛	12½
- Low	9¼	4	4¾	4¼	2⅝	2¼	3¼	5½	9⅞	7
P/E Ratio - High	61	44	NM	NM	NM	NM	NM	NM	32	26
- Low	22	12	NM	NM	NM	NM	NM	NM	18	15

Income Statement Analysis (Million $)

	1998	1997	1996	1995	1994	1993	1992	1991	1990	1989
Revs.	310	178	150	154	116	108	90.0	136	111	66.0
Oper. Inc.	48.4	19.7	-1.7	9.1	10.9	0.3	-11.2	18.6	23.6	18.9
Depr.	12.9	5.8	6.3	6.4	6.5	7.7	7.2	5.7	3.1	2.0
Int. Exp.	0.3	1.0	1.9	0.5	0.6	1.1	1.3	1.5	0.6	0.3
Pretax Inc.	23.7	13.0	-7.9	2.2	-21.4	-6.7	-23.9	5.0	20.0	17.7
Eff. Tax Rate	16%	10%	NM	10%	NM	NM	NM	25%	34%	35%
Net Inc.	19.9	11.7	-6.0	2.0	-22.5	-6.7	-19.7	3.8	13.2	11.6

Balance Sheet & Other Fin. Data (Million $)

	1998	1997	1996	1995	1994	1993	1992	1991	1990	1989
Cash	25.1	58.3	9.0	3.0	4.7	5.4	2.3	3.7	0.1	11.4
Curr. Assets	192	152	80.7	88.6	72.6	61.9	72.8	90.8	81.8	61.9
Total Assets	240	170	96.0	103	84.0	73.0	87.0	108	94.0	69.0
Curr. Liab.	61.7	52.5	43.3	61.6	54.6	26.5	33.6	35.0	26.5	17.1
LT Debt	0.2	0.2	2.8	6.4	0.5	0.2	0.6	0.9	0.1	0.5
Common Eqty.	178	118	49.7	34.6	28.6	46.3	53.0	72.6	67.7	51.9
Total Cap.	179	118	52.5	41.0	29.1	46.5	53.6	73.5	67.7	52.4
Cap. Exp.	22.6	8.5	4.5	8.1	5.9	4.5	3.7	9.6	8.1	6.1
Cash Flow	32.7	17.5	0.4	8.3	-16.0	1.0	-12.4	9.5	16.3	13.6
Curr. Ratio	3.1	2.9	1.9	1.4	1.3	2.3	2.2	2.6	3.1	3.6
% LT Debt of Cap.	0.1	0.1	5.3	15.5	1.6	0.4	1.2	1.3	0.1	1.0
% Net Inc.of Revs.	6.4	6.6	NM	1.3	NM	NM	NM	2.8	11.9	17.5
% Ret. on Assets	9.7	8.8	NM	2.1	NM	NM	NM	3.7	16.0	20.0
% Ret. on Equity	13.4	13.9	NM	6.1	NM	NM	NM	5.4	21.9	25.3

Data as orig. reptd.; bef. results of disc. opers. and/or spec. items. Per share data adj. for stk. divs. as of ex-div. date. Bold denotes diluted EPS (FASB 128). E-Estimated. NA-Not Available. NM-Not Meaningful. NR-Not Ranked.

Office—170 Rose Orchard Way, San Jose, CA 95134. **Reincorporated**—in Delaware in 1987. **Tel**—(408) 943-0777. **Website**—www.dmcwave.com **Chrmn, Pres & CEO**—C. D. Kissner. **VP, CFO & Secy**—C. A. Thomsen. **Pres & COO**—S. Smookler. **Investor Contact**—Rebecca Wallo. **Dirs**—R. C. Alberding, J. W. Combs, C. H. Higgerson, C. D. Kissner, J. D. Meindl, B. B. Oliver, H. Oringer. **Transfer Agent**—ChaseMellon Shareholder Services, SF. **Empl**—1,147. **S&P Analyst**: S.J.T.

STANDARD &POOR'S
STOCK REPORTS

DiMon Inc.

757P

NYSE Symbol **DMN**

In S&P SmallCap 600

03-OCT-98

Industry: Agricultural Products

Summary: DiMon believes that it is the world's second largest leaf tobacco dealer, and the largest importer and exporter of fresh cut flowers.

Quantitative Evaluations

Outlook (1 Lowest—5 Highest)
- **3⁻**

Fair Value
- **12⅝**

Risk
- **Average**

Earn./Div. Rank
- **NR**

Technical Eval.
- **Bullish** since 3/98

Rel. Strength Rank (1 Lowest—99 Highest)
- **63**

Insider Activity
- **NA**

Recent Price • 10⅜
52 Wk Range • 26⅛-8⅝
Yield • 6.6%
12-Mo. P/E • 10.6

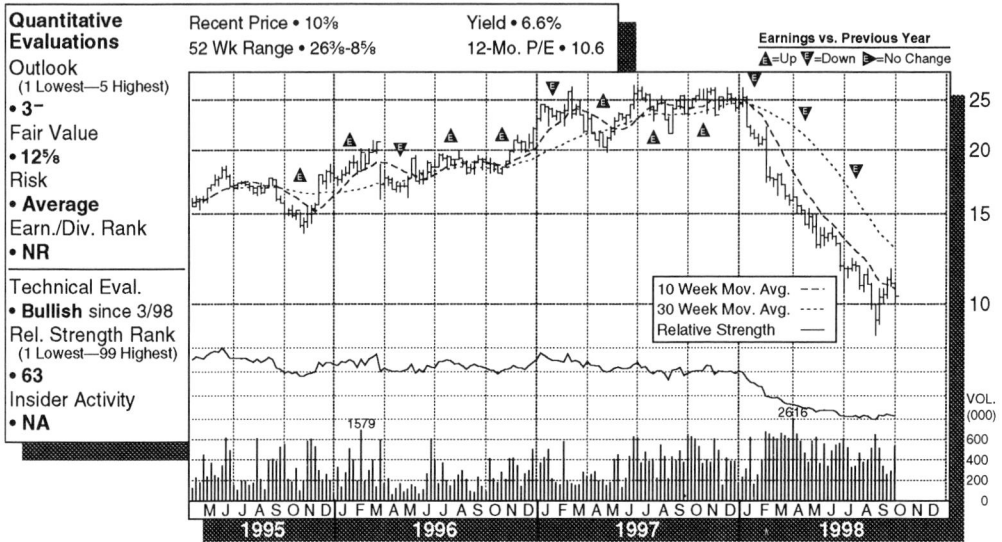

Earnings vs. Previous Year
▲=Up ▼=Down ▶=No Change

10 Week Mov. Avg. – – –
30 Week Mov. Avg. ·······
Relative Strength ——

Business Profile - 27-MAY-98

In April 1997, DiMon completed the largest acquisition in the history of the tobacco leaf industry when it purchased Intabex Holdings Worldwide S.A. (Intabex), the world's fourth largest leaf tobacco dealer, in a transaction valued at approximately $264 million. The acquisition made DiMon the world's second largest tobacco leaf dealer. FY 98 (Jun.) second quarter results were hurt by weak currencies in many Asian markets; this caused certain customers to delay shipments of leaf tobacco from the U.S. In addition, certain domestic customers have been cautious in their commitments for tobacco purchases, given the uncertainty of the proposed tobacco litigation settlement.

Operational Review - 27-MAY-98

Sales and other operating revenues in the nine months ended March 31, 1998, rose 5.2%, year to year, reflecting a 6.8% advance in tobacco sales, partly offset by a 3.2% drop in flower sales, due to a strong U.S. dollar. Tobacco sales were up, as healthy cigar leaf business boosted Intabex sales, and international sales were strong. Margins widened, on greater gross profits on tobacco from Europe, Asia and South America; operating income climbed 13%. After much higher interest expense and depreciation charges, pretax income fell 32%. After taxes at 26.3%, versus 39.3%, and equity in net income of investee companies, net income was down 18%, to $42,032,000 ($0.93 a share, on 15% more shares), from $51,143,000 ($1.20).

Stock Performance - 02-OCT-98

In the past 30 trading days, DMN's shares have increased 4%, compared to a 7% fall in the S&P 500. Average trading volume for the past five days was 105,800 shares, compared with the 40-day moving average of 102,072 shares.

Key Stock Statistics

Dividend Rate/Share	0.68	Shareholders	4,300
Shs. outstg. (M)	44.5	Market cap. (B)	$0.462
Avg. daily vol. (M)	0.074	Inst. holdings	56%
Tang. Bk. Value/Share	4.77		
Beta	0.41		

Value of $10,000 invested 5 years ago: NA

Fiscal Year Ending Jun. 30

	1998	1997	1996	1995	1994	1993
Revenues (Million $)						
1Q	513.1	410.7	339.7	272.9	--	--
2Q	688.5	771.3	763.4	631.5	—	--
3Q	744.6	668.1	577.1	644.1	—	--
4Q	513.1	663.0	487.3	380.2	—	--
Yr.	2,172	2,513	2,167	1,928	1,447	1,677
Earnings Per Share ($)						
1Q	**0.44**	0.36	0.16	-0.04	--	--
2Q	**0.25**	0.40	0.48	0.10	—	--
3Q	**0.22**	0.44	0.16	0.20	—	--
4Q	**0.05**	0.58	0.21	-1.05	—	--
Yr.	**0.94**	1.79	1.00	-0.79	-0.17	1.81

Next earnings report expected: mid November

Dividend Data (Dividends have been paid since 1995.)

Amount ($)	Date Decl.	Ex-Div. Date	Stock of Record	Payment Date
0.170	Nov. 14	Nov. 26	Dec. 01	Dec. 12 '97
0.170	Feb. 27	Mar. 05	Mar. 09	Mar. 13 '98
0.170	May. 26	Jun. 03	Jun. 05	Jun. 15 '98
0.170	Aug. 28	Sep. 03	Sep. 08	Sep. 15 '98

A Division of The McGraw-Hill Companies

STANDARD
&POOR'S
STOCK REPORTS

DiMon Incorporated

757P
03-OCT-98

Business Summary - 27-MAY 08

DiMon Inc. is the world's second largest leaf tobacco dealer, and the largest importer and exporter of fresh cut flowers. The great bulk of revenues flow from the sale of tobacco. Fresh-cut flower operations consist of buying flowers from sources throughout the world and transporting them to operating units for resale through wholly owned Florimex Worldwide.

Principally through its April 1997 acquisition of Intabex Holdings Worldwide in a transaction valued at over $265 million, DMN increased its tobacco-related revenues in FY 97 (Jun.) by 20%, and boosted its approximate market share in the established worldwide leaf tobacco market from 30% to 37% on a pro forma basis. DMN also strengthened its presence in several important tobacco growing regions, including Brazil, Argentina, Malawi, Thailand and Zimbabwe. Intabex, based in Wokingham, England, is a leaf tobacco dealer with annual sales of about $700 million; it owns and operates leaf tobacco buying, processing and exporting operations in principal tobacco markets around the world.

As one of the world's largest leaf tobacco merchants, DiMon selects, purchases, processes, stores, packs, ships, and in some markets provides agronomy expertise and financing for growing leaf tobacco. The company processes tobacco to meet each customer's specifications as to quality, yield, chemistry, particle size, moisture, content, and other characteristics. DiMon purchases tobacco in about 32 countries and sells it to manufacturers of cigarettes including Philip Morris, RJR Nabisco, Japan Tobacco, and other consumer tobacco product companies, in about 60 countries throughout the world.

The company's primary business objective is to capitalize on growth in worldwide consumption of American blend cigarettes by becoming the low-cost preferred supplier of leaf tobacco to the large multinational manufacturers of American blend cigarettes. Strategies to achieve this goal include increasing the company's operations in low-cost tobacco growing regions, capitalizing on outsourcing trends, improving efficiency while reducing operating costs, and expanding operations in new markets.

In FY 97, flower operations produced 15% of revenues, and, at June 30, 1997, represented approximately 5% of consolidated assets. DMN does not view its flowers operations as a core business, and will continue to evaluate its strategic alternatives with respect to Florimex.

Per Share Data ($)

(Year Ended Jun. 30)	1998	1997	1996	1995	1994	1993	1992	1991	1990	1989
Tangible Bk. Val.	4.77	4.46	6.03	4.52	5.85	NA	NA	NA	NA	NA
Cash Flow	1.91	2.65	1.86	0.04	0.58	2.47	2.25	NA	NA	NA
Earnings	0.94	1.79	1.00	-0.79	-0.17	1.81	1.57	NA	NA	NA
Dividends	0.66	0.58	0.54	Nil	NA	NA	NA	NA	NA	NA
Payout Ratio	70%	33%	54%	Nil	NA	NA	NA	NA	NA	NA
Prices - High	26¹/₄	26³/₄	23¹/₄	18⁵/₈	NA	NA	NA	NA	NA	NA
- Low	9³/₄	19³/₄	16	13³/₄	NA	NA	NA	NA	NA	NA
P/E Ratio - High	28	15	23	NM	NA	NA	NA	NA	NA	NA
- Low	10	11	16	NM	NA	NA	NA	NA	NA	NA

Income Statement Analysis (Million $)

	1998	1997	1996	1995	1994	1993	1992	1991	1990	1989
Revs.	2,172	2,513	2,167	1,928	1,447	1,677	1,698	NA	NA	NA
Oper. Inc.	183	218	164	69.3	49.0	138	135	NA	NA	NA
Depr.	43.5	37.2	33.8	31.9	28.8	24.5	24.0	NA	NA	NA
Int. Exp.	83.8	53.0	46.9	45.2	35.1	38.1	42.8	NA	NA	NA
Pretax Inc.	56.6	124	67.2	-24.0	-1.4	94.5	79.3	NA	NA	NA
Eff. Tax Rate	26%	38%	40%	NM	NM	29%	30%	NA	NA	NA
Net Inc.	41.8	77.2	39.9	-30.2	-6.6	67.0	54.1	NA	NA	NA

Balance Sheet & Other Fin. Data (Million $)

	1998	1997	1996	1995	1994	1993	1992	1991	1990	1989
Cash	18.7	107	53.8	42.3	22.7	NA	NA	NA	NA	NA
Curr. Assets	1,209	1,371	669	731	938	NA	NA	NA	NA	NA
Total Assets	1,797	1,988	1,020	1,094	1,307	NA	NA	NA	NA	NA
Curr. Liab.	503	671	246	454	741	NA	NA	NA	NA	NA
LT Debt	797	826	391	344	245	NA	NA	NA	NA	NA
Common Eqty.	422	408	316	239	277	NA	NA	NA	NA	NA
Total Cap.	1,256	1,272	729	640	566	NA	NA	NA	NA	NA
Cap. Exp.	61.2	60.9	41.3	27.0	NA	NA	NA	NA	NA	NA
Cash Flow	85.3	114	73.7	1.7	22.3	91.5	79.5	NA	NA	NA
Curr. Ratio	2.4	2.0	2.7	1.6	1.3	NA	NA	NA	NA	NA
% LT Debt of Cap.	63.4	64.9	53.6	54.5	43.3	NA	NA	NA	NA	NA
% Net Inc.of Revs.	1.9	3.1	1.8	NM	NM	4.0	3.2	NA	NA	NA
% Ret. on Assets	2.2	5.1	3.8	NM	NA	NA	NA	NA	NA	NA
% Ret. on Equity	10.1	21.3	21.3	NM	NA	NA	NA	NA	NA	NA

Data as orig. reptd.; bef. results of disc. opers. and/or spec. items. Data for 1994-1992 pro forma. Per share data adj. for stk. divs. as of ex-div. date. E-Estimated. NA-Not Available. NM-Not Meaningful. NR-Not Ranked.

Office—512 Bridge St., Danville, VA 24543-0681.**Tel**—(804) 792-7511. **Chrmn & CEO**—C. B. Owen, Jr. **Pres**—A. C. Monk III. **EVP & CFO**—B. J. Harker. **VP & Treas**—J. A. Cooley. **VP & Secy**—J. O. Hunnicutt III. **Dirs**—L. N. Dibrell III, R. S. Dickson, H. F. Frigon, J. M. Hines, J. E. Johnson, Jr., T. F. Keller, J. L. Lanier, Jr., A. C. Monk III, R. T. Monk, Jr., C. B. Owen, W. R. Slee, Jr, N. A. Scher, A. C. B. Taberer. **Transfer Agent & Registrar**—First Union National Bank, Charlotte, NC. **Incorporated**—Virginia in 1995.**Empl**— 6,700. **S&P Analyst:** Robert J. Izmirlian

Dionex Corp. 3692

NASDAQ Symbol **DNEX**

In S&P SmallCap 600

03-OCT-98

Industry:
Manufacturing (Specialized)

Summary: This company makes chromatography systems and related products that isolate and identify the components of chemical mixtures.

Quantitative Evaluations	
Outlook (1 Lowest—5 Highest)	• 2+
Fair Value	• 23⅛
Risk	• **Low**
Earn./Div. Rank	• **B+**
Technical Eval.	• **Bearish** since 5/98
Rel. Strength Rank (1 Lowest—99 Highest)	• 51
Insider Activity	• **NA**

Recent Price • 21¼
52 Wk Range • 30-20½

Yield • Nil
12-Mo. P/E • 18.1

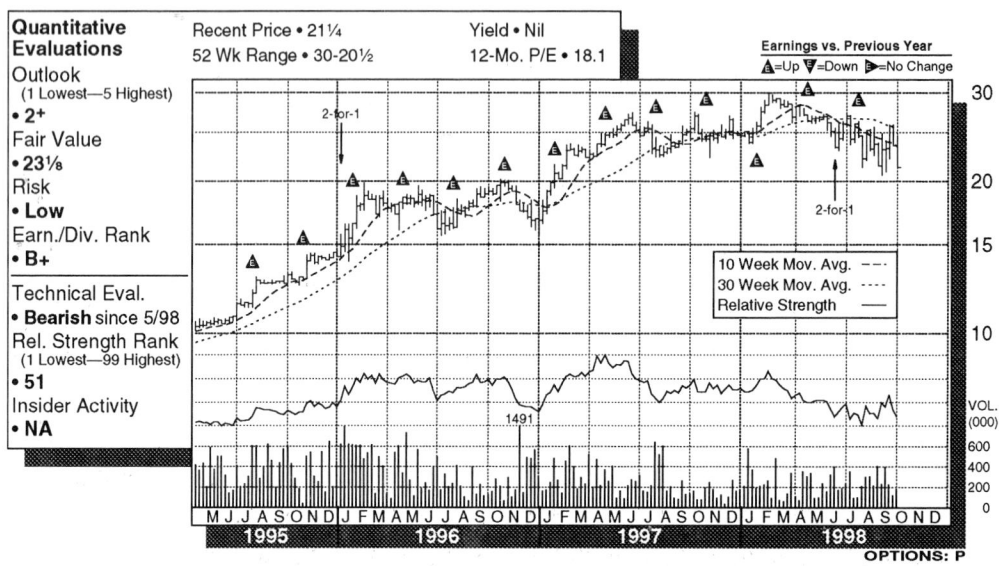

Earnings vs. Previous Year
▲=Up ▼=Down ▶=No Change

10 Week Mov. Avg. ---
30 Week Mov. Avg. ····
Relative Strength —

OPTIONS: P

Business Profile - 24-AUG-98

In FY 98 (Jun), this manufacturer, producer and marketer of chromatography systems for chemical analysis registered a 6% increase in sales. However, excluding the adverse effects of currency translations, sales advanced approximately 10%. DNEX believes that recent product introductions position the company well for a successful FY 99. In FY 98, the company purchased 1,851,460 of its common shares, versus 1,583,478 shares repurchased in FY 97. In June 1998, the shares were split two for one.

Operational Review - 24-AUG-98

Based on a preliminary report, net sales in the fiscal year ended June 30, 1998, rose 6.0%, driven by increases in the U.S. and Europe, partly offset by reduced demand in Asia. Despite unfavorable currency exchange, operating income grew 8.8%. After taxes at 34.0%, versus 34.4%, net income advanced 9.2%, to $28,650,000 ($1.18 a share, on 4.4% fewer shares), from $26,227,000 ($0.94).

Stock Performance - 02-OCT-98

In the past 30 trading days, DNEX's shares have declined 10%, compared to a 7% fall in the S&P 500. Average trading volume for the past five days was 36,480 shares, compared with the 40-day moving average of 53,059 shares.

Key Stock Statistics

Dividend Rate/Share	Nil	Shareholders	1,700
Shs. outstg. (M)	22.3	Market cap. (B)	$0.476
Avg. daily vol. (M)	0.046	Inst. holdings	63%
Tang. Bk. Value/Share	3.17		
Beta	0.44		

Value of $10,000 invested 5 years ago: $ 20,919

Fiscal Year Ending Jun. 30

	1998	1997	1996	1995	1994	1993
Revenues (Million $)						
1Q	33.93	31.51	30.06	27.04	25.46	25.10
2Q	39.42	36.60	34.01	30.62	28.13	26.90
3Q	38.40	36.65	34.03	30.58	27.72	26.65
4Q	38.76	37.30	34.91	31.78	28.22	26.98
Yr.	150.5	142.1	133.0	120.0	109.5	105.6
Earnings Per Share ($)						
1Q	0.23	0.20	0.16	0.14	0.11	0.11
2Q	0.32	0.27	0.21	0.17	0.14	0.13
3Q	**0.31**	0.28	0.26	0.18	0.15	0.13
4Q	**0.32**	0.28	0.24	0.19	0.15	0.13
Yr.	**1.18**	1.03	0.88	0.67	0.55	0.51

Next earnings report expected: mid October

Dividend Data

No cash has been paid. A two-for-one stock split was effected in 1986.

A Division of The McGraw-Hill Companies

Business Summary - 24-AUG-98

Dionex Corp. (DNEX) pioneered ion chromatography more than 20 years ago, providing chemists with a powerful new tool for analyzing the components of a wide range of samples. In 1995, the company introduced accelerated solvent extraction (ASE), a new technique for extracting compounds from solid materials such as soil and plastic prior to analysis. DNEX has also been extending the utility of high performance liquid chromatography (HPLC), another key technology, for biological and environmental applications. For example, the company is working with regulatory agencies in the U.S. and abroad to develop effective methods for analyzing organic contaminants that plague the environment.

The company's chromatography systems and its product development efforts are focused on these three technologies, led by ion chromatography (IC), a technique that separates ions, or charged molecules, and typically identifies them based on their electrical conductivity. The sale of IC systems and related products accounts for a majority of revenues. HPLC separates biological molecules such as proteins and pharmaceuticals and identifies them by measuring the amount of light they absorb or emit. DNEX's ASE 200 system, based on the company's new ASE technology, extracts solid samples using common solvents.

The company's chromatography systems and related products are used extensively in environmental analysis and by a broad range of industries to isolate and identify the individual components of complex chemical mixtures. In its important environmental market, DNEX's methods and instrumentation are used worldwide to analyze drinking water, waste water and air in accordance with governmental regulatory procedures. In addition, the company's ASE technology offers rapid extraction of difficult environmental samples such as soil and sludge.

DNEX's products are also used by industry to ensure the quality of their products and processes. DNEX's systems provide detailed information about chemical processes for customers in the chemical and petrochemical industries, for instance, and allow plant managers to monitor problematic contaminants in feedstocks, equipment and finished products. In semiconductor fabrication, where water purity is critical, the company's IC technology, which can detect and identify ions at part-per-trillion concentration levels, is used to monitor water for trace-level contaminants. DNEX also serves customers in the pharmaceutical, life science, biotechnology and power generation industries.

Net sales grew 6%, to $151 million, in FY 98 (Jun.), reflecting improved demand for DNEX's systems in North America and Europe. However, problems associated with Asian economies limited revenue growth in that region.

Per Share Data ($)

(Year Ended Jun. 30)	1998	1997	1996	1995	1994	1993	1992	1991	1990	1989
Tangible Bk. Val.	NA	3.55	3.33	3.79	3.67	3.12	2.96	2.42	2.19	2.04
Cash Flow	NA	1.13	0.98	0.76	0.63	0.57	0.50	0.47	0.41	0.38
Earnings	1.18	1.03	0.88	0.67	0.55	0.51	0.45	0.42	0.36	0.34
Dividends	Nil	Nil	Nil	Nil	Nil	Nil	Nil	Nil	Nil	Nil
Payout Ratio	Nil	Nil	Nil	Nil	Nil	Nil	Nil	Nil	Nil	Nil
Prices - High	30	27½	20¼	14⅝	9¾	11⅛	10¼	8½	7	6⅞
- Low	23	17¼	13⅞	9¼	7⅞	7¾	6¼	4⅝	3⅝	4¼
P/E Ratio - High	25	27	23	22	18	22	23	20	19	21
- Low	19	17	16	14	14	15	14	11	10	13

Income Statement Analysis (Million $)

	1998	1997	1996	1995	1994	1993	1992	1991	1990	1989
Revs.	NA	142	133	120	110	106	96.4	89.3	80.6	75.5
Oper. Inc.	NA	43.3	36.6	30.3	27.4	25.8	22.4	20.7	18.7	17.8
Depr.	NA	2.6	2.9	2.6	2.5	2.0	1.9	1.8	1.9	1.7
Int. Exp.	NA	0.1	0.1	0.1	0.3	0.5	0.7	0.6	0.3	0.2
Pretax Inc.	NA	40.0	36.7	31.7	26.1	24.9	22.5	21.8	19.9	20.3
Eff. Tax Rate	NA	34%	35%	38%	35%	35%	35%	35%	35%	37%
Net Inc.	NA	26.2	24.0	19.8	17.0	16.3	14.7	14.2	13.0	12.8

Balance Sheet & Other Fin. Data (Million $)

	1998	1997	1996	1995	1994	1993	1992	1991	1990	1989
Cash	NA	24.6	33.6	49.5	51.3	42.5	49.5	48.3	50.8	54.1
Curr. Assets	NA	79.8	77.8	93.5	92.5	82.9	84.7	80.6	80.4	78.8
Total Assets	NA	118	113	132	133	118	120	109	106	99
Curr. Liab.	NA	31.6	29.9	26.2	21.1	22.1	23.8	23.2	21.8	16.9
LT Debt	NA	Nil	Nil	0.1	0.1	0.1	0.1	0.1	0.2	0.2
Common Eqty.	NA	84.2	82.0	104	111	94.9	94.9	85.3	83.7	81.1
Total Cap.	NA	86.5	83.0	106	112	96.0	96.2	86.2	84.5	81.3
Cap. Exp.	NA	2.6	3.0	2.0	7.8	1.2	8.5	4.5	3.8	2.8
Cash Flow	NA	28.8	26.8	22.4	19.5	18.3	16.7	15.9	14.8	14.6
Curr. Ratio	NA	2.5	2.6	3.6	4.4	3.8	3.6	3.5	3.7	4.7
% LT Debt of Cap.	NA	Nil	Nil	0.1	0.1	0.1	0.1	0.2	0.2	0.2
% Net Inc.of Revs.	NA	18.5	18.1	16.5	15.6	15.4	15.3	15.9	16.1	17.0
% Ret. on Assets	NA	22.7	19.6	14.9	13.6	14.1	13.0	13.1	13.0	14.0
% Ret. on Equity	NA	31.5	25.8	18.4	16.6	17.6	16.6	16.8	16.1	17.1

Data as orig. reptd.; bef. results of disc. opers. and/or spec. items. Per share data adj. for stk. divs. as of ex-div. date. Bold denotes diluted EPS (FASB 128). E-Estimated. NA-Not Available. NM-Not Meaningful. NR-Not Ranked.

Office—1228 Titan Way, Sunnyvale, CA 94086. **Tel**—(408) 737-0700. **Pres & CEO**—A. B. Bowman. **Secy**—J. C. Gaither **VP, CFO & Investor Contact**—Michael W. Pope. **Dirs**—D. L. Anderson, J. F. Battey, A. B. Bowman, B. J. Moore. **Transfer Agent & Registrar**—Boston EquiServe. **Incorporated**—in California in 1980; reincorporated in Delaware in 1986. **Empl**— 685. **S&P Analyst:** S.J.T.

03-OCT-98   Industry:
Retail (Specialty)

Summary: DAP operates more than 400 stores in the Southeast, selling automotive replacement parts and maintenance items to the do-it-yourself customer.

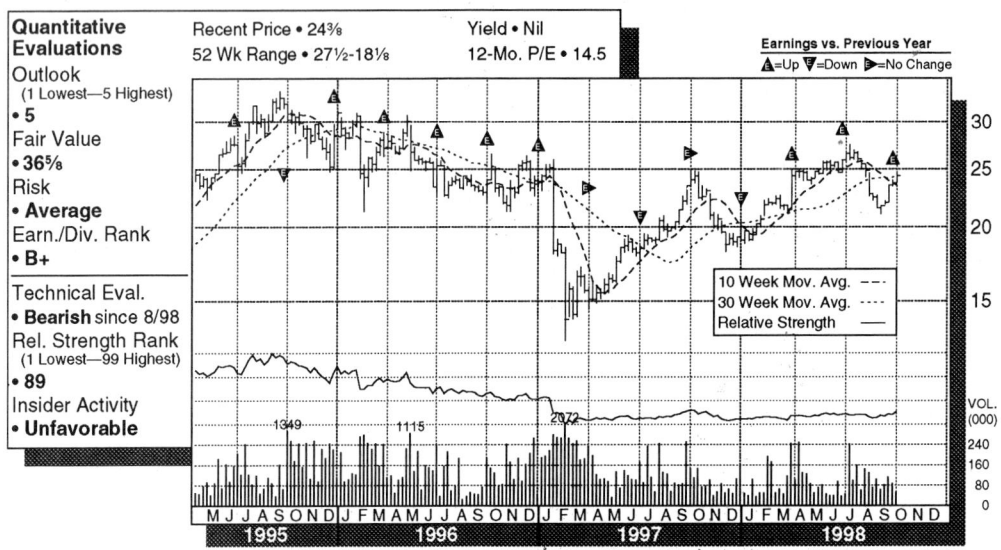

Quantitative Evaluations

Recent Price • 24⅜
52 Wk Range • 27½-18⅛

Yield • Nil
12-Mo. P/E • 14.5

Earnings vs. Previous Year
▲=Up ▼=Down ▶=No Change

Outlook
(1 Lowest—5 Highest)
• **5**

Fair Value
• **36⅝**

Risk
• **Average**

Earn./Div. Rank
• **B+**

Technical Eval.
• **Bearish** since 8/98

Rel. Strength Rank
(1 Lowest—99 Highest)
• **89**

Insider Activity
• **Unfavorable**

10 Week Mov. Avg. ---
30 Week Mov. Avg. ····
Relative Strength —

Business Profile - 31-MAR-98

Traditional Do-It-Yourself (DIY) comparable store sales and operating results have remained strong for DAP while certain competitors have reported weakness in selected markets in the overall automotive aftermarket. During the third quarter of FY 98 (May), the company opened 15 new mini-depot stores and closed one new depot store. DAP plans to open 60 to 65 stores for the full fiscal year. In December 1997, Hi-Lo Automotive terminated an agreement to be acquired by Discount Auto Parts in favor of a higher offer from O'Reilly Automotive. Hi-Lo paid a $4 million termination fee to DAP.

Operational Review - 31-MAR-98

Net sales for the 39 weeks ended March 3, 1997, rose 9.2%, over the 40 weeks ended March 4, 1997, reflecting a 25% advance of traditional Do-It-Yourself retail sales, partially offset by much lower commercial sales of R-12 freon. Same store sales grew 9.6%, but decreased 3.1% including commercial freon sales. Profitability was hurt by costs related to the development and roll-out of the commercial delivery program; operating income advanced 4.6%. Following higher interest expense and taxes at 38.5% in both periods, net income climbed 3.1% to $19,510,000 ($1.17 a diluted share) from $18,923,000 ($1.13).

Stock Performance - 02-OCT-98

In the past 30 trading days, DAP's shares have increased 9%, compared to a 7% fall in the S&P 500. Average trading volume for the past five days was 10,320 shares, compared with the 40-day moving average of 17,849 shares.

Key Stock Statistics

Dividend Rate/Share	Nil	Shareholders	700
Shs. outstg. (M)	16.6	Market cap. (B)	$0.405
Avg. daily vol. (M)	0.017	Inst. holdings	39%
Tang. Bk. Value/Share	15.45		
Beta	0.98		

Value of $10,000 invested 5 years ago: $ 9,512

Fiscal Year Ending May 31

	1999	1998	1997	1996	1995	1994
Revenues (Million $)						
1Q	123.0	109.7	90.10	71.35	57.81	48.64
2Q	—	105.2	105.8	73.77	59.97	49.53
3Q	—	110.3	101.9	75.43	63.92	52.23
4Q	—	122.2	107.4	86.93	72.00	57.18
Yr.	—	447.5	405.2	307.5	253.7	207.6
Earnings Per Share ($)						
1Q	0.44	0.39	0.39	0.34	0.52	0.26
2Q	—	0.37	0.42	0.36	0.29	0.20
3Q	—	0.42	0.34	0.34	0.31	0.25
4Q	—	0.46	-0.37	0.40	0.36	0.27
Yr.	—	1.63	0.77	1.44	1.48	1.03

Next earnings report expected: mid December

Dividend Data

No dividends have been paid, and the company has no plans to pay any, as it intends to retain all earnings for future operations and expansion of its business.

A Division of The McGraw·Hill Companies

Business Summary - 31-MAR-98

Discount Auto Parts (DAP) is now one of the Southeast's leading retailers of replacement parts, maintenance items, and accessories serving the car owner. The company was started as a single store in 1971 by the Fontaine family in Eloise, FL, and, as of March 3, 1998, supports 435 stores throughout Florida, Georgia, Alabama, South Carolina and Mississippi, up from 400 stores at the end of FY 97 (May) and 314 at the end of FY 96.

DAP is relying on its employees to continue to grow and avoid the hazards in the road ahead. DAP attributes its continuing growth (FY 97 was another year of record sales and operating income for the company) to its employee-centered management, team-building that results in building business. It has retained more than 90% of its managers and district managers and is determined not to become a bureaucracy no matter how successful it becomes. The company also points to its company wide goal of having parts in stock 99% of the time and its emphasis on team members' greeting customers within 20 feet or 20 seconds of entering.

The company's stores use two different formats: mini-depot and depot. The smaller standard-format stores have been phased out. Mini-depot stores (410 as of March 3, 1998) under DAP's new standardized format will average approximately 4,800 sq. ft. of selling space and 15,400 stock-keeping units (SKUs); depot stores (25) will average 10,000 sq. ft. of space and 20,000 SKUs. Although brandname products are emphasized, a number of private-label products are also carried under the Discount Auto and Power Pak names.

In March 1997, the company entered into a joint business agreement with Q Lube Inc., a subsidiary of Quaker State Corp., to jointly develop locations that provide fast lube and automotive maintenance services for the car owner. The service centers will primarily be located on properties owned or leased by DAP and adjacent to the retail stores. Previously, the company did not perform repairs and limited its offerings to parts and supplies for the home mechanic.

During the third quarter of FY 98 (May), DAP opened 15 new mini-depot stores and closed one depot store, for a year to date total of 36 new stores. The company plans to open a total of 60 to 65 new stores in FY 98, down from the 86 units (85 mini-depot and one depot) launched in FY 97.

Discount Auto relies on its parts management strategies, low operating costs, and increased direct importing to give it a competitive edge.

Per Share Data ($)

(Year Ended May 31)	1998	1997	1996	1995	1994	1993	1992	1991	1990	1989
Tangible Bk. Val.	15.45	13.80	13.04	8.47	6.99	5.96	4.84	NA	NA	NA
Cash Flow	2.52	1.52	2.07	2.00	1.39	1.39	0.95	NA	NA	NA
Earnings	1.63	0.77	1.44	1.48	1.03	0.89	0.66	NA	NA	NA
Dividends	Nil	Nil	Nil	Nil	Nil	Nil	NA	NA	NA	NA
Payout Ratio	Nil	Nil	Nil	Nil	Nil	Nil	NA	NA	NA	NA
Cal. Yrs.	1997	1996	1995	1994	1993	1992	1991	1990	1989	1988
Prices - High	26	31⅛	33⅞	27⅝	31⅛	28⅛	NA	NA	NA	NA
- Low	12⅞	21¼	17¾	13⅞	20⅝	18	NA	NA	NA	NA
P/E Ratio - High	16	40	24	19	30	32	NA	NA	NA	NA
- Low	8	28	12	9	20	28	NA	NA	NA	NA

Income Statement Analysis (Million $)

	1998	1997	1996	1995	1994	1993	1992	1991	1990	1989
Revs.	447	405	307	254	208	177	141	NA	NA	NA
Oper. Inc.	67.0	59.7	50.4	38.1	31.1	26.4	20.3	NA	NA	NA
Depr.	15.0	12.5	9.9	7.2	5.0	4.7	3.9	NA	NA	NA
Int. Exp.	10.2	6.1	5.1	6.3	5.1	3.6	2.9	NA	NA	NA
Pretax Inc.	44.2	20.7	36.6	30.6	23.3	18.9	14.0	NA	NA	NA
Eff. Tax Rate	38%	39%	39%	33%	39%	28%	37%	NA	NA	NA
Net Inc.	27.2	12.7	22.5	20.6	14.3	13.6	8.9	NA	NA	NA

Balance Sheet & Other Fin. Data (Million $)

	1998	1997	1996	1995	1994	1993	1992	1991	1990	1989
Cash	5.1	6.4	4.6	4.6	16.3	14.4	NA	NA	NA	NA
Curr. Assets	195	177	125	104	80.4	68.1	NA	NA	NA	NA
Total Assets	512	443	334	271	214	159	131	NA	NA	NA
Curr. Liab.	89.1	96.1	65.4	57.2	46.4	34.2	NA	NA	NA	NA
LT Debt	161	114	50.4	94.6	70.1	42.0	37.3	NA	NA	NA
Common Eqty.	257	229	216	118	97.2	82.8	65.8	NA	NA	NA
Total Cap.	423	347	269	214	167	125	103	NA	NA	NA
Cap. Exp.	64.6	70.2	58.2	42.3	47.9	22.5	NA	NA	NA	NA
Cash Flow	42.2	25.2	32.4	27.8	19.3	18.3	12.8	NA	NA	NA
Curr. Ratio	2.2	1.8	1.9	1.8	1.7	2.0	NA	NA	NA	NA
% LT Debt of Cap.	38.0	32.9	18.8	44.3	41.9	33.7	36.1	NA	NA	NA
% Net Inc.of Revs.	6.1	3.1	7.3	8.1	6.9	7.7	6.3	NA	NA	NA
% Ret. on Assets	5.7	3.3	7.5	8.5	7.7	8.2	NA	NA	NA	NA
% Ret. on Equity	11.2	5.7	13.5	19.2	15.9	20.6	NA	NA	NA	NA

Data as orig. reptd.; bef. results of disc. opers. and/or spec. items. Per share data adj. for stk. divs. as of ex-div. date. Bold denotes diluted EPS (FASB 128). E-Estimated. NA-Not Available. NM-Not Meaningful. NR-Not Ranked.

Office—4900 Frontage Road South, Lakeland, FL 33815. **Tel**—(941) 687-9226.**CEO**—P. J. Fontaine. **Pres & COO**—W. C. Perkins.**CFO, Secy & Investor Contact**—C. Michael Moore (941-284-2010). **Dirs**—P. J. Fontaine, W. C. Perkins, W. Shatzer, A. G. Tunstall, D. P. Walling, E. E. Wardlow.**Transfer Agent & Registrar**—ChaseMellon Shareholder Services, Ridgefield Park, NJ. **Incorporated**—in Florida in 1972. **Empl**— 3,677.
S&P Analyst: Ray Lam, CFA

Dixie Group
3708
NASDAQ Symbol **DXYN**

In S&P SmallCap 600

03-OCT-98

Industry:
Textiles (Specialty)

Summary: This company (formerly Dixie Yarns) makes value-added textile and floorcovering products for specialty markets.

Quantitative Evaluations		
Recent Price • 6⅜	Yield • 3.1%	
52 Wk Range • 15-6¼	12-Mo. P/E • NM	

Outlook
(1 Lowest—5 Highest)
• **3**

Fair Value
• **8⅜**

Risk
• **Average**

Earn./Div. Rank
• **C**

Technical Eval.
• **Neutral** since 7/98

Rel. Strength Rank
(1 Lowest—99 Highest)
• **22**

Insider Activity
• **NA**

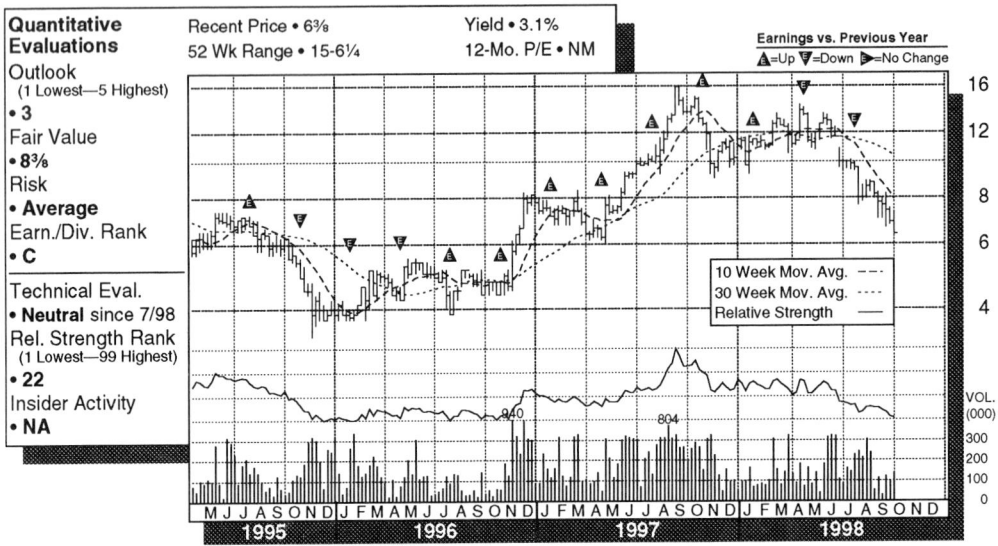

Earnings vs. Previous Year
▲=Up ▼=Down ▶=No Change

10 Week Mov. Avg. ---
30 Week Mov. Avg. ····
Relative Strength —

Business Profile - 25-AUG-98

Following its January 1997 purchase of Danube Carpet Mills ($75 million in annual sales), DXYN now derives approximately two-thirds of its revenues from floorcoverings. In May 1998, the company announced plans to spin off its textile/apparel operations so that each of its two businesses, floorcoverings and textiles/apparel, could pursue individual strategies. In June 1998, DXYN announced it would discontinue the knit fabric and apparel business. The company now consists of the specialty yarns business and the floorcovering business. The spin-off of the textile/apparel business (now specialty yarns) remain is expected to occur in late 1998 or early 1999.

Operational Review - 25-AUG-98

Revenues from continuing operations in the six months ended June 27, 1998, increased 10%, year to year, as higher floorcovering sales outweighed lower textile/apparel sales. Gross margins narrowed, and selling and administrative expenses rose faster than sales. With higher interest and other expenses, and taxes at 38.8%, versus 40.3%, income from continuing operations fell 5.2%, to $6,532,000 ($0.54 a share, diluted), from $6,887,000 ($0.60). Results exclude a loss of $0.11 a share from discontinued operations and a loss of $1.22 on the disposal of the knit fabric operations and the apparel segment in 1998, and a loss of $0.05 from discontinued operations in 1997.

Stock Performance - 02-OCT-98

In the past 30 trading days, DXYN's shares have declined 27%, compared to a 7% fall in the S&P 500. Average trading volume for the past five days was 27,380 shares, compared with the 40-day moving average of 29,228 shares.

Key Stock Statistics

Dividend Rate/Share	0.20	Shareholders	4,500
Shs. outstg. (M)	11.3	Market cap. (B)	$0.068
Avg. daily vol. (M)	0.020	Inst. holdings	61%
Tang. Bk. Value/Share	4.41		
Beta	0.83		

Value of $10,000 invested 5 years ago: $ 5,301

Fiscal Year Ending Dec. 31

	1998	1997	1996	1995	1994	1993
Revenues (Million $)						
1Q	167.9	162.4	161.5	181.7	164.8	120.8
2Q	167.7	169.2	168.0	177.8	178.3	161.4
3Q	—	159.9	145.4	161.3	173.9	152.5
4Q	—	170.4	140.2	150.1	171.5	159.9
Yr.	—	661.8	615.1	670.8	688.5	594.6
Earnings Per Share ($)						
1Q	0.21	0.26	-0.09	0.06	-0.33	0.10
2Q	0.28	0.29	0.12	0.03	0.01	-0.09
3Q	—	0.25	0.18	-0.53	0.04	0.07
4Q	—	0.19	-1.21	-4.24	0.04	0.07
Yr.	—	0.99	-1.00	-4.44	-0.24	0.41

Next earnings report expected: late October

Dividend Data (Dividends have been paid since 1998.)

Amount ($)	Date Decl.	Ex-Div. Date	Stock of Record	Payment Date
0.050	Feb. 19	Mar. 04	Mar. 06	Mar. 20 '98
0.050	May. 04	May. 13	May. 15	May. 29 '98
0.050	Aug. 31	Sep. 10	Sep. 14	Sep. 25 '98
0.050	Aug. 31	Sep. 10	Sep. 14	Sep. 25 '98

A Division of The McGraw·Hill Companies

Business Summary - 25-AUG-98

Once exclusively a maker of products (yarns, thread, textiles) sold to industrial customers for further processing, The Dixie Group (DXYN) has built a floorcovering operation, sold its threads business, and added finished apparel products in a strategic shift toward higher-margin items aimed at consumers. Such items now account for approximately 65% of the products sold by DXYN, which changed its name in May 1997 from Dixie Yarns, Inc. to highlight its new direction.

DXYN expanded into the floorcovering business (65% of net sales in 1997) through a series of acquisitions in 1993 and 1994. DXYN further expanded its floorcovering business by acquiring Danube Carpet Mills, Inc. in early fiscal 1997. In October 1997, the company acquired the needlebond and artificial turf assets and business of General Felt Industries, Inc.

The company supplies carpet to the manufactured/modular housing and recreational vehicles industries, produces indoor/outdoor needlebond carpet for high-traffic areas and makes high-end residential and commercial carpets and rugs. The Candlewick Yarns operation produces specialty yarns for the tufting industry, with 35% of its production used internally by the company's floorcovering businesses.

DXYN is also pursuing new markets in the floorcovering business by launching a new product line in 1998. The new line involves the manufacture and sale of carpet pad which will be made by recycling the company's synthetic material byproducts.

As the company expanded its floorcovering business, it also reduced its presence in the textile industry, in an effort to focus on higher-margin products, and in 1995 it established a finished knit apparel business. Today, DXYN's textile/apparel segment (35% of net sales in 1997) is a vertically integrated operation comprising three companies: Dixie Yarns, a spinner and dyer of cotton and synthetic yarns; Caro Knit, a producer of 100%-cotton knit fabrics; and C-Knit Apparel, which relies on fabric supplied by Caro Knit to produce "placket," or golf-type, shirts for sports apparel markets. The company believes that its vertical yarn and fabric capabilities give it greater control over the quality and delivery of its apparel products.

In May 1998, the company said it plans to spin off its textile/apparel operations so that each of its two businesses, floorcoverings and textiles/apparel, could pursue individual strategies. In June 1998, DXYN announced it would discontinue the knit fabric and apparel business. The company now consists of the specialty yarns business and the floorcovering business. The spin-off of the textile/apparel business (now specialty yarns) is expected to occur in late 1998 or early 1999.

Per Share Data ($)										
(Year Ended Dec. 31)	**1997**	**1996**	**1995**	**1994**	**1993**	**1992**	**1991**	**1990**	**1989**	**1988**
Tangible Bk. Val.	5.09	6.87	7.37	9.53	10.06	12.46	11.91	15.20	14.70	14.80
Cash Flow	3.07	1.52	1.38	2.41	2.96	3.26	-0.43	2.71	2.71	3.04
Earnings	0.99	-1.00	-4.44	-0.24	0.41	0.65	-2.88	0.71	1.13	1.80
Dividends	Nil	Nil	Nil	0.20	0.20	0.20	0.42	0.68	0.68	0.64
Payout Ratio	Nil	Nil	Nil	NM	49%	31%	NM	96%	57%	33%
Prices - High	16	8 1/4	7 3/8	11 1/4	16 3/4	14 1/4	15 1/4	16 1/4	22 1/2	22
- Low	6	3 3/4	3 3/8	6 3/4	8 3/4	8 3/4	7 1/2	7 7/8	14	16
P/E Ratio - High	16	NM	NM	NM	41	22	NM	23	20	12
- Low	6	NM	NM	NM	21	13	NM	11	12	9
Income Statement Analysis (Million $)										
Revs.	662	615	671	689	595	470	492	556	571	606
Oper. Inc.	58.6	54.0	51.4	41.3	36.8	44.5	28.7	45.2	46.0	56.2
Depr.	24.5	28.2	36.0	35.2	29.2	22.9	21.6	19.2	16.3	14.8
Int. Exp.	12.6	13.0	15.6	13.7	12.8	10.8	12.2	10.8	7.6	6.9
Pretax Inc.	18.8	-15.5	-64.7	-11.9	9.0	11.3	-31.6	12.7	24.1	34.8
Eff. Tax Rate	38%	NM	NM	NM	48%	50%	NM	46%	52%	38%
Net Inc.	11.6	-11.2	-52.2	-3.2	4.7	5.7	-25.4	6.8	11.7	21.5
Balance Sheet & Other Fin. Data (Million $)										
Cash	1.8	2.0	3.4	1.9	4.0	1.4	2.3	2.0	3.4	3.1
Curr. Assets	136	131	157	153	148	128	136	141	139	151
Total Assets	387	328	397	488	497	372	347	359	347	343
Curr. Liab.	67.9	58.5	46.0	63.8	59.2	45.0	37.0	43.8	37.8	63.9
LT Debt	161	129	192	182	182	165	154	126	111	64.0
Common Eqty.	121	109	118	171	176	145	141	174	185	204
Total Cap.	309	260	340	413	424	324	306	314	307	278
Cap. Exp.	26.5	17.6	30.0	36.0	116	26.0	38.0	31.0	33.0	26.0
Cash Flow	36.1	17.0	-16.2	32.0	33.9	28.5	-3.8	26.0	28.1	36.3
Curr. Ratio	2.0	2.2	3.4	2.4	2.5	2.9	3.7	3.2	3.7	2.4
% LT Debt of Cap.	52.1	49.5	56.6	44.0	43.0	50.9	50.3	40.1	36.1	23.1
% Net Inc.of Revs.	1.8	NM	NM	NM	0.8	1.2	NM	1.2	2.1	3.5
% Ret. on Assets	3.3	NM	NM	NM	1.0	1.6	NM	2.0	3.6	6.4
% Ret. on Equity	10.1	NM	NM	NM	2.6	3.9	NM	4.0	6.4	10.9

Data as orig. reptd.; bef. results of disc. opers. and/or spec. items. Per share data adj. for stk. divs. as of ex-div. date. Bold denotes diluted EPS (FASB 128). E-Estimated. NA-Not Available. NM-Not Meaningful. NR-Not Ranked.

Office—1100 S. Watkins St., Chattanooga, TN 37404. **Tel**—(423) 698-2501. **Chrmn, Pres, CEO**—D. K. Frierson. **EVP, CFO & Investor Contact**—Glenn A. Berry (423-493-7285). **EVP & COO**—W. N. Fry IV. **Treas**—G. A. Harmon. **Secy**—S. T. Klein. **Dirs**—J. D. Brock, P. K. Brock, L. A. Brooks Jr., D. K. Frierson, P. K. Frierson, W. N. Fry IV, J. W. Murrey III, P. L. Smith, R. J. Sudderth Jr. **Transfer Agent**—SunTrust Bank, Atlanta. **Incorporated**—in Tennessee in 1920. **Empl**— 4,600. **S&P Analyst:** Kathleen J. Fraser

03-OCT-98

Industry: Savings & Loan Companies

Summary: This company, through its Downey Savings and Loan subsidiary (assets of $5.8 billion), provides diversified savings and loan services in northern and southern California.

Quantitative Evaluations	
Recent Price • 22⅝	Yield • 1.4%
52 Wk Range • 35¼-21⅞	12-Mo. P/E • 11.2

Outlook (1 Lowest—5 Highest)
• **3**

Fair Value
• **25¾**

Risk
• **Low**

Earn./Div. Rank
• **B**

Technical Eval.
• **Bullish** since 9/98

Rel. Strength Rank (1 Lowest—99 Highest)
• **33**

Insider Activity
• **NA**

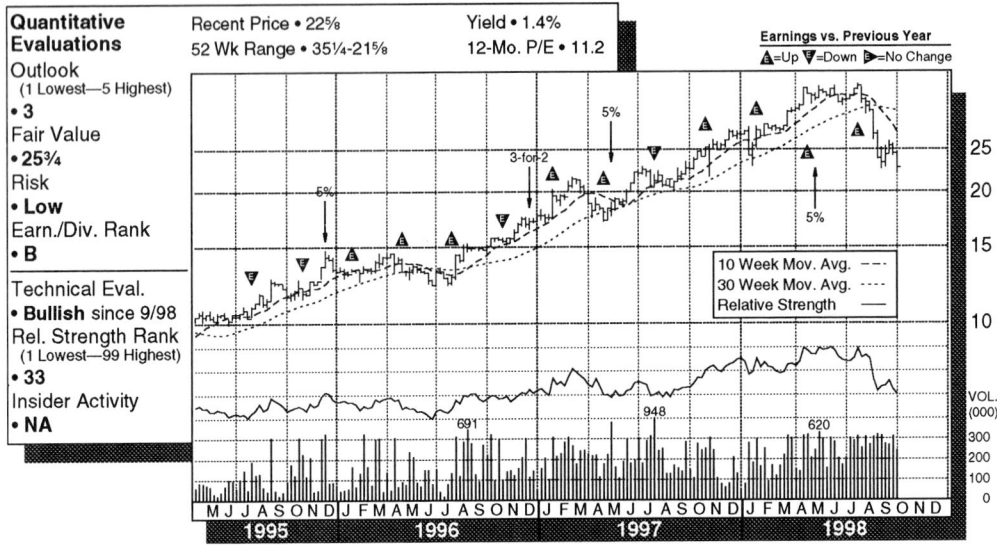

Earnings vs. Previous Year: ▲=Up ▼=Down ▷=No Change

10 Week Mov. Avg. – – –
30 Week Mov. Avg. · · · ·
Relative Strength —

Business Profile - 15-JUL-98

In the second quarter of 1998, Downey opened one new in-store branch, bringing total branches at quarter-end to 90, of which 27 are in supermarkets. The recent expansion, particularly into supermarket banking, has boosted the company's retail deposit franchise. At June 30, 1998, deposits were up 12%, year to year, to $5.2 billion. Loan originations in the second quarter reached a record $1.0 billion, 60% of which were single family loans originated for sale in the secondary market. Credit quality remains good, with nonperforming assets accounting for just 0.84% of total assets at June 30, 1998, down from 0.95% a year earlier.

Operational Review - 15-JUL-98

Net interest income in the first six months of 1998 rose 14%, year to year, on increased average earning assets and a wider effective interest rate spread (3.03%, versus 2.89%). The provision for loan losses was down sharply, to $1,734,000, from $4,028,000. Noninterest income was up 64% and noninterest expense advanced 4.7%. Results in the 1998 period were aided by the settlement of litigation regarding obligations of a prior venture partner, which added $8.3 million to pretax income. After taxes at 43.0%, versus 43.1%, net income climbed 58%, to $32,553,000 ($1.15 a share), from $20,640,000 ($0.74).

Stock Performance - 02-OCT-98

In the past 30 trading days, DSL's shares have declined 16%, compared to a 7% fall in the S&P 500. Average trading volume for the past five days was 48,120 shares, compared with the 40-day moving average of 73,200 shares.

Key Stock Statistics

Dividend Rate/Share	0.32	Shareholders	1,000
Shs. outstg. (M)	28.1	Market cap. (B)	$0.638
Avg. daily vol. (M)	0.063	Inst. holdings	36%
Tang. Bk. Value/Share	16.33		
Beta	1.15		

Value of $10,000 invested 5 years ago: $ 29,231

Fiscal Year Ending Dec. 31

	1998	1997	1996	1995	1994	1993
Revenues (Million $)						
1Q	124.7	108.6	92.16	79.91	54.71	58.90
2Q	121.7	108.6	87.15	84.24	58.76	62.85
3Q	—	117.1	93.12	85.67	62.24	60.06
4Q	—	121.3	99.1	89.60	70.99	53.97
Yr.	—	455.6	371.6	339.5	246.7	235.8
Earnings Per Share ($)						
1Q	**0.62**	0.44	0.37	0.12	0.21	0.25
2Q	**0.53**	0.30	0.28	0.15	0.23	0.33
3Q	—	0.37	-0.23	0.19	0.20	0.28
4Q	—	0.50	0.31	0.30	0.20	0.15
Yr.	—	1.61	0.73	0.75	0.84	1.01

Next earnings report expected: mid October

Dividend Data (Dividends have been paid since 1986.)

Amount ($)	Date Decl.	Ex-Div. Date	Stock of Record	Payment Date
0.080	Jan. 28	Feb. 09	Feb. 11	Feb. 27 '98
0.080	Apr. 22	May. 05	May. 07	May. 22 '98
5%	Apr. 22	May. 05	May. 07	May. 22 '98
0.080	Jul. 29	Aug. 10	Aug. 12	Aug. 27 '98

A Division of The McGraw-Hill Companies

Business Summary - 15-JUL-98

Downey Financial Corp. is a $5.8 billion asset savings and loan institution operating primarily in California. Historically, Downey has focused its lending activities on the origination of first mortgage loans secured by residential property and retail neighborhood shopping centers. To a lesser degree, it has also concentrated on originating real estate loans secured by multi-family and commercial and industrial properties, including office buildings, land and other properties with income producing capabilities.

In addition, Downey has provided construction loan financing for residential (both single family and multi-family) and commercial retail neighborhood shopping center projects, including loans to joint ventures where DSL Service Company or the bank was a participant.

Downey also originates loans to businesses through its commercial banking operations and loans on new and used automobiles through the purchase of motor vehicle sales contracts from auto dealers in California and other western states. The thrift's indirect auto lending program is in addition to automobile loans originated directly through Downey's branch network.

During 1998, Downey's primary focus will continue to be the origination of adjustable rate single family mortgage loans, particularly subprime loans which carry higher interest rates, and consumer loans. In addition, management expects to continue its secondary marketing activities of selling its production of certain fixed rate single family loans as well as certain adjustable rate mortgage (ARM) loan products.

Like most savings and loan institutions, Downey's primary source of revenue is interest earned on its loan and investment portfolios. It also generates income through fees connected with loans and deposit accounts, and through the sale of securities. Downey's net interest income (interest income less interest expense paid on deposit accounts and other borrowings) is a function of changes in prevailing interest rates and the company's levels of interest-earning assets and liabilities. Profitability can often be measured by the spread between the yield on earning assets and the rate paid on funds to support these assets.

Another important determinant of operating results is credit costs. It is Downey's policy to provide an allowance for loan and real estate losses through quarterly provisions, when the value of an asset has been impaired and the loss can be reasonably estimated. In 1997, nonperforming asset levels declined by 16%, to $52.1 million (0.89% of total assets). The loan loss provision declined to $8,640,000, from $9,137,000 in 1996.

Per Share Data ($)

(Year Ended Dec. 31)	1997	1996	1995	1994	1993	1992	1991	1990	1989	1988
Tangible Bk. Val.	16.10	13.75	13.47	12.81	12.21	10.89	9.53	8.81	7.46	7.11
Earnings	1.61	0.73	0.75	0.84	1.01	1.49	0.89	1.50	0.10	1.04
Dividends	0.30	0.29	0.28	0.28	0.20	0.18	0.18	0.16	0.16	0.15
Payout Ratio	19%	40%	37%	33%	20%	12%	20%	11%	159%	15%
Prices - High	27³/₄	18¹/₄	14³/₄	12¹/₂	16	10³/₈	10⁵/₈	11³/₈	13⁷/₈	7¹/₂
- Low	17	12¹/₄	8⁵/₈	8¹/₄	8¹/₄	6¹/₂	6¹/₂	5⁷/₈	5⁷/₈	4¹/₂
P/E Ratio - High	17	25	20	15	16	7	12	8	NM	7
- Low	11	17	11	10	8	4	7	4	NM	4

Income Statement Analysis (Million $)

	1997	1996	1995	1994	1993	1992	1991	1990	1989	1988
Net Int. Inc.	154	135	105	106	112	116	115	86.0	54.0	76.0
Loan Loss Prov.	8.6	9.1	9.0	4.2	1.1	9.0	5.7	3.8	7.0	1.6
Non Int. Inc.	35.2	19.7	20.4	17.6	14.1	15.3	-11.4	30.0	11.0	NA
Non Int. Exp.	101	114	79.2	79.7	76.4	73.2	67.3	68.5	65.7	NA
Pretax Inc.	79.4	36.5	36.7	40.2	48.4	49.5	30.8	44.1	-7.7	50.2
Eff. Tax Rate	43%	36%	43%	42%	41%	16%	19%	4.70%	NM	42%
Net Inc.	45.2	20.7	21.1	23.5	28.6	41.9	24.9	42.0	2.7	29.0
% Net Int. Marg.	2.83	2.96	2.33	2.99	3.44	3.53	3.11	2.39	2.10	1.74

Balance Sheet & Other Fin. Data (Million $)

	1997	1996	1995	1994	1993	1992	1991	1990	1989	1988
Total Assets	5,836	5,198	4,656	4,651	3,467	3,478	3,778	4,168	4,099	4,333
Loans	5,282	4,747	4,184	4,189	2,917	2,766	3,254	3,002	2,713	3,036
Deposits	4,870	4,173	3,790	3,557	3,069	3,108	3,355	3,361	3,511	3,500
Capitalization:										
Debt	365	397	240	477	13.7	15.0	97.0	262	22.0	210
Equity	430	392	384	366	351	313	277	257	219	210
Total	795	789	624	843	365	328	373	519	241	420
% Ret. on Assets	0.8	0.4	0.5	0.6	0.8	1.2	0.6	1.0	0.1	0.8
% Ret. on Equity	11.0	5.3	5.6	6.6	8.6	14.2	9.3	17.6	1.3	14.6
% Loan Loss Resv.	0.6	0.6	0.7	0.6	0.9	1.0	0.6	0.6	0.6	0.4
% Risk Based Capital	NA	NA	14.3	14.2	16.9	14.4	12.1	11.1	9.4	NA
Price Times Book Value:										
Hi	1.7	1.3	1.1	1.0	1.3	1.0	1.1	1.3	1.9	1.1
Low	1.1	0.9	0.6	0.6	0.7	0.6	0.6	0.7	0.8	0.6

Data as orig. reptd.; bef. results of disc. opers. and/or spec. items. Per share data adj. for stk. divs. as of ex-div. date. Bold denotes diluted EPS (FASB 128). E-Estimated. NA-Not Available. NM-Not Meaningful. NR-Not Ranked.

Office—3501 Jamboree Rd., Newport Beach, CA 92660. **Tel**—(714) 854-0300. **Chrmn**—M. L. McAlister. **Pres & CEO**—J. W. Lokey. **EVP, CFO & Investor Contact**—Thomas E. Prince. **Dirs**—D. J. Aigner, C. E. Jones, P. Kouri, J. W. Lokey, M. L. McAlister, B. McQuarrie, L. C. Smull, S. Yellen. **Transfer Agent & Registrar**—American Stock Transfer & Trust Co. **Incorporated**—in California in 1957; reincorporated in Delaware in 1994. **Empl**— 1,285. **S&P Analyst:** Michael Schneider

STANDARD &POOR'S
STOCK REPORTS

Dravo Corp.

772

NYSE Symbol **DRV**

In S&P SmallCap 600

03-OCT-98

Industry: Construction (Cement & Aggregates)

Summary: This company is the largest publicly owned U.S. supplier of lime and lime-related technologies.

Quantitative Evaluations

Recent Price • 12⅝
52 Wk Range • 12⅝-6½

Yield • Nil
12-Mo. P/E • 13.7

Outlook
(1 Lowest—5 Highest)
• **4**

Fair Value
• **18½**

Risk
• **Low**

Earn./Div. Rank
• **B-**

Technical Eval.
• **Bearish** since 4/96

Rel. Strength Rank
(1 Lowest—99 Highest)
• **99**

Insider Activity
• **NA**

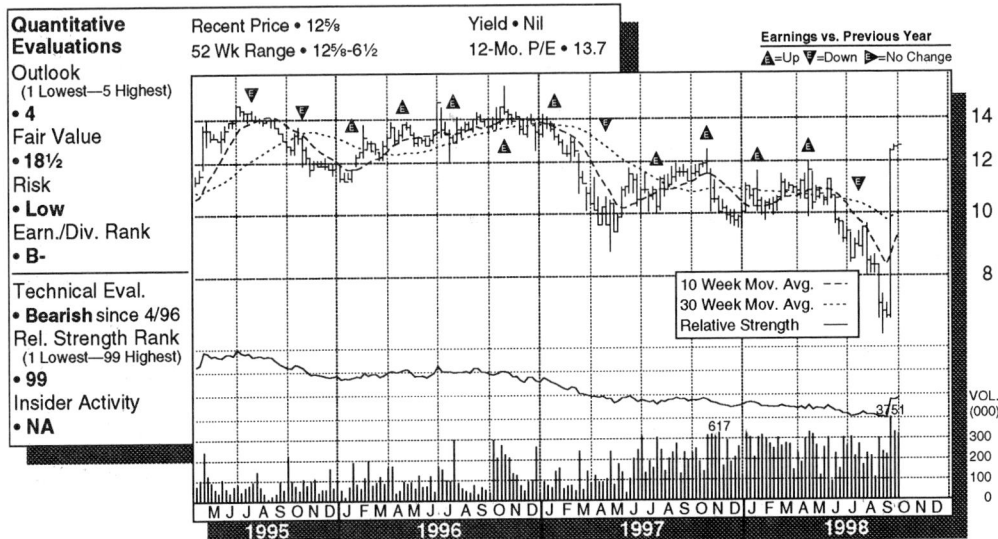

Earnings vs. Previous Year
▲=Up ▼=Down ▶=No Change

10 Week Mov. Avg. – – –
30 Week Mov. Avg. · · · ·
Relative Strength —

Business Profile - 26-MAR-98

Dravo is intent on streamlining its executive organization and further reducing its corporate overhead expenses. A hiring freeze went into effect in early January, and the company expects a savings in rent expense as a result of the relocation of the corporate and Dravo Lime Co. headquarters offices to the Westinghouse Building in downtown Pittsburgh. The company is also attempting to reduce costs in its plant operations. In order to realize additional return on advanced clean air technology investments, Dravo is in discussions with several existing customers regarding conversion of their existing flue gas desulfurization systems to Dravo's THIOCLEAR process. The company is also in preliminary discussions regarding overseas applications of its environmental technologies.

Operational Review - 26-MAR-98

Based on a preliminary report, revenues in 1997 edged up 2.8%, restricted by the effects of flooding in Kentucky during the first quarter. Margins narrowed, on the weaker volume; gross profit was up 2.2%. After a 14% jump in SG&A expenses, greater interest expense, and lower interest income, pretax income dropped 22%. After tax credits of $4,073,000, net income rose 7.0%, to $15,116,000 ($0.85 a share, after preferred dividends), from $14,128,000 ($0.79).

Stock Performance - 02-OCT-98

In the past 30 trading days, DRV's shares have increased 53%, compared to a 7% fall in the S&P 500. Average trading volume for the past five days was 109,600 shares, compared with the 40-day moving average of 157,610 shares.

Key Stock Statistics

Dividend Rate/Share	Nil	Shareholders	2,700
Shs. outstg. (M)	14.7	Market cap. (B)	$0.187
Avg. daily vol. (M)	0.266	Inst. holdings	47%
Tang. Bk. Value/Share	7.80		
Beta	0.59		

Value of $10,000 invested 5 years ago: $ 14,295

Fiscal Year Ending Dec. 31

	1998	1997	1996	1995	1994	1993
Revenues (Million $)						
1Q	42.37	37.62	38.22	33.91	57.68	61.81
2Q	41.88	42.44	39.35	35.70	72.63	70.19
3Q	—	40.97	40.75	37.77	75.31	76.13
4Q	—	41.45	39.81	38.69	72.50	69.46
Yr.	—	162.5	158.1	146.1	278.1	277.6
Earnings Per Share ($)						
1Q	**0.16**	**0.03**	0.17	0.13	-0.13	-0.02
2Q	**0.19**	**0.26**	0.10	0.11	0.17	0.21
3Q	—	**0.21**	0.20	0.15	0.22	0.24
4Q	—	**0.36**	0.22	0.15	-0.10	1.77
Yr.	—	**0.85**	0.78	0.57	0.16	2.20

Next earnings report expected: late October

Dividend Data

Common dividends were omitted in 1987, after having been paid since 1939. A poison pill stock purchase rights plan was adopted in 1986.

A Division of The **McGraw·Hill** *Companies*

Business Summary - 26-MAR-98

Dravo Corp. (DRV) is the largest publicly owned U.S. supplier of lime and lime-related technologies. In 1994, DRV sold substantially all the assets and certain liabilities of Dravo Basic Materials Co., its construction aggregates subsidiary, to Martin Marietta Materials, Inc.

Activities include production of lime for utility, metallurgical, pulp and paper, municipal, construction and miscellaneous chemical and industrial applications as well as the development and marketing of related environmental technologies, products and services. Operations are carried on principally by wholly owned Dravo Lime Co. All properties on which company reserves are located are physically accessible for mining and processing limestone into lime.

Dravo Lime, one of the largest U.S. lime producers, owns and operates three integrated lime production facilities -- two in Kentucky and one in Alabama. In 1995, the Black River plant in Butler, KY, completed a two-kiln expansion that boosted annual quicklime capacity to about 3,000,000 tons. Capacity will further increase, to slightly over 3,300,000 tons, when construction of a fourth 1,000-ton-per-day kiln in Maysville, KY, is completed.

The Maysville facility, currently a three-kiln,

1,050,000-ton-per-year plant, produces material marketed under the trade name Thiosorbic Lime. Product chemistry is ideally suited for removing sulfur dioxide from power plant stack gases. All of Maysville's output is committed under long-term contracts with utility companies in the Ohio Valley region. All contracts contain price escalation provisions. Owned reserves at the Maysville site are recovered from a mine 950 ft. underground and are considered adequate to sustain the future four kiln operations in excess of 75 years.

In conjunction with the sale of Dravo Basic Materials, Dravo Lime entered into agreements appointing Martin Marietta Materials the exclusive distributor of aggregate by-products produced by Dravo Lime in the lime production process. As part of the agreement covering Dravo Lime's Longview facility in Alabama, an aggregates processing facility was constructed in 1995 that is expected to produce from 500,000 to 1,000,000 tons of aggregates annually for purchase by Martin Marietta. DRV believes that a benefit of this installation is to make a marketable by-product out of limestone that is chemically unsuitable for lime production, thereby reducing the cost Dravo Lime incurs to recover the high calcium limestone reserves that are beneath the aggregate quality materials.

Per Share Data ($)

(Year Ended Dec. 31)	1997	1996	1995	1994	1993	1992	1991	1990	1989	1988
Tangible Bk. Val.	7.39	6.29	5.34	5.06	5.91	6.27	5.63	7.57	6.41	5.33
Cash Flow	1.56	1.46	1.38	1.35	3.41	1.78	1.85	1.99	1.86	1.83
Earnings	0.85	0.78	0.57	0.16	2.20	0.52	0.65	0.90	0.82	0.75
Dividends	Nil	Nil	Nil	Nil	Nil	Nil	Nil	Nil	Nil	Nil
Payout Ratio	Nil	Nil	Nil	Nil	Nil	Nil	Nil	Nil	Nil	Nil
Prices - High	14¹/₈	15³/₄	14³/₄	13³/₈	12¹/₂	10¹/₂	13³/₄	17¹/₄	22³/₄	17³/₈
- Low	8³/₄	11¹/₄	10	9¹/₂	8³/₄	6⁵/₈	5³/₄	9³/₄	13	11⁵/₈
P/E Ratio - High	17	20	26	84	6	20	21	19	28	23
- Low	10	14	18	59	4	13	9	11	16	16

Income Statement Analysis (Million $)

	1997	1996	1995	1994	1993	1992	1991	1990	1989	1988
Revs.	162	158	146	278	278	273	296	296	279	274
Oper. Inc.	27.5	29.1	24.8	32.0	35.6	38.2	42.7	39.9	41.9	36.9
Depr.	10.5	10.1	9.5	17.6	18.0	18.6	17.7	16.2	15.6	15.9
Int. Exp.	7.0	6.4	4.8	12.4	9.2	10.5	11.2	9.8	9.7	10.0
Pretax Inc.	11.0	14.1	11.3	5.5	10.5	12.7	16.1	19.7	17.8	16.0
Eff. Tax Rate	NA	NM	3.00%	11%	NM	19%	24%	20%	17%	26%
Net Inc.	15.1	14.1	11.0	4.9	35.1	10.3	12.3	15.8	14.7	11.8

Balance Sheet & Other Fin. Data (Million $)

	1997	1996	1995	1994	1993	1992	1991	1990	1989	1988
Cash	1.5	1.6	1.1	2.0	0.8	1.0	1.7	1.6	1.5	2.2
Curr. Assets	45.7	43.0	43.0	160	108	113	110	109	115	110
Total Assets	255	225	213	307	272	269	272	300	283	280
Curr. Liab.	41.7	35.0	33.0	154	49.0	53.0	64.0	99	80.0	74.0
LT Debt	74.4	63.5	64.3	42.4	88.5	88.0	90.0	55.0	62.0	71.0
Common Eqty.	110	92.8	78.4	75.0	88.0	93.0	83.0	112	95.0	78.0
Total Cap.	199	178	164	139	198	203	195	189	179	172
Cap. Exp.	27.2	20.0	33.1	44.8	13.6	8.5	19.7	29.1	12.4	12.7
Cash Flow	23.1	21.7	20.5	20.0	50.6	26.4	27.4	29.5	27.7	26.9
Curr. Ratio	1.1	1.2	1.3	1.0	2.2	2.1	1.7	1.1	1.4	1.5
% LT Debt of Cap.	37.4	35.8	39.2	30.5	44.7	43.4	46.0	28.9	34.5	41.3
% Net Inc.of Revs.	9.3	8.9	7.5	1.8	12.7	3.8	4.1	5.4	5.3	4.3
% Ret. on Assets	6.3	6.4	4.2	1.7	13.0	3.8	4.3	5.4	5.2	4.0
% Ret. on Equity	12.4	13.5	14.3	2.9	36.0	8.8	9.9	12.8	14.0	13.3

Data as orig. reptd.; bef. results of disc. opers. and/or spec. items. Per share data adj. for stk. divs. as of ex-div. date. Bold denotes diluted EPS (FASB 128). E-Estimated. NA-Not Available. NM-Not Meaningful. NR-Not Ranked.

Office—11 Stanwix St., Pittsburgh, PA 15222**Tel**—(412) 995-5500.**Chrmn**—A. E. Byrnes. **Pres & CEO**—C. A. Gilbert. **SVP & COO**—J. R. Major. **SVP-CFO & Secy**—E. J. Bellisario. **VP- Contr**—L. J. Walker.**VP-Treas & Investor Contact**—Richard E. Redlinger (412 995-5554).**Dirs**—A. E. Byrnes, C. A. Gilbert, J. C. Huntington Jr., W. E. Kassling, P. T. Kross, W. G. Roth.**Transfer Agent & Registrar**—Continental Stock Transfer & Trust Co., NYC. **Incorporated**—in Pennsylvania in 1936. **Empl**— 780. **S&P Analyst:** J.R.C.

Dress Barn — 3746

NASDAQ Symbol **DBRN**

In S&P SmallCap 600

03-OCT-98

Industry:
Retail (Discounters)

Summary: This retailer operates a chain of women's apparel stores, mainly in the East, offering moderate- to better-quality brand name merchandise at discount prices.

Quantitative Evaluations	
Outlook (1 Lowest—5 Highest)	• **4⁻**
Fair Value	• **16⅞**
Risk	• **Average**
Earn./Div. Rank	• **B+**
Technical Eval.	• **Bullish** since 7/98
Rel. Strength Rank (1 Lowest—99 Highest)	• **18**
Insider Activity	• **Neutral**

Recent Price • 14
52 Wk Range • 32⅜-11¼

Yield • Nil
12-Mo. P/E • 8.2

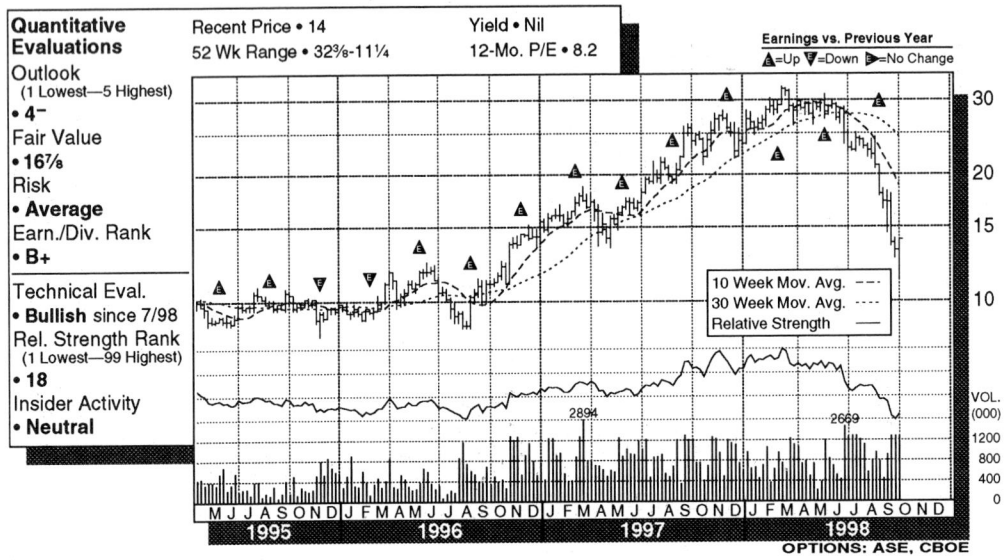

Earnings vs. Previous Year
▲=Up ▼=Down ▶=No Change

10 Week Mov. Avg. - - -
30 Week Mov. Avg. ·······
Relative Strength ——

OPTIONS: ASE, CBOE

Business Profile - 08-JUL-98

DBRN is placing primary emphasis on new store expansion using its new combo format, which combines its Dress Barn and Dress Barn Woman businesses in a single 9,000 sq. ft. location. The company expects that putting the two operating formats into one location will save it over $50,000 per store in annual expenses. During the first nine months of FY 98 (Jul.), DBRN opened or converted 50 stores to combos, and closed or moved 55 smaller stores. The larger stores represent about 34% of the total store base, accounting for approximately 50% of total store square footage.

Operational Review - 08-JUL-98

Net sales for the 39 weeks ended April 25, 1998, advanced 8.9%, year to year, reflecting consumer acceptance of the company's new merchandising strategy. Comparable-store sales grew 5%. Margins widened, due to higher initial margins resulting from the company's increased percentage of private brand merchandise and decreased markdowns; operating income was up 28%. With higher interest income, and after taxes at 36.5% in each period, net income climbed 41%, to $28,900,000 ($1.22 a share), from $20,554,000 ($0.88).

Stock Performance - 02-OCT-98

In the past 30 trading days, DBRN's shares have declined 33%, compared to a 7% fall in the S&P 500. Average trading volume for the past five days was 396,720 shares, compared with the 40-day moving average of 254,467 shares.

Key Stock Statistics

Dividend Rate/Share	Nil	Shareholders	2,000
Shs. outstg. (M)	23.2	Market cap. (B)	$0.325
Avg. daily vol. (M)	0.352	Inst. holdings	71%
Tang. Bk. Value/Share	11.38		
Beta	1.04		

Value of $10,000 invested 5 years ago: $ 7,724

Fiscal Year Ending Jul. 31

	1998	1997	1996	1995	1994	1993
Revenues (Million $)						
1Q	156.2	142.8	137.3	130.1	119.7	104.9
2Q	144.2	131.5	119.1	116.7	106.6	98.58
3Q	144.3	134.1	125.2	123.5	112.9	95.22
4Q	153.4	146.5	133.9	130.6	118.2	120.8
Yr.	598.2	554.8	515.5	500.8	457.3	419.6
Earnings Per Share ($)						
1Q	0.47	0.35	0.27	0.29	0.29	0.25
2Q	**0.34**	0.23	0.08	0.11	0.10	0.15
3Q	**0.41**	0.32	0.23	0.22	0.19	0.16
4Q	**0.48**	0.47	0.27	0.20	0.15	0.30
Yr.	**1.70**	1.35	0.84	0.82	0.73	0.86

Next earnings report expected: late November

Dividend Data

No cash has been paid.

A Division of The McGraw·Hill Companies

The Dress Barn, Inc.

Business Summary - 08-JUL-98

When it comes to women's fashions, Dress Barn feels that leaner is better. The Dress Barn, Inc. (DBRN) operates a national chain of value-priced specialty stores offering career fashion to the working woman. These stores offer in-season, moderate price fashion apparel at substantial discounts from department store prices.

The company that grew out of the store that Roslyn Jaffe opened and ran with her husband in 1962 operated 681 stores in 43 states as of April 25, 1998, versus 702 stores a year before. Store names include Dress Barn, Dress Barn Woman, and Westport and are located in strip centers and outlet centers. They offer three private labels, Atrium, Westport, and the newest, Dress Barn. Although the number of stores declined, as a result of the proliferation of the larger size, 9,000 sq. ft. to 10,000 sq. ft. combination stores that include Misses and Women's offerings, total square footage increased 3%.

The growth of the company will depend upon its ability to successfully execute its strategy of adding new combination stores and aggressively closing underperforming locations. Consistent with this lean operating style are plans to close or relocate 60 underperforming stores (primarily single-format stores) and replace them with 60 larger and more productive combination stores by the end of FY 98 (Jul.). By concentrating on opening larger stores that are combinations of both types of Dress Barn stores, the company can add petite and shoe departments and save an estimated $50,000 per store compared with the cost of operating two individual stores.

Also crucial to its success is its ability to spot and respond to trends in the marketplace. Company managers feel that by keeping store stock current they can stay in front of the competition. In the highly competitive field of women's apparel, Dress Barn intends to become the leader in national chains serving the moderate income working woman with value-priced specialty apparel. Its current strategy includes development of private brands, continued roll-out of combination stores, target marketing, maintaining merchandise focus, and improvement of customer service.

DBRN's main competitors are department stores, specialty stores and low price retailers.

During the first nine months of FY 98, DBRN opened or converted 50 stores to the combination format, and closed or moved 55 smaller stores.

Total sales for the five weeks ended June 27, 1998, were $58.6 million, up 2% from the year-ago period. Same-store sales declined 3%.

Per Share Data ($) (Year Ended Jul. 31)	1998	1997	1996	1995	1994	1993	1992	1991	1990	1989
Tangible Bk. Val.	NA	10.24	8.82	8.02	7.15	6.42	5.51	4.74	4.11	3.39
Cash Flow	NA	2.04	1.55	1.44	1.27	1.31	1.12	0.99	0.87	1.02
Earnings	1.70	1.35	0.84	0.82	0.73	0.86	0.74	0.68	0.64	0.85
Dividends	Nil	Nil	0.68	Nil	Nil	Nil	Nil	Nil	Nil	Nil
Payout Ratio	Nil	Nil	47%	Nil	Nil	Nil	Nil	Nil	Nil	Nil
Prices - High	32 3/8	28 3/8	15 3/4	11	14	23 1/2	20 1/8	15 1/2	12 3/4	17 3/8
- Low	13 1/2	13 3/8	8 5/8	8 1/4	8 1/4	10 1/4	7 3/4	6	4 3/4	10 3/4
P/E Ratio - High	19	21	19	13	19	27	27	23	20	20
- Low	8	10	10	10	11	12	10	9	7	13
Income Statement Analysis (Million $)										
Revs.	NA	555	516	501	457	420	363	325	284	249
Oper. Inc.	NA	61.4	45.3	40.1	35.9	37.3	30.1	27.5	25.4	31.2
Depr.	NA	16.1	15.8	14.0	12.0	9.8	8.1	6.8	5.2	3.7
Int. Exp.	NA	Nil	Nil	Nil	Nil	Nil	Nil	Nil	Nil	Nil
Pretax Inc.	Nil	50.0	30.0	29.0	25.6	29.7	25.0	23.7	22.8	29.7
Eff. Tax Rate	NA	37%	37%	37%	37%	36%	35%	37%	37%	36%
Net Inc.	NA	31.8	18.9	18.3	16.2	19.0	16.2	15.0	14.4	18.9
Balance Sheet & Other Fin. Data (Million $)										
Cash	NA	1.1	91.3	72.0	62.0	61.1	50.7	39.1	35.2	31.9
Curr. Assets	NA	226	184	163	146	143	125	95.0	86.0	71.0
Total Assets	NA	310	266	244	218	202	173	138	125	101
Curr. Liab.	NA	72.7	61.1	60.0	56.8	59.1	51.0	32.6	30.2	23.4
LT Debt	NA	3.5	3.5	3.5	Nil	Nil	Nil	Nil	Nil	Nil
Common Eqty.	Nil	233	199	179	159	142	120	103	93.0	76.0
Total Cap.	NA	237	205	184	161	143	122	105	95.0	78.0
Cap. Exp.	NA	16.5	17.1	22.0	25.5	21.9	14.9	10.1	14.5	11.8
Cash Flow	NA	47.9	34.7	32.0	28.1	28.9	24.3	21.7	19.6	22.6
Curr. Ratio	NA	3.1	3.0	2.7	2.6	2.4	2.4	2.9	2.8	3.0
% LT Debt of Cap.	NA	1.5	1.7	1.9	Nil	Nil	Nil	Nil	Nil	Nil
% Net Inc.of Revs.	Nil	5.7	3.7	3.7	3.5	4.5	4.5	4.6	5.1	7.6
% Ret. on Assets	NA	11.0	7.4	8.0	7.7	10.1	10.4	11.6	12.6	20.9
% Ret. on Equity	NA	14.7	10.0	10.9	10.7	14.4	14.5	15.6	16.9	28.6

Data as orig. reptd.; bef. results of disc. opers. and/or spec. items. Per share data adj. for stk. divs. as of ex-div. date. Bold denotes diluted EPS (FASB 128). E-Estimated. NA-Not Available. NM-Not Meaningful. NR-Not Ranked.

Office—30 Dunnigan Drive, Suffern, NY 10901. **Tel**—(914) 369-4500. **Chrmn & CEO**—E. S. Jaffe. **Pres & COO**—B. Steinberg. **SVP, CFO & Investor Contact**—Armand Correia. **Secy & Treas**—Roslyn S. Jaffe. **Dirs**—K. Eppler, M. S. Handler, E. S. Jaffe, R. S. Jaffe, D. Jonas, E. D. Solomon, B. Steinberg. **Transfer Agent & Registrar**—First City Transfer Co., Iselin, NJ. **Incorporated**—in Connecticut in 1966. **Empl**— 7,100. **S&P Analyst:** Ray Lam, CFA

STANDARD &POOR'S
STOCK REPORTS

Etec Systems

3815D

Nasdaq Symbol **ETEC**

In S&P SmallCap 600

03-OCT-98

Industry: Equipment (Semiconductor)

Summary: Etec is the leading producer of mask pattern generation equipment for the semiconductor industry.

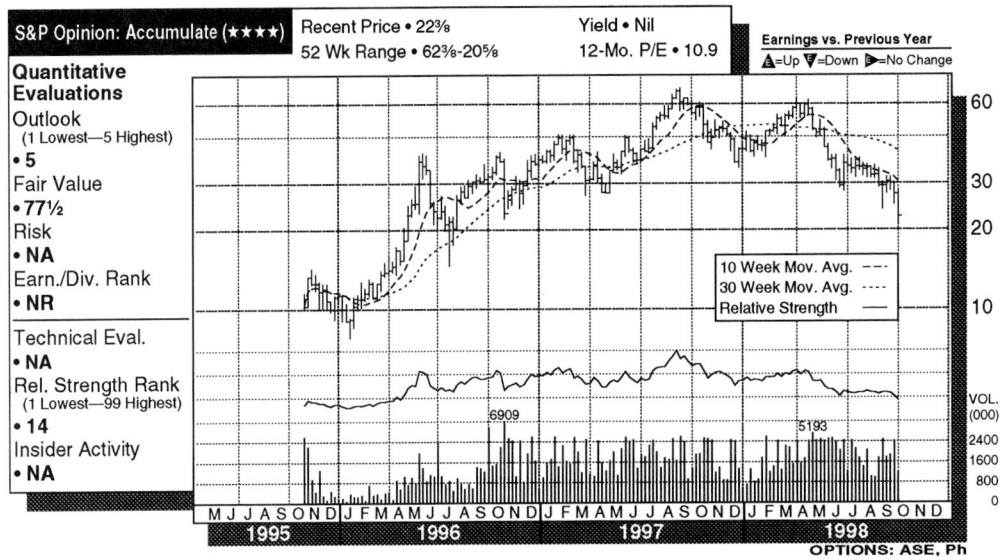

S&P Opinion: Accumulate (★★★★)	Recent Price • 22⅝	Yield • Nil
	52 Wk Range • 62⅜-20⅝	12-Mo. P/E • 10.9

Earnings vs. Previous Year
▲=Up ▼=Down ▶=No Change

Quantitative Evaluations

Outlook (1 Lowest—5 Highest)
• **5**

Fair Value
• **77½**

Risk
• **NA**

Earn./Div. Rank
• **NR**

Technical Eval.
• **NA**

Rel. Strength Rank (1 Lowest—99 Highest)
• **14**

Insider Activity
• **NA**

10 Week Mov. Avg. — — ‑
30 Week Mov. Avg. ‑ ‑ ‑ ‑
Relative Strength ————

6909   5193

VOL. (000)

OPTIONS: ASE, Ph

Overview - 08-SEP-98

Etec is the leading supplier of maskmaking equipment with a 75% worldwide market share. The company's most advanced systems can produce photomasks, used in the production of semiconductors, with circuit line widths of 0.25 micron and below. Although the shares have been affected by the general industry downturn, demand for photomasks, and consequently for Etec's systems, has historically remained high during similarly poor periods. Companies tend to increase their chip design activity during semiconductor recessions, and photomasks are critical elements in chip design. The Asian crisis has also affected sales to Japan and Korea, although Taiwan has remained strong. In September, the company reported solid fourth quarter earnings that were a few cents above analyst expectations, driven by the sale of high-margin leading edge equipment.

Valuation - 08-SEP-98

We continue to recommend accumulation of ETEC. The semiconductor recession and earlier earnings shortfalls have kept the stock from approaching a more reasonable valuation. The shortfalls resulted from system specification issues (since solved), not demand problems. Although Etec is susceptible to future shortfalls, because it sells only a limited number of high priced systems, we believe that the stock has already more than discounted this factor. The shares were recently trading at a very attractive level of only 11X our FY 99 (Jul.) EPS estimate of $2.75. We expect revenues to advance about 20% in FY 99, with wider gross margins, reflecting demand for more advanced systems. We are also optimistic about the company's attempt to diversify itself by developing systems for printed circuit board (PCB) manufacturers.

Key Stock Statistics

S&P EPS Est. 1998	NA	Tang. Bk. Value/Share	9.57
P/E on S&P Est. 1998	NA	Beta	NA
S&P EPS Est. 1999	2.75	Shareholders	400
Dividend Rate/Share	Nil	Market cap. (B)	$0.495
Shs. outstg. (M)	22.1	Inst. holdings	87%
Avg. daily vol. (M)	0.394		

Value of $10,000 invested 5 years ago: NA

Fiscal Year Ending Jul. 31

	1998	1997	1996	1995	1994	1993
Revenues (Million $)						
1Q	68.37	44.89	24.70	19.50	—	—
2Q	62.17	53.68	31.60	19.80	—	—
3Q	70.03	69.70	41.70	21.70	—	—
4Q	87.77	72.65	47.60	21.90	—	—
Yr.	288.3	240.9	145.6	82.90	68.70	58.58
Earnings Per Share ($)						
1Q	0.41	0.33	—	—	—	—
2Q	**0.38**	0.35	0.20	—	—	—
3Q	**0.47**	0.34	0.80	—	—	—
4Q	**0.80**	0.54	0.78	—	—	—
Yr.	**2.05**	1.57	2.07	0.31	0.12	-0.94

Next earnings report expected: late November

Dividend Data

No cash dividends have been paid, and the company does not anticipate paying any for the foreseeable future. It currently intends to retain its earnings for the development of its business. A shareholder rights plan was adopted in 1997.

STANDARD
&POOR'S
STOCK REPORTS

Etec Systems, Inc.

3815D
03-OCT-98

Business Summary - 08-SEP-98

Etec Systems believes that the products it makes are crucial to the success of the semiconductor and electronics industries. It is the leading supplier of electronic and laser-beam mask pattern generation (PG) equipment for the worldwide semiconductor industry. These systems create the master patterns that make semiconductor chip designs. Semiconductor chips going into every conceivable electronic product must deliver greater performance in less space as the electronic content of these products grows to meet the demands of manufacturers and consumers.

The company's pattern generation equipment transforms electronic design data into complex master patterns or masks, similar to a photographic negative, which are then used many times to create chips. Each chip needs an average of 16 to 24 different masks in the manufacturing process to create a unique electronic function. Semiconductor manufacturers use ETEC's products to help meet the challenge of shrinking feature sizes, greater device complexity, and the need for higher accuracy and throughput.

ETEC is the technology leader in the global semiconductor mask pattern generation market, holding a market share of more than 75%. The company is the only mask PG supplier with a dual technology strategy offering both electron-beam and laser-beam based systems. The different characteristics of these systems suit each to different segments of the mask pattern generation market. Electron beam systems have a much smaller beam spot size than laser beam systems and are best suited for leading-edge market segments that require the highest resolution and accuracy.

Most revenues are derived from the sale of a relatively small number of systems at prices ranging from about $3.0 million to $11.7 million. Consequently, results for any given period could be adversely affected by any delay in the recognition of revenue for a single system or upgrade. ETEC also derives significant revenues from service and support of its installed base of systems. Sales outside of the U.S. comprised about 36% and 45% of revenues in FY 97 (Jul.) and FY 96, respectively.

The Etec Polyscan subsidiary manufactures ultraviolet laser direct imaging systems for applications that require large area pattern generation, including printed circuit boards, multi-chip modules and flat panel displays.

In August 1997, the company purchased 15.2 acres of land in Oregon to construct a new manufacturing facility. Groundbreaking for the facility occurred in March 1998.

Per Share Data ($)

(Year Ended Jul. 31)	1998	1997	1996	1995	1994	1993	1992	1991	1990	1989
Tangible Bk. Val.	NA	9.12	5.91	NM	NM	NM	NA	NA	NA	NA
Cash Flow	NA	1.78	2.10	0.30	0.18	-0.49	NA	NA	NA	NA
Earnings	2.05	1.57	2.07	0.31	0.12	-0.94	-2.86	-0.23	NA	NA
Dividends	Nil	Nil	Nil	Nil	Nil	Nil	Nil	Nil	Nil	Nil
Payout Ratio	Nil	Nil	Nil	Nil	Nil	Nil	Nil	Nil	Nil	Nil
Prices - High	62³/₈	69¹/₈	39¹/₂	14¹/₄	NA	NA	NA	NA	NA	NA
- Low	23⁷/₈	27	7³/₄	9¹/₈	NA	NA	NA	NA	NA	NA
P/E Ratio - High	30	44	19	46	NA	NA	NA	NA	NA	NA
- Low	12	17	4	29	NA	NA	NA	NA	NA	NA

Income Statement Analysis (Million $)

	1998	1997	1996	1995	1994	1993	1992	1991	1990	1989
Revs.	NA	241	146	83.0	69.0	59.0	NA	NA	NA	NA
Oper. Inc.	NA	58.9	28.5	14.4	13.4	0.2	NA	NA	NA	NA
Depr.	NA	4.6	1.6	3.0	3.8	4.6	NA	NA	NA	NA
Int. Exp.	NA	1.0	1.8	4.2	5.1	5.9	NA	NA	NA	NA
Pretax Inc.	NA	53.3	21.3	6.8	3.9	-12.9	NA	NA	NA	NA
Eff. Tax Rate	NA	35%	NM	34%	59%	NM	NM	NM	NM	NM
Net Inc.	NM	34.4	37.8	4.5	1.6	-11.4	NA	NA	NA	NA

Balance Sheet & Other Fin. Data (Million $)

	1998	1997	1996	1995	1994	1993	1992	1991	1990	1989
Cash	NA	56.0	68.6	23.6	6.6	NA	NA	NA	NA	NA
Curr. Assets	NA	238	186	75.0	50.5	NA	NA	NA	NA	NA
Total Assets	NA	285	209	86.0	63.0	NA	NA	NA	NA	NA
Curr. Liab.	NA	82.2	74.4	52.1	44.3	NA	NA	NA	NA	NA
LT Debt	NA	Nil	6.7	16.9	31.3	NA	NA	NA	NA	NA
Common Eqty.	NA	198	116	-67.0	-76.0	NA	NA	NA	NA	NA
Total Cap.	NA	198	121	25.8	-45.0	NA	NA	NA	NA	NA
Cap. Exp.	NA	27.1	11.7	2.9	2.0	0.7	NA	NA	NA	NA
Cash Flow	NA	39.1	38.3	4.4	2.5	-6.8	NA	NA	NA	NA
Curr. Ratio	NA	2.9	2.5	1.4	1.1	NA	NA	NA	NA	NA
% LT Debt of Cap.	NA	Nil	5.5	65.3	NM	NM	NM	NM	NM	NM
% Net Inc.of Revs.	NM	14.3	25.9	5.4	2.3	NM	NM	NM	NM	NM
% Ret. on Assets	NM	14.0	25.6	6.0	NM	NM	NM	NM	NM	NM
% Ret. on Equity	NM	22.0	157.7	NM	NM	NM	NM	NM	NM	NM

Data as orig. reptd.; bef. results of disc. opers. and/or spec. items. Per share data adj. for stk. divs. as of ex-div. date. Bold denotes diluted EPS (FASB 128). E-Estimated. NA-Not Available. NM-Not Meaningful. NR-Not Ranked.

Office—26460 Corporate Ave., Hayward, CA 94545. **Tel**—(510) 783-9210. **Website**—http://www.etec.com **Chrmn, Pres & CEO**—S. E. Cooper. **VP & CFO**—W. Snyder. **Dirs**—S. E. Cooper, E. J. Gelbach, J. B. McBennett, W. Ryan, W. Siegle, T. Suzuki, T. M. Trent, R. L. Wehrli. **Transfer Agent & Registrar**—Bank of Boston. **Incorporated**—in Nevada in 1989. **Empl**— 902. **S&P Analyst:** Mark Cavallone

STANDARD &POOR'S
STOCK REPORTS

E*Trade Group

3766S

NASDAQ Symbol **EGRP**

In S&P SmallCap 600

03-OCT-98

Industry:
Investment Banking/
Brokerage

Summary: EGRP provides online discount brokerage services, including automated order placement, portfolio tracking, and related market information, news and other information services.

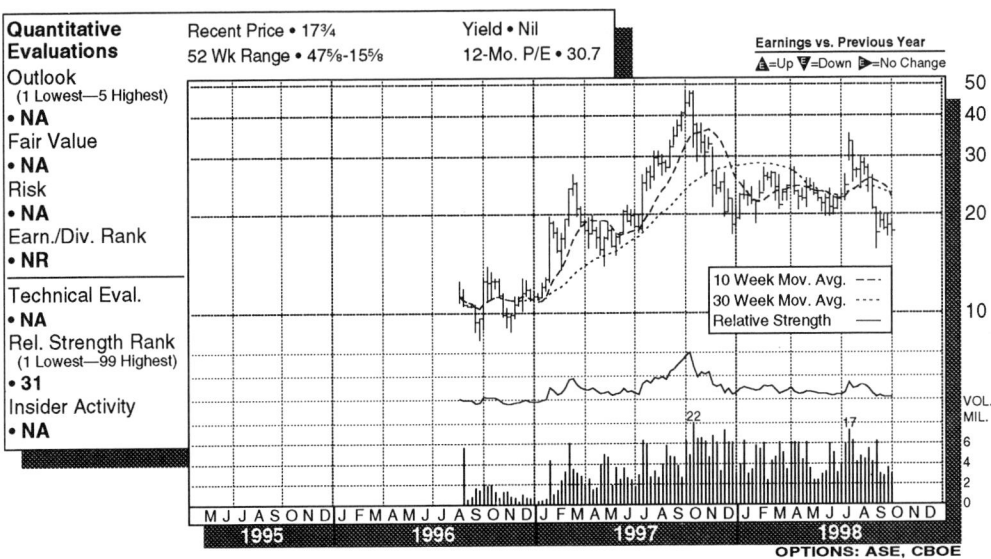

Quantitative Evaluations

Outlook
(1 Lowest—5 Highest)
• **NA**

Fair Value
• **NA**

Risk
• **NA**

Earn./Div. Rank
• **NR**

Technical Eval.
• **NA**

Rel. Strength Rank
(1 Lowest—99 Highest)
• **31**

Insider Activity
• **NA**

Recent Price • 17¾
52 Wk Range • 47⅝-15⅝

Yield • Nil
12-Mo. P/E • 30.7

Earnings vs. Previous Year
▲=Up ▼=Down ▶=No Change

10 Week Mov. Avg. ---
30 Week Mov. Avg. ....
Relative Strength —

OPTIONS: ASE, CBOE

Business Profile - 23-JUN-98

This company, which provides online discount brokerage services, continued its rapid growth in the second quarter of FY 98 (Sep.). EGRP added 80,000 net new accounts during the quarter, and passed the 400,000 account mark at March 31, 1998, up 178% from 145,000 a year earlier, and up 24% from 325,000 at the end of the first quarter. Assets held in customer accounts now exceed $10 billion. In April 1998, the company said it had launched a major international expansion effort designed to give it a presence throughout Europe, Southeast Asia and North Asia. It added that it had signed four master licensing agreements that, when fully implemented, would extend the E*TRADE brand name to more than 25 countries worldwide.

Operational Review - 23-JUN-98

Revenues in the first half of FY 98 soared 83%, year to year, paced by a 69% gain in transaction revenues (commissions and payments for order flow) and a 178% rise in net interest revenues. Cost of services increased 84%, but operating expenses rose less rapidly. Despite a $2.76 million pretax charge ($0.04 a share after tax) related to the acquisition of OptionsLink, a division of Hambrecht & Quist), net income surged 108%, to $11,032,000 ($0.27 a share, diluted, on 25% more shares), from $5,314,000 ($0.16).

Stock Performance - 02-OCT-98

In the past 30 trading days, EGRP's shares have declined 31%, compared to a 7% fall in the S&P 500. Average trading volume for the past five days was 603,640 shares, compared with the 40-day moving average of 903,821 shares.

Key Stock Statistics

Dividend Rate/Share	Nil	Shareholders	200
Shs. outstg. (M)	54.9	Market cap. (B)	$0.976
Avg. daily vol. (M)	0.686	Inst. holdings	43%
Tang. Bk. Value/Share	7.67		
Beta	NA		

Value of $10,000 invested 5 years ago: NA

Fiscal Year Ending Sep. 30

	1998	1997	1996	1995	1994	1993
Revenues (Million $)						
1Q	51.13	—	—	—	—	—
2Q	53.31	—	—	—	—	—
3Q	62.32	—	—	—	—	—
4Q	—	—	—	—	—	—
Yr.	—	142.7	51.60	23.34	10.91	2.97
Earnings Per Share ($)						
1Q	0.12	0.07	—	—	—	—
2Q	**0.15**	0.09	—	—	—	—
3Q	**0.16**	0.09	—	—	—	—
4Q	—	0.15	—	—	—	—
Yr.	—	0.40	-0.03	0.10	0.03	—

Next earnings report expected: mid October

Dividend Data

No cash dividends have been paid, and the company currently intends to retain all earnings for use in its business, and does not anticipate paying cash dividends in the foreseeable future.

A Division of The **McGraw·Hill** *Companies*

Business Summary - 23-JUN-98

Advances in telecommunications and information technology have made it possible to trade securities, track a portfolio, or obtain market information with a click of a mouse or by pushing a few buttons on a touch-tone phone. E*Trade Group Inc. (EGRP) is a leading provider of online investing services, and has established a popular, branded destination website for self-directed investors. The company offers automated order placement and execution, together with a suite of products and services that can be personalized, including portfolio tracking, Java-based charting and quote applications, real-time market commentary and analysis, news, and other information services. EGRP provides these services 24 hours a day, seven days a week, via the Internet, touch-tone telephone, online service providers, interactive television, and direct modem access.

The company's services are based on proprietary transaction-enabling technology, based on the E*TRADE engine, and are designed to serve the needs of the self-directed investor. Customers can directly place orders to buy and sell Nasdaq and listed securities, as well as equity and index options and mutual funds, through the E*TRADE automated order processing system. EGRP uses a combination of proprietary and industry standard security measures to protect customer accounts. It relies on encryption and authentication technology, and uses additional security measures as well. At the end of the FY 98 (Sep.) second quarter, the company had more than 400,000 customer accounts, holding total assets in excess of $10 billion.

In order to increase its access to online consumers, build brand-name recognition, and expand the range of products and services offered, EGRP pursues strategic relationships, with emphasis to date on alliances with Internet access, online service and content providers. The company has entered into alliances with America Online, AT&T, CompuServe, Intuit, Microsoft, Prodigy Services, USA Today, Yahoo!, Banc One and SinaNet, and has also established relationships with several information and content providers. In addition, it regards technology as a key component in efforts to maintain market leadership in the Internet arena, and has entered into partnerships with leading technology providers to support its products and services with up-to-date features and offer optimal solutions to customers.

Although the company has been growing rapidly, it faces significant competition, both from other discount brokerage firms, such as Charles Schwab & Co. and Fidelity Brokerage Services, and from established full-commission firms such as Merrill Lynch and PaineWebber.

Per Share Data ($)

(Year Ended Sep. 30)	1997	1996	1995	1994	1993	1992	1991	1990	1989	1988
Tangible Bk. Val.	7.28	2.35	NA	NA	NA	NA	NA	NA	NA	NA
Cash Flow	0.51	0.00	0.11	NA	NA	NA	NA	NA	NA	NA
Earnings	0.40	-0.03	0.10	0.03	NA	NA	NA	NA	NA	NA
Dividends	Nil	Nil	Nil	Nil	Nil	Nil	Nil	Nil	Nil	Nil
Payout Ratio	Nil	Nil	Nil	Nil	Nil	Nil	Nil	Nil	Nil	Nil
Prices - High	47⁷/₈	13⁷/₈	NA	NA	NA	NA	NA	NA	NA	NA
- Low	11	8¹/₄	NA	NA	NA	NA	NA	NA	NA	NA
P/E Ratio - High	119	NM	NA	NA	NA	NA	NA	NA	NA	NA
- Low	27	NM	NA	NA	NA	NA	NA	NA	NA	NA

Income Statement Analysis (Million $)

	1997	1996	1995	1994	1993	1992	1991	1990	1989	1988
Commissions	110	44.2	20.8	9.5	NA	NA	NA	NA	NA	NA
Int. Inc.	25.3	4.8	1.0	0.3	NA	NA	NA	NA	NA	NA
Total Revs.	143	51.6	23.3	10.9	NA	NA	NA	NA	NA	NA
Int. Exp.	14.9	2.2	Nil	Nil	Nil	Nil	Nil	Nil	Nil	Nil
Pretax Inc.	23.3	-1.4	4.3	0.2	NA	NA	NA	NA	NA	NA
Eff. Tax Rate	40%	NM	40%	NM	NM	NM	NM	NM	NM	NM
Net Inc.	13.9	-0.8	2.6	0.8	NA	NA	NA	NA	NA	NA

Balance Sheet & Other Fin. Data (Million $)

	1997	1996	1995	1994	1993	1992	1991	1990	1989	1988
Total Assets	990	990	14.2	NA	NA	NA	NA	NA	NA	NA
Cash Items	36.8	50.1	9.6	NA	NA	NA	NA	NA	NA	NA
Receivables	728	193	2.1	NA	NA	NA	NA	NA	NA	NA
Secs. Owned	191	35.0	NA	NA	NA	NA	NA	NA	NA	NA
Sec. Borrowed	NA	NA	NA	NA	NA	NA	NA	NA	NA	NA
Due Brokers & Cust.	0.7	0.2	NA	NA	NA	NA	NA	NA	NA	NA
Other Liabs.	18.1	6.1	NA	NA	NA	NA	NA	NA	NA	NA
Capitalization:										
Debt	9.4	0.0	0.1	NA	NA	NA	NA	NA	NA	NA
Equity	281	69.3	11.1	NA	NA	NA	NA	NA	NA	NA
Total	291	69.3	11.2	NA	NA	NA	NA	NA	NA	NA
% Return On Revs.	11.8	NM	11.6	8.3	NA	NA	NA	NA	NA	NA
% Ret. on Assets	2.2	NM	NA	NA	NA	NA	NA	NA	NA	NA
% Ret. on Equity	7.9	NM	NA	NA	NA	NA	NA	NA	NA	NA

Data as orig. reptd.; bef. results of disc. opers. and/or spec. items. Per share data adj. for stk. divs. as of ex-div. date. Bold denotes diluted EPS (FASB 128). E-Estimated. NA-Not Available. NM-Not Meaningful. NR-Not Ranked.

Office—Four Embarcadero Place, 2400 Geng Rd., Palo Alto, CA 94303. Tel—(650) 842-2500. Website—http://www.etrade.com Chrmn—W. A. Porter. Pres & CEO—C. M. Cotsakos. EVP & CFO—L. C. Purkis. Dirs—R. S. Braddock, C. M. Cotsakos, W. E. Ford, G. Hayter, K. Petty, W. A. Porter, L. E. Randall, L. C. Thurow. Transfer Agent & Registrar—American Stock Transfer & Trust Co., NYC. Incorporated—in California in 1982; reincorporated in Delaware in 1996. Empl— 499. S&P Analyst: P.M.W.

Eagle Hardware & Garden   3770G
Nasdaq Symbol EAGL
In S&P SmallCap 600

03-OCT-98

Industry: Retail (Building Supplies)

Summary: This home improvement retailer operates more than 30 warehouse centers, primarily in the western U.S., serving do-it-yourself customers as well as professional contractors.

S&P Opinion: Buy (★★★★)	Recent Price • 21	Yield • Nil
	52 Wk Range • 26¼-15¼	12-Mo. P/E • 19.1

Earnings vs. Previous Year
▲=Up ▼=Down ▶=No Change

Quantitative Evaluations

Outlook (1 Lowest—5 Highest)
• **4**

Fair Value
• **30**

Risk
• **High**

Earn./Div. Rank
• **NR**

Technical Eval.
• **Bullish** since 6/98

Rel. Strength Rank (1 Lowest—99 Highest)
• **69**

Insider Activity
• **NA**

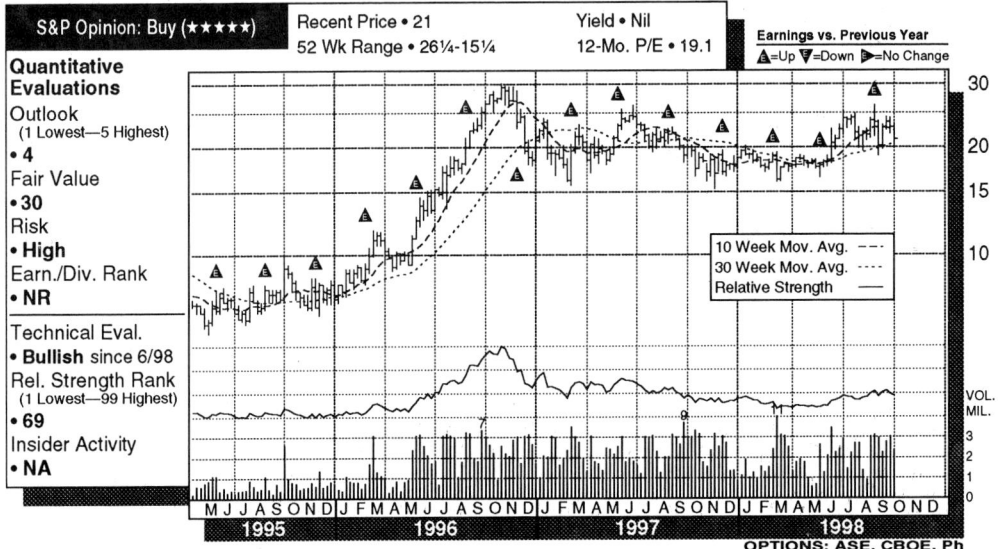

10 Week Mov. Avg. — — —
30 Week Mov. Avg. ·······
Relative Strength ——

VOL. MIL.

OPTIONS: ASE, CBOE, Ph

Overview - 29-MAY-98

Sales in FY 99 (Jan.) should increase about 24%, reflecting seven new units and a 5% to 6% gain in same-unit sales. Gross margins and operating expenses should remain at about the same percentage of sales as in FY 98. Operating income should increase about 20%. Interest expense should increase somewhat. EPS should advance about 18%. Although the home improvement industry is highly competitive, with Home Depot regarded as the 800 pound gorilla of the group, the industry remains highly fragmented, with the five largest competitors garnering only 30% of the estimated $142.5 billion market in 1997. This is up from 15% in 1991. Industry consolidation should continue, with Eagle becoming the beneficiary as smaller players exit markets unable to compete with the larger players. The company plans to spend $125 to $135 million for capital expenditures in FY 99, including seven new stores. This would be funded via cash, income from operations, bank borrowings and sale and leaseback financing.

Valuation - 29-MAY-98

We have upgraded the shares to a strong buy. Although earnings gains have been solid, the stock price has lagged behind the strong advance of HD and LOW. We believe that investors are discounting the company's ability to compete with HD, which it already does successfully in 40% of its locations. The share price has stayed in a trading range over the past year, well below its 1996 high. Growth will come from store expansion of seven to 10 new units in each of the next three years both in the company's existing trade area as well as by expansion into contiguous states. Eagle is conservatively financed, and plows its cash flow into store expansion. The company pays no cash dividends.

Key Stock Statistics

S&P EPS Est. 1999	1.15	Tang. Bk. Value/Share	12.32
P/E on S&P Est. 1999	18.3	Beta	0.64
S&P EPS Est. 2000	1.35	Shareholders	1,100
Dividend Rate/Share	Nil	Market cap. (B)	$0.611
Shs. outstg. (M)	29.1	Inst. holdings	56%
Avg. daily vol. (M)	0.548		

Value of $10,000 invested 5 years ago: $ 21,356

Fiscal Year Ending Jan. 31

	1999	1998	1997	1996	1995	1994
Revenues (Million $)						
1Q	250.2	221.1	161.1	130.2	104.0	53.60
2Q	308.0	278.2	209.1	167.8	144.8	85.30
3Q	—	249.7	198.7	159.8	148.2	91.60
4Q	—	222.4	192.1	157.9	121.8	92.40
Yr.	—	971.5	761.0	615.7	518.8	322.9
Earnings Per Share ($)						
1Q	0.21	0.16	0.13	0.12	0.10	0.09
2Q	**0.48**	0.41	0.35	0.20	0.15	0.12
3Q	**E0.33**	0.29	0.29	0.11	0.09	0.16
4Q	**E0.17**	0.12	0.11	0.07	-0.61	0.12
Yr.	**E1.15**	0.98	0.85	0.49	-0.28	0.50

Next earnings report expected: late November

Dividend Data

No cash dividends have been paid. The company intends to retain earnings for use in the expansion of its business and does not expect to pay cash dividends in the foreseeable future.

A Division of The **McGraw·Hill** Companies

Business Summary - 29-MAY-98

Eagle Hardware & Garden, Inc. has grown, since opening its first store in 1990, to 32 stores, mostly in the Northwest. Stores serve a wide range of do-it-yourself customers and professional contractors, featuring more than 60,000 stock keeping units (SKUs), which Eagle believes is greater than the number carried by its primary competitors. Net sales by product category in FY 98 (Jan.) were: plumbing, electrical and lighting 24%; lumber and building materials 26%; paint and decor 18%; tools and hardware 16%; and lawn and garden supplies 16%.

The company's typical home centers average 128,000 sq. ft. The Design Center is the central core of each home center. It features a kitchen and bath display area with 27 different styles of kitchen cabinets, brand name appliances and a large selection of bathroom fixtures. It also features a wide variety of countertops, wallpaper, floor coverings and window treatments, as well as a design coordinator who works with customers. The Design Center is complemented by surrounding departments, such as paint and decor, plumbing, hardware and tools, electrical, lighting, lawn and garden and lumber and building materials.

In FY 97, EAGL implemented a new store prototype designed for a single-store market. The prototype store has about 95,000 sq. ft., including a 60,000 sq. ft. lumber and building materials yard that customers can drive through. As with Eagle's larger home centers, these stores will also carry more than 60,000 SKUs. There are now four stores in operation.

Home centers also offer such specialized services as a cut shop, where customers can have window screen, fencing, glass, netting, chain, hose, rope and other materials custom cut; a licensed locksmith, for assistance with locks, keys and home and commercial security systems; an idea center that features do-it-yourself books, plans and video tapes; free or low-cost delivery service; personnel to assist in designing and planning projects and selecting appropriate materials; and a separate lumber and building materials cashier and loading area. In addition, most centers also offer professional product installation services.

Eagle's expansion strategy includes new markets such as southern California; EAGL plans on having at least seven locations in California by the end of 1999. A significant element of its strategy to achieve economies of scale by clustering stores in metropolitan markets, even though new stores tend to cannibalize sales of existing stores. The company plans to open a total of seven stores in FY 99 and 8-10 stores in FY 00.

Per Share Data ($)

(Year Ended Jan. 31)	1998	1997	1996	1995	1994	1993	1992	1991	1990	1989
Tangible Bk. Val.	11.58	10.55	6.77	6.30	6.56	4.07	0.65	NA	NA	NA
Cash Flow	1.30	1.30	0.89	0.02	0.65	0.36	0.12	NA	NA	NA
Earnings	0.98	0.85	0.49	-0.28	0.50	0.26	0.09	NA	NA	NA
Dividends	Nil	Nil	Nil	Nil	Nil	Nil	Nil	Nil	Nil	Nil
Payout Ratio	Nil	Nil	Nil	Nil	Nil	Nil	Nil	Nil	Nil	Nil
Cal. Yrs.	1997	1996	1995	1994	1993	1992	1991	1990	1989	1988
Prices - High	26¼	30¼	10	18¼	34¾	40½	NA	NA	NA	NA
- Low	15¼	7¼	6	7⅝	12¾	9⅜	NA	NA	NA	NA
P/E Ratio - High	27	36	20	NM	70	NM	NA	NA	NA	NA
- Low	16	9	12	NM	26	NM	NA	NA	NA	NA

Income Statement Analysis (Million $)

	1998	1997	1996	1995	1994	1993	1992	1991	1990	1989
Revs.	971	761	616	519	323	147	51.0	NA	NA	NA
Oper. Inc.	67.7	48.4	31.7	24.4	19.4	7.8	1.2	NA	NA	NA
Depr.	14.8	11.4	9.3	6.8	3.4	1.5	0.4	NA	NA	NA
Int. Exp.	8.6	9.4	9.0	6.5	0.4	0.3	0.0	NA	NA	NA
Pretax Inc.	46.8	32.8	17.0	0.5	16.8	6.4	1.1	NA	NA	NA
Eff. Tax Rate	37%	34%	34%	NM	36%	35%	Nil	Nil	Nil	Nil
Net Inc.	29.6	21.7	11.3	-6.3	10.8	4.2	1.1	NA	NA	NA

Balance Sheet & Other Fin. Data (Million $)

	1998	1997	1996	1995	1994	1993	1992	1991	1990	1989
Cash	63.6	52.0	6.6	5.4	2.5	1.3	0.2	NA	NA	NA
Curr. Assets	278	238	157	148	111	52.0	26.0	NA	NA	NA
Total Assets	602	519	367	322	212	103	37.0	NA	NA	NA
Curr. Liab.	105	94.7	102	68.9	54.7	29.8	14.1	NA	NA	NA
LT Debt	146	108	102	104	4.9	Nil	Nil	Nil	Nil	Nil
Common Eqty.	337	305	156	144	149	72.0	4.0	NA	NA	NA
Total Cap.	493	422	263	252	156	72.0	23.0	NA	NA	NA
Cap. Exp.	53.5	88.8	45.9	101	58.0	36.3	10.4	NA	NA	NA
Cash Flow	44.4	33.2	20.6	0.5	14.1	5.7	1.5	NA	NA	NA
Curr. Ratio	2.6	2.5	1.5	2.1	2.0	1.7	1.8	NA	NA	NA
% LT Debt of Cap.	29.6	25.6	38.8	41.3	3.1	Nil	Nil	Nil	Nil	Nil
% Net Inc.of Revs.	3.0	2.9	1.8	NM	3.3	2.8	2.2	NA	NA	NA
% Ret. on Assets	5.3	4.9	3.3	NM	6.2	3.8	NA	NA	NA	NA
% Ret. on Equity	9.2	9.4	7.5	NM	8.9	10.0	NA	NA	NA	NA

Data as orig. reptd.; bef. results of disc. opers. and/or spec. items. Per share data adj. for stk. divs. as of ex-div. date. Bold denotes diluted EPS (FASB 128). E-Estimated. NA-Not Available. NM-Not Meaningful. NR-Not Ranked.

Office—981 Powell Ave. S.W., Renton, WA 98055. **Tel**—(425) 227-5740. **Website**—www.eaglehardware.com. **Chrmn** —D. J. Heerensperger. **Pres & CEO**—R. T. Takata.**EVP-Fin & CFO**—R. P. Maccarone. **Dirs**—R. D. Crockett, H. D. Douglass, D. J. Heerensperger, H. Sarkowsky, R. T. Takata, T. M. Wight. **Transfer Agent & Registrar**—ChaseMellon Shareholder Services, Seattle.**Incorporated**—in Washington in 1989. **Empl**—6,300. **S&P Analyst:** Karen J. Sack, CFA

03-OCT-98

Industry: Foods

Summary: EGR produces and distributes fresh baked goods and refrigerated dough products in the U.S. and Europe.

Quantitative Evaluations

Outlook (1 Lowest—5 Highest)
• **1**

Fair Value
• **29½**

Risk
• **NA**

Earn./Div. Rank
• **NR**

Technical Eval.
• **NA**

Rel. Strength Rank (1 Lowest—99 Highest)
• **92**

Insider Activity
• **Neutral**

| Recent Price • 31½ | Yield • 0.5% |
| 52 Wk Range • 35⅜-18¾ | 12-Mo. P/E • 32.1 |

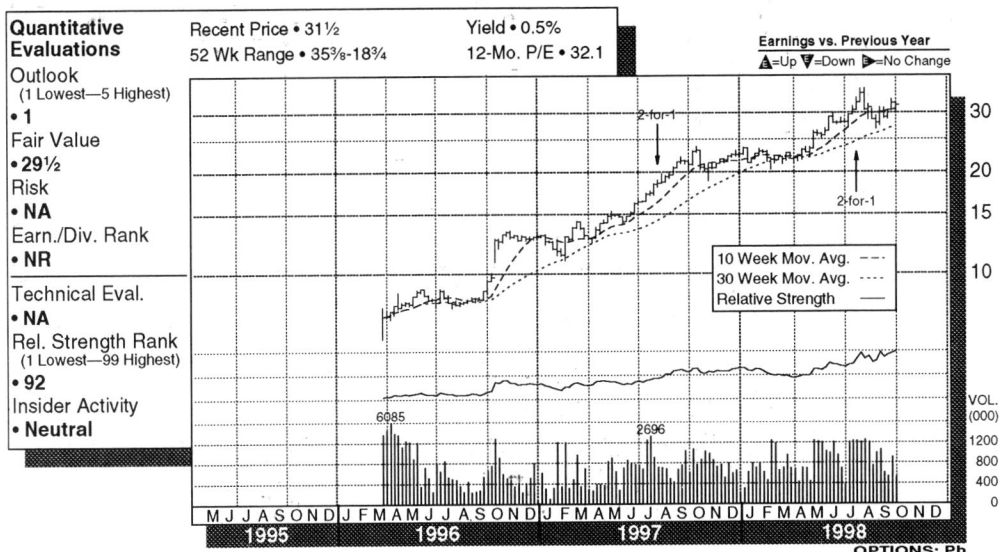

Earnings vs. Previous Year
▲=Up ▼=Down ▶=No Change

10 Week Mov. Avg. - - -
30 Week Mov. Avg. ....
Relative Strength —

OPTIONS: Ph

Business Profile - 29-JUL-98

EGR has been continuing its acquisition strategy, buying four companies during the past 19 months, with agreements pending to buy two more. The company seeks to eliminate redundancies and improve efficiencies in its operations, expand customer partnerships, leverage its investments in new product development, and expand its territory. In FY 97 (Mar.), results benefited from restructuring and consolidation efforts (including the elimination of facilities) and improvements in profit margins. In early 1998, EGR said it was making progress toward its operating margin goal of 5% and EBITDA margin goal of 10% by FY 2000. A two-for-one stock split was effected in July 1998, and the dividend was boosted 60%.

Operational Review - 29-JUL-98

Net sales in the 12 weeks ended June 23, 1998, rose 15%, year to year, as contributions from CooperSmith (acquired in January 1998) and San Luis Sourdough (March 1998), and improved refrigerated dough sales outweighed lower foreign sales. Gross margins widened, on a more favorable product mix. With improved operating efficiencies and lower raw material costs, pretax income soared 57%. After taxes at 40.1%, versus 40.5%, net income was 58%, to $10.9 million ($0.25, diluted, as adjusted), from $6.9 million ($0.17).

Stock Performance - 02-OCT-98

In the past 30 trading days, EGR's shares have increased 10%, compared to a 7% fall in the S&P 500. Average trading volume for the past five days was 102,600 shares, compared with the 40-day moving average of 170,777 shares.

Key Stock Statistics

Dividend Rate/Share	0.16	Shareholders	NA
Shs. outstg. (M)	42.9	Market cap. (B)	$ 1.4
Avg. daily vol. (M)	0.133	Inst. holdings	62%
Tang. Bk. Value/Share	7.21		
Beta	NA		

Value of $10,000 invested 5 years ago: NA

Fiscal Year Ending Mar. 31

	1999	1998	1997	1996	1995	1994
Revenues (Million $)						
1Q	433.0	377.4	370.5	—	—	—
2Q	—	382.5	381.8	—	—	—
3Q	—	514.7	522.7	—	—	—
4Q	—	444.4	387.6	—	—	—
Yr.	—	1,719	1,663	1,665	—	—
Earnings Per Share ($)						
1Q	0.26	0.17	0.02	—	—	—
2Q	—	0.23	0.11	—	—	—
3Q	—	0.33	0.23	—	—	—
4Q	—	0.17	0.05	—	—	—
Yr.	—	0.89	0.40	-0.63	—	—

Next earnings report expected: early October

Dividend Data (Dividends have been paid since 1996.)

Amount ($)	Date Decl.	Ex-Div. Date	Stock of Record	Payment Date
0.050	Jan. 23	Feb. 11	Feb. 13	Feb. 28 '98
0.050	May. 01	May. 13	May. 15	May. 31 '98
2-for-1	May. 26	Jul. 21	Jul. 10	Jul. 20 '98
0.040	Jul. 17	Aug. 12	Aug. 14	Aug. 31 '98

A Division of The McGraw-Hill Companies

Business Summary - 29-JUL-98

Earthgrains (EGR), the third largest U.S. bread and baked goods producer, is on the rise. In FY 97 (Mar.), its first full fiscal year as an independent company (EGR was spun off from brewing giant Anheuser-Busch in March 1996), the company was able to effect a significant turnaround, following a large loss in the preceding year. EGR improved revenue and profit margins in each of its businesses, and a continued focus on cost effectiveness (including a restructuring and consolidation program that involved plant consolidations and staff reorganization) resulted in lower costs of products sold and reduced operating expenses. Earnings continued to advanced in FY 98.

EGR is a leading producer and distributor of packaged bakery products for sale to retail grocers and food service companies in the U.S. and Europe. Its product lines include fresh, refrigerated and frozen baked goods, refrigerated and frozen dough products, and shelf stable toaster pastries.

In the U.S., the company's fresh-baked goods are produced at 44 bakeries and two refrigerated dough plants in 16 states, and are sold in 27 states in the Southeast, South, Southwest, Midwest and Northern and Central California. Its principal fresh baked goods are baked bread, rolls, cookies, snack cakes and other sweet goods. The majority of EGR's fresh baked goods are sold under the Colonial, Rainbo, Iron Kids, Heiner's, Grant's Farm, and Earth Grains brand names; snack cakes and other sweet goods are sold principally under the Bread Cake and Merico brand names. This segment also produces fresh baked goods for sale under the brand names of its customers. EGR also supplies specialty rolls, sandwich buns, and other products to fast-food chains such as Burger King, Pizza Hut, and Waffle House. In early 1998, EGR acquired Cooper-Smith, Inc., an Atlanta-based bakery holding company, for $193 million.

In addition to its leading position in the fresh-baked segment, EGR is the second largest maker of refrigerated and frozen dough products, which include biscuits, dinner rolls, sweet rolls, danish, cookies, crescent rolls and breadsticks. EGR is the only U.S. manufacturer of store-brand refrigerated dough products, which are sold nationwide under more than 100 store brands.

Outside the U.S., the company operates eight bakeries in Spain, and distributes fresh baked goods in Spain and Portugal. EGR's Spanish unit, Bimbo S.A., introduced American-style sliced bread to Spain. The principal products are baked breads, buns, snack cakes and sweet goods. In addition, the company operates one refrigerated dough plant in France, and sells refrigerated dough products throughout Europe. Sales in Europe accounted for 19% of FY 98 sales.

Per Share Data ($)

(Year Ended Mar. 31)	1998	1997	1996	1995	1994	1993	1992	1991	1990	1989
Tangible Bk. Val.	6.93	10.26	10.89	NA	NA	NA	NA	NA	NA	NA
Cash Flow	5.77	2.49	1.32	NA	NA	NA	NA	NA	NA	NA
Earnings	0.89	0.40	-0.63	NA	NA	NA	NA	NA	NA	NA
Dividends	0.10	0.04	Nil	NA	NA	NA	NA	NA	NA	NA
Payout Ratio	11%	9%	Nil	NA	NA	NA	NA	NA	NA	NA
Cal. Yrs.	1997	1996	1995	1994	1993	1992	1991	1990	1989	1988
Prices - High	23¾	13½	NA	NA	NA	NA	NA	NA	NA	NA
- Low	11	6⅜	NA	NA	NA	NA	NA	NA	NA	NA
P/E Ratio - High	27	34	NA	NA	NA	NA	NA	NA	NA	NA
- Low	12	16	NA	NA	NA	NA	NA	NA	NA	NA

Income Statement Analysis (Million $)

	1998	1997	1996	1995	1994	1993	1992	1991	1990	1989
Revs.	1,719	1,663	1,665	NA	NA	NA	NA	NA	NA	NA
Oper. Inc.	152	112	48.3	NA	NA	NA	NA	NA	NA	NA
Depr.	85.0	84.5	79.5	NA	NA	NA	NA	NA	NA	NA
Int. Exp.	8.2	6.3	7.3	NA	NA	NA	NA	NA	NA	NA
Pretax Inc.	62.0	22.7	-33.8	NA	NA	NA	NA	NA	NA	NA
Eff. Tax Rate	39%	29%	NM	NA	NA	NA	NA	NA	NA	NA
Net Inc.	37.8	16.2	-25.7	NA	NA	NA	NA	NA	NA	NA

Balance Sheet & Other Fin. Data (Million $)

	1998	1997	1996	1995	1994	1993	1992	1991	1990	1989
Cash	43.7	43.1	33.4	NA	NA	NA	NA	NA	NA	NA
Curr. Assets	326	297	256	NA	NA	NA	NA	NA	NA	NA
Total Assets	1,394	1,172	1,130	NA	NA	NA	NA	NA	NA	NA
Curr. Liab.	234	216	198	NA	NA	NA	NA	NA	NA	NA
LT Debt	267	103	81.5	NA	NA	NA	NA	NA	NA	NA
Common Eqty.	607	582	574	NA	NA	NA	NA	NA	NA	NA
Total Cap.	974	789	655	NA	NA	NA	NA	NA	NA	NA
Cap. Exp.	79.6	71.2	109	NA	NA	NA	NA	NA	NA	NA
Cash Flow	122	101	53.8	NA	NA	NA	NA	NA	NA	NA
Curr. Ratio	1.4	1.4	1.3	NA	NA	NA	NA	NA	NA	NA
% LT Debt of Cap.	27.4	13.1	12.4	NA	NA	NA	NA	NA	NA	NA
% Net Inc.of Revs.	2.2	1.0	NM	NA	NA	NA	NA	NA	NA	NA
% Ret. on Assets	2.9	1.4	NA	NA	NA	NA	NA	NA	NA	NA
% Ret. on Equity	6.4	NA	NA	NA	NA	NA	NA	NA	NA	NA

Data as orig. reptd.; bef. results of disc. opers. and/or spec. items. Per share data adj. for stk. divs. as of ex-div. date. Data for FY 96 refer to yr. ended December 31, 1995. Yr. end changed in 1996 from December 31 to March 31. EPS in bold/italic follow FASB 128 definition of Diluted EPS; all other EPS generally follow earlier use of Primary EPS.NA-Not Available. NM-Not Meaningful. NR-Not Ranked.

Office—8400 Maryland Ave., St. Louis, MO 63105. **Tel**—314-259-7000. **Chrmn & CEO**—B. H. Beracha. **VP & CFO**—M. H. Krieger. **VP & Secy**—J. M. Noelker. **VP & Investor Contact**—Molly Salky (314-259-7018). **Dirs**—J. J. Adorjan, P. F. Benoist, B. H. Beracha, M. K. Clark, J. Iglesias, J. E. Ritter, W. E. Stevens. **Transfer Agent & Registrar**—ChaseMellon Shareholder Services. **Incorporated**—in Delaware. **Empl**— 18,000. **S&P Analyst:** S.S.

03-OCT-98

Industry:
Electric Companies

Summary: This Boston-based holding company operates utilities in southeastern Massachusetts and Rhode Island and provides energy-related services across the U.S.

S&P Opinion: Hold (★★★)	Recent Price • 26⅞	Yield • 6.2%
	52 Wk Range • 27¾-20	12-Mo. P/E • 14.3

Quantitative Evaluations

Outlook
(1 Lowest—5 Highest)
• **1**

Fair Value
• **24½**

Risk
• **Low**

Earn./Div. Rank
• **B**

Technical Eval.
• **Bullish** since 9/98

Rel. Strength Rank
(1 Lowest—99 Highest)
• **91**

Insider Activity
• **NA**

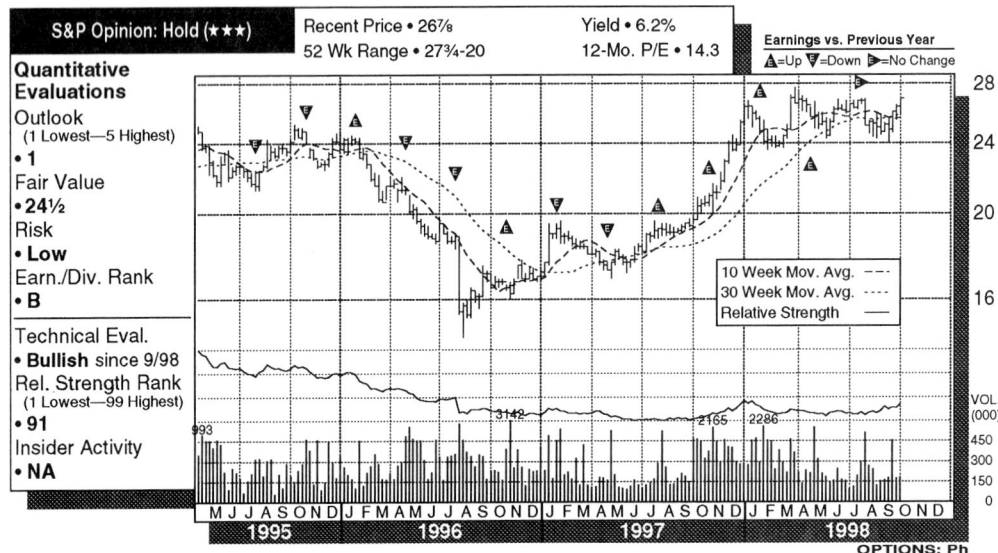

Earnings vs. Previous Year
▲=Up ▼=Down ▶=No Change

10 Week Mov. Avg. — - —
30 Week Mov. Avg. - - - -
Relative Strength ——

OPTIONS: Ph

Overview - 02-SEP-98

We expect low single-digit EPS growth in 1999. This will follow an anticipated decline in 1998 EPS, mainly reflecting a 10% rate reduction that went into effect on March 1, 1998, with the implementation of full customer choice legislation in Massachusetts. As part of a settlement agreement in December 1997, EUA will, in exchange for full recovery of its stranded costs, divest its power generation plants and a portion of its power purchase contracts. After initial bids for the generation assets proved disappointing, EUA reopened the auction process and was able to sell, in May 1998, its Canal Station interest for nearly twice its book value. Regulatory approvals and final sales should be realized in 1999. While 1998 results should benefit from a return to profitability at EUA Cogenex, EUA continues to consider the possible sale of the energy services unit.

Valuation - 02-SEP-98

We recommend holding EUA stock. After a sharp 51% surge in 1997 (significantly outperforming both the 31% gain for the S&P 500 and the nearly 20% increase for the S&P Index of Electric Companies), the shares are down 4.3% year to date. The strength of the shares in 1997 reflected the low interest rate environment, the turnaround at EUA Cogenex, and the passage of legislation permitting the full recovery of the company's stranded costs. While we remain concerned with EUA's high payout ratio (at 92% of our 1998 EPS estimate of $1.80), we believe that the company's strong cash flow will let it keep the dividend (recently yielding about 6.6%) at its current level. With the shares trading between 13X and 14X our 1999 EPS estimate of $1.85, the stock appears fairly valued for the near term.

Key Stock Statistics

S&P EPS Est. 1998	1.80	Tang. Bk. Value/Share	17.73
P/E on S&P Est. 1998	15.0	Beta	0.55
S&P EPS Est. 1999	1.85	Shareholders	12,000
Dividend Rate/Share	1.66	Market cap. (B)	$0.550
Shs. outstg. (M)	20.4	Inst. holdings	44%
Avg. daily vol. (M)	0.051		

Value of $10,000 invested 5 years ago: $ 15,882

Fiscal Year Ending Dec. 31

	1998	1997	1996	1995	1994	1993
Revenues (Million $)						
1Q	139.3	141.8	134.8	138.0	150.2	137.7
2Q	130.1	138.9	122.8	146.1	137.3	125.6
3Q	—	142.0	131.1	143.9	143.9	156.2
4Q	—	145.9	138.4	135.3	132.9	146.9
Yr.	—	568.5	527.1	563.4	564.3	566.5
Earnings Per Share ($)						
1Q	**0.54**	**0.51**	0.56	0.57	0.80	0.71
2Q	**0.29**	**0.29**	0.13	0.38	0.52	0.49
3Q	**E0.56**	**0.54**	0.43	0.15	0.67	0.74
4Q	**E0.41**	**0.52**	0.38	0.51	0.42	0.51
Yr.	**E1.80**	**1.86**	1.50	1.61	2.41	2.44

Next earnings report expected: early November

Dividend Data (Dividends have been paid since 1928.)

Amount ($)	Date Decl.	Ex-Div. Date	Stock of Record	Payment Date
0.415	Oct. 16	Oct. 29	Oct. 31	Nov. 15 '97
0.415	Jan. 20	Jan. 28	Jan. 30	Feb. 17 '98
0.415	Apr. 20	Apr. 29	May. 01	May. 15 '98
0.415	Jul. 20	Jul. 29	Jul. 31	Aug. 15 '98

*A Division of The **McGraw·Hill** Companies*

Business Summary - 02-SEP-98

With recent settlement agreements in Massachusetts and Rhode Island having removed many of the uncertainties related to the impact of industry restructuring, Eastern Utilities Associates believes that it will be able to insure the financial strength of its utility operations as it enters into an era of competitive electricity markets.

Eastern Utilities Associates supplies electricity to over 300,000 customers in southeastern Massachusetts and in Rhode Island. The core electric business (which accounted for 89% of revenues and 96% of operating income in 1997) consists of Montaup, a wholesale electric subsidiary that generates and transmits electricity to EUA's three wholly owned electric utilities: Blackstone, Eastern Edison and Newport. Electric revenues by customer class in recent years were:

	1997	1996	1995	1994
Residential	42%	42%	41%	41%
Commercial	35%	36%	36%	36%
Industrial	17%	18%	18%	18%
Other	6%	4%	5%	5%

Power sources in 1997 were oil 31% (20% in 1996), natural gas 28% (31%), coal 18% (15%), nuclear 17% (29%), and other 6% (5%).

In November 1997, Massachusetts passed legislation requiring, effective March 1, 1998, the states electric utilities to reduce rates by 10% (with an additional 5% reduction to be implemented on September 1, 1999) and to provide choice of supplier to all customers. The legislation also provided for the full recovery of stranded costs and called for the divestiture of Montaup's generation facilities, with the proceeds used to mitigate stranded cost recovery.

In August 1996, Rhode Island passed the Utility Restructuring Act of 1996 (URA). The legislation provided for unbundling of electric service into generation, transmission and distribution functions; the phasing in of choice of electricity supplier for all customer classes by July 1, 1998 (later moved up to January 1, 1998); and the full recovery of stranded costs through a non-bypassable transition charge.

Because of the limited growth prospects of its utility operations, EUA is focusing on the growth potential of its nonregulated subsidiaries. In 1997, these businesses broke even, with losses at the investment (-$0.18 a share) and energy services (-$0.02) units offset by earnings of $0.19 at EUA Ocean State (which owns a 29.9% interest in non-utility generating units) and $0.01 at EUA Cogenex (which provides energy efficiency products and energy management services).

In May 1998, EUA's Montauk subsidiary agreed to sell its 50% interest in Unit 2 of the Canal Generating Station in Sandwich, Massachusetts to Southern Energy, a subsidiary of Southern Company, for $75 million.

Per Share Data ($)

(Year Ended Dec. 31)	1997	1996	1995	1994	1993	1992	1991	1990	1989	1988
Tangible Bk. Val.	17.73	17.60	17.72	17.62	17.46	14.91	14.05	13.75	23.37	21.03
Earnings	1.86	1.50	1.61	2.41	2.44	2.00	1.58	-8.21	2.95	2.85
Dividends	1.66	1.65	1.58	1.51	1.42	1.36	1.45	2.58	2.48	2.38
Payout Ratio	89%	110%	98%	63%	58%	68%	92%	NM	84%	83%
Prices - High	26¾	24½	25¼	27¾	29⅞	25¼	25	41½	41¾	33⅛
- Low	16⅞	14½	21¼	21⅛	23⅝	20⅜	15¾	20¾	30⅜	21⅛
P/E Ratio - High	14	16	16	12	12	13	16	NM	14	12
- Low	9	10	13	9	10	10	10	NM	10	7

Income Statement Analysis (Million $)

	1997	1996	1995	1994	1993	1992	1991	1990	1989	1988
Revs.	569	527	563	564	566	526	524	452	409	374
Depr.	49.5	45.5	45.5	46.5	44.7	41.3	40.6	37.5	25.9	23.0
Maint.	30.4	25.0	23.5	23.5	25.1	20.0	20.9	22.5	18.3	17.3
Fxd. Chgs. Cov.	2.1	1.8	1.9	2.1	1.9	1.9	1.7	NM	3.3	2.8
Constr. Credits	1.0	2.2	3.2	2.1	2.4	2.0	2.5	55.6	85.4	60.6
Eff. Tax Rate	27%	25%	30%	29%	27%	32%	33%	NM	32%	32%
Net Inc.	38.0	30.6	32.6	47.4	44.9	34.1	26.3	-130	40.9	37.5

Balance Sheet & Other Fin. Data (Million $)

	1997	1996	1995	1994	1993	1992	1991	1990	1989	1988
Gross Prop.	1,156	1,071	1,045	1,029	1,025	1,008	998	992	1,363	1,207
Cap. Exp.	76.1	62.7	78.0	51.0	61.0	42.0	52.0	60.0	161	126
Net Prop.	780	720	721	725	728	733	746	751	1,159	1,020
Capitalization:										
LT Debt	333	406	435	455	497	463	488	444	606	555
% LT Debt	45	50	52	53	58	60	62	61	59	61
Pfd.	34.5	33.9	33.2	32.3	32.0	44.3	45.8	50.4	49.7	49.7
% Pfd.	4.70	4.20	3.90	3.80	3.70	5.70	5.80	6.90	4.80	5.50
Common	373	372	375	365	333	267	249	237	375	302
% Common	50	46	45	43	39	35	32	32	36	33
Total Cap.	904	981	984	991	999	935	928	871	1,202	1,059
% Oper. Ratio	90.1	89.4	87.3	87.0	86.7	87.8	87.6	87.7	85.7	82.6
% Earn. on Net Prop.	7.5	7.8	9.9	10.1	10.3	8.7	8.7	5.8	5.4	6.8
% Return On Revs.	6.7	5.8	5.8	8.4	7.9	6.5	5.0	NM	10.0	10.0
% Return On Invest. Capital	8.9	7.4	7.7	9.3	9.8	9.5	8.6	NM	5.9	6.9
% Return On Com. Equity	10.2	8.2	8.8	13.6	15.0	13.2	10.8	NM	12.1	12.8

Data as orig. reptd.; bef. results of disc opers. and/or spec. items. Per share data adj. for stk. divs. as of ex-div. date. Bold denotes diluted EPS (FASB 128). E-Estimated. NA-Not Available. NM-Not Meaningful. NR-Not Ranked.

Office—One Liberty Square, Boston, MA 02109. **Organized**—in Massachusetts in 1928. **Tel**—(617) 357-9590.**Website**—http://www.eua.com. **Chrmn & CEO**—D. G. Pardus. **Pres & COO**—J. R. Stevens. **Treas, Secy & Investor Contact**—Clifford J. Hebert Jr. **Trustees**—R. A. Boss, P. J. Choquette Jr., P. S. Damon, P. B. Freeman, L. A. Liebenow, J. Makowski, W. W. Marple Jr., D. G. Pardus, M. M. Stapleton, J. R. Stevens, W. N. Thorndike. **Transfer Agent & Registrar**—Boston EquiServe, Boston. **Empl**— 983. **S&P Analyst:** Justin McCann

STANDARD &POOR'S
STOCK REPORTS

Eaton Vance

804G

NYSE Symbol **EV**

In S&P SmallCap 600

03-OCT-98

Industry: Investment Management

Summary: This Boston-based holding company is primarily engaged in investment management.

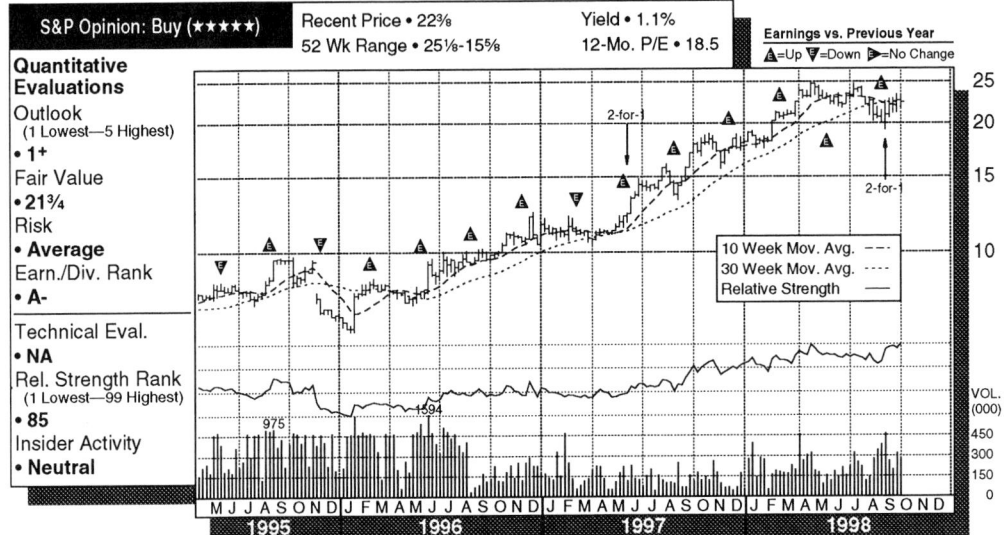

S&P Opinion: Buy (★★★★)	
Recent Price • 22⅝	Yield • 1.1%
52 Wk Range • 25⅛-15⅝	12-Mo. P/E • 18.5

Quantitative Evaluations

Outlook (1 Lowest—5 Highest)
• **1+**

Fair Value
• **21¾**

Risk
• **Average**

Earn./Div. Rank
• **A-**

Technical Eval.
• **NA**

Rel. Strength Rank (1 Lowest—99 Highest)
• **85**

Insider Activity
• **Neutral**

Earnings vs. Previous Year
▲=Up ▼=Down ▶=No Change

10 Week Mov. Avg. ---
30 Week Mov. Avg. ·····
Relative Strength —

Overview - 19-AUG-98

The pace of asset growth in EV's mutual fund group has increased sharply in recent years, particularly in its tax efficient equity and bank loan funds. Continuing this trend, sales of EV-managed funds increased 100% in the first nine months of FY 98 (Oct.), to $6.4 billion, from $3.2 billion in the FY 97 period. Combined with strong gains in asset valuations and flat fund redemptions, managed assets at the end of the period were up 31%, to $27.5 billion from $21.0 billion a year earlier. Operating expenses rose in line with revenues; excluding a FY 98 $2.6 million writedown of real estate to be sold, net income increased 25%. In the third quarter alone, revenues and net income climbed 31% and 30%, respectively. For the fourth quarter and into FY 99, we expect more of the same. We have raised our EPS projection for the fourth time this year, to $2.65, and upped our FY 99 estimate from $3.00 to $3.20. We have not adjusted for a two-for-one split to be effected September 1, 1998.

Valuation - 19-AUG-98

We think that EV's valuation is extremely compelling, and are upgrading our recommendation from accumulate to buy. Valuation remains at a discount relative to that of other asset management industry companies. Mutual fund cash inflows from 401(k) plans remain in a strong long-term pattern, as workers are convinced that they must save more for retirement. Along this line, EV has added "Investing for the 21st Century" as a major marketing theme to complement its existing "Mutual Funds for People Who Pay Taxes" program for its tax efficient funds. A one million share (pre-split) buyback authorization would likely be used to repurchase stock should the shares fall significantly in a market correction.

Key Stock Statistics

S&P EPS Est. 1998	1.32	Tang. Bk. Value/Share	6.23
P/E on S&P Est. 1998	16.9	Beta	1.00
S&P EPS Est. 1999	1.60	Shareholders	1,000
Dividend Rate/Share	0.24	Market cap. (B)	$0.805
Shs. outstg. (M)	35.9	Inst. holdings	35%
Avg. daily vol. (M)	0.055		

Value of $10,000 invested 5 years ago: NA

Fiscal Year Ending Oct. 31

	1998	1997	1996	1995	1994	1993
Revenues (Million $)						
1Q	55.27	47.81	44.50	41.54	53.89	42.88
2Q	59.99	47.44	45.46	40.73	54.25	46.25
3Q	67.00	47.74	45.06	42.69	54.81	49.38
4Q	—	53.86	46.34	42.96	55.83	50.65
Yr.	—	200.9	181.4	167.9	218.0	189.2
Earnings Per Share ($)						
1Q	**0.28**	0.26	0.26	0.15	0.17	0.15
2Q	**0.30**	0.24	0.23	0.16	0.20	0.21
3Q	**0.36**	0.24	0.24	0.23	0.16	0.30
4Q	**E0.38**	0.27	0.20	0.18	0.22	0.10
Yr.	**E1.32**	1.04	0.94	0.72	0.75	0.77

Next earnings report expected: late November

Dividend Data (Dividends have been paid since 1976.)

Amount ($)	Date Decl.	Ex-Div. Date	Stock of Record	Payment Date
0.120	Jan. 14	Jan. 28	Jan. 30	Feb. 09 '98
0.120	Apr. 09	Apr. 28	Apr. 30	May. 11 '98
0.120	Jul. 07	Jul. 29	Jul. 31	Aug. 10 '98
2-for-1	Jul. 07	Sep. 01	Aug. 14	Aug. 31 '98

A Division of The McGraw-Hill Companies

STANDARD
&POOR'S
STOCK REPORTS

Eaton Vance Corp.

804G
03-OCT-98

Business Summary - 19-AUG-98

Eaton Vance Corp. is a Boston-based investment advisory company. Historically, it has focused on offering products in the fixed-income sector, with particular emphasis on tax-free municipal bonds. However, with industry dynamics pushing an increasing number of investors to the stock market for superior investment returns, EV has targeted its equity business as a growth area. As of October 31, 1997, EV provided investment advisory or administration services to over 70 funds and to over 800 separately managed individual and institutional accounts. Separately managed accounts had assets of $2.4 billion at October 31, 1997. Fund managed assets at the end of FY 97 (Oct.) totaled $18.9 billion, and were divided as follows:

	FY 97
Non-taxable fixed income	40%
Equities	27%
Bank loans	21%
Taxable fixed income	11%
Money market	1%

The company derives the vast majority of its revenue from investment advisory and administration fees and distribution income received from the Eaton Vance funds and separately managed accounts. These fees are calculated as a percentage of assets under management, and as such, the company's operating results are largely dependent on its ability to attract and retain funds, and on the overall health of the securities markets. In FY 97, assets under management rose 23%, reflecting a strong rise in mutual fund sales and appreciation of the market value of managed assets.

Net fund sales were $1.4 billion in FY 97 ($0.5 billion in FY 96), reflecting a successful sales campaign. Eaton Vance employs two separate mutual fund sales teams that operate through different distribution channels. The company uses targeted marketing to push its funds through a wide variety of national and regional broker/dealers, independent broker/dealers and banks. To further improve distribution, EV has recently begun marketing its products through independent fee-based advisers.

In FY 96, Eaton Vance began to place particular emphasis on growing its equity fund business, and its efforts have begun to pay off. Equity fund assets under management were $5.2 billion in FY 97, up 68% over their level in FY 96. In addition, the company's strong balance sheet gives it the ability to seek acquisitions to fuel growth in its equity business.

Eaton Vance has committed to sell most of the assets of Northeast Properties, a real estate subsidiary with 662,000 sq. ft. of property in Massachusetts, New Hampshire and New York. In the first quarter of FY 98, a $2.6 million charge was recorded to reduce the value of certain of the properties to net realizable value.

Per Share Data ($)

(Year Ended Oct. 31)	1997	1996	1995	1994	1993	1992	1991	1990	1989	1988
Tangible Bk. Val.	6.04	5.54	5.17	4.49	3.89	2.51	1.94	1.56	1.41	1.18
Cash Flow	1.10	1.00	0.79	2.24	2.03	1.65	1.31	0.95	0.63	0.36
Earnings	1.04	0.94	0.72	0.75	0.77	0.62	0.44	0.26	0.25	0.34
Dividends	0.21	0.18	0.16	0.15	0.12	0.09	0.07	0.06	0.05	0.05
Payout Ratio	20%	19%	22%	20%	16%	14%	17%	23%	21%	14%
Prices - High	19⅛	12½	9⅞	9⅜	10⅜	7⅝	4⅛	3½	3½	3
- Low	10½	6½	6⅞	6⅛	7¼	3⅞	2	1¹³⁄₁₆	2¾	1⅞
P/E Ratio - High	18	13	14	13	13	12	9	14	14	9
- Low	10	7	9	8	9	6	5	7	11	5

Income Statement Analysis (Million $)

	1997	1996	1995	1994	1993	1992	1991	1990	1989	1988
Commissions	118	100	85.4	85.8	75.2	69.5	61.5	55.1	NA	NA
Int. Inc.	3.6	3.7	2.6	4.9	4.6	3.7	3.7	2.7	3.3	2.0
Total Revs.	201	181	168	218	189	153	120	94.0	64.0	47.0
Int. Exp.	4.0	3.7	4.7	5.3	4.9	3.3	3.1	3.6	NA	NA
Pretax Inc.	67.5	59.9	46.1	47.7	47.0	33.1	21.1	16.4	13.5	17.0
Eff. Tax Rate	40%	40%	38%	40%	42%	42%	40%	53%	46%	39%
Net Inc.	40.2	35.8	30.4	28.5	27.3	19.3	12.7	7.7	7.3	10.7

Balance Sheet & Other Fin. Data (Million $)

	1997	1996	1995	1994	1993	1992	1991	1990	1989	1988
Total Assets	387	360	358	456	426	318	278	224	242	77.0
Cash Items	141	116	79.0	34.0	28.7	25.5	17.1	15.7	91.0	11.0
Receivables	13.1	7.7	1.6	13.1	11.6	10.5	7.2	4.1	3.5	1.9
Secs. Owned	NA	NA	NA	88.3	80.2	64.0	50.8	36.1	NA	NA
Sec. Borrowed	NA	NA	Nil	Nil	Nil	Nil	Nil	Nil	Nil	Nil
Due Brokers & Cust.	NA	NA	Nil	Nil	Nil	Nil	Nil	Nil	Nil	Nil
Other Liabs.	121	125	138	226	205	162	153	124	NA	NA
Capitalization:										
Debt	50.9	54.5	56.1	60.3	73.2	78.4	64.0	50.6	14.2	14.2
Equity	226	211	195	166	145	77.5	59.6	47.9	43.9	37.4
Total	347	336	333	229	221	156	125	100	58.0	52.0
% Return On Revs.	20.0	19.8	16.1	13.1	14.5	12.6	10.6	8.2	11.4	23.1
% Ret. on Assets	10.8	10.0	6.6	6.5	7.4	6.4	5.1	3.3	3.6	13.6
% Ret. on Equity	18.4	17.7	15.0	18.3	24.7	28.0	23.5	16.9	17.9	29.1

Data as orig. reptd.; bef. results of disc opers. and/or spec. items. Per share data adj. for stk. divs. as of ex-div. date. Bold denotes diluted EPS (FASB 128). E-Estimated. NA-Not Available. NM-Not Meaningful. NR-Not Ranked.

Office—24 Federal St., Boston, MA 02110. **Tel**—(617) 482-8260. **Chrmn**—J. B. Hawkes. **Vice Chrmn**—M. D. Gardner. **Pres & CEO**—J. B. Hawkes. **VP & Secy**—T. Otis. **CFO & Investor Contact**—William M. Steul. **Dirs**—J. G. L. Cabot, M. D. Gardner, J. B. Hawkes, J. M. Nelson, B. A. Rowland, Jr., R. Z. Sorenson. **Transfer Agent & Registrar**—BostonEquiserve. **Incorporated**—in Maryland in 1959. **Empl**— 359. **S&P Analyst:** Mark S. Basham

STANDARD &POOR'S
STOCK REPORTS

Electro Scientific Industries 3787H

NASDAQ Symbol **ESIO**

In S&P SmallCap 600

03-OCT-98

Industry:
Electrical Equipment

Summary: ESIO makes products used in electronics manufacturing including: laser production systems; production and test equipment; laser trim systems; and laser and drilling systems.

Quantitative Evaluations	
Outlook (1 Lowest—5 Highest)	• **4⁻**
Fair Value	• 25⅛
Risk	• **High**
Earn./Div. Rank	• **B**
Technical Eval.	• **Bearish** since 11/97
Rel. Strength Rank (1 Lowest—99 Highest)	• 20
Insider Activity	• **Neutral**

Recent Price • 16¼
52 Wk Range • 63-14⅜

Yield • Nil
12-Mo. P/E • 9.3

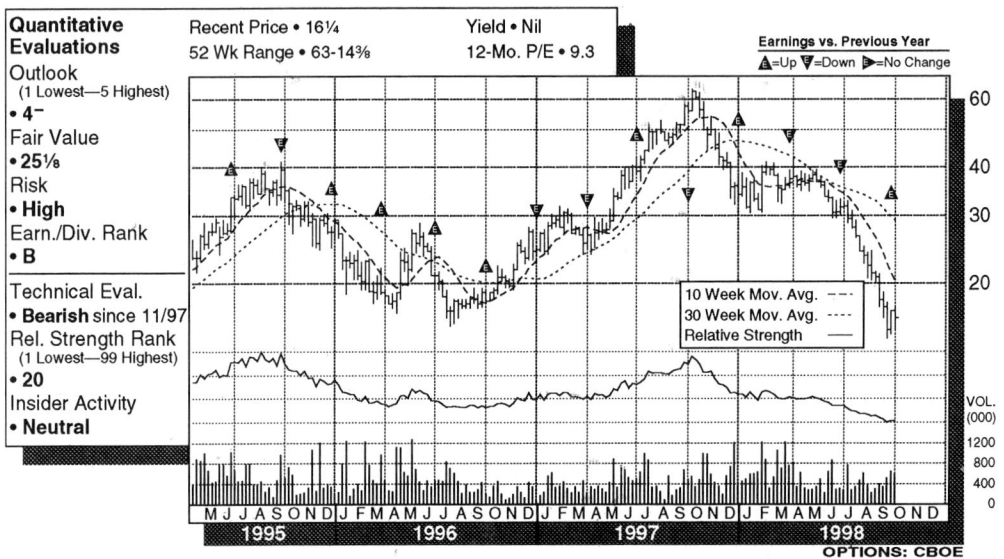

Earnings vs. Previous Year
▲=Up ▼=Down ▶=No Change

10 Week Mov. Avg. – – –
30 Week Mov. Avg. ·······
Relative Strength ——

VOL. (000)

OPTIONS: CBOE

Business Profile - 17-SEP-98

The company's business depends, in large part, upon the capital expenditures of manufacturers of electronic devices. In December 1997, ESIO acquired Applied Intelligent Systems, Inc. (AISI), a privately held company based in Ann Arbor, MI, in exchange for 1.4 million common shares. AISI provides machine vision solutions for automated process control and visual inspection to the semiconductor and electronics industries. AISI's sales in the three months ended August 31, 1997, were $8.7 million. Backlog, including AISI, as of May 31, 1998, was $21.8 million, down from $31.8 million on May 31, 1997.

Operational Review - 17-SEP-98

Net sales in the fiscal year ended May 31, 1998, rose 28%, on increased sales of advanced electronic packaging systems, electronic component equipment and machine visible systems. Margins widened, reflecting a more favorable sales mix; operating income grew 31%. Results were penalized by merger-related costs of $14.6 million, partly offset by higher interest income. After taxes at 37.1% in each period, net income fell 13%, to $16,883,000 ($1.47 a share, diluted, on 5.9% more shares), from $19,459,000 ($1.79).

Stock Performance - 02-OCT-98

In the past 30 trading days, ESIO's shares have declined 23%, compared to a 7% fall in the S&P 500. Average trading volume for the past five days was 118,300 shares, compared with the 40-day moving average of 85,662 shares.

Key Stock Statistics

Dividend Rate/Share	Nil	Shareholders	300
Shs. outstg. (M)	11.4	Market cap. (B)	$0.185
Avg. daily vol. (M)	0.107	Inst. holdings	65%
Tang. Bk. Value/Share	16.04		
Beta	1.60		

Value of $10,000 invested 5 years ago: $ 31,070

Fiscal Year Ending May 31

	1999	1998	1997	1996	1995	1994
Revenues (Million $)						
1Q	45.19	48.36	34.86	35.97	21.01	20.29
2Q	—	59.87	35.10	40.84	24.80	17.68
3Q	—	57.59	37.20	41.63	29.40	16.95
4Q	—	55.03	43.00	41.27	33.00	17.64
Yr.	—	229.6	150.2	159.7	108.2	72.55
Earnings Per Share ($)						
1Q	0.11	-0.17	0.51	0.06	0.33	0.22
2Q	—	0.70	0.53	0.57	0.36	0.48
3Q	—	0.40	0.56	0.61	0.39	0.26
4Q	—	0.54	0.59	0.63	0.43	0.27
Yr.	—	1.47	2.19	1.87	1.53	1.23

Next earnings report expected: mid December

Dividend Data

No cash dividends have been paid.

A Division of The McGraw·Hill Companies

Electro Scientific Industries, Inc.

3787H
03-OCT-98

Business Summary - 17-SEP-98

Electro Scientific Industries (ESIO) provides electronics manufacturers with equipment necessary to produce key components in wireless telecommmunications, computers, automotive electronics and many other electronic products. The company believes that it is the leading supplier of advanced laser systems used to fine tune electronic circuitry, to improve the yield of semiconductor memory devices, and of high-speed test and termination equipment used in the high-volume production of miniature capacitors. In addition, ESIO produces a family of mechanical and laser drilling systems for production of printed wiring boards for manufacturers of semiconductors, electronics and other products.

The company's test and production systems for miniature capacitors consist of automated test, production and handling equipment for the manufacture of miniature multi-layer ceramic capacitors (MLCCs) used in electronic circuits. Large numbers of MLCCs are used in circuits that process analog signals or operate at high frequencies such as in video products (VCRs and

camcorders), voice communication products, wireless telecommunication products and computers.

ESIO's fine-tuning systems are used to tune the precise frequency of electronic circuits that receive and transmit signals in pagers, cellular telephones and other wireless devices. Laser trimming systems are also used to tune automotive electronic assemblies such as engine control circuits.

The company's vision systems combine advanced computer technology, proprietary software and optical equipment to reduce application development time and provide machine vision inspection that facilitates quality products and fast throughput. ESIO's advanced laser technology provides a cost effective method for forming electrical connections between layers, called vias, in a multiple layer substrate.

Research and development spending in FY 98 (May) and FY 97 totaled $28.5 million and $22.7 million, respectively, excluding research and development expenditures funded by the Advanced Research Projects Agency of the U.S. government.

International sales accounted for 58% of the total in FY 98, and 64% in FY 97.

Per Share Data ($)

(Year Ended May 31)	1998	1997	1996	1995	1994	1993	1992	1991	1990	1989
Tangible Bk. Val.	16.04	15.42	13.28	11.28	8.34	7.11	6.79	7.74	7.58	8.41
Cash Flow	1.94	2.54	2.19	1.88	1.58	0.77	-0.56	0.64	-0.07	1.46
Earnings	1.47	2.19	1.87	1.53	1.23	0.37	-1.00	0.20	-0.52	1.05
Dividends	Nil	Nil	Nil	Nil	Nil	Nil	Nil	Nil	Nil	Nil
Payout Ratio	Nil	Nil	Nil	Nil	Nil	Nil	Nil	Nil	Nil	Nil
Cal. Yrs.	1997	1996	1995	1994	1993	1992	1991	1990	1989	1988
Prices - High	63¾	29	41½	21⅝	17	5½	7	9	14½	11¾
- Low	23¾	15½	17½	8⅝	5	2½	2¾	3⅛	7	6½
P/E Ratio - High	43	13	22	14	14	15	NM	45	NM	11
- Low	16	7	9	6	4	7	NM	16	NM	6

Income Statement Analysis (Million $)

	1998	1997	1996	1995	1994	1993	1992	1991	1990	1989
Revs.	230	150	160	108	72.6	67.9	58.2	66.7	73.9	83.1
Oper. Inc.	44.7	30.4	33.6	18.7	10.7	5.6	-2.7	4.0	-0.7	12.0
Depr.	5.5	3.1	2.8	2.6	2.3	2.5	2.7	2.7	2.7	2.5
Int. Exp.	Nil	Nil	Nil	NA	0.6	0.8	1.0	1.3	1.2	1.3
Pretax Inc.	26.9	28.7	25.3	16.5	10.0	2.6	-6.9	1.6	-4.3	9.3
Eff. Tax Rate	37%	34%	37%	30%	21%	14%	NM	23%	NM	32%
Net Inc.	16.9	18.9	16.1	11.5	7.9	2.2	-6.1	1.2	-3.2	6.3

Balance Sheet & Other Fin. Data (Million $)

	1998	1997	1996	1995	1994	1993	1992	1991	1990	1989
Cash	9.8	43.2	37.0	28.4	8.2	2.8	3.4	5.5	10.3	7.8
Curr. Assets	159	127	112	91.2	44.3	40.5	35.3	45.0	47,9	55.2
Total Assets	199	149	133	111	62.4	61.2	58.5	68.7	72.0	82.5
Curr. Liab.	17.2	13.7	17.6	15.1	8.1	11.6	11.5	11.9	16.0	22.7
LT Debt	Nil	Nil	Nil	Nil	Nil	4.8	5.0	7.6	8.4	8.7
Common Eqty.	182	135	115	94.4	53.5	44.0	41.5	47.3	46.1	51.0
Total Cap.	182	135	115	94.4	53.5	48.8	46.5	56.4	56.0	59.9
Cap. Exp.	12.5	3.4	3.6	3.0	2.1	0.8	2.8	2.5	3.0	2.3
Cash Flow	22.4	22.0	18.8	14.1	10.1	4.7	-3.4	3.9	-0.4	8.8
Curr. Ratio	9.3	9.3	6.4	6.0	5.5	3.5	3.1	3.8	3.0	2.4
% LT Debt of Cap.	Nil	Nil	Nil	Nil	Nil	9.9	10.7	13.4	15.1	14.5
% Net Inc.of Revs.	7.4	12.6	10.1	10.6	10.9	3.3	NM	1.8	NM	7.6
% Ret. on Assets	9.7	13.4	13.2	12.0	12.5	3.7	NM	1.7	NM	8.1
% Ret. on Equity	10.6	15.1	9.9	14.0	15.9	5.2	NM	2.6	NM	13.2

Data as orig. reptd.; bef. results of disc. opers. and/or spec. items. Per share data adj. for stk. divs. as of ex-div. date. Bold denotes diluted EPS (FASB 128). E-Estimated. NA-Not Available. NM-Not Meaningful. NR-Not Ranked.

Office—13900 N.W. Science Park Dr., Portland, OH 97229-5497. **Tel**—(503) 641-4141. **Fax**—(503) 643-4873.**Website**—http://www.elcsci.com **Chrmn**—D. F. Bolender. **Pres & CEO**—D. R. VanLuvanee. **SVP-Fin & CFO**—B. L. Harmon. **Secy & Investor Contact**—Larry T. Rapp (503-671-5446). **Dirs**—D. F. Bolender, L. L. Hänsen, W. A. Porter, V. B. Ryles Jr., D. C. Strain, J. D. Thompkins, K. Thomson, D. R. VanLuvanee. **Transfer Agent & Registrar**—First Chicago Trust Co. of New York, NYC. **Incorporated**—in Oregon in 1953. **Empl**— 900. **S&P Analyst:** S.J.T.

STANDARD &POOR'S
STOCK REPORTS

Electroglas, Inc.

3786T
Nasdaq Symbol EGLS
In S&P SmallCap 600

03-OCT-98

Industry: Equipment (Semiconductor)

Summary: This company is a leader in the development, manufacture, marketing and servicing of automatic wafer probing equipment for use in the testing of integrated circuit (IC) devices.

S&P Opinion: Hold (★★★)	Recent Price • 8⅛	Yield • Nil	Earnings vs. Previous Year
	52 Wk Range • 31⅜-8⅛	12-Mo. P/E • NM	▲=Up ▼=Down ▶=No Change

Quantitative Evaluations

Outlook
(1 Lowest—5 Highest)
• **NA**

Fair Value
• **NA**

Risk
• **High**

Earn./Div. Rank
• **NR**

Technical Eval.
• **Bearish** since 10/97

Rel. Strength Rank
(1 Lowest—99 Highest)
• **17**

Insider Activity
• **NA**

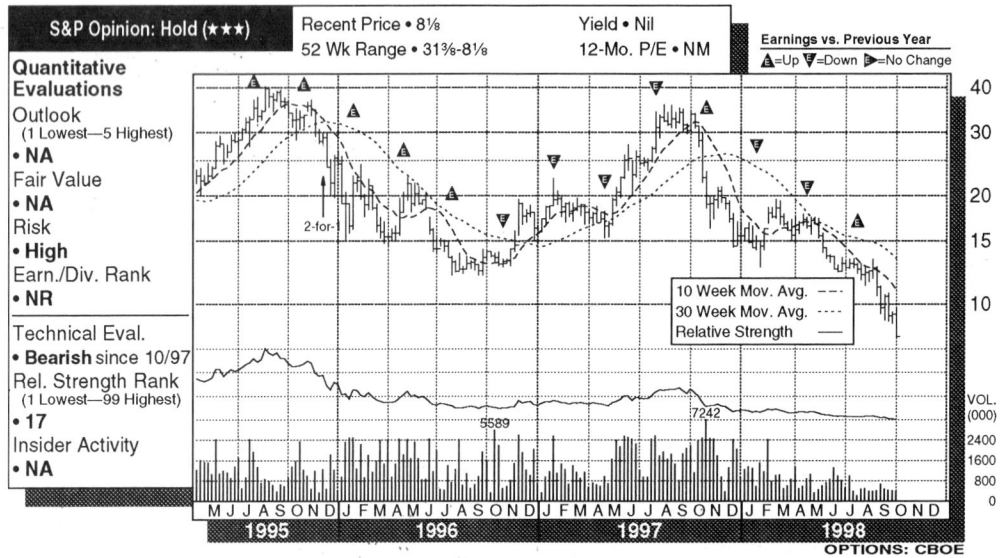

10 Week Mov. Avg. - - -
30 Week Mov. Avg. ·····
Relative Strength ——

2-for-1

5589   7242

VOL. (000)
2400
1600
800
0

M J J A S O N D J F M A M J J A S O N D J F M A M J J A S O N D J F M A M J J A S O N D
1995   1996   1997   1998

OPTIONS: CBOE

Overview - 27-JUL-98

Operating results are likely to trend lower over the next few quarters, reflecting the impact of the Asian financial crisis and weak semiconductor industry conditions. Chip makers have sharply reduced capital spending plans, and have pushed out or canceled orders for equipment. Gross margins will come under pressure as costs are spread over a smaller revenue base, but a shift in the product mix toward EGLS's newest prober, the 4090, will partially offset the impact. Despite higher selling prices, this product has taken market share from the competition. Interest income generated from the company's healthy cash balances will help buffer the poor operating results. In addition, EPS comparisons should benefit from a recently announced one million share repurchase program. Overall, we look for a loss of $0.58 a share for 1998, versus 1997's EPS of $0.66 (before charges).

Valuation - 27-JUL-98

The shares of this chip equipment maker have fallen sharply since early October 1997, reflecting investor concerns regarding semiconductor equipment industry conditions. We are maintaining our neutral recommendation on the shares, as we expect the Asian financial crisis and overcapacity in the chip industry to continue to hurt operating results over the next few quarters. EGLS is one of only three wafer-prober suppliers in the world, and maintains a strong position in a long-term growth market. As semiconductor complexity increases, longer test times per die are required, and therefore more probers are needed to maintain the same throughput. However, although the shares are trading at a low multiple of 1.2X book value, we see no near-term catalyst for share price outperformance, given current weakness in industry conditions.

Key Stock Statistics

S&P EPS Est. 1998	-0.58	Tang. Bk. Value/Share	9.23
P/E on S&P Est. 1998	NM	Beta	1.84
S&P EPS Est. 1999	-0.30	Shareholders	14,500
Dividend Rate/Share	Nil	Market cap. (B)	$0.160
Shs. outstg. (M)	19.7	Inst. holdings	59%
Avg. daily vol. (M)	0.091		

Value of $10,000 invested 5 years ago: NA

Fiscal Year Ending Dec. 31

	1998	1997	1996	1995	1994	1993
Revenues (Million $)						
1Q	36.87	25.55	51.84	33.92	24.63	16.20
2Q	27.54	36.08	48.87	39.40	27.58	18.60
3Q	—	44.26	31.47	45.34	29.36	21.70
4Q	—	44.15	19.78	50.58	30.74	22.81
Yr.	—	150.0	151.9	169.2	112.3	79.41
Earnings Per Share ($)						
1Q	-0.02	Nil	0.62	0.39	0.28	0.13
2Q	-0.26	-1.14	0.50	0.48	0.32	0.15
3Q	—	0.29	0.24	0.54	0.37	0.54
4Q	—	-0.05	Nil	0.64	0.34	0.24
Yr.	—	-0.86	1.36	2.05	1.31	1.07

Next earnings report expected: late October

Dividend Data

EGLS intends to retain earnings for use in its business and does not expect to pay cash dividends in the foreseeable future. A two-for-one stock split was effected in December 1995.

A Division of The McGraw·Hill Companies

Business Summary - 27-JUL-98

Electroglas, Inc. operates in a niche market in the rapidly growing semiconductor equipment industry: the manufacturing of automatic wafer probing equipment. The total worldwide market for wafer probing equipment is approximately $500 million, and the company has only two major competitors: Tokyo Electron Labs and Tokyo Seimitsu.

There are several elements to the company's strategy. These include a focus on technological innovation, as the company has invested heavily in engineering, research and development to add features and functionality to its products. Electroglas also seeks to maintain strong customer relationships, with the company working closely with its customers to determine their needs and specifications. To enhance its future growth, EGLS plans to increase its focus on the Japanese market, which has been difficult for EGLS to penetrate. In addition, EGLS seeks to expand its product offerings through new internally developed products and strategic alliances and acquisitions.

Semiconductor devices are fabricated by repeating a complex series of process steps on a wafer substrate, usually made of silicon and measuring three to eight inches in diameter. A wafer prober successfully positions each integrated circuit on a wafer so that the electrical contact points on the finished wafer align under and make contact with the probe pins, which are located on a probe card mounted on the wafer prober.

Parametric testing is performed during the wafer fabrication process ("in-line"), at the completion of the wafer fabrication process while the individual ICs are still intact on the wafer ("end-of-line"), and after the completion of the cutting and packaging of individual ICs ("wafer sort"), to identify ICs which do not conform to specifications. EGLS's probers are used for in-line and end-of-line testing.

The company's primary product lines are the 2000 series and Horizon 4000 wafer probers. The older 2000 Series products are used primarily for wafers whose diameters are six inches and less. The Horizon 4000 Series products, used primarily for eight inch wafers, consist of four models: the Horizon 4060X, which features wafer sizing, noncontact wafer realign, single wafer load and quick load stations and a robotic transfer mechanism; the Horizon 4080X Automatic Prober, targeted at high-volume semiconductor production lines of eight-inch wafers; and the Horizon 4085X Automatic Prober, developed to meet the exacting standards required for probing high-pin-count advanced logic devices; and the Horizon 4090, which was introduced in 1996.

EGLS is developing a range of software products named SORTnet, which is to be used for the management and control of data gained during the test process.

Per Share Data ($)

(Year Ended Dec. 31)	1997	1996	1995	1994	1993	1992	1991	1990	1989	1988
Tangible Bk. Val.	9.48	9.91	8.74	6.35	2.90	0.77	NA	NA	NA	NA
Cash Flow	-0.43	1.59	2.16	1.39	1.16	0.39	NA	NA	NA	NA
Earnings	-0.86	1.36	2.05	1.31	1.07	0.32	NA	NA	NA	NA
Dividends	Nil	Nil	Nil	Nil	Nil	Nil	Nil	Nil	Nil	Nil
Payout Ratio	Nil	Nil	Nil	Nil	Nil	Nil	Nil	Nil	Nil	Nil
Prices - High	35⅞	25¾	40¼	25¼	14⅜	NA	NA	NA	NA	NA
- Low	14⅜	12	13⅝	11½	6⅞	NA	NA	NA	NA	NA
P/E Ratio - High	NM	19	20	19	13	NA	NA	NA	NA	NA
- Low	NM	9	7	9	6	NA	NA	NA	NA	NA

Income Statement Analysis (Million $)

Revs.	150	152	169	112	79.0	55.0	59.8	64.8	64.5	66.8
Oper. Inc.	17.2	32.9	55.5	33.7	17.8	7.5	11.6	14.9	NA	NA
Depr.	8.0	4.1	2.0	1.3	1.2	1.0	1.0	0.8	NA	NA
Int. Exp.	Nil	Nil	Nil	Nil	Nil	Nil	Nil	Nil	Nil	Nil
Pretax Inc.	-13.0	33.7	57.5	35.4	17.1	7.0	11.3	14.1	16.1	16.7
Eff. Tax Rate	NM	27%	36%	37%	14%	37%	39%	37%	38%	39%
Net Inc.	-15.9	24.5	37.1	22.3	14.7	4.3	6.9	8.9	10.0	10.3

Balance Sheet & Other Fin. Data (Million $)

Cash	20.3	129	118	79.2	21.7	0.0	NM	NA	NA	NA
Curr. Assets	199	184	182	118	43.0	17.6	18.6	NA	NA	NA
Total Assets	230	198	192	132	53.0	20.0	21.4	21.0	18.8	20.8
Curr. Liab.	26.6	24.2	34.0	21.1	13.5	9.6	11.6	NA	NA	NA
LT Debt	Nil	Nil	Nil	Nil	Nil	Nil	Nil	Nil	Nil	Nil
Common Eqty.	200	174	157	111	39.0	10.5	9.7	10.5	10.5	11.8
Total Cap.	204	174	157	111	39.0	10.5	9.7	10.5	10.5	11.8
Cap. Exp.	10.7	8.0	3.5	2.1	0.7	0.7	0.7	1.2	NA	NA
Cash Flow	-7.9	28.6	39.1	23.6	15.8	5.3	7.9	9.7	NA	NA
Curr. Ratio	7.5	7.6	5.4	5.6	3.2	1.8	1.6	NA	NA	NA
% LT Debt of Cap.	Nil	Nil	Nil	Nil	Nil	Nil	Nil	Nil	Nil	Nil
% Net Inc.of Revs.	NM	16.1	22.0	19.9	18.5	8.0	11.6	13.7	15.5	15.4
% Ret. on Assets	NM	12.6	22.9	22.4	NM	20.7	16.3	44.5	50.0	NA
% Ret. on Equity	NM	14.8	27.7	27.7	NM	NM	NM	NM	NM	NM

Data as orig. reptd.; bef. results of disc. opers. and/or spec. items. Per share data adj. for stk. divs. as of ex-div. date. Bold denotes diluted EPS (FASB 128). E-Estimated. NA-Not Available. NM-Not Meaningful. NR-Not Ranked.

Office—2901 Coronado Dr., Santa Clara, CA 95054. **Tel**—(408) 727-6500. **Website**—http://www.electroglas.com **Chrmn**—N. R. Bonke. **CEO**—C. S. Wozniak. **VP-Fin, CFO, Treas, Secy & Investor Contact**—Armand J. Stegall. **Dirs**—N. R. Bonke, J. Dox, R. D. Emerick, R. J. Frankenberg, C. Wozniak. **Transfer Agent & Registrar**—Boston Equiserve LP. **Incorporated**—in Delaware in 1993. **Empl**— 607. **S&P Analyst:** B. McGovern

STANDARD &POOR'S
STOCK REPORTS

Energen Corp.

828R

NYSE Symbol **EGN**

In S&P SmallCap 600

03-OCT-98

Industry: Natural Gas

Summary: Through its Alabama Gas (Alagasco) unit, this company is the largest natural gas distributor in Alabama, serving about 460,000 customers.

Quantitative Evaluations

Outlook
(1 Lowest—5 Highest)
- **2⁻**

Fair Value
- **18¾**

Risk
- **Low**

Earn./Div. Rank
- **A**

Technical Eval.
- **Bearish** since 9/98

Rel. Strength Rank
(1 Lowest—99 Highest)
- **87**

Insider Activity
- **Neutral**

Recent Price • 18½
52 Wk Range • 22½-15⅛

Yield • 3.4%
12-Mo. P/E • 14.8

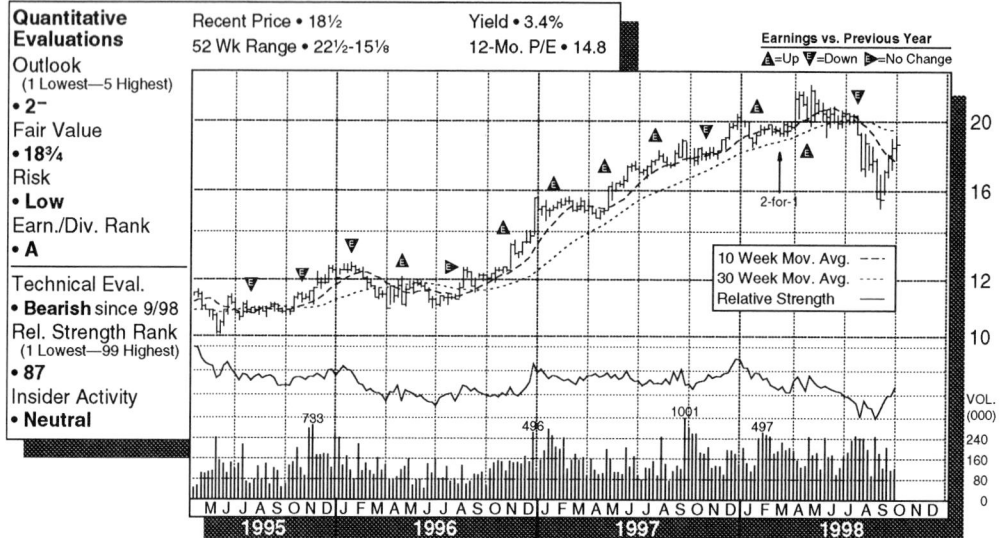

Earnings vs. Previous Year
▲=Up ▼=Down ▶=No Change

10 Week Mov. Avg. - - - -
30 Week Mov. Avg. · · · · ·
Relative Strength ———

Business Profile - 01-MAY-98

Under a diversified growth strategy, the Taurus Exploration unit invested during FY 96 (Sep.) and FY 97 a total of $280 million in producing property acquisitions, $32 million in related development, and $61 million for exploration and related development. Over this two-year period, proved reserves increased 600%, annual oil and gas production rose 260%, and Taurus's net income increased 185%. A January 1998 purchase of $17 million of Gulf of Mexico properties from Chateau Oil and Gas Inc. brought Taurus's acquisition expenditures in FY 98 to approximately $70 million, for estimated proved reserves of about 105 Bcf equivalent. Taurus planned to invest approximately $100 million in the acquisition of producing properties in FY 98.

Operational Review - 01-MAY-98

Revenues in the six months ended March 31, 1998, rose 16%, year to year, reflecting higher oil and gas E&P volume from acquisitions, aided by greater gas distribution revenues. Margins were unchanged, as slower growth in the cost of gas and O&M expenses offset an 83% jump in DD&A charges. After higher interest expense and a $3 million after-tax write down related to the recent decline in crude oil prices, pretax income was up only 7.1%. After taxes at 5.5% (reflecting greater recognition of fuel tax credits), versus 17.9%, net income surged 38%, to $46,419,000 ($1.59 a share, on 21% more shares), from $33,708,000 ($1.40).

Stock Performance - 02-OCT-98

In the past 30 trading days, EGN's shares have increased 5%, compared to a 7% fall in the S&P 500. Average trading volume for the past five days was 24,380 shares, compared with the 40-day moving average of 34,764 shares.

Key Stock Statistics

Dividend Rate/Share	0.64	Shareholders	7,700
Shs. outstg. (M)	29.2	Market cap. (B)	$0.543
Avg. daily vol. (M)	0.029	Inst. holdings	46%
Tang. Bk. Value/Share	11.70		
Beta	0.69		

Value of $10,000 invested 5 years ago: $ 25,596

Fiscal Year Ending Sep. 30

	1998	1997	1996	1995	1994	1993
Revenues (Million $)						
1Q	125.9	97.00	78.82	73.48	87.92	84.10
2Q	198.0	182.9	171.0	140.8	168.1	149.7
3Q	93.91	90.88	87.13	61.53	73.13	75.32
4Q	—	77.41	62.50	45.37	47.94	48.04
Yr.	—	448.2	399.4	321.2	377.1	357.1
Earnings Per Share ($)						
1Q	**0.21**	0.14	0.10	0.13	0.11	0.13
2Q	**1.37**	1.21	1.06	0.99	1.01	0.97
3Q	Nil	0.12	0.05	0.05	0.18	0.06
4Q	—	-0.29	-0.23	-0.29	-0.21	-0.28
Yr.	—	1.16	0.97	0.89	1.09	0.89

Next earnings report expected: late October

Dividend Data (Dividends have been paid since 1943.)

Amount ($)	Date Decl.	Ex-Div. Date	Stock of Record	Payment Date
0.310	Jan. 28	Feb. 11	Feb. 13	Mar. 02 '98
2-for-1	Jan. 28	Mar. 03	Feb. 13	Mar. 02 '98
0.155	Apr. 20	May. 13	May. 15	Jun. 01 '98
0.160	Jul. 22	Aug. 12	Aug. 14	Sep. 01 '98

A Division of The **McGraw·Hill** Companies

Business Summary - 01-MAY-98

Energen (EGN) is a diversified energy holding company engaged in natural gas distribution and oil and natural gas exploration and production; its two major subsidiaries are Alabama Gas Corp. (Alagasco) and Taurus Exploration Inc. (Taurus). While Alagasco earns within its allowed range of return of equity, the company's five-year plan, spanning FY 96 (Sep.) through FY 2000, calls for Energen to invest, through Taurus, $400 million in the acquisition of producing properties with development potential, and $100 million in offshore Gulf of Mexico exploration and development.

Alagasco, Alabama's largest gas distribution utility, purchases gas through interstate and intrastate marketers and suppliers and distributes the purchased gas through its distribution facilities for sale to end-users of natural gas. Alagasco also provides transportation services to industrial and commercial customers located on its distribution system. These customers purchase gas directly from producers, marketers or suppliers and arrange for delivery of the gas into the Alagasco distribution system; Alagasco charges a fee to transport the gas through its distribution system to the customer's facility. In FY 97, Alagasco served an average of 422,878 residential customers, 34,432 small commercial and in-

dustrial customers, and 54 large commercial and industrial customers. Deliveries of sales and transportation gas totaled 106,533 million cubic feet (MMcf) in FY 97, down from 111,423 MMcf in FY 96.

The Alagasco distribution system includes approximately 8,950 miles of main and more than 9,800 miles of service lines, odorization and regulation facilities, and customer meters. Alagasco also operates two liquefied natural gas facilities which its uses to meet peak demand. Alagasco's distribution system is connected to and has firm transportation contracts with two major interstate pipeline systems: Southern and Transcontinental Gas Pipe Line Corp.

Taurus Exploration, Inc. is involved in the exploration and production of natural gas and oil in the Gulf of Mexico, and through coalbed methane projects in Alabama's Black Warrior Coal Basin. At the end of FY 97, Taurus's remaining recoverable reserves totaled 673.3 billion cubic feet equivalent (Bcfe), and were located primarily in Alabama, New Mexico, Texas, Mississippi, Louisiana and the Gulf of Mexico. In FY 96 and FY 97, Taurus invested $357 million, adding an estimated 638 Bcfe of proved reserves. During FY 97, Taurus's nine months of production totaled 10.5 Bcfe, and production is expected to exceed 14.5 Bcfe in FY 98.

Per Share Data ($)

(Year Ended Sep. 30)	1997	1996	1995	1994	1993	1992	1991	1990	1989	1988
Tangible Bk. Val.	10.46	8.44	7.97	7.65	6.80	6.38	6.04	6.11	5.84	5.59
Earnings	1.16	0.97	0.89	1.09	0.89	0.77	0.71	0.68	0.59	0.83
Dividends	0.60	0.58	0.56	0.55	0.53	0.51	0.48	0.45	0.43	0.39
Payout Ratio	52%	60%	64%	50%	59%	66%	67%	66%	72%	46%
Prices - High	20⅝	15⅝	12⅝	12	13⅜	9⅝	9½	10¼	12¼	8⅝
- Low	14½	10⅞	10⅛	9⅝	9⅛	7½	8	8	7¾	6¼
P/E Ratio - High	18	16	14	11	15	13	13	15	20	10
- Low	13	11	11	9	10	10	11	12	13	7

Income Statement Analysis (Million $)

	1997	1996	1995	1994	1993	1992	1991	1990	1989	1988
Revs.	448	399	321	377	357	332	326	325	309	363
Depr.	59.7	41.1	29.6	28.0	25.3	26.3	24.1	23.0	22.4	21.1
Maint.	11.1	11.1	9.8	9.5	9.2	9.1	8.2	8.4	6.8	8.1
Fxd. Chgs. Cov.	2.4	2.9	3.0	3.5	3.0	2.5	2.5	2.5	2.6	3.0
Constr. Credits	NA	NA	NA	NA	NA	NA	NA	NA	NA	NA
Eff. Tax Rate	9.65%	19%	16%	22%	16%	2.40%	2.50%	8.90%	8.60%	16%
Net Inc.	29.0	21.5	19.3	23.8	18.1	15.7	14.1	13.2	11.1	12.8

Balance Sheet & Other Fin. Data (Million $)

	1997	1996	1995	1994	1993	1992	1991	1990	1989	1988
Gross Prop.	1,042	545	504	465	429	411	393	377	357	320
Cap. Exp.	283	168	68.9	45.5	43.7	22.5	46.9	41.9	59.5	25.6
Net Prop.	667	277	256	233	213	208	206	205	203	179
Capitalization:										
LT Debt	280	196	132	118	85.9	90.6	77.7	82.8	86.2	53.2
% LT Debt	48	51	43	42	38	41	39	40	43	37
Pfd.	Nil	Nil	Nil	Nil	Nil	1.8	1.8	1.8	2.5	2.5
% Pfd.	Nil	Nil	Nil	Nil	Nil	0.80	0.90	0.90	1.20	1.70
Common	301	188	174	167	140	130	122	121	113	89.0
% Common	52	49	57	59	62	58	61	59	56	62
Total Cap.	581	385	312	292	232	230	225	236	236	182
% Oper. Ratio	89.1	91.6	90.0	92.2	92.5	93.2	92.9	93.0	94.1	94.6
% Earn. on Net Prop.	9.4	12.7	13.2	13.1	12.7	10.8	11.2	11.9	9.6	11.3
% Return On Revs.	6.5	5.4	6.0	6.3	5.1	4.7	4.3	4.1	3.6	3.5
% Return On Invest. Capital	6.1	10.2	11.5	13.4	12.5	11.5	10.7	10.3	8.9	11.5
% Return On Com. Equity	11.8	11.9	11.3	15.5	13.4	12.5	12.0	11.3	11.0	16.5

Data as orig. reptd.; bef. results of disc opers. and/or spec. items. Per share data adj. for stk. divs. as of ex-div. date. Bold denotes diluted EPS (FASB 128). E-Estimated. NA-Not Available. NM-Not Meaningful. NR-Not Ranked.

Office—2101 Sixth Ave. North, Birmingham, AL 35203. **Tel**—(205) 326-2700. **Website**—http://www.energen.com **Chrmn, Pres & CEO**—W. M. Warren Jr. **EVP-Fin, Treas & CFO**—G. C. Ketcham. **Secy**—D. C. Reynolds. **Investor Contact**—Julie S. Ryland (205-326-2634). **Dirs**—S. D. Ban, J. W. Banton, R. D. Cash, J. M. Davis Jr., J. S. M. French, W. L. Luthy, R. J. Lysinger, J. M. Merritt, D. Nabers Jr., W. M. Warren Jr. **Transfer Agent & Registrar**—First Chicago Trust Company of New York. **Incorporated**—in Alabama in 1929. **Empl**— 1,469. **S&P Analyst:** J. Robert Cho

03-OCT-98

Industry: Insurance (Property-ty-Casualty)

Summary: This company provides financial guaranty insurance and reinsurance and other products and services utilizing its credit-related analytical skills.

S&P Opinion: Buy (★★★★)	Recent Price • 28¼	Yield • 0.8%
	52 Wk Range • 37⅝-24⅝	12-Mo. P/E • 14.3

Quantitative Evaluations

Outlook
(1 Lowest—5 Highest)
• **2**

Fair Value
• **32**

Risk
• **Low**

Earn./Div. Rank
• **B+**

Technical Eval.
• **Bullish** since 6/98

Rel. Strength Rank
(1 Lowest—99 Highest)
• **62**

Insider Activity
• **Neutral**

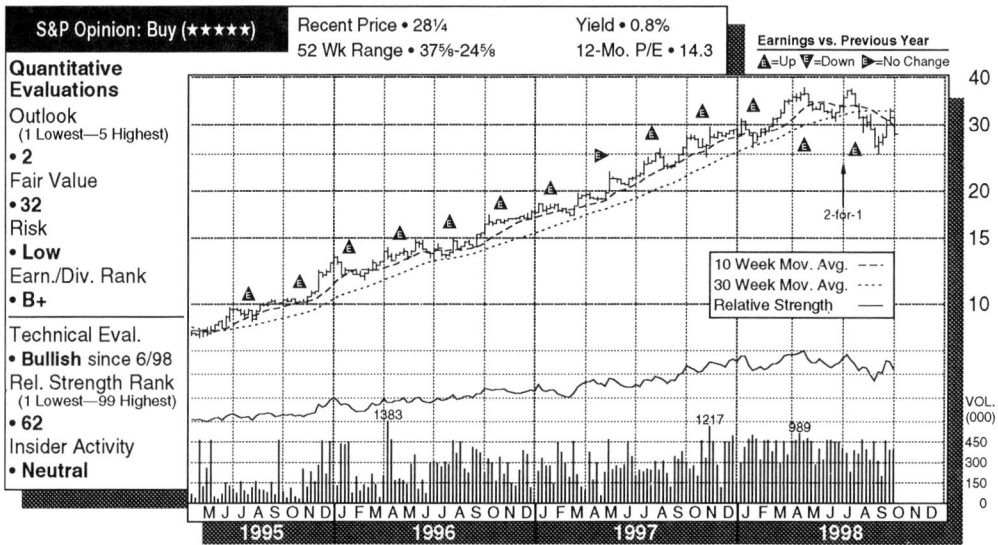

Earnings vs. Previous Year
▲=Up ▼=Down ▶=No Change

10 Week Mov. Avg. – – –
30 Week Mov. Avg. · · · ·
Relative Strength ——

2-for-1

VOL. (000)

1995   1996   1997   1998

Overview - 10-AUG-98

Enhance continued to post strong results in the second quarter of 1998. Diluted operating earnings per share advanced 21%, year to year. Enhance's strategy to leverage its core skills in analyzing credit based risks into businesses with higher growth and higher returns on equity continues to pay dividends, with Singer Asset Finance Company and C-BASS making nice contributions to earnings. In addition to making notable contributions to earnings, these businesses are beginning to develop new products and services themselves. For example, just two years ago, Singer had only one product and operated in just twelve states. Today, Singer has four products and operates nationwide. C-BASS, EFS's joint venture with MGIC Investment Corp., recently entered the seller-financed mortgage market, a large fragmented market that offers significant growth potential. Our EPS estimates are based on operating earnings; actual earnings per share are based on net income.

Valuation - 10-AUG-98

EFS's shares have been under pressure lately, as have the broader markets as a whole. We view this downturn as a great buying opportunity. EFS has demonstrated the ability to successfully leverage its core skills into high growth, high return businesses and the company is continually looking for innovative, creative ways to boost earnings and returns. We expect ROEs to continue to improve, as these new businesses account for a greater percentage of the bottom line. We see operating EPS growing at a compound annual rate of 18% a year going forward. At a recent price of 15X our 1998 operating EPS estimate and less than 13X our 1999 estimate, we feel the shares are undervalued. We recommend purchase of the shares for superior capital appreciation.

Key Stock Statistics

S&P EPS Est. 1998	2.10	Tang. Bk. Value/Share	16.42
P/E on S&P Est. 1998	13.5	Beta	1.08
S&P EPS Est. 1999	2.50	Shareholders	100
Dividend Rate/Share	0.24	Market cap. (B)	$ 1.1
Shs. outstg. (M)	37.4	Inst. holdings	58%
Avg. daily vol. (M)	0.077		

Value of $10,000 invested 5 years ago: $ 31,084

Fiscal Year Ending Dec. 31

	1998	1997	1996	1995	1994	1993
Revenues (Million $)						
1Q	48.31	32.48	32.62	25.54	24.21	26.60
2Q	51.42	45.16	28.91	26.30	22.81	27.95
3Q	—	42.08	31.93	27.57	26.04	31.51
4Q	—	50.68	38.84	33.35	23.38	24.28
Yr.	—	170.4	132.3	112.5	96.44	110.3
Earnings Per Share ($)						
1Q	**0.49**	**0.37**	0.38	0.30	0.29	0.34
2Q	**0.52**	**0.44**	0.33	0.32	0.23	0.10
3Q	—	**0.45**	0.39	0.34	0.24	0.34
4Q	—	**0.53**	0.45	0.41	-0.02	0.27
Yr.	**E2.10**	**1.78**	1.56	1.36	0.74	1.04

Next earnings report expected: early November

Dividend Data (Dividends have been paid since 1992.)

Amount ($)	Date Decl.	Ex-Div. Date	Stock of Record	Payment Date
0.110	Mar. 13	Mar. 19	Mar. 23	Mar. 27 '98
0.110	Jun. 03	Jun. 10	Jun. 12	Jun. 19 '98
2-for-1	Apr. 08	Jun. 29	Jun. 12	Jun. 26 '98
0.060	Sep. 17	Sep. 24	Sep. 28	Oct. 05 '98

A Division of The McGraw·Hill Companies

Business Summary - 10-AUG-98

Enhance Financial Services Group is transforming itself from a company that primarily provides financial guarantee reinsurance into a diversified financial services company that provides insurance, reinsurance and other products and services utilizing its credit-related analytical skills. EFS's primary business remains the reinsurance of financial guaranties of municipal debt obligations issued by monoline financial guaranty insurers. This business accounted for over 54% of EFS's gross premiums written in 1997. Financial guarantee insurance ensures the full and timely payment of principal and interest to holders of debt obligations.

The company's other insurance businesses include trade credit reinsurance, financial responsibility bonds, excess-SIPC insurance, and direct financial guaranty insurance. These insurance businesses collectively accounted for 46% of gross premiums written in 1997.

In recent years, EFS has moved to leverage its core skill of complex credit analysis and securitization into businesses it believes offer greater growth and profit potential than the company's traditional reinsurance business. Management anticipates that a significant portion of the company's future growth will come from these non-financial guaranty businesses.

In 1996, Enhance formed C-BASS, a joint venture with MGIC Investment, a leading provider of private mortgage insurance. C-BASS evaluates, purchases, services and securitizes sub-performing and non-performing residential mortgages.

Wholly owned Singer Asset Finance Company purchases state lottery prizes, structured settlement payment rights and other long-term payment streams from individuals. Singer then securitizes these assets and sells pools of these assets in the securities market.

In late-1997, EFS and Swiss Re each acquired a 25% interest in SBF, one of Brazil's largest surety companies. The remaining interest in SBF is held by Banco Pactual, S.A., one of Brazil's largest investment banks. Terms of the joint venture call for the expansion of SBF in the Latin American insurance and other credit-related markets and opportunities.

Enhance repurchased 226,394 common shares in the second quarter of 1998. Through June 30, 1998, under a December 1996 authorization to buy 1,500,000 shares, Enhance had purchased 812,244 shares.

Per Share Data ($)

(Year Ended Dec. 31)	1997	1996	1995	1994	1993	1992	1991	1990	1989	1988
Tangible Bk. Val.	15.04	13.52	12.29	10.22	10.07	9.14	8.23	7.23	6.33	5.58
Oper. Earnings	1.77	1.45	1.29	NA	NA	NA	NA	NA	NA	NA
Earnings	1.78	1.56	1.36	0.74	1.04	1.03	0.93	0.80	0.78	0.56
Dividends	0.22	0.20	0.18	0.16	0.14	0.12	NA	NA	NA	NA
Payout Ratio	12%	13%	13%	21%	13%	12%	NA	NA	NA	NA
Prices - High	31⅛	18¼	13½	10⅜	12½	10⅝	NA	NA	NA	NA
- Low	17⅛	11⅝	8	7¾	8¾	7¾	NA	NA	NA	NA
P/E Ratio - High	17	12	10	14	12	10	NA	NA	NA	NA
- Low	10	7	6	10	8	7	NA	NA	NA	NA

Income Statement Analysis (Million $)

	1997	1996	1995	1994	1993	1992	1991	1990	1989	1988
Premium Inc.	85.5	77.4	63.0	61.8	59.6	45.6	35.9	24.8	19.8	14.7
Net Invest. Inc.	50.6	48.1	44.2	39.0	32.8	30.3	27.2	22.6	17.5	14.1
Oth. Revs.	34.3	6.7	5.3	-4.3	17.9	9.3	6.7	0.4	0.5	-1.0
Total Revs.	170	132	113	96.4	110	85.2	69.8	47.8	37.8	27.8
Pretax Inc.	94.0	76.4	63.8	32.7	50.3	49.4	40.9	32.2	28.3	19.1
Net Oper. Inc.	68.4	51.7	44.7	NA	NA	NA	NA	NA	NA	NA
Net Inc.	68.8	55.7	47.3	26.6	38.0	37.6	32.4	25.1	23.0	15.3

Balance Sheet & Other Fin. Data (Million $)

	1997	1996	1995	1994	1993	1992	1991	1990	1989	1988
Cash & Equiv.	5.7	5.4	19.5	39.1	20.4	21.5	13.3	10.5	9.0	NA
Premiums Due	30.0	22.5	21.2	9.8	10.5	8.0	9.7	8.4	3.6	NA
Invest. Assets: Bonds	819	758	696	620	622	487	428	352	258	NA
Invest. Assets: Stocks	0.8	0.9	0.7	0.7	0.5	0.5	0.4	1.6	2.1	NA
Invest. Assets: Loans	Nil	Nil	Nil	Nil	Nil	Nil	Nil	Nil	Nil	Nil
Invest. Assets: Total	938	821	748	651	624	488	429	360	279	NA
Deferred Policy Costs	95.6	87.3	81.0	74.0	66.2	54.6	48.4	41.4	34.5	NA
Total Assets	1,148	983	881	765	735	584	509	430	330	289
Debt	75.0	75.0	78.4	79.8	81.2	7.6	9.0	Nil	Nil	NA
Common Eqty.	581	488	424	360	364	332	288	253	189	166
Prop. & Cas. Loss Ratio	11.4	11.9	15.1	37.0	37.0	20.4	14.2	9.1	0.1	Nil
Prop. & Cas. Expense Ratio	50.3	52.6	54.2	56.7	54.9	57.6	65.8	55.6	57.2	64.8
Prop. & Cas. Combined Ratio	61.7	64.5	69.3	93.7	91.9	78.0	80.0	64.7	57.3	64.8
% Return On Revs.	40.4	42.1	42.1	27.5	34.4	44.2	46.4	52.5	60.9	55.2
% Ret. on Equity	12.9	29.0	12.1	7.3	10.9	12.1	12.0	11.3	13.0	10.6

Data as orig. reptd.; bef. results of disc. opers. and/or spec. items. Per share data adj. for stk. divs. as of ex-div. date. Bold denotes diluted EPS (FASB 128). E-Estimated. NA-Not Available. NM-Not Meaningful. NR-Not Ranked.

Office—335 Madison Ave., New York, NY 10017. **Tel**—(212) 983-3100. **Website**—www.efsgroup.com **Chrmn**—A. R. Tessler. **Vice Chrmn**—W. O. Sellers. **Pres & CEO**—D. J. Gross. **EVP & CFO**—A. Dubroff. **EVP & Secy**—S. Bergman. **SVP & Investor Contact**—Sheila Brody. **Dirs**—D. J. Gross, B. W. Harries, D. R. Markin, R.P. Saltzman, W. O. Sellers, R. J. Shima, S. R. Stuart, A. U. Sulzer, A. R. Tessler, F. K. Wallison, J. Wind. **Transfer Agent & Registrar**—ChaseMellon Shareholder Services, Ridgefield Park, NJ. **Incorporated**—in New York in 1985. **Empl**— 232. **S&P Analyst:** Michael Schneider

Envoy Corporation   3810R

NASDAQ Symbol **ENVY**

In S&P SmallCap 600

03-OCT-98

Industry:
Services (Data Processing)

Summary: This company provides a variety of electronic processing services primarily to healthcare markets, including pharmacies, physicians, dentists and third-party payors.

Quantitative Evaluations	
Outlook (1 Lowest—5 Highest) • **5**	
Fair Value • **38⅝**	
Risk • **Average**	
Earn./Div. Rank • **C**	
Technical Eval. • **Neutral** since 8/98	
Rel. Strength Rank (1 Lowest—99 Highest) • **13**	
Insider Activity • **Favorable**	

Recent Price • 21½
52 Wk Range • 55⅝-17¼

Yield • Nil
12-Mo. P/E • NM

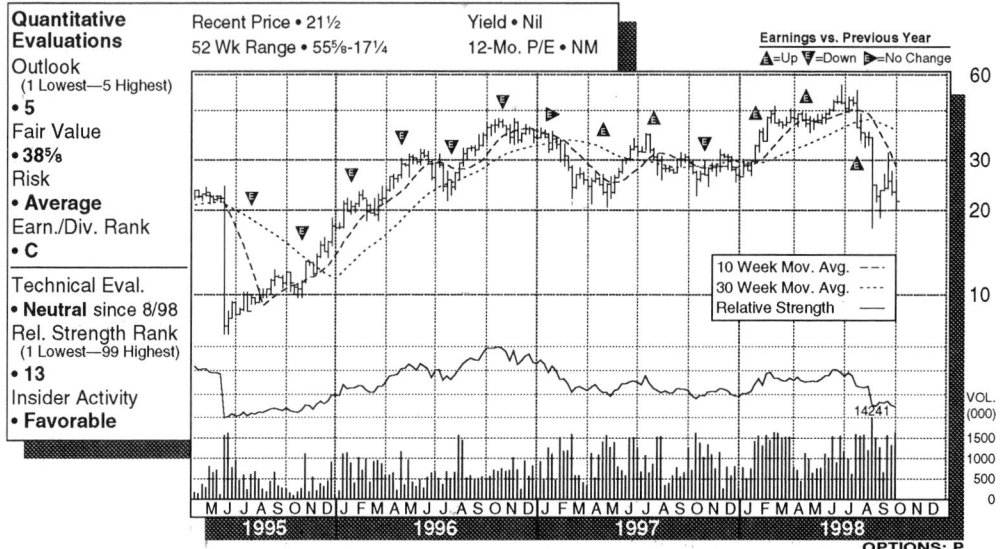

Earnings vs. Previous Year
▲=Up ▼=Down ▶=No Change

10 Week Mov. Avg. — — —
30 Week Mov. Avg. - - - -
Relative Strength ———

OPTIONS: P

Business Profile - 17-SEP-98

In August 1998, ENVY announced that it hired an additional independent appraisal firm to conduct additional valuation procedures of intangible assets acquired in certain acquisitions accounted for as purchases. The need for a new appraisal stemmed from the fact that the SEC in May 1998 commented on and questioned the valuations of purchased research and development costs, as well as the amortization periods for these acquisitions. ENVY said that if there are any significant changes as a result of the investigation, they could have a material adverse impact on the related noncash charges reflected in financial results for the 1998 first half, the years 1997 and 1996, as well as future operating results.

Operational Review - 17-SEP-98

Revenues in the six months ended June 30, 1998, climbed 36%, year to year, driven by internal growth as well as recent acquisitions. Profit comparisons benefited from smaller increases in cost of revenues and SG&A expense, and the absence of prior-year charges associated with the writeoff of acquired in-process technology; income from operations surged to $12,450,000 from $4,287,000. After taxes of $6,915,000, versus $2,662,000, the company reported net income of $5,043,000 ($0.20 a share, on 30% more shares), in contrast to a net loss of $1,044,000 ($0.05).

Stock Performance - 02-OCT-98

In the past 30 trading days, ENVY's shares have declined 12%, compared to a 7% fall in the S&P 500. Average trading volume for the past five days was 591,840 shares, compared with the 40-day moving average of 653,231 shares.

Key Stock Statistics

Dividend Rate/Share	Nil	Shareholders	300
Shs. outstg. (M)	21.2	Market cap. (B)	$0.456
Avg. daily vol. (M)	0.363	Inst. holdings	79%
Tang. Bk. Value/Share	0.04		
Beta	1.84		

Value of $10,000 invested 5 years ago: $ 19,545

Fiscal Year Ending Dec. 31

	1998	1997	1996	1995	1994	1993
Revenues (Million $)						
1Q	45.52	26.09	10.33	6.92	4.69	--
2Q	42.95	26.42	19.59	6.05	4.59	--
3Q	--	28.59	21.50	5.95	4.71	--
4Q	--	32.60	25.16	6.29	6.96	--
Yr.	--	113.7	76.58	25.21	20.95	14.00
Earnings Per Share ($)						
1Q	0.09	-0.14	-2.97	-0.02	0.01	--
2Q	0.11	-0.01	-0.12	-0.02	Nil	--
3Q	--	-1.28	-0.14	-0.03	0.01	--
4Q	--	-0.01	-0.11	-0.11	-0.02	--
Yr.	--	-1.47	-2.99	-0.18	-0.01	-0.07

Next earnings report expected: late October

Dividend Data

No dividends have been paid, and the company does not expect to pay dividends in the foreseeable future. A poison pill stock purchase rights plan was adopted in 1995.

A Division of The McGraw-Hill Companies

STANDARD
&POOR'S
STOCK REPORTS

Envoy Corporation

3810R

03-OCT-98

Business Summary - 17-SEP-98

Envoy Corp. (ENVY) provides electronic data interchange (EDI) services for pharmacies, physicians, hospitals, dentists, billing companies, insurance companies, managed care organizations, government agencies and others, through a real-time network and batch clearinghouse. Its transaction processing services for the healthcare market include managed care transactions, facilitating on-line pharmacy claims adjudication, electronic claims clearing for physician and dental claims and on-line Medicaid eligibility. ENVY's transaction network consists of approximately 206,000 physicians, 34,000 pharmacies and 38,000 dentists.

The company first introduced its system for the transfer of data for on-line eligibility verification and adjudication to the pharmacy insurance claims market. Today, ENVY provides real-time transaction processing for pharmacy claims and managed care transactions. As of December 31, 1997, the company's EDI network was linked to approximately 34,000 of the estimated 51,000 retail pharmacies in the U.S., including 40 of the top 50 retail pharmacy chains. ENVY's real-time managed care transactions transmit the following types of information between providers and payors: verification of patient enrollment, provider eligibility and treatment eligibility; filing of encounter data; and referral to a specialist.

ENVY has experienced tremendous revenue growth in the last two years, aided by an aggressive acquisition program. In March 1996, the company acquired National Electronic Information Corp., a clearinghouse of batch claims for commercial payors. In October 1996, Envoy acquired Professional Office Systems, Inc., the electronic data interchange clearinghouse for Blue Cross and Blue Shield of the National Capital Area. In August 1997, ENVY acquired Healthcare Data Interchange, Inc., the healthcare EDI subsidiary of Aetna U.S. Healthcare Inc. ENVY acquired ExpressBill Companies, which provides patient settlement services, in February 1998, and acquired Synergy Health Care, a provider of health care information products and services, in May 1998.

ENVY delivers its services through an integrated electronic transaction processing system that includes company-designed software, host computer hardware, network management, switching services and the ability to interact with customer personal computers and a variety of point of service devices. ENVY believes that its electronic systems lower claims processing costs, provide more efficient medical cost management, lower the risk of fraud and streamline procedures.

In May 1998, ENVY hired an additional independent appraiser following comments and questions from the SEC regarding the earlier valuations of purchased research and development costs, and amortization periods for certain acquisitions. Subsequently, a number of class action lawsuits were filed against ENVY on behalf of shareholders.

Per Share Data ($)

(Year Ended Dec. 31)	1997	1996	1995	1994	1993	1992	1991	1990	1989	1988
Tangible Bk. Val.	0.04	3.64	1.35	1.43	NA	NA	NA	NA	NA	NA
Cash Flow	0.12	-1.52	0.04	0.17	0.04	-0.05	NA	NA	NA	NA
Earnings	-1.47	-2.99	-0.18	-0.01	-0.07	-0.13	NA	NA	NA	NA
Dividends	Nil	Nil	Nil	Nil	Nil	Nil	Nil	Nil	Nil	Nil
Payout Ratio	Nil	Nil	Nil	Nil	Nil	Nil	Nil	Nil	Nil	Nil
Prices - High	38¼	42¼	24¼	23	17¾	17½	NA	NA	NA	NA
- Low	20⅜	17⅛	7¼	16¼	10¾	10¼	NA	NA	NA	NA
P/E Ratio - High	NM	NM	NM	NM	NM	NM	NM	NM	NM	NM
- Low	NM	NM	NM	NM	NM	NM	NM	NM	NM	NM

Income Statement Analysis (Million $)

	1997	1996	1995	1994	1993	1992	1991	1990	1989	1988
Revs.	114	76.6	25.2	21.0	14.0	NA	NA	NA	NA	NA
Oper. Inc.	34.4	19.4	1.5	1.8	-0.1	NA	NA	NA	NA	NA
Depr.	25.7	19.2	2.5	2.0	1.2	NA	NA	NA	NA	NA
Int. Exp.	1.4	2.6	0.5	Nil	Nil	Nil	Nil	Nil	Nil	Nil
Pretax Inc.	-29.3	-37.3	-0.2	-0.2	-1.4	NA	NA	NA	NA	NA
Eff. Tax Rate	NM	NM	NM	NM	NM	NM	NM	NM	NM	NM
Net Inc.	-23.8	-38.9	-2.0	-0.1	-0.8	NA	NA	NA	NA	NA

Balance Sheet & Other Fin. Data (Million $)

	1997	1996	1995	1994	1993	1992	1991	1990	1989	1988
Cash	8.4	36.4	5.3	NA	NA	NA	NA	NA	NA	NA
Curr. Assets	39.7	62.4	15.4	NA	NA	NA	NA	NA	NA	NA
Total Assets	127	134	29.8	20.9	NA	NA	NA	NA	NA	NA
Curr. Liab.	21.5	15.0	4.1	NA	NA	NA	NA	NA	NA	NA
LT Debt	0.1	8.4	10.0	0.7	NA	NA	NA	NA	NA	NA
Common Eqty.	56.0	68.3	15.3	15.8	NA	NA	NA	NA	NA	NA
Total Cap.	96.2	144	25.6	16.5	NA	NA	NA	NA	NA	NA
Cap. Exp.	7.7	4.8	NA	NA	NA	NA	NA	NA	NA	NA
Cash Flow	1.9	-19.7	0.5	1.9	0.4	NA	NA	NA	NA	NA
Curr. Ratio	1.8	4.2	3.7	NA	NA	NA	NA	NA	NA	NA
% LT Debt of Cap.	0.0	5.8	39.1	4.5	NA	NA	NA	NA	NA	NA
% Net Inc.of Revs.	NM	NM	NM	NM	NM	NM	NM	NM	NM	NM
% Ret. on Assets	NM	NM	NM	NM	NM	NM	NM	NM	NM	NM
% Ret. on Equity	NM	NM	NM	NM	NM	NM	NM	NM	NM	NM

Data as orig. reptd.; bef. results of disc. opers. and/or spec. items. Per share data adj. for stk. divs. as of ex-div. date. Bold denotes diluted EPS (FASB 128). E-Estimated. NA-Not Available. NM-Not Meaningful. NR-Not Ranked.

Office—15 Century Blvd., Suite 600, Nashville, TN 37214. **Tel**—(615) 885-3700. **Website**—http://www.envoy-neic.com **Chrmn & Co-CEO**— F. C. Goad Jr. **Pres & Co-CEO**—J. D. Kever. **CFO, Secy & Investor Contact**—Kevin M. McNamara. **Dirs**—W. E. Ford, F. C. Goad Jr., W. M. Gresham, L. E. Hirsch, J. D. Kever, K. M. McNamara, R. A. McStay, H. F. Seymour. **Transfer Agent & Registrar**—First Union National Bank, Charlotte, NC.**Incorporated**—in Tennessee in 1994.**Empl**— 583. **S&P Analyst:** W.H.D.

STANDARD &POOR'S
STOCK REPORTS

Enzo Biochem

7823

ASE Symbol **ENZ**

In S&P SmallCap 600

03-OCT-98 Industry: Biotechnology

Summary: This biotechnology company is engaged in research, manufacturing and marketing of diagnostic and research products based on molecular biology and genetic engineering.

Quantitative Evaluations

Outlook (1 Lowest—5 Highest)
- **NA**

Fair Value
- **NA**

Risk
- **Average**

Earn./Div. Rank
- **B-**

Technical Eval.
- **Bearish** since 12/97

Rel. Strength Rank (1 Lowest—99 Highest)
- **13**

Insider Activity
- **Neutral**

Recent Price • 6¾
52 Wk Range • 20¼-6⅜

Yield • Nil
12-Mo. P/E • 67.5

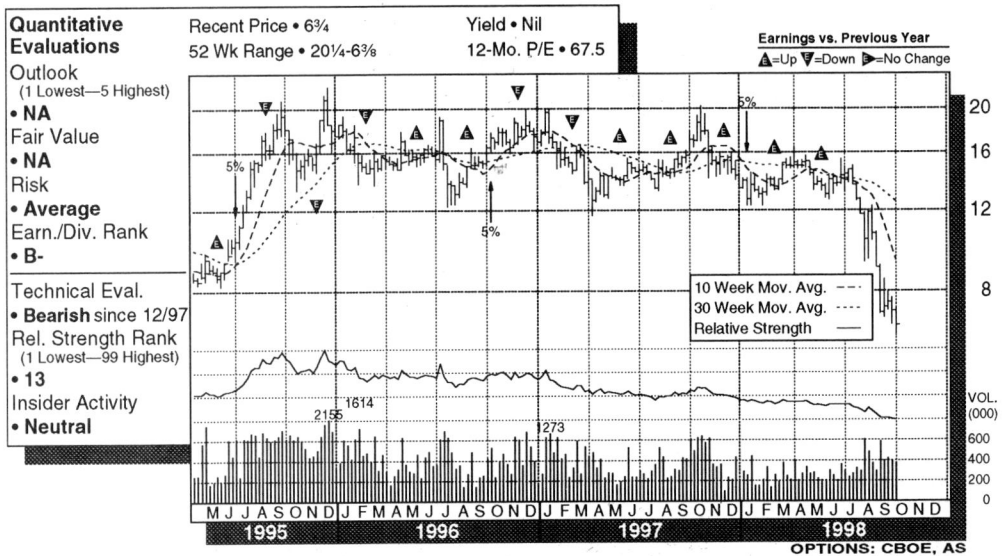

Earnings vs. Previous Year
▲=Up ▼=Down ▶=No Change

10 Week Mov. Avg. ---
30 Week Mov. Avg. ·····
Relative Strength ——

OPTIONS: CBOE, AS

Business Profile - 25-AUG-98

The company's primary current research focus is the development of products based on gene labeling and gene regulation. Enzo has increased its investment in research and development as it prepares for human clinical trials of medicines for AIDS and hepatitis, based on its proprietary gene regulation technology. The company is funding research programs through operating cash flows, cash and equivalents, and is also seeking joint ventures and collaborative relationships. Each of its three business activities is performed by one of three wholly owned subsidiaries; Enzo Diagnostics, Inc., Enzo Therapeutics, Inc., and Enzo Clinical Labs, Inc. The company recently initiated Phase I human clinical trials for a compound to treat HIV.

Operational Review - 25-AUG-98

Revenues in the nine months ended April 30, 1998, advanced 23%, year to year, on sharply higher sales at the clinical laboratory subsidiary. Gross margins widened, on the greater volume. Total operating expenses rose 18%, primarily reflecting high R&D spending, and a near doubling of the provision for uncollectable accounts receivable. Despite taxes at 4.8%, versus 2.6%, net income more than doubled, to $1,984,000 ($0.08 a share), from $934,000 ($0.04). Cash and equivalents totaled $32,024,000 at the end of the third quarter.

Stock Performance - 02-OCT-98

In the past 30 trading days, ENZ's shares have declined 37%, compared to a 7% fall in the S&P 500. Average trading volume for the past five days was 73,660 shares, compared with the 40-day moving average of 84,895 shares.

Key Stock Statistics

Dividend Rate/Share	Nil	Shareholders	1,400
Shs. outstg. (M)	24.5	Market cap. (B)	$0.166
Avg. daily vol. (M)	0.083	Inst. holdings	12%
Tang. Bk. Value/Share	2.15		
Beta	1.79		

Value of $10,000 invested 5 years ago: $ 10,595

Fiscal Year Ending Jul. 31

	1998	1997	1996	1995	1994	1993
Revenues (Million $)						
1Q	9.81	8.01	8.56	8.03	5.18	5.50
2Q	10.33	7.73	8.01	7.04	4.48	4.96
3Q	10.70	8.89	8.55	8.22	4.88	4.80
4Q	—	10.32	9.37	8.41	8.27	4.77
Yr.	—	34.94	34.49	31.70	22.80	20.03
Earnings Per Share ($)						
1Q	0.02	0.01	0.04	0.78	0.03	0.02
2Q	0.02	0.01	0.02	0.03	-0.03	0.01
3Q	0.04	0.03	0.02	Nil	-0.01	Nil
4Q	Nil	0.02	-0.41	-0.57	0.22	-0.34
Yr.	—	0.06	-0.32	0.24	0.22	-0.31

Next earnings report expected: late October

Dividend Data

Amount ($)	Date Decl.	Ex-Div. Date	Stock of Record	Payment Date
5%	Dec. 15	Jan. 07	Jan. 09	Jan. 23 '98

A Division of The McGraw·Hill Companies

Business Summary - 25-AUG-98

This biotechnology company studies the labels on genes. Enzo Biochem Inc. (ENZ) researches, develops, manufactures and markets innovative health care products based on molecular biology and genetic engineering techniques and also provides diagnostic services to the medical community. It currently focuses on development of products based on gene labeling and gene regulation.

ENZ has three subsidiaries, each of which performs one of the company's three business activities: diagnostic and research product development; therapeutic product research and development; and the operation of a clinical reference laboratory. In each of FY 97 (Jul.) and FY 96, 38% of revenues came from product sales and 62% from clinical reference laboratory services.

Enzo Diagnostics Inc. develops and markets biomedical products used largely to detect viral infections, using DNA probes. Its product development focuses on Bioprobe nucleic acid probes to detect sexually transmitted and other infectious diseases, such as AIDS, herpes, chlamydia, tuberculosis, hepatitis and cytomegalovirus. It has distribution agreements with Boehringer Mannheim, Amersham International, VWR Scientific Products, Sigma Chemical, Dako O/S, and Ortho Diagnostic Systems.

Enzo markets two BioProbe products: PathoGene DNA probe kits to detect a variety of specific viruses, and BioPap DNA probe kits to detect certain types of human papillomavirus (HPV) in pap smear samples. It also markets two Microplate Hybridization Assays (MHAs) to detect HIV-1 virus causing AIDS and a bacteria that causes tuberculosis. MHAs to detect HIV-2 and hepatitis B and C viruses are also available. In October 1994, Johnson & Johnson settled litigation with the company, and paid it $35 million in connection with an agreement to develop and market products using DNA probes and other technologies.

Enzo Therapeutics, Inc. is applying its technological capabilities for manipulating genetic material to the development of therapeutic treatments for a variety of cancers and infections. In the third quarter of FY 97, a patent covering ENZ's genetic antisense technology was issued in Japan and upheld in Europe. This technology makes it possible to regulate the function of any gene in any cell.

Enzo Clinical Labs, Inc. operates a clinical reference laboratory offering diagnostic services to the greater New York medical community. The services include a variety of tests to detect precancerous conditions, cervical cancers and sexually transmitted diseases.

In January 1998, ENZ entered into a licensing agreement with Japan Tobacco, Inc., for use of the company's patented genetic antisense technology in Japan. This agreement is the first agricultural licensing agreement involving Enzo's proprietary technology and involves upfront fees, commercialization payments plus royalties.

Per Share Data ($)

(Year Ended Jul. 31)	1997	1996	1995	1994	1993	1992	1991	1990	1989	1988
Tangible Bk. Val.	2.04	1.79	1.96	1.78	1.00	1.05	-0.82	0.03	0.19	1.34
Cash Flow	0.10	-0.28	0.28	0.26	-0.26	-0.01	-0.75	-0.25	-0.28	-0.24
Earnings	0.06	-0.32	0.24	0.22	-0.31	-0.08	-0.82	-0.31	-0.32	-0.27
Dividends	Nil	Nil	Nil	Nil	Nil	Nil	Nil	Nil	Nil	Nil
Payout Ratio	Nil	Nil	Nil	Nil	Nil	Nil	Nil	Nil	Nil	Nil
Prices - High	20$^1/_4$	20	22$^1/_4$	17$^1/_8$	18$^3/_4$	6$^5/_8$	7$^3/_8$	4	4$^3/_8$	4$^3/_4$
- Low	11$^5/_8$	12$^1/_4$	8$^1/_4$	6$^5/_8$	5$^1/_4$	2$^3/_4$	$^1/_2$	1$^1/_2$	2$^1/_4$	2$^3/_{16}$
P/E Ratio - High	NM	NM	93	79	NM	NM	NM	NM	NM	NM
- Low	NM	NM	35	30	NM	NM	NM	NM	NM	NM

Income Statement Analysis (Million $)

	1997	1996	1995	1994	1993	1992	1991	1990	1989	1988
Revs.	34.9	34.5	31.7	22.8	20.0	20.5	19.8	19.4	12.1	9.1
Oper. Inc.	1.0	0.3	-0.4	-2.7	-1.7	1.8	-1.6	-0.8	-1.5	0.3
Depr.	1.3	1.3	1.2	1.1	1.2	1.1	0.9	0.8	0.5	0.3
Int. Exp.	0.0	0.0	0.1	0.1	0.3	2.3	5.2	5.4	4.9	4.7
Pretax Inc.	1.6	-7.5	9.7	2.2	-6.3	-1.1	-10.8	-3.9	-4.0	-3.5
Eff. Tax Rate	7.10%	NM	42%	NM	NM	NM	NM	NM	NM	NM
Net Inc.	1.4	-7.7	5.6	5.1	-6.4	-1.2	-10.8	-4.1	-4.1	-3.5

Balance Sheet & Other Fin. Data (Million $)

	1997	1996	1995	1994	1993	1992	1991	1990	1989	1988
Cash	25.3	17.8	11.1	4.2	0.7	0.8	0.6	7.9	30.4	43.8
Curr. Assets	45.6	35.9	30.3	25.7	7.9	9.4	9.7	16.2	36.7	46.9
Total Assets	67.4	62.8	72.5	65.0	47.6	49.8	49.3	66.5	74.6	69.9
Curr. Liab.	2.4	6.5	5.8	8.6	10.3	12.1	43.4	5.6	5.5	2.2
LT Debt	0.1	0.1	4.7	4.4	4.2	4.2	4.5	48.1	53.9	48.3
Common Eqty.	64.0	55.3	61.1	51.2	32.4	33.0	1.1	12.7	15.1	19.3
Total Cap.	64.1	55.4	65.8	55.8	36.8	37.4	5.8	60.9	69.1	67.7
Cap. Exp.	0.7	0.7	1.0	1.8	3.5	2.4	9.0	8.2	4.2	1.7
Cash Flow	2.7	-6.4	6.8	6.2	-5.2	-0.2	-9.9	-3.3	-3.7	-3.2
Curr. Ratio	19.2	5.6	5.2	3.0	0.8	0.8	0.2	2.9	6.7	21.3
% LT Debt of Cap.	0.0	0.2	7.1	7.8	11.3	11.2	78.6	78.9	78.0	71.4
% Net Inc.of Revs.	4.2	NM	17.7	22.4	NM	NM	NM	NM	NM	NM
% Ret. on Assets	2.2	NM	8.2	8.7	NM	NM	NM	NM	NM	NM
% Ret. on Equity	2.4	NM	10.0	11.8	NM	NM	NM	NM	NM	NM

Data as orig. reptd.; bef. results of disc. opers. and/or spec. items. Per share data adj. for stk. divs. as of ex-div. date. Bold denotes diluted EPS (FASB 128). E-Estimated. NA-Not Available. NM-Not Meaningful. NH-Not Ranked.

Office—575 Fifth Avenue, New York, NY 10017. **Tel**—(212) 856-0100. **Chrmn & CEO**—E. Rabbani. **Pres**—B. W. Weiner. **COO & Secy**—S. K. Rabbani. **Dirs**—J. J. Delucca, E. Rabbani, S. K. Rabbani, J. B. Sias, B. W. Weiner. **Transfer Agent**—Continental Stock Transfer & Trust Co., NYC. **Incorporated**—in New York in 1976. **Empl**— 210. **S&P Analyst:** D.R.J.

Ethan Allen Interiors

840N

NYSE Symbol **ETH**

In S&P SmallCap 600

03-OCT-98

Industry: Household Furnishings & Appliances

Summary: This home furnishings manufacturer sells its products through Ethan Allen Galleries (most of which are owned by independent dealers).

S&P Opinion: Hold (★★★)	Recent Price • 33⅛	Yield • 0.5%
	52 Wk Range • 66⅝-30	12-Mo. P/E • 13.5

Quantitative Evaluations

Outlook (1 Lowest—5 Highest)
• **3**

Fair Value
• **45¾**

Risk
• **Average**

Earn./Div. Rank
• **NR**

Technical Eval.
• **Bearish** since 8/98

Rel. Strength Rank (1 Lowest—99 Highest)
• **31**

Insider Activity
• **Neutral**

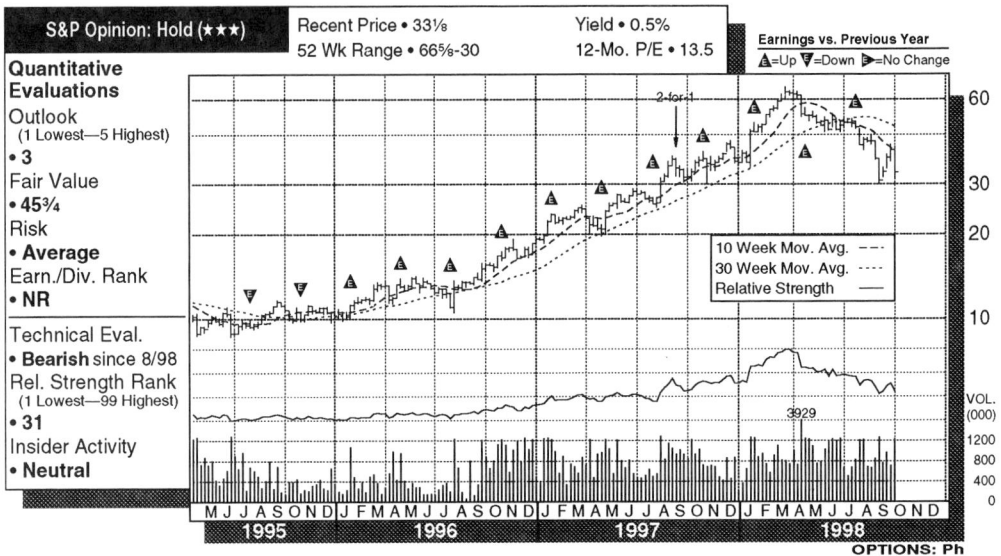

Earnings vs. Previous Year
▲=Up ▼=Down ▶=No Change

10 Week Mov. Avg. – – –
30 Week Mov. Avg. ······
Relative Strength ——

VOL. (000)

OPTIONS: Ph

Overview - 06-AUG-98

Ethan Allen, one of the 10 largest manufacturers of household furniture in the U.S., sells a full range of furniture products and decorative accessories through a network of 310 retail stores, of which 67 are company-owned. Within this fragmented industry, the company has the largest domestic furniture retail network utilizing the gallery concept. Comparable-store sales have benefited from a repositioning of the product mix to appeal to a broader consumer base, a program to renovate or relocate existing stores, and more frequent advertising and promotional campaigns. ETH is also pursuing an aggressive growth strategy, including investments in technology, employee training, and new stores. Margins have been aided by manufacturing efficiencies, lower interest expense, and a strengthening of the upholstery and accessory lines.

Valuation - 06-AUG-98

The shares of this well-managed company have advanced about four-fold since early 1996. A recent pullback from its highs has increased the attractiveness of the stock. However, given recent negative sentiment towards the shares, we would not rush to add to positions. although long-term investors may purchase on dips. The company continues to rack up impressive margins, and, given management's attention to all facets of the business (manufacturing, distribution, retail service and training, new product development, marketing, etc.), further efficiencies will likely be achieved over time. In light of a better than expected FY 98 (Jun.) fourth quarter, and a continued favorable economic environment, we recently increased our EPS estimate for FY 99 to $2.84, from $2.75, and are projecting $3.18 for FY 2000.

Key Stock Statistics

S&P EPS Est. 1998	NA	Tang. Bk. Value/Share	9.24
P/E on S&P Est. 1998	NA	Beta	0.80
S&P EPS Est. 1999	2.84	Shareholders	400
Dividend Rate/Share	0.16	Market cap. (B)	$0.943
Shs. outstg. (M)	28.5	Inst. holdings	69%
Avg. daily vol. (M)	0.213		

Value of $10,000 invested 5 years ago: NA

Fiscal Year Ending Jun. 30

	1998	1997	1996	1995	1994	1993
Revenues (Million $)						
1Q	152.5	132.4	116.9	113.5	96.77	85.60
2Q	172.7	138.3	127.2	125.7	108.3	96.80
3Q	171.4	144.7	134.6	123.6	115.9	99.2
4Q	182.7	156.4	131.0	113.2	116.3	102.6
Yr.	679.3	571.8	509.8	476.1	437.3	384.2
Earnings Per Share ($)						
1Q	0.48	0.30	0.15	0.20	0.14	0.10
2Q	0.65	0.42	0.27	0.24	0.20	0.14
3Q	0.64	0.44	0.28	0.23	0.21	0.16
4Q	0.68	0.51	0.26	0.10	0.21	0.16
Yr.	2.45	1.67	0.96	0.78	0.77	0.56

Next earnings report expected: NA

Dividend Data (Dividends have been paid since 1996.)

Amount ($)	Date Decl.	Ex-Div. Date	Stock of Record	Payment Date
0.030	Nov. 19	Jan. 07	Jan. 09	Jan. 26 '98
0.030	Jan. 30	Apr. 07	Apr. 10	Apr. 24 '98
0.040	Apr. 30	Jul. 08	Jul. 10	Jul. 24 '98
0.040	Aug. 06	Oct. 07	Oct. 09	Oct. 23 '98

A Division of The McGraw-Hill Companies

Business Summary - 06-AUG-98

Ethan Allen Interiors (ETH) focuses its growth strategy on realizing greater potential from its existing stores, opening new stores domestically and abroad, and improving service levels through a strengthened vertically integrated manufacturing and distribution system. In addition to new eye-catching store fronts, innovative products, such as ETH's new EA Organizer modular home office collection, and expanded spending on national television advertising campaigns, have increased the pace of sales.

Ethan Allen Interiors, through wholly owned Ethan Allen Inc., is a leading manufacturer and retailer of home furnishings. One of the 10 largest U.S. manufacturers of household furniture, ETH produces or assembles about 90% of its products at 20 manufacturing facilities and three saw mills, thereby maintaining greater control over cost, quality and service to its customers. The company has 10 regional distribution centers located throughout the U.S.

At June 30, 1998, ETH's products were sold through a network of 310 Ethan Allen Galleries. The galleries exclusively sell Ethan Allen products. The company owned and operated 67 galleries, while independent dealers owned and operated 243 galleries in North America and abroad. Sales to independent dealer owned stores accounted for 68% of net sales in FY 97 (Jun.).

The company's products are positioned in terms of selection, quality and value in what it considers to be the four currently most important style categories in home furnishings: Formal, American Country, Casual Contemporary and Classic Elegance. ETH has grouped its products into collections within these categories. Each collection includes case goods (58% of FY 97 sales), consisting primarily of wood furnishings such as bedroom and dining room furniture, wall units and tables; upholstered products (30%), consisting largely of sofas, loveseats, chairs, recliners and swivel rockers; and home furnishing accessories (12%), including carpeting and area rugs, lighting products, clocks, wall decor, bedding ensembles, draperies and decorative accessories.

The company employs a showcase gallery concept: products are displayed in complete room ensembles, including furnishings, wall decor, window treatments, floor coverings, accents and accessories. ETH believes that the gallery concept results in a higher sales, as it encourages customers to buy a complete home collection, including case goods, upholstery and accessories, and provides designers an opportunity to offer additional service. While the average gallery is 15,000 sq. ft., in May 1997, the company opened a three-stores-in-one 30,000 sq. ft. prototype store in Stamford, CT.

Per Share Data ($)

(Year Ended Jun. 30)	1998	1997	1996	1995	1994	1993	1992	1991	1990	1989
Tangible Bk. Val.	9.24	7.35	5.74	4.72	5.99	4.50	1.80	NA	NA	NA
Cash Flow	2.98	2.23	1.56	1.37	1.25	0.41	0.71	NA	NA	NA
Earnings	2.45	1.67	0.96	0.78	0.77	-0.10	-0.12	NA	NA	NA
Dividends	0.12	0.08	Nil	Nil	Nil	Nil	NA	NA	NA	NA
Payout Ratio	5%	5%	Nil	Nil	Nil	Nil	NA	NA	NA	NA
Prices - High	66⅝	42⅞	19½	12½	16	15¾	NA	NA	NA	NA
- Low	34¼	18½	9⅞	8⅝	9¾	8⅛	NA	NA	NA	NA
P/E Ratio - High	27	26	20	16	21	NM	NA	NA	NA	NA
- Low	14	11	10	11	13	NM	NA	NA	NA	NA

Income Statement Analysis (Million $)

	1998	1997	1996	1995	1994	1993	1992	1991	1990	1989
Revs.	679	572	510	476	437	384	351	NA	NA	NA
Oper. Inc.	136	102	73.1	64.9	62.8	50.7	32.5	NA	NA	NA
Depr.	15.9	16.4	17.5	17.2	13.3	13.8	19.6	NA	NA	NA
Int. Exp.	4.6	5.9	8.9	10.8	13.3	41.8	13.2	NA	NA	NA
Pretax Inc.	119	80.7	47.0	36.0	38.6	-3.4	1.1	NA	NA	NA
Eff. Tax Rate	39%	40%	40%	37%	42%	NM	69%	NA	NA	NA
Net Inc.	71.9	48.7	28.1	22.7	22.6	-2.3	0.3	NA	NA	NA

Balance Sheet & Other Fin. Data (Million $)

	1998	1997	1996	1995	1994	1993	1992	1991	1990	1989
Cash	19.4	39.8	9.1	7.5	6.7	4.8	4.6	NA	NA	NA
Curr. Assets	188	195	168	176	167	148	142	NA	NA	NA
Total Assets	433	428	396	408	413	396	391	NA	NA	NA
Curr. Liab.	73.6	63.3	59.1	53.5	64.4	57.4	48.5	NA	NA	NA
LT Debt	12.5	66.8	82.7	127	139	154	161	NA	NA	NA
Common Eqty.	314	265	220	193	171	116	95.2	NA	NA	NA
Total Cap.	359	365	336	354	347	337	340	NA	NA	NA
Cap. Exp.	29.7	23.4	13.3	11.2	12.2	7.7	NA	NA	NA	NA
Cash Flow	87.8	65.2	45.6	40.0	35.2	11.0	16.8	NA	NA	NA
Curr. Ratio	2.6	3.1	2.8	3.3	2.6	2.6	2.9	NA	NA	NA
% LT Debt of Cap.	35.0	18.3	24.6	35.9	40.1	45.6	47.6	NA	NA	NA
% Net Inc.of Revs.	10.6	8.5	5.5	4.8	5.2	NM	0.1	NA	NA	NA
% Ret. on Assets	16.7	11.8	7.0	5.5	5.3	NM	NA	NA	NA	NA
% Ret. on Equity	24.8	20.1	13.6	12.5	14.6	NM	NA	NA	NA	NA

Data as orig. reptd.; bef. results of disc. opers. and/or spec. items. Per share data adj. for stk. divs. as of ex-div. date. Bold denotes diluted FPS (FASB 128). Pro forma data in 1993 (Income & EPS tbls. only) & 1992. E-Estimated. NA-Not Available. NM-Not Meaningful. NR-Not Ranked.

Office—Ethan Allen Drive, Danbury, CT 06811. **Tel**—(203) 743-8000. **Website**—http://www.ethanallen.com **Chrmn, Pres & CEO**—M. F. Kathwari. **VP, Treas & Investor Contact**—Margaret W. Lupton.**Secy**—Roxanne Khazarian.**Dirs**—C. A. Clark, S. A. Galef, K. Gamble, M. F. Kathwari, H. G. McDonell, E. H. Meyer, W. W. Sprague. **Transfer Agent & Registrar**—Harris Trust Co. of Chicago. **Empl**— 5,991. **S&P Analyst:** Efraim Levy

Exabyte Corp.

3816T

Nasdaq Symbol **EXBT**

In S&P SmallCap 600

03-OCT-98

Industry: Computers (Peripherals)

Summary: Exabyte designs, develops, makes and markets high-capacity 8mm cartridge and other tape subsystems for cost-effective data storage solutions.

S&P Opinion: No Opinion	Recent Price • 6¼	Yield • Nil
	52 Wk Range • 12¾-5	12-Mo. P/E • NM

Earnings vs. Previous Year
▲=Up ▼=Down ▶=No Change

Quantitative Evaluations

Outlook
(1 Lowest—5 Highest)
• **1**

Fair Value
• **6⅛**

Risk
• **High**

Earn./Div. Rank
• **C**

Technical Eval.
• **Bearish** since 6/98

Rel. Strength Rank
(1 Lowest—99 Highest)
• **73**

Insider Activity
• **Neutral**

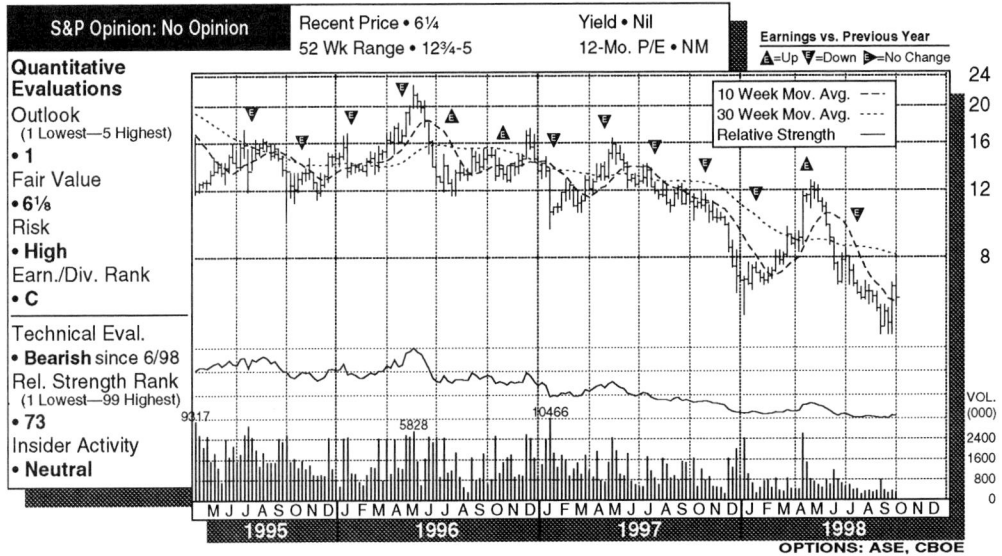

10 Week Mov. Avg. – – –
30 Week Mov. Avg. ·····
Relative Strength ——

OPTIONS: ASE, CBOE

Overview - 22-JUL-98

Revenues should decline in 1998, but could post sequential growth in the second half of the year. The company's second quarter results were hampered by general weakness in the tape storage industry, as well as continuing disk media supply constraints. Demand from OEMs has been weak because of these customers' exposure to Asia. The company is refocusing its efforts on the mid-range NT and UNIX applications server storage market. Margins will improve following the discontinuance of the lower-margin Eagle division. Exabyte is also taking aggressive actions to reduce costs. Manufacturing yields on Mammoth should improve, aiding sales of 8mm cartridge tape subsystems and libraries. Margins will benefit from manufacturing efficiencies, but will be hurt by higher marketing and research and development expenses. Per share results for 1997 included charges of $0.41 in the third quarter and $0.53 in the fourth quarter.

Valuation - 22-JUL-98

After rebounding sharply in early 1998, the shares have recently declined, as the company's progress was hurt by slower demand. EXBT recently recorded restructuring charges to reflect work force reductions and the phaseout of unprofitable product lines. These actions should lead to lower expenses, and have helped the company return to profitability. We view favorably the recent decision to sell the Eagle division and focus on higher growth opportunities in the server storage market. Demand for Mammoth and tape libraries is solid. The company still needs to address its media supply constraint issue, as it continues to seek a second source of tapes. EXBT should benefit from expanded marketing programs and improving inventory management. However, the company is faced with tough competition from larger companies.

Key Stock Statistics

S&P EPS Est. 1998	0.18	Tang. Bk. Value/Share	7.70
P/E on S&P Est. 1998	34.7	Beta	0.48
S&P EPS Est. 1999	0.30	Shareholders	900
Dividend Rate/Share	Nil	Market cap. (B)	$0.141
Shs. outstg. (M)	22.5	Inst. holdings	61%
Avg. daily vol. (M)	0.069		

Value of $10,000 invested 5 years ago: $ 3,424

Fiscal Year Ending Dec. 31

	1998	1997	1996	1995	1994	1993
Revenues (Million $)						
1Q	80.75	85.43	93.82	96.19	86.89	76.21
2Q	69.75	97.14	90.46	96.98	92.68	75.76
3Q	—	78.47	92.74	84.10	99.0	75.14
4Q	—	74.64	85.87	96.87	103.3	83.19
Yr.	—	335.7	362.9	374.1	381.8	310.3
Earnings Per Share ($)						
1Q	0.09	0.05	0.15	0.34	0.32	0.28
2Q	0.01	0.05	0.16	0.08	0.34	0.08
3Q	E0.03	-0.68	0.17	-1.13	0.40	0.12
4Q	E0.06	-0.79	-0.09	0.15	0.41	0.28
Yr.	E0.18	-1.38	0.39	-0.57	1.48	0.76

Next earnings report expected: mid October

Dividend Data

The company has never paid cash dividends on its common stock. A shareholder rights plan was adopted in 1991.

A Division of The McGraw-Hill Companies

Business Summary - 22-JUL-98

Exabyte was formed in 1985 to capitalize on its proprietary adaptation to the computer industry of 8mm helical scan recording technology, originally developed for video applications in the 1950s. EXBT is currently the world's largest company devoted solely to the design, manufacture and marketing of tape storage products. The company's products include cartridge tape subsystems based on 8mm helical scan and quarter-inch technologies and robotic tape libraries. Exabyte derives its name from the mathematical term "exa" (the largest named number) and "byte" (the memory space needed to store one character of computer information).

EXBT's strategic focus is the market for information storage and retrieval tape subsystems for workstations, midrange computer systems and networks, particularly for data backup and archival applications.

The Enterprise division manufacturers 8mm tape drive products and media, which address the midrange markets including UNIX and NT server. The company's 8mm tape drive products offer data capacities ranging from 5GB to 40GB with data compression. In 1997, sales of 8mm products accounted for 59% of total revenues, down from 65% in 1996. Products include the Mammoth and Eliant tape drives. EXBT provides various types of media cartridges, as well as cleaning cartridges and data cartridge holders, for its 8mm tape

drive products. Media sales accounted for 15% of 1997 sales (12% in 1995).

EXBT's Storage Automation Solutions division manufactures robotic tape libraries. These libraries automate the storage and retrieval of substantial amounts of data, and accounted for 18% of 1997 revenues (14% in 1996).

The company's Worldwide Service division provides a full range of support services for the company's library, tape drive, and media products. Services accounted for 7% of 1997 revenues (6% in 1996).

The Eagle division, which was created in 1995, was discontinued in December 1997. This division was responsible for Exabyte's line of minicartridge drives and media. The Eagle line provided 6% of revenues in 1997 (5% in 1996).

International sales provided 32% and 30% of revenues in 1997 and 1996, respectively. The three leading customers accounted for 39% of sales in 1997.

EXBT recorded charges of $9.2 million ($0.41 a share) in the third quarter of 1997, related to a work force reduction, the termination of certain development programs, and the phaseout of some unprofitable product lines. These actions were expected to result in approximately $3 million in quarterly savings. Fourth quarter charges totaling $11.9 million ($0.53) were primarily related to the decision to sell the Eagle division.

Per Share Data ($)

(Year Ended Dec. 31)	1997	1996	1995	1994	1993	1992	1991	1990	1989	1988
Tangible Bk. Val.	7.61	9.02	8.54	9.10	7.49	6.70	5.51	3.80	2.38	NA
Cash Flow	-0.50	1.15	0.22	2.07	1.36	1.36	1.78	1.47	0.73	0.13
Earnings	-1.38	0.39	-0.57	1.48	0.76	0.95	1.51	1.32	0.65	0.10
Dividends	Nil	Nil	Nil	Nil	Nil	Nil	Nil	Nil	Nil	Nil
Payout Ratio	Nil	Nil	Nil	Nil	Nil	Nil	Nil	Nil	Nil	Nil
Prices - High	16½	22¾	21⅝	24	18¾	40⅝	31⅝	25⅜	13⅛	NA
- Low	5⅝	11⅝	10	14	7¼	12	13⅛	6⅝	10	NA
P/E Ratio - High	NM	58	NM	16	25	43	21	19	20	NA
- Low	NM	30	NM	9	10	13	9	5	15	NA

Income Statement Analysis (Million $)

	1997	1996	1995	1994	1993	1992	1991	1990	1989	1988
Revs.	336	363	374	382	310	287	234	170	89.0	32.0
Oper. Inc.	-32.7	28.6	-7.4	61.3	35.3	59.4	54.2	43.7	19.2	2.8
Depr.	19.7	17.1	17.1	13.0	12.9	9.0	5.7	3.2	1.4	0.6
Int. Exp.	0.6	0.5	0.3	0.2	0.2	0.1	0.1	0.1	0.1	0.1
Pretax Inc.	-53.1	12.7	-23.0	47.8	23.9	38.9	50.2	42.9	19.4	2.8
Eff. Tax Rate	NM	32%	NM	32%	32%	47%	36%	36%	36%	38%
Net Inc.	-30.8	8.6	-12.4	32.4	16.2	20.5	32.2	27.6	12.4	1.7

Balance Sheet & Other Fin. Data (Million $)

	1997	1996	1995	1994	1993	1992	1991	1990	1989	1988
Cash	47.0	66.8	68.8	80.3	66.0	51.2	55.6	28.8	30.1	NA
Curr. Assets	176	196	197	204	168	155	135	89.0	58.0	NA
Total Assets	221	256	250	243	197	183	150	101	62.0	NA
Curr. Liab.	47.6	52.7	60.0	45.6	38.3	42.3	37.7	25.5	16.5	NA
LT Debt	3.0	3.5	4.2	0.2	0.5	0.5	0.1	0.2	0.2	NA
Common Eqty.	171	200	186	197	159	140	112	75.0	46.0	NA
Total Cap.	174	203	190	197	159	141	112	75.0	46.0	NA
Cap. Exp.	11.8	19.3	23.4	13.6	8.0	17.8	6.8	9.3	2.9	0.9
Cash Flow	-11.1	25.7	4.7	45.4	29.0	29.5	37.9	30.8	13.7	2.3
Curr. Ratio	3.7	3.7	3.3	4.5	4.4	3.7	3.6	3.5	3.5	NA
% LT Debt of Cap.	1.7	1.7	2.2	0.1	0.3	0.4	0.1	0.3	0.4	NA
% Net Inc.of Revs.	NM	2.3	NM	8.5	5.2	7.1	13.8	16.2	13.9	5.6
% Ret. on Assets	NM	3.4	NM	14.6	8.5	12.1	25.4	33.4	30.9	NA
% Ret. on Equity	NM	4.5	NM	18.1	10.8	16.0	34.0	45.2	43.9	NA

Data as orig. reptd.; bef. results of disc. opers. and/or spec. items. Per share data adj. for stk. divs. as of ex-div. date. Bold denotes diluted EPS (FASB 128). E-Estimated. NA-Not Available. NM-Not Meaningful. NR-Not Ranked.

Office—1685 38th St., Boulder, CO 80301-9803. **Tel**—(303) 442-4333. **Website**—http://www.exabyte.com **Chrmn**—P. D. Behrendt. **Pres & CEO**—W. L. Marriner. **EVP & COO**—D. L. Riegel. **Dirs**—P. D. Behrendt, B. M. Holland, T. E. Pardun, M. W. Perry, R. Z. Sorenson, T. G. Washing. **Transfer Agent & Registrar**—First National Bank of Boston. **Incorporated**—in Delaware in 1985. **Empl**— 1,300. **S&P Analyst:** Brian Goodstadt

Executive Risk

844M

NYSE Symbol **ER**

In S&P SmallCap 600

03-OCT-98

Industry:
Insurance (Property-Casualty)

Summary: This specialty insurance holding company markets and underwrites directors and officers liability, lawyers professional liability and miscellaneous liability insurance.

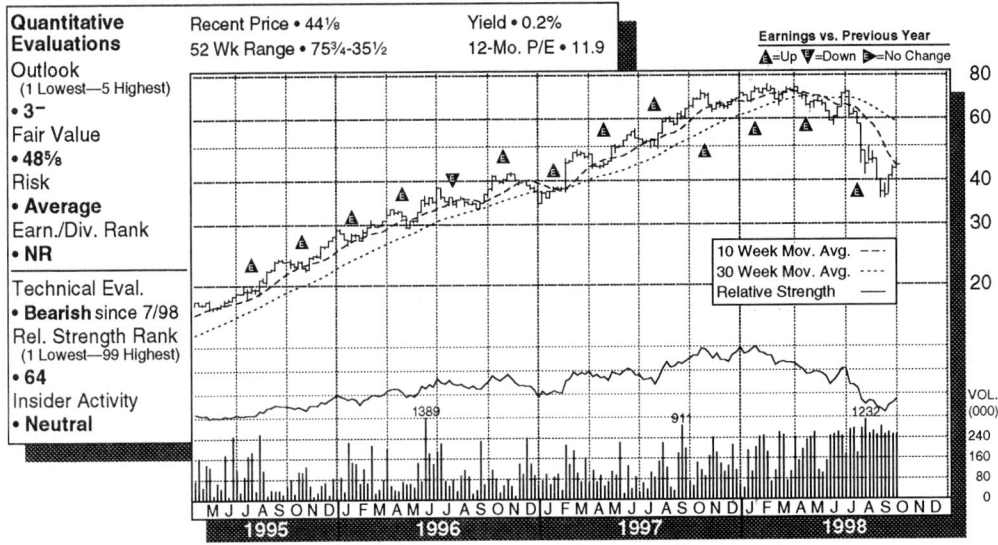

Quantitative Evaluations	
Outlook (1 Lowest—5 Highest)	• **3⁻**
Fair Value	• **48⅝**
Risk	• **Average**
Earn./Div. Rank	• **NR**
Technical Eval.	• **Bearish** since 7/98
Rel. Strength Rank (1 Lowest—99 Highest)	• **64**
Insider Activity	• **Neutral**

Recent Price • 44⅛
52 Wk Range • 75¾-35½

Yield • 0.2%
12-Mo. P/E • 11.9

Earnings vs. Previous Year
▲=Up ▼=Down ▷=No Change

10 Week Mov. Avg. ‑ ‑ ‑
30 Week Mov. Avg. ·······
Relative Strength ———

Business Profile - 14-JUL-98

In December 1997, the company announced that its UPEX joint venture would terminate at the end of 1997. During 1997, gross written premiums by UPEX totaled $21.3 million, in which ER had a 50% participation. The company plans to continue to serve the European market through its Dutch ERNV subsidiary. ER is committed to diversifying its business both within and outside the specialty liability arena. In September 1997, the company acquired the assets and business of Sullivan, Kelly & Associates, Inc., an underwriting manager specializing in hospital professional liability and liability insurance for managed care medical groups. In late 1997, ER sold publicly 1,150,000 common shares at $62.25 each, and also sold $75,000,000 of senior notes; combined net proceeds were $142 million.

Operational Review - 14-JUL-98

Net premiums earned in the three months ended March 31, 1998, increased 29%, year to year, aided by sales growth in miscellaneous professional liability errors and omissions insurance. With net investment income up 50%, total revenues advanced 34%. Loss and loss adjustment expense, as well as total expenses rose less rapidly than revenues; pretax income increased 45%. After taxes at 21.5%, versus 16.7%, net income advanced 36%, to $11,479,000 ($0.98 a share, based on 15% more shares), from $8,414,000 ($0.83).

Stock Performance - 02-OCT-98

In the past 30 trading days, ER's shares have declined 4%, compared to a 7% fall in the S&P 500. Average trading volume for the past five days was 77,740 shares, compared with the 40-day moving average of 96,431 shares.

Key Stock Statistics

Dividend Rate/Share	0.08	Shareholders	100
Shs. outstg. (M)	10.9	Market cap. (B)	$0.483
Avg. daily vol. (M)	0.091	Inst. holdings	77%
Tang. Bk. Value/Share	27.89		
Beta	NA		

Value of $10,000 invested 5 years ago: NA

Fiscal Year Ending Dec. 31

	1998	1997	1996	1995	1994	1993
Revenues (Million $)						
1Q	76.78	57.49	42.33	31.22	25.75	—
2Q	80.14	61.77	42.76	36.04	27.97	—
3Q	—	67.09	49.09	37.37	30.43	—
4Q	—	74.02	55.46	40.18	37.60	—
Yr.	—	258.3	189.6	144.8	117.1	91.32
Earnings Per Share ($)						
1Q	0.98	0.83	0.60	0.45	0.55	--
2Q	0.97	0.83	0.56	0.59	0.42	--
3Q	--	0.84	0.67	0.51	0.44	--
4Q	--	0.91	0.85	0.56	0.45	--
Yr.	--	3.41	2.67	2.11	1.80	2.40

Next earnings report expected: NA

Dividend Data (Dividends have been paid since 1995.)

Amount ($)	Date Decl.	Ex-Div. Date	Stock of Record	Payment Date
0.020	Nov. 21	Dec. 11	Dec. 15	Dec. 31 '97
0.020	Feb. 23	Mar. 11	Mar. 15	Mar. 31 '98
0.020	May. 11	Jun. 11	Jun. 15	Jun. 30 '98
0.020	Aug. 11	Sep. 11	Sep. 15	Sep. 30 '98

A Division of The **McGraw·Hill** Companies

Business Summary - 14-JUL-98

This insurer of directors and officers (D&O) also issues professional liability insurance. Executive Risk Inc. (ER) emphasizes industry specialization as part of its business strategy. It seeks to become a niche player in the D&O market by developing expertise in the commercial, financial institution and not-for-profit sectors. ER's underwriting philosophy stresses expert consideration of complex insurance submissions, including those from harder-to-insure applicants, and profitability over premium growth. Accordingly, the company prices premiums based primarily upon specific risk exposure, including loss experience, rather than market factors. The combined ratio (which measures claims losses and operating expenses against premiums) was 95.2% in 1997.

The demand for D&O insurance, which protects officers and directors from liabilities arising from their official responsibilities, grew dramatically during the late 1970s and in the 1980s, as corporate merger and acquisition activity, and attendant shareholder lawsuits, increased. Having suffered losses, a number of carriers reduced or ceased their D&O activities by the mid-80s, leaving a shortage of capacity in the market. Executive Re, a principal subsidiary of ER, was formed largely to capitalize on that decreased capacity. ER believes that the D&O market will continue to be affected by consolidating sectors, as well as by statutory, regulatory and case law developments that affect executive liabilities. In 1997, commercial entities accounted for 51% of ER's D&O premiums written, and the financial, healthcare and not-for-profit sectors contributed equally the remaining 49%. ER believes that it is a leading underwriter of primary D&O insurance in the U.S.

The company's other principal line is errors and omissions (E&O) insurance, which is most often sold to professionals, such as attorneys, psychologists, and insurance agents, where the primary sources of potential claims are dissatisfied clients alleging breaches of professional standards or ethical violations. A small, but growing percentage of ER's E&O coverage is being written through outside firms that have experience and expertise with respect to specific classes of risk.

ER has recently restructured its relationship with Aetna Casualty & Surety Company. Under a February 1997 agreement, ER relinquished its exclusive right to underwrite and issue D&O on Aetna policies through 1999. Although competition may increase, the company believes that it could benefit, particularly from cessation, under the agreement, of Aetna as a 12.5% quota share reinsurer on ER's direct D&O liability insurance business, which totaled about $225 million in 1996.

Per Share Data ($)

(Year Ended Dec. 31)	1997	1996	1995	1994	1993	1992	1991	1990	1989	1988
Tangible Bk. Val.	25.48	15.53	15.46	11.50	11.21	NA	NA	NA	NA	NA
Oper. Earnings	NA	2.60	2.02	1.72	NA	NA	NA	NA	NA	NA
Earnings	3.41	2.67	2.11	1.80	2.40	NA	NA	NA	NA	NA
Dividends	0.08	0.08	0.08	0.06	NA	NA	NA	NA	NA	NA
Payout Ratio	2%	3%	4%	3%	NA	NA	NA	NA	NA	NA
Prices - High	72³/₄	42³/₈	29	15⁷/₈	NA	NA	NA	NA	NA	NA
- Low	35⁵/₈	26¹/₈	13⁵/₈	10⁷/₈	NA	NA	NA	NA	NA	NA
P/E Ratio - High	21	16	14	9	NA	NA	NA	NA	NA	NA
- Low	10	10	6	6	NA	NA	NA	NA	NA	NA

Income Statement Analysis (Million $)

	1997	1996	1995	1994	1993	1992	1991	1990	1989	1988
Premium Inc.	211	156	116	95.0	69.0	NA	NA	NA	NA	NA
Net Invest. Inc.	47.0	32.6	26.7	22.5	20.7	NA	NA	NA	NA	NA
Oth. Revs.	3.3	1.2	1.7	-0.4	1.6	NA	NA	NA	NA	NA
Total Revs.	262	190	145	117	91.3	NA	NA	NA	NA	NA
Pretax Inc.	54.5	34.7	30.1	22.8	19.7	NA	NA	NA	NA	NA
Net Oper. Inc.	35.7	27.4	24.3	19.5	NA	NA	NA	NA	NA	NA
Net Inc.	36.5	28.1	25.3	19.2	16.3	NA	NA	NA	NA	NA

Balance Sheet & Other Fin. Data (Million $)

	1997	1996	1995	1994	1993	1992	1991	1990	1989	1988
Cash & Equiv.	88.5	34.8	29.7	32.4	NA	NA	NA	NA	NA	NA
Premiums Due	40.0	26.8	10.7	10.4	NA	NA	NA	NA	NA	NA
Invest. Assets: Bonds	934	620	503	383	NA	NA	NA	NA	NA	NA
Invest. Assets: Stocks	61.7	45.9	26.1	24.3	NA	NA	NA	NA	NA	NA
Invest. Assets: Loans	Nil	Nil	Nil	Nil	NA	NA	NA	NA	NA	NA
Invest. Assets: Total	997	666	530	407	400	NA	NA	NA	NA	NA
Deferred Policy Costs	34.6	22.7	16.2	10.9	NA	NA	NA	NA	NA	NA
Total Assets	1,486	941	688	517	459	NA	NA	NA	NA	NA
Debt	200	70.0	25.0	25.0	25.0	NA	NA	NA	NA	NA
Common Eqty.	396	145	178	131	129	NA	NA	NA	NA	NA
Prop. & Cas. Loss Ratio	67.1	67.6	67.4	67.6	NA	NA	NA	NA	NA	NA
Prop. & Cas. Expense Ratio	NA	25.1	23.3	30.0	NA	NA	NA	NA	NA	NA
Prop. & Cas. Combined Ratio	95.2	92.7	90.7	97.6	NA	NA	NA	NA	NA	NA
% Return On Revs.	14.0	14.5	17.5	16.4	17.8	NA	NA	NA	NA	NA
% Ret. on Equity	13.5	22.3	17.1	15.6	NA	NA	NA	NA	NA	NA

Data as orig. reptd.; bef. results of disc. opers. and/or spec. items. Per share data adj. for stk. divs. as of ex-div. date. Pro forma data in 1993. E-Estimated. NA-Not Available. NM-Not Meaningful. NR-Not Ranked.

Office—82 Hopmeadow St., P.O. Box 2002, Simsbury, CT 06070. **Tel**—(860) 408-2000.**Website**—http://www.execrisk.com **Chrmn & CEO**—L. A. Vander Putten. **Vice Chrmn & COO**—R. H. Kullas. **Pres**—S. J. Sills. **EVP, CFO & Treas**—R. V. Deutsch. **Dirs**—G. G. Benanav, B. G. Cohen, J. G. Crosby, P. A. Gerschel, P. Goldberg, R. H. Kullas, M. D. Rice, J. D. Sargent, S. J. Sills, L. A. Vander Putten, I. B. Yoskowitz. **Transfer Agent & Registrar**—Bank of New York. **Incorporated**—in Delaware in 1993. **Empl**— 480. **S&P Analyst:** B.G.

STANDARD &POOR'S
STOCK REPORTS

Expeditors International
3819

NASDAQ Symbol **EXPD**

In S&P SmallCap 600

03-OCT-98

Industry: Air Freight

Summary: This company is a global air and ocean freight forwarder and customs broker.

Quantitative Evaluations		
Recent Price • 26⅞	Yield • 0.5%	
52 Wk Range • 48¾-25	12-Mo. P/E • 16.3	

Outlook (1 Lowest—5 Highest)
• **4⁻**

Fair Value
• **35¼**

Risk
• **Average**

Earn./Div. Rank
• **B+**

Technical Eval.
• **Neutral** since 8/98

Rel. Strength Rank (1 Lowest—99 Highest)
• **26**

Insider Activity
• **Neutral**

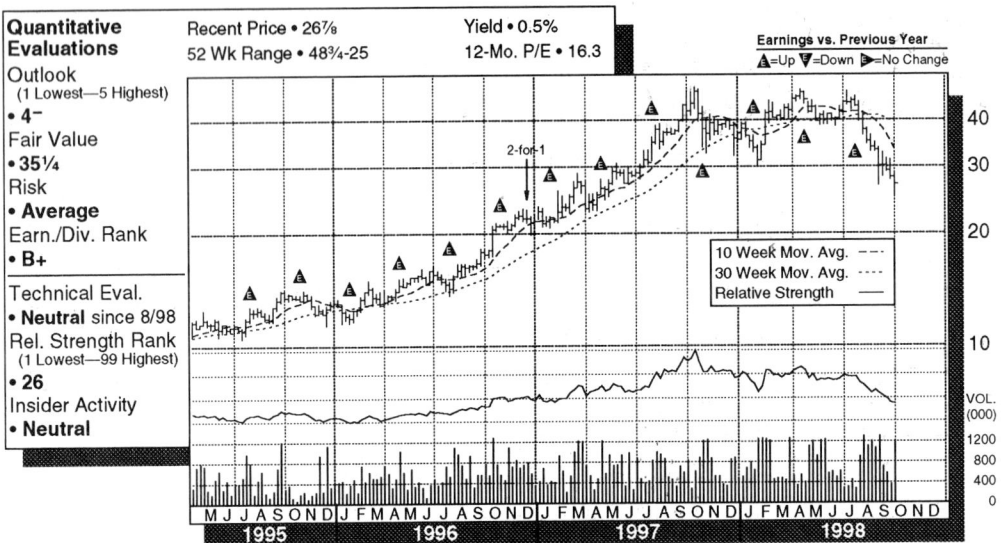

Earnings vs. Previous Year
▲=Up ▼=Down ▶=No Change

10 Week Mov. Avg. ---
30 Week Mov. Avg. ····
Relative Strength —

Business Profile - 04-SEP-98

Expeditors International provides logistics services worldwide through a network of over 100 offices. The company pursues a strategy of organic growth supplemented by certain strategic acquisitions, where economic benefits significantly exceed premiums. In the second quarter of 1998, EXPD opened three new offices in Milan, Italy, Prague, Czech Republic and McAllen, Texas. Historically, the company is subjected to seasonal trends with the first quarter the weakest and third quarter generally the strongest ahead of the holiday season. Same store revenue and operating income growth during the second quarter of 1998 was 19% and 30%, respectively, compared with 29% and 44% a year earlier.

Operational Review - 04-SEP-98

Consolidated revenues in the first half of 1998 rose 10% from those of the prior year, primarily due to EXPD's entry into the truck and rail border brokerage business in the U.S. and aggressive marketing of ocean freight rates for eastbound cargo from the Far East. Margins widened on a slight decline in airfreight consolidation expenses; operating income advanced 36%. Following a gain from the sale of a real estate asset, net income advanced 39%, to $19.1 million ($0.72 a share, on 1.9% more shares) from $13.8 million ($0.53).

Stock Performance - 02-OCT-98

In the past 30 trading days, EXPD's shares have declined 20%, compared to a 7% fall in the S&P 500. Average trading volume for the past five days was 257,260 shares, compared with the 40-day moving average of 225,285 shares.

Key Stock Statistics

Dividend Rate/Share	0.14	Shareholders	500
Shs. outstg. (M)	24.6	Market cap. (B)	$0.662
Avg. daily vol. (M)	0.150	Inst. holdings	77%
Tang. Bk. Value/Share	7.63		
Beta	1.63		

Value of $10,000 invested 5 years ago: $ 35,536

Fiscal Year Ending Dec. 31

	1998	1997	1996	1995	1994	1993
Revenues (Million $)						
1Q	223.3	196.0	137.7	122.9	93.09	73.80
2Q	242.0	225.6	166.2	141.5	106.1	81.90
3Q	—	262.3	204.9	159.2	123.8	99.0
4Q	—	270.1	221.3	161.1	127.6	106.8
Yr.	—	954.0	730.1	584.7	450.6	361.5
Earnings Per Share ($)						
1Q	**0.30**	0.20	0.15	0.13	0.10	0.08
2Q	**0.12**	0.21	0.01	0.17	0.10	0.10
3Q	—	**0.44**	0.30	0.20	0.16	0.12
4Q	—	**0.48**	0.29	0.20	0.15	0.12
Yr.	—	**1.46**	0.95	0.69	0.54	0.42

Next earnings report expected: NA

Dividend Data (Dividends have been paid since 1993.)

Amount ($)	Date Decl.	Ex-Div. Date	Stock of Record	Payment Date
0.050	Nov. 21	Nov. 26	Dec. 01	Dec. 15 '97
0.070	May. 13	May. 28	Jun. 01	Jun. 15 '98

A Division of The McGraw-Hill Companies

Business Summary - 04-SEP-98

Expeditors International's original focus was on air-freight shipments from the Far East to the U.S. Today, the company's capabilities include worldwide airfreight, ocean freight, and distribution services, with a complete range of global services through an integrated information management system. Services include freight forwarding, vendor consolidation, customs clearance, marine insurance, distribution and other international services.

Shipments of computer components, other electronic equipment, housewares, sporting goods, machine parts, and toys comprise a significant percentage of the company's business. Typical import customers include computer retailers and distributors of consumer electronics, department store chains, clothing and shoe wholesalers, manufacturers and catalogue stores.

Airfreight services accounted for 43% of net revenues in 1997. The company typically acts either as a freight consolidator (purchasing cargo space on airlines and reselling it to customers at lower rates than the airline would charge customers directly) or as an agent for the airlines (receiving shipments from suppliers, consolidating and forwarding them to the airlines). Because of the high cost of airfreight, shipments are usually characterized by a high value-to-weight ratio, such as computer components, and time sensitivity. EXPD also performs

breakbulk services, breaking down consolidated shipments and distributing each lot to its final destination.

In the Customs Brokerage and Import Services division, which accounted for 39% of the company's net revenues in 1997, EXPD assists importers in clearing shipments through customs by preparing documentation, calculating and providing payment of duties, and arranging government inspections. Domestic services also include temporary warehousing, inland transportation, inventory management, cargo insurance and distribution. Ocean Freight Services accounted for 18% of net revenues in 1997. Revenue comes from commissions paid by carriers and fees charged to customers for added services, including preparing documentation, procuring insurance, arranging packing and crating, and providing consultation. Expeditors Cargo Management Systems (ECMS) supplies a sophisticated ocean consolidation service to large volume customers that have signed service agreements with ocean carriers. Utilizing ECMS, the company obtains less than container load shipments and consolidates them into full container loads. ECMS customers pay a fee for access to the data and handling charges for shipments.

The company staffs its offices largely with managers and other key personnel who are citizens of the nations in which they operate and who have extensive experience in global logistics. Marketing and customer service staffs are responsible for marketing directly to local shippers and traffic managers.

Per Share Data ($) (Year Ended Dec. 31)	1997	1996	1995	1994	1993	1992	1991	1990	1989	1988
Tangible Bk. Val.	6.92	5.78	4.88	4.23	3.65	3.28	2.80	2.34	1.88	1.45
Cash Flow	1.88	1.26	0.95	0.75	0.58	0.60	0.53	0.49	0.48	0.38
Earnings	1.46	0.95	0.69	0.54	0.42	0.47	0.43	0.42	0.40	0.31
Dividends	0.10	0.08	0.06	0.05	0.05	Nil	Nil	Nil	Nil	Nil
Payout Ratio	7%	8%	9%	9%	12%	Nil	Nil	Nil	Nil	Nil
Prices - High	48¾	23¼	14⅛	11⅝	8⅞	9	8	7⅛	7⅛	4⅞
- Low	20⅝	11½	9⅞	7½	6¼	7	4⅛	3½	3⅞	3⅜
P/E Ratio - High	33	24	20	22	21	19	18	17	18	15
- Low	14	12	14	14	15	15	10	8	10	11

Income Statement Analysis (Million $)	1997	1996	1995	1994	1993	1992	1991	1990	1989	1988
Revs.	954	730	585	451	361	333	254	207	194	147
Oper. Inc.	71.1	45.6	33.5	26.5	21.1	17.7	14.9	13.0	12.5	9.6
Depr.	11.2	8.1	6.6	5.2	3.9	3.2	2.4	1.8	1.9	1.5
Int. Exp.	0.4	0.2	0.3	0.2	0.2	0.2	0.2	0.2	0.2	0.2
Pretax Inc.	62.6	39.6	28.4	22.4	17.1	15.7	14.3	13.5	12.3	9.1
Eff. Tax Rate	39%	39%	39%	41%	40%	28%	28%	28%	24%	21%
Net Inc.	38.4	24.3	17.4	13.2	10.2	11.3	10.2	9.7	9.3	7.2

Balance Sheet & Other Fin. Data (Million $)	1997	1996	1995	1994	1993	1992	1991	1990	1989	1988
Cash	42.1	37.3	36.6	18.4	28.5	28.1	27.6	26.0	20.5	14.8
Curr. Assets	260	215	168	126	118	92.5	86.8	72.1	53.2	42.3
Total Assets	342	272	204	157	145	118	107	91.0	65.0	52.0
Curr. Liab.	172	132	86.9	56.2	57.3	38.2	39.4	35.4	18.7	15.8
LT Debt	Nil	Nil	Nil	Nil	Nil	0.8	0.9	1.0	1.7	1.9
Common Eqty.	170	140	117	101	87.6	79.0	66.4	55.0	44.5	34.7
Total Cap.	170	140	117	101	87.6	79.8	67.3	56.1	46.2	36.6
Cap. Exp.	36.0	20.8	9.3	8.6	5.7	10.5	2.6	8.2	3.2	1.7
Cash Flow	49.6	32.4	24.0	18.4	14.0	14.5	12.6	11.5	11.2	8.7
Curr. Ratio	1.5	1.6	1.9	2.2	2.1	2.4	2.2	2.0	2.8	2.7
% LT Debt of Cap.	Nil	Nil	Nil	Nil	Nil	1.0	1.3	1.8	3.7	5.2
% Net Inc.of Revs.	4.0	3.3	3.0	2.9	2.8	3.4	4.0	4.7	4.8	4.9
% Ret. on Assets	12.5	10.2	9.5	8.7	7.7	10.0	10.3	12.4	15.8	14.6
% Ret. on Equity	24.8	18.9	16.0	13.9	12.2	15.4	16.7	19.5	23.5	23.0

Data as orig. reptd.; bef. results of disc. opers. and/or spec. items. Per share data adj. for stk. divs. as of ex-div. date. Bold denotes diluted EPS (FASB 128). E-Estimated. NA-Not Available. NM-Not Meaningful. NR-Not Ranked.

Office—999 Third Ave., Suite 2500, Seattle, WA 98104. **Tel**—(206) 674-3400. **Website**—http://www.expd.com **Chrmn & CEO**—P. J. Rose. **Pres & COO**—K. M. Walsh. **CFO & Treas & Investor Contact**—R. Jordan Gates.**Secy**—J. J. King.**Dirs**—G. M. Alger, J. J. Casey, M. R. Claydon, D. Kourkoumelis, J. W. Meisenbach, P. J. Rose, R. C. Saber, K. M. Walsh, J. K. Wang. **Transfer Agent & Registrar**—ChaseMellon Shareholder Services, Seattle.**Incorporated**—in Washington in 1979. **Empl**— 4,500. **S&P Analyst:** John A. Massey

STANDARD &POOR'S
STOCK REPORTS

Express Scripts
Nasdaq Symbol **ESRX**

3819L

In S&P SmallCap 600

03-OCT-98

Industry:
Health Care (Managed Care)

Summary: This company offers prescription benefits, eyecare, infusion therapy and disease state management services.

S&P Opinion: Accumulate (★★★★)	Recent Price • 77½	Yield • Nil
	52 Wk Range • 90½-50⅝	12-Mo. P/E • 34.9

Earnings vs. Previous Year
▲=Up ▼=Down ▶=No Change

Quantitative Evaluations

Outlook
(1 Lowest—5 Highest)
• 5

Fair Value
• 146

Risk
• Average

Earn./Div. Rank
• NR

Technical Eval.
• **Bullish** since 9/98

Rel. Strength Rank
(1 Lowest—99 Highest)
• 75

Insider Activity
• **Neutral**

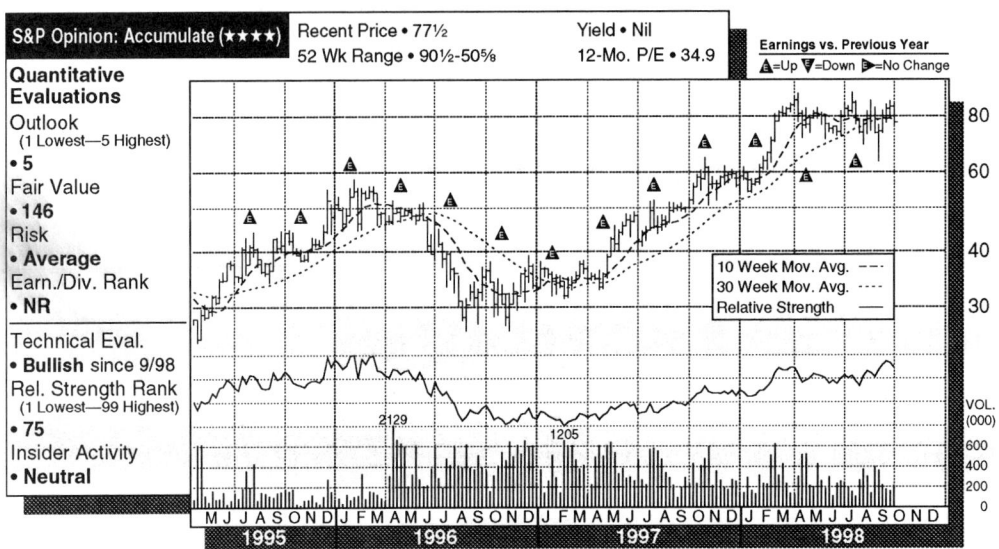

10 Week Mov. Avg. – – –
30 Week Mov. Avg. ·······
Relative Strength ——

VOL.
(000)

Overview - 05-JUN-98

Revenue growth in 1998 should approximate 40%, on enrollment expansion in the pharmacy benefits management (PBM) business and contributions from the vision and infusion therapy segments. Top-line comparisons will also benefit from the recent $445 million purchase of ValueRx, formerly the pharmacy benefits division of Columbia/HCA. The acquisition increased ESRX's processed network claims by 75%, and more than doubled the amount of annual mail order prescriptions. Gross margin pressures will continue to reflect heightened competition and increased usage of the company's own pharmacy network, which requires that these drug ingredient costs be included in the cost of goods sold. However, operating margins should benefit from the ValueRx merger, particularly as ESRX increasingly penetrates the more profitable large employer markets. Annual earnings growth in excess of 25% is anticipated over the coming three years.

Valuation - 05-JUN-98

We maintain an accumulate opinion on the thinly traded stock, and believe that ESRX is attractive both on a fundamental basis and as a potential takeover target. On the earnings front, the company is poised for another strong year in 1998, aided by expanding usage of its services by the existing client base, and the inclusion of ValueRx. Management continues to anticipate that the ValueRx acquisition will be a non-event for 1998 EPS, but we look for an approximate 5% boost to 1999 profits, as cost overlaps are eliminated and other operating synergies take hold. Accordingly, we have raised our 1999 EPS forecast to $3.50, from $3.35. Given the underlying strength in the company's earnings, we feel that the stock is underpriced at a recent level of 22X this estimate.

Key Stock Statistics

S&P EPS Est. 1998	2.55	Tang. Bk. Value/Share	NM
P/E on S&P Est. 1998	30.4	Beta	1.31
S&P EPS Est. 1999	3.50	Shareholders	200
Dividend Rate/Share	Nil	Market cap. (B)	$0.720
Shs. outstg. (M)	16.8	Inst. holdings	39%
Avg. daily vol. (M)	0.038		

Value of $10,000 invested 5 years ago: $ 119,230

Fiscal Year Ending Dec. 31

	1998	1997	1996	1995	1994	1993
Revenues (Million $)						
1Q	371.4	262.0	168.4	118.0	83.08	26.70
2Q	807.4	300.5	184.7	135.2	89.97	29.50
3Q	—	319.9	194.3	138.5	100.7	30.70
4Q	—	348.2	226.2	152.8	110.8	33.40
Yr.	—	1,231	773.6	544.5	384.5	120.3
Earnings Per Share ($)						
1Q	**0.60**	**0.40**	0.30	0.23	0.18	0.11
2Q	**0.57**	**0.50**	0.39	0.30	0.20	0.13
3Q	**E0.66**	**0.52**	0.42	0.31	0.22	0.15
4Q	**E0.68**	**0.54**	0.43	0.31	0.24	0.16
Yr.	**E2.55**	**2.02**	1.60	1.20	0.84	0.55

Next earnings report expected: late October

Dividend Data

No cash dividends have been paid. A two-for-one stock split was effected in 1994.

A Division of The **McGraw·Hill** *Companies*

Business Summary - 05-JUN-98

Express Scripts is one of the fastest growing companies in America, and stands as the largest pharmacy benefits manager (PBM) not owned by one of the large drug manufacturers. Revenues are primarily generated from the administration and distribution of pharmaceuticals through both retail and mail-order pharmacies, from the sale of pharmaceuticals, the provision of infusion therapy services and the sale of eyeglasses and contact lenses. As of December 31, 1997, the company provided PBM programs to about 12,600,000 individuals, up from 9,900,000 a year earlier.

The company's PBM unit manages outpatient prescription drug usage through the application of managed care principles and advanced information technologies. Core services include retail pharmacy network administration; formulary administration; electronic point-of-sale claims processing; drug utilization review; mail pharmacy service; and benefit plan design consultation. About 80% of the members served have access to prescription drugs through one ESRX's retail pharmacy networks and mail pharmacy facilities.

Express Scripts also offers advanced PBM services, including the development of formulary compliance and therapeutic substitution programs; therapy management

services such as prior authorization, therapy guidelines, step therapy protocols and disease management interventions; and sophisticated management information reporting and analytic capabilities.

The number of claims processed by ESRX through its pharmacy networks reached 73.2 million in 1997, up from 57.8 million in 1996, while the number of mail prescriptions processed rose to 3.9 million from 2.8 million.

The company is a major provider of PBM services to the managed care industry, and some of its largest HMO customers include NYLCare Health Plans Inc. and Coventry Corp. During March 1998, ESRX negotiated an agreement to extend its relationship with NYLCare Health Plans through December 31, 2003. NYLCare is in the process of being acquired by Aetna U.S. Healthcare.

ESRX also offers non-PBM services (4% of 1997 revenues) including disease management, informed decision counseling, medical information management, infusion therapy and vision care.

Outpatient infusion services include administration of prescription drugs and other products by catheter, feeding tube or intravenously at the home, a doctor's office or freestanding center. These services aid managed care clients by reducing the length of hospital stays.

Per Share Data ($)

(Year Ended Dec. 31)	1997	1996	1995	1994	1993	1992	1991	1990	1989	1988
Tangible Bk. Val.	12.34	10.07	5.15	3.56	2.60	2.05	0.33	NA	NA	NA
Cash Flow	2.65	2.01	1.48	1.06	0.68	0.44	0.34	NA	NA	NA
Earnings	2.02	1.60	1.20	0.84	0.55	0.36	0.28	NA	NA	NA
Dividends	Nil	Nil	Nil	Nil	Nil	Nil	Nil	Nil	Nil	Nil
Payout Ratio	Nil	Nil	Nil	Nil	Nil	Nil	Nil	Nil	Nil	Nil
Prices - High	64³/₄	58	55	38¹/₄	23¹/₂	16¹/₂	NA	NA	NA	NA
- Low	31¹/₄	26¹/₂	25	22	9³/₈	6¹/₄	NA	NA	NA	NA
P/E Ratio - High	32	36	46	46	43	46	NA	NA	NA	NA
- Low	15	17	21	26	17	17	NA	NA	NA	NA

Income Statement Analysis (Million $)

	1997	1996	1995	1994	1993	1992	1991	1990	1989	1988
Revs.	1,231	774	544	385	120	71.0	47.0	NA	NA	NA
Oper. Inc.	59.3	46.3	33.3	23.8	14.8	8.3	5.3	NA	NA	NA
Depr.	10.5	6.7	4.4	3.3	1.9	1.0	0.7	NA	NA	NA
Int. Exp.	0.2	0.1	0.1	0.1	0.1	0.1	0.1	NA	NA	NA
Pretax Inc.	54.7	43.1	29.6	20.8	13.0	7.4	4.7	NA	NA	NA
Eff. Tax Rate	39%	39%	38%	39%	38%	37%	38%	NA	NA	NA
Net Inc.	33.4	26.1	18.3	17.7	8.1	4.6	2.9	NA	NA	NA

Balance Sheet & Other Fin. Data (Million $)

	1997	1996	1995	1994	1993	1992	1991	1990	1989	1988
Cash	64.2	79.6	11.5	5.7	2.0	11.8	3.5	NA	NA	NA
Curr. Assets	364	263	144	92.8	63.3	40.1	16.6	NA	NA	NA
Total Assets	403	300	164	108	75.4	45.4	20.2	NA	NA	NA
Curr. Liab.	198	135	86.0	55.9	37.1	15.7	16.8	NA	NA	NA
LT Debt	Nil	Nil	Nil	Nil	Nil	Nil	Nil	Nil	Nil	Nil
Common Eqty.	204	164	77.4	52.5	38.3	29.7	3.4	NA	NA	NA
Total Cap.	204	166	78.3	52.5	38.3	29.7	3.4	NA	NA	NA
Cap. Exp.	13.0	9.5	8.1	6.3	7.1	2.5	1.8	NA	NA	NA
Cash Flow	43.9	32.9	22.7	16.0	10.0	5.6	3.6	NA	NA	NA
Curr. Ratio	1.8	2.0	1.7	1.7	1.7	2.6	1.0	NA	NA	NA
% LT Debt of Cap.	Nil	Nil	Nil	Nil	Nil	Nil	Nil	Nil	Nil	Nil
% Net Inc.of Revs.	2.7	3.4	3.4	3.3	6.7	6.5	6.1	NA	NA	NA
% Ret. on Assets	9.5	11.3	13.4	13.8	13.3	12.6	NA	NA	NA	NA
% Ret. on Equity	18.2	21.7	28.2	28.0	23.7	26.9	NA	NA	NA	NA

Data as orig. reptd.; bef. results of disc. opers. and/or spec. items. Per share data adj. for stk. divs. as of ex-div. date. Bold denotes diluted EPS (FASB 128). E-Estimated. NA-Not Available. NM-Not Meaningful. NR-Not Ranked.

Office—14000 Riverport Dr., Maryland Heights, MO 63043. **Tel**—(314) 770-1666. **Website**—http://www.express-scripts.com **Chrmn**—H. L. Waltman. **Pres & CEO**—B. A. Toan. **EVP**—S. L. Bascomb. **SVP & CFO**—G. Paz. **Dirs**—H. Atkins, J. E. Campbell, R. M. Kernan Jr., R. A. Norling, F. J. Sievert, N. Steinig, S. Sternberg, B. A. Toan, H. L. Waltman, N. Zachary. **Transfer Agent & Registrar**—American Stock Transfer & Trust Co., NYC. **Incorporated**—in Missouri in 1986; reincorporated in Delaware in 1992. **Empl**—3,000. **S&P Analyst:** Robert M. Gold

Fair, Isaac & Co. 852V

NYSE Symbol **FIC**

In S&P SmallCap 600

03-OCT-98

Industry:
Services (Data Processing)

Summary: FIC is a leading developer of predictive models, software systems, and marketing database management and decision services used in the credit, insurance and marketing industries.

Quantitative Evaluations	
Recent Price • 32⅛	Yield • 0.2%
52 Wk Range • 46-28⅛	12-Mo. P/E • 20.6

Outlook
(1 Lowest—5 Highest)
• **4−**

Fair Value
• **45¾**

Risk
• **Average**

Earn./Div. Rank
• **B+**

Technical Eval.
• **NA**

Rel. Strength Rank
(1 Lowest—99 Highest)
• **64**

Insider Activity
• **Neutral**

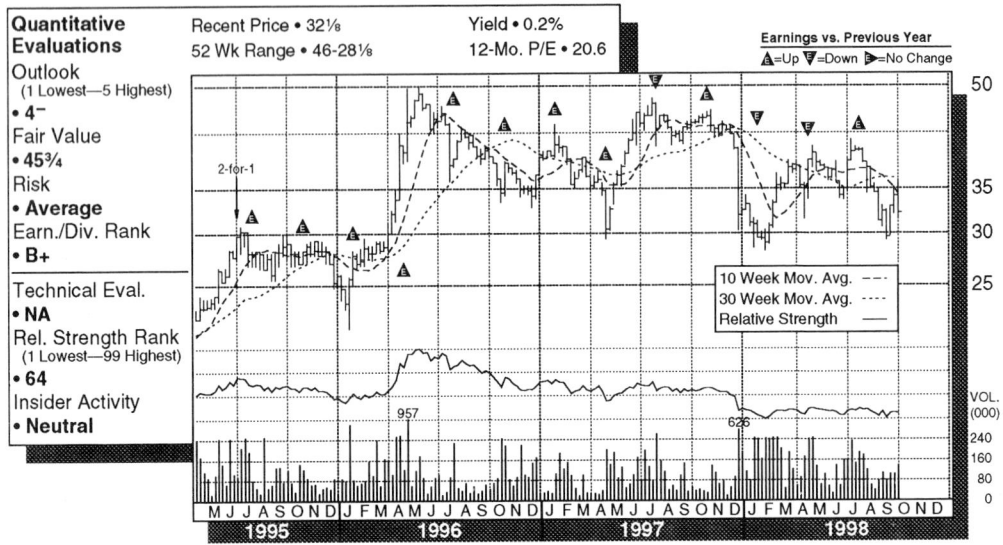

Earnings vs. Previous Year
▲=Up ▼=Down ►=No Change

10 Week Mov. Avg. ‑ ‑ ‑
30 Week Mov. Avg. ·······
Relative Strength ——

VOL. (000)

Business Profile - 30-JUL-98

By winning accounts with large banks and other credit issuers, FIC achieved above-average annual compound revenue growth of 34% over the past five fiscal years, when the U.S. bankcard industry was slowing and banks were consolidating. It believes that it now ranks first or second in all of its product categories. FIC has grown by expanding product functionality and entering new markets such as insurance, small business and mortgage lending, but caveats include potential government regulation and dependence on a few large credit bureaus. In July 1998, the company reported record third quarter revenues and earnings. Results were driven by better than 50% revenue growth from both the DynaMark and Insurance business units, as well as margin improvement.

Operational Review - 30-JUL-98

Revenues in the nine months ended June 00, 1000, rose 25%, year to year, reflecting strong performances from DynaMark and Insurance. Gross margins widened slightly, but R&D expenses surged 64%, and general and administrative costs were up 31%; operating profit increased 6.3%. After taxes at 41.8%, versus 40.0%, net income improved 10%, to $15,854,000 ($1.11 a share), from $14,362,000 ($1.01).

Stock Performance - 02-OCT-98

In the past 30 trading days, FIC's shares have declined 7%, compared to a 7% fall in the S&P 500. Average trading volume for the past five days was 27,360 shares, compared with the 40-day moving average of 18,169 shares.

Key Stock Statistics

Dividend Rate/Share	0.08	Shareholders	300
Shs. outstg. (M)	14.0	Market cap. (B)	$0.449
Avg. daily vol. (M)	0.022	Inst. holdings	32%
Tang. Bk. Value/Share	7.52		
Beta	0.86		

Value of $10,000 invested 5 years ago: $ 52,428

Fiscal Year Ending Sep. 30

	1998	1997	1996	1995	1994	1993
Revenues (Million $)						
1Q	53.51	41.53	32.63	25.63	21.02	13.35
2Q	59.66	46.46	35.28	26.38	21.00	15.08
3Q	64.64	49.04	37.12	28.67	22.64	17.90
4Q	—	56.23	43.73	33.19	25.51	20.34
Yr.	—	199.0	148.8	113.9	90.28	66.67
Earnings Per Share ($)						
1Q	**0.28**	0.35	0.28	0.22	0.18	0.10
2Q	**0.38**	0.39	0.34	0.23	0.17	0.09
3Q	**0.45**	0.32	0.34	0.25	0.20	0.11
4Q	—	0.44	0.31	0.30	0.24	0.13
Yr.	—	1.46	1.27	1.00	0.80	0.43

Next earnings report expected: late October

Dividend Data (Dividends have been paid since 1989.)

Amount ($)	Date Decl.	Ex-Div. Date	Stock of Record	Payment Date
0.020	Nov. 25	Dec. 03	Dec. 05	Dec. 22 '97
0.020	Feb. 03	Feb. 18	Feb. 20	Mar. 06 '98
0.020	May. 19	Jun. 10	Jun. 12	Jun. 29 '98
0.020	Aug. 04	Aug. 21	Aug. 25	Sep. 10 '98

A Division of The McGraw-Hill Companies

Business Summary - 30-JUL-98

Fair, Isaac and Company has been a pioneer in the development of statistical tools, called scoring algorithms, used mainly by grantors of credit to evaluate prospective credit customers, applicants for credit and existing credit customers. The company also produces software and stand-alone computers for the implementation of its scoring algorithms as well as credit and risk management consulting services (CRMA).

The company's best-known product, the Credit Application Scoring Algorithm, is used to calculate the risk of lending to individual credit applicants. The company's user base of over 600 companies includes more than 75 of the 100 largest banks in the U.S., each of the major travel and entertainment card companies, 40 banks in the U.K., more than 40 finance companies and more than 70 retailers. Products and services sold to the consumer credit industry have traditionally accounted for most of Fair, Isaac's revenues, but the company is actively promoting its products and services to other segments of the credit industry, including mortgage and small business lending; and to non-credit industries--particularly personal lines insurance and direct marketing. Consumer credit and direct marketing accounted for 77% and 15% of FY 97 (Sep.) revenues, respectively. DynaMark Inc., acquired in 1992, is engaged in developing and managing marketing databases.

Other key product offerings include: Behavior Scoring Algorithms, which permit managements to define rules for treatment of existing credit customers on an ongoing basis; PreScore Algorithms, used for screening mailings that solicit credit applications; and Automated Strategic Application Processing (ASAP) systems, which are stand-alone assemblies of hardware and software that automate the processing of credit applications.

The company's most advanced product is the Adaptive Control System, now generally marketed under the name TRIAD. An Adaptive Control System is a complex of behavior scoring algorithms, computer software and account management strategy addressed to one or more aspects of the management of a consumer credit or similar portfolio.

The percentage of revenues derived from customers outside the U.S. was 17% in FY 97, 17% in FY 96, and 14% in FY 95.

In June 1997, FIC acquired Risk Management Technologies, a leading provider of enterprise-wide risk management and performance measurement solutions, in exchange for stock valued at $46 million. In September 1997, the company signed an agreement with Brazil's largest credit reporting agency (Serasa Centralizaco de Servicos dos Bancos), which will result in the first bureau-based score delivery service in Brazil.

Per Share Data ($)

(Year Ended Sep. 30)	1997	1996	1995	1994	1993	1992	1991	1990	1989	1988
Tangible Bk. Val.	7.05	5.48	4.20	3.31	2.50	2.37	2.02	1.80	1.69	1.53
Cash Flow	2.28	1.88	1.50	1.15	0.69	0.41	0.32	0.21	0.23	0.24
Earnings	1.46	1.27	1.00	0.81	0.43	0.33	0.24	0.14	0.17	0.20
Dividends	0.08	0.08	0.08	0.07	0.07	0.07	0.05	0.05	0.05	Nil
Payout Ratio	5%	6%	8%	9%	16%	20%	21%	35%	28%	Nil
Prices - High	47⅞	50	30¾	28⅝	11¼	8	6	3⅜	4½	4⅛
- Low	29⅜	21½	17	10½	5⅞	4¾	2⅜	2¼	2½	2¼
P/E Ratio - High	33	39	31	36	26	24	26	24	26	20
- Low	20	17	17	13	14	14	10	16	15	11

Income Statement Analysis (Million $)

	1997	1996	1995	1994	1993	1992	1991	1990	1989	1988
Revs.	199	149	114	90.3	66.7	42.6	31.8	25.5	23.2	21.0
Oper. Inc.	49.5	35.8	26.0	20.1	12.2	6.6	4.0	1.7	2.4	3.1
Depr.	11.8	7.9	6.2	4.3	3.1	1.0	0.9	0.8	0.6	0.5
Int. Exp.	0.3	0.1	0.2	0.2	0.3	NM	Nil	Nil	Nil	0.0
Pretax Inc.	35.5	27.2	21.4	16.6	8.7	6.7	4.4	2.4	3.2	3.7
Eff. Tax Rate	42%	41%	41%	39%	39%	41%	37%	33%	38%	36%
Net Inc.	20.7	16.2	12.7	10.0	5.3	3.9	2.8	1.6	2.0	2.4

Balance Sheet & Other Fin. Data (Million $)

	1997	1996	1995	1994	1993	1992	1991	1990	1989	1988
Cash	13.2	15.7	8.3	14.9	10.7	12.1	16.3	17.2	13.5	14.3
Curr. Assets	81.8	61.5	47.8	38.3	32.0	24.7	24.6	24.4	20.8	21.9
Total Assets	145	113	88.3	70.9	54.2	41.9	31.4	27.6	25.9	24.5
Curr. Liab.	34.1	28.2	23.4	21.8	17.3	11.4	8.1	7.3	5.7	5.2
LT Debt	1.2	1.6	1.9	2.3	2.7	2.7	Nil	Nil	Nil	Nil
Common Eqty.	103	78.3	56.1	42.9	31.5	26.6	22.3	19.7	18.4	16.8
Total Cap.	104	80.9	64.9	45.3	34.2	29.3	22.3	20.1	19.8	18.9
Cap. Exp.	21.7	1.7	10.7	5.3	5.7	6.2	1.0	1.0	1.3	0.6
Cash Flow	32.4	24.0	18.9	14.3	8.4	4.9	3.6	2.4	2.6	2.8
Curr. Ratio	2.4	2.2	2.0	1.8	1.8	2.2	3.0	3.3	3.6	4.2
% LT Debt of Cap.	1.1	2.0	2.9	5.2	8.0	9.1	Nil	Nil	Nil	Nil
% Net Inc.of Revs.	10.4	10.9	11.2	11.1	7.9	9.2	8.7	6.1	8.5	11.3
% Ret. on Assets	16.0	16.1	16.0	15.8	10.8	10.6	9.3	5.8	7.8	10.5
% Ret. on Equity	22.8	24.1	25.7	26.6	17.9	15.9	13.1	8.2	11.2	15.1

Data as orig. reptd.; bef. results of disc. opers. and/or spec. items. Per share data adj. for stk. divs. as of ex-div. date. Bold denotes diluted EPS (FASB 128). E-Estimated. NA-Not Available. NM-Not Meaningful. NR-Not Ranked.

Office—120 N. Redwood Dr., San Rafael, CA 94903-1996. **Tel**—(415) 472-2211. **Website**—http://www.fairisaac.com **Chrmn**—R. M. Oliver. **Pres & CEO**—L. E. Rosenberger. **EVP & COO**—J. D. Woldrich. **SVP & CFO**—P. Cole **VP & Secy**—P. L. McCorkell. **Dirs**—A. G. Battle, B. J. Brooks, H. R. Heller, G. R. Henshaw, D. S. P. Hopkins, R. M. Oliver, L. E. Rosenberger, R. D. Sanderson, J. D. Woldrich. **Transfer Agent & Registrar**—ChaseMellon Shareholder Services, SF. **Incorporated**—in Delaware in 1987. **Empl**—1,200. **S&P Analyst:** Mark Cavallone

03-OCT-98

Industry: Leisure Time (Products)

Summary: This company is a leading consolidator and operator of golf centers in the U.S.

Quantitative Evaluations

Outlook (1 Lowest—5 Highest)
- **NA**

Fair Value
- **NA**

Risk
- **High**

Earn./Div. Rank
- **NR**

Technical Eval.
- **NA**

Rel. Strength Rank (1 Lowest—99 Highest)
- **33**

Insider Activity
- **NA**

Recent Price • 16¾
52 Wk Range • 31⅝-15⅛

Yield • Nil
12-Mo. P/E • 88.2

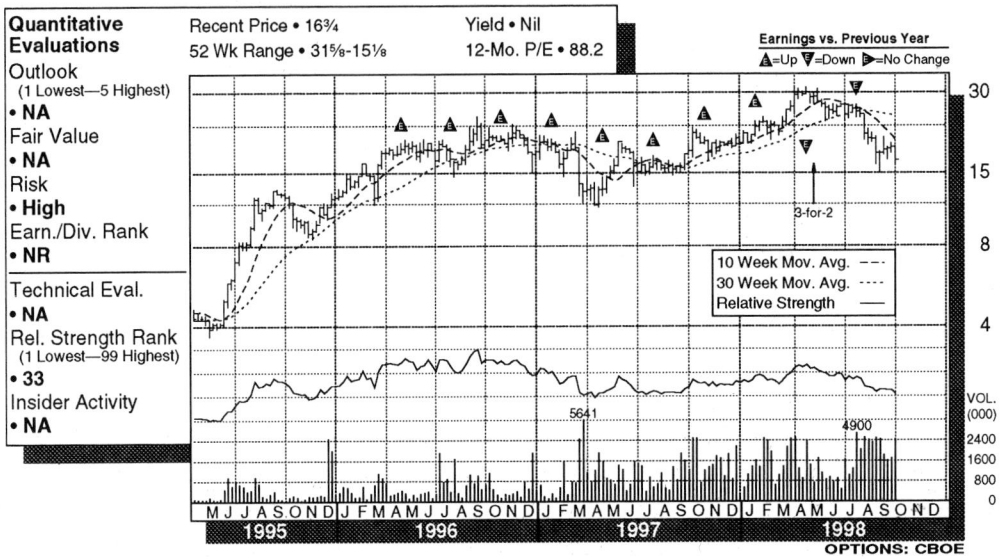

Earnings vs. Previous Year
▲=Up ▼=Down ▶=No Change

10 Week Mov. Avg. ---
30 Week Mov. Avg. ----
Relative Strength —

3-for-2

OPTIONS: CBOE

Business Profile - 02-SEP-98

The company's growth strategy is to continue to consolidate the golf center industry by identifying and acquiring well-located but underperforming golf ranges and building new golf centers. It also plans to develop complementary sports and family entertainment facilities and to augment its existing golf centers with amenities including ice rinks, video and virtual reality games, children's rides and batting cages. Eagle Quest Golf Centers, the second largest operator of golf driving ranges in North America with 20 in Texas, Washington and Canada, was acquired in June 1998. The company had a total of 97 golf centers in operation or under construction as of June 30, 1998.

Operational Review - 02-SEP-98

Total revenues in the first half of 1998 advanced 91%, year to year, reflecting additional golf centers in operation and contributions from ice rink and family sports supercenters. Operating expenses more than doubled, mainly due to costs of new locations, and following $7.8 million of merger, acquisition, integration and other charges, a pretax loss contrasted with pretax income. After taxes of $4.9 million, versus a tax rate of 58.9%, a net loss of $5,570,000 ($0.27 a share) replaced net income of $1,980,000 ($0.10).

Stock Performance - 02-OCT-98

In the past 30 trading days, FGCI's shares have declined 17%, compared to a 7% fall in the S&P 500. Average trading volume for the past five days was 550,460 shares, compared with the 40-day moving average of 486,121 shares.

Key Stock Statistics

Dividend Rate/Share	Nil	Shareholders	100
Shs. outstg. (M)	25.8	Market cap. (B)	$0.432
Avg. daily vol. (M)	0.401	Inst. holdings	57%
Tang. Bk. Value/Share	7.09		
Beta	NA		

Value of $10,000 invested 5 years ago: NA

Fiscal Year Ending Dec. 31

	1998	1997	1996	1995	1994	1993
Revenues (Million $)						
1Q	21.50	9.02	3.36	1.78	—	—
2Q	34.62	17.54	6.85	3.66	—	—
3Q	—	21.87	10.65	4.43	—	—
4Q	—	16.40	7.04	2.56	—	—
Yr.	—	64.83	27.90	12.43	6.36	2.63
Earnings Per Share ($)						
1Q	-0.09	0.02	0.01	Nil	Nil	Nil
2Q	-0.19	0.23	0.12	0.10	—	—
3Q	—	0.22	0.18	0.09	—	—
4Q	—	0.09	0.03	-0.02	—	—
Yr.	—	0.56	0.34	0.16	0.10	-0.15

Next earnings report expected: early November

Dividend Data

Amount ($)	Date Decl.	Ex-Div. Date	Stock of Record	Payment Date
3-for-2	Apr. 02	May. 05	Apr. 20	May. 04 '98

A Division of The McGraw-Hill Companies

Business Summary - 02-SEP-98

Having grown from one golf facility in 1992 to 73 as of March 31, 1998, through an aggressive acquisition program, Family Golf Centers is a leading consolidator and operator of golf centers in the U.S. It plans to continue to consolidate the golf center industry by identifying and acquiring well-located but underperforming golf ranges and building new golf centers.

The company's golf centers are designed to provide a wide variety of practice opportunities, including facilities for driving, chipping, putting, pitching and sand play. They also typically offer full-line pro shops, golf lessons instructed by PGA-certified golf professionals and other amenities such as miniature golf and snack bars.

Golf centers are designed around a driving range with target greens, bunkers and sand traps, to simulate golf course conditions, and are generally lighted to allow night play. In addition, golf centers typically include a number of amenities designed to appeal to golfers and their families, such as a clubhouse (with pro shop, lockers, restaurant or snack bar and video games), miniature golf courses and a short-game practice area. The company's pro shops are stocked with clubs, bags, shoes, apparel and videos and related accessories.

As of March 31, 1998, the company owned, leased or managed 73 golf facilities in 19 states, eight of which were under construction. These included three regulation 18-hole golf courses, one 27-hole golf course and 14 18-hole, 9-hole or executive golf courses. Seven of the facilities were operated under the name Great Bear under a non-exclusive license agreement with Great Bear Centers.

The company also owns, leases or manages four ice rink/family entertainment facilities in three states. Ice rinks are designed with rinks as the main attraction but with amenities including a pro shop (stocked with skates, hockey sticks, jerseys, protective equipment and other skating-related items), video games, a supervised play area for young children, restaurants and snack bars.

In December 1997, the company acquired Confidence Golf, Inc., a designer and assembler of premium grade golf clubs that are sold to large volume free-standing golf shop retailers as well as to the company's owned pro shops.

The company is converting its golf center in Denver, CO, to a family sports supercenter and plans to construct one additional family sports supercenter in 1998. Family sports supercenters provide a variety of sports-related and other entertainment, typically have two or more attractions such as golf centers, skating rinks, bowling centers and batting cages, and a variety of family entertainment such as games, rides and other amenities including snack and sports bars, gift shops, meeting rooms and conference facilities.

Per Share Data ($)

(Year Ended Dec. 31)	1997	1996	1995	1994	1993	1992	1991	1990	1989	1988
Tangible Bk. Val.	7.63	7.55	3.91	0.94	NA	NA	NA	NA	NA	NA
Cash Flow	0.86	0.48	0.25	0.19	-0.10	NA	NA	NA	NA	NA
Earnings	0.56	0.34	0.16	0.10	-0.15	NA	NA	NA	NA	NA
Dividends	Nil	Nil	Nil	Nil	Nil	Nil	Nil	Nil	Nil	Nil
Payout Ratio	Nil	Nil	Nil	Nil	Nil	Nil	Nil	Nil	Nil	Nil
Prices - High	22⅛	24⅜	13⅛	4⅞	NA	NA	NA	NA	NA	NA
- Low	11⅛	11⅜	3⅝	3⅜	NA	NA	NA	NA	NA	NA
P/E Ratio - High	40	71	81	48	NA	NA	NA	NA	NA	NA
- Low	20	33	22	33	NA	NA	NA	NA	NA	NA

Income Statement Analysis (Million $)

	1997	1996	1995	1994	1993	1992	1991	1990	1989	1988
Revs.	64.8	27.9	12.4	6.4	2.6	NA	NA	NA	NA	NA
Oper. Inc.	23.4	8.8	3.5	1.4	-0.4	NA	NA	NA	NA	NA
Depr.	5.7	2.2	0.7	0.6	0.3	NA	NA	NA	NA	NA
Int. Exp.	2.3	0.4	0.9	0.3	0.2	NA	NA	NA	NA	NA
Pretax Inc.	17.1	8.4	1.9	0.4	-0.8	NA	NA	NA	NA	NA
Eff. Tax Rate	38%	38%	35%	NM	Nil	Nil	Nil	Nil	Nil	Nil
Net Inc.	10.5	5.2	1.3	0.5	-0.8	NA	NA	NA	NA	NA

Balance Sheet & Other Fin. Data (Million $)

	1997	1996	1995	1994	1993	1992	1991	1990	1989	1988
Cash	6.0	4.6	23.1	2.3	0.4	NA	NA	NA	NA	NA
Curr. Assets	83.3	48.9	26.1	3.0	0.7	NA	NA	NA	NA	NA
Total Assets	326	158	61.6	16.1	7.7	NA	NA	NA	NA	NA
Curr. Liab.	17.4	12.2	5.5	3.3	2.5	NA	NA	NA	NA	NA
LT Debt	135	8.0	6.3	5.3	2.6	NA	NA	NA	NA	NA
Common Eqty.	168	137	49.4	7.2	1.1	NA	NA	NA	NA	NA
Total Cap.	307	146	55.7	12.5	4.5	NA	NA	NA	NA	NA
Cap. Exp.	66.6	58.8	15.2	NA	NA	NA	NA	NA	NA	NA
Cash Flow	16.3	7.4	2.0	1.1	-0.5	NA	NA	NA	NA	NA
Curr. Ratio	4.8	4.0	4.8	0.9	0.3	NA	NA	NA	NA	NA
% LT Debt of Cap.	44.0	5.5	11.4	42.0	58.7	NA	NA	NA	NA	NA
% Net Inc.of Revs.	16.2	18.7	10.1	7.7	NM	NM	NM	NM	NM	NM
% Ret. on Assets	4.4	4.7	3.2	NA	NM	NM	NM	NM	NM	NM
% Ret. on Equity	6.9	5.6	4.4	NA	NM	NM	NM	NM	NM	NM

Data as orig. reptd.; bef. results of disc. opers. and/or spec. items. Per share data adj. for stk. divs. as of ex-div. date. Bold denotes diluted EPS (FASB 128). E-Estimated. NA-Not Available. NM-Not Meaningful. NR-Not Ranked.

Office—538 Broadhollow Rd., Melville, NY 11747. **Tel**—http://www.familygolf.com **Chrmn & CEO**—D. Chang. **Pres, COO & Treas**—K. P. Thampi. **CFO**—J. C. Key. **Dirs**—D. Chang, J. Ganley, J. C. M. Hsu, K. P. Thampi, Y. Wang. **Transfer Agent & Registrar**—Continental Stock Transfer & Trust Co., NYC. **Incorporated**—in Delaware in 1994. **Empl**— 1,496. **S&P Analyst:** Stephen R. Biggar

STANDARD &POOR'S
STOCK REPORTS

Fedders Corp.

864

NYSE Symbol **FJC**

In S&P SmallCap 600

03-OCT-98

Industry:
Household Furnishings & Appliances

Summary: This manufacturer of room air conditioners has the largest share of the U.S. room air conditioner market.

Quantitative Evaluations

Recent Price • 4⅞
52 Wk Range • 7⅜-4¾

Yield • 2.0%
12-Mo. P/E • 70.5

Outlook
(1 Lowest—5 Highest)
• **NA**

Fair Value
• **NA**

Risk
• **Average**

Earn./Div. Rank
• **B-**

Technical Eval.
• **Bearish** since 7/98

Rel. Strength Rank
(1 Lowest—99 Highest)
• **42**

Insider Activity
• **Neutral**

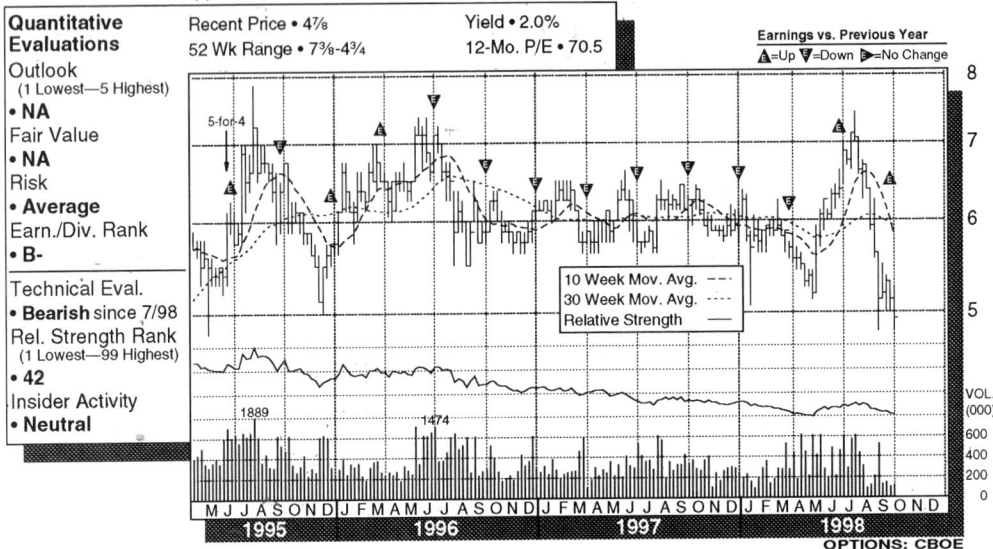

Earnings vs. Previous Year
▲=Up ▼=Down ▶=No Change

10 Week Mov. Avg. - - -
30 Week Mov. Avg. · · · ·
Relative Strength —

OPTIONS: CBOE

Business Profile - 14-JUL-98

Fourth quarter FY 98 (Aug.) sales will depend on weather conditions in major U.S. markets; in mid-June, FJC forecast that recent hot weather would boost June sales from last year's level. Also in June 1998, FJC said it plans to spin off its Melcor subsidiary, a manufacturer of thermoelectric modules, subject to an IRS tax ruling. If the transaction is approved, it is expected that shareholders will receive one share of Melcor for every 10 shares of FJC (common, Class A or Class B). In the third quarter of FY 98, FJC bought back 2.6 million shares of its common and Class A stock for $14.3 million. Directors have boosted the quarterly common and Class A dividend to $0.025 a share, from $0.02, and the Class B dividend to $0.0225 from $0.018, effective with the September 1998 payment.

Operational Review - 14-JUL-98

Sales in the nine months ended May 31, 1998, fell 2.7%, year to year, with recent quarterly fluctuations reflecting a seasonal shift in domestic sales into the second half of FY 00 (Aug.) as major retailers are scheduling deliveries closer to air conditioning season. Gross margins narrowed, but SG&A expenses declined 3.4%; after a $16.8 million restructuring charge, the operating profit dropped 84%. Interest expense climbed 151%, and after a tax benefit of $863,000, versus taxes at 34.0%, the net loss was $1,605,000 ($0.04 a share, on more shares), against net income of $13,905,000 ($0.29 a diluted share, after preferred dividends).

Stock Performance - 02-OCT-98

In the past 30 trading days, FJC's shares have declined 17%, compared to a 7% fall in the S&P 500. Average trading volume for the past five days was 23,140 shares, compared with the 40-day moving average of 36,685 shares.

Key Stock Statistics

Dividend Rate/Share	0.10	Shareholders	8,700
Shs. outstg. (M)	38.9	Market cap. (B)	$0.085
Avg. daily vol. (M)	0.026	Inst. holdings	18%
Tang. Bk. Value/Share	2.04		
Beta	0.53		

Value of $10,000 invested 5 years ago: $ 17,221

Fiscal Year Ending Aug. 31

	1998	1997	1996	1995	1994	1993
Revenues (Million $)						
1Q	25.49	33.09	27.81	20.13	10.53	13.30
2Q	33.58	60.59	88.33	72.36	36.96	36.60
3Q	172.1	143.8	173.9	145.9	95.81	50.46
4Q	—	76.64	81.77	78.14	88.27	58.24
Yr.	—	314.1	371.8	316.5	231.6	158.6
Earnings Per Share ($)						
1Q	-0.09	-0.05	0.01	-0.03	-0.10	-0.07
2Q	**-0.32**	0.04	0.15	0.14	0.03	-0.02
3Q	**0.37**	0.30	0.42	0.44	0.30	0.01
4Q	—	0.12	0.16	0.18	0.26	0.03
Yr.	—	0.40	0.74	0.72	0.49	-0.05

Next earnings report expected: NA

Dividend Data (Dividends have been paid since 1995.)

Amount ($)	Date Decl.	Ex-Div. Date	Stock of Record	Payment Date
0.020	Oct. 28	Nov. 10	Nov. 13	Dec. 02 '97
0.020	Dec. 16	Feb. 11	Feb. 13	Mar. 03 '98
0.020	Feb. 24	May. 13	May. 15	Jun. 02 '98
0.025	Jun. 23	Aug. 19	Aug. 21	Sep. 01 '98

A Division of The McGraw·Hill Companies

STANDARD
&POOR'S
STOCK REPORTS

Fedders Corporation

864

03-OCT-98

Business Summary - 14-JUL-98

Although earnings growth of this room air conditioner manufacturer cooled off in FY 97 (Aug.), the company plans to heat up international growth in the next century. Fedders (FJC), the largest U.S. manufacturer of room air conditioners, holds about a 30% domestic market share. However, the U.S. air conditioner market is a slow-growing, mature industry, with total shipments of about 3.5 million units in FY 97. Improved living standards and a growing middle class are leading to higher demand internationally, with more than 20 million units shipped outside of the U.S. In addition, most consumers outside of the U.S. prefer split-type units, which retail for about three times the typical U.S. room unit. Thus, the market abroad generates annual sales of about $18 billion, versus just $1.25 billion in the U.S.

This worldwide growth in demand is the cornerstone of FJC's long-term strategy. In November 1995, the company entered into a joint venture in China with the Ningbo General Air Conditioner Factory, in which FJC has a 60% interest. With its entry into these new markets, the company expects to receive 50% of its revenues internationally by 2001.

In August 1996, FJC acquired Rotorex, a manufacturer of heating and cooling systems parts. Fedders believes there is a worldwide shortage of compressors, a crucial part of air conditioners and the company's expansion plans, and that by acquiring Rotorex, it will lock in a supply of compressors.

Air conditioners are manufactured in models ranging in capacity from 5,000 to 32,000 BTUs. Products are sold under the brand names Fedders, Airtemp and Emerson Quiet Kool, as well as under private labels, primarily to retail chains and buying groups. NYCOR, through Rotorex, manufactures and markets a broad line of rotary compressors, primarily for use in Fedders room air conditioners. Its product line consists of two basic series of compressors, with capacities ranging from 5,100 to 18,500 BTUs. FJC's Melcor unit manufactures solid-state heat pump modules, selling them under the trademarks MELCOR and FRIGICHIP.

Fedders has several significantly larger competitors, including Frigidaire, Whirlpool, Matsushita and Mitsubishi, which sell a broad line of products. However, after 50 years of producing its narrow product line, FJC believes it is the lowest-cost producer of room air conditioners.

In June 1998, the company announced plans to spin off its Melcor subsidiary, subject to a favorable ruling from the IRS on the tax-free status of the distribution. Melcor, a leading manufacturer of thermoelectric modules, designs, manufactures and markets an extensive line of solid-state heat-pump products. If the transaction is approved, FJC shareholders will receive one share of Melcor for every 10 shares of FJC (common, Class A or Class B). The company expects that Melcor's sales in FY 98 will be approximately $12 million.

Per Share Data ($)

(Year Ended Aug. 31)	1997	1996	1995	1994	1993	1992	1991	1990	1989	1988
Tangible Bk. Val.	2.04	2.23	1.90	1.08	0.45	-0.44	0.14	0.77	0.93	0.70
Cash Flow	0.70	0.90	0.90	0.61	0.09	-0.32	-0.02	-0.02	0.92	0.52
Earnings	0.40	0.74	0.72	0.49	-0.05	-0.70	-0.32	-0.45	0.64	0.46
Dividends	0.08	0.08	0.02	Nil	Nil	Nil	0.19	0.26	0.21	0.16
Payout Ratio	20%	11%	3%	Nil	Nil	Nil	NM	NM	34%	33%
Prices - High	6⅝	7⅜	7⅞	4¾	4⅛	5⅜	5¾	9¼	9¾	6⅞
- Low	5⅝	5½	4¾	3⅜	2⁵/₁₆	1¹³/₁₆	3⅜	2⅝	6⅜	3¼
P/E Ratio - High	17	10	11	10	NM	NM	NM	NM	15	15
- Low	14	7	7	7	NM	NM	NM	NM	10	7

Income Statement Analysis (Million $)

	1997	1996	1995	1994	1993	1992	1991	1990	1989	1988
Revs.	314	372	316	232	159	192	191	241	368	221
Oper. Inc.	41.7	57.6	45.2	28.7	6.9	7.5	8.7	28.0	50.8	23.9
Depr.	9.9	6.6	7.5	4.8	5.0	13.6	10.6	15.1	9.2	1.5
Int. Exp.	4.3	2.4	2.7	4.1	4.2	15.6	11.8	12.6	6.2	0.2
Pretax Inc.	28.3	50.3	35.7	19.8	-2.3	-25.0	13.7	-17.0	35.8	24.1
Eff. Tax Rate	36%	38%	17%	3.00%	NM	NM	NM	NM	38%	38%
Net Inc.	18.8	31.2	29.5	19.2	-1.8	-24.9	-11.2	-15.6	22.1	14.9

Balance Sheet & Other Fin. Data (Million $)

	1997	1996	1995	1994	1993	1992	1991	1990	1989	1988
Cash	110	90.3	57.7	34.9	8.6	8.7	2.9	Nil	Nil	11.1
Curr. Assets	195	159	99	66.0	42.0	78.0	88.0	114	163	105
Total Assets	329	290	137	101	81.0	179	197	215	281	140
Curr. Liab.	53.6	72.0	43.0	28.0	25.0	106	95.0	56.0	108	42.0
LT Debt	113	38.5	4.5	17.3	23.4	45.0	49.0	88.4	81.6	22.4
Common Eqty.	139	152	82.5	49.3	24.2	19.0	44.2	61.5	82.6	30.6
Total Cap.	264	204	87.0	68.0	54.0	70.0	98.0	156	168	96.0
Cap. Exp.	9.2	7.0	9.0	3.6	2.7	3.7	3.6	7.1	8.9	2.7
Cash Flow	28.7	37.7	37.0	24.0	3.2	-11.3	-0.6	-0.5	30.6	13.4
Curr. Ratio	3.6	2.2	2.3	2.4	1.7	0.7	0.9	2.1	1.5	2.5
% LT Debt of Cap.	43.0	18.9	5.1	25.5	43.6	64.4	50.2	56.8	48.5	23.4
% Net Inc.of Revs.	6.0	8.4	9.3	8.3	NM	NM	NM	NM	6.0	6.7
% Ret. on Assets	6.1	14.6	24.8	20.6	NM	NM	NM	NM	9.3	13.1
% Ret. on Equity	12.9	25.8	44.7	51.4	NM	NM	NM	NM	34.3	51.8

Data as orig. reptd.; bef. results of disc. opers. and/or spec. items. Per share data adj. for stk. divs. as of ex-div. date. Bold denotes diluted EPS (FASB 128). E-Estimated. NA-Not Available. NM-Not Meaningful. NR-Not Ranked.

Office—Westgate Corporate Center, 505 Martinsville Rd., P.O. Box 813, Liberty Corner, NJ 07938. **Tel**—(908) 604-8686. **Web site**—www.fedders.com **Chrmn**—S. Giordano. **Vice Chrmn, Pres & CEO**—S. Giordano Jr. **EVP & CFO**—R. L. Laurent Jr. **Investor Contact**—Barbara H. VanBlarcum. **Secy**—K. E. Hansen. **Dirs**—W. J. Brennan, J. Giordano, S. Giordano, S. Giordano Jr., C. A. Keen, H. S. Modlin, C. R. Moll, S. A. Muscarnera, A. E. Puleo. **Transfer Agent & Registrar**—Bank of Boston. **Incorporated**—in New York in 1913; reincorporated in Delaware in 1984. **Empl**— 2,700. **S&P Analyst:** Kathleen J. Fraser

03-OCT-98

Industry:
Insurance (Property-ty-Casualty)

Summary: This company, through subsidiaries, is one of the largest U.S. title insurance underwriters, engaged in the business of issuing title insurance and other title-related services.

Quantitative Evaluations

Recent Price • 30½   Yield • 0.9%
52 Wk Range • 43⅝-16½   12-Mo. P/E • 9.8

Outlook
(1 Lowest—5 Highest)
• 3⁻

Fair Value
• 37¼

Risk
• Low

Earn./Div. Rank
• A-

Technical Eval.
• Bullish since 6/97

Rel. Strength Rank
(1 Lowest—99 Highest)
• 47

Insider Activity
• Neutral

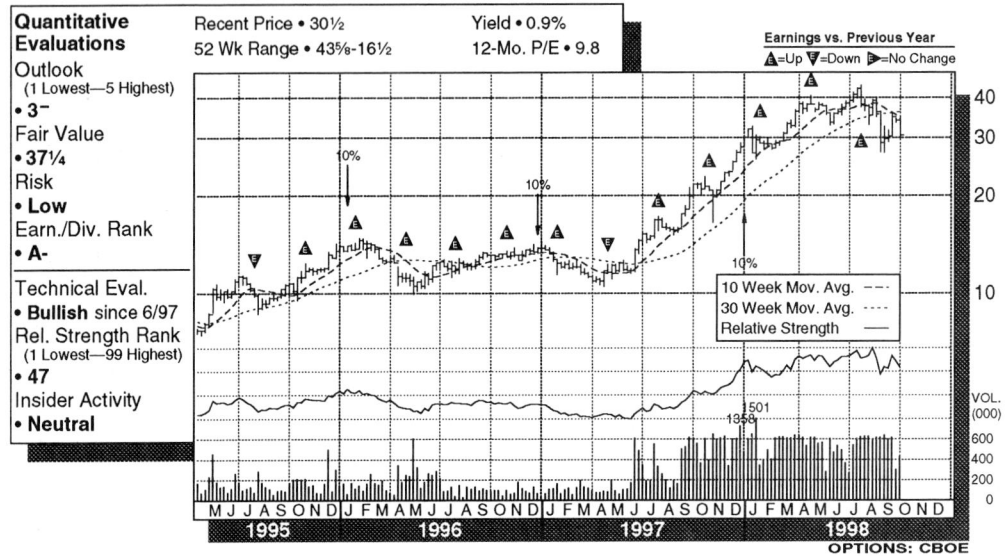

Earnings vs. Previous Year
▲=Up ▼=Down ▷=No Change

10 Week Mov. Avg. – – –
30 Week Mov. Avg. - - - -
Relative Strength —

OPTIONS: CBOE

Business Profile - 19-JUN-98

Continued strength in the overall economy, stability in mortgage interest rates, a thriving real estate market and recent acquisitions made by the company led to strong revenue growth. FNF has implemented aggressive cost-cutting measures designed to reduce expenses and maximize efficiency by maintaining expenses, including personnel costs and other operating expenses, at levels consistent with revenue production and business mix. In May 1998, FNF entered into an agreement to merge Alamo Title Holding Co. with a newly formed subsidiary, subject to Alamo shareholder approval. In March 1998, Fidelity executed an agreement to merge Matrix Capital Corp. with a newly formed subsidiary, and announced the sale of National Title Insurance of New York to American Title Co.

Operational Review - 19-JUN-98

First quarter 1998 revenues advanced 52% to $237 million, year to year, primarily a result of a 45% rise in title premiums and 100% increase in other fees, reflecting the purchase of Granite Financial in 1997. Operating margins improved, led by a decrease in personnel costs and other operating expenses as a percent of revenue. After taxes of 42.5% versus 40.7% in 1997, net income was up 266% to $16.0 million ($0.58 a share, on 18% more shares), from $4.4 million ($0.19).

Stock Performance - 02-OCT-98

In the past 30 trading days, FNF's shares have declined 15%, compared to a 7% fall in the S&P 500. Average trading volume for the past five days was 85,420 shares, compared with the 40-day moving average of 137,403 shares.

Key Stock Statistics

Dividend Rate/Share	0.28	Shareholders	900
Shs. outstg. (M)	25.1	Market cap. (B)	$0.766
Avg. daily vol. (M)	0.111	Inst. holdings	48%
Tang. Bk. Value/Share	12.13		
Beta	1.58		

Value of $10,000 invested 5 years ago: $ 37,351

Fiscal Year Ending Dec. 31

	1998	1997	1996	1995	1994	1993
Revenues (Million $)						
1Q	236.7	153.2	126.4	83.06	143.6	110.3
2Q	289.1	178.5	171.6	95.49	129.4	147.3
3Q	—	197.9	166.7	113.5	113.3	154.3
4Q	—	217.2	172.2	117.8	106.4	163.5
Yr.	—	746.7	636.9	409.9	492.8	575.4
Earnings Per Share ($)						
1Q	0.58	0.18	0.33	-0.16	0.32	0.23
2Q	1.08	0.48	0.45	0.07	0.17	0.47
3Q	—	0.78	0.41	0.38	0.12	0.50
4Q	—	0.62	0.37	0.21	-0.17	0.57
Yr.	—	2.08	1.55	0.49	0.49	1.78

Next earnings report expected: late October

Dividend Data (Dividends have been paid since 1987.)

Amount ($)	Date Decl.	Ex-Div. Date	Stock of Record	Payment Date
0.070	Mar. 19	Apr. 07	Apr. 10	May. 01 '98
0.070	Jun. 17	Jul. 09	Jul. 13	Jul. 24 '98
0.070	Sep. 23	Oct. 01	Oct. 05	Oct. 19 '98

Business Summary - 19-JUN-98

Fidelity National Financial, Inc. (FNF), headquartered in Irvine, CA, is one of the largest underwriters of title insurance policies in the U.S. and also performs other title-related services. Title insurance revenue is closely related to the level of real estate activity and the average price of real estate sales. Since late 1995, decreases in mortgage interest rates and the resulting improvement in the real estate market have had a favorable effect on the level of real estate activity.

FNF operates through a number of subsidiaries currently licensed to issue title insurance policies through direct operations and approximately 2,200 independent agents in all states (except Iowa) and the District of Columbia, the Bahamas, the Virgin Islands and Puerto Rico. For the entire industry, 12 states accounted for 72% of title premiums written in the U.S. in 1996, and California, the largest contributor, accounted for 17.5%. Title insurance premiums accounted for 71.4% of FNF's revenues in 1997, with about 38% of the insurance premium revenue coming from California.

FNF also provides other title-related services such as escrow, collection and trust activities, real estate information services, trustee sale guarantees, credit report-ing, attorney services, flood certification, tax monitoring, reconveyances, recordings, foreclosure publishing and posting services and exchange intermediary services in connection with real estate transactions.

Significant data for the title insurance operations follows:

	1997	1996	1995
Title insurance premiums: Direct	47%	50%	62%
Average fee per file	$853	$806	$790
Avg. pct. of premiums from agents	20.9%	21.3%	23.7%

On May 7, 1998, the company announced that it has entered into an agreement and plan of merger to merge Alamo Title Holding Company with a newly formed subsidiary of FNF for 2.1 million shares of its common stock. In March 1998, management announced an agreement to sell National Title Insurance of New York to American Title Co., and that it had executed an agreement to merge Matrix Capital Corp. with a newly formed subsidiary of FNF. In November 1997, FNF agreed to merge Granite Financial, Inc. with a newly formed subsidiary of Fidelity. Under the terms of the agreement, each Granite share will be converted into 0.701 shares of FNF.

Per Share Data ($)

(Year Ended Dec. 31)	1997	1996	1995	1994	1993	1992	1991	1990	1989	1988
Tangible Bk. Val.	9.17	6.32	4.98	5.80	5.45	3.30	2.28	1.83	1.62	1.39
Oper. Earnings	NA	NA	NA	NA	NA	NA	NA	NA	0.32	0.13
Earnings	2.61	1.55	0.49	0.49	1.78	0.88	0.44	0.37	0.33	0.15
Dividends	0.28	0.25	0.21	0.21	0.17	0.13	0.11	0.10	0.07	0.04
Payout Ratio	11%	16%	43%	43%	10%	15%	26%	27%	21%	25%
Prices - High	31³/₈	14⁷/₈	14¹/₄	20¹/₄	20¹/₂	9¹/₄	4¹/₂	2³/₄	2⁵/₁₆	1³/₄
- Low	10¹/₂	9⁷/₈	7³/₈	7³/₈	8³/₈	4¹/₂	1¹⁵/₁₆	1⁷/₈	1³/₈	1¹/₁₆
P/E Ratio - High	12	10	29	41	11	11	10	8	7	14
- Low	4	6	15	15	5	5	4	5	4	8

Income Statement Analysis (Million $)

	1997	1996	1995	1994	1993	1992	1991	1990	1989	1988
Premium Inc.	533	476	286	369	430	289	163	132	122	104
Net Invest. Inc.	33.5	8.3	8.4	3.3	12.1	4.3	2.3	2.2	2.0	2.0
Oth. Revs.	99	143	107	112	131	89.1	55.5	49.2	39.7	28.3
Total Revs.	747	637	410	493	575	382	221	183	163	135
Pretax Inc.	73.4	40.6	9.5	12.3	52.5	8.0	10.0	8.2	8.5	3.8
Net Oper. Inc.	NA	NA	NA	NA	NA	NA	NA	NA	4.9	2.2
Net Inc.	41.5	24.3	7.6	9.7	36.3	5.2	6.2	5.2	5.0	2.5

Balance Sheet & Other Fin. Data (Million $)

	1997	1996	1995	1994	1993	1992	1991	1990	1989	1988
Cash & Equiv.	54.0	64.0	47.4	34.7	42.7	48.5	21.0	11.3	10.1	11.3
Premiums Due	61.5	65.7	55.7	41.6	28.5	15.7	15.2	11.9	13.1	13.0
Invest. Assets: Bonds	217	166	129	176	212	84.1	3.6	5.2	4.0	3.8
Invest. Assets: Stocks	70.4	43.6	31.4	15.5	6.3	2.8	7.0	0.7	1.9	0.7
Invest. Assets: Loans	Nil	Nil	Nil	Nil	Nil	Nil	Nil	Nil	Nil	Nil
Invest. Assets: Total	326	228	180	218	226	94.1	10.9	5.9	5.9	4.4
Deferred Policy Costs	Nil	Nil	Nil	Nil	Nil	Nil	Nil	Nil	Nil	Nil
Total Assets	601	509	405	418	396	249	125	106	90.1	89.3
Debt	123	149	136	142	52.8	26.1	30.3	24.5	14.7	25.8
Common Eqty.	196	110	77.9	74.0	115	62.4	38.2	28.7	27.8	26.5
Prop. & Cas. Loss Ratio	6.6	7.8	9.2	6.3	4.2	7.2	6.0	5.2	4.5	9.2
Prop. & Cas. Expense Ratio	NA	NA	NA	NA	NA	NA	NA	NA	NA	NA
Prop. & Cas. Combined Ratio	NA	NA	NA	NA	NA	NA	NA	NA	NA	NA
% Return On Revs.	5.6	3.8	1.9	2.0	6.3	4.0	2.8	2.8	3.1	1.8
% Ret. on Equity	27.1	25.9	10.0	10.3	40.3	30.0	18.6	18.5	18.5	9.4

Data as orig. reptd.; bef. results of disc. opers. and/or spec. items. Per share data adj. for stk. divs. as of ex-div. date. Bold denotes diluted EPS (FASB 128). E-Estimated. NA-Not Available. NM-Not Meaningful. NR-Not Ranked.

Office—17911 Von Karman Ave., Irvine, CA 92614. **Reincorporated**—in Delaware in 1986. **Tel**—(714) 622-5000. **Chrmn & CEO**—W.P. Foley II. **Pres**—F. P. Willey. **Exec VP, CFO & Treas**—C. A. Strunk. **Sr VP & Secy**—M. Jones Kane.**VP & Investor Contact**—Jo Etta Bandy. **Dirs**—W. P. Foley II, W. A. Imparato, D. M. Kofl, D. D. Lane, S. C. Mahood, J. T. Talbot, C. H. Thompson, F. P. Willey. **Transfer Agent & Registrar**—Continental Stock Transfer & Trust Co., NYC. **Empl**— 5,200. **S&P Analyst:** J.A.M.

Filene's Basement

3869L

NASDAQ Symbol **BSMT**

In S&P SmallCap 600

03-OCT-98

Industry:
Retail (Discounters)

Summary: This company operates 47 off-price specialty stores offering focused assortments of fashionable, nationally recognized branded and private-label family apparel and accessories.

Quantitative Evaluations	
Outlook (1 Lowest—5 Highest)	• **5**
Fair Value	• 6¼
Risk	• **High**
Earn./Div. Rank	• **C**
Technical Eval.	• **Bearish** since 3/98
Rel. Strength Rank (1 Lowest—99 Highest)	• **4**
Insider Activity	• **Neutral**

Recent Price • 1⅞
52 Wk Range • 8⅜-1½
Yield • Nil
12-Mo. P/E • NM

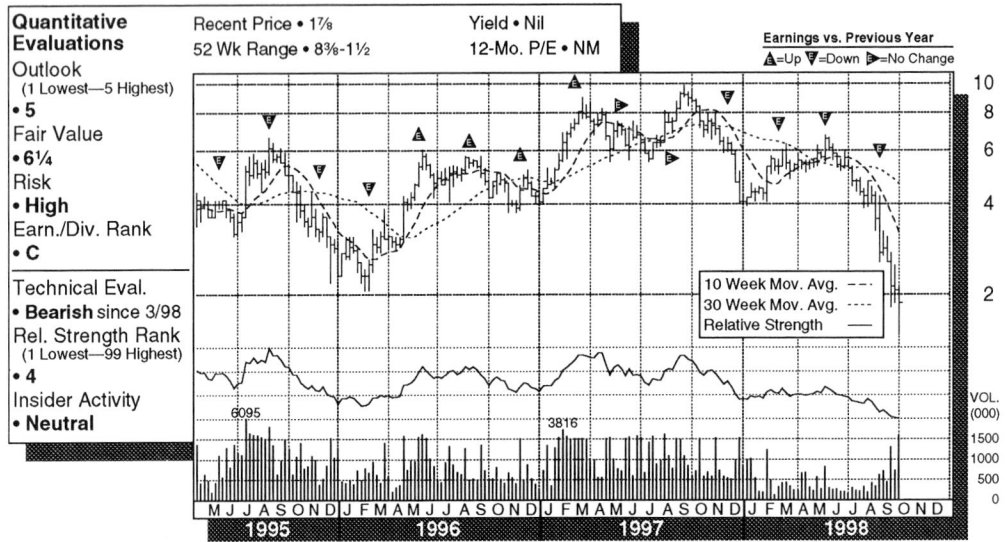

Earnings vs. Previous Year
▲=Up ▼=Down ▶=No Change

10 Week Mov. Avg. – – –
30 Week Mov. Avg. ....
Relative Strength ——

Business Profile - 17-SEP-98

Following a comparable-store sales decline of 1.0% in FY 98 (Jan.), Filene's Basement posted a 2.9% same-store sales increase in the first half of FY 99. In March 1998, BSMT said that its Year 2000 exposure will lead to the replacement of certain computer software, hardware and related assets before 2000. As a result, the company has readjusted its depreciation and amortization rates to reflect the shorter useful lives of these assets. Because of these additional non-cash charges, BSMT projected its tax rate for FY 99 at about 22%.

Operational Review - 17-SEP-98

Net sales in the 26 weeks ended August 1, 1998, rose 6.0%, year to year, reflecting more stores in operation, and a 2.9% increase in comparable-store sales. Margins narrowed, on a 10% increase in SG&A expenses related to the store openings; operating profit fell 47%. With higher interest expense, after taxes at 21.3%, versus 24.0%, net income plunged 85%, to $255,000 ($0.01 a share), from $1,750,000 ($0.08).

Stock Performance - 02-OCT-98

In the past 30 trading days, BSMT's shares have declined 47%, compared to a 7% fall in the S&P 500. Average trading volume for the past five days was 475,840 shares, compared with the 40-day moving average of 177,123 shares.

Key Stock Statistics

Dividend Rate/Share	Nil	Shareholders	1,700
Shs. outstg. (M)	21.0	Market cap. (B)	$0.039
Avg. daily vol. (M)	0.247	Inst. holdings	59%
Tang. Bk. Value/Share	3.48		
Beta	1.17		

Value of $10,000 invested 5 years ago: $ 931

Fiscal Year Ending Jan. 31

	1999	1998	1997	1996	1995	1994
Revenues (Million $)						
1Q	127.7	120.5	124.0	127.7	133.1	120.1
2Q	131.4	126.3	120.1	130.3	130.9	119.6
3Q	—	152.5	147.2	154.2	165.8	161.0
4Q	—	155.1	153.7	170.3	178.5	178.1
Yr.	—	554.3	545.0	582.5	608.3	578.8
Earnings Per Share ($)						
1Q	-0.04	0.00	0.00	0.00	0.01	-0.06
2Q	0.05	0.06	0.06	-0.02	Nil	-0.06
3Q	—	0.15	0.17	0.08	0.19	0.27
4Q	—	-0.51	0.06	-1.52	-0.16	-0.35
Yr.	—	-0.28	0.31	-1.56	0.05	-0.20

Next earnings report expected: mid November

Dividend Data

No cash has been paid. Filene's Basement intends to retain earnings for use in its business.

*A Division of The **McGraw·Hill** Companies*

STANDARD
&POOR'S
STOCK REPORTS

Filene's Basement Corp.

3869L
03-OCT-98

Business Summary - 17-SEP-98

Filene's Basement Corp. (BSMT), a leading off-price specialty store chain, seeks to propel its earnings from the basement to the penthouse by opening new stores. This represents a departure from the past few years, when the company closed 16 stores while opening only seven. BSMT has also emphasised improving comparable-store sales. Comparable-store sales decreased 1.0% in FY 98 (Jan.), but rebounded with a 2.9% increase in the first half of FY 99.

As of August 17, 1998, the company operated 47 stores, principally in the Northeast and Midwest, including the flagship store in Boston. The stores offer focused assortments of fashionable, nationally recognized branded and private-label family apparel and accessories. Prices are typically 20% to 60% below those of traditional department stores.

Filene's Boston store has become a landmark institution since it established itself in the downtown Boston shopping district in 1908. The store, located on Washington Street, occupies four floors totaling 65,300 sq. ft. of selling space. In FY 98, the Boston store accounted for 17% of BSMT's retail sales, and generated $1,478 in sales per sq. ft. it is the only Filene's store that oper-

ates under the Automatic Markdown Plan concept. Under the Automatic Markdown Plan, merchandise prices are reduced by previously determined percentages after set time periods in which an item does not sell. The company believes that this sales method generates a sense of urgency among its customers.

BSMT's 46 branch stores averaged 24,400 sq. ft., and accounted for 83% of retail sales in FY 98. The stores averaged $10.4 million in sales ($440 per sq. ft., higher than many competitors). Each store is on a single level, and employs a racetrack layout for merchandise. The stores sell merchandise similar to that of the Boston flagship store, but, due to operational complexity, do not use the Automatic Markdown Plan.

The company sees itself as occupying a market niche between traditional department stores and typical off-price stores. It offers products typically found at department stores, at prices competitive with those of the discount chains. Merchandise is purchased from major upscale retailers such as Bloomingdale's, Neiman Marcus and Bendel's during in-season overruns and end-of-season surpluses at attractive prices. More recently, the company has been offering more private label merchandise, because margins are wider and supply is more predictable.

Per Share Data ($)

(Year Ended Jan. 31)	1998	1997	1996	1995	1994	1993	1992	1991	1990	1989
Tangible Bk. Val.	2.88	3.13	2.63	4.40	4.36	4.42	3.53	1.61	NA	NA
Cash Flow	0.64	0.89	-0.91	0.69	0.39	1.40	1.34	1.16	1.00	-1.21
Earnings	-0.28	0.31	-1.56	0.05	-0.20	0.87	0.82	0.52	0.14	-1.82
Dividends	Nil	Nil	Nil	Nil	Nil	Nil	Nil	Nil	Nil	Nil
Payout Ratio	Nil	Nil	Nil	Nil	Nil	Nil	Nil	Nil	Nil	Nil
Cal. Yrs.	1997	1996	1995	1994	1993	1992	1991	1990	1989	1988
Prices - High	9⁷/₈	6	6⁵/₈	11³/₄	20¹/₂	37	30	NA	NA	NA
- Low	3⁷/₈	2¹/₁₆	2³/₁₆	4¹/₂	6³/₄	11³/₄	14¹/₂	NA	NA	NA
P/E Ratio - High	NM	20	NM	NM	NM	43	37	NA	NA	NA
- Low	NM	7	NM	NM	NM	14	18	NA	NA	NA

Income Statement Analysis (Million $)

Revs.	554	545	583	608	579	529	465	401	358	304
Oper. Inc.	15.9	26.4	-2.7	19.1	24.7	45.4	43.2	36.7	34.2	-3.4
Depr.	19.0	12.3	13.3	13.4	12.4	11.5	10.3	10.2	13.6	9.3
Int. Exp.	2.7	4.0	5.2	4.1	3.9	3.9	6.7	11.3	15.2	14.7
Pretax Inc.	-5.8	10.4	-32.2	2.1	-5.5	30.4	27.1	15.7	6.6	-27.0
Eff. Tax Rate	NM	38%	NM	47%	NM	39%	40%	43%	54%	Nil
Net Inc.	-5.8	6.5	-31.8	1.1	-4.2	18.7	16.3	9.1	3.0	-27.0

Balance Sheet & Other Fin. Data (Million $)

Cash	0.5	0.5	0.5	4.6	0.3	4.5	7.6	5.5	1.7	NA
Curr. Assets	105	99	113	142	141	133	120	84.0	66.0	NA
Total Assets	175	183	210	239	237	216	189	148	132	139
Curr. Liab.	73.7	80.2	84.0	83.9	87.9	75.0	64.3	57.1	49.1	NA
LT Debt	14.3	10.7	38.6	39.1	25.7	25.9	30.9	77.0	82.0	105
Common Eqty.	82.5	87.5	80.9	112	113	115	94.0	14.0	1.0	-5.0
Total Cap.	96.7	98.2	122	151	138	141	124	91.0	83.0	100
Cap. Exp.	12.5	8.2	14.4	NA	22.9	21.3	14.3	7.6	4.8	2.3
Cash Flow	13.2	18.7	-18.5	14.5	8.3	30.1	26.4	19.2	16.7	-17.6
Curr. Ratio	1.4	1.2	1.3	1.7	1.6	1.8	1.9	1.5	1.3	NA
% LT Debt of Cap.	14.7	10.9	31.8	25.9	18.6	18.4	24.9	85.7	98.8	105.0
% Net Inc.of Revs.	NM	1.2	NM	0.2	NM	3.5	3.5	2.3	0.8	NM
% Ret. on Assets	NM	3.3	NM	0.5	NM	9.2	NM	6.5	2.2	NM
% Ret. on Equity	NM	7.7	NM	1.0	NM	17.8	NM	31.5	NM	NM

Data as orig. reptd.; bef. results of disc. opers. and/or spec. items. Per share data adj. for stk. divs. as of ex-div. date. Bold denotes diluted EPS (FASB 128). E-Estimated. NA-Not Available. NM-Not Meaningful. NR-Not Ranked.

Office—40 Walnut St., Wellesley, MA 02181. **Tel**—(617) 348-7000. **Chrmn & CEO**—S. J. Gerson. **Pres & COO**—W. J. Carothers. **EVP, CFO, Treas, Secy & Investor Contact**—Steven R. Siegel. **Dirs**—M. Anathan III, W. J. Carothers, J. Eyler, D. R. Gardner, S. J. Gerson, R. P. Henderson, H. Leppo, P. D. Paganucci. **Transfer Agent & Registrar**—State Street Bank & Trust Co., Boston. **Incorporated**—in Massachusetts in 1988. **Empl**— 2,700. **S&P Analyst:** K.J.F.

STANDARD &POOR'S
STOCK REPORTS

FileNet Corp.

3869M
Nasdaq Symbol **FILE**

In S&P SmallCap 600

03-OCT-98

Industry: Computers (Peripherals)

Summary: This company specializes in imaging and business process automation solutions that electronically capture, store, retrieve, transmit and manage document images, data and text.

S&P Opinion: Accumulate (★★★★)	Recent Price • 12½ 52 Wk Range • 32⅞-9¼	Yield • Nil 12-Mo. P/E • 26.6

Earnings vs. Previous Year
▲=Up ▼=Down ▶=No Change

Quantitative Evaluations

Outlook (1 Lowest—5 Highest)
• **3⁻**

Fair Value
• **20½**

Risk
• **High**

Earn./Div. Rank
• **B-**

Technical Eval.
• **Bearish** since 7/98

Rel. Strength Rank (1 Lowest—99 Highest)
• **7**

Insider Activity
• **Neutral**

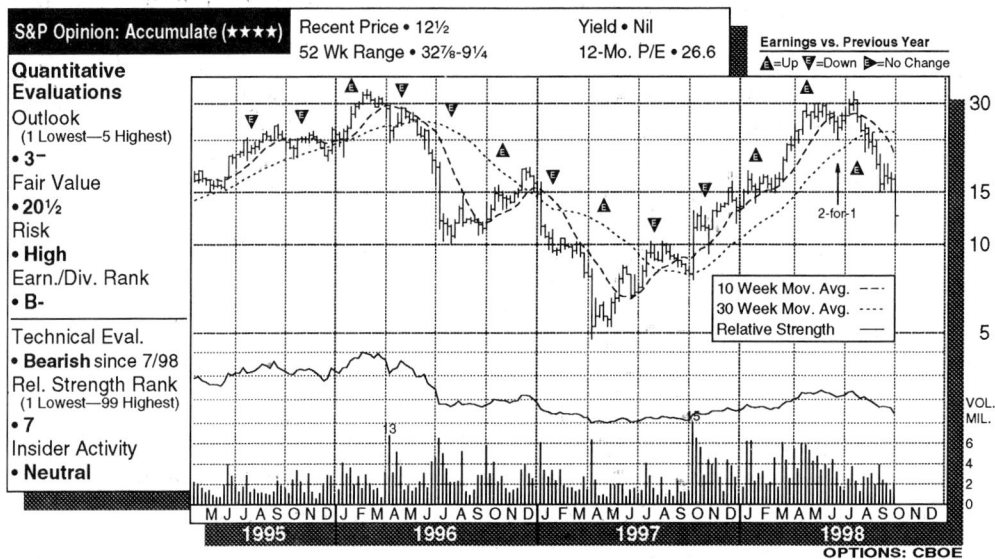

10 Week Mov. Avg. — — —
30 Week Mov. Avg. · · · · ·
Relative Strength —

2-for-1

VOL. MIL.

1995 1996 1997 1998

OPTIONS: CBOE

Overview - 20-JUL-98

FileNet reported EPS of $0.14 for the 1998 second quarter, exceeding the consensus expectation, on a 29% revenue rise. Software revenues were up an impressive 43%, year over year. It appears that FileNet's increased focus on enterprise sales has paid off, as the company once again booked several deals in excess of $1 million. FILE is firmly entrenched as a document imaging leader, but wishes to gain market share in the faster growing document management industry. In line with this strategy, the company introduced its Panagon product family in January 1998, which offers desktop users the ability to access and manage documents (including images, text, videos and faxes) via an Internet browser. Panagon integrates various stand-alone software products and consolidates them under a single brand name. Initial customer shipments of Panagon branded products began in February 1998.

Valuation - 20-JUL-98

We continue to recommend accumulation of FileNet. The company has completed a restructuring under new management, and we are looking forward to steady, consistent results and solid returns for shareholders. We believe FileNet will continue to grow software revenues at a minimum of 30% per quarter. As software revenues increase as a percentage of the total, the company's margins should approach those of typical software companies. Our new EPS estimates of $0.63 in 1998 and $1.00 in 1999 account for both improved profitability and strong revenue growth. Operating margins should hit 15% by the end of 1999. Although the stock is not inexpensive, FileNet's position and superior technology in the fast growing document management market (35% estimated CAGR over the next four years) warrant a premium valuation.

Key Stock Statistics

S&P EPS Est. 1998	0.63	Tang. Bk. Value/Share	4.14
P/E on S&P Est. 1998	19.8	Beta	1.65
S&P EPS Est. 1999	1.00	Shareholders	700
Dividend Rate/Share	Nil	Market cap. (B)	$0.394
Shs. outstg. (M)	31.5	Inst. holdings	65%
Avg. daily vol. (M)	0.437		

Value of $10,000 invested 5 years ago: $ 10,989

Fiscal Year Ending Dec. 31

	1998	1997	1996	1995	1994	1993
Revenues (Million $)						
1Q	73.61	47.56	66.74	45.06	38.75	34.70
2Q	80.37	62.45	65.00	53.29	44.90	38.26
3Q	—	65.01	64.62	53.55	42.59	39.96
4Q	—	76.40	72.55	63.58	53.45	45.85
Yr.	—	251.4	268.9	215.5	179.7	158.8
Earnings Per Share ($)						
1Q	0.09	-0.32	-0.40	0.12	0.10	0.01
2Q	0.14	-0.13	0.08	0.11	0.17	0.06
3Q	E0.15	0.06	0.11	0.01	0.17	0.10
4Q	E0.24	0.18	0.10	0.29	0.24	0.17
Yr.	E0.63	-0.18	-0.09	0.54	0.69	0.35

Next earnings report expected: late October

Dividend Data

Amount ($)	Date Decl.	Ex-Div. Date	Stock of Record	Payment Date
2-for-1	May. 15	Jun. 15	May. 29	Jun. 12 '98

STANDARD
&POOR'S
STOCK REPORTS

FileNet Corporation

3869M
03-OCT-98

Business Summary - 20-JUL-98

More than 90% of all information today arrives at the desktop in paper form. Although applications such as e-mail have greatly enhanced productivity in the workplace, information that originates on paper continues to be photocopied and sent by interoffice mail. In 1985, FileNet (FILE) pioneered workflow software for automating paper-based transactions, and has since produced other complementary products in the Integrated Document Management (IDM) field.

The company develops, markets and services an integrated family of software products for workflow, document imaging and document management applications. Document imaging software allows users to scan a paper document, make changes, link it to a corporate intranet (company-wide network based on Internet protocols) and share it with colleagues. Workflow systems perform electronically what interoffice envelopes were designed to do; gather information and deliver it to a predetermined destination.

The company's software products are used in a client/server environment, as opposed to the traditional mainframe model. Image Management Services (IMS) software is used to organize, store and access multiple types of information such as document images, data, text, graphics, voice and photographs. IMS software supports the IBM AIX/6000, Hewlett-Packard HP-UX and the Sun Solaris Unix operating systems.

In February 1998, FileNet introduced the Panagon family of IDM software that combines imaging, electronic document management and workflow into a unified architecture. Panagon allows companies to capture any type of document electronically, then easily access, manage and integrate the information with existing critical business applications. Companies can use familiar web browsers to search the entire enterprise network for information, and retrieve documents of all types. Panagon was built around Microsoft's component software architecture and FileNet maintains a development and marketing relationship with Microsoft.

Typical users of FILE's products have included companies that possess large, active document files in such businesses as mortgage loan servicing, credit card customer service, insurance claims processing, accounts payable and retirement account management.

The company also markets an optional integration service, which offers customers the option to purchase complete solutions, including industry standard hardware, directly from FileNet.

Per Share Data ($)

(Year Ended Dec. 31)	1997	1996	1995	1994	1993	1992	1991	1990	1989	1988
Tangible Bk. Val.	7.84	4.42	5.17	4.71	3.85	3.44	3.79	3.38	3.21	3.08
Cash Flow	0.51	0.30	0.89	1.03	0.66	-0.07	0.65	0.50	0.38	0.23
Earnings	-0.18	-0.09	0.54	0.69	0.35	-0.38	0.38	0.18	0.14	0.07
Dividends	Nil	Nil	Nil	Nil	Nil	Nil	Nil	Nil	Nil	Nil
Payout Ratio	Nil	Nil	Nil	Nil	Nil	Nil	Nil	Nil	Nil	Nil
Prices - High	16³/₈	33¹/₂	25¹/₂	14⁵/₈	11¹/₂	18³/₄	12¹/₂	10³/₄	6⁷/₈	8¹/₄
- Low	4³/₄	10	12⁵/₈	7¹/₈	4³/₈	5¹/₄	3³/₈	2¹/₂	3³/₄	3¹/₄
P/E Ratio - High	NM	NM	48	21	32	NM	33	58	47	NM
- Low	NM	NM	24	10	12	NM	9	14	26	NM

Income Statement Analysis (Million $)

	1997	1996	1995	1994	1993	1992	1991	1990	1989	1988
Revs.	251	269	215	180	159	138	122	103	83.0	63.0
Oper. Inc.	8.4	26.8	36.1	27.7	18.7	6.3	17.5	11.7	9.6	3.0
Depr.	13.3	11.8	9.6	8.1	6.6	6.5	5.8	6.5	4.8	3.2
Int. Exp.	Nil	Nil	Nil	0.1	0.4	0.6	0.4	0.4	0.3	NA
Pretax Inc.	-7.7	1.8	22.9	21.4	12.5	-9.8	12.5	5.1	3.9	1.5
Eff. Tax Rate	NM	245%	35%	25%	38%	NM	35%	27%	23%	9.20%
Net Inc.	-5.5	-2.6	14.8	16.1	7.8	-8.0	8.1	3.8	3.0	1.4

Balance Sheet & Other Fin. Data (Million $)

	1997	1996	1995	1994	1993	1992	1991	1990	1989	1988
Cash	37.3	50.5	68.8	41.0	43.5	29.3	32.8	22.3	19.7	24.6
Curr. Assets	144	149	138	95.1	96.3	77.2	76.3	66.7	62.5	56.5
Total Assets	180	196	182	142	123	102	104	91.0	82.0	71.0
Curr. Liab.	60.6	59.4	46.7	34.7	37.6	28.9	23.6	22.8	18.6	10.2
LT Debt	Nil	Nil	0.1	Nil	0.2	0.1	0.2	0.3	0.6	1.0
Common Eqty.	119	133	134	104	82.8	72.7	78.2	67.5	63.1	59.8
Total Cap.	119	136	136	107	85.1	73.5	80.2	67.8	63.7	61.2
Cap. Exp.	14.2	17.8	12.5	10.7	6.7	10.6	6.3	8.2	7.5	5.7
Cash Flow	7.8	9.2	24.5	24.2	14.4	-1.5	13.9	10.3	7.7	4.5
Curr. Ratio	2.4	2.5	3.0	2.7	2.6	2.7	3.2	2.9	3.4	5.5
% LT Debt of Cap.	Nil	Nil	0.1	Nil	0.2	0.1	0.3	0.4	0.9	1.6
% Net Inc.of Revs.	NM	NM	6.9	8.9	4.9	NM	6.6	3.7	3.6	2.2
% Ret. on Assets	NM	NM	9.1	12.0	6.9	NM	8.2	4.3	3.9	1.9
% Ret. on Equity	NM	NM	12.8	16.9	9.9	NM	11.0	5.7	4.8	2.3

Data as orig. reptd.; bef. results of disc. opers. and/or spec. items. Per share data adj. for stk. divs. as of ex-div. date. Bold denotes diluted EPS (FASB 128). E-Estimated. NA-Not Available. NM-Not Meaningful. NR-Not Ranked.

Office—3565 Harbor Blvd., Costa Mesa, CA 92626. **Tel**—(714) 966-3400. **Website**—http://www.filenet.com **Chrmn** —T. J. Smith. **Pres & CEO**—L.D. Roberts. **SVP-Fin, CFO & Investor Contact**—Mark S. St. Clare. **Dirs**—F. K. Fluegel, J. B. Jamieson, W. P. Lyons, J. C. Savage, T. J. Smith. **Transfer Agent & Registrar**—First National Bank of Boston. **Incorporated**—in California in 1982; reincorporated in Delaware in 1987. **Empl**— 1,490. **S&P Analyst:** Mark Cavallone

03-OCT-98

Industry:
Insurance (Property-Casualty)

Summary: Through subsidiaries, First American Financial provides real estate financial services, including title insurance, home warranty, tax monitoring, and trust services.

Quantitative Evaluations

Outlook
(1 Lowest—5 Highest)
• **1**⁻

Fair Value
• **30**

Risk
• **Average**

Earn./Div. Rank
• **B**

Technical Eval.
• **Bullish** since 6/97

Rel. Strength Rank
(1 Lowest—99 Highest)
• **93**

Insider Activity
• **NA**

Recent Price • 32¾
52 Wk Range • 43-13⅛

Yield • 0.7%
12-Mo. P/E • 13.4

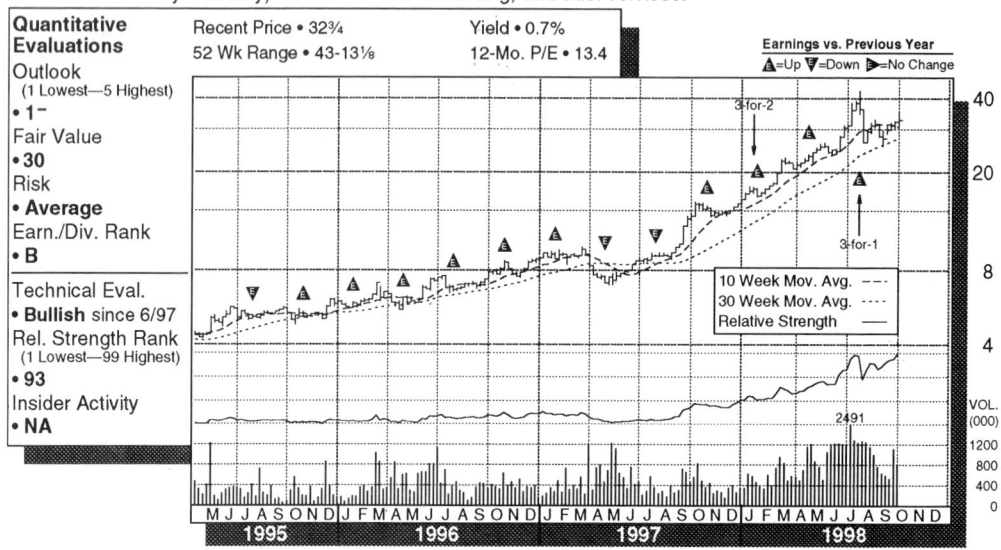

Earnings vs. Previous Year
▲=Up ▼=Down ▶=No Change

10 Week Mov. Avg. ---
30 Week Mov. Avg. ····
Relative Strength —

Business Profile - 30-JUL-98

This California-based holding company is a leading provider of real estate related financial and informational services to real property buyers and mortgage lenders. Subsidiaries include First American Title Insurance Co., a national and international title insurer; First American Real Estate Information Services, Inc., which offers tax monitoring, credit reporting, flood certification, mortgage loan servicing systems and property information services; and First American Home Buyers Protection Corp., a home warranty company. The company also provides trust and limited banking services. In May 1998, FAF acquired Wisconsin-based, Evans Title Companies, Inc. In June, FAF acquired Data Tree Corporation for about 1,900,000 shares (adjusted). Data Tree provides database management and document imaging systems to county recorders, governmental agencies and the title industry. Also in June, FAF acquired Florida Title & Abstract Co.

Operational Review - 30-JUL-98

Revenues in the first half of 1998 rose 57%, year to year, reflecting a robust national economy and exceptionally strong real estate activity in California. Total expenses were up less sharply (44%), on higher salaries and other personnel costs, increased premiums retained by agents and greater other operating expenses; pretax income more than quadrupled. After taxes and minority interests, net income surged to $90,071,000 ($1.63 a share), from $21,382,000 ($0.40), adjusted.

Stock Performance - 02-OCT-98

In the past 30 trading days, FAF's shares have increased 4%, compared to a 7% fall in the S&P 500. Average trading volume for the past five days was 157,320 shares, compared with the 40-day moving average of 167,341 shares.

Key Stock Statistics

Dividend Rate/Share	0.24	Shareholders	3,100
Shs. outstg. (M)	57.3	Market cap. (B)	$ 1.9
Avg. daily vol. (M)	0.154	Inst. holdings	39%
Tang. Bk. Value/Share	7.50		
Beta	0.92		

Value of $10,000 invested 5 years ago: $ 62,169

Fiscal Year Ending Dec. 31

	1998	1997	1996	1995	1994	1993
Revenues (Million $)						
1Q	605.0	382.9	347.4	261.1	372.4	279.0
2Q	704.3	450.4	413.4	293.2	369.0	333.5
3Q	—	501.9	411.3	331.3	334.9	376.8
4Q	—	552.4	425.5	364.5	300.1	409.1
Yr.	—	1,887	1,598	1,250	1,376	1,398
Earnings Per Share ($)						
1Q	**0.83**	**0.05**	0.17	-0.25	0.18	0.09
2Q	**0.80**	**0.35**	0.38	0.02	0.15	0.34
3Q	—	**0.39**	0.27	0.18	0.09	0.38
4Q	—	**0.42**	0.23	0.19	-0.06	0.40
Yr.	—	**1.21**	1.04	0.15	0.37	1.22

Next earnings report expected: late October

Dividend Data (Dividends have been paid since 1909.)

Amount ($)	Date Decl.	Ex-Div. Date	Stock of Record	Payment Date
0.150	Feb. 27	Mar. 27	Mar. 31	Apr. 15 '98
0.150	Jun. 26	Jul. 01	Jul. 06	Jul. 17 '98
3-for-1	Jun. 26	Jul. 20	Jul. 07	Jul. 17 '98
0.060	Aug. 28	Sep. 28	Sep. 30	Oct. 15 '98

A Division of The McGraw-Hill Companies

Business Summary - 30-JUL-98

With operations throughout the U.S. and abroad, First American Financial has emerged as a leading provider of real estate related financial and information services. Its growth has been achieved primarily through an active acquisition strategy, which has emphasized geographic expansion and the development of new products and markets. Looking forward, First American sees significant opportunities to expand on its operations overseas, where the markets for the company's primary services are underdeveloped.

In 1997, title insurance operations accounted for 79% of operating revenues and 62% of pretax profits. Title insurance protects lenders against challenges to the title claim to a property, and it protects policyholders against loss from a prior occurrence, such as a forged deed somewhere in the chain of title. In 1996, the most recent data available, First American had the largest market share of title insurance written in the U.S.

In 1996, low mortgage interest rates and an improved national real estate economy helped produce high volumes of new home sales and residential resales. This favorable environment continued in 1997, and contributed to record setting residential resale transactions, an increase in new home sales and renewed commercial activity. Combined with higher refinance and home equity transactions, FAF's title insurance segment produced pretax profits of $95.6 million in 1997 ($66.1 million in 1996), on revenues of $1.5 billion ($1.3 billion).

The bulk of the company's remaining revenues and profits were generated by FAF's real estate information business. This segment provides services such as real estate tax monitoring, mortgage credit reporting and flood zone determination and was almost entirely built through acquisitions. This segment accounted for 29% of pretax profits in 1997 (40% in 1996) and 18% of total revenues (16%).

In December 1997, FAF and Experian Group completed the merger of their respective real estate subsidiaries. The new company is owned 80% by FAF and 20% by Experian. The merger created the largest and most diverse U.S. provider of information technology and decision support solutions for the mortgage and real estate industries, with revenues exceeding $450 million, and a staff of 4,000. In 1998's first quarter, FAF recorded a $32.4 million investment gain associated with the Experian joint venture. On an after-tax basis, the gain amounted to $19.6 million, or $0.36 a share, adjusted for the 3-for-1 stock split distributed on July 17, 1998.

Per Share Data ($)

(Year Ended Dec. 31)	1997	1996	1995	1994	1993	1992	1991	1990	1989	1988
Tangible Bk. Val.	5.35	5.10	4.50	4.50	4.49	3.20	2.07	2.73	2.74	2.80
Oper. Earnings	NA	NA	0.13	0.38	1.21	NA	NA	NA	NA	NA
Earnings	1.21	1.04	0.15	0.37	1.22	1.01	0.07	0.07	0.29	0.27
Dividends	0.17	0.15	0.13	0.13	0.11	0.09	0.09	0.09	0.08	0.07
Payout Ratio	14%	15%	90%	36%	9%	9%	120%	117%	27%	28%
Prices - High	16⁵/₈	9¹/₈	6¹/₈	8³/₈	8³/₄	6	2⁷/₈	3¹/₈	3³/₄	3³/₈
- Low	7	5¹/₂	3⁵/₈	3¹/₂	5	2⁵/₈	1³/₈	1⁷/₁₆	2⁷/₁₆	2³/₈
P/E Ratio - High	14	9	41	23	7	6	40	43	13	13
- Low	6	5	25	10	4	3	20	20	9	9

Income Statement Analysis (Million $)

	1997	1996	1995	1994	1993	1992	1991	1990	1989	1988
Premium Inc.	1,860	1,268	1,035	1,222	1,249	998	738	688	681	630
Net Invest. Inc.	27.3	26.4	23.0	19.4	19.9	13.1	19.2	19.7	16.0	12.5
Oth. Revs.	Nil	303	192	135	129	0.1	Nil	Nil	2.0	1.5
Total Revs.	1,887	1,598	1,250	1,376	1,398	1,115	757	708	699	644
Pretax Inc.	106	89.2	13.8	32.0	104	71.5	6.1	-6.1	20.7	20.0
Net Oper. Inc.	NA	NA	6.6	19.3	61.8	NA	NA	NA	NA	NA
Net Inc.	64.7	53.6	7.6	18.9	62.1	43.3	3.0	3.3	13.5	12.3

Balance Sheet & Other Fin. Data (Million $)

	1997	1996	1995	1994	1993	1992	1991	1990	1989	1988
Cash & Equiv.	182	173	146	154	130	120	77.4	67.2	72.8	80.2
Premiums Due	128	89.4	75.1	47.1	64.6	48.2	38.5	27.1	35.8	32.2
Invest. Assets: Bonds	152	131	129	149	166	138	68.1	81.6	72.8	66.1
Invest. Assets: Stocks	13.9	8.5	21.4	21.8	21.1	7.6	2.7	8.0	10.1	6.8
Invest. Assets: Loans	63.4	54.3	46.1	40.5	33.3	30.8	26.8	15.0	NA	NA
Invest. Assets: Total	293	245	240	255	262	219	136	138	144	116
Deferred Policy Costs	25.0	24.8	24.3	26.6	23.5	18.4	Nil	Nil	Nil	Nil
Total Assets	1,168	980	874	829	786	691	520	465	451	386
Debt	42.0	71.3	77.2	89.6	85.0	82.0	93.0	102	97.0	86.0
Common Eqty.	411	352	303	292	284	217	138	146	147	148
Prop. & Cas. Loss Ratio	NA	NA	NA	9.0	10.1	9.8	10.3	11.3	9.4	11.6
Prop. & Cas. Expense Ratio	NA	NA	NA	99.7	92.2	93.4	90.2	91.1	89.0	86.0
Prop. & Cas. Combined Ratio	NA	NA	NA	108.7	102.3	103.2	100.5	102.4	98.4	97.6
% Return On Revs.	3.4	3.4	0.6	1.4	4.4	3.9	0.4	0.5	1.9	1.9
% Ret. on Equity	16.9	16.4	2.6	6.6	24.8	24.4	2.1	2.3	9.7	8.6

Data as orig. reptd.; bef. results of disc. opers. and/or spec. items. Per share data adj. for stk. divs. as of ex-div. date. Bold denotes diluted EPS (FASB 128). E-Estimated. NA-Not Available. NM-Not Meaningful. NR-Not Ranked.

Office—114 East 5th St., Santa Ana, CA 92701-4642. **Tel**—(714) 558-3211. **Website**—http://www.firstam.com **Chrmn**—D. P. Kennedy. **Pres**—P. S. Kennedy. **EVP, CFO & Investor Contact**—Thomas A. Klemens. **VP & Secy**—M. R. Arnesen. **Dirs**—G. L. Argyros, G.J. Beban, J. D. Chatham, W. G. Davis, J. L. Doti, L. W. Douglas Jr., P. B. Fay Jr., D.F. Frey, D. P. Kennedy, P. S. Kennedy, A. R. Moiso, R. J. Munzer, F. E. O'Bryan, R. B. Payne, D. V. Skilling, V. M. Ueberroth. **Transfer Agent & Registrar**—First American Trust Co., Santa Ana. **Incorporated**—in California in 1894. **Empl**—12,149. **S&P Analyst:** Michael Schneider

STANDARD &POOR'S
STOCK REPORTS

First BanCorp

887J

NYSE Symbol **FBP**

In S&P SmallCap 600

03-OCT-98

Industry:
Banks (Regional)

Summary: FBP is the holding company for Firstbank Puerto Rico, a Puerto Rico-chartered commercial bank.

Quantitative Evaluations	
Outlook (1 Lowest—5 Highest)	
• **NA**	
Fair Value	
• **NA**	
Risk	
• **Low**	
Earn./Div. Rank	
• **B**	
Technical Eval.	
• **NA**	
Rel. Strength Rank (1 Lowest—99 Highest)	
• **80**	
Insider Activity	
• **NA**	

Recent Price • 25¾
52 Wk Range • 29⅝-15⅛

Yield • 1.2%
12-Mo. P/E • 15.7

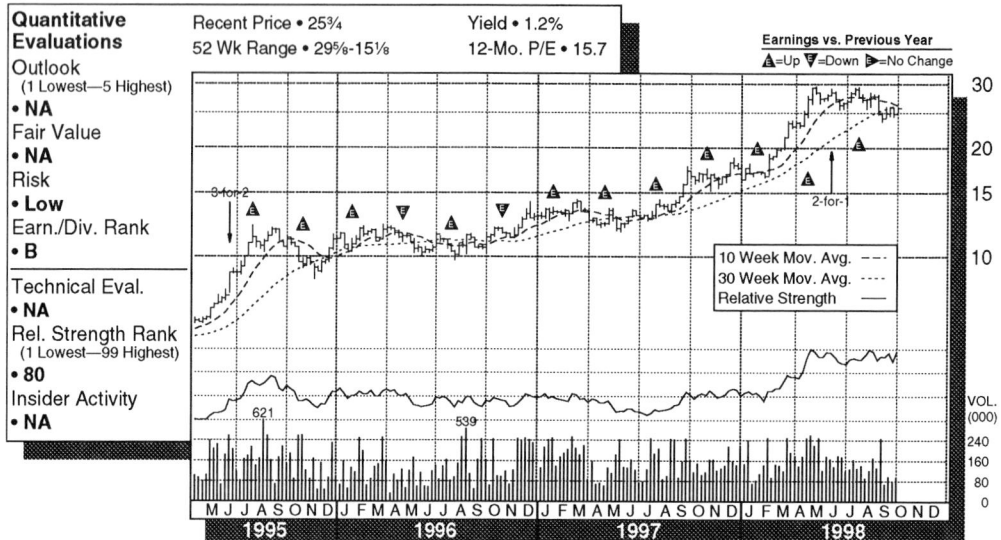

Earnings vs. Previous Year
▲=Up ▼=Down ▶=No Change

10 Week Mov. Avg. ---
30 Week Mov. Avg. ....
Relative Strength ——

Business Profile - 31-AUG-98

Effective October 1, 1998, FBP reorganized into a bank holding company, named First BanCorp., which is now the holding company for FirstBank Puerto Rico. Management expects the change in structure to greatly increase FBP's flexibility to take advantage of future business opportunities. The bank is exploring options for diversification, including introducing new products and expanding its geographic reach to the U.S. mainland and neighboring Caribbean islands. The bank has been investing significantly in new technology and infrastructure to support new products on the commercial lending side, and new consumer credit monitoring systems.

Operational Review - 31-AUG-98

Net interest income in the six months ended June 30, 1998, rose 6.0%, year to year. Other income increased 62%, but the provision for possible loan losses climbed 51%. Pretax income was up 0.7%. After taxes at 9.8%, versus 14.9%, net income rose 6.8%, to $25,061,000 ($0.04 a share) from $23,461,000 ($0.77, as adjusted).

Stock Performance - 02-OCT-98

In the past 30 trading days, FBP's shares have declined 7%, compared to a 7% fall in the S&P 500. Average trading volume for the past five days was 18,780 shares, compared with the 40-day moving average of 27,441 shares.

Key Stock Statistics

Dividend Rate/Share	0.30	Shareholders	700
Shs. outstg. (M)	29.8	Market cap. (B)	$0.769
Avg. daily vol. (M)	0.018	Inst. holdings	21%
Tang. Bk. Value/Share	7.91		
Beta	0.84		

Value of $10,000 invested 5 years ago: $ 115,388

Fiscal Year Ending Dec. 31

	1998	1997	1996	1995	1994	1993
Revenues (Million $)						
1Q	94.15	76.77	65.21	—	45.50	—
2Q	—	—	68.23	—	47.94	—
3Q	—	—	74.02	—	50.94	43.36
4Q	—	—	47.94	—	54.10	
Yr.	—	325.0	286.1	256.8	198.5	176.6
Earnings Per Share ($)						
1Q	**0.41**	0.39	0.34	0.37	0.23	0.10
2Q	**0.43**	0.39	0.35	0.30	0.25	0.12
3Q		0.40	0.15	0.58	0.26	0.18
4Q	—	0.41	0.38	0.33	0.27	0.22
Yr.	—	**1.57**	1.22	1.58	1.00	0.63

Next earnings report expected: early October

Dividend Data (Dividends have been paid since 1995.)

Amount ($)	Date Decl.	Ex-Div. Date	Stock of Record	Payment Date
0.150	Apr. 30	May. 13	May. 15	May. 29 '98
2-for-1	Apr. 30	Jun. 01	May. 15	May. 29 '98
0.075	May. 26	Jun. 11	Jun. 15	Jun. 30 '98
0.075	Aug. 21	Sep. 11	Sep. 15	Sep. 30 '98

A Division of The **McGraw·Hill** *Companies*

STANDARD
&POOR'S
STOCK REPORTS

First BanCorp

887J
03-OCT-98

Business Summary - 31-AUG-98

First BanCorp (FBP) is the holding company for FirstBank Puerto Rico, the second largest independently owned commercial bank in Puerto Rico, with total assets of $3.3 billion as of December 31, 1997. The bank specializes in consumer lending in the Puerto Rican market, offering an array of financial services to a growing number of consumer and commercial customers.

Although the bank's $1.1 billion consumer loan portfolio is concentrated in auto loans, personal loans and credit cards, FBP also provides other consumer products such as marine financing and credit line accounts. In addition, the bank has a $585 million commercial loan portfolio, including real estate commercial loans, serving a wide range of small and medium sized businesses as well as professional practices.

The bank's strategy is to emphasize consumer lending, primarily auto loans, personal loans and credit cards. FBP continues to develop commercial mortgage lending as a secondary area of concentration. In pursuing growth in these selected lines of business, the bank has strengthened its capital base, built reserves for possible loan losses and improved asset/liability management. During the past three years, the bank has increased its portfolio of asset based commercial loans and commercial real estate loans as a way to diversify the portfolio.

The bank operates 36 branches (including two in the U.S. Virgin Islands), 12 loan origination offices in Puerto Rico focusing on personal loans and credit cards, and five loan origination offices focusing on auto loans. It plans to open five new branches during 1998. In addition, FBP, through subsidiaries, operates 26 loan offices in Puerto Rico specializing in small personal loans and three offices specializing in vehicle rental.

As of December 31, 1997, the allowance for loan losses totaled $57,712,000 (equal to 2.95% of total loans and loans held for sale), compared with $55,254,000 (2.91%) a year earlier. Net chargeoffs amounted to $53,217,000 (2.79% of average loans) in 1997, versus $31,337,000 (1.80%) in 1996. At the end of 1997, nonperforming assets aggregated $74,317,000 (2.23% of total assets), compared with $70,176,000 (2.49%) a year earlier.

During 1997, the bank purchased 495,650 of its common shares (as adjusted), at a total cost of $6.9 million. Under a share repurchase program that began more than two years ago, the bank had acquired a total of 1,345,850 shares (adjusted) at a total cost of $15.9 million as of December 31, 1997.

October 1, 1998, FBP reorganized itself into a bank holding company named First BanCorp. Stockholders of FirstBank Puerto Rico became shareholders of First BanCorp, in the same proportion of shares owned before the conversion.

Per Share Data ($)

(Year Ended Dec. 31)	1997	1996	1995	1994	1993	1992	1991	1990	1989	1988
Tangible Bk. Val.	15.82	6.30	5.49	3.98	3.02	1.80	1.26	0.89	1.52	1.34
Earnings	1.57	1.22	1.58	1.00	0.63	0.37	0.28	-0.72	0.30	0.33
Dividends	0.48	0.20	0.08	Nil	Nil	Nil	Nil	0.02	0.07	NA
Payout Ratio	31%	16%	5%	Nil	Nil	Nil	Nil	NM	23%	NA
Prices - High	18⅞	14¼	12¼	6⅜	5¾	2⁵/₁₆	1	1⅜	1⁹/₁₆	NA
- Low	11¾	9¾	5½	4½	2¼	¹⁵/₁₆	¾	¹¹/₁₆	1⅛	NA
P/E Ratio - High	12	12	8	6	9	6	4	NM	5	NA
- Low	7	8	3	4	4	2	3	NM	4	NA

Income Statement Analysis (Million $)

	1997	1996	1995	1994	1993	1992	1991	1990	1989	1988
Net Int. Inc.	155	143	112	104	87.0	73.0	61.8	59.5	58.8	55.5
Tax Equiv. Adj.	9.7	4.9	7.8	5.4	NA	NA	NA	NA	NA	NA
Non Int. Inc.	28.5	24.8	25.2	18.2	17.1	13.6	18.9	12.6	13.2	8.9
Loan Loss Prov.	55.7	31.6	30.9	17.7	18.7	13.6	16.4	32.0	11.3	8.5
Exp./Op. Revs.	45%	48%	48%	50%	NA	NA	NA	NA	NA	NA
Pretax Inc.	55.7	49.9	63.4	43.4	28.5	18.3	12.9	-17.6	12.5	13.0
Eff. Tax Rate	15%	25%	23%	29%	23%	16%	11%	NM	6.40%	4.20%
Net Inc.	47.5	37.6	49.1	31.0	22.0	15.3	11.5	-17.7	11.7	12.5
% Net Int. Marg.	5.83	6.03	5.59	5.65	4.81	4.04	3.39	3.20	3.20	3.46

Balance Sheet & Other Fin. Data (Million $)

	1997	1996	1995	1994	1993	1992	1991	1990	1989	1988
Earning Assets:										
Money Mkt	0.5	126	Nil	18.9	NA	NA	NA	NA	NA	NA
Inv. Securities	1,266	694	766	563	NA	NA	NA	NA	NA	NA
Com'l Loans	278	233	189	127	NA	NA	NA	NA	NA	NA
Other Loans	1,681	1,663	1,367	1,374	NA	NA	NA	NA	NA	NA
Total Assets	3,327	2,822	2,433	2,175	1,914	1,889	1,898	1,908	1,928	1,819
Demand Deposits	140	136	129	127	NA	NA	NA	NA	NA	NA
Time Deposits	1,455	1,568	1,389	1,367	NA	NA	NA	NA	NA	NA
LT Debt	142	286	218	155	NA	NA	NA	NA	NA	NA
Common Eqty.	236	191	171	120	NA	NA	NA	NA	NA	NA
% Ret. on Assets	1.5	1.4	2.2	1.5	1.1	0.8	0.6	NM	0.6	0.7
% Ret. on Equity	22.2	20.8	33.2	29.1	29.8	26.9	24.6	NM	19.1	NA
% Loan Loss Resv.	3.0	2.9	3.5	2.5	2.5	2.7	2.3	2.0	0.5	0.4
% Loans/Deposits	116.9	107.1	102.5	100.5	NA	NA	NA	NA	NA	NA
% Equity to Assets	7.0	6.9	6.7	5.3	5.1	2.5	1.8	2.1	2.4	NA

Data as orig. reptd.; bef. results of disc opers. and/or spec. items. Per share data adj. for stk. divs. as of ex-div. date. Bold denotes diluted EPS (FASB 128). E-Estimated. NA-Not Available. NM-Not Meaningful. NR-Not Ranked.

Organized—in Puerto Rico in 1948.**Office**—1519 Ponce de Leon Ave., Stop 23-1/2, Santurce, PR 00908. **Tel**—(787) 729-8200. **Website**—http://www.1bankpr.com**Chrmn**—G. E. Malaret.**Pres & CEO**—A. Alvarez-Perez. **EVP, CFO & Investor Contact**—Annie Astor de Carbonell (787-729-8200). **Dirs**—A. Alvarez-Perez, J. J. Alvarez, A. A. de Carbonell, F. D. Fernandez, A. Lopez, G. E. Malaret, H. M. Nevares, A. Pavia-Villamil, J. Teixidor, A. L. Umpierre. **Transfer Agent & Registrar**—Bank of New York, NYC. **Empl**— 1,600. **S&P Analyst:** J.J.S.

First Midwest Bancorp   3886

NASDAQ Symbol **FMBI**

In S&P SmallCap 600

03-OCT-98

Industry: Banks (Regional)

Summary: This company, the third largest publicly traded bank holding company in Illinois, engages in commercial banking, trust, investment management and mortgage activities.

Quantitative Evaluations

Recent Price • 39⅝	Yield • 2.3%
52 Wk Range • 52-34⅛	12-Mo. P/E • 19.5

Outlook (1 Lowest—5 Highest)
• **1**⁻

Fair Value
• **36⅛**

Risk
• **Low**

Earn./Div. Rank
• **A-**

Technical Eval.
• **Bullish** since 8/98

Rel. Strength Rank (1 Lowest—99 Highest)
• **71**

Insider Activity
• **Neutral**

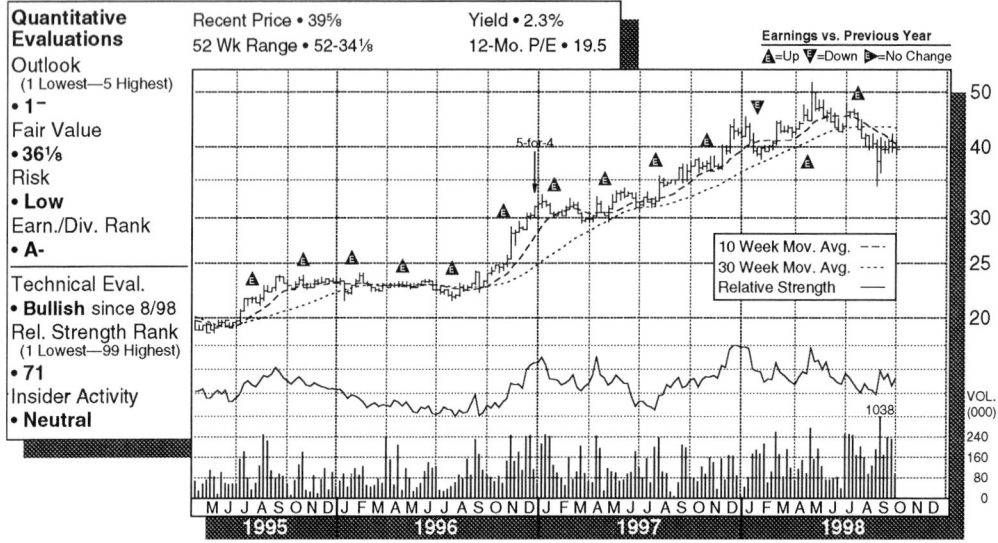

Earnings vs. Previous Year
▲=Up ▼=Down ▶=No Change

10 Week Mov. Avg. ---
30 Week Mov. Avg. ....
Relative Strength —

Business Profile - 20-AUG-98

On July 1, 1998, the company completed the acquisition of Heritage Financial Services, a $1.3 billion bank holding company with 17 offices serving 15 communities in southwest suburban Chicago. FMBI issued 9.7 million shares to conclude the transaction, which was accounted for as a pooling of interests. Heritage operations will be counted in FMBI's third quarter results and a pretax merger related charge of about $15.4 million is expected. The acquisition increases FMBI's deposit base in the Chicago area 48%, lifts overall deposits 40%, and raises FMBI's assets to $5.1 billion. The addition of Heritage should help FMBI continue a record of efficiency gains from acquisitions and centralization of administrative functions. In the first quarter of 1998, FMBI completed the integration of recently acquired SparBank, the parent of McHenry State Bank, with $445 million in assets.

Operational Review - 20-AUG-98

In the first half of 1998, net interest income fell 1.4%, year to year, as the net interest margin narrowed to 4.30%, from 4.59%. The provision for loan losses decreased to $1.8 million, from $3.3 million. Noninterest income was up 15%, as all major categories rose, and noninterest expense rose 2.4%, led by a 6.9% increase in salaries and wages. After taxes at 31.0%, versus 34.5%, net income advanced 12%, to $23,305,000 ($1.14 a share), from $20,862,000 ($1.03).

Stock Performance - 02-OCT-98

In the past 30 trading days, FMBI's shares have declined 2%, compared to a 7% fall in the S&P 500. Average trading volume for the past five days was 19,220 shares, compared with the 40-day moving average of 55,867 shares.

Key Stock Statistics

Dividend Rate/Share	0.90	Shareholders	3,000
Shs. outstg. (M)	29.8	Market cap. (B)	$ 1.2
Avg. daily vol. (M)	0.062	Inst. holdings	19%
Tang. Bk. Value/Share	17.18		
Beta	0.75		

Value of $10,000 invested 5 years ago: $ 29,104

Fiscal Year Ending Dec. 31

	1998	1997	1996	1995	1994	1993
Revenues (Million $)						
1Q	78.28	75.10	74.70	—	—	—
2Q	77.96	74.70	75.00	—	—	—
3Q	—	79.10	75.60	—	—	—
4Q	—	78.84	77.80	—	—	—
Yr.	—	307.7	303.1	309.4	265.4	247.9
Earnings Per Share ($)						
1Q	0.56	0.51	0.46	0.39	0.36	0.30
2Q	0.58	0.52	0.48	0.42	0.37	0.33
3Q	—	0.56	0.50	0.45	0.38	0.35
4Q	—	0.33	0.53	0.26	0.23	0.36
Yr.	—	1.92	1.95	1.51	1.34	1.34

Next earnings report expected: mid October

Dividend Data (Dividends have been paid since 1983.)

Amount ($)	Date Decl.	Ex-Div. Date	Stock of Record	Payment Date
0.225	Nov. 20	Dec. 23	Dec. 26	Jan. 22 '98
0.225	Feb. 18	Mar. 25	Mar. 27	Apr. 21 '98
0.225	May. 29	Jul. 06	Jul. 08	Jul. 21 '98
0.225	Aug. 19	Sep. 23	Sep. 25	Oct. 20 '98

A Division of The **McGraw·Hill** Companies

Business Summary - 20-AUG-98

First Midwest Bancorp, Inc. is the third largest independent publicly traded Illinois bank holding company. Following the July 1, 1998, completion of the acquisition of Heritage Financial Services, a $1.3 billion bank holding company based in Tinely Park, IL, FMBI operates 72 banking offices in northern Illinois and eastern Iowa. Fifty-six of the offices are located in suburban Chicago, where FMBI ranks ninth in overall share of deposits. FMBI ranks first or second in deposit share in four of the nine counties in the Chicago metropolitan statistical area. The company also operates in the Quad Cities area of Moline and Rock Island, IL, and Davenport and Bettendorf, IA.

In 1994, FMBI consolidated all support, administrative and clerical functions formerly spread across the company. As of June 30, 1995, FMBI's four banking regions had been merged to create the First Midwest Bank, with $3.6 billion in assets at December 31, 1997. The First Midwest Trust subsidiary administered about $1.6 billion in assets at year-end 1997. With the addition of Heritage, FMBI had assets of $5.1 billion and a market capitalization of $1.3 billion at July 1, 1998.

FMBI's gross loans outstanding at the end of 1997 totaled $2.3 billion. The bank serves a diverse customer base, with 30% of loans in the real estate-commercial sector, 28% consumer, 25% commercial & industrial, 10% real estate-1 to 4 family, 5% real estate-construction, 2% agricultural, and 1% in other areas at year-end 1997.

FMBI's credit quality has been improving. At December 31, 1997, nonperforming assets amounted to $15,193,000 (0.65% of loans plus foreclosed real estate), down from $19,524,000 (0.83%) a year earlier. The reserve for loan losses at the end of 1997 was $37,344,00 (1.60% of net loans outstanding), versus $32,202,000 (1.37%) a year earlier.

FMBI's July 1998 acquisition of Heritage was accomplished through an exchange of stock in which each share of Heritage stock was converted into 0.7695 shares of FMBI, resulting in the issuance of 9.7 million shares of FMBI. Three former Heritage directors joined the FMBI board. Earlier, in February, FMBI completed the merger and integration of SparBank, Inc., the holding company for the $445 million McHenry State Bank. McHenry State has a 14% share of deposits in the northwest suburban Chicago county of McHenry.

Per Share Data ($) (Year Ended Dec. 31)	1997	1996	1995	1994	1993	1992	1991	1990	1989	1988
Tangible Bk. Val.	16.82	16.08	14.58	11.17	11.97	12.12	11.38	10.60	9.74	8.58
Earnings	1.92	1.97	1.51	1.34	1.34	1.14	1.14	1.44	1.60	1.04
Dividends	0.82	0.70	0.61	0.54	0.48	0.42	0.42	0.42	0.38	0.32
Payout Ratio	43%	36%	40%	41%	36%	36%	37%	29%	24%	31%
Prices - High	45 1/4	33	23 3/4	23	22 5/8	16 1/4	16	18 3/8	20	13 1/4
- Low	29 3/8	21 3/8	18 5/8	17 5/8	15 3/8	11 3/8	10 3/8	9 3/8	13 1/8	7 1/2
P/E Ratio - High	24	17	16	17	17	14	14	13	13	13
- Low	15	11	12	13	11	10	9	7	8	7
Income Statement Analysis (Million $)										
Net Int. Inc.	145	123	119	108	104	97.6	94.3	88.3	83.2	71.8
Tax Equiv. Adj.	5.0	2.2	1.2	1.4	1.6	2.3	2.8	3.0	3.1	4.0
Non Int. Inc.	36.2	30.8	27.9	25.2	27.9	23.4	20.4	14.6	19.1	11.9
Loan Loss Prov.	8.8	7.5	11.3	8.5	11.4	15.4	15.5	8.5	6.0	7.2
Exp./Op. Revs.	63%	61%	64%	70%	84%	88%	90%	87%	83%	88%
Pretax Inc.	59.4	53.4	40.5	32.1	31.4	25.5	23.6	30.7	34.7	19.7
Eff. Tax Rate	35%	36%	37%	37%	34%	30%	25%	26%	32%	23%
Net Inc.	38.8	33.7	25.7	20.4	20.8	17.9	17.8	22.6	23.5	15.1
% Net Int. Marg.	4.54	4.33	4.04	4.24	4.60	4.80	4.50	4.60	4.80	4.80
Balance Sheet & Other Fin. Data (Million $)										
Earning Assets:										
Money Mkt	31.1	23.1	7.9	NA	2.3	Nil	Nil	35.1	28.6	84.0
Inv. Securities	995	792	859	865	893	640	704	749	578	511
Com'l Loans	1,273	571	657	548	516	540	543	626	587	504
Other Loans	1,061	1,514	1,449	1,237	1,073	917	848	745	614	656
Total Assets	3,614	3,119	3,207	2,875	2,687	2,297	2,311	2,368	2,082	1,931
Demand Deposits	473	350	361	347	331	305	269	254	255	276
Time Deposits	2,323	1,911	1,911	1,648	1,603	1,577	1,547	1,683	1,298	1,390
LT Debt	Nil	Nil	Nil	Nil	Nil	Nil	Nil	Nil	12.1	13.4
Common Eqty.	338	262	249	186	200	189	178	166	143	125
% Ret. on Assets	1.2	1.1	0.8	0.7	0.8	0.8	0.8	1.0	1.2	0.9
% Ret. on Equity	12.9	13.2	11.2	10.6	10.8	9.8	10.3	14.3	17.5	12.7
% Loan Loss Resv.	1.6	1.4	1.4	1.4	1.4	1.5	1.5	1.3	1.3	1.3
% Loans/Deposits	83.5	92.2	92.7	89.5	82.2	77.4	74.6	70.8	76.6	68.8
% Equity to Assets	8.9	8.1	7.3	6.9	7.8	8.0	7.4	7.3	6.7	6.9

Data as orig. reptd.; bef. results of disc. opers. and/or spec. items. Per share data adj. for stk. divs. as of ex-div. date. Bold denotes diluted EPS (FASB 128). E-Estimated. NA-Not Available. NM-Not Meaningful. NR-Not Ranked.

Office—300 Park Blvd., Suite 405, P.O. Box 459, Itasca, IL 60143-0459. **Tel**—(630) 875-7450. **Chrmn & CEO**—R. P. O'Meara. **Pres & COO**—J. M. O'Meara. **EVP & CFO**—D. J. Swistowicz. **Investor Contact**—James M. Roolf (630-875-7452). **Dirs**—A. B. Barber, V. A. Brunner, B. S. Chelberg, W. J. Cowlin, O. R. Edwards, J. W. England, T. M. Garvin, J. M. O'Meara, R. P. O'Meara, J. Payan, J. L. Sterling, J. S. Vanderwoude, R. T. Wojcik. **Transfer Agent**—American Securities Transfer, Lakewood, Colorado. **Incorporated**—in Delaware in 1982. **Empl**— 1,250. **S&P Analyst:** T. W. Smith, CFA

FirstMerit Corp.   3894M

NASDAQ Symbol **FMER**

In S&P SmallCap 600

10-OCT-98

Industry: Banks (Regional)

Summary: This bank holding company, with about $6.2 billion in assets, operates about 130 offices, primarily in northeastern Ohio.

Quantitative Evaluations	
Outlook (1 Lowest—5 Highest) • **1⁻**	
Fair Value • **22**	
Risk • **Low**	
Earn./Div. Rank • **A-**	
Technical Eval. • **Bearish** since 8/98	
Rel. Strength Rank (1 Lowest—99 Highest) • **58**	
Insider Activity • **Favorable**	

Recent Price • 21⅞   Yield • 2.9%
52 Wk Range • 34⅜-20¾   12-Mo. P/E • 15.2

Earnings vs. Previous Year
▲=Up ▼=Down ▷=No Change

10 Week Mov. Avg. ---
30 Week Mov. Avg. ····
Relative Strength —

2-for-1

Business Profile - 11-SEP-98

In August 1998, FMER announced an agreement to acquire Signal Corp. (NASDAQ: SGNL), a $1.9 billion Ohio-based bank holding company, for $470 million in stock. The transaction is set to close in early 1999. In April 1998, FMER agreed to acquire Security First Corp., in a stock swap valued at around $256 million. The acquisition of Security First, with $678 million in assets and 14 branches in northeastern Ohio, is set to close in late 1998. The deal will solidify FMER's presence in six counties and offer cross selling opportunities. Results in 1997 benefited from FMER's move to reduce the level of low-yielding loans and increase commercial and consumer loans, as higher net interest margins more than offset a decline in earning assets and greater loss provisions. The recent corporate restructuring program, which included back-office consolidation, staff reductions and replacement of computer systems and equipment, has led to improved efficiencies.

Operational Review - 11-SEP-98

Net interest income in the first six months of 1998 rose 4.1%, year to year, as growth in earning assets more than offset a slight decline in the net interest margin (5.25% versus 5.31%). The provision for loan losses climbed 18%, to $10.9 million, from $9.2 million. Noninterest income grew 22%, thanks to strong fee income growth, while noninterest expense grew 10%. Net income advanced 11% to $46.1 million ($0.73 per share, diluted), from $41.6 million ($0.65).

Stock Performance - 09-OCT-98

In the past 30 trading days, FMER's shares have declined 4%, compared to a 4% fall in the S&P 500. Average trading volume for the past five days was 85,720 shares, compared with the 40-day moving average of 123,036 shares.

Key Stock Statistics

Dividend Rate/Share	0.64	Shareholders	7,000
Shs. outstg. (M)	69.3	Market cap. (B)	$ 1.5
Avg. daily vol. (M)	0.143	Inst. holdings	20%
Tang. Bk. Value/Share	9.91		
Beta	0.93		

Value of $10,000 invested 5 years ago: $ 22,240

Fiscal Year Ending Dec. 31

	1998	1997	1996	1995	1994	1993
Revenues (Million $)						
1Q	125.8	118.1	121.3	120.9	80.64	83.40
2Q	136.1	122.0	121.1	121.5	88.86	84.41
3Q	—	125.0	122.2	122.8	95.32	83.03
4Q	—	70.33	129.7	119.9	108.9	81.23
Yr.	—	435.6	494.2	485.1	373.7	332.1
Earnings Per Share ($)						
1Q	0.35	0.32	0.29	-0.02	0.28	0.26
2Q	0.38	0.33	0.29	0.19	0.28	0.28
3Q	—	0.35	0.21	0.25	0.28	0.28
4Q	—	0.36	0.29	-0.04	0.28	0.47
Yr.	—	1.36	1.09	0.39	1.11	1.09

Next earnings report expected: mid October

Dividend Data (Dividends have been paid since 1939.)

Amount ($)	Date Decl.	Ex-Div. Date	Stock of Record	Payment Date
0.160	Nov. 20	Nov. 26	Dec. 01	Dec. 15 '97
0.160	Feb. 19	Feb. 26	Mar. 02	Mar. 16 '98
0.160	May. 21	May. 28	Jun. 01	Jun. 15 '98
0.160	Aug. 20	Aug. 27	Aug. 31	Sep. 21 '98

A Division of The McGraw-Hill Companies

FirstMerit Corporation

Business Summary - 11-SEP-98

After spending almost two years streamlining its operations to increase productivity and profitability, FirstMerit Corporation (FMER) re-entered the consolidation market in May 1997, with the acquisition of Abell & Associates, a nationally known life insurance and financial consulting firm. Subsequently, in October 1997, this bank holding company agreed to purchase three branches from First Western Bank. On May 22, 1998, FMER acquired Elyria-based CoBancorp, for about $174 million. FirstMerit, which now operates 129 offices throughout 11 counties in Ohio, recently consolidated administrative and processing functions, cut staff levels, and implemented a $9.5 million platform/teller technology. Additionally, FMER created a stand-alone mortgage company, to complement the bank's existing credit card and trust businesses.

FMER aims to capitalize on its community banking orientation by adhering to high customer service standards in its banking network. Its principal subsidiary is First National Bank of Ohio, which has over 60 offices. Other units include Old Phoenix National Bank of Medina, EST National Bank, Peoples National Bank, Citizens National Bank and Peoples Bank, N.A. The company also owns FirstMerit Mortgage Co.

One of the more important recent undertakings was the shifting of the company's loan portfolio toward higher yielding commercial and consumer loans (which also have higher loss ratios), away from the traditional residential portfolio. Total loans, which grew to $3.83 billion at December 31, 1997, were divided in recent years:

	1997	1996	1995
Commercial, financial & agricultural	23%	20%	15%
Real estate	51%	53%	59%
Consumer / installment	22%	22%	21%
Lease financing	4%	5%	5%

The net yield on a bank's earning assets, or the net interest margin, is affected by changes in the volume and mix of assets and liabilities, as well as changes in interest rates. FMER earned higher net interest income in 1997, as a higher net interest margin (5.25%, versus 4.94% in 1996), due largely to a shift to higher yielding loans, outweighed a decline in the overall level of earning assets. Unfortunately, the price of moving to higher yielding loans involved taking on a greater level of risk -- net chargeoffs (amount of loans written off as uncollectible) rose to 0.45% of average loans in 1997, from 0.40% in 1996, while nonperforming assets climbed to 0.35% of total loans, from 0.29% a year earlier.

Per Share Data ($) (Year Ended Dec. 31)	1997	1996	1995	1994	1993	1992	1991	1990	1989	1988
Tangible Bk. Val.	8.56	8.20	8.11	7.95	7.75	6.67	6.01	6.13	6.13	5.94
Earnings	1.36	1.09	0.39	1.11	1.09	1.01	0.79	0.69	0.80	0.78
Dividends	0.61	0.55	0.51	0.49	0.45	0.41	0.40	0.38	0.37	0.34
Payout Ratio	44%	50%	132%	44%	41%	41%	51%	55%	46%	44%
Prices - High	30¾	18	15¼	13⅞	15⅜	11¾	9½	7½	8⅝	8⅜
- Low	17⅜	13⅞	10¾	10⅞	10⅜	9	5⅛	4⅛	6⅝	6¼
P/E Ratio - High	23	17	40	13	14	12	12	11	11	11
- Low	13	13	28	10	9	9	7	6	8	8
Income Statement Analysis (Million $)										
Net Int. Inc.	255	251	236	201	184	180	152	141	129	108
Tax Equiv. Adj.	3.2	3.0	3.8	4.6	5.3	5.6	6.9	9.1	10.2	10.7
Non Int. Inc.	81.6	84.3	68.0	56.9	54.3	49.2	44.1	37.9	34.2	30.2
Loan Loss Prov.	21.6	17.8	19.8	4.5	6.6	17.4	11.4	11.7	7.1	5.0
Exp./Op. Revs.	57%	62%	74%	64%	62%	60%	64%	65%	62%	61%
Pretax Inc.	126	106	56.7	86.4	80.7	73.1	55.0	46.1	50.0	42.1
Eff. Tax Rate	32%	33%	55%	30%	32%	31%	28%	24%	23%	19%
Net Inc.	86.3	70.9	25.7	60.3	55.2	50.7	39.6	34.9	38.6	33.9
% Net Int. Marg.	5.25	4.98	4.56	4.85	5.28	5.37	4.68	4.53	4.71	4.85
Balance Sheet & Other Fin. Data (Million $)										
Earning Assets:										
Money Mkt	33.1	15.6	12.6	4.0	59.0	95.0	82.0	NA	NA	NA
Inv. Securities	1,117	1,188	1,403	1,378	1,210	1,167	1,119	1,046	914	876
Com'l Loans	1,020	908	769	626	487	442	419	422	546	481
Other Loans	2,815	2,748	3,001	2,554	1,909	1,881	1,832	1,739	1,406	1,251
Total Assets	5,307	5,228	5,597	4,924	3,997	3,916	3,766	3,722	3,334	3,049
Demand Deposits	1,240	1,250	1,243	1,080	688	639	531	529	500	464
Time Deposits	3,015	2,955	3,259	2,783	2,739	2,745	2,737	2,700	2,344	2,184
LT Debt	Nil	Nil	Nil	Nil	Nil	Nil	Nil	Nil	16.9	21.2
Common Eqty.	530	524	543	432	392	358	327	308	297	258
% Ret. on Assets	1.6	1.3	0.5	1.3	1.4	1.3	1.1	1.0	1.2	1.3
% Ret. on Equity	16.4	13.3	4.8	14.1	14.7	14.8	12.5	11.7	13.6	14.2
% Loan Loss Resv.	1.4	1.3	1.2	1.2	1.3	1.3	1.1	1.1	1.0	1.0
% Loans/Deposits	90.1	85.3	83.8	82.3	69.9	68.6	68.8	66.7	68.4	65.4
% Equity to Assets	10.0	9.9	9.4	9.3	9.5	9.1	8.6	8.3	8.8	9.2

Data as orig. reptd.; bef. results of disc opers. and/or spec. items. Per share data adj. for stk. divs. as of ex-div. date. Bold denotes diluted EPS (FASB 128). E-Estimated. NA-Not Available. NM-Not Meaningful. NR-Not Ranked.

Office—III Cascade Plaza, 7th Floor, Akron, OH 44308. **Tel**—(330) 996-6300. **Website**—http://www.firstmerit.com **Chrm & CEO**—J. R. Cochran. **Pres & COO**—S. A. Bostic.**SVP & Investor Contact**—G. J. Elek. **EVP, Fin & Admn**—J.R. Gravo. **SVP & Secy**—T. E. Patton.**Dirs**—K. S. Belden, R. C. Blair, J. C. Blickle, R. W. Briggs, R. M. Carter, J. R. Cochran, R. Collela, E. A. Dalton, T. L. Haines, C. J. Isroff, P. A. Lloyd II, R. G. Merzweiler, S. E. Myers, G. H. Neal, R. T. Read, J. T. Rogers, Jr., R. N. Seaman, D. Spitzer. **Transfer Agent**—First National Bank of Ohio. **Incorporated**—in Ohio in 1962. **Empl**— 2,300. **S&P Analyst:** C. A. S.

STANDARD &POOR'S
STOCK REPORTS

Fleming Cos.

903K

NYSE Symbol **FLM**

In S&P SmallCap 600

10-OCT-98

Industry:
Distributors (Food & Health)

Summary: Fleming, one of the largest food wholesalers in the U.S., is in the process of consolidating facilities and re-engineering operating processes to increase efficiency.

S&P Opinion: Hold (★★★)	Recent Price • 11¼	Yield • 0.7%
	52 Wk Range • 20¾-10¾	12-Mo. P/E • 8.7

Quantitative Evaluations

Outlook
(1 Lowest—5 Highest)
• **5**

Fair Value
• **20¾**

Risk
• **Average**

Earn./Div. Rank
• **B**

Technical Eval.
• **Bullish** since 1/98

Rel. Strength Rank
(1 Lowest—99 Highest)
• **48**

Insider Activity
• **NA**

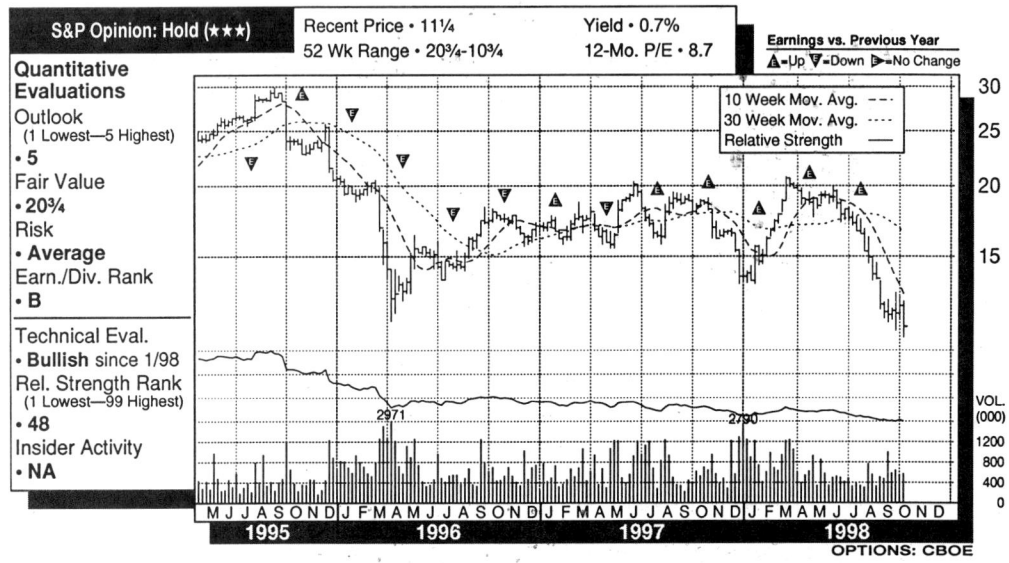

Earnings vs. Previous Year
▲=Up ▼=Down ▷=No Change

10 Week Mov. Avg. – – –
30 Week Mov. Avg. · · · ·
Relative Strength —

OPTIONS: CBOE

Overview - 05-AUG-98

We expect sales to decline at a low single-digit pace in 1998, reflecting increased competition in existing markets and a loss of customers due to stricter credit policies instituted by FLM. Margins will continue to widen in 1998, driven by penetration into more profitable business segments and a decline in credit loss expense, as a result of tighter credit granting policies with clients. Profitability in 1998 should benefit from the planned building of 20 company-owned stores, which typically generate higher margins than FLM's food distribution segment. The recent recapitalization of the company at less favorable interest rates will push interest expense to higher levels. However, a decline in legal costs will bolster the bottom line. We see 1998 EPS increasing fractionally to $1.34, from $1.32 in 1997, before a one-time charge associated with a litigation settlement.

Valuation - 05-AUG-98

We maintain our hold recommendation on Fleming, given the potential for improving results in the next year. Although the company is losing some of its food distribution business from Randall's and Furr's, this is lower than average margin business. In addition, the company is still contracting to do some business for Randall's, to help Randall's as it becomes more self-sufficient in its distribution needs. Meanwhile, the company has made progress in developing new distribution accounts. Fleming should also benefit from about 350 remodelings projected at company owned and customer stores which should help boost distribution revenues as these stores become more profitable at retail. The shares, recently trading at 12 times our 1998 EPS estimate, are a worthwhile holding given the potential for operational improvements.

Key Stock Statistics

S&P EPS Est. 1998	1.34	Tang. Bk. Value/Share	4.76
P/E on S&P Est. 1998	8.4	Beta	0.37
S&P EPS Est. 1999	1.45	Shareholders	13,500
Dividend Rate/Share	0.08	Market cap. (B)	$0.432
Shs. outstg. (M)	38.4	Inst. holdings	71%
Avg. daily vol. (M)	0.117		

Value of $10,000 invested 5 years ago: $ 4,302

Fiscal Year Ending Dec. 31

	1998	1997	1996	1995	1994	1993
Revenues (Million $)						
1Q	4,567	4,752	5,168	5,459	4,032	4,045
2Q	3,506	3,551	3,742	4,000	2,884	2,965
3Q	—	3,453	3,706	3,898	4,142	2,936
4Q	—	3,617	3,870	4,144	4,696	3,147
Yr.	—	15,373	16,487	17,502	15,753	13,092
Earnings Per Share ($)						
1Q	0.40	0.14	0.16	0.52	0.66	1.02
2Q	0.36	0.34	0.25	0.39	0.50	0.73
3Q	E0.27	0.26	0.03	0.10	0.07	0.55
4Q	E0.31	0.29	0.27	0.11	0.28	-1.28
Yr.	E1.34	1.02	0.71	1.12	1.51	1.02

Next earnings report expected: late October

Dividend Data (Dividends have been paid since 1927.)

Amount ($)	Date Decl.	Ex-Div. Date	Stock of Record	Payment Date
0.020	Oct. 20	Nov. 18	Nov. 20	Dec. 10 '97
0.020	Jan. 20	Feb. 18	Feb. 20	Mar. 10 '98
0.020	Apr. 27	May. 18	May. 20	Jun. 10 '98
0.020	Jul. 29	Aug. 18	Aug. 20	Sep. 10 '98

Business Summary - 05-AUG-98

Fleming Companies (FLM) turned a corner in 1997. Following significant challenges in 1995 and 1996, including lower profits and several lawsuits, the company was able to improve margins and grow earnings in 1997.

In late 1996, Fleming settled lawsuits with Premium Sales Corp. and Megafoods Stores Inc.. In addition, a $208 million judgment was set aside in its case with David's Supermarkets, and the case was settled in early 1997. In October 1997, FLM settled its lawsuit with 30%-owned Furr's Supermarkets, Inc., which had accused the company of overcharging for its products. Under the agreement, FLM's supply contract will be terminated in 19 months at the latest, and Fleming will pay Furr's $800,000 a month until the contract ends. FLM is currently in arbitration hearings with Randall's Food Markets, Inc., which is also accusing Fleming of charging inflated prices. In April 1998, 20 retailers in Kansas and Missouri filed suit against Fleming, also alleging intentional overcharging on the part of FLM.

FLM is one of the largest food wholesalers in the U.S., having grown mainly through acquisitions. At May 1, 1998, the company served over 3,000 retail food stores in 42 states, the District of Columbia, the Caribbean, Mexico, and Central and South American countries with a wide variety of inventory, including groceries, meats, produce, frozen foods, dairy products and general merchandise. Retail stores served by the company range in size from small convenience outlets to conventional supermarkets to large superstores, combination units and price-impact stores.

FLM offers a wide variety of support services to its retail customers designed to provide modern systems and programs to support the operation of their business.

In addition to providing food distribution, Fleming also operates over 275 company-owned retail food stores, which generated more than 20% of of revenues in 1997. The company is committed to growing this part of the business, given its higher profitability relative to the wholesale business.

The company has recently completed an extensive re-engineering process. The primary objectives were to lower the cost of goods to its retail customers; to align the retailers, manufacturers and FLM's business systems through technology; to maximize marketing capabilities by using the company's size and purchasing power; and to lower system costs through shared efficiencies.

The company has attributed lower year-to-year sales comparisons in recent periods to "cherry picking" by existing customers; the loss of Megafoods Stores as a customer; normal attrition; tightened credit standards; closed corporate stores; and negative press that has hurt prospecting.

Per Share Data ($)

(Year Ended Dec. 31)	1997	1996	1995	1994	1993	1992	1991	1990	1989	1988
Tangible Bk. Val.	3.29	2.10	1.65	2.42	15.93	16.19	14.44	9.98	7.18	7.48
Cash Flow	5.79	5.66	5.87	5.42	3.77	5.33	4.22	5.78	4.78	4.22
Earnings	1.02	0.71	1.12	1.51	1.02	3.33	2.06	3.06	2.54	2.43
Dividends	0.08	0.36	1.20	1.20	1.20	1.20	1.14	1.03	1.00	1.00
Payout Ratio	8%	51%	107%	79%	118%	37%	58%	34%	40%	44%
Prices - High	20⅜	20⅞	29⅞	30	34⅜	35⅛	40⅝	37⅝	40	35½
- Low	13⅜	11½	19⅛	22⅝	23¾	27¼	29⅞	28	27½	26½
P/E Ratio - High	20	29	27	20	34	11	20	12	16	15
- Low	13	16	17	15	23	8	15	9	11	11

Income Statement Analysis (Million $)

	1997	1996	1995	1994	1993	1992	1991	1990	1989	1988
Revs.	15,373	16,487	17,502	15,753	13,092	12,938	12,902	11,933	12,045	10,467
Oper. Inc.	418	396	402	329	293	348	350	325	302	218
Depr.	181	188	181	146	101	71.8	72.7	66.9	65.8	48.2
Int. Exp.	163	163	176	121	78.0	81.1	93.5	93.8	97.4	76.2
Pretax Inc.	83.0	54.6	85.9	112	72.0	195	117	165	139	117
Eff. Tax Rate	53%	51%	51%	50%	48%	39%	38%	41%	43%	44%
Net Inc.	39.0	26.7	42.0	56.0	37.0	119	72.3	97.3	80.1	65.4

Balance Sheet & Other Fin. Data (Million $)

	1997	1996	1995	1994	1993	1992	1991	1990	1989	1988
Cash	30.0	63.7	4.4	28.4	1.6	4.7	21.1	21.3	37.2	37.3
Curr. Assets	1,495	1,564	1,651	1,820	1,361	1,403	1,343	1,208	1,141	1,138
Total Assets	3,924	4,055	4,297	4,608	3,103	3,118	2,956	2,768	2,689	2,559
Curr. Liab.	1,155	1,343	1,286	1,324	919	875	915	830	778	850
LT Debt	1,494	1,453	1,717	1,995	1,004	1,038	952	981	692	935
Common Eqty.	1,094	1,076	1,083	1,079	1,060	1,060	957	764	692	634
Total Cap.	2,649	2,567	2,840	3,125	2,092	2,138	1,935	1,839	1,774	1,632
Cap. Exp.	129	129	117	150	56.0	114	82.0	69.0	137	278
Cash Flow	220	215	223	202	139	191	142	160	140	114
Curr. Ratio	1.3	1.2	1.3	1.4	1.5	1.6	1.5	1.5	1.5	1.3
% LT Debt of Cap.	56.4	56.6	60.5	63.8	48.0	48.6	49.2	53.4	55.8	57.3
% Net Inc.of Revs.	0.3	0.2	0.2	0.4	0.3	0.9	0.6	0.8	0.7	0.6
% Ret. on Assets	1.0	0.6	0.9	1.4	1.2	3.8	2.3	3.5	3.0	3.3
% Ret. on Equity	3.6	2.5	3.9	5.2	3.5	11.6	7.5	12.7	11.1	10.9

Data as orig. reptd.; bef. results of disc. opers. and/or spec. items. Per share data adj. for stk. divs. as of ex-div. date. Bold denotes diluted EPS (FASB 128). E-Estimated. NA-Not Available. NM-Not Meaningful. NR-Not Ranked.

Office—6301 Waterford Blvd., P.O. Box 26647, Oklahoma City, OK 73126. **Tel**—(405) 840-7200. **Chrmn & CEO**—R. E. Stauth. **Pres & COO**—W. Dowd. **EVP & CFO**—H. L. Winn, Jr. **VP-Treas & Investor Contact**—J. M. Thompson (405-841-8170). **SVP & Secy**—D. R. Almond. **Dirs**—J. W. Baker, A. R. Dykes, C. B. Hallett, J. G. Harlow, Jr., L. M. Jones, E. C. Joullian, III, G. A. Osborn, A. Peterson, R. E. Stauth, E. D. Werries. **Transfer Agent & Registrar**—Liberty National Bank & Trust Co., Oklahoma City. **Incorporated**—in Kansas in 1915; reincorporated in Oklahoma in 1981. **Empl**— 39,700. **S&P Analyst:** Stephen J. Tekirian

03-OCT-98

Industry:
Construction (Cement & Aggregates)

Summary: FRK is a major basic construction materials company concentrating in the Southeastern and Mid-Atlantic states.

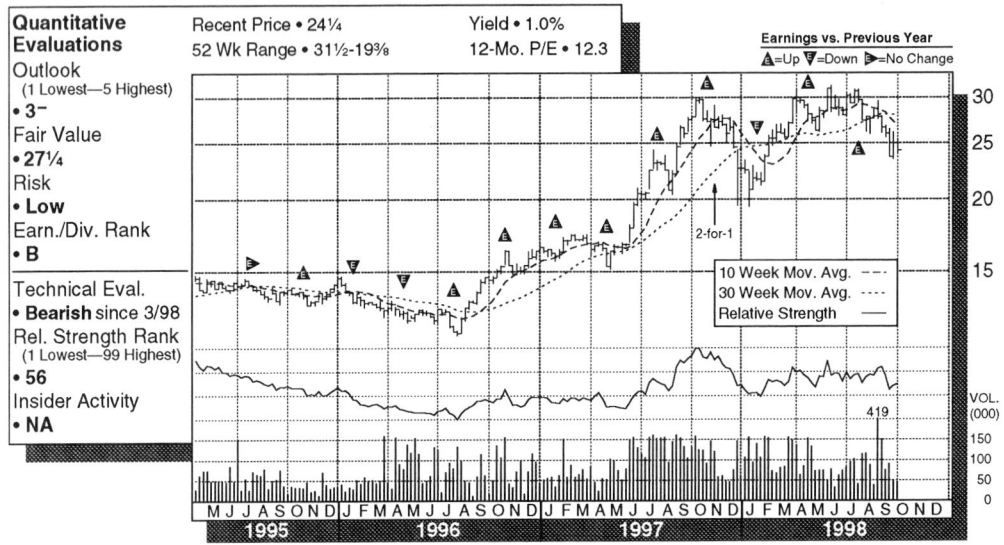

Quantitative Evaluations

Outlook
(1 Lowest—5 Highest)
• **3⁻**

Fair Value
• 27¼

Risk
• **Low**

Earn./Div. Rank
• **B**

Technical Eval.
• **Bearish** since 3/98

Rel. Strength Rank
(1 Lowest—99 Highest)
• **56**

Insider Activity
• **NA**

Recent Price • 24¼
52 Wk Range • 31½-19⅜

Yield • 1.0%
12-Mo. P/E • 12.3

Earnings vs. Previous Year
▲=Up ▼=Down ▶=No Change

10 Week Mov. Avg. — — —
30 Week Mov. Avg. ·········
Relative Strength ———

2-for-1

419

VOL. (000)

1995 1996 1997 1998

Business Profile - 26-AUG-98

FRK has been modernizing and expanding operations where cost savings and/or long-term growth plans justify the outlays. The company also continues to explore opportunities that will permit it to maximize its position in markets that are expected to experience long-term secular growth. It is building a 750,000 ton capacity cement plant near Newberry, FL; the plant is about 35% completed and is expected to be operational by the fourth quarter of FY 99 (Sep.). The shares were split two for one in late 1997.

Operational Review - 26-AUG-98

Net sales in the nine months ended June 30, 1998, rose 5.9%, year to year, reflecting the continuation of strong construction activity and demand for construction materials, as well as modest price increases. Profitability was restricted by a 10% increase in selling, general and administrative expense, which was related to the higher sales, and various special projects including a program to upgrade FRK's computer systems and processes. Pretax income was up 3.0%. After taxes at 35.2%, versus 35.0%, net income rose 2.7%, to $27,352,000 ($1.43 a share, based on 3.3% more shares), from $26,626,000 ($1.43).

Stock Performance - 02-OCT-98

In the past 30 trading days, FRK's shares have declined 13%, compared to a 7% fall in the S&P 500. Average trading volume for the past five days was 9,180 shares, compared with the 40-day moving average of 24,459 shares.

Key Stock Statistics

Dividend Rate/Share	0.25	Shareholders	1,100
Shs. outstg. (M)	18.9	Market cap. (B)	$0.459
Avg. daily vol. (M)	0.014	Inst. holdings	49%
Tang. Bk. Value/Share	15.29		
Beta	0.78		

Value of $10,000 invested 5 years ago: $ 22,290

Fiscal Year Ending Sep. 30

	1998	1997	1996	1995	1994	1993
Revenues (Million $)						
1Q	111.6	106.4	92.27	89.61	75.91	66.90
2Q	107.7	101.6	85.80	84.68	67.00	63.77
3Q	132.0	123.9	110.3	98.26	95.60	82.68
4Q	—	124.9	110.3	96.41	98.03	81.10
Yr.	—	456.8	398.7	369.0	336.5	294.4
Earnings Per Share ($)						
1Q	**0.38**	0.43	0.29	0.33	0.15	0.01
2Q	**0.38**	0.35	0.14	0.17	0.01	0.00
3Q	**0.66**	0.65	0.48	0.37	0.37	0.23
4Q	—	0.55	0.52	0.39	0.37	0.22
Yr.	—	1.98	1.43	1.25	0.91	0.42

Next earnings report expected: NA

Dividend Data (Dividends have been paid since 1978.)

Amount ($)	Date Decl.	Ex-Div. Date	Stock of Record	Payment Date
2-for-1	Oct. 01	Nov. 03	Oct. 15	Oct. 31 '97
0.125	Dec. 01	Dec. 12	Dec. 16	Jan. 02 '98
0.125	May. 06	Jun. 10	Jun. 12	Jul. 01 '98

A Division of The McGraw-Hill Companies

Business Summary - 26-AUG-98

Florida Rock Industries produces and sells ready mixed concrete and mines, processes and sells sand, gravel and crushed stone (construction aggregates). The company also produces and sells concrete block and prestressed concrete and sells other building materials. Substantially all operations are conducted in the Southeast, primarily in Florida, Georgia, Virginia, Maryland, Washington, DC, and North Carolina.

Sales contributions by product line in recent fiscal years (Sep.) were:

	FY 97	FY 96	FY 95
Ready mixed concrete	59%	58%	58%
Construction aggregates	37%	41%	40%
Other concrete products & building materials	10%	10%	10%
Less: Intercompany	-6%	-9%	-8%

At the end of FY 97, FRK was operating 87 ready mixed concrete plants, 10 concrete block plants and a delivery fleet of 962 ready mix and block trucks.

Ready mixed concrete is produced and sold throughout peninsula Florida; southern Georgia; central Maryland; Richmond, Norfolk-Virginia Beach and northeastern Virginia; and Washington, DC.

Since ready mixed concrete hardens rapidly, delivery is generally confined to a radius of about 20 miles to 25 miles from the producing plant. The bulk weight of concrete block limits its delivery to approximately 40 miles from the plant.

During FY 97, 48% of the coarse aggregates and 57% of the sand used in concrete operations were produced by the company. Remaining aggregates were purchased from other suppliers.

FRK has received all necessary building, zoning and environmental permits for construction of a $100 million, 750,000 ton capacity cement plant near Newberry, FL; construction began in April 1997, with the plant expected to be operational by the fourth quarter of FY 99. An aggregate plant in Paulding County, GA, is being constructed to serve FRK's customers in northwest Georgia.

A total of $114.2 million of capital expenditures was projected for FY 98, with 28% slated for plant and equipment replacements and modernization, 67% for expansion and new projects (including $46.2 million for the new cement plant), and 5% for new plant sites and deposits.

Per Share Data ($)

(Year Ended Sep. 30)	1997	1996	1995	1994	1993	1992	1991	1990	1989	1988
Tangible Bk. Val.	13.49	11.77	10.60	9.57	8.74	8.55	8.58	8.70	8.01	6.96
Cash Flow	3.61	2.96	2.65	2.25	1.31	1.66	1.75	2.58	2.85	2.85
Earnings	1.98	1.43	1.25	0.91	0.42	0.21	0.11	0.93	1.26	1.51
Dividends	0.25	0.25	0.25	0.25	0.25	0.25	0.25	0.25	0.25	0.25
Payout Ratio	13%	17%	20%	27%	59%	119%	225%	27%	20%	17%
Prices - High	30	16⅞	15	17¼	15⅜	14⅜	14⅝	16⅜	20⅞	17
- Low	15⅛	11⅝	13⅛	11⅞	11⅞	10¼	9⅛	8¼	14⅞	10⅜
P/E Ratio - High	15	12	12	19	36	68	NM	18	17	11
- Low	8	8	10	13	28	49	NM	9	12	7

Income Statement Analysis (Million $)

Revs.	457	399	368	337	294	272	296	391	420	409
Oper. Inc.	86.8	71.1	65.7	52.9	36.9	33.2	35.5	63.6	71.8	72.0
Depr.	30.7	28.8	26.5	25.4	25.5	26.7	30.2	29.9	29.4	24.7
Int. Exp.	0.9	2.0	2.1	2.3	3.0	3.3	4.8	5.8	8.0	6.0
Pretax Inc.	56.4	41.1	36.4	25.5	12.2	4.3	1.7	25.1	34.9	42.8
Eff. Tax Rate	34%	34%	34%	33%	36%	11%	NM	32%	33%	35%
Net Inc.	37.1	27.0	23.9	17.2	7.8	3.9	2.0	17.1	23.3	27.8

Balance Sheet & Other Fin. Data (Million $)

Cash	18.4	5.0	0.9	0.8	4.1	1.2	1.7	1.5	1.8	0.7
Curr. Assets	104	87.1	78.8	75.7	73.0	65.9	62.6	71.2	79.0	78.6
Total Assets	383	347	326	311	312	297	300	305	318	313
Curr. Liab.	55.7	51.9	57.6	49.3	52.0	46.6	47.7	48.6	55.0	49.5
LT Debt	10.9	16.9	9.7	23.1	43.9	39.4	41.4	41.7	60.2	77.8
Common Eqty.	265	228	211	192	172	168	170	172	160	141
Total Cap.	304	275	252	246	246	239	242	247	255	253
Cap. Exp.	46.5	44.9	40.2	23.0	34.0	27.0	24.0	27.0	44.0	146
Cash Flow	67.8	55.8	50.4	42.6	33.3	30.5	32.3	47.0	52.7	52.5
Curr. Ratio	1.9	1.7	1.4	1.5	1.4	1.4	1.3	1.5	1.4	1.6
% LT Debt of Cap.	3.6	6.1	3.8	9.4	17.8	16.4	17.1	16.9	23.6	30.8
% Net Inc.of Revs.	8.1	6.8	6.5	5.1	2.6	1.4	0.7	4.4	5.5	6.8
% Ret. on Assets	10.2	8.0	7.5	5.4	2.6	1.3	0.7	5.5	7.4	11.4
% Ret. on Equity	15.1	12.3	11.8	9.3	4.6	2.3	1.2	10.3	15.5	21.6

Data as orig. reptd.; bef. results of disc. opers. and/or spec. items. Per share data adj. for stk. divs. as of ex-div. date. Bold denotes diluted EPS (FASB 128). E-Estimated. NA-Not Available. NM-Not Meaningful. NR-Not Ranked.

Office—155 E. 21st St., Jacksonville, FL 32206; P.O. Box 4667, Jacksonville 32201. Tel—(904) 355-1781. Chrmn—E. L. Baker. Pres & CEO—J. D. Baker II. Secy—D. D. Frick.VP, Treas & CFO—James J. Gilstrap.Dirs—E. L. Baker, J. D. Baker II, T. S. Baker II, A. R. Carpenter, C. H. Denny III, A. D. Ernest Jr., L. E. Fichthorn III, G. K. Thompson, F. X. Knott, R. D. Lovett, C. J. Shepherdson. Transfer Agent & Registrar—First Union National Bank of North Carolina, Charlotte.Incorporated—in Florida in 1945. Empl— 2,448. S&P Analyst: J.J.S.

03-OCT-98

Industry: Manufacturing (Specialized)

Summary: Flow is the world's leading manufacturer of ultrahigh-pressure waterjet technology for advanced commercial applications, and a leading provider of robotics and assembly equipment.

Quantitative Evaluations

Recent Price • 9
52 Wk Range • 13½-7⅞

Yield • Nil
12-Mo. P/E • 17.6

Outlook
(1 Lowest—5 Highest)
• **4**

Fair Value
• **12¼**

Risk
• **Average**

Earn./Div. Rank
• **B**

Technical Eval.
• **Bearish** since 8/98

Rel. Strength Rank
(1 Lowest—99 Highest)
• **50**

Insider Activity
• **Neutral**

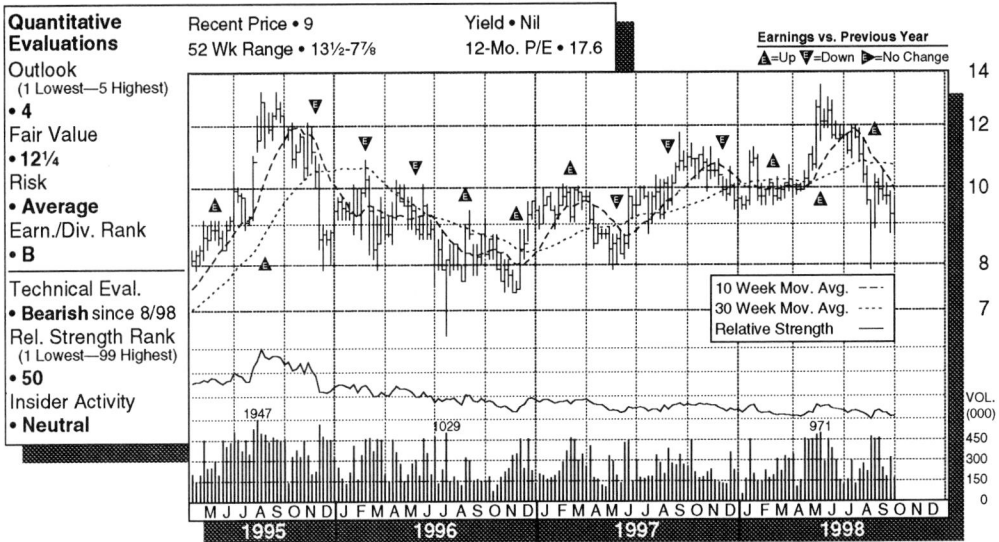

Earnings vs. Previous Year
▲=Up ▼=Down ▶=No Change

10 Week Mov. Avg. ---
30 Week Mov. Avg. ·····
Relative Strength —

1947   1029   971

1995   1996   1997   1998

Business Profile - 15-JUN-98

Reflecting the strong growth and high profitability of FLOW'S ultrahigh-pressure (UHP) waterjet products, the company has chosen to focus on this segment as its core business. The non-core access and service operations were divested in October 1997. FLOW believes its UHP technologies have tremendous potential for use in the rapidly growing fresh food market. The process essentially eliminates bacteria and other organisms, extending the shelf life of fresh foods without affecting flavor or texture. The company also aims to grow through international expansion, with sales outside the U.S. (which accounted for 38% of FY 98 revenues) providing about 50% of total revenues. To accelerate growth in Asia, the company formed a 51%-owned joint venture in Japan and recently opened an office in China.

Operational Review - 15-JUN-98

Based on a preliminary report, sales in FY 98 (Apr.) fell 5.2%, reflecting the divestiture of slower growth businesses. Margins widened reflecting the focus on the more profitable ultrahigh-pressure core operations. Following $4.91 million in restructuring charges, versus $8.95 million in FY 97, and slightly lower net interest and other expense, there was pretax income of $6,505,000 versus $963,000. After taxes at 26.2%, versus 24.7%, net income rose to $4,803,000 ($0.32 a diluted share), from $725,000 ($0.05).

Stock Performance - 02-OCT-98

In the past 30 trading days, FLOW's shares were unchanged, compared to a 7% fall in the S&P 500. Average trading volume for the past five days was 33,080 shares, compared with the 40-day moving average of 71,095 shares.

Key Stock Statistics

Dividend Rate/Share	Nil	Shareholders	1,500
Shs. outstg. (M)	14.9	Market cap. (B)	$0.135
Avg. daily vol. (M)	0.046	Inst. holdings	45%
Tang. Bk. Value/Share	3.09		
Beta	0.29		

Value of $10,000 invested 5 years ago: $ 13,584

Fiscal Year Ending Apr. 30

	1999	1998	1997	1996	1995	1994
Revenues (Million $)						
1Q	36.42	47.51	40.93	33.01	24.51	19.36
2Q	—	35.16	41.32	35.62	26.76	24.59
3Q	—	34.46	39.66	35.64	27.19	20.56
4Q	—	42.34	46.28	40.63	31.56	24.13
Yr.	—	159.5	168.2	144.9	110.0	88.63
Earnings Per Share ($)						
1Q	0.12	-0.07	0.15	0.14	0.12	0.08
2Q	—	0.12	0.16	0.12	0.15	0.13
3Q	—	0.12	0.09	0.08	0.11	-0.13
4Q	—	0.14	-0.36	0.14	0.15	0.10
Yr.	—	0.32	0.05	0.47	0.53	0.18

Next earnings report expected: NA

Dividend Data

No cash dividends have been paid. A "poison pill" stock purchase rights plan was adopted in 1990.

 *A Division of The* **McGraw·Hill** *Companies*

Business Summary - 15-JUN-98

Which is stronger, water or metal? The correct answer depends, in part, on how the water is handled. By pressurizing water to as much as 100,000 pounds per square inch and shooting an intense stream, the ultrahigh-pressure waterjet systems produced by Flow International Corp. (FLOW) are capable of cutting metal and other materials (the abrasive garnet is added to the waterjet stream for the hardest substances). FLOW's waterjet systems are also used in industrial cleaning applications such as paint removal and surface preparation. In addition, FLOW makes the robotic articulation equipment used in the cutting and cleaning processes, as well as other factory automation systems for assembly, "pick and place" and load/unload operations.

Other businesses that included the manufacture and sale of scaffolding "access" systems for maintenance and construction applications, and services that use waterjets to remove debris from bridges and airport runways were sold to SafeWorks, LLC in October 1997. These secondary operations, which together accounted for 31% of FLOW's revenues in FY 97 (Apr.), were divested as part of the company's plan to refocus on its core ultrahigh-pressure (UHP) technology and associated automation business. In connection with the planned sale of these businesses, FLOW recorded restructuring charges of $9 million in FY 97, and $5 million in FY 98.

FLOW is emphasizing four strategic priorities -- its "total solutions" capability, new products, expanded applications and technology leadership -- as the company sharpens its focus on UHP technology. It is using new products, such as the BENGAL 4 x 4 abrasivejet cutting system introduced in 1997, to position waterjets as a mainstream machine tool. FLOW has extended the use of UHP technology in the key automotive market beyond its original application in carpet cutting to include additional cutting applications (most recently composite parts and castings) and automated UHP surface preparation. FLOW is now bringing its technology to an entirely new market -- food processing. UHP processing equipment produced by FLOW extends the shelf life of pumpable foods by exposing them to microorganism-destroying pressures. Under an agreement signed in May 1997, the company's "Fresher Under Pressure" equipment will put the squeeze on guacamole for a Texas-based supplier of avocado products.

Per Share Data ($) (Year Ended Apr. 30)	1998	1997	1996	1995	1994	1993	1992	1991	1990	1989
Tangible Bk. Val.	3.01	3.03	2.89	2.54	2.58	2.43	2.30	2.11	2.20	1.81
Cash Flow	0.61	0.54	0.93	0.89	0.45	0.54	0.47	0.14	0.44	0.45
Earnings	0.32	0.05	0.47	0.53	0.18	0.30	0.23	-0.08	0.20	0.24
Dividends	Nil	Nil	Nil	Nil	Nil	Nil	Nil	Nil	Nil	Nil
Payout Ratio	Nil	Nil	Nil	Nil	Nil	Nil	Nil	Nil	Nil	Nil
Cal. Yrs.	1997	1996	1995	1994	1993	1992	1991	1990	1989	1988
Prices - High	11 3/4	10 7/8	13 1/4	8 1/2	8 3/4	7 1/4	4 1/8	5	4 3/8	3 5/8
- Low	7 7/8	6 1/2	6 1/2	4 5/8	5	3	1 3/8	1 1/8	2 3/4	1 7/8
P/E Ratio - High	37	NM	28	16	49	24	18	NM	22	15
- Low	25	NM	14	9	28	10	6	NM	14	8
Income Statement Analysis (Million $)										
Revs.	159	168	145	110	88.6	79.1	48.4	41.5	46.1	39.4
Oper. Inc.	19.5	21.3	18.6	16.9	7.9	10.3	7.5	3.8	8.5	7.3
Depr.	4.4	7.5	6.9	5.2	3.9	3.4	2.7	2.5	3.0	2.6
Int. Exp.	3.2	3.8	3.5	2.4	1.8	1.4	1.0	1.8	1.7	0.8
Pretax Inc.	6.5	1.0	8.9	9.3	3.1	5.8	4.1	-0.4	3.7	4.2
Eff. Tax Rate	26%	25%	20%	17%	18%	28%	25%	NM	33%	31%
Net Inc.	4.8	0.7	7.1	7.7	2.5	4.2	3.1	-0.5	2.5	2.9
Balance Sheet & Other Fin. Data (Million $)										
Cash	3.0	2.5	3.9	1.1	1.4	0.1	0.8	1.5	0.7	1.1
Curr. Assets	87.7	90.7	80.8	66.0	55.1	47.4	28.2	28.5	33.8	27.6
Total Assets	121	133	127	106	78.2	69.3	43.7	41.0	48.4	38.9
Curr. Liab.	27.8	22.6	23.0	21.4	29.7	22.3	12.5	13.2	13.2	10.9
LT Debt	32.1	53.6	45.6	33.4	10.6	12.5	4.4	4.6	10.4	3.9
Common Eqty.	61.2	56.8	57.1	49.8	35.4	31.7	26.6	22.7	23.8	21.8
Total Cap.	93.4	112	104	84.1	48.5	46.9	31.2	27.7	35.2	26.5
Cap. Exp.	6.6	9.2	8.8	5.6	6.2	7.8	3.9	2.3	4.0	4.0
Cash Flow	9.2	8.2	13.9	12.9	6.4	7.3	5.4	1.6	5.4	5.5
Curr. Ratio	3.2	4.0	3.5	3.1	1.9	2.1	2.3	2.2	2.6	2.5
% LT Debt of Cap.	34.4	47.9	44.0	39.7	21.8	26.7	14.1	16.7	29.6	14.8
% Net Inc.of Revs.	3.0	0.4	4.9	7.0	2.9	5.3	6.4	NM	5.4	7.5
% Ret. on Assets	3.8	0.6	6.1	8.4	3.4	7.1	7.0	NM	6.0	8.8
% Ret. on Equity	8.1	1.3	13.3	17.6	7.3	13.6	10.5	NM	10.9	12.8

Data as orig. reptd.; bef. results of disc. opers. and/or spec. items. Per share data adj. for stk. divs. as of ex-div. date. Bold denotes diluted EPS (FASB 128). Data for 1Q 1998 incl. discont. ops. E-Estimated. NA-Not Available. NM-Not Meaningful. NR-Not Ranked.

Office—23500-64th Ave. South, Kent, WA 98032. **Tel**—(253) 850-3500. **Chrmn, Pres & CEO**—R. W. Tarrant. **EVP & COO**—R. B. Lawrence. **CFO**—S. D. Reichenbach. **Secy**—J. S. Leness. **Dirs**—R. D. Barbaro, D. J. Evans, K. L. Munro, A. I. Prentice, J. M. Ribaudo, K. M. Roberts, S. F. Rorem, R. W. Tarrant, D. D. Thornton. **Transfer Agent & Registrar**—ChaseMellon Shareholder Services LLC, NYC. **Incorporated**—in Washington in 1980; reincorporated in Delaware in 1983. **Empl**— 805. **S&P Analyst:** E. J. H.

03-OCT-98　**Industry:** Restaurants

Summary: This company operates and franchises Jack In The Box, a leading regional fast-food chain.

Quantitative Evaluations

Outlook
(1 Lowest—5 Highest)
• **5**

Fair Value
• **24½**

Risk
• **Average**

Earn./Div. Rank
• **NR**

Technical Eval.
• **Bullish** since 11/97

Rel. Strength Rank
(1 Lowest—99 Highest)
• **91**

Insider Activity
• **NA**

Recent Price • 15⅜
52 Wk Range • 21-12½

Yield • Nil
12-Mo. P/E • 9.1

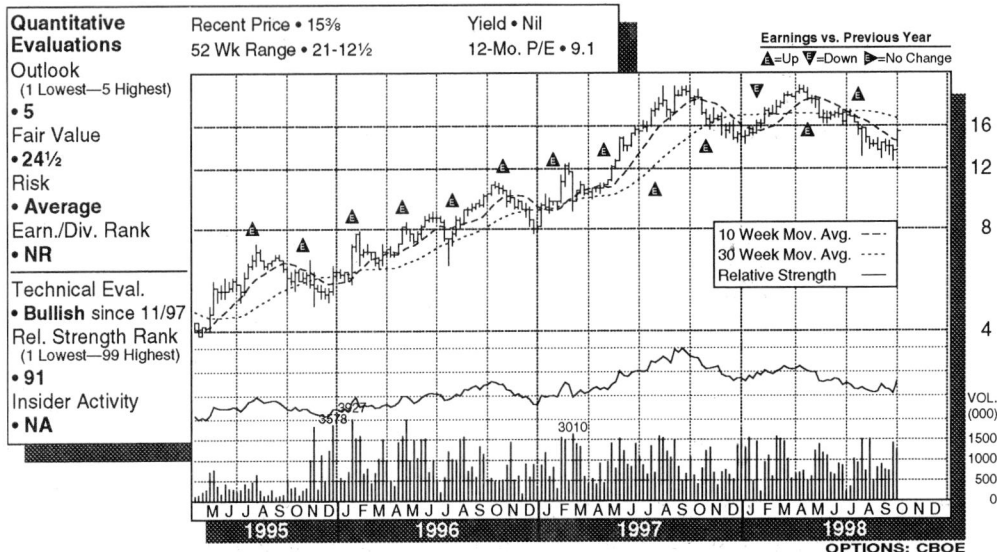

Earnings vs. Previous Year
▲=Up ▼=Down ▶=No Change

10 Week Mov. Avg. - - -
30 Week Mov. Avg. ·····
Relative Strength ——

OPTIONS: CBOE

Business Profile - 29-MAY-98

FM operates and franchises Jack In The Box fast-food restaurants. It is seeking to strengthen its brand identity and to introduce new products, promotions and advertising in order to boost sales. The company has now posted 13 straight quarters of increased per store average (PSA) sales at comparable company restaurants. Recent success has been achieved by the company's marketing strategy, which focuses on its core products as a tool to build preference for its products with its customers. The company utilized proceeds from the recent settlement of litigation to reduce long-term debt.

Operational Review - 29-MAY-98

Revenues in the 28 weeks ended April 12, 1998, rose 15%, year to year, reflecting a 12% jump in restaurant sales and a $45.8 million gain on settlement of the Hamburger Patty Cases litigation against Vons in connection with a 1993 incidence of food-borne illness attributed to hamburgers served at Jack In The Box restaurants, partially offset by a 65% decline in distribution sales after franchisees formed their own purchasing cooperative. Per store average sales were up as transactions and the average transaction size grew. Following a 13% decline in interest expense, pretax income grew to $67.6 million from $20.2 million. After taxes at 31.9%, versus 22.3%, net income jumped to $46,021,000 ($1.14 a share), from $15,722,000 ($0.40).

Stock Performance - 02-OCT-98

In the past 30 trading days, FM's shares have increased 9%, compared to a 7% fall in the S&P 500. Average trading volume for the past five days was 248,640 shares, compared with the 40-day moving average of 200,974 shares.

Key Stock Statistics

Dividend Rate/Share	Nil	Shareholders	600
Shs. outstg. (M)	39.1	Market cap. (B)	$0.604
Avg. daily vol. (M)	0.215	Inst. holdings	76%
Tang. Bk. Value/Share	1.35		
Beta	0.94		

Value of $10,000 invested 5 years ago: $ 11,026

Fiscal Year Ending Sep. 30

	1998	1997	1996	1995	1994	1993
Revenues (Million $)						
1Q	343.8	323.5	330.6	293.7	381.6	403.0
2Q	309.9	247.0	250.0	229.7	218.7	244.9
3Q	280.6	251.7	243.2	244.1	225.8	280.2
4Q	—	249.6	239.1	251.3	227.2	312.2
Yr.	—	1,072	1,063	1,020	1,053	1,241
Earnings Per Share ($)						
1Q	**0.17**	0.23	0.12	-1.87	-0.11	0.29
2Q	**0.85**	0.17	0.10	-0.08	-0.59	-0.58
3Q	**0.31**	0.25	0.14	0.07	0.00	0.91
4Q	—	0.24	0.15	0.10	-0.14	-0.07
Yr.	—	0.89	0.51	-1.77	-0.94	-1.15

Next earnings report expected: early November

Dividend Data

No dividends have been paid, and the company does not intend to pay any in the foreseeable future.

A Division of The **McGraw·Hill** *Companies*

STANDARD
&POOR'S
STOCK REPORTS

Foodmaker, Inc.

915

03-OCT-98

Business Summary - 29-MAY-98

Jack's Back -- and so is Foodmaker, Inc. (FM), which features its clown-headed "founder" Jack in television commercials for Jack in the Box restaurants, FM's regional fast-food hamburger chain with locations concentrated in the West and Southwest. FM credits its "Jack's Back" advertising campaign with helping to build its brand and grow its sales, which rose 9.0% systemwide in FY 96 (Sep.) and grew almost 9.0% in FY 97. Sales at company-operated restaurants advanced 11% to $892 million in FY 96 and advanced another 11% to $987 million in FY 97.

The Jack in the Box chain started in 1950 as a single drive-thru restaurant, and drive-thru sales still account for the lion's share (over 64%) of sales at company-operated restaurants. Systemwide, there are 1,323 Jack in the Box units (as of September 28, 1997), including 360 operated by franchisees. After growing 7.2% in FY 96, per store average sales increased 6.5% in FY 97, despite a fiercely competitive environment that included heavy discounting and major product introductions. FM uses a two-tier marketing strategy which emphasizes adult-oriented premium sandwiches and hamburgers as well as lower-priced value selections to broaden its appeal among three core customer groups: hamburger lovers, consumers who prefer higher quality levels, and individuals who shop for price. FM believes its willingness to offer certain distinctive, premium foods, such as its Chicken Teriyaki Bowl and Chicken Fajita Pita, is unique among quick-serve restaurants, and, along with its focus on the adult market, has helped Jack in the Box develop a niche in an overcrowded industry. In order to showcase value, FM introduced its "Under a Buck" menu featuring, among other items, its Jumbo Jack hamburgers and tacos. Although discounting reduced average check amounts by 0.5% in FY 96, the average check grew 1.4% in FY 97 and the company experienced a 5.1% improvement in customer transactions.

Over the next five years, FM plans to open approximately 400 to 500 new restaurants. About 15% of this new development will be through confronting consumer demand for convenience head-on by including nontraditional locations such as gas stations and supermarkets in its growth plans. FM is also looking at dual branding, which provides consumers with two brands in a single location, and in this regard it is developing its own Mexican-brand line of foods to offer along with Jack in the Box products.

Per Share Data ($)

(Year Ended Sep. 30)	1997	1996	1995	1994	1993	1992	1991	1990	1989	1988
Tangible Bk. Val.	0.46	NM	NM	0.18	-1.49	1.24	0.83	NA	NA	NA
Cash Flow	1.84	1.44	-0.85	-0.12	-0.05	1.83	1.87	NA	NA	NA
Earnings	0.89	0.51	-1.77	-0.94	-1.15	0.67	0.57	NA	NA	NA
Dividends	Nil	Nil	Nil	Nil	Nil	Nil	NA	NA	NA	NA
Payout Ratio	Nil	Nil	Nil	Nil	NM	Nil	NA	NA	NA	NA
Prices - High	21	11	7¼	10¾	14	18½	NA	NA	NA	NA
- Low	8¾	5½	3¼	3⅜	7½	9⅛	NA	NA	NA	NA
P/E Ratio - High	21	22	NM	NM	NM	28	NA	NA	NA	NA
- Low	10	11	NM	NM	NM	14	NA	NA	NA	NA

Income Statement Analysis (Million $)

	1997	1996	1995	1994	1993	1992	1991	1990	1989	1988
Revs.	1,072	1,063	1,019	1,053	1,241	1,219	1,157	NA	NA	NA
Oper. Inc.	123	108	73.0	57.0	86.0	149	150	NA	NA	NA
Depr.	37.9	36.5	35.8	31.6	42.4	37.8	50.3	NA	NA	NA
Int. Exp.	41.0	46.3	48.6	55.9	57.8	73.2	59.3	NA	NA	NA
Pretax Inc.	45.2	25.4	-68.5	-33.3	-66.2	38.7	40.6	NA	NA	NA
Eff. Tax Rate	22%	21%	NM	NM	NM	43%	46%	NA	NA	NA
Net Inc.	35.3	20.1	-69.0	-36.3	-44.1	21.9	22.0	NA	NA	NA

Balance Sheet & Other Fin. Data (Million $)

	1997	1996	1995	1994	1993	1992	1991	1990	1989	1988
Cash	28.5	42.0	36.0	36.0	4.5	20.0	1.4	NA	NA	NA
Curr. Assets	100	96.5	98.0	107	94.0	106	67.0	NA	NA	NA
Total Assets	682	654	663	740	890	915	845	NA	NA	NA
Curr. Liab.	193	147	132	148	203	167	159	NA	NA	NA
LT Debt	346	396	440	448	500	501	505	NA	NA	NA
Common Eqty.	87.9	51.4	31.3	100	139	247	182	NA	NA	NA
Total Cap.	434	455	481	553	657	748	687	NA	NA	NA
Cap. Exp.	59.7	33.2	27.0	92.0	59.0	77.0	NA	NA	NA	NA
Cash Flow	73.2	56.5	-33.1	-4.6	-1.7	59.7	72.3	NA	NA	NA
Curr. Ratio	0.5	0.7	0.7	0.7	0.5	0.6	0.4	NA	NA	NA
% LT Debt of Cap.	79.7	87.0	91.6	81.0	76.2	67.0	73.5	NA	NA	NA
% Net Inc.of Revs.	3.3	1.9	NM	NM	NM	1.8	1.9	NA	NA	NA
% Ret. on Assets	5.3	3.0	NM	NM	NM	1.1	NA	NA	NA	NA
% Ret. on Equity	50.7	48.5	NM	NM	NM	NM	NA	NA	NA	NA

Data as orig. reptd.; bef. results of disc. opers. and/or spec. items. Per share data adj. for stk. divs. as of ex-div. date. Bold denotes diluted EPS (FASB 128). E-Estimated. NA-Not Available. NM-Not Meaningful. NR-Not Ranked.

Office—9330 Balboa Ave., San Diego, CA 92123. **Tel**—(619) 571-2121. **Website**—http://www.foodmaker.com **Chrmn**—J. W. Goodall. **CEO & Pres**—R. J. Nugent. **EVP, CFO & Investor Contact**—Charles W. Duddles. **EVP & Secy**—L. E. Schauf. **Dirs**—M. E. Alpert, J. W. Brown, P. T. Carter, C. W. Duddles, E. Gibbons, J. W. Goodall, R. J. Nugent, L. R. Payne. **Transfer Agent & Registrar**—ChaseMellon Shareholder Services, Ridgefield Park, NJ. **Incorporated**—in Delaware in 1971. **Empl**— 29,000. **S&P Analyst:** Robert J. Izmirlian

STANDARD &POOR'S
STOCK REPORTS

Footstar, Inc.

916R

NYSE Symbol **FTS**

In S&P SmallCap 600

03-OCT-98

Industry: Retail (Specialty)

Summary: This company, spun off by Melville Corp. in October 1996, is a leading retailer of discount footwear and branded athletic footwear and apparel.

S&P Opinion: Accumulate (★★★★)			
Recent Price • 23⅞		Yield • Nil	
52 Wk Range • 49¼-22		12-Mo. P/E • 8.1	

Quantitative Evaluations

Outlook
(1 Lowest—5 Highest)
• **NA**

Fair Value
• **NA**

Risk
• **NA**

Earn./Div. Rank
• **NR**

Technical Eval.
• **NA**

Rel. Strength Rank
(1 Lowest—99 Highest)
• **23**

Insider Activity
• **Favorable**

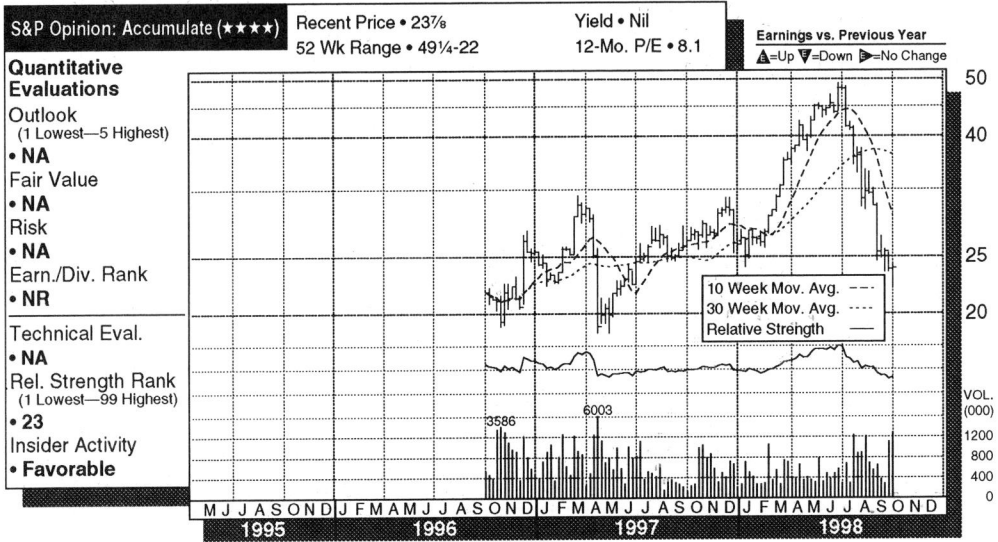

Earnings vs. Previous Year
▲=Up ▼=Down ▶=No Change

10 Week Mov. Avg.
30 Week Mov. Avg. - - - -
Relative Strength ——

Overview - 04-AUG-98

We expect this footwear retailer to have approximately 5% sales growth in 1998. Growth is expected to come from improvements at Meldisco, the company's discount retailer, which operates a low-overhead business that yields high cash flow. In the balance of the year, Meldisco's sales will continue to benefit from the re-modeling of over 1,100 Kmart stores; renovations were already completed at 667 stores at the end of 1997. Footaction, the company's retailer of branded footwear and apparel stores, has had higher sales, driven by sales of Nike's Jordan sneakers; branded apparel sales have improved slightly. Also fueling the sales growth at Footaction is the ongoing shift to a larger format store. After successfully managing inventory, the company's total inventory levels were off 2.9%, year to year, at the end of the second quarter, leaving FTS well positioned. Thus, we expect to see less promotional selling activity in the immediate term. We expect earnings to grow 40% in 1998.

Valuation - 04-AUG-98

The shares have climbed approximately 40% since the beginning of 1998. In the first half of the year, sales were up 7.5%, on higher sales at Meldisco and Footaction. The company's operating profit improved, as better results at Meldisco outweighed contracting operating profits at Footaction due to the division's higher occupancy costs and competitive pricing. Earnings in the first half were fueled by an aggressive share repurchase program, which was completed during the second quarter. Following this impressive first half, we look forward to a year of higher sales and profits. We believe the stock remains attractive at 14X our 1998 estimated EPS of $2.78 and 12X our 1999 estimated EPS of $3.05.

Key Stock Statistics

S&P EPS Est. 1998	2.78	Tang. Bk. Value/Share	11.68
P/E on S&P Est. 1998	8.6	Beta	NA
S&P EPS Est. 1999	3.05	Shareholders	NA
Dividend Rate/Share	Nil	Market cap. (B)	$0.586
Shs. outstg. (M)	24.5	Inst. holdings	90%
Avg. daily vol. (M)	0.197		

Value of $10,000 invested 5 years ago: NA

Fiscal Year Ending Dec. 31

	1998	1997	1996	1995	1994	1993
Revenues (Million $)						
1Q	400.9	376.9	336.9	—	—	—
2Q	462.6	426.0	419.0	—	—	—
3Q	—	464.0	432.7	—	—	—
4Q	—	528.0	483.7	—	—	—
Yr.	—	1,795	1,672	1,615	1,613	1,475
Earnings Per Share ($)						
1Q	0.20	0.16	—	—	—	—
2Q	0.69	0.50	0.61	—	—	—
3Q	E0.72	0.66	0.49	—	—	—
4Q	E1.15	0.70	0.79	—	—	—
Yr.	E2.78	1.99	1.90	0.94	—	—

Next earnings report expected: mid October

Dividend Data

The company anticipates that future earnings will be used principally to support operations and finance growth of its business. It does not intend to pay cash dividends on its common shares for the foreseeable future.

A Division of The McGraw·Hill Companies

Business Summary - 04-AUG-98

Footstar is a leading retailer of discount footwear and branded athletic footwear and apparel. The company was spun off by Melville Corp. in October 1996, with Melville shareholders receiving 0.2879 of a Footstar common share for each Melville common share owned. As of January 3, 1998, the company operated 2,136 Meldisco leased footwear departments and 550 Footaction stores. Sales in recent years were derived as follows:

	1997	1996	1995
Meldisco	66%	69%	74%
Footaction	34%	31%	26%

Meldisco is the leading operator of leased footwear departments in the U.S. As of January 3, 1998, Meldisco operated leased footwear departments in 2,136 Kmart department stores, 400 PayLess Drug Stores and Thrifty Drug Stores, and 14 Tesco department stores (in the Czech Republic, Slovakia and Hungary).

In its Kmart departments, Meldisco sells a wide variety of family footwear, including men's, women's and children's dress, casual and athletic footwear, workshoes and slippers. Most of the shoes offered are private label

brands, although some brand-name merchandise is sold at discount prices. In its PayLess Drug and Thrifty Drug operations, Meldisco leases approximately 100 ft. of selling space to display merchandise.

In 1997, Kmart operations accounted for 96% of Meldisco's net sales and 64% of Footstar's combined net sales.

Footaction is a leading mall-based specialty retailer of branded athletic footwear, apparel and related accessories. It offers the latest and most popular products and uses celebrity endorsements to appeal to its 12- to 24-year old target customers. Stores offer a wide variety of footwear including Nike, Reebok, Fila, Adidas, Converse, New Balance, Asics, and outdoor brands such as Timberland.

Footstar recorded an $85 million charge in the first quarter of 1996, related to its decision to discontinue operating Thom McAn stores, which were mall-based specialty retailers. The Thom McAn line of men's footwear is now being sold by Meldisco. The company converted 76 Thom McAn stores to Footaction stores, and sold or closed the remaining stores. In January 1998, the company said it was able to exit the business at a substantially lower cost than previously estimated. Consequently, FTS reversed some $34 million ($21.4 million after taxes) of the original reserve in the fourth quarter of 1997.

Per Share Data ($)

(Year Ended Dec. 31)	1997	1996	1995	1994	1993	1992	1991	1990	1989	1988
Tangible Bk. Val.	13.45	11.63	NA	NA	NA	NA	NA	NA	NA	NA
Cash Flow	3.13	2.71	NA	NA	NA	NA	NA	NA	NA	NA
Earnings	1.99	1.90	0.94	NA	NA	NA	NA	NA	NA	NA
Dividends	Nil	Nil	Nil	Nil	Nil	Nil	Nil	Nil	Nil	Nil
Payout Ratio	Nil	Nil	Nil	Nil	Nil	Nil	Nil	Nil	Nil	Nil
Prices - High	31¾	27¾	NA	NA	NA	NA	NA	NA	NA	NA
- Low	18½	19	NA	NA	NA	NA	NA	NA	NA	NA
P/E Ratio - High	16	15	NA	NA	NA	NA	NA	NA	NA	NA
- Low	9	10	NA	NA	NA	NA	NA	NA	NA	NA

Income Statement Analysis (Million $)

	1997	1996	1995	1994	1993	1992	1991	1990	1989	1988
Revs.	1,795	NA	NA	NA	NA	NA	NA	NA	NA	NA
Oper. Inc.	183	NA	NA	NA	NA	NA	NA	NA	NA	NA
Depr.	33.5	NA	NA	NA	NA	NA	NA	NA	NA	NA
Int. Exp.	Nil	NA	NA	NA	NA	NA	NA	NA	NA	NA
Pretax Inc.	136	NA	NA	NA	NA	NA	NA	NA	NA	NA
Eff. Tax Rate	30%	NA	NA	NA	NA	NA	NA	NA	NA	NA
Net Inc.	58.6	58.2	43.5	NA	NA	NA	NA	NA	NA	NA

Balance Sheet & Other Fin. Data (Million $)

	1997	1996	1995	1994	1993	1992	1991	1990	1989	1988
Cash	152	165	NA	NA	NA	NA	NA	NA	NA	NA
Curr. Assets	529	584	NA	NA	NA	NA	NA	NA	NA	NA
Total Assets	771	832	NA	NA	NA	NA	NA	NA	NA	NA
Curr. Liab.	244	325	NA	NA	NA	NA	NA	NA	NA	NA
LT Debt	Nil	0.2	NA	NA	NA	NA	NA	NA	NA	NA
Common Eqty.	403	384	NA	NA	NA	NA	NA	NA	NA	NA
Total Cap.	468	449	NA	NA	NA	NA	NA	NA	NA	NA
Cap. Exp.	59.1	68.3	NA	NA	NA	NA	NA	NA	NA	NA
Cash Flow	92.1	83.0	NA	NA	NA	NA	NA	NA	NA	NA
Curr. Ratio	2.2	1.8	NA	NA	NA	NA	NA	NA	NA	NA
% LT Debt of Cap.	Nil	0.0	NA	NA	NA	NA	NA	NA	NA	NA
% Net Inc.of Revs.	3.3	NA	NA	NA	NA	NA	NA	NA	NA	NA
% Ret. on Assets	7.3	NA	NA	NA	NA	NA	NA	NA	NA	NA
% Ret. on Equity	14.9	NA	NA	NA	NA	NA	NA	NA	NA	NA

Data as orig. reptd.; bef. results of disc. opers. and/or spec. items. Per share data adj. for stk. divs. as of ex-div. date. Bold denotes diluted EPS (FASB 128). E-Estimated. NA-Not Available. NM-Not Meaningful. NR-Not Ranked.

Office—933 MacArthur Boulevard, Mahwah, NJ 07430. **Tel**—(201) 934-2000. **Chrmn & CEO**—J. M. Robinson. **CFO**—C. E. Alberini.**Secy**—M. Richards.**Investor Contact**—Carlos Alberini (201-760-4008). **Dirs**—R. A. Davies III, G. S. Day, S. P. Goldstein, T. R. Lautenbach, B. M. Musham, K. S. Olshan, J. M. Robinson. **Transfer Agent**—ChaseMellon Shareholder Services, Ridgefield Park, NJ. **Incorporated**—in Delaware in 1996.**Empl**— 15,200. **S&P Analyst:** Kathleen J. Fraser

Franklin Covey

922C

NYSE Symbol **FC**

In S&P SmallCap 600

03-OCT-98

Industry: Consumer (Jewelry, Novelties & Gifts)

Summary: This company (formerly Franklin Quest) provides time management products and training seminars for corporations, government agencies and the general public.

Quantitative Evaluations

Outlook (1 Lowest—5 Highest)
- **1+**

Fair Value
- **18¼**

Risk
- **Average**

Earn./Div. Rank
- **B**

Technical Eval.
- **NA**

Rel. Strength Rank (1 Lowest—99 Highest)
- **73**

Insider Activity
- **NA**

Recent Price • 19⅛
52 Wk Range • 26⅛-18¼
Yield • Nil
12-Mo. P/E • 11.3

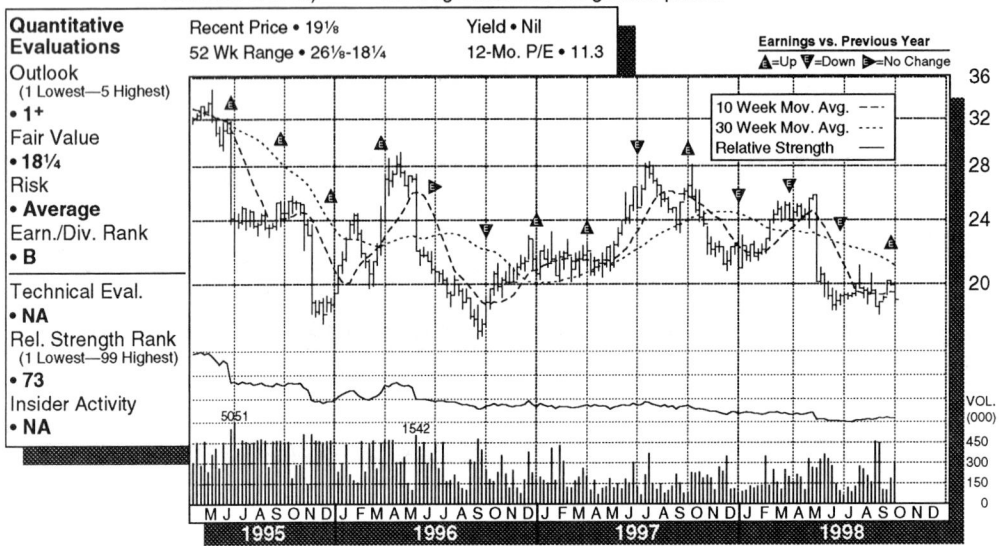

Business Profile - 26-MAR-98

In the first half of FY 98 (Aug.), net income fell 8%, due in part to an $0.08 a share charge associated with a change in accounting rules. However, operating income grew over 20%, driven by strong revenue growth. In the second quarter of 1998, same-store sales advanced 6%. Furthermore, the company has plans to open an additional 5 to 10 stores in the remainder of FY 98. In May 1997, FC acquired Covey Leadership Center for 5 million common shares. Management expects the combined company to generate over $500 million in fiscal 1998. In March 1998, directors authorized the repurchase of an additional 3 million shares of FC common stock.

Operational Review - 26-MAR-98

Revenues in the six months ended February 28, 1998, rose 36%, year to year, fueled by a 17% increase in sales of products and a 110% rise in training sales. Despite a smaller increase in cost of sales, margins narrowed, reflecting a jump in SG&A expense, stemming from costs associated with the Premier acquisition; operating income grew 23%. Following significantly higher depreciation and amortization charges, coupled with greater net interest expense, pretax income was up 2.2%. After taxes at 41.5%, versus 40.2%, net income fell 8.0%, to $23,993,000 ($0.94 a share, on 22% more shares), from $26,068,000 ($1.25). Results in the FY 98 interim include a loss of $0.08 a share related to a change in method of accounting.

Stock Performance - 02-OCT-98

In the past 30 trading days, FC's shares have declined 3%, compared to a 7% fall in the S&P 500. Average trading volume for the past five days was 60,920 shares, compared with the 40-day moving average of 50,931 shares.

Key Stock Statistics

Dividend Rate/Share	Nil	Shareholders	400
Shs. outstg. (M)	22.9	Market cap. (B)	$0.438
Avg. daily vol. (M)	0.035	Inst. holdings	49%
Tang. Bk. Value/Share	3.66		
Beta	0.70		

Value of $10,000 invested 5 years ago: $ 9,622

Fiscal Year Ending Aug. 31

	1998	1997	1996	1995	1994	1993
Revenues (Million $)						
1Q	143.9	102.4	91.85	71.06	56.44	44.00
2Q	138.6	106.0	93.60	74.67	56.17	44.48
3Q	107.5	79.80	72.47	59.38	48.91	36.62
4Q	156.6	145.1	74.07	72.01	54.42	40.43
Yr.	546.6	433.3	332.0	277.1	215.9	165.5
Earnings Per Share ($)						
1Q	0.53	0.62	0.57	0.56	0.46	0.36
2Q	**0.49**	0.63	0.57	0.53	0.41	0.32
3Q	**0.02**	0.15	0.28	0.28	0.24	0.19
4Q	**0.67**	0.37	0.10	0.35	0.30	0.24
Yr.	**1.70**	1.76	1.53	1.71	1.40	1.10

Next earnings report expected: NA

Dividend Data

No cash dividends have been paid.

A Division of The **McGraw·Hill** *Companies*

STANDARD
&POOR'S
STOCK REPORTS

Franklin Covey Co.

922C
03-OCT-98

Business Summary - 26-MAR-98

Franklin Covey Co. (formerly Franklin Quest Co.) is the world's leading productivity and time management training company. In FY 97 (Aug.), FC provided products and services to 82 of the Fortune 100 companies and to over 60% of Fortune 500 firms. In addition, the company serves both the governmental and educational markets. Franklin Covey also offers its products and services in 38 countries through company-owned or licensed operations.

On May 30, 1997, Franklin Quest acquired for about 5,000,000 common shares Covey Leadership Center, whose products include books, seminar, videos, corporate consulting and training programs The company adopted its present corporate title in connection with the acquisition. Management expects the combined company to have revenues of over $500 million in FY 98.

FC's seminars and products are based upon its proprietary time management system, which it believes enables individuals to better manage their time by identifying goals and prioritizing tasks. The linchpin of this system is the Franklin Day Planner. In 1991, FC developed its Ascend software product, which can be used by itself or in conjunction with the Day Planner. Historically, a large portion of the users of FC's products re-

purchase the planner each year, generating substantial recurring sales. Sales of the planner and related accessories accounted for 70% of FC's total revenues in FY 97 (Aug.). Beginning in January 1997, the company's TimeQuest seminar was added to the personal enrichment and development programs offered by the Disney Institute in Orlando, FL.

FC also provides training, consulting services and products designed to improve written and oral business communication skills. Through recent acquisitions, FC also offers fitness training services, books and commercial printing services. These services comprised the remaining 30% of total revenues in FY 97.

FC markets its products and services through its own catalog and a network of 110 (as of December 1997) retail stores throughout the U.S. In FY 97, FC opened 20 new stores, which matched the 20 stores opened in fiscal 1996.

In March 1997, the company said it had acquired, for approximately $23 million, Premier Agendas, Inc. and Premier School Agendas, Ltd., leading providers of academic and personal planners for a wide range of students. The two companies, based in Washington state and British Columbia, had combined revenues of about $35 million in 1996.

Per Share Data ($)

(Year Ended Aug. 31)	1998	1997	1996	1995	1994	1993	1992	1991	1990	1989
Tangible Bk. Val.	NA	13.49	8.80	8.11	6.61	5.55	4.15	3.64	NA	NA
Cash Flow	NA	2.82	2.26	2.22	1.64	1.30	1.08	0.70	0.25	0.12
Earnings	1.70	1.76	1.53	1.71	1.40	1.10	0.93	0.61	0.18	0.09
Dividends	Nil	Nil	Nil	Nil	Nil	Nil	Nil	Nil	NA	NA
Payout Ratio	Nil	Nil	Nil	Nil	Nil	Nil	Nil	NA	NA	NA
Prices - High	$25^3/_4$	$28^1/_4$	$29^1/_8$	$35^7/_8$	$40^1/_2$	$35^1/_4$	$21^7/_8$	NA	NA	NA
- Low	$18^1/_4$	$20^1/_8$	$17^1/_8$	$17^7/_8$	$27^1/_4$	$19^1/_8$	$14^5/_8$	NA	NA	NA
P/E Ratio - High	15	16	19	21	29	32	24	NA	NA	NA
- Low	11	11	11	10	19	17	16	NA	NA	NA

Income Statement Analysis (Million $)

	1998	1997	1996	1995	1994	1993	1992	1991	1990	1989
Revs.	NA	433	332	277	216	165	121	82.0	53.0	31.0
Oper. Inc.	NA	96.4	72.9	73.6	54.9	41.9	30.5	18.7	8.2	3.9
Depr.	NA	23.6	16.2	11.7	5.3	4.3	2.7	1.5	1.3	0.6
Int. Exp.	NA	2.3	0.6	0.6	0.9	1.1	1.3	1.2	1.4	0.6
Pretax Inc.	NA	66.4	58.2	64.2	51.0	38.7	27.4	16.6	5.7	2.9
Eff. Tax Rate	NA	41%	41%	40%	39%	40%	39%	35%	39%	39%
Net Inc.	NA	38.9	34.2	38.7	30.9	23.4	16.6	10.8	3.5	1.8

Balance Sheet & Other Fin. Data (Million $)

	1998	1997	1996	1995	1994	1993	1992	1991	1990	1989
Cash	NA	20.4	24.0	35.0	49.7	63.5	58.2	53.0	NA	NA
Curr. Assets	NA	170	113	120	113	108	89.4	NA	NA	NA
Total Assets	NA	572	268	263	198	145	114	102	NA	NA
Curr. Liab.	NA	86.9	28.6	32.2	28.0	23.5	20.6	NA	NA	NA
LT Debt	NA	94.1	5.5	4.5	7.6	8.2	10.6	8.0	NA	NA
Common Eqty.	NA	355	232	224	162	113	82.4	71.1	NA	NA
Total Cap.	NA	485	240	231	170	121	93.1	79.1	NA	NA
Cap. Exp.	NA	20.2	19.4	32.7	24.6	13.0	16.3	4.4	4.0	4.9
Cash Flow	NA	62.4	50.4	50.4	36.2	27.7	19.3	12.4	4.8	2.3
Curr. Ratio	NA	2.0	4.0	3.7	4.0	4.6	4.3	NA	NA	NA
% LT Debt of Cap.	NA	19.4	2.3	1.9	4.5	6.8	11.4	10.1	NA	NA
% Net Inc.of Revs.	NA	9.0	10.3	14.0	14.3	14.2	13.7	13.2	6.6	5.7
% Ret. on Assets	NA	9.2	12.9	16.8	17.9	17.9	20.1	NA	NA	NA
% Ret. on Equity	NA	13.2	15.0	20.0	22.3	23.7	32.3	NA	NA	NA

Data as orig. reptd.; bef. results of disc. opers. and/or spec. items. Per share data adj. for stk. divs. as of ex-div. date. Bold denotes diluted EPS (FASB 128). E-Estimated. NA-Not Available. NM-Not Meaningful. NR-Not Ranked.

Office—2200 West Parkway Blvd., Salt Lake City, UT 84119-2331. **Tel**—(801) 975-1776. **Website**—http://www.franklincovey.com **Chrmn**—H. W. Smith.**Co-Chrmn**—S. R. Covey. **CEO, Pres & COO**—J. Rowberry. **CFO**—J. L. Theler. **Investor Contact**—Richard Putnam.**Dirs**—R. F. Bennett, B. B. Campbell, S. R. Covey, R. H. Daines, E. J. Garn, D. G. Heiner, T. H. Lenagh, J. C. Peterson, J. H. Rowberry, H. W. Smith, E. Kay Stepp, J. L. Theler, S. Wheelwright, R. A. Whitman. **Transfer Agent & Registrar**—Zions First National Bank, Salt Lake City. **Incorporated**—In Utah in 1983. **Empl**— 4,741. **S&P Analyst:** Stephen J. Tekirian

Fremont General 926

NYSE Symbol **FMT**

In S&P SmallCap 600

03-OCT-98

Industry:
Insurance (Proper-ty-Casualty)

Summary: Through subsidiaries, this company provides insurance and financial services, including workers' compensation, malpractice and life insurance and asset-based lending.

Quantitative Evaluations

Recent Price • 49⅛
52 Wk Range • 62⅛-37¾

Yield • 1.2%
12-Mo. P/E • 13.8

Outlook
(1 Lowest—5 Highest)
• **2⁻**

Fair Value
• **48**

Risk
• **Low**

Earn./Div. Rank
• **A-**

Technical Eval.
• **Bearish** since 4/98

Rel. Strength Rank
(1 Lowest—99 Highest)
• **82**

Insider Activity
• **Neutral**

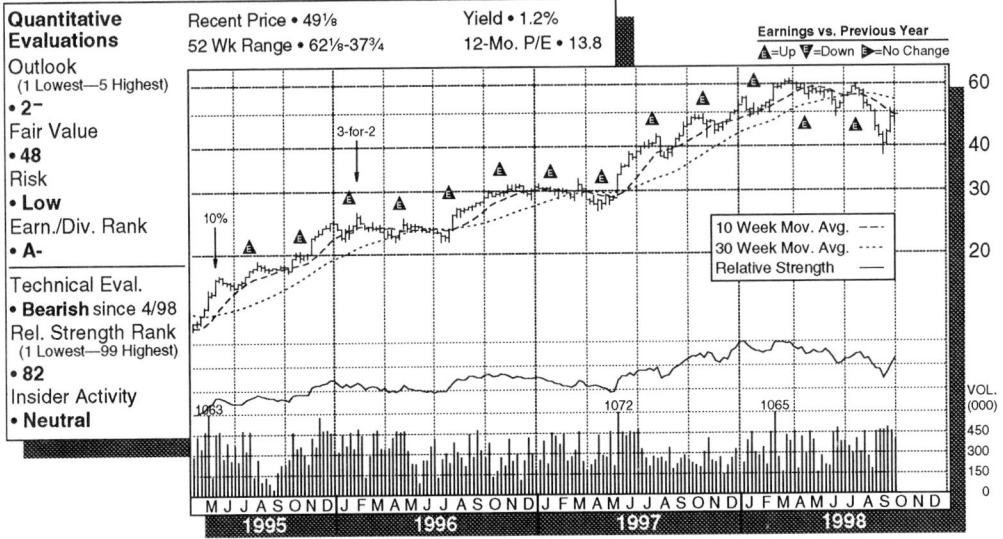

Earnings vs. Previous Year
▲=Up ▼=Down ▶=No Change

10 Week Mov. Avg. - - -
30 Week Mov. Avg. · · · ·
Relative Strength —

Business Profile - 26-MAY-98

Consistent with its core operating strategy , Fremont General completed the acquisition of Industrial Indemnity Holdings in mid-1997, expanding its underwriting of workers' compensation insurance into the western U.S. Fremont, a holding company with some $6.2 billion in assets, has subsidiaries that provide insurance and financial services, including workers' compensation, malpractice and life insurance and asset-based lending. During the first quarter of 1998, the combined ratio deteriorated to a still profitable 96.9%, from 91.2% a year earlier, due mainly to underwriting expenses at Industrial and higher incurred losses. However, recent strength in real estate lending has helped bolster results.

Operational Review - 26-MAY-98

Total revenues advanced 33% year to year in the first quarter of 1998, largely on higher workers' compensation insurance premiums and net interest income due to the acquisition of Industrial Indemnity and higher loan interest in the financial services segment. Margins were virtually flat, as a small reduction in underwriting profitability in the property and casualty division was offset by solid results in the financial services businesses. Following well-controlled interest and corporate expenses, and taxes at 32.8%, versus 32.0%, net income advanced 30%, to $31.7 million ($0.91 a share, on 3.4% more shares), from $24.4 million ($0.75).

Stock Performance - 02-OCT-98

In the past 30 trading days, FMT's shares have declined 2%, compared to a 7% fall in the S&P 500. Average trading volume for the past five days was 78,760 shares, compared with the 40-day moving average of 100,554 shares.

Key Stock Statistics

Dividend Rate/Share	0.60	Shareholders	1,600
Shs. outstg. (M)	34.8	Market cap. (B)	$ 1.7
Avg. daily vol. (M)	0.126	Inst. holdings	54%
Tang. Bk. Value/Share	21.52		
Beta	1.23		

Value of $10,000 invested 5 years ago: $ 39,564

Fiscal Year Ending Dec. 31

	1998	1997	1996	1995	1994	1993
Revenues (Million $)						
1Q	263.3	194.7	203.6	199.2	156.1	151.5
2Q	238.3	206.2	199.7	253.0	158.0	169.3
3Q	—	267.3	197.4	238.5	173.8	167.1
4Q	—	306.1	195.1	233.2	165.3	163.5
Yr.	—	974.3	795.8	923.8	653.1	651.4
Earnings Per Share ($)						
1Q	**0.91**	0.75	0.72	0.55	0.52	0.44
2Q	**0.93**	0.75	0.85	0.65	0.55	0.47
3Q	—	0.85	0.85	0.70	0.55	0.47
4Q	—	0.88	0.83	0.71	0.55	0.49
Yr.	—	**3.23**	3.26	2.61	2.17	1.85

Next earnings report expected: late October

Dividend Data (Dividends have been paid since 1977.)

Amount ($)	Date Decl.	Ex-Div. Date	Stock of Record	Payment Date
0.150	Oct. 30	Dec. 29	Dec. 31	Jan. 30 '98
0.150	Feb. 13	Mar. 27	Mar. 31	Apr. 30 '98
0.150	May. 19	Jun. 26	Jun. 30	Jul. 31 '98
0.150	Aug. 14	Sep. 28	Sep. 30	Oct. 31 '98

A Division of The McGraw-Hill Companies

Business Summary - 26-MAY-98

Fremont General Corp. (FMT) began the 1990s as an underwriter of workers' compensation insurance operating almost exclusively in California. However, through acquisitions, it has become one of the largest underwriters of workers' compensation in the nation, and, since 1990, it has also built a complementary financial services business that contributed about one-quarter of its income in 1997. Although operations in California and Illinois remain significant (61% of total inforce premiums in 1997), the addition of Industrial Indemnity in 1997 has further diversified the company geographically.

This product and market diversification served the company well in 1997. Despite California's abandonment at the start of 1995 of minimum rates for workers' compensation premiums, a legislative move that precipitated severe price competition among carriers, FMT achieved a 23% increase in property and casualty pretax income in 1997.

Workers' compensation is a statutory system requiring employers to buy insurance or self-insure in order to provide workers with medical care and other benefits for work-related injuries or illnesses. Generally, employers provide for this potential liability by purchasing

workers' compensation insurance from insurance carriers such as the company. Since the adoption of an "open" rating system in California in 1995, insurance companies there have set significantly lower premium rates, hurting profitability on the company's California policies, and causing it to withdraw from this market in 1995 and 1996. In 1997, FMT saw an emerging trend toward a more orderly market. Determined to survive recent consolidation in the workers' compensation industry as it pursues its key geographical diversification strategy, FMT acquired two workers' compensation providers in the summer of 1997. Industrial Indemnity Holdings, Inc., the larger of the two companies acquired, was purchased for $365 million in cash and the assumption of $79 million of debt.

Real estate lending operations began in 1990, with the acquisition of a California thrift and loan and now serve more than 42,000 deposit accounts through 13 branch offices. FMT's national commercial finance operation makes working capital loans to small and medium sized companies. The company believes that wider margins and less competition in the under $1 million loan market will make its recent emphasis on these smaller loans a profitable move.

Per Share Data ($)

(Year Ended Dec. 31)	1997	1996	1995	1994	1993	1992	1991	1990	1989	1988
Tangible Bk. Val.	19.77	17.51	16.83	12.69	13.35	13.84	10.35	9.14	8.21	7.71
Oper. Earnings	NA	NA	NA	NA	NA	NA	NA	NA	NA	0.79
Earnings	3.23	3.26	2.61	2.16	1.85	1.72	1.57	1.28	0.88	0.65
Dividends	0.60	0.60	0.51	0.45	0.44	0.39	0.34	0.32	0.28	0.24
Payout Ratio	19%	18%	20%	21%	24%	23%	22%	25%	32%	38%
Prices - High	55¼	31½	24⅞	15¾	17⅜	14	10¼	9⅛	8⅜	5½
- Low	26⅜	21½	11½	13	12¾	6⅞	5½	4⅛	4⅞	3½
P/E Ratio - High	17	10	10	7	9	8	7	7	9	7
- Low	8	7	4	6	7	4	4	3	6	4

Income Statement Analysis (Million $)

	1997	1996	1995	1994	1993	1992	1991	1990	1989	1988
Premium Inc.	601	487	607	448	470	429	434	430	350	305
Net Invest. Inc.	150	124	120	77.0	77.0	71.0	74.0	83.0	80.0	69.0
Oth. Revs.	223	185	197	128	104	99	73.3	60.7	40.5	37.8
Total Revs.	974	796	924	653	651	599	581	573	467	408
Pretax Inc.	159	128	100	81.6	64.3	48.6	41.0	39.0	22.2	23.2
Net Oper. Inc.	NA	NA	NA	NA	NA	NA	NA	NA	NA	20.1
Net Inc.	108	87.3	68.0	55.8	42.7	35.2	32.1	26.1	17.7	16.4

Balance Sheet & Other Fin. Data (Million $)

	1997	1996	1995	1994	1993	1992	1991	1990	1989	1988
Cash & Equiv.	65.0	82.2	70.0	44.7	48.6	62.6	41.8	47.7	64.6	84.3
Premiums Due	146	99	108	48.6	76.7	64.8	62.0	64.0	71.0	49.0
Invest. Assets: Bonds	2,059	1,124	1,659	697	996	780	770	761	994	754
Invest. Assets: Stocks	379	355	277	190	57.0	Nil	Nil	Nil	Nil	Nil
Invest. Assets: Loans	1,984	1,688	1,499	1,441	846	689	520	432	188	253
Invest. Assets: Total	2,443	3,172	3,437	2,330	1,902	1,472	1,293	1,205	1,195	1,022
Deferred Policy Costs	38.0	25.6	76.6	59.3	55.2	57.5	60.7	59.6	54.9	37.4
Total Assets	6,091	4,308	4,477	3,067	2,601	2,080	1,964	1,982	1,489	1,240
Debt	717	653	765	645	530	309	249	187	214	289
Common Eqty.	833	559	498	351	369	281	210	187	165	155
Prop. & Cas. Loss Ratio	64.7	68.9	76.0	63.1	70.0	80.4	72.7	73.7	64.6	75.6
Prop. & Cas. Expense Ratio	27.5	25.9	24.5	23.4	21.3	22.5	24.5	24.4	24.4	23.6
Prop. & Cas. Combined Ratio	93.0	94.8	100.0	86.5	91.3	102.9	97.2	98.1	89.0	99.2
% Return On Revs.	11.1	11.0	7.4	8.5	6.6	5.9	5.5	4.6	3.8	4.0
% Ret. on Equity	15.6	16.5	16.1	15.5	13.3	14.3	16.2	14.8	11.0	9.9

Data as orig. reptd.; bef. results of disc. opers. and/or spec. items. Per share data adj. for stk. divs. as of ex-div. date. Bold denotes diluted EPS (FASB 128). E-Estimated. NA-Not Available. NM-Not Meaningful. NR-Not Ranked.

Office—2020 Santa Monica Blvd., Suite 600, Santa Monica, CA 90404. **Tel**—(310) 315-5500. **Chrmn & CEO**—J. A. McIntyre. **Pres & COO**—L. J. Rampino. **EVP, Treas, CFO & Investor Contact**—Wayne R. Bailey. **Secy**—A. W. Faigin. **Dirs**—W. R. Bailey, H. I. Flournoy, C. D. Kranwinkle, J. A. McIntyre, D. W. Morrisroe, L. J. Rampino, D. C. Ross. **Transfer Agent & Registrar**—ChaseMellon Shareholder Services, Ridgefield Park, NJ. **Incorporated**—in Nevada in 1972. **Empl**— 2,843. **S&P Analyst:** L. A. Olive

Fritz Companies   3928Q

Nasdaq Symbol **FRTZ**

In S&P SmallCap 600

03-OCT-98   Industry:
Air Freight

Summary: This company provides integrated global transportation and distribution services encompassing ocean and air freight forwarding, customs brokerage and warehousing.

S&P Opinion: Hold (★★★)	Recent Price • 7¼	Yield • Nil	Earnings vs. Previous Year
	52 Wk Range • 16¾-5⅞	12-Mo. P/E • 12.6	▲=Up ▼=Down ▶=No Change

Quantitative Evaluations

Outlook
(1 Lowest—5 Highest)
• **5**

Fair Value
• **18⅝**

Risk
• **High**

Earn./Div. Rank
• **NR**

Technical Eval.
• **Bearish** since 6/98

Rel. Strength Rank
(1 Lowest—99 Highest)
• **33**

Insider Activity
• **Unfavorable**

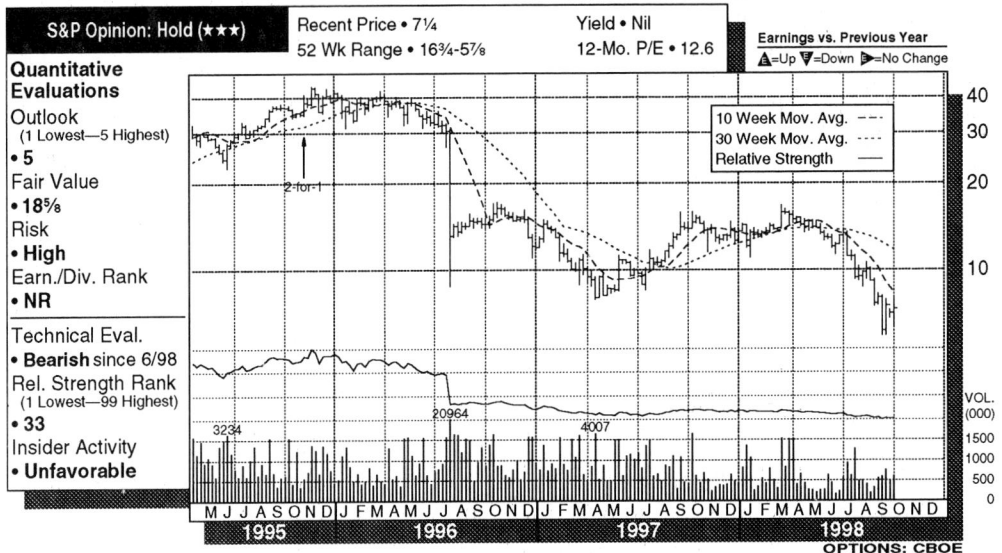

- 10 Week Mov. Avg. ---
- 30 Week Mov. Avg. ····
- Relative Strength —

2-for-1

VOL. (000)

3234   20964   4007

1500
1000
500
0

M J J A S O N D | J F M A M J J A S O N D | J F M A M J J A S O N D | J F M A M J J A S O N D
1995   **1996**   **1997**   **1998**

OPTIONS: CBOE

Overview - 23-JUL-98

Profits are expected to continue to improve in FY 99 (May). FRTZ is attracting new clients and having better success retaining its accounts, following the upgrading of its information systems to include Internet shipment tracking. FRTZ landed a new account in June 1998 to provide direct-to-store transportation services for K-B Toys. Air freight forwarding could grow at a double-digit pace, aided by increased demand in domestic markets. Ocean freight forwarding will see good growth from existing customers and the addition of new accounts. Strength in eastbound movements from Asia will be offset by few exports from the U.S., with the net effect to penalize margins. Asia's currency crisis also will manifest itself in a surge in customs filings for Asian imports, countered by increased pricing pressure. Increased movement of goods is anticipated between Canada and the U.S. Limiting the improvement will be lower fees. Warehousing and logistics will benefit from new contracts such as those recently signed with Mannatech and Brooks Sports, strength in Latin American markets and improved pricing. Comparisons will benefit from lower interest expense and stable labor costs.

Valuation - 23-JUL-98

FRTZ's shares appear to be in the process of re-testing their 1997 lows. We think the low will hold. FRTZ first fell sharply in 1996 when it revealed that its acquisition of Intertrans Corp. was not going well and then in 1997 when it disclosed that it was incurring heavy costs to develop shipment tracking and other services already offered by its competitors. FRTZ's investment in technology lagged while it went on an acquisition binge to expand its network. Fritz has been making solid progress in growing its business profitably, and the stock, now at the lower end of its trading range and no longer at a premium to its peers, is fairly priced.

Key Stock Statistics

S&P EPS Est. 1999	0.75	Tang. Bk. Value/Share	3.83
P/E on S&P Est. 1999	9.7	Beta	1.08
S&P EPS Est. 2000	1.00	Shareholders	600
Dividend Rate/Share	Nil	Market cap. (B)	$0.262
Shs. outstg. (M)	35.9	Inst. holdings	55%
Avg. daily vol. (M)	0.124		

Value of $10,000 invested 5 years ago: $ 8,477

Fiscal Year Ending May 31

	1999	1998	1997	1996	1995	1994
Revenues (Million $)						
1Q	145.2	139.2	129.7	115.7	--	46.29
2Q	—	145.2	130.8	119.0	—	55.25
3Q	—	132.3	118.0	103.8	—	69.22
4Q	—	141.6	130.9	119.1	—	74.69
Yr.	—	558.3	509.4	457.6	165.7	245.4
Earnings Per Share ($)						
1Q	**0.19**	0.11	0.22	0.36	--	0.13
2Q	—	0.19	0.26	0.36	—	0.18
3Q	—	**0.07**	-0.48	0.09	—	0.28
4Q	—	**0.13**	Nil	-0.10	—	0.27
Yr.	**E0.75**	**0.50**	0.01	0.70	-0.26	0.86

Next earnings report expected: late December

Dividend Data

No cash dividends have been paid to the public. A two-for-one common stock split was effected in 1995.

A Division of The McGraw-Hill Companies

Fritz Companies, Inc.

Business Summary - 23-JUL-98

A third-party provider of transportation and logistics services, Fritz Companies (FRTZ) is a technology and communications-driven company, having no assets tied up in transportation equipment. FRTZ embarked on a major acquisition binge during the early 1990s to establish a network of 480 offices in 115 nations. Its focus now is to reclaim its leadership in technology and build the business of its existing network.

FRTZ is the largest customs broker in the U.S. (accounting for 30% of revenues in FY 97; May). Customs brokerage services also are provided in Australia, Canada and the U.K. As a customs broker, FRTZ coordinates all steps in the movement of imported goods via ocean or air modes. Its services include the preparation of all documentation required for the import of merchandise, obtaining customs bonds, arranging payment of collect freight charges and depositing import duties with the U.S. Customs Service. Through its "Automated Broker Interface," clients can monitor their shipments and electronically interact on-line with FRTZ.

FRTZ is one of the largest U.S. forwarders of international ocean and air freight (21% and 29%, respectively, of net revenue in FY 97). A forwarder consolidates many small shipments bound for a single destination, procuring transportation at a discount to the fee per pound charged to its clients.

FRTZ established its network of forwarders in recent years through acquisitions. The acquisition pace has slowed as FRTZ's global network is essentially complete. In FY 97, FRTZ spent just $10 million for acquisitions, versus $37.1 million in FY 96. FRTZ's shares fell sharply in 1996 when it developed a severe case of indigestion accompanying the $210 million stock-based acquisition of Intertrans in May 1995. Intertrans's problems included an incompatible accounting system, bad debts and poor documentation of transactions.

The company invested heavily in software development in FY 97 preparing for the launch of several service enhancements. In June 1997, FRTZ unveiled its Ocean Export System, a program that allows shippers to automatically keep track of their account with FRTZ and price services. Also in June, FRTZ rolled out Internet-based tracking services for both air and ocean forwarding customers.

FRTZ also provides a wide variety of warehousing and distribution services (20% of revenues) for import and export customers utilizing some 6.3 million sq. ft. of owned and leased space. Some of the services offered include receiving, deconsolidation, cargo loading and unloading, and inventory management.

Per Share Data ($) (Year Ended May 31)	1998	1997	1996	1995	1994	1993	1992	1991	1990	1989
Tangible Bk. Val.	3.83	3.50	4.07	3.34	2.76	1.48	0.90	-1.24	-1.36	NA
Cash Flow	1.23	0.70	1.26	-0.06	1.25	0.86	1.01	0.70	0.52	NA
Earnings	0.50	0.01	0.70	-0.26	0.86	0.66	0.64	0.35	0.29	NA
Dividends	Nil	Nil	Nil	Nil	Nil	Nil	Nil	Nil	Nil	Nil
Payout Ratio	Nil	Nil	Nil	Nil	Nil	Nil	Nil	Nil	Nil	Nil
Cal. Yrs.	1997	1996	1995	1994	1993	1992	1991	1990	1989	1988
Prices - High	16	42¼	23⅝	23⅝	15¼	13⅜	NA	NA	NA	NA
- Low	7⅞	8¾	13	13	10¼	7½	NA	NA	NA	NA
P/E Ratio - High	32	NM	34	NM	18	20	NA	NA	NA	NA
- Low	16	NM	19	NM	12	11	NA	NA	NA	NA
Income Statement Analysis (Million $)										
Revs.	558	509	458	165	516	342	249	121	108	94.0
Oper. Inc.	52.2	27.5	73.4	24.2	40.3	25.3	20.7	17.8	13.7	13.3
Depr.	26.4	24.6	20.2	6.5	8.9	4.2	3.7	5.4	3.6	2.6
Int. Exp.	Nil	Nil	NA	NA	2.2	0.3	0.9	3.2	2.6	3.1
Pretax Inc.	26.6	0.5	38.4	-12.5	30.1	21.6	16.2	9.1	7.5	NA
Eff. Tax Rate	32%	35%	35%	NM	35%	35%	14%	40%	40%	NA
Net Inc.	18.1	0.3	25.0	-8.3	19.6	14.0	13.1	5.4	4.5	NA
Balance Sheet & Other Fin. Data (Million $)										
Cash	53.9	43.4	86.4	74.3	39.8	8.3	19.8	14.9	13.5	NA
Curr. Assets	500	496	520	422	291	152	136	121	103	NA
Total Assets	722	724	733	577	400	191	157	136	114	119
Curr. Liab.	359	394	408	361	252	143	131	132	110	NA
LT Debt	101	84.9	89.5	33.6	33.0	2.2	Nil	17.3	19.7	28.4
Common Eqty.	250	235	231	174	107	39.1	21.1	-17.4	-19.6	-22.6
Total Cap.	353	321	322	210	143	43.6	22.1	-0.1	-0.2	5.7
Cap. Exp.	21.8	42.5	42.6	13.1	35.5	15.2	7.5	6.0	2.9	2.1
Cash Flow	44.5	24.9	45.2	-1.8	28.5	18.2	16.8	10.8	8.1	NA
Curr. Ratio	1.4	1.3	1.3	1.2	1.2	1.1	1.0	0.9	0.9	NA
% LT Debt of Cap.	28.7	26.4	27.8	16.0	23.0	5.1	Nil	NM	NM	NM
% Net Inc.of Revs.	3.2	0.1	5.5	NM	3.8	4.1	5.3	4.5	4.1	NA
% Ret. on Assets	2.5	0.0	3.8	NM	6.3	8.0	7.6	4.3	3.9	NA
% Ret. on Equity	7.5	0.1	12.3	NM	25.7	46.5	NM	NM	NM	NM

Data as orig. reptd.; bef. results of disc. opers. and/or spec. items. Per share data adj. for stk. divs. as of ex-div. date. Bold denotes diluted EPS (FASB 128). Prior to 1995 (five mos.), yrs. ended Dec. 31. E-Estimated. NA-Not Available. NM-Not Meaningful. NR-Not Ranked.

Office—706 Mission St., Suite 900, San Francisco, CA 94103. **Tel**—(415) 904-8360. **Website**—http://www.fritz.com **Chrmn & CEO**—L. C. Fritz. **Pres & COO**—D. L. Pelino. **EVP-CFO**—R. Arovas. **SVP & Secy**—J. H. Raymond. **Investor Contact**—Graeme Stewart (415-538-0444). **Dirs**—L. C. Fritz, J. Gilleran, P. Martin, P. Otellini, D. L. Pelino, W. J. Razzouk. **Transfer Agent & Registrar**—ChaseMellon Shareholder Services, Ridgefield Park, NJ. **Incorporated**—in Delaware in 1988. **Empl**— 10,000. **S&P Analyst:** Stephen R. Klein

03-OCT-98   **Industry:** Insurance (Property-ty-Casualty)

Summary: FTR is a specialty property and casualty insurer and reinsurer.

Quantitative Evaluations	
Outlook (1 Lowest—5 Highest)	• **5**
Fair Value	• **23¼**
Risk	• **Low**
Earn./Div. Rank	• **B+**
Technical Eval.	• **Bearish** since 5/98
Rel. Strength Rank (1 Lowest—99 Highest)	• **26**
Insider Activity	• **Neutral**

Recent Price • 12¾   52 Wk Range • 33½-12⅛
Yield • 2.2%   12-Mo. P/E • 12.8

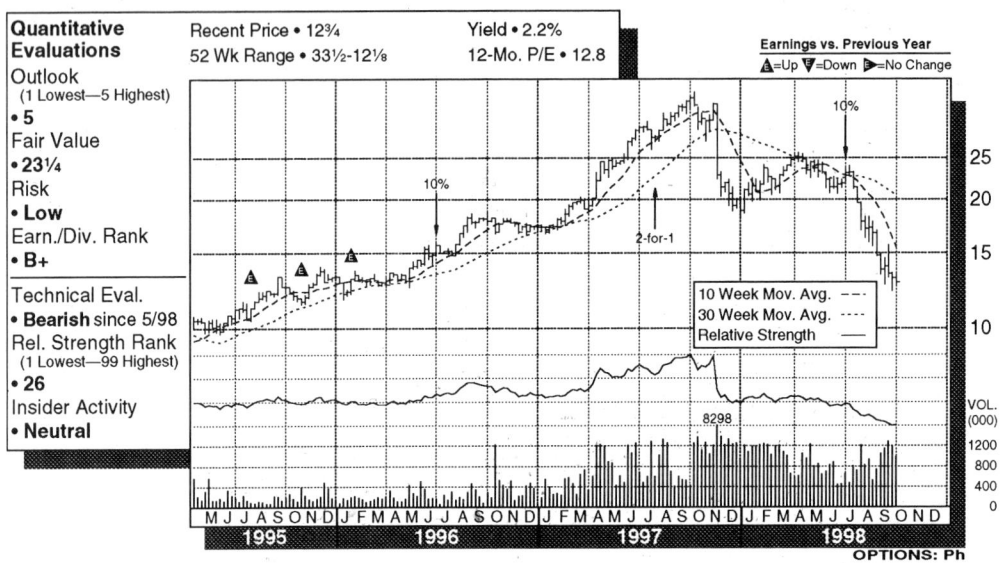

Earnings vs. Previous Year
▲=Up ▼=Down ▶=No Change

10 Week Mov. Avg. ---
30 Week Mov. Avg. ····
Relative Strength —

VOL. (000)

OPTIONS: Ph

Business Profile - 24-AUG-98

Frontier's growth strategy calls for the development of new insurance programs, the expansion of existing lines of business, and the acquisition of other specialty insurers. In June 1998, FTR formed an underwriting division called Creative Risk to focus on professional liability lines. In July, FTR formed the Frontier Financial division to consolidate FTR's existing surety and fidelity products with those of recently acquired Acceleration Life Insurance Co. and Lyndon Insurance Group. Also in July, FTR acquired 85% of the capital stock of London & European Title Insurance Services Limited, the leading provider of title insurance to mortgage lenders in the United Kingdom. The company paid a 10% stock dividend on July 20 in addition to the regular cash dividend. Directors and officers own over 8% of the stock.

Operational Review - 24-AUG-98

In the first half of 1998, total revenues climbed 59%, year to year, reflecting growth in the majority of core and new program business and the impact of several acquisitions. Expenses rose 68%, led by an 89% increase in insurance losses, and pretax income was up 25%. After taxes at 25.4%, versus 27.8%, net income rose 29%, to $35.2 million ($0.85 a share, on 14% more shares), from $27.3 million ($0.77).

Stock Performance - 02-OCT-98

In the past 30 trading days, FTR's shares have declined 23%, compared to a 7% fall in the S&P 500. Average trading volume for the past five days was 196,520 shares, compared with the 40-day moving average of 226,959 shares.

Key Stock Statistics

Dividend Rate/Share	0.28	Shareholders	900
Shs. outstg. (M)	37.5	Market cap. (B)	$0.480
Avg. daily vol. (M)	0.287	Inst. holdings	61%
Tang. Bk. Value/Share	11.55		
Beta	0.99		

Value of $10,000 invested 5 years ago: $ 12,886

Fiscal Year Ending Dec. 31

	1998	1997	1996	1995	1994	1993
Revenues (Million $)						
1Q	142.5	90.44	66.80	51.77	41.16	36.78
2Q	143.3	89.32	75.30	53.91	37.95	34.80
3Q	—	118.0	79.77	58.07	46.44	36.14
4Q	—	128.7	83.05	62.65	54.43	31.44
Yr.	—	426.4	305.0	226.4	180.0	139.2
Earnings Per Share ($)						
1Q	**0.43**	**0.34**	0.29	0.22	0.21	0.21
2Q	**0.42**	**0.40**	0.31	0.26	0.24	0.23
3Q	—	**0.38**	0.30	0.26	-0.16	0.19
4Q	—	**-0.18**	0.36	0.26	0.25	0.20
Yr.	—	**0.92**	1.25	0.99	0.54	0.84

Next earnings report expected: mid November

Dividend Data (Dividends have been paid since 1992.)

Amount ($)	Date Decl.	Ex-Div. Date	Stock of Record	Payment Date
0.070	Feb. 24	Mar. 27	Mar. 31	Apr. 21 '98
0.070	May. 28	Jun. 26	Jun. 30	Jul. 20 '98
10%	May. 28	Jun. 29	Jul. 01	Jul. 20 '98
0.070	Sep. 21	Sep. 28	Sep. 30	Oct. 20 '98

STANDARD
&POOR'S
STOCK REPORTS

Frontier Insurance Group, Inc.

926M
03-OCT-98

Business Summary - 24-AUG-98

Frontier Insurance Group, Inc., through its Frontier Insurance Company and other subsidaries, is engaged in specialty insurance and reinsurance businesses, and performs claims adjusting and management services. It has operations in all 50 states. In 1997, gross and net premiums written rose to $587.6 million and $389.0 million, respectively, from $402.8 million and $311.9 million in 1996. Growth came both from stronger core and new program business, and from the company's ongoing acquisition campaign. Contributions to gross and net written premiums in 1997:

	Gross premiums	Net premiums
General liability	29.1%	33.6%
Medical malpractice	20.6%	25.8%
Surety	13.0%	15.9%
Specialty personal lines	12.8%	9.0%
Credit related products	7.8%	3.3%
Workers compensation	4.2%	1.9%
Commericial earthquake	2.5%	2.0%
Other	10.0%	8.5%

FTR markets its products directly and through independent agents. In 1997, 13.6% of FTR's gross premiums were generated directly, and 86.4% came through independent insurance agencies and brokerage firms.

The statutory combined ratio is a traditional measure of underwriting success for insurance companies. Generally, if the ratio is below 100%, an insurance company has generated a profit for a given period, and if it's over 100%, the insurer has experienced an underwriting loss. Using the combined ratio as a measure of underwriting expertise, FTR has consistently outperformed the industry since 1993; in 1997, its combined ratio was 100.9%, while the industry's was about 101.8%.

Total net investment income accounted for 14% of FTR's total revenues in 1997. At December 31, 1997, the company's invested assets were valued at $1,249.5 million, up from $838.3 million a year before.

In June 1997, the company acquired St. Louis-based Lyndon Property Insurance Co. and its six subsidiaries, providers of credit-related and specialty insurance for financial institutions, for $92 million. In December, FTR acquired Houston-based Western Indemnity Insurance Co., a provider of insurance for health care providers, for $48 million, and FTR's United Capitol subsidiary acquired Environmental and Commercial Insurance Agency, Inc., of Columbus, Ohio, for $4.5 million. In early 1998, FTR acquired Acceleration Life Insurance Co. for $40.5 million.

In January 1998, FTR's founder and longtime CEO Walter Rhulen passed away after a five-month battle with leukemia. His son, Harry Rhulen, was named chairman and CEO in February.

Per Share Data ($)

(Year Ended Dec. 31)	1997	1996	1995	1994	1993	1992	1991	1990	1989	1988
Tangible Bk. Val.	12.49	7.97	7.29	6.05	5.93	4.09	3.52	2.42	1.90	1.44
Oper. Earnings	NA	1.23	0.99	0.57	0.84	0.72	0.61	0.52	0.44	0.36
Earnings	0.92	1.26	0.99	0.54	0.84	0.73	0.63	0.53	0.46	0.35
Dividends	0.31	0.23	0.20	0.19	0.16	0.15	Nil	Nil	Nil	Nil
Payout Ratio	34%	18%	20%	35%	19%	20%	Nil	Nil	Nil	Nil
Prices - High	35⅝	18¾	14	15½	13¾	11	6⅝	7⅛	4¼	2⅜
- Low	16⅝	11⅝	8⅜	6⅞	10⅛	6⅛	3⅞	3⅛	2³⁄₁₆	1⅛
P/E Ratio - High	39	15	14	29	16	15	11	14	9	7
- Low	18	9	8	13	12	8	6	6	5	3

Income Statement Analysis (Million $)

	1997	1996	1995	1994	1993	1992	1991	1990	1989	1988
Premium Inc.	367	266	196	157	116	105	78.0	72.3	55.0	39.3
Net Invest. Inc.	56.1	37.2	30.0	24.5	22.5	19.9	15.9	12.1	8.6	6.0
Oth. Revs.	4.2	0.1	0.1	-1.2	0.3	1.7	2.4	1.6	Nil	Nil
Total Revs.	427	305	226	180	139	127	96.3	86.0	63.6	45.3
Pretax Inc.	56.9	56.5	43.3	21.3	30.3	25.2	20.1	14.7	12.8	10.0
Net Oper. Inc.	NA	NA	31.2	17.9	23.0	NA	NA	10.4	9.2	7.4
Net Inc.	32.3	40.0	31.2	17.0	23.2	19.0	15.0	10.8	9.4	7.2

Balance Sheet & Other Fin. Data (Million $)

	1997	1996	1995	1994	1993	1992	1991	1990	1989	1988
Cash & Equiv.	11.8	8.3	12.6	11.4	17.8	5.0	14.4	4.1	3.8	2.8
Premiums Due	95.2	76.6	50.0	41.1	28.4	28.2	24.7	26.6	18.0	18.4
Invest. Assets: Bonds	1,080	685	521	346	276	242	208	153	114	72.0
Invest. Assets: Stocks	20.3	16.2	21.0	48.6	7.5	9.9	1.1	3.8	4.9	6.2
Invest. Assets: Loans	Nil	Nil	Nil	Nil	Nil	Nil	Nil	Nil	Nil	Nil
Invest. Assets: Total	1,249	702	553	408	344	262	235	165	131	90.0
Deferred Policy Costs	55.6	32.8	18.8	13.2	6.8	6.0	3.2	2.2	Nil	Nil
Total Assets	1,976	1,246	773	599	522	341	300	215	170	122
Debt	167	NM	25.0	Nil	Nil	Nil	Nil	Nil	Nil	Nil
Common Eqty.	454	269	230	190	186	107	91.2	49.7	39.0	29.4
Prop. & Cas. Loss Ratio	65.2	58.7	NA	70.8	66.7	71.2	69.7	73.7	75.1	75.6
Prop. & Cas. Expense Ratio	35.7	32.2	NA	27.0	26.5	25.6	26.3	24.0	23.7	17.8
Prop. & Cas. Combined Ratio	100.9	90.9	91.5	97.8	93.3	96.8	96.0	97.7	98.8	93.4
% Return On Revs.	7.6	13.1	13.8	9.4	16.7	15.0	15.6	12.5	14.8	16.3
% Ret. on Equity	8.9	16.1	14.9	9.1	15.8	19.2	21.3	24.3	27.5	28.8

Data as orig. reptd.; bef. results of disc. opers. and/or spec. items. Per share data adj. for stk. divs. as of ex-div. date. Bold denotes diluted EPS (FASB 128). E-Estimated. NA-Not Available. NM-Not Meaningful. NR-Not Ranked.

Office—195 Lake Louise Marie Rd., Rock Hill, NY 12775-8000. **Tel**—(914) 796-2100. **Fax**—(914) 796-1902. **Website**—http://www.frontierins.com **Chrmn, CEO & Pres**—H. W. Rhulen. **VP-CFO & Treas**—M.H. Mishler. **Secy**—J. P. Loughlin. **Investor Contact**—Jeanne Jennings (914-796-2100). **Dirs**—A. Gerry, P. B. Guenther, J. Loughlin, S. Rhulen Loughlin, D. C. Moat, L. E. O'Brien, H. W. Rhulen, P. L. Rhulen. **Transfer Agent & Registrar**—American Stock Transfer & Trust Co., NYC. **Incorporated**—in Delaware in 1986. **Empl**—1,180. **S&P Analyst:** T. W. Smith, CFA

Frozen Food Express

3929R

NASDAQ Symbol **FFEX**

In S&P SmallCap 600

03-OCT-98

Industry: Truckers

Summary: FFEX is the largest publicly owned, full-service motor carrier of perishable commodities in North America.

Quantitative Evaluations		
Outlook (1 Lowest—5 Highest)	• 4	
Fair Value	• 8⅜	
Risk	• Average	
Earn./Div. Rank	• A-	
Technical Eval.	• **Bearish** since 7/98	
Rel. Strength Rank (1 Lowest—99 Highest)	• 90	
Insider Activity	• NA	

Recent Price • 7¾
52 Wk Range • 10½-5⅝

Yield • 1.5%
12-Mo. P/E • 13.2

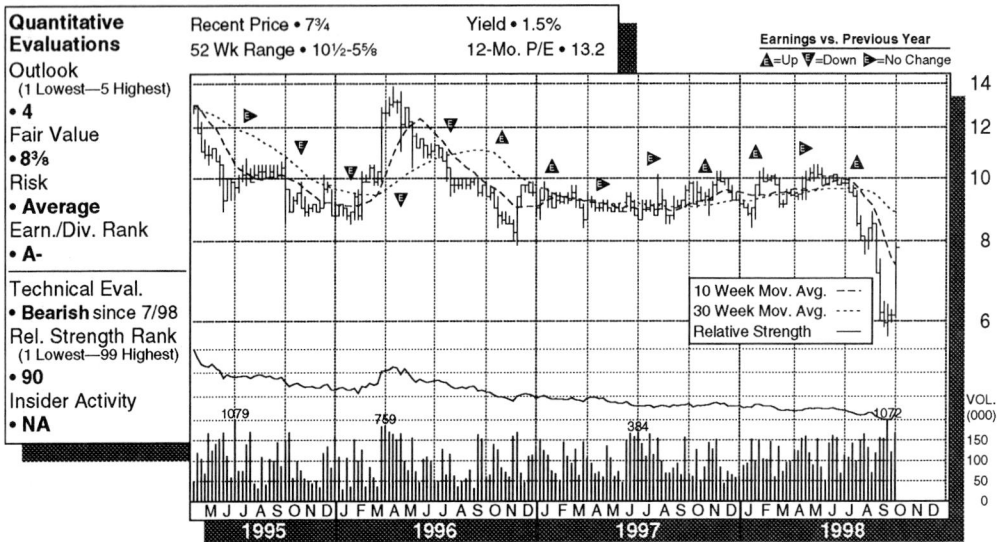

Earnings vs. Previous Year
▲=Up ▼=Down ▶=No Change

10 Week Mov. Avg. – – –
30 Week Mov. Avg. · · · ·
Relative Strength ——

Business Profile - 06-JUL-98

Over the years, Frozen Food Express has pursued a strategy combining both internal growth and acquisitions. The company is continuing to expand international and domestic transportation and logistics services, which involve railroad-based intermodal long-haul transportation (intermodal means a blend of two or more modes of transportation, such as railcar and truck). The company plans to add about 100 tractors during 1998, and to replace about 350 more. Share earnings were in a long-term uptrend until peaking in 1994 at $0.72. The company has a strong balance sheet, with minimal long term debt.

Operational Review - 06-JUL-98

Revenues in the three months ended March 31, 1998, advanced 6.6%, year to year, on gains of 4.2% and 41% in freight and non freight revenues, respectively. Although interest and other expense fell sharply, profitability was restricted by increases in salaries, wages and related expenses; pretax income rose only 4.1%. After taxes at 32.0%, versus 30.4%, net income was up 1.8%, to $1,395,000 ($0.08 a share), from $1,371,000 ($0.08).

Stock Performance - 02-OCT-98

In the past 30 trading days, FFEX's shares have declined 8%, compared to a 7% fall in the S&P 500. Average trading volume for the past five days was 81,840 shares, compared with the 40-day moving average of 59,310 shares.

Key Stock Statistics

Dividend Rate/Share	0.12	Shareholders	7,500
Shs. outstg. (M)	16.9	Market cap. (B)	$0.132
Avg. daily vol. (M)	0.093	Inst. holdings	25%
Tang. Bk. Value/Share	5.74		
Beta	0.59		

Value of $10,000 invested 5 years ago: $ 8,301

Fiscal Year Ending Dec. 31

	1998	1997	1996	1995	1994	1993
Revenues (Million $)						
1Q	77.51	72.69	74.17	66.98	60.30	48.96
2Q	88.42	81.26	79.41	73.84	70.30	57.03
3Q	—	82.98	80.82	75.78	72.54	60.56
4Q	—	79.65	77.02	75.75	71.48	60.85
Yr.	—	316.6	311.4	292.4	274.6	227.4
Earnings Per Share ($)						
1Q	**0.08**	**0.08**	0.08	0.11	0.10	0.08
2Q	**0.18**	**0.16**	0.16	0.23	0.23	0.18
3Q	—	0.17	0.15	0.13	0.21	0.17
4Q	—	**0.15**	0.12	0.10	0.18	0.14
Yr.	—	**0.57**	0.52	0.57	0.72	0.58

Next earnings report expected: NA

Dividend Data (Dividends have been paid since 1971.)

Amount ($)	Date Decl.	Ex-Div. Date	Stock of Record	Payment Date
0.030	Nov. 12	Nov. 24	Nov. 26	Dec. 05 '97
0.030	Feb. 11	Feb. 24	Feb. 26	Mar. 05 '98
0.030	May. 13	May. 19	May. 21	Jun. 01 '98
0.030	Aug. 14	Aug. 17	Aug. 26	Sep. 04 '98

A Division of The **McGraw·Hill** *Companies*

Frozen Food Express Industries, Inc.

Business Summary - 06-JUL-98

In late 1946, a couple of World War II veterans scraped up enough money to buy two used trucks. From this beginning, Frozen Food Express Industries (FFEX) has grown to become the largest temperature-controlled trucking company in North America, with operations that extend from Montreal throughout the continental U.S. to Mexico City. FFEX offers both less-than-truckload (LTL) and full truckload service.

More than 80% of the company's cargo is temperature sensitive. Its primary cargo includes meat, poultry, seafood, processed foods, candy, dairy products, pharmaceuticals, medical supplies, fruits and vegetables, film and heat-sensitive aerospace manufacturing materials.

With full truckload service (67% of 1997 freight revenues), loads typically weigh between 20,000 lbs. and 40,000 lbs., and are usually from a single shipper, filling the trailer. Prior to 1987, FFEX's truckload operations were conducted mostly through the use of equipment and drivers under agreements with independent contractors. Most of FFEX's full truckload operations are currently conducted with company-operated equipment.

LTL loads (33% of 1997 freight revenues) consist of multiple shipments (usually between 18 and 30), weigh-ing as little as 50 lbs. or as much as 20,000 lbs., from multiple shippers, destined for various deliveries across North America. The company's temperature-controlled LTL operation is the largest in the U.S., and the only one that offers continent-wide service that provides pickups and deliveries on a regular schedule, like a bus line. FFEX is also the only major LTL carrier that uses multi-compartment refrigerated trailers to carry different goods at different temperatures. Scheduling, billing and climate control information is provided through an on-line computer system.

During 1996, FFEX expanded its use of a satellite-based tracking and communication system that provides automatic hourly updates of the position of each full-truckload tractor and permits real-time communication between operations personnel and drivers. The company is also continuing to expand its international and domestic transportation and logistics services, which involve railroad-based intermodal long-haul transportation.

At the end of 1997, equipment in service included 1,220 company-operated tractors, 628 owner-operated tractors, and 2,784 company-provided tractors, plus 23 tractors provided by owner-operators. FFEX plans to add about 100 tractors to its company-operated, full truckload fleet during 1998.

Per Share Data ($)

(Year Ended Dec. 31)	1997	1996	1995	1994	1993	1992	1991	1990	1989	1988
Tangible Bk. Val.	5.53	5.04	4.59	4.03	3.31	2.72	2.03	2.06	1.88	1.69
Cash Flow	1.13	1.09	1.24	1.31	1.19	0.95	0.89	0.82	0.69	0.64
Earnings	0.57	0.52	0.57	0.72	0.58	0.45	0.34	0.25	0.26	0.26
Dividends	0.12	0.12	0.12	0.10	0.10	0.08	0.06	0.06	0.05	0.04
Payout Ratio	21%	23%	21%	14%	16%	17%	20%	24%	18%	14%
Prices - High	10¹/₄	13⁷/₈	13⁷/₈	15	15	11¹/₂	4¹/₈	2³/₄	3¹/₂	2⁵/₈
- Low	8³/₈	7⁷/₈	8¹/₂	11	7¹/₄	4	1¹³/₁₆	1¹³/₁₆	2¹/₈	1¹/₁₆
P/E Ratio - High	18	27	24	21	26	26	12	11	13	9
- Low	15	15	15	15	12	9	5	7	8	4

Income Statement Analysis (Million $)

	1997	1996	1995	1994	1993	1992	1991	1990	1989	1988
Revs.	317	311	292	275	227	195	177	160	122	102
Oper. Inc.	23.6	48.9	25.5	28.5	24.7	19.6	17.6	15.7	11.8	10.6
Depr.	9.6	9.5	10.7	9.8	9.9	8.0	8.3	8.2	6.2	5.3
Int. Exp.	NM	3.4	NA	NA	0.8	0.4	1.3	1.9	1.2	0.8
Pretax Inc.	13.8	11.7	13.2	17.8	14.4	11.2	8.6	5.8	5.5	5.0
Eff. Tax Rate	30%	28%	30%	33%	35%	36%	39%	38%	31%	26%
Net Inc.	9.7	8.5	9.3	11.9	9.4	7.1	5.2	3.6	3.8	3.7

Balance Sheet & Other Fin. Data (Million $)

	1997	1996	1995	1994	1993	1992	1991	1990	1989	1988
Cash	23.3	6.7	7.5	4.4	3.8	3.7	3.2	0.5	1.6	0.3
Curr. Assets	77.0	65.4	61.6	57.1	48.1	37.4	29.9	26.9	18.9	13.8
Total Assets	143	130	124	117	109	86.0	66.9	74.3	58.8	47.9
Curr. Liab.	32.0	31.3	36.6	31.4	27.2	20.4	14.3	13.8	9.3	8.3
LT Debt	Nil	NM	NM	9.0	17.0	12.0	7.1	21.3	14.0	8.6
Common Eqty.	93.1	83.9	75.0	64.3	52.0	41.8	35.1	30.0	27.3	24.3
Total Cap.	101	90.8	75.0	77.8	72.5	58.2	47.4	56.5	46.5	38.3
Cap. Exp.	14.7	13.7	10.7	13.6	23.6	20.3	2.2	17.7	13.5	17.2
Cash Flow	19.3	18.0	19.9	21.6	19.4	15.2	13.5	11.9	10.0	9.0
Curr. Ratio	2.4	2.1	1.7	1.8	1.8	1.8	2.1	1.9	2.0	1.7
% LT Debt of Cap.	NM	NM	NM	11.6	23.4	20.6	15.0	37.8	30.2	22.4
% Net Inc.of Revs.	3.1	2.7	3.2	4.3	4.2	3.7	2.9	2.3	3.1	3.6
% Ret. on Assets	7.1	6.7	7.7	10.5	9.6	9.8	6.6	5.4	7.0	8.7
% Ret. on Equity	10.9	10.7	12.1	20.3	19.9	19.6	14.5	12.5	14.5	16.2

Data as orig. reptd.; bef. results of disc. opers. and/or spec. items. Per share data adj. for stk. divs. as of ex-div. date. Bold denotes diluted EPS (FASB 128). E-Estimated. NA-Not Available. NM-Not Meaningful. NR-Not Ranked.

Office—1145 Empire Central Place, Dallas, TX 75247-4309; P.O. Box 655888, Dallas 75265-5888.**Tel**—(214) 630-8090. **Chrmn & Pres**—S. M. Stubbs Jr. **Vice Chrmn**—E. O. Weller.**SVP & CFO**—B. G. Cott. **Secy**—L. W. Bartholomew. **Treas**—T. G. Yetter. **Dirs**—W. M. Baggett, B. R. Blackmarr, B. G. Cott, L. Hallman, W. G. Lord, T. M. O'Connor, C. G. Robertson, S. M. Stubbs Jr., E. O. Weller. **Transfer Agent**—First National Bank of Boston. **Incorporated**—in Texas in 1969. **Empl**— 2,738. **S&P Analyst:** J.J.S.

G & K Services

3933

NASDAQ Symbol **GKSRA**

In S&P SmallCap 600

03-OCT-98

Industry:
Services (Commercial & Consumer)

Summary: This company is one of the leading U.S. suppliers of uniforms and related textile products used in a wide range of businesses and institutions.

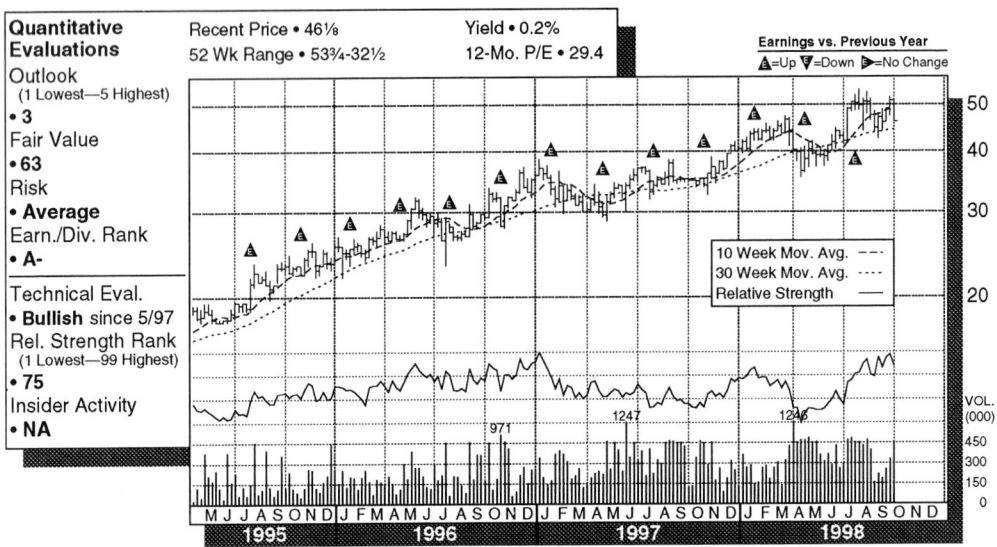

Quantitative Evaluations	
Outlook (1 Lowest—5 Highest)	• 3
Fair Value	• 63
Risk	• Average
Earn./Div. Rank	• A-
Technical Eval.	• Bullish since 5/97
Rel. Strength Rank (1 Lowest—99 Highest)	• 75
Insider Activity	• NA

Recent Price • 46⅛
52 Wk Range • 53¾-32½
Yield • 0.2%
12-Mo. P/E • 29.4

Earnings vs. Previous Year
▲=Up ▼=Down ▶=No Change

10 Week Mov. Avg. – – –
30 Week Mov. Avg. .....
Relative Strength ——

Business Profile - 16-SEP-98

Operations were significantly expanded with the July 1997 acquisition of National Linen Services (NLS). The company divested 11 business locations during FY 98 (Jun.) acquired through the NLS acquisition, that were not compatible with the firm's strategic goals. In addition, GKSRA sold seven of the nine linen rental plants and three of the 20 uniform rental plants originally acquired with National Linen Services. Management feels that they are taking positive steps in integrating the acquisition and reducing the number of redundant routes and plants in the two systems.

Operational Review - 16-SEP-98

Based on a preliminary report, total revenues for the twelve months ended June 27, 1998, rose 43%, reflecting a significant contribution from the National Linen Services acquisition and double digit growth in existing operations. Despite higher merchandise and production costs associated with the newly acquired locations, margins expanded due to well-controlled selling and administrative expenses from the leveraging of corporate costs and growth in start-up locations; operating income climbed 45%. After sharply higher amortization and depreciation charges, interest expense, and taxes at 39.2%, versus 39.5%, net income increased 11% to $32,058,000 ($1.57 a share), from $29,002,000 ($1.42).

Stock Performance - 02-OCT-98

In the past 30 trading days, GKSRA's shares have declined 3%, compared to a 7% fall in the S&P 500. Average trading volume for the past five days was 109,580 shares, compared with the 40-day moving average of 71,033 shares.

Key Stock Statistics

Dividend Rate/Share	0.07	Shareholders	600
Shs. outstg. (M)	20.5	Market cap. (B)	$0.877
Avg. daily vol. (M)	0.067	Inst. holdings	60%
Tang. Bk. Value/Share	6.31		
Beta	0.74		

Value of $10,000 invested 5 years ago: $ 40,764

Fiscal Year Ending Jun. 30

	1998	1997	1996	1995	1994	1993
Revenues (Million $)						
1Q	118.4	83.31	70.95	60.53	53.35	49.40
2Q	128.3	87.44	75.09	65.55	55.53	50.70
3Q	127.5	88.47	77.48	66.72	57.13	51.00
4Q	128.4	91.69	81.89	69.67	59.22	56.75
Yr.	502.6	350.9	305.4	262.5	225.2	207.9
Earnings Per Share ($)						
1Q	0.36	0.34	0.25	0.21	0.17	0.12
2Q	0.38	0.35	0.27	0.23	0.18	0.10
3Q	0.39	0.36	0.28	0.22	0.18	0.13
4Q	0.43	0.37	0.31	0.24	0.20	0.18
Yr.	1.57	1.42	1.11	0.90	0.73	0.55

Next earnings report expected: early November

Dividend Data (Dividends have been paid since 1968.)

Amount ($)	Date Decl.	Ex-Div. Date	Stock of Record	Payment Date
0.018	Oct. 31	Dec. 09	Dec. 11	Jan. 02 '98
0.018	Feb. 19	Mar. 17	Mar. 19	Apr. 02 '98
0.018	May. 21	Jun. 02	Jun. 04	Jun. 18 '98
0.018	Aug. 27	Sep. 15	Sep. 17	Oct. 01 '98

A Division of The McGraw·Hill Companies

STANDARD
&POOR'S
STOCK REPORTS

G & K Services, Inc.

3933

03-OCT-98

Business Summary - 16-SEP-98

G&K Services believes that its uniform program can help improve a company's image, promote teamwork among workers, provide protection from wear and tear on employees' clothing, create walking advertising, and increase company morale. Across America, over 90,000 local businesses and half of all Fortune 100 businesses have chosen G&K for their uniform service needs.

Over the past 10 years, G&K's net income has advanced at a 19% annual rate. During this time, the company's shares have risen nearly tenfold, from under $4 a share (as adjusted) in 1987 to a recent price of about $40.

Among the key elements of the company's strategy for continued revenue and earnings growth is entering new markets through acquisitions. In July 1997, G&K acquired for approximately $280 million uniform rental assets and selected linen rental assets of National Linen Service, a division of National Service Industries (NYSE: NSI). The 29 processing facilities, located primarily in the Southeast, have annual revenues of about $205 million. In May 1998, GKSRA sold 10 of the facilities for $81 million to Tartan Textile Services.

G&K also hopes to improve performance through start-ups, adding customers that currently do not have uniform programs, and reducing costs through technology and innovation. The company targets its marketing efforts to focus on customers, industries and geographic locations that are expanding. G&K believes that its existing and potential customers are willing to pay a premium price for its services.

The company's full-service rental program supplies a broad range of work garments, specialized uniforms for corporate identity programs, anti-static garments, ultra-clean particle-free garments, and dress clothing for supervisors and sales personnel. Assistance is provided in selecting fabrics, styles and colors. Professional cleaning, finishing, repair and replacement are provided as part of the normal service.

GKSRA believes that uniform leasing provides customers with significant advantages over ownership. Leasing eliminates investment in uniforms and offers flexibility in styles, colors and quantities as customer requirements change. Furthermore, leasing assures professional cleaning, repair and replacement of items.

In addition to uniforms, many of the company's customers lease other items, including floor mats, dust mops and linens.

Per Share Data ($)

(Year Ended Jun. 30)	1998	1997	1996	1995	1994	1993	1992	1991	1990	1989
Tangible Bk. Val.	1.17	6.31	5.19	3.65	2.76	1.97	1.29	0.75	3.04	2.59
Cash Flow	3.31	2.49	2.11	1.75	1.50	1.26	1.12	0.91	0.83	0.69
Earnings	1.57	1.42	1.11	0.90	0.73	0.55	0.43	0.35	0.51	0.41
Dividends	0.07	0.07	0.07	0.09	0.07	0.07	0.07	0.07	0.07	0.06
Payout Ratio	4%	5%	6%	10%	10%	12%	16%	19%	13%	15%
Prices - High	53³/₄	42¹/₄	38⁵/₈	26	17¹/₄	16	13³/₈	12³/₈	11	10
- Low	35³/₈	28³/₄	21⁷/₈	15	12¹/₂	10⁷/₈	8⁵/₈	7¹/₈	5⁷/₈	6³/₄
P/E Ratio - High	34	30	35	29	24	29	31	35	22	24
- Low	23	20	20	17	17	20	20	20	12	16

Income Statement Analysis (Million $)

Revs.	503	350	305	262	225	208	195	176	119	109
Oper. Inc.	108	74.7	65.6	53.5	45.5	39.5	35.6	28.0	24.7	20.0
Depr.	35.6	22.0	20.4	17.4	15.8	14.5	14.0	11.3	7.8	7.0
Int. Exp.	21.8	6.8	8.0	7.1	5.8	7.3	8.5	8.3	0.5	0.4
Pretax Inc.	52.7	47.9	37.2	30.3	25.3	19.1	14.1	12.3	16.5	13.4
Eff. Tax Rate	39%	39%	39%	40%	42%	42%	39%	43%	38%	38%
Net Inc.	32.1	29.0	22.7	18.3	14.8	11.1	8.6	7.1	10.2	8.3

Balance Sheet & Other Fin. Data (Million $)

Cash	12.0	6.9	6.9	3.0	5.1	4.6	2.1	2.2	0.6	2.6
Curr. Assets	153	113	100	87.3	63.5	59.0	52.3	56.7	32.5	30.2
Total Assets	532	312	282	253	205	202	200	206	101	83.0
Curr. Liab.	80.1	72.3	49.8	42.4	34.2	36.4	33.9	28.7	16.1	13.8
LT Debt	235	54.3	75.1	76.5	54.7	59.8	68.4	85.9	9.1	3.8
Common Eqty.	198	168	141	119	101	90.2	82.4	76.8	69.9	61.0
Total Cap.	442	222	226	206	167	162	164	175	84.0	70.0
Cap. Exp.	37.4	35.6	36.2	36.5	17.6	14.4	16.3	18.4	21.8	14.2
Cash Flow	67.7	51.0	43.1	35.7	30.6	25.6	22.6	18.4	18.0	15.3
Curr. Ratio	1.9	1.6	2.0	2.1	1.9	1.6	1.5	2.0	2.0	2.2
% LT Debt of Cap.	53.1	24.5	33.3	37.2	32.8	36.9	41.8	49.1	10.8	5.4
% Net Inc.of Revs.	6.4	8.3	7.4	7.0	6.6	5.4	4.4	4.0	8.6	7.6
% Ret. on Assets	NA	9.7	8.5	8.0	7.3	5.5	4.2	4.6	11.1	10.4
% Ret. on Equity	NA	18.9	17.5	16.7	15.5	12.9	10.8	9.6	15.6	14.5

Data as orig. reptd.; bef. results of disc. opers. and/or spec. items. Per share data adj. for stk. divs. as of ex-div. date. Bold denotes diluted EPS (FASB 128). E-Estimated. NA-Not Available. NM-Not Meaningful. NR-Not Ranked.

Office—5995 Opus Parkway, Suite 500, Minnetonka, MN 55343. **Tel**—(612) 912-5500. **Website**—http://www.gkcares.com **Chrmn**—R. M. Fink. **CEO**—W. Hope. **Pres & COO**—T. Moberly. **CFO, Treas, Secy & Investor Contact**—Timothy W. Kuck. **Dirs**—B. G. Allbright, P. Baszucki, R. Fink, W. Fortun, D. Goldfus, W. Hope, B. Sweet. **Transfer Agent & Registrar**—Norwest Bank, Minneapolis. **Incorporated**—in Minnesota in 1934. **Empl**— 5,666. **S&P Analyst:** Jordan Horoschak

03-OCT-98

Industry: Entertainment

Summary: GCX operates 1,148 screens at 175 motion picture theatres in 24 states, as well as 74 screens at seven locations in Mexico and Argentina; it also manages investments.

Quantitative Evaluations		
Outlook (1 Lowest—5 Highest)	Recent Price • 39⅜	Yield • Nil
• **1**	52 Wk Range • 53-36	12-Mo. P/E • 63.5

Fair Value
• **19¼**

Risk
• **Low**

Earn./Div. Rank
• **NR**

Technical Eval.
• **Bullish** since 3/98

Rel. Strength Rank
(1 Lowest—99 Highest)
• **54**

Insider Activity
• **NA**

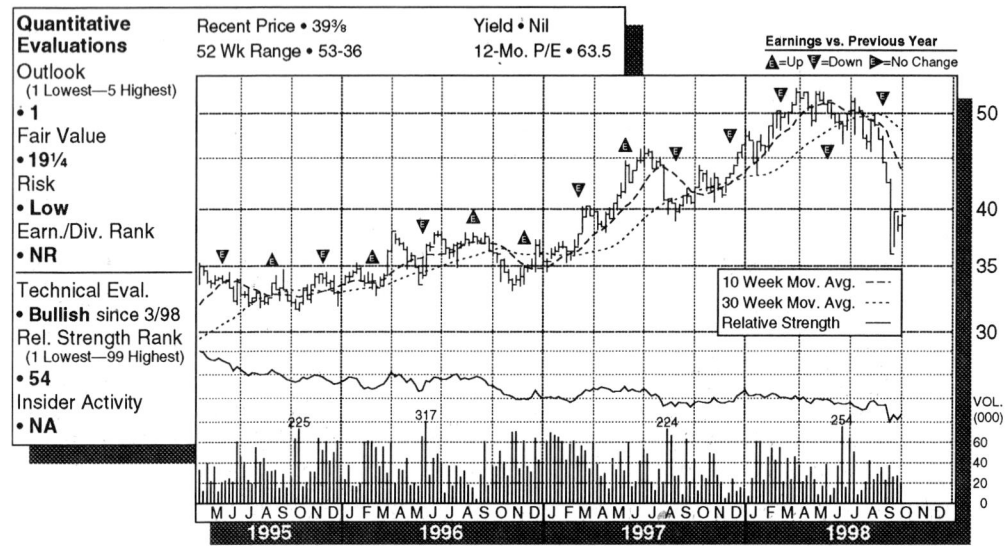

Business Profile - 01-APR-98

The company is continuing to focus on its long-term strategic plan of building state-of-the-art megaplex theatres in densely populated urban and suburban areas, while closing or selling older, less profitable units. As of January 31, 1998, it was operating 1,148 screens at 175 locations in 24 states as well as 74 screens at seven locations in Mexico and Argentina. It plans to add an additional 87 screens by the end of FY 98 (Oct.). In August 1997, GCX entered into a joint venture agreement with actor Robert Redford to create Sundance Cinemas, a stand-alone theatre circuit dedicated to exhibiting the growing number of independent films.

Operational Review - 01-APR-98

Revenues for the three months ended January 31, 1998, declined 2.3%, year to year, as a 3.6% decrease in admissions revenues and lower other revenues more than offset 1.1% higher concessions revenues. Profitability was penalized by a reduction in the number of screens (mainly reflecting dispositions of theatres in 1997's fourth quarter), and by a $314,000 investment loss, which contrasted with $1,026,000 of investment income. Pretax income fell 45%. After taxes at 40.0%, versus 41.0%, net income was down 44%, to $3,105,000 ($0.40 a share, diluted), from $5,590,000 ($0.71).

Stock Performance - 02-OCT-98

In the past 30 trading days, GCX's shares have declined 16%, compared to a 7% fall in the S&P 500. Average trading volume for the past five days was 3,960 shares, compared with the 40-day moving average of 5,621 shares.

Key Stock Statistics

Dividend Rate/Share	Nil	Shareholders	7,700
Shs. outstg. (M)	7.7	Market cap. (B)	$0.304
Avg. daily vol. (M)	0.006	Inst. holdings	63%
Tang. Bk. Value/Share	28.82		
Beta	NA		

Value of $10,000 invested 5 years ago: NA

Fiscal Year Ending Oct. 31

	1998	1997	1996	1995	1994	1993
Revenues (Million $)						
1Q	122.8	126.2	126.5	124.2	116.2	135.4
2Q	89.03	108.8	95.57	86.88	92.02	96.10
3Q	114.6	123.1	137.3	138.8	138.3	148.7
4Q	—	89.02	86.65	101.4	106.1	114.9
Yr.	—	447.1	446.0	451.3	452.6	495.0
Earnings Per Share ($)						
1Q	**0.40**	0.71	0.72	0.50	0.71	--
2Q	**-0.52**	0.20	-0.10	-0.12	0.05	
3Q	**0.26**	0.50	1.07	1.02	0.92	--
4Q	--	0.48	0.58	-0.30	0.06	
Yr.	--	1.90	2.20	1.11	1.73	NA

Next earnings report expected: early December

Dividend Data

No cash dividends have been paid. The company does not contemplate paying cash dividends on its common stock in the foreseeable future.

A Division of The McGraw-Hill Companies

Business Summary - 01-APR-98

As an outgrowth of a motion picture exhibition business credited with opening two of the first drive-in movies in 1938 and one of the first indoor shopping center movie theatres in 1951, GC Companies (GCX) has a long tradition of providing cutting-edge entertainment to movie-goers. As of January 1998, it was operating 175 state-of-the-art movie theatres, mostly megaplexes, with a total of 1,148 screens, in 24 states. About a third of the theatres were located in California, Florida and Texas.

The company's theatres offer the latest in audio and visual technology, including digital sound systems. Concession stands at the theatres sell traditional movie fare, as well as specialty products, such as Starbuck's coffee and other brand name fast foods, and movie memorabilia. Concession sales are the second largest source of revenues, providing 30% of revenues in FY 97 (Oct.); box office receipts provided 67%.

The disposition of theatres is part of the company's strategy of improving margins through measures that also include building theatres with more screens per location, adding new screens to existing theatres, expanding concession operations and continuing cost containment practices.

During the first quarter of FY 98 (Oct.), the company opened a 9-screen theatre in Mexico and a 12-screen theatre in Argentina. As of January 31, 1998, it was operating 74 screens at seven locations in Mexico and Argentina, compared with 53 screens in five locations at the end of FY 97. GCX plans to build or add an additional 30 screens in Latin America by the end of FY 98.

The company has formed a joint venture with Sundance Group to create Sundance Cinemas, a stand-alone theatre circuit dedicated to the exhibition of a growing number of independent films. The joint venture plans to open a large number of state-of-the-art Sundance Cinemas across the country in urban, suburban and college locations, aiming to add substantially to the number of screens dedicated to specialty films.

GCX manages a portfolio of investments that it hopes will provide substantial returns, as well as opportunities for business diversification. During the fourth quarter of FY 97, the company made a $30 million minority investment in a newly formed financial guaranty insurance company. GCX also increased its investment in an international telecommunications service provider (Global TeleSystems Group, Inc.) with a $5.0 million follow-on investment, raising its equity in that company to $25.2 million. In addition, GCX's investment portfolio includes minority investments in a German cable television systems operator and an optical and photo service retailer. The aggregate cost of its investment portfolio was about $87.1 million at the end of FY 97.

Per Share Data ($)

(Year Ended Oct. 31)	1997	1996	1995	1994	1993	1992	1991	1990	1989	1988
Tangible Bk. Val.	24.23	22.52	20.32	19.16	NA	16.56	NA	NA	NA	NA
Cash Flow	4.38	4.66	3.60	4.24	NA	3.29	NA	NA	NA	NA
Earnings	1.90	2.20	1.11	1.73	NA	0.56	NA	NA	NA	NA
Dividends	Nil	Nil	Nil	Nil	NA	NA	NA	NA	NA	NA
Payout Ratio	Nil	Nil	Nil	Nil	NA	NA	NA	NA	NA	NA
Prices - High	47⁷/₈	38	35¹/₄	38¹/₂	40	NA	NA	NA	NA	NA
- Low	34⁵/₈	32⁵/₈	26	24³/₄	32	NA	NA	NA	NA	NA
P/E Ratio - High	25	17	32	22	NA	NA	NA	NA	NA	NA
- Low	18	15	23	14	NA	NA	NA	NA	NA	NA

Income Statement Analysis (Million $)

	1997	1996	1995	1994	1993	1992	1991	1990	1989	1988
Revs.	447	446	451	453	495	457	NA	NA	NA	NA
Oper. Inc.	27.5	40.1	37.5	36.5	40.3	28.1	NA	NA	NA	NA
Depr.	19.2	19.4	19.4	19.6	22.0	20.9	NA	NA	NA	NA
Int. Exp.	0.6	0.6	0.6	0.7	0.6	0.7	NA	NA	NA	NA
Pretax Inc.	25.0	29.2	14.8	23.0	17.2	7.0	NA	NA	NA	NA
Eff. Tax Rate	41%	41%	41%	41%	39%	38%	NA	NA	NA	NA
Net Inc.	14.8	17.2	8.7	13.6	10.5	4.3	NA	NA	NA	NA

Balance Sheet & Other Fin. Data (Million $)

	1997	1996	1995	1994	1993	1992	1991	1990	1989	1988
Cash	30.0	73.3	71.3	85.0	7.8	64.0	NA	NA	NA	NA
Curr. Assets	62.4	97.1	79.8	92.8	10.4	66.9	NA	NA	NA	NA
Total Assets	340	314	300	297	211	267	NA	NA	NA	NA
Curr. Liab.	113	93.7	95.5	100	88.6	85.8	NA	NA	NA	NA
LT Debt	2.3	3.1	3.6	4.2	5.3	5.5	NA	NA	NA	NA
Common Eqty.	187	176	159	150	NA	128	NA	NA	NA	NA
Total Cap.	196	192	176	NA	NA	152	NA	NA	NA	NA
Cap. Exp.	18.7	10.8	17.3	9.5	19.3	12.7	NA	NA	NA	NA
Cash Flow	34.0	36.6	28.1	33.2	32.5	25.2	NA	NA	NA	NA
Curr. Ratio	0.6	1.0	0.8	0.9	0.1	0.8	NA	NA	NA	NA
% LT Debt of Cap.	1.2	1.6	2.0	2.5	NA	3.6	NA	NA	NA	NA
% Net Inc.of Revs.	3.3	3.9	1.9	3.0	2.1	0.9	NA	NA	NA	NA
% Ret. on Assets	4.5	5.6	2.9	4.5	NA	NA	NA	NA	NA	NA
% Ret. on Equity	8.1	10.3	5.6	9.1	NA	NA	NA	NA	NA	NA

Data as orig. reptd.; bef. results of disc. opers. and/or spec. items. Per share data adj. for stk. divs. as of ex-div. date. Bold denotes diluted EPS (FASB 128). E-Estimated. NA-Not Available. NM-Not Meaningful. NR-Not Ranked.

Office—27 Boylston St., Chestnut Hill, MA, 02167.**Tel**—(617) 278-5600. **Chrmn & CEO**—Richard A. Smith. **Pres & COO**—Robert A. Smith. **VP, Treas & CFO**—G. G. Edwards. **VP & Secy**—P. J. Szabla.**Investor Contact**—Joanne W. Parker. **Dirs**—W. L. Brown, P. C. Read, L. A. Schlesinger, Richard A. Smith, F. E. Sutherby. **Transfer Agent & Registrar**—First National Bank of Boston. **Incorporated**—in Delaware in 1993. **Empl**— 7,200.
S&P Analyst: J.J.S.

Galey & Lord

935E

NYSE Symbol **GNL**

In S&P SmallCap 600

03-OCT-98

Industry: Textiles (Specialty)

Summary: This company is a leading manufacturer of high-quality woven cotton and cotton-blended apparel fabrics sold principally to manufacturers of sportswear and commercial uniforms.

Quantitative Evaluations	
Outlook (1 Lowest—5 Highest)	• **5**
Fair Value	• **19¾**
Risk	• **Average**
Earn./Div. Rank	• **NR**
Technical Eval.	• **Bearish** since 6/98
Rel. Strength Rank (1 Lowest—99 Highest)	• **78**
Insider Activity	• **Favorable**

Recent Price • 11⅞
52 Wk Range • 28⅞-8¾
Yield • Nil
12-Mo. P/E • 13.4

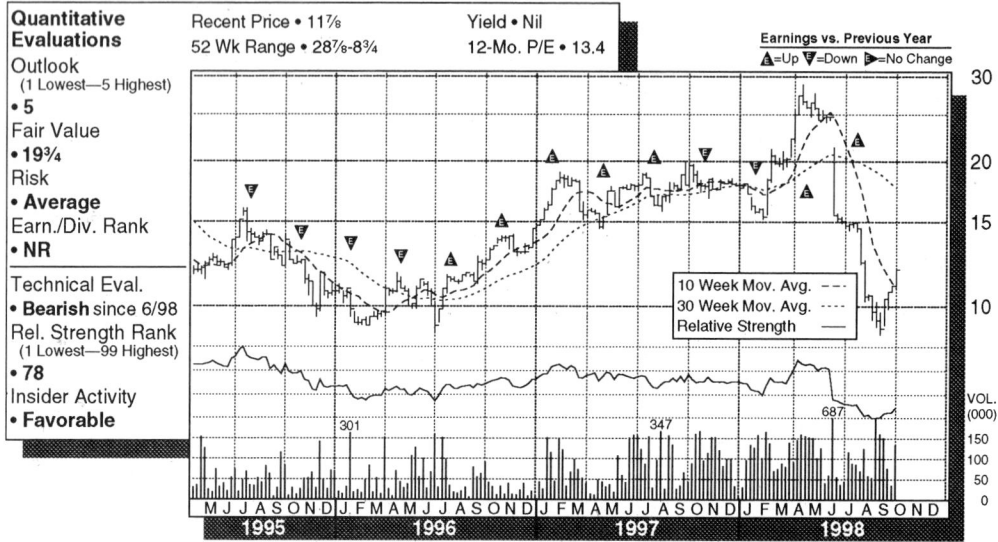

Earnings vs. Previous Year
▲=Up ▼=Down ►=No Change

10 Week Mov. Avg. - - -
30 Week Mov. Avg. ·····
Relative Strength —

Business Profile - 04-AUG-98

In the first quarter of FY 98 (Sep.), GNL incurred non-recurring charges of about $4 million related to the acquisition of the apparel fabrics businesses of Dominion Textile, Inc. from DT Acquisition, Inc. (a subsidiary of Polymer Group, Inc.). As a result of the acquisition, GNL's sales have soared. However, pretax charges related to the acquisition hampered earnings. In July 1998, the company said that the majority of the consolidation had been completed. At the end of the third quarter of FY 98, total backlog was down 14%, year to year, including a 14% decline in apparel backlog and a 7% decrease in home fabrics backlog. GNL recently expanded operations by entering into a joint venture with Litton Mills, a denim producer in the Philippines.

Operational Review - 04-AUG-98

Sales in the nine months ended June 27, 1998, advanced 70%, year to year, primarily reflecting the January 1998 acquisition of Dominion Textiles, and to a lesser extent, higher sales in woven sportswear. Margins widened, as expenses rose less rapidly; operating profit was up 84%. However, interest expense rose significantly, and profitability was hurt by bridge financing interest expenses and a loss on foreign currency hedges. After taxes at 41.3%, versus 38.5%, income dropped 24%, to $8,707,000 ($0.67 a share, diluted), from $11,506,000 ($0.96). Results in the FY 98 period exclude a charge of $0.04 a share for debt refinancing.

Stock Performance - 02-OCT-98

In the past 30 trading days, GNL's shares have increased 22%, compared to a 7% fall in the S&P 500. Average trading volume for the past five days was 26,520 shares, compared with the 40-day moving average of 37,669 shares.

Key Stock Statistics

Dividend Rate/Share	Nil	Shareholders	2,600
Shs. outstg. (M)	11.8	Market cap. (B)	$0.141
Avg. daily vol. (M)	0.021	Inst. holdings	83%
Tang. Bk. Value/Share	NM		
Beta	0.54		

Value of $10,000 invested 5 years ago: $ 11,645

Fiscal Year Ending Sep. 30

	1998	1997	1996	1995	1994	1993
Revenues (Million $)						
1Q	127.2	110.9	85.13	127.2	99.1	84.70
2Q	237.7	129.4	100.4	133.3	111.5	102.4
3Q	275.3	135.1	115.4	127.2	120.8	102.5
4Q	—	117.9	110.5	114.4	119.8	96.27
Yr.	—	493.4	411.5	502.2	451.1	385.8
Earnings Per Share ($)						
1Q	-0.01	0.30	-0.06	0.40	0.36	0.34
2Q	0.34	0.32	0.22	0.34	0.38	0.29
3Q	0.38	0.35	0.34	0.17	0.42	0.26
4Q	—	0.18	0.30	-0.46	0.41	0.24
Yr.	—	1.14	0.80	0.44	1.56	1.12

Next earnings report expected: late October

Dividend Data

The company has never paid dividends on its common stock and it intends to retain earnings for the operation and expansion of its business.

A Division of The McGraw·Hill Companies

Business Summary - 04-AUG-98

Although most consumers have never heard of Galey & Lord, Inc. (GNL), a leading manufacturer of fabrics, the company's customer list includes some of the most widely recognized names in the apparel industry. Galey & Lord sells its fabrics to apparel manufacturers such as Levi Strauss, Polo Ralph Lauren, Tommy Hilfiger, Calvin Klein and Liz Claiborne for use in the production of clothing. The company entered the home furnishing fabrics industry in FY 94 (Sep.) by acquiring the Decorative Prints business of Burlington Industries. Net sales by product line in recent fiscal years were:

	FY 97	FY 96	FY 95
Apparel fabrics	93%	89%	88%
Home fabrics	7%	11%	12%

The company's principal products are spun woven medium-weight cotton and cotton blended apparel fabrics. GNL manufactures a relatively limited number of basic fabric styles, and it enhances the value of the fabrics to its customers through a wide variety of mechanical and chemical finishing processes, including dyeing, napping, sueding and prewashing. Fabrics are offered in a variety of finishes including wrinkle resistant and soil release finishes in an array of colors. Woven fabrics are sold primarily to manufacturers of men-swear, uniforms, and branded and private-label womenswear.

The company makes corduroy to customer order in various wales and widths, for sale to manufacturers of menswear, womenswear and childrenswear. GNL believes it is the only vertically integrated domestic producer of corduroy.

In its uniform fabric product line, GNL stresses durability, fitness for use, continuity of color and customer service. The company also sells chemically treated fabrics, including a fire-retardant finish and an antibacterial finish. Uniform fabrics are distributed to the industrial laundry, hospitality and health care markets.

The Home Fashion Fabrics unit sells greige, dyed and printed fabrics to the home furnishings trade for use in bedspreads, comforters, curtains and accessories.

In June 1996, the company formed a new subsidiary, G&L Service Co., and also acquired Mexico-based Dimmit Industries, S.A. de C.V. for $22.5 million. Dimmit sews and finishes pants and shorts for the casualwear market. Its six plants will produce finished products from GNL fabrics. The location of this manufacturing facility allows the company to respond quickly to the needs of its domestic apparel customer and to compete effectively with competitors in the Far East. In response to the rising demand for the Company's garments, GNL plans to open a new garment manufacturing facility in Monclova, Mexico during FY 98.

Per Share Data ($)

(Year Ended Sep. 30)	1997	1996	1995	1994	1993	1992	1991	1990	1989	1988
Tangible Bk. Val.	5.69	4.34	4.45	4.02	4.98	3.80	0.26	NA	NA	NA
Cash Flow	2.40	1.80	1.37	2.27	1.69	2.01	1.08	NA	NA	NA
Earnings	1.14	0.80	0.44	1.56	1.12	1.30	0.26	NA	NA	NA
Dividends	Nil	Nil	Nil	Nil	Nil	Nil	Nil	Nil	Nil	Nil
Payout Ratio	Nil	Nil	Nil	Nil	Nil	Nil	Nil	Nil	Nil	Nil
Prices - High	20	15	16	23½	15	14¾	NA	NA	NA	NA
- Low	14½	8⅞	9½	12¾	8½	9½	NA	NA	NA	NA
P/E Ratio - High	18	19	36	15	13	11	NA	NA	NA	NA
- Low	13	11	22	8	8	7	NA	NA	NA	NA

Income Statement Analysis (Million $)

	1997	1996	1995	1994	1993	1992	1991	1990	1989	1988
Revs.	493	411	502	451	386	353	329	NA	NA	NA
Oper. Inc.	49.5	40.0	45.0	47.5	34.7	36.3	25.5	NA	NA	NA
Depr.	15.2	11.6	11.0	8.5	6.8	6.8	6.5	NA	NA	NA
Int. Exp.	12.3	11.6	13.1	8.4	6.5	9.7	14.3	NA	NA	NA
Pretax Inc.	22.0	15.5	8.7	30.7	21.4	19.9	4.7	NA	NA	NA
Eff. Tax Rate	38%	39%	39%	39%	37%	34%	36%	NA	NA	NA
Net Inc.	13.7	9.5	5.4	18.9	13.4	13.1	3.0	NA	NA	NA

Balance Sheet & Other Fin. Data (Million $)

	1997	1996	1995	1994	1993	1992	1991	1990	1989	1988
Cash	2.3	3.8	4.4	6.0	2.7	3.5	5.2	NA	NA	NA
Curr. Assets	181	157	182	173	141	116	105	NA	NA	NA
Total Assets	349	305	305	299	202	173	164	NA	NA	NA
Curr. Liab.	50.4	49.7	46.8	58.3	42.2	45.0	42.7	NA	NA	NA
LT Debt	177	149	162	150	95.0	80.0	106	NA	NA	NA
Common Eqty.	104	89.6	81.9	77.7	59.1	45.2	4.4	NA	NA	NA
Total Cap.	299	255	258	24.0	160	127	121	NA	NA	NA
Cap. Exp.	36.6	13.5	15.0	22.4	11.7	7.3	4.3	NA	NA	NA
Cash Flow	28.9	21.1	16.4	27.4	20.2	19.2	8.4	NA	NA	NA
Curr. Ratio	3.6	3.2	3.9	3.0	3.3	2.6	2.5	NA	NA	NA
% LT Debt of Cap.	59.2	58.4	62.8	62.4	59.6	63.0	88.1	NA	NA	NA
% Net Inc.of Revs.	2.8	2.3	1.1	4.2	3.5	3.7	0.9	NA	NA	NA
% Ret. on Assets	4.2	3.1	1.8	7.5	7.1	6.4	NA	NA	NA	NA
% Ret. on Equity	14.1	11.1	6.8	27.3	25.6	48.2	NA	NA	NA	NA

Data as orig. reptd.; bef. results of disc. opers. and/or spec. items. Per share data adj. for stk. divs. as of ex-div. date. Bold denotes diluted EPS (FASB 128). E-Estimated. NA-Not Available. NM-Not Meaningful. NR-Not Ranked.

Office—980 Ave. of the Americas, New York, NY 10018. **Tel**—(212) 465-3000. **Chrmn, Pres & CEO**—A. C. Wiener. **EVP, CFO, Secy, Treas & Investor Contact**—Michael R. Harmon (910-665-3037). **Dirs**—L. Abraham, P. G. Gillease, W. deR. Holt, H. S. Jacobs, W. M. R. Mapel, S. C. Sherrill, D. F. Thomas. **Transfer Agent & Registrar**—First Union National Bank of North Carolina, Charlotte. **Incorporated**—in Delaware in 1987. **Empl**—3,868. **S&P Analyst:** Kathleen J. Fraser

STANDARD
&POOR'S
STOCK REPORTS

Gallagher (Arthur J.) 935H

NYSE Symbol **AJG**

In S&P SmallCap 600

03-OCT-98

Industry: Insurance Brokers

Summary: This company provides insurance brokerage, risk management and other insurance-related services for commercial, industrial, individual and other clients.

Quantitative Evaluations	
Outlook (1 Lowest—5 Highest)	• **2⁻**
Fair Value	• **43¾**
Risk	• **Low**
Earn./Div. Rank	• **A**
Technical Eval.	• **Bullish** since 7/98
Rel. Strength Rank (1 Lowest—99 Highest)	• **78**
Insider Activity	• **NA**

Recent Price • 40 Yield • 3.5%
52 Wk Range • 46½-33½ 12-Mo. P/E • 13.4

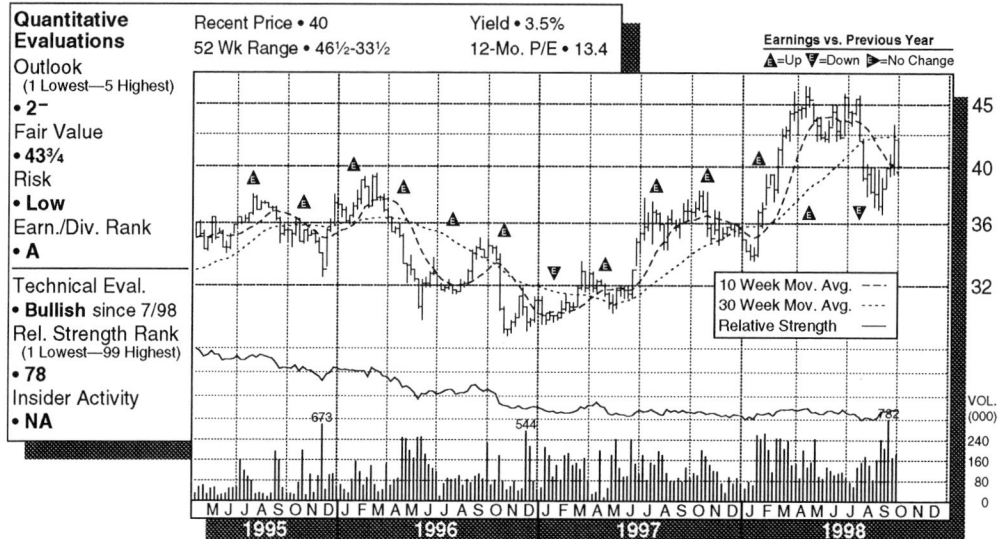

Earnings vs. Previous Year
▲=Up ▼=Down ►=No Change

10 Week Mov. Avg. ----
30 Week Mov. Avg. ·····
Relative Strength —

1995 1996 1997 1998

Business Profile - 06-AUG-98

This company conducts insurance brokerage and risk management services through offices in seven countries, and through correspondent brokers in more than 80 countries. Operations continue to expand, reflecting an aggressive acquisition program that began in 1986. Most recently, AJG acquired three insurance brokers: Martin, Gordon & Jones, of Jackson, MS; Employee Benefits of the Carolinas, of Charlotte, NC; and Gardner Marine Agency, of St. Louis, MO. Although extremely competitive pricing has put pressure on revenue growth over the past few years, future results could benefit from expected sales growth in the risk management, benefits and self-insurance service areas in addition to growth through acquisitions.

Operational Review - 06-AUG-98

Total revenues in the first six months of 1998 rose 7.9%, year to year, on 13% growth in fee revenue and a 4.6% rise in commission income, in the face of a continued soft insurance market. Net investment and other income advanced 5.5%. Margins widened, as total expenses rose 5.5%; higher salary and benefit costs were partly offset by well controlled other operating expenses. After taxes at 34.0% in each period, net operating income increased 28%, to $20.34 million ($1.15 a share, on 4.8% more shares), from $15.87 million ($0.94). Results exclude a gain of $6.2 million ($0.36) in the 1997 period.

Stock Performance - 02-OCT-98

In the past 30 trading days, AJG's shares have increased 5%, compared to a 7% fall in the S&P 500. Average trading volume for the past five days was 36,560 shares, compared with the 40-day moving average of 50,746 shares.

Key Stock Statistics

Dividend Rate/Share	1.40	Shareholders	700
Shs. outstg. (M)	17.2	Market cap. (B)	$0.691
Avg. daily vol. (M)	0.069	Inst. holdings	48%
Tang. Bk. Value/Share	10.17		
Beta	0.41		

Value of $10,000 invested 5 years ago: $ 16,883

Fiscal Year Ending Dec. 31

	1998	1997	1996	1995	1994	1993
Revenues (Million $)						
1Q	120.3	111.5	106.8	95.61	82.95	71.44
2Q	121.0	116.6	108.6	94.89	80.94	73.64
3Q	—	130.4	121.7	110.6	97.65	89.07
4Q	—	129.6	119.5	110.9	94.83	83.52
Yr.	—	488.0	456.7	412.0	356.4	317.7
Earnings Per Share ($)						
1Q	**0.63**	**0.54**	0.51	0.41	0.32	0.27
2Q	**0.52**	**0.76**	0.44	0.36	0.28	0.45
3Q	—	**1.09**	1.02	0.94	0.81	0.74
4Q	—	**0.74**	0.65	0.83	0.77	0.56
Yr.	—	**3.13**	2.52	2.54	2.17	2.02

Next earnings report expected: mid October

Dividend Data (Dividends have been paid since 1985.)

Amount ($)	Date Decl.	Ex-Div. Date	Stock of Record	Payment Date
0.310	Nov. 20	Dec. 29	Dec. 31	Jan. 15 '98
0.350	Jan. 22	Mar. 27	Mar. 31	Apr. 15 '98
0.350	May. 19	Jun. 26	Jun. 30	Jul. 15 '98
0.350	Sep. 17	Sep. 28	Sep. 30	Oct. 15 '98

A Division of The McGraw-Hill Companies

Business Summary - 06-AUG-98

Arthur J. Gallagher & Co. provides insurance brokerage, risk management and related services in the U.S. and abroad. Because of the fiercely competitive pricing of premiums in the domestic market, AJG has been focusing on international expansion through acquisitions and joint ventures. Its two major sources of operating revenues are commissions from brokerage and risk management operations, and service fees from risk management operations. Total revenues in recent years were derived as follows:

	1997	1996	1995
Commissions	56%	57%	57%
Fees	37%	38%	39%
Investment income	7%	5%	4%

The company's principal activity is the negotiation and placement of insurance for its clients (corporations, organizations and individuals). It acts as an agent in soliciting, negotiating and effecting contracts of insurance through insurance companies worldwide and also as a broker in procuring contracts of insurance on behalf of insureds. Specific coverages include property and casualty, marine, employee benefits, pension and life insurance products. AJG also places surplus lines coverage

(coverage not available from insurance companies licensed by the states in which the risks are located) for various specialized risks and provides reinsurance services to its clients.

The company provides professional consulting services to assist clients in analyzing risks and determining whether proper protection is best obtained through the purchase of insurance or through retention of all or a portion of those risks and the adoption of risk management policies and cost-effective loss control and prevention programs.

In connection with its risk management services, AJG provides self-insurance programs for large institutions, risk-sharing pools and associations, and large commercial and industrial customers.

AJG aims to be at the forefront of the global claims and risk control service market. In keeping with this goal, the company has been very active in acquiring selected businesses worldwide, as well as in forming joint ventures. Expansion has recently focused on Australia and Canada. During 1997, AJG formed a joint venture with the Wyatt Group in Australia, to provide loss adjusting, marine and aviation surveying and risk control consulting for the Australian market. Separately, the company teamed up with American Re to offer risk management for workers' compensation exposure in Canada.

Per Share Data ($) (Year Ended Dec. 31)	1997	1996	1995	1994	1993	1992	1991	1990	1989	1988
Tangible Bk. Val.	9.25	7.58	7.17	6.01	7.49	5.88	5.72	6.35	5.88	5.33
Cash Flow	3.78	3.13	3.03	2.63	2.42	1.99	1.72	1.86	1.70	1.64
Earnings	3.13	2.63	2.54	2.17	2.02	1.57	1.31	1.42	1.42	1.41
Dividends	1.24	1.16	1.00	0.88	0.72	0.64	0.64	0.60	0.52	0.48
Payout Ratio	40%	44%	39%	41%	36%	39%	46%	40%	35%	32%
Prices - High	38¼	39½	38	36⅜	37⅜	29¼	28⅜	25	26½	19⅛
- Low	29¾	29⅛	30⅛	28⅛	25½	21	19	19¾	16⅛	13⅞
P/E Ratio - High	12	15	15	17	19	19	22	18	19	14
- Low	10	11	12	13	13	13	15	14	11	10

Income Statement Analysis (Million $)

	1997	1996	1995	1994	1993	1992	1991	1990	1989	1988
Revs.	488	457	412	356	318	272	232	198	173	156
Oper. Inc.	91.8	79.2	70.9	62.3	59.2	43.7	35.6	34.8	32.0	28.8
Depr.	11.1	9.8	8.0	7.4	6.4	6.2	5.9	5.5	3.5	2.7
Int. Exp.	Nil	Nil	NA	1.7	1.9	2.4	2.3	2.0	2.0	2.1
Pretax Inc.	80.8	69.4	62.9	53.2	51.2	36.1	26.5	27.2	26.5	24.0
Eff. Tax Rate	34%	34%	34%	35%	37%	35%	29%	35%	35%	30%
Net Inc.	53.3	45.8	41.5	34.5	32.3	23.5	18.8	17.7	17.3	16.9

Balance Sheet & Other Fin. Data (Million $)

	1997	1996	1995	1994	1993	1992	1991	1990	1989	1988
Cash	148	144	167	151	130	112	116	112	69.0	84.0
Curr. Assets	469	464	382	351	364	274	257	227	195	192
Total Assets	642	590	496	451	464	401	376	320	294	277
Curr. Liab.	466	445	364	342	306	275	256	206	190	180
LT Debt	Nil	1.1	2.3	3.4	24.5	20.0	20.0	20.0	20.0	20.0
Common Eqty.	164	135	118	97.0	121	91.2	85.8	81.9	74.2	67.5
Total Cap.	164	136	120	100	146	111	106	102	94.0	88.0
Cap. Exp.	11.3	10.1	9.4	7.4	7.0	5.8	7.7	7.2	4.7	3.3
Cash Flow	64.4	55.6	49.5	41.9	38.7	29.7	24.7	23.2	20.7	19.6
Curr. Ratio	1.0	1.0	1.0	1.0	1.2	1.0	1.0	1.1	1.0	1.1
% LT Debt of Cap.	Nil	0.8	1.9	3.4	16.8	18.0	18.9	19.6	21.2	22.9
% Net Inc.of Revs.	10.9	10.1	10.1	9.7	10.2	8.6	8.1	8.9	10.0	10.8
% Ret. on Assets	8.7	8.0	8.7	7.7	7.4	5.9	5.1	5.7	6.0	6.2
% Ret. on Equity	35.7	35.3	38.7	32.1	30.1	26.1	20.9	22.3	24.3	25.3

Data as orig. reptd.; bef. results of disc. opers. and/or spec. items. Per share data adj. for stk. divs. as of ex-div. date. Bold denotes diluted EPS (FASB 128). E-Estimated. NA-Not Available. NM-Not Meaningful. NR-Not Ranked.

Office—Two Pierce Place, Itasca, IL 60143-3141. **Founded**—in 1927; reincorporated in Delaware in 1972. **Tel**—(630) 773-3800. **Fax**—(630) 285-4000. **Website**—http://www.ajg.com **Chrmn**—R. E. Gallagher. **Pres & CEO**—J. P. Gallagher Jr. **VP-Fin, CFO & Investor Contact**—Michael J. Cloherty. **Secy**—C. E. Fasig. **Dirs**—T. K. Brooker, J. G. Campbell, M. J. Cloherty, F. M. Heffernan, J. P. Gallagher Jr., R. E. Gallagher, J. M. Greenberg, P. A. Marineau, W. F. McClure, J. R. Wimmer. **Transfer Agent & Registrar**—Harris Trust & Savings Bank, Chicago. **Empl**—3,890. **S&P Analyst:** L. A. Olive

STANDARD &POOR'S
STOCK REPORTS

Galoob Toys

935N

NYSE Symbol **GAL**

In S&P SmallCap 600

03-OCT-98

Industry: Leisure Time (Products)

Summary: Galoob designs and markets a wide variety of toy products, including Star Wars Action Fleet Micro Machines.

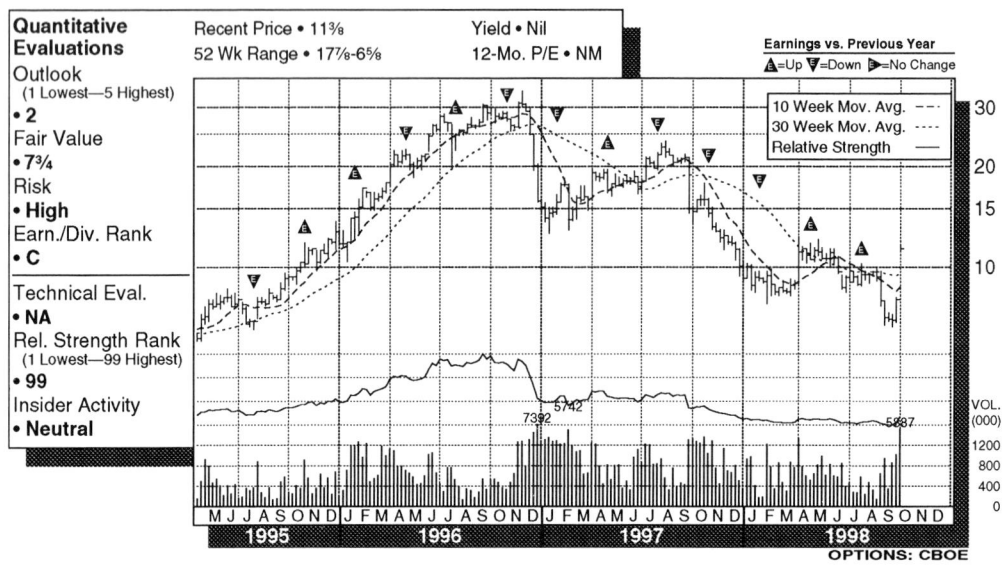

Quantitative Evaluations	
Outlook (1 Lowest—5 Highest)	**• 2**
Fair Value	**• 7¾**
Risk	**• High**
Earn./Div. Rank	**• C**
Technical Eval.	**• NA**
Rel. Strength Rank (1 Lowest—99 Highest)	**• 99**
Insider Activity	**• Neutral**

Recent Price • 11⅜
52 Wk Range • 17⅞-6⅝
Yield • Nil
12-Mo. P/E • NM

Earnings vs. Previous Year
▲=Up ▼=Down ▶=No Change

10 Week Mov. Avg. ---
30 Week Mov. Avg. ....
Relative Strength —

OPTIONS: CBOE

Business Profile - 25-MAR-98

Following a lack of revenue growth and net losses in the first nine months of 1997, GAL announced the restructuring of its product line and changes in its product selection strategy. The company has discontinued all of its male action lines that were introduced in 1996 and 1997, and will now focus on its most profitable line - Star Wars. GAL's 1998 product line features Micro Machines, Star Wars and Pound Puppies, all having proven records as toy lines over the past 10 to 15 years. In June 1997, GAL acquired all the rights to its Micro Machines line, eliminating future royalty payments and ending litigation regarding past royalties.

Operational Review - 25-MAR-98

Based on a preliminary report, net revenues fell 16% in 1997, as reduced product shipments in the fourth quarter dragged down results for the full year. With total operating expenses up 1.1%, an operating loss contracted with operating income. Following a $22,949,000 charge related to the purchase of the Micro Machines license rights, a tax benefit of $18,054,000, versus taxes at 11.9%, and despite the absence of a $24,279,000 after-tax charge related to the exchange of preferred stock, the net loss widened to $29,450,000 ($1.63 a share, on 11% more shares), from $5,849,000 ($0.41).

Stock Performance - 02-OCT-98

In the past 30 trading days, GAL's shares have increased 21%, compared to a 7% fall in the S&P 500. Average trading volume for the past five days was 1,177,480 shares, compared with the 40-day moving average of 260,846 shares.

Key Stock Statistics

Dividend Rate/Share	Nil	Shareholders	1,200
Shs. outstg. (M)	18.1	Market cap. (B)	$0.206
Avg. daily vol. (M)	0.422	Inst. holdings	41%
Tang. Bk. Value/Share	6.42		
Beta	1.55		

Value of $10,000 invested 5 years ago: $ 35,000

Fiscal Year Ending Dec. 31

	1998	1997	1996	1995	1994	1993
Revenues (Million $)						
1Q	30.26	40.60	37.52	33.34	30.24	27.30
2Q	40.02	52.36	49.20	38.22	33.72	26.77
3Q	—	83.25	88.55	65.52	50.27	37.69
4Q	—	63.35	109.6	82.97	64.57	42.53
Yr.	—	239.6	284.9	220.0	178.8	134.3
Earnings Per Share ($)						
1Q	**-0.12**	**-0.13**	-2.71	-0.49	-0.25	-0.23
2Q	**-0.04**	**-0.73**	0.02	-0.48	0.91	-0.45
3Q	—	**-0.62**	0.57	0.58	0.30	-0.12
4Q	—	**-0.16**	0.74	0.93	0.55	-0.67
Yr.	—	**-1.63**	-0.41	0.60	1.51	-1.47

Next earnings report expected: late October

Dividend Data

No cash dividends have been paid on the publicly held common stock.

Business Summary - 25-MAR-98

With both Luke Skywalker and Darth Vader leading the charge, Galoob Toys, Inc. (GAL) in 1996 expanded beyond its traditional Micro Machines small-scale toys and saw net revenues rise 29% to $285 million from those of 1995, following the introduction of Star Wars toys in the company's new, larger-scale segment--Action Fleet. In 1996, GAL successfully mined its Star Wars license with a broad range of toys based on the movies. These toys are also produced in the miniature Micro Machines scale. Sales of Star Wars toys received a lift in 1997 from the release of a special edition of the movie trilogy. GAL is a contender for a license covering a new generation of Star Wars movies, to be released starting in 1999. Worldwide sales of Micro Machines and Star Wars Action Fleet toys grew 58% in 1996.

Beginning in 1991, following a period of irregular revenues and earnings, GAL instituted a recovery plan that focused on restoring and expanding its core Micro Machines business, exploiting new product areas and reducing its cost structure. New products are the life-blood of a toy company, as older toys eventually face product attrition--dwindling sales--as part of their life cycle. In 1996, higher sales and reduced costs led to a 96% gain in net income to $18.5 million, before a $24.3 million charge related to the exchange of pre-

ferred for common stock, which resulted in a per-share loss for the year.

The company designs toys--Micro Machines and other toys for boys and Sky Dancers and other mini-dolls for girls--and sells them to retailers in the U.S. and distributors overseas. GAL's toys are made by foreign contractors, mainly in China. GAL's gross margins rose to 49.4% in 1996 from 44.7% in 1995 as the contribution to net revenues from domestic sales, which carry higher margins than foreign sales, grew to 69% from 63%.

Substantially all of GAL's toys are produced under licenses. While the company's Star Wars license is certainly its most visible arrangement, GAL holds several other licenses that permit it to make toys based on the characters or other aspects of a movie or television program. GAL's 1998 product line features Micro Machines, Star Wars and Pound Puppies, all having proven records as toy lines over the past 10 to 15 years.

In October 1997, following a lack of revenue growth and net losses in the first three quarters of 1997, Galoob announced a restructuring of its product portfolio to feature toys based on Star Wars, on agreements with Lucasfilm Ltd. and Twentieth Century Fox, on its Micro Machines core brand, on continuing and new product lines in miniature dolls, and on additional product categories of toys. The company discontinued its male action lines and took a $17.6 million charge.

Per Share Data ($)

(Year Ended Dec. 31)	1997	1996	1995	1994	1993	1992	1991	1990	1989	1988
Tangible Bk. Val.	6.56	8.36	0.56	0.48	-1.86	-0.73	-0.18	0.95	4.36	2.63
Cash Flow	-1.57	1.34	0.90	1.58	-1.40	-0.50	-1.03	-3.35	2.07	0.88
Earnings	-1.63	-0.41	0.60	1.51	-1.47	-0.59	-1.14	-3.48	1.95	0.72
Dividends	Nil	Nil	Nil	Nil	Nil	Nil	Nil	Nil	Nil	Nil
Payout Ratio	Nil	Nil	Nil	Nil	Nil	Nil	Nil	Nil	Nil	Nil
Prices - High	23³/₄	33⁵/₈	13³/₄	10⁵/₈	11¹/₂	6¹/₈	6¹/₈	13⁷/₈	14³/₄	7⁵/₈
- Low	9¹/₈	10³/₈	5¹/₄	4¹/₄	2³/₈	2¹/₄	2⁵/₈	2¹/₄	6³/₈	2³/₄
P/E Ratio - High	NM	NM	23	7	NM	NM	NM	NM	8	11
- Low	NM	NM	9	3	NM	NM	NM	NM	3	4

Income Statement Analysis (Million $)

	1997	1996	1995	1994	1993	1992	1991	1990	1989	1988
Revs.	240	285	220	179	134	166	151	127	228	140
Oper. Inc.	-20.8	24.4	14.0	10.0	-4.5	2.2	-2.0	-28.6	28.4	12.9
Depr.	1.0	0.8	0.5	0.6	0.7	0.9	1.0	1.2	1.1	1.5
Int. Exp.	0.6	3.2	3.4	2.6	1.8	1.6	1.8	3.0	5.4	5.2
Pretax Inc.	-47.5	20.9	10.0	19.2	-10.9	-2.2	-7.5	-29.2	23.6	7.2
Eff. Tax Rate	NM	12%	1.70%	4.10%	NM	NM	NM	NM	17%	7.50%
Net Inc.	-29.4	18.4	9.4	18.4	-10.9	-2.4	-7.5	-29.2	19.6	6.6

Balance Sheet & Other Fin. Data (Million $)

	1997	1996	1995	1994	1993	1992	1991	1990	1989	1988
Cash	3.4	27.9	2.0	2.2	2.3	1.4	6.8	21.8	25.7	1.2
Curr. Assets	124	180	107	91.0	61.0	61.0	53.0	62.0	101	63.0
Total Assets	208	197	120	101	71.0	72.0	64.0	76.0	117	75.0
Curr. Liab.	41.4	46.0	51.9	37.6	30.2	34.4	23.7	24.4	33.6	42.1
LT Debt	4.0	Nil	14.0	18.4	18.6	4.9	5.2	5.5	5.7	8.8
Common Eqty.	162	150	NM	4.9	-17.8	-6.9	-1.7	8.8	40.5	23.8
Total Cap.	166	151	31.4	63.2	40.8	37.2	40.3	51.2	83.0	32.7
Cap. Exp.	1.4	2.3	1.0	0.5	0.1	0.1	0.2	0.5	1.5	0.7
Cash Flow	-28.4	19.2	9.9	15.9	-13.4	-4.7	-9.6	31.2	20.0	8.1
Curr. Ratio	3.0	3.9	2.1	2.4	2.0	1.8	2.2	2.6	3.0	1.5
% LT Debt of Cap.	2.4	Nil	44.6	29.1	45.6	13.3	13.0	10.8	6.9	27.1
% Net Inc.of Revs.	NM	6.5	4.3	10.3	NM	NM	NM	NM	8.6	4.7
% Ret. on Assets	NM	11.6	8.5	21.0	NM	NM	NM	NM	20.3	8.9
% Ret. on Equity	NM	18.0	NM	NM	NM	NM	NM	NM	58.1	32.7

Data as orig. reptd.; bef. results of disc. opers. and/or spec. items. Per share data adj. for stk. divs. as of ex-div. date. Bold denotes diluted EPS (FASB 128). E-Estimated. NA-Not Available. NM-Not Meaningful. NR-Not Ranked.

Office—500 Forbes Blvd., South San Francisco, CA 94080. **Tel**—(415) 952-1678. **Fax**—(415) 952-7084. **Website**—http://www.galoob.com **Pres & CEO**—M. D. Goldman. **EVP & COO**—L. R. Novak. **EVP & Secy**—W. G. Catron. **SVP & CFO**—K. R. McElwee.**Dirs**—A. J. Cavanaugh, P. A. Gliebe, Jr., M. D. Goldman, S. R. Heldfond, S. L. Kling, R. Kowalsky. **Transfer Agent & Registrar**—Continental Stock Transfer & Trust Co., NYC. **Incorporated**—in California in 1957; reincorporated in Delaware in 1987. **Empl**— 235. **S&P Analyst:** M.I.

03-OCT-98 | **Industry:** Machinery (Diversified) | **Summary:** GDI, formerly Gardner Denver Machinery Inc., manufactures air compressors and blowers for industrial use, and pumps for oil and gas production, well servicing and drilling.

Quantitative Evaluations

Outlook
(1 Lowest—5 Highest)
- **NA**

Fair Value
- **NA**

Risk
- **Average**

Earn./Div. Rank
- **NR**

Technical Eval.
- **NA**

Rel. Strength Rank
(1 Lowest—99 Highest)
- **11**

Insider Activity
- **Neutral**

Recent Price • 13½   Yield • Nil
52 Wk Range • 30⅜-13⅛   12-Mo. P/E • 6.7

Earnings vs. Previous Year
▲=Up ▼=Down ▶=No Change

10 Week Mov. Avg. ---
30 Week Mov. Avg. ····
Relative Strength —

VOL. (000)

Business Profile - 12-JAN-98

Higher oil and natural gas prices and related increases in drilling activity have led to strong demand for GDI's petroleum products. The company, expects demand in the compressed air products segment to continue to increase at a rate slightly greater than that of the general expansion in the U.S. economy. In December 1997, GDI signed a definitive agreement to acquire for about $24 million Champion Pneumatic Machinery Company, Inc., a leading manufacturer of lubricated and nonlubricated single acting, single and two-stage compressors. The company expects Champion to generate revenues of about $31 million in 1997, to be slightly accretive in 1998, and to provide it with a more complete product offering to penetrate the low horsepower compressor market. In May 1998, GDI changed its name from Gardner Denver Machinery Inc. to Gardner Denver, Inc.

Operational Review - 12-JAN-98

Revenues in the nine months ended September 30, 1997, advanced 38%, year to year, with acquisitions contributing importantly to the gain. Profitability benefited from significantly increased order levels for the company's petroleum products, growth in demand for compressed air products, and the performance of recent acquisitions. Despite sharply higher interest expense, pretax income climbed 69%. After taxes at 40.3% in each period, net income was also up 69%, to $19,102,000 ($1.21 a share. as adjusted), from $11,287,000 ($0.74).

Stock Performance - 02-OCT-98

In the past 30 trading days, GDI's shares have declined 34%, compared to a 7% fall in the S&P 500. Average trading volume for the past five days was 35,720 shares, compared with the 40-day moving average of 54,946 shares.

Key Stock Statistics

Dividend Rate/Share	Nil	Shareholders	9,600
Shs. outstg. (M)	16.2	Market cap. (B)	$0.220
Avg. daily vol. (M)	0.052	Inst. holdings	56%
Tang. Bk. Value/Share	1.20		
Beta	NA		

Value of $10,000 invested 5 years ago: NA

Fiscal Year Ending Dec. 31

	1998	1997	1996	1995	1994	1993
Revenues (Million $)						
1Q	89.79	66.08	48.57	49.97	39.16	—
2Q	103.5	69.45	48.91	49.21	42.41	—
3Q	—	76.45	56.52	44.89	44.63	—
4Q	—	79.57	64.00	47.46	49.64	—
Yr.	—	291.6	218.0	191.5	175.8	158.2
Earnings Per Share ($)						
1Q	**0.49**	**0.34**	0.26	0.20	0.01	—
2Q	**0.55**	**0.43**	0.24	0.17	0.03	—
3Q		**0.44**	0.24	0.13	0.06	—
4Q	—	**0.53**	0.36	0.30	-6.46	—
Yr.	—	**1.74**	1.11	0.79	-6.41	—

Next earnings report expected: late October

Dividend Data

Amount ($)	Date Decl.	Ex-Div. Date	Stock of Record	Payment Date
3-for-2	Nov. 05	Dec. 30	Dec. 08	Dec. 29 '97

A Division of The **McGraw·Hill** *Companies*

Business Summary - 12-JAN-98

Gardner Denver, Inc. (GDI; formerly Gardner Denver Machinery Inc.) began its business of manufacturing industrial and petroleum equipment in 1859, when Robert W. Gardner redesigned the fly-ball governor to provide speed control for steam engines. By 1900, the then Gardner Co. had broadened its product offerings to include steam pumps and vertical high-speed air compressors. In 1927, Gardner Co. merged with Denver Rock Drill, a manufacturer of equipment for oil wells and mining and construction, and became Gardner-Denver Co. Cooper Industries, Inc. acquired Gardner-Denver Co. in 1979, and spun it off as an independent company to Cooper shareholders in April 1994. In May 1998, the company changed its name from Gardner Denver Machinery Inc. to Gardner Denver, Inc.

The company's operations are now organized into two segments: compressed air products and petroleum products. The compressed air products segment (which accounted for over 85% of both revenues and operating income in 1996) designs, manufactures, markets and services rotary screw and reciprocating compressors and blowers to serve all aspects of the industrial air market. Markets served are mainly in the U.S., but a growing portion of revenues are from exports.

The largest markets for GDI's compressors and blowers are durable goods manufacturers; process industries such as petroleum, primary metals, pharmaceuti-

cals, food and paper; original equipment manufacturers; manufacturers of carpet cleaning equipment, pneumatic conveying equipment and dry bulk trailers; and wastewater treatment facilities.

The much smaller but rapidly growing petroleum products segment (which accounted for the balance of 1996 revenues and operating income) designs, manufactures, markets and services a diverse group of pump products used in oil and gas production, well servicing, well stimulation and oil and gas drilling markets. Typical applications include oil transfer, salt water disposal, ammine pumping for gas processing, enhanced oil recovery, hydraulic power, and other liquid transfer requirements.

In 1996, the petroleum products business recorded significant revenue growth and returned to profitability for the first time since 1981. Management anticipated at least comparable revenue growth and continuing improvement in margins in 1997.

GDI made two acquisitions in August 1996, adding revenues of about $24.3 million in 1996. It purchased NORAMPTCO, Inc. (renamed Gardner Denver Holdings Inc.), a manufacturer of multistage centrifugal blowers and exhausters, for $26.8 million; and TCM Investments, Inc., an oil field pump manufacturer, for $7.2 million.

Sales outside the U.S. accounted for 25% of revenues in 1996, with the largest contributions coming from Asia and Canada.

Per Share Data ($) (Year Ended Dec. 31)	1997	1996	1995	1994	1993	1992	1991	1990	1989	1988
Tangible Bk. Val.	1.17	0.26	0.84	NA	NA	NA	NA	NA	NA	NA
Cash Flow	2.35	1.46	1.35	-5.48	NA	NA	NA	NA	NA	NA
Earnings	1.74	1.11	0.78	-6.40	NA	NA	NA	NA	NA	NA
Dividends	Nil	Nil	Nil	Nil	Nil	Nil	Nil	Nil	Nil	Nil
Payout Ratio	Nil	Nil	Nil	Nil	Nil	Nil	Nil	Nil	Nil	Nil
Prices - High	28³/₈	12⁷/₈	6³/₈	3⁵/₈	NA	NA	NA	NA	NA	NA
- Low	10¹/₈	5⁷/₈	3³/₈	2¹/₂	NA	NA	NA	NA	NA	NA
P/E Ratio - High	16	11	8	d	d	d	d	d	d	d
- Low	6	5	4	d	d	d	d	d	d	d

Income Statement Analysis (Million $)

	1997	1996	1995	1994	1993	1992	1991	1990	1989	1988
Revs.	292	218	192	176	158	NA	NA	NA	NA	NA
Oper. Inc.	60.0	37.0	33.0	23.1	NA	NA	NA	NA	NA	NA
Depr.	9.7	5.4	8.3	12.9	NA	NA	NA	NA	NA	NA
Int. Exp.	3.9	3.1	5.0	4.7	NA	NA	NA	NA	NA	NA
Pretax Inc.	46.2	28.4	19.8	-94.2	NA	NA	NA	NA	NA	NA
Eff. Tax Rate	40%	41%	42%	NM	NM	NM	NM	NM	NM	NM
Net Inc.	27.7	16.9	11.6	-89.6	1.8	NA	NA	NA	NA	NA

Balance Sheet & Other Fin. Data (Million $)

	1997	1996	1995	1994	1993	1992	1991	1990	1989	1988
Cash	8.8	8.6	1.9	NA	NA	NA	NA	NA	NA	NA
Curr. Assets	125	109	90.3	NA	NA	NA	NA	NA	NA	NA
Total Assets	269	236	184	23.3	NA	NA	NA	NA	NA	NA
Curr. Liab.	58.9	49.3	31.6	NA	NA	NA	NA	NA	NA	NA
LT Debt	51.2	55.1	36.7	56.1	NA	NA	NA	NA	NA	NA
Common Eqty.	104	74.1	55.2	42.3	NA	NA	NA	NA	NA	NA
Total Cap.	155	129	91.9	98.4	NA	NA	NA	NA	NA	NA
Cap. Exp.	9.8	4.2	3.3	4.3	NA	NA	NA	NA	NA	NA
Cash Flow	37.3	22.4	19.9	-6.7	NA	NA	NA	NA	NA	NA
Curr. Ratio	2.1	2.2	2.9	NA	NA	NA	NA	NA	NA	NA
% LT Debt of Cap.	33.0	42.7	39.9	57.0	NA	NA	NA	NA	NA	NA
% Net Inc.of Revs.	9.5	7.8	6.1	NM	1.1	NA	NA	NA	NA	NA
% Ret. on Assets	11.0	NM	6.0	NM	NM	NM	NM	NM	NM	NM
% Ret. on Equity	31.0	26.1	23.8	NM	NM	NM	NM	NM	NM	NM

Data as orig. reptd.; bef. results of disc. opers. and/or spec. items. Per share data adj. for stk. divs. as of ex-div. date. Bold denotes diluted EPS (FASB 128). E-Estimated. NA-Not Available. NM-Not Meaningful. NR-Not Ranked.

Office—1800 Gardner Expressway, Quincy, IL 62301.**Tel**—(217) 222-5400.**Fax**—(217) 228-8260.**Website**—http://www.gardnerdenver.com **Pres & CEO**—R. J. Centanni. **VP-Fin & CFO**—P. R. Roth.**VP, Treas & Secy** —H. W. Cornell.**Dirs**—D. G. Barger Jr., R. J. Centanni, T. M. McKenna, A. E. Riedel, M. J. Sebastian.**Transfer Agent & Registrar**—First Chicago Trust Co. of New York, Jersey City, NJ. **Incorporated**—in Delaware in 1993. **Empl**— 1,154. **S&P Analyst:** J. J. Schemitsch

03-OCT-98

Industry:
Telecommunications
(Long Distance)

Summary: Through subsidiaries, this MCI affiliate provides long-distance and other telecommunications services, including cable television, to the state of Alaska.

Quantitative Evaluations	
Outlook (1 Lowest—5 Highest)	• **NA**
Fair Value	• **NA**
Risk	• **High**
Earn./Div. Rank	• **B**
Technical Eval.	• **Bearish** since 5/98
Rel. Strength Rank (1 Lowest—99 Highest)	• **48**
Insider Activity	• **Favorable**

Recent Price • 3½
52 Wk Range • 8⅜-2⅝
Yield • Nil
12-Mo. P/E • NM

Earnings vs. Previous Year
▲=Up ▼=Down ▶=No Change

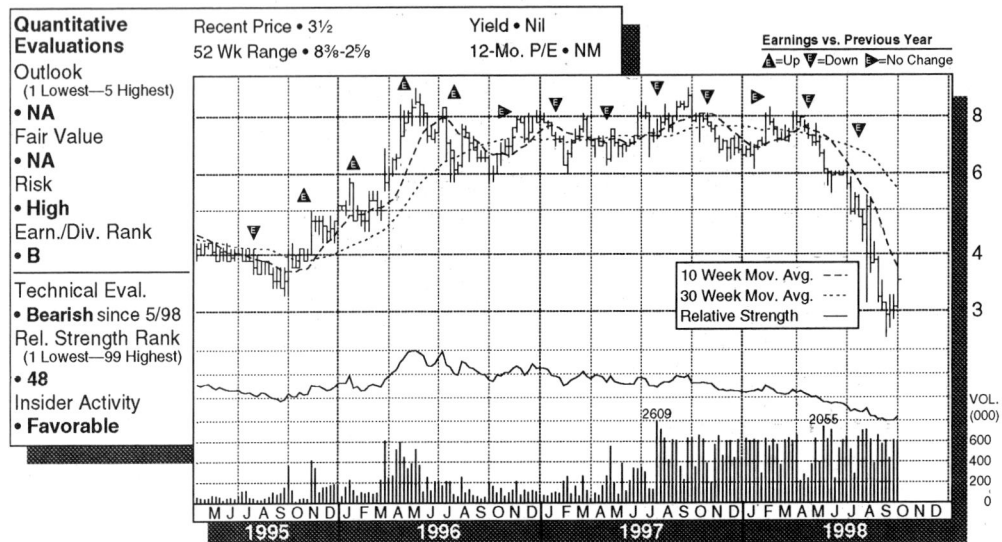

10 Week Mov. Avg. - - -
30 Week Mov. Avg. ·····
Relative Strength —

Business Profile - 11-SEP-98

General Communication's strategy is to be a one-stop provider of voice, video and data transmission services. GNCMA has a leading position in facilities-based long distance service in the state of Alaska and is that state's largest cable operator with over 109,000 subscribers. The company began offering retail Internet services in 1998, and as of August 12, 1998, had 3,000 wholesale and retail subscribers.

Operational Review - 11-SEP-98

Revenues in the first half of 1998 rose 11%, year to year, on higher calling volumes, an increase in revenues from other common carriers and the advent of local access services in Anchorage. Margins widened on the provision of local access in Anchorage as well as reduced charges paid to other carriers to provide local access in other areas. The company continued to invest in expansion of its network and the introduction of new products and services, resulting in 28% higher SG&A expenses. Following sharply higher interest expense and depreciation and amortization charges, the net loss widened to $3,682,000 ($0.08 a share, on 13% more shares) from $1,357,000 ($0.03).

Stock Performance - 02-OCT-98

In the past 30 trading days, GNCMA's shares have declined 10%, compared to a 7% fall in the S&P 500. Average trading volume for the past five days was 117,080 shares, compared with the 40-day moving average of 136,005 shares.

Key Stock Statistics

Dividend Rate/Share	Nil	Shareholders	2,500
Shs. outstg. (M)	49.5	Market cap. (B)	$0.159
Avg. daily vol. (M)	0.119	Inst. holdings	41%
Tang. Bk. Value/Share	NM		
Beta	1.23		

Value of $10,000 invested 5 years ago: $ 14,356

Fiscal Year Ending Dec. 31

	1998	1997	1996	1995	1994	1993
Revenues (Million $)						
1Q	58.15	52.88	37.97	29.69	28.19	23.60
2Q	62.94	56.19	37.20	31.86	28.97	24.70
3Q	—	57.96	38.66	33.36	30.68	26.95
4Q	—	56.78	51.06	34.37	28.93	26.92
Yr.	—	223.8	164.9	129.3	117.0	102.2
Earnings Per Share ($)						
1Q	-0.03	-0.01	0.09	0.07	0.07	0.03
2Q	-0.04	-0.02	0.09	0.08	0.09	0.02
3Q	—	-0.01	0.09	0.09	0.08	0.05
4Q	—	Nil	Nil	0.07	0.06	0.07
Yr.	—	-0.04	0.27	0.31	0.30	0.17

Next earnings report expected: NA

Dividend Data

No cash dividends have been paid.

Business Summary - 11-SEP-98

Alaska-based General Communication, Inc. (GNCMA) supplies common-carrier long distance and other telecommunication products and services to residential, commercial and government users. Following the October 1996 acquisition of the three leading Alaskan cable operators, the company now provides video broadcast services to about 78% of Alaskan households. Competition for the company is restricted due to its location in Alaska. Major competitors include AT&T Alascom, a subsidiary of AT&T, Anchorage Telephone Utility, and Pacific Telecom, Inc.

GNCMA offers a broad spectrum of telecommunication services to customers primarily throughout Alaska. Long distance consists of switched message and data transmission (MTS) services on both an interstate and intrastate level in Alaska and with the rest of the U.S. and foreign countries. The MTS business generated about 70% of 1997 revenue, down from 87% in 1996. Private line and private network communication services is provided between major cities. In addition, the unit sells data communication equipment and provides technical support, consulting and outsourcing services (5% of 1997 revenues). Its two largest customers, MCI and Sprint, accounted for 15% and 11% of 1997 sales, respectively. GNCMA's MTS subscribers fell 5.2% to about 89,000 at December 31, 1997. Systemwide minutes of use climbed 9.1% in 1997 to 753,983 minutes.

Cable services are offered to 21 communities and areas In Alaska, including the three largest urban areas, Anchorage, Fairbanks and Juneau. The cable system passed approximately 167,500 homes and served approximately 108,000 subscribers, implying a 64% penetration rate. The system consisted of about 1,820 miles of installed cable plant having 300 to 450 MHz of channel capacity. Cable services provided 25% of total revenues in 1997.

Other communications offerings include wireless services provided through a cellular reseller agreement, satellite earth stations that operate in rural, hard-to-reach areas, and from an as yet to be developed PCS network, the license for which was purchased from the FCC in 1995 for $1.7 million. The company also entered the local services market in Anchorage in 1997, and can access 95% of Anchorage area local loops from its facilities. The company resells its competitors' local service where the company does not have access to loop facilities.

The company is constructing a new undersea fiber optic cable connecting Anchorage, Fairbanks, and Juneau with the lower 48 states. GNCMA will use half the capacity of the cable for its own traffic. In August, 1998, AT&T informed the company that it would not purchase capacity on the cable, but the company said that efforts to sell the remaining capacity will continue.

Per Share Data ($)

(Year Ended Dec. 31)	1997	1996	1995	1994	1993	1992	1991	1990	1989	1988
Tangible Bk. Val.	NM	NM	1.76	1.42	1.12	0.65	0.58	0.64	0.57	0.46
Cash Flow	0.49	0.61	0.56	0.58	0.47	0.43	0.28	0.33	0.35	1.24
Earnings	-0.05	0.27	0.31	0.30	0.17	0.02	-0.12	0.04	0.08	0.90
Dividends	Nil	Nil	Nil	Nil	Nil	Nil	Nil	Nil	Nil	Nil
Payout Ratio	Nil	Nil	Nil	Nil	Nil	Nil	Nil	Nil	Nil	Nil
Prices - High	9¼	9¼	5⅛	5⅞	5½	2⅝	3¼	3	3⅝	1¾
- Low	6	4½	3¼	3⅛	2¼	1⁵/₁₆	1⅝	1⅝	1½	⅞
P/E Ratio - High	NM	34	17	20	32	NM	NM	75	45	2
- Low	NM	17	10	10	13	NM	NM	41	19	1

Income Statement Analysis (Million $)

	1997	1996	1995	1994	1993	1992	1991	1990	1989	1988
Revs.	224	165	129	117	102	96.5	75.5	63.4	52.1	42.3
Oper. Inc.	39.1	25.9	19.7	19.7	15.5	12.3	7.4	8.3	10.1	5.1
Depr.	23.8	9.5	6.2	6.7	6.7	7.0	5.8	5.0	4.7	4.4
Int. Exp.	17.6	4.8	1.0	1.5	2.3	4.0	3.2	2.6	3.5	3.5
Pretax Inc.	-2.2	12.7	12.6	11.7	6.7	1.5	-1.4	1.0	1.9	18.0
Eff. Tax Rate	NM	41%	41%	39%	41%	42%	NM	44%	34%	34%
Net Inc.	-1.7	7.5	7.5	7.1	4.0	0.9	-1.1	0.5	1.3	11.9

Balance Sheet & Other Fin. Data (Million $)

	1997	1996	1995	1994	1993	1992	1991	1990	1989	1988
Cash	42.5	13.3	4.0	1.6	2.6	3.0	0.9	0.8	1.8	4.9
Curr. Assets	44.2	47.1	29.2	21.5	23.4	20.8	19.5	13.6	11.0	12.2
Total Assets	545	447	84.8	74.2	71.6	72.4	70.2	54.4	47.8	53.9
Curr. Liab.	49.2	69.9	24.1	19.8	17.6	38.0	38.7	16.5	9.8	15.8
LT Debt	249	192	9.1	12.0	19.8	14.9	12.7	21.8	23.3	26.7
Common Eqty.	204	150	43.0	35.1	27.2	11.6	10.3	10.3	9.3	6.6
Total Cap.	492	375	59.1	53.6	53.4	33.9	30.8	37.2	37.0	37.2
Cap. Exp.	64.6	38.6	8.9	10.6	5.7	4.8	16.1	8.5	3.4	0.7
Cash Flow	22.1	16.9	13.7	13.9	10.5	7.3	4.1	5.5	5.9	16.4
Curr. Ratio	0.9	0.7	1.2	1.1	1.3	0.5	0.5	0.8	1.1	0.8
% LT Debt of Cap.	50.5	51.0	15.3	22.4	37.0	43.9	41.3	58.5	62.9	71.7
% Net Inc.of Revs.	NM	4.5	5.8	6.1	3.9	0.9	NM	0.9	2.4	28.2
% Ret. on Assets	NM	2.8	9.4	9.6	4.4	1.2	NM	1.0	2.4	20.1
% Ret. on Equity	NM	7.7	19.2	22.6	17.1	2.4	NM	5.4	15.6	NM

Data as orig. reptd.; bef. results of disc. opers. and/or spec. items. Per share data adj. for stk. divs. as of ex-div. date. Bold denotes diluted EPS (FASB 128). E-Estimated. NA-Not Available. NM-Not Meaningful. NR-Not Ranked.

Office—2550 Denali St., Suite 1000, Anchorage, AK 99503. **Tel**—(907) 265-5600. **Chrmn**—C. F. Page. **Vice Chrmn**—R. M. Walp. **Pres & CEO**—R. A. Duncan. **SVP, CFO, Secy & Treas**—J. M. Lowber. **Dirs**—R. A. Duncan, D. F. Fisher, J. C. Garvey, J. W, Gerdelman, W. P. Glasgow, D. Lynch, C. F. Page, L. E. Romrell, J. M. Schneider, R. M. Walp. **Transfer Agent**—ChaseMellon Shareholder Services, SF. **Incorporated**—in Alaska in 1979. **Empl**— 950. **S&P Analyst:** M.S.B.

03-OCT-98

Industry:
Electronics (Semiconductors)

Summary: This company, the successor to General Instrument's semiconductor business, is a leading manufacturer of discrete semiconductors.

Quantitative Evaluations	
Outlook (1 Lowest—5 Highest)	• **NA**
Fair Value	• **NA**
Risk	• **NA**
Earn./Div. Rank	• **NR**
Technical Eval.	• **NA**
Rel. Strength Rank (1 Lowest—99 Highest)	• **24**
Insider Activity	• **NA**

Recent Price • 6¼
52 Wk Range • 15⅛-5¾

Yield • Nil
12-Mo. P/E • 18.9

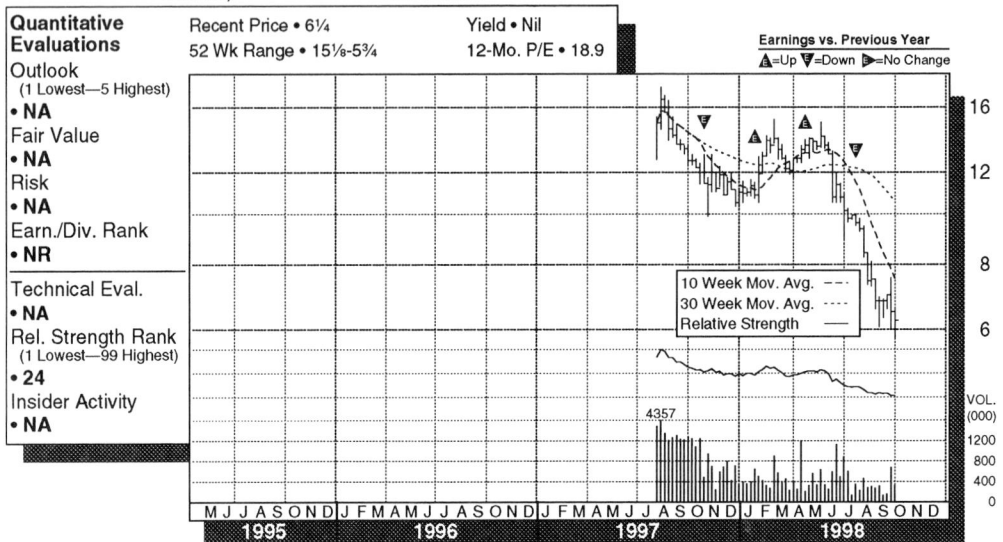

Earnings vs. Previous Year
▲=Up ▼=Down ▶=No Change

10 Week Mov. Avg. - - -
30 Week Mov. Avg. · · · ·
Relative Strength ——

4357

VOL. (000)

Business Profile - 21-SEP-98

Formerly the Power Semiconductor division of General Instrument Corp., the company derived about 70% of its sales in 1997 from outside the U.S. During the second quarter of 1998, SEM, like many of its competitors, experienced a reduction in new orders in all geographic areas, due partly to continuing economic weakness in the Far East and reduced end-market demand in the computer, computer peripheral and related industries. These conditions are exacerbated by industrywide excess capacity which has resulted in significant competitive pricing pressures. SEM expects earnings for the second half of 1998 to decrease from those reported in the first half.

Operational Review - 21-SEP-98

Net sales for the six months ended June 30, 1998, advanced 13%, year to year, mainly reflecting increased volume shipments as well as the inclusion of small signal product revenues (this business was acquired October 1, 1997), partly offset by lower average selling prices and unfavorable foreign exchange rate fluctuations. In the absence of $32.7 million of charges for severance and other costs, and with well controlled SG&A expenses, operating income rose sharply. Following higher net interest expense, and after taxes at 35.0% versus 17.9%, income from continuing operations of $16,311,000 ($0.44 a share) contrasted with a loss of $8,709,000 ($0.25, excluding income from discontinued operations of $0.53).

Stock Performance - 02-OCT-98

In the past 30 trading days, SEM's shares have declined 17%, compared to a 7% fall in the S&P 500. Average trading volume for the past five days was 65,020 shares, compared with the 40-day moving average of 62,495 shares.

Key Stock Statistics

Dividend Rate/Share	Nil	Shareholders	700
Shs. outstg. (M)	36.8	Market cap. (B)	$0.230
Avg. daily vol. (M)	0.065	Inst. holdings	80%
Tang. Bk. Value/Share	NM		
Beta	NA		

Value of $10,000 invested 5 years ago: NA

Fiscal Year Ending Dec. 31

	1998	1997	1996	1995	1994	1993
Revenues (Million $)						
1Q	106.4	85.37	97.90	90.00	67.76	61.21
2Q	98.76	95.51	100.0	111.5	77.26	67.24
3Q	—	95.57	84.70	109.7	83.50	70.18
4Q	—	103.6	79.34	103.1	87.17	69.14
Yr.	—	380.0	361.9	414.3	315.7	267.8
Earnings Per Share ($)						
1Q	**0.26**	0.14	0.29	—	—	—
2Q	**0.19**	0.24	0.36	—	—	—
3Q	—	0.22	0.25	—	—	—
4Q	—	0.25	0.02	—	—	—
Yr.	—	0.84	0.93	1.41	0.43	0.13

Next earnings report expected: late October

Dividend Data

No dividends have been paid, and the company does not anticipate paying any in the foreseeable future. A "poison pill" shareholder rights plan was adopted in 1997.

Business Summary - 21-SEP-98

General Semiconductor Inc. (SEM) became a stand-alone company in July 1997 with the restructuring of General Instrument Corp. At that time, NextLevel Systems Inc. and CommScope Inc. were spun off from General Instrument, and the remaining business was renamed General Semiconductor. The company is a world leader in the design, manufacture and sale of low- to medium-power rectifiers and transient voltage suppression components. It produces some 10 billion discrete semiconductors annually in manufacturing facilities located in China, Europe, Taiwan and the U.S. More than two-thirds of the company's sales are derived from outside North America.

The company's products are used throughout the electrical and electronics industries to condition current and voltage and to protect electrical circuits from power surges. Applications for General Semiconductor's products include consumer electronics, telecommunications, computers, lighting ballasts, home appliances, and automotive and industrial products.

On October 1, 1997, the company purchased certain assets and assumed certain liabilities related to the discrete semiconductor business of ITT Industries, Inc.

for $8.0 million. The acquisition was accounted for as a purchase transaction. By broadening the company's served market to include small signal transistors and zener diodes, this acquisition enabled the company to participate in approximately 50% of the $14.0 billion worldwide discrete semiconductor market compared to the 17% in which the company participated prior to the acquisition.

The company believes that the demand for discrete semiconductors will be driven by several factors including (i) increased electronic content in a broad range of products, devices and systems, including automotive, consumer products and industrial equipment; (ii) greater demand for voice and data communications products; (iii) growth in personal computers and peripheral products; (iv) the rapid replacement of heavier and less efficient magnetic lighting ballasts with electronic ballasts; and (v) increasing international demand for all discrete products.

Research and development expenditures totaled $6.0 million in 1997, up from $5.8 million the year before. R&D spending reflects continued development and the advancement of new product and packaging technologies targeted for the automotive, telecommunications and computer end-market applications.

Per Share Data ($)

(Year Ended Dec. 31)	1997	1996	1995	1994	1993	1992	1991	1990	1989	1988
Tangible Bk. Val.	NM	NA	NA	NA	NA	NA	NA	NA	NA	NA
Cash Flow	0.93	1.89	2.55	NA	NA	NA	NA	NA	NA	NA
Earnings	0.84	0.93	1.41	NA	NA	NA	NA	NA	NA	NA
Dividends	Nil	Nil	Nil	Nil	Nil	Nil	Nil	Nil	Nil	Nil
Payout Ratio	Nil	Nil	Nil	Nil	Nil	Nil	Nil	Nil	Nil	Nil
Prices - High	17½	NA	NA	NA	NA	NA	NA	NA	NA	NA
- Low	9⅞	NA	NA	NA	NA	NA	NA	NA	NA	NA
P/E Ratio - High	21	NA	NA	NA	NA	NA	NA	NA	NA	NA
- Low	12	NA	NA	NA	NA	NA	NA	NA	NA	NA

Income Statement Analysis (Million $)

	1997	1996	1995	1994	1993	1992	1991	1990	1989	1988
Revs.	380	362	414	NA	NA	NA	NA	NA	NA	NA
Oper. Inc.	68.7	77.6	97.8	NA	NA	NA	NA	NA	NA	NA
Depr.	24.2	22.6	21.3	NA	NA	NA	NA	NA	NA	NA
Int. Exp.	19.6	19.6	19.6	NA	NA	NA	NA	NA	NA	NA
Pretax Inc.	49.1	57.9	77.9	NA	NA	NA	NA	NA	NA	NA
Eff. Tax Rate	37%	41%	35%	NA	NA	NA	NA	NA	NA	NA
Net Inc.	31.0	34.0	50.6	NA	NA	NA	NA	NA	NA	NA

Balance Sheet & Other Fin. Data (Million $)

	1997	1996	1995	1994	1993	1992	1991	1990	1989	1988
Cash	5.2	20.2	36.4	NA	NA	NA	NA	NA	NA	NA
Curr. Assets	118	169	156	NA	NA	NA	NA	NA	NA	NA
Total Assets	550	2,057	1,799	NA	NA	NA	NA	NA	NA	NA
Curr. Liab.	101	100	88.6	NA	NA	NA	NA	NA	NA	NA
LT Debt	264	688	728	NA	NA	NA	NA	NA	NA	NA
Common Eqty.	93.7	1,181	924	NA	NA	NA	NA	NA	NA	NA
Total Cap.	358	1,869	1,652	NA	NA	NA	NA	NA	NA	NA
Cap. Exp.	29.2	60.3	34.9	NA	NA	NA	NA	NA	NA	NA
Cash Flow	55.2	56.7	71.9	NA	NA	NA	NA	NA	NA	NA
Curr. Ratio	1.2	1.7	1.8	NA	NA	NA	NA	NA	NA	NA
% LT Debt of Cap.	74.4	36.9	44.0	NA	NA	NA	NA	NA	NA	NA
% Net Inc.of Revs.	8.2	9.4	12.2	NA	NA	NA	NA	NA	NA	NA
% Ret. on Assets	3.3	2.4	NA	NA	NA	NA	NA	NA	NA	NA
% Ret. on Equity	1.4	NA	NA	NA	NA	NA	NA	NA	NA	NA

Data as orig. reptd. Per share data adj. for stk. divs. as of ex-div. date. Bold denotes diluted EPS (FASB 128). E-Estimated. NA-Not Available. NM-Not Meaningful. NR-Not Ranked.

Office—10 Melville Park Road, Melville, NY 11747. **Tel**—(516) 847-3000. **Fax**—(516) 847-3236. **Website**—www.gensemi.com **Chrmn, Pres & CEO**—R. A. Ostertag. **SVP & CFO**—A. M. Caggia. **SVP & Secy**—S. B. Paige. **VP-Investor Contact**—Pamela A. Jameson (516) 847-3169.**Dirs**—S. B. Klinsky, R. A. Ostertag, R. Rosenzweig, P. Schwartz, S. L. Simmons, G. T. Wrixon. **Transfer Agent & Registrar**—ChaseMellon Shareholder Services, South Hackensack, NJ**Incorporated**—in Delaware. **Empl**— 5,000. **S&P Analyst**: C.C.P.

Genesis Health Ventures   1001

NYSE Symbol **GHV**

In S&P SmallCap 600

03-OCT-98

Industry:
Health Care
(Long-Term Care)

Summary: This company provides basic and specialty health care services to the elderly through health care networks serving five geographic markets in the eastern U.S.

Quantitative Evaluations

Outlook
(1 Lowest—5 Highest)
• **5**

Fair Value
• **44¼**

Risk
• **Average**

Earn./Div. Rank
• **NR**

Technical Eval.
• **Bearish** since 11/97

Rel. Strength Rank
(1 Lowest—99 Highest)
• **19**

Insider Activity
• **Neutral**

Recent Price • 12¼
52 Wk Range • 39⅝-11⅛

Yield • Nil
12-Mo. P/E • 8.6

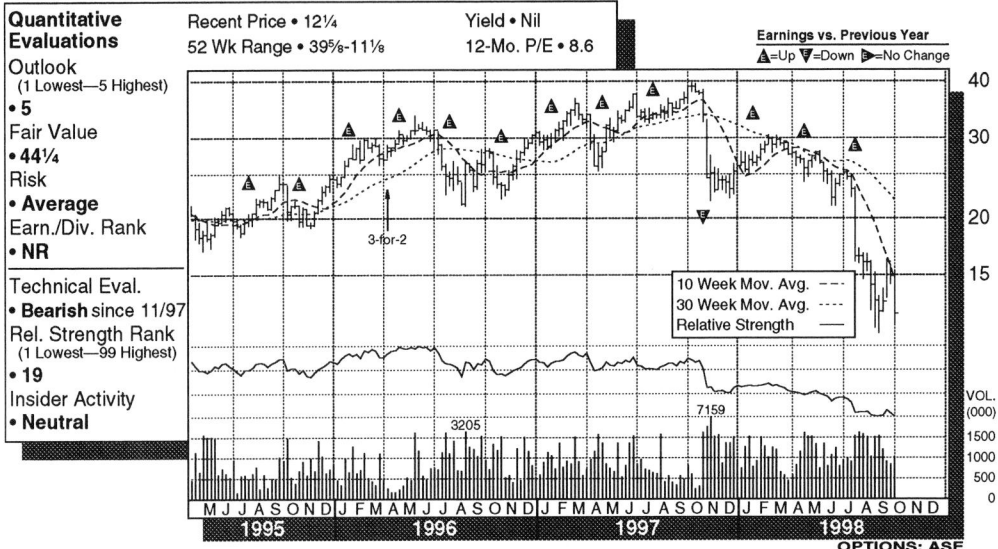

Earnings vs. Previous Year
▲=Up ▼=Down ▶=No Change

10 Week Mov. Avg. – – –
30 Week Mov. Avg. ⋯⋯
Relative Strength ——

3-for-2

3205   7159

VOL. (000)

OPTIONS: ASE

Business Profile - 08-SEP-98

In August 1998, the company acquired Vitalink Pharmacy Services Inc., for approximately $680 million, including $80 million of assumed debt. About $295 million of the consideration was in the form of perpetual, convertible preferred stock having an initial dividend of 5.94%, and convertible into Genesis common shares after three years, provided the Genesis stock price reaches certain trading levels. Vitalink provides medications, consulting, infusion and other ancillary services to 170,000 institutional beds in 36 states, as well as home infusion patients. Genesis will merge Vitalink with its NeighborCare pharmacy operations, resulting in over 100 institutional and community-based pharmacies with annual revenues of about $900 million.

Operational Review - 08-SEP-98

Revenues in the nine months ended June 30, 1998, were up 22%, year to year, due to higher revenues in the Multicare pharmacy and rehabilitation therapy businesses, and volume growth in institutional pharmacy, medical supply and contract therapy sales. Margins widened, due to lower costs from the de-consolidation of the physician services business, and the termination of operations of three eldercare centers. After higher interest and depreciation expenses relating to acquisitions, and taxes at 36.5% in both periods, net income rose 7.0%, to $43.4 million ($1.22 per share), from $40.6 million ($1.14). Results exclude special charges of $0.05 and $0.02 a share in the respective periods.

Stock Performance - 02-OCT-98

In the past 30 trading days, GHV's shares have declined 14%, compared to a 7% fall in the S&P 500. Average trading volume for the past five days was 205,860 shares, compared with the 40-day moving average of 259,956 shares.

Key Stock Statistics

Dividend Rate/Share	Nil	Shareholders	700
Shs. outstg. (M)	35.2	Market cap. (B)	$0.434
Avg. daily vol. (M)	0.221	Inst. holdings	55%
Tang. Bk. Value/Share	6.47		
Beta	1.36		

Value of $10,000 invested 5 years ago: $ 11,192

Fiscal Year Ending Sep. 30

	1998	1997	1996	1995	1994	1993
Revenues (Million $)						
1Q	302.6	258.5	132.8	111.5	71.91	52.30
2Q	344.3	273.3	154.7	117.0	98.64	53.25
3Q	352.5	284.5	172.8	126.0	105.4	55.59
4Q	—	283.6	211.1	131.9	112.7	58.62
Yr.	—	1,100	671.5	486.4	388.6	219.8
Earnings Per Share ($)						
1Q	**0.36**	0.34	0.25	0.21	0.15	0.13
2Q	**0.41**	0.37	0.30	0.25	0.19	0.15
3Q	**0.45**	0.43	0.37	0.28	0.23	0.17
4Q	—	0.47	0.43	0.31	0.27	0.21
Yr.	—	1.35	1.35	1.13	0.89	0.67

Next earnings report expected: mid November

Dividend Data

No cash dividends have been paid. A poison pill stock purchase rights plan was adopted in April 1995.

A Division of The McGraw·Hill Companies

Business Summary - 08-SEP-98

Genesis Health Ventures (GHV) has aggressively expanded its Genesis ElderCare healthcare and support services for the elderly to capitalize on the increasing numbers of older Americans. Its strategy is to enhance eldercare networks, establish new eldercare networks in markets it deems attractive and broaden its array of high margin specialty medical services through internal development and selected acquisitions.

Consistent with its strategy, in October 1997, the company, in collaboration with the Cypress Group, LLC, and the Texas Pacific Group (TPG), acquired Multicare Companies, Inc. (MUL), a New Jersey-based long-term care concern, in a transaction valued at about $1.4 billion, and formed a new company, Genesis ElderCare Acquisition Corp. (GEAC). GHV owns 42% of GEAC, while Cypress and TPG each own about 29%. GEAC is now a consolidated subsidiary of GHV, and GHV acquired Multicare's rehabilitation therapy business. GHV also entered into a multi-year management services contract with GEAC to manage Multicare's operations, for an annual management fee of 6.0% of total revenues.

The company has 175,000 customers in more than five regional markets in the eastern U.S. (New England; Mid-Atlantic; Chesapeake; Southern; and Allegheny), in which over 6 million people over the age of 65 reside. As of September 1997, GHV's networks included 340 eldercare centers, about 100 physicians and physician assistants and nurse practitioners, 22 institutional phar-

macies and 7 medical supply distribution centers, 29 community-based pharmacies and 8 home healthcare agencies.

Revenue contributions in FY 97 were derived from basic health care (50% of total revenues), specialty medical (46%), and management services and other products and services (4%). The payor mix of basic and specialty medical services revenue in FY 97 was 39% private pay and other, 24% Medicare, and 37% Medicaid. Specialty medical services revenues have increased at a 61% compounded annual rate over the past four fiscal years. Specialty medical services typically generate higher profit margins than basic healthcare services and are less capital intensive.

Basic health care services are offered at three levels: skilled care (provides 24-hour per day professional services of a registered nurse), intermediate care (provides less intensive nursing care), and personal care (provides for the needs of customers requiring minimal supervision and assistance). Specialty medical services provided by the company include pharmacy and medical supply, rehabilitation, subacute care, physician services, home health care, and other services. GHV also provides management, development and marketing services to 210 eldercare centers.

In August 1998, the company acquired Vitalink Pharmacy Services, Inc., for approximately $680 million, including $80 million of assumed debt. The acquisition will result in more than 100 institutional and community-based pharmacies throughout the U.S.

Per Share Data ($)

(Year Ended Sep. 30)	1997	1996	1995	1994	1993	1992	1991	1990	1989	1988
Tangible Bk. Val.	7.07	8.29	4.84	4.15	5.78	4.19	2.57	-0.61	NA	NA
Cash Flow	2.53	2.27	1.96	1.43	0.99	1.03	0.95	0.86	NA	NA
Earnings	1.60	1.35	1.13	0.89	0.67	0.53	0.37	0.08	NA	NA
Dividends	Nil	Nil	Nil	Nil	Nil	Nil	Nil	Nil	Nil	Nil
Payout Ratio	Nil	Nil	Nil	Nil	Nil	Nil	Nil	Nil	Nil	Nil
Prices - High	39³/₄	33³/₄	25	21³/₈	16¹/₈	11³/₈	8¹/₂	NA	NA	NA
- Low	21³/₄	21¹/₄	16⁷/₈	14¹/₂	7⁵/₈	4¹/₈	4¹/₂	NA	NA	NA
P/E Ratio - High	29	25	22	24	24	21	23	NA	NA	NA
- Low	16	16	15	16	12	8	12	NA	NA	NA

Income Statement Analysis (Million $)

Revs.	1,100	671	486	389	220	196	171	144	NA	NA
Oper. Inc.	200	128	93.2	53.9	29.7	28.4	21.8	18.0	NA	NA
Depr.	41.9	254	18.8	10.9	5.8	7.2	4.9	4.4	NA	NA
Int. Exp.	39.1	24.9	20.4	15.7	5.1	8.8	11.1	11.4	NA	NA
Pretax Inc.	75.2	58.1	40.2	27.7	18.9	12.4	5.8	1.1	NA	NA
Eff. Tax Rate	36%	36%	37%	36%	37%	38%	38%	37%	NA	NA
Net Inc.	48.1	37.2	25.5	17.7	11.9	7.7	3.6	0.7	NA	NA

Balance Sheet & Other Fin. Data (Million $)

Cash	11.7	18.3	10.3	4.3	4.0	1.3	1.3	1.1	NA	NA
Curr. Assets	352	233	191	120	69.7	51.9	40.7	32.8	NA	NA
Total Assets	1,434	951	600	512	237	189	173	150	NA	NA
Curr. Liab.	126	77.2	56.9	53.3	19.6	19.9	26.0	25.6	NA	NA
LT Debt	652	339	308	251	83.8	80.2	89.8	97.7	NA	NA
Common Eqty.	608	515	222	195	125	82.7	37.7	12.1	NA	NA
Total Cap.	1,297	867	544	456	216	167	145	122	NA	NA
Cap. Exp.	61.1	38.6	24.7	26.6	23.5	7.3	18.2	16.9	NA	NA
Cash Flow	90.1	62.5	44.3	28.6	17.7	14.9	8.0	4.9	NA	NA
Curr. Ratio	2.8	3.0	3.4	2.3	3.6	2.6	1.6	1.3	NA	NA
% LT Debt of Cap.	50.3	39.1	56.6	55.1	38.9	48.1	61.8	80.1	NA	NA
% Net Inc.of Revs.	4.4	5.5	5.2	4.6	5.4	3.9	2.1	0.5	NA	NA
% Ret. on Assets	4.0	4.8	4.6	4.5	5.1	3.3	1.1	NA	NA	NA
% Ret. on Equity	8.6	10.1	12.2	10.3	10.6	10.8	8.5	NA	NA	NA

Data as orig. reptd.; bef. results of disc. opers. and/or spec. items. Per share data adj. for stk. divs. as of ex-div. date. Bold denotes diluted EPS (FASB 128). E-Estimated. NA-Not Available. NM-Not Meaningful. NR-Not Ranked.

Office—148 West State St., Kennett Square, PA 19348. **Tel**—(610) 444-6350. **Website**—http://www.ghv.com **Chrmn & CEO**—M. R. Walker. **Pres** —R. R. Howard. **EVP & COO**—D. C. Barr. **SVP, CFO & Investor Contact**—G. V. Hager Jr. **VP & Treas**—G. K. Kuhnle. **Secy**—I. C. Gubernick.**Dirs**—A. R. Freedman, R. R. Howard, S. H. Howard, R. C. Lipitz, S. E. Luongo, A. B. Miller, M. R. Walker. **Transfer Agent**—ChaseMellon Shareholder Services, NYC. **Incorporated**—in Pennsylvania in 1985. **Empl**— 43,400. **S&P Analyst:** John J. Arege

Gentex Corp.

3978C

NASDAQ Symbol **GNTX**

In S&P SmallCap 600

03-OCT-98

Industry:
Auto Parts & Equipment

Summary: Gentex manufactures automatic-dimming rearview mirrors for the automotive industry and fire protection products for commercial applications.

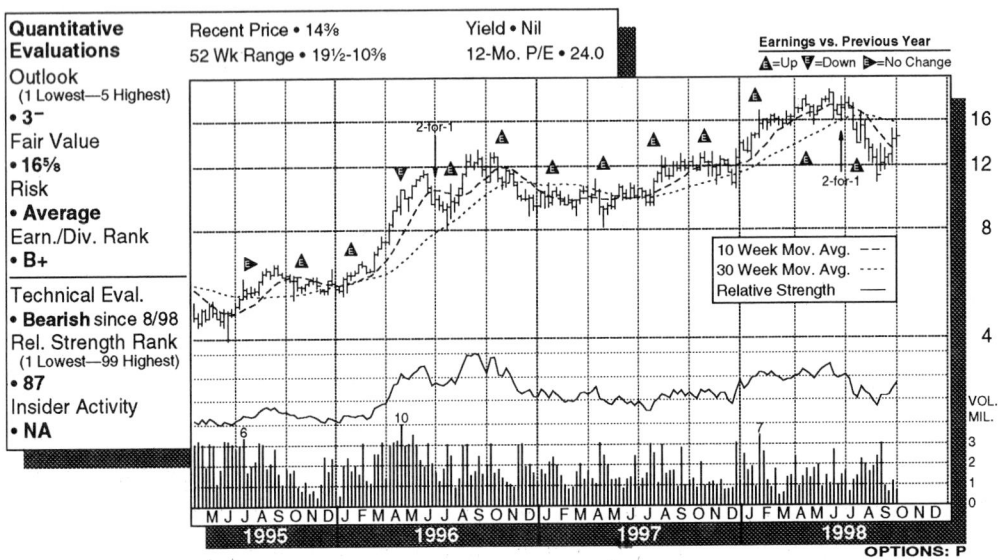

Quantitative Evaluations	Recent Price • 14⅜	Yield • Nil
	52 Wk Range • 19½-10⅜	12-Mo. P/E • 24.0

Quantitative Evaluations

Outlook (1 Lowest—5 Highest)
• **3⁻**

Fair Value
• **16⅝**

Risk
• **Average**

Earn./Div. Rank
• **B+**

Technical Eval.
• **Bearish** since 8/98

Rel. Strength Rank (1 Lowest—99 Highest)
• **87**

Insider Activity
• **NA**

Earnings vs. Previous Year
▲=Up ▼=Down ▶=No Change

10 Week Mov. Avg. — - —
30 Week Mov. Avg. - - - -
Relative Strength ——

OPTIONS: P

Business Profile - 15-JUL-98

Gentex is the leading producer of automatic rearview mirrors, with a dominant 90% market share worldwide. Following record revenues and earnings in 1997, on 64% higher shipment levels for exterior mirrors, the positive trend continued into the first half of 1998, with the posting once again of record sales and net income. In July 1998, GNTX said that sales in the second quarter reached record levels, despite the impact of the strike at GM. The company estimates that the strike cost it about $0.02 a share in the second quarter. A two-for-one split was effected in June 1998. In May 1997, directors authorized the repurchase of one million common shares, expected to be completed within 12 months.

Operational Review - 15-JUL-98

Sales advanced 25% in the six months ended June 30, 1998, reflecting a 36% increase in total automotive mirror unit shipments. Gross margins widened significantly, as cost of goods sold, R&D spending and SG&A expenses rose less rapidly. Aided by higher other income, after taxes at 32.7%, versus 32.5%, net income soared 51%, to $23,265,801 ($0.32 a share), from $15,385,125 ($0.21, as adjusted).

Stock Performance - 02-OCT-98

In the past 30 trading days, GNTX's shares have increased 14%, compared to a 7% fall in the S&P 500. Average trading volume for the past five days was 137,120 shares, compared with the 40-day moving average of 312,805 shares.

Key Stock Statistics

Dividend Rate/Share	Nil	Shareholders		2,000
Shs. outstg. (M)	71.8	Market cap. (B)		$ 1.0
Avg. daily vol. (M)	0.193	Inst. holdings		58%
Tang. Bk. Value/Share	2.85			
Beta	0.58			

Value of $10,000 invested 5 years ago: $ 54,117

Fiscal Year Ending Dec. 31

	1998	1997	1996	1995	1994	1993
Revenues (Million $)						
1Q	56.98	41.90	35.91	26.04	21.16	15.27
2Q	51.37	44.87	38.67	26.02	20.71	13.74
3Q	—	46.97	36.80	26.80	23.09	15.47
4Q	—	52.58	37.33	32.70	24.80	19.19
Yr.	—	186.3	148.7	111.6	89.76	63.66
Earnings Per Share ($)						
1Q	**0.17**	0.10	0.05	0.07	0.06	0.03
2Q	**0.15**	0.11	0.10	0.06	0.06	0.03
3Q	—	0.12	0.09	0.07	0.06	0.03
4Q	—	**0.15**	0.10	0.08	0.07	0.05
Yr.	—	**0.49**	**0.34**	0.28	0.24	0.15

Next earnings report expected: mid October

Dividend Data

Amount ($)	Date Decl.	Ex-Div. Date	Stock of Record	Payment Date
2-for-1	May. 21	Jun. 22	Jun. 05	Jun. 19 '98

Business Summary - 15-JUL-98

Gentex Corp. (GNTX) has derived about 85% of net sales in recent years from the manufacture of automatic rearview mirrors for automobiles. The company's Night Vision Safety (NVS) mirrors are active, crash-avoidance safety features, the same designation given to anti-lock brake systems (ABS). These mirrors use electrochromic technology and sophisticated electronic circuitry and sensors to automatically vary the reflectance of interior and exterior rearview mirrors in proportion to the amount of glare from the headlights of following vehicles. Driver safety is enhanced, because glare from following vehicles is eliminated, while optimum driver vision is preserved.

In 1987, GNTX was the first company to introduce a commercial automatic-dimming mirror to the worldwide auto industry, and it is currently the dominant supplier of these mirrors, with a 90% market share.

The company's NVS mirrors are offered as standard or optional equipment on more than 100 1998 vehicle models worldwide. During 1997, Gentex sold 2.8 million interior NVS mirrors, compared with 2.4 million in 1996 and 1.8 million in 1995. Sales of exterior NVS mirror subassemblies rose to 1,079,000 units in 1997, up from 656,000 in 1996.

The company said that it is producing NVS mirrors at an annual rate of about 4,000,000 units. Advanced-feature NVS mirrors developed by the company include an automatic-dimming mirror with an electric compass, one with map lights, one with remote keyless entry control, and one with electronics to turn a vehicle's head- and tail-lamps on and off at dusk and dawn.

GNTX currently supplies NVS mirrors to GM, Chrysler, Ford, Toyota, Mercedes-Benz, BMW, Toyota/Lexus, Nissan/Infiniti, Opel, Fiat, Audi, Bentley, Rolls Royce, Honda, Hyundai, Daewoo, Kia Motors, and to GM and Fiat in Brazil.

The company has derived about 15% of net sales in recent years from its line of fire protection products, which consist of more than 60 different models of smoke detectors and more than 160 different models of signaling devices. During 1996, GNTX made several revisions to its products, including weather-proofing the mechanical horn and strobe for outdoor use, increasing the power taps on their speaker series, adding three new candela ratings to their visual signals, and adding terminal blocks to the remote signaling appliances to meet new code requirements. In 1997, the company launched a new visual and audible signaling product line. GNTX was also the first company in the fire alarm market to implement the temporal code 3 pattern on fire alarm products.

Per Share Data ($)

(Year Ended Dec. 31)	1997	1996	1995	1994	1993	1992	1991	1990	1989	1988
Tangible Bk. Val.	2.44	1.84	1.40	1.08	0.76	0.52	0.45	0.42	0.40	0.17
Cash Flow	0.58	0.40	0.32	0.28	0.18	0.10	0.05	0.04	0.05	0.03
Earnings	0.49	0.34	0.28	0.24	0.15	0.08	0.03	0.02	0.04	0.02
Dividends	Nil	Nil	Nil	Nil	Nil	Nil	Nil	Nil	Nil	Nil
Payout Ratio	Nil	Nil	Nil	Nil	Nil	Nil	Nil	Nil	Nil	Nil
Prices - High	14⅛	13⅜	6⅞	8⅞	8⅞	3¼	1¹¹/₁₆	1¹³/₁₆	1¹³/₁₆	⅝
- Low	8⅛	5¼	4	4½	2½	1⅝	⅝	⅝	⁹/₁₆	⁷/₁₆
P/E Ratio - High	29	40	25	36	60	41	56	95	47	43
- Low	17	16	14	19	17	21	20	34	15	29

Income Statement Analysis (Million $)

	1997	1996	1995	1994	1993	1992	1991	1990	1989	1988
Revs.	186	149	112	89.8	63.7	45.1	26.9	21.2	23.8	14.7
Oper. Inc.	53.9	39.8	28.1	26.0	16.0	8.5	3.1	1.6	3.5	1.5
Depr.	6.4	3.9	3.2	3.0	2.1	1.6	1.3	1.0	0.8	0.5
Int. Exp.	Nil	Nil	Nil	Nil	0.0	0.2	0.5	0.5	0.3	Nil
Pretax Inc.	52.2	35.5	27.9	24.7	14.7	7.6	2.7	1.2	3.1	1.1
Eff. Tax Rate	33%	33%	32%	33%	33%	33%	30%	5.50%	32%	35%
Net Inc.	35.2	24.0	18.9	16.5	9.8	5.1	1.9	1.1	2.1	0.7

Balance Sheet & Other Fin. Data (Million $)

	1997	1996	1995	1994	1993	1992	1991	1990	1989	1988
Cash	41.1	48.5	34.2	19.3	13.3	7.8	14.3	10.9	14.1	0.5
Curr. Assets	75.9	72.7	56.0	36.4	27.1	17.8	20.8	15.6	20.1	5.8
Total Assets	190	140	109	80.5	55.2	40.3	37.2	33.9	32.5	10.7
Curr. Liab.	14.6	11.4	14.0	8.7	5.5	4.0	8.6	1.7	1.9	2.2
LT Debt	Nil	Nil	Nil	Nil	Nil	Nil	0.1	6.1	6.1	0.3
Common Eqty.	173	128	94.7	71.4	49.5	35.5	28.2	25.9	24.2	7.9
Total Cap.	175	129	95.2	71.8	49.7	36.2	28.6	32.2	30.7	8.5
Cap. Exp.	16.4	16.4	4.9	6.2	3.4	4.2	2.2	2.4	4.1	2.8
Cash Flow	41.6	27.9	22.1	19.5	12.0	6.7	3.1	2.2	2.9	1.2
Curr. Ratio	5.2	6.4	4.0	4.2	4.9	4.4	2.4	9.3	10.9	2.6
% LT Debt of Cap.	Nil	Nil	Nil	Nil	Nil	Nil	0.3	18.9	19.9	3.8
% Net Inc.of Revs.	18.9	16.1	16.9	18.3	15.5	11.2	6.9	5.3	8.8	4.6
% Ret. on Assets	21.3	19.2	19.9	24.1	20.4	12.9	5.2	3.3	9.1	6.9
% Ret. on Equity	23.4	21.5	22.8	27.0	23.0	15.8	6.8	4.5	12.2	9.1

Data as orig. reptd.; bef. results of disc. opers. and/or spec. items. Per share data adj. for stk. divs. as of ex-div. date. Bold denotes diluted EPS (FASB 128). E-Estimated. NA-Not Available. NM-Not Meaningful. NR-Not Ranked.

Office—600 N. Centennial, Zeeland, MI 49464. Tel—(616) 772-1800. Fax—(616) 772-7348. Website—http://www.gentex.com Chrmn & CEO—F. Bauer. EVP—K. LaGrand. VP-Fin & Treas—E. Jen. Secy & Investor Contact—Connie Hamblin.Dirs—F. Bauer, M. E. Fouts, K. LaGrand, A. Lanting, J. Mulder, T. Thompson, L. L. Weber. Transfer Agent—American Stock Transfer & Trust Co., NYC. Incorporated—in Michigan in 1974. Empl— 1,250. S&P Analyst: Kathleen J. Fraser

STANDARD &POOR'S
STOCK REPORTS

Geon Co.

1005P

NYSE Symbol **GON**

In S&P SmallCap 600

06-OCT-98

Industry: Chemicals

Summary: This company, the world's largest supplier of PVC compounds, intends to joint venture its PVC resins business with Occidental Petroleum.

S&P Opinion: Hold (★★★)	Recent Price • 18⅛	Yield • 2.7%
	52 Wk Range • 26-17⅜	12-Mo. P/E • 17.5

Quantitative Evaluations

Outlook
(1 Lowest—5 Highest)
• **3**

Fair Value
• **21½**

Risk
• **Average**

Earn./Div. Rank
• **NR**

Technical Eval.
• **Neutral** since 9/98

Rel. Strength Rank
(1 Lowest—99 Highest)
• **52**

Insider Activity
• **Neutral**

Earnings vs. Previous Year
▲=Up ▼=Down ▶=No Change

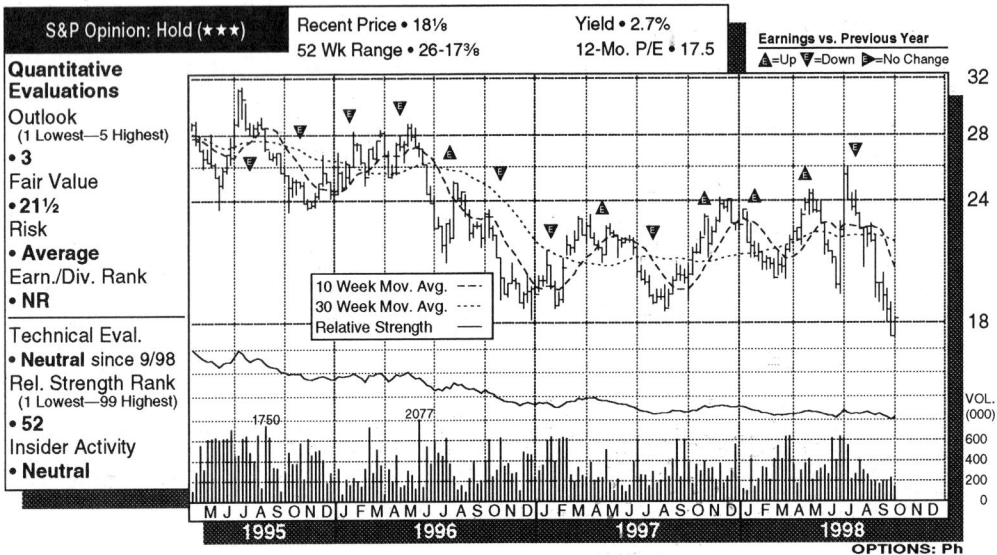

10 Week Mov. Avg. – – –
30 Week Mov. Avg. – – – –
Relative Strength ——

OPTIONS: Ph

Overview - 06-OCT-98

Geon plans to focus on its compound and specialty resins businesses. In June 1998, GON and Occidental Petroleum agreed to merge their PVC suspension resins operations. The venture, to be formed by early 1999 and 24% owned by GON, will be the largest PVC resin producer. The venture projects to reduce annual costs by $80 million. Geon will also acquire OXY's vinyl compound unit (annual sales of about $200 million) and receive $110 million. The two companies will retain their specialty PVC resin businesses. Following the formation of the joint venture, Geon's annual revenues will be about $1.2 billion, consisting of vinyl compounds and dispersion resins, and non-vinyl plastic compounds. GON's existing compounds and specialty resins accounted for about 63% of its sales in 1998's first half and for all of its operating income. Operating income for this group of businesses exists in the industry range of 7% to 9% of sales. The commodity PVC industry will continue to have difficult conditions for at least through the end of 1998. Prices and margins for PVC resins have declined since mid-1997 and prices could remain under pressure until the normal seasonal pick-up in demand in early 1999, offset by lower raw material costs. GON expected to achieve another $30 million of productivity and cost benefits in 1998.

Valuation - 06-OCT-98

The stock retreated in the third quarter of 1998 after jumping on the news of GON's intention to form a joint venture in PVC resins. GON's plan to focus on its performance polymers, a business with consistent earnings growth and margins, should be viewed as a positive. We remain concerned, however, about the PVC industry's poor profitability, with margins remaining at or near historical lows, largely because of increased industry capacity and weakened Asian demand.

Key Stock Statistics

S&P EPS Est. 1998	0.85	Tang. Bk. Value/Share	9.79
P/E on S&P Est. 1998	21.4	Beta	0.29
S&P EPS Est. 1999	1.60	Shareholders	7,000
Dividend Rate/Share	0.50	Market cap. (B)	$0.419
Shs. outstg. (M)	23.3	Inst. holdings	92%
Avg. daily vol. (M)	0.038		

Value of $10,000 invested 5 years ago: NA

Fiscal Year Ending Dec. 31

	1998	1997	1996	1995	1994	1993
Revenues (Million $)						
1Q	324.5	301.0	245.7	336.2	261.3	224.6
2Q	330.7	333.0	311.8	357.6	284.5	245.1
3Q	—	303.7	307.8	310.2	312.3	254.5
4Q	—	312.3	279.1	263.8	350.5	248.3
Yr.	—	1,250	1,144	1,268	1,209	972.5
Earnings Per Share ($)						
1Q	**0.25**	**0.10**	-0.22	0.80	0.25	-0.15
2Q	**0.20**	**0.26**	0.40	0.21	0.46	0.20
3Q	**E0.22**	**0.45**	0.25	0.56	0.71	311.80
4Q	**E0.18**	**0.15**	0.07	0.18	0.65	-0.17
Yr.	**0.85**	**0.95**	0.50	1.24	2.06	0.08

Next earnings report expected: mid October

Dividend Data (Dividends have been paid since 1993.)

Amount ($)	Date Decl.	Ex-Div. Date	Stock of Record	Payment Date
0.125	Nov. 05	Nov. 26	Dec. 01	Dec. 15 '97
0.125	Feb. 05	Feb. 25	Feb. 27	Mar. 16 '98
0.125	May. 07	May. 28	Jun. 01	Jun. 15 '98
0.125	Aug. 06	Aug. 28	Sep. 01	Sep. 15 '98

A Division of The **McGraw·Hill** *Companies*

STANDARD
&POOR'S
STOCK REPORTS

The Geon Company

1005P
06-OCT-98

Business Summary - 06-OCT-98

Geon Co. (GON), a part of B.F. Goodrich until the company's 1993 IPO, makes one of the world's most widely used plastics-- polyvinyl chloride, popularly known as PVC. GON is a leading North American producer of PVC resins and the world's largest producer of PVC compounds. It also makes the intermediate precursor to PVC--vinyl chloride monomer (VCM). About 44% of 1997 revenues were attributed to commodity PVC suspension resins, 9% to specialty resins, 40% to compounds, and the remaining 7% to VCM sales. About 75% of PVC shipments (in lbs.) in 1997 were sold as resins, with 25% sold as compounds.

During the first half of the 1990s, Geon focused on strengthening its competitiveness. It closed old, high cost plants, streamlined its product lines, and re-engineered its business practices. GON more than replaced lost resin capacity through efficiency improvements. Margins for PVC resins in 1997 were considerably less than in the last cyclical bottom in 1992. Nonetheless, operating income in 1997 was $52.0 million versus 1992's operating loss of $22.9 million.

GON now plans to focus on its more profitable compound and specialty businesses. As part of this strategy, GON plans to merge its PVC suspension resin and VCM operations by the end of 1998 with Occidental Petroleum. The new venture will be 24% owned by GON. The two partners expect the venture to reduce annual costs by $80 million. GON completed its first major acquisition in October 1997 with the purchase of Synergistics Industries, a major plastics compounder with sales of $240 million in 1997.

PVC is the world's second most widely used plastic, with about two-thirds of sales going to infrastructure and construction applications such as pipe, siding and window components. Other uses include consumer durable goods, packaging, and business machine housings. Geon expects global demand for PVC to rise by about 6% per year through 2000. Resin, the base form of PVC, is made from ethylene and chlorine in a two-step process. Before resin can be processed into finished goods, it is combined with other ingredients to create a compound with specific processing or end-use properties. Compound demand generally is less cyclical than resin demand and compound prices are typically more stable than for resins. At year-end 1997, GON's North American PVC resin capacity was 2.8 billion lbs. (18% of total industry capacity), while PVC compound capacity was 1.1 billion lbs.

GON has increased its backward integration in order to reduce raw material costs. It now produces nearly 90% of its VCM needs at its 2.4 billion pound per year plant in LaPorte, TX. In late 1997, Geon and Olin Corp. completed a 250,00 ton per year chlor-alkali plant, providing 35% of GON's chlorine needs. GON plans to use hydrogen chloride from Bayer Corp. to produce VCM; GON will then have 65% of its chlorine needs supplied at below market costs.

Per Share Data ($)

(Year Ended Dec. 31)	1997	1996	1995	1994	1993	1992	1991	1990	1989	1988
Tangible Bk. Val.	9.65	9.55	8.46	9.13	7.64	6.14	NA	NA	NA	NA
Cash Flow	3.21	2.70	3.43	4.13	2.43	NA	NA	NA	NA	NA
Earnings	0.95	0.50	1.24	2.06	0.08	-0.92	NA	NA	NA	NA
Dividends	0.50	0.50	0.50	0.50	0.38	NA	NA	NA	NA	NA
Payout Ratio	53%	100%	40%	24%	NM	NA	NA	NA	NA	NA
Prices - High	24⅛	28¾	31⅜	31⅝	24⅜	NA	NA	NA	NA	NA
- Low	18½	18⅛	23⅜	23¼	17¾	NA	NA	NA	NA	NA
P/E Ratio - High	25	57	25	15	NM	NA	NA	NA	NA	NA
- Low	19	36	19	11	NM	NA	NA	NA	NA	NA

Income Statement Analysis (Million $)

	1997	1996	1995	1994	1993	1992	1991	1990	1989	1988
Revs.	1,250	1,144	1,268	1,209	983	894	NA	NA	NA	NA
Oper. Inc.	120	84.0	184	160	87.1	NA	NA	NA	NA	NA
Depr.	53.3	54.1	56.6	58.2	58.8	NA	NA	NA	NA	NA
Int. Exp.	11.9	10.8	6.2	8.2	7.4	11.1	NA	NA	NA	NA
Pretax Inc.	34.6	20.7	52.4	94.8	9.9	-36.6	NA	NA	NA	NA
Eff. Tax Rate	35%	41%	39%	39%	39%	NM	NM	NM	NM	NM
Net Inc.	22.5	12.2	32.2	57.9	6.0	-24.2	NA	NA	NA	NA

Balance Sheet & Other Fin. Data (Million $)

	1997	1996	1995	1994	1993	1992	1991	1990	1989	1988
Cash	49.1	17.9	61.1	47.5	20.0	5.0	NA	NA	NA	NA
Curr. Assets	314	234	283	295	214	157	NA	NA	NA	NA
Total Assets	873	737	752	792	721	697	NA	NA	NA	NA
Curr. Liab.	314	204	193	247	189	175	NA	NA	NA	NA
LT Debt	136	137	138	93.0	88.3	119	NA	NA	NA	NA
Common Eqty.	224	222	209	240	230	181	NA	NA	NA	NA
Total Cap.	356	393	384	380	343	340	NA	NA	NA	NA
Cap. Exp.	50.9	73.4	70.0	61.5	44.1	NA	NA	NA	NA	NA
Cash Flow	75.8	66.3	88.8	116	64.8	NA	NA	NA	NA	NA
Curr. Ratio	1.0	1.1	1.5	1.2	1.1	0.9	NA	NA	NA	NA
% LT Debt of Cap.	34.4	34.9	35.9	24.5	25.7	35.0	NA	NA	NA	NA
% Net Inc.of Revs.	1.8	1.1	2.5	4.8	0.6	NM	NM	NM	NM	NM
% Ret. on Assets	2.8	1.6	4.2	7.8	NM	NA	NA	NA	NA	NA
% Ret. on Equity	10.1	5.6	7.2	25.2	NM	NA	NA	NA	NA	NA

Data as orig. reptd.; bef. results of disc. opers. and/or spec. items. Per share data adj. for stk. divs. as of ex-div. date. Bold denotes diluted EPS (FASB 128). Pro forma data in 1993 (except Income Statement, Bal. Sheet and Ratio) and 1992. E-Estimated. NA-Not Available. NM-Not Meaningful. NR-Not Ranked.

Office—One Geon Center, Avon Lake, OH 44012. **Tel**—(440) 930-1000. **Website**—http://www.geon.com **Chrmn & CEO**—W. F. Patient. **Pres**—T. A. Waltermire. **VP & Secy**—G. L. Rutman. **VP & CFO**—W. D. Wilson.**VP & Investor Contact**—Dennis Cocco. **Dirs**—J. K. Baker, J. A. Brothers, J. D. Campbell, G. Duff-Bloom, D. L. Moore, J. D. Ong, W. F. Patient, R. G. P. Styles, T. A. Waltermire, F. M. Walters. . **Transfer Agent & Registrar**—Bank of New York, NYC. **Incorporated**—in Delaware in 1993. **Empl**— 2,400. **S&P Analyst**: Richard O'Reilly, CFA

Gerber Scientific

1007E

NYSE Symbol **GRB**

In S&P SmallCap 600

03-OCT-98

Industry:
Services (Computer Systems)

Summary: This company manufactures and services computer-aided design and computer-aided manufacturing systems that automate design and production processes in a broad range of industries.

Quantitative Evaluations	
Outlook (1 Lowest—5 Highest)	• NA
Fair Value	• NA
Risk	• Low
Earn./Div. Rank	• B
Technical Eval.	• Bearish since 3/98
Rel. Strength Rank (1 Lowest—99 Highest)	• 83
Insider Activity	• Neutral

Recent Price • 26¼
52 Wk Range • 29⅞-17⅝

Yield • 1.2%
12-Mo. P/E • 62.6

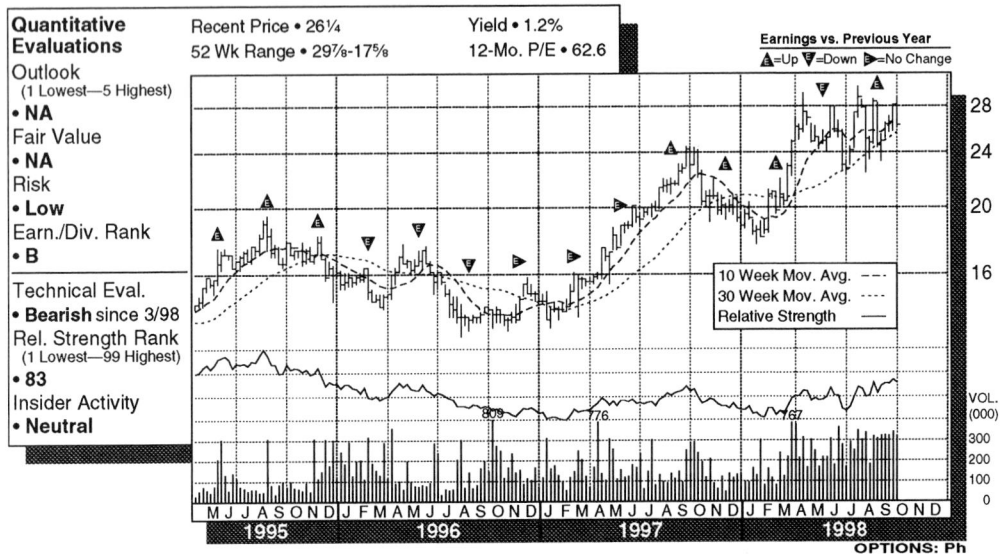

Earnings vs. Previous Year
▲=Up ▼=Down ▶=No Change

10 Week Mov. Avg. – – –
30 Week Mov. Avg. ········
Relative Strength ——

OPTIONS: Ph

Business Profile - 05-JUN-98

Sales in FY 98 (Apr.) reached an all-time high, aided by positive trends in the core optical, signmaking and specialty graphics group and in apparel and flexible goods, as well. Earnings were hurt, however, by a fourth quarter special charge for the write-down of assets related to the sale of the Gerber Systems unit to the BARCO Group of Belgium. The recent acquisitions of Coburn Optical (in February 1998) and Spandex PLC (May 1998), have enhanced the company's global presence and will provide diversification in core markets. The largest distributor of signmaking systems and supplies in Europe and North America, UK-based Spandex PLC had sales of about $167 million in the year ended December 31, 1997, and was acquired by Gerber in a $173 million tender offer.

Operational Review - 05-JUN-98

Based on a preliminary report, revenues in FY 98 (Apr.) rose 13% from those of FY 97, reflecting a 15% advance in product sales and a 1.4% increase in service revenues. Costs and expenses were well controlled, but after a $25 million non-recurring charge in the FY 98 fourth quarter for a writedown of assets in connection with the sale of the Gerber Systems unit, operating profit dropped 64%. With taxes at 25.3%, versus 27.9%, net income was down 54% to $7.4 million ($0.32 per share) from $16.0 million ($0.69).

Stock Performance - 02-OCT-98

In the past 30 trading days, GRB's shares have declined 7%, compared to a 7% fall in the S&P 500. Average trading volume for the past five days was 108,060 shares, compared with the 40-day moving average of 99,174 shares.

Key Stock Statistics

Dividend Rate/Share	0.32	Shareholders	1,600
Shs. outstg. (M)	22.7	Market cap. (B)	$0.598
Avg. daily vol. (M)	0.117	Inst. holdings	66%
Tang. Bk. Value/Share	NM		
Beta	0.90		

Value of $10,000 invested 5 years ago: $ 25,963

Fiscal Year Ending Apr. 30

	1999	1998	1997	1996	1995	1994
Revenues (Million $)						
1Q	153.7	98.96	85.81	88.19	70.03	64.93
2Q	—	106.4	94.95	90.16	72.94	63.31
3Q	—	104.8	94.59	86.88	82.81	63.78
4Q	—	120.3	105.6	93.89	96.92	68.72
Yr.	—	430.5	380.9	359.1	322.7	260.7
Earnings Per Share ($)						
1Q	0.29	0.19	0.07	0.19	0.13	0.08
2Q	—	0.24	0.22	0.23	0.17	0.11
3Q	—	0.27	0.18	0.22	0.20	0.25
4Q	—	-0.38	0.22	0.20	0.26	0.17
Yr.	—	0.32	0.69	0.84	0.76	0.61

Next earnings report expected: mid November

Dividend Data (Dividends have been paid since 1978.)

Amount ($)	Date Decl.	Ex-Div. Date	Stock of Record	Payment Date
0.080	Nov. 03	Nov. 12	Nov. 14	Nov. 28 '97
0.080	Feb. 03	Feb. 11	Feb. 13	Feb. 27 '98
0.080	May. 06	May. 13	May. 15	May. 29 '98
0.080	Aug. 10	Aug. 13	Aug. 17	Aug. 31 '98

A Division of The McGraw·Hill Companies

Gerber Scientific, Inc.

Business Summary - 05-JUN-98

What do the apparel and sewn goods, signmaking, commercial printing and electronics, and eyeglass lens industries have in common? They all use Gerber Scientific's (GRB) computer-aided design and computer-aided manufacturing (CAD/CAM) systems to automate design and production processes. Connecticut-based GRB operates mainly through four wholly owned operating subsidiaries.

Gerber Garment Technology (GGT) produces computer-controlled systems and software for product design, marker-making (nesting), spreading, labeling, cutting and handling flexible materials, such as fabrics and composites, in the apparel, aerospace, automotive, furniture and other industries. GGT accounted for 51% of sales in FY 97 (Apr.). The company initiated a plan to increase GGT's profitability, which included a targeted $9 million in cost reductions in FY 98, and growth in new high-margin software products. As part of this strategy, in February 1997, GGT acquired Cutting Edge Inc., a maker of high-performance single layer fabric cutting systems, for $7.8 million, diversifying into non-apparel markets such as industrial fabric, and aerospace and composite materials.

Gerber Scientific Products (30% of FY 97 sales) is the world's largest supplier of computerized signmaking systems and supplies. Its microprocessor- and PC-controlled production systems, software and aftermarket supplies are used in the signmaking, graphic arts and screenprinting industries, with typical end users being small businesses.

Gerber Systems Corp. (12% of FY 97 sales) makes interactive imaging and inspection systems for the electronics and commercial printing industries. The company is making a major investment in computer-to-plate imaging systems that streamline the prepress phase of the printing process.

Gerber Optical, Inc. (7% of FY 97 sales), GRB's smallest subsidiary, makes computer-controlled production systems and aftermarket supplies for the ophthalmic lens manufacturing industry. Gerber Optical sells to each segment of the optical market: retail chains (LensCrafters and Pearle Vision); wholesale optical laboratories; and individual practitioners.

GRB's revenues (preliminary) rose 13% in FY 98, to an all-time annual high of $430.5 million. The core optical, signmaking and specialty graphics groups showed improvement and Coburn Optical, acquired in February 1998, added about $12.5 million to revenues. Net income, however, was down 54%, after a fourth quarter $16.3 million (after-tax) charge related to the sale of the Gerber Systems unit. New orders in FY 98 rose 13% to a record $437.8 million.

Per Share Data ($) (Year Ended Apr. 30)	1998	1997	1996	1995	1994	1993	1992	1991	1990	1989
Tangible Bk. Val.	6.17	8.67	8.62	8.32	8.38	8.33	8.35	8.26	8.24	7.18
Cash Flow	0.90	1.19	1.29	1.23	1.01	0.77	0.69	0.69	1.71	1.67
Earnings	0.32	0.69	0.84	0.76	0.61	0.35	0.31	0.34	1.36	1.35
Dividends	0.32	0.32	0.32	0.30	0.23	0.20	0.20	0.20	0.16	0.12
Payout Ratio	100%	46%	38%	39%	38%	57%	64%	59%	12%	9%
Cal. Yrs.	1997	1996	1995	1994	1993	1992	1991	1990	1989	1988
Prices - High	24½	17¾	19½	16⅜	14¾	15¼	14¾	15⅞	21	21¼
- Low	13⅜	13	12⅝	11⅞	10¾	9¾	8	7	14⅛	13⅞
P/E Ratio - High	77	26	23	22	24	44	48	47	15	16
- Low	42	19	15	16	18	28	26	21	10	10
Income Statement Analysis (Million $)										
Revs.	430	381	359	323	261	254	250	268	307	299
Oper. Inc.	45.0	29.7	34.1	31.0	20.6	18.0	16.2	16.1	53.6	54.9
Depr.	13.6	11.7	10.8	11.4	9.7	10.1	9.1	8.3	8.3	7.7
Int. Exp.	0.7	0.3	0.4	0.5	0.3	0.5	1.8	1.9	1.7	1.7
Pretax Inc.	9.9	22.2	27.8	25.1	21.4	12.2	11.3	12.3	49.8	50.9
Eff. Tax Rate	25%	28%	29%	28%	32%	32%	34%	35%	35%	35%
Net Inc.	7.4	16.0	19.9	18.1	14.5	8.3	7.4	8.0	32.4	32.9
Balance Sheet & Other Fin. Data (Million $)										
Cash	27.0	9.5	8.7	10.2	15.6	17.3	50.6	48.8	29.7	33.9
Curr. Assets	185	178	158	147	130	121	186	197	197	181
Total Assets	339	325	313	324	286	270	277	288	277	255
Curr. Liab.	90.7	58.9	56.2	68.4	41.9	38.1	42.9	55.0	51.5	54.2
LT Debt	7.0	7.2	7.3	7.5	7.7	7.9	8.1	9.2	9.5	11.5
Common Eqty.	231	248	239	237	225	215	214	210	205	181
Total Cap.	248	266	257	254	244	232	231	228	224	200
Cap. Exp.	15.9	13.1	12.6	12.5	4.6	6.5	8.8	6.3	6.9	10.3
Cash Flow	21.0	27.7	30.7	29.5	24.2	18.4	16.5	16.2	40.8	40.6
Curr. Ratio	2.0	3.0	2.8	2.1	3.1	3.2	4.3	3.6	3.8	3.3
% LT Debt of Cap.	2.8	2.7	2.9	3.0	3.2	3.4	3.5	4.0	4.2	5.7
% Net Inc.of Revs.	1.7	4.2	5.5	5.6	5.6	3.3	3.0	3.0	10.6	11.0
% Ret. on Assets	2.2	5.0	6.2	5.9	5.2	3.0	2.6	2.8	12.3	13.4
% Ret. on Equity	3.1	27.8	8.3	7.8	6.6	3.9	3.5	3.8	16.9	19.1

Data as orig. reptd.; bef. results of disc. opers. and/or spec. items. Per share data adj. for stk. divs. as of ex-div. date. Bold denotes diluted EPS (FASB 128). E-Estimated. NA-Not Available. NM-Not Meaningful. NR-Not Ranked.

Office—83 Gerber Rd. West, South Windsor, CT 06074. **Tel**—(203) 644-1551. **Fax**—(203) 643-7039. **Website**—www.gerberscientific.com **Chrmn**—G. M. Gentile. **Pres & CEO**—M.J. Cheshire. **SVP-Fin & CFO**—G. K. Bennett. **Secy**—D. J. Gerber. **Dirs**—D. P. Aiken, M. J. Cheshire, G. M. Gentile, D. J. Gerber, E. E. Hood, D. J. Logan, C. F. St. Mark, A. R. Towbin, W. J. Vereen. **Transfer Agent & Registrar**—ChaseMellon Shareholder Services, East Hartford, CT. **Incorporated**—in Connecticut in 1948. **Empl**— 1,900. **S&P Analyst:** S.A.H.

Getchell Gold

7986

ASE Symbol **GGO**

In S&P SmallCap 600

03-OCT-98

Industry: Gold & Precious Metals Mining

Summary: Getchell Gold explores for, develops, mines and process-es gold ore from operations in north central Nevada.

Quantitative Evaluations	
Outlook (1 Lowest—5 Highest)	• 1⁻
Fair Value	• 14¾
Risk	• NA
Earn./Div. Rank	• C
Technical Eval.	• NA
Rel. Strength Rank (1 Lowest—99 Highest)	• 99
Insider Activity	• NA

Recent Price • 20⅝
52 Wk Range • 42¼-8⅞
Yield • Nil
12-Mo. P/E • NM

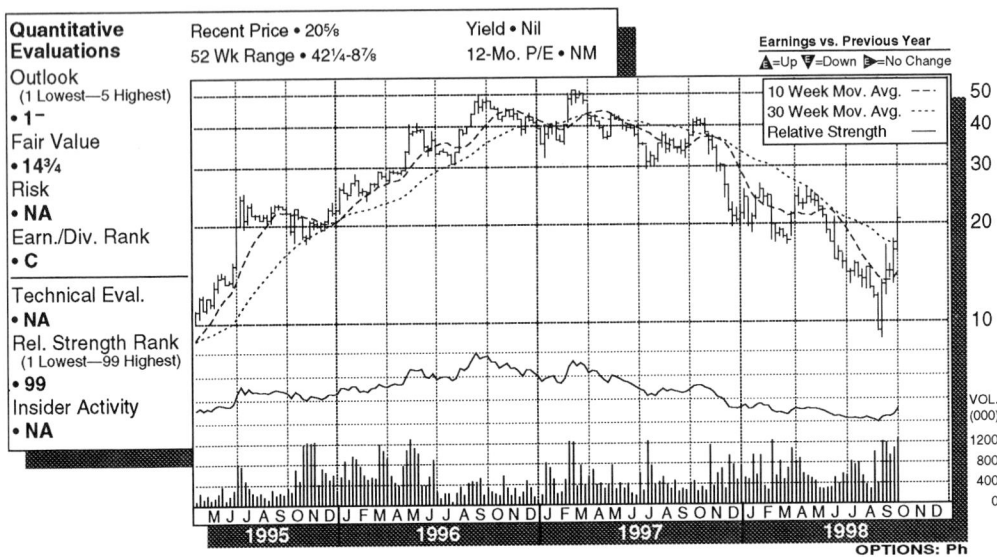

Earnings vs. Previous Year
▲=Up ▼=Down ▶=No Change

10 Week Mov. Avg. ---
30 Week Mov. Avg. ·····
Relative Strength —

OPTIONS: Ph

Business Profile - 02-SEP-98

The shares have fallen in 1998, reflecting unfavorable conditions affecting all participants in the gold industry. In the first half of 1998, GGO sold 66,213 oz. of gold, down 23%, year to year. Over the same period, the average market price per oz. of gold decreased 13%, to $298. In March 1998, the company completed an equity offering, with net proceeds of $69.8 million to be used for the completion of the Turquoise Ridge Mine, an increase in mill capacity, and exploration projects.

Operational Review - 02-SEP-98

Net sales in the six months ended June 30, 1998, fell 33%, year to year, on lower gold prices and a decision to suspend the processing of low-grade stockpile ore. Aided by reductions in cost of sales, G&A expenditures and exploration costs, the operating loss narrowed to $3,119,000, from $7,691,000. With lower interest income and greater depreciation and amortization charges, the net loss widened to $7,244,000 ($0.25 a share, on 11% more shares), from $11,063,000 ($0.42).

Stock Performance - 02-OCT-98

In the past 30 trading days, GGO's shares have increased 73%, compared to a 7% fall in the S&P 500. Average trading volume for the past five days was 406,960 shares, compared with the 40-day moving average of 209,349 shares.

Key Stock Statistics

Dividend Rate/Share	Nil	Shareholders	12,300
Shs. outstg. (M)	30.8	Market cap. (B)	$0.635
Avg. daily vol. (M)	0.274	Inst. holdings	72%
Tang. Bk. Value/Share	7.87		
Beta	0.93		

Value of $10,000 invested 5 years ago: $ 33,673

Fiscal Year Ending Dec. 31

	1998	1997	1996	1995	1994	1993
Revenues (Million $)						
1Q	10.80	14.86	14.66	—	21.51	20.84
2Q	11.81	18.68	17.19	—	16.52	24.50
3Q	—	17.59	17.02	17.61	15.79	24.66
4Q	—	13.67	19.01	16.82	17.67	25.16
Yr.	—	64.80	67.88	34.43	66.14	95.15
Earnings Per Share ($)						
1Q	-0.18	-0.31	-0.07	—	0.03	-0.01
2Q	-0.08	-0.12	-0.08	—	•0.10	0.10
3Q	—	-0.18	-0.16	-0.07	-0.03	0.12
4Q	—	-0.13	-0.23	-0.18	-0.91	0.03
Yr.	—	-0.73	-0.54	-0.25	-1.01	0.24

Next earnings report expected: late October

Dividend Data

No dividends have been declared since the company's initial public offering in May 1988, and the company does not anticipate paying dividends in the near future. It intends to retain earnings to support current operations and to fund exploration and development projects.

STANDARD
&POOR'S
STOCK REPORTS

Getchell Gold Corporation

7986

03-OCT-98

Business Summary - 02-SEP-98

Getchell Gold Corp. (formerly FirstMiss Gold Corp.) is engaged in the exploration, development, mining and processing of gold ore from the 33,000 acre Getchell Property, located in north central Nevada. The company was an 81%-owned subsidiary of First Mississippi Corp. (FMC) until October 1995, when FMC distributed to its shareholders all of its 14,750,000 GGO common shares on the basis of 0.70846 of a GGO common share for each FMC common share held.

The Getchell Property consists of approximately 18,900 acres of unpatented lode and mill site mining claims and 14,100 acres of fee land owned by GGO. Proven and probable reserves at December 31, 1996, totaled 12.8 million tons of underground ore graded at 0.343 oz./ton, or about 4.4 million contained ounces of gold. There are also some 2.1 million tons of surface ore on the Getchell Property averaging 0.065 oz./ton, or 0.1 million contained oz. Approximately 65% of the Getchell Property, including all current proven and probable reserves, is subject to a 2% net smelter royalty owned by a third party. The company's operations on the Getchell property include a pressure oxidation (autoclave) mill facility, a heap leach facility and an underground mine known as the Getchell Underground mine. Prior to July 1, 1995, and for a nine-month period in

1996, operations also included open pit mining of oxide and sulfide ores.

GGO's current ore production comes primarily from Getchell Underground, which began commercial production in May 1995. During 1996, production from Getchell Underground averaged 1,188 tons of ore per operating day with an average gold grade of 0.301 oz./ ton, or 127,687 contained oz.

The Getchell Property is in the midst of a transition from a predominantly open pit operation to a predominantly underground operation. The continued transition away from stockpiled surface ores will be dependent on the successful development of a second underground mine on the Getchell Property known as Turquoise Ridge. Estimated capital required to bring the Turquoise Ridge mine into commercial production at 2,000 tons of ore per day will be will be approximately $90 million, of which $46 million had been spent through September 30, 1997. The company expects net revenue from the Turquoise Ridge mine development ore to be offset against the capital costs of the mine until it is declared to be in commercial production, which is expected no earlier than 1998's second half.

The company sold 1,000,000 common shares in March 1997 at $50 a share, providing funds for further exploration and development.

Per Share Data ($)

(Year Ended Dec. 31)	1997	1996	1995	1994	1993	1992	1991	1990	1989	1988
Tangible Bk. Val.	6.72	5.87	6.40	1.75	2.75	2.43	2.55	NA	NA	NA
Cash Flow	-0.32	-0.18	-0.05	-0.21	1.52	0.62	NA	NA	NA	NA
Earnings	-0.73	-0.54	-0.25	-1.01	0.24	-0.14	0.24	NM	NM	NM
Dividends	Nil	Nil	Nil	Nil	Nil	Nil	Nil	Nil	Nil	Nil
Payout Ratio	Nil	Nil	Nil	Nil	Nil	Nil	Nil	Nil	Nil	Nil
Prices - High	51½	50¼	25	25	10½	8	6⅜	4⅞	NA	NA
- Low	19½	21¾	7¾	7¾	5⅞	4⅝	2⅝	2⅝	NA	NA
P/E Ratio - High	NM	NM	NM	NM	44	NM	26	NM	NM	NM
- Low	NM	NM	NM	NM	24	NM	11	NM	NM	NM

Income Statement Analysis (Million $)

	1997	1996	1995	1994	1993	1992	1991	1990	1989	1988
Revs.	64.8	67.9	34.4	71.5	95.2	78.8	83.0	73.5	NA	NA
Oper. Inc.	-17.6	-9.4	-0.1	-1.7	30.6	12.4	NA	NA	NA	NA
Depr.	11.0	9.8	4.1	14.5	23.4	13.7	NA	NA	NA	NA
Int. Exp.	0.8	2.4	3.0	3.0	1.8	1.7	2.3	2.9	NA	NA
Pretax Inc.	-25.4	-14.8	-5.9	-17.9	5.6	-3.1	5.9	NM	NM	NM
Eff. Tax Rate	NM	NM	NM	NM	23%	NM	28%	NM	NM	NM
Net Inc.	-19.4	-14.0	-5.0	-18.4	4.3	-2.5	4.3	0.1	NA	NA

Balance Sheet & Other Fin. Data (Million $)

	1997	1996	1995	1994	1993	1992	1991	1990	1989	1988
Cash	34.2	64.1	115	0.6	2.0	NA	NA	NA	NA	NA
Curr. Assets	50.0	79.0	131	15.2	19.7	NA	NA	NA	NA	NA
Total Assets	238	209	210	85.1	88.7	92.2	93.3	104	NA	NA
Curr. Liab.	19.4	11.9	6.5	9.4	6.7	NA	NA	NA	NA	NA
LT Debt	6.5	34.4	28.2	40.9	29.3	23.6	14.2	13.1	NA	NA
Common Eqty.	180	151	164	31.7	49.7	44.1	46.1	41.8	NA	NA
Total Cap.	187	193	201	72.6	79.0	67.7	60.3	54.9	NA	NA
Cap. Exp.	66.8	51.7	10.7	26.9	10.5	5.6	NA	NA	NA	NA
Cash Flow	-8.4	-4.2	-0.9	-3.8	27.7	11.3	NA	NA	NA	NA
Curr. Ratio	2.6	6.6	20.1	1.6	2.9	NA	NA	NA	NA	NA
% LT Debt of Cap.	3.6	17.8	14.0	56.3	37.1	34.8	23.5	23.9	NA	NA
% Net Inc.of Revs.	NM	NM	NM	NM	4.5	NM	5.1	0.1	NA	NA
% Ret. on Assets	NM	NM	NM	NM	4.8	NM	4.3	NM	NM	NM
% Ret. on Equity	NM	NM	NM	NM	9.2	NM	9.7	NM	NM	NM

Data as orig. reptd.; bef. results of disc. opers. and/or spec. items. Per share data adj. for stk. divs. as of ex-div. date. Yrs. ended Jun. 30 of foll. cal. yr. prior to 1995. Data for 1995 is for 6 mos. ended Dec. 31, 1995. E-Estimated. NA-Not Available. NM-Not Meaningful. NR-Not Ranked.

Office—5460 S. Quebec St., Suite 240, Englewood, CO 80111. **Tel**—(303) 771-9000. **Chrmn**—J. K. Williams. **Pres & CEO**—G. W. Thompson. **VP, CFO & Secy**—D. S. Robson. **Dirs**—W. A. Drexel, R. C. Horton, P. Ingersoll, J. Racich, C. E. Stott Jr., R. M. Summerford, G. W. Thompson, J. K. Williams, A. Winters, R. L. Zerga. **Transfer Agents & Registrars**—KeyCorp Shareholder Services, Inc.; R-M Trust Co. **Incorporated**—in Nevada in 1987; reincorporated in Delaware in 1996. **Empl**— 437. **S&P Analyst**: S.J.T.

03-OCT-98

Industry: Consumer (Jewelry, Novelties & Gifts)

Summary: Gibson Greetings is the third largest producer of greeting cards in the U.S.

S&P Opinion: Avoid (★★)	Recent Price • 19⅞
	52 Wk Range • 29¼-16

Yield • Nil
12-Mo. P/E • 51.0

Quantitative Evaluations

Outlook
(1 Lowest—5 Highest)
• 2

Fair Value
• 21¼

Risk
• **Average**

Earn./Div. Rank
• **B-**

Technical Eval.
• **Neutral** since 8/98

Rel. Strength Rank
(1 Lowest—99 Highest)
• **64**

Insider Activity
• **NA**

Earnings vs. Previous Year
▲=Up ▼=Down ▶=No Change

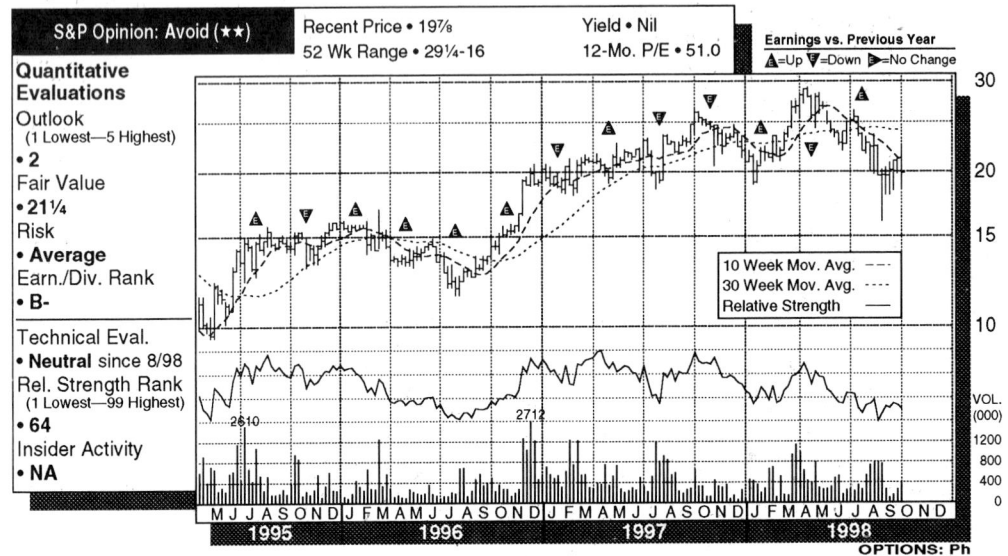

10 Week Mov. Avg. - - -
30 Week Mov. Avg. ····
Relative Strength —

VOL. (000)

OPTIONS: Ph

Overview - 05-AUG-98

Revenues in 1998 are projected to rise 10% or more. Continued healthy growth is seen for international cards, while domestic cards should benefit from new product introductions, such as Silly Slammers, and new licensing agreements. Gibson's overall strategic plan for growth in an industry that has long been stagnant includes getting faster to market with new products, such as the "Buzzcuts" card line introduced in early 1998; moving quickly into licensed products, including non-card products tied to movies; and shifting away from traditional card outlets and toward mass channels that sell entertainment products. Acquisitions are a critical part of GIBG's strategy, and would likely be in areas that complement greeting cards. Results for 1998's first quarter included a pretax restructuring charge of $26.1 million, or $0.92 per share.

Valuation - 05-AUG-98

We recently upgraded our opinion on Gibson to avoid, from sell, following the release of second quarter 1998 results. Q2 EPS rose 3.1% on a 13% advance in revenues. Excluding a $0.92 restructuring charge, EPS rose 5.5% on a 2.1% revenue gain. GIBG's ability to meet its 10% revenue growth target in a long stagnant industry looks to be achievable, particularly in the next year or so, but the domestic card market is expected to remain competitive, which will keep pressure on top-line growth. With margins expected to be squeezed by investments in the company's infrastructure, there is the possibility of EPS disappointments in the near term. While the downside potential of the stock looks to be limited in the short term, the shares are currently fully valued and are likely to underperform the market over the next six months or so.

Key Stock Statistics

S&P EPS Est. 1998	1.47	Tang. Bk. Value/Share	16.88
P/E on S&P Est. 1998	13.5	Beta	1.04
S&P EPS Est. 1999	1.70	Shareholders	7,800
Dividend Rate/Share	Nil	Market cap. (B)	$0.326
Shs. outstg. (M)	16.4	Inst. holdings	76%
Avg. daily vol. (M)	0.045		

Value of $10,000 invested 5 years ago: $ 11,093

Fiscal Year Ending Dec. 31

	1998	1997	1996	1995	1994	1993
Revenues (Million $)						
1Q	101.7	99.6	97.78	100.3	93.43	84.91
2Q	105.0	92.66	88.59	97.47	90.65	83.96
3Q	—	92.15	92.55	144.3	153.0	142.3
4Q	—	113.3	111.3	198.7	211.5	235.8
Yr.	—	397.7	390.3	540.8	548.8	546.9
Earnings Per Share ($)						
1Q	-0.54	0.30	0.04	0.00	1.13	0.11
2Q	0.33	0.32	0.36	0.04	-0.85	0.08
3Q	—	0.15	0.25	-3.41	0.02	0.26
4Q	—	0.44	0.39	0.49	0.39	1.16
Yr.	—	1.27	1.34	-2.86	-1.77	1.61

Next earnings report expected: early November

Dividend Data

Dividends, paid since 1983, were omitted in February 1995.

Business Summary - 05-AUG-98

Gibson Greetings, Inc., whose predecessors date from 1850, is the third largest U.S. manufacturer of greeting cards. It also owns The Paper Factory, which operates over 190 retail party goods stores located primarily in manufacturers' outlet malls. A line of gift wrap and related accessories is also produced by Gibson.

Gibson's growth strategy is to market relationship-fostering products that provide strong entertainment value. This is being achieved by developing proprietary new products, negotiating major licensing agreements and deploying high-energy shopping environments in a wide spectrum of major retail stores. Gibson manufactures and distributes more than 24,000 individual relationship communication products, of which over 5,000 were introduced in the 12 months through May 1998.

Among Gibson's newest products is Silly Slammers, a brand of beanbag toys introduced in late 1997 that say funny things when dropped or slammed. Marketed by the new Entertainment Division, the toys have proven to be enormously popular. As of late May, 1998, Gibson has introduced six generations of Silly Slammers with dozens of characters. The newest lines include The Office Group of five characters, and the Summer Sports group for soccer, baseball, and golf, all introduced in late May 1998. New greeting card lines include Chef'n Around, featuring recipes from well-known chefs, and Buzzcuts, with cutting-edge humor for Baby Boomers.

About 7% of 1997 revenues were derived from international sources, most notably in Europe. Gibson's products are sold through more than 25,000 retail outlets worldwide, primarily supermarkets, deep discounters, mass merchandisers, card and specialty shops and variety stores. In 1997, the five largest customers accounted for 32% of net sales, and the largest customer, Winn-Dixie Stores, accounted for 15%.

In December 1997, Gibson announced on-line merchandising alliances with Greet Street, the largest retailer of on-line electronics greetings in the U.S., and on-line technical provider Firefly Greetings L.L.C. Through Greet Street, E-mail greetings featuring Gibson content are available (www.greetst.com). Gibson cards may be purchased, inscribed and mailed on-line through Firefly (www.fireflygreet.com).

The Paper Factory operates retail stores under the names The Paper Factory, Greetings N' More and Great Party, which offer broad product assortments of branded gift wrap, greeting cards, paper decorations, wedding supplies and other paper products. Gibson plans to eventually divest The Paper Factory.

Other products include paper partywares, candles, calendars, gift items and holiday decorations. Gibson's products often incorporate well-known persons or characters. Net sales associated with licensed properties accounted for 13% of 1997 net sales.

In July 1998, Gibson acquired 60% of Ink Group's operating companies in Australia and New Zealand and 100% of its U.K. subsidiary. Ink Group, a greeting card company, had 1997 revenues of $17.5 million.

Per Share Data ($)

(Year Ended Dec. 31)	1997	1996	1995	1994	1993	1992	1991	1990	1989	1988
Tangible Bk. Val.	15.89	15.81	14.31	17.24	20.15	18.92	18.86	16.58	14.15	11.99
Cash Flow	2.63	2.72	-1.21	NM	NM	NM	3.76	3.46	3.54	3.03
Earnings	1.27	1.34	-2.86	-1.77	1.61	0.50	2.61	2.51	2.68	2.25
Dividends	Nil	Nil	Nil	Nil	0.40	0.39	0.35	0.34	0.33	0.29
Payout Ratio	Nil	Nil	Nil	Nil	25%	78%	14%	13%	12%	13%
Prices - High	26¾	20¾	16⅛	23⅝	22¾	32	29½	26⅞	28¾	23⅜
- Low	18	11½	8	11¾	17¾	15⅝	21⅜	19⅞	21	12½
P/E Ratio - High	21	15	NM	NM	14	64	11	11	11	10
- Low	14	9	NM	NM	11	32	8	8	8	6

Income Statement Analysis (Million $)

	1997	1996	1995	1994	1993	1992	1991	1990	1989	1988
Revs.	397	389	540	549	547	502	524	513	465	404
Oper. Inc.	58.3	60.5	58.4	NA	NA	NA	95.7	86.7	80.8	74.4
Depr.	22.9	22.8	26.9	NA	NA	NA	18.5	15.0	13.6	12.2
Int. Exp.	5.4	8.8	13.2	10.6	7.7	7.9	10.6	10.2	3.9	6.9
Pretax Inc.	36.3	33.1	-63.1	-45.6	44.0	13.1	68.2	63.9	66.5	56.7
Eff. Tax Rate	41%	34%	NM	NM	41%	39%	39%	38%	36%	38%
Net Inc.	21.6	22.0	-46.5	-28.6	25.9	8.0	41.9	39.8	42.4	35.0

Balance Sheet & Other Fin. Data (Million $)

	1997	1996	1995	1994	1993	1992	1991	1990	1989	1988
Cash	114	98.0	16.0	2.0	9.5	9.5	9.8	25.0	5.5	15.4
Curr. Assets	250	253	215	382	377	334	368	379	311	269
Total Assets	443	452	426	612	580	501	544	553	439	326
Curr. Liab.	103	119	109	231	163	110	153	250	164	108
LT Debt	24.2	40.9	46.5	63.2	74.4	70.2	71.1	21.8	30.4	18.6
Common Eqty.	282	256	230	278	324	303	301	261	226	186
Total Cap.	306	297	277	341	397	376	383	295	265	214
Cap. Exp.	17.7	26.5	19.9	35.4	31.0	31.0	31.7	42.7	32.0	17.8
Cash Flow	44.5	44.7	-19.6	NM	NM	NM	60.4	54.8	55.9	47.3
Curr. Ratio	2.4	2.1	2.0	1.7	2.3	3.0	2.4	1.5	1.9	2.5
% LT Debt of Cap.	7.9	13.8	16.9	18.6	18.7	18.7	18.5	7.4	11.5	8.7
% Net Inc.of Revs.	5.4	5.6	NM	NM	4.7	1.6	8.0	7.8	9.1	8.7
% Ret. on Assets	4.8	5.0	NM	NM	4.8	1.5	7.6	8.0	11.0	11.3
% Ret. on Equity	8.0	9.0	NM	NM	8.2	2.6	14.8	16.3	20.5	20.5

Data as orig. reptd.; bef. results of disc. opers. and/or spec. items. Per share data adj. for stk. divs. as of ex-div. date. Bold denotes diluted EPS (FASB 128). E-Estimated. NA-Not Available. NM-Not Meaningful. NR-Not Ranked.

Office—2100 Section Rd., Cincinnati, OH 45237. **Tel**—(513) 841-6600. **Chrmn, Pres & CEO**—F. J. O'Connell. **EVP-Fin, CFO & Investor Contact**—James T. Wilson. **Secy**—H. L. Caldwell. **Dirs**—G. M. Gibson, R. P. Kirby, C. D. Lindberg, F. J. O'Connell, A. R. Pezzillo, C. A. St. Martin, C. A. Wainwright. **Transfer Agent & Registrar**—Bank of New York, NYC. **Incorporated**—in Delaware in 1982. **Empl**— 2,300. **S&P Analyst**: William H. Donald

STANDARD &POOR'S
STOCK REPORTS

Glamis Gold

1011M
NYSE Symbol **GLG**

In S&P SmallCap 600

03-OCT-98

Industry: Gold & Precious Metals Mining

Summary: GLG is a Canadian mining company that operates gold mines in California.

Quantitative Evaluations

Outlook (1 Lowest—5 Highest)
• **NA**

Fair Value
• **NA**

Risk
• **Average**

Earn./Div. Rank
• **C**

Technical Eval.
• **Neutral** since 9/98

Rel. Strength Rank (1 Lowest—99 Highest)
• **89**

Insider Activity
• **NA**

Recent Price • 2⅞   Yield • Nil
52 Wk Range • 6⅝-1¹³/₁₆   12-Mo. P/E • NM

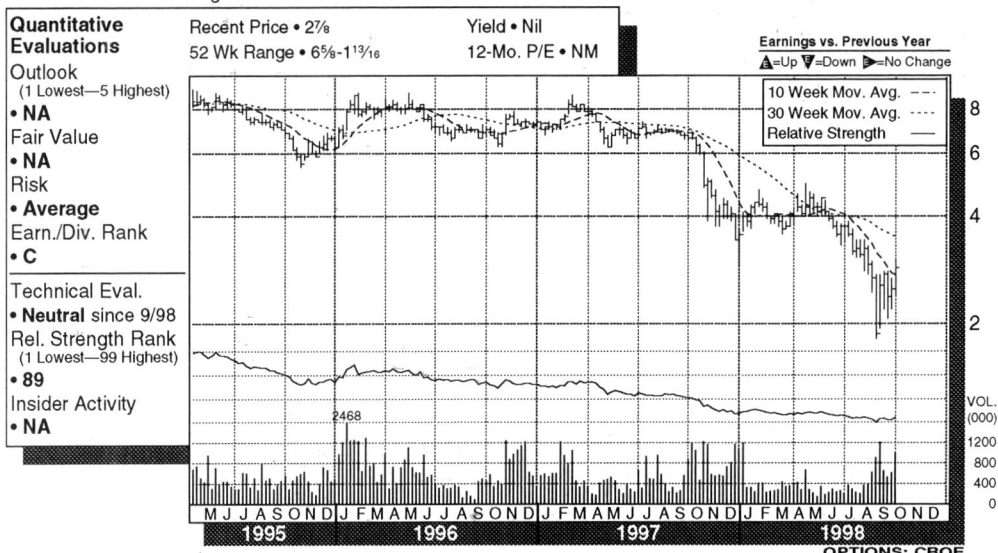

Earnings vs. Previous Year
▲=Up ▼=Down ▶=No Change

10 Week Mov. Avg. – – –
30 Week Mov. Avg. ‥‥
Relative Strength ——

VOL. (000)

OPTIONS: CBOE

Business Profile - 08-DEC-97

The company said it was concerned about the downturn in the price of gold thus far in 1997. GLG's strategy is to remain a low cost profitable producer and while the company has achieved greater production at lower costs, it has initiated a cost containment program at all facilities in an attempt to keep costs to a minimum. In the third quarter of 1997, Glamis implemented a policy of hedging a maximum of 50,000 ozs. of future gold production. As a result, GLG has acquired put options for 42,000 ozs. of gold at a strike price of $325 per oz. expiring through April 1998; the company also held call options at the end of the third quarter for 8,100 ozs. of gold at $415 per oz. expiring through December 1997.

Operational Review - 08-DEC-97

Revenues in the nine months ended September 30, 1997, rose 2.5%, year to year, as an 11% increase in gold production was largely offset by a 14% drop in the price per oz. of gold ($334, versus $389). Gross margins narrowed, as cost of production increased with the greater gold production and coupled with a drop in the price per oz. of gold . Operating expenses were up 9.4%, and despite sharply higher other income, a pretax loss of $168,000, contrasted with pretax income of $2,870,000. After taxes of $174,000, versus 31.2%, a net loss of $342,000 ($0.01 a share) contrasted with net income of $1,975,000 ($0.07 per share, on 17% more shares) from $1,975,000 ($0.07).

Stock Performance - 02-OCT-98

In the past 30 trading days, GLG's shares have increased 7%, compared to a 7% fall in the S&P 500. Average trading volume for the past five days was 201,040 shares, compared with the 40-day moving average of 151,900 shares.

Key Stock Statistics

Dividend Rate/Share	Nil	Shareholders	2,000
Shs. outstg. (M)	31.2	Market cap. (B)	$0.090
Avg. daily vol. (M)	0.154	Inst. holdings	14%
Tang. Bk. Value/Share	2.97		
Beta	0.79		

Value of $10,000 invested 5 years ago: $ 7,351

Fiscal Year Ending Dec. 31

	1998	1997	1996	1995	1994	1993
Revenues (Million $)						
1Q	8.96	11.36	9.95	—	10.85	7.98
2Q	8.19	11.09	11.35	—	8.99	13.75
3Q	—	10.30	12.29	—	9.97	13.94
4Q	—	9.49	13.15	—	9.23	16.77
Yr.	—	42.24	46.74	17.16	39.03	52.44
Earnings Per Share ($)						
1Q	0.01	0.04	Nil	—	0.04	0.05
2Q	Nil	-0.02	0.02	—	Nil	0.08
3Q	—	-0.03	0.05	—	Nil	0.12
4Q	—	-0.26	0.08	—	0.06	0.07
Yr.	—	-0.27	0.15	-0.07	0.10	0.32

Next earnings report expected: NA

Dividend Data (Dividends have been paid since 1997.)

Amount ($)	Date Decl.	Ex-Div. Date	Stock of Record	Payment Date

A Division of The **McGraw·Hill** *Companies*

Business Summary - 08-DEC-97

Since its formation in 1972 as Renniks Resources Ltd., Glamis Gold Ltd. (GLG; current name adopted in 1977) has undergone several capital reorganizations. It is currently engaged in the mining and extraction of precious metals by open-pit mining and the heap leaching method and has an active program of exploration and development of precious metals. It initiated heap leaching in California in 1981 and is recognized as a leader in the use of this process.

Heap leaching is generally used to extract gold from low-grade ores. The process involves piling relatively coarse ore on an impervious membrane and allowing a dissolving fluid (a weak cyanide solution in the case of gold recovery) to seep down through the pile. The valuable metals are contained in the leaching solution that drains from the bottom of the pile and is subsequently collected on carbon and then recovered by electrolysis and smelting.

The company's approach to the acquisition of mining properties has generally been to limit its review to undeveloped precious metal properties that others have explored in sufficient detail to demonstrate that the properties have significant gold mineralization or to review companies that own such properties. Of particular interest to the company are properties on which reserves have been established by major companies.

While such properties may not be economical for other companies to develop, GLG's expertise in the profitable exploitation of low-grade ores through the heap leaching process may make the properties attractive to GLG.

GLG currently produces gold from two operating mines in California: the Picacho mine in Imperial County (34,621 oz. produced in 1996; 39,501 oz. of contained gold at year end), and the Rand mine (consisting of the Yellow Aster and Baltic mines) in Kern County (85,762 oz.; 1,414,655 oz.).

The company also has a 100% interest in a property located in Imperial County (the Imperial Project) that is currently being permitted for future mining activities. Gold production is expected to begin in 1998 (reserves at 1996 year end amounted to 1,515,545 contained ounces).

GLG also has a 60% interest in a venture that has the right to acquire a 100% interest in the Cieneguita property in the State of Chihuahua, Mexico (minimal production in 1996).

In 1996, Glamis acquired 2 million units of Paramount Ventures & Finance Inc. at C$2.25 a unit and agreed to acquire 50% of Paramount's interest in the Gunung Pani Gold Project on North Sulawesi Island, Indonesia, in exchange for funding all exploration and development costs up to the time of delivery of a positive feasibility study.

Per Share Data ($)

(Year Ended Dec. 31)	1997	1996	1995	1994	1993	1992	1991	1990	1989	1988
Tangible Bk. Val.	2.96	3.25	2.44	2.56	2.41	2.30	1.55	1.55	1.32	1.04
Cash Flow	0.09	NA	0.11	0.43	0.61	0.39	0.46	0.58	0.42	0.11
Earnings	-0.27	0.15	-0.07	0.10	0.24	0.04	0.09	0.24	0.26	-0.27
Dividends	0.05	0.06	0.06	0.06	0.06	0.05	0.05	0.03	Nil	Nil
Payout Ratio	NM	40%	NM	60%	25%	118%	58%	14%	Nil	Nil
Prices - High	8¾	8⅞	9⅜	10⅛	9¾	9¾	4⅛	4⅛	2⅞	2¾
- Low	2⅞	6¼	5½	5½	3¾	3¾	2⅝	2	1⅝	⅞
P/E Ratio - High	NM	59	NM	NM	41	NM	46	17	11	NM
- Low	NM	42	NM	NM	16	NM	29	8	6	NM

Income Statement Analysis (Million $)

	1997	1996	1995	1994	1993	1992	1991	1990	1989	1988
Revs.	42.2	46.7	17.2	39.0	52.4	32.8	32.8	29.0	19.4	14.1
Oper. Inc.	7.1	15.3	2.8	11.8	18.4	9.3	10.3	12.5	9.0	-0.2
Depr.	11.0	10.6	4.7	8.6	12.3	7.8	7.4	6.5	3.0	7.3
Int. Exp.	0.0	0.2	0.1	0.2	Nil	Nil	1.1	1.1	0.7	0.7
Pretax Inc.	-7.9	5.3	-2.3	3.5	9.6	1.8	2.0	5.7	6.6	-7.4
Eff. Tax Rate	NM	23%	NM	24%	17%	53%	18%	19%	24%	NM
Net Inc.	-8.3	4.1	-1.9	2.7	7.9	0.9	1.6	4.7	5.0	-5.2

Balance Sheet & Other Fin. Data (Million $)

	1997	1996	1995	1994	1993	1992	1991	1990	1989	1988
Cash	26.9	26.5	4.2	14.1	17.7	22.4	6.1	0.1	5.6	2.9
Curr. Assets	40.9	43.1	17.7	25.9	31.7	29.8	15.8	5.1	10.1	9.2
Total Assets	102	108	69.8	73.8	92.1	81.8	55.5	41.8	34.5	33.5
Curr. Liab.	4.5	4.4	2.5	3.6	3.6	3.9	2.5	3.0	8.0	7.0
LT Debt	Nil	Nil	Nil	Nil	Nil	9.7	19.0	8.4	0.6	NM
Common Eqty.	94.6	101	64.6	67.6	86.7	66.4	32.2	29.8	25.3	20.1
Total Cap.	94.9	102	66.1	69.2	87.2	77.0	52.1	38.2	26.1	20.3
Cap. Exp.	8.4	17.6	4.1	5.3	17.7	16.8	10.5	18.8	10.2	11.2
Cash Flow	2.8	14.6	2.8	11.3	20.2	8.7	9.1	11.2	8.0	2.1
Curr. Ratio	9.1	9.9	7.0	7.3	8.7	7.6	6.2	1.7	1.3	1.3
% LT Debt of Cap.	Nil	Nil	Nil	Nil	Nil	12.6	36.5	21.9	2.2	NM
% Net Inc.of Revs.	NM	8.7	NM	6.9	15.1	2.6	5.0	16.1	25.8	NM
% Ret. on Assets	NM	4.6	NM	3.8	9.1	1.3	3.4	12.2	14.7	NM
% Ret. on Equity	NM	4.9	NM	4.1	10.3	1.8	5.3	16.9	22.0	NM

Data as orig. reptd.; bef. results of disc. opers. and/or spec. items. Per share data adj. for stk. divs. as of ex-div. date. Prior to 1995, qtrly. revs., EPS, inc. and bal. sheet tables in Can. $. Data for 1995 represents six mos end December 31. Prior to 1995, fiscal yrs. ended Jun. 30 of fol. cal yr. E-Estimated. NA-Not Available. NM-Not Meaningful. NR-Not Ranked.

Office—5190 Nell Rd., Suite 310, Reno, Nevada 89560 **Tel**—(702) 827-4600. **Website**—http://www.glamis.com. **Chrmn**—C. F. Millar. **Pres & CEO**—C. K. McArthur. **CFO, Treas, Secy & Investor Contact**—Dan Forbush. **Dirs**—I. S. Davidson, J. Depatie, C. F. Millar, C. K. McArthur, F. S. O'Kelly, H. von Michaelis. **Transfer Agents & Registrars**—Montreal Trust, Vancouver; United Missouri Trust Co., NYC. **Incorporated**—in British Columbia in 1972. **Empl**— 125. **S&P Analyst**: G.A.S.

03-OCT-98

Industry:
Machinery (Diversified)

Summary: This company manufactures specialty equipment, refractory products, minerals, forged products and industrial tools used by a wide range of industries.

Quantitative Evaluations	
Outlook (1 Lowest—5 Highest)	• **3+**
Fair Value	• **8⅛**
Risk	• **Average**
Earn./Div. Rank	• **NR**
Technical Eval.	• **Bullish** since 7/98
Rel. Strength Rank (1 Lowest—99 Highest)	• **17**
Insider Activity	• **NA**

Recent Price • 7⅜
52 Wk Range • 20⅞-5½
Yield • Nil
12-Mo. P/E • 1.9

Earnings vs. Previous Year
▲=Up ▼=Down ▶=No Change

10 Week Mov. Avg. – – –
30 Week Mov. Avg. ⋯⋯
Relative Strength ——

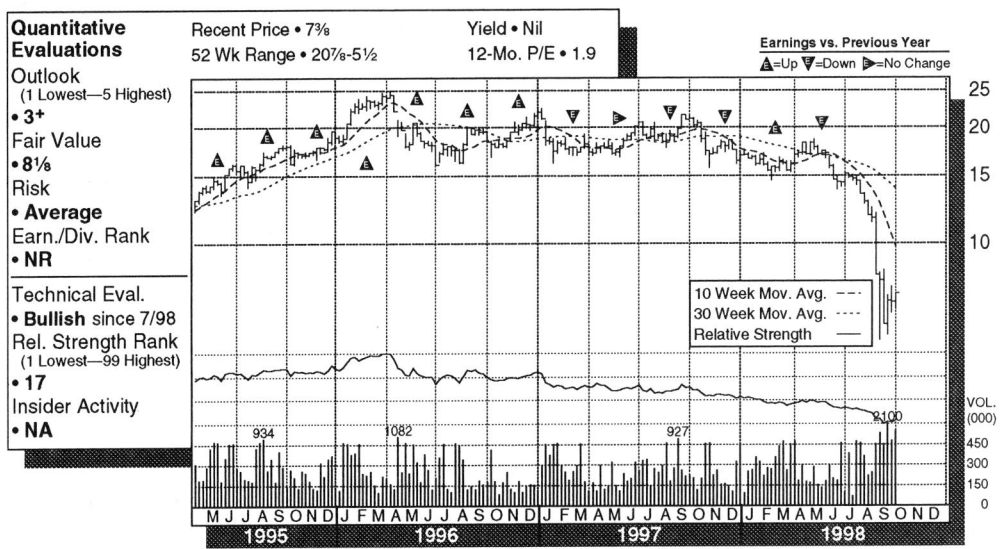

Business Profile - 05-JUN-98

In March 1998, GIX announced the acquisition of A.P. Green Industries, Inc., for approximately $195 million in cash. A.P. Green manufactures refractory products and lime. The company expects the acquisition to lead to annual cost savings of $15-20 million. It also anticipates that the deal will be accretive to earnings in FY 98 (Oct.) and beyond. In March 1998, the company sold its industrial tool division for $217.5 million. Earlier divestitures, in 1997, included Marion Power Shovel, the underground mining segment of British Jeffrey Diamond, and a partnership interest in Komdresco, a South African heavy equipment distributor.

Operational Review - 05-JUN-98

Total revenues in the six months ended April 30, 1998, declined 1.4%, year to year. Margins narrowed, but in the absence of a $20.5 million special charge, the loss from continuing operations narrowed to $1.4 million ($0.07 a share) from $6.2 million ($0.27). Results exclude earnings from discontinued operations of $5.1 million in the current period, versus $5.0 million in the year-earlier period. Also excluded was a gain on the sale of the industrial tool division of $86.1 million in the current period.

Stock Performance - 02-OCT-98

In the past 30 trading days, GIX's shares have declined 37%, compared to a 7% fall in the S&P 500. Average trading volume for the past five days was 304,820 shares, compared with the 40-day moving average of 181,733 shares.

Key Stock Statistics

Dividend Rate/Share	Nil	Shareholders	8,200
Shs. outstg. (M)	22.0	Market cap. (B)	$0.163
Avg. daily vol. (M)	0.248	Inst. holdings	73%
Tang. Bk. Value/Share	14.34		
Beta	1.24		

Value of $10,000 invested 5 years ago: $ 7,283

Fiscal Year Ending Oct. 31

	1998	1997	1996	1995	1994	1993
Revenues (Million $)						
1Q	137.5	132.3	149.9	126.3	99.9	123.1
2Q	121.9	153.6	155.2	142.0	106.3	134.0
3Q	—	155.1	171.1	155.0	108.4	127.5
4Q	—	161.4	171.7	173.8	126.2	155.4
Yr.	—	602.4	647.9	597.1	440.8	540.0
Earnings Per Share ($)						
1Q	**0.10**	-0.50	0.25	0.14	0.04	-0.16
2Q	**0.03**	0.45	0.45	0.43	0.21	0.13
3Q	—	-0.64	0.58	0.50	0.35	0.20
4Q	—	0.49	0.73	0.63	0.42	0.61
Yr.	—	-0.20	2.01	1.70	1.02	0.78

Next earnings report expected: NA

Dividend Data

No cash dividends have been paid. "Poison pill" stock purchase rights were distributed with the company's common stock in 1992.

A Division of The McGraw-Hill Companies

Business Summary - 05-JUN-98

In February 1997, Global Industrial Technology (GIX; formerly Indresco) announced a reorganization into five segments: refractory products (56% of FY 97 (Oct.) revenues); minerals (8%); industrial tools (19%); specialty equipment products (11%); and forged products (9%). Three units (Marion Power Shovel, the underground mining segment of British Jeffrey Diamond and a partnership interest in Komdresco, a South African heavy equipment distributor) were divested in 1997.

The refractory products division includes Harbinson-Walker Refractories (HWR), a leading supplier of refractory products and an overseas licensor of technology. HWR manufactures over 200 refractory products. Refractories, which are made from magnesite, graphite, bauxite, quartzite and fire clays, are used in virtually every industrial process requiring heating or containment of a solid, liquid or gas at a high temperature. Iron and steel producers account for a substantial portion of refractory sales.

In the minerals segment, Harbinson-Walker collects and processed certain minerals, including high-purity magnesite, which is used in the manufacture of premium refractory products. Previously an internal source of magnesite, the company now sells raw materials to refractory manufacturers worldwide.

The industrial tool division was sold in March 1998 for $217.5 million. This division, through INTOOL, Inc., manufactures Cleco pneumatic tools (such as assembly tools used in electronic, aircraft and automotive markets) and maintenance and fabrication tools (supplied to petroleum refineries, chemical plants, foundries and steel mills); and Quackenbush pneumatic and hydraulic precision drilling equipment (used in the aircraft and aerospace industries and in mobile machining applications), and airtool cleaners and expanders (used in heat exchangers and boilers).

The specialty equipment division manufactures equipment for various industrial applications. Products include the Unicell, a polymer concrete cell used in the refining of non-ferrous metals; and shredders, crushers, vibrating feeders and coal jigs, which are sold to the processing and recycling, forest products, quarrying, coal processing and waste processing and recycling markets.

The forged products segment, through Ameri-Forge Corp., manufactures forged steel flanges used to connect components of closed systems for processing and transporting liquids and gases. Products serve oil and gas, petrochemical, construction, food and water treatment and heavy equipment manufacturers and users.

Per Share Data ($)

(Year Ended Oct. 31)	1997	1996	1995	1994	1993	1992	1991	1990	1989	1988
Tangible Bk. Val.	9.26	9.60	10.60	11.81	11.15	12.70	NA	NA	NA	NA
Cash Flow	0.80	2.84	2.33	1.41	1.29	-1.40	0.24	NA	NA	NA
Earnings	-0.20	2.01	1.70	1.02	0.78	-1.84	-0.18	NA	NA	NA
Dividends	Nil	Nil	Nil	Nil	Nil	Nil	NA	NA	NA	NA
Payout Ratio	Nil	Nil	Nil	Nil	Nil	Nil	NA	NA	NA	NA
Prices - High	22	25	19⁵/₈	15¹/₂	15¹/₂	10¹/₈	NA	NA	NA	NA
- Low	15⁵/₈	16	10⁷/₈	10¹/₄	9	6³/₈	NA	NA	NA	NA
P/E Ratio - High	NM	12	12	15	20	NM	NA	NA	NA	NA
- Low	NM	8	6	10	12	NA	NA	NA	NA	NA

Income Statement Analysis (Million $)

	1997	1996	1995	1994	1993	1992	1991	1990	1989	1988
Revs.	602	648	597	437	538	559	618	NA	NA	NA
Oper. Inc.	71.0	72.2	56.0	27.7	32.3	21.2	-2.3	NA	NA	NA
Depr.	22.3	18.7	16.1	9.3	13.7	12.2	11.0	NA	NA	NA
Int. Exp.	10.1	7.0	NM	NM	Nil	Nil	NA	NA	NA	NA
Pretax Inc.	-6.7	55.4	42.5	24.6	11.1	-50.8	3.5	NA	NA	NA
Eff. Tax Rate	NM	18%	8.90%	Nil	NM	NM	234%	NA	NA	NA
Net Inc.	-4.4	45.4	38.7	24.6	21.4	-50.1	-4.7	NA	NA	NA

Balance Sheet & Other Fin. Data (Million $)

	1997	1996	1995	1994	1993	1992	1991	1990	1989	1988
Cash	14.9	11.5	21.1	27.0	116	32.4	8.0	NA	NA	NA
Curr. Assets	356	376	319	277	307	249	234	NA	NA	NA
Total Assets	807	753	584	478	461	491	516	NA	NA	NA
Curr. Liab.	245	207	218	130	110	131	115	NA	NA	NA
LT Debt	152	137	2.3	2.0	Nil	1.9	2.7	NA	NA	NA
Common Eqty.	284	300	262	274	288	352	396	NA	NA	NA
Total Cap.	453	444	269	289	288	355	401	NA	NA	NA
Cap. Exp.	64.4	53.7	34.8	13.0	10.4	15.3	NA	NA	NA	NA
Cash Flow	17.9	64.1	54.8	33.9	35.1	-37.9	6.3	NA	NA	NA
Curr. Ratio	1.5	1.8	1.5	2.1	2.8	1.9	2.0	NA	NA	NA
% LT Debt of Cap.	33.6	30.8	1.0	0.7	Nil	0.5	0.7	NA	NA	NA
% Net Inc.of Revs.	NM	7.0	6.5	5.6	4.0	NM	NM	NM	NM	NM
% Ret. on Assets	NM	6.8	7.3	5.6	4.7	NM	NA	NA	NA	NA
% Ret. on Equity	NM	16.2	14.5	9.4	6.9	NM	NA	NA	NA	NA

Data as orig. reptd.; bef. results of disc. opers. and/or spec. items. Per share data adj. for stk. divs. as of ex-div. date. Bold denotes diluted EPS (FASB 128). E-Estimated. NA-Not Available. NM-Not Meaningful. NR-Not Ranked.

Office—2121 San Jacinto St., Suite 2500, Dallas, TX 75201. **Tel**—(214) 953-4500. **Chrmn, Pres & CEO**—J. L. Jackson. **VP-Fin Treas & CFO**—G. G. Garrison. **Secy**—S. G. Barnett. **Dirs**—D. H. Blake, S. B. Casey Jr., R. Fulgham, J. L. Jackson, R. W. Vieser. **Transfer Agent & Registrar**—Bank of New York, NYC. **Incorporated**—in Delaware in 1995. **Empl**—2,612. **S&P Analyst:** B.G.

Global Motorsport Group 4002M

NASDAQ Symbol **CSTM**

In S&P SmallCap 600

03-OCT-98

Industry:
Auto Parts & Equipment

Summary: This provider of motorcycle aftermarket parts has entered into a definitive merger agreement to be acquired by Fremont Partners for $21.75 a share in cash.

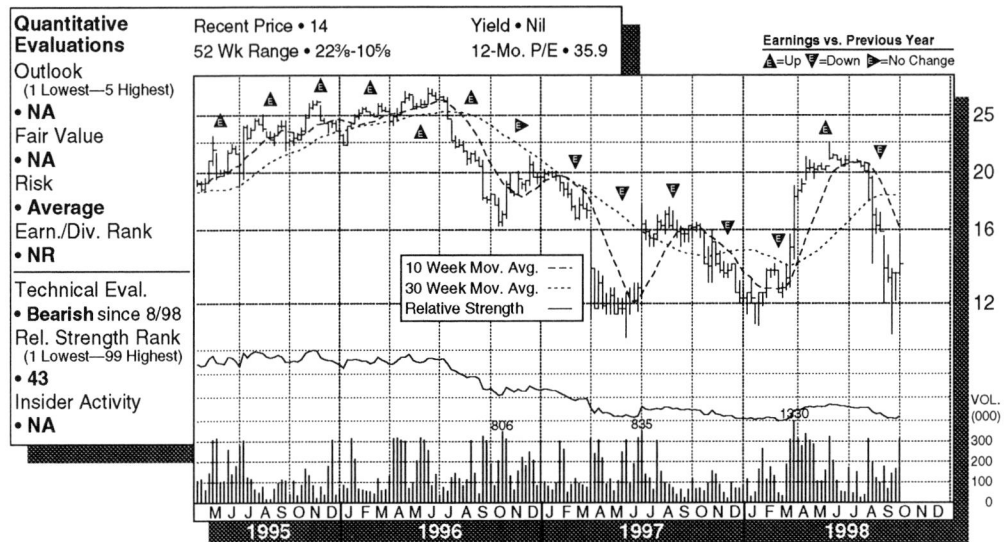

Quantitative Evaluations

Outlook (1 Lowest—5 Highest)
• **NA**

Fair Value
• **NA**

Risk
• **Average**

Earn./Div. Rank
• **NR**

Technical Eval.
• **Bearish** since 8/98

Rel. Strength Rank (1 Lowest—99 Highest)
• **43**

Insider Activity
• **NA**

Recent Price • 14
52 Wk Range • 22⅜-10⅝

Yield • Nil
12-Mo. P/E • 35.9

Earnings vs. Previous Year
▲=Up ▼=Down ▶=No Change

10 Week Mov. Avg. – – –
30 Week Mov. Avg. · · · ·
Relative Strength —

Business Profile - 16-SEP-98

In June 1998, this provider of motorcycle aftermarket parts entered into a definitive merger agreement with Fremont Partners, a private investment company. CSTM will be acquired for $21.75 a share in cash. A tender offer was extended through September 25, 1998. Since March 1998, CSTM was in a takeover battle with Golden Cycle, L.L.C. The company changed its name from Custom Chrome Inc., and in September 1997 purchased Chrome Specialties, Inc. (CSI), a wholesale distributor of aftermarket parts and accessories for Harley-Davidson motorcycles, for $36 million in cash.

Operational Review - 16-SEP-98

Net sales in the six months ended July 31, 1998, rose 41%, year to year. Gross margins were essentially flat. Despite a 42% increase in SG&A expenses and $1.7 million in costs associated with the unsolicited tend offer, against none, the operating profit was up 22%. However, after a 201% jump in interest expense, and taxes at 41.7%, versus 39.7%, net income slipped fractionally to $4,837,000 ($0.88 a share, diluted and on 4.9% more shares), from $4,867,000 ($0.93).

Stock Performance - 02-OCT-98

In the past 30 trading days, CSTM's shares have declined 14%, compared to a 7% fall in the S&P 500. Average trading volume for the past five days was 82,560 shares, compared with the 40-day moving average of 35,228 shares.

Key Stock Statistics

Dividend Rate/Share	Nil	Shareholders	300
Shs. outstg. (M)	5.2	Market cap. (B)	$0.072
Avg. daily vol. (M)	0.041	Inst. holdings	52%
Tang. Bk. Value/Share	12.62		
Beta	1.28		

Value of $10,000 invested 5 years ago: $ 14,545

Fiscal Year Ending Jan. 31

	1999	1998	1997	1996	1995	1994
Revenues (Million $)						
1Q	44.80	31.71	30.63	24.49	21.10	18.23
2Q	45.33	32.30	30.36	25.95	20.00	19.04
3Q	—	30.45	26.19	23.57	17.55	15.79
4Q	—	28.27	21.38	19.89	16.27	14.19
Yr.	—	122.7	108.6	93.91	74.90	67.25
Earnings Per Share ($)						
1Q	**0.46**	**0.45**	0.58	0.50	0.42	0.33
2Q	**0.43**	**0.49**	0.52	0.51	0.41	0.40
3Q	—	**0.02**	0.30	0.30	0.25	0.20
4Q	—	**-0.52**	0.10	0.23	0.20	0.16
Yr.	—	**0.44**	1.48	1.52	1.27	1.10

Next earnings report expected: mid December

Dividend Data

No dividends have been paid. Global Motorsport intends to retain all earnings for use in the expansion of its business and, therefore, does not expect to pay any dividends in the foreseeable future.

A Division of The **McGraw·Hill** *Companies*

STANDARD
&POOR'S
STOCK REPORTS

Global Motorsport Group, Inc.

4002M
03-OCT-98

Business Summary - 16-SEP-98

There are over one million Harley-Davidson motorcycles in use worldwide, and annual production of new Harleys was approximately 132,000 in 1997. This is good news for Global Motorsport Group (CSTM), formerly Custom Chrome Inc., whose sole mission is to supply aftermarket parts and accessories for Harley-Davidson motorcycles. CSTM is the largest independent supplier to this market niche, whose recent growth the company attributes not only to the popularity of Harley-Davidson motorcycles but also to the desire and ability of Harley-Davidson enthusiasts to customize their bikes and the tendency for Harley-Davidson motorcycles to change hands several times during their useful lives.

CSTM distributes some 15,000 different items, including replacement parts, custom parts, accessories and apparel, across a broad range of product categories. CSTM's strategy emphasizes the introduction of new, company-designed, proprietary products, and in FY 98 (Jan.) the company added 500 of these higher-margin items to its product line. Proprietary products accounted for 20% of CSTM's net sales in FY 98.

CSTM promotes market awareness through the use of company brand names, which also serve to identify particular products with specific features or performance

characteristics. For example, the RevTech name identifies products designed to enhance the performance of Harley-Davidson motorcycles, such as carburetors, cylinder heads, ignition and exhaust systems, oil pumps and cams. In all, CSTM derived 62% of its net sales in FY 98 from proprietary and non-proprietary products sold under the company's brand names, which also include Premium, C.C. Rider, Dyno Power, Tour Ease, Bullskins and Custom Chrome.

The company also distributes a number of products, such as Champion spark plugs, Dunlop tires, Crane cams, Accel electrical parts and Russell braided lines and tubing, under the manufacturer's brand name, and in FY 97 products sold under brand names other than the company's accounted for 38% of CSTM's net sales.

In September 1997, Global Motorsport acquired Chrome Specialties, Inc., a wholesale distributor of proprietary brand and aftermarket parts for Harley-Davidson motorcycles, for $36 million in cash.

After declining an offer of $18 a share in March 1998 from Golden Cycle L.L.C., CSTM entered a definitive merger agreement with Fremont Partners. Fremont Partners, a unit of the the Fremont Group, is a private investment company which offered CSTM $21.75 a share in cash. The tender offer will be extended through September 25, 1998.

Per Share Data ($)

(Year Ended Jan. 31)	1998	1997	1996	1995	1994	1993	1992	1991	1990	1989
Tangible Bk. Val.	5.13	9.81	7.81	7.71	6.54	5.08	2.31	-2.75	NA	NA
Cash Flow	1.03	1.83	1.83	1.58	1.40	1.00	0.68	0.06	NA	NA
Earnings	0.44	1.48	1.52	1.27	1.10	0.78	0.33	-1.03	NA	NA
Dividends	Nil	Nil	Nil	Nil	Nil	Nil	Nil	Nil	Nil	Nil
Payout Ratio	Nil	Nil	Nil	Nil	Nil	Nil	Nil	Nil	Nil	Nil
Cal. Yrs.	1997	1996	1995	1994	1993	1992	1991	1990	1989	1988
Prices - High	20¼	27⅞	26½	28	27	11¾	10½	NA	NA	NA
- Low	10½	16¼	15¾	12¼	9¼	6	6	NA	NA	NA
P/E Ratio - High	46	19	17	22	25	15	32	NA	NA	NA
- Low	24	11	10	10	8	8	18	NA	NA	NA

Income Statement Analysis (Million $)

	1998	1997	1996	1995	1994	1993	1992	1991	1990	1989
Revs.	123	109	93.9	74.9	67.3	52.4	43.6	39.6	NA	NA
Oper. Inc.	10.4	16.9	15.6	12.9	11.5	8.3	8.6	7.4	NA	NA
Depr.	3.1	1.9	1.6	1.6	1.5	1.1	1.1	2.7	NA	NA
Int. Exp.	3.0	1.9	1.6	0.7	0.8	0.8	3.3	4.5	NA	NA
Pretax Inc.	4.4	13.0	12.3	10.6	9.2	6.4	1.4	-2.6	NA	NA
Eff. Tax Rate	48%	40%	36%	40%	40%	40%	27%	NM	NM	NM
Net Inc.	2.3	7.9	7.9	6.4	5.5	3.9	1.0	-2.6	NA	NA

Balance Sheet & Other Fin. Data (Million $)

	1998	1997	1996	1995	1994	1993	1992	1991	1990	1989
Cash	1.4	0.0	0.3	9.0	Nil	Nil	Nil	Nil	Nil	Nil
Curr. Assets	88.3	67.5	67.4	45.1	29.6	23.3	16.4	16.2	NA	NA
Total Assets	142	91.5	89.7	64.3	47.3	40.5	32.8	34.4	NA	NA
Curr. Liab.	29.4	14.7	21.7	5.8	10.8	11.6	9.0	13.5	NA	NA
LT Debt	52.3	16.2	19.5	19.5	4.8	4.7	4.6	26.9	NA	NA
Common Eqty.	59.3	59.8	48.0	38.6	31.7	24.1	19.2	-6.0	NA	NA
Total Cap.	113	76.8	68.0	58.6	36.5	28.8	23.8	20.9	NA	NA
Cap. Exp.	4.0	3.6	4.7	3.3	1.5	1.6	0.5	0.2	NA	NA
Cash Flow	5.4	9.8	9.5	8.0	7.0	5.0	2.1	0.1	NA	NA
Curr. Ratio	3.0	4.6	3.1	7.8	2.7	2.0	1.8	1.2	NA	NA
% LT Debt of Cap.	46.2	21.0	28.6	33.3	13.0	16.3	19.4	128.9	NA	NA
% Net Inc.of Revs.	1.9	7.3	8.4	8.6	8.2	7.4	2.4	NM	NM	NM
% Ret. on Assets	2.0	8.7	10.3	11.4	12.4	10.6	1.9	NM	NM	NM
% Ret. on Equity	3.8	14.6	18.3	18.0	19.5	17.9	NM	NM	NM	NM

Data as orig. reptd.; bef. results of disc. opers. and/or spec. items. Per share data adj. for stk. divs. as of ex-div. date. Bold denotes diluted EPS (FASB 128). E-Estimated. NA-Not Available. NM-Not Meaningful. NR-Not Ranked.

Office—16100 Jacqueline Court, Morgan Hill, CA 95037. **Tel**—(408) 778-0500. **Chrmn**—J. F. Keenan. **Pres & CEO**— J. Piazza. **EVP-Fin, CFO, Secy & Investor Contact**—James J. Kelly, Jr. **Dirs**—L. M Allan, J. F. Keenan, J. J. Kelly, Jr., I. J. Panzica, J. Piazza. **Transfer Agent & Registrar**—Bank of Boston, NYC. **Incorporated**—in California in 1970; reincorporated in Delaware in 1990. **Empl**— 497. **S&P Analyst:** Kathleen J. Fraser

Goody's Family Clothing 4020M

NASDAQ Symbol **GDYS**

In S&P SmallCap 600

03-OCT-98

Industry:
Retail (Special-
ty-Apparel)

Summary: This company is a retailer of moderately priced apparel for women, men and children, with more than 200 stores in 15 states in the Southeast and Midwest.

Quantitative Evaluations

Outlook
(1 Lowest—5 Highest)
• **5**

Fair Value
• **20¾**

Risk
• **High**

Earn./Div. Rank
• **B**

Technical Eval.
• **Bearish** since 10/96

Rel. Strength Rank
(1 Lowest—99 Highest)
• **4**

Insider Activity
• **Neutral**

Recent Price • 10½
52 Wk Range • 29-10

Yield • Nil
12-Mo. P/E • 9.2

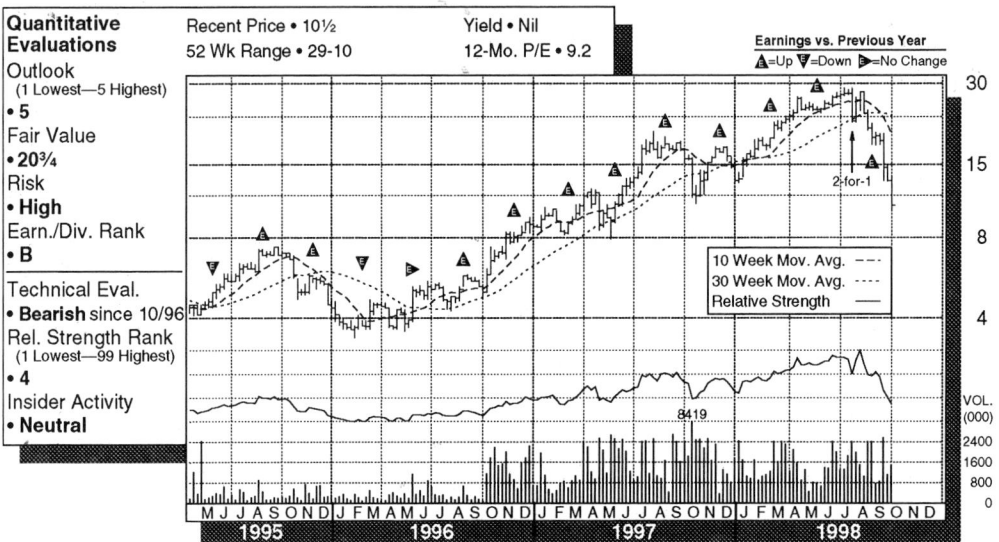

Earnings vs. Previous Year
▲=Up ▼=Down ▶=No Change

10 Week Mov. Avg. – – –
30 Week Mov. Avg. ·······
Relative Strength ——

2-for-1

Business Profile - 01-SEP-98

With an objective to be the leading retailer of brand name apparel in each of the markets it serves, this company plans to appeal to value-conscious customers, offer a broad range of merchandise for the entire family, emphasize current-season and quality brands, use private label merchandise and focus on small to midsize markets. Capital expenditures are planned at $30 million for fiscal 1999, most of which is allocated to the opening of 28 new stores and the relocation or remodeling of 10 to 12 stores. The company also intends to close two stores. Plans call for continued expansion in the Southeast and Midwest, as well as outside these traditional boundaries.

Operational Review - 01-SEP-98

Sales in the 26 weeks ended August 1, 1998, advanced 18%, year to year, aided by the opening of new stores and a 6.9% rise in same-store sales. Gross margins widened on the higher volume, and following 16% higher operating expenses to support expansion, pretax income climbed 57%. After taxes at 37.7%, versus 37.5%, net income was also up 57%, to $16,426,000 ($0.47 a share) from $10,476,000 ($0.31).

Stock Performance - 02-OCT-98

In the past 30 trading days, GDYS's shares have declined 48%, compared to a 7% fall in the S&P 500. Average trading volume for the past five days was 298,380 shares, compared with the 40-day moving average of 375,318 shares.

Key Stock Statistics

Dividend Rate/Share	Nil	Shareholders	500
Shs. outstg. (M)	33.3	Market cap. (B)	$0.352
Avg. daily vol. (M)	0.393	Inst. holdings	58%
Tang. Bk. Value/Share	5.53		
Beta	1.52		

Value of $10,000 invested 5 years ago: $ 9,261

Fiscal Year Ending Jan. 31

	1999	1998	1997	1996	1995	1994
Revenues (Million $)						
1Q	226.7	190.1	150.8	144.9	—	96.70
2Q	249.5	212.2	183.4	155.1	132.4	110.6
3Q	—	234.9	211.4	168.1	147.4	123.6
4Q	—	33.75	273.5	228.7	209.6	174.1
Yr.	—	971.9	819.1	696.9	613.7	505.0
Earnings Per Share ($)						
1Q	0.23	0.15	0.07	0.07	0.09	0.07
2Q	0.25	0.16	0.04	0.03	0.01	0.07
3Q	—	0.17	0.10	0.07	-0.07	0.04
4Q	—	0.51	0.31	0.16	0.18	0.25
Yr.	—	0.99	0.52	0.33	0.21	0.43

Next earnings report expected: mid November

Dividend Data

Amount ($)	Date Decl.	Ex-Div. Date	Stock of Record	Payment Date
2-for-1	Jun. 17	Jul. 20	Jul. 01	Jul. 17 '98

A Division of The **McGraw·Hill** Companies

Business Summary - 01-SEP-98

As a retailer of moderately priced apparel for women, men and children, Goody's Family Clothing operated 223 stores in 15 Southeastern and Midwestern states as of January 31, 1998. To meet the changing tastes and lifestyles of its customer base, the company continually develops and refines its merchandising strategy. The stores are generally located in strip shopping centers in small to midsize markets.

The company has experienced strong growth in the past several years, aided by a new store opening strategy that has increased the number of stores from 146 in fiscal 1994. The stores are now located in Alabama, Arkansas, Florida, Georgia, Illinois, Indiana, Kentucky, Mississippi, Missouri, North Carolina, Ohio, South Carolina, Tennessee, Virginia and West Virginia.

Goody's offers merchandise at prices targeted at 10% to 30% below those of traditional department stores. Stores are segmented into departments by women's (juniors, misses, intimate apparel, swimwear and outerwear; 42% of sales in fiscal 1998), denim (23%), men's (sportswear, activewear, young men's and men's

furnishings; 20%), children's (infants and toddlers, boys and girls; 7%), accessories (jewelry, handbags, belts and gift items; 4%) and shoes (3%). The company also offers tuxedo rentals (1%).

Goody's sells products with key brand names including Adidas, Alfred Dunner, Bugle Boy, Dockers, Lee, Leslie Fay, Levi's, Nike, Reebok, Requirements and Sag Harbor. It also offers products under its own private label names such as Chandler Hill, Electro Sport, GFC Trading Co., Intimate Classics, Montana Blue Jean Company and Mountain Lake for women; Authentic GFC, Bobby by Ivy Crew, GFC, Ivy Crew, Old College Inn and OCI -- Quality Clothing for men; and GoodKidz for children.

Goody's plans to increase its gross store square footage by at least 10% per year in each of the next four fiscal years by opening new stores and relocating existing stores. Its current plans for fiscal 1999 are to open a total of 28 new stores, including the first stores in Texas, relocate or remodel 10 to 12 stores and close two stores. During fiscal 1998, the company opened 24 new stores, expanding its store base by 10%.

Per Share Data ($)

(Year Ended Jan. 31)	1998	1997	1996	1995	1994	1993	1992	1991	1990	1989
Tangible Bk. Val.	4.37	3.83	3.29	2.96	2.75	2.37	1.86	NA	NA	NA
Cash Flow	1.34	0.84	0.61	0.41	0.60	NA	1.04	0.42	NA	NA
Earnings	0.99	0.52	0.33	0.21	0.43	0.50	NA	NA	NA	NA
Dividends	Nil	Nil	Nil	0.01	NA	NA	NA	NA	NA	NA
Payout Ratio	Nil	Nil	Nil	0%	NA	NA	NA	NA	NA	NA
Cal. Yrs.	1997	1996	1995	1994	1993	1992	1991	1990	1989	1988
Prices - High	19⁷/₈	9⁵/₈	7³/₈	10	12¹/₂	12¹/₂	8⁷/₈	NA	NA	NA
- Low	7⁷/₈	3³/₈	4¹/₈	3³/₄	5⁷/₈	7⁵/₈	5	NA	NA	NA
P/E Ratio - High	20	18	22	46	29	25	22	NA	NA	NA
- Low	8	6	12	17	13	15	13	NA	NA	NA

Income Statement Analysis (Million $)

	1998	1997	1996	1995	1994	1993	1992	1991	1990	1989
Revs.	972	821	697	614	505	NA	362	273	NA	NA
Oper. Inc.	63.7	37.3	25.0	24.4	25.1	NA	22.1	11.7	NA	NA
Depr.	11.6	10.6	9.1	6.2	5.6	NA	4.6	4.3	NA	NA
Int. Exp.	0.5	0.8	0.6	1.2	1.5	NA	2.4	3.3	NA	NA
Pretax Inc.	53.4	27.4	16.5	10.8	21.2	NA	17.0	5.7	NA	NA
Eff. Tax Rate	38%	38%	37%	36%	35%	NA	12%	40%	NA	NA
Net Inc.	33.3	17.2	10.5	6.9	13.8	NA	15.0	3.4	NA	NA

Balance Sheet & Other Fin. Data (Million $)

	1998	1997	1996	1995	1994	1993	1992	1991	1990	1989
Cash	64.2	43.3	33.0	23.1	18.1	NA	31.4	23.2	NA	NA
Curr. Assets	228	162	119	97.6	108	NA	73.4	58.2	NA	NA
Total Assets	328	254	208	186	164	NA	115	96.2	NA	NA
Curr. Liab.	154	118	91.5	82.5	68.4	NA	50.3	39.3	NA	NA
LT Debt	0.6	0.9	NA	NA	NA	NA	NA	NA	NA	NA
Common Eqty.	160	124	106	95.4	88.4	NA	60.4	26.6	NA	NA
Total Cap.	171	135	NA	NA	NA	NA	NA	NA	NA	NA
Cap. Exp.	21.2	16.1	NA	NA	NA	NA	NA	NA	NA	NA
Cash Flow	44.9	27.7	19.6	13.1	19.4	NA	19.5	7.6	NA	NA
Curr. Ratio	1.5	1.4	1.3	1.2	1.6	NA	1.5	1.5	NA	NA
% LT Debt of Cap.	0.4	0.6	NA	NA	NA	NA	NA	NA	NA	NA
% Net Inc.of Revs.	3.4	2.1	1.5	1.1	2.7	NA	4.1	1.2	NA	NA
% Ret. on Assets	11.4	7.4	5.3	3.9	NA	NA	14.2	NA	NA	NA
% Ret. on Equity	7.7	14.9	10.4	7.5	NA	NA	34.4	NA	NA	NA

Data as orig. reptd.; bef. results of disc. opers. and/or spec. items. Per share data adj. for stk. divs. as of ex-div. date. Bold denotes diluted EPS (FASB 128). E-Estimated. NA-Not Available. NM-Not Meaningful. NR-Not Ranked.

Office—400 Goody's Lane, Knoxville, TN 37922. **Tel**—(423) 966-2000. **Chrmn & CEO**—R. M. Goodfriend. **Pres & COO**—H. M. Call. **EVP, CFO & Treas**—E. R. Carlin. **Dirs**—H. M. Call, E. R. Carlin, S. J. Furrow, R. M. Goodfriend, R. F. Koppel, I. L. Lowenstein, C. L. Turnbull. **Transfer Agent & Registrar**—Wachovia Bank of North Carolina, Winston-Salem, NC. **Incorporated**—in Tennessee in 1954. **Empl**— 8,800. **S&P Analyst:** Stephen R. Biggar

Gottschalks Inc.

1032M

NYSE Symbol **GOT**

In S&P SmallCap 600

03-OCT-98

Industry: Retail (Department Stores)

Summary: This company operates 46 department stores and 22 specialty stores in non-major metropolitan areas in California, Washington, Oregon and Nevada.

Quantitative Evaluations

Recent Price • 6¾
52 Wk Range • 9¼-6½

Yield • Nil
12-Mo. P/E • 42.6

Outlook (1 Lowest—5 Highest)
• 2

Fair Value
• 7

Risk
• Average

Earn./Div. Rank
• B-

Technical Eval.
• **Bearish** since 9/98

Rel. Strength Rank (1 Lowest—99 Highest)
• 49

Insider Activity
• NA

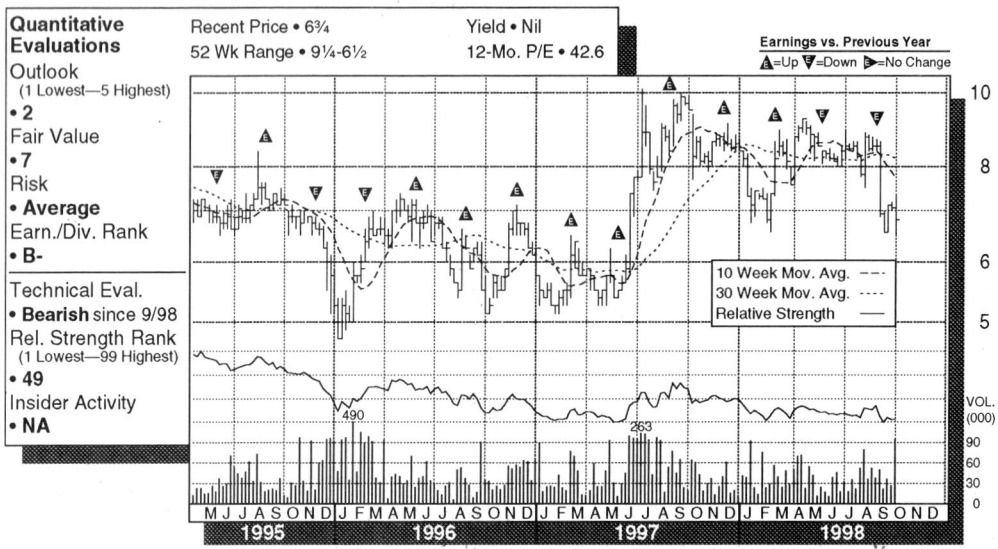

Earnings vs. Previous Year
▲=Up ▼=Down ▶=No Change

10 Week Mov. Avg. ---
30 Week Mov. Avg. ----
Relative Strength —

Business Profile - 24-SEP-98

This regional department store chain derives most of its revenues from Gottschalks stores, which are located mainly in smaller California cities. Management generally seeks to open two new stores annually. In August 1998, GOT purchased the assets of The Harris Co. from El Corte Ingles. Harris operated nine department stores in the Southern California area and had sales of $97.4 million in its fiscal year ended January 31, 1998. GOT's business is seasonal, with the major portion of net sales, gross profit and operating results realized during the Christmas selling months (November and December), and, to a lesser extent, during the Easter and Back-to-School selling seasons.

Operational Review - 24-SEP-98

Net sales in the 26 weeks ended August 1, 1998, rose 4.8%, year to year, primarily reflecting sales from two new stores opened in the third quarter of FY 98 (Jan.). Same-store sales were down 0.2%. Net credit revenues were up 5.6%. Margins narrowed on higher markdowns as a percentage of sales taken in an attempt to improve sales of spring and summer merchandise which were sluggish due to adverse weather conditions caused by El Nino; operating income was down 48%. Despite tax benefits of $2,372,000, versus $860,000, the net loss widened to $3,346,000 ($0.32 a share), from $1,235,000 ($0.12).

Stock Performance - 02-OCT-98

In the past 30 trading days, GOT's shares have declined 20%, compared to a 7% fall in the S&P 500. Average trading volume for the past five days was 29,440 shares, compared with the 40-day moving average of 10,405 shares.

Key Stock Statistics

Dividend Rate/Share	Nil	Shareholders	1,000
Shs. outstg. (M)	12.6	Market cap. (B)	$0.086
Avg. daily vol. (M)	0.012	Inst. holdings	28%
Tang. Bk. Value/Share	7.90		
Beta	-0.11		

Value of $10,000 invested 5 years ago: $ 7,465

Fiscal Year Ending Jan. 31

	1999	1998	1997	1996	1995	1994
Revenues (Million $)						
1Q	95.47	90.51	85.56	77.93	72.50	65.83
2Q	104.1	100.0	95.68	91.88	80.52	76.22
3Q	—	101.5	95.68	86.07	78.84	75.75
4Q	—	156.2	145.3	145.2	134.0	124.6
Yr.	—	448.2	422.2	401.0	363.6	342.4
Earnings Per Share ($)						
1Q	-0.19	-0.09	-0.13	-0.30	-0.22	-0.35
2Q	-0.13	-0.02	-0.07	-0.19	-0.38	-0.23
3Q	—	-0.14	-0.15	-0.30	-0.05	-0.17
4Q	—	0.62	0.52	0.25	0.81	0.49
Yr.	—	0.36	0.18	-0.54	0.15	-0.26

Next earnings report expected: mid November

Dividend Data

No cash dividends have been paid. A two-for-one stock split was effected in April 1987.

A Division of The McGraw-Hill Companies

Business Summary - 24-SEP-98

Fresno, CA-based Gottschalks (GOT; currently the largest independent department store chain based in California) and its predecessor, E. Gottschalk & Co., have operated continuously for more than 93 years, since their founding by Emil Gottschalk in 1904. Since the company first offered its stock to the public in 1986, it has added 38 of its 46 Gottschalks stores, opened 20 of its 22 Village East specialty stores, and constructed its distribution center. GOT stores are located primarily in non-major metropolitan cities throughout California, and in Oregon, Washington and Nevada.

Gottschalks department stores typically offer a wide range of brand-name and private-label merchandise, including men's, women's, junior's and children's apparel; cosmetics and accessories; shoes and jewelry; home furnishings including china, housewares, electronics and small electric appliances; and other consumer goods. Village East specialty stores offer apparel for larger women. Gottschalks stores are generally anchor tenants of regional shopping malls, with Village East specialty stores generally located in the regional malls in which a Gottschalks department store is located or as a separate department within some of the company's larger Gottschalks stores. The company's stores carry primarily moderately priced brand-name merchandise, complemented with private-label merchandise and a mix of higher and budget-priced merchandise.

GOT's stores are located primarily in diverse, growing, non-major metropolitan areas. GOT believes that it has a competitive advantage in offering brand-name merchandise and a high level of service to customers in secondary markets in the western U.S., where there is a strong demand for nationally advertised, brand-name merchandise and fewer competitors offering such merchandise. Some of the company's stores are located in agricultural areas and cater to mature customers with above average levels of disposable income. Gottschalks strives to be the "hometown store" in each of the communities it serves.

GOT generally seeks to open two new stores a year, and invests in the renovation and refixturing of its existing store locations in order to maintain and improve market share in those market areas.

In August 1998, GOT purchased the assets of The Harris Co. from El Corte Ingles. Harris operated nine department stores in the Southern California area and had sales of $97.4 million in its fiscal year ended January 31, 1998. The purchase price consisted of about 2.1 million GOT common shares, an 8% extendable subordinated note due 2003 in the principal amount of $22.2 million, and the assumption of certain liabilities of Harris.

Per Share Data ($)

(Year Ended Jan. 31)	1998	1997	1996	1995	1994	1993	1992	1991	1990	1989
Tangible Bk. Val.	7.90	7.53	7.35	7.90	7.73	7.98	9.02	7.01	6.29	5.83
Cash Flow	0.99	0.83	0.24	0.71	0.33	-0.19	0.94	1.34	0.88	0.94
Earnings	0.36	0.18	-0.54	0.15	-0.26	-0.77	0.44	0.80	0.46	0.61
Dividends	Nil	Nil	Nil	Nil	Nil	Nil	Nil	Nil	Nil	Nil
Payout Ratio	Nil	Nil	Nil	Nil	Nil	Nil	Nil	Nil	Nil	Nil
Cal. Yrs.	1997	1996	1995	1994	1993	1992	1991	1990	1989	1988
Prices - High	10⅛	7⅜	8⅜	13	10⅜	22½	26⅜	15	13⅜	13¼
- Low	5⅛	4¾	5⅛	7	6⅛	7½	11⅝	8⅝	8	8⅛
P/E Ratio - High	28	41	NM	87	NM	NM	60	19	29	22
- Low	14	26	NM	47	NM	NM	26	11	17	13

Income Statement Analysis (Million $)

Revs.	455	422	401	373	351	340	324	295	243	202
Oper. Inc.	19.1	8.4	-0.9	21.5	13.3	7.9	16.9	21.4	15.9	15.5
Depr.	6.7	6.9	8.1	5.9	6.1	6.0	4.9	4.3	3.5	2.7
Int. Exp.	7.3	11.7	11.3	10.3	8.6	7.0	7.0	9.8	8.4	5.5
Pretax Inc.	6.4	3.1	-8.6	2.3	-3.9	-12.0	7.0	10.4	5.7	8.1
Eff. Tax Rate	42%	41%	NM	35%	NM	NM	39%	38%	35%	38%
Net Inc.	3.7	1.8	-5.6	1.5	-2.7	-8.0	4.3	6.4	3.7	5.0

Balance Sheet & Other Fin. Data (Million $)

Cash	1.6	6.7	7.4	5.5	1.2	1.1	3.3	1.4	2.8	0.9
Curr. Assets	135	134	139	127	140	131	131	121	99	87.0
Total Assets	242	233	239	253	248	240	234	208	166	142
Curr. Liab.	67.1	64.0	96.0	89.0	108	114	62.6	84.9	60.8	44.2
LT Debt	62.4	60.2	34.9	33.7	31.5	15.0	50.3	41.6	44.8	40.1
Common Eqty.	83.9	80.1	77.9	83.6	82.1	84.5	95.7	58.7	51.8	49.7
Total Cap.	150	143	117	123	120	106	152	106	99	91.0
Cap. Exp.	15.0	6.8	12.8	4.5	6.5	12.1	15.0	25.8	38.0	21.4
Cash Flow	10.4	8.7	2.5	7.4	3.4	-2.0	9.2	10.8	7.1	7.8
Curr. Ratio	2.0	2.1	1.4	1.4	1.3	1.1	2.1	1.4	1.6	2.0
% LT Debt of Cap.	41.6	42.0	29.9	27.3	26.3	14.2	33.2	39.3	45.3	43.9
% Net Inc.of Revs.	0.8	0.4	NM	0.4	NM	NM	1.3	2.2	1.5	2.5
% Ret. on Assets	1.6	0.8	NM	0.6	NM	NM	1.7	3.4	2.4	4.0
% Ret. on Equity	4.5	2.3	NM	1.8	NM	NM	5.0	11.6	7.3	10.4

Data as orig. reptd.; bef. results of disc. opers. and/or spec. items. Per share data adj. for stk. divs. as of ex-div. date. Bold denotes diluted EPS (FASB 128). E-Estimated. NA-Not Available. NM-Not Meaningful. NR-Not Ranked.

Office—7 River Park Place East, Fresno, CA 93720. **Registrar & Transfer Agent**—ChaseMellon Shareholder Services, SF. **Tel**—(209) 434-8000. **Website**—www.gottschalks.com **Chrmn & CEO**—J. W. Levy. **Vice Chrmn**—G. H. Blum. **Pres & COO**—James Famalette. **SVP & CFO**—A. A. Weinstein. **Dirs**—J. R. Famalette, M. Gutmann, B. W Levy, J. W. Levy, S. Levy, J. J. Penbera, F. R. Ruiz, O. J. Woodward III. **Transfer Agent & Registrar**—ChaseMellon Shareholder Services, SF. **incorporated**—in California in 1912; reincorporated in Delaware in 1986. **Empl**—5,661. **S&P Analyst:** M.I.

03-OCT-98

Industry:
Manufacturing (Diversified)

Summary: This company is a U.S.-based global producer of industrial pumps, valves, meters and accessories.

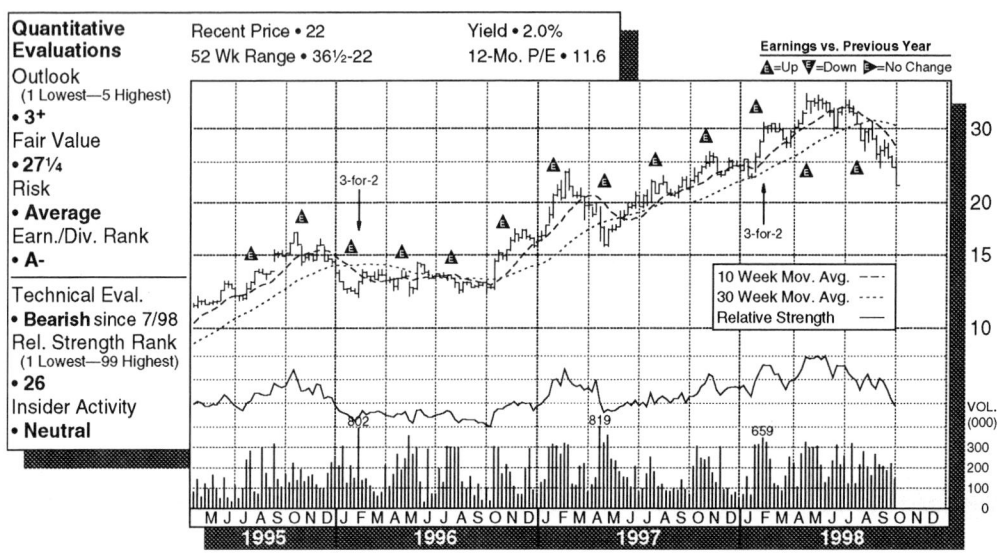

Quantitative Evaluations		
Outlook (1 Lowest—5 Highest) • **3+**		
Fair Value • **27¼**		
Risk • **Average**		
Earn./Div. Rank • **A-**		
Technical Eval. • **Bearish** since 7/98		
Rel. Strength Rank (1 Lowest—99 Highest) • **26**		
Insider Activity • **Neutral**		

Recent Price • 22
52 Wk Range • 36½-22
Yield • 2.0%
12-Mo. P/E • 11.6

Business Profile - 30-SEP-98

This company operates in the consolidating but still fragmented industrial pump and valve industry. Graco's financial objectives are to increase revenues at an average annual rate of 10% to 12%, expand net income at an annualized rate of 12% to 15%, and generate net profit margins of 6%. Management plans to achieve these objectives by capitalizing on favorable trends in GGG's targeted global markets, investing in facilities and new products, and making judicious acquisitions. As the third quarter of 1998 began, Graco was optimistic about the balance of the year with strong order levels in the Contractor and Industrial/Automotive Equipment Divisions. At June 26, 1998, the company's backlog stood at $25 million, up 19% from the beginning of 1998.

Operational Review - 30-SEP-98

Revenues in the first half of 1998 rose 8.4%, year to year, primarily due to strong Contractor and Industrial/Automotive demand in the Americas and Europe. Margins widened, aided by improvements in manufacturing processes, discipline purchasing, increased sales volumes and price increases; operating income advanced 25%. Following a decline in interest and other expenses, net income rose 31%, to $21.7 million ($0.82 a share), from $16.6 million ($0.64, as adjusted).

Stock Performance - 02-OCT-98

In the past 30 trading days, GGG's shares have declined 22%, compared to a 7% fall in the S&P 500. Average trading volume for the past five days was 28,420 shares, compared with the 40-day moving average of 41,103 shares.

Key Stock Statistics

Dividend Rate/Share	0.44	Shareholders	2,000
Shs. outstg. (M)	20.0	Market cap. (B)	$0.441
Avg. daily vol. (M)	0.039	Inst. holdings	88%
Tang. Bk. Value/Share	6.90		
Beta	1.02		

Value of $10,000 invested 5 years ago: $ 40,187

Fiscal Year Ending Dec. 31

	1998	1997	1996	1995	1994	1993
Revenues (Million $)						
1Q	105.7	92.10	90.15	95.53	80.93	77.81
2Q	115.2	111.7	97.10	103.4	94.18	79.42
3Q	—	101.9	97.68	94.80	89.05	81.75
4Q	—	108.2	106.8	92.59	95.87	83.63
Yr.	—	413.9	391.8	386.3	360.0	322.6
Earnings Per Share ($)						
1Q	0.34	0.24	0.21	0.21	0.07	0.10
2Q	0.48	0.40	0.38	0.32	0.16	0.10
3Q	—	0.49	0.39	0.25	0.16	0.13
4Q	—	0.59	0.40	0.27	0.20	-0.03
Yr.	—	1.71	1.38	1.06	0.59	0.36

Next earnings report expected: early October

Dividend Data (Dividends have been paid since 1970.)

Amount ($)	Date Decl.	Ex-Div. Date	Stock of Record	Payment Date
0.110	Dec. 12	Jan. 05	Jan. 07	Feb. 04 '98
0.110	Feb. 20	Mar. 30	Apr. 01	May. 06 '98
0.110	May. 18	Jun. 29	Jul. 01	Aug. 05 '98
0.110	Sep. 11	Oct. 05	Oct. 07	Nov. 04 '98

A Division of The **McGraw·Hill** Companies

Business Summary - 30-SEP-98

Graco is a U.S.-based global producer of industrial and commercial pumps, valves, meters and related accessories. It also produces a line of portable painting and cleaning equipment. GGG's products are sold to the manufacturing, processing, construction and maintenance industries. Segment revenues and gross profit margins in recent years were derived as follows:

	1997	1996	1995
REVENUES			
Commercial & Industrial equipment	55%	53%	54%
Accessories & replacement parts	45%	47%	46%
GROSS PROFIT MARGINS			
Commercial & Industrial equipment	44%	45%	44%
Accessories & replacement parts	55%	56%	55%

In 1997, the Americas accounted for 67% of revenues and $87 million in operating profit (65% and $72 million in 1996), Europe 20% and $7 million (20% and $9 million) and Asia/Pacific 13% and $3 million (15% and $6 million).

Commercial and industrial equipment includes specialized pumps, air and airless spray units, manual finishing equipment and fluid-handling systems.

Replacement parts and accessories (aftermarket prod-ucts) are sold for use with the company's equipment. Packings, seals and hoses for Graco pumps and related equipment must be replaced periodically to maintain efficiency and prevent loss of the material being handled. Graco offers its customers hoses, couplings, various flow regulators and valves, agitators, filters, meters, gauges and a variety of spray guns and tips. Typically, aftermarket products are more profitable than original equipment products. Over the last three years, sales of replacement parts and accessories have averaged 47% of total GGG revenues.

Primary applications of the company's products include product coating and finishing; mixing, metering, dispensing and applying adhesive, chemical bonding and sealant materials; professional cleaning and spray painting of architectural structures; lubrication and maintenance of vehicles and industrial machinery; and transferring and dispensing various fluids such as chemicals, inks, food and plastics.

Graco emphasizes research and development. In each of 1997, 1996 and 1995, the company spent about 4% of total revenues for R&D. One of GGG's stated financial goals is to generate 30% of annual sales from products introduced in the prior three years. To this end, Graco has substantially increased new product design, expanded its engineering staff, and doubled the size of the company's R&D center.

Per Share Data ($)

(Year Ended Dec. 31)	1997	1996	1995	1994	1993	1992	1991	1990	1989	1988
Tangible Bk. Val.	6.17	4.93	4.00	3.09	2.82	3.86	3.82	3.72	3.12	2.61
Cash Flow	2.22	1.86	1.49	0.99	0.72	0.74	0.67	1.04	0.89	0.85
Earnings	1.71	1.38	1.06	0.59	0.36	0.43	0.35	0.72	0.60	0.56
Dividends	0.39	0.33	0.27	1.46	0.32	0.27	0.20	0.18	0.16	0.15
Payout Ratio	23%	24%	25%	NM	87%	62%	58%	25%	27%	26%
Prices - High	26¹/₂	17³/₈	17	11	10³/₄	8³/₄	9¹/₈	7¹/₂	6¹/₈	7
- Low	15⁵/₈	11⁷/₈	8³/₄	7¹/₂	6⁷/₈	6⁷/₈	5⁷/₈	4⁵/₈	4¹/₂	4¹/₂
P/E Ratio - High	15	13	16	19	30	20	26	10	10	13
- Low	9	9	8	13	19	16	17	6	8	8

Income Statement Analysis (Million $)

	1997	1996	1995	1994	1993	1992	1991	1990	1989	1988
Revs.	414	392	386	360	323	320	312	321	298	268
Oper. Inc.	79.0	65.7	56.3	36.8	27.9	27.4	29.8	41.9	37.1	32.7
Depr.	13.5	12.6	11.0	10.4	9.3	7.9	8.0	7.7	7.0	6.8
Int. Exp.	0.9	0.8	2.3	1.9	2.3	2.7	3.7	3.5	4.5	4.2
Pretax Inc.	63.5	52.7	43.5	23.4	13.8	18.0	15.3	29.0	24.5	21.8
Eff. Tax Rate	30%	31%	37%	35%	31%	38%	42%	39%	41%	39%
Net Inc.	44.7	36.1	27.7	15.3	9.5	11.1	8.9	17.7	14.5	13.3

Balance Sheet & Other Fin. Data (Million $)

	1997	1996	1995	1994	1993	1992	1991	1990	1989	1988
Cash	13.5	6.5	1.6	2.4	37.4	38.2	24.0	6.0	4.5	2.0
Curr. Assets	156	144	128	144	147	162	150	151	133	124
Total Assets	265	248	218	228	216	220	206	209	182	172
Curr. Liab.	69.0	80.6	71.5	89.5	100	77.1	74.9	84.0	69.9	66.6
LT Debt	6.2	8.1	10.0	26.8	13.9	17.8	19.6	23.9	28.5	34.0
Common Eqty.	158	126	104	80.4	73.2	99	96.0	90.3	74.7	61.6
Total Cap.	164	134	114	109	89.0	118	119	117	108	103
Cap. Exp.	20.1	30.0	19.8	23.1	16.2	10.2	8.4	14.7	12.3	9.8
Cash Flow	58.2	48.8	38.8	25.7	18.7	19.0	16.9	25.4	21.5	20.1
Curr. Ratio	2.3	1.8	1.8	1.6	1.5	2.1	2.0	1.8	1.9	1.9
% LT Debt of Cap.	3.8	6.0	8.8	24.7	15.7	15.1	16.4	20.4	26.4	33.1
% Net Inc.of Revs.	10.8	9.2	7.2	4.3	2.9	3.5	2.9	5.5	4.9	5.0
% Ret. on Assets	17.5	15.4	12.4	6.9	4.3	5.2	4.2	9.0	8.1	8.2
% Ret. on Equity	25.7	31.5	NA	19.9	10.9	11.3	9.4	21.3	21.0	23.0

Data as orig. reptd.; bef. results of disc. opers. and/or spec. items. Per share data adj. for stk. divs. as of ex-div. date. Bold denotes diluted EPS (FASB 128). E-Estimated. NA-Not Available. NM-Not Meaningful. NR-Not Ranked.

Office—4050 Olson Memorial Highway, Golden Valley, MN 55422-2332. **Tel**—(612) 623-6000. **Website**—http://www.graco.com **Chrmn**—D. A. Koch. **CEO**—G. Aristides. **Pres & COO**—C. M. Osborne. **Treas**—M. W. Sheahan. **VP & Secy**—R. M. Mattison. **Investor Contact**—Mark Sheahan (612-623-6656). **Dirs**—G. Aristides, R. O. Baukol, D. A. Koch, R. D. McFarland, L. R. Mitau, M. Morfitt, D. R. Olseth, C. M. Osborne, J. L. Scott, W. G. Van Dyke. **Transfer Agent & Registrar**—Norwest Bank Minnesota, St. Paul. **Incorporated**—in Minnesota in 1947. **Empl**— 2,100. **S&P Analyst:** John A. Massey

Grand Casinos

1043M

NYSE Symbol **GND**

In S&P SmallCap 600

03-OCT-98

Industry: Gaming, Lottery & Pari-mutuel Cos.

Summary: This casino entertainment company develops, constructs and manages land-based and dockside casinos in emerging gaming markets.

Quantitative Evaluations

Outlook (1 Lowest—5 Highest)
• **5**

Fair Value
• **21⅜**

Risk
• **High**

Earn./Div. Rank
• **NR**

Technical Eval.
• **Bearish** since 7/98

Rel. Strength Rank (1 Lowest—99 Highest)
• **14**

Insider Activity
• **NA**

Recent Price • 7⅝
52 Wk Range • 19⅛-7⅛

Yield • Nil
12-Mo. P/E • 4.7

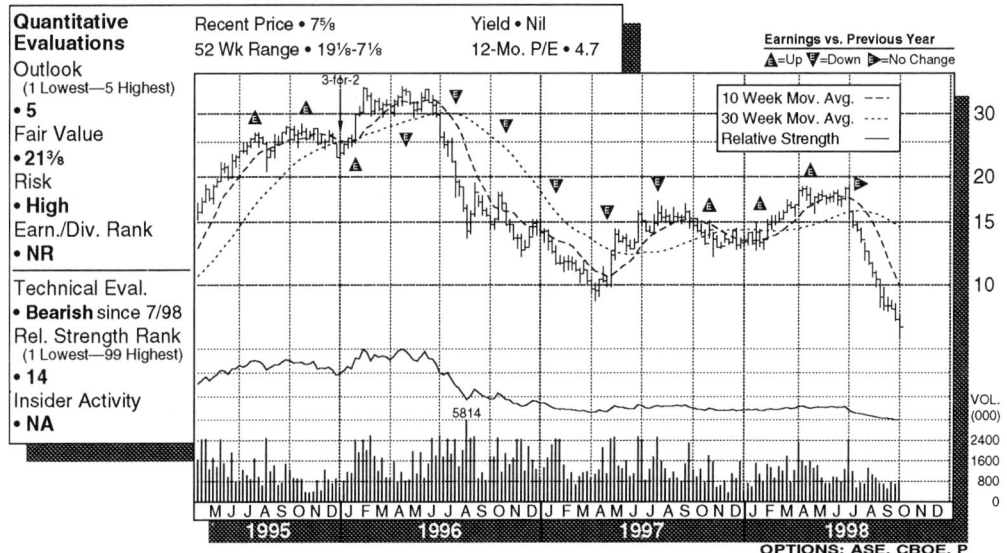

Earnings vs. Previous Year
▲=Up ▼=Down ▶=No Change

10 Week Mov. Avg. ----
30 Week Mov. Avg. ·····
Relative Strength ——

OPTIONS: ASE, CBOE, P

Business Profile - 22-APR-98

This casino entertainment company owns and operates the three largest casino resorts in the state of Mississippi. In recent years, GND has been successfully expanding its operations and amenities in Tunica, Mississippi. In 1996, GND opened Grand Casino Tunica which is the largest dockside casino in Mississippi. Thus far in 1998, GND has opened a 500-room luxury hotel at its Grand Casino Biloxi facility and the Cottonwoods Golf Club at Grand Casino Tunica. The company is currently developing a third hotel at Tunica, a 600-room property which is scheduled to open in the first quarter of 1999. The company recently announced that it plans to relocate its corporate headquarters from Minneapolis to the Mississippi Gulf Coast.

Operational Review - 22-APR-98

Net revenues for the three months ended March 31, 1998, increased 17%, year to year, reflecting GND's two Gulf Coast casinos generating nearly 10% higher revenues, the opening of a 500-room hotel at Grand Casino Biloxi and 37% higher revenues at Grand Casino Tunica. Profitability was helped by higher management fees, as all four of the company's managed properties benefited from expansions and new amenities that recently opened. Net income advanced 19%, to $17.4 million ($0.40 per share), from $14.6 million ($0.34).

Stock Performance - 02-OCT-98

In the past 30 trading days, GND's shares have declined 27%, compared to a 7% fall in the S&P 500. Average trading volume for the past five days was 166,740 shares, compared with the 40-day moving average of 155,838 shares.

Key Stock Statistics

Dividend Rate/Share	Nil	Shareholders	1,600
Shs. outstg. (M)	42.3	Market cap. (B)	$0.322
Avg. daily vol. (M)	0.142	Inst. holdings	54%
Tang. Bk. Value/Share	12.29		
Beta	1.78		

Value of $10,000 invested 5 years ago: $ 6,931

Fiscal Year Ending Dec. 31

	1998	1997	1996	1995	1994	1993
Revenues (Million $)						
1Q	165.5	142.2	103.8	81.09	66.80	0.70
2Q	162.3	150.8	113.0	93.98	76.18	24.40
3Q	—	167.6	146.7	102.2	76.39	49.30
4Q	—	146.8	126.5	95.56	66.42	42.60
Yr.	—	607.4	490.0	372.9	285.8	117.0

	1998	1997	1996	1995	1994	1993
Earnings Per Share ($)						
1Q	**0.40**	0.34	0.41	0.45	0.17	-0.07
2Q	**0.43**	0.43	0.45	0.52	0.23	0.17
3Q	—	0.51	0.08	0.61	0.29	0.32
4Q	—	**0.26**	-3.39	0.44	0.18	0.23
Yr.	—	**1.54**	-2.43	1.98	0.87	0.71

Next earnings report expected: late October

Dividend Data

A three-for-two stock split was effected in December 1995.

A Division of The McGraw-Hill Companies

Grand Casinos 1043M
NYSE Symbol **GND**
In S&P SmallCap 600

03-OCT-98

Industry: Gaming, Lottery & Parimutuel Cos.

Summary: This casino entertainment company develops, constructs and manages land-based and dockside casinos in emerging gaming markets.

Quantitative Evaluations

Outlook
(1 Lowest—5 Highest)
• **5**

Fair Value
• **21⅛**

Risk
• **High**

Earn./Div. Rank
• **NR**

Technical Eval.
• **Bearish** since 7/98

Rel. Strength Rank
(1 Lowest—99 Highest)
• **14**

Insider Activity
• **NA**

Recent Price • 7⅝
52 Wk Range • 19⅛-7⅛
Yield • Nil
12-Mo. P/E • 4.7

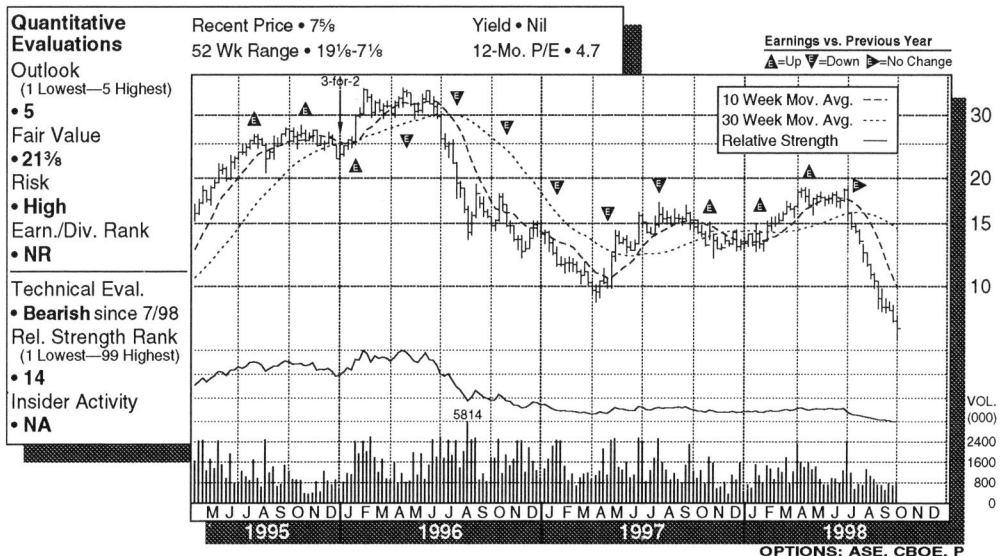

OPTIONS: ASE, CBOE, P

Business Profile - 22-APR-98

This casino entertainment company owns and operates the three largest casino resorts in the state of Mississippi. In recent years, GND has been successfully expanding its operations and amenities in Tunica, Mississippi. In 1996, GND opened Grand Casino Tunica which is the largest dockside casino in Mississippi. Thus far in 1998, GND has opened a 500-room luxury hotel at its Grand Casino Biloxi facility and the Cottonwoods Golf Club at Grand Casino Tunica. The company is currently developing a third hotel at Tunica, a 600-room property which is scheduled to open in the first quarter of 1999. The company recently announced that it plans to relocate its corporate headquarters from Minneapolis to the Mississippi Gulf Coast.

Operational Review - 22-APR-98

Net revenues for the three months ended March 31, 1998, increased 17%, year to year, reflecting GND's two Gulf Coast casinos generating nearly 10% higher revenues, the opening of a 500-room hotel at Grand Casino Biloxi and 37% higher revenues at Grand Casino Tunica. Profitability was helped by higher management fees, as all four of the company's managed properties benefited from expansions and new amenities that recently opened. Net income advanced 19%, to $17.4 million ($0.40 per share), from $14.6 million ($0.34).

Stock Performance - 02-OCT-98

In the past 30 trading days, GND's shares have declined 27%, compared to a 7% fall in the S&P 500. Average trading volume for the past five days was 166,740 shares, compared with the 40-day moving average of 155,838 shares.

Key Stock Statistics

Dividend Rate/Share	Nil	Shareholders	1,600
Shs. outstg. (M)	42.3	Market cap. (B)	$0.322
Avg. daily vol. (M)	0.142	Inst. holdings	54%
Tang. Bk. Value/Share	12.29		
Beta	1.78		

Value of $10,000 invested 5 years ago: $ 6,931

Fiscal Year Ending Dec. 31

	1998	1997	1996	1995	1994	1993
Revenues (Million $)						
1Q	165.5	142.2	103.8	81.09	66.80	0.70
2Q	162.3	150.8	113.0	93.98	76.18	24.40
3Q	—	167.6	146.7	102.2	76.39	49.30
4Q	—	146.8	126.5	95.56	66.42	42.60
Yr.	—	607.4	490.0	372.9	285.8	117.0
Earnings Per Share ($)						
1Q	**0.40**	0.34	0.41	0.45	0.17	-0.07
2Q	**0.43**	0.43	0.45	0.52	0.23	0.17
3Q	—	0.51	0.08	0.61	0.29	0.32
4Q	—	**0.26**	-3.39	0.44	0.18	0.23
Yr.	—	**1.54**	-2.43	1.98	0.87	0.71

Next earnings report expected: late October

Dividend Data

A three-for-two stock split was effected in December 1995.

A Division of The McGraw-Hill Companies

STANDARD
&POOR'S
STOCK REPORTS

Graco Inc.

1037
03-OCT-98

Business Summary - 30-SEP-98

Graco is a U.S.-based global producer of industrial and commercial pumps, valves, meters and related accessories. It also produces a line of portable painting and cleaning equipment. GGG's products are sold to the manufacturing, processing, construction and maintenance industries. Segment revenues and gross profit margins in recent years were derived as follows:

	1997	1996	1995
REVENUES			
Commercial & Industrial equipment	55%	53%	54%
Accessories & replacement parts	45%	47%	46%
GROSS PROFIT MARGINS			
Commercial & Industrial equipment	44%	45%	44%
Accessories & replacement parts	55%	56%	55%

In 1997, the Americas accounted for 67% of revenues and $87 million in operating profit (65% and $72 million in 1996), Europe 20% and $7 million (20% and $9 million) and Asia/Pacific 13% and $3 million (15% and $6 million).

Commercial and industrial equipment includes specialized pumps, air and airless spray units, manual finishing equipment and fluid-handling systems.

Replacement parts and accessories (aftermarket prod-

ucts) are sold for use with the company's equipment. Packings, seals and hoses for Graco pumps and related equipment must be replaced periodically to maintain efficiency and prevent loss of the material being handled. Graco offers its customers hoses, couplings, various flow regulators and valves, agitators, filters, meters, gauges and a variety of spray guns and tips. Typically, aftermarket products are more profitable than original equipment products. Over the last three years, sales of replacement parts and accessories have averaged 47% of total GGG revenues.

Primary applications of the company's products include product coating and finishing; mixing, metering, dispensing and applying adhesive, chemical bonding and sealant materials; professional cleaning and spray painting of architectural structures; lubrication and maintenance of vehicles and industrial machinery; and transferring and dispensing various fluids such as chemicals, inks, food and plastics.

Graco emphasizes research and development. In each of 1997, 1996 and 1995, the company spent about 4% of total revenues for R&D. One of GGG's stated financial goals is to generate 30% of annual sales from products introduced in the prior three years. To this end, Graco has substantially increased new product design, expanded its engineering staff, and doubled the size of the company's R&D center.

Per Share Data ($)

(Year Ended Dec. 31)	1997	1996	1995	1994	1993	1992	1991	1990	1989	1988
Tangible Bk. Val.	6.17	4.93	4.00	3.09	2.82	3.86	3.82	3.72	3.12	2.61
Cash Flow	2.22	1.86	1.49	0.99	0.72	0.74	0.67	1.04	0.89	0.85
Earnings	1.71	1.38	1.06	0.59	0.36	0.43	0.35	0.72	0.60	0.56
Dividends	0.39	0.33	0.27	1.46	0.32	0.27	0.20	0.18	0.16	0.15
Payout Ratio	23%	24%	25%	NM	87%	62%	58%	25%	27%	26%
Prices - High	26$\frac{1}{2}$	17$\frac{3}{8}$	17	11	10$\frac{3}{4}$	8$\frac{3}{4}$	9$\frac{1}{8}$	7$\frac{1}{2}$	6$\frac{1}{8}$	7
- Low	15$\frac{5}{8}$	11$\frac{7}{8}$	8$\frac{3}{4}$	7$\frac{1}{2}$	6$\frac{7}{8}$	6$\frac{7}{8}$	5$\frac{7}{8}$	4$\frac{5}{8}$	4$\frac{1}{2}$	4$\frac{1}{2}$
P/E Ratio - High	15	13	16	19	30	20	26	10	10	13
- Low	9	9	8	13	19	16	17	6	8	8

Income Statement Analysis (Million $)

	1997	1996	1995	1994	1993	1992	1991	1990	1989	1988
Revs.	414	392	386	360	323	320	312	321	298	268
Oper. Inc.	79.0	65.7	56.3	36.8	27.9	27.4	29.8	41.9	37.1	32.7
Depr.	13.5	12.6	11.0	10.4	9.3	7.9	8.0	7.7	7.0	6.8
Int. Exp.	0.9	0.8	2.3	1.9	2.3	2.7	3.7	3.5	4.5	4.2
Pretax Inc.	63.5	52.7	43.5	23.4	13.8	18.0	15.3	29.0	24.5	21.8
Eff. Tax Rate	30%	31%	37%	35%	31%	38%	42%	39%	41%	39%
Net Inc.	44.7	36.1	27.7	15.3	9.5	11.1	8.9	17.7	14.5	13.3

Balance Sheet & Other Fin. Data (Million $)

	1997	1996	1995	1994	1993	1992	1991	1990	1989	1988
Cash	13.5	6.5	1.6	2.4	37.4	38.2	24.0	6.0	4.5	2.0
Curr. Assets	156	144	128	144	147	162	150	151	133	124
Total Assets	255	219	219	228	216	220	206	209	182	172
Curr. Liab.	69.0	80.6	71.5	89.5	100	77.1	74.9	84.0	69.9	66.6
LT Debt	6.2	8.1	10.0	26.8	13.9	17.8	19.6	23.9	28.5	34.0
Common Eqty.	158	126	104	80.4	73.2	99	96.0	90.3	74.7	61.6
Total Cap.	164	134	114	109	89.0	118	119	117	108	103
Cap. Exp.	20.1	30.0	19.8	23.1	16.2	10.2	8.4	14.7	12.3	9.8
Cash Flow	58.2	48.8	38.8	25.7	18.7	19.0	16.9	25.4	21.5	20.1
Curr. Ratio	2.3	1.8	1.8	1.6	1.5	2.1	2.0	1.8	1.9	1.9
% LT Debt of Cap.	3.8	6.0	8.8	24.7	15.7	15.1	16.4	20.4	26.4	33.1
% Net Inc.of Revs.	10.8	9.2	7.2	4.3	2.9	3.5	2.9	5.5	4.9	5.0
% Ret. on Assets	17.5	15.4	12.4	6.9	4.3	5.2	4.2	9.0	8.1	8.2
% Ret. on Equity	25.7	31.5	NA	19.9	10.9	11.3	9.4	21.3	21.0	23.0

Data as orig. reptd.; bef. results of disc. opers. and/or spec. items. Per share data adj. for stk. divs. as of ex-div. date. Bold denotes diluted EPS (FASB 128). E-Estimated. NA-Not Available. NM-Not Meaningful. NR-Not Ranked.

Office—4050 Olson Memorial Highway, Golden Valley, MN 55422-2332. **Tel**—(612) 623-6000. **Website**—http://www.graco.com **Chrmn**—D. A. Koch. **CEO**—G. Aristides. **Pres & COO**—C. M. Osborne. **Treas**—M. W. Sheahan. **VP & Secy**—R. M. Mattison. **Investor Contact**—Mark Sheahan (612-623-6656). **Dirs**—G. Aristides, R. O. Baukol, D. A. Koch, R. D. McFarland, L. R. Mitau, M. Morfitt, D. R. Olseth, C. M. Osborne, J. L. Scott, W. G. Van Dyke. **Transfer Agent & Registrar**—Norwest Bank Minnesota, St. Paul. **Incorporated**—in Minnesota in 1947. **Empl**—2,100. **S&P Analyst:** John A. Massey

03-OCT-98

Industry: Electric Companies

Summary: This small electric utility provides service to about 83,000 customers in north central Vermont. Electric generation is primarily hydropower and nuclear.

Quantitative Evaluations

Recent Price • 11½
52 Wk Range • 20-11

Yield • 9.6%
12-Mo. P/E • 33.8

Outlook
(1 Lowest—5 Highest)
• **NA**

Fair Value
• **NA**

Risk
• **Low**

Earn./Div. Rank
• **B**

Technical Eval.
• **Neutral** since 5/98

Rel. Strength Rank
(1 Lowest—99 Highest)
• **56**

Insider Activity
• **Favorable**

Earnings vs. Previous Year
▲=Up ▼=Down ▷=No Change

10 Week Mov. Avg. - - -
30 Week Mov. Avg. - - - -
Relative Strength —

Business Profile - 19-JUN-98

This public utility is faced with the changing environment of the electric utility industry. Electrical utilities have historically been regulated exclusive franchises, but this is changing across the country. In April of 1997, the Vermont Senate passed a electric utility restructuring bill. The bill is to be considered by the House of Representatives in 1998, and if passed would implement retail competition for Vermont electrical utilities. This legislation has been opposed by the GMP, which sees major risk factors arising from this restructuring including its ability to recover costs, regulatory and legal decisions, the market price of power and the amount of market share retained by the company.

Operational Review - 19-JUN-98

Operating revenues in the three months ended March 31, 1998, decreased slightly, year to year, due to warmer weather. Power supply expenses increased 28.3% due to an increase in generation expenses incurred during a severe ice storm and a $4.6 million pretax expense relating to a long term Hydro-Quebec power contract following an adverse decision from the Vermont Public Service Board. Primarily due to the Hydro-Quebec pretax loss and a one time charge of $1.3 million relating to an investment in a wind facility, the net loss was $3,405,000 ($0.66 per share, after preferred dividends) compared to net income of $2,941,000 ($0.58). Cash dividends decreased to $0.275 per share versus $0.53.

Stock Performance - 02-OCT-98

In the past 30 trading days, GMP's shares have declined 10%, compared to a 7% fall in the S&P 500. Average trading volume for the past five days was 16,860 shares, compared with the 40-day moving average of 10,577 shares.

Key Stock Statistics

Dividend Rate/Share	1.10	Shareholders	6,500
Shs. outstg. (M)	5.2	Market cap. (B)	$0.060
Avg. daily vol. (M)	0.011	Inst. holdings	17%
Tang. Bk. Value/Share	21.01		
Beta	0.28		

Value of $10,000 invested 5 years ago: $ 5,452

Fiscal Year Ending Dec. 31

	1998	1997	1996	1995	1994	1993
Revenues (Million $)						
1Q	46.93	47.20	48.42	40.02	40.61	40.75
2Q	43.73	42.68	40.47	37.13	33.60	33.43
3Q	—	43.57	44.42	39.78	36.68	35.65
4Q	—	45.86	45.70	44.61	37.30	37.43
Yr.	—	179.3	179.0	161.5	148.2	147.3
Earnings Per Share ($)						
1Q	-0.66	0.58	0.80	0.65	0.85	0.93
2Q	0.18	0.17	0.17	0.38	0.23	0.17
3Q	—	0.59	0.67	0.60	0.54	0.41
4Q	—	0.23	0.58	0.63	0.61	0.69
Yr.	—	1.57	2.22	2.26	2.23	2.20

Next earnings report expected: mid November

Dividend Data (Dividends have been paid since 1951.)

Amount ($)	Date Decl.	Ex-Div. Date	Stock of Record	Payment Date
0.275	Dec. 08	Dec. 15	Dec. 17	Dec. 31 '97
0.275	Feb. 09	Mar. 13	Mar. 17	Mar. 31 '98
0.275	May. 20	Jun. 11	Jun. 15	Jun. 30 '98
0.275	Aug. 10	Sep. 11	Sep. 15	Sep. 30 '98

Business Summary - 22-APR-98

Grand Casinos is a casino entertainment company that develops, constructs and manages land-based and dockside casinos in emerging and established gaming markets. The company distinguishes its facilities with the inclusion of extensive non-gaming amenities, such as hotels, theaters, and recreational vehicle parks. GND owns and operates Grand Casino Biloxi and Grand Casino Gulfport, both located on the Mississippi Gulf Coast. In addition, the company also owns and operates Grand Casino Tunica, the largest dockside casino in Mississippi and one of the largest casinos in the U.S.

GND is continuing its development of Grand Casino Tunica into a themed destination resort. Tunica currently features two hotels offering a total of 766 rooms, six restaurants and a live entertainment lounge. Other amenities include a convention center, a Grand Casino Kids Quest child care facility, a Grand Arcade, and valet and self-parking for approximately 5,400 vehicles. Under construction are a 18-hole golf course and driving range as well as a convention center. Grand Casino Tunica offers a 400,000 sq. ft., three-story, multi-themed casino complex that contains about 140,000 sq. ft. of gaming space with approximately 3,000 slot machines and 108 gaming tables.

Grand Casino Gulfport is located in the Gulfport har-

bor. It is a three-story building set upon moored steel linked barges consisting of approximately 225,000 sq. ft. of interior space and 3,500 parking spaces available for guests. The casino consists of 110,000 sq. ft. of gaming space and features 2,100 slot machines and 97 table games.

Grand Casino Biloxi, located 15 miles east of Gulfport, is the largest dockside casino on the Mississippi Gulf Coast. Grand Casino Biloxi is a three-story building built upon a moored steel barge with about 250,000 sq. ft. of interior space and 3,500 parking spaces. The casino area includes approximately 115,000 sq. ft. of gaming space and features 2,300 slot machines and approximately 121 table games. GND opened a 400-room hotel at the Gulfport casino in late 1995, and later opened a 500-room hotel next to the Biloxi casino.

In addition to owning and operating casinos, GND also manages four casinos. Grand Casino Mille Lacs in Onamia, MI and Grand Casino Hinckley in Hinckley, MI are both managed on behalf of Indian gaming enterprises. However, the management contract for Grand Casinos Mille Lacs expires in April 1988 and will not be renewed. The company also manages two land-based, Indian-owned casinos in Louisiana: Grand Casino Avoyelles, in Marksville and Grand Casino Coushatta, in Kinder.

Per Share Data ($)

(Year Ended Dec. 31)	1997	1996	1995	1994	1993	1992	1991	1990	1989	1988
Tangible Bk. Val.	11.36	9.97	12.33	7.90	7.42	2.47	0.35	NA	NA	NA
Cash Flow	2.69	-1.33	2.65	1.39	0.87	0.19	0.14	NA	NA	NA
Earnings	1.54	-2.43	1.98	0.87	0.71	0.19	0.15	NA	NA	NA
Dividends	Nil	Nil	Nil	Nil	Nil	Nil	Nil	Nil	Nil	Nil
Payout Ratio	Nil	Nil	Nil	Nil	Nil	Nil	Nil	Nil	Nil	Nil
Prices - High	17¹/₈	35³/₄	28¹/₈	21⁷/₈	34⁵/₈	14⁵/₈	5⁷/₈	NA	NA	NA
- Low	9	12	9¹/₈	8	10¹/₂	4³/₄	3	NA	NA	NA
P/E Ratio - High	11	NM	14	25	49	78	40	NA	NA	NA
- Low	6	NM	5	9	15	25	20	NA	NA	NA

Income Statement Analysis (Million $)

	1997	1996	1995	1994	1993	1992	1991	1990	1989	1988
Revs.	607	490	373	286	117	7.0	2.0	NA	NA	NA
Oper. Inc.	187	143	140	69.3	33.7	3.9	2.0	NA	NA	NA
Depr.	49.5	45.5	24.0	17.5	4.4	0.1	Nil	Nil	Nil	Nil
Int. Exp.	42.8	32.7	26.2	14.1	10.6	0.1	Nil	Nil	Nil	Nil
Pretax Inc.	107	-83.2	111	44.5	28.3	4.7	2.1	NA	NA	NA
Eff. Tax Rate	38%	NM	39%	35%	34%	28%	Nil	Nil	Nil	Nil
Net Inc.	66.2	-100	70.1	29.0	18.8	3.3	2.1	NA	NA	NA

Balance Sheet & Other Fin. Data (Million $)

	1997	1996	1995	1994	1993	1992	1991	1990	1989	1988
Cash	244	147	335	30.0	158	30.0	1.0	NA	NA	NA
Curr. Assets	290	194	380	66.0	183	39.0	2.0	NA	NA	NA
Total Assets	1,334	1,123	1,128	484	427	58.0	5.0	NA	NA	NA
Curr. Liab.	168	100	55.0	56.3	47.3	3.2	0.5	NA	NA	NA
LT Debt	566	455	459	123	119	Nil	Nil	Nil	Nil	Nil
Common Eqty.	503	440	526	277	248	54.0	4.0	NA	NA	NA
Total Cap.	1,167	966	1,060	428	367	55.0	4.0	NA	NA	NA
Cap. Exp.	163	309	186	89.0	210	10.0	Nil	Nil	Nil	Nil
Cash Flow	116	-55.4	94.0	46.5	23.2	3.5	2.1	NA	NA	NA
Curr. Ratio	1.7	1.9	6.9	1.2	3.9	12.2	4.4	NA	NA	NA
% LT Debt of Cap.	48.5	10.3	43.3	28.8	32.3	0.5	Nil	Nil	Nil	Nil
% Net Inc.of Revs.	10.1	NM	18.8	10.1	16.0	47.1	85.8	NA	NA	NA
% Ret. on Assets	5.4	NM	8.7	6.4	7.3	10.0	NA	NA	NA	NA
% Ret. on Equity	14.0	NM	17.5	11.0	11.3	10.8	NA	NA	NA	NA

Data as orig. reptd.; bef. results of disc. opers. and/or spec. items. Per share data adj. for stk. divs. as of ex-div. date. Bold denotes diluted EPS (FASB 128). E-Estimated. NA-Not Available. NM-Not Meaningful. NR-Not Ranked.

Office—130 Cheshire Lane, Minnetonka, Minneapolis, MN 55305. **Tel**—(612) 449-9092. **Website**—http://www.grandcasinos.com **Chrmn**—L. Berman. **Pres & CEO**—T. J. Brosig. **EVP & CFO**—T. J. Cope. **Investor Contact**—Lawrence Taylor. **Dirs**—L. Berman, T. J. Brosig, T. J. Cope, M. Goldfarb, R. J. Kramer, D. L. Rogers, N. I. Sell, J. Waller. **Transfer Agent & Registrar**—Norwest Bank Minnesota, South St. Paul. **Incorporated**—in Minnesota in 1991. **Empl**— 7,300. **S&P Analyst:** Robert J. Izmirlian

Business Summary - 19-JUN-98

Green Mountain Power is an investor-owned, independent energy services company serving one fourth of the population of Vermont totaling approximately 83,000 customers. In 1997 the company's sources of revenue were as follows: 34% from residential customers; 54% from commercial and industrial accounts; and 12% from utilities and other sources.

In September 1997, the company said it would reduce its common stock dividend by 50%, as a result of three years of flat earnings growth, and lower forecasted earnings for 1997 and 1998, due to warmer weather, higher power costs, and losses from nonregulated energy businesses. Improvement to GMP's finances is contingent on stable nuclear operations at the Vermont Yankee unit (17.3% equity interest; supplies about 28% of GMP's electric power), and rate relief to recover increased power costs. In June 1997, the company filed a request for a 16.7% rate increase with the Vermont Public Service Board (VPSB). On March 2, 1998, the VPSB authorized a 3.6% rate increase which the company indicates will increase annual revenues by $5.6 million.

GMP has a 30% interest in Vermont Electric Power Co. (VELCO), which owns nearly all the transmission network serving Vermont and interconnects with the New England transmission system. The company's unregulated businesses include: Green Mountain Propane Gas, Mountain Energy, and a water heater leasing unit.

A major GMP financial investment has been its 33% interest in a new retail energy marketing business, Green Mountain Energy Resources. Along with the Wyly family of Texas, the company announced in August 1997 that GMER would compete in the emerging consumer retail energy market, starting in California where customers will begin choosing their electricity supplier as early as November 1997.

In 1997, the Vermont Senate passed legislation to allow competitive retail sales of electricity in the state. The House, which must also approve the bill, is scheduled to review the legislation during the 1998 session. The company has opposed this legislation and sees major risk factors arising from this restructuring including its ability to recover costs, regulatory and legal decisions, the market price of power and the amount of market share retained by the company.

Per Share Data ($)

(Year Ended Dec. 31)	1997	1996	1995	1994	1993	1992	1991	1990	1989	1988
Tangible Bk. Val.	21.68	21.71	21.48	21.01	20.65	20.15	19.38	19.10	18.79	18.39
Earnings	1.57	2.22	2.26	2.23	2.20	2.54	2.45	2.29	2.36	2.41
Dividends	1.61	2.12	2.12	2.12	2.11	2.08	2.04	2.00	1.95	1.89
Payout Ratio	103%	95%	94%	95%	96%	82%	83%	87%	83%	78%
Prices - High	26¼	29⅛	28⅝	31¼	36⅝	33⅝	30¼	27⅛	27⅞	26¾
- Low	17½	22¾	23⅞	23⅜	30¾	29	22	21¼	22⅛	22
P/E Ratio - High	17	14	13	14	17	13	12	12	12	11
- Low	11	11	11	10	14	11	9	9	9	9

Income Statement Analysis (Million $)

Revs.	179	179	162	148	147	145	144	148	144	129
Depr.	16.3	16.3	14.1	10.7	8.6	8.1	7.0	6.8	5.9	5.4
Maint.	4.9	4.5	4.2	4.5	4.3	4.7	4.3	4.4	4.8	5.5
Fxd. Chgs. Cov.	2.5	2.6	2.6	3.0	3.1	3.3	3.0	2.9	3.4	3.7
Constr. Credits	0.7	0.6	0.6	0.8	0.6	0.4	0.4	0.5	0.5	0.2
Eff. Tax Rate	43%	27%	25%	33%	29%	29%	29%	28%	28%	24%
Net Inc.	9.4	12.0	11.5	11.0	10.6	11.8	10.5	9.0	9.0	9.2

Balance Sheet & Other Fin. Data (Million $)

Gross Prop.	284	271	258	245	236	223	215	204	179	160
Cap. Exp.	16.4	17.5	15.3	13.5	15.9	15.3	14.8	14.3	20.2	14.2
Net Prop.	197	190	182	176	171	165	160	152	132	118
Capitalization:										
LT Debt	102	104	101	85.2	90.8	79.6	68.9	73.4	57.0	41.6
% LT Debt	44	44	47	44	46	44	42	47	44	37
Pfd.	17.7	19.3	8.9	9.1	9.4	9.6	9.8	10.1	3.4	3.7
% Pfd.	7.60	8.20	4.10	4.70	4.80	5.30	5.90	6.50	2.60	3.20
Common	114	112	106	101	97.1	92.6	87.5	71.9	69.5	67.9
% Common	49	48	49	52	49	51	53	46	54	60
Total Cap.	261	266	246	223	224	203	185	173	145	128
% Oper. Ratio	90.9	91.0	90.6	90.2	89.9	88.7	89.9	90.7	91.5	91.4
% Earn. on Net Prop.	8.0	8.7	8.6	8.4	8.8	10.1	9.3	9.6	9.8	9.7
% Return On Revs.	5.3	6.7	7.1	7.4	7.2	8.2	7.3	6.1	6.3	7.2
% Return On Invest. Capital	6.5	7.5	3.4	8.1	8.2	9.6	9.7	9.9	10.6	10.7
% Return On Com. Equity	7.1	10.0	10.4	10.3	10.3	12.2	12.5	12.0	12.5	13.0

Data as orig. reptd.; bef. results of disc opers. and/or spec. items. Per share data adj. for stk. divs. as of ex-div. date. Bold denotes diluted EPS (FASB 128). E-Estimated. NA-Not Available. NM-Not Meaningful. NR-Not Ranked.

Office—25 Green Mountain Dr., South Burlington, VT 05403. **Tel**—(802) 864-5731. **Pres & CEO**—C. L. Dutton. **EVP & COO**—A. N. Terreri. **Secy**—D. S. Laffan. **VP, CFO & Treas**—E. M. Norse. **Investor Contact**—Bonnie W. Fairbanks. **Dirs**—T. P. Salmon (Chrmn), N. L. Brue, W. B. Bruett, M. O. Burns, L. E. Chickering, J. V. Cleary, R. I. Fricke, D. G. Hyde, E. A. Irving, M. L. Johnson, R. W. Page. **Transfer Agent & Registrar**—ChaseMellon Shareholder Services, Ridgefield Park, NJ. **Incorporated**—in Vermont in 1893. **Empl**— 321. **S&P Analyst:** John J. Arege

Griffon Corporation

1064G

NYSE Symbol **GFF**

In S&P SmallCap 600

03-OCT-98

Industry: Manufacturing (Diversified)

Summary: Griffon is a diversified manufacturer of building products, electronic information and communication systems and specialty plastic films.

Quantitative Evaluations

Outlook
(1 Lowest—5 Highest)
• **NA**

Fair Value
• **NA**

Risk
• **Average**

Earn./Div. Rank
• **B**

Technical Eval.
• **Bearish** since 4/98

Rel. Strength Rank
(1 Lowest—99 Highest)
• **37**

Insider Activity
• **NA**

Recent Price • 8½
52 Wk Range • 17½-7⅞

Yield • Nil
12-Mo. P/E • 8.7

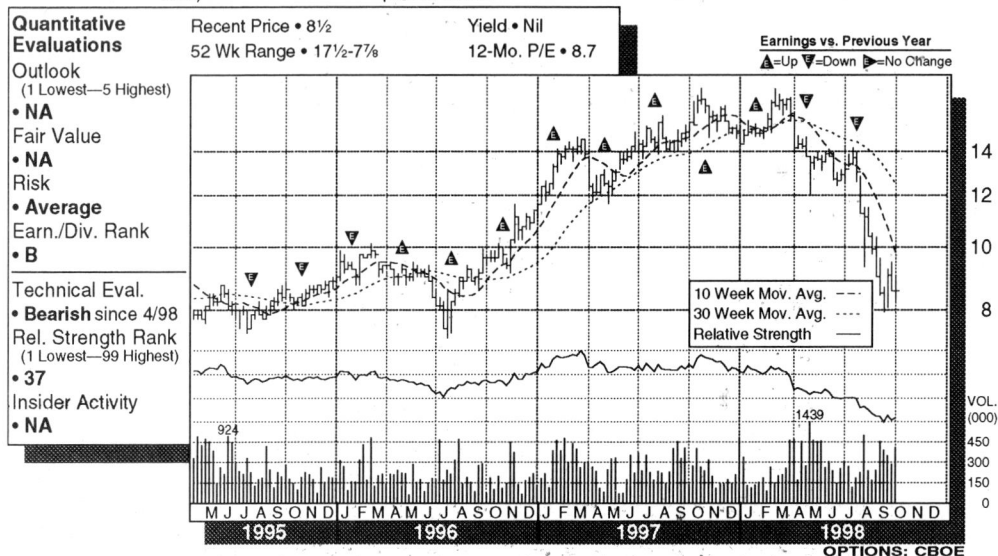

Earnings vs. Previous Year
▲=Up ▼=Down ▶=No Change

10 Week Mov. Avg. - - -
30 Week Mov. Avg. ••••
Relative Strength —

OPTIONS: CBOE

Business Profile - 18-SEP-98

Despite strong demand in the garage door business, near-term capacity constraints and continued pricing pressures have hurt results at the building products unit. Recent acquisitions have resulted in an increased number of production facilities, putting pressure on margins in this segment. In response, the company is currently reviewing its manufacturing structure, with a view toward consolidation of certain operations. Sales decreases and pricing competition also affected the specialty plastic films unit, although anticipated volume growth, plus the benefit of a recent acquisition, are expected to lead to improved operating results. In July 1998, GFF purchased a German manufacturer of plastic packaging and specialty films, with annual sales of approximately $35 million.

Operational Review - 18-SEP-98

Net sales in the nine months ended June 30, 1998, rose 23%, year to year, as acquisitions in building products business outweighed a sales decrease in specialty plastic films division. Profitability weakened, on competitive pricing pressures in both business lines, and production and manufacturing inefficiencies in the building products division; operating income fell 1.5%. With a significant rise in depreciation and amortization, net interest expense, and other expense, pretax income was down 13%. After taxes at 37.0%, versus 37.7%, net income decreased 12%, to $18,386,000 ($0.59 a share), from $20,785,000 ($0.67).

Stock Performance - 02-OCT-98

In the past 30 trading days, GFF's shares have declined 14%, compared to a 7% fall in the S&P 500. Average trading volume for the past five days was 81,280 shares, compared with the 40-day moving average of 65,115 shares.

Key Stock Statistics

Dividend Rate/Share	Nil	Shareholders	16,000
Shs. outstg. (M)	31.0	Market cap. (B)	$0.265
Avg. daily vol. (M)	0.074	Inst. holdings	75%
Tang. Bk. Value/Share	5.41		
Beta	0.93		

Value of $10,000 invested 5 years ago: $ 13,978

Fiscal Year Ending Sep. 30

	1998	1997	1996	1995	1994	1993
Revenues (Million $)						
1Q	229.0	181.7	153.4	133.6	116.2	104.0
2Q	199.9	160.8	139.1	120.2	105.9	94.73
3Q	229.4	193.1	168.9	135.2	125.3	108.2
4Q	—	234.6	193.7	157.4	141.7	130.5
Yr.	—	770.2	655.1	546.4	489.0	436.9
Earnings Per Share ($)						
1Q	**0.27**	0.24	0.18	0.22	0.18	0.15
2Q	**0.10**	0.14	0.12	0.10	0.13	0.13
3Q	**0.22**	0.29	0.25	0.15	0.20	0.18
4Q	—	0.40	0.34	0.24	0.29	0.25
Yr.	—	1.06	0.88	0.71	0.80	0.70

Next earnings report expected: early November

Dividend Data

No dividends have been paid on the common stock. A poison pill stock purchase rights plan was adopted in 1986.

A Division of The **McGraw·Hill** Companies

STANDARD
&POOR'S
STOCK REPORTS

Griffon Corporation

1064G
03-OCT-98

Business Summary - 18-SEP-98

In 1995, this company (formerly Instrument Systems Corp.) adopted the name Griffon Corp., after the composite beast of mythology (half eagle and half lion), to symbolize the combined strength of its diverse operations. No longer primarily a manufacturer of electronic information and communication systems, Griffon (GFF) is also a leading provider of building products and specialty plastic films.

GFF's building products unit, Clopay, accounted for 62% of FY 97 (Sep.). Clopay is one of the largest manufacturers of residential and industrial garage doors in the U.S. Clopay is focusing on increasing its market share by introducing new products, expanding its distribution, sales and marketing programs and through strategic acquisitions. In July 1997, the company acquired for $35 million in cash Holmes-Hally Industries, a major West Coast manufacturer and installer of residential garage doors and related hardware, with annual sales of about $80 million. Acquisitions completed in FY 95 and FY 96 contributed abouty $80 million to FY 97 revenues. AcquClopay also operates a service company that installs and services garage doors and openers, fireplaces and a range of related products.

Through its electronics information and communication systems unit (17% of FY 97 sales), GFF manufactures a variety of electronic systems used in commercial and government markets worldwide. The division, known as Telephonics, also provides audio and communication systems for use on aircraft and trains and produces custom large-scale integrated circuits. A substantial portion of the unit's FY 97 sales (50%) were to U.S. government agencies. Telephonics is increasing its emphasis on non-military markets such as transit and air traffic control. At September 30, 1997, the unit's backlog was $182 million (up from $78 million a year earlier), of which 36% was expected to be shipped in FY 98.

GFF is a leader in the development of specialty plastic films (21% of FY 97 sales) used in the disposable diaper, adult incontinence, feminine napkin and healthcare markets. Its strategy is to offer technologically advanced products for use in niche markets to major consumer and healthcare product companies. A substantial portion of the unit's sales over the past five years has been to Procter & Gamble Co.

In February 1997, GFF approved the redemption of its second preferred stock at $10.17 a share. On the March 10 redemption date, holders of the preferred stock converted their shares into 1,524,429 common shares, while 45,165 preferred shares were redeemed.

Per Share Data ($)

(Year Ended Sep. 30)	1997	1996	1995	1994	1993	1992	1991	1990	1989	1988
Tangible Bk. Val.	5.41	5.18	4.33	4.17	3.56	3.06	1.52	0.90	0.31	0.80
Cash Flow	1.43	1.19	0.97	1.06	0.95	0.97	0.88	0.65	0.38	0.20
Earnings	1.06	0.88	0.71	0.80	0.70	0.66	0.51	0.32	0.13	-0.02
Dividends	Nil	Nil	Nil	Nil	Nil	Nil	Nil	Nil	Nil	Nil
Payout Ratio	Nil	Nil	Nil	Nil	Nil	Nil	Nil	Nil	Nil	Nil
Prices - High	17$\frac{1}{2}$	12$\frac{1}{4}$	9$\frac{1}{2}$	9$\frac{3}{4}$	9$\frac{1}{8}$	8$\frac{1}{4}$	6$\frac{3}{8}$	2$\frac{3}{8}$	2	1$\frac{3}{4}$
- Low	11$\frac{5}{8}$	7$\frac{1}{4}$	7$\frac{3}{8}$	6$\frac{5}{8}$	6	4$\frac{1}{8}$	1$\frac{3}{8}$	1$\frac{1}{4}$	1	$\frac{7}{8}$
P/E Ratio - High	17	14	13	12	13	13	13	7	15	NM
- Low	11	8	10	8	9	6	3	4	8	NM

Income Statement Analysis (Million $)

	1997	1996	1995	1994	1993	1992	1991	1990	1989	1988
Revs.	770	655	546	489	437	500	494	459	405	381
Oper. Inc.	65.9	57.8	48.3	59.7	53.7	58.1	50.1	42.6	31.7	23.5
Depr.	11.5	10.3	8.7	9.8	9.5	11.1	11.2	9.8	7.3	7.0
Int. Exp.	3.5	3.4	2.2	1.8	1.9	7.0	13.5	14.8	14.3	5.7
Pretax Inc.	53.0	45.9	39.0	50.3	44.3	42.9	28.8	21.5	10.7	12.0
Eff. Tax Rate	37%	39%	39%	41%	40%	40%	40%	42%	43%	49%
Net Inc.	33.2	28.1	23.8	29.7	26.6	24.1	15.4	9.5	4.8	6.1

Balance Sheet & Other Fin. Data (Million $)

	1997	1996	1995	1994	1993	1992	1991	1990	1989	1988
Cash	15.4	22.1	21.9	58.4	37.6	24.4	23.5	27.5	33.4	14.9
Curr. Assets	264	229	212	223	200	152	202	193	185	147
Total Assets	385	311	286	293	270	247	304	295	271	223
Curr. Liab.	129	106	97.8	102	82.8	74.0	78.1	79.4	71.6	66.9
LT Debt	53.9	32.5	16.2	16.0	25.0	25.0	105	119	123	29.0
Common Eqty.	202	172	155	159	145	128	66.0	49.0	33.0	48.0
Total Cap.	256	205	188	192	186	170	224	214	198	154
Cap. Exp.	25.8	9.4	8.1	9.2	8.4	13.4	15.2	19.5	25.4	4.6
Cash Flow	44.6	37.9	32.5	39.5	36.0	35.1	26.6	19.3	11.2	6.0
Curr. Ratio	2.0	2.2	2.2	2.2	2.4	2.1	2.6	2.4	2.6	2.2
% LT Debt of Cap.	21.1	15.8	8.6	8.1	13.2	14.9	47.1	55.6	62.3	18.6
% Net Inc.of Revs.	4.3	4.3	4.4	6.1	6.1	4.8	3.1	2.1	1.2	1.6
% Ret. on Assets	9.5	9.8	8.2	10.8	10.3	7.7	5.1	3.3	1.9	2.9
% Ret. on Equity	17.7	16.1	15.1	20.0	19.5	22.9	26.7	23.2	9.7	NM

Data as orig. reptd.; bef. results of disc. opers. and/or spec. items. Per share data adj. for stk. divs. as of ex-div. date. Bold denotes diluted EPS (FASB 128). E-Estimated. NA-Not Available. NM-Not Meaningful. NR-Not Ranked.

Office—100 Jericho Quadrangle, Jericho, NY 11753. **Reincorporated**—in Delaware in 1970. **Tel**—(516) 938-5544. **Website**—http://www.telephonics.com **Chrmn & CEO**—H. R. Blau. **Pres & CFO**—R. Balemian. **Secy**—S. E. Rowland. **VP, Treas & Investor Contact**—Patrick L. Alesia. **Dirs**—H.A. Alpert, R. Balemian, B. M. Bell, H. R. Blau, R. Bradley, A. M. Buchman, C. A. Hill Jr., R. J. Kramer, J. W. Stansberry, M. S. Sussman, W. H. Waldorf, L. L. Wolff. **Transfer Agent & Registrar**—American Stock Transfer & Trust Co., NYC. **Empl**— 5,000. **S&P Analyst**: Jordan Horoschak

03-OCT-98 | Industry: Textiles (Specialty)

Summary: Guilford is a leading producer of warp knit fabrics used to manufacture apparel, automobile interiors and home furnishings.

Quantitative Evaluations

Outlook (1 Lowest—5 Highest)
• **4⁻**

Fair Value
• **21**

Risk
• **Low**

Earn./Div. Rank
• **B+**

Technical Eval.
• **Neutral** since 6/98

Rel. Strength Rank (1 Lowest—99 Highest)
• **44**

Insider Activity
• **NA**

Recent Price • 14⅞
52 Wk Range • 29⅝-13¾

Yield • 3.0%
12-Mo. P/E • 7.8

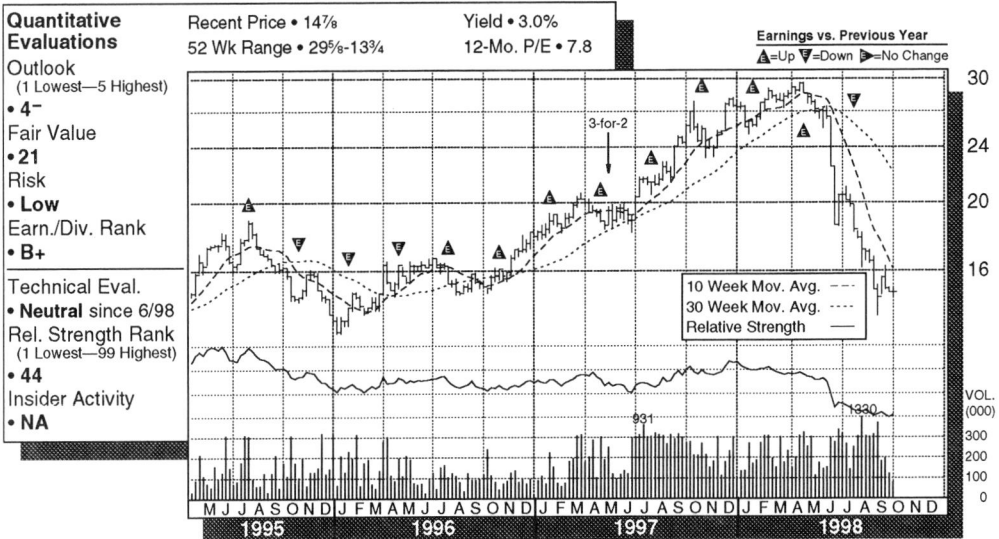

Earnings vs. Previous Year
▲=Up ▼=Down ▶=No Change

10 Week Mov. Avg. ---
30 Week Mov. Avg. ·····
Relative Strength

Business Profile - 04-AUG-98

This company is a major producer of value-added fabrics used for apparel, home furnishings, automotive and industrial applications. Known as one of the major innovators in the textile industry, Guilford, which is the world's largest warp knitter, has excelled in creating highly specialized apparel fabrics. In addition, the company's automotive fabric division is a market leader. In fiscal 1998's third quarter, GFD's results were hurt by softness in apparel and specialty fabric sales, including an adverse impact on apparel fabric sales from lower-priced Asian goods. Also, in June 1998, GFD said that its directors had authorized the repurchase of up 2.5 million common shares (close to 10% of the amount outstanding).

Operational Review - 04-AUG-98

Net sales for the nine months ended June 28, 1998, were up 0.9%, year to year, as increases of 22% in home fashion products and 4% in automotive fabrics more than offset a decline of about 27% in sales to what GFD calls the industrial/specialty markets, and a decline of about 3% to the apparel market. Net income was up 8.3%, to $29.7 million, from $27.4 million, and diluted earning per share were $1.15 in both periods. However, net income was down 15% in FY 98's third quarter, following a 35% rise in the first half of FY 98.

Stock Performance - 02-OCT-98

In the past 30 trading days, GFD's shares have declined 10%, compared to a 7% fall in the S&P 500. Average trading volume for the past five days was 15,320 shares, compared with the 40-day moving average of 70,382 shares.

Key Stock Statistics

Dividend Rate/Share	0.44	Shareholders	500
Shs. outstg. (M)	25.7	Market cap. (B)	$0.382
Avg. daily vol. (M)	0.036	Inst. holdings	63%
Tang. Bk. Value/Share	16.58		
Beta	0.65		

Value of $10,000 invested 5 years ago: $ 10,171

Fiscal Year Ending Sep. 30

	1998	1997	1996	1995	1994	1993
Revenues (Million $)						
1Q	213.4	210.9	174.2	182.0	158.0	157.0
2Q	228.4	219.1	207.1	202.0	156.0	153.0
3Q	232.8	238.4	232.2	210.8	183.0	192.0
4Q	—	226.3	216.8	187.4	207.0	141.0
Yr.	—	894.7	830.3	782.5	704.0	643.0

	1998	1997	1996	1995	1994	1993
Earnings Per Share ($)						
1Q	**0.30**	0.25	0.13	0.29	0.19	0.25
2Q	**0.37**	0.34	0.27	0.45	0.19	0.30
3Q	**0.48**	0.66	0.58	0.53	0.43	0.52
4Q	—	0.66	0.60	0.33	0.41	-0.05
Yr.	—	1.91	1.59	1.61	1.21	--

Next earnings report expected: mid November

Dividend Data (Dividends have been paid since 1973.)

Amount ($)	Date Decl.	Ex-Div. Date	Stock of Record	Payment Date
0.110	Nov. 13	Nov. 20	Nov. 24	Dec. 08 '97
0.110	Jan. 20	Jan. 28	Jan. 30	Feb. 10 '98
0.110	Apr. 20	Apr. 28	Apr. 30	May. 12 '98
0.110	Jul. 20	Jul. 28	Jul. 30	Aug. 11 '98

Business Summary - 04-AUG-98

In 1946, the year that James M. Hornaday founded Guilford Mills (GFD) with two warp knitting machines in the warehouse of his Hornaday Feed and Seed Store in Greensboro, NC, the company racked up sales of $90,000. Five decades later, in FY 97 (Sep.), its sales had reached a record $895 million. This astounding growth was achieved by a combination of internal expansion and acquisitions that led the company into various areas of the warp knitting business. GFD knits synthetic yarn, primarily nylon, acetate and polyester, on warp knitting machinery into warp knit fabrics, which it then dyes and finishes. Finished fabrics are sold to customers for use in a broad range of apparel, automotive, industrial and home fashions products. The company also designs, knits, dyes, prints and finishes elastomeric and circular knit fabrics for sale primarily to swimwear, dress and sportswear manufacturers. In addition, GFD has introduced woven velour fabric capabilities in its expanding automotive business.

In January 1996, the company acquired Hoffman Laces, Ltd., Raschel Fashion Interknitting, Ltd. and Curtains and Fabrics, Inc., makers of knitted lace fabrics for the apparel, intimate apparel and home furnishings market. The purchase price consisted of $22 million in cash, 300,000 (adjusted) common shares, and a contingent payment, payable in cash or shares, or a combination of cash and shares, based on a formula, for a five-year period ending December 31, 2000.

International sales accounted for 21% of sales in FY 97, up from 20% in FY 96.

Contributions to sales in recent fiscal years were:

	FY 97	FY 96	FY 95
Apparel	39%	41%	45%
Automotive	37%	41%	43%
Home fashions	15%	12%	7%
Other	9%	7%	6%

In late 1997, GFD had 27 manufacturing and/or warehousing facilities in the U.S., plus seven such facilities in England or Mexico. Some of GFD's facilities are leased.

GFD's research and development department works closely with customers to develop patterns and create new fabrics and styles. Expenditures for research and development totaled $14.9 million in FY 97, compared to $14.5 million in FY 96, and $13.4 million in FY 95.

The company owns 95% (increased from 75% in mid-1997) of the outstanding stock of Grupo Ambar, S.A. de C.V., a leading manufacturer of knit textile fabrics in Mexico, and 100% of Guilford Europe in the U.K. Also, GFD was operating 12 retail stores in the U.S. or Mexico.

Per Share Data ($)

(Year Ended Sep. 30)	1997	1996	1995	1994	1993	1992	1991	1990	1989	1988
Tangible Bk. Val.	15.88	14.57	12.64	11.63	10.59	10.05	8.85	8.75	9.41	8.69
Cash Flow	4.54	4.18	3.83	3.12	2.74	2.56	1.99	0.89	2.21	2.03
Earnings	1.91	1.59	1.61	1.21	1.41	1.23	0.68	-0.38	1.19	1.17
Dividends	0.42	0.40	0.40	0.40	0.40	0.38	0.36	0.36	0.36	0.36
Payout Ratio	22%	25%	25%	33%	28%	31%	53%	NM	30%	29%
Prices - High	28¼	18⅛	18⅞	16⅛	18⅝	19	14⅞	11¼	15¼	13
- Low	17¾	13	13⅜	12⅜	12⅝	11⅞	7⅝	6⅛	10⅜	10⅝
P/E Ratio - High	15	11	12	13	13	15	22	NM	13	11
- Low	9	8	8	10	9	10	11	NM	9	9

Income Statement Analysis (Million $)

	1997	1996	1995	1994	1993	1992	1991	1990	1989	1988
Revs.	895	830	783	704	654	615	529	544	620	578
Oper. Inc.	146	127	115	91.2	79.8	76.2	56.8	57.1	69.0	66.0
Depr.	59.6	55.4	46.7	39.3	27.4	26.8	26.4	26.9	22.8	19.6
Int. Exp.	16.2	17.0	14.1	12.4	8.2	7.0	8.4	8.4	8.6	9.1
Pretax Inc.	65.8	50.9	50.2	38.9	43.9	34.1	20.1	-15.5	41.7	41.5
Eff. Tax Rate	34%	33%	33%	35%	34%	27%	32%	NM	37%	36%
Net Inc.	43.2	34.0	33.6	25.1	28.9	24.9	13.6	-8.0	26.3	26.7

Balance Sheet & Other Fin. Data (Million $)

	1997	1996	1995	1994	1993	1992	1991	1990	1989	1988
Cash	24.3	31.0	18.0	6.1	17.9	15.9	14.3	25.4	40.2	29.9
Curr. Assets	349	352	286	264	249	227	204	227	255	247
Total Assets	730	729	586	565	507	414	375	390	410	379
Curr. Liab.	135	174	108	111	96.6	87.5	80.0	88.9	76.8	63.2
LT Debt	135	209	166	165	147	77.0	80.0	92.0	96.0	100
Common Eqty.	409	298	268	244	220	206	178	176	208	192
Total Cap.	566	530	454	429	386	301	278	287	319	303
Cap. Exp.	57.6	65.0	58.0	48.0	102	35.8	26.6	31.3	46.6	39.2
Cash Flow	103	89.4	80.3	64.5	56.2	51.7	39.9	18.9	49.1	46.3
Curr. Ratio	2.6	2.0	2.7	2.4	2.6	2.6	2.6	2.6	3.3	3.9
% LT Debt of Cap.	23.9	39.5	36.7	38.4	38.2	25.5	28.8	32.1	30.1	33.1
% Net Inc.of Revs.	4.8	4.1	4.3	3.6	4.4	4.0	2.6	NM	4.2	4.6
% Ret. on Assets	5.9	5.2	5.8	4.7	6.2	6.2	3.5	NM	6.7	7.3
% Ret. on Equity	12.1	12.1	13.1	10.8	13.5	12.8	7.7	NM	13.2	14.5

Data as orig. reptd.; bef. results of disc. opers. and/or spec. items. Co. changed its fiscal yr. end to Sep. 30 from Jun. 30 in fiscal 1994. Per share data adj. for stk. divs. as of ex-div. date. Bold denotes diluted EPS (FASB 128). E-Estimated. NA-Not Available. NM-Not Meaningful. NR-Not Ranked.

Reincorporated—in Delaware in 1971.**Office**—4925 W. Market St., Greensboro, NC 27407. **Tel**—(910) 316-4000. **Website**—http://www.guilfordmills.com.**Chrmn & CEO**—C. A. Hayes. **Pres & COO**—J. Emrich. **EVP & CFO**—T. E. Geremski. **Treas**—M. E. Cook. **Investor Contact**—Jaime Vasquez.**Dirs**—T. Adachi, D. B. Dixon, J. Emrich, M. Fishman, T. E. Geremski, P. G. Gillease, G. Greenberg, S. C. Hassenfelt, C. A. Hayes, B. Hofmann, S. R. Jacobs, S. R. Kry, G. M. Wilson, J. Zaidenweber. **Transfer Agent & Registrar**—Wachovia Bank of North Carolina, Winston-Salem. **Empl**— 6,571. **S&P Analyst:** Tom Graves, CFA

Gymboree Corp.

4059

Nasdaq Symbol **GYMB**

In S&P SmallCap 600

03-OCT-98 **Industry:** Retail (Specialty)

Summary: This company sells apparel and accessories for children ages newborn to seven, and operates and franchises directed parent-child developmental play programs.

S&P Opinion: Avoid (★★)	Recent Price • 7½ Yield • Nil 52 Wk Range • 30⅞-7⅛ 12-Mo. P/E • 7.4

Quantitative Evaluations

Outlook
(1 Lowest—5 Highest)
• **5+**

Fair Value
• **18⅜**

Risk
• **High**

Earn./Div. Rank
• **B**

Technical Eval.
• **Bullish** since 3/98

Rel. Strength Rank
(1 Lowest—99 Highest)
• **17**

Insider Activity
• **NA**

Earnings vs. Previous Year
▲=Up ▼=Down ▶=No Change

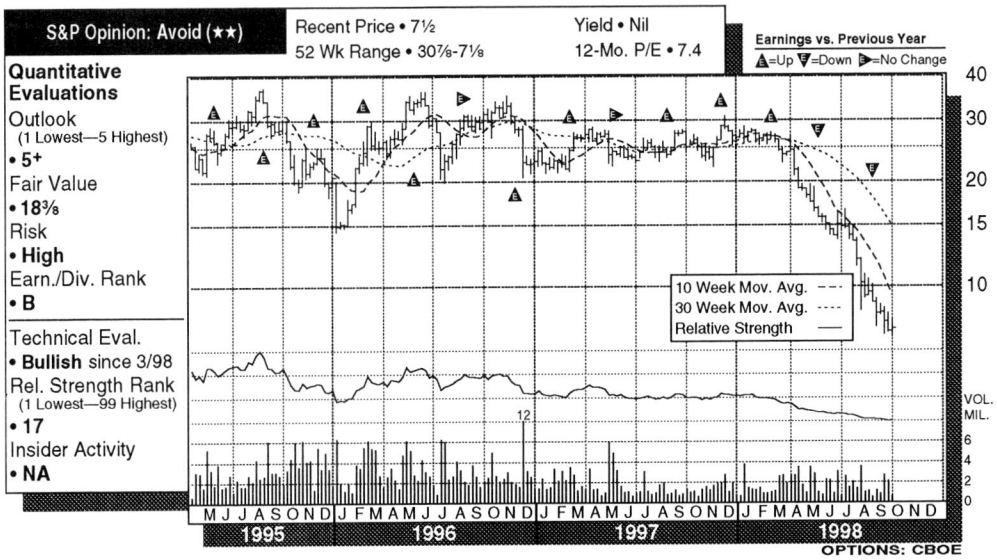

10 Week Mov. Avg. - - -
30 Week Mov. Avg. ·····
Relative Strength ——

VOL. MIL.

OPTIONS: CBOE

Overview - 10-SEP-98

Gymboree posted a net loss of $0.03 for its second quarter of FY 99 (Jan.), markedly lower than last year's $0.19 earnings per share and our estimate of $0.01. Significant summer promotional activity adversely impacted GYMB's second quarter results, and will hurt performance in the third quarter and perhaps the fourth quarter. The company hopes to improve its revenue growth by opening stores in Japan, and introducing Kid Cool, a new retail concept targeting children ages six to 12. Although these initiatives may have long-term potential, they call for significant capital expenditures as GYMB tries to emphasize improving its core business. Kid Cool strays somewhat from GYMB's target customers (children under seven), and the Japanese retail environment remains poor. Although management hopes its new line of boys clothing will spearhead a turn-around in domestic sales growth, we do not believe mere merchandising will enable GYMB to rekindle the former success of its U.S. business.

Valuation - 10-SEP-98

We continue to recommend investors avoid GYMB, following another disappointing quarter. GYMB's excessive fall inventory and the competitive retail environment for children's clothing will likely pressure GYMB's margins for at least another quarter or two. High inventory levels and signficant promotions caused second quarter cost of goods sold and SG&A each to increase as a percentage of sales. At a time when its relative costs are rising and pressuring margins and earnings, GYMB intends to add to those costs by entering new markets. We expect GYMB shares to underperform the market over the next six to 12 months, as the company attempts to turn around its core domestic business while implementing its international and Kid Cool plans.

Key Stock Statistics

S&P EPS Est. 1999	0.80	Tang. Bk. Value/Share	6.77
P/E on S&P Est. 1999	9.5	Beta	0.95
S&P EPS Est. 2000	1.03	Shareholders	800
Dividend Rate/Share	Nil	Market cap. (B)	$0.183
Shs. outstg. (M)	24.2	Inst. holdings	74%
Avg. daily vol. (M)	0.320		

Value of $10,000 invested 5 years ago: NA

Fiscal Year Ending Jan. 31

	1999	1998	1997	1996	1995	1994
Revenues (Million $)						
1Q	103.1	85.24	69.10	55.08	—	26.62
2Q	99.8	71.68	57.90	49.39	34.86	24.01
3Q	—	101.1	84.69	66.23	51.46	34.23
4Q	—	115.4	91.42	88.69	62.77	44.72
Yr.	—	373.4	303.1	259.4	188.4	129.6
Earnings Per Share ($)						
1Q	**0.17**	0.34	0.34	0.25	0.17	0.12
2Q	**-0.03**	0.19	0.17	0.17	0.10	0.06
3Q	**E0.23**	0.44	0.35	0.28	0.27	0.17
4Q	**E0.43**	0.46	0.39	0.35	0.33	0.22
Yr.	**E0.80**	1.41	1.24	1.04	0.88	0.57

Next earnings report expected: mid November

Dividend Data

The company has never paid cash dividends on its common stock and anticipates that all future earnings will be retained for development of its business.

A Division of The **McGraw·Hill** *Companies*

Business Summary - 10-SEP-98

Gymboree sells apparel and accessories for children ages newborn to seven years old. As of August 12, 1998, GYMB operated 495 retail stores, with 468 outlets in 48 states across the U.S., 13 locations in Canada, and 14 in the United Kingdom and Ireland. Stores are decorated with bright colors and bold prints. The company designs and manufactures its own exclusive line of active-wear, which often places it in the role of toddler fashion trend-setter. Gymboree also adds to the value of its brand name with its branded parent-child developmental play programs for children ages newborn to five years old at, as of August 12, 1998, 390 centers. GYMB recently decided to discontinue its short-lived catalog which included popular items from its stores, focusing on other new diversification ideas.

Gymboree's business strategy includes several principal elements: horizontal efficiency via integrated design, production and retail operations; high-quality products; exclusive distribution channels; responsive customer service; and a recognized and respected brand name. The company seeks to significantly increase its store base by opening new domestic and international locations. In FY 98 (Jan.), GYMB opened 81 new stores, up from 75 in FY 97. For FY 99, GYMB plans to open a total of 120 new Gymboree stores. GYMB also plans to

open 10 to 15 new Kid Cool stores, which will cater to the clothing needs of children ages 6 to 12, in early 1999. New Japanese stores are expected to be opened in late FY 00.

Some 60 independent companies, located primarily in the Far East, and, to a lesser extent, Honduras, Israel and the U.S, manufacture GYMB's apparel to company specifications. GYMB currently outsources its purchasing operations, but plans to open its own buying office in Hong Kong in late 1999. GYMB expects its in-house purchasing facility to reduce inefficiencies and cut costs going forward.

At the end of FY 98, GYMB's Play Programs facilities included some 13 company-operated play centers in Northern California, and about 377 franchisee-operated play centers, 80% of which were located in the U.S., and the remaining 20% in Australia, Canada, Colombia, France, Indonesia, Mexico, Singapore, South Korea and Taiwan. The company believes that its Play Programs centers provide attractive cross-marketing opportunities for its stores, and strengthens the Gymboree brand. Programs entail parents playing with their children under the direction of an instructor. The programs are designed to enhance early childhood development through fun-filled sensory and motor activities. Each play program generally entails ten weekly 45-minute classes, which are offered year-round.

Per Share Data ($)

(Year Ended Jan. 31)	1998	1997	1996	1995	1994	1993	1992	1991	1990	1989
Tangible Bk. Val.	6.57	6.39	4.96	3.77	2.64	1.95	NA	NA	NA	NA
Cash Flow	2.00	1.59	1.25	1.01	0.68	0.39	NA	NA	NA	NA
Earnings	1.41	1.24	1.04	0.88	0.57	0.31	0.13	NA	NA	NA
Dividends	Nil	Nil	Nil	Nil	Nil	Nil	Nil	Nil	Nil	Nil
Payout Ratio	Nil	Nil	Nil	Nil	Nil	Nil	Nil	Nil	Nil	Nil
Cal. Yrs.	1997	1996	1995	1994	1993	1992	1991	1990	1989	1988
Prices - High	30⅞	36⅜	37¼	33	26¼	NA	NA	NA	NA	NA
- Low	21⅛	14⅜	18	17⅜	10	NA	NA	NA	NA	NA
P/E Ratio - High	22	29	36	38	46	NA	NA	NA	NA	NA
- Low	15	12	17	20	18	NA	NA	NA	NA	NA

Income Statement Analysis (Million $)

	1998	1997	1996	1995	1994	1993	1992	1991	1990	1989
Revs.	373	303	259	188	130	86.0	NA	NA	NA	NA
Oper. Inc.	66.9	56.4	45.5	38.6	25.5	12.9	NA	NA	NA	NA
Depr.	13.5	8.9	5.4	3.3	2.5	1.6	NA	NA	NA	NA
Int. Exp.	Nil	Nil	Nil	Nil	Nil	Nil	Nil	Nil	Nil	Nil
Pretax Inc.	55.8	51.2	43.2	37.0	23.9	11.6	NA	NA	NA	NA
Eff. Tax Rate	37%	38%	39%	40%	41%	40%	NA	NA	NA	NA
Net Inc.	35.2	31.7	26.4	22.2	14.1	6.9	NA	NA	NA	NA

Balance Sheet & Other Fin. Data (Million $)

	1998	1997	1996	1995	1994	1993	1992	1991	1990	1989
Cash	17.9	90.3	73.6	63.1	46.8	NA	NA	NA	NA	NA
Curr. Assets	121	146	116	101	71.0	NA	NA	NA	NA	NA
Total Assets	229	217	160	127	88.0	NA	NA	NA	NA	NA
Curr. Liab.	49.9	40.4	26.6	27.5	20.8	NA	NA	NA	NA	NA
LT Debt	Nil	Nil	Nil	Nil	Nil	Nil	Nil	Nil	Nil	Nil
Common Eqty.	158	162	124	92.6	63.3	NA	NA	NA	NA	NA
Total Cap.	158	162	124	92.6	63.3	NA	NA	NA	NA	NA
Cap. Exp.	NA	37.0	Nil	11.6	6.9	5.3	NA	NA	NA	NA
Cash Flow	48.7	40.6	31.7	25.5	16.6	8.5	NA	NA	NA	NA
Curr. Ratio	2.4	3.6	4.4	3.7	3.4	NA	NA	NA	NA	NA
% LT Debt of Cap.	Nil	Nil	Nil	Nil	Nil	Nil	Nil	Nil	Nil	Nil
% Net Inc.of Revs.	9.4	10.5	10.2	11.8	10.9	8.0	NA	NA	NA	NA
% Ret. on Assets	15.8	16.8	18.4	20.6	16.0	NA	NA	NA	NA	NA
% Ret. on Equity	22.0	22.2	24.4	28.5	35.8	NA	NA	NA	NA	NA

Data as orig. reptd.; bef. results of disc. opers. and/or spec. items. Per share data adj. for stk. divs. as of ex-div. date. Bold denotes diluted EPS (FASB 128). E-Estimated. NA-Not Available. NM-Not Meaningful. NR-Not Ranked.

Office—700 Airport Blvd., Suite 200, Burlingame, CA 94010-1912. **Tel**—(650) 579-0600. **Website**—http://www.gymboree.com. **Chrmn**—S. G. Moldaw. **Pres & CEO**—G. White. **CFO & SVP**—L. H. Meyer. **Treas & VP**—F. M. Petrocco. **Dirs**—A. S. Berliner, J. A. Chazen, W. F. Loeb, S. G. Moldaw, B. L. Rambo, P. I. Thigpen, W. U. Westerfield, G. White. **Transfer Agent**—BankBoston. **Incorporated**—in California in 1979; reincorporated in Delaware in 1992. **Empl**— 6,500. **S&P Analyst:** Scott H. Kessler.

03-OCT-98

Industry: Services (Data Processing)

Summary: This company develops, markets and supports advanced decision software based on computational intelligence.

Quantitative Evaluations

Outlook (1 Lowest—5 Highest)
- **NA**

Fair Value
- **NA**

Risk
- **High**

Earn./Div. Rank
- **NR**

Technical Eval.
- **Bullish** since 9/98

Rel. Strength Rank (1 Lowest—99 Highest)
- **47**

Insider Activity
- **Unfavorable**

Recent Price • 35⅜
52 Wk Range • 47⅛-30

Yield • Nil
12-Mo. P/E • NM

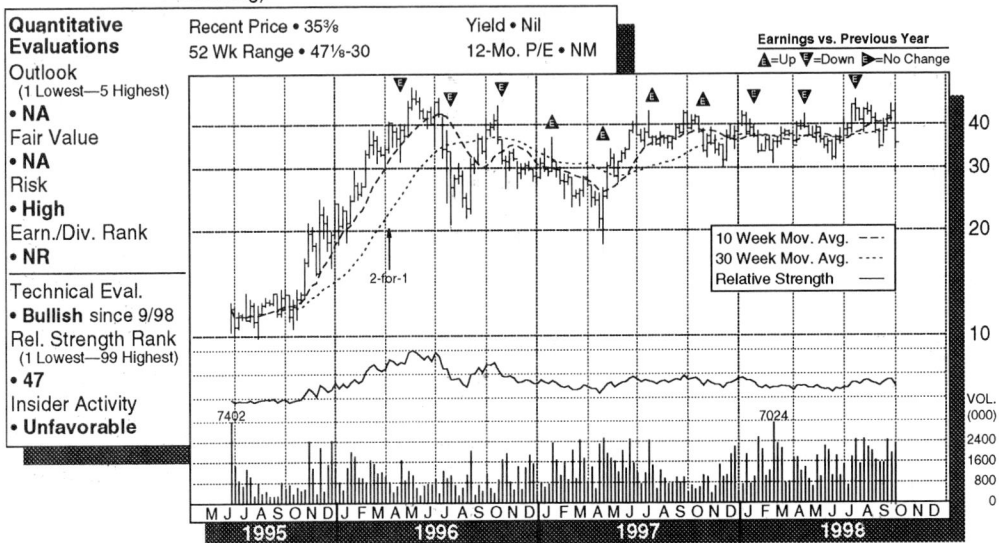

Earnings vs. Previous Year
▲=Up ▼=Down ▷=No Change

10 Week Mov. Avg. ---
30 Week Mov. Avg. ····
Relative Strength ——

2-for-1

Business Profile - 15-SEP-98

HNCS seeks to obtain recurring revenues through long-term contracts; to broaden its product line into new applications and markets, such as medical payments, Internet commerce and database marketing; to leverage its database to provide complete industry-specific modeling solutions; to expand its worldwide distribution; and to commit resources to maintain technology leadership in developed solutions. In November 1997, it acquired CompReview Inc., a developer of integrated payment systems and medical bill review software, for about 5 million common shares. The acquisitions of Financial Technology Inc. (April 1998) and the Advanced Telecommunications Abuse Control System product line (June) led to a $19.1 million 1998 second quarter charge to write off in-process research and development.

Operational Review - 15-SEP-98

Revenues in the first half of 1998 rose 51% from those of the year-earlier period, as restated for CompReview, mostly reflecting a 49% gain in software license and maintenance revenue. Margins narrowed, as operating expenses grew faster than revenues; the gain in operating income was held to 32%. After $23.5 million in acquisition related costs, a net loss of $10,701,000 ($0.43 per share, diluted) contrasted with net income of $9,171,000 ($0.36). Excluding acquisition costs, and assuming a tax rate of 37% in each year, EPS would have been $0.40, versus $0.30.

Stock Performance - 02-OCT-98

In the past 30 trading days, HNCS's shares have declined 15%, compared to a 7% fall in the S&P 500. Average trading volume for the past five days was 462,240 shares, compared with the 40-day moving average of 408,856 shares.

Key Stock Statistics

Dividend Rate/Share	Nil	Shareholders	200
Shs. outstg. (M)	25.7	Market cap. (B)	$0.908
Avg. daily vol. (M)	0.440	Inst. holdings	83%
Tang. Bk. Value/Share	4.65		
Beta	NA		

Value of $10,000 invested 5 years ago: NA

Fiscal Year Ending Dec. 31

	1998	1997	1996	1995	1994	1993
Revenues (Million $)						
1Q	35.08	24.07	9.90	5.09	—	—
2Q	43.14	27.59	12.56	5.92	—	—
3Q	—	29.99	14.60	6.91	—	—
4Q	—	32.08	16.78	7.25	—	—
Yr.	—	113.7	53.83	25.17	16.47	—
Earnings Per Share ($)						
1Q	0.08	0.17	-0.04	0.03	—	—
2Q	-0.50	0.20	0.02	0.04	—	—
3Q	—	0.21	0.07	0.18	—	—
4Q	—	0.13	0.26	0.06	—	—
Yr.	—	0.68	0.31	0.31	0.16	0.02

Next earnings report expected: mid October

Dividend Data

No cash dividends have been paid. A two-for-one stock split was effected in April 1996.

A Division of The McGraw·Hill Companies

STANDARD
&POOR'S
STOCK REPORTS

HNC Software Inc.

4072N
03-OCT-98

Business Summary - 15-SEP-98

The leading supplier of predictive software, HNC Software, Inc. enables customers to optimize revenues and profit, cut costs, and provide protection against business risk and fraud. HNCS develops, markets and supports intelligent client-server software solutions for mission-critical decision applications in real-time environments. It also performs contract research and development using neural networks and other computational intelligence models. HNCS has clients in the financial services, health care/insurance and retail industries. Revenues in recent years were derived as follows:

	1997	1996	1995
License and maintenance	79%	68%	56%
Installation and implementation	10%	9%	11%
Contracts and other	7%	16%	21%
Service bureau	4%	7%	12%

In the financial service industry, HNCS's products are used to detect, predict and prevent credit card fraud, as well as to manage credit card portfolios and automate the selection of new customers. In August 1997, the company announced a strategic alliance with Equifax Inc., a provider of financial information and processing solutions, to jointly develop and market new products to the financial services, retail and electronic commerce industries.

In the health care/insurance industry, the company's products are used to automate workers' compensation bill review, predict loss reserves and prevent workers' compensation fraud. In November 1997, the company acquired CompReview, Inc., a provider of software solutions that assist in the management and containment of the costs of workers' compensation and automobile accident medical claims.

In the retail industry, HNCS's products are used in inventory management, sales forecasting, price/promotion management and purchasing/receiving.

In the first half of 1998, the company received proceeds of $100 million from the sale of 4.75% convertible subordinated notes due 2003, and net proceeds of $4.9 million from the issuance of common stock. From March through June 1998, HNCS acquired PCS, a supplier of fully integrated distribution center management software, in exchange for 142,868 common shares; FTI, a provider of profitability measurement and decision-support software to the financial services industry, in exchange for 396,617 shares and $1.5 million in cash; and the ATACS product line, a fraud-management software solution for wireline, wireless and Internet telecommunication service providers, from a wholly owned subsidiary of British Airways plc, for $4.75 million in cash.

The company intends to continue to develop and introduce new products and enhance the performance of existing predictive models through research and development.

Per Share Data ($)

(Year Ended Dec. 31)	1997	1996	1995	1994	1993	1992	1991	1990	1989	1988
Tangible Bk. Val.	4.23	4.31	3.28	NM	NM	NM	NM	NM	NM	NM
Cash Flow	0.87	0.48	0.39	0.18	NA	NA	NA	NA	NA	NA
Earnings	0.68	0.31	0.31	0.16	NA	NA	NA	NA	NA	NA
Dividends	Nil	Nil	Nil	Nil	Nil	Nil	Nil	Nil	Nil	Nil
Payout Ratio	Nil	Nil	Nil	Nil	Nil	Nil	Nil	Nil	Nil	Nil
Prices - High	43⅝	51	24½	NA	NA	NA	NA	NA	NA	NA
- Low	18¼	18¼	7	NA	NA	NA	NA	NA	NA	NA
P/E Ratio - High	64	NM	79	NA	NA	NA	NA	NA	NA	NA
- Low	27	NM	23	NA	NA	NA	NA	NA	NA	NA

Income Statement Analysis (Million $)

	1997	1996	1995	1994	1993	1992	1991	1990	1989	1988
Revs.	114	53.8	25.2	16.5	NA	NA	NA	NA	NA	NA
Oper. Inc.	27.9	7.5	4.2	1.7	NA	NA	NA	NA	NA	NA
Depr.	4.8	3.3	1.1	0.3	NA	NA	NA	NA	NA	NA
Int. Exp.	0.1	0.5	0.0	0.1	NA	NA	NA	NA	NA	NA
Pretax Inc.	25.0	0.1	3.9	1.5	NA	NA	NA	NA	NA	NA
Eff. Tax Rate	29%	NM	15%	31%	NA	NA	NA	NA	NA	NA
Net Inc.	17.6	6.3	4.5	1.9	NA	NA	NA	NA	NA	NA

Balance Sheet & Other Fin. Data (Million $)

	1997	1996	1995	1994	1993	1992	1991	1990	1989	1988
Cash	18.1	14.9	34.5	6.0	NA	NA	NA	NA	NA	NA
Curr. Assets	90.0	42.6	42.0	10.0	NA	NA	NA	NA	NA	NA
Total Assets	120	94.2	53.4	12.2	NA	NA	NA	NA	NA	NA
Curr. Liab.	15.7	11.1	5.2	2.6	NA	NA	NA	NA	NA	NA
LT Debt	Nil	Nil	Nil	0.4	NA	NA	NA	NA	NA	NA
Common Eqty.	104	82.4	48.3	-4.0	NA	NA	NA	NA	NA	NA
Total Cap.	104	82.4	48.3	9.6	NA	NA	NA	NA	NA	NA
Cap. Exp.	9.6	3.9	1.8	1.4	NA	NA	NA	NA	NA	NA
Cash Flow	22.4	9.7	5.6	2.2	NA	NA	NA	NA	NA	NA
Curr. Ratio	5.7	3.8	8.1	3.8	NA	NA	NA	NA	NA	NA
% LT Debt of Cap.	Nil	Nil	Nil	4.2	NA	NA	NA	NA	NA	NA
% Net Inc.of Revs.	15.4	11.8	17.7	11.7	NA	NA	NA	NA	NA	NA
% Ret. on Assets	16.4	8.3	13.6	22.6	NA	NA	NA	NA	NA	NA
% Ret. on Equity	18.9	9.8	10.1	NM	NM	NM	NM	NM	NM	NM

Data as orig. reptd.; bef. results of disc. opers. and/or spec. items. Per share data adj. for stk. divs. as of ex-div. date. Bold denotes diluted EPS (FASB 128). E-Estimated. NA-Not Available. NM-Not Meaningful. NR-Not Ranked.

Office—5930 Cornerstone Court West, San Diego, CA 92121. **Tel**—(619) 546-8877. **Website**—http://www.hnc.com **Pres & CEO**—R. L. North. **VP-Fin & CFO**—R. V. Thomas. **Dirs**—E. K. Chandler, O. D. Curme, T. F. Farb, C. H. Gaylord, Jr., R. L. North. **Transfer Agent & Registrar**—First National Bank of Boston. **Incorporated**—in Delaware in 1995. **Empl**— 385. **S&P Analyst:** M.G.H.

HS Resources

1082Y

NYSE Symbol **HSE**

In S&P SmallCap 600

03-OCT-98

Industry:
Oil & Gas (Exploration & Production)

Summary: This independent oil and gas exploration and production company focuses on the Rocky Mountain area, New Mexico, Oklahoma and Texas.

Quantitative Evaluations		
Recent Price • 11⅛	Yield • Nil	
52 Wk Range • 18¾-7⅜	12-Mo. P/E • NM	

Outlook
(1 Lowest—5 Highest)
• **3⁻**

Fair Value
• **12¾**

Risk
• **Average**

Earn./Div. Rank
• **NR**

Technical Eval.
• **Bearish** since 6/98

Rel. Strength Rank
(1 Lowest—99 Highest)
• **78**

Insider Activity
• **NA**

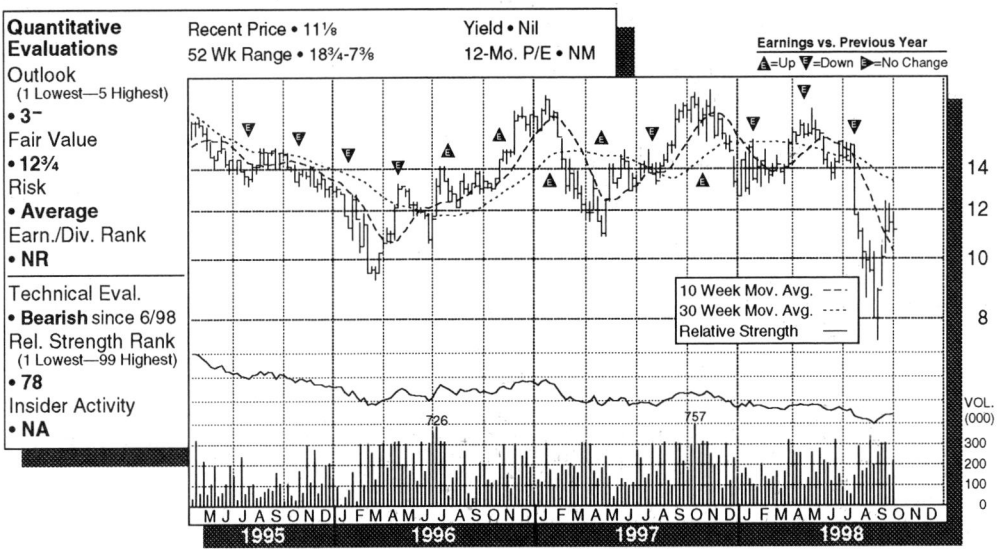

Earnings vs. Previous Year ▲=Up ▼=Down ▶=No Change

10 Week Mov. Avg. ---
30 Week Mov. Avg. ····
Relative Strength —

Business Profile - 28-JUL-98

This independent oil and gas exploration and production company's drilling program is concentrated in the Wattenberg Field area of the Denver-Julesberg Basin in Colorado, where it has a significant acreage position. HSE undertakes projects on strict financial measures, with the company attempting to establish competitive advantages by managing risk with technology and/or capital structure. Projects are located in areas where HSE has technical expertise, that provide a balanced commodity mix, and that are characterized by multi-pay potential, low entry costs and strong operating efficiencies. Proceeds of $24 million from the sale of non-core properties in July 1997 were to be used to pay bank debt. In December 1997, HSE acquired for about $333 million all of Amoco's upstream oil and gas properties in the Denver-Julesburg Basin. The properties included estimated proved reserves of 15,200,000 bbl. of oil and 330,000 MMcf of gas.

Operational Review - 28-JUL-98

Revenues in the three months ended March 31, 1998 declined 3.7%, year to year, despite higher oil and gas production, reflecting lower oil and gas prices, reduced trading and transportation activity and lower interest income. After higher depreciation, depletion and amortization (DD&A) charges, and a sharp increase in interest expense, net income fell 25%, to $3,291,372 ($0.18 a share, on 6.5% more shares), from $4,367,506 ($0.25).

Stock Performance - 02-OCT-98

In the past 30 trading days, HSE's shares have increased 16%, compared to a 7% fall in the S&P 500. Average trading volume for the past five days was 43,420 shares, compared with the 40-day moving average of 53,903 shares.

Key Stock Statistics

Dividend Rate/Share	Nil	Shareholders	400
Shs. outstg. (M)	18.9	Market cap. (B)	$0.211
Avg. daily vol. (M)	0.052	Inst. holdings	59%
Tang. Bk. Value/Share	10.28		
Beta	1.08		

Value of $10,000 invested 5 years ago: $ 7,946

Fiscal Year Ending Dec. 31

	1998	1997	1996	1995	1994	1993
Revenues (Million $)						
1Q	63.77	70.16	14.19	15.75	14.09	10.14
2Q	52.20	55.16	26.83	14.84	15.01	12.41
3Q	—	54.37	47.74	11.98	15.79	13.75
4Q	—	67.47	68.20	12.77	15.51	11.19
Yr.	—	233.7	157.0	55.34	60.40	47.48
Earnings Per Share ($)						
1Q	**0.18**	0.25	0.02	0.06	0.15	0.27
2Q	**-1.89**	0.07	0.14	0.02	0.14	0.28
3Q	—	0.09	0.08	-0.03	0.14	0.27
4Q	—	0.24	0.37	-0.01	0.11	0.12
Yr.	—	**0.64**	0.61	0.02	0.53	0.93

Next earnings report expected: late October

Dividend Data

Dividends have never been paid on the common stock. The company does not intend to declare cash dividends on its common stock for the foreseeable future and will retain earnings to support the growth of its business.

A Division of The **McGraw·Hill** Companies

STANDARD
&POOR'S
STOCK REPORTS

HS Resources, Inc.

1082Y

03-OCT-98

Business Summary - 28-JUL-98

HS Resources is one of the most active domestic independent oil and gas operators. Since 1995, the company has articulated a strategy that included (i) consolidating its core geographic areas, particularly the Denver-Julesburg Basin (D-J Basin), (ii) diversifying its asset base outside the D-J Basin, (iii) capturing more of the value stream by marketing its production and (iv) maximizing its financial flexibility.

In addition to the core D-J Basin, HSE is active in exploration and development in the Rocky Mountain, Mid-Continent and Gulf Coast regions of the U.S. In December 1997, the company purchased from Amoco production Co. all of its oil and gas producing property located in the D-J Basin. Estimated proved reserves on the acquired properties are approximately 15,200,000 bbl. of oil and 330,000 MMcf of gas. The properties included more than 800 operated wells located on 411,000 gross (311,000 net) acres, with an average working interest of 91%, plus smaller interests in about 1,200 wells operated by others, including more than 500 operated by HSE. The company earlier expanded its position in the D-J Basin through the June 1996 acquisition of Basin Exploration, Inc.'s properties. Also in 1996, by merging with Tide West Oil Co., the company significantly expanded its activities in the Mid-Continent, specifically in the Anadarko and Arkoma Basins. Finally, financial strength and flexibility were fostered by the

placement of $150 million of 10-year subordinated notes in the fall of 1996.

HSE is committed to using advanced technologies, having developed drilling and completion techniques intended to maximize production. The company has conducted detailed reservoir studies. It also utilizes extensive geoscientific databases. In addition, HSE actively employs 3-D seismic surveys.

At December 31, 1997, estimated proved reserves totaled 192,000,000 bbl. of oil equivalent (boe), consisting of 45,400,000 bbl. of crude oil and 880,000 MMcf of natural gas. The net increase of 50,000,000 boe included 70,200,000 boe of reserves purchased from Amoco. Production in 1997 totaled 9,254,000 boe, versus 1996's 7,617,000 boe. Average prices were $19.71 a bbl. and $2.19 per Mcf ($20.90 and $1.96).

In 1998, HSE anticipates that it will undertake more than 500 exploitation activities. Including the wells acquired from Amoco, the company's extensive base of D-J Basin producing wells totals more than 4,000.

Substantially all company wells produce both oil and gas. Development, exploration and acquisition expenditures declined to $50.6 million in 1996, from $62.1 million in 1995. HSE planned 1997 capital spending of about $65 million, to be allocated in varying amounts in the D-J Basin, the Anadarko and Arkoma Basins and the onshore Gulf Coast. The balance sheet at year-end 1997 reflected bank debt used as an interim financial structure to fund the Amoco transaction.

Per Share Data ($)

(Year Ended Dec. 31)	1997	1996	1995	1994	1993	1992	1991	1990	1989	1988
Tangible Bk. Val.	12.04	11.26	10.92	10.94	10.38	8.31	10.30	NA	NA	NA
Cash Flow	3.67	3.51	2.35	2.68	2.34	2.00	1.35	NA	NA	NA
Earnings	0.64	0.61	0.02	0.53	0.93	0.69	0.16	NA	NA	NA
Dividends	Nil	Nil	Nil	Nil	Nil	Nil	Nil	Nil	Nil	Nil
Payout Ratio	Nil	Nil	Nil	Nil	Nil	Nil	Nil	Nil	Nil	Nil
Prices - High	18¾	17⅝	17½	24¾	29	14¾	NA	NA	NA	NA
- Low	10⅞	9¼	12⅝	17⅛	13¾	12¾	NA	NA	NA	NA
P/E Ratio - High	29	29	NM	47	31	21	NA	NA	NA	NA
- Low	17	15	NM	32	15	18	NA	NA	NA	NA

Income Statement Analysis (Million $)

	1997	1996	1995	1994	1993	1992	1991	1990	1989	1988
Revs.	234	157	55.2	60.2	47.3	27.4	12.8	NA	NA	NA
Oper. Inc.	103	79.7	37.1	42.5	34.5	20.2	8.0	NA	NA	NA
Depr. Depl. & Amort.	53.2	42.3	26.6	25.1	15.3	8.8	4.4	NA	NA	NA
Int. Exp.	31.2	26.2	12.2	9.4	3.7	5.5	4.7	NA	NA	NA
Pretax Inc.	18.3	14.5	12.2	10.1	16.2	7.6	1.0	NA	NA	NA
Eff. Tax Rate	38%	38%	39%	38%	38%	38%	40%	NA	NA	NA
Net Inc.	11.3	8.9	0.3	6.3	10.1	4.7	0.6	NA	NA	NA

Balance Sheet & Other Fin. Data (Million $)

	1997	1996	1995	1994	1993	1992	1991	1990	1989	1988
Cash	6.9	9.3	0.1	0.7	21.1	7.1	7.4	NA	NA	NA
Curr. Assets	54.7	59.8	11.2	13.4	32.4	12.3	11.3	NA	NA	NA
Total Assets	1,035	731	302	269	228	120	83.0	NA	NA	NA
Curr. Liab.	63.7	46.1	27.2	15.8	16.2	8.7	9.0	NA	NA	NA
LT Debt	637	400	126	103	74.4	20.6	36.3	NA	NA	NA
Common Eqty.	224	193	119	119	113	79.0	28.0	NA	NA	NA
Total Cap.	951	678	269	246	207	109	73.0	NA	NA	NA
Cap. Exp.	1.9	182	62.9	86.0	100	45.0	19.0	NA	NA	NA
Cash Flow	64.6	51.2	26.9	31.3	25.4	13.5	5.0	NA	NA	NA
Curr. Ratio	0.9	1.3	40.8	0.8	2.0	1.4	1.3	NA	NA	NA
% LT Debt of Cap.	66.9	59.0	46.8	42.0	35.9	18.9	50.0	NA	NA	NA
% Ret. on Assets	1.3	1.7	0.2	2.5	5.5	2.3	NA	NA	NA	NA
% Ret. on Equity	5.4	5.7	0.2	5.4	9.9	5.3	NA	NA	NA	NA

Data as orig. reptd.; bef. results of disc opers. and/or spec. items. Per share data adj. for stk. divs. as ex-div. date. Bold denotes diluted EPS (FASB 128). E-Estimated. NA-Not Available. NM-Not Meaningful. NR-Not Ranked.

Office—One Maritime Plaza, 15th Fl., San Francisco CA 94111. **Tel**—(415) 433-5795. **Website**—http://www.hsresources.com **Chrmn & CEO**—N. J. Sutton. **Pres**—P. M. Highum. **VP-Fin & CFO**—J. E. Duffy. **VP & Secy**—J. M. Piccone. **investor Contact**—T. Gazulis. **Dirs**—J. E. Duffy, K. A. Hersh, P. M. Highum, M. J. Savage, P. B. Smith, N. J. Sutton. **Transfer Agent & Registrar**—Harris Trust Co. of California, LA. **Incorporated**—in Delaware in 1987. **Empl**— 260. **S&P Analyst:** NR

HUBCO, Inc.

4073B

NASDAQ Symbol **HUBC**

In S&P SmallCap 600

03-OCT-98

Industry: Banks (Regional)

Summary: HUBCO is the holding company for Hudson United Bank, Lafayette American Bank and Trust and Bank of the Hudson.

Quantitative Evaluations

Outlook (1 Lowest—5 Highest)
- **NA**

Fair Value
- **NA**

Risk
- **Low**

Earn./Div. Rank
- **A-**

Technical Eval.
- **Bearish** since 8/98

Rel. Strength Rank (1 Lowest—99 Highest)
- **50**

Insider Activity
- **Neutral**

Recent Price • 26¼   Yield • 3.7%
52 Wk Range • 39⅛-24⅝   12-Mo. P/E • 17.0

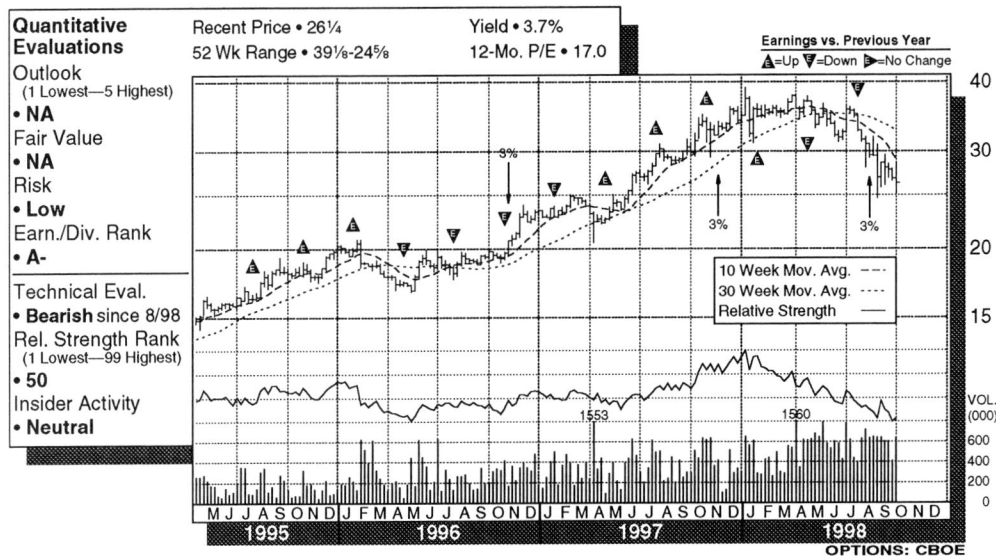

Earnings vs. Previous Year
△=Up ▽=Down ▷=No Change

- 10 Week Mov. Avg. - - -
- 30 Week Mov. Avg. ·····
- Relative Strength ——

OPTIONS: CBOE

Business Profile - 28-JUL-98

HUBC is the third largest bank holding company based in New Jersey. The company has completed a number of acquisitions over the past few years, boosting its total asset base to over $5.1 billion at June 30, 1998, from $1.6 billion at year end 1995. During the second quarter of 1998, HUBC completed the acquisitions of Poughkeepsie Financial Corp., MSB Bancorp, Inc. and 21 First Union National Bank branches. HUBC also has pending mergers with Community Financial Holding Corporation, IBS Financial Corp. and Dime Financial Corporation. Following completion of all pending acquisitions, HUBC will have roughly 160 offices and total assets of some $6.5 billion.

Operational Review - 28-JUL-98

Net interest income (as restated) in the first six months of 1998 fell 2.1%, year to year, largely reflecting a 3.9% decrease in loans. The provision for loan losses jumped 88%, to $8,794,000, from $4,680,000. Noninterest income, excluding security gains, grew 21%. Noninterest expense was up 36%, and included $28.1 million in merger related expenses and restructuring charges; pretax income was down sharply. After taxes at 40.4%, versus 39.9%, net income declined 61%, to $10,841,000 ($0.37 a share, on 5.4% fewer shares), from $27,665,000 ($0.89).

Stock Performance - 02-OCT-98

In the past 30 trading days, HUBC's shares have declined 11%, compared to a 7% fall in the S&P 500. Average trading volume for the past five days was 202,580 shares, compared with the 40-day moving average of 180,402 shares.

Key Stock Statistics

Dividend Rate/Share	0.97	Shareholders	3,500
Shs. outstg. (M)	43.3	Market cap. (B)	$ 1.1
Avg. daily vol. (M)	0.143	Inst. holdings	28%
Tang. Bk. Value/Share	6.87		
Beta	1.07		

Value of $10,000 invested 5 years ago: $ 30,317

Fiscal Year Ending Dec. 31

	1998	1997	1996	1995	1994	1993
Revenues (Million $)						
1Q	94.64	63.05	53.25	24.20	--	16.39
2Q	98.79	66.15	63.32	24.45	36.10	16.32
3Q	—	65.04	50.72	24.93	23.40	17.62
4Q	—	67.17	64.92	—	17.43	
Yr.	—	259.1	234.5	65.04	93.89	73.37
Earnings Per Share ($)						
1Q	**0.35**	**0.47**	0.33	0.38	0.35	0.28
2Q	**0.01**	**0.50**	0.31	0.42	0.37	0.31
3Q	—	**0.52**	0.08	0.42	0.40	0.33
4Q	—	**0.55**	0.15	0.44	0.41	0.34
Yr.	—	**2.04**	0.85	1.67	1.55	1.25

Next earnings report expected: mid October

Dividend Data (Dividends have been paid since 1952.)

Amount ($)	Date Decl.	Ex-Div. Date	Stock of Record	Payment Date
0.200	Jan. 22	Feb. 12	Feb. 17	Mar. 02 '98
0.200	Apr. 22	May. 14	May. 18	Jun. 01 '98
0.250	Jul. 17	Aug. 12	Aug. 14	Sep. 04 '98
3%	Jul. 17	Aug. 12	Aug. 14	Sep. 01 '98

STANDARD
&POOR'S
STOCK REPORTS

HUBCO, Inc.

4073B
03-OCT-98

Business Summary - 28-JUL-98

HUBCO, Inc. is the holding company for Hudson United Bank, which operates offices throughout northern New Jersey, Lafayette American Bank and Trust, which operates offices in southwestern Connecticut and Bank of the Hudson, which operates in New York State. In addition, HUBC is the indirect owner, through Hudson United and Lafayette, of three investment subsidiaries and five real estate holding companies. HUBCO also owns, through Hudson United, a 50% interest in a data processing and imaged check processing company.

Acquisitions have played a key role in the bank's development. Through its philosophy of seeking intramarket and contiguous market opportunities that can be accomplished with little or no dilution to earnings, HUBC has boosted EPS at a compound annual growth rate of over 25% over the past few years. From October 1990 to December 1997, HUBC acquired 17 institutions, adding over $2.7 billion to assets and expanding its branch network from 15 branches to over 80 branches. HUBCO completed two acquisitions in the first quarter of 1998 and three acquisitions in the second quarter. HUBC has a number of pending acquisitions, including Community Financial Holding Corporation, Dime Financial Corporation and IBS Financial Corp. The bank also has two New York branches of First Union National Bank scheduled to be acquired in July 1998. After closing all pending acquisitions, HUBC will have roughly 160 offices and total assets of $6.5 billion.

Interest income advanced 6.8% in 1997, to $218.0 million, and accounted for 84% of total revenues. Average earning assets, from which interest income is derived, increased 3.6% in 1997 and was comprised mainly of loans (67%) and federal funds sold (32%). The net interest margin (the ratio of net interest income to average earning assets) is a key measure of profitability of the bank's lending operations. In 1997, HUBC's net interest margin widened 15 basis points, to 5.20%. This margin expansion, combined with the growth in earning assets, drove net interest income up 6.7%.

Noninterest income climbed 36% in 1997, to $41.1 million, and accounted for 16% of revenues (13% of revenues in 1996.) This increase was largely the result of sharply higher securities gains and increased Shoppers Charge fee income.

Per Share Data ($)

(Year Ended Dec. 31)	1997	1996	1995	1994	1993	1992	1991	1990	1989	1988
Tangible Bk. Val.	7.17	7.55	8.55	7.60	7.16	5.48	4.53	4.22	4.13	4.00
Earnings	2.04	-0.85	1.67	1.55	1.26	0.97	0.61	0.27	0.37	0.58
Dividends	0.73	0.68	0.55	0.33	0.29	0.24	0.21	0.20	0.18	0.18
Payout Ratio	36%	80%	33%	21%	23%	25%	34%	73%	49%	30%
Prices - High	39$\frac{1}{8}$	24	20$\frac{1}{4}$	14$\frac{1}{2}$	15$\frac{3}{8}$	9$\frac{1}{2}$	4$\frac{7}{8}$	4$\frac{3}{8}$	6$\frac{1}{4}$	8$\frac{1}{8}$
- Low	20$\frac{1}{2}$	16$\frac{3}{4}$	13$\frac{3}{8}$	11$\frac{1}{2}$	9$\frac{3}{4}$	4$\frac{5}{8}$	2$\frac{3}{16}$	2$\frac{1}{8}$	4	5$\frac{7}{8}$
P/E Ratio - High	19	28	12	9	12	10	8	16	17	14
- Low	10	20	8	7	8	5	4	8	11	10

Income Statement Analysis (Million $)

	1997	1996	1995	1994	1993	1992	1991	1990	1989	1988
Net Int. Inc.	140	131	81.1	58.0	47.0	41.0	26.5	23.0	23.3	22.2
Tax Equiv. Adj.	0.5	0.3	0.7	0.9	0.8	0.7	1.0	0.9	0.7	NA
Non Int. Inc.	32.6	29.3	16.8	10.0	8.6	7.7	5.4	4.6	4.1	3.4
Loan Loss Prov.	7.3	12.3	4.2	3.0	3.6	4.1	2.4	4.2	1.9	0.5
Exp./Op. Revs.	54%	72%	61%	55%	53%	70%	68%	70%	71%	70%
Pretax Inc.	80.4	33.1	34.5	27.0	22.1	10.2	7.4	3.4	5.8	7.3
Eff. Tax Rate	39%	35%	31%	37%	36%	5.50%	32%	34%	43%	28%
Net Inc.	49.3	21.5	23.7	16.9	14.2	9.6	5.0	2.2	3.3	5.3
% Net Int. Marg.	5.20	5.05	5.46	5.09	5.20	4.97	4.94	4.55	4.77	4.90

Balance Sheet & Other Fin. Data (Million $)

	1997	1996	1995	1994	1993	1992	1991	1990	1989	1988
Earning Assets:										
Money Mkt	218	24.2	46.7	Nil	9.8	23.3	6.0	11.9	40.1	29.8
Inv. Securities	778	936	566	537	427	323	139	151	89.0	54.0
Com'l Loans	496	482	245	188	179	154	159	144	134	140
Other Loans	1,278	1,402	609	545	356	367	317	370	363	263
Total Assets	3,047	3,116	1,613	1,377	1,042	932	673	595	548	507
Demand Deposits	622	623	311	210	205	171	128	103	102	92.0
Time Deposits	1,692	1,969	1,114	990	730	672	481	410	382	353
LT Debt	100	100	25.0	25.0	Nil	Nil	0.8	0.8	0.8	0.9
Common Eqty.	186	203	130	100	79.0	68.3	41.1	37.6	37.4	35.8
% Ret. on Assets	1.6	0.7	1.4	1.4	1.4	1.1	0.8	0.4	0.6	1.1
% Ret. on Equity	25.1	9.8	20.6	19.4	19.3	17.4	12.8	5.9	8.9	15.3
% Loan Loss Resv.	2.1	1.9	1.9	2.3	2.0	1.5	1.4	1.4	0.8	0.6
% Loans/Deposits	74.6	70.2	59.9	61.1	56.6	60.9	78.2	72.5	76.3	85.1
% Equity to Assets	6.3	7.2	6.0	6.9	7.4	6.0	6.5	6.3	7.0	7.0

Data as orig. reptd.; bef. results of disc opers. and/or spec. items. Per share data adj. for stk. divs. as of ex-div. date. Bold denotes diluted EPS (FASB 128). E-Estimated. NA-Not Available. NM-Not Meaningful. NR-Not Ranked.

Office—1000 MacArthur Blvd., Mahwah, NJ 07430. **Organized**—in New Jersey in 1982. **Tel**—(201) 236-2600. **Chrmn, Pres & CEO**—K. T. Neilson. **EVP, CFO & Investor Contact**—Joseph F. Hurley (201-236-6141). **EVP & Secy**—D. L. Van Borkulo-Nuzzo. **Dirs**—R. J. Burke, D. P. Calcagnini, J. David, T. Farley, B. D. Malcom, W. P. McBride, K. T. Neilson, C. F. X. Poggi, D. A. Rosow, J. E. Schierloh, G. F. Strauber, J. H. Tatigian Jr. **Transfer Agent**—American Stock Transfer & Trust Co., NYC. **Empl**— 833. **S&P Analyst:** Michael Schneider

HA-LO Industries 1084N

NYSE Symbol **HMK**

In S&P SmallCap 600

03-OCT-98

Industry:
Services (Advertising & Marketing)

Summary: This leading marketer and distributor of advertising specialty and promotional products also provides telemarketing services to large corporations.

Quantitative Evaluations	
Outlook (1 Lowest—5 Highest)	• NA
Fair Value	• NA
Risk	• High
Earn./Div. Rank	• B-
Technical Eval.	• NA
Rel. Strength Rank (1 Lowest—99 Highest)	• 60
Insider Activity	• Neutral

Recent Price • 25⅜
52 Wk Range • 38⅜-22¼

Yield • Nil
12-Mo. P/E • 34.8

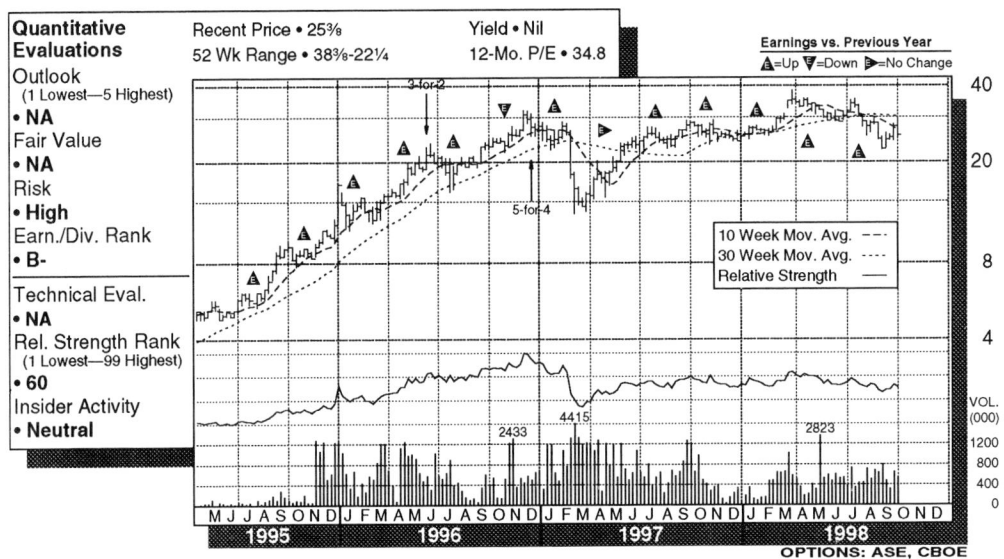

Earnings vs. Previous Year
▲=Up ▼=Down ▶=No Change

10 Week Mov. Avg. - - -
30 Week Mov. Avg. · · · ·
Relative Strength —

VOL. (000)

OPTIONS: ASE, CBOE

Business Profile - 12-SEP-98

Results for the first half of 1998 include $4.5 million in non-recurring charges relating to the completion of an acquisition and a fire at one of the firm's office and distribution facilities. Since reporting second quarter 1998 results, HMK has made two acquisitions: UP-SHOT, a Chicago promotion marketing agency, and Lipson Alport Glass and Associates (LAGA), the nation's largest independent brand identity and package design firm. UPSHOT and LAGA have projected 1998 revenues of $35 million and $21 million, respectively, and both are profitable operations. In May 1998, the company completed a public offering of 3.9 million shares of common stock and received proceeds of approximately $118 million, which it used to pay off debt.

Operational Review - 12-SEP-98

Net sales for the six months ended June 30, 1998, rose 30%, year to year, due to internal growth and acquisitions. A more favorable product mix enhanced gross margins and improved profitability. Despite higher selling expense and a rise in acquisition-related charges, comparisons benefited from more efficient leverage of the firm's cost structure; operating profit surged 57%. After a decline in interest expense, pro forma net income was up 57%, to $5,833,745 ($0.23 per share, on 9.5% more shares), from $3,377,366 ($0.14).

Stock Performance - 02-OCT-98

In the past 30 trading days, HMK's shares have declined 11%, compared to a 7% fall in the S&P 500. Average trading volume for the past five days was 106,780 shares, compared with the 40-day moving average of 117,418 shares.

Key Stock Statistics

Dividend Rate/Share	Nil	Shareholders	800
Shs. outstg. (M)	27.7	Market cap. (B)	$0.704
Avg. daily vol. (M)	0.100	Inst. holdings	54%
Tang. Bk. Value/Share	6.79		
Beta	1.36		

Value of $10,000 invested 5 years ago: $ 69,204

Fiscal Year Ending Dec. 31

	1998	1997	1996	1995	1994	1993
Revenues (Million $)						
1Q	109.4	78.59	49.91	20.80	12.60	--
2Q	127.9	90.95	60.79	25.40	15.50	--
3Q	--	98.30	65.11	36.70	16.90	--
4Q	--	135.7	79.07	58.60	23.70	14.40
Yr.	—	413.8	254.9	172.9	68.60	35.70
Earnings Per Share ($)						
1Q	0.09	0.03	0.05	0.02	0.02	--
2Q	0.15	0.13	0.12	0.04	0.02	--
3Q	--	0.17	0.10	0.09	0.04	--
4Q	--	0.32	0.27	0.11	0.09	0.03
Yr.	—	0.64	0.54	0.29	0.16	0.03

Next earnings report expected: late October

Dividend Data

Since its November 1992 initial public offering, the company has not paid any dividends on its common stock and does not anticipate paying any cash dividends in the foreseeable future.

A Division of The **McGraw-Hill** *Companies*

STANDARD
&POOR'S
STOCK REPORTS

HA-LO Industries, Inc.

1084N
03-OCT-98

Business Summary - 12-SEP-98

HA-LO Industries is the largest and one of the fastest growing marketers and distributors of promotional products in the U.S. The company utilizes a system of 25 showrooms throughout the U.S. It displays products provided by its network of more than 2,500 vendors and marketed by its approximately 700 sales representatives. Under the name Market USA, the company provides telemarketing services, employing 2,100 telephone representatives and 300 insurance agents.

HA-LO develops customized products, generally articles of merchandise with a customer's name, logo or message, for marketing, sales incentives and awards and development of goodwill for a targeted audience. Products include: (i) apparel items such as jackets, sweaters, hats and golf shirts; (ii) business accessories such as clocks, portfolios, briefcases, blotters, and pen and pencil sets; (iii) recognition awards such as trophies and plaques; and (iv) other miscellaneous items such as etched crystalware, calendars, golf accessories, key chains, watches and mugs.

Among the company's more notable clients are Champion Products, Inc., Sony Signatures, Ford, Abbott Laboratories, General Electric, Allied Signal, Ameritech Corporation, General Mills, and the Green Bay Packers. In 1997, no single customer accounted for more than 10% of total revenues.

In September 1996, HMK acquired Market USA and Marusa Marketing, Ltd. (together MUSA). MUSA creates, manages and conducts large scale telephone marketing programs for corporate clients throughout the U.S. and Canada. It provides script development, direct sales, database analysis and management, consultation and program design, and customer lead acquisition primarily for insurance and financial services companies. Telemarketing services generated 15% and 19% of revenues in 1997 and 1996, respectively.

In 1997, the company made several acquisitions. In January, it purchased Creative Concepts in Advertising, a privately held advertising and licensing company that expected to generate $100 million in sales in 1997. In February, the company acquired Entertel, Inc., a privately held telemarketing firm based in Kansas City with annual revenues of roughly $5.5 million. In April, HMK acquired Bradley Marketing Group, a Detroit-based promotional products company with $9.7 million in annual revenues. In June, HMK purchased Lees/Keystone, a private promotional products distributor based in New York, with projected annual revenues of $10 million. In July, HMK acquired The Corporate Choice/Red Sail Merchandising, Inc., a private promotional products distributor with offices in San Francisco, Chicago, and New Jersey, and 1996 revenues of $14 million.

Per Share Data ($)

(Year Ended Dec. 31)	1997	1996	1995	1994	1993	1992	1991	1990	1989	1988
Tangible Bk. Val.	2.79	3.01	2.44	0.40	0.46	0.85	NA	NA	NA	NA
Cash Flow	0.91	0.76	0.50	0.28	0.09	0.14	NA	NA	NA	NA
Earnings	0.64	0.53	0.29	0.16	0.03	0.09	0.16	-0.01	NA	NA
Dividends	Nil	Nil	Nil	Nil	Nil	Nil	Nil	Nil	Nil	Nil
Payout Ratio	Nil	Nil	Nil	Nil	Nil	Nil	Nil	Nil	Nil	Nil
Prices - High	29³/₈	32¹/₄	16³/₈	4¹/₈	3³/₄	4	NA	NA	NA	NA
- Low	12¹/₂	10³/₄	3¹/₄	2⁵/₈	1¹⁵/₁₆	2⁷/₈	NA	NA	NA	NA
P/E Ratio - High	46	61	57	26	NM	47	NA	NA	NA	NA
- Low	20	20	11	17	NM	34	NA	NA	NA	NA

Income Statement Analysis (Million $)

	1997	1996	1995	1994	1993	1992	1991	1990	1989	1988
Revs.	414	255	173	68.6	35.7	23.5	NA	NA	NA	NA
Oper. Inc.	34.7	19.1	8.4	3.9	0.9	1.2	NA	NA	NA	NA
Depr.	5.8	3.9	2.1	1.0	0.5	0.3	NA	NA	NA	NA
Int. Exp.	1.9	0.2	1.3	0.7	0.0	0.3	NA	NA	NA	NA
Pretax Inc.	23.1	15.6	5.0	2.1	0.4	0.8	NA	NA	NA	NA
Eff. Tax Rate	40%	40%	40%	40%	40%	37%	NA	NA	NA	NA
Net Inc.	13.9	9.4	3.0	1.3	0.2	0.5	NA	NA	NA	NA

Balance Sheet & Other Fin. Data (Million $)

	1997	1996	1995	1994	1993	1992	1991	1990	1989	1988
Cash	2.7	6.8	1.5	0.0	0.1	NA	NA	NA	NA	NA
Curr. Assets	162	68.0	54.7	27.2	15.5	NA	NA	NA	NA	NA
Total Assets	211	88.0	68.8	36.1	22.0	NA	NA	NA	NA	NA
Curr. Liab.	84.2	26.0	27.2	13.5	7.8	NA	NA	NA	NA	NA
LT Debt	43.6	2.9	Nil	12.0	5.5	NA	NA	NA	NA	NA
Common Eqty.	81.4	57.2	39.6	8.9	7.3	NA	NA	NA	NA	NA
Total Cap.	125	60.1	39.6	21.2	13.7	NA	NA	NA	NA	NA
Cap. Exp.	8.2	5.0	2.2	0.5	1.0	0.1	NA	NA	NA	NA
Cash Flow	19.7	13.3	5.1	2.3	0.7	0.8	NA	NA	NA	NA
Curr. Ratio	1.9	2.6	2.0	2.0	2.0	NA	NA	NA	NA	NA
% LT Debt of Cap.	34.8	4.8	Nil	56.5	40.2	NA	NA	NA	NA	NA
% Net Inc.of Revs.	3.4	3.7	1.7	1.9	0.6	2.0	NA	NA	NA	NA
% Ret. on Assets	9.3	11.2	5.3	4.4	1.4	NA	NA	NA	NA	NA
% Ret. on Equity	20.0	18.4	12.1	15.9	3.2	NA	NA	NA	NA	NA

Data as orig. reptd.; bef. results of disc. opers. and/or spec. items. Per share data adj. for stk. divs. as of ex-div. date. Bold denotes diluted EPS (FASB 128). E-Estimated. NA-Not Available. NM-Not Meaningful. NR-Not Ranked.

Office—5980 W. Touhy Ave., Niles, IL 60714. **Tel**—(847) 647-2300. **Website**—http://www.ha-lo.com **Chrmn, Pres & CEO**—L. Weisbach. **Treas & COO**—R. A. Magid. **CFO**—G. J. Kilrea. **VP & Secy**—B. G. Berman. **VP-Fin**—B. T. Margolin. **VP & Investor Contact**—Michael P. Nemlich. **Dirs**—T Herskovits, J. R. Katz, M. J. Katz, R. A. Magid, L. D. Nelson, S. N. Okner, N. A. Ramo, D. C. Robbins, R. Sosnick, L. Weisbach. **Transfer Agent & Registrar**—Harris Trust & Savings Bank, Chicago. **Incorporated**—in Illinois in 1986. **Empl**—4,000. **S&P Analyst:** Jordan Horoschak

STANDARD
&POOR'S
STOCK REPORTS

HADCO Corp.

4073T

NASDAQ Symbol **HDCO**

In S&P SmallCap 600

03-OCT-98

Industry:
Electrical Equipment

Summary: This company is a leading supplier of electronic interconnect products and services.

Quantitative Evaluations	
Outlook (1 Lowest—5 Highest) • **5**	
Fair Value • **34⅝**	
Risk • **High**	
Earn./Div. Rank • **B**	
Technical Eval. • **Bullish** since 8/98	
Rel. Strength Rank (1 Lowest—99 Highest) • **77**	
Insider Activity • **Favorable**	

Recent Price • 24⅛
52 Wk Range • 65¼-17½

Yield • Nil
12-Mo. P/E • NM

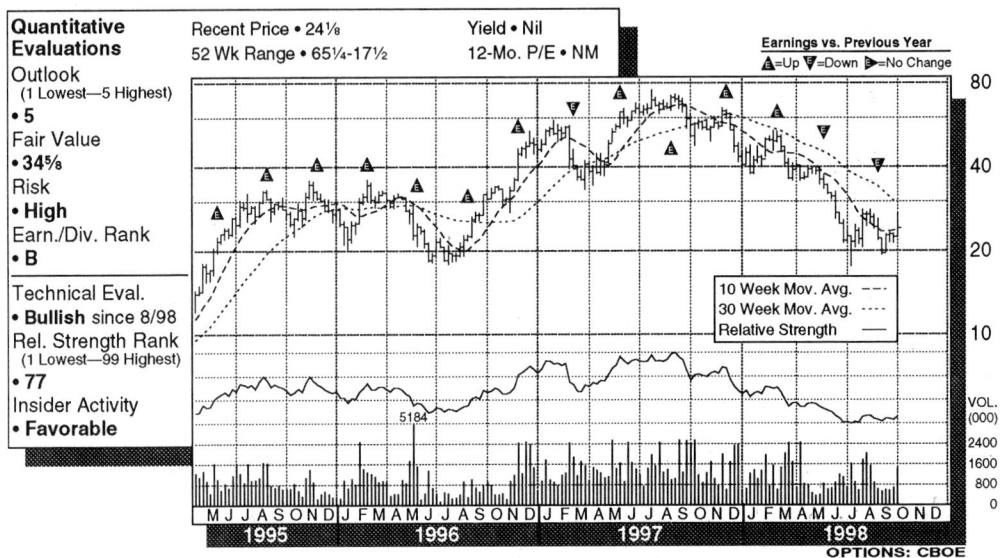

Earnings vs. Previous Year
▲=Up ▼=Down ▶=No Change

10 Week Mov. Avg. – – –
30 Week Mov. Avg. ·····
Relative Strength ——

5184

VOL. (000)

OPTIONS: CBOE

Business Profile - 11-AUG-98

In July 1998, HADCO Corp. announced that net sales
for the third quarter of FY 98 (Oct.) are expected to be
approximately $194 million, resulting in an expected net
loss per share (excluding any non-recurring costs) in
the range of approximately $0.45 to $0.50. Backlog was
approximately $107 million as of July 3, 1998, down
from $126 million (including Continental Circuits) at the
end of the second quarter. Management noted that the
slowdown in sales is the result of several factors including the general slowdown in the broad electronics industry, customer product transitions, customer inventory
adjustments and the economic situation in Asia. Responding to this slowdown, the company is reducing its
workforce by 3%.

Operational Review - 11-AUG-98

Net sales in the first half of FY 98 (Oct.) rose 40%,
year to year, reflecting the acquisitions of Zycon and
Continental. Gross margin narrowed to 19% of sales,
from 22%, due primarily to lower capacity utilization.
Following non-recurring write-offs of $63 million and
$78 million in the respective periods, the net loss nar-
rowed to $47,612,000 ($3.63 a share, on 26% more
shares), from $59,212,000 ($5.67).

Stock Performance - 02-OCT-98

In the past 30 trading days, HDCO's shares have declined 0.52%, compared to a 7% fall in the S&P 500.
Average trading volume for the past five days was
286,780 shares, compared with the 40-day moving average of 174,677 shares.

Key Stock Statistics

Dividend Rate/Share	Nil	Shareholders	400
Shs. outstg. (M)	13.4	Market cap. (B)	$0.322
Avg. daily vol. (M)	0.169	Inst. holdings	65%
Tang. Bk. Value/Share	NM		
Beta	1.66		

Value of $10,000 invested 5 years ago: $ 26,081

Fiscal Year Ending Oct. 31

	1998	1997	1996	1995	1994	1993
Revenues (Million $)						
1Q	198.3	111.5	76.48	56.83	46.46	44.30
2Q	209.6	180.7	88.10	67.64	56.20	51.20
3Q	201.4	183.3	88.23	67.75	59.27	46.50
4Q	—	173.2	97.89	72.95	59.64	47.54
Yr.	—	648.7	350.7	265.2	221.6	189.5
Earnings Per Share ($)						
1Q	0.90	-6.64	0.65	0.29	0.10	0.15
2Q	-4.54	0.91	0.71	0.49	0.22	0.25
3Q	-0.52	0.93	0.72	0.56	0.27	0.14
4Q	—	0.84	0.81	0.63	0.34	0.22
Yr.	—	-3.18	2.89	1.98	0.93	0.76

Next earnings report expected: late November

Dividend Data

No cash dividends have been paid. The company plans
to continue to retain earnings for use in its business. A
stockholder rights plan was adopted in August 1995.

A Division of The **McGraw·Hill** *Companies*

Business Summary - 11-AUG-98

With the January 1997 acquisition of Zycon (valued at $212 million), a manufacturer of electronic interconnect products, HADCO became the largest publicly owned electronic interconnect supplier in North America. In order to solidify its position, the company in March 1998 acquired Continental Circuits Corp. (Nasdaq: CCIR) for approximately $185 million in cash, plus the assumption of approximately $33 million in debt. Continental is a leading manufacturer of complex multilayer printed circuits and will improve HADCO's position in the complex multilayer circuit board segment, one of the fastest growing segments of the interconnect industry.

HADCO offers a wide array of sophisticated manufacturing, engineering and systems integration services to meet its customers' electronic interconnect needs. The company's principal products are complex multilayer rigid printed circuits and backplane assemblies. Printed circuits are the basic platforms used to interconnect microprocessors, integrated circuits and other components essential to the functioning of electronic products. Backplane assemblies are generally larger and thicker printed circuits on which connectors are mounted to interconnect printed circuits, integrated circuits and other electronic components. Net sales of backplane assemblies accounted for 11% and 17% of the total company net sales in FY 97 (Oct.) and FY 96, respectively, and for 10% on a pro forma basis including Zycon during FY 97.

In keeping with its strategy of developing and commercializing technologies that increase density and improve electrical performance, HADCO has focused its efforts in four key areas: high-density interconnect solutions; high-performance materials; buried passive components; and emerging technologies. HADCO's customers are OEMs and contract manufacturers in the computing (mainly workstations, servers, mainframes, storage and notebooks), data communications/telecommunications and industrial automation industries, including process controls, automotive, medical and instrumentation. HADCO's largest customers during FY 97 included leading companies in the electronics industry, such as Cabletron systems, Compaq Computer, Lucent Technologies, Solectron and Sun Microsystems.

In response to a slowdown in sales in the third quarter of FY 98, HADCO announced in July 1998 a 3% overall reduction in the workforce. Management attributes the slowdown to several factors, including the general slowdown in the broad electronics industry, customer product transitions, customer inventory adjustments and the economic situation in Asia.

Per Share Data ($)

(Year Ended Oct. 31)	1997	1996	1995	1994	1993	1992	1991	1990	1989	1988
Tangible Bk. Val.	10.61	13.37	10.14	7.95	7.03	6.13	5.33	4.74	4.01	3.50
Cash Flow	-2.24	4.45	3.20	2.25	1.98	1.92	1.52	1.50	1.29	1.14
Earnings	-3.18	2.89	1.98	0.93	0.76	0.75	0.52	0.65	0.40	0.36
Dividends	Nil	Nil	Nil	Nil	Nil	Nil	Nil	Nil	Nil	Nil
Payout Ratio	Nil	Nil	Nil	Nil	Nil	Nil	Nil	Nil	Nil	Nil
Prices - High	75⅝	54	35⅞	9¼	10½	11	6½	6⅛	7	6⅝
- Low	33⅛	17⅞	8⅜	5⅞	7¼	5⅛	3⅜	3⅝	3⅜	3⅛
P/E Ratio - High	NM	19	18	10	14	15	13	9	18	18
- Low	NM	6	4	6	10	7	6	6	8	9

Income Statement Analysis (Million $)

	1997	1996	1995	1994	1993	1992	1991	1990	1989	1988
Revs.	649	351	265	222	189	183	153	161	156	144
Oper. Inc.	88.0	68.9	47.1	30.7	26.9	26.1	20.5	23.9	20.9	18.4
Depr.	11.2	17.3	13.2	14.2	13.2	12.7	10.9	10.1	10.7	9.6
Int. Exp.	10.9	0.3	0.5	0.9	1.4	2.0	2.1	2.5	2.7	1.9
Pretax Inc.	-9.2	52.5	35.0	16.4	12.9	12.2	8.6	12.4	8.0	7.4
Eff. Tax Rate	NM	39%	39%	40%	36%	34%	35%	38%	40%	39%
Net Inc.	-36.9	32.0	21.4	9.9	8.2	8.1	5.6	7.7	4.8	4.5

Balance Sheet & Other Fin. Data (Million $)

	1997	1996	1995	1994	1993	1992	1991	1990	1989	1988
Cash	12.2	42.2	36.5	31.6	27.4	25.9	23.3	20.7	19.6	8.5
Curr. Assets	167	114	93.6	71.6	60.7	55.6	51.3	48.3	47.1	37.2
Total Assets	503	220	163	126	111	104	99	92.0	90.0	78.0
Curr. Liab.	113	70.0	52.5	39.8	30.1	32.4	29.7	27.9	26.2	21.9
LT Debt	110	1.5	2.4	4.5	9.4	11.0	17.4	13.8	17.8	16.5
Common Eqty.	240	139	101	77.4	68.4	59.4	50.6	48.2	44.1	38.2
Total Cap.	380	140	103	82.0	77.8	71.1	69.5	64.0	63.4	56.2
Cap. Exp.	70.0	54.0	28.9	19.5	14.3	13.0	15.1	11.4	12.7	16.1
Cash Flow	-25.7	49.3	34.5	24.2	21.4	20.8	16.5	17.8	15.5	14.0
Curr. Ratio	1.5	1.6	1.8	1.8	2.0	1.7	1.7	1.7	1.8	1.7
% LT Debt of Cap.	28.8	1.1	2.3	5.5	12.1	15.5	25.0	21.6	28.1	29.3
% Net Inc.of Revs.	NM	9.1	8.1	4.5	4.3	4.4	3.7	4.8	3.1	3.1
% Ret. on Assets	NM	16.7	14.8	8.4	7.6	7.9	6.1	8.8	5.7	5.5
% Ret. on Equity	NM	26.7	24.0	13.6	12.8	14.5	11.7	17.3	11.6	11.1

Data as orig. reptd.; bef. results of disc. opers. and/or spec. items. Per share data adj. for stk. divs. as of ex-div. date. Bold denotes diluted EPS (FASB 128). E-Estimated. NA-Not Available. NM-Not Meaningful. NR-Not Ranked.

Office—12A Manor Pkwy., Salem, NH 03079. **Organized**—in Massachusetts in 1966. **Tel**—(603) 898-8000. **Website**—http://www.hadco.com **Chrmn**—H. H. Irvine II. **Pres & CEO**—A. E. Lietz. **VP, CFO, Treas & Investor Contact**—Timothy P. Losik. **Clerk**—J. C. Hamilton. **Dirs**—L. Coolidge, J. S. Hill, H. H. Irvine II, A. E. Lietz, J. E. Pomeroy, J. F. Smith, P. Sweeney, J. C. Taylor, O. O. Ward. **Transfer Agent**—BankBoston, N.A., Boston. **Empl**— 6,142. **S&P Analyst:** J. Robert Cho

03-OCT-98

Industry:
Textiles (Apparel)

Summary: This company designs, makes, imports and markets men's casual and dress apparel products primarily under the Haggar and Reed St. James brand names.

Quantitative Evaluations

Outlook
(1 Lowest—5 Highest)
• **4**

Fair Value
• **14½**

Risk
• **Average**

Earn./Div. Rank
• **NR**

Technical Eval.
• **Bearish** since 3/98

Rel. Strength Rank
(1 Lowest—99 Highest)
• **65**

Insider Activity
• **NA**

Recent Price • 10¾
52 Wk Range • 18-10⅛

Yield • 1.9%
12-Mo. P/E • 12.5

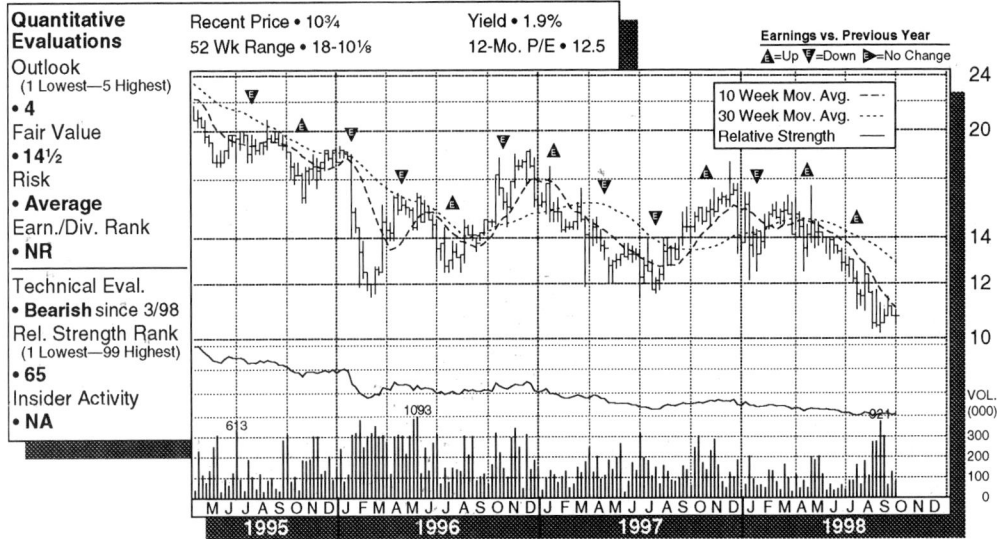

Earnings vs. Previous Year
▲=Up ▼=Down ▶=No Change

10 Week Mov. Avg. ---
30 Week Mov. Avg. ····
Relative Strength —

Business Profile - 05-AUG-98

In October 1996, Haggar announced a restructuring of its worldwide manufacturing capacity. The restructuring, which was completed in FY 97 (Sep.) aided gross margins in FY 97 and the first half of FY 98. HGGR expects the restructuring to result in about 15% of all FY 98 manufacturing occurring in the U.S., with the remaining 85% in foreign countries (versus 25% and 75%, respectively, in FY 97). In the fall of 1997, the company launched its Black Label collection, a premium line of its finest dress and casual pants, as well as a new fabrication called Cotton Flex. Lower earnings in the first quarter of FY 98 reflected softness in the retail industry, although results exceeded analyst expectations. The weak retail environment continued into the second quarter of FY 98, although earnings recovered from the prior year's depressed levels. In the third quarter, the Haggar brand sold well, despite mixed retail results, and earnings beat analyst expectations for the fourth consecutive quarter.

Operational Review - 05-AUG-98

Net sales in the nine months ended June 30, 1998, slid 1.2%, year to year. Gross margins widened significantly, on a more favorable sourcing mix. SG&A expense fell slightly, and royalty income was up; operating profit climbed 603%. Despite lower other income, and taxes at 38.5%, versus tax credits of $69,000, net income of $3,535,000 ($0.41 a share) contrasted with a net loss of $103,000 ($0.01).

Stock Performance - 02-OCT-98

In the past 30 trading days, HGGR's shares have increased 2%, compared to a 7% fall in the S&P 500. Average trading volume for the past five days was 15,540 shares, compared with the 40-day moving average of 54,928 shares.

Key Stock Statistics

Dividend Rate/Share	0.20	Shareholders	300
Shs. outstg. (M)	8.6	Market cap. (B)	$0.092
Avg. daily vol. (M)	0.050	Inst. holdings	60%
Tang. Bk. Value/Share	19.49		
Beta	0.37		

Value of $10,000 invested 5 years ago: $ 6,278

Fiscal Year Ending Sep. 30

	1998	1997	1996	1995	1994	1993
Revenues (Million $)						
1Q	102.5	104.2	98.42	121.0	110.2	82.00
2Q	94.68	98.61	110.8	121.1	118.3	104.9
3Q	90.19	88.00	103.8	85.18	120.2	83.40
4Q	—	115.3	124.9	121.2	142.5	123.8
Yr.	—	406.0	437.9	448.5	491.2	394.1
Earnings Per Share ($)						
1Q	**0.13**	**0.16**	0.12	0.62	0.51	0.18
2Q	**0.14**	0.06	0.19	0.25	0.92	0.75
3Q	0.14	0.22	0.10	-2.00	0.65	0.26
4Q	—	0.45	-0.71	2.57	0.86	0.70
Yr.	—	0.44	-0.28	1.14	2.95	1.88

Next earnings report expected: early November

Dividend Data (Dividends have been paid since 1993.)

Amount ($)	Date Decl.	Ex-Div. Date	Stock of Record	Payment Date
0.050	Nov. 04	Nov. 06	Nov. 03	Nov. 17 '97
0.050	Jan. 21	Jan. 29	Feb. 02	Feb. 16 '98
0.050	Apr. 29	May. 07	May. 11	May. 25 '98
0.050	Jul. 22	Jul. 30	Aug. 03	Aug. 17 '98

 A Division of The McGraw·Hill Companies

Business Summary - 05-AUG-98

Haggar Corp. introduced its wrinkle-free, 100% cotton pants in FY 93 (Sep.), helping to midwife the phenomenon known worldwide as "Casual Friday." The launch gave the apparel maker the leading position in the wrinkle-resistant category, and the second slot in the total casual pants category. In October 1996, in an effort to eliminate the wrinkles from its own operations, Haggar initiated a restructuring designed to keep it competitive in the global apparel industry and improve its gross margins. The plan included consolidation of three Texas plants into one; Haggar believed that this could cut $12 million to $14 million in annual manufacturing costs. It recorded a related charge of $14 million to cover the restructuring, resulting in a net loss for FY 96, only the third in its 70-year history.

the company designs, makes, imports and markets men's casual and dress apparel products, including pants, shorts, suits, sportcoats and shirts. HGGR sells its apparel products directly to retailers throughout the U.S., primarily under the Haggar and Reed St. James brand names, as well as under retailers' own labels. During FY 97, 25% of products were produced in the U.S., with the balance manufactured in other countries.

The company's apparel lines are focused on basic, recurring styles that are less susceptible to fashion obso-

lescence. Haggar-brand products, which accounted for 77% of apparel sales in FY 97, are sold nationwide mainly to major department stores and include dress and casual pants, sportcoats, suits, shirts and shorts. Haggar has developed specific product lines (such as Haggar Wrinkle-Free Cottons and Haggar City Casuals) intended to keep it in the forefront of the trend among men toward more casual clothing, while maintaining its traditional strength in men's dress apparel. Besides the epochal wrinkle-free cotton trousers, HGGR continues to emphasize its shirt lines which are designed to complement its casual product lines.

HGGR also markets Reed St. James branded products, including dress slacks, casual slacks, shorts, suits, sportcoats and shirts. Reed St. James products are offered at lower prices than the Haggar line and are generally sold to mass-market retailers. The company also markets Mustang brand jeans and shorts, and Reed Stretch jeans; and manufactures specialty-label men's apparel, mainly for major department stores and mass merchandisers.

Haggar branded products are sold throughout the U.S., primarily in major department stores. The company also operates retail outlet stores that market Haggar branded men's clothing. As of January 21, 1998, 47 outlet stores were in operation.

Per Share Data ($)

(Year Ended Sep. 30)	1997	1996	1995	1994	1993	1992	1991	1990	1989	1988
Tangible Bk. Val.	19.24	19.00	19.46	18.51	15.70	11.15	NA	NA	NA	NA
Cash Flow	1.78	0.52	1.52	3.31	2.28	2.26	NA	NA	NA	NA
Earnings	0.44	-0.28	1.14	2.95	1.88	1.70	NA	NA	NA	NA
Dividends	0.20	0.20	0.20	0.20	0.10	Nil	Nil	Nil	Nil	Nil
Payout Ratio	45%	NM	18%	7%	6%	Nil	Nil	Nil	Nil	Nil
Prices - High	18	19	26¼	40½	25½	21½	NA	NA	NA	NA
- Low	11½	11½	15¾	20½	15½	16½	NA	NA	NA	NA
P/E Ratio - High	40	NM	23	14	14	13	NA	NA	NA	NA
- Low	26	NM	14	7	8	10	NA	NA	NA	NA

Income Statement Analysis (Million $)

	1997	1996	1995	1994	1993	1992	1991	1990	1989	1988
Revs.	406	438	449	491	394	381	NA	NA	NA	NA
Oper. Inc.	17.0	16.3	15.4	42.3	24.2	24.1	NA	NA	NA	NA
Depr.	11.4	6.8	3.3	3.2	3.1	3.7	NA	NA	NA	NA
Int. Exp.	3.5	4.3	5.0	1.3	1.5	4.0	NA	NA	NA	NA
Pretax Inc.	6.0	-3.4	15.8	42.0	23.3	19.5	NA	NA	NA	NA
Eff. Tax Rate	38%	NM	38%	39%	36%	36%	NA	NA	NA	NA
Net Inc.	3.7	-2.4	9.8	25.7	15.0	12.4	NA	NA	NA	NA

Balance Sheet & Other Fin. Data (Million $)

	1997	1996	1995	1994	1993	1992	1991	1990	1989	1988
Cash	2.2	2.9	2.2	2.6	17.9	0.4	NA	NA	NA	NA
Curr. Assets	192	210	249	215	179	146	NA	NA	NA	NA
Total Assets	262	278	315	257	206	170	NA	NA	NA	NA
Curr. Liab.	65.7	73.7	70.4	84.3	67.4	49.3	NA	NA	NA	NA
LT Debt	31.8	42.1	78.6	15.0	5.5	28.2	NA	NA	NA	NA
Common Eqty.	165	162	166	158	133	93.0	NA	NA	NA	NA
Total Cap.	196	205	245	173	139	121	NA	NA	NA	NA
Cap. Exp.	15.0	16.0	30.6	15.4	6.5	NA	NA	NA	NA	NA
Cash Flow	15.2	4.4	13.1	28.8	18.1	15.1	NA	NA	NA	NA
Curr. Ratio	2.9	2.9	3.5	2.6	2.7	3.0	NA	NA	NA	NA
% LT Debt of Cap.	16.2	20.5	32.1	8.7	3.9	23.2	NA	NA	NA	NA
% Net Inc.of Revs.	0.9	NM	2.2	5.2	3.8	3.3	NA	NA	NA	NA
% Ret. on Assets	1.4	NM	3.4	11.1	7.9	NA	NA	NA	NA	NA
% Ret. on Equity	2.3	NM	6.0	17.6	13.2	NA	NA	NA	NA	NA

Data as orig. reptd.; bef. results of disc. opers. and/or spec. items. Per share data adj. for stk. divs. as of ex-div. date. Bold denotes diluted EPS (FASB 128). E-Estimated. NA-Not Available. NM-Not Meaningful. NR-Not Ranked.

Office—6113 Lemmon Ave., Dallas, TX 75209. Tel—(214) 352-8481. Chrmn & CEO—J. M. Haggar III. Pres & COO—F. D. Bracken. SVP & CFO—D. Tehle. Dirs—F. D. Bracken, N. E. Brinker, R. F. Evans, J. M. Haggar III, R. W. Heath, J. C. Tolleson. Transfer Agent & Registrar—ChaseMellon Shareholder Services, Ridgefield Park, NJ. Incorporated—in Nevada in 1989. Empl— 4,300. S&P Analyst: Kathleen J. Fraser

Halter Marine Group   8068

ASE Symbol **HLX**

In S&P SmallCap 600

03-OCT-98

Industry:
Manufacturing (Specialized)

Summary: This company specializes in the construction, repair and conversion of oceangoing and inland waterway vessels for commercial and governmental markets.

Quantitative Evaluations

Recent Price • 9¾	Yield • Nil
52 Wk Range • 41½-8½	12-Mo. P/E • 12.3

Outlook (1 Lowest—5 Highest)
• **NA**

Fair Value
• **NA**

Risk
• **Average**

Earn./Div. Rank
• **NR**

Technical Eval.
• **NA**

Rel. Strength Rank (1 Lowest—99 Highest)
• **22**

Insider Activity
• **Neutral**

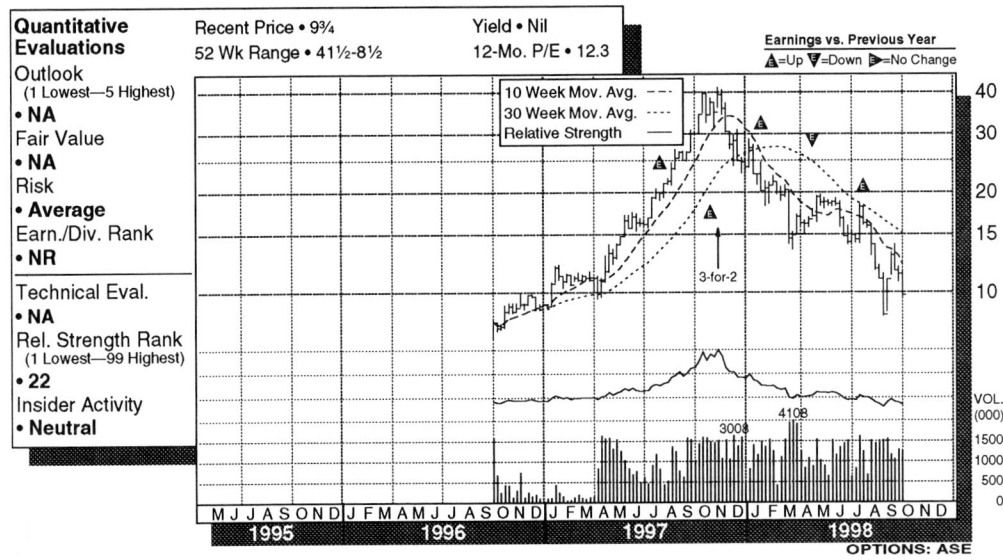

Earnings vs. Previous Year
▲=Up ▼=Down ▶=No Change

10 Week Mov. Avg. ---
30 Week Mov. Avg. ....
Relative Strength ----

3-for-2

OPTIONS: ASE

Business Profile - 22-SEP-98

In November 1997, HLX acquired for $60 million in cash and stock three companies that formed the basis for a new Engineered Products Group. The companies make and market winches, cranes, mooring systems, and other related equipment used in the construction and modification of vessels and drilling rigs. In May 1998, HLX formed a joint venture to build marine vessels in China. Separately, the company acquired from Trinity Industries that company's Orange, TX, shipyard, significantly increasing HLX's rig building capability. Backlog at June 30, 1998, totaled $988 million, up 73% from the level a year earlier. A three-for-two stock split was effected in October 1997.

Operational Review - 22-SEP-98

Contract revenues in the three months ended June 30, 1998, advanced 41%, year to year, reflecting contributions from the recently acquired engineered products group, and higher revenues from the rigs segment. Gross margins narrowed, on a decreased percentage of higher-margin revenues generated from the government customer group. With a rise in SG&A expense, and higher amortization of excess of cost over net assets acquired, pretax income slid fractionally. After taxes at 30.0%, versus 38.3%, net income rose 13%, to $6,128,000 ($0.21 a share, diluted), from $5,411,000 ($0.19, as adjusted).

Stock Performance - 02-OCT-98

In the past 30 trading days, HLX's shares have declined 11%, compared to a 7% fall in the S&P 500. Average trading volume for the past five days was 254,220 shares, compared with the 40-day moving average of 296,069 shares.

Key Stock Statistics

Dividend Rate/Share	Nil	Shareholders	NA
Shs. outstg. (M)	28.9	Market cap. (B)	$0.283
Avg. daily vol. (M)	0.259	Inst. holdings	62%
Tang. Bk. Value/Share	2.05		
Beta	NA		

Value of $10,000 invested 5 years ago: NA

Fiscal Year Ending Mar. 31

	1999	1998	1997	1996	1995	1994
Revenues (Million $)						
1Q	209.8	149.1	85.98	—	—	—
2Q	—	151.2	94.50	—	—	—
3Q	—	180.6	112.5	—	—	—
4Q	—	189.4	113.9	—	—	—
Yr.	—	670.2	406.8	254.3	—	—
Earnings Per Share ($)						
1Q	**0.21**	0.19	0.13	—	—	—
2Q	—	0.27	0.15	—	—	—
3Q	—	**0.29**	0.15	—	—	—
4Q	—	**0.02**	0.17	—	—	—
Yr.	—	**0.78**	0.59	0.47	—	—

Next earnings report expected: mid October

Dividend Data

Amount ($)	Date Decl.	Ex-Div. Date	Stock of Record	Payment Date
3-for-2	Sep. 29	Nov. 03	Oct. 15	Oct. 31 '97

A Division of The **McGraw·Hill** Companies

Business Summary - 22-SEP-98

In May 1997, shortly after completing its first fiscal year as a public company, Halter Marine Group, Inc. (HLX) acquired Texas Drydock, Inc. (TDI), launching the shipbuilder into the related, and promising, business of building, converting and mending offshore drilling rigs. HLX believes that increased drilling activity and the demand for rigs that can drill in deeper waters will keep the offshore drilling rig market booming. Its new capabilities complement its existing energy-related activities, including the construction of offshore support vessels and ocean going fuel barges.

Ranked fourth among U.S. shipbuilders, HLX is the leader in the construction of small- to medium-sized ocean-going vessels in the U.S. that range in length from 50 ft. to 400 ft. With a varied product line that serves government, energy, commercial and other markets, the company considers its shipbuilding versatility to be among its greatest strengths. The vessels segment operates nine shipyards mainly dedicated to the new construction of marine vessels. HLX has 21 shipyards strategically located along the Gulf Coast from Florida to Texas.

In FY 98 (Mar.), HLX entered the engineered products market through the acquisition of four companies (AmClyde Engineered Products, Inc. of St. Paul, MN; Utility Steel Fabrication, Inc. of Slidell, LA; Fritz Culver, Inc. of Covington, LA; and McElroy Machine & Manufacturing

Co.) which manufacture market cranes, derrricks, winches, holsts, control systems and other related products.

Sales to government customers accounted for 26% of total revenues in FY 98, verusus 53% in FY 97. The decline in government revenues in the vessels segment in FY 98 reflected the absence of a major contract that aided revenues in FY 97.

Customers in the energy industry accounted for 51% of FY 98 revenues, up from 21% in FY 97, with 24% derived from the addition of the rigs segment. Products sold to this market include offshore supply vessels and large anchor handling tug/supply vessels, tug boats and double hull ocean going fuel barges. Rising demand for these products is reflected in HLX's strong energy backlog of $515 million (including $229 million from rigs) at March 31, 1998, up from $156 million at the end of FY 97.

Products sold to the commercial market include harbor and ocean going tugs, tow boats and hopper barges, and accounted for 9.4% of FY 98 revenues, down from 20% a year earlier.

In April 1998, HLX signed two contracts, valued at a total of $170 million, to construct two drilling rigs for Petrodrill Construction, Inc. The rigs will be delivered in late 1999 and early 2000. At March 31, 1998, HLX had 30 offshore support vessels, three rigs, and six drill barges under contract.

Per Share Data ($)

(Year Ended Mar. 31)	1998	1997	1996	1995	1994	1993	1992	1991	1990	1989
Tangible Bk. Val.	2.05	5.06	2.98	NA	NA	NA	NA	NA	NA	NA
Cash Flow	1.30	1.32	0.71	NA	NA	NA	NA	NA	NA	NA
Earnings	0.78	0.59	0.47	NA	NA	NA	NA	NA	NA	NA
Dividends	Nil	Nil	Nil	Nil	Nil	Nil	Nil	Nil	Nil	Nil
Payout Ratio	Nil	Nil	Nil	Nil	Nil	Nil	Nil	Nil	Nil	Nil
Cal. Yrs.	1997	1996	1995	1994	1993	1992	1991	1990	1989	1988
Prices - High	41½	10	NA	NA	NA	NA	NA	NA	NA	NA
- Low	9	7⅜	NA	NA	NA	NA	NA	NA	NA	NA
P/E Ratio - High	53	17	NA	NA	NA	NA	NA	NA	NA	NA
- Low	12	12	NA	NA	NA	NA	NA	NA	NA	NA

Income Statement Analysis (Million $)

	1998	1997	1996	1995	1994	1993	1992	1991	1990	1989
Revs.	670	407	254	NA	NA	NA	NA	NA	NA	NA
Oper. Inc.	54.5	38.1	30.6	NA	NA	NA	NA	NA	NA	NA
Depr.	15.2	7.9	6.7	NA	NA	NA	NA	NA	NA	NA
Int. Exp.	6.6	3.2	3.3	NA	NA	NA	NA	NA	NA	NA
Pretax Inc.	31.7	27.0	20.6	NA	NA	NA	NA	NA	NA	NA
Eff. Tax Rate	29%	40%	39%	NA	NA	NA	NA	NA	NA	NA
Net Inc.	22.5	16.1	12.5	NA	NA	NA	NA	NA	NA	NA

Balance Sheet & Other Fin. Data (Million $)

	1998	1997	1996	1995	1994	1993	1992	1991	1990	1989
Cash	51.1	7.1	0.7	NA	NA	NA	NA	NA	NA	NA
Curr. Assets	273	148	102	NA	NA	NA	NA	NA	NA	NA
Total Assets	500	209	158	NA	NA	NA	NA	NA	NA	NA
Curr. Liab.	122	62.1	62.7	NA	NA	NA	NA	NA	NA	NA
LT Debt	218	52.0	31.1	NA	NA	NA	NA	NA	NA	NA
Common Eqty.	151	93.3	80.4	NA	NA	NA	NA	NA	NA	NA
Total Cap.	369	145	112	NA	NA	NA	NA	NA	NA	NA
Cap. Exp.	40.9	14.5	5.6	NA	NA	NA	NA	NA	NA	NA
Cash Flow	37.7	24.0	19.2	NA	NA	NA	NA	NA	NA	NA
Curr. Ratio	2.2	2.4	1.6	NA	NA	NA	NA	NA	NA	NA
% LT Debt of Cap.	57.9	35.8	27.9	NA	NA	NA	NA	NA	NA	NA
% Net Inc.of Revs.	3.4	4.0	4.9	NA	NA	NA	NA	NA	NA	NA
% Ret. on Assets	6.4	9.2	NA	NA	NA	NA	NA	NA	NA	NA
% Ret. on Equity	18.4	20.1	NA	NA	NA	NA	NA	NA	NA	NA

Data as orig. reptd.; bef. results of disc. opers. and/or spec. items. Per share data adj. for stk. divs. as of ex-div. date. Bold denotes diluted EPS (FASB 128). E-Estimated. NA-Not Available. NM-Not Meaningful. NR-Not Ranked.

Office—13085 Industrial Seaway Rd., Gulfport, MS 39503. **Tel**—(601) 896-0029. **Website**—http://www.haltermarine.com **Chrmn, Pres & CEO**—J. Dane III. **EVP & COO**—D. J. Mortimer. **SVP, CFO & Investor Contact**—Keith L. Voigts. **Dirs**—A. R. Cooper, J. Dane III, B. J. Galt, B. H. Keenan, K. W. Lewis, D. J. Mortimer, R. S. Rees. **Transfer Agent & Registrar**—Bank of New York, NYC. **Incorporated**—in Delaware in 1996. **Empl**—6,744. **S&P Analyst:** Stewart Scharf

Hancock Fabrics

1090M

NYSE Symbol **HKF**

In S&P SmallCap 600

03-OCT-98

Industry: Retail (Specialty)

Summary: This company, which sells fabrics and related items primarily at retail to the home sewing market, operates about 470 stores in 39 states.

Quantitative Evaluations

Recent Price • 9¼	Yield • 4.3%
52 Wk Range • 17⅛-9⅛	12-Mo. P/E • 14.3

Outlook (1 Lowest—5 Highest)
• **4+**

Fair Value
• 12⅛

Risk
• **Average**

Earn./Div. Rank
• **B-**

Technical Eval.
• **Bearish** since 6/96

Rel. Strength Rank (1 Lowest—99 Highest)
• **51**

Insider Activity
• **NA**

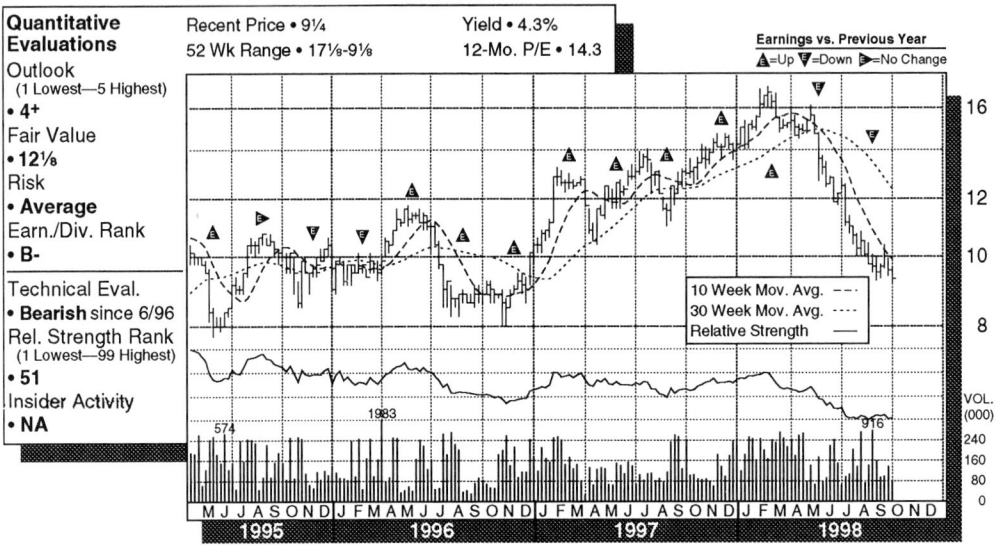

Earnings vs. Previous Year ▲=Up ▼=Down ▶=No Change

10 Week Mov. Avg. - - -
30 Week Mov. Avg. ....
Relative Strength —

VOL. (000)

1995   1996   1997   1998

Business Profile - 01-OCT-98

The company's growth strategy includes emphasizing new products, expansion into under-served markets, and strategic acquisitions. In keeping with its strategy, HKF has altered its merchandising mix by reducing its dependence on fashion apparel and emphasizing home decorating, quilting, special occasion and seasonal fabrics and goods. The company planned to open 25 stores and close 25 in FY 99 (Jan.); in the first half of the year, it opened 10 stores and closed 21, lowering the total number of stores in operation to 470. Approximately 120 stores were remodeled through September 1998. In November 1997, HKF acquired 48 Northwest Fabrics and Crafts stores from Silas Creek Retail, L.P., for about $20.9 million. Directors have authorized the repurchase of up to 1 million common shares; in the first half of FY 99, $12.6 million was spent on stock purchases.

Operational Review - 01-OCT-98

Sales in the 26 weeks ended August 2, 1998, rose 6.5%, year to year, as the inclusion of sales from recently acquired Northwest Fabrics and Crafts stores outweighed a 2.0% decline in same-store sales, as well as lower sales from net store openings and closings. Gross margins narrowed slightly; with SG&A expenses up 9.6%, and 14% higher interest expense, pretax income fell 39%. After taxes at 36.2%, versus 38.4%, net income declined 37%, to $2,549,000 ($0.12 a share), from $4,028,000 ($0.19).

Stock Performance - 02-OCT-98

In the past 30 trading days, HKF's shares have declined 4%, compared to a 7% fall in the S&P 500. Average trading volume for the past five days was 15,620 shares, compared with the 40-day moving average of 43,431 shares.

Key Stock Statistics

Dividend Rate/Share	0.40	Shareholders	9,400
Shs. outstg. (M)	20.5	Market cap. (B)	$0.191
Avg. daily vol. (M)	0.022	Inst. holdings	61%
Tang. Bk. Value/Share	4.67		
Beta	0.87		

Value of $10,000 invested 5 years ago: $ 9,397

Fiscal Year Ending Jan. 31

	1999	1998	1997	1996	1995	1994
Revenues (Million $)						
1Q	97.80	92.00	91.63	90.10	92.90	92.80
2Q	85.37	79.95	82.78	81.60	81.80	83.60
3Q	—	96.46	94.37	95.90	96.50	99.0
4Q	—	113.5	109.4	96.70	95.60	92.30
Yr.	—	381.9	378.2	364.2	366.8	367.8
Earnings Per Share ($)						
1Q	**0.10**	0.11	0.08	0.06	0.05	0.04
2Q	**0.02**	0.08	0.06	0.04	0.04	Nil
3Q	Nil	0.23	0.18	0.16	0.10	0.10
4Q	—	**0.30**	0.26	0.16	0.21	0.06
Yr.	—	**0.72**	0.58	0.42	0.48	0.26

Next earnings report expected: mid November

Dividend Data (Dividends have been paid since 1987.)

Amount ($)	Date Decl.	Ex-Div. Date	Stock of Record	Payment Date
0.100	Dec. 11	Dec. 29	Jan. 01	Jan. 15 '98
0.100	Mar. 24	Mar. 30	Apr. 01	Apr. 15 '98
0.100	Jun. 11	Jun. 29	Jul. 01	Jul. 15 '98
0.100	Sep. 10	Sep. 29	Oct. 01	Oct. 15 '98

A Division of The McGraw·Hill Companies

Business Summary - 01-OCT-98

Hancock Fabrics caters to the woman who makes clothing for her family and decorations for her home. Stores sell fabrics and related items at retail to the home sewing and home decorating markets. Wholesale operations accounted for less than 2% of sales in FY 98 (Jan.). As of August 2, 1998, the company operated 470 fabric stores in 39 states, under the names Hancock Fabrics, Minnesota Fabrics and Fabric Warehouse, and supplied approximately 100 independent wholesale customers.

Retail stores are usually located in neighborhood shopping centers and offer a wide selection of clothing fabrics. Each store maintains an inventory of cotton, wool and synthetic fabrics such as broadcloth, poplin, gabardine, unbleached muslin and corduroy, as well as seasonal and current fashions. Notions (including sewing aids and accessories such as zippers, buttons, threads and ornamentation), patterns, quilting materials and supplies, decorative fabrics (including drapery and upholstery), craft items and related supplies are also available. The company's business is slightly seasonal. Peak sale periods occur during the fall and pre-Easter weeks, while the lowest sales periods occur before Christmas and midsummer.

Hancock is one of the largest U.S. fabric retailers, but its business has become increasingly competitive in certain geographic areas as a result of the entry and expansion of other fabric stores. As a result, the company has been pruning its store base, closing 90 underperforming stores in FY 98 and FY 97. Store closings and the associated inventory liquidations by competitors slowed in 1997, as piece goods retail capacity adjusted more closely to customer demand. During FY 99, Hancock planned to open approximately 25 stores and close 25. In the first half of FY 99, HKF opened 10 stores and closed 21.

HKF targets its customers primarily through promotional advertising in newspapers, direct mail and television. Typically 8 to 10 direct mail pieces are circulated to approximately 1.2 million households annually. The direct mailer includes the company's magazine Directions, which offers discount coupons, sewing instructions and fashion ideas.

During 1994, the company entered into an agreement with the Home and Garden Television Network to sponsor a weekly sewing show called Sew Perfect. The program, which reaches 40 million U.S. households, is designed for the beginning and intermediate seamstress.

In November, 1997, Hancock acquired 48 Northwest Fabrics & Crafts stores for approximately $20.9 million. The Northwest Stores were sold as part of the Chapter 11 bankruptcy of Solas Creek Retail, L.P., and its affiliates.

Per Share Data ($)

(Year Ended Jan. 31)	1998	1997	1996	1995	1994	1993	1992	1991	1990	1989
Tangible Bk. Val.	5.05	4.94	4.67	4.54	4.37	4.44	4.41	4.18	3.71	4.15
Cash Flow	0.87	0.75	0.61	0.68	0.46	0.77	1.21	1.40	1.20	0.99
Earnings	0.72	0.58	0.42	0.48	0.26	0.57	1.03	1.23	1.06	0.86
Dividends	0.46	0.32	0.32	0.32	0.32	0.32	0.32	0.28	0.24	0.20
Payout Ratio	64%	55%	76%	67%	123%	56%	31%	22%	21%	23%
Cal. Yrs.	1997	1996	1995	1994	1993	1992	1991	1990	1989	1988
Prices - High	15	11¾	11¾	10	14½	19	27¾	20⅝	17⅛	9¼
- Low	10⅛	8	7¾	6½	8	9	14¼	15½	9	6⅜
P/E Ratio - High	21	20	28	21	56	33	27	17	16	11
- Low	14	14	18	14	31	16	14	13	9	7

Income Statement Analysis (Million $)

	1998	1997	1996	1995	1994	1993	1992	1991	1990	1989
Revs.	382	378	364	367	368	380	388	387	346	315
Oper. Inc.	28.3	25.0	20.6	23.2	15.0	25.8	42.6	51.2	46.5	40.1
Depr.	3.3	3.7	3.9	4.2	4.2	4.3	4.0	3.8	3.7	3.4
Int. Exp.	0.4	1.2	2.3	2.4	2.3	2.6	2.8	3.8	2.9	2.7
Pretax Inc.	24.8	20.3	14.7	16.8	8.7	19.1	36.6	44.5	41.3	35.0
Eff. Tax Rate	38%	39%	39%	40%	37%	37%	37%	37%	37%	37%
Net Inc.	15.3	12.5	9.0	10.1	5.4	12.1	23.0	28.1	26.0	22.0

Balance Sheet & Other Fin. Data (Million $)

	1998	1997	1996	1995	1994	1993	1992	1991	1990	1989
Cash	7.1	6.9	5.0	3.9	4.3	9.0	4.1	8.8	7.0	15.5
Curr. Assets	165	161	174	180	180	185	189	173	154	150
Total Assets	196	188	202	209	209	214	218	196	176	170
Curr. Liab.	55.9	57.8	51.5	56.0	53.3	47.4	58.5	64.4	51.6	36.3
LT Debt	10.0	3.0	30.0	37.0	45.0	58.0	50.3	35.5	35.8	26.1
Common Eqty.	107	105	100	97.0	94.0	95.0	97.0	93.0	86.0	106
Total Cap.	117	108	130	131	139	153	148	131	124	134
Cap. Exp.	2.7	2.3	1.9	4.0	2.8	4.2	6.3	4.9	5.0	5.1
Cash Flow	18.6	16.2	12.9	14.3	9.7	16.4	26.9	31.9	29.6	25.4
Curr. Ratio	2.9	2.8	3.4	3.2	3.4	3.9	3.2	2.7	3.0	4.1
% LT Debt of Cap.	8.6	2.8	23.0	27.0	32.5	38.0	34.1	27.1	29.0	19.5
% Net Inc.of Revs.	4.0	3.3	2.5	2.8	1.5	3.2	5.9	7.3	7.5	7.0
% Ret. on Assets	8.0	6.4	4.4	4.9	2.6	5.7	11.2	15.4	15.8	13.0
% Ret. on Equity	14.5	12.1	9.1	10.6	5.8	12.9	24.3	31.9	28.6	22.6

Data as orig. reptd.; bef. results of disc. opers. and/or spec. items. Per share data adj. for stk. divs. as of ex-div. date. Bold denotes diluted EPS (FASB 128). E-Estimated. NA-Not Available. NM-Not Meaningful. NR-Not Ranked.

Office—3406 W. Main St., Tupelo, MS 38803. **Tel**—(601) 842-2834. **Chrmn & CEO**—L. G. Kirk. **Pres & COO**—J. W. Busby Jr. **SVP, CFO, Treas & Investor Contact**—Bruce D. Smith (601-842-2834 Ext. 112). **Dirs**—J. W. Busby Jr., R. R. Devening, D. L. Fruge, L. G. Kirk, D. L. Weaver. **Transfer Agent & Registrar**—Continental Stock Transfer & Trust Co., NYC. **Incorporated**—in Delaware in 1987. **Empl**— 6,700. **S&P Analyst:** Kathleen J. Fraser

Harbinger Corp. 4100

Nasdaq Symbol **HRBC**

In S&P SmallCap 600

03-OCT-98

Industry:
Computer (Software & Services)

Summary: HRBC produces software and provides computer communications network and consulting services designed to enable businesses to engage in electronic commerce.

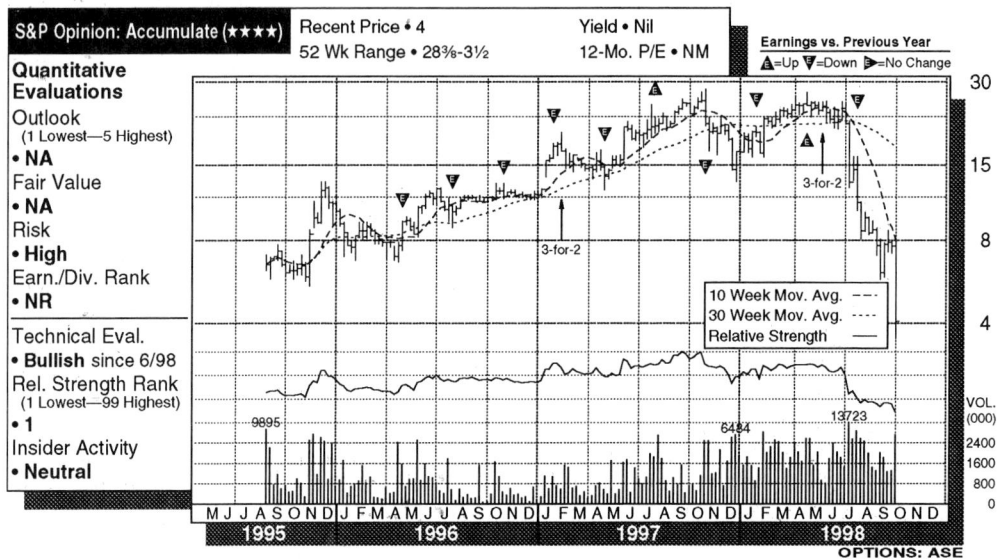

S&P Opinion: Accumulate (★★★★)	Recent Price ◆ 4	Yield ● Nil
	52 Wk Range ● 28⅜-3½	12-Mo. P/E ● NM

Earnings vs. Previous Year
▲=Up ▼=Down ▶=No Change

Quantitative Evaluations

Outlook
(1 Lowest—5 Highest)
● **NA**

Fair Value
● **NA**

Risk
● **High**

Earn./Div. Rank
● **NR**

Technical Eval.
● **Bullish** since 6/98

Rel. Strength Rank
(1 Lowest—99 Highest)
● **1**

Insider Activity
● **Neutral**

10 Week Mov. Avg. – – –
30 Week Mov. Avg. - - - -
Relative Strength —

OPTIONS: ASE

Overview - 24-AUG-98

An aggressive acquisition strategy and a lack of sufficient procedures to handle business integration issues caught up with HRBC in the 1998 second quarter, when it failed to ship about $1.0 million of software representing 20 new software licenses. The software was subsequently shipped on July 1. However, the underlying problem remained, which led HRBC to initiate a new review of acquisitions and the revenue goals of each business line. As a result of the review (expected to be completed by late August), HRBC expects growth in operating income, which was 121% in the first half of 1998, to slow to the 50% range in the second half, and to about 45% in 1999. Thus, we now expect 1998 net income, excluding non-recurring charges that may include a reserve for restructuring later this year, to approach $0.49 per share. In 1999, we expect a strong upturn in operating net to $0.76 a share.

Valuation - 24-AUG-98

The operating difficulties Harbinger is experiencing appear to be fully discounted in the stock price. The numerous acquisitions in the past three years have perhaps distracted management from the core issue of managing the transition in the company's line of products and services, from private network-based electronic commerce, which appeared to offer the best combination of cost and security features in the mid-90s, to emerging Internet based e-commerce technologies. We think Harbinger has recognized its problems and identified the solutions. With these solutions likely to be implemented quickly, we expect a rebound in the shares. Currently trading at a multiple of 1999 earnings that is a substantial discount to the market and a steep markdown versus other e-commerce firms, HRBC is ranked accumulate.

Key Stock Statistics

S&P EPS Est. 1998	0.35	Tang. Bk. Value/Share	2.92
P/E on S&P Est. 1998	11.6	Beta	NA
S&P EPS Est. 1999	0.70	Shareholders	200
Dividend Rate/Share	Nil	Market cap. (B)	$0.171
Shs. outstg. (M)	42.2	Inst. holdings	64%
Avg. daily vol. (M)	0.566		

Value of $10,000 invested 5 years ago: NA

Fiscal Year Ending Dec. 31

	1998	1997	1996	1995	1994	1993
Revenues (Million $)						
1Q	31.10	24.32	7.16	4.54	—	—
2Q	34.27	28.42	10.08	5.29	—	—
3Q	—	30.24	11.15	6.10	—	—
4Q	—	37.70	13.33	7.19	—	—
Yr.	—	120.7	41.73	23.12	13.65	10.54
Earnings Per Share ($)						
1Q	-0.23	-0.39	-0.36	0.01	—	—
2Q	0.04	0.07	0.00	0.01		
3Q	—	-0.23	-0.01	0.01	—	—
4Q	—	-0.31	0.01	0.02		
Yr.	—	-0.85	-0.35	0.05	-0.14	0.21

Next earnings report expected: NA

Dividend Data

Amount ($)	Date Decl.	Ex-Div. Date	Stock of Record	Payment Date
3-for-2	Apr. 24	May. 18	May. 01	May. 15 '98

A Division of The McGraw-Hill Companies

STANDARD
&POOR'S
STOCK REPORTS

Harbinger Corporation

4100

03-OCT-98

Business Summary - 24-AUG-98

Harbinger Corp. (HRBC) is a leading worldwide provider of products, services and solutions to the rapidly expanding business-to-business electronic commerce market. HRBC offers solutions that enable businesses of all sizes to move goods and services along their supply chain. These electronic commerce solutions are provided over the Harbinger value-added network (VAN) or the company's Internet Value-Added Server (IVAS), or directly over standard telephone lines, the Internet, or private internal computer networks known as intranets.

Harbinger offers software products that operate on multiple computer platforms, computer networks to facilitate the transmission of business information and transactions, and value-added products and services to enable businesses of all sizes to maximize the number and value of their electronic trading relationships.

The method of document exchange is user configurable by trading partner and by document type (such as purchase order, invoice, quote and similar business documents). Both the Harbinger VAN and IVAS provide encryption and other document management and security methods to allow documents to be exchanged securely and reliably.

Harbinger facilitates the electronic link to its computer communications network through its electronic commerce software packages for use in a broad range of computing environments, including DOS, Windows (3.x, 95 and NT), UNIX, IBM AS/400 midrange and IBM MVS mainframe platforms. Professional services are also provided to assist businesses in the installation and customization, operation and maintenance of their electronic trading relationships.

The company's objective is to be a leading worldwide provider of electronic commerce solutions by enabling customer transactions on the Internet, intranets or Harbinger networks. Focus is placed on building trading partner relationships and generating recurring revenue by increasing the number of subscribers to its network.

The strategy to achieve this objective includes the following key elements: focusing on marketing to trading communities; providing a comprehensive range of integrated products and services; delivering superior customer support services; capitalizing on electronic commerce on the Internet; pursuing strategic acquisitions and alliances; and penetrating international markets.

HRBC has aggressively pursued acquisitions as part of its strategy to enter new vertical markets, penetrate additional geographic markets and expand its product and service offerings. In 1997, it completed five such purchases, with the largest being that of Premenos for about 5.4 million HRBC shares. In 1998 through July, HRBC made two additional acquisitions, including that of the Materials Management division of MACTEC, Inc., and of EDI Works!.

Per Share Data ($)

(Year Ended Dec. 31)	1997	1996	1995	1994	1993	1992	1991	1990	1989	1988
Tangible Bk. Val.	2.75	0.81	0.93	0.30	0.28	NM	NM	NM	NM	NM
Cash Flow	-0.57	-0.19	0.13	-0.08	0.25	0.01	NA	NA	NA	NA
Earnings	-0.85	-0.35	0.05	-0.14	0.21	-0.04	-0.01	NA	NA	NA
Dividends	Nil	Nil	Nil	Nil	Nil	Nil	Nil	Nil	Nil	Nil
Payout Ratio	Nil	Nil	Nil	Nil	Nil	Nil	Nil	Nil	Nil	Nil
Prices - High	28³/₈	12⁷/₈	13¹/₈	NA	NA	NA	NA	NA	NA	NA
- Low	11¹/₂	6⁵/₈	5³/₈	NA	NA	NA	NA	NA	NA	NA
P/E Ratio - High	NM	NM	NM	NM	NA	NA	NA	NA	NA	NA
- Low	NM	NM	NM	NM	NA	NA	NA	NA	NA	NA

Income Statement Analysis (Million $)

	1997	1996	1995	1994	1993	1992	1991	1990	1989	1988
Revs.	121	41.7	23.1	13.7	10.5	6.7	NA	NA	NA	NA
Oper. Inc.	29.6	11.4	4.8	2.5	1.8	0.6	NA	NA	NA	NA
Depr.	10.9	3.8	1.7	0.9	0.6	0.4	NA	NA	NA	NA
Int. Exp.	Nil	Nil	0.1	0.1	0.2	0.1	NA	NA	NA	NA
Pretax Inc.	-29.4	-8.4	1.9	-3.0	1.0	-0.1	NA	NA	NA	NA
Eff. Tax Rate	NM	NM	36%	NM	NM	Nil	Nil	Nil	Nil	Nil
Net Inc.	-32.5	-8.2	1.3	-1.9	3.6	-0.1	NA	NA	NA	NA

Balance Sheet & Other Fin. Data (Million $)

	1997	1996	1995	1994	1993	1992	1991	1990	1989	1988
Cash	69.8	8.4	11.9	4.6	0.8	NA	NA	NA	NA	NA
Curr. Assets	148	22.5	20.8	10.0	6.7	NA	NA	NA	NA	NA
Total Assets	184	184	40.3	15.7	12.2	4.8	NA	NA	NA	NA
Curr. Liab.	53.5	11.2	6.5	7.3	2.9	NA	NA	NA	NA	NA
LT Debt	Nil	Nil	Nil	Nil	2.0	4.2	NA	NA	NA	NA
Common Eqty.	130	31.3	29.1	5.4	4.2	-4.5	NA	NA	NA	NA
Total Cap.	130	31.3	29.1	8.3	9.2	2.7	NA	NA	NA	NA
Cap. Exp.	8.6	6.0	3.3	1.3	1.7	NA	NA	NA	NA	NA
Cash Flow	-21.6	-4.5	2.7	-1.2	3.9	0.1	NA	NA	NA	NA
Curr. Ratio	2.8	2.0	3.2	1.4	2.3	NA	NA	NA	NA	NA
% LT Debt of Cap.	Nil	Nil	Nil	Nil	21.6	154.0	NA	NA	NA	NA
% Net Inc.of Revs.	NM	NM	5.4	NM	33.9	NM	NM	NM	NM	NM
% Ret. on Assets	NM	NM	4.5	NM	13.8	NM	NM	NM	NM	NM
% Ret. on Equity	NM	NM	6.1	NM	NM	NM	NM	NM	NM	NM

Data as orig. reptd.; bef. results of disc. opers. and/or spec. items. Per share data adj. for stk. divs. as of ex-div. date. Bold denotes diluted EPS (FASB 128). E-Estimated. NA-Not Available. NM-Not Meaningful. NR-Not Ranked.

Organized—in Georgia in 1994. **Office**—1277 Lenox Park Blvd., Atlanta, GA 30319. **Tel**—(404) 467-3000. **Website**—http://www.harbinger.com **Chrmn & CEO**—C. T. Howle. **Pres**—D. T. Leach. **VP-Fin, Secy & Investor Contact**—Joel G. Katz. **Dirs**—S. L. Bell, J. C. Davis, D. Hildes, C. T. Howle, W. B. King, B. R. Konsynski, T. Leach, J. Lowenberg, A. Nederlof, K. Neugebauer, W. D. Savoy. **Transfer Agent & Registrar**—First Union National Bank of North Carolina, Charlotte. **Empl**— 1,032. **S&P Analyst:** Mark S. Basham

Harland (John H.)

1096P

NYSE Symbol **JH**

In S&P SmallCap 600

03-OCT-98

Industry:
Specialty Printing

Summary: This leading supplier of bank checks, business documents and forms also produces optical mark reading and optical character recognition forms and equipment.

S&P Opinion: Avoid (★★)	Recent Price • 12⅞	Yield • 2.3%
	52 Wk Range • 23⅞-12½	12-Mo. P/E • 24.8

Quantitative Evaluations

Outlook
(1 Lowest—5 Highest)
• **4**

Fair Value
• **18½**

Risk
• **Average**

Earn./Div. Rank
• **B+**

Technical Eval.
• **Neutral** since 7/98

Rel. Strength Rank
(1 Lowest—99 Highest)
• **48**

Insider Activity
• **NA**

Earnings vs. Previous Year
▲=Up ▼=Down ▶=No Change

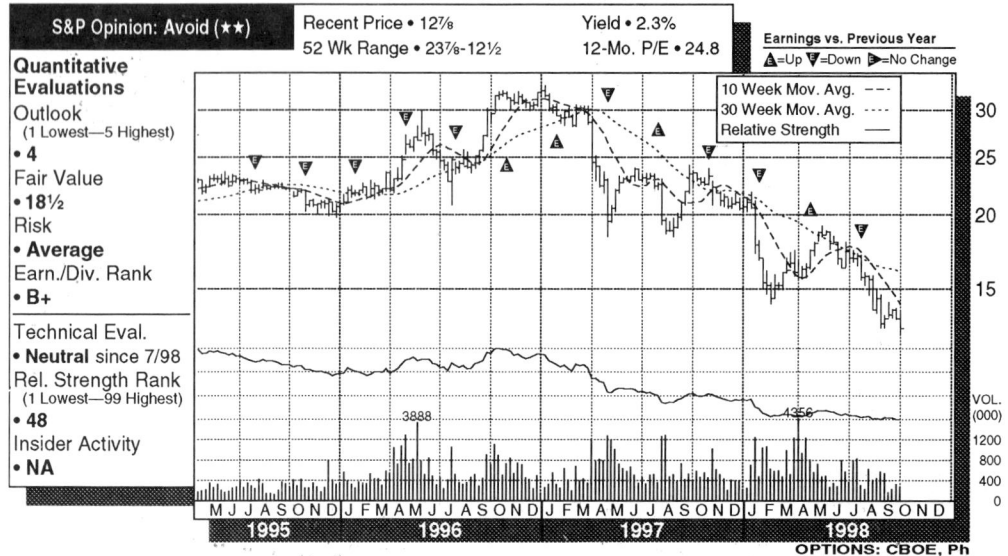

- 10 Week Mov. Avg. – – –
- 30 Week Mov. Avg. ·····
- Relative Strength ——

OPTIONS: CBOE, Ph

Overview - 08-JUN-98

JH reported diluted Q1'98 EPS of $0.20, which included a net special gain of $0.03, on a 3% rise in revenues. Check volume gained over 10% , but check revenues rose less than 3% reflecting continuation of fiercely competitive conditions in the check printing business. Transition costs associated with rebuilding JH's printing infrastructure are expected to continue in 1998. The rebuilding of JH's manufacturing operations continues as planned. The majority of plant consolidations are completed, and the regional printing network was recently producing 75% of all orders. The network is now focused on implementing more than $40 million in new check business. Progress also continued to be made in other areas, including marketing services, systems and work process. Although a partial recovery appears to be under way, the outlook is clouded by a spate of large bank mergers, including JH customers.

Valuation - 08-JUN-98

JH's shares have been depressed since late March 1007, reflecting disappointing revenues and earnings which, even with guidance from the company, consistently fell short of analysts' consensus opinion in each quarter of 1997. The market, already wary of JH, which has been restructuring its business since 1991, has taken a "wait and see" attitude before championing the stock. Thus, the shares are likely to remain under a cloud through much of 1998, given that management's aim to restore double-digit revenue and earnings growth by the end of 1997 has been pushed further into the future. The new strategies are designed to improve competitiveness and boost profitability by consolidating printing facilities and combining various sales and marketing functions into a single, multi-product organization, focused on serving the needs of financial institutions.

Key Stock Statistics

S&P EPS Est. 1998	0.87	Tang. Bk. Value/Share	2.86
P/E on S&P Est. 1998	14.8	Beta	0.60
S&P EPS Est. 1999	1.20	Shareholders	8,200
Dividend Rate/Share	0.30	Market cap. (B)	$0.400
Shs. outstg. (M)	31.1	Inst. holdings	68%
Avg. daily vol. (M)	0.050		

Value of $10,000 invested 5 years ago: $ 6,048

Fiscal Year Ending Dec. 31

	1998	1997	1996	1995	1994	1993
Revenues (Million $)						
1Q	143.5	139.3	152.3	138.3	131.0	133.5
2Q	135.3	139.7	149.7	136.1	130.8	130.0
3Q	—	142.1	155.9	141.3	129.2	129.9
4Q	—	141.7	151.6	145.9	130.3	126.1
Yr.	—	562.7	609.4	561.6	521.3	519.5
Earnings Per Share ($)						
1Q	**0.20**	0.16	0.28	0.43	0.42	0.00
2Q	**0.13**	0.21	-1.66	0.41	0.42	0.42
3Q	**E0.31**	0.16	0.45	0.36	0.43	0.42
4Q	**E0.20**	0.03	0.47	0.32	0.40	0.39
Yr.	**E0.87**	0.56	-0.45	1.51	1.68	1.62

Next earnings report expected: late October

Dividend Data (Dividends have been paid since 1932.)

Amount ($)	Date Decl.	Ex-Div. Date	Stock of Record	Payment Date
0.075	Oct. 27	Nov. 18	Nov. 20	Dec. 04 '97
0.075	Feb. 05	Feb. 17	Feb. 19	Mar. 05 '98
0.075	Apr. 21	May. 19	May. 21	Jun. 04 '98
0.075	Jul. 25	Aug. 18	Aug. 20	Sep. 03 '98

A Division of The McGraw-Hill Companies

John H. Harland Company

Business Summary - 08-JUN-98

John H. Harland is mainly a financial stationer, engaged primarily in printing checks and related items. With about 30% of the market, it is among the three largest U.S. printers of personalized checks. The company, which has been involved in restructuring activities since 1991, announced in April 1996 a new strategic plan. Checks will continue to generate significant cash flow, and will be linked to JH's marketing services, but the company plans to transform itself from a checks and forms printer into a financial marketing services company.

As part of its strategy to restore double-digit revenue and earnings growth, JH is taking measures to improve service and increase profitability of its check printing business by standardizing products and pricing and consolidating and restructuring manufacturing operations. It is completing the consolidation of its 40 core printing plants into a network of seven regional facilities incorporating advanced manufacturing technology and systems. This strategy includes creating a communications network linking the check printing business with marketing services. It also will require the development of additional marketing services to enhance JH's database management capabilities.

In order to more closely align the company's dividend payout with its overall business strategy, in February 1997, directors reduced the dividend to $0.30 a share annually, from $1.02. Also, JH's 1997 operating results included $0.15 of severance-related and equipment development costs. In 1996, JH incurred a second quarter restructuring charge of $92.5 million ($1.80), and an $8.0 million ($0.26) charge related to an acquisition.

The company's principal products are MICR encoded checks designed to be processed on automatic sorting and posting equipment, deposit tickets and related forms for financial institutions and their customers. JH also produces customer-designed printed, lithographed and engraved business forms and other stationery items for banks and other accounts. JH also markets checks directly to consumers through a subsidiary as a means of augmenting financial institution sales. The direct check market is growing 10% to 12% annually.

Scantron Corp. (acquired in 1988) designs, develops and produces optical mark reading (OMR) equipment and scannable forms used to score tests and tabulate data. Datascan, headquartered in Switzerland, is a leading producer of OMR equipment and optical character recognition (OCR) check reader equipment.

JH entered a third line of business with the 1994 purchase of Marketing Profiles, a database marketing and consulting firm that provides software products and related marketing services to the financial industry.

Per Share Data ($) (Year Ended Dec. 31)	1997	1996	1995	1994	1993	1992	1991	1990	1989	1988
Tangible Bk. Val.	2.49	1.78	2.91	3.34	4.25	6.42	7.99	7.92	7.26	6.48
Cash Flow	1.80	0.93	3.09	3.04	2.70	2.42	1.94	2.08	2.01	1.83
Earnings	0.56	-0.45	1.51	1.68	1.62	1.59	1.33	1.52	1.54	1.41
Dividends	0.30	1.02	1.02	0.98	0.94	0.90	0.86	0.78	0.68	0.58
Payout Ratio	54%	NM	68%	58%	58%	57%	65%	51%	44%	41%
Prices - High	$32\frac{7}{8}$	33	$23\frac{5}{8}$	$24\frac{3}{4}$	$28\frac{1}{8}$	$27\frac{1}{4}$	$24\frac{3}{8}$	$26\frac{1}{8}$	25	$24\frac{1}{4}$
- Low	$18\frac{3}{8}$	$20\frac{3}{4}$	$19\frac{1}{8}$	$19\frac{3}{8}$	$20\frac{7}{8}$	$20\frac{1}{2}$	$17\frac{7}{8}$	$17\frac{7}{8}$	$19\frac{1}{2}$	$19\frac{1}{4}$
P/E Ratio - High	59	NM	16	15	17	17	18	17	16	17
- Low	33	NM	13	12	13	13	13	12	13	14
Income Statement Analysis (Million $)										
Revs.	563	609	562	521	519	445	379	371	345	333
Oper. Inc.	77.7	129	132	134	122	113	109	106	104	93.0
Depr.	39.3	42.7	48.3	41.5	35.1	29.7	22.6	20.9	18.0	16.4
Int. Exp.	8.4	10.3	8.7	7.8	NA	NA	NA	NA	NA	NA
Pretax Inc.	29.6	-15.5	76.9	85.1	85.7	88.3	79.7	90.6	91.8	81.3
Eff. Tax Rate	42%	NM	40%	40%	39%	36%	38%	37%	37%	34%
Net Inc.	17.3	-13.9	46.0	51.2	52.5	56.6	49.8	57.2	58.1	53.3
Balance Sheet & Other Fin. Data (Million $)										
Cash	9.8	22.7	13.2	15.3	28.1	19.3	71.4	44.6	78.9	57.8
Curr. Assets	148	148	144	117	135	111	150	138	163	138
Total Assets	426	455	475	414	356	340	352	357	321	295
Curr. Liab.	110	145	121	79.3	44.0	59.5	35.1	28.4	24.0	29.7
LT Debt	109	114	115	115	112	12.6	11.7	12.6	11.3	11.2
Common Eqty.	193	182	222	203	184	256	292	296	273	244
Total Cap.	302	296	342	323	302	271	308	323	294	256
Cap. Exp.	45.4	28.9	33.4	37.5	27.1	18.7	17.5	29.0	28.7	32.6
Cash Flow	56.6	28.9	94.3	92.8	87.6	86.3	72.4	78.0	76.0	69.5
Curr. Ratio	1.4	1.0	1.2	1.5	3.1	1.9	4.3	4.9	6.8	4.6
% LT Debt of Cap.	36.2	38.5	33.6	35.6	37.0	4.7	3.8	3.9	3.8	4.4
% Net Inc.of Revs.	3.1	NM	8.2	9.8	10.1	12.7	13.2	15.4	16.8	16.0
% Ret. on Assets	3.9	NM	10.3	13.3	15.9	17.0	14.2	16.9	18.9	19.7
% Ret. on Equity	9.2	NM	21.6	26.5	25.4	21.4	17.1	20.2	22.5	23.6

Data as orig. reptd.; bef. results of disc. opers. and/or spec. items. Per share data adj. for stk. divs. as of ex-div. date. Bold denotes diluted EPS (FASB 128). E-Estimated. NA-Not Available. NM-Not Meaningful. NR-Not Ranked.

Office—2939 Miller Rd. (P.O. Box 105250), Decatur, GA 30035 (30348). **Tel**—(800) 723-3690. **Website**—http://www.harland.net. **Chrmn, CEO**—J. H. Weitnauer. **SVP, CFO**—S. D. Passman III. **VP, Secy & Investor Contact**—Victoria P. Weyand (770) 593-5128. **Dirs**—J. P. Baranco, E. J. Hawie, J. J. McMahon, G. H. Northrop, H. G. Pattillo, L. L. Prince, J. H. Weitnauer, Jr., R. R. Woodson, R. A. Yellowlees. **Transfer Agent & Registrar**—First Chicago Trust Co. of New York. **Incorporated**—in Georgia in 1923. **Empl**— 5,997. **S&P Analyst:** William H. Donald

03-OCT-98

Industry:
Electrical Equipment

Summary: Harman is a leading worldwide manufacturer and distributor of high fidelity audio system components for consumer, OEM and professional markets.

Quantitative Evaluations

Outlook
(1 Lowest—5 Highest)
• **4**

Fair Value
• **51⅝**

Risk
• **Average**

Earn./Div. Rank
• **B**

Technical Eval.
• **Bearish** since 3/98

Rel. Strength Rank
(1 Lowest—99 Highest)
• **65**

Insider Activity
• **Neutral**

Recent Price • 35¼

52 Wk Range • 57-32½

Yield • 0.6%

12-Mo. P/E • 12.3

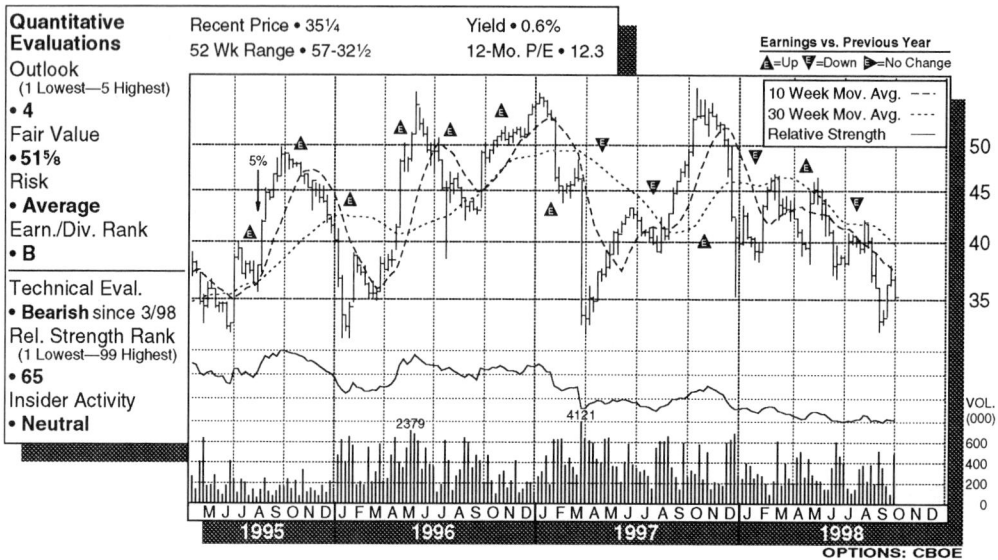

Earnings vs. Previous Year
△=Up ▽=Down ▷=No Change

10 Week Mov. Avg. – · –
30 Week Mov. Avg. – – – –
Relative Strength ——

OPTIONS: CBOE

Business Profile - 22-SEP-98

In FY 98 (Jun.), HAR reported record sales during a year dominated by the economic collapse of Asia. The company stated that, in the face of a soft market for consumer electronics and intense competition from Asian competitors, it produced good results. During the year, HAR strengthened its balance sheet and retired high interest debt replacing it with newly issued investment grade notes. In addition, HAR completed the sale of its distribution companies in Germany, Japan, France and Great Britain. In June 1998, HAR announced that its Board of Directors had approved a stock repurchase program for up to 1.5 million shares in FY 98.

Operational Review - 22-SEP-98

Net sales in FY 98 (Jun.) rose 2.7%, primarily driven by growth in the OEM Group, partially offset by lower Consumer Group and Professional Group sales resulting from the weakness in Asia and soft markets for audio products elsewhere. Gross margins narrowed, reflecting weakness in Asia, pricing pressures in the consumer and professional audio markets associated with currency effects and unstable market conditions, and the divestiture of the company's distribution operations in Germany, the U.K., France and Japan; pretax income declined 2.8%. After taxes at 28.9%, versus 29.5%, net income was down 1.8%, to $53,826,000 ($2.86 a share), from $54,832,000 ($2.90). Results in FY 98 exclude a $0.19 a share extraordinary charge.

Stock Performance - 02-OCT-98

In the past 30 trading days, HAR's shares have declined 5%, compared to a 7% fall in the S&P 500. Average trading volume for the past five days was 96,960 shares, compared with the 40-day moving average of 61,467 shares.

Key Stock Statistics

Dividend Rate/Share	0.20	Shareholders	200
Shs. outstg. (M)	18.6	Market cap. (B)	$0.657
Avg. daily vol. (M)	0.067	Inst. holdings	88%
Tang. Bk. Value/Share	18.79		
Beta	0.55		

Value of $10,000 invested 5 years ago: $ 24,712

Fiscal Year Ending Jun. 30

	1998	1997	1996	1995	1994	1993
Revenues (Million $)						
1Q	329.3	338.0	300.5	228.6	163.7	144.7
2Q	403.0	401.3	348.7	288.7	222.7	177.3
3Q	391.9	358.1	339.3	310.5	222.9	167.6
4Q	389.1	376.6	373.1	342.4	252.8	175.3
Yr.	1,513	1,474	1,362	1,170	862.1	664.9
Earnings Per Share ($)						
1Q	0.46	0.41	0.36	0.28	0.10	-0.12
2Q	**0.84**	1.05	0.95	0.80	0.56	0.30
3Q	**0.80**	0.56	0.86	0.75	0.52	0.35
4Q	**0.76**	0.94	0.97	0.88	0.61	0.47
Yr.	**2.86**	2.96	3.16	2.72	1.89	0.99

Next earnings report expected: late October

Dividend Data (Dividends have been paid since 1994.)

Amount ($)	Date Decl.	Ex-Div. Date	Stock of Record	Payment Date
0.050	Oct. 30	Nov. 07	Nov. 12	Nov. 26 '97
0.050	Jan. 30	Feb. 09	Feb. 11	Feb. 25 '98
0.050	May. 05	May. 11	May. 13	May. 27 '98
0.050	Aug. 04	Aug. 10	Aug. 12	Aug. 26 '98

A Division of The **McGraw·Hill** Companies

Business Summary - 22-SEP-98

Harman International Industries, Incorporated (HAR), is a worldwide leader in the design, manufacture and marketing of high-quality high-fidelity audio products targeted primarily at the consumer, professional and original equipment manufacturer (OEM) markets. HAR's historical reputation for ingenuity and quality dates back to 1953, when Dr. Sidney Harman co-founded Harman/Kardon, the first domestic company to design and manufacture the high-fidelity receiver.

HAR has developed, internally and through a series of strategic acquisitions, a broad range of product offerings sold under renowned brand names in each of its three major markets. The objective of HAR's development efforts has been to secure engineering, manufacturing and marketing leadership in its three major markets and to strengthen its ability to provide total audio system solutions to its customers.

Harman serves three major audio markets: consumer, professional and OEM. In the consumer audio market, HAR's range of product offerings has grown from the traditional base of two-channel stereo loudspeakers and electronics to include multi-channel, surround-sound electronics and loudspeaker systems, powered loudspeakers, mini-systems and audio systems for computers. In the professional audio market, HAR offers a complete range of audio products for the sound reinforcement, broadcast and recording, and music instru-

ment segments. In the OEM audio market, HAR offers branded and non-branded audio systems for installation as original equipment in automobiles and computers.

In FY 98 (Jun.), the Consumer Group accounted for 32% of HAR's sales, of which 76% was attributable to home loudspeaker and automotive aftermarket systems, 21% was from home electronic components and 3% was from audio systems for computer manufacturers. The Professional Group contributed 30% of FY 98 sales, of which 45% was attributable to sound reinforcement, 25% was from broadcast and recording and 30% was from musical instrument support. OEM Group sales to the automakers produced 38% of FY 98 sales.

Based on its experience in, and knowledge of, the audio industry, HAR believes that the consumer, professional and OEM markets, both domestic and international, have grown in recent years. In 1997 and 1998, the consumer and professional audio markets slowed somewhat due to uncertainty associated with technology transitions. The transition from analog to digital audio technology has transformed music recording and reproduction and has led to the development of a new generation of consumer and professional audio products. Although this transition has created near-term market weakness due to customer confusion and hesitancy, HAR believes that the evolution of digital audio will fuel long-term growth in the consumer and professional audio markets.

Per Share Data ($) (Year Ended Jun. 30)	1998	1997	1996	1995	1994	1993	1992	1991	1990	1989
Tangible Bk. Val.	18.79	19.35	16.46	10.80	12.50	7.10	6.82	5.60	7.79	7.34
Cash Flow	6.16	5.82	6.32	5.73	4.28	3.13	2.88	0.08	3.73	3.30
Earnings	2.86	2.96	3.16	2.72	1.89	0.99	0.37	-2.15	1.53	1.70
Dividends	0.20	0.20	0.20	0.17	Nil	Nil	Nil	Nil	Nil	Nil
Payout Ratio	7%	7%	6%	6%	Nil	Nil	Nil	Nil	Nil	Nil
Prices - High	46¾	57	56½	49¾	36¼	27⅞	14⅝	10⅝	19¾	22⅞
- Low	36¾	32⅜	32	32⅜	23⅜	13¾	8½	4¼	6	15⅛
P/E Ratio - High	16	19	18	18	19	28	39	NM	13	13
- Low	13	11	10	12	12	14	23	NM	4	9

Income Statement Analysis (Million $)

	1998	1997	1996	1995	1994	1993	1992	1991	1990	1989
Revs.	1,513	1,474	1,362	1,170	862	665	604	587	557	524
Oper. Inc.	163	155	157	133	100	65.3	50.9	24.1	63.0	57.1
Depr.	62.5	53.1	52.0	45.7	33.6	24.4	23.4	20.5	20.1	14.5
Int. Exp.	24.9	23.6	27.5	25.3	22.1	23.6	21.1	23.9	20.3	16.3
Pretax Inc.	75.7	77.9	75.0	61.2	42.7	18.6	5.9	-20.6	23.0	25.8
Eff. Tax Rate	29%	30%	32%	32%	38%	39%	41%	NM	39%	40%
Net Inc.	53.8	54.8	52.0	41.4	26.4	11.2	3.5	-19.8	14.1	15.4

Balance Sheet & Other Fin. Data (Million $)

	1998	1997	1996	1995	1994	1993	1992	1991	1990	1989
Cash	16.2	4.2	0.3	11.3	9.7	2.2	2.8	3.8	2.9	1.9
Curr. Assets	695	679	652	553	490	289	269	220	256	212
Total Assets	1,131	1,014	996	887	681	432	416	359	393	315
Curr. Liab.	327	251	275	295	274	141	167	139	148	99
LT Debt	260	266	255	266	157	176	133	133	133	123
Common Eqty.	512	467	436	289	232	111	111	81.0	102	85.0
Total Cap.	772	734	692	560	389	287	244	214	235	207
Cap. Exp.	57.5	68.4	80.6	54.7	40.7	25.6	21.0	24.6	40.7	29.5
Cash Flow	116	108	104	87.1	60.0	35.6	26.9	0.7	34.1	29.9
Curr. Ratio	2.1	2.7	2.4	1.9	1.8	2.0	1.6	1.6	1.7	2.1
% LT Debt of Cap.	33.6	36.2	36.8	47.5	40.3	61.2	54.4	62.2	56.7	59.2
% Net Inc.of Revs.	3.6	3.7	3.8	3.5	3.0	1.7	0.6	NM	2.5	2.9
% Ret. on Assets	5.0	5.5	5.5	5.3	4.7	2.6	0.8	NM	4.0	5.0
% Ret. on Equity	11.0	12.1	14.3	15.9	15.3	10.1	3.3	NM	15.0	19.5

Data as orig. reptd.; bef. results of disc. opers. and/or spec. items. Per share data adj. for stk. divs. as of ex-div. date. Bold denotes diluted EPS (FASB 128). E-Estimated. NA-Not Available. NM-Not Meaningful. NR-Not Ranked.

Office—1101 Pennsylvania Ave. N.W., Suite 1010, Washington, DC 20004. **Tel**—(202) 393-1101. **Website**—http://www.harman.com. **Chrmn & CEO**—S. Harman. **Pres, COO & Secy**—B. A. Girod. **VP & CFO**—F. Meredith. **Investor Contact**—Sandra Robinson. **Dirs**—B. A. Girod, S. Harman, S. M. Hufstedler, A. McLaughlin, E. H. Meyer, G. P. Stapleton, S. A. Weiss. **Transfer Agent & Registrar**—ChaseMellon Shareholder Services, Encino, CA. **Incorporated**—in Delaware in 1980. **Empl**— 10,010. **S&P Analyst:** M.I.

Harmon Industries   4108
NASDAQ Symbol **HRMN**
In S&P SmallCap 600

03-OCT-98   Industry:
Electrical Equipment

Summary: This comp :p / is a leading supplier of signal, inspection and control products for the rail freight and transit industries.

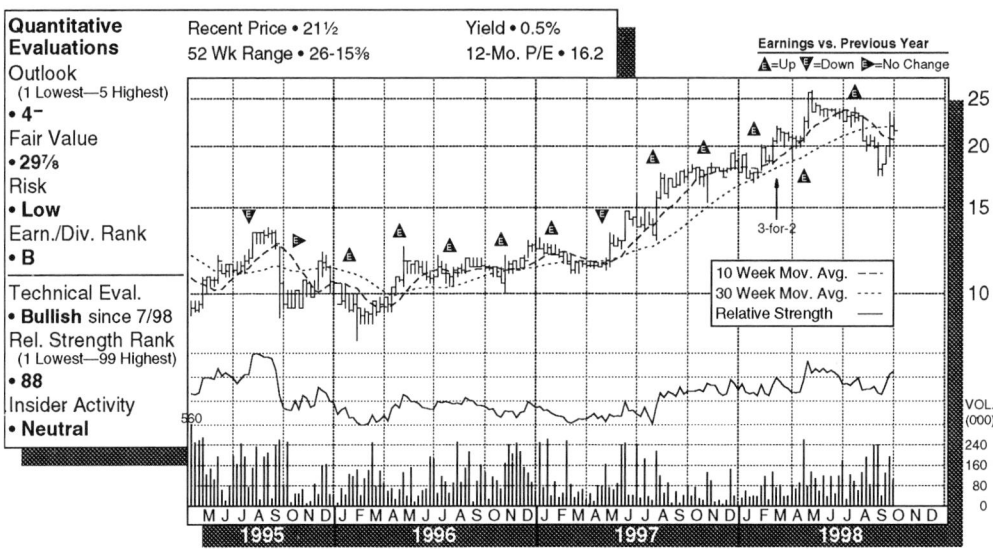

Quantitative Evaluations	
Recent Price • 21½	Yield • 0.5%
52 Wk Range • 26-15⅜	12-Mo. P/E • 16.2

Outlook
(1 Lowest—5 Highest)
• **4⁻**

Fair Value
• **29⅞**

Risk
• **Low**

Earn./Div. Rank
• **B**

Technical Eval.
• **Bullish** since 7/98

Rel. Strength Rank
(1 Lowest—99 Highest)
• **88**

Insider Activity
• **Neutral**

Earnings vs. Previous Year
▲=Up ▼=Down ▶=No Change

10 Week Mov. Avg. – – –
30 Week Mov. Avg. ·····
Relative Strength ——

3-for-2

Business Profile - 13-SEP-98

This company primarily supplies controls and systems for the North American rail freight market. In recent years it has expanded into commuter and urban transit markets and established operations in international markets. Internationally, HRMN has targeted those countries that are privatizing railroads. In addition, HRMN is shifting its product mix from sales of individual products to customized integrated systems. Harmon is benefiting from the long-term trend for railroads to outsource their engineering and maintenance tasks and the creation of new short-line railroads from major trunk systems.

Operational Review - 13-SEP-98

Net sales in the six months ended June 30, 1998, rose 61%, year to year, aided by increased demand for products and services designed to increase rail system capacity and efficiency. Additionally, Harmon expanded its share of the cross warning systems market. Gross margins narrowed as the mix changed favoring services. Operating margins improved, however, reflecting good control over administrative costs and the absence of 1997's equity losses from an affiliate; operating profits advanced 66%. Despite reduced investment income and greater interest expense, a lower tax rate helped net income rise 67% to $7,414,000 ($0.70 a share) from $4,434,000 ($0.43, adjusted for the February 1998 3-for-2 split).

Stock Performance - 02-OCT-98

In the past 30 trading days, HRMN's shares have increased 5%, compared to a 7% fall in the S&P 500. Average trading volume for the past five days was 20,460 shares, compared with the 40-day moving average of 31,110 shares.

Key Stock Statistics

Dividend Rate/Share	0.11	Shareholders	600
Shs. outstg. (M)	10.5	Market cap. (B)	$0.227
Avg. daily vol. (M)	0.023	Inst. holdings	39%
Tang. Bk. Value/Share	6.51		
Beta	0.72		

Value of $10,000 invested 5 years ago: $ 27,779

Fiscal Year Ending Dec. 31

	1998	1997	1996	1995	1994	1993
Revenues (Million $)						
1Q	60.56	35.99	38.40	29.42	25.90	20.62
2Q	73.71	47.62	39.11	32.85	32.17	22.85
3Q	—	56.13	41.96	38.03	29.45	27.13
4Q	—	73.80	55.98	36.49	32.19	28.69
Yr.	—	213.5	175.4	136.8	119.7	99.3
Earnings Per Share ($)						
1Q	**0.27**	0.14	0.20	0.07	0.15	0.11
2Q	**0.43**	0.29	0.26	0.20	0.24	0.19
3Q	—	0.25	0.24	0.22	0.22	0.23
4Q	—	**0.37**	0.21	0.18	0.17	0.20
Yr.	—	**1.06**	0.91	0.67	0.77	0.74

Next earnings report expected: NA

Dividend Data (Dividends have been paid since 1994.)

Amount ($)	Date Decl.	Ex-Div. Date	Stock of Record	Payment Date
0.075	Nov. 24	Nov. 26	Nov. 28	Dec. 12 '97
3-for-2	Jan. 23	Mar. 02	Feb. 13	Feb. 27 '98
0.055	May. 12	May. 27	May. 29	Jun. 19 '98

Business Summary - 22-SEP-98

Harman International Industries, Incorporated (HAR), is a worldwide leader in the design, manufacture and marketing of high-quality high-fidelity audio products targeted primarily at the consumer, professional and original equipment manufacturer (OEM) markets. HAR's historical reputation for ingenuity and quality dates back to 1953, when Dr. Sidney Harman co-founded Harman/ Kardon, the first domestic company to design and manufacture the high-fidelity receiver.

HAR has developed, internally and through a series of strategic acquisitions, a broad range of product offerings sold under renowned brand names in each of its three major markets. The objective of HAR's development efforts has been to secure engineering, manufacturing and marketing leadership in its three major markets and to strengthen its ability to provide total audio system solutions to its customers.

Harman serves three major audio markets: consumer, professional and OEM. In the consumer audio market, HAR's range of product offerings has grown from the traditional base of two-channel stereo loudspeakers and electronics to include multi-channel, surround-sound electronics and loudspeaker systems, powered loudspeakers, mini-systems and audio systems for computers. In the professional audio market, HAR offers a complete range of audio products for the sound reinforcement, broadcast and recording, and music instru-

ment segments. In the OEM audio market, HAR offers branded and non-branded audio systems for installation as original equipment in automobiles and computers.

In FY 98 (Jun.), the Consumer Group accounted for 32% of HAR's sales, of which 76% was attributable to home loudspeaker and automotive aftermarket systems, 21% was from home electronic components and 3% was from audio systems for computer manufacturers. The Professional Group contributed 30% of FY 98 sales, of which 45% was attributable to sound reinforcement, 25% was from broadcast and recording and 30% was from musical instrument support. OEM Group sales to the automakers produced 38% of FY 98 sales.

Based on its experience in, and knowledge of, the audio industry, HAR believes that the consumer, professional and OEM markets, both domestic and international, have grown in recent years. In 1997 and 1998, the consumer and professional audio markets slowed somewhat due to uncertainty associated with technology transitions. The transition from analog to digital audio technology has transformed music recording and reproduction and has led to the development of a new generation of consumer and professional audio products. Although this transition has created near-term market weakness due to customer confusion and hesitancy, HAR believes that the evolution of digital audio will fuel long-term growth in the consumer and professional audio markets.

Per Share Data ($)

(Year Ended Jun. 30)	1998	1997	1996	1995	1994	1993	1992	1991	1990	1989
Tangible Bk. Val.	18.79	19.35	16.46	10.80	12.50	7.10	6.82	5.60	7.79	7.34
Cash Flow	6.16	5.82	6.32	5.73	4.28	3.13	2.88	0.08	3.73	3.30
Earnings	2.86	2.96	3.16	2.72	1.89	0.99	0.37	-2.15	1.53	1.70
Dividends	0.20	0.20	0.20	0.17	Nil	Nil	Nil	Nil	Nil	Nil
Payout Ratio	7%	7%	6%	6%	Nil	Nil	Nil	Nil	Nil	Nil
Prices - High	46¾	57	56½	49¾	36¼	27⅞	14⅝	10⅝	19¾	22⅞
- Low	36¾	32⅜	32	32⅜	23⅜	13¾	8½	4¼	6	15⅛
P/E Ratio - High	16	19	18	18	19	28	39	NM	13	13
- Low	13	11	10	12	12	14	23	NM	4	9

Income Statement Analysis (Million $)

	1998	1997	1996	1995	1994	1993	1992	1991	1990	1989
Revs.	1,513	1,474	1,362	1,170	862	665	604	587	557	524
Oper. Inc.	163	155	157	133	100	65.3	50.9	24.1	63.0	57.1
Depr.	62.5	53.1	52.0	45.7	33.6	24.4	23.4	20.5	20.1	14.5
Int. Exp.	24.9	23.6	27.5	25.3	22.1	23.6	21.1	23.9	20.3	16.3
Pretax Inc.	75.7	77.9	75.0	61.2	42.7	18.6	5.9	-20.6	23.0	25.8
Eff. Tax Rate	29%	30%	32%	32%	38%	39%	41%	NM	39%	40%
Net Inc.	53.8	54.8	52.0	41.4	26.4	11.2	3.5	-19.8	14.1	15.4

Balance Sheet & Other Fin. Data (Million $)

	1998	1997	1996	1995	1994	1993	1992	1991	1990	1989
Cash	16.2	4.2	0.3	11.3	9.7	2.2	2.8	3.8	2.9	1.9
Curr. Assets	695	679	652	553	490	289	269	220	256	212
Total Assets	1,131	1,014	996	887	681	432	416	359	393	315
Curr. Liab.	327	251	275	295	274	141	167	139	148	99
LT Debt	260	266	255	266	157	176	133	133	133	123
Common Eqty.	512	467	436	289	232	111	111	81.0	102	85.0
Total Cap.	772	734	692	560	389	287	244	214	235	207
Cap. Exp.	57.5	68.4	80.6	54.7	40.7	25.6	21.0	24.6	40.7	29.5
Cash Flow	116	108	104	87.1	60.0	35.6	26.9	0.7	34.1	29.9
Curr. Ratio	2.1	2.7	2.4	1.9	1.8	2.0	1.6	1.6	1.7	2.1
% LT Debt of Cap.	33.6	36.2	36.8	47.5	40.3	61.2	54.4	62.2	56.7	59.2
% Net Inc.of Revs.	3.6	3.7	3.8	3.5	3.0	1.7	0.6	NM	2.5	2.9
% Ret. on Assets	5.0	5.5	5.5	5.3	4.7	2.6	0.8	NM	4.0	5.0
% Ret. on Equity	11.0	12.1	14.3	15.9	15.3	10.1	3.3	NM	15.0	19.5

Data as orig. reptd.; bef. results of disc. opers. and/or spec. items. Per share data adj. for stk. divs. as of ex-div. date. Bold denotes diluted EPS (FASB 128). E-Estimated. NA-Not Available. NM-Not Meaningful. NR-Not Ranked.

Office—1101 Pennsylvania Ave. N.W., Suite 1010, Washington, DC 20004. **Tel**—(202) 393-1101. **Website**—http://www.harman.com. **Chrmn & CEO**—S. Harman. **Pres, COO & Secy**—B. A. Girod. **VP & CFO**—F. Meredith. **Investor Contact**—Sandra Robinson. **Dirs**—B. A. Girod, S. Harman, S. M. Hufstedler, A. McLaughlin, E. H. Meyer, G. P. Stapleton, S. A. Weiss. **Transfer Agent & Registrar**—ChaseMellon Shareholder Services, Encino, CA. **Incorporated**—in Delaware in 1980. **Empl**— 10,010. **S&P Analyst:** M.I.

03-OCT-98

Industry:
Electrical Equipment

Summary: This comp :p / is a leading supplier of signal, inspection and control products for the rail freight and transit industries.

Quantitative Evaluations

Outlook
(1 Lowest—5 Highest)
• **4⁻**

Fair Value
• **29⅞**

Risk
• **Low**

Earn./Div. Rank
• **B**

Technical Eval.
• **Bullish** since 7/98

Rel. Strength Rank
(1 Lowest—99 Highest)
• **88**

Insider Activity
• **Neutral**

Recent Price • 21½
52 Wk Range • 26-15⅝

Yield • 0.5%
12-Mo. P/E • 16.2

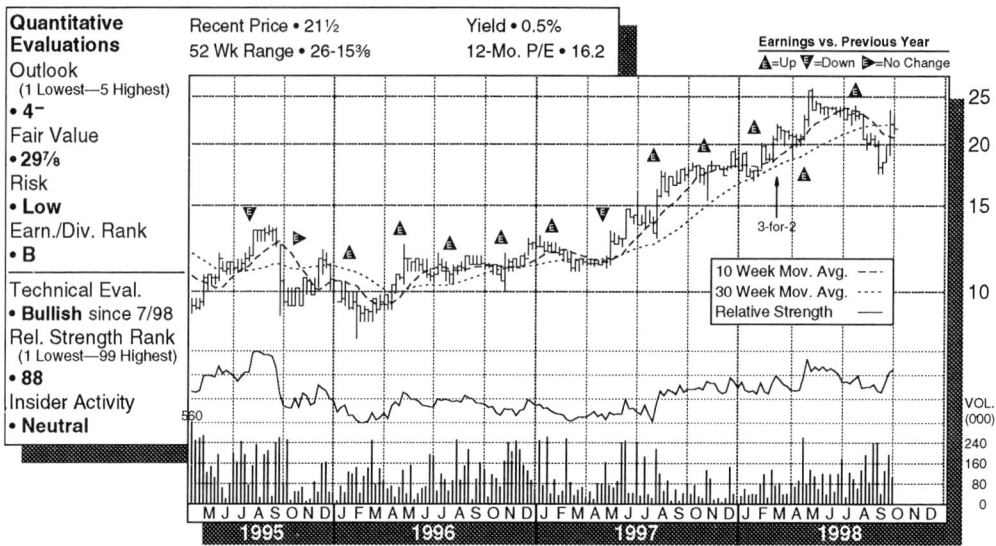

Earnings vs. Previous Year
▲=Up ▼=Down ▶=No Change

10 Week Mov. Avg. ---
30 Week Mov. Avg. ·······
Relative Strength ——

Business Profile - 13-SEP-98

This company primarily supplies controls and systems for the North American rail freight market. In recent years it has expanded into commuter and urban transit markets and established operations in international markets. Internationally, HRMN has targeted those countries that are privatizing railroads. In addition, HRMN is shifting its product mix from sales of individual products to customized integrated systems. Harmon is benefiting from the long-term trend for railroads to outsource their engineering and maintenance tasks and the creation of new short-line railroads from major trunk systems.

Operational Review - 13-SEP-98

Net sales in the six months ended June 30, 1998, rose 61%, year to year, aided by increased demand for products and services designed to increase rail system capacity and efficiency. Additionally, Harmon expanded its share of the cross warning systems market. Gross margins narrowed as the mix changed favoring services. Operating margins improved, however, reflecting good control over administrative costs and the absence of 1997's equity losses from an affiliate; operating profits advanced 66%. Despite reduced investment income and greater interest expense, a lower tax rate helped net income rise 67% to $7,414,000 ($0.70 a share) from $4,434,000 ($0.43, adjusted for the February 1998 3-for-2 split).

Stock Performance - 02-OCT-98

In the past 30 trading days, HRMN's shares have increased 5%, compared to a 7% fall in the S&P 500. Average trading volume for the past five days was 20,460 shares, compared with the 40-day moving average of 31,110 shares.

Key Stock Statistics

Dividend Rate/Share	0.11	Shareholders	600
Shs. outstg. (M)	10.5	Market cap. (B)	$0.227
Avg. daily vol. (M)	0.023	Inst. holdings	39%
Tang. Bk. Value/Share	6.51		
Beta	0.72		

Value of $10,000 invested 5 years ago: $ 27,779

Fiscal Year Ending Dec. 31

	1998	1997	1996	1995	1994	1993
Revenues (Million $)						
1Q	60.56	35.99	38.40	29.42	25.90	20.62
2Q	73.71	47.62	39.11	32.85	32.17	22.85
3Q	—	56.13	41.96	38.03	29.45	27.13
4Q	—	73.80	55.98	36.49	32.19	28.69
Yr.	—	213.5	175.4	136.8	119.7	99.3
Earnings Per Share ($)						
1Q	**0.27**	0.14	0.20	0.07	0.15	0.11
2Q	**0.43**	0.29	0.26	0.20	0.24	0.19
3Q	—	0.25	0.24	0.22	0.22	0.23
4Q	—	0.37	0.21	0.18	0.17	0.20
Yr.	—	**1.06**	0.91	0.67	0.77	0.74

Next earnings report expected: NA

Dividend Data (Dividends have been paid since 1994.)

Amount ($)	Date Decl.	Ex-Div. Date	Stock of Record	Payment Date
0.075	Nov. 24	Nov. 26	Nov. 28	Dec. 12 '97
3-for-2	Jan. 23	Mar. 02	Feb. 13	Feb. 27 '98
0.055	May. 12	May. 27	May. 29	Jun. 19 '98

A Division of The **McGraw·Hill** Companies

STANDARD
&POOR'S
STOCK REPORTS

Harmon Industries, Inc.

4108

03-OCT-98

Business Summary - 13-SEP-98

Harmon Industries is a leading supplier of signal, inspection and train control systems, products and services to railroads primarily in North America. HRMN sells its products and services to major freight railroads, short-lines, commuter and urban mass transit operators. Harmon's products are used principally to increase asset utilization, enhance safety and improve communications. Recently, the company has begun to focus on shifting its revenue mix from sales generated strictly from individual products, to complete systems that are tailored to the specific needs of the individual customer.

Harmon's future growth may be rooted in a planned international expansion. HRMN estimates that the international market is roughly eight times as large as the current domestic market. Harmon's new Mexican subsidiary was awarded an $8 million contract in July 1998 from TFM for centralized traffic control systems. In June 1997, HRMN bought out the minority interest in its Canadian affiliate, Vale-Harmon Enterprises Ltd. In 1996 Harmon established a foothold in the European market with the purchase of Vaughan Systems, Ltd., a UK-based manufacturer of train control products.

Harmon's largest product line (47.4% of 1997 revenue) is its Train Control Systems. These include signal control track circuits, interlocking control equipment and computer-based dispatch and traffic control equipment. Railroads use HRMN products to direct the movement of trains over vast distances, allow remote switching of trains to other tracks and permit communication and remote control of locomotives.

Crossing Systems (25.9% of revenue) includes rail/highway cross warning systems, motion detectors, flashing lights and cantilevers. Asset Management Services (14.0%) involves the rapid delivery of packaged rail components. One of HRMN's most popular offerings is a containerized construction kit containing all the materials needed by a railroad for a signal installation project.

Train Inspection Systems (6.2% of revenue) include products that generate information by monitoring moving trains. HRMN increased its share of this market in November 1997 with the acquisition of Devtronics, Inc. Harmon's hot-bearing detector helps railroads avoid costly and lethal train derailments. Other business segments include the production of custom designed printed wiring boards and mobile and stationary two-way radios.

Harmon has benefited from cost reduction measures adopted by large Class I railroads. As the big companies cut employment, HRMN provided products to monitor the condition of moving trains, help ensure safe switching and passage of trains, and facilitate better communication among crew members and between moving trains. The reduction in cars in service prompted HRMN to make products that permit railroads to track the location and performance of a particular train.

Per Share Data ($)

(Year Ended Dec. 31)	1997	1996	1995	1994	1993	1992	1991	1990	1989	1988
Tangible Bk. Val.	5.84	4.91	4.07	3.48	3.48	1.85	0.94	0.73	1.81	1.57
Cash Flow	1.67	1.39	1.05	1.04	0.97	0.82	0.65	0.93	0.63	0.79
Earnings	1.06	0.91	0.67	0.77	0.74	0.58	0.38	0.43	0.17	0.37
Dividends	0.10	0.10	0.10	0.10	Nil	Nil	Nil	0.04	0.08	0.08
Payout Ratio	10%	11%	15%	13%	Nil	Nil	Nil	10%	50%	23%
Prices - High	19⅝	13	13⅝	16⅛	15½	8⅜	4⅞	4⅞	5⅞	5½
- Low	11	8	8⅞	11	7¾	2¼	2⁵⁄₁₆	2⁵⁄₁₆	3⅞	3½
P/E Ratio - High	19	14	20	21	21	15	13	11	36	15
- Low	10	9	13	14	10	4	6	5	23	10

Income Statement Analysis (Million $)

	1997	1996	1995	1994	1993	1992	1991	1990	1989	1988
Revs.	214	175	137	120	99	81.9	70.9	72.7	73.3	64.6
Oper. Inc.	25.0	21.1	16.1	15.5	13.6	10.2	9.7	10.8	6.1	8.0
Depr.	6.3	5.0	3.9	2.6	2.1	1.9	2.0	3.5	3.2	2.8
Int. Exp.	1.2	0.7	0.7	0.3	0.4	1.3	2.2	1.5	2.5	2.0
Pretax Inc.	17.6	15.1	11.1	12.7	11.1	7.1	4.6	5.1	1.3	3.5
Eff. Tax Rate	38%	38%	38%	40%	38%	35%	37%	40%	48%	37%
Net Inc.	11.0	9.3	6.9	7.6	6.9	4.6	2.9	3.1	1.2	2.5

Balance Sheet & Other Fin. Data (Million $)

	1997	1996	1995	1994	1993	1992	1991	1990	1989	1988
Cash	6.7	Nil	Nil	0.3	3.1	0.4	0.4	0.5	0.4	0.5
Curr. Assets	96.4	73.0	56.8	42.7	37.0	25.6	23.3	24.3	27.9	23.1
Total Assets	136	105	86.8	68.4	53.0	38.5	36.6	41.4	50.4	46.1
Curr. Liab.	46.0	39.4	21.8	21.1	16.2	14.8	13.7	16.4	13.4	16.1
LT Debt	15.5	3.4	12.0	0.7	0.4	4.9	11.9	17.2	19.9	14.4
Common Eqty.	69.8	57.9	49.2	43.1	33.1	15.2	7.4	5.7	14.8	13.6
Total Cap.	85.3	61.3	61.3	43.8	33.5	20.1	19.3	23.0	35.3	28.8
Cap. Exp.	10.5	6.4	5.5	3.2	3.6	2.1	1.1	2.2	5.9	9.9
Cash Flow	17.3	14.3	10.8	10.3	9.0	6.5	4.9	6.6	4.3	5.3
Curr. Ratio	2.1	1.9	2.6	2.0	2.3	1.7	1.7	1.5	2.1	1.4
% LT Debt of Cap.	18.2	5.6	19.6	1.7	1.3	24.4	61.8	75.0	56.4	50.0
% Net Inc.of Revs.	5.1	5.3	5.0	6.4	6.9	5.6	4.1	4.3	1.6	3.9
% Ret. on Assets	9.1	9.7	8.9	12.2	14.0	11.8	7.3	6.6	2.4	5.9
% Ret. on Equity	17.2	17.4	8.9	19.5	27.0	39.6	43.7	29.5	8.1	19.7

Data as orig. reptd.; bef. results of disc. opers. and/or spec. items. Per share data adj. for stk. divs. as of ex-div. date. Bold denotes diluted EPS (FASB 128). E-Estimated. NA-Not Available. NM-Not Meaningful. NR-Not Ranked.

Office—1300 Jefferson Ct., Blue Springs, MO 64015. **Tel**—(816) 229-3345. **Chrmn**—R. E. Harmon. **Pres & CEO**—B. E. Olsson. **EVP-Fin, CFO, Treas, Secy & Investor Contact**—Charles M. Foudree. **Dirs**—B. M. Flohr, C. M. Foudree, R. L. Gray, R. E. Harmon, H. M. Kohn, D. W. List, G. E. Myers, B. E. Olsson, S. A. Sprague, J. C. Whittaker. **Transfer Agent & Registrar**—United Missouri Bank, Kansas City. **Incorporated**—in Missouri in 1961. **Empl**— 1,510. **S&P Analyst:** S. R. Klein

03-OCT-98

Industry:
Textiles (Apparel)

Summary: This company manufactures and markets men's and women's business, casual and golfing apparel under a number of leading brand names.

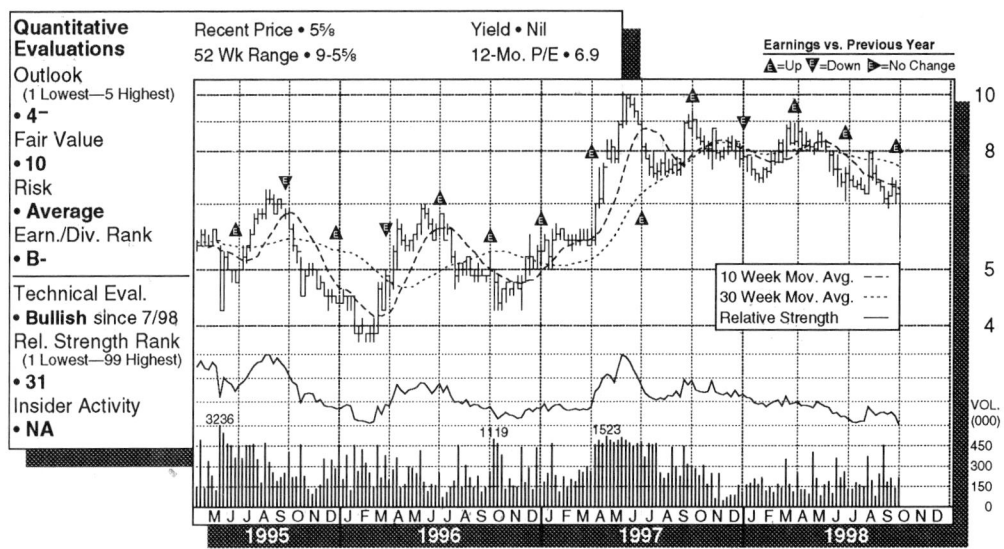

Quantitative Evaluations			
Recent Price • 5⅝		Yield • Nil	
52 Wk Range • 9-5⅝		12-Mo. P/E • 6.9	

Outlook
(1 Lowest—5 Highest)
• **4⁻**

Fair Value
• **10**

Risk
• **Average**

Earn./Div. Rank
• **B-**

Technical Eval.
• **Bullish** since 7/98

Rel. Strength Rank
(1 Lowest—99 Highest)
• **31**

Insider Activity
• **NA**

Earnings vs. Previous Year: ▲=Up ▼=Down ▶=No Change

10 Week Mov. Avg. – – –
30 Week Mov. Avg. · · · · ·
Relative Strength ——

Business Profile - 01-OCT-98

After soaring 153% in FY 97 (Nov.), pretax earnings continued to improve in the first nine months of FY 98, climbing 52%, year to year. Although retail sales have softened, the company's key brands, led by Hart Schaffner & Marx and Hickey-Freeman, produced an 11% sales increase in the third quarter of FY 98. HMX anticipates that higher revenues, improved gross margins, and ongoing cost control efforts will continue to enhance earnings in FY 98. In November 1996, the company acquired Plaid Clothing Group Inc., a major supplier of men's tailored clothing to better specialty and department stores. The acquisition included license rights to manufacture under the Burberrys, Claiborne, and Evan-Picone brands, as well as ownership of other brand names. HMX is actively considering other opportunities in sportswear and casualwear.

Operational Review - 01-OCT-90

Net sales in the nine months ended August 31, 1998, rose 1.7%, year to year. Gross margins widened on a shift in product mix to higher margin premium tailored clothing and sportswear. After taxes at 38.0% in each period, net income climbed 52%, to $8,765,000 ($0.25 a share on 5.3% more shares), from $5,770,000 ($0.17).

Stock Performance - 02-OCT-98

In the past 30 trading days, HMX's shares have declined 19%, compared to a 7% fall in the S&P 500. Average trading volume for the past five days was 42,900 shares, compared with the 40-day moving average of 44,172 shares.

Key Stock Statistics

Dividend Rate/Share	Nil	Shareholders	6,200
Shs. outstg. (M)	34.4	Market cap. (B)	$0.196
Avg. daily vol. (M)	0.039	Inst. holdings	57%
Tang. Bk. Value/Share	5.75		
Beta	0.60		

Value of $10,000 invested 5 years ago: $ 8,920

Fiscal Year Ending Nov. 30

	1998	1997	1996	1995	1994	1993
Revenues (Million $)						
1Q	179.3	177.1	150.9	149.3	177.9	187.0
2Q	167.5	169.7	134.3	135.0	164.0	171.9
3Q	195.2	185.9	164.9	166.7	196.1	189.0
4Q	—	185.4	160.2	144.3	179.7	184.2
Yr.	—	718.1	610.2	595.3	717.7	732.0
Earnings Per Share ($)						
1Q	0.07	0.01	-0.05	Nil	-0.02	-0.04
2Q	0.03	0.01	-0.05	-0.09	-0.10	-0.11
3Q	0.15	0.12	0.09	0.07	0.11	0.06
4Q	—	0.57	0.73	0.68	0.63	0.29
Yr.	—	0.74	0.72	0.66	0.62	0.20

Next earnings report expected: late January

Dividend Data

Dividends, paid since 1939, were omitted in 1992. A poison pill stock purchase rights plan was adopted in 1986.

A Division of The **McGraw·Hill** *Companies*

Business Summary - 01-OCT-98

For more than 100 years, Hartmarx (HMX) has been outfitting American men. The company, which was established in 1872, believes itself to be the largest U.S. maker and marketer of men's suits, sportcoats and slacks. It also manufactures men's and women's sportswear, including golfwear, and women's career apparel. In FY 97 (Nov.), tailored clothing accounted for 65% of sales, sportswear and slacks for 26%, and women's apparel for 9%.

In FY 97, Hartmarx's business consisted of two groups. The larger, the Men's Apparel group (92% of total sales), designs, manufactures and markets well-known, prestigious brands of men's tailored clothing, slacks and sportswear. The Women's Apparel group (8%) consists of International Women's Apparel (IWA), which designs and markets women's career apparel to department and specialty stores under owned and licensed brand names, and Barrie Pace, a direct-mail catalog company that offers a wide range of apparel and accessories to the business and professional woman.

Hartmarx owns two of the most recognized brands in men's tailored clothing: Hart Schaffner & Marx, which was introduced in 1887; and Hickey-Freeman, which

began in 1899. The company also offers its products under other brands it owns, such as Sansabelt, Racquet Club, Palm Beach, Brannoch, Barrie Pace, Hawksley & Wight, and Desert Classic; and under exclusive license agreements for specified product lines, including Tommy Hilfiger, Jack Nicklaus, Bobby Jones, Burberrys, Austin Reed, Perry Ellis, Kenneth Cole, Evan-Picone, Daniel Hechter, Robert Comstock, Gieves & Hawkes, Claiborne, KM by Krizia, Pierre Cardin and Nino Cerruti.

In November 1996, HMX acquired Plaid Clothing Group Inc., a major supplier of men's tailored clothing to better specialty and department stores. Plaid had been operating under Chapter 11 bankruptcy protection since July 1995. In July 1995, the company completed its exit from the retail business with the disposition of its Kuppenheimer operation, the vertically integrated factory-direct-to-consumer manufacturer of popular-priced men's tailored clothing whose products were sold exclusively through Kuppenheimer-operated retail stores.

Hartmarx's current strategy involves distributing its apparel to a broader base. The company has entered into several license agreements with third parties to produce, market and distribute products in 13 foreign countries. Hartmarx has also begun direct marketing of its golfwear in 28 countries, primarily in Europe and Asia.

Per Share Data ($)

(Year Ended Nov. 30)	1997	1996	1995	1994	1993	1992	1991	1990	1989	1988
Tangible Bk. Val.	5.62	4.85	4.11	3.95	3.41	2.72	11.32	14.60	18.37	19.21
Cash Flow	0.99	1.00	0.96	1.05	0.65	-7.54	-0.21	-1.33	2.48	3.37
Earnings	0.74	0.72	0.66	0.62	0.20	-8.59	-1.74	-3.11	0.89	2.03
Dividends	Nil	Nil	Nil	Nil	Nil	Nil	0.60	0.90	1.18	1.07
Payout Ratio	Nil	Nil	Nil	Nil	Nil	Nil	NM	NM	132%	53%
Prices - High	10⅛	6½	6⅞	7⅜	8¼	8⅝	13¼	19⅞	28⅛	29¾
- Low	5	3¾	4¼	5	5⅛	3	6⅞	5½	18¾	20¾
P/E Ratio - High	14	9	10	12	41	NM	NM	NM	32	15
- Low	7	5	6	8	26	NM	NM	NM	21	10

Income Statement Analysis (Million $)

	1997	1996	1995	1994	1993	1992	1991	1990	1989	1988
Revs.	718	610	595	718	732	1,054	1,215	1,296	1,297	1,174
Oper. Inc.	39.3	28.2	25.0	38.1	37.4	2.5	0.3	32.7	72.3	84.1
Depr.	8.6	9.3	10.0	13.8	14.1	26.9	33.8	35.2	31.0	25.0
Int. Exp.	17.5	16.7	19.9	21.2	22.9	21.1	23.8	29.0	28.4	14.5
Pretax Inc.	16.5	6.5	1.6	11.0	6.0	-226	-60.0	-95.0	28.0	60.0
Eff. Tax Rate	NM	NM	NM	NM	3.00%	NM	NM	NM	37%	37%
Net Inc.	25.2	23.8	21.4	20.0	6.0	-219	-38.0	-62.0	17.0	38.0

Balance Sheet & Other Fin. Data (Million $)

	1997	1996	1995	1994	1993	1992	1991	1990	1989	1988
Cash	1.6	2.8	5.7	2.8	1.5	22.4	6.6	2.7	2.9	5.0
Curr. Assets	357	320	279	312	338	430	579	578	698	578
Total Assets	470	430	377	392	405	512	740	762	908	734
Curr. Liab.	120	120	89.4	97.0	89.0	193	347	243	277	240
LT Debt	158	148	153	167	207	249	105	227	271	135
Common Eqty.	192	162	134	128	109	70.0	287	293	360	358
Total Cap.	350	310	287	295	316	319	393	519	631	494
Cap. Exp.	10.1	8.2	8.4	7.1	6.0	9.5	15.2	16.1	52.3	33.7
Cash Flow	33.9	33.1	31.4	34.0	20.0	-192	-5.0	-26.0	48.0	63.0
Curr. Ratio	3.0	2.7	3.1	3.2	3.8	2.2	1.7	2.4	2.5	2.4
% LT Debt of Cap.	45.1	47.7	53.2	56.6	65.6	77.9	26.9	43.7	42.9	27.4
% Net Inc.of Revs.	3.5	3.9	3.6	2.8	0.8	NM	NM	NM	1.3	3.2
% Ret. on Assets	5.6	5.9	5.6	5.0	1.2	NM	NM	NM	2.1	5.5
% Ret. on Equity	14.2	16.1	16.3	16.7	6.4	NM	NM	NM	4.7	10.9

Data as orig. reptd.; bef. results of disc. opers. and/or spec. items. Per share data adj. for stk. divs. as of ex-div. date. Bold denotes diluted EPS (FASB 128). E-Estimated. NA-Not Available. NM-Not Meaningful. NR-Not Ranked.

Office—101 N. Wacker Dr., Chicago, IL 60606. **Tel**—(312) 372-6300. **Chrmn & CEO**—E. O. Hand. **Pres**—H. B. Patel. **EVP & CFO**—G. R. Morgan. **EVP & Secy**—M. D. Allen. **VP & Treas**—James E. Condon. **Investor Contact**—Adriana Schmeling (212-840-4772). **Dirs**—A. R. Abboud, S. A. Bakhsh, J. A. Cole, R. F. Farley, E. O. Hand, D. P. Jacobs, C. Marshall, H. B. Patel, M. B. Rohlfs, S. L. Scott. **Transfer Agents & Registrars**—First National Bank of Chicago; First Chicago Trust Co. of New York, Jersey City, NJ. **Incorporated**—in New York in 1911; reincorporated in Delaware in 1983. **Empl**— 8,100. **S&P Analyst:** Kathleen J. Fraser

03-OCT-98

Industry: Chemicals (Specialty)

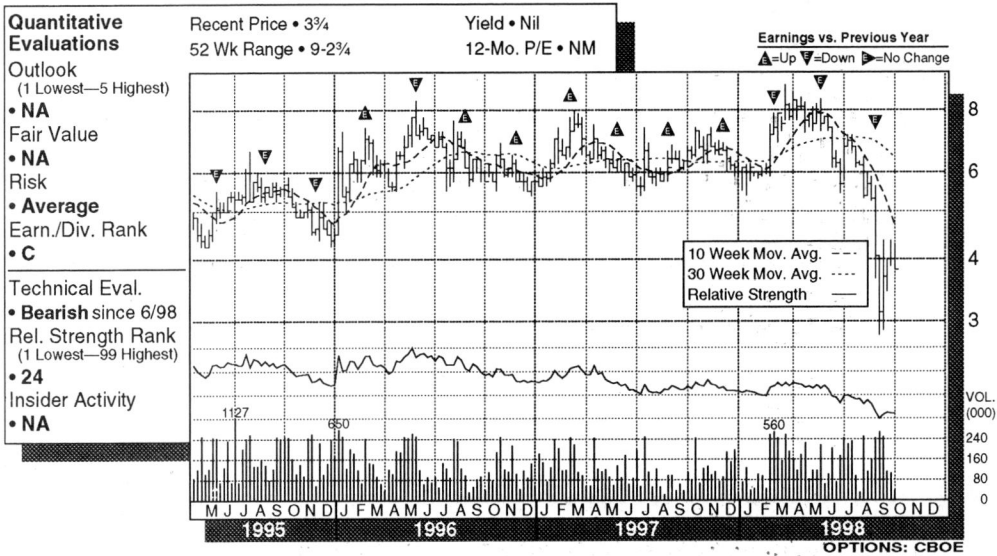

Summary: This company (formerly Hauser Chemical Research) produces natural flavor extracts for the food and beverage industry, and natural compounds for pharmaceutical and other uses.

Quantitative Evaluations

Outlook (1 Lowest—5 Highest)
• **NA**

Fair Value
• **NA**

Risk
• **Average**

Earn./Div. Rank
• **C**

Technical Eval.
• **Bearish** since 6/98

Rel. Strength Rank (1 Lowest—99 Highest)
• **24**

Insider Activity
• **NA**

Recent Price • 3¾
52 Wk Range • 9-2¾

Yield • Nil
12-Mo. P/E • NM

10 Week Mov. Avg. ----
30 Week Mov. Avg. ·····
Relative Strength ——

OPTIONS: CBOE

Business Profile - 06-SEP-98

In June 1998, HAUS indicated that it is continuing to build its NaturEnhance and Technical Services businesses, which produced 43% and 45% of sales in fiscal 1998 (Apr.), respectively. During fiscal 1998, HAUS signed a $20 million contract with PharmaPrint Inc., to manufacture botanical extracts and provide R&D services. In July 1997, HAUS's customer, Immunex Corp., received Canadian marketing approval for the cancer drug paclitaxel. In August 1998, the company signed a new agreement to supply paclitaxel for the collaborative arrangement between Immunex and IVAX Corp., which is awaiting FDA approval for Paclitaxel Injection. HAUS also supplies bulk paclitaxel to American Home Products and Yew Tree Pharmaceuticals.

Operational Review - 06-SEP-98

Total revenues in the first three months of FY 99 (Apr.), declined 7%, year to year, due to late completion of the paclitaxel contract with Immunex, and reduced demand for nutraceuticals because of customer inventory build-ups and a seasonal slowdown. Technical Services sales, however, rose 44%, largely offsetting the other declines. With general and administrative costs, and R&D expenditures decreasing by 17% and 30%, respectively, and sales and marketing expenses increasing by 33%, the net loss widened to $1,061,924 ($0.10 a share) from $181,737 ($0.02). Cash and equivalents totaled $958,581 on July 31, 1998.

Stock Performance - 02-OCT-98

In the past 30 trading days, HAUS's shares have declined 28%, compared to a 7% fall in the S&P 500. Average trading volume for the past five days was 6,580 shares, compared with the 40-day moving average of 42,115 shares.

Key Stock Statistics

Dividend Rate/Share	Nil	Shareholders	700
Shs. outstg. (M)	10.5	Market cap. (B)	$0.040
Avg. daily vol. (M)	0.035	Inst. holdings	43%
Tang. Bk. Value/Share	5.60		
Beta	1.25		

Value of $10,000 invested 5 years ago: $ 1,540

Fiscal Year Ending Apr. 30

	1999	1998	1997	1996	1995	1994
Revenues (Million $)						
1Q	7.05	7.54	4.92	4.04	5.18	22.80
2Q	—	6.10	5.89	7.02	6.72	14.46
3Q	—	7.12	7.96	6.50	5.61	13.04
4Q	—	11.28	7.55	8.11	5.39	10.14
Yr.	—	32.04	25.23	25.67	22.90	60.38
Earnings Per Share ($)						
1Q	-0.10	-0.02	-0.12	-0.17	0.01	0.30
2Q	—	-0.10	-0.12	-0.15	0.09	0.20
3Q	—	-0.06	Nil	-0.16	-0.19	0.23
4Q	—	-0.12	-0.02	-0.27	-0.16	0.25
Yr.	—	-0.30	-0.38	-0.75	-0.26	0.98

Next earnings report expected: late November

Dividend Data

No cash dividends have been paid.

A Division of The McGraw-Hill Companies

STANDARD
&POOR'S
STOCK REPORTS

Hauser, Inc.

4124

03-OCT-98

Business Summary - 06-SEP-98

Business comes naturally for Hauser, Inc. (formerly Hauser Chemical Research), a company with good taste. Colorado-based Hauser (HAUS) produces natural compounds for pharmaceuticals and makes nutraceuticals, natural flavor extracts, and natural food ingredients. HAUS also performs testing and contract research services.

For the three years prior to fiscal 1995 (Apr.), almost all of HAUS's revenues came from a contract to supply the non-patented compound paclitaxel to Bristol-Myers Squibb. Paclitaxel is an anti-tumor agent that has shown promise for the treatment of ovarian, breast and other cancers. After the expiration of the Bristol-Myers contract, HAUS embarked on a plan to rebuild its market base for paclitaxel products, increase its presence in natural ingredients markets, and strengthen its technical services area.

In 1994, HAUS signed a 10 year agreement to supply American Home Products with bulk paclitaxel. In July 1997, HAUS's customer, Immunex Corp., received Canadian marketing approval for paclitaxel in treating cancer. In August 1998, the company reported that it signed a new agreement to supply paclitaxel for the collaborative arrangement between Immunex and IVAX Corp., which is awaiting FDA approval for Paclitaxel In-

jection. Also in August, the firm announced that it had severed the exclusivity portion of its relationship with Yew Tree Pharmaceuticals, enabling HAUS to supply other companies in European markets. Haus's pharmaceutical business unit, comprised mainly of the paclitaxel product, generated 12% of total revenues in fiscal 1998.

The NaturEnhance business unit, consisting of flavor extracts, food ingredients, and nutraceuticals (natural products used to supplement the diet), accounted for 43% of total revenues in fiscal 1998. HAUS's NaturEnhance brand natural flavor extracts include hibiscus, rosehips, and chicory for use in ready-to-drink beverages, yogurt, dressings, ethnic foods, teas and other natural foods. The company's natural food ingredients act as preservatives, stabilizers, antioxidants and nutritional additives in foods. The company began development of nutraceuticals in fiscal 1995. HAUS's products, which may be consumed as supplements in liquids, capsules, or tablets, or as ingredients in processed foods, include herbal extracts of ecinacea, valerian, ginseng, rosemary, and chamomile.

HAUS's Technical Services unit provides laboratory testing and analysis services; contract research; and product development in a variety of chemical, engineering, and food technology applications. Technical Services provided 45% of total revenues in fiscal 1998.

Per Share Data ($)

(Year Ended Apr. 30)	1998	1997	1996	1995	1994	1993	1992	1991	1990	1989
Tangible Bk. Val.	5.60	5.90	6.42	7.34	7.69	6.68	5.73	0.58	0.25	0.20
Cash Flow	0.09	0.03	-0.40	0.07	1.42	1.17	0.38	0.15	0.02	0.07
Earnings	-0.30	-0.38	-0.75	-0.26	0.98	0.80	0.31	0.08	-0.04	NM
Dividends	Nil	Nil	Nil	Nil	Nil	Nil	Nil	Nil	Nil	Nil
Payout Ratio	Nil	Nil	Nil	Nil	Nil	Nil	Nil	Nil	Nil	Nil
Cal. Yrs.	1997	1996	1995	1994	1993	1992	1991	1990	1989	1988
Prices - High	8	8³⁄₈	6⁵⁄₈	10¹⁄₂	25¹⁄₄	31	23¹⁄₂	2⁷⁄₈	NA	NA
- Low	5³⁄₈	4¹⁄₂	4¹⁄₄	4¹⁄₄	4¹⁄₂	8¹⁄₄	2¹⁄₈	1³⁄₈	NA	NA
P/E Ratio - High	NM	NM	NM	NM	26	39	76	36	NM	NA
- Low	NM	NM	NM	NM	5	10	7	17	NM	NA

Income Statement Analysis (Million $)

	1998	1997	1996	1995	1994	1993	1992	1991	1990	1989
Revs.	32.0	25.2	25.7	22.9	60.4	59.3	25.6	7.4	3.0	2.2
Oper. Inc.	-0.6	-1.9	-9.1	-2.8	19.5	15.9	5.1	1.2	0.2	0.3
Depr.	4.0	4.2	3.6	3.4	4.6	3.7	0.7	0.4	0.2	0.1
Int. Exp.	0.0	0.0	0.1	0.0	Nil	0.0	0.0	0.1	0.1	0.1
Pretax Inc.	-4.0	-5.5	-12.7	-4.4	16.1	13.1	5.0	0.7	-0.2	0.1
Eff. Tax Rate	NM	NM	NM	NM	36%	38%	40%	42%	NM	27%
Net Inc.	-3.1	-3.9	-7.7	-2.7	10.3	8.2	3.0	0.4	-0.1	0.1

Balance Sheet & Other Fin. Data (Million $)

	1998	1997	1996	1995	1994	1993	1992	1991	1990	1989
Cash	2.2	8.4	15.2	24.7	23.2	12.6	18.8	0.8	Nil	0.1
Curr. Assets	23.7	24.1	35.0	39.4	39.6	27.7	29.1	5.6	2.1	1.1
Total Assets	68.3	66.8	74.9	82.6	84.6	73.4	45.6	8.1	3.4	1.7
Curr. Liab.	7.0	3.0	1.5	2.3	1.9	2.5	2.2	2.1	1.3	0.4
LT Debt	0.7	0.1	0.2	0.1	Nil	Nil	0.1	0.3	1.1	0.8
Common Eqty.	60.6	63.7	70.2	77.4	80.8	69.7	39.8	2.6	1.0	0.5
Total Cap.	61.2	63.8	71.9	80.3	82.6	70.9	43.4	5.9	2.1	1.3
Cap. Exp.	2.1	2.7	2.2	4.0	9.4	11.5	12.5	0.8	0.7	0.3
Cash Flow	0.9	0.3	-4.1	0.7	14.9	11.9	3.8	0.8	0.1	0.2
Curr. Ratio	3.4	8.1	22.7	17.3	20.5	11.1	13.1	2.6	1.6	3.2
% LT Debt of Cap.	1.1	0.2	0.3	0.1	Nil	Nil	0.2	5.0	51.0	56.4
% Net Inc.of Revs.	NM	NM	NM	NM	17.1	13.7	11.8	5.9	NM	3.7
% Ret. on Assets	NM	NM	NM	NM	13.1	11.5	10.3	7.0	NM	5.7
% Ret. on Equity	NM	NM	NM	NM	13.7	12.6	13.7	21.9	NM	18.0

Data as orig. reptd.; bef. results of disc. opers. and/or spec. items. Per share data adj. for stk. divs. as of ex-div. date. Bold denotes diluted EPS (FASB 128). E-Estimated. NA-Not Available. NM-Not Meaningful. NR-Not Ranked.

Reincorporated—in Colorado in 1996. **Office**—5555 Airport Blvd., Boulder, CO 80301. **Tel**—(303) 443-4662. **E-mail**—relations@hauser.com **Chrmn, Pres & CEO**—D. P. Stull. **EVP & COO**—M. C. Wehr. **CFO & Treas**—D. I. Rosenthal. **Secy**—P. A. Roberts. **Investor Contact**—Joanna Manley.**Dirs**—W. E. Coleman, S. J. Cristol, R. J. Daughenbaugh, B. J. Haddon, R. F. Saydah, D. P. Stull, B. M. Tolbert. **Transfer Agent & Registrar**—American Securities Transfer Inc., Denver. **Incorporated**—in Delaware in 1985; reincorporated in Colorado in 1996. **Empl**— 320. **S&P Analyst:** David Moskowitz

Heartland Express
4131N
NASDAQ Symbol HTLD
In S&P SmallCap 600

03-OCT-98

Industry: Truckers

Summary: Heartland Express is a short-to-medium haul truckload carrier based near Iowa City, IA.

Quantitative Evaluations

Recent Price • 16
52 Wk Range • 30⅞-15½

Yield • Nil
12-Mo. P/E • 15.1

Outlook (1 Lowest—5 Highest)
• 3

Fair Value
• 17¾

Risk
• **Average**

Earn./Div. Rank
• **B+**

Technical Eval.
• **Neutral** since 5/98

Rel. Strength Rank (1 Lowest—99 Highest)
• 50

Insider Activity
• NA

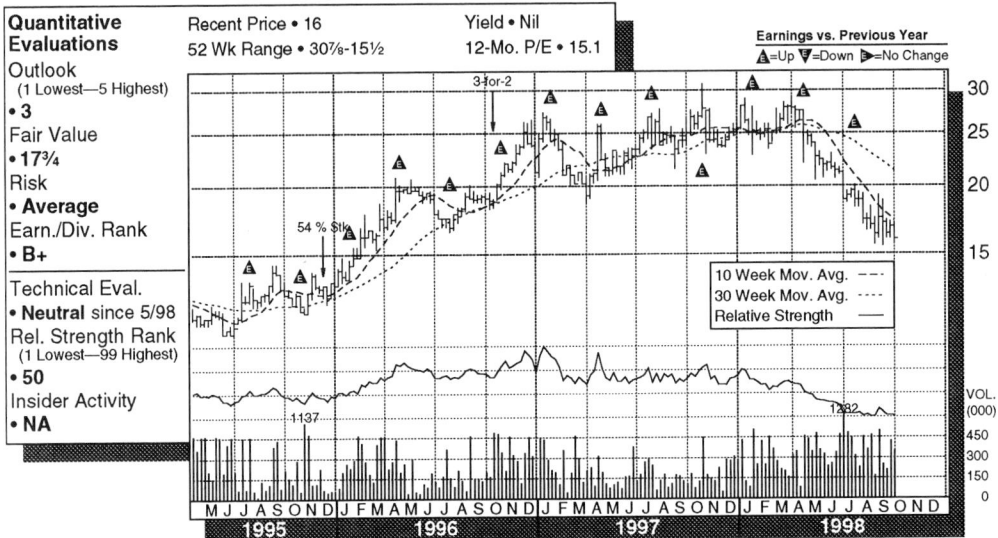

Business Profile - 24-AUG-98

This short-to-medium haul truckload carrier has grown rapidly in recent years, largely as a result of expanding service for existing customers and acquiring new customers. As of the second quarter of 1998, the company had registered 14 consecutive quarters of earnings growth. In the first half of 1998, revenues and earnings rose 9% and 14%, respectively, aided by the July 1997 acquisition of A&M Express, which operates with a predominance of company tractors, targeting both van and flatbed transportation markets.

Operational Review - 24-AUG-98

Operating revenue in the six months ended June 30, 1998, rose 8.6%, year to year, driven by recent acquisitions, expansion of the customer base and increased sales to existing customers. Margins widened, reflecting lower rent costs, partially offset by a rise in compensation expense; operating income grew 16%. Following a significant jump in depreciation and amortization charges, pretax income was up 10%. After taxes at 35.0%, versus 37.0%, net income advanced 14%, to $16,323,444 ($0.54 a share), from $14,357,637 ($0.48).

Stock Performance - 02-OCT-98

In the past 30 trading days, HTLD's shares have declined 6%, compared to a 7% fall in the S&P 500. Average trading volume for the past five days was 70,000 shares, compared with the 40-day moving average of 85,223 shares.

Key Stock Statistics

Dividend Rate/Share	Nil	Shareholders	300
Shs. outstg. (M)	30.0	Market cap. (B)	$0.480
Avg. daily vol. (M)	0.065	Inst. holdings	44%
Tang. Bk. Value/Share	5.67		
Beta	0.98		

Value of $10,000 invested 5 years ago: $ 10,713

Fiscal Year Ending Dec. 31

	1998	1997	1996	1995	1994	1993
Revenues (Million $)						
1Q	66.84	59.89	54.36	47.58	61.35	27.08
2Q	69.22	65.38	59.38	46.97	59.30	29.38
3Q	—	70.18	58.18	47.53	53.88	29.23
4Q	—	67.06	57.09	49.42	49.69	30.32
Yr.	—	262.5	229.0	191.5	224.3	116.0
Earnings Per Share ($)						
1Q	0.26	0.22	0.19	0.15	-0.06	
2Q	0.28	0.26	0.21	0.17	0.14	
3Q	—	0.28	0.22	0.19	0.15	
4Q	—	0.24	0.21	0.17	0.10	0.11
Yr.	—	1.00	0.83	0.69	0.33	0.48

Next earnings report expected: mid October

Dividend Data

No cash has been paid. The most recent stock split was 3-for-2, effected in October 1996.

A Division of The McGraw·Hill Companies

Business Summary - 24-AUG-98

Heartland Express, Inc. (HTLD) is a short-to-medium haul truckload carrier that provides nationwide transportation service to major shippers, using late-model tractors and a uniform fleet of 53-foot aluminum plate dry vans. The company's primary traffic lanes are between customer locations east of the Rocky Mountains, with selected service to the West.

Since becoming a public company in 1986, HTLD has grown from $22 million in revenues to $263 million in 1997, while net income has grown from $3 million to $30 million. The company attributes this growth to expanding service for existing customers and acquiring new customers, which Heartland's sales personnel solicit by emphasizing premium service, regular monitoring of customer needs, and coordinating of customer requirements with operations personnel. Management believes that the company's uniform fleet of 53-foot aluminum plate dry van trailers offers a marketing advantage because of these trailers' 11% greater capacity than 48-foot trailers. In addition, the standardized fleet allows customers to know load dimensions in advance of all shipments, rather than preparing different loads for trailers of varying lengths.

The company targets customers in its operating area that require multiple, time-sensitive shipments, including those employing "just-in-time" manufacturing and inventory management. In seeking those customers, HTLD has positioned itself as a provider of premium service at compensatory rates, rather than competing solely on the basis of price.

The company's 25, 10 and five largest customers accounted for 70%, 54% and 39% of revenues, respectively, in 1997. Major customers represent the consumer appliance, food products and automotive industries. Sears Logistics Services accounted for 15% of revenues.

In addition to its own operations department, the company operates three specialized regional distribution operations for major customers near Atlanta, GA; Columbus, OH; and Iowa City, IA. These short-haul operations concentrate on freight movements generally within a 400-mile radius of the regional terminal, and are designed to meet the needs of significant customers in those regions.

Operations were significantly expanded in 1994 with the acquisition of Munson Transportation, an unprofitable truckload carrier serving customers primarily in the Midwest, Northeast and West. In July 1997, HTLD acquired A&M Express of Kingsport, TN ($28 million in sales), which operates with a predominance of company tractors, targeting both van and flatbed transportation markets.

Per Share Data ($)

(Year Ended Dec. 31)	1997	1996	1995	1994	1993	1992	1991	1990	1989	1988
Tangible Bk. Val.	5.13	4.12	3.29	2.59	2.32	1.81	1.60	1.38	NA	NA
Cash Flow	1.59	1.30	1.19	1.00	1.10	1.01	0.85	0.77	NA	NA
Earnings	1.00	0.83	0.69	0.33	0.48	0.33	0.24	0.21	NA	NA
Dividends	Nil	Nil	Nil	Nil	Nil	Nil	Nil	Nil	Nil	Nil
Payout Ratio	Nil	Nil	Nil	Nil	Nil	Nil	Nil	Nil	Nil	Nil
Prices - High	30⅞	26½	14⅜	15⅞	13	12⅛	11½	7⅛	NA	NA
- Low	18½	13⅛	10¾	10½	8⅝	6¼	5⅞	4⅛	NA	NA
P/E Ratio - High	31	32	21	48	27	37	48	34	NA	NA
- Low	18	16	16	31	18	19	24	20	NA	NA

Income Statement Analysis (Million $)

	1997	1996	1995	1994	1993	1992	1991	1990	1989	1988
Revs.	263	229	192	224	116	97.0	74.0	NA	NA	NA
Oper. Inc.	60.6	50.7	46.1	47.2	45.5	40.3	34.8	NA	NA	NA
Depr.	17.5	14.0	15.1	20.1	22.8	20.7	18.5	NA	NA	NA
Int. Exp.	0.1	0.0	Nil	2.2	5.3	5.4	4.7	NA	NA	NA
Pretax Inc.	47.0	39.7	32.7	21.8	18.3	15.6	12.2	NA	NA	NA
Eff. Tax Rate	36%	37%	37%	54%	44%	40%	42%	NA	NA	NA
Net Inc.	30.1	25.0	20.6	10.1	10.2	9.4	7.1	NA	NA	NA

Balance Sheet & Other Fin. Data (Million $)

	1997	1996	1995	1994	1993	1992	1991	1990	1989	1988
Cash	76.2	59.6	46.6	10.2	9.4	NA	NA	NA	NA	NA
Curr. Assets	138	121	83.9	44.4	57.9	NA	NA	NA	NA	NA
Total Assets	225	191	158	136	169	150	135	NA	NA	NA
Curr. Liab.	55.8	51.6	42.1	41.6	69.0	NA	NA	NA	NA	NA
LT Debt	Nil	Nil	Nil	0.7	21.4	NA	NA	NA	NA	NA
Common Eqty.	154	124	99	78.1	68.0	57.0	48.0	NA	NA	NA
Total Cap.	170	140	116	94.8	100	NA	NA	NA	NA	NA
Cap. Exp.	22.4	7.5	NA	3.7	28.0	32.0	NA	NA	NA	NA
Cash Flow	47.6	39.0	35.7	30.1	33.1	30.1	25.7	NA	NA	NA
Curr. Ratio	2.5	2.4	2.0	1.1	0.8	NA	NA	NA	NA	NA
% LT Debt of Cap.	Nil	Nil	Nil	0.7	21.4	NA	NA	NA	NA	NA
% Net Inc.of Revs.	11.5	10.9	10.7	4.5	4.3	4.6	4.0	NA	NA	NA
% Ret. on Assets	14.4	14.3	14.0	6.6	6.4	6.6	5.7	NA	NA	NA
% Ret. on Equity	21.5	22.5	23.3	13.8	16.4	17.9	15.9	NA	NA	NA

Data as orig. reptd.; bef. results of disc. opers. and/or spec. items. Per share data adj. for stk. divs. as of ex-div. date. Bold denotes diluted EPS (FASB 128). E-Estimated. NA-Not Available. NM-Not Meaningful. NR-Not Ranked.

Office—2777 Heartland Drive, Coralville, IA 52241. **Tel**—(319) 645-2728. **Chrmn, Pres & Secy**—R. A. Gerdin. **EVP-Fin & Treas**—J. P. Cosaert. **Dirs**—B. J. Allen, M. J. Gerdin, R. A. Gerdin, R. O. Jacobson. **Transfer Agent & Registrar**—Boatmen's Trust Co., St. Louis. **Incorporated**—in Nevada in 1978. **Empl**— 1,009. **S&P Analyst**: S.J.T.

STANDARD &POOR'S
STOCK REPORTS

Hecla Mining

1125

NYSE Symbol **HL**

In S&P SmallCap 600

03-OCT-98

Industry:
Gold & Precious Metals
Mining

Summary: This company produces gold, silver, lead and zinc from properties in the U.S. and Mexico. It also produces kaolin, ball clay and other industrial minerals.

S&P Opinion: Accumulate (★★★★)	Recent Price • 4¾	Yield • Nil		Earnings vs. Previous Year
	52 Wk Range • 7⅛-3⅛	12-Mo. P/E • NM		▲=Up ▼=Down ▶=No Change

Quantitative Evaluations

Outlook
(1 Lowest—5 Highest)
• **NA**

Fair Value
• **NA**

Risk
• **Average**

Earn./Div. Rank
• **C**

Technical Eval.
• **Bullish** since 6/98

Rel. Strength Rank
(1 Lowest—99 Highest)
• **91**

Insider Activity
• **Neutral**

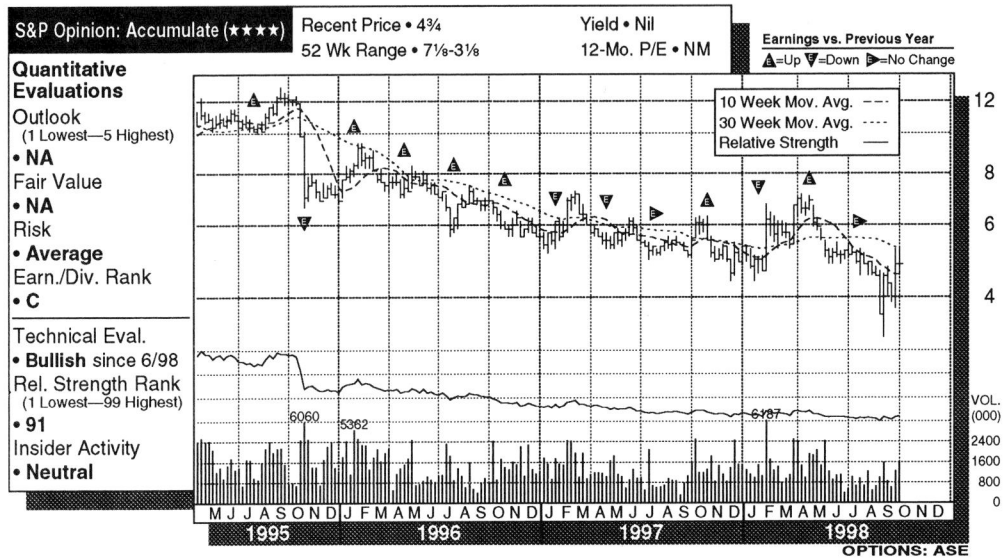

10 Week Mov. Avg. — — —
30 Week Mov. Avg. ·······
Relative Strength ——

OPTIONS: ASE

Overview - 13-AUG-98

EPS for 1998's second quarter were aided by an asset sale totaling $1.2 million; excluding the gain, HL broke even for the quarter. Operating results for the quarter were mixed. Cash costs for gold rose both sequentially and year over year on lower production. Silver cash costs were down sequentially, reflecting higher production; however, compared with 1997's second quarter, cash costs rose as lower by-product credits for lead and zinc offset higher production. For all of 1998, silver cash costs should decline as output rises and ore grades improve in the second half.

Valuation - 13-AUG-98

Following second quarter 1998 EPS, we still rate HL accumulate based on our positive outlook for silver. HL has gold and non precious metals operations but it can still be viewed as a proxy for silver. Fundamentals have been favorable for silver for quite some time as fabrication demand has exceeded mine production and scrap recovery since 1989. This gap has been made up by liquidation of above ground supplies. For the ninth consecutive year, such inventories were liquidated in 1997 to bridge the gap. From the end of 1996 to August 11, 1998, Comex inventories declined from 205.1 million oz. to 79.1 million oz. So far in 1998, silver has averaged $5.80/oz., versus $4.90/oz. for all of 1997. In the first week of February, silver rose to over $7/oz. for the first time in nine years on news that Berkshire Hathaway, the investment company led by Warren Buffett, had accumulated 129.3 million oz. of silver between July 25, 1997, and January 12, 1998. Subsequently, the metal declined sharply, to the $5.17/oz. level as of mid-August. Notwithstanding the volatile trading, we believe the fundamentals will push silver, and ultimately HL to higher levels.

Key Stock Statistics

S&P EPS Est. 1998	0.05	Tang. Bk. Value/Share	0.82
P/E on S&P Est. 1998	96.2	Beta	1.31
S&P EPS Est. 1999	0.10	Shareholders	11,300
Dividend Rate/Share	Nil	Market cap. (B)	$0.265
Shs. outstg. (M)	55.1	Inst. holdings	27%
Avg. daily vol. (M)	0.239		

Value of $10,000 invested 5 years ago: $ 6,209

Fiscal Year Ending Dec. 31

	1998	1997	1996	1995	1994	1993
Revenues (Million $)						
1Q	40.13	42.46	42.95	35.71	26.34	20.87
2Q	47.00	46.07	40.52	42.24	38.00	23.09
3Q	—	41.20	37.66	41.20	35.28	19.54
4Q	—	34.22	37.12	36.73	29.08	18.35
Yr.	—	163.9	158.3	155.9	128.8	81.85
Earnings Per Share ($)						
1Q	0.02	-0.03	-0.01	-0.09	-0.19	-0.15
2Q	0.02	0.02	0.02	0.01	-0.03	-0.06
3Q	E Nil	-0.02	-0.76	-2.17	-0.03	-0.09
4Q	E0.01	-0.13	-0.04	-0.02	-0.47	-0.17
Yr.	E0.05	-0.16	-0.79	-2.28	-0.74	-0.48

Next earnings report expected: late October

Dividend Data

Common dividends were omitted in 1991.

A Division of The **McGraw·Hill** *Companies*

Hecla Mining Company

Business Summary - 13-AUG-98

Hecla produces gold, silver, lead and zinc from properties in the U.S. and Mexico and kaolin clay and other industrial minerals. In 1997 gold accounted for 34% of sales and $15 million of gross profit, silver 20% of sales and $3.8 million of losses, and industrial minerals 46% of sales and $5.0 million of profit.

Hecla's main business strategy is to increase its silver production to a rate of about 8 million oz. per year by the end of 1998, and to replace its gold reserves. Its strategy also entails using the industrial minerals segment to offset the earnings and cash flow volatility of the precious metals business. Operating and reserve data for recent years (reserve data as of year end):

	1997	1996
Silver production (oz.)	5,147,009	3,024,911
Cash cost	$3.58	$4.24
Total cost	$5.42	$5.47
Silver reserves	63,378,168	71,992,619
Gold production (oz.)	174,164	169,376
Cash cost	$173	$276
Total cost	$239	$364
Gold reserves	613,538	787,249
Lead production (tons)	24,995	22,660
Lead reserves	253,704	260,704
Zinc production (tons)	16,830	7,464
Zinc reserves	343,200	360,721
Industrial mineral shipments	1,025,993	1,072,319

HL's strategy for reserve replacement is to concentrate on existing operations where an infrastructure already exists. In addition, it will focus on advanced-stage exploration properties that have been identified as having potential for additional discoveries. HL is currently concentrating its exploration activities at the Lucky Friday and Greens Creek silver mines, the 50%-owned Rosebud gold mine, the La Choya mine and gold properties in Mexico, including the Pinos, La Jojoba and Porvenir properties. Exploration expenditures for 1998 are expected to total $3.9 million, down from $7.4 million in 1997.

The industrial minerals segment produces ball clay, kaolin and sodium feldspar, three of the four ingredients needed to produce ceramic products.

Gold production in 1998's first half totaled 66,956 oz., versus 89,333 oz. in 1997; cash costs for the period were $181/oz., versus $175/oz. Silver production was 3,221,649 oz., versus 2,524,504 oz. in 1997; cash costs were $4.06/oz., versus $3.40/oz., reflecting lower ore grades and decreased by-product credits for lead and zinc. Shipments for industrial minerals totaled 592,927 tons, up from 519,463 tons in 1997's first half.

Per Share Data ($) (Year Ended Dec. 31)	1997	1996	1995	1994	1993	1992	1991	1990	1989	1988
Tangible Bk. Val.	0.79	0.56	0.98	3.34	3.56	3.60	4.95	4.95	4.79	5.29
Cash Flow	0.23	-0.23	-1.62	-0.39	-0.11	-1.14	0.17	0.84	-0.17	1.06
Earnings	-0.16	-0.79	-2.28	-0.74	-0.48	-1.59	-0.51	0.19	-0.83	0.61
Dividends	Nil	Nil	Nil	Nil	Nil	Nil	Nil	0.05	0.05	0.05
Payout Ratio	Nil	Nil	Nil	Nil	Nil	Nil	Nil	26%	NM	8%
Prices - High	7¼	9½	13	15	15¼	12¼	12⅝	16⅜	16⅛	17⅞
- Low	4⅜	5½	6⅝	9¼	7⅜	7¼	6⅝	6⅝	11½	11¾
P/E Ratio - High	NM	NM	NM	NM	NM	NM	NM	86	NM	29
- Low	NM	NM	NM	NM	NM	NM	NM	35	NM	19
Income Statement Analysis (Million $)										
Revs.	164	158	156	129	82.0	101	118	133	99	102
Oper. Inc.	20.2	17.2	13.6	-3.3	0.4	-28.5	10.1	16.8	4.2	22.9
Depr.	21.3	20.8	23.8	14.8	12.2	13.9	20.5	17.6	17.9	11.9
Int. Exp.	1.7	3.1	2.0	2.6	5.0	6.9	7.0	5.8	4.7	1.8
Pretax Inc.	1.4	-31.7	-100	-24.2	-12.7	-49.6	-18.5	2.3	-25.9	13.5
Eff. Tax Rate	NM	NM	NM	NM	NM	NM	NM	NM	NM	NM
Net Inc.	-0.5	-32.4	-101	-23.8	-11.7	-49.2	-15.4	5.1	-22.4	16.6
Balance Sheet & Other Fin. Data (Million $)										
Cash	3.8	8.3	4.0	7.3	65.4	3.3	5.6	16.4	15.5	0.3
Curr. Assets	52.6	58.8	53.3	51.3	97.2	33.0	46.9	48.4	49.2	30.0
Total Assets	251	268	258	335	333	222	258	232	222	189
Curr. Liab.	25.0	32.7	26.0	23.5	19.6	12.7	12.6	11.7	14.4	11.9
LT Debt	22.1	38.2	36.1	2.0	49.5	70.4	76.9	70.2	65.0	17.3
Common Eqty.	160	145	164	161	123	114	150	134	129	143
Total Cap.	183	184	201	280	290	186	232	210	198	169
Cap. Exp.	24.8	33.7	45.3	66.6	58.7	23.2	19.5	29.9	40.6	26.0
Cash Flow	12.8	-11.6	-77.9	-17.1	-3.6	-35.3	5.1	22.7	-4.5	28.5
Curr. Ratio	2.1	1.8	2.0	2.2	5.0	2.6	3.7	4.1	3.4	2.5
% LT Debt of Cap.	12.1	20.8	18.0	0.7	17.1	37.9	33.2	33.4	32.8	10.2
% Net Inc.of Revs.	NM	NM	NM	NM	NM	NM	NM	3.9	NM	16.2
% Ret. on Assets	NM	NA	NM	NM	NM	NM	NM	2.3	NM	9.2
% Ret. on Equity	NM	NM	NM	NM	NM	NM	NM	3.9	NM	12.1

Data as orig. reptd.; bef. results of disc. opers. and/or spec. items. Per share data adj. for stk. divs. as of ex-div. date. Bold denotes diluted EPS (FASB 128). E-Estimated. NA-Not Available. NM-Not Meaningful. NR-Not Ranked.

Office—6500 Mineral Dr., Coeur d'Alene, ID 83814-8788. **Tel**—(208) 769-4100. **Fax**—(208) 769-4107. **Website**—http://www.hecla-mining.com **Chrmn, Pres & CEO**—A. Brown. **VP & Secy**—M. B. White. **VP-Fin & Treas**—J. P. Stilwell. **VP & Investor Contact**—William B. Booth. **Dirs**—A. Brown, J. E. Clute, J. Coors Jr., T. Crumley, L. O. Erdahl, C. L. McAlpine, T. J. O'Neil, J. E. Ordonez, P. A. Redmond. **Transfer Agent & Registrar**—American Stock Transfer & Trust Co., NYC. **Incorporated**—in Washington in 1898; reincorporated in Delaware in 1983. **Empl**— 1,202. **S&P Analyst:** Leo J. Larkin

STANDARD &POOR'S
STOCK REPORTS

Helix Technology
4136

Nasdaq Symbol **HELX**

In S&P SmallCap 600

03-OCT-98

Industry: Equipment (Semiconductor)

Summary: This company makes, sells and services products based on cryogenic and vacuum technology.

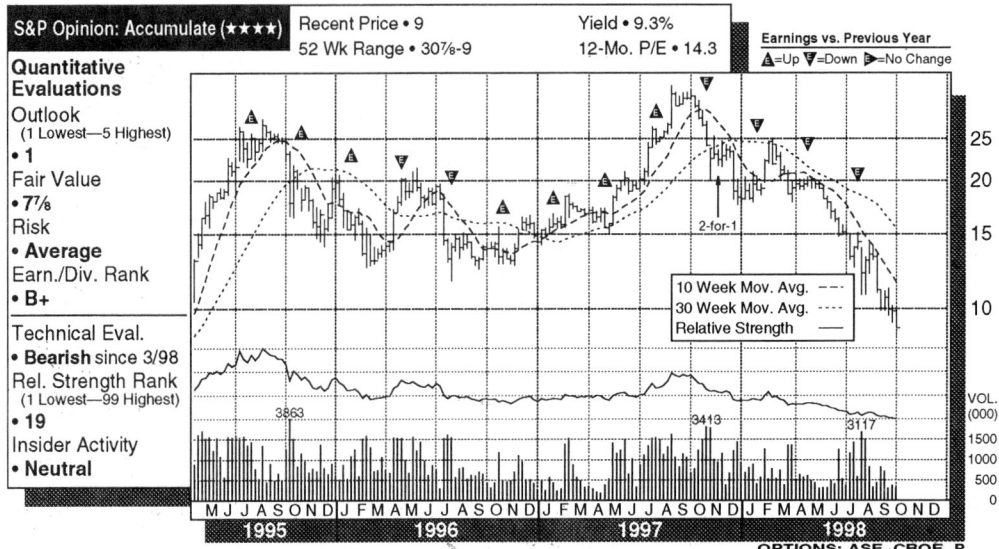

S&P Opinion: Accumulate (★★★★)	Recent Price • 9	Yield • 9.3%	Earnings vs. Previous Year
	52 Wk Range • 30⅞-9	12-Mo. P/E • 14.3	▲=Up ▼=Down ▶=No Change

Quantitative Evaluations

Outlook (1 Lowest—5 Highest)
• 1

Fair Value
• 7⅞

Risk
• Average

Earn./Div. Rank
• B+

Technical Eval.
• Bearish since 3/98

Rel. Strength Rank (1 Lowest—99 Highest)
• 19

Insider Activity
• Neutral

OPTIONS: ASE, CBOE, P

Overview - 16-SEP-98

Based on a weakening outlook for global semiconductor capital equipment spending, we expect HELX's revenues to be down about 35% in 1998. Spending for capital equipment is currently being restrained by the Asian financial crisis, and by persistent overcapacity in the market for dynamic random access memory (DRAM) and other semiconductors. We expect revenues to flatten in 1999, however, as industry conditions stabilize, and chip-makers migrate to next-generation technologies. In prior capital spending cycle downturns, HELX demonstrated an impressive ability to maintain profit margins. The company's liberal use of temporary workers in its manufacturing process provides it with greater flexibility in managing production costs. Based on HELX's weak near-term prospects, we expect 1998 EPS to fall to $0.24, from 1997's $1.07 (excluding charges, and pro forma to include the May 1998 acquisition of Granville-Phillips Co.).

Valuation - 16-SEP-98

The shares have fallen sharply this year, reflecting deteriorating semiconductor equipment industry conditions. We are maintaining our accumulate recommendation, however, as we believe that much of the bad news regarding near-term prospects has already been discounted in the stock price. Although we remain cautious about overcapacity and prospects for slower capital spending over the next few quarters, long-term fundamentals remain intact. HELX continues to command a dominant position in the market for cryogenic vacuum pumps, and is well positioned to benefit from semiconductor industry growth. We believe that the shares, recently trading at 1.8X trailing 12-month sales, are attractively valued. In addition, the dividend yield (recently about 5.8%) offers some downside protection.

Key Stock Statistics

S&P EPS Est. 1998	0.24	Tang. Bk. Value/Share	3.38
P/E on S&P Est. 1998	37.5	Beta	1.23
S&P EPS Est. 1999	0.35	Shareholders	700
Dividend Rate/Share	0.84	Market cap. (B)	$0.200
Shs. outstg. (M)	22.2	Inst. holdings	42%
Avg. daily vol. (M)	0.087		

Value of $10,000 invested 5 years ago: $ 52,951

Fiscal Year Ending Dec. 31

	1998	1997	1996	1995	1994	1993
Revenues (Million $)						
1Q	25.87	29.02	40.21	27.15	18.79	15.19
2Q	25.71	32.93	39.35	29.03	21.25	16.51
3Q	—	35.62	25.12	32.25	22.36	16.04
4Q	—	33.94	23.70	35.23	24.37	16.12
Yr.	—	131.5	128.4	123.7	86.76	63.86
Earnings Per Share ($)						
1Q	**0.15**	**0.21**	0.37	0.21	0.09	0.05
2Q	**-0.02**	**0.26**	0.38	0.25	0.13	0.06
3Q	—	**0.30**	0.20	0.28	0.14	0.07
4Q	—	**0.30**	0.16	0.31	0.17	0.07
Yr.	—	**1.07**	1.10	1.05	0.54	0.26

Next earnings report expected: mid October

Dividend Data (Dividends have been paid since 1987.)

Amount ($)	Date Decl.	Ex-Div. Date	Stock of Record	Payment Date
0.210	Oct. 16	Oct. 28	Oct. 30	Nov. 13 '97
0.210	Feb. 19	Mar. 03	Mar. 05	Mar. 19 '98
0.210	Apr. 16	Apr. 27	Apr. 29	May. 13 '98
0.210	Jul. 17	Jul. 28	Jul. 30	Aug. 13 '98

A Division of The **McGraw·Hill** *Companies*

Business Summary - 16-SEP-98

Helix Technology Corp. is a leader in the development and application of cyrogenic (low-temperature) and vacuum technology. Using proprietary engineering and unique manufacturing competence, the company delivers innovative solutions to meet customer requirements in selected markets worldwide. Helix believes it is the world's leading producer of cryogenic vacuum pumping systems.

Thin film deposition and ion implantation systems are dependent on Helix's vacuum products. These systems in turn are used in the production of rapidly growing high-technology products, including semiconductors, flat panel displays, magnetic recording heads, and optics. The company's cryogenic systems are are also facilitating the commercialization of emerging applications for superconducting electronics in the growing wireless telecommunications market.

CTI's On-Board pumping systems incorporate built-in microprocessor capabilities to provide online performance monitoring and diagnostics to enhance vacuum processing system uptime. The On-Board system allows users to set and control all key parameters of pump status, such as temperature or pumping speed, and it provides comprehensive, real time parameter monitoring with programmable alarms. This substantially increases control over the process environment, and gives the user the ability to optimize system perform-

ance for specific applications. The On-Board product line includes On-Board Cryopumps, On-Board Waterpumps, an increasing range of computer networking products and an expanding set of innovative, user friendly software offerings.

Cryopumps are designed to pump various gases from a vacuum chamber by freezing the gases onto refrigerated surfaces. These captured gases are periodically vented by shutting down the chamber and warming the condensed gases, allowing them to escape into the atmosphere. Waterpumps are high-performance cryo pumps which increase water vapor pumping speed in the vacuum process, providing improved throughput and better process results.

Helix also applies its unique talents to provide specialized solutions to customer requirements for low-temperature refrigeration applications, including the cooling of infrared detectors and of advanced electronic circuits and superconducting materials.

Helix's GUTS rapid-response, global customer support network ensures customers direct, 24-hour-a-day access to customer support resources.

In May 1998, HELX acquired, in exchange for 2.38 million common shares, Granville-Phillips Co., a Boulder, CO-based company that develops and manufactures instrumentation for vacuum measurement and control. Granville-Phillips had total sales in 1997 of $25.6 million.

Per Share Data ($)

(Year Ended Dec. 31)	1997	1996	1995	1994	1993	1992	1991	1990	1989	1988
Tangible Bk. Val.	3.38	3.04	2.63	1.77	1.31	1.15	1.08	1.01	1.06	1.01
Cash Flow	1.23	1.26	1.18	0.64	0.35	0.24	0.25	0.14	0.22	0.26
Earnings	1.07	1.10	1.05	0.54	0.26	0.15	0.16	0.06	0.13	0.18
Dividends	0.73	0.65	0.29	0.14	0.10	0.10	0.10	0.10	0.09	0.58
Payout Ratio	68%	59%	27%	26%	67%	63%	58%	158%	67%	321%
Prices - High	33³/₈	21¹/₂	27⁷/₈	9¹/₂	4³/₈	3⁷/₈	2³/₄	1¹³/₁₆	2⁷/₁₆	3³/₄
- Low	14¹/₈	11⁵/₈	7³/₈	3³/₈	2¹/₈	1⁷/₈	1⁵/₁₆	⁷/₈	1⁹/₁₆	2¹/₈
P/E Ratio - High	31	19	27	18	17	26	17	30	18	21
- Low	13	11	7	6	8	12	6	15	11	12

Income Statement Analysis (Million $)

	1997	1996	1995	1994	1993	1992	1991	1990	1989	1988
Revs.	132	128	124	86.8	63.9	50.8	55.8	52.4	54.6	55.2
Oper. Inc.	32.4	34.9	34.4	17.7	9.0	5.8	6.1	3.5	5.3	6.4
Depr.	3.2	3.2	2.6	2.0	1.8	1.7	1.6	1.7	1.7	1.6
Int. Exp.	NA	Nil	Nil	Nil	0.1	0.2	0.3	0.6	0.5	0.2
Pretax Inc.	32.5	34.4	33.7	16.4	7.4	4.1	4.8	1.9	4.1	5.6
Eff. Tax Rate	34%	36%	38%	36%	34%	30%	36%	36%	35%	34%
Net Inc.	21.3	22.0	21.0	10.6	4.9	2.9	3.1	1.2	2.7	3.6

Balance Sheet & Other Fin. Data (Million $)

	1997	1996	1995	1994	1993	1992	1991	1990	1989	1988
Cash	33.4	29.4	21.7	8.1	1.7	1.6	1.2	2.2	1.3	2.0
Curr. Assets	65.3	57.5	55.4	32.9	21.0	20.5	19.6	22.0	22.3	23.0
Total Assets	81.7	71.8	69.1	45.4	32.7	32.0	29.1	30.7	31.1	31.6
Curr. Liab.	14.6	11.9	17.1	10.4	7.0	9.4	7.8	10.8	8.9	9.8
LT Debt	Nil	Nil	Nil	0.0	0.1	0.1	0.2	0.2	0.4	0.7
Common Eqty.	67.0	59.8	51.6	34.3	25.0	21.8	20.5	19.1	21.1	20.2
Total Cap.	67.0	59.8	51.9	34.9	25.7	22.6	21.3	19.9	22.3	21.8
Cap. Exp.	4.5	3.3	3.0	2.2	1.7	3.4	1.8	1.1	1.4	1.9
Cash Flow	24.5	25.2	23.6	12.7	6.7	4.6	4.7	2.9	4.3	5.3
Curr. Ratio	4.5	4.8	3.2	3.1	3.0	2.2	2.5	2.0	2.5	2.3
% LT Debt of Cap.	Nil	NM	NM	0.1	0.3	0.5	0.8	1.0	1.7	3.1
% Net Inc.of Revs.	16.2	17.1	17.0	12.2	7.7	5.6	5.5	2.3	4.9	6.6
% Ret. on Assets	27.8	31.2	36.7	27.0	15.2	9.4	10.3	3.9	8.6	10.9
% Ret. on Equity	33.6	39.4	48.9	25.5	20.9	13.6	15.6	6.0	13.0	15.1

Data as orig. reptd.; bef. results of disc. opers. and/or spec. items. Per share data adj. for stk. divs. as of ex-div. date. Bold denotes diluted EPS (FASB 128). E-Estimated. NA-Not Available. NM-Not Meaningful. NR-Not Ranked.

Office—Mansfield Corporate Center, 9 Hampshire St., Mansfield, MA 02048-9171. **Tel**—(508) 337-5500. **Chrmn**—M. G. Schorr. **Pres & CEO**—R. J. Lepofsky. **SVP & CFO**—M. El-Hillow. **Treas**—L. G. Greenberg. **Secy & Investor Contact**—Beverly L. Armell. **Dirs**—R. E. Anastasi, A. R. Buckland, M. O. Diggs, Jr., F. Gabron, R. J. Lepofsky, C. Moody, M. G. Schorr, W. Skinner, M. S. Wrighton. **Transfer Agent & Registrar**—BankBoston, N.A. **Incorporated**—in Delaware in 1967. **Empl**— 442. **S&P Analyst:** B. McGovern

Henry (Jack) & Associates   4139R

NASDAQ Symbol **JKHY**

In S&P SmallCap 600

03-OCT-98

Industry:
Computer (Software & Services)

Summary: This company provides integrated computer systems for in-house data processing, as well as ATM networking products, to banks and other financial institutions.

Quantitative Evaluations

Recent Price • 39⅛	Yield • 0.7%
52 Wk Range • 50¼-22¾	12-Mo. P/E • 36.0

Outlook
(1 Lowest—5 Highest)
• **3⁻**

Fair Value
• **55⅞**

Risk
• **Average**

Earn./Div. Rank
• **B+**

Technical Eval.
• **Bullish** since 12/97

Rel. Strength Rank
(1 Lowest—99 Highest)
• **58**

Insider Activity
• **NA**

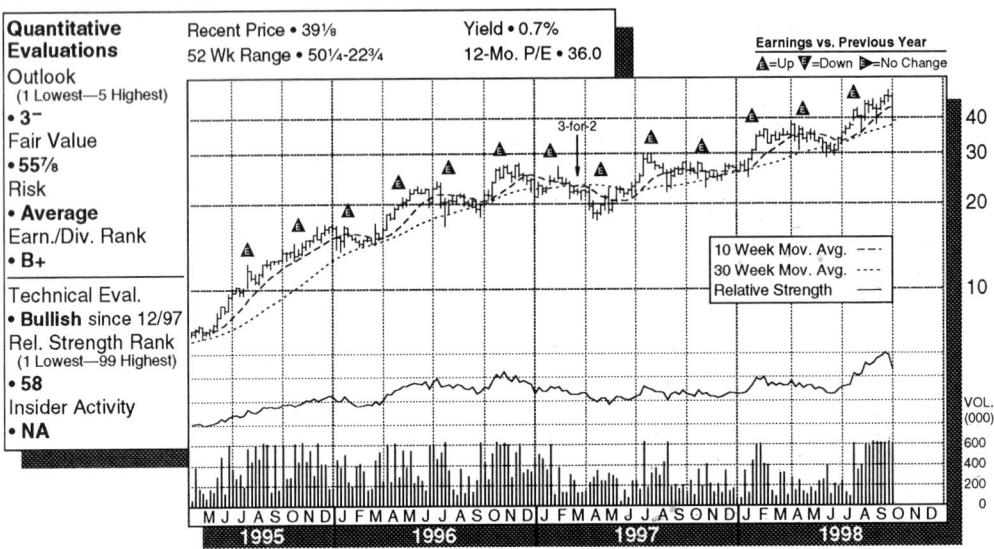

Earnings vs. Previous Year
▲=Up ▼=Down ▶=No Change

10 Week Mov. Avg. – – –
30 Week Mov. Avg. · · · · ·
Relative Strength ——

Business Profile - 24-JUL-98

Jack Henry & Associates, one of the largest providers of integrated computer systems that perform data processing for banks and other financial institutions, believes that it compares favorably to competitors in the primary competitive factors in the industry: comprehensiveness of applications, features and functions, flexibility and ease of use, customer support, references of existing customers, and hardware preferences and pricing. Recent results have been driven by strong sales of software systems and IBM hardware, coupled with growth in outsourcing. In July 1998, JKHY acquired Hewlett Computer Services for $2.25 million in cash.

Operational Review - 24-JUL-98

Based on a preliminary report, revenues from continuing operations advanced 37% in FY 98 (Jun.), reflecting 44% higher software licensing and installation revenues, a 29% rise in maintenance/support and service revenues, and 40% growth in hardware sales and commissions. Margins widened, on the greater volume; income from continuing operations was up 41%, to $22,237,000 ($1.13 a share, on 3.6% more shares), from $15,755,000 ($0.83). Results exclude losses from discontinued operations of $0.04 and $0.03 a share in the respective years.

Stock Performance - 02-OCT-98

In the past 30 trading days, JKHY's shares have declined 11%, compared to a 7% fall in the S&P 500. Average trading volume for the past five days was 118,180 shares, compared with the 40-day moving average of 144,754 shares.

Key Stock Statistics

Dividend Rate/Share	0.26	Shareholders	5,400
Shs. outstg. (M)	18.9	Market cap. (B)	$0.742
Avg. daily vol. (M)	0.150	Inst. holdings	34%
Tang. Bk. Value/Share	2.69		
Beta	0.54		

Value of $10,000 invested 5 years ago: $ 66,018

Fiscal Year Ending Jun. 30

	1998	1997	1996	1995	1994	1993
Revenues (Million $)						
1Q	20.06	18.35	16.15	9.65	9.22	6.40
2Q	27.38	21.35	16.52	11.41	10.14	9.90
3Q	27.25	22.06	16.56	10.41	8.85	6.75
4Q	38.73	20.84	18.33	14.66	10.18	9.52
Yr.	113.4	82.60	67.56	46.12	38.39	32.59
Earnings Per Share ($)						
1Q	0.23	0.20	0.17	0.10	0.08	0.07
2Q	**0.26**	0.20	0.15	0.11	0.09	0.07
3Q	**0.27**	0.20	0.15	0.10	0.07	0.07
4Q	**0.37**	0.23	0.19	0.13	0.10	0.09
Yr.	**1.13**	0.83	0.65	0.44	0.35	0.30

Next earnings report expected: mid October

Dividend Data (Dividends have been paid since 1990.)

Amount ($)	Date Decl.	Ex-Div. Date	Stock of Record	Payment Date
0.055	Oct. 31	Nov. 14	Nov. 18	Dec. 09 '97
0.065	Feb. 02	Feb. 17	Feb. 19	Mar. 12 '98
0.065	Apr. 29	May. 08	May. 12	May. 27 '98
0.065	Aug. 26	Sep. 03	Sep. 08	Sep. 24 '98

A Division of The **McGraw·Hill** Companies

Business Summary - 24-JUL-98

Jack Henry & Associates (JKHY), founded in 1976 by John W. Henry (currently vice chairman), and headed since October 1994 by his son Michael E. Henry, is a computer software company that has developed several banking software systems. Revenues are earned by marketing these systems, together with the computer equipment (hardware), to financial institutions nationwide, and by providing conversion and software customization services necessary for a financial institution to install a JKHY software system. The company also provides continuing support and maintenance services to customers using the system.

Revenue contributions in recent fiscal years (Jun.) were:

	FY 97	FY 96	FY 95
Software	28%	27%	33%
Maintenance/support	33%	33%	23%
Hardware	39%	40%	44%

Software includes development and licensing of applications software and conversion, installation and customization services. Maintenance/support consists of ongoing services to operate the systems and to modify and update software. Hardware relates to the sale of computer equipment and maintenance.

The company's primary systems are CIF 20/20 and Silverlake. Each has several fully integrated applications software modules that can interface with peripherals used in banks. CIF 20/20 is designed for community banks, savings banks and thrifts with up to $300 million in assets and runs on IBM AS/400 and IBM System 36 computers. Silverlake is aimed at larger banks, with assets of $100 million to $10 billion, and is designed to take advantage of the relational database capabilities of the IBM System 38 and AS/400.

JKHY licenses its systems under agreements that provide the customer with a fully paid, nontransferable right to use the software for 25 years on one computer at one location.

Wholly owned subsidiaries include Jack Henry International, Ltd., which markets products outside of the U.S.; BankVision Software, Ltd., which has installations in Colombia, Indonesia, the Caribbean and the Philippines; Liberty Software, Inc., which sells software and hardware to commercial banks (acquired as the community banking business of Broadway & Seymour in June 1995); and CommLink Corp. and Central Interchange, Inc., which market ATM switching products and services. JKHY also has a 25% ownership interest in Silverlake System Sdn Bhd, which markets, installs and supports the Asian Pacific Version of Silverlake.

Per Share Data ($)

(Year Ended Jun. 30)	1998	1997	1996	1995	1994	1993	1992	1991	1990	1989
Tangible Bk. Val.	3.07	2.02	1.16	0.67	1.17	0.90	0.66	0.47	0.40	0.41
Cash Flow	1.38	1.04	0.85	0.55	0.45	0.39	0.31	0.21	0.13	0.04
Earnings	1.13	0.83	0.65	0.44	0.35	0.30	0.24	0.14	0.06	-0.02
Dividends	0.24	0.20	0.17	0.14	0.12	0.13	0.09	0.10	Nil	Nil
Payout Ratio	21%	24%	26%	33%	36%	41%	38%	71%	Nil	Nil
Prices - High	42$\frac{1}{2}$	30$\frac{1}{4}$	27	17	7$\frac{7}{8}$	8$\frac{1}{2}$	6$\frac{1}{2}$	2$\frac{1}{2}$	1$\frac{3}{16}$	$\frac{7}{8}$
- Low	24$\frac{3}{4}$	17$\frac{1}{2}$	13$\frac{5}{8}$	5$\frac{7}{8}$	4$\frac{3}{8}$	5$\frac{1}{8}$	2$\frac{5}{16}$	$\frac{7}{16}$	$\frac{5}{16}$	$\frac{1}{4}$
P/E Ratio - High	38	36	41	39	23	28	27	19	13	NM
- Low	22	21	21	13	13	17	10	3	6	NM

Income Statement Analysis (Million $)

	1998	1997	1996	1995	1994	1993	1992	1991	1990	1989
Revs.	113	82.6	67.6	46.1	38.4	32.6	23.5	20.7	15.2	11.4
Oper. Inc.	38.9	28.3	22.8	14.0	10.7	8.8	6.1	4.3	2.6	1.4
Depr.	5.1	4.1	3.6	2.0	1.8	1.5	1.2	1.2	1.2	1.0
Int. Exp.	NA	Nil	Nil	Nil	0.0	0.0	Nil	0.0	0.0	0.1
Pretax Inc.	35.4	25.1	19.9	12.6	9.8	7.9	6.1	3.5	1.6	-0.5
Eff. Tax Rate	37%	37%	38%	37%	36%	33%	36%	38%	40%	NM
Net Inc.	22.2	15.8	12.3	8.0	6.3	5.3	3.9	2.2	0.9	-0.3

Balance Sheet & Other Fin. Data (Million $)

	1998	1997	1996	1995	1994	1993	1992	1991	1990	1989
Cash	23.3	13.9	8.1	8.0	11.7	9.4	8.8	5.7	2.7	1.4
Curr. Assets	69.1	42.7	28.1	27.4	25.2	19.4	15.6	11.6	7.1	5.6
Total Assets	115	82.1	60.4	58.7	38.3	29.9	22.1	17.6	14.4	12.8
Curr. Liab.	39.3	27.2	21.3	28.1	14.0	12.0	9.4	8.2	5.1	2.9
LT Debt	Nil	Nil	Nil	Nil	Nil	Nil	Nil	Nil	0.1	0.3
Common Eqty.	73.5	52.8	37.4	29.4	23.7	17.6	12.4	9.2	8.5	9.3
Total Cap.	76.0	54.8	39.2	30.5	24.3	17.9	12.7	9.5	9.3	9.9
Cap. Exp.	7.8	10.3	5.0	2.6	2.4	3.7	0.6	0.2	0.7	0.8
Cash Flow	27.3	19.8	15.8	10.0	8.1	6.8	5.1	3.4	2.1	0.7
Curr. Ratio	1.8	1.6	1.3	1.0	1.8	1.6	1.7	1.4	1.4	1.9
% LT Debt of Cap.	Nil	Nil	Nil	Nil	Nil	Nil	Nil	Nil	1.6	3.0
% Net Inc.of Revs.	19.6	19.1	18.2	17.3	16.3	16.2	16.5	10.5	6.2	NM
% Ret. on Assets	NM	22.1	20.6	16.4	18.3	20.0	19.3	13.6	7.0	NM
% Ret. on Equity	NM	34.9	36.7	30.1	30.3	34.7	35.6	24.6	10.7	NM

Data as orig. reptd.; bef. results of disc. opers. and/or spec. items. Per share data adj. for stk. divs. as of ex-div. date. Bold denotes diluted EPS (FASB 128). E-Estimated. NA-Not Available. NM-Not Meaningful. NR-Not Ranked.

Office—663 West Highway 60, P.O. Box 807, Monett, MO 65708. **Tel**—(417) 235-6652. **Fax**—(417) 235-4281.**Website**—http://www.jackhenry.com **Chrmn & CEO**—M. E. Henry.**Vice Chrmn & SVP**—J. W. Henry. **Pres & COO**—M. R. Wallace. **VP, CFO, Treas & Investor Contact**—Terry W. Thompson. **Secy**—Janet E. Gray. **Dirs**—G. R. Curry, J. J. Ellis, B. O. George, J. D. Hall, J. W. Henry, M. E. Henry, M. R. Wallace. **Transfer Agent & Registrar**—United Missouri Bank, Kansas City. **Incorporated**—in Missouri in 1977; reincorporated in Delaware in 1985. **Empl**— 447. **S&P Analyst:** Jim Corridore

03-OCT-98

Industry:
Insurance Brokers

Summary: This company provides insurance agency services to a broad range of clients through a network of 66 insurance agencies in both the U.S. and Canada.

Quantitative Evaluations		
Outlook (1 Lowest—5 Highest) • **2+**		
Fair Value • **18¾**		
Risk • **Low**		
Earn./Div. Rank • **B+**		
Technical Eval. • **Bearish** since 7/98		
Rel. Strength Rank (1 Lowest—99 Highest) • **82**		
Insider Activity • **Favorable**		

Recent Price • 18⅛
52 Wk Range • 19⅝-15⅜

Yield • 3.5%
12-Mo. P/E • 16.5

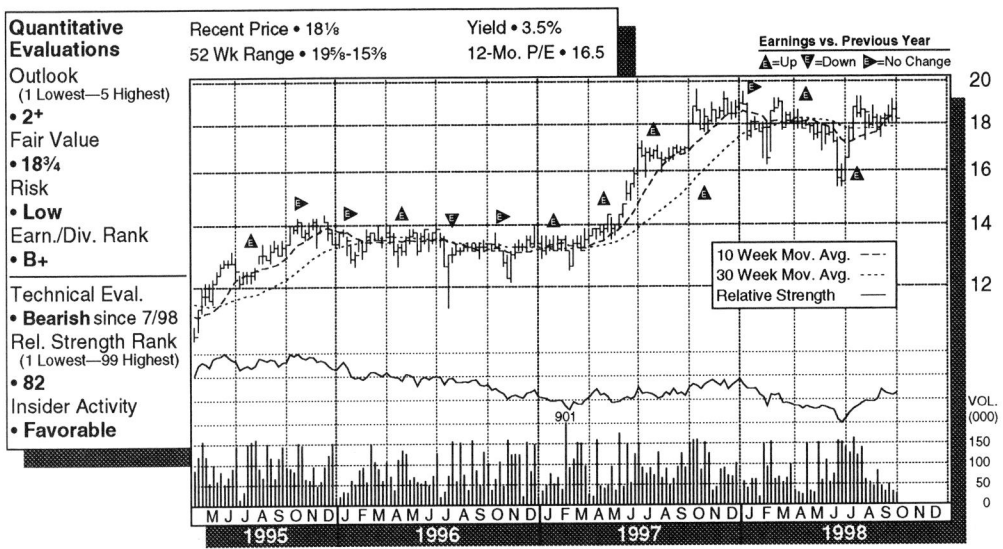

Earnings vs. Previous Year
▲=Up ▼=Down ▶=No Change

10 Week Mov. Avg. — - —
30 Week Mov. Avg. - - - -
Relative Strength ———

VOL. (000)

Business Profile - 13-MAY-98

HRH, ranked as the eighth largest U.S. insurance agency, has grown rapidly by acquiring independent agencies. From 1984 through 1997, it acquired 167 independent agencies. However, since late 1995, HRH has chosen a less aggressive acquisition strategy in order to focus more on building a stronger, more operationally-sound organization. During the three months ended March 31, 1998, HRH repurchased 132,000 common shares under a stock repurchase program. HRH is authorized to repurchase an additional 591,000 shares and expects to continue to repurchase shares during the remainder of 1998.

Operational Review - 13-MAY-98

Total revenues in the three months ended March 31, 1998, edged up 1.6%, year to year, as acquisitions of new insurance agencies led to a 1.5% gain in commissions and fees; investment and other income rose slightly. Operating expenses fell fractionally, as lower compensation and employee benefits costs outweighed the effects of higher interest and other expenses; pretax income was up 11%. After taxes at 41.0%, versus 40.5%, net income increased 10%, to $5,945,543 ($0.46 a diluted share, on 2.8% fewer shares), from $5,406,716 ($0.40).

Stock Performance - 02-OCT-98

In the past 30 trading days, HRH's shares have declined 0.35%, compared to a 7% fall in the S&P 500. Average trading volume for the past five days was 5,160 shares, compared with the 40-day moving average of 9,297 shares.

Key Stock Statistics

Dividend Rate/Share	0.64	Shareholders	700
Shs. outstg. (M)	12.2	Market cap. (B)	$0.222
Avg. daily vol. (M)	0.007	Inst. holdings	68%
Tang. Bk. Value/Share	NM		
Beta	0.32		

Value of $10,000 invested 5 years ago: $ 14,492

Fiscal Year Ending Dec. 31

	1998	1997	1996	1995	1994	1993
Revenues (Million $)						
1Q	48.70	47.91	43.07	39.46	39.33	37.02
2Q	45.92	44.32	37.94	36.57	35.19	32.82
3Q	—	41.85	38.31	36.39	34.14	32.39
4Q	—	39.62	38.92	35.72	32.16	32.73
Yr.	—	173.7	158.2	148.2	140.8	134.9
Earnings Per Share ($)						
1Q	**0.46**	**0.40**	0.38	0.33	0.32	0.29
2Q	**0.35**	**0.27**	0.20	0.20	0.20	0.10
3Q	—	**0.19**	0.17	0.17	0.17	0.12
4Q	—	**0.10**	0.10	0.09	0.09	0.10
Yr.	—	**0.97**	0.85	0.82	0.77	0.61

Next earnings report expected: mid October

Dividend Data (Dividends have been paid since 1987.)

Amount ($)	Date Decl.	Ex-Div. Date	Stock of Record	Payment Date
0.155	Nov. 04	Dec. 11	Dec. 15	Dec. 31 '97
0.155	Feb. 03	Mar. 13	Mar. 17	Mar. 31 '98
0.160	May. 05	Jun. 12	Jun. 16	Jun. 30 '98
0.160	Aug. 04	Sep. 14	Sep. 16	Sep. 30 '98

A Division of The **McGraw-Hill** *Companies*

Business Summary - 13-MAY-98

Late in 1995, this fast-growing insurance brokerage concern began to apply the brakes on its aggressive merger and acquisition strategy, a strategy which had added more than 160 independent agencies since the company's founding in 1982. In a shift in focus, Hilb, Rogal and Hamilton consolidated the majority of its dozens of decentralized independent agencies into six regional operating units. Each unit developed its own strategic plan, suited to the local marketplace environment, and designed to coordinate and objectify all sales and service activities.

By creating these regional operating units, HRH believes it has been able to better respond to the needs of clients and deal more effectively with trading partners. Additionally, the company has been able to streamline operations by merging multiple agency locations in the same city into a single profit center and converting smaller locations into sales offices of a larger profit center in the same region.

Currently, the company's agencies operate 66 offices in the U.S. and Canada. The agencies are organized into six U.S regions and the Canada region.

HRH primarily places insurance, such as property, casualty, marine, aviation and employee benefits, with insurance carriers and underwriters on behalf of its cli-

ents. Although the company's client base ranges from personal to large national accounts, it primarily targets medium-size commercial and industrial accounts. Revenues derived from the sale of insurance products to clients, typically coming in the form of commissions paid by insurance carriers with which clients' insurance is placed, accounted for 91% of total revenues in 1997.

HRH also advises clients on risk management and employee benefits and provides claims administration and loss control consulting services to clients, which contributed about 6% of revenues in 1997. Investment and other income, including the sale of certain insurance accounts and other assets, made up the remaining 3% of sales in 1997.

In the foreign arena, HRH has been able to establish direct access to certain overseas insurance markets without the need to share commissions with excess and surplus lines brokers. This direct access has allowed the company to enhance revenues from insurance products written by foreign insurers and provide a broader array of insurance products to clients.

While HRH's acquisition strategy has slowed, it has not stopped altogether. In 1997, the company acquired a total of 6 agencies, each deemed a fit into the new regional infrastructure. More acquisitions are expected, though they will be less frequent and more selective than in the past.

Per Share Data ($)

(Year Ended Dec. 31)	1997	1996	1995	1994	1993	1992	1991	1990	1989	1988
Tangible Bk. Val.	NM	NM	NM	1.21	1.05	NM	NM	NM	NM	NM
Cash Flow	1.85	1.65	1.49	1.40	1.29	1.48	1.37	1.40	1.55	1.58
Earnings	0.97	0.85	0.82	0.77	0.61	0.71	0.57	0.65	0.76	0.86
Dividends	0.62	0.60	0.57	0.50	0.45	0.41	0.37	0.30	0.19	0.09
Payout Ratio	64%	71%	70%	65%	74%	58%	65%	47%	25%	11%
Prices - High	19⅝	14	14⅜	13⅜	16⅞	15⅝	17½	19	20⅝	11⅛
- Low	12½	11⅜	10½	11	11⅜	11	11¼	11¼	10¾	7⅛
P/E Ratio - High	20	16	18	17	28	22	31	29	27	13
- Low	13	13	13	14	19	15	20	17	14	8

Income Statement Analysis (Million $)

	1997	1996	1995	1994	1993	1992	1991	1990	1989	1988
Revs.	174	158	148	141	135	126	115	97.0	78.0	49.0
Oper. Inc.	43.7	31.1	29.9	29.4	24.4	24.5	21.2	19.4	17.8	11.9
Depr.	11.7	3.3	2.8	9.3	9.5	9.2	8.8	7.2	6.0	3.7
Int. Exp.	2.0	1.3	0.6	0.8	1.2	1.7	2.1	2.7	2.4	1.9
Pretax Inc.	21.8	19.0	19.6	18.8	13.2	13.1	9.6	8.8	8.5	6.3
Eff. Tax Rate	42%	40%	40%	39%	36%	36%	35%	31%	32%	30%
Net Inc.	12.8	11.4	11.8	11.4	8.4	8.4	6.2	6.1	5.8	4.4

Balance Sheet & Other Fin. Data (Million $)

	1997	1996	1995	1994	1993	1992	1991	1990	1989	1988
Cash	26.2	24.9	28.1	35.7	12.1	26.6	23.2	23.7	24.4	21.6
Curr. Assets	76.8	76.3	78.6	84.9	81.1	76.9	72.2	73.5	66.0	47.7
Total Assets	182	182	163	159	156	139	132	133	113	82.0
Curr. Liab.	88.3	89.1	87.3	87.1	81.9	85.2	77.5	79.0	63.8	45.2
LT Debt	32.5	27.2	11.8	3.2	7.0	13.0	14.7	18.1	22.3	17.1
Common Eqty.	51.3	55.3	56.6	66.4	64.3	38.8	37.1	33.7	25.6	18.5
Total Cap.	83.8	84.5	68.4	69.6	71.3	53.8	51.8	51.8	48.5	36.3
Cap. Exp.	2.1	5.0	4.0	2.2	3.0	2.4	2.2	2.9	6.7	1.6
Cash Flow	24.5	22.3	21.6	20.7	17.9	17.6	15.0	13.3	11.8	8.1
Curr. Ratio	0.9	0.9	0.9	1.0	1.0	0.9	0.9	0.9	1.0	1.1
% LT Debt of Cap.	38.8	32.1	17.3	4.6	9.9	24.2	28.4	34.9	46.1	47.1
% Net Inc.of Revs.	7.4	7.2	8.0	8.1	6.2	6.7	5.4	6.3	7.4	8.9
% Ret. on Assets	7.0	6.6	7.3	7.5	5.5	5.9	4.4	4.4	4.9	5.7
% Ret. on Equity	24.0	20.4	19.2	17.4	16.5	21.2	16.5	18.5	21.8	25.3

Data as orig. reptd.; bef. results of disc. opers. and/or spec. items. Per share data adj. for stk. divs. as of ex-div. date. Bold denotes diluted EPS (FASB 128). E-Estimated. NA-Not Available. NM-Not Meaningful. NR-Not Ranked.

Office—4235 Innslake Drive, P. O. Box 1220, Glen Allen, VA 23060-1220. **Tel**—(804) 747-6500.**Fax**—(804) 747-6046.**Website**—http://www.hrh.com **Chrmn**—R. H. Hilb.**Pres & CEO**—A. L. Rogal. **SVP, CFO, Treas & Investor Contact**—Carolyn Jones.**EVP-Fin**—T. J. Korman.**VP-Secy**—W. L. Smith.**Dirs**—T. L. Chandler, Jr., N. H. Davis, Jr., P. J. Faccenda, J. S. M. French, R. H. Hilb, A. F. Markel, T. H. O'Brien, A. L. Rogal, R. S. Ukrop. **Transfer Agent & Registrar**—ChaseMellon Securities Trust Co., Ridgefield Park, NJ. **Incorporated**—in Virginia in 1982. **Empl**— 1,770. **S&P Analyst:** M.I.

Hollywood Park

1144

NYSE Symbol **HPK**

In S&P SmallCap 600

03-OCT-98

Industry: Gaming, Lottery & Pari-mutuel Cos.

Summary: This gaming and entertainment company has agreed to merge with Casino Magic Corp. (Nasdaq: CMAG).

Quantitative Evaluations

Recent Price • 10⅛
52 Wk Range • 22¾-9¾

Yield • Nil
12-Mo. P/E • 26.6

Outlook
(1 Lowest—5 Highest)
• **5**

Fair Value
• **17⅝**

Risk
• **Average**

Earn./Div. Rank
• **NR**

Technical Eval.
• **NA**

Rel. Strength Rank
(1 Lowest—99 Highest)
• **61**

Insider Activity
• **NA**

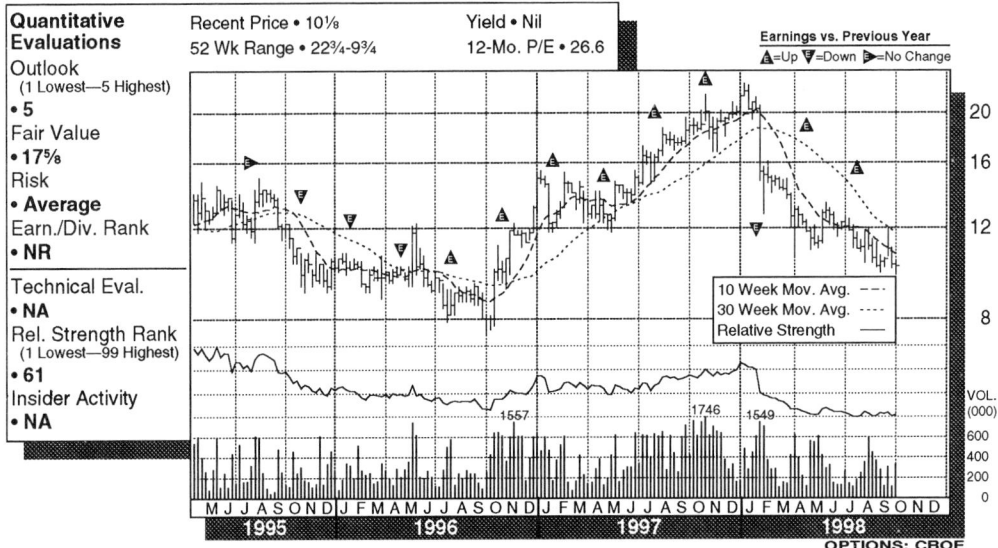

Earnings vs. Previous Year
▲=Up ▼=Down ▶=No Change

10 Week Mov. Avg. – – –
30 Week Mov. Avg. ·······
Relative Strength ——

1557   1746   1549

VOL. (000)
600
400
200
0

M J J A S O N D | J F M A M J J A S O N D | J F M A M J J A S O N D | J F M A M J J A S O N D
1995 | 1996 | 1997 | 1998

OPTIONS: CBOE

Business Profile - 16-SEP-98

In September 1998, the Indiana Gaming Commission awarded HPK the last remaining riverboat gaming license for the Ohio River. Operations are expected to begin in 18 months, and will include a cruising riverboat, plus land-based facilities, including a 309-room hotel and 18-hole golf course. In September 1998, shareholders of Casino Magic Corp. (Nasdaq: CMAG) agreed for CMAG to be acquired by HPK for cash and assumed debt with an aggregate value of $340 million. The transaction is expected to close before the end of October 1998. CMAG operates gaming casinos in Mississippi, Louisiana and Argentina. The combined company will have six operating casinos in three states, own two card club casinos in California and operate three pari-mutuel race tracks, with total revenues and assets of more than $600 million and $800 million, respectively. On August 5, 1998, directors authorized the repurchase of up to 20% of HPK's 26.2 million shares outstanding.

Operational Review - 16-SEP-98

In the six months ended June 30, 1998, revenues surged 148%, year to year, boosted by the June 1997 acquisition of Boomtown. EBITDA advanced 138%. After other items, including higher non-cash charges, interest expense, and taxes at 40.3%, versus 39.7%, net income advanced 84% to $6,895,000 ($0.26 a share on more shares), from $3,746,000 ($0.20).

Stock Performance - 02-OCT-98

In the past 30 trading days, HPK's shares have declined 4%, compared to a 7% fall in the S&P 500. Average trading volume for the past five days was 66,140 shares, compared with the 40-day moving average of 65,251 shares.

Key Stock Statistics

Dividend Rate/Share	Nil	Shareholders	3,600
Shs. outstg. (M)	26.3	Market cap. (B)	$0.266
Avg. daily vol. (M)	0.045	Inst. holdings	44%
Tang. Bk. Value/Share	6.79		
Beta	0.71		

Value of $10,000 invested 5 years ago: $10,771

Fiscal Year Ending Dec. 31

	1998	1997	1996	1995	1994	1993
Revenues (Million $)						
1Q	78.16	26.82	27.85	24.46	12.91	5.78
2Q	103.1	46.32	46.43	42.83	35.98	26.47
3Q	—	85.21	30.25	26.59	30.10	16.09
4Q	—	89.78	38.70	36.69	38.34	14.90
Yr.	—	236.0	143.2	130.6	117.3	63.24
Earnings Per Share ($)						
1Q	**-0.05**	-0.07	-0.74	-0.06	-0.10	-0.34
2Q	**0.31**	0.28	0.26	0.24	0.24	0.54
3Q	—	0.08	0.01	-0.33	-0.16	0.05
4Q	—	**0.05**	0.15	-0.01	0.12	0.01
Yr.	—	**0.32**	-0.33	-0.17	0.10	0.25

Next earnings report expected: NA

Dividend Data

The most recent cash dividend on the common stock was paid in 1992. The company does not anticipate paying cash dividends on its common stock in the near future.

A Division of The McGraw·Hill Companies

STANDARD
&POOR'S
STOCK REPORTS

Hollywood Park, Inc.

1144

03-OCT-98

Business Summary - 16-SEP-98

By the end of October 1998, this company plans to acquire Casino Magic Corp. (Nasdaq: CMAG) for cash and assumed debt with an aggregate value of $340 million. CMAG operates gaming casinos in Bay Saint Louis and Biloxi, Mississippi, Bossier City, Louisiana, and Neuquen City and San Martin de los Andes, Argentina. The combined company will have six operating casinos, own two card club casinos in California and operate three pari-mutuel race tracks, creating a company with revenues and assets in excess of $600 million and $800 million, respectively.

In September 1998, the Indiana Gaming Commission awarded HPK the last remaining riverboat gaming license for the Ohio River. Operations are expected to begin in 18 months, and will include a cruising riverboat with 38,000 square feet of gaming space, plus land-based facilities that will include 309 hotel rooms and suites, an 18-hole golf course, a multi-purpose special events center, and several restaurants and retail operations.

In 1997, HPK acquired three of the four Boomtown properties. Boomtown Reno is a 40,000 square foot western-themed casino. Boomtown New Orleans conducts gaming on a riverboat. Boomtown Biloxi occupies 19 acres on Mississippi's historic Back Bay of the Mississippi gulf Coast, a major tourist destination.

The Hollywood Park racetrack, HPK's main race track, located on 378 acres in Inglewood, CA, is the site of two live on-track horse race meets per year, and had a total of 102 race days in 1997. HPK also simulcasts its live races to 861 locations in 40 states and four countries. In addition, HPK accepts the simulcast signal from live races conducted at other tracks, including the four other local Southern California tracks, helping to mitigate the seasonality of its horse racing business by allowing for year-round operations.

HPK also owns and operates the Turf Paradise thoroughbred track in Phoenix, AZ. Turf Paradise has one continuous live horse race meet per year, and operates as a simulcast facility from late May to early September. The Hollywood Park Casino, also located on HPK's Inglewood property, is a casino card club that also offers pari-mutuel wagering on simulcast races.

The company opened the Radisson Crystal Park Hotel & Casino in Crystal City, CA, in 1996, which is leased to an unaffiliated operator.

In September 1998, the company announced that four top executives from Horsehoe Gaming agreed to join Hollywood in similar positions when their current contracts expire. At year-end 1998, Paul Alanis will become president and COO of HPK; Loren Ostrow will become SVP and general counsel; and Cliff Kortman will become VP in charge of construction and development within the gaming division. In May 1999, J. Michael Allen will become SVP-COO of HPK's gaming division.

Per Share Data ($)

(Year Ended Dec. 31)	1997	1996	1995	1994	1993	1992	1991	1990	1989	1988
Tangible Bk. Val.	7.18	7.50	7.48	8.79	8.65	NA	NA	NA	NA	NA
Cash Flow	1.13	0.24	0.45	0.63	0.73	0.72	NA	NA	NA	NA
Earnings	0.33	-0.33	-0.17	0.10	0.30	0.27	NA	NA	NA	NA
Dividends	Nil	Nil	Nil	Nil	Nil	0.04	NA	NA	NA	NA
Payout Ratio	Nil	Nil	Nil	Nil	Nil	15%	NA	NA	NA	NA
Prices - High	22¾	15½	15	30¾	35	11⅞	NA	NA	NA	NA
- Low	11¾	7½	9	9¼	8⅝	5⅝	NA	NA	NA	NA
P/E Ratio - High	69	NM	NM	NM	117	44	NA	NA	NA	NA
- Low	36	NM	NM	NM	29	21	NA	NA	NA	NA

Income Statement Analysis (Million $)

Revs.	236	136	123	111	75.0	78.0	NA	NA	NA	NA
Oper. Inc.	27.8	15.0	13.8	14.6	12.0	14.4	NA	NA	NA	NA
Depr.	18.2	10.7	11.4	9.6	6.4	5.9	NA	NA	NA	NA
Int. Exp.	7.3	0.9	3.9	3.1	1.5	4.9	NA	NA	NA	NA
Pretax Inc.	14.5	-0.8	-0.5	5.3	7.4	6.7	NA	NA	NA	NA
Eff. Tax Rate	40%	NM	NM	29%	14%	47%	NA	NA	NA	NA
Net Inc.	8.7	-4.2	-1.2	3.8	6.4	3.5	NA	NA	NA	NA

Balance Sheet & Other Fin. Data (Million $)

Cash	24.2	21.2	32.0	37.8	80.6	NA	NA	NA	NA	NA
Curr. Assets	60.2	41.0	48.6	66.0	87.7	NA	NA	NA	NA	NA
Total Assets	419	206	287	247	176	NA	NA	NA	NA	NA
Curr. Liab.	57.3	35.3	75.2	26.1	17.7	NA	NA	NA	NA	NA
LT Debt	132	0.3	15.6	42.8	0.3	NA	NA	NA	NA	NA
Common Eqty.	221	158	166	167	154	NA	NA	NA	NA	NA
Total Cap.	361	171	195	221	164	NA	NA	NA	NA	NA
Cap. Exp.	32.5	23.8	NA	27.6	12.9	5.3	NA	NA	NA	NA
Cash Flow	25.3	4.5	8.3	11.4	11.3	9.4	NA	NA	NA	NA
Curr. Ratio	1.1	1.2	0.6	2.5	5.0	NA	NA	NA	NA	NA
% LT Debt of Cap.	36.6	0.2	8.0	19.4	0.2	NA	NA	NA	NA	NA
% Net Inc.of Revs.	3.7	NM	NM	3.4	8.5	4.5	NA	NA	NA	NA
% Ret. on Assets	2.8	NM	NM	1.8	4.8	NA	NA	NA	NA	NA
% Ret. on Equity	3.8	NM	NM	2.4	7.8	NA	NA	NA	NA	NA

Data as orig. reptd.; bef. results of disc. opers. and/or spec. items. Per share data adj. for stk. divs. as of ex-div. date. Bold denotes diluted EPS (FASB 128). E-Estimated. NA-Not Available. NM-Not Meaningful. NR-Not Ranked.

Office—1050 South Prairie Ave., Inglewood, CA 90301. **Tel**—(310) 419-1500. **Website**—http://www.racetech.com **Chrmn & CEO**—R. D. Hubbard. **EVP, CFO & Treas**—G. M. Finnigan. **Dirs**—P. L. Harris, R. D. Hubbard, J. R. Johnson, R. T. Manfuso, T. J. Parrott, L. P. Reitnouer, H. Sarkowsky, W.B. Williamson. D. W. Yocam. **Transfer Agent & Registrar**—ChaseMellon Shareholder Services, NYC.**Incorporated**—in Delaware in 1981. **Empl**— 5,926. **S&P Analyst:** W.H.D.

STANDARD &POOR'S
STOCK REPORTS

Hologic, Inc.

4160H

NASDAQ Symbol **HOLX**

In S&P SmallCap 600

03-OCT-98

Industry:
Health Care (Medical Products & Supplies)

Summary: This company makes and distributes proprietary X-ray bone densitometer systems to diagnose and monitor osteoporosis and other metabolic bone diseases.

Quantitative Evaluations

Outlook
(1 Lowest—5 Highest)
• **NA**

Fair Value
• **NA**

Risk
• **High**

Earn./Div. Rank
• **B-**

Technical Eval.
• **Bearish** since 5/98

Rel. Strength Rank
(1 Lowest—99 Highest)
• **19**

Insider Activity
• **NA**

Recent Price • 10⅞
52 Wk Range • 30¾-9⅞

Yield • Nil
12-Mo. P/E • 11.5

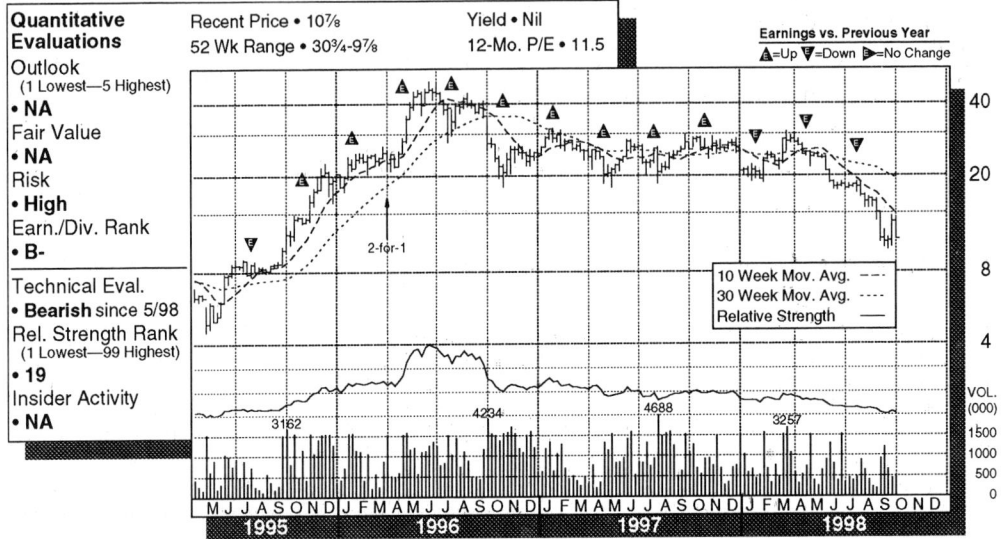

Earnings vs. Previous Year
▲=Up ▼=Down ▶=No Change

10 Week Mov. Avg. - - -
30 Week Mov. Avg. · · · ·
Relative Strength —

2-for-1

Business Profile - 16-JUL-98

In FY 97 (Sep.), this maker of X-ray bone densitometer systems attained record sales for its dual-energy X-ray bone densitometry (DXA) system. In addition, the company has experienced increased sales of its X-ray bone densitometers, in the second quarter of FY 98 (Sep.), reflecting greater interest in bone disease detection and treatment, such as osteoporosis, and the availability of new drug therapies to treat the disease. In the U.S., demand has also been driven by an increase in the recommended Medicare reimbursement rates for bone densitometry examinations. In March 1998, HOLX became the first U.S. company to receive FDA pre-market approval for its Sahara Clinical Bone Sonometer, an ultrasound bone sonometer that estimates bone density of the heel, assisting physicians in diagnosing osteoporosis and estimating the risk for future fractures.

Operational Review - 16-JUL-98

In the six months ended March 28, 1998, total revenues increased 2.2%, year to year, primarily due to greater domestic sales of DXA bone densitometer products and higher international sales of the Sahara, partially offset by decreased sales of DXA densitometers in Asia and Japan. Margins narrowed, primarily due to a less favorable product mix and a 23% rise in R&D expenses. After taxes at 36.1%, versus 36.4%, net income fell 47%, to $4.8 million ($0.35 a share), from $9.1 million ($0.66).

Stock Performance - 02-OCT-98

In the past 30 trading days, HOLX's shares have declined 30%, compared to a 7% fall in the S&P 500. Average trading volume for the past five days was 97,720 shares, compared with the 40-day moving average of 115,695 shares.

Key Stock Statistics

Dividend Rate/Share	Nil	Shareholders	400
Shs. outstg. (M)	13.4	Market cap. (B)	$0.146
Avg. daily vol. (M)	0.171	Inst. holdings	57%
Tang. Bk. Value/Share	10.33		
Beta	1.12		

Value of $10,000 invested 5 years ago: $ 37,232

Fiscal Year Ending Sep. 30

	1998	1997	1996	1995	1994	1993
Revenues (Million $)						
1Q	26.12	27.11	14.76	10.20	7.65	5.44
2Q	30.20	28.00	18.76	9.03	9.91	6.43
3Q	34.43	26.95	22.83	11.30	10.95	6.63
4Q	—	24.63	24.37	12.87	9.98	6.34
Yr.	—	106.7	91.59	43.40	38.48	24.85
Earnings Per Share ($)						
1Q	**0.15**	0.32	0.14	0.08	0.05	-0.06
2Q	**0.20**	0.34	0.27	0.02	0.10	-0.02
3Q	**0.31**	0.35	0.32	0.06	0.14	-0.02
4Q	—	0.29	0.15	0.07	0.06	-0.12
Yr.	—	1.30	0.91	0.21	0.35	-0.23

Next earnings report expected: mid November

Dividend Data

No cash dividends have been paid, and HOLX does not expect to pay dividends in the foreseeable future. A "poison pill" stock purchase rights plan was adopted in 1992.

A Division of The McGraw·Hill Companies

Business Summary - 16-JUL-98

This pioneer of the dual energy X-ray densitometer (DXA) develops, makes and markets proprietary X-ray systems. With more than 5,100 installations worldwide, the company's Quantitative Digital Radiography (QDR) and ultrasound bone densitometers are used for precise measurement of bone density to assist in diagnosing and monitoring osteoporosis and other metabolic bone diseases. Since its introduction, the DXA system has become the standard in measuring bone density.

In March 1998, HOLX became the first U.S. company to receive FDA pre-market approval for its Sahara Clinical Bone Sonometer, an ultrasound bone sonometer that estimates bone density of the heel. The Sahara aides physicians in diagnosing osteoporosis and estimating the risk for future fractures.

Osteoporosis, characterized by decreased bone density and increased risk of fractures, occurs mainly in older women. The National Osteoporosis Foundation estimates that osteoporosis afflicts more than 25 million people in the U.S. and a much larger number worldwide. Prior to 1995, there were only two drug treatments for osteoporosis in the U.S.: hormone replacement therapy and calcitonin. However, these were not proven to restore bone mass. In September 1995, the FDA approved Merck's Fosamax drug, used for the treatment of established osteoporosis in post-menopausal women; Fosamax has the ability to restore bone mass. In August 1997, a Medicare Bone

Mass Measurement Coverage Standardization Act was approved the President Clinton, which will require Medicare to cover bone density diagnostic tests, effective July 1998. With the established reimbursement levels in the U.S. and the FDA approval of additional osteoporosis drug therapies, the company believes that the U.S. market for bone densitometers and other methods of bone mineral assessment will expand to the larger .potential market of primary care providers.

The QDR 4500 ACCLAIM series has replaced the company's QDR 1500, QDR 2000 and QDR 2000-plus products. It accounted for more 73% of product sales in FY 97 (Sep.). The ACCLAIM series integrates HOLX's most advanced technology into a compact package that facilitates installation in a standard examination room. An important feature of the QDR 4500A and QDR 4500SL is the ability to perform lateral scans of the lower spine, without turning patients on their sides, in addition to posterior-anterior measurements.

In FY 97, about 61% of product sales were generated in the U.S., 20% in Europe, 10% in Asia and 9% in other international markets.

In August 1996, HOLX entered the mini C-arm market by acquiring FluoroScan Imaging Systems, Inc., a manufacturer of mini C-arm imaging systems for minimally invasive surgery. FluoroScan's systems are primarily used by orthopedic surgeons to perform minimally invasive surgical procedures on patient's extremities at a cost well below those of conventional X-ray and fluoroscopic equipment.

Per Share Data ($)

(Year Ended Sep. 30)	1997	1996	1995	1994	1993	1992	1991	1990	1989	1988
Tangible Bk. Val.	9.67	8.33	2.75	2.47	2.06	2.32	2.15	2.04	-0.38	-0.90
Cash Flow	1.39	0.98	0.28	0.43	-0.17	0.22	0.12	0.41	0.28	0.02
Earnings	1.30	0.92	0.21	0.35	-0.23	0.18	0.09	0.37	0.26	Nil
Dividends	Nil	Nil	Nil	Nil	Nil	Nil	Nil	Nil	Nil	Nil
Payout Ratio	Nil	Nil	Nil	Nil	Nil	Nil	Nil	Nil	Nil	Nil
Prices - High	31¾	49½	22¾	9⅛	3⅛	7⅛	6⅛	15½	NA	NA
- Low	17⅞	17¼	4½	2	1¹¹⁄₁₆	2³⁄₁₆	2⅜	3⅝	NA	NA
P/E Ratio - High	24	54	NM	26	NM	39	72	42	NA	NA
- Low	14	19	NM	6	NM	12	28	10	NA	NA

Income Statement Analysis (Million $)

	1997	1996	1995	1994	1993	1992	1991	1990	1989	1988
Revs.	107	91.6	43.4	38.5	24.8	26.2	17.1	19.8	11.4	4.6
Oper. Inc.	23.6	18.4	5.3	4.7	-0.6	1.6	1.7	3.4	2.0	0.1
Depr.	1.3	0.9	0.6	0.6	0.4	0.3	0.3	0.2	0.1	0.1
Int. Exp.	Nil	Nil	Nil	0.1	Nil	Nil	Nil	0.0	0.1	0.1
Pretax Inc.	27.6	17.1	2.5	4.3	-2.1	2.1	1.0	3.8	1.7	0.0
Eff. Tax Rate	36%	33%	26%	31%	NM	30%	31%	30%	17%	Nil
Net Inc.	17.7	11.4	1.9	3.0	-1.8	1.5	0.7	2.6	1.4	0.0

Balance Sheet & Other Fin. Data (Million $)

	1997	1996	1995	1994	1993	1992	1991	1990	1989	1988
Cash	28.1	75.6	9.9	9.4	10.1	10.5	11.9	13.4	2.0	0.5
Curr. Assets	131	113	30.6	26.3	20.4	21.0	18.6	19.2	5.1	2.1
Total Assets	145	123	33.9	28.5	22.2	22.7	19.8	20.3	5.4	2.3
Curr. Liab.	17.9	15.8	11.2	8.6	5.8	4.6	3.1	4.6	2.7	0.7
LT Debt	Nil	Nil	Nil	Nil	Nil	Nil	Nil	Nil	1.0	1.0
Common Eqty.	127	107	22.7	19.9	16.3	18.1	16.7	15.7	-0.8	-1.9
Total Cap.	127	107	22.7	19.9	16.3	18.1	16.7	15.7	2.7	1.6
Cap. Exp.	2.1	0.9	0.2	0.5	0.2	0.6	0.4	0.9	0.3	0.0
Cash Flow	19.0	12.3	2.4	3.6	-1.4	1.8	1.0	2.9	1.5	0.1
Curr. Ratio	7.3	7.2	2.7	3.1	3.5	4.6	5.9	4.1	1.9	3.1
% LT Debt of Cap.	Nil	Nil	Nil	Nil	Nil	Nil	Nil	Nil	37.5	62.8
% Net Inc.of Revs.	16.6	12.4	4.5	7.8	NM	5.6	4.1	13.2	12.3	0.3
% Ret. on Assets	13.2	13.7	6.0	11.7	NM	6.9	3.5	13.4	36.3	0.6
% Ret. on Equity	15.2	16.5	8.8	16.4	NM	8.5	4.3	35.4	NM	NM

Data as orig. reptd.; bef. results of disc. opers. and/or spec. items. Per share data adj. for stk. divs. as of ex-div. date. Bk. val. figs. in Per Share Data incl. intangibles. Bold denotes diluted EPS (FASB 128). NA-Not Available. NM-Not Meaningful. NR-Not Ranked.

Office—590 Lincoln St., Waltham, MA 02154. **Tel**—(617) 890-2300. **Chrmn & CEO**—S. D. Ellenbogen. **Pres & COO**—S. L. Nakashige. **Secy**—L. M. Levy. **VP-Fin & Treas**—G. P. Muir. **Dirs**—S. D. Ellenbogen, I. Jacobs, W. A. Peck, G. Segel, J. A. Stein, E. Ullian. **Transfer Agent & Registrar**—American Stock Transfer & Trust Co., NYC. **Incorporated**—in Massachusetts in 1985; reincorporated in Delaware in 1990. **Empl**— 339. **S&P Analyst:** John J. Arege

03-OCT-98

Industry: Leisure Time (Products)

Summary: This leading manufacturer of bicycles also makes basketball backboards and lawn and garden tools, and provides inventory, assembly and supplier services.

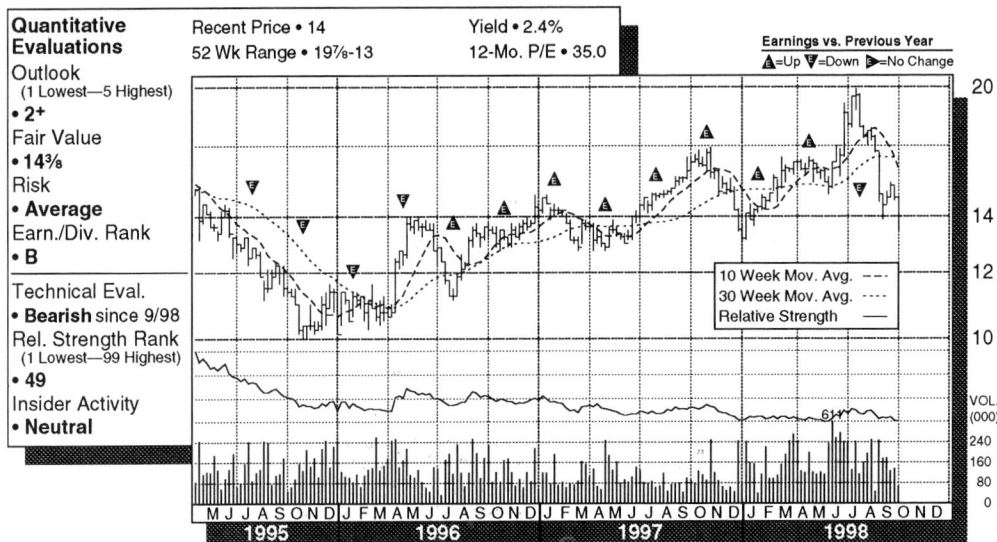

Quantitative Evaluations

Recent Price • 14
52 Wk Range • 19⅞-13
Yield • 2.4%
12-Mo. P/E • 35.0

Outlook (1 Lowest—5 Highest)
• **2+**

Fair Value
• **14⅜**

Risk
• **Average**

Earn./Div. Rank
• **B**

Technical Eval.
• **Bearish** since 9/98

Rel. Strength Rank (1 Lowest—99 Highest)
• **49**

Insider Activity
• **Neutral**

Earnings vs. Previous Year
▲=Up ▼=Down ►=No Change

10 Week Mov. Avg. ---
30 Week Mov. Avg. ·····
Relative Strength —

Business Profile - 21-APR-98

Results for the first quarter of 1998 marked the ninth consecutive quarter of earnings improvement over the prior year. Huffy believes that its product innovation and brand/channel management strategies led to a more favorable product mix in a very competitive industry. The company's cost cutting efforts, particularly its Continuous Rapid Improvement program (CRI), continue to drive earnings growth. CRI controls expenses related to the manufacturing and delivery of products and services, such as raw material sourcing and product fabrication.

Operational Review - 21-APR-98

Net sales for the three months ended March 31, 1998, rose 6.0%, year to year, reflecting strong seasonal sales for bicycles and basketball systems and continued channel diversification in the lawn and garden tools business. Margins widened, as a higher-margin product mix outweighed unfavorable pricing pressures; operating income advanced 12%. After lower interest expense, and taxes at 38.3%, versus 35.5%, net income climbed 29%, to $3,786,000 ($0.30 a share, diluted) from $2,944,000 ($0.22). Results in 1997 exclude earnings of $0.03 from discontinued operations.

Stock Performance - 02-OCT-98

In the past 30 trading days, HUF's shares have declined 16%, compared to a 7% fall in the S&P 500. Average trading volume for the past five days was 12,760 shares, compared with the 40-day moving average of 34,510 shares.

Key Stock Statistics

Dividend Rate/Share	0.34	Shareholders	3,100
Shs. outstg. (M)	12.2	Market cap. (B)	$0.171
Avg. daily vol. (M)	0.025	Inst. holdings	56%
Tang. Bk. Value/Share	5.75		
Beta	0.68		

Value of $10,000 invested 5 years ago: $ 9,947

Fiscal Year Ending Dec. 31

	1998	1997	1996	1995	1994	1993
Revenues (Million $)						
1Q	182.3	171.9	186.5	200.7	189.2	215.0
2Q	220.3	213.1	199.6	200.4	214.9	220.1
3Q	—	150.0	151.6	148.9	153.3	167.2
4Q	—	159.5	164.2	134.8	162.0	155.5
Yr.	—	694.5	701.9	684.8	719.5	757.9
Earnings Per Share ($)						
1Q	0.30	0.22	0.22	0.33	0.33	0.38
2Q	Nil	0.49	0.34	0.03	0.53	0.54
3Q	—	0.08	-0.02	-0.33	0.18	0.18
4Q	—	0.02	-0.06	-0.80	0.14	-1.26
Yr.	—	0.80	0.48	-0.78	1.20	-0.30

Next earnings report expected: mid October

Dividend Data (Dividends have been paid since 1950.)

Amount ($)	Date Decl.	Ex-Div. Date	Stock of Record	Payment Date
0.085	Dec. 11	Jan. 13	Jan. 15	Feb. 02 '98
0.085	Feb. 12	Apr. 13	Apr. 15	May. 01 '98
0.085	Jun. 11	Jul. 13	Jul. 15	Aug. 03 '98
0.085	Aug. 21	Oct. 13	Oct. 15	Nov. 02 '98

A Division of The McGraw-Hill Companies

STANDARD
&POOR'S
STOCK REPORTS

Huffy Corporation

1173

03-OCT-98

Business Summary - 21-APR-98

While maintaining its position as the leading U.S. maker of bicycles, Huffy has also expanded its product line and now offers a diverse mix of well known products in the sporting goods, juvenile products and lawn and garden industries. A separate division of the company provides services to the retail industry.

Huffy's consumer products segment accounts for about 18% of the nearly $3 billion spent in the bicycle, juvenile, basketball and lawn and garden markets in which it competes. Product innovation has strengthened HUF's position as the number one or two provider of products or services in each market segment and remains a key element in the company's turnaround. In 1997, new products and services, such as BMX bicycles, expanded in-home assembly services and the Hercules basketball system, delivered sales in higher-margin markets.

Huffy Bicycle Company is the largest seller of bicycles in the U.S., with a full line of adult bicycles and children's bicycles and tricycles. The company is committed to remaining the market share leader through an extensive advertising campaign and the use of licensed trademarks, such as Warner Brothers' Looney Tunes and World Triathalon Corp.'s Ironman.

True Temper Hardware is the largest wheelbarrow supplier in the U.S., and one of the three leading suppliers of non-powered lawn and garden tools and snow tools. Products are sold to national and regional retail and hardware stores.

Huffy Sports Company is the leading supplier of basketball backboards, poles, goals, and related products. The company's promotional campaign highlights its connection with the National Basketball Association. The NBA logo adorns many of Huffy Sports' products.

Huffy's retail services division, which consists of Huffy Service First, Inc. and Washington Inventory Service, provides assembly and repair, in-store display services and physical inventory services on a nationwide basis.

Percentage of sales from each product or service segment in 1997 were: bicycles (44.4%), lawn and garden tools (16.4%), basketball backboards (12.3%) and retail services (26.0%).

In 1997, Huffy expanded its portfolio of companies by acquiring Royce Union Bicycle Company, Inc. and Sure Shot International, Inc. Each brings recognized brand names and new distribution channels further strengthening Huffy's market leading position and leveraging time-tested core brands. HUF also divested Gerry Baby Products because it did not meet the company's criteria of being number one or two in its industry.

Per Share Data ($)

(Year Ended Dec. 31)	1997	1996	1995	1994	1993	1992	1991	1990	1989	1988
Tangible Bk. Val.	7.19	6.87	6.78	7.94	7.46	6.78	7.17	5.89	5.23	4.18
Cash Flow	2.15	2.18	0.89	2.59	1.26	2.31	2.76	2.26	1.96	0.93
Earnings	0.80	0.48	-0.78	1.20	-0.30	0.92	1.52	1.37	1.17	0.36
Dividends	0.34	0.34	0.34	0.34	0.30	0.30	0.28	0.27	0.23	0.20
Payout Ratio	42%	71%	NM	28%	NM	32%	18%	19%	19%	56%
Prices - High	16⁷/₈	14⁷/₈	15⁷/₈	19¹/₂	20³/₈	24³/₈	22¹/₄	17¹/₈	15³/₈	12¹/₂
- Low	12³/₄	10¹/₄	10	14	14⁵/₈	12	9⁷/₈	8¹/₂	8³/₄	8
P/E Ratio - High	21	31	NM	16	NM	26	15	13	13	34
- Low	16	21	NM	12	NM	13	7	6	7	22

Income Statement Analysis (Million $)

	1997	1996	1995	1994	1993	1992	1991	1990	1989	1988
Revs.	694	702	685	719	758	703	679	517	449	336
Oper. Inc.	38.7	38.5	20.5	52.1	56.1	45.4	56.2	43.2	36.9	24.5
Depr.	17.7	22.9	22.4	20.2	20.3	18.0	16.2	11.8	10.3	7.2
Int. Exp.	5.7	7.3	8.0	6.4	8.7	9.6	9.0	6.7	6.6	4.9
Pretax Inc.	14.5	8.9	-15.0	27.6	-3.1	18.6	31.5	28.6	23.8	7.8
Eff. Tax Rate	28%	27%	NM	37%	NM	36%	37%	37%	37%	42%
Net Inc.	10.4	6.5	-10.5	17.4	-3.8	11.8	19.8	18.0	15.0	4.5

Balance Sheet & Other Fin. Data (Million $)

	1997	1996	1995	1994	1993	1992	1991	1990	1989	1988
Cash	2.1	2.1	2.6	1.6	4.1	3.5	8.5	21.9	51.9	15.4
Curr. Assets	213	186	163	189	197	207	197	177	153	103
Total Assets	323	316	299	322	319	335	317	292	235	183
Curr. Liab.	140	121	100	99	104	116	98.0	90.0	73.0	57.0
LT Debt	36.2	43.9	51.2	58.6	43.2	74.9	80.2	84.3	57.5	37.2
Common Eqty.	117	116	116	133	136	118	125	107	96.0	81.0
Total Cap.	149	160	167	192	179	193	205	191	153	118
Cap. Exp.	17.5	17.7	24.4	35.7	21.3	23.9	21.1	9.5	13.8	14.2
Cash Flow	28.1	29.4	12.0	37.6	16.4	29.8	36.0	29.8	25.2	11.7
Curr. Ratio	1.5	1.5	1.6	1.9	1.9	1.8	2.0	2.0	2.1	1.8
% LT Debt of Cap.	24.3	27.5	30.6	30.5	24.1	38.9	39.1	44.1	37.6	31.5
% Net Inc.of Revs.	1.5	0.9	NM	2.4	NM	1.7	2.9	3.5	3.3	1.4
% Ret. on Assets	3.3	2.1	NM	5.7	NM	3.7	6.5	6.9	7.1	2.7
% Ret. on Equity	8.8	5.6	NM	13.5	NM	9.9	17.0	17.9	16.7	5.7

Data as orig. reptd.; bef. results of disc. opers. and/or spec. items. Per share data adj. for stk. divs. as of ex-div. date. Bold denotes diluted EPS (FASB 128). E-Estimated. NA-Not Available. NM-Not Meaningful. NR-Not Ranked.

Office—225 Byers Rd., Miamisburg, OH 45342. **Tel**—(937) 866-6251. **Chrmn, Pres & CEO**—D. R. Graber. **VP-Fin & CFO**—T. A. Frederick. **VP & Secy**—N. A. Michaud. **Asst Treas & Investor Contact**—Paul E. Fisher (937 865-5494). **Dirs**—W. A. Huffman, L. B. Keene, J. D. Michaels, D. K. Miller, D. R. Graber, J. F. Robeson, P. W. Rooney, G. W. Smith, T. C. Sullivan, J. P. Viviano. **Transfer Agent & Registrar**—Harris Trust & Savings Bank, Chicago. **Incorporated**—in Ohio in 1928. **Empl**— 7,000. **S&P Analyst:** Ray Lam, CFA

03-OCT-98

Industry:
Retail (Building Supplies)

Summary: This wholesale distributor of materials, equipment and supplies to the construction industry has more than 400 locations, in 27 states, Mexico, and Puerto Rico.

Quantitative Evaluations	
Recent Price • 28⅛	Yield • 1.2%
52 Wk Range • 39¾-25⅛	12-Mo. P/E • 11.6

Outlook
(1 Lowest—5 Highest)
• **3⁻**

Fair Value
• **30⅞**

Risk
• **Average**

Earn./Div. Rank
• **B+**

Technical Eval.
• **Bearish** since 3/98

Rel. Strength Rank
(1 Lowest—99 Highest)
• **68**

Insider Activity
• **NA**

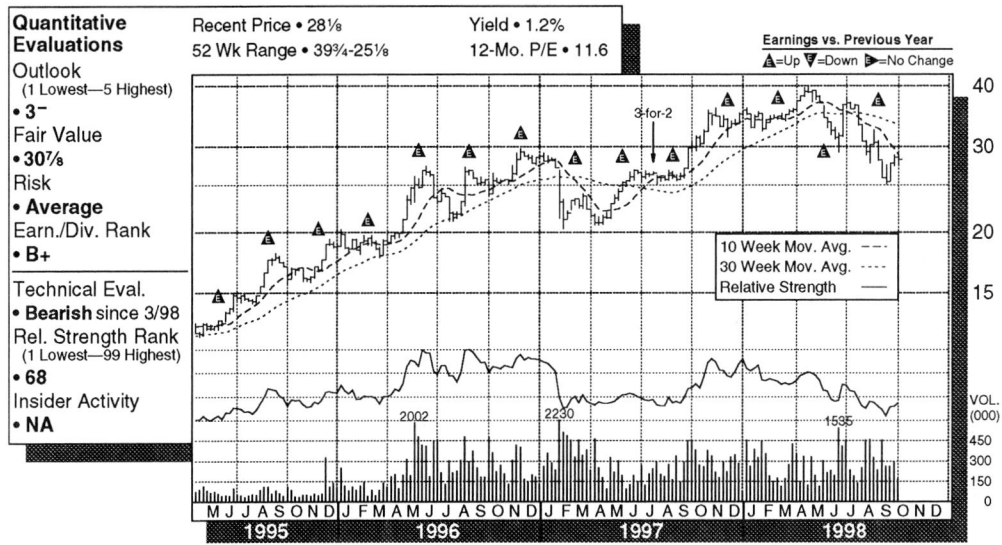

Earnings vs. Previous Year
△=Up ▽=Down ▷=No Change

10 Week Mov. Avg. ---
30 Week Mov. Avg. ·····
Relative Strength —

Business Profile - 02-JUL-98

FY 98 (Jan.) marked the sixth consecutive year in which HUG posted earnings growth in excess of 25%. The company's acquisition strategy includes geographical diversification into the industrial and replacement markets with the goal of becoming a leading national distributor in each of its nine product groups. Since January 1993, HUG has completed more than 50 acquisitions; the company now has operations in 27 states, Mexico, and Puerto Rico. In September 1997, Hughes closed an $80 million private placement, and also increased its bank lending facility by $30 million.

Operational Review - 02-JUL-98

Net sales in the three months ended April 30, 1998, advanced 34%, year to year, as higher same-store sales (up 6%) were augmented by the inclusion of newly opened and acquired wholesale outlets. Gross profit margins narrowed slightly, to 21.5% of revenues, from 21.6%, reflecting weaker stainless steel pricing in the industrial pipe, plate, valves and fittings product group; operating income was up 31%. With sharply higher net interest expense, and after taxes at 39.5%, versus 37.0%, net income rose 24%, to $10,746,000 ($0.47 a share, on 23% more shares), from $8,663,000 ($0.46, as adjusted).

Stock Performance - 02-OCT-98

In the past 30 trading days, HUG's shares have declined 8%, compared to a 7% fall in the S&P 500. Average trading volume for the past five days was 33,220 shares, compared with the 40-day moving average of 65,767 shares.

Key Stock Statistics

Dividend Rate/Share	0.34	Shareholders	1,100
Shs. outstg. (M)	24.0	Market cap. (B)	$0.676
Avg. daily vol. (M)	0.052	Inst. holdings	51%
Tang. Bk. Value/Share	12.81		
Beta	0.67		

Value of $10,000 invested 5 years ago: $ 31,121

Fiscal Year Ending Jan. 31

	1999	1998	1997	1996	1995	1994
Revenues (Million $)						
1Q	582.0	434.5	349.5	253.9	184.0	141.6
2Q	674.5	478.2	395.8	282.4	202.6	163.9
3Q	—	505.6	405.4	284.1	210.6	179.0
4Q	—	460.5	365.4	261.8	205.3	169.5
Yr.	—	1,879	1,516	1,082	802.5	660.9
Earnings Per Share ($)						
1Q	0.47	0.46	0.42	0.29	0.21	0.10
2Q	0.00	0.71	0.57	0.40	0.34	0.26
3Q	—	0.69	0.61	0.41	0.31	0.27
4Q	—	0.43	0.42	0.37	0.32	0.26
Yr.	—	2.30	2.05	1.56	1.19	0.90

Next earnings report expected: mid November

Dividend Data (Dividends have been paid since 1976.)

Amount ($)	Date Decl.	Ex-Div. Date	Stock of Record	Payment Date
0.080	Jan. 27	Feb. 04	Feb. 06	Feb. 20 '98
0.080	Mar. 18	Apr. 29	May. 01	May. 15 '98
0.080	Jul. 27	Aug. 05	Aug. 07	Aug. 21 '98
0.085	Aug. 19	Nov. 04	Nov. 06	Nov. 20 '98

A Division of The McGraw-Hill Companies

Business Summary - 02-JUL-98

More than 70 years ago, Russell and Harry Hughes, and their father Clarence, started a wholesale building supply business with a single premise: "You can't do business out of an empty wagon." Since then, Hughes Supply, Inc. (HUG) has grown into one of the largest U.S. wholesalers of construction materials, with more than 400 branches in 27 states, Puerto Rico, and Mexico.

In FY 98 (Jan.), this diversified wholesale distributor of products for construction and industrial markets completed a record 15 acquisitions, with combined annual sales of about $440 million. Each of the 15 acquisitions was expected to become accretive to earnings during FY 99. As of mid-May 1998, HUG had more than 404 locations in 27 states, Mexico, and Puerto Rico, up from 212 outlets at the start of FY 97. The largest geographic market is Florida (34% of FY 98 net sales), one of the largest commercial and residential construction markets in the U.S.

HUG distributes materials, equipment and supplies in nine major groups: electrical; plumbing; water and sewer; air conditioning and heating; industrial pipe, valves and fittings; buildings materials; electric utilities; water systems; and pool equipment and supplies. These products (about 210,000 in all) are used by contractors, utilities, municipalities and manufacturers in new construction and for replacement and renovation projects. The company's products span all of the major sectors of the construction market, including commercial building, single- and multi-family housing, infrastructure (including electric utility and water and sewer applications), and industrial.

HUG uses acquisitions to enhance diversification in three key areas: its products, its markets and its geographic presence. Over the past several years, the company has increasingly focused on new market acquisitions, with the goal of adding products and product groups with wider gross margins, increasing sales to the replacement and industrial markets (which tend to be less cyclical than new construction markets), achieving greater geographic diversification, and developing additional opportunities for future "fill-in" acquisitions (generally smaller in size, and representing new branches within existing product groups and existing geographic markets), and new branch openings. In early March 1998, HUG acquired San Antonio Plumbing Distributors, Inc., a wholesale distributor of plumbing supplies and equipment, with annual sales of about $55 million.

HUG believes that it has sufficient borrowing capacity to take advantage of growth and business acquisition opportunities, while still funding operating requirements and anticipated capital expenditures.

Per Share Data ($)

(Year Ended Jan. 31)	1998	1997	1996	1995	1994	1993	1992	1991	1990	1989
Tangible Bk. Val.	11.61	10.95	15.11	14.50	13.52	13.29	13.01	13.81	13.26	12.59
Cash Flow	3.24	2.99	2.59	2.21	1.97	1.40	0.49	1.73	2.15	2.52
Earnings	2.30	2.05	1.56	1.19	0.83	0.36	-0.65	0.33	0.89	1.33
Dividends	0.29	0.25	0.18	0.14	0.09	0.08	0.20	0.24	0.23	0.20
Payout Ratio	13%	12%	12%	12%	11%	22%	NM	70%	25%	15%
Cal. Yrs.	1997	1996	1995	1994	1993	1992	1991	1990	1989	1988
Prices - High	36⅛	29¾	19⅜	21½	13⅛	10⅞	9¼	12¼	14⅝	12⅞
- Low	20⅜	17¾	11⅞	10⅝	8⅞	7	6¾	6½	11⅝	10¾
P/E Ratio - High	16	14	12	18	16	30	NM	38	16	10
- Low	9	9	8	9	11	19	NM	20	13	8

Income Statement Analysis (Million $)

Revs.	1,879	1,516	1,082	802	661	528	481	548	530	502
Oper. Inc.	102	74.2	40.5	28.2	19.8	11.4	6.4	16.8	24.3	27.7
Depr.	18.4	15.0	10.6	8.8	7.5	6.5	7.1	9.2	9.1	8.7
Int. Exp.	18.5	13.5	7.5	4.9	4.6	4.7	5.9	8.0	7.3	6.5
Pretax Inc.	70.9	51.7	27.0	17.4	10.6	3.7	-6.1	3.6	10.6	15.8
Eff. Tax Rate	37%	37%	41%	41%	41%	39%	NM	41%	40%	39%
Net Inc.	44.8	32.5	16.1	10.3	6.3	2.3	-4.0	2.1	6.4	9.7

Balance Sheet & Other Fin. Data (Million $)

Cash	7.7	6.3	3.4	3.2	1.1	2.3	5.5	3.2	2.1	3.0
Curr. Assets	664	477	297	260	204	170	165	164	176	165
Total Assets	942	650	379	329	263	225	216	220	236	224
Curr. Liab.	190	146	117	95.1	68.6	60.3	56.9	46.1	58.5	54.2
LT Debt	335	222	106	101	99	79.9	76.3	85.6	82.8	76.0
Common Eqty.	414	279	154	131	94.4	83.3	81.5	86.5	92.7	91.3
Total Cap.	749	501	260	232	194	163	159	173	177	169
Cap. Exp.	27.7	16.1	11.9	11.8	8.3	8.5	4.9	7.2	10.7	9.8
Cash Flow	63.3	47.5	26.7	19.1	13.8	8.8	3.1	11.3	15.5	18.5
Curr. Ratio	3.5	3.3	2.5	2.7	3.0	2.8	2.9	3.6	3.0	3.0
% LT Debt of Cap.	44.7	44.4	41.7	43.5	51.2	49.0	48.1	49.4	46.8	44.8
% Net Inc.of Revs.	2.4	2.2	1.5	1.3	1.0	0.4	NM	0.4	1.2	1.9
% Ret. on Assets	5.6	6.0	4.4	3.5	2.4	1.0	NM	1.0	2.8	4.6
% Ret. on Equity	12.9	14.5	11.1	9.2	6.7	2.7	NM	2.5	7.1	11.1

Data as orig. reptd.; bef. results of disc. opers. and/or spec. items. Per share data adj. for stk. divs. as of ex-div. date. Bold denotes diluted EPS (FASB 128). E-Estimated. NA-Not Available. NM-Not Meaningful. NR-Not Ranked.

Office—20 N. Orange Ave., Suite 200, Orlando, FL 32801. **Tel**—(407) 841-4755. **Website**—http://www.hughessupply.com **Chrmn, CEO & Investor Contact**—David H. Hughes. **Pres & COO**—A. S. Hall Jr. **CFO & Treas**—J. S. Zepf. **Secy**—B. P. Butterfield.**Dirs**—J. D. Baker II, R. N. Blackford, H. C. Day, J. B. Ellis, A. S. Hall Jr., C. M. Hames, D. H. Hughes, R. V. Hughes, V. S. Hughes, D. C. Martin, H. B. McManaway.**Transfer Agent & Registrar**—American Stock Transfer & Trust Co., NYC. **Incorporated**—in Florida in 1947. **Empl**— 6,000. **S&P Analyst:** M.I.

03-OCT-98

Industry:
Computers (Peripherals)

Summary: This company is the leading producer of suspension assemblies for manufacturers of rigid disk drives.

Quantitative Evaluations	
Outlook (1 Lowest—5 Highest)	• **4⁻**
Fair Value	• **23⅜**
Risk	• **High**
Earn./Div. Rank	• **B**
Technical Eval.	• **Bearish** since 6/98
Rel. Strength Rank (1 Lowest—99 Highest)	• **31**
Insider Activity	• **Neutral**

Recent Price • 15⅞
52 Wk Range • 36⅛-12⅝

Yield • Nil
12-Mo. P/E • NM

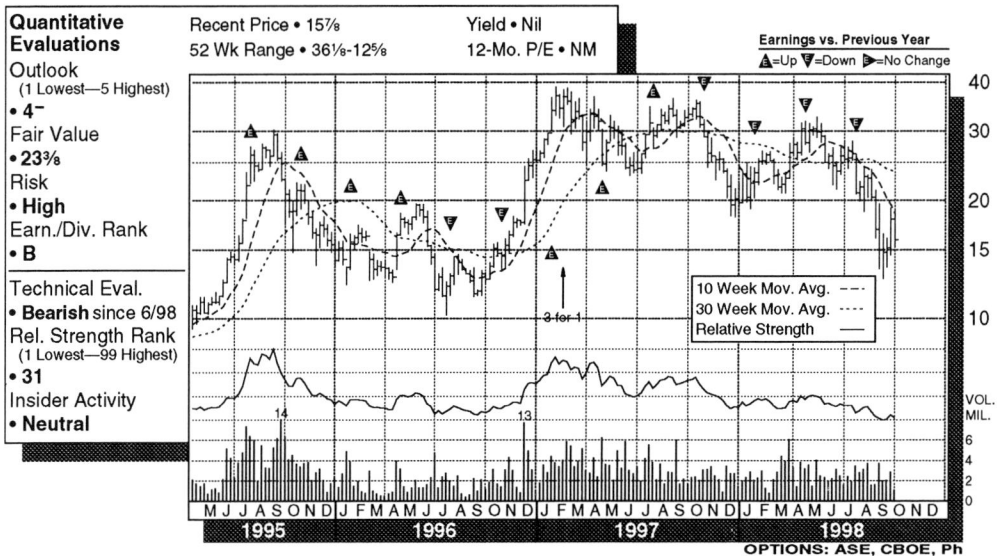

Earnings vs. Previous Year
▲=Up ▼=Down ▷=No Change

10 Week Mov. Avg. ----
30 Week Mov. Avg. ········
Relative Strength ——

OPTIONS: ASE, CBOE, Ph

Business Profile - 12-SEP-98

Results of this leading supplier of suspension assemblies for disk drives have been hurt by the continuing weak demand from the major disk drive manufacturers. Higher production volumes and improved manufacturing efficiency at all plants helped boost sales 28% in FY 97 (Sep.), although declining demand in the fourth quarter partially offset the company's earnings increase. However, in the first three quarters of FY 98, Hutchinson has recorded losses, mainly due to continued low demand and the costs related to the development and production ramp-up of its TSA suspensions. Management noted that although its TSA production should break even at the gross profit level in the fourth quarter of FY 98, the projected level of shipments is expected to result in a net loss for the quarter.

Operational Review - 12-SEP-98

Net sales in the nine months ended June 28, 1998, declined 17%, year to year, due primarily to weak demand for conventional suspensions as a result of inventory reduction among the major disk drive makers. Margins narrowed, reflecting the drop in sales volume; an operating loss contrasted with an operating profit. A net loss of $35,149,000 ($1.79 per diluted share, on 6.3% more shares), contrasted with net income of $41,498,000 ($2.24 per diluted share).

Stock Performance - 02-OCT-98

In the past 30 trading days, HTCH's shares have declined 22%, compared to a 7% fall in the S&P 500. Average trading volume for the past five days was 220,060 shares, compared with the 40-day moving average of 475,456 shares.

Key Stock Statistics

Dividend Rate/Share	Nil	Shareholders	1,000
Shs. outstg. (M)	19.8	Market cap. (B)	$0.314
Avg. daily vol. (M)	0.408	Inst. holdings	70%
Tang. Bk. Value/Share	12.64		
Beta	1.65		

Value of $10,000 invested 5 years ago: $ 11,107

Fiscal Year Ending Sep. 30

	1998	1997	1996	1995	1994	1993
Revenues (Million $)						
1Q	88.98	106.9	83.33	63.50	46.96	50.40
2Q	95.13	124.3	86.55	67.89	58.64	55.70
3Q	107.1	121.7	91.42	81.89	62.79	49.07
4Q	—	100.3	91.89	86.72	70.41	43.57
Yr.	—	453.2	353.2	300.0	238.8	198.7
Earnings Per Share ($)						
1Q	**-0.58**	0.66	0.17	0.14	-0.15	0.36
2Q	**-0.73**	0.91	0.26	0.25	0.11	0.34
3Q	**-0.47**	0.68	0.31	0.36	0.14	0.00
4Q	—	0.02	0.08	0.52	0.25	-0.16
Yr.	—	2.21	0.82	1.28	0.36	0.53

Next earnings report expected: early November

Dividend Data

No cash dividends have been paid. The company does not anticipate paying cash dividends in the foreseeable future.

Business Summary - 12-SEP-98

Hutchinson Technology (HTCH) is the world's leading supplier of suspension assemblies for rigid disk drives. The additional data storage capacity required by complex computer applications is provided primarily by rigid disk drives. HTCH is a supplier to nearly all domestic and many non-U.S. users of suspension assemblies, including Applied Magnetics, IBM, Maxtor, Quantum, Read-Rite, TDK/SAE Magnetics, Seagate Technology, Toshiba, Western Digital and Yamaha Corp. In recent fiscal years (ended September), HTCH's product sales were derived as follows:

	FY 97	FY 96	FY 95
Suspension assemblies	99%	98%	97%
Other	1%	2%	3%

Making use of sophisticated manufacturing capabilities, including photoetching, stamping, precision forming, laser welding and proprietary cleaning processes, the company has become a leading supplier of suspension assemblies, which hold the recording heads in position above the disk surface in rigid disk drives. Hutchinson also produces certain of the photoetched or stamped precision components constituting parts of suspension assemblies.

Hutchinson's current research and development efforts are principally focused on continuing the development

and prototype production of new high-precision conventional and TSA suspension assemblies to meet changing market demands, performance standards and electrical connectivity requirements. During the next several years, the company anticipates increasing acceptance by the disk drive industry of its TSA suspensions, which integrate into the suspension thin electrical conductors that connect directly with the recording head. The company also is evaluating product opportunities in the medical devices market but does not expect any medical-related revenues in FY 98 (Sep.)

The company entered into an agreement with IBM during FY 95, under which IBM made available to HTCH the results of research by IBM into a new type of suspension. HTCH contributed its existing TSA suspension technology to the joint effort. The company and IBM will continue to pursue joint R&D efforts to complete the commercialization of integrated lead suspension designs. As of September 28, 1997, HTCH had made payments totaling $3,500,000 to IBM and will make additional payments over the next two fiscal years totaling $4,500,000, all of which have been recorded as an expense by the company.

Seagate Technology, Read-Rite Corp. and Yamaha accounted for about 33%, 14% and 14% of FY 97 net sales, respectively. TDK/SAE Magnetics and IBM have also been significant customers in recent years. Exports made up 38% of net sales in FY 97 and 33% in FY 96.

Per Share Data ($)

(Year Ended Sep. 30)	1997	1996	1995	1994	1993	1992	1991	1990	1989	1988
Tangible Bk. Val.	14.42	8.47	7.33	5.91	5.55	4.96	2.81	2.43	1.98	2.48
Cash Flow	4.23	2.82	2.99	1.83	1.50	1.82	1.31	1.25	0.54	1.04
Earnings	2.21	0.82	1.28	0.36	0.53	0.91	0.37	0.45	-0.48	0.36
Dividends	Nil	Nil	Nil	Nil	Nil	Nil	Nil	Nil	Nil	Nil
Payout Ratio	Nil	Nil	Nil	Nil	Nil	Nil	Nil	Nil	Nil	Nil
Prices - High	39	26⁷/₈	30³/₈	13⁵/₈	17¹/₈	15¹/₈	5	4¹/₂	5¹/₈	4³/₄
- Low	18¹/₈	10¹/₈	7⁷/₈	7¹/₈	6³/₈	4⁵/₈	2³/₄	1¹³/₁₆	1¹¹/₁₆	2⁵/₈
P/E Ratio - High	18	33	24	38	32	17	13	10	NM	13
- Low	8	12	6	20	12	5	7	4	NM	7

Income Statement Analysis (Million $)

	1997	1996	1995	1994	1993	1992	1991	1990	1989	1988
Revs.	453	353	300	239	199	160	143	122	92.0	114
Oper. Inc.	91.0	51.8	57.1	31.8	25.8	26.5	18.5	18.2	4.8	14.5
Depr.	38.2	33.6	28.0	24.0	15.8	12.9	11.2	9.6	12.1	8.0
Int. Exp.	3.1	2.1	2.6	2.1	0.3	1.2	1.8	2.1	2.1	1.1
Pretax Inc.	53.7	17.3	27.7	8.0	11.1	13.8	6.0	7.3	-8.9	6.5
Eff. Tax Rate	22%	20%	24%	26%	23%	7.10%	25%	27%	NM	34%
Net Inc.	41.9	13.8	21.1	5.9	8.6	12.8	4.5	5.3	-5.7	4.3

Balance Sheet & Other Fin. Data (Million $)

	1997	1996	1995	1994	1993	1992	1991	1990	1989	1988
Cash	119	26.0	31.7	18.6	8.4	33.7	6.3	8.1	0.9	0.8
Curr. Assets	243	109	90.5	70.8	44.1	67.3	31.4	36.7	25.0	26.3
Total Assets	430	239	191	151	117	109	66.0	65.0	56.0	63.0
Curr. Liab.	70.1	46.6	36.2	18.8	17.9	18.3	13.3	14.0	9.2	13.6
LT Debt	76.6	53.2	34.9	37.7	10.1	13.0	16.7	19.3	20.5	19.1
Common Eqty.	283	134	120	94.6	88.7	77.0	33.5	28.8	23.4	28.9
Total Cap.	360	187	155	132	99	90.8	52.7	50.7	46.5	49.5
Cap. Exp.	82.6	77.1	44.5	82.2	73.9	25.5	18.3	7.0	6.9	19.3
Cash Flow	80.2	47.4	49.3	29.9	24.4	25.7	15.7	15.0	6.4	12.3
Curr. Ratio	3.5	2.3	2.5	3.8	2.5	3.7	2.4	2.6	2.7	1.9
% LT Debt of Cap.	21.3	28.4	22.5	28.5	10.2	14.3	31.8	38.1	44.1	38.6
% Net Inc.of Revs.	9.2	3.9	7.0	2.5	4.3	8.0	3.1	4.4	NM	3.8
% Ret. on Assets	12.5	6.4	12.3	4.4	7.5	13.2	6.9	8.9	NM	7.8
% Ret. on Equity	20.1	10.9	19.6	6.4	10.2	21.3	14.4	20.4	NM	15.9

Data as orig. reptd.; bef. results of disc. opers. and/or spec. items. Per share data adj. for stk. divs. as of ex-div. date. Bold denotes diluted EPS (FASB 128). E-Estimated. NA-Not Available. NM-Not Meaningful. NR-Not Ranked.

Office—40 W. Highland Park, Hutchinson, MN 55350. **Tel**—(320) 587-3797. **Chrmn**—J. W. Green. **Pres, CEO & COO**—W. M. Fortun. **VP, CFO, Secy & Investor Contact**—John A. Ingleman. **Dirs**—W. T. Brunberg, A. Cox Jr., J. E. Donaghy, H. C. Ervin Jr., W. M. Fortun, J. W. Green, S. E. Landsburg, R. N. Rosett. **Transfer Agent & Registrar**—Norwest Bank Minnesota, St. Paul. **Incorporated**—in Minnesota in 1965.**Empl**— 7,181. **S&P Analyst:** J. M.

13-OCT-98

Industry:
Computer (Software & Services)

Summary: Formed through the August 1998, merger of Arbor Software and Hyperion Software, HYSL provides analytic application software for reporting, analysis, modeling and planning.

Quantitative Evaluations		
Outlook (1 Lowest—5 Highest) • **5**	Recent Price • 17	Yield • Nil
Fair Value • **44%**	52 Wk Range • 51⅛-12	12-Mo. P/E • 25.4

Risk • **High**

Earn./Div. Rank • **NR**

Technical Eval. • **NA**

Rel. Strength Rank (1 Lowest—99 Highest) • **13**

Insider Activity • **NA**

Earnings vs. Previous Year
▲=Up ▼=Down ▶=No Change

10 Week Mov. Avg. – – –
30 Week Mov. Avg. ·····
Relative Strength ——

VOL. (000)

4025   7064

OPTIONS: CBOE

Business Profile - 14-JUL-98

On August 24, 1998, Arbor Software Corp. and Hyperion Software Corp. announced the completion of the merger of the two companies. The combined company, named Hyperion Solutions Corp. (HYSL), is a global leader in the rapidly emerging analytic applications marketplace, with more than $375 million in annual revenues. HYSL's products are in use by more than 4,000 customers worldwide and the company has about 1,800 employees in 26 countries. The merger was effected by the issuance of 0.95 shares of Arbor Software common stock for each share of Hyperion Software Corp. common stock. Former Arbor Software and Hyperion Software shareholders hold approximately 40% and 60%, respectively, of HYSL common stock.

Operational Review - 14-JUL-98

Total revenues for Arbor Software advanced 74% in FY 98 (Mar.), as license revenues increased 71% and maintenance, support and other revenues advanced 87%. Gross margins narrowed slightly, and with $3 million of acquired in-process technology expenses in the current year only, the gain in operating income was held to 63%. After taxes at 45.7%, versus 35.0%, net income was up 19%, to $6,916,000 ($0.58 a share, on 2.2% more shares), from $5,826,000 ($0.50).

Stock Performance - 09-OCT-98

In the past 30 trading days, HYSL's shares have declined 42%, compared to a 4% fall in the S&P 500. Average trading volume for the past five days was 1,412,860 shares, compared with the 40-day moving average of 675,005 shares.

Key Stock Statistics

Dividend Rate/Share	Nil	Shareholders	200
Shs. outstg. (M)	29.5	Market cap. (B)	$0.579
Avg. daily vol. (M)	0.879	Inst. holdings	27%
Tang. Bk. Value/Share	5.05		
Beta	NA		

Value of $10,000 invested 5 years ago: NA

Fiscal Year Ending Mar. 31

	1999	1998	1997	1996	1995	1994
Revenues (Million $)						
1Q	27.11	16.11	9.27	—	—	—
2Q	—	18.01	10.80	—	—	—
3Q	—	21.38	12.47	6.76	—	—
4Q	—	26.74	14.84	8.23	—	—
Yr.	—	82.24	47.38	25.13	11.52	—
Earnings Per Share ($)						
1Q	0.24	0.15	0.10	—	—	—
2Q		0.18	0.12			
3Q	—	-0.02	0.13	—	—	—
4Q	—	0.27	0.15	0.12	—	—
Yr.	—	0.58	0.50	0.27	0.04	—

Next earnings report expected: late October

Dividend Data

No cash dividends have been paid.

A Division of The McGraw·Hill Companies

Business Summary - 14-JUL-98

On August 24, 1998, Arbor Software Corp. (ARSW) and Hyperion Software Corp. announced the completion of the merger of the two companies. The combined company, Hyperion Solutions Corp., provides analytic software for reporting, analysis, modeling and planning. In the merger, 0.95 ARSW common shares were issued for each share of Hyperion Software common stock.

ARSW developed and marketed enterprise on-line analytical processing (OLAP) software for management reporting, analysis and planning applications. Its Arbor Essbase software is a powerful OLAP server that integrates data from throughout an enterprise, including data from relational databases, data warehouses and other data repositories, and allows users to perform multidimensional analysis on this data utilizing spreadsheets, query tools, report writers and web browsers.

Revenues in recent fiscal years (ended Mar.) were derived as follows:

	1998	1997
License	81%	83%
Maintenance, support & other	19%	17%

OLAP software is a category of software specifically designed for business planning and analysis. OLAP provides a basis for strategic and tactical decision making by allowing users to work with large volumes of historical and projected data located throughout the enterprise and transform such data into useful information. OLAP software is designed to facilitate planning and analysis by enabling users to organize easily and view data in multiple dimensions, rapidly perform interactive scenario analyses and share data with other users, without significant utilization of MIS resources.

Arbor Essbase users can easily access and organize large volumes of historical and projected data, rapidly perform interactive what-if scenario analyses and share this information with users throughout the enterprise. Arbor's product family consists principally of Arbor Essbase OLAP Server, and complementary products that extend and enhance the functionality of the Arbor Essbase solution, including user tools, developer tools, server management and data integration modules, and application modules. Arbor Essbase also has the flexibility to reorganize and present data from a variety of perspectives without disturbing the integrity of the underlying historical data or causing the degradation of network performance.

ARSW markets and sells its products in the U.S., Canada and Europe through its direct sales force and worldwide through original equipment manufacturers, value added resellers and distributors.

Per Share Data ($)

(Year Ended Mar. 31)	1998	1997	1996	1995	1994	1993	1992	1991	1990	1989
Tangible Bk. Val.	4.67	3.83	3.16	0.97	NA	NA	NA	NA	NA	NA
Cash Flow	0.97	0.70	0.38	0.09	NA	NA	NA	NA	NA	NA
Earnings	0.58	0.50	0.27	0.04	NA	NA	NA	NA	NA	NA
Dividends	Nil	Nil	Nil	Nil	Nil	Nil	Nil	Nil	Nil	Nil
Payout Ratio	Nil	Nil	Nil	Nil	Nil	Nil	Nil	Nil	Nil	Nil
Cal. Yrs.	1997	1996	1995	1994	1993	1992	1991	1990	1989	1988
Prices - High	53¼	82¾	48½	NA	NA	NA	NA	NA	NA	NA
- Low	17	21	17	NA	NA	NA	NA	NA	NA	NA
P/E Ratio - High	92	NM	NM	NM	NM	NM	NM	NM	NM	NM
- Low	29	NM	NM	NM	NM	NM	NM	NM	NM	NM

Income Statement Analysis (Million $)

	1998	1997	1996	1995	1994	1993	1992	1991	1990	1989
Revs.	82.2	47.4	25.1	11.5	4.3	NA	NA	NA	NA	NA
Oper. Inc.	16.1	9.9	4.2	1.0	1.9	NA	NA	NA	NA	NA
Depr.	4.8	2.4	1.1	0.5	0.3	NA	NA	NA	NA	NA
Int. Exp.	0.3	0.2	0.3	0.2	0.1	NA	NA	NA	NA	NA
Pretax Inc.	12.7	9.0	3.6	0.4	-2.2	NA	NA	NA	NA	NA
Eff. Tax Rate	46%	35%	20%	6.10%	Nil	Nil	Nil	Nil	Nil	Nil
Net Inc.	6.9	5.8	2.9	0.4	-2.2	NA	NA	NA	NA	NA

Balance Sheet & Other Fin. Data (Million $)

	1998	1997	1996	1995	1994	1993	1992	1991	1990	1989
Cash	102	28.9	10.7	2.7	NA	NA	NA	NA	NA	NA
Curr. Assets	166	47.0	42.6	4.9	NA	NA	NA	NA	NA	NA
Total Assets	186	59.6	45.9	6.5	NA	NA	NA	NA	NA	NA
Curr. Liab.	30.1	16.7	10.5	3.4	NA	NA	NA	NA	NA	NA
LT Debt	100	0.3	1.1	0.8	NA	NA	NA	NA	NA	NA
Common Eqty.	56.1	42.6	34.3	2.3	NA	NA	NA	NA	NA	NA
Total Cap.	156	42.9	35.4	3.1	NA	NA	NA	NA	NA	NA
Cap. Exp.	6.0	10.8	1.3	0.1	0.0	NA	NA	NA	NA	NA
Cash Flow	11.7	8.2	3.9	0.9	NA	NA	NA	NA	NA	NA
Curr. Ratio	5.5	2.8	4.1	1.4	NA	NA	NA	NA	NA	NA
% LT Debt of Cap.	64.1	0.7	3.1	26.8	NA	NA	NA	NA	NA	NA
% Net Inc.of Revs.	8.4	12.3	11.5	3.2	NA	NA	NA	NA	NA	NA
% Ret. on Assets	5.6	5.5	11.0	NA	NA	NA	NA	NA	NA	NA
% Ret. on Equity	14.0	15.2	15.7	NA	NA	NA	NA	NA	NA	NA

Data as orig. reptd.; bef. results of disc. opers. and/or spec. items. Per share data adj. for stk. divs. as of ex-div. date. Bold denotes diluted EPS (FASB 128). E-Estimated. NA-Not Available. NM-Not Meaningful. NR-Not Ranked.

Office—1344 Crossman Ave., Sunnyvale, CA 94089. **Tel**—(408) 744-9500. **Website**—http://www.hyperion.com.**Chrmn**—J. Dorrian. **Pres & CEO**—J. M. Dillon. **SVP & CFO**—S. V. Imbler. **Dirs**—J. M. Dillon, J. A. Dorrian, M. W. Perry, J. R. Rodek, A. L. Winblad. **Transfer Agent & Registrar**—Boston EquiServe, Palo Alto, CA. **Incorporated**—in Delaware in 1991. **Empl**— 1,800. **S&P Analyst:** M.I.

IHOP Corp.

4231B

NASDAQ Symbol **IHOP**

In S&P SmallCap 600

03-OCT-98

Industry:
Restaurants

Summary: This company develops, franchises and operates International House of Pancakes restaurants, one of the best-known national family restaurant chains in the U.S.

Quantitative Evaluations

Outlook
(1 Lowest—5 Highest)
• **4**–

Fair Value
• **50¾**

Risk
• **Average**

Earn./Div. Rank
• **B+**

Technical Eval.
• **Bullish** since 8/98

Rel. Strength Rank
(1 Lowest—99 Highest)
• **66**

Insider Activity
• **Neutral**

Recent Price • 37⅛
52 Wk Range • 47½-31

Yield • Nil
12-Mo. P/E • 15.6

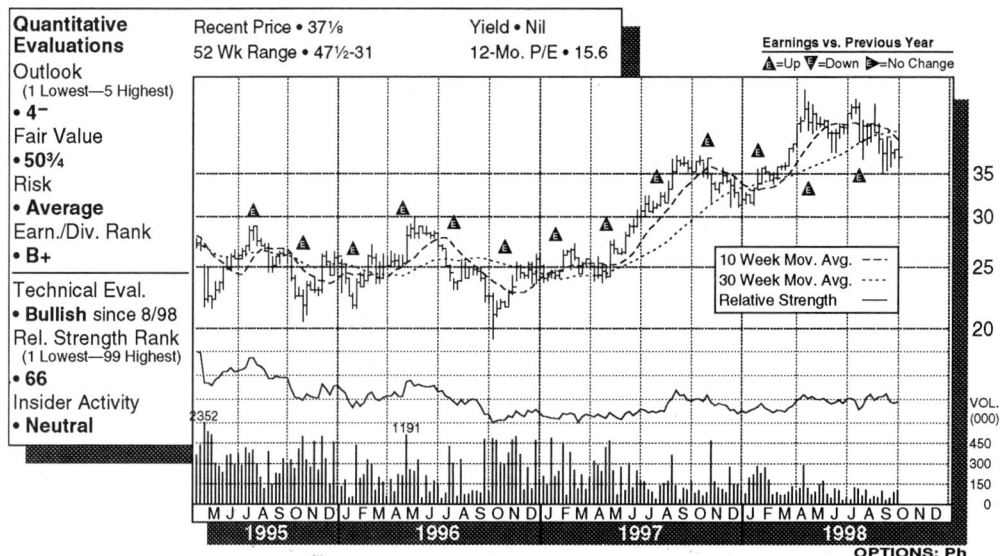

OPTIONS: Ph

Business Profile - 10-SEP-98

Although the restaurant industry has been suffering from weakness in comparable-store sales and cost pressures in the ingredients and labor markets, IHOP has been able to post higher same-store sales and improved earnings, year to year. Revenues in recent periods benefited from additional units in operation, and from higher comparable-store sales. In addition, results have been sparked by the recent success of the company's "Cliff at IHOP" series of television commercials. IHOP opened 30 restaurants in the first quarter of 1998, and plans to open a total of 70 to 85 units in 1998. Officers and directors own nearly 12% of the stock.

Operational Review - 10-SEP-98

Revenues in the six months ended June 30, 1998, climbed 24%, year to year, reflecting 55 additional units in operation and a system-wide sales increase of 14%; comparable-store sales were up 3.4%. Margins widened, due primarily to the leveraging of corporate and franchise expenses over higher sales dollars; operating income grew 37%. Following higher depreciation and interest charges, pretax income was up 30%. After taxes at 39.0% in each period, net income was also up 30%, to $11,164,000 ($1.12 a share), from $8,588,000 ($0.89).

Stock Performance - 02-OCT-98

In the past 30 trading days, IHOP's shares have declined 8%, compared to a 7% fall in the S&P 500. Average trading volume for the past five days was 21,120 shares, compared with the 40-day moving average of 13,049 shares.

Key Stock Statistics

Dividend Rate/Share	Nil	Shareholders	2,200
Shs. outstg. (M)	9.9	Market cap. (B)	$0.366
Avg. daily vol. (M)	0.015	Inst. holdings	78%
Tang. Bk. Value/Share	16.13		
Beta	0.64		

Value of $10,000 invested 5 years ago: $ 17,921

Fiscal Year Ending Dec. 31

	1998	1997	1996	1995	1994	1993
Revenues (Million $)						
1Q	55.88	46.44	40.29	33.20	32.80	30.20
2Q	65.59	51.57	44.47	40.10	37.20	35.50
3Q	—	56.31	51.57	42.57	37.30	38.20
4Q	—	61.13	53.77	48.45	42.80	38.60
Yr.	—	215.5	190.1	164.3	150.0	142.6
Earnings Per Share ($)						
1Q	0.47	0.37	0.32	0.19	0.24	0.16
2Q	0.04	0.31	0.40	0.40	0.00	0.15
3Q	—	0.58	0.56	0.50	0.40	0.37
4Q	—	0.67	0.61	0.59	0.57	0.48
Yr.	—	2.15	1.95	1.70	1.60	1.15

Next earnings report expected: late October

Dividend Data

No cash dividends have been paid.

A Division of The McGraw·Hill Companies

STANDARD
&POOR'S
STOCK REPORTS

IHOP Corp.

4231B

03-OCT-98

Business Summary - 10-SEP-98

IHOP's pancakes may be flat, but Its recent growth trend is not. Systemwide sales (the retail sales of all International House of Pancakes restaurants) totaled $903 million in 1997, up 13% from the 1996 level. Comparable average sales per restaurant, an important measure of operating performance trends, increased 1.7% in 1996; the growth rate accelerated to 3.7% in 1997. Restaurant additions form the other part of the company's growth recipe: since the beginning of 1992, the IHOP chain has added about 100 restaurants every two years; as of June 30, 1998, there were 804 IHOP restaurants in 36 states, Canada, and Japan. IHOP started with one restaurant in 1958.

IHOP operates fewer than 10% of the chain's restaurants, relying instead on a franchise system that stresses the active involvement of franchisees in the day-to-day management of their restaurants. IHOP views franchising as a way of putting qualified, equity-involved managers in charge of a business venture. Unlike other franchisors, the company removes much of the downside risk for the franchisee by buying or leasing the site itself, building the restaurant, and then becoming the franchisee's landlord. IHOP collects a hefty

fee (between $200,000 and $350,000) for each newly developed restaurant it franchises, and it also receives a recurring revenue stream that includes rental income on the property and equipment it leases, as well as royalties and advertising fees.

As of March 31, 1998, 570 of the chain's restaurants were operated by franchisees, and 145 units (located principally in Florida and Japan) were operated under area license agreements. In 1997, franchise operations (including royalties from area licensees, but excluding sales of franchises and equipment) generated revenues of $114 million, about 53% of total revenues.

IHOP's marketing efforts have helped make International House of Pancakes one of the most recognizable names of any restaurant chain in the U.S. Most IHOP franchisees and company-operated restaurants contribute approximately 2.0% of their revenues to local advertising cooperatives, which purchase television advertising time and place advertisements in printed media or direct mail. For many years, IHOP's television advertising has featured Cliff Bemis as IHOP's affable spokesman. In more recent commercials, the company has been emphasizing the appetizing appearance, quality and taste of IHOP food.

Per Share Data ($)

(Year Ended Dec. 31)	1997	1996	1995	1994	1993	1992	1991	1990	1989	1988
Tangible Bk. Val.	14.80	12.30	10.13	8.12	6.26	4.81	3.76	NA	NA	NA
Cash Flow	3.18	2.82	2.43	2.28	1.77	1.54	1.45	NA	NA	NA
Earnings	2.15	1.95	1.70	1.60	1.15	0.98	0.73	0.53	NA	NA
Dividends	Nil	Nil	Nil	Nil	Nil	Nil	Nil	NA	NA	NA
Payout Ratio	Nil	Nil	Nil	Nil	Nil	Nil	Nil	NA	NA	NA
Prices - High	37⅜	29⅞	30½	33¾	31¼	21½	15⅛	NA	NA	NA
- Low	23⅝	19¼	20½	22½	18⅜	11⅞	9⅜	NA	NA	NA
P/E Ratio - High	17	15	18	21	27	22	21	NA	NA	NA
- Low	11	10	12	14	16	12	13	NA	NA	NA

Income Statement Analysis (Million $)

	1997	1996	1995	1994	1993	1992	1991	1990	1989	1988
Revs.	216	190	164	145	139	112	103	NA	NA	NA
Oper. Inc.	59.0	50.7	43.3	33.6	29.0	22.2	17.6	NA	NA	NA
Depr.	10.0	8.3	6.9	6.4	5.7	5.0	4.9	NA	NA	NA
Int. Exp.	14.6	11.7	8.9	6.8	5.6	4.8	5.7	NA	NA	NA
Pretax Inc.	34.3	30.8	26.7	25.0	18.6	14.8	9.0	NA	NA	NA
Eff. Tax Rate	39%	40%	40%	40%	42%	41%	41%	NA	NA	NA
Net Inc.	20.9	18.6	16.2	15.1	10.7	8.8	5.3	NA	NA	NA

Balance Sheet & Other Fin. Data (Million $)

	1997	1996	1995	1994	1993	1992	1991	1990	1989	1988
Cash	6.0	8.7	3.9	2.0	1.2	5.7	2.7	NA	NA	NA
Curr. Assets	40.8	41.3	27.5	21.2	19.9	21.7	15.9	NA	NA	NA
Total Assets	383	329	252	203	180	150	113	NA	NA	NA
Curr. Liab.	39.3	35.1	28.7	17.2	16.6	18.1	15.1	NA	NA	NA
LT Debt	158	139	93.5	78.0	66.4	53.8	38.8	NA	NA	NA
Common Eqty.	156	156	108	88.3	71.2	58.0	48.7	NA	NA	NA
Total Cap.	343	269	223	184	162	130	97.0	NA	NA	NA
Cap. Exp.	59.7	57.2	42.0	30.5	40.9	29.3	20.3	NA	NA	NA
Cash Flow	30.9	26.9	23.1	21.5	16.5	13.8	10.1	NA	NA	NA
Curr. Ratio	1.0	1.2	1.0	1.2	1.2	1.2	1.0	NA	NA	NA
% LT Debt of Cap.	46.1	51.9	41.9	42.4	41.0	41.3	39.9	NA	NA	NA
% Net Inc.of Revs.	9.7	9.8	9.8	10.4	7.7	7.9	5.1	NA	NA	NA
% Ret. on Assets	5.9	6.4	7.1	7.9	6.5	6.6	4.0	NA	NA	NA
% Ret. on Equity	14.6	15.7	16.4	18.9	16.5	16.4	14.7	NA	NA	NA

Data as orig. reptd.; bef. results of disc. opers. and/or spec. items. Per share data adj. for stk. divs. as of ex-div. date. Bold denotes diluted EPS (FASB 128). E-Estimated. NA-Not Available. NM-Not Meaningful. NR-Not Ranked.

Office—525 N. Brand Blvd., Glendale, CA 91203-1903. **Tel**—(818) 240-6055. **Chrmn, Pres & CEO**—R. K. Herzer. **EVP & COO**—D. M. Leifheit.**VP-Fin, CFO, Treas & Investor Contact**—Frederick G. Silny. **VP & Secy**—M. D. Weisberger. **Dirs**—H. F. Christie, F. Edelstein, M. S. Gordon, R. K. Herzer, N. C. Hulsey, L. A. Kay, D. M. Leifheit, C. W. Nahas, P. W. Rose. **Transfer Agent**—ChaseMellon Shareholder Services, Ridgefield Park, NJ. **Incorporated**—in Delaware in 1976. **Empl**— 2,600. **S&P Analyst:** R.J.I.

STANDARD &POOR'S
STOCK REPORTS

IMCO Recycling

1179V
NYSE Symbol **IMR**

In S&P SmallCap 600

10-OCT-98 Industry: Metal Fabricators

Summary: IMCO is the world's largest aluminum recycler and also processes zinc and magnesium.

Quantitative Evaluations	
Outlook (1 Lowest—5 Highest)	**5**
Fair Value	**23½**
Risk	**Average**
Earn./Div. Rank	**B+**
Technical Eval.	**Bullish** since 9/98
Rel. Strength Rank (1 Lowest—99 Highest)	**52**
Insider Activity	**Neutral**

Recent Price • 12⅜ Yield • 1.6%
52 Wk Range • 21-10¼ 12-Mo. P/E • 10.6

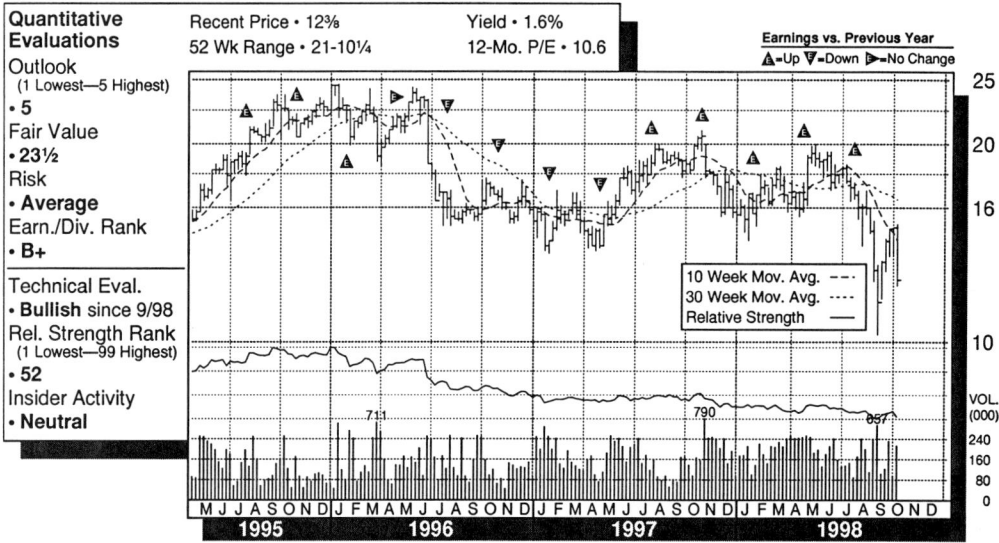

Earnings vs. Previous Year
▲=Up ▼=Down ▷=No Change

10 Week Mov. Avg. ---
30 Week Mov. Avg. ····
Relative Strength —

Business Profile - 13-MAY-98

The world's largest aluminum recycler, IMR increased its participation in the auto industry and the transportation sector, the largest and fastest growing aluminum market, through the November 1997 acquisition of Al-chem Aluminum, Inc. In April 1998, it signed a letter of intent to acquire U.S. Zinc Corp. for about $75,000,000 in cash, assumption of debt, and new IMR common shares, plus contingent payments and warrants. U.S. Zinc, headquartered in Houston, is the world's largest zinc recycler, and the second largest supplier of zinc oxide and zinc dust; it operates five production facilities, in Illinois, Texas and Tennessee, with annual processing capacity of 200,000,000 lbs. of zinc. The acquisition is expected to increase IMR's total annual processing capacity in 1998 to approximately 2.7 billion lbs.

Operational Review - 13-MAY-98

Revenues climbed 54% year to year in the first quarter of 1998; income before special items more than doubled, to $4,611,000 ($0.28 a share, on 33% more shares), from $2,280,000 ($0.18). Results benefited from greater processing volume stemming from acquisitions and new plant construction completed in 1997. In addition, IMR's joint venture in Germany significantly improved its contribution to net earnings. Results for 1997 are before a charge of $0.10 a share from early extinguishment of debt,

Stock Performance - 09-OCT-98

In the past 30 trading days, IMR's shares have declined 3%, compared to a 4% fall in the S&P 500. Average trading volume for the past five days was 42,500 shares, compared with the 40-day moving average of 45,269 shares.

Key Stock Statistics

Dividend Rate/Share	0.20	Shareholders	600
Shs. outstg. (M)	17.0	Market cap. (B)	$0.211
Avg. daily vol. (M)	0.033	Inst. holdings	54%
Tang. Bk. Value/Share	6.25		
Beta	1.21		

Value of $10,000 invested 5 years ago: $ 8,612

Fiscal Year Ending Dec. 31

	1998	1997	1996	1995	1994	1993
Revenues (Million $)						
1Q	127.2	82.53	50.72	30.75	21.68	15.74
2Q	124.5	76.60	50.47	29.72	23.07	18.64
3Q	—	77.46	53.69	32.11	26.21	19.04
4Q	—	102.8	55.99	48.59	30.16	20.80
Yr.	—	339.4	210.9	141.2	101.1	74.22
Earnings Per Share ($)						
1Q	0.28	0.18	0.24	0.24	0.18	0.15
2Q	0.30	0.28	0.21	0.25	0.09	0.17
3Q	—	0.32	-0.07	0.27	0.22	0.19
4Q	—	0.28	0.17	0.27	0.24	0.19
Yr.	—	1.06	0.55	1.03	0.73	0.70

Next earnings report expected: mid October

Dividend Data (Dividends have been paid since 1995.)

Amount ($)	Date Decl.	Ex-Div. Date	Stock of Record	Payment Date
0.050	Nov. 12	Dec. 10	Dec. 12	Dec. 31 '97
0.050	Feb. 26	Mar. 18	Mar. 20	Mar. 31 '98
0.050	May. 14	Jun. 10	Jun. 12	Jun. 30 '98
0.050	Aug. 20	Sep. 09	Sep. 11	Sep. 30 '98

A Division of The McGraw-Hill Companies

STANDARD
&POOR'S
STOCK REPORTS

IMCO Recycling Inc.

1179V

10-OCT-98

Business Summary - 13-MAY-98

This company is not a fan of heavy metal. IMCO Recycling Inc. (IMR), based in Irving, TX, is the world's largest recycler of secondary aluminum, which includes used aluminum beverage cans (UBCs), scrap and dross (a by-product of aluminum production). IMR converts UBCs, scrap and dross into molten metal, which is then delivered to customers in molten form or ingots. The company also recovers magnesium via a relatively similar process and also recycles zinc.

Recycled metal has gained a larger share of the overall U.S. aluminum market in the past two decades. Recycled aluminum, which performs as well as primary aluminum in most applications, saves the aluminum industry 95% of the energy costs and 90% of the capital and labor involved in making aluminum from bauxite.

Most of the company's processing consists of aluminum, magnesium and zinc tolled for its customers. To a lesser (but increasing) extent, the company's processing also consists of buy/sell business, which involves purchasing scrap metal and dross for processing and resale. IMR's aluminum alloying facility (acquired in November 1997) is primarily engaged in buy/sell business, as opposed to tolling; therefore, the company has experienced higher levels of buy/sell business relative to tolling during 1998. The higher level of buy/sell business has increased IMR's working capital requirements, and subjected it to greater risks associated with price fluctuations in the aluminum market. The proposed acquisition of U.S. Zinc is also expected to increase the level of overall buy/sell business.

IMR's customers include most of the major U.S. aluminum producers, aluminum diecasters, extruders, and other processors of aluminum products. Although the company's traditional role is as a supplier to the container and construction markets, a principal element of IMR's strategy involves expansion into new markets, specifically the rapidly expanding aluminum automotive market. Aluminum is an attractive alternative to steel in the automobile industry because it is recyclable, corrosion-resistant, and lighter in weight.

The company intends to continue to expand in the U.S. and abroad by establishing additional aluminum recycling facilities, expanding its existing facilities and acquiring other recycling businesses. IMR has a 50% interest in a German joint venture that owns and operates two recycling and foundry alloy facilities mainly serving the European automotive markets, and owns an aluminum recycling plant in Wales (built in 1997). The January 1997, $58 million acquisition of IMSAMET, Inc., a subsidiary of EnviroSource, Inc., added three aluminum recycling facilities, in Idaho, Arizona and Utah, strengthening IMR's ability to serve customers in the western U.S. As of April 1998, the company had 16 domestic recycling plants.

Per Share Data ($)

(Year Ended Dec. 31)	1997	1996	1995	1994	1993	1992	1991	1990	1989	1988
Tangible Bk. Val.	5.72	6.64	6.13	5.38	4.50	3.83	2.92	2.34	1.84	0.11
Cash Flow	2.30	1.46	1.80	1.36	1.23	1.01	0.84	0.80	0.69	0.77
Earnings	1.06	0.55	1.03	0.73	0.70	0.67	0.52	0.53	0.54	0.58
Dividends	0.20	0.20	0.10	0.10	Nil	Nil	Nil	Nil	Nil	Nil
Payout Ratio	19%	36%	10%	14%	Nil	Nil	Nil	Nil	Nil	Nil
Prices - High	21	24⅝	24½	16⅞	16¾	15⅛	11⅜	6⅞	8½	5¼
- Low	13⅝	14⅜	13⅜	12⅛	10⅞	6½	5⅜	4	4¾	1⅜
P/E Ratio - High	20	45	24	23	24	23	22	13	16	9
- Low	13	26	13	17	16	10	10	8	9	2

Income Statement Analysis (Million $)

	1997	1996	1995	1994	1993	1992	1991	1990	1989	1988
Revs.	339	211	141	101	74.2	60.2	49.2	54.6	37.1	46.7
Oper. Inc.	46.8	25.1	30.3	23.6	17.9	14.2	10.7	10.9	8.6	8.8
Depr.	16.5	11.3	9.3	7.4	6.2	3.8	3.5	3.0	1.6	1.3
Int. Exp.	7.3	3.4	1.5	1.3	1.4	1.4	1.4	1.6	2.3	2.7
Pretax Inc.	23.5	10.9	20.4	13.7	11.1	9.8	6.5	7.1	5.8	5.0
Eff. Tax Rate	39%	38%	39%	38%	28%	23%	15%	19%	7.30%	6.20%
Net Inc.	14.1	6.7	12.5	8.5	8.0	7.5	5.6	5.7	5.4	4.0

Balance Sheet & Other Fin. Data (Million $)

	1997	1996	1995	1994	1993	1992	1991	1990	1989	1988
Cash	0.4	5.1	8.7	2.9	1.7	12.0	9.2	6.1	6.3	3.8
Curr. Assets	91.7	53.3	47.9	27.9	19.8	19.9	18.1	17.1	15.9	10.5
Total Assets	333	165	140	96.8	79.4	68.9	53.0	47.7	45.1	33.4
Curr. Liab.	33.8	20.7	19.9	10.6	10.7	8.6	3.4	3.8	5.9	7.1
LT Debt	109	48.2	29.8	11.9	8.0	10.5	13.0	13.0	13.0	18.1
Common Eqty.	169	88.3	83.3	68.3	57.1	48.9	35.8	29.9	25.3	7.4
Total Cap.	289	142	119	85.0	68.1	60.3	49.6	44.0	39.3	26.3
Cap. Exp.	37.2	16.7	15.5	6.6	11.9	16.9	7.1	4.8	8.9	1.5
Cash Flow	30.6	18.0	21.8	15.8	14.2	11.3	9.1	8.8	6.9	5.3
Curr. Ratio	2.7	2.6	2.4	2.6	1.9	2.3	5.4	4.5	2.7	1.5
% LT Debt of Cap.	37.7	33.9	25.1	14.0	11.8	17.4	26.2	29.6	33.1	69.1
% Net Inc.of Revs.	4.2	3.2	8.9	8.4	10.8	12.4	11.4	10.5	14.5	8.6
% Ret. on Assets	5.7	4.4	10.5	9.5	10.9	12.0	11.0	12.4	12.2	11.0
% Ret. on Equity	11.0	7.8	16.5	13.3	15.1	17.2	17.0	20.8	30.9	73.1

Data as orig. reptd.; bef. results of disc. opers. and/or spec. items. Per share data adj. for stk. divs. as of ex-div. date. Bold denotes diluted EPS (FASB 128). E-Estimated. NA-Not Available. NM-Not Meaningful. NR-Not Ranked.

Office—5215 N. O'Connor Blvd., Suite 940, Irving, TX 75039. **Tel**—(972) 401-7200. **Chrmn & CEO**—D. V. Ingram. **Pres & COO**—R. L. Kerr. **EVP, CFO, Secy & Investor Contact**—Paul V. Dufour. **Dirs**—S. Bartlett, J. M. Brundrett, R. L. Cheek, J. J. Fleming, D. V. Ingram, D. Navarro, J. C. Page. **Transfer Agent & Registrar**—ChaseMellon Shareholder Services, Ridgefield Park, NJ.**Incorporated**—in 1985 in Delaware. **Empl**— 1,586. **S&P Analyst:** C.F.B.

STANDARD &POOR'S
STOCK REPORTS

IDEXX Laboratories
NASDAQ Symbol **IDXX**

4230X
In S&P SmallCap 600

10-OCT-98

Industry:
Biotechnology

Summary: This company provides veterinary practice management software and diagnostic products for a broad range of veterinary, food and environmental testing applications.

Quantitative Evaluations

Outlook
(1 Lowest—5 Highest)
• **5**

Fair Value
• **35¼**

Risk
• **Average**

Earn./Div. Rank
• **B**

Technical Eval.
• **Bullish** since 9/98

Rel. Strength Rank
(1 Lowest—99 Highest)
• **65**

Insider Activity
• **Neutral**

Recent Price • 19½
52 Wk Range • 25½-12¼

Yield • Nil
12-Mo. P/E • NM

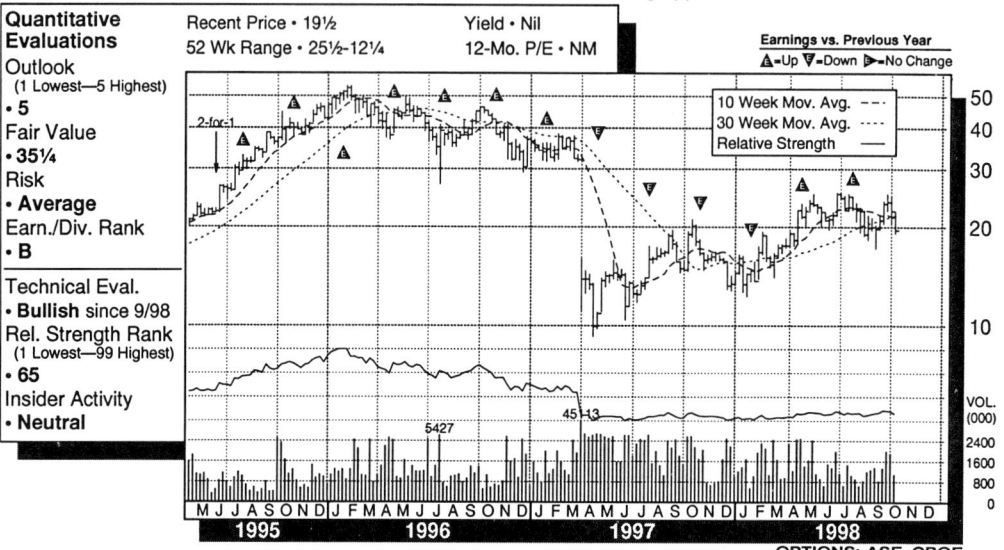

Earnings vs. Previous Year
▲=Up ▼=Down ▷=No Change

10 Week Mov. Avg. – – –
30 Week Mov. Avg. ·····
Relative Strength ——

OPTIONS: ASE, CBOE

Business Profile - 06-AUG-98

During 1998, IDXX has seen strong revenue growth from increased sales in existing and recently acquired product lines. In 1997, IDXX acquired Professionals' Software, Inc. and Advanced Veterinary Systems, leaders in the veterinary practice management software business. Through these acquisitions, the company has become the leading U.S. supplier of veterinary practice management software systems. Results in 1997 were hurt by $9 million ($0.14 a share) of nonrecurring charges related to restructuring costs and the writeoff of acquired in-process R&D. The company plans to implement additional operating improvements over the coming quarters as well as evaluate acquisition, licensing and other opportunities in the veterinary market.

Operational Review - 06-AUG-98

Based on a brief report, revenues for the six months ended June 30, 1998, rose 33%, year to year, primarily reflecting increased sales of veterinary test kits, consumables, reference and laboratory services. Sales were also higher in the practice management software division, due in part to the Professionals' Software acquisition, partially offset by lower sales of veterinary instruments. Gross margins widened to 50.3%, from 48.2%, and sales and marketing expenses were 20% of revenues, versus 28%. After taxes at 39%, versus a tax credit, net income of $8,859,000 ($0.22 a share, on 2.6% fewer shares) contrasted with a net loss of $1,174,000 ($0.03).

Stock Performance - 09-OCT-98

In the past 30 trading days, IDXX's shares have declined 2%, compared to a 4% fall in the S&P 500. Average trading volume for the past five days was 213,640 shares, compared with the 40-day moving average of 278,190 shares.

Key Stock Statistics

Dividend Rate/Share	Nil	Shareholders	1,300
Shs. outstg. (M)	38.6	Market cap. (B)	$0.755
Avg. daily vol. (M)	0.313	Inst. holdings	70%
Tang. Bk. Value/Share	8.13		
Beta	1.23		

Value of $10,000 invested 5 years ago: $ 23,892

Fiscal Year Ending Dec. 31

	1998	1997	1996	1995	1994	1993
Revenues (Million $)						
1Q	77.79	60.53	57.40	39.20	27.40	19.50
2Q	80.89	58.89	65.88	46.50	31.10	23.10
3Q	—	71.73	69.84	48.70	31.90	23.80
4Q	—	71.82	74.57	54.20	35.90	26.70
Yr.	—	263.0	267.7	188.6	126.4	93.10
Earnings Per Share ($)						
1Q	0.10	0.02	0.18	0.12	0.09	0.04
2Q	0.13	-0.05	0.20	0.15	0.08	0.07
3Q	—	-0.44	0.22	0.16	0.11	0.08
4Q	—	-0.08	0.23	0.18	0.13	0.11
Yr.	—	-0.56	0.83	0.61	0.40	0.29

Next earnings report expected: mid October

Dividend Data

The company has never paid cash dividends on its common stock, and does not expect to pay any in the foreseeable future. The common stock was split two for one in 1993 and in 1995.

A Division of The McGraw-Hill Companies

IDEXX Laboratories   4230X

NASDAQ Symbol **IDXX**

In S&P SmallCap 600

10-OCT-98

Industry: Biotechnology

Summary: This company provides veterinary practice management software and diagnostic products for a broad range of veterinary, food and environmental testing applications.

Quantitative Evaluations	
Outlook (1 Lowest—5 Highest)	• **5**
Fair Value	• **35¼**
Risk	• **Average**
Earn./Div. Rank	• **B**
Technical Eval.	• **Bullish** since 9/98
Rel. Strength Rank (1 Lowest—99 Highest)	• **65**
Insider Activity	• **Neutral**

Recent Price • 19½
52 Wk Range • 25½–12¼
Yield • Nil
12-Mo. P/E • NM

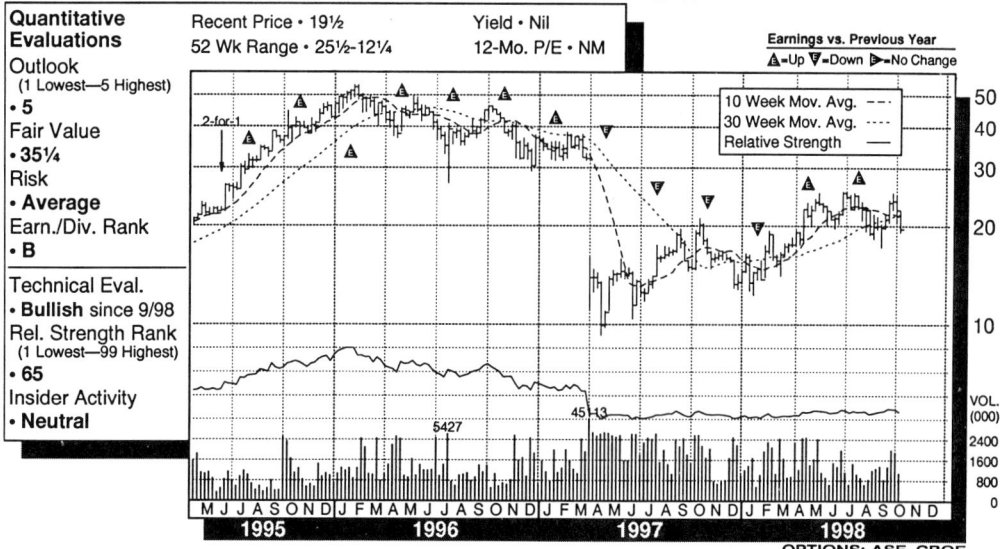

Earnings vs. Previous Year
▲=Up ▼=Down ▷=No Change

10 Week Mov. Avg. – – –
30 Week Mov. Avg. ·····
Relative Strength —

OPTIONS: ASE, CBOE

Business Profile - 06-AUG-98

During 1998, IDXX has seen strong revenue growth from increased sales in existing and recently acquired product lines. In 1997, IDXX acquired Professionals' Software, Inc. and Advanced Veterinary Systems, leaders in the veterinary practice management software business. Through these acquisitions, the company has become the leading U.S. supplier of veterinary practice management software systems. Results in 1997 were hurt by $9 million ($0.14 a share) of nonrecurring charges related to restructuring costs and the writeoff of acquired in-process R&D. The company plans to implement additional operating improvements over the coming quarters as well as evaluate acquisition, licensing and other opportunities in the veterinary market.

Operational Review - 06-AUG-98

Based on a brief report, revenues for the six months ended June 30, 1998, rose 33%, year to year, primarily reflecting increased sales of veterinary test kits, consumables, reference and laboratory services. Sales were also higher in the practice management software division, due in part to the Professionals' Software acquisition, partially offset by lower sales of veterinary instruments. Gross margins widened to 50.3%, from 48.2%, and sales and marketing expenses were 20% of revenues, versus 28%. After taxes at 39%, versus a tax credit, net income of $8,859,000 ($0.22 a share, on 2.6% fewer shares) contrasted with a net loss of $1,174,000 ($0.03).

Stock Performance - 09-OCT-98

In the past 30 trading days, IDXX's shares have declined 2%, compared to a 4% fall in the S&P 500. Average trading volume for the past five days was 213,640 shares, compared with the 40-day moving average of 278,190 shares.

Key Stock Statistics

Dividend Rate/Share	Nil	Shareholders	1,300
Shs. outstg. (M)	38.6	Market cap. (B)	$0.755
Avg. daily vol. (M)	0.313	Inst. holdings	70%
Tang. Bk. Value/Share	8.13		
Beta	1.23		

Value of $10,000 invested 5 years ago: $ 23,892

Fiscal Year Ending Dec. 31

	1998	1997	1996	1995	1994	1993
Revenues (Million $)						
1Q	77.79	60.53	57.40	39.20	27.40	19.50
2Q	80.89	58.89	65.88	46.50	31.10	23.10
3Q	—	71.73	69.84	48.70	31.90	23.80
4Q	—	71.82	74.57	54.20	35.90	26.70
Yr.	—	263.0	267.7	188.6	126.4	93.10
Earnings Per Share ($)						
1Q	0.10	0.02	0.18	0.12	0.09	0.04
2Q	0.13	-0.05	0.20	0.15	0.08	0.07
3Q	—	-0.44	0.22	0.16	0.11	0.08
4Q	—	-0.08	0.23	0.18	0.13	0.11
Yr.	—	-0.56	0.83	0.61	0.40	0.29

Next earnings report expected: mid October

Dividend Data

The company has never paid cash dividends on its common stock, and does not expect to pay any in the foreseeable future. The common stock was split two for one in 1993 and in 1995.

A Division of The McGraw-Hill Companies

Business Summary - 13-MAY-98

This company is not a fan of heavy metal. IMCO Recycling Inc. (IMR), based in Irving, TX, is the world's largest recycler of secondary aluminum, which includes used aluminum beverage cans (UBCs), scrap and dross (a by-product of aluminum production). IMR converts UBCs, scrap and dross into molten metal, which is then delivered to customers in molten form or ingots. The company also recovers magnesium via a relatively similar process and also recycles zinc.

Recycled metal has gained a larger share of the overall U.S. aluminum market in the past two decades. Recycled aluminum, which performs as well as primary aluminum in most applications, saves the aluminum industry 95% of the energy costs and 90% of the capital and labor involved in making aluminum from bauxite.

Most of the company's processing consists of aluminum, magnesium and zinc tolled for its customers. To a lesser (but increasing) extent, the company's processing also consists of buy/sell business, which involves purchasing scrap metal and dross for processing and resale. IMR's aluminum alloying facility (acquired in November 1997) is primarily engaged in buy/sell business, as opposed to tolling; therefore, the company has experienced higher levels of buy/sell business relative to tolling during 1998. The higher level of buy/sell business has increased IMR's working capital requirements,

and subjected it to greater risks associated with price fluctuations in the aluminum market. The proposed acquisition of U.S. Zinc is also expected to increase the level of overall buy/sell business.

IMR's customers include most of the major U.S. aluminum producers, aluminum diecasters, extruders, and other processors of aluminum products. Although the company's traditional role is as a supplier to the container and construction markets, a principal element of IMR's strategy involves expansion into new markets, specifically the rapidly expanding aluminum automotive market. Aluminum is an attractive alternative to steel in the automobile industry because it is recyclable, corrosion-resistant, and lighter in weight.

The company intends to continue to expand in the U.S. and abroad by establishing additional aluminum recycling facilities, expanding its existing facilities and acquiring other recycling businesses. IMR has a 50% interest in a German joint venture that owns and operates two recycling and foundry alloy facilities mainly serving the European automotive markets, and owns an aluminum recycling plant in Wales (built in 1997). The January 1997, $58 million acquisition of IMSAMET, Inc., a subsidiary of EnviroSource, Inc., added three aluminum recycling facilities, in Idaho, Arizona and Utah, strengthening IMR's ability to serve customers in the western U.S. As of April 1998, the company had 16 domestic recycling plants.

Per Share Data ($)

(Year Ended Dec. 31)	1997	1996	1995	1994	1993	1992	1991	1990	1989	1988
Tangible Bk. Val.	5.72	6.64	6.13	5.38	4.50	3.83	2.92	2.34	1.84	0.11
Cash Flow	2.30	1.46	1.80	1.36	1.23	1.01	0.84	0.80	0.69	0.77
Earnings	1.06	0.55	1.03	0.73	0.70	0.67	0.52	0.53	0.54	0.58
Dividends	0.20	0.20	0.10	0.10	Nil	Nil	Nil	Nil	Nil	Nil
Payout Ratio	19%	36%	10%	14%	Nil	Nil	Nil	Nil	Nil	Nil
Prices - High	21	24⅝	24½	16⅞	16¾	15⅛	11⅜	6⅞	8½	5¼
- Low	13⅝	14⅜	13⅜	12⅛	10⅞	6½	5⅜	4	4¾	1⅜
P/E Ratio - High	20	45	24	23	24	23	22	13	16	9
- Low	13	26	13	17	16	10	10	8	9	2

Income Statement Analysis (Million $)

Revs.	339	211	141	101	74.2	60.2	49.2	54.6	37.1	46.7
Oper. Inc.	46.8	25.1	30.3	23.6	17.9	14.2	10.7	10.9	8.6	8.8
Depr.	16.5	11.3	9.3	7.4	6.2	3.8	3.5	3.0	1.6	1.3
Int. Exp.	7.3	3.4	1.5	1.3	1.4	1.4	1.4	1.6	2.3	2.7
Pretax Inc.	23.5	10.9	20.4	13.7	11.1	9.8	6.5	7.1	5.8	5.0
Eff. Tax Rate	39%	38%	39%	38%	28%	23%	15%	19%	7.30%	6.20%
Net Inc.	14.1	6.7	12.5	8.5	8.0	7.5	5.6	5.7	5.4	4.0

Balance Sheet & Other Fin. Data (Million $)

Cash	0.4	5.1	8.7	2.9	1.7	12.0	9.2	6.1	6.3	3.8
Curr. Assets	91.7	53.3	47.9	27.9	19.8	19.9	18.1	17.1	15.9	10.5
Total Assets	333	165	140	96.8	79.4	68.9	53.0	47.7	45.1	33.4
Curr. Liab.	33.8	20.7	19.9	10.6	10.7	8.6	3.4	3.8	5.9	7.1
LT Debt	109	48.2	29.8	11.9	8.0	10.5	13.0	13.0	13.0	18.1
Common Eqty.	169	88.3	83.3	68.3	57.1	48.9	35.8	29.9	25.3	7.4
Total Cap.	289	142	119	85.0	68.1	60.3	49.6	44.0	39.3	26.3
Cap. Exp.	37.2	16.7	15.5	6.6	11.9	16.9	7.1	4.8	8.9	1.5
Cash Flow	30.6	18.0	21.8	15.8	14.2	11.3	9.1	8.8	6.9	5.3
Curr. Ratio	2.7	2.6	2.4	2.6	1.9	2.3	5.4	4.5	2.7	1.5
% LT Debt of Cap.	37.7	33.9	25.1	14.0	11.8	17.4	26.2	29.6	33.1	69.1
% Net Inc.of Revs.	4.2	3.2	8.9	8.4	10.8	12.4	11.4	10.5	14.5	8.6
% Ret. on Assets	5.7	4.4	10.5	9.5	10.9	12.0	11.0	12.4	12.2	11.0
% Ret. on Equity	11.0	7.8	16.5	13.3	15.1	17.2	17.0	20.8	30.9	73.1

Data as orig. reptd.; bef. results of disc. opers. and/or spec. items. Per share data adj. for stk. divs. as of ex-div. date. Bold denotes diluted EPS (FASB 128). E-Estimated. NA-Not Available. NM-Not Meaningful. NR-Not Ranked.

Office—5215 N. O'Connor Blvd., Suite 940, Irving, TX 75039. **Tel**—(972) 401-7200. **Chrmn & CEO**—D. V. Ingram. **Pres & COO**—R. L. Kerr. **EVP, CFO, Secy & Investor Contact**—Paul V. Dufour. **Dirs**—S. Bartlett, J. M. Brundrett, R. L. Cheek, J. J. Fleming, D. V. Ingram, D. Navarro, J. C. Page. **Transfer Agent & Registrar**—ChaseMellon Shareholder Services, Ridgefield Park, NJ.**Incorporated**—in 1985 in Delaware. **Empl**—1,586. **S&P Analyst:** C.F.B.

Immune Response   4233K

NASDAQ Symbol **IMNR**

In S&P SmallCap 600

10-OCT-98

Industry: Biotechnology

Summary: This company is developing immune-based therapies that induce T cell responses to treat HIV infection, autoimmune disease, and cancer.

Quantitative Evaluations	
Outlook (1 Lowest—5 Highest) • **NA**	
Fair Value • **NA**	
Risk • **High**	
Earn./Div. Rank • **C**	
Technical Eval. • **Bearish** since 7/98	
Rel. Strength Rank (1 Lowest—99 Highest) • **96**	
Insider Activity • **NA**	

Recent Price • 11½
52 Wk Range • 19⅝-7⅜

Yield • Nil
12-Mo. P/E • NM

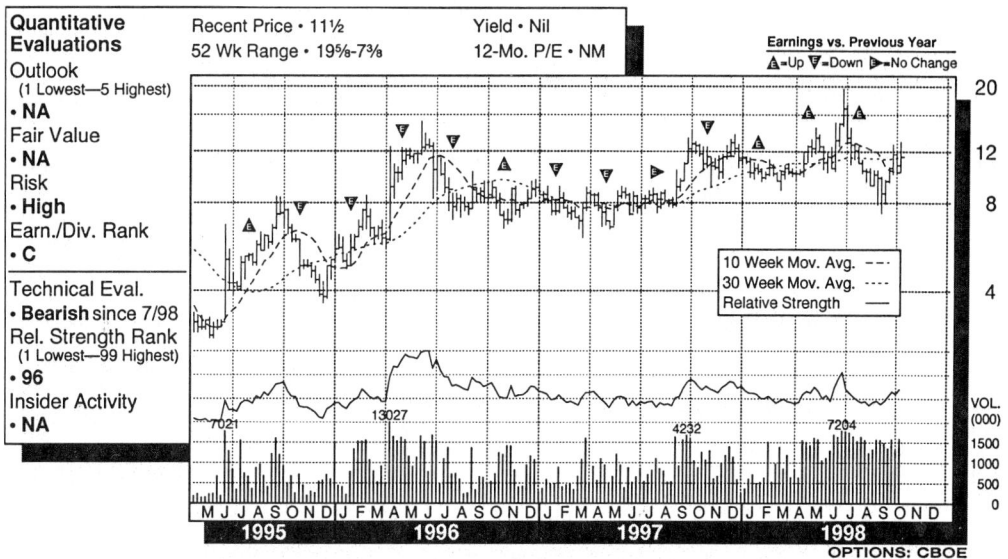

Earnings vs. Previous Year
▲=Up ▼=Down ▶=No Change

10 Week Mov. Avg. - - -
30 Week Mov. Avg. ·····
Relative Strength —

OPTIONS: CBOE

Business Profile - 16-SEP-98

This company has not recorded any product sales to date, and derives its revenues from contract research, licensing agreements and investment income. In June 1998, IMNR signed an agreement with Agouron Pharmaceuticals, Inc. (AGPH) under which Remune, the company's immune-based treatment for HIV infection, was licensed to AGPH for development and marketing rights. AGPH initially paid $10 million in fees and purchased $2 million of IMNR common shares, and will make quarterly payments for Remune's development. In July 1998, the company announced a research collaboration with Schering-Plough Corp. (SGP) to combine IMNR's GeneDrug gene delivery technology with SGP genes for treating hepatitis B and C, and other diseases. Under the initial agreement, IMNR could receive $5 million in fees, reimbursement expenses, and milestone payments.

Operational Review - 16-SEP-98

Revenues in the first half of 1998 increased to $11,667,000 from $1,000,000 the year before, due to initial licensed research revenue from an agreement with Agouron Pharmaceuticals. G&A costs rose 2.8%, while R&D expenditures declined 8.0% on lower clinical trial costs and changes in 1998 clinical trial payment schedules. Despite lower investment income, the net loss narrowed to $6,413,000 ($0.28 a share) from $17,916,000 ($0.85).

Stock Performance - 09-OCT-98

In the past 30 trading days, IMNR's shares have increased 18%, compared to a 4% fall in the S&P 500. Average trading volume for the past five days was 489,040 shares, compared with the 40-day moving average of 374,331 shares.

Key Stock Statistics

Dividend Rate/Share	Nil	Shareholders	1,000
Shs. outstg. (M)	23.2	Market cap. (B)	$0.267
Avg. daily vol. (M)	0.371	Inst. holdings	25%
Tang. Bk. Value/Share	1.32		
Beta	1.95		

Value of $10,000 invested 5 years ago: $ 5,974

Fiscal Year Ending Dec. 31

	1998	1997	1996	1995	1994	1993
Revenues (Million $)						
1Q	1.00	1.00	Nil	1.31	1.24	1.12
2Q	10.67	Nil	Nil	0.13	1.40	1.17
3Q	—	1.00	7.00	Nil	2.59	1.18
4Q	—	Nil	Nil	0.13	1.81	1.30
Yr.	—	2.00	7.00	1.56	7.03	4.77
Earnings Per Share ($)						
1Q	-0.35	-0.39	-0.33	-0.27	-0.28	-0.23
2Q	0.06	-0.45	-0.45	-0.26	-0.32	-0.26
3Q	—	-0.31	-0.01	-0.31	-0.20	-0.19
4Q	—	-0.38	-0.40	-0.35	-0.25	-0.27
Yr.	—	-1.53	-1.19	-1.19	-1.05	-0.95

Next earnings report expected: late October

Dividend Data

Cash dividends have never been paid, and the company does not expect to pay any for the foreseeable future.

Business Summary - 06-AUG-98

This world leader in diagnostic and detection systems for veterinary, food and environmental applications offers over 400 products to customers in more than 50 countries. IDXX operates in two primary business areas: veterinary products and services; and food, hygiene and environmental products and services. Products range from single-sample hand-held tests and sophisticated laboratory instrument systems, to veterinary practice management software.

In 1997, IDXX acquired Professionals' Software, Inc. and Advanced Veterinary Systems, leaders in the veterinary practice management software business. Through these acquisitions, the company has become the leading U.S. supplier of veterinary practice management software systems. As of December 1997, IDXX software was installed in more than 8,000 clinics in the U.S.

A majority of the company's revenues are derived from animal health diagnostic products and services, provided through its Professional Office Diagnostics Division (POD). Diagnostic testing for animal health purposes includes the detection and monitoring of diseases, physiologic disorders, immune status, hormone and enzyme levels, blood chemistry, electrolyte levels and other conditions. Approximately 57% and 73% of the company's total revenues were derived from sales of POD products in 1997 and 1996, respectively.

IDXX's food, hygiene and environmental testing products are used to detect contaminants, residues and toxins in various types of food, food processing plants, water, and other environments. The company believes that growth for these types of test products will be spurred by the trend toward total quality control in manufacturing processes, which is resulting in more intensive testing of food, food processing environments and other environmental conditions. Commercial test kits can also be easier to use, provide quicker test results and offer potential cost savings.

Veterinary Services was formed in 1996 when it acquired veterinary service companies located in Texas and California and combined them with the company's consulting service known as Cardiopet, Inc. In the U.S., IDXX Veterinary Services currently offers commercial veterinary and laboratory services to approximately 4,500 clinics through facilities located in eight states. Through subsidiaries in the U.K., Japan and Australia, the company offers these services to 4,000 clinics in these countries.

Customers include veterinarians, animal health laboratory managers and technicians, government laboratory officials, quality control personnel, food producers and water laboratory personnel. The company markets, sells and services its products worldwide through its own marketing, sales and technical services group, as well as through independent distributors and other re-sellers. International sales accounted for 32% of the total in 1997.

Per Share Data ($)

(Year Ended Dec. 31)	1997	1996	1995	1994	1993	1992	1991	1990	1989	1988
Tangible Bk. Val.	6.60	7.79	7.32	2.90	2.40	2.17	1.53	NA	NA	NA
Cash Flow	-0.18	1.09	0.77	0.53	0.41	0.29	NA	NA	NA	NA
Earnings	-0.56	0.83	0.61	0.40	0.29	0.17	0.15	NA	NA	NA
Dividends	Nil	Nil	Nil	Nil	Nil	Nil	Nil	Nil	Nil	Nil
Payout Ratio	Nil	Nil	Nil	Nil	Nil	Nil	Nil	Nil	Nil	Nil
Prices - High	38¹/₂	53³/₄	47¹/₂	18⁵/₈	16	8¹/₄	7¹/₄	NA	NA	NA
- Low	9¹/₄	26⁷/₈	16⁷/₈	12⁵/₈	6⁵/₈	4¹/₂	3³/₈	NA	NA	NA
P/E Ratio - High	NM	65	78	47	55	47	48	NA	NA	NA
- Low	NM	32	28	32	23	32	22	NA	NA	NA

Income Statement Analysis (Million $)

	1997	1996	1995	1994	1993	1992	1991	1990	1989	1988
Revs.	263	268	189	126	93.0	61.0	29.0	NA	NA	NA
Oper. Inc.	10.0	57.4	38.7	27.2	18.4	9.6	NA	NA	NA	NA
Depr.	14.4	10.4	5.7	4.5	3.8	3.6	NA	NA	NA	NA
Int. Exp.	Nil	Nil	Nil	Nil	Nil	Nil	Nil	Nil	Nil	Nil
Pretax Inc.	-32.3	55.3	37.0	22.8	15.0	7.0	3.3	NA	NA	NA
Eff. Tax Rate	NM	41%	42%	42%	36%	22%	10%	NA	NA	NA
Net Inc.	-21.1	32.6	21.5	13.3	9.7	5.4	3.0	NA	NA	NA

Balance Sheet & Other Fin. Data (Million $)

	1997	1996	1995	1994	1993	1992	1991	1990	1989	1988
Cash	107	174	184	50.4	39.4	NA	NA	NA	NA	NA
Curr. Assets	274	302	202	99	76.8	NA	NA	NA	NA	NA
Total Assets	377	374	313	122	98.0	83.0	NA	NA	NA	NA
Curr. Liab.	74.3	51.1	33.4	22.0	14.3	NA	NA	NA	NA	NA
LT Debt	Nil	Nil	Nil	Nil	Nil	Nil	Nil	Nil	Nil	Nil
Common Eqty.	303	323	279	100	83.6	71.7	NA	NA	NA	NA
Total Cap.	303	323	279	100	83.6	71.7	NA	NA	NA	NA
Cap. Exp.	12.5	11.8	15.9	4.4	2.1	2.4	NA	NA	NA	NA
Cash Flow	-6.7	43.0	27.2	17.9	13.4	9.0	NA	NA	NA	NA
Curr. Ratio	3.7	5.9	7.8	4.5	5.4	NA	NA	NA	NA	NA
% LT Debt of Cap.	Nil	Nil	Nil	Nil	Nil	Nil	Nil	Nil	Nil	Nil
% Net Inc.of Revs.	NM	12.2	11.4	10.6	10.4	8.8	10.6	NA	NA	NA
% Ret. on Assets	NM	9.6	9.9	12.1	10.7	8.9	NA	NA	NA	NA
% Ret. on Equity	NM	10.9	11.3	14.5	12.4	10.4	NA	NA	NA	NA

Data as orig. reptd.; bef. results of disc. opers. and/or spec. items. Per share data adj. for stk. divs. as of ex-div. date. Bold denotes diluted EPS (FASB 128). E-Estimated. NA-Not Available. NM-Not Meaningful. NR-Not Ranked.

Office—One IDEXX Dr., Westbrook, ME 04092. **Tel**—(207) 856-0300. **Fax**—(207) 856-0347. **Website**—http//:www.idexx.com **Chrmn & CEO**—D. E. Shaw. **SVP & CFO**—R. K. Carlton. **Pres & COO**—J.J. Langan **Secy**—R. B. Thorp.**VP-Fin, Treas & Investor Contact**—Merilee Raines. **Dirs**—M. L. Good, J. R. Hesse, E. R. Kinney, J. J. Langan, J. L. Moody Jr., K. Paigen, W. F. Pounds, D. E. Shaw, E. F. Workman Jr. **Transfer Agent & Registrar**—First National Bank of Boston. **Incorporated**—in Delaware in 1983. **Empl**— 2,100. **S&P Analyst:** John J. Arege

Business Summary - 16-SEP-98

The Immune Response Corp. (IMNR) has proprietary technologies in four therapeutic areas: Human Immunodeficiency Virus (HIV), autoimmune disease, gene therapy and cancer.

Remune, IMNR's most advanced therapy in clinical trials, is designed to stimulate natural defense mechanisms in HIV-infected individuals. Remune is composed of inactivated HIV, which elicits a potent immune response in individuals. IMNR believes that Remune has been shown to be safe and well tolerated, and is an appropriate treatment for HIV-infected individuals taken alone or in combination with other antiviral HIV therapies.

In March 1996, IMNR began a Phase III clinical trial for Remune, with an enrollment of 2,500 HIV-infected individuals at 74 sites around the U.S. The company anticipates the trial will conclude in the second quarter of 1999. Additional clinical trials for Remune are being conducted in Thailand (Phase II); Spain, Switzerland, and the U.K. (Phase II trials in combination with antivirals); and in the U.S. (Phase I pediatric trial). In February 1997, IMNR began a 32-week Phase II trial using Remune in combination with AZT, 3TC and Crixivan, designed to examine the potential synergy between triple antiviral drug therapy and Remune.

In June 1998, IMNR signed an agreement with Agouron Pharmaceuticals, Inc. (AGPH), under which Remune was licensed to AGPH for development and exclusive marketing rights in North America, Europe and certain other countries.

IMNR's autoimmune disease treatments are designed to inhibit the autoreactive T cells that IMNR believes cause the tissue damage in certain autoimmune conditions. In August 1998, the company initiated a long term follow-up clinical trial for IR501, IMNR's therapy for rheumatoid arthritis, to evaluate long-term safety and activity, while allowing Phase IIb patients to extend treatment. IMNR is conducting a second Phase II trial for IR502 (to treat psoriasis), and has completed a Phase I clinical trial for IR208 (to treat multiple sclerosis), both of which, have yielded promising results.

The company is using its immune-based vaccine technology in combination with molecular gene therapy to develop cancer treatments, which enable the immune system to recognize and control tumor growth. IMNR is conducting preclinical research on its prostate cancer therapy, has initiated Phase I trials for its colon cancer treatment, and has filed an IND to begin trials for its brain tumor treatment.

The company's GeneDrug products are based on a patented gene delivery technology, which enables the targeted delivery of gene products to liver cells. In 1996, IMNR entered into an agreement with Bayer AG to develop gene therapy products to treat hemophilia A. In July 1998, the company announced a research collaboration with Schering-Plough Corp. (SGP) to combine IMNR's gene delivery technology with SGP genes to treat hepatitis B and C, and other diseases.

Per Share Data ($) (Year Ended Dec. 31)	1997	1996	1995	1994	1993	1992	1991	1990	1989	1988
Tangible Bk. Val.	1.54	2.54	2.89	4.01	5.13	6.09	7.10	2.90	-1.24	NA
Cash Flow	-1.48	-1.14	-1.13	-0.97	-0.88	-2.15	-0.20	-0.12	-0.62	-0.35
Earnings	-1.53	-1.19	-1.19	-1.05	-0.95	-2.19	-0.23	-0.12	-0.63	-0.35
Dividends	Nil	Nil	Nil	Nil	Nil	Nil	Nil	Nil	Nil	Nil
Payout Ratio	Nil	Nil	Nil	Nil	Nil	Nil	Nil	Nil	Nil	Nil
Prices - High	14 1/4	15 1/4	8 3/8	13 3/4	28 1/2	47 1/4	62 3/4	7 3/8	NA	NA
- Low	6	4 3/4	2 5/8	5 3/8	9 1/4	12 1/4	2 7/8	2 3/4	NA	NA
P/E Ratio - High	NM	NM	NM	NM	NM	NM	NM	NM	NM	NM
- Low	NM	NM	NM	NM	NM	NM	NM	NM	NM	NM
Income Statement Analysis (Million $)										
Revs.	2.0	7.0	1.6	7.0	4.8	4.0	4.3	4.3	3.3	1.2
Oper. Inc.	-34.7	-22.8	-20.6	-10.8	-10.0	-6.5	-4.1	-1.7	-1.8	-1.4
Depr.	1.3	0.8	1.0	1.3	1.2	0.6	0.4	0.1	0.1	0.0
Int. Exp.	Nil	Nil	Nil	NA	NA	Nil	Nil	Nil	Nil	Nil
Pretax Inc.	-33.6	-21.0	-19.9	-17.4	-15.7	-33.8	-3.0	-1.2	-4.7	-1.9
Eff. Tax Rate	NM	NM	NM	NM	NM	NM	Nil	Nil	Nil	Nil
Net Inc.	-33.6	-21.0	-19.9	-17.4	-15.7	-33.8	-3.0	-1.2	-4.7	-1.9
Balance Sheet & Other Fin. Data (Million $)										
Cash	30.4	47.8	44.6	59.0	75.0	90.0	104	25.0	7.0	NA
Curr. Assets	31.2	48.5	45.6	61.0	77.0	93.0	106	28.0	9.0	NA
Total Assets	37.4	54.1	50.4	68.0	87.0	103	110	33.0	10.0	NA
Curr. Liab.	2.3	2.8	2.0	1.4	1.5	2.0	1.4	0.7	0.4	NA
LT Debt	Nil	Nil	Nil	Nil	0.3	0.5	Nil	Nil	Nil	Nil
Common Eqty.	35.1	51.3	48.4	67.0	85.0	101	108	32.0	-6.0	NA
Total Cap.	35.1	51.3	48.4	67.0	85.0	101	108	32.0	10.0	NA
Cap. Exp.	2.5	1.6	0.4	0.8	0.9	4.2	0.7	2.9	0.0	0.4
Cash Flow	-32.3	-20.2	-18.9	-16.1	-14.6	-33.1	-2.6	-1.2	-4.6	-1.9
Curr. Ratio	13.7	17.4	22.9	43.4	50.8	45.9	74.1	40.8	23.7	NA
% LT Debt of Cap.	Nil	Nil	Nil	Nil	0.3	0.5	Nil	Nil	Nil	Nil
% Net Inc.of Revs.	NM	NM	NM	NM	NM	NM	NM	NM	NM	NM
% Ret. on Assets	NM	NM	NM	NM	NM	NM	NM	NM	NM	NM
% Ret. on Equity	NM	NM	NM	NM	NM	NM	NM	NM	NM	NM

Data as orig. reptd.; bef. results of disc. opers. and/or spec. items. Per share data adj. for stk. divs. as of ex-div. date. Bold denotes diluted EPS (FASB 128). E-Estimated. NA-Not Available. NM-Not Meaningful. NR-Not Ranked.

Office—5935 Darwin Ct., Carlsbad, CA 92008. **Tel**—(619) 431-7080. **Fax**—(619) 431-8636. **Website**—http://www.imnr.com **Chrmn**—J. B. Glavin. **Pres & CEO**—D. J. Carlo. **COO**—S. P. Richieri. **SVP-Fin, CFO, Secy & Treas**—C. J. Cashion. **Investor Contact**—Debra L. Altman. **Dirs**—D. J. Carlo, J. B. Glavin, K. B. Kimberlin, G. S. Omenn, M. Perelman, J. Simon, W. M. Sullivan, P. M. Young. **Transfer Agent & Registrar**—First Interstate Bank, LA. **Incorporated**—in Delaware in 1986. **Empl**— 143. **S&P Analyst:** David Moskowitz

STANDARD &POOR'S
STOCK REPORTS

Incyte Pharmaceuticals   4233X
NASDAQ Symbol **INCY**

In S&P SmallCap 600

10-OCT-98

Industry: Biotechnology

Summary: This company is a leading provider of an integrated platform of genomic technologies designed to aid in the understanding of the molecular basis of disease.

Quantitative Evaluations

Recent Price • 25
52 Wk Range • 51-17⅜

Yield • Nil
12-Mo. P/E • 37.9

Outlook (1 Lowest—5 Highest)
• **3⁻**

Fair Value
• **27⅛**

Risk
• **High**

Earn./Div. Rank
• **NR**

Technical Eval.
• **NA**

Rel. Strength Rank (1 Lowest—99 Highest)
• **77**

Insider Activity
• **NA**

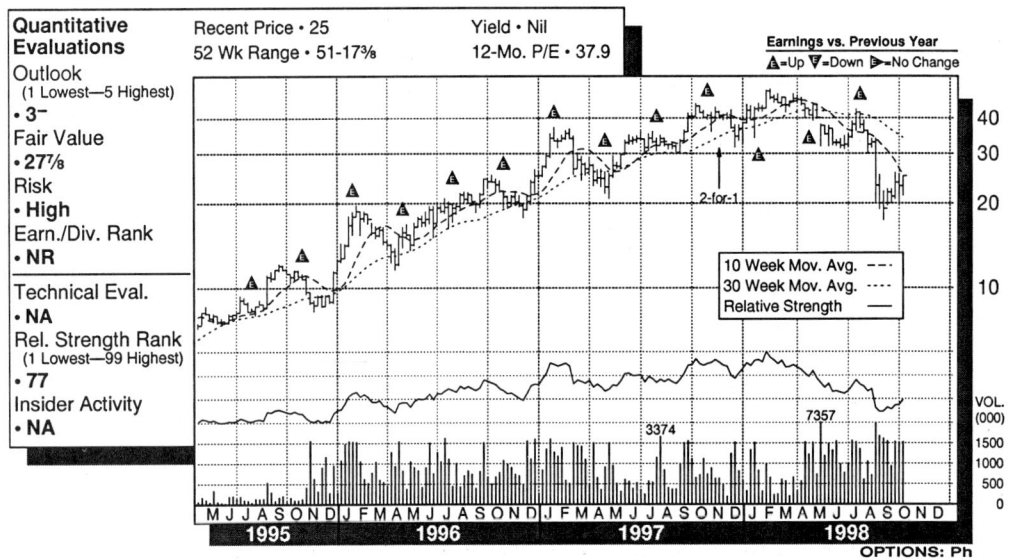

Earnings vs. Previous Year
▲=Up ▼=Down ▶=No Change

10 Week Mov. Avg. ---
30 Week Mov. Avg. ····
Relative Strength —

OPTIONS: Ph

Business Profile - 05-OCT-98

The company's genomic products and services are designed to meet the needs of the pharmaceutical and biotechnology industries to use genomic information for the acceleration of the discovery and development of new diagnostic and therapeutic products. Incyte has made substantial investments in research and technology development since its inception in 1991, and is currently evaluating new technologies relating to tissue processing, DNA amplification, microarray production, advanced automated sequencing and expression profiling to expand the productivity, efficiency and quality of its database products.

Operational Review - 05-OCT-98

Revenues in the first half of 1998 advanced 61%, year to year, reflecting new and expanded collaborative database agreements. Total expenses were up 46%, mainly on higher research and development costs and $1.2 million of acquisition-related charges. After sharply higher other income (net), and taxes at 14.0%, versus 8.4%, net income increased to $8,773,000 ($0.30 a share) from $1,728,000 ($0.07, as restated).

Stock Performance - 09-OCT-98

In the past 30 trading days, INCY's shares have increased 25%, compared to a 4% fall in the S&P 500. Average trading volume for the past five days was 352,340 shares, compared with the 40-day moving average of 550,621 shares.

Key Stock Statistics

Dividend Rate/Share	Nil	Shareholders	200
Shs. outstg. (M)	26.7	Market cap. (B)	$0.667
Avg. daily vol. (M)	0.310	Inst. holdings	64%
Tang. Bk. Value/Share	6.07		
Beta	NA		

Value of $10,000 invested 5 years ago: NA

Fiscal Year Ending Dec. 31

	1998	1997	1996	1995	1994	1993
Revenues (Million $)						
1Q	30.38	17.86	5.58	1.48	Nil	0.28
2Q	33.09	21.19	7.63	1.95	Nil	Nil
3Q	Nil	22.66	12.92	2.26	Nil	Nil
4Q	Nil	26.64	14.18	4.21	0.24	Nil
Yr.	Nil	88.35	41.79	9.91	0.24	0.28
Earnings Per Share ($)						
1Q	0.12	0.05	-0.10	-0.13	-0.17	0.23
2Q	0.18	0.09	-0.08	-0.18	-0.20	-0.32
3Q	—	0.13	-0.17	-0.19	-0.21	-0.41
4Q	—	0.17	0.01	-0.13	-0.26	-0.17
Yr.	—	0.43	-0.33	-0.62	-0.84	-1.13

Next earnings report expected: mid October

Dividend Data

No cash dividends have been paid, and the company does not anticipate paying any in the foreseeable future.

Business Summary - 05-OCT-98

A leading provider of an integrated platform of genomic technologies designed to aid in the understanding of the molecular basis of disease, Incyte Pharmaceuticals, Inc. designs, develops and markets genomic database products, genomic data management software tools and related reagents and services to the biotechnology, pharmaceutical and agricultural industries. In building its databases, the company uses high-throughput, computer-aided gene sequencing and analysis technologies to identify and characterize the expressed genes of the human genome, as well as certain animal, plant and microbial genomes.

The company provides access to its genomic databases through collaborations with companies worldwide. By searching the genomic databases, collaborators can integrate and analyze genetic information from multiple sources in order to discover genes that may represent the basis for new biological targets, therapeutic proteins, or gene therapy, antisense or diagnostic products. The company's products and services assist with gene and target discovery, as well as with functional genomic studies, preclinical pharmacology and toxicology studies and understanding and analyzing the results of clinical development studies.

Incyte's portfolio of database modules includes the LifeSeq human gene sequence and expression database, the LifeSeq FL database of full-length human genes, the LifeSeq Atlas mapping database, the PathoSeq microbial genomic database, the ZooSeq animal genomic database, the LifeTools suite of bioinformatics software programs, LifeSeq 3D data mining and visualization software, and a variety of custom database and sequencing services.

The company also offers a variety of DNA clone and other services designed to assist its collaborators in using information from its database in internal lab-based experiments. In addition, it produces a broad line of genomic research products, such as DNA clones and insert libraries, and offers technical support services including high-throughput DNA screening, custom robotic services, contract DNA preparation, and fluorescent in-situ hybridization, to assist researchers in the identification and isolation of novel genes.

As of 1997 year end, Incyte had entered into database collaboration agreements with 19 companies, including Abbott Laboratories, Monsanto, Bristol-Myers Squibb, Eli Lilly, Pfizer, Glaxo Wellcome, Johnson & Johnson, Pharmacia & Upjohn, Rhone-Poulenc, Schering and SmithKline Beecham.

In September 1998, the company acquired privately-held Hexagen Limited, which has developed leading edge technology for rapid discovery of single nucleotide polymorphisms, for $5 million in cash and 976,130 common shares.

Per Share Data ($)

(Year Ended Dec. 31)	1997	1996	1995	1994	1993	1992	1991	1990	1989	1988
Tangible Bk. Val.	6.07	2.16	2.39	1.51	1.26	NA	NA	NA	NA	NA
Cash Flow	0.86	-0.01	-0.46	-0.77	-1.03	-0.23	NA	NA	NA	NA
Earnings	0.43	-0.33	-0.62	-0.84	-1.13	-0.24	NA	NA	NA	NA
Dividends	Nil	Nil	Nil	Nil	Nil	Nil	Nil	Nil	Nil	Nil
Payout Ratio	Nil	Nil	Nil	Nil	Nil	Nil	Nil	Nil	Nil	Nil
Prices - High	45¼	26½	12⅝	8⅛	6	NA	NA	NA	NA	NA
- Low	20¾	11⅝	6½	3⅜	3¾	NA	NA	NA	NA	NA
P/E Ratio - High	NM	NM	NM	NM	NM	NA	NA	NA	NA	NA
- Low	NM	NM	NM	NM	NM	NA	NA	NA	NA	NA

Income Statement Analysis (Million $)

	1997	1996	1995	1994	1993	1992	1991	1990	1989	1988
Revs.	88.4	41.8	9.9	0.2	0.3	1.6	0.3	NA	NA	NA
Oper. Inc.	17.7	-2.6	-8.6	-11.1	-4.5	-1.9	-1.4	NA	NA	NA
Depr.	10.4	6.5	2.6	0.9	0.4	0.2	0.1	NA	NA	NA
Int. Exp.	0.2	0.2	0.1	0.2	0.1	0.0	Nil	Nil	Nil	Nil
Pretax Inc.	11.0	-6.8	-10.1	-11.5	-4.9	-2.1	-1.4	NA	NA	NA
Eff. Tax Rate	5.00%	NM	NM	NM	NM	Nil	Nil	Nil	Nil	Nil
Net Inc.	10.4	-6.8	-10.1	-11.5	-4.9	-2.1	-1.4	NA	NA	NA

Balance Sheet & Other Fin. Data (Million $)

	1997	1996	1995	1994	1993	1992	1991	1990	1989	1988
Cash	57.2	7.6	10.4	6.8	15.5	4.8	1.6	NA	NA	NA
Curr. Assets	138	43.2	49.0	25.3	15.7	5.5	2.0	NA	NA	NA
Total Assets	193	66.9	57.8	28.7	17.6	6.8	2.5	NA	NA	NA
Curr. Liab.	46.6	21.1	10.4	4.6	1.0	0.6	0.5	NA	NA	NA
LT Debt	Nil	Nil	0.0	0.1	0.5	0.4	Nil	Nil	Nil	Nil
Common Eqty.	146	45.2	46.8	24.0	16.1	5.9	2.0	NA	NA	NA
Total Cap.	146	45.2	46.9	24.1	16.6	6.2	2.0	NA	NA	NA
Cap. Exp.	26.1	20.2	7.9	2.6	0.4	0.4	0.6	NA	NA	NA
Cash Flow	20.8	-0.3	-7.6	-10.6	-4.5	-1.9	-1.4	NA	NA	NA
Curr. Ratio	3.0	2.0	4.7	5.5	16.2	9.2	3.8	NA	NA	NA
% LT Debt of Cap.	Nil	Nil	0.0	0.4	3.1	6.0	Nil	Nil	Nil	Nil
% Net Inc.of Revs.	11.8	NM	NM	NM	NM	NM	NM	NM	NM	NM
% Ret. on Assets	8.0	NM	NM	NM	NM	NM	NM	NM	NM	NM
% Ret. on Equity	10.9	NM	NM	NM	NM	NM	NM	NM	NM	NM

Data as orig. reptd.; bef. results of disc. opers. and/or spec. items. Per share data adj. for stk. divs. as of ex-div. date. Bold denotes diluted EPS (FASB 128). E-Estimated. NA-Not Available. NM-Not Meaningful. NR-Not Ranked.

Office—3174 Porter Dr., Palo Alto, CA 94304. **Tel**—(650) 855-0555. **Website**—http://www.incyte.com **Chrmn**—J. J. Collinson. **CEO**—R. A. Whitfield. **EVP-Fin & CFO**—D. M. Gilbert. **Dirs**—B. M. Bloom, J. J. Collinson, F. B. Craves, J. S. Saxe, R. W. Scott, R. A. Whitfield. **Transfer Agent & Registrar**—ChaseMellon Shareholder Services, San Francisco. **Incorporated**—in Delaware in 1991. **Empl**— 676. **S&P Analyst:** SRB

Innovex, Inc.

4248G

Nasdaq Symbol **INVX**

In S&P SmallCap 600

03-OCT-98

Industry: Computers (Peripherals)

Summary: This company manufactures lead wire assemblies for the disk drive industry and other high precision electrical components.

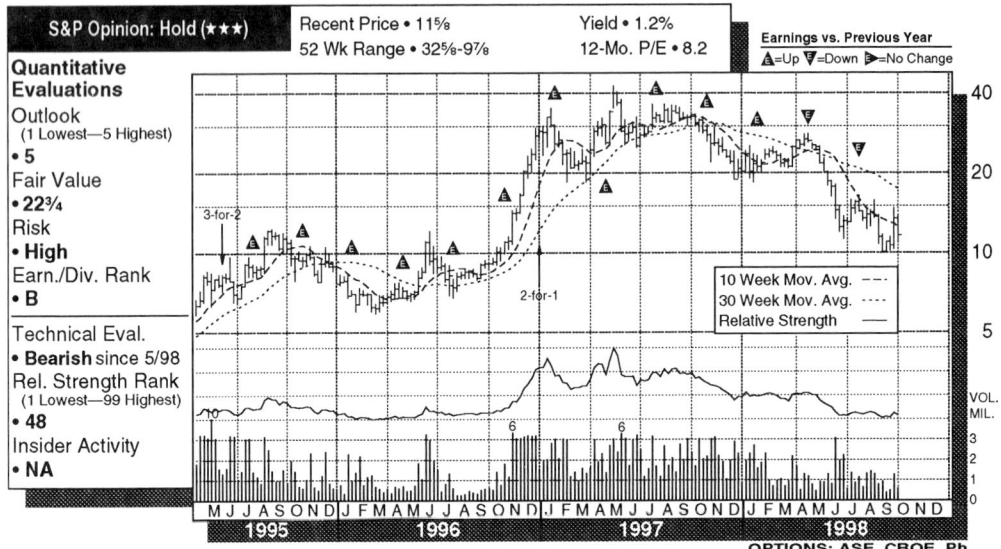

S&P Opinion: Hold (★★★)	Recent Price • 11⅝	Yield • 1.2%
	52 Wk Range • 32⅝-9⅞	12-Mo. P/E • 8.2

Quantitative Evaluations

Outlook (1 Lowest—5 Highest)
• **5**

Fair Value
• **22¾**

Risk
• **High**

Earn./Div. Rank
• **B**

Technical Eval.
• **Bearish** since 5/98

Rel. Strength Rank (1 Lowest—99 Highest)
• **48**

Insider Activity
• **NA**

Earnings vs. Previous Year
▲=Up ▼=Down ▶=No Change

10 Week Mov. Avg. – – –
30 Week Mov. Avg. ·····
Relative Strength ——

3-for-2

2-for-1

VOL. MIL.

OPTIONS: ASE, CBOE, Ph

Overview - 15-SEP-98

Revenues in the nine months ended June 30, 1998, fell 29% from the corresponding year-earlier level. Overcapacity and excess inventories at the company's customers in the disk drive industry have continued to hurt orders. Earnings declined 49% to $0.92 a diluted share from $1.81, reflecting lower margins due to decreased unit volumes and start-up costs related to INVX's new high volume flexible circuit production facility. While we previously had looked for a rebound in orders some time in late 1998 or early 1999, signs of a recovery remain illusive. We cut our earnings estimates further in September, and now expect $1.12 for FY 98 (Sep.). Tentatively, we think the PC industry may recover in mid-FY 99, and INVX's earnings will rebound to $1.45 a share.

Valuation - 15-SEP-98

Our view that INVX is only a market performer has not changed since we upgraded our opinion in late spring from avoid after a sharp decline in the stock price. Further improvement in the recommendation is predicated on conditions in the parts and components supply channel for the PC industry, specifically the disk drive industry. Global economic conditions do not appear to be supportive of a resumption of more normal industry conditions; as such, there remains considerable uncertainty as to the timing of the industry rebound. Our view, which we first stated earlier this year, that it would take longer for conditions to get better, now appears to be more likely than the case for an early fall turnaround. Still, with most of the bad news already reflected in the stock price, we don't think there is much downside at this point.

Key Stock Statistics

S&P EPS Est. 1998	1.12	Tang. Bk. Value/Share	6.65
P/E on S&P Est. 1998	10.4	Beta	1.15
S&P EPS Est. 1999	1.45	Shareholders	600
Dividend Rate/Share	0.14	Market cap. (B)	$0.172
Shs. outstg. (M)	14.8	Inst. holdings	26%
Avg. daily vol. (M)	0.139		

Value of $10,000 invested 5 years ago: $ 70,335

Fiscal Year Ending Sep. 30

	1998	1997	1996	1995	1994	1993
Revenues (Million $)						
1Q	33.01	29.31	13.11	9.98	5.66	5.87
2Q	25.11	38.39	14.67	11.69	6.45	7.10
3Q	20.30	41.96	19.25	14.03	8.44	7.15
4Q	—	32.34	22.53	14.50	10.01	6.48
Yr.	—	142.0	69.57	50.19	30.56	26.60
Earnings Per Share ($)						
1Q	**0.48**	0.42	0.19	0.12	0.04	0.06
2Q	**0.28**	0.66	0.20	0.15	0.04	0.08
3Q	**0.16**	0.72	0.24	0.20	0.07	0.08
4Q	**E0.20**	0.51	0.27	0.23	0.11	0.05
Yr.	**E1.12**	2.31	0.90	0.70	0.26	0.27

Next earnings report expected: early November

Dividend Data (Dividends have been paid since 1993.)

Amount ($)	Date Decl.	Ex-Div. Date	Stock of Record	Payment Date
0.030	Oct. 23	Nov. 07	Nov. 12	Nov. 26 '97
0.035	Jan. 29	Feb. 09	Feb. 11	Feb. 25 '98
0.035	Apr. 30	May. 11	May. 13	May. 27 '98
0.035	Aug. 03	Aug. 10	Aug. 12	Aug. 26 '98

A Division of The McGraw-Hill Companies

Innovex, Inc.

Business Summary - 15-SEP-98

Innovex, Inc. designs, develops and manufactures specialty components, primarily lead wire assemblies, for the disk drive industry. In May 1996, INVX acquired privately held Litchfield Precision Components, Inc., a designer and manufacturer of intricate flexible circuitry, chemically machined parts, and film and optical components. After operating as a separate division since being acquired, in July 1998, Litchfield was consolidated with INVX's main Precision Products division as part of a strategy to combine core competencies in high volume precision manufacturing, flexible circuitry, and chemical etching, to the disk drive market and the emerging chip packaging and medical applications markets. The company also makes pacemaker lead wires and other medical devices, and software for document storage retrieval and management.

The company produces a variety of small, thin-wire computer subassemblies that often involve specialized tasks and cannot be economically produced by its customers. Products are manufactured according to individual customer orders and specifications. Lead assembly sales constituted 80% of consolidated revenues from continuing operations in the past three fiscal years.

Ramp up of a newly constructed flexible circuit production facility is expected to gain momentum as the disk drive industry transitions to using integrated lead suspensions. It also affords the company an opportunity to diversify into other product areas which use high end flexible circuits with line and spacing tolerances of less than two mils.

On June 1, 1998, the company sold nearly all the assets of its Innomedica medical products division. Terms were not disclosed for the transaction. The division never achieved the profitability which management had hoped for and we believe it no longer fit into the company's future growth plans.

In November 1993, Innovex bought from Syntactic Analyzer, Inc. and ZH Computer, Inc. a technologically advanced software product line for preparing indexes and abstracts of documents stored in computer hard drives and CD-ROM systems, for $835,000. A new wholly owned subsidiary, Iconovex, currently handles the software business. In April 1995, AnchorPage, an automatic hypertext software program for use with the Internet, was unveiled. In October 1997, Iconovex became the 51% owner of Smart Solution, a joint venture with Solutions Corp. of America, which intends to target the corporate intranet market with a product to manage email and eventually perform the same functions for corporate databases.

Exports, principally to Pacific Rim customers, accounted for 86% of net sales in FY 97, up from 74% in FY 96. Often these accounts are with the foreign operations of U.S. based companies. Five customers accounted for 84% of total revenues in FY 97, up from 82% in FY 96 and FY 95.

Per Share Data ($)

(Year Ended Sep. 30)	1997	1996	1995	1994	1993	1992	1991	1990	1989	1988
Tangible Bk. Val.	5.81	6.48	2.55	1.82	1.65	1.42	1.41	1.36	1.23	1.15
Cash Flow	2.66	1.94	0.92	0.40	0.37	0.96	0.14	0.20	0.14	0.19
Earnings	2.31	0.91	0.70	0.26	0.27	0.06	0.05	0.13	0.08	0.13
Dividends	0.11	0.09	0.08	0.07	0.07	Nil	Nil	Nil	Nil	Nil
Payout Ratio	5%	10%	11%	28%	24%	Nil	Nil	Nil	Nil	Nil
Prices - High	42⁷/₈	30¹/₄	12³/₈	5⁵/₈	4¹/₂	1³/₄	1¹³/₁₆	1⁹/₁₆	1⁵/₈	1¹⁵/₁₆
- Low	18¹/₂	5⁷/₈	4³/₄	2¹/₂	1¹¹/₁₆	¹⁵/₁₆	¹³/₁₆	1	1	1¹/₈
P/E Ratio - High	19	34	18	21	16	31	37	12	19	14
- Low	8	6	7	10	6	16	17	8	12	9

Income Statement Analysis (Million $)

	1997	1996	1995	1994	1993	1992	1991	1990	1989	1988
Revs.	142	69.6	50.1	30.6	26.6	35.2	35.0	34.4	28.2	26.0
Oper. Inc.	53.5	22.0	17.4	6.9	6.7	3.4	2.0	3.7	2.2	3.2
Depr.	4.9	3.6	3.1	2.0	1.3	1.4	1.1	1.0	0.8	0.7
Int. Exp.	0.1	0.1	0.1	0.1	0.1	0.1	0.1	0.1	0.1	0.1
Pretax Inc.	50.0	18.7	14.8	5.2	5.5	1.1	0.8	2.5	1.7	2.7
Eff. Tax Rate	30%	30%	32%	32%	34%	33%	18%	34%	35%	32%
Net Inc.	35.1	13.1	10.0	3.5	3.7	0.8	0.7	1.7	1.1	1.8

Balance Sheet & Other Fin. Data (Million $)

	1997	1996	1995	1994	1993	1992	1991	1990	1989	1988
Cash	37.9	21.8	22.4	13.1	9.5	4.2	2.9	2.6	1.8	2.4
Curr. Assets	71.3	42.0	32.2	21.0	19.2	18.1	15.8	16.4	14.9	13.5
Total Assets	97.3	58.2	41.2	29.9	26.6	25.2	22.9	22.5	20.4	18.7
Curr. Liab.	9.5	8.5	3.9	3.4	2.2	5.2	3.0	3.2	3.4	2.6
LT Debt	0.9	1.1	1.2	1.5	1.9	0.9	1.0	1.1	0.6	0.7
Common Eqty.	86.8	48.4	36.0	24.7	22.2	18.7	18.6	17.9	16.2	15.2
Total Cap.	87.8	49.5	37.2	26.6	24.4	20.0	19.9	19.3	17.0	16.0
Cap. Exp.	15.6	4.2	3.0	1.8	4.0	1.9	2.3	2.0	0.9	1.4
Cash Flow	40.0	14.0	13.1	5.5	4.9	2.2	1.8	2.6	1.9	2.5
Curr. Ratio	7.5	5.0	8.3	6.2	8.7	3.5	5.2	5.1	4.4	5.1
% LT Debt of Cap.	1.1	2.2	3.1	5.8	7.7	4.5	5.2	6.0	3.6	4.1
% Net Inc.of Revs.	24.7	18.9	20.0	11.5	13.7	2.1	1.9	4.8	3.9	7.0
% Ret. on Assets	45.1	26.4	28.1	12.4	14.0	3.1	2.9	7.8	5.6	9.5
% Ret. on Equity	51.9	31.1	32.9	14.9	17.7	4.0	3.6	9.8	6.9	12.7

Data as orig. reptd.; bef. results of disc. opers. and/or spec. items. Per share data adj. for stk. divs. as of ex-div. date. Bold denotes diluted EPS (FASB 128). E-Estimated. NA-Not Available. NM-Not Meaningful. NR-Not Ranked.

Office—1313 S. Fifth St., Hopkins, MN 55343-9904. Tel—(612) 938-4155. Website—http://www.innovexinc.com Chrmn & CEO—T. W. Haley. Pres & COO—W. P. Murnane. VP-Fin—D. W. Keller. Dirs—G. M. Bestler, M. E. Curtin, W. K. Drake, T. W. Haley, W. J. Miller, M. C. Slagle, B. M\. Tessem. Transfer Agent & Registrar—Norwest Bank Minnesota, South St. Paul. Incorporated—in Minnesota in 1972. Empl— 893. S&P Analyst: Mark S. Basham

STANDARD &POOR'S
STOCK REPORTS

Input/Output, Inc.

1198L

NYSE Symbol **IO**

In S&P SmallCap 600

03-OCT-98

Industry:
Oil & Gas (Drilling & Equipment)

Summary: This company designs and manufactures seismic data acquisition products used in land and marine environments.

S&P Opinion: Hold (★★★)	Recent Price • 7⅝	Yield • Nil	Earnings vs. Previous Year
	52 Wk Range • 32⅞-7⅜	12-Mo. P/E • 7.1	▲=Up ▼=Down ▶=No Change

Quantitative Evaluations

Outlook
(1 Lowest—5 Highest)
• **5**

Fair Value
• **21½**

Risk
• **Average**

Earn./Div. Rank
• **B+**

Technical Eval.
• **Bearish** since 5/98

Rel. Strength Rank
(1 Lowest—99 Highest)
• **6**

Insider Activity
• **Favorable**

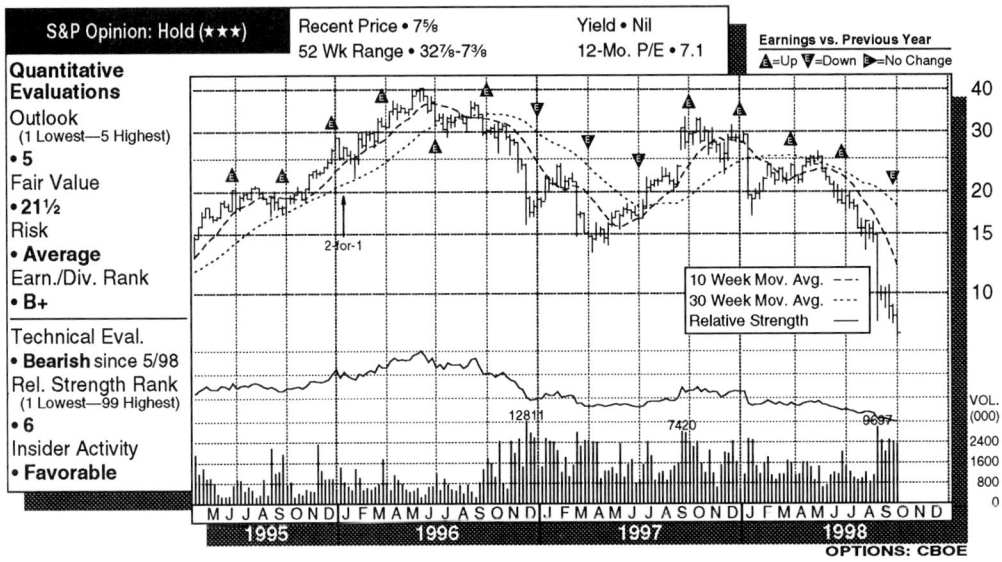

10 Week Mov. Avg. – – –
30 Week Mov. Avg. · · · ·
Relative Strength ——

2-for-1

128¹¹   7420   9697

VOL. (000)
2400
1600
800
0

OPTIONS: CBOE

Overview - 04-SEP-98

Input/Output's seismic data acquisition products are crucial to the exploration activities of the oil and gas industry. Sales are to contractors, who collect customer-specified data, and to major, independent and foreign oil and gas companies. Recently, the company has been hurt by weak oil prices, as exploration budgets have been slashed. On August 24, 1998, IO announced that its first quarter earnings for FY 99 (May) will come in below expectations. We have since lowered our FY 99 earnings estimate to $1.15 from $1.40. The company's financial results may also be hurt by a $350 million product agreement with Western Atlas International that will probably expire during the first quarter. In June, IO announced an agreement with Mitcham Industries whereby Mitcham will purchase a minimum of $90 to $100 million of IO's products over a five year period. Input/Output went through several organizational changes in the past year, including a newly appointed president, chairman and CEO, and directors. The company's recent acquisitions of CompuSeis and Green Mountain Geophysical, which are engaged in recording system integration and producing 3-D survey planning software, respectively, should complement IO's existing product line.

Valuation - 04-SEP-98

With shares already 70% off their high, and trading at only 8.7 times estimated FY 99 earnings, IO may look like a bargain. However, with the oil and gas sector temporary out of favor, we would not add to positions. The stock may prove of longer term interest, when oil prices improve. Meanwhile, oil services are in less demand, which directly affects Input/Output. In addition, the company derives a significant portion of its revenues abroad, an area beset by financial turmoil.

Key Stock Statistics

S&P EPS Est. 1999	0.95	Tang. Bk. Value/Share	7.79
P/E on S&P Est. 1999	8.0	Beta	1.72
Dividend Rate/Share	Nil	Shareholders	200
Shs. outstg. (M)	44.6	Market cap. (B)	$0.340
Avg. daily vol. (M)	0.525	Inst. holdings	76%

Value of $10,000 invested 5 years ago: $ 28,372

Fiscal Year Ending May 31

	1999	1998	1997	1996	1995	1994
Revenues (Million $)						
1Q	67.00	82.97	73.00	54.76	27.32	16.78
2Q	—	103.7	67.04	70.53	34.22	20.80
3Q	—	95.27	64.77	77.07	34.51	26.70
4Q	—	103.9	77.02	75.92	38.65	31.47
Yr.	—	385.9	281.9	278.3	134.7	95.75
Earnings Per Share ($)						
1Q	0.05	0.26	0.22	0.17	0.13	0.00
2Q	—	0.34	0.11	0.21	0.16	0.12
3Q	—	0.34	0.14	0.27	0.18	0.17
4Q	—	0.34	-0.09	0.28	0.18	0.15
Yr.	E0.95	1.28	0.38	0.94	0.65	0.53

Next earnings report expected: early December

Dividend Data

No cash has been paid, and no payments are expected in the foreseeable future. A two-for-one stock split was effected in 1994.

A Division of The McGraw·Hill Companies

STANDARD
&POOR'S
STOCK REPORTS

Input/Output, Inc.

1198L
03-OCT-98

Business Summary - 04-SEP-98

Input/Output (IO) designs and manufacturers seismic data acquisition products used on land, in transition zones (marshes and shallow bays), and in marine environments. The company's principal customers are seismic data contractors, which collect seismic data to meet customer specifications. In addition, IO markets its systems to major, independent, and foreign oil and gas companies. During FY 98 (May), approximately 35% of revenues were derived from foreign customers. Western Atlas International (WAI) accounted for approximately 28% of FY 98 revenues.

Companies use seismic data while mapping subsurface conditions in order to increase drilling success rates. In particular, demand for 3-D seismic data has increased substantially, as advances in technology have reduced cost requirements and improved data quality. Input/Output believes that its I/O SYSTEM product line is the most technologically advanced seismic data acquisition system. IO shipped 49 I/O SYSTEMs in FY 98. Depending on the system's configuration, the price of a land I/O SYSTEM typically ranges from $800,000 to $4.5 million.

On land, the company offers the I/O SYSTEM TWO, MRX, and RSR systems, as well as its Vibrators, a land energy source, and Geophones. Versions of the MRX

and RSR systems are available for transition zones. IO's marine data acquisition systems consist primarily of marine steamers and shipboard electronics that collect seismic data in deep-water environments.

IO's growth strategy consists of technological leadership and complementary acquisitions. The company allocates approximately 8% to 10% of its revenue forecast for research and development. Most of those expenses are dedicated to I/O SYSTEM enhancements; however, IO is also investigating new technologies, such as 4-D seismic and multicomponent recording. The 4-D process, or time lapse 3-D, involves the repeated recording of 3-D image volumes at different times in the life of a producing hydrocarbon reservoir.

Input/Output has expanded its product line through several complementary acquisitions. In 1998, IO acquired CompuSeis and Green Mountain Geophysical, which are engaged in recording system integration and producing 3-D survey planning software, respectively.

In connection with Input/Output's 1995 acquisition of WAI's Western Geophysical Exploration Products Group, WAI agreed to purchase $350 million of IO's products. IO expects the product agreement to expire in the first quarter of FY 99. In June 1998, IO entered into an agreement with Mitcham Industries, whereby Mitcham will purchase a minimum $90 to $100 million of IO's products within a five year period.

Per Share Data ($)

(Year Ended May 31)	1998	1997	1996	1995	1994	1993	1992	1991	1990	1989
Tangible Bk. Val.	7.79	6.41	5.89	4.04	3.02	1.60	1.29	1.01	0.52	0.05
Cash Flow	1.66	0.67	1.18	0.75	0.58	0.35	0.30	0.28	0.20	0.13
Earnings	1.28	0.38	0.94	0.66	0.53	0.31	0.27	0.25	0.17	0.09
Dividends	Nil	Nil	Nil	Nil	Nil	Nil	Nil	Nil	Nil	Nil
Payout Ratio	Nil	Nil	Nil	Nil	Nil	Nil	Nil	Nil	Nil	Nil
Cal. Yrs.	1997	1996	1995	1994	1993	1992	1991	1990	1989	1988
Prices - High	33⅛	40½	28⅞	13⅝	6⅛	4½	3½	NA	NA	NA
- Low	13¼	16	11	6	2⁷⁄₁₆	2⅜	1⅜	NA	NA	NA
P/E Ratio - High	26	NM	31	21	12	14	13	NA	NA	NA
- Low	10	NM	12	9	5	8	5	NA	NA	NA

Income Statement Analysis (Million $)

	1998	1997	1996	1995	1994	1993	1992	1991	1990	1989
Revs.	386	282	278	135	95.8	54.2	45.5	36.0	28.8	21.4
Oper. Inc.	94.3	49.6	65.9	35.1	24.6	13.8	12.1	9.8	7.3	4.9
Depr.	16.8	12.6	10.1	3.6	1.9	1.4	1.1	0.8	0.8	1.1
Int. Exp.	1.1	0.8	2.5	0.0	0.2	0.2	0.3	1.0	1.1	1.0
Pretax Inc.	83.7	24.3	56.3	35.4	24.0	13.3	11.9	8.7	5.5	2.9
Eff. Tax Rate	32%	32%	31%	31%	31%	32%	34%	34%	34%	34%
Net Inc.	56.9	16.6	38.6	24.5	16.6	9.1	7.8	5.7	3.7	1.9

Balance Sheet & Other Fin. Data (Million $)

	1998	1997	1996	1995	1994	1993	1992	1991	1990	1989
Cash	72.3	2.6	34.2	57.4	58.4	4.5	9.0	6.3	1.3	2.7
Curr. Assets	302	203	200	121	101	40.1	29.2	26.1	16.7	19.0
Total Assets	490	385	355	105	132	61.5	46.3	40.8	30.9	30.2
Curr. Liab.	62.8	32.4	35.2	15.9	13.5	10.4	7.4	8.0	12.7	10.5
LT Debt	10.0	11.0	Nil	Nil	Nil	0.4	0.6	2.1	5.9	8.4
Common Eqty.	416	339	317	147	116	47.9	37.4	29.3	11.2	7.7
Total Cap.	406	350	317	147	117	49.5	38.9	32.9	18.2	19.7
Cap. Exp.	7.0	27.0	10.2	6.0	4.0	3.7	1.8	4.7	2.1	1.4
Cash Flow	73.7	29.2	48.8	28.1	18.4	10.6	8.9	6.6	4.3	3.0
Curr. Ratio	4.8	6.3	5.7	7.6	7.5	3.8	3.9	3.3	1.3	1.8
% LT Debt of Cap.	2.4	3.1	Nil	Nil	Nil	0.9	1.4	6.3	32.3	42.7
% Net Inc.of Revs.	14.7	5.9	13.9	18.2	17.3	16.9	17.2	15.9	12.7	9.0
% Ret. on Assets	13.0	4.5	14.8	16.3	16.2	16.7	18.0	14.0	12.0	8.3
% Ret. on Equity	15.1	5.1	16.7	18.5	19.2	21.1	23.5	25.9	37.9	27.3

Data as orig. reptd.; bef. results of disc. opers. and/or spec. items. Per share data adj. for stk. divs. as of ex-div. date. Bold denotes diluted EPS (FASB 128). E-Estimated. NA-Not Available. NM-Not Meaningful. NR-Not Ranked.

Office—11104 West Airport Blvd., Stafford, TX 77477. **Tel**—(281) 933-3339. **Fax**—(281) 933-9826. **Website**—http://www.i-o.com **Chrmn & CEO**—W. J. Zeringue. **Pres & COO**—A. M. Sigmar. **VP & CFO**—G. S. Mayeux. **VP & Secy**—Chris E. Wolfe. **Investor Contact**—Gregory A. Rosenstein.**Dirs**—R. P. Brindley, S. H. Carter Jr., E. E. Cook, T. H. Elliott Jr., G. T. Graves III, C. E. Selecman, A. M. Sigmar, W. F. Wallace, W. J. Zeringue. **Transfer Agent**—Harris Trust and Savings Bank, Houston, TX. **Incorporated**—in Delaware in 1979. **Empl**— 1,300. **S&P Analyst**: Ephraim Juskowicz

Insituform Technologies 4248L

NASDAQ Symbol **INSUA**

In S&P SmallCap 600

03-OCT-98

Industry: Manufacturing (Specialized)

Summary: This company provides patented methods of reconstructing deteriorated pipelines and manholes with little or no excavation.

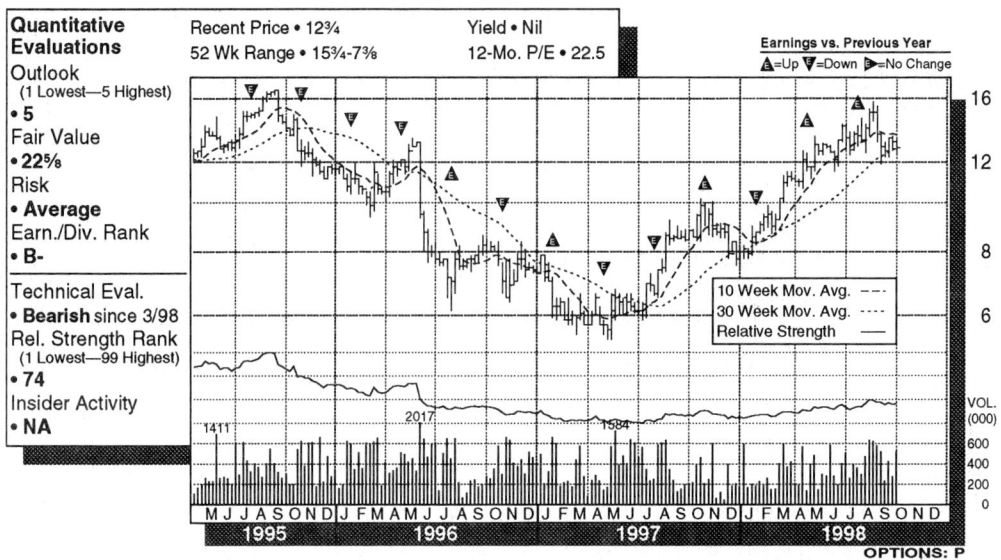

Quantitative Evaluations

Outlook (1 Lowest—5 Highest)
• **5**

Fair Value
• **22⅝**

Risk
• **Average**

Earn./Div. Rank
• **B-**

Technical Eval.
• **Bearish** since 3/98

Rel. Strength Rank (1 Lowest—99 Highest)
• **74**

Insider Activity
• **NA**

Recent Price • 12¾
52 Wk Range • 15¾-7⅞
Yield • Nil
12-Mo. P/E • 22.5

Earnings vs. Previous Year
▲=Up ▼=Down ▶=No Change

10 Week Mov. Avg. – – –
30 Week Mov. Avg. ⋯⋯
Relative Strength —

OPTIONS: P

Business Profile - 29-SEP-98

The company plans to continue to develop and acquire new technologies, significantly increase its rate of penetration of the industrial market, and exploit its broad international presence and worldwide rights to the Insituform process and other technologies. It expects to focus on the Far East, Japan and India. The Insituform Process accounted for 63% of revenues in 1997. In March 1998, the company acquired the 40% minority interest in its Chilean unit for $2.1 million. In July 1998, INSUA authorized the repurchase of up to 2.7 million of its common shares, or 10% of those outstanding.

Operational Review - 29-SEP-98

Total revenues in the first half of 1998 fell 8.6%, year to year, primarily reflecting lower corrosion and abrasion volume in the U.S. and Latin America. Gross margins widened on improved productivity and efficiencies in the pipeline rehabilitation business, and with well controlled strategic marketing and product development costs, and in the absence of $3.8 million of unusual items, pretax income more than quadrupled. After taxes at 39.7%, versus 43.0%, minority interest, and equity in earnings of affiliates, income advanced to $7,455,000 ($0.27 a diluted share), from $1,295,000 ($0.06). Results in the 1997 period exclude a loss of $0.01 a share on early retirement of debt.

Stock Performance - 02-OCT-98

In the past 30 trading days, INSUA's shares have declined 15%, compared to a 7% fall in the S&P 500. Average trading volume for the past five days was 104,180 shares, compared with the 40-day moving average of 111,767 shares.

Key Stock Statistics

Dividend Rate/Share	Nil	Shareholders	2,200
Shs. outstg. (M)	27.0	Market cap. (B)	$0.346
Avg. daily vol. (M)	0.075	Inst. holdings	48%
Tang. Bk. Value/Share	2.44		
Beta	0.23		

Value of $10,000 invested 5 years ago: $ 5,024

Fiscal Year Ending Dec. 31

	1998	1997	1996	1995	1994	1993
Revenues (Million $)						
1Q	63.76	77.08	68.11	62.27	30.48	16.08
2Q	75.50	75.32	71.77	69.62	31.80	20.78
3Q	—	85.49	70.65	69.89	40.95	32.20
4Q	—	82.75	79.41	70.42	45.02	31.45
Yr.	—	320.6	289.9	272.2	148.3	100.5
Earnings Per Share ($)						
1Q	0.11	0.05	0.08	0.13	0.10	0.18
2Q	0.16	0.01	0.14	0.08	0.15	0.10
3Q	—	0.16	0.13	0.15	0.25	0.21
4Q	—	0.14	-0.19	-0.40	0.18	0.02
Yr.	—	0.36	0.17	-0.04	0.68	0.51

Next earnings report expected: early November

Dividend Data

No cash has been paid.

A Division of The McGraw-Hill Companies

STANDARD
&POOR'S
STOCK REPORTS

Insituform Technologies, Inc.

4248L
03-OCT-98

Business Summary - 29-SEP-98

From a company deriving all of its revenues from royalties and product sales to its licensees just six years ago, Insituform Technologies (INSUA) has become an integrated pipe rehabilitation company which derived 92% of its revenues in 1997 from contracting using its non-disruptive technologies. Formerly Insituform of North America, INSUA believes the domestic and international market remains strong for the trenchless rehabilitation business, as well as for the tunneling and United Pipeline companies. INSUA plans to transform the company by increasing operational efficiency and cutting fixed costs.

The company provides a trenchless means of rehabilitating sewers, tunnels and pipelines. It also offers the NuPipe Process in the U.S. and overseas, and was engaged in the rehabilitation of downhole tubulars for the oil industry under the UltraPipe name from April 1992 until December 1993, when it discontinued the tubular business. INSUA's Tite Liner Process lines new and existing steel pipelines with a corrosion and abrasion resistant polyethylene pipe. The company expanded its operations significantly through the October 1995 acquisition of Insituform Mid-America (INSMA) for 12,450,896 common shares.

Pipeline technology primarily involves licensing, selling and servicing trenchless pipeline reconstruction technology and products. Construction consists mainly of the installation of trenchless pipeline reconstruction materials.

The Insituform technology utilizes the INSUA manufactured Insitutube that serves as a carrier for liquid thermosetting plastic resins. At the job site, this tube is positioned in the pipe to be reconstructed through a manhole. Once the tube is in place and positioned tightly against the inner walls of the old pipe, heated water is used to cure the resin, forming a jointless, structural, corrosion-resistant new pipe (the Insitupipe) inside the old pipe.

The NuPipe subsidiary repairs pipe by first heating material which is then pulled into the pipe to be repaired. Once in place, the NuPipe is expanded tightly against the walls of the old pipe, forming a jointless, corrosion resistant pipe-within-a-pipe.

INSUA receives royalties from a network of sublicensees that distribute and install Insituform and NuPipe in the U.S. The NuPipe Ltd. subsidiary markets and installs NuPipe in the U.K., while NuPipe International is responsible for worldwide licensing outside the U.S.

In July 1997, the company moved its headquarters to Chesterfield, MO, from Memphis, TN, and combined it with its engineering and development center and North American contracting headquarters. INSUA expects to save more than $1 million a year in operating costs from the combination.

Per Share Data ($)

(Year Ended Dec. 31)	1997	1996	1995	1994	1993	1992	1991	1990	1989	1988
Tangible Bk. Val.	2.37	1.99	1.69	5.15	4.45	3.91	5.74	3.77	3.58	2.51
Cash Flow	1.07	0.87	0.59	1.20	0.95	-0.15	1.97	0.35	0.55	0.57
Earnings	0.36	0.17	-0.04	0.68	0.51	-0.45	1.77	0.22	0.46	0.52
Dividends	Nil	Nil	Nil	Nil	Nil	Nil	Nil	Nil	Nil	Nil
Payout Ratio	Nil	Nil	Nil	Nil	Nil	Nil	Nil	Nil	Nil	Nil
Prices - High	10⅛	13⅜	16⅝	15⅜	25¾	26½	20⅝	8⅝	11½	11½
- Low	5⅜	6⅛	11⅛	10½	11¼	14	3¼	2⁷⁄₁₆	6⅞	5⅛
P/E Ratio - High	28	79	NM	23	50	NM	12	39	25	22
- Low	15	36	NM	15	22	NM	2	11	15	10

Income Statement Analysis (Million $)

	1997	1996	1995	1994	1993	1992	1991	1990	1989	1988
Revs.	321	290	272	148	101	95.8	30.4	22.0	21.1	19.0
Oper. Inc.	48.9	40.0	43.1	26.1	16.4	12.8	5.7	2.8	3.8	4.5
Depr.	19.2	19.2	16.8	7.5	6.3	4.2	1.6	1.1	0.7	0.3
Int. Exp.	8.8	6.2	6.4	3.1	1.4	0.2	NA	NA	0.7	0.1
Pretax Inc.	17.2	9.9	4.3	16.5	11.0	-2.0	24.4	2.4	5.0	5.5
Eff. Tax Rate	41%	51%	NM	37%	30%	NM	42%	29%	28%	31%
Net Inc.	9.6	4.5	-1.0	9.8	7.3	-6.2	14.3	1.7	3.7	3.8

Balance Sheet & Other Fin. Data (Million $)

	1997	1996	1995	1994	1993	1992	1991	1990	1989	1988
Cash	45.7	13.5	11.4	17.7	16.1	14.3	25.9	13.9	13.0	7.0
Curr. Assets	161	131	121	71.7	56.3	43.7	37.8	20.7	19.5	14.0
Total Assets	298	268	260	162	129	87.4	58.1	41.9	40.2	35.2
Curr. Liab.	47.0	52.0	51.0	38.9	28.0	24.0	5.8	5.4	4.3	3.4
LT Debt	111	82.4	82.8	47.3	36.3	7.3	6.4	6.7	7.3	7.8
Common Eqty.	132	123	117	73.9	63.4	54.5	45.6	29.4	27.9	23.3
Total Cap.	250	209	208	124	101	63.4	52.2	36.5	35.6	31.4
Cap. Exp.	16.6	18.2	16.5	9.0	5.3	6.1	1.5	1.7	2.8	4.8
Cash Flow	28.9	23.7	15.8	17.3	13.6	-2.1	15.9	2.7	4.3	4.1
Curr. Ratio	3.4	2.5	2.4	1.8	2.0	1.8	6.5	3.8	4.5	4.1
% LT Debt of Cap.	44.4	39.4	39.8	38.3	35.9	11.6	12.3	18.3	20.5	24.8
% Net Inc.of Revs.	3.0	1.5	NM	6.6	7.2	NM	46.9	7.7	17.0	20.0
% Ret. on Assets	3.4	1.7	NM	6.7	6.6	NM	28.3	4.1	9.4	12.7
% Ret. on Equity	7.6	3.7	NM	14.2	12.2	NM	37.8	5.9	13.9	18.4

Data as orig. reptd.; bef. results of disc. opers. and/or spec. items. Per share data adj. for stk. divs. as of ex-div. date. Bold denotes diluted EPS (FASB 128). E-Estimated. NA-Not Available. NM-Not Meaningful. NR-Not Ranked.

Office—702 Spirit 40 Park Drive, Chesterfield, MO 63005. **Tel**—(314) 530-8000. **Chrmn, Pres & CEO**—A. W. Hooper. **Vice Chrmn**—J. Kalishman.**SVP & CFO**—W. A. Martin. **Secy**—H. Kailes. **Dirs**—R. W. Affholder, P. A. Biddelman, S. Cortinovis, A. W. Hooper, J. Kalishman, S. Spengler, S. Weinig, R. B. Wight, Jr., A.L. Woods. **Transfer Agent & Registrar**—American Stock Transfer & Trust Co., NYC. **Incorporated**—in Delaware in 1980. **Empl**— 1,420. **S&P Analyst:** Stewart Scharf

STANDARD &POOR'S
STOCK REPORTS

Insteel Industries
1199

NYSE Symbol **III**

In S&P SmallCap 600

03-OCT-98

Industry: Manufacturing (Specialized)

Summary: This company produces concrete wire reinforcing products, industrial wire, agricultural fencing, nails, specialty wire fabrics and building panels.

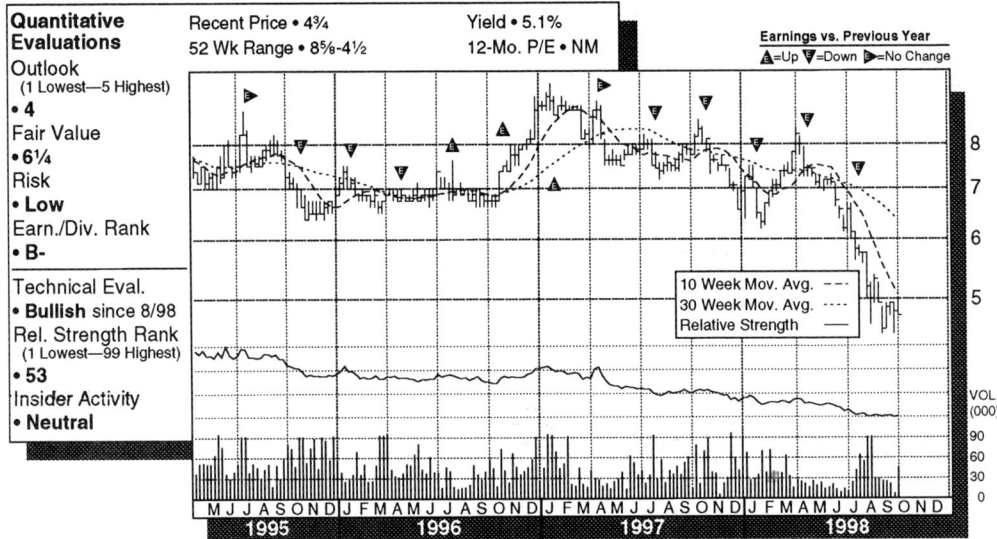

Quantitative Evaluations

Recent Price • 4¾

52 Wk Range • 8⅝-4½

Yield • 5.1%

12-Mo. P/E • NM

Outlook
(1 Lowest—5 Highest)
• **4**

Fair Value
• **6¼**

Risk
• **Low**

Earn./Div. Rank
• **B-**

Technical Eval.
• **Bullish** since 8/98

Rel. Strength Rank
(1 Lowest—99 Highest)
• **53**

Insider Activity
• **Neutral**

Earnings vs. Previous Year
▲=Up ▼=Down ▷=No Change

10 Week Mov. Avg. – – –
30 Week Mov. Avg. ⋯⋯
Relative Strength ——

VOL.
(000)

Business Profile - 12-AUG-98

Insteel's strategy continues to be focused on further expansion into higher value products that offer the potential to generate significantly more attractive returns than its traditional business. During 1994-1997, the company built two new production facilities and reconfigured an existing operation in order to develop the manufacturing capabilities to enter the PC strand, collated fasteners, tire bead wire, and welding wire markets. Insteel expects sales of these new products to increase from $33 million in 1997 to $100 million in 2000 when fully operational. However, it expects operating results to continue to be negatively impacted until sales of the new products rise to significant levels.

Operational Review - 12-AUG-98

Revenues in the first nine months of FY 98 (Sep.) rose 0.2%, year to year. The gross profit margin narrowed significantly, due to higher raw material costs and insufficient revenues to cover operating costs at the company's new Virginia manufacturing facility. Despite a $2.5 million pretax gain from the sale of its agricultural fencing business and after tax credits of $1.1 million, a loss from continuing operations of $2.1 million ($0.24 a share) contrasted with income of $1.9 million ($0.22). Results exclude a special charge of $0.05 a share from the early extinguishment of debt in the FY 98 period, and a loss from discontinued operations of $0.34 in the FY 97 period.

Stock Performance - 02-OCT-98

In the past 30 trading days, III's shares have declined 11%, compared to a 7% fall in the S&P 500. Average trading volume for the past five days was 9,080 shares, compared with the 40-day moving average of 7,269 shares.

Key Stock Statistics

Dividend Rate/Share	0.24	Shareholders	700
Shs. outstg. (M)	8.4	Market cap. (B)	$0.040
Avg. daily vol. (M)	0.005	Inst. holdings	39%
Tang. Bk. Value/Share	7.98		
Beta	0.64		

Value of $10,000 invested 5 years ago: $ 5,207

Fiscal Year Ending Sep. 30

	1998	1997	1996	1995	1994	1993
Revenues (Million $)						
1Q	59.92	58.43	57.51	58.62	50.56	53.92
2Q	63.00	65.25	63.76	66.00	56.27	65.43
3Q	69.28	68.13	72.99	69.36	71.54	63.15
4Q	—	70.52	72.51	66.36	69.30	63.25
Yr.	—	262.3	266.8	260.3	247.7	245.8
Earnings Per Share ($)						
1Q	-0.20	Nil	-0.07	0.08	Nil	0.07
2Q	-0.04	0.08	0.08	0.48	0.09	0.17
3Q	Nil	0.14	0.25	0.19	0.19	0.19
4Q	—	0.08	0.24	0.01	0.18	0.34
Yr.	—	0.30	0.50	0.76	0.45	0.80

Next earnings report expected: mid October

Dividend Data (Dividends have been paid since 1986.)

Amount ($)	Date Decl.	Ex-Div. Date	Stock of Record	Payment Date
0.060	Nov. 05	Dec. 10	Dec. 12	Jan. 02 '98
0.060	Feb. 06	Mar. 09	Mar. 11	Apr. 01 '98
0.060	Apr. 30	Jun. 08	Jun. 10	Jul. 01 '98
0.060	Aug. 12	Sep. 08	Sep. 10	Oct. 01 '98

A Division of The **McGraw·Hill** *Companies*

STANDARD
&POOR'S
STOCK REPORTS

Insteel Industries, Inc.

1199

03-OCT-98

Business Summary - 12-AUG-98

Over the last several years, Insteel has been making serious efforts to expand its product line to offer more profitable, value-added wire and related products. During the past five years, the company invested about $75 million to expand into new products and markets, as well as upgrade existing production operations. In addition, management plans to enter the tire reinforcement business. To this end, Insteel recently reconfigured and expanded its Fredricksburg, VA, plant to make bead wire. Bead wire, which is located in the inside of a tire, is used as a tire reinforcement. The upgraded Fredricksburg plant began operations in the third quarter of FY 97 (Sep.).

Consistent with III's efforts to focus on offering higher-margin wire and related products, the company sold its money-losing Construction Systems division in mid-1997. The Insteel Construction Systems division makes a wire-reinforced building panel known as the Insteel 3-D system, used in the construction of buildings, prisons, apartments and homes. In the past seven years, the Construction Systems division has reported modest losses.

At FY 97 year-end, Insteel offered two related product lines: Wire products (56% of FY 97 sales) and concrete reinforcing products (44%). Insteel's core Wire Products (IWP) division produces the company's concrete reinforcing products, wire, fencing and nails. IWP sells its products to the construction, home furnishing, appliance and agricultural industries. The company also makes prestressed concrete strand (PC strand), a reinforcing product used in construction of structural members, bridges, buildings, parking decks and other structural components.

Important profitability statistics from recent fiscal years (Sep.) are:

	FY 97	FY 96	FY 95
Gross margins	7.2%	8.4%	8.4%
Operating margins	2.5%	3.3%	3.4%
Free cash flow (000's)	-$15,516	-$11,668	$6,290
Free cash flow/share	-$1.84	-$1.39	$0.75

Insteel operates in a highly competitive industry. Competitors include integrated steelmakers and smaller wire mills. Most company products are commodity items, so that it competes primarily on price. Raw material costs heavily influence selling prices, and technology has become critical in lowering production costs. Insteel believes that it is the leading low-cost producer, because of its high-tech facilities.

Per Share Data ($)

(Year Ended Sep. 30)	1997	1996	1995	1994	1993	1992	1991	1990	1989	1988
Tangible Bk. Val.	8.45	8.74	8.48	7.98	7.61	7.04	6.56	6.47	6.15	5.23
Cash Flow	1.28	1.46	1.69	1.22	1.52	1.73	1.32	1.55	1.59	1.44
Earnings	0.30	0.50	0.76	0.45	0.80	0.68	0.26	0.55	1.07	0.95
Dividends	0.24	0.24	0.30	0.24	0.23	0.21	0.19	0.17	0.15	0.10
Payout Ratio	80%	48%	39%	53%	29%	31%	72%	31%	14%	11%
Prices - High	9⅝	9¼	8⅞	12⅛	12¾	12⅛	8⅛	8½	9⅛	6¾
- Low	6¼	6½	6⅝	7⅜	8⅝	7⅝	5⅛	4	5⅝	3¾
P/E Ratio - High	32	19	12	27	16	18	31	15	8	7
- Low	21	13	9	16	11	11	20	7	5	4

Income Statement Analysis (Million $)

	1997	1996	1995	1994	1993	1992	1991	1990	1989	1988
Revs.	262	267	260	247	245	240	240	252	197	195
Oper. Inc.	-14.7	17.0	16.5	13.3	13.4	13.1	10.7	13.5	13.3	12.8
Depr.	8.2	8.1	7.8	6.3	5.7	6.8	6.7	6.2	3.3	3.0
Int. Exp.	2.3	2.3	2.3	2.4	1.5	2.5	3.0	3.4	2.1	2.4
Pretax Inc.	4.0	6.6	6.3	5.3	7.1	4.8	1.6	3.6	8.7	7.8
Eff. Tax Rate	36%	35%	NM	41%	19%	19%	30%	13%	23%	24%
Net Inc.	2.5	4.2	6.3	3.8	6.3	4.3	1.7	3.5	6.7	6.0

Balance Sheet & Other Fin. Data (Million $)

	1997	1996	1995	1994	1993	1992	1991	1990	1989	1988
Cash	1.1	1.4	0.3	1.2	9.3	0.4	3.8	Nil	10.2	1.0
Curr. Assets	80.2	68.8	73.9	64.5	64.3	57.2	55.6	62.5	54.2	48.9
Total Assets	171	146	146	139	133	113	109	119	90.0	79.0
Curr. Liab.	43.5	35.2	47.8	39.3	33.9	30.0	27.1	35.6	18.9	18.3
LT Debt	49.7	29.7	22.1	26.8	29.2	30.4	32.1	33.7	27.3	23.2
Common Eqty.	71.3	73.7	71.2	66.5	62.9	44.9	41.7	41.1	38.4	32.6
Total Cap.	127	110	98.3	100	99	82.8	81.8	83.1	70.9	60.4
Cap. Exp.	27.1	13.2	5.5	10.7	19.7	9.8	3.4	10.9	4.5	3.2
Cash Flow	10.8	12.3	14.1	10.1	12.0	11.2	8.3	9.7	10.0	8.9
Curr. Ratio	1.8	2.0	1.5	1.6	1.9	1.9	2.1	1.8	2.9	2.7
% LT Debt of Cap.	39.1	27.1	22.5	26.9	29.5	36.8	39.3	40.5	38.5	38.5
% Net Inc.of Revs.	1.0	1.6	2.4	1.5	2.6	1.8	0.7	1.4	3.4	3.1
% Ret. on Assets	1.6	2.0	4.4	2.8	4.5	3.9	1.5	3.4	8.0	7.6
% Ret. on Equity	3.5	5.9	9.2	5.8	10.4	10.0	4.0	8.8	18.9	21.0

Data as orig. reptd.; bef. results of disc. opers. and/or spec. items. Per share data adj. for stk. divs. as of ex-div. date. Bold denotes diluted EPS (FASB 128). E-Estimated. NA-Not Available. NM-Not Meaningful. NR-Not Ranked. Free cash flow defined as net operating income plus depreciation/amortization, less capital expenditures, increases in working capital and preferred dividends.

Office—1373 Boggs Drive, Mount Airy, NC 27030. **Tel**—(910) 786-2141. **Chrmn**—H. O. Woltz Jr. **Pres & CEO**—H. O. Woltz III. **CFO & Treas**—M. C. Gazmarian. **VP & Secy**—G. D. Kniskern. **Dirs**—T. J. Cumby, L. E. Hannen, F. H. Johnson, C. B. Newsome, J. D. Noell III, W. A. Rogers II, C. R. Vaughn, H. O. Woltz Jr., H. O. Woltz III, J. E. Woltz. **Transfer Agent**—First Union National Bank of North Carolina, Charlotte. **Incorporated**—in North Carolina in 1953. **Empl**— 1,100. **S&P Analyst:** John A. Massey

Insurance Auto Auctions 4248M

NASDAQ Symbol **IAAI**

In S&P SmallCap 600

03-OCT-98

Industry:
Services (Commercial & Consumer)

Summary: IAAI sells automobile salvage in the U.S., providing insurance companies a means to process and sell total-loss and recovered theft vehicles.

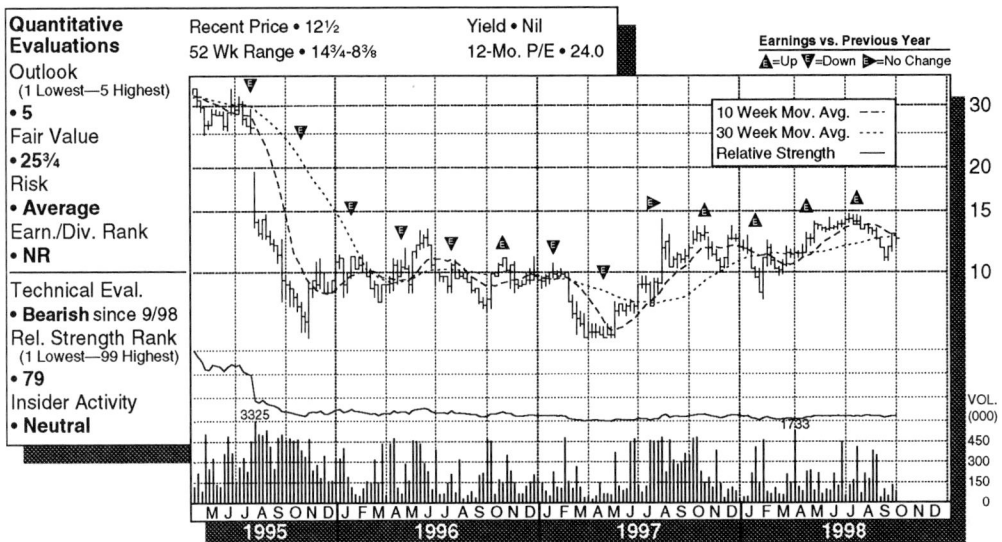

Quantitative Evaluations	
Outlook (1 Lowest—5 Highest)	• **5**
Fair Value	• **25¾**
Risk	• **Average**
Earn./Div. Rank	• **NR**
Technical Eval.	• **Bearish** since 9/98
Rel. Strength Rank (1 Lowest—99 Highest)	• **79**
Insider Activity	• **Neutral**

Recent Price • 12½
52 Wk Range • 14¾-8⅜
Yield • Nil
12-Mo. P/E • 24.0

Earnings vs. Previous Year
▲=Up ▼=Down ▶=No Change

10 Week Mov. Avg. – – –
30 Week Mov. Avg. · · · ·
Relative Strength —

Business Profile - 04-AUG-98

Insurance Auto Auctions has grown, and expects to continue to grow, mostly through acquisitions of salvage pools throughout the U.S. In February 1998, it acquired Auto Disposal Company, operator of two salvage pools in Alabama. Auto Disposal processes 9,000 units per year, and the acquisition increased IAAI's total number of sites to 48. The company believes that this acquisition, coupled with a site planned for a Southeast metropolitan area, will strengthen its market penetration in the region. Earnings improved in 1997 and the first half of 1998 on improved margins and cost containment.

Operational Review - 04-AUG-98

Net sales in the six months ended June 30, 1998, advanced 7.5%, year to year, reflecting a 9.9% increase in vehicle sales and a 2.6% rise in fee income. Unit volume was essentially flat. Gross profit per unit increased $24 to $154. Despite an increase in direct operating expenses as a percent of sales, and special charges of $1,564,000, against $750,000, operating profit advanced 50%. After taxes at 46.0% versus 43.0%, net income was up 64% to $3,366,000 ($0.30 a share), from $2,050,000 ($0.18).

Stock Performance - 02-OCT-98

In the past 30 trading days, IAAI's shares have declined 5%, compared to a 7% fall in the S&P 500. Average trading volume for the past five days was 16,520 shares, compared with the 40-day moving average of 33,041 shares.

Key Stock Statistics

Dividend Rate/Share	Nil	Shareholders	200
Shs. outstg. (M)	11.3	Market cap. (B)	$0.141
Avg. daily vol. (M)	0.018	Inst. holdings	70%
Tang. Bk. Value/Share	2.12		
Beta	0.73		

Value of $10,000 invested 5 years ago: $ 5,434

Fiscal Year Ending Dec. 31

	1998	1997	1996	1995	1994	1993
Revenues (Million $)						
1Q	68.56	67.89	72.82	60.24	37.63	21.32
2Q	75.40	65.98	76.04	65.19	42.37	26.32
3Q	—	61.40	68.68	64.98	41.38	28.54
4Q	—	64.06	64.36	67.59	50.75	27.91
Yr.	—	259.3	281.9	258.0	172.1	104.1
Earnings Per Share ($)						
1Q	**0.08**	**0.05**	0.07	0.24	0.18	0.15
2Q	**0.22**	**0.13**	0.13	0.17	0.27	0.21
3Q	—	**0.09**	0.07	-0.20	0.27	0.22
4Q	—	**0.13**	0.01	0.07	0.26	0.16
Yr.	—	**0.40**	0.27	0.27	0.98	0.74

Next earnings report expected: late October

Dividend Data

No dividends have been paid, and the company plans to retain all earnings to support the development and expansion of its business.

A Division of The McGraw-Hill Companies

Business Summary - 04-AUG-98

Have you ever wondered what happens to cars that have been declared "totaled"? Many of them end up being sold by Insurance Auto Auctions, Inc., the largest vehicle salvage services company in the U.S. Insurance Auto Auctions believes it provides insurance companies with a cost-effective way to process and sell "total loss" and recovered theft vehicles. (The size of the market for the processing and sale of total loss and recovered theft vehicles in the U.S. is estimated at $3 billion a year.) The company buys such vehicles from insurance companies for resale and also sells vehicles on consignment for insurers. Vehicles are sold at live or closed bid auctions on a competitive basis. As of April 1998, the company was selling vehicles at 48 auction sites throughout the country.

Insurance Auto Auctions processes salvage vehicles under three methods: purchase agreement, fixed fee consignment, and percentage of sale consignment.

Under the purchase agreement method, IAAI generally purchases the vehicles from the insurance companies at a percentage of actual cash value (ACV) and then resells these vehicles for its own account. By assuming some of the risk in owning the salvage vehicle, the company can potentially increase profits by improving the value of the salvage vehicle prior to the sale. Under the fixed fee and percentage of sale consignment methods, the company sells vehicles on behalf of insurance companies, and costs associated with processing and sales are proportionately lower. IAAI receives agreed upon sales fees under the consignment methods and charges for other services such as towing and storage.

The volume of vehicles processed increased to 440,000 in 1997, down fractionally from 443,000 in the previous year. In 1997, 30% of vehicles processed by Insurance Auto Auctions were sold under purchase agreements, down from 33% in 1996.

Historically, the conversion from consignment sales to purchase agreement sales generally benefited the company. However, in recent years, used car prices and ACVs have risen significantly, while prices at salvage auctions have not. Because of this, Insurance Auto Auctions has renegotiated some of its purchase agreements and is seeking to renegotiate others at lower percentages of ACV than previously offered to customers. IAAI has also added adjustment and risk-sharing clauses to its new purchase agreement contracts to provide further protection from material changes in the ACV/salvage price relationship. In 1997, the company began to shift from purchase agreements to consignment contracts.

Vehicles from Insurance Auto Auctions' three largest suppliers, Allstate Insurance Co., Farmers Insurance Group and State Farm Insurance Co., accounted for 46% of unit sales in 1997.

Per Share Data ($)

(Year Ended Dec. 31)	1997	1996	1995	1994	1993	1992	1991	1990	1989	1988
Tangible Bk. Val.	1.75	0.93	12.72	12.43	11.18	5.38	2.24	-0.29	0.76	0.43
Cash Flow	1.50	1.36	0.85	1.47	0.97	0.71	0.44	0.83	0.33	0.02
Earnings	0.40	0.27	0.27	0.98	0.74	0.61	-3.13	-0.19	0.21	0.08
Dividends	Nil	Nil	Nil	Nil	Nil	Nil	Nil	Nil	Nil	Nil
Payout Ratio	Nil	Nil	Nil	Nil	Nil	Nil	Nil	Nil	Nil	Nil
Prices - High	14¼	13⅜	36	38⅝	45½	23	20	NA	NA	NA
- Low	6½	7¾	6½	24½	17½	12⅛	11	NA	NA	NA
P/E Ratio - High	36	50	NM	39	61	38	NM	NA	NA	NA
- Low	16	29	NM	25	24	20	NA	NA	NA	NA

Income Statement Analysis (Million $)

	1997	1996	1995	1994	1993	1992	1991	1990	1989	1988
Revs.	259	282	258	172	104	60.5	41.8	35.8	32.3	17.6
Oper. Inc.	23.4	21.3	21.1	24.6	12.7	6.4	3.9	3.0	1.9	0.7
Depr.	12.5	8.6	6.6	5.5	2.0	0.7	1.2	1.5	0.3	0.2
Int. Exp.	2.7	3.0	2.4	0.5	0.1	0.1	1.5	1.2	0.2	0.1
Pretax Inc.	8.3	5.4	5.5	19.1	11.0	6.3	-11.7	0.5	1.4	0.5
Eff. Tax Rate	46%	43%	43%	43%	40%	31%	NM	44%	43%	43%
Net Inc.	4.5	3.1	3.1	11.0	6.6	4.4	-11.5	0.3	0.8	0.3

Balance Sheet & Other Fin. Data (Million $)

	1997	1996	1995	1994	1993	1992	1991	1990	1989	1988
Cash	9.6	5.9	7.2	10.4	30.4	17.3	10.7	3.0	0.3	NM
Curr. Assets	52.3	54.1	50.4	41.4	48.0	26.1	15.8	6.6	3.6	2.5
Total Assets	207	212	211	174	144	51.9	18.6	12.3	4.7	3.3
Curr. Liab.	26.5	34.4	38.2	29.3	19.2	6.5	4.9	4.7	2.5	2.0
LT Debt	20.2	26.7	24.6	0.2	1.1	0.9	Nil	6.9	0.3	0.2
Common Eqty.	151	147	143	140	124	44.4	13.7	-0.7	1.9	1.1
Total Cap.	177	173	168	140	125	45.4	13.7	6.2	2.2	1.3
Cap. Exp.	4.6	5.9	11.0	5.5	4.1	0.9	0.6	0.7	0.6	0.3
Cash Flow	17.0	15.5	9.7	16.5	8.7	5.1	1.8	3.1	1.2	0.0
Curr. Ratio	2.0	1.6	1.3	1.4	2.5	4.0	3.2	1.4	1.4	1.3
% LT Debt of Cap.	11.4	15.4	14.6	0.2	0.8	2.0	Nil	111.5	13.3	16.8
% Net Inc.of Revs.	1.7	1.1	1.2	6.4	6.4	7.2	NM	0.7	2.4	1.7
% Ret. on Assets	2.1	1.5	1.6	6.9	6.2	11.4	NM	7.9	17.0	9.1
% Ret. on Equity	3.0	2.1	2.2	8.3	7.2	13.9	NM	NA	42.3	27.5

Data as orig. reptd.; bef. results of disc. opers. and/or spec. items. Per share data adj. for stk. divs. as of ex-div. date. Bold denotes diluted EPS (FASB 128). E-Estimated. NA-Not Available. NM-Not Meaningful. NR-Not Ranked.

Office—850 E. Algonquin Rd., Suite 100, Schaumburg, IL 60173. **Tel**— (847) 839-3939. **Website**—http://www.iaai.com **Pres & CEO**—J. P. Alampi. **VP-CFO & Investor Contact**—Linda C. Larrabee. **Dirs**—J. P. Alampi, M. A. Cocca, S. B. Gould, C. G. Knowles, M. R. Martin, T. J. O'Malia, G. E. Tullman, J. K. Wilcox. **Transfer Agent**—Bank of Boston, Boston, MA, and Palo Alto, CA. **Incorporated**—in California in 1982. **Empl**— 670. **S&P Analyst:** Kathleen J. Fraser

03-OCT-98

Industry:
Electronics (Semiconductors)

Summary: This company makes and sells mixed-signal integrated circuits for frequency timing, multimedia and data communications applications.

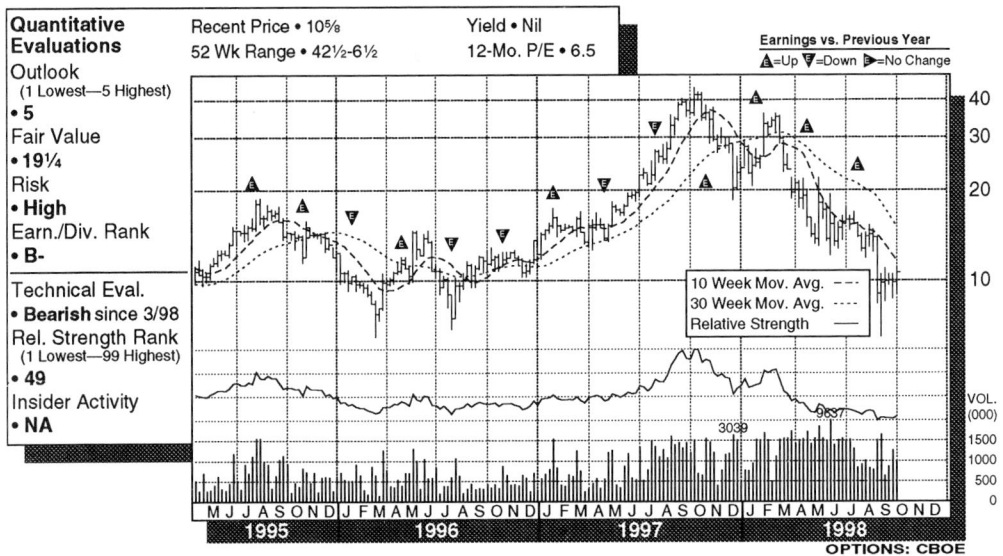

Quantitative Evaluations	
Outlook (1 Lowest—5 Highest)	• **5**
Fair Value	• **19¼**
Risk	• **High**
Earn./Div. Rank	• **B-**
Technical Eval.	• **Bearish** since 3/98
Rel. Strength Rank (1 Lowest—99 Highest)	• **49**
Insider Activity	• **NA**

Recent Price • 10⅝
52 Wk Range • 42½-6½

Yield • Nil
12-Mo. P/E • 6.5

Earnings vs. Previous Year
▲=Up ▼=Down ▶=No Change

10 Week Mov. Avg. – – –
30 Week Mov. Avg. - - - -
Relative Strength ——

VOL. (000)

OPTIONS: CBOE

Business Profile - 10-SEP-98

Following two sales and an acquisition, ICST is focusing on data communications, frequency timing generation and custom products, its three primary businesses. The company has recently experienced a decline in demand for its networking transceivers and motherboard frequency timing products and in response is focusing its resources on making existing products more competitive and on developing new products based on its core technology. However, ICST is unable to predict when revenues and earnings from these new products will contribute materially to its existing earnings stream.

Operational Review - 10-SEP-98

Based on a preliminary report, revenues in FY 98 (Jun.) advanced 54% from those of the prior year, reflecting strong gains in frequency timing products and network transceivers. Gross margins widened, and in the absence of an $11.2 million in process research and development charge and $7.8 million of minority interest and equity investment expense, a pretax loss contrasted with pretax income. After taxes at 37.5%, versus $6.3 million, net income of $21,374,000 ($1.63 a share) replaced a net loss of $7,509,000 ($0.65). Results in the FY 97 period exclude a loss from discontinued operations of $0.08 a share.

Stock Performance - 02-OCT-98

In the past 30 trading days, ICST's shares have declined 24%, compared to a 7% fall in the S&P 500. Average trading volume for the past five days was 196,140 shares, compared with the 40-day moving average of 260,133 shares.

Key Stock Statistics

Dividend Rate/Share	Nil	Shareholders	200
Shs. outstg. (M)	12.3	Market cap. (B)	$0.131
Avg. daily vol. (M)	0.195	Inst. holdings	54%
Tang. Bk. Value/Share	7.28		
Beta	1.61		

Value of $10,000 invested 5 years ago: $ 5,448

Fiscal Year Ending Jun. 30

	1998	1997	1996	1995	1994	1993
Revenues (Million $)						
1Q	38.59	21.38	28.29	22.55	19.29	15.10
2Q	43.05	27.45	33.12	25.88	22.61	19.24
3Q	43.55	25.12	17.35	27.79	25.04	21.10
4Q	35.46	30.41	21.73	28.16	26.89	19.52
Yr.	160.6	104.4	100.5	104.4	93.82	74.91
Earnings Per Share ($)						
1Q	0.00	0.09	0.35	0.26	0.26	0.23
2Q	**0.45**	0.24	0.16	0.30	0.26	0.25
3Q	**0.48**	-0.68	-0.18	-0.47	0.31	0.35
4Q	**0.33**	-0.27	0.01	0.34	0.27	0.31
Yr.	**1.63**	-0.65	0.34	0.45	1.11	1.15

Next earnings report expected: NA

Dividend Data

Under terms of credit agreements, the company is prohibited from paying cash dividends without prior bank approval. A 3-for-2 stock split was effected in 1992.

A Division of The McGraw-Hill Companies

Business Summary - 10-SEP-98

In an effort to enhance its strategic focus on its primary timing, data communications and custom products operations, Integrated Circuit Systems has jettisoned certain business units. In September 1996, it sold its battery charge controller business. Later in 1996, it sold its 87% interest in Turtle Beach Systems Inc., a provider of PC-based sound generation and editing hardware and software, to Voyetra Technologies Inc., a leading supplier of music and audio software, in exchange for about 35% of Voyetra's common stock. In June 1997, the company sold approximately 80% of its share holdings in ARK Logic, Inc., and recorded a one-time gain of about $2.3 million ($0.20 a share) in the fourth quarter of FY 97 (Jun.).

Intel, Compaq, IBM, Hewlett-Packard and Seagate were the company's major frequency timing generator (FTG) customers in FY 97. FTG products are mixed analog/digital integrated circuits that produce the high-frequency video dot timing function required by the video graphics array (VGA) display adaptors of IBM-compatible computers. FTG products also control multiple functions by providing and synchronizing the timing of the computer system. After a decline in the percentage of total revenues provided by FTG components in FY 96, the company increased its presence in new and growing applications for FTG in wireless communications and other non-PC applications which comprised less than 10% of its total FTG revenues in FY 97. FTG products made up about 54%, 45% and 52% of revenues in FY 97, FY 96 and FY 95, respectively.

The company has also developed and, since late FY 95, marketed transceiver chipsets for data communications applications, including ATM and SONET. New product introductions in FY 96 continued to address these applications and the Fast Ethernet market. The company believes that transition to Fast Ethernet in the LAN marketplace still offers opportunities for the firm's communication products. The company derived about 15% of total revenue in FY 97 from data communications applications, which were sold to customers such as Compaq, Hitachi, Hewlett Packard, Lexmark, Racore and Silicon Graphics.

Revenue from advanced technologies comprised 24%, 31% and 36% of total revenue in FY 97, FY 96 and FY 95, respectively, including engineering and design revenue representing reimbursement of research and development expenditures. The declining contribution of this segment reflects the overall increases in revenue from FTG and data communications components.

In FY 97, international sales, primarily to the Pacific Rim area, rose 13%, to 60% of revenues from 47% in FY 96.

Per Share Data ($)

(Year Ended Jun. 30)	1998	1997	1996	1995	1994	1993	1992	1991	1990	1989
Tangible Bk. Val.	7.28	5.64	5.93	5.62	5.15	4.19	2.09	1.61	0.37	NA
Cash Flow	1.97	-0.34	0.62	0.73	1.28	1.33	0.52	0.42	0.15	NA
Earnings	1.63	-0.65	0.34	0.45	1.11	1.15	0.43	0.33	0.07	NA
Dividends	Nil	Nil	Nil	Nil	Nil	Nil	Nil	Nil	Nil	Nil
Payout Ratio	Nil	Nil	Nil	Nil	Nil	Nil	Nil	Nil	Nil	Nil
Prices - High	36	44	14¾	18⅞	15¾	25	20⅜	7	NA	NA
- Low	12⅛	12⅝	6½	7⅜	6¾	9¾	6⅜	4⅜	NA	NA
P/E Ratio - High	22	NM	43	42	14	22	47	21	NA	NA
- Low	7	NM	19	16	6	8	15	13	NA	NA

Income Statement Analysis (Million $)

	1998	1997	1996	1995	1994	1993	1992	1991	1990	1989
Revs.	161	104	100	104	93.8	74.9	22.6	12.5	7.3	NA
Oper. Inc.	36.9	20.2	9.4	25.0	20.3	21.0	5.4	3.2	0.9	NA
Depr.	4.6	3.7	3.3	3.1	1.9	1.8	0.6	0.4	0.3	NA
Int. Exp.	0.1	0.6	0.7	0.8	0.5	0.3	0.0	0.1	0.1	NA
Pretax Inc.	34.2	-1.4	5.3	10.7	18.5	18.2	5.0	2.7	0.5	NA
Eff. Tax Rate	38%	NM	26%	49%	34%	38%	37%	37%	32%	NA
Net Inc.	21.4	-7.5	3.9	4.9	12.2	11.3	3.2	1.7	0.3	NA

Balance Sheet & Other Fin. Data (Million $)

	1998	1997	1996	1995	1994	1993	1992	1991	1990	1989
Cash	25.3	18.4	30.5	22.5	9.6	17.6	6.1	7.6	0.0	NA
Curr. Assets	80.8	66.2	68.5	63.9	48.3	41.3	15.0	12.3	2.8	NA
Total Assets	108	90.6	91.0	82.2	73.5	54.8	18.4	13.9	4.2	NA
Curr. Liab.	15.7	18.0	15.5	11.9	13.0	8.2	3.5	2.6	1.3	NA
LT Debt	1.4	1.5	1.6	3.5	3.8	3.3	0.1	0.2	1.1	NA
Common Eqty.	89.8	70.1	69.2	62.5	55.7	42.7	14.6	10.9	1.7	NA
Total Cap.	92.4	72.6	75.5	70.3	60.4	46.6	14.9	11.3	2.9	NA
Cap. Exp.	8.1	3.4	4.7	3.7	4.6	7.6	2.5	0.9	0.5	NA
Cash Flow	26.0	-3.9	7.2	8.1	14.1	13.0	3.8	2.1	0.7	NA
Curr. Ratio	5.2	3.7	4.4	5.4	3.7	5.1	4.3	4.7	2.2	NA
% LT Debt of Cap.	1.5	2.1	2.2	5.0	6.2	7.1	0.8	1.6	40.1	NA
% Net Inc.of Revs.	13.3	NM	3.9	4.7	13.0	15.1	14.1	13.7	4.7	NA
% Ret. on Assets	21.5	NM	4.5	6.3	18.6	27.6	19.5	16.8	NA	NA
% Ret. on Equity	26.7	NM	5.9	8.3	24.2	35.2	24.7	25.3	NA	NA

Data as orig. reptd.; bef. results of disc. opers. and/or spec. items. Per share data adj. for stk. divs. as of ex-div. date. Bold denotes diluted EPS (FASB 128). E-Estimated. NA-Not Available. NM-Not Meaningful. NR-Not Ranked.

Office—2435 Boulevard of the Generals, Norristown, PA 19403. **Tel**—(610) 630-5300. **Website**—http://www.icst.com **Chrmn**—H. I. Boreen.**Pres & CEO**—Dr. S. Prodromou.**SVP, CFO & COO**—H. E. Tan. **Dirs**—H. I. Boreen, E. M. Esber, R. Gassner, J. L. Pickitt, S. E. Prodromou. **Transfer Agent & Registrar**—StockTrans, Inc., Ardmore, PA. **Incorporated**—in Pennsylvania in 1976. **Empl**— 177. **S&P Analyst:** SRB

03-OCT-98

Industry:
Health Care
(Long-Term Care)

Summary: This company provides a broad range of medical services in medical specialty units located within nursing home facilities.

S&P Opinion: Hold (★★★)	Recent Price • 15⅞	Yield • 0.1%
	52 Wk Range • 39⅞-15⅜	12-Mo. P/E • 99.6

Quantitative Evaluations

Outlook
(1 Lowest—5 Highest)
• **5**

Fair Value
• **32**

Risk
• **Average**

Earn./Div. Rank
• **NR**

Technical Eval.
• **Bullish** since 9/98

Rel. Strength Rank
(1 Lowest—99 Highest)
• **8**

Insider Activity
• **Neutral**

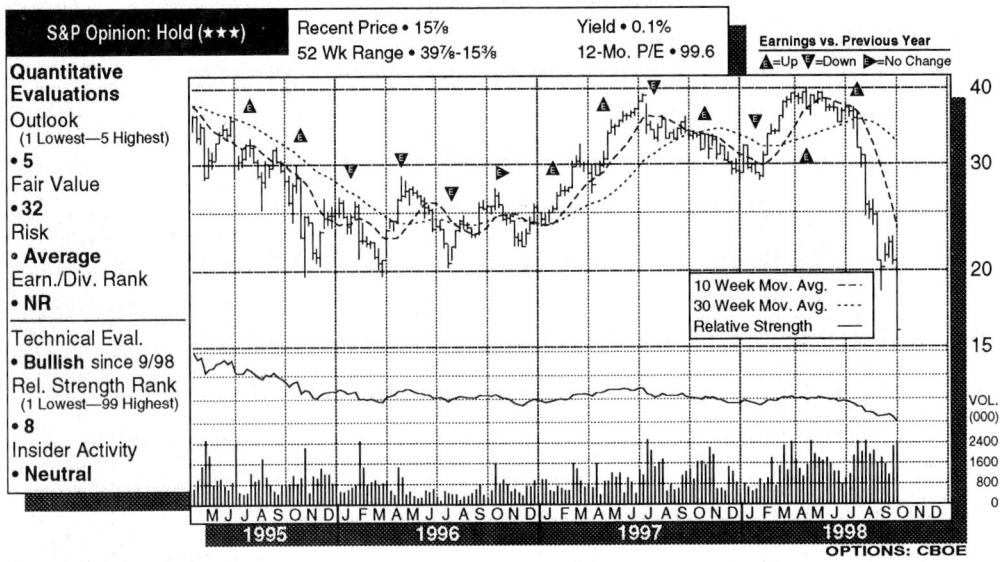

Earnings vs. Previous Year
▲=Up ▼=Down ▶=No Change

10 Week Mov. Avg. - - - -
30 Week Mov. Avg. - - - -
Relative Strength ——

OPTIONS: CBOE

Overview - 26-AUG-98

Revenues in 1998 should top the $3.0 billion level, reflecting the inclusion of the contract rehabilitation and long-term care operations recently acquired from HEALTHSOUTH Corp., expanding contributions from the home health care division (which should account for about one-third of total revenues) and increased demand for rehabilitation and other ancillary service offerings. Management has been actively divesting "noncore" assets in recent months, with proceeds used to retire outstanding debt. Efforts to streamline the operating cost structure should help the company sustain its margins as Medicare reimbursement changes take effect, while a more diversified revenue stream (specialty medical services account for about 70% of total revenues) offers added margin support. We look for diluted EPS of $3.05 in 1998 and $3.40 in 1999.

Valuation - 26-AUG-98

Although the stock appears inexpensive with a recent P/E of under 10 times our 1998 EPS estimate and less than 0.5 times projected 1998 sales, we do not expect IHS to outperform the broader market indices in coming months due to ongoing fears regarding the impact of Medicare reimbursement changes. The long term care group has been hurt by the lower earnings visibility resulting from Medicare changes implemented as part of the Balanced Budget Act of 1997, and the related uncertainties may continue to restrict upside moves. Although IHS's recent earnings reports were in line with our expectations, there may be some shortfalls ahead as demand for contract therapies, home nursing and other ancillary services wanes, while revenue growth on a "same-store" basis is not expected to rise materially in 1998.

Key Stock Statistics

S&P EPS Est. 1998	3.05	Tang. Bk. Value/Share	NM
P/E on S&P Est. 1998	5.2	Beta	1.28
S&P EPS Est. 1999	3.40	Shareholders	600
Dividend Rate/Share	0.02	Market cap. (B)	$0.861
Shs. outstg. (M)	54.1	Inst. holdings	92%
Avg. daily vol. (M)	0.413		

Value of $10,000 invested 5 years ago: $ 6,461

Fiscal Year Ending Dec. 31

	1998	1997	1996	1995	1994	1993
Revenues (Million $)						
1Q	854.8	460.9	327.3	265.4	132.3	57.60
2Q	816.7	458.0	335.8	278.1	138.7	63.00
3Q	—	472.9	360.0	299.5	177.2	72.20
4Q	—	602.2	445.7	319.2	235.4	89.47
Yr.	—	1,993	1,436	1,179	683.6	282.2
Earnings Per Share ($)						
1Q	**0.74**	**0.64**	0.62	0.61	0.41	0.30
2Q	**0.76**	**0.32**	0.64	0.62	0.44	0.33
3Q	—	**0.63**	0.69	0.60	0.52	0.35
4Q	—	**-1.55**	0.08	-3.03	0.59	0.38
Yr.	—	**-0.39**	2.03	-1.21	1.96	1.36

Next earnings report expected: late October

Dividend Data (Dividends have been paid since 1995.)

Amount ($)	Date Decl.	Ex-Div. Date	Stock of Record	Payment Date
0.020	Dec. 22	Dec. 26	Dec. 30	Jan. 09 '98

A Division of The **McGraw·Hill** Companies

STANDARD
&POOR'S
STOCK REPORTS

Integrated Health Services, Inc.

1203

03-OCT-98

Business Summary - 26-AUG-98

Integrated Health Services has grown dramatically in the past few years as it has capitalized on opportunities created by changes in the health care landscape. These have included limitations on reimbursement of hospital costs imposed by the federal government, along with pressures from private insurers and managed care organizations to lower inpatient hospital expenditures. The company ranks as one of the largest providers of "post-acute" health care services, offering a wide range of cost-effective medical and rehabilitative services more typically delivered in the acute care hospital setting and using home health care to provide those services that do not require 24-hour monitoring. IHS's post-acute care network consists of over 2,000 service locations in 47 states.

IHS provides subacute care through medical specialty units (MSUs), which typically have 20 to 75 beds with physical identities, specialized medical technology and staffs separate from the geriatric care facilities in which they are located. At 1997 year end, IHS operated 312 geriatric care facilities (260 owned or leased and 52 managed) and 158 MSUs located within 84 of these facilities. MSUs are designed to provide care similar to, but at per diem treatment costs believed to be generally 30% to 60% below, that in acute care hospitals.

Services provided to all patients at IHS's geriatric facilities, which are licensed as skilled care nursing homes, include nursing care, room and board, special diets and other services that may be ordered by a patient's physician. Specialty medical services include complex care programs; ventilator programs; wound management programs; cardiac care programs; rehabilitative services; oncology; HIV; Alzheimer's disease programs; and hospice services.

IHS also provides contract management services to 52 geriatric care facilities in return for a management fee generally equal to 4% to 8% of gross revenues of the facility.

Through acquisitions and organic growth, the company has expanded its home health care operations to take advantage of health care payors' increasing desire to deliver services in the lowest-cost setting possible, advances in medical technology that have facilitated the delivery of medical services in alternative sites, and the preference of many patients to be treated at home. Services include skilled nursing, infusion therapy, home health aid, mental health nursing, medical social services, and physical, speech and occupational therapies, respiratory therapy and infusion therapy.

IHS also owns a controlling interest in 10 lithotripsy partnerships (primarily consisting of physicians), and fully owns two lithotripsy partnerships and a lithotripter maintenance company. Its lithotripsy business consists of about 35 lithotripsy machines that provide services in 170 locations in 17 states.

Patient revenues in 1997 were derived from private pay sources (34%), Medicare (49%) and Medicaid (17%).

Per Share Data ($)

(Year Ended Dec. 31)	1997	1996	1995	1994	1993	1992	1991	1990	1989	1988
Tangible Bk. Val.	NM	-1.58	6.23	22.24	12.28	12.38	9.75	-149.48	NA	NA
Cash Flow	1.40	3.79	0.65	3.41	1.71	1.28	1.13	0.94	NA	NA
Earnings	-0.39	2.03	-1.20	1.96	1.36	1.04	0.82	0.42	NA	NA
Dividends	0.02	0.02	0.02	0.02	Nil	Nil	Nil	Nil	Nil	Nil
Payout Ratio	NM	1%	NM	1%	Nil	Nil	Nil	Nil	Nil	Nil
Prices - High	39⅛	28¾	42½	41⅛	31⅜	29¼	22½	NA	NA	NA
- Low	23¾	19⅝	19⅝	28⅛	19⅞	16¾	13¾	NA	NA	NA
P/E Ratio - High	NM	14	NM	21	23	28	27	NA	NA	NA
- Low	NM	10	NM	14	15	16	17	NA	NA	NA

Income Statement Analysis (Million $)

	1997	1996	1995	1994	1993	1992	1991	1990	1989	1988
Revs.	1,993	1,435	1,179	682	281	195	144	82.0	NA	NA
Oper. Inc.	332	202	168	102	38.2	23.4	14.6	8.1	NA	NA
Depr.	70.8	41.7	40.0	26.0	4.6	2.8	2.2	1.7	NA	NA
Int. Exp.	123	66.3	40.8	24.7	9.8	3.6	6.1	5.7	NA	NA
Pretax Inc.	13.3	111	-42.3	56.3	29.1	18.8	8.0	1.6	NA	NA
Eff. Tax Rate	183%	57%	NM	38%	39%	38%	26%	8.00%	NA	NA
Net Inc.	-11.1	47.8	-26.0	35.2	17.5	11.7	5.9	1.4	NA	NA

Balance Sheet & Other Fin. Data (Million $)

	1997	1996	1995	1994	1993	1992	1991	1990	1989	1988
Cash	53.0	39.0	41.3	60.0	60.0	104	16.0	2.0	NA	NA
Curr. Assets	718	415	314	240	161	168	61.0	22.0	NA	NA
Total Assets	5,063	1,993	1,434	1,238	768	312	156	102	NA	NA
Curr. Liab.	654	358	177	170	100	22.7	19.1	19.7	NA	NA
LT Debt	3,202	1,038	766	542	388	140	47.0	56.0	NA	NA
Common Eqty.	1,088	535	432	443	209	146	87.0	-162	NA	NA
Total Cap.	4,290	1,595	1,250	1,060	667	288	135	81.0	NA	NA
Cap. Exp.	127	146	60.0	91.0	343	41.0	8.3	14.7	NA	NA
Cash Flow	59.6	89.4	14.0	61.2	22.4	14.4	8.1	3.1	NA	NA
Curr. Ratio	1.1	1.2	1.8	1.4	1.6	7.4	3.2	1.1	NA	NA
% LT Debt of Cap.	74.6	65.1	61.3	51.1	58.2	48.8	35.0	68.9	NA	NA
% Net Inc.of Revs.	NM	3.3	NM	5.2	6.3	6.0	4.1	1.7	NA	NA
% Ret. on Assets	NM	2.8	NM	3.0	3.1	4.5	1.3	NA	NA	NA
% Ret. on Equity	NM	9.9	NM	9.4	9.3	8.9	NM	NA	NA	NA

Data as orig. reptd.; bef. results of disc. opers. and/or spec. items. Per share data adj. for stk. divs. as of ex-div. date. Bold denotes diluted EPS (FASB 128). E-Estimated. NA-Not Available. NM-Not Meaningful. NR-Not Ranked.

Office—10065 Red Run Blvd., Owings Mills, MD 21117. **Tel**—(410) 998-8400. **Website**—http://www.ihs-inc.com **Chrmn & CEO**—R. N. Elkins. **EVP-COO**—C. C. Winkle. **EVP-Fin**—Eleanor C. Harding. **EVP-Investor Relations & Secy**—Marc B. Levin. **Dirs**—L. P. Cirka, E. M. Crawford, R. N. Elkins, K. M. Mazik, R. A. Mitchell, C. N. Newhall III, T. F. Nicholson, J. L. Silverman, G. H. Strong. **Transfer Agent & Registrar**—American Stock Transfer & Trust Co., NYC. **Incorporated**—in Delaware in 1986.**Empl**— 59,000. **S&P Analyst:** Robert M. Gold

STANDARD &POOR'S
STOCK REPORTS
Inter-Tel, Inc.
4249N
NASDAQ Symbol **INTL**
In S&P SmallCap 600

03-OCT-98

Industry:
Communications
Equipment

Summary: Inter-Tel designs, produces and markets telephone systems, applications and services to businesses requiring small to medium-size telephone system installations.

Quantitative Evaluations

Recent Price • 11⅜	Yield • 0.4%
52 Wk Range • 32⅜-11¼	12-Mo. P/E • 66.9

Outlook
(1 Lowest—5 Highest)
• **5**

Fair Value
• **25**

Risk
• **High**

Earn./Div. Rank
• **B**

Technical Eval.
• **Bearish** since 3/98

Rel. Strength Rank
(1 Lowest—99 Highest)
• **17**

Insider Activity
• **Neutral**

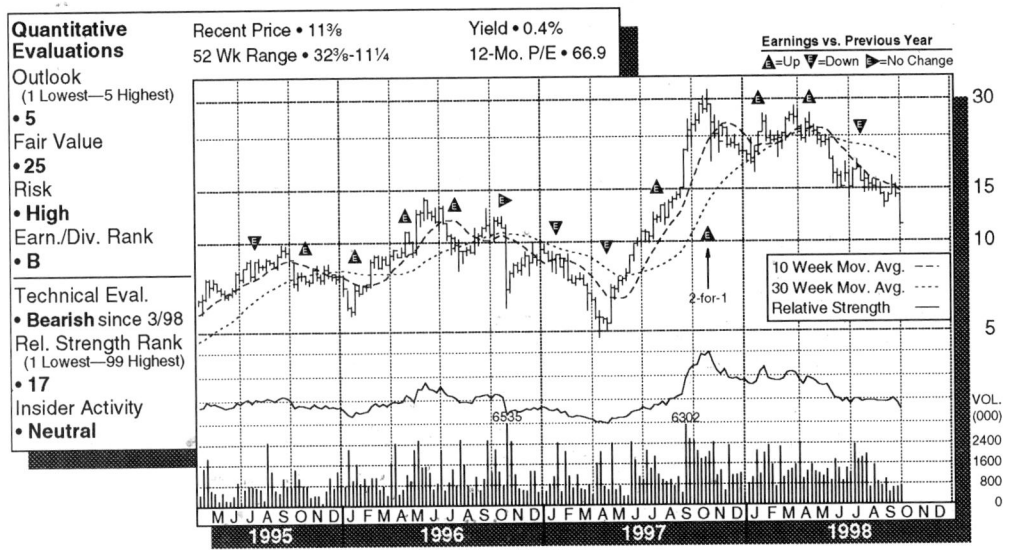

Earnings vs. Previous Year
▲=Up ▼=Down ▶=No Change

10 Week Mov. Avg. - - -
30 Week Mov. Avg. ·····
Relative Strength ——

2-for-1

Business Profile - 31-JUL-98

In June 1998, the company acquired for $25 million in cash Telecom Multimedia Systems Inc., a California-based provider of communications solutions. During the second quarter of 1998, Inter-Tel also acquired Kentucky-based Integrated Telecom Services Corp. In June 1998, directors approved the repurchase of up to 2.5 million INTL common shares. In December 1997, 3,070,00 common shares (3 million new) were sold at $21 a share, with net proceeds slated for private telephone network expansion, potential acquisitions, and general corporate purposes.

Operational Review - 31-JUL-98

Net sales in the six months ended June 30, 1998, rose 30%, year to year, aided by recent acquisitions. Margins widened significantly, reflecting a smaller rise in cost of sales, partly offset by greater R&D and SG&A expenditures. Results were penalized by a $24.2 million charge associated with purchased in-process R&D and other acquisition costs. Despite tax credits of $2,638,000, versus taxes at 40.2%, a net loss of $4,601,000 ($0.17 a share, on more shares) contrasted with net income of $6,094,000 ($0.24, as adjusted).

Stock Performance - 02-OCT-98

In the past 30 trading days, INTL's shares have declined 24%, compared to a 7% fall in the S&P 500. Average trading volume for the past five days was 142,540 shares, compared with the 40-day moving average of 165,103 shares.

Key Stock Statistics

Dividend Rate/Share	0.04	Shareholders	1,000
Shs. outstg. (M)	27.1	Market cap. (B)	$0.308
Avg. daily vol. (M)	0.125	Inst. holdings	46%
Tang. Bk. Value/Share	5.23		
Beta	1.89		

Value of $10,000 invested 5 years ago: $ 50,043

Fiscal Year Ending Dec. 31

	1998	1997	1996	1995	1994	1993
Revenues (Million $)						
1Q	63.76	50.32	42.20	34.56	25.47	18.70
2Q	70.51	54.82	43.74	36.33	27.76	22.25
3Q	—	56.92	47.44	37.76	27.63	23.40
4Q	—	61.51	52.50	40.19	31.32	24.97
Yr.	—	223.6	185.9	148.8	112.2	89.26
Earnings Per Share ($)						
1Q	0.19	0.10	0.11	0.08	0.06	0.04
2Q	-0.37	0.13	0.10	0.06	0.08	0.05
3Q	—	0.16	0.10	0.10	0.07	0.06
4Q	—	0.18	0.03	0.11	0.10	0.08
Yr.	—	0.57	0.34	0.35	0.29	0.23

Next earnings report expected: late October

Dividend Data (Dividends have been paid since 1998.)

Amount ($)	Date Decl.	Ex-Div. Date	Stock of Record	Payment Date
0.010	Sep. 25	Dec. 29	Dec. 31	Jan. 15 '98
0.010	Mar. 23	Mar. 27	Mar. 31	Apr. 15 '98
0.010	Jul. 22	Jul. 24	Jun. 30	Jul. 15 '98
0.010	Sep. 17	Sep. 28	Sep. 30	Oct. 15 '98

Business Summary - 31-JUL-98

Inter-Tel is a single point of contact, full-service provider of digital business telephone systems, call processing software, voice processing software, call accounting software, Internet Protocol (IP) telephony software, computer telephone integration applications, and long distance calling services. The company also provides maintenance, leasing and support services for its products.

The company has developed a distribution network of direct sales offices, dealers and value-added resellers that sell INTL's products to small-to-medium size organizations and to divisions of larger companies, including Fortune 500 firms, large service organizations and governmental agencies. Inter-Tel has 30 sales offices in the U.S., and one each in the U.K. and Japan.

INTL offers an extensive line of digital communication systems, including hardware platforms and C++ software applications. The company's primary product, the AXXESS platform, incorporates advanced technology for computer and telephone integration providing businesses with ability to customize applications to enhance their operations and increase productivity. In the second half of 1998, Inter-Tel expects to introduce AXX-ESS 5.1, which is designed to allow two or more systems to operate as one, and to increase capacity to 20,000 ports.

The company's gateway products are designed as transition points between two different networks, such as between a telephone network and the Internet. Gateway products convert regular voice transmissions to or from the compressed data packets that travel over networks. In September 1997, INTL unveiled Inter-Tel Vocal 'Net, a stand-alone IP network telephony solution available for use with the AXXESS system or other traditional telephone systems. Vocal 'Net allows customers to bridge their telephone network to the company's intranet or Internet.

Inter-Tel's computer-telephone integration products enable users to receive phone calls through their desktop PC. In addition, the system can collect, analyze and report real-time call processing information for staff forecasting and analysis. INTL also offers Visual Mail, a messaging software system which supports both voice mail and facsimile mail, providing another means for improving productivity and retrieving messages from a PC connected to a modem.

In June 1998, the company acquired Telecom Multimedia Systems Inc., paying $25 million in cash for the California-based provider of communications solutions.

In December 1997, 3,070,000 common shares (including 70,000 for selling shareholders) were sold at $21 a share. Company proceeds were targeted to expand INTL's private telephone network, for potential acquisitions, and for general corporate purposes.

Per Share Data ($)

(Year Ended Dec. 31)	1997	1996	1995	1994	1993	1992	1991	1990	1989	1988
Tangible Bk. Val.	5.29	3.50	3.33	2.12	1.81	1.09	0.95	1.23	1.13	1.09
Cash Flow	0.74	0.49	0.45	0.36	0.30	0.29	0.20	0.21	0.14	0.19
Earnings	0.57	0.34	0.35	0.29	0.23	0.18	0.06	0.08	0.03	0.10
Dividends	0.01	Nil	Nil	Nil	Nil	Nil	Nil	Nil	Nil	Nil
Payout Ratio	2%	Nil	Nil	Nil	Nil	Nil	Nil	Nil	Nil	Nil
Prices - High	32³/₈	14¹/₄	9⁷/₈	6¹/₈	6	2⁵/₈	³/₄	1¹/₄	1³/₈	2⁵/₈
- Low	4³/₄	5³/₄	3¹/₂	3	2	⁷/₁₆	⁵/₁₆	¹/₂	⁹/₁₆	1
P/E Ratio - High	57	42	28	21	27	14	13	16	46	26
- Low	8	17	10	10	9	3	6	6	19	10

Income Statement Analysis (Million $)

	1997	1996	1995	1994	1993	1992	1991	1990	1989	1988
Revs.	224	186	149	112	89.3	78.8	66.1	67.4	61.6	62.6
Oper. Inc.	27.8	22.0	15.7	10.5	7.6	6.7	4.3	5.4	4.0	4.8
Depr.	4.6	4.1	2.2	1.5	1.3	1.8	2.4	2.0	1.8	1.6
Int. Exp.	0.0	0.1	0.1	0.1	0.4	0.7	0.9	1.4	1.6	1.1
Pretax Inc.	24.6	15.3	13.7	9.8	6.1	4.9	1.5	2.5	0.8	3.0
Eff. Tax Rate	40%	41%	38%	38%	38%	38%	40%	46%	39%	42%
Net Inc.	14.7	9.0	8.4	6.1	3.8	3.0	0.9	1.3	0.5	1.8

Balance Sheet & Other Fin. Data (Million $)

	1997	1996	1995	1994	1993	1992	1991	1990	1989	1988
Cash	88.8	38.9	39.6	15.3	14.5	2.2	1.3	0.7	3.3	1.0
Curr. Assets	157	105	97.8	50.9	45.7	25.2	23.8	21.1	25.5	23.2
Total Assets	195	133	118	64.1	53.4	35.3	39.6	40.7	45.8	44.2
Curr. Liab.	33.6	25.8	22.3	13.3	11.6	13.0	16.0	11.3	16.8	14.9
LT Debt	Nil	Nil	Nil	Nil	Nil	1.8	5.9	7.8	8.6	8.3
Common Eqty.	146	94.9	85.2	45.3	38.1	19.2	16.6	20.9	20.4	21.0
Total Cap.	157	104	92.4	47.9	39.3	21.0	22.5	28.7	29.0	29.3
Cap. Exp.	12.5	7.0	7.9	4.1	1.4	0.6	0.9	2.0	1.6	4.5
Cash Flow	19.3	13.1	10.7	7.6	5.1	4.8	3.3	3.4	2.3	3.3
Curr. Ratio	4.7	4.1	4.4	3.8	3.9	1.9	1.5	1.9	1.5	1.6
% LT Debt of Cap.	Nil	Nil	Nil	Nil	Nil	8.8	26.1	27.0	29.5	28.4
% Net Inc.of Revs.	6.6	4.9	5.7	5.4	4.3	3.8	1.4	2.0	0.8	2.8
% Ret. on Assets	9.0	7.2	9.1	10.2	7.8	8.0	2.3	3.2	1.2	3.9
% Ret. on Equity	12.2	10.1	12.9	14.4	12.3	16.8	4.9	6.6	2.6	8.7

Data as orig. reptd.; bef. results of disc. opers. and/or spec. items. Per share data adj. for stk. divs. as of ex-div. date. E-Estimated. NA-Not Available. NM-Not Meaningful. NR-Not Ranked.

Office—120 North 44th St., Suite 200, Phoenix, AZ 85034-1822. **Tel**—(602) 302-8900. **Website**—http://www.inter-tel.com. **Chrmn & CEO**—S. G. Mihaylo. **Pres & COO**—T. C. Parise. **VP, CFO, Treas & Secy**—K. R. Kneip. **Dirs**—J. R. Anderson, G. D. Edens, M. S. Esperseth, C. R. Haden, S. G. Mihaylo, N. Stout. **Transfer Agent & Registrar**—First Interstate Bank of California, LA. **Incorporated**—in Arizona in 1969. **Empl**— 1,248. **S&P Analyst:** Stephen J. Tekirian

03-OCT-98

Industry: Textiles (Home Furnishings)

Summary: The company is a leader in the worldwide commercial interiors market, offering floorcoverings, fabrics, specialty chemicals and interior architectural products.

Quantitative Evaluations	
Outlook (1 Lowest—5 Highest)	• **4⁻**
Fair Value	• **15¾**
Risk	• **Average**
Earn./Div. Rank	• **A-**
Technical Eval.	• **NA**
Rel. Strength Rank (1 Lowest—99 Highest)	• **16**
Insider Activity	• **Neutral**

Recent Price • 10½
52 Wk Range • 22⅞-10⅛
Yield • 1.7%
12-Mo. P/E • 12.1

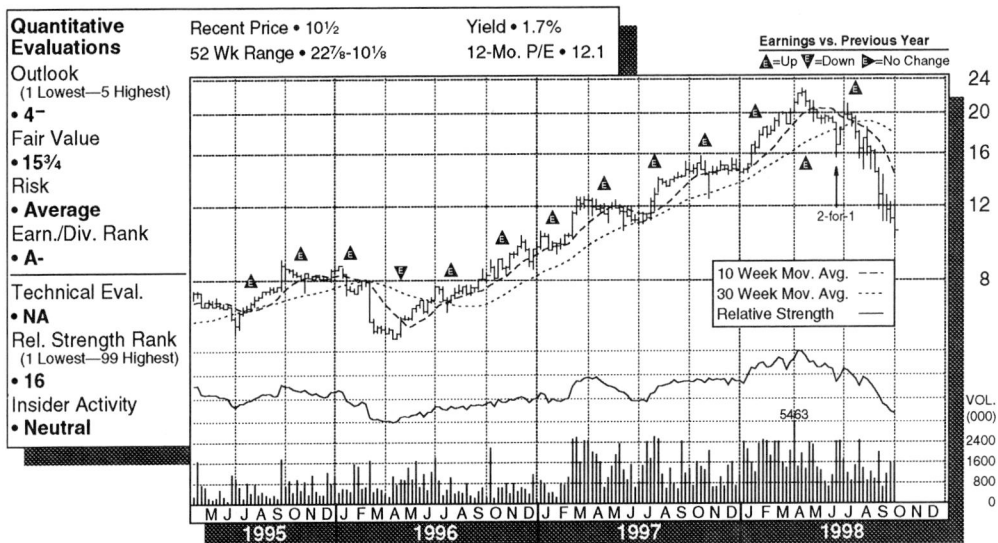

Earnings vs. Previous Year ▲=Up ▼=Down ▶=No Change

10 Week Mov. Avg. - - -
30 Week Mov. Avg. · · · ·
Relative Strength —

2-for-1

Business Profile - 05-AUG-98

IFSIA, the world's largest manufacturer of modular carpet, also makes broadloom carpeting, interior fabrics for open-plan office furniture systems and certain specialty chemicals. In June 1997, the company purchased a manufacturer of textiles for the office and contract furnishings industry. The Interface Specialty Resources Group combined IFSIA's chemical and specialty surfaces companies, Intersept licensing program and Architectural Resources business unit. In December 1997, IFSIA acquired the European carpet businesses of Readicut International plc (Firth Carpets Ltd). In April 1998 public offerings, $150 million of debt and 1.7 million Class A common shares were sold. Directors have authorized the repurchase of up to 600,000 shares. The dividend was boosted 20% with the August 1998 payment.

Operational Review - 05-AUG-98

Net sales in the six months ended July 5, 1998, advanced 20%, year to year, on strong U.S. floor covering and fabric sales, and higher sales at Interface Americas Workplace Solutions. Despite the negative effect of currency translations, and increased SG&A expense, operating profit advanced 30%. After taxes at 38.6%, versus 38.7%, net income climbed 53%, to $21,947,000 ($0.42 a share, diluted, on 15% more shares), from $14,313,000 ($0.31).

Stock Performance - 02-OCT-98

In the past 30 trading days, IFSIA's shares have declined 35%, compared to a 7% fall in the S&P 500. Average trading volume for the past five days was 316,200 shares, compared with the 40-day moving average of 253,851 shares.

Key Stock Statistics

Dividend Rate/Share	0.18	Shareholders	500
Shs. outstg. (M)	52.4	Market cap. (B)	$0.490
Avg. daily vol. (M)	0.250	Inst. holdings	74%
Tang. Bk. Value/Share	0.78		
Beta	1.29		

Value of $10,000 invested 5 years ago: $ 18,412

Fiscal Year Ending Dec. 31

	1998	1997	1996	1995	1994	1993
Revenues (Million $)						
1Q	318.9	257.4	205.0	191.3	160.7	135.0
2Q	316.9	271.8	237.5	202.8	181.7	150.1
3Q	—	297.4	275.0	203.3	185.0	167.6
4Q	—	308.9	284.5	204.7	196.9	172.4
Yr.	—	1,135	1,002	802.1	725.3	625.1
Earnings Per Share ($)						
1Q	**0.20**	0.14	0.09	0.10	0.07	0.07
2Q	**0.22**	0.17	0.14	0.13	0.09	0.08
3Q	—	0.22	0.17	0.11	0.10	0.10
4Q	—	**0.26**	0.20	0.15	0.14	0.13
Yr.	—	**0.76**	0.61	0.51	0.41	0.38

Next earnings report expected: late October

Dividend Data (Dividends have been paid since 1977.)

Amount ($)	Date Decl.	Ex-Div. Date	Stock of Record	Payment Date
0.075	Feb. 25	Mar. 11	Mar. 13	Mar. 27 '98
0.075	Apr. 27	May. 06	May. 08	May. 22 '98
2-for-1	May. 21	Jun. 16	Jun. 01	Jun. 15 '98
0.045	Jul. 30	Aug. 12	Aug. 14	Aug. 28 '98

STANDARD
&POOR'S
STOCK REPORTS

Interface, Inc.

4249X
03-OCT-98

Business Summary - 05-AUG-98

Interface, Inc. (IFSIA) is involved in an office coverup. IFSIA (formerly Interface Flooring Systems) is a leader in the worldwide commercial and institutional interiors market, providing floor coverings, fabrics, specialty chemicals, and interior architectural products in over 100 countries. The company is the world's largest manufacturer in the modular carpet segment, with a 40% market share in 1997.

IFSIA's traditional core business has been the manufacture, marketing and servicing of modular carpet, including carpet tile and two meter roll goods, which offers advantages over broadloom carpet and other soft surface flooring, such as greater design options and flexibility, longer average life and easy access to under floor wiring.

Modular carpet is offered under the international brands Interface and Heuga, which are the leading names in carpet tiles for commercial and institutional use. IFSIA has a large share of the high end, designer oriented broadloom carpet segment and combines innovative product design and styling capabilities. Production and delivery times are short and the company's marketing strategy involves serving and working with interior designers, architects and other specifiers. The company's Bentley Mills unit makes broadloom carpet-

ing used primarily for commercial and institutional applications, and its Prince Street Technologies unit makes technically advanced tufted broadloom carpeting used mainly in the U.S. commercial market. Firth Carpets manufactures high quality woven and tufted products. Vebe Floorcoverings is one of Europe's largest needlepunch carpet producers that focuses on volume sales to large distributors of carpet products.

The carpet segment also includes Re:Source Americas, a network of floorcovering dealers and Renovisions, a nationwide carpet installation firm which also created innovative methods of carpet replacement.

The interior fabrics segment designs, manufactures and markets specialty fabrics for use in open-plan office furniture systems and commercial interiors. It also makes fabrics for seating fabrics, wall covering fabrics, fabrics used for vertical blinds in office interiors and fabrics used for cubicle curtains in health care facilities. The Interface Specialty Products Group develops specialty chemical products and an antimicrobial chemical compound called Intersept. Additionally, Pandel produces vinyl carpet tile backing and specialty mat and foam products while Interface Architectural Resources offers products for raised/access flooring systems.

In July 1998, Interface acquired Atlantic Access Flooring, Inc., a manufacturer of steel panel/raised access systems (1997 sales of under $5 million).

Per Share Data ($)

(Year Ended Dec. 31)	1997	1996	1995	1994	1993	1992	1991	1990	1989	1988
Tangible Bk. Val.	0.78	0.56	0.35	0.31	-0.21	1.53	1.64	1.48	0.54	0.06
Cash Flow	1.54	1.50	1.30	1.19	0.96	0.75	0.90	1.19	1.14	0.97
Earnings	0.77	0.61	0.51	0.41	0.38	0.35	0.26	0.69	0.71	0.59
Dividends	0.14	0.12	0.12	0.12	0.12	0.12	0.12	0.12	0.10	0.08
Payout Ratio	18%	20%	24%	29%	32%	34%	46%	18%	15%	13%
Prices - High	15⅞	10¼	9	8½	7¾	8¼	7⅛	9⅞	9¾	8⅜
- Low	9¼	5⅞	5⅞	4⅞	4⅞	4⅞	4	3⅜	7⅜	4¼
P/E Ratio - High	21	17	18	21	21	23	27	14	14	14
- Low	12	9	11	12	13	14	15	5	10	7

Income Statement Analysis (Million $)

	1997	1996	1995	1994	1993	1992	1991	1990	1989	1988
Revs.	1,135	1,002	802	725	625	594	582	623	582	397
Oper. Inc.	136	114	90.5	79.0	66.6	54.1	59.9	76.8	78.4	58.9
Depr.	38.6	35.3	28.9	28.2	20.5	13.6	22.0	17.3	14.5	13.2
Int. Exp.	35.0	32.9	26.8	24.1	22.8	21.9	23.3	25.2	23.8	11.2
Pretax Inc.	61.3	43.4	31.7	25.7	21.3	18.6	14.3	37.7	40.6	34.1
Eff. Tax Rate	39%	39%	36%	36%	35%	34%	38%	37%	40%	41%
Net Inc.	37.5	26.4	20.3	16.5	13.8	12.3	8.9	23.6	24.5	20.2

Balance Sheet & Other Fin. Data (Million $)

	1997	1996	1995	1994	1993	1992	1991	1990	1989	1988
Cash	10.2	8.8	8.8	7.1	8.7	10.2	10.4	10.1	18.7	14.0
Curr. Assets	375	353	274	292	267	232	263	271	244	225
Total Assets	930	863	714	688	642	534	569	582	526	493
Curr. Liab.	192	164	115	117	126	94.0	112	114	112	97.0
LT Debt	390	379	324	314	292	235	240	255	244	249
Common Eqty.	316	273	232	214	182	186	199	198	157	136
Total Cap.	735	863	599	570	516	441	457	468	414	395
Cap. Exp.	38.7	36.4	42.1	21.3	28.7	13.7	15.9	32.8	23.0	60.1
Cash Flow	76.1	60.0	47.5	42.9	33.4	25.9	30.9	40.9	39.1	33.4
Curr. Ratio	2.0	2.2	2.4	2.5	2.1	2.5	2.3	2.4	2.2	2.3
% LT Debt of Cap.	53.1	44.0	54.1	55.0	56.5	53.5	52.5	54.4	59.0	63.1
% Net Inc.of Revs.	3.3	2.6	2.6	2.3	2.2	2.1	1.5	3.8	4.2	5.1
% Ret. on Assets	4.2	3.3	2.2	2.4	2.3	2.2	1.5	4.3	4.8	5.6
% Ret. on Equity	12.7	9.8	6.8	7.3	7.0	6.4	4.5	13.3	16.7	16.0

Data as orig. reptd.; bef. results of disc. opers. and/or spec. items. Per share data adj. for stk. divs. as of ex-div. date. Bold denotes diluted EPS (FASB 128). E-Estimated. NA-Not Available. NM-Not Meaningful. NR-Not Ranked.

Office—2859 Paces Ferry Rd., Suite 2000, Atlanta, GA 30339. **Tel**—(770) 437-6800. **Chrmn & CEO**—R. C. Anderson. **Pres & COO**—C. R. Eitel. **SVP-Fin, CFO, Treas & Investor Contact**—Daniel T. Hendrix. **Secy**—R. S. Willoch. **Dirs**—R. C. Anderson, B. L. DeMoura, D. Dillon-Ridgley, C. R. Eitel, C. I. Gable, D. T. Hendrix, J. M. Henton, J. S. Lanier II, T. R. Oliver, L. G. Saulter, C. C. van Andel, J. H. Walker, G. D. Whitener. **Transfer Agent**—Wachovia Bank & Trust Co., Winston-Salem, NC. **Incorporated**—in Georgia in 1981. **Empl**— 7,200. **S&P Analyst:** Kathleen J. Fraser

STANDARD &POOR'S
STOCK REPORTS

Interim Services
1207M

NYSE Symbol **IS**

In S&P SmallCap 600

03-OCT-98

Industry:
Services (Employment)

Summary: This company provides staffing solutions in technology, legal, accounting, human resources, marketing, search and outplacement, as well as clerical and light industrial.

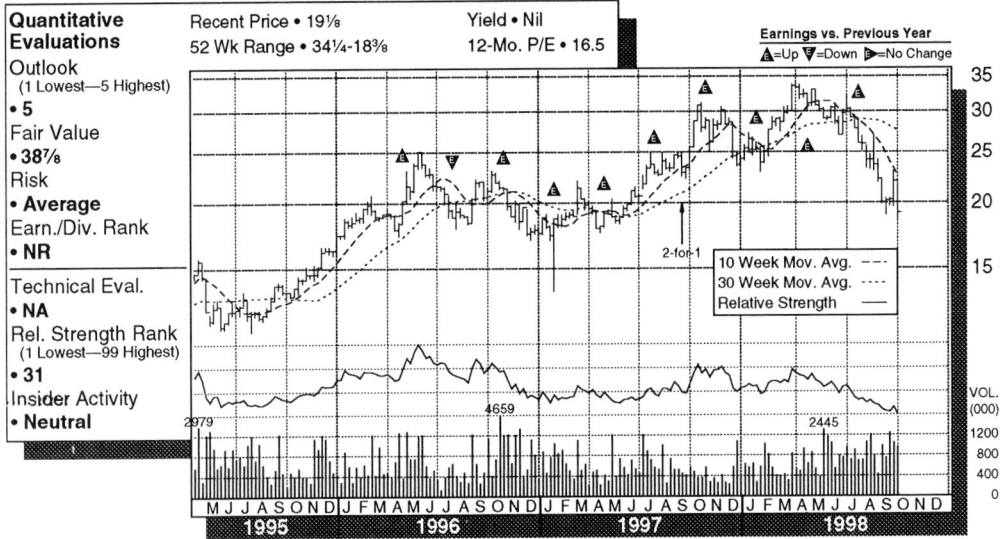

Quantitative Evaluations	
Outlook (1 Lowest—5 Highest)	**• 5**
Fair Value	**• 38⅞**
Risk	**• Average**
Earn./Div. Rank	**• NR**
Technical Eval.	**• NA**
Rel. Strength Rank (1 Lowest—99 Highest)	**• 31**
Insider Activity	**• Neutral**

Recent Price • 19⅛
52 Wk Range • 34¼-18⅜

Yield • Nil
12-Mo. P/E • 16.5

Earnings vs. Previous Year
▲=Up ▼=Down ▷=No Change

10 Week Mov. Avg. ---
30 Week Mov. Avg. ·····
Relative Strength —

2-for-1

Business Profile - 17-SEP-98

Several acquisitions have provided growth for the company over the past year, and IS continued its campaign into the third quarter of 1998, with the purchase of three additional businesses. The companies that were acquired were the Saratoga Institute, a human performance measurement firm, AGO Uitzendbureau, a Netherlands commercial staffing company, and Clarke, Poynton and Associates, a privately held outplacement services provider. The professional services unit of IS now accounts for more than half of the company's revenues and is responsible for expanding overall gross margins. In May 1998, IS completed the sale of 7 million shares of common stock and $207 million of convertible subordinated debt.

Operational Review - 17-SEP-98

Revenues for the six months ended June 30, 1998, rose 19%, year to year, due to internal growth and the benefit of several acquisitions. Despite substantially higher interest expense from funding acquisitions, profitability improved on a larger contribution from higher-margin professional services revenue; operating income increased 33%. Following greater depreciation and amortization charges resulting from acquisitions, and taxes at 44.2% in both periods, income climbed 31%, to $24,139,000 ($0.57 per share, on 8.1% more shares), from $18,447,000 ($0.46). Results in the 1998 period exclude an extraordinary loss from the early extinguishment of debt of $0.06 per share.

Stock Performance - 02-OCT-98

In the past 30 trading days, IS's shares have declined 19%, compared to a 7% fall in the S&P 500. Average trading volume for the past five days was 191,640 shares, compared with the 40-day moving average of 200,703 shares.

Key Stock Statistics

Dividend Rate/Share	Nil	Shareholders	700
Shs. outstg. (M)	47.3	Market cap. (B)	$0.904
Avg. daily vol. (M)	0.225	Inst. holdings	90%
Tang. Bk. Value/Share	NM		
Beta	NA		

Value of $10,000 invested 5 years ago: NA

Fiscal Year Ending Dec. 31

	1998	1997	1996	1995	1994	1993
Revenues (Million $)						
1Q	416.2	316.8	264.7	147.6	—	—
2Q	461.6	422.8	281.2	182.8	—	—
3Q	—	455.8	294.7	201.2	—	—
4Q	—	412.9	306.5	223.4	—	—
Yr.	—	1,608	1,147	780.9	634.4	515.0
Earnings Per Share ($)						
1Q	**0.26**	0.21	0.18	0.14	—	—
2Q	**0.31**	0.25	-0.01	0.17	—	—
3Q	—	0.30	0.25	0.20	—	—
4Q	—	0.29	0.27	0.23	—	—
Yr.	—	**1.05**	0.69	0.75	0.62	0.47

Next earnings report expected: early November

Dividend Data

No cash dividends have been paid.

A Division of The **McGraw·Hill** Companies

Business Summary - 17-SEP-98

Interim Services is a $1.6 billion employment staffing and consulting company with 706 offices in North America, Europe, Asia and Australia. It has two major divisions: Professional Services and Commercial Staffing. Professional Services (42% of 1997 revenues) provides staffing and consulting solutions, information technology, legal, accounting, human resources, sales and marketing, search and outplacement. Commercial Staffing (46%) specializes in administrative, clerical and light industrial employees; its major driver is Interim On-Premise, a service in which the company establishes an office at the client's site and manages the entire flexible work force.

Interim was founded in 1946 to provide temporary industrial services. In 1978, a company known as Personnel Pool of America was acquired by H&R Block, which also acquired Interim. The two businesses were combined and expanded to serve both corporate and health care clients under the Interim name. IS had its IPO in 1994; since then, the company has acquired 13 flexible staffing companies, including five companies in 1995, three in 1996, and four in 1997.

In March 1997, Interim acquired Aim Executive Holdings for about $33 million; the acquired company will operate under the Interim banner as three divisions

called Interim Career Consulting, Interim Executive Recruiting, and Interim Technical Staffing. IS announced recently that Career Consulting had won a significant exclusive contract to provide career transition assistance for 10,000 employees of one of the largest U.S. retailers.

In April 1997, IS purchased a 75% interest in U.K.-based Michael Page Group, a staffing and recruitment company operating throughout eight countries in Europe and Asia; the purchase raised Interim's stake in Michael Page to 92%.

As part of an effort to focus on its professional and commercial staffing units, Interim sold its health care business in September 1997 for $134 million in cash. Proceeds were used to reduce debt.

Interim, headquartered in Fort Lauderdale, FL, is led by its chairman and CEO Ray Marcy, who noted that the divestiture of the health care business would enable management to focus on the core commercial business and future growth. IS has outlined its strategies for growth: to increase revenue through network expansion, aggressively expand professional services, replicate domestic success globally, leverage common brand identity, deliver services through specialized offices, support an entrepreneurial environment, and provide total human resource solutions.

Per Share Data ($)

(Year Ended Dec. 31)	1997	1996	1995	1994	1993	1992	1991	1990	1989	1988
Tangible Bk. Val.	NM	12.33	1.08	3.78	2.48	3.74	3.29	NA	NA	NA
Cash Flow	1.92	2.51	1.34	1.12	1.00	0.84	NA	NA	NA	NA
Earnings	1.05	0.69	0.75	0.62	0.47	0.39	0.34	NA	NA	NA
Dividends	Nil	Nil	Nil	Nil	Nil	Nil	Nil	Nil	Nil	Nil
Payout Ratio	Nil	Nil	Nil	Nil	Nil	Nil	Nil	Nil	Nil	Nil
Prices - High	31⅛	25⅛	17¾	14⅛	NA	NA	NA	NA	NA	NA
- Low	13½	17	11⅜	10	NA	NA	NA	NA	NA	NA
P/E Ratio - High	30	36	24	23	NA	NA	NA	NA	NA	NA
- Low	13	25	15	16	NA	NA	NA	NA	NA	NA

Income Statement Analysis (Million $)

	1997	1996	1995	1994	1993	1992	1991	1990	1989	1988
Revs.	1,608	1,147	781	634	515	429	382	NA	NA	NA
Oper. Inc.	135	78.3	53.8	44.5	37.1	32.2	NA	NA	NA	NA
Depr.	34.9	18.9	13.7	11.5	10.6	9.0	NA	NA	NA	NA
Int. Exp.	24.3	5.7	1.8	0.5	0.5	Nil	NA	NA	NA	NA
Pretax Inc.	81.4	45.1	31.4	26.5	18.6	16.0	14.0	NA	NA	NA
Eff. Tax Rate	48%	49%	44%	47%	50%	51%	52%	NA	NA	NA
Net Inc.	42.5	23.0	17.5	14.2	9.4	7.8	6.8	NA	NA	NA

Balance Sheet & Other Fin. Data (Million $)

	1997	1996	1995	1994	1993	1992	1991	1990	1989	1988
Cash	15.6	18.9	2.1	0.8	10.0	NA	NA	NA	NA	NA
Curr. Assets	308	264	191	141	122	NA	NA	NA	NA	NA
Total Assets	1,092	512	407	261	229	220	207	NA	NA	NA
Curr. Liab.	235	95.0	150	82.0	62.0	NA	NA	NA	NA	NA
LT Debt	379	Nil	60.0	Nil	30.0	89.1	94.3	NA	NA	NA
Common Eqty.	474	415	196	179	136	75.0	66.0	NA	NA	NA
Total Cap.	857	418	256	179	166	164	160	NA	NA	NA
Cap. Exp.	24.9	33.0	9.9	8.4	5.0	4.0	NA	NA	NA	NA
Cash Flow	77.4	41.9	31.2	25.6	20.0	16.8	NA	NA	NA	NA
Curr. Ratio	1.3	2.8	1.3	1.7	2.0	NA	NA	NA	NA	NA
% LT Debt of Cap.	44.2	Nil	23.4	Nil	18.1	54.3	58.9	NA	NA	NA
% Net Inc.of Revs.	2.6	2.0	2.2	2.2	1.8	1.8	1.8	NA	NA	NA
% Ret. on Assets	5.3	5.0	5.3	5.8	4.2	3.7	3.4	NA	NA	NA
% Ret. on Equity	9.6	7.5	9.3	9.0	8.9	11.1	6.6	NA	NA	NA

Data as orig. reptd.; bef. results of disc. opers. and/or spec. items. Per share data adj. for stk. divs. as of ex-div. date. Bold denotes diluted EPS (FASB 128). E-Estimated. NA-Not Available. NM-Not Meaningful. NR-Not Ranked.

Office—2050 Spectrum Blvd., Fort Lauderdale, FL 33309. **Tel**—(954) 938-7600. **Website**—http://www.interim.com **Chrmn, Pres & CEO**—R. Marcy. **EVP & COO**—R. Livonius. **EVP & CFO**—R. G. Krause. **Dirs**—S. S. Elbaum, W. Evans, J. Grossman, C. A. Hallman, R. Marcy, J. I. Morrison, A. M. Victory. **Transfer Agent & Registrar**—Boatmen's Trust Co., St. Louis, MO. **Incorporated**—in Delaware in 1987. **Empl**—4,000. **S&P Analyst:** Jordan Horoschak

Intermagnetics General   8207N

ASE Symbol **IMG**

In S&P SmallCap 600

03-OCT-98

Industry:
Manufacturing (Special-ized)

Summary: IMG manufactures superconducting magnet systems and superconducting wire used in medical diagnostic imaging systems; it also produces cryogenic refrigeration equipment.

Quantitative Evaluations		
Recent Price • 6½	Yield • Nil	
52 Wk Range • 11⅝-5¾	12-Mo. P/E • 27.1	

Outlook
(1 Lowest—5 Highest)
• **NA**

Fair Value
• **NA**

Risk
• **Average**

Earn./Div. Rank
• **B**

Technical Eval.
• **Bearish** since 6/98

Rel. Strength Rank
(1 Lowest—99 Highest)
• **46**

Insider Activity
• **Favorable**

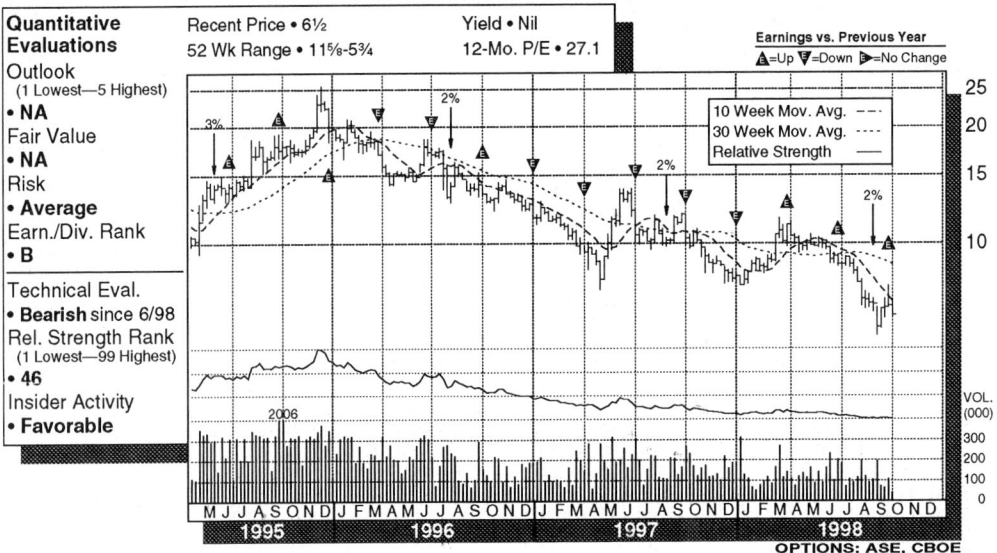

Earnings vs. Previous Year
▲=Up ▼=Down ▶=No Change

10 Week Mov. Avg. ---
30 Week Mov. Avg. ....
Relative Strength —

OPTIONS: ASE, CBOE

Business Profile - 27-AUG-98

In November 1997, Intermagnetics General completed the acquisition of privately held Polycold Systems International, Inc., a leading maker of low-temperature refrigeration systems, for about $16.5 million. The company expects several factors to yield future operating improvements: continuing cost-containment efforts; a recently improved product mix; the building of a better infrastructure to handle distribution of new products; and increased research and development efforts. Also, the integration of recent acquisitions should boost FY 99 (May) results.

Operational Review - 27-AUG-98

Based on a preliminary report, sales rose 10% in the fiscal year ended May 31, 1998, primarily reflecting acquisitions. The integration of recent acquisitions, a better product mix and cost reductions aided gross margins. This improvement outweighed higher R&D, marketing, general & administrative expenses, and amortization charges related to the acquisitions; operating income climbed 58%. After higher equity in the loss of affiliates and taxes at 42.0%, versus 35.2%, net income increased only 5.3%, to $2.8 million ($0.21 per share, on more shares) from $2.6 million ($0.21).

Stock Performance - 02-OCT-98

In the past 30 trading days, IMG's shares have declined 7%, compared to a 7% fall in the S&P 500. Average trading volume for the past five days was 8,000 shares, compared with the 40-day moving average of 20,141 shares.

Key Stock Statistics

Dividend Rate/Share	Nil	Shareholders	1,900
Shs. outstg. (M)	12.8	Market cap. (B)	$0.083
Avg. daily vol. (M)	0.015	Inst. holdings	13%
Tang. Bk. Value/Share	4.53		
Beta	1.55		

Value of $10,000 invested 5 years ago: $ 10,761

Fiscal Year Ending May 31

	1999	1998	1997	1996	1995	1994
Revenues (Million $)						
1Q	26.49	21.02	21.37	20.72	14.90	11.01
2Q	—	22.22	23.26	21.75	19.79	12.01
3Q	—	25.74	17.32	21.21	21.65	12.28
4Q	—	27.42	25.10	24.79	27.54	15.95
Yr.	—	95.89	87.05	88.47	83.88	51.24
Earnings Per Share ($)						
1Q	**0.07**	0.04	0.08	0.06	0.02	0.02
2Q	—	0.05	0.07	0.00	0.00	0.01
3Q	—	**0.07**	Nil	0.06	0.09	0.03
4Q	—	**0.07**	0.06	0.14	0.15	0.04
Yr.	—	**0.21**	0.21	0.33	0.33	0.11

Next earnings report expected: mid December

Dividend Data

Amount ($)	Date Decl.	Ex-Div. Date	Stock of Record	Payment Date
2%	Jul. 29	Aug. 25	Aug. 27	Sep. 17 '98

A Division of The McGraw-Hill Companies

Business Summary - 27-AUG-98

Superconductivity is the phenomenon where certain materials lose all resistance to the flow of electrical current when cooled below a critical temperature. Intermagnetics General Corp. (IMG) is a leader in the development and application of this technology. IMG manufactures superconductive magnets, wires and cable, and radio frequency (RF) coils used mainly for magnetic resonance imaging (MRI) systems; and other "cool" products including low temperature refrigerants and refrigeration equipment.

IMG's superconductive MRI magnet systems (43% of FY 97 (May) net sales) are solenoid magnets that are sold to MRI systems integrators for use in mobile and stationary MRI systems. Superconductive niobium-titanium wire and niobium-tin wire (12% of FY 97 net sales) are commercially available for the construction of superconductive magnets. Medical Advances, Inc. (acquired in March 1997) makes and sells RF coils for use in MRI systems. IMG's permanent magnet systems are used in low field-strength MRI systems. Other superconductive magnetic systems have applications in scientific and defense areas.

The company produces specialty cryogenic refrigeration equipment for use in medical diagnostic equipment, laboratory research and semiconductor manufacturing. Products include specialized shield coolers and recondensers (refrigerators) that reduce or eliminate liquid helium and liquid nitrogen boil-off during normal operation of conventional superconductive MRI magnet systems; laboratory cryogenic systems for use in applications such as spectroscopy and X-ray diffraction, where they are used to reduce the temperatures of materials under study; and cryogenic vacuum pumps mainly used in the semiconductor industry. In November 1997, the company acquired Polycold Systems International, a manufacturer of low temperature refrigeration systems, whose products complement those of IMG's subsidiary APD Cryogenics.

IMG's FRIGC FR-12 product is the first of a planned line of environmentally friendly refrigerants developed for use as replacements for ozone depleting chlorofluorocarbons (CFCs). This product is marketed for mobile air conditioning applications and certain stationary refrigerant applications.

IMG is working to develop materials inspection systems using magnetic resonance technology for the food and beverages, explosives and narcotics, and other industries. The company is encouraged by the early success of the technology.

Per Share Data ($)

(Year Ended May 31)	1998	1997	1996	1995	1994	1993	1992	1991	1990	1989
Tangible Bk. Val.	4.53	4.99	5.51	4.59	4.07	3.75	3.59	3.06	2.78	2.69
Cash Flow	0.61	0.52	0.60	0.59	0.38	0.54	0.64	0.49	0.27	0.32
Earnings	0.21	0.21	0.34	0.33	0.11	0.30	0.41	0.28	0.09	0.17
Dividends	Nil	Nil	Nil	Nil	Nil	Nil	Nil	Nil	Nil	Nil
Payout Ratio	Nil	Nil	Nil	Nil	Nil	Nil	Nil	Nil	Nil	Nil
Cal. Yrs.	1997	1996	1995	1994	1993	1992	1991	1990	1989	1988
Prices - High	13⁷/₈	21	25¹/₂	18⁵/₈	16¹/₄	6³/₄	9¹/₂	5	5⁵/₈	4³/₈
- Low	7⁵/₈	11¹/₈	9³/₈	9	4¹/₂	3⁷/₈	3⁵/₈	3	3⁵/₈	2⁵/₈
P/E Ratio - High	66	NM	76	57	NM	23	23	18	65	25
- Low	36	NM	28	27	NM	13	9	11	41	15

Income Statement Analysis (Million $)

	1998	1997	1996	1995	1994	1993	1992	1991	1990	1989
Revs.	95.9	87.1	88.5	83.9	51.2	56.3	58.2	60.8	46.6	42.3
Oper. Inc.	10.9	7.3	7.9	10.7	6.2	6.9	7.6	6.0	3.6	4.2
Depr.	5.4	4.0	3.2	3.3	3.3	2.7	2.5	2.2	1.9	1.4
Int. Exp.	2.1	2.1	2.6	2.8	NA	NA	NA	1.4	1.3	1.1
Pretax Inc.	4.7	4.0	6.9	6.5	2.1	3.9	4.8	3.1	1.0	2.0
Eff. Tax Rate	42%	35%	36%	39%	40%	20%	11%	10%	15%	15%
Net Inc.	2.8	2.6	4.4	4.0	1.3	3.1	4.3	2.8	0.8	1.7

Balance Sheet & Other Fin. Data (Million $)

	1998	1997	1996	1995	1994	1993	1992	1991	1990	1989
Cash	3.0	12.7	18.7	13.0	13.2	1.6	1.0	0.5	0.8	0.7
Curr. Assets	60.3	62.8	67.8	62.1	56.3	31.2	32.4	32.4	35.5	29.4
Total Assets	128	116	112	104	93.8	58.4	53.2	49.3	50.8	42.4
Curr. Liab.	14.8	13.5	14.2	9.4	7.0	11.6	7.5	9.5	13.6	8.5
LT Debt	28.8	29.1	29.4	39.8	39.9	5.0	10.7	9.7	10.4	8.2
Common Eqty.	76.8	73.1	67.3	53.3	46.9	41.8	35.1	30.1	26.7	25.8
Total Cap.	113	103	98.2	94.3	86.8	46.8	45.7	39.8	37.2	34.0
Cap. Exp.	3.1	5.5	4.1	3.9	9.4	3.1	4.9	3.9	4.3	2.4
Cash Flow	8.2	6.6	7.6	7.3	4.5	5.9	6.8	5.0	2.7	3.1
Curr. Ratio	4.1	4.7	4.8	6.6	8.1	2.7	4.3	3.4	2.6	3.5
% LT Debt of Cap.	25.6	28.3	29.9	42.3	45.9	10.7	23.3	24.4	28.1	24.1
% Net Inc.of Revs.	2.9	3.0	5.0	4.8	2.5	5.6	7.3	4.6	1.8	4.0
% Ret. on Assets	2.3	2.3	4.1	4.1	1.7	5.4	8.2	5.6	1.8	4.1
% Ret. on Equity	3.7	3.7	7.4	8.0	2.8	7.8	12.9	9.8	3.2	6.8

Data as orig. reptd.; bef. results of disc. opers. and/or spec. items. Per share data adj. for stk. divs. as of ex-div. date. Bold denotes diluted EPS (FASB 128). E-Estimated. NA-Not Available. NM-Not Meaningful. NR-Not Ranked.

Office—450 Old Niskayuna Rd., Latham, NY 12110-0461. **Tel**—(518) 782-1122. **Website**—http://www.igc.com **Chrmn & CEO**—C. H. Rosner. **Pres & COO**—G. Epstein. **SVP-CFO**—M. C. Zeigler. **Investor Contact**—Cathy Yudzevich.**Secy**—Catherine E. Arduini. **Dirs**—J. C. Abeles, J. M. Albertine, E. E. David, Jr., G. H. Epstein, J. S. Hyde, T. L. Kempner, C. H. Rosner, S. A. Shikiar, S. Weinig. **Transfer Agent & Registrar**—American Stock Transfer & Trust Co., NYC. **Incorporated**—in New York in 1971. **Empl**— 537. **S&P Analyst:** E.P.L.

03-OCT-98 Industry: Auto Parts & Equipment

Summary: This company provides precision iron and aluminum parts to automotive and industrial customers in North America and Europe.

Quantitative Evaluations	
Outlook (1 Lowest—5 Highest)	• 5
Fair Value	• 23⅞
Risk	• Average
Earn./Div. Rank	• B-
Technical Eval.	• **Bearish** since 9/98
Rel. Strength Rank (1 Lowest—99 Highest)	• 66
Insider Activity	• NA

Recent Price • 15⅞
52 Wk Range • 23¾-12⅝

Yield • 1.0%
12-Mo. P/E • 9.9

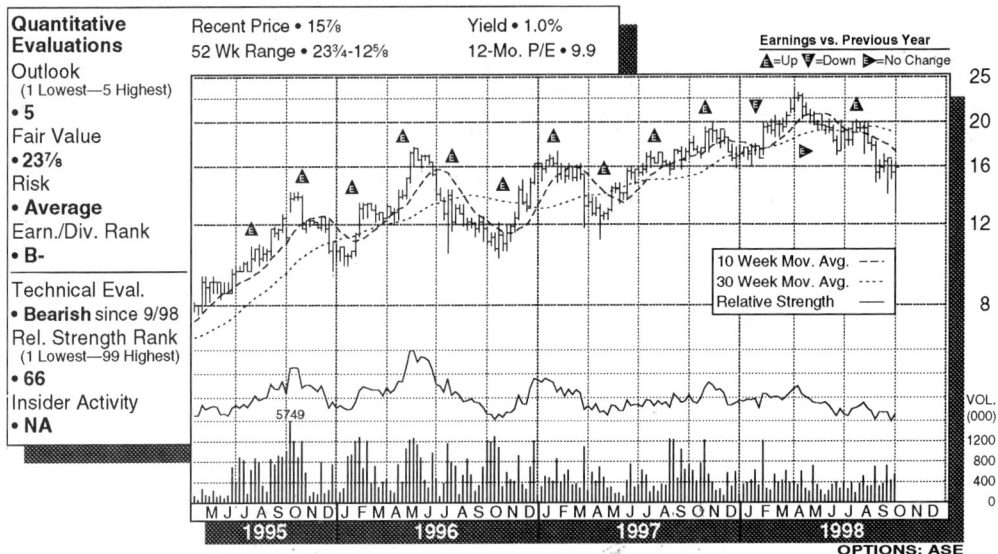

Earnings vs. Previous Year
▲=Up ▼=Down ▶=No Change

10 Week Mov. Avg. ---
30 Week Mov. Avg. ·····
Relative Strength —

OPTIONS: ASE

Business Profile - 26-AUG-98

Intermet continues its focus on growing the company, having improved productivity at each of its four operations. INMT has been increasing its orders, and expects the new business to ramp up sharply in the second half of 1998 and continue to phase in through 2002. During 1997, INMT integrated Sudbury, a newly acquired iron and aluminum parts maker, into the company, rebalanced its domestic foundries' workload and reduced its product launch expenses. In early 1998, INMT received a major order to supply cast ductile iron steering knuckles for General Motors vehicles. INMT believes that the North American car build in 1998 will be in the 14.5 million to 15 million range, which should continue to fuel sales growth.

Operational Review - 26-AUG-98

Net sales in the first half of 1998 advanced 5.6%, year to year, primarily reflecting increased sales from the iron foundry operations. Operating costs and expenses were well controlled, and pretax income rose 10%. After taxes at 38.5%, versus 35.4%, and minority interest in 1998, the gain in net income was held to 6.9%, to $23,608,000 ($0.91 a diluted share), from $22,086,000 ($0.86). The company expects the automotive industry to continue at its current pace through 1999, but is implementing measures to balance capacity with sales should there be a downturn going into 2000.

Stock Performance - 02-OCT-98

In the past 30 trading days, INMT's shares have declined 11%, compared to a 7% fall in the S&P 500. Average trading volume for the past five days was 108,620 shares, compared with the 40-day moving average of 94,472 shares.

Key Stock Statistics

Dividend Rate/Share	0.16	Shareholders	600
Shs. outstg. (M)	25.7	Market cap. (B)	$0.408
Avg. daily vol. (M)	0.103	Inst. holdings	71%
Tang. Bk. Value/Share	4.35		
Beta	1.03		

Value of $10,000 invested 5 years ago: $ 16,431

Fiscal Year Ending Dec. 31

	1998	1997	1996	1995	1994	1993
Revenues (Million $)						
1Q	224.0	209.5	134.2	153.3	118.9	122.8
2Q	219.9	210.9	143.8	149.0	124.6	122.7
3Q	—	189.5	130.3	117.3	121.0	92.69
4Q	—	203.8	126.3	122.1	136.8	106.1
Yr.	—	813.7	534.5	541.8	501.3	444.2
Earnings Per Share ($)						
1Q	**0.43**	0.43	0.35	0.26	0.07	0.03
2Q	**0.47**	0.43	0.42	0.39	0.10	0.05
3Q	—	0.29	0.27	0.14	0.02	-0.87
4Q	—	0.41	0.65	0.24	-0.63	-0.05
Yr.	—	1.55	1.69	1.02	-0.45	-0.83

Next earnings report expected: mid October

Dividend Data (Dividends have been paid since 1996.)

Amount ($)	Date Decl.	Ex-Div. Date	Stock of Record	Payment Date
0.040	Oct. 16	Nov. 26	Dec. 01	Dec. 30 '97
0.040	Feb. 02	Feb. 26	Mar. 02	Mar. 31 '98
0.040	Apr. 16	May. 28	Jun. 01	Jun. 30 '98
0.040	Jul. 16	Aug. 28	Sep. 01	Sep. 30 '98

Business Summary - 26-AUG-98

Intermet Corp. (INMT) continues to review acquisition opportunities to complement its existing business, maintain its growth focus, and benefit its shareholders by increasing earnings. The company is a world leader in the manufacture of precision iron castings for automotive and industrial equipment producers, producing a wide array of ductile and gray iron castings at seven foundries in Georgia, Minnesota, Ohio, Virginia and Portugal. Sales by market in recent years were:

	1997	1996
U.S. passenger cars & light trucks	66%	76%
U.S. industrial	17%	7%
Foreign	17%	17%

Products manufactured for the automotive, light-truck and heavy-truck industries include brake parts, steering system components, differential cases, camshafts and crankshafts. INMT also makes products for construction equipment manufacturers, valve and air-conditioning equipment producers and farm equipment makers. The company expanded its product offerings to include aluminum castings through its November 1995 acquisition of the Bodine-Robinson aluminum foundry ($25 million annual sales) in Alexander City, AL. In early 1997, INMT acquired Sudbury, Inc. (SUDS; Nasdaq) for $156 million. Sudbury ($302 million in sales in FY 96) manufactures iron and aluminum parts for the automotive and industrial markets.

Intermet's marketing strategy emphasizes complex castings requiring precise metallurgical and dimensional standards. The six largest customers contributed 58% of 1997 sales, down from 72% in 1996, with Chrysler, Ford and General Motors accounting for 18%, 18% and 8%, respectively.

In May 1998, INMT formed a joint venture with an iron foundry in Portugal, adding much needed capacity in Europe. In April 1998, INMT terminated an agreement to purchase a 50% stake in Polcast SP, a foundry in Poland. Also in the second quarter of 1998, INMT ended its joint venture agreement with German machinery maker IWESA GmbH and sold its Industrial Powder coatings unit. INMT said the termination and the sale had minimal impact on second quarter earnings.

In 1997, shipments of castings totaled 539,000 tons, up from 458,000 tons in 1996. INMT's foundries operated at 87% of average annual capacity. Sales of ductile iron castings in 1997 represented 89% of total castings sales. Total castings sales in 1997 amounted to 76%, down from 94% in 1996.

In August 1997, company founder and former chairman George W. Mathews, Jr. reduced his family's stake in INMT from 21% to 7.2% through a secondary offering at $15.75 a share.

Per Share Data ($)

(Year Ended Dec. 31)	1997	1996	1995	1994	1993	1992	1991	1990	1989	1988
Tangible Bk. Val.	3.69	2.10	3.91	2.24	2.84	3.91	4.93	4.84	6.31	5.85
Cash Flow	2.96	2.78	2.06	0.73	0.18	0.90	1.36	0.65	1.52	1.50
Earnings	1.55	1.69	1.02	-0.45	-0.83	-0.06	0.42	-0.49	0.68	0.76
Dividends	0.16	0.08	Nil	Nil	0.12	0.16	0.14	0.20	0.20	0.20
Payout Ratio	10%	5%	Nil	Nil	NM	NM	33%	NM	29%	22%
Prices - High	19⁷/₈	17⁵/₈	14¹/₈	10¹/₂	12	13¹/₄	9	9⁵/₈	13¹/₄	14
- Low	11¹/₈	9³/₄	6¹/₄	4³/₄	6	7¹/₄	4¹/₂	3⁵/₈	6⁷/₈	8
P/E Ratio - High	13	10	14	NM	NM	NM	21	NM	19	18
- Low	7	6	6	NM	NM	NM	11	NM	10	11

Income Statement Analysis (Million $)

	1997	1996	1995	1994	1993	1992	1991	1990	1989	1988
Revs.	814	534	542	501	444	402	320	386	397	357
Oper. Inc.	114	83.0	81.0	41.7	25.4	27.8	27.4	37.6	46.1	49.7
Depr.	36.3	26.9	28.1	29.0	24.9	22.0	19.8	24.1	17.7	15.9
Int. Exp.	12.4	3.1	6.5	7.6	6.7	4.3	4.3	7.1	5.6	4.0
Pretax Inc.	61.4	54.3	45.5	-5.1	-29.1	2.3	11.9	-5.0	25.3	31.2
Eff. Tax Rate	35%	21%	44%	NM	NM	187%	26%	NM	48%	54%
Net Inc.	40.0	43.2	25.4	-11.0	-20.5	-1.5	8.8	-10.4	14.5	16.3

Balance Sheet & Other Fin. Data (Million $)

	1997	1996	1995	1994	1993	1992	1991	1990	1989	1988
Cash	7.0	23.5	11.2	13.7	11.2	6.1	8.5	7.3	6.4	19.7
Curr. Assets	193	189	103	123	109	89.3	76.1	81.1	96.8	99
Total Assets	539	526	274	306	307	274	214	215	277	229
Curr. Liab.	136	171	91.0	93.5	69.0	58.9	58.9	48.3	60.4	50.8
LT Debt	167	149	32.3	88.0	102	69.5	32.9	45.1	74.8	47.3
Common Eqty.	175	141	98.0	68.0	76.0	101	105	104	114	106
Total Cap.	345	293	130	159	185	174	153	165	214	177
Cap. Exp.	40.6	26.0	24.4	24.9	43.6	59.7	25.9	25.0	69.9	42.8
Cash Flow	76.3	70.0	53.5	18.1	4.4	20.5	28.6	13.7	32.2	32.1
Curr. Ratio	1.4	1.1	1.1	1.3	1.6	1.5	1.3	1.7	1.6	2.0
% LT Debt of Cap.	48.5	50.9	24.8	55.3	55.1	39.8	21.5	27.3	35.0	26.8
% Net Inc.of Revs.	4.9	8.1	4.7	NM	NM	NM	2.8	NM	3.7	4.6
% Ret. on Assets	7.5	10.8	8.8	NM	NM	NM	4.2	NM	5.8	8.0
% Ret. on Equity	25.3	36.1	30.6	NM	NM	NM	8.5	NM	13.3	16.3

Data as orig. reptd.; bef. results of disc. opers. and/or spec. items. Per share data adj. for stk. divs. as of ex-div. date. Bold denotes diluted EPS (FASB 128). E-Estimated. NA-Not Available. NM-Not Meaningful. NR-Not Ranked.

Office—5445 Corporate Dr., Suite 200, Troy, MI 48098-2683. **Tel**—(248) 952-2500. **Fax**—(248) 952-2501. **Website**—http://www.intermet.com **Chrmn & CEO**—J. Doddridge. **VP-Fin, CFO & Secy**—Doretha Christoph. **Investor Contact**—Bytha Mills. **Dirs**—J. P. Crecine, J. Doddridge, N. Enlers, W. E. Gross Jr., A. W. Hardy, J. R. Horne, T. H. Jeffs II, H. C. McKenzie Jr., J. H. Reed. **Transfer Agent & Registrar**—SunTrust Bank, Atlanta. **Incorporated**—in Georgia in 1984. **Empl**— 5,700. **S&P Analyst:** Stewart Scharf

03-OCT-98 | **Industry:** Electronics (Semiconductors) | **Summary:** This major worldwide supplier of power semiconductors is the leading producer in the power MOSFET (metal oxide semiconductor field effect transistor) market.

Quantitative Evaluations

Outlook
(1 Lowest—5 Highest)
• **1**

Fair Value
• 4½

Risk
• **High**

Earn./Div. Rank
• **B-**

Technical Eval.
• **Bearish** since 3/98

Rel. Strength Rank
(1 Lowest—99 Highest)
• **19**

Insider Activity
• **NA**

Recent Price • 4⅞
52 Wk Range • 22⅝-4¼
Yield • Nil
12-Mo. P/E • 15.2

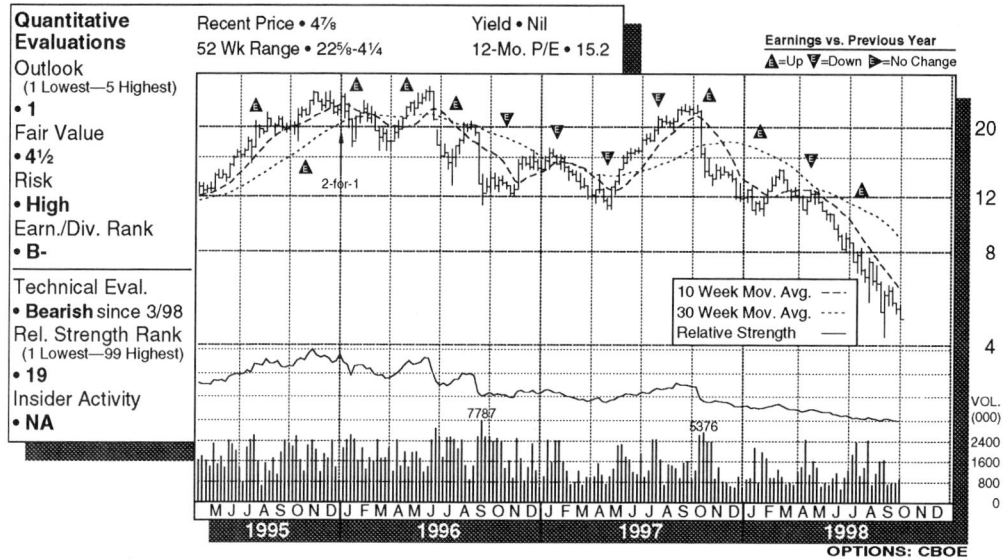

Earnings vs. Previous Year
▲=Up ▼=Down ▶=No Change

10 Week Mov. Avg. — –
30 Week Mov. Avg. ----
Relative Strength —

OPTIONS: CBOE

Business Profile - 30-JUN-98

After three years of rapid growth, FY 97 (Jun.) results were hurt by industry conditions and attempts by distributors to lower inventory. In response to this trend, IRF took a $71 million charge in the fourth quarter of FY 97 to improve its competitive position and accelerate earnings growth. The plan called for cutting IRF's work force by about 4%, transferring production operations into a more advanced plant, moving R&D activity to a new facility, and consolidating administrative and service functions. The restructuring was expected to result in annual savings of about $20 million. Strong earnings during FY 98 primarily reflect benefits from the initiative.

Operational Review - 30-JUN-98

Revenues in the nine months ended March 31, 1998, rose 17%, year to year, reflecting demand in North America and increasing sales in Europe, which offset adverse market conditions in Asia and exchange rate losses. Results benefited from the increased volume and cost reduction measures under the restructuring program, and despite higher interest expense, pretax earnings were up 60%. After taxes at 33.0%, versus 31.0%, net income advanced 56%, to $16,078,000 ($0.31 a share), from $10,335,000 ($0.20).

Stock Performance - 02-OCT-98

In the past 30 trading days, IRF's shares have declined 23%, compared to a 7% fall in the S&P 500. Average trading volume for the past five days was 175,640 shares, compared with the 40-day moving average of 207,744 shares.

Key Stock Statistics

Dividend Rate/Share	Nil	Shareholders	1,800
Shs. outstg. (M)	51.3	Market cap. (B)	$0.250
Avg. daily vol. (M)	0.161	Inst. holdings	60%
Tang. Bk. Value/Share	7.77		
Beta	1.83		

Value of $10,000 invested 5 years ago: $ 8,125

Fiscal Year Ending Jun. 30

	1998	1997	1996	1995	1994	1993
Revenues (Million $)						
1Q	133.1	115.2	126.1	92.25	73.09	65.00
2Q	144.6	118.0	141.0	102.8	79.10	70.50
3Q	140.4	122.8	154.1	111.9	84.25	70.60
4Q	133.8	130.2	155.7	122.1	92.43	75.73
Yr.	551.9	486.1	576.9	429.0	328.9	281.7
Earnings Per Share ($)						
1Q	0.12	0.06	0.25	0.16	0.05	-0.05
2Q	**0.13**	0.07	0.30	0.18	0.08	-0.05
3Q	**0.06**	0.08	0.35	0.21	0.10	0.01
4Q	**0.01**	**-0.13**	0.40	0.27	0.16	0.02
Yr.	**0.32**	**-0.84**	1.29	0.84	0.39	-0.08

Next earnings report expected: early October

Dividend Data

Annual dividends, paid since 1973, were omitted in 1982. The shares were split two for one in 1995.

A Division of The McGraw-Hill Companies

STANDARD
&POOR'S
STOCK REPORTS

International Rectifier Corporation

1226K
03-OCT-98

Business Summary - 30-JUN-98

International Rectifier Corporation is a major worldwide supplier of power semiconductors for a broad spectrum of commercial and industrial applications.

Products offered by the company include power MOS-FETs (metal oxide semiconductor field effect transistors) and IGBTs (insulated gate bipolar transistors), which serve the switch function in power conversion to provide an even, usable flow of power for electronic equipment; high-voltage control ICs, which serve the control function of power conversion; and a broad line of rectifiers, diodes and thyristors that serve the output rectification and input rectification functions of power conversion.

Based on statistics from the Semiconductor Industry Association, IRF believes that it is the leader in the power MOSFET segment. Industrywide sales of power MOSFETs have grown at an average annual rate of 27% over the past five years. The company's power MOSFET and IGBT products accounted for about 70% of sales in FY 97 (Jun.)

The company's products serve all major market sectors. Applications for power semiconductors in automobiles include anti-lock braking and fuel injection systems, power accessories and air bags. Computer/

peripheral applications include power supplies, disk drives and printers. Office equipment applications include copiers and facsimile machines. Consumer electronics and lighting applications include home entertainment, household appliances and electronic lighting ballasts. Communications applications include portable phones, telephone networks and modems. Power semiconductors are also used widely in industrial applications such as motor-driven production lines, machine tools, fork lifts and welders. Major customers in the automotive segment include Delco, Ford, Siemens and Bosch; and major computer customers include IBM, Hewlett-Packard and Compaq.

Sales by region in FY 97 were: North America 47%; Europe 25%; and Asia 28%. Foreign operations accounted for 51% of sales in FY 97.

In order to address the fastest-growing segments of the power transistor market--high-density MOSFETs and IGBTs--the company installed a second wafer fabrication unit. Phase one, completed in September 1995, and Phase two, completed in the second half of FY 97, combined are expected to add about $297 million in annual revenues at full utilization. In FY 97, the company spent about $35.5 million on R&D, up from $27.0 million in FY 96.

Per Share Data ($)

(Year Ended Jun. 30)	1998	1997	1996	1995	1994	1993	1992	1991	1990	1989
Tangible Bk. Val.	NA	7.48	8.29	6.86	4.99	4.60	4.81	4.53	0.94	0.73
Cash Flow	NA	-0.12	1.88	1.33	0.78	0.28	0.61	1.08	0.58	-0.08
Earnings	0.32	-0.84	1.29	0.84	0.39	-0.08	0.23	0.65	0.09	-0.56
Dividends	Nil	Nil	Nil	Nil	Nil	Nil	Nil	Nil	Nil	Nil
Payout Ratio	Nil	Nil	Nil	Nil	Nil	Nil	Nil	Nil	Nil	Nil
Prices - High	14¾	23¾	27	26	12¼	7½	8⅛	12⅝	6⅛	3¼
- Low	6¾	10⅞	11¼	11⅛	6½	4⅞	3¾	4⅝	2⅛	1¹¹⁄₁₆
P/E Ratio - High	46	NM	21	31	31	NM	35	19	67	NM
- Low	21	NM	9	13	17	NM	16	7	24	NM

Income Statement Analysis (Million $)

Revs.	NM	486	577	429	329	282	265	253	230	195
Oper. Inc.	NA	58.7	127	71.8	39.4	16.5	26.2	38.1	31.1	14.2
Depr.	NA	37.1	30.1	23.4	15.9	14.2	15.4	11.4	11.5	11.0
Int. Exp.	NA	4.0	0.4	0.4	3.6	3.6	1.4	13.7	17.2	16.4
Pretax Inc.	NA	-52.7	95.9	47.5	18.9	-2.6	10.5	18.2	2.6	-12.1
Eff. Tax Rate	NA	NM	31%	17%	17%	NM	12%	6.00%	18%	NM
Net Inc.	NM	-43.2	66.5	39.4	15.7	-3.0	9.2	17.1	2.2	-12.7

Balance Sheet & Other Fin. Data (Million $)

Cash	NA	53.4	53.8	53.8	13.1	8.5	8.5	24.3	2.4	2.1
Curr. Assets	NA	316	277	234	157	128	136	125	92.0	83.0
Total Assets	NA	680	629	496	331	278	286	250	218	212
Curr. Liab.	NA	113	125	106	89.7	69.8	68.4	49.8	66.3	60.0
LT Debt	NA	143	48.0	23.9	27.0	12.0	12.0	12.0	120	127
Common Eqty.	NA	382	421	345	203	186	192	180	22.0	17.0
Total Cap.	NA	538	488	379	230	198	204	192	143	145
Cap. Exp.	NA	100	112	107	37.1	21.8	33.0	14.2	5.6	5.8
Cash Flow	NA	-6.1	96.6	62.8	31.6	11.1	24.6	28.6	13.6	-1.7
Curr. Ratio	NA	2.8	2.2	2.2	1.7	1.8	2.0	2.5	1.4	1.4
% LT Debt of Cap.	NA	26.7	9.8	6.3	11.6	6.0	5.7	6.2	84.2	87.6
% Net Inc.of Revs.	NA	NM	11.5	9.2	4.8	NM	3.5	6.8	0.9	NM
% Ret. on Assets	NM	NM	11.8	9.5	5.2	NM	3.4	5.5	1.0	NM
% Ret. on Equity	NM	NM	17.3	14.4	8.1	NM	5.0	15.8	11.2	NM

Data as orig. reptd.; bef. results of disc. opers. and/or spec. items. Per share data adj. for stk. divs. as of ex-div. date. Bold denotes diluted EPS (FASB 128). E-Estimated. NA-Not Available. NM-Not Meaningful. NR-Not Ranked.

Office—233 Kansas St., El Segundo, CA 90245. **Tel**—(310) 726-8000. **Fax**—(310) 322-3332. **Website**—http://www.irf.com.**Chrmn** —E. Lidow. **Co-CEOs**—A. Lidow, D. B. Lidow. **VP & CFO**—M. P. McGee. **Investor Contact**—Shelley Wagers (310) 726-8512. **Dirs**—D. S. Burns, G. Krsek, A. Lidow, D. B. Lidow, E. Lidow, M. Matsuda, R. J. Mueller, J. D. Plummer, J. O. Vance, R. E. Vogt. **Transfer Agent & Registrar**—ChaseMellon Shareholder Services, Los Angeles. **Incorporated**—in California in 1947; reincorporated in Delaware in 1979. **Empl**—4,385. **S&P Analyst:** S.S.

10-OCT-98

Industry: Services (Computer Systems)

Summary: This company develops, sells and services automated call processing solutions, with an emphasis on interactive voice response.

Quantitative Evaluations

Recent Price · 20⅜

52 Wk Range · 25¼-6¾

Yield · Nil

12-Mo. P/E · NM

Outlook (1 Lowest—5 Highest)
- **4+**

Fair Value
- **27⅞**

Risk
- **High**

Earn./Div. Rank
- **B-**

Technical Eval.
- **Bullish** since 4/98

Rel. Strength Rank (1 Lowest—99 Highest)
- **93**

Insider Activity
- **Neutral**

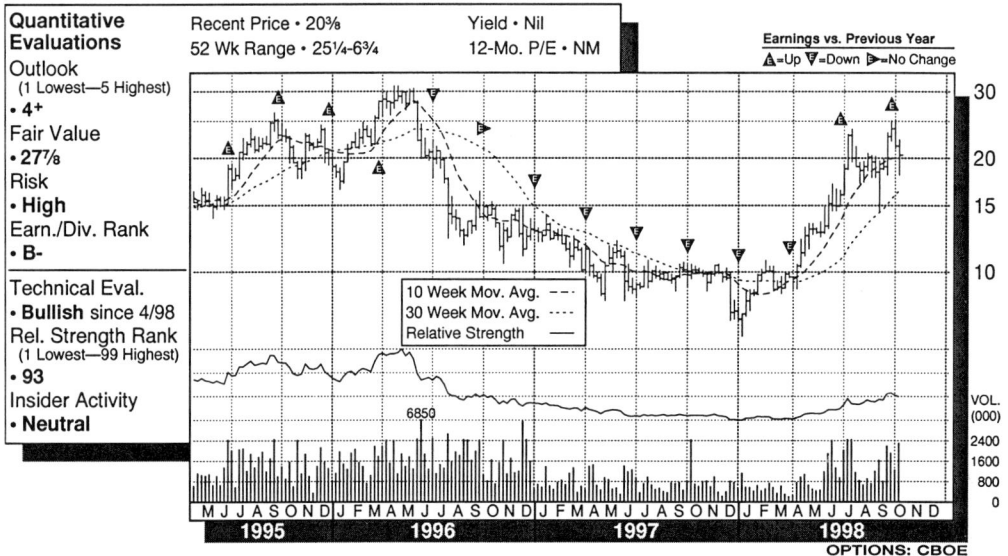

Earnings vs. Previous Year
△=Up ▽=Down ▷=No Change

10 Week Mov. Avg. – – –
30 Week Mov. Avg. · · · ·
Relative Strength ——

6850

VOL. (000)

OPTIONS: CBOE

Business Profile - 21-AUG-98

This leading global supplier of automated call processing solutions has improved year-over-year results significantly in the first quarter of FY 99 (Feb.). In a June 1998 announcement, the company noted that its sales performance exceeded consensus analyst expectations which called for flat sales. InterVoice's annualized sales growth rate during the quarter was over 25%, year to year. Also, the company met an expense reduction target, and generated net cash flow of nearly $2.5 million as a result of cost reductions and tightened credit practices.

Operational Review - 21-AUG-98

Sales in the first quarter of FY 99 (Feb.) increased 21%, year to year, reflecting a significant improvement in Worldwide Telecommunications sales and higher domestic Customer Premises Equipment sales. Margins widened, due primarily to the higher volume and cost control efforts; operating income jumped considerably. Following income taxes at 34.4%, versus 35.0%, net income surged to $3,002,588 ($0.21 per share), from $270,862 ($0.02).

Stock Performance - 09-OCT-98

In the past 30 trading days, INTV's shares have increased 11%, compared to a 4% fall in the S&P 500. Average trading volume for the past five days was 458,420 shares, compared with the 40-day moving average of 306,474 shares.

Key Stock Statistics

Dividend Rate/Share	Nil	Shareholders	1,000
Shs. outstg. (M)	13.9	Market cap. (B)	$0.282
Avg. daily vol. (M)	0.381	Inst. holdings	47%
Tang. Bk. Value/Share	3.90		
Beta	1.51		

Value of $10,000 invested 5 years ago: $ 25,076

Fiscal Year Ending Feb. 28

	1999	1998	1997	1996	1995	1994
Revenues (Million $)						
1Q	30.00	24.74	25.56	22.02	16.60	13.80
2Q	33.07	29.28	27.30	23.68	18.00	14.50
3Q	—	25.55	24.34	25.15	20.10	16.10
4Q	—	22.74	27.65	26.26	21.60	16.50
Yr.	—	102.3	104.8	97.10	76.30	60.90
Earnings Per Share ($)						
1Q	0.21	0.02	0.24	0.25	0.16	0.15
2Q	0.30	0.14	0.26	0.26	-0.47	0.16
3Q	—	0.02	0.08	0.27	0.22	0.17
4Q	—	-0.55	0.20	0.28	0.24	0.17
Yr.	—	-0.33	0.77	1.05	0.15	0.64

Next earnings report expected: mid December

Dividend Data

No cash dividends have been paid. A shareholder rights plan was adopted in 1991. Two-for-one stock splits were effected in 1992 and 1993.

Business Summary - 21-AUG-98

InterVoice, Inc. develops, sells and services call automation systems under the trade names OneVoice and InterDial. According to the company, the number of telephone calls requesting information or requiring operator services that must be handled by businesses, telecommunications service providers and other organizations has increased dramatically in recent years. This would normally be a very labor-intensive enterprise, were it not for call automation systems, such as OneVoice and InterDial. The company believes that OneVoice enables its customers to handle more calls with fewer delays and errors at lower costs than through the use of customer service representatives. InterDial allows the company's customers to contact a large number of people in applications such as collections and telemarketing.

INTV's product strategy emphasizes leveraging industry-standard computer platforms and operating systems to allow the company to take advantage of hardware and software technology offered by third parties. This strategy also provides customers the option to select the computer platform and operating system of their choice.

The company competes primarily on the basis of a broad range of product capabilities and features, professional services and customer support services. Its principal competitors are Lucent Technologies, Periphonics, Brite Voice, Edify, Davox, EIS, Mosaix, Boston Technology and Comverse Technology. The company also believes that it may face market entry from non-traditional competitors, including telephone switching equipment manufacturers and independent interactive voice response (IVR) service bureaus.

InterVoice markets its products through direct and indirect sales channels. During FY 98 (Feb.), approximately 52% and 48% of the company's total sales were attributable to direct sales to end-users and to sales to distributors, respectively. In addition, sales to existing customers, as a percentage of total sales, were 65% in FY 98, unchanged from FY 97. One customer, Siemens AG, an InterVoice distributor, accounted for 10.2% of the company's total sales in FY 97, but no one customer accounted for 10% of total sales in FY 98. INTV offers its products outside the U.S. through a network of more than 45 distributors and direct sales offices, which together currently sell INTV's products in 10 countries. The company anticipates that the international market for IVR systems will grow as foreign countries overcome regulatory, technological and other barriers. International sales in FY 98 declined 14% and as a percentage of total sales were 21%.

Per Share Data ($)

(Year Ended Feb. 28)	1998	1997	1996	1995	1994	1993	1992	1991	1990	1989
Tangible Bk. Val.	3.66	5.04	4.08	3.05	3.56	2.77	2.54	2.51	2.41	0.65
Cash Flow	0.29	1.07	1.32	0.29	0.73	0.54	0.20	0.21	0.38	0.16
Earnings	-0.33	0.77	1.05	0.15	0.64	0.45	0.16	0.19	0.37	0.15
Dividends	Nil	Nil	Nil	Nil	Nil	Nil	Nil	Nil	Nil	Nil
Payout Ratio	Nil	Nil	Nil	Nil	Nil	Nil	Nil	Nil	Nil	Nil
Cal. Yrs.	1997	1996	1995	1994	1993	1992	1991	1990	1989	1988
Prices - High	14¼	31⅛	26⅜	17	22½	8½	5	7⅛	8½	2¾
- Low	6¾	10½	12⅜	5⅞	6⅜	3⅛	1¹³⁄₁₆	1¹³⁄₁₆	2⅜	½
P/E Ratio - High	NM	40	25	113	35	19	32	39	23	18
- Low	NM	14	12	39	10	7	12	10	7	3

Income Statement Analysis (Million $)

Revs.	102	105	97.1	76.3	60.9	44.6	30.2	20.6	24.4	11.1
Oper. Inc.	8.7	24.2	29.4	22.2	18.8	12.6	4.3	3.1	8.8	3.0
Depr.	9.7	5.0	4.4	2.3	1.8	1.6	0.8	0.5	0.2	0.1
Int. Exp.	Nil	Nil	Nil	Nil	Nil	Nil	Nil	Nil	Nil	Nil
Pretax Inc.	-7.6	18.2	25.6	9.7	17.7	11.5	4.3	4.6	10.1	3.1
Eff. Tax Rate	NM	30%	33%	74%	34%	32%	31%	18%	31%	32%
Net Inc.	-5.1	12.7	17.3	2.5	11.7	7.8	2.9	3.8	7.0	2.1

Balance Sheet & Other Fin. Data (Million $)

Cash	4.2	24.1	23.6	10.3	36.2	25.0	25.9	27.9	41.9	6.7
Curr. Assets	46.4	75.0	63.8	40.0	58.7	41.1	40.1	39.5	50.4	11.5
Total Assets	84.9	109	90.2	62.7	74.2	52.6	49.6	46.8	56.1	12.3
Curr. Liab.	27.6	21.2	19.5	15.9	11.1	8.6	5.0	2.5	2.1	2.3
LT Debt	Nil	0.1	Nil	Nil	Nil	Nil	Nil	Nil	Nil	Nil
Common Eqty.	56.6	86.1	70.0	46.8	63.2	44.1	44.7	44.3	54.0	10.0
Total Cap.	57.3	87.8	70.7	46.8	63.2	44.1	44.7	44.3	54.0	10.0
Cap. Exp.	9.2	11.4	4.6	9.2	5.6	0.9	2.0	1.3	4.8	0.3
Cash Flow	4.6	17.7	21.7	4.8	13.5	9.5	3.7	4.3	7.2	2.2
Curr. Ratio	1.7	3.5	3.3	2.5	5.3	4.8	8.1	15.6	23.5	5.0
% LT Debt of Cap.	Nil	Nil	Nil	Nil	Nil	Nil	Nil	Nil	Nil	Nil
% Net Inc.of Revs.	NM	12.2	17.8	3.3	19.2	17.6	9.7	18.4	28.5	19.4
% Ret. on Assets	NM	12.8	22.6	4.0	17.6	16.1	6.1	8.4	18.8	21.8
% Ret. on Equity	NM	NM	29.5	5.0	20.8	18.6	6.6	8.8	20.3	26.8

Data as orig. reptd.; bef. results of disc. opers. and/or spec. items. Per share data adj. for stk. divs. as of ex-div. date. Bold denotes diluted EPS (FASB 128). E-Estimated. NA-Not Available. NM-Not Meaningful. NR-Not Ranked.

Office—17811 Waterview Parkway, Dallas, TX 75252. **Tel**—(214) 454-8000. **Website**—http://www.intervoice.com **Chrmn & CEO**—D. D. Hammond. **CFO, Secy & Investor Contact**—Rob-Roy J. Graham. **Dirs**—G. A. Dove, D. D. Hammond, J. J. Pietropaolo, G. C. Platt. **Transfer Agent**—KeyCorp Shareholder Services, Dallas. **Incorporated**—in Texas in 1984. **Empl**— 662. **S&P Analyst:** Robert Cho

Invacare Corp.   4277

NASDAQ Symbol **IVCR**

In S&P SmallCap 600

03-OCT-98

Industry: Health Care (Medical Products & Supplies)

Summary: This company is a leading manufacturer and marketer of of a broad line of home health care products.

Quantitative Evaluations	
Outlook (1 Lowest—5 Highest)	• 4
Fair Value	• 33¼
Risk	• Average
Earn./Div. Rank	• B+
Technical Eval.	• Bearish since 8/98
Rel. Strength Rank (1 Lowest—99 Highest)	• 66
Insider Activity	• Neutral

Recent Price • 22¼   Yield • 0.2%
52 Wk Range • 28¾-19⅛   12-Mo. P/E • NM

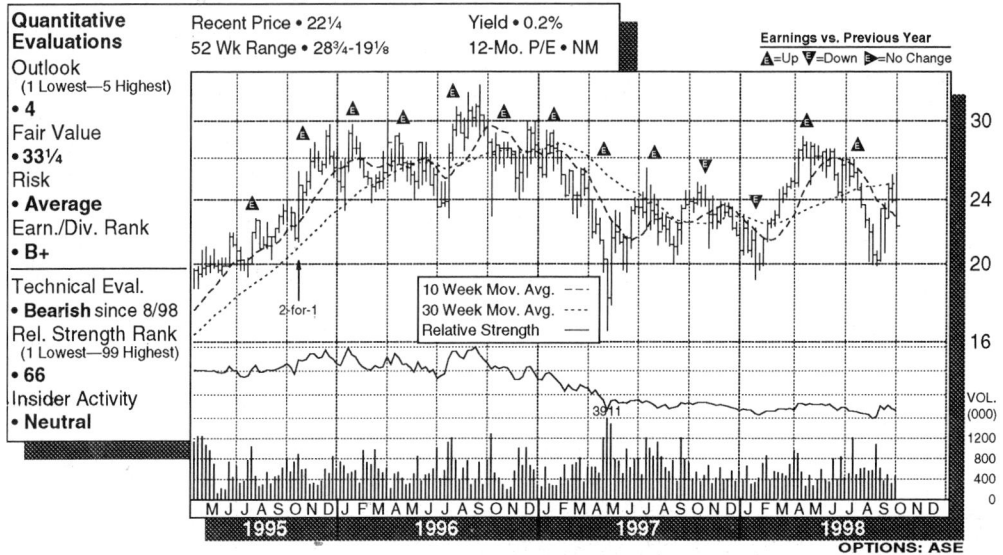

Earnings vs. Previous Year
▲=Up ▼=Down ▶=No Change

10 Week Mov. Avg. ----
30 Week Mov. Avg. ····
Relative Strength —

2-for-1

OPTIONS: ASE

Business Profile - 15-JUL-98

In January 1998, the company signed two-year agreements to supply home health care products to RoTech Medical Corp., and Apria Healthcare Group. IVCR also recently entered the medical supplies business, and further strengthened its industry-leading "one stop shopping" strategy by acquiring Suburban Ostomy Supply Co., a wholesaler of medical supplies and related home health care products. Invacare said it expects slower sales growth to continue in the 1998 first half, reflecting reimbursement cuts that have caused its provider customers to become cautious about purchasing new equipment. In 1997, Invacare initiated strategic initiatives, including the consolidation of manufacturing operations, to lower its operating cost structure and improve manufacturing efficiency beginning in 1998.

Operational Review - 15-JUL-98

Sales for the three months ended March 31, 1998, rose 19%, year to year, primarily due to acquisitions and growth in rehabilitation product sales. Results were negatively impacted by a substantial reduction in purchases from IVCR's largest customer, the negative impact of a strong dollar, and continued pricing pressures. Gross margins narrowed slightly on higher costs. SG&A expenses increased 18%, and operating income was up 13%. After greater interest expense, and taxes at 39.0% in both periods, net income increased 4.5%, to $7.5 million ($0.25 a share), from $7.2 million ($0.24).

Stock Performance - 02-OCT-98

In the past 30 trading days, IVCR's shares have increased 9%, compared to a 7% fall in the S&P 500. Average trading volume for the past five days was 92,760 shares, compared with the 40-day moving average of 113,172 shares.

Key Stock Statistics

Dividend Rate/Share	0.05	Shareholders	3,800
Shs. outstg. (M)	30.0	Market cap. (B)	$0.635
Avg. daily vol. (M)	0.083	Inst. holdings	45%
Tang. Bk. Value/Share	0.93		
Beta	0.47		

Value of $10,000 invested 5 years ago: $ 18,505

Fiscal Year Ending Dec. 31

	1998	1997	1996	1995	1994	1993
Revenues (Million $)						
1Q	181.1	151.5	134.5	107.7	87.90	78.77
2Q	202.8	165.0	159.2	122.3	98.89	90.31
3Q	—	166.1	158.2	130.6	109.0	95.68
4Q	—	170.8	167.7	143.5	115.3	100.7
Yr.	—	653.4	619.5	504.0	411.1	365.5
Earnings Per Share ($)						
1Q	0.25	0.24	0.20	0.16	0.13	0.11
2Q	0.36	0.33	0.32	0.26	0.21	0.18
3Q	—	-0.64	0.35	0.30	0.25	0.21
4Q	—	-0.11	0.41	0.05	0.00	0.26
Yr.	—	0.05	1.28	1.07	0.89	0.75

Next earnings report expected: late October

Dividend Data (Dividends have been paid since 1994.)

Amount ($)	Date Decl.	Ex-Div. Date	Stock of Record	Payment Date
0.013	Nov. 18	Dec. 30	Jan. 02	Jan. 15 '98
0.013	Feb. 16	Mar. 30	Apr. 01	Apr. 15 '98
0.013	May. 28	Jun. 29	Jul. 01	Jul. 15 '98
0.013	Aug. 18	Sep. 29	Oct. 01	Oct. 15 '98

A Division of The **McGraw·Hill** Companies

Business Summary - 15-JUL-98

This innovative manufacturer and marketer of the broadest line of home medical equipment for the home health care, retail and extended care markets has experienced 21.5% compound average annual sales growth since inception in 1979. The company has grown from $19.5 million in sales in 1979, with a limited product line of standard wheelchairs and patient aids, to become the largest home medical equipment manufacturer, based upon its distribution channels through more than 10,000 provider locations worldwide, the breadth of its product line, and sales of $653 million in 1997.

With a 20% global marketshare, IVCR's products now include standard manual wheelchairs, motorized and lightweight prescription wheelchairs, motorized scooters, patient aids, home care beds, low air loss therapy products, home respiratory products, seating and positioning products and ambulatory infusion pumps. IVCR continuously revises and expands product lines to meet changing demand.

The company's complete line of wheelchairs includes standard wheelchairs, as well as prescription wheelchairs custom built for long-term use by one individual, based on specifications prescribed by a medical professional.

Invacare also makes and markets three- and four-wheeled motorized scooters; seat and positioning products such as cushions and back positioners; a wide variety of manual, semi-electric and fully electric hospital-type beds; home respiratory products; low air loss therapy products; patient transport products such as lifts, slings and multi-position recliners, and institutional and accessory products. Other products include microprocessor electronic control systems and ambulatory infusion pumps and accessories. The company also distributes medical care products made by others, including incontinence products and bedding.

Products are marketed in the U.S. primarily to home health care and medical equipment dealers, who then sell or rent directly to end-users or health care institutions. Although the primary customers are dealers, products are also marketed to medical professionals, including physical, occupational and respiratory therapists, who refer patients to dealers to purchase specific types of home medical equipment.

The company has continued to make strategic acquisitions. In 1997, IVCR completed two acquisitions that extended or added new product lines and expanded distribution capabilities. In January 1998, the company acquired Suburban Ostomy, a wholesaler of medical supplies and related products to the home health care industry, for approximately $132 million.

The company expects that sales of domestic home medical equipment products will continue to grow during the next decade. According to IVCR, sales will be helped by growth in the population over age 65, increasing trends toward home health care treatment, technological advancement making medical equipment adaptable for home use, and continued health care cost containment.

Per Share Data ($) (Year Ended Dec. 31)	1997	1996	1995	1994	1993	1992	1991	1990	1989	1988
Tangible Bk. Val.	4.38	3.91	3.38	3.13	2.59	2.21	3.17	1.81	1.43	1.34
Cash Flow	0.66	1.87	1.54	1.31	1.17	0.97	0.83	0.61	0.33	0.37
Earnings	0.05	1.28	1.07	0.89	0.75	0.63	0.53	0.33	0.12	0.23
Dividends	0.05	0.05	0.05	0.02	Nil	Nil	Nil	Nil	Nil	Nil
Payout Ratio	100%	4%	5%	2%	Nil	Nil	Nil	Nil	Nil	Nil
Prices - High	29¼	33¼	29¾	18⅛	13⅞	15½	16⅛	5½	4⅜	2½
- Low	16½	22¾	16⅛	12⅝	10⅝	8¼	4¾	2⅛	2³⁄₁₆	1⅝
P/E Ratio - High	NM	26	28	20	19	25	30	17	38	11
- Low	NM	18	15	14	14	13	9	7	19	7

Income Statement Analysis (Million $)

	1997	1996	1995	1994	1993	1992	1991	1990	1989	1988
Revs.	653	619	504	411	365	305	263	230	186	161
Oper. Inc.	56.8	83.2	68.3	56.4	49.1	37.6	31.7	24.2	13.8	14.1
Depr.	18.4	17.8	14.2	12.7	12.3	10.0	8.1	6.6	5.0	3.2
Int. Exp.	3.2	11.2	9.6	8.2	8.6	4.6	4.3	5.7	5.4	3.7
Pretax Inc.	5.2	63.7	51.8	41.9	33.5	27.6	22.9	13.9	5.0	8.4
Eff. Tax Rate	70%	39%	38%	37%	34%	36%	38%	45%	48%	40%
Net Inc.	1.6	38.9	32.2	26.4	22.1	17.7	14.1	7.6	2.6	5.1

Balance Sheet & Other Fin. Data (Million $)

	1997	1996	1995	1994	1993	1992	1991	1990	1989	1988
Cash	5.7	8.0	6.6	10.4	13.5	10.7	3.2	3.9	3.2	2.4
Curr. Assets	275	259	205	180	156	152	120	104	92.0	76.0
Total Assets	530	510	409	337	286	262	162	138	123	102
Curr. Liab.	110	97.7	84.9	70.4	60.9	68.2	42.1	42.8	29.7	25.8
LT Debt	184	173	122	103	90.4	78.6	31.8	51.5	58.8	44.3
Common Eqty.	236	239	201	164	135	114	86.7	41.9	32.1	30.1
Total Cap.	420	412	324	267	225	194	120	96.0	93.0	76.0
Cap. Exp.	38.5	22.5	11.2	10.9	12.0	14.5	12.0	8.7	10.9	9.0
Cash Flow	20.0	56.8	46.3	39.1	34.4	27.7	22.2	14.2	7.6	8.3
Curr. Ratio	2.5	2.6	2.4	2.6	2.6	2.2	2.8	2.4	3.1	2.9
% LT Debt of Cap.	43.8	41.9	37.7	38.5	40.1	40.5	26.4	53.9	63.1	58.0
% Net Inc.of Revs.	0.2	6.3	6.4	6.4	6.1	5.8	5.4	3.3	1.4	3.1
% Ret. on Assets	0.3	8.4	8.6	8.4	8.0	8.2	8.7	5.8	2.3	5.5
% Ret. on Equity	0.7	17.7	17.6	17.6	17.7	17.3	20.7	20.4	8.4	18.4

Data as orig. reptd.; bef. results of disc. opers. and/or spec. items. Per share data adj. for stk. divs. as of ex-div. date. Bold denotes diluted EPS (FASB 128). E-Estimated. NA-Not Available. NM-Not Meaningful. NR-Not Ranked.

Office—One Invacare Way, P.O. Box 4028, Elyria, OH 44036. **Tel**—(216) 329-6000. **Website**—http://www.invacare.com **Chrmn & CEO**—A. M. Mixon III. **Pres & COO**—B. B. Blouch. **CFO, Treas, Secy & Investor Contact**—Thomas R. Miklich. **Dirs**—G. B. Blouch, F. J. Callahan, F. B. Carr, M. F. Delaney, W. Evans, B. P. Healy, A. M. Mixon III, D. T. Moore III, E. P. Nalley, J. B. Richey II, W. M. Weber. **Transfer Agent**—National City Bank, Cleveland. **Incorporated**—in Ohio in 1971. **Empl**—4,550. **S&P Analyst:** John J. Arege

Ionics, Inc.

1243M

NYSE Symbol **ION**

In S&P SmallCap 600

03-OCT-98

Industry: Manufacturing (Specialized)

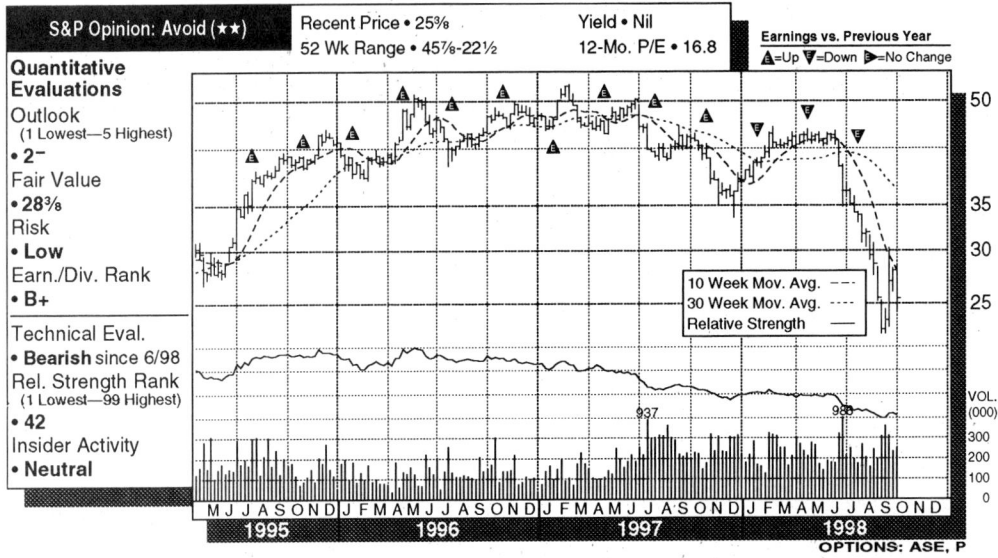

Summary: Ionics manufactures and sells or leases products, systems and services for the treatment of water and other liquids. Applications include water desalination and bottled water.

S&P Opinion: Avoid (★★)	
Recent Price • 25⅝	Yield • Nil
52 Wk Range • 45⅞-22½	12-Mo. P/E • 16.8

Earnings vs. Previous Year
▲=Up ▼=Down ▶=No Change

Quantitative Evaluations

Outlook (1 Lowest—5 Highest)
• **2⁻**

Fair Value
• **28⅜**

Risk
• **Low**

Earn./Div. Rank
• **B+**

Technical Eval.
• **Bearish** since 6/98

Rel. Strength Rank (1 Lowest—99 Highest)
• **42**

Insider Activity
• **Neutral**

10 Week Mov. Avg. - - -
30 Week Mov. Avg. - - -
Relative Strength —

VOL. (000)

OPTIONS: ASE, P

Overview - 06-AUG-98

This provider of water purification products and services operates in the fragmented and consolidating $13 billion water equipment and chemicals industry. Growth will be limited into 1999, due to Asia's deepening economic problems, slumping semiconductor equipment orders, and strong U.S. dollar translations of international business. International sales represent 41% of Ionics's total. However, the company should regain momentum as it continues to execute its strategic diversification and acquisition programs, which have transformed ION's traditional equipment operation into a more diversified business, and the Asian and microelectronics markets stabilize.

Valuation - 06-AUG-98

Revenues should be down modestly in 1998, but we expect double-digit growth in the Consumer Products division (21% of total sales) as a result of continued volume growth at Aqua Cool, as well as the probable expansion of the bottled water and bleach business. Overall profitability will be under pressure from deteriorating margins. However, ION has shown significant improvement in its free cash flow recently; $0.51 a share in 1997, compared with -$0.46, and -$0.75, for the full years 1996, and 1995 respectively. The shares are trading at about 26X our 1998 and 21X our 1999 EPS estimates, a sizeable premium to the company's five-year projected compound average EPS growth rate of 16%. Net income should decline 20% to 30% in 1998, but should return to historical growth rates when the semiconductor industry and Asian economies rebound. The drop in earnings prospects has been reflected in share prices, but we believe estimates do not yet fully reflect the depth and length of Asia's impact. Therefore, we recommend avoiding ION until its prospects improve.

Key Stock Statistics

S&P EPS Est. 1998	1.25	Tang. Bk. Value/Share	20.39
P/E on S&P Est. 1998	20.3	Beta	0.81
S&P EPS Est. 1999	1.50	Shareholders	1,800
Dividend Rate/Share	Nil	Market cap. (B)	$0.409
Shs. outstg. (M)	16.1	Inst. holdings	55%
Avg. daily vol. (M)	0.088		

Value of $10,000 invested 5 years ago: $ 7,495

Fiscal Year Ending Dec. 31

	1998	1997	1996	1995	1994	1993
Revenues (Million $)						
1Q	78.97	87.10	77.84	56.87	53.04	41.16
2Q	80.27	87.11	74.90	56.54	49.83	45.62
3Q	—	85.11	84.51	62.95	56.45	42.79
4Q	—	93.14	89.41	72.25	63.06	45.71
Yr.	—	352.5	326.7	248.6	222.4	175.3
Earnings Per Share ($)						
1Q	**0.37**	**0.43**	0.38	0.29	0.24	0.24
2Q	**0.28**	**0.44**	0.40	0.32	0.26	0.25
3Q	—	**0.44**	0.43	0.36	0.29	0.25
4Q	—	**0.42**	0.44	0.38	0.30	0.24
Yr.	—	**1.73**	1.65	1.35	1.09	0.98

Next earnings report expected: late October

Dividend Data

No cash dividends have been paid. The shares were split two for one in January 1995. A "poison pill" stock purchase rights plan was adopted in 1987.

A Division of The McGraw-Hill Companies

STANDARD
&POOR'S
STOCK REPORTS

Ionics, Incorporated

1243M

03-OCT-98

Business Summary - 06-AUG-98

This provider of water purification products and services operates in the fragmented and consolidating $13 billion water equipment and chemicals industry. Ionics derives about 80% of its revenues from industrial customers and 20% from consumer markets. In 1997, the company obtained 41% of its revenues from foreign sales of water-related products or operations of water treatment plants. Important profitability statistics from recent years are as follows:

	1997	1996	1995
Gross profit margins	32.8%	32.7%	32.8%
Operating profit margins	12.0%	11.8%	11.7%
Net profit margins	8.0%	8.1%	8.2%
Free cash flow (000)	$8,391	-$7,479	-$11,331
Free cash flow per share	$0.51	-$0.46	-$0.75

The company's products and services are used by ION or its customers to desalt brackish water and seawater, to purify and supply bottled water, to treat water in the home, to manufacture and supply water treatment chemicals and ultrapure water, to process food products, recycle and reclaim process water and wastewater, and to measure levels of water-borne contaminants and pollutants.

ION's membranes and related equipment business accounted for 47% of revenues in 1997. Products include reverse-osmosis systems and instruments for monitoring and on-line detection of pollution levels.

The water, food and chemical supply business accounted for 32% of revenues in 1997. Operations in this segment include sale of desalted water for municipal and industrial use, sale of ultrapure water for electronics and other industries, processing of food products and sale of sodium hypochlorite and related chemicals.

Consumer products, which accounted for 21% of revenues in 1997, include bottled water, over- and under-the-sink point-of-use devices and point-of-entry systems for treating the entire home water supply. The company has about 29 Aqua Cool distribution centers and 8 bottling facilities, with a ninth coming on line in 1998, in the U.S. and overseas.

Ionics principally competes with $3.2 billion U.S. Filter, the largest U.S. water treatment equipment maker; $165 million Osmonics, Inc.; and $506 million Culligan Water Technologies. The balance of the water equipment and chemicals industry consists of about 50,000 small operations around the U.S.

On June 30, 1998, long-term debt stood at $1,431,000.

Per Share Data ($)

(Year Ended Dec. 31)	1997	1996	1995	1994	1993	1992	1991	1990	1989	1988
Tangible Bk. Val.	17.39	16.50	15.51	13.94	12.67	13.78	11.05	8.84	8.00	7.54
Cash Flow	3.37	3.27	2.75	2.36	2.06	1.83	1.44	1.35	1.18	1.02
Earnings	1.73	1.65	1.35	1.09	0.98	0.93	0.72	0.55	0.42	0.32
Dividends	Nil	Nil	Nil	Nil	Nil	Nil	Nil	Nil	Nil	Nil
Payout Ratio	Nil	Nil	Nil	Nil	Nil	Nil	Nil	Nil	Nil	Nil
Prices - High	53	51¼	45½	31⅜	34	34¼	24¼	16	13⅜	10⅞
- Low	33½	38⅛	26¼	21⅜	19¼	21⅛	13¼	9⅞	7¾	6
P/E Ratio - High	31	31	34	29	35	37	33	29	31	34
- Low	19	23	19	20	20	23	18	18	18	19

Income Statement Analysis (Million $)

	1997	1996	1995	1994	1993	1992	1991	1990	1989	1988
Revs.	352	327	249	222	175	155	138	128	109	88.0
Oper. Inc.	69.5	64.7	48.6	39.1	32.4	27.4	18.4	16.5	14.7	10.9
Depr.	27.0	26.1	20.6	18.1	15.3	12.6	8.2	7.2	6.4	5.5
Int. Exp.	0.9	Nil	Nil	0.1	0.2	0.7	2.6	5.0	4.1	3.1
Pretax Inc.	43.2	39.5	29.6	22.7	19.7	18.2	11.6	6.4	5.3	3.9
Eff. Tax Rate	33%	33%	34%	32%	30%	29%	28%	25%	27%	27%
Net Inc.	28.3	26.5	19.7	15.4	13.8	12.8	8.3	4.7	3.6	2.5

Balance Sheet & Other Fin. Data (Million $)

	1997	1996	1995	1994	1993	1992	1991	1990	1989	1988
Cash	25.8	12.2	8.1	20.6	30.1	41.8	7.8	3.9	8.1	11.9
Curr. Assets	166	144	118	113	110	109	72.3	66.6	67.0	61.7
Total Assets	407	377	317	277	250	225	178	144	135	123
Curr. Liab.	66.0	68.1	58.1	54.9	46.1	30.5	36.5	51.7	44.8	32.4
LT Debt	0.8	2.1	0.2	0.1	0.1	0.4	5.6	8.0	14.4	17.7
Common Eqty.	320	292	250	219	200	190	128	76.0	68.0	64.0
Total Cap.	338	309	258	222	203	194	141	91.0	88.0	89.0
Cap. Exp.	33.5	46.0	49.1	38.2	30.1	24.7	36.7	8.7	13.7	16.1
Cash Flow	55.4	52.6	40.3	33.5	29.1	25.4	16.4	11.6	10.0	7.9
Curr. Ratio	2.5	2.1	2.0	2.1	2.4	3.6	2.0	1.3	1.5	1.9
% LT Debt of Cap.	0.2	0.7	Nil	Nil	0.1	0.2	4.0	8.8	16.4	20.0
% Net Inc.of Revs.	8.0	8.1	7.9	6.9	7.9	8.3	6.0	3.7	3.3	2.8
% Ret. on Assets	7.2	7.6	6.6	5.8	5.8	5.8	4.4	3.4	2.8	2.1
% Ret. on Equity	9.3	9.7	8.4	7.4	7.1	7.4	7.2	6.6	5.4	4.0

Data as orig. reptd.; bef. results of disc. opers. and/or spec. items. Per share data adj. for stk. divs. as of ex-div. date. E-Estimated. NA-Not Available. NM-Not Meaningful. NR-Not Ranked. Free cash flow defined as: Net income plus depreciation/amortization, less net capital expenditures, increases in working capital and preferred dividends.

Office—65 Grove St., Watertown, MA 02172. **Tel**—(617) 926-2500. **Website**—http://www.ionics.com **Chrmn, Pres & CEO**—A. L. Goldstein. **Exec VP**—W. E. Katz. **VP-Fin & CFO**—R. Halliday. **Treas**—J.P. Bergeron. **Dirs**—D. R. Brown, W. L. Brown, A. de Vitry d'Avaucourt, K. Feldstein, A. L. Goldstein, W. E. Katz, R. B. Luick, J. J. Shields, C. S. Sloane, D. I. Wang, M. S. Wrighton, A. S. Wyett. **Transfer Agent & Registrar**—State Street Bank & Trust Co., Boston. **Incorporated**—in Massachusetts in 1948. **Empl**—2,000. **S&P Analyst:** John A. Massey

STANDARD &POOR'S

STOCK REPORTS

Itron, Inc.

4286K

NASDAQ Symbol **ITRI**

In S&P SmallCap 600

03-OCT-98

Industry:
Electrical Equipment

Summary: Itron is a leading provider of energy information, communications and management solutions to electric, gas and water utilities worldwide.

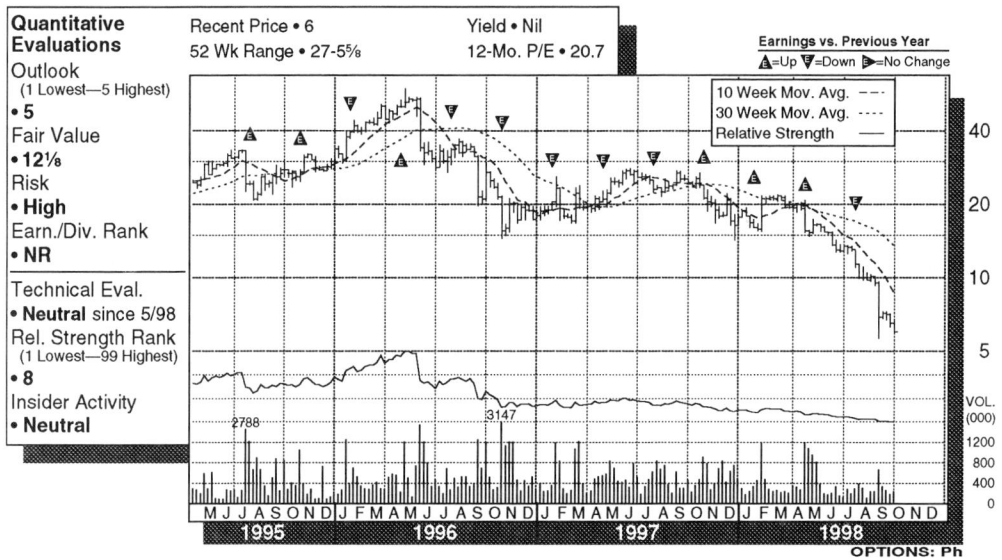

Quantitative Evaluations	Recent Price • 6	Yield • Nil
	52 Wk Range • 27-5⅝	12-Mo. P/E • 20.7

Outlook
(1 Lowest—5 Highest)
• **5**

Fair Value
• **12⅛**

Risk
• **High**

Earn./Div. Rank
• **NR**

Technical Eval.
• **Neutral** since 5/98

Rel. Strength Rank
(1 Lowest—99 Highest)
• **8**

Insider Activity
• **Neutral**

Earnings vs. Previous Year
▲=Up ▼=Down ▶=No Change

10 Week Mov. Avg. – – –
30 Week Mov. Avg. ·······
Relative Strength ——

OPTIONS: Ph

Business Profile - 14-SEP-98

This company seeks to provide cost-effective automatic meter reading (AMR) solutions to its base of handheld systems customers, as well as to utility customers not previously served. In June 1997, ITRI acquired Design Concepts International, a supplier of telephone-based AMR systems to electric utilities. ITRI and Schlumberger (NYSE: SLB), the world's largest provider of metering systems and solutions, announced the signing of a memorandum of understanding in October 1997. The intent of the alliance is to obtain AMR business in Europe. A pretax charge of from $2 million to $3 million will be recorded in the 1998 third quarter for a corporate restructuring designed to improve efficiency and financial performance.

Operational Review - 14-SEP-98

Total revenues in the six months ended June 30, 1998, rose 33%, year to year, as sharply higher AMR systems sales, reflecting electric meter module shipments under a fixed network contract, outweighed reduced revenues due to completion or near completion of large handheld systems and outsourcing contracts. Gross margins narrowed, but with well-controlled SG&A and product development expenses, operating income contrasted with an operating loss. Despite higher other expense, the net loss narrowed to $923,000 ($0.06 a share), from $3,934,000 ($0.28).

Stock Performance - 02-OCT-98

In the past 30 trading days, ITRI's shares have declined 41%, compared to a 7% fall in the S&P 500. Average trading volume for the past five days was 46,720 shares, compared with the 40-day moving average of 57,615 shares.

Key Stock Statistics

Dividend Rate/Share	Nil	Shareholders	10,700
Shs. outstg. (M)	14.7	Market cap. (B)	$0.088
Avg. daily vol. (M)	0.056	Inst. holdings	52%
Tang. Bk. Value/Share	6.75		
Beta	NA		

Value of $10,000 invested 5 years ago: NA

Fiscal Year Ending Dec. 31

	1998	1997	1996	1995	1994	1993
Revenues (Million $)						
1Q	63.71	40.58	48.05	36.06	25.21	18.38
2Q	60.77	52.73	48.20	37.73	28.62	22.44
3Q	—	58.43	38.74	39.33	31.95	23.32
4Q	—	64.38	42.59	42.24	34.88	24.48
Yr.	—	216.1	177.6	155.3	120.7	88.61
Earnings Per Share ($)						
1Q	**0.01**	-0.24	0.21	0.18	0.11	0.02
2Q	**-0.07**	-0.05	0.17	0.20	0.14	0.08
3Q	—	0.11	-0.34	0.20	0.19	0.1/
4Q	—	0.22	-0.17	0.21	0.23	0.18
Yr.	—	0.07	-0.11	0.79	0.67	0.46

Next earnings report expected: mid October

Dividend Data

No cash dividends have been paid on the common stock.

A Division of The McGraw·Hill Companies

STANDARD
&POOR'S
STOCK REPORTS

Itron, Inc.

4286K
03-OCT-98

Business Summary - 14-SEP-98

This electronic meter reading system maker is yards ahead of its competition. Spokane, WA-based Itron, Inc. (ITRI) is the world's leading supplier of automatic meter reading (AMR) and hand-held computer-based electronic meter reading (EMR) systems for the utility industry. ITRI's systems are used for collecting, communicating and analyzing electric, gas and water usage for all classes of a utility's customers - residential, commercial and industrial.

Did you ever wonder why you rarely see the meter man anymore? The company's AMR products and systems (66% of sales in 1997), known as Genesis by Itron, involve the use of radio and, in some instances, telephone technology to remotely collect meter data for all types of utilities. ITRI's ERT (encoder, receiver, transmitter) radio meter modules attach to utility meters and allow meters to receive communications, encode consumption and tamper information and communicate that data remotely. ERT meter modules can be read off-site by a person up to 800 feet away with a hand-held computer; by a data collection device mounted in a vehicle; or through a fixed network AMR which eliminates the need to send meter readers to or near customer premises. ITR has shipped some 11.1 million AMR meter modules to over 300 utilities through December 31, 1997.

ITRI has been the leading supplier of hand-held computer-based EMR systems since the early 1980s. Its systems (23% of sales in 1997) are installed at over 1,500 utility customers in more than 40 countries, including 80% of North American utilities with more than 50,000 customer meters. ITRI's systems allow the automation of a substantial portion of visual meter reading and billing functions, including data acquisition, storage and transfer.

The company also offers its products and services through outsourcing arrangements with utilities, performing meter reading and other services for periods of 15 years or more, in return for a fixed amount.

ITRI's Utility Transfer Systems Inc., subsidiary is the leading U.S. provider of software systems for metering data acquisition and analysis for the large commercial and industrial customers of electric and gas utilities. In June 1997, ITRI acquired Design Concepts International, a supplier of telephone-based AMR systems to electric utilities, for 759,297 common shares.

While 1996 revenues increased 10% from those of 1995, to $177.6 million (on increased AMR system sales), ITRI had a net loss of $1.5 million, reflecting higher operating expenses. Profitability was restored during the third quarter of 1997, as orders increased and costs were well managed. To further reduce costs, a corporate restructuring will be implemented during 1998; it is expected to provide additional savings of from $6 million to $8 million annually.

Per Share Data ($)

(Year Ended Dec. 31)	1997	1996	1995	1994	1993	1992	1991	1990	1989	1988
Tangible Bk. Val.	6.78	6.86	7.29	6.24	4.84	NA	NA	NA	NA	NA
Cash Flow	1.22	0.68	1.42	1.23	1.12	0.52	NA	NA	NA	NA
Earnings	0.07	-0.11	0.79	0.67	0.46	0.02	NA	NA	NA	NA
Dividends	Nil	Nil	Nil	Nil	Nil	Nil	Nil	Nil	Nil	Nil
Payout Ratio	Nil	Nil	Nil	Nil	Nil	Nil	Nil	Nil	Nil	Nil
Prices - High	28$\frac{1}{8}$	60	34$\frac{1}{2}$	23$\frac{1}{2}$	18	NA	NA	NA	NA	NA
- Low	14$\frac{1}{4}$	14$\frac{1}{2}$	18	14	13$\frac{1}{2}$	NA	NA	NA	NA	NA
P/E Ratio - High	NM	NM	43	35	39	NA	NA	NA	NA	NA
- Low	NM	NM	23	21	29	NA	NA	NA	NA	NA

Income Statement Analysis (Million $)

	1997	1996	1995	1994	1993	1992	1991	1990	1989	1988
Revs.	216	178	155	121	88.6	67.9	NA	NA	NA	NA
Oper. Inc.	21.5	8.8	21.6	17.5	14.0	9.8	NA	NA	NA	NA
Depr.	16.8	10.5	8.0	6.6	6.1	4.6	NA	NA	NA	NA
Int. Exp.	3.9	1.2	0.2	0.1	0.7	0.5	NA	NA	NA	NA
Pretax Inc.	1.6	-2.1	15.3	11.9	7.4	0.9	NA	NA	NA	NA
Eff. Tax Rate	38%	NM	34%	33%	42%	NM	NM	NM	NM	NM
Net Inc.	1.0	-1.5	10.1	8.0	4.3	0.1	NA	NA	NA	NA

Balance Sheet & Other Fin. Data (Million $)

	1997	1996	1995	1994	1993	1992	1991	1990	1989	1988
Cash	3.0	2.2	31.5	41.7	25.1	NA	NA	NA	NA	NA
Curr. Assets	112	90.7	92.5	85.2	68.6	NA	NA	NA	NA	NA
Total Assets	240	187	147	119	99	NA	NA	NA	NA	NA
Curr. Liab.	44.1	64.5	28.8	22.9	25.5	NA	NA	NA	NA	NA
LT Debt	69.8	6.4	5.6	0.1	0.3	NA	NA	NA	NA	NA
Common Eqty.	120	114	109	94.0	71.0	NA	NA	NA	NA	NA
Total Cap.	193	120	116	94.0	71.0	NA	NA	NA	NA	NA
Cap. Exp.	9.3	27.5	16.5	7.3	3.8	NA	NA	NA	NA	NA
Cash Flow	17.8	9.1	18.1	14.6	10.3	4.7	NA	NA	NA	NA
Curr. Ratio	2.5	1.4	3.2	3.7	2.7	NA	NA	NA	NA	NA
% LT Debt of Cap.	36.2	5.3	4.8	Nil	0.4	NA	NA	NA	NA	NA
% Net Inc.of Revs.	0.5	NM	6.5	6.6	4.8	0.2	NA	NA	NA	NA
% Ret. on Assets	0.5	NM	7.6	7.3	NA	NA	NA	NA	NA	NA
% Ret. on Equity	0.9	NM	9.9	9.6	NA	NA	NA	NA	NA	NA

Data as orig. reptd.; bef. results of disc. opers. and/or spec. items. Per share data adj. for stk. divs. as of ex-div. date. Bold denotes diluted EPS (FASB 128). E-Estimated. NA-Not Available. NM-Not Meaningful. NR-Not Ranked.

Office—2818 N. Sullivan Rd., Spokane, WA 99216-1897.**Tel**—(509) 924-9900. **Chrmn**—P. A. Redmond. **Pres & CEO**—J. M. Humphreys. **EVP & COO**—C. R. Aron. **VP & CFO**—D. G. Remington. **Secy**—MariLyn R. Blair. **Treas & Investor Contact**—Mima G. Scarpelli (509-891-3565). **Dirs**—M. B. Bracy, T. C. DeMerritt, J. E. Eliassen, J. M. Humphreys, M. A. Peters, P. A. Redmond, S. E. White, G. M. Wilson. **Transfer Agent & Registrar**—ChaseMellon Shareholder Services, SF. **Incorporated**—in Delaware in 1981. **Empl**— 1,213. **S&P Analyst:** S.A.H.

J & J Snack Foods   4288K

NASDAQ Symbol **JJSF**

In S&P SmallCap 600

03-OCT-98   Industry:
Foods

Summary: This company manufactures and markets snack foods and baked goods, and distributes frozen beverage products to the foodservice, retail grocery and supermarket industries.

Quantitative Evaluations

Outlook
(1 Lowest—5 Highest)
• **4⁻**

Fair Value
• **24¼**

Risk
• **Average**

Earn./Div. Rank
• **B**

Technical Eval.
• **Bullish** since 8/98

Rel. Strength Rank
(1 Lowest—99 Highest)
• **51**

Insider Activity
• **Neutral**

Recent Price • 17
52 Wk Range • 22¼-12½

Yield • Nil
12-Mo. P/E • 15.7

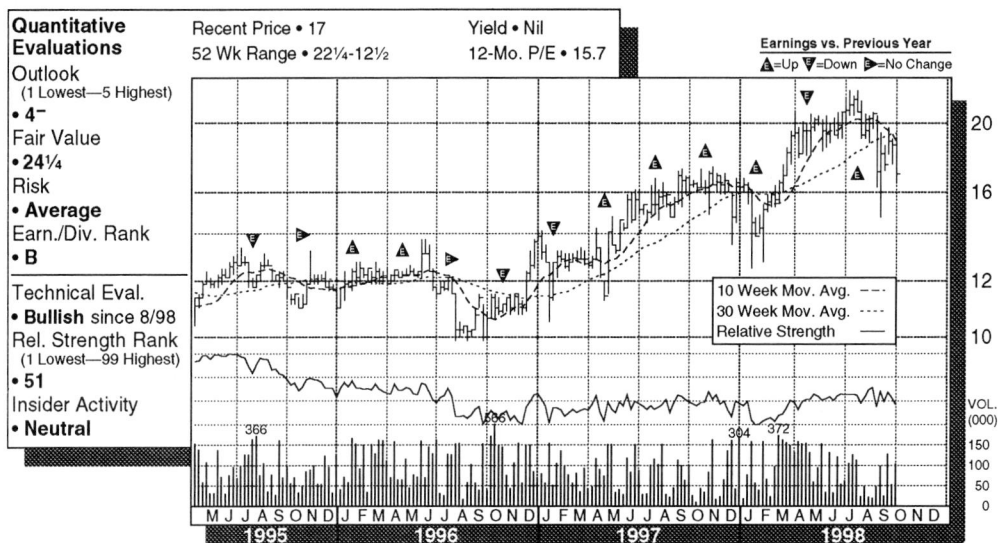

10 Week Mov. Avg. - - -
30 Week Mov. Avg. ·······
Relative Strength ——

Business Profile - 18-SEP-98

In December 1997, this manufacturer of snack foods acquired a controlling interest in National ICEE Corp. (annual revenues of about $40 million), which markets and distributes frozen carbonated beverages under the tradename ICEE in the eastern half of the U.S. The company believed that the acquisition would enable it to further develop the frozen beverage category and the ICEE brand on a national basis. Gross margins expanded to 53% in the fiscal third quarter (from 49% in the year earlier period), as higher margins at National ICEE and lower flour costs offset higher manufacturing costs of approximately $1 million incurred during the startup of JJSF's expanded Italian ice and frozen dessert plant in Scranton, PA. G.B. Shreiber, the company's president and CEO, owns 34% of the shares.

Operational Review - 18-SEP-98

Net sales in the nine months ended June 27, 1998, advanced 17%, year to year, aided by the acquisition of National ICEE. Margins widened on lower flour costs and an improved product mix, and despite sharply higher interest and sundry expenses, pretax income rose 44%. After taxes at 37.0% in both periods, net income was also up 44%, to $6,007,000 ($0.64 a diluted share, on 4.4% more shares), from $4,175,000 ($0.47).

Stock Performance - 02-OCT-98

In the past 30 trading days, JJSF's shares have declined 18%, compared to a 7% fall in the S&P 500. Average trading volume for the past five days was 20,780 shares, compared with the 40-day moving average of 12,718 shares.

Key Stock Statistics

Dividend Rate/Share	Nil	Shareholders	NA
Shs. outstg. (M)	9.0	Market cap. (B)	$0.153
Avg. daily vol. (M)	0.016	Inst. holdings	47%
Tang. Bk. Value/Share	8.28		
Beta	0.81		

Value of $10,000 invested 5 years ago: $ 18,854

Fiscal Year Ending Sep. 30

	1998	1997	1996	1995	1994	1993
Revenues (Million $)						
1Q	52.19	43.60	42.86	41.22	38.41	30.79
2Q	58.87	50.31	42.14	40.32	40.27	32.73
3Q	73.28	63.45	49.09	47.88	45.17	39.42
4Q	—	62.96	51.93	55.95	50.58	44.25
Yr.	—	220.3	186.0	185.4	174.4	147.2
Earnings Per Share ($)						
1Q	**0.06**	0.01	0.09	0.06	0.12	0.05
2Q	**0.08**	0.10	0.07	0.05	0.15	0.13
3Q	**0.50**	0.35	0.21	0.21	0.25	0.27
4Q	—	0.43	0.29	0.30	0.30	0.34
Yr.	—	0.91	0.65	0.61	0.82	0.80

Next earnings report expected: early November

Dividend Data

The company has not paid any cash dividends.

A Division of The **McGraw·Hill** *Companies*

STANDARD
&POOR'S
STOCK REPORTS

J & J Snack Foods Corporation

4288K
03-OCT-98

Business Summary - 18-SEP-98

From just $400,000 in annual sales in 1971, when president and CEO Gerald B. Shreiber purchased J & J Snack Foods Corporation out of bankruptcy, the company reported revenues of $220 million in FY 97 (Sep.). The company's principal snack food products are soft pretzels marketed primarily under the brand name Superpretzel. J & J also manufactures frozen carbonated beverages, frozen juice treats and desserts, churros, baked goods, and other products. All products are sold to the foodservice and retail supermarket industries. The company's strategy is to produce niche quality products, be the low-cost producer and develop strong marketing and distribution channels.

In the early 1970s, J & J sold one product, soft pretzels, in only two varieties: raw and baked. Today, the company's soft-pretzel products are sold under the Superpretzel, Mr. Twister, Soft Pretzel Bites, Softstix, Soft Pretzel Buns, Hot Knots, Dutch Twist, Texas Twist and Sandwich Twist brand names and, to a lesser extent, under private labels. Pretzels are sold to foodservice industry customers and to the retail grocery and supermarket industries. Pretzels are also sold direct to the public through its Bavarian Pretzel Bakery and Pretzel Gourmet snack food retail outlet chains. Soft pretzel sales accounted for 40% of total sales in FY 97, down from 45% in FY 96.

Frozen carbonated beverages are sold under the ICEE and Artic Blast names in 15 western states, Mexico and Canada, and under the brand names Frozen Coke and Artic Blast in 32 midwestern and eastern states. Frozen carbonated beverages are also sold through the company's Bavarian Pretzel Bakery and Pretzel Gourmet snack food chains. Frozen carbonated beverage sales accounted for 20% of total FY 97 revenues, down from 23% in FY 96.

The company's frozen juice treat and desserts are sold under the Super Juice, Mazzone, Frostar, Shape-ups, Luigi's and Mama Tish's brand names. Frozen juice treat and dessert sales were 19% and 15% of total revenues in FY 97 and FY 96, respectively.

Frozen churros are sold under the Tio Pepe's brand name and are marketed primarily in the western and southwestern states. Churro revenues accounted for 5% and 6% of sales in FY 97 and FY 96, respectively.

Baked goods, such as cookies, muffins and other baked products, are sold under private labels by contract for third parties. In addition, the company markets baked goods under the Danish Mill and Pretzelcookie brand names. Baked goods sales amounted to 8% and 4% of sales in FY 97 and FY 96, respectively. J & J also sells soft drinks and funnel cakes under the Funnel Cake Factory name, as well as popcorn under the Airport brand name.

Per Share Data ($)

(Year Ended Sep. 30)	1997	1996	1995	1994	1993	1992	1991	1990	1989	1988
Tangible Bk. Val.	9.54	9.99	9.58	9.18	8.59	7.68	7.07	4.65	4.45	1.91
Cash Flow	3.01	2.47	2.18	2.14	1.93	1.39	1.45	1.10	1.45	1.36
Earnings	0.91	0.65	0.61	0.82	0.80	0.55	0.67	0.44	0.81	0.68
Dividends	Nil	Nil	Nil	Nil	Nil	Nil	Nil	Nil	Nil	Nil
Payout Ratio	Nil	Nil	Nil	Nil	Nil	Nil	Nil	Nil	Nil	Nil
Prices - High	17⅜	14⅛	13⅜	20¾	20¾	14¾	15⅞	13¼	17⅛	12
- Low	10½	9⅞	10	10⅞	8¾	7½	7⅝	4⅞	10¾	6⅝
P/E Ratio - High	19	22	22	25	26	27	24	30	21	18
- Low	12	15	16	13	11	14	11	11	13	10

Income Statement Analysis (Million $)

	1997	1996	1995	1994	1993	1992	1991	1990	1989	1988
Revs.	220	186	185	174	147	127	110	96.0	87.0	71.0
Oper. Inc.	30.5	24.5	22.9	26.2	24.0	17.1	16.5	12.2	15.0	11.6
Depr.	18.9	16.5	15.0	13.8	11.8	9.1	7.2	5.6	4.7	4.3
Int. Exp.	0.4	0.4	0.4	0.5	0.4	0.4	0.8	0.9	1.8	2.2
Pretax Inc.	12.0	9.0	9.8	13.7	13.1	9.0	9.3	5.8	9.4	6.4
Eff. Tax Rate	32%	35%	38%	38%	36%	34%	35%	36%	37%	37%
Net Inc.	8.2	5.8	5.8	8.5	8.3	5.9	6.1	3.7	5.9	4.2

Balance Sheet & Other Fin. Data (Million $)

	1997	1996	1995	1994	1993	1992	1991	1990	1989	1988
Cash	1.4	11.7	14.5	11.1	15.8	15.7	23.7	2.4	6.8	6.9
Curr. Assets	41.2	44.2	44.5	41.4	43.5	41.0	46.3	22.7	24.2	21.9
Total Assets	137	123	123	127	121	112	104	75.0	67.0	62.0
Curr. Liab.	22.0	17.4	16.5	16.4	13.6	12.9	11.2	15.0	9.9	10.9
LT Debt	5.0	5.0	5.0	5.0	5.0	5.1	2.4	5.9	6.7	27.4
Common Eqty.	106	96.7	96.1	101	98.0	90.1	86.4	50.5	47.5	22.5
Total Cap.	114	105	106	110	108	100	93.2	60.2	56.7	51.4
Cap. Exp.	19.6	14.4	12.9	18.6	15.4	21.8	13.2	12.4	8.1	10.6
Cash Flow	27.0	22.3	20.8	22.3	20.2	15.0	13.3	9.3	10.6	8.5
Curr. Ratio	1.9	2.5	2.7	2.5	3.2	3.2	4.1	1.5	2.4	2.0
% LT Debt of Cap.	4.4	4.8	4.8	4.6	4.7	5.1	2.6	9.7	11.8	53.3
% Net Inc.of Revs.	3.7	3.1	3.2	4.9	5.7	4.7	5.5	3.8	6.8	5.9
% Ret. on Assets	6.3	4.8	4.7	7.0	7.2	5.5	6.0	5.2	7.9	7.0
% Ret. on Equity	8.1	6.1	5.9	8.8	8.9	6.8	8.0	7.6	15.3	21.6

Data as orig. reptd.; bef. results of disc. opers. and/or spec. items. Per share data adj. for stk. divs. as of ex-div. date. Bold denotes diluted EPS (FASB 128). E-Estimated. NA-Not Available. NM-Not Meaningful. NR-Not Ranked.

Office—6000 Central Hwy., Pennsauken, NJ 08109. **Tel**—(609) 665-9533. **Chrmn, Pres & CEO**—G. B. Shreiber. **SVP & COO**—R. M. Radano. **SVP, CFO, Secy, Treas & Investor Contact**—Dennis G. Moore. **Dirs**—S. N. Frankel, L. M. Lodish, D. G. Moore, R. M. Radano, G. B. Shreiber, P. G. Stanley. **Transfer Agent & Registrar**—American Stock Transfer & Trust Co., Brooklyn. **Incorporated**—in New Jersey in 1971. **Empl**— 1,700.
S&P Analyst: K.S.

JLG Industries

1255T

NYSE Symbol **JLG**

In S&P SmallCap 600

10-OCT-98

Industry:
Manufacturing (Specialized)

Summary: This company is a leading manufacturer, distributor and international marketer of mobile aerial work platforms.

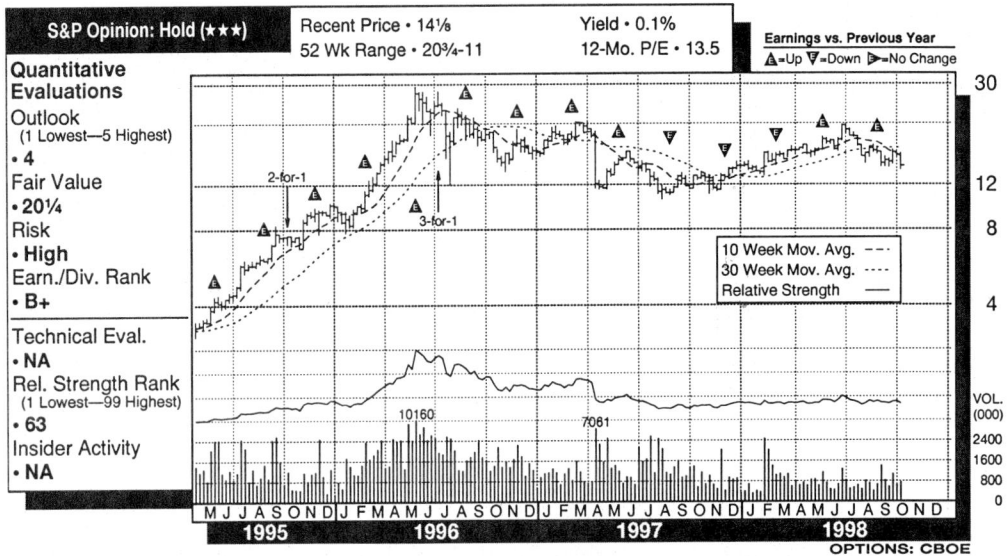

S&P Opinion: Hold (★★★)		
Recent Price • 14⅛		Yield • 0.1%
52 Wk Range • 20¾-11		12-Mo. P/E • 13.5

Earnings vs. Previous Year
▲=Up ▼=Down ►=No Change

Quantitative Evaluations

Outlook
(1 Lowest—5 Highest)
• **4**

Fair Value
• 20¼

Risk
• **High**

Earn./Div. Rank
• **B+**

Technical Eval.
• **NA**

Rel. Strength Rank
(1 Lowest—99 Highest)
• **63**

Insider Activity
• **NA**

10 Week Mov. Avg. – – –
30 Week Mov. Avg. · · · ·
Relative Strength ——

VOL. (000)
2400
1600
800
0

OPTIONS: CBOE

Overview - 08-SEP-98

EPS in FY 98 (Jul.) were $1.05, versus $1.04 in FY 97, exceeding analyst estimates. Sales in the fourth quarter benefited from improved unit volume, despite a relatively flat pricing environment. While it appears that pricing levels may have bottomed, we believe that competition in the industry will keep prices under pressure. After a difficult transitional period in FY 98, we see improved prospects for JLG. The company believes that it is well positioned to pick up market share and continue to increase international sales, despite the volatile global economic environment. International expansion strategies have recently focused on Asia and Europe, where self propelled aerial work platforms are gaining acceptance. In addition, rental fleets have been experiencing robust growth, with utilization rates up, year to year. However, JLG noted that its production schedule has recently been constrained by supplier issues, but would not comment on specifics. Management also reaffirmed that it is seeking an acquisition with about $300 million to $400 million in revenues. The company expects sales growth of 15% in FY 99, with earnings up at a somewhat faster rate.

Valuation - 08-SEP-98

We continue to recommend holding JLG. Although incredible momentum experienced in recent years has clearly slowed, we believe that JLG is in a better competitive position, following aggressive restructuring measures in FY 98. We also expect additional cost reduction benefits to be realized in FY 99. Although JLG aims for sales and earnings growth of at least 15% in FY 99, we remain neutral on the shares, recently trading at about 13X our FY 99 EPS estimate of $1.20, reflecting uncertainty over supplier issues, and a possible slowdown in the U.S. economy.

Key Stock Statistics

S&P EPS Est. 1998	NA	Tang. Bk. Value/Share	4.30
P/E on S&P Est. 1998	NA	Beta	0.64
S&P EPS Est. 1999	1.20	Shareholders	4,300
Dividend Rate/Share	0.02	Market cap. (B)	$0.625
Shs. outstg. (M)	44.1	Inst. holdings	56%
Avg. daily vol. (M)	0.149		

Value of $10,000 invested 5 years ago: $ 152,643

Fiscal Year Ending Jul. 31

	1998	1997	1996	1995	1994	1993
Revenues (Million $)						
1Q	95.64	120.2	86.70	53.72	36.76	25.00
2Q	111.7	121.3	87.56	52.18	34.17	27.10
3Q	146.3	143.6	113.2	75.81	50.14	32.98
4Q	177.2	141.2	125.9	87.50	55.37	37.99
Yr.	530.9	526.3	413.4	269.2	176.4	123.0
Earnings Per Share ($)						
1Q	0.11	0.28	0.18	0.09	0.03	0.01
2Q	**0.17**	0.26	0.19	0.09	0.03	0.01
3Q	**0.32**	0.30	0.28	0.14	0.08	0.03
4Q	**0.46**	0.22	0.30	0.17	0.09	0.03
Yr.	**1.05**	1.06	0.95	0.49	0.23	0.07

Next earnings report expected: mid November

Dividend Data (Dividends have been paid since 1993.)

Amount ($)	Date Decl.	Ex-Div. Date	Stock of Record	Payment Date
0.005	Nov. 17	Dec. 12	Dec. 16	Jan. 02 '98
0.005	Feb. 19	Mar. 11	Mar. 13	Apr. 01 '98
0.005	May. 21	Jun. 10	Jun. 12	Jul. 01 '98
0.005	Sep. 03	Sep. 11	Sep. 15	Oct. 01 '98

A Division of The McGraw-Hill Companies

Business Summary - 08-SEP-98

JLG Industries is the world's leading manufacturer, distributor and international marketer of mobile aerial work platforms (the development of which it pioneered). These products are used primarily for construction, industrial, commercial, and institutional applications.

JLG specializes in three types of aerial work platforms: boom-type, scissor-type and push-around (vertical) lifts. They are powered by electric motors or gasoline, diesel, or propane engines. The self-propelled telescoping boom-lifts, which have lift capacity of up to 1,000 lbs., can reach heights of 150 ft., and may be rotated 360 degrees in either direction. Scissor-lifts, which can reach heights of 50 ft., provide larger work areas, and lift capacity of up to 2,500 lbs. Push-around units consist of an aluminum or steel base that holds a work platform up to 36 ft., with a lift capacity of up to 750 lbs.

The company believes that the dramatic growth experienced by the industry over the last five years was driven by five factors: a national movement by businesses to improve productivity through the reduction of cycle times and labor costs; changes in workplace safety rules (such as an OSHA requirement for fall restraints in work done more than six ft. above the ground); growing acceptance of these machines in the developing world as a more efficient alternative to scaffolding and ladders; a strong economic environment

and the growth in capital spending; and increased demand for rental equipment, along with the greater ability of rental companies to purchase equipment.

In July 1997, a slowdown in domestic orders and competitive market conditions led to the announcement of a restructuring plan aimed at improving productivity and profitability. With an apparent slowdown in the tremendous growth experienced by the industry in recent years, JLG is now taking measures to reduce its exposure to the market's inherent cyclicality. Its plan includes: improving manufacturing efficiencies and processes, reducing costs, and shortening manufacturing lead times; accelerating new product development; expanding global distribution; enhancing customer support services; expanding its own rental fleet and used equipment business; strengthening employee involvement; and pursuing strategic acquisitions.

The company's products are sold mainly to independent distributors that rent and service the equipment. The North American distributor network consists of about 100 companies operating nearly 300 branches, while the European base includes approximately 80 locations. JLG also has a presence in the Asia/Pacific region, Australia, Japan and Latin America, including a Brazilian joint venture established in FY 97. In FY 98 (Jul.), international sales were 32% of total net sales (versus 30% in FY 97 and 24% in FY 96).

Per Share Data ($)

(Year Ended Jul. 31)	1998	1997	1996	1995	1994	1993	1992	1991	1990	1989
Tangible Bk. Val.	NA	3.70	2.61	1.60	1.09	0.89	0.86	0.90	1.04	0.84
Cash Flow	NA	1.30	1.09	0.58	0.29	0.13	-0.01	-0.03	0.24	0.22
Earnings	1.05	1.06	0.95	0.49	0.23	0.07	-0.07	-0.08	0.20	0.18
Dividends	0.02	0.02	0.02	0.01	0.01	Nil	0.01	0.02	0.02	0.01
Payout Ratio	2%	2%	2%	2%	3%	Nil	Nil	NM	8%	7%
Prices - High	20¾	21⅜	29½	10⅛	3½	2¹/₁₆	1	1⁵/₁₆	2⁷/₁₆	1¹⁵/₁₆
- Low	13	10½	7¾	2⁷/₈	2	⁷/₈	⁵/₈	¹³/₁₆	⁵/₈	1¼
P/E Ratio - High	20	20	31	21	15	28	NM	NM	12	11
- Low	12	10	8	6	9	12	NM	NM	3	7

Income Statement Analysis (Million $)

	1998	1997	1996	1995	1994	1993	1992	1991	1990	1989
Revs.	NA	526	413	269	176	123	110	94.0	149	121
Oper. Inc.	NA	84.2	64.7	36.6	17.8	7.4	3.1	0.5	16.7	15.0
Depr.	NA	10.4	6.5	3.9	2.8	2.5	2.6	1.9	1.8	1.6
Int. Exp.	NA	0.4	0.3	0.4	0.4	0.5	1.2	1.5	2.3	1.4
Pretax Inc.	NA	71.2	65.7	32.7	14.6	4.6	-5.8	-6.4	13.4	12.4
Eff. Tax Rate	NA	35%	36%	37%	35%	30%	NM	NM	37%	39%
Net Inc.	NA	46.1	42.1	20.8	9.5	3.2	-3.0	-3.2	8.5	7.5

Balance Sheet & Other Fin. Data (Million $)

	1998	1997	1996	1995	1994	1993	1992	1991	1990	1989
Cash	NA	25.4	30.4	13.0	8.1	4.8	4.9	0.9	4.5	2.1
Curr. Assets	NA	156	129	84.6	62.5	49.4	53.1	58.4	70.5	57.2
Total Assets	NA	249	249	120	91.6	72.5	73.8	74.9	86.7	70.6
Curr. Liab.	NA	71.1	57.1	39.2	30.1	24.0	20.8	21.9	23.2	22.5
LT Debt	NA	3.7	2.0	2.3	6.3	3.2	10.2	8.8	15.5	9.2
Common Eqty.	NA	162	113	68.4	45.7	38.9	37.2	38.6	44.0	35.3
Total Cap.	NA	166	115	70.7	52.0	42.1	47.3	48.1	60.2	45.4
Cap. Exp.	NA	29.8	16.7	11.0	7.8	3.6	5.1	2.2	2.3	4.7
Cash Flow	NA	56.5	48.6	24.6	12.3	5.7	-0.5	-1.3	10.3	9.2
Curr. Ratio	NA	2.2	2.3	2.2	2.1	2.1	2.5	2.7	3.0	2.5
% LT Debt of Cap.	NA	2.2	1.7	3.2	12.1	7.5	21.4	18.4	25.8	20.3
% Net Inc.of Revs.	NA	8.8	10.2	7.7	5.4	2.6	NM	NM	5.7	6.2
% Ret. on Assets	NA	21.4	27.8	19.6	11.9	4.4	NM	NM	10.8	11.7
% Ret. on Equity	NA	33.5	46.4	36.4	23.0	8.4	NM	NM	21.4	23.6

Data as orig. reptd.; bef. results of disc. opers. and/or spec. items. Per share data adj. for stk. divs. as of ex-div. date. Bold denotes diluted EPS (FASB 128). E-Estimated. NA-Not Available. NM-Not Meaningful. NR-Not Ranked.

Office—JLG Drive, McConnellsburg, PA 17233. **Tel**—(717) 485-5161. **Website**—http://www.jlg.com **Chrmn, Pres & CEO**—L. D. Black. **EVP, CFO & Investor Contact**—Charles H. Diller Jr. **Dirs**—L. D. Black, C. H. Diller Jr., G. R. Kempton, J. A. Mezera, G. Palmer, S. Rabinowitz, T. C. Wajnert; C. O. Wood III. **Transfer Agent**—ChaseMellon Shareholder Services, Ridgefield Park, NJ. **Incorporated**—in Pennsylvania in 1969. **Empl**— 2,686.
S&P Analyst: Eric J. Hunter

STANDARD &POOR'S
STOCK REPORTS
JSB Financial
1256M
NYSE Symbol **JSB**
In S&P SmallCap 600

06-OCT-98

Industry:
Savings & Loan Companies

Summary: JSB is the holding company for the $1.6 billion-asset Jamaica Savings Bank, which conducts business from 13 offices located mainly in the New York City borough of Queens.

Quantitative Evaluations	
Outlook (1 Lowest—5 Highest)	**• NA**
Fair Value	**• NA**
Risk	**• Low**
Earn./Div. Rank	**• NR**
Technical Eval.	**• NA**
Rel. Strength Rank (1 Lowest—99 Highest)	**• 77**
Insider Activity	**• Favorable**

Recent Price • 50⅝
52 Wk Range • 60-44¾

Yield • 3.2%
12-Mo. P/E • 11.1

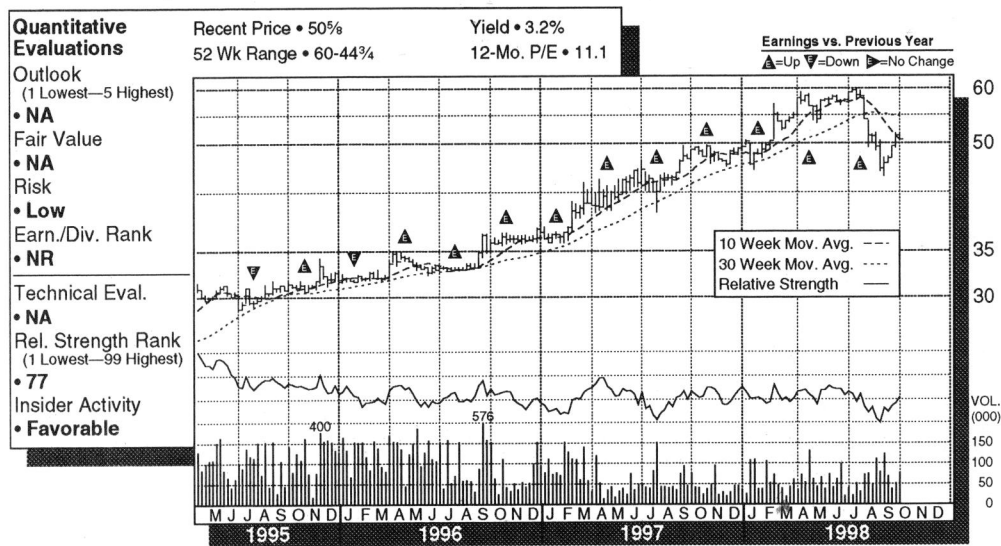

Earnings vs. Previous Year
▲=Up ▼=Down ▶=No Change

10 Week Mov. Avg. — — —
30 Week Mov. Avg. ·······
Relative Strength ———

Business Profile - 06-OCT-98

In 1998's second quarter, JSB received the final settlement on a $12.8 million delinquent mortgage loan, whereby all contracted principal, interest, legal and other fees were received. As a result, the ratio of nonperforming loans to total loans decreased to 0.02% at June 30, 1998, from 1.26% at March 31, 1998. In connection with the settlement of the loan, JSB recognized additional pretax income of $3.3 million in the second quarter, increasing earnings per share by $0.18. During 1997, JSB sold equity securities with a cost of $823,000, generating pretax gains of $7.0 million, including $4.1 million recorded in the fourth quarter. The sale of these securities, net of tax, increased net income by $3.9 million, and added $0.39 to 1997 EPS.

Operational Review - 056OCT-98

Net interest income for the six months ended June 30, 1998, rose 6.7%, year to year. The provision for possible loan losses fell 91%, and noninterest income increased to $7,460,000 from $2,650,000 mainly reflecting the recognition of $4,300,000 from the settlement of a previously delinquent mortgage loan. Following virtually flat noninterest expense, pretax income was up 32%. After taxes at 24.0%, versus 40.3%, with the lower rate stemming from a realignment of operations involving a bank operating subsidiary, net income advanced 69%, to $22,850,000 ($2.24 a share) from $13,557,000 ($1.33).

Stock Performance - 02-OCT-98

In the past 30 trading days, JSB's shares have increased 2%, compared to a 7% fall in the S&P 500. Average trading volume for the past five days was 15,180 shares, compared with the 40-day moving average of 15,118 shares.

Key Stock Statistics

Dividend Rate/Share	1.60	Shareholders	2,200
Shs. outstg. (M)	9.9	Market cap. (B)	$0.492
Avg. daily vol. (M)	0.014	Inst. holdings	36%
Tang. Bk. Value/Share	38.65		
Beta	0.56		

Value of $10,000 invested 5 years ago: $ 28,537

Fiscal Year Ending Dec. 31

	1998	1997	1996	1995	1994	1993
Revenues (Million $)						
1Q	29.05	27.79	28.12	27.53	25.90	30.21
2Q	34.08	28.53	27.73	28.09	26.16	27.66
3Q	—	31.31	28.59	28.12	27.26	26.35
4Q	—	42.04	27.89	27.98	30.46	26.23
Yr.	—	129.7	112.7	111.7	109.8	110.4
Earnings Per Share ($)						
1Q	**0.75**	**0.63**	0.56	0.50	0.42	0.46
2Q	**1.49**	**0.70**	0.63	0.39	0.46	0.38
3Q	—	**0.84**	0.64	0.56	0.50	0.35
4Q	—	**1.46**	0.71	0.54	0.65	0.38
Yr.	—	**3.64**	2.54	1.99	2.02	1.57

Next earnings report expected: late October

Dividend Data (Dividends have been paid since 1990.)

Amount ($)	Date Decl.	Ex-Div. Date	Stock of Record	Payment Date
0.350	Oct. 22	Nov. 03	Nov. 05	Nov. 19 '97
0.400	Jan. 07	Feb. 02	Feb. 04	Feb. 18 '98
0.400	Apr. 15	May. 04	May. 06	May. 20 '98
0.400	Jul. 21	Aug. 03	Aug. 05	Aug. 19 '98

A Division of The McGraw-Hill Companies

STANDARD
&POOR'S
STOCK REPORTS

JSB Financial, Inc.

1256M
06-OCT-98

Business Summary - 06-OCT-98

JSB Financial, Inc. is the holding company for Jamaica Savings Bank FSB, which serves the New York City borough of Queens through 10 full service branches. The bank, which also operates one branch office in each of Manhattan and suburban Nassau (its headquarters) and Suffolk counties, NY, had assets of $1.54 billion at the end of 1997.

Founded in 1866, Jamaica Savings primarily seeks to attract deposits from the residents in the neighborhoods surrounding its branch offices and invest those deposits, together with funds generated from operations, mainly in first mortgage loans secured by real estate, CMOs, and U.S. government and agency securities.

Total deposits have been declining over the past five years, a trend the bank attributes to the relatively low interest rate levels that have prevailed over this period. Deposits totaled $1.12 billion at the end of 1997, compared with $1.14 billion and $1.16 billion at the end of 1996 and 1995, respectively. Although JSB believes that its interest rates are competitive with other financial institutions in its market, it has shied away from paying rates that would potentially lower net income, and has chosen instead to allow deposits to decline.

The bank's loan portfolio consists mainly of first mortgage loans secured by multi-family rental properties, cooperative buildings, one-to-four family residence, commercial property, and, to a lesser extent, construction loans. Other loans offered by the bank include property improvement loans, loans secured by deposit accounts, student loans, and various types of consumer loans, including auto and personal loans.

Loans receivable totaled $1.01 billion at the end of 1997, with multi-family and underlying cooperative mortgage loans comprising 58% and 27% of this total, respectively. The allowance for possible loan losses totaled $5,880,000 (0.58% of total loans) at the end of 1997, versus $5,327,000 (0.62%) a year earlier. As of December 31, 1997, the ratio of non-performing loans to total loans was 1.32%, compared with 1.64% a year earlier.

The average yield on total interest-earning assets was 7.51% in 1997 (7.47% in 1996), while the average rate paid on total interest-bearing liabilities was 3.63% (3.57%), for a net interest rate spread of 3.88% (3.90%).

Faced with the challenges of stiff competition, a potentially volatile interest rate environment, and increased consolidation within the industry, Jamaica Savings hopes to distinguish itself through its community-oriented approach and an increased service offering, which includes the introduction of home banking services.

Per Share Data ($)

(Year Ended Dec. 31)	1997	1996	1995	1994	1993	1992	1991	1990	1989	1988
Tangible Bk. Val.	37.05	34.27	32.38	30.67	27.87	25.56	23.33	21.96	NA	NA
Earnings	3.64	2.54	1.99	2.02	1.57	1.89	1.00	0.43	NA	NA
Dividends	1.40	1.20	1.00	0.72	0.60	0.52	0.44	0.20	NA	NA
Payout Ratio	38%	47%	50%	36%	38%	28%	44%	47%	NA	NA
Prices - High	50⅝	38⅜	34¼	27½	26⅞	21⅛	19⅞	13⅝	NA	NA
- Low	36	31½	23¾	22	20⅞	16⅛	12	10	NA	NA
P/E Ratio - High	14	15	17	14	17	11	20	32	NA	NA
- Low	10	12	12	11	13	9	12	23	NA	NA

Income Statement Analysis (Million $)

	1997	1996	1995	1994	1993	1992	1991	1990	1989	1988
Net Int. Inc.	67.9	67.4	67.0	66.4	68.5	76.5	62.1	48.7	39.6	19.9
Loan Loss Prov.	0.6	0.6	0.6	0.6	0.6	0.6	1.7	0.6	1.0	0.0
Non Int. Inc.	14.9	5.0	4.0	6.8	2.2	4.0	NA	NA	NA	NA
Non Int. Exp.	27.4	27.6	29.6	30.9	33.7	34.7	NA	NA	NA	NA
Pretax Inc.	61.7	46.3	38.8	41.6	36.4	45.2	30.1	21.9	26.2	2.2
Eff. Tax Rate	40%	42%	43%	43%	43%	42%	49%	47%	53%	31%
Net Inc.	37.1	26.7	22.2	23.6	20.6	26.4	15.4	11.6	12.4	1.5
% Net Int. Marg.	4.73	4.68	4.60	4.40	4.30	4.80	4.00	NA	NA	NA

Balance Sheet & Other Fin. Data (Million $)

	1997	1996	1995	1994	1993	1992	1991	1990	1989	1988
Total Assets	1,535	1,516	1,545	1,565	1,636	1,698	1,675	1,628	1,458	1,426
Loans	1,000	855	768	711	668	642	598	565	486	407
Deposits	1,121	1,145	1,163	1,204	1,274	1,324	1,302	1,250	1,230	1,205
Capitalization:										
Debt	Nil	Nil	Nil	Nil	Nil	NA	NA	NA	NA	NA
Equity	368	335	340	328	325	232	330	334	NA	NA
Total	368	335	340	328	325	NA	NA	NA	NA	NA
% Ret. on Assets	2.4	1.7	1.4	1.5	1.2	1.6	0.9	0.7	0.9	0.1
% Ret. on Equity	10.6	7.9	6.6	7.2	6.2	8.1	4.6	NA	NA	NA
% Loan Loss Resv.	0.6	0.6	0.6	0.6	0.6	NA	0.5	0.4	NM	NA
% Risk Based Capital	21.7	20.0	21.3	NA	NA	NA	NA	NA	NA	NA
Price Times Book Value:										
Hi	1.4	1.1	1.1	0.9	1.0	0.8	0.9	0.6	NA	NA
Low	1.0	0.9	0.7	0.7	0.7	0.6	0.5	0.5	NA	NA

Data as orig. reptd.; bef. results of disc opers. and/or spec. items. Per share data adj. for stk. divs. as of ex-div. date. Bold denotes diluted EPS (FASB 128). E-Estimated. NA-Not Available. NM-Not Meaningful. NR-Not Ranked.

Office—303 Merrick Rd., Lynbrook, NY 11563.**Tel**—(516) 887-7000.**Website**—http://www.jsbf.com **Chrmn & CEO**—P. T. Adikes.**Pres**—E. P. Henson.**VP, CFO & Treas**—T. R. Lehmann. **Secy**—J. Corrigan.**Dirs**—P. T. Adikes, J. C. Cantwell, R. M. Cummins, H. J. Dirkes Jr., C. Gibbons, J. E. Gibbons Jr., E. P. Henson, A. F. Kelly, R. W. Meyer, A. B. Pritcher, P. R. Screvane.**Transfer Agent & Registrar**—ChaseMellon Shareholder Services LLC, Ridgefield, NJ. **Incorporated**—in Delaware in 1990.**Empl**— 429. **S&P Analyst:** J.J.S.

Jan Bell Marketing
8253

ASE Symbol **JBM**

In S&P SmallCap 600

03-OCT-98

Industry:
Consumer (Jewelry, Novelties & Gifts)

Summary: Jan Bell markets fine jewelry, watches and other consumer products primarily through over 440 leased departments of Sam's Club stores.

Quantitative Evaluations

Recent Price • 5½
52 Wk Range • 7⅞-2⁵⁄₁₆

Yield • Nil
12-Mo. P/E • 11.0

Outlook
(1 Lowest—5 Highest)
• **NA**

Fair Value
• **NA**

Risk
• **High**

Earn./Div. Rank
• **B-**

Technical Eval.
• **Bullish** since 7/97

Rel. Strength Rank
(1 Lowest—99 Highest)
• **52**

Insider Activity
• **Neutral**

Earnings vs. Previous Year
▲=Up ▼=Down ▶=No Change

10 Week Mov. Avg. ---
30 Week Mov. Avg. ----
Relative Strength —

OPTIONS: ASE, CBOE

Business Profile - 08-SEP-98

The second quarter of FY 99 (Jan.) was the company's first profitable quarter (excluding the fourth quarter of every year, when JBM generates 41% of its yearly sales) since 1993. Efforts to enhance the company's merchandise assortment, marketing presentations and control expenses, led to $461,000 in net income. During the quarter, the company closed the acquisition of Mayor's Jewelers, for $18 million in cash, 2 million shares of JBM stock and assumption of debt. The company also announced a marketing and distribution agreement with Value America, an internet-based retailer offering a wide variety of products for sale at its internet site.

Operational Review - 08-SEP-98

Net sales for the twenty-six weeks ended August 2, 1998, rose 13%, year over year, due to sales volume increases. Profitability improved tremendously through the firm's efforts to enhance inventory turn and improve operating efficiencies, which lowered general and administrative expenses on an absolute basis and cost of sales as a percentage of revenues. Following a 30% reduction in depreciation and amortization (partially offset by a sharp increase in currency exchange loss from the firm's Mexican operations) and an 82% increase in interest income, pretax income contrasted with a loss. After taxes of $142,000, versus $108,000, the net loss narrowed to $111,000 ($0.00 per share), from $2,949,000 ($0.11).

Stock Performance - 02-OCT-98

In the past 30 trading days, JBM's shares have declined 19%, compared to a 7% fall in the S&P 500. Average trading volume for the past five days was 54,740 shares, compared with the 40-day moving average of 67,708 shares.

Key Stock Statistics

Dividend Rate/Share	Nil	Shareholders	800
Shs. outstg. (M)	28.3	Market cap. (B)	$0.156
Avg. daily vol. (M)	0.041	Inst. holdings	42%
Tang. Bk. Value/Share	4.24		
Beta	0.63		

Value of $10,000 invested 5 years ago: $ 2,716

Fiscal Year Ending Jan. 31

	1999	1998	1997	1996	1995	1994
Revenues (Million $)						
1Q	52.49	46.98	47.45	50.02	63.01	45.57
2Q	60.35	53.31	55.15	55.45	60.08	49.85
3Q	—	45.22	44.71	46.21	68.59	42.60
4Q	—	102.4	95.77	102.3	114.0	137.2
Yr.	—	247.9	243.1	254.0	305.7	275.2
Earnings Per Share ($)						
1Q	-0.02	-0.09	-0.20	-0.22	-0.23	-0.40
2Q	0.02	-0.02	-0.05	-0.07	-0.19	-0.01
3Q	—	-0.09	-0.11	-0.11	-0.18	-0.11
1Q		0.59	0.38	0.28	-2.32	-0.90
Yr.	—	0.39	0.03	-0.13	-2.92	-1.40

Next earnings report expected: mid November

Dividend Data

No cash dividends have been paid on the common stock. Three-for-two stock splits were effected in 1989 and 1988.

A Division of The **McGraw-Hill** *Companies*

Business Summary - 08-SEP-98

Jan Bell Marketing, Inc. markets fine jewelry, watches and other non-jewelry consumer products (including perfumes, sunglasses, writing instruments, and collectible and giftware items). The company markets its products primarily through Sam's Club, a division of Wal-Mart, pursuant to an arrangement whereby JBM operates an exclusive leased department at all Sam's domestic locations through February 1, 2001. Sales through Sam's accounted for 93% of total sales in the fiscal year ended January 31, 1998.

Each Sam's location is staffed by JBM employees, with the inventory owned by JBM. In exchange for the right to operate the department and the use of retail space, the company pays a tenancy fee of 9% of net sales. While Sam's is responsible for paying utility costs, maintenance and certain other expenses associated with operation of the departments, JBM provides and maintains all fixtures and other equipment necessary to operate the departments.

Over the last three fiscal years, the company's strategy has been to achieve cost reductions at all levels. JBM has implemented merchandise strategies that emphasize higher margin diamond, semi-precious gem,

gold and watch products in place of other lower margin non-jewelry products. The company has also taken action to lower its reliance on borrowings, balance inventories, reduce discounted stock, and improve inventory returns. Management believes that additional opportunities to improve sales, gross margins, and expense savings still exist within its business with Sam's.

JBM also operates four Manhattan Diamond stores in shopping mall locations, which were acquired in September 1996. The company is presently reviewing its strategy for the stores since management believes that the four locations do not generate an acceptable rate of return on capital employed. The firm will either open additional locations to achieve economies of scale or will seek the sale of the business.

In January 1997, the company decided to close both of its Jewelry Depot stores in Massachusetts, which had been opened in FY 95, citing a lack of success.

In the second quarter of FY 99, Jan Bell consummated the acquisition of Mayor's Jewelers, Inc., a leading provider of luxury jewelry in the Southeast. Total consideration consisted of approximately $18 million in cash, 2 million shares of Jan Bell Marketing, Inc. stock and the refinancing of Mayor's outstanding debt.

Per Share Data ($)

(Year Ended Jan. 31)	1998	1997	1996	1995	1994	1993	1992	1991	1990	1989
Tangible Bk. Val.	5.12	4.73	4.74	4.84	6.87	8.10	7.28	8.11	7.81	2.95
Cash Flow	0.65	0.35	0.21	-2.57	-1.14	-0.79	0.51	0.37	0.86	0.61
Earnings	0.39	0.03	-0.13	-2.92	-1.40	-0.59	0.33	0.30	0.80	0.57
Dividends	Nil	Nil	Nil	Nil	Nil	Nil	Nil	Nil	Nil	Nil
Payout Ratio	Nil	Nil	Nil	Nil	Nil	Nil	Nil	Nil	Nil	Nil
Cal. Yrs.	1997	1996	1995	1994	1993	1992	1991	1990	1989	1988
Prices - High	3¼	3⅝	4¼	20⅝	23	17	26⅝	34	13⅜	6¾
- Low	1¹⁵/₁₆	1¾	2³/₁₆	8½	12½	5¾	6¼	12⅛	3⅝	2⅜
P/E Ratio - High	8	NM	NM	NM	39	2	89	43	24	20
- Low	5	NM	NM	NM	21	17	20	15	6	7

Income Statement Analysis (Million $)

	1998	1997	1996	1995	1994	1993	1992	1991	1990	1989
Revs.	248	243	254	306	175	334	224	177	181	120
Oper. Inc.	13.3	14.5	7.7	-9.2	-10.9	26.9	12.3	21.0	25.0	14.9
Depr.	6.9	8.2	8.7	9.2	6.8	5.1	3.9	1.8	1.2	0.7
Int. Exp.	Nil	1.0	3.2	3.5	3.2	0.9	2.4	0.8	0.4	0.0
Pretax Inc.	7.8	0.9	-3.3	-74.7	-47.4	-21.5	11.3	13.2	25.6	14.8
Eff. Tax Rate	NM	17%	NM	NM	NM	31%	27%	30%	38%	37%
Net Inc.	10.0	0.8	-3.4	-75.1	-35.7	-14.8	7.5	6.6	16.0	4.4

Balance Sheet & Other Fin. Data (Million $)

	1998	1997	1996	1995	1994	1993	1992	1991	1990	1989
Cash	48.4	23.5	15.0	28.2	30.2	49.0	17.4	51.2	46.6	18.0
Curr. Assets	128	111	117	148	248	232	161	186	179	62.0
Total Assets	152	139	153	187	312	302	228	207	193	67.0
Curr. Liab.	16.1	14.0	20.4	59.4	73.4	33.9	20.4	32.9	19.8	16.7
LT Debt	Nil	Nil	7.5	Nil	33.5	33.0	Nil	Nil	Nil	Nil
Common Eqty.	136	125	125	127	205	235	208	172	173	50.0
Total Cap.	136	125	133	127	239	268	208	175	173	5.0
Cap. Exp.	1.7	2.3	1.8	6.3	12.6	6.7	4.4	5.9	10.2	3.7
Cash Flow	17.0	9.0	5.2	-65.9	-29.0	-19.9	11.4	8.4	17.2	9.9
Curr. Ratio	7.9	7.9	5.7	2.5	3.4	6.8	7.9	5.7	9.1	3.7
% LT Debt of Cap.	Nil	Nil	5.7	Nil	14.0	12.3	Nil	Nil	Nil	Nil
% Net Inc.of Revs.	4.1	0.3	NM	NM	NM	3.4	4.4	3.7	8.8	7.7
% Ret. on Assets	6.9	0.5	NM	NM	NM	5.6	3.2	3.4	11.4	17.5
% Ret. on Equity	7.7	0.6	NM	NM	NM	6.7	3.7	3.9	13.4	24.3

Data as orig. reptd.; bef. results of disc. opers. and/or spec. items. Per share data adj. for stk. divs. as of ex-div. date. Yrs. end. Dec. 31 of preceding cal yr. pr. to 1995. E-Estimated. NA-Not Available. NM-Not Meaningful. NR-Not Ranked.

Office—14051 N.W. 14th St., Sunrise, FL 33323. **Tel**—(954) 846-2703. **Chrmn & CEO**—I. Arguetty. **SEVP & Secy**—R. W. Bowers. **SVP-Fin, CFO, Treas & Investor Contact**—D. Boudreau. **Dirs**—I. Arguetty, H. Bashan, G. Bedol, T. Epstein, M. Gilliam, W. Grayson, P. Offerman, R. G. Robison. **Transfer Agent & Registrar**—Sun Bank, Miami. **Incorporated**—in Delaware in 1987. **Empl**— 1,016. **S&P Analyst**: Jordan Horoschak

Jo-Ann Stores

852A

NYSE Symbol **JAS.A**

In S&P SmallCap 600

13-OCT-98

Industry:
Retail (Specialty)

Summary: This leading U.S. fabric and craft retailer operates 1,065 stores, under the names Jo-Ann Fabrics and Crafts, Cloth World, House of Fabrics and New York Fabrics and Crafts.

Quantitative Evaluations	
Outlook (1 Lowest—5 Highest)	• NA
Fair Value	• NA
Risk	• NA
Earn./Div. Rank	• B
Technical Eval.	• NA
Rel. Strength Rank (1 Lowest—99 Highest)	• 26
Insider Activity	• NA

Recent Price • 16⅞
52 Wk Range • 31⅞-16⅞

Yield • Nil
12-Mo. P/E • 18.0

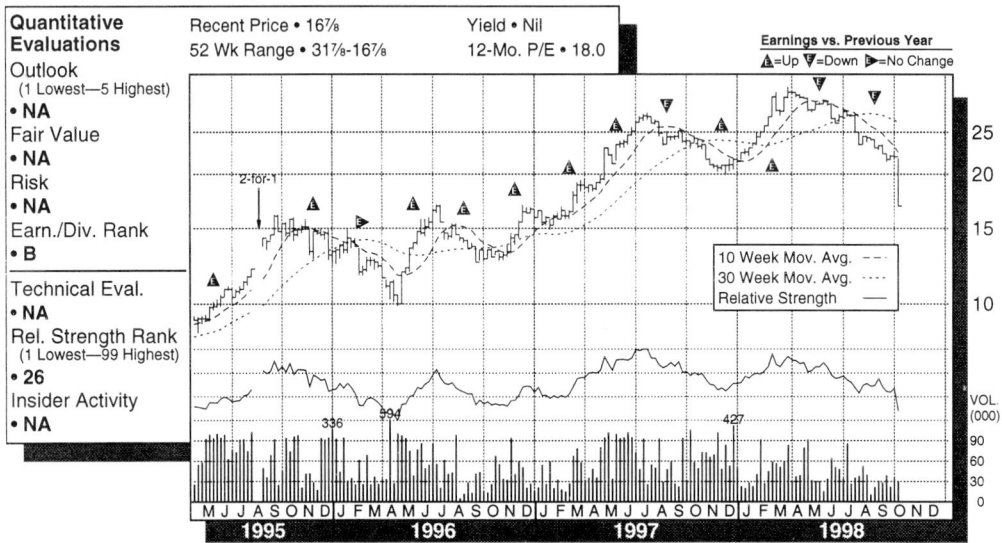

Earnings vs. Previous Year
▲=Up ▼=Down ▶=No Change

10 Week Mov. Avg. - - -
30 Week Mov. Avg. ·····
Relative Strength —

Business Profile - 13-OCT-98

In September 1998, the company changed its name to Jo-Ann Stores, Inc. from Fabri-Centers of America, Inc., in order to more closely align its corporate identity with its retail locations. In April 1998, the company acquired the 261-store House of Fabrics chain for $4.25 a share, or a total of about $100 million, including the assumption of debt. JAS.A plans to continue to operate 171 of the stores, while closing the remaining locations. As a result of the closings and integration of stores, the company recorded a $7.5 million ($0.37 a share) after-tax charge in the first quarter.

Operational Review - 10-SEP-98

Net sales for the 13 weeks ended May 2, 1998, advanced 16%, year to year, due to additional sales from the acquisition of House of Fabrics. Same-store sales grow 1.3%. Margins widened, reflecting improved gross margins, partly offset by higher SG&A expense as a percent of sales; operating income was up 19%. Following a $12.2 million pretax charge related to the acquisition, a net loss of $4,400,000 ($0.23 a share) contrasted with net income of $2,600,000 ($0.14). Earnings per share without the charge would have been $0.15.

Stock Performance - 09-OCT-98

In the past 30 trading days, JAS.A's shares have declined 27%, compared to a 4% fall in the S&P 500. Average trading volume for the past five days was 5,880 shares, compared with the 40-day moving average of 5,331 shares.

Key Stock Statistics

Dividend Rate/Share	Nil	Shareholders	1,700
Shs. outstg. (M)	19.0	Market cap. (B)	$0.161
Avg. daily vol. (M)	0.006	Inst. holdings	24%
Tang. Bk. Value/Share	14.43		
Beta	0.63		

Value of $10,000 invested 5 years ago: $ 23,549

Fiscal Year Ending Jan. 31

	1999	1998	1997	1996	1995	1994
Revenues (Million $)						
1Q	252.9	218.8	203.0	183.3	132.7	139.8
2Q	251.6	197.5	188.9	168.5	112.8	113.2
3Q	—	247.2	229.6	214.4	175.4	147.1
4Q	—	311.5	307.5	268.4	256.3	182.1
Yr.	—	975.0	929.0	834.6	677.3	582.1

Earnings Per Share ($)						
1Q	-0.23	0.14	0.06	0.02	-0.07	-0.09
2Q	-0.34	-0.05	-0.13	-0.17	0.00	0.00
3Q	—	0.47	0.43	0.31	0.22	0.19
4Q	—	1.07	0.95	0.75	0.75	0.56
Yr.	—	1.60	1.30	0.91	0.63	0.38

Next earnings report expected: mid November

Dividend Data

Cash dividends were omitted in 1987, after having been paid since 1969. A "poison pill" stock purchase rights plan was adopted in 1990. A two-for-one stock split was effected in August 1995.

A Division of The **McGraw·Hill** *Companies*

Business Summary - 10-SEP-98

Jo-Ann Stores, Inc. (formerly Fabri-Centers of America, Inc.) operates retail fabric stores that sell a wide variety of fashion and decorator fabrics, notions, crafts, patterns, seasonal merchandise, and silk and dried flowers. JAS.A's stores operate under the names Jo-Ann Fabrics and Crafts, Jo-Ann etc, Cloth World, New York Fabrics, and House of Fabrics. Including its recent purchase of 171 House of Fabrics stores, the company operated 1,065 stores in 49 states, as of June 2, 1998. For the balance of FY 99 (Jan.), JAS.A plans to open 25 new stores, relocate 21 and close 13 smaller stores. Sales from continuing operations in recent fiscal years were derived as follows:

	FY 98	FY 97	FY 96
Fabric	48%	47%	48%
Notions	21%	21%	22%
Crafts & Floral	15%	17%	16%
Seasonal	12%	11%	10%
Other	4%	4%	4%

The company's stores offer a wide range of products for customers to make their own clothing, or to complete home decorating and craft projects. Fabrics consists of apparel fabrics, quilting, crafting fabrics, drapery and upholstery. Notions include cutting implements, trimmings, buttons, threads and ribbons. Crafts & Floral include stenciling, woodworking, doll making, and artificial floral arranging. Merchandise also includes seasonal and holiday offerings for Easter, Halloween, Thanksgiving and Christmas.

The company's stores are mostly positioned in high-traffic strip shopping centers and the stores average 13,400 square feet. In FY 97, JAS.A opened an experimental store in Hudson, OH under the name Jo-Ann etc. The store featured 45,000 square feet and offers considerably more merchandise than Fabri-Centers normal stores. The company has since opened 10 additional mega-stores, including four in the first quarter of FY 99.

In April 1998, the company acquired House of Fabrics, Inc. for $4.25 per share, or a total of $100 million, including the assumption of debt. An after-tax charge of $7.5 million ($0.37 a share) was recorded during the first quarter of FY 99, due to nonrecurring integration costs.

Per Share Data ($)

(Year Ended Jan. 31)	1998	1997	1996	1995	1994	1993	1992	1991	1990	1989
Tangible Bk. Val.	14.43	12.54	10.37	8.53	8.19	8.00	7.67	5.16	4.50	3.92
Cash Flow	2.61	2.45	1.87	1.31	0.96	0.73	1.27	1.03	0.86	0.61
Earnings	1.60	1.30	0.91	0.63	0.38	0.27	0.95	0.71	0.56	0.34
Dividends	Nil	Nil	Nil	Nil	Nil	Nil	Nil	Nil	Nil	Nil
Payout Ratio	Nil	Nil	Nil	Nil	Nil	Nil	Nil	Nil	Nil	Nil
Cal. Yrs.	1997	1996	1995	1994	1993	1992	1991	1990	1989	1988
Prices - High	27¾	17	16⅛	9⅜	9⅝	23⅝	23	8⅝	4⅞	4
- Low	14⅞	9⅞	7⅞	5⅞	6¼	5	7½	4⅝	3⅝	2¼
P/E Ratio - High	17	13	18	15	26	88	24	12	9	12
- Low	9	8	9	9	17	19	8	6	6	7

Income Statement Analysis (Million $)

	1998	1997	1996	1995	1994	1993	1992	1991	1990	1989
Revs.	975	929	835	677	582	574	469	386	333	291
Oper. Inc.	78.7	71.6	58.4	40.3	27.6	22.8	36.7	26.9	23.0	15.2
Depr.	21.7	21.5	18.5	12.8	10.9	9.0	6.0	5.0	4.6	4.2
Int. Exp.	5.9	10.7	12.0	8.4	5.5	5.5	3.4	5.1	4.6	3.0
Pretax Inc.	51.2	39.4	27.9	19.1	11.1	8.3	27.4	18.0	14.1	8.0
Eff. Tax Rate	38%	38%	38%	39%	38%	38%	36%	38%	38%	36%
Net Inc.	32.0	24.6	17.5	11.7	7.0	5.2	17.5	11.2	8.8	5.1

Balance Sheet & Other Fin. Data (Million $)

	1998	1997	1996	1995	1994	1993	1992	1991	1990	1989
Cash	14.8	12.6	11.6	21.9	7.7	6.6	8.6	5.2	5.0	6.6
Curr. Assets	322	318	361	326	246	242	221	166	129	110
Total Assets	448	429	480	427	337	352	286	205	158	135
Curr. Liab.	165	141	129	127	76.6	93.6	99	72.2	58.3	49.3
LT Debt	24.7	72.0	155	127	103	104	40.1	52.1	28.6	23.0
Common Eqty.	241	199	181	162	149	148	143	77.0	68.2	59.6
Total Cap.	280	285	349	299	260	258	186	132	99	85.0
Cap. Exp.	36.6	13.2	34.7	11.7	8.5	32.3	19.7	15.9	9.8	3.4
Cash Flow	53.7	46.1	35.9	24.5	17.9	14.1	23.5	16.3	13.3	9.3
Curr. Ratio	2.0	2.3	2.8	2.6	3.2	2.6	2.2	2.3	2.2	2.2
% LT Debt of Cap.	8.8	25.3	44.5	42.5	39.4	40.4	21.5	39.3	28.8	27.1
% Net Inc.of Revs.	3.3	2.7	2.1	1.7	1.2	0.9	3.7	2.9	2.6	1.8
% Ret. on Assets	7.3	5.5	3.9	3.1	2.0	1.6	6.5	6.2	6.0	3.9
% Ret. on Equity	14.5	13.0	10.2	7.5	4.7	3.6	14.7	15.6	13.7	8.9

Data as orig. reptd.; bef. results of disc. opers. and/or spec. items. Per share data adj. for stk. divs. as of ex-div. date. Bold denotes diluted EPS (FASB 128). E-Estimated. NA-Not Available. NM-Not Meaningful. NR-Not Ranked.

Office—5555 Darrow Rd., Hudson, OH 44236. **Tel**—(216) 656-2600. **Chrmn, Pres, CEO**—Alan Rosskamm. **EVP, CFO & Investor Contact**—Brian Carney. **SVP & Secy**—Betty Rosskamm. **Dirs**—S. S. Cowen, I. Gumberg, F. A, Newman, A. Rosskamm, B. Rosskamm, G. Searle, A. Zimmerman. **Transfer Agent & Registrar**—Harris Trust and Savings Bank, Chicago.**Incorporated**—in Ohio in 1951. **Empl**— 16,400. **S&P Analyst:** Ray Lam, CFA.

Johnston Industries

1268M

NYSE Symbol **JII**

In S&P SmallCap 600

03-OCT-98

Industry:
Textiles (Specialty)

Summary: This company (34% owned by Redlaw Industries) makes woven and nonwoven textile fabrics for industrial, home furnishing and apparel markets.

Quantitative Evaluations

Recent Price • 3

52 Wk Range • 6¾-3

Yield • Nil

12-Mo. P/E • NM

Outlook
(1 Lowest—5 Highest)
• 4

Fair Value
• 4⅛

Risk
• **Low**

Earn./Div. Rank
• **C**

Technical Eval.
• **Bearish** since 7/96

Rel. Strength Rank
(1 Lowest—99 Highest)
• **24**

Insider Activity
• **Neutral**

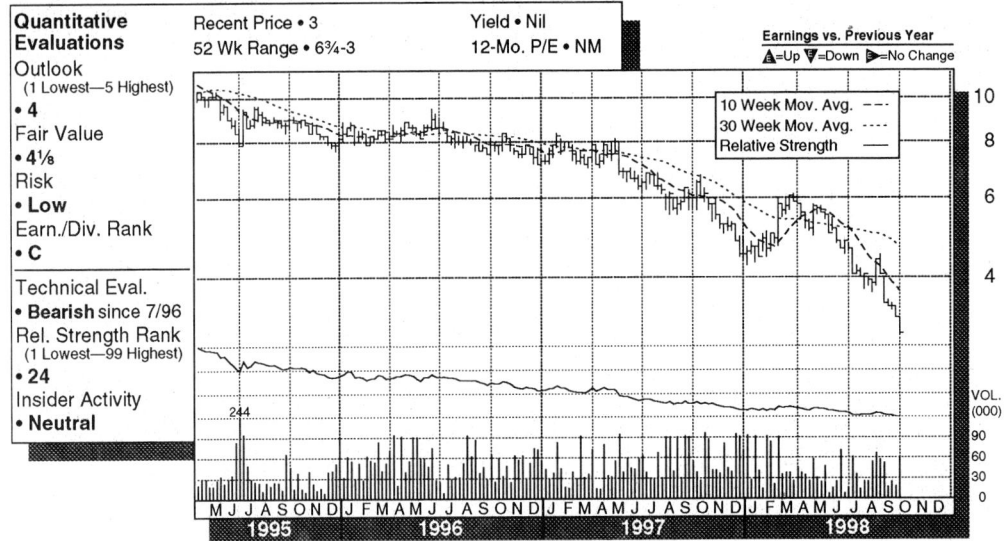

Earnings vs. Previous Year
▲=Up ▼=Down ▶=No Change

10 Week Mov. Avg. ---
30 Week Mov. Avg. ----
Relative Strength —

Business Profile - 24-SEP-98

During 1997, JII implemented a restructuring program that involved integrating its former Wellington Sears division into other business units, closing production at its Langdale mill and shifting it to its more modern Southern Phoenix plant, and converting the Langdale facility into a light manufacturing, warehousing and distribution center. In May 1998, JII said that the integration of Wellington Sears had been substantially completed during the 1998 first quarter. The company added that three of its four divisions were profitable during the quarter. A number of initiatives are under way at the unprofitable division, finished fabrics. Redlaw Industries owns 34% of the shares. The dividend has been suspended.

Operational Review - 24-SEP-98

Net sales in the six months ended July 4, 1998, fell 15%, year to year, reflecting the discontinuation of unprofitable businesses and product lines in the second half of 1997, one less operating week in the first half of 1998, versus the first half of 1997, and lower sales in the greige fabrics division. Gross margins widened significantly. The operating profit soared reflecting $7 million less in restructuring and impairment charges. After tax credits, the loss from continuing operations narrowed to $1,503,000 ($0.14 a share), from $5,085,000 ($0.50, after preferred dividends). Results in the 1997 period exclude a gain from discontinued operations of $126,000 ($0.01).

Stock Performance - 02-OCT-98

In the past 30 trading days, JII's shares have declined 31%, compared to a 7% fall in the S&P 500. Average trading volume for the past five days was 12,020 shares, compared with the 40-day moving average of 8,882 shares.

Key Stock Statistics

Dividend Rate/Share	Nil	Shareholders	700
Shs. outstg. (M)	10.7	Market cap. (B)	$0.032
Avg. daily vol. (M)	0.006	Inst. holdings	29%
Tang. Bk. Value/Share	3.22		
Beta	0.49		

Value of $10,000 invested 5 years ago: $ 4,178

Fiscal Year Ending Dec. 31

	1998	1997	1996	1995	1994	1993
Revenues (Million $)						
1Q	79.84	86.78	84.03	—	40.77	35.70
2Q	69.06	87.72	81.74	—	44.20	38.30
3Q	—	78.49	77.07	—	91.00	42.60
4Q	—	79.55	79.04	—	87.36	43.32
Yr.	—	332.5	321.9	150.0	263.3	159.9
Earnings Per Share ($)						
1Q	-0.09	0.14	0.12	—	0.16	0.20
2Q	-0.05	-0.63	-0.01	—	0.24	0.10
3Q		0.31	0.02	—	0.25	0.23
4Q	—	-0.02	-0.09	—	0.10	0.08
Yr.	—	-0.81	Nil	-0.59	0.74	0.60

Next earnings report expected: early November

Dividend Data (Dividends have been paid since 1988.)

The most recent dividend payment was $0.10 a share in June 1997.

A Division of The McGraw-Hill Companies

Business Summary - 24-SEP-98

This diversified textile maker viewed 1997 as a year of transition. Its business operations were realigned into four divisions: greige (unfinished cotton) fabrics, finished fabrics, fiber products, and Johnston Industries Composite Reinforcements (JICR).

JII is a leading designer, manufacturer and marketer of finished and unfinished cotton, synthetic and blended fabrics used for a variety of industrial and consumer applications. Fabric products are sold to niche markets, including segments of the home furnishings, hospitality, industrial, automotive and specialty markets. The company believes that it is one of the largest domestic manufacturers of fabrics used of upholstery backing, automotive belts and hoses and abrasive applications. In addition, JII reprocesses and markets waste textile fiber and off-quality fabrics for sale to a variety of specialty markets. Fabrics are also manufactured for use in engineered composite materials for primarily recreation and construction markets.

The greige fabrics division makes cotton, synthetic and poly-cotton (blended) unfinished fabric which is unbleached and undyed. Its product line includes upholstery backing manufactured for the home furnishings market (such as upholstery, window treatments and bedding), decorative and print base unfinished goods for the home furnishings market and hospitality markets and fabric used in a variety of products manufactured for automotive and industrial uses such as belts, hosing and abrasives.

The finished fabrics division is a vertically integrated manufacturer of finished products, primarily synthetic finished fabrics (dyed, treated or coated). Greige fabrics manufactured by the division are processed through the application of value-added dyeing and finishing.

Waste textile fiber and off-quality fabrics are reprocessed and marketed through the fiber products division. Millions of pounds of waste are converted into raw materials that an be recycled in the textile manufacturing process or used as a low cost substitute in a wide range of consumer and industrial applications. Such products can be used for padding (used in a variety of applications from mattresses to sound proofing in automobiles), clean and reprocessed fiber reintroduced into textile yarn manufacturing process, wiper cloth and reworked off-quality textile products, such as towels and sheets.

The company also operates JI Composite Reinforcements, which produces a variety of non-crimp multi-axial fabrics from fiberglass, carbon and aramid fibers which are sold to specialty markets. JICR's products are used in engineered composite material to replace traditional fiberglass and metal components when superior performance or specific weight characteristics are required.

Per Share Data ($)

(Year Ended Dec. 31)	1997	1996	1995	1994	1993	1992	1991	1990	1989	1988
Tangible Bk. Val.	3.33	4.16	4.99	5.75	5.33	5.37	4.93	4.70	5.00	5.35
Cash Flow	1.20	2.21	0.27	2.04	1.54	1.68	1.45	0.66	0.73	1.13
Earnings	-0.81	-0.01	-0.59	0.74	0.60	0.81	0.62	-0.10	0.17	0.69
Dividends	0.20	0.40	0.40	0.39	0.34	0.32	0.24	0.22	0.22	0.15
Payout Ratio	NM	NM	NM	53%	58%	39%	39%	NM	128%	20%
Prices - High	8⅜	9½	12	12	13¾	13⅛	10	5⅝	4⅞	6½
- Low	4¼	7⅛	7⅜	7⅜	8¼	8⅜	5⅜	3	2⅞	4½
P/E Ratio - High	NM	NM	NM	16	23	16	16	NM	29	9
- Low	NM	NM	NM	11	14	10	9	NM	17	7

Income Statement Analysis (Million $)

	1997	1996	1995	1994	1993	1992	1991	1990	1989	1988
Revs.	333	322	150	263	160	154	138	117	119	116
Oper. Inc.	30.0	31.3	4.9	31.8	25.3	21.2	19.7	9.9	11.2	17.8
Depr.	21.4	19.7	9.0	13.9	10.2	9.5	9.0	8.1	6.4	5.2
Int. Exp.	13.7	11.2	4.9	5.9	3.0	2.9	2.7	2.6	1.5	1.7
Pretax Inc.	-11.7	-0.4	-14.8	16.7	10.6	14.1	10.6	-1.3	2.8	13.0
Eff. Tax Rate	NM	NM	NM	43%	39%	37%	36%	NM	32%	40%
Net Inc.	-8.6	3.4	-6.2	7.9	6.5	8.9	6.8	-1.0	1.9	7.8

Balance Sheet & Other Fin. Data (Million $)

	1997	1996	1995	1994	1993	1992	1991	1990	1989	1988
Cash	2.3	1.7	25.5	19.2	3.9	4.1	3.9	4.5	5.1	10.7
Curr. Assets	103	121	143	111	48.8	49.1	50.6	39.9	41.0	42.0
Total Assets	235	272	264	255	141	134	128	112	101	94.0
Curr. Liab.	105	46.0	48.4	49.6	23.3	34.7	26.9	21.7	20.8	12.1
LT Debt	61.7	144	126	99	36.2	22.5	30.0	25.0	11.5	13.0
Common Eqty.	49.1	59.2	55.2	63.4	60.1	61.3	57.7	53.1	56.7	59.5
Total Cap.	121	214	201	191	100	90.3	91.7	81.2	72.0	76.5
Cap. Exp.	10.3	21.0	18.0	22.0	12.7	10.4	9.4	18.0	12.6	13.8
Cash Flow	12.7	23.1	2.8	21.8	16.7	18.4	15.7	7.1	8.3	13.0
Curr. Ratio	1.0	2.6	3.0	2.2	2.1	1.4	1.9	1.8	2.0	3.5
% LT Debt of Cap.	51.0	67.1	62.6	51.7	36.0	24.9	32.7	30.8	16.0	17.0
% Net Inc.of Revs.	NM	1.1	NM	3.0	4.1	5.8	4.9	NM	1.6	6.7
% Ret. on Assets	NM	1.3	NM	4.0	4.7	6.8	5.6	NM	1.9	8.4
% Ret. on Equity	NM	5.9	NM	12.8	10.8	15.0	12.1	NM	3.3	14.1

Data as orig. reptd.; bef. results of disc. opers. and/or spec. items. Per share data adj. for stk. divs. as of ex-div. date. Yrs. ended Jun. 30 of the foll. cal. yr. prior to 1995. Qtrs. ended Sep., Dec., Mar., Jun. prior to 1995. Data for 1995 is for 6 mos. ended Dec. 31, 1995. E-Estimated. NA-Not Available. NM-Not Meaningful. NR-Not Ranked.

Office—105 13th St., Columbus, GA 31901. **Tel**—(706) 641-3140. **CEO & Pres**—D. C. Ogle. **EVP & COO**—W. I. Henry. **CFO & Investor Contact**—James J. Murphy.**Secy & Treas**—F. F. Walton..**Dirs**—J. R. Bingham, J. A. Friedman, W. J. Hart, G. R. Jeffcoat, D. C. Ogle, C. P. Stanley. **Transfer Agent & Registrar**—Bank of New York, NYC. **Incorporated**—in New York in 1948; reincorporated in Delaware in 1987. **Empl**— 2,700. **S&P Analyst:** Kathleen J. Fraser

03-OCT-98

Industry: Health Care (Drugs - Generic & Other)

Summary: This company offers a line of niche-oriented, specialty prescription pharmaceuticals.

Quantitative Evaluations	
Recent Price • 29	Yield • 0.4%
52 Wk Range • 40⅞-20½	12-Mo. P/E • 20.6

Outlook (1 Lowest—5 Highest)
• **3**

Fair Value
• **35½**

Risk
• **High**

Earn./Div. Rank
• **B+**

Technical Eval.
• **Bearish** since 4/98

Rel. Strength Rank (1 Lowest—99 Highest)
• **87**

Insider Activity
• **Neutral**

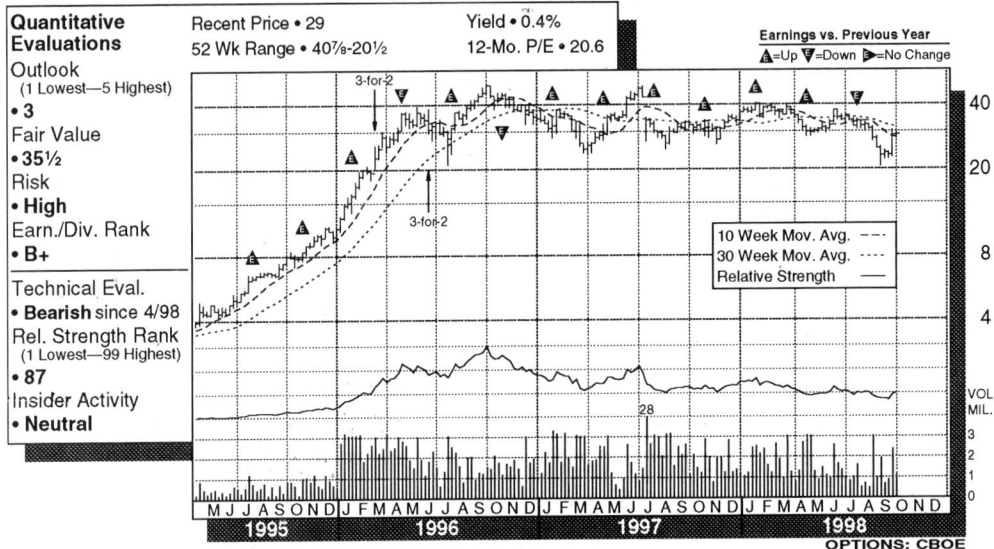

Earnings vs. Previous Year
▲=Up ▼=Down ▶=No Change

10 Week Mov. Avg. – – –
30 Week Mov. Avg. ·····
Relative Strength ——

OPTIONS: CBOE

Business Profile - 14-SEP-98

This specialty pharmaceutical company has chalked up a long-term record of profit growth. JMED's strategy has been to build a portfolio of growing products through the acquisition of under-promoted, approved products from other firms. The most recent acquisitions included Triostat and Cytomel endocrine drugs from SmithKline Beecham in June 1997; Tapazole anti-thyroid agent from Eli Lilly in March 1996; and the hypothyroidism product Levoxyl, acquired with the purchase of Daniels Pharmaceuticals in August 1996. In April 1998, the company sold its nutritional supplements business to Twinlab Corp. for $55 million.

Operational Review - 14-SEP-98

Sales from continuing operations in the six months ended June 30, 1998, advanced 24%, year to year. The gain reflected a 47% increase in endocrine product sales, a 20% rise in veterinarian drug sales and a 1% gain in critical care care product sales. Gross margins widened on the rise in sales of higher-margined products, and gross profits rose 34%. However, following a $10.5 million writedown of certain lower-margined drug products, income from continuing operations dropped 52%, to $5,269,000 ($0.18 a share), from $11,051,000 ($0.38). Results exclude income from discontinued operations of $0.64 a share, versus $0.12. Cash and equivalents totaled $115 million at the end of the second quarter.

Stock Performance - 02-OCT-98

In the past 30 trading days, JMED's shares have increased 4%, compared to a 7% fall in the S&P 500. Average trading volume for the past five days was 216,420 shares, compared with the 40-day moving average of 291,492 shares.

Key Stock Statistics

Dividend Rate/Share	0.12	Shareholders	500
Shs. outstg. (M)	28.7	Market cap. (B)	$0.833
Avg. daily vol. (M)	0.254	Inst. holdings	53%
Tang. Bk. Value/Share	5.09		
Beta	1.46		

Value of $10,000 invested 5 years ago: $ 94,738

Fiscal Year Ending Dec. 31

	1998	1997	1996	1995	1994	1993
Revenues (Million $)						
1Q	23.74	21.64	21.85	11.46	12.14	6.78
2Q	26.68	19.00	25.74	13.28	11.59	12.28
3Q	—	22.17	26.22	15.25	12.16	12.04
4Q	—	25.98	26.34	16.41	11.67	12.11
Yr.	—	88.78	100.2	56.40	47.55	43.22
Earnings Per Share ($)						
1Q	**0.25**	**0.22**	0.15	0.09	0.08	0.05
2Q	**-0.07**	**0.16**	0.20	0.10	0.06	0.08
3Q	—	**0.22**	0.06	0.11	0.08	0.08
4Q	—	**0.26**	0.24	0.13	0.06	0.09
Yr.	—	**0.85**	0.65	0.43	0.27	0.29

Next earnings report expected: late October

Dividend Data (Dividends have been paid since 1989.)

Amount ($)	Date Decl.	Ex-Div. Date	Stock of Record	Payment Date
0.025	Oct. 13	Dec. 18	Dec. 22	Jan. 02 '98
0.025	Feb. 19	Mar. 19	Mar. 23	Apr. 01 '98
0.030	May. 20	Jun. 11	Jun. 15	Jul. 01 '98
0.030	Jul. 08	Sep. 14	Sep. 16	Oct. 01 '98

Business Summary - 14-SEP-98

JONES PHARMA INCORPORATED (formerly Jones Medical Industries) manufactures and distributes specialty pharmaceuticals under its own trademarks and tradenames. In 1997, about 60% of total sales were generated from products manufactured by the company and 40% from products manufactured for the company by third parties. In March 1998, the company's directors approved a plan to discontinue the nutritional supplements product line and contract manufacturing operations. In April 1998, the company sold its nutritional business to Twinlab Corp. for $55 million. A net gain of $17 million from the sale was recorded in 1998 second quarter results.

Since it was founded in 1981, JMED has produced a long-term record of almost uninterrupted sales and profit growth. This consistent growth has been driven by the acquisition of under-promoted, approved specialty product lines from other firms. This strategy has allowed the company to avoid the risks associated with new drug development and the lengthy and costly FDA approval process. JMED intends to leverage its existing marketing and sales capabilities through additional strategic acquisitions of complementary products and businesses, by expanding and increasing the market share for current products, and by new product introductions.

Endocrine pharmaceuticals are the company's largest single product category. Key products include Levoxyl (sales of $22.2 million in 1997), a synthetic thyroid hormone used to treat hypothyroidism; Tapazole ($18.3 million), an anti-thyroid agent for hyperthyroidism; Cytomel ($2.6 million), a thyroid replacement hormone in tablet form used to treat chronic thyroid disorders; and Triostat ($1.8 million), an injectable thyroid replacement hormone for acute thyroid disorders ($1.8 million). The latter two drugs were purchased from SmithKline Beecham in June 1997 for $22.8 million in cash.

Critical care pharmaceuticals represents the company's second largest product category. Principal products consist of Thrombin ($19.4 million), a topical hemostat used to arrest bleeding during surgical procedures; and Brevital Sodium ($9.1 million), an intravenous anesthetic agent used in both minor and major surgical procedures.

Veterinary pharmaceuticals ($7.9 million) include Soloxine, used to treat hypothyroidism in pets; Tussigon for pain management and kennel cough; and Pancrezyme, an animal digestive aid.

The company maintains distribution facilities in Canton, OH, and St. Louis, MO. A plant in St. Petersburg, FL, manufactures pharmaceuticals. The company makes thrombin products for itself and for Johnson & Johnson at a plant in Middleton, WI.

Per Share Data ($)

(Year Ended Dec. 31)	1997	1996	1995	1994	1993	1992	1991	1990	1989	1988
Tangible Bk. Val.	3.57	3.24	0.80	0.89	0.46	0.78	0.52	0.63	0.00	0.28
Cash Flow	1.07	0.79	0.54	0.37	0.37	0.24	0.20	0.20	0.14	0.10
Earnings	0.85	0.65	0.43	0.27	0.29	0.18	0.16	0.16	0.10	0.08
Dividends	0.10	0.08	0.05	0.04	0.04	0.03	0.03	0.02	0.02	0.00
Payout Ratio	12%	12%	11%	17%	14%	19%	16%	13%	17%	5%
Prices - High	48¾	50½	11	6⅞	7¾	4¼	5⅝	3⅜	2⁷/₁₆	1¼
- Low	23⅝	10⅜	2¾	2⅞	2¼	2⅝	2¼	2	1¹/₁₆	¹¹/₁₆
P/E Ratio - High	57	78	26	26	27	24	35	21	24	15
- Low	28	16	7	11	8	15	14	13	10	8

Income Statement Analysis (Million $)

	1997	1996	1995	1994	1993	1992	1991	1990	1989	1988
Revs.	88.8	100	56.4	47.5	43.2	24.1	20.5	19.7	13.3	10.2
Oper. Inc.	44.2	38.4	17.7	11.6	11.8	6.7	5.7	5.6	3.6	2.6
Depr.	6.1	4.0	2.4	2.2	1.8	1.3	0.9	0.8	0.6	0.4
Int. Exp.	0.2	0.6	0.5	0.5	0.3	0.1	0.3	0.4	0.4	0.2
Pretax Inc.	40.4	30.4	14.9	9.0	9.9	6.0	5.2	4.8	2.7	2.0
Eff. Tax Rate	38%	40%	38%	37%	38%	38%	36%	41%	41%	39%
Net Inc.	25.0	18.1	9.3	5.7	6.2	3.7	3.3	2.8	1.6	1.2

Balance Sheet & Other Fin. Data (Million $)

	1997	1996	1995	1994	1993	1992	1991	1990	1989	1988
Cash	49.9	52.2	5.4	7.2	2.3	11.8	11.1	9.5	1.3	1.0
Curr. Assets	85.1	81.0	25.0	20.8	18.3	19.8	18.0	15.4	5.3	4.9
Total Assets	204	177	74.7	54.9	51.8	35.2	33.4	26.2	16.4	10.4
Curr. Liab.	6.6	10.0	11.6	5.8	6.3	3.8	3.3	4.6	3.3	1.3
LT Debt	Nil	Nil	9.1	3.8	5.4	0.5	2.7	1.5	4.4	2.0
Common Eqty.	192	162	49.9	39.2	31.2	24.7	20.0	19.9	8.3	7.0
Total Cap.	198	167	63.1	49.1	45.5	31.4	30.1	21.5	13.1	9.1
Cap. Exp.	5.6	7.4	4.7	3.2	5.0	0.6	0.2	0.4	0.2	0.8
Cash Flow	31.2	22.1	11.7	7.9	8.0	5.0	4.2	3.6	2.2	1.6
Curr. Ratio	12.9	8.1	2.2	3.6	2.9	5.2	5.5	3.3	1.6	3.9
% LT Debt of Cap.	Nil	Nil	14.4	7.7	11.9	1.6	9.1	7.0	33.9	22.1
% Net Inc.of Revs.	28.2	18.1	16.5	12.1	14.4	15.5	16.1	14.4	12.0	11.9
% Ret. on Assets	13.1	13.8	14.4	10.6	14.2	10.8	11.0	12.2	11.9	14.3
% Ret. on Equity	14.2	167.0	20.9	16.0	21.9	16.4	16.2	18.8	20.9	19.1

Data as orig. reptd.; bef. results of disc. opers. and/or spec. items. Per share data adj. for stk. divs. as of ex-div. date. Bold denotes diluted EPS (FASB 128). E-Estimated. NA-Not Available. NM-Not Meaningful. NR-Not Ranked.

Office—1945 Craig Rd., St. Louis, MO 63146. **Tel**—(314) 576-6100. **Chrmn, Pres & CEO**—D. M. Jones. **EVP, Treas & Secy**—J. A. Jones. **Dirs**—M. T. Bramblett, E. A. Chod, G. A. Franz, D. M. Jones, J. A. Jones, S. L. Lopata, D. A. McLaughlin, T. F. Patton, L. J. Polite Jr. **Transfer Agent**—Mark Twain Bank, St. Louis. **Incorporated**—in Delaware in 1981. **Empl**— 562. **S&P Analyst:** Herman Saftlas

Juno Lighting   4316

NASDAQ Symbol **JUNO**

In S&P SmallCap 600

10-OCT-98

Industry:
Electrical Equipment

Summary: This company is a leading maker of track lighting, recessed lighting and exit signs.

Quantitative Evaluations	
Outlook (1 Lowest—5 Highest)	**2**
Fair Value	**22⅛**
Risk	**Average**
Earn./Div. Rank	**A-**
Technical Eval.	**Bullish** since 8/98
Rel. Strength Rank (1 Lowest—99 Highest)	**81**
Insider Activity	**NA**

Recent Price • 20⅛
52 Wk Range • 24¼-15¾

Yield • 1.8%
12-Mo. P/E • 14.9

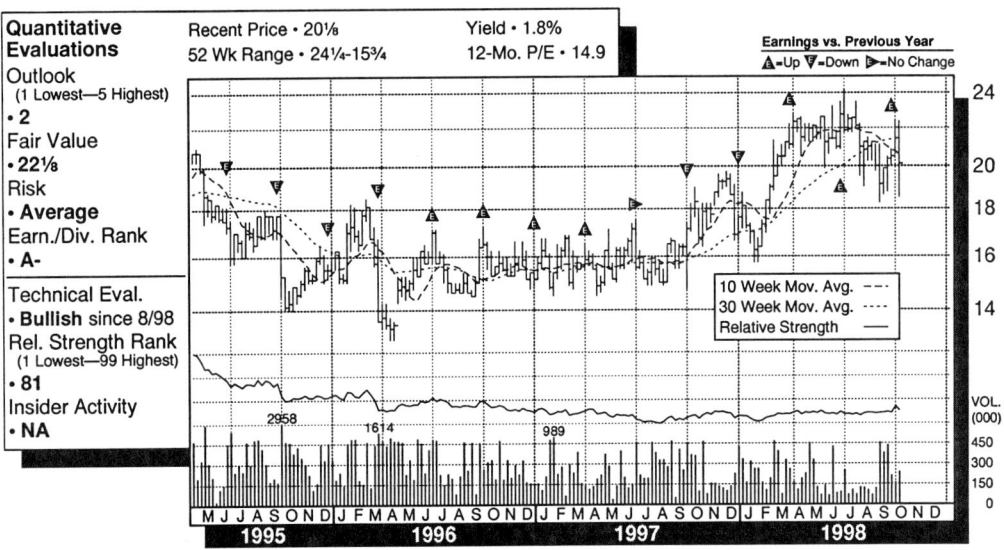

Earnings vs. Previous Year
▲=Up ▼=Down ▶=No Change

10 Week Mov. Avg. ---
30 Week Mov. Avg. ....
Relative Strength —

Business Profile - 09-SEP-98

Many of Juno's recessed and track lighting fixtures are moderately priced, to attract the high-volume commercial and residential markets. As part of management's efforts to boost market share, Juno seeks to continually introduce innovative new products and enter new markets. As part of JUNO's strategy of entering new, yet complementary markets, the company acquired a maker of fiberoptic lighting products in mid-1997. Juno's growth strategy, as well as management's emphasis on product design and service, seems to have paid off, as the company has achieved solid profitability over the past several years. Since FY 95 (Nov.), the company has recorded average gross, operating and net profit margins of 50%, 22% and 15%, respectively, as well as a three-year average return on equity of 14%.

Operational Review - 09-SEP-98

Net sales for the six months ended May 31, 1998, advanced 13%, year to year, with solid economic conditions and new product introductions boosting demand. Operating margins widened on increased productivity, stable raw materials costs, benefits resulting from the redesign and retooling of high volume parts, and economies of scale. Pretax income gained 28%. After taxes at 35.6%, against 34.6%, net income was ahead by 26%, at $11,587,000 ($0.62 a share), versus $9,188,000 ($0.50).

Stock Performance - 09-OCT-98

In the past 30 trading days, JUNO's shares have increased 0.63%, compared to a 4% fall in the S&P 500. Average trading volume for the past five days was 47,060 shares, compared with the 40-day moving average of 52,897 shares.

Key Stock Statistics

Dividend Rate/Share	0.36	Shareholders	300
Shs. outstg. (M)	18.6	Market cap. (B)	$0.374
Avg. daily vol. (M)	0.052	Inst. holdings	78%
Tang. Bk. Value/Share	8.95		
Beta	0.53		

Value of $10,000 invested 5 years ago: $ 12,434

Fiscal Year Ending Nov. 30

	1998	1997	1996	1995	1994	1993
Revenues (Million $)						
1Q	34.39	30.80	28.19	31.50	27.70	24.60
2Q	40.85	35.83	35.04	33.26	33.30	26.20
3Q	44.42	37.24	34.87	31.12	34.20	29.60
4Q	—	35.98	33.38	30.48	31.55	28.70
Yr.	—	139.9	131.5	126.4	126.8	109.1
Earnings Per Share ($)						
1Q	**0.26**	0.21	0.16	0.29	0.26	0.23
2Q	**0.37**	0.29	0.29	0.28	0.33	0.23
3Q	**0.43**	0.31	0.32	0.24	0.33	0.26
4Q	—	0.29	0.31	0.27	0.32	0.26
Yr.	—	1.10	1.08	1.08	1.23	0.98

Next earnings report expected: late January

Dividend Data (Dividends have been paid since 1987.)

Amount ($)	Date Decl.	Ex-Div. Date	Stock of Record	Payment Date
0.090	Oct. 22	Dec. 11	Dec. 15	Jan. 15 '98
0.090	Mar. 02	Mar. 12	Mar. 16	Apr. 15 '98
0.090	Jun. 01	Jun. 11	Jun. 15	Jul. 15 '98
0.090	Sep. 01	Sep. 11	Sep. 15	Oct. 15 '98

A Division of The McGraw-Hill Companies

Business Summary - 09-SEP-98

As part of its efforts to increase market share, Juno Lighting's recessed and track lighting fixtures are moderately priced, to attract the high-volume commercial and residential markets. JUNO also seeks to continually introduce new products and enter new, yet complementary markets. Important profitability performance statistics from recent years are as follows:

	FY 97	FY 96	FY 95
Gross profit margins	49%	51%	51%
Operating profit margins	20%	22%	24%
Free cash flow per share	$0.43	$0.43	$0.33

Juno sells its products primarily to electrical distributors and certain wholesale lighting outlets. Distributors resell company products to the new residential and commercial construction markets and the remodeling industry. As a result, Juno's sales are partly dependent on new construction and remodeling activity.

Juno sells recessed lighting mostly under variants of the Down-Lites brand name. The company also sells energy-efficient recessed lighting under the Air-Loc brand name.

The company's principal track lighting system, sold

under the Trac-Master name, consists of a wide variety of spot lights that can be connected at any point on a track. These lights are available in different styles, light source sizes and finishes. Juno also sells track lighting under the more moderately priced Vector By Juno name, to complement the Trac-Master brand. Track lighting products were originally developed for use in store displays, although they have also become popular in the remodeling and do-it-yourself markets.

The company's Indy Lighting subsidiary produces lighting fixtures for department and chain stores. Indy's Danalite lighting fixture produces low-voltage halogen and fluorescent linear strip lighting fixtures for merchandise showcases. Several years ago, JUNO entered the Exit and Emergency lighting market with the introduction of a line of electronically powered and protected lighting products.

The company emphasizes new product development. In FY 97, FY 96 and FY 95, spending on R&D and new product testing represented 3.4%, 3.3% and 2.9% of total revenues, respectively.

Juno believes that it is one of the five largest track and recessed lighting producers in the U.S. Two competitors have substantially higher sales. The company estimates that it competes with a total of about 50 track and recessed lighting makers.

Per Share Data ($)

(Year Ended Nov. 30)	1997	1996	1995	1994	1993	1992	1991	1990	1989	1988
Tangible Bk. Val.	8.95	8.18	7.43	6.63	5.62	4.84	4.25	3.90	3.29	2.60
Cash Flow	1.28	1.24	1.23	1.41	1.10	0.95	0.81	0.88	0.80	0.66
Earnings	1.10	1.08	1.08	1.23	0.98	0.83	0.70	0.77	0.70	0.61
Dividends	0.32	0.32	0.30	0.26	0.22	0.17	0.14	0.12	0.09	0.07
Payout Ratio	29%	30%	28%	21%	22%	20%	20%	16%	13%	11%
Prices - High	19¾	18½	21	21	21	18¼	12⅛	11⅝	10⅛	12⅞
- Low	14½	13	14	16¼	15¼	10	8¼	6	6½	7¼
P/E Ratio - High	18	17	19	17	21	22	17	15	15	21
- Low	13	12	13	13	16	12	12	8	9	12

Income Statement Analysis (Million $)

	1997	1996	1995	1994	1993	1992	1991	1990	1989	1988
Revs.	140	131	126	127	109	97.0	80.0	85.0	77.0	58.0
Oper. Inc.	30.9	29.5	30.4	36.9	28.4	23.4	19.5	22.5	20.2	16.9
Depr.	3.5	3.1	2.8	3.2	2.2	2.3	2.2	2.0	1.9	1.0
Int. Exp.	0.2	0.3	0.4	0.3	0.3	0.2	0.3	0.3	0.4	0.3
Pretax Inc.	31.4	30.1	30.9	36.4	28.5	23.3	19.2	21.6	19.9	17.4
Eff. Tax Rate	35%	34%	35%	37%	36%	34%	34%	35%	36%	36%
Net Inc.	20.3	20.0	20.0	22.9	18.2	15.3	12.8	14.1	12.8	11.1

Balance Sheet & Other Fin. Data (Million $)

	1997	1996	1995	1994	1993	1992	1991	1990	1989	1988
Cash	6.8	71.1	6.6	58.4	45.3	44.0	38.2	32.5	23.6	18.2
Curr. Assets	123	120	113	100	81.5	75.8	63.6	56.7	48.0	38.2
Total Assets	187	178	160	146	125	111	93.0	86.0	73.0	61.0
Curr. Liab.	11.6	16.0	10.6	10.6	9.2	8.6	6.4	8.8	6.5	5.3
LT Debt	3.4	4.4	6.0	6.4	6.9	7.3	3.8	4.1	4.5	5.1
Common Eqty.	171	156	141	127	108	94.0	82.0	72.0	60.0	49.0
Total Cap.	174	160	149	135	116	103	87.0	76.0	65.0	54.0
Cap. Exp.	13.2	13.3	3.7	4.4	10.1	5.8	1.8	2.5	2.9	5.3
Cash Flow	23.8	23.0	22.8	26.1	20.4	17.6	15.0	16.1	14.7	12.1
Curr. Ratio	10.5	7.5	10.6	9.5	8.9	8.8	9.9	6.5	7.4	7.3
% LT Debt of Cap.	1.9	2.8	4.0	4.7	5.9	7.1	4.3	5.4	7.0	9.3
% Net Inc.of Revs.	14.5	15.1	15.8	18.1	16.7	15.9	16.1	16.5	16.6	19.1
% Ret. on Assets	11.1	11.8	13.1	16.9	15.4	15.0	14.2	17.7	19.0	19.7
% Ret. on Equity	12.4	13.4	14.9	19.5	18.0	17.4	16.7	21.3	23.3	25.2

Data as orig. reptd.; bef. results of disc. opers. and/or spec. items. Per share data adj. for stk. divs. as of ex-div. date. Bold denotes diluted EPS (FASB 128). E-Estimated. NA-Not Available. NM-Not Meaningful. NR-Not Ranked. Free cash flow defined as net income plus depreciation/amortization and decreases in working capital; less net capital expenditures, increases in working capital and preferred stock dividends.

Office—1300 S. Wolf Rd., P. O. Box 5065, Des Plaines, IL 60017-5065. **Tel**—(847) 827-9880. **Fax**—(847) 827-2925. **Chrmn & CEO**—R. S. Fremont. **VP-Fin, Treas & Investor Contact**—George J. Bilek. **Secy**—J. Lewis. **Dirs**—G. M. Ball, A. Coleman, R. S. Fremont, J. Lewis, T. W. Tomsovic. **Transfer Agent**—First Chicago Trust Co., NYC. **Incorporated**—in Delaware in 1983. **Empl**— 1,061. **S&P Analyst:** MWJ

STANDARD &POOR'S
STOCK REPORTS

Just For Feet

4316G

Nasdaq Symbol **FEET**

In S&P SmallCap 600

10-OCT-98

Industry: Retail (Specialty)

Summary: This company operates retail stores that sell brand-name athletic and outdoor footwear.

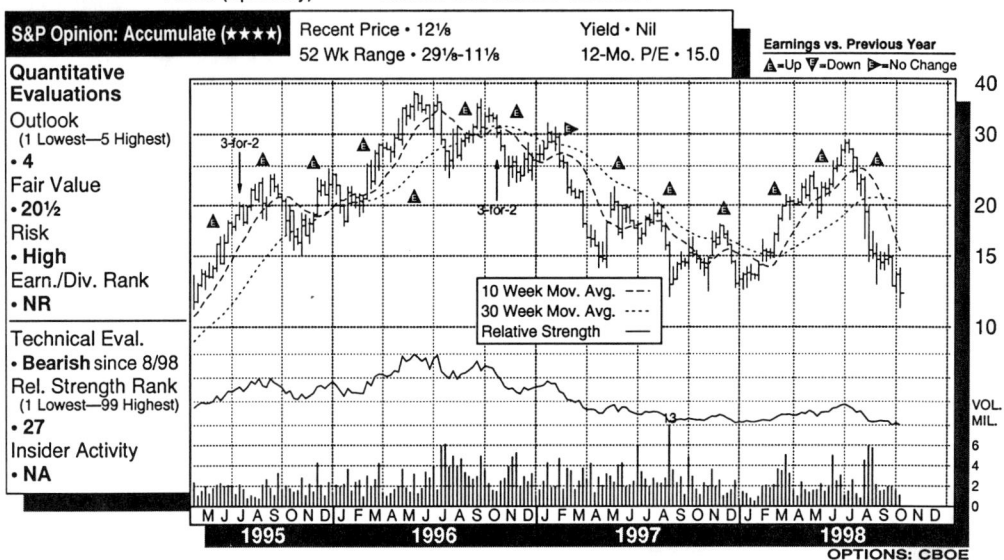

S&P Opinion: Accumulate (★★★★)

Recent Price • 12⅛
52 Wk Range • 29⅛-11⅛

Yield • Nil
12-Mo. P/E • 15.0

Earnings vs. Previous Year
▲=Up ▽=Down ▶=No Change

Quantitative Evaluations

Outlook
(1 Lowest—5 Highest)
• **4**

Fair Value
• **20½**

Risk
• **High**

Earn./Div. Rank
• **NR**

Technical Eval.
• **Bearish** since 8/98

Rel. Strength Rank
(1 Lowest—99 Highest)
• **27**

Insider Activity
• **NA**

10 Week Mov. Avg. ---
30 Week Mov. Avg. ·····
Relative Strength —

OPTIONS: CBOE

Overview - 01-SEP-98

Driven by a combination of the acquisition of Sneaker Stadium, the opening of approximately 17 superstores and 30 smaller specialty stores, and low to mid-single digit comparable-store growth, we expect sales of this footwear retailer to surge about 75% in FY 99 (Jan.). Sneaker Stadium was acquired in July 1998, adding 39 stores to FEET's superstore base. This followed the acquisition of Athletic Attic and Imperial Sports in the first half of FY 98, adding about 140 smaller-type specialty stores to the company's portfolio, and contributing about $60 million to sales in FY 98. Despite a slowdown in industry growth, FEET has consistently outperformed the domestic footwear industry, spurred by the success of its superstore format, which appeals to a wide audience. As FEET adjusts its infrastructure for the recently acquired stores, SG&A expenses are expected to decline as a percentage of sales in FY 99. We expect annual EPS growth in excess of 20% over the next three years.

Valuation - 01-SEP-98

Like those of other athletic footwear retailers, shares of FEET have fallen sharply since July. However, we believe that the company is better positioned than its competitors. First, FEET's inventory levels are well managed, while others have struggled to get rid of excess inventory. Second, sluggish sales of athletic apparel continue to hurt many athletic footwear retailers. However, only 12% of FEET's annualized sales are derived from apparel (most of this occurs in the fourth quarter). The company has a proven superstore concept, and we believe that FEET is still poised for rapid growth in coming years. The acquisition of Sneaker Stadium is expected to be neutral to earnings in FY 99, but it should boost earnings beginning in FY 2000. With the shares recently trading at 14X our FY 99 EPS estimate of $1.01, we continue to regard them as attractive.

Key Stock Statistics

S&P EPS Est. 1999	1.01	Tang. Bk. Value/Share	7.84
P/E on S&P Est. 1999	12.0	Beta	NA
S&P EPS Est. 2000	1.40	Shareholders	200
Dividend Rate/Share	Nil	Market cap. (B)	$0.378
Shs. outstg. (M)	31.2	Inst. holdings	57%
Avg. daily vol. (M)	0.314		

Value of $10,000 invested 5 years ago: NA

Fiscal Year Ending Jan. 31

	1999	1998	1997	1996	1995	1994
Revenues (Million $)						
1Q	151.9	92.80	49.15	21.14	—	—
2Q	175.3	112.4	58.38	25.43	12.52	—
3Q	—	131.0	69.74	34.77	16.48	—
4Q	—	142.4	79.13	38.48	18.43	6.98
Yr.	—	478.6	256.4	119.8	56.36	23.68
Earnings Per Share ($)						
1Q	0.19	0.18	0.11	0.06	0.03	—
2Q	0.25	0.16	0.10	0.09	0.04	—
3Q	E0.28	0.18	0.17	0.11	0.06	—
4Q	E0.28	0.20	0.17	0.16	0.06	-0.05
Yr.	E1.01	0.70	0.55	0.38	0.18	-0.02

Next earnings report expected: mid November

Dividend Data

The company has not paid any dividends on the common stock, and it does not anticipate paying cash dividends for the foreseeable future. FEET intends to retain its earnings to finance growth and development of its business.

Business Summary - 01-SEP-98

Just For Feet is a rapidly growing operator of super-stores specializing in brand-name athletic and outdoor footwear and apparel. The company's goal is to become the leading athletic and outdoor footwear retailer in each of its markets by offering the largest selection of brand-name shoes, superior customer service and technical sales assistance in a high-energy, entertaining store environment. As of January 31, 1998, there were 82 superstores operating in 20 states and Puerto Rico, including 9 franchises, and 140 small stores, including 48 franchises.

FEET's prototype superstore occupies 15,000 sq. ft. to 20,000 sq. ft., and offers approximately 2,500 to 4,500 styles of footwear, versus 200 to 700 typically offered by conventional mall-based footwear retailers, department stores and sporting goods superstores. Leading brands include Nike, Reebok, New Balance, Adidas, Fila, K-Swiss, Asics and Converse, as well as outdoor footwear brands such as Timberland and Rockport. The company seeks to carry virtually all styles in the brands it carries. The company's superstores offer shoes for practically every sport and recreational activity. Brand name apparel and accessories are also offered and include products such as warm-up suits, t-shirts, athletic shorts, caps, socks and shoe care products. The stores are primarily freestanding and are typically located on outparcels of or adjacent to shopping malls.

The company tries to create an exciting, high-energy shopping experience in its superstores through the use of bright colors, upbeat music, an enclosed half court basketball court for use by customers, a multi-screen video bank and appearances by sports celebrities. FEET emphasizes the training and testing of its sales associates in the technology employed by manufacturers, allowing it to provide a higher level of customer service than that offered by most traditional footwear retailers.

FEET's expansion strategy is to open approximately 17 superstores in FY 98 (Jan.), in new and existing metropolitan markets, including those markets with potential for multiple sites, allowing for advertising and operating efficiencies.

In March 1997, the company entered the small store segment with the acquisition of two privately owned footwear and apparel retailers, Athletic Attic and Imperial Sports. At that time, Athletic Attic operated 30 stores in eight states and had 48 franchised stores in 16 states and Puerto Rico. Imperial Sports operated 57 stores in the Midwest. FEET plans to open 30 new specialty stores in FY 99.

To reflect a change to more conservative accounting methods for store opening costs, FEET restated its FY 97 EPS to $0.55, from $0.66.

In July 1998, the company acquired Sneaker Stadium, a privately held athletic retailer operating 39 super-stores. FEET plans to convert Sneaker Stadium stores to the Just For Feet name and format.

Per Share Data ($)

(Year Ended Jan. 31)	1998	1997	1996	1995	1994	1993	1992	1991	1990	1989
Tangible Bk. Val.	7.64	7.56	5.55	3.01	1.38	NA	NA	NA	NA	NA
Cash Flow	0.99	0.69	0.47	0.47	0.01	0.07	NA	NA	NA	NA
Earnings	0.70	0.55	0.38	0.18	-0.02	0.05	-0.02	NA	NA	NA
Dividends	Nil	Nil	Nil	Nil	Nil	Nil	Nil	Nil	Nil	Nil
Payout Ratio	Nil	Nil	Nil	Nil	Nil	Nil	Nil	Nil	Nil	Nil
Cal. Yrs.	1997	1996	1995	1994	1993	1992	1991	1990	1989	1988
Prices - High	32	38¼	24⅝	10⅜	NA	NA	NA	NA	NA	NA
- Low	11⅞	17¾	7⅝	3⅛	NA	NA	NA	NA	NA	NA
P/E Ratio - High	46	NM	65	58	NA	NA	NA	NA	NA	NA
- Low	17	NM	20	18	NA	NA	NA	NA	NA	NA

Income Statement Analysis (Million $)

	1998	1997	1996	1995	1994	1993	1992	1991	1990	1989
Revs.	479	256	120	56.4	23.7	17.2	NA	NA	NA	NA
Oper. Inc.	42.0	24.2	13.4	5.3	-0.2	0.9	NA	NA	NA	NA
Depr.	8.8	4.0	2.2	0.9	0.3	0.2	NA	NA	NA	NA
Int. Exp.	1.4	0.8	0.7	0.3	0.2	0.2	NA	NA	NA	NA
Pretax Inc.	34.2	24.7	14.6	5.2	0.0	0.9	NA	NA	NA	NA
Eff. Tax Rate	37%	36%	33%	38%	NM	38%	NA	NA	NA	NA
Net Inc.	21.4	16.0	9.7	3.2	-0.2	0.6	NA	NA	NA	NA

Balance Sheet & Other Fin. Data (Million $)

	1998	1997	1996	1995	1994	1993	1992	1991	1990	1989
Cash	82.5	173	129	48.7	3.0	NA	NA	NA	NA	NA
Curr. Assets	311	315	194	76.6	12.6	NA	NA	NA	NA	NA
Total Assets	448	376	244	89.5	16.0	7.3	NA	NA	NA	NA
Curr. Liab.	156	147	85.4	12.0	10.4	NA	NA	NA	NA	NA
LT Debt	16.6	6.5	6.7	3.1	0.9	0.9	NA	NA	NA	NA
Common Eqty.	268	219	149	73.0	1.5	0.9	NA	NA	NA	NA
Total Cap.	285	226	157	77.0	4.5	1.9	NA	NA	NA	NA
Cap. Exp.	43.4	33.7	14.2	6.0	1.9	0.7	NA	NA	NA	NA
Cash Flow	30.2	19.9	11.9	11.9	0.1	0.7	NA	NA	NA	NA
Curr. Ratio	2.0	2.1	2.3	6.4	1.2	NA	NA	NA	NA	NA
% LT Debt of Cap.	5.8	2.9	4.3	4.0	20.1	48.3	NA	NA	NA	NA
% Net Inc.of Revs.	4.5	6.2	8.1	5.7	NM	3.3	NA	NA	NA	NA
% Ret. on Assets	5.2	5.2	5.8	6.1	NM	9.7	NA	NA	NA	NA
% Ret. on Equity	8.8	8.7	8.8	8.6	NM	57.0	NA	NA	NA	NA

Data as orig. reptd.; bef. results of disc. opers. and/or spec. items. Per share data adj. for stk. divs. as of ex-div. date. Bold denotes diluted EPS (FASB 128). E-Estimated. NA-Not Available. NM-Not Meaningful. NR-Not Ranked.

Office—7400 Cahaba Valley Rd., Birmingham, AL 35242.**Tel**—(205) 408-3000. **Chrmn, Pres & CEO**—H. Ruttenberg. **EVP & CFO**—E. L. Tyra. **VP & Secy**—S. C. Wynne.**Dirs**—D. F. Bellet, E. S. Croft III, R. L. Haines, M. P. Lazarus, H. Ruttenberg, B. Starr Sr.**Transfer Agent**—AmSouth Bank, Birmingham.**Incorporated**—in Alabama in 1977. **Empl**— 7,975. **S&P Analyst:** Kathleen J. Fraser

STANDARD &POOR'S
STOCK REPORTS

Justin Industries
4317K

NASDAQ Symbol **JSTN**

In S&P SmallCap 600

03-OCT-98 **Industry:** Footwear

Summary: This company produces western-style footwear, face brick, concrete blocks and other building materials.

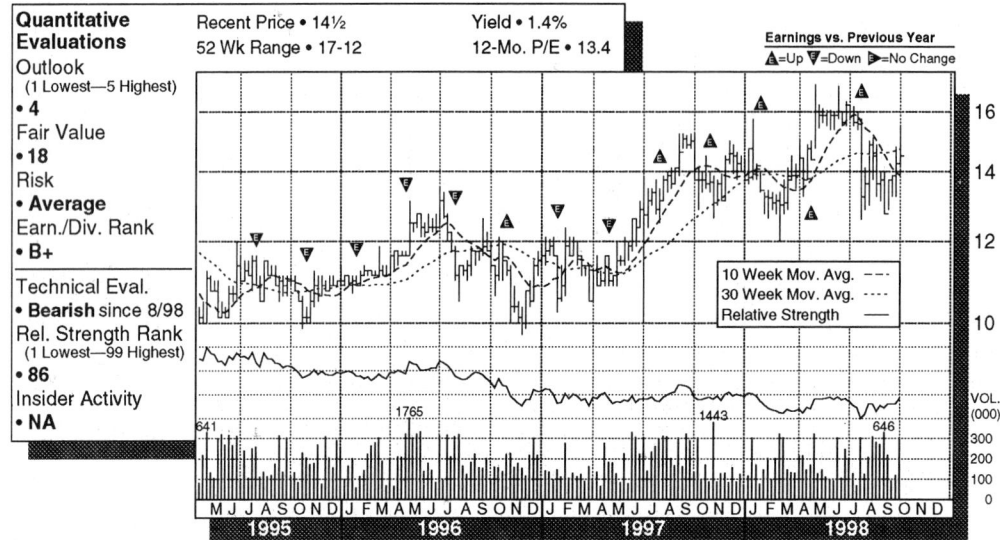

Quantitative Evaluations

Outlook (1 Lowest—5 Highest)
• **4**

Fair Value
• **18**

Risk
• **Average**

Earn./Div. Rank
• **B+**

Technical Eval.
• **Bearish** since 8/98

Rel. Strength Rank (1 Lowest—99 Highest)
• **86**

Insider Activity
• **NA**

Recent Price • 14½
52 Wk Range • 17-12

Yield • 1.4%
12-Mo. P/E • 13.4

Business Profile - 01-SEP-98

Higher levels of construction activity in the company's primary building territory boosted revenues and earnings for the building materials segment in the first half of 1998. This was an improvement compared to the 6% decline in residential construction in 1997, which led to a 1% decrease in brick shipments. However, the decline was outweighed by higher pricing and sales of products including floor and wall tile, bagged goods, limestone, and glazed products. Additional distribution locations for the building materials division are scheduled for 1998, and the company is also planning future expansion of production. In the 1997 second quarter, Justin introduced the Justin Original Workboot, which somewhat offset declining sales of the western boot in 1997. JSTN plans to introduce new lines of the workboot, and other footwear products.

Operational Review - 01-SEP-98

Sales in the six months ended June 30, 1998, rose 6.0%, reflecting a 10% rise in the sale of building materials and a 12% increase in the footwear business. Gross margins widened, as improvements at Acme Brick, which had higher volume and unit pricing, offset flat gross margins at the footwear division. SG&A and interest expenses rose only slightly, and after taxes at 36.5% in both periods, net income climbed 20%, to $12,719,000 ($0.48 a share), from $10,576,000 ($0.39).

Stock Performance - 02-OCT-98

In the past 30 trading days, JSTN's shares have increased 6%, compared to a 7% fall in the S&P 500. Average trading volume for the past five days was 65,760 shares, compared with the 40-day moving average of 59,849 shares.

Key Stock Statistics

Dividend Rate/Share	0.20	Shareholders	1,800
Shs. outstg. (M)	26.4	Market cap. (B)	$0.383
Avg. daily vol. (M)	0.044	Inst. holdings	36%
Tang. Bk. Value/Share	10.47		
Beta	0.35		

Value of $10,000 invested 5 years ago: $ 8,475

Fiscal Year Ending Dec. 31

	1998	1997	1996	1995	1994	1993
Revenues (Million $)						
1Q	103.8	97.61	104.3	113.7	109.9	110.1
2Q	119.1	110.9	110.7	109.9	114.9	116.1
3Q	—	114.2	110.4	112.4	119.7	118.3
4Q	—	117.1	122.4	125.5	138.5	130.4
Yr.	—	439.8	447.8	461.4	483.0	474.9
Earnings Per Share ($)						
1Q	0.17	0.12	0.14	0.19	0.24	0.20
2Q	0.31	0.28	0.21	0.22	0.34	0.28
3Q	—	0.27	0.22	0.21	0.34	0.35
4Q	—	0.32	0.30	0.32	0.41	0.46
Yr.	—	0.99	0.87	0.94	1.33	1.29

Next earnings report expected: NA

Dividend Data (Dividends have been paid since 1984.)

Amount ($)	Date Decl.	Ex-Div. Date	Stock of Record	Payment Date
0.050	Dec. 17	Dec. 24	Dec. 29	Jan. 07 '98
0.050	Mar. 20	Mar. 30	Apr. 01	Apr. 08 '98
0.050	Jun. 18	Jun. 25	Jun. 29	Jul. 07 '98
0.050	Sep. 15	Sep. 24	Sep. 28	Oct. 06 '98

A Division of The McGraw·Hill Companies

Justin Industries, Inc.

Business Summary - 01-SEP-98

Justin Industries, Inc., which traces its history to a company that began making boots in 1879, today operates two principal business segments -- western-style footwear and building materials.

Sales and operating profits in 1997 were derived as follows:

	Sales	Profits
Building materials	60%	90%
Footwear	40%	10%

In the footwear segment, Justin designs, manufactures and distributes men's, women's and children's western-style safety, work and sports boots and shoes. Footwear products, made by Justin Boot Co., Nocona Boot Co. and Tony Lama Co., are sold primarily in the U.S. under the trade names Justin, Chippewa, Nocona, Tony Lama, Sport Lace-R and Diamond J.

Building materials include clay brick (primarily face brick) manufactured by Acme Brick Co. for use in residential and commercial construction; concrete building block sold under the trade name Featherlite Building Products Corp.; and cut limestone manufactured under the name Texas Quarries. The company also represents other manufacturers as a distributor of clay brick, glass block, glazed and unglazed tile and masonry units, fireplace equipment and masonry tools and related items. Justin also provides evaporative coolers produced by Tradewind Technologies Inc., which are used primarily for central residential, light commercial and spot cooling.

In April 1997, Justin was named a defendant in a lawsuit that alleges that Tradewinds has designed, manufactured, and sold defective evaporative coolers that have a propensity to start or spread fires. Justin recorded $500,000 in litigation related expenses through the third quarter of 1997.

In August 1994, the Acme Brick unit acquired American Tile Supply, a Dallas-based distributor of ceramic tile and marble, for about $16 million in cash and notes. American had annual revenues of about $32 million.

In December 1991, Justin sold Ceramic Cooling Tower Co., which was engaged in the design, installation and marketing of water-cooling systems, at a gain of approximately $9.8 million. As a result, Justin's industrial segment was eliminated and operations of Tradewind Technologies were incorporated into the building materials segment.

Justin also operates Northland Publishing Co., which publishes books about the history and art of the West.

Per Share Data ($) (Year Ended Dec. 31)	1997	1996	1995	1994	1993	1992	1991	1990	1989	1988
Tangible Bk. Val.	9.76	9.01	8.32	8.15	6.95	5.75	4.92	4.30	4.15	3.98
Cash Flow	1.65	1.47	1.47	1.83	1.77	1.48	0.81	0.69	0.69	0.77
Earnings	0.99	0.87	0.94	1.33	1.29	0.98	0.32	0.28	0.28	0.29
Dividends	0.18	0.16	0.16	0.16	0.16	0.14	0.13	0.13	0.10	0.09
Payout Ratio	18%	18%	17%	12%	12%	14%	41%	47%	36%	30%
Prices - High	15 1/4	13 1/2	12 1/8	16 3/4	25 3/8	19	6 1/8	6	5 5/8	3 3/4
- Low	10	9 3/4	9 1/2	9 3/4	11 3/4	5 5/8	3 5/8	3 3/4	3 1/8	2 5/8
P/E Ratio - High	15	16	13	13	20	19	19	21	20	13
- Low	10	11	10	7	9	6	11	13	11	9
Income Statement Analysis (Million $)										
Revs.	440	448	461	483	475	453	368	315	278	250
Oper. Inc.	60.2	56.3	60.0	75.4	73.5	61.4	36.0	28.2	26.8	27.0
Depr.	17.7	16.3	14.7	13.9	13.5	13.8	12.8	10.7	10.5	10.7
Int. Exp.	1.8	3.4	5.0	4.1	4.0	5.2	9.5	6.6	6.0	4.4
Pretax Inc.	40.7	36.6	40.2	57.5	56.0	42.4	13.7	10.9	10.7	11.0
Eff. Tax Rate	35%	36%	36%	36%	36%	36%	38%	33%	33%	32%
Net Inc.	26.3	23.4	25.7	36.9	36.0	27.1	8.5	7.3	7.2	7.5
Balance Sheet & Other Fin. Data (Million $)										
Cash	5.1	3.2	2.2	6.1	10.6	2.4	4.1	1.5	3.3	2.0
Curr. Assets	230	226	251	260	240	224	201	199	137	141
Total Assets	376	360	376	375	347	316	296	293	211	214
Curr. Liab.	63.9	60.9	69.2	73.8	54.9	54.1	44.9	47.9	38.9	35.9
LT Debt	23.8	32.9	57.1	65.0	89.0	100	116	125	56.0	70.0
Common Eqty.	273	253	236	222	189	155	128	111	106	99
Total Cap.	312	299	307	301	292	262	251	245	172	178
Cap. Exp.	21.8	24.7	26.0	18.6	17.3	12.0	11.0	13.2	9.0	9.4
Cash Flow	44.0	39.7	40.3	50.8	49.5	40.9	21.3	18.0	17.7	19.1
Curr. Ratio	3.6	3.7	3.6	3.5	4.4	4.1	4.5	4.1	3.5	3.9
% LT Debt of Cap.	7.6	11.0	18.6	21.7	30.3	38.3	46.2	50.9	32.6	39.0
% Net Inc.of Revs.	6.0	5.2	5.5	7.6	7.6	6.0	2.3	2.3	2.6	3.0
% Ret. on Assets	7.2	6.3	6.8	10.2	10.8	8.7	2.9	2.9	3.3	3.4
% Ret. on Equity	10.0	9.5	11.2	17.9	20.9	18.8	7.1	6.7	6.9	7.8

Data as orig. reptd.; bef. results of disc. opers. and/or spec. items. Per share data adj. for stk. divs. as of ex-div. date. Bold denotes diluted EPS (FASB 128). E-Estimated. NA-Not Available. NM-Not Meaningful. NR-Not Ranked.

Office—2821 W. 7th St., P.O. Box 425, Fort Worth, TX 76107. **Tel**—(817) 336-5125. **Website**—http://www.justinind.com **Chrmn & CEO**—J. S. Justin. **Pres & COO**—J. T. Dickenson. **VP & Secy**—J. M. Bennett. **VP-Fin, CFO & Investor Contact**—Richard J. Savitz (817-390-2412). **Dirs**—J. T. Dickenson, B. H. Friedman, M. Gearhart, R. E. Glaze, J. S. Justin, D. J. Kelly, J. R. Musolino, J. V. Roach, W. E. Tucker. **Transfer Agent**—Bank of New York, NYC. **Incorporated**—in Texas in 1916. **Empl**— 4,222. **S&P Analyst:** Kathleen J. Fraser

STANDARD &POOR'S
STOCK REPORTS

KCS Energy

1272R
NYSE Symbol **KCS**

In S&P SmallCap 600

03-OCT-98

Industry:
Oil & Gas (Exploration & Production)

Summary: KCS is engaged primarily in the acquisition, exploration, development and production of natural gas and crude oil.

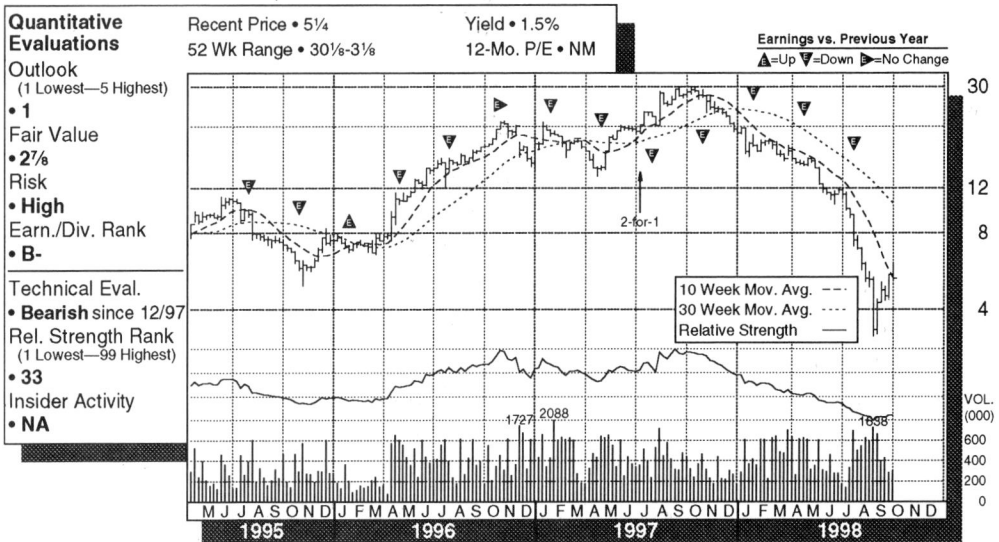

Quantitative Evaluations

Outlook
(1 Lowest—5 Highest)
• 1

Fair Value
• 2⅞

Risk
• **High**

Earn./Div. Rank
• **B-**

Technical Eval.
• **Bearish** since 12/97

Rel. Strength Rank
(1 Lowest—99 Highest)
• 33

Insider Activity
• **NA**

Recent Price • 5¼
52 Wk Range • 30⅛-3⅛

Yield • 1.5%
12-Mo. P/E • NM

Earnings vs. Previous Year
▲=Up ▼=Down ▷=No Change

10 Week Mov. Avg. ---
30 Week Mov. Avg. ....
Relative Strength —

Business Profile - 21-MAY-98

KCS Energy is an independent energy company focused on oil and gas exploration and production. Historically, the company's most significant field was the Bob West field in south Texas. The company had been the beneficiary of a take or pay contract with Tennessee Gas Pipeline Co., which was to expire in January 1999. KCS gave up the lucrative contract, effective January 1997, to settle a lawsuit brought by Tennessee Gas. As part of the settlement, KCS will not have to pay the $143 million verdict awarded in the lawsuit. The company in January 1997 completed the public offering of 6,000,000 shares (giving effect to a June 1997 stock split), raising approximately $111 million that was used to reduce outstanding indebtedness under KCS's bank credit facilities. As of March 31, 1997, the company sold its intrastate pipeline system located north of Houston, together with related marketing assets, and a joint venture gathering system, for $28 million in cash.

Operational Review - 21-MAY-98

Revenues from continuing operations in the first quarter of 1998 declined 21%, year to year, on significantly lower oil, gas and liquids prices and decreased oil and liquids production. Total costs and expenses fell less rapidly. With higher interest expense, and despite a tax benefit, versus taxes at 36.9%, a loss from continuing operations of $140,000 (nil per share, on 7.7% more shares) contrasted with income of $5,404,000 ($0.20 a share).

Stock Performance - 02-OCT-98

In the past 30 trading days, KCS's shares have increased 1%, compared to a 7% fall in the S&P 500. Average trading volume for the past five days was 59,780 shares, compared with the 40-day moving average of 147,785 shares.

Key Stock Statistics

Dividend Rate/Share	0.08	Shareholders	1,200
Shs. outstg. (M)	29.6	Market cap. (B)	$0.157
Avg. daily vol. (M)	0.079	Inst. holdings	65%
Tang. Bk. Value/Share	3.58		
Beta	1.25		

Value of $10,000 invested 5 years ago: $ 10,367

Fiscal Year Ending Dec. 31

	1998	1997	1996	1995	1994	1993
Revenues (Million $)						
1Q	31.31	39.88	146.6	96.04	85.19	52.58
2Q	33.66	32.55	96.49	126.6	85.17	52.27
3Q	—	31.67	73.56	109.7	84.49	77.28
4Q	—	39.59	81.41	117.7	80.74	89.55
Yr.	—	143.7	398.0	450.0	335.6	271.7
Earnings Per Share ($)						
1Q	Nil	0.20	0.27	0.30	0.27	0.06
2Q	-1.32	0.08	0.23	0.27	0.26	0.13
3Q	—	0.05	0.17	0.23	0.29	0.18
4Q	—	-3.63	0.22	0.17	0.17	0.23
Yr.	—	-3.37	0.91	0.97	0.98	0.59

Next earnings report expected: early November

Dividend Data (Dividends have been paid since 1992.)

Amount ($)	Date Decl.	Ex-Div. Date	Stock of Record	Payment Date
0.020	Dec. 05	Jan. 08	Jan. 12	Feb. 25 '98
0.020	Apr. 17	Apr. 29	May. 01	May. 20 '98
0.020	May. 28	Jul. 08	Jul. 10	Aug. 25 '98
0.020	Sep. 25	Oct. 07	Oct. 09	Nov. 25 '98

A Division of The McGraw-Hill Companies

Business Summary - 21-MAY-98

With its acquisition of InterCoast Oil and Gas Co. in December 1996, KCS Energy Co. (KCS) not only doubled its oil and gas production and reserves, it also added a third core operating area -- the Mid-Continent region of the U.S. KCS is engaged in the acquisition, exploration, development and production of natural gas and crude oil in the Onshore Gulf Coast region, the Rocky Mountains, and now the Mid-Continent region, encompassing west Texas, the Texas Panhandle, northwest Oklahoma, and northern Louisiana.

Through its volumetric production payment (VPP) program, KCS also participates with other oil and gas operators mainly in the Gulf of Mexico and Michigan's Niagaran Reef trend. Under the VPP, KCS is entitled to a specified volume of oil and gas reserves scheduled to be produced and delivered over a stated period of time.

On December 23, 1996, KCS and Tennessee Gas Pipeline Co. entered into a settlement ending six years of litigation and claims related to an above-market, take-or-pay contract. The contract (covering the Bob West Field in Texas) was terminated effective January 1, 1997, approximately two years prior to its expiration date, and the parties also agreed to the dismissal of a contract dispute that resulted in a November 1996 jury award that was unfavorable to KCS.

KCS's strategy has now shifted from Bob West Field development and reserve acquisitions to a more balanced approach combining acquisitions with broad-based development drilling and increased exploration. Areas of intense drilling activity include the Manderson Field of the Big Horn Basin in the Rocky Mountains, the Langham Creek Field in Texas and the Anadarko, ArkLaTex, Arkoma and Permian basins in the Mid-Continent. KCS also plans to expand its VPP program targeting small to medium size independent oil and gas companies whose capital requirements exceed their own cash flow and credit capacity. In January 1998, a VPP agreement was reached for 10,800,000 Mcf of offshore reserves with Hall-Houston Oil Co.

Production in 1997 totaled 1,696,000 bbl. of oil and 43,700 MMcf of gas, up from 758,000 bbl. and 25,581 MMcf in 1996. Average sales prices were $18.57 per bbl. of oil ($20.69 in 1996) and $2.40 per Mcf of gas ($3.61). Total proved reserves were estimated at 19,063,000 bbl. of oil and 326,168 MMcf of natural gas. At December 31, 1997, the present value of future net revenues (discounted at 10%) was estimated at $374.9 million, versus $437.6 million a year earlier. KCS had working interests in 2,836 gross producing wells.

In early 1997, KCS sold its 150-mile intrastate natural gas pipeline system in Texas, together with related marketing assets and a joint venture gathering system, for $28 million.

Per Share Data ($)

(Year Ended Dec. 31)	1997	1996	1995	1994	1993	1992	1991	1990	1989	1988
Tangible Bk. Val.	4.93	5.42	4.42	3.23	2.26	1.34	1.21	1.09	0.98	0.48
Cash Flow	-1.27	2.79	2.58	1.63	0.85	0.33	0.25	0.20	0.15	0.13
Earnings	-3.37	0.91	0.97	0.98	0.59	0.15	0.12	0.12	0.06	0.04
Dividends	0.07	0.06	0.06	0.04	0.02	0.01	Nil	Nil	Nil	Nil
Payout Ratio	NM	7%	7%	4%	3%	8%	Nil	Nil	Nil	Nil
Prices - High	30¼	22	11⅛	14½	16⅜	5⅞	1⅛	1⅛	1¼	¹³/₁₆
- Low	13⅜	6½	5	6⅛	4½	1¹/₁₆	¾	⅞	⁹/₁₆	⁷/₁₆
P/E Ratio - High	NM	26	12	15	28	38	9	10	22	21
- Low	NM	8	5	6	8	7	6	8	10	12

Income Statement Analysis (Million $)

	1997	1996	1995	1994	1993	1992	1991	1990	1989	1988
Revs.	144	398	450	336	272	144	99	72.2	73.1	55.3
Oper. Inc.	97.7	91.0	75.0	51.4	26.1	9.1	6.6	3.7	1.4	1.8
Depr.	60.6	46.6	39.2	15.2	6.0	3.9	2.9	1.9	2.0	2.0
Int. Exp.	21.9	18.0	7.7	2.4	1.8	1.3	1.2	0.2	0.1	0.2
Pretax Inc.	-148	31.5	31.9	35.0	19.0	4.7	3.4	3.5	1.9	1.1
Eff. Tax Rate	NM	37%	33%	34%	28%	28%	26%	32%	35%	26%
Net Inc.	-97.4	19.9	21.3	23.3	13.7	3.3	2.5	2.4	1.2	0.8

Balance Sheet & Other Fin. Data (Million $)

	1997	1996	1995	1994	1993	1992	1991	1990	1989	1988
Cash	4.8	5.1	5.1	5.1	11.3	3.2	2.2	3.2	25.3	6.9
Curr. Assets	51.7	126	68.0	47.7	70.3	27.4	18.9	17.3	31.8	15.4
Total Assets	502	570	361	181	153	74.7	60.5	51.1	42.2	25.6
Curr. Liab.	64.0	96.0	64.0	42.1	65.0	23.2	15.5	14.4	18.0	12.8
LT Debt	292	310	166	48.6	30.9	17.8	16.0	10.7	0.2	0.7
Common Eqty.	145	126	102	73.8	51.4	29.0	25.7	23.1	20.8	10.6
Total Cap.	438	470	293	137	87.1	50.2	42.8	34.6	21.5	12.4
Cap. Exp.	277	277	125	66.1	41.3	9.8	9.0	26.8	3.8	1.1
Cash Flow	-36.8	66.5	60.5	38.4	19.7	7.2	5.4	4.3	3.2	2.8
Curr. Ratio	0.8	1.3	1.1	1.1	1.1	1.2	1.2	1.2	1.8	1.2
% LT Debt of Cap.	66.8	66.0	56.4	35.5	35.5	35.4	37.4	31.0	0.8	5.7
% Net Inc.of Revs.	NM	5.0	4.7	6.9	5.0	2.3	2.5	3.3	1.7	1.5
% Ret. on Assets	NM	4.3	7.4	13.9	11.8	4.9	4.5	5.1	3.6	NA
% Ret. on Equity	NM	17.5	51.8	37.2	33.4	12.2	10.2	10.9	7.9	NA

Data as orig. reptd.; bef. results of disc. opers. and/or spec. items. Per share data adj. for stk. divs. as of ex-div. date. Prior to 1995, yrs. ended Sep. 30 of fol. cal yr. Bold denotes diluted EPS (FASB 128). E-Estimated. NA-Not Available. NM-Not Meaningful. NR-Not Ranked.

Office—379 Thornall St., Edison, NJ 08837.**Tel**—(732) 632-1770. **Website**—http://www.kcsenergy.com **Chrmn**—S. B. Kean.**Pres & CEO**—J. W. Christmas. **SVP & CFO**—P. S. Samett . **VP & Treas**—K. M. Kinnamon. **Dirs**—J. W. Christmas, G. S. Geary, S. B. Kean, J. E. Murphy Jr., R. G. Raynolds, J. D. Siegel, C. A. Viggiano.**Transfer Agent & Registrar**—Registrar & Transfer Co., Cranford, NJ. **Incorporated**—in Delaware in 1988.**Empl**— 209. **S&P Analyst:** S.A.H.

K-Swiss Inc. 4318T
NASDAQ Symbol **KSWS**
In S&P SmallCap 600

03-OCT-98 Industry: Footwear

Summary: This company designs, develops and markets high-performance and casual athletic footwear.

Quantitative Evaluations

Outlook
(1 Lowest—5 Highest)
• **3+**

Fair Value
• **24¾**

Risk
• **Average**

Earn./Div. Rank
• **B**

Technical Eval.
• **Bearish** since 9/98

Rel. Strength Rank
(1 Lowest—99 Highest)
• **90**

Insider Activity
• **Unfavorable**

Recent Price • 24
52 Wk Range • 29-15¾

Yield • 0.3%
12-Mo. P/E • 15.7

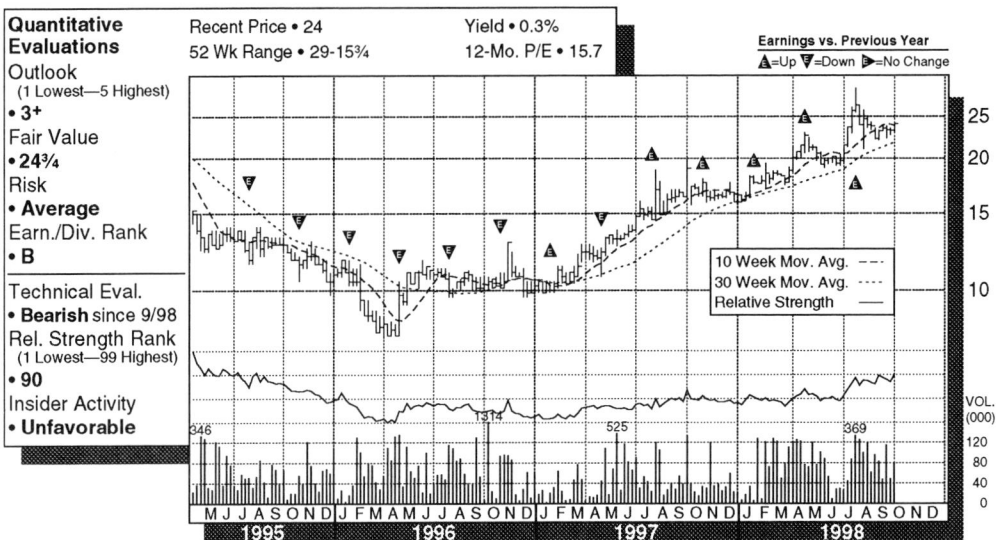

Earnings vs. Previous Year
▲=Up ▼=Down ▶=No Change

10 Week Mov. Avg. ---
30 Week Mov. Avg. ····
Relative Strength —

Business Profile - 10-SEP-98

Although KSWS has conducted an ambitious expansion of international operations, foreign sales accounted for only 10% of revenues in the first half of 1998, down from 24% in the 1997 period -- due to the Asian currency crisis. Approximately 97% of production capacity is now located in China and Indonesia. KSWS's primary operating strategy is to design products with longer life cycles and introduce fewer new models than its competition. The company continues to focus the majority of its advertising and promotion on tennis, where it is attempting to take advantage of high brand awareness. Biltrite Corp. holds approximately 9.8% of the company's shares outstanding.

Operational Review - 10-SEP-98

Revenues in the six months ended June 30, 1998, advanced 40%, year to year, reflecting increases in both footwear volumes and average wholesale prices per pair. Domestic revenues rose 64%, while international revenues decreased 40%. Gross margins widened, on favorable changes in the geographic and product mix, as well as a reduction in close-out sales. With only a 29% increase in SG&A expenses, operating income climbed to $8,759,000, from $1,158,000. After taxes at 39.9%, versus 41.2%, net income soared to $5,800,000 ($1.02 a diluted share, on 5.3% fewer shares), from $1,160,000 ($0.19).

Stock Performance - 02-OCT-98

In the past 30 trading days, KSWS's shares have increased 1%, compared to a 7% fall in the S&P 500. Average trading volume for the past five days was 15,940 shares, compared with the 40-day moving average of 16,559 shares.

Key Stock Statistics

Dividend Rate/Share	0.08	Shareholders	100
Shs. outstg. (M)	5.4	Market cap. (B)	$0.077
Avg. daily vol. (M)	0.015	Inst. holdings	36%
Tang. Bk. Value/Share	13.59		
Beta	0.55		

Value of $10,000 invested 5 years ago: $ 11,203

Fiscal Year Ending Dec. 31

	1998	1997	1996	1995	1994	1993
Revenues (Million $)						
1Q	42.27	31.20	34.37	42.76	45.55	43.56
2Q	41.02	28.42	26.02	29.73	36.27	38.30
3Q	—	32.84	28.78	29.36	48.74	43.92
4Q	—	23.76	17.67	18.40	24.38	23.79
Yr.	—	116.2	106.8	120.3	154.9	149.6
Earnings Per Share ($)						
1Q	**0.62**	**0.25**	0.32	0.60	0.68	0.52
2Q	**0.40**	**-0.06**	-0.11	0.23	0.52	0.46
3Q	—	**0.29**	0.04	0.15	0.78	0.67
4Q	—	**0.22**	-0.16	-0.71	0.22	0.22
Yr.	—	**0.70**	0.11	0.28	2.20	1.87

Next earnings report expected: late October

Dividend Data (Dividends have been paid since 1994.)

Amount ($)	Date Decl.	Ex-Div. Date	Stock of Record	Payment Date
0.020	Dec. 04	Dec. 29	Dec. 31	Jan. 15 '98
0.020	Feb. 26	Mar. 27	Mar. 31	Apr. 15 '98
0.020	May. 21	Jun. 26	Jun. 30	Jul. 15 '98
0.020	Aug. 31	Sep. 28	Sep. 30	Oct. 15 '98

A Division of The McGraw-Hill Companies

Business Summary - 10-SEP-98

Tennis enthusiasts quickly recognize the name K-Swiss. As a company, KSWS develops and markets a growing array of athletic footwear for high-performance sports use and fitness activities. It was founded in 1966 by two Swiss brothers, who introduced one of the first leather tennis shoes in the U.S. The company was acquired on December 30, 1986, in a leveraged transaction by an investment group led by the current chairman and president. Subsequently, several new footwear products were introduced, and manufacturing was shifted to independent suppliers primarily in China and Indonesia.

Revenues in recent years were derived as follows:

	1997	1996	1995
Classic	58%	48%	56%
Tennis/court shoes	18%	24%	18%
Children's	19%	18%	16%
Other	5%	10%	10%

K-Swiss derives the bulk of sales from its Classic leather tennis shoes. The Classic, little changed from its original design, has become popular as a casual shoe for men and women, while continuing to sell well as a tennis shoe. In recent years, the company has developed new product categories whose initial styles were extensions of the Classic. It believes that the use of classic styling reduces the effect of changes in consumer preferences. In 1997, a total of 4,870,000 pairs of footwear were sold, up from 4,697,000 pairs in 1996.

Men's footwear accounted for 42% of revenues in 1997 (42% in 1996), and women's footwear accounted for 36% (34%).

The company sells a line of apparel and accessories manufactured by third parties. The line consists of warm-ups, skirts, shorts and shirts, fleece tops and pants, T-shirts, caps, bags and socks. All apparel and accessories carry the K-Swiss logo and name.

K-Swiss sells its products in the U.S. through independent sales representatives, primarily to specialty athletic footwear stores, pro shops, sporting goods stores and upscale department stores. It also sells to a number of foreign distributors. The Foot Locker group of stores accounted for 17% of total revenues in 1997 (11% in 1996), while international sales provided 21% (28%).

Per Share Data ($)

(Year Ended Dec. 31)	1997	1996	1995	1994	1993	1992	1991	1990	1989	1988
Tangible Bk. Val.	12.72	12.26	12.00	11.77	9.50	7.40	6.00	4.64	0.90	-0.11
Cash Flow	0.85	0.30	0.46	2.39	2.06	1.68	1.51	1.34	1.05	0.63
Earnings	0.70	0.11	0.28	2.20	1.87	1.49	1.34	1.22	0.91	0.52
Dividends	0.08	0.08	0.08	0.08	Nil	Nil	Nil	Nil	Nil	Nil
Payout Ratio	11%	73%	29%	4%	Nil	Nil	Nil	Nil	Nil	Nil
Prices - High	19⁷/₈	12⁷/₈	21	25³/₄	27¹/₄	24³/₄	28⁷/₈	30¹/₄	NA	NA
- Low	9⁷/₈	7³/₄	9³/₄	18¹/₄	18¹/₄	14¹/₄	11¹/₄	10¹/₂	NA	NA
P/E Ratio - High	28	NM	75	12	15	17	22	25	NA	NA
- Low	14	NM	35	8	10	10	8	9	NA	NA

Income Statement Analysis (Million $)

	1997	1996	1995	1994	1993	1992	1991	1990	1989	1988
Revs.	116	107	120	155	150	128	119	98.0	69.0	40.0
Oper. Inc.	6.3	2.3	7.6	25.8	21.1	18.1	17.9	17.0	12.5	6.3
Depr.	0.9	1.2	1.2	1.2	1.3	1.3	1.1	0.7	0.7	0.6
Int. Exp.	NA	NA	NA	NA	0.4	2.0	2.9	3.7	3.6	1.9
Pretax Inc.	7.2	2.6	7.2	24.8	19.4	14.8	13.9	12.6	8.2	3.8
Eff. Tax Rate	42%	72%	74%	40%	36%	34%	37%	42%	42%	29%
Net Inc.	4.2	0.7	1.9	14.9	12.5	9.8	8.8	7.2	4.8	2.7

Balance Sheet & Other Fin. Data (Million $)

	1997	1996	1995	1994	1993	1992	1991	1990	1989	1988
Cash	36.1	34.3	31.4	15.8	14.4	10.6	1.1	0.1	0.6	NM
Curr. Assets	91.5	90.5	92.8	90.1	75.7	68.3	54.8	57.7	43.9	24.2
Total Assets	102	100	102	100	86.9	80.2	67.1	68.5	52.7	31.8
Curr. Liab.	16.0	11.2	9.6	12.9	15.1	23.2	10.9	17.0	26.8	17.8
LT Debt	0.1	0.2	0.5	0.5	0.6	1.4	10.9	13.8	16.3	9.6
Common Eqty.	75.9	79.6	84.1	82.8	68.0	53.7	45.0	36.1	8.5	3.8
Total Cap.	85.7	89.1	92.8	87.4	71.8	57.0	56.2	51.5	25.9	13.4
Cap. Exp.	1.6	1.0	0.4	0.7	0.8	0.7	1.6	1.0	0.4	0.1
Cash Flow	5.1	1.9	3.0	16.1	13.8	11.1	9.9	8.0	5.5	3.3
Curr. Ratio	5.7	8.1	9.7	7.0	5.0	2.9	5.0	3.4	1.6	1.4
% LT Debt of Cap.	0.2	0.2	0.5	0.6	0.9	2.5	19.5	26.7	63.0	71.8
% Net Inc.of Revs.	3.6	0.7	1.5	9.6	8.4	7.7	7.4	8.0	6.9	6.8
% Ret. on Assets	4.1	0.7	1.8	15.9	14.9	13.3	13.0	9.4	11.3	10.6
% Ret. on Equity	5.4	0.9	2.2	19.7	20.4	19.8	21.7	29.0	77.3	114.9

Data as orig. reptd.; bef. results of disc. opers. and/or spec. items. Per share data adj. for stk. divs. as of ex-div. date. Bold denotes diluted EPS (FASB 128). E-Estimated. NA-Not Available. NM-Not Meaningful. NR-Not Ranked.

Office—20664 Bahama St., Chatsworth, CA 91311. **Tel**—(818) 998-3388. **Chrmn & Pres**—S. Nichols. **VP-Fin, CFO, Secy & Investor Contact**—George Powlick. **Dirs**—L. Feldman, J. K. Layne, S. Nichols, G. Powlick, M. Wilford. **Transfer Agent & Registrar**—Bank of New York, NYC. **Incorporated**—in Delaware in 1990. **Empl**— 144. **S&P Analyst:** K.S.

STANDARD &POOR'S
STOCK REPORTS

K2 Inc.

1272P

NYSE Symbol **KTO**

In S&P SmallCap 600

05-OCT-98

Industry: Leisure Time (Products)

Summary: K2 is a leading designer, manufacturer and marketer of brand name sporting goods and recreational and industrial products.

Quantitative Evaluations

Outlook (1 Lowest—5 Highest)
• 3

Fair Value
• 19⅛

Risk
• **Average**

Earn./Div. Rank
• **B+**

Technical Eval.
• **NA**

Rel. Strength Rank (1 Lowest—99 Highest)
• **56**

Insider Activity
• **NA**

Recent Price • 16½
52 Wk Range • 29¾-15

Yield • 2.7%
12-Mo. P/E • 14.8

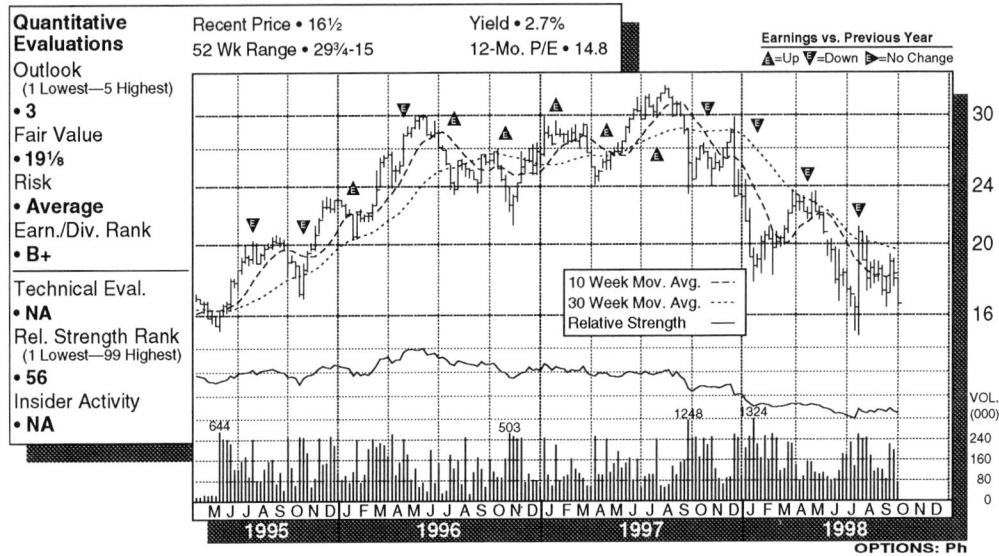

10 Week Mov. Avg. -- -
30 Week Mov. Avg. .....
Relative Strength —

Earnings vs. Previous Year
▲=Up ▼=Down ▶=No Change

OPTIONS: Ph

Business Profile - 05-OCT-98

Long recognized for its top-selling brand of K2 alpine skis, this company has entered several other rapidly growing sports markets, including in-line skates, snowboards and mountain bikes. Due to the current competitive environment, management has warned that both sales and earnings may remain under pressure, resulting in possibly no overall growth this year. However, the company has been introducing innovative new products, such as split frame in-line skates, children's skates and recreational ice skates, which it hopes will lead to resumed growth.

Operational Review - 05-OCT-98

Net sales rose 3.2%, year to year, in the first half of 1998, as gains for snowboards and fishing tackle were offset by declines in skates and skis. Gross profit margins were restricted by a less favorable sales mix of higher margin products, margin pressures from closeout sales of certain skate and bike inventories and higher manufacturing costs and competitive pricing pressures in certain segments of the industrial group. With significantly higher interest expense, net income fell 23%, to $11,224,000 ($0.68 a diluted share), from $14,549,000 ($0.87).

Stock Performance - 02-OCT-98

In the past 30 trading days, KTO's shares have declined 8%, compared to a 7% fall in the S&P 500. Average trading volume for the past five days was 14,100 shares, compared with the 40-day moving average of 28,218 shares.

Key Stock Statistics

Dividend Rate/Share	0.44	Shareholders	1,700
Shs. outstg. (M)	16.6	Market cap. (B)	$0.274
Avg. daily vol. (M)	0.029	Inst. holdings	59%
Tang. Bk. Value/Share	11.63		
Beta	0.50		

Value of $10,000 invested 5 years ago: $ 16,337

Fiscal Year Ending Dec. 31

	1998	1997	1996	1995	1994	1993
Revenues (Million $)						
1Q	173.2	171.5	158.8	138.0	109.7	97.98
2Q	180.9	171.5	143.4	135.9	131.8	112.9
3Q	—	142.3	147.7	134.7	127.9	114.0
4Q	—	161.5	152.8	135.7	133.1	106.8
Yr.	—	646.9	602.7	544.3	502.4	431.6
Earnings Per Share ($)						
1Q	**0.19**	**0.35**	0.29	0.30	0.04	0.08
2Q	**0.49**	**0.52**	0.42	0.41	0.42	0.34
3Q	—	**0.18**	0.43	0.36	0.38	0.32
4Q	—	**0.26**	0.38	0.29	0.25	0.20
Yr.	—	**1.31**	1.51	1.37	1.09	0.94

Next earnings report expected: late October

Dividend Data (Dividends have been paid since 1978.)

Amount ($)	Date Decl.	Ex-Div. Date	Stock of Record	Payment Date
0.110	Dec. 18	Dec. 23	Dec. 26	Jan. 02 '98
0.110	Feb. 23	Mar. 10	Mar. 12	Apr. 01 '98
0.110	May. 08	Jun. 01	Jun. 03	Jul. 01 '98
0.110	Sep. 10	Sep. 24	Sep. 28	Oct. 06 '98

Business Summary - 05-OCT-98

K2 Inc. (KTO), founded in 1946 as Anthony Pools, has been transformed through acquisitions and internal growth into a $650 million (sales) designer and manufacturer of sporting goods and other recreational products. These include the widely recognized brand names K2 and Olin alpine skis, K2 snowboards, boots and bindings, K2 in-line skates, K2 full-suspension mountain bikes, SHAKESPEARE fishing rods and reels, STEARNS personal flotation devices, rainwear and wet suits and DANA DESIGN and K2 backpacks and hydration systems. The company also produces and markets HILTON corporate casual apparel and K2 ski apparel. K2 Inc.'s industrial products consist primarily of SHAKESPEARE monofilament line which is used mostly in weed trimmers, in paper mills and as fishing line; SHAKESPEARE fiberglass and composite marine antennas, light, transmission and distribution poles; and SIMPLEX coated and laminated products. The swimming pool and motorized pool cover business was sold to General Aquatics Inc. in March 1996.

Foreign markets accounted for 24% of net sales and 16% of operating profits in 1997.

The company's sporting goods and other recreational products (69% of net sales and 56% of pretax profits in 1997) include alpine skis sold under the names K2 and Olin in the three major ski markets of the world: the U.S., Europe and Japan. In recent years, the company has aggressively expanded into several new sporting goods markets in the U.S., Europe and Japan, including in-line skates, snowboards and full-suspension mountain bikes. Management believes these newer products have benefited from the market share positions of other company products, several of which are now among the top brands in their respective markets. For example, in the United States, K2 has the #2 market position in alpine skis, snowboards, boots and bindings, and management believes that STEARNS has the #1 market position in personal flotation devices and that Shakespeare's UGLY STIK is the top selling line of moderately-priced fishing rods.

The industrial products group (31% of net sales and 44% of pretax profits in 1997) consists of SHAKESPEARE monofilament line, fiberglass utility and decorative light poles, marine radio antennas, coated laminated paperboard products, protective building wrap, and synthetic commercial building coatings.

Per Share Data ($)

(Year Ended Dec. 31)	1997	1996	1995	1994	1993	1992	1991	1990	1989	1988
Tangible Bk. Val.	12.21	10.43	9.75	7.02	6.19	5.84	5.61	5.33	5.79	5.03
Cash Flow	2.08	2.17	2.07	1.74	1.71	1.56	1.32	0.98	1.95	1.80
Earnings	1.31	1.51	1.37	1.09	0.94	0.73	0.57	0.24	1.23	1.11
Dividends	0.44	0.44	0.44	0.42	0.40	0.38	0.37	0.35	0.33	0.27
Payout Ratio	34%	29%	32%	39%	43%	53%	64%	149%	27%	25%
Prices - High	32$^7/_8$	30$^1/_8$	23$^1/_4$	17$^1/_2$	15$^3/_4$	12$^3/_4$	9$^5/_8$	13$^1/_2$	15$^3/_8$	10
- Low	22$^3/_8$	20$^3/_8$	15$^1/_8$	13$^7/_8$	10$^7/_8$	8$^5/_8$	5$^1/_4$	4$^7/_8$	8$^1/_2$	5$^1/_2$
P/E Ratio - High	25	20	17	16	17	17	17	57	13	9
- Low	17	13	11	13	12	12	9	21	7	5

Income Statement Analysis (Million $)

	1997	1996	1995	1994	1993	1992	1991	1990	1989	1988
Revs.	647	603	544	502	432	402	370	377	382	308
Oper. Inc.	56.4	55.5	47.3	33.9	30.5	28.2	25.0	20.3	34.9	26.6
Depr.	12.9	11.2	10.2	7.7	9.1	9.7	8.7	8.4	6.8	5.8
Int. Exp.	10.6	9.3	9.9	7.5	5.8	6.8	6.9	8.8	7.9	5.4
Pretax Inc.	31.1	36.5	28.6	20.3	17.0	12.9	10.7	4.5	21.3	16.1
Eff. Tax Rate	30%	31%	31%	36%	34%	34%	38%	39%	37%	36%
Net Inc.	21.9	25.2	19.8	13.0	11.1	8.5	6.6	2.7	13.4	10.3

Balance Sheet & Other Fin. Data (Million $)

	1997	1996	1995	1994	1993	1992	1991	1990	1989	1988
Cash	5.9	10.9	7.4	7.7	5.9	2.1	3.1	2.6	2.8	3.7
Curr. Assets	330	274	300	233	188	169	152	147	144	124
Total Assets	429	368	384	304	257	236	222	221	210	180
Curr. Liab.	123	74.0	121	82.6	70.0	73.1	87.2	78.8	78.6	70.2
LT Debt	88.7	89.1	75.1	110	87.3	68.5	43.5	53.8	44.0	37.8
Common Eqty.	203	189	176	99	88.7	83.6	80.7	78.1	78.1	62.9
Total Cap.	307	294	264	222	187	163	134	142	131	110
Cap. Exp.	23.7	18.8	17.3	11.6	8.7	7.1	5.1	14.0	13.5	16.8
Cash Flow	34.8	36.4	30.0	20.7	20.2	18.2	15.3	11.1	20.3	16.1
Curr. Ratio	2.7	3.7	2.5	2.8	2.7	2.3	1.7	1.9	1.8	1.8
% LT Debt of Cap.	28.9	30.3	28.4	49.6	46.6	42.0	32.3	37.9	33.5	34.4
% Net Inc.of Revs.	3.4	4.2	3.6	2.6	2.6	2.1	1.8	0.7	3.5	3.3
% Ret. on Assets	5.5	6.7	5.8	4.6	4.5	3.7	3.0	1.2	6.6	6.3
% Ret. on Equity	11.2	13.8	14.4	13.9	12.9	10.3	8.3	3.4	18.1	17.4

Data as orig. reptd.; bef. results of disc. opers. and/or spec. items. Per share data adj. for stk. divs. as of ex-div. date. Bold denotes diluted EPS (FASB 128). E-Estimated. NA-Not Available. NM-Not Meaningful. NR-Not Ranked.

Office—4900 South Eastern Ave., Los Angeles, CA 90040.**Tel**—(323) 724-2800. **Chrmn**—B. I. Forester. **Pres & CEO**—R. M. Rodstein. **SVP-Fin & Investor Contact**—John J. Rangel. **Secy**—Susan E. McConnell. **Dirs**—S. E. Engel, B. I. Forester, W. D. Godbold, J. E. Goldress, R. J. Heckmann, S. M. Kasen, J. H. Offermans, R. M. Rodstein, J. B. Simon. **Transfer Agent & Registrar**—Harris Trust Co. of California, LA. **Incorporated**—in Delaware in 1959. **Empl**— 3,800. **S&P Analyst:** C.F.B.

Kaman Corporation
4324

NASDAQ Symbol **KAMNA**

In S&P SmallCap 600

03-OCT-98

Industry: Manufacturing (Diversified)

Summary: This company provides products and services for defense markets, and distributes industrial and commercial products.

Quantitative Evaluations	
Outlook (1 Lowest—5 Highest)	• **NA**
Fair Value	• **NA**
Risk	• **Average**
Earn./Div. Rank	• **B**
Technical Eval.	• **Bullish** since 3/98
Rel. Strength Rank (1 Lowest—99 Highest)	• **82**
Insider Activity	• **NA**

Recent Price • 16½
52 Wk Range • 20⅜-13

Yield • 2.7%
12-Mo. P/E • 4.8

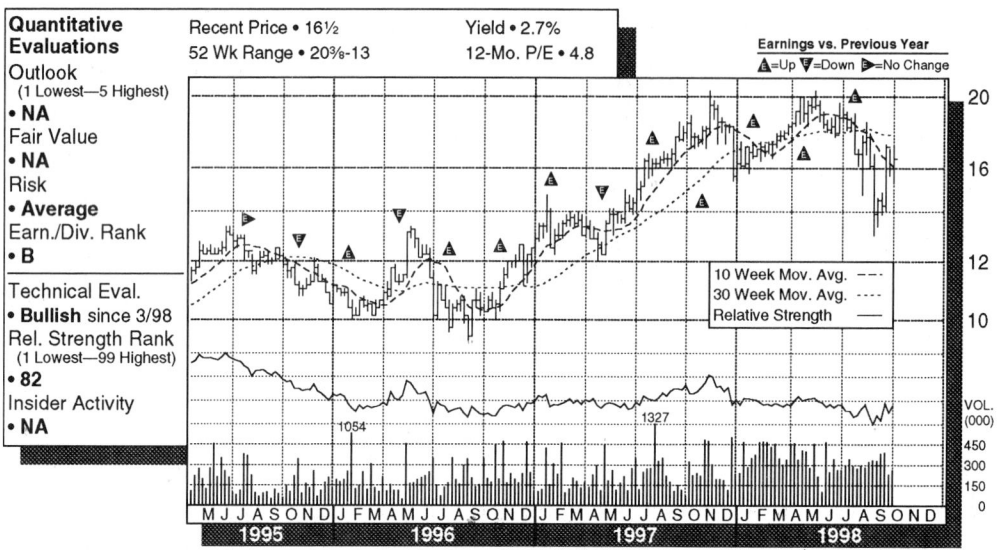

Earnings vs. Previous Year
▲=Up ▼=Down ▷=No Change

10 Week Mov. Avg. – – –
30 Week Mov. Avg. ·····
Relative Strength —

Business Profile - 27-JUL-98

Kaman has been making a transition from being primarily a U.S. defense contractor to operating as a company serving international markets. The diversified technologies segment grew in 1997, aided by aerospace industry trends and the success of certain products. In foreign markets, Kaman signed contracts for SH-2G helicopters, plus support, valued at over $900 million.The Government of Australia ordered 11 Super Seasprites and support, the Arab Republic of Egypt ordered 10 of the multi-mission naval helicopters, and the Government of New Zealand ordered four of the helicopters. In December 1997, the company sold its Kaman Sciences Corp. subsidiary to ITT Industries, Inc. (NYSE: ITT), for $135 million in cash.

Operational Review - 27-JUL-98

Revenues in the six months ended June 30, 1998, declined 3.2%, year to year, in the absence of reveneus from Kaman Sciences Corp. Gross margins widened, but operating expenses rose as a percentage of sales. However, in the absence of a pretax charge of $10.4 million reflecting a loss on the sale of the amplifier business, pretax income soared to $24.7 million, from $4.8 million. After taxes at 40.9%, versus 52.2%, net income surged to $14,593,000 ($0.60 a share), from $445,000 ($0.02, after preferred dividends).

Stock Performance - 02-OCT-98

In the past 30 trading days, KAMNA's shares have increased 2%, compared to a 7% fall in the S&P 500. Average trading volume for the past five days was 52,100 shares, compared with the 40-day moving average of 64,779 shares.

Key Stock Statistics

Dividend Rate/Share	0.44	Shareholders	7,600
Shs. outstg. (M)	23.7	Market cap. (B)	$0.380
Avg. daily vol. (M)	0.066	Inst. holdings	56%
Tang. Bk. Value/Share	12.66		
Beta	0.77		

Value of $10,000 invested 5 years ago: $ 20,287

Fiscal Year Ending Dec. 31

	1998	1997	1996	1995	1994	1993
Revenues (Million $)						
1Q	239.1	252.2	240.0	208.0	198.0	197.9
2Q	247.4	250.3	246.5	221.5	208.6	194.9
3Q	—	270.0	228.0	225.6	198.9	202.5
4Q	—	272.4	239.1	241.3	21.04	197.9
Yr.	—	1,045	953.6	896.4	820.8	794.1
Earnings Per Share ($)						
1Q	0.29	-0.28	0.23	0.25	0.18	0.22
2Q	0.01	0.28	0.24	0.20	0.20	0.26
3Q	—	0.29	0.26	0.20	0.22	-2.36
4Q	—	2.43	0.33	0.21	-1.53	0.23
Yr.	—	2.86	1.06	0.86	-0.93	-1.63

Next earnings report expected: mid October

Dividend Data (Dividends have been paid since 1972.)

Amount ($)	Date Decl.	Ex-Div. Date	Stock of Record	Payment Date
0.110	Nov. 18	Dec. 24	Dec. 29	Jan. 12 '98
0.110	Feb. 10	Mar. 26	Mar. 30	Apr. 13 '98
0.110	Jun. 09	Jun. 25	Jun. 29	Jul. 13 '98
0.110	Aug. 11	Oct. 01	Oct. 05	Oct. 19 '98

A Division of The **McGraw-Hill** Companies

Business Summary - 27-JUL-98

Kaman Corporation (KAMNA) has been reshaping itself, focusing on the development of those of its core areas with the greatest potential, including the aircraft manufacturing, sciences and industrial distribution businesses. The company and its subsidiaries serve defense, industrial and commercial markets in two industry segments: diversified technologies and distribution. Segment contributions to sales and operating profits (in 000s) in 1997 were:

	Sales	Profits
Diversified technologies	41.5%	$44,941
Distribution	58.5%	18,738

The diversified technologies segment provides design and manufacture of advanced technology products and systems, mostly for use on aircraft; and advanced technology services to customers including all branches of the armed forces, government agencies, defense contractors and industrial organizations, including software engineering and maintenance. The segment also provides aircraft manufacturing, including the development and manufacture of helicopters and the integration of systems related to helicopters. The company is the prime contractor for the SH-2 series helicopter, a multi-mission aircraft for the U.S. Navy.

Kaman is a national distributor of industrial products, operating through more than 195 service centers located in 38 states and British Columbia. It supplies a broad range of industries with original equipment, repair and replacement products needed to maintain traditional manufacturing processes and, increasingly, with products of higher technological content that are required to support automated production processes. This segment serves nearly every sector of heavy and light industry, including automobile, agriculture, food processing, pulp and paper, mining, chemicals and electronics. Products include bearings, power transmission equipment, motors, belts and pulleys. The segment also distributes aviation fuel and provides aviation services at Jacksonville International Airport in Florida. Until closing the division in the first quarter of 1997, KAMNA distributed more than 10,000 music instruments and accessories in the U.S. and overseas.

In October 1997, the company rolled out the first of 10 SH-2G Super Seasprite helicopters for delivery to the Arab Republic of Egypt, the first international customer for the aircraft. The value of the contract exceeds $150 million for aircraft and support. Two additional aircraft were delivered by the end of 1997, with the remaining seven scheduled to be delivered in 1998. Other international customers for the SH-2G include Australia and New Zealand, which signed contracts in June 1997 with Kaman for a total of 15 aircraft and support valued at a total of $785 million.

Per Share Data ($)

(Year Ended Dec. 31)	1997	1996	1995	1994	1993	1992	1991	1990	1989	1988
Tangible Bk. Val.	12.12	8.72	8.08	7.60	7.83	9.88	9.33	8.81	8.19	7.94
Cash Flow	3.84	1.72	1.54	-0.21	-0.88	1.68	1.67	1.79	1.19	2.05
Earnings	2.86	1.06	0.86	-0.93	-1.63	0.95	0.93	1.06	0.48	1.42
Dividends	0.44	0.44	0.44	0.44	0.44	0.44	0.44	0.44	0.44	0.42
Payout Ratio	15%	42%	51%	NM	NM	46%	47%	42%	92%	30%
Prices - High	20³/₈	13³/₈	13³/₈	11¹/₈	12¹/₈	10³/₄	9⁵/₈	9¹/₂	14⁷/₈	18¹/₂
- Low	12	9³/₈	10	8¹/₈	8⁵/₈	7⁷/₈	7³/₈	6	7⁵/₈	12¹/₄
P/E Ratio - High	7	13	16	NM	NM	11	10	9	31	13
- Low	4	9	12	NM	NM	8	8	6	16	9

Income Statement Analysis (Million $)

	1997	1996	1995	1994	1993	1992	1991	1990	1989	1988
Revs.	1,043	954	896	819	793	783	778	825	801	767
Oper. Inc.	58.9	58.2	51.7	46.6	44.1	48.0	48.6	56.0	41.1	63.2
Depr.	12.2	12.4	12.7	13.1	13.5	13.4	13.6	13.5	12.8	11.2
Int. Exp.	7.9	10.0	8.8	4.7	7.0	7.1	8.2	11.3	12.1	10.1
Pretax Inc.	120	40.7	32.7	-14.2	-40.5	29.0	28.3	32.8	16.6	42.2
Eff. Tax Rate	41%	42%	40%	NM	NM	40%	40%	41%	48%	40%
Net Inc.	70.5	23.6	19.6	-13.2	-28.8	17.4	17.0	19.2	8.7	25.3

Balance Sheet & Other Fin. Data (Million $)

	1997	1996	1995	1994	1993	1992	1991	1990	1989	1988
Cash	110	5.5	4.1	3.7	3.8	2.5	3.3	3.2	8.7	10.1
Curr. Assets	535	434	405	339	317	335	310	327	319	298
Total Assets	598	522	500	443	440	443	422	444	441	420
Curr. Liab.	260	196	206	193	167	122	111	117	119	110
LT Debt	29.9	83.9	66.4	37.0	38.0	101	102	123	131	123
Common Eqty.	253	171	157	147	171	210	202	193	183	179
Total Cap.	320	312	294	241	266	317	307	323	321	310
Cap. Exp.	13.7	8.0	11.5	21.6	20.4	10.6	8.6	9.6	12.4	19.5
Cash Flow	79.0	32.2	28.6	-3.8	-16.0	30.7	30.6	32.7	21.5	36.5
Curr. Ratio	2.1	2.2	2.0	1.8	1.9	2.7	2.8	2.8	2.7	2.7
% LT Debt of Cap.	9.4	26.9	22.6	15.5	14.3	31.8	33.2	38.2	40.7	39.8
% Net Inc.of Revs.	6.8	2.5	2.2	NM	NM	2.2	2.2	2.3	1.1	3.3
% Ret. on Assets	12.6	4.7	4.2	NM	NM	4.0	3.9	4.3	2.0	6.3
% Ret. on Equity	31.4	12.2	12.9	NM	NM	8.5	8.6	10.2	4.8	14.9

Data as orig. reptd.; bef. results of disc. opers. and/or spec. items. Per share data adj. for stk. divs. as of ex-div. date. E-Estimated. NA-Not Available. NM-Not Meaningful. NR-Not Ranked.

Office—1332 Blue Hills Ave., P.O. Box 1, Bloomfield, CT 06002. **Tel**—(860) 243-7100. **Website**—http://www.kaman.com **Chrmn, Pres & CEO**—C. H. Kaman. **EVP & CFO**—R. M. Garneau. **VP & Secy**—G. M. Messemer. **Investor Contact**—J. Kenneth Nasshan (860-243-7319). **Dirs**—B. E. Barents, F. A. Breidenback, E. R. Callaway III, F. C. Carlucci, L. J. Chouest, J. A. DiBiaggio, E. J. Gaines, H. Hardisty, C. H. Kaman, C. W. Kaman II, E. S. Kraus, H. Z. Lebed, W. H. Monteith Jr., J. S. Murtha, W. L. Rogers. **Transfer Agent**—Chase Bank, NYC. **Incorporated**—in Connecticut in 1945. **Empl**— 4,318. **S&P Analyst:** M.C.C.

STANDARD &POOR'S
STOCK REPORTS

Kellwood Co.

1289M

NYSE Symbol **KWD**

In S&P SmallCap 600

03-OCT-98

Industry: Textiles (Apparel)

Summary: This global manufacturer and marketer of apparel and recreational camping products offers branded apparel, as well as private-label products.

S&P Opinion: Accumulate (★★★★)

| Recent Price • 26½ | Yield • 2.4% |
| 52 Wk Range • 37-26¼ | 12-Mo. P/E • 13.5 |

Earnings vs. Previous Year
▲=Up ▼=Down ▶=No Change

Quantitative Evaluations

Outlook
(1 Lowest—5 Highest)
• **4⁻**

Fair Value
• **35⅛**

Risk
• **Low**

Earn./Div. Rank
• **B+**

Technical Eval.
• **Bullish** since 1/98

Rel. Strength Rank
(1 Lowest—99 Highest)
• **50**

Insider Activity
• **Neutral**

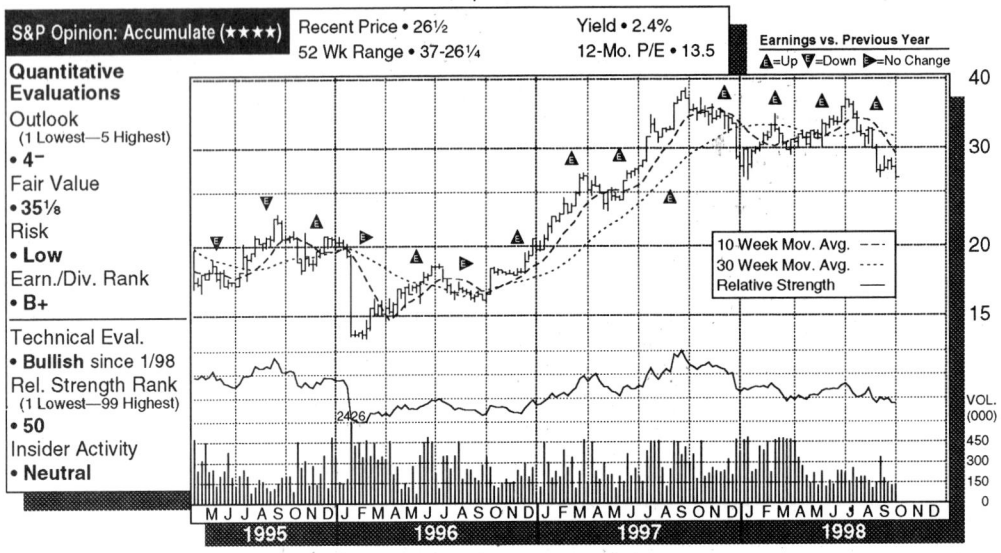

10 Week Mov. Avg. - - - -
30 Week Mov. Avg. · · · ·
Relative Strength ——

VOL. (000)

MJJASONDJFMAMJJASONDJFMAMJJASONDJFMAMJJASOND
1995 1996 1997 1998

Overview - 17-SEP-98

Propelled by new customers, marketing initiatives, the turnaround of restructured divisions, and market share gains, we expect approximately 5% sales growth for FY 99 (Apr.). With strong demand for popular-to-moderate brand names such as Sag Harbor, Kathie Lee and Cricket Lane, Kellwood continues to gain market share with leading retailers. The company believes that its largest brand, Sag Harbor, could reach sales of $900 million in FY 00, an achievable goal considering its past success. In FY 99, we expect margins to be restricted by Vision 2000 spending, particularly in the first half of the year. In FY 99, total spending for Vision 2000, a cost saving program, is expected to be approximately $0.48 a share, $0.10 higher than in FY 98. However, margins should widen due to improved efficiencies, aided by the Vision 2000 program. Increased interest expense will also hamper profitability. However, given the solid business trends, we anticipate FY 99 EPS growth of about 18%.

Valuation - 17-SEP-98

We recommend accumulation of KWD shares based on KWD's ability to grow faster than the overall apparel industry and to improve its cost structure. The Sag Harbor brand is gaining market share and growing revenues at a brisk pace. We expect this trend to continue. Furthermore, KWD is aggressively pursuing additional strategies which should ensure solid revenue and earnings growth for the next few years. Kellwood's efforts to diversify its product mix, strengthen its presence in every channel of distribution, and increase its overseas sourcing leads us to believe that it is one of the best positioned apparel makers to benefit from a push by mass merchandisers and discounters to broaden their apparel offerings. With a 2.3% yield, the stock remains attractive at 12X our FY 99 estimate of $2.30.

Key Stock Statistics

S&P EPS Est. 1999	2.30	Tang. Bk. Value/Share	12.96
P/E on S&P Est. 1999	11.5	Beta	0.38
Dividend Rate/Share	0.64	Shareholders	1,600
Shs. outstg. (M)	21.6	Market cap. (B)	$0.573
Avg. daily vol. (M)	0.031	Inst. holdings	76%

Value of $10,000 invested 5 years ago: $ 17,024

Fiscal Year Ending Apr. 30

	1999	1998	1997	1996	1995	1994
Revenues (Million $)						
1Q	427.7	400.6	327.4	340.6	300.9	298.5
2Q	—	502.9	429.4	425.6	376.0	342.1
3Q	—	373.7	315.8	288.5	291.5	251.6
4Q	—	504.4	448.3	411.3	396.3	310.9
Yr.	—	1,782	1,521	1,466	1,365	1,203
Earnings Per Share ($)						
1Q	**0.35**	0.34	0.27	0.27	0.51	0.48
2Q	**E0.80**	0.77	0.68	0.66	0.53	0.51
3Q	**E0.15**	0.11	0.10	-0.10	-0.10	0.17
4Q	**E1.00**	0.76	0.73	0.49	-0.41	0.55
Yr.	**E2.30**	1.95	1.78	1.32	0.53	1.71

Next earnings report expected: late November

Dividend Data (Dividends have been paid since 1962.)

Amount ($)	Date Decl.	Ex-Div. Date	Stock of Record	Payment Date
0.160	Nov. 25	Dec. 03	Dec. 05	Dec. 19 '97
0.160	Feb. 26	Mar. 05	Mar. 09	Mar. 20 '98
0.160	May. 28	Jun. 04	Jun. 08	Jun. 19 '98
0.160	Aug. 27	Sep. 03	Sep. 08	Sep. 18 '98

A Division of The McGraw-Hill Companies

Business Summary - 17-SEP-98

Growing through 14 acquisitions since 1985, Kellwood has become one of the leading manufacturers of women's apparel. The company has expanded due to the success of its business strategy which began in the mid-1980's and continued through the mid-1990's. KWD's goals were to increase its branded label products, its customer base, its channels of distribution and its global sourcing. As a result of achieving these goals, KWD now has revenues of over $1.7 billion annually.

Kellwood traces its origins to 1961, when the company was created to manufacture clothing lines strictly for Sears. KWD has evolved into a diverse company, with 33 operating plants worldwide. By FY 98 (Apr.), Sears accounted for only 8% of total revenues, compared with 50% in FY 85.

Its three divisions are: brandname apparel (accounting for 74% of FY 98 sales), domestic private-label apparel (16%) and the Far East (10%). In addition, the company sells camping products through American Recreational Products and Slumberjack.

The branded apparel business includes women's labels such as Sag Harbor, Kathie Lee and Cricket Lane. The Far East operations produce private label shirts and blouses in Hong Kong, China and Sri Lanka. During the fourth quarter of FY 97 (Apr.), KWD began shipping products for Polo Ralph Lauren.

In recent years, consumption in the apparel industry has risen only slightly. However, due to the strength of its popular-to-moderate line of apparel, Kellwood managed to increase its sales by 17% in FY 98 and 4% in FY 97. To reduce costs, offshore sourcing has increased over the years. In addition to manufacturing products at its own manufacturing facilities, KWD also sources products through outside contractors.

In 1995, KWD embarked on a restructuring plan called Vision 2000, designed to align internal capabilities with customer needs. Under phase one of Vision 2000, which was largely completed at the end of FY 96, KWD restructured its assets and consolidated certain divisions. Phase two, which involves operational functions such as systems, logistics, warehousing, distribution and finance, began in FY 97, and will be the main focus of Vision 2000 initiative. In FY 98, Vision 2000 spending was approximately $14.4 million, up $11.1 million from FY 97. For FY 99, it is anticipated that spending for Vision 2000 will increase sharply, with most of the spending in the first half of the year.

Per Share Data ($)

(Year Ended Apr. 30)	1998	1997	1996	1995	1994	1993	1992	1991	1990	1989
Tangible Bk. Val.	12.96	11.08	9.65	8.36	9.51	8.87	9.40	7.68	7.51	7.42
Cash Flow	3.99	3.12	2.66	1.87	2.91	2.42	2.29	1.70	1.78	2.72
Earnings	1.95	1.78	1.32	0.53	1.71	1.39	1.26	0.71	0.80	1.93
Dividends	0.64	0.60	0.60	0.60	0.55	0.53	0.53	0.53	0.53	0.49
Payout Ratio	33%	34%	45%	113%	32%	38%	48%	76%	67%	26%
Cal. Yrs.	1997	1996	1995	1994	1993	1992	1991	1990	1989	1988
Prices - High	38½	20⅞	22⅞	26⅞	27⅛	22⅛	17⅞	15¼	23⅝	20⅝
- Low	19⅝	13⅝	16½	19⅛	15⅞	14¼	6¼	3½	13⅝	12
P/E Ratio - High	20	12	17	51	16	16	14	22	29	11
- Low	10	8	12	36	9	10	5	5	17	6

Income Statement Analysis (Million $)

	1998	1997	1996	1995	1994	1993	1992	1991	1990	1989
Revs.	1,782	1,521	1,466	1,365	1,203	1,078	915	808	780	754
Oper. Inc.	146	128	113	87.4	96.1	80.0	66.0	48.0	47.9	71.4
Depr.	44.8	28.3	28.2	28.3	25.1	21.3	18.5	17.6	17.3	13.7
Int. Exp.	28.9	21.6	22.9	19.1	15.6	13.8	14.2	16.1	17.1	15.5
Pretax Inc.	73.9	64.8	48.5	28.5	61.0	51.9	41.5	22.6	21.6	49.3
Eff. Tax Rate	42%	42%	42%	61%	42%	45%	45%	45%	35%	32%
Net Inc.	42.7	37.6	28.0	11.1	35.6	28.7	22.8	12.4	14.0	33.5

Balance Sheet & Other Fin. Data (Million $)

	1998	1997	1996	1995	1994	1993	1992	1991	1990	1989
Cash	31.8	22.5	25.0	11.1	17.7	39.2	40.8	41.3	44.1	30.0
Curr. Assets	759	622	544	511	413	426	364	321	310	298
Total Assets	1,016	875	797	768	642	636	538	484	469	447
Curr. Liab.	343	374	306	274	151	228	145	143	128	149
LT Debt	243	110	125	145	153	103	111	120	128	94.0
Common Eqty.	384	348	325	308	307	280	260	200	197	191
Total Cap.	673	500	490	491	490	407	389	338	337	295
Cap. Exp.	18.4	11.6	16.4	11.7	12.5	16.8	12.6	10.4	9.7	7.4
Cash Flow	87.5	65.9	56.2	39.4	60.7	50.0	41.4	30.0	31.3	47.2
Curr. Ratio	2.2	1.7	1.8	1.9	2.7	1.9	2.5	2.2	2.4	2.0
% LT Debt of Cap.	36.1	21.9	25.6	29.5	31.2	25.3	28.4	35.5	38.0	31.9
% Net Inc.of Revs.	2.4	2.5	1.9	0.8	3.0	2.7	2.5	1.5	1.8	4.4
% Ret. on Assets	4.5	4.5	3.6	1.6	5.5	4.9	4.2	2.6	3.0	7.8
% Ret. on Equity	11.7	11.2	8.8	3.6	12.1	10.6	9.3	6.3	7.2	18.7

Data as orig. reptd.; bef. results of disc. opers. and/or spec. items. Per share data adj. for stk. divs. as of ex-div. date. Bold denotes diluted EPS (FASB 128). E-Estimated. NA-Not Available. NM-Not Meaningful. NR-Not Ranked.

Office—600 Kellwood Parkway, P.O. Box 14374, St. Louis, MO 63178. **Tel**—(314) 576-3100. **Website**—http://www.kwdco.com **Chrmn** —W. J. McKenna. **Vice Chrmn**—J. C. Jacobsen. **Pres, CEO & COO**—H. J. Upbin. **VP, Treas & Investor Contact**—Roger D. Joseph. **VP & Secy**—T. H. Pollihan. **Dirs**—R. F. Bentele, E. S. Bottum, K. G. Dickerson, L. Genovese, J. M. Hunter, J. C. Jacobsen, J. S. Marcus, W. J. McKenna, H. J. Upbin, F. W. Wenzel (Chrmn Emeritus). **Transfer Agent & Registrar**—KeyCorp Shareholder Services, Cleveland. **Incorporated**—in Delaware in 1961. **Empl**— 18,400. **S&P Analyst:** Kathleen J. Fraser

KEMET Corp. 4339

Nasdaq Symbol **KMET**

In S&P SmallCap 600

03-OCT-98

Industry: Electrical Equipment

Summary: KEMET manufactures and supplies solid tantalum capacitors and multilayer ceramic capacitors.

S&P Opinion: Hold (★★★)	Recent Price • 10	Yield • Nil
	52 Wk Range • 30¼-8¾	12-Mo. P/E • 10.8

Quantitative Evaluations

Outlook (1 Lowest—5 Highest)
• 4

Fair Value
• 17

Risk
• High

Earn./Div. Rank
• NR

Technical Eval.
• Bearish since 9/98

Rel. Strength Rank (1 Lowest—99 Highest)
• 32

Insider Activity
• NA

Earnings vs. Previous Year
▲=Up ▼=Down ▶=No Change

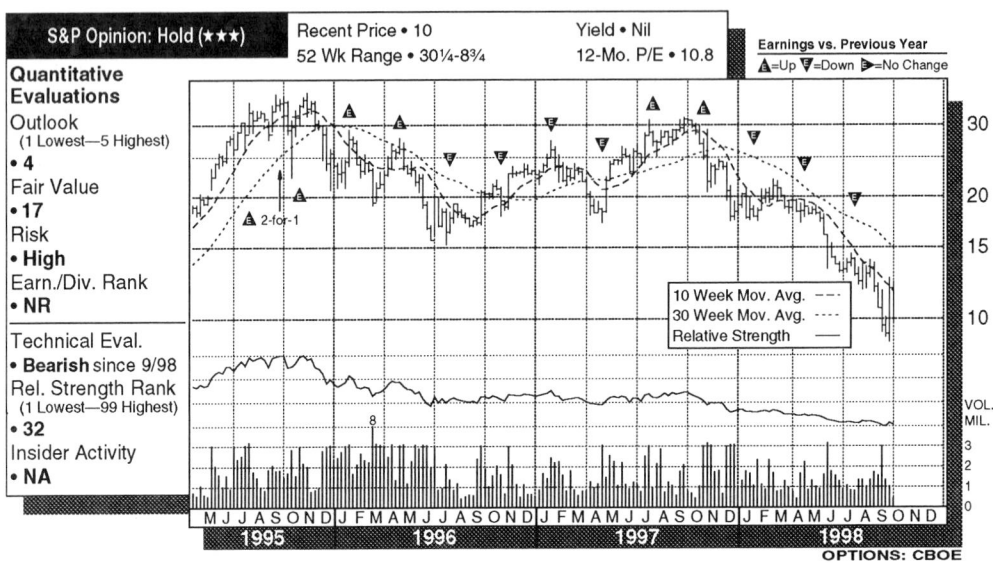

10 Week Mov. Avg. -- -
30 Week Mov. Avg. - - - -
Relative Strength —

OPTIONS: CBOE

Overview - 30-JUL-98

We expect revenues to fall approximately 8% in FY 99 (Mar.), as demand for surface-mount products is restricted by excess inventory at OEMs and distributors. Capacitor prices, which generally fall throughout the product life cycle, declined twice as fast as normal in FY 97, as high industry-wide inventories led to weak demand. Although business conditions improved over the course of FY 98, a further inventory build-up in the PC industry limits near-term prospects. We expect continued pricing pressures and unfavorable currency fluctuations to limit top-line growth. While margins have been negatively affected by sharply higher palladium prices, the company plans a 30% reduction in palladium content per unit in FY 99, in order to mitigate the future impact. In addition, a recent restructuring is expected to result in annual savings of $14 million. Overall, we expect EPS to decline to $0.65 in FY 99, from FY 98's $1.43 (before charges).

Valuation - 30 JUL 08

We are maintaining our neutral recommendation on the shares, reflecting weak near-term demand for the company's capacitor products, as well as limited visibility. Although KMET's products are used for a broad base of applications in a variety of industries with good growth prospects, excess inventory levels will result in slower bookings and shipments. To counter the impact of this cyclical downturn, KMET has taken proactive steps, such as cutting headcount and capital expenditures. As a result, we expect the company's financial condition to remain strong. However, given the overall unfavorable tenor of business conditions, we believe that the shares are fully valued at a recent level of 19X our FY 99 EPS estimate of $0.65.

Key Stock Statistics

S&P EPS Est. 1999	0.65	Tang. Bk. Value/Share	6.62
P/E on S&P Est. 1999	15.4	Beta	1.09
Dividend Rate/Share	Nil	Shareholders	200
Shs. outstg. (M)	39.2	Market cap. (B)	$0.381
Avg. daily vol. (M)	0.296	Inst. holdings	61%

Value of $10,000 invested 5 years ago: $ 18,390

Fiscal Year Ending Mar. 31

	1999	1998	1997	1996	1995	1994
Revenues (Million $)						
1Q	142.5	161.2	125.7	152.5	110.2	96.20
2Q	—	165.5	130.2	160.7	110.2	90.50
3Q	—	170.4	143.6	160.1	112.3	95.04
4Q	—	170.7	155.8	160.8	140.4	103.4
Yr.	—	667.7	555.3	634.2	473.2	385.1
Earnings Per Share ($)						
1Q	0.04	0.36	0.25	0.33	0.17	0.13
2Q	E0.17	0.31	0.01	0.38	0.17	0.08
3Q	E0.20	0.19	0.31	0.44	0.17	0.10
4Q	E0.25	0.34	0.38	0.52	0.29	0.15
Yr.	E0.65	1.25	0.95	1.67	0.80	0.46

Next earnings report expected: late October

Dividend Data

No cash dividends have been paid. The company has said it does not expect to pay cash dividends in the foreseeable future.

A Division of The McGraw·Hill Companies

Business Summary - 30-JUL-98

As the world's largest manufacturer of solid tantalum capacitors and the second largest manufacturer of ceramic capacitors, KEMET is well positioned to participate in the continued rapid growth of the electronics industry. Capacitors are used in virtually all electronics applications and products to store, filter and regulate electrical energy and current flow. For example, these components are used in computers, cellular phones and watches, as well as in communications, data processing, automotive, military and aerospace systems.

Following a challenging year in FY 97 (Mar.), the company's operations recovered somewhat in FY 98, as sales increased by 20%. The major contributor to improved performance was increased demand for tantalum and ceramic surface-mount products. During the year, surface-mount capacitor sales rose 29%, accounting for over 77% of total revenues. This growth reflected KMET's investment in surface-mount capacity to meet increasing customer demand. In the first quarter of FY 99, however, the company reported that the financial crisis in Asia, combined with excess channel inventory, had depressed shipments. Furthermore, lower average selling prices due to supply/demand imbalances, and elevated palladium prices contributed to lower earnings.

Despite the uncertainty in the marketplace, KMET has prepared for the future during the last two years. It has spent a total of $114.5 million in capital expansion for the tantalum and ceramic business units, thereby increasing its capacity to more than 26 billion units annually. The company expects to spend an additional $60 million in FY 99.

Currently, the vast majority of the company's manufacturing efforts are focused on the fastest growing segments of the capacitor industry: tantalum and ceramic capacitors. Both types of capacitors are commonly used in conjunction with integrated circuits and are best suited for applications requiring lower- to medium-capacitance values. Generally, ceramic capacitors are more cost-effective at lower capacitance values, while tantalum capacitors are more cost-effective at medium capacitance values. Demand for both products tends to reflect general demand for electronic components.

In November 1997, KMET reorganized its corporate structure along the tantalum and ceramic business units, in order to facilitate better response to its customer needs. In addition, the company announced plans to phase out the manufacture of multilayer ceramic chips at its North Carolina facility over a 10-month period. The restructuring is expected to generate annual savings of approximately $14 million.

Per Share Data ($)

(Year Ended Mar. 31)	1998	1997	1996	1995	1994	1993	1992	1991	1990	1989
Tangible Bk. Val.	6.63	5.25	3.84	1.92	1.09	1.68	-2.02	NA	NA	NA
Cash Flow	2.23	1.80	2.63	2.97	1.11	1.44	1.84	NA	NA	NA
Earnings	1.25	0.95	1.67	0.80	0.46	0.44	-2.19	NA	NA	NA
Dividends	Nil	Nil	Nil	Nil	Nil	Nil	Nil	Nil	Nil	Nil
Payout Ratio	Nil	Nil	Nil	Nil	Nil	Nil	Nil	Nil	Nil	Nil
Cal. Yrs.	1997	1996	1995	1994	1993	1992	1991	1990	1989	1988
Prices - High	$31^3/_8$	$29^1/_4$	$36^1/_8$	$14^7/_8$	10	$7^1/_4$	NA	NA	NA	NA
- Low	$17^1/_4$	$15^1/_4$	$12^7/_8$	7	$6^1/_2$	5	NA	NA	NA	NA
P/E Ratio - High	25	31	22	18	22	16	NA	NA	NA	NA
- Low	14	16	8	9	14	11	NA	NA	NA	NA

Income Statement Analysis (Million $)

Revs.	668	555	634	473	385	348	294	NA	NA	NA
Oper. Inc.	132	111	158	89.5	61.3	62.2	45.7	NA	NA	NA
Depr.	38.9	33.5	37.9	26.3	24.5	23.3	54.0	NA	NA	NA
Int. Exp.	7.3	5.7	4.9	6.9	8.9	19.1	24.6	NA	NA	NA
Pretax Inc.	70.8	54.4	105	50.3	26.4	20.9	-35.4	NA	NA	NA
Eff. Tax Rate	31%	32%	38%	39%	37%	37%	NM	NM	NM	NM
Net Inc.	49.2	37.2	65.2	31.0	16.7	11.1	-28.2	NA	NA	NA

Balance Sheet & Other Fin. Data (Million $)

Cash	1.8	2.2	3.4	4.2	2.6	2.3	1.7	NA	NA	NA
Curr. Assets	195	170	155	128	115	103	86.0	NA	NA	NA
Total Assets	642	543	490	387	362	353	339	NA	NA	NA
Curr. Liab.	146	107	122	97.7	71.2	78.2	60.8	NA	NA	NA
LT Debt	104	103	78.1	77.0	107	147	188	NA	NA	NA
Common Eqty.	306	252	212	139	108	52.5	-29.5	NA	NA	NA
Total Cap.	426	368	318	246	250	232	229	NA	NA	NA
Cap. Exp.	115	84.8	120	42.8	29.3	23.1	23.3	NA	NA	NA
Cash Flow	88.0	70.7	103	57.3	41.3	33.6	24.6	NA	NA	NA
Curr. Ratio	1.3	1.6	1.3	1.3	1.6	1.3	1.4	NA	NA	NA
% LT Debt of Cap.	24.4	28.0	24.5	31.1	43.0	63.3	82.2	NA	NA	NA
% Net Inc.of Revs.	7.4	6.7	10.3	6.5	4.3	3.2	NM	NM	NM	NM
% Ret. on Assets	8.3	7.2	14.9	8.3	4.3	2.1	NM	NM	NM	NM
% Ret. on Equity	17.6	16.0	37.2	25.1	19.5	NM	NM	NM	NM	NM

Data as orig. reptd.; bef. results of disc. opers. and/or spec. items. Per share data adj. for stk. divs. as of ex-div. date. Bold denotes diluted EPS (FASB 128). E-Estimated. NA-Not Available. NM-Not Meaningful. NR-Not Ranked.

Office—2835 Kemet Way, Simpsonville, SC 29681. **Tel**—(864) 963-6300. **Website**—http://www.kemet.com **Chrmn, Pres & CEO**—D. E. Maguire. **SVP & Treas**—D. R. Cash. **SVP & Secy & Investor Contact**—Glenn H. Spears (864-963-6674). **Dirs**—S. A. Kohl, E. E. Maddrey II, D. E. Maguire, P. C. Schorr IV, C. E. Volpe. **Transfer Agent & Registrar**—Wachovia Corp., Winston-Salem, NC. **Incorporated**—in Delaware in 1990.**Empl**—10,700. **S&P Analyst:** B. McGovern

Kent Electronics

1292M

NYSE Symbol **KNT**

In S&P SmallCap 600

10-OCT-98

Industry:
Electronics (Component Distributors)

Summary: Kent is a national specialty electronics distributor and a multi-plant custom contract manufacturer.

Quantitative Evaluations

Recent Price · 8½

Yield · Nil

52 Wk Range · 41⅝-7½

12-Mo. P/E · 7.8

Outlook
(1 Lowest—5 Highest)
· **5**

Fair Value
· 16¾

Risk
· **High**

Earn./Div. Rank
· **B+**

Technical Eval.
· **Bearish** since 11/97

Rel. Strength Rank
(1 Lowest—99 Highest)
· **21**

Insider Activity
· **Neutral**

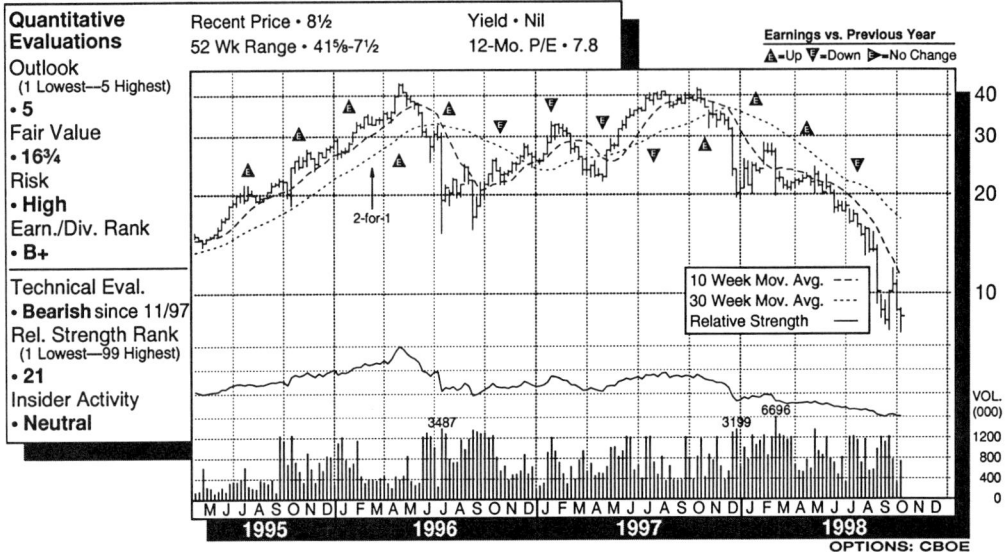

Earnings vs. Previous Year
▲=Up ▼=Down ▶=No Change

10 Week Mov. Avg. - - -
30 Week Mov. Avg. ·····
Relative Strength —

OPTIONS: CBOE

Business Profile - 19-AUG-98

KNT shares have been plunging since October 1997, as results have been penalized by lower manufacturing revenues, facility underutilization and pricing pressure in the semiconductor and computer industries. Looking forward, management expects FY 99 (Mar.) second quarter earnings to fall below the first quarter level. However, the company believes results will begin to improve, on a sequential basis, beginning in the third quarter.

Operational Review - 19-AUG-98

Net sales in the 13 weeks ended June 27, 1998, rose 3.3%, year to year, driven by an increase in distribution sales, largely offset by a decline in manufacturing revenues. Margins narrowed significantly, reflecting underutilization of facilities, a less favorable product mix and pricing pressure; operating income fell 41%. Further penalized by a jump in depreciation and amortization charges, and after taxes at 39.2%, versus 39.5%, net income plummeted 53%, to $4,108,000 ($0.15 a share), from $8,775,000 ($0.32).

Stock Performance - 09-OCT-98

In the past 30 trading days, KNT's shares have declined 16%, compared to a 4% fall in the S&P 500. Average trading volume for the past five days was 145,400 shares, compared with the 40-day moving average of 180,064 shares.

Key Stock Statistics

Dividend Rate/Share	Nil	Shareholders	137,800
Shs. outstg. (M)	27.3	Market cap. (B)	$0.232
Avg. daily vol. (M)	0.159	Inst. holdings	47%
Tang. Bk. Value/Share	11.17		
Beta	1.90		

Value of $10,000 invested 5 years ago: $ 10,049

Fiscal Year Ending Mar. 31

	1999	1998	1997	1996	1995	1994
Revenues (Million $)						
1Q	157.1	152.1	125.1	77.59	56.53	43.25
2Q	—	167.5	124.0	90.19	60.34	46.91
3Q	—	177.4	126.4	100.1	64.46	49.24
4Q	—	162.4	141.2	104.2	72.16	53.49
Yr.	—	659.4	516.8	372.0	253.5	192.9
Earnings Per Share ($)						
1Q	0.15	0.32	0.34	0.23	0.14	0.11
2Q	—	0.34	0.25	0.28	0.16	0.12
3Q	—	0.36	0.25	0.33	0.17	0.13
4Q	—	0.25	0.16	0.36	0.19	0.13
Yr.	—	1.26	1.00	1.22	0.66	0.48

Next earnings report expected: early October

Dividend Data

The company has not paid any cash dividends. A three-for-two stock split was effected March 1, 1995, for shareholders of record February 15. A two-for-one stock split was effected March 1, 1996, for shareholders of record February 15.

A Division of The McGraw-Hill Companies

Business Summary - 19-AUG-98

Kent Electronics is a national specialty distributor of electronic products and a manufacturer of custom-made electronic products. The company has strategically aligned its operations into four distinct, yet complementary, business units — Kent Components, Kent Datacom, Futronix Systems and K*TEC.

Kent Components distributes electronic connectors, wire and cable, capacitors, resistors and other passive and electromechanical components to original equipment manufacturers (OEMs) and industrial customers.

Kent Datacomm designs, delivers, installs and supports a broad range of networking products used in local area networks (LANs) and wide area networks (WANs). The unit offers a variety of voice and data communications products, such as network interface cards, switches, hubs, routers, modems, connectivity devices, fiber optics and copper cabling.

Futronix Systems is a redistributor of specialty wire and cable to electrical distributors worldwide. The unit provides just-in-time availability of exact quantities of specialty wire and cable products, as well as limited quantities of complementary products.

KNT's contract manufacturing subsidiary, K*TEC Electronics, produces a wide array of products, including electronic interconnect assemblies, printed circuit board assemblies, sheet metal fabrication, powder painting and plastic injection molding, among others.

Among the company's strategic initiatives is the provision of a continuum of services, from order fulfillment to direct distribution, to OEMs. Looking forward, KNT expects to experience a shift toward technology-based materials management services. Another aspect of Kent's strategic plan is the pursuit of acquisitions, which will arise as a result of increasing demand on suppliers by OEMs for integrated, technology-based solutions. The company has also expanded its professional services, which includes product configuration and network monitoring, in response to greater demand for value-added services. Finally, KNT believes it will be able to achieve synergies among its four operating units, including cross-selling opportunities, purchasing discounts, ease of geographic expansion and shared warehousing and materials handling capabilities.

Per Share Data ($)

(Year Ended Mar. 31)	1998	1997	1996	1995	1994	1993	1992	1991	1990	1989
Tangible Bk. Val.	10.91	9.37	8.88	4.87	4.08	3.33	2.84	1.93	1.56	1.70
Cash Flow	1.67	1.28	1.41	0.85	0.64	0.55	0.45	0.43	0.34	0.30
Earnings	1.26	1.00	1.22	0.66	0.48	0.40	0.34	0.31	0.26	0.23
Dividends	Nil	Nil	Nil	Nil	Nil	Nil	Nil	Nil	Nil	Nil
Payout Ratio	Nil	Nil	Nil	Nil	Nil	Nil	Nil	Nil	Nil	Nil
Cal. Yrs.	1997	1996	1995	1994	1993	1992	1991	1990	1989	1988
Prices - High	42⅛	43¾	30	13½	9⅝	8⅝	6¾	5	3⅛	2¾
- Low	19½	15¼	12⅞	8⅞	6⅝	5⅝	3⅝	2⁷/₁₆	1⅞	1¹³/₁₆
P/E Ratio - High	33	44	25	20	20	22	20	16	12	12
- Low	15	15	11	13	14	14	10	8	7	8

Income Statement Analysis (Million $)

	1998	1997	1996	1995	1994	1993	1992	1991	1990	1989
Revs.	659	517	372	253	193	155	94.7	71.0	47.5	36.5
Oper. Inc.	68.0	54.6	47.0	24.8	17.8	14.3	9.7	7.0	4.8	3.6
Depr.	11.6	7.5	4.3	3.8	3.2	2.8	1.8	1.3	0.9	0.6
Int. Exp.	5.3	1.2	0.0	0.0	0.0	0.0	0.0	0.1	0.1	0.1
Pretax Inc.	58.2	45.1	46.9	22.1	15.4	12.2	9.2	6.0	4.6	3.4
Eff. Tax Rate	39%	39%	40%	39%	38%	37%	37%	37%	35%	35%
Net Inc.	35.4	27.6	28.0	13.4	9.5	7.7	5.8	3.8	3.0	2.2

Balance Sheet & Other Fin. Data (Million $)

	1998	1997	1996	1995	1994	1993	1992	1991	1990	1989
Cash	180	25.0	112	21.3	26.6	22.2	22.9	6.1	4.7	8.8
Curr. Assets	437	212	217	91.1	77.9	63.1	55.7	23.0	18.9	18.3
Total Assets	592	326	277	134	115	100	85.9	35.9	30.6	23.7
Curr. Liab.	70.3	61.5	51.0	24.8	22.0	16.7	13.6	6.7	5.9	3.1
LT Debt	209	1.7	Nil	Nil	Nil	Nil	Nil	0.7	0.8	1.0
Common Eqty.	313	262	225	109	92.5	81.7	71.6	28.1	23.7	19.4
Total Cap.	522	264	226	109	92.5	83.0	72.4	29.2	24.7	20.6
Cap. Exp.	46.9	50.8	21.0	10.0	5.8	9.2	5.7	1.9	2.0	2.0
Cash Flow	47.0	35.1	32.3	17.2	12.7	10.6	7.5	5.1	3.8	2.8
Curr. Ratio	6.2	3.5	4.2	3.7	3.5	3.8	4.1	3.4	3.2	5.9
% LT Debt of Cap.	40.0	0.6	NM	Nil	Nil	Nil	Nil	2.5	3.2	4.9
% Net Inc.of Revs.	5.4	5.3	7.5	5.3	4.9	5.0	6.1	5.3	6.2	6.0
% Ret. on Assets	7.7	8.7	13.6	10.7	8.9	8.2	8.1	11.3	10.7	9.7
% Ret. on Equity	12.3	11.1	16.8	13.2	10.9	10.0	9.9	14.4	13.4	12.5

Data as orig. reptd.; bef. results of disc. opers. and/or spec. items. Per share data adj. for stk. divs. as of ex-div. date. Bold denotes diluted EPS (FASB 128). E-Estimated. NA-Not Available. NM-Not Meaningful. NR-Not Ranked.

Office—1111 Gillingham Lane, Sugar Land, TX 77478.**Tel**—(281) 243-4000. **Chrmn, Pres & CEO**—M. K. Abramson. **VP, Treas, Secy & Investor Contact**—Stephen J. Chapko. **Dirs**—M. K. Abramson, T. M. Hunt, M. S. Levit, L. D. Olson, D. Siegel, R. C. Webb, A. L. Zimmerman. **Transfer Agent & Registrar**—Society National Bank, Dallas. **Incorporated**—in Texas in 1973. **Empl**—1,830. **S&P Analyst:** Stephen J. Tekirian

Keystone Financial

4351M

NASDAQ Symbol **KSTN**

In S&P SmallCap 600

03-OCT-98

Industry: Banks (Regional)

Summary: Harrisburg-based Keystone Financial is the third largest bank holding company headquartered in Pennsylvania.

Quantitative Evaluations	
Outlook (1 Lowest—5 Highest)	**• 2+**
Fair Value	**• 29¼**
Risk	**• Low**
Earn./Div. Rank	**• A-**
Technical Eval.	**• Neutral** since 8/98
Rel. Strength Rank (1 Lowest—99 Highest)	**• 57**
Insider Activity	**• Neutral**

Recent Price • 29¼
52 Wk Range • 42¼-27
Yield • 3.8%
12-Mo. P/E • 15.4

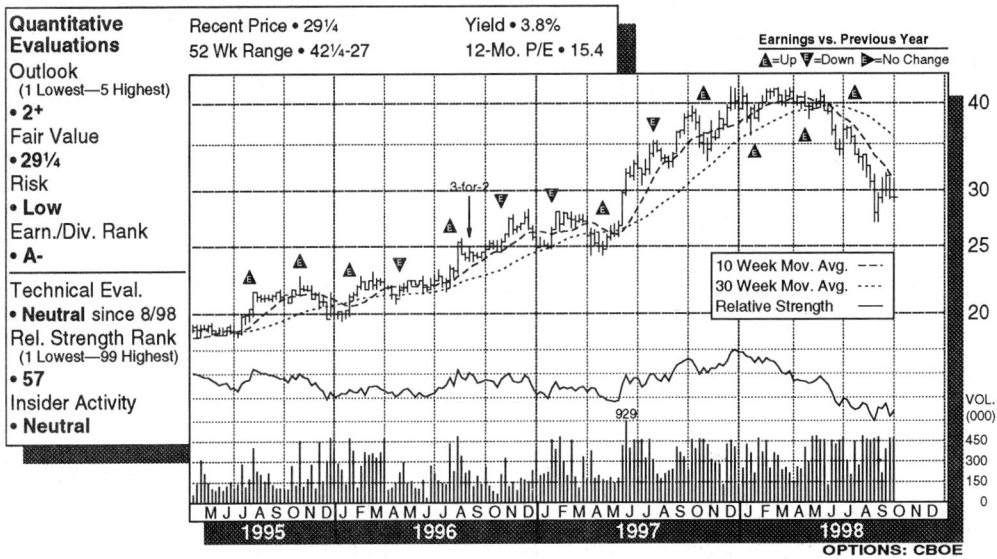

Earnings vs. Previous Year
▲=Up ▼=Down ▶=No Change

10 Week Mov. Avg. - - -
30 Week Mov. Avg. ——
Relative Strength ———

OPTIONS: CBOE

Business Profile - 24-JUL-98

The third largest bank holding company in Pennsylvania, Keystone practices a supercommunity banking policy, delivering personalized services to customers through local community banks, while creating broad, highly competitive product lines and managing costs efficiently through its centralized banking operation. It also operates several nonbanking companies to provide brokerage, investment, mortgage banking and other services. In 1997, the company exited the indirect auto loan business, in order to focus on lines of business more consistent with its relationship-based banking strategy. However, it will offer auto loans and leases directly to consumers through KeyBuy, a new direct auto loan and service package. In March 1998, directors authorized the repurchase of up to 500,000 common shares.

Operational Review - 24-JUL-98

Net interest income rose 2.5%, year to year, in the first six months of 1998, as loan growth outweighed a narrower net interest margin (4.49%, versus 4.60%). The provision for loan losses increased 40%, to $10,436,000, from $7,453,000. Following 13% greater noninterest income and 3.1% lower noninterest expense, net income climbed 31%, to $49,417,000 ($0.94 a share), from $37,753,000 ($0.72). Results in the 1997 period included merger and portfolio restructuring charges of $8,600,000 ($0.17 a share).

Stock Performance - 02-OCT-98

In the past 30 trading days, KSTN's shares have declined 5%, compared to a 7% fall in the S&P 500. Average trading volume for the past five days was 132,160 shares, compared with the 40-day moving average of 110,723 shares.

Key Stock Statistics

Dividend Rate/Share	1.12	Shareholders	10,800
Shs. outstg. (M)	51.4	Market cap. (B)	$ 1.5
Avg. daily vol. (M)	0.097	Inst. holdings	25%
Tang. Bk. Value/Share	13.01		
Beta	0.85		

Value of $10,000 invested 5 years ago: $ 18,626

Fiscal Year Ending Dec. 31

	1998	1997	1996	1995	1994	1993
Revenues (Million $)						
1Q	153.3	120.4	110.8	100.2	73.02	64.12
2Q	160.2	126.8	109.4	102.5	75.80	63.81
3Q	—	132.2	112.0	104.5	90.20	64.45
4Q	—	155.8	114.5	107.0	95.08	63.79
Yr.	—	600.7	447.2	414.3	357.8	256.2
Earnings Per Share ($)						
1Q	**0.46**	**0.43**	0.44	0.42	0.40	0.41
2Q	**0.48**	**0.29**	0.47	0.43	0.40	0.41
3Q	—	**0.47**	0.45	0.43	0.27	0.42
4Q	—	**0.49**	0.47	0.45	0.40	0.42
Yr.	—	**1.68**	**1.70**	1.72	1.46	1.66

Next earnings report expected: mid October

Dividend Data (Dividends have been paid since 1985.)

Amount ($)	Date Decl.	Ex-Div. Date	Stock of Record	Payment Date
0.280	Nov. 21	Jan. 07	Jan. 09	Jan. 20 '98
0.280	Mar. 27	Apr. 07	Apr. 09	Apr. 20 '98
0.280	May. 21	Jul. 07	Jul. 09	Jul. 20 '98
0.280	Jul. 23	Oct. 07	Oct. 09	Oct. 20 '98

A Division of The McGraw-Hill Companies

STANDARD
&POOR'S
STOCK REPORTS

Keystone Financial, Inc.

4351M
03-OCT-98

Business Summary - 24-JUL-98

After completing two mergers in as many days, Harrisburg-based Keystone Financial, Inc. (KSTN) became one of the largest Pennsylvania-based bank holding companies. The May 29, 1997, merger of First Financial Corp. of Western Maryland, boosted KSTN's market share in that state. The next day, the company acquired Financial Trust Corp., a four-bank holding company with 48 community offices and $1.2 billion in assets, strengthening KSTN's Harrisburg market while extending the company's franchise into high-growth areas of central Pennsylvania and Maryland. At December 31, 1997, KSTN had $6.6 billion in assets.

In practicing its super community banking philosophy, KSTN delivers personalized service to customers through its local banks, while creating broad, highly competitive product lines and managing costs efficiently through its centralized banking operations. Because Keystone acknowledges the importance customers place on convenience, efficiency and speed of service, it is continually looking to expand and enhance the ways in which it delivers products and services to customers. The bank's ATM network, with over 450 stations, is the 38th largest network in the country.

Following its mission to become the financial institution of choice for consumers and businesses in its markets, Keystone has developed a consultative selling model, targeting consumers based on where they are in their financial life cycle. The company's KeySource package, for instance, combines investment management with basic banking for people who need to save for future expenses, such as children's education.

In 1997, net income fell 1.8%, to $87.9 million, from $89.5 million in 1996. This decline was the result of $11.4 million in one-time charges associated with the Financial Trust Corp. merger. Excluding the charges, net income in 1997 would have been $96.5 million. Net interest income rose 6%, to $278 million, but the most significant improvement in the company's performance occurred in the area of noninterest income, which KSTN has been emphasizing. Noninterest income grew 26%, to $89.9 million, in 1997.

In 1997, average earning assets, from which interest income is derived, amounted to $6.2 billion and consisted mainly of real estate loans (36%), consumer loans (24%), commercial loans (13%) and investment securities (24%).

Per Share Data ($)

(Year Ended Dec. 31)	1997	1996	1995	1994	1993	1992	1991	1990	1989	1988
Tangible Bk. Val.	13.18	13.38	12.68	11.64	12.53	NA	10.82	NA	NA	NA
Earnings	1.68	1.83	1.72	1.46	1.66	NA	1.54	NA	NA	NA
Dividends	1.04	0.96	0.92	0.87	NA	NA	NA	NA	NA	NA
Payout Ratio	62%	52%	53%	60%	NA	NA	NA	NA	NA	NA
Prices - High	42¼	28¼	22⅝	21½	23	NA	17½	NA	NA	NA
- Low	24¼	19½	17½	18⅛	18⅞	NA	9⅝	NA	NA	NA
P/E Ratio - High	25	15	13	15	14	NA	11	NA	NA	NA
- Low	14	11	10	12	11	NA	6	NA	NA	NA

Income Statement Analysis (Million $)

	1997	1996	1995	1994	1993	1992	1991	1990	1989	1988
Net Int. Inc.	278	210	197	188	128	NA	NA	NA	NA	NA
Tax Equiv. Adj.	8.8	4.9	5.6	6.3	NA	NA	NA	NA	NA	NA
Non Int. Inc.	83.9	62.1	49.0	43.8	NA	NA	NA	NA	NA	NA
Loan Loss Prov.	15.3	9.9	7.9	9.5	5.6	NA	NA	NA	NA	NA
Exp./Op. Revs.	62%	59%	60%	64%	NA	NA	NA	NA	NA	NA
Pretax Inc.	127	100	89.2	71.8	54.6	NA	NA	NA	NA	NA
Eff. Tax Rate	31%	31%	31%	29%	28%	NA	NA	NA	NA	NA
Net Inc.	87.9	69.5	61.3	51.4	39.4	NA	NA	NA	NA	NA
% Net Int. Marg.	4.59	4.49	4.49	4.63	4.63	NA	NA	NA	NA	NA

Balance Sheet & Other Fin. Data (Million $)

	1997	1996	1995	1994	1993	1992	1991	1990	1989	1988
Earning Assets:										
Money Mkt	27.2	78.3	109	50.0	NA	NA	NA	NA	NA	NA
Inv. Securities	1,619	1,236	1,223	1,174	NA	NA	NA	NA	NA	NA
Com'l Loans	2,297	1,575	1,511	1,430	NA	NA	NA	NA	NA	NA
Other Loans	2,416	1,979	1,855	1,763	NA	NA	NA	NA	NA	NA
Total Assets	6,841	5,231	5,075	4,706	3,151	NA	NA	NA	NA	NA
Demand Deposits	637	512	533	513	NA	NA	NA	NA	NA	NA
Time Deposits	4,596	3,585	3,529	3,314	NA	NA	NA	NA	NA	NA
LT Debt	102	146	100	55.9	NA	NA	NA	NA	NA	NA
Common Eqty.	685	507	481	408	297	NA	NA	NA	NA	NA
% Ret. on Assets	1.5	1.4	1.3	1.3	1.3	NA	NA	NA	NA	NA
% Ret. on Equity	14.7	14.1	13.8	14.6	13.8	NA	NA	NA	NA	NA
% Loan Loss Resv.	1.4	1.3	1.3	1.3	NA	NA	NA	NA	NA	NA
% Loans/Deposits	90.1	86.7	82.9	83.4	NA	NA	NA	NA	NA	NA
% Equity to Assets	9.9	9.7	9.1	9.0	NA	NA	NA	NA	NA	NA

Data as orig. reptd.; bef. results of disc opers. and/or spec. items. Per share data adj. for stk. divs. as of ex-div. date. Bold denotes diluted EPS (FASB 128). E-Estimated. NA-Not Available. NM-Not Meaningful. NR-Not Ranked.

Office—P. O. Box 3660, One Keystone Plaza, Front and Market Streets, Harrisburg, PA 17105-3660. **Tel**—(717) 233-1555. **Website**—www.keyfin.com **Chrmn & CEO**—C. L. Campbell. **Pres & COO**—M. L. Pulaski. **Vice Chrmn & Secy**—B. G. Rooke. **Dirs**—A. J. Antanavage, J. B. Barry, C. L. Campbell, P. I. Detwiler Jr., D. Devorris, G. E. Field, P. C. Herr II, A. W. Holman, R. G. King, U. H. Martz Jr., M. A. Messenger, W. L. Miller, M. L. Pulaski, D. A. Rosini, J. I. Scheiner, M. D. Shepard, F. D. Schoeneman, R. C. Unterberger, G. W. Ward, R. L. Wolfe. **Transfer Agent & Registrar**—American Stock Transfer & Trust Co., NYC. **Incorporated**—in Pennsylvania in 1983. **Empl**— 3,126. **S&P Analyst:** Michael Schneider.

STANDARD &POOR'S
STOCK REPORTS

Kirby Corp.

1304G
NYSE Symbol **KEX**

In S&P SmallCap 600

03-OCT-98

Industry: Shipping

Summary: This company provides inland and offshore marine transportation, performs marine and rail diesel engine services and has a 45% voting interest in Universal Insurance Co.

Quantitative Evaluations	
Recent Price • 20⅜	Yield • Nil
52 Wk Range • 25⅝-17⅞	12-Mo. P/E • 23.5

Outlook (1 Lowest—5 Highest)
• **3+**

Fair Value
• **24⅛**

Risk
• **Low**

Earn./Div. Rank
• **B**

Technical Eval.
• **NA**

Rel. Strength Rank (1 Lowest—99 Highest)
• **65**

Insider Activity
• **NA**

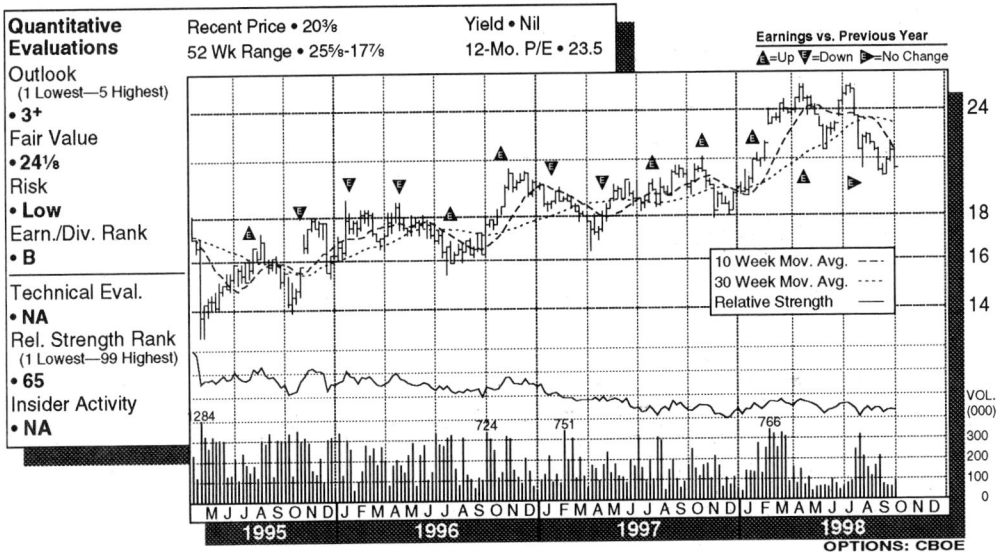

Earnings vs. Previous Year ▲=Up ▼=Down ▷=No Change

10 Week Mov. Avg. ---
30 Week Mov. Avg. ·····
Relative Strength —

OPTIONS: CBOE

Business Profile - 27-JUL-98

Kirby's 1998 second quarter results were hurt by a short liquid fertilizer season, resulting from high inventory levels in distribution terminals at the beginning of the season. This was partly offset by record profits by the diesel repair segment reflecting continued strong engine overhauls and direct parts sales and reduced administrative and other expenses. Excluding the liquid fertilizer market, the transportation segment performed well, on strong movements of chemicals, petrochemicals and refined products. In March 1998, the company sold selected offshore tankers and its harbor services operation for $38.6 million in cash. As of March 31, 1998, 1.8 million shares remained under an authorization to repurchase 6.3 million shares.

Operational Review - 27-JUL-98

Revenues in the six months ended June 30, 1998, slid 1.2%, year to year, as lower marine transportation revenues outweighed increased diesel repair revenues. Operating profits rose 13%, on gains at both segments. Despite sharply lower equity in the earnings of the insurance affiliate, after taxes at 37.7%, versus 37.9%, income from continuing operations gained 14%, to $11,715,000 ($0.52 a share), from $10,313,000 ($0.42). Results exclude income of $0.11 a share from discontinued operations in the 1997 period.

Stock Performance - 02-OCT-98

In the past 30 trading days, KEX's shares have declined 7%, compared to a 7% fall in the S&P 500. Average trading volume for the past five days was 18,640 shares, compared with the 40-day moving average of 23,867 shares.

Key Stock Statistics

Dividend Rate/Share	Nil	Shareholders	1,900
Shs. outstg. (M)	21.1	Market cap. (B)	$0.432
Avg. daily vol. (M)	0.016	Inst. holdings	68%
Tang. Bk. Value/Share	6.16		
Beta	0.46		

Value of $10,000 invested 5 years ago: $ 15,571

Fiscal Year Ending Dec. 31

	1998	1997	1996	1995	1994	1993
Revenues (Million $)						
1Q	82.75	80.26	92.90	118.6	101.8	74.38
2Q	84.88	88.97	97.90	123.0	104.7	94.35
3Q	—	84.22	100.3	104.3	108.1	97.94
4Q	—	57.64	99.5	94.20	118.5	111.9
Yr.	—	336.5	386.8	440.1	433.1	368.6
Earnings Per Share ($)						
1Q	0.21	0.11	0.20	0.17	0.10	0.17
2Q	0.31	0.01	0.01	0.18	0.11	0.16
3Q	—	0.24	0.28	-0.24	0.13	0.18
4Q	—	0.46	0.27	0.23	0.24	0.26
Yr.	—	0.92	1.05	0.34	0.58	0.86

Next earnings report expected: late October

Dividend Data

Special cash dividends of $0.10 a share were paid in 1988 and 1989.

A Division of The **McGraw·Hill** Companies

Business Summary - 27-JUL-98

Kirby Corp. operates in the highly competitive marine transportation market for commodities transported on the Mississippi River System, the Gulf Intracoastal Waterway and the Houston Ship Channel. the company is the leading inland tank barge carrier, based on its 519 barges and approximately 9.4 million bbl. of available capacity. Over the last five years, through consolidations within the inland barge market, the company has expanded its distribution capabilities and gained economies of scale to better match barges, towboats, products and destinations.

The marine transportation segment (76% of revenues in 1997) provides inland transportation of industrial chemicals, petrochemical feedstocks, agricultural chemicals and refined petroleum products by tank barges, and the offshore transportation of refined petroleum products by tanker and tank barge and dry-bulk, container and palletized cargoes by barges. In 1997, results of this segment were hurt by flooding on the Mississippi River System from February through April, which resulted in reduced revenues and increased expenses. The company said that the unfavorable weather conditions reduced EPS by $0.11 for the year.

KEX estimates that the total number of tank barges operating in U.S. inland waters has fallen from 4,200 in 1981 to 2,900 in 1997. As the supply of inland tank barges has declined, domestic production of petrochemicals (an important revenue source for the company) has risen. KEX believes that a continuation of these trends will lead to higher rates.

During the fourth quarter of 1997, the company said it would review alternative strategies regarding certain offshore assets. In January 1998, it agreed to sell its U.S. flag offshore operation and harbor service operation. In March 1998, it sold a total of seven harbor tugboats and seven tankers, for a total of $38.6 million in cash.

In 1996, the Diesel Repair division (24% of revenues) purchased the assets of MKW Power Systems, Inc., adding $25 million in annual sales. With the acquisition, the company became the East Coast distributor for the GM Electro-Motive division parts, engines and aftermarket services. The Diesel Repair division also serves marine and industrial markets in other regions of the U.S.

KEX owns a 45% voting interest in Universal Insurance Co., a property-casualty insurer operating in Puerto Rico. It recorded equity in the earnings of Universal of $4,609,000 in 1997.

Per Share Data ($)

(Year Ended Dec. 31)	1997	1996	1995	1994	1993	1992	1991	1990	1989	1988
Tangible Bk. Val.	12.83	7.97	7.63	7.41	7.04	4.96	4.99	4.31	3.65	3.43
Cash Flow	2.07	2.39	1.73	1.75	1.78	1.45	1.21	1.16	0.82	0.58
Earnings	0.92	1.05	0.34	0.58	0.86	0.60	0.61	0.60	0.39	0.33
Dividends	Nil	Nil	Nil	Nil	Nil	Nil	Nil	Nil	0.10	0.10
Payout Ratio	Nil	Nil	Nil	Nil	Nil	Nil	Nil	Nil	25%	30%
Prices - High	21⅛	20½	19¾	23⅜	22	15½	16⅛	11⅛	9¾	4⅞
- Low	16⅜	15⅜	13	15½	11⅜	10	7	6⅛	4⅜	2½
P/E Ratio - High	23	20	58	40	26	26	26	19	25	15
- Low	18	15	38	27	13	17	11	10	11	8

Income Statement Analysis (Million $)

Revs.	335	387	432	433	378	269	187	174	140	94.0
Oper. Inc.	69.0	81.6	59.5	74.6	69.3	46.6	34.8	36.3	26.9	14.4
Depr.	28.1	34.8	38.9	33.8	24.5	19.3	13.3	12.9	9.9	6.1
Int. Exp.	13.4	13.3	12.5	8.8	8.4	9.4	6.0	6.3	5.1	2.1
Pretax Inc.	36.5	43.4	20.6	30.3	36.9	18.7	17.8	19.1	11.3	10.1
Eff. Tax Rate	38%	37%	43%	34%	34%	27%	26%	29%	21%	24%
Net Inc.	22.7	27.2	9.4	16.7	22.8	13.6	13.3	13.5	8.9	7.7

Balance Sheet & Other Fin. Data (Million $)

Cash	23.8	19.7	17.1	35.9	40.1	20.3	30.1	28.9	49.3	64.9
Curr. Assets	136	130	105	NA	NA	NA	NA	NA	NA	NA
Total Assets	518	525	498	667	563	446	286	254	247	172
Curr. Liab.	95.6	89.7	69.4	NA	NA	NA	35.5	33.9	31.4	18.7
LT Debt	149	177	174	149	110	148	80.0	67.0	76.0	17.0
Common Eqty.	218	206	205	223	212	123	112	97.0	88.0	79.0
Total Cap.	1,272	42.0	379	432	377	309	199	169	165	98.0
Cap. Exp.	24.5	37.2	49.5	31.0	71.0	128	37.2	18.1	73.9	9.0
Cash Flow	50.8	62.0	48.3	50.5	47.3	32.9	26.6	26.4	18.8	13.8
Curr. Ratio	1.4	1.4	1.5	NA	NA	NA	NA	NA	NA	NA
% LT Debt of Cap.	35.8	41.3	45.9	34.4	29.1	47.8	40.0	39.8	45.9	17.4
% Net Inc.of Revs.	6.8	7.0	2.2	3.8	6.0	5.1	7.1	7.8	6.4	8.2
% Ret. on Assets	4.4	5.3	1.6	2.7	4.1	3.7	4.9	5.5	4.3	6.2
% Ret. on Equity	10.7	13.2	3.1	7.6	12.5	11.4	12.8	14.9	10.7	12.2

Data as orig. reptd.; bef. results of disc. opers. and/or spec. items. Per share data adj. for stk. divs. as of ex-div. date. Bold denotes diluted EPS (FASB 128). E-Estimated. NA-Not Available. NM-Not Meaningful. NR-Not Ranked.

Office—1775 St. James Place, Suite 200, Houston, TX 77056-3453. **Tel**—(713) 435-1000. **Chrmn**—G. A. Peterkin Jr. **Pres & CEO**—J. H. Pyne. **SVP & Treas**—B. K. Harrington. **Secy**—H. Gilchrist. **Investor Contact**—Steve Holcomb. **Dirs**—G. F. Clements Jr., C. S. Day, B. G. Gower, W. M. Lamont Jr., G. A. Peterkin Jr., J. H. Pyne, R. G. Stone Jr., T. M. Taylor, J. V. Waggoner. **Transfer Agent & Registrar**—Bank of Boston. **Incorporated**—in Nevada in 1969. **Empl**— 1,350. **S&P Analyst**: S.A.H.

Komag, Inc.

4376

Nasdaq Symbol **KMAG**

In S&P SmallCap 600

03-OCT-98

Industry:
Computers (Peripherals)

Summary: This company is the largest independent maker of sputtered thin-film media used in Winchester disk drives.

S&P Opinion: Avoid (★★)	Recent Price • 3⅛	Yield • Nil
	52 Wk Range • 21¾-2¼	12-Mo. P/E • NM

Quantitative Evaluations

Outlook
(1 Lowest—5 Highest)
• **NA**

Fair Value
• **NA**

Risk
• **High**

Earn./Div. Rank
• **B**

Technical Eval.
• **Bullish** since 2/98

Rel. Strength Rank
(1 Lowest—99 Highest)
• **20**

Insider Activity
• **Favorable**

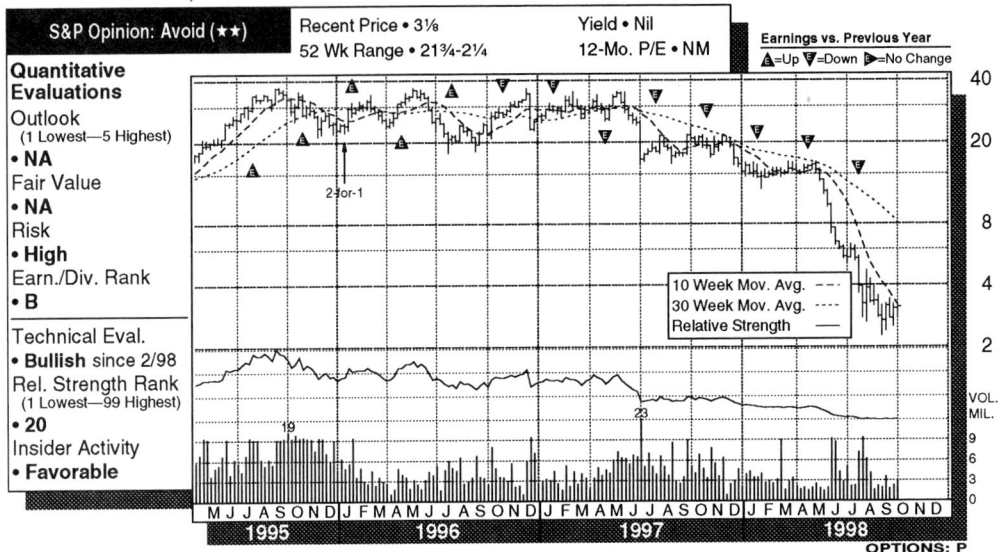

Earnings vs. Previous Year
▲=Up ▼=Down ▶=No Change

10 Week Mov. Avg. — - -
30 Week Mov. Avg. - - - -
Relative Strength

OPTIONS: P

Overview - 24-JUL-98

This disk manufacturer's revenues should decline sharply in 1998. Revenues fell 55% in the second quarter as a result of a continued supply/demand imbalance in the industry, as well as intense pricing pressures. Revenues could show modest sequential improvements in the second half of 1998, on slowly improving industry conditions. Low utilization rates and pricing pressures should continue to restrict profit margins in 1998. KMAG continues to cut costs, and is reducing its capital expenditures. The company has also lost money recently from its Japanese joint venture, reflecting MR-based product transition problems, as well as weakness in Asian markets. Results in the 1997 third quarter were penalized by pretax charges of $63 million for the consolidation of U.S. manufacturing operations and inventory writedowns. We project a substantial net loss for all of 1998.

Valuation - 24-JUL-98

The shares of this leading vendor of magnetic media dropped sharply in late June 1997, when the company announced that earnings would be significantly lower than expected for the balance of 1997. The shares have plummeted further since then, reflecting the impact of an industry-wide oversupply problem. The company produced 55 million disks in 1997 (accounting for over 13% of all disks produced worldwide), up from 49 million disks in 1996 (a 14% share). While we believe that Komag is making progress in addressing its problems, we anticipate continued intense pricing pressures from a continuation of difficult industry conditions, and we estimate a large net loss in 1998. Due to the mounting losses, the company may need more capital, and may be forced to issue more shares. As a result, we recommend avoiding the shares until there are signs of a turnaround.

Key Stock Statistics

S&P EPS Est. 1998	-7.59	Tang. Bk. Value/Share	6.87
P/E on S&P Est. 1998	NM	Beta	1.52
S&P EPS Est. 1999	-0.57	Shareholders	500
Dividend Rate/Share	Nil	Market cap. (B)	$0.167
Shs. outstg. (M)	53.4	Inst. holdings	68%
Avg. daily vol. (M)	0.547		

Value of $10,000 invested 5 years ago: $ 3,571

Fiscal Year Ending Dec. 31

	1998	1997	1996	1995	1994	1993
Revenues (Million $)						
1Q	76.06	167.2	152.8	105.1	97.70	93.56
2Q	78.81	175.1	152.2	120.8	97.77	103.2
3Q	—	129.7	131.5	132.8	98.17	97.45
4Q	—	159.0	141.2	153.5	98.74	91.19
Yr.	—	631.1	577.8	512.3	392.4	385.4
Earnings Per Share ($)						
1Q	-1.10	0.33	0.80	0.31	0.34	0.17
2Q	-4.95	0.22	0.80	0.48	0.30	0.18
3Q	E-0.87	-1.01	0.31	0.61	0.33	0.10
4Q	E-0.67	0.02	0.16	0.72	0.30	-0.69
Yr.	E-7.59	-0.42	2.07	2.14	1.27	-0.23

Next earnings report expected: late October

Dividend Data

No cash dividends have been paid.

A Division of The **McGraw·Hill** *Companies*

Business Summary - 24-JUL-98

Komag is the world's largest independent manufacturer of thin-film media (disks) for use in computer hard disk drives. The company designs, manufactures and markets thin-film media for use in high-capacity, high-performance 5.25-inch, 3.5-inch and smaller disk drive storage devices. Komag exited the thin-film recording head business in the third quarter of 1994.

International Data Corp. (IDC) forecasts that worldwide disk drive unit shipments will grow at a 17% compound annual rate from 1998 through 2001. The need for higher performance disk drives result from greater processing power, more sophisticated operating systems and application software, high-resolution graphics, and larger databases.

Media products are the disks or platters within a disk drive onto which information is recorded and stored, and from which it is retrieved. High density media are essential to the performance of high-capacity hard disk drives. The company's media products are primarily used in disk arrays, network file servers, high-end personal computers and engineering workstations.

Komag's production volume of media products depends on available capacity, utilization of capacity and production yield performance. By the end of 1998, KMAG expects to have the capacity to produce in excess of 25 million units per quarter.

Disk sales to the company's 50%-owned Asahi Komag Co. joint venture accounted for 14% of sales in 1997.

The company sells its products to independent OEM disk drive manufacturers for incorporation into rigid disk drives marketed under the manufacturers' own labels. It also sells media to computer system manufacturers that produce their own disk drives.

In 1997, five customers accounted for 96% of total revenues: Western Digital (38%), Maxtor (19%), Quantum (15%), Seagate (14%) and IBM (10%). Nearly half of Komag's 1997 revenues came from magnetoresistive media, versus inductive media.

After spending $199 million in 1997, KMAG projects capital expenditures of $120 million in 1998, as well as $50 million for research and development.

Results in the third quarter of 1997 included pretax charges of $52.2 million for the consolidation of U.S. manufacturing operations and $10.8 million for inventory write-downs.

Per Share Data ($)

(Year Ended Dec. 31)	1997	1996	1995	1994	1993	1992	1991	1990	1989	1988
Tangible Bk. Val.	13.00	13.50	11.33	7.23	5.87	5.90	4.93	3.92	2.92	2.58
Cash Flow	2.04	3.71	3.45	2.31	0.92	1.24	1.08	1.04	0.27	0.65
Earnings	-0.42	2.07	2.14	1.27	-0.23	0.40	0.37	0.44	-0.23	0.29
Dividends	Nil	Nil	Nil	Nil	Nil	Nil	Nil	Nil	Nil	Nil
Payout Ratio	Nil	Nil	Nil	Nil	Nil	Nil	Nil	Nil	Nil	Nil
Prices - High	35³/₈	37	37¹/₂	14¹/₂	12	11⁵/₈	12¹/₄	8¹/₈	5³/₄	7¹/₈
- Low	13¹/₂	17⁵/₈	11¹/₈	7⁷/₈	6⁷/₈	5³/₈	5³/₈	4¹/₄	3¹/₄	4¹/₈
P/E Ratio - High	NM	18	17	11	NM	29	33	18	NM	25
- Low	NM	9	5	6	NM	14	15	10	NM	14

Income Statement Analysis (Million $)

	1997	1996	1995	1994	1993	1992	1991	1990	1989	1988
Revs.	631	578	512	392	385	327	279	150	85.0	84.0
Oper. Inc.	143	199	195	125	82.7	56.6	59.0	36.9	4.0	21.2
Depr.	129	86.9	65.5	47.6	49.0	36.3	29.4	18.2	13.0	9.0
Int. Exp.	9.1	0.6	1.9	2.9	5.5	3.8	5.6	3.0	3.0	2.0
Pretax Inc.	-42.7	131	143	82.8	-2.5	25.8	30.7	19.2	-8.0	11.8
Eff. Tax Rate	NM	16%	24%	28%	NM	71%	48%	35%	NM	37%
Net Inc.	-22.1	110	107	58.5	-9.9	16.9	15.1	13.4	-6.1	7.5

Balance Sheet & Other Fin. Data (Million $)

	1997	1996	1995	1994	1993	1992	1991	1990	1989	1988
Cash	134	93.2	214	93.9	91.6	89.3	91.0	45.2	37.8	22.2
Curr. Assets	372	251	323	172	178	153	149	82.0	64.0	54.0
Total Assets	1,085	938	686	424	382	356	277	163	122	100
Curr. Liab.	75.6	109	70.9	53.3	85.9	55.5	51.7	24.0	19.3	13.8
LT Debt	245	70.0	Nil	16.3	29.5	27.6	16.5	19.9	21.8	20.7
Common Eqty.	686	698	575	331	255	249	202	115	77.0	62.0
Total Cap.	1,008	829	615	370	296	300	225	138	102	86.0
Cap. Exp.	199	403	166	102	86.0	109	60.2	40.3	24.7	31.2
Cash Flow	106	197	172	106	39.1	53.2	44.5	31.6	7.0	16.5
Curr. Ratio	4.9	2.3	4.6	3.2	2.1	2.8	2.9	3.4	3.3	3.9
% LT Debt of Cap.	24.3	8.4	Nil	4.4	10.0	9.2	7.3	14.4	21.4	24.1
% Net Inc.of Revs.	NM	19.0	20.9	14.9	NM	5.2	5.4	8.9	NM	9.0
% Ret. on Assets	NM	13.5	19.3	14.2	NM	5.3	6.0	9.0	NM	8.5
% Ret. on Equity	NM	17.3	23.6	19.5	NM	7.4	8.3	13.3	NM	12.9

Data as orig. reptd.; bef. results of disc. opers. and/or spec. items. Per share data adj. for stk. divs. as of ex-div. date. Bold denotes diluted EPS (FASB 128). E-Estimated. NA-Not Available. NM-Not Meaningful. NR-Not Ranked.

Office—1704 Automation Parkway, San Jose, CA 95131-1873. **Tel**—(408) 576-2000. **Website**—http://www.komag.com **Pres & CEO**—S. C. Johnson. **Chrmn**—T. Chen. **SVP, CFO & Secy**—W. L. Potts, Jr. **Investor Contact**—David H. Allen. **Dirs**—C. R. Barrett, T. Chen, C. A. Eyre, I. Federman, S. C. Johnson, G. A. Neil, M. Palevsky, A. Sun, M. Takebayashi. **Transfer Agent & Registrar**—ChaseMellon Shareholder Services, SF. **Incorporated**—in Delaware in 1986. **Empl**—4,738. **S&P Analyst:** Brian Goodstadt

10-OCT-98

Industry: Computer (Software & Services)

Summary: This company designs, develops, manufactures and markets integrated time accounting and other data collection systems.

Quantitative Evaluations	
Outlook (1 Lowest—5 Highest)	• **4⁻**
Fair Value	• 54⅞
Risk	• **Average**
Earn./Div. Rank	• **B+**
Technical Eval.	• **Bullish** since 10/97
Rel. Strength Rank (1 Lowest—99 Highest)	• **31**
Insider Activity	• **Neutral**

Recent Price • 27
52 Wk Range • 40-19¼

Yield • Nil
12-Mo. P/E • 16.7

Earnings vs. Previous Year
▲=Up ▼=Down ▷=No Change

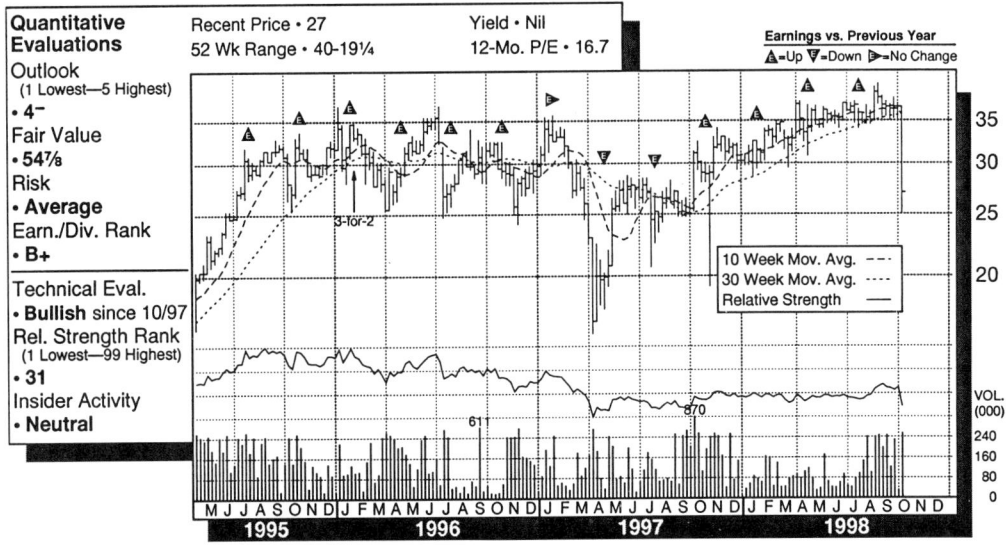

10 Week Mov. Avg. - - -
30 Week Mov. Avg. ......
Relative Strength ——

Business Profile - 13-AUG-98

Kronos manufactures data collection and integrated time accounting systems that consist of intelligent hardware and fully integrated software, designed to enhance productivity and efficiency. The company is actively expanding its product line, and is strengthening its distribution network through acquisitions. KRON has just completed a transition to Windows and client/server technologies, which now makes up the majority of software sales. Kronos is also attempting to expand its products into the manufacturing, retail, health care, government and education markets. KRON recently acquired Visionware labor productivity software from Cost Systems Group, part of the company's goal to providing labor management solutions in all its key markets.

Operational Review - 13-AUG-98

In the first nine months of FY 98 (Sep.), revenues advanced 20%, year to year, reflecting strong growth in Windows, client/server and AS/400 time and labor management software products, as well as products for the government and education markets. Gross margins widened slightly and operating expenses declined as a percentage of revenues due to a restructuring and refocusing of the sales and service organizations; pretax income was up 38%. After taxes at 38.2% in both periods, net income was also up 38%, to $8,971,000 ($1.05 per share), from $6,498,000 ($0.77).

Stock Performance - 09-OCT-98

In the past 30 trading days, KRON's shares have declined 29%, compared to a 4% fall in the S&P 500. Average trading volume for the past five days was 79,900 shares, compared with the 40-day moving average of 47,354 shares.

Key Stock Statistics

Dividend Rate/Share	Nil	Shareholders	3,000
Shs. outstg. (M)	8.3	Market cap. (B)	$0.224
Avg. daily vol. (M)	0.039	Inst. holdings	70%
Tang. Bk. Value/Share	8.64		
Beta	0.46		

Value of $10,000 invested 5 years ago: $ 18,837

Fiscal Year Ending Sep. 30

	1998	1997	1996	1995	1994	1993
Revenues (Million $)						
1Q	44.57	37.11	31.47	26.15	19.02	15.30
2Q	46.47	39.40	33.10	29.21	21.05	15.80
3Q	52.68	43.30	36.25	31.07	23.49	16.99
4Q	—	50.73	42.14	33.95	29.36	19.01
Yr.	—	170.5	143.0	120.4	92.92	67.09
Earnings Per Share ($)						
1Q	0.29	0.26	0.26	0.14	0.07	0.09
2Q	0.34	0.21	0.28	0.19	0.11	0.11
3Q	0.43	0.30	0.35	0.28	0.16	0.12
4Q	—	0.57	0.47	0.42	0.27	0.18
Yr.	—	1.34	1.37	1.03	0.62	0.51

Next earnings report expected: early November

Dividend Data

No cash dividends have been paid. The company intends to retain earnings for use in the development of its business. A "poison pill" stock purchase rights plan was adopted in 1995.

A Division of The McGraw·Hill Companies

STANDARD
&POOR'S
STOCK REPORTS

Kronos Incorporated

4381

10-OCT-98

Business Summary - 13-AUG-98

Kronos (Greek for time) began operations in 1977, when the company's founders saw timekeeping as an industry that could benefit from the introduction of computerized automation. Today Kronos designs, makes and markets time and attendance, work force management and shop floor data collection systems and application software that enhances workplace productivity. Its systems consist of fully integrated software and intelligent data collection terminals. The company also maintains an extensive service and support organization that provides on-site and remote maintenance, as well as professional and educational services. Net revenues in recent fiscal years (Sep.) were derived as follows:

	FY 97	FY 96	FY 95
Product	68%	71%	73%
Service	32%	29%	27%

Major systems include Timekeeper Central, Timekeeper/AS and Timekeeper C/S Systems, which are designed to reduce payroll preparation time, improve labor scheduling and control labor costs; ShopTrac Data Collection System, marketed primarily to manufacturing plants, which collects a wide variety of labor and material data to provide real-time information on cost, loca-

tion and product completion time; and WorkForce Management System, a labor management system designed for the retail and hospitality markets that consists of several integrated modules, including Business Forecaster and WorkForce Planner, which predict the level of store activity and generate correct staffing levels required. This information is then integrated with Timekeeper Central System, which enables management to compare actual versus budgeted labor costs.

Optional application software includes Kronos Scheduling Module, which assists in creating employee schedules; the Kronos Archive Program, which performs long-term record keeping; the Kronos CardSaver, which records employees' in and out data for wage and hour inquiries; the Kronos Accruals Module, which calculates each employees' available benefit time; and the Kronos Attendance Tracker, which records and documents employee absences.

Other products include the Time Bank, which interfaces with commonly used payroll, human resources and scheduling software; Gatekeeper terminals, which control employee access to a facility; Kronos TeleTime System, which allows customer telephones to serve as data input devices; and ImageKeeper, which stores digital photographs and signatures of employees, and items such as badges, time cards, bar code labels and modems.

Per Share Data ($)

(Year Ended Sep. 30)	1997	1996	1995	1994	1993	1992	1991	1990	1989	1988
Tangible Bk. Val.	7.92	6.63	5.14	3.87	4.01	3.41	1.66	NA	NA	NA
Cash Flow	2.66	2.34	1.80	1.24	0.90	0.81	0.58	0.42	NA	NA
Earnings	1.34	1.37	1.03	0.62	0.51	0.54	0.37	0.23	0.23	0.05
Dividends	Nil	Nil	Nil	Nil	Nil	Nil	Nil	Nil	Nil	Nil
Payout Ratio	Nil	Nil	Nil	Nil	Nil	Nil	Nil	Nil	Nil	Nil
Prices - High	35¾	37	33⅝	18	15½	16	NA	NA	NA	NA
- Low	16¼	24⅛	16⅜	9⅝	9⅛	7⅞	NA	NA	NA	NA
P/E Ratio - High	27	27	33	29	31	30	NA	NA	NA	NA
- Low	12	18	16	16	18	15	NA	NA	NA	NA

Income Statement Analysis (Million $)

	1997	1996	1995	1994	1993	1992	1991	1990	1989	1988
Revs.	171	143	120	92.9	67.1	58.1	47.8	39.6	32.9	25.9
Oper. Inc.	29.5	26.9	20.3	13.4	8.3	7.4	4.6	3.4	NA	NA
Depr.	11.2	8.2	6.3	4.9	3.3	1.8	1.4	1.1	NA	NA
Int. Exp.	Nil	Nil	Nil	0.0	0.1	0.1	0.2	0.2	NA	NA
Pretax Inc.	18.3	18.7	13.6	7.8	6.0	5.7	3.6	2.3	NA	NA
Eff. Tax Rate	38%	39%	38%	38%	36%	38%	38%	36%	NA	NA
Net Inc.	11.3	11.4	8.4	4.9	3.8	3.5	2.3	1.4	1.4	0.3

Balance Sheet & Other Fin. Data (Million $)

	1997	1996	1995	1994	1993	1992	1991	1990	1989	1988
Cash	20.7	32.8	21.4	8.7	12.2	13.8	4.1	NA	NA	NA
Curr. Assets	90.2	74.4	57.2	40.7	35.0	30.3	16.9	NA	NA	NA
Total Assets	128	105	77.8	59.4	46.0	37.3	22.3	17.2	15.2	14.0
Curr. Liab.	49.0	38.1	30.4	22.7	16.0	12.5	10.9	NA	NA	NA
LT Debt	Nil	Nil	Nil	Nil	0.2	0.5	0.9	1.1	1.3	NA
Common Eqty.	72.5	61.1	46.6	35.9	29.8	24.3	10.1	6.6	5.4	NA
Total Cap.	75.1	63.3	46.6	35.9	30.0	24.8	11.5	10.1	9.0	NA
Cap. Exp.	8.7	9.7	4.1	4.8	4.6	3.4	1.5	1.4	NA	NA
Cash Flow	22.4	19.6	14.7	9.8	6.8	5.3	3.6	2.6	NA	NA
Curr. Ratio	1.8	1.9	1.9	1.8	2.2	2.4	1.6	NA	NA	NA
% LT Debt of Cap.	Nil	Nil	Nil	Nil	0.5	2.1	7.9	10.7	13.9	NA
% Net Inc.of Revs.	6.6	8.0	7.0	5.3	5.7	6.1	4.7	3.7	4.3	1.2
% Ret. on Assets	9.7	12.5	12.3	9.1	9.0	10.7	11.4	8.9	9.6	NA
% Ret. on Equity	16.9	21.3	20.4	14.6	13.9	18.8	24.4	20.5	NA	NA

Data as orig. reptd.; bef. results of disc. opers. and/or spec. items. Per share data adj. for stk. divs. as of ex-div. date. Bold denotes diluted EPS (FASB 128). E-Estimated. NA-Not Available. NM-Not Meaningful. NR-Not Ranked.

Office—400 Fifth Ave., Waltham, MA 02154. **Tel**—(781) 890-3232. **Website**—http://www.kronos.com **Chrmn & CEO**—M. S. Ain. **Pres & COO**—W. P. Decker. **VP-Fin & Treas**—P. A. Lacy. **Investor Contact**—Marie Harris (617-487-4809). **Dirs**—M. S. Ain, R. J. Dumler, T. G. Johnson, D. B. Kiser, D. S. Levy, D. B. McWilliams, L. Portner, S. Rubinovitz. **Transfer Agent & Registrar**—State Street Bank & Trust Co., Boston. **Incorporated**—in Massachusetts in 1977. **Empl**— 1,341. **S&P Analyst:** Jim Corridore

03-OCT-98

Industry:
Electrical Equipment

Summary: This holding company primarily manufactures electrical transformers, wire and cable products and engine components.

Quantitative Evaluations

Outlook
(1 Lowest—5 Highest)
• **5**

Fair Value
• **41⅜**

Risk
• **Average**

Earn./Div. Rank
• **B+**

Technical Eval.
• **Neutral** since 8/98

Rel. Strength Rank
(1 Lowest—99 Highest)
• **59**

Insider Activity
• **Neutral**

Recent Price • 28⅜

52 Wk Range • 51⅜-23⅜

Yield • 2.1%

12-Mo. P/E • 14.0

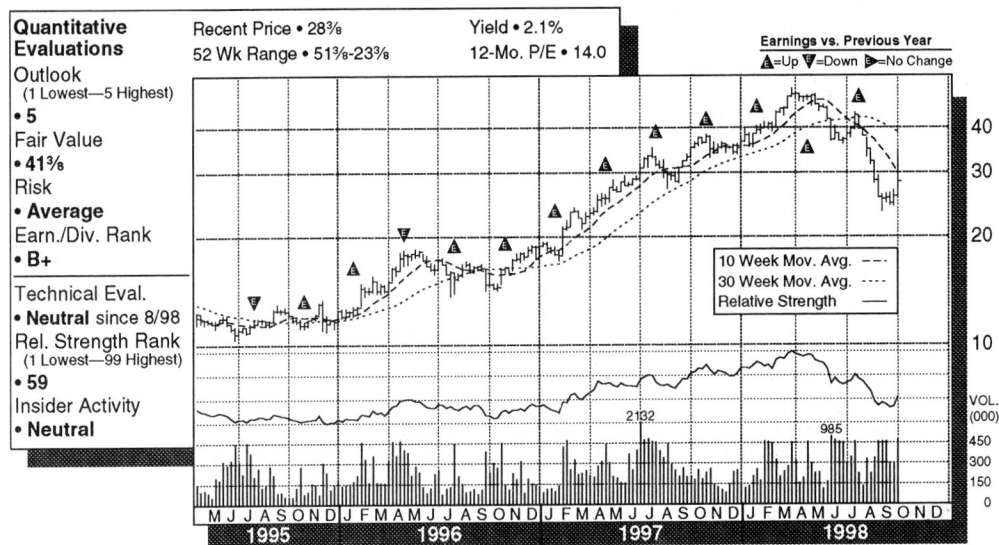

Earnings vs. Previous Year
▲=Up ▼=Down ▶=No Change

10 Week Mov. Avg. - - -
30 Week Mov. Avg. ‧‧‧‧
Relative Strength ——

Business Profile - 28-MAY-98

The strong growth in profits recorded in the industrial products segment in 1998's first quarter reflected record shipments of engine component products and fuel tanks, improved operating efficiencies and the full period impact of the March and November 1997 acquisitions of Kysor Industrial and Snyder Tank, respectively. Strong gains in both transformers and wire and cable products led to higher profits in the electrical products segment. In mid-1997, Kuhlman generated about $68.2 million of net proceeds from the public sale of 2.5 million common shares at $28.875 each. About $59.0 million of this capital was used to reduce debt, and $9.2 million was utilized to redeem outstanding warrants.

Operational Review - 28-MAY-98

Net sales in the three months ended March 31, 1998, rose 37%, year to year, mainly reflecting robust demand in the industrial products segment and the inclusion of the Kysor and Snyder Tank acquisitions in all of the 1998 period. Profitability benefited from record sales volume and improved gross profit margins for certain products. Following a 4.5% decrease in interest expense (net), pretax income was up 61%. After taxes at 39.2%, versus 41.3%, net income rose 67%, to $8,817,000 ($0.51 a share, diluted and based on 20% more average shares) from $5,282,000 ($0.36).

Stock Performance - 02-OCT-98

In the past 30 trading days, KUH's shares have declined 0.65%, compared to a 7% fall in the S&P 500. Average trading volume for the past five days was 134,000 shares, compared with the 40-day moving average of 85,785 shares.

Key Stock Statistics

Dividend Rate/Share	0.60	Shareholders	6,000
Shs. outstg. (M)	16.8	Market cap. (B)	$0.477
Avg. daily vol. (M)	0.091	Inst. holdings	57%
Tang. Bk. Value/Share	4.33		
Beta	1.38		

Value of $10,000 invested 5 years ago: $ 26,128

Fiscal Year Ending Dec. 31

	1998	1997	1996	1995	1994	1993
Revenues (Million $)						
1Q	184.1	134.2	103.5	106.9	62.42	27.24
2Q	194.1	170.2	112.2	102.8	56.99	28.95
3Q	—	164.4	119.2	108.6	64.13	29.99
4Q	—	174.7	121.6	107.1	59.31	31.92
Yr.	—	643.4	456.5	425.4	242.8	118.1
Earnings Per Share ($)						
1Q	0.51	0.36	0.26	0.27	0.19	-0.80
2Q	0.57	0.43	0.27	-0.06	0.05	0.13
3Q	—	0.45	0.37	0.26	0.21	0.21
4Q	—	0.51	0.36	0.29	-0.18	0.15
Yr.	—	1.75	1.26	0.76	0.27	-0.29

Next earnings report expected: mid October

Dividend Data (Dividends have been paid since 1990.)

Amount ($)	Date Decl.	Ex-Div. Date	Stock of Record	Payment Date
0.150	Nov. 25	Dec. 09	Dec. 11	Jan. 09 '98
0.150	Feb. 19	Mar. 09	Mar. 11	Apr. 10 '98
0.150	Apr. 23	Jun. 09	Jun. 11	Jul. 10 '98
0.150	Jul. 31	Sep. 09	Sep. 11	Oct. 09 '98

A Division of The **McGraw·Hill** *Companies*

STANDARD
&POOR'S
STOCK REPORTS

Kuhlman Corporation

1315D
03-OCT-98

Business Summary - 28-MAY-98

By acquiring or merging with six businesses since 1993, Kuhlman Corp. (KUH), once a producer primarily of electric power transformers, has re-made itself into a diversified manufacturer with varied product lines in each of its two segments: Electrical Products (46% of net sales in 1997) and Industrial Products (54%). The acquisitions allowed KUH to boost net sales from 1993's $118 million to $643 million in 1997. The company has deliberately pursued the twin goals of size and diversity, determined to avoid the cyclical character of more narrowly focused organizations whose fortunes rise or fall with those of a single industry or product.

In 1993, the company acquired Coleman Holding Co., adding wire and cable products. The 1995 combination with Schwitzer, Inc. expanded the scope of KUH's operations to include the manufacture of engine components. The acquisition of two wire-and-cable firms in 1996 expanded KUH's participation in some of the faster-growing areas of this industry. The size of the Industrial Products segment has been greatly broadened by two 1997 acquisitions. These were the March 1997 purchase of Kysor Industrial Corp.'s Transportation Products Group (net sales of $136 million in 1996) and the November 1997 purchase of Snyder Tank Corp. (annual sales of about $46 million). The Group's

products (fans, fan clutches, engine monitoring devices, fuel tanks) are used in commercial and industrial transportation applications, as are the products of KUH's Schwitzer subsidiary.

KUH's distribution, power and instrument transformers are sold mainly to electric utilities, although commercial and industrial markets are also served. Profits of Kuhlman Electric rose 50% in 1997, aided by a shift in sales mix toward higher margin products and services and efforts to improve manufacturing efficiencies at key locations. Overall, the segment increased operating earnings by 5% over 1996, with strength at Kuhlman Electric partly offset by a decline at Coleman Cable, stemming from costs related to efforts to strengthen manufacturing operations.

The company's Schwitzer subsidiary makes a variety of products that improve the performance of diesel and gasoline engines by enhancing horsepower, durability and fuel and emissions efficiency. KUH's turbochargers, which accounted for 26% of its net sales in 1997, are found on engines used in trucks and farm and construction equipment. The acquisition of Kysor and continued robust demand worldwide for various industrial engine components contributed to a 108% increase in the operating earnings of KUH's Industrial Products segment over 1996.

Per Share Data ($)

(Year Ended Dec. 31)	1997	1996	1995	1994	1993	1992	1991	1990	1989	1988
Tangible Bk. Val.	3.08	2.42	2.81	1.54	1.39	9.15	8.71	8.06	6.88	5.93
Cash Flow	3.00	2.17	1.62	1.18	0.18	1.51	1.78	1.84	1.94	-0.67
Earnings	1.75	1.26	0.76	0.27	-0.29	1.05	1.21	1.03	0.92	-1.88
Dividends	0.60	0.60	0.60	0.60	0.60	0.60	0.60	0.31	0.03	Nil
Payout Ratio	34%	48%	79%	NM	NM	55%	48%	30%	3%	Nil
Prices - High	40	19³/₈	13¹/₂	19³/₈	17¹/₄	18	18	12⁵/₈	16¹/₂	13
- Low	17¹/₈	11⁷/₈	10³/₈	11	13¹/₄	11¹/₂	9³/₄	8¹/₂	9	6¹/₄
P/E Ratio - High	23	15	18	72	NM	17	15	12	18	NM
- Low	10	9	14	41	NM	11	8	8	10	NM

Income Statement Analysis (Million $)

	1997	1996	1995	1994	1993	1992	1991	1990	1989	1988
Revs.	643	456	425	243	118	122	126	118	166	172
Oper. Inc.	77.1	50.9	40.8	11.8	4.6	11.6	14.7	16.7	15.6	10.7
Depr.	19.9	12.5	11.3	5.6	2.8	2.8	3.4	4.6	5.7	6.7
Int. Exp.	8.6	7.0	7.1	4.2	1.0	0.5	1.0	1.5	3.1	3.3
Pretax Inc.	46.5	29.3	18.1	2.9	-5.1	10.3	12.3	10.5	6.4	-13.7
Eff. Tax Rate	40%	41%	44%	45%	NM	40%	42%	45%	21%	NM
Net Inc.	27.9	17.3	10.0	1.6	-1.7	6.2	7.2	5.8	5.1	-10.3

Balance Sheet & Other Fin. Data (Million $)

	1997	1996	1995	1994	1993	1992	1991	1990	1989	1988
Cash	6.5	2.2	0.6	0.6	18.4	21.6	18.6	15.1	1.5	2.2
Curr. Assets	200	136	107	68.7	87.5	54.0	54.0	55.1	46.7	52.6
Total Assets	461	277	215	147	164	77.0	75.0	75.0	83.0	93.0
Curr. Liab.	140	81.5	67.4	40.7	45.6	15.5	15.4	17.1	21.4	25.8
LT Debt	116	92.3	63.7	55.0	67.4	8.5	9.1	9.5	20.4	34.5
Common Eqty.	175	91.6	74.2	48.7	48.9	52.7	49.8	46.0	39.0	32.7
Total Cap.	291	184	138	104	116	61.2	59.2	58.3	61.8	67.2
Cap. Exp.	20.2	11.0	15.2	7.0	2.8	5.2	6.5	5.2	5.2	3.8
Cash Flow	47.8	29.8	21.4	7.2	1.1	9.0	10.6	10.4	10.8	-3.7
Curr. Ratio	1.4	1.7	1.6	1.7	1.9	3.5	3.5	3.2	2.2	2.0
% LT Debt of Cap.	39.9	50.2	46.1	53.0	57.9	13.9	15.3	16.3	33.0	51.4
% Net Inc.of Revs.	4.3	3.8	2.4	0.7	NM	5.1	5.7	4.9	3.1	NM
% Ret. on Assets	7.6	7.0	4.5	1.0	NM	8.2	9.6	7.3	5.7	NM
% Ret. on Equity	21.0	20.9	13.6	3.3	NM	12.1	15.0	13.6	14.1	NM

Data as orig. reptd.; bef. results of disc. opers. and/or spec. items. Per share data adj. for stk. divs. as of ex-div. date. Bold denotes diluted EPS (FASB 128). E-Estimated. NA-Not Available. NM-Not Meaningful. NR-Not Ranked.

Office—Three Skidaway Village Square, Savannah, GA 31411. **Tel**—(912) 598-7809. **Chrmn & CEO**—R. S. Jepson Jr. **Pres & COO**—C. G. Anderson. **EVP & Secy**—R. A. Walker. **EVP, CFO, Treas & Investor Contact**—Vernon J. Nagel. **Dirs**—C. G. Anderson, W. E. Burch, S. Cenko, G. G. Dillon, A. W. Dreyfoos Jr., R. S. Jepson Jr., W. M. Kearns Jr., G. J. Michel Jr., H. N. Schwarzkopf. **Transfer Agent & Registrar**—Harris Trust, Chicago. **Incorporated**—in Michigan in 1915; reincorporated in Delaware in 1993. **Empl**— 4,194. **S&P Analyst**: J.J.S.

10-OCT-98

Industry:
Equipment (Semicon-ductor)

Summary: This company is the world's largest producer of semiconductor assembly equipment, including wafer dicing, die bonding and wire bonding products and systems.

S&P Opinion: Hold (★★★)	Recent Price • 11½	Yield • Nil	Earnings vs. Previous Year
	52 Wk Range • 39¼-9⅜	12-Mo. P/E • 9.7	▲-Up ▼-Down ▶-No Change

Quantitative Evaluations

Outlook
(1 Lowest—5 Highest)
• **NA**

Fair Value
• **NA**

Risk
• **High**

Earn./Div. Rank
• **B-**

Technical Eval.
• **Bearish** since 3/98

Rel. Strength Rank
(1 Lowest—99 Highest)
• **41**

Insider Activity
• **NA**

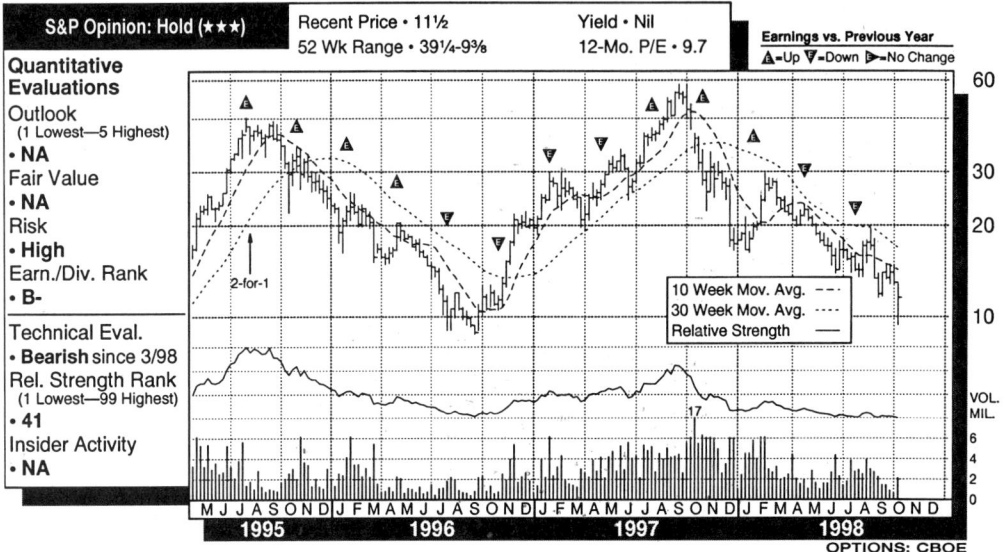

2-for-1

10 Week Mov. Avg. ---
30 Week Mov. Avg. ····
Relative Strength —

MJJASOND J FMAMJJASOND J FMAMJJASOND J FMAMJJASOND J FMAMJJASOND
1995   1996   1997   1998

VOL. MIL.

OPTIONS: CBOE

Overview - 28-JUL-98

Following sharp sequential revenue declines in the first three quarters of FY 98 (Sep.), we expect overall sales to be down about 22% for the full year. We expect a modest recovery to begin in the second half of FY 99. In recent months, the company's semiconductor customers have cancelled or deferred orders for equipment, as the Asian financial crisis has clouded end-market demand for chips. In the third quarter of FY 98, bookings were down 60% from the level of the first quarter. Gross margins will be hurt by the lower near-term volume, but should improve into FY 99, aided by an ongoing shift in the product mix toward the 8000 series of wire bonders. In light of the near-term uncertainty for new order growth, we expect EPS to fall to $0.05 in FY 98, from FY 97's $1.78. With prospects for continued weak market conditions over the next few quarters, we project a loss of $1.00 a share for FY 99.

Valuation - 28-JUL-98

With the vast majority of the company's sales being derived from the troubled Asia/Pacific region, KLIC's shares have been among the hardest hit during recent market turbulence. We are maintaining our hold rating on the stock, reflecting the company's market leading position for semiconductor assembly equipment. However, given the limited visibility for operating results over the next few quarters, we do not recommend that investors add to positions at this time. Semiconductor equipment industry conditions have deteriorated considerably over the past few months, and we do not expect a recovery to emerge until the second half of 1999. With the shares recently trading at just 1.1X book value, we recommend that patient investors hold the stock, as the company remains well positioned for the next industry upcycle.

Key Stock Statistics

S&P EPS Est. 1998	0.05	Tang. Bk. Value/Share	11.39
P/E on S&P Est. 1998	NM	Beta	2.63
S&P EPS Est. 1999	-1.00	Shareholders	700
Dividend Rate/Share	Nil	Market cap. (B)	$0.269
Shs. outstg. (M)	23.3	Inst. holdings	51%
Avg. daily vol. (M)	0.245		

Value of $10,000 invested 5 years ago: $ 36,998

Fiscal Year Ending Sep. 30

	1998	1997	1996	1995	1994	1993
Revenues (Million $)						
1Q	123.1	81.84	127.2	51.46	38.26	27.90
2Q	120.1	121.5	115.4	64.79	43.77	30.50
3Q	91.69	146.4	76.91	87.30	40.84	38.53
4Q	—	152.2	61.70	101.0	50.44	43.97
Yr.	—	501.9	381.2	304.5	173.3	140.9
Earnings Per Share ($)						
1Q	0.29	0.02	0.82	0.22	0.14	0.03
2Q	0.39	0.46	0.54	0.40	0.19	0.12
3Q	-0.13	0.62	-0.13	0.76	0.07	0.23
4Q	E-0.50	0.63	-0.65	0.85	0.23	0.27
Yr.	E0.05	1.78	0.60	2.38	0.63	0.67

Next earnings report expected: mid November

Dividend Data

Cash dividends were omitted in 1985.

A Division of The McGraw-Hill Companies

Business Summary - 28-JUL-98

Founded back in 1951 to design industrial equipment, Kulicke & Soffa Industries (KLIC) is today the world's largest producer of semiconductor assembly equipment. It is estimated that the company has a 16% share of the worldwide assembly equipment market. KLIC, based in Willow Grove, PA, also supplies packaging materials used in the semiconductor assembly process. In FY 97 (Sept.), about 85% of revenues were from customers for delivery outside the U.S.

The company's sales and earnings are affected by the level of capital investment by the semiconductor (IC) industry. Demand for assembly equipment usually lags IC plant (fab) construction by 18 months to 24 months.

Principal products are computerized automatic wire bonders, which determine the location of the semiconductor devices being assembled and position the wires being attached to them automatically rather than manually. KLIC is currently the market leader in all geographic regions except Japan.

KLIC's principal wire bonders are its 1488 model turbo ball bonder and its 1474f wedge bonder. In the second half of 1997, the company introduced a new generation of wire bonders, the 8000 family. Demand for bonders is driven largely by new fab construction.

The company makes other semiconductor assembly equipment, including precision dicing saws used to cut silicon, ceramics and other materials to extremely close tolerances and die bonders used to attach an individual semiconductor die to the package to which it is wire bonded. KLIC also offers spare parts and services for its equipment.

The company's principal strategy is to improve and broaden the range of its products. Along with enhancing its leadership position in the wire bonder market with the development of the 8000 family of products, KLIC has been forging alliances that enable it to develop new technologies. In February 1996, the company formed a joint venture with Delco Electronics Corp. called Flip Chip Technologies, L. L. C. (FCT), which provides wafer bumping services. KLIC believes that by 2002, flip chip technologies will begin to take incremental market share from wire bonding technologies in the high end of the market. In February 1997, KLIC formed an alliance with PRI Automation Inc., to develop technology to integrate and automate semiconductor assembly equipment.

The packaging materials business was greatly expanded by the 1995 acquisition of American Fine Wire Corp., a maker of gold and aluminum bonding wire, and the 1996 acquisition of Semitec, Inc., a maker of saw blades. KLIC plans to continue to expand this business, which has a less volatile revenue pattern than its equipment segment.

Per Share Data ($) (Year Ended Sep. 30)	1997	1996	1995	1994	1993	1992	1991	1990	1989	1988
Tangible Bk. Val.	10.73	5.42	6.92	3.75	3.17	2.46	3.19	3.24	3.02	2.64
Cash Flow	2.30	1.09	2.65	0.86	0.85	-0.60	0.10	0.30	0.56	0.49
Earnings	1.78	0.60	2.38	0.63	0.67	-0.78	-0.08	0.13	0.38	0.28
Dividends	Nil	Nil	Nil	Nil	Nil	Nil	Nil	Nil	Nil	Nil
Payout Ratio	Nil	Nil	Nil	Nil	Nil	Nil	Nil	Nil	Nil	Nil
Prices - High	$58\frac{3}{8}$	$25\frac{3}{4}$	$45\frac{3}{8}$	11	$15\frac{5}{8}$	$4\frac{1}{4}$	$5\frac{1}{8}$	6	5	$7\frac{3}{8}$
- Low	$16\frac{1}{2}$	$8\frac{3}{4}$	$9\frac{1}{8}$	$4\frac{3}{4}$	$3\frac{1}{8}$	$1\frac{7}{8}$	$2\frac{5}{8}$	$2\frac{3}{16}$	$3\frac{1}{4}$	$3\frac{5}{8}$
P/E Ratio - High	33	43	19	18	24	NM	NM	48	13	26
- Low	9	15	4	7	5	NM	NM	18	9	13
Income Statement Analysis (Million $)										
Revs.	502	381	305	173	141	95.0	100	103	96.0	84.0
Oper. Inc.	69.0	27.1	60.4	17.9	17.3	-4.8	3.5	11.3	9.5	9.9
Depr.	11.3	9.7	5.0	3.9	3.1	2.8	2.8	2.8	2.9	3.1
Int. Exp.	2.3	3.3	1.4	2.2	2.2	2.3	2.4	2.7	3.1	3.1
Pretax Inc.	51.8	15.6	55.6	13.0	12.1	-13.1	-1.6	2.7	5.8	4.4
Eff. Tax Rate	26%	24%	23%	20%	10%	NM	NM	28%	NM	0.50%
Net Inc.	38.3	11.8	42.8	10.4	10.8	-12.3	-1.2	1.9	5.8	4.4
Balance Sheet & Other Fin. Data (Million $)										
Cash	108	45.3	38.2	21.7	22.8	22.0	21.9	22.4	22.4	11.8
Curr. Assets	272	163	160	91.6	84.3	63.6	71.9	77.3	76.4	70.0
Total Assets	377	250	191	121	105	84.0	93.0	97.0	95.0	91.0
Curr. Liab.	82.0	48.9	56.2	30.1	26.1	17.7	14.6	17.5	12.9	13.9
LT Debt	0.2	50.7	0.2	26.5	26.7	26.8	27.7	28.5	35.2	35.9
Common Eqty.	292	147	134	63.2	51.5	39.0	50.2	50.6	46.8	40.6
Total Cap.	292	198	134	90.4	78.6	65.8	77.9	79.2	82.0	76.6
Cap. Exp.	13.5	18.0	10.8	6.2	4.4	3.6	3.8	2.4	2.6	1.7
Cash Flow	49.6	21.5	47.8	14.4	13.9	-9.5	1.6	4.8	8.7	7.5
Curr. Ratio	3.3	3.3	2.9	3.0	3.2	3.6	4.9	4.4	5.9	5.0
% LT Debt of Cap.	0.1	25.6	Nil	29.3	34.0	40.7	35.6	36.0	42.9	46.9
% Net Inc.of Revs.	7.6	3.1	14.1	6.0	7.7	NM	NM	1.9	6.0	5.2
% Ret. on Assets	12.2	5.4	27.5	9.1	11.3	NM	NM	2.0	6.3	5.0
% Ret. on Equity	17.4	8.4	43.6	18.0	23.7	NM	NM	4.0	13.3	11.3

Data as orig. reptd.; bef. results of disc. opers. and/or spec. items. Per share data adj. for stk. divs. as of ex-div. date. Bold denotes diluted EPS (FASB 128). E-Estimated. NA-Not Available. NM-Not Meaningful. NR-Not Ranked.

Office—2101 Blair Mill Rd., Willow Grove, PA 19090. **Tel**—(215) 784-6750. **Fax**—(215) 659-6167. **Website**—http://www.kns.com **Chrmn & CEO**—C. S. Kulicke. **SVP & CFO** —C. G. Sprague. **Investor Contact** —Jim Chiafery (215-784-6436). **Dirs**—J. W. Bagley, C. S. Kulicke, F. W. Kulicke Jr., J. A. O'Steen, A. F. Page, M. Roehm Jr., L. D. Striplin, C. W. Zadel. **Transfer Agent & Registrar**—American Stock Transfer & Trust Co., NYC. **Incorporated**—in Pennsylvania in 1956. **Empl**— 2,229. **S&P Analyst:** B. McGovern

LSB Industries

1319

NYSE Symbol **LSB**

In S&P SmallCap 600

03-OCT-98

Industry:
Chemicals (Diversified)

Summary: This diversified manufacturing, engineering and marketing company primarily makes and sells chemicals and air-conditioning, automotive and industrial products.

Quantitative Evaluations	
Outlook (1 Lowest—5 Highest)	
• **NA**	
Fair Value	
• **NA**	
Risk	
• **High**	
Earn./Div. Rank	
• **B-**	
Technical Eval.	
• **Bearish** since 6/98	
Rel. Strength Rank (1 Lowest—99 Highest)	
• **55**	
Insider Activity	
• **Neutral**	

Recent Price • 3⅛
52 Wk Range • 5-3

Yield • 0.6%
12-Mo. P/E • NM

Earnings vs. Previous Year
▲=Up ▼=Down ▶=No Change

10 Week Mov. Avg. – – –
30 Week Mov. Avg. - - - -
Relative Strength —

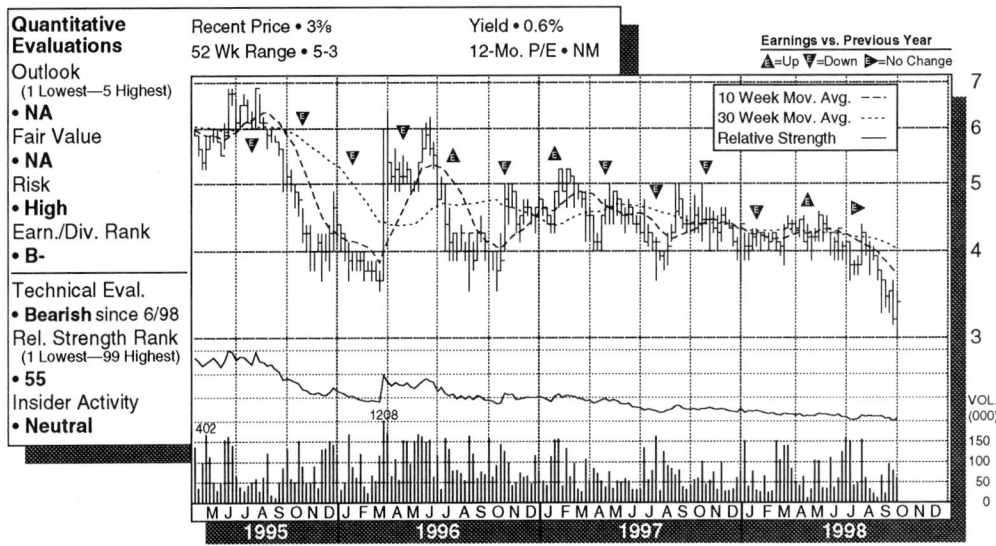

Business Profile - 11-JUN-98

LSB has reduced its investment in automotive and industrial products in order to focus on its chemical and environmental business. The company lowered its investment to $52.6 million in 1997, from $61.2 million in 1996, and plans to realize further reductions as a result of the disposal of non-core assets. By contrast, LSB increased its investment in its chemical business to $137.6 million in 1997, from $111.9 million in 1996. The company achieved improved profitability in the first quarter of 1998, and management has implemented a company-wide cost reduction program to further reduce operating expenses.

Operational Review - 11-JUN-98

Revenues in the three months ended March 31, 1998, rose 6.5%, year to year, primarily reflecting a 38% increase in climate control sales, which was partially offset by an 18% drop in chemical sales. Gross margins widened, and operating costs, expenses and interest were well controlled; an operating profit of $3,252,000 contrasted with a loss of $985,000. After a $12.8 million pretax gain on the sale of an office building, net income of $9,278,000 contrasted with a net loss of $6,241,000. After preferred dividends, income per share was $0.53, on 35% more shares, versus a loss per share of $0.48.

Stock Performance - 02-OCT-98

In the past 30 trading days, LSB's shares have declined 14%, compared to a 7% fall in the S&P 500. Average trading volume for the past five days was 12,080 shares, compared with the 40-day moving average of 9,803 shares.

Key Stock Statistics

Dividend Rate/Share	0.02	Shareholders	1,200
Shs. outstg. (M)	12.2	Market cap. (B)	$0.041
Avg. daily vol. (M)	0.013	Inst. holdings	17%
Tang. Bk. Value/Share	NM		
Beta	0.39		

Value of $10,000 invested 5 years ago: $ 5,243

Fiscal Year Ending Dec. 31

	1998	1997	1996	1995	1994	1993
Revenues (Million $)						
1Q	78.04	74.86	70.91	65.93	64.35	63.42
2Q	87.65	91.44	91.46	79.93	69.74	78.42
3Q	—	77.93	76.84	65.53	60.14	68.73
4Q	—	75.96	74.83	62.73	55.73	66.03
Yr.	—	320.2	314.1	274.1	250.0	276.6
Earnings Per Share ($)						
1Q	0.53	-0.48	-0.10	0.05	0.08	0.25
2Q	0.05	0.05	0.12	0.05	0.17	0.40
3Q	—	-0.44	-0.31	-0.20	-0.12	0.09
4Q	—	-0.82	-0.25	-0.44	-0.27	0.05
Yr.	—	-1.68	-0.54	-0.53	-0.16	0.77

Next earnings report expected: early November

Dividend Data (Dividends have been paid since 1993.)

Amount ($)	Date Decl.	Ex-Div. Date	Stock of Record	Payment Date
0.030	Dec. 22	Dec. 29	Dec. 31	Jan. 15 '98
0.010	Jun. 08	Jun. 11	Jun. 15	Jul. 01 '98

A Division of The McGraw·Hill Companies

Business Summary - 11-JUN-98

The high cost of ammonia--a key raw material in this company's Chemical business--and continuing losses in Automotive and Industrial Products combined to produce an $18.4 million net loss for LSB Industries, Inc. (LSB) in 1997. LSB lost $3.8 million in 1996. LSB in 1998 will focus on businesses and products that have emerged as leaders in specific markets or have the potential of becoming market leaders. In connection with this strategy, the company intends to dispose of all non-core and/or non-earning assets. In addition, LSB has been liquidating certain slow moving inventory in the Industrial Products business.

In its Chemical business (50% of sales in 1997), LSB manufactures three principal product lines that are derived from anhydrous ammonia: fertilizer grade ammonium nitrate for the agricultural industry; explosive grade ammonium nitrate for the mining industry; and concentrated, blended and mixed nitric acid for commercial applications. These products are sold in niche markets where the company can establish a position as a market leader.

The company's Environmental Control business (34% of sales), which makes products used in air conditioning and heating systems, enjoys leadership positions in markets for fan coils and water source and geothermal heat pumps.

In its Automotive Products business (11% of sales), which has recorded mounting losses in recent years, LSB has been focusing on product lines it believes have strategic advantages in certain markets.

Through sales of slow-moving inventory, LSB has reduced the size of its Industrial Products business (5% of sales) and intends to narrow its product offering to a limited selection of machine tool lines.

LSB's Chemical business buys 220,000 tons of anhydrous ammonia a year and uses this raw material in the manufacture of its ammonium nitrate products (fertilizer and explosives) and the production of nitric acid. During 1995, 1996 and 1997, there were substantial increases in the price of anhydrous ammonia, and the company was unable to increase its sales prices to cover all of the higher costs.

Per Share Data ($)

(Year Ended Dec. 31)	1997	1996	1995	1994	1993	1992	1991	1990	1989	1988
Tangible Bk. Val.	NM	1.68	2.25	2.90	0.34	-2.27	-5.34	-5.22	-3.35	-3.20
Cash Flow	-0.72	0.46	0.40	0.42	1.61	1.99	0.91	-0.79	1.13	0.57
Earnings	-1.68	-0.54	-0.53	-0.16	0.77	0.94	-0.48	-2.30	0.32	-0.06
Dividends	0.06	0.06	0.06	0.03	0.06	Nil	Nil	Nil	Nil	Nil
Payout Ratio	NM	NM	NM	NM	8%	Nil	Nil	Nil	Nil	Nil
Prices - High	5¼	6⅜	6⅞	10	12⅜	7¾	2⅜	1⅞	3¼	2⅛
- Low	3⅝	3½	3⅝	5¼	6¾	1¼	1	1	1½	1⅛
P/E Ratio - High	NM	NM	NM	NM	16	8	NM	NM	10	NM
- Low	NM	NM	NM	NM	9	1	NM	NM	5	NM

Income Statement Analysis (Million $)

	1997	1996	1995	1994	1993	1992	1991	1990	1989	1988
Revs.	314	307	267	245	277	247	234	248	264	216
Oper. Inc.	2.5	9.2	8.9	13.9	34.0	31.9	23.8	18.6	24.9	16.9
Depr.	12.4	9.8	9.1	8.1	11.2	8.9	8.6	8.3	6.3	4.8
Int. Exp.	14.7	12.4	11.5	7.4	9.5	13.2	16.1	16.9	14.5	8.1
Pretax Inc.	-18.4	-3.7	-3.6	0.3	13.3	9.8	-1.0	-7.9	4.6	4.0
Eff. Tax Rate	NM	NM	NM	NM	6.60%	5.30%	NM	NM	12%	64%
Net Inc.	-18.4	-3.9	-3.7	1.0	12.4	9.3	-1.1	-8.2	4.0	1.5

Balance Sheet & Other Fin. Data (Million $)

	1997	1996	1995	1994	1993	1992	1991	1990	1989	1988
Cash	4.9	1.6	1.4	2.6	13.0	33.7	24.1	50.0	7.7	28.3
Curr. Assets	133	128	117	111	NA	NA	NA	NA	NA	NA
Total Assets	271	261	238	221	598	582	606	652	662	546
Curr. Liab.	60.9	68.1	53.1	48.6	NA	NA	NA	NA	NA	NA
LT Debt	165	119	103	82.0	19.6	41.1	47.7	55.6	39.2	89.0
Common Eqty.	-3.5	25.6	33.6	42.6	26.9	3.1	-7.0	-3.8	7.1	5.5
Total Cap.	210	193	185	173	95.0	60.0	58.0	68.0	233	126
Cap. Exp.	12.6	19.9	17.8	15.6	10.5	5.3	3.9	16.3	14.9	6.5
Cash Flow	-9.2	5.9	5.3	5.8	21.6	16.3	5.5	-1.9	8.3	4.1
Curr. Ratio	2.2	1.9	2.2	2.3	NA	NA	NA	NA	NA	NA
% LT Debt of Cap.	78.6	61.7	55.7	47.5	20.8	69.0	81.9	76.2	89.1	80.2
% Net Inc.of Revs.	NM	NM	NM	0.4	4.5	3.8	NM	NM	1.5	0.7
% Ret. on Assets	NM	NM	NM	0.2	1.5	1.3	NM	NM	0.7	0.4
% Ret. on Equity	NM	NM	NM	NM	63.6	NM	NM	NM	31.7	NM

Data as orig. reptd.; bef. results of disc. opers. and/or spec. items. Per share data adj. for stk. divs. as of ex-div. date. Bold denotes diluted EPS (FASB 128). E-Estimated. NA-Not Available. NM-Not Meaningful. NR-Not Ranked.

Office—16 S. Pennsylvania Ave., Oklahoma City, OK 73107. **Reincorporated**—in Delaware in 1977. **Tel**—(405) 235-4546. **Fax**—(405) 235-5067.**Chrmn & Pres**—J. E. Golsen. **SVP-Fin, CFO & Investor Contact**—Tony M. Shelby. **VP & Treas**—J. D. Jones. **VP & Secy**—D. M. Shear. **Dirs**—R. B. Ackerman, R. C. Brown, G. J. Gagner, B. H. Golsen, J. E. Golsen, D. R. Goss, B. G. Ille, D. W. Munson, H. Rhodes, J. D. Shaffer, T. M. Shelby. **Transfer Agent & Registrar**—Liberty National Bank, Oklahoma City. **Empl**— 1,685. **S&P Analyst:** M.J.C.

Landry's Seafood Restaurants 4402K

Nasdaq Symbol **LDRY**

In S&P SmallCap 600

10-OCT-98

Industry: Restaurants

Summary: This company owns and operates full-service and take-out seafood restaurants, primarily using the Landry's Seafood House and Joe's Crab Shack names.

S&P Opinion: Avoid (★★)	Recent Price • 5¾	Yield • Nil
	52 Wk Range • 34⅜-5⅛	12-Mo. P/E • 5.0

Quantitative Evaluations

Outlook
(1 Lowest—5 Highest)
• **5**

Fair Value
• **19⅞**

Risk
• **Average**

Earn./Div. Rank
• **NR**

Technical Eval.
• **Bearish** since 5/98

Rel. Strength Rank
(1 Lowest—99 Highest)
• **7**

Insider Activity
• **NA**

Earnings vs. Previous Year
△=Up ▽=Down ▷=No Change

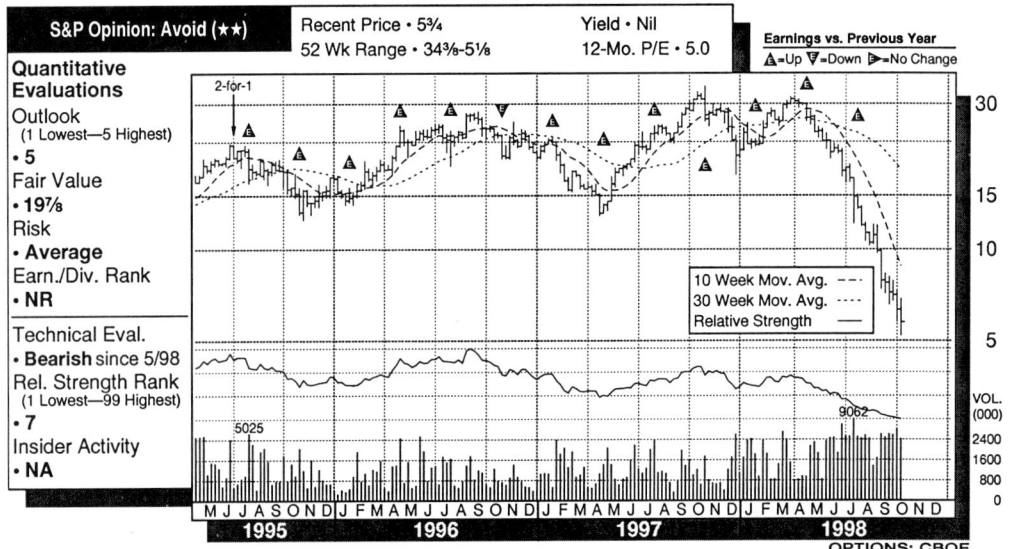

10 Week Mov. Avg. ---
30 Week Mov. Avg. ····
Relative Strength —

VOL. (000)

OPTIONS: CBOE

Overview - 12-SEP-98

Revenues grew 32% in 1997, driven primarily by the August 1996 acquisition of Bayport Restaurant Group and the addition of 40 restaurants, 30 of which were Joe's units. In 1998, sales growth should approximate 35% as the company plans to add at least 30 restaurants, bringing the total number of units to about 150. As in 1997, most of the new restaurants will be Joe's Crab Shack units. Landry's has been focusing on its Joe's concept because these restaurants are cheaper to build and offer better returns on investment. In addition, the company has been successful in converting older units to the Joe's concept, providing a 60% return on their conversion investment. As the company continually strives to become more efficient, it is experimenting with only opening certain restaurants at dinner by eliminating its lunch hours. As a result, 50% of the units opened in 1998 will not feature lunch hours.

Valuation - 12-SEP-98

We maintain our avoid rating on the shares. The shares have fallen precipitously in tandem with the overall market and as revenue growth has moderated. The company projects consolidated revenue growth of 25% in the third quarter of 1998, well below the 38% gain in the first half of 1998. As a result, we have lowered out earnings estimate for 1998 by about 10%. In addition, the company does not generate enough cash flow from operations to fund its expansion plans and we believe that additional equity will be needed to provide for expansion in 1999 and 2000. The March 1998 stock offering will enable the company to administer its expansion plans this year, however. Nevertheless, we remain concerned about the company's continual need to finance new growth via equity offerings.

Key Stock Statistics

S&P EPS Est. 1998	1.00	Tang. Bk. Value/Share	14.03
P/E on S&P Est. 1998	5.8	Beta	1.69
S&P EPS Est. 1999	1.25	Shareholders	6,100
Dividend Rate/Share	Nil	Market cap. (B)	$0.174
Shs. outstg. (M)	30.3	Inst. holdings	81%
Avg. daily vol. (M)	0.892		

Value of $10,000 invested 5 years ago: NA

Fiscal Year Ending Dec. 31

	1998	1997	1996	1995	1994	1993
Revenues (Million $)						
1Q	90.05	64.30	53.07	20.61	11.39	6.71
2Q	111.0	81.18	66.29	27.74	15.72	8.82
3Q	—	89.81	64.39	29.01	19.69	9.66
4Q	—	76.38	52.36	26.66	15.72	9.05
Yr.	—	311.7	236.1	104.0	62.53	34.24
Earnings Per Share ($)						
1Q	0.28	0.22	0.17	0.12	0.08	0.00
2Q	0.36	0.30	0.22	0.16	0.11	0.09
3Q	E0.20	0.32	-0.40	0.17	0.13	0.09
4Q	E0.16	0.19	0.14	0.10	0.08	0.05
Yr.	E1.00	1.03	0.06	0.55	0.40	0.28

Next earnings report expected: NA

Dividend Data

The company currently does not pay dividends. A two-for-one stock split was effected in June 1995.

A Division of The McGraw·Hill Companies

Business Summary - 12-SEP-98

In 1988, the company's current chairman Tilman Fertitta acquired two existing Landry's restaurants and, through an aggressive has growth plan, the chain has grown to over 120 restaurants. Restaurants are operated under the divisional names Joe's Crab Shack (58 units at February 19, 1998), Landry's Seafood House (43), and The Crab House (21). At March 31, 1998, there were 127 units in operation, mainly in southern states.

The company's strategy is based on an aggressive growth plan within a unique segment of the market. Management believes that there are a small number of regional and national seafood chains competing within the restaurant industry in comparison to other restaurant segments. As a result, the company believes it has an opportunity to capitalize on its casual dining, value-oriented restaurant concepts.

Since 1990, the company has pursued an aggressive expansion strategy via the opening of new units, conversions of existing restaurants and the August 1996 acquisition 17 Crab House restaurants via the acquisition of Bayport Restaurant Group, Inc. The company plans to open at least 45 units in 1998 and another 45 units in 1999. Expansion efforts will primarily be focused in the southern and Midwestern states of the U.S., with select development or acquisitions outside these areas. The primary driver of this expansion will primarily utilize the Joe's Crab Shack concept, given its strong economics and appeal to customers.

Landry's has always emphasized the distinctive design and locations of its units. The Joe's Crab Shack units are designed to resemble an old fishing camp with a wood facade, tin roof and a raised outside deck, while the Landry's Seafood Houses typically can be identified by its large theatre-style marquee over the entrance and its distinctive brick and wood facade. The Crab House restaurants are highlighted by their nautical themes, many of which include a fresh seafood salad bar. Many of the restaurants also feature outdoor patio service for an open-air dining experience that often features waterfront views. Restaurants are generally located in markets which provide a balanced mix of tourist, convention, business and residential traffic. Factors the company considers in its site selection are local market demographics, site visibility, aesthetics (including waterfront views), and proximity to significant generators of potential customers.

Restaurants are typically 5,000 sq. ft. to 16,000 sq. ft. in size, averaging 8,000 sq. ft., with seating capacity for approximately 215 customers and bar seating for approximately 10 to 20 additional patrons. The menu offers a wide variety of high quality, broiled, grilled and fried seafood at moderate prices, including red snapper, shrimp, crawfish, lump crabmeat, lobster, oysters, scallops, flounder, and other traditional seafood offerings.

Per Share Data ($)

(Year Ended Dec. 31)	1997	1996	1995	1994	1993	1992	1991	1990	1989	1988
Tangible Bk. Val.	11.30	10.05	6.59	3.96	1.36	NA	NA	NA	NA	NA
Cash Flow	1.67	0.60	0.87	0.61	0.40	0.30	NA	NA	NA	NA
Earnings	1.03	0.06	0.55	0.40	0.28	0.22	NA	NA	NA	NA
Dividends	Nil	Nil	Nil	Nil	Nil	Nil	NA	NA	NA	NA
Payout Ratio	Nil	Nil	Nil	Nil	Nil	Nil	NA	NA	NA	NA
Prices - High	34³⁄₈	28³⁄₈	22¹⁄₄	15³⁄₈	12¹⁄₈	NA	NA	NA	NA	NA
- Low	12⁷⁄₈	14	12¹⁄₂	8⁵⁄₈	6	NA	NA	NA	NA	NA
P/E Ratio - High	33	NM	40	38	43	NA	NA	NA	NA	NA
- Low	12	NM	23	22	21	NA	NA	NA	NA	NA

Income Statement Analysis (Million $)

	1997	1996	1995	1994	1993	1992	1991	1990	1989	1988
Revs.	312	236	104	62.5	34.2	22.4	NA	NA	NA	NA
Oper. Inc.	58.5	39.2	18.5	10.8	5.5	3.7	NA	NA	NA	NA
Depr.	17.1	13.0	5.5	2.9	1.2	0.6	NA	NA	NA	NA
Int. Exp.	Nil	Nil	0.1	0.1	0.3	0.2	NA	NA	NA	NA
Pretax Inc.	42.8	2.3	14.8	8.8	4.3	3.1	NA	NA	NA	NA
Eff. Tax Rate	36%	34%	35%	36%	11%	4.40%	NA	NA	NA	NA
Net Inc.	27.4	1.5	9.6	5.7	2.7	2.0	NA	NA	NA	NA

Balance Sheet & Other Fin. Data (Million $)

	1997	1996	1995	1994	1993	1992	1991	1990	1989	1988
Cash	17.2	57.3	16.6	19.5	6.7	NA	NA	NA	NA	NA
Curr. Assets	62.2	85.4	23.7	22.9	8.2	NA	NA	NA	NA	NA
Total Assets	382	281	140	71.1	24.9	NA	NA	NA	NA	NA
Curr. Liab.	27.1	21.0	15.2	8.1	4.5	NA	NA	NA	NA	NA
LT Debt	50.2	0.2	0.4	0.7	1.8	NA	NA	NA	NA	NA
Common Eqty.	297	256	122	62.0	18.4	NA	NA	NA	NA	NA
Total Cap.	347	257	123	62.7	20.2	NA	NA	NA	NA	NA
Cap. Exp.	136	64.5	71.3	32.1	9.4	2.6	NA	NA	NA	NA
Cash Flow	44.5	14.5	15.1	8.6	3.9	2.6	NA	NA	NA	NA
Curr. Ratio	2.3	4.1	1.6	2.8	1.8	NA	NA	NA	NA	NA
% LT Debt of Cap.	14.5	0.1	0.3	1.2	8.9	NA	NA	NA	NA	NA
% Net Inc.of Revs.	8.8	0.6	9.2	9.1	8.0	8.8	NA	NA	NA	NA
% Ret. on Assets	8.3	0.6	9.1	11.8	15.5	NA	NA	NA	NA	NA
% Ret. on Equity	9.9	0.8	10.4	14.1	25.2	NA	NA	NA	NA	NA

Data as orig. reptd.; bef. results of disc. opers. and/or spec. items. Per share data adj. for stk. divs. as of ex-div. date. Bold denotes diluted EPS (FASB 128). E-Estimated. NA-Not Available. NM-Not Meaningful. NR-Not Ranked.

Office—1400 Post Oak Blvd., Suite 1010, Houston, TX 77056.**Tel**—(713) 850-1010.**Chrmn, Pres & CEO**—T. J. Fertitta.**EVP & COO**—E. A. Jaksa, Jr.**VP & CFO**—P. S. West. **VP & Secy**—S. L. Scheinthal.**Dirs**—T. J. Fertitta, A. Jaska, Jr., J. E. Masucci, S. L. Scheinthal, J. M. Taylor, P. S. West.**Transfer Agent & Registrar**—American Stock Transfer, New York.**Incorporated**—in Delaware in 1993.**Empl**— 8,200. **S&P Analyst:** Robert J. Izmirlian

La-Z-Boy

1319Z
NYSE Symbol **LZB**

In S&P SmallCap 600

03-OCT-98

Industry:
Household Furnishings
& Appliances

Summary: LZB manufactures residential and office upholstered seating products, including recliners and motion chairs, and solid-wood bedroom/dining room products.

Quantitative Evaluations

Outlook
(1 Lowest—5 Highest)
• **2**

Fair Value
• **21**

Risk
• **Low**

Earn./Div. Rank
• **A-**

Technical Eval.
• **Bullish** since 9/98

Rel. Strength Rank
(1 Lowest—99 Highest)
• **75**

Insider Activity
• **Neutral**

Recent Price • 18½
52 Wk Range • 22⅝-12

Yield • 1.7%
12-Mo. P/E • 18.0

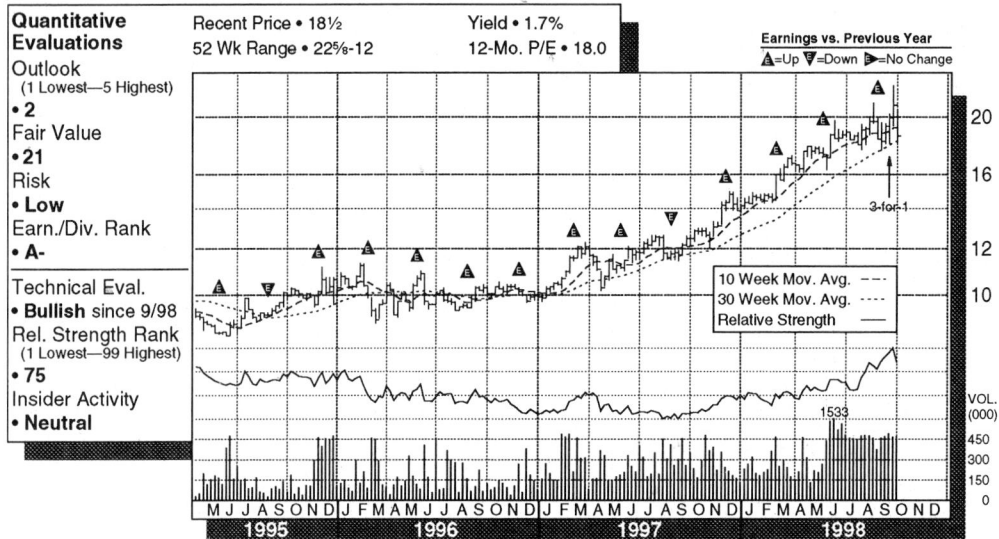

Earnings vs. Previous Year
▲=Up ▼=Down ▶=No Change

10 Week Mov. Avg. – – –
30 Week Mov. Avg. · · · ·
Relative Strength —

Business Profile - 17-SEP-98

One of the world's largest furniture producers, La-Z-Boy (LZB) continued to report record revenue and earnings. According to management, strong product demand during the spring contributed to robust sales and profits. LZB aims for growth exceeding that of the furniture industry, with a benchmark of 10% annually. Other goals include an earnings growth rate more rapid than that of sales and a 20% return on capital. Management expects strong revenue growth to continue in August and September 1998. LZB has a strong balance sheet; at the end of FY 1998 (Apr.), the debt to capital ratio stood at 16%, and the current ratio totaled 3.5 to 1.

Operational Review - 17-SEP-98

For the quarter ended July 25, 1998, revenues rose 27%, year to year, reflecting strong sales, three acquisitions, price increases, and a more profitable product mix. Significant growth in unit sales permitted fixed costs to be absorbed more efficiently, leading to higher gross margins. Selling, general and administrative costs increased 13%, as a result of lower bad debt expense. Interest expense grew 16%, while interest income rose 20%. The income tax rate decreased to 39.7%, from 42.3%. Net income more than tripled to $7.2 million ($0.40 a share), from $1.7 million ($0.10).

Stock Performance - 02-OCT-98

In the past 30 trading days, LZB's shares have declined 6%, compared to a 7% fall in the S&P 500. Average trading volume for the past five days was 138,320 shares, compared with the 40-day moving average of 131,423 shares.

Key Stock Statistics

Dividend Rate/Share	0.32	Shareholders	12,700
Shs. outstg. (M)	53.2	Market cap. (B)	$0.988
Avg. daily vol. (M)	0.150	Inst. holdings	16%
Tang. Bk. Value/Share	6.33		
Beta	0.69		

Value of $10,000 invested 5 years ago: $ 24,194

Fiscal Year Ending Apr. 30

	1999	1998	1997	1996	1995	1994
Revenues (Million $)						
1Q	268.9	212.3	202.2	195.8	174.4	162.1
2Q	—	293.2	271.6	258.3	230.6	209.0
3Q	—	280.5	244.6	226.3	210.8	192.7
4Q	—	322.0	287.5	266.8	234.5	241.1
Yr.	—	1,108	1,006	947.3	850.3	804.9
Earnings Per Share ($)						
1Q	0.13	0.03	0.08	0.06	0.08	0.07
2Q	—	0.31	0.20	0.20	0.22	0.10
3Q	—	0.21	0.18	0.14	0.13	0.15
4Q	—	0.37	0.29	0.25	0.24	0.22
Yr.	—	0.93	0.83	0.71	0.67	0.63

Next earnings report expected: NA

Dividend Data (Dividends have been paid since 1963.)

Amount ($)	Date Decl.	Ex-Div. Date	Stock of Record	Payment Date
0.210	Jan. 13	Feb. 18	Feb. 20	Mar. 10 '98
0.210	May. 12	May. 20	May. 22	Jun. 10 '98
0.240	Jul. 27	Aug. 19	Aug. 21	Sep. 10 '98
3-for-1	Jul. 27	Sep. 15	Aug. 21	Sep. 14 '98

A Division of The **McGraw·Hill** *Companies*

Business Summary - 17-SEP-98

In 1928, Edward Knabusch and Edwin Shoemaker invented the wood slat reclining chair, enhancing the prospects of the furniture company they founded a year earlier. The 1961 introduction by the company (known since 1941 as La-Z-Boy Chair) of the three-position Reclina Rocker caused sales to explode. While reclining chairs remain an important part of its business--La-Z-Boy is the world's leading producer--the company has since expanded its product line to include a full range of upholstered and wood furniture products across six operating divisions, and it believes that most of its growth opportunities lie outside the recliner market segment. In order to better reflect the true breadth of its furniture lines, which now take La-Z-Boy into every room in the home (and into offices as well), the company in 1996 dropped the word "Chair" from its title and is now known simply as La-Z-Boy Inc. (LZB), the nation's third largest furniture maker.

The company's La-Z-Boy Residential division, which accounts for the majority of sales, produces numerous upholstered products, including stationary chairs, sofas and loveseats, recliners, reclining sofas, sleep sofas and modular seating groups. LZB's Hammary unit makes occasional tables, living room cabinets, wall entertainment units and upholstered furniture, and the company's Kincaid division specializes in solid-wood bedroom and dining room furniture. Other units include England/Corsair (upholstered furniture), La-Z-Boy Canada and the company's contract furniture group, which makes furniture for office and institutional settings. Upholstered products for the home accounted for 77% of sales in FY 98 (Apr.) and residential wood furniture 17%; contract furniture contributed the remaining 6%. LZB ranks number one in the U.S. in both upholstered furniture and solid-wood furniture. The company's products are sold through a vast retail network that includes free-standing La-Z-Boy Furniture Gallery stores, In-Store Gallery stores, Sears HomeLife stores, regional furniture chains and thousands of independent dealers.

LZB's marketing efforts are pursued at the national, local and store level. In its national advertising campaign, the company uses the slogan "We Make the Rooms that Make a Home" to help reposition LZB as a total home furnishings resource. LZB also assists dealers with local advertising and in-store promotional tools.

Sales surpassed $1.1 billion in FY 98, and net income advanced 10% to $49.9 million. On August 5, 1998, LZB announced a 14% dividend increase to $0.24.

Per Share Data ($)

(Year Ended Apr. 30)	1998	1997	1996	1995	1994	1993	1992	1991	1990	1989
Tangible Bk. Val.	6.33	5.97	5.49	5.06	4.92	4.43	4.11	3.81	3.54	3.16
Cash Flow	1.32	1.21	1.07	0.95	0.89	0.76	0.74	0.69	0.78	0.75
Earnings	0.93	0.83	0.71	0.67	0.63	0.50	0.46	0.43	0.53	0.51
Dividends	0.28	0.26	0.25	0.23	0.21	0.20	0.19	0.19	0.18	0.15
Payout Ratio	30%	31%	35%	34%	34%	40%	42%	43%	34%	30%

Cal. Yrs.	1997	1996	1995	1994	1993	1992	1991	1990	1989	1988
Prices - High	15	11³/₈	11¹/₈	13³/₈	13	9⁵/₈	8³/₈	7³/₈	7³/₄	6³/₈
- Low	9⁷/₈	9	8¹/₂	8³/₈	8³/₈	5⁷/₈	5	4¹/₈	5⁵/₈	4¹/₂
P/E Ratio - High	16	14	16	20	20	19	18	17	15	12
- Low	11	11	12	13	13	12	11	10	11	9

Income Statement Analysis (Million $)

	1998	1997	1996	1995	1994	1993	1992	1991	1990	1989
Revs.	1,108	1,006	947	850	805	684	619	608	592	553
Oper. Inc.	98.2	94.3	87.6	78.0	73.3	60.9	58.4	57.3	64.0	61.1
Depr.	21.0	20.4	20.1	15.2	14.0	14.1	14.8	14.0	13.7	12.6
Int. Exp.	4.2	4.4	5.3	3.3	2.8	3.3	5.3	6.4	7.2	7.6
Pretax Inc.	79.3	73.8	66.2	62.0	58.2	45.3	39.9	38.4	45.5	44.0
Eff. Tax Rate	37%	39%	41%	42%	40%	40%	37%	39%	38%	38%
Net Inc.	49.9	45.3	39.2	36.3	34.7	27.3	25.1	23.4	28.3	27.5

Balance Sheet & Other Fin. Data (Million $)

	1998	1997	1996	1995	1994	1993	1992	1991	1990	1989
Cash	28.7	25.0	27.0	27.0	25.9	28.8	21.7	13.0	6.7	18.2
Curr. Assets	383	343	337	325	296	279	254	238	240	236
Total Assets	580	528	528	504	430	401	377	363	362	349
Curr. Liab.	108	97.7	96.5	88.1	71.5	77.5	69.1	65.2	70.1	76.9
LT Debt	67.3	54.7	61.2	76.4	52.5	55.4	55.9	62.2	69.1	70.6
Common Eqty.	388	359	343	324	291	263	246	229	215	194
Total Cap.	461	420	411	407	350	324	308	298	292	272
Cap. Exp.	22.0	17.8	18.1	19.0	17.5	12.2	12.2	21.4	22.4	9.3
Cash Flow	70.9	65.7	59.4	51.5	48.7	41.3	39.9	37.4	42.0	40.1
Curr. Ratio	3.5	3.5	3.5	3.7	4.1	3.6	3.7	3.7	3.4	3.1
% LT Debt of Cap.	14.6	13.0	14.9	18.8	15.0	17.1	18.2	20.9	23.7	26.0
% Net Inc.of Revs.	4.5	4.5	4.1	4.3	4.3	4.0	4.1	3.8	4.8	5.0
% Ret. on Assets	9.0	8.7	7.7	7.8	8.3	7.0	6.8	6.4	7.9	8.1
% Ret. on Equity	13.4	12.9	11.7	11.9	12.5	10.7	10.5	10.5	13.8	14.8

Data as orig. reptd.; bef. results of disc. opers. and/or spec. items. Per share data adj. for stk. divs. as of ex-div. date. Bold denotes diluted EPS (FASB 128). E-Estimated. NA-Not Available. NM-Not Meaningful. NR-Not Ranked.

Office—1284 N. Telegraph Rd., Monroe, MI 48162-3390. **Tel**—(734) 241-4414. **Website**—http://www.lazboy.com **Chrmn**—P. H. Norton. **Pres**—G. L. Kiser. **VP-Fin**—F. H. Jackson. **Secy, Treas & Investor Contact**—Gene M. Hardy. **Dirs**— G. M. Hardy, D. K. Hehl, F. H. Jackson, J. W. Johnston, G. L. Kiser, H.G. Levy, R. E. Lipford, P. H. Norton, L. G. Stevens, J. F. Weaver. **Transfer Agent & Registrar**—American Stock Transfer & Trust, NYC. **Incorporated**—in Michigan in 1941. **Empl**— 12,155. **S&P Analyst:** J. Staszak

Landstar System   4402N

Nasdaq Symbol **LSTR**

In S&P SmallCap 600

03-OCT-98 | Industry: Truckers

Summary: Landstar is one of the largest truckload carriers in North America. With the sale of its Poole unit, LSTR operates entirely with independent contractors and commission agents.

S&P Opinion: Accumulate (★★★★)	Recent Price • 28⅝	Yield • Nil
	52 Wk Range • 37¼-23⅝	12-Mo. P/E • 61.0

Quantitative Evaluations

Outlook
(1 Lowest—5 Highest)
• **4+**

Fair Value
• **36¾**

Risk
• **Average**

Earn./Div. Rank
• **NR**

Technical Eval.
• **Bearish** since 9/98

Rel. Strength Rank
(1 Lowest—99 Highest)
• **57**

Insider Activity
• **NA**

Earnings vs. Previous Year
▲=Up ▼=Down ▶=No Change

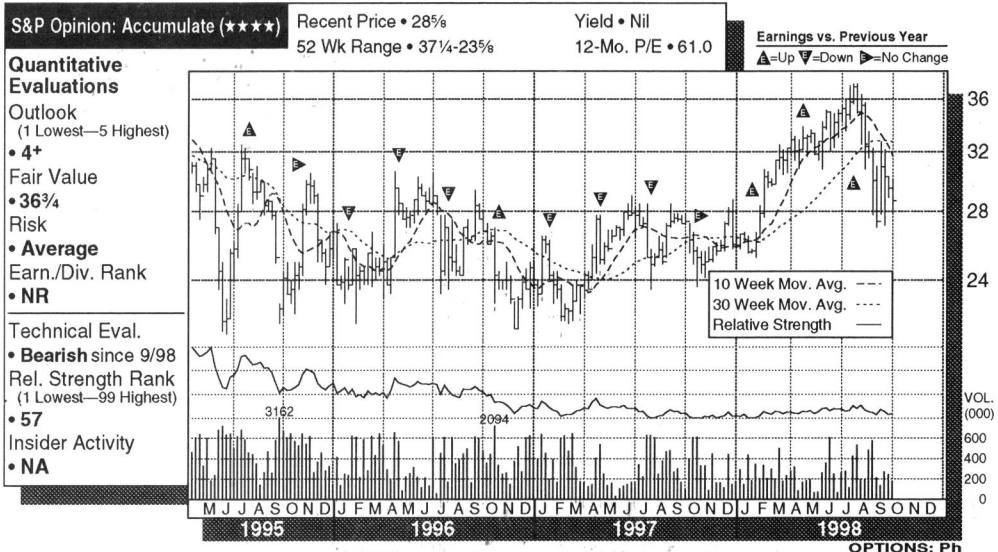

10 Week Mov. Avg. ---
30 Week Mov. Avg. ·····
Relative Strength —

OPTIONS: Ph

Overview - 29-JUL-98

A solid profit from continuing operations is projected for 1998. Volume growth will resume in 1998, after slipping in 1997, reflecting the consolidation of operations. LSTR's management projects that it can add about 100 contractors per quarter, indicating at least a 5% increase in capacity. Good growth is projected for LSTR's logistics business, as it expands its share of business from existing clients, and attracts new customers in the automotive and food service industries. Landstar Express will grow rapidly, and should move into the black, reflecting the significant increase in the number of Express Centers opened in 1997. Aiding margins will be increased utilization for LSTR's contractors, following installation of a new computer system and reduced cargo claims. Revenue per load will increase reflecting an improved freight mix. A solid contribution is anticipated from the insurance unit. Comparisons will benefit from the absence of restructuring charges, and from 11% fewer shares outstanding.

Valuation - 29-JUL-98

In July, the shares of this truckload carrier were challenging highs set in 1995. Investors applauded LSTR's agreement to sell its last salaried driver carrier unit. This move should free up capital that is likely to be used to fund additional share repurchases. LSTR has purchased $34.3 million of its stock in 1998, at an average price of $30.83 a share. Excess cash flow has also been used to cut debt. Management currently believes that it can expand its contractor base by 5% in 1998. We view this as realistic, given new policies, such as providing greater training and financial assistance for drivers and passing through savings in the area of fuel and insurance. The shares, recently trading in line with the P/Es of other truckload carriers, are still worth accumulating.

Key Stock Statistics

S&P EPS Est. 1998	2.60	Tang. Bk. Value/Share	6.79
P/E on S&P Est. 1998	11.0	Beta	0.39
S&P EPS Est. 1999	2.85	Shareholders	100
Dividend Rate/Share	Nil	Market cap. (B)	$0.311
Shs. outstg. (M)	10.9	Inst. holdings	89%
Avg. daily vol. (M)	0.042		

Value of $10,000 invested 5 years ago: NA

Fiscal Year Ending Dec. 31

	1998	1997	1996	1995	1994	1993
Revenues (Million $)						
1Q	320.2	305.6	295.5	295.7	207.2	171.1
2Q	327.5	333.7	329.1	308.1	250.2	197.0
3Q	—	326.3	330.2	298.7	247.6	200.6
4Q	—	347.1	329.0	302.1	279.4	211.7
Yr.	—	1,313	1,284	1,205	984.4	780.5
Earnings Per Share ($)						
1Q	**0.38**	**0.24**	0.25	0.37	0.26	0.01
2Q	**0.79**	**0.51**	0.55	0.61	0.51	0.33
3Q	**E0.70**	**0.60**	0.60	0.56	0.56	0.37
4Q	**E0.69**	**0.62**	0.08	0.41	0.57	0.39
Yr.	**E2.60**	**1.96**	1.48	1.95	1.90	1.14

Next earnings report expected: mid October

Dividend Data

The company has not paid cash dividends on the common stock and does not intend to pay dividends for the foreseeable future.

Business Summary - 29-JUL-98

Landstar System, Inc., which operates through several major subsidiaries, is collectively the third largest truckload carrier in North America. Truckload carriers transport large shipments from origin to destination and hence have few, if any, terminal facilities. Landstar transports a wide variety of items ranging from bulk raw materials to finished manufactured goods. LSTR's operating strategy is to limit its investment in fixed assets by harnessing the services of independent owner-operator drivers and commission sales agents. It will realize its goal of a 100% variable cost operation with the planned sale of Landstar Poole in August 1998.

In 1997, 93% of revenues were generated from independent contractor drivers. LSTR will derive all of its revenues from independent drivers effective August 1998, following the sale of Poole. LSTR provides its 6,500 contractors with 60% to 70% of the revenues generated per load, if they supply the tractor, and with up to 75% if a trailer is included. By using contractors, LSTR avoids investment in rolling stock, has little exposure to fuel price changes, and is relatively insulated from industry downturns.

The second component of Landstar's "variable cost" strategy is to use the services of independent commission sales agents in place of salaried personnel. LSTR's 1,000 agents earn a base commission of 7% of revenues, and up to 10% after certain volume incentives have been attained.

LSTR's carrier group (72% of 1997 revenues) includes the Ranger, Inway and Ligon units. These carriers operate almost exclusively with independent contractors and agents. Ranger and Inway operate nationwide and in parts of Canada and Mexico while Ligon primarily serves the eastern and midwestern U.S.

In July 1998, LSTR agreed to sell Landstar Poole (7% of 1997 revenues), which primarily provides truckload services in the eastern U.S., to Schneider National, Inc., for $41 million. LSTR recorded a $21.5 million loss on the pending sale in the 1998 second quarter income statement. The sale of Poole, expected to close by late August 1998, completes LSTR's plan to operate exclusively with independent contractors and commission agents.

The multimodal group (19% of 1997 revenues) includes Landstar Logistics and Landstar Express America. Landstar Logistics provides contract logistics and intermodal services. Logistics involves providing a single source solution for large customers for all of their transportation and distribution needs. Intermodal services involves the arrangement of transportation (both rail and truck) to provide door-to-door coverage. Landstar Express provides expedited air and ground transportation services. Signature Insurance Co., established in 1997 (2% of revenues), cuts insurance costs for LSTR's owner-operators, and also contributes to the bottom line.

Per Share Data ($)

(Year Ended Dec. 31)	1997	1996	1995	1994	1993	1992	1991	1990	1989	1988
Tangible Bk. Val.	8.21	7.28	5.58	5.66	3.69	2.07	NA	NA	NA	NA
Cash Flow	3.63	3.36	3.58	2.95	2.22	0.98	NA	NA	NA	NA
Earnings	1.96	1.48	1.95	1.90	1.14	0.67	0.22	NA	NA	NA
Dividends	Nil	Nil	Nil	Nil	Nil	Nil	Nil	Nil	Nil	Nil
Payout Ratio	Nil	Nil	Nil	Nil	Nil	Nil	Nil	Nil	Nil	Nil
Prices - High	29	30⅝	37¾	36	22⅛	NA	NA	NA	NA	NA
- Low	21¾	21½	21¼	19¾	12¼	NA	NA	NA	NA	NA
P/E Ratio - High	15	21	19	19	19	NA	NA	NA	NA	NA
- Low	11	15	11	10	11	NA	NA	NA	NA	NA

Income Statement Analysis (Million $)

	1997	1996	1995	1994	1993	1992	1991	1990	1989	1988
Revs.	1,313	1,284	1,205	984	781	672	NA	NA	NA	NA
Oper. Inc.	71.3	71.2	70.8	59.3	43.0	34.7	NA	NA	NA	NA
Depr.	20.9	24.0	20.8	13.5	12.8	11.8	NA	NA	NA	NA
Int. Exp.	4.6	7.5	17.5	4.1	5.7	9.7	NA	NA	NA	NA
Pretax Inc.	42.6	32.4	42.5	41.6	24.5	13.2	NA	NA	NA	NA
Eff. Tax Rate	42%	41%	41%	41%	45%	52%	NA	NA	NA	NA
Net Inc.	24.7	19.0	25.0	24.4	13.6	6.4	NA	NA	NA	NA

Balance Sheet & Other Fin. Data (Million $)

	1997	1996	1995	1994	1993	1992	1991	1990	1989	1988
Cash	18.0	4.2	3.4	17.8	15.1	NA	NA	NA	NA	NA
Curr. Assets	218	201	179	155	124	NA	NA	NA	NA	NA
Total Assets	357	371	353	267	219	NA	NA	NA	NA	NA
Curr. Liab.	139	130	127	113	87.0	NA	NA	NA	NA	NA
LT Debt	36.2	67.2	73.2	30.5	36.4	NA	NA	NA	NA	NA
Common Eqty.	152	148	128	105	81.0	NA	NA	NA	NA	NA
Total Cap.	190	215	202	136	117	NA	NA	NA	NA	NA
Cap. Exp.	9.8	12.8	7.3	7.5	6.7	3.5	NA	NA	NA	NA
Cash Flow	45.6	42.9	45.8	37.9	26.3	18.2	NA	NA	NA	NA
Curr. Ratio	1.6	1.5	1.4	1.2	1.4	NA	NA	NA	NA	NA
% LT Debt of Cap.	19.1	31.3	36.3	22.5	31.2	NA	NA	NA	NA	NA
% Net Inc.of Revs.	1.9	1.5	2.1	2.5	1.7	0.9	NA	NA	NA	NA
% Ret. on Assets	6.8	5.2	8.1	10.1	6.8	NA	NA	NA	NA	NA
% Ret. on Equity	16.5	13.7	21.4	26.2	24.2	NA	NA	NA	NA	NA

Data as orig. reptd.; bef. results of disc. opers. and/or spec. items. Per share data adj. for stk. divs. as of ex-div. date. Bold denotes diluted EPS (FASB 128). E-Estimated. NA-Not Available. NM-Not Meaningful. NR-Not Ranked.

Office—4160 Woodcock Dr., Jacksonville, FL 32207.**Tel**—(904) 390-1234.**Website**—http://www.landstar.com**Chrmn, Pres & CEO**—J. C. Crowe.**EVP & CFO**—H. H. Gerkens.**VP**—M. L. Harvey.**Investor Contact**—Pamela J. Miller (904-390-1530).**Dirs**—D. G. Bannister, J. B. Bowron, J. C. Crowe, R. W. Drucker, W. S. Elston, M. J. Mott, D. M. Murphy.**Transfer Agent**—ChaseMellon Shareholder Services, NYC.**Incorporated**—in Delaware in 1991.**Empl**— 2,050. **S&P Analyst:** Stephen R. Klein

Lattice Semiconductor   4407

NASDAQ Symbol **LSCC**

In S&P SmallCap 600

03-OCT-98

Industry:
Electronics (Semicon-
ductors)

Summary: This company designs, develops and markets both high and low performance programmable logic devices (PLDs) and related development system software.

Quantitative Evaluations	
Outlook (1 Lowest—5 Highest)	• **5**
Fair Value	• **39¾**
Risk	• **High**
Earn./Div. Rank	• **B+**
Technical Eval.	• **NA**
Rel. Strength Rank (1 Lowest—99 Highest)	• **31**
Insider Activity	• **Favorable**

Recent Price • 23½
52 Wk Range • 67½-23¼

Yield • Nil
12-Mo. P/E • 10.8

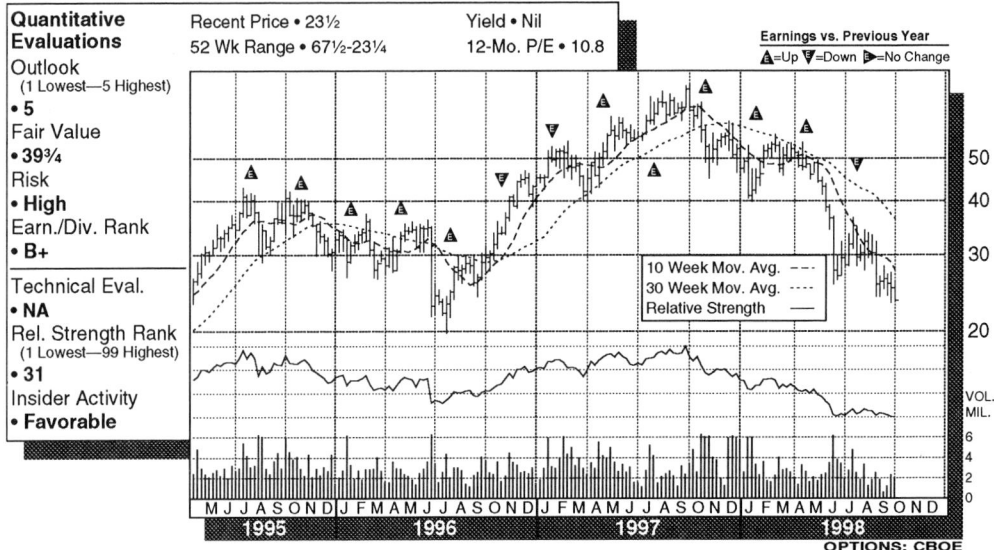

Earnings vs. Previous Year
▲=Up ▼=Down ▶=No Change

10 Week Mov. Avg. - - -
30 Week Mov. Avg. ·····
Relative Strength —

OPTIONS: CBOE

Business Profile - 07-AUG-98

This company's programmable logic devices (PLDs) shorten design cycles and reduce development costs by allowing their users to quickly and efficiently incorporate different logic functions on a single device. LSCC, a "fabless" semiconductor company, maintains relationships with other companies to source its finished silicon wafers and assemble it products. Lattice products are sold worldwide through an extensive network of independent sales representatives and distributors, primarily to original equipment manufacturers (OEMs) of communications, computing, industrial controls, and military systems.

Operational Review - 07-AUG-98

Revenues in the three months ended June 27, 1998, fell 22%, year to year, reflecting a shortfall in direct OEM business from the data communications and computing end markets. Aided by a more favorable product mix and reductions in manufacturing costs, gross margins improved by 80 basis points, to 60.2%. Operating margins declined, however, as relatively flat R&D and 8% lower SG&A expenses were spread over a much smaller sales base. With no change in other income, and despite taxes at a lower rate, net income fell 31%, to $9,816,000 ($0.41 a share, diluted), from $14,168,000 ($0.60).

Stock Performance - 02-OCT-98

In the past 30 trading days, LSCC's shares have declined 22%, compared to a 7% fall in the S&P 500. Average trading volume for the past five days was 389,380 shares, compared with the 40-day moving average of 348,900 shares.

Key Stock Statistics

Dividend Rate/Share	Nil	Shareholders	300
Shs. outstg. (M)	23.5	Market cap. (B)	$0.554
Avg. daily vol. (M)	0.314	Inst. holdings	88%
Tang. Bk. Value/Share	19.03		
Beta	1.56		

Value of $10,000 invested 5 years ago: $ 14,137

Fiscal Year Ending Mar. 31

	1999	1998	1997	1996	1995	1994
Revenues (Million $)						
1Q	48.03	61.62	48.17	45.01	32.91	33.35
2Q	—	64.07	48.64	48.61	34.56	34.14
3Q	—	60.04	51.02	51.54	36.29	28.57
4Q	—	60.17	56.26	53.01	40.32	30.19
Yr.	—	245.9	204.1	198.2	144.1	126.2
Earnings Per Share ($)						
1Q	**0.41**	0.60	0.46	0.45	0.32	0.30
2Q	—	0.62	0.46	0.49	0.34	0.32
3Q	—	0.57	0.49	0.52	0.36	0.27
4Q	—	0.58	0.55	0.53	0.40	0.30
Yr.	—	2.37	1.96	1.99	1.41	1.19

Next earnings report expected: NA

Dividend Data

No cash dividends have been paid. A three-for-two stock split was distributed in July 1993.

A Division of The McGraw-Hill Companies

Lattice Semiconductor Corporation

Business Summary - 07-AUG-98

Lattice Semiconductor Corporation is the world's leading supplier of in-system programmable (ISP) logic devices. The company pioneered the application of electrically erasable CMOS (E2CMOS) technology to programmable logic. LSCC designs, develops and markets both high- and low-density, high performance E2CMOS programmable logic devices (PLDs) and related development system software. PLDs are standard semiconductor components that can be custom configured by the customer to perform specific logic functions. PLDs enable the customer to shorten design cycle times and reduce development costs. LSCC's proprietary generic array logic (GAL), pLSI (programmable large scale integration) and ispLSI (in-system programmable large scale integration) devices give customers quickly designed, easily configured components.

Company products are marketed worldwide through a network of independent sales representatives and indirectly through a network of distributors, primarily to original equipment manufacturers of communications, computing, industrial controls, and military systems.

As a "fabless" semiconductor company, Lattice does not manufacture its silicon wafers. Rather, it maintains strategic relationships with large semiconductor-makers, in order to source its finished product. This lets the company focus on product, process, and market development. The majority of LSCC's silicon wafer requirements are supplied by Seiko Epson Corp. in Japan, under an agreement with S MOS Systems, Inc., an affiliated U.S. distributor. United Microelectronics Corp. of Taiwan also provides wafers to the company. Wafer volumes, prices and terms are negotiated periodically with these suppliers. Assembly and final testing of the chips are performed by independent contractors in the Asia/Pacific region and in the U.S.

While outsourcing the chip-manufacturing process reduces the capital-intensive nature of the business and frees up resources to focus on product development and design, the strategy also adds the risk that the company will be unable to obtain wafers to meet demand.

In the in-system programmable logic device market, Lattice competes directly with Altera, Advanced Micro Devices (AMD) and Xilinx, all of which offer competing products. In the non-in-system, low density, programmable logic device market, Lattice competes primarily with AMD, a licensee of the company's GAL patents. Atmel and Cypress Semiconductor offer products based on similar and competing CMOS technologies and architectures, but these companies do not offer full product lines.

Per Share Data ($)

(Year Ended Mar. 31)	1998	1997	1996	1995	1994	1993	1992	1991	1990	1989
Tangible Bk. Val.	18.56	15.76	13.50	8.57	6.79	5.49	4.44	3.79	2.09	0.91
Cash Flow	2.77	2.33	2.33	1.73	1.49	1.20	0.77	0.79	0.65	0.34
Earnings	2.37	1.96	1.99	1.41	1.19	0.94	0.61	0.61	0.51	0.20
Dividends	Nil	Nil	Nil	Nil	Nil	Nil	Nil	Nil	Nil	Nil
Payout Ratio	Nil	Nil	Nil	Nil	Nil	Nil	Nil	Nil	Nil	Nil
Cal. Yrs.	1997	1996	1995	1994	1993	1992	1991	1990	1989	1988
Prices - High	74½	47	43	20⅛	26¾	17¼	10	11½	4⅝	NA
- Low	39¾	19¾	16⅜	14	12¼	7¼	3⅝	3¼	3⅜	NA
P/E Ratio - High	31	24	22	14	22	18	16	19	9	NA
- Low	17	10	8	10	10	8	6	5	7	NA

Income Statement Analysis (Million $)

	1998	1997	1996	1995	1994	1993	1992	1991	1990	1989
Revs.	246	204	198	144	126	103	71.0	64.5	38.9	21.5
Oper. Inc.	84.6	67.6	64.9	43.3	35.8	27.5	16.1	14.9	8.3	3.5
Depr.	9.6	8.6	7.1	6.0	5.8	4.7	2.8	2.8	1.8	1.5
Int. Exp.	Nil	Nil	Nil	Nil	Nil	Nil	0.1	0.2	0.3	0.3
Pretax Inc.	85.7	67.8	63.2	40.6	32.6	25.2	15.7	14.6	7.1	2.2
Eff. Tax Rate	34%	34%	34%	34%	31%	31%	31%	29%	4.90%	Nil
Net Inc.	56.6	45.0	41.8	27.0	22.5	17.4	10.9	10.3	6.8	2.2

Balance Sheet & Other Fin. Data (Million $)

	1998	1997	1996	1995	1994	1993	1992	1991	1990	1989
Cash	60.3	229	215	88.7	93.6	80.9	63.3	51.3	23.8	6.1
Curr. Assets	338	311	289	141	126	110	80.1	67.1	35.1	14.0
Total Assets	489	403	343	193	146	129	91.7	79.1	40.8	18.4
Curr. Liab.	54.4	43.0	44.2	35.0	21.0	30.4	15.8	15.3	9.6	5.8
LT Debt	Nil	Nil	Nil	Nil	Nil	Nil	0.2	0.6	1.2	2.6
Common Eqty.	435	360	299	158	125	99	75.6	63.2	29.9	-7.0
Total Cap.	435	360	299	158	125	99	75.8	63.8	31.2	12.6
Cap. Exp.	18.8	10.6	12.6	6.3	7.2	11.7	2.4	9.2	3.5	3.2
Cash Flow	66.1	53.6	48.9	33.0	28.3	22.1	13.6	13.1	8.6	3.7
Curr. Ratio	6.2	7.2	6.5	4.0	6.0	3.6	5.1	4.4	3.7	2.4
% LT Debt of Cap.	Nil	Nil	Nil	Nil	Nil	Nil	0.3	0.9	3.9	21.0
% Net Inc.of Revs.	23.0	22.1	21.1	18.8	17.8	16.8	15.3	16.0	17.5	10.3
% Ret. on Assets	12.7	12.1	15.6	15.9	16.2	15.4	12.6	16.3	5.7	NA
% Ret. on Equity	14.2	13.7	18.3	19.1	19.9	19.5	15.5	21.0	34.1	34.9

Data as orig. reptd.; bef. results of disc. opers. and/or spec. items. Per share data adj. for stk. divs. as of ex-div. date. Bold denotes diluted EPS (FASB 128). E-Estimated. NA-Not Available. NM-Not Meaningful. NR-Not Ranked.

Office—5555 N.E. Moore Ct., Hillsboro, OR 97124-6421. Tel—(503) 681-0118. Website—http://www.latticesemi.com Fax—(503) 681-0347. Chrmn, Pres & CEO—C. Y. Tsui. SVP, CFO & Secy—S. A. Skaggs. VP-Fin, Investor Contact—Rodney F. Sloss. Dirs—M. O. Hatfield. S. Hauer, H. A. Merlo, L. W. Sonsini, D. C. Strain, C. Y. Tsui. Transfer Agent & Registrar—First Interstate Bank, Seattle. Incorporated—in Delaware in 1985. Empl— 569. S&P Analyst: B. McGovern

STANDARD &POOR'S
STOCK REPORTS

Lawson Products
NASDAQ Symbol **LAWS**

4410F
In S&P SmallCap 600

03-OCT-98

Industry: Manufacturing (Diversified)

Summary: LAWS primarily distributes replacement fasteners and other parts and supplies used for the repair and maintenance of capital equipment, buildings and automobiles.

Quantitative Evaluations

Recent Price • 21½
52 Wk Range • 31⅞-20¼

Yield • 2.6%
12-Mo. P/E • 11.9

Outlook
(1 Lowest—5 Highest)
• **NA**

Fair Value
• **NA**

Risk
• **Low**

Earn./Div. Rank
• **B+**

Technical Eval.
• **Neutral** since 6/98

Rel. Strength Rank
(1 Lowest—99 Highest)
• **61**

Insider Activity
• **NA**

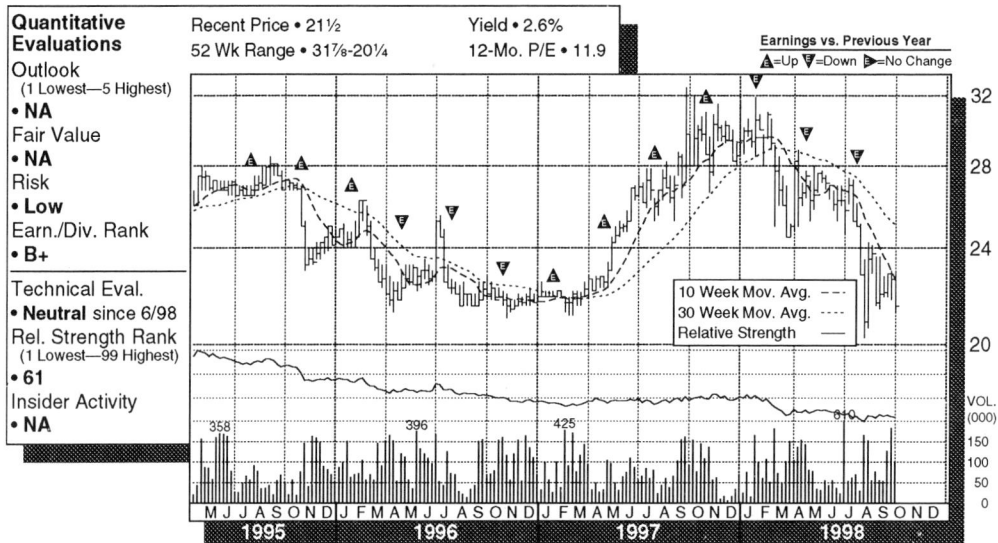

Business Profile - 08-SEP-98

Lawson Products has marketing programs in place that are designed to enable the company to expand into new markets and broaden existing ones with a CD-ROM catalog. The company expects this electronic catalog to have a positive impact on revenue growth. The balance sheet is strong, with no long term debt, and a current ratio of over 5.0 at June 30, 1998. S.L. Port, the company's founder, owns more than 30% of the shares outstanding.

Operational Review - 08-SEP-98

Net sales in the first half of 1998 advanced 4.9%, year to year, reflecting increased contributions from virtually all of operations. Gross margins narrowed somewhat, and with higher SG&A expenses, due to a rise in selling costs resulting from a restructuring of the sales force, pretax income fell 8.1%. After taxes at 42.2%, versus 40.4%, net income declined 11%, to $9,252,000 ($0.83 a share, diluted), from $10,371,000 ($0.93).

Stock Performance - 02-OCT-98

In the past 30 trading days, LAWS's shares have declined 9%, compared to a 7% fall in the S&P 500. Average trading volume for the past five days was 19,760 shares, compared with the 40-day moving average of 28,451 shares.

Key Stock Statistics

Dividend Rate/Share	0.56	Shareholders	1,200
Shs. outstg. (M)	11.1	Market cap. (B)	$0.239
Avg. daily vol. (M)	0.038	Inst. holdings	36%
Tang. Bk. Value/Share	13.15		
Beta	0.42		

Value of $10,000 invested 5 years ago: $ 9,597

Fiscal Year Ending Dec. 31

	1998	1997	1996	1995	1994	1993
Revenues (Million $)						
1Q	70.36	65.88	56.11	54.85	49.77	47.05
2Q	72.54	70.39	63.90	56.10	53.75	49.59
3Q	—	71.42	66.30	56.18	55.54	49.84
4Q	—	70.45	64.40	56.42	54.04	49.25
Yr.	—	278.1	250.3	223.5	213.1	195.7
Earnings Per Share ($)						
1Q	**0.40**	**0.42**	0.35	0.40	0.30	0.34
2Q	**0.42**	**0.51**	0.41	0.43	0.38	0.36
3Q	—	**0.53**	0.42	0.43	0.40	0.34
4Q	—	**0.46**	0.56	0.49	0.47	0.27
Yr.	—	**1.91**	1.73	1.75	1.55	1.32

Next earnings report expected: late October

Dividend Data (Dividends have been paid since 1973.)

Amount ($)	Date Decl.	Ex-Div. Date	Stock of Record	Payment Date
0.140	Dec. 10	Dec. 30	Jan. 02	Jan. 16 '98
0.140	Mar. 17	Apr. 01	Apr. 03	Apr. 17 '98
0.140	May. 12	Jun. 30	Jul. 02	Jul. 16 '98
0.140	Aug. 11	Sep. 29	Oct. 01	Oct. 15 '98

Lawson Products, Inc.

Business Summary - 08-SEP-98

This distributor of fasteners, fittings and other expendable parts and supplies already serves more than 213,000 customers, and hopes to expand sales further with the help of a new electronic catalog its agents now bring on sales calls. Using a laptop computer and a compact disk, agents can selectively display only those products relevant to a particular customer. Boasting a product line that includes some 46,000 individual items, Lawson Products, Inc. (LAWS) will be able to show more of its wares in greater detail and in less time as the static printed catalog gives way to the virtual sales presentation at the dawn of the 21st century.

LAWS distributes a wide variety of maintenance, repair and replacement products and distributes (and, in some cases, makes) production components for the OEM (original equipment manufacturer) marketplace. The company's products fall into three broad categories. Fasteners, fittings and related parts (46% of 1997 net sales) include screws, nuts, rivets and other fasteners. Industrial supplies (49%) consist of hoses and hose fittings, lubricants, cleansers, adhesives and other chemicals, as well as files, drills, welding products and other shop supplies. LAWS also furnishes automotive and equipment maintenance parts (5%) such as primary wiring, connectors and other electrical supplies, exhaust and other automotive parts. About 90% of the com-

pany's products are sold under its own label. Maintenance items are purchased by the company in bulk and then repackaged in smaller quantities.

The company's two largest markets are the heavy-duty equipment and in-plant and building maintenance markets, which accounted for 40% and 39% of 1997 sales, respectively. Customers in the heavy-duty equipment maintenance market include operators of trucks, buses, agricultural implements, construction and road building equipment, mining, logging and drilling equipment, and other off-the-road equipment. The in-plant and building maintenance market includes plants engaged in a broad range of manufacturing and processing activities as well as institutions such as hospitals, universities, school districts and governmental units. LAWS also serves the passenger car maintenance and OEM markets.

Through mid-August 1998, the company had repurchased 514,500 common shares, under a 1996 authorization to buy back up to 1,000,000 shares. In August, LAWS said it planned to buy an additional 500,000 common shares in the open market or in negotiated transactions. Capital expenditures in 1998 reflect costs incurred for the construction of a new facility in Atlanta, and purchases of computer related equipment. The new plant, expected to be completed during 1999 at a cost of $7 million, will replace another facility in Norcross, GA.

Per Share Data ($)

(Year Ended Dec. 31)	1997	1996	1995	1994	1993	1992	1991	1990	1989	1988
Tangible Bk. Val.	12.57	11.38	10.51	10.41	10.37	9.50	8.87	8.04	6.74	5.85
Cash Flow	2.36	2.08	1.94	1.78	1.55	1.35	1.41	1.82	1.76	1.56
Earnings	1.91	1.73	1.75	1.55	1.32	1.13	1.23	1.67	1.61	1.42
Dividends	0.54	0.52	0.51	0.48	0.44	0.40	0.40	0.37	0.33	0.25
Payout Ratio	28%	30%	29%	31%	33%	35%	33%	22%	20%	18%
Prices - High	32½	26¼	28½	31	30¾	31¾	35¼	30½	26	30½
- Low	21⅛	21	23	21¾	23¼	21½	22½	22¾	18½	18⅞
P/E Ratio - High	17	15	16	20	23	28	29	18	16	21
- Low	11	12	13	14	18	19	18	14	11	13

Income Statement Analysis (Million $)

	1997	1996	1995	1994	1993	1992	1991	1990	1989	1988
Revs.	278	250	224	213	196	187	182	186	177	166
Oper. Inc.	38.9	36.1	35.5	35.4	27.8	27.5	26.7	35.7	34.9	30.4
Depr.	5.0	4.0	3.3	3.1	3.2	3.0	2.4	2.1	2.0	2.0
Int. Exp.	0.0	0.0	NM	0.1	0.0	0.0	0.1	0.0	0.0	0.0
Pretax Inc.	35.7	33.9	34.8	34.0	27.8	25.4	26.4	35.2	34.7	31.0
Eff. Tax Rate	40%	41%	39%	40%	36%	40%	37%	36%	37%	34%
Net Inc.	21.4	20.0	21.1	20.5	17.8	15.3	16.6	22.6	21.9	20.3

Balance Sheet & Other Fin. Data (Million $)

	1997	1996	1995	1994	1993	1992	1991	1990	1989	1988
Cash	21.9	28.8	26.5	31.7	71.9	59.6	61.3	52.3	39.1	32.5
Curr. Assets	104	103	88.0	92.0	127	112	110	102	86.0	78.0
Total Assets	189	175	161	168	171	158	150	138	119	106
Curr. Liab.	24.5	24.4	18.5	19.8	15.6	16.0	18.4	18.7	18.8	17.1
LT Debt	Nil	Nil	NM	Nil	Nil	Nil	Nil	Nil	Nil	Nil
Common Eqty.	140	129	123	131	141	129	120	109	91.0	81.0
Total Cap.	140	129	123	131	141	129	120	120	92.0	81.0
Cap. Exp.	5.9	4.8	3.0	6.9	1.4	8.2	4.8	6.4	7.9	1.0
Cash Flow	26.4	24.0	24.4	23.6	21.0	18.3	19.1	24.7	23.9	22.4
Curr. Ratio	4.2	4.2	4.8	4.7	8.1	7.0	6.0	5.4	4.6	4.5
% LT Debt of Cap.	Nil	Nil	NM	Nil	Nil	Nil	Nil	Nil	Nil	Nil
% Net Inc.of Revs.	7.7	8.0	9.4	9.6	9.1	8.2	9.2	12.2	12.3	12.2
% Ret. on Assets	11.8	11.9	12.8	12.5	10.8	10.0	11.6	17.6	19.7	19.6
% Ret. on Equity	15.9	15.9	16.6	15.7	13.2	12.3	14.5	22.5	25.6	25.4

Data as orig. reptd.; bef. results of disc. opers. and/or spec. items. Per share data adj. for stk. divs. as of ex-div. date. Bold denotes diluted EPS (FASB 128). E-Estimated. NA-Not Available. NM-Not Meaningful. NR-Not Ranked.

Office—1666 E. Touhy Ave., Des Plaines, IL 60018. **Tel**—(847) 827-9666. **Website**—http://www.lawsonprod.com **Chrmn & CEO**—B. Kalish. **Pres** —P. G. Smith. **VP, CFO & Treas** —J. Shaffer. **Secy**—R. J. Washlow. **VP & Investor Contact**—Joseph L. Pawlick. **Dirs**—H. Allen, J. T. Brophy, B. Kalish, R. B. Port, S. L. Port, R. G. Rettig, J. Shaffer, P. G. Smith. **Transfer Agent**—First National Bank of Chicago. **Incorporated**—in Illinois in 1952; reincorporated in Delaware in 1982. **Empl**— 1,103. **S&P Analyst:** K.S.

Lechters, Inc. 4415

NASDAQ Symbol **LECH**

In S&P SmallCap 600

03-OCT-98

Industry: Retail (Specialty)

Summary: This retailer operates more than 612 stores, mainly in regional malls, featuring a large selection of basic housewares, table-top items and kitchen textiles at competitive prices.

Quantitative Evaluations	
Outlook (1 Lowest—5 Highest)	• 4
Fair Value	• 4
Risk	• High
Earn./Div. Rank	• B-
Technical Eval.	• Bearish since 7/98
Rel. Strength Rank (1 Lowest—99 Highest)	• 33
Insider Activity	• NA

Recent Price • 3⅛
52 Wk Range • 7⅜-2⅝

Yield • Nil
12-Mo. P/E • NM

Earnings vs. Previous Year
▲=Up ▼=Down ▶=No Change

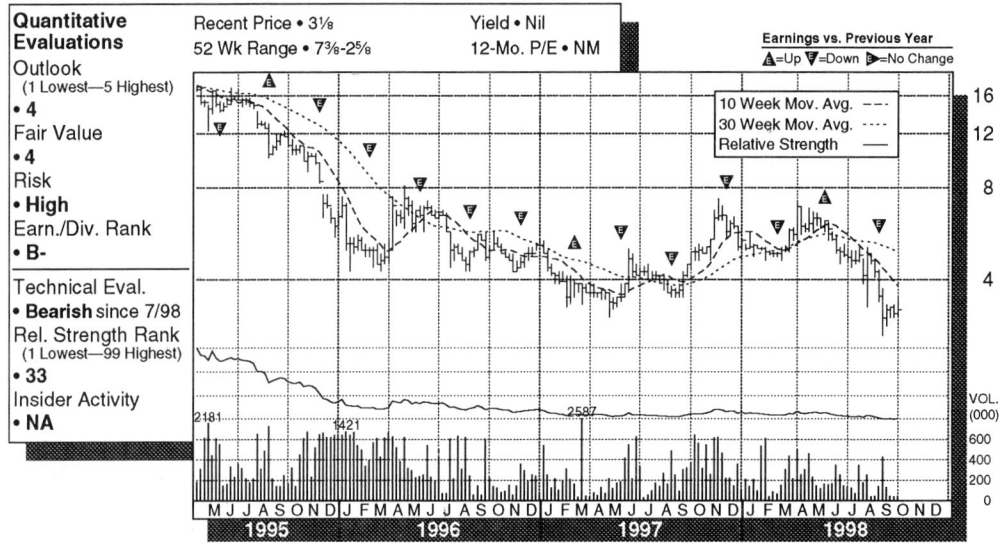

- 10 Week Mov. Avg. – – –
- 30 Week Mov. Avg. ·······
- Relative Strength ——

Business Profile - 18-SEP-98

Following a modest 1.4% total same-store sales increase in FY 98 (Jan.), Lechters reported a mere 0.8% increase in th first half of FY 99, with a 2.8% increase at Lechters Housewares offsetting a 5.3% decline at Famous Brands Housewares Outlets. In the second quarter of FY 99, the company opened four stores and closed seven, ending the quarter with 612 stores, comprised of 453 Lechters Housewares locations and 159 Famous Brands Housewares Outlets.

Operational Review - 18-SEP-98

Net sales in the 26 weeks ended August 1, 1998, slipped 1.5%, year to year, reflecting a 0.1% decrease for Lechters Housewares and a decline of 5.9% for Famous Brands Housewares Outlets. Margins narrowed on higher SG&A expenses, but with 79% higher interest income, the net loss narrowed to $7,476,000 ($0.46 a share, after preferred dividends), from $7,958,000 ($0.49).

Stock Performance - 02-OCT-98

In the past 30 trading days, LECH's shares have declined 25%, compared to a 7% fall in the S&P 500. Average trading volume for the past five days was 8,620 shares, compared with the 40-day moving average of 22,882 shares.

Key Stock Statistics

Dividend Rate/Share	Nil	Shareholders	1,100
Shs. outstg. (M)	17.2	Market cap. (B)	$0.055
Avg. daily vol. (M)	0.017	Inst. holdings	51%
Tang. Bk. Value/Share	8.00		
Beta	1.01		

Value of $10,000 invested 5 years ago: $ 1,603

Fiscal Year Ending Jan. 31

	1999	1998	1997	1996	1995	1994
Revenues (Million $)						
1Q	86.19	85.13	84.99	80.32	73.70	64.44
2Q	91.42	95.11	92.73	88.67	81.58	71.33
3Q	—	99.7	98.50	95.15	91.08	80.71
4Q	—	165.4	165.0	167.9	152.9	133.7
Yr.	—	445.3	441.2	432.1	399.3	350.2
Earnings Per Share ($)						
1Q	**-0.23**	**-0.29**	-0.21	-0.13	-0.07	0.02
2Q	**-0.24**	**-0.21**	-0.18	-0.11	-0.41	0.01
3Q	—	**-0.15**	-0.11	-0.05	0.07	0.10
4Q	—	**0.31**	0.64	0.56	0.60	0.52
Yr.	—	**-0.28**	0.15	0.26	0.20	0.65

Next earnings report expected: NA
Dividend Data

No cash dividends have been paid on the common stock.

A Division of The **McGraw·Hill** Companies

Business Summary - 18-SEP-98

Operating 612 stores in 44 states, Lechters, Inc. (LECH), a specialty retailer of brandname basic and decorative housewares, is a major presence in shopping malls and outlet centers throughout the United States. The large majority of the company's stores are being operated under the Lechters Housewares name, with the remainder operating under the Famous Brands Housewares Outlet name. Sales by product category in recent fiscal years (Jan.) were:

	FY 98	FY 97	FY 96
Basic housewares	61%	62%	60%
Decorative housewares	39%	38%	40%

Lechters Housewares stores (453 at August 1, 1998), averaging about 3,700 square feet in size, offer a large, attractively presented assortment of merchandise at prices below those customarily charged by department stores. Each unit stocks more than 4,000 items categorized as cookware, bakeware, kitchen gadgets, utensils, small electrics, table top, textiles, household storage and organization, frames and other decorative housewares. The products offered by the store are ei-

ther private label or national brands, including Rubbermaid, Durand, Ecko, Farberware, Henckels, Krups, OXO, Pyrex, Revere and T-Fal. Generally, prices range from $1.00 to $200.00; most items sell for under $10.00. Lechters Housewares stores are primarily in regional malls, but some are also in strip centers and downtown cities.

Famous Brands Housewares Outlets (159 at August 1, 1998) are off-price housewares outlets that are positioned in outlet malls. These stores average 3,900 square feet and offer an assortment of liquidated, discontinued or slow-selling housewares, as well as basic Lechters Housewares merchandise. The outlet stores generally have lower occupancy expenses and can offer lower price points to their customers.

LECH opened seven stores in FY 98 and closed 30 stores, versus 16 stores opened and nine closed in FY 97. Given the company's already high penetration of attractive shopping malls and outlet centers, expansion in the near future should be limited, with improvement of same-store sales a primary focus. The company believes that its best opportunity for new store development lies in strip malls, where the company already has a small presence.

Per Share Data ($)

(Year Ended Jan. 31)	1998	1997	1996	1995	1994	1993	1992	1991	1990	1989
Tangible Bk. Val.	8.20	8.41	8.25	8.38	8.14	7.48	6.55	4.71	4.00	2.25
Cash Flow	0.73	1.19	1.19	1.03	1.30	1.36	1.18	1.03	0.95	0.80
Earnings	-0.28	0.15	0.26	0.20	0.65	0.90	0.80	0.70	0.68	0.58
Dividends	Nil	Nil	Nil	Nil	Nil	Nil	Nil	Nil	Nil	Nil
Payout Ratio	Nil	Nil	Nil	Nil	Nil	Nil	Nil	Nil	Nil	Nil
Cal. Yrs.	1997	1996	1995	1994	1993	1992	1991	1990	1989	1988
Prices - High	7⅜	8⅛	19	19	24¼	25¼	22	13⅞	12⅛	NA
- Low	3	4¼	5½	10¾	9	16¾	7¼	5⅝	8⅝	NA
P/E Ratio - High	NM	54	73	95	37	28	28	20	18	NA
- Low	NM	28	21	54	14	19	9	8	13	NA

Income Statement Analysis (Million $)

	1998	1997	1996	1995	1994	1993	1992	1991	1990	1989
Revs.	445	441	432	399	350	306	234	188	157	121
Oper. Inc.	21.8	25.0	28.5	36.8	34.8	34.9	28.4	22.9	20.3	16.2
Depr.	17.3	17.1	16.1	14.3	11.1	8.0	6.2	4.8	3.6	2.6
Int. Exp.	4.6	5.0	6.9	7.2	7.3	7.2	4.1	1.8	2.1	2.2
Pretax Inc.	-6.2	4.5	7.7	5.7	18.7	24.2	20.3	16.3	14.6	11.3
Eff. Tax Rate	NM	26%	41%	41%	41%	37%	36%	38%	38%	38%
Net Inc.	-3.8	3.3	4.5	3.4	11.1	15.4	13.0	10.1	9.0	7.0

Balance Sheet & Other Fin. Data (Million $)

	1998	1997	1996	1995	1994	1993	1992	1991	1990	1989
Cash	91.1	61.1	41.8	58.1	48.1	64.6	97.9	7.3	14.2	1.7
Curr. Assets	197	173	163	167	157	158	163	57.0	57.0	35.0
Total Assets	277	272	272	271	257	240	220	102	90.0	62.0
Curr. Liab.	33.4	20.9	26.7	31.9	19.1	20.1	20.1	15.5	14.7	12.6
LT Debt	60.0	58.9	75.0	77.8	85.9	85.0	84.2	15.0	15.0	20.0
Common Eqty.	146	150	149	144	137	125	109	67.0	57.0	27.0
Total Cap.	437	246	241	235	222	210	194	82.0	72.0	48.0
Cap. Exp.	7.5	8.5	22.6	20.6	29.2	32.7	16.3	16.4	10.7	9.6
Cash Flow	12.5	20.4	20.6	17.6	22.2	23.4	19.2	14.9	12.7	9.6
Curr. Ratio	5.9	8.3	6.1	5.2	8.2	7.9	8.1	3.7	3.9	2.8
% LT Debt of Cap.	25.3	24.0	31.2	33.1	38.6	40.5	43.5	18.2	20.8	41.5
% Net Inc.of Revs.	NM	0.8	1.1	0.8	3.2	5.0	5.6	5.4	5.8	5.8
% Ret. on Assets	NM	1.2	1.7	1.3	4.5	6.7	7.7	10.5	11.9	13.2
% Ret. on Equity	NM	1.6	4.1	2.4	8.5	13.1	13.9	16.2	21.3	29.4

Data as orig. reptd.; bef. results of disc. opers. and/or spec. items. Per share data adj. for stk. divs. as of ex-div. date. Bold denotes diluted EPS (FASB 128). E-Estimated. NA-Not Available. NM-Not Meaningful. NR-Not Ranked.

Office—1 Cape May St., Harrison, NJ 07029-9998. **Tel**—(201) 481-1100. **Chrmn, Pres & CEO**—D. Jonas. **SVP & CFO**—J. W. Smolak. **VP & Secy**—I. S. Rosenberg. **VP & Treas**—Kathleen M. Guinnessey. **Dirs**—M. S. Begun, C. A. Davis, B. D. Fischman, D. Jonas, R Knox, A. Lechter, A. E. Malkin, R. S. Maneker, N. Matthews, L. Pfeffer, S. Westerfield, J. Wolff. **Transfer Agent**—Harris Trust Co. of New York. **Incorporated**—in New Jersey in 1975. **Empl**— 6,364. **S&P Analyst:** K.J.F.

Legg Mason

1334

NYSE Symbol **LM**

In S&P SmallCap 600

03-OCT-98

Industry:
Investment Banking/
Brokerage

Summary: Headquartered in Baltimore, this multi-regional broker-dealer and investment banking concern serves individual and institutional investors through offices in 21 states.

Quantitative Evaluations

Recent Price • 24
52 Wk Range • 32¼-20⅛

Yield • 1.1%
12-Mo. P/E • 16.7

Outlook
(1 Lowest—5 Highest)
• **1⁻**

Fair Value
• **51⅝**

Risk
• **Average**

Earn./Div. Rank
• **A**

Technical Eval.
• **Bearish** since 9/98

Rel. Strength Rank
(1 Lowest—99 Highest)
• **49**

Insider Activity
• **Neutral**

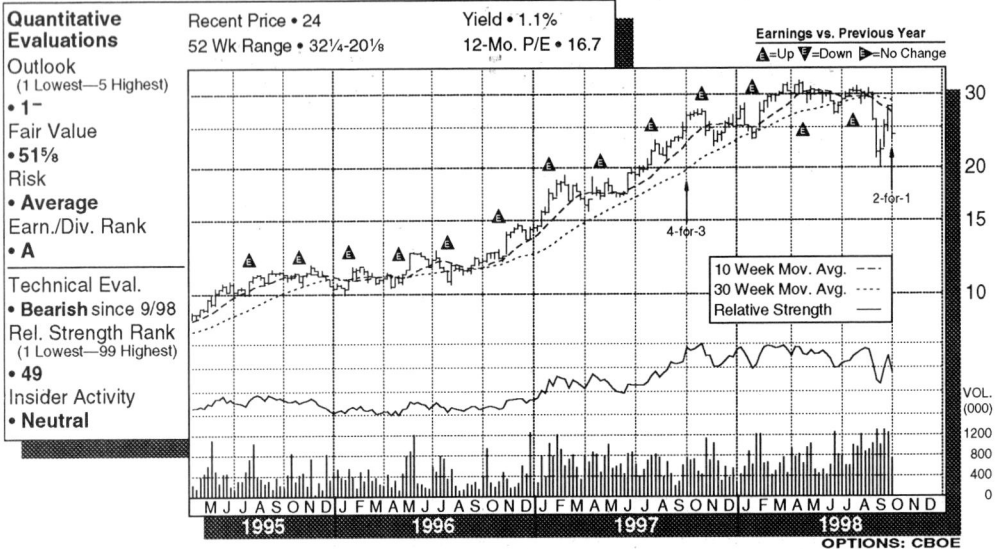

Earnings vs. Previous Year
▲=Up ▼=Down ▶=No Change

10 Week Mov. Avg. ----
30 Week Mov. Avg. ····
Relative Strength ——

2-for-1

4-for-3

VOL.
(000)

OPTIONS: CBOE

Business Profile - 27-MAY-98

Demand for the company's value-oriented research, brokerage and investment advisory activities should continue to expand in tandem with growth in the number of high-net-worth individuals and do-it-yourself retirement planners. LM focuses its corporate finance activities on the middle market, which is underserved by most large investment banks. In early 1998, the company issued approximately 2.6 million shares of stock to acquire privately held, Delaware-based Brandywine Asset Management, Inc. Brandywine has $7 billion in assets under management. LM currently manages over $71 billion of assets for individual and institutional accounts and mutual funds.

Operational Review - 27-MAY-98

Based on a preliminary report, revenues for FY 98 (Mar.) rose 34%, year to year, reflecting solid growth in each of LM's core businesses. Security brokerage commissions were up 27%, benefiting from record trading volumes and equity prices; investment advisory revenues increased 42% on growth in assets under management; and investment banking fees were up 35%, reflecting an increase in fees from managed municipal finance offerings. Margins were flat, as total expenses rose in line with revenues. After taxes at 40.7%, versus 40.6%, net income was up 33%, to $76.1 million ($2.63 a share, diluted, on 3.6% more shares), from $57.2 million ($2.05, as restated).

Stock Performance - 02-OCT-98

In the past 30 trading days, LM's shares have declined 20%, compared to a 7% fall in the S&P 500. Average trading volume for the past five days was 147,360 shares, compared with the 40-day moving average of 275,010 shares.

Key Stock Statistics

Dividend Rate/Share	0.26	Shareholders	1,600
Shs. outstg. (M)	55.4	Market cap. (B)	$ 1.3
Avg. daily vol. (M)	0.291	Inst. holdings	54%
Tang. Bk. Value/Share	8.36		
Beta	1.54		

Value of $10,000 invested 5 years ago: $ 33,215

Fiscal Year Ending Mar. 31

	1999	1998	1997	1996	1995	1994
Revenues (Million $)						
1Q	248.7	179.2	148.8	116.0	89.84	91.35
2Q	—	212.8	147.3	124.7	88.45	106.8
3Q	—	227.1	167.3	127.5	92.89	103.1
4Q	—	246.3	176.3	147.8	100.4	96.29
Yr.	—	889.1	639.7	516.0	371.6	397.5
Earnings Per Share ($)						
1Q	0.41	0.31	0.30	0.30	0.15	0.26
2Q	—	0.36	0.29	0.20	0.09	0.35
3Q	—	0.39	0.30	0.23	0.12	0.30
4Q	—	0.40	0.28	0.21	0.12	0.21
Yr.	—	1.31	1.18	0.93	0.49	1.12

Next earnings report expected: mid October

Dividend Data (Dividends have been paid since 1983.)

Amount ($)	Date Decl.	Ex-Div. Date	Stock of Record	Payment Date
0.110	Feb. 02	Mar. 03	Mar. 05	Apr. 06 '98
0.110	Apr. 28	Jun. 12	Jun. 16	Jul. 13 '98
2-for-1	Jul. 23	Sep. 28	Sep. 09	Sep. 25 '98
0.065	Jul. 23	Oct. 07	Oct. 09	Oct. 26 '98

A Division of The McGraw-Hill Companies

STANDARD
&POOR'S
STOCK REPORTS

Legg Mason, Inc.

1334

03-OCT-98

Business Summary - 27-MAY-98

At the start of the decade, Legg Mason, Inc. (LM), a holding company for numerous securities firms, embarked on a plan to lift the contribution of its investment management business to 25% of total revenues over a ten-year period. At the time, investment management provided only 18% of the company's revenues, and assets under management were under $10 billion. Pursuing a strategy that combined targeted acquisitions (such as the purchase of asset manager Batterymarch Financial Management, Inc. in January 1995) and the expansion of its mutual fund offerings, LM reached its goal in 1995 -- five years early. In FY 97 (Mar.), investment advisory revenues accounted for 29% of the total, and LM closed the year with $44 billion in assets under management. Now, LM has set a new goal for itself: to increase assets under management to $100 billion in three to five years.

LM provides securities brokerage, investment advisory, corporate and public finance and commercial mortgage banking services to individuals, institutions, corporations, and municipalities. Revenues totaled $640 million in FY 97, up 24% over the previous year, and net earnings advanced 49% to $56.6 million. The company's principal broker-dealer subsidiary, Legg Mason Wood Walker, Inc., operates primarily in the eastern and mid-south regions of the U.S. Howard, Weil, Labouisse, Friedrichs Inc., another broker-dealer subsidiary, specializes in energy-related investment banking and institutional brokerage. LM's core securities brokerage business accounted for 41% of total revenues in FY 97. Investment banking contributed 11%, and interest and other 19%.

Through its investment advisory subsidiaries, LM manages 17 Legg Mason mutual funds with combined assets exceeding $7 billion (at the end of March 1997), numerous offshore funds with another $1 billion in assets, and some 2,000 institutional and private client accounts holding assets of more than $32 billion. About 74% of assets under management at the end of FY 97 were fixed income assets. LM plans to leverage existing fund management resources by introducing a new family of institutional mutual funds for the 401(k) marketplace in 1997.

The company's securities brokerage business serves investors from 109 offices in the East, Midwest and South, as well as institutional offices in Europe. Total assets in retail client accounts exceed $35 billion. LM is placing greater emphasis on fee-based services to lessen its dependence on volume-driven commissions.

Per Share Data ($)

(Year Ended Mar. 31)	1998	1997	1996	1995	1994	1993	1992	1991	1990	1989
Tangible Bk. Val.	7.97	7.33	5.64	4.71	6.01	5.04	4.06	3.39	3.30	2.86
Cash Flow	1.31	NA	NA	NA	NA	NA	NA	NA	NA	NA
Earnings	1.31	1.17	0.93	0.49	1.12	0.98	0.70	0.46	0.41	0.21
Dividends	0.16	0.19	0.18	0.16	0.14	0.12	0.10	0.09	0.08	0.07
Payout Ratio	12%	16%	19%	33%	13%	12%	15%	20%	20%	34%

Cal. Yrs.	1997	1996	1995	1994	1993	1992	1991	1990	1989	1988
Prices - High	28⅛	14¾	11¾	9½	9½	8⅛	7⅜	5	4⅞	3⅞
- Low	14⅛	10	7¾	6¾	7¼	5¾	3¾	3⅛	3⅛	2⅞
P/E Ratio - High	21	13	13	19	8	8	11	11	12	18
- Low	11	8	8	14	7	6	5	7	8	14

Income Statement Analysis (Million $)

Commissions	241	190	169	121	141	117	113	91.0	100	80.0
Int. Inc.	127	84.1	57.1	39.3	30.0	24.0	25.6	27.8	30.8	29.7
Total Revs.	648	640	516	372	398	336	292	243	244	213
Int. Exp.	73.7	43.4	26.2	17.1	15.4	11.6	13.4	14.2	17.1	18.5
Pretax Inc.	128	95.2	63.9	27.7	59.2	49.0	35.0	21.2	19.5	9.6
Eff. Tax Rate	41%	41%	41%	41%	39%	38%	40%	39%	39%	38%
Net Inc.	76.1	56.6	37.9	16.3	36.0	30.2	21.1	12.9	11.8	6.0

Balance Sheet & Other Fin. Data (Million $)

Total Assets	2,832	1,879	1,315	817	811	640	580	496	433	419
Cash Items	1,128	593	258	87.0	167	131	145	139	22.0	34.0
Receivables	713	527	398	371	353	305	259	216	291	269
Secs. Owned	81.5	78.9	84.2	51.9	57.6	112	94.6	64.6	53.3	42.4
Sec. Borrowed	448	264	197	120	96.0	90.0	100	48.0	17.0	47.0
Due Brokers & Cust.	1,568	968	569	325	310	282	243	248	212	197
Other Liabs.	85.4	57.4	50.0	58.6	64.1	56.6	53.4	39.2	52.3	32.5
Capitalization:										
Debt	114	100	168	103	103	34.6	35.0	35.1	35.1	35.5
Equity	500	419	299	226	212	177	148	126	116	108
Total	600	519	467	329	314	212	183	161	151	143
% Return On Revs.	11.8	8.8	7.3	4.4	9.1	9.0	7.2	5.3	4.9	2.8
% Ret. on Assets	3.2	3.5	3.5	2.0	5.0	4.9	3.9	2.8	2.8	1.4
% Ret. on Equity	16.6	15.8	14.3	7.4	18.6	18.6	15.2	10.7	10.6	5.7

Data as orig. reptd.; bef. results of disc opers. and/or spec. items. Per share data adj. for stk. divs. as of ex-div. date. Bold denotes diluted EPS (FASB 128). E-Estimated. NA-Not Available. NM-Not Meaningful. NR-Not Ranked.

Office—111 South Calvert St., Baltimore, MD 21203-1476. Tel—(410) 539-0000. Website—http://www.leggmason.com Chrmn, Pres & CEO—R. A. Mason. Vice Chrmn & Investor Contact—John F. Curley, Jr. VP-Fin—F. B. Bilson. SVP & Secy—C. A. Bacigalupo. Dirs—H. L. Adams, C. A. Bacigalupo, K. S. Battye, J. W. Brinkley, E. J. Cashman, Jr., J. F. Curley, Jr., H. M. Ford, Jr., R. J. Himelfarb, J. E. Koerner, III, J. B. Levert, Jr., W. C. Livingston, R. A. Mason, E. I. O'Brien, P. F. O'Malley,— N. J. St. George, R. W. Schipke, M. DeB. Tutwiler, J. E. Ukrop, W. Wirth. Transfer Agent—First Union National Bank of North Carolina, Charlotte. Incorporated—in Maryland in 1981. Empl— 3,200. S&P Analyst: L. A. Olive

STANDARD &POOR'S
STOCK REPORTS

Libbey Inc.

1348F

NYSE Symbol **LBY**

In S&P SmallCap 600

14-OCT-98

Industry: Housewares

Summary: This leading manufacturer of glass tableware has one of the most extensive product portfolios in the domestic glassware industry.

Quantitative Evaluations

Outlook
(1 Lowest—5 Highest)
• **5**

Fair Value
• **49½**

Risk
• **Low**

Earn./Div. Rank
• **NR**

Technical Eval.
• **Bullish** since 3/98

Rel. Strength Rank
(1 Lowest—99 Highest)
• **89**

Insider Activity
• **NA**

Recent Price • 32⅛
52 Wk Range • 42¼-28¼

Yield • 0.9%
12-Mo. P/E • 13.3

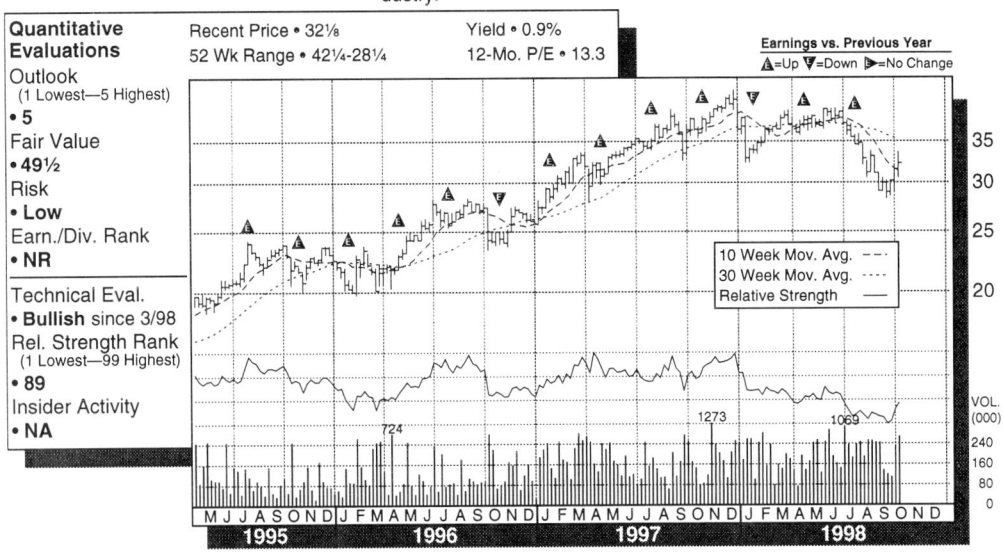

Earnings vs. Previous Year
▲=Up ▼=Down ▶=No Change

10 Week Mov. Avg. – – –
30 Week Mov. Avg. ·······
Relative Strength ——

Business Profile - 14-OCT-98

A disappointing performance at the core glassware operations in 1997, primarily reflecting a slowdown of orders from certain mass merchandisers late in the holiday selling season, prompted Libbey to devise a plan to accelerate sales growth and improve its cost structure. The cost improvements include a headcount reduction of about 50 salaried positions, the elimination of redundant warehouse operations and LBY's exiting from the factory outlet mall business. Strategic expansion in 1997, notably a new partnership with the largest tableware manufacturer in Mexico and the acquisition of a metal flatware manufacturer, offset some of the unfavorable results from core operations. In November 1997, LBY sold 2.6 million common shares to the public at $37.875 per share.

Operational Review - 14-OCT-98

Net sales in the first six months of 1998 advanced 12%, year to year, reflecting incremental sales from the August 1997 World Tableware acquisition and distribution agreement with Vitrocrisa and the new joint venture in Mexico, offset partially by lower export sales. Margins narrowed on greater sales of lower-margin products and higher distribution costs related to acquisitions; income from operations was up 6.2%. Following much higher other income reflecting equity in the Mexican joint venture, net income climbed 34%, to $19,852,000 ($1.10 a share, on 16% more shares), from $14,778,000 ($0.95).

Stock Performance - 09-OCT-98

In the past 30 trading days, LBY's shares have increased 4%, compared to a 4% fall in the S&P 500. Average trading volume for the past five days was 111,700 shares, compared with the 40-day moving average of 51,810 shares.

Key Stock Statistics

Dividend Rate/Share	0.30	Shareholders	400
Shs. outstg. (M)	17.6	Market cap. (B)	$0.575
Avg. daily vol. (M)	0.051	Inst. holdings	82%
Tang. Bk. Value/Share	3.97		
Beta	0.42		

Value of $10,000 invested 5 years ago: NA

Fiscal Year Ending Dec. 31

	1998	1997	1996	1995	1994	1993
Revenues (Million $)						
1Q	90.09	78.48	84.48	71.02	68.32	57.81
2Q	113.7	104.0	103.8	84.01	74.75	67.88
3Q	—	104.8	95.58	89.14	85.17	77.89
4Q	—	124.7	115.0	113.4	105.8	99.3
Yr.	—	412.0	397.7	357.6	334.0	302.9

Earnings Per Share ($)						
1Q	0.34	0.30	0.26	0.23	0.19	0.28
2Q	0.76	0.65	0.56	0.51	0.44	0.38
3Q	—	0.74	0.65	0.66	0.58	0.56
4Q	—	0.50	0.05	0.00	0.57	0.40
Yr.	—	2.27	2.12	2.00	1.78	1.58

Next earnings report expected: mid October

Dividend Data (Dividends have been paid since 1993.)

Amount ($)	Date Decl.	Ex-Div. Date	Stock of Record	Payment Date
0.075	Oct. 30	Oct. 31	Nov. 03	Dec. 04 '97
0.075	Feb. 03	Feb. 23	Feb. 25	Mar. 11 '98
0.075	Apr. 08	May. 11	May. 13	Jun. 03 '98
0.075	Jul. 22	Aug. 10	Aug. 12	Sep. 02 '98

A Division of The McGraw-Hill Companies

Business Summary - 14-OCT-98

Libbey, Inc. (LBY), which was wholly owned by Owens-Illinois, Inc., prior to its June 1993 IPO, makes an extensive line of glass beverageware and other glass tableware, for sale under the well-recognized Libbey name, to foodservice, retail and special markets. With the acquisition of Syracuse China in late 1995, the company added ceramic dinnerware to its product offerings. The acquisition in 1997 of the stainless steel flatware and holloware businesses of Vitro S.A. of Mexico, makes it possible now for one to set a whole table using LBY's products.

According to management's estimates, Libbey makes 64% of the glass tableware sales to the U.S. foodservice market, which includes restaurants, bars and institutions. Sales to foodservice customers represent about one-half of LBY's total sales. LBY serves this market through a network of about 500 independent distributors who are supported by a company sales force utilizing comprehensive product catalogs. The company enhanced its industry standing in 1997 with the acquisition of World Tableware. The acquisition provides Libbey with a greater number of foodservice supply-related products, an expanded customer base and the opportunity to realize synergies among World Tableware and other operating units, such as the Syracuse China unit, a leading supplier of ceramic dinnerware.

While Libbey's retail market has consisted mostly of mass merchants and discount stores, the company is increasing its distribution to department stores and specialty housewares stores. Libbey is one of the three leading suppliers of glass beverageware to retail markets in the U.S. In addition, it is one of the leading suppliers of glassware to industrial customers who use glassware for candle and gift packaging, floral purposes and lighting applications. Libbey decided in late 1997 to discontinue its factory outlet mall store business; 17 stores were closed in 1997 and the remaining 15 mall stores were expected to be closed during 1998.

Although 1997 results benefited from the addition of new businesses, the new businesses generally operate at lower profit margins than Libbey's average. In January 1998, LBY announced plans to increase its profitability through personnel reductions and the elimination of redundant warehouse space through improved inventory management.

In August 1997, Libbey entered into a joint venture with Vitro S.A., with respect to that company's glass tableware operations in Mexico, and purchased Vitro's WorldCrisa business (subsequently renamed World Tableware), a Dallas-based manufacturer of metal flatware, holloware and serving accessories. LBY believes the transaction, in which it paid a total of $100 million in cash, will provide it with an additional $60 million of sales in North America and place it prominently in the Mexican market.

Per Share Data ($)

(Year Ended Dec. 31)	1997	1996	1995	1994	1993	1992	1991	1990	1989	1988
Tangible Bk. Val.	2.91	-3.73	-5.78	-7.11	-8.65	-9.91	NA	NA	NA	NA
Cash Flow	3.52	3.52	3.21	2.86	2.15	3.01	NA	NA	NA	NA
Earnings	2.27	2.12	2.00	1.78	1.57	2.03	NA	NA	NA	NA
Dividends	0.30	0.30	0.30	0.30	0.08	NA	NA	NA	NA	NA
Payout Ratio	13%	14%	15%	17%	5%	NA	NA	NA	NA	NA
Prices - High	42¼	28⅜	24¼	19⅞	17⅝	NA	NA	NA	NA	NA
- Low	26¾	19¾	14⅜	14	11⅞	NA	NA	NA	NA	NA
P/E Ratio - High	19	13	12	11	11	NA	NA	NA	NA	NA
- Low	12	9	7	8	8	NA	NA	NA	NA	NA

Income Statement Analysis (Million $)

	1997	1996	1995	1994	1993	1992	1991	1990	1989	1988
Revs.	415	398	360	336	305	279	NA	NA	NA	NA
Oper. Inc.	90.4	88.7	81.3	75.5	68.2	59.8	NA	NA	NA	NA
Depr.	19.9	21.5	18.2	16.3	14.5	14.6	NA	NA	NA	NA
Int. Exp.	14.8	15.0	14.2	14.0	23.5	14.6	NA	NA	NA	NA
Pretax Inc.	58.5	53.5	49.7	45.2	30.7	51.6	NA	NA	NA	NA
Eff. Tax Rate	38%	39%	40%	41%	42%	41%	NA	NA	NA	NA
Net Inc.	36.1	32.6	30.0	26.7	17.7	30.5	NA	NA	NA	NA

Balance Sheet & Other Fin. Data (Million $)

	1997	1996	1995	1994	1993	1992	1991	1990	1989	1988
Cash	2.6	2.0	2.1	3.7	1.8	Nil	Nil	Nil	Nil	Nil
Curr. Assets	161	127	131	103	93.7	66.7	NA	NA	NA	NA
Total Assets	450	316	322	256	249	218	NA	NA	NA	NA
Curr. Liab.	81.9	66.0	56.0	62.1	55.1	47.2	NA	NA	NA	NA
LT Debt	200	203	249	214	237	234	NA	NA	NA	NA
Common Eqty.	100	-18.4	-47.1	-73.0	-95.0	-112	NA	NA	NA	NA
Total Cap.	300	185	202	141	153	120	NA	NA	NA	NA
Cap. Exp.	18.4	15.4	20.2	17.4	17.5	NA	NA	NA	NA	NA
Cash Flow	56.0	54.0	48.2	43.0	32.2	45.1	NA	NA	NA	NA
Curr. Ratio	2.0	1.9	2.3	1.7	1.7	1.4	NA	NA	NA	NA
% LT Debt of Cap.	66.5	109.7	123.0	151.9	155.0	194.0	NA	NA	NA	NA
% Net Inc.of Revs.	8.7	8.2	8.4	7.9	5.8	10.9	NA	NA	NA	NA
% Ret. on Assets	9.4	10.2	10.4	10.6	NA	NA	NA	NA	NA	NA
% Ret. on Equity	88.6	NM	NM	NM	NM	NA	NA	NA	NA	NA

Data as orig. reptd.; bef. results of disc. opers. and/or spec. items. Per share data adj. for stk. divs. as of ex-div. date. Bold denotes diluted EPS (FASB 128). E-Estimated. NA-Not Available. NM-Not Meaningful. NR-Not Ranked.

Office—300 Madison Ave., Toledo, OH 43699.**Tel**—(419) 325-2100.**Chrmn & CEO**—J. F. Meier.**EVP & COO**—R. I. Reynolds. **VP, CFO, Treas & Investor Contact**—Kenneth G. Wilkes. **VP & Secy**—A. H. Smith. **Dirs**—W. A. Foley, P. C. M. Howell, J. F. Meier, C. B. Moerdyk, G. L. Moreau, R. I. Reynolds, T. P. Stewart, T. L. Wilkison. **Transfer Agent & Registrar**—Bank of New York, NYC. **Incorporated**—in Delaware in 1987. **Empl**— 4,136. **S&P Analyst**: S.A.H.

Life Re Corp.

1351K

NYSE Symbol **LRE**

In S&P SmallCap 600

03-OCT-98

Industry: Insurance (Life & Health)

Summary: Life Re Corp., a leading provider of ordinary life and group life reinsurance through its Life Reassurance Corp. of America unit, has agreed to be acquired by Swiss Reinsurance Co.

Quantitative Evaluations	
Outlook (1 Lowest—5 Highest)	• **2⁻**
Fair Value	• **94¾**
Risk	• **Low**
Earn./Div. Rank	• **NR**
Technical Eval.	• **Bullish** since 10/96
Rel. Strength Rank (1 Lowest—99 Highest)	• **89**
Insider Activity	• **NA**

Recent Price • 91⅜   Yield • 0.7%
52 Wk Range • 92⅞-52   12-Mo. P/E • 23.9

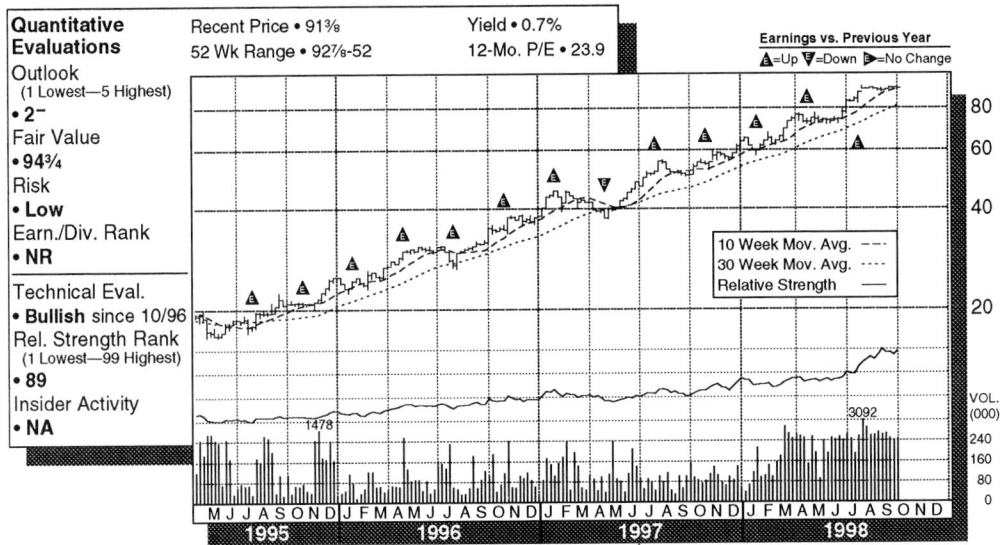

Earnings vs. Previous Year
▲=Up ▼=Down ▷=No Change

10 Week Mov. Avg. – – –
30 Week Mov. Avg. · · · ·
Relative Strength ——

Business Profile - 04-AUG-98

On July 27, 1998, Life Re reached a definitive agreement to be acquired by Swiss Reinsurance Company for $95 per share; equal to about $1.8 billion in cash. The deal, subject to approvals by LRE shareholders and by regulators, is expected to close by January 1999. In 1997, 65% of LRE's policy income came from traditional life reinsurance, including ordinary and group life, 10% from administrative reinsurance, and 25% from group accident and health reinsurance. LRE is presently exiting the accident and health business following a strategic decision to pursue higher margin activities in the life reinsurance and administrative reinsurance areas.

Operational Review - 04-AUG-98

In the six months ended June 30, 1998, total revenues rose 32%, year to year, reflecting 27% higher policy revenues, 48% higher investment income, and lower realized investment gains. Total benefits and expenses were up 30%, paced by a 22% rise in policy benefits, 25% higher policy acquisition costs, 42% higher other operating expenses, and $6.7 million in distributions on capital securities, against $0.6 million. After taxes at 35.0% in both periods, net income rose 44%, to $31,913,000 ($1.92 a share, on 18% more shares), from $22,095,000 ($1.57).

Stock Performance - 02-OCT-98

In the past 30 trading days, LRE's shares have increased 0.48%, compared to a 7% fall in the S&P 500. Average trading volume for the past five days was 65,120 shares, compared with the 40-day moving average of 114,441 shares.

Key Stock Statistics

Dividend Rate/Share	0.60	Shareholders	3,400
Shs. outstg. (M)	17.3	Market cap. (B)	$ 1.6
Avg. daily vol. (M)	0.097	Inst. holdings	82%
Tang. Bk. Value/Share	36.55		
Beta	0.94		

Value of $10,000 invested 5 years ago: $ 33,521

Fiscal Year Ending Dec. 31

	1998	1997	1996	1995	1994	1993
Revenues (Million $)						
1Q	189.7	150.4	143.6	114.5	102.2	85.20
2Q	218.8	160.0	133.6	116.3	108.8	90.54
3Q	—	163.4	157.3	121.9	106.6	112.2
4Q	—	172.0	158.0	132.9	115.8	95.35
Yr.	—	645.8	592.5	485.6	433.4	383.3
Earnings Per Share ($)						
1Q	**0.95**	**0.71**	1.43	0.29	0.48	0.31
2Q	**0.97**	**0.85**	0.74	0.63	0.57	0.61
3Q	—	**0.90**	0.76	0.61	0.51	1.07
4Q	—	**1.01**	0.95	0.87	0.65	0.50
Yr.	—	**3.48**	3.89	2.39	2.21	2.50

Next earnings report expected: late October

Dividend Data (Dividends have been paid since 1993.)

Amount ($)	Date Decl.	Ex-Div. Date	Stock of Record	Payment Date
0.130	Nov. 10	Nov. 26	Dec. 01	Dec. 17 '97
0.150	Feb. 12	Mar. 02	Mar. 04	Mar. 25 '98
0.150	Apr. 30	Jun. 01	Jun. 03	Jun. 24 '98
0.150	Aug. 03	Sep. 04	Sep. 09	Sep. 30 '98

A Division of The **McGraw-Hill** Companies

Business Summary - 04-AUG-98

Life Re Corp. (LRE), a leading life reinsurer, agreed on July 27, 1998, to be acquired by Swiss Reinsurance Company for $95 per share, equal to approximately $1.8 billion in cash. The deal remains subject to approvals by the company's shareholders and by regulators.

Through its principal subsidiary, Life Reassurance Corp., LRE has specialized in providing life reinsurance since its formation in 1967. Life reinsurance is the insurance purchased by a primary life insurer, the ceding company, from a second life insurer, the reinsurer, through which the ceding company passes to the reinsurer some or all of the risks that the ceding company has assumed through its direct underwriting of insurance policies. Reinsurance is bought by primary insurers as a tool through which they mitigate the risk of having to pay more than a fixed amount on any single claim; consequently, the principal benefit for the ceding company is reduced claim volatility resulting from several large losses in a given period of time. LRE serves as a holding company for all of the common stock of TexasRe Life Insurance Co., which in turn owns all of the common stock of Life Reassurance. LRE acquired all the common stock of Life Reassurance from General Re in late 1988.

The company's two core lines of business are tradi-

tional life reinsurance, wherein mortality risks on new sales from primary (ceding) life insurance companies are transferred to LRE, and administrative reinsurance, in which the company acquires blocks of life insurance in force and, often, assumes administrative responsibility. Administrative reinsurance is a fast growing component of total policy revenues, as shown below, and will assume more importance following LRE's decision in 1997 to leave the accident/health/special risk reinsurance field:

	1997	1996	1995
Traditional life reinsurance	65.2%	64.8%	70.0%
Administrative reinsurance	10.1%	4.2%	0.7%
Group accident and health reinsurance	24.7%	31.0%	29.3%

LRE's marketing efforts are grounded in a strategy that calls for its competing on the basis of service and price. The majority of sales are made through direct marketing relationships established over years of responsive service. As a rule, senior management is directly involved in all aspects of the company's marketing efforts.

Investment income accounted for 23% of LRE's total revenues in 1997. At December 31, 1997, the company's invested assets had an aggregate fair value of $2.78 billion, up from $1.83 billion a year earlier. At year-end 1997, 88% of assets in the portfolio were investment grade, fixed maturity securities.

Per Share Data ($)

(Year Ended Dec. 31)	1997	1996	1995	1994	1993	1992	1991	1990	1989	1988
Tangible Bk. Val.	27.42	21.44	16.14	9.61	11.71	7.58	-0.16	NA	NA	NA
Oper. Earnings	3.28	2.66	2.14	2.21	NA	1.88	NA	NA	NA	NA
Earnings	3.48	3.89	2.39	2.21	2.50	3.45	1.72	NA	NA	NA
Dividends	0.52	0.40	0.28	0.24	0.20	Nil	NA	NA	NA	NA
Payout Ratio	15%	10%	12%	11%	8%	Nil	NA	NA	NA	NA
Prices - High	65⅜	38⅞	25	23¼	39¼	29¾	NA	NA	NA	NA
- Low	37⅜	22⅜	16½	14⅞	19⅛	22	NA	NA	NA	NA
P/E Ratio - High	19	10	10	11	16	9	NA	NA	NA	NA
- Low	11	6	7	7	8	6	NA	NA	NA	NA

Income Statement Analysis (Million $)

	1997	1996	1995	1994	1993	1992	1991	1990	1989	1988
Life Ins. In Force	158	116	91.3	81.0	79.4	74.1	81.1	NA	NA	NA
Prem. Inc.: Life	319	433	383	351	289	NA	NA	NA	NA	NA
Prem. Inc.: A & H	121	Nil	Nil	Nil	Nil	Nil	Nil	Nil	Nil	Nil
Prem. Inc.: Other	50.0	18.0	Nil	Nil	Nil	Nil	Nil	Nil	Nil	Nil
Net Invest. Inc.	151	124	99	82.4	73.5	72.6	66.6	NA	NA	NA
Total Revs.	646	593	486	433	383	355	310	NA	NA	NA
Pretax Inc.	76.2	76.1	54.8	52.8	60.6	68.6	38.7	NA	NA	NA
Net Oper. Inc.	46.6	37.0	31.9	34.2	NA	27.2	NA	NA	NA	NA
Net Inc.	49.5	54.2	35.6	34.3	39.2	45.1	26.6	NA	NA	NA

Balance Sheet & Other Fin. Data (Million $)

	1997	1996	1995	1994	1993	1992	1991	1990	1989	1988
Cash & Equiv.	60.2	38.3	30.0	21.4	23.1	22.1	18.9	NA	NA	NA
Premiums Due	159	121	NA	NA	NA	NA	NA	NA	NA	NA
Invest. Assets: Bonds	2,336	1,636	1,330	847	908	777	752	NA	NA	NA
Invest. Assets: Stocks	26.8	21.5	16.6	12.1	11.8	48.1	14.4	NA	NA	NA
Invest. Assets: Loans	146	58.2	31.4	24.0	25.2	20.6	18.8	NA	NA	NA
Invest. Assets: Total	2,675	1,833	1,504	999	945	845	785	NA	NA	NA
Deferred Policy Costs	326	224	113	119	96.0	NA	NA	NA	NA	NA
Total Assets	3,700	2,519	2,024	1,442	1,340	1,078	1,021	NA	NA	NA
Debt	125	125	140	140	150	165	165	NA	NA	NA
Common Eqty.	374	290	279	195	231	171	125	NA	NA	NA
% Return On Revs.	7.7	9.1	7.3	7.9	10.2	12.7	8.6	NA	NA	NA
% Ret. on Assets	1.6	2.4	2.1	2.5	3.2	NA	NA	NA	NA	NA
% Ret. on Equity	14.9	19.0	15.0	16.1	19.5	30.5	NA	NA	NA	NA
% Invest. Yield	6.7	7.5	7.2	8.1	8.2	8.9	9.4	NA	NA	NA

Data as orig. reptd.; bef. results of disc. opers. and/or spec. items. Per share data adj. for stk. divs. as of ex-div. date. Bold denotes diluted EPS (FASB 128). E-Estimated. NA-Not Available. NM-Not Meaningful. NR-Not Ranked.

Office—969 High Ridge Rd., Stamford, CT 06905. **Tel**—(203) 321-3000. **Chrmn & CEO**—R. A. Hawes Jr. **Pres & COO**—J. E. Dubois. **EVP & CFO**—C. C. Stroup. **EVP & Secy**—W. W. Wilson. **Investor Contact**—Bruce I. Weiser (203-321-3084). **Dirs**—J. E. Dubois, R. A. Hawes Jr., C. K. McCandless, D. M. Schair, K. F. Skousen, C.C. Stroup, T. B. Woodbury II. **Transfer Agent**—Bank of New York, NYC. **Incorporated**—in Delaware in 1988. **Empl**— 130. **S&P Analyst:** Thomas W. Smith, CFA

Lillian Vernon

8400

ASE Symbol **LVC**

In S&P SmallCap 600

03-OCT-98

Industry:
Retail (Home Shopping)

Summary: LVC is a direct-mail specialty catalog marketer of household, gift, and other consumer products.

Quantitative Evaluations

Recent Price • 13	Yield • 2.5%
52 Wk Range • 18⅝-13	12-Mo. P/E • 18.1

Outlook (1 Lowest—5 Highest)
• **4+**

Fair Value
• **19¾**

Risk
• **Average**

Earn./Div. Rank
• **B**

Technical Eval.
• **Bullish** since 3/98

Rel. Strength Rank (1 Lowest—99 Highest)
• **31**

Insider Activity
• **Neutral**

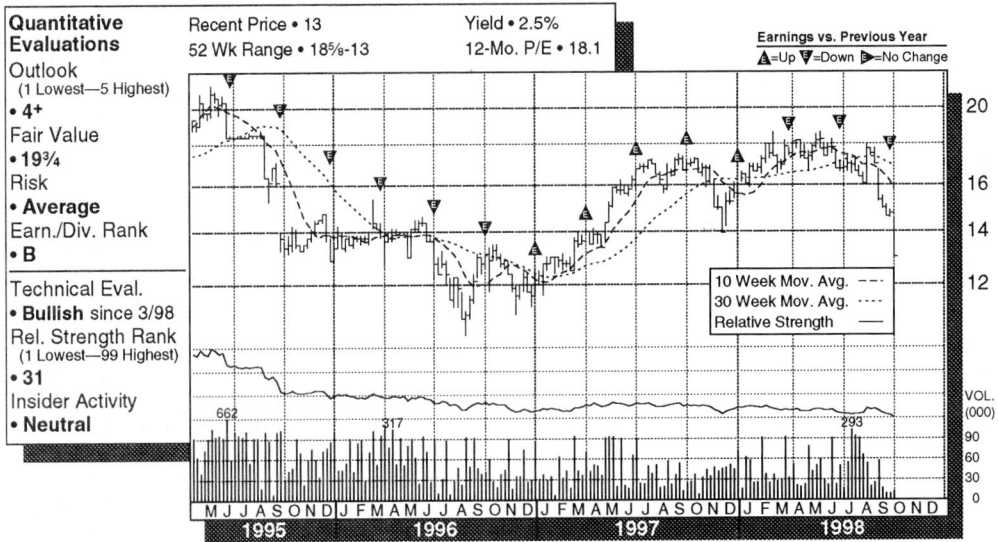

Earnings vs. Previous Year
▲=Up ▼=Down ▶=No Change

10 Week Mov. Avg. – – –
30 Week Mov. Avg. · · · · ·
Relative Strength ——

Business Profile - 29-JUL-98

LVC introduced its ninth catalog title, Lillian Vernon Gardening, in March 1998, and it added new Spring editions of its Personalized Gift and Lilly's Kids catalogs. These new mailings helped increase the customer database, and the company expects these initiatives to improve revenues and profits in the future. Directors raised the quarterly cash dividend 14%, to $0.08 a share from $0.07, with the March 2, 1998, payment. As of June 26, 1998, LVC had repurchased 725,700 common shares as part of its ongoing open market stock repurchase program.

Operational Review - 29-JUL-98

Revenues for the three months ended May 30, 1998, advanced 15%, year to year, mainly reflecting a 17% increase in pages circulated. A large portion of the increased circulation stemmed from the introduction of a new catalog title, Lillian Vernon Gardening. Results were penalized by start-up expenses for the new catalog launch, additional catalog mailings and higher overhead costs. The seasonal net loss widened to $2,650,000 ($0.28 a share) from $2,345,000 ($0.24).

Stock Performance - 02-OCT-98

In the past 30 trading days, LVC's shares have declined 26%, compared to a 7% fall in the S&P 500. Average trading volume for the past five days was 2,380 shares, compared with the 40-day moving average of 5,131 shares.

Key Stock Statistics

Dividend Rate/Share	0.32	Shareholders	400
Shs. outstg. (M)	9.3	Market cap. (B)	$0.121
Avg. daily vol. (M)	0.003	Inst. holdings	42%
Tang. Bk. Value/Share	12.08		
Beta	-0.01		

Value of $10,000 invested 5 years ago: $ 10,286

Fiscal Year Ending Feb. 28

	1999	1998	1997	1996	1995	1994
Revenues (Million $)						
1Q	32.01	27.75	26.31	29.61	26.00	20.84
2Q	39.39	37.26	32.97	36.92	33.66	29.70
3Q	—	106.3	100.3	97.45	91.92	83.21
4Q	—	86.92	80.43	74.21	70.63	62.59
Yr.	—	258.2	240.1	238.2	222.2	196.3
Earnings Per Share ($)						
1Q	-0.28	-0.24	-0.38	-0.29	-0.10	0.11
2Q	-0.21	-0.04	-0.22	-0.05	0.08	0.06
3Q	—	0.99	0.90	0.86	0.98	0.95
4Q	—	0.23	0.25	0.06	0.42	0.48
Yr.	—	0.93	0.55	0.59	1.38	1.35

Next earnings report expected: mid December

Dividend Data (Dividends have been paid since 1992.)

Amount ($)	Date Decl.	Ex-Div. Date	Stock of Record	Payment Date
0.070	Sep. 23	Nov. 12	Nov. 14	Dec. 01 '97
0.080	Dec. 18	Feb. 11	Feb. 16	Mar. 02 '98
0.080	Apr. 21	May. 13	May. 15	Jun. 01 '98
0.080	Jul. 15	Aug. 13	Aug. 17	Sep. 01 '98

A Division of The **McGraw·Hill** Companies

Business Summary - 29-JUL-98

Lillian Vernon Corp. (LVC) is a direct mail specialty catalog company concentrating on the marketing of gift, household, gardening, kitchen, Christmas and children's products. LVC, which traces its roots back to 1951, seeks to provide customers with reasonably priced products that can be differentiated from competitive products either by design, price or personalization.

LVC has developed a proprietary customer data base containing information about its customers, including such data as order frequency, size and date of last order, and type of items purchased. These and other factors are analyzed by computer to rank and segment customers to determine those most likely to purchase products offered in LVC's catalogs. The data base contains information with respect to about 21.8 million people, approximately 3.3 million of whom have placed orders with LVC during the last fiscal year.

Catalog and order activity (in millions) in recent years (ended on or about February 28):

	1998	1997	1996	1995
Catalogs mailed	178.9	175.2	179.5	179.4
Orders received	4.9	4.6	4.9	4.9
Avg. revenue/order	$54.13	$52.57	$49.31	$44.61

LVC's catalogs are designed to capture the reader's interest through the use of distinctive covers, colorful product presentations and product descriptions that highlight significant features. The catalogs are created and produced by LVC's in-house creative staff, which includes designers, writers and production assistants. LVC also hires free-lance designers and photographers, as needed. The combination of in-house and free-lance staff enables LVC to maintain both high quality control and flexibility in the production of its catalogs.

LVC varies the quantity of its catalog mailings based on the selling season, anticipated revenue per catalog, the price of paper and its capacity to process and fill orders. In FY 98, LVC produced 34 different catalog editions.

Orders are executed from and products are stored in LVC's national distribution center in Virginia Beach, VA. Products are obtained from approximately 1,100 suppliers, with 76% of the items sold purchased abroad, mostly in the Far East. Business is seasonal, with volume heaviest from September through February.

The retail business in general, and mail order in particular, is highly competitive. LVC competes primarily with other mail order catalogs and secondarily with retail stores, including specialty shops and department stores. LVC competes on the basis of its product selection, personalization, its proprietary customer list, the quality of its customer service and its unconditional guarantee.

Per Share Data ($)

(Year Ended Feb. 28)	1998	1997	1996	1995	1994	1993	1992	1991	1990	1989
Tangible Bk. Val.	12.45	11.90	11.75	11.44	10.22	9.07	8.10	7.08	6.06	4.89
Cash Flow	1.43	1.03	1.00	1.77	1.68	1.45	1.29	1.28	1.47	1.11
Earnings	0.93	0.55	0.59	1.38	1.35	1.15	1.02	1.00	1.17	0.88
Dividends	0.29	0.28	0.28	0.26	0.20	0.20	Nil	Nil	Nil	Nil
Payout Ratio	31%	51%	47%	19%	15%	17%	Nil	Nil	Nil	Nil
Cal. Yrs.	1997	1996	1995	1994	1993	1992	1991	1990	1989	1988
Prices - High	17$\frac{1}{2}$	15$\frac{3}{8}$	22$\frac{1}{4}$	22$\frac{5}{8}$	18$\frac{7}{8}$	17	14$\frac{1}{2}$	17$\frac{1}{2}$	17	8$\frac{3}{4}$
- Low	12	10$\frac{3}{8}$	12$\frac{7}{8}$	14$\frac{1}{2}$	11$\frac{1}{2}$	10$\frac{1}{2}$	7$\frac{3}{4}$	6$\frac{1}{2}$	8$\frac{1}{8}$	5$\frac{3}{8}$
P/E Ratio - High	19	28	38	16	14	15	14	18	15	10
- Low	13	19	22	11	9	9	8	7	7	6

Income Statement Analysis (Million $)

	1998	1997	1996	1995	1994	1993	1992	1991	1990	1989
Revs.	258	240	238	222	196	173	162	160	155	141
Oper. Inc.	19.3	12.7	12.6	22.6	22.5	18.9	16.4	16.5	20.6	16.6
Depr.	4.8	4.5	4.0	3.9	3.1	2.8	2.5	2.6	2.8	2.1
Int. Exp.	0.5	0.7	0.6	0.7	0.9	1.2	1.4	2.0	2.3	2.2
Pretax Inc.	13.6	8.1	8.4	19.1	19.5	16.3	14.3	13.9	17.2	12.9
Eff. Tax Rate	34%	34%	31%	29%	35%	34%	34%	33%	37%	37%
Net Inc.	9.0	5.3	5.7	13.6	12.8	10.8	9.5	9.3	10.8	8.1

Balance Sheet & Other Fin. Data (Million $)

	1998	1997	1996	1995	1994	1993	1992	1991	1990	1989
Cash	25.1	22.7	25.8	38.8	52.9	51.1	43.5	35.7	36.8	23.4
Curr. Assets	96.9	89.7	93.3	99	101	83.6	76.6	72.9	68.9	55.8
Total Assets	144	139	136	138	131	115	105	102	99	88.0
Curr. Liab.	22.5	18.9	16.6	19.4	26.6	20.7	15.9	20.9	21.8	19.0
LT Debt	Nil	1.4	2.5	4.3	5.8	7.2	11.0	12.5	18.9	21.6
Common Eqty.	120	114	113	110	97.3	85.1	75.5	65.8	56.2	45.1
Total Cap.	118	116	116	115	104	94.3	88.7	80.9	77.6	69.2
Cap. Exp.	3.1	10.3	7.7	6.3	1.8	7.5	1.8	1.5	2.3	8.0
Cash Flow	13.8	9.9	9.7	17.5	15.9	13.6	12.0	11.9	13.6	10.2
Curr. Ratio	4.3	4.8	5.6	5.1	3.8	4.0	4.8	3.5	3.2	2.9
% LT Debt of Cap.	Nil	1.2	2.1	3.8	5.5	7.6	12.4	15.5	24.4	31.3
% Net Inc.of Revs.	3.5	2.3	2.4	6.1	6.5	6.2	5.8	5.8	7.0	5.8
% Ret. on Assets	6.4	3.9	4.2	10.1	10.3	9.8	9.2	9.2	11.5	9.8
% Ret. on Equity	7.5	4.7	5.1	13.1	13.9	13.4	13.4	15.2	21.3	19.9

Data as orig. reptd.; bef. results of disc. opers. and/or spec. items. Per share data adj. for stk. divs. as of ex-div. date. Bold denotes diluted EPS (FASB 128). E-Estimated. NA-Not Available. NM-Not Meaningful. NR-Not Ranked.

Office—1 Theall Road, Rye, NY 10580 **Tel**—(914) 925-1200. **Website**—http://www.lillianvernon.com. **Chrmn & CEO**—Lillian Vernon. **Pres & COO**—H. P. Goldberg. **VP & CFO**—R. S. Mednick. **Secy**—S. C. Handler. **Dirs**—R. Berman, E. Eveillard, J. Gitlitz, H. P. Goldberg, D. C. Hochberg, L. Salon, L. Vernon, B. W. Wasserman. **Transfer Agent & Registrar**—Continental Stock Transfer & Trust Co., NYC. **Incorporated**—in New York in 1965; reincorporated in Delaware in 1987. **Empl**—1,500. **S&P Analyst:** J.J.S.

STANDARD &POOR'S
STOCK REPORTS

Lilly Industries

1354M

NYSE Symbol **LI**

In S&P SmallCap 600

03-OCT-98

Industry: Chemicals (Specialty)

Summary: This company is a leading producer of industrial paints and coatings for use on furniture, automotive parts, business machines, appliances and a wide variety of metal products.

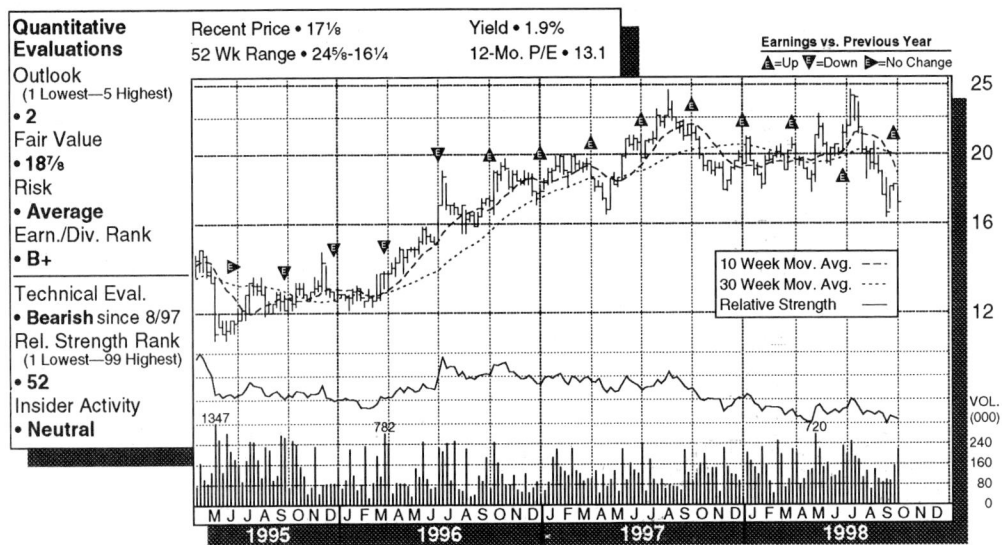

Quantitative Evaluations	
Outlook (1 Lowest—5 Highest)	**• 2**
Fair Value	**• 18⅞**
Risk	**• Average**
Earn./Div. Rank	**• B+**
Technical Eval.	**• Bearish** since 8/97
Rel. Strength Rank (1 Lowest—99 Highest)	**• 52**
Insider Activity	**• Neutral**

Recent Price • 17⅛   Yield • 1.9%
52 Wk Range • 24⅝-16¼   12-Mo. P/E • 13.1

Earnings vs. Previous Year
▲=Up ▼=Down ▶=No Change

10 Week Mov. Avg. - - - -
30 Week Mov. Avg. ·······
Relative Strength ——

Business Profile - 02-SEP-98

Lilly Industries, one of the five largest manufacturers of industrial coatings and specialty chemical products in North America, acquired Guardsman Products in April 1996. In 1997, the company successfully lowered the combined companies' costs by approximately $25 million. To remain competitive and on the cutting edge of technological advances, LI has reorganized its operations into six strategic business units, with each responsible for achieving growth within its own targeted market. The company is concentrating on paying down debt, consolidating older facilities to improve efficiencies, opening new plants and expanding its international presence. In December 1997, LI acquired a German industrial coatings concern, with annual revenues of about $15 million, as part of its globalization strategy.

Operational Review - 02-SEP-98

Revenues in the first half of FY 97 (Nov.) rose 2.1%, as sales from the recent German acquisition outweighed unfavorable foreign currency translation and lost sales from the divestiture of the retail paint business. Margins widened on the higher sales volume. Following lower net interest expense, pretax income was up 8.5%. After taxes at 42.0% versus 45.0%, net income rose 14%, to $13,855,000 ($0.59 a share), from $12,111,000 ($0.52).

Stock Performance - 02-OCT-98

In the past 30 trading days, LI's shares have declined 11%, compared to a 7% fall in the S&P 500. Average trading volume for the past five days was 43,480 shares, compared with the 40-day moving average of 24,131 shares.

Key Stock Statistics

Dividend Rate/Share	0.32	Shareholders	2,100
Shs. outstg. (M)	23.2	Market cap. (B)	$0.390
Avg. daily vol. (M)	0.028	Inst. holdings	46%
Tang. Bk. Value/Share	NM		
Beta	0.69		

Value of $10,000 invested 5 years ago: $ 18,680

Fiscal Year Ending Nov. 30

	1998	1997	1996	1995	1994	1993
Revenues (Million $)						
1Q	143.3	142.2	73.27	80.45	73.97	54.52
2Q	159.2	154.2	131.7	85.41	84.52	65.83
3Q	159.3	150.9	150.9	79.70	86.64	82.81
4Q	—	154.0	153.1	82.79	86.18	81.17
Yr.	—	601.3	509.0	328.4	331.3	284.3
Earnings Per Share ($)						
1Q	**0.22**	0.20	0.15	0.20	0.13	0.10
2Q	**0.37**	0.32	0.03	0.25	0.25	0.18
3Q	**0.37**	0.33	0.30	0.20	0.30	0.20
4Q	—	**0.35**	0.33	0.23	0.32	0.22
Yr.	—	**1.20**	0.81	0.88	1.00	0.70

Next earnings report expected: late January

Dividend Data (Dividends have been paid since 1957.)

Amount ($)	Date Decl.	Ex-Div. Date	Stock of Record	Payment Date
0.080	Jan. 26	Mar. 09	Mar. 11	Apr. 01 '98
0.080	Mar. 23	Jun. 08	Jun. 10	Jul. 01 '98
0.080	Jun. 22	Sep. 08	Sep. 10	Oct. 01 '98
0.080	Sep. 28	Dec. 08	Dec. 10	Jan. 04 '99

 A Division of The McGraw-Hill Companies

Business Summary - 02-SEP-98

A leading North American manufacturer of industrial coatings and specialty chemical products, Lilly Industries (LI) believes that the most significant transaction in its 131-year history occurred in April 1996 when it acquired Guardsman Products, Inc. for $235 million. The acquisition brought complementary technology and related products to Lilly with little customer overlap.

Guardsman's strengths are in specialty coatings for appliances and furniture, and two-component coatings for construction and agricultural equipment. The combined operations and technologies will result in significant cost reductions, and access to an expanded customer base. In 1997, LI successfully reduced the combined companies' operating costs by approximately $25 million through improved raw material procurement, facility rationalization, and workforce reductions. In FY 96 (Nov.), LI recorded a one-time pretax restructuring charge of $9.6 million ($0.23 a share, after tax) related to consolidation of manufacturing facilities.

The company aims its products at four end use markets: metal coatings, wood coatings, glass coatings and the Guardsman products. Lilly believes it is one of the fivo largest North American manufacturers of industrial coatings, based on annual sales to industrial customers. The company believes that its competitive advantage is gained primarily by meeting customer-specific industrial coating demands, at a competitive price and with prompt delivery.

Principal markets for industrial coatings include wood coatings for furniture, flooring, kitchen cabinets and paneling; coil coatings for appliances, aluminum siding and components, automotive parts, doors, windows and metal buildings; and general metal coatings for a variety of metal products, including extrusions, appliances, caskets, office furniture and truck trailers.

The company's glass coatings include silver and copper plating solutions sold to mirror manufacturers, and specialty coatings, including gelcoats, mold release agents and adhesives in the fiberglass-reinforced products industry, and automotive finishes for the automotive aftermarket.

Lilly's customers are primarily in the U.S. and Canada, with the remainder in Asia and Europe. Foreign operations accounted for approximately 21% of sales in FY 97.

Per Share Data ($)

(Year Ended Nov. 30)	1997	1996	1995	1994	1993	1992	1991	1990	1989	1988
Tangible Bk. Val.	NM	NM	2.75	2.13	1.14	1.98	3.16	3.09	3.00	2.65
Cash Flow	2.14	1.48	1.23	1.39	1.01	0.86	0.44	0.57	0.64	0.58
Earnings	1.20	0.81	0.88	1.00	0.70	0.55	0.27	0.40	0.50	0.45
Dividends	0.32	0.32	0.31	0.28	0.24	0.22	0.21	0.20	0.17	0.15
Payout Ratio	27%	40%	35%	28%	33%	41%	78%	47%	35%	34%
Prices - High	24⅝	19¾	15	18	16⅛	10¾	6	7¼	7⅜	6⅞
- Low	16½	12⅛	11	11¾	9½	5¾	3⅞	3⅞	5⅛	4⅝
P/E Ratio - High	21	24	17	18	23	20	22	18	15	15
- Low	14	15	12	12	14	11	14	9	10	10

Income Statement Analysis (Million $)

	1997	1996	1995	1994	1993	1992	1991	1990	1989	1988
Revs.	601	509	328	331	284	236	213	232	212	197
Oper. Inc.	92.1	73.1	43.6	51.0	36.5	29.6	16.4	21.3	23.7	21.0
Depr.	22.0	15.6	8.2	9.0	6.9	6.8	4.0	4.0	3.4	3.1
Int. Exp.	19.3	14.5	2.2	2.9	1.9	1.7	2.4	2.6	1.4	0.8
Pretax Inc.	51.2	34.1	33.8	39.7	27.9	21.9	10.8	16.9	20.7	18.5
Eff. Tax Rate	45%	45%	40%	41%	42%	42%	41%	41%	41%	41%
Net Inc.	28.1	18.8	20.3	23.3	16.2	12.7	6.4	10.0	12.6	11.3

Balance Sheet & Other Fin. Data (Million $)

	1997	1996	1995	1994	1993	1992	1991	1990	1989	1988
Cash	10.1	6.8	20.3	26.6	7.5	10.8	14.1	5.0	10.6	11.9
Curr. Assets	147	159	76.9	93.1	70.2	55.3	60.7	56.5	67.2	56.4
Total Assets	502	522	184	190	167	117	127	125	129	101
Curr. Liab.	94.5	108	41.4	51.5	37.0	28.2	30.3	22.0	26.8	20.0
LT Debt	224	245	21.2	28.0	40.6	10.4	16.6	23.0	21.1	5.8
Common Eqty.	142	122	109	99	81.1	70.1	74.2	73.2	74.5	66.0
Total Cap.	367	367	131	127	122	81.5	92.0	98.2	97.9	77.2
Cap. Exp.	12.7	19.2	15.6	6.7	7.6	3.3	1.9	4.1	2.5	2.9
Cash Flow	50.1	34.4	28.4	32.3	23.0	19.5	10.4	14.0	16.0	14.4
Curr. Ratio	1.6	1.5	1.9	1.8	1.9	2.0	2.0	2.6	2.5	2.8
% LT Debt of Cap.	61.2	66.8	16.2	22.0	33.4	12.7	18.1	23.4	21.6	7.6
% Net Inc.of Revs.	4.7	3.7	6.2	7.0	5.7	5.4	3.0	4.3	5.9	5.7
% Ret. on Assets	5.5	5.3	10.8	13.0	11.3	10.7	5.0	8.1	10.9	11.4
% Ret. on Equity	21.3	16.3	19.4	25.7	21.2	18.1	8.7	13.9	17.9	18.2

Data as orig. reptd.; bef. results of disc. opers. and/or spec. items. Per share data adj. for stk. divs. as of ex-div. date. Bold denotes diluted EPS (FASB 128). E-Estimated. NA-Not Available. NM-Not Meaningful. NR-Not Ranked.

Office—733 S. West St., Indianapolis, IN 46225. **Tel**—(317) 687-6700. **Chrmn, Pres & CEO**—D. W. Huemme. **VP, CFO & Secy**—J. C. Elbin. **Treas & Asst Secy**—K. L. Mills. **Dirs**— J. M. Cornelius, W. C. Dorris, P. K. Gaston, D. W. Huemme, H. Morrison, N. J. Oman, J. D. Peterson, T. E. Reilly Jr., V. P. Smith, R. A. Taylor. **Transfer Agent & Registrar**—KeyCorp Shareholder Services, Cleveland. **Incorporated**—in Indiana in 1888. **Empl**—2,140. **S&P Analyst:** E. Hunter

Lindsay Manufacturing 1358

NYSE Symbol **LNN**

In S&P SmallCap 600

10-OCT-98

Industry:
Manufacturing (Specialized)

Summary: Lindsay is one of the two leading manufacturers and marketers of automated, center pivot and lateral move irrigation systems. It also provides outsource manufacturing.

Quantitative Evaluations

Outlook
(1 Lowest—5 Highest)
• **3+**

Fair Value
• **14⅝**

Risk
• **Average**

Earn./Div. Rank
• **B+**

Technical Eval.
• **NA**

Rel. Strength Rank
(1 Lowest—99 Highest)
• **12**

Insider Activity
• **Neutral**

Recent Price • 12⅛
52 Wk Range • 33½-11¼

Yield • 1.1%
12-Mo. P/E • 7.5

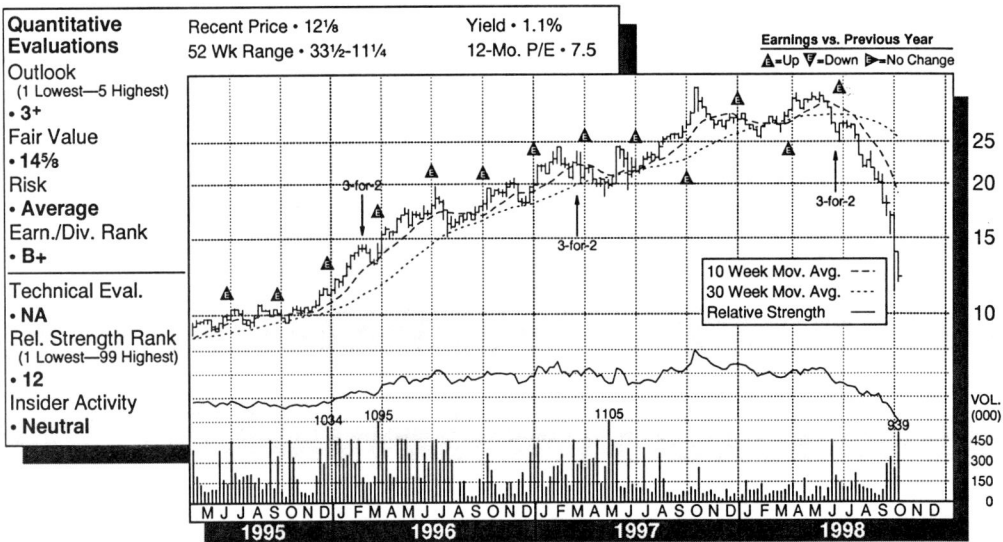

Earnings vs. Previous Year
△=Up ▽=Down ▷=No Change

10 Week Mov. Avg. ---
30 Week Mov. Avg. ····
Relative Strength —

Business Profile - 15-JUN-98

Revenues rose 16% in FY 97 (Aug.), exceeding LNN's annual goal of 5% to 10%. With low U.S. grain reserves giving support to higher commodity prices, the company sees its North American irrigation equipment segment continuing to benefit from a strong farm economy. Aided by greater demand from Europe and Latin America, exports revenue climbed 41% in FY 97. After declining in FY 96, sales of the diversified products segment were up 32% in FY 97, reflecting stronger demand for large diameter steel tubing, and increased revenue from outsource manufacturing services. In October 1997, trading in the company's shares shifted to the NYSE, from the Nasdaq Stock Market.

Operational Review - 15-JUN-98

Revenues in the first nine months of FY 98 rose 3.3%, year to year, reflecting strength in domestic irrigation sales. Gross margins widened, on productivity improvements. Despite higher SG&A, engineering and research and interest expenses, with $4 million in extraordinary pretax income from a litigation settlement, pretax income climbed 23%. After taxes at 32.5%, versus 32.0%, net income rose 22%, to $20,652,000 ($1.41 a share, as adjusted), from $16,958,000 ($1.13).

Stock Performance - 09-OCT-98

In the past 30 trading days, LNN's shares have declined 40%, compared to a 4% fall in the S&P 500. Average trading volume for the past five days was 187,740 shares, compared with the 40-day moving average of 52,721 shares.

Key Stock Statistics

Dividend Rate/Share	0.14	Shareholders	300
Shs. outstg. (M)	13.9	Market cap. (B)	$0.169
Avg. daily vol. (M)	0.089	Inst. holdings	57%
Tang. Bk. Value/Share	7.03		
Beta	0.25		

Value of $10,000 invested 5 years ago: $ 13,264

Fiscal Year Ending Aug. 31

	1998	1997	1996	1995	1994	1993
Revenues (Million $)						
1Q	37.45	39.47	27.33	22.14	25.57	24.90
2Q	49.71	45.69	38.14	30.35	27.56	21.50
3Q	43.90	41.66	41.14	37.45	37.72	27.50
4Q	—	31.50	29.63	21.90	21.84	28.15
Yr.	—	158.3	136.2	111.8	112.7	102.1

Earnings Per Share ($)						
1Q	0.32	0.32	0.20	0.12	0.15	0.14
2Q	0.49	0.41	0.34	0.19	0.17	0.14
3Q	0.60	0.41	0.37	0.31	0.27	0.22
4Q	—	0.21	0.16	0.12	0.09	0.15
Yr.	—	1.34	1.09	0.73	0.68	0.65

Next earnings report expected: NA

Dividend Data (Dividends have been paid since 1996.)

Amount ($)	Date Decl.	Ex-Div. Date	Stock of Record	Payment Date
0.050	Jan. 23	Feb. 11	Feb. 13	Feb. 27 '98
0.050	Apr. 15	May. 13	May. 15	May. 29 '98
3-for-2	May. 06	Jun. 16	Jun. 05	Jun. 15 '98
0.035	Jul. 15	Aug. 12	Aug. 14	Aug. 31 '98

A Division of The McGraw-Hill Companies

Business Summary - 15-JUN-98

As one of the two leading manufacturers of automatic systems for the irrigation of agricultural crops, Lindsay Manufacturing believes that it is positioned to benefit from an extremely favorable market environment.

Lindsay believes that, driven by a potent combination of record demand for grain and a near record low in grain reserves, grain prices, although off their FY 97 (Aug.) peak levels, should stabilize in a range still sufficient for farmers to generate profits in 1998. This should maintain the income and cash reserves of North American farmers, allowing them the means to invest in the kind of capital equipment that will further enhance their operating efficiencies.

More than 95% of Lindsay's irrigation system sales (83% of FY 97 revenues) are of the center-pivot type, which is lower in price and simpler to operate than the lateral-move type. Both products are automatic continuous-move systems that consist of sprinklers mounted on a water-carrying pipeline supported about 11 ft. off the ground by a truss system suspended between moving towers. The systems will enable farmers to conserve water and energy, reduce labor and variable costs, and help ensure reliability of crop production.

A typical center-pivot system, fully installed, requires an investment of approximately $60,000 to $70,000. About half of the cost is for the pivot itself, with the remainder for installation of additional equipment such as wells, pumps, underground water pipe, electrical supply and a concrete pad upon which the pivot is anchored. The company also has a significant replacement-parts business.

In addition to the factors favoring domestic growth (which include the consolidation of U.S. farms, low interest rates, and favorable farm legislation), LNN expects to benefit from the growing global demand for irrigation equipment. Exports accounted for 18% of total revenues in FY 97 (up from 15% in FY 96). The international market is currently strongest in Western Europe, Mexico, Latin America, Australia and South Africa.

The national and international distribution network consists of approximately 350 dealer locations. The major markets for domestic irrigation systems include the Pacific Northwest, Idaho, Texas, Colorado, Nebraska, Georgia and Alabama.

The diversified products segment, which accounted for 17% of FY 97 sales (up from 15% in FY 96), manufactures large-diameter tubing and performs outsource manufacturing. Lindsay offers agricultural and industrial capital goods makers services that include welding, machining, painting, punching, forming, galvanizing and hydraulic, electrical and mechanical assembly.

In October 1997, LNN said that 16% revenue growth in FY 97 reflected gains of 8% in North American irrigation equipment, 41% export irrigation equipment, and 32% in diversified products.

Per Share Data ($)										
(Year Ended Aug. 31)	1997	1996	1995	1994	1993	1992	1991	1990	1989	1988
Tangible Bk. Val.	6.16	5.39	4.66	4.28	3.51	2.82	2.09	1.53	1.02	0.51
Cash Flow	1.47	1.18	0.81	0.76	0.73	0.74	0.63	0.60	0.53	0.30
Earnings	1.34	1.08	0.73	0.68	0.65	0.68	0.57	0.54	0.47	0.24
Dividends	0.09	0.07	Nil	Nil	Nil	Nil	Nil	Nil	Nil	NA
Payout Ratio	7%	6%	Nil	Nil	Nil	Nil	Nil	Nil	Nil	NA
Prices - High	33½	19¾	11½	11	10⅝	13	9	5	3⅞	2⅝
- Low	18⅝	11⅛	8⅜	8¼	8	8⅛	3¼	2⅜	2⅜	1⁵⁄₁₆
P/E Ratio - High	25	18	16	16	16	19	16	9	8	11
- Low	14	10	11	12	12	12	6	4	5	5

Income Statement Analysis (Million $)										
Revs.	158	136	112	113	102	109	99	103	93.0	76.0
Oper. Inc.	28.5	20.9	15.2	15.4	14.3	13.9	12.0	15.0	11.3	5.8
Depr.	2.0	1.5	1.3	1.2	1.2	1.0	0.9	0.9	1.0	1.0
Int. Exp.	NA	NA	NM	NM	Nil	Nil	Nil	Nil	Nil	Nil
Pretax Inc.	29.9	23.9	17.1	16.8	15.7	15.7	12.6	12.9	11.1	5.0
Eff. Tax Rate	33%	31%	32%	33%	32%	30%	29%	35%	34%	24%
Net Inc.	20.1	16.5	11.7	11.2	10.7	11.0	8.9	8.4	7.4	3.8

Balance Sheet & Other Fin. Data (Million $)										
Cash	4.2	26.3	23.3	13.6	15.6	18.3	18.7	16.9	12.8	3.1
Curr. Assets	49.8	57.9	43.7	36.4	39.5	35.8	39.3	38.7	27.3	19.2
Total Assets	108	96.8	86.1	88.4	79.9	71.4	60.4	46.9	31.7	24.0
Curr. Liab.	19.5	18.7	16.0	19.0	23.7	26.2	26.9	22.2	15.2	15.4
LT Debt	0.3	Nil	Nil	Nil	Nil	Nil	Nil	Nil	Nil	Nil
Common Eqty.	87.0	76.8	68.7	68.1	55.5	44.4	32.8	24.0	16.0	8.0
Total Cap.	87.2	76.8	68.7	68.1	55.5	44.4	32.8	24.0	16.0	8.0
Cap. Exp.	3.3	4.0	2.8	1.3	0.9	1.7	1.7	1.2	0.8	2.3
Cash Flow	22.1	18.0	12.9	12.5	11.9	12.0	9.8	9.3	8.4	4.8
Curr. Ratio	2.6	3.1	2.8	1.9	1.7	1.4	1.5	1.7	1.8	1.2
% LT Debt of Cap.	0.3	Nil	Nil	Nil	Nil	Nil	Nil	Nil	Nil	Nil
% Net Inc.of Revs.	12.7	12.1	10.0	10.0	10.5	10.1	9.0	8.2	8.0	5.0
% Ret. on Assets	19.6	18.1	13.5	13.3	14.2	16.7	16.6	21.3	26.5	17.6
% Ret. on Equity	24.5	22.7	17.1	18.1	21.4	28.5	31.3	41.9	61.5	51.1

Data as orig. reptd.; bef. results of disc. opers. and/or spec. items. Per share data adj. for stk. divs. as of ex-div. date. Bold denotes diluted EPS (FASB 128). E-Estimated. NA-Not Available. NM-Not Meaningful. NR-Not Ranked.

Office—E. Hwy 91, P.O. Box 156, Lindsay, NE 68644. **Tel**—(402) 428-2131. **Chrmn, Pres & CEO**—G. D. Parker. **VP-Fin, Treas & Secy**—Bruce C. Karsk (402-428-7250). **Dirs**—V.L. Beals, H. G. Buffett, J. W. Croghan, J. D. Dunn, G. D. Parker, G. W. Plossl. **Transfer Agent & Registrar**—First National Bank of Omaha. **Incorporated**—in Nebraska in 1969; reincorporated in Delaware in 1974. **Empl**— 553. **S&P Analyst:** E. Hunter

Linens 'n Things

1359

NYSE Symbol **LIN**

In S&P SmallCap 600

10-OCT-98

Industry: Retail (Specialty)

Summary: This retailer operates a nationwide chain of superstores selling home textiles, housewares and home accessories at everyday low prices.

S&P Opinion: Hold (★★★)

Recent Price • 21⅞	Yield • Nil
52 Wk Range • 35⅞-15¼	12-Mo. P/E • 30.0

Quantitative Evaluations

Outlook (1 Lowest—5 Highest)
• **NA**

Fair Value
• **NA**

Risk
• **NA**

Earn./Div. Rank
• **NR**

Technical Eval.
• **NA**

Rel. Strength Rank (1 Lowest—99 Highest)
• **44**

Insider Activity
• **NA**

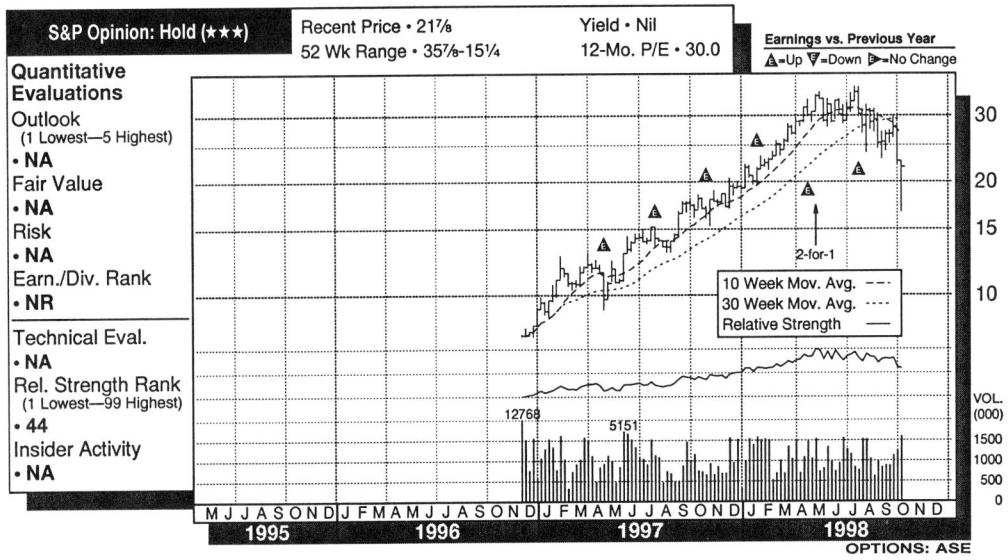

Earnings vs. Previous Year
▲=Up ▽=Down ▷=No Change

10 Week Mov. Avg. ---
30 Week Mov. Avg. ----
Relative Strength —

2-for-1

VOL. (000)

OPTIONS: ASE

Overview - 21-JUL-98

In recent years, Linens has emerged as a major category killer and destination superstore catering to the time-pressed and value-seeking shopper in the home furnishings product segment. The company allows consumers to one-stop shop by offering a broad selection of practical and decorative merchandise at prices below those of department stores. In the next three to four years, LIN aims to grow the "things" portion of its business, which primarily consists of housewares and home accessories, to 50% of its sales mix, up from the current 35%. This merchandising initiative should not only improve gross margins, but also widen the company's product offerings and reinforce Linens 'n Things as a destination superstore. We expect 20% annual sales growth and 25% earnings gains over the next five years.

Valuation - 21-JUL-98

The shares have doubled over the past nine months, due to better than expected sales growth. LIN continues to capture market share from department stores and weaker specialty chain store competitors by offering quality merchandise at low prices. We believe sales will increase 21% in 1998, reflecting same-store sales growth of 5% to 7% and 30 new superstores. Operating margins will be up 40 to 60 basis points, due to operating leverage and more favorable product mix. The long-term outlook for the industry remains favorable, as the top three superstore operators account for less than 5% of the $60 billion home furnishings industry. We believe that there is still room for expansion, especially in the western U.S. We have raised our 1998 EPS estimate to $0.91 from $0.85. However, with the stock recently trading at 38X our 1998 EPS estimate, we recommend holding the shares.

Key Stock Statistics

S&P EPS Est. 1998	0.91	Tang. Bk. Value/Share	6.84
P/E on S&P Est. 1998	24.0	Beta	NA
S&P EPS Est. 1999	1.07	Shareholders	2,000
Dividend Rate/Share	Nil	Market cap. (B)	$0.852
Shs. outstg. (M)	39.0	Inst. holdings	87%
Avg. daily vol. (M)	0.285		

Value of $10,000 invested 5 years ago: NA

Fiscal Year Ending Dec. 31

	1998	1997	1996	1995	1994	1993
Revenues (Million $)						
1Q	218.0	179.9	138.1	—	—	—
2Q	222.1	185.2	147.7	—	—	—
3Q	—	225.2	180.4	—	—	—
4Q	—	283.4	229.8	—	—	—
Yr.	—	874.2	696.1	555.1	440.1	333.2
Earnings Per Share ($)						
1Q	**0.04**	0.01	0.05	—	—	—
2Q	**0.07**	0.03	-0.01	—	—	—
3Q	**E0.24**	0.19	0.13	—	—	—
4Q	**E0.55**	0.42	0.32	—	—	—
Yr.	**E0.91**	0.65	0.39	Nil	0.45	0.30

Next earnings report expected: mid October

Dividend Data

Amount ($)	Date Decl.	Ex-Div. Date	Stock of Record	Payment Date
2-for-1	Apr. 15	May. 08	Apr. 24	May. 07 '98

A Division of The McGraw-Hill Companies

Business Summary - 21-JUL-98

Founded in 1975, Linens 'n Things (LIN) was acquired by CVS Corp. (formerly Melville Corp.) in 1983 and spun off in November 1996. CVS still owns 32.5% of the common shares. LIN's strategy is to offer a broad assortment of high-quality, brand name merchandise at everyday low prices, while providing efficient customer service and maintaining low operating costs. Prices are substantially below regular department store prices and comparable to or lower than store sale prices. The company offers over 25,000 items across six departments: bath, home accessories, housewares, storage, bedding and window treatments.

Linens 'n Things' growth strategy includes new superstore expansion and increased productivity of the existing store base. As of June 27, 1998, the company operated 178 stores, including 160 superstores, in 38 states. After opening a net of seven stores in 1997, the company expects to open about 18 net new stores in 1998. Total square footage at the end of 1997 was 5.5 million, up from 1.2 million in January 1991. Most new market opportunities exist in the western U.S., but the company will also add stores in markets in which it already has a presence.

To increase existing-store productivity, the company expects to increase sales of "things" merchandise (i.e., housewares and home accessories) to 50% of total sales (up from 10% in 1991 and 38% in the third quar-

ter of 1997). These "things" carry higher margins than "linens" products (i.e., bedding, towels and pillows) and are more impulse driven items. In July 1995, the company opened a 275,000 sq. ft. distribution center in Greensboro, NC, which supplies approximately 80% of store merchandise. Linens 'n Things believes that this centralized infrastructure will result in lower average freight costs, more efficient scheduling of inventory shipments and improved inventory turnover. A second distribution center is scheduled to open in mid-1999. In addition, the company plans to continue to convert its traditional stores to its new superstore format. Currently, there are 160 superstores (averaging 35,000 sq. ft.) and 18 traditional stores (averaging between 7,000 and 10,000 sq. ft.). The company also sells private-label merchandise, which accounts for about 10% of sales.

Total sales in the home textiles, housewares and decorative furnishings industry are over $60 billion. The industry is fragmented and highly competitive, with competition coming from department stores, mass merchandisers, specialty retailers and other stores. Specialty superstores are the fastest growing segment in the industry. However, the three largest specialty retailers (including LIN) account for less than 5% of total unit sales. Sales in the industry are highly seasonal, with most of the company's sales and earnings coming during the third and fourth quarters. Sales may also be impacted by trends in the housing market.

Per Share Data ($)

(Year Ended Dec. 31)	1997	1996	1995	1994	1993	1992	1991	1990	1989	1988
Tangible Bk. Val.	6.69	5.90	5.58	1.60	NA	NA	NA	NA	NA	NA
Cash Flow	1.11	0.77	0.34	0.69	0.49	NA	NA	NA	NA	NA
Earnings	0.65	0.39	Nil	0.45	0.30	NA	NA	NA	NA	NA
Dividends	Nil	Nil	Nil	Nil	Nil	Nil	Nil	Nil	Nil	Nil
Payout Ratio	Nil	Nil	Nil	Nil	Nil	Nil	Nil	Nil	Nil	Nil
Prices - High	22¼	9⅞	NA	NA	NA	NA	NA	NA	NA	NA
- Low	8¾	7¾	NA	NA	NA	NA	NA	NA	NA	NA
P/E Ratio - High	34	25	NA	NA	NA	NA	NA	NA	NA	NA
- Low	13	20	NA	NA	NA	NA	NA	NA	NA	NA

Income Statement Analysis (Million $)

	1997	1996	1995	1994	1993	1992	1991	1990	1989	1988
Revs.	874	696	555	440	333	NA	NA	NA	NA	NA
Oper. Inc.	63.5	45.2	32.0	41.8	29.1	NA	NA	NA	NA	NA
Depr.	18.0	14.5	12.9	9.6	7.4	NA	NA	NA	NA	NA
Int. Exp.	1.0	4.7	7.1	3.2	1.4	NA	NA	NA	NA	NA
Pretax Inc.	44.5	25.9	1.1	29.1	20.3	NA	NA	NA	NA	NA
Eff. Tax Rate	42%	42%	103%	41%	42%	NA	NA	NA	NA	NA
Net Inc.	25.8	15.0	0.0	17.2	11.7	NA	NA	NA	NA	NA

Balance Sheet & Other Fin. Data (Million $)

	1997	1996	1995	1994	1993	1992	1991	1990	1989	1988
Cash	39.9	26.9	2.9	NA	NA	NA	NA	NA	NA	NA
Curr. Assets	290	257	234	NA	NA	NA	NA	NA	NA	NA
Total Assets	472	424	400	NA	NA	NA	NA	NA	NA	NA
Curr. Liab.	167	146	177	NA	NA	NA	NA	NA	NA	NA
LT Debt	Nil	13.5	13.5	NA	NA	NA	NA	NA	NA	NA
Common Eqty.	280	250	237	NA	NA	NA	NA	NA	NA	NA
Total Cap.	306	281	251	NA	NA	NA	NA	NA	NA	NA
Cap. Exp.	35.3	46.4	41.3	39.1	30.6	NA	NA	NA	NA	NA
Cash Flow	43.8	29.6	12.8	26.8	19.1	NA	NA	NA	NA	NA
Curr. Ratio	1.7	1.8	3.0	NA	NA	NA	NA	NA	NA	NA
% LT Debt of Cap.	Nil	4.8	5.4	NA	NA	NA	NA	NA	NA	NA
% Net Inc.of Revs.	3.0	2.2	NM	3.9	3.5	NA	NA	NA	NA	NA
% Ret. on Assets	5.8	3.9	NA	NA	NA	NA	NA	NA	NA	NA
% Ret. on Equity	9.7	9.2	NA	NA	NA	NA	NA	NA	NA	NA

Data as orig. reptd.; bef. results of disc. opers. and/or spec. items. Per share data adj. for stk. divs. as of ex-div. date. Bold denotes diluted EPS (FASB 128). E-Estimated. NA-Not Available. NM-Not Meaningful. NR-Not Ranked.

Office—6 Brighton Rd., Clifton, NJ 07015. **Tel**—(973) 778-1300. **Website**—http://www.lnthings.com **Pres, Chrmn & CEO**—N. Axelrod. **CFO & Investor Contact**—William T. Giles (973) 815-2929. **Dirs**—N. Axelrod, P. E. Beekman, H. F. Compton, C. C. Conaway, S. P. Goldstein. **Transfer Agent**—BankBoston, NA. **Incorporated**—in Delaware in 1996. **Empl**— 7,700. **S&P Analyst**: Ray Lam, CFA

Liposome Co.

4440P

NASDAQ Symbol **LIPO**

In S&P SmallCap 600

10-OCT-98

Industry:
Health Care (Drugs - Generic & Other)

Summary: This company develops and makes proprietary liposome and lipid-complex based pharmaceuticals for the treatment, prevention and diagnosis of life-threatening illnesses.

Quantitative Evaluations

Outlook
(1 Lowest—5 Highest)
- **NA**

Fair Value
- **NA**

Risk
- **High**

Earn./Div. Rank
- **C**

Technical Eval.
- **Bearish** since 6/98

Rel. Strength Rank
(1 Lowest—99 Highest)
- **99**

Insider Activity
- **Neutral**

Recent Price • 6
52 Wk Range • 8⅝-3⅜

Yield • Nil
12-Mo. P/E • NM

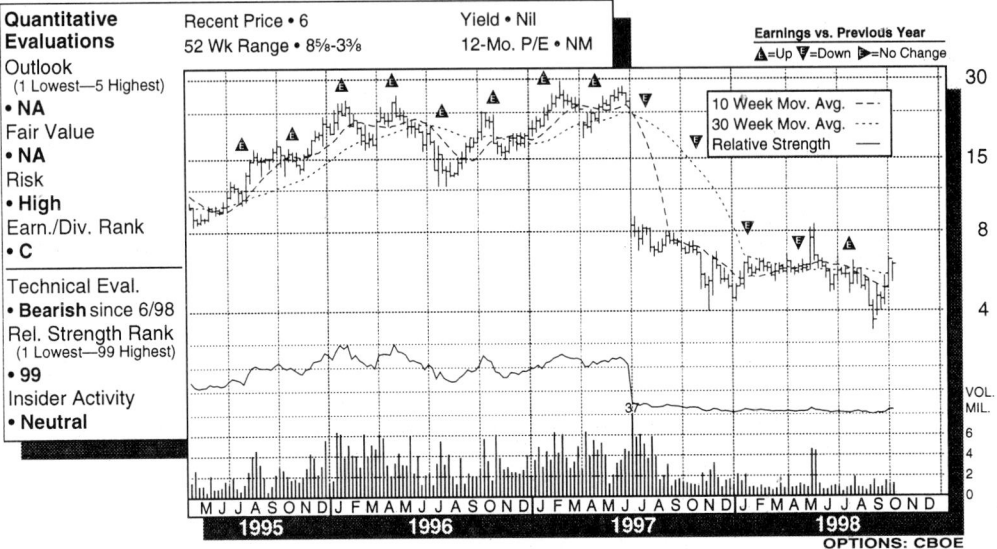

Earnings vs. Previous Year
▲=Up ▼=Down ▶=No Change

10 Week Mov. Avg. ---
30 Week Mov. Avg. ....
Relative Strength —

OPTIONS: CBOE

Business Profile - 01-OCT-98

This firm began selling its lead drug, Abelcet, for the treatment of systemic fungal infections, in the U.S. during the fourth quarter of 1995. Worldwide sales of Abelcet advanced 11% in 1997, to $58.5 million, from $52.8 million in 1996. LIPO reported marketing approvals for Abelcet in Sweeden and Australia in July and September 1998, respectively. The shares fell sharply in June 1997, after the company announced disappointing Phase III trial results for Ventus, its product candidate for the treatment of Acute Respiratory Distress Syndrome (ARDS). Interim analyses of Phase III studies of Evacet (a treatment for metastatic breast cancer) produced positive data, and LIPO intends to file for FDA approval in 1998.

Operational Review - 01-OCT-98

Total revenues in the six months ended June 28, 1998, rose 15%, year to year, primarily driven by higher U.S. sales volume of Abelcet and additional marketing clearance of the product in major European countries and Canada. However, sharply higher unit shipments were offset by lower prices. Gross margins improved slightly as the increase in cost of goods sold was well contained. After a modest 6% rise in R&D expenses, and a 22% decline in SG&A costs from the absence of a restructuring charge in the prior year, the net loss narrowed to $5,924,000 ($0.16 a share, on 4% more shares), from $13,019,000 ($0.36). Cash and equivalents totaled $25.4 million on June 28, 1998.

Stock Performance - 09-OCT-98

In the past 30 trading days, LIPO's shares have increased 44%, compared to a 4% fall in the S&P 500. Average trading volume for the past five days was 230,600 shares, compared with the 40-day moving average of 208,477 shares.

Key Stock Statistics

Dividend Rate/Share	Nil	Shareholders	1,400
Shs. outstg. (M)	38.0	Market cap. (B)	$0.228
Avg. daily vol. (M)	0.225	Inst. holdings	15%
Tang. Bk. Value/Share	1.80		
Beta	1.04		

Value of $10,000 invested 5 years ago: $ 5,106

Fiscal Year Ending Dec. 31

	1998	1997	1996	1995	1994	1993
Revenues (Million $)						
1Q	17.09	15.85	12.41	1.85	3.04	2.85
2Q	20.23	16.65	14.40	3.72	2.94	3.56
3Q	—	16.05	14.91	3.50	2.45	3.48
4Q	—	16.54	18.21	6.65	2.02	3.16
Yr.	—	65.10	59.93	15.72	10.89	13.04
Earnings Per Share ($)						
1Q	-0.13	-0.12	-0.16	-0.49	-0.34	-0.21
2Q	-0.02	-0.23	-0.17	-0.38	-0.40	-0.21
3Q	—	-0.17	-0.16	-0.35	-0.42	-0.37
4Q	—	-0.19	-0.09	-0.31	-0.47	-0.39
Yr.	—	-0.71	-0.57	-1.50	-1.64	-1.18

Next earnings report expected: late October

Dividend Data

No cash dividends have been paid.

A Division of The McGraw·Hill Companies

Business Summary - 01-OCT-98

The Liposome Company, both independently and in collaboration with others, is a leading developer of proprietary liposome and lipid-complex based pharmaceuticals for the treatment, prevention and diagnosis of serious illnesses. Leading products are focused on cancer treatments and fungal infections in immunocompromised patients.

Liposomes are microscopic synthetic spheres composed of lipids (fat molecules) that can be engineered to entrap drugs or other biologically active molecules within the lipid membranes of the spheres or in the aqueous spaces between them.

LIPO's research activities focus on developing enhanced liposomal drugs for the treatment of cancer, infections and inflammatory diseases.

The company's first commercialized product, Abelcet (Amphotericin B Lipid Complex), was approved in the U.S. in November 1995. Abelcet is being used to treat refractory aspergillosis, or systemic fungal infections. Abelcet is also being sold in several European countries for the same indication. Conventional amphotericin B is very toxic, but LIPO's formulation has demonstrated lower liver toxicity levels in patients undergoing treatment.

LIPO is conducting Phase III clinical trials of TLC D-99, for first-line treatment of metastatic breast cancer. The company reacquired all development, manufacturing and marketing rights to Evacet (formerly TLC D-99, liposomal doxorubicin) from Pfizer Inc. in July 1997. Pfizer will provide a credit line of up to $10 million to continue development, and will receive royalties worldwide (except Japan) on any commercial sales of Evacet. Interim analyses of the Phase III studies have produced positive data, and the company anticipates filing for marketing approval in the U.S. in 1998. Other products in development include TLC ELL-12, a cancer treatment expected to enter Phase I trials in the second half of 1998.

A Phase III clinical trial for Ventus in the treatment of Acute Respiratory Distress Syndrome produced unfavorable results in June 1997, with no significant difference between patients receiving Ventus or a placebo. In response, the company was forced to restructure operations, eliminating 137 positions. LIPO expects to save approximately $8 million annually as a result of this restructuring.

In August 1997, the company reached a settlement with NeXstar Pharmaceuticals, Inc. in connection with all of their outstanding patent litigation. As part of the settlement, NeXstar agreed to make certain payments to LIPO, and the companies granted each other options to take licenses under other patented technology.

Per Share Data ($)

(Year Ended Dec. 31)	1997	1996	1995	1994	1993	1992	1991	1990	1989	1988
Tangible Bk. Val.	1.95	2.06	0.68	0.37	4.87	3.54	2.38	0.52	0.86	1.40
Cash Flow	-0.57	-0.46	-1.29	-1.50	-1.11	-0.40	-0.19	-0.29	-0.48	-0.40
Earnings	-0.71	-0.57	-1.50	-1.64	-1.18	-0.43	-0.22	-0.35	-0.54	-0.47
Dividends	Nil	Nil	Nil	Nil	Nil	Nil	Nil	Nil	Nil	Nil
Payout Ratio	Nil	Nil	Nil	Nil	Nil	Nil	Nil	Nil	Nil	Nil
Prices - High	29¹/₂	26¹/₈	21³/₄	10³/₄	12¹/₈	27³/₈	14³/₈	3¹/₄	3¹/₂	4⁵/₈
- Low	4	11⁷/₈	7⁷/₈	4³/₄	5¹/₈	7³/₈	2³/₄	⁷/₈	⁷/₈	1³/₄
P/E Ratio - High	NM	NM	NM	NM	NM	NM	NM	NM	NM	NM
- Low	NM	NM	NM	NM	NM	NM	NM	NM	NM	NM

Income Statement Analysis (Million $)

	1997	1996	1995	1994	1993	1992	1991	1990	1989	1988
Revs.	60.8	56.1	12.8	5.9	5.4	6.1	6.3	3.9	2.5	3.2
Oper. Inc.	-24.9	-17.6	-35.0	-34.8	-28.2	-13.6	-6.0	-7.0	-7.1	-7.7
Depr.	5.1	3.8	3.4	3.1	1.6	0.8	0.7	0.9	0.9	0.8
Int. Exp.	0.7	0.3	0.3	0.3	0.3	0.1	0.0	0.0	0.0	Nil
Pretax Inc.	-26.4	-17.9	-35.7	-33.7	-22.5	-9.7	-4.1	-5.0	-7.6	-6.3
Eff. Tax Rate	NM	NM	NM	NM	NM	NM	Nil	Nil	Nil	Nil
Net Inc.	-26.4	-17.9	-35.7	-33.7	-22.5	-9.7	-4.1	-5.0	-7.6	-6.3

Balance Sheet & Other Fin. Data (Million $)

	1997	1996	1995	1994	1993	1992	1991	1990	1989	1988
Cash	30.6	30.1	54.4	58.0	110	75.4	45.7	7.7	10.6	17.8
Curr. Assets	49.5	48.8	65.1	61.0	112	78.5	46.9	8.2	11.4	18.6
Total Assets	91.5	94.6	106	93.0	140	92.8	50.8	11.0	14.9	22.7
Curr. Liab.	11.0	12.1	12.0	8.9	9.6	6.6	3.3	2.9	2.0	1.8
LT Debt	17.8	19.7	4.1	5.9	7.7	2.4	Nil	0.0	0.1	0.2
Common Eqty.	73.7	74.9	89.8	9.0	115	83.2	46.9	7.4	12.2	19.7
Total Cap.	91.5	82.4	93.9	84.0	130	85.6	46.9	7.5	12.3	19.9
Cap. Exp.	1.9	9.6	8.0	2.9	7.7	9.8	1.3	0.3	0.3	0.4
Cash Flow	-21.3	-15.3	-32.3	-35.9	-26.2	-8.9	-3.4	-4.1	-6.7	-5.5
Curr. Ratio	4.5	4.0	5.4	6.8	11.7	11.9	14.1	2.8	5.8	10.5
% LT Debt of Cap.	19.5	9.2	4.4	7.0	5.9	2.8	Nil	0.2	1.0	1.1
% Net Inc.of Revs.	NM	NM	NM	NM	NM	NM	NM	NM	NM	NM
% Ret. on Assets	NM	NM	NM	NM	NM	NM	NM	NM	NM	NM
% Ret. on Equity	NM	NM	NM	NM	NM	NM	NM	NM	NM	NM

Data as orig. reptd.; bef. results of disc. opers. and/or spec. items. Per share data adj. for stk. divs. as of ex-div. date. Bold denotes diluted EPS (FASB 128). E-Estimated. NA-Not Available. NM-Not Meaningful. NR-Not Ranked.

Office—One Research Way, Princeton Forrestal Center, Princeton, NJ 08540. **Tel**—(609) 452-7060. **Website**—http://www.lipo.com **Chrmn, Pres & CEO**—C. A. Baker. **VP-Fin & CFO**—B. J. Geiger. **VP & Secy**—C. Gillespie. **Dirs**—J. G. Andress, C. A. Baker, M. Collins, S. F. Feiner, R. F. Hendrickson, B. Samuelsson, J. T. Stewart Jr., G. Weissmann, H. Witzel. **Transfer Agent & Registrar**—American Stock Transfer & Trust, NYC.**Incorporated**—in Delaware in 1981. **Empl**— 280. **S&P Analyst:** David Moskowitz

Lone Star Industries   1372

NYSE Symbol **LCE**

In S&P SmallCap 600

10-OCT-98

Industry: Construction (Cement & Aggregates)

Summary: LCE produces cement, concrete, sand, gravel, crushed stone and precast concrete products.

Quantitative Evaluations	
Outlook (1 Lowest—5 Highest) • **NA**	
Fair Value • **NA**	
Risk • **Average**	
Earn./Div. Rank • **NR**	
Technical Eval. • **Bearish** since 9/98	
Rel. Strength Rank (1 Lowest—99 Highest) • **73**	
Insider Activity • **NA**	

Recent Price • 59
52 Wk Range • 84⅞-48⅞

Yield • 0.3%
12-Mo. P/E • 10.8

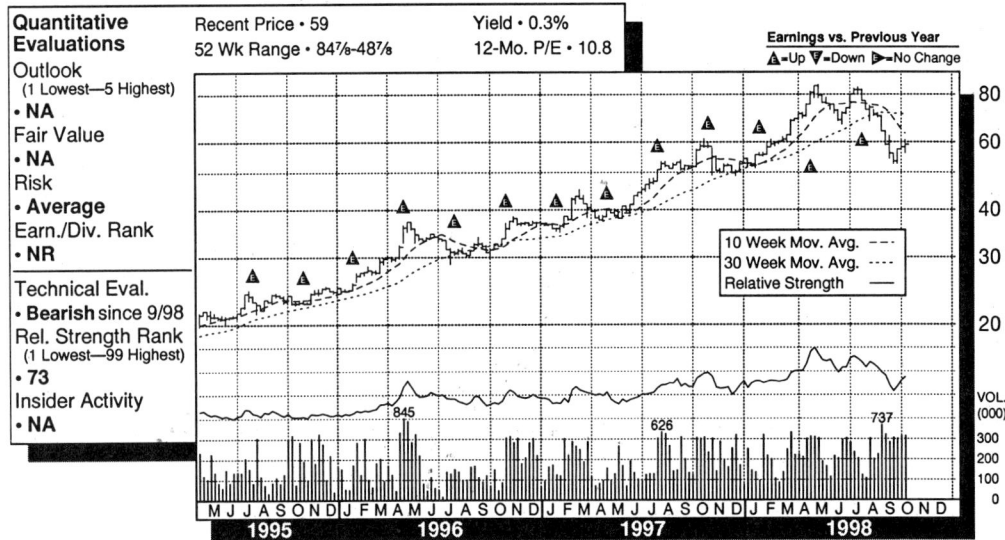

Earnings vs. Previous Year
▲=Up ▼=Down ▶=No Change

10 Week Mov. Avg. ---
30 Week Mov. Avg. ....
Relative Strength —

Business Profile - 11-SEP-98

Results in 1997 and early 1998 benefited from higher cement prices, reflecting Lone Star's decision to implement price increases of $1 to $2 per ton in most markets effective April 1, 1997. Losses in 1997 in the construction aggregates business were due to less favorable product mix and higher production and distribution costs. The company's business is cyclical and seasonal. Risks and uncertainties include changes in general economic conditions or conditions specific to any one or more of Lone Star's markets (such as the local real estate markets and the availability of public funds for construction.)

Operational Review - 11-SEP-98

Revenues in the first half of 1998 fell 3.1%, year to year, primarily reflecting the sale of the New York construction aggregates and central Illinois ready-mixed concrete operations in March 1997. Cement shipments from continuing operations were up 4%, reflecting strong demand in most markets. Margins widened on higher average net realized cement selling prices. With a $1.5 million gain on sale of real estate, and much lower interest and depreciation charges, and after taxes at 33.8%, versus 34.0%, net income advanced 44%, to $29,473,000 ($2.15 a share), from $20,445,000 ($1.55).

Stock Performance - 09-OCT-98

In the past 30 trading days, LCE's shares have declined 8%, compared to a 4% fall in the S&P 500. Average trading volume for the past five days was 93,900 shares, compared with the 40-day moving average of 85,656 shares.

Key Stock Statistics

Dividend Rate/Share	0.20	Shareholders	2,200
Shs. outstg. (M)	10.7	Market cap. (B)	$0.630
Avg. daily vol. (M)	0.078	Inst. holdings	93%
Tang. Bk. Value/Share	33.66		
Beta	0.99		

Value of $10,000 invested 5 years ago: $ 218,374

Fiscal Year Ending Dec. 31

	1998	1997	1996	1995	1994	1993
Revenues (Million $)						
1Q	57.79	60.84	52.97	52.71	–	32.00
2Q	97.70	104.6	102.3	87.55	87.00	71.00
3Q	—	111.8	118.3	100.6	95.97	73.00
4Q	—	80.34	94.03	82.13	78.68	64.00
Yr.	—	357.6	367.7	323.0	261.6	240.0
Earnings Per Share ($)						
1Q	0.52	0.02	0.20	-0.42	–	-0.94
2Q	1.63	1.53	1.26	0.89	0.62	-1.78
3Q	—	2.04	1.86	1.30	0.99	0.61
4Q	—	1.27	1.13	0.79	0.61	-0.37
Yr.	—	4.87	3.96	2.66	2.22	-2.42

Next earnings report expected: late October

Dividend Data (Dividends have been paid since 1995.)

Amount ($)	Date Decl.	Ex-Div. Date	Stock of Record	Payment Date
0.050	Nov. 20	Nov. 26	Dec. 01	Dec. 15 '97
0.050	Feb. 19	Feb. 25	Mar. 01	Mar. 16 '98
0.050	May. 14	May. 28	Jun. 01	Jun. 15 '98
0.050	Aug. 14	Aug. 28	Sep. 01	Sep. 15 '98

A Division of The McGraw-Hill Companies

Business Summary - 11-SEP-98

Lone Star Industries (LCE) has been steadily profitable (save for losses in the seasonally weak first quarters of 1996 and 1995) ever since it emerged from Chapter 11 bankruptcy proceedings in April 1994. In accordance with its post-bankruptcy strategic plan, LCE began concentrating on the manufacture, distribution and sale of cement and related materials throughout the Midwest and Southwest regions of the U.S. In addition to its cement operations, LCE quarries and processes construction aggregates (11% of net sales in 1997) and makes ready-mixed concrete in the Memphis, TN, area (6%).

The company's five wholly owned cement plants produced 3.9 million tons of cement in 1997. Portland cement, the primary binding material used in the production of concrete, is LCE's main cement product, although it also makes masonry and oil well cement. One of these plants uses a "wet" production process, but the other four employ the newer, more fuel-efficient "dry" cement production process. Portland cement is a commodity product, and suppliers compete largely on the basis of price. LCE also has a plant in New Orleans where it grinds and distributes slag cement, a

by product of iron blast furnaces sometimes used in place of portland cement; it produced 190,000 tons of slag cement in 1997. In addition, LCE has a 25% interest in Kosmos Cement Co., which operates one cement plant in Kentucky and another in Pennsylvania.

LCE sold 4.2 million tons of construction aggregates in 1997.

Used in almost all construction, ready-mixed concrete is produced by mixing stone, sand, water and chemicals with cement. The proximity of LCE's ready-mixed concrete business to the company's large cement complex at Cape Girardeau, MO has resulted in a vertically integrated operation.

Benefiting from a favorable combination of price increases and higher shipments in its core cement business, LCE in 1997 reported a 19% gain in net income. Also contributing to higher net income was a gain on the sale of surplus real estate, higher interest income and lower interest expense. Net sales were lower due to the sale of its New York construction aggregates and central Illinois ready-mixed concrete operations in March 1997.

In February 1998, Lone Star recorded a gain of $1.5 million from the sale of a piece of surplus real estate in Massachusetts.

Per Share Data ($)

(Year Ended Dec. 31)	1997	1996	1995	1994	1993	1992	1991	1990	1989	1988
Tangible Bk. Val.	31.11	24.67	13.92	10.21	-0.96	2.15	12.44	15.37	19.82	37.52
Cash Flow	6.63	5.70	4.14	3.88	-0.85	-1.47	0.91	-2.88	-14.37	4.06
Earnings	4.87	4.02	2.66	2.22	-2.42	-3.03	-0.64	-4.34	-16.68	2.00
Dividends	0.20	0.20	0.15	Nil	Nil	Nil	Nil	Nil	1.90	1.90
Payout Ratio	4%	5%	6%	Nil	Nil	Nil	Nil	Nil	NM	95%
Prices - High	61¼	38½	25¼	19¾	2⅞	5⅜	6⅛	18⅛	37	36¾
- Low	34⅞	24¼	17¼	1⅞	1⅜	2½	2½	1⅞	16¼	21¾
P/E Ratio - High	13	10	9	NM	NM	NM	NM	NM	NM	18
- Low	7	6	6	NM	NM	NM	NM	NM	NM	11

Income Statement Analysis (Million $)

	1997	1996	1995	1994	1993	1992	1991	1990	1989	1988
Revs.	358	368	323	262	240	230	239	254	338	371
Oper. Inc.	109	102	75.3	60.9	5.0	1.0	-7.0	-4.0	-22.0	-14.0
Depr.	24.0	24.0	23.6	17.2	26.3	26.1	25.7	24.3	38.3	33.9
Int. Exp.	5.0	6.6	9.4	6.8	1.8	2.4	4.6	45.2	53.8	60.1
Pretax Inc.	99	81.7	53.4	45.1	-42.0	-31.0	-4.0	-88.0	-342	50.0
Eff. Tax Rate	34%	34%	33%	35%	NM	NM	NM	NM	NM	24%
Net Inc.	65.4	54.2	35.8	29.3	-35.0	-45.0	-5.5	-67.0	-270	38.0

Balance Sheet & Other Fin. Data (Million $)

	1997	1996	1995	1994	1993	1992	1991	1990	1989	1988
Cash	154	71.2	50.0	55.0	244	169	136	97.0	52.0	121
Curr. Assets	233	165	142	137	355	264	244	220	305	224
Total Assets	599	562	481	553	925	953	914	942	1,146	1,424
Curr. Liab.	63.4	88.2	60.6	65.0	80.0	75.0	56.0	53.0	198	93.0
LT Debt	50.0	50.0	82.4	182	Nil	Nil	Nil	Nil	431	467
Common Eqty.	334	264	160	122	-0.5	47.0	219	267	340	646
Total Cap.	384	314	249	311	53.0	113	276	321	856	1,290
Cap. Exp.	42.0	42.6	36.6	16.5	19.0	22.0	18.0	38.0	31.0	22.0
Cash Flow	89.4	78.2	59.4	46.5	-14.0	-24.0	15.0	-48.0	-237	67.0
Curr. Ratio	3.7	1.9	2.3	2.1	4.5	3.5	4.4	4.2	1.5	2.4
% LT Debt of Cap.	15.0	15.9	33.1	58.5	Nil	Nil	Nil	0.1	50.4	36.2
% Net Inc.of Revs.	18.3	14.7	11.1	11.2	NM	NM	NM	NM	NM	10.3
% Ret. on Assets	11.3	10.4	7.0	NM	NM	NM	NM	NM	NM	2.6
% Ret. on Equity	21.9	25.5	25.4	NM	NM	NM	NM	NM	NM	5.1

Data as orig. reptd.; bef. results of disc. opers. and/or spec. items. Per share data adj. for stk. divs. as of ex-div. date. 1994 data for 9 mos. ended Dec. 1994. E-Estimated. NA-Not Available. NM-Not Meaningful. NR-Not Ranked.

Office—300 First Stamford Place, P.O. Box 120014, Stamford, CT 06912-0014. **Tel**—(203) 969-8600. **Fax**—(203) 969-8546. **Chrmn**—D. W. Wallace. **Pres & CEO**—W. M. Troutman. **VP, CFO, Contr & Treas**—W. E. Roberts. **VP & Secy**—J. W. Langham.**Investor Contact**—William E. Roberts.**Dirs**—J. E. Bacon, T. F. Brophy, A. B. Newman, A. E. Puckett, R. G. Schwartz, W. M. Troutman, D. W. Wallace, J. R. Wentworth. **Transfer Agent & Registrar**—ChaseMellon Shareholder Services, NYC. **Incorporated**—in Maine in 1919; reincorporated in Delaware in 1969. **Empl**—1,060. **S&P Analyst:** E.P.L.

Luby's Cafeterias

1386P

NYSE Symbol **LUB**

In S&P SmallCap 600

03-OCT-98

Industry: Restaurants

Summary: This company owns and operates more than 230 cafeterias, primarily in Texas.

Quantitative Evaluations		
Outlook (1 Lowest—5 Highest)		• **3**
Fair Value		• **17⅛**
Risk		• **Low**
Earn./Div. Rank		• **A**
Technical Eval.		• **Bullish** since 2/98
Rel. Strength Rank (1 Lowest—99 Highest)		• **72**
Insider Activity		• **NA**

Recent Price • 15⅝   Yield • 5.1%
52 Wk Range • 21⅛-14⅞   12-Mo. P/E • 15.3

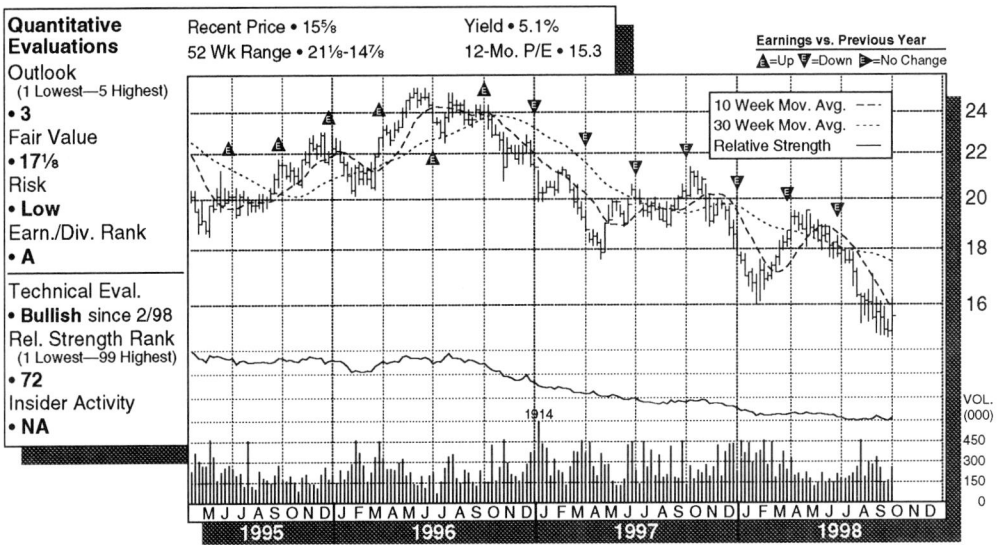

Earnings vs. Previous Year
▲=Up ▼=Down ▶=No Change

10 Week Mov. Avg. – – –
30 Week Mov. Avg. ·······
Relative Strength ——

Business Profile - 16-JUN-98

Same-store sales and customer counts have been hurt in the past year by competitor openings and a difficult industry environment. As a result, Luby's has decided to reduce the number of new units to be opened in the next few years to concentrate on remodelings and increasing operational efficiency. The company plans to open only seven units in FY 98 (Aug.) and seven more units in FY 99 in order to focus on same store sales and customer counts. In May 1998, the company completed a broad review of its overall business and plans to implement its plans for growth identified in its strategic review. Currently, LUB is conducting tests of its new breakfast service, extended hours and expanded beverage offerings.

Operational Review - 16-JUN-98

Net sales for the nine months ended May 31, 1998, rose 2.8%, year to year, reflecting more units in operation. Margins narrowed, due to higher food costs, product promotions and increased payroll expenses stemming from the federal minimum wage hike in October 1996; operating income was down 13%. Following a 42% rise in interest expense, pretax income fell 18%. After taxes at 35.6%, versus 34.8%, net income slid 19%, to $21,295,000 ($0.92 a share), from $26,153,000 ($1.12).

Stock Performance - 02-OCT-98

In the past 30 trading days, LUB's shares have declined 3%, compared to a 7% fall in the S&P 500. Average trading volume for the past five days was 51,080 shares, compared with the 40-day moving average of 48,882 shares.

Key Stock Statistics

Dividend Rate/Share	0.80	Shareholders	4,100
Shs. outstg. (M)	23.3	Market cap. (B)	$0.364
Avg. daily vol. (M)	0.043	Inst. holdings	41%
Tang. Bk. Value/Share	9.72		
Beta	0.55		

Value of $10,000 invested 5 years ago: $ 8,684

Fiscal Year Ending Aug. 31

	1998	1997	1996	1995	1994	1993
Revenues (Million $)						
1Q	124.7	122.3	108.3	101.5	94.17	88.60
2Q	123.2	118.8	108.8	100.6	93.72	88.30
3Q	131.2	127.6	117.1	106.9	101.1	94.79
4Q	—	126.7	115.8	110.1	101.8	96.07
Yr.	—	495.4	450.1	419.0	390.7	367.8
Earnings Per Share ($)						
1Q	0.27	0.35	0.37	0.35	0.32	0.29
2Q	**0.30**	0.30	0.40	0.30	0.33	0.29
3Q	**0.35**	0.41	0.46	0.42	0.40	0.36
4Q	—	0.10	0.43	0.42	0.40	0.37
Yr.	—	1.22	1.66	1.55	1.45	1.31

Next earnings report expected: early October

Dividend Data (Dividends have been paid since 1965.)

Amount ($)	Date Decl.	Ex-Div. Date	Stock of Record	Payment Date
0.200	Oct. 17	Dec. 17	Dec. 19	Jan. 02 '98
0.200	Jan. 09	Mar. 11	Mar. 13	Mar. 30 '98
0.200	May. 15	Jun. 10	Jun. 12	Jun. 29 '98
0.200	Jul. 24	Sep. 09	Sep. 11	Sep. 28 '98

A Division of The McGraw·Hill Companies

Luby's Cafeterias, Inc.

Business Summary - 16-JUN-98

Demographic trends indicate that people are increasingly eating away from home and dining out. Luby's Cafeteria's, Inc. hopes to capitalize on this development by providing freshly prepared foods in an attractive and informal environment that appeals to value-oriented consumers.

Luby's is one of the largest cafeteria chain companies in the U.S. As of August 31, 1997, it was operating 232 cafeterias in 11 states, including 168 in Texas, 14 in Arizona, 12 in Tennessee, eight in Oklahoma, seven in both Arkansas and Florida, five in New Mexico, four in Missouri, three in Kansas, and two in both Louisiana and Mississippi.

In FY 98 and FY 99 (Aug.), the company plans to open only seven new units in each year after opening 25 net new units in FY 97. The company has chosen to focus on improving customer counts and same store sales in an effort to help restore the company's operational efficiency. In FY 96, LUB's experienced lower customer counts for the first time since 1992. The negative trend in customer counts continued in FY 97, which contributed to a 2.0% decline in same-store sales, despite a menu price increase in September 1996. In addition, the company plans to remodel many of its older units to update their appearance.

A typical Luby's cafeteria seats 250 to 300 persons and contains 9,000 to 10,500 square feet of floor space. The cafeterias cater primarily to shoppers and office or store personnel for lunch and to families for dinner. In recent years, the estimated cost of constructing, equipping and furnishing a new Luby's cafeteria in a freestanding building under normal conditions (including land acquisition costs) was $2.5 million to $2.7 million. The cost to finish out, equip and furnish a new cafeteria on a leased site has ranged from $1.2 million to $1.4 million.

Cafeterias combine the food quality and atmosphere of a good restaurant with the convenience and visual food selection of a cafeteria. Food is prepared in small quantities, offering a broad and varied menu which typically consists of 12 to 14 entrees, 12 to 14 vegetable dishes, 22 to 25 salads and 18 to 22 desserts. The cafeterias are open for lunch and dinner seven days a week and offer take-out services which accounted for 11% of sales in FY 97.

The company and a joint-venture partner, Water Street Inc., plan to open five initial Water Street Oyster Bar seafood restaurants over five years. The venture was formed in January 1996, and after five years, LUB will have an option to buy the existing restaurants. In FY 97, the company opened one seafood restaurant and plans to open two more units in FY 98.

Per Share Data ($)

(Year Ended Aug. 31)	1997	1996	1995	1994	1993	1992	1991	1990	1989	1988
Tangible Bk. Val.	9.41	9.41	8.27	8.50	8.78	8.01	7.40	6.68	5.95	5.25
Cash Flow	2.08	2.41	2.24	2.06	1.87	1.72	1.66	1.59	1.44	1.32
Earnings	1.22	1.66	1.55	1.45	1.31	1.19	1.18	1.17	1.08	1.01
Dividends	0.80	0.72	0.66	0.60	0.54	0.50	0.46	0.43	0.37	0.33
Payout Ratio	66%	43%	43%	41%	41%	42%	39%	36%	35%	33%
Prices - High	21³/₈	25¹/₄	23¹/₄	24⁵/₈	25⁷/₈	23¹/₂	20³/₄	21¹/₄	18⁷/₈	17¹/₈
- Low	17⁵/₈	19⁷/₈	18¹/₂	21⁵/₈	19³/₄	14	12	15⁵/₈	15³/₈	13¹/₂
P/E Ratio - High	18	15	15	17	20	20	18	18	18	17
- Low	14	12	12	15	15	12	10	13	14	13

Income Statement Analysis (Million $)

	1997	1996	1995	1994	1993	1992	1991	1990	1989	1988
Revs.	495	450	419	391	368	346	328	311	283	254
Oper. Inc.	77.3	80.7	7.3	74.8	70.1	63.7	60.3	58.3	52.2	47.8
Depr.	20.2	17.7	16.4	15.7	15.4	14.5	13.0	11.4	9.9	8.6
Int. Exp.	4.0	2.1	1.7	0.3	0.3	0.3	0.3	0.3	0.4	0.4
Pretax Inc.	42.7	62.5	58.9	60.4	56.2	50.5	48.8	48.5	44.4	41.2
Eff. Tax Rate	33%	37%	37%	38%	37%	36%	34%	34%	34%	33%
Net Inc.	28.4	39.2	37.0	37.8	35.5	32.6	32.3	32.1	29.5	27.5

Balance Sheet & Other Fin. Data (Million $)

	1997	1996	1995	1994	1993	1992	1991	1990	1989	1988
Cash	6.4	2.7	12.4	10.9	34.3	12.3	14.2	12.3	15.3	20.2
Curr. Assets	16.0	11.4	20.2	18.1	43.8	18.4	21.2	18.4	21.9	25.9
Total Assets	369	335	312	290	302	274	261	235	210	185
Curr. Liab.	45.7	46.5	100	56.4	43.3	38.9	40.4	32.5	28.6	23.0
LT Debt	84.0	41.0	Nil	Nil	Nil	1.4	1.9	2.3	2.8	3.5
Common Eqty.	219	226	193	214	239	217	203	183	163	144
Total Cap.	323	289	213	230	254	233	218	201	180	160
Cap. Exp.	50.8	42.8	29.7	26.3	17.8	27.1	28.8	33.7	30.0	23.6
Cash Flow	48.6	56.9	53.4	53.5	50.9	47.0	45.3	43.5	39.3	36.1
Curr. Ratio	0.3	0.2	0.2	0.3	1.0	0.5	0.5	0.6	0.8	1.1
% LT Debt of Cap.	26.0	14.2	Nil	Nil	Nil	0.6	0.8	1.2	1.6	2.2
% Net Inc.of Revs.	5.7	8.7	8.9	9.7	9.7	9.4	9.9	10.3	10.4	10.8
% Ret. on Assets	8.1	12.1	12.3	13.3	12.3	12.3	13.0	14.4	14.9	15.9
% Ret. on Equity	12.8	18.7	18.3	17.4	15.6	15.6	16.8	18.6	19.2	20.4

Data as orig. reptd.; bef. results of disc. opers. and/or spec. items. Per share data adj. for stk. divs. as of ex-div. date. Bold denotes diluted EPS (FASB 128). E-Estimated. NA-Not Available. NM-Not Meaningful. NR-Not Ranked.

Office—2211 Northeast Loop 410, P.O. Box 33069, San Antonio, TX 78265-3069. **Tel**—(210) 654-9000. **Chrmn**—D. B. Daviss. **CEO & Pres**—B. J. C. Parker. **VP & Treas**—R. E. Riemenschneider. **Secy**—J. R. Hale. **Investor Contact**—Laura M. Bishop. **Dirs**—L. F. Cavazos, D. B. Daviss, R. R. Hemminghaus, J. B. Lahourcade, B. J. C. Parker, W. J. Salmon, G. H. Wenglein, J. Winik. **Transfer Agent & Registrar**—American Stock Transfer & Trust Co.**Incorporated**—in Texas in 1959; reincorporated in Delaware in 1991.**Empl**— 13,000. **S&P Analyst:** Robert J. Izmirlian

Lydall, Inc.

1388M
NYSE Symbol **LDL**

In S&P SmallCap 600

03-OCT-98

Industry: Manufacturing (Specialized)

Summary: Lydall's fiber-based materials are used in demanding specialty applications, including filtration media, thermal barriers, electrical insulation, and materials handling products.

Quantitative Evaluations		
Outlook (1 Lowest—5 Highest) • **5+**	Recent Price • 10⅞	Yield • Nil
Fair Value • **16½**	52 Wk Range • 24⅛-9⅞	12-Mo. P/E • 10.2

Risk • **Average**

Earn./Div. Rank • **B+**

Technical Eval. • **Bearish** since 11/97

Rel. Strength Rank (1 Lowest—99 Highest) • **35**

Insider Activity • **Neutral**

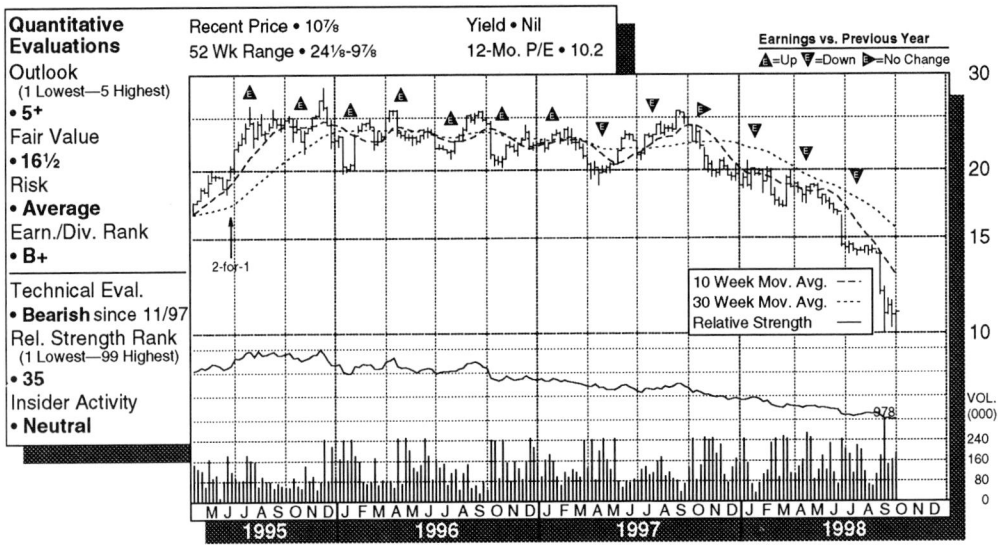

Earnings vs. Previous Year
▲=Up ▼=Down ▶=No Change

10 Week Mov. Avg. − − −
30 Week Mov. Avg. · · · · ·
Relative Strength ———

2-for-1

Business Profile - 20-MAR-98

Although results for this manufacturer of fiber materials and composites have been negatively impacted by a slowdown in demand from the semiconductor and other industries, Lydall believes that many of the factors contributing to its sales and earnings woes in 1997 are temporary. LDL is expanding its efforts in the automotive sector of the barrier materials business, its primary focus for future growth, and has intensified new product development in all business segments. It believes that its air filtration business will pick up once an expected strengthening of the semiconductor market in 1998 takes hold. In April 1997, Lydall's directors authorized management to repurchase up to one million common shares.

Operational Review - 20-MAR-98

Net sales in 1997 (preliminary) slipped 3.3% from those of 1996, primarily reflecting unfavorable market conditions. Cost of sales declined less rapidly, and selling, product development and administrative expenses increased; operating income fell 17%. With higher investment income and reduced interest expense, and after taxes at 36.4%, versus 37.9%, net income was down 11%, to $21,911,000 ($1.27 a share, diluted and on 3.7% fewer shares), from $ 24,736,000 ($1.38).

Stock Performance - 02-OCT-98

In the past 30 trading days, LDL's shares have declined 23%, compared to a 7% fall in the S&P 500. Average trading volume for the past five days was 36,980 shares, compared with the 40-day moving average of 47,985 shares.

Key Stock Statistics

Dividend Rate/Share	Nil	Shareholders	1,900
Shs. outstg. (M)	15.7	Market cap. (B)	$0.172
Avg. daily vol. (M)	0.076	Inst. holdings	69%
Tang. Bk. Value/Share	5.84		
Beta	0.42		

Value of $10,000 invested 5 years ago: $ 11,028

Fiscal Year Ending Dec. 31

	1998	1997	1996	1995	1994	1993
Revenues (Million $)						
1Q	56.54	61.97	65.79	62.74	48.12	38.20
2Q	59.24	64.02	67.67	65.55	53.56	40.42
3Q	—	59.38	59.71	61.49	54.45	38.84
4Q	—	58.92	59.48	62.35	56.95	39.93
Yr.	—	244.3	252.7	252.1	213.1	157.4
Earnings Per Share ($)						
1Q	**0.22**	0.32	0.33	0.29	0.20	0.14
2Q	**0.24**	0.33	0.38	0.32	0.21	0.14
3Q	—	0.32	0.32	0.30	0.21	0.13
4Q	—	**0.30**	0.34	0.32	0.24	0.15
Yr.	—	**1.27**	1.37	1.23	0.86	0.57

Next earnings report expected: late October

Dividend Data

Cash dividends were omitted in 1982, following substantial charges related to plant closings and reorganizations.

A Division of The **McGraw·Hill** Companies

Business Summary - 20-MAR-98

Although this diversified maker of engineered fiber materials and composites enjoyed record earnings for the twelfth consecutive year in 1996, as well as an increase in sales, albeit a modest one, for the sixth consecutive year, Lydall's momentum was somewhat restrained by less-than-favorable market conditions during the year.

In particular, difficult market conditions in 1996 helped slow the sales tempo of Lydall's air and liquid filtration business (24% of total sales in 1996), which dropped off from the strong pace experienced in 1995 and 1994. This was due mainly to the downturn in the semiconductor market, which uses LDL's filters for clean-room applications. Additionally, sales for electrical insulation products (6% of sales) stumbled, mainly on the further decline in battery separator product demand in Europe, as did receipts for materials-handling products (13% of sales), which were hampered by deflationary pressures. However, Lydall did experience solid growth in its thermal barrier products business (38% of sales), primarily for automotive heat-shield applications, which helped offset weaknesses in other products.

While LDL's top line grew fractionally in 1996, its bottom line advanced at a more substantial 10%, boosted by a record gross margin of 32.5% of sales. Management believes its comprehensive quality program has been the underlying factor driving strong gross margin results. This program is focused on constant enhancement of products and processes, elimination of waste, and better customer service.

Drawing from its extensive fiber and fiber-composite knowledge-base, as well as from a variety of proprietary manufacturing processes, Lydall has been able to design and produce technologically advanced, unique materials for high-performance applications. Its major offerings comprise air filtration products, including high-efficiency air filtration media, sold under the name Lydair, for use in clean-room applications; patented biomedical liquid filtration systems; automotive thermal barrier and heat shielding components; and cryogenic insulation for use in trucks which transport liquid gases. Other important lines include a broad range of materials-handling products, which are used in place of wooden pallets for shipping, electrical insulation materials, speciality shoeboard composites, and paperboard.

Over the past ten years, Lydall has depended on acquisitions to help drive long-term growth. During this period, sales have increased at a compound annual rate of 13%, and acquisitions accounted for about 40% of this growth. LDL will continue to actively seek companies and product lines that complement existing businesses and expand its strategic focus, and intends to further its efforts to streamline operations and improve efficiencies.

Per Share Data ($)

(Year Ended Dec. 31)	1997	1996	1995	1994	1993	1992	1991	1990	1989	1988
Tangible Bk. Val.	5.84	5.71	5.27	3.90	3.63	3.08	2.50	2.34	1.83	1.34
Cash Flow	1.82	1.87	1.70	1.28	0.91	0.82	0.68	0.65	0.61	0.49
Earnings	1.27	1.37	1.23	0.86	0.57	0.52	0.47	0.47	0.45	0.30
Dividends	Nil	Nil	Nil	Nil	Nil	Nil	Nil	Nil	Nil	Nil
Payout Ratio	Nil	Nil	Nil	Nil	Nil	Nil	Nil	Nil	Nil	Nil
Prices - High	25³/₄	25⁷/₈	28¹/₂	18⁵/₈	11³/₄	11¹/₈	8¹/₄	5³/₈	6¹/₈	3³/₈
- Low	18¹/₂	19³/₄	14³/₄	10¹/₈	9³/₈	8	4¹/₈	3⁵/₈	2¹/₂	2³/₁₆
P/E Ratio - High	20	19	23	22	21	21	17	11	14	11
- Low	15	14	12	12	16	15	9	8	6	7

Income Statement Analysis (Million $)

	1997	1996	1995	1994	1993	1992	1991	1990	1989	1988
Revs.	244	253	252	213	157	151	135	123	128	115
Oper. Inc.	42.3	48.6	45.7	36.2	23.9	22.6	19.2	18.2	18.1	14.1
Depr.	9.6	9.2	8.6	7.5	5.9	5.3	3.8	3.2	2.8	3.0
Int. Exp.	0.4	0.5	0.8	1.3	1.5	2.1	2.2	2.0	1.9	2.3
Pretax Inc.	34.5	39.9	36.9	26.5	16.9	14.6	13.3	13.2	12.6	8.0
Eff. Tax Rate	36%	38%	39%	42%	41%	38%	36%	37%	37%	36%
Net Inc.	21.9	24.7	22.4	15.5	10.0	9.0	8.5	8.3	7.9	5.1

Balance Sheet & Other Fin. Data (Million $)

	1997	1996	1995	1994	1993	1992	1991	1990	1989	1988
Cash	8.9	38.2	28.7	14.6	16.8	9.1	1.5	10.2	5.9	3.0
Curr. Assets	67.4	96.4	82.5	64.1	53.2	46.7	40.4	40.9	37.0	29.9
Total Assets	160	182	158	137	108	99	93.2	83.1	74.7	64.7
Curr. Liab.	28.2	43.0	29.7	33.3	21.4	22.1	20.6	14.8	15.9	13.7
LT Debt	2.1	5.0	7.8	10.6	11.2	16.2	22.7	20.4	20.6	21.0
Common Eqty.	117	118	102	76.2	60.1	50.1	39.1	38.5	30.1	21.2
Total Cap.	128	136	124	99	81.6	72.3	67.8	65.1	56.6	48.5
Cap. Exp.	17.1	10.9	12.0	8.0	6.3	6.2	4.1	8.2	6.4	3.4
Cash Flow	31.5	33.9	31.1	23.0	15.9	14.3	13.0	12.3	11.2	8.0
Curr. Ratio	2.4	2.2	2.8	1.9	2.5	2.1	2.0	2.8	2.3	2.2
% LT Debt of Cap.	1.9	3.7	6.3	10.8	13.7	22.4	33.6	31.3	36.4	43.3
% Net Inc.of Revs.	9.0	9.8	8.9	7.3	6.4	6.0	6.3	6.8	6.2	4.5
% Ret. on Assets	12.8	14.5	15.2	12.6	9.6	9.2	9.9	10.6	11.2	6.3
% Ret. on Equity	18.4	22.5	25.2	22.7	18.0	19.9	22.5	24.3	30.1	15.5

Data as orig. reptd.; bef. results of disc. opers. and/or spec. items. Per share data adj. for stk. divs. as of ex-div. date. Bold denotes diluted EPS (FASB 128). E-Estimated. NA-Not Available. NM-Not Meaningful. NR-Not Ranked.

Office—One Colonial Rd. (P.O. Box 151), Manchester, CT 06045-0151.**Tel**—(860) 646-1233. **Fax**—(860) 646-4917. **Website**—http://www.lydall.com **Chrmn, Pres & CEO**—L. R. Jaskol. **VP-Fin & Treas**—J. E. Hanley.**Secy**—Mary Adamowicz Tremblay.**VP & Investor Contact**—Carole F. Butenas.**Dirs**—L. A. Asseo, P. S. Buddenhagen, J. P. Carolan, S. P. Cooley, W. L. Duffy, L. R. Jaskol, W. P. Lyons, J. Schiavone, C. R. Skomonoski, E. F. Whitely, R. M. Widmann, A. E. Wolf.**Transfer Agent**—American Stock Transfer & Trust Co., NYC.**Incorporated**—in Connecticut in 1913; reincorporated in Delaware in 1987. **Empl**— 1,272. **S&P Analyst:** S.A.H.

M.D.C. Holdings   1397

NYSE Symbol **MDC**

In S&P SmallCap 600

10-OCT-98   Industry:
Homebuilding

Summary: MDC builds and sells residential housing. In addition, the company supports its building activities by originating, buying, and servicing mortgages for its customers and others.

Quantitative Evaluations	
Recent Price • 13⅝	Yield • 1.2%
52 Wk Range • 24-9⅞	12-Mo. P/E • 8.1

Outlook
(1 Lowest—5 Highest)
• **3⁻**

Fair Value
• **21¼**

Risk
• **Average**

Earn./Div. Rank
• **B**

Technical Eval.
• **Bullish** since 10/96

Rel. Strength Rank
(1 Lowest—99 Highest)
• **29**

Insider Activity
• **Neutral**

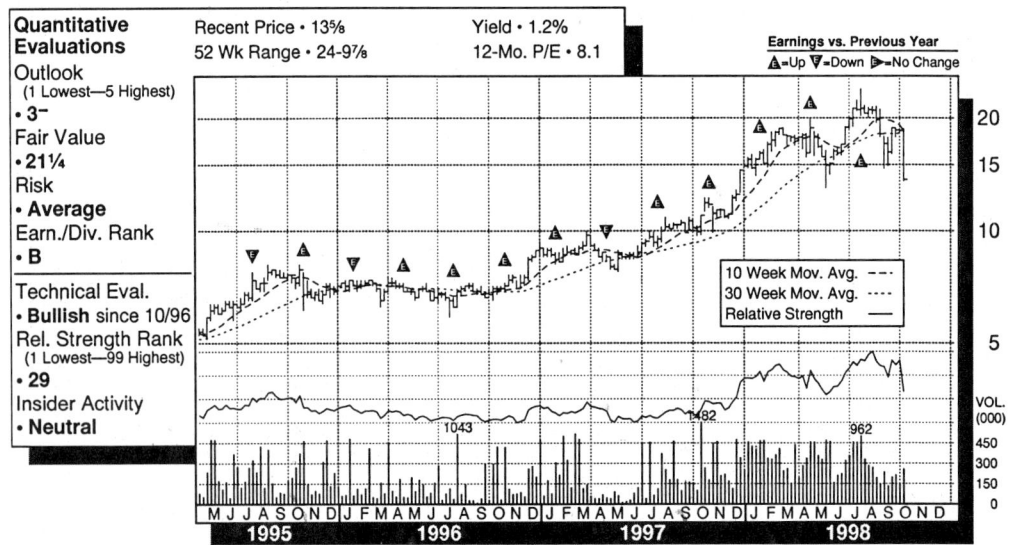

Earnings vs. Previous Year
▲=Up ▼=Down ▶=No Change

10 Week Mov. Avg. ---
30 Week Mov. Avg. ·····
Relative Strength —

Business Profile - 23-JUN-98

M.D.C. Holdings' strategy is to build homes generally for the first-time and move-up buyer, the largest segments of prospective home buyers. As part of its land inventory policy, MDC generally limits new projects to fewer than 150 lots to avoid overexposure to any single sub-market. In this regard, the company's priority is to acquire finished lots using rolling options and finished lots in phases for cash. If potential returns justify the risk, land is acquired for development. MDC recently reduced the interest expense on a major portion of its long term debt. In January 1998, it sold $175 million of 8.375% senior notes due 2008, with most of the proceeds used to replace higher cost debt. Larry A. Mizel, chairman and president of MDC, owns about 25% of the shares.

Operational Review - 23-JUN-98

In the first three months of 1998, total revenues were up 26%, year to year, principally reflecting more home closings, higher selling prices, and wider margins on home sales. Expenses rose 23%, and pretax income was up 24%. After taxes at 38.5%, versus 37.8%, net income advanced 121%, to $7,928,000 ($0.37 a share), from $3,586,000 ($0.18). Results were before special charges for early extinguishment of debt of $0.68 a share and $0.10. Backlog at March 31, 1998, was 3,038 units, up sharply from 1,942 a year earlier.

Stock Performance - 09-OCT-98

In the past 30 trading days, MDC's shares have declined 24%, compared to a 4% fall in the S&P 500. Average trading volume for the past five days was 50,780 shares, compared with the 40-day moving average of 38,500 shares.

Key Stock Statistics

Dividend Rate/Share	0.16	Shareholders	1,600
Shs. outstg. (M)	18.2	Market cap. (B)	$0.250
Avg. daily vol. (M)	0.040	Inst. holdings	68%
Tang. Bk. Value/Share	13.16		
Beta	0.92		

Value of $10,000 invested 5 years ago: $ 35,127

Fiscal Year Ending Dec. 31

	1998	1997	1996	1995	1994	1993
Revenues (Million $)						
1Q	243.5	193.8	199.3	191.1	168.7	117.3
2Q	303.9	237.3	237.8	214.1	197.8	161.2
3Q	—	266.6	233.3	233.5	214.3	192.7
4Q	—	271.8	252.3	227.2	244.2	185.3
Yr.	—	969.6	922.6	865.9	824.9	652.1
Earnings Per Share ($)						
1Q	0.37	0.18	0.22	0.20	0.19	0.04
2Q	0.58	0.26	0.23	0.21	0.28	0.14
3Q	—	0.35	0.30	0.28	0.26	0.14
4Q	—	0.39	0.34	0.17	0.21	0.13
Yr.	—	1.18	0.98	0.86	0.94	0.45

Next earnings report expected: late October

Dividend Data (Dividends have been paid since 1994.)

Amount ($)	Date Decl.	Ex-Div. Date	Stock of Record	Payment Date
0.030	Nov. 05	Nov. 14	Nov. 18	Nov. 28 '97
0.030	Jan. 28	Jan. 30	Feb. 02	Feb. 20 '98
0.040	Apr. 21	Apr. 29	May. 01	May. 20 '98
0.040	Jul. 27	Jul. 29	Jul. 31	Aug. 14 '98

A Division of The McGraw-Hill Companies

STANDARD
&POOR'S
STOCK REPORTS

M.D.C. Holdings, Inc.

1397
10-OCT-98

Business Summary - 23-JUN-98

M.D.C. Holdings, Inc. is engaged in the construction and sale of residential housing. The company also provides mortgage loans primarily to its home buyers.
Business segment contributions in 1997:

	Revs.	Profits
Home building	99%	82%
Financial services	1%	18%

Homebuilding operations involve the design, construction and sale of single-family residential homes. M.D.C. Holdings builds its homes principally on finished lots acquired using rolling options, phased acquisitions or bulk purchases. To a lesser extent, the company acquires land for development for use in its homebuilding activities.

M.D.C. Holdings is one of the largest homebuilders in the U.S., building and selling homes under the name, Richmond American Homes. MDC is a major regional homebuilder, with a significant presence in a number of selected growth markets.

The company is the largest homebuilder in metropolitan Denver; the largest builder of detached homes in Riverside County, CA; among the top five builders in Northern Virginia, Tucson, and Colorado Springs; among the top ten builders in suburban Maryland and Phoenix; and has a growing presence in Orange, Los Angeles, Ventura, San Bernardino, and San Diego Counties, CA and Las Vegas. MDC also builds homes in the San Francisco Bay Area. The company believes a significant presence in its markets enables it to compete effectively for home sales, land acquisition opportunities, and subcontractor labor.

MDC builds its homes generally for the first-time and move-up buyer. Approximately 41% of its homes that closed in 1997 were in subdivisions targeted to the first-time buyer.

Financial services operations are conducted through the HomeAmerican Mortgage subsidiary, which is a full-service mortgage lender. HomeAmerican originates mortgage loans primarily for MDC's home buyers and, to a lesser extent, for others on a spot basis through offices located in each of MDC's markets. HomeAmerican is the principal originator of mortgage loans for MDC's home buyers.

HomeAmerican is authorized to originate Federal Housing Administration-insured (FHA), Veterans Administration-guaranteed (VA), Federal National Mortgage Association (FNMA), Federal Home Loan Mortgage Corp. (FHLMC) and conventional mortgage loans. Substantially all of the mortgage loans originated or purchased by HomeAmerican are sold to private investors within 40 days of origination or purchase.

Per Share Data ($)

(Year Ended Dec. 31)	1997	1996	1995	1994	1993	1992	1991	1990	1989	1988
Tangible Bk. Val.	12.91	11.83	10.54	10.19	9.64	8.08	8.00	8.25	7.89	11.21
Cash Flow	1.79	1.72	1.37	1.44	0.81	0.59	-0.23	-0.06	-4.68	-4.52
Earnings	1.18	1.09	0.86	0.94	0.45	0.22	-0.62	-0.63	-5.66	-5.01
Dividends	0.12	0.12	0.11	0.06	Nil	Nil	Nil	Nil	Nil	0.25
Payout Ratio	10%	11%	13%	6%	Nil	Nil	Nil	Nil	Nil	NM
Prices - High	15¼	9⅜	8⅛	7⅞	7	4½	2¼	1½	3¾	6⅞
- Low	7¾	5⅞	4⅞	4½	3¾	1¾	¼	⅛	1	2⅝
P/E Ratio - High	13	9	9	8	16	20	NM	NM	NM	NM
- Low	7	5	6	5	8	8	NM	NM	NM	NM

Income Statement Analysis (Million $)

	1997	1996	1995	1994	1993	1992	1991	1990	1989	1988
Revs.	970	923	866	825	652	517	422	507	719	816
Oper. Inc.	55.1	48.6	44.8	58.4	57.4	84.5	73.2	90.6	39.5	25.7
Depr.	15.1	12.1	10.3	10.1	8.0	8.2	8.1	10.9	15.6	8.6
Int. Exp.	0.8	44.5	48.1	44.0	45.0	77.0	103	123	170	205
Pretax Inc.	39.3	32.8	26.7	31.0	15.0	7.0	-14.0	-13.0	-115	-144
Eff. Tax Rate	38%	37%	35%	38%	33%	27%	NM	NM	NM	NM
Net Inc.	24.2	20.8	17.3	19.3	10.1	4.8	-12.9	-12.0	-90.1	-86.7

Balance Sheet & Other Fin. Data (Million $)

	1997	1996	1995	1994	1993	1992	1991	1990	1989	1988
Cash	11.7	11.3	20.8	49.0	82.0	106	91.0	83.0	91.0	60.0
Curr. Assets	NA	NA	NA	NA	NA	NA	NA	NA	NA	NA
Total Assets	622	617	635	725	777	859	1,316	1,477	1,664	1,993
Curr. Liab.	NA	NA	NA	NA	NA	NA	NA	NA	NA	NA
LT Debt	202	232	240	322	412	510	976	1,131	1,297	1,547
Common Eqty.	230	214	205	192	176	164	160	157	150	180
Total Cap.	431	446	445	515	587	676	1,163	1,315	1,464	1,737
Cap. Exp.	Nil	Nil	Nil	Nil	Nil	Nil	Nil	Nil	Nil	Nil
Cash Flow	39.3	32.9	27.5	29.4	18.1	12.9	-4.8	-1.1	-74.5	-78.1
Curr. Ratio	NA	NA	NA	NA	NA	NA	NA	NA	NA	NA
% LT Debt of Cap.	46.9	52.1	54.0	62.6	70.1	75.4	83.9	86.0	88.6	89.0
% Net Inc.of Revs.	2.5	2.3	2.0	2.3	1.5	0.9	NM	NM	NM	NM
% Ret. on Assets	3.9	3.3	2.7	2.5	1.3	0.4	NM	NM	NM	NM
% Ret. on Equity	10.9	9.9	8.7	10.3	6.2	2.9	NM	NM	NM	NM

Data as orig. reptd.; bef. results of disc. opers. and/or spec. items. Per share data adj. for stk. divs. as of ex-div. date. Bold denotes diluted EPS (FASB 128). E-Estimated. NA-Not Available. NM-Not Meaningful. NR-Not Ranked.

Office—3600 South Yosemite St., Suite 900, Denver, CO 80237. Tel—(303) 773-1100. Website—http://www.mdcholdings.com Chrmn & Pres—L. A. Mizel. EVP-COO—D. D. Mandarich. SVP-CFO & Investor Contact—P. G. Reece III. Secy—D. S. Japha. Dirs—S. J. Borick, H. T. Buchwald, G. Goldstein, W. B. Kemper, D. D. Mandarich, L. A. Mizel. Transfer Agent—Continental Stock Transfer & Trust Co., NYC. Incorporated—in Colorado in 1972; reincorporated in Delaware in 1985. Empl— 1,200. S&P Analyst: T. W. Smith, CFA

03-OCT-98

Industry:
Savings & Loan Companies

Summary: MAFB is the parent company of Mid America Bank, which operates a network of retail banking offices primarily in the western suburbs of Chicago.

Quantitative Evaluations

Recent Price • 23¼
52 Wk Range • 29¼-18¾

Yield • 1.2%
12-Mo. P/E • 14.7

Outlook
(1 Lowest—5 Highest)
• **NA**

Fair Value
• **NA**

Risk
• **Low**

Earn./Div. Rank
• **NR**

Technical Eval.
• **Bearish** since 8/98

Rel. Strength Rank
(1 Lowest—99 Highest)
• **87**

Insider Activity
• **Neutral**

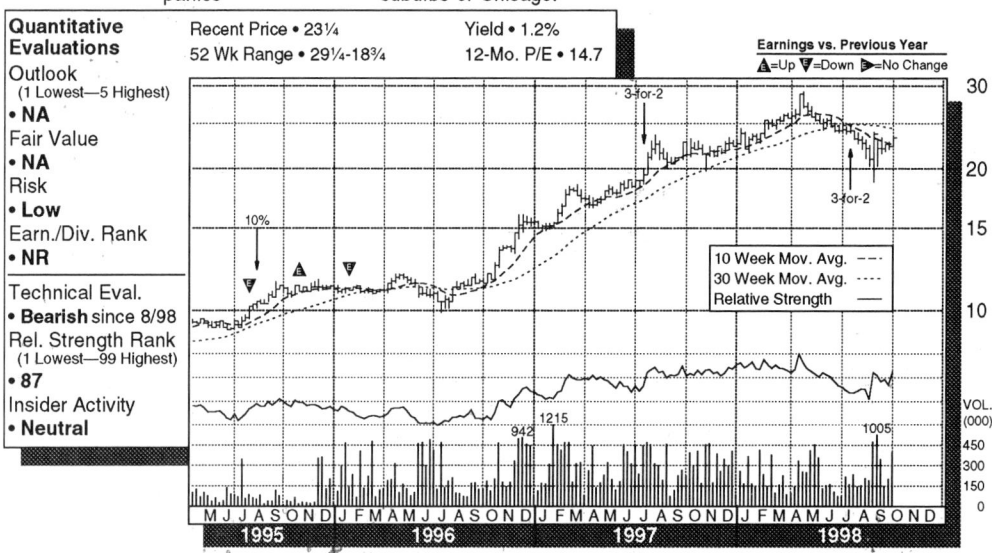

Earnings vs. Previous Year
▲=Up ▼=Down ▶=No Change

10 Week Mov. Avg. ---
30 Week Mov. Avg. ····
Relative Strength —

Business Profile - 10-SEP-98

MAFB offers a variety of financial services through 23 retail banking offices mainly in the western suburbs of Chicago. On August 17, 1998, MAFB agreed to acquire Westco Bancorp of Westchester, IL for stock. Westco's subsidiary First Federal Savings and Loan Association of Westchester has $320 million in assets and operates one office and a drive-up facility. If completed as expected in late 1998 or early 1999, the deal would make MAFB the market share leader in the Westchester-LaGrange Park area. Subsequent to the merger announcement, MAFB said it would buy back up to 1.25 million, or 5.5%, of its outstanding common shares and Westco would buy back about 6% of Westco shares, with the result that the merger would be accounted for as a purchase, rather than as a pooling of interests.

Operational Review - 10-SEP-98

In the first half of 1998, net interest income rose 2.9%, year to year, reflecting 8.5% more interest-earning assets and a narrower net interest margin (2.88% versus 3.04%). The provision for loan losses was reduced to $400,000, from $600,000. Noninterest income grew 17%, led by higher gains on sales of loans receivable and investment instruments, and noninterest expense was up 11%, reflecting higher compensation and benefits. After taxes at 38.5%, versus 35.7%, net income fell 2.8%, to $18,947,000 ($0.81 a share, based on fewer shares, adjusted for the 3-to-2 split), from $19,496,000 ($0.81).

Stock Performance - 02-OCT-98

In the past 30 trading days, MAFB's shares have increased 11%, compared to a 7% fall in the S&P 500. Average trading volume for the past five days was 79,460 shares, compared with the 40-day moving average of 81,815 shares.

Key Stock Statistics

Dividend Rate/Share	0.28	Shareholders	1,800
Shs. outstg. (M)	22.6	Market cap. (B)	$0.527
Avg. daily vol. (M)	0.062	Inst. holdings	47%
Tang. Bk. Value/Share	11.34		
Beta	0.81		

Value of $10,000 invested 5 years ago: $ 41,772

Fiscal Year Ending Dec. 31

	1998	1997	1996	1995	1994	1993
Revenues (Million $)						
1Q	66.74	62.98	—	37.36	29.92	31.54
2Q	68.67	64.25	—	38.28	33.21	31.50
3Q	—	66.56	—	38.67	32.36	31.71
4Q	—	67.85	—	45.88	36.13	28.68
Yr.	—	261.6	124.8	209.3	131.6	123.4
Earnings Per Share ($)						
1Q	**0.39**	0.38	—	0.32	0.21	0.25
2Q	**0.42**	0.43	—	0.31	0.34	0.27
3Q	—	0.39	—	0.33	0.25	0.26
4Q	—	**0.39**	—	0.31	0.33	0.19
Yr.	—	**1.59**	0.93	1.26	1.13	0.99

Next earnings report expected: late October

Dividend Data (Dividends have been paid since 1994.)

Amount ($)	Date Decl.	Ex-Div. Date	Stock of Record	Payment Date
0.070	Feb. 25	Mar. 12	Mar. 16	Apr. 03 '98
0.105	Apr. 29	Jun. 16	Jun. 18	Jul. 03 '98
3-for-2	Apr. 29	Jul. 13	Jun. 18	Jul. 10 '98
0.070	Aug. 26	Sep. 11	Sep. 15	Oct. 29 '98

A Division of The McGraw-Hill Companies

Business Summary - 10-SEP-98

MAF Bancorp, Inc. is the parent company of Mid America Bank, fsb, a federally chartered savings bank which operates a network of retail banking offices primarily in the western suburbs of Chicago. MAFB is a leading provider of residential mortgage loans in its market. With assets of $3.5 billion and 22 branch offices (at year-end 1997), MAFB offers a wide range of personal banking services to the communities it serves. Gross loans outstanding at December 31, 1997, were $2.73 billion, up from $2.43 billion at year-end 1996, and were divided as follows:

	1997	1996
Real estate loans:		
One-to four-family	88.5%	88.2%
Multi-family	3.9%	3.8%
Commercial	1.3%	1.9%
Construction	0.6%	0.7%
Land	0.9%	1.1%
Other loans:		
Consumer	4.7%	4.3%
Commercial business	0.1%	0.1%

The allowance for loan losses totaled $15,475,000

(0.57% of loans receivable) at December 31, 1997, down from $17,914,000 (0.73%) a year earlier. Net chargeoffs were $3,589,000 (0.14%) in 1997. Nonperforming assets were $11,144,000 (0.32% of total assets) at December 31, 1997, versus $14,721,000 (0.46%) a year earlier.

Interest on loans receivable provided 76% of total income in 1997, interest on mortgage-backed securities 8%, other interest 7%, income from real estate operations 3%, deposit account servicing fees 3%, and other noninterest income 3%.

Total deposits at December 31, 1997, were $1.4 billion, and were apportioned: certificate accounts 55.5%, passbook accounts 27.8%, money-market accounts 6.0%, NOW accounts 7.0%, and other accounts 3.7%.

The average yield on total interest-earning assets was 7.57% in 1997, while the average rate paid on total interest-bearing liabilities was 4.95%, for a net interest rate spread of 2.62%. The net interest margin was 2.98%.

MAFB also operates a real estate development unit, a full-service insurance agency and an independent brokerage operation.

MAFB acquired N.S. Bancorp Inc. for about $270 million in cash and stock in May 1996.

Per Share Data ($)

(Year Ended Dec. 31)	1997	1996	1995	1994	1993	1992	1991	1990	1989	1988
Tangible Bk. Val.	10.61	9.50	9.25	8.53	7.45	6.44	5.35	4.57	4.16	NA
Earnings	1.59	0.36	1.26	1.13	0.99	0.98	0.67	0.37	0.37	NA
Dividends	0.18	0.15	0.14	0.14	Nil	Nil	Nil	Nil	Nil	Nil
Payout Ratio	11%	41%	11%	13%	Nil	Nil	Nil	Nil	Nil	Nil
Prices - High	24½	16	16	11⅝	9¾	9⅞	6¼	3	2⁷/₁₆	NA
- Low	14¾	9⅞	9⅞	7⅝	7¼	5¾	2⅝	1¼	1³/₁₆	NA
P/E Ratio - High	15	NM	13	10	10	9	9	8	7	NA
- Low	9	NM	8	7	7	6	4	3	3	NA

Income Statement Analysis (Million $)

	1997	1996	1995	1994	1993	1992	1991	1990	1989	1988
Net Int. Inc.	93.7	44.2	49.9	41.6	34.1	38.5	35.3	31.6	27.2	27.3
Loan Loss Prov.	1.1	0.7	0.7	0.5	1.2	2.7	4.1	1.1	0.6	0.6
Non Int. Inc.	22.3	12.0	17.1	16.7	19.6	14.3	15.8	6.0	10.1	14.1
Non Int. Exp.	54.6	26.9	37.8	33.4	31.3	28.2	29.7	28.1	29.1	28.6
Pretax Inc.	60.7	14.4	28.5	24.4	21.2	21.9	17.3	8.4	7.6	12.2
Eff. Tax Rate	37%	39%	38%	38%	37%	38%	49%	41%	37%	37%
Net Inc.	37.9	8.8	17.7	15.0	13.5	13.5	8.9	4.9	4.7	7.7
% Net Int. Marg.	2.62	2.62	2.62	2.62	2.29	2.65	2.55	2.23	1.84	1.86

Balance Sheet & Other Fin. Data (Million $)

	1997	1996	1995	1994	1993	1992	1991	1990	1989	1988
Total Assets	3,458	3,230	3,117	1,783	1,586	1,544	1,513	1,473	1,597	1,536
Loans	2,701	2,430	2,712	1,575	1,359	1,326	1,267	1,202	1,220	1,265
Deposits	2,337	2,262	2,254	1,313	1,293	1,290	1,269	1,237	1,208	1,164
Capitalization:										
Debt	797	660	564	327	170	138	151	153	310	318
Equity	263	251	242	105	95.2	85.0	70.2	59.8	54.4	25.0
Total	1,060	910	807	433	265	223	221	212	365	343
% Ret. on Assets	1.1	0.3	0.7	0.9	0.8	0.9	0.7	0.3	0.3	0.6
% Ret. on Equity	14.8	3.6	10.2	15.0	14.8	17.8	15.0	8.7	13.1	43.5
% Loan Loss Resv.	0.6	0.7	0.6	0.6	0.6	0.6	0.5	0.2	0.1	NM
% Risk Based Capital	15.1	14.3	8.0	12.1	13.2	12.8	11.1	7.8	7.1	NA
Price Times Book Value:										
Hi	2.3	1.7	1.3	1.2	1.3	1.4	1.2	0.6	0.6	NA
Low	1.4	1.0	1.1	0.9	1.1	0.9	0.5	0.3	0.3	NA

Data as orig. reptd.; bef. results of disc opers. and/or spec. items. Per share data adj. for stk. divs. as of ex-div. date. Rev and Inc. data for 1996 is for 6 mos. ended Dec. 31, 1996. Prior to 1996, fisc. yrs. ended Jun. 30. Bold denotes diluted EPS (FASB) 128. E-Estimated. NA-Not Available. NM-Not Meaningful. NR-Not Ranked.

Office—55th St. & Holmes Ave., Clarendon Hills, IL 60514. **Tel**—(630) 325-7300. **Chrmn & CEO**—A. H. Koranda. **Pres**—K. Koranda. **EVP-CFO**—J. A. Weberling. **VP-Secy**—C. Pihera. **SVP-Investor Contact**—Michael J. Janssen. **Dirs**—R. Bowles, T. Ekl, J. F. Hanauer, A. H. Koranda, K. Koranda, H. Smogolski, F. W. Trescott, L. B. Vasto, J. A. Weberling, A. J. Zych. **Transfer Agent & Registrar**—Harris Trust & Savings Bank, Chicago. **Incorporated**—in Delaware in 1989. **Empl**— 855. **S&P Analyst**: T. W. Smith, CFA

M.S. Carriers

4475T

NASDAQ Symbol **MSCA**

In S&P SmallCap 600

03-OCT-98

Industry:
Truckers

Summary: This irregular-route truckload carrier transports a wide range of general commodities, primarily in the eastern two-thirds of the U.S. and in parts of Canada and Mexico.

Quantitative Evaluations

Outlook
(1 Lowest—5 Highest)
• **4**–

Fair Value
• **30¼**

Risk
• **Average**

Earn./Div. Rank
• **B+**

Technical Eval.
• **NA**

Rel. Strength Rank
(1 Lowest—99 Highest)
• **17**

Insider Activity
• **NA**

Recent Price • 18¼
52 Wk Range • 35⅜-17⅛

Yield • Nil
12-Mo. P/E • 10.1

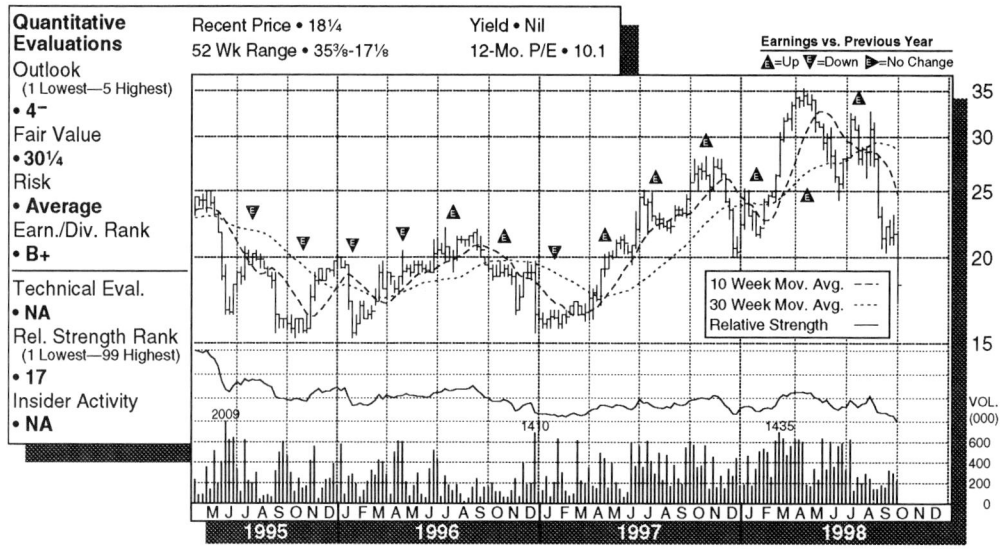

Earnings vs. Previous Year
▲=Up ▼=Down ▶=No Change

10 Week Mov. Avg. – – –
30 Week Mov. Avg. ·····
Relative Strength —

Business Profile - 24-AUG-98

In March 1998, the company acquired the U.S. operations of Challenger Motor Freight, adding 195 tractors and 481 trailors to MSCA's fleet. As a result of the Challenger acquisition, combined with the September 1997 purchase of Hi-Way Express and solid internal growth, MSCA added 786 units in the 12 months ended June 30, 1998. Results in the first half of 1998 also benefited from a strong freight environment, favorable fuel prices, marketing strategies and fleet optimization.

Operational Review - 24-AUG-98

Operating revenues in the six months ended June 30, 1998, climbed 29%, year to year, driven by an increase in domestic linehaul business, partly offset by a decline in regional revenues. Margins remained steady, as a less rapid rise in compensation expenses was offset by an increase in rent expenditures; operating income grew 29%. Results benefited from increased gains on asset sales, and a significant jump in other income. After taxes at 36.5%, versus 35.9%, net income advanced 44%, to $11,336,629 ($0.89 a share, on 2.9% more shares), from $12,444,208 ($0.63).

Stock Performance - 02-OCT-98

In the past 30 trading days, MSCA's shares have declined 35%, compared to a 7% fall in the S&P 500. Average trading volume for the past five days was 43,320 shares, compared with the 40-day moving average of 43,162 shares.

Key Stock Statistics

Dividend Rate/Share	Nil	Shareholders	3,000
Shs. outstg. (M)	12.3	Market cap. (B)	$0.224
Avg. daily vol. (M)	0.050	Inst. holdings	58%
Tang. Bk. Value/Share	15.48		
Beta	1.15		

Value of $10,000 invested 5 years ago: $ 8,390

Fiscal Year Ending Dec. 31

	1998	1997	1996	1995	1994	1993
Revenues (Million $)						
1Q	117.2	92.70	79.69	81.70	60.42	49.90
2Q	133.6	101.5	84.27	84.54	69.56	55.20
3Q	—	107.5	85.82	84.33	80.30	59.30
4Q	—	114.3	90.46	82.50	82.59	60.43
Yr.	—	415.9	340.2	333.1	292.9	224.7
Earnings Per Share ($)						
1Q	0.35	0.26	0.14	0.29	0.18	0.24
2Q	0.54	0.40	0.34	0.31	0.34	0.31
3Q	—	0.45	0.35	0.20	0.41	0.30
4Q	—	0.44	0.19	0.22	0.38	0.28
Yr.	—	1.54	1.02	1.01	1.31	1.13

Next earnings report expected: mid October

Dividend Data

No cash dividends have been paid, and the company has expressed its intention to retain earnings to finance expansion of its business. Two-for-one stock splits were effected in 1992 and 1987.

A Division of The McGraw·Hill Companies

STANDARD
&POOR'S
STOCK REPORTS

M.S. Carriers, Inc.

4475T

03-OCT-98

Business Summary - 24-AUG-98

This Memphis-based motor carrier has been boosting revenues and profits by expanding both the capacity and utilization of its fleet of trucks. M.S. Carriers, Inc. (MSCA) ended 1997 with 3,141 tractors, up 27% from 2,465 at the end of 1996. Utilization of equipment improved in 1997; revenue per tractor per week increased to $2,652 from $2,592 in 1996.

The company's emphasis on owner-operators, independent contractors who supply their own tractors and drivers, has allowed it to grow its fleet and generate additional revenue without swelling its capital budget. Owner-operators accounted for 771 of the company's tractors at December 31, 1997, up from 419 a year earlier.

MSCA hauls truckload shipments of general commodities throughout the U.S. and the Canadian provinces of Ontario and Quebec (the term "truckload" refers to shipments exceeding 10,000 lbs.). The company's main traffic flows are between the middle southern and the southwestern, midwestern, central, southeastern and northeastern portions of the U.S. Freight shipments originating or terminating in Mexico accounted for 9.3% of operating revenues in 1997.

The principal types of freight transported by MSCA are packages, retail goods, nonperishable foodstuffs, paper and paper products, household appliances, furniture

and packaged petroleum products. Revenues are derived mainly from the medium to long line-haul and the regional short-haul segments of the dry van truckload market.

The company provides premium services and charges compensating rates, preferring to serve customers for whom the quality and range of service are more important than price. MSCA believes that its late-model equipment and the availability of extra trailers that can be placed in service for the convenience of customers help it to compete effectively in the service-sensitive segment of the market.

MSCA's marketing efforts concentrate on attracting customers that ship multiple loads from numerous locations that complement the company's existing traffic flows. As shipping patterns of existing customers expand or change, the company attempts to obtain additional customers to complement the new traffic flows. Thus, the effort to attract new customers varies from time to time, depending on growth or changes in the shipping patterns of existing customers.

In September 1997, MSCA acquired Hi-Way Express, an Arkansas-based dry van carrier operating 261 conventional tractors and 486 trailers. In March 1998, the company acquired the U.S. operations of Challenger Motor Freight, adding 195 tractors and 481 trailors to its fleet.

Per Share Data ($)

(Year Ended Dec. 31)	1997	1996	1995	1994	1993	1992	1991	1990	1989	1988
Tangible Bk. Val.	14.53	12.84	12.24	11.49	10.25	6.74	5.75	5.02	4.43	3.64
Cash Flow	4.79	4.04	4.02	3.88	3.40	2.97	2.44	2.10	1.95	1.38
Earnings	1.54	1.02	1.01	1.31	1.13	0.97	0.73	0.60	0.79	0.61
Dividends	Nil	Nil	Nil	Nil	Nil	Nil	Nil	Nil	Nil	Nil
Payout Ratio	Nil	Nil	Nil	Nil	Nil	Nil	Nil	Nil	Nil	Nil
Prices - High	28¹/₈	22¹/₈	25¹/₄	28¹/₂	26¹/₂	22³/₄	16	10³/₄	12	8³/₄
- Low	15³/₄	15¹/₄	15¹/₄	17³/₄	18¹/₄	12¹/₂	6³/₄	4⁵/₈	8	5³/₈
P/E Ratio - High	18	22	25	22	23	23	22	18	15	14
- Low	10	15	15	14	16	13	9	8	10	9

Income Statement Analysis (Million $)

	1997	1996	1995	1994	1993	1992	1991	1990	1989	1988
Revs.	416	340	333	293	225	181	153	124	97.0	68.0
Oper. Inc.	74.5	58.4	63.8	63.4	52.4	42.2	33.6	29.0	27.7	18.9
Depr.	40.1	37.0	39.1	33.7	27.4	21.9	18.2	15.9	12.3	8.2
Int. Exp.	5.8	4.8	5.5	1.8	2.1	2.6	3.0	3.0	2.2	0.8
Pretax Inc.	29.4	19.5	20.5	28.0	23.1	18.0	13.0	10.6	13.6	10.5
Eff. Tax Rate	36%	36%	36%	39%	41%	41%	40%	40%	39%	38%
Net Inc.	19.0	12.4	13.2	17.2	13.6	10.6	7.8	6.4	8.3	6.4

Balance Sheet & Other Fin. Data (Million $)

	1997	1996	1995	1994	1993	1992	1991	1990	1989	1988
Cash	0.4	1.1	0.5	30.8	0.1	0.1	0.1	0.0	0.1	1.9
Curr. Assets	60.5	50.2	42.9	73.8	32.0	25.0	20.3	17.0	16.4	11.5
Total Assets	362	291	280	276	199	151	122	111	95.0	64.0
Curr. Liab.	46.8	43.0	42.3	44.9	22.7	24.6	16.7	17.7	17.6	8.4
LT Debt	80.0	45.4	47.4	51.2	18.0	32.7	26.8	25.6	18.2	7.6
Common Eqty.	177	154	153	148	132	72.0	61.3	53.4	46.8	38.5
Total Cap.	257	248	238	231	176	126	106	94.0	77.0	55.0
Cap. Exp.	96.0	57.9	76.6	100	70.1	46.5	35.3	36.9	39.9	27.6
Cash Flow	59.1	49.4	52.2	50.8	41.0	32.4	25.9	22.3	20.6	14.6
Curr. Ratio	1.3	1.2	1.0	1.6	1.4	1.0	1.2	1.0	0.9	1.4
% LT Debt of Cap.	31.1	18.3	19.9	22.1	10.2	25.9	25.4	27.4	23.6	13.8
% Net Inc.of Revs.	4.6	3.7	3.9	5.9	6.1	5.8	5.1	5.2	8.6	9.4
% Ret. on Assets	5.8	4.4	4.7	7.2	7.1	7.7	6.6	6.2	10.5	11.8
% Ret. on Equity	11.4	8.1	8.7	12.3	12.4	15.9	13.5	12.7	19.5	18.2

Data as orig. reptd.; bef. results of disc. opers. and/or spec. items. Per share data adj. for stk. divs. as of ex-div. date. Bold denotes diluted EPS (FASB 128). E-Estimated. NA-Not Available. NM-Not Meaningful. NR-Not Ranked.

Office—3171 Directors Row, Memphis, TN 38116. Tel—(901) 332-2500. Chrmn, Pres & CEO—M. S. Starnes. SVP-Fin, Secy & Treas—M. J. Barrow. Dirs—M. J. Barrow, M. H. Fair, J. H. Morris III, C. Mungenast, M. S. Starnes, J. W. Welch. Transfer Agent & Registrar—Sun Trust Bank, Atlanta. Incorporated—in Tennessee in 1977. Empl— 3,112. S&P Analyst: S.J.T.

STANDARD &POOR'S
STOCK REPORTS

MacDermid, Inc.

1404C
NYSE Symbol **MRD**

In S&P SmallCap 600

03-OCT-98

Industry: Chemicals (Specialty)

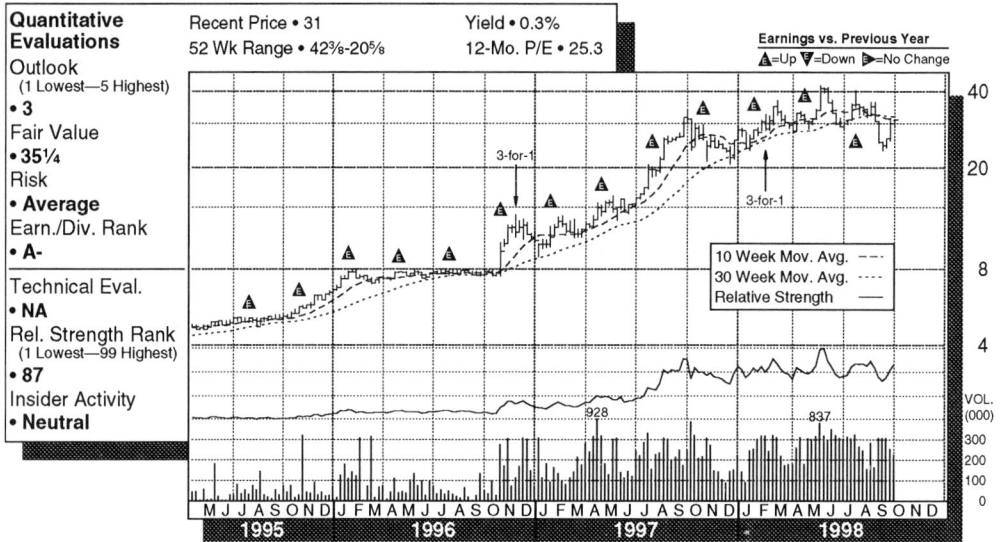

Quantitative Evaluations

Outlook (1 Lowest—5 Highest)
• **3**

Fair Value
• **35¼**

Risk
• **Average**

Earn./Div. Rank
• **A-**

Technical Eval.
• **NA**

Rel. Strength Rank (1 Lowest—99 Highest)
• **87**

Insider Activity
• **Neutral**

Recent Price • 31
52 Wk Range • 42⅝-20⅝
Yield • 0.3%
12-Mo. P/E • 25.3

Earnings vs. Previous Year ▲=Up ▼=Down ▶=No Change

10 Week Mov. Avg. – – –
30 Week Mov. Avg. ·······
Relative Strength —

Business Profile - 19-JUN-98

MRD continues to seek growth through acquisitions and the development of its product line. In April 1998, MRD acquired a 30% interest in an Italian maker of metal finishing chemicals, with the intent of acquiring a majority interest in 1999. In June 1995, MRD acquired the remaining 50% interest in Hollmuller America and renamed it MacDermid Equipment. The December 1995 acquisition of the electronics and printing division of Hercules, Inc. increased annual sales by more than $70 million. Also, MRD will continue to place a high priority on its R&D program. The shares began trading on the New York Stock Exchange on February 23, 1998.

Operational Review - 19-JUN-98

Based on a preliminary report, revenues in FY 98 (Mar.) advanced 6.9%, year to year, as increased sales of proprietary chemicals outweighed the negative effects of foreign currency translation. Margins widened and pretax income was up 24%. After taxes at 36.0%, versus 39.0%, net income increased 38.4%, to $30,488,000 ($1.20 a share, after preferred dividends), from $22,010,000 ($0.85, as adjusted).

Stock Performance - 02-OCT-98

In the past 30 trading days, MRD's shares have declined 11%, compared to a 7% fall in the S&P 500. Average trading volume for the past five days was 44,600 shares, compared with the 40-day moving average of 56,844 shares.

Key Stock Statistics

Dividend Rate/Share	0.08	Shareholders	800
Shs. outstg. (M)	25.1	Market cap. (B)	$0.781
Avg. daily vol. (M)	0.065	Inst. holdings	59%
Tang. Bk. Value/Share	0.95		
Beta	0.84		

Value of $10,000 invested 5 years ago: $ 113,088

Fiscal Year Ending Mar. 31

	1999	1998	1997	1996	1995	1994
Revenues (Million $)						
1Q	81.07	74.72	72.66	48.97	42.59	39.85
2Q	—	75.00	74.04	53.36	46.50	37.76
3Q	—	83.81	74.37	58.28	44.55	34.81
4Q	—	80.53	72.66	75.29	48.47	37.61
Yr.	—	314.1	293.7	235.9	182.1	150.0
Earnings Per Share ($)						
1Q	0.32	0.29	0.17	0.11	0.10	0.06
2Q	—	0.29	0.20	0.12	0.09	0.06
3Q	—	0.30	0.21	0.12	0.10	0.05
4Q	—	0.32	0.27	0.15	0.10	0.08
Yr.	—	1.20	0.85	0.50	0.39	0.24

Next earnings report expected: NA

Dividend Data (Dividends have been paid since 1946.)

Amount ($)	Date Decl.	Ex-Div. Date	Stock of Record	Payment Date
3-for-1	Jan. 15	Feb. 09	Jan. 26	Feb. 06 '98
0.020	Jan. 15	Mar. 12	Mar. 16	Apr. 01 '98
0.020	May. 18	Jun. 11	Jun. 15	Jul. 01 '98
0.020	Jul. 22	Sep. 11	Sep. 15	Oct. 01 '98

A Division of The McGraw-Hill Companies

MacDermid, Incorporated

Business Summary - 19-JUN-98

MacDermid develops, produces and markets a broad line of specialty chemical products used in the metal and plastic finishing and electronics industries. It also markets chemical supplies and equipment produced by others.

Sales in recent fiscal years (Mar.) were derived:

	1997	1996
Proprietary chemicals	88%	88%
Resale chemicals & supplies	6%	6%
Equipment	6%	6%

In FY 97, North American operations accounted for 58% of net sales, while Asia Pacific accounted for 23%, and Europe 19%.

The company produces more than 1,000 proprietary chemical compounds. The chemicals are used for cleaning, activating and polishing, mechanical plating, mechanical galvanizing, electroplating and phosphatizing metal surfaces, stripping of metal and final coating of metal surfaces, filtering, antitarnishing and rust retarding in the metal finishing industry, and etching, imaging, deposition of metal, and other chemical processes in the manufacture of printed circuits and other electronic parts.

MRD markets its products through more than 220 sales personnel in the U.S., Europe and Asia/Pacific. It owns and operates manufacturing facilities in Australia, Great Britain, Spain and Taiwan.

Chemicals, supplies and equipment manufactured by others and resold by the company include basic chemicals, automatic plating conveyors, barrel plating and pollution control equipment, rectifiers, pumps and filters. MRD markets resale items primarily in conjunction with and as an aid to the sale of its proprietary chemicals. It also resells equipment used in the production of printed circuit boards and in chemical machining.

In December 1995, the company acquired the electronics and printing division of Hercules, Inc. and formed a new wholly owned subsidiary, MacDermid Imaging Technology. The subsidiary manufactures photoresists used to imprint electrical patterns on circuit boards. In June 1995, MRD acquired the remaining 50% interest in Hollmuller America, Inc., and renamed it MacDermid Equipment. The unit markets chemical supplies and equipment produced by others.

Outlays for R&D totaled $10,850,000 in FY 97, versus $10,042,000 in FY 96 and $9,644,000 in FY 95.

Per Share Data ($)

(Year Ended Mar. 31)	1998	1997	1996	1995	1994	1993	1992	1991	1990	1989
Tangible Bk. Val.	0.70	0.15	NM	2.17	2.12	2.03	1.90	1.74	1.55	1.46
Cash Flow	1.64	1.32	0.80	0.57	0.42	0.39	0.37	0.38	0.34	0.37
Earnings	1.20	0.85	0.50	0.39	0.24	0.24	0.23	0.21	0.17	0.21
Dividends	0.07	0.07	0.07	0.07	0.07	0.07	0.07	0.07	0.07	0.06
Payout Ratio	6%	8%	13%	17%	28%	28%	30%	32%	40%	31%
Cal. Yrs.	1997	1996	1995	1994	1993	1992	1991	1990	1989	1988
Prices - High	34	13⅛	6⅝	4⅝	3½	3¼	3	2⅝	3⅛	3⅛
- Low	9⅛	6½	4	2⅝	2¾	2⅝	2¼	1¾	1¹¹⁄₁₆	2½
P/E Ratio - High	40	15	13	12	14	14	13	13	19	15
- Low	11	8	8	7	11	11	10	8	10	12

Income Statement Analysis (Million $)

	1998	1997	1996	1995	1994	1993	1992	1991	1990	1989
Revs.	314	294	236	182	150	156	145	151	149	143
Oper. Inc.	66.8	57.0	37.0	25.2	18.7	20.3	15.8	18.5	18.8	18.0
Depr.	11.2	10.2	7.8	5.0	5.6	4.8	4.8	5.3	5.7	5.3
Int. Exp.	7.8	7.3	4.4	2.0	1.4	1.9	1.6	2.0	3.1	2.3
Pretax Inc.	48.1	38.7	23.6	18.1	12.4	12.3	11.0	11.3	9.2	11.1
Eff. Tax Rate	36%	38%	42%	39%	38%	38%	34%	40%	42%	40%
Net Inc.	30.8	23.8	13.8	11.1	7.8	7.7	7.2	6.8	5.3	6.7

Balance Sheet & Other Fin. Data (Million $)

	1998	1997	1996	1995	1994	1993	1992	1991	1990	1989
Cash	3.5	6.5	8.8	7.6	6.5	6.3	5.1	6.0	3.9	2.9
Curr. Assets	132	116	119	81.2	68.4	71.5	66.1	67.8	64.0	57.9
Total Assets	300	261	265	123	106	107	101	103	102	100
Curr. Liab.	86.0	68.8	59.0	46.5	33.5	40.5	38.5	44.5	48.0	44.6
LT Debt	104	75.1	105	18.2	0.9	1.0	1.4	1.9	2.7	6.2
Common Eqty.	106	80.0	65.8	53.7	68.2	65.2	61.1	55.8	49.7	47.1
Total Cap.	210	188	202	72.9	69.2	66.7	62.7	58.8	53.7	55.4
Cap. Exp.	8.3	6.9	4.3	4.0	7.5	4.7	5.4	3.2	3.5	9.0
Cash Flow	41.7	34.0	21.0	16.2	13.4	12.4	12.0	12.1	11.0	12.0
Curr. Ratio	1.5	1.7	2.0	1.7	2.0	1.8	1.7	1.5	1.3	1.3
% LT Debt of Cap.	49.5	39.9	52.1	25.0	1.3	1.5	2.1	3.3	5.0	11.1
% Net Inc.of Revs.	9.8	8.1	5.8	6.1	5.2	4.9	5.0	4.5	3.6	4.7
% Ret. on Assets	11.0	9.0	7.1	9.7	7.3	7.4	7.1	6.6	5.3	7.0
% Ret. on Equity	32.9	32.6	22.1	18.3	11.7	12.2	12.4	12.8	11.0	14.8

Data as orig. reptd.; bef. results of disc. opers. and/or spec. items. Per share data adj. for stk. divs. as of ex-div. date. Bold denotes diluted EPS (FASB 128). E-Estimated. NA-Not Available. NM-Not Meaningful. NR-Not Ranked.

Office—245 Freight St., Waterbury, CT 06702-0671. **Tel**—(203) 575-5700. **Chrmn & Investor Contact**—Harold Leever. **Pres & CEO**—D. H. Leever. **EVP & CFO**—A. J. LoVetere, Jr. **Secy**—J. L. Cordani. **Dirs**—D. H. Leever, H. Leever, D. G. Ogilvie, J. C. Smith, T. W. Smith. **Transfer Agent & Registrar**—Harris Trust Co. of New York, NYC. **Incorporated**—in Connecticut in 1922. **Empl**—1,086. **S&P Analyst**: E. Hunter

STANDARD &POOR'S
STOCK REPORTS

Macromedia, Inc.

NASDAQ Symbol **MACR**

4487M

In S&P SmallCap 600

03-OCT-98

Industry: Computer (Software & Services)

Summary: Macromedia is a leading provider of software tools for Web publishing, multimedia and graphics.

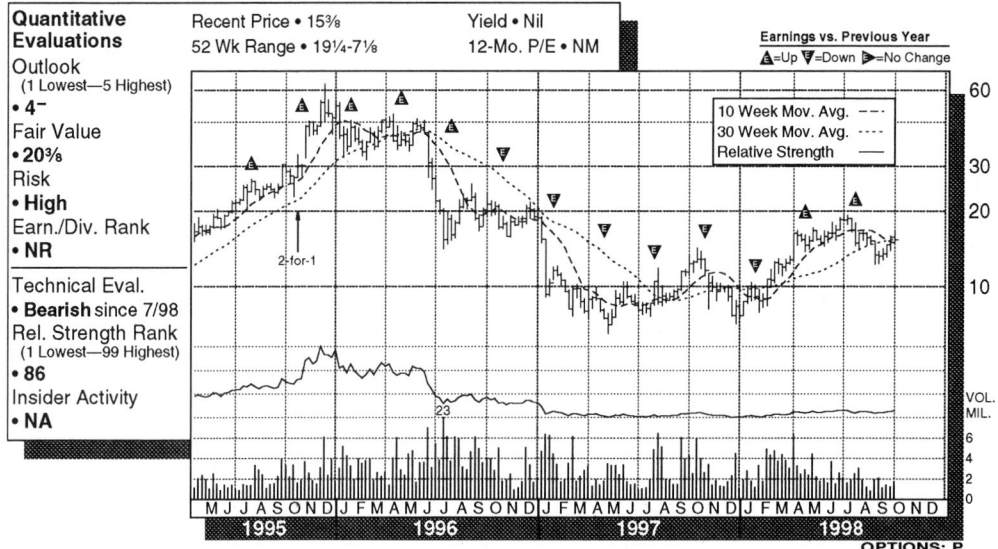

Quantitative Evaluations	
Outlook (1 Lowest—5 Highest)	• **4⁻**
Fair Value	• **20⅝**
Risk	• **High**
Earn./Div. Rank	• **NR**
Technical Eval.	• **Bearish** since 7/98
Rel. Strength Rank (1 Lowest—99 Highest)	• **86**
Insider Activity	• **NA**

Recent Price • 15⅜
52 Wk Range • 19¼-7⅛

Yield • Nil
12-Mo. P/E • NM

Earnings vs. Previous Year
▲=Up ▼=Down ▶=No Change

10 Week Mov. Avg. — —
30 Week Mov. Avg. ·····
Relative Strength ——

OPTIONS: P

Business Profile - 09-SEP-98

This company's products are used by a variety of industries to publish content on the Internet. Recent results have been driven by the release of new products including the latest version of its Dreamweaver product. Dreamweaver enables Web developers to deploy high-impact Web pages over low-bandwidth Internet connections. During the first quarter of FY 99 (Mar.), the company announced that Netscape has licensed Macromedia Flash technology and will include the Flash player with every copy of its Netscape Navigator browser software. Macromedia's Shockwave and Flash players are pre-installed with every copy of Microsoft's newly released Windows 98 operating system.

Operational Review - 09-SEP-98

In the first three months of FY 99 (Mar.), revenues rose 18%, year to year, primarily reflecting revenue streams from new Web related products and services. Gross margins widened, and operating expenses advanced less rapidly than sales; operating income of $5,064,000 contrasted with a loss of $516,000. After taxes at 31.0% versus tax credits of $557,000, net income of $2,959,000 ($0.07 a share, on 16% more shares) contrasted with a net loss of $1,239,000 ($0.03).

Stock Performance - 02-OCT-98

In the past 30 trading days, MACR's shares have increased 0.82%, compared to a 7% fall in the S&P 500. Average trading volume for the past five days was 339,760 shares, compared with the 40-day moving average of 290,308 shares.

Key Stock Statistics

Dividend Rate/Share	Nil	Shareholders	600
Shs. outstg. (M)	39.6	Market cap. (B)	$0.609
Avg. daily vol. (M)	0.284	Inst. holdings	54%
Tang. Bk. Value/Share	3.47		
Beta	NA		

Value of $10,000 invested 5 years ago: NA

Fiscal Year Ending Mar. 31

	1999	1998	1997	1996	1995	1994
Revenues (Million $)						
1Q	32.34	27.33	35.01	23.85	8.55	6.80
2Q	—	29.17	31.03	27.30	9.55	7.32
3Q	—	26.58	28.10	30.93	10.70	7.90
4Q	—	30.01	13.23	34.61	19.63	8.12
Yr.	—	113.1	107.4	116.7	53.70	30.13
Earnings Per Share ($)						
1Q	0.07	-0.03	0.18	0.13	0.03	0.02
2Q	—	0.01	0.12	0.16	0.06	0.04
3Q	—	-0.19	-0.06	0.18	0.05	0.05
4Q	—	0.05	-0.41	0.15	0.05	0.05
Yr.	—	-0.16	-0.16	0.59	0.19	0.14

Next earnings report expected: late October

Dividend Data

No cash dividends have been paid and the company does not plan to pay dividends for the foreseeable future.

STANDARD
&POOR'S
STOCK REPORTS

Macromedia, Inc.

4487M
03-OCT-98

Business Summary - 09-SEP-98

Macromedia, Inc. aims to become the preferred, high-volume supplier of software tools for graphics, multimedia, video and Web publishing. It develops, markets and supports an integrated line of graphics, multimedia and online publishing software for both Windows and Macintosh platforms; revenues in FY 98 (Mar.) were divided 56% Windows-based and 44% Macintosh-based. The company is currently seeing a shift in its product mix toward the Windows platform.

The company's products are used to create interactive multimedia applications and printed materials for business communications, the arts and entertainment, and education. They are used by multimedia, graphic arts, Web and learning professionals working independently or in organizations ranging from large corporations to small companies, as well as in educational institutions. During FY 98, the company increased its focus on Web-related products. Macromedia's three principal products -- Director, FreeHand and Authorware (together accounting for 84% of FY 98 sales) -- were updated for the Internet.

The Macromedia Studios, each consisting of a suite of Macromedia products, meet the needs of individuals who develop and deliver multimedia and graphics con-

tent by providing a complete, integrated set of tools. The company's Director Multimedia Studio gives developers the capability to create visuals, animation and interactivity, all within a single working environment. MACR's design and illustration FreeHand Graphics Studio software package provides a complete set of tools for graphic arts and design. The company provides software tools for building Websites through its Backstage Internet Studio. The Authorware Interactive Studio consists of software authoring tools for creating interactive information applications. Macromedia Flash is the first tool for creating and animating vector-based, resolution-independent graphics without programming.

With Macromedia's Shockwave technology, users of the company's products are adapting and developing interactive content for use on Websites. Authorware, Director, FreeHand and Flash files can be translated or "shocked" for use on Websites as well as corporate intranets, and other networks.

The company sells and distributes its products mainly through large national software distributors which in turn distribute them through large retail chains, mail order, national corporate resellers and small independent dealers. With more than 80 distributors in more than 50 countries worldwide, international sales accounted for 48% of total revenues in FY 98.

Per Share Data ($)

(Year Ended Mar. 31)	1998	1997	1996	1995	1994	1993	1992	1991	1990	1989
Tangible Bk. Val.	3.35	3.50	3.66	1.28	NA	NA	NA	NA	NA	NA
Cash Flow	0.04	0.05	0.69	0.25	NA	NA	NA	NA	NA	NA
Earnings	-0.16	-0.16	0.59	0.19	0.14	-0.01	NA	NA	NA	NA
Dividends	Nil	Nil	Nil	Nil	Nil	Nil	Nil	Nil	Nil	Nil
Payout Ratio	Nil	Nil	Nil	Nil	Nil	Nil	Nil	Nil	Nil	Nil
Cal. Yrs.	1997	1996	1995	1994	1993	1992	1991	1990	1989	1988
Prices - High	18¼	53¾	63¾	13⅞	8⅞	NA	NA	NA	NA	NA
- Low	6½	14⅛	10⅝	3¾	6⅜	NA	NA	NA	NA	NA
P/E Ratio - High	NM	NM	NM	73	31	NA	NA	NA	NA	NA
- Low	NM	NM	NM	20	22	NA	NA	NA	NA	NA

Income Statement Analysis (Million $)

Revs.	113	107	117	53.7	30.1	25.3	24.7	15.3	NA	NA
Oper. Inc.	5.3	-5.9	34.3	12.4	NA	NA	NA	NA	NA	NA
Depr.	7.7	7.8	4.1	2.1	NA	NA	NA	NA	NA	NA
Int. Exp.	Nil	Nil	Nil	Nil	Nil	Nil	Nil	Nil	Nil	Nil
Pretax Inc.	-5.4	-9.4	31.8	7.6	3.3	-0.2	-12.0	-7.6	NA	NA
Eff. Tax Rate	NM	NM	28%	14%	5.60%	NM	NM	NM	NM	NM
Net Inc.	-6.2	-5.9	23.0	6.5	3.1	-0.2	-12.0	-7.6	NA	NA

Balance Sheet & Other Fin. Data (Million $)

Cash	10.0	15.4	117	34.0	NA	NA	NA	NA	NA	NA
Curr. Assets	107	118	141	46.0	NA	NA	NA	NA	NA	NA
Total Assets	154	157	155	52.0	NA	NA	NA	NA	NA	NA
Curr. Liab.	25.1	25.0	22.0	12.6	NA	NA	NA	NA	NA	NA
LT Debt	Nil	Nil	Nil	Nil	Nil	Nil	Nil	Nil	Nil	Nil
Common Eqty.	128	132	133	40.0	NA	NA	NA	NA	NA	NA
Total Cap.	128	132	133	40.0	NA	NA	NA	NA	NA	NA
Cap. Exp.	12.4	27.2	9.5	4.3	NA	NA	NA	NA	NA	NA
Cash Flow	1.5	1.8	27.1	8.6	10.4	NA	NA	NA	NA	NA
Curr. Ratio	4.3	4.7	6.4	3.7	NA	NA	NA	NA	NA	NA
% LT Debt of Cap.	Nil	Nil	Nil	Nil	Nil	Nil	Nil	Nil	Nil	Nil
% Net Inc.of Revs.	NM	NM	19.7	12.2	10.4	NM	NM	NM	NM	NM
% Ret. on Assets	NM	NM	22.2	NA	NA	NA	NA	NA	NA	NA
% Ret. on Equity	NM	NM	26.6	NA	NA	NA	NA	NA	NA	NA

Data as orig. reptd.; bef. results of disc. opers. and/or spec. items. Per share data adj. for stk. divs. as of ex-div. date. Bold denotes diluted EPS (FASB 128). E-Estimated. NA-Not Available. NM-Not Meaningful. NR-Not Ranked.

Office—600 Townsend St., San Francisco, CA 94103.**Tel**—(415) 252-2000.**Fax**—(415) 626-0554.**E-Mail**—ir@macromedia.com**Website**—http:// www.macromedia.com**Chrmn**—J. C. Colligan.**CEO & Pres**—R.K. Burgess.**VP-Fin & CFO**—E. A. Nelson**Dirs**—R.K. Burgess, J. C. Colligan, I. J. Doerr, J. Giffen, C. R. Kramlich, D. L. Lucas, J. R. Von Ehr II, W. B. Welty. **Transfer Agent**—ChaseMellon Shareholder Services, SF. **Incorporated**—in Delaware in 1992.**Empl**— 491. **S&P Analyst:** M.J.C.

03-OCT-98   Industry:
Health Care (Hospital
Management)

Summary: This company provides a broad range of behavioral
healthcare services in the U.S. and Europe.

S&P Opinion: Hold (★★★)	

Recent Price • 10¼   Yield • Nil
52 Wk Range • 31⅝-9⅝   12-Mo. P/E • 13.5

Quantitative Evaluations

Outlook
(1 Lowest—5 Highest)
• **5+**

Fair Value
• **25⅝**

Risk
• **Average**

Earn./Div. Rank
• **NR**

Technical Eval.
• **NA**

Rel. Strength Rank
(1 Lowest—99 Highest)
• **11**

Insider Activity
• **Favorable**

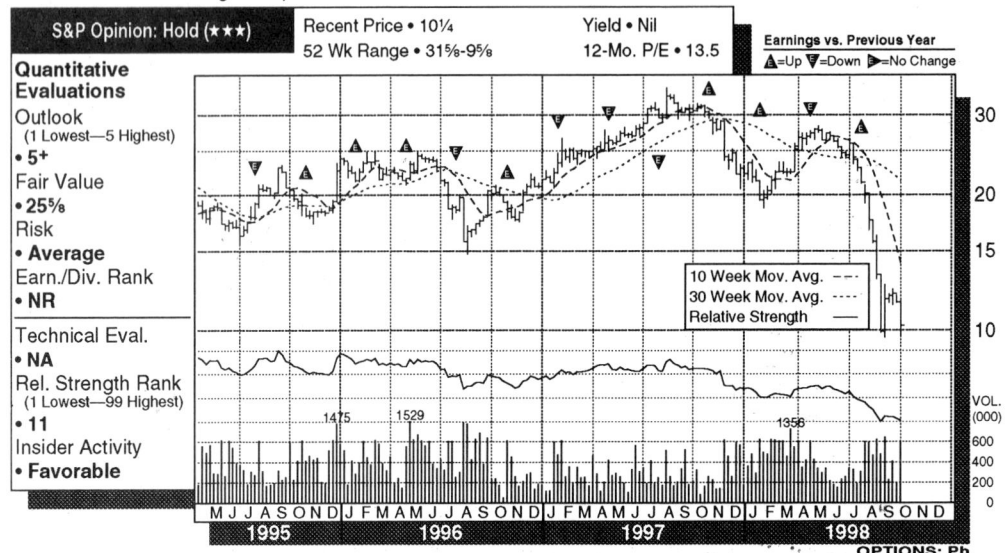

Earnings vs. Previous Year
▲=Up ▼=Down ▷=No Change

10 Week Mov. Avg. — · —
30 Week Mov. Avg. · · · ·
Relative Strength —

VOL. (000)

OPTIONS: Ph

Overview - 01-JUL-98

The company's long-term prospects have been enhanced by a strategic shift away from the operation of
inpatient psychiatric facilities and toward the pure provision of managed behavioral care services. The inpatient
business continues to be hurt by falling Medicare rates,
while the migration of commercial customers to HMOs
has affected service utilization and lengths of stay,
while putting additional pressure on pricing. However,
we anticipate that revenue comparisons in coming
quarters will increasingly benefit both from internal
growth at the managed behavioral health operations
and from acquisitions; revenues in FY 99 (Sep.) should
approach $2 billion. Our EPS estimates for FY 98 and
FY 99 are $1.00 and $1.20, respectively, but these projections are somewhat at risk, given the prospect that
franchise fees from the Crescent joint venture could fall
up to $20 million below original expectations.

Valuation - 01-JUL-98

We are maintaining an accumulate opinion on the
stock, and feel that both revenue and earnings comparisons in coming quarters should benefit from the company's increased presence in the managed behavioral
care industry. The recent purchase of Merit Behavioral
Care should be the last major acquisition for the near
future; management now intends to shift its focus toward integrating the operations of Merit, Allied Health
Group, and Human Affairs International, all of which
were purchased since the start of December 1997.
Magellan expects to realize about $60 million of cost
savings by eliminating expense overlaps over the next
18 months; despite lower than expected franchise fees,
we look for three-year EPS growth of about 20%. Despite uncertainties created by the Crescent situation,
the stock significantly outperformed the S&P 500 during
the first half of 1998.

Key Stock Statistics

S&P EPS Est. 1998	1.00	Tang. Bk. Value/Share	NM
P/E on S&P Est. 1998	10.3	Beta	1.71
S&P EPS Est. 1999	1.45	Shareholders	9,600
Dividend Rate/Share	Nil	Market cap. (B)	$0.324
Shs. outstg. (M)	31.6	Inst. holdings	71%
Avg. daily vol. (M)	0.079		

Value of $10,000 invested 5 years ago: $ 12,812

Fiscal Year Ending Sep. 30

	1998	1997	1996	1995	1994	1993
Revenues (Million $)						
1Q	216.1	346.8	296.0	264.0	209.0	226.0
2Q	372.2	349.9	354.9	300.0	213.0	233.0
3Q	474.8	324.9	346.4	305.0	221.0	232.0
4Q	—	189.0	348.3	283.0	262.0	207.0
Yr.	—	1,211	1,345	1,152	905.0	898.0
Earnings Per Share ($)						
1Q	**0.26**	0.25	0.35	0.01	-0.15	-0.16
2Q	**-0.07**	0.41	0.63	-0.53	0.04	-0.68
3Q	**0.23**	-0.85	-0.18	0.06	0.18	-0.10
4Q	**E0.56**	0.35	0.26	-1.07	-1.72	-0.65
Yr.	**E1.00**	0.16	1.04	-1.54	-1.78	-1.59

Next earnings report expected: mid November

Dividend Data

Cash dividend payments, suspended since 1988, are
currently prohibited under terms of certain debt
agreements.

A Division of The **McGraw·Hill** Companies

Business Summary - 01-JUL-98

Magellan Health Services (formerly Community Psychiatric) has transformed itself from the largest domestic operator of psychiatric hospitals into one of the leading providers of managed behavioral healthcare services in the U.S. The company's change in direction was driven by increased usage by third party healthcare payors of managed care programs as their principal cost control measure, which continues to place pressure on inpatient lengths of stay and pricing. In order to facilitate the development of its managed care business, Magellan sold substantially all of its domestic acute care psychiatric facilities and residential treatment facilities to Crescent Real Estate Equities L.P., for $417 million in cash. The two parties subsequently created an equally owned joint venture to operate the 90 facilities; original terms call for MGL to receive $78.3 million in annual franchise fees, while Crescent leases the real estate to the venture at an initial annual rate of $41.7 million.

The managed care division consists of four operating subsidiaries. Green Spring (61% owned) is one of the largest managed behavioral care companies in the U.S., and the largest such provider to the Blue Cross/Blue Shield networks, covering about 16.6 million lives.

Allied Health Group (acquired in December 1997) provides specialty risk-based products and administrative services to various insurance companies and other customers, including CIGNA, Blue Cross of New Jersey and NYLCare, for about 3.4 million individuals. Human Affairs International (HAI, acquired from Aetna/U.S. Healthcare in December 1997) manages the care of more than 16 million individuals through employee assistance programs and other managed behavioral healthcare plans. Merit Behavioral Care Corp. (acquired in February 1998) manages healthcare programs covering more than 21 million people, for about 800 clients including HMOs, Blue Cross/Blue Shield organizations and other insurers, corporations and labor unions, government agencies and various state Medicaid programs.

Magellan also offers specialty products related to the management of chronic medical conditions and franchises the CHARTER system of behavioral healthcare to the psychiatric and other facilities operated by Charter Behavioral Health System, an equally owned joint venture with Crescent Real Estate Equities L.P.

Through National Mentor Inc., the company provides specialty home-based behavioral healthcare services to more than 2,800 individuals in 84 government-sponsored programs in 20 states.

Per Share Data ($)

(Year Ended Sep. 30)	1997	1996	1995	1994	1993	1992	1991	1990	1989	1988
Tangible Bk. Val.	NM	-1.68	0.96	1.06	2.29	0.42	3.09	NA	NA	NA
Cash Flow	1.69	2.62	0.76	-0.75	-0.53	0.05	2.08	NA	NA	NA
Earnings	0.16	1.04	-1.54	-1.78	-1.59	-1.50	-1.43	NA	NA	NA
Dividends	Nil	Nil	Nil	Nil	Nil	Nil	Nil	Nil	Nil	Nil
Payout Ratio	Nil	Nil	Nil	Nil	Nil	Nil	Nil	Nil	Nil	Nil
Prices - High	34½	25	23¼	28½	27	8¾	NA	NA	NA	NA
- Low	20⅝	14¾	13⅞	21¼	8	4⅝	NA	NA	NA	NA
P/E Ratio - High	NM	24	NM	NM	NM	NM	NA	NA	NA	NA
- Low	NM	14	NM	NM	NM	NM	NM	NM	NM	NM

Income Statement Analysis (Million $)

Revs.	1,211	1,345	1,152	905	898	1,275	1,195	NA	NA	NA
Oper. Inc.	182	198	196	111	108	246	218	NA	NA	NA
Depr.	44.9	48.9	64.1	27.2	26.4	38.6	87.2	NA	NA	NA
Int. Exp.	55.5	58.5	58.9	44.0	78.0	88.5	98.3	NA	NA	NA
Pretax Inc.	23.1	64.2	-54.3	-58.0	-38.0	-9.6	-27.0	NA	NA	NA
Eff. Tax Rate	40%	40%	NM	NM	NM	NM	NM	NM	NM	NM
Net Inc.	4.8	32.3	-43.0	-47.0	-40.0	-37.7	-35.4	NA	NA	NA

Balance Sheet & Other Fin. Data (Million $)

Cash	373	121	106	130	86.0	144	117	NA	NA	NA
Curr. Assets	507	338	306	325	232	355	345	NA	NA	NA
Total Assets	896	1,140	984	961	838	1,306	1,428	NA	NA	NA
Curr. Liab.	219	274	214	215	273	315	227	NA	NA	NA
LT Debt	392	566	539	533	350	846	991	NA	NA	NA
Common Eqty.	241	122	88.6	56.0	57.0	10.4	76.7	NA	NA	NA
Total Cap.	611	753	627	602	446	877	1,068	NA	NA	NA
Cap. Exp.	33.4	38.8	20.2	105	11.0	28.0	NA	NA	NA	NA
Cash Flow	49.6	81.3	21.1	-20.0	-13.0	1.3	51.8	NA	NA	NA
Curr. Ratio	2.3	1.2	1.4	1.5	0.9	1.1	1.5	NA	NA	NA
% LT Debt of Cap.	64.1	75.2	86.0	88.6	78.5	96.5	92.8	NA	NA	NA
% Net Inc.of Revs.	0.4	2.4	NM	NM	NM	NM	NM	NM	NM	NM
% Ret. on Assets	0.5	3.0	NM	NM	NM	NM	NM	NM	NM	NM
% Ret. on Equity	2.1	30.7	NM	NM	NM	NM	NM	NM	NM	NM

Data as orig. reptd.; bef. results of disc. opers. and/or spec. items. Per share data adj. for stk. divs. as of ex-div. date. Bold denotes diluted EPS (FASB 128). E-Estimated. NA-Not Available. NM-Not Meaningful. NR-Not Ranked.

Office—3414 Peachtree Rd., Suite 1400, Atlanta, GA 30326. Tel—(404) 841-9200. Website—http://www.magellanhealth.com Chrmn, Pres, CEO & COO—E. M. Crawford. EVP & CFO—C. L. McKnight.SVP & Contr—H. A. McLure. Investor Contact—Kevin Helmintoller (404-814-5742). Dirs—E. M. Banks, E. M. Crawford, F. Dibona Jr., A. C. Dimitriadis, A. D. Frazier Jr., R. H. Kiefer, D. S. Messina, G. L. McManis, D. D. Moore, J. A. Sonnenfeld. Transfer Agent & Registrar—First Union National Bank of North Carolina, Charlotte.Incorporated—in Delaware in 1969. Empl—5,000. S&P Analyst: Robert M. Gold

Manitowoc Co.   1411

NYSE Symbol **MTW**

In S&P SmallCap 600

10-OCT-98

Industry:
Machinery (Diversified)

Summary: This company manufactures cranes, excavators and ice cube machines. It also provides ship-repair services.

Quantitative Evaluations

Outlook
(1 Lowest—5 Highest)
• **3**

Fair Value
• **35¼**

Risk
• **Average**

Earn./Div. Rank
• **B**

Technical Eval.
• **Bearish** since 7/98

Rel. Strength Rank
(1 Lowest—99 Highest)
• **46**

Insider Activity
• **Neutral**

Recent Price • 25⅞   Yield • 1.7%
52 Wk Range • 47-24½   12-Mo. P/E • 10.6

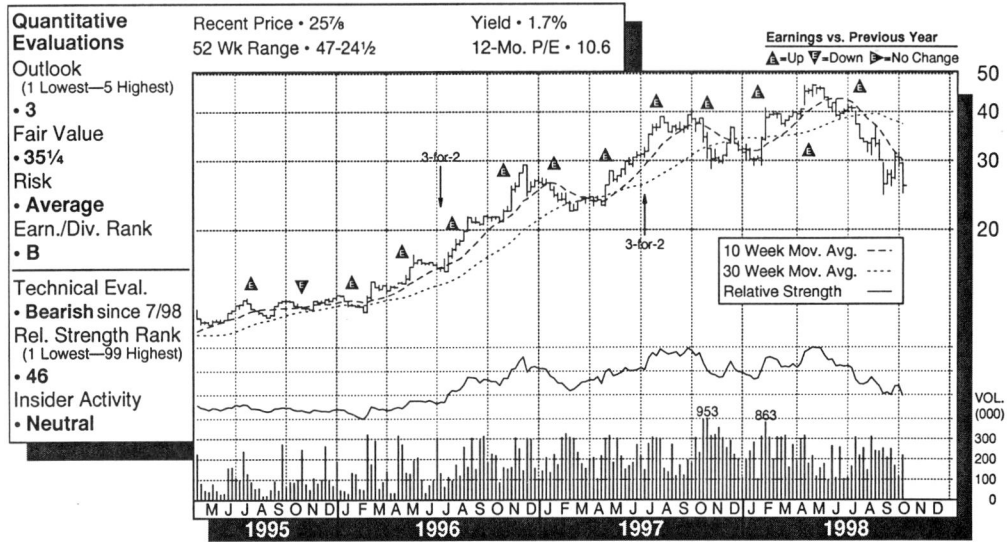

10 Week Mov. Avg. - - -
30 Week Mov. Avg. ·······
Relative Strength —

Earnings vs. Previous Year
▲=Up ▼=Down ▷=No Change

Business Profile - 30-SEP-98

MTW recently acquired SerVend International, a major manufacturer of ice/beverage dispensers and dispensing valves for the soft drink industry. The company also sold its Tonka unit, a manufacturer of walk-in refrigerators and freezers, which was part of the December 1995 acquisition of The Shannon Group. That acquisition more than doubled the size of the foodservice segment, which provided 45% of sales and 48% of profits in 1997. The company's plans for its foodservice and crane operations include continued development of international markets, continued widening of distribution channels, and improved productivity through expansion of some operations and the consolidation of others.

Operational Review - 30-SEP-98

Revenues rose 31% year to year in the first half of 1998, reflecting higher sales of foodservice products, cranes and related products and marine products. Margins widened, primarily reflecting improved profitability in the foodservice segment. With sharply higher interest expense, and net other expense, versus net other income, pretax income advanced 34%. After taxes at 36.7%, versus 37.0%, net income also climbed about 34%, to $24,745,000 ($1.42 a share), from $18,407,000 ($1.06).

Stock Performance - 09-OCT-98

In the past 30 trading days, MTW's shares have declined 14%, compared to a 4% fall in the S&P 500. Average trading volume for the past five days was 43,360 shares, compared with the 40-day moving average of 43,021 shares.

Key Stock Statistics

Dividend Rate/Share	0.45	Shareholders	2,500
Shs. outstg. (M)	17.3	Market cap. (B)	$0.447
Avg. daily vol. (M)	0.037	Inst. holdings	59%
Tang. Bk. Value/Share	NM		
Beta	1.35		

Value of $10,000 invested 5 years ago: $ 26,533

Fiscal Year Ending Dec. 31

	1998	1997	1996	1995	1994	1993
Revenues (Million $)						
1Q	154.1	116.0	114.1	69.10	60.61	62.87
2Q	188.9	145.0	139.2	82.29	85.95	100.6
3Q	—	133.9	132.0	80.09	66.04	61.06
4Q	—	150.9	115.1	81.67	57.87	67.77
Yr.	—	545.9	500.5	313.1	–	–
Earnings Per Share ($)						
1Q	0.54	0.37	0.24	0.10	0.08	-0.22
2Q	0.88	0.69	0.51	0.31	0.28	-0.37
3Q	—	0.55	0.49	0.21	0.22	-0.20
4Q	—	0.49	0.24	0.22	-0.52	0.16
Yr.	—	2.09	1.49	0.85	–	–

Next earnings report expected: mid October

Dividend Data (Dividends have been paid since 1945.)

Amount ($)	Date Decl.	Ex-Div. Date	Stock of Record	Payment Date
0.113	Feb. 10	Feb. 26	Mar. 02	Mar. 10 '98
0.113	May. 05	May. 28	Jun. 01	Jun. 10 '98
0.113	Jul. 21	Aug. 28	Sep. 01	Sep. 10 '98
0.113	Oct. 07	Nov. 27	Dec. 01	Dec. 10 '98

Business Summary - 30-SEP-98

Once thought of as a stodgy old rust-belt manufacturer in a cyclical business, Manitowoc (MTW) is taking steps to minimize the impact of economic swings on its fortunes. The company intends to build on its strength as a leader in the manufacture of cranes. In addition, management intends to expand MTW's less cyclical foodservice equipment business in order to add stability to its growth and greater predictability to earnings. Manitowoc designs and manufactures commercial ice machines and refrigeration products, cranes and related products, and provides marine vessel conversion and repair services.

In December 1995, Manitowoc acquired The Shannon Group, which more than doubled the company's foodservice equipment sales and made it a major player in commercial food cooling. Foodservice equipment represented 45% of the company's sales and 48% of profits in 1997; cranes and related products accounted for 48% of sales and 45% of profits, and the marine segment made up 7% of sales and 7% of profits. Shannon, headquartered in Brentwood, TN, supplies refrigerator/freezers to leading restaurants and grocery chains in the U.S. Manitowoc has also been growing its sales and service networks in Europe, and in China, the company is involved in a joint venture with the Hangzhou Household Electric Appliance Industrial Corp., which management believes gives the company a leading position in local restaurants.

MTW sells a diversified line of crawler, truck, fixed-base mounted and hydraulically powered cranes under the Manitowoc, Manitex and West-Manitowoc, Inc. names, designed for use by the energy, pulp and paper, mining, construction and other industries. Cranes have lifting capabilities ranging from 10 tons to 1,500 tons and excavating capacities of three cubic yards to 15 cubic yards. The company has developed a line of hydraulically driven, electronically controlled M-Series cranes, which are easier to transport, operate and maintain. In 1995, MTW introduced the 230 ton capacity Model 888. As a result of the model's initial success, MTW introduced two new attachments in 1996, and introduced the Model 777 liftcrane (a smaller version of Model 888) in 1997.

MTW also remanufactures older cranes and performs machining and assembly subcontract work. The company serves smaller independent contractors and rental fleet customers through West-Manitowoc. Replacement parts for cranes, draglines and other heavy equipment are produced by Femco Machine Co.

The Bay Shipbuilding Corp. unit operates a shipyard at Sturgeon Bay, WI, where it performs inspection, repair, reconstruction and conversion work on existing vessels. Merce Industries operates ship repair facilities in Toledo and Cleveland, OH.

Per Share Data ($) (Year Ended Dec. 31)	1997	1996	1995	1994	1993	1992	1991	1990	1989	1988
Tangible Bk. Val.	NM	0.47	NM	4.89	5.66	6.97	7.18	6.93	6.90	6.56
Cash Flow	2.77	2.14	1.23	1.04	0.56	0.63	0.91	1.13	0.93	0.28
Earnings	2.11	1.49	0.84	0.72	0.29	0.36	0.67	0.91	0.73	0.00
Dividends	0.45	0.45	0.45	0.44	0.44	0.44	0.44	0.89	0.36	0.36
Payout Ratio	21%	30%	53%	62%	145%	125%	67%	98%	49%	991%
Prices - High	40⅝	29⅜	13⅝	14⅜	14¾	12¼	12½	9⅞	11⅝	10
- Low	22¼	12¼	9⅜	10¾	10⅞	8⅜	7⅝	7½	7⅝	7⅜
P/E Ratio - High	19	20	16	20	51	34	19	11	16	NM
- Low	11	8	11	15	38	23	12	8	11	NM
Income Statement Analysis (Million $)										
Revs.	546	500	313	275	279	246	236	226	201	172
Oper. Inc.	76.7	63.7	30.0	27.4	31.5	16.8	24.0	23.2	24.4	13.3
Depr.	11.7	11.6	6.8	6.3	5.9	6.3	5.7	4.7	4.7	6.7
Int. Exp.	6.2	9.1	1.9	Nil	Nil	Nil	Nil	NA	NA	NA
Pretax Inc.	57.8	42.5	23.1	22.6	8.9	11.6	20.5	30.4	24.2	-1.2
Eff. Tax Rate	37%	40%	37%	38%	29%	29%	25%	31%	30%	NM
Net Inc.	36.4	25.6	14.6	14.0	6.3	8.3	15.4	21.0	16.9	0.1
Balance Sheet & Other Fin. Data (Million $)										
Cash	11.9	16.0	16.6	30.0	49.0	37.0	29.0	39.0	50.0	67.0
Curr. Assets	146	128	135	118	148	168	165	159	163	154
Total Assets	396	318	325	186	208	225	219	213	217	211
Curr. Liab.	171	110	111	63.6	58.4	43.8	42.6	41.4	36.5	35.5
LT Debt	66.4	76.5	101	Nil	Nil	Nil	Nil	Nil	Nil	Nil
Common Eqty.	129	100	81.6	94.0	119	166	167	162	161	154
Total Cap.	195	177	183	95.0	122	169	170	164	162	156
Cap. Exp.	12.0	8.4	19.2	13.9	11.2	5.1	6.3	4.3	2.7	3.1
Cash Flow	48.1	37.3	21.4	20.3	12.2	14.6	21.1	25.8	21.6	6.7
Curr. Ratio	0.9	1.2	1.2	1.8	2.5	3.8	3.9	3.9	4.5	4.3
% LT Debt of Cap.	34.1	43.3	55.6	Nil	Nil	Nil	Nil	Nil	Nil	Nil
% Net Inc.of Revs.	6.7	5.1	4.7	5.1	2.3	3.4	6.5	9.3	8.4	0.1
% Ret. on Assets	10.2	8.0	4.5	7.6	3.1	3.7	7.1	9.8	7.9	NM
% Ret. on Equity	31.8	28.2	17.9	14.1	4.7	5.0	9.4	13.0	10.7	0.1

Data as orig. reptd.; bef. results of disc. opers. and/or spec. items. Per share data adj. for stk. divs. as of ex-div. date. Yrs. ended Jun. 30 prior to 1995. Bold denotes diluted EPS (FASB 128). E-Estimated. NA-Not Available. NM-Not Meaningful. NR-Not Ranked.

Office—500 South 16th Street (P.O. Box 66), Manitowoc, WI 54220 (54221-0066). **Tel**—(414) 684-4410. **Pres & CEO**—T. D. Growcock.**SVP, CFO & Investor Contact**—Robert R. Friedl. **Secy**—E. D. Flynn. **Dirs**—D. H. Anderson, G. E. Fischer, J. P. McCann, G. T. McCoy, G. R. Rahr, Jr., G. F. Rankin, Jr., R. S. Throop. **Transfer Agent & Registrar**—First Chicago Trust Co. of New York, Jersey City, NJ. **Incorporated**—in Wisconsin in 1902. **Empl**— 3,000. **S&P Analyst:** E. Hunter

10-OCT-98 Industry: Lodging - Hotels

Summary: This company operates hotels and motels, movie theatres and restaurants, primarily in the Midwest.

Quantitative Evaluations	
Outlook (1 Lowest—5 Highest)	• **4-**
Fair Value	• **21**
Risk	• **Low**
Earn./Div. Rank	• **A**

Technical Eval.
• **Bearish** since 7/98

Rel. Strength Rank (1 Lowest—99 Highest)
• **91**

Insider Activity
• **Neutral**

Recent Price • 15⅛
52 Wk Range • 20⅜-12⅜

Yield • 1.5%
12-Mo. P/E • 15.9

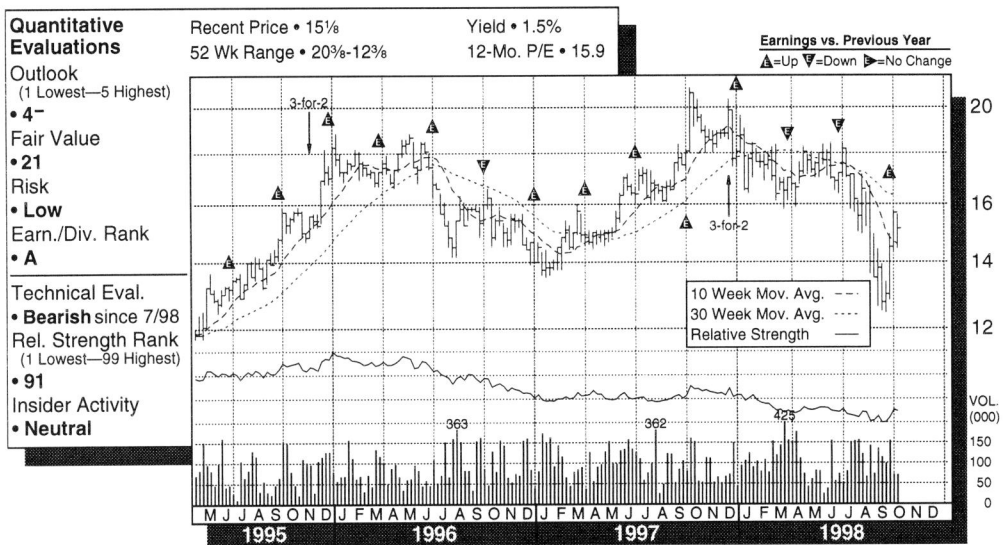

Earnings vs. Previous Year
▲=Up ▼=Down ▶=No Change

10 Week Mov. Avg. – – –
30 Week Mov. Avg. ·······
Relative Strength ——

Business Profile - 06-MAR-98

The company's long-term objectives include increasing to 300 the number of Budgetel Inns by 2000, continued expansion of Woodfield Suites, increasing the number of theatre screens to 500 by 2000, adding one or two hotel properties annually, and expanding the number of KFC franchise outlets. Recent results for the company's Budgetel Inns were hurt by overbuilding in the limited service segment. In December 1997, MCS agreed to acquire six suburban Minneapolis/St. Paul theatres with a total of 44 screens from Guetschoff Theatre Management Corp. A 6.7% dividend increase in August 1997 marked the 10th consecutive year of higher dividends. The shares were split three for two in December 1997.

Operational Review - 06-MAR-98

Total revenues in the 36 weeks ended February 5, 1998, rose 13%, year to year, on an 11% advance in hotel room revenues, a 19% jump in theatre sales, and a 20% increase in other income. Margins narrowed, as administrative and marketing expenses, as well as other operating expenses, rose more rapidly; EBITDA rose 7.7%. After higher interest expense and depreciation charges, pretax income was up 4.0%. After taxes at 40.0% in each period, net income was also up 4.0%, to $23,017,000 ($0.76 a share), from $22,125,000 ($0.74, as adjusted).

Stock Performance - 09-OCT-98

In the past 30 trading days, MCS's shares have increased 12%, compared to a 4% fall in the S&P 500. Average trading volume for the past five days was 13,820 shares, compared with the 40-day moving average of 22,567 shares.

Key Stock Statistics

Dividend Rate/Share	0.22	Shareholders	1,700
Shs. outstg. (M)	30.2	Market cap. (B)	$0.266
Avg. daily vol. (M)	0.021	Inst. holdings	41%
Tang. Bk. Value/Share	10.00		
Beta	0.95		

Value of $10,000 invested 5 years ago: $ 17,764

Fiscal Year Ending May 31

	1999	1998	1997	1996	1995	1994
Revenues (Million $)						
1Q	107.4	90.05	77.82	73.57	76.35	64.75
2Q	—	71.18	64.83	59.09	64.74	55.46
3Q	—	71.22	63.21	51.98	59.26	51.75
4Q	—	103.3	97.50	77.66	77.64	74.36
Yr.	—	335.8	303.4	244.3	278.0	246.3
Earnings Per Share ($)						
1Q	0.47	0.44	0.39	0.85	0.31	0.27
2Q	—	0.23	0.23	0.22	0.19	0.15
3Q	—	0.10	0.13	0.09	0.08	0.08
4Q	—	0.18	0.29	0.27	0.24	0.22
Yr.	—	0.94	1.04	1.43	0.82	0.71

Next earnings report expected: mid December

Dividend Data (Dividends have been paid since 1983.)

Amount ($)	Date Decl.	Ex-Div. Date	Stock of Record	Payment Date
0.055	Mar. 20	Apr. 23	Apr. 27	May. 15 '98
0.055	Mar. 20	Apr. 23	Apr. 27	May. 15 '98
0.055	Jul. 08	Jul. 23	Jul. 27	Aug. 17 '98
0.055	Sep. 28	Oct. 22	Oct. 26	Nov. 16 '98

A Division of The **McGraw·Hill** *Companies*

Business Summary - 06-MAR-98

With operations in the lodging, movie theatre and restaurant fields, The Marcus Corp. (MCS) is at once diversified and highly focused. The company strives to bring relaxation and entertainment to patrons in a variety of settings. In each of its businesses, MCS is introducing amenities designed to further enhance the comfort or convenience of its clientele: home delivery for customers of many of its KFC restaurants, tiered stadium seating (which provides unobstructed viewing) for moviegoers, and a host of new conveniences for business travelers who stay at the company's Budgetel Inns. An aggressive expansion program in MCS's motel and theatre divisions promises to double the number of Budgetel Inns to 300 and add 200 theatre screens for a total count of 500 by the end of the century.

At March 5, 1998, MCS's motel division operated or franchised 153 Budgetel Inns in 30 states, and operated five mid-priced, all-suite hotels under the name Woodfield Suites. Hotel and resort operations include three hotels and a resort in Wisconsin, a hotel in Minnesota, a hotel in California and a resort in Michigan. The remaining divisions operate exclusively in the Midwest. At March 5, 1998, the company had 309 theatre screens at 40 locations in Wisconsin and Illinois, and operated 31 KFC (Kentucky Fried Chicken) restaurants

in Wisconsin. MCS also operates a family entertainment center in Appleton, WI.

The company differentiates its Budgetel Inn chain from other limited-service motels by providing conveniences not typically found in this segment of the lodging industry. Under its Business First program introduced in FY 97 (May), MCS added a package of business amenities such as a speakerphone, an ergonomic chair, and a larger desk to 10% of the rooms at every Budgetel location. In addition to expanding its Budgetel chain, the motel division (45% of FY 97 revenues) hopes to have as many as 50 Woodfield Suites (including franchised units) by the end of FY 2002.

MCS's hotels and resorts division (20% of revenues) plans to add 250 rooms to its 500-room Milwaukee Hilton to create Wisconsin's largest hotel.

The theatre division (26% of revenues) is pursuing a growth strategy that emphasizes multi-screen theatres with eight to 20 screens. It will enter Ohio in the spring of 1998 with two 16-screen theatres.

MCS's restaurant division (9% of revenues) now offers home delivery at 14 of its 31 KFCs.

Revenue increases were recorded in all divisions in FY 97. Net income of $30.9 million was down from FY 96's $42.3 million, which included a large gain on the sale of certain restaurant locations.

Per Share Data ($)

(Year Ended May 31)	1998	1997	1996	1995	1994	1993	1992	1991	1990	1989
Tangible Bk. Val.	10.00	9.37	8.51	7.29	6.61	5.96	4.97	4.54	4.16	3.83
Cash Flow	2.03	2.01	2.27	1.62	1.40	1.32	1.21	1.06	0.98	0.92
Earnings	0.94	1.04	1.43	0.82	0.71	0.63	0.52	0.45	0.42	0.39
Dividends	0.33	0.20	0.31	0.15	0.12	0.11	0.10	0.09	0.08	0.07
Payout Ratio	35%	19%	22%	18%	18%	18%	18%	20%	19%	19%
Cal. Yrs.	1997	1996	1995	1994	1993	1992	1991	1990	1989	1988
Prices - High	20⅞	18⅞	18¼	13⅛	12¼	9⅛	5¼	5⅜	5⅞	4⅞
- Low	13½	13⅞	11⅜	10⅝	8¾	4⅞	3⅜	2⅞	4	3⅞
P/E Ratio - High	22	18	13	16	17	14	10	12	14	13
- Low	14	13	8	13	12	8	7	6	10	10

Income Statement Analysis (Million $)

Revs.	311	282	244	263	233	214	204	188	169	158
Oper. Inc.	69.5	68.1	58.9	55.6	48.5	42.5	43.0	36.2	32.6	28.6
Depr.	32.9	28.9	25.1	23.6	20.3	18.2	17.5	15.6	14.5	13.9
Int. Exp.	12.6	12.9	8.7	8.6	7.7	7.3	9.2	9.6	7.4	5.6
Pretax Inc.	47.4	51.2	70.1	40.2	34.7	27.0	22.0	18.9	16.4	15.3
Eff. Tax Rate	40%	40%	40%	40%	39%	39%	40%	38%	34%	35%
Net Inc.	28.4	30.9	42.3	24.1	21.0	16.5	13.3	11.6	10.8	10.0

Balance Sheet & Other Fin. Data (Million $)

Cash	4.7	8.0	15.5	8.8	10.0	15.8	8.1	7.4	10.2	6.4
Curr. Assets	28.4	18.2	31.6	21.6	27.4	33.4	24.7	19.5	22.1	16.7
Total Assets	609	522	455	407	362	309	274	255	231	198
Curr. Liab.	66.0	46.7	50.7	52.3	40.7	37.2	34.0	29.8	24.1	22.2
LT Debt	206	168	127	116	108	79.0	100	96.0	86.0	64.0
Common Eqty.	303	277	251	214	194	174	125	115	107	98.0
Total Cap.	535	468	398	350	318	269	239	225	207	176
Cap. Exp.	116	108	83.7	77.0	75.8	47.2	41.8	39.9	42.4	35.7
Cash Flow	61.3	59.8	67.4	47.7	41.3	34.7	30.8	27.2	25.3	23.9
Curr. Ratio	0.4	0.4	0.6	0.4	0.7	0.9	0.7	0.7	0.9	0.8
% LT Debt of Cap.	38.5	35.9	31.9	33.1	33.9	29.4	41.8	42.8	41.4	36.5
% Net Inc.of Revs.	9.2	11.0	17.3	9.2	9.0	8.1	6.8	6.5	6.4	6.3
% Ret. on Assets	5.0	6.3	9.8	6.3	6.3	5.2	5.0	4.8	5.0	5.3
% Ret. on Equity	9.8	11.7	18.2	11.8	11.4	10.3	11.1	10.6	10.5	10.6

Data as orig. reptd.; bef. results of disc. opers. and/or spec. items. Per share data adj. for stk. divs. as of ex-div. date. Bold denotes diluted EPS (FASB 128). E-Estimated. NA-Not Available. NM-Not Meaningful. NR-Not Ranked.

Office—250 E. Wisconsin Ave., Suite 1700, Milwaukee, WI 53202-4200. **Reincorporated**—in Wisconsin in 1992. **Tel**—(414) 905-1000. **Chrmn, Pres & CEO**—S. H. Marcus. **CFO, Treas & Investor Contact**—Douglas A. Neis (414 905-1100). **Secy**—T. F. Kissinger. **Dirs**—D. M. Gershowitz, T. E. Hoeksema, S. H. Marcus, P. L. Milstein, D. F. McKeithan Jr., B. J. Olson, A. H. Selig, G. R. Slater. **Transfer Agent**—Firstar Trust Co., Milwaukee. **Empl**— 6,800. **S&P Analyst:** Robert J. Izmirlian

Mariner Post-Acute Network   1759Q

NYSE Symbol **MPN**

In S&P SmallCap 600

13-OCT-98

Industry:
Health Care
(Long-Term Care)

Summary: This diversified health care services provider was formed in July 1998 as a result of a merger between Paragon Health Network Inc. and Mariner Health Group Inc.

Quantitative Evaluations

Recent Price • 3⅞
52 Wk Range • 21½-2¾

Yield • Nil
12-Mo. P/E • NM

Outlook
(1 Lowest—5 Highest)
• **4**

Fair Value
• 5¾

Risk
• **Average**

Earn./Div. Rank
• **NR**

Technical Eval.
• **NA**

Rel. Strength Rank
(1 Lowest—99 Highest)
• **3**

Insider Activity
• **Favorable**

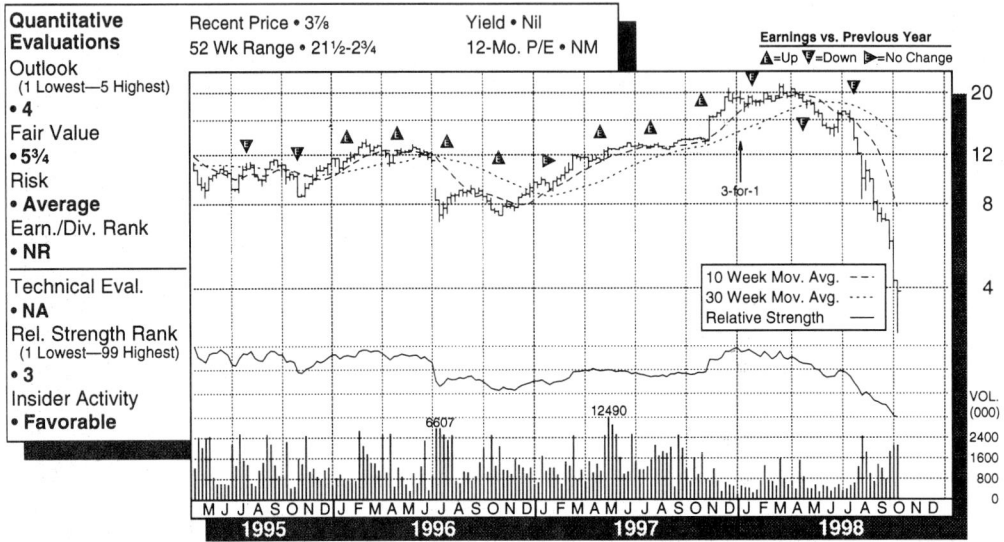

Earnings vs. Previous Year
▲=Up ▼=Down ▶=No Change

10 Week Mov. Avg. ---
30 Week Mov. Avg. ·····
Relative Strength —

Business Profile - 13-OCT-98

This company changed its name to Mariner Post-Acute Network, Inc. from Paragon Health Network, Inc. on July 31, 1998, concurrent with the merger with Mariner Health Group, in a stock-for-stock transaction. MPN is now the second largest provider of long term care in the U.S., with pro forma annual revenues approaching $3 billion. The new company is headquartered in Atlanta, and has over 430 skilled nursing and assisted living facilities with more than 50,000 beds throughout the U.S. In August 1998, the company announced the acquisition of 12 post-acute care facilities in California totaling 1,500 beds.

Operational Review - 13-OCT-98

In the nine months ended June 30, 1998, net revenues rose 64%, year to year, primarily due to revenue from nursing home operations following recent acquisitions. With substantially higher salaries and wages, greater general and administrative expenses, and indirect merger and transition costs of $80.7 million, income from operations fell to $23,640,000 from $75,928,000. After significantly higher interest expense ($83,598,000, up from $16,302,000), and a tax credit of $8,432,000 versus taxes at 41.9%, a net loss of $43.9 million ($1.00 per share, on 27% fewer shares), contrasted with net income of $36.2 million ($0.61, adjusted). Results for the FY 98 period exclude an extraordinary charge of $11.3 million ($0.26 a share).

Stock Performance - 09-OCT-98

In the past 30 trading days, MPN's shares have declined 52%, compared to a 4% fall in the S&P 500. Average trading volume for the past five days was 413,320 shares, compared with the 40-day moving average of 277,759 shares.

Key Stock Statistics

Dividend Rate/Share	Nil	Shareholders	500
Shs. outstg. (M)	71.0	Market cap. (B)	$0.280
Avg. daily vol. (M)	0.348	Inst. holdings	40%
Tang. Bk. Value/Share	NM		
Beta	1.32		

Value of $10,000 invested 5 years ago: $ 5,344

Fiscal Year Ending Sep. 30

	1998	1997	1996	1995	1994	1993
Revenues (Million $)						
1Q	421.6	280.2	270.4	202.1	118.8	92.58
2Q	487.2	285.3	278.1	208.1	122.8	94.42
3Q	494.1	288.4	281.2	215.8	125.6	99.2
4Q	—	286.3	284.8	267.8	131.5	102.7
Yr.	—	1,140	1,114	893.9	498.6	388.9
Earnings Per Share ($)						
1Q	-1.40	0.18	0.18	0.13	0.12	0.10
2Q	0.10	0.21	0.20	0.14	0.15	0.13
3Q	0.17	0.23	0.21	0.09	0.16	0.14
4Q	—	0.12	0.12	0.07	0.16	0.13
Yr.	—	0.74	0.71	0.42	0.59	0.49

Next earnings report expected: late December

Dividend Data

Amount ($)	Date Decl.	Ex-Div. Date	Stock of Record	Payment Date
3-for-1	Nov. 26	Dec. 31	Dec. 15	Dec. 30 '97

A Division of The **McGraw·Hill** Companies

Business Summary - 13-OCT-98

Mariner Post-Acute Network (MPN), is the second largest provider of long term care in the U.S., with pro forma annual revenues approaching $3 billion. The company changed its name from Paragon Health Network, Inc. concurrent with the July 31, 1998, merger with Mariner Health Group, in a stock-for-stock transaction.

The new company is headquartered in Atlanta, and has over 430 skilled nursing and assisted living facilities with more than 50,000 beds throughout the U.S. The company's institutional pharmacy group, American Pharmaceutical Services, operates 43 institutional pharmacies serving more than 1,000 facilities comprising approximately 125,000 beds.

Prism Rehab Systems, the company's contract therapy provider, offers therapy and rehabilitation staffing services to more than 1,000 long-term care facilities.

The Specialty Hospitals group operates 11 long term acute care hospitals. Mariner Specialty Services and Cornerstone Health Management collectively manage more than 100 programs for long-term care providers and acute care hospitals, provide physician management services, and operate more than 50 branches that provide home health, hospice and private duty nursing services.

Contributions to patient revenues in recent years were derived from Medicaid, private pay and Medicare. There is an increasing trend in the percentage of revenues derived from private pay and Medicare sources reflecting the growth in pharmacy and therapy operations.

In August 1998, the company announced the acquisition of 12 post-acute care facilities in California, totaling 1,500 beds. Historically, these facilities had generated annual revenues of about $40 million.

In July 1998, MPN announced the acquisition of four long term acute care hospitals and two acute rehabilitation hospitals comprising approximately 300 beds in Texas, Arizona and Louisiana from Summit Medical Holdings, Ltd.

According to the company, the merger will add value to patients and shareholders immediately through in-sourcing of key services and cross-selling in strategic marketplaces. The company also anticipates achieving synergies, principally from cost savings of approximately $30 million by the end of the first full year of combined operations and $40 million by the end of the following year.

Per Share Data ($)

(Year Ended Sep. 30)	1997	1996	1995	1994	1993	1992	1991	1990	1989	1988
Tangible Bk. Val.	3.05	2.41	2.61	3.36	2.98	2.52	1.88	NA	NA	NA
Cash Flow	1.40	1.35	1.03	1.33	1.02	0.86	0.74	NA	NA	NA
Earnings	0.74	0.71	0.42	0.59	0.49	0.39	0.30	NA	NA	NA
Dividends	Nil	Nil	Nil	Nil	Nil	Nil	NA	NA	NA	NA
Payout Ratio	Nil	Nil	Nil	Nil	Nil	Nil	NA	NA	NA	NA
Prices - High	20¾	13⅝	12¾	11	9¼	7½	NA	NA	NA	NA
- Low	8⅞	6⅞	8⅜	8⅜	5⅛	3⅝	NA	NA	NA	NA
P/E Ratio - High	28	19	30	19	19	19	NA	NA	NA	NA
- Low	12	10	20	14	10	9	NA	NA	NA	NA

Income Statement Analysis (Million $)

	1997	1996	1995	1994	1993	1992	1991	1990	1989	1988
Revs.	1,140	1,114	894	499	389	351	306	NA	NA	NA
Oper. Inc.	137	128	101	56.8	39.7	34.5	28.8	NA	NA	NA
Depr.	39.3	39.2	31.2	23.5	15.0	13.0	11.2	NA	NA	NA
Int. Exp.	21.5	20.1	18.3	10.6	6.9	7.7	6.5	NA	NA	NA
Pretax Inc.	77.5	77.1	46.2	28.8	22.2	17.2	11.0	NA	NA	NA
Eff. Tax Rate	43%	44%	47%	35%	39%	39%	37%	NA	NA	NA
Net Inc.	43.9	43.2	24.2	18.7	13.6	10.5	7.8	NA	NA	NA

Balance Sheet & Other Fin. Data (Million $)

	1997	1996	1995	1994	1993	1992	1991	1990	1989	1988
Cash	14.4	21.4	17.9	8.5	5.8	12.6	0.1	NA	NA	NA
Curr. Assets	287	282	227	105	63.7	64.5	44.4	NA	NA	NA
Total Assets	874	822	731	410	244	226	208	NA	NA	NA
Curr. Liab.	185	181	192	96.4	62.9	57.3	45.1	NA	NA	NA
LT Debt	253	263	182	111	60.0	69.3	84.2	NA	NA	NA
Common Eqty.	375	329	304	154	107	97.3	75.4	NA	NA	NA
Total Cap.	629	592	486	265	167	167	160	NA	NA	NA
Cap. Exp.	37.0	53.4	38.9	91.2	30.9	11.6	NA	NA	NA	NA
Cash Flow	83.2	82.4	55.4	42.2	28.6	23.5	19.1	NA	NA	NA
Curr. Ratio	1.6	1.6	1.2	1.1	1.0	1.1	1.0	NA	NA	NA
% LT Debt of Cap.	40.2	44.4	37.5	41.9	35.7	41.6	52.8	NA	NA	NA
% Net Inc.of Revs.	3.9	3.9	2.7	3.8	3.5	3.0	2.6	NA	NA	NA
% Ret. on Assets	5.2	5.6	3.9	5.4	5.9	4.4	NA	NA	NA	NA
% Ret. on Equity	12.5	13.7	10.2	13.5	13.5	11.2	NA	NA	NA	NA

Data as orig. reptd.; bef. results of disc. opers. and/or spec. items. Per share data adj. for stk. divs. as of ex-div. date. Bold denotes diluted EPS (FASB 128). E-Estimated. NA-Not Available. NM-Not Meaningful. NR-Not Ranked.

Office—1 Ravinia Drive, Suite 1500, Atlanta, GA, 30346. **Tel**—(678) 443-7000. **Chrmn & CEO**—K. B. Pitts. **Vice Chrmn, Pres & COO**—A.W. Stratton. **Exec VP & CFO**—C. B. Carden. **Sr VP & Secy**—S. T. Whittle. **Dirs**—L. M. Berg, G.E. Burleson, P. P. Copses, J.M. Gellert, J. S. Kanter, J.H. Kissick, J. H. Kissick, W. G. Petty, Jr., K. B. Pitts, R. L. Rosen, A.W. Stratton. **Transfer Agent & Registrar**—ChaseMellon Shareholder Services, Dallas. **Incorporated**—in Delaware in 1977; reincorporated in 1998. **Empl**—29,000. **S&P Analyst:** John J. Arege

STANDARD &POOR'S
STOCK REPORTS

Marquette Medical Systems   4529

NASDAQ Symbol **MARQ**

In S&P SmallCap 600

03-OCT-98

Industry:
Health Care (Medical Products & Supplies)

Summary: Marquette is a leading manufacturer of medical equipment systems for diagnostic cardiology, patient monitoring and integration of clinical information.

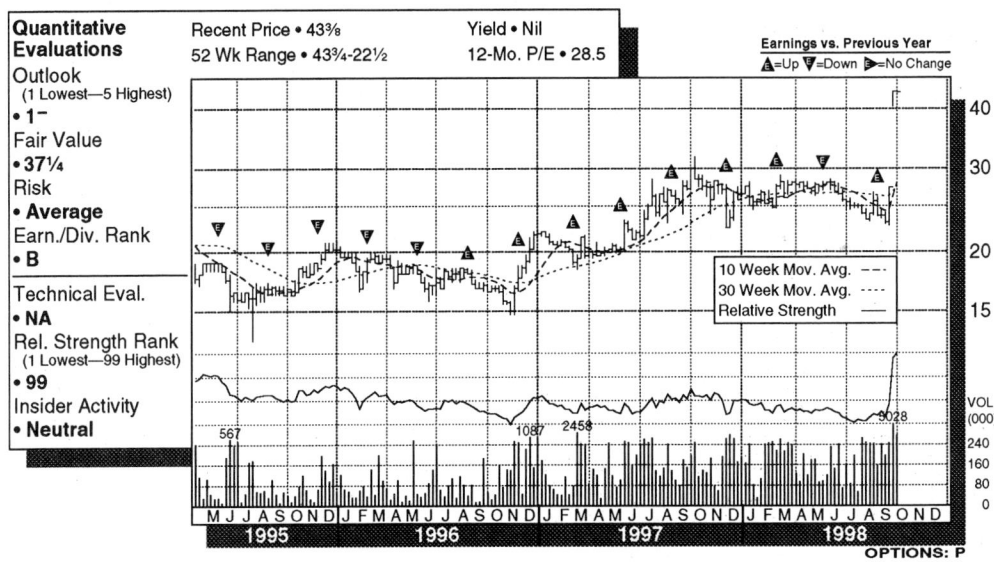

Quantitative Evaluations	
Outlook (1 Lowest—5 Highest)	• **1⁻**
Fair Value	• **37¼**
Risk	• **Average**
Earn./Div. Rank	• **B**
Technical Eval.	• **NA**
Rel. Strength Rank (1 Lowest—99 Highest)	• **99**
Insider Activity	• **Neutral**

Recent Price • 43⅜
52 Wk Range • 43¾-22½

Yield • Nil
12-Mo. P/E • 28.5

Earnings vs. Previous Year
▲=Up ▼=Down ▶=No Change

10 Week Mov. Avg. - - -
30 Week Mov. Avg. - - - -
Relative Strength ——

OPTIONS: P

Business Profile - 29-JUL-98

The company expects its monitoring group to continue to provide it with opportunities for growth, based on a continued strong level of incoming orders, especially for its modular bedside monitors. MARQ believes that ongoing efforts to increase manufacturing efficiencies will enable it to maintain its gross margins even as product mix and geographic mix may cause a shift toward lower gross margins. The company also expects future results to be bolstered by new products currently under development, and by the increased customer focused orientation of its new group operating structure.

Operational Review - 29-JUL-98

Net sales in the fiscal year ended April 30, 1998, rose 6.4% from those of the preceding year, entirely reflecting growth in the monitoring group that stemmed from strong domestic demand, especially for modular bedside monitors. Profitability benefited from a shift toward higher-margin products, especially in the monitoring group, and from a 29% drop in interest expense. Net income climbed 26%, to $26,639,000 ($1.46 a share), from $21,191,000 ($1.27).

Stock Performance - 02-OCT-98

In the past 30 trading days, MARQ's shares have increased 69%, compared to a 7% fall in the S&P 500. Average trading volume for the past five days was 319,540 shares, compared with the 40-day moving average of 207,774 shares.

Key Stock Statistics

Dividend Rate/Share	Nil	Shareholders	600
Shs. outstg. (M)	18.0	Market cap. (B)	$0.779
Avg. daily vol. (M)	0.358	Inst. holdings	43%
Tang. Bk. Value/Share	9.33		
Beta	-0.03		

Value of $10,000 invested 5 years ago: $ 22,532

Fiscal Year Ending Apr. 30

	1999	1998	1997	1996	1995	1994
Revenues (Million $)						
1Q	143.6	132.1	124.8	81.13	76.57	56.72
2Q	—	148.6	136.9	84.51	86.72	64.31
3Q	—	143.7	137.7	110.3	92.97	64.52
4Q	—	153.9	143.9	140.3	85.92	68.25
Yr.	—	578.3	543.3	416.3	342.2	253.8
Earnings Per Share ($)						
1Q	0.30	0.24	0.20	0.00	0.00	0.21
2Q	—	0.38	0.32	0.25	0.34	0.27
3Q	—	0.41	0.37	-1.89	0.38	0.33
4Q	—	0.36	0.40	0.05	0.23	0.35
Yr.	—	1.46	1.29	-1.53	1.21	1.16

Next earnings report expected: mid November

Dividend Data

No cash dividends have been paid.

A Division of The McGraw-Hill Companies

STANDARD
&POOR'S
STOCK REPORTS

Marquette Medical Systems, Inc.

4529

03-OCT-98

Business Summary - 29-JUL-98

The objective of Marquette Medical Systems (MARQ) is to be the premier provider of medical systems for patient monitoring and diagnostic cardiology across the continuum of care. To achieve this objective, the company plans to: enter new care areas, broaden and enhance its existing product line, continue development of clinical information systems, penetrate international markets, and increase recurring revenue streams.

MARQ is a worldwide leader in the development and manufacture of medical equipment and integrated systems for patient monitoring and diagnostic cardiology applications. The company also develops clinical information systems, designed to be integrated with medical equipment, consisting of hardware and software used by integrated health care delivery networks and individual hospitals to electronically acquire, record, store, analyze and distribute patient medical data.

Sales contributions by product line in recent fiscal years (Apr.) were:

	FY 98	FY 97
Cardiology group	31.6%	32.8%
Monitoring group	50.8%	48.0%
Supplies & service	17.6%	19.2%

The company's products are sold in more than 65 countries throughout the world. International markets accounted for 36% of sales in FY 98.

Marquette believes that its ability to offer integrated clinical information systems with patient monitoring and diagnostic cardiology equipment provides it with significant competitive advantages over companies that market only equipment or clinical information systems.

MARQ's diagnostic cardiology products are used to diagnose cardiac disorders through the detection, recording and analysis of electrical signals and other information relating to the heart. Coronary artery disease is the leading cause of death of adult Americans today, and accounts for over 20% of the national health care budget. MARQ estimates that the worldwide market for diagnostic cardiology products is about $1 billion.

Marquette's patient monitoring systems continuously acquire, analyze, store, display and print patient physiological information such as ECGs, pulse rate, blood pressure, temperature, gas measurements, respiration rate and oxygen saturation in the blood. This information provides attending medical personnel a means to continuously evaluate a patient's condition. The company estimates that the worldwide market for patient monitoring systems is about $1.65 billion.

The company manufactures, markets and distributes a broad spectrum of disposable supplies and disposables used mainly in conjunction with its large installed base of patient monitoring systems and diagnostic cardiology products.

Per Share Data ($)

(Year Ended Apr. 30)	1998	1997	1996	1995	1994	1993	1992	1991	1990	1989
Tangible Bk. Val.	9.34	7.20	1.93	NA	NA	NA	2.61	1.90	NA	NA
Cash Flow	2.56	2.63	-0.79	NA	NA	NA	NA	NA	NA	NA
Earnings	1.46	1.29	-1.53	1.21	1.16	1.08	NA	NA	NA	NA
Dividends	Nil	Nil	Nil	NA	NA	NA	NA	NA	NA	NA
Payout Ratio	Nil	Nil	Nil	NA	NA	NA	NA	NA	NA	NA
Cal. Yrs.	1997	1996	1995	1994	1993	1992	1991	1990	1989	1988
Prices - High	31³/₄	22³/₈	NA	NA	NA	23	23¹/₂	NA	NA	NA
- Low	18³/₈	14³/₄	NA	NA	NA	15⁵/₈	16¹/₄	NA	NA	NA
P/E Ratio - High	22	NM	NA	NA	NA	24	29	NA	NA	NA
- Low	13	NM	NA	NA	NA	16	25	NA	NA	NA

Income Statement Analysis (Million $)

	1998	1997	1996	1995	1994	1993	1992	1991	1990	1989
Revs.	578	543	416	NA	NA	NA	NA	NA	NA	NA
Oper. Inc.	69.8	61.0	37.9	NA	NA	NA	NA	NA	NA	NA
Depr.	20.1	22.0	12.0	NA	NA	NA	NA	NA	NA	NA
Int. Exp.	6.0	8.4	4.4	NA	NA	NA	NA	NA	NA	NA
Pretax Inc.	44.0	34.1	-17.0	NA	NA	NA	NA	NA	NA	NA
Eff. Tax Rate	39%	38%	NM	NM	NM	NM	NM	NM	NM	NM
Net Inc.	26.6	21.2	-24.9	NA	NA	NA	NA	NA	NA	NA

Balance Sheet & Other Fin. Data (Million $)

	1998	1997	1996	1995	1994	1993	1992	1991	1990	1989
Cash	5.1	2.7	2.9	NA	NA	NA	NA	NA	NA	NA
Curr. Assets	290	267	261	NA	NA	NA	NA	NA	NA	NA
Total Assets	459	428	432	NA	NA	NA	NA	NA	NA	NA
Curr. Liab.	128	118	128	NA	NA	NA	NA	NA	NA	NA
LT Debt	37.5	57.0	81.3	NA	NA	NA	NA	NA	NA	NA
Common Eqty.	214	183	148	NA	NA	NA	NA	NA	NA	NA
Total Cap.	268	257	251	NA	NA	NA	NA	NA	NA	NA
Cap. Exp.	25.5	18.2	11.4	NA	NA	NA	NA	NA	NA	NA
Cash Flow	46.8	43.2	-12.8	NA	NA	NA	NA	NA	NA	NA
Curr. Ratio	2.3	2.3	2.0	NA	NA	NA	NA	NA	NA	NA
% LT Debt of Cap.	14.0	22.2	32.4	NA	NA	NA	NA	NA	NA	NA
% Net Inc.of Revs.	4.6	3.9	NM	NM	NM	NM	NM	NM	NM	NM
% Ret. on Assets	6.0	4.9	NM	NM	NM	NM	NM	NM	NM	NM
% Ret. on Equity	13.4	12.2	NM	NM	NM	NM	NM	NM	NM	NM

Data as orig. reptd.; bef. results of disc. opers. and/or spec. items. Per share data adj. for stk. divs. as of ex-div. date. Bold denotes diluted EPS (FASB 128). E-Estimated. NA-Not Available. NM-Not Meaningful. NR-Not Ranked.

Office—8200 West Tower Ave., Milwaukee, WI 53223. **Tel**—(414) 355-5000.**Fax**—(414) 355-3790. **Website**—http://www.mei.com**Chrmn**—M. J. Cudahy.**CEO**—F. A. Robertson.**Secy**—G. W. Petersen.**SVP,,CFO, Treas & Investor Contact**—Mary M. Kabacinski.**Dirs**—J. G. Bollinger, M. J. Cudahy, F. G. Luber, M. S. Newman, W. L. Robb, F. A. Robertson. **Transfer Agent & Registrar**—Firstar Trust Co., Milwaukee.**Incorporated**—in Wisconsin in 1965.**Empl**— 2,371. **S&P Analyst:** J. J. Schemitsch

STANDARD &POOR'S

STOCK REPORTS

Marshall Industries

1421M

NYSE Symbol **MI**

In S&P SmallCap 600

03-OCT-98

Industry: Electronics (Component Distributors)

Summary: This company is among the largest U.S. distributors of electronic components and industrial production supplies.

Quantitative Evaluations

Outlook (1 Lowest—5 Highest)
• **1**

Fair Value
• **26**

Risk
• **Low**

Earn./Div. Rank
• **B**

Technical Eval.
• **Bearish** since 5/98

Rel. Strength Rank (1 Lowest—99 Highest)
• **49**

Insider Activity
• **NA**

Recent Price • 23¾
52 Wk Range • 39¾-22

Yield • Nil
12-Mo. P/E • 12.4

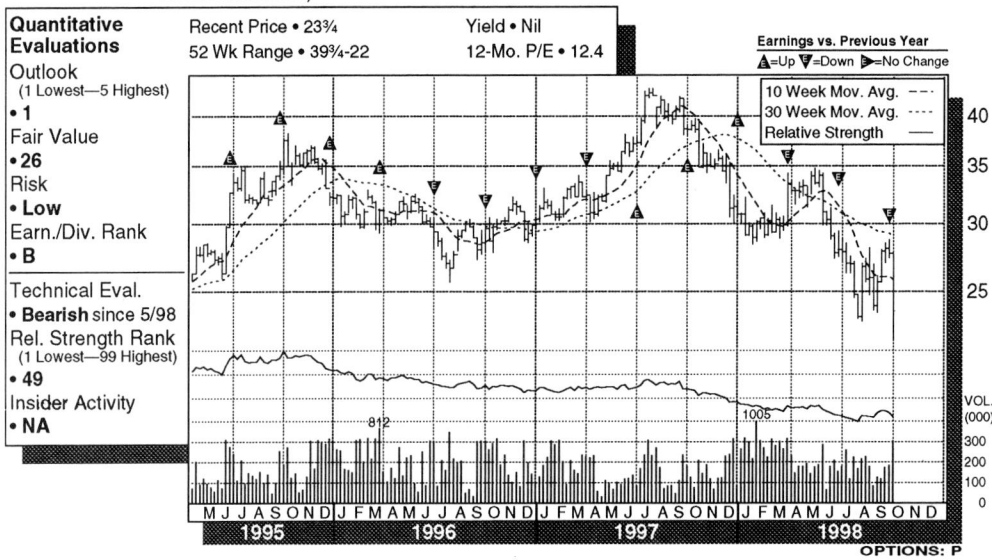

OPTIONS: P

Business Profile - 18-MAR-98

This company focuses on obtaining franchises with the leading manufacturers in product categories that it distributes (semiconductor products; passive components; computer systems and peripherals; and industrial production supplies), in order to meet rising customer demand in the face of product shortages. Key strategic programs now deliver mass-customized and individually made-to-order solutions and on-line access for product information and purchasing. Results in the first half of FY 98 (May) were hurt by a sales shift toward lower margin mass storage and microprocessor products. In January 1998, MI acquired Sterling Electronics Corp., an electronics parts distributor with branches in the U.S. and Canada, for about $162 million.

Operational Review - 18-MAR-98

Net sales in the six months ended November 30, 1997, rose 22%, year to year, largely on increased sales of mass storage and microprocessor products, as the company added new suppliers. Margins narrowed on a higher proportion of sales of low-margin mass storage products and microprocessors, and reduced margins on DRAMs; operating income rose 9.0%. After interest expense of $1.2 million, versus income, and taxes at 42.1% in both periods, net income was up 3.0%, to $18.7 million ($1.11 a share, on 1.9% fewer shares), from $18.1 million ($1.05). Results exclude an extraordinary gain of $0.86 per share in 1997 related to the termination of a joint venture.

Stock Performance - 02-OCT-98

In the past 30 trading days, MI's shares have declined 8%, compared to a 7% fall in the S&P 500. Average trading volume for the past five days was 67,800 shares, compared with the 40-day moving average of 36,677 shares.

Key Stock Statistics

Dividend Rate/Share	Nil	Shareholders	5,000
Shs. outstg. (M)	16.6	Market cap. (B)	$0.395
Avg. daily vol. (M)	0.041	Inst. holdings	81%
Tang. Bk. Value/Share	16.83		
Beta	0.64		

Value of $10,000 invested 5 years ago: $ 12,500

Fiscal Year Ending May 31

	1999	1998	1997	1996	1995	1994
Revenues (Million $)						
1Q	460.9	324.4	269.3	275.9	223.1	199.8
2Q	—	351.2	286.4	295.5	243.8	200.6
3Q	—	368.1	304.0	288.0	261.6	197.6
4Q	—	417.6	325.0	305.4	280.8	224.5
Yr.	—	1,461	1,185	1,165	1,009	822.5
Earnings Per Share ($)						
1Q	0.47	0.55	0.51	0.70	0.50	0.43
2Q	—	0.56	0.55	0.78	0.54	0.50
3Q		0.48	0.58	0.70	0.58	0.45
4Q	—	0.40	0.70	0.68	0.70	0.53
Yr.	—	1.99	2.32	2.86	2.32	1.91

Next earnings report expected: mid December

Dividend Data

No cash dividends have been paid. The stock was split two for one in 1983, 1986 and 1994.

A Division of The McGraw-Hill Companies

Business Summary - 18-MAR-98

Marshall Industries (MI) must listen every day to its customers to anticipate their needs, in order to survive and thrive in an increasingly competitive marketplace. Customers say they need lower costs, higher quality, and faster delivery to deal with shortening product life cycles. As the fifth largest U.S. distributor of electronic components and industrial production supplies, the company must anticipate and master the accelerating forces in its industry. The most sweeping series of changes at MI has come in anticipating the developing importance of supply chain management for its customers. To support these critical engineering requirements, MI provides both manned technical field resources and high-technology capabilities including parametric part number searching, on-line engineering design lab, on-line training, and 24-hour-a-day support.

MI provides suppliers with nationwide coverage of customers in major electronics manufacturing areas of the U.S. and Canada. To its 30,000 customers, MI offers a broad range of franchised, brand name products (more than 125,000) from more than 50 major suppliers, including Advanced Micro Devices, Atmel, Cypress Semiconductor, IBM Technology, Lattice Semiconductor, Lin-

ear Technology, Philips, Siemens, TI, and Xilinx. MI is a major U.S. distributor of Japanese semiconductor products, which accounted for 17% and 23% of total sales in FY 97 (May) and FY 96, respectively. MI also holds a 16% equity position in Sonepar Electronique International, a Paris-based electronics distributor with coverage in 24 countries and alliances that total $800 million in sales.

General product areas include semiconductor products (76% and 73% of revenues in FY 97 and FY 96, respectively), passive components (11% and 11%), computer systems and peripherals (7% and 10%), and industrial production supplies (6% and 6%).

In FY 97, net sales rose 1.7%, to $1.18 billion, from $1.16 billion in FY 96. Net income fell to $39.7 million, from $50.1 million, mainly on a shift in the mix of products sold, with an increase in the sales of mass storage products and microprocessors, which are lower margin products.

In January 1998, MI acquired Sterling Electronics Corp. for about $162 million in cash, plus about $55 million in debt assumption. Sterling, with net income of $9.6 million on sales of $343.8 million in its FY 97 (Mar.), is an international broad-line electronic parts distributor, with 39 branches in the U.S. and Canada.

Per Share Data ($)

(Year Ended May 31)	1998	1997	1996	1995	1994	1993	1992	1991	1990	1989
Tangible Bk. Val.	16.83	21.00	19.10	16.20	13.85	11.90	10.48	9.35	8.32	7.29
Cash Flow	2.54	2.84	3.31	2.75	2.28	1.75	1.51	1.43	1.40	1.40
Earnings	1.99	2.32	2.86	2.32	1.91	1.38	1.13	1.01	1.13	1.16
Dividends	Nil	Nil	Nil	Nil	Nil	Nil	Nil	Nil	Nil	Nil
Payout Ratio	Nil	Nil	Nil	Nil	Nil	Nil	Nil	Nil	Nil	Nil
Cal. Yrs.	1997	1996	1995	1994	1993	1992	1991	1990	1989	1988
Prices - High	43⅛	32⅞	38¼	29½	25	21⅛	13⅜	15⅛	9¾	9½
- Low	30	25⅝	24⅜	20¼	16⅞	12¾	10	8½	7	6¾
P/E Ratio - High	22	14	13	13	13	15	12	15	9	8
- Low	15	11	9	9	9	9	9	8	6	6

Income Statement Analysis (Million $)

	1998	1997	1996	1995	1994	1993	1992	1991	1990	1989
Revs.	1,461	1,185	1,165	1,009	823	653	575	583	544	533
Oper. Inc.	75.0	76.1	94.2	79.0	65.4	48.0	41.2	40.1	41.6	43.8
Depr.	9.2	8.8	7.9	7.6	6.3	6.5	6.6	7.0	4.9	4.4
Int. Exp.	7.9	1.4	2.7	3.1	1.9	2.0	2.7	5.3	4.2	4.3
Pretax Inc.	58.3	68.6	85.3	69.5	56.3	39.5	31.9	28.7	33.3	36.0
Eff. Tax Rate	43%	42%	41%	42%	41%	40%	40%	40%	40%	41%
Net Inc.	33.3	39.7	50.1	40.4	33.2	23.9	19.3	17.3	20.1	21.4

Balance Sheet & Other Fin. Data (Million $)

	1998	1997	1996	1995	1994	1993	1992	1991	1990	1989
Cash	4.8	1.7	2.2	3.5	3.7	1.6	1.8	1.9	2.0	1.8
Curr. Assets	642	469	398	348	314	275	210	200	194	180
Total Assets	854	540	473	423	364	331	268	254	250	224
Curr. Liab.	206	138	114	93.8	84.8	67.6	53.2	48.8	57.9	48.9
LT Debt	246	50.0	25.0	45.2	34.7	54.5	36.2	47.0	51.5	40.5
Common Eqty.	400	349	330	279	239	203	178	158	141	135
Total Cap.	648	402	359	329	279	263	215	205	192	175
Cap. Exp.	12.2	2.7	5.3	2.9	1.8	3.2	6.4	7.2	16.3	7.1
Cash Flow	42.5	48.5	57.9	48.0	39.5	30.3	25.9	24.3	25.0	25.8
Curr. Ratio	3.1	3.4	3.5	3.7	3.7	4.1	3.9	4.1	3.4	3.7
% LT Debt of Cap.	37.9	12.4	7.0	13.7	12.5	20.7	16.9	22.9	26.8	23.1
% Net Inc.of Revs.	2.3	3.4	4.3	4.0	4.0	3.7	3.4	3.0	3.7	4.0
% Ret. on Assets	4.8	7.8	11.2	10.3	9.5	8.0	7.4	6.8	8.8	10.1
% Ret. on Equity	8.9	11.7	15.6	15.6	14.9	12.5	11.4	11.5	15.2	17.3

Data as orig. reptd.; bef. results of disc. opers. and/or spec. items. Per share data adj. for stk. divs. as of ex-div. date. Bold denotes diluted EPS (FASB 128). E-Estimated. NA-Not Available. NM-Not Meaningful. NR-Not Ranked.

Office—9320 Telstar Ave., El Monte, CA 91731-2895. **Tel**—(626) 307-6000. **Website**—http://www.marshall.com **Chrmn**—G. S. Marshall. **Pres & CEO**—R. Rodin. **VP-Fin, CFO, Secy & Investor Contact**—Henry W. Chin. **Dirs**—R. D. Bentley, R. C. Colyear, J. Fribourg, L. Hoffman, G. S. Marshall, J. Menendez, R. G. Rinehart, R. Rodin, H. C. White. **Transfer Agent & Registrar**—First Union National Bank, Charlotte, NC. **Incorporated**—in California in 1954. **Empl**—1,400. **S&P Analyst**: L. A. Olive.

STANDARD &POOR'S
STOCK REPORTS

Material Sciences

1432

NYSE Symbol **MSC**

In S&P SmallCap 600

10-OCT-98

Industry: Chemicals (Specialty)

Summary: MSC produces coil-coated and composite materials, electroplated sheet steel, and metallized, coated and laminated films.

Quantitative Evaluations

Outlook (1 Lowest—5 Highest)
• **NA**

Fair Value
• **NA**

Risk
• **Average**

Earn./Div. Rank
• **B**

Technical Eval.
• **Bearish** since 8/98

Rel. Strength Rank (1 Lowest—99 Highest)
• **60**

Insider Activity
• **NA**

Recent Price • 7⅞
52 Wk Range • 15⅜-6½

Yield • Nil
12-Mo. P/E • 20.7

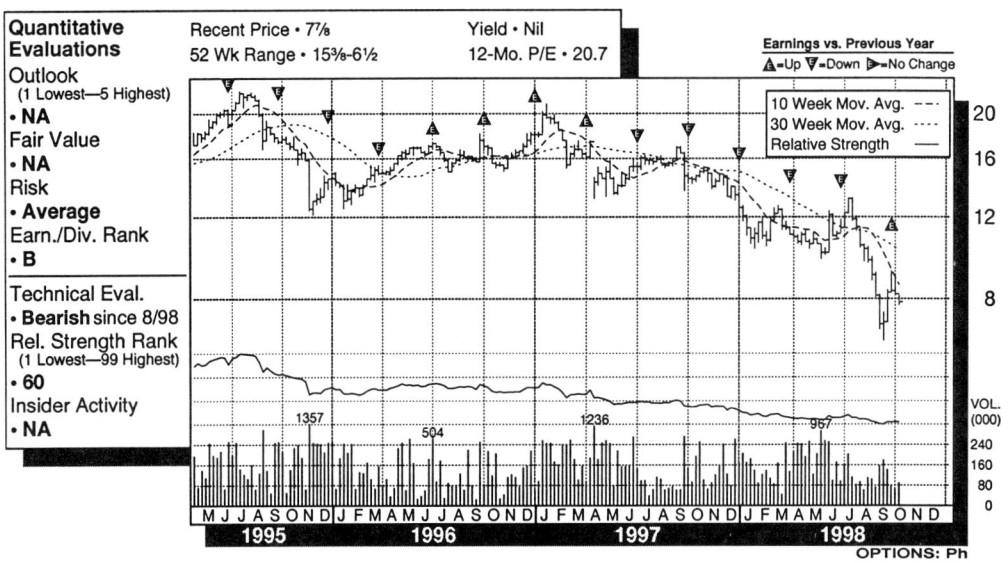

Earnings vs. Previous Year
▲=Up ▼=Down ▷=No Change

10 Week Mov. Avg. - - -
30 Week Mov. Avg. ·······
Relative Strength ——

OPTIONS: Ph

Business Profile - 08-JUL-98

In June 1998, Sequa Corp. (Nasdaq: SQAA), an aerospace, chemical and automobile products company, purchased an 8.8% stake in MSC. It was reported that this could lead to merger or acquisition talks between the two parties, as MSC provides specialty coatings for steel and plastics, while Sequa's precoat metals unit also specializes in applying protective coating to steel and aluminum coil. In December 1997, MSC acquired Colorstrip, Inc., a West Coast hot-dip galvanizing and coil coating business with $195 million in annual sales, for $127 million. The transaction expanded MSC's product line and markets, and the company expected the inclusion of Colorstrip to be accretive to earnings in FY 99 (Feb.).

Operational Review - 08-JUL-98

Net sales in the three months ended May 31, 1998, advanced 54%, year to year, reflecting contributions from Colorstrip, and growth in specialty films, coil coating and electrogalvanizing; same-store sales, excluding Colorstrip, rose 1.6%. Gross margins narrowed, and, with higher SG&A expense and interest expense, net income fell 36%, to $1,638,000 ($0.11 a share), from $2,562,000 ($0.17).

Stock Performance - 09-OCT-98

In the past 30 trading days, MSC's shares have declined 3%, compared to a 4% fall in the S&P 500. Average trading volume for the past five days was 17,700 shares, compared with the 40-day moving average of 22,464 shares.

Key Stock Statistics

Dividend Rate/Share	Nil	Shareholders	1,000
Shs. outstg. (M)	15.4	Market cap. (B)	$0.121
Avg. daily vol. (M)	0.018	Inst. holdings	58%
Tang. Bk. Value/Share	7.72		
Beta	0.96		

Value of $10,000 invested 5 years ago: $ 7,745

Fiscal Year Ending Feb. 28

	1999	1998	1997	1996	1995	1994
Revenues (Million $)						
1Q	112.9	73.10	68.88	60.41	58.80	41.62
2Q	119.2	70.54	70.42	58.65	59.42	47.66
3Q	—	75.11	69.66	58.02	56.80	48.28
4Q	—	101.4	69.06	59.07	52.62	50.15
Yr.	—	320.2	278.0	236.2	227.7	187.7
Earnings Per Share ($)						
1Q	**0.11**	0.17	0.26	0.20	0.27	0.17
2Q	**0.10**	0.11	0.07	0.23	0.20	0.21
3Q	—	0.14	0.27	-0.04	0.30	0.19
4Q	—	Nil	0.24	0.16	0.24	0.22
Yr.	—	**0.42**	1.04	0.55	1.10	0.79

Next earnings report expected: mid December

Dividend Data

No cash dividends have been paid. The shares were split three for two in 1994 and 1992. A new poison pill shareholder rights plan was adopted in 1996.

A Division of The McGraw·Hill Companies

Material Sciences Corporation

Business Summary - 08-JUL-98

This company makes a range of special materials, from solar control window film to "quiet steel" composites that can silence the valves on a Ford Explorer. Specular, its film-and-metal laminate for fluorescent lighting fixtures, uses the unique reflective properties of pure silver to produce the same amount of light with far fewer bulbs, reducing energy costs. Cutting across the various laminating and coating operations conducted by Material Sciences Corp. (MSC) is its continuous roll-to-roll process, a manufacturing technique in which the trailing end of a coil of material in process is attached to the leading end of a new coil, eliminating the need to stop or slow down production.

The company's products and processes offer energy savings and environmental advantages to customers in the automotive, appliance, energy conservation and building and construction industries. In its laminates and composites and specialty films groups, MSC is primarily a manufacturer and marketer of its own proprietary products. These higher value-added specialty products address the needs of faster-growing markets by displacing older, less effective technologies. In its coil coating and electrogalvanizing groups, the company generally acts as a toll coater, processing customer metal for a fee, without taking ownership of the metal. MSC estimates that there are 85 companies operating coil coating lines in North America.

MSC's disc brake noise dampers are multilayer composites of coated metal and other materials that reduce brake noise. The market for these materials developed as brake manufacturers moved away from asbestos to noisier semi-metallic brake linings. The company sees significant opportunities for growth in the largely untapped replacement market. In addition, MSC's polycore composite "sandwiches" help reduce noise and vibration in a wide variety of products.

Specialty films include solar control and safety window films and sputter coated films for paper copier photoreceptor belts.

Coil coating is a continuous and highly automated process for painting sheet metal before it is fabricated into a final product. In late 1997, MSC expanded into the western U.S. market by acquiring Colorstrip, Inc., a hot-dipped galvanizing and coil coating line operating in the San Francisco Bay area, for $129 million. MSC's electrogalvanizing business is conducted through a joint venture with two steel makers.

Per Share Data ($) (Year Ended Feb. 28)	1998	1997	1996	1995	1994	1993	1992	1991	1990	1989
Tangible Bk. Val.	7.60	7.86	7.08	6.75	5.81	5.00	3.57	2.71	2.29	3.89
Cash Flow	1.74	1.96	1.26	1.67	1.27	1.15	1.20	0.93	-2.27	1.26
Earnings	0.42	1.04	0.55	1.10	0.79	0.67	0.63	0.42	-2.71	0.70
Dividends	Nil	Nil	Nil	Nil	Nil	Nil	Nil	Nil	Nil	Nil
Payout Ratio	Nil	Nil	Nil	Nil	Nil	Nil	Nil	Nil	Nil	Nil
Cal. Yrs.	1997	1996	1995	1994	1993	1992	1991	1990	1989	1988
Prices - High	21	18 1/4	22 3/8	17 5/8	17 3/8	10 5/8	7 7/8	7 5/8	7 3/4	8 7/8
- Low	12	12 1/2	12 1/8	13 5/8	9 3/4	7 1/4	4 3/8	4 1/8	6 3/8	5 1/8
P/E Ratio - High	50	33	29	16	22	16	12	18	NM	13
- Low	29	23	16	13	12	11	7	10	NM	7
Income Statement Analysis (Million $)										
Revs.	320	278	236	228	188	156	143	139	153	172
Oper. Inc.	36.2	41.2	29.1	35.2	25.6	20.3	18.6	16.6	8.9	20.7
Depr.	20.4	14.3	11.1	8.8	7.3	6.5	6.4	5.7	4.9	6.1
Int. Exp.	6.1	2.2	0.6	0.1	0.1	0.3	1.2	2.5	2.6	2.0
Pretax Inc.	10.5	26.4	13.8	27.2	19.0	14.1	11.7	7.8	-39.0	13.0
Eff. Tax Rate	39%	39%	38%	39%	38%	37%	39%	40%	NM	39%
Net Inc.	6.5	16.2	8.5	16.7	11.8	8.9	7.1	4.7	-30.4	7.9
Balance Sheet & Other Fin. Data (Million $)										
Cash	3.6	2.1	3.4	5.8	11.9	23.5	Nil	0.9	3.5	2.1
Curr. Assets	126	75.0	66.7	61.8	62.3	62.1	35.1	40.5	49.4	47.9
Total Assets	418	254	200	172	152	129	101	104	111	130
Curr. Liab.	65.5	43.9	43.0	39.1	33.2	24.4	25.8	23.2	30.7	23.8
LT Debt	188	54.8	16.8	6.9	8.9	10.7	13.8	29.4	42.4	37.4
Common Eqty.	141	133	118	105	86.5	73.3	42.0	30.9	25.5	56.6
Total Cap.	341	200	146	123	108	96.0	69.0	73.0	78.0	105
Cap. Exp.	19.1	55.6	27.5	29.4	49.4	7.6	8.4	7.6	23.0	9.7
Cash Flow	26.8	30.6	19.6	25.5	19.1	15.4	13.5	10.4	-25.5	14.2
Curr. Ratio	1.9	1.7	1.6	1.6	1.9	2.5	1.4	1.7	1.6	2.0
% LT Debt of Cap.	55.1	27.4	11.5	5.6	8.2	11.2	20.1	40.4	54.6	35.7
% Net Inc.of Revs.	2.0	5.8	3.6	7.4	6.3	5.7	5.0	3.4	NM	4.6
% Ret. on Assets	1.9	7.2	4.6	10.3	8.5	7.0	6.9	4.3	NM	6.3
% Ret. on Equity	4.7	12.9	7.6	17.4	14.9	14.2	19.3	16.5	NM	15.0

Data as orig. reptd.; bef. results of disc. opers. and/or spec. items. Per share data adj. for stk. divs. as of ex-div. date. Bold denotes diluted EPS (FASB 128). E-Estimated. NA-Not Available. NM-Not Meaningful. NR-Not Ranked.

Office—2300 E. Pratt Blvd., Elk Grove Village, IL 60007. **Tel**—(847) 439-8270. **Website**—http://www.matsci.com **Chrmn, Pres & CEO**—G. G. Nadig. **EVP & COO**—T. E. Moore. **SVP, CFO & Secy**—J. J. Waclawik Sr. **Contr**—D. J. DeNeve. **VP & Investor Contact**—Robert J. Mataya. **Dirs**—J. B. Cohen, R. J. Decyk, E. W. Emmerich, G. R. Evans, E. F. Heizer Jr., G. G. Nadig, I. P. Pochter, H. B. Witt. **Transfer Agent & Registrar**—Mellon Securities Transfer Services, Ridgefield Park, NJ. **Incorporated**—in Delaware in 1983 to succeed to the business of a company founded in 1971. **Empl**— 1,269. **S&P Analyst:** S.S.

03-OCT-98

Industry:
Chemicals (Specialty)

Summary: This company is a leading specialty chemical manufacturer of liquid and powder resins for the coatings industry and of composite polymers for the fiberglass industry.

Quantitative Evaluations		
Recent Price • 20⅛	Yield • Nil	
52 Wk Range • 28⅜-19¾	12-Mo. P/E • 12.8	

Outlook
(1 Lowest—5 Highest)
• **5+**

Fair Value
• **31½**

Risk
• **Low**

Earn./Div. Rank
• **NR**

Technical Eval.
• **Bearish** since 5/97

Rel. Strength Rank
(1 Lowest—99 Highest)
• **54**

Insider Activity
• **NA**

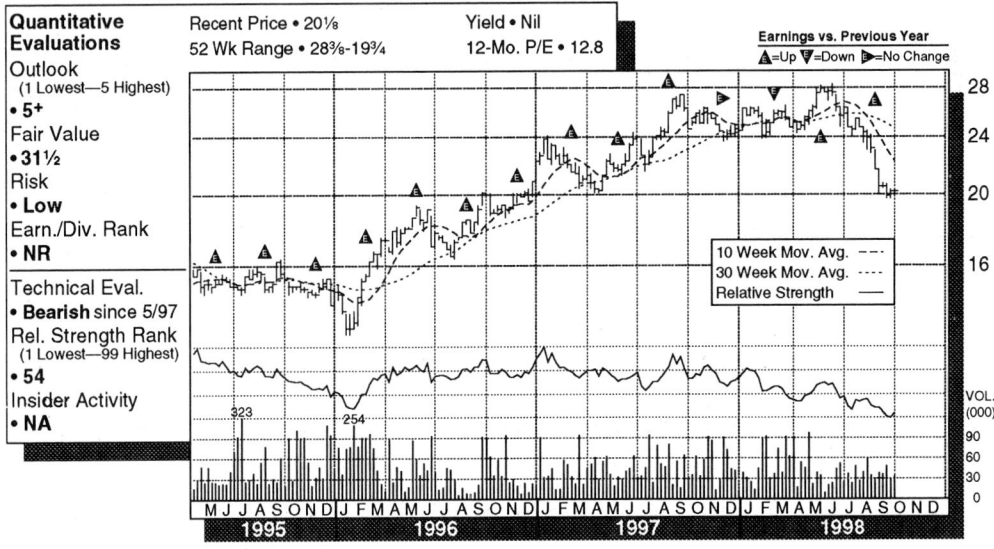

Earnings vs. Previous Year
▲=Up ▼=Down ▷=No Change

10 Week Mov. Avg. – – –
30 Week Mov. Avg. ·······
Relative Strength ——

Business Profile - 01-SEP-98

This former subsidiary of Valspar Corp. became an independent company in April 1994, when it was spun off to Valspar shareholders. In 1995, it substantially streamlined its product line, and, to capitalize on a trend toward environmentally friendly products, separated its rapidly growing powder business from its liquid coatings business. In August 1997, MWT acquired Syntech S.p.A., an Italy-based liquid and powder resins concern. This transaction is expected to increase MWT's global presence and lead to improved performance across all business units in 1998. In April 1998, MWT acquired Accurate Coatings and Dispersions, Inc., a manufacturer of dispersed pigments for the coatings industry. In August 1998, the company decided to close its Chicago Heights, IL manufacturing facility, and to writedown its investment in the McWhorter Thailand joint venture.

Operational Review - 01-SEP-98

Revenues in the first nine months of FY 98 (Oct.) rose 43%, year to year, primarily reflecting the August 1007 acquisition of Syntech S.p.A., and the April 1998 acquisition of Accurate Coatings and Dispersions. Margins narrowed, reflecting increased SG&A expenses. Following sharply higher interest expense, pretax income was down 2.3%. After taxes at 29.0% (reflecting a beneficial change in Italian income tax law), versus 37.3%, net income rose 11%, to $12,421,000 ($1.19 a share), from $11,222,000 ($1.08).

Stock Performance - 02-OCT-98

In the past 30 trading days, MWT's shares have declined 13%, compared to a 7% fall in the S&P 500. Average trading volume for the past five days was 6,560 shares, compared with the 40-day moving average of 7,851 shares.

Key Stock Statistics

Dividend Rate/Share	Nil	Shareholders	1,400
Shs. outstg. (M)	10.4	Market cap. (B)	$0.209
Avg. daily vol. (M)	0.008	Inst. holdings	48%
Tang. Bk. Value/Share	2.92		
Beta	NA		

Value of $10,000 invested 5 years ago: NA

Fiscal Year Ending Oct. 31

	1998	1997	1996	1995	1994	1993
Revenues (Million $)						
1Q	98.12	71.53	65.24	67.31	25.39	55.90
2Q	115.6	80.88	76.92	79.12	63.11	67.70
3Q	125.8	85.58	87.14	82.97	79.24	74.70
4Q	—	93.47	86.62	82.00	74.59	70.70
Yr.	—	331.5	315.9	311.4	242.3	269.0
Earnings Per Share ($)						
1Q	**0.12**	0.24	0.20	0.17	-0.03	0.01
2Q	**0.61**	0.37	0.31	0.26	0.23	0.23
3Q	**0.47**	0.46	0.42	0.30	0.29	0.25
4Q	—	0.40	0.40	0.29	0.28	0.44
Yr.	—	1.47	1.32	1.02	0.78	0.93

Next earnings report expected: mid November

Dividend Data

No dividends have been paid. A "poison pill" stock purchase rights plan was adopted at the time of the company's spinoff from Valspar.

Business Summary - 01-SEP-98

McWhorter Technologies, spun off from Valspar Corp. in April 1994, is a leading U.S. manufacturer of surface coating resins and also makes resins used in the reinforced fiberglass plastics industry. In September 1996, MWT completed the joint venture McWhorter Technologies Europe, which provided the company an opportunity to enter the European market in phases. McWhorter intends to identify additional channels of distribution outside North America and grow internally and through acquisitions.

Another step in that direction came with the August 1997 acquisition of Syntech S.p.A., an Italy-based liquid and powder resins company with 1996 sales of approximately $85 million. The addition of Syntech gave the company an expanded presence in Europe, Asia and North America. Syntech's growing European and North American powder resins business is being combined with MWT's current powder resins and curatives to create a significant global powder coatings supplier. The company believes it is now well positioned in North America and Europe to serve the needs of multinational coatings companies.

The company's products include alkyds, copolymers, polyurethanes, polyester resins, unsaturated polyesters, powder resins, acrylic emulsions, polyvinyl acetate emulsions, solution acrylics, curing agents and a number of small-volume specialty resins.

Customers require a variety of resins to meet application and product performance characteristics. Alkyd resins and copolymers, MWT's largest product category, have uses from house paint to protective coatings for machinery to special-purpose coatings such as traffic striping paints and automotive refinish coatings. Polyester resins are used for coil coated metal buildings and metal office furniture. Acrylic emulsion resins, used in trim paints and exterior applications, meet or exceed environmental regulations because of their low solvent content. Powder resins emit no solvents, and are the fastest growing segment of the industrial coatings industry.

The paint and coatings industry is a mature market, growing at an estimated 2% annually, about the same rate as durable goods. MWT believes that there are more than 800 active companies purchasing resins and selling paint and coatings for a variety of end uses. While many paint and coating manufacturers have captive resin manufacturing capabilities, with increasing costs of product reformulation and updating resin manufacturing processes to comply with environmental regulations, there has been a shift toward outsourcing. MWT believes this trend will give it additional sales opportunities in the future.

MWT's business is somewhat seasonal, with sales volume traditionally highest in the fiscal third quarter.

Per Share Data ($)

(Year Ended Oct. 31)	1997	1996	1995	1994	1993	1992	1991	1990	1989	1988
Tangible Bk. Val.	5.36	8.00	6.66	5.72	4.94	NA	NA	NA	NA	NA
Cash Flow	2.46	2.19	1.74	1.35	1.70	NA	NA	NA	NA	NA
Earnings	1.47	1.32	1.02	0.78	0.93	NA	NA	NA	NA	NA
Dividends	Nil	Nil	Nil	Nil	Nil	Nil	Nil	Nil	Nil	Nil
Payout Ratio	Nil	Nil	Nil	Nil	Nil	Nil	Nil	Nil	Nil	Nil
Prices - High	27³/₈	20¹/₈	16³/₈	19¹/₄	NA	NA	NA	NA	NA	NA
- Low	20¹/₈	12⁷/₈	14	13¹/₄	NA	NA	NA	NA	NA	NA
P/E Ratio - High	19	15	16	25	NA	NA	NA	NA	NA	NA
- Low	14	10	14	17	NA	NA	NA	NA	NA	NA

Income Statement Analysis (Million $)

	1997	1996	1995	1994	1993	1992	1991	1990	1989	1988
Revs.	331	316	311	242	269	NA	NA	NA	NA	NA
Oper. Inc.	38.4	34.0	28.7	24.1	26.7	NA	NA	NA	NA	NA
Depr.	10.4	9.1	7.9	6.2	8.3	NA	NA	NA	NA	NA
Int. Exp.	2.2	1.6	2.3	1.1	2.0	NA	NA	NA	NA	NA
Pretax Inc.	25.0	23.2	18.6	14.0	16.3	NA	NA	NA	NA	NA
Eff. Tax Rate	38%	41%	41%	40%	38%	NA	NA	NA	NA	NA
Net Inc.	15.4	13.8	11.1	8.4	10.1	NA	NA	NA	NA	NA

Balance Sheet & Other Fin. Data (Million $)

	1997	1996	1995	1994	1993	1992	1991	1990	1989	1988
Cash	3.9	1.0	1.9	1.4	1.6	NA	NA	NA	NA	NA
Curr. Assets	107	71.4	60.5	67.1	30.7	NA	NA	NA	NA	NA
Total Assets	259	153	138	139	103	NA	NA	NA	NA	NA
Curr. Liab.	82.2	46.9	38.5	40.2	13.2	NA	NA	NA	NA	NA
LT Debt	57.2	13.1	19.1	30.1	34.1	NA	NA	NA	NA	NA
Common Eqty.	91.7	79.7	71.5	62.1	53.6	NA	NA	NA	NA	NA
Total Cap.	171	103	97.3	95.6	88.4	NA	NA	NA	NA	NA
Cap. Exp.	11.2	7.0	6.5	4.7	NA	NA	NA	NA	NA	NA
Cash Flow	25.8	22.9	19.0	14.6	18.5	NA	NA	NA	NA	NA
Curr. Ratio	1.3	1.5	1.6	1.7	2.3	NA	NA	NA	NA	NA
% LT Debt of Cap.	33.4	13.4	19.7	31.5	38.6	NA	NA	NA	NA	NA
% Net Inc.of Revs.	4.7	4.4	3.6	3.5	3.8	NA	NA	NA	NA	NA
% Ret. on Assets	7.5	9.5	8.0	NA	NA	NA	NA	NA	NA	NA
% Ret. on Equity	18.0	18.3	16.6	NA	NA	NA	NA	NA	NA	NA

Data as orig. reptd.; bef. results of disc. opers. and/or spec. items. Per share data adj. for stk. divs. as of ex-div. date. Bold denotes diluted EPS (FASB 128). E-Estimated. NA-Not Available. NM-Not Meaningful. NR-Not Ranked.

Office—400 E. Cottage Place, Carpentersville, IL 60110. **Tel**—(847) 428-2657. **Chrmn & CEO**—J. R. Stevenson. **Pres, COO**—Jeffrey M. Nodland. **VP & CFO & Secy**—Louise M. Tonozzi-Frederick. **Dirs**—M. L. Collins, E.M. Giles, D. G. Harris, J. G. Johnson Jr., J. M. Nodland, J. R. Stevenson, H. F. Tomfohrde III. **Transfer Agent & Registrar**—Wachovia Bank of North Carolina, Winston-Salem. **Incorporated**—in Delaware in 1993. **Empl**—791. **S&P Analyst:** E. Hunter

MedImmune, Inc.   4567T

NASDAQ Symbol **MEDI**

In S&P SmallCap 600

03-OCT-98

Industry:
Health Care (Drugs - Generic & Other)

Summary: This company develops, manufactures and markets therapeutics and vaccines to treat and prevent certain infectious diseases and cancer.

Quantitative Evaluations

Recent Price • 66
52 Wk Range • 69½-31

Yield • Nil
12-Mo. P/E • NM

Outlook (1 Lowest—5 Highest)
• **NA**

Fair Value
• **NA**

Risk
• **Average**

Earn./Div. Rank
• **NR**

Technical Eval.
• **Bullish** since 6/97

Rel. Strength Rank (1 Lowest—99 Highest)
• **96**

Insider Activity
• **Neutral**

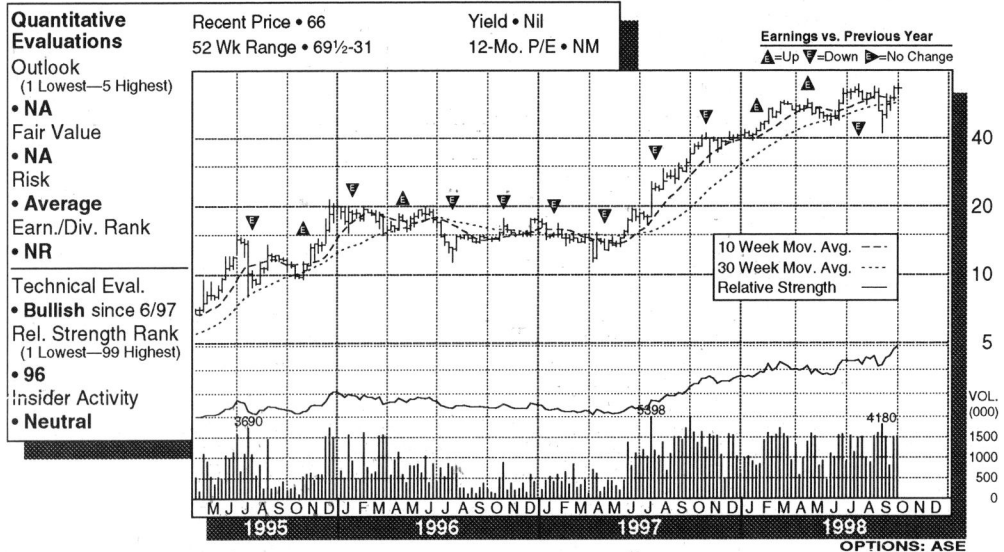

Earnings vs. Previous Year
▲=Up ▼=Down ▷=No Change

10 Week Mov. Avg. ---
30 Week Mov. Avg. ····
Relative Strength —

OPTIONS: ASE

Business Profile - 17-SEP-98

In June 1998, MedImmune received marketing approval from the FDA for Synagis, for the prevention of serious RSV disease in certain high risk infants. The company currently markets two other products: CytoGam, for the prevention of cytomegalovirus disease associated with kidney transplantation; and RespiGam, for the prevention of respiratory syncytial virus (RSV) infection in infants. In addition, MedImmune has four products undergoing clinical trials, and several product candidates in development. The company has received $30 million in milestone payments and $5 million equity investment from SmithKline Beecham, associated with the initiation of an alliance to develop MEDI's HPV vaccine candidates and for regulatory approval of Synagis.

Operational Review - 17-SEP-98

Revenues in the six months ended June 30, 1998, increased to $83.9 million, from $16.5 million in the year-earlier period, reflecting strong sales of RespiGam and CytoGam, and $30 million in milestone payments from SmithKline Beecham. Results were hurt by one-time charges totaling $18 million related to buying certain royalty obligations and reserving against inventories of RespiGam. However, SG&A costs rose 50%, and R&D expenses were down substantially due to the completion of a clinical trial. The net loss narrowed to $5,363,000 ($0.20 a share, on 19% more shares), from $26,531,000 ($1.20).

Stock Performance - 02-OCT-98

In the past 30 trading days, MEDI's shares have increased 4%, compared to a 7% fall in the S&P 500. Average trading volume for the past five days was 354,540 shares, compared with the 40-day moving average of 389,554 shares.

Key Stock Statistics

Dividend Rate/Share	Nil	Shareholders	400
Shs. outstg. (M)	26.6	Market cap. (B)	$ 1.8
Avg. daily vol. (M)	0.293	Inst. holdings	80%
Tang. Bk. Value/Share	4.13		
Beta	1.29		

Value of $10,000 invested 5 years ago: $ 28,695

Fiscal Year Ending Dec. 31

	1998	1997	1996	1995	1994	1993
Revenues (Million $)						
1Q	59.34	10.14	11.43	5.93	3.28	2.08
2Q	24.59	6.41	6.93	7.86	4.00	2.35
3Q	—	10.66	4.78	6.66	3.89	2.71
4Q	—	53.76	17.96	6.99	7.41	7.94
Yr.	—	80.96	41.10	27.44	18.86	15.08
Earnings Per Share ($)						
1Q	0.44	-0.65	-0.08	-0.37	-0.31	-0.27
2Q	-0.70	-0.55	-0.33	-0.32	-0.29	-0.25
3Q	—	-0.57	-0.47	-0.22	-0.29	-0.26
4Q	—	0.18	-0.50	-0.49	-0.41	-0.17
Yr.	—	-1.59	-1.41	-1.41	-1.29	-0.96

Next earnings report expected: late October

Dividend Data

Cash dividends have never been paid.

A Division of The McGraw-Hill Companies

STANDARD
&POOR'S
STOCK REPORTS

MedImmune, Inc.

4567T
03-OCT-98

Business Summary - 17-SEP-98

MedImmune focuses on developing and marketing products for infectious diseases and transplantation medicine. Since the start of operations in 1988, the company has sought to establish an initial commercial base using proven technologies and targeting well-understood diseases to support longer-term product development. This strategy has relied on the advancement of an internally developed pipeline of product candidates and on in-licensing products from third parties.

In June 1998, the company received marketing approval from the U.S. Food and Drug Administration for Synagis, a humanized monoclonal antibody that has demonstrated an ability to neutralize RSV. MedImmune submitted a regulatory application the European authorities in August 1998, and expects to submit an application for regulatory approval in Canada before the end of 1998.

MEDI is currently marketing two products, CytoGam and RespiGam Intravenous. The company has established core competencies in transplantation and infectious diseases, and has a research and development portfolio which includes five products undergoing clinical trials, and a number of product candidates in preclinical development.

Cytomegalovirus (CMV) is a major cause of illness and death in patients with weakened immune systems associated with organ transplantation or immunosuppressive diseases such as AIDS. MedImmune's first commercial product for CMV infections, CytoGam, is an injectable immune globulin made from human plasma containing high concentrations of naturally occurring antibodies to CMV. CytoGam is sold for the prevention of disease caused by CMV infection in kidney transplant patients. In 1997, sales of CytoGam totaled $20.3 million, up from $18.4 million in 1996.

As a result of the FDA approval and expected market acceptance of Synagis, the company reserved $9.2 million against its RespiGam inventory, as it does not expect any further product sales to result from this inventory. RespiGam was launched for sale in January 1996 for the prevention of respiratory syncytial virus (RSV) in infants with bronchopulmonary dysplasia or a history of prematurity. RSV causes annual epidemics of bronchiolitis and pneumonia and can be fatal. RespiGam is also injectable immune globulin, but contains naturally occurring antibodies to RSV. Sales of RespiGam were $45.0 million in 1997, and $17.3 million in 1996.

The company has a royalty agreement with American Home Products (AHP) on sales of RespiGam. AHP paid $4.5 million to MEDI as a milestone payment after the U.S. FDA approved RespiGam. Other research agreements include those with Human Genome Sciences for development of a Haemophilus influenzae therapeutic and Baxter Healthcare Corp., which will market RespiGam overseas.

Per Share Data ($)

(Year Ended Dec. 31)	1997	1996	1995	1994	1993	1992	1991	1990	1989	1988
Tangible Bk. Val.	1.66	3.34	2.47	2.34	3.63	3.49	4.15	-12.08	NA	NA
Cash Flow	-1.48	-1.32	-1.31	-1.19	-0.88	-0.46	0.13	-0.94	-0.64	-0.32
Earnings	-1.59	-1.41	-1.41	-1.29	-0.96	-0.51	0.11	-1.02	-0.69	-0.33
Dividends	Nil	Nil	Nil	Nil	Nil	Nil	Nil	Nil	NA	NA
Payout Ratio	Nil	Nil	Nil	Nil	Nil	Nil	Nil	Nil	NA	NA
Prices - High	43¹/₂	20¹/₈	21¹/₂	13¹/₄	32⁵/₈	50¹/₂	55	NA	NA	NA
- Low	11³/₈	11³/₈	3¹/₂	3³/₈	10	12¹/₂	10	NA	NA	NA
P/E Ratio - High	NM	NM	NM	NM	NM	NM	NM	NA	NA	NA
- Low	NM	NM	NM	NM	NM	NM	NM	NM	NM	NM

Income Statement Analysis (Million $)

	1997	1996	1995	1994	1993	1992	1991	1990	1989	1988
Revs.	81.0	41.1	27.4	18.9	15.1	13.1	14.0	3.3	1.1	0.1
Oper. Inc.	-34.7	-31.1	-22.5	-18.5	-13.9	-3.9	0.8	-3.6	-2.4	-1.3
Depr.	2.7	1.8	1.6	1.5	1.1	0.7	0.4	0.3	0.2	0.1
Int. Exp.	3.5	2.3	0.3	0.3	0.3	0.3	0.1	0.3	0.2	0.0
Pretax Inc.	-36.9	-29.5	-22.7	-18.8	-13.2	-8.4	1.7	-4.1	-2.8	-1.3
Eff. Tax Rate	NM	NM	NM	NM	NM	NM	2.20%	Nil	Nil	Nil
Net Inc.	-36.9	-29.5	-22.7	-18.8	-13.2	-8.5	1.6	-4.1	-2.8	-1.3

Balance Sheet & Other Fin. Data (Million $)

	1997	1996	1995	1994	1993	1992	1991	1990	1989	1988
Cash	30.0	115	38.0	22.5	44.4	46.9	55.8	4.6	0.5	1.6
Curr. Assets	100	133	49.0	32.3	51.9	52.6	59.6	6.0	0.5	NA
Total Assets	170	164	57.3	44.7	61.2	60.2	65.3	7.5	1.8	2.7
Curr. Liab.	43.7	20.0	11.0	7.8	5.7	11.1	7.9	5.9	1.9	NA
LT Debt	85.3	70.9	2.0	2.1	2.2	2.2	2.2	0.1	0.3	0.1
Common Eqty.	40.5	72.9	43.8	34.2	53.0	46.8	55.1	-18.6	-0.5	2.2
Total Cap.	126	144	45.8	36.3	55.2	48.9	57.3	1.1	-0.2	2.4
Cap. Exp.	36.7	22.7	1.1	1.4	3.8	2.2	4.2	0.3	0.1	0.6
Cash Flow	-34.1	-27.7	-21.1	-17.3	-12.2	-7.7	1.9	-3.8	-2.6	-1.2
Curr. Ratio	2.3	6.7	4.4	4.1	9.2	4.7	7.5	1.0	0.2	NA
% LT Debt of Cap.	67.7	49.3	4.3	5.8	4.0	4.4	3.8	12.0	NM	6.4
% Net Inc.of Revs.	NM	NM	NM	NM	NM	NM	11.6	NM	NM	NM
% Ret. on Assets	NM	NM	NM	NM	NM	NM	1.6	NM	NM	NM
% Ret. on Equity	NM	NM	NM	NM	NM	NM	NM	NM	NM	NM

Data as orig. reptd.; bef. results of disc. opers. and/or spec. items. Per share data adj. for stk. divs. as of ex-div. date. Bold denotes diluted EPS (FASB 128). E-Estimated. NA-Not Available. NM-Not Meaningful. NR-Not Ranked.

Office—35 W. Watkins Mill Rd., Gaithersburg, MD 20878. **Tel**—(301) 417-0770. **Website**—http://www.medimmune.com **Chrmn & CEO**—W. T. Hockmeyer. **Pres & COO**—M. D. Booth.**Vice-Chrmn & CFO**—D. M. Mott. **Investor Contact**—Mark E. Kaufmann. **Dirs**—M. J. Barrett, M. D. Booth, J. H. Cavanaugh, B. H. Franklin, W. T. Hockmeyer, L. C. Hoff, G. S. Macklin, D. M. Mott, F. H. Top Jr. **Transfer Agent & Registrar**—American Stock Transfer & Trust Co., NYC. **Incorporated**—in Delaware in 1987. **Empl**— 344. **S&P Analyst:** Richard Joy

MedQuist Inc   4567V
NASDAQ Symbol **MEDQ**
In S&P SmallCap 600

17-OCT-98

Industry: Services (Data Processing)

Summary: This company is a leading national provider of electronic transcription and health care information management solutions.

Quantitative Evaluations

Outlook (1 Lowest—5 Highest)
- **NA**

Fair Value
- **NA**

Risk
- **High**

Earn./Div. Rank
- **B**

Technical Eval.
- **NA**

Rel. Strength Rank (1 Lowest—99 Highest)
- **99**

Insider Activity
- **Neutral**

Recent Price • 33
52 Wk Range • 33⅛-11⅜

Yield • Nil
12-Mo. P/E • 76.9

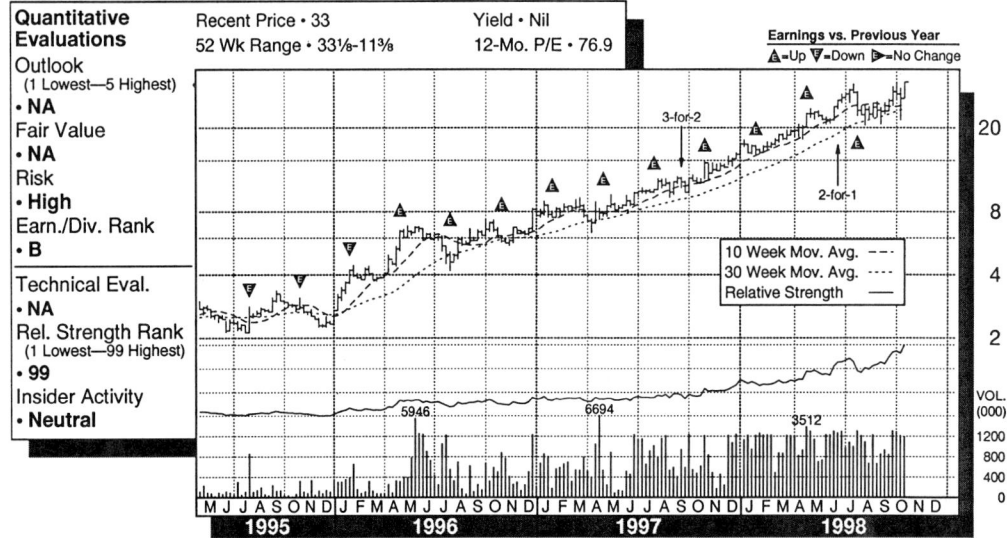

Earnings vs. Previous Year
▲=Up ▼=Down ▶=No Change

- 10 Week Mov. Avg. ‑ ‑ ‑
- 30 Week Mov. Avg. ·····
- Relative Strength ——

Business Profile - 12-OCT-98

The company's strategy is to expand existing client relationships with hospital medical record departments and to penetrate the direct care departments at hospitals; pursue new clients such as health maintenance organizations, out-patient clinics and physician practice groups; create value added services for its clients through relationships with developers and end users of emerging technologies such as voice-recognition, data mining and outcomes analysis and Internet-based telecommunications; and pursue acquisitions of other transcription companies.

Operational Review - 12-OCT-98

Revenues in the first half of 1998 advanced 46%, year to year, reflecting additional revenues generated by new and existing clients as well as medical transcription acquisitions. Margins widened on the higher volume, and despite $750,000 of non-recurring merger costs, pretax income climbed 49%. After taxes at 38.3%, versus 38.7%, net income was up 50%, to $5,535,000 ($0.23 a share) from $3,693,000 ($0.16).

Stock Performance - 16-OCT-98

In the past 30 trading days, MEDQ's shares have increased 38%, compared to a 8% rise in the S&P 500. Average trading volume for the past five days was 237,560 shares, compared with the 40-day moving average of 263,805 shares.

Key Stock Statistics

Dividend Rate/Share	Nil	Shareholders	100
Shs. outstg. (M)	23.1	Market cap. (B)	$0.764
Avg. daily vol. (M)	0.351	Inst. holdings	74%
Tang. Bk. Value/Share	1.73		
Beta	1.34		

Value of $10,000 invested 5 years ago: $ 149,714

Fiscal Year Ending Dec. 31

	1998	1997	1996	1995	1994	1993
Revenues (Million $)						
1Q	27.40	18.62	13.98	10.43	5.80	8.20
2Q	32.21	20.19	14.37	10.81	11.70	8.50
3Q	—	21.90	15.51	11.54	14.30	7.40
4Q	—	23.88	17.62	12.35	14.61	5.00
Yr.	—	84.59	61.48	45.13	46.35	29.10
Earnings Per Share ($)						
1Q	0.12	0.08	0.05	Nil	0.03	0.04
2Q	0.10	0.08	0.01	0.02	0.05	0.05
3Q	—	0.09	0.06	0.04	0.06	0.08
4Q	—	0.10	0.07	0.03	0.06	0.03
Yr.	—	0.34	0.20	0.10	0.19	0.21

Next earnings report expected: late October

Dividend Data

Amount ($)	Date Decl.	Ex-Div. Date	Stock of Record	Payment Date
2-for-1	May. 11	Jun. 16	Jun. 01	Jun. 15 '98

A Division of The McGraw-Hill Companies

STANDARD
&POOR'S
STOCK REPORTS

MedQuist Inc

4567V
17-OCT-98

Business Summary - 12-OCT-98

Having sold its outpatient health care businesses over the past several years, MedQuist Inc., following several acquisitions, is now a leading national provider of electronic transcription and data management services to the health care industry.

Using its proprietary software, open architecture environment and network of more than 2,800 transcriptionists, the company converts free-form medical dictation into electronically formatted patient records that health care providers use in connection with patient care and for other administrative purposes. Its customized outsourcing services enable clients to improve the accuracy of transcribed medical reports, reduce report turnaround times, shorten billing cycles, and reduce overhead and other costs.

The company provides clients with its Medical Transcription System (MTS), an integrated transcription and document management system based on proprietary software. MedQuist customizes MTS to address initial data capture, conversion of data into electronic format, editing of data and routing of electronically formatted reports to the client's host computer. The company also offers the Dictation Tracking System, which enables clients to track the status of particular patient data and transcribed reports at any time, and can be used as an integral management tool to monitor physician timeliness in the dictation, review and sign-off process.

MedQuist integrates proprietary software with digital dictation equipment, a health care provider's host system and its network of more than 2,800 transcriptionists to provide customized solutions for hospitals and other health care providers. The company captures and stores free-form medical dictation, professionally transcribes the dictation into accurate reports, and electronically receives, reviews and distributes final reports to clients by up-loading them into the client's computer system for placement into a patient's medical record.

The company's client base includes more than 800 hospitals and other health care organizations and physician practice groups. In 1997, hospital medical records departments accounted for 68% of revenues, other hospital departments 22%, HMOs, out-patient clinics and other health care providers 8%, and physician practice groups 2%.

Between May and July 1998, the company acquired all of the outstanding shares of Digital Dictation, Inc. for 912,000 MEDQ common shares. In September 1998, the company said it signed a definitive agreement to acquire MRC Group Inc., a national provider of medical transcription services, for 8.5 million MEDQ common shares.

Per Share Data ($)

(Year Ended Dec. 31)	1997	1996	1995	1994	1993	1992	1991	1990	1989	1988
Tangible Bk. Val.	1.35	1.13	NM	NM	NM	NM	0.38	NA	NA	NA
Cash Flow	0.56	0.65	0.69	0.56	0.51	0.67	0.52	NA	NA	NA
Earnings	0.34	0.20	0.10	0.19	0.20	0.18	0.17	NA	NA	NA
Dividends	Nil	Nil	Nil	Nil	Nil	Nil	Nil	Nil	Nil	Nil
Payout Ratio	Nil	Nil	Nil	Nil	Nil	Nil	Nil	Nil	Nil	Nil
Prices - High	17⅝	8⅜	3⅜	3	2⅝	2½	NA	NA	NA	NA
- Low	6⅜	2¾	2⅛	1½	1⁵/₁₆	1½	NA	NA	NA	NA
P/E Ratio - High	52	42	34	15	12	13	NA	NA	NA	NA
- Low	19	13	21	7	6	8	NA	NA	NA	NA

Income Statement Analysis (Million $)

	1997	1996	1995	1994	1993	1992	1991	1990	1989	1988
Revs.	84.6	61.5	45.1	46.3	29.1	27.4	22.5	NA	NA	NA
Oper. Inc.	17.7	12.3	8.7	7.4	3.1	5.3	3.7	NA	NA	NA
Depr.	5.1	3.6	4.0	2.3	1.9	2.1	1.2	NA	NA	NA
Int. Exp.	0.2	1.6	3.7	2.8	1.4	0.6	0.5	NA	NA	NA
Pretax Inc.	12.4	7.0	1.0	2.4	4.0	2.7	2.0	NA	NA	NA
Eff. Tax Rate	39%	40%	42%	40%	54%	44%	41%	NA	NA	NA
Net Inc.	7.6	4.2	0.6	1.4	1.9	1.5	1.2	NA	NA	NA

Balance Sheet & Other Fin. Data (Million $)

	1997	1996	1995	1994	1993	1992	1991	1990	1989	1988
Cash	12.3	8.9	1.8	2.4	2.5	2.2	0.9	NA	NA	NA
Curr. Assets	33.0	23.5	13.3	14.9	9.0	10.1	5.9	NA	NA	NA
Total Assets	90.8	74.3	58.1	55.1	29.6	30.6	11.1	NA	NA	NA
Curr. Liab.	10.3	5.1	8.4	11.9	6.9	4.5	2.5	NA	NA	NA
LT Debt	1.4	1.7	33.3	30.7	12.4	13.9	4.0	NA	NA	NA
Common Eqty.	76.3	65.7	15.0	10.7	9.1	12.4	5.0	NA	NA	NA
Total Cap.	80.0	68.6	48.9	42.2	21.7	25.9	8.5	NA	NA	NA
Cap. Exp.	4.6	3.2	0.7	1.0	0.9	2.0	1.6	NA	NA	NA
Cash Flow	12.7	7.8	4.6	3.7	3.7	3.6	2.4	NA	NA	NA
Curr. Ratio	3.2	4.6	1.6	1.3	1.3	2.2	2.3	NA	NA	NA
% LT Debt of Cap.	1.8	2.5	68.1	72.6	57.3	53.9	46.9	NA	NA	NA
% Net Inc.of Revs.	9.0	6.8	1.3	3.1	6.4	5.5	5.1	NA	NA	NA
% Ret. on Assets	9.2	6.3	1.1	3.4	6.1	7.2	NA	NA	NA	NA
% Ret. on Equity	10.7	10.4	4.7	14.6	17.3	17.4	NA	NA	NA	NA

Data as orig. reptd.; bef. results of disc. opers. and/or spec. items. Per share data adj. for stk. divs. as of ex-div. date. Bold denotes diluted EPS (FASB 128). E-Estimated. NA-Not Available. NM-Not Meaningful. NR-Not Ranked.

Office—Five Greentree Centre, Suite 311, Marlton, NJ 08053. **Tel**—(609) 596-8877. **Website**—http://www.medquist.com **Chrmn, Pres & CEO**—D. A. Cohen. **VP, CFO & Treas**—J. R. Emery. **Dirs**—W. T. Carson, Jr., J. T. Casey, R. J. Censits, D. A. Cohen, J. F. Conway, J. A. Donohue, J. R. Emshoff, T. J. Mulligan, A. F. Ruttenberg, R. T. Stack, J. H. Underwood. **Transfer Agent & Registrar**—American Stock Transfer & Trust Co., NYC. **Incorporated**—in New Jersey in 1987. **Empl**— 857. **S&P Analyst:** Stephen R. Biggar

Men's Wearhouse   4569M
NASDAQ Symbol **SUIT**
In S&P SmallCap 600

03-OCT-98

Industry:
Retail (Special-ty-Apparel)

Summary: One of the largest off-price specialty retailers of men's tailored business attire, this company operates more than 400 stores, many of which are in California and Texas.

Quantitative Evaluations

Outlook
(1 Lowest—5 Highest)
• **5**

Fair Value
• **35**

Risk
• **High**

Earn./Div. Rank
• **B+**

Technical Eval.
• **NA**

Rel. Strength Rank
(1 Lowest—99 Highest)
• **13**

Insider Activity
• **Neutral**

Recent Price • 18½
52 Wk Range • 36⅞–14¾

Yield • Nil
12-Mo. P/E • 18.5

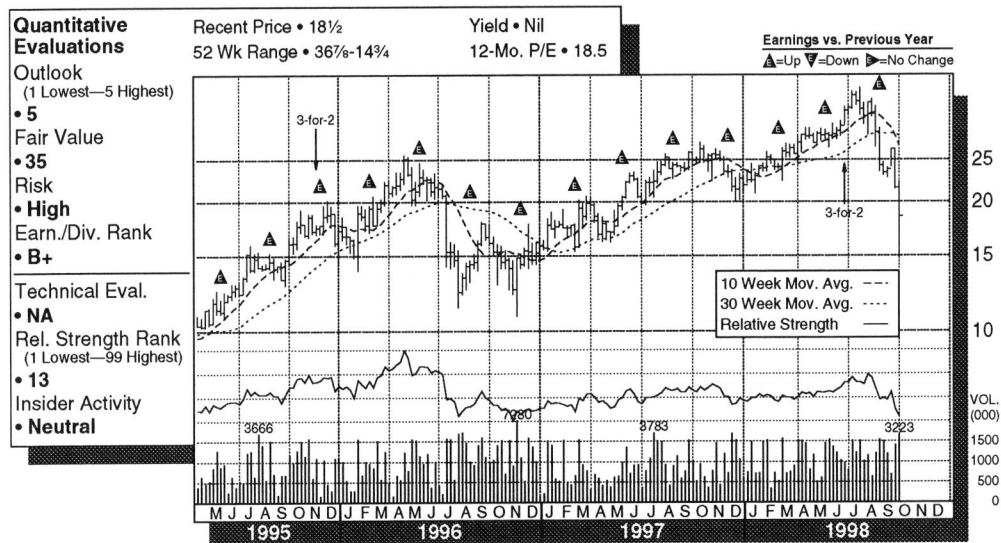

Business Profile - 25-AUG-98

This specialty retailer operates more than 400 stores, emphasizing apparel and footwear for men, at prices which the company believes are generally below the regular prices of traditional department and specialty stores. Most of SUIT's stores are part of its flagship Men's Wearhouse chain, which places an emphasis on tailored business attire. The price of suits at this chain generally ranges from $199 to $499. Also, SUIT has a smaller Value Priced Clothing (VPC) division, with about 28 stores, which addresses the market for a more price-sensitive consumer. Suits at VPC stores generally are priced from $99 to $199. Also, in August 1998, SUIT signed a letter of intent to acquire Moores Retail Group, a retailer of 112 men's apparel stores (largely in Canada).

Operational Review - 25-AUG-98

Net sales for the six months ended August 1, 1998, increased 26%, year to year, boosted by more stores and a 12.9% rise in comparable-store sales. Operating profit was up 52%, and after a 13% decline in interest expense, pretax profit increased 57%. After taxes at 41.3% in both periods, net income also rose 57%, to $14,732,000 ($0.43 a share, diluted, on more shares), from $9,372,000 ($0.30).

Stock Performance - 02-OCT-98

In the past 30 trading days, SUIT's shares have declined 36%, compared to a 7% fall in the S&P 500. Average trading volume for the past five days was 644,520 shares, compared with the 40-day moving average of 301,621 shares.

Key Stock Statistics

Dividend Rate/Share	Nil	Shareholders	200
Shs. outstg. (M)	33.3	Market cap. (B)	$0.616
Avg. daily vol. (M)	0.338	Inst. holdings	69%
Tang. Bk. Value/Share	6.62		
Beta	1.32		

Value of $10,000 invested 5 years ago: $ 49,952

Fiscal Year Ending Jan. 31

	1999	1998	1997	1996	1995	1994
Revenues (Million $)						
1Q	170.9	130.6	103.7	81.36	63.93	44.01
2Q	162.9	133.9	98.89	85.71	67.20	50.21
3Q	—	146.3	110.3	92.86	73.32	56.18
4Q	—	220.2	170.7	146.4	112.7	90.00
Yr.	—	631.1	483.6	406.3	317.1	240.4
Earnings Per Share ($)						
1Q	**0.20**	0.13	0.10	0.07	0.06	0.04
2Q	**0.23**	0.17	0.13	0.10	0.08	0.06
3Q	—	0.17	0.12	0.10	0.08	0.06
4Q	—	**0.40**	0.33	0.27	0.21	0.16
Yr.	—	**0.87**	0.67	0.55	0.42	0.32

Next earnings report expected: mid November

Dividend Data

Amount ($)	Date Decl.	Ex-Div. Date	Stock of Record	Payment Date
3-for-2	Jun. 02	Jun. 22	Jun. 12	Jun. 19 '98

A Division of The McGraw-Hill Companies

Business Summary - 25-AUG-98

The Men's Wearhouse is one of the largest U.S. off-price retailers of men's tailored business attire. It has grown from its one store in Houston, TX, in 1973, to 396 stores in 37 states and the District of Columbia as of January 31, 1998. This included 371 Men's Wearhouse stores and 25 stores which were part of its newer Value Priced Clothing (VPC) business. Of all the stores operated by SUIT, about 37% were located in Texas or California. In FY 98 (Jan.), 71% of net sales were attributable to tailored apparel, down from 72% in FY 97.

SUIT's expansion strategy includes opening traditional stores in existing and new markets, and increasing sales and profitability in existing markets. Also, in August 1998, SUIT signed a letter of intent to acquire Moores Retail Group Inc., which operates 112 men's apparel stores, including 104 in Canada. SUIT would issue about 2.4 million common shares, and also assume about $87 million (Can.) of debt, which SUIT expects to refinance. SUIT intends to account for the acquisition as a pooling of interests.

The Men's Wearhouse stores target middle- to upper-middle-income men, and offer designer brand name and private label merchandise at prices that SUIT believes are typically 20% to 30% below the regular retail prices of traditional department and specialty stores. SUIT's merchandise, which it considers conservative, includes suits, sport coats, slacks, outerwear, dress shirts, shoes and accessories. Suits are generally offered in a price range of $199 to $499. In 1995, SUIT expanded its inventory to include "business casual" merchandise. In doing so, SUIT could seek to meet increased demand for such product resulting from a trend toward more relaxed dress codes in the workplace.

SUIT launched its VPC business in late 1996 to address the market for more price-sensitive customers. VPC stores generally offer suits that range in price from $99 to $199. Through its VPC business, SUIT is seeking to integrate and develop three acquisitions made between January 1997 and February 1998. This process is expected to include a move toward a common average store size, ranging from 10,000 sq. ft. to 15,000 sq. ft., with hours of operation from Friday through Sunday only in most markets.

SUIT's advertising expenditures in the fiscal year ended January 1998 totaled $38 million. SUIT advertises principally on television and radio.

Starting the day after Christmas, Men's Wearhouse has a once-a-year sale that runs through January. During this period, prices on many items are reduced 20% to 50% from everyday prices. This sale reduces SUIT stock for the arrival of the new season's merchandise.

Per Share Data ($)

(Year Ended Jan. 31)	1998	1997	1996	1995	1994	1993	1992	1991	1990	1989
Tangible Bk. Val.	9.97	5.07	4.39	2.97	2.13	1.54	1.34	NA	NA	NA
Cash Flow	1.94	1.06	0.85	0.67	0.53	0.38	0.31	0.26	0.22	NA
Earnings	0.87	0.67	0.55	0.42	0.32	0.24	0.19	0.16	0.14	0.14
Dividends	Nil	Nil	Nil	Nil	Nil	Nil	Nil	Nil	Nil	Nil
Payout Ratio	Nil	Nil	Nil	Nil	Nil	Nil	Nil	Nil	Nil	Nil
Cal. Yrs.	1997	1996	1995	1994	1993	1992	1991	1990	1989	1988
Prices - High	27½	25⅝	20⅛	15½	14½	5¼	NA	NA	NA	NA
- Low	15⅜	10⅞	8	7	4¾	2½	NA	NA	NA	NA
P/E Ratio - High	32	38	37	37	45	22	NA	NA	NA	NA
- Low	18	16	15	17	15	11	NA	NA	NA	NA

Income Statement Analysis (Million $)

Revs.	631	484	406	317	240	170	133	105	80.0	57.0
Oper. Inc.	68.3	50.7	40.0	29.5	21.4	14.4	11.0	8.9	7.2	NA
Depr.	16.8	12.6	9.4	7.1	5.6	3.6	2.6	2.1	1.5	NA
Int. Exp.	3.6	3.4	2.5	1.8	1.1	1.0	1.5	1.4	1.0	NA
Pretax Inc.	49.2	36.0	28.1	20.6	14.8	9.8	6.9	5.4	4.7	NA
Eff. Tax Rate	41%	41%	41%	41%	41%	40%	39%	38%	37%	NA
Net Inc.	28.9	21.1	16.5	12.1	8.7	5.9	4.2	3.4	2.9	2.8

Balance Sheet & Other Fin. Data (Million $)

Cash	59.9	34.1	2.5	1.2	1.6	2.4	1.1	1.8	NA	NA
Curr. Assets	278	208	145	115	83.1	56.9	39.8	32.5	NA	NA
Total Assets	379	295	204	160	112	78.7	54.7	43.7	30.2	22.2
Curr. Liab.	95.0	71.5	56.2	46.8	40.4	28.6	18.9	18.1	NA	NA
LT Debt	57.5	57.5	4.7	24.6	10.8	8.9	14.8	9.8	6.5	3.7
Common Eqty.	220	159	137	84.9	57.9	38.4	18.3	14.1	10.8	7.9
Total Cap.	278	217	142	110	68.7	47.4	33.1	24.0	17.3	11.6
Cap. Exp.	27.4	26.2	22.5	23.7	12.6	10.6	5.1	3.6	3.6	2.2
Cash Flow	45.7	33.7	25.4	19.2	14.3	9.5	6.8	5.5	4.5	NA
Curr. Ratio	2.9	2.9	2.6	2.5	2.1	2.0	2.1	1.8	NA	NA
% LT Debt of Cap.	20.6	26.5	3.3	22.4	15.7	18.8	44.7	41.0	37.5	31.7
% Net Inc.of Revs.	4.6	4.4	4.1	3.8	3.6	3.5	3.1	3.2	3.7	4.9
% Ret. on Assets	8.6	8.5	9.1	8.7	8.8	7.9	8.5	9.1	11.2	15.3
% Ret. on Equity	15.2	14.3	14.9	16.6	27.5	18.9	25.7	26.9	31.5	43.3

Data as orig. reptd.; bef. results of disc. opers. and/or spec. items. Per share data adj. for stk. divs. as of ex-div. date. Bold denotes diluted EPS (FASB 128). E-Estimated. NA-Not Available. NM-Not Meaningful. NR-Not Ranked.

Offices—5803 Glenmont Dr., Houston, TX 77081; 40650 Encyclopedia Circle, Fremont, CA 94538. **Tels**—(713) 592-7200; (510) 657-9821. **Website**—www.menswearhouse.com **Chrmn & CEO**—G. Zimmer. **Pres**—David H. Edwab. **EVP**—R. E. Goldman. **Dirs**—R. Brutoco, D. H. Edwab, R. E. Goldman, H. M. Levy, M. L. Ray, S. I. Stein, G. Zimmer, J. E. Zimmer, R. E. Zimmer. **Transfer Agent & Registrar**—American Stock Transfer & Trust Co., NYC. **Incorporated**—in Texas in 1974. **Empl**— 6,000. **S&P Analyst:** Tom Graves, CFA

Mentor Corp. 4570
Nasdaq Symbol **MNTR**
In S&P SmallCap 600

10-OCT-98

Industry:
Health Care (Medical Products & Supplies)

Summary: This company makes products for plastic surgery, urology and ophthalmology, including implantable devices, diagnostic and surgical instruments and disposable products.

S&P Opinion: Hold (★★★)

Recent Price • 11	Yield • 0.9%
52 Wk Range • 41-9⅜	12-Mo. P/E • 12.1

Quantitative Evaluations

Outlook
(1 Lowest—5 Highest)
• **5**

Fair Value
• **28¼**

Risk
• **Average**

Earn./Div. Rank
• **B**

Technical Eval.
• **Bearish** since 2/98

Rel. Strength Rank
(1 Lowest—99 Highest)
• **20**

Insider Activity
• **Neutral**

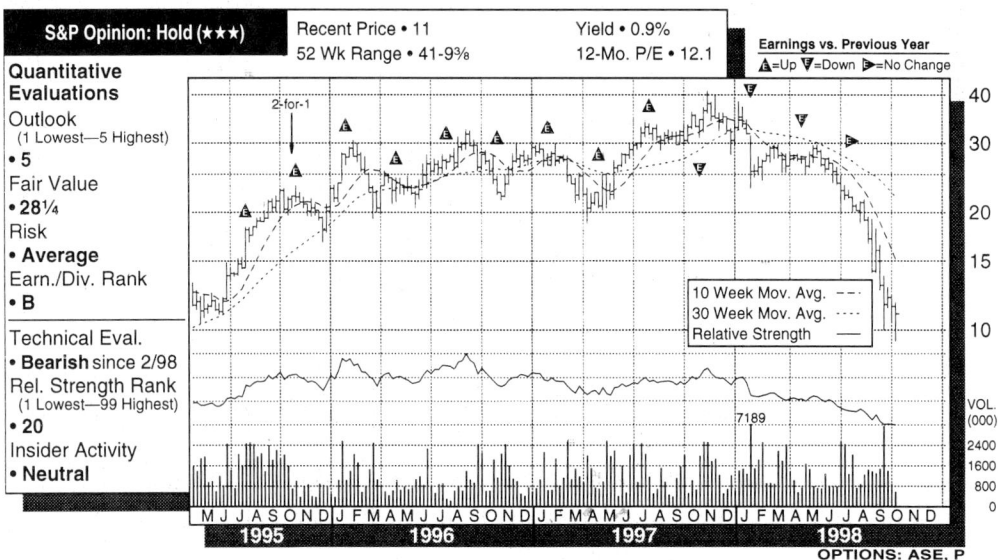

Earnings vs. Previous Year
▲=Up ▼=Down ▶=No Change

10 Week Mov. Avg. ---
30 Week Mov. Avg. ····
Relative Strength —

OPTIONS: ASE, P

Overview - 04-AUG-98

During the first three months of FY 99 (Mar.), Mentor's sales increased 3%, and EPS were unchanged, year to year. Plastic surgery sales (which accounted for 50% of FY 98 sales) fell 4%, due in part to a factory fire in the summer of 1997. Moreover, penile prostheses sales fell 22%, due to competition from Viagra, the impotence drug introduced by Pfizer earlier this year. Mentor has had recent success with MemoryLens, a foldable intraocular lens for cataract patients, launched in January 1998. Sales of MemoryLens have been offset by reduced sales of older intraocular lenses. The company has also reported positive acceptance of its recently launched IoGold brachytherapy seeds for treatment of prostate cancer. While Mentor has projected sales growth expansion toward the end of FY 99, we expect sales growth in the 15% range through the end of the fiscal year. We are therefore reducing our FY 99 EPS estimate to $1.27 from $1.39.

Valuation - 04-AUG-98

The shares declined recently, due to reduced sales growth prospects. As a result of back-orders for breast implants, plastic surgery sales are down from a year ago, but have increased 12% sequentially. We expect this trend to continue through the end of the year. We are also encouraged by the January 1998 launch of MNTR's MemoryLens, providing the company with a complete line of advanced products for all phases of cataract surgery. Urology sales have been boosted by the recent introduction of IoGold radioactive seeds for prostate cancer, but have been somewhat offset by reduced demand for penile implants. The shares, recently trading at 16X our reduced FY 99 EPS estimate of $1.27, are in line with the company's projected growth rate, and we see MNTR as a market performer.

Key Stock Statistics

S&P EPS Est. 1999	1.27	Tang. Bk. Value/Share	6.13
P/E on S&P Est. 1999	8.7	Beta	0.95
Dividend Rate/Share	0.10	Shareholders	1,700
Shs. outstg. (M)	24.8	Market cap. (B)	$0.273
Avg. daily vol. (M)	0.482	Inst. holdings	75%

Value of $10,000 invested 5 years ago: $ 16,460

Fiscal Year Ending Mar. 31

	1999	1998	1997	1996	1995	1994
Revenues (Million $)						
1Q	57.02	55.29	50.39	43.73	34.73	31.03
2Q	—	48.82	48.16	42.33	32.69	29.33
3Q	—	54.08	50.50	45.00	38.13	31.18
4Q	—	57.11	54.33	46.76	40.85	32.05
Yr.	—	215.3	203.4	177.8	146.4	123.6
Earnings Per Share ($)						
1Q	0.30	0.30	0.27	0.23	0.17	0.11
2Q	E0.31	0.12	0.24	0.21	0.15	0.12
3Q	E0.32	0.22	0.27	0.23	0.19	0.14
4Q	E0.34	0.27	0.28	0.25	0.20	0.14
Yr.	E1.27	0.91	1.06	0.92	0.70	0.51

Next earnings report expected: late October

Dividend Data (Dividends have been paid since 1987.)

Amount ($)	Date Decl.	Ex-Div. Date	Stock of Record	Payment Date
0.025	Jan. 05	Jan. 14	Jan. 16	Feb. 06 '98
0.025	Mar. 31	Apr. 07	Apr. 10	May. 01 '98
0.025	Jun. 15	Jun. 24	Jun. 26	Jul. 17 '98
0.025	Sep. 18	Sep. 23	Sep. 25	Oct. 16 '98

A Division of The **McGraw·Hill** *Companies*

STANDARD
&POOR'S
STOCK REPORTS

Mentor Corporation

4570
10-OCT-98

Business Summary - 04-AUG-98

Mentor develops, makes and markets a broad range of products for plastic and reconstructive surgery (50% of sales in FY 98; Mar.), urology (32%), ophthalmology (16%), and general surgery (2%). International sales accounted for 26% of FY 98 sales.

The company makes an extensive line of implants for cosmetic and reconstructive surgery, including a line of breast implants; skin and tissue expanders, which are used to generate additional tissue for reconstruction and skin graft procedures; and facial and dermal implants, which are injected into the skin to correct scars and other skin defects. In September 1997, MNTR launched the Contour Genesis Ultrasonic Assisted Liposuction system, a liposuction surgery device.

In the area of urology, MNTR offers a line of implantable products, including penile implants for the treatment of male sexual impotence and vacuum constriction devices, used as a first-line nonsurgical treatment of male sexual impotence. Other urology products include disposable products for the management of urinary incontinence or retention and surgical products which aid in curing the problem, including Urethrin, an injectable implant that is currently sold outside of the U.S.

In May 1997, Mentor began marketing the Cinch bond anchor system, for women suffering from stress incontinence. In January 1998, the company launched the IoGold brachytherapy seeds for treatment of prostate cancer.

Ophthalmic products include intraocular lenses, for replacement of a lens following cataract surgery, surgical equipment, primarily coagulators used to control bleeding during ophthalmic and other microsurgery, and diagnostic equipment, used to evaluate disorders of the eye.

In January 1998, MNTR launched the MemoryLens, a foldable intraocular lens used with cataract patients, in the U.S. The MemoryLens has been available internationally since early 1996. The company continues to manufacture a fixed hard plastic lens, in addition to the new proprietary foldable lens.

As of March 1998, Mentor employed 113 people engaged in full-time research and development. The company continues to work on new and improved products in many of its principle product lines, including general surgery and ophthalmology. MNTR is also partially funding Phase III clinical trials of the BCI-Immune Activator bladder cancer treatment. Mentor believes that its future growth is dependant upon the introduction of new products that provide superior benefits, premium prices and significant growth potential.

Per Share Data ($)

(Year Ended Mar. 31)	1998	1997	1996	1995	1994	1993	1992	1991	1990	1989
Tangible Bk. Val.	5.82	4.82	3.97	2.35	2.56	2.04	2.25	2.07	1.90	1.27
Cash Flow	1.26	1.35	1.20	1.04	0.80	0.13	0.42	0.45	0.51	0.37
Earnings	0.91	1.06	0.92	0.70	0.51	-0.14	0.21	0.27	0.39	0.27
Dividends	0.08	0.10	0.10	0.10	0.02	0.06	0.10	0.08	0.08	0.08
Payout Ratio	8%	9%	11%	14%	4%	NM	47%	29%	20%	30%
Cal. Yrs.	1997	1996	1995	1994	1993	1992	1991	1990	1989	1988
Prices - High	41	32¹/₂	23³/₈	9³/₈	8	9⁵/₈	14⁷/₈	10⁷/₈	7¹/₄	6³/₈
- Low	18³/₄	19¹/₄	8¹/₂	6³/₈	4¹/₂	4	4³/₄	5	4³/₄	4⁵/₈
P/E Ratio - High	45	31	25	13	16	NM	71	40	19	24
- Low	21	18	9	9	9	NM	23	18	12	17

Income Statement Analysis (Million $)

Revs.	215	203	178	146	124	115	89.4	73.8	50.4	43.1
Oper. Inc.	43.8	50.0	44.3	33.8	26.1	24.3	13.5	15.0	13.9	11.3
Depr.	9.1	7.8	7.2	6.8	6.2	5.6	4.7	3.9	2.4	2.3
Int. Exp.	0.0	0.6	1.1	3.1	3.7	2.5	2.3	2.2	1.8	1.9
Pretax Inc.	36.3	42.4	36.1	24.2	16.8	-4.7	6.7	8.9	12.6	8.8
Eff. Tax Rate	34%	34%	34%	35%	35%	NM	33%	33%	33%	34%
Net Inc.	23.9	27.9	23.8	15.7	11.0	-2.8	4.5	5.9	8.4	5.8

Balance Sheet & Other Fin. Data (Million $)

Cash	27.9	27.8	18.5	11.3	10.3	8.2	6.1	9.7	31.0	31.9
Curr. Assets	128	116	102	81.0	70.1	61.4	47.0	42.9	50.5	47.3
Total Assets	201	167	150	129	121	110	90.3	84.5	74.3	68.2
Curr. Liab.	32.6	27.6	31.7	27.3	30.4	26.3	18.2	14.6	7.7	7.6
LT Debt	Nil	0.0	0.1	24.6	25.4	24.4	24.4	26.0	26.0	26.0
Common Eqty.	165	138	116	71.1	54.7	43.4	47.7	43.9	40.3	34.0
Total Cap.	169	139	118	95.8	80.0	67.8	72.1	69.9	66.6	60.5
Cap. Exp.	15.8	8.3	NA	NA	NA	7.3	NA	NA	NA	NA
Cash Flow	33.0	35.6	31.0	22.6	17.2	2.8	9.2	9.9	10.8	8.1
Curr. Ratio	3.9	4.2	3.2	3.0	2.3	2.3	2.6	2.9	6.6	6.2
% LT Debt of Cap.	NM	--	0.1	25.7	31.7	35.9	33.8	37.1	39.0	42.9
% Net Inc.of Revs.	11.1	13.8	13.4	10.7	8.9	NM	5.0	8.0	16.7	13.5
% Ret. on Assets	13.0	17.7	17.1	12.6	9.5	NM	5.2	7.5	11.9	8.7
% Ret. on Equity	15.8	21.9	25.4	25.1	22.4	NM	9.8	14.1	22.7	17.7

Data as orig. reptd.; bef. results of disc. opers. and/or spec. items. Per share data adj. for stk. divs. as of ex-div. date. Bold denotes diluted EPS (FASB 128). E-Estimated. NA-Not Available. NM-Not Meaningful. NR-Not Ranked.

Office—5425 Hollister Ave., Santa Barbara, CA 93111. **Tel**—(805) 681-6000. **Chrmn & CEO**—C. J. Conway. **Pres, COO & Secy**—A. R. Gette. **VP-Fin, CFO & Treas**—G. E. Mistlin. **Dirs**—C. J. Conway, W. W. Faster, A. R. Gette, E. G. Glover, M. Nakonechny, B. G. Shaffer, R. W. Young. **Transfer Agent & Registrar**—American Stock Transfer & Trust Co., NYC. **Incorporated**—in Minnesota in 1969. **Empl**— 1,612. **S&P Analyst:** John J. Arege

STANDARD
&POOR'S
STOCK REPORTS

Mercury Interactive 4580U

Nasdaq Symbol **MERQ**

In S&P SmallCap 600

03-OCT-98

Industry:
Computer (Software & Services)

Summary: MERQ develops, markets and supports a family of automated client/server and Web-based system software tools for testing business-critical enterprise applications.

S&P Opinion: Hold (★★★)	Recent Price • 32⅜	Yield • Nil
	52 Wk Range • 45¾-17⅞	12-Mo. P/E • 62.3

Quantitative Evaluations

Outlook
(1 Lowest—5 Highest)
• **3⁻**

Fair Value
• **49¼**

Risk
• **High**

Earn./Div. Rank
• **NR**

Technical Eval.
• **Bullish** since 5/97

Rel. Strength Rank
(1 Lowest—99 Highest)
• **32**

Insider Activity
• **Unfavorable**

Earnings vs. Previous Year
▲=Up ▼=Down ▷=No Change

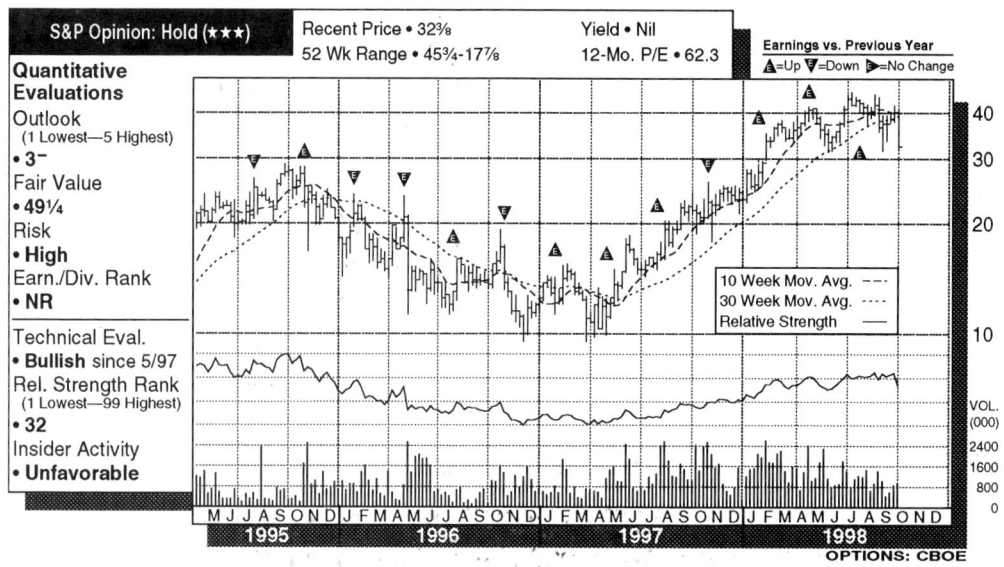

10 Week Mov. Avg. ---
30 Week Mov. Avg. ·····
Relative Strength ——

VOL. (000)

OPTIONS: CBOE

Overview - 25-SEP-98

Automated software testing is increasingly being viewed as a strategic decision to accelerate information technology development (IT) and implementation, as well as avoid or minimize unnecessary IT expenditures. IT spending continues to accelerate as corporations and institutions make the transition to Internet Protocol-based applications, as well as to packaged, enterprise software applications from SAP, Oracle, Baan, PeopleSoft and other concerns. This trend, as well as a tremendous acceleration of Year 2000 software certification and preparations for adoption of the euro, continue to be the primary forces behind demand for MERQ's automated software testing tools. We forecast 40% revenue growth in 1998, to be followed by 35% in 1999. Earnings gains are likely to exceed revenue gains in 1998 due to expanding margins, with operating EPS rising 50% to $0.93, and 35% to $1.25 in 1999. The company has $109 million in cash and equivalents with which it may acquire technologies which add to or enhance its current product offerings.

Valuation - 25-SEP-98

We rate MERQ a hold at this point. Although the shares merit their premium valuation relative to the overall market, we think the near-term upside is limited, particularly in the wake of increased volatility in equity markets. While the shares have held up well amid the market correction, a sharp pullback remains a distinct possibility if operating results do not meet current aggressive growth expectations. We think that long-term investors should wait before making any changes to their current positions.

Key Stock Statistics

S&P EPS Est. 1998	0.93	Tang. Bk. Value/Share	7.22
P/E on S&P Est. 1998	34.8	Beta	NA
S&P EPS Est. 1999	1.25	Shareholders	5,300
Dividend Rate/Share	Nil	Market cap. (B)	$0.564
Shs. outstg. (M)	17.4	Inst. holdings	86%
Avg. daily vol. (M)	0.144		

Value of $10,000 invested 5 years ago: NA

Fiscal Year Ending Dec. 31

	1998	1997	1996	1995	1994	1993
Revenues (Million $)						
1Q	22.20	15.40	11.00	7.70	4.30	2.60
2Q	27.20	17.50	12.10	9.00	5.25	3.00
3Q	—	19.60	14.20	10.25	6.40	3.30
4Q	—	24.20	17.25	12.50	7.50	4.10
Yr.	—	76.70	54.55	39.45	23.45	13.00
Earnings Per Share ($)						
1Q	**0.15**	**0.11**	-0.04	0.08	0.06	0.01
2Q	**0.21**	**0.13**	0.05	-0.14	0.08	0.02
3Q	**E0.25**	-0.14	0.09	0.16	0.10	0.04
4Q	**E0.32**	**0.28**	0.19	-0.44	0.14	0.05
Yr.	**E0.93**	**0.39**	0.28	-0.38	0.38	0.12

Next earnings report expected: late October

Dividend Data

No cash dividends have been paid. The company intends to retain earnings for use in its business and does not expect to pay cash dividends in the foreseeable future. A stockholder rights plan was adopted in July 1996.

STANDARD
&POOR'S
STOCK REPORTS

Mercury Interactive Corporation

4580U
03-OCT-98

Business Summary - 25-SEP-98

Mercury Interactive Corp. develops, markets and supports a family of automated client/server and Web-based (Internet and intranets) tools for testing business-critical applications. MERQ's products allow corporate development organizations, system integrators and independent software developers to identify client/server system problems with greater accuracy, speed and efficiency than traditional methods allow. The company is committed to its research and development efforts in order to achieve its strategy of offering advanced and innovative testing solutions for evolving business needs. Research and development costs rose to $10.9 million in 1997, from $9.4 million in 1996.

Mercury's automated software quality products allow developers of client/server software to compress software development cycles, reduce costs and improve software quality throughout the development, maintenance and porting process by automating the tedious, highly structured and error-prone manual testing process.

The company's XRunner product is an automated GUI regression tool that tests X Window applications running under UNIX. XRunner makes test development easier by incorporating simplified test script management, point-and-click selection and interactive debugging. WinRunner tests client/server GUI applications on

Windows 3.1, Windows 95 and Windows NT platforms. LoadRunner is an integrated client/server and Web load testing tool. It provides a scalable load testing solution for managing the risks of client/server systems. The company's TestDirector is a workgroup test management software that directs the quality assurance process for software development. SQLInspector, a tool for viewing application function calls to databases, includes performance data so that developers can analyze their application's database access and better understand how to tune the application. WebTest is designed specifically for testing Web applications.

The company markets its products primarily through its direct sales and service organization, which focuses on major accounts. Current customers include Allstate Insurance, Citibank, DHL Airways, Gap, Inc., Michelin, Nabisco, and Quebec/Hydro, among others. International sales accounted for 36%, 37% and 29% of total revenues in 1997, 1996 and 1995, respectively.

In addition to its own sales force, MERQ has an indirect sales channel of value added resellers and major system integrators, including Andersen Consulting, Deloitte & Touche, EDS and KPMG Peat Marwick. The indirect sales channel accounted for 47%, 43% and 23% of total license revenues in 1997, 1996 and 1995, respectively. The company believes that the indirect sales channel will account for an increasingly significant portion of total revenue in future periods.

Per Share Data ($)

(Year Ended Dec. 31)	1997	1996	1995	1994	1993	1992	1991	1990	1989	1988
Tangible Bk. Val.	6.75	6.17	5.89	3.07	2.65	-4.37	NA	NA	NA	NA
Cash Flow	0.61	0.48	-0.22	0.47	0.17	-1.32	NA	NA	NA	NA
Earnings	0.39	0.28	-0.38	0.38	0.12	-1.50	NA	NA	NA	NA
Dividends	Nil	Nil	Nil	Nil	Nil	Nil	Nil	Nil	Nil	Nil
Payout Ratio	Nil	Nil	Nil	Nil	Nil	Nil	Nil	Nil	Nil	Nil
Prices - High	28⅛	24	29	21¾	23	NA	NA	NA	NA	NA
- Low	9½	9½	11¾	7	13	NA	NA	NA	NA	NA
P/E Ratio - High	NM	86	NM	57	NM	NA	NA	NA	NA	NA
- Low	NM	34	NM	18	NA	NA	NA	NA	NA	NA

Income Statement Analysis (Million $)

	1997	1996	1995	1994	1993	1992	1991	1990	1989	1988
Revs.	76.7	54.6	39.5	23.5	13.0	4.3	NA	NA	NA	NA
Oper. Inc.	10.3	6.1	-4.3	5.8	1.8	-3.0	NA	NA	NA	NA
Depr.	3.7	3.3	2.2	1.2	0.6	0.4	NA	NA	NA	NA
Int. Exp.	Nil	Nil	Nil	0.0	0.1	0.0	NA	NA	NA	NA
Pretax Inc.	9.6	5.8	-4.3	5.9	1.4	-3.3	NA	NA	NA	NA
Eff. Tax Rate	30%	20%	NM	15%	3.90%	Nil	Nil	Nil	Nil	Nil
Net Inc.	6.7	4.6	-5.3	5.0	1.4	-3.3	NA	NA	NA	NA

Balance Sheet & Other Fin. Data (Million $)

	1997	1996	1995	1994	1993	1992	1991	1990	1989	1988
Cash	57.2	71.0	77.8	33.3	33.7	6.3	NA	NA	NA	NA
Curr. Assets	119	96.5	95.7	44.1	39.4	9.3	NA	NA	NA	NA
Total Assets	143	117	113	49.6	41.7	11.1	NA	NA	NA	NA
Curr. Liab.	30.4	18.5	20.2	10.4	8.2	4.8	NA	NA	NA	NA
LT Debt	Nil	Nil	Nil	Nil	0.4	0.5	NA	NA	NA	NA
Common Eqty.	113	99	92.6	39.2	33.0	-7.0	NA	NA	NA	NA
Total Cap.	112	99	92.6	39.2	33.4	6.2	NA	NA	NA	NA
Cap. Exp.	11.8	4.6	7.0	3.2	1.3	0.9	NA	NA	NA	NA
Cash Flow	10.4	7.9	3.1	6.2	2.0	-2.9	NA	NA	NA	NA
Curr. Ratio	3.9	5.2	4.7	4.2	4.8	1.9	NA	NA	NA	NA
% LT Debt of Cap.	Nil	Nil	Nil	Nil	1.3	7.7	NA	NA	NA	NA
% Net Inc.of Revs.	8.7	8.5	NM	21.5	10.5	NM	NM	NM	NM	NM
% Ret. on Assets	5.1	4.0	NM	10.9	2.1	NM	NM	NM	NM	NM
% Ret. on Equity	6.3	4.8	NM	13.8	NM	NM	NM	NM	NM	NM

Data as orig. reptd.; bef. results of disc. opers. and/or spec. items. Per share data adj. for stk. divs. as of ex-div. date. Bold denotes diluted EPS (FASB 128). E-Estimated. NA-Not Available. NM-Not Meaningful. NR-Not Ranked.

Office—1325 Borregas Ave., Sunnyvale, CA 94089. **Tel**—(408) 822-5200. **Fax**—(408) 523-9911. **Website**—http://www.merc-int.com **Chrmn**—A. Finegold. **Pres & CEO**—A. Landan **VP-Fin, CFO & Secy**—Sharlene Abrams. **Investor Contact**—Ann Marie McCauley (408) 822-5359.**Dirs**—A. Finegold, I. Kohavi, A. Landan, Y. Shamir, G. Yaron. **Transfer Agent & Registrar**—ChaseMellon Shareholder Services, SF. **Incorporated**—in Delaware in 1989. **Empl**— 437. **S&P Analyst:** Mark Basham

STANDARD &POOR'S
STOCK REPORTS

Merrill Corp.

4581E

NASDAQ Symbol **MRLL**

In S&P SmallCap 600

03-OCT-98

Industry:
Specialty Printing

Summary: MRLL provides typesetting, printing, document management and reproduction, distribution and marketing communication services to financial, legal, funds and corporate markets.

Quantitative Evaluations	
Outlook (1 Lowest—5 Highest)	**• NA**
Fair Value	**• NA**
Risk	**• Average**
Earn./Div. Rank	**• B+**
Technical Eval.	**• NA**
Rel. Strength Rank (1 Lowest—99 Highest)	**• 22**
Insider Activity	**• Unfavorable**

Recent Price • 15¼
52 Wk Range • 24¾-13¼

Yield • 0.5%
12-Mo. P/E • 9.2

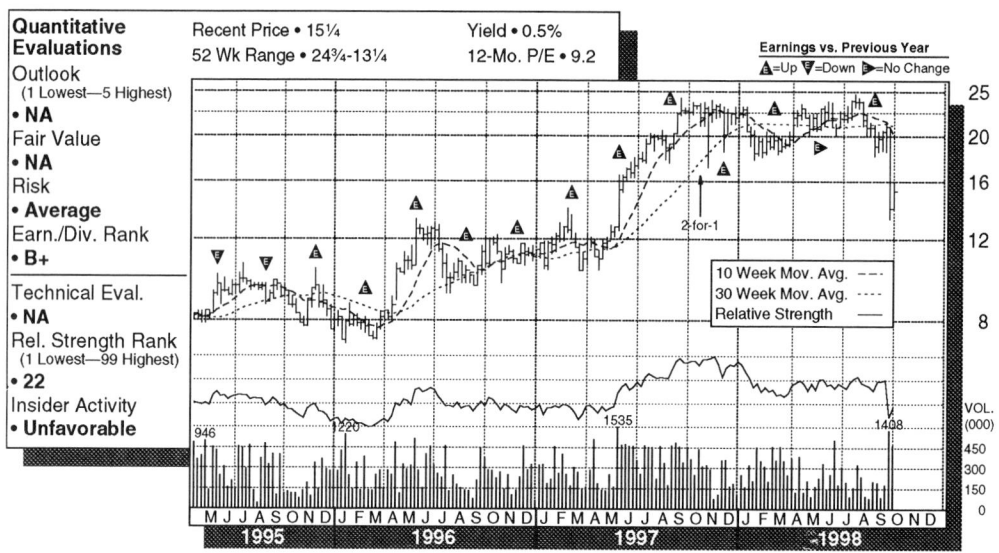

Earnings vs. Previous Year
▲=Up ▼=Down ▶=No Change

10 Week Mov. Avg. ----
30 Week Mov. Avg. ·······
Relative Strength ——

2-for-1

Business Profile - 01-SEP-98

In the second quarter of FY 99 (Jan.), the company benefited from strong demand in all business segments, led by 52% growth in financial transactions revenues and a 42% advance in document service center business. Management continues to focus their efforts on the document service business line with the acquisition of Executech in June 1998. Commercial and other revenue also grew as a result of the election year ballot production business, which is completed primarily in the second quarter. Fast growth and the rapid addition of clients has led MRLL to invest in both the sales force and marketing activities, additions which the company expects will continue throughout the year.

Operational Review - 01-SEP-98

Revenues for the six months ended July 31, 1998, rose 21%, year to year, due to double digit growth in all business sectors. Margins narrowed, as investments in the sales force and information technology staffing triggered higher selling, general and administrative costs. Following a decline in other expenses (net), and taxes at 44.5% in both periods, net income increased 19% to $16,718,000 ($0.97 per share), from $14,066,000 ($0.85).

Stock Performance - 02-OCT-98

In the past 30 trading days, MRLL's shares have declined 27%, compared to a 7% fall in the S&P 500. Average trading volume for the past five days was 127,680 shares, compared with the 40-day moving average of 73,528 shares.

Key Stock Statistics

Dividend Rate/Share	0.08	Shareholders	1,800
Shs. outstg. (M)	16.3	Market cap. (B)	$0.249
Avg. daily vol. (M)	0.117	Inst. holdings	64%
Tang. Bk. Value/Share	6.03		
Beta	1.41		

Value of $10,000 invested 5 years ago: $ 21,679

Fiscal Year Ending Jan. 31

	1999	1998	1997	1996	1995	1994
Revenues (Million $)						
1Q	123.5	109.9	71.20	57.43	61.46	41.24
2Q	148.5	115.6	87.57	62.70	63.68	44.91
3Q	—	112.1	93.78	62.47	57.47	42.54
4Q	—	122.0	101.2	62.70	54.26	52.89
Yr.	—	459.5	353.8	245.3	236.9	181.6
Earnings Per Share ($)						
1Q	0.47	0.47	0.27	0.13	0.29	0.21
2Q	0.50	0.38	0.28	0.17	0.28	0.22
3Q	—	0.33	0.27	0.19	0.14	0.19
4Q	—	0.36	0.28	0.18	0.05	0.20
Yr.	—	1.54	1.09	0.67	0.75	0.82

Next earnings report expected: late November

Dividend Data (Dividends have been paid since 1993.)

Amount ($)	Date Decl.	Ex-Div. Date	Stock of Record	Payment Date
0.020	Dec. 18	Dec. 29	Dec. 31	Jan. 15 '98
0.020	Mar. 19	Mar. 27	Mar. 31	Apr. 15 '98
0.020	Jun. 19	Jun. 26	Jun. 30	Jul. 15 '98
0.020	Sep. 21	Sep. 28	Sep. 30	Oct. 15 '98

A Division of The **McGraw·Hill** Companies

Business Summary - 01-SEP-98

Based in St. Paul, Minnesota, this company provides on demand, 24-hour-a-day typesetting, printing, document management and reproduction, distribution and marketing services to financial, legal, funds and corporate markets. MRLL operates through over 30 U.S. locations and is involved in joint ventures in Canada, Europe and Asia.

Financial printing (38% of revenues in FY 98 -Jan.) involves the production and distribution of time-sensitive financial documents, such as registration statements and prospectuses. Corporate printing, which accounted for 32% of revenues, consists of documents that are provided at regular intervals, including annual and quarterly reports and proxy statements. The financial and corporate printing process begins with the transfer of information to Merrill, which performs several rounds of editing. Interim versions are then distributed to relevant parties, such as corporate executives, investment bankers, attorneys and accountants. The final document is filed with the proper regulatory authorities and then prepared for printed distribution. MRLL also has the capability to distribute documents via the Internet.

Document management services (12% of revenues) can be performed at either the client's location or an

MRLL facility. On-site services are characterized by three-year agreements to provide a range of services including determination of needs, equipment, staffing and management. Merrill's own facilities are geared to handle time-sensitive and other special projects, such as photocopying for large litigation matters. These sites are outfitted with qualified personnel and equipped with high-performance document management machines.

Commercial services, which generated 18% of revenues, include services provided by Merrill/May, Inc. and FMC Resource Management Corporation (FMC). Merrill/May provides marketing, printing and distribution services designed to promote corporate identity of large national customers with multiple franchises, members, divisions or affiliates, such as real estate companies, fast-food restaurants and credit card companies. FMC provides manufacturing, distribution and inventory management services of marketing items for large, geographically diverse companies, such as department stores.

In April 1997, MRLL directors authorized the company to repurchase as many as 750,000 shares of its common stock.

In October 1997, the company said it had acquired certain assets of Total Management, a provider of outsourcing services in the Midwest and Northeast.

Per Share Data ($)

(Year Ended Jan. 31)	1998	1997	1996	1995	1994	1993	1992	1991	1990	1989
Tangible Bk. Val.	4.98	3.92	4.28	4.28	2.80	2.68	2.06	1.60	1.41	1.42
Cash Flow	2.45	1.92	1.35	1.36	1.17	0.82	0.64	0.43	0.06	0.30
Earnings	1.54	1.09	0.67	0.75	0.82	0.56	0.43	0.18	-0.09	0.20
Dividends	0.07	0.06	0.06	0.06	0.05	Nil	Nil	Nil	Nil	Nil
Payout Ratio	5%	5%	9%	8%	6%	Nil	Nil	Nil	Nil	Nil
Cal. Yrs.	1997	1996	1995	1994	1993	1992	1991	1990	1989	1988
Prices - High	24¼	13¼	10⅝	16¼	14	7⅞	6⅝	2¾	2⅞	2³⁄₁₆
- Low	10¼	7⅛	7	6⅞	6¾	4⅛	1¾	1⅜	1⁹⁄₁₆	1⁹⁄₁₆
P/E Ratio - High	16	12	16	22	17	14	15	15	NM	11
- Low	7	7	10	9	8	7	4	7	NM	8

Income Statement Analysis (Million $)

	1998	1997	1996	1995	1994	1993	1992	1991	1990	1989
Revs.	460	354	245	237	182	148	125	101	69.0	63.0
Oper. Inc.	65.4	50.0	30.3	31.5	27.5	18.2	14.2	7.6	2.6	6.7
Depr.	15.4	13.4	10.8	9.8	5.5	4.1	3.1	3.5	2.1	1.5
Int. Exp.	4.3	4.1	1.1	1.1	0.3	0.3	0.5	0.6	0.3	0.4
Pretax Inc.	46.5	32.5	18.7	21.2	22.0	14.2	10.8	4.1	-0.9	5.2
Eff. Tax Rate	44%	45%	43%	43%	40%	39%	40%	38%	NM	41%
Net Inc.	26.0	17.8	10.7	12.0	13.2	8.6	6.5	2.7	-1.2	3.0

Balance Sheet & Other Fin. Data (Million $)

	1998	1997	1996	1995	1994	1993	1992	1991	1990	1989
Cash	2.5	5.2	12.1	10.0	2.6	9.6	6.3	1.2	1.2	7.0
Curr. Assets	150	127	79.2	63.5	59.4	48.0	37.7	30.6	24.3	21.6
Total Assets	246	202	126	202	100	66.0	53.0	46.9	40.6	35.6
Curr. Liab.	71.1	57.4	39.9	31.9	36.9	23.3	21.0	21.2	16.4	11.2
LT Debt	40.2	40.9	6.5	7.5	8.7	2.1	2.2	2.3	2.4	2.5
Common Eqty.	126	96.2	77.7	66.1	53.6	39.3	29.1	22.5	20.5	20.8
Total Cap.	67.5	139	84.2	73.6	62.9	42.7	32.0	25.7	24.2	24.4
Cap. Exp.	17.1	9.2	12.5	10.1	7.9	7.5	2.6	2.8	5.0	2.1
Cash Flow	41.5	31.2	21.5	21.8	18.7	12.7	9.7	6.2	0.8	4.5
Curr. Ratio	2.1	2.2	2.0	2.0	1.6	2.0	1.8	1.4	1.5	1.9
% LT Debt of Cap.	24.0	29.4	7.7	10.2	13.8	5.0	7.0	9.0	9.9	10.3
% Net Inc.of Revs.	5.7	5.0	4.4	5.1	7.3	5.8	5.2	2.6	NM	4.7
% Ret. on Assets	11.6	10.9	9.2	11.5	15.7	14.2	13.0	6.2	NM	8.7
% Ret. on Equity	23.5	20.5	14.9	19.9	28.1	24.8	25.2	12.6	NM	15.0

Data as orig. reptd.; bef. results of disc. opers. and/or spec. items. Per share data adj. for stk. divs. as of ex-div. date. Bold denotes diluted EPS (FASB 128). E-Estimated. NA-Not Available. NM-Not Meaningful. NR-Not Ranked.

Office—One Merrill Circle, St. Paul, MN 55108. **Tel**—(612) 646-4501. **Website**—http://www.merrillcorp.com **Chrmn**—P. G. Miller. **Pres & CEO**—J. W. Castro. **VP-Fin, CFO & Treas**—K. A. Barber. **Secy**—S. J. Machov. **Dirs**—R. R. Atterbury, J. R. Campbell, J. W. Castro, R. N. Hege, F. W. Kanner, R. G. Lareau, P. G. Miller, M. S. Morton, R. F. Nienhouse. **Transfer Agent & Registrar**—First Trust Co. Inc., St. Paul. **Incorporated**—in Minnesota in 1968. **Empl**—3,626. **S&P Analyst:** Jordan Horoschak

Mesa Air Group   4586B

NASDAQ Symbol **MESA**

In S&P SmallCap 600

10-OCT-98

Industry: Airlines

Summary: Mesa is one of the largest independently owned regional airlines in the world, serving over 100 cities in the U. S. and Canada.

Quantitative Evaluations

Outlook (1 Lowest—5 Highest)
- **2**

Fair Value
- **5⅛**

Risk
- **High**

Earn./Div. Rank
- **B-**

Technical Eval.
- **Bearish** since 8/98

Rel. Strength Rank (1 Lowest—99 Highest)
- **23**

Insider Activity
- **Neutral**

Recent Price • 4⅛
52 Wk Range • 9¾-3⅞

Yield • Nil
12-Mo. P/E • NM

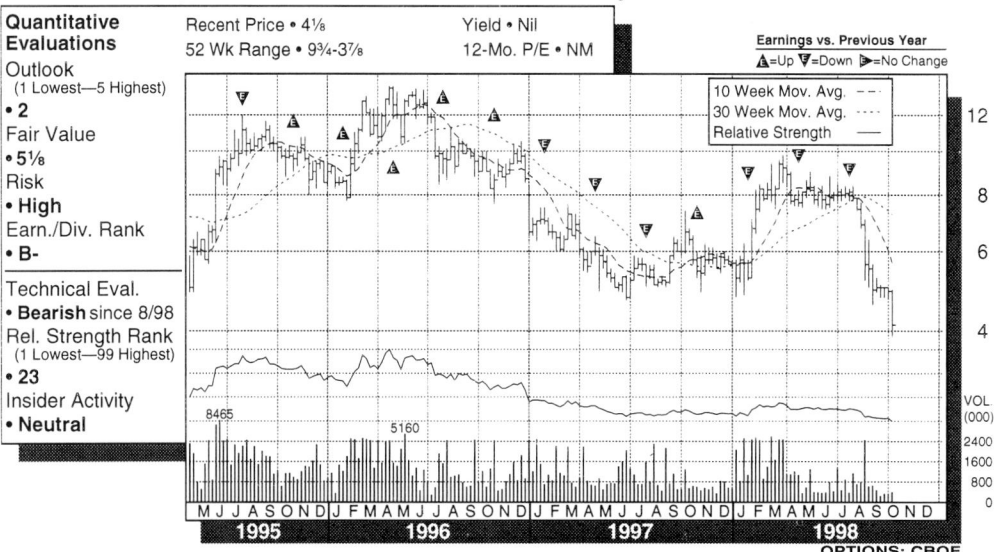

Earnings vs. Previous Year
▲=Up ▼=Down ▶=No Change

10 Week Mov. Avg. – –
30 Week Mov. Avg. ·····
Relative Strength ——

Business Profile - 28-AUG-98

This regional airline serves 113 cities in 29 states, Canada and the District of Columbia primarily via "through fare" arrangements with larger airlines. Following a large charge in 1998's first quarter resulting from the termination of two code-sharing agreements with UAL Corp. in May 1998, which accounted for some 44% of FY 97 revenues, Mesa announced that as of June 30, 1998 it was not in compliance with some secured debt covenants required by a bank credit agreement. However, the bank has waived compliance with such covenants. The company believes it will maintain compliance or obtain waivers through September 30, 1998. As of June 30, 1998 the company had aggregate indebtedness of about $259.4 million payable to various parties under promissory notes issued in connection with the purchase of aircraft.

Operational Review - 28-AUG-98

Total operating revenues in the first nine months of FY 98 (Sep.) fell 8.7%, year to year, primarily reflecting the discontinuation of the company's United Airlines Express operations and independent jet operations in Ft Worth, Texas. Results were negatively impacted by a $33.9 million loss provision related to the discontinuation of the code-sharing agreement with United Airlines, a $4.0 million charge related to the shutdown of Ft. Worth operations and a $2.5 million provision for anticipated settlement of a class action lawsuit. The net loss widened significantly, to $56,711,000 ($2.00 a share), from $4,368,000 ($0.15).

Stock Performance - 09-OCT-98

In the past 30 trading days, MESA's shares have declined 25%, compared to a 4% fall in the S&P 500. Average trading volume for the past five days was 73,900 shares, compared with the 40-day moving average of 143,990 shares.

Key Stock Statistics

Dividend Rate/Share	Nil	Shareholders	1,400
Shs. outstg. (M)	28.4	Market cap. (B)	$0.117
Avg. daily vol. (M)	0.060	Inst. holdings	58%
Tang. Bk. Value/Share	3.42		
Beta	1.49		

Value of $10,000 invested 5 years ago: $ 2,509

Fiscal Year Ending Sep. 30

	1998	1997	1996	1995	1994	1993
Revenues (Million $)						
1Q	124.6	121.4	120.0	102.0	92.00	--
2Q	119.6	125.4	121.0	106.0	94.00	--
3Q	99.5	129.4	130.3	118.0	102.0	--
4Q	--	134.7	129.1	128.0	108.0	--
Yr.	--	511.0	500.4	455.0	396.0	354.0
Earnings Per Share ($)						
1Q	**-1.38**	-0.03	0.12	0.08	0.21	--
2Q	**-0.33**	-0.03	0.39	Nil	0.17	--
3Q	**-0.15**	-0.09	0.23	0.11	0.20	--
4Q	--	-1.57	0.29	0.23	0.17	--
Yr.	--	-1.72	1.00	0.42	0.75	0.73

Next earnings report expected: NA

Dividend Data

Mesa has never paid cash dividends and does not intend to pay cash dividends in the future. The shares were split two for one in March 1993 and three for two in August and January 1992.

A Division of The McGraw·Hill Companies

STANDARD
&POOR'S
STOCK REPORTS

Mesa Air Group, Inc.

4586B
10-OCT-98

Business Summary - 28-AUG-98

One of the nation's largest independently-owned regional airlines, Mesa Air Group, Inc. and its subsidiaries operate as America West Express, Mesa Airlines, US Airways Express and, through May 31, 1998, United Express. The company serves 113 cities in 29 states, Canada and the District of Columbia through a fleet of 107 aircraft with about 1,000 daily departures.

Mesa's long-term strategy is to profitably service routes not directly served by major air carriers and to supplement service of major carriers' code partners on certain routes. The company evaluates market demand and utilizes its fleet of aircraft to meet that demand. Code-sharing agreements (where the smaller airline typically adopts the code of the larger airline in the computer reservations systems used by travel agents) with certain of the major carriers provide benefits from the name recognition, reservation systems, marketing and promotional efforts of these carriers. For instance, code sharing permits use of the logo, service marks, exterior aircraft paint schemes and uniforms similar to the code-sharing partner's, and provides coordinated schedules and joint advertising. Also, Mesa's passengers receive mileage credits in the respective frequent flyer programs, and credits in those programs can be used on the company's flights. The company operates a fleet of new and efficient aircraft and perfoms much of its own maintenance and overhaul work.

Mesa has historically relied on generating much of its revenues by use of a "through fare" arrangement with its major code sharing partners. A "through fare" is a combined fare offered to passengers who connect to Mesa from a major code sharing partner and vice versa. As an alternative to this arrangement, the company, in certain markets, has utilized fee per departure arrangements. A fee per departure allows Mesa to obtain a fee based on a proprietary formula for each flight operated.

As a result of the termination of two code sharing agreements by UAL Corp. on April 22 and May 31, 1998, respectively, which together accounted for some 44% of FY 97 revenues, the company incurred a loss provision totaling $106 million to provide for costs to dispose of certain aircraft and equipment, and other costs to shut down the entire United Express system. The company said the termination of all of the code-sharing agreements with UAL could have a material negative impact on its financial position and cash flow.

Mesa has ordered 32 CRJ aircraft for use in its AmericaWest Express operation in Phoenix, Arizona, as USAirways on the East Coast and in other markets that management believes have the potential for profitable operations. As of June 30, 1998, the company had received 16 of the 32 aircraft on order, and expects to take delivery of the remaining 16 aircraft by the end of 1999.

Per Share Data ($)

(Year Ended Sep. 30)	1997	1996	1995	1994	1993	1992	1991	1990	1989	1988
Tangible Bk. Val.	5.48	6.06	5.84	6.43	5.74	2.81	2.25	NA	NA	NA
Cash Flow	-0.49	1.80	1.05	1.16	1.12	0.98	0.85	NA	NA	NA
Earnings	-0.15	1.00	0.42	0.75	0.73	0.50	0.39	NA	NA	NA
Dividends	Nil	Nil	Nil	Nil	Nil	Nil	Nil	Nil	Nil	Nil
Payout Ratio	Nil	Nil	Nil	Nil	Nil	Nil	Nil	Nil	Nil	Nil
Prices - High	7⅝	13⅞	12	23	24	16⅝	5¼	NA	NA	NA
- Low	4⅝	6½	4⅞	6	14	4⅝	1⅞	NA	NA	NA
P/E Ratio - High	NM	14	29	31	33	33	13	NA	NA	NA
- Low	NM	6	12	8	19	9	5	NA	NA	NA

Income Statement Analysis (Million $)

Revs.	511	500	455	396	354	317	NA	NA	NA	NA
Oper. Inc.	48.3	75.3	50.5	63.5	61.2	37.5	NA	NA	NA	NA
Depr.	34.9	24.3	20.9	15.1	13.1	11.9	NA	NA	NA	NA
Int. Exp.	27.8	12.8	6.4	7.9	5.4	4.9	NA	NA	NA	NA
Pretax Inc.	-79.2	49.5	23.0	44.0	40.3	22.5	NA	NA	NA	NA
Eff. Tax Rate	NM	39%	39%	38%	38%	36%	NA	NA	NA	NA
Net Inc.	-48.6	30.4	14.0	27.3	25.0	14.3	NA	NA	NA	NA

Balance Sheet & Other Fin. Data (Million $)

Cash	57.2	60.0	109	99	135	NA	NA	NA	NA	NA
Curr. Assets	167	134	176	174	186	NA	NA	NA	NA	NA
Total Assets	650	678	447	420	399	NA	NA	NA	NA	NA
Curr. Liab.	98.1	63.6	55.6	43.7	60.5	NA	NA	NA	NA	NA
LT Debt	338	338	78.4	91.8	91.7	NA	NA	NA	NA	NA
Common Eqty.	177	225	256	234	215	NA	NA	NA	NA	NA
Total Cap.	517	585	363	351	323	NA	NA	NA	NA	NA
Cap. Exp.	4.6	20.3	92.3	32.6	38.9	30.0	NA	NA	NA	NA
Cash Flow	-13.7	54.7	34.9	42.4	38.2	26.2	NA	NA	NA	NA
Curr. Ratio	1.7	2.1	3.2	4.0	3.1	NA	NA	NA	NA	NA
% LT Debt of Cap.	65.4	57.8	21.6	26.1	28.4	NA	NA	NA	NA	NA
% Net Inc.of Revs.	NM	6.1	3.1	6.9	7.1	4.5	NA	NA	NA	NA
% Ret. on Assets	NM	5.4	3.2	6.6	6.7	NA	NA	NA	NA	NA
% Ret. on Equity	NM	12.7	5.7	12.1	11.5	NA	NA	NA	NA	NA

Data as orig. reptd.; bef. results of disc. opers. and/or spec. items. Per share data adj. for stk. divs. as of ex-div. date. Bold denotes diluted EPS (FASB 128). E-Estimated. NA-Not Available. NM-Not Meaningful. NR-Not Ranked.

Office—3753 Howard Hughes Parkway, Suite 200, Las Vegas, NV 89109. **Tel**—(702) 892-3773. **Website**—http://www.mesa-air.com **Chrmn**—P. R. Madden.**CEO**—J. Ornstein.**CFO, Treas, VP-Fin & Investor Contact**—W. Stephen Jackson (505-326-4410). **VP & Secy**—G. E. Risley. **Dirs**—D. J. Altobello, J. Braly, H. A. Denton, R. R. Fogleman, P. R. Madden, J. Ornstein, L. L. Risley, J. Swigart.**Transfer Agent & Registrar**—American Securities Transfer, Denver. **Incorporated**—in Nevada in 1996; originally organized in New Mexico in 1983. **Empl**—4,800. **S&P Analyst:** P.L.H.

Methode Electronics   4588

NASDAQ Symbol **METHA**

In S&P SmallCap 600

10-OCT-98

Industry: Electronics (Instrumentation)

Summary: Methode manufactures component devices for OEMs of electronic data processing equipment, communication systems and automobiles.

Quantitative Evaluations

Outlook
(1 Lowest—5 Highest)
• **4**

Fair Value
• **20¼**

Risk
• **Average**

Earn./Div. Rank
• **A-**

Technical Eval.
• **NA**

Rel. Strength Rank
(1 Lowest—99 Highest)
• **76**

Insider Activity
• **NA**

Recent Price • 13	Yield • 1.5%
52 Wk Range • 27⅛-10⅝	12-Mo. P/E • 13.5

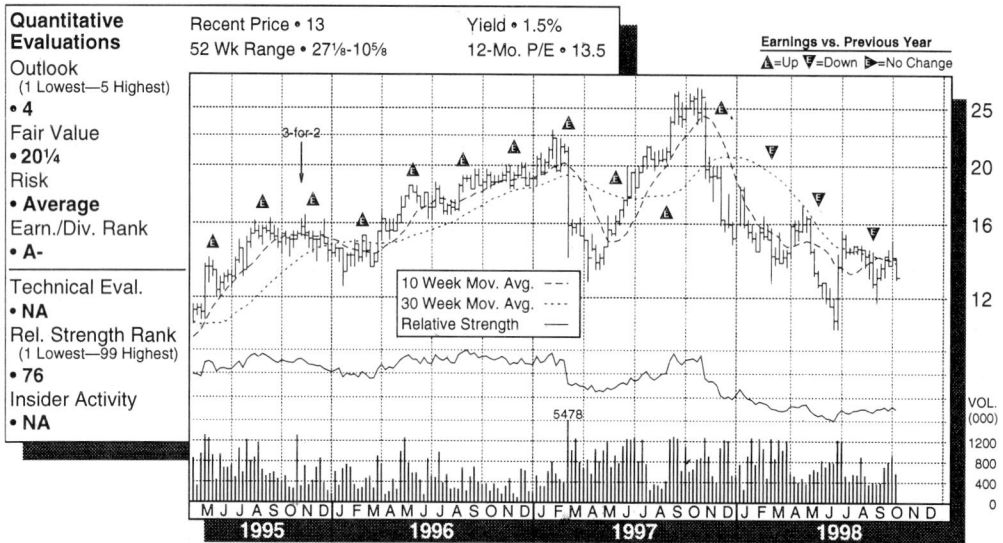

Earnings vs. Previous Year
▲=Up ▼=Down ►=No Change

10 Week Mov. Avg. ---
30 Week Mov. Avg. ·····
Relative Strength —

Business Profile - 26-JUN-98

METHA believes that it will benefit in FY 99 (Apr.) from strong demand for fiber optics and intelligent connectors, as well as improved demand for its Network Buss technology which has been repositioned to serve a broader range of markets, lessening its dependence on the mainframe computer market. METHA is hopeful that the disk drive industry will recover in the second quarter and beyond as well. Double digit sales are expected to continue in its domestic automotive division, primarily related to additional products for sport utility vehicles. However, the company expects to start the fiscal year off slower than last year, as opportunities in optoelectronics will not kick in until late summer, and later in the year for other products.

Operational Review - 26-JUN-98

Net sales (preliminary) rose 11% in FY 98 (Apr.), reflecting the acquisition of Merit-Malta Methode in February 1997 and Adam Technologies in May 1997. Sales of network buss products to the mainframe computer industry continued to decline, and sales of automotive interconnect devices and controls to the domestic automotive industry were down. Margins narrowed, due to additional manufacturing costs, increased staffing levels, a less favorable product mix, and customer pricing pressures; pretax income declined 8.3%. After taxes at 34.2%, versus 36.3%, net income was down 5.2%, to $35,266,000 ($1.00 a share), from $37,219,000 ($1.06).

Stock Performance - 09-OCT-98

In the past 30 trading days, METHA's shares have increased 2%, compared to a 4% fall in the S&P 500. Average trading volume for the past five days was 113,200 shares, compared with the 40-day moving average of 113,644 shares.

Key Stock Statistics

Dividend Rate/Share	0.20	Shareholders	1,800
Shs. outstg. (M)	35.6	Market cap. (B)	$0.447
Avg. daily vol. (M)	0.147	Inst. holdings	60%
Tang. Bk. Value/Share	5.22		
Beta	0.98		

Value of $10,000 invested 5 years ago: $ 19,940

Fiscal Year Ending Apr. 30

	1999	1998	1997	1996	1995	1994
Revenues (Million $)						
1Q	87.96	91.90	78.97	68.22	57.76	43.51
2Q	—	99.9	85.19	78.64	66.78	52.97
3Q	—	90.74	85.94	75.73	67.39	52.99
4Q	—	96.73	92.99	84.95	78.81	63.83
Yr.	—	379.3	343.1	307.5	270.8	213.3
Earnings Per Share ($)						
1Q	0.22	0.26	0.23	0.19	0.17	0.11
2Q	—	0.27	0.26	0.22	0.17	0.14
3Q	—	0.20	0.26	0.22	0.17	0.15
4Q	—	0.27	0.31	0.30	0.24	0.21
Yr.	—	1.00	1.06	0.93	0.75	0.61

Next earnings report expected: late November

Dividend Data (Dividends have been paid since 1983.)

Amount ($)	Date Decl.	Ex-Div. Date	Stock of Record	Payment Date
0.050	Dec. 09	Jan. 13	Jan. 15	Jan. 30 '98
0.050	Mar. 17	Apr. 13	Apr. 15	Apr. 30 '98
0.050	Jun. 26	Jul. 13	Jul. 15	Jul. 31 '98
0.050	Sep. 08	Oct. 13	Oct. 15	Oct. 30 '98

A Division of The **McGraw·Hill** *Companies*

Business Summary - 26-JUN-98

A long-established (1946) manufacturer of components that connect, convey and control electrical signal, digital pulse and energy, Methode Electronics, Inc. (METHA) is positioned to benefit from the continuing trend toward increased electronic content in modern products. Items manufactured by the company include connectors, controls, interconnect devices, printed circuits and current-carrying distribution systems.

Products made by Methode are sold to manufacturers of electronic data processing equipment, instruments, voice and data communications, and the automotive industry.

The company's serialized optical links are becoming increasingly critical for high-speed data transfer. Power and signal busses are used in mainframe computers and in automation, robotics and cellular communications equipment. Methode's connectors contain sophisticated circuits that enhance high-speed signal transmission between computers and peripheral equipment such as printers, scanners and disc drives. Automotive components include a wide range of electromechanical and electronic controls used in both cars and trucks. Sales to Chrysler and Ford accounted for 42%, 40% and 42%

of net sales in FY 97 (Apr.), FY 96 and FY 95, respectively.

Methode's operating units specialize in segments of the interconnect and controls markets. The concept of relatively small product-oriented groupings supported by a wide range of corporate resources has proved to be a successful strategy for the company.

The company's products are sold through a direct sales staff, by independent manufacturers' representatives with offices throughout the world, and through a number of distributor organizations. Foreign sales accounted for 19% of the total in FY 97, up from 18% in FY 96 and 17% in FY 95.

Methode operates 21 electronic and fiber optic connector and cable assembly manufacturing plants that serve the electronics industry in the U.S., Malta, the U.K., Ireland and Singapore. METHA also operates three service facilities.

Recent acquisitions included Adam Technologies, a broad-line supplier of connectors (May 1997), Merit Elektrik, a Maltese automotive switch manufacturer (February 1997), and 75% of Sentorque, which owns a portfolio of intellectual property covering innovative advances in circularly magnetized non-contact torque sensors (February 1997).

Per Share Data ($)

(Year Ended Apr. 30)	1998	1997	1996	1995	1994	1993	1992	1991	1990	1989
Tangible Bk. Val.	5.22	4.51	4.59	3.75	2.97	2.29	1.80	1.85	1.65	1.51
Cash Flow	1.49	1.47	1.27	1.06	0.87	0.67	0.50	0.44	0.33	0.23
Earnings	1.00	1.06	0.93	0.75	0.61	0.43	0.29	0.24	0.15	0.07
Dividends	0.20	0.20	0.16	0.08	0.03	0.02	0.02	0.02	0.02	0.02
Payout Ratio	20%	19%	17%	11%	5%	6%	8%	10%	15%	35%
Cal. Yrs.	1997	1996	1995	1994	1993	1992	1991	1990	1989	1988
Prices - High	27$\frac{1}{8}$	20$\frac{1}{4}$	16$\frac{1}{2}$	13$\frac{5}{8}$	9$\frac{7}{8}$	7$\frac{1}{8}$	4$\frac{1}{8}$	2$\frac{5}{8}$	1$\frac{15}{16}$	2$\frac{1}{4}$
- Low	12$\frac{3}{4}$	12$\frac{1}{2}$	8$\frac{5}{8}$	8$\frac{3}{4}$	6$\frac{7}{8}$	3$\frac{1}{4}$	1$\frac{15}{16}$	1$\frac{9}{16}$	1$\frac{5}{16}$	1$\frac{5}{16}$
P/E Ratio - High	27	19	18	18	23	17	15	11	13	34
- Low	13	12	9	12	14	8	7	7	10	20

Income Statement Analysis (Million $)

	1998	1997	1996	1995	1994	1993	1992	1991	1990	1989
Revs.	379	343	308	271	213	172	148	149	133	122
Oper. Inc.	65.7	167	58.5	48.1	40.4	28.7	20.8	17.5	14.1	8.8
Depr.	17.6	14.7	12.1	10.6	9.0	7.8	7.3	6.6	5.7	5.1
Int. Exp.	0.3	0.2	0.3	0.4	0.4	0.3	0.2	0.6	0.7	0.7
Pretax Inc.	53.6	58.4	51.0	40.8	33.5	22.5	13.6	12.0	8.6	3.6
Eff. Tax Rate	34%	36%	37%	36%	37%	35%	30%	34%	41%	39%
Net Inc.	35.3	37.2	32.4	26.1	21.0	14.7	9.5	7.9	5.1	2.2

Balance Sheet & Other Fin. Data (Million $)

	1998	1997	1996	1995	1994	1993	1992	1991	1990	1989
Cash	24.2	23.1	50.2	40.8	26.8	21.9	19.8	11.1	9.4	2.3
Curr. Assets	145	123	137	120	97.0	72.0	59.6	53.9	51.4	42.3
Total Assets	288	254	223	191	161	129	107	90.0	84.8	74.3
Curr. Liab.	50.4	44.5	46.0	43.7	38.2	34.0	28.5	21.5	21.9	16.1
LT Debt	Nil	Nil	Nil	Nil	0.1	0.2	0.3	0.4	2.8	3.9
Common Eqty.	226	198	165	135	108	84.7	67.6	62.3	54.8	49.9
Total Cap.	226	198	165	135	108	85.3	69.0	64.6	59.6	55.6
Cap. Exp.	23.2	20.4	22.1	17.4	13.3	17.3	10.1	8.0	6.2	8.0
Cash Flow	52.9	51.9	44.5	36.7	30.0	22.6	16.8	14.5	10.8	7.3
Curr. Ratio	2.8	2.8	3.0	2.7	2.5	2.1	2.1	2.5	2.3	2.6
% LT Debt of Cap.	Nil	Nil	Nil	Nil	0.1	0.2	0.4	0.6	4.7	6.9
% Net Inc.of Revs.	9.3	10.9	10.5	9.6	9.8	8.6	6.4	5.3	3.8	1.8
% Ret. on Assets	13.0	15.7	15.6	14.8	14.4	12.4	9.6	9.1	6.4	3.0
% Ret. on Equity	16.7	20.6	21.6	21.5	21.7	19.3	14.6	13.5	9.7	4.4

Data as orig. reptd.; bef. results of disc. opers. and/or spec. items. Per share data adj. for stk. divs. as of ex-div. date. Bold denotes diluted EPS (FASB 128). E-Estimated. NA-Not Available. NM-Not Meaningful. NR-Not Ranked.

Office—7444 W. Wilson Ave, Harwood Heights, IL 60656. **Tel**—(708) 867-9600. **Website**—http://www.methode.com **Chrmn & Pres**—W. J. McGinley. **EVP & CFO**—K. J. Hayes.**Secy**—J. W. Ashley. **Dirs**—M. G. Andre, J. W. Ashley, J. R. Cannon, W. C. Croft, K. J. Hayes, J. W. McGinley, W. J. McGinley, R. J. Roberts, G. C. Wright. **Transfer Agent & Registrar**—ChaseMellon Shareholder Services, Ridgefield Park, NJ. **Incorporated**—in Illinois in 1946; reincorporated in Delaware in 1966. **Empl**— 3,650. **S&P Analyst:** Jim Corridore

STANDARD &POOR'S
STOCK REPORTS

Metro Networks

4588D

Nasdaq Symbol **MTNT**

In S&P SmallCap 600

10-OCT-98

Industry: Broadcasting (Television, Radio & Cable)

Summary: This company, the largest provider of traffic reporting services, also supplies news, sports and weather information to the television and radio broadcast industries:

S&P Opinion: Accumulate (★★★★)	

Recent Price • 30	Yield • Nil
52 Wk Range • 45½-27⅞	12-Mo. P/E • 29.4

Quantitative Evaluations

Outlook (1 Lowest—5 Highest)
• **NA**

Fair Value
• **NA**

Risk
• **NA**

Earn./Div. Rank
• **NR**

Technical Eval.
• **NA**

Rel. Strength Rank (1 Lowest—99 Highest)
• **44**

Insider Activity
• **NA**

Earnings vs. Previous Year
▲=Up ▼=Down ▶=No Change

10 Week Mov. Avg. — — —
30 Week Mov. Avg. · · · · ·
Relative Strength ———

1995 1996 1997 1998

Overview - 14-AUG-98

We expect revenues to advance at a 18%-22% pace through 1999, driven by Metro's dominant position in the traffic reporting services industry. The company currently provides traffic reports in 47 of the 50 largest Metro Survey Areas (MSA's). In addition, the top-line should benefit from recent efforts to expand its information services to include news, sports and weather. In the long term, we believe emerging avenues of communication, such as the Internet and the wireless communications field, offer MTNT with a tremendous opportunity to offer existing services in new markets. Margins should widen on the larger revenue base, as well as efforts to control marketing expenditures. Following a decline in the effective tax rate, we see 1998 EPS rising nearly 30%, to $1.20 from 1997's $0.93, and expect EPS to increase 30% to $1.56 in 1999.

Valuation - 14-AUG-98

The shares have recently pulled back with the rest of the market and are currently selling at about 33 times our 1998 EPS estimate of $1.20 (25X our 1999 estimate of $1.56). We feel this generous valuation is warranted, given MTNT's above-average earnings growth expectations and its industry leading position. Additionally, we feel the shares offer skittish investors a safe haven from the problems plaguing many other fast-growing companies, such as unfavorable economic conditions in Asia and negative currency translations. As a result, we continue to recommend accumulation of the stock. We believe MTNT's future growth will be driven by penetration of the untapped international arena and through offering expanded, real-time news services via the Internet and wireless communication devices. These fast-growing markets will become increasingly important as organizations and individuals seek the most efficient method of information exchange.

Key Stock Statistics

S&P EPS Est. 1998	1.20	Tang. Bk. Value/Share	4.66
P/E on S&P Est. 1998	25.0	Beta	NA
S&P EPS Est. 1999	1.56	Shareholders	NA
Dividend Rate/Share	Nil	Market cap. (B)	$0.498
Shs. outstg. (M)	16.6	Inst. holdings	50%
Avg. daily vol. (M)	0.029		

Value of $10,000 invested 5 years ago: NA

Fiscal Year Ending Dec. 31

	1998	1997	1996	1995	1994	1993
Revenues (Million $)						
1Q	34.39	29.37	—	—	—	—
2Q	42.95	34.71	—	—	—	—
3Q	—	34.99	29.00	—	—	—
4Q	—	40.06	30.16	—	—	—
Yr.	—	139.1	109.2	72.43	60.05	47.91
Earnings Per Share ($)						
1Q	0.09	0.09	—	—	—	—
2Q	0.33	0.24	—	—	—	—
3Q	E0.35	0.27	0.32	—	—	—
4Q	E0.44	0.33	0.34	—	—	—
Yr.	E1.20	0.93	0.94	0.23	—	—

Next earnings report expected: NA

Dividend Data

No cash dividends have been paid. The company intends to retain its earnings to finance the development and expansion of its business and does not anticipate paying cash dividends in the foreseeable future.

A Division of The **McGraw·Hill** *Companies*

STANDARD
&POOR'S
STOCK REPORTS

Metro Networks, Inc.

4588D
10-OCT-98

Business Summary - 14-AUG-98

If you listened to the radio this morning, perhaps you caught the local traffic report. Whose voice was that, telling you to avoid the freeway, warning you of sluggish service on your rail or bus line? There's a good chance it belonged to a broadcaster with Metro Networks, Inc. (MTNT), the nation's largest provider of traffic reporting services. MTNT is also a leading supplier of local news, sports and weather to the radio broadcast industry, and it provides traffic and news services to television stations as well.

MTNT operates in over 70 markets across the U.S. (including nearly all of the country's top 50 markets), servicing more than 1,500 radio station affiliates and 100 TV station affiliates. That translates into well over 100 million pairs of ears that listen daily to the company's reports.

MTNT began its business nearly 20 years ago, offering individual radio stations customized broadcast reports on local traffic conditions. In return, the company received commercial advertising inventory; the packaging and sale of such inventory today accounts for substantially all of MTNT's revenues. MTNT later reached out to the television industry with similar traffic reporting services. In 1994, the company broadened its service offering to the radio broadcast field by adding news, sports and weather (collectively, "expanded radio services"), and it began providing video news services to TV affiliates the following year.

The progressive expansion of services to the broadcast industry has continued, and in September 1997 the company unveiled a new digital information system, Metro Source, which allows its affiliates to receive via satellite, view, write, edit and report news and features in text and audio formats.

Although MTNT has grown rapidly in recent years, the company believes there is still plenty of room for expansion. MTNT's core radio traffic services are used by about half of the stations in its existing markets, leaving untapped a large base of potential customers. Through strategic acquisitions and start-ups, MTNT is expanding into new markets as well. The September 1997 acquisition of Traffax Traffic Network and Freecom Newsnet, for example, added over 100 radio and TV affiliates in seven eastern markets to the number of stations served. All but one of these markets represented new entries for MTNT.

MTNT believes this continued expansion also benefits the company's advertisers by allowing them to reach potential customers in one market, a region or throughout the country with a single advertising purchase.

Per Share Data ($)

(Year Ended Dec. 31)	1997	1996	1995	1994	1993	1992	1991	1990	1989	1988
Tangible Bk. Val.	4.27	3.50	NA	NA	NA	NA	NA	NA	NA	NA
Cash Flow	1.46	1.41	0.55	NA	NA	NA	NA	NA	NA	NA
Earnings	0.93	0.94	0.23	NA	NA	NA	NA	NA	NA	NA
Dividends	Nil	Nil	Nil	Nil	Nil	Nil	Nil	Nil	Nil	Nil
Payout Ratio	Nil	Nil	Nil	Nil	Nil	Nil	Nil	Nil	Nil	Nil
Prices - High	37¾	25¾	NA	NA	NA	NA	NA	NA	NA	NA
- Low	21⅝	16	NA	NA	NA	NA	NA	NA	NA	NA
P/E Ratio - High	41	27	NA	NA	NA	NA	NA	NA	NA	NA
- Low	23	17	NA	NA	NA	NA	NA	NA	NA	NA

Income Statement Analysis (Million $)

	1997	1996	1995	1994	1993	1992	1991	1990	1989	1988
Revs.	139	109	72.4	NA	47.9	42.0	NA	NA	NA	NA
Oper. Inc.	34.0	27.0	9.4	NA	4.7	2.3	NA	NA	NA	NA
Depr.	8.9	6.2	4.0	NA	1.8	1.8	NA	NA	NA	NA
Int. Exp.	0.2	1.8	1.3	NA	0.1	0.1	NA	NA	NA	NA
Pretax Inc.	26.7	19.4	4.3	NA	2.5	0.4	NA	NA	NA	NA
Eff. Tax Rate	42%	38%	36%	NA	43%	NM	NM	NM	NM	NM
Net Inc.	15.5	12.0	2.8	NA	0.9	-2.3	NA	NA	NA	NA

Balance Sheet & Other Fin. Data (Million $)

	1997	1996	1995	1994	1993	1992	1991	1990	1989	1988
Cash	25.1	43.4	3.0	NA	NA	NA	NA	NA	NA	NA
Curr. Assets	72.5	80.0	21.7	NA	NA	NA	NA	NA	NA	NA
Total Assets	115	106	42.4	NA	16.5	22.4	NA	NA	NA	NA
Curr. Liab.	24.4	30.7	13.8	NA	NA	NA	NA	NA	NA	NA
LT Debt	0.5	0.5	21.9	NA	2.2	0.6	NA	NA	NA	NA
Common Eqty.	88.3	71.9	4.5	NA	4.2	5.2	NA	NA	NA	NA
Total Cap.	89.5	72.4	28.4	NA	NA	NA	NA	NA	NA	NA
Cap. Exp.	16.6	6.8	2.0	NA	0.3	NA	NA	NA	NA	NA
Cash Flow	24.4	18.2	6.8	NA	2.7	-0.4	NA	NA	NA	NA
Curr. Ratio	3.0	2.6	1.6	NA	NA	NA	NA	NA	NA	NA
% LT Debt of Cap.	0.6	0.6	77.1	NA	NA	NA	NA	NA	NA	NA
% Net Inc.of Revs.	11.2	11.0	3.9	NA	1.8	NA	NA	NA	NA	NA
% Ret. on Assets	14.1	16.2	8.0	NA	4.4	NA	NA	NA	NA	NA
% Ret. on Equity	19.4	31.6	40.3	NA	18.3	NA	NA	NA	NA	NA

Data as orig. reptd.; bef. results of disc. opers. and/or spec. items. Per share data adj. for stk. divs. as of ex-div. date. Bold denotes diluted EPS (FASB 128). E-Estimated. NA-Not Available. NM-Not Meaningful. NR-Not Ranked.

Office—2800 Post Oak Blvd., Suite 4000, Houston, TX 77056. **Tel**—(713) 407-6000. **Website**—http://www.metronetworks.com **Chrmn & CEO**—D. Saperstein. **Pres**—C. I. Bortnick. **SVP, CFO & Investor Contact**—Timothy D. McMillin. **Dirs**—J. A. Arcara, C. I. Bortnick, S. E. Coppola, D. F. Holt, T. D. McMillin, R. M. Miggins, D. Saperstein, K. M. Spivak, G. L. Worobow. **Transfer Agent**—American Stock Transfer & Trust Co. NYC. **Incorporated**—in Delaware in 1996. **Empl**— 1,759. **S&P Analyst:** Stephen J. Tekirian

03-OCT-98

Industry:
Retail (Specialty)

Summary: This company is the leading arts and crafts retailer in the U.S., with a chain of 483 Michaels stores in 45 states, Canada and Puerto Rico, and 75 Aaron Brothers stores.

S&P Opinion: Hold (★★★)	Recent Price • 24¾	Yield • Nil
	52 Wk Range • 37⅞-23	12-Mo. P/E • 20.0

Quantitative Evaluations

Outlook
(1 Lowest—5 Highest)
• **2⁻**

Fair Value
• **29⅛**

Risk
• **High**

Earn./Div. Rank
• **C**

Technical Eval.
• **Bearish** since 8/98

Rel. Strength Rank
(1 Lowest—99 Highest)
• **39**

Insider Activity
• **Neutral**

Earnings vs. Previous Year
▲=Up ▼=Down ▶=No Change

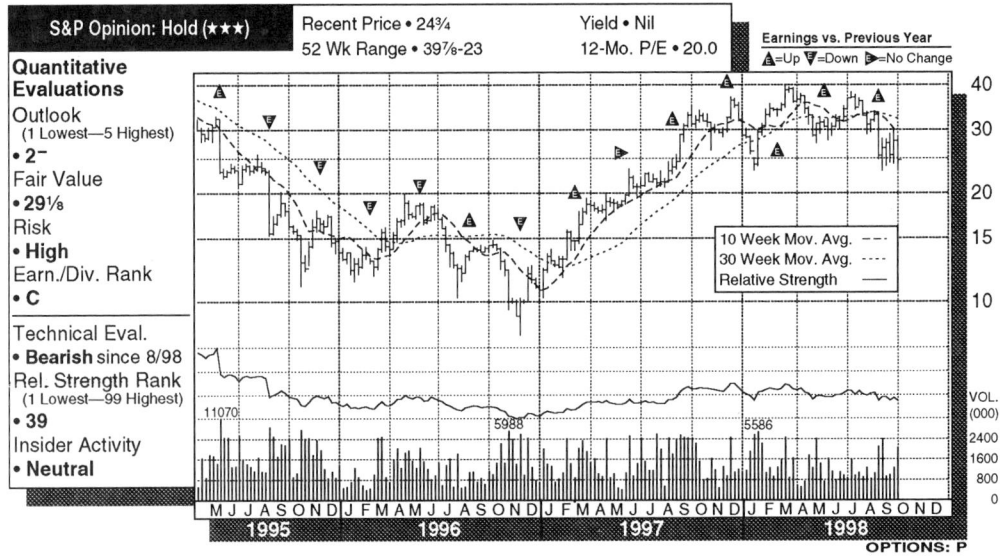

10 Week Mov. Avg. ---
30 Week Mov. Avg. - - -
Relative Strength ——

OPTIONS: P

Overview - 20-SEP-98

MIKE is aggressively expanding, expecting to have 43 more Michaels locations in FY 99 (Jan.) than it had last year, and 50 to 55 more by the end of FY 00. MIKE is currently completing the implementation of an extensive point-of-sale (POS) system, and at 1998's end, we expect its Michaels outlets to have full electronic inventory and merchandise management capabilities, enabling stores to quickly improve its in-stock position of best selling items and more adequately react to prevailing sales trends. We anticipate significant sales growth, cost cutting and margin benefits to accrue as a result of the successful deployment of the POS system, as well as the second quarter completion of a new distribution center. MIKE derives some 60% of sales and 80% of earnings during its holiday-rich third and fourth quarters, which we believe will be the best in the company's history, because of MIKE's high inventory position and strong marketing plans. MIKE is also considering a national roll-out of its 75-store Aaron Brothers custom framing and arts supplies chain, which we believe could be quite successful considering the stores' solid and improving same-store sales.

Valuation - 20-SEP-98

We currently rate shares of MIKE a hold. Though the company is executing its business plan quite effectively, we believe the ever-changing tastes of arts and crafts customers tend to reduce the consistency of MIKE's sales and earnings, as well as the multiple at which such shares trade relative to expected earnings. At a recent $25.50 a share, the stock was trading at a reasonable 18 times our FY 99 (Jan.) estimate, and 14 times our FY 00 estimate, considering our expected long-term earnings growth rate of some 20%.

Key Stock Statistics

S&P EPS Est. 1999	1.40	Tang. Bk. Value/Share	11.08
P/E on S&P Est. 1999	17.7	Beta	0.90
S&P EPS Est. 2000	1.82	Shareholders	1,000
Dividend Rate/Share	Nil	Market cap. (B)	$0.734
Shs. outstg. (M)	29.7	Inst. holdings	84%
Avg. daily vol. (M)	0.280		

Value of $10,000 invested 5 years ago: $ 7,279

Fiscal Year Ending Jan. 31

	1999	1998	1997	1996	1995	1994
Revenues (Million $)						
1Q	335.8	321.3	301.9	265.6	159.8	113.0
2Q	314.2	278.0	260.5	259.9	174.2	115.4
3Q	—	350.1	322.2	312.7	283.1	155.8
4Q	—	507.1	493.7	456.7	377.5	235.6
Yr.	—	1,457	1,378	1,295	994.6	619.7
Earnings Per Share ($)						
1Q	**0.18**	0.12	0.12	0.35	0.28	0.22
2Q	**0.02**	-0.11	-0.34	-1.55	0.04	0.28
3Q	**E0.22**	0.15	-1.45	0.14	0.36	0.28
4Q	**E0.98**	0.79	0.35	0.10	1.01	0.75
Yr.	**E1.40**	1.05	-1.34	-0.95	1.77	1.53

Next earnings report expected: late November

Dividend Data

No dividends have been paid.

Business Summary - 20-SEP-98

Michaels Stores, Inc. is the largest U.S. specialty retailer of arts, crafts and decorative items. Its stores offer a selection of more than 35,000 competitively priced products, including picture framing materials and services; dried flowers and other floral items; art, craft and hobby supplies; and party, holiday and seasonal merchandise. The company's primary customers are women aged 25 to 54 with above-average household incomes.

As of September 3, 1998, MIKE was operating 483 Michaels outlets in 45 states, Canada and Puerto Rico, having an average of 16,500 square feet of selling space. The company expects to add 43 stores to the Michaels chain during FY 99, and 50 to 55 stores in FY 00. By the end of FY 99, Michaels expects to convert one-third of its stores to a new prototype format, featuring modern layouts with oval racetrack-style aisles.

Stores are located in clusters or on a single-store basis in geographic areas where rent, freight and advertising expenditures are not cost-prohibitive. Stores currently in operation are located primarily in strip shopping centers with ample parking in areas easily accessible to customer traffic.

Substantially all products sold are manufactured in the U.S., the Far East or Mexico. Goods manufactured in the Far East generally require long lead times, and are ordered four to six months in advance of delivery. In the past, about 40% of merchandise was shipped to the stores via the company's distribution facilities, and MIKE hopes to increase this percentage to 65.

As of September 3, 1998, the company was operating 75 Aaron Brothers stores, primarily in California, offering frames, related materials and equipment, as well as art supplies. The company expects to open 7 new Aaron Brothers stores in FY 99. Stores average some 6,500 square feet, and have started to feature do-it-yourself framing areas. MIKE's management has recently been considering a national roll-out of Aaron Brothers in light of the chain's three consecutive years of improving high single-digit same-store sales growth, and the significantly-fragmented nature of the custom framing market.

Management expects the implementation of an extensive point-of-sale (POS) system to be complete by year's end. This system will provide Michaels outlets with full electronic inventory and merchandise management capabilities, enabling stores to quickly replenish best selling items and react to prevailing sales trends. The deployment of the POS system and the second quarter opening of MIKE's new distribution center should make the company's management of inventory more effective and efficient.

Per Share Data ($)

(Year Ended Jan. 31)	1998	1997	1996	1995	1994	1993	1992	1991	1990	1989
Tangible Bk. Val.	10.51	8.11	8.94	11.17	9.70	7.96	6.90	2.39	1.70	4.05
Cash Flow	2.64	0.45	0.49	2.84	2.25	1.83	1.65	1.34	0.68	0.99
Earnings	1.05	-1.34	-0.95	1.76	1.53	1.22	0.90	0.57	Nil	0.50
Dividends	Nil	Nil	Nil	Nil	Nil	Nil	Nil	Nil	Nil	Nil
Payout Ratio	Nil	Nil	Nil	Nil	Nil	Nil	Nil	Nil	Nil	Nil
Cal. Yrs.	1997	1996	1995	1994	1993	1992	1991	1990	1989	1988
Prices - High	37	19⁷/₈	37	46¹/₂	39	34	17¹/₈	6¹/₂	10¹/₄	7⁵/₈
- Low	11¹/₄	8	11	29¹/₂	25¹/₄	16	3⁵/₈	2⁷/₈	4⁷/₈	3⁷/₈
P/E Ratio - High	35	NM	NM	26	25	28	19	11	NM	15
- Low	11	NM	NM	17	17	13	4	5	NM	8

Income Statement Analysis (Million $)

	1998	1997	1996	1995	1994	1993	1992	1991	1990	1989
Revs.	1,457	1,378	1,295	995	620	493	411	362	290	250
Oper. Inc.	115	20.7	15.9	92.6	53.8	44.4	34.5	27.5	21.5	21.9
Depr.	45.6	41.7	30.9	21.5	12.5	10.2	8.9	7.8	7.2	5.1
Int. Exp.	23.4	21.0	16.8	9.1	6.4	0.3	7.0	9.7	9.9	8.6
Pretax Inc.	48.5	-41.1	-34.8	57.2	42.6	33.5	17.8	9.7	0.6	8.4
Eff. Tax Rate	38%	NM	NM	38%	38%	39%	40%	40%	98%	38%
Net Inc.	30.1	-31.2	-20.4	35.6	26.3	20.4	10.7	5.9	NM	5.2

Balance Sheet & Other Fin. Data (Million $)

	1998	1997	1996	1995	1994	1993	1992	1991	1990	1989
Cash	162	59.1	2.9	16.9	68.8	42.1	27.4	0.1	1.2	1.4
Curr. Assets	573	438	416	419	291	170	126	85.0	92.0	79.0
Total Assets	908	784	740	686	398	322	181	144	151	135
Curr. Liab.	214	198	187	186	109	65.6	51.1	40.5	33.5	21.2
LT Debt	222	222	184	138	97.8	97.8	Nil	54.2	74.2	72.0
Common Eqty.	442	333	336	356	185	155	126	47.0	40.0	39.0
Total Cap.	664	555	520	494	283	253	126	104	117	114
Cap. Exp.	44.0	33.6	54.9	68.1	46.8	19.8	5.5	6.8	9.5	15.2
Cash Flow	75.7	10.5	10.5	57.2	38.8	30.5	19.6	13.7	7.2	10.3
Curr. Ratio	2.7	2.2	2.2	2.2	2.7	2.6	2.5	2.1	2.8	3.7
% LT Debt of Cap.	34.8	40.0	35.4	27.9	34.5	38.6	Nil	52.2	63.3	63.4
% Net Inc.of Revs.	2.1	NM	NM	3.6	4.2	4.1	2.6	1.6	NM	2.1
% Ret. on Assets	3.6	NM	NM	6.0	7.3	7.8	5.4	4.0	NM	4.3
% Ret. on Equity	7.8	NM	NM	12.0	15.3	13.9	10.9	13.4	NM	14.2

Data as orig. reptd.; bef. results of disc. opers. and/or spec. items. Per share data adj. for stk. divs. as of ex-div. date. Bold denotes diluted EPS (FASB 128). E-Estimated. NA-Not Available. NM-Not Meaningful. NR-Not Ranked.

Office—8000 Brent Branch Drive, Irving, TX 75063; P.O. Box 619566, DFW, TX 75261-9566. **Tel**—(972) 409-1300. **Website**—http://www.michaels.com **Chrmn**—S. Wyly. **Vice Chrmn**—C. J. Wyly Jr. **Pres & CEO**—R. M. Rouleau. **EVP & CFO**—B. M. DeCordova. **VP-Fin**—C. J. Holland. **VP & Secy**—M. V. Beasley. **Dirs**—K. Elliot; M. C. French; D. R. Miller, Jr.; C. J. Wyly, Jr.; E. A. Wyly; S. Wyly. **Transfer Agent & Registrar**—Harris Trust & Savings Bank, NYC. **Incorporated**—in Delaware in 1983. **Empl**— 17,900. **S&P Analyst**: Scott H. Kessler.

STANDARD &POOR'S
STOCK REPORTS

MicroAge, Inc.

4606M

NASDAQ Symbol **MICA**

In S&P SmallCap 600

10-OCT-98

Industry:
Retail (Computers &
Electronics)

Summary: This franchisor of computer stores and distributor of
microcomputer systems has an international network of outlets that
sell, support and service office information products.

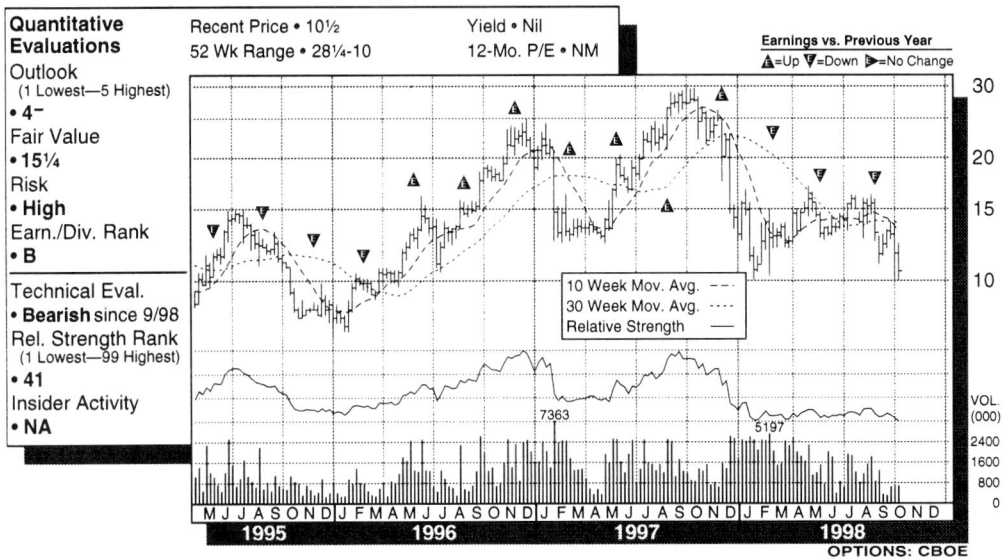

Quantitative Evaluations	
Outlook (1 Lowest—5 Highest)	• **4**-
Fair Value	• **15¼**
Risk	• **High**
Earn./Div. Rank	• **B**
Technical Eval.	• **Bearish** since 9/98
Rel. Strength Rank (1 Lowest—99 Highest)	• **41**
Insider Activity	• **NA**

Recent Price • 10½
52 Wk Range • 28¼-10

Yield • Nil
12-Mo. P/E • NM

Earnings vs. Previous Year
▲=Up ▼=Down ▶=No Change

10 Week Mov. Avg. ---
30 Week Mov. Avg. ....
Relative Strength —

OPTIONS: CBOE

Business Profile - 14-SEP-98

This global provider of efficient technology solutions restored modest levels of profits in the third quarter of FY
98 (Oct.). During the second quarter, MicroAge created
a separate entity for its distribution business. The new
unit, named Pinacor, will be the third largest technology
distributor in the U.S. MICA believes the separation of
its distribution and integration business into autonomous
units will allow each division to be more competitive in
its respective markets. As a result of the restructuring, a
pretax charge of $5.6 million was recorded in the sec-
ond quarter. The company continues to explore all financial options for Pinacor as part of an effort to maximize shareholder value.

Operational Review - 14-SEP-98

Revenues for the nine months ended August 2, 1998,
rose 25%, year to year, reflecting strong demand for
new products and growth of microcomputer products.
Gross profit margins narrowed to 6.2% from 7.1%,
largely reflecting competitive pricing pressures, and results were adversely impacted by sharply higher operating expenses, the inclusion of a $5.6 million restructur-
ing charge and higher other expenses. Despite a tax
benefit of $6.5 million, versus taxes at 41.6%, a net
loss of $9.941,000 ($0.51 a share) contrasted with net
income of $18,210,000 ($1.01).

Stock Performance - 09-OCT-98

In the past 30 trading days, MICA's shares have declined 20%, compared to a 4% fall in the S&P 500.
Average trading volume for the past five days was
131,240 shares, compared with the 40-day moving average of 165,821 shares.

Key Stock Statistics

Dividend Rate/Share	Nil	Shareholders	400
Shs. outstg. (M)	20.2	Market cap. (B)	$0.213
Avg. daily vol. (M)	0.113	Inst. holdings	43%
Tang. Bk. Value/Share	9.11		
Beta	1.25		

Value of $10,000 invested 5 years ago: $ 19,803

Fiscal Year Ending Oct. 31

	1998	1997	1996	1995	1994	1993
Revenues (Million $)						
1Q	1,179	890.8	780.3	674.3	470.4	328.0
2Q	1,327	1,086	863.6	743.5	529.6	365.0
3Q	1,441	1,148	842.7	759.1	583.4	392.1
4Q	—	1,322	1,030	764.2	637.4	425.2
Yr.	—	4,446	3,516	2,941	2,221	1,510
Earnings Per Share ($)						
1Q	-0.28	0.29	0.11	0.20	0.36	0.20
2Q	-0.27	0.37	0.20	0.17	0.41	0.23
3Q	0.04	0.39	0.24	0.05	0.23	0.33
4Q	—	0.40	0.34	-0.40	0.25	0.38
Yr.	—	1.40	0.89	0.02	1.22	1.15

Next earnings report expected: **early December**

Dividend Data

No cash has been paid. Under its credit agreements,
the company is prohibited from paying dividends without bank consent. A three-for-two stock split was effected in January 1994.

A Division of The McGraw-Hill Companies

STANDARD
&POOR'S
STOCK REPORTS

MicroAge, Inc.

4606M
10-OCT-98

Business Summary - 14-SEP-98

When many companies enter the information superhighway, they turn to MicroAge (MICA) for help in getting into the fast lane. The company is a global systems integrator and distributor of information technology (IT) products and services, providing an all-inclusive range of hardware and software products, along with logistics, integration and installation services.

The company markets itself as an interconnected chain, comprising products, resources and skills required to implement complex IT solutions. The various business groups of MicroAge work together to sell, ship, engineer, install and service the company's products.

MICA's computer centers distribute more than 20,000 technology hardware and software products and value-added services to reseller customers (who sell the products to others, hence the name reseller) worldwide. Resellers include franchisees, which operate under the company's proprietary name, as well as non-franchised resellers. MICA provides distribution and support services to the resellers, allowing them to realize operating efficiencies and benefit from economies of scale. Sales to value-added resellers have been one of the fastest growing segments for the company.

The integration group provides computing solutions to large corporations, government agencies and educational institutions through a network of qualified resel-

lers (including 51 resellers owned and operated by the company). Advanced technical support and expertise is available from more than 1,250 field engineers, including 325 certified Novell engineers throughout the U.S. and in 29 foreign countries.

The logistics group fulfills and ships product orders from distribution centers in Arizona, Ohio and Nevada for delivery anywhere in the continental U.S. in one to three business days. The group also provides systems set-up, local area network set-up and testing, and other installation and testing services.

The services group provides value added services to MICA's customers, allowing them to configure, place and track orders. Orders can be placed over the Internet as well as through other electronic linkages. The group's software enables users to determine product compatibility, develop custom proposals, and place orders.

MICA's distribution strategy focuses on the products of major microcomputer and peripheral manufacturers. In FY 97 (Oct.), Compaq, Hewlett-Packard and IBM together accounted for 57% of the company's product sales.

In May 1998, MicroAge completed a restructuring plan to consolidate operations into two separate units: a distribution business renamed Pinacor and an integration business. In an effort to enhance shareholder value, the company hired an investment banking firm to help explore options for Pinacor.

Per Share Data ($)

(Year Ended Oct. 31)	1997	1996	1995	1994	1993	1992	1991	1990	1989	1988
Tangible Bk. Val.	10.93	11.56	10.96	11.11	13.48	6.32	4.87	4.27	3.66	3.37
Cash Flow	2.75	2.26	1.09	1.91	2.77	1.20	1.05	1.41	0.98	0.90
Earnings	1.40	0.89	0.02	1.22	1.15	0.59	0.50	0.97	0.64	0.62
Dividends	Nil	Nil	Nil	Nil	Nil	Nil	Nil	Nil	Nil	Nil
Payout Ratio	Nil	Nil	Nil	Nil	Nil	Nil	Nil	Nil	Nil	Nil
Prices - High	29¾	25	15	32½	26⅝	10½	10⅛	12⅜	7⅛	6⅛
- Low	12¼	7½	7¼	9¼	5⅜	3⅞	3⅞	4⅛	4⅛	2⅞
P/E Ratio - High	21	28	NM	27	23	18	20	13	11	10
- Low	9	8	NM	8	5	6	8	4	6	5

Income Statement Analysis (Million $)

	1997	1996	1995	1994	1993	1992	1991	1990	1989	1988
Revs.	4,446	3,516	2,941	2,221	1,510	1,017	787	613	360	252
Oper. Inc.	94.7	56.8	41.1	41.8	25.1	13.4	10.0	4.7	6.2	6.5
Depr.	24.0	20.3	15.4	9.3	6.4	4.8	3.5	2.9	2.2	1.8
Int. Exp.	5.9	1.3	3.4	1.3	0.7	1.6	1.6	0.3	1.4	1.0
Pretax Inc.	43.3	23.1	1.0	27.0	17.5	7.8	5.8	11.0	7.0	5.9
Eff. Tax Rate	42%	43%	78%	39%	40%	40%	44%	41%	40%	33%
Net Inc.	25.0	13.3	0.2	16.3	10.5	4.7	3.2	6.5	4.2	4.0

Balance Sheet & Other Fin. Data (Million $)

	1997	1996	1995	1994	1993	1992	1991	1990	1989	1988
Cash	24.0	20.5	13.7	11.1	20.2	23.2	14.7	2.5	3.0	2.6
Curr. Assets	844	610	508	456	298	205	141	100	82.0	47.0
Total Assets	974	690	573	510	323	227	162	113	92.0	54.0
Curr. Liab.	701	499	400	342	214	161	117	74.0	58.0	20.0
LT Debt	35.2	3.9	4.1	2.1	1.2	9.3	11.0	8.8	6.4	10.1
Common Eqty.	238	186	168	166	108	56.9	33.5	29.7	27.0	23.9
Total Cap.	273	190	173	168	109	66.2	44.5	38.5	33.4	34.1
Cap. Exp.	36.5	24.0	22.9	17.6	7.9	4.9	8.4	4.9	1.6	2.2
Cash Flow	49.0	33.6	15.7	25.6	16.9	9.5	6.8	9.4	6.3	5.8
Curr. Ratio	1.2	1.2	1.3	1.3	1.4	1.3	1.2	1.3	1.4	2.3
% LT Debt of Cap.	12.8	2.0	2.4	1.2	1.1	14.1	24.7	22.9	19.2	29.7
% Net Inc.of Revs.	0.6	0.4	NM	0.7	0.7	0.5	0.4	1.1	1.2	1.6
% Ret. on Assets	3.0	2.1	0.1	3.7	3.3	2.1	2.4	6.4	5.7	7.2
% Ret. on Equity	11.8	7.5	0.2	11.1	11.3	9.1	10.2	23.1	16.5	18.0

Data as orig. reptd.; bef. results of disc. opers. and/or spec. items. Per share data adj. for stk. divs. as of ex-div. date. Bold denotes diluted EPS (FASB 128). E-Estimated. NA-Not Available. NM-Not Meaningful. NR-Not Ranked.

Office—2400 South MicroAge Way, Tempe, AZ 85282-1896. **Tel**—(602) 366-2000. **Website**—http://www.microage.com **Chrmn & CEO**—J. D. McKeever. **Secy**—A. P. Hald. **SVP, CFO, Treas & Investor Contact**—James R. Daniel (602-929-2410). **Dirs**—L. M. Applegate, C. F. Friedheim, R. A. Herberger Jr., F. Israel, J. D. McKeever, W. H. Mallender, S. G. Mihaylo. **Transfer Agent & Registrar**—First Interstate Bank of Arizona, LA. **Incorporated**—in Delaware in 1987. **Empl**—4,400. **S&P Analyst**: R.M.G.

MICROS Systems 4607V

NASDAQ Symbol **MCRS**

In S&P SmallCap 600

03-OCT-98

Industry:
Computers (Peripherals)

Summary: This company is a leading worldwide designer, manufacturer, supplier and servicer of restaurant point-of-sale computer systems and hotel management systems.

Quantitative Evaluations		
Outlook (1 Lowest—5 Highest) • **5**	Recent Price • 30¾ 52 Wk Range • 39½-21¼	Yield • Nil 12-Mo. P/E • 25.6

Fair Value • **54¾**

Risk • **High**

Earn./Div. Rank • **B+**

Technical Eval. • **Bullish** since 3/98

Rel. Strength Rank (1 Lowest—99 Highest) • **80**

Insider Activity • **NA**

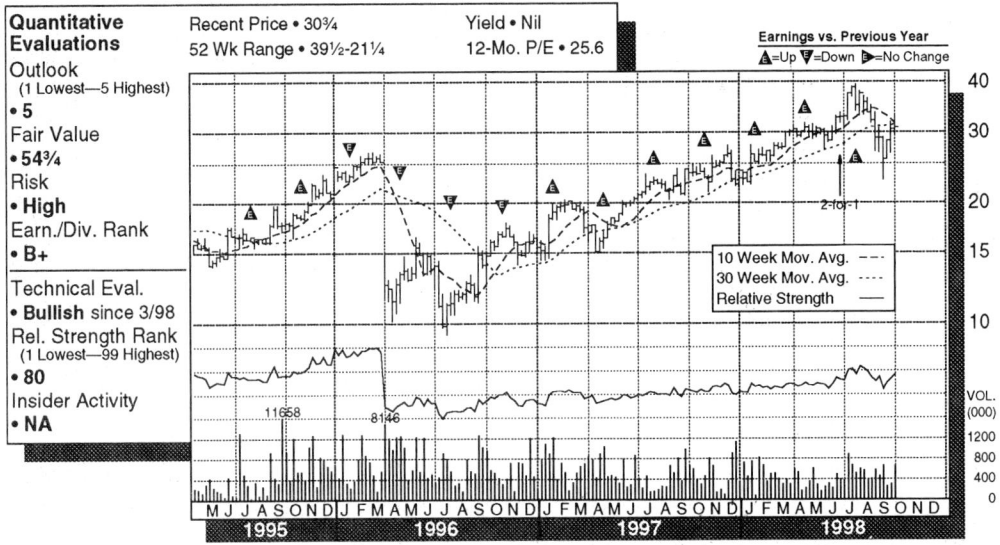

Earnings vs. Previous Year
▲=Up ▼=Down ▶=No Change
10 Week Mov. Avg. – – –
30 Week Mov. Avg. ·······
Relative Strength ———

Business Profile - 31-AUG-98

MICROS has posted revenue growth rates in recent periods significantly in excess of the global market for POS computer systems, although it does not expect to maintain growth at these levels. MCRS expects increased competition to continue to put pressure on gross margins. New target markets for the company's POS systems include casinos, cruise ships, sports arenas, theme parks, institutional food service organizations and specialty retail shops. In the fourth quarter of FY 98 (Jun.), the company recorded a $2.2 million charge to close its European headquarters in Munich, Germany, in order to reduce expenses and centralize operations.

Operational Review - 31-AUG-98

Revenues advanced 23% in FY 98 (preliminary), reflecting a 23% increase in hardware and software sales and a 22% gain in service revenues. Gross margins narrowed, but after well controlled SG&A expenses, operating income was up 27%. Following $2.2 million in office closure costs and 16% higher depreciation and amortization charges, net income was up 23%, to $20,053,000 ($1.20 a share, on 3.7% more shares), from $16,332,000 ($1.01). Results in FY 98 exclude a charge of $0.02 a share for an accounting change; per share amounts in both periods are adjusted for a 2-for-1 stock split in June 1998.

Stock Performance - 02-OCT-98

In the past 30 trading days, MCRS's shares have declined 4%, compared to a 7% fall in the S&P 500. Average trading volume for the past five days was 131,060 shares, compared with the 40-day moving average of 94,990 shares.

Key Stock Statistics

Dividend Rate/Share	Nil	Shareholders	500
Shs. outstg. (M)	16.0	Market cap. (B)	$0.493
Avg. daily vol. (M)	0.098	Inst. holdings	78%
Tang. Bk. Value/Share	4.08		
Beta	1.34		

Value of $10,000 invested 5 years ago: $ 30,370

Fiscal Year Ending Jun. 30

	1998	1997	1996	1995	1994	1993
Revenues (Million $)						
1Q	59.59	47.51	32.36	24.47	16.40	11.43
2Q	66.27	55.96	42.89	27.12	19.32	13.11
3Q	71.08	56.71	47.31	25.19	19.28	12.27
4Q	83.31	67.99	55.50	35.24	24.27	18.50
Yr.	280.3	228.2	178.1	112.0	79.26	55.31
Earnings Per Share ($)						
1Q	0.18	0.14	0.20	0.19	0.13	0.07
2Q	**0.30**	0.25	-0.32	0.18	0.12	0.08
3Q	**0.35**	0.28	0.08	0.14	0.13	0.08
4Q	**0.36**	0.34	0.19	0.21	0.18	0.14
Yr.	**1.20**	1.01	0.15	0.73	0.55	0.37

Next earnings report expected: early November

Dividend Data

Amount ($)	Date Decl.	Ex-Div. Date	Stock of Record	Payment Date
2-for-1	Apr. 29	Jun. 23	May. 22	Jun. 22 '98

A Division of The **McGraw·Hill** *Companies*

Business Summary - 31-AUG-98

MICROS Systems, Inc. is a leading worldwide designer, manufacturer, supplier and servicer of point-of-sale (POS) computer systems for hospitality providers, primarily full service and fast food restaurants and hotels. It also markets and distributes property management information systems products and offers service and support for both systems.

The company's POS systems, which as of June 30, 1997, were installed in over 37,000 independent, national and international table service restaurants and over 6,500 quick service restaurants, consist of terminals, display devices, printers, computer and software that provide transaction processing, in-store control and information management capabilities. Such systems enable users to control operations and inventory, enhance customer service efficiency, reduce labor costs, increase productivity and improve planning and reporting. POS products include the 8700 Hospitality Management System (HMS), which is designed for hotels, resorts, casinos, airports, sports arenas, theme parks and large local and chain restaurants. Features include customized workstations, flexible guest check printing, table and check tracking, automatic credit card authorization and system-wide reporting of sales mix, sales balancing, serving periods and table turns.

Other POS products include the 2700 HMS, a stand-alone intelligent terminal designed for small to large full service restaurants and certain fast food operations; 2400 HMS, a stand-alone system for the quick service restaurant sector; 3700 HMS, a PC-driven system for operations control of full service dining operations; and the Handheld Touchscreen terminal, a small remote order entry computer device that allows a server to enter a food and beverage order at the table or seat-side.

The company's property management information systems (PMS) products provide reservation, guest accounting and other information management capabilities to hotels and other lodging establishments. In addition to PMS products for the hotel industry, the company offers central reservation systems (CRS) software, which allows hotel companies to provide instantaneous updating of reservations for member hotels.

MICROS also offers service and support for its POS, PMS and CRS products, including installations, training, hardware and software maintenance, spare parts, media supplies and consulting services. Such services accounted for 35% of revenues in FY 97 (Jun.).

Products are marketed and sold through company-owned domestic and foreign sales offices as well as through international distributors. Foreign sales accounted for 51% of revenues in FY 97.

Per Share Data ($)

(Year Ended Jun. 30)	1998	1997	1996	1995	1994	1993	1992	1991	1990	1989
Tangible Bk. Val.	NA	3.19	2.23	3.29	2.44	1.89	1.57	1.27	1.07	0.79
Cash Flow	NA	1.58	0.45	0.83	0.63	0.43	0.33	0.28	0.24	0.17
Earnings	1.20	1.01	0.15	0.73	0.55	0.37	0.27	0.22	0.18	0.11
Dividends	Nil	Nil	Nil	Nil	Nil	Nil	Nil	Nil	Nil	Nil
Payout Ratio	Nil	Nil	Nil	Nil	Nil	Nil	Nil	Nil	Nil	Nil
Prices - High	39½	27¾	26⅞	24⅞	20⅝	13	11⅜	3⅝	2¾	2½
- Low	22¼	14⅜	9⅜	13⅞	11¼	5⅞	2⅞	1⅝	1⅜	11/16
P/E Ratio - High	33	27	179	26	38	35	43	16	15	23
- Low	18	14	63	19	21	16	10	7	8	6

Income Statement Analysis (Million $)

	1998	1997	1996	1995	1994	1993	1992	1991	1990	1989
Revs.	NA	228	178	112	79.0	55.3	44.3	39.6	35.2	25.5
Oper. Inc.	NA	37.0	25.1	18.2	13.6	10.3	6.8	5.6	4.8	2.7
Depr.	NA	9.2	4.8	1.6	1.2	0.9	1.0	1.0	0.9	0.7
Int. Exp.	NA	1.4	1.6	0.4	0.2	0.1	0.1	0.1	0.1	0.2
Pretax Inc.	NA	27.6	2.7	17.7	12.6	8.8	6.0	5.0	4.1	2.0
Eff. Tax Rate	NA	38%	13%	35%	32%	35%	35%	34%	38%	37%
Net Inc.	NA	16.3	2.4	11.6	8.7	5.8	4.0	3.3	2.6	1.3

Balance Sheet & Other Fin. Data (Million $)

	1998	1997	1996	1995	1994	1993	1992	1991	1990	1989
Cash	NA	10.9	15.2	26.4	16.3	12.8	14.0	9.7	6.7	1.8
Curr. Assets	NA	108	87.9	66.6	46.7	33.6	29.7	23.9	20.9	12.0
Total Assets	NA	164	137	89.6	66.2	48.1	37.4	30.1	26.6	16.9
Curr. Liab.	NA	79.9	67.2	29.6	19.6	15.3	11.3	9.1	8.8	5.5
LT Debt	NA	7.1	10.2	5.3	5.5	1.6	1.7	1.8	2.0	2.0
Common Eqty.	NA	71.7	56.2	53.5	39.9	30.0	23.6	19.2	15.8	9.3
Total Cap.	NA	83.6	69.6	60.0	46.6	32.7	26.1	21.1	17.9	11.4
Cap. Exp.	NA	8.1	4.8	2.6	1.2	0.7	0.4	1.1	0.8	0.3
Cash Flow	NA	25.5	7.2	13.2	9.9	6.7	5.0	4.3	3.5	2.0
Curr. Ratio	NA	1.3	1.3	2.3	2.3	2.2	2.6	2.6	2.4	2.2
% LT Debt of Cap.	NA	8.5	14.6	8.8	11.8	5.0	6.4	8.8	11.3	17.4
% Net Inc.of Revs.	NA	7.2	1.3	10.3	11.0	10.4	9.1	8.3	7.3	5.0
% Ret. on Assets	NA	10.9	2.1	14.9	15.2	13.5	11.8	11.6	11.8	8.2
% Ret. on Equity	NA	25.5	4.4	24.8	24.9	21.5	18.8	18.7	20.4	14.8

Data as orig. reptd.; bef. results of disc. opers. and/or spec. items. Per share data adj. for stk. divs. as of ex-div. date. Bold denotes diluted EPS (FASB 128). E-Estimated. NA-Not Available. NM-Not Meaningful. NR-Not Ranked.

Office—12000 Baltimore Ave., Beltsville, MD 20705-1291. **Tel**—(301) 210-6000. **Chrmn**—L. M. Brown, Jr. **Pres & CEO**—A. L. Giannopoulos. **EVP & COO**—R. J. Kolson. **SVP-Fin & CFO**—G. C. Kaufman. **Secy**—J. F. Wilbert. **Dirs**—L. M. Brown, Jr., D. A. Cohen, A. L. Giannopoulos, F. S. Jenniches, J. G. Puente, D. S. Taylor, A. M. Voorhees, E. T. Wilson. **Transfer Agent & Registrar**—Registrar and Transfer Co., Cranford, NJ. **Incorporated**—in Maryland in 1977. **Empl**—1,534. **S&P Analyst:** Jim Corridore

Midway Games
1494M

NYSE Symbol **MWY**

In S&P SmallCap 600

10-OCT-98

Industry: Leisure Time (Products)

Summary: The company designs, publishes and markets interactive entertainment software played in both the coin operated and home markets.

Quantitative Evaluations

Recent Price • 10¾
52 Wk Range • 25⅝-9¼

Yield • Nil
12-Mo. P/E • 9.8

Outlook (1 Lowest—5 Highest)
• **NA**

Fair Value
• **NA**

Risk
• **NA**

Earn./Div. Rank
• **NR**

Technical Eval.
• **NA**

Rel. Strength Rank (1 Lowest—99 Highest)
• **46**

Insider Activity
• **Neutral**

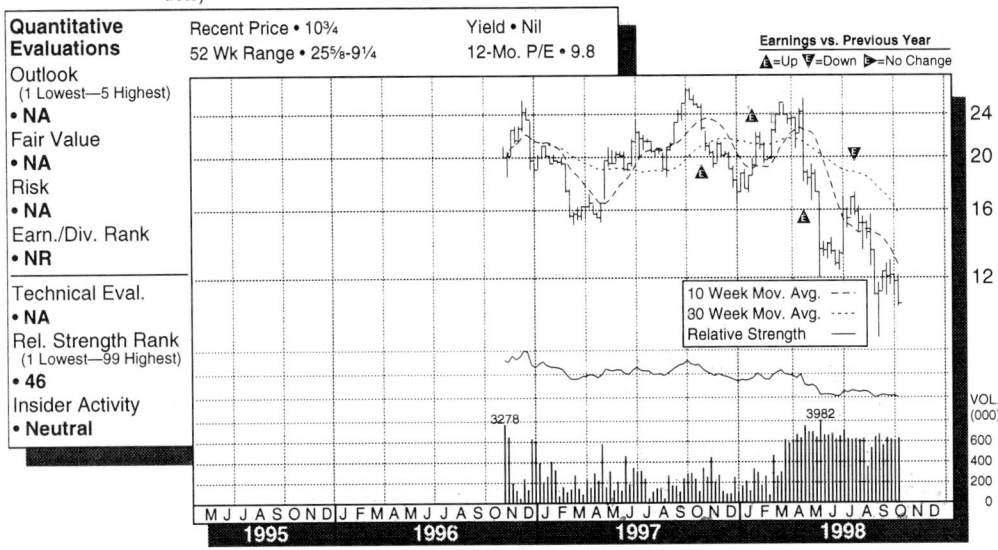

Earnings vs. Previous Year
▲=Up ▼=Down ▶=No Change

10 Week Mov. Avg. - - -
30 Week Mov. Avg. ·····
Relative Strength ——

Business Profile - 08-OCT-98

Midway's business strategy is to create a portfolio of exciting, popular video games. It seeks to utilize the coin-operated market as a meaningful indicator for how successful a game will be in the home market; maintain platform independence; exploit franchise and library value opportunities for its games; develop multi-site game playing networks; and continue to invest in advanced technology. For the first quarter of FY 99 (Jun.), Midway expects to launch four new home video game products and three new coin-operated games. During the June 1998 quarter, directors authorized the repurchase of up to 1,000,000 shares of the company's common stock, and through mid-August, MWY had repurchased 893,800 shares.

Operational Review - 08-OCT-98

Revenues for the fiscal year ended June 30, 1998, rose 0.8% from those of the prior year, reflecting a stronger contribution from next generation home videos, offset for the most part by lower sales of home video games in the 16 bit cartridge category. Gross margins widened, aided by more favorable sales mix and lower parts costs. Despite higher research and development and selling costs, pretax income was up 8.6%. After taxes at 38.1%, versus 38.0%, net income increased 8.4%, to $42,122,000 ($1.10 a share, on 4.6% more shares outstanding), from $38,851,000 ($1.06). FY 97 results exclude an $0.08 a share special credit from the early extinguishment of debt.

Stock Performance - 09-OCT-98

In the past 30 trading days, MWY's shares have declined 4%, compared to a 4% fall in the S&P 500. Average trading volume for the past five days was 172,880 shares, compared with the 40-day moving average of 170,269 shares.

Key Stock Statistics

Dividend Rate/Share	Nil	Shareholders	700
Shs. outstg. (M)	37.4	Market cap. (B)	$0.402
Avg. daily vol. (M)	0.157	Inst. holdings	54%
Tang. Bk. Value/Share	3.46		
Beta	NA		

Value of $10,000 invested 5 years ago: NA

Fiscal Year Ending Jun. 30

	1998	1997	1996	1995	1994	1993
Revenues (Million $)						
1Q	73.74	65.56	—	—	—	—
2Q	125.1	125.5	—	—	—	—
3Q	94.35	99.1	—	—	—	—
4Q	98.09	98.09	—	—	—	—
Yr.	391.2	388.2	329.4	—	—	—
Earnings Per Share ($)						
1Q	0.19	0.18	—	—	—	—
2Q	0.48	0.41	—	—	—	—
3Q	0.18	0.17	—	—	—	—
4Q	0.25	0.29	—	—	—	—
Yr.	1.10	1.06	0.74	—	—	—

Next earnings report expected: late October

Dividend Data

The company does not intend to pay any dividends on its common stock in the foreseeable future. MWY intends to retain any earnings for the development and expansion of its business.

A Division of The **McGraw-Hill** Companies

STANDARD
&POOR'S
STOCK REPORTS

Midway Games Inc.

1494M
10-OCT-98

Business Summary - 08-OCT-98

Midway Games Inc. designs, publishes and markets interactive entertainment software played in both the coin-operated and home markets. Prior to its initial public offering of 5.1 million common shares in October 1996, the company was a wholly-owned subsidiary of WMS Industries Inc. WMS continues to provide certain administrative, accounting, and information services and facilities to the company, and acts as a contract manufacturer for MWY's coin-operated video games. Revenue contributions in recent fiscal years (ending June 30) were:

	1998	1997	1996
Home Video	59%	57%	63%
Coin Operated Video	41%	43%	37%

The company believes that a successful video game may present the opportunity to exploit ancillary rights such as film, television and merchandising rights.

Like coin-operated video games, interactive software programs for the home allow the consumer to participate actively in the outcome of the game. The interactive software publishing business involves the creation or the acquisition of titles or intellectual property rights, the development of interactive software products based on those titles or rights, and the publication, marketing, merchandising, distribution and licensing of the resulting software products. The business is highly dependant on consumer tastes and preferences and on the commercial success of the hardware platform for which the software is produced. Home video games have suggested retail prices ranging from $39.95-$59.95.

Coin-operated video games, which are sold to distributors at prices ranging from $3,000 to $7,000 are made in self-contained cabinetry containing large video screens that display the game. Multiple players can play the same game simultaneously, and games are generally designed to permit the players to play against each other, in addition to being able to play against the game itself. Most coin-operated video games cost $0.50 to play a game of about two minutes in duration.

Since the late 1970s, Midway has released many of the industry's leading games including the Mortal Kombat line (which line of games has sold over 15 million copies and accounted for 19% of revenues in FY 98), Cruis'n USA, Cruis'n World, NBA Jam, Joust, Defender, Pacman and Space Invaders, and through its subsidiary Atari Games Corp. such games as San Francisco Rush Extreme Racing, The NHLPA & NHL Present Wayne Gretzky's 3D Hockey, Area 51, Gauntlet, Centipede, Asteroids and Pong. The company's games are generally available for play on all major dedicated home video game platforms, including those of Nintendo, Sony and Sega and personal computers.

Per Share Data ($)

(Year Ended Jun. 30)	1998	1997	1996	1995	1994	1993	1992	1991	1990	1989
Tangible Bk. Val.	3.46	2.38	1.98	NA	NA	NA	NA	NA	NA	NA
Cash Flow	1.33	1.23	0.89	NA	NA	NA	NA	NA	NA	NA
Earnings	1.10	1.06	0.74	NA	NA	NA	NA	NA	NA	NA
Dividends	Nil	Nil	Nil	Nil	Nil	Nil	Nil	Nil	Nil	Nil
Payout Ratio	Nil	Nil	Nil	Nil	Nil	Nil	Nil	Nil	Nil	Nil
Prices - High	25⅝	26⅞	25½	NA	NA	NA	NA	NA	NA	NA
- Low	12	15	18⅜	NA	NA	NA	NA	NA	NA	NA
P/E Ratio - High	23	25	34	NA	NA	NA	NA	NA	NA	NA
- Low	11	14	25	NA	NA	NA	NA	NA	NA	NA

Income Statement Analysis (Million $)

	1998	1997	1996	1995	1994	1993	1992	1991	1990	1989
Revs.	391	388	329	NA	NA	NA	NA	NA	NA	NA
Oper. Inc.	74.0	66.8	45.7	NA	NA	NA	NA	NA	NA	NA
Depr.	8.9	6.3	5.1	NA	NA	NA	NA	NA	NA	NA
Int. Exp.	Nil	2.4	0.8	NA	NA	NA	NA	NA	NA	NA
Pretax Inc.	68.0	62.7	39.9	NA	NA	NA	NA	NA	NA	NA
Eff. Tax Rate	38%	38%	38%	NA	NA	NA	NA	NA	NA	NA
Net Inc.	42.1	38.9	24.7	NA	NA	NA	NA	NA	NA	NA

Balance Sheet & Other Fin. Data (Million $)

	1998	1997	1996	1995	1994	1993	1992	1991	1990	1989
Cash	26.1	61.9	52.9	NA	NA	NA	NA	NA	NA	NA
Curr. Assets	162	154	NA	NA	NA	NA	NA	NA	NA	NA
Total Assets	227	214	162	NA	NA	NA	NA	NA	NA	NA
Curr. Liab.	43.9	68.1	NA	NA	NA	NA	NA	NA	NA	NA
LT Debt	Nil	Nil	7.9	NA	NA	NA	NA	NA	NA	NA
Common Eqty.	177	141	99	NA	NA	NA	NA	NA	NA	NA
Total Cap.	181	144	107	NA	NA	NA	NA	NA	NA	NA
Cap. Exp.	4.4	4.7	4.1	NA	NA	NA	NA	NA	NA	NA
Cash Flow	51.0	45.1	29.8	NA	NA	NA	NA	NA	NA	NA
Curr. Ratio	3.7	2.3	NA	NA	NA	NA	NA	NA	NA	NA
% LT Debt of Cap.	Nil	Nil	7.3	NA	NA	NA	NA	NA	NA	NA
% Net Inc.of Revs.	10.8	10.0	7.5	NA	NA	NA	NA	NA	NA	NA
% Ret. on Assets	19.1	23.4	NA	NA	NA	NA	NA	NA	NA	NA
% Ret. on Equity	26.5	32.4	NA	NA	NA	NA	NA	NA	NA	NA

Data as orig. reptd.; bef. results of disc. opers. and/or spec. items. Per share data adj. for stk. divs. as of ex-div. date. Bold denotes diluted EPS (FASB 128). E-Estimated. NA-Not Available. NM-Not Meaningful. NR-Not Ranked.

Office—3401 North California Ave., Chicago, IL 60618. **Tel**—(773) 961-2222. **Chrmn, Pres, CEO & COO**—N. D. Nicastro. **EVP, CFO & Treas**—H. H. Bach, Jr. **VP & Secy**—O. J. Edidin. **Dirs**—H. H. Bach, Jr., W. C. Bartholomay, B. C. Cook, K. J. Fedesna, W. E. McKenna, N. J. Menell, L. J. Nicastro, N. D. Nicastro, H. Reich, I. S. Sheinfeld, G. O. Sweeney, Jr., R. D. White. **Transfer Agent & Registrar**—Bank of New York, NYC. **Incorporated**—in Delaware in 1988. **Empl**— 550. **S&P Analyst:** P.L.H.

03-OCT-98   Industry: Chemicals

Summary: This major manufacturer of fertilizers produces and markets all three primary crop nutrients, including nitrogen, phosphate and potash.

Quantitative Evaluations	
Recent Price • 12⅜	Yield • 3.2%
52 Wk Range • 20⅛-11½	12-Mo. P/E • 14.8

Outlook (1 Lowest—5 Highest)
• **3+**

Fair Value
• **15¼**

Risk
• **Low**

Earn./Div. Rank
• **NR**

Technical Eval.
• **NA**

Rel. Strength Rank (1 Lowest—99 Highest)
• **48**

Insider Activity
• **NA**

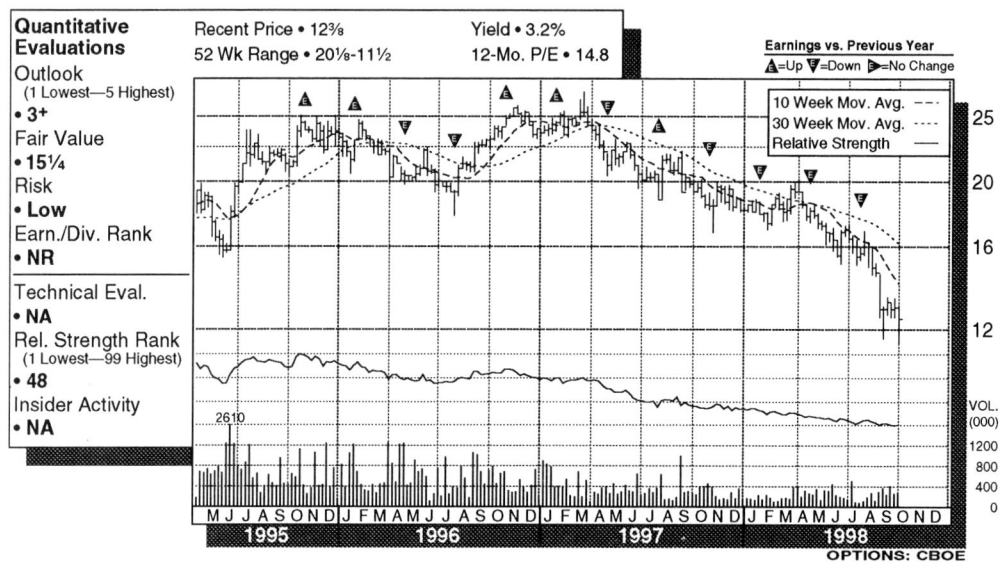

Earnings vs. Previous Year
▲=Up ▼=Down ▶=No Change

10 Week Mov. Avg. ---
30 Week Mov. Avg. ····
Relative Strength —

OPTIONS: CBOE

Business Profile - 21-SEP-98

While the company is looking forward to the benefits resulting from a series of recent expansions, a key issue currently is the direction of nitrogen pricing. Soft Asian market conditions, pricing policies out of Russia, and recent capacity expansions will exert downward pressure on prices. While most analysts expect nitrogen prices to retreat from fourth quarter highs, they believe that prices, on average, will remain above the deeply depressed levels seen during late calendar 1997 and early 1998. Since the inception of a stock repurchase program in May 1995, the company has repurchased approximately 2,800,000 shares of its common stock out of the 3,000,000 shares authorized; authorization for the buyback of another 5,000,000 shares was announced in September 1998.

Operational Review - 21-SEP-98

Net sales (preliminary) were little changed in FY 98 (Jun.), as the acquisition of First Mississippi in December 1996 was offset by lower nitrogen prices. With profitability severely affected by the weak prices, net income plunged 59%, to $23.0 million ($0.84 per share, diluted), from $55.8 million ($2.29).

Stock Performance - 02-OCT-98

In the past 30 trading days, GRO's shares have declined 15%, compared to a 7% fall in the S&P 500. Average trading volume for the past five days was 55,980 shares, compared with the 40-day moving average of 56,462 shares.

Key Stock Statistics

Dividend Rate/Share	0.40	Shareholders	10,700
Shs. outstg. (M)	27.3	Market cap. (B)	$0.340
Avg. daily vol. (M)	0.063	Inst. holdings	59%
Tang. Bk. Value/Share	9.42		
Beta	NA		

Value of $10,000 invested 5 years ago: NA

Fiscal Year Ending Jun. 30

	1998	1997	1996	1995	1994	1993
Revenues (Million $)						
1Q	110.6	91.29	96.57	72.75	—	—
2Q	118.0	113.2	99.9	83.71	—	—
3Q	125.4	142.6	107.7	114.7	—	—
4Q	165.1	173.5	124.6	117.0	—	—
Yr.	519.1	520.6	428.8	388.1	309.4	—
Earnings Per Share ($)						
1Q	0.16	0.44	0.43	0.27	—	—
2Q	**0.02**	0.56	0.53	0.46	—	—
3Q	**0.02**	0.38	0.72	0.75	—	—
4Q	**0.65**	0.86	0.79	0.82	—	—
Yr.	**0.84**	2.29	2.46	2.34	—	—

Next earnings report expected: late October

Dividend Data (Dividends have been paid since 1995.)

Amount ($)	Date Decl.	Ex-Div. Date	Stock of Record	Payment Date
0.100	Oct. 20	Oct. 31	Nov. 04	Nov. 24 '97
0.100	Jan. 22	Jan. 29	Feb. 02	Feb. 13 '98
0.100	Apr. 23	May. 01	May. 05	May. 19 '98
0.100	Jul. 23	Jul. 31	Aug. 04	Aug. 18 '98

A Division of The **McGraw·Hill** *Companies*

Business Summary - 21-SEP-98

Originally organized as a cooperative by 600 farmers in 1948, Mississippi Chemical Corp. (GRO) is a major manufacturer of fertilizers. GRO is a leading producer and supplier of nitrogen fertilizers in the southern U.S. and also manufactures phosphate and potash fertilizers, making it a full product line fertilizer supplier. GRO sells its nitrogen and potash fertilizer products to farmers, fertilizer dealers and distributors mainly for use in the southern farming regions of the U.S., and in areas served by the Mississippi River system.

Sales contributions by product categories in recent fiscal years (Jun.) were:

	FY 97	FY 96
Nitrogen	59%	60%
DAP	25%	33%
Potash	16%	7%

GRO's principal nitrogen products include ammonia; fertilizer-grade ammonium nitrate, which is sold under the company's trade name Amtrate; and UAN solutions, which are sold under the trade name N-Sol; and urea. In FY 97, the company produced about 1,151,000 tons of anhydrous ammonia at its Yazoo City, MS, and Donaldson, LA facilities, and purchased about 59,000 tons. In GRO's markets, ammonia is used mainly as a pre-emergent fertilizer for most row crops. The company is the largest U.S. manufacturer and marketer of ammonium nitrate fertilizer. In FY 97, it sold about 725,000 tons of solid ammonium nitrate fertilizer. In FY 97, GRO sold about 457,000 tons of N-Sol, a 32% nitrogen product used in direct application to cotton, corn, grains and pastures as well as for use in liquid fertilizer blends. In FY 97, the company sold about 297,000 tons of prilled urea and about 127,000 tons of urea melt.

GRO produces diammonium phosphate fertilizers (DAP), the most common form of phosphate fertilizer; in FY 97, it sold about 723,000 tons of DAP, mainly into international markets. DAP is an important fertilizer for both direct application and for use in blended fertilizers applied to all major types of row crops.

In FY 97, GRO sold about 1,020,000 tons of potash primarily in granular form and mainly to customers located west of the Mississippi River. In August 1996, the company acquired the potash assets of Trans-Resources, Inc. for $45 million.

In December 1996, GRO acquired the fertilizer operations of First Mississippi Corp.'s (FMC) in exchange for 6.9 million common shares and the assumption of debt. The transaction, representing a total value of $311 million, was closed following the spinoff by FMC of its non-fertilizer assets into a new, publicly traded company called ChemFirst Inc. As part of the transaction, GRO received the remaining 50% interest in Triad Chemical that it did not already own. FMC's name has since been changed to Triad Nitrogen, Inc.

Per Share Data ($)

(Year Ended Jun. 30)	1998	1997	1996	1995	1994	1993	1992	1991	1990	1989
Tangible Bk. Val.	NA	9.43	11.61	10.19	7.87	NA	NA	NA	NA	NA
Cash Flow	NA	3.32	3.28	3.10	NA	NA	NA	NA	NA	NA
Earnings	0.84	2.29	2.46	2.34	NA	NA	NA	NA	NA	NA
Dividends	0.40	0.30	0.36	0.16	Nil	Nil	Nil	Nil	Nil	Nil
Payout Ratio	48%	13%	15%	7%	Nil	Nil	Nil	Nil	Nil	Nil
Prices - High	20⅛	27¼	24¾	25¼	19¼	NA	NA	NA	NA	NA
- Low	11⅝	16¾	17¾	15⅜	14¾	NA	NA	NA	NA	NA
P/E Ratio - High	24	12	10	11	NA	NA	NA	NA	NA	NA
- Low	14	7	7	7	NA	NA	NA	NA	NA	NA

Income Statement Analysis (Million $)

	1998	1997	1996	1995	1994	1993	1992	1991	1990	1989
Revs.	NA	521	429	388	309	289	NA	NA	NA	NA
Oper. Inc.	NA	119	103	98.0	61.0	44.0	NA	NA	NA	NA
Depr.	NA	28.0	17.8	17.1	17.0	14.4	NA	NA	NA	NA
Int. Exp.	NA	8.9	0.7	2.0	4.7	6.0	NA	NA	NA	NA
Pretax Inc.	NA	90.6	88.5	81.4	32.9	26.4	NA	NA	NA	NA
Eff. Tax Rate	NA	38%	39%	36%	18%	14%	NA	NA	NA	NA
Net Inc.	NA	55.8	54.2	52.2	26.9	22.7	NA	NA	NA	NA

Balance Sheet & Other Fin. Data (Million $)

	1998	1997	1996	1995	1994	1993	1992	1991	1990	1989
Cash	NA	8.2	60.2	29.6	23.2	NA	NA	NA	NA	NA
Curr. Assets	NA	149	142	115	100	NA	NA	NA	NA	NA
Total Assets	NA	859	341	302	298	NA	NA	NA	NA	NA
Curr. Liab.	NA	95.1	60.0	44.5	64.4	NA	NA	NA	NA	NA
LT Debt	NA	245	Nil	2.5	57.2	NA	NA	NA	NA	NA
Common Eqty.	NA	439	248	227	90.0	NA	NA	NA	NA	NA
Total Cap.	NA	743	263	243	156	NA	NA	NA	NA	NA
Cap. Exp.	NA	93.8	NA	22.3	11.2	26.4	NA	NA	NA	NA
Cash Flow	NA	80.8	72.0	69.3	43.9	37.1	NA	NA	NA	NA
Curr. Ratio	NA	1.6	2.4	2.6	1.6	NA	NA	NA	NA	NA
% LT Debt of Cap.	NA	33.0	Nil	1.0	36.7	NA	NA	NA	NA	NA
% Net Inc.of Revs.	NA	10.7	12.6	13.5	8.7	7.9	NA	NA	NA	NA
% Ret. on Assets	NA	9.3	16.8	17.4	NA	NA	NA	NA	NA	NA
% Ret. on Equity	NA	16.2	22.8	32.6	NA	NA	NA	NA	NA	NA

Data as orig. reptd.; bef. results of disc. opers. and/or spec. items. Per share data adj. for stk. divs. as of ex-div. date. Bold denotes diluted EPS (FASB 128). E-Estimated. NA-Not Available. NM-Not Meaningful. NR-Not Ranked.

Office—Highway 49 East, P. O. Box 388, Yazoo City, MS 39194. **Tel**—(601) 746-4131.**Website**—http://www.misschem.com **Chrmn**—C. L. Bailey. **Pres & CEO**—C. O. Dunn. **VP-Fin**—T. A. Dawson.**Secy**—R. B. Glascoe. **Dirs**—J. W. Anderson, C. L. Bailey, H. Barbour, F. R. Burnside Jr., R. P. Dixon, C. O. Dunn, W. R. Dyess, W. E. Eastland, J. S. Howie, G. D. Penick Jr., D. M. Ratcliffe, W. Thames. **Transfer Agent & Registrar**—Harris Trust & Savings Bank, Chicago.**Incorporated**—in Mississippi in 1994.**Empl**— 1,700. **S&P Analyst:** C.F.B.

10-OCT-98

Industry: Textiles (Home Furnishings)

Summary: This producer of woven and tufted broadloom carpeting and rugs for residential and commercial applications is among the world's largest manufacturers of carpeting.

Quantitative Evaluations	
Recent Price • 23⅞	Yield • Nil
52 Wk Range • 35½-18¼	12-Mo. P/E • 14.6

Outlook (1 Lowest—5 Highest)
• 2

Fair Value
• 27⅞

Risk
• Average

Earn./Div. Rank
• NR

Technical Eval.
• NA

Rel. Strength Rank (1 Lowest—99 Highest)
• 52

Insider Activity
• Unfavorable

Earnings vs. Previous Year ▲=Up ▼=Down ▶=No Change

10 Week Mov. Avg. ---
30 Week Mov. Avg. ····
Relative Strength —

OPTIONS: P

Business Profile - 21-JUL-98

This producer of carpet for residential and commercial applications is among the world's largest carpet makers. MHK expanded its rug operations with the July 1998 acquisition of Newmark & James, Inc., a manufacturer of high-end washable bath rugs. Newmark & James, with annualized sales of over $35 million, is expected to be accretive to earnings immediately. In July 1997, the company acquired selected assets of Diamond Rug and Carpet Mills, Inc. for $36 million. Trading in the shares moved from the Nasdaq Stock Market to the NYSE in December 1997, following a three-for-two stock split.

Operational Review - 21-JUL-98

Sales in the six months ended June 27, 1998, rose 14%, year to year, reflecting growth for all major product categories as a result of favorable industry conditions. Gross margins widened significantly, on improved manufacturing efficiencies stemming from restructuring. SG&A expenses declined as a percentage of sales; the operating profit climbed 40%. Profitability benefited from sharp declines in interest and other expense. After taxes at 39.5% in each period, net income soared 63%, to $45,362,000 ($0.86 a share, diluted), from $27,854,000 ($0.53, as adjusted).

Stock Performance - 09-OCT-98

In the past 30 trading days, MHK's shares have declined 17%, compared to a 4% fall in the S&P 500. Average trading volume for the past five days was 43,820 shares, compared with the 40-day moving average of 140,687 shares.

Key Stock Statistics

Dividend Rate/Share	Nil	Shareholders	400
Shs. outstg. (M)	52.4	Market cap. (B)	$ 1.3
Avg. daily vol. (M)	0.106	Inst. holdings	52%
Tang. Bk. Value/Share	8.67		
Beta	1.23		

Value of $10,000 invested 5 years ago: $ 35,224

Fiscal Year Ending Dec. 31

	1998	1997	1996	1995	1994	1993
Revenues (Million $)						
1Q	459.8	412.8	383.7	379.1	327.1	140.5
2Q	546.4	479.2	474.6	429.1	370.5	156.9
3Q	—	500.8	471.2	425.3	377.6	216.9
4Q	—	516.1	465.6	415.1	362.1	219.7
Yr.	—	1,901	1,795	1,649	1,437	734.0
Earnings Per Share ($)						
1Q	0.28	0.17	0.11	0.09	-0.01	0.08
2Q	0.50	0.07	0.02	0.11	0.25	0.21
3Q	—	0.40	0.29	0.13	0.27	0.24
4Q	—	0.37	0.24	-0.21	0.15	0.24
Yr.	—	1.30	0.95	0.13	0.66	0.77

Next earnings report expected: mid October

Dividend Data

Amount ($)	Date Decl.	Ex-Div. Date	Stock of Record	Payment Date
3-for-2	Oct. 23	Dec. 05	Nov. 04	Dec. 04 '97

Business Summary - 21-JUL-98

Mohawk Industries is a leading maker of both woven and tufted broadloom carpets and rugs for residential and commercial markets. It is the second largest U.S. carpet and rug manufacturer. The company competes in three market segments: residential broadloom, commercial carpet, and residential rugs.

The company designs, makes and markets hundreds of carpet styles in a broad range of colors, textures and patterns, with the products positioned in all price ranges. It also offers a broad line of washable accent and bath rugs and area rugs.

The residential broadloom market is the largest segment of the industry, and accounts for a significant portion of the company's sales. This segment sells approximately 370 carpet styles in all price ranges, with most shipments consisting of tufted broadloom carpet. The brands of Mohawk, Alexander Smith, Galaxy, New Visions, Horizon, Karastan and Bigelow sell mainly in the medium-to-high price range. These lines also sell under private labels.

The commercial market is segmented into several sub-markets: educational institutions, corporate office space, hospitality facilities, retail space and health care facilities. Mohawk also sells carpet for the export market, the federal government and other niche markets. Brand names include Mohawk Commercial, Harbinger, Aladdin, Karastan Contract and Bigelow Commercial.

The machine-made residential rug market is currently the fastest growing segment in the carpet and rug industry, with an annual growth rate estimated at 7% in 1997. Much of this growth has occurred in the low to middle retail price ranges. The company emphasizes the fast growing lower retail price ranges through its American Rug Craftsmen brand name. It also sells to the bath mat and washable bath rug segments of the rug market through its Aladdin brand name. Karastan brand name rugs represent the higher retail price ranges, and Mohawk considers Karastan one of the most valuable brand names in the industry.

In January 1995, Mohawk acquired the Galaxy Carpet Mills unit (annual sales of about $200 million) of Peerless Carpet Corp. for $43.3 million in cash. Galaxy makes broadloom carpet for sale mainly in the mid-to-upper price points of the residential market.

In July 1997, the company acquired certain assets of Diamond Rug and Carpet Mills, Inc., for $36 million in cash and notes. The assets were complementary to current manufacturing capabilities, and were expected to help Mohawk significantly expand its polyester product line, enter into a new line of cut pile polypropylene products, and continue its move toward becoming the low cost producer in the industry. By late 1997, the Diamond acquisition had been largely assimilated into Mohawk's operations.

MHK expanded its rug operations with the July 1998 acquisition of Newmark & James, Inc., a manufacturer of high-end washable bath rugs. Newmark & James has annualized sales of over $35 million, and the deal is expected to be accretive to earnings immediately.

Per Share Data ($) (Year Ended Dec. 31)	1997	1996	1995	1994	1993	1992	1991	1990	1989	1988
Tangible Bk. Val.	6.78	6.65	4.43	4.25	3.86	2.90	0.97	NA	NA	NA
Cash Flow	2.43	2.01	1.17	1.65	1.55	0.89	0.66	NA	NA	NA
Earnings	1.30	0.95	0.13	0.66	0.77	0.57	0.34	NA	NA	NA
Dividends	Nil	Nil	Nil	Nil	Nil	Nil	Nil	Nil	Nil	Nil
Payout Ratio	Nil	Nil	Nil	Nil	Nil	Nil	Nil	Nil	Nil	Nil
Prices - High	22	18 5/8	12 7/8	24 3/8	23 1/8	9 5/8	NA	NA	NA	NA
- Low	12 7/8	8 3/8	7 1/4	7 1/8	8 3/4	4 7/8	NA	NA	NA	NA
P/E Ratio - High	17	20	NM	37	30	17	NA	NA	NA	NA
- Low	10	9	NM	11	11	8	NA	NA	NA	NA
Income Statement Analysis (Million $)										
Revs.	1,901	1,795	1,649	1,437	734	353	279	NA	NA	NA
Oper. Inc.	209	179	137	148	74.4	33.5	25.9	NA	NA	NA
Depr.	59.3	55.1	52.6	49.5	22.7	7.1	5.3	NA	NA	NA
Int. Exp.	26.5	31.5	35.0	27.1	13.7	5.2	9.9	NA	NA	NA
Pretax Inc.	112	82.7	10.5	58.2	39.3	21.6	10.5	NA	NA	NA
Eff. Tax Rate	39%	41%	39%	43%	42%	40%	39%	NA	NA	NA
Net Inc.	68.0	49.0	6.4	33.0	22.7	13.1	6.4	NA	NA	NA
Balance Sheet & Other Fin. Data (Million $)										
Cash	Nil	Nil	Nil	Nil	Nil	Nil	2.9	NA	NA	NA
Curr. Assets	573	556	508	454	287	166	78.0	NA	NA	NA
Total Assets	961	961	903	855	561	278	116	NA	NA	NA
Curr. Liab.	236	245	263	162	134	67.9	33.4	NA	NA	NA
LT Debt	257	346	342	394	244	114	59.0	NA	NA	NA
Common Eqty.	406	333	275	264	159	89.3	15.9	NA	NA	NA
Total Cap.	692	706	638	691	426	208	81.0	NA	NA	NA
Cap. Exp.	31.7	42.0	36.0	78.0	33.9	7.7	4.8	NA	NA	NA
Cash Flow	127	104	59.0	82.5	45.4	20.0	11.0	NA	NA	NA
Curr. Ratio	2.4	2.3	1.9	2.8	2.2	2.4	2.3	NA	NA	NA
% LT Debt of Cap.	37.2	49.0	53.5	57.0	57.2	54.7	72.1	NA	NA	NA
% Net Inc.of Revs.	3.6	2.7	0.4	2.3	3.1	3.7	2.3	NA	NA	NA
% Ret. on Assets	7.1	5.3	0.7	3.6	5.1	5.8	5.3	NA	NA	NA
% Ret. on Equity	18.4	16.1	2.4	12.3	17.1	23.0	43.7	NA	NA	NA

Data as orig. reptd.; bef. results of disc. opers. and/or spec. items. Per share data adj. for stk. divs. as of ex-div. date. Bold denotes diluted EPS (FASB 128). E-Estimated. NA-Not Available. NM-Not Meaningful. NR-Not Ranked.

Office—160 S. Industrial Blvd., P.O. Box 12069, Calhoun, GA 30703. **Tel**—(706) 629-7721. **Chrmn & CEO**—D. L. Kolb. **Pres & COO**—J. S. Lorberbaum. **VP-Fin, CFO & Investor Contact**—John D. Swift. **Secy**—B. B. Lance. **Dirs**—L. Benatar, B. C. Bruckmann, D. L. Kolb, A. S. Lorberbaum, J. S. Lorberbaum, L. W. McCurdy, R. N. Pokelwaldt. **Transfer Agent & Registrar**—First Union National Bank of North Carolina, Charlotte. **Incorporated**—in Delaware in 1988. **Empl**— 12,600. **S&P Analyst:** Kathleen J. Fraser

Molecular Biosystems   1533

NYSE Symbol **MB**

In S&P SmallCap 600

10-OCT-98

Industry:
Health Care (Medical Products & Supplies)

Summary: This company is developing ultrasound contrast agents for medical imaging.

Quantitative Evaluations		
Outlook (1 Lowest—5 Highest) • **NA**	Recent Price • 3¾	Yield • Nil
Fair Value • **NA**	52 Wk Range • 12¼-3¼	12-Mo. P/E • NM

Outlook
(1 Lowest—5 Highest)
• **NA**

Fair Value
• **NA**

Risk
• **High**

Earn./Div. Rank
• **C**

Technical Eval.
• **Bullish** since 8/98

Rel. Strength Rank
(1 Lowest—99 Highest)
• **22**

Insider Activity
• **Favorable**

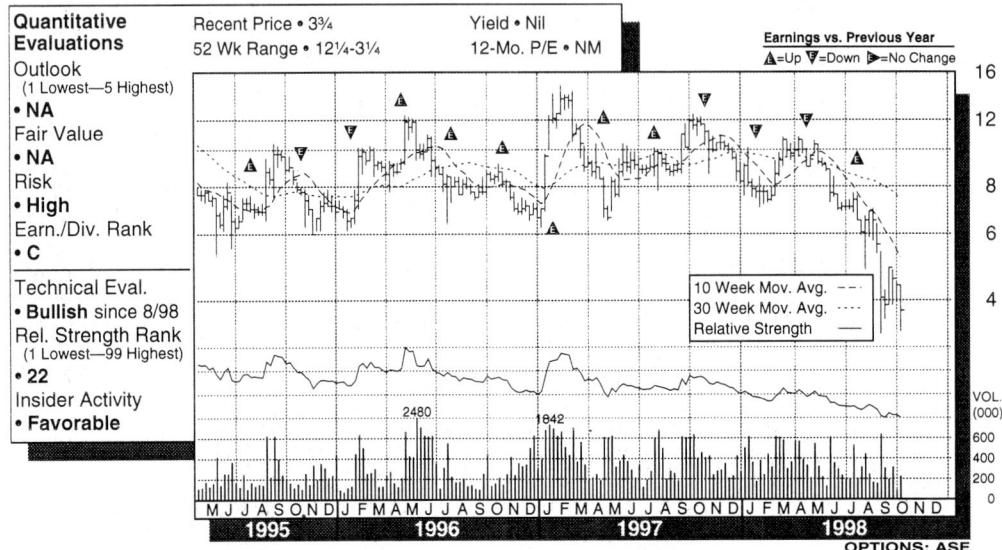

Earnings vs. Previous Year
▲=Up ▼=Down ▶=No Change

10 Week Mov. Avg. – – –
30 Week Mov. Avg. ‥‥‥
Relative Strength ——

VOL. (000)

OPTIONS: ASE

Business Profile - 12-AUG-98

In 1995, Molecular Biosystems restructured operations to focus on ultrasound-related products, significantly reducing staff and research expenditures. The company's second-generation ultrasound contrasting agent, Optison, received marketing approval from the U.S. Food and Drug Administration (FDA) in January 1998. Mallinckrodt has been granted distribution rights for Optison, with MB to receive 40% of net product sales. In April 1998, the company granted Chugai Pharmaceutical a license to market Optison and Oralex in Japan, Taiwan and South Korea. In return, the company received up-front payments of over $22 million, will receive milestone payments of up to $20 million based on certain product development goals, and will receive royalties of 28% of end user sales.

Operational Review - 12-AUG-98

Revenues for the three months ended June 30, 1998, climbed to $18,988,000 from $1,474,000 in the prior-year period, reflecting license fees of $16,371,000 in connection with a partnership announced in April 1998, and a sharp increase in product and royalty revenues. Despite a steep rise in operating expenses, which included $9.4 million of nonrecurring charges in 1998, and after a foreign income tax provision of $1,400,000, against no taxes, net income of $740,000 ($0.04) contrasted with a net loss of $4,799,000 ($0.27). Cash and equivalents totaled $33.6 million as of June 30, 1998.

Stock Performance - 09-OCT-98

In the past 30 trading days, MB's shares have declined 33%, compared to a 4% fall in the S&P 500. Average trading volume for the past five days was 43,640 shares, compared with the 40-day moving average of 61,326 shares.

Key Stock Statistics

Dividend Rate/Share	Nil	Shareholders	2,100
Shs. outstg. (M)	18.6	Market cap. (B)	$0.070
Avg. daily vol. (M)	0.040	Inst. holdings	27%
Tang. Bk. Value/Share	2.02		
Beta	1.44		

Value of $10,000 invested 5 years ago: $ 1,796

Fiscal Year Ending Mar. 31

	1999	1998	1997	1996	1995	1994
Revenues (Million $)						
1Q	18.99	1.47	1.18	0.35	0.53	2.36
2Q	—	1.43	1.22	0.35	8.79	0.37
3Q	—	1.37	7.01	1.25	6.91	5.53
4Q	—	1.97	1.45	1.14	0.71	0.52
Yr.	—	6.25	10.85	3.08	16.94	8.78
Earnings Per Share ($)						
1Q	0.04	-0.27	-0.30	-0.37	-0.49	-0.23
2Q	—	-0.26	-0.21	-0.42	0.17	-0.49
3Q	—	-0.33	-0.05	-0.50	-0.19	-0.09
4Q	—	-0.33	-0.24	-0.33	-0.51	-0.76
Yr.	—	-1.19	-0.78	-1.62	-1.02	-1.58

Next earnings report expected: late October

Dividend Data

No cash dividend has ever been paid.

Business Summary - 12-AUG-98

Incorporated in 1980, Molecular Biosystems is viewed as a leading developer and manufacturer of ultrasound contrast imaging agents. Its products are designed to increase the diagnostic usefulness of ultrasound examinations through enhanced visualization and to reduce the need for diagnostic procedures that may be more expensive, time consuming or invasive.

The company's business strategy is to obtain regulatory approval for its Optison imaging agent for the diagnosis of multiple cardiac indications and then expand the product's application by seeking approval for non-cardiac indications. Additionally, the company plans to utilize its imaging expertise in the development of new, proprietary imaging products.

In August 1994 (following FDA approval), Albunex became the first ultrasound contrast imaging agent available for U.S. sale. The product was approved in the U.S. to assess cardiac function. The product is being sold by Mallinckrodt Medical Inc. in the U.S. and Europe and by Shionogi & Co. Ltd. in Japan. The company believes that, other than in niche markets, it is likely Albunex will be replaced by Optison because of the latter's superior performance characteristics.

MB's second-generation imaging agent, Optison (FS069), received FDA marketing approval in January 1998. Optison, an improvement over Albunex in terms of efficacy, is used to detect heart disease by assessing blood flow within the heart chambers and by identifying the location of the chamber borders and the movement of the chamber walls. In June 1998, the company announced results from Phase II myocardial perfusion clinical trials which indicated that Optison may be a useful contrast agent for the evaluation of myocardial perfusion.

The company also completed Phase II clinical trials for an oral ultrasound contrast agent, known as Oralex, which may be used to enhance the ultrasound image of the abdominal area and improve the ability to detect stomach lesions and pancreatic tumors. In April 1998, the company entered into a strategic alliance with Chugai Pharmaceutical Co. Ltd. to market Oralex in japan, Taiwan and South Korea. The company is currently seeking a partner for the development of Oralex in the U.S.

MB has a collaboration with Mallinckrodt Medical Inc. for the development and commercialization of Albunex and Optison. Mallinckrodt has been granted exclusive marketing rights to Albunex and Optison in the United States, Europe, Africa, India and parts of Asia in exchange for funding for clinical development and milestone payments. Under the distribution agreement, the company is responsible for manufacturing the licensed products for Mallinckrodt, and is entitled to 40% of net product sales.

Per Share Data ($)

(Year Ended Mar. 31)	1998	1997	1996	1995	1994	1993	1992	1991	1990	1989
Tangible Bk. Val.	1.73	0.74	2.16	2.89	3.88	5.38	6.62	3.58	3.53	2.92
Cash Flow	-1.13	-0.70	-1.45	-0.76	-1.46	-0.89	0.03	0.05	0.63	0.27
Earnings	-1.19	-0.78	-1.62	-1.02	-1.58	-1.01	-0.05	-0.02	0.43	0.24
Dividends	Nil	Nil	Nil	Nil	Nil	Nil	Nil	Nil	Nil	Nil
Payout Ratio	Nil	Nil	Nil	Nil	Nil	Nil	Nil	Nil	Nil	Nil
Cal. Yrs.	1997	1996	1995	1994	1993	1992	1991	1990	1989	1988
Prices - High	14⅞	12⅜	11⅜	20¾	27⅝	40⅞	39¼	24⅜	26¼	17
- Low	6½	6⅛	5¼	8⅝	16¼	17	13⅛	13⅛	15⅜	11⅛
P/E Ratio - High	NM	NM	NM	NM	NM	NM	NM	NM	61	71
- Low	NM	NM	NM	NM	NM	NM	NM	NM	36	46

Income Statement Analysis (Million $)

	1998	1997	1996	1995	1994	1993	1992	1991	1990	1989
Revs.	6.2	10.9	3.1	16.9	8.8	3.7	10.7	10.6	16.7	8.9
Oper. Inc.	-21.4	-13.4	-18.8	-9.7	-15.3	-14.4	-3.3	-1.0	6.9	2.0
Depr.	1.1	1.4	2.2	3.0	1.4	1.4	0.8	0.7	1.9	0.4
Int. Exp.	0.7	0.8	0.8	0.7	0.3	0.3	0.5	0.5	0.5	NA
Pretax Inc.	-21.3	-13.3	-20.7	-12.2	-18.8	-13.0	-0.9	-0.4	7.2	3.3
Eff. Tax Rate	NM	NM	NM	Nil	NM	NM	NM	NM	42%	33%
Net Inc.	-21.3	-13.3	-20.7	-12.2	-18.8	-11.8	-0.6	-0.2	4.2	2.2

Balance Sheet & Other Fin. Data (Million $)

	1998	1997	1996	1995	1994	1993	1992	1991	1990	1989
Cash	1.1	41.4	20.6	19.7	29.5	51.2	67.5	24.4	27.9	25.6
Curr. Assets	33.6	51.4	24.9	26.7	32.6	54.7	71.0	26.7	30.7	27.9
Total Assets	51.3	70.2	43.8	50.6	56.5	71.8	87.0	43.2	47.6	38.8
Curr. Liab.	12.6	7.6	6.3	5.8	4.5	2.9	5.9	2.7	7.2	5.6
LT Debt	6.1	7.3	8.6	8.4	3.9	4.0	4.0	4.6	4.6	4.6
Common Eqty.	225	51.7	29.0	36.4	48.1	64.9	77.2	34.4	33.4	27.2
Total Cap.	37.2	59.1	37.4	44.8	52.0	68.9	81.2	39.4	38.0	31.9
Cap. Exp.	1.4	0.7	2.4	2.5	8.2	1.8	1.1	0.7	1.9	8.5
Cash Flow	-20.2	-11.8	-18.5	-9.2	-17.4	-10.4	0.3	0.5	6.1	2.6
Curr. Ratio	2.7	6.8	4.0	4.6	7.3	18.8	12.1	10.0	4.3	5.0
% LT Debt of Cap.	16.3	12.4	23.0	18.8	7.5	5.8	4.9	11.7	12.1	14.6
% Net Inc.of Revs.	NM	NM	NM	NM	NM	NM	NM	NM	24.9	24.9
% Ret. on Assets	NM	NM	NM	NM	NM	NM	NM	NM	9.6	7.2
% Ret. on Equity	NM	NM	NM	NM	NM	NM	NM	NM	13.6	9.0

Data as orig. reptd.; bef. results of disc. opers. and/or spec. items. Per share data adj. for stk. divs. as of ex-div. date. Bold denotes diluted EPS (FASB 128). E-Estimated. NA-Not Available. NM-Not Meaningful. NR-Not Ranked.

Office—10070 Barnes Canyon Rd., San Diego, CA 92121. **Tel**—(619) 824-2200. **Website**—http://www.mobi.com **Chrmn**—K. J. Widder. **Pres & CEO**—B. Venkatadri. **VP-Fin & CFO**—G. A. Wills. **Investor Contact**—Bob Giargiari (619-812-7179). **Dirs**—D. W. Barry, R. W. Brightfelt, C. C. Edwards, J. T. Jackson, G. C. Luce, D. Rubinfien, B. Venkatadri, K. J. Widder. **Transfer Agent & Registrar**—Continental Stock Transfer & Trust Co., NYC. **Incorporated**—in Delaware in 1980. **Empl**— 148. **S&P Analyst:** C.C.P.

Morrison Knudsen 1554S

NYSE Symbol **MK**

In S&P SmallCap 600

03-OCT-98

Industry: Engineering & Construction

Summary: MK provides a range of engineering and construction management services.

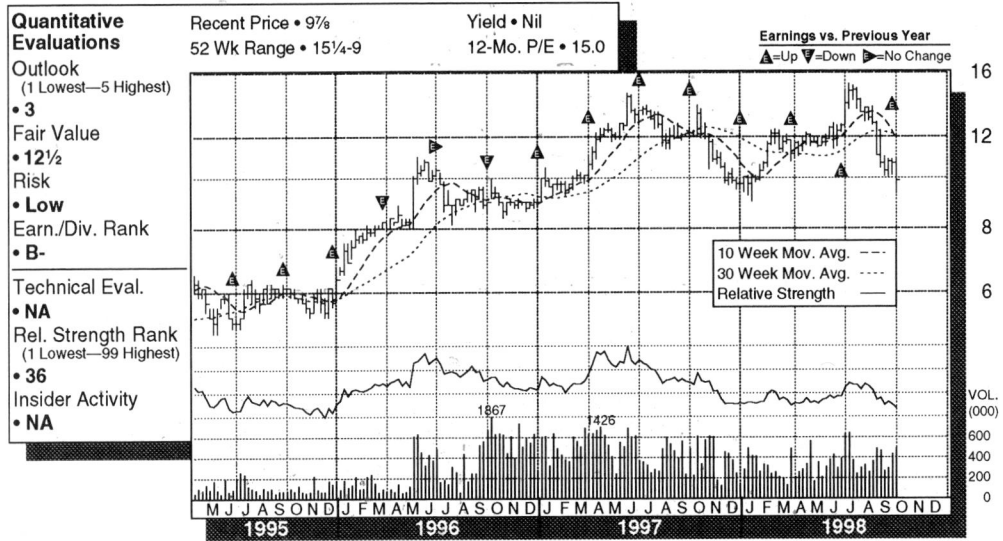

Quantitative Evaluations	Recent Price • 9⅞	Yield • Nil	Earnings vs. Previous Year
	52 Wk Range • 15¼-9	12-Mo. P/E • 15.0	▲=Up ▼=Down ▶=No Change

Quantitative Evaluations

Outlook (1 Lowest—5 Highest)
• 3

Fair Value
• 12½

Risk
• **Low**

Earn./Div. Rank
• **B-**

Technical Eval.
• **NA**

Rel. Strength Rank (1 Lowest—99 Highest)
• **36**

Insider Activity
• **NA**

Chart legend:
- 10 Week Mov. Avg. ---
- 30 Week Mov. Avg. ·····
- Relative Strength —

Business Profile - 11-MAR-98

Following the merger of the old Morrison Knudsen (MK) and Washington Construction Group (WCGI), the combined company now plans to continue to focus on its core businesses and the markets in which WCGI and MK have historically performed best in order to maximize the combined company's efficiency and effectiveness in those markets. The company has noted that it may pursue opportunities to complement existing operations through business combinations and ownership interests in ventures.

Operational Review - 11-MAR-98

Revenues climbed 154% in FY 97 (Nov.), reflecting the combination of the old Morrison Knudson with Washington Construction Group. Gross margins narrowed on unexpected losses on contracts. Operating expenses were well controlled, and with results further benefiting from the absence of an $18.2 million impairment loss on long-lived assets, pretax income compared with a loss. After taxes at 46.5%, versus a tax benefit of $494,000, net income of $32,031,000 ($0.59 a share, on 55% more shares), contrasted with a loss of $4,780,000 ($0.14).

Stock Performance - 02-OCT-98

In the past 30 trading days, MK's shares have declined 23%, compared to a 7% fall in the S&P 500. Average trading volume for the past five days was 96,720 shares, compared with the 40-day moving average of 78,115 shares.

Key Stock Statistics

Dividend Rate/Share	Nil	Shareholders	1,600
Shs. outstg. (M)	53.4	Market cap. (B)	$0.527
Avg. daily vol. (M)	0.075	Inst. holdings	42%
Tang. Bk. Value/Share	4.22		
Beta	1.39		

Value of $10,000 invested 5 years ago: $ 10,239

Fiscal Year Ending Nov. 30

	1998	1997	1996	1995	1994	1993
Revenues (Million $)						
1Q	385.0	389.5	62.00	36.78	50.50	14.80
2Q	436.1	414.2	82.69	51.60	63.75	29.50
3Q	497.8	434.3	97.75	71.87	78.49	74.20
4Q	—	439.3	416.6	68.28	65.96	91.70
Yr.	—	1,700	659.1	228.5	258.7	210.2
Earnings Per Share ($)						
1Q	**0.15**	0.13	-0.03	0.02	0.04	0.17
2Q	**0.17**	0.14	0.06	0.06	-0.08	0.17
3Q	**0.18**	0.15	-0.38	0.10	0.09	0.14
4Q	—	0.17	0.11	0.10	-0.03	0.01
Yr.	—	**0.59**	-0.14	0.28	0.02	0.39

Next earnings report expected: late January

Dividend Data

Cash distributions were omitted in 1985, resumed in 1989 on a semiannual basis and omitted again in 1994.

*A Division of The **McGraw·Hill** Companies*

Business Summary - 11-MAR-98

Effective September 11, 1996, the old Morrison Knudsen Corp. merged into Washington Construction Group, Inc. (WCGI), with WCGI continuing as the surviving corporation and concurrently changing its name to Morrison Knudsen Corp. The merger was effected pursuant to a prepackaged plan of reorganization of old Morrison Knudsen under Chapter 11 of the Federal bankruptcy code. MK's decision to seek a prepackaged plan of reorganization stemmed from its conclusion in early 1996 that it could not meet its debt obligations coming due during the year. MK had been experiencing significant losses and negative cash flow problems since 1994 and was in default under its credit facilities.

The company is an international provider of engineering and construction management services to industrial companies, electric utilities and public agencies; comprehensive environmental and hazardous substance remediation services to governmental and private-sector clients; diverse heavy construction services for the highway, airport, water resource, railway and commercial building industries; and mine planning, engineering and contract mining services for diverse customers.

In providing such services, the company enters into three basic types of contracts: fixed-price or lump-sum contracts providing for a single price for the total amount of work to be performed and unit-price contracts providing for a fixed price for each unit of work performed. Engineering, construction management and environmental and hazardous substance remediation contracts are typically awarded on a cost-plus-fee basis.

MK also participates in construction joint ventures, often as sponsor and manager of projects, which are formed for the sole purpose of bidding, negotiating and completing specific projects. In addition, it participates in the following mining ventures: Westmoreland Resources, Inc., a coal mining company in Montana, and MIBRAG mbH, a company that operates lignite coal mines, process and power plants in Germany.

The combined company plans to continue to focus on its core businesses and the markets in which WCGI and MK have historically performed best in order to maximize the combined company's efficiency and effectiveness in those markets.

Backlog of all uncompleted contracts at November 30, 1997 was $3.70 billion, up from $3.52 billion at fiscal 1996 year end. More than 35% of MK is owned by Dennis R. Washington, its chairman.

Per Share Data ($)

(Year Ended Nov. 30)	1997	1996	1995	1994	1993	1992	1991	1990	1989	1988
Tangible Bk. Val.	3.82	3.18	3.84	3.53	3.53	4.31	3.68	2.50	2.11	1.94
Cash Flow	1.01	0.23	0.58	0.34	0.96	0.90	0.91	0.68	0.48	0.63
Earnings	0.59	-0.14	0.28	0.02	0.39	0.65	0.61	0.39	0.18	0.30
Dividends	Nil	Nil	Nil	0.05	0.10	0.10	0.09	0.07	0.07	Nil
Payout Ratio	Nil	Nil	Nil	NM	33%	15%	16%	17%	38%	Nil
Prices - High	14⅝	11	6¾	10¾	11¼	13⅜	15½	9⅛	7½	6⅞
- Low	9	6½	4⅜	3⅞	7	6⅝	7⅜	5⅝	5	4⅛
P/E Ratio - High	25	NM	24	NM	38	21	25	23	42	23
- Low	15	NM	16	NM	23	10	12	14	28	14

Income Statement Analysis (Million $)

	1997	1996	1995	1994	1993	1992	1991	1990	1989	1988
Revs.	1,677	659	229	259	210	162	195	153	115	107
Oper. Inc.	75.6	22.5	16.0	6.7	18.9	10.7	9.5	5.1	3.4	5.7
Depr.	22.8	12.9	8.9	9.2	10.1	2.5	2.8	2.2	2.3	2.5
Int. Exp.	0.9	1.0	0.2	0.1	0.1	Nil	0.3	1.1	1.4	1.1
Pretax Inc.	59.9	-5.3	12.2	1.0	11.2	9.9	8.7	4.8	2.2	3.8
Eff. Tax Rate	47%	NM	33%	35%	38%	35%	35%	35%	38%	39%
Net Inc.	32.0	-4.8	8.2	0.7	6.9	6.5	5.7	3.1	1.4	2.3

Balance Sheet & Other Fin. Data (Million $)

	1997	1996	1995	1994	1993	1992	1991	1990	1989	1988
Cash	53.2	48.3	30.0	44.9	53.0	45.1	47.5	44.9	33.0	22.8
Curr. Assets	405	459	93.7	114	118	66.4	73.9	67.9	55.3	40.8
Total Assets	770	840	185	182	181	78.8	85.9	79.8	65.4	52.6
Curr. Liab.	300	401	42.2	46.4	52.5	32.9	46.9	46.3	28.1	17.2
LT Debt	Nil	18.0	5.0	5.5	Nil	Nil	Nil	11.2	18.5	18.5
Common Eqty.	343	312	129	120	120	43.3	36.7	19.9	16.5	14.7
Total Cap.	361	330	143	136	129	45.8	39.0	33.4	37.4	35.4
Cap. Exp.	19.7	26.2	22.3	14.8	35.2	3.4	3.9	4.0	1.9	2.9
Cash Flow	54.8	8.2	17.1	9.9	17.0	9.0	8.5	5.3	3.7	4.8
Curr. Ratio	1.4	1.1	2.2	2.5	2.3	2.0	1.6	1.5	2.0	2.4
% LT Debt of Cap.	Nil	5.5	3.6	4.0	Nil	Nil	Nil	33.5	49.5	52.3
% Net Inc.of Revs.	1.9	NM	3.6	0.3	3.3	4.0	2.9	2.0	1.2	2.1
% Ret. on Assets	4.0	NM	4.5	0.4	3.4	7.8	6.1	4.2	2.3	4.2
% Ret. on Equity	9.8	NM	6.6	0.5	5.6	16.1	18.4	16.9	8.7	17.0

Data as orig. reptd.; bef. results of disc. opers. and/or spec. items. Per share data adj. for stk. divs. as of ex-div. date. Bold denotes diluted EPS (FASB 128). E-Estimated. NA-Not Available. NM-Not Meaningful. NR-Not Ranked.

Office—Morrison Knudsen Plaza, Box 73, Boise, ID 83729. **Tel**—(208) 386-5000. **Fax**—(208) 386-5065. **Website**—http:// www.mk.com.**Chrmn**—D. R. Washington.**Pres & CEO**—R. A. Tinstman. **EVP-Secy**—S. G. Hanks. **EVP & CFO**—A. S. Cleberg. **Asst. Treas-Investor Contact**—Lisa Ross(208) 386-5120. **Dirs**—D. H. Batchelder, L. R. Judd, W. C. Langley, R. S. Miller, D. Parkinson, T. W. Payne, J. D. C. Roach, R. A. Tinstman, D. R. Washington. **Transfer Agent & Registrar**—Norwest Bank Minnesota. **Incorporated**—in California in 1961; reincorporated in Delaware in 1993. **Empl**— 8,900. **S&P Analyst:** M.I.

10-OCT-98

Industry:
Metal Fabricators

Summary: Through subsidiaries, this company fabricates brass, bronze, copper, plastic and aluminum products, owns a short-line railroad, and mines gold.

Quantitative Evaluations

Outlook
(1 Lowest—5 Highest)
- **2⁻**

Fair Value
- **22**

Risk
- **Average**

Earn./Div. Rank
- **NR**

Technical Eval.
- **Bearish** since 9/98

Rel. Strength Rank
(1 Lowest—99 Highest)
- **17**

Insider Activity
- **Neutral**

Recent Price • 18¾	Yield • Nil
52 Wk Range • 40-15¼	12-Mo. P/E • 9.7

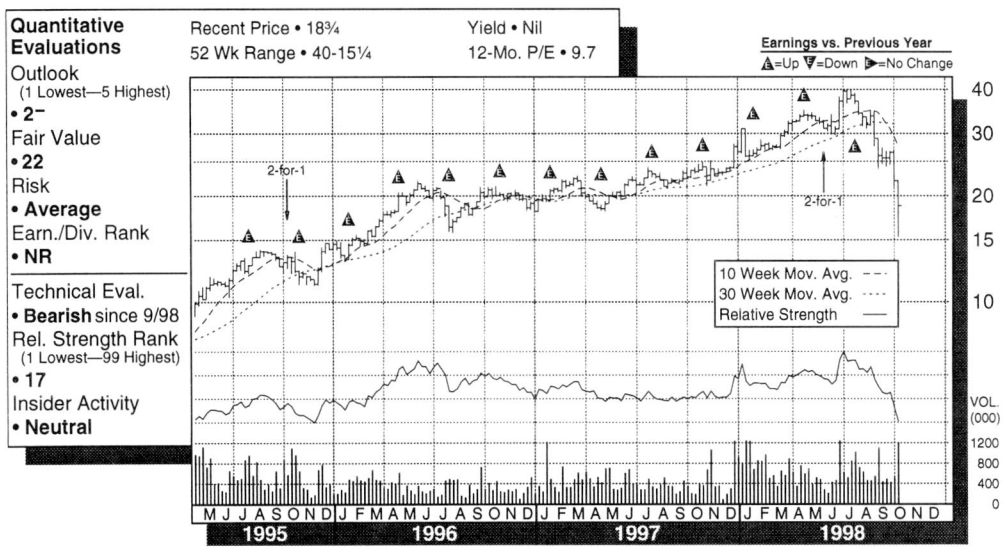

Earnings vs. Previous Year
▲=Up ▼=Down ▶=No Change

10 Week Mov. Avg. ---
30 Week Mov. Avg. ·····
Relative Strength —

Business Profile - 16-MAR-98

Major capital investments over the past few years have resulted in expanded capacity, higher yields and improved efficiency at MLI's manufacturing operations. MLI intends to continue enhancing its manufacturing productivity and expects that the current strength in its business will continue, provided that interest rates do not spike upward. In May 1997, it completed the acquisition of Desnoyers S.A., a copper tube manufacturer based in France, with 1996 revenues of about $100 million, for approximately $13.5 million in cash. Product shipments totaled 147.7 million pounds in the fourth quarter of 1997, up 34% from the year-earlier level.

Operational Review - 16-MAR-98

Based on a preliminary report, net sales for 1997 rose 24% from those of 1996, as a result of a strong housing market that reflected favorable U.S. economic conditions. Profitability was restricted by increases in the cost of goods sold and environmental reserves. Pretax income was up 14%. After taxes at 30.8% in both years, net income also rose 14%, to $69,770,000 ($3.56 a share, diluted) from $61,173,000 ($3.14).

Stock Performance - 09-OCT-98

In the past 30 trading days, MLI's shares have declined 35%, compared to a 4% fall in the S&P 500. Average trading volume for the past five days was 242,080 shares, compared with the 40-day moving average of 131,236 shares.

Key Stock Statistics

Dividend Rate/Share	Nil	Shareholders	4,200
Shs. outstg. (M)	35.6	Market cap. (B)	$0.668
Avg. daily vol. (M)	0.131	Inst. holdings	51%
Tang. Bk. Value/Share	12.93		
Beta	1.42		

Value of $10,000 invested 5 years ago: $ 32,786

Fiscal Year Ending Dec. 31

	1998	1997	1996	1995	1994	1993
Revenues (Million $)						
1Q	226.7	201.4	180.5	171.8	120.8	131.0
2Q	225.9	215.4	189.6	181.4	136.6	127.3
3Q	—	229.1	176.0	171.6	138.0	122.1
4Q	—	243.1	172.3	154.1	154.6	121.4
Yr.	—	889.0	718.3	678.8	550.0	501.9
Earnings Per Share ($)						
1Q	0.48	0.40	0.04	0.07	0.10	0.10
2Q	0.50	0.41	0.35	0.28	0.14	0.13
3Q	—	0.46	0.41	0.30	0.23	0.14
4Q	—	0.50	0.46	0.33	0.25	0.14
Yr.	—	1.78	1.57	1.17	0.72	0.51

Next earnings report expected: mid October

Dividend Data

Amount ($)	Date Decl.	Ex-Div. Date	Stock of Record	Payment Date
2-for-1	Apr. 15	May. 28	May. 12	May. 27 '98

A Division of The **McGraw·Hill** Companies

Mueller Industries, Inc.

Business Summary - 16-MAR-98

Since emerging from bankruptcy in 1990, Mueller Industries (MLI) has rebounded strongly. Profitability was restored in 1992, and earnings have continued to advance. In 1997, this fabricator of brass, bronze, copper, plastic and aluminum fittings, tubing and extrusions reported net income of $69.8 million, up 14% from that of 1996 and significantly above the 1992 level. Part of this recovery is attributable to the expanded capacity, higher yields and improved efficiencies of Mueller's manufacturing operations, which have benefited from a strong capital investment program.

In addition to its fabrication business (97% of net sales in 1996), MLI operates a short-line railroad in Utah and a placer mining operation in Alaska.

The fabrication business, referred to as the "manufacturing segment," produces industrial and standard products. Industrial products include brass rod, nonferrous forgings and impact extrusions, which are sold mainly to other manufacturers and distributors. Standard products include a broad line of copper tube, water tube and coils, copper and plastic fittings and related components for the plumbing and heating industry, and valves, wrot copper and brass fittings, filter driers and other related assemblies for the commercial air-conditioning and refrigeration industry. A majority of these products are ultimately used in residential and commercial construction markets and, to a lesser extent, in the on- and off-road vehicle markets.

With a significant portion of MLI's products used in the construction of single- and multi-family housing and commercial buildings, new housing starts and commercial construction are important determinants of the company's sales. Mueller remains optimistic about its sales growth in 1998, due to prevailing low mortgage interest rates, which historically have stimulated the housing market.

Mueller's Utah Railway Co. subsidiary operates about 100 miles of railroad track in Utah. It serves four major customers pursuant to long-term contracts and transports more than six million tons of coal a year. Another subsidiary, Alaska Gold, mines placer gold in Nome, AK. It produced 22,918 net oz. of gold in 1996, up from 18,731 net oz. in 1995. Mueller also holds interests in various other mineral properties in the U.S., including coal properties in Utah, but none are considered significant to its business.

Mueller's future focus is to continue with its efforts to improve its existing operations and pursue additional areas of growth. MLI intends to enhance its refining processes, thereby improving the utilization of scrap metal, broaden its plastics offering and streamline its distribution network. MLI also continues to seek external growth through acquisitions.

Per Share Data ($) (Year Ended Dec. 31)	1997	1996	1995	1994	1993	1992	1991	1990	1989	1988
Tangible Bk. Val.	23.88	9.98	8.24	6.95	5.79	5.30	3.95	5.00	5.38	NA
Cash Flow	4.63	2.04	1.57	1.01	0.82	0.71	-0.78	NA	0.71	NA
Earnings	1.78	1.57	1.17	0.70	0.51	0.40	-1.12	NA	0.39	NA
Dividends	Nil	Nil	Nil	Nil	Nil	Nil	Nil	NA	NA	NA
Payout Ratio	Nil	Nil	Nil	Nil	Nil	Nil	Nil	NA	NA	NA
Prices - High	29 3/4	22 1/8	14 3/4	9 5/8	9 3/8	5 3/4	3 1/2	NA	NA	NA
- Low	18 1/8	13	7 1/8	6 3/4	5	1 3/4	1 3/4	NA	NA	NA
P/E Ratio - High	17	14	13	14	18	14	NM	NA	NA	NA
- Low	10	8	6	10	10	4	NM	NA	NA	NA
Income Statement Analysis (Million $)										
Revs.	889	718	679	550	502	517	441	505	511	NA
Oper. Inc.	121	109	79.0	56.0	51.3	41.8	11.7	8.8	35.7	NA
Depr.	21.0	18.5	15.5	12.1	13.3	12.5	13.3	13.3	13.1	NA
Int. Exp.	5.0	5.3	4.2	6.7	5.8	5.7	6.0	5.0	2.0	NA
Pretax Inc.	101	88.4	64.5	41.0	33.0	24.0	-50.0	9.0	27.0	NA
Eff. Tax Rate	31%	31%	31%	32%	37%	33%	NM	12%	43%	NA
Net Inc.	69.8	61.2	45.0	28.0	21.0	16.0	-44.0	8.0	15.0	NA
Balance Sheet & Other Fin. Data (Million $)										
Cash	70.0	97.0	48.4	34.5	77.3	44.0	8.0	41.0	39.0	NA
Curr. Assets	309	275	211	184	194	182	152	201	229	NA
Total Assets	611	509	451	431	370	373	335	416	385	NA
Curr. Liab.	101	79.0	68.0	67.0	51.0	62.0	89.0	113	84.0	NA
LT Debt	NA	44.8	59.7	76.1	54.3	62.0	45.0	54.0	55.0	NA
Common Eqty.	418	348	291	242	222	204	153	200	215	NA
Total Cap.	NA	396	353	321	280	271	211	261	269	NA
Cap. Exp.	NA	18.9	NA	48.2	11.1	11.0	11.8	9.9	NA	NA
Cash Flow	90.8	79.6	60.3	40.0	34.0	29.0	-30.0	21.0	29.0	NA
Curr. Ratio	3.1	3.5	3.1	2.7	3.8	3.0	1.7	1.8	2.7	NA
% LT Debt of Cap.	NA	11.4	16.9	23.7	19.4	23.0	21.4	20.7	20.2	NA
% Net Inc.of Revs.	7.8	8.6	6.6	5.1	4.2	3.1	NM	1.6	3.0	NA
% Ret. on Assets	12.5	12.8	10.2	7.3	5.7	4.6	NM	NM	NA	NA
% Ret. on Equity	18.2	19.3	16.8	12.6	9.9	9.1	NM	NM	NA	NA

Data as orig. reptd.; bef. results of disc. opers. and/or spec. items. Per share data adj. for stk. divs. as of ex-div. date. Bold denotes diluted EPS (FASB 128). E-Estimated. NA-Not Available. NM-Not Meaningful. NR-Not Ranked.

Office—6799 Great Oaks Rd., Memphis, TN 38138-2572. **Tel**—(901) 753-3200. **Chrmn**—H. L. Karp. **Pres & CEO**—W. D. O'Hagan. **Exec VP & CFO**—E. W. Bunkers. **VP & Secy**—W. H. Hensley. **VP & Investor Contact**—Kent A. McKee. **Dirs**—R. B. Hodes, H. L. Karp, A. Mactier, W. D. O'Hagan, R. J. Pasquarelli. **Transfer Agent & Registrar**—Continental Stock Transfer & Trust Co., NYC. **Incorporated**—in Pennsylvania in 1900; reincorporated in Delaware in 1990. **Empl**— 2,350. **S&P Analyst:** J.J.S.

STANDARD &POOR'S
STOCK REPORTS

Mutual Risk Management 1565

NYSE Symbol **MM**

In S&P SmallCap 600

10-OCT-98

Industry: Financial (Diversified)

Summary: MM provides risk management services to clients seeking alternatives to traditional commercial insurance for certain risk exposure.

Quantitative Evaluations		
Outlook (1 Lowest—5 Highest) • **3⁻**	Recent Price • 27½	Yield • 0.7%
Fair Value • **36⅞**	52 Wk Range • 39⅞-25⅜	12-Mo. P/E • 21.3

Risk
• **Average**

Earn./Div. Rank
• **A-**

Technical Eval.
• **Bearish** since 8/98

Rel. Strength Rank (1 Lowest—99 Highest)
• **41**

Insider Activity
• **NA**

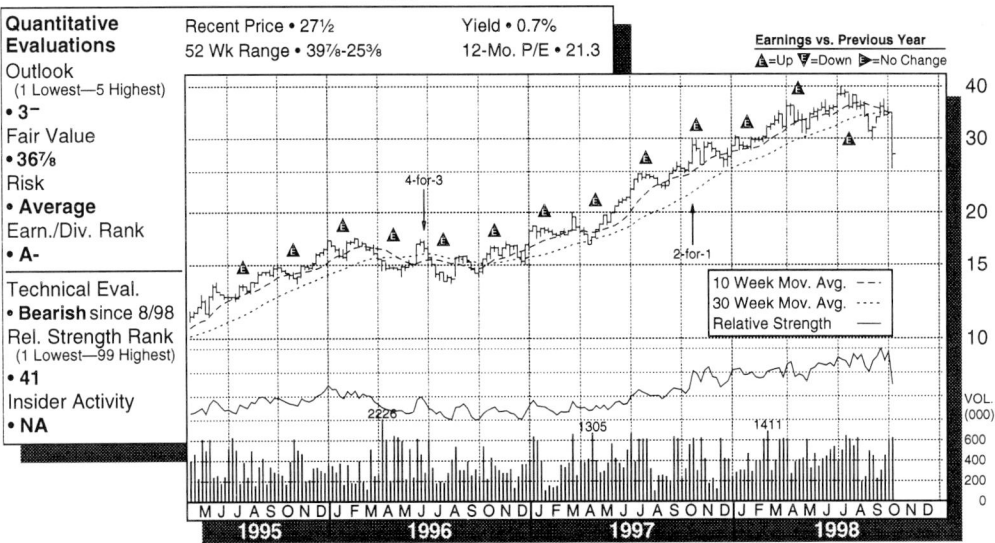

Earnings vs. Previous Year
▲=Up ▼=Down ▶=No Change

4-for-3

2-for-1

10 Week Mov. Avg. - - -
30 Week Mov. Avg. ·····
Relative Strength —

Business Profile - 11-AUG-98

MM is a leader in the alternative insurance market (one of the fastest growing segments of the insurance industry), which includes self-insurance and captive insurance programs, representing about one-third of the U.S. commercial lines insurance market. MM's income is principally derived from fees for services provided to clients; typically, MM earns 11% to 13% of a client's premium in fee income. Pretax profit margins on fees are consistently from 40% to 45%. In recent periods, the company has diversified its product line to include program business, financial services, and specialty brokerage for alternative risk transfer insurers and reinsurers. In July 1998, MM announced the acquisition of two specialty insurers: CompFirst, Inc. of Georgia, with 1997 annual revenues of $3 million; and Avreco Corp. of Chicago, with revenues of $4 million.

Operational Review - 11-AUG-98

In the first half of 1998, total revenues advanced 34%, year to year, on a 32% increase in fee income, 42% higher premiums earned, and a 10% rise in net investment income. Program business fees, which represent over half of total fee income, climbed 73%, while corporate risk management fees declined 8%, due to a soft commercial insurance market. Total expenses were up 38%, reflecting higher losses and loss expenses; pretax income rose 24%. After taxes at 12.9%, versus 18.3%, net income climbed 33%, to $29,068,000 ($0.67 a share on 3.6% more shares), from $21,894,000 ($0.54).

Stock Performance - 09-OCT-98

In the past 30 trading days, MM's shares have declined 12%, compared to a 4% fall in the S&P 500. Average trading volume for the past five days was 159,960 shares, compared with the 40-day moving average of 89,590 shares.

Key Stock Statistics

Dividend Rate/Share	0.20	Shareholders	400
Shs. outstg. (M)	39.7	Market cap. (B)	$ 1.1
Avg. daily vol. (M)	0.106	Inst. holdings	87%
Tang. Bk. Value/Share	6.43		
Beta	1.05		

Value of $10,000 invested 5 years ago: $ 28,427

Fiscal Year Ending Dec. 31

	1998	1997	1996	1995	1994	1993
Revenues (Million $)						
1Q	68.09	47.19	36.69	28.77	29.53	26.01
2Q	59.97	48.48	40.61	32.70	30.49	20.82
3Q	—	62.21	32.78	34.78	33.61	31.38
4Q	—	56.91	47.62	26.99	35.18	27.93
Yr.	—	214.8	157.7	123.2	128.7	106.1
Earnings Per Share ($)						
1Q	0.34	0.27	0.24	0.19	0.17	0.13
2Q	0.33	0.28	0.23	0.22	0.16	0.14
3Q	—	0.33	0.24	0.21	0.18	0.16
4Q	—	0.31	0.24	0.20	0.17	0.16
Yr.	—	1.16	0.96	0.82	0.68	0.58

Next earnings report expected: NA

Dividend Data (Dividends have been paid since 1991.)

Amount ($)	Date Decl.	Ex-Div. Date	Stock of Record	Payment Date
0.050	Sep. 16	Nov. 05	Nov. 07	Nov. 21 '97
0.050	Jan. 28	Feb. 06	Feb. 10	Feb. 20 '98
0.050	Apr. 23	May. 06	May. 08	May. 22 '98
0.050	Jul. 22	Aug. 05	Aug. 07	Aug. 21 '98

A Division of The **McGraw-Hill** Companies

Business Summary - 11-AUG-98

Mutual Risk Management provides risk management services to clients seeking alternatives to traditional commercial insurance for certain risk exposures. Risk management involves analyzing loss exposure and developing risk financing methods to reduce exposure. The use of loss financing methods in place of traditional insurance, known as the alternative market, involves client self-funding of a significant amount of loss exposure, transferring only unpredictable excess risk to insurers. Revenues in recent years (revenues rose 36% in 1997) were derived as follows:

	1997	1996
Fee income	49%	51%
Premiums earned	39%	36%
Net investment income	13%	14%
Realized capital losses	-1%	-1%

MM's principal source of profits is fees received for services provided to clients in connection with its programs. The structure of the company's programs places most underwriting risk with the client. For regulatory and other reasons, however, MM is required to assume a limited amount of risk. It does not seek to earn income from underwriting risk, but from fees for services provided. Through its subsidiaries, MM provides risk management services in the U.S., Bermuda, Barbados, the Cayman Islands, and Europe.

In connection with many programs, Legion Insurance Co., admitted in 50 states, the District of Columbia and Puerto Rico, issues an insurance policy to the client and reinsures the premium and liability related to the client's chosen retention. For most programs, Legion retains only the relatively small portion of the premium associated with its retention of a portion of the specific and aggregate excess risk, ceding the majority of premiums and risk to the client's IPC (Insurance Profit Center) Program and the balance to unaffiliated excess reinsurers.

Subsidiaries include Park International Ltd., a wholesale insurance broker; MRM Hancock Ltd., a reinsurance broker; Captive Managers, which provides a full range of administrative and accounting services to unaffiliated captive insurers; The Worksafe Group, Inc., which operates a proprietary loss control system; IPC Companies, multiple-line insurance and reinsurance companies; and Commonwealth Risk Services, Inc., a marketing subsidiary. During 1996, MM acquired The Hemisphere Group Ltd., which provides administrative services to offshore mutual funds, Professional Underwriters Corp. and Legion Indemnity.

In July 1998, MM announced the acquisition of CompFirst, Inc., a Georgia-based managing general agent specializing in workers' compensation and excess medical stop loss, and Avreco Corp., a Chicago-based brokerage operation specializing in medical malpractice, excess property, and professional liability.

Per Share Data ($)

(Year Ended Dec. 31)	1997	1996	1995	1994	1993	1992	1991	1990	1989	1988
Tangible Bk. Val.	5.99	5.11	4.46	3.42	3.23	2.65	1.95	1.25	0.87	NA
Oper. Earnings	1.19	1.02	0.84	0.69	0.58	0.44	0.34	NA	NA	NA
Earnings	1.16	0.96	0.82	0.68	0.58	0.44	0.34	0.23	0.15	0.11
Dividends	0.18	0.16	0.13	0.11	0.08	0.06	0.03	Nil	Nil	Nil
Payout Ratio	16%	17%	16%	16%	14%	14%	7%	Nil	Nil	Nil
Prices - High	29⅞	18⅝	17⅛	11⅛	12¼	10⅛	8⅞	NA	NA	NA
- Low	16¾	13½	9⅜	7⅞	8	6½	4¼	NA	NA	NA
P/E Ratio - High	26	19	21	17	21	23	26	NA	NA	NA
- Low	14	14	11	12	14	15	12	NA	NA	NA

Income Statement Analysis (Million $)

	1997	1996	1995	1994	1993	1992	1991	1990	1989	1988
Premium Inc.	84.2	56.4	48.2	68.2	55.2	50.4	24.4	17.5	13.4	12.6
Net Invest. Inc.	26.2	22.5	16.1	11.4	9.5	9.2	6.6	3.5	2.6	2.4
Oth. Revs.	104	79.1	58.9	49.0	41.4	31.7	23.3	18.1	13.2	9.3
Total Revs.	215	158	123	129	106	91.4	54.3	39.1	29.2	24.2
Pretax Inc.	58.5	45.6	39.3	32.3	27.2	21.7	15.6	8.2	5.6	4.0
Net Oper. Inc.	NA	39.2	30.6	24.5	20.5	15.4	10.0	NA	NA	NA
Net Inc.	47.9	37.2	29.9	24.0	20.7	15.6	10.3	5.5	3.9	2.7

Balance Sheet & Other Fin. Data (Million $)

	1997	1996	1995	1994	1993	1992	1991	1990	1989	1988
Cash & Equiv.	78.9	57.2	83.1	48.0	32.4	51.7	24.8	25.5	13.7	NA
Premiums Due	156	73.6	39.2	19.0	15.9	10.1	6.2	3.3	2.9	NA
Invest. Assets: Bonds	395	400	352	235	205	148	120	65.0	41.0	NA
Invest. Assets: Stocks	Nil	Nil	Nil	Nil	Nil	Nil	Nil	Nil	Nil	Nil
Invest. Assets: Loans	Nil	Nil	Nil	Nil	Nil	0.6	0.6	1.2	1.5	NA
Invest. Assets: Total	405	400	352	235	205	149	120	66.0	43.0	NA
Deferred Policy Costs	29.9	20.6	19.1	9.5	8.0	6.8	3.6	1.5	1.0	NA
Total Assets	2,147	1,639	1,374	1,018	859	499	405	310	253	NA
Debt	129	122	116	3.0	6.0	8.0	9.0	10.0	4.0	NA
Common Eqty.	1,166	208	167	122	114	95.6	62.6	34.0	23.9	NA
Prop. & Cas. Loss Ratio	NA	NA	NA	56.4	73.0	84.4	93.4	99.2	95.4	NA
Prop. & Cas. Expense Ratio	NA	NA	NA	83.9	64.7	45.7	51.6	72.7	81.4	NA
Prop. & Cas. Combined Ratio	NA	NA	NA	140.3	137.7	130.1	145.0	171.9	176.8	NA
% Return On Revs.	25.4	23.6	24.1	18.6	19.5	17.1	19.0	14.1	13.4	11.3
% Ret. on Equity	5.1	19.9	20.3	20.2	19.8	19.6	20.9	18.2	16.5	13.2

Data as orig. reptd.; bef. results of disc. opers. and/or spec. items. Per share data adj. for stk. divs. as of ex-div. date. Bold denotes diluted EPS (FASB 128). E-Estimated. NA-Not Available. NM-Not Meaningful. NR-Not Ranked.

Office—44 Church St., P. O. Box HM 2064, Hamilton, Bermuda. **Tel**—(441) 295-5688. **Website**—http://www.mutrisk.com **Chrmn & CEO**—R. A. Mulderig. **Pres**—J. Kessock Jr. **SVP, CFO & Investor Contact**—James C. Kelly. **Dirs**—R. E. Dailey, D. J. Doyle, A. E. Engel, A. W. Fulkerson, W. F. Galtney Jr., J. Kessock Jr., R. A. Mulderig, G. R. Partridge, B. H. Patrick, J. S. Rosenbloom, N. L. Rosenthal, J. D. Sargent, R. G. Turner. **Transfer Agent & Registrar**—Boston EquiServe L.P., Canton, MA. **Incorporated**—in Bermuda in 1977. **Empl**— 617. **S&P Analyst:** T.W. Smith, CFA

Myers Industries 8601

ASE Symbol **MYE**

In S&P SmallCap 600

03-OCT-98 **Industry:** Manufacturing (Diversified)

Summary: This diversified maker of polymer and metal products is also a specialized distributor of tools, equipment and supplies for the tire service and transportation industries.

Quantitative Evaluations	Recent Price • 23¾	Yield • 1.0%
	52 Wk Range • 26¾-16¼	12-Mo. P/E • 16.3

Outlook (1 Lowest—5 Highest)
• **3+**

Fair Value
• **25¾**

Risk
• **Average**

Earn./Div. Rank
• **A**

Technical Eval.
• **Bearish** since 9/98

Rel. Strength Rank (1 Lowest—99 Highest)
• **91**

Insider Activity
• **NA**

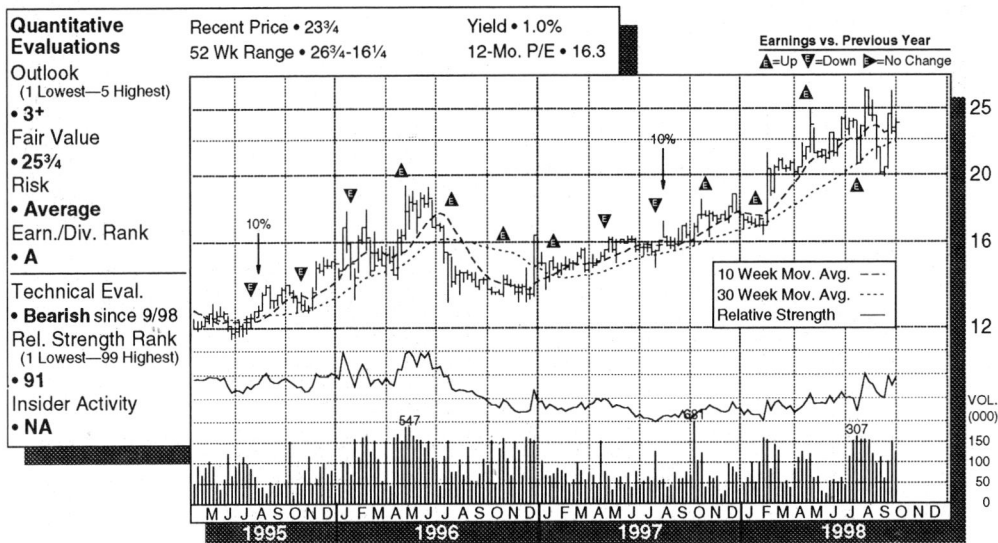

Earnings vs. Previous Year
▲=Up ▼=Down ▶=No Change

10 Week Mov. Avg. - - -
30 Week Mov. Avg. ·······
Relative Strength ——

Business Profile - 20-JUL-98

The company anticipates annual capital spending of $15 million to $20 million over the next five years, primarily for increased polymer manufacturing capacity. Myers believes that available credit and cash flow from operations will be sufficient to meet its needs. In April 1997, the company acquired Molded Solutions, Inc., a manufacturer of custom engineered molded rubber products. MYE has said that a pause in spiraling polymer prices in the third quarter provided some relief from margin pressures that plagued the company for most of 1997. The company is optimistic about its prospects for 1998, as a result of the recent expansion of manufacturing capacity and a new European enterprise that will add new products, customers and markets.

Operational Review - 20-JUL-98

Net sales in the six months ended June 30, 1998, advanced 16%, year to year, reflecting sales growth in the manufacturing and distribution business segments. After taxes at 40.9%, versus 41.3%, net income climbed 44% to $14,587,937 ($0.80 a share, as adjusted), from $10,121,972 ($0.55).

Stock Performance - 02-OCT-98

In the past 30 trading days, MYE's shares have declined 3%, compared to a 7% fall in the S&P 500. Average trading volume for the past five days was 25,000 shares, compared with the 40-day moving average of 24,805 shares.

Key Stock Statistics

Dividend Rate/Share	0.24	Shareholders	2,000
Shs. outstg. (M)	18.3	Market cap. (B)	$0.435
Avg. daily vol. (M)	0.023	Inst. holdings	44%
Tang. Bk. Value/Share	8.91		
Beta	0.65		

Value of $10,000 invested 5 years ago: $ 18,583

Fiscal Year Ending Dec. 31

	1998	1997	1996	1995	1994	1993
Revenues (Million $)						
1Q	88.19	76.80	72.55	67.50	59.69	54.40
2Q	101.1	86.18	79.95	75.58	68.44	63.56
3Q	—	81.14	77.88	74.65	66.19	61.19
4Q	—	95.51	90.56	82.96	79.73	65.98
Yr.	—	339.6	320.9	300.7	274.1	245.1
Earnings Per Share ($)						
1Q	**0.38**	**0.26**	0.28	0.20	0.19	0.18
2Q	**0.42**	**0.29**	0.30	0.24	0.28	0.25
3Q	—	0.21	0.20	0.18	0.21	0.17
4Q	—	**0.45**	0.35	0.25	0.29	0.25
Yr.	—	**1.21**	1.13	0.86	0.96	0.85

Next earnings report expected: NA

Dividend Data (Dividends have been paid since 1966.)

Amount ($)	Date Decl.	Ex-Div. Date	Stock of Record	Payment Date
0.050	Oct. 23	Dec. 10	Dec. 12	Jan. 02 '98
0.050	Jan. 15	Mar. 11	Mar. 13	Apr. 01 '98
0.050	Apr. 30	Jun. 10	Jun. 12	Jul. 01 '98
0.060	Jul. 30	Sep. 09	Sep. 11	Oct. 01 '98

A Division of The McGraw-Hill Companies

Business Summary - 20-JUL-98

Founded in 1933, Myers Industries, Inc. (MYE) is a leading manufacturer of reusable plastic containers and distributor of equipment, tools and supplies used for tire servicing and automotive underbody repair.

The Manufacturing segment, which accounted for 58.1% of total sales in 1997, and 59.1% in 1996, designs, manufactures and markets reusable plastic containers under the brand names NesTier, Akro-Bins and Buckhorn. These products are used in industrial applications including the distribution of food items, such as poultry, meat and baked goods, and the distribution of non-food items, such as apparel, electronic, automotive, and industrial components, health and beauty aids and hardware. Consumer products include the Keepbox line of household storage containers, plastic tool boxes and other products to organize the home workshop, plastic containers to facilitate consumer recycling, and a line of plastic pots, planters and urns sold to consumers through lawn and garden retailers and other similar specialty outlets.

MYE also designs, manufactures and markets molded rubber products, such as air intake hoses, rubber boots, mounts, and hood hold-down latches for diesel-powered vehicles and equipment used in the transportation, construction and agricultural industries.

The Distribution segment, which accounted for 41.9% of total sales in 1997, and 40.9% in 1996, distributes equipment, tools and supplies used for tire servicing and automotive underbody repair. Its business is conducted primarily through the Myers Tire Supply division. Products distributed include air compressors, mechanic's hand tools, tire changers, tire display and storage equipment, valves, tire balancing and wheel alignment equipment, curing rims and presses, retread presses and tire repair materials for the retreading industry. The company believes that it is the only nationwide distributor supplying such products. Customers include independent tire dealers, tire retreaders, tire service centers, automotive supply chains and rubber companies.

Myers Tire Supply's domestic distribution system includes 42 owned branch warehouse distributors in 31 states. Internationally, it has two wholly owned warehouse distributors located in Canada and owns an interest in several other foreign warehouse distributors. Its main distribution center stocks approximately 10,000 items which are purchased from numerous suppliers.

Per Share Data ($)

(Year Ended Dec. 31)	1997	1996	1995	1994	1993	1992	1991	1990	1989	1988
Tangible Bk. Val.	8.41	7.85	6.73	6.40	5.53	4.12	3.67	3.08	2.43	1.85
Cash Flow	1.88	1.74	1.43	1.47	1.29	1.14	0.99	0.99	0.99	0.86
Earnings	1.21	1.13	0.86	0.97	0.85	0.77	0.63	0.64	0.58	0.49
Dividends	0.19	0.16	0.15	0.14	0.11	0.10	0.09	0.08	0.08	0.07
Payout Ratio	16%	15%	17%	15%	13%	13%	15%	13%	13%	14%
Prices - High	18³/₄	19³/₈	15¹/₄	15¹/₄	16⁷/₈	13⁷/₈	8	8¹/₄	7⁵/₈	6¹/₄
- Low	13⁵/₈	13¹/₈	10⁷/₈	10⁵/₈	12⁵/₈	7³/₈	5¹/₂	5¹/₂	6	3¹/₈
P/E Ratio - High	15	17	18	16	20	18	13	13	13	13
- Low	11	12	13	11	15	10	9	9	10	6

Income Statement Analysis (Million $)

	1997	1996	1995	1994	1993	1992	1991	1990	1989	1988
Revs.	340	321	301	274	245	229	196	202	195	184
Oper. Inc.	50.8	47.2	38.3	40.1	34.2	29.5	25.6	26.5	25.3	22.4
Depr.	12.5	11.3	10.5	9.4	7.6	6.3	6.0	5.7	5.4	4.9
Int. Exp.	0.6	0.6	1.0	0.8	1.2	1.5	2.0	3.1	4.2	4.3
Pretax Inc.	38.1	35.6	27.1	30.0	25.4	21.8	17.8	18.0	16.2	13.9
Eff. Tax Rate	41%	41%	41%	41%	40%	40%	41%	40%	41%	42%
Net Inc.	22.3	21.0	16.0	17.8	15.4	13.1	10.5	10.8	9.6	8.1

Balance Sheet & Other Fin. Data (Million $)

	1997	1996	1995	1994	1993	1992	1991	1990	1989	1988
Cash	6.3	5.6	3.4	1.8	1.7	3.4	3.2	2.5	2.5	1.6
Curr. Assets	107	106	101	94.7	78.9	74.9	60.7	63.3	61.5	58.9
Total Assets	224	207	194	172	152	142	113	116	111	110
Curr. Liab.	39.6	36.9	32.4	34.1	24.4	31.7	25.3	26.3	26.4	24.8
LT Debt	4.3	4.6	13.3	4.2	10.7	24.9	14.6	25.4	29.8	38.4
Common Eqty.	177	162	145	131	115	83.9	72.5	63.2	53.3	44.8
Total Cap.	181	170	161	138	128	110	88.0	90.0	85.0	85.0
Cap. Exp.	18.8	21.5	12.0	12.5	14.1	16.7	6.3	11.0	6.4	8.6
Cash Flow	34.8	32.3	26.4	27.2	23.0	19.4	16.5	16.5	15.0	13.0
Curr. Ratio	2.7	2.9	3.1	2.8	3.2	2.4	2.4	2.4	2.3	2.4
% LT Debt of Cap.	2.4	2.7	8.3	3.0	8.3	22.6	16.6	28.2	35.2	45.3
% Net Inc.of Revs.	6.6	6.5	5.3	6.5	6.3	5.7	5.4	5.3	4.9	4.4
% Ret. on Assets	10.4	10.5	8.7	11.0	10.0	10.2	9.2	9.4	8.7	7.5
% Ret. on Equity	13.2	13.7	11.6	14.5	14.9	16.7	15.5	18.5	19.6	19.4

Data as orig. reptd.; bef. results of disc. opers. and/or spec. items. Per share data adj. for stk. divs. as of ex-div. date. Bold denotes diluted EPS (FASB 128). E-Estimated. NA-Not Available. NM-Not Meaningful. NR-Not Ranked.

Office—1293 S. Main St., Akron, OH 44301. **Tel**—(330) 253-5592. **Pres & CEO**—S. E. Myers. **SVP & Secy**—M. I. Wiskind. **VP-Fin, CFO & Investor Contact**—Gregory J. Stodnick. **Dirs**—K. A. Brown, K. S. Hay, R. P. Johnston, S. E. Myers, R. L. Osborne, J. H. Outcalt, S. Salem, E. P. Schrank, M. I. Wiskind. **Transfer Agent & Registrar**—First Chicago Trust of New York, NYC. **Incorporated**—in Ohio in 1955. **Empl**— 2,083. **S&P Analyst:** Kathleen J. Fraser

NBTY, Inc.

4675H

NASDAQ Symbol **NBTY**

In S&P SmallCap 600

03-OCT-98

Industry:
Personal Care

Summary: NBTY (formerly Nature's Bounty) manufactures and distributes vitamins, food supplements and health and beauty aids under its own and private labels.

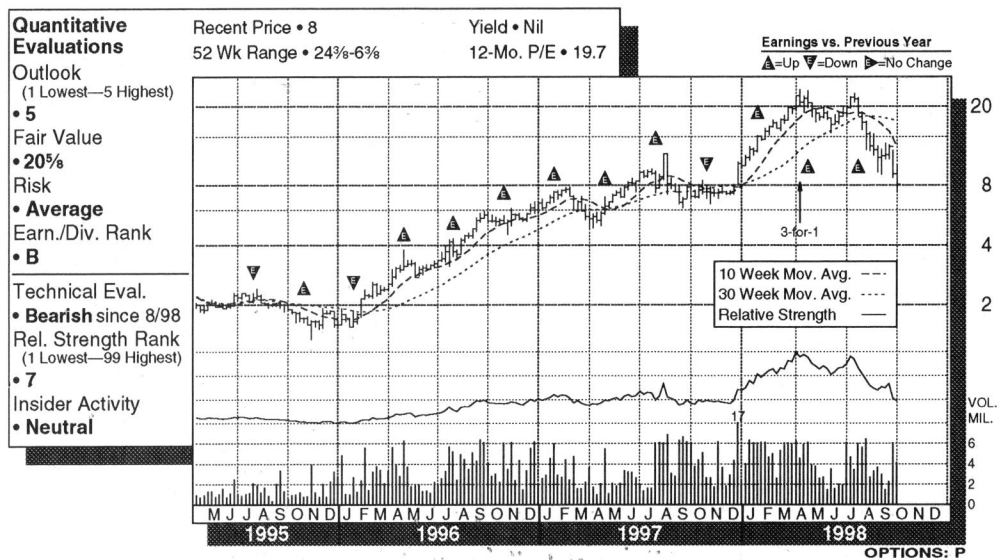

Quantitative Evaluations	
Recent Price • 8	Yield • Nil
52 Wk Range • 24⅜-6⅜	12-Mo. P/E • 19.7

Outlook
(1 Lowest—5 Highest)
• **5**

Fair Value
• **20⅝**

Risk
• **Average**

Earn./Div. Rank
• **B**

Technical Eval.
• **Bearish** since 8/98

Rel. Strength Rank
(1 Lowest—99 Highest)
• **7**

Insider Activity
• **Neutral**

Earnings vs. Previous Year
▲=Up ▼=Down ▶=No Change

3-for-1

10 Week Mov. Avg. ---
30 Week Mov. Avg. ·····
Relative Strength ——

VOL. MIL.

OPTIONS: P

Business Profile - 15-SEP-98

In August 1997, NBTY acquired Holland & Barrett (H&B), the United Kingdom's largest chain of vitamin and health food stores, for $169 million, financed through long-term debt. The chain was established in 1920 and has approximate annual revenues of $400 million. NBTY's strategy with H&B is to replace products made by other manufacturers, currently being sold by H&B, with NBTY's own manufactured products. Earnings growth in the first nine months of FY 98 (Sep.) was aided by sooner than anticipated accretive results at H&B. Sales and operating income derived from the United Kingdom account for approximately 34% and 17%, respectively, of the company's total.

Operational Review - 15-SEP-98

Net sales in the nine months ended June 30, 1998, rose 78%, year to year, primarily reflecting the Holland & Barrett (H&B) acquisition coupled with robust performance at domestic retail stores. Margins widened on the increased volume, but following sharply higher acquisition-related depreciation & amortization charges, interest expense and other costs, pretax profits advanced 38%. After taxes at 33.6%, versus 31.4%, net income was up 34%, to $31,768,000 ($0.46 a share), from $23,696,000 ($0.34, adjusted).

Stock Performance - 02-OCT-98

In the past 30 trading days, NBTY's shares have declined 33%, compared to a 7% fall in the S&P 500. Average trading volume for the past five days was 823,940 shares, compared with the 40-day moving average of 681,813 shares.

Key Stock Statistics

Dividend Rate/Share	Nil	Shareholders	600
Shs. outstg. (M)	67.7	Market cap. (B)	$0.546
Avg. daily vol. (M)	0.713	Inst. holdings	46%
Tang. Bk. Value/Share	0.27		
Beta	1.88		

Value of $10,000 invested 5 years ago: $ 26,505

Fiscal Year Ending Sep. 30

	1998	1997	1996	1995	1994	1993
Revenues (Million $)						
1Q	109.4	47.33	38.59	37.48	32.74	25.60
2Q	135.0	75.02	55.61	50.95	47.00	36.65
3Q	138.9	61.76	47.90	41.65	35.86	34.06
4Q	—	97.30	52.31	48.69	40.45	42.13
Yr.	—	281.4	194.4	178.8	156.1	138.4
Earnings Per Share ($)						
1Q	**0.08**	0.05	0.00	0.02	0.03	0.02
2Q	**0.10**	0.10	0.00	0.04	0.07	0.00
3Q	**0.12**	0.09	0.06	0.02	0.03	0.03
4Q	—	0.02	0.09	0.01	Nil	0.07
Yr.	—	0.29	0.22	0.09	0.13	0.18

Next earnings report expected: mid November

Dividend Data

Amount ($)	Date Decl.	Ex-Div. Date	Stock of Record	Payment Date
3-for-1	Mar. 10	Apr. 06	Mar. 23	Apr. 03 '98

A Division of The McGraw·Hill Companies

Business Summary - 15-SEP-98

NBTY, Inc. (formerly Nature's Bounty, Inc.) is engaged primarily in the manufacture and distribution of vitamins and nutritional supplements. The company emphasizes sales of its own products and, to a lesser extent, sales under private label. Products are distributed through direct mail, wholesale and retail channels.

In August 1997, NBTY acquired Holland & Barrett (H&B), the largest chain of vitamin and healthfood stores in the United Kingdom for $168.8 million financed through long-term debt. Holland & Barrett was established in 1920 and has approximate annual sales of $400 million.

NBTY markets more than 650 products consisting of vitamins and other nutritional supplements such as minerals, amino acids and herbs. Vitamins, minerals and amino acids are sold as a single vitamin and in multi-vitamin combinations and in varying potency levels in powder, tablet, soft gel, chewable and hard shell capsule form.

NBTY sells through direct mail, offering its full line of vitamins and other nutritional supplements as well as personal care items. Products are sold under its Puritan's Pride brand name at prices that are generally discounted to similar products sold in retail stores.

The Nature's Bounty line, the company's leading brand, is distributed to drug store chains and supermarkets, independent pharmacies, health food stores, health food store wholesalers and other retailers such as mass merchandisers. Clients include Genovese Drug Stores, Walgreens, Lucky Stores and Bergen Brunswig. NBTY also offers private label products under the brand name Natural Wealth. In addition, a comprehensive line of over-the-counter products such as cold remedies and analgesic formulas are sold to independent pharmacies under the Hudson brand name.

The company operates 127 Vitamin World retail stores in 38 states and the territory of Guam. In addition, the company plans to open 80 new stores by year-end 1998. These retail stores carry a full line of NBTY's products under the Vitamin World brand name as well as products from other manufacturers.

Holland & Barrett operates 420 stores in the United Kingdom. Holland & Barrett classifies its products into two categories: nutritional supplement products and food products. Nutritional supplement products accounted for approximately 58% of sales in FY 97 (Sep.) and include herbal and alternative remedies, sports nutrition, aromatherapy and diet products. Food products accounted for 42% of FY 97 sales and include fruits and nuts, confectionery, chilled and frozen foods, beverages and milk, vegetarian foods, herbal teas, water and juices, honeys and spreads, breakfast foods, condiments and biscuits.

Per Share Data ($)

(Year Ended Sep. 30)	1997	1996	1995	1994	1993	1992	1991	1990	1989	1988
Tangible Bk. Val.	NM	1.67	1.44	1.38	1.21	0.33	0.31	0.25	0.19	0.29
Cash Flow	0.42	0.32	0.17	0.20	0.25	0.17	0.11	0.11	0.07	0.05
Earnings	0.29	0.22	0.09	0.13	0.18	0.09	0.03	0.02	0.01	0.01
Dividends	Nil	Nil	Nil	Nil	Nil	Nil	Nil	Nil	Nil	Nil
Payout Ratio	Nil	Nil	Nil	Nil	Nil	Nil	Nil	Nil	Nil	Nil
Prices - High	11½	6⅞	2¾	8⅛	7⅛	4	¼	¼	3/16	5/16
- Low	4¾	1⁹/₁₆	1⁵/₁₆	1⁹/₁₆	2⁵/₁₆	3/16	⅛	⅛	⅛	⅛
P/E Ratio - High	40	31	32	64	41	43	8	12	32	45
- Low	17	7	15	13	13	2	3	6	16	16

Income Statement Analysis (Million $)

	1997	1996	1995	1994	1993	1992	1991	1990	1989	1988
Revs.	281	194	179	156	138	101	74.0	71.0	63.0	51.0
Oper. Inc.	47.9	28.2	13.7	17.7	20.2	10.5	5.8	5.4	4.1	2.6
Depr.	8.2	5.6	4.8	4.2	4.0	3.1	2.5	3.0	2.1	1.4
Int. Exp.	6.7	1.4	1.1	0.9	1.2	1.3	1.4	1.4	1.3	0.9
Pretax Inc.	28.7	22.4	8.4	12.5	15.7	5.9	1.7	1.3	0.4	0.4
Eff. Tax Rate	40%	40%	39%	38%	38%	35%	40%	42%	39%	39%
Net Inc.	17.2	13.3	5.1	7.8	9.8	3.8	1.0	0.7	0.2	0.2

Balance Sheet & Other Fin. Data (Million $)

	1997	1996	1995	1994	1993	1992	1991	1990	1989	1988
Cash	26.8	20.3	10.4	5.9	10.8	2.4	2.4	0.3	0.2	0.3
Curr. Assets	143	78.8	67.7	66.6	63.7	32.7	24.2	17.1	20.0	15.7
Total Assets	543	146	124	115	102	58.3	43.5	36.3	35.8	27.3
Curr. Liab.	79.9	26.6	27.1	27.2	21.7	19.6	15.5	12.4	13.1	8.7
LT Debt	337	18.4	10.9	7.6	8.3	21.0	14.2	11.4	11.2	7.5
Common Eqty.	117	96.9	82.6	78.0	70.0	16.5	12.8	11.8	11.4	11.2
Total Cap.	462	118	96.3	87.5	79.2	38.0	27.6	23.8	22.7	18.6
Cap. Exp.	21.1	15.8	11.5	11.6	14.2	5.1	3.1	6.4	2.4	1.4
Cash Flow	25.4	19.0	10.0	12.0	13.7	6.9	3.6	3.7	2.4	1.6
Curr. Ratio	1.8	3.0	2.5	2.5	2.9	1.7	1.6	1.4	1.5	1.8
% LT Debt of Cap.	73.0	15.6	11.3	8.7	10.4	55.3	51.4	48.0	49.5	40.1
% Net Inc.of Revs.	6.1	6.9	2.9	5.0	7.1	3.8	1.4	1.0	0.4	0.4
% Ret. on Assets	5.0	10.0	4.3	7.2	10.0	7.5	2.6	2.1	0.7	0.8
% Ret. on Equity	16.1	14.9	6.4	10.5	20.2	26.2	8.3	6.4	2.1	2.0

Data as orig. reptd.; bef. results of disc. opers. and/or spec. items. Per share data adj. for stk. divs. as of ex-div. date. Bold denotes diluted EPS (FASB 128). E-Estimated. NA-Not Available. NM-Not Meaningful. NR-Not Ranked.

Office—90 Orville Dr., Bohemia, NY 11716. **Tel**—(516) 567-9500. **Chrmn, Pres & CEO**—S. Rudolph. **EVP, CFO, Secy & Investor Contact**—Harvey Kamil. **Dirs**—G. Cohen, M. Daly, A. Garabedian, B. G. Owen, N. Rosenblatt, A. Rudolph, S. Rudolph, A. Sacks, B. Solk. **Transfer Agent & Registrar**—American Stock Transfer Co., NYC. **Incorporated**—in Delaware in 1980. **Empl**—3,655. **S&P Analyst:** K.S.

STANDARD &POOR'S
STOCK REPORTS

NCS HealthCare

4675K

NASDAQ Symbol **NCSS**

In S&P SmallCap 600

03-OCT-98

Industry:
Health Care (Special-
ized Services)

Summary: This company is a leading independent provider of pharmacy services to long-term care institutions.

Quantitative Evaluations

Outlook
(1 Lowest—5 Highest)
• **NA**

Fair Value
• **NA**

Risk
• **Average**

Earn./Div. Rank
• **NR**

Technical Eval.
• **NA**

Rel. Strength Rank
(1 Lowest—99 Highest)
• **11**

Insider Activity
• **Neutral**

Recent Price • 14⅝
52 Wk Range • 34-13¾

Yield • Nil
12-Mo. P/E • 25.2

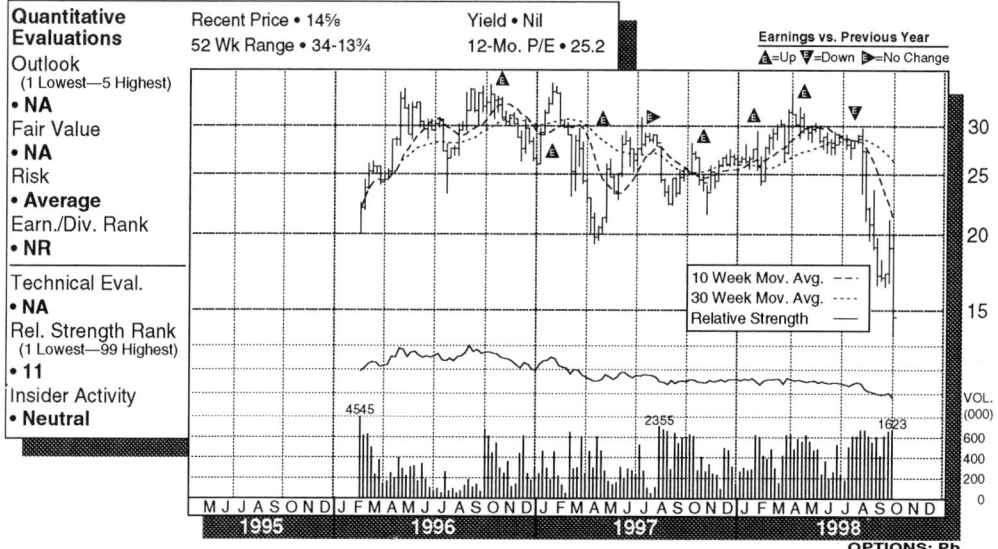

Earnings vs. Previous Year
△=Up ▽=Down ▷=No Change

10 Week Mov. Avg. ---
30 Week Mov. Avg. ----
Relative Strength —

VOL. (000)

OPTIONS: Ph

Business Profile - 01-SEP-98

The company's strategy is to capitalize on industry
trends to strengthen its position as a leading provider of
integrated pharmacy and related services to institutional
clients. Key elements of this strategy include continuing
an aggressive acquisition and development program,
identifying and standardizing best practices, cross marketing services across the customer base to generate
internal growth, using technology to deliver information,
and providing ancillary health care services to complement core pharmacy services. In June 1998, NCSS acquired the long-term care pharmacy assets of Walgreen
Co., with annual revenues of $40 million, for an undis-
closed amount.

Operational Review - 01-SEP-98

Based on a preliminary report, revenues in FY 98 (Jun.)
advanced 85% from the prior fiscal year, aided by acquisitions and internal growth. Costs and expenses
were well controlled, however, following $8.9 million of
non-recurring charges in the FY 98 fourth quarter, operating income was up 42%. With interest expense, versus income, and after taxes at 44.3%, versus 43.4%,
net income rose slightly, to $11,331,000 ($0.58, diluted,
on 15% more shares) from $11,272,000 ($0.69). Excluding non-recurring charges, which reflected strategic
restructuring and consolidation initiatives, earnings in
FY 98 amounted to $0.86 per share.

Stock Performance - 02-OCT-98

In the past 30 trading days, NCSS's shares have declined 30%, compared to a 7% fall in the S&P 500.
Average trading volume for the past five days was
324,600 shares, compared with the 40-day moving average of 190,972 shares.

Key Stock Statistics

Dividend Rate/Share	Nil	Shareholders	300
Shs. outstg. (M)	19.6	Market cap. (B)	$0.189
Avg. daily vol. (M)	0.207	Inst. holdings	60%
Tang. Bk. Value/Share	0.15		
Beta	NA		

Value of $10,000 invested 5 years ago: NA

Fiscal Year Ending Jun. 30

	1998	1997	1996	1995	1994	1993
Revenues (Million $)						
1Q	103.7	43.04	22.43	—	—	—
2Q	114.5	59.32	27.60	—	—	—
3Q	137.7	78.54	30.21	—	—	—
4Q	153.2	94.14	33.05	—	—	—
Yr.	509.1	275.0	113.3	65.60	48.20	33.60
Earnings Per Share ($)						
1Q	0.20	0.15	-0.15	—	—	—
2Q	**0.21**	0.17	0.10	—	—	—
3Q	**0.22**	0.18	0.12	—	—	—
4Q	**-0.03**	0.19	0.19	—	—	—
Yr.	**0.58**	0.70	0.26	0.28	0.13	0.11

Next earnings report expected: early November

Dividend Data

No cash dividends have been paid. The company intends to retain its earnings for use in its business and
does not anticipate paying cash dividends in the foreseeable future.

A Division of The McGraw-Hill Companies

STANDARD
&POOR'S

STOCK REPORTS

NCS HealthCare, Inc.

4675K

03-OCT-98

Business Summary - 01-SEP-98

Traditionally providing institutional pharmacy and infusion products and services to long-term care facility residents, NCS Health Care, Inc. in more recent years has developed an array of services that address the needs of long-term care facilities to accommodate higher acuity admissions and manage costs. It remains a leading independent provider of pharmacy services to long-term care institutions that include skilled nursing facilities, assisted living facilities and other institutional health care settings. At June 30, 1997, the company had contracts to provide services to about 152,000 residents in 23 states.

The company purchases and dispenses prescriptions and non-prescription pharmaceuticals and provides client facilities with related management services, automated medical record keeping, drug therapy evaluation and regulatory assistance. It also provides a broad range of ancillary health care services including infusion therapy, physical, speech and occupational therapies and nutrition management and other services.

The company's core business is providing pharmaceutical dispensing services to residents of long-term care facilities and other institutions. It purchases, repackages and dispenses prescription and non-prescription medication in accordance with physician orders and delivers the prescriptions at least daily to long-term care facili-

ties for administration to residents by nursing home staffs. At FY 97 (Jun.) year end, the company provided its services from 52 sites in 23 states. It also provides services through the management of third party institutional pharmacies.

NCS provides consulting services that help clients comply with federal and state regulations applicable to long-term care facilities. Services include reviewing each patient's drug regimen, inspecting medication carts and storage rooms, monitoring and reporting on facility-wide drug usage and administration systems and practices, and developing and maintaining a client's pharmaceutical policy and procedure manuals. Pharmacy and consulting pharmacy services to long-term care facilities provided 75% of revenues in FY 97.

The company also provides infusion therapy (intravenous delivery of medication) services including pain management, antibiotic therapy and chemotherapy for long-term care residents and home care patients. In 1993, it began offering physical, speech and occupational therapy services.

Nutrition management services involve assisting long-term care facilities in menu planning, purchasing and managing their dietary operations. Other services include providing long-term care facilities with assistance in complying with regulations concerning healthy and sanitary environments.

Per Share Data ($)

(Year Ended Jun. 30)	1998	1997	1996	1995	1994	1993	1992	1991	1990	1989
Tangible Bk. Val.	NA	4.01	4.27	4.67	NA	NA	NA	NA	NA	NA
Cash Flow	NA	1.25	0.62	0.46	NA	NA	NA	NA	NA	NA
Earnings	0.58	0.70	0.26	0.28	0.13	0.11	0.11	NA	NA	NA
Dividends	Nil	Nil	Nil	Nil	Nil	Nil	Nil	Nil	Nil	Nil
Payout Ratio	Nil	Nil	Nil	Nil	Nil	Nil	Nil	Nil	Nil	Nil
Prices - High	34	35¼	35	NA	NA	NA	NA	NA	NA	NA
- Low	23¼	19¼	16½	NA	NA	NA	NA	NA	NA	NA
P/E Ratio - High	59	50	NA	NA	NA	NA	NA	NA	NA	NA
- Low	40	27	NA	NA	NA	NA	NA	NA	NA	NA

Income Statement Analysis (Million $)

	NA	1997	1996	1995	1994	1993	1992	1991	1990	1989
Revs.	NA	275	113	65.6	48.2	33.6	28.5	NA	NA	NA
Oper. Inc.	NA	27.2	9.0	5.7	NA	NA	NA	NA	NA	NA
Depr.	NA	8.9	3.2	1.2	NA	NA	NA	NA	NA	NA
Int. Exp.	NA	1.1	2.3	1.1	NA	NA	NA	NA	NA	NA
Pretax Inc.	NA	19.9	4.2	3.4	NA	NA	NA	NA	NA	NA
Eff. Tax Rate	NA	43%	43%	45%	NA	NA	NA	NA	NA	NA
Net Inc.	NA	11.3	2.4	1.9	1.5	0.8	0.7	NA	NA	NA

Balance Sheet & Other Fin. Data (Million $)

Cash	NA	8.2	21.5	0.0	NA	NA	NA	NA	NA	NA
Curr. Assets	NA	107	59.2	20.4	NA	NA	NA	NA	NA	NA
Total Assets	NA	321	111	38.6	NA	NA	NA	NA	NA	NA
Curr. Liab.	NA	54.3	10.9	9.8	NA	NA	NA	NA	NA	NA
LT Debt	NA	12.9	8.5	20.4	NA	NA	NA	NA	NA	NA
Common Eqty.	NA	253	91.1	8.1	NA	NA	NA	NA	NA	NA
Total Cap.	NA	267	100	28.7	NA	NA	NA	NA	NA	NA
Cap. Exp.	NA	9.9	4.7	2.8	NA	NA	NA	NA	NA	NA
Cash Flow	NA	20.2	5.6	3.1	NA	NA	NA	NA	NA	NA
Curr. Ratio	NA	2.0	5.5	2.1	NA	NA	NA	NA	NA	NA
% LT Debt of Cap.	NA	4.8	8.5	71.1	NA	NA	NA	NA	NA	NA
% Net Inc.of Revs.	NA	4.1	2.1	2.9	3.1	2.4	2.5	NA	NA	NA
% Ret. on Assets	NA	5.2	3.2	NA	NA	NA	NA	NA	NA	NA
% Ret. on Equity	NA	6.6	4.8	NA	NA	NA	NA	NA	NA	NA

Data as orig. reptd.; bef. results of disc. opers. and/or spec. items. Per share data adj. for stk. divs. as of ex-div. date. Bold denotes diluted EPS (FASB 128). E-Estimated. NA-Not Available. NM-Not Meaningful. NR-Not Ranked.

Office—3201 Enterprise Parkway, Suite 220, Beachwood, OH 44122. **Tel**—(216) 514-3350. **Website**—http://www.ncshealth.com **Chrmn**—J. H. Outcalt. **Pres & CEO**—K. B. Shaw. **SVP & CFO**—J. R. Steinhilber. **Dirs**—A. M. Mixon III, J. B. Naylor, R. L. Osborne, J. H. Outcalt, B. A. Sells, K. B. Shaw, P. K. Wilson. **Transfer Agent & Registrar**—National City Bank, Cleveland. **Incorporated**—in Delaware. **Empl**— 2,350. **S&P Analyst:** S.A.H.

NAC Re Corp.

1568B

NYSE Symbol **NRC**

In S&P SmallCap 600

03-OCT-98

Industry:
Insurance (Property-Casualty)

Summary: One of the largest reinsurers in the U.S., NRC underwrites property and casualty reinsurance coverage in the U.S. and abroad.

S&P Opinion: Accumulate (★★★★)

Recent Price • 49⅞	Yield • 0.7%
52 Wk Range • 55⅞-43½	12-Mo. P/E • 10.9

Quantitative Evaluations

Outlook
(1 Lowest—5 Highest)
• **3+**

Fair Value
• **52¼**

Risk
• **Average**

Earn./Div. Rank
• **A-**

Technical Eval.
• **Bearish** since 8/96

Rel. Strength Rank
(1 Lowest—99 Highest)
• **83**

Insider Activity
• **NA**

Earnings vs. Previous Year
▲=Up ▼=Down ▶=No Change

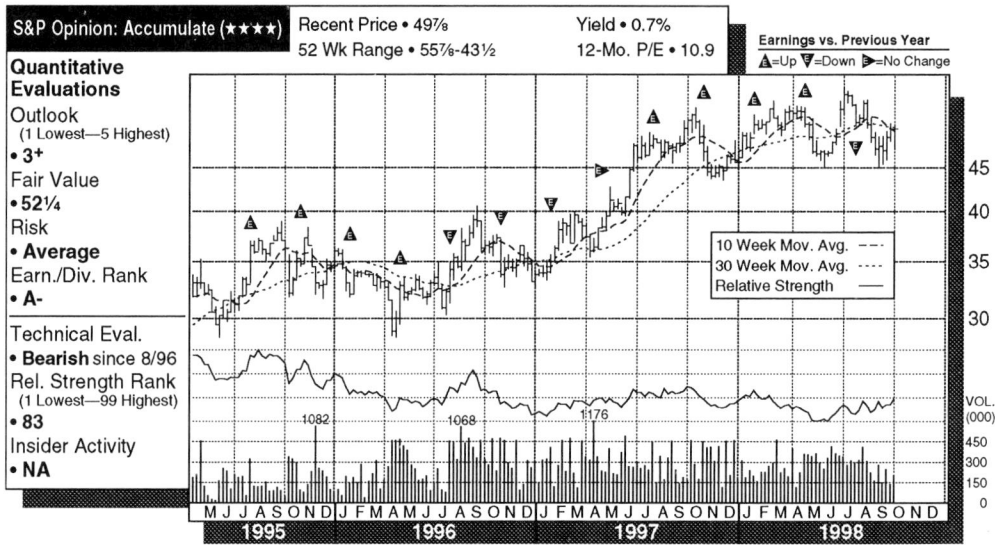

10 Week Mov. Avg. — — —
30 Week Mov. Avg. ‥‥‥
Relative Strength —

Overview - 12-AUG-98

Net written premiums will likely advance around 5% in 1998, reflecting extremely competitive market conditions (due mainly to an industry-wide oversupply of underwriting capacity), particularly in most treaty lines of business. Although pricing in most sectors of the reinsurance market remains very competitive, NRC is well positioned to benefit from a consolidation trend emerging in the reinsurance industry. Also, growth in the casualty area has been driven by increased emphasis on complex lines of business, where competition is based more on service and underwriting skill than on premium rates. Property reinsurance pricing, though down from its peak, is still decent. Growth here increases NRC's exposure to catastrophes. But under a relatively new program, its net retention is $5 million per catastrophe, down from $10 million in 1993. Assuming a "normal" level of catastrophe and weather-related losses, underwriting results should approach breakeven.

Valuation - 12-AUG-98

The shares of this property-casualty reinsurer recovered from a correction in early 1996 that was driven primarily by concerns over rising interest rates and increased competitive pricing pressures in the U.S. reinsurance market. Renewed concerns over slowing premium growth sent the shares tumbling in late 1997. They have since recovered, but remain attractively valued at approximately 12 times our 1999 operating earnings estimate (which excludes realized investment gains) of $4.15 a share. NRC is a high-quality reinsurer, well positioned over the long term. Moreover, as the reinsurance industry consolidates, NRC may become a takeover target.

Key Stock Statistics

S&P EPS Est. 1998	3.75	Tang. Bk. Value/Share	37.98
P/E on S&P Est. 1998	13.3	Beta	0.74
S&P EPS Est. 1999	4.15	Shareholders	400
Dividend Rate/Share	0.36	Market cap. (B)	$0.908
Shs. outstg. (M)	18.2	Inst. holdings	75%
Avg. daily vol. (M)	0.040		

Value of $10,000 invested 5 years ago: $ 12,752

Fiscal Year Ending Dec. 31

	1998	1997	1996	1995	1994	1993
Revenues (Million $)						
1Q	173.3	165.8	152.4	130.8	102.3	90.86
2Q	173.9	190.1	158.7	146.4	109.0	102.6
3Q	—	185.4	167.4	164.1	131.6	104.8
4Q	—	199.1	171.8	165.1	135.4	103.9
Yr.	—	740.4	650.2	606.5	478.4	402.1
Earnings Per Share ($)						
1Q	1.14	1.00	1.06	0.64	0.57	0.67
2Q	1.10	1.42	0.85	0.82	0.32	0.61
3Q	—	1.03	0.84	0.98	0.58	0.47
4Q	—	1.32	0.92	1.04	0.53	0.54
Yr.	—	4.77	3.69	3.47	1.99	2.30

Next earnings report expected: late October

Dividend Data (Dividends have been paid since 1989.)

Amount ($)	Date Decl.	Ex-Div. Date	Stock of Record	Payment Date
0.075	Dec. 10	Dec. 22	Dec. 24	Jan. 07 '98
0.075	Mar. 11	Mar. 23	Mar. 25	Apr. 08 '98
0.090	Jun. 10	Jun. 22	Jun. 24	Jul. 08 '98
0.090	Sep. 16	Sep. 28	Sep. 30	Oct. 14 '98

A Division of The McGraw·Hill Companies

NAC Re Corp.

1568B

03-OCT-98

Business Summary - 12-AUG-98

NAC Re Corp. (formerly North American Company for Property and Casualty Insurance) provides treaty and facultative reinsurance to primary insurers of casualty risks (principally general liability, professional liability, automobile and workers' compensation) and commercial and personal property risks. Greenwich Insurance Co. offers a limited number of specialized primary insurance products to NAC Re's reinsurance clients. NAC Re International Ltd. underwrites reinsurance outside the U.S.

Net premiums written in recent years were derived:

	1997	1996
Casualty	53%	57%
Property	20%	21%
Specialty	18%	13%
International	9%	9%

During 1997, 54% of NRC's business was written on an excess-of-loss basis, which means that its liability arises only after the loss incurred by the primary insurer exceeds a specified sum. The balance of NRC's business is generally written on a pro rata basis, under which NRC assumes from the primary insurer a percentage specified in the treaty of each risk in the reinsured class.

The company obtains substantially all of its treaty business--an agreement between a reinsurer and an insurance company that provides for the reinsurance of an entire class of risks specified within the agreement--through reinsurance brokers. During 1997, three brokers -- AON Reinsurance Agency, Guy Carpenter and E.W. Blanch, Inc. -- accounted for 52% of NRC's premiums assumed from client companies.

Net written premiums increased 3.4% in 1997, to $593.7 million, from about $574.0 million in 1996. The somewhat tepid growth in written premiums was primarily due to NRC's refusal to write inadequately priced business in the face of an extremely competitive operating environment, particularly in treaty business. Underwriting results deteriorated slightly, and the combined ratio equaled 103.6% at year-end 1997, up from 101.6% at year-end 1996. (A combined ratio under 100% indicates an underwriting profit; one in excess of 100% points to an underwriting loss.) Competitive market conditions continued into the first half of 1998, and net written premiums for the six months ended June 30, 1998, declined 2.6%, year to year, to $277.5 million from $284.8 million in 1997. Despite a higher level of industry-wide weather losses, NRC's underwriting results were stable, and the combined ratio for the period was 103.3%, versus 103.4% in the 1997 interim.

Per Share Data ($)

(Year Ended Dec. 31)	1997	1996	1995	1994	1993	1992	1991	1990	1989	1988
Tangible Bk. Val.	35.71	29.87	26.44	17.98	20.87	17.07	15.34	12.60	11.69	10.14
Oper. Earnings	3.42	3.03	2.53	1.95	1.63	0.24	1.92	1.63	1.45	1.11
Earnings	4.77	3.69	3.47	1.99	2.30	0.57	2.20	1.57	1.62	1.12
Dividends	0.28	0.23	0.19	0.16	0.16	0.16	0.15	0.13	0.10	Nil
Payout Ratio	6%	6%	5%	8%	7%	28%	7%	8%	6%	Nil
Prices - High	52⁷/₈	40⁵/₈	39	34	44³/₄	42	31¹/₂	25⁷/₈	27³/₈	14¹/₈
- Low	33¹/₄	28¹/₂	28¹/₄	24	28	21³/₄	19³/₈	17	13³/₄	8¹/₄
P/E Ratio - High	740	11	11	17	19	74	14	16	17	13
- Low	7	8	8	12	12	38	9	11	9	7

Income Statement Analysis (Million $)

	1997	1996	1995	1994	1993	1992	1991	1990	1989	1988
Premium Inc.	575	526	492	396	306	251	229	215	191	162
Net Invest. Inc.	123	104	89.3	80.5	76.6	65.6	58.7	51.9	45.5	35.6
Oth. Revs.	42.7	19.6	25.4	2.2	19.1	9.1	5.5	-1.1	2.5	0.4
Total Revs.	617	650	606	478	402	325	294	266	239	198
Pretax Inc.	123	89.0	78.8	42.3	49.5	3.6	41.7	29.4	29.5	19.9
Net Oper. Inc.	NA	57.8	45.8	34.9	29.9	4.4	30.4	25.9	23.0	NA
Net Inc.	95.7	70.5	62.8	35.6	42.4	10.4	34.8	25.0	25.6	17.7

Balance Sheet & Other Fin. Data (Million $)

	1997	1996	1995	1994	1993	1992	1991	1990	1989	1988
Cash & Equiv.	8.4	47.3	37.3	29.7	24.9	22.1	17.3	16.3	13.2	18.9
Premiums Due	228	200	155	121	75.9	71.2	45.7	38.0	35.5	45.0
Invest. Assets: Bonds	2,089	1,704	1,594	1,145	1,158	1,072	761	696	621	479
Invest. Assets: Stocks	143	180	127	124	102	40.3	34.3	22.2	8.5	0.9
Invest. Assets: Loans	Nil	Nil	Nil	Nil	Nil	141	Nil	Nil	Nil	Nil
Invest. Assets: Total	2,340	1,965	1,853	1,405	1,405	1,254	889	778	689	536
Deferred Policy Costs	92.7	85.2	70.5	60.0	44.5	30.0	20.6	17.5	14.3	13.9
Total Assets	2,985	2,745	2,462	1,917	1,779	1,490	1,017	914	781	637
Debt	313	300	300	200	200	200	52.0	52.0	52.0	52.0
Common Eqty.	657	553	512	319	376	309	241	203	186	163
Prop. & Cas. Loss Ratio	65.9	63.7	65.1	66.6	69.9	86.7	71.8	74.3	74.7	77.0
Prop. & Cas. Expense Ratio	37.2	37.5	38.0	39.1	41.0	40.2	36.4	33.9	33.8	29.8
Prop. & Cas. Combined Ratio	103.1	101.1	103.0	105.7	110.9	126.9	108.2	108.2	108.5	106.8
% Return On Revs.	15.5	10.8	10.4	7.4	10.5	3.2	11.9	9.4	10.7	9.0
% Ret. on Equity	15.8	13.2	15.1	10.2	12.4	3.8	15.7	12.8	14.7	13.4

Data as orig. reptd.; bef. results of disc. opers. and/or spec. items. Per share data adj. for stk. divs. as of ex-div. date. Bold denotes diluted EPS (FASB 128). E-Estimated. NA-Not Available. NM-Not Meaningful. NR-Not Ranked.

Office—One Greenwich Plaza, P.O. Box 2568, Greenwich, CT 06836-2568. **Tel**—(203) 622 5200. **Website**—http://www.nacre.com **Chrmn & CEO**—R. L. Bornhuetter. **Pres**—N. M. Brown Jr. **VP-CFO & Treas**—J. T. Fadden. **Secy**—Celia R. Brown. **Dirs**—R. A. Belfer, J. P. Birkelund, R. L. Bornhuetter, N. M. Brown Jr., D. Ciampa, C. W. Carson Jr., T. G. Cole, M. G. Fitt, D. J. McNamara, S. Robert, H. S. Winokur Jr. **Transfer Agent**—American Stock Transfer & Trust Co., NYC. **Incorporated**—in New York in 1929. **Empl**— 315. **S&P Analyst:** Catherine A. Seifert

NFO Worldwide, Inc. 4676C

NYSE Symbol **NFO**

In S&P SmallCap 600

03-OCT-98

Industry: Services (Advertising & Marketing)

Summary: This company is a leading provider of custom and syndicated market information to major U.S. and international businesses.

Quantitative Evaluations

Outlook (1 Lowest—5 Highest)
• **5**

Fair Value
• **17¼**

Risk
• **Average**

Earn./Div. Rank
• **NR**

Technical Eval.
• **NA**

Rel. Strength Rank (1 Lowest—99 Highest)
• **9**

Insider Activity
• **NA**

Recent Price • 8⅞
52 Wk Range • 22-8½

Yield • Nil
12-Mo. P/E • 13.2

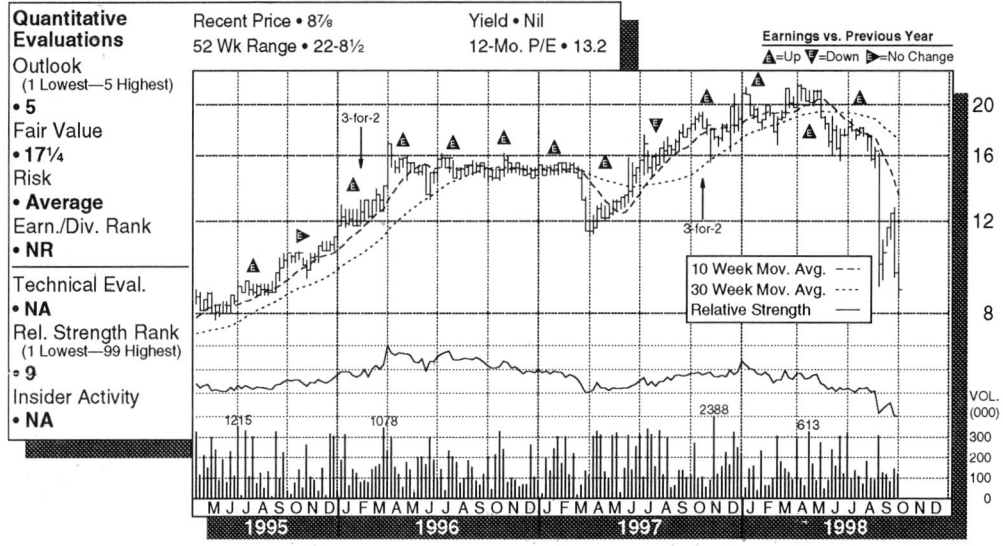

Earnings vs. Previous Year
▲=Up ▼=Down ▶=No Change

10 Week Mov. Avg. - - -
30 Week Mov. Avg. .....
Relative Strength —

Business Profile - 08-SEP-98

Acquisitions have aided the company's transition to a broader, more far-reaching marketing information business. NFO provides custom and syndicated market information in 24 countries to more than 2,000 clients in key market segments. Continuing to make acquisitions, it recently purchased CF Group, Inc., Canada's largest market research firm, with CN$31 million in annual revenues. It also acquired Ross-Cooper-Lund, a strategic market reseach firm, and MarketMind Technologies, developer of MarketMind continuous information tracking system.

Operational Review - 08-SEP-98

Revenues in the first half of 1998 advanced 29%, year to year, reflecting strong contributions from high tech/telecommunications, health care and international business units, as well as acquisitions. Gross margins narrowed slightly due to the higher cost base of acquisitions; operating income rose 27%. Following substantially higher net interest expense, pretax income was up only 16%. After taxes at 39.5%, versus 43.2%, net income climbed 35%, to $6,848,000 ($0.32 a share, based on 4.8% more shares), from $5,073,000 ($0.25).

Stock Performance - 02-OCT-98

In the past 30 trading days, NFO's shares have declined 46%, compared to a 7% fall in the S&P 500. Average trading volume for the past five days was 23,780 shares, compared with the 40-day moving average of 29,356 shares.

Key Stock Statistics

Dividend Rate/Share	Nil	Shareholders	200
Shs. outstg. (M)	21.3	Market cap. (B)	$0.189
Avg. daily vol. (M)	0.024	Inst. holdings	54%
Tang. Bk. Value/Share	0.96		
Beta	1.44		

Value of $10,000 invested 5 years ago: NA

Fiscal Year Ending Dec. 31

	1998	1997	1996	1995	1994	1993
Revenues (Million $)						
1Q	50.24	30.12	24.11	16.22	14.00	12.19
2Q	65.00	35.92	25.64	17.35	15.11	12.91
3Q	—	49.34	26.84	18.56	14.96	12.87
4Q	—	51.84	32.57	20.96	17.47	13.92
Yr.	—	190.2	109.2	73.10	61.54	51.89
Earnings Per Share ($)						
1Q	0.12	0.11	0.11	0.09	0.07	0.06
2Q	0.20	0.13	0.14	0.12	0.10	0.07
3Q	—	0.15	0.15	0.12	0.12	0.06
4Q	—	0.20	0.16	0.13	0.11	0.09
Yr.	—	0.60	0.55	0.46	0.39	0.29

Next earnings report expected: early November

Dividend Data

Amount ($)	Date Decl.	Ex-Div. Date	Stock of Record	Payment Date
3-for-2	Sep. 18	Oct. 16	Sep. 30	Oct. 15 '97

A Division of The **McGraw-Hill** Companies

STANDARD
&POOR'S
STOCK REPORTS

NFO Worldwide, Inc.

4676C
03-OCT-98

Business Summary - 08-SEP-98

NFO Worldwide, Inc. (formerly NFO Research, Inc.) makes it its business to know what consumers are thinking. It helps some of the largest American corporations and the international community launch, market and advertise their products for competitive advantage. It does this through specialized databases and a pre-recruited consumer panel, offering access to more than 575,000 households and 1.5 million consumers. NFO reaches over 100,000 additional households though a European joint venture. The company also conducts the consumer confidence survey for the Conference Board, recognized by the U.S. Commerce Department as a leading economic indicator.

The company focuses on fast-growing niche markets, mainly pharmaceuticals, financial services, telecommunications and travel and leisure. The centerpiece of its business is NFO Panel, which is comprised of a group of more than 525,000 households in the continental U.S., matching the general U.S. population in several important geographic and demographic characteristics. In its panel market research, NFOR surveys a population sample from its proprietary panel which meets the specific criteria targeted by a client. In 1996, through a joint venture, the company extended its panel to the global market, with the introduction of Select Panels of Europe, a market research panel comprised of 100,000 households in Germany, the U.K. and France. Also during the year, it introduced NFO Interactive, an on-line panel of more than 75,000 households and 175,000 consumers accessed through the Internet.

The company continued its aggressive growth-via-acquisition strategy in 1998 with the separate purchases of MarketMind Technologies and Ross-Cooper-Lund. Subsequently, NFO purchased Toronto-based CF Group, Inc., Canada's largest market research firm.

In 1997, the company acquired Prognostics, one of the leading providers of survey-based quantitative customer satisfaction research to information technology companies. Also in 1997, NFO expanded its presence in the financial services industry through the acquisition of Access Research by The Spectrem Group. In addition to its domestic acquisition activity, the company took significant steps to expand its presence overseas when it acquired The MBL Group Plc, a leading international market research firm. The MBL Group Plc has 19 companies and 27 offices in 17 countries throughout the world, including the U.K., the Middle East, Asia, Mainland China and Southeast Asia. With this acquisition, the company became the largest U.S.-based custom market research firm and the ninthlargest market research organization in the world. NFO concluded its 1997 merger activity in December by acquiring New Zealand-based CM Research Group, the leading provider of custom market researchin that country and one of the largest market research organizations in Australia.

Per Share Data ($)

(Year Ended Dec. 31)	1997	1996	1995	1994	1993	1992	1991	1990	1989	1988
Tangible Bk. Val.	1.08	1.13	1.24	0.26	0.26	NA	NA	NA	NA	NA
Cash Flow	0.93	0.83	0.69	0.61	0.55	0.57	NA	NA	NA	NA
Earnings	0.60	0.55	0.46	0.39	0.29	0.22	NA	NA	NA	NA
Dividends	Nil	Nil	Nil	Nil	Nil	Nil	Nil	Nil	Nil	Nil
Payout Ratio	Nil	Nil	Nil	Nil	Nil	Nil	Nil	Nil	Nil	Nil
Prices - High	21⅝	17	11¾	7⅝	6⅝	NA	NA	NA	NA	NA
- Low	11⅛	11⅝	6⅜	5⅝	4¼	NA	NA	NA	NA	NA
P/E Ratio - High	36	31	26	19	23	NA	NA	NA	NA	NA
- Low	19	21	14	14	15	NA	NA	NA	NA	NA

Income Statement Analysis (Million $)

	1997	1996	1995	1994	1993	1992	1991	1990	1989	1988
Revs.	190	109	73.1	61.5	51.9	47.1	NA	NA	NA	NA
Oper. Inc.	30.2	21.6	15.2	12.4	11.0	10.0	NA	NA	NA	NA
Depr.	6.9	4.6	3.4	3.1	3.3	3.5	NA	NA	NA	NA
Int. Exp.	0.9	0.5	0.3	0.3	0.9	0.3	NA	NA	NA	NA
Pretax Inc.	21.4	16.3	11.8	9.0	6.9	4.3	NA	NA	NA	NA
Eff. Tax Rate	42%	45%	43%	38%	47%	48%	NA	NA	NA	NA
Net Inc.	12.5	9.0	6.7	5.8	3.6	2.3	NA	NA	NA	NA

Balance Sheet & Other Fin. Data (Million $)

	1997	1996	1995	1994	1993	1992	1991	1990	1989	1988
Cash	8.1	4.1	5.7	6.3	5.3	NA	NA	NA	NA	NA
Curr. Assets	70.8	36.1	27.2	21.0	15.7	NA	NA	NA	NA	NA
Total Assets	170	102	68.2	60.2	48.8	NA	NA	NA	NA	NA
Curr. Liab.	42.4	25.3	19.3	19.1	12.1	NA	NA	NA	NA	NA
LT Debt	24.8	4.8	1.4	2.0	4.4	NA	NA	NA	NA	NA
Common Eqty.	96.7	66.7	44.0	36.4	27.9	NA	NA	NA	NA	NA
Total Cap.	124	71.6	45.4	38.4	32.3	NA	NA	NA	NA	NA
Cap. Exp.	NA	3.3	2.1	1.4	1.5	0.6	NA	NA	NA	NA
Cash Flow	19.4	13.6	10.1	8.6	6.9	5.7	NA	NA	NA	NA
Curr. Ratio	1.7	1.4	1.4	1.1	1.3	NA	NA	NA	NA	NA
% LT Debt of Cap.	25.6	6.7	3.1	5.3	13.5	NA	NA	NA	NA	NA
% Net Inc.of Revs.	6.6	8.3	9.2	9.4	7.0	4.8	NA	NA	NA	NA
% Ret. on Assets	9.3	10.7	10.5	10.7	7.3	NA	NA	NA	NA	NA
% Ret. on Equity	15.2	16.3	16.7	18.1	11.4	NA	NA	NA	NA	NA

Data as orig. reptd.; bef. results of disc. opers. and/or spec. items. Per share data adj. for stk. divs. as of ex-div. date. Bold denotes diluted EPS (FASB 128). E-Estimated. NA-Not Available. NM-Not Meaningful. NR-Not Ranked.

Office—2 Pickwick Plaza, Greenwich, CT 06830. **Tel**—(203) 629-8888. **Chrmn, Pres & CEO**—W. E. Lipner. **CFO, Secy & Investor Contact**—Patrick G. Healy (203-618-8502). **Dirs**—W. A. Forbes, S. J. Gilbert, E. A. Hajim, W. E. Lipner, J. Sculley. **Transfer Agent & Registrar**—Fleet Bank, Providence, RI. **Incorporated**—in Delaware in 1991. **Empl**— 6,500. **S&P Analyst:** P.D.W.

STANDARD &POOR'S
STOCK REPORTS

Nash-Finch Co.

4680K

NASDAQ Symbol **NAFC**

In S&P SmallCap 600

03-OCT-98

Industry: Distributors (Food & Health)

Summary: This leading food wholesaler supplies products to more than 1,400 supermarkets, other retail outlets and institutional accounts.

Quantitative Evaluations

Recent Price • 14⅛	Yield • 5.1%
52 Wk Range • 24⅜-13¼	12-Mo. P/E • NM

Outlook (1 Lowest—5 Highest)
• **2**

Fair Value
• **15⅛**

Risk
• **Low**

Earn./Div. Rank
• **B+**

Technical Eval.
• **Bullish** since 7/98

Rel. Strength Rank (1 Lowest—99 Highest)
• **66**

Insider Activity
• **Neutral**

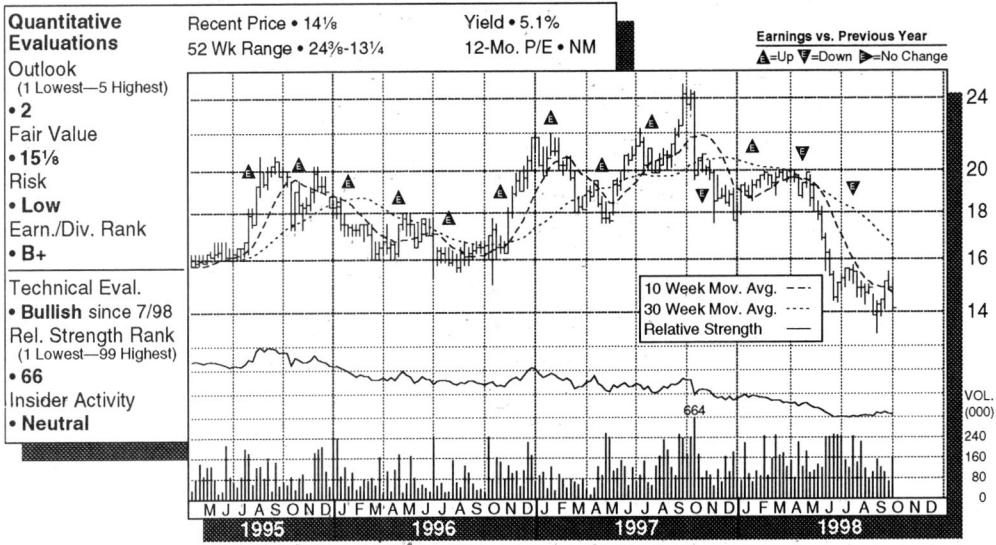

Earnings vs. Previous Year
▲=Up ▼=Down ▶=No Change

10 Week Mov. Avg. - - -
30 Week Mov. Avg. ·····
Relative Strength —

Business Profile - 14-SEP-98

The company is seeking to improve the results and operations of both its retail and its wholesale businesses. NAFC's goal for its retail operations is to have 85% of its stores in markets where it is first or second in market share by 2000. The company is focusing on building critical mass in target markets, while selling or closing stores that do not fit its strategy. NAFC is also reshaping its wholesale operations by focusing on selling, rather than buying. Rather than being in the warehousing business, the company is focusing on implementation of information systems to provide more efficient delivery of products to wholesale customers.

Operational Review - 14-SEP-98

Total sales and revenues in the 24 weeks ended June 20, 1998, slid 0.2%, year to year, reflecting lower retail sales stemming from the closure of 15 underperforming stores, partly offset by higher wholesale revenues due to the 1997 acquisition of United-A.G. Cooperative. Despite continued focus on cost savings, results were affected by an increased proportion of wholesale business versus retail business; operating income fell 14%. Following a $1.3 million special charge associated with a sale and leaseback transaction, pretax income fell 35%. After taxes at 41.5%, versus 41.9%, net income was down 34%, to $6,243,000 ($0.55 a share), from $9,520,000 ($0.84). Results in the 1998 period exclude a charge of $0.49 a share from the early retirement of debt.

Stock Performance - 02-OCT-98

In the past 30 trading days, NAFC's shares have declined 5%, compared to a 7% fall in the S&P 500. Average trading volume for the past five days was 32,180 shares, compared with the 40-day moving average of 23,067 shares.

Key Stock Statistics

Dividend Rate/Share	0.72	Shareholders	2,200
Shs. outstg. (M)	11.3	Market cap. (B)	$0.160
Avg. daily vol. (M)	0.023	Inst. holdings	51%
Tang. Bk. Value/Share	13.32		
Beta	0.42		

Value of $10,000 invested 5 years ago: $ 9,630

Fiscal Year Ending Dec. 31

	1998	1997	1996	1995	1994	1993
Revenues (Million $)						
1Q	937.1	947.8	684.5	623.6	618.2	601.0
2Q	982.8	975.5	735.2	676.5	670.4	631.3
3Q	—	1,354	1,004	918.8	887.0	856.5
4Q	—	1,114	951.9	669.9	656.5	634.6
Yr.	—	4,392	3,375	2,889	2,832	2,724
Earnings Per Share ($)						
1Q	**0.23**	**0.27**	0.26	0.25	0.24	0.23
2Q	**0.32**	**0.57**	0.56	0.54	0.48	0.46
3Q	—	**-0.15**	0.61	0.46	0.37	0.27
4Q	—	**0.50**	0.38	0.35	0.33	0.50
Yr.	—	**-0.11**	1.81	1.60	1.42	1.46

Next earnings report expected: mid November

Dividend Data (Dividends have been paid since 1926.)

Amount ($)	Date Decl.	Ex-Div. Date	Stock of Record	Payment Date
0.180	Nov. 19	Nov. 25	Nov. 28	Dec. 12 '97
0.180	Feb. 18	Feb. 25	Feb. 27	Mar. 13 '98
0.180	May. 13	May. 20	May. 22	Jun. 05 '98
0.180	Jul. 15	Aug. 19	Aug. 21	Sep. 04 '98

Nash-Finch Company

4680K

03-OCT-98

Business Summary - 14-SEP-98

Nash-Finch Company is one of the largest U.S. food wholesalers. The company' principal operations include wholesale distribution and operation of conventional and warehouse supermarkets. In addition, through its Nash-DeCamp subsidiary, NAFC packages, ships and markets fresh produce from California, and from Chile and Mexico, to buyers across the U.S., Canada, and overseas. Contributions in 1997 were:

	Revs.	Profits
Wholesale distribution	80%	124%
Retail distribution	19%	-23%
Produce marketing & other	1%	-1%

Wholesale operations serve primarily the Midwest and Southeast. NAFC's wholesale business serves the supermarket industry (70% of 1997 wholesale sales) and military commissaries (30%) by offering a wide array of national brand and private label products. Product offerings include dry groceries, fresh fruits and vegetables, frozen foods, fresh and processed meat products and dairy products, as well as a wide variety of non-food products including health and beauty care, tobacco, paper products, cleaning supplies and small household items. Private label products are sold primarily under the Our Family and Fame brand names.

The company's 21 distribution centers serve about 2,250 affiliated and independent supermarkets, U.S. military commissaries and other customers. Customers served by NAFC's wholesale operations range in size from small stores to large warehouse stores with over 100,000 sq. ft. of space.

At the end of 1997, the company owned and operated 97 retail outlets, consisting of 66 supermarkets, 27 warehouse stores, and four combination general merchandise/food stores. Conventional supermarkets are operated principally under the Sun Mart, Easter Foods and Food Folks names and typically range in size up to 46,000 sq. ft. Warehouse stores are operated under the Econofoods name and range in size up to 106,000 sq. ft. The four combination stores are operated under the Family Thrift Center name and average approximately 60,000 sq. ft.

Wholly owned Nash-DeCamp Co. grows, packs, ships and markets fresh fruits and vegetables from California, Mexico and Chile to customers across the U.S., Canada, and overseas. For regulatory reasons, business between Nash-DeCamp and the company is limited.

Per Share Data ($)

(Year Ended Dec. 31)	1997	1996	1995	1994	1993	1992	1991	1990	1989	1988
Tangible Bk. Val.	13.68	13.54	19.22	18.25	17.45	17.59	16.45	15.40	14.43	13.87
Cash Flow	4.13	4.96	4.29	4.35	4.12	4.31	4.13	4.20	3.32	3.50
Earnings	-0.11	1.81	1.60	1.42	1.46	1.85	1.75	1.64	1.21	1.67
Dividends	0.72	0.75	0.74	0.73	0.72	0.71	0.70	0.69	0.67	0.65
Payout Ratio	NM	41%	46%	51%	49%	38%	40%	42%	55%	39%
Prices - High	24⅞	22	20¾	18½	23¼	19⅞	20¼	25¼	26	27½
- Low	17½	15	15¼	15	17	16¼	16⅛	15¾	21	17½
P/E Ratio - High	NM	12	13	13	16	11	12	15	21	16
- Low	NM	8	10	11	12	9	9	10	17	10

Income Statement Analysis (Million $)

	1997	1996	1995	1994	1993	1992	1991	1990	1989	1988
Revs.	4,392	3,375	2,831	2,822	2,716	2,509	2,338	2,369	2,219	2,092
Oper. Inc.	112	83.3	68.8	59.3	57.9	62.7	59.9	59.6	51.4	51.1
Depr.	47.7	34.8	29.4	31.8	28.9	26.8	25.8	27.8	22.9	19.9
Int. Exp.	32.8	14.9	10.8	11.4	10.1	9.3	9.0	8.7	8.3	8.1
Pretax Inc.	-0.2	33.7	28.6	25.8	26.7	32.6	30.8	29.0	21.2	29.0
Eff. Tax Rate	NM	41%	39%	40%	41%	38%	38%	38%	38%	37%
Net Inc.	-1.0	20.0	17.4	15.5	15.9	20.1	19.1	17.8	13.2	18.2

Balance Sheet & Other Fin. Data (Million $)

	1997	1996	1995	1994	1993	1992	1991	1990	1989	1988
Cash	0.9	0.9	26.0	1.1	0.9	0.8	0.6	0.6	12.8	0.7
Curr. Assets	494	526	312	310	295	310	240	234	212	220
Total Assets	905	945	514	532	522	514	430	416	381	388
Curr. Liab.	294	297	208	220	215	214	155	158	128	153
LT Debt	364	404	81.1	96.0	97.9	94.1	82.5	74.3	78.0	66.2
Common Eqty.	226	233	215	206	199	191	179	167	157	151
Total Cap.	590	637	297	302	297	285	263	246	240	224
Cap. Exp.	67.7	51.3	33.2	35.0	52.0	46.3	36.8	43.8	34.6	52.0
Cash Flow	-46.7	54.8	46.8	47.3	44.8	46.8	44.9	45.6	36.1	38.1
Curr. Ratio	1.7	1.8	1.5	1.4	1.4	1.4	1.5	1.5	1.7	1.4
% LT Debt of Cap.	61.7	63.4	27.3	31.8	32.9	33.0	31.3	30.3	32.5	29.6
% Net Inc.of Revs.	NM	0.6	0.6	0.5	0.6	0.8	0.8	0.8	0.6	0.9
% Ret. on Assets	NM	2.7	3.3	2.9	3.1	4.3	4.5	4.5	3.4	4.9
% Ret. on Equity	NM	8.9	8.2	7.6	8.1	10.8	11.0	11.0	8.5	12.5

Data as orig. reptd.; bef. results of disc. opers. and/or spec. items. Per share data adj. for stk. divs. as of ex-div. date. Bold denotes diluted EPS (FASB 128). E-Estimated. NA-Not Available. NM-Not Meaningful. NR-Not Ranked.

Office—7600 France Ave. South, P.O. Box 355, Minneapolis, MN 55440-0355. **Tel**—(612) 832-0534. **Website**—http://www.nashfinch.com **CEO & Pres**—A. N. Flaten Jr. **EVP COO**—W. E. May Jr. **VP, Secy & Investor Contact**—Norman R. Soland. **VP & CFO**—J. R. Scherer. **Treas**—Suzanne S. Allen. **Dirs**—C. F. Bitter, R. A. Fisher, A. N. Flaten Jr., J. L. Ford, A. P. Graham, J. H. Grunewald, R. G. Lareau, D. E. Marsh, D. R. Miller, R. F. Nash, J. O. Rodysill. **Transfer Agent & Registrar**—Norwest Bank Minnesota, St. Paul. **Incorporated**—in Delaware in 1921. **Empl**— 12,200. **S&P Analyst:** R.J.I.

10-OCT-98

Industry:
Office Equipment & Supplies

Summary: This company provides a diverse mix of products including specialty coated paper products, imaging supplies and pressure-sensitive labels.

Quantitative Evaluations

Outlook
(1 Lowest—5 Highest)
- **NA**

Fair Value
- **NA**

Risk
- **Average**

Earn./Div. Rank
- **B-**

Technical Eval.
- **Bullish** since 9/98

Rel. Strength Rank
(1 Lowest—99 Highest)
- **67**

Insider Activity
- **Neutral**

Recent Price • 13⅜
52 Wk Range • 17½-11¼

Yield • Nil
12-Mo. P/E • NM

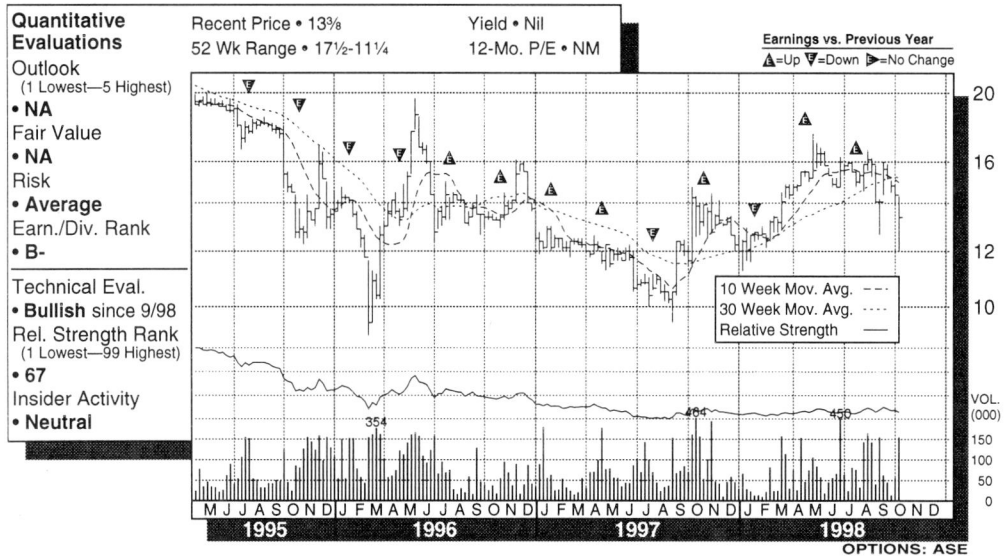

OPTIONS: ASE

Business Profile - 28-MAY-98

After completing a strategic assessment during 1997, the company decided in March 1998 to exit the photofinishing business and focus its resources on the label, imaging supplies and specialty coated products divisions. In early April 1998, the company completed the sale of its entire photofinishing business, with net after tax proceeds of $42 million, and its United Kingdom-based Microsharp imaging technology operation. Both sales resulted in a small gain to be recognized in the 1998 second quarter.

Operational Review - 28-MAY-98

Net sales for the three months ended April 3, 1998, rose fractionally, year to year, as sales growth in the label and specialty coated products divisions offset a sales decline in the imaging supplies division. Although gross margins were lower (21.9% versus 22.9%), research, selling, distribution and administrative expenses fell 9.2%, and after an income tax benefit in both periods, the loss from continuing operations narrowed, to $643,000 ($0.10 a share) from $841,000 ($0.13). Results exclude a loss from discontinued operations of $0.02 a share in 1998 and $0.09 a share in 1997.

Stock Performance - 09-OCT-98

In the past 30 trading days, NSH's shares have declined 5%, compared to a 4% fall in the S&P 500. Average trading volume for the past five days was 36,600 shares, compared with the 40-day moving average of 18,254 shares.

Key Stock Statistics

Dividend Rate/Share	Nil	Shareholders	1,400
Shs. outstg. (M)	6.7	Market cap. (B)	$0.090
Avg. daily vol. (M)	0.015	Inst. holdings	74%
Tang. Bk. Value/Share	14.03		
Beta	0.93		

Value of $10,000 invested 5 years ago: $ 5,271

Fiscal Year Ending Dec. 31

	1998	1997	1996	1995	1994	1993
Revenues (Million $)						
1Q	44.49	44.40	101.5	109.6	112.8	141.1
2Q	40.08	43.20	103.6	122.2	122.7	141.7
3Q	—	42.60	100.9	121.7	127.8	147.9
4Q	—	43.00	83.71	98.74	115.2	125.0
Yr.	—	173.2	389.7	452.2	478.6	555.7
Earnings Per Share ($)						
1Q	-0.10	-0.13	-0.35	0.01	-0.18	0.42
2Q	-0.35	-0.45	2.91	0.23	0.46	0.61
3Q	—	-0.17	0.08	-1.14	0.37	0.69
4Q	—	-0.19	-0.07	-1.53	0.05	-5.14
Yr.	—	-0.94	2.58	-2.43	0.70	-3.42

Next earnings report expected: NA

Dividend Data

Omitted in 1983, cash dividends were resumed in 1986 and paid regularly through October 1995. Cash dividends were suspended in November 1995.

A Division of The McGraw·Hill Companies

Business Summary - 28-MAY-98

After several years of weak results (including losses in 1993, 1995 and 1997), management of Nashua Corporation (NSH) undertook major steps to return the company to profitability. In March 1998, the company decided to exit the photofinishing business and focus on expanding niche markets where the company's set of imaging products can be differentiated, add value and generate consistent, sustainable, profitable growth. As a result, NSH sold its international photofinishing business and its United Kingdom-based Microsharp imaging technology operations in April 1998.

The company's continuing operations consist of three divisions: imaging supplies, specialty coated products, and label products. The company also owns a 37.1% interest in Cerion Technologies, Inc., which makes and markets precision-machined aluminum disk substrates that are used in the production of magnetic thin-film disks for hard disk drives of portable and desktop computers.

The imaging supplies division, which accounted for about 42% of sales from continuing operations, makes and sells a variety of consumable products used in the process of reproducing and transferring readable images. Imaging supplies include toners, developers, remanufactured laser printer cartridges and copy paper, and are marketed to national and government accounts

through a network of approximately 150 dealers located throughout the United States.

The specialty coated products division (17% of sales) makes and sells thermal and non-thermal, thermosensitive label, Davac dry-gummed label paper and carbonless papers. Thermal papers develop an image upon contact with either a heated stylus or a thermal print head and are used in point of sale printers, airline and package identification systems, gaming systems, medical and industrial recording charts and for use in thermal facsimile machines. Thermosensitive label papers are coated with an adhesive that is activated when heat is applied, and are used by printers who convert the papers into labels for use primarily in the pharmaceutical industry. Davac dry-gummed label paper is coated with a moisture-activated adhesive and is sold primarily to fine paper merchants and business forms manufacturers, where it is converted into various types of labels and stamps. Carbonless paper is a coated paper used in the production of multi-part business forms which produce multiple copies without carbon paper.

The label products division (41% of sales) sells pressure-sensitive labels through distributors and directly to end-users, and are used in grocery scale marking, inventory control and address labels. This division is a major supplier of labels to the supermarket industry and of labels used in the distribution and manufacture of a wide variety of other products.

Per Share Data ($)

(Year Ended Dec. 31)	1997	1996	1995	1994	1993	1992	1991	1990	1989	1988
Tangible Bk. Val.	14.15	12.34	6.53	12.25	12.25	14.74	15.60	15.83	23.84	22.01
Cash Flow	0.24	5.30	0.30	3.10	0.07	4.56	3.47	5.63	4.13	6.92
Earnings	-0.94	2.58	-2.43	0.70	-3.42	0.84	0.09	2.73	1.84	3.38
Dividends	Nil	Nil	0.54	0.72	0.72	0.72	0.72	0.69	0.57	0.43
Payout Ratio	Nil	Nil	NM	103%	NM	86%	NM	21%	30%	12%
Prices - High	14¾	19⅝	21	30⅞	31¾	31¼	37	44⅞	42⅞	42
- Low	9½	9⅛	12¼	19⅜	25¼	21	18	30½	28¾	26½
P/E Ratio - High	NM	8	NM	44	NM	37	NM	16	23	12
- Low	NM	4	NM	28	NM	25	NM	11	16	8

Income Statement Analysis (Million $)

	1997	1996	1995	1994	1993	1992	1991	1990	1989	1988
Revs.	173	390	452	479	556	552	526	589	549	989
Oper. Inc.	1.3	16.1	18.3	27.2	41.0	33.6	26.0	58.0	53.0	98.0
Depr.	7.6	17.5	17.4	15.3	22.1	23.6	21.4	22.1	21.8	34.1
Int. Exp.	0.1	2.7	5.5	2.5	2.1	2.7	1.7	1.7	3.5	12.9
Pretax Inc.	-10.0	28.6	-20.1	7.5	-31.4	10.5	3.5	33.9	28.5	52.9
Eff. Tax Rate	NM	43%	NM	41%	NM	49%	84%	39%	38%	39%
Net Inc.	-6.0	16.5	-15.5	4.4	-21.7	5.3	0.6	20.8	17.6	32.5

Balance Sheet & Other Fin. Data (Million $)

	1997	1996	1995	1994	1993	1992	1991	1990	1989	1988
Cash	3.7	20.0	8.4	10.2	5.9	12.2	30.0	7.5	10.8	22.0
Curr. Assets	45.8	72.2	99	108	110	111	113	104	178	297
Total Assets	147	177	231	228	219	237	243	239	319	450
Curr. Liab.	26.9	51.0	67.0	61.0	86.0	71.0	77.0	87.0	64.0	168
LT Debt	3.5	2.0	68.4	49.2	20.3	27.9	25.4	10.4	19.4	51.9
Common Eqty.	95.0	102	75.0	93.0	93.0	117	130	134	236	228
Total Cap.	99	104	143	142	113	145	155	145	255	282
Cap. Exp.	4.4	12.8	13.2	16.8	35.7	23.6	33.1	49.8	36.8	48.7
Cash Flow	1.5	34.0	1.9	19.7	0.5	28.9	22.0	42.9	39.4	66.6
Curr. Ratio	1.7	1.4	1.5	1.8	1.3	1.6	1.5	1.2	2.8	1.8
% LT Debt of Cap.	3.5	1.9	47.8	34.7	17.9	19.2	16.4	7.2	7.6	18.4
% Net Inc.of Revs.	NM	4.2	NM	0.9	NM	1.0	0.1	3.5	3.2	3.3
% Ret. on Assets	NM	8.1	NM	2.0	NM	2.2	0.2	9.1	4.6	7.6
% Ret. on Equity	NM	18.7	NM	4.8	NM	4.3	0.4	14.1	7.7	15.0

Data as orig. reptd.; bef. results of disc. opers. and/or spec. items. Per share data adj. for stk. divs. as of ex-div. date. Bold denotes diluted EPS (FASB 128). E-Estimated. NA-Not Available. NM-Not Meaningful. NR-Not Ranked.

Office—44 Franklin St., P.O. Box 2002, Nashua, NH 03061-2002. **Tel**—(603) 880-2323. **Website**—http://www.nashua.com **Chrmn, Pres & CEO**—G. G. Garbacz. **VP-Fin, Treas & CFO**—D. Junius. **VP, CFO & Treas**—D. M. Junius. **VP & Gen Counsel**—P. Anastos. **Dirs**—S. A. Buckler, G. G. Garbacz, C. S. Hoppin, J. M. Kucharski, D. C. Miller, Jr., P. J. Murphy, J. F. Orr III. **Transfer Agent & Registrar**—Bank Boston, N.A. **Incorporated**—in Delaware in 1957. **Empl**— 1,811. **S&P Analyst:** C.C.P.

03-OCT-98

Industry:
Services (Data Processing)

Summary: This information services company provides data collection services and systems to selected segments of the education, business, government and health care markets.

Quantitative Evaluations	
Recent Price • 28	**Yield • 0.7%**
52 Wk Range • 30¼-15½	**12-Mo. P/E • 30.8**

Outlook
(1 Lowest—5 Highest)
• **2⁻**

Fair Value
• **28½**

Risk
• **Average**

Earn./Div. Rank
• **B+**

Technical Eval.
• **NA**

Rel. Strength Rank
(1 Lowest—99 Highest)
• **96**

Insider Activity
• **Neutral**

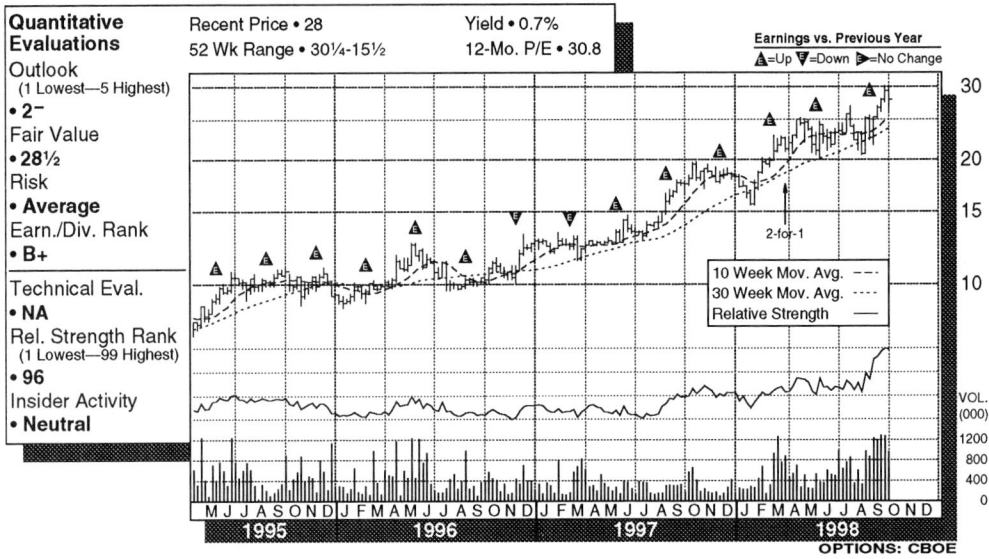

Earnings vs. Previous Year
▲=Up ▼=Down ▶=No Change

2-for-1

10 Week Mov. Avg. – – –
30 Week Mov. Avg. ·····
Relative Strength ——

VOL. (000)

1995 1996 1997 1998

OPTIONS: CBOE

Business Profile - 25-AUG-98

NLCS continues to build upon its systems and services in the educational, professional assessment and employee testing markets through selective acquisitions. In June 1998, the company acquired a 19% stake in Learning Ventures International, Inc., a leading provider of distance learning programs. The investment, in the form of convertible preferred stock, is valued at $4.6 million. Shares of NLCS have performed well since early 1997, driven by strong growth of revenues and earnings.

Operational Review - 25-AUG-98

Revenues in the six months ended July 31, 1998, rose 29%, year to year, driven by an increase in information systems revenues and, to a lesser extent, revenues derived from maintenance and support services. Margins widened, reflecting cost controls in all operating units and a less rapid rise in sales and marketing expenditures; operating income grew 34%. After taxes at 40.3%, versus 39.8%, net income also advanced 34%, to $14,837,000 ($0.46 a share, based on 3.0% more shares), from $11,059,000 ($0.35).

Stock Performance - 02-OCT-98

In the past 30 trading days, NLCS's shares have increased 11%, compared to a 7% fall in the S&P 500. Average trading volume for the past five days was 192,380 shares, compared with the 40-day moving average of 256,049 shares.

Key Stock Statistics

Dividend Rate/Share	0.20	Shareholders	1,900
Shs. outstg. (M)	31.2	Market cap. (B)	$0.874
Avg. daily vol. (M)	0.338	Inst. holdings	60%
Tang. Bk. Value/Share	5.30		
Beta	0.33		

Value of $10,000 invested 5 years ago: $ 37,140

Fiscal Year Ending Jan. 31

	1999	1998	1997	1996	1995	1994
Revenues (Million $)						
1Q	97.90	78.97	70.51	74.30	68.80	68.51
2Q	128.1	96.03	80.96	88.44	80.13	75.67
3Q	—	115.4	88.78	97.32	94.61	77.65
4Q	—	115.6	90.91	98.92	93.45	83.63
Yr.	—	406.0	331.2	359.0	336.9	305.4

Earnings Per Share ($)						
1Q	0.16	0.13	0.10	0.08	0.07	0.06
2Q	0.30	0.22	0.19	0.18	0.15	0.14
3Q	—	0.19	0.16	0.20	0.15	0.05
4Q	—	0.26	-0.01	0.26	0.07	-0.33
Yr.	—	0.80	0.44	0.71	0.44	-0.08

Next earnings report expected: mid November

Dividend Data (Dividends have been paid since 1976.)

Amount ($)	Date Decl.	Ex-Div. Date	Stock of Record	Payment Date
0.050	Mar. 03	Mar. 12	Mar. 16	Mar. 26 '98
2-for-1	Mar. 03	Mar. 27	Mar. 16	Mar. 26 '98
0.050	May. 22	Jun. 04	Jun. 08	Jun. 18 '98
0.050	Aug. 26	Sep. 03	Sep. 08	Sep. 17 '98

A Division of The McGraw-Hill Companies

Business Summary - 25-AUG-98

NLCS is a global information services company that provides quality services, software and systems for the collection, management and interpretation of data. The company's services include data capture and processing, analysis, data management, reporting, network services and hardware maintenance. NLCS's application software products are focused on targeted markets, specifically elementary education. The company's products and services are offered through two operating segments: education and data management.

NLCS develops and markets data collection services and systems that provide optical scanning, image-based or electronic data collection and computer processing services for the high accuracy, large volume, complex processing needs of major test publishers, state education agencies, universities, colleges and local school districts. In addition, the company offers application software for the administration and management of curriculum, student instruction and financial data at the classroom, school, school district and state levels. Recently, NLCS has begun providing network services and Internet utilization services to its customers. By utilizing

NLCS's optical scanning and image-based systems, individual school districts can perform in-house student assessment testing applications, including teacher created tests and administrative functions, such as attendance, scheduling and grade reporting.

The company's data management services consist of complex data collection, processing and reporting services and products. These applications include sales and marketing, billing, quality management, product warranty and customer satisfaction surveys. NLCS also offers human resource services, such as applicant tracking, employee attitude surveys, benefits enrollment and employee evaluation. The company provides scanners and forms for customers to do their own paper-based data collection. For more sophisticated information management needs, NLCS offers comprehensive data collection technologies, software development, telecommunications support and information dissemination systems.

In April 1997, the company acquired Virtual University Enterprises, an electronic course registration firm, complementing NLCS's participation in testing services for the K-12 market while providing an avenue for entry into the electronic testing market for professionals.

Per Share Data ($)

(Year Ended Jan. 31)	1998	1997	1996	1995	1994	1993	1992	1991	1990	1989
Tangible Bk. Val.	4.81	5.33	4.09	3.60	3.17	3.62	3.28	2.90	2.57	3.00
Cash Flow	1.74	1.25	1.59	0.99	0.45	1.08	1.03	1.01	0.76	0.74
Earnings	0.80	0.44	0.71	0.44	-0.08	0.52	0.48	0.41	0.23	0.46
Dividends	0.18	0.18	0.18	0.18	0.18	0.17	0.14	0.14	0.14	0.13
Payout Ratio	23%	41%	25%	41%	NM	32%	30%	34%	60%	27%
Cal. Yrs.	1997	1996	1995	1994	1993	1992	1991	1990	1989	1988
Prices - High	19¾	13¼	11	8⅜	9	9⅝	8⅞	4⅞	7⅝	7⅝
- Low	11⅜	8¾	7⅜	5⅛	5⅜	6¼	4⅝	3	3⅞	6⅛
P/E Ratio - High	25	30	15	19	17	19	18	12	33	17
- Low	14	20	10	12	10	12	10	7	17	13

Income Statement Analysis (Million $)

	1998	1997	1996	1995	1994	1993	1992	1991	1990	1989
Revs.	406	331	359	337	305	300	303	315	284	242
Oper. Inc.	73.2	59.8	67.1	51.2	39.0	45.7	46.6	47.2	35.1	40.3
Depr.	30.1	25.3	27.4	16.7	16.3	18.4	17.9	19.1	11.4	16.6
Int. Exp.	1.4	1.7	3.3	3.6	2.5	2.1	4.0	7.0	6.1	3.5
Pretax Inc.	42.0	26.5	37.0	19.1	-2.9	26.6	24.2	21.0	11.5	24.0
Eff. Tax Rate	40%	49%	40%	30%	NM	38%	36%	38%	37%	36%
Net Inc.	25.2	13.7	22.2	13.4	-2.5	16.5	15.5	13.0	7.3	15.4

Balance Sheet & Other Fin. Data (Million $)

	1998	1997	1996	1995	1994	1993	1992	1991	1990	1989
Cash	23.3	58.1	5.2	1.2	1.7	10.8	2.4	3.3	2.8	2.1
Curr. Assets	147	161	115	111	104	99	96.0	104	114	109
Total Assets	315	274	235	241	220	215	218	225	250	205
Curr. Liab.	103	82.2	74.0	75.1	67.5	60.0	56.4	52.7	63.1	45.3
LT Debt	12.4	16.3	24.5	45.3	44.7	23.9	37.2	56.0	82.3	47.3
Common Eqty.	194	170	128	113	100	121	112	101	90.0	104
Total Cap.	213	192	161	166	153	155	161	172	187	160
Cap. Exp.	25.2	14.9	14.0	29.2	23.9	14.4	11.5	11.0	37.8	16.5
Cash Flow	55.3	38.9	49.7	30.1	13.8	34.9	33.3	32.1	24.3	25.1
Curr. Ratio	1.4	2.0	1.6	1.5	1.5	1.6	1.7	2.0	1.8	2.4
% LT Debt of Cap.	5.8	8.5	15.2	27.4	29.3	15.4	23.1	32.5	44.0	29.5
% Net Inc.of Revs.	6.2	4.1	6.2	4.0	NM	5.5	5.1	4.1	2.6	6.4
% Ret. on Assets	8.5	5.5	9.3	5.8	NM	7.7	7.0	5.4	3.3	7.7
% Ret. on Equity	13.8	9.2	18.4	12.4	NM	14.2	14.5	13.6	7.7	15.1

Data as orig. reptd.; bef. results of disc. opers. and/or spec. items. Per share data adj. for stk. divs. as of ex-div. date. Bold denotes diluted EPS (FASB 128). E-Estimated. NA-Not Available. NM-Not Meaningful. NR-Not Ranked.

Office—11000 Prairie Lakes Dr., Eden Prairie, MN 55344. **Tel**—(612) 829-3000. **Website**—http://www.ncs.com **Chrmn, Pres & CEO**—R. A. Gullotti. **VP & CFO**—J. W. Taylor. **Secy & Treas**—J. W. Fenton Jr. **Investor Contact**—Yolanda Scharton (612-829-3203). **Dirs**—D. C. Cox, R. A. Gullotti, M. Joseph, J. B. Keffeler, C. W. Oswald, S. G. Shank, J. E. Steuri, J. W. Vessey. **Transfer Agent & Registrar**—Norwest Bank Minnesota, Minneapolis. **Incorporated**—in Minnesota in 1962. **Empl**— 3,500. **S&P Analyst:** S.J.T.

National Data Corp.

1595

NYSE Symbol **NDC**

In S&P SmallCap 600

03-OCT-98

Industry:
Services (Data
Processing)

Summary: This company is a leading provider of high-volume transaction processing services and application systems to the health care and payment systems markets.

Quantitative Evaluations

Recent Price • 28⅝   Yield • 1.0%
52 Wk Range • 46-27⅞   12-Mo. P/E • NM

Outlook
(1 Lowest—5 Highest)
• **4⁻**

Fair Value
• 38½

Risk
• **Average**

Earn./Div. Rank
• **B-**

Technical Eval.
• **Bullish** since 9/98

Rel. Strength Rank
(1 Lowest—99 Highest)
• **21**

Insider Activity
• **Neutral**

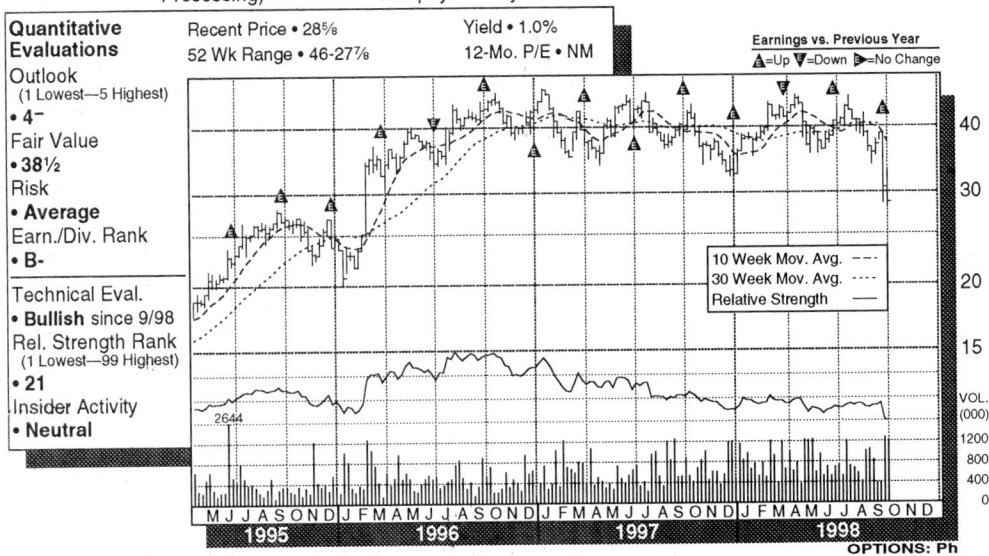

Earnings vs. Previous Year
▲=Up ▼=Down ►=No Change

10 Week Mov. Avg. ---
30 Week Mov. Avg. ······
Relative Strength ——

2644

VOL.
(000)
1200
800
400
0

M J J A S O N D | J F M A M J J A S O N D | J F M A M J J A S O N D | J F M A M J J A S O N D
1995   1996   1997   1998

OPTIONS: Ph

Business Profile - 24-JUL-98

The company now processes payments over the Internet, and has begun processing bankcard transactions in conjunction with CyberCash. NDC expanded its position in the health care services market with the October 1996 acquisition of Equifax's Health EDI Services and the January 1997 purchase of HCS, a provider of data processing services for the health care industry. In addition, in December 1997, NDC acquired two related health care database information management businesses, as well as Physician and Hospital Support Services, Inc., a provider of business management solutions to physicians and hospitals. The combined purchase price was $35.74 million in cash and 6,994,713 common shares.

Operational Review - 24-JUL-98

Based on a preliminary report, revenues in FY 98 (May) increased 24%, as restated for acquisitions, primarily driven by growth in health care (34%, net of a divestiture), and integrated payment systems (21%). Gross margins were virtually flat, but after $120 million in nonrecurring charges, versus $9.5 million, an operating loss of $25.9 million contrasted with profit of $60.8 million. Following higher interest expense, minority interests, and taxes of $21.6 million, versus $23.8 million, a net loss of $61,326,000 ($1.90 a share) contrasted with net income of $29,398,000 ($0.91). Excluding the nonrecurring charges, earnings would have been $1.48 per share, versus $1.23.

Stock Performance - 02-OCT-98

In the past 30 trading days, NDC's shares have declined 26%, compared to a 7% fall in the S&P 500. Average trading volume for the past five days was 280,080 shares, compared with the 40-day moving average of 191,315 shares.

Key Stock Statistics

Dividend Rate/Share	0.30	Shareholders	3,500
Shs. outstg. (M)	33.6	Market cap. (B)	$0.965
Avg. daily vol. (M)	0.212	Inst. holdings	80%
Tang. Bk. Value/Share	NM		
Beta	0.66		

Value of $10,000 invested 5 years ago: $ 34,447

Fiscal Year Ending May 31

	1999	1998	1997	1996	1995	1994
Revenues (Million $)						
1Q	191.7	120.1	101.2	78.29	55.97	50.20
2Q	—	120.0	102.6	78.06	59.81	50.30
3Q	—	171.6	112.0	77.62	62.16	50.40
4Q	—	185.3	118.2	91.83	64.09	53.00
Yr.	—	649.0	433.9	325.8	242.0	204.0
Earnings Per Share ($)						
1Q	0.47	0.38	0.30	0.18	0.15	0.11
2Q	—	0.41	0.34	0.25	0.17	0.13
3Q	—	-2.77	0.36	0.22	0.19	0.13
4Q	—	0.47	0.38	-0.96	0.24	0.19
Yr.	—	-1.90	1.38	-0.31	0.76	0.57

Next earnings report expected: mid December

Dividend Data (Dividends have been paid since 1977.)

Amount ($)	Date Decl.	Ex-Div. Date	Stock of Record	Payment Date
0.075	Oct. 23	Nov. 12	Nov. 14	Nov. 28 '97
0.075	Feb. 06	Feb. 13	Feb. 18	Feb. 27 '98
0.075	May. 04	May. 13	May. 15	May. 29 '98
0.075	Aug. 07	Aug. 19	Aug. 21	Aug. 31 '98

A Division of The **McGraw·Hill** Companies

Business Summary - 24-JUL-98

Each day, National Data Corp. (NDC) provides information and systems that help thousands of health care providers meet the needs of their patients. In addition, millions of individuals throughout North America pay for restaurant bills, shop for groceries and buy retail merchandise through the company's electronic payment systems. NDC was processing health care and integrated payment transactions at an annualized rate of 3 billion at the end of FY 97 (May). The company is a worldwide provider of value-added information systems and services for health care, government and retail markets. Revenue contributions in recent fiscal years were:

	FY 98	FY 97	FY 96	FY 95
Health care	55%	41%	44%	43%
Integrated payment systems	24%	30%	33%	32%
Global payment systems	25%	35%	23%	25%
Intercompany	-4%	-6%	0%	0%

The health care application systems and services segment, the fastest growing operation, offers NDC's Data-Stat pharmacy practice management systems, which provide solutions for independent and chain pharmacies, HMOs, clinics and hospitals. DataStat systems enable users to manage and perform patient registration, private and third-party billing, inventory, automatic price updating, management reporting and drug record-keeping. The company's EasyClaim services, offered to pharmacies, dentists, hospitals, preferred provider organizations and HMOs, include eligibility verification, patient-specific benefit coverage, claims data capture and adjudication, and drug utilization review. In September 1997, the company established a long-term strategic alliance with Medical Manager Corp. to provide expanded service to Medical Manager's customer base of 23,600 physician practice systems, representing 110,000 physicians nationwide.

The integrated payment systems segment provides a wide range of payment alternatives to the retail, health care and government markets. Services provided include credit card, debit card and check processing and verification services, data capture and product and customer support functions, primarily for VISA and Master-Card bank cards. NDC markets its retail application products and services principally through bank relationships and its own personnel.

The global payment systems unit, in addition to the services offered by the integrated segment, offers cash management solutions for multinational corporations and purchase card services aimed at high-volume corporate and government purchases.

Per Share Data ($)

(Year Ended May 31)	1998	1997	1996	1995	1994	1993	1992	1991	1990	1989
Tangible Bk. Val.	NM	NM	0.39	2.30	3.60	3.00	2.41	2.16	2.63	4.61
Cash Flow	-0.40	1.90	0.74	1.80	1.51	1.55	1.63	0.74	2.03	2.47
Earnings	-1.90	1.38	-0.31	0.76	0.57	0.47	0.41	-0.80	0.11	1.17
Dividends	0.30	0.30	0.30	0.30	0.29	0.29	0.29	0.29	0.29	0.29
Payout Ratio	NM	22%	NM	39%	51%	63%	71%	NM	263%	25%
Cal. Yrs.	1997	1996	1995	1994	1993	1992	1991	1990	1989	1988
Prices - High	47½	46⅝	28	17⅝	13	11⅞	10	23	23⅜	21½
- Low	32⅛	20	15⅜	10⅜	8⅞	5⅜	6⅛	5⅜	15⅜	12⅝
P/E Ratio - High	NM	34	NM	23	23	25	24	NM	NM	18
- Low	NM	14	NM	14	15	11	15	NM	NM	11

Income Statement Analysis (Million $)

	1998	1997	1996	1995	1994	1993	1992	1991	1990	1989
Revs.	649	434	326	242	204	205	219	230	276	227
Oper. Inc.	143	81.2	60.8	45.9	36.6	34.7	36.2	38.7	64.7	57.4
Depr.	48.4	14.5	28.6	21.0	18.2	19.7	21.6	27.2	34.0	22.8
Int. Exp.	12.9	6.8	3.8	2.5	1.5	2.2	4.2	5.6	7.4	5.4
Pretax Inc.	-37.1	60.6	-11.7	24.0	17.4	14.6	12.8	-23.9	6.4	31.5
Eff. Tax Rate	NM	36%	NM	36%	36%	42%	42%	NM	69%	36%
Net Inc.	-61.3	38.8	-8.5	15.4	11.2	8.5	7.4	-14.1	2.0	20.2

Balance Sheet & Other Fin. Data (Million $)

	1998	1997	1996	1995	1994	1993	1992	1991	1990	1989
Cash	3.2	19.2	9.8	30.8	38.0	17.8	2.9	5.4	4.0	4.1
Curr. Assets	172	109	81.4	98.0	100	86.0	74.0	83.0	108	87.0
Total Assets	731	522	368	217	183	175	195	212	277	236
Curr. Liab.	186	67.3	102	67.6	51.0	45.0	58.0	83.0	112	75.0
LT Debt	1,679	152	7.6	19.7	16.3	14.1	20.8	13.3	12.8	12.8
Common Eqty.	348	277	233	123	109	101	96.0	93.0	111	110
Total Cap.	535	450	241	146	127	126	128	118	145	151
Cap. Exp.	228	16.8	16.4	10.4	15.4	8.1	7.3	13.0	25.3	25.7
Cash Flow	-13.0	53.3	20.2	36.4	29.4	28.2	29.0	13.1	36.0	43.1
Curr. Ratio	0.9	1.6	0.8	1.5	2.0	1.9	1.3	1.0	1.0	1.2
% LT Debt of Cap.	31.4	33.8	3.1	13.5	12.8	11.2	16.3	11.3	8.8	8.5
% Net Inc.of Revs.	NM	8.9	NM	6.4	5.5	4.2	3.4	NM	0.7	8.9
% Ret. on Assets	NM	8.7	NM	7.7	6.1	4.5	3.6	NM	0.8	10.1
% Ret. on Equity	NM	15.2	NM	13.3	10.4	8.5	7.8	NM	1.8	19.9

Data as orig. reptd.; bef. results of disc. opers. and/or spec. items. Per share data adj. for stk. divs. as of ex-div. date. Bold denotes diluted EPS (FASB 128). E-Estimated. NA-Not Available. NM-Not Meaningful. NR-Not Ranked.

Office—National Data Plaza, Corporate Square, Atlanta, GA 30329-2010. **Tel**—(404) 728-2000. **Chrmn & CEO**—R. A. Yellowlees.**CFO**—R.L. Walker.**SVP & Secy**—E. M. Ingram. **Dirs**—E. L. Barlow, J. V. Biggins, J. B. Edwards, D. W. Sands, R. A. Yellowlees. **Transfer Agent**—Wachovia Bank of North Carolina, Winston-Salem. **Incorporated**—in Delaware in 1967. **Empl**— 2,900. **S&P Analyst:** Mark Cavallone

National Instruments 4712N
NASDAQ Symbol **NATI**
In S&P SmallCap 600

10-OCT-98

Industry:
Computers (Hardware)

Summary: NATI manufactures software and hardware products that scientists and engineers use to build measurement and automation systems in various applications and industries.

Quantitative Evaluations

Outlook
(1 Lowest—5 Highest)
• **4**

Fair Value
• **29**

Risk
• **Average**

Earn./Div. Rank
• **NR**

Technical Eval.
• **Neutral** since 8/98

Rel. Strength Rank
(1 Lowest—99 Highest)
• **41**

Insider Activity
• **Unfavorable**

Recent Price • 20¼
52 Wk Range • 36½-17½

Yield • Nil
12-Mo. P/E • 19.3

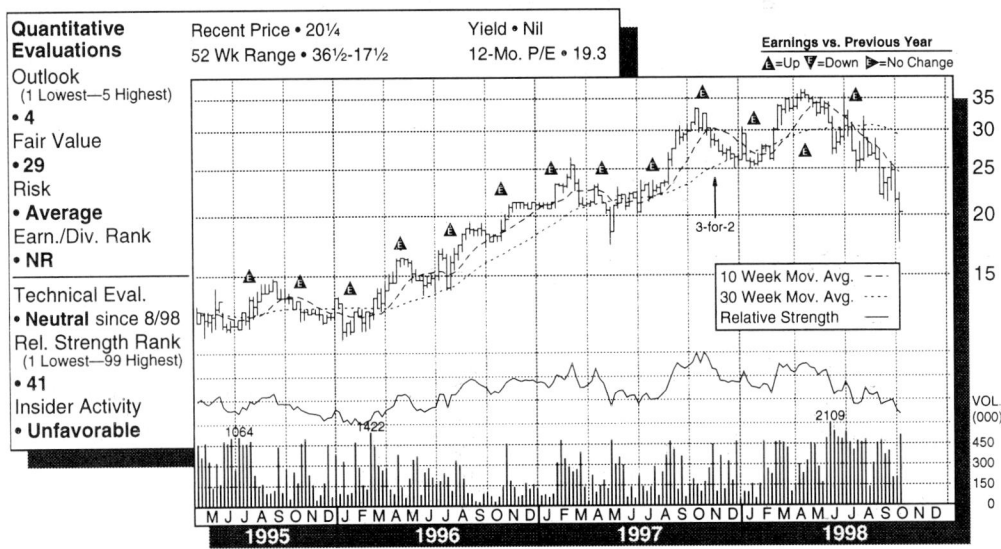

Earnings vs. Previous Year
▲=Up ▼=Down ►=No Change

10 Week Mov. Avg. – – –
30 Week Mov. Avg. ·····
Relative Strength —

3-for-2

Business Profile - 13-JUL-98

Sales of the company's LabVIEW 5.0 application software reached record levels in March 1998, surpassing the previous monthly record by over 20%. NATI's earnings growth rate in 1998's first quarter was impacted by a slight reduction in gross margins, due to the release of LabVIEW 5.0 late in the quarter and the delayed release of LabWindows/CVI 5.0 application software into the second quarter. The sales growth rate in the Asia Pacific market was limited to 3% in 1998's first quarter, due to the economic difficulties occurring in that region.

Operational Review - 13-JUL-98

Net sales for the three months ended March 31, 1998, advanced 20%, year to year. The gain mainly reflected the introduction of new and upgraded products and increased sales and marketing efforts. Despite sharply lower foreign exchange losses, profitability was restricted by the timing of the LabVIEW 5.0 release which started shipping toward the end of 1998's first quarter, and by higher sales and marketing expenses related to the LabVIEW. After taxes at 33.0% in both periods, net income rose 17%, to $8,831,000 ($0.26 a share, diluted) from $7,568,000 ($0.23, adjusted).

Stock Performance - 09-OCT-98

In the past 30 trading days, NATI's shares have declined 22%, compared to a 4% fall in the S&P 500. Average trading volume for the past five days was 226,180 shares, compared with the 40-day moving average of 96,226 shares.

Key Stock Statistics

Dividend Rate/Share	Nil	Shareholders	600
Shs. outstg. (M)	32.8	Market cap. (B)	$0.665
Avg. daily vol. (M)	0.096	Inst. holdings	25%
Tang. Bk. Value/Share	5.53		
Beta	NA		

Value of $10,000 invested 5 years ago: NA

Fiscal Year Ending Dec. 31

	1998	1997	1996	1995	1994	1993
Revenues (Million $)						
1Q	65.35	54.57	46.41	39.84	29.78	25.10
2Q	67.77	60.09	50.24	40.48	30.17	25.60
3Q	—	60.60	49.68	40.12	30.86	25.58
4Q	—	65.62	54.39	44.38	36.16	29.25
Yr.	—	240.9	200.7	164.8	127.0	105.5
Earnings Per Share ($)						
1Q	0.26	0.23	0.17	0.16	0.13	
2Q	0.27	0.26	0.17	0.12	0.11	—
3Q	—	0.23	0.19	0.12	0.09	—
4Q	—	0.29	0.25	0.17	0.15	—
Yr.	—	1.00	0.77	0.55	0.47	0.37

Next earnings report expected: late October

Dividend Data

Amount ($)	Date Decl.	Ex-Div. Date	Stock of Record	Payment Date
3-for-2	Oct. 21	Nov. 13	Oct. 28	Nov. 12 '97

A Division of The McGraw-Hill Companies

Business Summary - 13-JUL-98

Using the software and hardware products manufactured by National Instruments (NATI), engineers and scientists can customize PCs to measure and automate the collection of data from the world around us, perform analysis on that data, and present it in an easy-to-understand manner.

Engineers and scientists have long used instruments to observe, better understand and manage the real-world phenomena, events and processes related to their industries or areas of expertise. NATI pioneered a new instrumentation approach called virtual instrumentation in 1986 when it introduced its LabVIEW application software, which is a graphical programming environment.

While a traditional instrument bundles the data acquisition, analysis and presentation functions in a single, stand-alone unit, a "virtual instrument" consists of an industry standard computer or workstation equipped with the company's user-friendly application software, cost-effective hardware and driver software that together perform the functions of traditional instruments.

By unbundling the key instrumentation functions, virtual instruments represent a fundamental shift from traditional hardware-centered instrumentation systems to software-centered systems that exploit the computational, display, productivity and connectivity capabilities of popular desktop computers and workstations.

NATI's virtual instrumentation application software products give users the power and flexibility to define, implement, modify and control each of the three core instrumentation functions. Users can mix and match their choice of the company's DAQ and instrument control hardware/driver software with GPIB, VXI, PXI, image acquisition, motion control or serial instruments to create virtual instrumentation systems that meet their specific instrumentation needs. Because much of the instrumentation functionality resides in the software, in a significant sense, the software is the instrument.

The objective of the company is to be a leading supplier of virtual instrumentation products and solutions to engineers and scientists in both the test and measurement (T&M) and industrial automation (IA). markets. In research and development settings, scientists and engineers use T&M instruments to collect and analyze experimental data, and IA instruments and instrumentation systems to simulate manufacturing processes or techniques. In manufacturing systems, engineers use T&M instruments to test and verify the proper operation of the products being manufactured, while IA instruments and instrumentation systems monitor and control the manufacturing machines and processes.

The company directly markets and sells its products in the United States, Canada and many European and Asia Pacific countries. International sales accounted for over 40% revenues in recent years. NATI expects that a significant portion of its total revenues will continue to be derived from international sales.

Per Share Data ($)

(Year Ended Dec. 31)	1997	1996	1995	1994	1993	1992	1991	1990	1989	1988
Tangible Bk. Val.	4.95	3.91	3.07	2.26	NA	NA	NA	NA	NA	NA
Cash Flow	1.26	1.05	0.78	0.65	NA	NA	NA	NA	NA	NA
Earnings	1.00	0.77	0.55	0.47	NA	NA	NA	NA	NA	NA
Dividends	Nil	Nil	Nil	Nil	Nil	Nil	Nil	Nil	Nil	Nil
Payout Ratio	Nil	Nil	Nil	Nil	Nil	Nil	Nil	Nil	Nil	Nil
Prices - High	33½	21⅜	15⅛	NA	NA	NA	NA	NA	NA	NA
- Low	17⅜	11	9⅝	NA	NA	NA	NA	NA	NA	NA
P/E Ratio - High	33	27	27	NA	NA	NA	NA	NA	NA	NA
- Low	17	14	17	NA	NA	NA	NA	NA	NA	NA

Income Statement Analysis (Million $)

	1997	1996	1995	1994	1993	1992	1991	1990	1989	1988
Revs.	241	201	165	127	NA	NA	NA	NA	NA	NA
Oper. Inc.	58.6	46.5	33.5	24.8	NA	NA	NA	NA	NA	NA
Depr.	8.7	9.2	7.0	5.0	NA	NA	NA	NA	NA	NA
Int. Exp.	0.5	0.8	0.9	0.3	NA	NA	NA	NA	NA	NA
Pretax Inc.	50.2	38.0	27.4	21.1	NA	NA	NA	NA	NA	NA
Eff. Tax Rate	33%	33%	36%	39%	NA	NA	NA	NA	NA	NA
Net Inc.	33.6	25.5	17.4	13.0	NA	NA	NA	NA	NA	NA

Balance Sheet & Other Fin. Data (Million $)

	1997	1996	1995	1994	1993	1992	1991	1990	1989	1988
Cash	31.9	30.2	12.0	7.5	NA	NA	NA	NA	NA	NA
Curr. Assets	149	132	101	45.2	NA	NA	NA	NA	NA	NA
Total Assets	204	169	137	70.8	NA	NA	NA	NA	NA	NA
Curr. Liab.	37.1	32.3	26.1	18.4	NA	NA	NA	NA	NA	NA
LT Debt	5.2	9.2	11.6	9.1	NA	NA	NA	NA	NA	NA
Common Eqty.	162	127	99	40.5	NA	NA	NA	NA	NA	NA
Total Cap.	167	137	111	49.5	NA	NA	NA	NA	NA	NA
Cap. Exp.	22.0	6.8	16.2	9.9	NA	NA	NA	NA	NA	NA
Cash Flow	42.3	34.7	24.4	18.0	NA	NA	NA	NA	NA	NA
Curr. Ratio	4.0	4.1	3.9	2.5	NA	NA	NA	NA	NA	NA
% LT Debt of Cap.	3.1	6.7	10.5	18.3	NA	NA	NA	NA	NA	NA
% Net Inc.of Revs.	14.0	12.7	10.6	10.2	NA	NA	NA	NA	NA	NA
% Ret. on Assets	18.0	16.6	16.7	NA	NA	NA	NA	NA	NA	NA
% Ret. on Equity	23.3	22.6	25.0	NA	NA	NA	NA	NA	NA	NA

Data as orig. reptd.; bef. results of disc. opers. and/or spec. items. Per share data adj. for stk. divs. as of ex-div. date. Bold denotes diluted EPS (FASB 128). E-Estimated. NA-Not Available. NM-Not Meaningful. NR-Not Ranked.

Office—11500 N. Mopac Expwy., Building B, Austin, TX 78759-3504. **Tel**—(512) 794-0100. **Website**—http://www.natinst.com **Chrmn & Pres**—J. J. Truchard. **CFO & Treas**—A. M. Davern. **Secy**—D. G. Hugley. **Investor Contact**—Tara Mason (512-685-6873). **Dirs**—L. W. Ashby, D. M. Carlton, J. L. Kodosky, W. C. Nowlin Jr., B. G. Streetman, J. J. Truchard. **Transfer Agent & Registrar**—First National Bank of Boston, c/o Boston EquiServe. **Incorporated**—in Texas in 1976; reincorporated in Delaware in 1994. **Empl**— 1,465. **S&P Analyst:** J. J. Schemitsch

National Presto 1618

NYSE Symbol **NPK**

In S&P SmallCap 600

03-OCT-98

Industry:
Housewares

Summary: This company makes small electrical appliances and housewares, including comfort appliances, pressure cookers and canners, and private-label and premium sales products.

Quantitative Evaluations

Outlook
(1 Lowest—5 Highest)
• **NA**

Fair Value
• **NA**

Risk
• **Low**

Earn./Div. Rank
• **B**

Technical Eval.
• **Bearish** since 8/98

Rel. Strength Rank
(1 Lowest—99 Highest)
• **74**

Insider Activity
• **NA**

Recent Price • 37⅜
52 Wk Range • 44-36⅛

Yield • 5.3%
12-Mo. P/E • 15.9

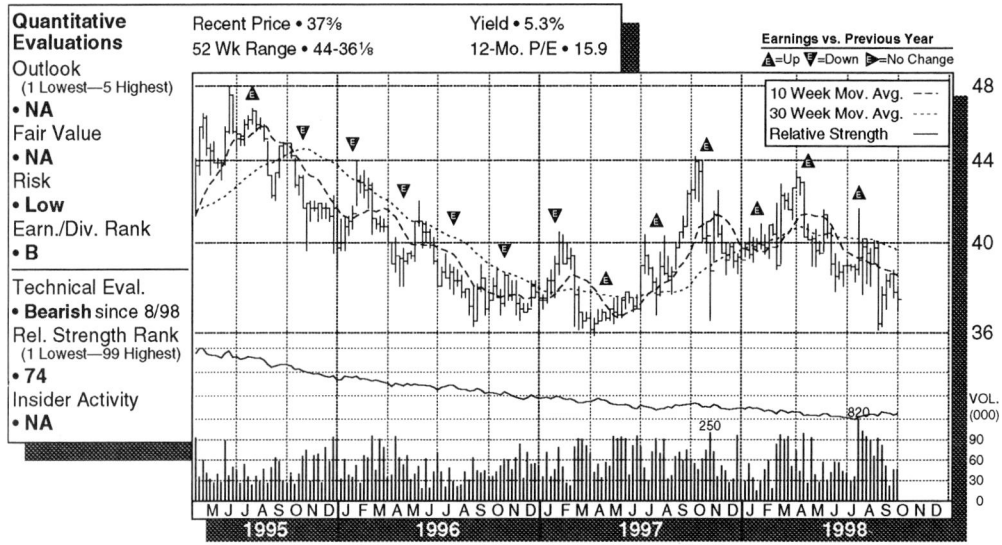

Earnings vs. Previous Year
▲=Up ▼=Down ▶=No Change

10 Week Mov. Avg. ---
30 Week Mov. Avg. ····
Relative Strength ——

Business Profile - 29-SEP-98

This company now focuses on its housewares business, having exited modestly successful efforts in door-to-door selling, graphic arts, tool and die fabrication, and trucking. Elimination of defense business and the loss of Kmart as a major customer restricted earnings in recent years. Successful new product introductions and higher consumer spending are seen as keys to future growth. Results in 1997 were helped by a higher rate of return on invested funds.

Operational Review - 29-SEP-98

Sales in the six months ended July 5, 1998, advanced 1.3%, year to year, reflecting the closeout of the electric barbecue grill. Gross margins widened on improved manufacturing efficiencies. After a 4.2% decline in SG&A expenses, the operating profit soared 261%. Despite the absence of last year's litigation judgments/settlements, pretax income was up 9.0%. After taxes at 11.4%, versus 9.6%, net income climbed 6.7% to $5,570,000 ($0.76 a share), from $5,218,000 ($0.71).

Stock Performance - 02-OCT-98

In the past 30 trading days, NPK's shares have declined 6%, compared to a 7% fall in the S&P 500. Average trading volume for the past five days was 9,260 shares, compared with the 40-day moving average of 13,092 shares.

Key Stock Statistics

Dividend Rate/Share	2.00	Shareholders	1,100
Shs. outstg. (M)	7.4	Market cap. (B)	$0.275
Avg. daily vol. (M)	0.009	Inst. holdings	44%
Tang. Bk. Value/Share	32.64		
Beta	0.49		

Value of $10,000 invested 5 years ago: $ 9,480

Fiscal Year Ending Dec. 31

	1998	1997	1996	1995	1994	1993
Revenues (Million $)						
1Q	18.97	17.95	17.11	17.96	16.20	22.37
2Q	16.29	16.87	16.97	15.88	16.49	14.28
3Q	—	24.92	23.00	29.04	35.49	24.66
4Q	—	49.81	48.93	57.29	59.89	57.27
Yr.	—	109.5	106.0	120.2	128.1	118.6
Earnings Per Share ($)						
1Q	**0.38**	**0.35**	0.26	0.35	0.31	0.43
2Q	**0.38**	**0.36**	0.31	0.35	0.30	0.36
3Q	—	**0.48**	0.38	0.65	0.66	0.60
4Q	—	**1.12**	1.05	1.26	1.65	1.16
Yr.	—	**2.31**	2.00	2.61	2.92	2.55

Next earnings report expected: NA

Dividend Data (Dividends have been paid since 1994.)

Amount ($)	Date Decl.	Ex-Div. Date	Stock of Record	Payment Date
2.000	Feb. 20	Feb. 26	Mar. 02	Mar. 12 '98

A Division of The **McGraw·Hill** *Companies*

Business Summary - 29-SEP-98

With a 92-year history that included defense contracting (including the production of 105 mm and 8-inch projectiles), National Presto Industries, Inc. (NPK) is today fighting its battles in a hotly competitive marketplace: small electrical appliances and housewares. NPK manufactures and distributes such gadgets under the well-known Presto name, and its offerings include pressure cookers and canners, fry pans, griddles, deep fryers, can openers, slicer/shredders, slicer/shredder/mixers, electric heaters, corn poppers, microwave bacon cookers, electronic toasters, coffee makers, electric tea kettles, electric knives, bread slicing systems, electric knife sharpeners and timers.

In 1997, 56% of consolidated net sales were provided by cast products (fry pans, griddles, deep fryers and electric multi-cookers), 15% by motorized nonthermal appliances (can openers, knife sharpeners, slicer/shredders, electric knives and bread slicing systems), and 25% by noncast/thermal appliances (stamped cookers and canners, stainless steel cookers, electronic toasters, corn poppers, coffee makers, microwave bacon cookers, tea kettles and heaters). Wal-Mart accounted for 43% of consolidated net sales in 1997, versus 38% in 1996.

Net sales increased 3.3% in 1997, to $109.5 million from $106.0 million in 1996. Net consolidated earnings were $17.0 million, up 15% from $14.7 million. During the year, NPK expanded its dealer and consumer choices in styles and sizes of pressure cookers. In August 1997, a new five-model line of cookers was introduced. Furthermore, this product line was enhanced through the addition of "Eurostyled" handles. The Presto Salad Shooter line was expanded with the introduction of the Salad Shooter Mixer Too, an electric slicer/shredder/mixer. The Presto Pride line offered products to be sold exclusively in department stores, thereby differentiating its product offerings. In October 1997, new products launched in this category included a 6-cup stainless steel coffee maker and a 12-cup deluxe stainless steel pressure cooker. NPK also introduced a new electronic clock/timer that can count either up or down.

NPK's commercial business is highly competitive and seasonal with the normal peak sales period occurring in the fourth quarter of the year, prior to the holiday season. New product introductions are an important part of the company's efforts to offset the eventual demise of older products.

Per Share Data ($) (Year Ended Dec. 31)	1997	1996	1995	1994	1993	1992	1991	1990	1989	1988
Tangible Bk. Val.	33.88	33.56	33.57	33.11	32.08	29.53	29.79	27.48	27.66	25.99
Cash Flow	2.59	2.27	2.79	3.03	2.67	3.65	5.11	4.06	3.99	2.86
Earnings	2.31	2.00	2.61	2.92	2.55	3.53	4.98	3.94	3.89	2.74
Dividends	2.00	2.00	2.15	1.90	Nil	3.80	2.70	4.15	2.25	1.25
Payout Ratio	87%	100%	82%	65%	Nil	108%	54%	104%	57%	45%
Prices - High	44 1/8	44	48	48	60 1/8	83	62 1/4	44 1/2	40 5/8	36
- Low	35 7/8	36 1/4	38 3/4	39 1/8	45 1/2	45 1/4	39 5/8	33 1/2	32 1/2	26 1/4
P/E Ratio - High	19	22	18	16	24	24	13	11	10	13
- Low	16	18	15	13	18	13	8	9	8	10
Income Statement Analysis (Million $)										
Revs.	110	106	120	128	119	128	162	127	127	108
Oper. Inc.	14.3	12.3	16.6	25.4	21.8	30.7	43.8	29.4	28.0	17.5
Depr.	2.1	2.0	1.5	1.2	1.1	1.3	1.3	1.2	1.1	1.2
Int. Exp.	0.0	Nil	0.7	0.5	0.8	0.7	0.6	0.6	0.6	0.6
Pretax Inc.	22.0	19.2	25.4	30.5	26.2	36.7	52.4	39.6	39.0	26.7
Eff. Tax Rate	23%	23%	25%	30%	29%	30%	30%	26%	26%	24%
Net Inc.	17.0	15.0	19.0	21.5	18.7	25.9	36.7	29.1	28.7	20.3
Balance Sheet & Other Fin. Data (Million $)										
Cash	91.6	228	204	222	221	206	201	191	179	178
Curr. Assets	272	269	270	279	273	249	259	234	235	224
Total Assets	292	285	285	291	283	260	266	242	243	231
Curr. Liab.	42.7	38.5	38.1	43.0	42.6	38.2	43.0	35.4	34.1	34.7
LT Debt	Nil	Nil	Nil	5.1	5.1	5.1	5.1	5.1	6.0	6.0
Common Eqty.	249	247	247	243	235	217	218	201	203	191
Total Cap.	249	247	247	248	240	222	223	207	209	197
Cap. Exp.	4.0	2.0	4.5	1.7	1.0	1.5	0.8	1.2	1.4	1.1
Cash Flow	19.0	16.7	20.5	22.6	19.8	27.1	38.0	30.4	29.8	21.5
Curr. Ratio	6.4	6.9	7.1	6.5	6.4	6.5	6.0	6.6	6.9	6.5
% LT Debt of Cap.	Nil	Nil	Nil	2.1	2.1	2.3	2.3	2.5	2.9	3.1
% Net Inc.of Revs.	15.5	13.9	15.8	16.8	15.7	20.2	22.7	22.9	22.5	18.8
% Ret. on Assets	5.9	5.2	6.6	7.5	6.9	9.8	14.4	12.0	12.1	9.1
% Ret. on Equity	6.8	6.0	7.7	9.0	8.3	11.9	17.5	14.4	14.6	10.9

Data as orig. reptd.; bef. results of disc. opers. and/or spec. items. Per share data adj. for stk. divs. as of ex-div. date. Bold denotes diluted EPS (FASB 128). E-Estimated. NA-Not Available. NM-Not Meaningful. NR-Not Ranked.

Office—3925 North Hastings Way, Eau Claire, WI 54703-3703. **Tel**—(715) 839-2121. **Chrmn**—M. S. Cohen. **Pres, CEO, CFO & Investor Contact**—Maryjo Cohen. **Treas**—R. F. Lieble. **Secy**—J. F. Bartl. **Dirs**—J. F. Bartl, M. Cohen, M. S. Cohen, M. J. O'Meara, W. G. Ryberg, J. M. Sirianni. **Transfer Agent & Registrar**—Harris Trust & Savings Bank, Chicago. **Incorporated**—in Wisconsin in 1905. **Empl**— 577. **S&P Analyst:** Kathleen J. Fraser

Nature's Sunshine Products 4747K

NASDAQ Symbol **NATR**

In S&P SmallCap 600

03-OCT-98

Industry: Personal Care

Summary: This company is a leading international manufacturer and marketer of encapsulated and tableted herbal products, high-quality natural vitamins and other complementary products.

Quantitative Evaluations	Recent Price • 15⅝	Yield • 0.9%
	52 Wk Range • 28⅝-13⅝	12-Mo. P/E • 13.5

Outlook (1 Lowest—5 Highest)
• **NA**

Fair Value
• **NA**

Risk
• **Average**

Earn./Div. Rank
• **A**

Technical Eval.
• **NA**

Rel. Strength Rank (1 Lowest—99 Highest)
• **42**

Insider Activity
• **Neutral**

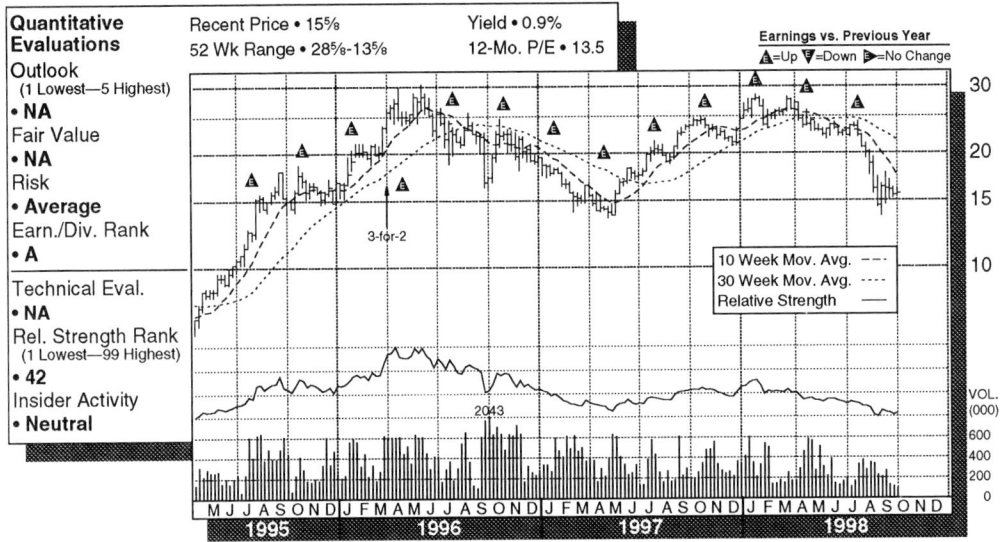

Earnings vs. Previous Year
▲=Up ▼=Down ▶=No Change

10 Week Mov. Avg. — — —
30 Week Mov. Avg. · · · ·
Relative Strength ——

3-for-2

VOL. (000)

Business Profile - 14-SEP-98

Nature's Sunshine has expanded its revenue base substantially in recent years, mainly as a result of its growing number of distributors. At the end of the second quarter of 1998, the number of distributors worldwide totaled 652,000, up about 8% from the year-earlier level. Earnings growth has been impressive, aided by healthy demand for nutritional and herbal products in the U.S. and abroad. Results in recent quarters have benefited from an ongoing program to control costs. NATR has distributors in the rapidly growing markets of Japan, Colombia, Venezuela, Brazil and Malaysia. In January 1998, company directors authorized the acquisition of 500,000 shares of NATR common stock. During the first half of 1998, the company repurchased 236,000 shares of its common stock under this repurchase plan.

Operational Review - 14-SEP-98

Sales in the six months ended June 30, 1998, rose 9.5%, year to year, reflecting expansion of the company's independent sales force, increased penetration in international markets, and strong demand for NATR's products in the U.S. Margins widened, despite a higher level of volume incentives; operating profit advanced 19%. Other income fell modestly, and after taxes at 38.5%, versus 39.3%, net income also advanced 19%, to $10,972,000 ($0.58 a share), from $9,256,000 ($0.48).

Stock Performance - 02-OCT-98

In the past 30 trading days, NATR's shares have declined 3%, compared to a 7% fall in the S&P 500. Average trading volume for the past five days was 17,960 shares, compared with the 40-day moving average of 43,928 shares.

Key Stock Statistics

Dividend Rate/Share	0.13	Shareholders	1,300
Shs. outstg. (M)	18.4	Market cap. (B)	$0.287
Avg. daily vol. (M)	0.030	Inst. holdings	41%
Tang. Bk. Value/Share	3.93		
Beta	0.84		

Value of $10,000 invested 5 years ago: $ 19,165

Fiscal Year Ending Dec. 31

	1998	1997	1996	1995	1994	1993
Revenues (Million $)						
1Q	75.28	67.83	60.11	47.06	37.34	29.83
2Q	77.20	71.41	63.18	50.73	38.31	31.62
3Q	—	71.59	63.03	53.16	41.00	32.46
4Q	—	70.08	62.72	54.62	44.25	33.29
Yr.	—	280.9	249.1	205.6	160.9	127.2
Earnings Per Share ($)						
1Q	**0.26**	0.21	0.17	0.11	0.09	0.06
2Q	**0.32**	0.28	0.22	0.16	0.12	0.10
3Q	—	0.29	0.23	0.17	0.12	0.12
4Q	—	**0.29**	0.24	0.19	0.12	0.12
Yr.	—	**1.06**	0.86	0.63	0.45	0.40

Next earnings report expected: mid October

Dividend Data (Dividends have been paid since 1988.)

Amount ($)	Date Decl.	Ex-Div. Date	Stock of Record	Payment Date
0.033	Nov. 03	Nov. 13	Nov. 17	Nov. 25 '97
0.033	Feb. 18	Feb. 26	Mar. 02	Mar. 11 '98
0.033	May. 05	May. 14	May. 18	May. 29 '98
0.033	Jul. 29	Aug. 06	Aug. 10	Aug. 19 '98

A Division of The McGraw-Hill Companies

Business Summary - 14-SEP-98

Nature's Sunshine Products, Inc. primarily manufactures and sells nutritional and personal care products. Nutritional products include herbs, vitamins, beverages, diet and weight loss plans, and mineral and food supplements. Personal care products include natural skin, hair and beauty care items. The company also sells a line of homeopathic remedies and a reverse-osmosis water purification system (Nature's Spring).

The company sells its products primarily through an independent sales force of managers and distributors; managers numbered 15,606 at June 30, 1998, and distributors numbered 619,000. For domestic sales, NATR generally sells its products on a cash or credit card basis. For certain international operations, the company uses independent distribution centers, and offers credit terms consistent with industry standards. Managers resell the products to the distributors in their sales group or to consumers, or use the products themselves. Many distributors sell on a part-time basis to friends or associates, or consume the products themselves. Demand for the products is created largely by the number of active members of the independent distributor sales force.

NATR buys herbs and other raw materials in bulk, and, after quality control testing, encapsulates, tabulates or concentrates them, and then packages them for shipment. Most products are made at the company headquarters in Spanish Fork, UT. Certain personal care products are manufactured for the company by contract manufacturers in accordance with company specifications. NATR also operates regional warehouses in Columbus, OH, Dallas, TX, and Atlanta, GA.

The company's direct sales of nutritional and personal care products are established internationally in Brazil, Colombia, Mexico, Venezuela, Japan, Canada, the United Kingdom, Argentina, South Korea, Costa Rica, El Salvador, Panama, Peru, Guatemala, Nicaragua, Honduras and Ecuador. NATR also exports its products to other countries, including Australia, New Zealand, Norway, the Philippines and, most recently, the Peoples Republic of China. International sales accounted for 37% of revenues in 1997, up from 36% in 1996 and 34% in 1995.

Per Share Data ($)

(Year Ended Dec. 31)	1997	1996	1995	1994	1993	1992	1991	1990	1989	1988
Tangible Bk. Val.	3.60	3.30	2.26	1.81	1.58	1.32	1.07	0.90	0.79	0.68
Cash Flow	1.28	1.03	0.82	0.61	0.50	0.41	0.32	0.25	0.26	0.21
Earnings	1.06	0.86	0.63	0.45	0.40	0.32	0.25	0.19	0.21	0.18
Dividends	0.13	0.13	0.13	0.12	0.12	0.09	0.07	0.07	0.07	0.03
Payout Ratio	13%	15%	21%	27%	30%	28%	28%	34%	31%	16%
Prices - High	26¾	30½	18⅝	10⅞	9	8¾	6	4¼	4¼	2³/₁₆
- Low	13½	15⅛	6½	6⅝	5⅛	3⅝	2¹/₁₆	1¹¹/₁₆	1¹¹/₁₆	1⅛
P/E Ratio - High	25	35	30	24	22	27	24	21	20	13
- Low	13	18	10	15	13	11	8	8	8	6

Income Statement Analysis (Million $)

	1997	1996	1995	1994	1993	1992	1991	1990	1989	1988
Revs.	281	249	206	161	127	101	72.6	60.1	52.1	44.5
Oper. Inc.	35.3	30.0	21.0	17.3	13.4	10.1	7.7	6.0	6.6	5.5
Depr.	4.3	3.4	3.5	3.1	1.9	1.6	1.1	1.0	0.8	0.7
Int. Exp.	0.2	0.1	0.2	0.1	Nil	0.1	0.0	0.0	0.1	0.1
Pretax Inc.	32.7	27.9	20.2	13.9	12.2	9.9	7.3	5.8	6.4	5.1
Eff. Tax Rate	40%	40%	41%	44%	40%	40%	36%	38%	38%	36%
Net Inc.	20.1	16.8	11.9	8.4	7.5	5.9	4.6	3.6	4.0	3.3

Balance Sheet & Other Fin. Data (Million $)

	1997	1996	1995	1994	1993	1992	1991	1990	1989	1988
Cash	27.8	27.9	14.2	11.2	8.7	6.3	9.2	8.5	7.3	6.6
Curr. Assets	66.0	67.1	47.2	36.6	26.5	20.5	17.8	14.6	13.0	11.2
Total Assets	95.8	92.0	65.2	52.5	41.5	34.0	27.4	22.0	20.1	17.5
Curr. Liab.	27.5	27.5	22.7	17.8	12.3	9.4	7.6	5.1	5.3	4.2
LT Debt	Nil	Nil	Nil	Nil	Nil	Nil	Nil	0.0	0.0	0.0
Common Eqty.	66.9	63.2	41.5	33.3	28.9	23.9	19.6	16.5	14.4	12.9
Total Cap.	68.4	64.0	42.5	34.7	29.3	24.6	19.8	16.9	14.8	13.3
Cap. Exp.	7.5	10.5	6.1	2.6	2.9	2.8	1.5	1.5	1.3	0.9
Cash Flow	24.4	20.3	15.4	11.5	9.4	7.5	5.8	4.6	4.8	4.0
Curr. Ratio	2.4	2.4	2.1	2.1	2.2	2.2	2.3	2.9	2.5	2.6
% LT Debt of Cap.	Nil	Nil	Nil	Nil	Nil	Nil	Nil	0.1	0.2	0.3
% Net Inc.of Revs.	7.2	6.7	5.8	5.3	5.9	5.9	6.4	6.0	7.6	7.4
% Ret. on Assets	21.4	21.4	20.2	18.0	19.7	19.3	18.7	17.1	21.2	19.8
% Ret. on Equity	30.9	32.2	31.9	27.2	28.2	27.2	25.6	23.3	29.3	28.6

Data as orig. reptd.; bef. results of disc. opers. and/or spec. items. Per share data adj. for stk. divs. as of ex-div. date. Bold denotes diluted EPS (FASB 128). E-Estimated. NA-Not Available. NM-Not Meaningful. NR-Not Ranked.

Office—75 E. 1700 S., Provo, UT 84606. **Tel**—(801) 342-4300. **Chrmn**—Kristine F. Hughes. **Pres & CEO**—D. P. Howells. **COO**—D. Faggioli. **VP-Fin, Treas & CFO**—C. D. Huff. **VP & Secy**—B. F. Ashworth. **Dirs**—R. H. Daines, D. Faggioli, M. Gappmayer, D. P. Howells, E. L. Hughes, K. F. Hughes, P. T. Hughes. **Transfer Agent & Registrar**—American Stock Transfer & Trust Co., NYC. **Incorporated**—in Utah in 1976. **Empl**— 994.
S&P Analyst: Richard Joy

Nautica Enterprises

4747M

Nasdaq Symbol **NAUT**

In S&P SmallCap 600

03-OCT-98

Industry: Textiles (Apparel)

Summary: NAUT designs, sources and markets men's sportswear, outerwear and activewear apparel through retail and wholesale operations.

S&P Opinion: Hold (★★★)

| Recent Price • 17½ | Yield • Nil |
| 52 Wk Range • 32½-15 | 12-Mo. P/E • 12.5 |

Earnings vs. Previous Year
▲=Up ▼=Down ▶=No Change

Quantitative Evaluations

Outlook (1 Lowest—5 Highest)
• **5**

Fair Value
• **36⅞**

Risk
• **Average**

Earn./Div. Rank
• **B+**

Technical Eval.
• **Bearish** since 8/98

Rel. Strength Rank (1 Lowest—99 Highest)
• **23**

Insider Activity
• **NA**

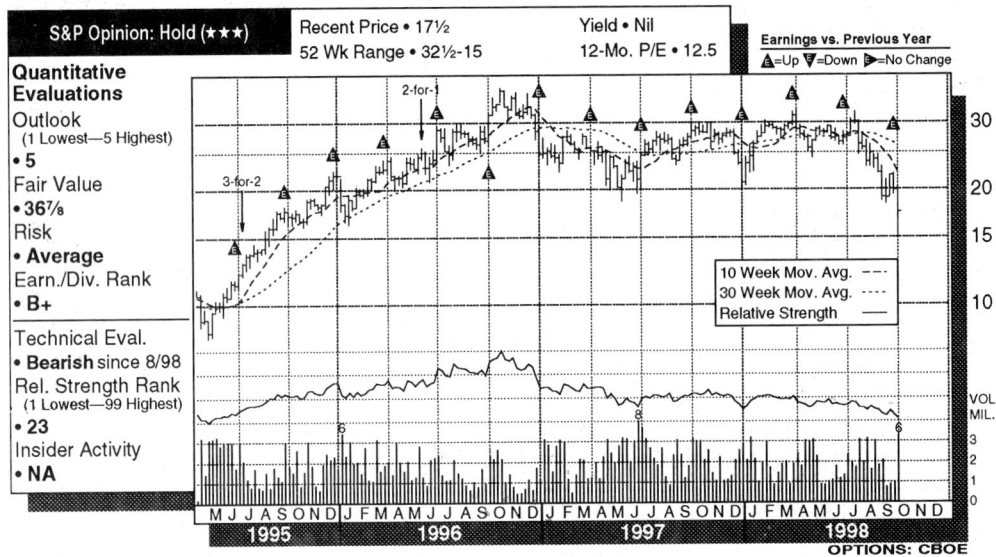

10 Week Mov. Avg. ---
30 Week Mov. Avg. ·····
Relative Strength

OPTIONS: CBOE

Overview - 01-OCT-98

We expect sales of this well known brand name apparel maker to rise about 15% during FY 99 (Feb.), far below the pace of 25% of FY 98. Sales in the first half of FY 99 were up 15%, driven by increases in both wholesale and retail operations. Wholesale business has grown, due to the addition of new shops, as well as the expansion of existing shops. Retail sales have benefited from modestly higher same-store sales at Nautica factory outlet stores, and from the addition of new stores. Gross margins have benefited from a more favorable sales mix, and we expect this trend to continue in the second half of FY 99. However, costs associated with new business initiatives, including the acquisition of its denim licensee, the upcoming introduction of the NST line, Nautica Sport Tech, and the launch of women's robes and sleepwear, will lead to increased SG&A expenses in the latter half of the year. We project profits to outpace sales growth, rising about 20% a year for the next several years, as Nautica expands and diversifies its product lines.

Valuation - 01-OCT-98

Since late July 1998, the shares have fallen sharply, on concerns about a difficult retail environment for the overall apparel industry. The company's plans to expand its product offerings will diversify its product lines and fuel 15% sales growth. However, due to startup costs associated with the three new businesses, we have lowered our earnings estimates for the FY 99 second half. For the longer term, prospects appear bright for NAUT, with EPS expected to grow approximately 20% annually over the next several years. With the stock recently trading at 11X our FY 99 EPS estimate of $1.62, we view the shares as fairly valued, and believe the stock is likely to be only a market performer over the next six to 12 months.

Key Stock Statistics

S&P EPS Est. 1999	1.62	Tang. Bk. Value/Share	6.63
P/E on S&P Est. 1999	10.8	Beta	0.84
S&P EPS Est. 2000	1.90	Shareholders	400
Dividend Rate/Share	Nil	Market cap. (B)	$0.691
Shs. outstg. (M)	39.5	Inst. holdings	73%
Avg. daily vol. (M)	0.439		

Value of $10,000 invested 5 years ago: $ 51,639

Fiscal Year Ending Feb. 28

	1999	1998	1997	1996	1995	1994
Revenues (Million $)						
1Q	111.0	95.81	76.14	61.40	44.60	30.70
2Q	150.9	132.3	103.3	80.60	63.30	51.90
3Q	—	145.7	116.6	90.80	87.00	67.60
4Q	—	111.0	90.51	69.72	52.80	42.80
Yr.	—	484.8	386.6	302.5	247.7	192.9
Earnings Per Share ($)						
1Q	**0.23**	0.18	0.13	0.09	0.06	0.03
2Q	**0.46**	0.36	0.26	0.18	0.14	0.12
3Q	E0.53	0.48	0.37	0.28	0.23	0.18
4Q	E0.40	**0.33**	0.26	0.20	0.15	0.13
Yr.	E1.62	**1.35**	1.02	0.75	0.57	0.45

Next earnings report expected: NA

Dividend Data

No cash has been paid. Three-for-two stock splits were effected in July 1995, November 1993 and March 1992.

A Division of The McGraw·Hill Companies

Business Summary - 01-OCT-98

Nautica Enterprises is sailing ahead of the competition by marketing its popular apparel in "concept stores" within department stores. A key part of the company's rapid growth has its strategy of selling its products in Nautica Shops, designed to NAUT's specifications and dedicated to the exclusive merchandising and sale of the Nautica collection, which the company believes achieve sales productivity significantly higher than that of sales of Nautica products in standard department store settings.

New York City-based Nautica designs, manufactures and markets men's apparel. By licensing the Nautica name, the company has extended its global distribution and the depth of its product offerings. Licensed products include tailored clothing, accessories, swimwear, watches, apparel for women, children and infants, footwear, a denim collection, a home collection, fragrances for men and women, luggage, and a Lincoln-Mercury Villager minivan.

The company was founded in 1971 as State-O-Maine, a company that offered shirts, robes, loungewear and sportswear under the Bayou Sport Label. This division operated as a subsidiary and was recently sold.

The company really took off with the yachting-inspired sportswear designed by Nautica founder and principal designer David Chu; the line was so successful that the company changed its name to Nautica in 1984. The collection includes sportswear (sweaters, shirts, pants and shorts), outerwear (jackets and parkas) and activewear (tops, pants, shorts, tee shirts and swimwear). Nautica is sold at more than 1,200 in-store shops, three flagship stores, and 58 U.S. factory outlets. The factory outlet stores are used to distribute excess and out of season merchandise. The company does not own or operate any manufacturing facilities; clothing is made by contracted overseas producers.

The company endeavors to leave its rivals in its wake with aggressive expansion into overseas markets, new label introductions, developing more in-store shops, and increased licensing agreements.

During FY 98 (Feb.), NAUT acquired The E. Magrath Apparel Co., a golf apparel company that designs, markets and distributes quality golf sportswear to top golf resorts and has an exclusive license to market sportswear under the name of legendary golf champion Byron Nelson.

Per Share Data ($)

(Year Ended Feb. 28)	1998	1997	1996	1995	1994	1993	1992	1991	1990	1989
Tangible Bk. Val.	6.26	5.10	4.31	3.50	2.90	1.79	1.47	1.32	NA	NA
Cash Flow	1.60	1.17	0.85	0.65	0.53	0.35	NA	NA	NA	NA
Earnings	1.35	1.02	0.75	0.57	0.45	0.30	0.22	0.10	NA	NA
Dividends	Nil	Nil	Nil	Nil	Nil	Nil	Nil	Nil	Nil	Nil
Payout Ratio	Nil	Nil	Nil	Nil	Nil	Nil	Nil	Nil	Nil	Nil
Cal. Yrs.	1997	1996	1995	1994	1993	1992	1991	1990	1989	1988
Prices - High	30	37	22¾	10⅞	9⅛	4⅛	NA	NA	NA	NA
- Low	18⅝	16¼	8⅛	6½	3¼	2⁵⁄₁₆	NA	NA	NA	NA
P/E Ratio - High	22	36	30	19	20	14	NA	NA	NA	NA
- Low	14	16	11	11	7	8	NA	NA	NA	NA

Income Statement Analysis (Million $)

	1998	1997	1996	1995	1994	1993	1992	1991	1990	1989
Revs.	485	387	303	248	193	151	NA	NA	NA	NA
Oper. Inc.	93.6	71.8	52.5	39.3	27.0	19.5	NA	NA	NA	NA
Depr.	10.5	6.3	4.3	3.1	3.0	1.8	NA	NA	NA	NA
Int. Exp.	Nil	Nil	0.0	0.0	0.3	0.3	NA	NA	NA	NA
Pretax Inc.	92.6	72.3	52.9	38.6	28.6	18.3	NA	NA	NA	NA
Eff. Tax Rate	40%	40%	40%	38%	41%	43%	NA	NA	NA	NA
Net Inc.	56.4	44.0	32.0	24.0	16.8	10.5	NA	NA	NA	NA

Balance Sheet & Other Fin. Data (Million $)

	1998	1997	1996	1995	1994	1993	1992	1991	1990	1989
Cash	34.6	71.9	61.0	49.2	44.9	NA	NA	NA	NA	NA
Curr. Assets	246	204	170	143	118	NA	NA	NA	NA	NA
Total Assets	310	251	209	168	137	NA	NA	NA	NA	NA
Curr. Liab.	58.8	47.6	36.0	28.8	22.6	NA	NA	NA	NA	NA
LT Debt	0.1	0.1	0.2	0.3	0.3	NA	NA	NA	NA	NA
Common Eqty.	251	203	173	139	114	NA	NA	NA	NA	NA
Total Cap.	252	204	173	140	114	NA	NA	NA	NA	NA
Cap. Exp.	22.9	17.7	15.9	7.2	7.5	1.9	NA	NA	NA	NA
Cash Flow	66.9	50.3	36.3	27.1	19.8	12.3	NA	NA	NA	NA
Curr. Ratio	4.2	4.3	4.7	5.0	5.2	NA	NA	NA	NA	NA
% LT Debt of Cap.	Nil	0.1	0.1	0.2	0.3	NA	NA	NA	NA	NA
% Net Inc.of Revs.	11.6	11.4	10.6	9.7	8.7	6.9	NA	NA	NA	NA
% Ret. on Assets	20.1	19.1	16.9	15.7	15.6	NA	NA	NA	NA	NA
% Ret. on Equity	24.8	23.4	20.5	18.9	19.4	NA	NA	NA	NA	NA

Data as orig. reptd.; bef. results of disc. opers. and/or spec. items. Per share data adj. for stk. divs. as of ex-div. date. Bold denotes diluted EPS (FASB 128). E-Estimated. NA-Not Available. NM-Not Meaningful. NR-Not Ranked.

Office— 40 West 57th St., New York, NY 10019. **Tel**—(212) 541-5990. **Chrmn, Pres & CEO**—H. Sanders. **VP-Fin & CFO**—N. S. Nackman. **Investor Contact**—Don Pennington (212-541-5757). **Dirs**—R. B. Bank, D. Chu, G. Greenberg, I. Rosenzweig, H. Sanders, C. H. Scherer, R. G. Weiner. **Transfer Agent & Registrar**—Harris Trust Co. of New York, NYC. **Incorporated**—in Delaware in 1971. **Empl**— 1,700. **S&P Analyst:** Kathleen J. Fraser

Thomas Nelson, Inc. 2227J

NYSE Symbol **TNM**

In S&P SmallCap 600

10-OCT-98

Industry: Publishing

Summary: This company is a leading publisher, producer and distributor of books with primarily religious themes, as well as a seller of a broad line of gift and and stationery products.

Quantitative Evaluations		
Outlook (1 Lowest—5 Highest)	Recent Price • 13⅛	Yield • 1.2%
• **3+**	52 Wk Range • 15⅝-10¼	12-Mo. P/E • 17.5

Fair Value
• **13¾**

Risk
• **Average**

Earn./Div. Rank
• **B+**

Technical Eval.
• **Bearish** since 9/98

Rel. Strength Rank (1 Lowest—99 Highest)
• **85**

Insider Activity
• **Favorable**

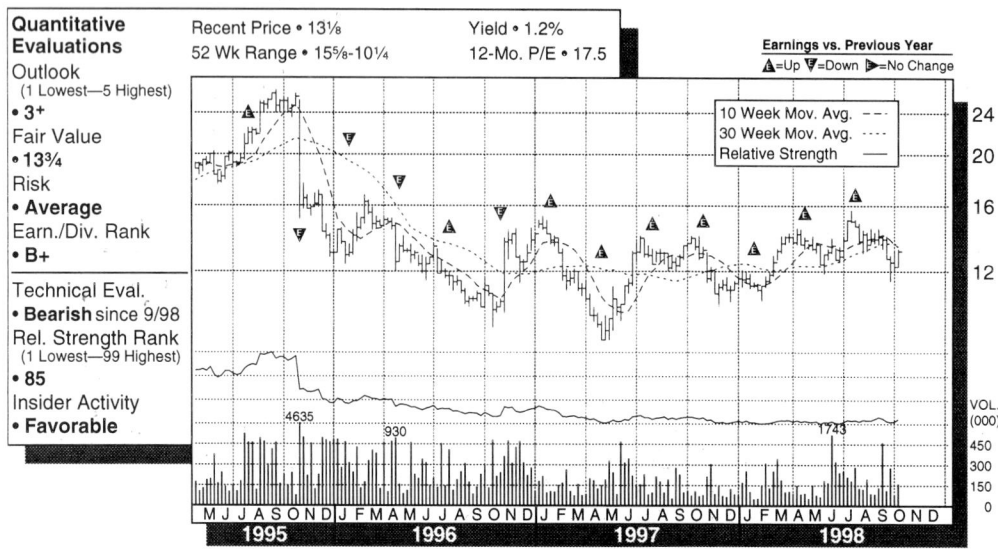

Earnings vs. Previous Year
▲=Up ▼=Down ▶=No Change

10 Week Mov. Avg. ---
30 Week Mov. Avg. ····
Relative Strength —

Business Profile - 18-AUG-98

After selling its music division in the fourth quarter of FY 97 (Mar.) and discontinuing the operations of its Royal Media division in the fourth quarter of FY 96, Thomas Nelson is focusing on its core book publishing (65% of FY 98 net revenues) and gift (35%) businesses, which appear to be rebounding after a difficult FY 96. TNM plans to grow by continuing to offer popular Christian and inspirational products; in FYs 96-98, the company published more than half of the top-ten Christian and inspirational non-fiction best-sellers as determined by the Christian Booksellers' Association. In June 1998, TNM's directors authorized the repurchase of up to 3 million shares, or about 18% of outstanding common shares.

Operational Review - 18-AUG-98

Revenues in FY 98 rose 3.9%, year-to-year, reflecting primarily a rebound in TNM's book publishing business, particularly in Christian and inspirational titles. Gross margins narrowed, reflecting lower licensing revenues, yet operating margins widened, due to reduced advertising and fulfillment costs. Following a 28% drop in interest expense and taxes of 37.5%, versus 37.0%, net income was up 33% to $12,673,000 ($0.74 a share), from $9,522,000 ($0.56). Results in FY 97 exclude income of $0.96 per share from the discontinued operations of the Royal Media division.

Stock Performance - 09-OCT-98

In the past 30 trading days, TNM's shares have declined 5%, compared to a 4% fall in the S&P 500. Average trading volume for the past five days was 31,140 shares, compared with the 40-day moving average of 36,146 shares.

Key Stock Statistics

Dividend Rate/Share	0.16	Shareholders	2,000
Shs. outstg. (M)	15.2	Market cap. (B)	$0.185
Avg. daily vol. (M)	0.030	Inst. holdings	39%
Tang. Bk. Value/Share	4.97		
Beta	0.49		

Value of $10,000 invested 5 years ago: $ 9,559

Fiscal Year Ending Mar. 31

	1999	1998	1997	1996	1995	1994
Revenues (Million $)						
1Q	55.99	54.46	55.18	60.30	49.10	46.10
2Q	—	68.62	65.21	80.53	70.51	64.40
3Q	—	64.66	63.56	86.24	71.09	60.70
4Q	—	65.22	59.49	81.34	74.41	56.50
Yr.	—	253.0	243.4	308.4	265.1	227.7
Earnings Per Share ($)						
1Q	0.08	0.06	0.01	-0.01	-0.04	-0.09
2Q	—	0.27	0.21	0.25	0.42	0.34
3Q	—	0.24	0.20	0.13	0.36	0.24
4Q	—	0.16	0.14	-0.72	0.14	0.11
Yr.	—	0.73	0.56	-0.39	0.88	0.66

Next earnings report expected: NA

Dividend Data (Dividends have been paid since 1989.)

Amount ($)	Date Decl.	Ex-Div. Date	Stock of Record	Payment Date
0.040	Nov. 20	Jan. 29	Feb. 02	Feb. 16 '98
0.040	Feb. 20	May. 07	May. 11	May. 25 '98
0.040	May. 21	Jul. 30	Aug. 03	Aug. 17 '98
0.040	Aug. 21	Oct. 29	Nov. 02	Nov. 16 '98

A Division of The **McGraw·Hill** Companies

Business Summary - 18-AUG-98

Thomas Nelson, Inc. (TNM) is a leading publisher and distributor of books emphasizing Christian, inspirational and family value themes. TNM's publishing business accounted for 65% of FY 98 (Mar.) revenues. The company also produces specialty gift items, including journals, photo albums, kitchen accessories and stationery, whose sale was responsible for 35% of TNM's FY 98 revenues. Over the past two years, the company began emphasizing its core book and gift businesses. Notably, TNM sold its music division in January 1997 for $120 million and discontinued the operations of its Royal Media division in the fourth quarter of 1996.

Year after year, the company's books, published under imprints including Nelson and Word, dominate the Christian Booksellers' Association's monthly best-seller lists for hardcover non-fiction. In FYs 96-98, TNM annually released over 200 new book titles. The company publishes books by well-known communicators such as Billy Graham and Pat Robertson, and famous athletes and celebrities, including Bobby Bowden, Joe Gibbs, Evander Holyfield, Nolan Ryan, Reggie White and Zig Ziglar.

The company's book publishing business is enhanced by its extensive marketing and distribution channels, which enable TNM to more successfully sign and renew contracts with popular authors than its competitors because of its ability to reach a wider audience. TNM's distribution network includes major bookstores and retailers (such as Barnes & Noble and Wal-Mart), Christian bookstores and a direct marketing infrastructure including 225 sales people and 24-hour-a-day telemarketing capabilities. TNM also distributes its products internationally in Canada, Mexico, South America, Europe, Australia and Asia.

TNM believes it is the largest commercial publisher of English translations of the Bible. Of the 13 major current Bible translations, nine are published by the company, with four being exclusive to TNM due to copyright ownership or licensing arrangements. The company's Bible franchise includes its publishing operations, with editorial and design functions, as well as the production of Bible reference products including commentaries, study guides and self-help texts.

TNM's gift division more than doubled in size in FY 96, as a result of the acquisition of C.R. Gibson, and nearly doubled in size again in FY 97. In FY 98, however, gift revenues declined slightly due to a change in product focus away from the mass merchandise stationery category. The company believes that its gift division has significant growth potential because of the variety of complementary gift items not currently offered, and the breadth of the company's distribution channels.

Per Share Data ($)

(Year Ended Mar. 31)	1998	1997	1996	1995	1994	1993	1992	1991	1990	1989
Tangible Bk. Val.	5.84	5.18	2.38	2.74	1.93	0.87	3.68	2.62	2.26	2.10
Cash Flow	1.24	1.05	0.18	1.31	0.97	0.67	0.60	0.50	0.41	0.33
Earnings	0.73	0.56	-0.39	0.88	0.66	0.49	0.48	0.42	0.32	0.25
Dividends	0.16	0.16	0.16	0.13	0.13	0.11	0.09	0.07	0.03	Nil
Payout Ratio	22%	29%	NM	15%	20%	22%	19%	18%	10%	Nil
Cal. Yrs.	1997	1996	1995	1994	1993	1992	1991	1990	1989	1988
Prices - High	$15^{1}/_{4}$	$16^{3}/_{4}$	$26^{1}/_{2}$	$20^{1}/_{4}$	$20^{3}/_{4}$	$15^{3}/_{4}$	$9^{1}/_{2}$	$5^{7}/_{8}$	$4^{3}/_{4}$	$3^{5}/_{8}$
- Low	$8^{7}/_{8}$	$9^{3}/_{8}$	$12^{1}/_{2}$	$14^{1}/_{4}$	$11^{3}/_{8}$	$8^{1}/_{4}$	$5^{3}/_{8}$	$3^{1}/_{4}$	$3^{1}/_{4}$	$2^{1}/_{8}$
P/E Ratio - High	21	30	NM	23	32	32	20	14	15	15
- Low	12	17	NM	16	17	17	11	8	10	9

Income Statement Analysis (Million $)

Revs.	253	243	308	265	228	138	93.1	73.6	59.4	49.1
Oper. Inc.	33.4	33.4	8.7	31.9	24.2	14.6	11.0	8.5	6.9	6.0
Depr.	8.6	8.4	9.0	5.9	4.2	2.4	1.5	1.0	0.9	0.9
Int. Exp.	6.1	8.4	10.7	8.6	6.9	2.9	0.9	1.3	0.9	1.0
Pretax Inc.	20.3	15.1	-10.4	18.3	13.3	9.4	9.0	6.7	5.6	4.4
Eff. Tax Rate	37%	37%	NM	36%	34%	33%	35%	36%	41%	42%
Net Inc.	12.7	9.5	-6.2	11.7	8.8	6.4	5.9	4.3	3.3	2.6

Balance Sheet & Other Fin. Data (Million $)

Cash	39.7	43.5	0.7	0.8	0.8	0.8	0.7	1.3	0.3	4.8
Curr. Assets	185	197	237	184	150	119	61.7	49.7	35.1	31.8
Total Assets	285	302	374	250	216	192	76.8	58.4	41.6	38.4
Curr. Liab.	44.8	65.5	65.6	54.2	45.9	36.7	17.4	16.9	13.2	12.5
LT Debt	79.6	83.5	180	120	103	92.8	9.7	13.9	4.6	4.0
Common Eqty.	156	147	122	72.7	62.7	55.4	49.1	26.9	23.8	21.9
Total Cap.	239	234	306	194	167	150	59.4	41.5	28.4	25.9
Cap. Exp.	3.3	1.9	4.2	2.2	3.2	11.1	3.2	2.4	0.5	0.2
Cash Flow	21.3	18.0	2.8	17.6	12.9	8.8	7.4	5.3	4.2	3.5
Curr. Ratio	4.1	3.0	3.6	3.4	3.3	3.2	3.5	2.9	2.7	2.5
% LT Debt of Cap.	33.2	35.7	58.9	61.8	62.0	62.0	16.3	33.4	16.2	15.5
% Net Inc.of Revs.	5.0	4.0	NM	4.4	3.8	4.6	6.4	5.6	5.6	5.3
% Ret. on Assets	4.3	2.9	NM	5.0	4.3	4.7	7.9	8.7	8.3	7.2
% Ret. on Equity	8.4	7.1	NM	17.3	14.7	12.1	14.2	17.2	14.5	12.5

Data as orig. reptd.; bef. results of disc. opers. and/or spec. items. Per share data adj. for stk. divs. as of ex-div. date. Bold denotes diluted EPS (FASB 128). E-Estimated. NA-Not Available. NM-Not Meaningful. NR-Not Ranked.

Office—501 Nelson Place, Nashville, TN 37214-1000. **Tel**—(615) 889-9000. **Website**—http://www.thomasnelson.com.**Chrmn, Pres & CEO**—S. Moore. **VP-Fin**—V. Lawson.**EVP & Secy**—J. L. Powers. **Treas & Investor Contact**—P. E. Williams. (615) 902-1305.**Dirs**—B. O. Currey, Jr.; W. L. Davis, Jr;, S. J. Moore; S. Moore; R. J. Niebel; M. V. Oakley; J. M. Rodgers; C. Turner, Jr.; A. Young. **Transfer Agent**—SunTrust Co. Bank, Atlanta, GA. **Incorporated**—in Tennessee in 1961. **Empl**— 1,200. **S&P Analyst:** Scott H. Kessler

12-OCT-98

Industry: Computers (Network-ing)

Summary: This company is a leading designer, developer, manufac-turer and supplier of WANs and associated services used by enter-prises, government organizations and carriers.

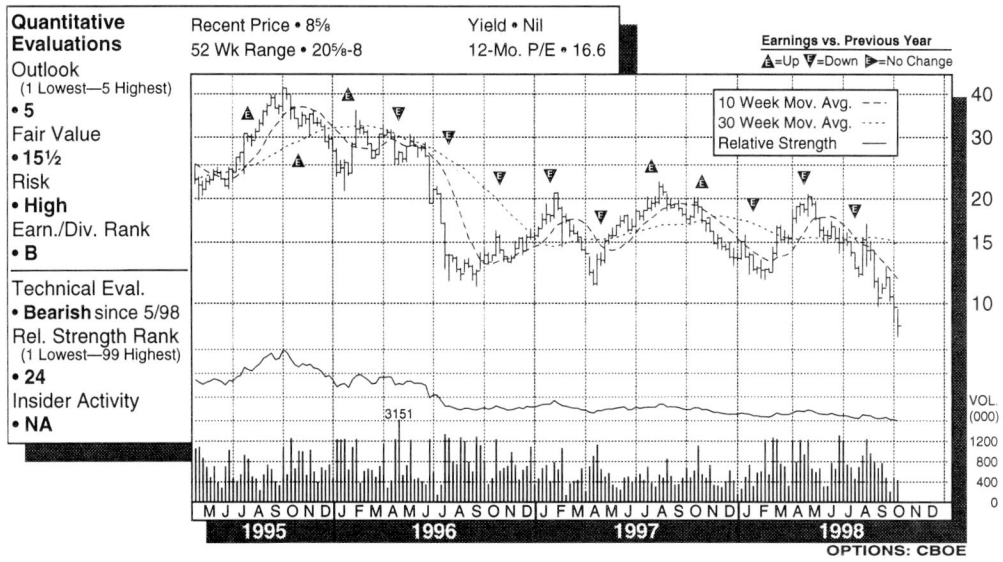

Quantitative Evaluations	
Outlook (1 Lowest—5 Highest)	• 5
Fair Value	• 15½
Risk	• High
Earn./Div. Rank	• B
Technical Eval.	• Bearish since 5/98
Rel. Strength Rank (1 Lowest—99 Highest)	• 24
Insider Activity	• NA

Recent Price • 8⅝
52 Wk Range • 20⅝-8
Yield • Nil
12-Mo. P/E • 16.6

Earnings vs. Previous Year
▲=Up ▼=Down ▶=No Change

10 Week Mov. Avg. – – –
30 Week Mov. Avg. ·······
Relative Strength —

OPTIONS: CBOE

Business Profile - 12-OCT-98

By the end of FY 98 (Mar.), over 1,500 of NWK's cus-tomers installed over 20,000 of its switches in over 70 countries throughout the world. The company's products and services provide sophisticated, high-value-added transmission, network management, connectivity appli-cations and solutions. NWK recently expanded its Promina product line with the introduction of the Promina 100 family. During the first quarter of FY 99, over two-thirds of NWK's product revenues were from the Promina 800 Series which was launched in late 1997. As a result of relocating its headquarters in May 1998, the company recorded a $3.3 million charge in the fourth quarter of FY 98 (Mar.). In September, direc-tors authorized a share repurchase program.

Operational Review - 12-OCT-98

Revenues in the three months ended June 28, 1998, declined 11%, year to year, reflecting a decrease in product sales through the Asia Pacific/Latin America channel. Gross margins were unchanged. Lower sales and marketing expenses were outweighed by higher re-search and development expenses and an increase in general and administrative expenses; income from op-erations fell 57%. After taxes at 29.7%, versus 32.0%, net income dropped 48%, to $2,948,000 ($0.13 a share, diluted), from $5,655,000 ($0.26).

Stock Performance - 09-OCT-98

In the past 30 trading days, NWK's shares have de-clined 25%, compared to a 4% fall in the S&P 500. Average trading volume for the past five days was 84,920 shares, compared with the 40-day moving aver-age of 120,756 shares.

Key Stock Statistics

Dividend Rate/Share	Nil	Shareholders	900
Shs. outstg. (M)	21.6	Market cap. (B)	$0.187
Avg. daily vol. (M)	0.078	Inst. holdings	75%
Tang. Bk. Value/Share	11.22		
Beta	1.78		

Value of $10,000 invested 5 years ago: $ 8,625

Fiscal Year Ending Mar. 31

	1999	1998	1997	1996	1995	1994
Revenues (Million $)						
1Q	71.43	79.97	76.47	79.61	61.54	54.58
2Q	—	77.85	78.40	82.96	66.85	55.01
3Q	—	71.96	83.30	84.56	73.84	61.25
4Q	—	78.95	86.27	91.77	81.81	66.84
Yr.	—	308.7	324.4	338.9	284.0	237.7
Earnings Per Share ($)						
1Q	0.13	0.26	0.21	0.32	0.08	-0.06
2Q	—	0.26	0.24	0.36	0.16	-0.09
3Q	—	0.11	0.31	0.39	0.27	0.02
4Q	—	0.02	0.33	0.43	0.87	-0.24
Yr.	—	0.65	1.08	1.50	1.44	-0.38

Next earnings report expected: mid October

Dividend Data

No cash has been paid. A "poison pill" stock purchase rights plan was adopted in 1989.

 A Division of The McGraw-Hill Companies

Business Summary - 12-OCT-98

Network Equipment Technologies offers a variety of solutions for mission-critical wide-area network (WAN) applications, primarily through sales of networking hardware and software. NWK provides expertise in systems integration, network design, installation, implementation and ongoing service and support. Products are based on a range of technologies and standards which are used throughout the industry and provide support such as switching, adaptation and aggregation for packet-, frame-, cell- and circuit-based applications. NWK allows customers to integrate diverse applications, including voice, data, video, multimedia and imaging across single network infrastructures. The company also offers efficient, cost effective and manageable backbones for wide area networks (WANs), along with a range of access capabilities. NWK allows carriers to provide a wide range of competitive service offerings such as native frame relay and Asynchronous Transfer Mode (ATM) services and enterprise customers to access those services or build their own networks.

The company competes primarily in the WAN markets. This segment provides the infrastructure and capability to link local area networks (LANs), campus networks, voice traffic, video and other applications to each other by public carrier-provided transmission facilities. In

WANs, the center, or core, is the high-capacity backbone or transmission infrastructure developed and maintained by a major carrier or network service provider. Typically, these are high-speed, high-capacity links using ATM, SONET or other technology and built on switches characterized by high capacity, high reliability and other considerations. Beyond and around the core is an edge layer which defines the area at the boundary between a carrier or service provider and its enterprise customer or other user. This is the area where significant value is added by switches providing features to help manage traffic, service levels, concentration, and with capabilities such as support of traffic from multiple interfaces such as Frame Relay and native ATM.

Target markets and industries for NWK include carriers or network service providers; enterprises such as financial institutions, manufacturers, utilities and retailers; and governmental agencies.

In 1997, NWK introduced the Promina product family, delivering on its promise to bring ATM technology to its customers. NWK's ATM products include the Promina 800 Series, the Promina 2000 and the Promina 4000.

Sales to the U.S. government and agencies accounted for 33% of net sales in FY 98 (Mar.), versus 29% in the prior year. International sales accounted for 37% of net sales in FY 98, up from 35% in FY 97.

Per Share Data ($)

(Year Ended Mar. 31)	1998	1997	1996	1995	1994	1993	1992	1991	1990	1989
Tangible Bk. Val.	11.03	10.11	8.85	5.43	3.45	3.82	4.15	4.29	7.45	6.21
Cash Flow	1.52	1.89	2.25	2.23	0.56	0.28	0.17	-2.65	1.55	1.65
Earnings	0.65	1.08	1.50	1.44	-0.38	-0.71	-0.76	-3.47	0.93	1.15
Dividends	Nil	Nil	Nil	Nil	Nil	Nil	Nil	Nil	Nil	Nil
Payout Ratio	Nil	Nil	Nil	Nil	Nil	NA	Nil	Nil	Nil	Nil
Cal. Yrs.	1997	1996	1995	1994	1993	1992	1991	1990	1989	1988
Prices - High	22³⁄₈	36	42	24³⁄₄	11¹⁄₂	18¹⁄₄	15⁷⁄₈	34³⁄₈	31⁷⁄₈	22⁵⁄₈
- Low	11¹⁄₄	11¹⁄₈	19³⁄₄	7³⁄₈	5³⁄₈	8⁷⁄₈	4	5	16¹⁄₂	14
P/E Ratio - High	34	33	28	17	NM	NA	NM	NM	34	20
- Low	17	10	13	5	NM	NA	NM	NM	18	12

Income Statement Analysis (Million $)

	1998	1997	1996	1995	1994	1993	1992	1991	1990	1989
Revs.	309	324	339	284	238	219	181	135	181	137
Oper. Inc.	36.3	49.8	62.9	40.8	13.5	25.4	17.4	-30.3	30.8	33.7
Depr.	19.2	17.4	15.5	14.8	15.8	15.5	13.7	11.6	9.1	7.0
Int. Exp.	2.0	2.3	4.7	5.2	5.3	5.3	5.8	6.2	6.3	1.8
Pretax Inc.	21.1	35.8	48.2	23.3	-6.3	-11.1	-12.6	-58.8	21.4	26.6
Eff. Tax Rate	32%	35%	35%	NM	NM	NM	NM	NM	37%	40%
Net Inc.	14.3	23.3	31.4	27.1	-6.3	-11.1	-11.2	-49.6	13.5	16.0

Balance Sheet & Other Fin. Data (Million $)

	1998	1997	1996	1995	1994	1993	1992	1991	1990	1989
Cash	59.5	139	112	86.6	41.6	52.1	44.8	49.8	66.6	20.4
Curr. Assets	270	258	238	190	137	132	118	111	159	69.0
Total Assets	335	62.9	282	232	187	187	177	170	234	122
Curr. Liab.	70.1	25.8	64.0	61.8	59.1	54.8	42.9	34.6	42.7	26.7
LT Debt	25.8	25.8	33.5	68.6	68.6	68.7	69.8	71.5	80.3	8.4
Common Eqty.	237	213	184	102	59.0	61.0	64.0	62.0	105	84.0
Total Cap.	265	292	218	170	128	132	134	135	191	95.0
Cap. Exp.	30.3	13.9	17.2	8.3	14.2	15.2	11.1	10.1	20.7	17.9
Cash Flow	33.6	40.7	46.8	41.9	9.4	4.4	2.4	-38.0	22.6	23.0
Curr. Ratio	3.9	4.1	3.7	3.1	2.3	2.4	2.8	3.2	3.7	2.6
% LT Debt of Cap.	9.7	10.8	15.4	40.3	53.7	52.1	52.2	52.8	42.1	8.9
% Net Inc.of Revs.	4.6	7.2	9.3	9.5	NM	NM	NM	NM	7.5	11.7
% Ret. on Assets	4.5	8.0	12.2	12.4	NM	NM	NM	NM	7.4	14.4
% Ret. on Equity	6.4	11.7	21.9	32.6	NM	NM	NM	NM	14.0	21.3

Data as orig. reptd.; bef. results of disc. opers. and/or spec. items. Per share data adj. for stk. divs. as of ex-div. date. Bold denotes diluted EPS (FASB 128). E-Estimated. NA-Not Available. NM-Not Meaningful. NR-Not Ranked.

Office—6500 Paseo Padre Parkway, Fremont, CA 94555.**Tel**—(510) 713-7300. **Website**—http://www.net.com **Chrmn**—H.A. Wolf. **Pres & CEO**—J. J. Francesconi. **Dirs**—D. R. Doll, J. K. Dutton, J. J. Francesconi, W. J. Gill, G. M. Scalise, H. A. Wolf. **Transfer Agent & Registrar**—First National Bank of Boston. **Incorporated**—in California in 1983; reincorporated in Delaware in 1986. **Empl**— 1,408. **S&P Analyst:** K.J.F.

New England Business Service   1645
NYSE Symbol **NEB**
In S&P SmallCap 600

07-OCT-98

Industry:
Office Equipment & Supplies

Summary: NEB supplies standardized business forms, software and related printed products, selling primarily by mail order to small businesses throughout the U.S., Canada and the U.K.

Quantitative Evaluations

Recent Price • 29⅞
52 Wk Range • 34½-26⅞

Yield • 2.7%
12-Mo. P/E • 16.9

Outlook
(1 Lowest—5 Highest)
• **4−**

Fair Value
• **34¾**

Risk
• **Average**

Earn./Div. Rank
• **B+**

Technical Eval.
• **Neutral** since 9/98

Rel. Strength Rank
(1 Lowest—99 Highest)
• **87**

Insider Activity
• **Neutral**

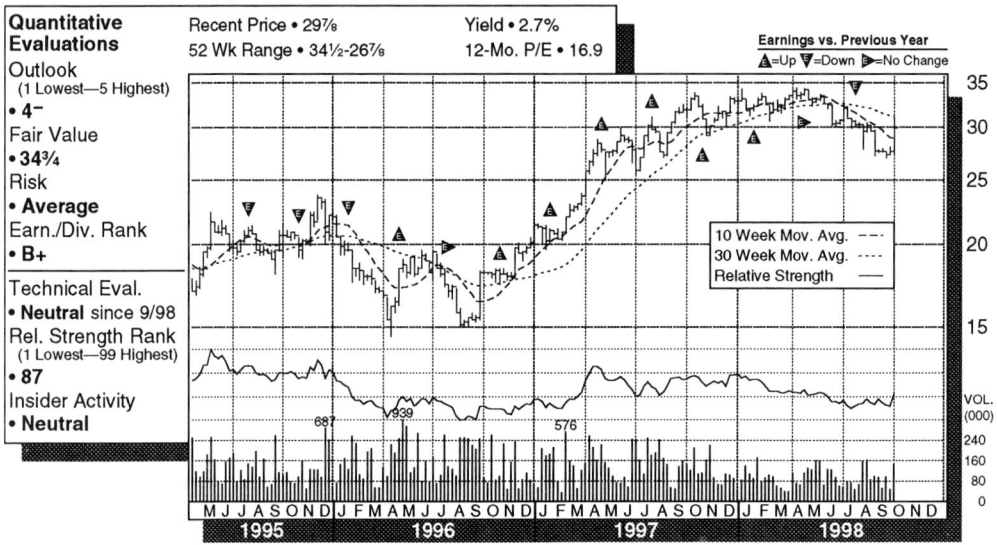

Earnings vs. Previous Year
▲=Up ▼=Down ▷=No Change

10 Week Mov. Avg. - - -
30 Week Mov. Avg. ......
Relative Strength —

Business Profile - 07-OCT-98

Four acquisitions during the past two fiscal years accounted for 92% of the revenue rise during FY 98 (Jun.). The company expects to achieve revenue growth in excess of 30% for FY 99, as the full impact of the acquisitions materialize. NEB's acquisition activity continued with the June 1998 purchase of McBee Systems. The purchase price for this manufacturer of small business products was $63 million in cash and stock. Despite the lower-margin products sold through the new acquisitions, management believes cost savings initiatives will be realized that will counter the unfavorable product mix. In addition, the company expects general and administrative expenses to fall as a percentage of revenues in the coming fiscal year.

Operational Review - 07-OCT-98

Net sales for the year ended June 27, 1998, rose 35%, year to year, due to acquisitions and price increases. Despite a rise in revenue from lower-margin products, profitability improved on a reduction in general and administrative expenses, partially attributable to economies gained from the acquisitions; operating income jumped 57%. Following greater depreciation and amortization charges, higher interest expense, and taxes at 39.8%, versus 40.6%, net income climbed 34%, to $24,934,000 ($1.77 per share), from $18,649,000 ($1.38).

Stock Performance - 02-OCT-98

In the past 30 trading days, NEB's shares have increased 1%, compared to a 7% fall in the S&P 500. Average trading volume for the past five days was 28,840 shares, compared with the 40-day moving average of 19,926 shares.

Key Stock Statistics

Dividend Rate/Share	0.80	Shareholders	700
Shs. outstg. (M)	13.8	Market cap. (B)	$0.394
Avg. daily vol. (M)	0.016	Inst. holdings	80%
Tang. Bk. Value/Share	2.10		
Beta	0.60		

Value of $10,000 invested 5 years ago: $ 20,769

Fiscal Year Ending Jun. 30

	1998	1997	1996	1995	1994	1993
Revenues (Million $)						
1Q	75.62	60.70	63.79	62.08	59.82	57.30
2Q	81.65	63.20	67.16	69.48	65.55	60.30
3Q	98.00	64.13	63.10	68.83	63.42	59.38
4Q	100.5	75.39	60.91	63.33	62.46	60.16
Yr.	355.8	263.4	254.9	263.7	251.3	237.1
Earnings Per Share ($)						
1Q	0.42	0.05	0.04	0.30	0.05	0.21
2Q	0.46	0.43	0.26	0.31	0.02	0.22
3Q	**0.45**	0.45	0.25	0.17	0.32	0.22
4Q	**0.43**	0.45	0.26	0.26	0.32	0.28
Yr.	**1.77**	1.37	0.81	1.07	1.01	0.93

Next earnings report expected: late October

Dividend Data (Dividends have been paid since 1965.)

Amount ($)	Date Decl.	Ex-Div. Date	Stock of Record	Payment Date
0.200	Oct. 24	Nov. 05	Nov. 07	Nov. 21 '97
0.200	Jan. 23	Feb. 04	Feb. 06	Feb. 20 '98
0.200	Apr. 28	May. 08	May. 12	May. 26 '98
0.200	Jul. 24	Aug. 05	Aug. 07	Aug. 21 '98

A Division of The **McGraw·Hill** Companies

Business Summary - 07-OCT-98

New England Business Service (NEB) markets office and business products primarily by mail order to small businesses. Products include more than 1,000 standardized imprinted manual and computer business forms, check writing systems, stationery, labels, custom forms and other printed products principally designed and imprinted in-house.

The company's proprietary software consists of user-friendly forms-filling packages. The software is developed to perform a variety of tasks required to manage a small business and is compatible with all of NEB's business forms and other printed products.

NEB's standard manual business forms include billing forms, work orders, job proposals, purchase orders, invoices and personnel forms. Standard business forms provide small businesses with the financial and other business records necessary to efficiently run a business. NEB's stationery products, which include letterhead, envelopes and business cards, are available in a variety formats and colors and are designed to give small businesses a more professional image.

The company provides a broad range of printed products compatible with the software NEB distributes and with over 3,500 other third-party small business software packages. Computer business forms include checks, billing forms and work orders, among others.

In addition, NEB offers promotional products, such as labels and pricing tags, and packaging material, including boxes and wrapping material.

NEB's primary channel of distribution is mail order. Promotional materials are delivered to 1,922,000 customers and 9,400,000 prospects every year. The retail channel includes a broad network of 30,000 dealers. The company considers its marketing database and customer/prospect list as a key competitive advantage.

NEB's growth is strongly correlated to the strength of its target small business market. The cost of paper accounts for approximately 20% of NEB's total revenues. In addition, NEB is heavily reliant on the U.S. Postal Service for the delivery of most of its promotional materials. To date, the company has been able to offset increases in paper prices and postal rates through cost reduction programs and selected price increases. NEB has recently faced increasing competition from low-price, high volume office supply chain stores and smaller local printers who have access to newly available low cost, high quality printing technology.

In June 1998, NEB acquired McBee Systems, Inc., for approximately $48.5 million in cash and $12.6 million in NEB stock. McBee manufactures and markets a line of checks and related products to small business in the United States and Canada through a dedicated field sales force. Although accretive in the longer term, NEB expects the acquisition will reduce FY 99 EPS by $0.07.

Per Share Data ($) (Year Ended Jun. 30)	1998	1997	1996	1995	1994	1993	1992	1991	1990	1989
Tangible Bk. Val.	NM	3.58	5.42	6.16	6.43	6.19	6.18	6.61	6.27	6.01
Cash Flow	2.85	2.03	1.51	1.90	1.77	1.58	1.63	1.73	1.81	1.65
Earnings	1.77	1.37	0.81	1.07	1.01	0.93	1.02	1.24	1.23	1.40
Dividends	0.80	0.80	0.80	0.80	0.80	0.80	0.80	0.80	0.76	0.66
Payout Ratio	45%	58%	99%	75%	79%	86%	77%	64%	61%	47%
Prices - High	34½	34¼	22⅛	23¾	21¾	20¼	19¾	20¼	19¾	23¾
- Low	29¾	19⅝	14½	16¾	17¼	14¾	13½	12¼	10½	17
P/E Ratio - High	19	25	27	22	22	22	19	16	16	17
- Low	17	14	18	16	17	16	13	10	9	12
Income Statement Analysis (Million $)										
Revs.	356	263	255	264	251	237	232	232	233	226
Oper. Inc.	60.1	42.2	32.8	41.8	43.4	32.8	32.2	39.8	38.9	44.5
Depr.	15.2	9.1	10.3	12.7	11.6	9.9	9.5	7.9	7.6	7.1
Int. Exp.	4.6	0.5	Nil	Nil	Nil	0.0	0.3	0.4	0.8	1.3
Pretax Inc.	41.4	31.4	20.0	28.1	27.6	24.1	24.9	34.1	33.4	39.1
Eff. Tax Rate	40%	41%	41%	42%	44%	41%	36%	40%	38%	39%
Net Inc.	24.9	18.6	11.9	16.3	15.6	14.2	15.9	20.3	20.6	24.0
Balance Sheet & Other Fin. Data (Million $)										
Cash	10.8	7.8	18.4	23.0	41.0	28.1	31.6	45.2	39.1	43.3
Curr. Assets	101	68.4	71.3	77.5	85.3	69.0	74.8	87.5	84.3	84.4
Total Assets	308	141	104	125	132	121	121	134	130	130
Curr. Liab.	50.7	33.3	27.3	32.2	30.1	25.3	25.6	24.1	21.6	20.0
LT Debt	141	27.0	Nil	Nil	Nil	Nil	Nil	Nil	3.3	6.7
Common Eqty.	115	80.6	76.0	92.0	99	95.0	94.0	108	104	102
Total Cap.	256	108	76.0	92.0	101	95.0	95.0	109	108	110
Cap. Exp.	13.3	9.6	9.4	10.8	6.1	6.5	9.7	9.2	8.8	11.1
Cash Flow	40.2	27.7	22.3	29.0	27.2	24.2	25.5	28.2	28.2	31.1
Curr. Ratio	2.0	2.0	2.6	2.4	2.8	2.7	2.9	3.6	3.9	4.2
% LT Debt of Cap.	55.2	25.0	Nil	Nil	Nil	Nil	Nil	Nil	3.1	6.1
% Net Inc.of Revs.	7.0	7.1	4.7	6.2	6.2	6.0	6.9	8.8	8.8	10.6
% Ret. on Assets	11.1	15.2	10.5	13.0	12.3	11.7	13.0	15.5	16.0	19.1
% Ret. on Equity	25.6	23.8	14.3	17.4	15.9	15.0	16.4	19.3	20.3	24.3

Data as orig. reptd.; bef. results of disc. opers. and/or spec. items. Per share data adj. for stk. divs. as of ex-div. date. Bold denotes diluted EPS (FASB 128). E-Estimated. NA-Not Available. NM-Not Meaningful. NR-Not Ranked.

Office—500 Main St., Groton, MA 01471. **Tel**—(978) 448-6111. **Website**—http://www.nebs.com **Chrmn, Pres & CEO**—R.J. Murray. **VP-CFO**—John F. Fairbanks. **Investor Contact**—Timothy D. Althof VP (978) 449-3425.**Dirs**—P. A. Brooke, R. L. Gable, B. H. Lacy, H. W. Moller, R. J. Murray, J. R. Rhoads Jr., R. H. Rhoads, M. A. Szostak, B. E. Stern. **Transfer Agent & Registrar**—BankBoston, c/o Boston EquiServe. **Incorporated**—in Massachusetts in 1955; reincorporated in Delaware in 1986. **Empl**— 3,738. **S&P Analyst:** Jordan Horoschak

03-OCT-98 Industry:
Natural Gas

Summary: Through New Jersey Natural Gas Co., this utility holding company supplies gas to some 380,000 customers in central and northern New Jersey.

Quantitative Evaluations

Recent Price • 36⅞
52 Wk Range • 42-31½

Yield • 4.4%
12-Mo. P/E • 15.8

Outlook
(1 Lowest—5 Highest)
• **2**

Fair Value
• **35¾**

Risk
• **Low**

Earn./Div. Rank
• **B+**

Technical Eval.
• **Bearish** since 8/98

Rel. Strength Rank
(1 Lowest—99 Highest)
• **93**

Insider Activity
• **Favorable**

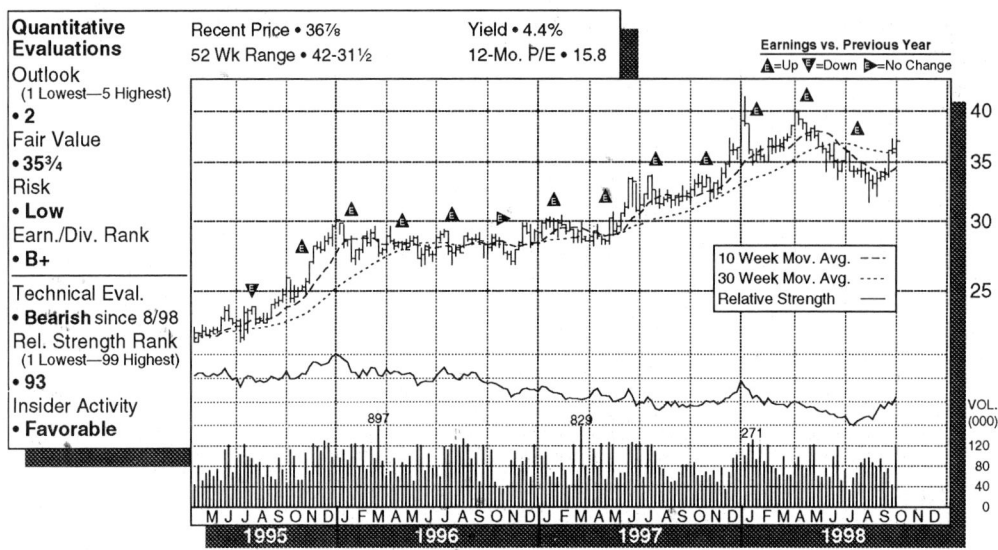

Business Profile - 05-AUG-98

NJR's strategy for future growth in a changing industry is based on providing customers with smart energy choices. Sales and earnings continue to benefit from an annual customer growth rate of 3%, well above the national average for natural gas distribution companies. In the first nine months of FY 98 (Sep.), the company added 9,375 new customers, 38% of whom converted to gas from other fuels. In October 1997, NJR sold its last significant operating real estate asset, bringing the total proceeds from real estate sales over the past two years to $107 million. Management believes that the real estate sales will allow the company to focus on its core energy services business.

Operational Review - 05-AUG-98

Revenues in the nine months ended June 30, 1998, were up only slightly, year to year. Residential sales slid 0.8%, while commercial, industrial and other sales fell 22%; off-system sales rose 16%. Weather was 11% warmer than normal. Profitability benefited from continued customer growth at New Jersey Natural Gas, cost control measures and a gain from the sale of a real estate property. Net income advanced 3.8%, to $45,621,000 ($2.55 a share), from $43,971,000 ($2.43).

Stock Performance - 02-OCT-98

In the past 30 trading days, NJR's shares have increased 12%, compared to a 7% fall in the S&P 500. Average trading volume for the past five days was 28,040 shares, compared with the 40-day moving average of 17,413 shares.

Key Stock Statistics

Dividend Rate/Share	1.64	Shareholders	18,500
Shs. outstg. (M)	17.8	Market cap. (B)	$0.658
Avg. daily vol. (M)	0.017	Inst. holdings	34%
Tang. Bk. Value/Share	15.57		
Beta	0.43		

Value of $10,000 invested 5 years ago: $ 20,569

Fiscal Year Ending Sep. 30

	1998	1997	1996	1995	1994	1993
Revenues (Million $)						
1Q	220.4	188.6	159.7	126.0	136.2	132.6
2Q	266.6	285.4	233.9	197.2	222.8	189.5
3Q	113.4	121.2	94.46	74.36	75.61	75.70
4Q	—	101.4	60.40	56.98	64.22	56.90
Yr.	—	696.5	548.5	454.6	498.8	454.7
Earnings Per Share ($)						
1Q	**0.79**	**0.71**	0.69	0.65	0.62	0.61
2Q	**1.60**	1.58	1.50	1.46	1.37	1.37
3Q	**0.16**	-0.15	0.12	0.07	0.19	0.06
4Q	—	-0.23	-0.25	-0.25	-0.28	-0.30
Yr.	—	2.22	2.06	1.93	1.89	1.72

Next earnings report expected: late October

Dividend Data (Dividends have been paid since 1951.)

Amount ($)	Date Decl.	Ex-Div. Date	Stock of Record	Payment Date
0.410	Nov. 19	Dec. 11	Dec. 15	Jan. 01 '98
0.410	Feb. 06	Mar. 12	Mar. 16	Apr. 01 '98
0.410	May. 14	Jun. 11	Jun. 15	Jul. 01 '98
0.410	Jul. 07	Sep. 11	Sep. 15	Oct. 01 '98

A Division of The McGraw-Hill Companies

Business Summary - 05-AUG-98

A 3% rise in gas-utility customers and higher profits from emerging energy markets fueled earnings growth for this marketer of natural gas and related energy services in FY 97 (Sep.). New Jersey Resources Corp.'s (NJR) utility subsidiary, New Jersey Natural Gas Co. (NJNG), added 11,500 new customers in FY 97, with similar additions expected in each of the next several years.

Through its NJNG subsidiary, the company provides regulated natural gas service to about 383,000 customers in central and northern New Jersey. In addition to customer growth through new construction, the utility pursues conversions from other fuels, such as oil, and in FY 97 it converted the heating systems of some 1,000 existing customers. Firm sales of gas totaled 51 Bcf in FY 97. NJNG also participates in "capacity release" and "off-system" sales programs whereby NJNG releases some of the capacity it has secured on interstate pipelines and sells excess gas supplies when demand is not at its peak. These programs reach wholesale customers as far away as Texas, well beyond NJNG's local franchise area. In FY 97, capacity release and off-system sales totaled 83 Bcf. Under a margin-sharing formula approved by state regulators, NJNG retains 20% of the gross margin earned from these transactions, and the balance is credited to firm utility customers to help stabilize utility prices. These programs generated gross margins of $5.4 million for the company in FY 97.

The New Jersey Natural Energy Co. (NJNE) unit was formed in 1995 to participate in the unregulated marketing of natural gas and energy services. NJNE must compete for its retail gas customers against a score of other marketers, and as of the end of FY 97, NJNE supplied gas to some 7,000 retail customers. NJNE's retail sales and gas under management totaled 76 Bcf in FY 97, double the volume sold or managed in FY 96.

Starting in January 1998, NJNG opened its Natural Solutions supplier choice program to an additional 25,000 residential customers. In April 1997, the first phase of the program was fully subscribed, with 5,000 NJNG customers enrolling. By unbundling, or separating, the sale of gas from its delivery, the program permits NJNG's residential and small commercial customers to choose another gas supplier, an option already available to industrial and large commercial customers. Under a fixed-price option, residential customers will also be allowed to lock in the unit price of gas before the start of the winter season.

Per Share Data ($)

(Year Ended Sep. 30)	1997	1996	1995	1994	1993	1992	1991	1990	1989	1988
Tangible Bk. Val.	15.34	15.12	14.55	14.46	14.72	14.16	12.85	13.27	13.65	12.40
Earnings	2.22	2.06	1.93	1.89	1.72	1.64	0.83	0.97	1.45	1.67
Dividends	1.60	1.55	1.52	1.52	1.52	1.52	1.50	1.44	1.36	1.28
Payout Ratio	72%	75%	98%	80%	88%	93%	181%	148%	94%	77%
Prices - High	42	29⅞	30½	27⅜	29½	25⅛	21⅛	20⅞	21½	20⅝
- Low	28⅛	26⅝	21½	19¾	24	18¼	17	17⅛	17⅛	16¾
P/E Ratio - High	19	15	16	14	17	15	25	22	15	12
- Low	13	13	11	10	14	11	20	18	12	10

Income Statement Analysis (Million $)

	1997	1996	1995	1994	1993	1992	1991	1990	1989	1988
Revs.	697	549	455	499	455	412	335	325	330	295
Depr.	25.8	23.2	23.0	27.6	25.4	24.3	21.7	18.3	16.1	13.5
Maint.	Nil	NA	NA	NA	NA	6.4	7.3	8.0	6.5	5.4
Fxd. Chgs. Cov.	3.8	3.7	2.8	3.0	2.8	2.5	1.7	1.9	2.3	2.6
Constr. Credits	Nil	Nil	Nil	Nil	3.2	3.3	3.6	2.6	2.2	1.9
Eff. Tax Rate	34%	34%	32%	30%	30%	31%	31%	31%	32%	34%
Net Inc.	39.9	37.1	33.9	33.9	28.5	23.5	11.3	13.0	16.4	16.0

Balance Sheet & Other Fin. Data (Million $)

	1997	1996	1995	1994	1993	1992	1991	1990	1989	1988
Gross Prop.	878	856	786	859	831	770	725	673	588	503
Cap. Exp.	47.0	56.1	53.8	58.6	70.4	47.6	57.4	83.2	84.8	84.0
Net Prop.	659	655	596	640	633	592	567	533	463	391
Capitalization:										
LT Debt	291	303	352	324	311	252	263	228	209	155
% LT Debt	49	51	57	54	54	49	55	54	52	51
Pfd.	20.8	21.0	21.0	22.1	22.3	32.6	32.9	13.2	13.4	13.7
% Pfd.	3.50	3.50	3.30	3.70	3.90	6.30	6.90	3.10	3.30	4.50
Common	278	274	259	250	248	231	179	179	180	136
% Common	47	46	41	42	43	45	38	43	45	45
Total Cap.	591	598	632	661	642	577	529	475	451	349
% Oper. Ratio	91.2	89.1	86.9	89.2	89.0	88.7	89.6	89.5	89.5	89.7
% Earn. on Net Prop.	9.4	9.5	9.5	8.7	8.2	8.0	6.3	6.8	8.1	8.5
% Return On Revs.	5.7	6.8	7.4	6.8	6.3	5.7	3.4	4.0	5.0	5.4
% Return On Invest. Capital	10.4	11.5	10.8	8.6	8.4	8.6	7.0	7.4	8.8	9.7
% Return On Com. Equity	14.5	13.9	13.3	13.4	11.9	11.4	6.3	7.2	10.4	13.8

Data as orig. reptd.; bef. results of disc opers. and/or spec. items. Per share data adj. for stk. divs. as of ex-div. date. Bold denotes diluted EPS (FASB 128). E-Estimated. NA-Not Available. NM-Not Meaningful. NR-Not Ranked.

Office—1415 Wyckoff Road, P.O. Box 1468, Wall, NJ 07719. **Tel**—(732) 938-1480. **Website**—http://www.njresources.com **Chrmn, Pres & CEO**—L. M. Downes. **SVP & CFO**—G. C. Lockwood. **SVP & Secy**—Oleta J. Harden. **Investor Contact**—Dennis Puma (732-938-1229). **Dirs**—B. G. Coe, L. S. Coleman, L. M. Downes, J. B. Foster, H. F. Gluck, L. D. Johnson, D. K. Light, D. E. O'Neill, C. G. Stalon, J. J. Unkles, Jr., G. W. Wolf, G. R. Zoffinger. **Transfer Agent & Registrar**—Bank of Boston. **Incorporated**—in New Jersey in 1922. **Empl**— 824. **S&P Analyst**: S.A.H.

03-OCT-98

Industry:
Oil & Gas (Exploration & Production)

Summary: This independent oil and natural gas exploration and production company operates primarily in the Gulf of Mexico offshore Louisiana and Texas.

Quantitative Evaluations

Recent Price • 22⅜	Yield • Nil
52 Wk Range • 33-15⅜	12-Mo. P/E • 27.3

Outlook (1 Lowest—5 Highest)
• **1⁻**

Fair Value
• **21½**

Risk
• **Average**

Earn./Div. Rank
• **NR**

Technical Eval.
• **Bullish** since 9/98

Rel. Strength Rank (1 Lowest—99 Highest)
• **96**

Insider Activity
• **Neutral**

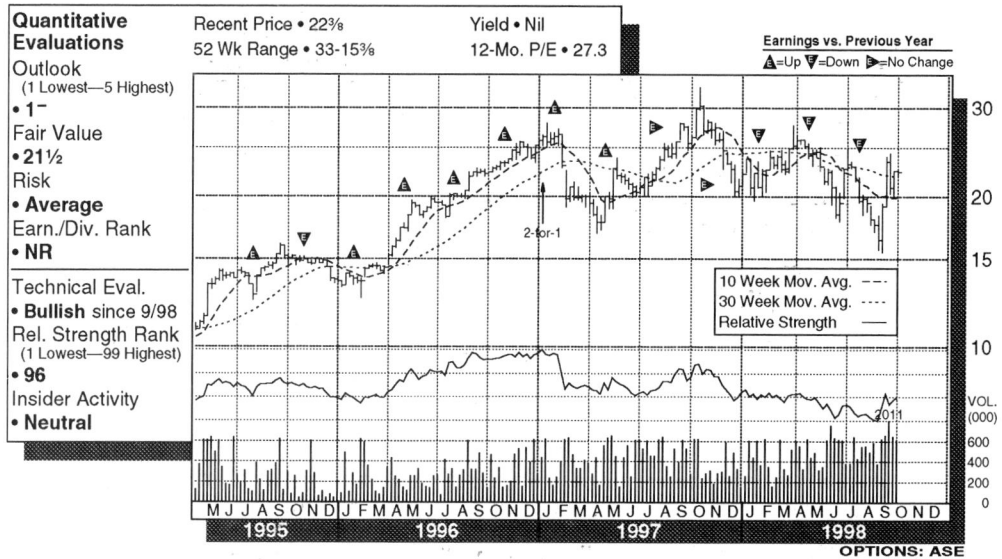

Earnings vs. Previous Year
▲=Up ▼=Down ▶=No Change

10 Week Mov. Avg. – – –
30 Week Mov. Avg. ·····
Relative Strength —

2-for-1

OPTIONS: ASE

Business Profile - 13-MAY-98

This independent oil and gas producer has focused its operations on the Gulf of Mexico offshore Louisiana and Texas. Revenues, profitability and future rate of growth are highly dependent on prevailing prices for natural gas and oil. NFX plans to continue to expand its reserve base and increase its cash flow through exploration, acquisition of proved properties and development of its properties. In October 1997, NFX placed privately $125 million principal amount of senior notes, with the proceeds used to pay down borrowings under the company's revolving credit facility. The company has increased its planned 1998 capital expenditures to $200 million from its original $153 million budget. Early 1998 success has resulted in an increase in planned development and construction activity.

Operational Review - 13-MAY-98

For the first three months of 1998, oil and gas revenues climbed 6.5%, year to year, reflecting increases in oil and gas production, partly offset by lower oil prices. Oil and gas production was 20.1 Bcf of natural gas equivalent, up 24% from the year-earlier level. Net income was down 44%, to $6,712,000 ($0.18 a share, diluted), from $11,887,000 ($0.31).

Stock Performance - 02-OCT-98

In the past 30 trading days, NFX's shares have increased 27%, compared to a 7% fall in the S&P 500. Average trading volume for the past five days was 147,800 shares, compared with the 40-day moving average of 187,418 shares.

Key Stock Statistics

Dividend Rate/Share	Nil	Shareholders	2,000
Shs. outstg. (M)	36.2	Market cap. (B)	$0.810
Avg. daily vol. (M)	0.267	Inst. holdings	62%
Tang. Bk. Value/Share	8.41		
Beta	NA		

Value of $10,000 invested 5 years ago: NA

Fiscal Year Ending Dec. 31

	1998	1997	1996	1995	1994	1993
Revenues (Million $)						
1Q	49.98	46.93	32.96	19.03	13.86	12.94
2Q	49.90	42.35	33.01	24.81	16.40	16.43
3Q	—	49.86	35.80	24.62	18.95	14.17
4Q	—	60.26	47.48	26.14	20.53	16.65
Yr.	—	199.4	149.3	94.60	69.73	60.18
Earnings Per Share ($)						
1Q	**0.18**	**0.31**	0.21	0.10	0.08	0.11
2Q	**0.10**	**0.21**	0.21	0.12	0.10	0.12
3Q	—	**0.23**	0.23	0.10	0.12	0.13
4Q	—	**0.32**	0.37	0.13	0.10	0.13
Yr.	—	**1.07**	1.03	0.45	0.40	0.49

Next earnings report expected: late October

Dividend Data

The company does not intend to pay cash dividends on its common stock in the foreseeable future, but to retain any earnings for the future operation and development of the business.

A Division of The McGraw·Hill Companies

Business Summary - 13-MAY-98

Newfield Exploration is an independent oil and gas concern engaged in the exploration, development and acquisition of oil and natural gas properties located in the Gulf of Mexico, primarily offshore Louisiana in water depths of less than 300 ft. Its strategy is to expand its reserve base and increase cash flow through a balanced program of exploring and developing existing properties and acquiring properties which it believes offer a significant drilling upside. At the end of 1997, the company owned interests in 440 wells and operated 95 platforms.

Revenues, operating cash flow and net income all improved in 1997, bolstered by a combination of robust oil and gas prices and a 31% jump in production volumes, to 74.0 Bcf of natural gas equivalent (Bcfe), from 456.7 Bcfe in 1996. Revenues rose 31% in 1997, while operating cash flow advanced 29%, and EPS increased 3.8% ($1.07, versus $1.03).

Since the company's inception in 1988, and its first discovery and acquisition of oil and gas reserves in 1990, NFX has added a total of 706 Bcfe of proved reserves. Exploration and development activities, accounted for 37% of the added reserves, while acquisitions accounted for 38%, and exploitation of acquired opportunities made up the balance. NFX had estimated oil and gas net proved reserves of 435.3 Bcfe at December 31, 1997, consisting of 16.3 MMBbls of oil and 337.5 Bcf of natural gas. Proved reserve replacement as a percent of production was 251% in 1997.

Newfield's current capital budget for 1998 is $200 million, a figure that represents work the company knows will be done, as opposed to being an estimate of how much it would like to invest. Therefore, NFX may very well spend additional funds for capital projects. NFX's capital expenditures totaled $253 million in 1997, compared with $164 million in the previous year. Part of Newfield's 1998 capital funding budget will be meted out on 15-20 exploratory drilling prospects. During 1996, the company had a 50% success rate with its exploratory drilling program, with 9 of the 18 wells drilled being productive.

As in the past, NFX intends to develop additional exploratory drilling prospects on its existing properties through the extensive application of 3-D seismic and other advanced technologies. In concert with its balanced capital program strategy, the company will also continue to pursue proved property additions through acquisitions.

Per Share Data ($)

(Year Ended Dec. 31)	1997	1996	1995	1994	1993	1992	1991	1990	1989	1988
Tangible Bk. Val.	8.12	6.81	5.63	5.08	4.62	4.29	NA	NA	NA	NA
Cash Flow	3.54	2.75	1.83	1.35	1.36	1.57	NA	NA	NA	NA
Earnings	1.07	1.03	0.45	0.40	0.49	0.49	NA	NA	NA	NA
Dividends	Nil	Nil	Nil	Nil	Nil	NA	NA	NA	NA	NA
Payout Ratio	Nil	Nil	Nil	Nil	Nil	NA	NA	NA	NA	NA
Prices - High	33	26½	16⅛	13	9¼	NA	NA	NA	NA	NA
- Low	16⅞	12½	9	8¾	7⅞	NA	NA	NA	NA	NA
P/E Ratio - High	31	26	36	32	19	NA	NA	NA	NA	NA
- Low	16	12	20	22	16	NA	NA	NA	NA	NA

Income Statement Analysis (Million $)

	1997	1996	1995	1994	1993	1992	1991	1990	1989	1988
Revs.	199	149	94.6	69.7	60.2	59.6	NA	NA	NA	NA
Oper. Inc.	159	123	74.1	56.4	49.4	49.7	NA	NA	NA	NA
Depr. Depl. & Amort.	94.0	64.0	50.0	34.1	25.1	28.6	NA	NA	NA	NA
Int. Exp.	3.3	0.4	0.2	0.4	0.1	1.5	NA	NA	NA	NA
Pretax Inc.	62.4	59.3	25.0	22.5	21.8	19.7	NA	NA	NA	NA
Eff. Tax Rate	35%	35%	35%	36%	36%	34%	NA	NA	NA	NA
Net Inc.	40.6	38.5	16.3	14.4	14.0	13.0	NA	NA	NA	NA

Balance Sheet & Other Fin. Data (Million $)

	1997	1996	1995	1994	1993	1992	1991	1990	1989	1988
Cash	8.2	13.3	12.5	18.6	65.0	NA	NA	NA	NA	NA
Curr. Assets	64.8	61.3	42.8	35.9	88.3	NA	NA	NA	NA	NA
Total Assets	554	396	227	216	184	NA	NA	NA	NA	NA
Curr. Liab.	64.4	49.8	31.6	24.9	18.1	NA	NA	NA	NA	NA
LT Debt	130	60.0	25.2	0.6	0.5	0.6	NA	NA	NA	NA
Common Eqty.	292	145	194	169	153	137	NA	NA	NA	NA
Total Cap.	486	249	245	190	165	NA	NA	NA	NA	NA
Cap. Exp.	243	159	107	115	43.8	NA	NA	NA	NA	NA
Cash Flow	135	103	66.3	48.6	39.1	41.6	NA	NA	NA	NA
Curr. Ratio	1.0	1.2	1.4	1.4	4.9	NA	NA	NA	NA	NA
% LT Debt of Cap.	26.7	24.1	10.3	0.3	0.3	NA	NA	NA	NA	NA
% Ret. on Assets	8.6	11.4	6.6	7.2	9.1	NA	NA	NA	NA	NA
% Ret. on Equity	15.3	17.8	9.0	8.9	11.1	NA	NA	NA	NA	NA

Data as orig. reptd.; bef. results of disc opers. and/or spec. items. Per share data adj. for stk. divs. as of ex-div. date. Bold denotes diluted EPS (FASB 128). E-Estimated. NA-Not Available. NM-Not Meaningful. NR-Not Ranked.

Office—363 North Sam Houston Parkway East, Suite 2020, Houston, TX 77060. Tel—(281) 847-6000. Fax—(281) 847-6006. Chrmn, CEO & Pres—J. B. Foster. Treas—J. P. Ulm II. VP-Secy—T. W. Rathert. Investor Contact—J. P. Ulm, II. Dirs—P. J. Burguieres, C. W. Duncan, Jr., J. B. Foster, D. Hendrix, T. Huffington, H. H. Newman, T. G. Ricks, J. C. Sawhill, C. E. Shultz, R. W. Waldrup. Transfer Agent & Registrar—ChaseMellon Shareholders Services, Ridgefield Park, NJ. Incorporated—in Delaware in 1988. Empl— 86. S&P Analyst: M.J.C.

STANDARD &POOR'S

STOCK REPORTS

Norrell Corp.

1686R

NYSE Symbol **NRL**

In S&P SmallCap 600

03-OCT-98

Industry:
Services (Employment)

Summary: This company provides a broad range of temporary personnel and outsourcing services through a national network of company-owned and franchised locations.

Quantitative Evaluations

Outlook
(1 Lowest—5 Highest)
• **5**

Fair Value
• **29¾**

Risk
• **Average**

Earn./Div. Rank
• **NR**

Technical Eval.
• **Neutral** since 9/98

Rel. Strength Rank
(1 Lowest—99 Highest)
• **47**

Insider Activity
• **Neutral**

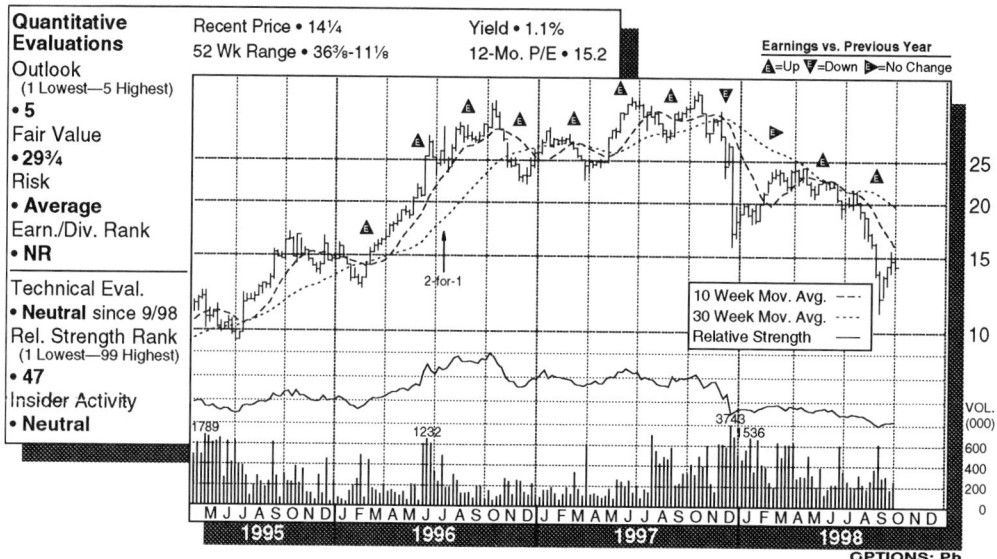

Recent Price • 14¼
52 Wk Range • 36⅜-11⅛
Yield • 1.1%
12-Mo. P/E • 15.2

Earnings vs. Previous Year
▲=Up ▼=Down ▶=No Change

10 Week Mov. Avg. -----
30 Week Mov. Avg. ······
Relative Strength ——

2-for-1

OPTIONS: Ph

Business Profile - 22-SEP-98

Growth in staffing services has been adversely affected by difficulty in recruiting employees in a tight labor market. However, this has been offset by strength in the professional services division, aided by acquisitions. Improved results thus far in FY 98 (Oct.) reflected three acquisitions: Imcor, The Trattner Network, and Carson Associates. NRL looks to continue professional services acquisitions in the U.S. and Europe. During September 1998, directors authorized the repurchase of up to 3.8 million common shares (approximately 15% of the shares outstanding).

Operational Review - 22-SEP-98

Revenues in the nine months ended August 2, 1998, rose 11%, year to year, reflecting strong growth in the professional services division. Despite gross margin decreases in staffing and outsourcing services, overall gross margins improved, on professional services acquisitions, which contributed a greater portion of higher margin information technology consulting services. However, results were restricted by acquisition costs, Year 2000 remediation, and expenses to support internal growth; operating income was up 7.3%. A sharp reduction in interest expense outweighed higher depreciation and amortization charges. After taxes at 37.5%, versus 38.0%, net income climbed 14%, to $28,448,000 ($0.99 a share, on 10% more shares), from $24,855,000 ($0.96).

Stock Performance - 02-OCT-98

In the past 30 trading days, NRL's shares have declined 12%, compared to a 7% fall in the S&P 500. Average trading volume for the past five days was 50,500 shares, compared with the 40-day moving average of 65,487 shares.

Key Stock Statistics

Dividend Rate/Share	0.16	Shareholders	200
Shs. outstg. (M)	27.5	Market cap. (B)	$0.392
Avg. daily vol. (M)	0.054	Inst. holdings	43%
Tang. Bk. Value/Share	2.73		
Beta	NA		

Value of $10,000 invested 5 years ago: NA

Fiscal Year Ending Oct. 31

	1998	1997	1996	1995	1994	1993
Revenues (Million $)						
1Q	334.3	281.2	229.3	186.1	154.0	123.0
2Q	352.3	317.9	250.3	196.7	167.0	135.0
3Q	351.2	332.7	255.3	202.2	173.0	144.0
4Q	—	368.2	279.0	227.6	187.0	161.0
Yr.	—	1,300	1,014	812.6	681.0	562.0
Earnings Per Share ($)						
1Q	**0.28**	0.28	0.21	0.16	--	--
2Q	**0.35**	0.33	0.25	0.17	--	--
3Q	**0.37**	0.35	0.26	0.19	--	--
4Q	--	-0.01	0.28	0.20	--	--
Yr.	--	0.91	1.00	0.72	0.69	0.11

Next earnings report expected: early December

Dividend Data (Dividends have been paid since 1994.)

Amount ($)	Date Decl.	Ex-Div. Date	Stock of Record	Payment Date
0.040	Dec. 09	Dec. 17	Dec. 19	Jan. 02 '98
0.040	Mar. 03	Mar. 12	Mar. 16	Apr. 01 '98
0.040	Jun. 02	Jun. 12	Jun. 16	Jul. 01 '98
0.040	Sep. 01	Sep. 11	Sep. 15	Oct. 01 '98

A Division of The McGraw·Hill Companies

Business Summary - 22-SEP-98

Norrell Corp. is a strategic management company and a leading provider of staffing, outsourcing and professional services through a network of 468 company-owned, franchised and outsourcing locations. NRL employs more than 8,000 associates, and in FY 97 (Oct.) placed more than 236,000 people in both temporary and long-term assignments.

The company's overall business strategy is focused on: (i) providing a seamless "spectrum of strategic work force management solutions" to its clients including traditional temporary services, short-term and long-term staffing, value-added outsourcing solutions, and professional services; (ii) establishing itself as a recognized high-quality service provider; (iii) continuing to grow its existing base of business by developing new product offerings from existing services, expanding into additional skill classes, functional areas and technology, and entering into selected new markets; and (iv) pursuing strategic acquisition opportunities that allow the company to develop new services, obtain additional management expertise or enter key geographic markets. Since July 1995, NRL has purchased three information technology services firms, three staffing companies, an accounting services firm and a provider of temporary and permanent executive placements. Norrell believes acquisitions in the area of professional services offer growth and profitability potential which exceeds that of its core staffing business.

As a national provider of temporary personnel and staffing services (68% of FY 97 sales), the company supplies its 19,000 clients with the services of individuals having a wide variety of office, light industrial and other skills, including secretarial, word processing, data entry, telemarketing, assembly, picking, packing and sorting, and shipping and receiving. In addition to providing temporary personnel and staffing services, the company provides its clients with outsourcing solutions (19% of FY 97 sales) in a similar range of office and business functions.

The professional services division (13% of FY 97 sales) grew revenues by 153% in 1997. The division offers information technology services, as well as professional services in the financial area, including providing accounting, bookkeeping and other financial services. The company believes the ongoing shift in revenue mix toward professional services indicates progress in its strategy to expand its faster-growing and higher-margin businesses.

During FY 97, revenues generated from contracts with IBM and UPS accounted for 13.2% and 8.0%, respectively, of total revenues. As a result of the 1997 UPS strike, several UPS locations have not resumed service, and bill rates have been reduced in certain cases.

Per Share Data ($)

(Year Ended Oct. 31)	1997	1996	1995	1994	1993	1992	1991	1990	1989	1988
Tangible Bk. Val.	2.64	2.25	2.56	2.15	0.82	0.14	NA	NA	NA	NA
Cash Flow	1.33	1.25	0.91	0.94	0.43	0.46	0.18	NA	NA	NA
Earnings	0.91	1.00	0.72	0.69	0.11	0.11	-0.21	0.19	NA	NA
Dividends	0.16	0.14	0.12	0.03	Nil	Nil	Nil	Nil	Nil	Nil
Payout Ratio	18%	14%	17%	4%	Nil	Nil	Nil	Nil	Nil	Nil
Prices - High	36³/₈	34¹/₂	17	9⁷/₈	NA	NA	NA	NA	NA	NA
- Low	15⁷/₈	12⁵/₈	9	7	NA	NA	NA	NA	NA	NA
P/E Ratio - High	40	34	24	14	NA	NA	NA	NA	NA	NA
- Low	17	13	12	10	NA	NA	NA	NA	NA	NA

Income Statement Analysis (Million $)

	1997	1996	1995	1994	1993	1992	1991	1990	1989	1988
Revs.	1,300	1,014	813	681	562	399	351	375	374	NA
Oper. Inc.	77.2	50.1	35.1	29.0	26.9	19.7	19.8	NA	NA	NA
Depr.	11.0	6.3	4.4	5.3	7.6	7.9	8.3	NA	NA	NA
Int. Exp.	7.0	1.2	0.2	1.8	3.7	4.5	6.2	6.5	7.3	NA
Pretax Inc.	39.5	51.1	29.0	26.5	5.8	6.4	-3.7	7.5	10.7	NA
Eff. Tax Rate	38%	39%	42%	43%	45%	55%	NM	44%	39%	NA
Net Inc.	24.5	25.3	16.8	15.1	3.1	2.9	-4.5	4.2	6.5	NA

Balance Sheet & Other Fin. Data (Million $)

	1997	1996	1995	1994	1993	1992	1991	1990	1989	1988
Cash	6.7	8.9	5.1	7.4	3.7	3.9	NA	NA	NA	NA
Curr. Assets	238	167	133	107	118	80.0	69.0	73.0	82.0	NA
Total Assets	439	263	176	148	163	135	125	143	155	NA
Curr. Liab.	125	103	79.8	62.1	88.4	53.9	47.2	42.1	51.2	NA
LT Debt	60.1	23.3	2.1	0.4	19.2	27.7	45.3	60.9	59.3	NA
Common Eqty.	207	98.0	70.2	65.1	42.1	43.2	24.8	33.9	36.1	NA
Total Cap.	267	121	72.3	65.5	61.2	70.9	70.1	94.8	95.4	NA
Cap. Exp.	10.9	6.9	5.8	2.0	3.1	1.2	1.6	NA	NA	NA
Cash Flow	35.5	31.6	21.2	20.4	10.7	10.8	3.8	NA	NA	NA
Curr. Ratio	1.9	1.6	1.7	1.7	1.3	1.5	1.5	1.7	1.6	NA
% LT Debt of Cap.	22.5	19.2	2.8	0.6	31.3	39.1	64.6	64.2	62.1	NA
% Net Inc.of Revs.	1.9	2.5	2.1	2.2	0.6	0.7	NM	1.1	1.7	NA
% Ret. on Assets	7.0	11.4	10.4	9.7	2.1	2.2	NM	2.8	4.0	NA
% Ret. on Equity	16.1	29.6	24.8	28.2	7.4	8.5	NM	11.9	16.3	NA

Data as orig. reptd.; bef. results of disc. opers. and/or spec. items. Per share data adj. for stk. divs. as of ex-div. date. Bold denotes diluted EPS (FASB 128). E-Estimated. NA-Not Available. NM-Not Meaningful. NR-Not Ranked.

Office—3535 Piedmont Rd. N.E., Atlanta, GA 30305. **Tel**—(404) 240-3000. **Website**—http://www.norrell.com **Chrmn**—G. W. Millner. **Pres & CEO**—C. D. Miller. **COO**—J. R. Riddle. **SVP & CFO**—S. L. Colabuono. **VP & Secy**—M. H. Hain. **Dirs**—L. J. Bryan, L. E. Burch III, K. Johnson-Street, D. A. McMahon, F. A. Metz Jr., C. D. Miller, G. W. Millner, N. C. Reynolds, C. E. Sanders, T. A. Vadnais. **Transfer Agent & Registrar**—First Union National Bank of North Carolina, Charlotte. **Incorporated**—in Georgia in 1965. **Empl**—8,866. **S&P Analyst:** Jordan Horoschak

03-OCT-98

Industry:
Health Care (Drugs - Generic & Other)

Summary: NVX is engaged in research, development and manufacture of vaccines to prevent human infectious diseases.

Quantitative Evaluations

Recent Price • 10⅛
52 Wk Range • 30¼-6¼

Yield • Nil
12-Mo. P/E • NM

Outlook
(1 Lowest—5 Highest)
• **NA**

Fair Value
• **NA**

Risk
• **High**

Earn./Div. Rank
• **NR**

Technical Eval.
• **Bullish** since 9/98

Rel. Strength Rank
(1 Lowest—99 Highest)
• **60**

Insider Activity
• **NA**

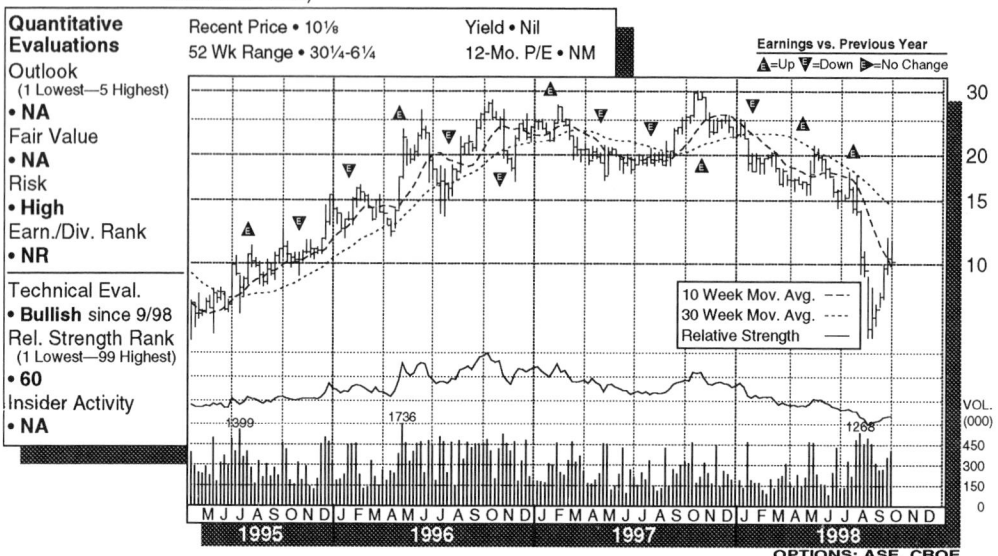

Earnings vs. Previous Year
▲=Up ▼=Down ▶=No Change

10 Week Mov. Avg. ---
30 Week Mov. Avg. ---
Relative Strength —

OPTIONS: ASE, CBOE

Business Profile - 25-AUG-98

North American Vaccine received FDA approval in July 1998 to manufacture and market Certiva, a combined diphtheria, tetanus and acellular pertussis vaccine. Designed for infants and children six weeks to seven years of age, Certiva is to be marketed and distributed in the U.S. by Abbott Laboratories to private physicians and managed care markets, and by NVX to state governments and the Centers for Disease Control and Prevention. Separately, in June 1998, NVX was advised that the registration process for marketing authorization of its DTaP-IPV vaccine (diphtheria, tetanus, pertussis, and polio) has been satisfactorily completed in several European countries, including Germany and Austria. The product was expected to be available for launch following marketing authorizations in each participating country. Officers and directors own more than 20% of NVX.

Operational Review - 25-AUG-98

Revenues for the first half of 1998 declined 3.5%, year to year. Expenses again exceeded revenues, but the loss from operations narrowed slightly to $20.5 million, from $21.7 million. After lower other expenses (net), the net loss decreased to $22.7 million ($0.71 a share on 1.6% more shares) from $23.4 million ($0.74). Cash and equivalents were $18.3 million at June 30, 1998. NVX said in its second quarter 10-Q report that it expected to incur a net loss of $9-$11 million in the 1998 third quarter.

Stock Performance - 02-OCT-98

In the past 30 trading days, NVX's shares have increased 54%, compared to a 7% fall in the S&P 500. Average trading volume for the past five days was 80,980 shares, compared with the 40-day moving average of 92,695 shares.

Key Stock Statistics

Dividend Rate/Share	Nil	Shareholders	300
Shs. outstg. (M)	32.2	Market cap. (B)	$0.328
Avg. daily vol. (M)	0.070	Inst. holdings	36%
Tang. Bk. Value/Share	NM		
Beta	1.41		

Value of $10,000 invested 5 years ago: $ 10,061

Fiscal Year Ending Dec. 31

	1998	1997	1996	1995	1994	1993
Revenues (Million $)						
1Q	0.83	1.08	0.23	Nil	Nil	0.04
2Q	1.23	1.06	0.50	Nil	Nil	Nil
3Q	—	6.95	Nil	Nil	Nil	0.08
4Q	—	0.61	9.82	3.00	Nil	0.03
Yr.	—	9.70	10.55	3.00	—	0.14
Earnings Per Share ($)						
1Q	**-0.37**	**-0.38**	-0.08	-0.12	-0.11	-0.11
2Q	**-0.34**	**-0.36**	0.18	-0.13	-0.11	-0.11
3Q		**-0.23**	-0.28	-0.20	-0.18	-0.11
4Q	—	**-0.41**	-0.01	-0.05	0.24	-0.11
Yr.	—	**-1.39**	-0.63	-0.17	-0.14	-0.44

Next earnings report expected: early November

Dividend Data

No cash dividends have been paid. A two-for-one stock split was effected in 1992.

 A Division of The **McGraw·Hill** *Companies*

Business Summary - 25-AUG-98

North American Vaccine, Inc. researches, develops, produces, and sells vaccines for the prevention of human infectious diseases. The company's first product is a patented, monocomponent acellular pertussis (aP) vaccine for the prevention of whooping cough. The aP vaccine has been combined with diphtheria and tetanus toxoids as a combined diphtheria-tetanus-acellular pertussis (DTaP) vaccine to be marketed in the U.S. under the trade name Certiva. In July 1998, NVX was granted FDA approval to manufacture and market Certiva.

Regulatory approvals were granted in 1996 in Sweden for a European formulation of Certiva and in Denmark for a DTaP-IPV vaccine, which combines the European formulation of Certiva with an enhanced, inactivated polio vaccine (IPV). In addition, regulatory approval was granted in Sweden in April 1997 for the company's aPvaccine for children and young adolescents at risk for pertussis, thereby expanding the indications and usage of the aP vaccine. The company has numerous other vaccines in various stages of development,

The company was, as of year-end 1997, focused on three categories of vaccines: acellular pertussis, combination, and conjugate.

Acellular pertussis vaccines consisted of Certiva (designed to treat diphtheria, tetanus, and pertussis or whooping cough); aP (pertussis); and TdaP (tetanus, diphtheria, and pertussis).

Combination vaccines consisted of DTaP-IPV (designed to treat diphtheria, tetanus, and pertussis); DTaP-HIB (diphtheria, tetanus, pertussis); and DTaP-IPV-HIB (diphtheria, tetanus, pertussis).

Conjugate vaccines consisted of Group B Streptococcal (designed to treat neonatal sepsis and meningitis); Group B Meningococcal (meningitis); Group C Meningococcal (meningitis); Group A/C Meningococcal (meningitis); Group A/B/C Meningococcal (meningitis); Haemophilus Influenzae type b (meningitis); Group A Streptococcal (streptococcal pharyngitis, or strep throat, and skin infections); Pneumococcal (otitis media, or middle ear infection); and Pneumococcal (pneumococcal pneumonia).

Utilizing patented and proprietary technologies, the company isperforming R&D on other adult and pediatric vaccines that are selected for development based on anticipated need for a particular product, the nature of the competition, and the ability of NVX to develop the product. NVX's R&D efforts are being conducted independently and in conjunction or in collaboration with governmental agencies and universities.

To maximize market penetration for its first commercial products within the least amount of time, NVX has been implementinga marketing strategy aimed at establishing marketing alliances in the U.S., Europe, and other territories, with well-established local partners on a country-by-country basis.

Per Share Data ($)

(Year Ended Dec. 31)	1997	1996	1995	1994	1993	1992	1991	1990	1989	1988
Tangible Bk. Val.	NM	0.37	0.94	1.38	2.07	1.29	1.63	0.23	0.34	NA
Cash Flow	-1.04	-0.43	-0.09	-0.06	-0.36	-0.32	-0.17	0.03	-0.13	NA
Earnings	-1.39	-0.63	-0.17	-0.14	-0.44	-0.40	-0.26	-0.11	-0.14	NA
Dividends	Nil	Nil	Nil	Nil	Nil	Nil	Nil	Nil	Nil	Nil
Payout Ratio	Nil	Nil	Nil	Nil	Nil	Nil	Nil	Nil	Nil	Nil
Prices - High	30¼	28⅜	15½	15½	12⅞	17⅛	14	3⅛	NA	NA
- Low	17	11¾	5¼	7¾	7⅝	7	1⅛	1	NA	NA
P/E Ratio - High	NM	NM	NM	NM	NM	NM	NM	NM	NA	NA
- Low	NM	NM	NM	NM	NM	NM	NM	NM	NM	NM

Income Statement Analysis (Million $)

	1997	1996	1995	1994	1993	1992	1991	1990	1989	1988
Revs.	9.7	10.5	3.0	Nil	0.1	1.5	0.9	3.7	1.9	NA
Oper. Inc.	-29.2	-16.4	-18.0	-12.5	-10.6	-9.7	-4.5	0.7	-1.0	NA
Depr.	11.0	6.2	2.2	2.2	2.2	2.1	2.1	2.3	0.2	NA
Int. Exp.	6.8	4.1	Nil	Nil	Nil	0.0	0.3	0.4	0.3	NA
Pretax Inc.	-43.8	-19.4	-5.0	-3.9	-12.1	-10.7	-5.8	-1.8	-2.5	NA
Eff. Tax Rate	NM	NM	NM	NM	NM	NM	NM	NM	NM	NM
Net Inc.	-43.8	-19.4	-5.0	-3.9	-12.1	-10.7	-5.8	-1.8	-2.5	NA

Balance Sheet & Other Fin. Data (Million $)

	1997	1996	1995	1994	1993	1992	1991	1990	1989	1988
Cash	45.5	70.9	10.4	20.9	17.2	28.2	39.9	1.0	5.5	NA
Curr. Assets	49.2	77.4	13.5	21.5	17.9	29.3	40.3	1.7	6.2	NA
Total Assets	84.5	123	41.2	49.6	63.8	42.6	51.0	13.2	19.1	NA
Curr. Liab.	14.0	10.9	7.8	5.4	2.1	2.5	3.1	3.4	6.0	NA
LT Debt	87.8	91.9	Nil	Nil	Nil	Nil	Nil	0.5	2.0	NA
Common Eqty.	-23.9	14.8	28.2	40.4	57.5	35.7	43.1	4.4	6.2	NA
Total Cap.	70.5	112	33.2	43.9	61.3	39.6	47.4	9.3	12.5	NA
Cap. Exp.	2.1	21.1	10.3	6.4	1.6	4.7	1.6	8.5	4.8	NA
Cash Flow	-32.8	-13.3	-2.8	-1.7	-10.0	-8.6	-3.7	0.5	-2.3	NA
Curr. Ratio	3.5	7.1	1.7	4.0	8.5	11.6	12.8	0.5	1.1	NA
% LT Debt of Cap.	125.0	82.1	Nil	Nil	Nil	Nil	Nil	5.8	15.9	NA
% Net Inc.of Revs.	NM	NM	NM	NM	NM	NM	NM	NM	NM	NM
% Ret. on Assets	NM	NM	NM	NM	NM	NM	NM	NM	NM	NM
% Ret. on Equity	NM	NM	NM	NM	NM	NM	NM	NM	NM	NM

Data as orig. reptd.; bef. results of disc. opers. and/or spec. items. Per share data adj. for stk. divs. as of ex-div. date. Bold denotes diluted EPS (FASB 128). E-Estimated. NA-Not Available. NM-Not Meaningful. NR-Not Ranked.

Office—12103 Indian Creek Court, Beltsville, MD 20705. **Tel**—(301) 419-8400. **Website**—http://www.nava.com **Chrmn**—N. W. Flanzraich. **Co-Vice Chrmn**—F. Bellini, P. Frost. **Pres**—S. Mates. **Sr VP & COO**—A. Y. Elliott. **VP-Fin & Investor Contact**—Lawrence J. Hineline. **Sr VP & Secy**—D. J. Abdun-Nabi. **Dirs**—F. Bellini, A. Cousineau, J. Deitcher, D. Dionne, G. Dionne, N. Flanzraich, P. Frost, L. Kasprick, F. Legault, S. Mates, R. Pfenniger. **Transfer Agent**—American Stock Transfer & Trust Co., NYC. **Incorporated**—in Canada in 1989. **Empl**— 260. **S&P Analyst:** N.J. DeVita

Northwest Natural Gas   4837

NASDAQ Symbol **NWNG**

In S&P SmallCap 600

03-OCT-98   Industry:
Natural Gas

Summary: NWNG distributes natural gas in the Pacific Northwest and also explores for and produces natural gas.

Quantitative Evaluations	
Outlook (1 Lowest—5 Highest)	• 2⁻
Fair Value	• 26¾
Risk	• Low
Earn./Div. Rank	• B+
Technical Eval.	• Bullish since 8/98
Rel. Strength Rank (1 Lowest—99 Highest)	• 92
Insider Activity	• NA

Recent Price • 27¾   Yield • 4.4%
52 Wk Range • 31⅜-24¼   12-Mo. P/E • 16.1

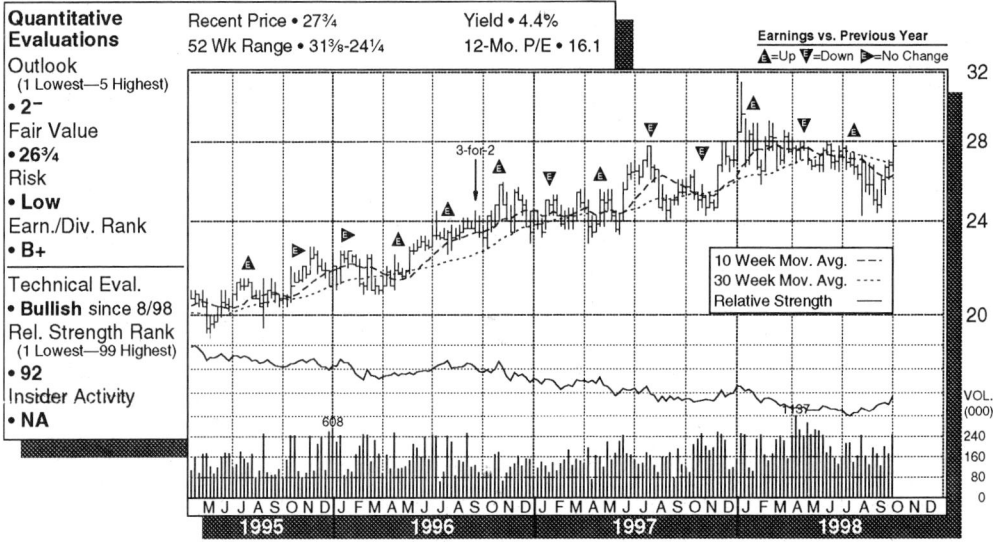

Earnings vs. Previous Year
▲=Up ▼=Down ▶=No Change

10 Week Mov. Avg. – – –
30 Week Mov. Avg. • • •
Relative Strength ——

VOL. (000)

1995 1996 1997 1998

Business Profile - 10-JUL-98

The company plans to continue its focus on distributing natural gas in its thriving service territory. Five-year performance goals include increasing earnings by 30%, most of which is expected to come from the company's core business--gas distribution. Although the sale and transportation of natural gas will remain its primary activity, NWNG hopes to sell a wider array of products and services by forming strategic alliances with other utilities. In July 1997, NWNG formed an alliance with PacifiCorp to jointly market natural gas and electric commodity and energy services to commercial and industrial customers in Oregon and Washington. In April 1998, NWNG sold 1.5 million common shares at $26.81 each, plus 225,000 shares to cover overallotments.

Operational Review - 10-JUL-98

Revenues in the first quarter of 1998 rose 1.0%, year to year, reflecting the adverse impact of 8.5% warmer than average weather on residential and commercial gas sales. Gross margins narrowed on higher cost of sales, and following higher operating expenses and interest charges, pretax earnings were down 16%. After taxes at 31.3%, versus 38.3%, net income decreased 6.3%, to $23.2 million ($0.97 a share, diluted, after preferred and preference dividends), from $24.8 million ($1.04).

Stock Performance - 02-OCT-98

In the past 30 trading days, NWNG's shares have increased 8%, compared to a 7% fall in the S&P 500. Average trading volume for the past five days was 61,540 shares, compared with the 40-day moving average of 37,241 shares.

Key Stock Statistics

Dividend Rate/Share	1.22	Shareholders	12,300
Shs. outstg. (M)	24.7	Market cap. (B)	$0.687
Avg. daily vol. (M)	0.041	Inst. holdings	34%
Tang. Bk. Value/Share	15.24		
Beta	0.47		

Value of $10,000 invested 5 years ago: $ 19,312

Fiscal Year Ending Dec. 31

	1998	1997	1996	1995	1994	1993
Revenues (Million $)						
1Q	135.7	134.3	137.6	125.4	128.5	128.7
2Q	83.65	65.86	71.88	71.03	66.51	61.79
3Q	—	46.28	50.59	48.64	48.47	47.45
4Q	—	115.3	120.3	111.2	124.8	120.8
Yr.	—	361.8	380.3	356.3	368.3	358.7
Earnings Per Share ($)						
1Q	0.97	1.04	1.02	0.88	0.91	1.21
2Q	0.14	0.07	0.22	0.13	0.09	0.10
3Q	—	-0.14	-0.02	-0.23	-0.23	-0.27
4Q	—	0.76	0.76	0.86	0.86	0.70
Yr.	—	1.76	1.94	1.61	1.63	1.74

Next earnings report expected: late October

Dividend Data (Dividends have been paid since 1952.)

Amount ($)	Date Decl.	Ex-Div. Date	Stock of Record	Payment Date
0.305	Jan. 15	Jan. 28	Jan. 30	Feb. 13 '98
0.305	Jan. 15	Jan. 28	Jan. 30	Feb. 13 '98
0.305	Feb. 27	Apr. 28	Apr. 30	May. 15 '98
0.305	Jul. 07	Jul. 29	Jul. 31	Aug. 14 '98

A Division of The McGraw-Hill Companies

STANDARD
&POOR'S
STOCK REPORTS

Northwest Natural Gas Company

4837

03-OCT-98

Business Summary - 10-JUL-98

Long associated with the lumber and paper industries, the Pacific Northwest is also attracting a different breed of business, companies that make computer chips instead of wood chips. These high-tech firms have brought thousands of new jobs to the region, fueling a population growth rate that exceeds the national average. With 78% of Oregon's population residing within its service area, natural gas distributor Northwest Natural Gas Co. (NWNG) is a major beneficiary of these emerging demographics. While many chipmakers have operated in NWNG's territories for years, the scheduled addition of billions of dollars in new semiconductor and silicon wafer plants through 1998 promises to sustain the region's rapid growth in the years ahead.

NWNG distributes natural gas to about 458,000 customers in 16 Oregon counties and three Washington counties encompassing the Portland-Vancouver metropolitan area, the Willamette Valley, the northern Oregon coast and the Columbia River Gorge. In 1997, NWNG derived some 75% of its utility operating revenues from gas sales to weather-sensitive residential and commercial customers. Variations in temperature have a profound impact on sales to these customers, and in

1997 weather conditions in NWNG's service area were much warmer than they were the year before. However, natural gas sales volumes to residential and commercial customers were about the same as in 1996, largely due to new customer acquisitions.

In 1997, NWNG maintained its competitive price advantage over electricity. Throughout the year, natural gas rates continued to be substantially lower than rates for electricity provided by the investor-owned utilities. The company derived 94% of its gas deliveries and its utility operating revenues from Oregon customers, with the balance from Washington customers. The company plans to file for a general rate hike in Oregon in late 1998.

The advent of competition and customer choice is forcing electric and gas utilities alike to adopt new ways of doing business. Although the sale and transportation of natural gas will remain its primary activity, NWNG hopes to sell a wider array of products and services by forming strategic alliances with other utilities. In July 1997, NWNG announced the formation of an alliance with PacifiCorp to jointly market natural gas and electric commodity and energy services to commercial and industrial customers in Oregon and Washington.

Per Share Data ($)

(Year Ended Dec. 31)	1997	1996	1995	1994	1993	1992	1991	1990	1989	1988
Tangible Bk. Val.	16.02	15.37	14.55	2.13	13.08	12.41	12.23	12.61	12.04	11.25
Earnings	1.76	1.97	1.61	1.63	1.74	0.74	0.67	1.62	1.58	1.33
Dividends	1.21	1.20	1.18	1.17	1.17	1.15	1.13	1.10	1.07	1.05
Payout Ratio	68%	61%	73%	72%	67%	155%	167%	68%	68%	79%
Prices - High	31³/₈	25⁷/₈	22⁷/₈	24³/₈	25⁷/₈	22⁵/₈	22³/₈	17⁷/₈	17⁷/₈	14¹/₂
- Low	23	20⁷/₈	18³/₈	18⁷/₈	19	17¹/₈	16¹/₂	13⁷/₈	12¹/₂	12³/₄
P/E Ratio - High	18	13	14	15	15	31	33	11	11	11
- Low	13	11	11	12	11	23	25	9	8	10

Income Statement Analysis (Million $)

	1997	1996	1995	1994	1993	1992	1991	1990	1989	1988
Revs.	362	380	356	368	359	274	296	296	261	278
Depr.	44.6	43.0	40.6	38.1	39.7	33.0	33.6	28.0	23.2	23.3
Maint.	NA	NA	NA	NA	NA	NA	NA	NA	7.5	7.4
Fxd. Chgs. Cov.	2.8	3.3	3.0	2.9	3.0	1.7	1.5	2.4	2.2	2.1
Constr. Credits	1.7	0.8	0.6	0.3	0.2	NM	Nil	NM	NM	NM
Eff. Tax Rate	33%	37%	37%	37%	37%	31%	14%	31%	35%	34%
Net Inc.	43.1	46.8	38.1	35.5	37.6	15.8	14.4	30.7	28.4	23.7

Balance Sheet & Other Fin. Data (Million $)

	1997	1996	1995	1994	1993	1992	1991	1990	1989	1988
Gross Prop.	1,165	1,055	969	908	840	779	722	669	623	567
Cap. Exp.	NA	83.4	67.2	77.7	70.4	60.7	58.4	50.5	57.6	45.0
Net Prop.	798	719	660	629	585	546	515	485	459	420
Capitalization:										
LT Debt	344	272	280	291	273	254	253	215	221	182
% LT Debt	46	41	44	48	48	46	51	46	48	46
Pfd.	37.4	38.7	39.8	42.2	44.0	55.0	31.0	32.1	33.9	36.1
% Pfd.	5.00	5.90	6.20	6.90	7.60	10	6.20	6.90	7.30	9.10
Common	366	347	324	274	259	242	216	219	206	180
% Common	49	53	50	45	45	44	43	47	45	45
Total Cap.	900	793	775	734	694	601	552	524	519	452
% Oper. Ratio	81.0	32.8	85.0	85.9	82.8	84.4	86.6	81.6	82.4	85.6
% Earn. on Net Prop.	9.1	9.5	8.3	8.5	10.9	9.4	7.9	11.6	10.5	10.1
% Return On Revs.	11.9	12.3	10.7	9.6	10.5	5.7	4.9	10.4	10.9	8.5
% Return On Invest. Capital	8.3	9.4	8.5	8.5	9.7	8.6	7.6	10.5	9.7	9.3
% Return On Com. Equity	11.3	13.1	11.8	12.2	13.7	5.8	5.4	13.1	13.3	12.1

Data as orig. reptd.; bef. results of disc opers. and/or spec. items. Per share data adj. for stk. divs. as of ex-div. date. Bold denotes diluted EPS (FASB 128). E-Estimated. NA-Not Available. NM-Not Meaningful. NR-Not Ranked.

Office—One Pacific Square, 220 N.W. Second Ave., Portland, OR 97209. **Tel**—(503) 226-4211. **Website**—http://www.nng.com **Chrmn**—R. L. Ridgley. **Pres & CEO**—R. G. Reiten. **Secy**—C. J. Rue. **VP & CFO**—B. R. De Bolt. **Investor Contact**—James Boehlke (503-226-4211; ext. 2451). **Dirs**—M. A. Arnstad, T. E. Dewey, Jr., T. R. Hamachek, R. B. Keller, W. D. Kunl, R. C. Pape, R. G. Reiten, R. L. Ridgley, D. A. Sangrey, M. C. Teppola, R. F. Tromley, B. R. Whiteley. **Transfer Agent & Registrar**—Co.'s office. **Incorporated**—in Oregon in 1910. **Empl**—1,337. **S&P Analyst:** S.S.

Northwestern Steel and Wire   4838D

NASDAQ Symbol **NWSW**

In S&P SmallCap 600

03-OCT-98

Industry: Iron & Steel

Summary: Following the April 1998 termination of a merger agreement, this maker of structural steel and rod and wire products announced tentative plans to exit several product lines.

Quantitative Evaluations

Outlook
(1 Lowest—5 Highest)
• **5**

Fair Value
• **6⅞**

Risk
• **Average**

Earn./Div. Rank
• **NR**

Technical Eval.
• **Bearish** since 6/98

Rel. Strength Rank
(1 Lowest—99 Highest)
• **19**

Insider Activity
• **Favorable**

Recent Price • 2
52 Wk Range • 4⅞-1⅝

Yield • Nil
12-Mo. P/E • NM

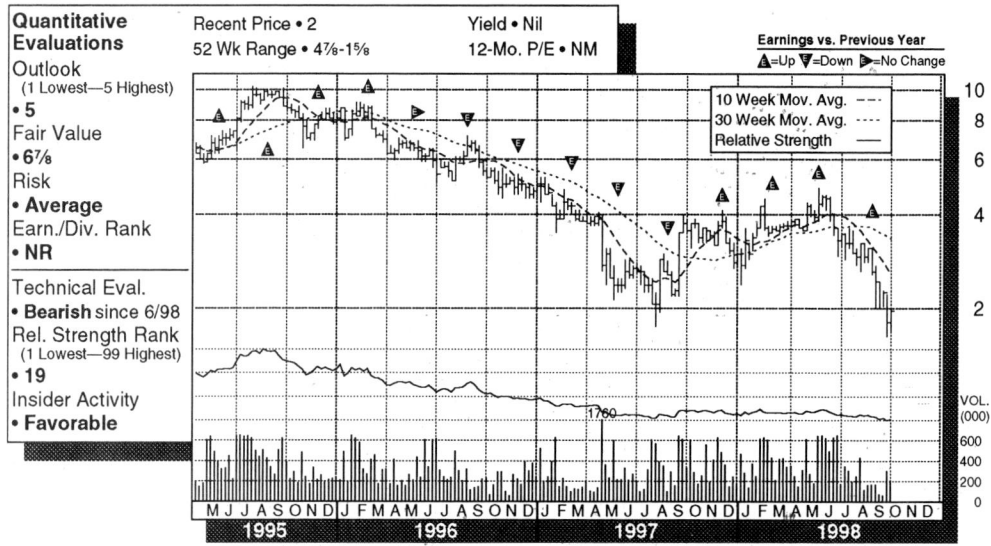

Business Profile - 04-SEP-98

In April 1998, following more than two months of merger talks with Bayou Steel Corp., the company said it had been unable to agree on mutually acceptable terms and conditions, and discussions were terminated. In August 1998, NWSW announced tentative plans to exit the majority of its wire products business by the end of 1998, in a move that would affect about 450 of its 2,000 employees. Management said the action reflected the fact that the company's wire products operations are at a competitive disadvantage to lower cost imports and other domestic suppliers. The decision remains subject to further financial analysis, and to contract discussions with NWSW's union.

Operational Review - 04-SEP-98

Based on a preliminary report, net sales in the fiscal year ended July 31, 1998, declined 6.9%, reflecting the closure of the Houston rolling mill in the 1997 fourth quarter. In the absence of a $92.9 million charge related to the shutdown of the Houston mill, and aided by lower depreciation charges and almost $15 million of income from legal and tax settlements, pretax income contrasted with a pretax loss of $98,420,000. After taxes at 39.5%, versus tax credits of $35,300,000, net income of $41,696,000 ($1.70 a share) contrasted with a net loss of $63,120,000 ($2.54).

Stock Performance - 02-OCT-98

In the past 30 trading days, NWSW's shares have declined 37%, compared to a 7% fall in the S&P 500. Average trading volume for the past five days was 41,300 shares, compared with the 40-day moving average of 32,110 shares.

Key Stock Statistics

Dividend Rate/Share	Nil	Shareholders	1,300
Shs. outstg. (M)	24.5	Market cap. (B)	$0.048
Avg. daily vol. (M)	0.034	Inst. holdings	16%
Tang. Bk. Value/Share	3.07		
Beta	0.38		

Value of $10,000 invested 5 years ago: NA

Fiscal Year Ending Jul. 31

	1998	1997	1996	1995	1994	1993
Revenues (Million $)						
1Q	138.9	145.2	160.9	153.6	156.0	—
2Q	140.4	143.7	149.2	145.8	140.3	—
3Q	168.3	171.7	173.2	166.6	150.4	—
4Q	148.8	180.4	177.8	172.5	157.0	—
Yr.	596.4	640.8	661.1	638.4	603.6	539.2
Earnings Per Share ($)						
1Q	0.32	-0.08	0.19	0.17	0.13	—
2Q	0.30	0.00	0.10	0.09	0.07	—
3Q	0.39	-0.02	0.14	0.14	0.06	—
4Q	0.69	-2.35	0.40	0.67	0.14	—
Yr.	1.70	-2.54	0.83	1.07	0.40	-0.08

Next earnings report expected: NA

Dividend Data

No cash dividends have been paid, and the company does not intend to pay any in the foreseeable future.

A Division of The **McGraw·Hill** Companies

Business Summary - 04-SEP-98

In 1936, Northwestern Steel and Wire Co. (NWSW) pioneered the use of electric arc furnaces for steelmaking. Today, this company is a major mini-mill producer of structural steel products and rod and wire products. In contrast to integrated mills, which produce steel from coke and iron ore by using blast furnaces and basic oxygen furnaces, mini-mills use electric arc furnaces to melt steel scrap and cast the resulting molten steel into long strands of various shapes in a continuous casting process. NWSW's steel products include wide flange beams, light structural shapes, merchant bars and semi-finished steel. The company's rod and wire products include nails, concrete reinforcing mesh, residential and agricultural fencing and a wide range of other wire products.

NWSW's two 400-ton electric arc furnaces are among the largest in the world, providing it with considerable economies of scale in its steel scrap melting operations. NWSW's operations are located in Sterling and neighboring Rock Falls, IL; a concrete reinforcing mesh facility, located in Hickman, KY, began operations in FY 96 (Jul.). After determining that its Houston, TX, facility would not return to profitability, it was closed during the fourth quarter of FY 97, and is being prepared to be sold. The mill closure resulted in a non-recurring charge of $92.9 million during the fourth quarter of FY 97.

The steel division (which accounted for 68% of FY 97 net sales) produces raw steel using the electric arc furnace process. Semi-finished products are then continuously cast into billets and blooms. Finished products are rolled from the semi-finished steel through a series of reduction mill processes. These products include wide flange beams, channels and angle products and merchant bar and bar shapes, which are sold nationally to steel fabricators, distributors and original equipment manufacturers.

The rod and wire products division (32%) produces rods for use in drawing to various wire gauges to produce nails, fence and a wide range of other fabricated wire products for shipments to hardware jobbers, agricultural cooperatives and the construction industry. NWSW has recently made capital improvements including the construction of a high-speed reinforcing mesh facility in Hickman, KY, and an upgraded powder coating process for lawn and garden products.

Over the past several years, approximately 40% to 50% of the company's steel rod production has been used to manufacture its rod and wire products, with the remaining rod production sold to other manufacturers of wire products.

Per Share Data ($)

(Year Ended Jul. 31)	1998	1997	1996	1995	1994	1993	1992	1991	1990	1989
Tangible Bk. Val.	NA	1.93	4.34	3.14	1.77	2.23	0.85	2.30	NA	NA
Cash Flow	NA	-1.50	1.86	1.99	1.28	1.13	-0.22	-0.39	NA	NA
Earnings	1.70	-2.54	0.83	1.07	0.40	-0.08	-1.72	-1.53	NA	NA
Dividends	Nil	Nil	Nil	Nil	Nil	Nil	Nil	Nil	Nil	Nil
Payout Ratio	Nil	Nil	Nil	Nil	Nil	Nil	Nil	Nil	Nil	Nil
Prices - High	4⁷/₈	5¹/₄	9¹/₈	10¹/₄	13¹/₈	10⁷/₈	NA	NA	NA	NA
- Low	2	1³/₄	4¹/₂	5³/₄	5¹/₂	7¹/₄	NA	NA	NA	NA
P/E Ratio - High	3	NM	11	10	33	NM	NA	NA	NA	NA
- Low	1	NM	5	5	14	NM	NA	NA	NA	NA

Income Statement Analysis (Million $)

	1998	1997	1996	1995	1994	1993	1992	1991	1990	1989
Revs.	NA	641	661	638	604	539	470	477	NA	NA
Oper. Inc.	NA	40.2	60.4	63.8	52.0	43.5	26.5	32.4	NA	NA
Depr.	NA	25.8	25.0	23.0	22.2	21.9	22.1	19.3	NA	NA
Int. Exp.	NA	20.0	18.9	19.7	19.2	23.2	27.1	27.5	NA	NA
Pretax Inc.	NA	-98.4	17.1	21.2	10.7	-1.5	-22.4	-19.8	NA	NA
Eff. Tax Rate	NA	NM	NM	NM	6.70%	Nil	Nil	Nil	Nil	Nil
Net Inc.	Nil	-63.1	21.0	27.0	10.0	-1.5	-22.4	-19.8	NA	NA

Balance Sheet & Other Fin. Data (Million $)

	1998	1997	1996	1995	1994	1993	1992	1991	1990	1989
Cash	NA	4.1	6.6	14.3	12.8	NA	NA	NA	NA	NA
Curr. Assets	NA	184	190	186	169	144	102	93.0	NA	NA
Total Assets	NA	383	443	421	394	372	340	343	NA	NA
Curr. Liab.	NA	86.5	106	96.6	90.1	80.9	107	52.3	NA	NA
LT Debt	NA	164	154	162	167	164	200	228	NA	NA
Common Eqty.	NA	50.5	106	82.9	50.5	54.9	10.3	29.3	NA	NA
Total Cap.	NA	214	260	250	225	227	210	257	NA	NA
Cap. Exp.	NA	17.4	36.2	35.6	22.9	12.3	7.1	26.1	NA	NA
Cash Flow	NA	-37.3	45.5	50.0	32.2	20.6	-0.3	-0.5	NA	NA
Curr. Ratio	NA	2.1	1.8	1.9	1.9	1.8	0.9	1.8	NA	NA
% LT Debt of Cap.	NA	76.5	59.2	64.8	74.2	72.2	95.2	88.7	NA	NA
% Net Inc.of Revs.	NA	NM	3.2	4.2	1.7	NM	NM	NM	NM	NM
% Ret. on Assets	NM	NM	4.8	6.6	2.6	NM	NM	NM	NM	NM
% Ret. on Equity	NM	NM	21.9	15.0	19.0	NM	NM	NM	NM	NM

Data as orig. reptd.; bef. results of disc. opers. and/or spec. items. Per share data adj. for stk. divs. as of ex-div. date. Bold denotes diluted EPS (FASB 128). E-Estimated. NA-Not Available. NM-Not Meaningful. NR-Not Ranked.

Office—121 Wallace St., Sterling, IL 61081.**Tel**—(815) 625-2500. **Chrmn & CEO**—T. A. Gildehaus. **Pres & COO**—R. D. Way. **Investor Contact**—T. M. Vercillo. **Dirs**—W. F. Andrews, W. C. Frazier, D. W. Gaskins Jr., T. A. Gildehaus, J. A. Kohlberg, C. Lacovara, M. E. Lubbs, A. G. Pastino, G. W. Peck IV. **Transfer Agent & Registrar**—Fleet National Bank, Providence, RI. **Incorporated**—in Illinois in 1979. **Empl**—2,000. **S&P Analyst:** P.L.H.

Novellus Systems — 4842T

Nasdaq Symbol **NVLS**
In S&P SmallCap 600

03-OCT-98

Industry: Equipment (Semiconductor)

Summary: This company manufactures, markets and services automated wafer fabrication systems for the deposition of thin films.

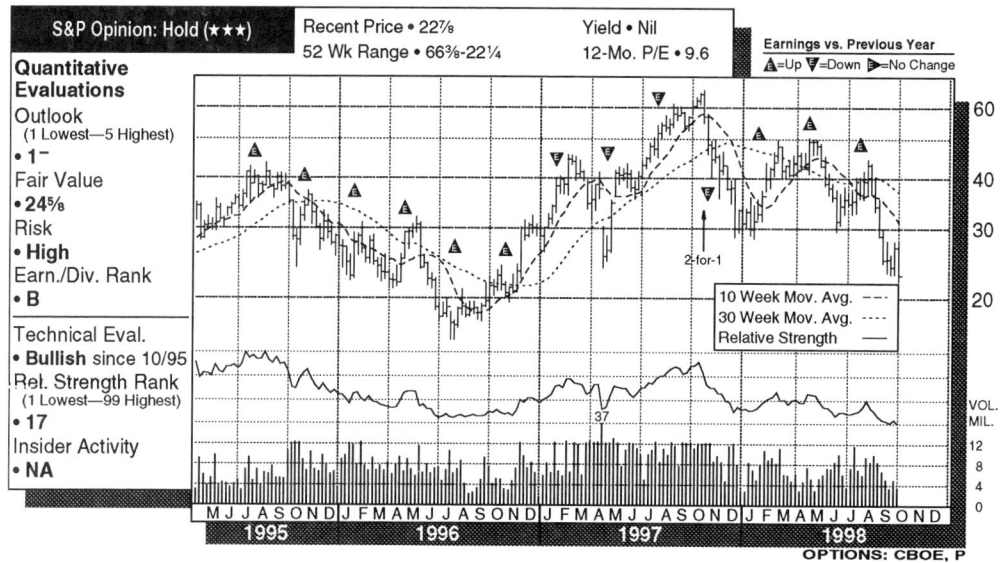

S&P Opinion: Hold (★★★)	Recent Price • 22⅞	Yield • Nil
	52 Wk Range • 66⅜-22¼	12-Mo. P/E • 9.6

Earnings vs. Previous Year
▲=Up ▼=Down ▶=No Change

Quantitative Evaluations

Outlook (1 Lowest—5 Highest)
• **1⁻**

Fair Value
• **24⅝**

Risk
• **High**

Earn./Div. Rank
• **B**

Technical Eval.
• **Bullish** since 10/95

Rel. Strength Rank (1 Lowest—99 Highest)
• **17**

Insider Activity
• **NA**

10 Week Mov. Avg. ---
30 Week Mov. Avg. ····
Relative Strength —

2-for-1

OPTIONS: CBOE, P

Overview - 22-JUL-98

We expect revenues to be flat in 1998, as a slowdown in capital spending from semiconductor companies results in weak demand for the company's deposition products. Overall order trends have slowed sharply, as evidenced by a below 1:1 book to bill ratio in each of the last two quarters. The ongoing Asian financial crisis and a general industry slowdown are likely to result in continued sluggish order trends over the next few quarters, as well. Due to the lower revenues expected in the second half, we expect margins to contract on a sequential basis, as fixed costs are absorbed over a smaller base. Overall, we look for EPS to fall to $1.40 in 1998, from the $2.17 recorded in 1997 (which excludes nonrecurring charges of $5.05 a share). Based on prospects for strong demand for the company's copper technology, we expect EPS to improve to $1.65 in 1999.

Valuation - 22-JUL-00

Following a sharp sell-off in late 1997, the shares of this leading semiconductor equipment maker have been volatile in 1998. We are maintaining our hold recommendation, however, as we believe semiconductor capital spending will drop sharply over the next few quarters. With approximately 47% of the company's sales derived from Japan and Asia Pacific last quarter, NVLS remains vulnerable to poor economic conditions in that region. We continue to believe that the shares are an attractive long-term holding for aggressive investors, as the company's technological strength, particularly in emerging copper interconnect solutions, should allow it to remain a major player in cyclical, semiconductor capital equipment industry.

Key Stock Statistics

S&P EPS Est. 1998	1.40	Tang. Bk. Value/Share	10.06
P/E on S&P Est. 1998	16.3	Beta	2.18
S&P EPS Est. 1999	1.65	Shareholders	600
Dividend Rate/Share	Nil	Market cap. (B)	$0.780
Shs. outstg. (M)	34.1	Inst. holdings	80%
Avg. daily vol. (M)	0.888		

Value of $10,000 invested 5 years ago: $ 25,068

Fiscal Year Ending Dec. 31

	1998	1997	1996	1995	1994	1993
Revenues (Million $)						
1Q	163.2	101.6	115.3	76.13	42.44	20.96
2Q	142.8	114.5	120.3	87.40	51.03	25.28
3Q	—	155.1	121.6	100.4	59.53	29.97
4Q	—	162.8	104.6	109.8	71.68	37.33
Yr.	—	534.0	461.7	373.7	224.7	113.5
Earnings Per Share ($)						
1Q	**0.60**	0.46	0.78	0.49	0.23	0.08
2Q	**0.46**	-4.66	0.80	0.56	0.30	0.13
3Q	**E0.16**	0.57	0.77	0.64	0.38	0.16
4Q	**E0.18**	0.64	0.51	0.72	0.45	0.19
Yr.	**E1.40**	-2.88	2.92	2.41	1.36	0.55

Next earnings report expected: mid October

Dividend Data

Amount ($)	Date Decl.	Ex-Div. Date	Stock of Record	Payment Date
2-for-1	Sep. 22	Oct. 14	Sep. 29	Oct. 13 '97

A Division of The **McGraw·Hill** *Companies*

Business Summary - 22-JUL-98

Novellus Systems designs, manufactures, markets and services chemical vapor deposition (CVD) equipment used in fabricating integrated circuits (ICs). Deposition is a process in which a film of either electrically insulating (dielectric) or electrically conductive material is deposited on the surface of a silicon wafer. Intermetal dielectrics are required to insulate conductive layers, which help transfer information among an IC's transistors, from each other.

The company's objective is to increase its market share in the worldwide CVD market and strengthen its position as a leading supplier of semiconductor processing equipment. To attain this goal, the company's strategy is to provide its customers with systems that achieve the highest levels of wafer throughput, yield (the percentage of functioning ICs to the total produced), and film quality. In addition, the company plans to maintain a leadership position in CVD technology, to allow its systems to utilize the most advanced CVD processes. Finally, NVLS will focus its marketing efforts on major semiconductor manufacturers. The company has sold at least one CVD system to each of the 20 largest semiconductor manufacturers in the world.

The company's CVD products include the Concept One-Dielectric system, which can deposit a variety of insulating films on a wafer. A modified version, the Concept One-W, deposits tungsten metal on wafers. The tungsten acts as a metal interconnect between conductor layers in an IC. The Concept Two is a modular, integrated CVD system that can deposit both dielectric and conductive metal layers by combining one or more processing chambers around a common, automated robotic wafer handler. The Concept Two-ALTUS combines the modular architecture of the Concept Two system with an advanced tungsten CVD process chamber. The Concept Two-Dual ALTUS, with a dual advanced tungsten CVD process chamber, addresses state-of-the-art, 0.35-micron linewidth processing needs. In 1996, NVLS introduced Speed, its high-density plasma deposition tool for 0.35-micron linewidth ICs and below.

Novellus settled a longstanding legal matter with Applied Materials (Nasdaq: AMAT), the company's chief competitor, in May 1997. In April 1997, a jury in a U.S. District Court ruled against the company in a patent infringement suit filed by AMAT. Under terms of the agreement, NVLS agreed to pay AMAT $80 million and a royalty for all future revenues of TEOS-based systems, which is the process that was the subject of the lawsuit.

In June 1997, NVLS entered the market for physical vapor deposition systems (PVD) through the acquisition of the Thin Film Systems business of Varian Associates Inc. (NYSE: VAR) for $150 million in cash.

Per Share Data ($)

(Year Ended Dec. 31)	1997	1996	1995	1994	1993	1992	1991	1990	1989	1988
Tangible Bk. Val.	8.93	11.49	8.55	6.63	3.72	3.02	2.87	2.09	1.53	0.77
Cash Flow	-2.33	3.19	2.63	1.48	0.68	0.33	0.64	0.56	0.47	0.15
Earnings	-2.88	2.85	2.41	1.36	0.55	0.22	0.57	0.51	0.43	0.13
Dividends	Nil	Nil	Nil	Nil	Nil	Nil	Nil	Nil	Nil	Nil
Payout Ratio	Nil	Nil	Nil	Nil	Nil	Nil	Nil	Nil	Nil	Nil
Prices - High	66³/₈	32¹/₄	43⁵/₈	28¹/₄	18¹/₂	13¹/₄	13⁵/₈	9	5	2¹/₄
- Low	23⁷/₈	15³/₄	21³/₈	12⁷/₈	7	3⁷/₈	5¹/₄	2³/₄	2³/₁₆	1³/₈
P/E Ratio - High	NM	11	18	21	34	60	24	18	11	18
- Low	NM	6	9	9	13	18	9	5	5	11

Income Statement Analysis (Million $)

	1997	1996	1995	1994	1993	1992	1991	1990	1989	1988
Revs.	534	462	374	225	114	69.8	80.0	67.1	51.0	23.2
Oper. Inc.	112	148	123	67.7	27.1	10.9	24.7	20.6	16.4	4.5
Depr.	18.3	11.3	7.7	4.0	3.7	3.2	1.9	1.4	0.9	0.6
Int. Exp.	2.7	0.5	0.2	0.3	0.1	0.3	0.1	0.1	0.2	0.1
Pretax Inc.	-120	145	125	68.1	24.8	9.4	25.4	21.7	17.3	4.2
Eff. Tax Rate	NM	35%	34%	34%	35%	34%	34%	36%	35%	40%
Net Inc.	-95.7	94.0	82.5	44.9	16.1	6.2	16.8	14.0	11.2	2.5

Balance Sheet & Other Fin. Data (Million $)

	1997	1996	1995	1994	1993	1992	1991	1990	1989	1988
Cash	59.3	177	150	137	48.6	43.0	40.5	39.8	30.0	11.8
Curr. Assets	351	374	318	234	109	79.2	79.3	62.8	45.6	21.1
Total Assets	493	460	365	265	131	97.3	94.7	68.9	50.5	23.9
Curr. Liab.	127	86.1	92.0	50.8	25.7	13.9	12.8	12.4	10.1	6.4
LT Debt	65.0	Nil	Nil	Nil	Nil	0.8	1.0	0.4	0.8	0.7
Common Eqty.	301	374	273	214	105	82.7	80.9	56.1	39.5	16.6
Total Cap.	366	374	273	214	105	83.4	81.9	56.5	40.3	17.4
Cap. Exp.	36.2	35.2	19.3	6.9	6.6	5.1	10.2	2.5	2.5	0.9
Cash Flow	-77.4	105	90.2	48.9	19.8	9.5	18.7	15.5	12.2	3.1
Curr. Ratio	2.8	4.3	3.5	4.6	4.3	5.7	6.2	5.1	4.5	3.3
% LT Debt of Cap.	17.8	NM	NM	Nil	Nil	0.9	1.2	0.7	1.9	4.2
% Net Inc.of Revs.	NM	20.4	22.1	20.0	14.2	8.9	21.0	20.9	22.1	11.0
% Ret. on Assets	NM	22.8	26.0	21.7	13.9	6.6	20.1	23.1	28.6	9.4
% Ret. on Equity	NM	29.1	33.9	26.9	16.9	7.7	24.0	28.8	38.0	NM

Data as orig. reptd.; bef. results of disc. opers. and/or spec. items. Per share data adj. for stk. divs. as of ex-div. date. Bold denotes diluted EPS (FASB 128). E-Estimated. NA-Not Available. NM-Not Meaningful. NR-Not Ranked.

Office—3970 North First Street, San Jose, CA 95134. **Tel**—(408) 943-9700. **Chrmn, Pres & CEO**—R. S. Hill. **VP & CFO**—R. H. Smith **Treas**—T. Foy. **Dirs**— D. J. Guzy, R. S. Hill, J.D. Lister, T. Long, G. Possley, R. H. Smith, W. R. Spivey. **Transfer Agent & Registrar**—Chasemellon Shareholder Services, San Francisco. **Incorporated**—in California in 1984. **Empl**— 1,776. **S&P Analyst**: B. McGovern

Noven Pharmaceuticals   4842V

NASDAQ Symbol **NOVN**

In S&P SmallCap 600

03-OCT-98

Industry: Health Care (Drugs - Generic & Other)

Summary: Noven is a leader in the development and commercialization of transdermal and transmucosal drug delivery systems.

Quantitative Evaluations

Outlook (1 Lowest—5 Highest)
• **2-**

Fair Value
• **5**

Risk
• **High**

Earn./Div. Rank
• **C**

Technical Eval.
• **Bullish** since 9/98

Rel. Strength Rank (1 Lowest—99 Highest)
• **27**

Insider Activity
• **Neutral**

Recent Price • 4
52 Wk Range • 9¼-2⅝

Yield • Nil
12-Mo. P/E • NM

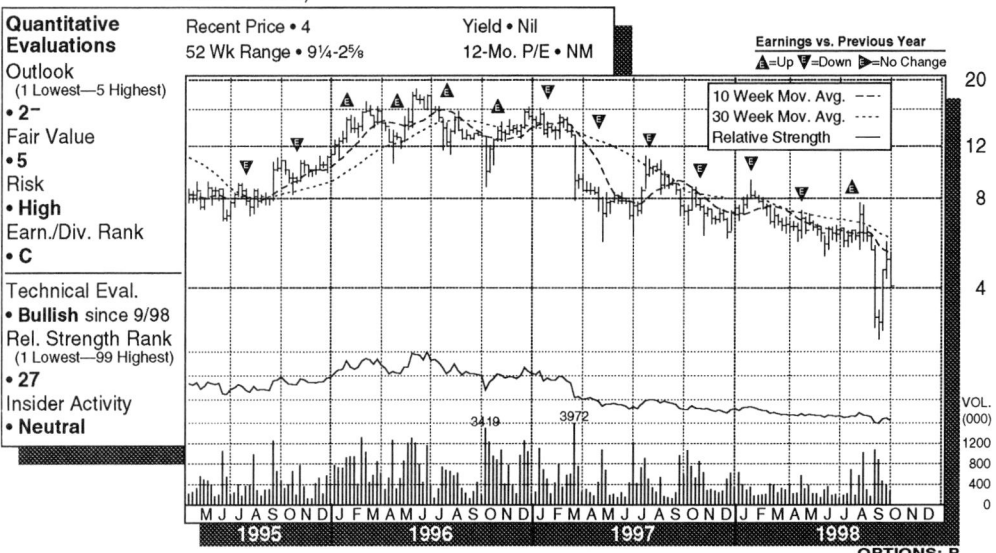

Earnings vs. Previous Year
▲=Up ▼=Down ▶=No Change

10 Week Mov. Avg. - - -
30 Week Mov. Avg. · · · ·
Relative Strength ——

OPTIONS: P

Business Profile - 02-SEP-98

Although product sales are increasing, this company anticipates further net losses for 1998, due to the fact that product sales will still not be sufficient to offset operating costs. During May 1998, the company entered into a joint venture with Novartis Pharmaceuticals Corp., focusing on the commercialization of Vivelle and other women's healthcare products. In June 1998, NOVN announced that the joint venture, Vivelle Ventures, LLC, has hired a contract sales force and is planning to double U.S. sales of Vivelle ($30 million in 1997) in the next two to three years. In August 1998, the FDA approved CombiPatch, the first transdermal patch system combining both estrogen and progestin, manufactured by NOVN and marketed by Rhone-Poulenc Rorer Pharmaceuticals, Inc.

Operational Review - 02-SEP-98

Total revenues in the first six months of 1998 advanced 58%, year to year, resulting from an increase in product sales of the company's estrogen delivery system, its DontiPatch system, and shipments of NOVN's combination estrogen/progestin delivery system. Gross margins narrowed reflecting a less favorable product mix. Cost of goods and SG&A rose 94% and 35%, respectively, and R&D expenditures declined 4%, resulting in total expenses of $14 million versus $10.6 million. The net loss widened to $4,833,856 ($0.24 a share, on 3% more shares), from $4,788,743 ($0.24). Cash and equivalents totaled $5,737,720 on June 30, 1998.

Stock Performance - 02-OCT-98

In the past 30 trading days, NOVN's shares have declined 32%, compared to a 7% fall in the S&P 500. Average trading volume for the past five days was 54,080 shares, compared with the 40-day moving average of 116,174 shares.

Key Stock Statistics

Dividend Rate/Share	Nil	Shareholders	500
Shs. outstg. (M)	21.5	Market cap. (B)	$0.087
Avg. daily vol. (M)	0.117	Inst. holdings	17%
Tang. Bk. Value/Share	1.21		
Beta	1.36		

Value of $10,000 invested 5 years ago: $ 3,154

Fiscal Year Ending Dec. 31

	1998	1997	1996	1995	1994	1993
Revenues (Million $)						
1Q	2.74	1.68	5.56	1.24	0.95	1.32
2Q	6.48	4.16	5.75	2.04	1.17	0.86
3Q	—	5.98	5.78	3.33	1.12	0.92
4Q	—	3.37	4.58	5.53	2.80	0.99
Yr.	—	15.19	20.47	12.18	6.04	4.09
Earnings Per Share ($)						
1Q	-0.16	-0.14	-0.03	-0.09	-0.06	-0.05
2Q	-0.08	-0.14	0.01	-0.11	-0.07	-0.04
3Q	—	Nil	0.03	-0.09	-0.07	-0.05
4Q	—	-0.23	-0.11	-0.05	-0.08	-0.07
Yr.	—	-0.47	-0.10	-0.34	-0.28	-0.21

Next earnings report expected: NA

Dividend Data

No dividends have been paid.

A Division of The McGraw-Hill Companies

Business Summary - 02-SEP-98

A leading developer and manufacturer of transdermal and transoral drug delivery systems, Noven Pharmaceuticals (NOVN) is focusing on the women's healthcare segment of the hormone replacement therapy (HRT) market. NOVN's technology delivers drugs into the bloodstream across the skin or oral mucosa, and is adaptable to numerous drug entities.

Noven's first product, an estrogen patch for the treatment of menopausal symptoms, was launched in the U.S. in March 1996 by Ciba-Geigy Corp. (now part of Novartis S.A.) under the trade name Vivelle. Rhone-Poulenc Rorer, Inc. (RPR) has received regulatory approval to market Vivelle for the treatment of menopausal symptoms in 38 countries, and has launched the product under the name Menorest in 19 countries. Menorest has also been approved in 36 countries as a preventative treatment for osteoporosis. Novartis is conducting clinical trials for this indication in the U.S.

In May 1998, the firm entered into a joint venture with Novartis Pharmaceuticals Corp., focusing on the commercialization of Vivelle and other women's healthcare products. In June 1998, the joint venture, Vivelle Ventures, LLC, hired a U.S. contract sales force to market the Vivelle product.

In August 1998, the company's other major development, CombiPatch, a transdermal patch combining estrogen and progestin, was approved by the FDA. Com-

biPatch, marketed by RPR and manufactured by NOVN, is the first patch of its kind enabling menopausal women to benefit from combination therapy with one drug product. NOVN's matrix technology allows the patch to be discreet in appearance, requires changing only twice per week, and releases two hormones that provide women with relief from menopausal symptoms and protection from endometrial hyperplasia (a condition linked to endometrial cancer). In low dosage forms, taken over several months, CombiPatch may eliminate bleeding in menopausal women.

In July 1998, NOVN announced that it had filed a Market Authorization Application in the U.K. for a transdermal patch system with matrix technology that is smaller, more comfortable, and nearly transparent. Marketing authorization is also pending at the FDA to utilize the new system with the firm's estrogen patch, which will be sold by Vivelle Ventures, LLC.

Transoral drug delivery systems use a bio-adhesive patch containing medication which, when moistened, adheres to the buccal mucosa. The buccal mucosa is a thin and highly vascular structure that allows larger drug molecules, including peptides, proteins, and carbohydrates, to be delivered into the bloodstream. DentiPatch, Noven's transoral anesthetic delivery system, was launched on a national basis in 1997. DentiPatch, which contains lidocaine, is indicated for the prevention of pain from oral injection, and soft-tissue dental procedures.

Per Share Data ($)

(Year Ended Dec. 31)	1997	1996	1995	1994	1993	1992	1991	1990	1989	1988
Tangible Bk. Val.	1.38	1.74	1.87	2.31	1.23	1.30	NA	NA	NA	NA
Cash Flow	-0.42	-0.06	-0.27	-0.23	-0.16	-0.19	NA	NA	NA	NA
Earnings	-0.47	-0.10	-0.34	-0.28	-0.21	-0.21	-0.25	NA	NA	NA
Dividends	Nil	Nil	Nil	Nil	Nil	Nil	Nil	Nil	Nil	Nil
Payout Ratio	Nil	Nil	Nil	Nil	Nil	Nil	Nil	Nil	Nil	Nil
Prices - High	16¹/₈	18³/₄	12³/₈	19¹/₄	15¹/₂	13¹/₂	9¹/₄	NA	NA	NA
- Low	5³/₄	8³/₄	6¹/₂	10¹/₄	10	6³/₄	1³/₄	NA	NA	NA
P/E Ratio - High	NM	NM	NM	NM	NM	NM	NM	NM	NM	NM
- Low	NM	NM	NM	NM	NM	NM	NM	NM	NM	NM

Income Statement Analysis (Million $)

	1997	1996	1995	1994	1993	1992	1991	1990	1989	1988
Revs.	14.3	20.5	10.5	4.5	3.1	1.9	0.1	NA	NA	NA
Oper. Inc.	-9.5	-2.3	-7.0	-5.6	-3.5	-3.8	NA	NA	NA	NA
Depr.	1.0	0.9	1.3	0.9	0.8	0.2	NA	NA	NA	NA
Int. Exp.	NA	Nil	Nil	Nil	Nil	Nil	NA	NA	NA	NA
Pretax Inc.	-9.6	-2.0	-6.6	-4.9	-3.3	-3.0	-3.1	NA	NA	NA
Eff. Tax Rate	NM	NM	Nil	Nil	Nil	Nil	Nil	Nil	Nil	Nil
Net Inc.	-9.6	-2.0	-6.6	-4.9	-3.3	-3.0	-3.1	NA	NA	NA

Balance Sheet & Other Fin. Data (Million $)

	1997	1996	1995	1994	1993	1992	1991	1990	1989	1988
Cash	11.3	19.1	24.0	35.5	14.7	NA	NA	NA	NA	NA
Curr. Assets	21.2	26.9	31.9	37.6	16.0	NA	NA	NA	NA	NA
Total Assets	38.2	44.2	48.6	53.7	29.9	23.3	3.5	NA	NA	NA
Curr. Liab.	2.5	2.1	4.3	2.6	1.1	NA	NA	NA	NA	NA
LT Debt	Nil	Nil	Nil	Nil	Nil	Nil	Nil	Nil	Nil	Nil
Common Eqty.	29.9	36.1	38.0	44.5	20.7	20.7	1.6	NA	NA	NA
Total Cap.	29.9	36.1	38.0	44.5	20.7	20.7	1.6	NA	NA	NA
Cap. Exp.	0.6	1.1	NA	2.8	3.2	0.3	NA	NA	NA	NA
Cash Flow	-8.5	-1.1	-5.3	-4.0	-2.5	-2.8	NA	NA	NA	NA
Curr. Ratio	8.6	12.8	7.4	14.7	14.0	NA	NA	NA	NA	NA
% LT Debt of Cap.	Nil	Nil	Nil	Nil	Nil	Nil	Nil	Nil	Nil	Nil
% Net Inc.of Revs.	NM	NM	NM	NM	NM	NM	NM	NM	NM	NM
% Ret. on Assets	NM	NM	NM	NM	NM	NM	NM	NM	NM	NM
% Ret. on Equity	NM	NM	NM	NM	NM	NM	NM	NM	NM	NM

Data as orig. reptd.; bef. results of disc. opers. and/or spec. items. Per share data adj. for stk. divs. as of ex-div. date. Bold denotes diluted EPS (FASB 128). E-Estimated. NA-Not Available. NM-Not Meaningful. NR-Not Ranked.

Office—11960 S.W. 144th St., Miami, FL 33186. **Tel**—(305) 253-5099. **Chrmn**—S. Sablotsky. **CEO & Pres**—R. C. Strauss. **EVP**—M. Goldberg. **VP-Fin & CFO**—W. A. Pecora. **Secy**—Noreen Sablotsky. **Dirs**—S. H. Becher, S. Braginsky, L. J. Dubow, M. Goldberg, S. Sablotsky, R. C. Strauss. **Transfer Agent & Registrar**—American Stock Transfer & Trust Co., NYC. **Incorporated**—in Delaware in 1987. **Empl**— 146. **S&P Analyst:** David Moskowitz

STANDARD &POOR'S
STOCK REPORTS

OM Group

1710P

NYSE Symbol **OMP**

In S&P SmallCap 600

03-OCT-98

Industry: Chemicals (Specialty)

Summary: This company is a leading producer and international marketer of value-added metal-based specialty chemicals.

Quantitative Evaluations		
Outlook (1 Lowest—5 Highest)	Recent Price • 28⅝	Yield • 1.3%
• **2**	52 Wk Range • 46-26⅞	12-Mo. P/E • 15.0

Outlook (1 Lowest—5 Highest)
• **2**

Fair Value
• **27⅝**

Risk
• **Low**

Earn./Div. Rank
• **NR**

Technical Eval.
• **NA**

Rel. Strength Rank (1 Lowest—99 Highest)
• **46**

Insider Activity
• **Neutral**

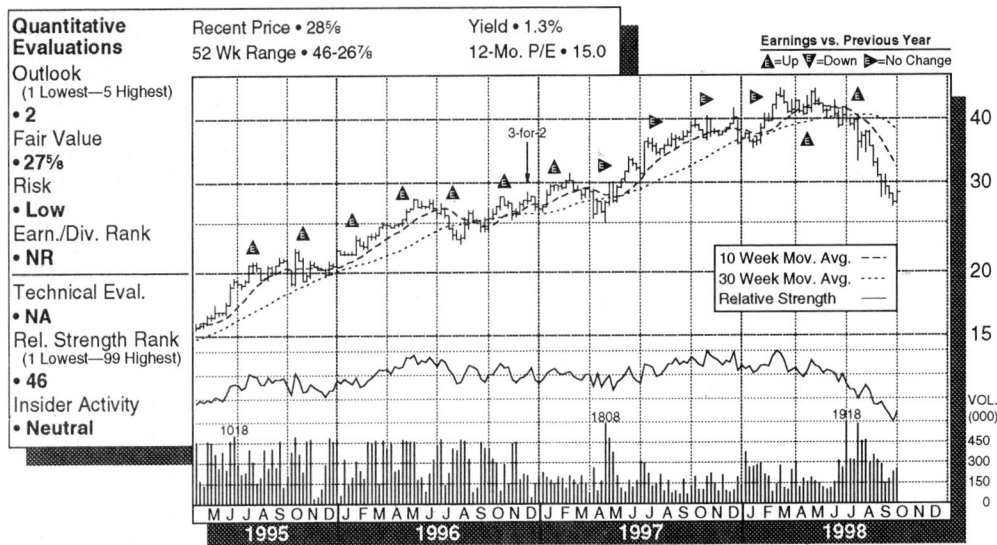

Business Profile - 16-SEP-98

Although OMP's new carboxylate and spherical nickel hydroxide facilities in Finland have not yet achieved significant revenues in the European coatings market and the Asia/Pacific rechargeable battery market, the company expects the facilities to enhance future results. In addition, it believes that earnings should benefit from increased capacity for cobalt fine powders. OMP also expects its January 1997 acquisition of SCM Metals to offer significant growth opportunities, through geographic expansion and new product development. The company, together with two foreign partners, has also committed to constructing a smelter in the Democratic Republic of Congo. The smelter, expected to be completed by mid-1999, will concentrate converter slags to cobalt-copper alloy, which will be shipped to Finland for further processing.

Operational Review - 16-SEP-98

Revenues in the first half of 1998 advanced 18%, year to year, reflecting higher sales volumes of carboxylates, salts and fine powders, as well as the January 1998 acquisition of Auric Corp. Margins widened, in part due to a more favorable product mix and lower pricing on nickel, copper and cobalt. Despite higher interest expense, pretax income climbed 27%. After taxes at 33.5%, versus 33.6%, net income was up 28%, to $22,705,000 ($1.00 a share, diluted and on 11% more shares), from $17,795,000 ($0.87).

Stock Performance - 02-OCT-98

In the past 30 trading days, OMP's shares have declined 13%, compared to a 7% fall in the S&P 500. Average trading volume for the past five days was 49,700 shares, compared with the 40-day moving average of 52,441 shares.

Key Stock Statistics

Dividend Rate/Share	0.36	Shareholders	5,700
Shs. outstg. (M)	23.8	Market cap. (B)	$0.682
Avg. daily vol. (M)	0.041	Inst. holdings	93%
Tang. Bk. Value/Share	6.17		
Beta	NA		

Value of $10,000 invested 5 years ago: NA

Fiscal Year Ending Dec. 31

	1998	1997	1996	1995	1994	1993
Revenues (Million $)						
1Q	138.1	110.1	102.8	89.43	54.86	47.50
2Q	139.2	124.3	101.5	84.97	59.06	48.60
3Q	—	126.3	89.07	80.97	59.52	43.03
4Q	—	126.6	94.59	105.6	77.84	40.38
Yr.	—	487.3	388.0	361.0	251.3	179.5
Earnings Per Share ($)						
1Q	**0.49**	0.43	0.37	0.32	0.23	0.39
2Q	**0.51**	0.44	0.39	0.35	0.28	0.12
3Q	—	0.45	0.40	0.35	0.29	0.25
4Q	—	**0.46**	0.40	0.34	0.29	0.20
Yr.	—	**1.78**	1.56	1.35	1.09	0.95

Next earnings report expected: late October

Dividend Data (Dividends have been paid since 1994.)

Amount ($)	Date Decl.	Ex-Div. Date	Stock of Record	Payment Date
0.080	Oct. 27	Nov. 12	Nov. 14	Nov. 28 '97
0.090	Feb. 03	Feb. 11	Feb. 13	Feb. 27 '98
0.090	Apr. 24	May. 13	May. 15	May. 29 '98
0.090	Aug. 04	Aug. 12	Aug. 14	Aug. 31 '98

A Division of The McGraw·Hill Companies

STANDARD
&POOR'S
STOCK REPORTS

OM Group, Inc.

1710P

03-OCT-98

Business Summary - 16-SEP-98

OM Group, Inc. is a leading producer and international marketer of value-added metal-based specialty chemicals, including metal carboxylates, salts and powders derived primarily from cobalt and nickel. It manufactures and sells more than 400 specialty chemical products for diverse applications in more than 25 industries.

Major products include custom catalysts used in petroleum refining and chemical processing; specialty additives used to accelerate the drying of paints and inks; bonding agents used in steel-belted radial tires; coloring agents used in pigments, ceramics and glass; specialty powders used to make machine, mining and drilling cutting tools; and heat stabilizers used in flexible polyvinyl chloride products.

OM Group believes that it is the only producer that manufactures and markets all three categories of metal-based specialty chemicals: carboxylates, inorganic salts and powders. The company believes it is the world's leading producer of cobalt carboxylates and cobalt and nickel specialty inorganic salts, and the second largest producer of cobalt extra-fine powders. In 1997, it sold 50.3 million lbs. of carboxylates, 61.0 million lbs. of salts, and 38.6 million lbs. of powders.

The company serves more than 1,000 customers in diverse industries, including catalysts, ceramics, coatings, electronics, magnetic tapes, petroleum refining, plating, plastics and other specialty chemicals. In 1996, the geographic breakdown of net sales was: North and South America 50%, Europe 33% and Asia/Pacific 17%.

Research and development efforts are focused on adapting proprietary technologies to develop new products and working with customers to meet their specific requirements. New products under development include new chemical formulations, concentrations of various components, product forms and packaging methods. Research and development expenditures amounted to $6.7 million in 1997, up from $3.8 million in 1996.

In January 1998, OMP said it had acquired Auric Corp., New Jersey, and Dussek Campbell, Ltd., Ontario, Canada. Auric is a leading producer of electroless nickel, electroplating chemicals, and metal concentrates, while Dussek Campbell manufactures metal carboxylates.

In April 1998, the company said it had acquired the rapid carbothermal reduction technology from Dow Chemical. The technology, which produces fine metal-based powders, has high value added applications that include rotary cutting dies and shear knives for cutting medical and industrial X-ray film.

Per Share Data ($)

(Year Ended Dec. 31)	1997	1996	1995	1994	1993	1992	1991	1990	1989	1988
Tangible Bk. Val.	8.36	8.71	7.39	6.50	5.55	NA	NA	NA	NA	NA
Cash Flow	2.76	2.44	2.07	1.65	1.55	NA	NA	NA	NA	NA
Earnings	1.78	1.56	1.35	1.09	0.95	0.77	NA	NA	NA	NA
Dividends	0.32	0.29	0.24	0.19	Nil	Nil	Nil	Nil	Nil	Nil
Payout Ratio	18%	19%	18%	17%	Nil	Nil	Nil	Nil	Nil	Nil
Prices - High	42	28³/₄	22³/₈	16¹/₂	14	NA	NA	NA	NA	NA
- Low	25	21⁵/₈	14¹/₂	12¹/₂	9³/₈	NA	NA	NA	NA	NA
P/E Ratio - High	24	18	17	15	15	NA	NA	NA	NA	NA
- Low	14	14	11	12	10	NA	NA	NA	NA	NA

Income Statement Analysis (Million $)

	1997	1996	1995	1994	1993	1992	1991	1990	1989	1988
Revs.	487	388	361	251	180	201	NA	NA	NA	NA
Oper. Inc.	91.8	67.2	57.7	45.9	34.8	NA	NA	NA	NA	NA
Depr.	21.2	15.8	13.7	10.7	9.6	NA	NA	NA	NA	NA
Int. Exp.	13.4	7.5	5.5	3.1	3.9	NA	NA	NA	NA	NA
Pretax Inc.	58.0	44.4	38.5	31.0	23.1	18.8	NA	NA	NA	NA
Eff. Tax Rate	34%	32%	33%	33%	34%	36%	NA	NA	NA	NA
Net Inc.	38.4	30.0	25.9	20.7	15.4	12.0	NA	NA	NA	NA

Balance Sheet & Other Fin. Data (Million $)

	1997	1996	1995	1994	1993	1992	1991	1990	1989	1988
Cash	13.2	7.8	9.1	8.6	NA	NA	NA	NA	NA	NA
Curr. Assets	325	271	234	157	110	89.0	NA	NA	NA	NA
Total Assets	601	439	358	278	217	173	NA	NA	NA	NA
Curr. Liab.	101	97.0	86.9	74.5	35.4	36.6	NA	NA	NA	NA
LT Debt	170	109	89.8	46.6	30.6	48.5	NA	NA	NA	NA
Common Eqty.	301	185	161	141	125	80.0	NA	NA	NA	NA
Total Cap.	492	312	270	202	156	129	NA	NA	NA	NA
Cap. Exp.	34.4	28.1	31.2	19.7	8.7	NA	NA	NA	NA	NA
Cash Flow	59.7	45.9	39.7	31.4	25.0	NA	NA	NA	NA	NA
Curr. Ratio	3.2	2.8	2.7	2.1	3.1	2.4	NA	NA	NA	NA
% LT Debt of Cap.	34.6	34.9	33.3	23.0	19.6	37.6	NA	NA	NA	NA
% Net Inc.of Revs.	7.9	7.7	7.2	8.3	8.6	6.0	NA	NA	NA	NA
% Ret. on Assets	7.4	7.5	8.2	8.4	7.9	6.9	NA	NA	NA	NA
% Ret. on Equity	15.8	17.3	13.7	15.6	15.0	15.7	NA	NA	NA	NA

Data as orig. reptd.; bef. results of disc. opers. and/or spec. items. Per share data adj. for stk. divs. as of ex-div. date. Bold denotes diluted EPS (FASB 128). E-Estimated. NA-Not Available. NM-Not Meaningful. NR-Not Ranked.

Office—50 Public Square, 3800 Terminal Tower, Cleveland, OH 44113-2204. **Tel**—(216) 781-0083. **Chrmn & CEO**—J. P. Mooney. **Pres & COO**—E. Bak. **CFO**—J. M. Materna. **VP & Secy**—M. J. Scott. **Investor Contact**—Kristine A. Marks. **Dirs**—L. R. Brodeur, F. Butler, T. R. Miklich, J. E. Mooney, J. P. Mooney, M. Toivanen. **Transfer Agent & Registrar**—National City Bank, Cleveland. **Incorporated**—in Delaware in 1991. **Empl**—758. **S&P Analyst**: K.J.F.

Oak Industries

1711M

NYSE Symbol **OAK**

In S&P SmallCap 600

10-OCT-98

Industry:
Electrical Equipment

Summary: This company is a leading supplier of components to manufacturers and service providers in the communications industry.

S&P Opinion: Hold (★★★)	Recent Price • 22⅜	Yield • Nil
	52 Wk Range • 41¼-21¾	12-Mo. P/E • 15.6

Quantitative Evaluations

Outlook
(1 Lowest—5 Highest)
• **3⁻**

Fair Value
• **28¾**

Risk
• **Average**

Earn./Div. Rank
• **B-**

Technical Eval.
• **NA**

Rel. Strength Rank
(1 Lowest—99 Highest)
• **28**

Insider Activity
• **NA**

Earnings vs. Previous Year
▲=Up ▼=Down ▶=No Change

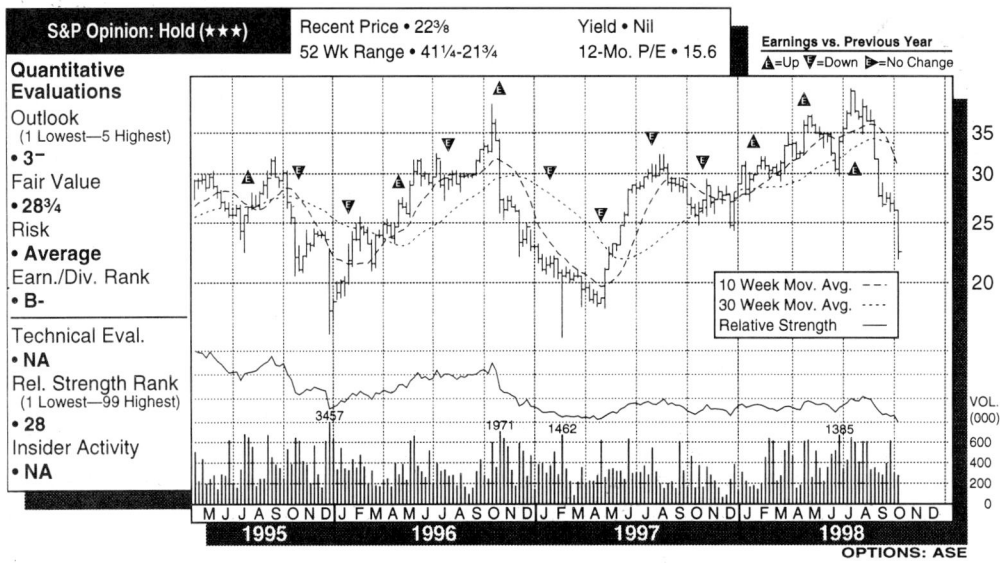

10 Week Mov. Avg. – – –
30 Week Mov. Avg. · · · · ·
Relative Strength ——

OPTIONS: ASE

Overview - 06-OCT-98

Uncertainty regarding capital spending by the communications industry increased as the third quarter drew to a close, as several leading systems suppliers indicated that their business is slowing. We had been expecting spending on high bandwidth fiber optic networks to remain robust, and for spending by cable firms to strengthen as 1998 progressed. We now expect moderate revenue growth for OAK at the lower end of our target 7%-9% in 1998, and have trimmed our earnings forecast this year from $1.55 to $1.50. Earnings visibility for 1999 has diminished as well, in light of the warnings from a few top firms in the industry. Thus, we have cut our revenue growth expectations for 1999 from 12%-14% to the 9%-11% range, and see earnings growth in the mid-teens, resulting in a reduction in our EPS estimate from $1.95 to $1.75.

Valuation - 06-OCT-98

Given our more conservative earnings growth forecast, we have lowered OAK from accumulate to hold. The overall market is discounting a greater level of risk into stock prices due to earnings concerns in the U.S., as economic weakness in nearly every other part of the world except Europe creeps nearer. Despite the Federal Reserve's cut in the overnight bank lending rate by a quarter point and the prospect for further rate cuts later this year, stocks have fallen out of favor at least in the short term. While a further decline in OAK's share price may at some point present a buying opportunity, we would not add to long positions at this time, as the shares may only trade in line with the market during the short term.

Key Stock Statistics

S&P EPS Est. 1998	1.50	Tang. Bk. Value/Share	1.55
P/E on S&P Est. 1998	15.0	Beta	0.89
S&P EPS Est. 1999	1.75	Shareholders	5,700
Dividend Rate/Share	Nil	Market cap. (B)	$0.407
Shs. outstg. (M)	18.1	Inst. holdings	92%
Avg. daily vol. (M)	0.084		

Value of $10,000 invested 5 years ago: $ 18,894

Fiscal Year Ending Dec. 31

	1998	1997	1996	1995	1994	1993
Revenues (Million $)						
1Q	79.21	73.04	78.74	71.60	61.79	59.22
2Q	88.66	80.31	80.59	66.93	65.68	58.22
3Q	—	76.98	74.09	65.04	58.40	51.58
4Q	—	84.07	70.12	73.01	63.14	50.54
Yr.	—	314.4	303.5	276.6	249.0	219.6
Earnings Per Share ($)						
1Q	0.35	0.22	0.92	0.58	0.40	0.28
2Q	0.11	0.30	0.34	0.58	0.56	0.31
3Q	E0.36	0.32	0.39	-4.08	0.40	0.35
4Q	E0.39	0.36	0.06	0.23	0.94	0.53
Yr.	E1.50	1.20	1.71	-2.74	2.31	1.47

Next earnings report expected: mid October

Dividend Data

Cash dividends, paid since 1934, were omitted in 1983. A one-for-five reverse stock split was effected in 1993. A "poison pill" stock purchase rights plan was adopted in 1995.

A Division of The McGraw-Hill Companies

Business Summary - 06-OCT-98

Oak Industries Inc., through its family of companies, is a leading supplier of highly engineered components to the communications and selected other industries. The company also manufactures controls components for the gas appliance industry and switches and encoders for use in commercial, medical and military applications.

The communications components segment is a leading manufacturer of highly engineered components that it designs and sells to manufacturers and service providers in the communications industry. Oak's precision components for the communications infrastructure include: fiber optic pumps, transmitters and detectors for telephony; oscillators and crystals for wireless base stations and digital switches; and coaxial connectors for CATV and microwave applications. The communications components group consists of Gilbert Engineering Co., Inc. (96.25% owned), Oak Frequency Control Group (OFCG) and Lasertron, Inc. Communications components accounted for 69% of 1997 revenues (70% in 1996).

Within the controls components group, Harper-Wyman Co. is a leading supplier of components to original equipment manufacturers of gas range appliances and also supplies components for outdoor grills. OakGrigsby Inc. manufactures optical, rotary and appliance switches and encoders for applications in the test and measure-

ment, communications, medical and other markets. Controls components accounted for 31% of 1997 revenues (30%).

Two key aspects of the company's business strategy are to develop new products and increase market share, and to grow through strategic acquisitions. To support these initiatives, Lasertron recently introduced advanced transmission products that will be marketed to the same customer base that purchases Lasertron's pump lasers for amplification of fiber-optic signals; and OFCG has recently introduced a voltage controlled oscillator product line, expanding its customer base to include manufacturers of switching and transmission equipment in addition to OFCG's traditional customer base of manufacturers of wireless base stations and military and satellite equipment.

Oak's sales have increased in part through acquisitions, including Gilbert in 1992, Cabel-Con A/S in 1994, Lasertron in 1995 and Piezo Crystal Co. in 1997. Oak also has divested non-strategic businesses in order to make more effective use of available capital. The company plans to continue pursuing strategic acquisitions that complement its existing businesses. Oak believes that the benefits of acquisitions include expanding its product lines and increasing its customer base.

On February 25, 1998, OAK issued $100 million of 4 7/8% convertible subordinated notes due 2008. The conversion price is $38.66 a share.

Per Share Data ($)

(Year Ended Dec. 31)	1997	1996	1995	1994	1993	1992	1991	1990	1989	1988
Tangible Bk. Val.	0.16	0.28	2.24	5.23	3.25	1.55	5.10	4.75	4.05	6.10
Cash Flow	2.33	2.08	2.11	2.89	2.04	0.95	0.60	0.35	-0.85	1.30
Earnings	1.20	1.71	-2.74	2.31	1.47	0.60	0.35	0.10	-1.15	0.85
Dividends	Nil	Nil	Nil	Nil	Nil	Nil	Nil	Nil	Nil	Nil
Payout Ratio	Nil	Nil	Nil	Nil	Nil	Nil	Nil	Nil	Nil	Nil
Prices - High	32¼	39	32	29⅞	29	14⅜	5⅝	6⅞	8¾	6¼
- Low	16¼	18¾	16½	15⅝	10⅝	4⅜	3⅛	1¼	3¾	3¾
P/E Ratio - High	27	23	NM	13	20	24	16	69	NM	7
- Low	14	11	NM	7	7	7	9	16	NM	4

Income Statement Analysis (Million $)

	1997	1996	1995	1994	1993	1992	1991	1990	1989	1988
Revs.	314	304	277	249	220	143	124	139	160	198
Oper. Inc.	66.3	54.3	-13.1	61.0	47.0	10.1	6.7	4.4	0.6	10.4
Depr.	19.1	7.3	11.7	10.6	10.3	5.3	4.6	5.2	5.0	6.5
Int. Exp.	11.0	5.8	6.3	6.6	7.8	1.4	1.8	2.1	4.6	5.8
Pretax Inc.	36.7	62.0	-27.8	43.4	26.3	9.0	2.0	2.0	-19.0	10.0
Eff. Tax Rate	38%	37%	NM	NM	NM	NM	NM	23%	NM	NM
Net Inc.	21.7	32.0	-50.5	42.4	26.7	10.0	5.0	1.0	-19.0	13.0

Balance Sheet & Other Fin. Data (Million $)

	1997	1996	1995	1994	1993	1992	1991	1990	1989	1988
Cash	8.6	6.1	16.9	37.6	27.4	24.9	37.6	44.5	21.8	29.9
Curr. Assets	126	125	134	120	96.0	90.0	82.0	93.0	82.0	120
Total Assets	388	374	313	282	238	229	125	131	131	181
Curr. Liab.	40.8	45.5	53.7	47.5	27.0	35.0	20.0	29.0	33.0	39.0
LT Debt	151	138	91.6	34.0	62.0	77.0	11.0	11.0	17.0	35.0
Common Eqty.	188	172	119	167	127	98.1	84.0	78.0	67.0	92.0
Total Cap.	339	321	247	228	203	182	95.0	90.0	84.0	127
Cap. Exp.	14.6	23.2	17.5	6.8	7.0	4.1	4.7	6.5	5.4	7.5
Cash Flow	40.8	39.3	-38.8	53.1	37.0	16.0	10.0	6.0	-14.0	19.0
Curr. Ratio	3.1	2.7	2.5	2.5	3.6	2.6	4.0	3.2	2.5	3.1
% LT Debt of Cap.	44.7	43.0	37.1	15.1	30.3	42.2	11.8	12.6	20.7	27.7
% Net Inc.of Revs.	6.9	NM	NM	17.0	12.1	7.3	4.2	1.0	NM	6.5
% Ret. on Assets	5.7	9.3	NM	16.2	11.2	5.9	4.1	1.1	NM	7.1
% Ret. on Equity	11.9	22.0	NM	28.7	23.3	11.4	6.5	1.9	NM	15.1

Data as orig. reptd.; bef. results of disc. opers. and/or spec. items. Per share data adj. for stk. divs. as of ex-div. date. Bold denotes diluted EPS (FASB 128). E-Estimated. NA-Not Available. NM-Not Meaningful. NR-Not Ranked.

Office—1000 Winter St., Waltham, MA 02154. **Tel**—(617) 890-0400. **Website**—http://www.oakind.com **Chrmn, Pres & CEO**—W. S Antle III. **Vice Chrmn**—R. M. Hills. **SVP & CFO**—C. S. Hicks. **VP & Secy**—M. Lew. **Dirs**—W. S. Antle III, B. L. Bronner, D. W. Derbes, R. M. Hills, G. W. Leisz, G. E. Matthews, C. H. B. Mills, E. L. Richardson. **Transfer Agent & Registrar**—Bank of Boston. **Incorporated**—in Delaware in 1960. **Empl**— 3,373. **S&P Analyst:** Mark S. Basham

Oakwood Homes

1712A

NYSE Symbol **OH**

In S&P SmallCap 600

03-OCT-98 **Industry:** Homebuilding

Summary: This vertically integrated producer and retailer of manufactured homes also derives substantial profits from related financial services.

S&P Opinion: Hold (★★★)	Recent Price • 13⅛ Yield • 0.3%
	52 Wk Range • 42¼-12½ 12-Mo. P/E • 10.9

Quantitative Evaluations

Outlook (1 Lowest—5 Highest)
• **5**

Fair Value
• **26¼**

Risk
• **Average**

Earn./Div. Rank
• **A**

Technical Eval.
• **Bearish** since 5/98

Rel. Strength Rank (1 Lowest—99 Highest)
• **14**

Insider Activity
• **Favorable**

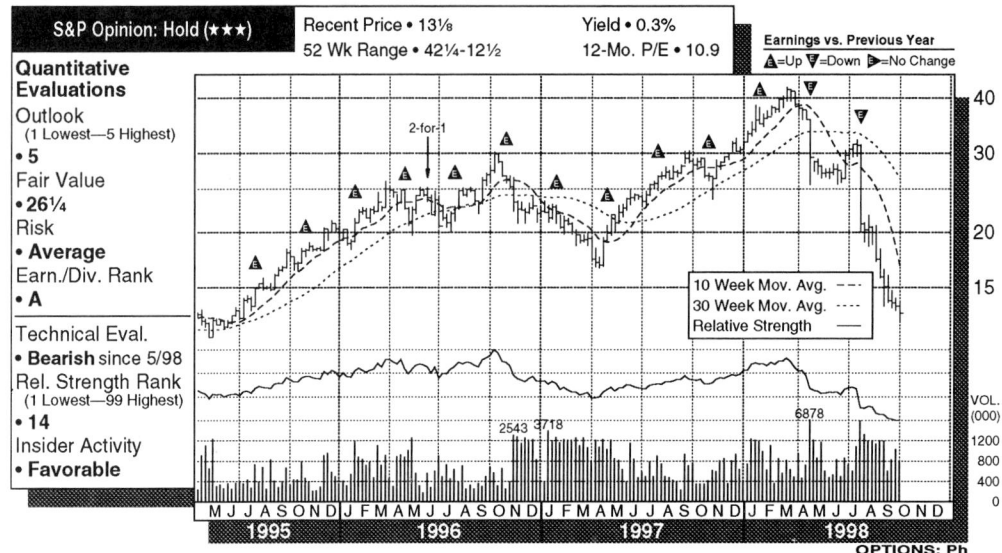

Earnings vs. Previous Year
▲=Up ▼=Down ▶=No Change

10 Week Mov. Avg. – – –
30 Week Mov. Avg. ····
Relative Strength —

OPTIONS: Ph

Overview - 28-JUL-98

We expect solid sales growth in FY 99 (Sep.), on OH's aggressive retail network expansion, its capacity re-alignment toward higher-priced multi-section homes, and the full-year inclusion of Schult Homes (acquired in April 1998). We expect margins to narrow a bit, as OH's proportion of lower-margin wholesale sales will increase with the inclusion of Schult. That factor will be partly offset by production efficiencies and higher operating levels. Despite the narrower margins accorded to sales made by Schult, the unit should still add considerably to OH's bottom line in FY 99 after having only a slight impact in FY 98. Comparisons will be distorted by $0.67 a share of charges taken to date in FY 98 for the writedown of interests in securitized loans and OH's investment in a financial services joint venture.

Valuation - 28-JUL-98

The shares weakened sharply in April and July 1998, when OH reported disappointing results for FY 98's second and third quarters, respectively. The shortfalls stemmed largely from charges related to a sloppy lending program between 1994 and 1996, excess loan prepayments generated by lower interest rates, and poor results in a financing joint venture (in which OH will sell its interest). In April, we expected a quick recovery of the shares, as management took aggressive steps to overcome its problems on the financing side, and told analysts that the troubles were behind it. However, when the situation grew even worse in the third quarter, it caused many to lose faith in OH's management. Although that situation caused us to downgrade our accumulate recommendation on Oakwood, we would still hold our shares. We base that opinion on the fact that despite its troubles in the financing arena, Oakwood still boasts a very solid manufactured housing operation.

Key Stock Statistics

S&P EPS Est. 1998	1.26	Tang. Bk. Value/Share	11.14
P/E on S&P Est. 1998	10.4	Beta	1.45
S&P EPS Est. 1999	2.25	Shareholders	1,000
Dividend Rate/Share	0.04	Market cap. (B)	$0.612
Shs. outstg. (M)	46.7	Inst. holdings	70%
Avg. daily vol. (M)	0.169		

Value of $10,000 invested 5 years ago: $ 13,221

Fiscal Year Ending Sep. 30

	1998	1997	1996	1995	1994	1993
Revenues (Million $)						
1Q	221.9	207.2	204.4	167.1	113.0	56.40
2Q	264.9	220.3	221.2	187.1	129.7	68.00
3Q	440.5	292.4	263.5	226.1	164.2	89.30
4Q	—	350.1	284.8	241.1	172.1	108.7
Yr.	—	1,070	973.9	821.4	579.1	322.4
Earnings Per Share ($)						
1Q	**0.38**	**0.33**	0.30	0.18	0.15	0.13
2Q	**0.16**	0.38	0.35	0.21	0.17	0.13
3Q	**0.10**	0.48	0.38	0.27	0.23	0.17
4Q	**E0.62**	0.56	0.44	0.33	0.23	0.20
Yr.	**E1.26**	1.75	1.47	0.98	0.77	0.63

Next earnings report expected: early November

Dividend Data (Dividends have been paid since 1976.)

Amount ($)	Date Decl.	Ex-Div. Date	Stock of Record	Payment Date
0.010	Oct. 22	Nov. 06	Nov. 10	Nov. 26 '97
0.010	Jan. 26	Feb. 06	Feb. 10	Feb. 25 '98
0.010	Apr. 29	May. 08	May. 12	May. 27 '98
0.010	Jul. 23	Aug. 07	Aug. 11	Aug. 26 '98

A Division of The McGraw-Hill Companies

Business Summary - 28-JUL-98

Oakwood Homes produces and sells manufactured homes (90% of revenues and 63% of operating profits in FY 97--Sep.). OH's manufacturing, sales and financing activities are completely integrated, giving it control of all important homebuying elements. Oakwood's retail home sales expanded twice as fast as the industry growth rate over the five years through FY 97.

OH's homes are constructed and furnished at its factories and transported by truck to the homesite. OH makes single- and multi-section homes, whose retail prices ranged from $13,000 to $124,000 in FY 97. Oakwood sold 25,135 new homes in FY 97 (22,088 at its own retailers) and produced 95% of the homes it sold at retail. In recent years, OH boosted its emphasis on multi-section homes, whose larger living area is attractive to consumers. Multi-sections represented 47% of retail unit sales in FY 97, up from 32% in FY 96.

Oakwood sells its homes through company-owned dealers (90% of manufactured housing sales in FY 97) and other channels (mainly independent dealers; 10%). OH's retail network nearly tripled in size in the five years through FY 97 year-end, through both expansion and acquisitions. After adding 45 net centers during the year, Oakwood was operating 300 company-owned retail centers at FY 97 year-end (339 at June 30, 1998), spanning 28 states. OH had planned to add about 50 centers per year over the next few years, focusing on the Deep South, Southwest and Pacific Northwest; its

April 1998 takeover of Schult Homes (annual sales of $348 million), for $101 million, will probably cause OH to increase the number of targeted openings. Schult produces manufactured and modular homes, and gives OH a leading position in the Midwest.

Oakwood also sold homes through 93 independent dealers at FY 97 year-end. It obtained those wholesale operations through the acquisitions of Destiny Industries (June 1995) and Golden West Homes (September 1994). Schult Homes also markets its product through over 900 independent dealers. However, OH believes it is much better served to be vertically integrated and control its retail distribution, and has been moving the Destiny and Golden West operations in that direction.

Most of OH's home sales are now financed through installment contracts with its finance unit. The division allows full-service one-stop shopping and also lets Oakwood achieve greater earnings stability, as it generates fee income from its servicing portfolio.

Oakwood recorded $0.46 a share of charges in FY 98's third quarter to reduce the carrying value of its interests in loan securitizations (group of loans pooled and sold in secondary markets) and its investment in a joint venture (DFC venture); it took $0.21 of charges in the prior quarter to writedown securitization interests. The latest charges stemmed from higher prepayment assumptions, a worse than expected performance of DFC securitizations, and OH's decision to terminate its interest in DFC, which offers financing to independent manufactured home retailers.

Per Share Data ($)

(Year Ended Sep. 30)	1997	1996	1995	1994	1993	1992	1991	1990	1989	1988
Tangible Bk. Val.	10.45	8.74	7.18	6.42	5.63	3.96	3.50	2.96	2.70	2.54
Cash Flow	2.06	1.70	1.20	0.86	0.70	0.64	0.53	0.43	0.27	0.14
Earnings	1.75	1.47	0.98	0.77	0.63	0.50	0.39	0.28	0.14	0.02
Dividends	0.04	0.04	0.04	0.04	0.04	0.03	0.02	0.02	0.02	0.02
Payout Ratio	2%	3%	4%	5%	7%	6%	7%	8%	15%	100%
Prices - High	33⅝	30¼	21¼	15	14⅜	10¾	5½	3¼	2⅜	2⅝
- Low	16⅝	18¼	10⅞	9⅝	8⅝	5⅛	2⅞	1¹¹/₁₆	1⅝	1½
P/E Ratio - High	19	21	22	19	23	21	14	11	17	NM
- Low	9	12	11	13	14	10	7	6	11	NM

Income Statement Analysis (Million $)

	1997	1996	1995	1994	1993	1992	1991	1990	1989	1988
Revs.	1,055	954	804	575	317	228	160	134	100	77.0
Oper. Inc.	153	125	88.3	56.1	37.4	47.2	35.0	25.0	14.8	-6.1
Depr.	14.3	10.4	8.3	4.3	2.9	3.7	3.1	3.0	2.6	2.5
Int. Exp.	19.8	22.4	24.9	24.3	26.1	25.3	20.3	16.2	14.6	4.1
Pretax Inc.	133	111	73.0	53.9	38.9	21.4	14.3	8.8	4.0	0.1
Eff. Tax Rate	39%	38%	36%	37%	37%	34%	38%	38%	29%	NM
Net Inc.	81.9	68.3	46.6	33.9	24.5	14.0	8.9	5.5	2.8	0.4

Balance Sheet & Other Fin. Data (Million $)

	1997	1996	1995	1994	1993	1992	1991	1990	1989	1988
Cash	28.7	28.6	6.2	12.6	23.9	17.2	16.3	12.8	14.8	38.6
Curr. Assets	NA	NA	NA	NA	NA	NA	NA	NA	NA	72.0
Total Assets	905	842	783	575	557	432	345	275	229	137
Curr. Liab.	NA	NA	NA	NA	NA	NA	NA	NA	NA	10.8
LT Debt	78.8	134	199	173	223	258	182	169	122	59.0
Common Eqty.	484	392	318	271	229	104	89.7	57.9	52.7	51.7
Total Cap.	563	526	517	444	452	364	274	232	179	116
Cap. Exp.	38.4	41.3	41.9	27.2	13.0	5.3	2.3	3.4	6.3	7.7
Cash Flow	96.2	78.8	54.9	38.2	27.4	17.7	12.0	8.5	5.3	3.0
Curr. Ratio	NA	NA	NA	NA	NA	NA	NA	NA	NA	6.7
% LT Debt of Cap.	14.0	25.5	38.5	39.0	49.3	70.8	66.3	73.1	68.1	50.4
% Net Inc.of Revs.	7.8	7.2	5.8	5.9	7.7	6.1	5.5	4.1	2.8	0.6
% Ret. on Assets	9.4	8.4	6.8	5.9	4.0	3.6	2.5	2.2	1.6	0.3
% Ret. on Equity	18.7	19.2	15.7	13.3	12.6	14.3	10.7	9.9	5.5	0.8

Data as orig. reptd.; bef. results of disc. opers. and/or spec. items. Per share data adj. for stk. divs. as of ex-div. date. Bold denotes diluted EPS (FASB 128). Revs. in Inc. Statement excl. certain oth. inc. E-Estimated. NA-Not Available. NM-Not Meaningful. NR-Not Ranked.

Mailing Address—P.O. Box 27081, Greensboro, NC 27425-7081. **Tel**—(336) 664-2400. **Website**—http://www.oakwoodhomes.com **Chrmn, Pres & CEO**—N. J. St. George. **EVP & CFO**—C. M. Kilbourne. **Dirs**—W. G. Edwards, C. M. Kilbourne, D. I. Meyer, K. G. Phillips II, N. J. St. George, H. W. Schipke, L. L. Smith, S. C. Streeter, F. T. Vincent Jr., C. W. Walker, H. M. Weaver. **Transfer Agent & Registrar**—First Union National Bank of North Carolina, Charlotte. **Incorporated**—in North Carolina in 1971. **Empl**— 7,078. **S&P Analyst:** Michael W. Jaffe

03-OCT-98

Industry:
Oil & Gas (Drilling & Equipment)

Summary: This company provides offshore services to the oil and gas industries, as well as various services to companies that operate in other harsh environments.

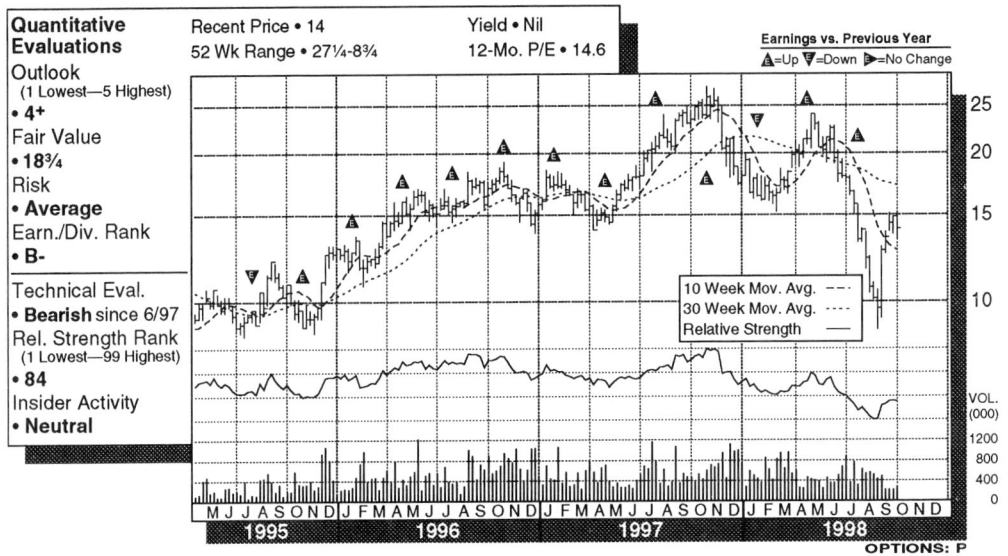

Quantitative Evaluations

Outlook (1 Lowest—5 Highest)
• **4+**

Fair Value
• **18¾**

Risk
• **Average**

Earn./Div. Rank
• **B-**

Technical Eval.
• **Bearish** since 6/97

Rel. Strength Rank (1 Lowest—99 Highest)
• **84**

Insider Activity
• **Neutral**

Recent Price • 14
52 Wk Range • 27¼-8¾

Yield • Nil
12-Mo. P/E • 14.6

Earnings vs. Previous Year
▲=Up ▼=Down ▶=No Change

10 Week Mov. Avg. — — —
30 Week Mov. Avg. ········
Relative Strength ————

VOL. (000)

OPTIONS: P

Business Profile - 13-JUL-98

Through several acquisitions and contracts awarded since 1990, Oceaneering International (OII) has grown to become one of the world's largest providers of services to companies that operate in harsh environments, such as the ocean and space. The company announced in December 1997 that it will begin construction of a second multiservice vehicle for deepwater installation work in the Gulf of Mexico. In January 1998, OII purchased a production barge for $7 million. A turnkey contract was granted in March to provide services to Kerr-McGee Oil and Gas. Also in March, the company announced that it will manufacture fourteen remotely operated vehicles.

Operational Review - 13-JUL-98

Revenues for the fiscal year ending March 31, 1998, decreased 3% to $358.1 million from $368.8 million. The Offshore Field Development and Advanced Technologies segments were responsible for the declines, the former due to the absence of a 1997 gain on the sale of a Floating Production, Storage and Offloading system, and the latter due to fewer telecommunications and civil projects. After taxes at 38.1%, versus 52.9%, net income climbed 15% to $22 million ($0.93 per share) from $19.4 million ($0.81).

Stock Performance - 02-OCT-98

In the past 30 trading days, OII's shares have increased 39%, compared to a 7% fall in the S&P 500. Average trading volume for the past five days was 53,180 shares, compared with the 40-day moving average of 74,256 shares.

Key Stock Statistics

Dividend Rate/Share	Nil	Shareholders	600
Shs. outstg. (M)	23.0	Market cap. (B)	$0.324
Avg. daily vol. (M)	0.050	Inst. holdings	67%
Tang. Bk. Value/Share	6.53		
Beta	0.97		

Value of $10,000 invested 5 years ago: $ 10,921

Fiscal Year Ending Mar. 31

	1999	1998	1997	1996	1995	1994
Revenues (Million $)						
1Q	98.91	95.16	80.54	71.54	63.37	59.39
2Q	—	90.58	96.76	77.09	66.90	65.54
3Q	—	86.23	94.12	74.24	55.20	55.49
4Q	—	86.15	97.36	66.64	54.47	49.34
Yr.	—	358.1	368.8	289.5	239.9	229.8
Earnings Per Share ($)						
1Q	0.28	0.25	0.16	0.12	0.15	0.20
2Q	—	0.28	0.21	0.20	0.18	0.20
3Q	—	0.21	0.28	0.15	-0.12	0.16
4Q	—	0.19	0.16	0.06	0.02	0.06
Yr.	—	0.93	0.81	0.53	0.23	0.62

Next earnings report expected: NA

Dividend Data

No dividends have been paid since 1977. A "poison pill" stock purchase rights plan was adopted in November 1992.

Business Summary - 13-JUL-98

From under water to outer space, Oceaneering International (OII) provides engineered services and hardware to help its customers deal with the unique challenges presented when operating in harsh environments. One of the world's largest underwater services contractors, OII's primary market is the offshore oil and gas industry. The company supplies a comprehensive range of services to that industry, including subsea construction, drilling support, production systems, facilities maintenance and repair, surveys and positioning, and specialized onshore and offshore engineering and inspection. OII breaks its business structure into three segments: Oilfield Marine Services, Offshore Field Developments, and Advanced Technologies.

Oilfield Marine Services consist of underwater intervention, and above-water inspection, maintenance and repair. Underwater intervention support is provided for all phases of offshore oil and gas operations. During exploration, OII provides positioning, placement and monitoring of subsea exploration equipment, collects data on seafloor characteristics at proposed drilling sites, and assists with navigational placements of drilling rigs. For development, OII aids in installing production platforms and connecting pipelines. In the production phase, OII inspects, maintains, and repairs offshore platforms, pipelines and equipment. These services are performed by divers or remotely operated vehicles (ROV's) The company believes that it operates the most technically advanced fleet of work class ROV's in the world, with a 25% market share. Oceaneering also supplies the oil and gas industry with survey and navigational positioning services, as well as ocean search and recovery projects. Above-water inspection services are provided for customers required to obtain third party inspections.

The Offshore Field Development segment provides subsea intervention services and the engineering, procurement, construction, installation, and operation of mobile offshore production systems (MOPS). Through its Advanced Technologies (AdTech) segment, OII provides underwater intervention, topside inspection, and engineering services to meet a variety of non-oilfield industrial requirements, including ship husbandry, search and recovery, subsea telecommunications cable installation, maintenance and repair, civil work projects, and commercial theme parks. AdTech customers include the U.S. Navy and NASA.

Per Share Data ($) (Year Ended Mar. 31)	1998	1997	1996	1995	1994	1993	1992	1991	1990	1989
Tangible Bk. Val.	6.54	6.06	4.95	4.43	4.14	4.17	3.78	3.08	2.23	1.44
Cash Flow	1.92	1.84	1.42	0.90	1.13	1.30	1.01	1.00	0.76	0.44
Earnings	0.93	0.81	0.53	0.23	0.62	0.82	0.70	0.72	0.47	0.06
Dividends	Nil	Nil	Nil	Nil	Nil	Nil	Nil	Nil	Nil	Nil
Payout Ratio	Nil	Nil	Nil	Nil	Nil	Nil	Nil	Nil	Nil	Nil
Cal. Yrs.	1997	1996	1995	1994	1993	1992	1991	1990	1989	1988
Prices - High	27 1/4	19 1/4	13	14 5/8	18 1/2	18 1/8	14 1/8	18 7/8	11 3/8	3 5/8
- Low	14	10 3/4	7 3/4	9 3/4	10 3/4	8 7/8	8 1/2	8 3/4	2 1/2	1
P/E Ratio - High	29	24	25	64	30	22	20	26	24	60
- Low	15	13	15	42	17	11	12	12	5	33
Income Statement Analysis (Million $)										
Revs.	358	369	290	240	230	216	168	147	183	133
Oper. Inc.	59.5	57.2	40.8	29.0	33.1	38.4	26.7	23.5	21.0	11.2
Depr.	23.2	24.7	20.6	16.2	12.2	11.5	7.2	6.3	6.5	8.3
Int. Exp.	0.6	2.0	2.3	0.7	0.9	1.4	NM	NM	NM	NM
Pretax Inc.	35.6	41.3	19.9	12.5	20.8	25.4	22.0	22.3	15.0	2.8
Eff. Tax Rate	38%	53%	38%	56%	28%	23%	26%	26%	30%	53%
Net Inc.	22.0	19.4	12.4	5.5	14.9	19.4	15.9	16.3	10.2	1.2
Balance Sheet & Other Fin. Data (Million $)										
Cash	9.1	23.0	9.3	12.9	26.5	34.0	23.3	40.1	37.8	23.9
Curr. Assets	131	149	110	75.8	80.8	88.8	66.9	72.1	71.6	57.3
Total Assets	317	268	256	188	172	155	136	113	96.0	77.0
Curr. Liab.	86.2	95.8	68.0	52.7	46.4	46.3	38.3	30.3	32.5	36.0
LT Debt	54.6	Nil	48.0	9.5	0.2	0.2	0.3	0.4	Nil	0.6
Common Eqty.	160	156	127	115	113	98.3	85.2	68.9	49.6	31.4
Total Cap.	215	157	176	126	115	101	89.5	73.2	52.6	34.6
Cap. Exp.	94.4	79.6	57.2	32.1	36.7	12.0	34.6	19.9	11.5	8.4
Cash Flow	45.2	44.2	32.9	21.7	27.1	30.9	23.1	22.6	16.7	9.6
Curr. Ratio	1.5	1.6	1.6	1.4	1.7	1.9	1.7	2.4	2.2	1.6
% LT Debt of Cap.	25.4	Nil	27.3	7.5	0.1	0.2	0.4	0.6	Nil	1.7
% Net Inc.of Revs.	6.1	5.3	4.3	2.3	6.5	9.0	9.5	11.1	5.6	0.9
% Ret. on Assets	7.5	7.4	5.6	3.1	9.1	13.1	12.7	15.5	11.6	1.8
% Ret. on Equity	13.9	13.7	10.2	4.8	14.1	20.7	20.6	27.4	24.9	3.9

Data as orig. reptd.; bef. results of disc. opers. and/or spec. items. Per share data adj. for stk. divs. as of ex-div. date. Bold denotes diluted EPS (FASB 128). E-Estimated. NA-Not Available. NM-Not Meaningful. NR-Not Ranked.

Office—11911 F.M. 529, Houston, TX 77041. **Tel**—(713) 329-4500.**Website**—http://www.oceaneering.com **Chrmn, Pres & CEO**—J. R. Huff. **SVP & CFO**—M. J. Migura. **VP & Secy**—G. R. Haubenreich, Jr. **Investor Contact**—Jack Jurkoshek, (713)329-4670.**Dirs**— C. B. Evans, D. S. Hooker, J. R. Huff, D. M. Hughes, H. J. Pappas. **Transfer Agent & Registrar**—First Chicago Trust Co. of New York, Jersey City, NJ. **Incorporated**—in Delaware in 1969. **Empl**— 2,600. **S&P Analyst:** Ephraim Juskowicz.

Offshore Logistics 4856

NASDAQ Symbol **OLOG**

In S&P SmallCap 600

10-OCT-98

Industry:
Oil & Gas (Drilling & Equipment)

Summary: This company provides helicopter transportation and related services to the offshore oil and gas industry worldwide, principally in the Gulf of Mexico.

Quantitative Evaluations		
Outlook (1 Lowest—5 Highest) • **4⁻**		
Fair Value • **16¾**		
Risk • **Average**		
Earn./Div. Rank • **B-**		
Technical Eval. • **Bullish** since 10/98		
Rel. Strength Rank (1 Lowest—99 Highest) • **57**		
Insider Activity • **Favorable**		

Recent Price • 11¼
52 Wk Range • 25¾-8¾
Yield • Nil
12-Mo. P/E • 8.3

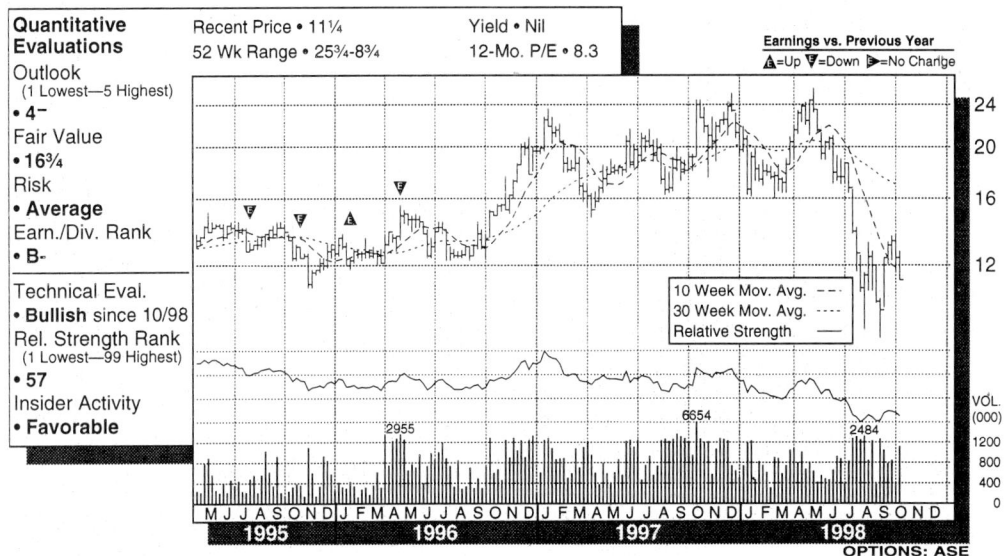

Earnings vs. Previous Year
▲=Up ▼=Down ▶=No Change

10 Week Mov. Avg. ---
30 Week Mov. Avg. ·····
Relative Strength —

OPTIONS: ASE

Business Profile - 27-JUL-98

This company's main business segment provides helicopter transportation services to the worldwide offshore oil and gas industry. Revenues have recently been boosted by increased activity in the Gulf of Mexico, and this trend should continue over the long term, with the added emphasis by the exploration and production industry in the Gulf. However, the recent deterioration of oil prices has led to a decline in drilling activity in the Gulf of Mexico. In December 1996, the company acquired 49% of the capital stock of Bristow Helicopter Group, Ltd., a U.K.-headquartered company. In May 1997, OLOG changed its fiscal year end to March 31, from June 30.

Operational Review - 27-JUL-98

Revenues from continuing operations in the fiscal year ended March 31, 1998, more than doubled from those of the preceding fiscal year, which included only the nine months ended March 31, 1997, resulting from a change in the company's fiscal year end from June 30 to March 31. Revenue growth reflected increased flight hours and higher helicopter rates in the Gulf of Mexico, and the inclusion of Bristow. Income from continuing operations was up 77%, to $31,254,000 ($1.35 a share), from $17,625,000 ($0.85).

Stock Performance - 09-OCT-98

In the past 30 trading days, OLOG's shares have increased 10%, compared to a 4% fall in the S&P 500. Average trading volume for the past five days was 220,400 shares, compared with the 40-day moving average of 194,977 shares.

Key Stock Statistics

Dividend Rate/Share	Nil	Shareholders	2,000
Shs. outstg. (M)	21.9	Market cap. (B)	$0.246
Avg. daily vol. (M)	0.154	Inst. holdings	79%
Tang. Bk. Value/Share	13.08		
Beta	1.46		

Value of $10,000 invested 5 years ago: $ 10,344

Fiscal Year Ending Mar. 31

	1999	1998	1997	1996	1995	1994
Revenues (Million $)						
1Q	117.5	100.0	NA	38.77	26.23	21.98
2Q	—	107.6	42.22	39.94	41.70	23.03
3Q	—	113.0	32.90	37.80	36.51	25.79
4Q	—	106.2	94.02	39.72	39.80	23.88
Yr.	—	426.7	167.1	156.2	144.2	94.68
Earnings Per Share ($)						
1Q	0.29	0.30	NA	0.19	0.28	0.25
2Q	—	0.35	0.29	0.18	0.27	0.23
3Q	—	0.34	0.08	0.21	0.20	0.27
4Q	—	0.37	0.30	0.20	0.22	0.22
Yr.	—	1.35	0.86	0.77	0.96	0.96

Next earnings report expected: NA

Dividend Data

No cash dividends have been paid on the common shares since 1984.

*A Division of The **McGraw·Hill** Companies*

Business Summary - 27-JUL-98

As oil and gas production moves further from the shore, simply "getting there" will take on increased significance. As one of the largest suppliers of helicopter transportation to the offshore oil and gas industry, Offshore Logistics (OLOG) has been transporting personnel and equipment to offshore production sites for nearly 30 years. With offshore production accounting for an ever larger proportion of total oil and gas production, the company hopes that its business is only beginning to "take off."

Not content with its status as one of the leading helicopter operators in the Gulf of Mexico, OLOG in December 1996 acquired 49% of the common stock of Bristow Aviation Holdings, which owns Bristow Helicopter Group, Ltd. Bristow, which operates 128 helicopters and other aircraft, provides helicopter services in the North Sea, which, like the Gulf of Mexico, is one of the world's hottest offshore markets.

Helicopter operations, involving 301 aircraft as of March 31, 1998, are conducted through the Air Logistics (Air Log) and Bristow subsidiaries. Air Log operates 173 aircraft. Domestic helicopter services are provided primarily from facilities along the Gulf of Mexico, where 142 aircraft were being operated. Air Log was also operating 12 aircraft in Alaska. Internationally, Air Log operates 19 helicopters in several countries, including

Brazil, Colombia, Egypt and Mexico. Bristow operates 26 aircraft in Africa, and 29 aircraft elsewhere throughout the world.

Historically, demand for the company's services has been influenced by the level of worldwide offshore oil and gas production and drilling activity. However, a secondary market for its fleet includes emergency medical transportation, agricultural and forestry support and general aviation activities. The company believes that this secondary market makes OLOG less vulnerable to oil and gas industry downturns than other oilfield equipment and services companies.

The company also provides production management services to the offshore oil and gas industry. Its wholly owned Grasso Production Management, Inc. subsidiary is the leading independent operator of oil and gas production facilities in the Gulf of Mexico. In addition, it also provides services for certain onshore facilities.

In July 1997, the company sold its 75% interest in Cathodic Protection Services Co. (CPS) to Corrpro Companies, Inc., which also purchased the 25% of CPS not currently held by OLOG. CPS, which manufactures, installs and maintains cathodic systems to arrest corrosion in oil and gas drilling and production facilities, pipelines, oil and gas well casings, hydrocarbon processing plants and other metal structures, had sales of approximately $30 million in the 12 months ended March 31, 1997.

Per Share Data ($)

(Year Ended Mar. 31)	1998	1997	1996	1995	1994	1993	1992	1991	1990	1989
Tangible Bk. Val.	11.97	10.09	10.24	8.13	8.04	7.06	6.09	5.10	3.81	1.27
Cash Flow	2.43	1.51	1.26	1.46	1.38	1.27	1.36	1.31	1.34	0.98
Earnings	1.35	0.86	0.77	0.96	0.96	0.90	1.00	0.97	0.98	0.67
Dividends	Nil	Nil	Nil	Nil	Nil	Nil	Nil	Nil	Nil	Nil
Payout Ratio	Nil	Nil	Nil	Nil	Nil	Nil	Nil	Nil	Nil	Nil
Cal. Yrs.	1997	1996	1995	1994	1993	1992	1991	1990	1989	1988
Prices - High	25¼	20⅞	20⅞	15⅛	16⅛	19¼	12⅛	10¾	14¾	12
- Low	14¾	11¾	11¾	12¼	11⅝	10⅜	7	6⅜	6⅝	3¼
P/E Ratio - High	19	NM	27	16	17	21	12	11	15	18
- Low	11	NM	15	11	12	12	7	7	7	5

Income Statement Analysis (Million $)

Revs.	427	167	157	144	92.0	80.0	82.0	95.0	98.0	81.0
Oper. Inc.	88.9	37.2	23.9	28.4	25.5	24.1	25.9	25.4	22.1	15.3
Depr.	32.2	13.2	9.2	9.7	7.5	6.5	6.4	6.1	6.3	5.5
Int. Exp.	20.5	5.5	0.8	0.9	1.1	1.5	1.9	2.1	2.6	2.0
Pretax Inc.	46.1	25.6	21.5	25.4	23.6	21.5	24.3	21.3	20.1	12.1
Eff. Tax Rate	30%	31%	29%	29%	27%	25%	28%	20%	14%	2.10%
Net Inc.	31.3	17.6	15.3	18.5	17.2	16.0	17.5	17.0	17.2	11.8

Balance Sheet & Other Fin. Data (Million $)

Cash	56.1	29.8	77.0	68.0	47.2	46.9	40.7	30.2	16.1	10.6
Curr. Assets	223	196	134	125	87.3	82.2	72.3	64.7	54.7	42.7
Total Assets	736	674	242	229	174	164	145	138	112	97.0
Curr. Liab.	101	139	18.0	18.0	10.0	16.0	19.0	27.0	17.0	17.0
LT Debt	252	200	0.8	5.6	2.0	9.3	10.0	19.0	25.0	31.0
Common Eqty.	280	235	200	184	142	124	107	88.9	66.4	18.2
Total Cap.	635	535	220	209	162	146	123	112	93.0	78.0
Cap. Exp.	70.5	10.1	12.5	3.0	12.0	7.9	9.2	33.4	11.8	12.3
Cash Flow	63.5	30.8	24.5	28.1	24.8	22.0	24.0	23.1	23.5	17.3
Curr. Ratio	2.2	1.4	7.4	6.8	8.6	5.2	3.8	2.4	3.2	2.5
% LT Debt of Cap.	39.7	37.4	1.0	2.7	1.2	6.4	8.2	17.0	26.4	39.8
% Net Inc.of Revs.	7.3	10.5	9.8	12.9	18.8	20.0	21.4	17.9	17.6	14.5
% Ret. on Assets	4.4	NM	6.5	9.2	10.2	10.4	12.4	13.6	14.9	11.8
% Ret. on Equity	12.2	NM	8.0	11.4	13.0	13.9	17.9	21.9	38.9	95.7

Data as orig. reptd.; bef. results of disc. opers. and/or spec. items. Yrs. ended Jun. 30 prior to 1997 (9 mos.). Per share data adj. for stk. divs. as of ex-div. date. Bold denotes diluted EPS (FASB 128). E-Estimated. NA-Not Available. NM-Not Meaningful. NR-Not Ranked.

Reincorporated—in Delaware in 1988. **Office**—224 Rue de Jean, P.O. Box 5C, Lafayette, LA 70505. **Tel**—(318) 233-1221. **Chrmn**—L. F. Crane. **Pres**—G. M. Small. **VP, CFO & Secy**—D. A. Milke. **Investor Contact**—Ann Alesi. **Dirs**— P. N. Buckley, J. H. Cartwright, L. F. Crane, D. M. Johnson, K. M. Jones, H. C. Sager, G. M. Small, H. Wolf. **Transfer Agent & Registrar**—ChaseMellon Shareholder Services, NYC. **Empl**—3,140. **S&P Analyst:** N.R.

10-OCT-98

Industry:
Retail (Specialty)

Summary: This specialty retailer and supplier of automotive aftermarket parts, tools, supplies and accessories operates 462 stores in 9 states.

Quantitative Evaluations

Recent Price • 33⅝
52 Wk Range • 39½-21

Yield • Nil
12-Mo. P/E • 28.3

Outlook
(1 Lowest—5 Highest)
• 4

Fair Value
• 47¾

Risk
• Low

Earn./Div. Rank
• B+

Technical Eval.
• NA

Rel. Strength Rank
(1 Lowest—99 Highest)
• 85

Insider Activity
• Neutral

Earnings vs. Previous Year
▲=Up ▼=Down ▶=No Change

2-for-1

10 Week Mov. Avg. – – –
30 Week Mov. Avg. ·····
Relative Strength —

VOL.
(000)

OPTIONS: Ph

Business Profile - 07-AUG-98

After opening 21 new stores in the first half of 1998, the company plans to open 29 more in the second half of the year. An additional 80 stores are planned for 1999. A new distribution center located in Iowa is scheduled to open in early 1999. In order to accelerate its growth, ORLY acquired Hi-Lo Automotive, Inc. in late January 1998; Hi-Lo shareholders received $4.35 per share in cash (some 10.8 million Hi-Lo shares were outstanding). The acquisition included a distribution center in Texas and 189 automotive aftermarket parts stores in Texas, Louisiana and California. As of June 30, 1998, ORLY operated 462 stores in 9 states. Total comparable-store sales gains were 4.1% in the first half of 1998. The O'Reilly family owns about 40% of the common shares.

Operational Review - 07-AUG-98

Sales in the six months ended June 30, 1998, rose 88%, year to year, mostly reflecting the acquisition of Hi-Lo Automotive. Gross margins were about the same but profitability was restricted as operating costs almost doubled; operating profit grew 41%. After other expense, versus other income, and taxes at 38.0%, versus 37.2%, net income increased 22% to $13,502,000 ($0.62 a diluted share), from $11,089,000 ($0.52).

Stock Performance - 09-OCT-98

In the past 30 trading days, ORLY's shares have increased 3%, compared to a 4% fall in the S&P 500. Average trading volume for the past five days was 82,120 shares, compared with the 40-day moving average of 117,203 shares.

Key Stock Statistics

Dividend Rate/Share	Nil	Shareholders	5,500
Shs. outstg. (M)	21.3	Market cap. (B)	$0.715
Avg. daily vol. (M)	0.118	Inst. holdings	50%
Tang. Bk. Value/Share	9.30		
Beta	0.72		

Value of $10,000 invested 5 years ago: NA

Fiscal Year Ending Dec. 31

	1998	1997	1996	1995	1994	1993
Revenues (Million $)						
1Q	118.3	68.47	55.32	42.77	36.70	28.50
2Q	165.2	82.45	68.78	50.64	43.30	35.40
3Q	—	87.52	70.43	57.18	44.69	37.80
4Q	—	77.96	64.71	50.90	42.36	35.40
Yr.	—	316.4	259.2	201.5	167.1	137.2
Earnings Per Share ($)						
1Q	0.27	0.24	0.20	0.17	0.14	0.14
2Q	0.35	0.29	0.23	0.20	0.17	0.14
3Q	—	0.31	0.26	0.23	0.18	0.15
4Q	—	0.25	0.21	0.19	0.14	0.07
Yr.	—	1.09	0.91	0.79	0.64	0.50

Next earnings report expected: late October

Dividend Data

No cash dividends have been paid, and the company does not expect to pay cash dividends on its ordinary shares for the foreseeable future. It intends to retain earnings, if any, to finance the development of its future business.

Business Summary - 07-AUG-98

Founded in 1957 by Charles F. O'Reilly and his son, Charles H. "Chub" O'Reilly, Sr., O'Reilly Automotive, Inc. (ORLY) began as a single store in Springfield, MO. As a specialty retailer and supplier of automotive aftermarket parts, tools, supplies, equipment and accessories, ORLY appeals to both do-it-yourself consumers and professional mechanics and service technicians. As of December 31, 1997, ORLY operated 259 stores in six midwestern states.

The company carries an extensive product line of new and remanufactured automotive hard parts (alternators, starters, fuel pumps, water pumps, brake shoes and pads), maintenance items (oil, antifreeze, fluids, engine additives, appearance products), accessories (floor mats, seat covers), and a complete line of autobody paint, automotive tools and professional service equipment. Merchandise consists of nationally recognized brands: A.C.Delco, Prestone, Quaker State, STP and Turtle Wax. ORLY also carries a wide variety of private label products under the O'Reilly Auto Parts, Super Start, Brake Best, Ultima and Omnispark brands. ORLY offers engine machining services through its O'Reilly stores, but does not sell tires or perform automotive repairs or installations.

ORLY believes that, because it aggressively pursues both the do-it-yourself consumer and the professional installer, it can successfully compete not only in large metropolitan markets, but also in less densely populated areas. In 1997, 50% of sales were to the do-it-yourself market and 50% to professional installers.

The company believes that its broad selection of more than 105,000 SKUs (stock keeping units) is an important competitive advantage. ORLY feels that offering superior in-store service with technically proficient professional parts people who undergo an extensive and ongoing training program, same day or overnight availability of products, and competitive pricing are all fundamental to meeting its customers' needs.

Management believes that ORLY's ability to open new stores at an accelerated rate will be a significant factor in achieving its growth objectives in the future. Fifty new store openings are planned for 1998 and 80 for 1999. ORLY's competition in the do-it-yourself market includes AutoZone, Parts America and Pep Boys, while automotive dealers and national warehouse distributors and associations such as National Automotive Parts Association (NAPA), Carquest and Parts Plus are rivals for the professional installer portion of its business.

In January 1998, ORLY acquired Hi-Lo Automotive, Inc., for about $47 million. The acquisition of Hi-Lo added 189 stores in Texas, Louisiana and California to ORLY's base of retail stores.

Per Share Data ($)

(Year Ended Dec. 31)	1997	1996	1995	1994	1993	1992	1991	1990	1989	1988
Tangible Bk. Val.	8.62	7.44	6.46	4.04	3.35	1.99	NA	NA	NA	NA
Cash Flow	1.48	1.20	1.01	0.82	0.68	0.62	NA	NA	NA	NA
Earnings	1.09	0.91	0.79	0.64	0.50	0.43	NA	NA	NA	NA
Dividends	Nil	Nil	Nil	Nil	Nil	Nil	Nil	Nil	Nil	Nil
Payout Ratio	Nil	Nil	Nil	Nil	Nil	Nil	Nil	Nil	Nil	Nil
Prices - High	28	20³⁄₈	16⁷⁄₈	17⁵⁄₈	16¹⁄₄	NA	NA	NA	NA	NA
- Low	15¹⁄₂	14³⁄₈	11¹⁄₂	11⁵⁄₈	8³⁄₄	NA	NA	NA	NA	NA
P/E Ratio - High	26	22	21	28	33	NA	NA	NA	NA	NA
- Low	14	16	15	18	18	NA	NA	NA	NA	NA

Income Statement Analysis (Million $)

	1997	1996	1995	1994	1993	1992	1991	1990	1989	1988
Revs.	316	259	201	167	137	110	NA	NA	NA	NA
Oper. Inc.	45.4	35.0	26.1	20.4	15.4	12.6	NA	NA	NA	NA
Depr.	8.3	6.1	4.0	3.3	2.9	2.7	NA	NA	NA	NA
Int. Exp.	0.1	0.0	0.3	0.1	0.2	0.4	NA	NA	NA	NA
Pretax Inc.	37.6	30.0	22.3	17.5	12.8	10.1	NA	NA	NA	NA
Eff. Tax Rate	38%	37%	37%	37%	36%	37%	NA	NA	NA	NA
Net Inc.	23.1	19.0	14.1	11.1	8.2	6.4	NA	NA	NA	NA

Balance Sheet & Other Fin. Data (Million $)

	1997	1996	1995	1994	1993	1992	1991	1990	1989	1988
Cash	2.3	2.2	26.2	5.4	12.0	1.6	NA	NA	NA	NA
Curr. Assets	134	100	99	57.2	55.2	32.1	NA	NA	NA	NA
Total Assets	248	184	154	87.3	73.1	58.9	NA	NA	NA	NA
Curr. Liab.	40.4	26.0	18.2	15.8	14.0	16.5	NA	NA	NA	NA
LT Debt	22.6	0.2	0.4	0.5	0.7	2.7	NA	NA	NA	NA
Common Eqty.	182	156	134	70.2	57.8	29.3	NA	NA	NA	NA
Total Cap.	207	156	135	71.1	58.7	32.1	NA	NA	NA	NA
Cap. Exp.	37.2	34.5	28.6	13.7	8.5	4.5	NA	NA	NA	NA
Cash Flow	31.4	25.1	18.1	14.3	11.1	9.1	NA	NA	NA	NA
Curr. Ratio	3.3	3.8	5.4	3.6	3.9	1.9	NA	NA	NA	NA
% LT Debt of Cap.	10.9	0.2	0.3	0.6	1.2	8.3	NA	NA	NA	NA
% Net Inc.of Revs.	7.3	7.3	7.0	6.6	6.0	5.8	NA	NA	NA	NA
% Ret. on Assets	10.7	11.3	11.7	13.8	11.6	11.8	NA	NA	NA	NA
% Ret. on Equity	13.7	13.1	13.8	17.2	17.9	24.5	NA	NA	NA	NA

Data as orig. reptd.; bef. results of disc. opers. and/or spec. items. Per share data adj. for stk. divs. as of ex-div. date. Bold denotes diluted EPS (FASB 128). E-Estimated. NA-Not Available. NM-Not Meaningful. NR-Not Ranked.

Office—233 S. Patterson, Springfield, MO 65801. Tel—(417) 862-6708. Website—www.oreillyauto.com Chrmn—C. H. O'Reilly Jr. Pres & CEO—D. E. O'Reilly. Pres & COO—L. P. O'Reilly. CFO & Investor Contact—James R. Batten. Secy—A. Drennan. Dirs—J. D. Burchfield, J. C. Greene, C. H. O'Reilly Jr., C. H. O'Reilly Sr., D. E. O'Reilly, L. P. O'Reilly, R. O'Reilly Wooten. Transfer Agent & Registrar—Boatmen's Trust Co., St. Louis. Incorporated—in Missouri in 1957. Empl— 3,945. S&P Analyst: Kathleen J. Fraser

Orange & Rockland Utilities   1719

NYSE Symbol **ORU**

In S&P SmallCap 600

03-OCT-98

Industry:
Electric Companies

Summary: This electric-gas utility, serving areas to the north of New York City, has agreed to be acquired by Consolidated Edison Inc. for $58.50 a share.

Quantitative Evaluations	
Recent Price • 54½	Yield • 4.7%
52 Wk Range • 55-35	12-Mo. P/E • 18.7

Outlook (1 Lowest—5 Highest)
• **1+**

Fair Value
• **52⅜**

Risk
• **Low**

Earn./Div. Rank
• **B+**

Technical Eval.
• **Bullish** since 9/97

Rel. Strength Rank (1 Lowest—99 Highest)
• **85**

Insider Activity
• **Neutral**

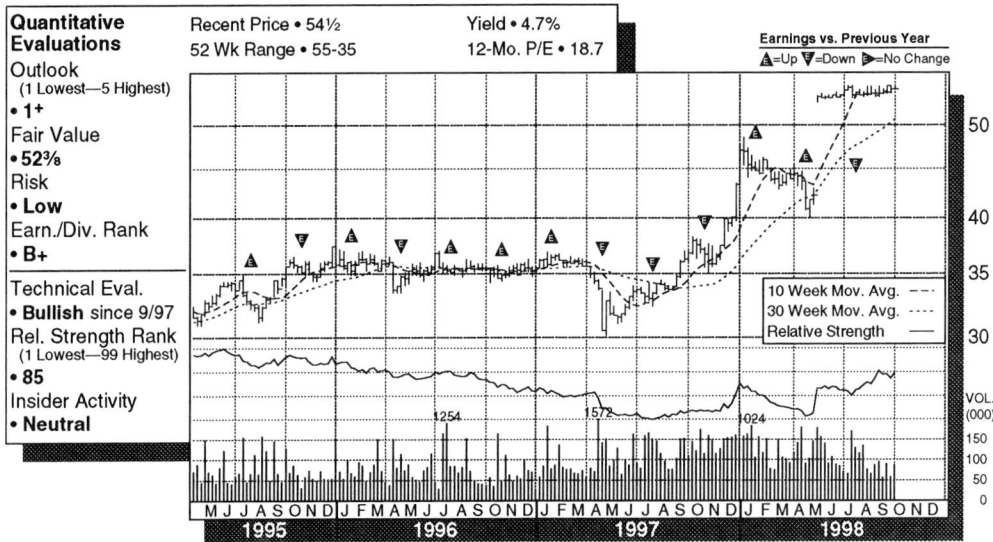

Earnings vs. Previous Year
▲=Up ▼=Down ▶=No Change

10 Week Mov. Avg. - - -
30 Week Mov. Avg. · · · ·
Relative Strength ——

Business Profile - 14-MAY-98

This electric-gas utility's service territory covers about 1,350 square miles, and extends north and west of New York City. As New York State prepares to open its electricity sales up to competition, Consolidated Edison, Inc. (NYSE: ED), the giant power company serving the five boroughs of New York City and Westchester County, NY, has agreed to acquire ORU for $58.50 a share in cash. The transaction is subject to approval by ORU shareholders. With ORU's New York service area adjacent to ED's, the companies estimate the combination would provide ED with cost savings of some $50 million annually. In response to the changing industry environment, ORU in 1997 announced plans to sell all of its electric generating assets and provide full retail choice to its customers by May 1,1999.

Operational Review - 14-MAY-98

Revenues in the first quarter of 1998 fell 11%, year to year, on 2.9% lower electric revenues reflecting electric base rate reductions, and a 25% decrease in gas revenues due to warmer winter weather and lower gas cost recoveries. With reduced operating and maintenance expenses, and absent costs incurred in 1997 for litigation with the company's former chairman and CEO, earnings available to common shares from continuing operations were up 21%, to $13,104,321 ($0.97 a share), from $10,814,000 ($0.79). Results in 1997 exclude a loss of $0.33 a share from discontinued operations.

Stock Performance - 02-OCT-98

In the past 30 trading days, ORU's shares have increased 1%, compared to a 7% fall in the S&P 500. Average trading volume for the past five days was 17,200 shares, compared with the 40-day moving average of 15,633 shares.

Key Stock Statistics

Dividend Rate/Share	2.58	Shareholders	21,300
Shs. outstg. (M)	13.5	Market cap. (B)	$0.737
Avg. daily vol. (M)	0.015	Inst. holdings	24%
Tang. Bk. Value/Share	26.86		
Beta	0.21		

Value of $10,000 invested 5 years ago: $ 19,027

Fiscal Year Ending Dec. 31

	1998	1997	1996	1995	1994	1993
Revenues (Million $)						
1Q	165.1	185.3	285.7	311.9	292.7	264.0
2Q	139.6	137.2	212.4	245.4	229.7	215.1
3Q	—	159.7	215.6	231.9	239.2	237.6
4Q	—	166.5	211.4	241.0	255.3	254.7
Yr.	—	648.8	925.0	1,030	1,017	971.4
Earnings Per Share ($)						
1Q	**0.97**	0.79	1.01	1.06	0.98	1.05
2Q	**0.32**	0.37	0.41	0.22	0.19	0.43
3Q	—	1.17	1.31	1.03	1.14	1.22
4Q	—	**0.70**	0.44	0.20	0.10	0.36
Yr.	—	**3.09**	3.30	2.60	2.50	3.06

Next earnings report expected: late October

Dividend Data (Dividends have been paid since 1908.)

Amount ($)	Date Decl.	Ex-Div. Date	Stock of Record	Payment Date
0.645	Jan. 06	Jan. 14	Jan. 19	Feb. 01 '98
0.645	Apr. 02	Apr. 16	Apr. 20	May. 01 '98
0.645	Jun. 25	Jul. 16	Jul. 20	Aug. 01 '98
0.645	Oct. 01	Oct. 15	Oct. 19	Nov. 01 '98

A Division of The McGraw-Hill Companies

STANDARD
&POOR'S
STOCK REPORTS

Orange & Rockland Utilities, Inc.

1719

03-OCT-98

Business Summary - 14-MAY-98

Orange & Rockland Utilities, established nearly 100 years ago, generates, distributes and sells electricity and distributes and sells natural gas. ORU and its subsidiaries, Rockland Electric company and Pike County Power & Light, serve an area of 1,350 square miles and a population of more than 680,000 in southwestern New York State, northern New Jersey, and northeastern Pennsylvania. In 1997, electricity accounted for 74% of revenues and 85% of operating income, gas for 26% and 15%, and non-utility subsidiaries for less than 1% of revenues and a loss.

In 1997, the company discontinued the unprofitable gas marketing operations of NORSTAR Management Inc., to further its strategy of positioning its operational and financial resources into selective competitive markets. A restructuring plan for the company's electric operations in New York State, under which ORU would sell at auction its generating plants, was approved in December 1997. Similar restructuring plans were submitted to regulatory authorities in New Jersey and Pennsylvania during 1997. Once the generating plants are sold, Orange & Rockland would no longer produce electricity; it would purchase electricity for resale to its

electric customers as a regulated delivery company (as the so called "provider of last resort"). The company planned to make retail access to a competitive energy and capacity market available to all electric customers by May 1, 1999. To facilitate the transition, ORU extended its PowerPick program, whereby customers can purchase energy (but not capacity) from suppliers other than the company, to all New York State customers on May 1, 1998.

The approved restructuring plan provided for electric price reductions of approximately $32.4 million over a four-year period. On December 1, 1997, the company implemented the initial electric rate reduction in the amount of $5.9 million. Additional rate reductions of $8.8 million would take effect in each of the next three years. The plan also provided for the company's recovery, through a competitive transition charge, of above-market generation costs should the transfer of title to its generating assets not occur before May 1, 1999.

In mid-May 1998, ORU agreed to be acquired by New York State power utility Consolidated Edison Inc., for $58.50 a share in cash (or a total of $790 million in cash). The transaction is subject to approval by ORU shareholders.

Per Share Data ($)

(Year Ended Dec. 31)	1997	1996	1995	1994	1993	1992	1991	1990	1989	1988
Tangible Bk. Val.	26.86	27.66	26.96	26.98	27.08	25.18	24.12	22.89	21.36	20.12
Earnings	3.09	3.17	2.60	2.50	3.06	3.15	3.12	2.99	3.14	3.18
Dividends	2.58	2.58	2.57	2.54	2.49	2.43	2.37	2.32	2.28	2.24
Payout Ratio	83%	81%	99%	102%	81%	77%	76%	78%	73%	70%
Prices - High	48⅝	37⅛	37⅜	41¼	47½	41⅞	39	32⅜	32	33½
- Low	30⅛	33⅜	30⅞	28⅜	38⅝	32⅜	30⅞	26⅛	27¼	27⅞
P/E Ratio - High	16	12	14	17	16	13	13	11	10	11
- Low	10	11	12	11	13	10	10	9	9	9

Income Statement Analysis (Million $)

	1997	1996	1995	1994	1993	1992	1991	1990	1989	1988
Revs.	649	925	1,030	1,017	971	844	732	559	536	487
Depr.	37.4	33.6	38.9	35.9	34.5	34.5	32.1	24.2	27.8	26.9
Maint.	35.3	36.7	41.2	44.0	42.9	42.5	40.3	36.7	32.1	32.6
Fxd. Chgs. Cov.	2.9	3.0	2.8	2.6	2.9	2.6	2.6	2.4	2.7	2.9
Constr. Credits	1.4	0.6	0.8	0.5	0.3	0.4	1.5	1.7	1.7	6.4
Eff. Tax Rate	33%	35%	40%	35%	33%	32%	29%	25%	30%	33%
Net Inc.	44.9	46.3	38.6	37.2	44.8	45.8	44.9	42.6	44.1	44.2

Balance Sheet & Other Fin. Data (Million $)

	1997	1996	1995	1994	1993	1992	1991	1990	1989	1988
Gross Prop.	1,419	1,340	1,294	1,255	1,204	1,163	1,118	1,067	1,013	970
Cap. Exp.	74.0	59.4	55.0	61.0	54.0	56.0	60.5	63.7	54.8	60.2
Net Prop.	947	900	874	856	832	815	792	765	722	694
Capitalization:										
LT Debt	358	282	360	360	381	381	379	374	293	290
% LT Debt	46	40	46	46	47	48	49	49	44	45
Pfd.	42.8	43.2	44.6	46.0	47.4	48.8	50.3	51.7	57.1	58.9
% Pfd.	5.50	6.10	5.70	5.90	5.90	6.10	6.50	6.80	8.60	9.10
Common	376	388	380	379	376	368	351	334	313	296
% Common	48	54	48	48	47	46	45	44	47	46
Total Cap.	969	899	1,014	975	999	918	894	872	776	757
% Oper. Ratio	88.2	914.0	93.0	92.5	91.5	90.6	89.4	86.7	86.0	84.7
% Earn. on Net Prop.	8.3	8.9	8.4	9.0	10.0	9.9	9.9	10.0	10.6	11.0
% Return On Revs.	6.9	5.0	3.7	3.7	4.6	5.4	6.1	7.6	8.2	9.1
% Return On Invest. Capital	10.9	16.5	7.0	7.2	8.2	9.0	8.9	9.3	9.9	9.8
% Return On Com. Equity	11.0	11.3	9.3	9.0	11.2	11.9	12.1	14.5	13.4	14.1

Data as orig. reptd.; bef. results of disc opers. and/or spec. items. Per share data adj. for stk. divs. as of ex-div. date. Bold denotes diluted EPS (FASB 128). E-Estimated. NA-Not Available. NM-Not Meaningful. NR-Not Ranked.

Office—One Blue Hill Plaza, Pearl River, NY 10965. **Tel**—(914) 352-6000. **Website**—http://www.oru.com **Chrmn**—M. J. Del Giudice. **Vice Chrmn & CEO**—D. L. Peoples. **SVP & CFO**—R. L. Haney. **VP & Secy**—G. D. Caliendo. **Treas & Investor Contact**—Robert J. McBennett. **Dirs**—R. M. Baruch, J. F. Creamer, M. J. Del Giudice, J. F. Hanson, K. D. McPherson, R. E. Mulcahy III, J. F. O'Grady Jr., D. L. Peoples, F. V. Salerno, L. C. Taliaferro, H. K. Vanderhoef. **Transfer Agent & Registrar**—Bank of New York, NYC. **Incorporated**—in New York in 1926. **Empl**— 1,473. **S&P Analyst:** S.A.H.

STANDARD &POOR'S
STOCK REPORTS

Orbital Sciences

1719J
NYSE Symbol **ORB**
In S&P SmallCap 600

03-OCT-98 Industry: Aerospace/Defense

Summary: This space technology company produces small satellites, launch vehicles and ground equipment, and operates satellite communications and imaging systems.

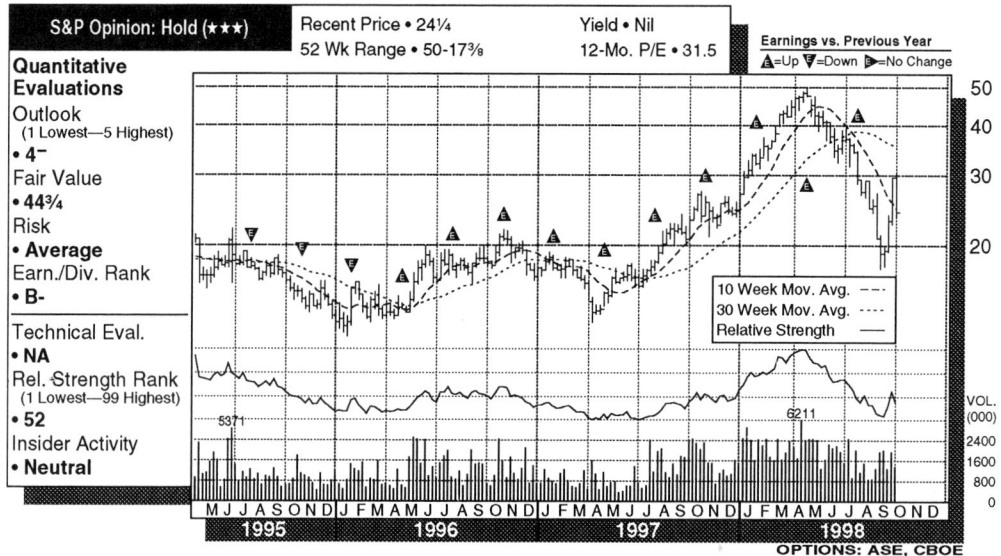

S&P Opinion: Hold (★★★)	Recent Price • 24¼	Yield • Nil
	52 Wk Range • 50-17⅜	12-Mo. P/E • 31.5

Earnings vs. Previous Year
▲=Up ▼=Down ▶=No Change

Quantitative Evaluations

Outlook (1 Lowest—5 Highest)
• **4⁻**

Fair Value
• **44¾**

Risk
• **Average**

Earn./Div. Rank
• **B-**

Technical Eval.
• **NA**

Rel. Strength Rank (1 Lowest—99 Highest)
• **52**

Insider Activity
• **Neutral**

10 Week Mov. Avg. - - -
30 Week Mov. Avg. ·····
Relative Strength ——

OPTIONS: ASE, CBOE

Overview - 04-AUG-98

Revenues are expected to grow at least 30% through 1998, benefiting from new orders and acquisitions in the satellite launch vehicles and access products areas. Satellite access product sales should advance mainly from strong GPS equipment volume resulting from Magellan's late 1997 acquisition of Ashtech. Near-term losses will persist in the division due to consolidation and restructuring costs, but Magellan could turn a profit by the end of the year. Gross margins are widening on increased unit pricing and lower costs in the infrastructure area. R&D will likely remain in the 12% to 14% range for 1998, while SG&A expenses drop significantly as a percentage of sales as revenues increase in the second half. Backlog is solid, up 45% (firm) and 60% (total) year-to-year through mid-1998. Start-up losses at ORBCOMM and ORBIMAGE are narrowing sequentially.

Valuation - 04-AUG-98

Following an almost 70% rise during the first half of 1998, the shares have since fallen close to 50%, reflecting unsettled market conditions and the recently postponed spinoff of its ORBCOMM unit as the weak state of new issues in the public market led to a sub-par valuation price placed on the unit. Although results should continue to benefit from strong orders and well controlled R&D and SG&A expenses, as well as proceeds raised from a recent common stock offering, and an equity and debt placement for ORBIMAGE, we expect the stock to continue its erratic behavior. With the shares trading at 30 times our 1998 estimate, and 17 times our recently reduced 1999 projection, we continue to advise investors against adding to their positions.

Key Stock Statistics

S&P EPS Est. 1998	0.90	Tang. Bk. Value/Share	9.32
P/E on S&P Est. 1998	26.9	Beta	1.38
S&P EPS Est. 1999	1.45	Shareholders	1,500
Dividend Rate/Share	Nil	Market cap. (B)	$0.892
Shs. outstg. (M)	36.8	Inst. holdings	49%
Avg. daily vol. (M)	0.342		

Value of $10,000 invested 5 years ago: $ 20,208

Fiscal Year Ending Dec. 31

	1998	1997	1996	1995	1994	1993
Revenues (Million $)						
1Q	186.2	122.1	104.9	89.00	50.30	50.50
2Q	184.5	142.2	116.5	81.80	48.40	60.40
3Q	—	164.7	119.6	95.80	58.20	57.70
4Q	—	177.0	120.5	97.80	65.10	54.50
Yr.	—	606.0	461.4	364.3	221.9	223.1
Earnings Per Share ($)						
1Q	0.20	0.16	0.12	0.12	0.12	0.07
2Q	0.21	0.17	0.14	-0.07	0.03	0.12
3Q	E0.24	0.18	0.15	0.06	0.08	0.12
4Q	E0.25	0.18	0.14	-0.14	0.06	0.13
Yr.	E0.90	0.69	0.55	-0.03	0.28	0.43

Next earnings report expected: late October

Dividend Data

The company has not paid dividends.

A Division of The McGraw-Hill Companies

STANDARD
&POOR'S
STOCK REPORTS

Orbital Sciences Corporation

1719J
03-OCT-98

Business Summary - 04-AUG-98

Orbital Sciences Corp. (ORB) is a space technology and satellite services company whose main objectives include launch success on its Pegasus and Taurus missions, on-schedule deployment of its ORBCOMM satellites, and continued progress with domestic customers as well as international partners for its satellite network services. Contributions (profits in million $) by segment in 1997:

	Revenues	Profits
Space and ground infrastructure systems	88%	$47.95
Satellite access products	12%	-11.75
Satellite-delivered services	Nil	-6.71

In August 1997, ORB acquired CTA, Inc.'s space systems and communications services business for $12 million. International sales comprised 26% of total revenues in 1997. The U.S. government accounted for 38%. Firm backlog at March 31, 1998, was up 44%, year to year, to $1.15 billion, while total backlog rose 58%, to $3.4 billion.

The space and ground infrastructure systems segment includes launch vehicles, satellites, electronics and sensors, and ground systems and software. Through mid-1998, ORB had completed about 180 space missions since 1982. A mission's success depends on the particular mission requirements designated by the customer.

MacDonald Dettwiler and Associates (MDA), acquired in 1995, manufactures commercial space remote sensing ground stations and related information processing software.

Satellite access products, provided by the Magellan unit, include hand-held Global Positioning System (GPS) navigators that provide users with precise positioning and location information. Through the satellite services division, ORBCOMM Global and ORBIMAGE are developing services to address markets for global two-way data communications and information derived from remote imaging of the atmosphere, oceans and land surfaces. In December 1997, Magellan acquired Ashtech, Inc., a provider of GPS equipment, for $25 million. ORB owns 66% of the combined company. ORB is planning a $50 million expansion of its satellite-related manufacturing operations facility.

In early 1998, ORB completed financings of $330 million, including a 3,000,000 share public offering at $45.81 a share in April, and a $173 million equity and debt placement for ORBIMAGE in February. With these recent financings, ORB is well positioned to reduce debt-to-equity below 25%. On July 10, 1998, ORB's shares began trading on the New York Stock Exchange, shifting from the Nasdaq Stock Market.

Per Share Data ($)

(Year Ended Dec. 31)	1997	1996	1995	1994	1993	1992	1991	1990	1989	1988
Tangible Bk. Val.	5.33	8.12	6.74	6.60	7.94	NA	NA	NA	NA	NA
Cash Flow	1.38	1.41	0.72	1.03	0.96	0.81	NA	NA	NA	NA
Earnings	0.69	0.55	-0.03	0.28	0.43	0.27	0.13	-0.21	NA	NA
Dividends	Nil	Nil	Nil	Nil	Nil	Nil	Nil	Nil	Nil	Nil
Payout Ratio	Nil	Nil	Nil	Nil	Nil	Nil	Nil	Nil	Nil	Nil
Prices - High	30¾	21⅞	22	26½	23½	19	NA	NA	NA	NA
- Low	12¾	11¾	12⅛	14	9½	10¾	NA	NA	NA	NA
P/E Ratio - High	45	40	NM	95	55	70	NA	NA	NA	NA
- Low	18	21	NM	50	22	40	NA	NA	NA	NA

Income Statement Analysis (Million $)

	1997	1996	1995	1994	1993	1992	1991	1990	1989	1988
Revs.	606	461	364	222	223	204	162	123	NA	NA
Oper. Inc.	53.3	48.9	19.9	22.9	18.4	12.5	NA	NA	NA	NA
Depr.	23.9	25.1	22.2	14.3	7.9	7.7	NA	NA	NA	NA
Int. Exp.	0.4	2.5	3.8	1.5	1.0	0.1	NA	NA	NA	NA
Pretax Inc.	22.4	17.7	-2.0	7.5	8.5	5.6	4.1	-2.2	NA	NA
Eff. Tax Rate	9.08%	10%	NM	28%	27%	29%	56%	NM	NM	NM
Net Inc.	23.0	15.9	-0.7	5.4	6.2	3.9	1.8	-2.4	NA	NA

Balance Sheet & Other Fin. Data (Million $)

	1997	1996	1995	1994	1993	1992	1991	1990	1989	1988
Cash	12.6	32.7	15.3	33.6	76.7	15.0	38.7	12.7	NA	NA
Curr. Assets	264	211	199	160	179	NA	NA	NA	NA	NA
Total Assets	772	505	467	403	322	176	169	103	NA	NA
Curr. Liab.	212	127	112	108	91.0	NA	NA	NA	NA	NA
LT Debt	198	33.1	96.7	81.2	61.6	0.6	0.2	2.7	NA	NA
Common Eqty.	355	331	239	202	166	108	103	57.0	NA	NA
Total Cap.	557	362	335	283	227	109	103	59.0	NA	NA
Cap. Exp.	45.0	43.5	17.2	27.1	35.6	41.7	NA	NA	NA	NA
Cash Flow	46.9	41.0	21.5	19.6	14.1	11.6	NA	NA	NA	NA
Curr. Ratio	1.2	1.7	1.8	1.5	2.0	NA	NA	NA	NA	NA
% LT Debt of Cap.	35.5	9.1	28.9	28.7	27.1	0.5	0.2	4.6	NA	NA
% Net Inc.of Revs.	3.8	3.4	NM	2.4	2.8	1.9	1.1	NM	NM	NM
% Ret. on Assets	3.6	3.3	NM	1.5	2.5	2.3	1.3	NA	NA	NA
% Ret. on Equity	6.7	5.6	NM	2.9	4.5	3.7	2.3	NA	NA	NA

Data as orig. reptd.; bef. results of disc. opers. and/or spec. items. Per share data adj. for stk. divs. as of ex-div. date. Bold denotes diluted EPS (FASB 128). E-Estimated. NA-Not Available. NM-Not Meaningful. NR-Not Ranked.

Office—21700 Atlantic Boulevard, Dulles, VA 20166. **Tel**—(703) 406-5000. **Website**—http://www.orbital.com **Chrmn, Pres & CEO**—D. W. Thompson. **SVP & Secy**—L. C. Seeman. **EVP & CFO**—J. V. Pirone. **Investor Contact**—Maureen O'Kane (703-406-5697). **Dirs**—F. C. Alcorn, K. H. Burke, B. W. Ferguson, D. J. Fink, L. A. Fisk, J. L. Kerrebrock, D. S. Luke, J. L. McLucas, J. Obuchowski, F. L. Salizzoni, H. H. Schmitt, D. W. Thompson, J. R. Thompson, S. L. Webster. **Transfer Agent & Registrar**—First National Bank of Boston. **Incorporated**—in Delaware in 1987. **Empl**— 4,000. **S&P Analyst:** Stewart Scharf

Orion Capital

1720M

NYSE Symbol **OC**

In S&P SmallCap 600

10-OCT-98

Industry: Insurance (Property-ty-Casualty)

Summary: Through subsidiaries, this insurance holding company is engaged in the specialty property and casualty insurance business.

Quantitative Evaluations

Recent Price • 32	Yield • 2.3%
52 Wk Range • 59¼-28	12-Mo. P/E • 6.4

Outlook (1 Lowest—5 Highest)
• 1

Fair Value
• 32⅞

Risk
• **Low**

Earn./Div. Rank
• **A**

Technical Eval.
• **Bearish** since 8/98

Rel. Strength Rank (1 Lowest—99 Highest)
• **35**

Insider Activity
• **NA**

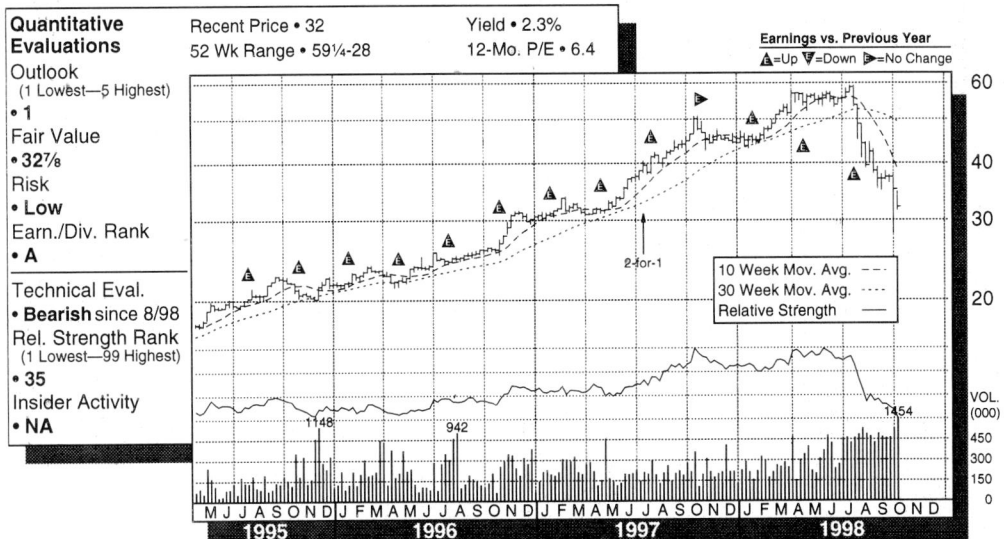

Earnings vs. Previous Year
▲=Up ▼=Down ▶=No Change

10 Week Mov. Avg. - - -
30 Week Mov. Avg. ......
Relative Strength ——

Business Profile - 04-AUG-98

This insurance holding company underwrites and sells specialty insurance products and services, including workers compensation products and related services, professional liability coverage for architects, engineers, environmental consultants, lawyers, and accountants, special property and casualty insurance, nonstandard automobile insurance, and property insurance. The underwriting segment of OC's operations focuses on ocean cargo, inland marine and commercial property coverage. In July 1998, OC acquired Grocers Insurance Group for $36.25 million in cash. Grocers is a specialty insurance holding company serving the grocery and food service industry in 35 states. In 1997, Grocers had revenues of approximately $34 million.

Operational Review - 04-AUG-98

Total revenues in the six months ended June 30, 1998, rose 12%, year to year, reflecting sharply higher realized investment gains and a 9.1% increase in premiums earned. Total expenses climbed 7.8%, as greater policy acquisition costs and other insurance expenses and increased dividends paid to policyholders offset lower interest expense; pretax income grew 44%. After taxes at 27.4%, versus 25.1%, and minority interest, net income advanced 46%, to $80,347,000 ($2.85 a share), from $54,859,000 ($1.97).

Stock Performance - 09-OCT-98

In the past 30 trading days, OC's shares have declined 17%, compared to a 4% fall in the S&P 500. Average trading volume for the past five days was 290,800 shares, compared with the 40-day moving average of 158,413 shares.

Key Stock Statistics

Dividend Rate/Share	0.72	Shareholders	1,800
Shs. outstg. (M)	27.6	Market cap. (B)	$0.882
Avg. daily vol. (M)	0.181	Inst. holdings	71%
Tang. Bk. Value/Share	22.06		
Beta	1.09		

Value of $10,000 invested 5 years ago: $ 25,246

Fiscal Year Ending Dec. 31

	1998	1997	1996	1995	1994	1993
Revenues (Million $)						
1Q	424.8	384.9	347.8	201.8	188.7	176.1
2Q	442.6	390.1	367.2	212.1	183.6	180.8
3Q	—	398.4	380.4	222.2	204.8	175.4
4Q	—	417.2	398.1	238.2	203.8	187.9
Yr.	—	1,591	1,493	874.3	781.0	720.2
Earnings Per Share ($)						
1Q	1.50	1.06	0.64	0.60	0.46	0.48
2Q	1.36	0.91	0.71	0.56	0.40	0.47
3Q	—	0.88	0.88	0.60	0.54	0.44
4Q	—	1.30	0.86	0.61	0.54	0.55
Yr.	—	4.15	3.12	2.38	1.93	1.94

Next earnings report expected: late October

Dividend Data (Dividends have been paid since 1978.)

Amount ($)	Date Decl.	Ex-Div. Date	Stock of Record	Payment Date
0.160	Nov. 07	Dec. 11	Dec. 15	Jan. 02 '98
0.160	Feb. 06	Mar. 12	Mar. 16	Apr. 01 '98
0.180	May. 28	Jun. 11	Jun. 15	Jul. 01 '98
0.180	Sep. 02	Sep. 10	Sep. 14	Oct. 01 '98

A Division of The **McGraw·Hill** Companies

Business Summary - 04-AUG-98

Orion Capital Corporation seeks to distinguish itself from its many competitors in the property and casualty insurance business by focusing on niche markets. Through its operating subsidiaries, the company is engaged in workers compensation, professional liability, nonstandard automobile insurance and ocean marine, inland marine and property insurance. Orion reports its insurance operations in three different segments: Regional Operations, Special Programs and Guaranty National.

Regional Operations, through EBI Companies, consist of workers' compensation, which accounted for 27%, 26% and 44% of net written premiums in 1997, 1996 and 1995, respectively. Targeting manufacturing and service establishments too small to employ risk management staffs, EBI focuses on building a "Zero Accident Culture" at each insured's workplace, to reduce claims payments. Premiums written increased 3% in 1997. This segment operates nationwide through 44 offices located in 24 states. Management plans on expanding into more states in the coming year.

Special Programs is made up of five units each of which operate in highly specialized lines of business in the property and casualty insurance field. DPIC Companies writes specialized liability insurance for niche markets such as architects, engineers, environmental consultants, accountants and lawyers. Orion Specialty focuses exclusively on specialty commercial insurance. Wm. H. McGee & Co., Inc., is a leading ocean cargo, inland marine and commercial property insurance underwriter. The Special Programs segment also contains the company's 24.7% interest in Intercargo Corporation, an insurance holding company that specializes in international trade and transportation coverages. Net written premiums in this segment fell 11% in 1997, and accounted for 32% of total net written premiums, versus 37% in 1996.

Guaranty National Companies, which became a wholly owned subsidiary in late 1997, writes nonstandard personal automobile insurance, surplus lines insurance, and specialty property and casualty coverages which are not readily available in traditional insurance markets. Guaranty National's net written premiums advanced 15% in 1997, and accounted for 41% of total net written premiums, compared to 37% in 1996.

Per Share Data ($)

(Year Ended Dec. 31)	1997	1996	1995	1994	1993	1992	1991	1990	1989	1988
Tangible Bk. Val.	15.79	17.89	15.79	11.96	12.64	9.58	7.84	3.69	4.06	3.19
Oper. Earnings	NA	2.63	2.11	1.84	1.61	1.66	2.06	1.26	1.06	0.86
Earnings	4.15	3.12	2.38	1.93	1.94	1.80	1.88	0.89	1.11	0.96
Dividends	0.92	0.52	0.43	0.38	0.34	0.30	0.29	0.29	0.26	0.24
Payout Ratio	22%	17%	18%	20%	18%	17%	16%	32%	24%	25%
Prices - High	51	31½	22⅝	17⅝	18¾	14⅜	10¾	7¾	9⅛	5⅝
- Low	30	21¼	17⅛	14⅛	13⅝	9¼	5¼	4⅛	4⅞	4¼
P/E Ratio - High	12	10	9	9	10	8	6	9	8	6
- Low	7	7	7	7	7	5	3	5	4	4

Income Statement Analysis (Million $)

	1997	1996	1995	1994	1993	1992	1991	1990	1989	1988
Premium Inc.	1,358	1,301	749	691	617	560	701	688	719	674
Net Invest. Inc.	165	145	99	84.9	91.8	82.5	100	96.9	95.4	80.2
Oth. Revs.	68.0	47.0	26.0	4.8	10.9	5.5	35.8	-1.0	7.8	7.8
Total Revs.	1,426	1,493	874	781	720	648	837	784	822	762
Pretax Inc.	176	127	88.0	71.5	72.5	46.7	46.1	26.8	32.8	34.8
Net Oper. Inc.	85.7	72.9	59.9	52.8	47.5	42.7	46.5	32.8	29.5	23.8
Net Inc.	116	86.6	67.6	55.2	57.0	45.8	44.7	25.5	30.3	25.9

Balance Sheet & Other Fin. Data (Million $)

	1997	1996	1995	1994	1993	1992	1991	1990	1989	1988
Cash & Equiv.	9.3	37.3	22.9	23.6	24.1	30.9	29.3	30.7	29.5	21.4
Premiums Due	189	181	137	125	111	102	96.0	113	114	108
Invest. Assets: Bonds	1,783	1,532	1,235	1,002	1,029	934	915	1,005	970	779
Invest. Assets: Stocks	439	362	305	264	243	186	130	105	104	124
Invest. Assets: Loans	Nil	Nil	Nil	Nil	Nil	Nil	2.0	4.0	4.0	4.0
Invest. Assets: Total	2,733	2,310	1,603	1,319	1,322	1,157	1,075	1,134	1,102	928
Deferred Policy Costs	147	136	77.7	70.1	57.5	56.1	58.9	64.9	70.3	65.5
Total Assets	3,884	3,464	2,474	2,113	2,117	1,554	1,455	1,500	1,471	1,281
Debt	435	311	209	152	160	130	142	175	175	152
Common Eqty.	723	577	491	365	394	283	188	130	141	125
Prop. & Cas. Loss Ratio	66.7	67.9	68.4	72.1	74.4	75.7	79.1	77.0	77.8	75.5
Prop. & Cas. Expense Ratio	31.2	30.1	29.0	27.0	26.8	27.3	30.2	28.7	28.1	28.6
Prop. & Cas. Combined Ratio	97.9	98.0	97.4	99.1	101.2	103.0	109.3	105.7	105.9	104.1
% Return On Revs.	8.1	5.8	7.7	7.1	7.9	7.1	5.3	3.2	3.7	3.4
% Ret. on Equity	17.8	16.2	15.8	14.5	16.8	19.7	20.2	12.9	15.6	16.4

Data as orig. reptd.; bef. results of disc. opers. and/or spec. items. Per share data adj. for stk. divs. as of ex-div. date. Bold denotes diluted EPS (FASB 128). E-Estimated. NA-Not Available. NM-Not Meaningful. NR-Not Ranked.

Office—9 Farm Springs Road, Farmington, CN, 06032.**Tel**—(860) 674-6600. **Chrmn & CEO**—W. M. Becker. **EVP & CFO**—D. W. Ebbert, Jr. **SVP & Secy**—J. J. McCann. **VP, Treas**—C. A. Nyman. **Investor Contact**—Jeanne S. Hotchkiss (860) 674-6754. **Dirs**—W. M. Becker, G.F. Cheesbrough, J. C. Colman, D. H. Elliott, V.R. Fash, R. H. Jeffrey, G. W. Kreh, W. R. Lyons, J. K. McWilliams, R. W. Moore, W.B. Weaver. **Transfer Agent & Registrar**—First Chicago Trust Co. of NY. **Incorporated**—in Delaware in 1960. **Empl**— 3,600. **S&P Analyst:** Michael Schneider

03-OCT-98

Industry: Health Care (Specialized Services)

Summary: This company develops and manages orthodontic practices on a national basis pursuant to long-term agreements.

S&P Opinion: Hold (★★★)	Recent Price • 15¼	Yield • Nil
	52 Wk Range • 24-13	12-Mo. P/E • 25.4

Quantitative Evaluations

Outlook (1 Lowest—5 Highest)
• **3⁻**

Fair Value
• **20¼**

Risk
• **High**

Earn./Div. Rank
• **NR**

Technical Eval.
• **NA**

Rel. Strength Rank (1 Lowest—99 Highest)
• **58**

Insider Activity
• **NA**

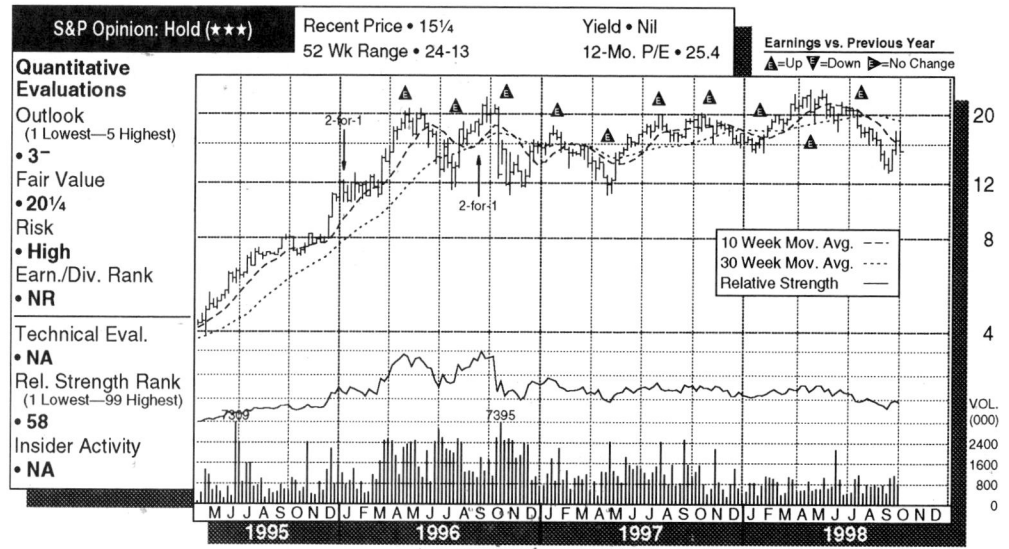

Earnings vs. Previous Year
▲=Up ▼=Down ▶=No Change

10 Week Mov. Avg. - - -
30 Week Mov. Avg. - - - -
Relative Strength ——

Overview - 05-AUG-98

OCA should generate 1998 revenues of about $175 million, reflecting an ongoing acquisition program and same-facility revenue growth of approximately 10%. The acquisition pipeline remains full in the $4 billion orthodontic market, in which an estimated 90% of the approximately 9,100 orthodontists are sole practitioners. After adding 24 net new centers during the second quarter of 1998, the company had 413 centers, and was affiliated with 238 orthodontists as of June 30, 1998. Cash flow is reliable and steady, aided by the company's 26-month patient contracts, which are payable in monthly installments (averaging $98 in 1997), except for a final payment ($398) due at the end of the contract. After posting 1998 second quarter EPS of $0.17, in line with our estimate, we look for full year EPS of $0.71, and project a gain for 1999 to $0.95.

Valuation - 05-AUG-98

We would continue to hold the stock, and expect OCA to provide returns in line with those of the S&P 500 over the coming six months. Although strong year to year revenue and earnings comparisons are expected in coming quarters, upside moves in the stock could be restricted by the company's association with the struggling physician practice management sector, where eroding physician relationships and some margin pressures have resulted in some bankruptcy filings and sharply lower stock valuations. The fundamentals of the orthodontics business differ from those of the primary care markets, but investor sentiment may remain weak, and we have some concern regarding OCA's reliance on acquisitions for revenue and EPS expansion. Given our growth expectations for the existing facility base, the stock looks fairly priced at recent levels.

Key Stock Statistics

S&P EPS Est. 1998	0.71	Tang. Bk. Value/Share	1.61
P/E on S&P Est. 1998	21.5	Beta	NA
S&P EPS Est. 1999	0.95	Shareholders	300
Dividend Rate/Share	Nil	Market cap. (B)	$0.728
Shs. outstg. (M)	47.7	Inst. holdings	81%
Avg. daily vol. (M)	0.175		

Value of $10,000 invested 5 years ago: NA

Fiscal Year Ending Dec. 31

	1998	1997	1996	1995	1994	1993
Revenues (Million $)						
1Q	37.69	24.90	13.72	8.46	—	—
2Q	41.53	27.48	15.51	9.24	—	—
3Q	—	31.44	18.88	11.49	—	—
4Q	—	33.51	23.16	12.37	—	—
Yr.	—	117.3	71.27	41.56	25.36	18.81
Earnings Per Share ($)						
1Q	0.16	0.11	0.07	0.06	—	—
2Q	0.17	0.12	0.08	0.05	—	—
3Q	E0.18	0.13	0.10	0.06	—	—
4Q	E0.20	0.14	0.10	0.07	—	—
Yr.	E0.71	0.50	0.34	0.24	0.11	—

Next earnings report expected: late October

Dividend Data

No cash dividends have been paid.

Business Summary - 05-AUG-98

Orthodontic Centers of America Inc. (OCA) develops, acquires and manages orthodontic practices on a national basis pursuant to long-term agreements. At 1997 year-end, OCA had management or consulting contracts with 205 orthodontists practicing in 360 centers in 39 states. Of these centers, 199 were developed internally and 161 (net of 56 which were consolidated) were existing practices acquired by the company. OCA provides capital for the development and growth of orthodontic centers and manages the business and marketing aspects of the practices, allowing affiliated orthodontists to focus on delivering quality patient care.

The company generally manages all operations of its orthodontic centers other than the provision of orthodontic services. It provides financial, accounting, billing and collection services and employs the orthodontic center's business personnel. OCA provides advertising and marketing services, personnel recruiting and training services, management and financial information systems, and purchasing and distribution services.

Comprehensive management and marketing services are provided to affiliated orthodontists pursuant to service or consulting agreements. Under these agreements, OCA manages the business and marketing aspects of orthodontic centers, provides capital, facilities and equipment (including utilities, maintenance and rental), implements a marketing program, prepares budgets and financial statements, orders and purchases inventory and supplies, provides a patient scheduling system and staff, bills and collects patient fees, maintains files and records, and arranges for certain legal and accounting services.

The orthodontic centers are generally located either in shopping centers or in professional office buildings, and substantially all include private treatment rooms and large patient waiting areas, allowing the centers to locate in a broader range of office space than a traditional orthodontic practice.

OCA believes that the average cost of developing a new orthodontic center is about $250,000, including the cost of equipment, leasehold improvements, working capital and funding of losses with the initial operation of the orthodontic center.

During 1997, the company created a new division focusing on affiliations with traditional, internally-marketed orthodontic practices that generate relatively large amounts of patient fees. At 1997 year-end, there were 13 orthodontic centers operating in the new division, and management believes that affiliating with selected traditional practices will provide the company with additional opportunities for growth.

Per Share Data ($)

(Year Ended Dec. 31)	1997	1996	1995	1994	1993	1992	1991	1990	1989	1988
Tangible Bk. Val.	1.91	1.42	1.71	0.78	NA	NA	NA	NA	NA	NA
Cash Flow	0.62	0.41	0.27	0.12	NA	NA	NA	NA	NA	NA
Earnings	0.50	0.34	0.24	0.11	NA	NA	NA	NA	NA	NA
Dividends	Nil	Nil	Nil	Nil	Nil	Nil	Nil	Nil	Nil	Nil
Payout Ratio	Nil	Nil	Nil	Nil	Nil	Nil	Nil	Nil	Nil	Nil
Prices - High	20¼	22⅝	12	3⅛	NA	NA	NA	NA	NA	NA
- Low	11	10⅜	2⅞	2¾	NA	NA	NA	NA	NA	NA
P/E Ratio - High	40	67	50	28	NA	NA	NA	NA	NA	NA
- Low	22	31	12	25	NA	NA	NA	NA	NA	NA

Income Statement Analysis (Million $)

	1997	1996	1995	1994	1993	1992	1991	1990	1989	1988
Revs.	117	71.3	41.6	25.4	18.8	14.5	NA	NA	NA	NA
Oper. Inc.	41.6	24.5	13.7	9.7	7.8	6.4	NA	NA	NA	NA
Depr.	5.6	2.8	1.4	0.9	1.1	1.2	NA	NA	NA	NA
Int. Exp.	0.2	0.4	0.5	0.3	0.2	0.2	NA	NA	NA	NA
Pretax Inc.	37.1	23.6	14.2	4.7	6.4	5.1	NA	NA	NA	NA
Eff. Tax Rate	39%	39%	36%	57%	5.10%	11%	NA	NA	NA	NA
Net Inc.	22.6	14.4	9.0	2.0	6.1	4.5	NA	NA	NA	NA

Balance Sheet & Other Fin. Data (Million $)

	1997	1996	1995	1994	1993	1992	1991	1990	1989	1988
Cash	9.9	24.4	33.6	17.1	1.5	0.8	NA	NA	NA	NA
Curr. Assets	84.9	56.1	54.4	28.9	9.3	5.7	NA	NA	NA	NA
Total Assets	229	145	92.6	37.5	12.5	7.2	NA	NA	NA	NA
Curr. Liab.	16.7	15.9	10.7	8.0	3.4	2.6	NA	NA	NA	NA
LT Debt	6.5	2.5	3.4	3.7	1.5	1.2	NA	NA	NA	NA
Common Eqty.	191	115	77.3	25.7	7.6	3.4	NA	NA	NA	NA
Total Cap.	212	129	81.9	29.5	9.1	4.6	NA	NA	NA	NA
Cap. Exp.	15.0	12.3	8.2	4.7	1.8	0.3	NA	NA	NA	NA
Cash Flow	28.3	17.2	10.5	3.0	7.2	5.7	NA	NA	NA	NA
Curr. Ratio	5.1	3.5	5.1	3.6	2.7	2.2	NA	NA	NA	NA
% LT Debt of Cap.	3.1	1.9	4.1	12.6	16.1	26.2	NA	NA	NA	NA
% Net Inc.of Revs.	19.3	20.2	21.7	8.0	32.5	31.1	NA	NA	NA	NA
% Ret. on Assets	12.1	12.1	13.9	8.1	62.1	NA	NA	NA	NA	NA
% Ret. on Equity	14.8	15.0	17.5	12.2	111.0	NA	NA	NA	NA	NA

Data as orig. reptd.; bef. results of disc. opers. and/or spec. items. Per share data adj. for stk. divs. as of ex-div. date. Bold denotes diluted EPS (FASB 128). E-Estimated. NA-Not Available. NM-Not Meaningful. NR-Not Ranked.

Office—5000 Sawgrass Village, Suite 25, Ponte Vedra Beach, FL 32082. **Tel**—(904) 280-6285. **Chrmn, Pres & CEO**—G. Lazzara Jr. **SVP, CFO, Treas & Secy**—B. F. Palmisano Sr. **VP & Investor Contact**—John Glover **Dirs**—G. L. Faux, M. C. Johnsen, G. Lazzara Jr., B. F. Palmisano Sr., A. J. Ryan Jr., A. G. Tunstall, E. J. Walters Jr. **Transfer Agent**—First Union National Bank of North Carolina, Charlotte. **Incorporated**—in Delaware in 1994. **Empl**— 1,721. **S&P Analyst:** Robert M. Gold.

Oshkosh B'Gosh 4880
NASDAQ Symbol **GOSHA**
In S&P SmallCap 600

03-OCT-98

Industry:
Textiles (Apparel)

Summary: This company designs, makes, sources and markets apparel for children, youth and men.

Quantitative Evaluations

Outlook
(1 Lowest—5 Highest)
• **NA**

Fair Value
• **NA**

Risk
• **Average**

Earn./Div. Rank
• **B-**

Technical Eval.
• **NA**

Rel. Strength Rank
(1 Lowest—99 Highest)
• **73**

Insider Activity
• **NA**

Recent Price • 19⅞
52 Wk Range • 24¾-13⅜

Yield • 1.0%
12-Mo. P/E • 15.8

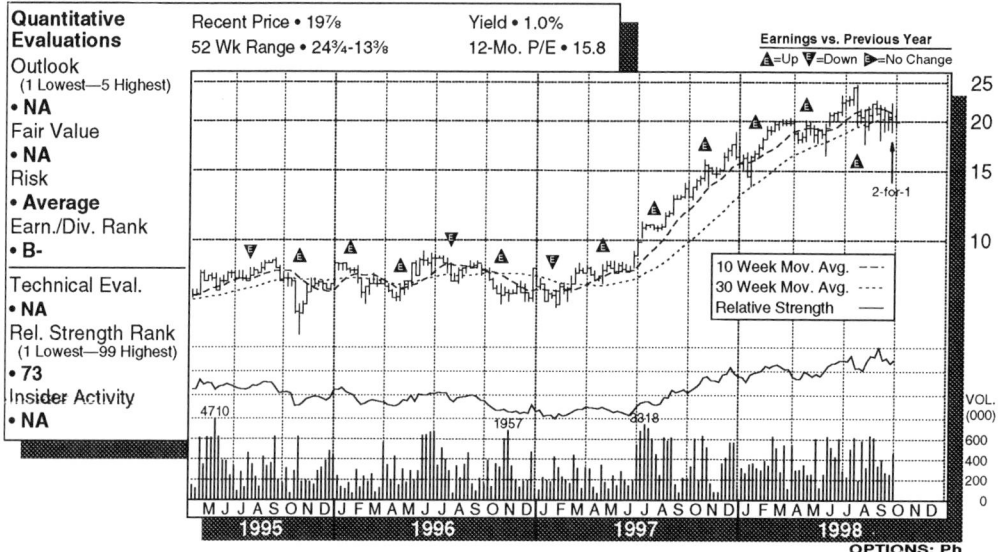

Earnings vs. Previous Year
▲=Up ▼=Down ▶=No Change

10 Week Mov. Avg. – – –
30 Week Mov. Avg. ·······
Relative Strength —

2-for-1

OPTIONS: Ph

Business Profile - 26-MAY-98

This company, which is best known for its children's clothing, sells products such as bib overalls, pants, shirts and dresses. Sales comparisons in 1997 were limited by several strategic decisions to scale back operations. In its wholesale business, which accounts for the majority of sales, Oshkosh has increasingly been focusing on a customer base of traditional department stores and selected national specialty store chains. The Genuine Kids retail chain has been discontinued, but GOSHA has a growing chain of more than 100 Oshkosh B'Gosh factory outlet or mall stores. An increased portion of GOSHA's manufactured product is likely to come from offshore contractors, and its European business has been transferred to a licensee.

Operational Review - 26-MAY-98

Net sales for the three months ended April 4, 1998, were up 5.3%, year to year, helped by three additional days of wholesale shipments, and a 10.6% rise in comparable-store sales from retail stores operated by GOSHA. Profitability improved, including benefits from using alternative sourcing for product, and improved operating efficiencies at GOSHA's domestic sewing facilities. Net income was up 28%, to $5.3 million from $4.2 million. With 15% fewer share share equivalents, diluted earnings per share rose 51%, to $0.53 from $0.35.

Stock Performance - 02-OCT-98

In the past 30 trading days, GOSHA's shares have declined 10%, compared to a 7% fall in the S&P 500. Average trading volume for the past five days was 91,820 shares, compared with the 40-day moving average of 96,903 shares.

Key Stock Statistics

Dividend Rate/Share	0.20	Shareholders	1,500
Shs. outstg. (M)	19.2	Market cap. (B)	$0.335
Avg. daily vol. (M)	0.069	Inst. holdings	30%
Tang. Bk. Value/Share	5.75		
Beta	0.35		

Value of $10,000 invested 5 years ago: $ 20,116

Fiscal Year Ending Dec. 31

	1998	1997	1996	1995	1994	1993
Revenues (Million $)						
1Q	102.5	97.36	120.9	108.5	87.39	93.23
2Q	82.29	71.14	82.58	74.93	66.16	63.31
3Q	—	124.9	136.7	142.9	118.4	103.1
4Q	—	101.8	104.6	105.9	91.41	80.53
Yr.	—	395.2	444.8	432.3	363.4	340.2
Earnings Per Share ($)						
1Q	0.27	0.17	0.14	0.10	0.03	0.14
2Q	0.14	-0.02	-0.40	-0.07	-0.03	0.05
3Q	—	0.57	0.41	0.33	0.19	0.18
4Q	—	0.32	-0.11	0.07	0.06	-0.21
Yr.	—	1.01	0.05	0.42	0.25	0.15

Next earnings report expected: NA

Dividend Data (Dividends have been paid since 1985.)

Amount ($)	Date Decl.	Ex-Div. Date	Stock of Record	Payment Date
0.070	Feb. 05	Feb. 11	Feb. 16	Mar. 02 '98
0.070	May. 01	May. 13	May. 15	Jun. 01 '98
0.100	Aug. 10	Aug. 13	Aug. 17	Sep. 01 '98
2-for-1	Aug. 10	Sep. 21	Sep. 02	Sep. 19 '98

A Division of The **McGraw·Hill** *Companies*

Business Summary - 26-MAY-98

This Wisconsin-based apparel company, which is best known for its children's clothing, sells products such as bib overalls, pants, shirts and dresses. Children's wear and youth wear accounted for about 95% of 1997 revenues. In 1998, a new licensing agreement with Evenflo Inc. is expected to result in a new OshKosh juvenile product line being available at more than 100 Babies "R" Us stores.

While GOSHA operates more than 100 retail outlets, most of its sales in recent periods have come from wholesale operations. In 1997, GOSHA's domestic wholesale business had net sales of about $214 million (54% of GOSHA's total), while net sales from GOSHA's domestic retail operations totaled approximately $174 million (44%).

GOSHA has taken steps to improve product marketability, streamline operations, reduce its capital base and cost structure, and improve its delivery performance. These steps include narrowing the distribution channels for GOSHA's children's wear, discontinuing underperforming business units, and closing certain domestic manufacturing facilities. GOSHA's 1996 results

included one-time charges totaling about $1.24 a share related to the discontinuance of the Genuine Kids retail chain, the wind down of GOSHA's European subsidiaries and the transfer of the European business to a licensee, and the closing of three U.S. manufacturing or sewing facilities.

GOSHA's business is seasonal, with sales and income likely to be highest in the third quarter, the peak wholesale shipping period and a major retail selling season at Oshkosh's retail outlet stores. Second-quarter sales and earnings are likely to be the lowest, because of relatively low domestic wholesale unit shipments and relatively modest retail outlet store sales in the period.

In August 1997, in connection with a self tender offer, the company repurchased 1,656,578 Class A common shares and 41,524 Class B shares, for approximately $37.7 million, including related expenses. Also in August, directors approved a program to buy up to 500,000 Class A shares. As of January 1, 1998, a group that included GOSHA's CEO and COO owned about 88% of the company's Class B shares, owners of which determine who is elected to seven of the seats on GOSHA's board of directors.

Per Share Data ($)

(Year Ended Dec. 31)	1997	1996	1995	1994	1993	1992	1991	1990	1989	1988
Tangible Bk. Val.	5.74	5.86	6.03	5.88	5.89	6.00	5.74	5.18	4.41	3.33
Cash Flow	1.60	0.52	0.86	0.63	0.45	0.81	1.02	1.19	1.44	0.76
Earnings	1.01	0.05	0.42	0.25	0.15	0.54	0.81	1.01	1.29	0.65
Dividends	0.14	0.14	0.14	0.19	0.26	0.26	0.26	0.24	0.21	0.17
Payout Ratio	14%	NM	33%	75%	165%	48%	32%	24%	17%	27%
Prices - High	18¾	9⅜	9	10⅞	11¼	15⅜	21⅛	21¾	22	14¾
- Low	6¾	6⅞	5¾	6⅛	6¾	9⅝	11¼	8½	10	10¼
P/E Ratio - High	18	NM	21	43	73	28	26	21	17	23
- Low	7	NM	14	24	44	18	14	8	8	16

Income Statement Analysis (Million $)

	1997	1996	1995	1994	1993	1992	1991	1990	1989	1988
Revs.	395	445	432	363	340	346	365	323	315	253
Oper. Inc.	42.0	33.9	30.0	19.7	25.2	28.2	47.0	51.1	66.9	34.1
Depr.	13.0	11.7	11.4	10.7	8.4	7.9	6.1	5.0	4.3	3.4
Int. Exp.	0.3	1.1	1.8	1.3	0.6	0.8	1.1	1.8	3.0	1.6
Pretax Inc.	38.2	-4.1	20.2	13.0	9.3	26.5	39.1	48.1	61.4	30.5
Eff. Tax Rate	41%	NM	46%	46%	51%	41%	41%	40%	39%	38%
Net Inc.	22.6	1.1	10.9	7.0	4.5	15.7	23.6	29.6	37.6	18.8

Balance Sheet & Other Fin. Data (Million $)

	1997	1996	1995	1994	1993	1992	1991	1990	1989	1988
Cash	13.8	41.2	2.4	10.5	17.9	21.1	14.4	6.8	3.3	0.1
Curr. Assets	131	149	137	142	152	146	141	129	116	94.0
Total Assets	175	196	209	217	229	226	215	189	163	139
Curr. Liab.	48.3	44.3	42.0	39.8	40.1	35.2	33.9	28.7	27.2	34.1
LT Debt	Nil	Nil	Nil	0.5	0.8	1.3	2.4	3.5	4.5	5.7
Common Eqty.	113	138	150	159	172	175	167	151	129	97.0
Total Cap.	113	138	153	162	176	180	174	155	134	104
Cap. Exp.	6.6	7.3	9.7	9.9	9.0	14.4	19.6	15.5	7.3	18.2
Cash Flow	35.6	12.8	22.3	17.7	12.9	23.6	29.7	34.5	41.9	22.2
Curr. Ratio	2.7	3.4	3.3	3.6	3.8	4.2	4.1	4.5	4.3	2.8
% LT Debt of Cap.	Nil	Nil	Nil	0.3	0.4	0.7	1.4	2.2	3.4	5.5
% Net Inc.of Revs.	5.7	0.3	2.5	1.9	1.3	4.5	6.5	9.1	11.9	7.4
% Ret. on Assets	12.2	0.6	5.1	3.3	2.0	7.1	11.7	16.8	24.9	14.9
% Ret. on Equity	18.0	0.8	7.1	4.4	2.6	9.2	14.8	21.1	33.3	20.8

Data as orig. reptd.; bef. results of disc. opers. and/or spec. items. Per share data adj. for stk. divs. as of ex-div. date. Bold denotes diluted EPS (FASB 128). E-Estimated. NA-Not Available. NM-Not Meaningful. NR-Not Ranked.

Office—112 Otter Ave., Oshkosh, WI 54901. **Tel**—(920) 231-8800. **Website**—http://www.oshkoshbgosh.com **Chrmn, Pres & CEO**—D. W. Hyde. **EVP & COO**—M. D. Wachtel. **VP-Fin, Treas & CFO**—D. L. Omachinski. **Secy**—S. R. Duback. **Dirs**—O. J. Bradley, S. A. Dawe, S. R. Duback, J. M. Hiegel, D. W. Hyde, S. A. Kry, D. L. Omachinski, M. D. Wachtel, W. F. Wyman. **Transfer Agent**—Harris Trust & Savings Bank, Chicago. **Incorporated**—in Delaware in 1929. **Empl**— 4,000. **S&P Analyst:** Tom Graves, CFA

03-OCT-98 **Industry:** Manufacturing (Diversified)

Summary: OSL produces smooth-rolled plastic products for the automotive and specialty plastics manufacturing industries.

Quantitative Evaluations

Recent Price • 8¼
52 Wk Range • 11-8⅛

Yield • 3.9%
12-Mo. P/E • 23.6

Outlook
(1 Lowest—5 Highest)
• **NA**

Fair Value
• **NA**

Risk
• **Average**

Earn./Div. Rank
• **B-**

Technical Eval.
• **Bullish** since 2/98

Rel. Strength Rank
(1 Lowest—99 Highest)
• **57**

Insider Activity
• **NA**

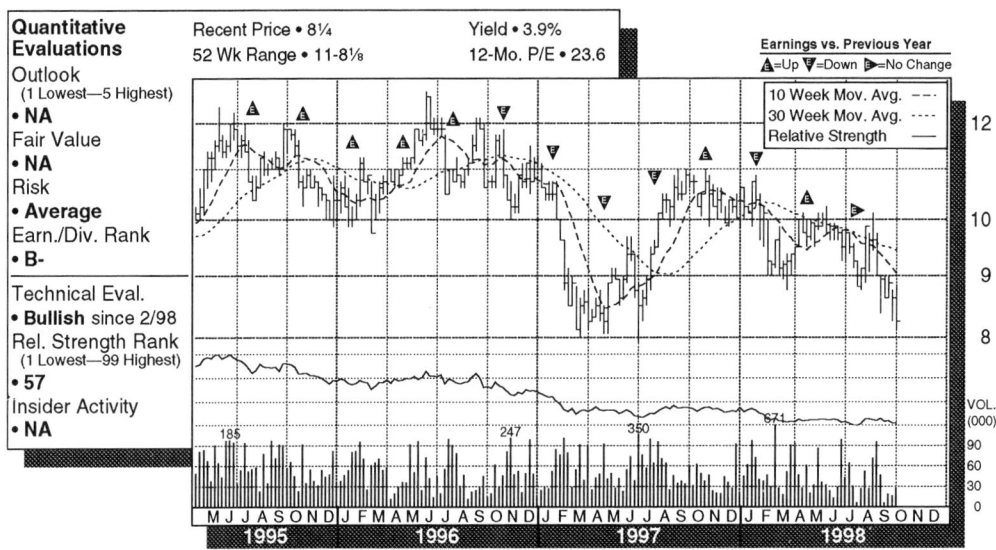

Earnings vs. Previous Year
▲=Up ▼=Down ▶=No Change

10 Week Mov. Avg. – – –
30 Week Mov. Avg. ·····
Relative Strength —

Business Profile - 14-SEP-98

O'Sullivan Corp. makes a variety of smooth-rolled plastic products for the automotive and pastics manufacturing industries. Despite lower sales in the first half of 1998 partly due to the auto workers strike, the company managed to post modestly higher earnings, reflecting efficiency gains and a lower tax rate. The company anticipates that capital expenditures for the remainder of 1998 will be substantially in excess of 1997 levels because of funding required to complete a coating facility and continue installation of additional laminating equipment. Management estimated total capital spending for 1998 in the range of $12 to $14 million.

Operational Review - 14-SEP-98

Net sales in the six months ended June 30, 1998, fell 1.3%, year to year, reflecting a decline in automotive-related products due to the auto workers strike and a less favorable product mix. Gross margins widened on improved manufacturing efficiencies and stable raw material costs, which offset higher costs for advertising and sales consultants; pretax income was up 4.1%. After taxes at 36.4%, versus 39.0%, income from continuing operations climbed 8.5%, to $6,417,096 ($0.41 a share), from $5,915,328 ($0.38). Results in the 1997 period exclude a loss from the discontinued Melnor subsidiary of $0.03 a share.

Stock Performance - 02-OCT-98

In the past 30 trading days, OSL's shares have declined 14%, compared to a 7% fall in the S&P 500. Average trading volume for the past five days was 5,400 shares, compared with the 40-day moving average of 9,241 shares.

Key Stock Statistics

Dividend Rate/Share	0.32	Shareholders	3,000
Shs. outstg. (M)	15.6	Market cap. (B)	$0.129
Avg. daily vol. (M)	0.004	Inst. holdings	22%
Tang. Bk. Value/Share	7.38		
Beta	0.16		

Value of $10,000 invested 5 years ago: $ 10,313

Fiscal Year Ending Dec. 31

	1998	1997	1996	1995	1994	1993
Revenues (Million $)						
1Q	41.95	40.46	48.49	55.05	47.41	70.80
2Q	42.14	44.71	59.00	57.07	57.03	80.24
3Q	—	38.83	61.21	48.55	44.70	66.51
4Q	—	39.60	44.24	49.05	45.85	74.66
Yr.	—	163.6	211.4	209.7	195.0	292.3
Earnings Per Share ($)						
1Q	**0.19**	**0.16**	0.14	0.25	0.17	0.14
2Q	**0.22**	**0.22**	0.23	0.24	0.23	0.26
3Q	—	**0.18**	0.19	0.17	0.16	0.13
4Q	—	Nil	0.04	0.19	0.12	0.09
Yr.	—	**0.56**	**0.87**	**0.85**	**0.67**	**0.59**

Next earnings report expected: mid October

Dividend Data (Dividends have been paid since 1960.)

Amount ($)	Date Decl.	Ex-Div. Date	Stock of Record	Payment Date
0.080	Nov. 26	Dec. 10	Dec. 12	Jan. 09 '98
0.080	Jan. 27	Mar. 05	Mar. 09	Apr. 10 '98
0.080	Apr. 29	Jun. 03	Jun. 05	Jul. 12 '98
0.080	Jul. 28	Sep. 09	Sep. 11	Oct. 09 '98

A Division of The McGraw·Hill Companies

STANDARD
&POOR'S
STOCK REPORTS

O'Sullivan Corporation

8735

03-OCT-98

Business Summary - 14-SEP-98

In 1896, Humphrey O'Sullivan's sore feet led to his invention of rubber heels and the founding of O'Sullivan Corporation (OSL). While it no longer makes rubber products, over 100 years later OSL is determined to cushion the impact of some of its recent difficulties. OSL makes calendered plastic products for the automotive and specialty plastics manufacturing industries. Consumer products operations were sold in August 1997.

Calendered (smooth-olled) plastic products made by OSL include vinyl sheeting for automobile dashboard pads and door panels, swimming pool linings and covers, notebook binders, luggage, upholstered furniture, golf bags, floor tile, pond liners, protective clothing, mine curtains, boat and automobile windows and medical-grade materials. Ford Motor accounted for more than 10% of 1997 sales.

OSL has a 49% equity interest in Keifel Technologies, Inc. Keifel designs, manufactures and distributes thermoforming and radio frequency welding machines and related machinery and tools.

Until its sale in August 1997, OSL's Consumer Products segment, through Melnor Inc., produced and sold oscillating, rotary and traveling sprinklers, hose storage units, watering timers, aqua guns, air spray tanks and snow shovels. To a much lesser extent, this segment also distributed ceiling fans and thermostats.

After a significant loss in 1996, a number of initiatives were implemented in order to get Melnor back on its feet. A new management team was installed with an emphasis on quality and on-time delivery, and four warehouses were consolidated into one to reduce costs and improve inventory control. After sales fell 31.5% at Melnor during the first six months of 1997, O'Sullivan sold the struggling subsidiary for approximately $21 million in August 1997. Following the divestiture, O'Sullivan had no debt and more than $30 million in cash with which to explore several small acquisitions related to its core plastics business.

Per Share Data ($)

(Year Ended Dec. 31)	1997	1996	1995	1994	1993	1992	1991	1990	1989	1988
Tangible Bk. Val.	7.16	7.19	6.98	6.42	6.54	6.23	5.88	6.09	5.48	4.77
Cash Flow	0.91	1.11	1.26	1.32	1.28	1.33	0.69	1.30	1.30	1.32
Earnings	0.56	0.66	0.85	0.67	0.61	0.66	0.09	0.89	0.98	1.03
Dividends	0.32	0.32	0.31	0.28	0.28	0.28	0.28	0.28	0.27	0.22
Payout Ratio	57%	48%	36%	42%	46%	43%	300%	31%	27%	21%
Prices - High	11	12¾	12⅜	10¾	12⅝	9⅞	11½	11¼	16¼	17
- Low	7⅞	9¾	9¼	8⅝	8½	7½	6⅝	7⅜	10	11
P/E Ratio - High	20	19	15	16	21	15	NM	13	17	16
- Low	14	15	11	13	14	11	NM	8	10	11

Income Statement Analysis (Million $)

	1997	1996	1995	1994	1993	1992	1991	1990	1989	1988
Revs.	164	211	210	195	292	218	196	199	219	202
Oper. Inc.	16.3	24.2	30.1	29.5	29.4	28.8	17.8	29.8	29.6	31.4
Depr.	5.5	7.3	6.8	10.9	11.4	11.1	9.9	6.7	5.3	4.7
Int. Exp.	0.0	0.1	0.1	0.9	2.5	0.8	1.6	1.8	0.9	0.6
Pretax Inc.	13.7	17.6	23.7	18.1	16.8	17.5	2.4	23.5	26.1	27.4
Eff. Tax Rate	36%	39%	41%	39%	42%	38%	36%	38%	38%	38%
Net Inc.	8.8	10.7	14.0	11.0	9.7	10.8	1.5	14.7	16.1	17.0

Balance Sheet & Other Fin. Data (Million $)

	1997	1996	1995	1994	1993	1992	1991	1990	1989	1988
Cash	35.4	6.5	10.4	9.7	3.1	3.5	2.0	1.0	2.5	4.3
Curr. Assets	86.1	84.5	88.9	89.0	103	76.9	60.2	58.3	53.7	59.5
Total Assets	138	141	150	145	205	172	151	157	140	118
Curr. Liab.	16.0	20.3	28.0	30.7	47.6	35.6	32.6	27.6	27.1	28.2
LT Debt	Nil	NM	0.1	1.7	39.6	25.5	13.7	19.8	16.5	4.5
Common Eqty.	113	114	116	107	109	104	97.0	100	90.0	79.0
Total Cap.	114	117	119	112	156	135	116	127	113	88.0
Cap. Exp.	4.9	6.8	10.2	8.8	17.3	14.5	7.5	16.5	33.7	12.6
Cash Flow	14.3	18.0	20.9	21.8	21.1	21.9	11.4	21.4	21.4	21.7
Curr. Ratio	5.4	4.2	3.2	2.9	2.2	2.2	1.8	2.1	2.0	2.1
% LT Debt of Cap.	Nil	NM	0.0	1.5	25.4	18.9	11.8	15.6	14.6	5.1
% Net Inc.of Revs.	5.4	5.1	6.7	5.6	3.3	4.9	0.8	7.4	7.4	8.4
% Ret. on Assets	6.3	7.4	9.6	6.3	5.2	6.7	1.0	9.9	12.5	15.7
% Ret. on Equity	7.8	9.4	12.7	10.2	9.1	10.7	1.6	15.4	19.0	23.5

Data as orig. reptd.; bef. results of disc. opers. and/or spec. items. Per share data adj. for stk. divs. as of ex-div. date. Bold denotes diluted EPS (FASB 128). E-Estimated. NA-Not Available. NM-Not Meaningful. NR-Not Ranked.

Office—1944 Valley Ave., P.O. Box 3510, Winchester, VA 22601. **Tel**—(540) 667-6666. **Fax**—(540) 722-2695. **Chrmn**—A. H. Bryant II. **Pres & CEO**—J. T. Holland. **Treas, Secy & CFO**—C. B. Nickerson. **Dirs**—C. H. Bloom Jr., A. H. Bryant II, M. O. Bryant, R. L. Burrus Jr., M. C. Chapman Jr., J. T. Holland, R. M. McCullough, S. P. Munn, T. J. Sandker, L. W. Smith, Jr. **Transfer Agent & Registrar**—Mellon Securities Trust Co., Pittsburgh. **Incorporated**—in Virginia in 1945. **Empl**— 900. **S&P Analyst:** P.L.H.

Owens & Minor

1723V

NYSE Symbol **OMI**

In S&P SmallCap 600

03-OCT-98

Industry: Distributors (Food & Health)

Summary: This company is a nationwide wholesale distributor of medical and surgical supplies.

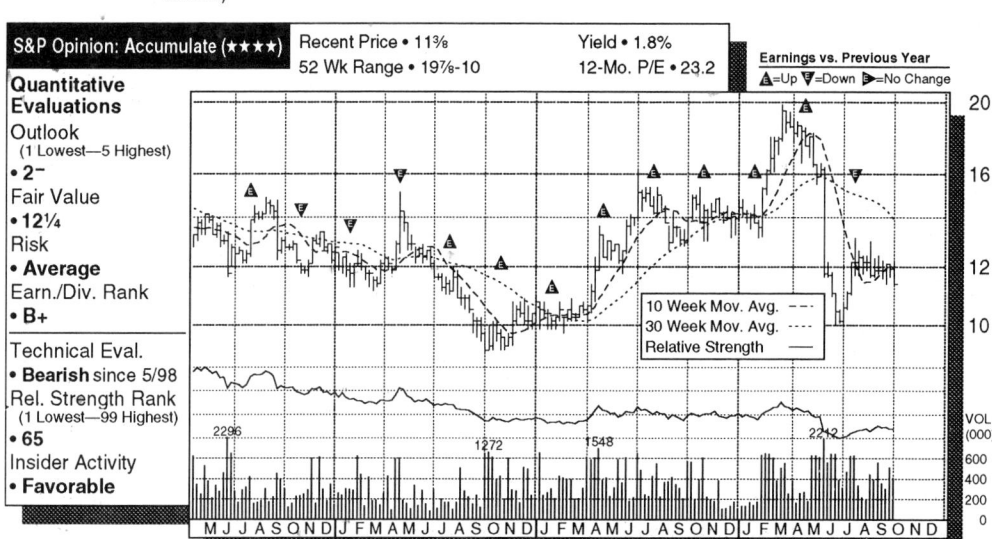

S&P Opinion: Accumulate (★★★★)	Recent Price • 11⅜	Yield • 1.8%	Earnings vs. Previous Year
	52 Wk Range • 19⅞-10	12-Mo. P/E • 23.2	▲=Up ▼=Down ▶=No Change

Quantitative Evaluations

Outlook (1 Lowest—5 Highest)
• **2⁻**

Fair Value
• **12¼**

Risk
• **Average**

Earn./Div. Rank
• **B+**

Technical Eval.
• **Bearish** since 5/98

Rel. Strength Rank (1 Lowest—99 Highest)
• **65**

Insider Activity
• **Favorable**

10 Week Mov. Avg. ----
30 Week Mov. Avg. ·······
Relative Strength ——

Overview - 20-JUL-98

The company's revenues will be hurt by the termination of a distribution pact with Columbia/HCA (11% of 1997 sales). However, expansion into surgicenter and nursing home markets, along with several new contracts pending with medical centers, should help moderate the negative impact of the Columbia cancellation during the second half of 1998 and into 1999. The Columbia cancelation will lower operating earnings by about $1.5 million in 1998 and $3.0 million in 1999, and OMI incurred a net charge of $6.6 million in the second quarter to downsize those warehouse operations with the greatest exposure to the Columbia contract. The development will somewhat hamper the earnings recovery in coming quarters, and now we look for sustained three-year EPS growth (before charges) of 15%, below earlier expectations for growth upwards of 20%.

Valuation - 20-JUL-98

While the stock has been punished by Columbia/HCA's decision to switch medical/surgical product vendors, we believe the stock remains attractive at 18 times our revised 1998 EPS estimate of $0.70 for 1998 (before second quarter charges of $0.20) and 14 times our 1999 forecast of $0.80. In addition, the stock should receive some consideration as a potential takeover target in the increasingly consolidating medical product distribution sector. Much like its peer group and despite the Columbia development, OMI's strong earnings outlook is fueled by improving margins as a result of more streamlined inventory management procedures, while improving cash flow allows for debt reductions and possible share buybacks. During the second quarter of 1998, OMI retired all outstanding (1.150,000) shares of Series B preferred stock, and this transaction will lower annual financing costs by about $5.2 million.

Key Stock Statistics

S&P EPS Est. 1998	0.50	Tang. Bk. Value/Share	NM
P/E on S&P Est. 1998	22.8	Beta	0.51
S&P EPS Est. 1999	0.80	Shareholders	17,000
Dividend Rate/Share	0.20	Market cap. (B)	$0.370
Shs. outstg. (M)	32.5	Inst. holdings	71%
Avg. daily vol. (M)	0.083		

Value of $10,000 invested 5 years ago: $ 12,503

Fiscal Year Ending Dec. 31

	1998	1997	1996	1995	1994	1993
Revenues (Million $)						
1Q	798.0	749.6	771.3	747.1	390.8	318.0
2Q	799.0	776.7	749.9	743.7	581.8	341.2
3Q	—	785.8	744.1	739.0	693.0	362.0
4Q	—	804.7	753.6	746.6	730.2	376.0
Yr.	—	3,117	3,019	2,976	2,396	1,397
Earnings Per Share ($)						
1Q	**0.17**	**0.12**	0.01	0.11	0.15	0.13
2Q	**-0.01**	**0.14**	0.05	0.01	0.10	0.14
3Q	**E0.16**	**0.16**	0.08	-0.32	0.01	0.15
4Q	**E0.18**	**0.18**	0.11	-0.33	0.18	0.18
Yr.	**E0.50**	**0.60**	0.25	-0.53	0.15	0.60

Next earnings report expected: mid October

Dividend Data (Dividends have been paid since 1926.)

Amount ($)	Date Decl.	Ex-Div. Date	Stock of Record	Payment Date
0.045	Oct. 27	Dec. 11	Dec. 15	Dec. 31 '97
0.050	Feb. 24	Mar. 12	Mar. 16	Mar. 31 '98
0.050	Apr. 28	Jun. 10	Jun. 12	Jun. 30 '98
0.050	Jul. 20	Sep. 10	Sep. 14	Sep. 30 '98

A Division of The **McGraw·Hill** Companies

STANDARD
&POOR'S
STOCK REPORTS

Owens & Minor, Inc.

1723V
03-OCT-98

Business Summary - 20-JUL-98

Founded in 1882 as a wholesale drug company, Owens & Minor Inc. has become one of the largest distributors of medical/surgical supplies in the U.S. The company stocks and distributes about 140,000 finished medical and surgical products produced by 2,400 manufacturers to 4,000 customers nationwide. Acute care hospitals account for more than 90% of net sales, but OMI also sells to alternate care facilities such as nursing homes, clinics, surgery centers, rehabilitation facilities, physicians' offices and home health care centers.

The majority of sales consist of dressings, endoscopic products, intravenous products, disposable gloves, needles and syringes, sterile procedure trays, surgical products and gowns, urological products and wound closure products.

The medical/surgical supply industry's recent expansion reflects, in part, increased consumption by an aging population, new health care procedures and new health care products. In addition, manufacturers and customers are seeking to take advantage of the cost savings achievable through the use of distributors that can purchase in bulk and achieve economies of scale. Increasingly, distributors are assuming the roles of asset managers, where they offer enhanced inventory management services that provide a continuous inventory replenishment process (CRP), asset management consulting and stockless, just in-time inventory programs.

Aside from its core distribution services, OMI offers flexible delivery alternatives that are supported by inventory management services to meet the widely varied needs of its customers. The company's information technology systems allow it to offer customers several services to minimize their inventory holding requirements. These include PANDAC, a wound closure management system that provides customers with an accurate evaluation of their current wound closure inventories and usage levels in order to reduce costs for these products; CostTrack, an activity-based costing and pricing model that allows management to identify the cost drivers in specific distribution activities; the FOCUS program, which helps customers standardize and consolidate their purchasing decisions to gain efficiencies from volume purchases; and DSS, a database used to help customers standardize the inventory management decisions within all of the facilities in an integrated network.

OMI believes it is one of the top two medical/surgical distributors in the U.S. This competitive industry consists of three major, nationwide participants, including OMI, Allegiance Corp. and McKesson Corp.

Per Share Data ($)

(Year Ended Dec. 31)	1997	1996	1995	1994	1993	1992	1991	1990	1989	1988
Tangible Bk. Val.	NA	NM	-1.67	-1.13	3.93	3.46	2.87	2.62	2.34	2.72
Cash Flow	1.15	0.75	0.13	0.57	0.84	0.72	0.50	0.49	0.22	0.40
Earnings	0.60	0.25	-0.53	0.15	0.60	0.52	0.33	0.31	0.09	0.30
Dividends	0.18	0.18	0.18	0.19	0.14	0.11	0.09	0.08	0.08	0.08
Payout Ratio	30%	72%	NM	125%	23%	21%	26%	25%	87%	25%
Prices - High	16¼	15⅛	14⅞	18⅛	15⅝	10¹/₈	10³/₄	4½	4³/₈	4¹/₂
- Low	9³/₄	9¹/₈	11⅝	13¼	8³/₈	7³/₈	4¹/₈	3¹/₈	3³/₈	2¹/₂
P/E Ratio - High	27	60	NM	NM	26	19	32	15	53	15
- Low	16	36	NM	NM	14	14	12	10	38	9

Income Statement Analysis (Million $)

	1997	1996	1995	1994	1993	1992	1991	1990	1989	1988
Revs.	3,117	3,019	2,976	2,396	1,397	1,177	1,027	1,220	953	732
Oper. Inc.	81.9	64.7	41.9	68.7	40.9	34.3	25.9	27.1	17.5	19.7
Depr.	17.7	16.1	15.4	13.0	7.6	5.9	5.0	5.3	3.6	3.1
Int. Exp.	18.8	23.7	29.3	12.1	2.9	2.5	4.5	7.6	6.7	2.9
Pretax Inc.	41.9	23.1	-16.4	14.0	30.4	25.9	16.5	14.2	4.7	13.7
Eff. Tax Rate	42%	44%	NM	43%	39%	41%	41%	38%	47%	39%
Net Inc.	24.3	13.0	-11.3	7.9	18.5	15.4	9.8	8.8	2.5	8.4

Balance Sheet & Other Fin. Data (Million $)

	1997	1996	1995	1994	1993	1992	1991	1990	1989	1988
Cash	0.6	0.7	0.2	0.5	2.0	7.1	0.8	3.3	3.3	0.6
Curr. Assets	499	456	624	641	282	229	267	249	226	171
Total Assets	713	680	858	869	334	275	312	290	259	190
Curr. Liab.	265	263	292	359	143	129	144	131	93.0	64.0
LT Debt	183	168	323	248	50.8	25.0	67.7	71.3	85.3	46.8
Common Eqty.	144	127	120	141	137	117	97.1	85.0	77.6	77.2
Total Cap.	442	410	558	505	188	142	165	156	163	124
Cap. Exp.	7.5	6.2	13.9	6.6	6.3	5.0	6.0	4.8	5.3	3.3
Cash Flow	36.8	23.9	4.1	17.6	26.1	21.3	14.7	14.1	6.1	11.5
Curr. Ratio	1.9	1.7	2.1	1.8	2.0	1.8	1.9	1.9	2.4	2.7
% LT Debt of Cap.	41.4	40.9	57.9	49.2	27.0	17.6	41.1	45.6	52.4	37.8
% Net Inc.of Revs.	0.8	0.4	NM	0.3	1.3	1.3	0.9	0.7	0.3	1.1
% Ret. on Assets	3.5	1.7	NM	1.3	6.0	5.2	3.2	3.2	1.1	4.9
% Ret. on Equity	14.1	6.3	NM	3.3	14.4	14.4	10.6	10.8	3.2	11.3

Data as orig. reptd.; bef. results of disc. opers. and/or spec. items. Per share data adj. for stk. divs. as of ex-div. date. Bold denotes diluted EPS (FASB 128). E-Estimated. NA-Not Available. NM-Not Meaningful. NR-Not Ranked.

Office—4800 Cox Rd., Glen Allen, VA 23060. **Tel**—(804) 747-9794. **Website**—http://www.owens-minor.com **Chrmn, Pres & CEO**—G. G. Minor III. **EVP & COO**—C. R. Smith. **SVP & Secy**—D. St. J. Carneal. **SVP & CFO**—A. G. Rector. **Investor Contact**—Elizabeth A. Hamilton (804-967-2848). **Dirs**—H. A. Berling, J. Bunting III, R. E. Cabell Jr., J. B. Farinholt Jr., W. F. Fife, C. G. Grefenstette, V. W. Henley, E. M. Massey, G. G. Minor III, J. E. Rogers, J. E. Ukrop, A. M. Whittemore. **Transfer Agent**—The Bank of New York, NYC. **Incorporated**—in Virginia in 1926. **Empl**— 3,000. **S&P Analyst:** Robert M. Gold

Oxford Industries　1727

NYSE Symbol **OXM**

In S&P SmallCap 600

03-OCT-98　**Industry:** Textiles (Apparel)

Summary: OXM manufactures and distributes brand-name and private-label apparel for men and women in the medium-to-higher-price range.

Quantitative Evaluations	
Outlook (1 Lowest—5 Highest)	**• NA**
Fair Value	**• NA**
Risk	**• Average**
Earn./Div. Rank	**• B+**
Technical Eval.	**• Bearish** since 7/98
Rel. Strength Rank (1 Lowest—99 Highest)	**• 79**
Insider Activity	**• NA**

Recent Price • 29⅞
52 Wk Range • 38¾-25½

Yield • 2.7%
12-Mo. P/E • 10.7

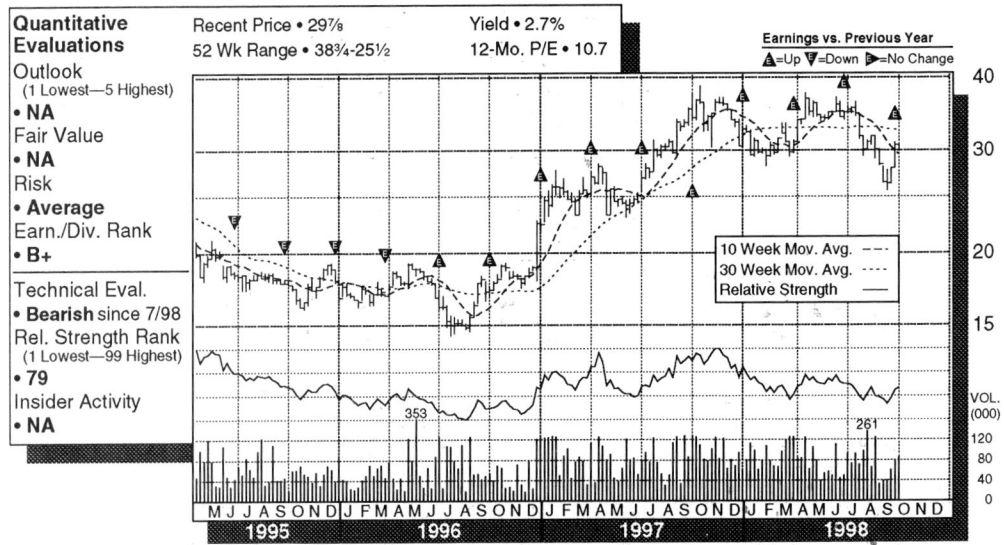

Earnings vs. Previous Year
▲=Up ▼=Down ▶=No Change

10 Week Mov. Avg. — — —
30 Week Mov. Avg. ········
Relative Strength ——

Business Profile - 16-JUL-98

OXM's strategy for dealing with a highly competitive apparel market environment includes reducing the cost of goods by shifting to global manufacturing and sourcing; cutting expenses as a percentage of sales; pursuing higher profit margin opportunities through licensing or acquisition of important brand or designer names; and focusing on asset management. In June 1998, OXM agreed to acquire the assets of Next Day Apparel, Inc., a manufacturer and marketer of private label womenswear for mass-market retailers. Next Day, headquartered in Walhalla, SC, with marketing offices in New York City and manufacturing plants in Honduras, has annual sales in excess of $100,000,000. OXM expects continued record results in FY 99 (May), but does not expect gains to be as strong as in FY 98.

Operational Review - 16-JUL-98

Based on a preliminary report, net sales rose 10% in FY 98, primarily reflecting growth in the company's licensed designer menswear lines and in OxSport and Oxford Womenswear. Gross margins widened, on faster growth in the higher-margin designer licensed businesses, improved manufacturing performance, and increased off-shore sourcing. With lower interest expense, net income climbed 25%, to $24,623,000 ($2.75 a share) from $19,647,000 ($2.23).

Stock Performance - 02-OCT-98

In the past 30 trading days, OXM's shares have declined 0.42%, compared to a 7% fall in the S&P 500. Average trading volume for the past five days was 16,980 shares, compared with the 40-day moving average of 14,659 shares.

Key Stock Statistics

Dividend Rate/Share	0.80	Shareholders	800
Shs. outstg. (M)	8.8	Market cap. (B)	$0.264
Avg. daily vol. (M)	0.014	Inst. holdings	60%
Tang. Bk. Value/Share	18.11		
Beta	0.12		

Value of $10,000 invested 5 years ago: $ 17,413

Fiscal Year Ending May 31

	1999	1998	1997	1996	1995	1994
Revenues (Million $)						
1Q	198.6	193.2	172.5	189.3	165.3	148.7
2Q	—	208.1	203.2	187.1	192.2	178.7
3Q	—	178.7	167.5	138.6	153.1	143.1
4Q	—	194.5	160.0	149.5	146.4	154.0
Yr.	—	774.5	703.2	664.4	657.0	624.6
Earnings Per Share ($)						
1Q	0.67	0.61	0.40	0.03	0.56	0.46
2Q	—	0.88	0.75	0.30	0.70	0.68
3Q	—	0.60	0.51	-0.23	0.21	0.52
4Q	—	0.67	0.59	0.15	-0.25	0.57
Yr.	—	2.75	2.25	0.25	1.22	2.23

Next earnings report expected: mid December

Dividend Data (Dividends have been paid since 1960.)

Amount ($)	Date Decl.	Ex-Div. Date	Stock of Record	Payment Date
0.200	Oct. 06	Nov. 12	Nov. 14	Nov. 29 '97
0.200	Jan. 05	Feb. 11	Feb. 13	Feb. 28 '98
0.200	Apr. 06	May. 13	May. 15	May. 30 '98
0.200	Jul. 13	Aug. 13	Aug. 17	Aug. 29 '98

A Division of The McGraw-Hill Companies

STANDARD
&POOR'S
STOCK REPORTS

Oxford Industries, Inc.

1727

03-OCT-98

Business Summary - 16-JUL-98

Oxford Industries, a diversified manufacturer and whole sale marketer of apparel for men, women and children, was able to drive down its costs in FY 97 (May), and in doing so was able to boost net earnings to $19.6 million from the depressed FY 96 amount of $2.2 million. Net sales rose 6% over FY 96 to $703 million in FY 97.

A number of factors were responsible for OXM's improved showing. Growth in the company's higher margin business, better internal control and lower manufacturing costs swelled OXM's gross margin to 19.5% from 17.4% the year before. Better management of inventory and receivables resulted in a 32% decline in interest expense. A $4.5 million provision for environmental remediation in FY 96 also enhanced year-to-year comparisons.

FY 97 was a recovery year for OXM's largest operating group, Oxford Shirt, whose products encompass not only men's shirts but also a broad range of men's and boys' sportswear. Although sales fell slightly in FY 97, the group returned to profitability after two years of losses. The group's Tommy Hilfiger Dress Shirts division recorded a strong sales increase and now occupies the number one position in all-cotton designer dress shirts. Another licensed division, Polo/Ralph Lauren for Boys, also had a strong sales gain. Sales were down at Oxford Shirtings, OXM's private label

dress shirt division, and at OxSport, its private label sport shirt division, but profitability of both units was significantly improved.

Lanier Clothes, a leading producer of suits, sportcoats, suit separates and dress slacks, achieved a 9% sales increase in FY 97, with the improvement balanced between Oscar de la Renta tailored clothing and private label business. Oxford Slacks, the leading U.S. maker of private label dress and casual slacks for men, posted sales increases in its Specialty Catalog, Mature Mens and Young Mens divisions.

The company's Oxford Womenswear Group improved its position as a leading supplier of private label womenswear to major national retailers in FY 97. Higher sales in the Sportswear Collections and Sportswear Separates divisions more than offset lower Dress division sales. In FY 97, womenswear accounted for 23% of net sales, and menswear 77%.

OXM has developed a number of operating strategies in the face of tough competition in its apparel markets. As part of an effort to lower product costs through global sourcing, the company invested in new and expanded production facilities in Mexico and the Philippines in FY 97. OXM will also continue to pursue higher profit margin opportunities through licensing or acquisition of important brand or designer names. It planned to launch Geoffrey Beene Tailored Clothing in FY 98.

Per Share Data ($)

(Year Ended May 31)	1998	1997	1996	1995	1994	1993	1992	1991	1990	1989
Tangible Bk. Val.	18.11	16.12	14.65	15.25	14.79	13.28	12.28	11.43	11.19	10.89
Cash Flow	3.71	3.28	1.26	2.12	3.05	2.45	2.13	1.30	1.50	1.74
Earnings	2.75	2.25	0.25	1.22	2.23	1.70	1.42	0.62	0.82	0.99
Dividends	0.80	0.80	0.80	0.76	0.69	0.63	0.55	0.50	0.50	0.50
Payout Ratio	29%	36%	NM	62%	31%	37%	39%	80%	58%	50%
Cal. Yrs.	1997	1996	1995	1994	1993	1992	1991	1990	1989	1988
Prices - High	38³/₄	24³/₈	22	34³/₄	25³/₈	27¹/₈	18³/₈	13	13³/₈	12³/₄
- Low	23	14³/₈	16	21⁷/₈	15	14³/₈	6⁷/₈	6¹/₂	10¹/₂	9¹/₈
P/E Ratio - High	14	11	88	28	11	16	13	21	16	13
- Low	8	6	64	18	7	8	5	10	13	9

Income Statement Analysis (Million $)

Revs.	775	703	664	657	625	573	528	506	550	566
Oper. Inc.	51.9	45.4	23.0	29.6	23.0	33.3	28.5	18.2	23.0	27.6
Depr.	8.1	9.1	8.9	7.8	7.0	6.5	6.3	6.2	6.6	7.5
Int. Exp.	3.4	4.1	6.1	4.1	2.3	2.3	1.7	3.0	3.5	4.0
Pretax Inc.	40.4	32.2	3.7	17.6	32.3	24.5	20.5	9.0	12.8	16.1
Eff. Tax Rate	39%	39%	40%	40%	41%	40%	39%	38%	38%	39%
Net Inc.	24.6	19.6	2.2	10.6	19.2	14.8	12.5	5.5	7.9	9.9

Balance Sheet & Other Fin. Data (Million $)

Cash	10.1	3.3	1.0	2.2	3.2	3.3	8.4	19.2	2.5	10.1
Curr. Assets	271	247	236	269	205	186	167	154	175	178
Total Assets	311	287	279	309	240	218	199	187	208	213
Curr. Liab.	102	96.3	99	126	96.1	81.8	66.2	56.8	70.0	67.8
LT Debt	41.4	41.8	45.0	47.0	12.4	17.8	22.7	27.3	32.0	36.8
Common Eqty.	160	142	129	133	128	115	108	101	104	108
Total Cap.	205	187	176	183	144	136	133	130	138	145
Cap. Exp.	8.8	7.6	7.6	14.8	9.4	8.1	5.4	6.4	5.8	5.8
Cash Flow	32.7	28.7	11.1	18.4	26.2	21.2	18.8	11.7	14.5	17.4
Curr. Ratio	2.7	2.6	2.4	2.1	2.1	2.3	2.5	2.7	2.5	2.6
% LT Debt of Cap.	20.1	27.9	25.6	25.7	8.6	13.0	17.1	20.9	23.1	25.4
% Net Inc.of Revs.	3.2	2.8	0.3	1.6	3.1	2.6	2.4	1.1	1.4	1.7
% Ret. on Assets	8.2	6.9	0.7	3.9	8.4	7.1	6.5	2.9	3.9	4.6
% Ret. on Equity	16.3	14.5	1.7	8.1	15.8	13.3	12.0	5.5	7.8	9.4

Data as orig. reptd.; bef. results of disc. opers. and/or spec. items. Per share data adj. for stk. divs. as of ex-div. date. Bold denotes diluted EPS (FASB 128). E-Estimated. NA-Not Available. NM-Not Meaningful. NR-Not Ranked.

Office—222 Piedmont Ave. N.E., Atlanta, GA 30308. **Tel**—(404) 659-2424. **Chrmn, Pres & CEO**—J. H. Lanier. **VP-Fin & Treas**—J. W. Wold. **VP & Secy**—D. K. Ginn. **Investor Contact**—Ben B. Blount Jr. (404-653-1433). **Dirs**—B. B. Blount Jr., C. D. Conlee, T. Gallagher, J. H. Lanier, J. R. Lanier, K. J. O'Reilly, C. B. Rogers Jr., R. E. Shaw, E. J. Wood. **Transfer Agent & Registrar**—SunTrust Bank, Atlanta. **Incorporated**—in Georgia in 1960. **Empl**—8,413. **S&P Analyst:** C.F.B.

STANDARD &POOR'S
STOCK REPORTS

P-Com, Inc.

4886M
NASDAQ Symbol **PCMS**
In S&P SmallCap 600

10-OCT-98

Industry:
Communications
Equipment

Summary: This company makes short-haul millimeter wave radio systems and spread spectrum microwave radio systems for use in the worldwide wireless telecommunications market.

Quantitative Evaluations

Recent Price • 2⅞	Yield • Nil
52 Wk Range • 29⅜-2⁵/₁₆	12-Mo. P/E • NM

Outlook
(1 Lowest—5 Highest)
• **NA**

Fair Value
• **NA**

Risk
• **High**

Earn./Div. Rank
• **NR**

Technical Eval.
• **Bearish** since 9/96

Rel. Strength Rank
(1 Lowest—99 Highest)
• **5**

Insider Activity
• **NA**

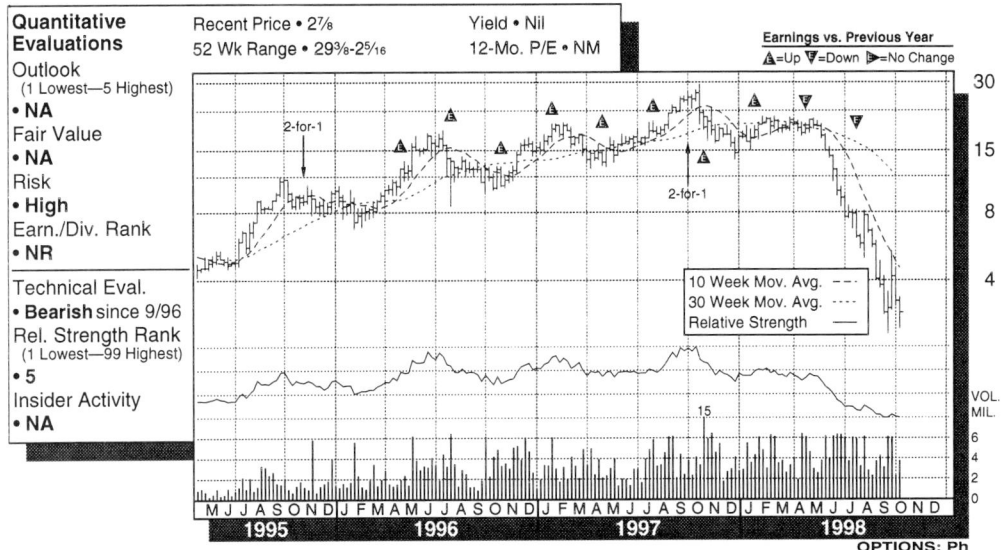

Earnings vs. Previous Year
▲=Up ▼=Down ▶=No Change

10 Week Mov. Avg. - - -
30 Week Mov. Avg. ·······
Relative Strength ——

OPTIONS: Ph

Business Profile - 15-SEP-98

This company provides point-to-point, spread spectrum, and point-to-multipoint radio links designed to satisfy the network requirements of cellular and personal communications services, corporate communications, public utilities and local governments. P-Com has consistently expanded through acquisitions, with nine purchases completed since April 1996. The March 1998 acquisition of Cylink Corp.'s wireless communications group for $60.5 million expanded distribution channels in Latin America and China, and added lower bandwidth services to P-Com's product portfolio. Spending on research and development is expected to remain high, as PCMS aggressively invests to roll out new microwave products. In September, the company announced a restructuring plan and a 10% reduction in its work force.

Operational Review - 15-SEP-98

Net sales in the first six months of 1998 advanced 23% from those of the year-earlier period, as restated, reflecting recent acquisitions. Gross margins widened, on the higher volume. Operating expenses were up 35%, and results were penalized by $33.8 million in acquisition-related charges; a pretax loss of $25,614,000 contrasted with pretax income of $10,159,000. After taxes of $8,711,000, versus taxes at 33.2%, a net loss of $16,903,000 ($0.39 a share) contrasted with net income of $6,790,000 ($0.16, as adjusted). Excluding acquisition charges, income would have been $0.12.

Stock Performance - 09-OCT-98

In the past 30 trading days, PCMS's shares have declined 29%, compared to a 4% fall in the S&P 500. Average trading volume for the past five days was 736,160 shares, compared with the 40-day moving average of 829,687 shares.

Key Stock Statistics

Dividend Rate/Share	Nil	Shareholders	NA
Shs. outstg. (M)	43.5	Market cap. (B)	$0.125
Avg. daily vol. (M)	0.958	Inst. holdings	50%
Tang. Bk. Value/Share	3.48		
Beta	NA		

Value of $10,000 invested 5 years ago: NA

Fiscal Year Ending Dec. 31

	1998	1997	1996	1995	1994	1993
Revenues (Million $)						
1Q	58.64	38.14	17.55	4.35	—	—
2Q	63.46	48.91	19.79	8.55	—	—
3Q	—	51.47	26.43	13.49	—	—
4Q	—	64.23	33.74	16.42	—	—
Yr.	—	220.7	97.52	42.81	9.24	0.74
Earnings Per Share ($)						
1Q	-0.40	0.07	0.04	-0.05	—	—
2Q	0.01	0.10	0.07	Nil	Nil	Nil
3Q	—	0.12	0.10	0.05	—	—
4Q	—	0.10	0.16	0.07	—	—
Yr.	—	0.43	0.22	0.08	-0.29	-0.98

Next earnings report expected: mid October

Dividend Data

The company has never paid cash dividends on its common stock. Two-for-one stock splits were effected in 1995 and 1996.

STANDARD
&POOR'S
STOCK REPORTS

P-Com, Inc.

4886M
10-OCT-98

Business Summary - 15-SEP-98

P-Com, Inc., which manufactures and markets short-haul millimeter wave radio systems and spread spectrum microwave radio systems, has benefited from strong demand for mobile high performance voice, data and facsimile communications. Its Tel-Link systems are used as digital links in applications that include interconnecting base stations and mobile switching centers in microcellular and personal communications services networks and providing local telephone company connectivity in the local loop. PCMS also markets a line of Windows-based software products that are complementary to its systems as diagnostic, maintenance and system configuration tools.

Millimeter wave systems have been increasingly used for short-haul wireless connections, since they can be implemented using lower cost, higher frequency systems, which do not require the longer transmission distances possible at lower frequencies used in long distance wireless connectivity. Products are based on a common system architecture and are designed to carry combinations of voice, data and video traffic and to be configurable based on the needs of customers. Tel-Link systems operate at both E1 and T1/T3 data rates and lower. Typical transmission distances for the company's systems range from one to forty miles, depending on the specific frequency at which the system operates, antenna size and local climate conditions.

The company's Tel-Link millimeter wave radio systems and proprietary software offer telecommunications service providers wireless connection for short-haul applications. Millimeter wave and spread spectrum microwave radios are comprised of three primary assemblies: the indoor unit and software, the outdoor unit and the antenna. The indoor unit houses the digital signal processing and modem functions, and interfaces to the outdoor unit via a single coaxial cable. The outdoor unit, a radio frequency enclosure, establishes the specific transmit and receive frequencies and houses a proprietary P-Com frequency converter. The antenna interfaces directly to the outdoor unit via a proprietary P-Com waveguide transition technology.

Winstar and Orange Personal Communications Ltd. accounted for 16% and 11% of 1997 sales, respectively. As of December 1997, seven customers accounted for over 64% of P-Com's backlog scheduled for shipment in 1998.

In June 1998, P-Com received purchase orders from a PCS service provider in the U.K. for the supply of digital millimeter waveradio systems. These orders, valued in excess of $5 million, represent additional business under an existing customer contract. As with previously purchased P-Com radio systems, these systems are being utilized as part of a nationwide network rollout in the U.K.

Per Share Data ($)

(Year Ended Dec. 31)	1997	1996	1995	1994	1993	1992	1991	1990	1989	1988
Tangible Bk. Val.	3.48	2.92	1.26	NA	NA	NA	NA	NA	NA	NA
Cash Flow	0.61	0.49	0.12	-0.27	NA	NA	NA	NA	NA	NA
Earnings	0.43	0.37	0.08	-0.29	NA	NA	NA	NA	NA	NA
Dividends	Nil	Nil	Nil	Nil	Nil	Nil	Nil	Nil	Nil	Nil
Payout Ratio	Nil	Nil	Nil	Nil	Nil	Nil	Nil	Nil	Nil	Nil
Prices - High	29⅜	18½	11⅜	NA	NA	NA	NA	NA	NA	NA
- Low	12⅜	6¾	3¾	NA	NA	NA	NA	NA	NA	NA
P/E Ratio - High	68	50	NM	NM	NM	NM	NM	NM	NM	NM
- Low	29	18	NM	NM	NM	NM	NM	NM	NM	NM

Income Statement Analysis (Million $)

	1997	1996	1995	1994	1993	1992	1991	1990	1989	1988
Revs.	221	97.5	42.8	9.2	0.7	Nil	Nil	Nil	Nil	Nil
Oper. Inc.	37.9	18.7	3.5	-6.1	NA	NA	NA	NA	NA	NA
Depr.	8.2	4.8	1.1	0.5	NA	NA	NA	NA	NA	NA
Int. Exp.	Nil	0.1	0.3	0.2	NA	NA	NA	NA	NA	NA
Pretax Inc.	29.9	15.1	2.7	-6.7	-6.4	-2.3	NA	NA	NA	NA
Eff. Tax Rate	37%	7.00%	5.10%	Nil	Nil	Nil	Nil	Nil	Nil	Nil
Net Inc.	18.9	14.1	2.6	-6.7	-6.4	-2.3	NA	NA	NA	NA

Balance Sheet & Other Fin. Data (Million $)

	1997	1996	1995	1994	1993	1992	1991	1990	1989	1988
Cash	88.1	41.9	7.7	1.3	3.6	1.0	NA	NA	NA	NA
Curr. Assets	230	119	46.6	NA	NA	NA	NA	NA	NA	NA
Total Assets	306	140	54.0	9.5	5.5	2.6	NA	NA	NA	NA
Curr. Liab.	54.9	27.4	12.3	NA	NA	NA	NA	NA	NA	NA
LT Debt	102	Nil	Nil	3.4	0.6	0.2	NA	NA	NA	NA
Common Eqty.	148	112	41.8	1.7	3.4	2.0	NA	NA	NA	NA
Total Cap.	251	113	41.8	NA	NA	NA	NA	NA	NA	NA
Cap. Exp.	16.9	13.6	6.8	0.2	NA	NA	NA	NA	NA	NA
Cash Flow	27.1	18.8	3.7	-6.2	NA	NA	NA	NA	NA	NA
Curr. Ratio	4.2	4.3	3.8	NA	NA	NA	NA	NA	NA	NA
% LT Debt of Cap.	40.6	Nil	Nil	NA	NA	NA	NA	NA	NA	NA
% Net Inc.of Revs.	8.6	14.4	6.0	NM	NM	NM	NM	NM	NM	NM
% Ret. on Assets	8.5	14.5	8.1	NM	NM	NM	NM	NM	NM	NM
% Ret. on Equity	14.5	3.4	11.9	NM	NM	NM	NM	NM	NM	NM

Data as orig. reptd.; bef. results of disc. opers. and/or spec. items. Per share data adj. for stk. divs. as of ex-div. date. Bold denotes diluted EPS (FASB 128). E-Estimated. NA-Not Available. NM-Not Meaningful. NR-Not Ranked.

Office—3175 S. Winchester Blvd., Campbell, CA 95008. **Tel**—(408) 866-3666. **Website**—http://www.p-com.com. **Chrmn & CEO**—G. P. Roberts. **Pres & COO**—P. Antoniucci. **VP-Fin & CFO**—M. Sophie. **Dirs**—G. Cogan, J. A. Hawkins, M. B. Puckett, G. P. Roberts, J. J. Sobczak. **Transfer Agent & Registrar**—U.S. Stock Transfer Corp., Glendale, CA. **Incorporated**—in Delaware in 1991. **Empl**— 754. **S&P Analyst:** Mark Cavallone

03-OCT-98   **Industry:** Health Care (Specialized Services)

Summary: This company provides knowledge-based product development and product launch services to pharmaceutical, biotechnology and medical device industries.

Quantitative Evaluations

Recent Price • 36⅛
52 Wk Range • 43½-24¾

Yield • Nil
12-Mo. P/E • 95.1

Outlook (1 Lowest—5 Highest)
• **NA**

Fair Value
• **NA**

Risk
• **High**

Earn./Div. Rank
• **NR**

Technical Eval.
• **NA**

Rel. Strength Rank (1 Lowest—99 Highest)
• **91**

Insider Activity
• **NA**

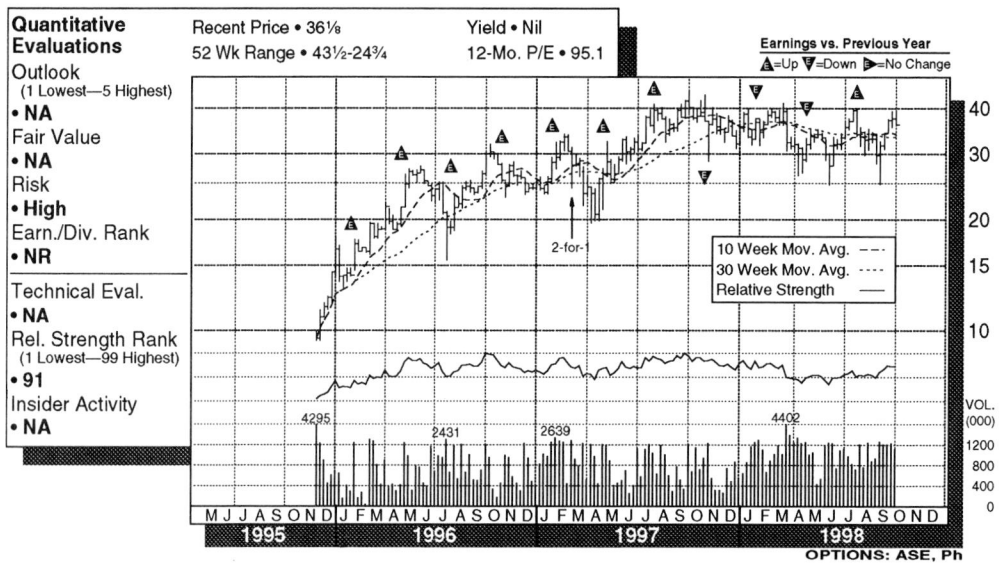

OPTIONS: ASE, Ph

Business Profile - 15-JUL-98

The company's primary objective is to help clients quickly obtain regulatory approvals of their products and optimize market penetration. PRXL has expertise in clinical trials management, data management, biostatistical analysis, medical and regulatory consulting, clinical pharmacology and other drug development consulting services. In March 1998, the company acquired PPS Europe Ltd. a U.K. marketing and clinical communications firm servicing the international pharmaceutical industry; Mirai B.V., a pan-European contract research organization based in the Netherlands; Genesis Pharma Strategies limited, a physician-focused marketing and clinical communications firm; and LOGOS GmbH, a provider of regulatory services to pharmaceutical manufacturers.

Operational Review - 15-JUL-98

Net revenue in the nine months ended March 31, 1998, advanced 41.7%, year to year, primarily attributable to an increase in the volume and average contract value of contract research projects. Gross margins widened, and SG&A decreased as a percentage of revenues. However, after $10.3 million of acquisition related charges, pre-tax income decreased 39.4%. After taxes of 55.5%, versus 39.4%, net income decreased 55.4%, to $3,876,000 ($0.16 a share, based on 15% more shares), from $8,697,000 ($0.40).

Stock Performance - 02-OCT-98

In the past 30 trading days, PRXL's shares have increased 9%, compared to a 7% fall in the S&P 500. Average trading volume for the past five days was 220,860 shares, compared with the 40-day moving average of 271,444 shares.

Key Stock Statistics

Dividend Rate/Share	Nil	Shareholders	100
Shs. outstg. (M)	24.6	Market cap. (B)	$0.888
Avg. daily vol. (M)	0.275	Inst. holdings	74%
Tang. Bk. Value/Share	6.88		
Beta	NA		

Value of $10,000 invested 5 years ago: NA

Fiscal Year Ending Jun. 30

	1998	1997	1996	1995	1994	1993
Revenues (Million $)						
1Q	51.21	33.03	—	13.20	12.90	—
2Q	58.62	37.17	20.62	14.30	14.90	—
3Q	73.07	42.26	22.51	14.80	15.00	—
4Q	81.39	47.22	26.91	16.30	15.60	—
Yr.	285.4	159.7	88.01	58.57	58.00	54.00
Earnings Per Share ($)						
1Q	-0.58	0.11	0.07	-0.58	—	—
2Q	0.06	0.13	0.08	0.03	—	—
3Q	-0.10	0.15	0.09	-0.30	—	—
4Q	0.22	0.17	0.10	0.07	—	—
Yr.	0.38	0.57	0.34	-6.31	—	—

Next earnings report expected: NA

Dividend Data

No cash dividends have been paid.

A Division of The McGraw-Hill Companies

Business Summary - 15-JUL-98

PAREXEL believes that it is the world's fourth largest contract research organization. It provides a wide range of knowledge-based product development and product launch services to the worldwide pharmaceutical, biotechnology and medical device industries. It aims to help clients obtain necessary regulatory approvals of their products and optimize the market penetration of those products.

The company's service offerings include clinical trials management, data management, biostatistical analysis, medical marketing, clinical pharmacology, regulatory and medical consulting, performance improvement, industry training and publishing, and other drug development consulting services. Operations are largely divided into three business units: drug development, medical marketing, and consulting services.

PRXL's drug development unit (accounting for 70% of revenues) offers complete services for the design, initiation and management of clinical trial programs, a critical element in obtaining regulatory approval for drugs. The company has performed services in connection with trials in most therapeutic areas. PRXL can manage all aspects of clinical trials, including study and protocol design, placement, initiation, monitoring, report preparation and strategy development. The company also offers data management services, which include designing case report forms and training manuals for

investigators to ensure that data are collected in an organized and consistent format, and biostatistical services aimed at helping clients with all phases of drug development, including biostatistical consulting, database design, data analysis and statistical reporting.

In the medical marketing segment, the company assists clients in developing product launch strategies, defining product attributes, product positioning and promotion, interpreting clinical results, pricing and reimbursement issues, justifying the cost-effectiveness and outcome of proposed treatments, post-approval studies, training physicians, sales force, patients and payors, managing patient registries, hotlines and other assistance programs, and advocating appropriate public policy.

In December 1997, PRXL acquired Kemper-Masterson, Inc., a leading management consulting firm on FDA and other regulatory matters to the worldwide pharmaceutical, biotechnology and medical device industries, in exchange for 582,000 PRXL common shares.

In March 1998, the company acquired PPS Europe Ltd. a U.K. marketing and clinical communications firm servicing the international pharmaceutical industry; Mirai B.V., a pan-European contract research organization based in the Netherlands; Genesis Pharma Strategies limited, a physician-focused marketing and clinical communications firm; and LOGOS GmbH, a provider of regulatory services to pharmaceutical manufacturers.

Per Share Data ($)

(Year Ended Jun. 30)	1998	1997	1996	1995	1994	1993	1992	1991	1990	1989
Tangible Bk. Val.	NA	6.88	3.93	NA	NA	NA	NA	NA	NA	NA
Cash Flow	NA	0.84	0.51	-4.97	NA	NA	NA	NA	NA	NA
Earnings	0.38	0.57	0.34	-6.31	NA	NA	NA	NA	NA	NA
Dividends	Nil	Nil	Nil	Nil	Nil	Nil	Nil	Nil	Nil	Nil
Payout Ratio	Nil	Nil	Nil	Nil	Nil	Nil	Nil	Nil	Nil	Nil
Prices - High	41¼	44¾	31⅞	18	NA	NA	NA	NA	NA	NA
- Low	24¾	19½	13	9⅜	NA	NA	NA	NA	NA	NA
P/E Ratio - High	NM	71	84	NM	NM	NM	NM	NM	NM	NM
- Low	NM	34	38	NM	NM	NM	NM	NM	NM	NM

Income Statement Analysis (Million $)

	1998	1997	1996	1995	1994	1993	1992	1991	1990	1989
Revs.	NM	160	88.0	58.6	NA	NA	NA	NA	NA	NA
Oper. Inc.	NA	18.7	8.8	3.1	NA	NA	NA	NA	NA	NA
Depr.	NA	5.0	2.3	2.3	NA	NA	NA	NA	NA	NA
Int. Exp.	NA	0.2	0.2	0.2	NA	NA	NA	NA	NA	NA
Pretax Inc.	NA	16.9	7.7	-10.3	NA	NA	NA	NA	NA	NA
Eff. Tax Rate	NA	36%	40%	NM	NM	NM	NM	NM	NM	NM
Net Inc.	NM	10.8	4.6	-10.6	2.4	-2.2	1.5	NA	NA	NA

Balance Sheet & Other Fin. Data (Million $)

	1998	1997	1996	1995	1994	1993	1992	1991	1990	1989
Cash	NA	30.3	17.1	6.7	NA	NA	NA	NA	NA	NA
Curr. Assets	NA	172	92.6	36.9	NA	NA	NA	NA	NA	NA
Total Assets	NA	201	102	43.3	NA	NA	NA	NA	NA	NA
Curr. Liab.	NA	61.4	39.2	25.3	NA	NA	NA	NA	NA	NA
LT Debt	NA	Nil	0.0	0.1	NA	NA	NA	NA	NA	NA
Common Eqty.	NA	138	61.2	15.5	NA	NA	NA	NA	NA	NA
Total Cap.	NA	138	61.2	15.6	NA	NA	NA	NA	NA	NA
Cap. Exp.	NA	22.0	5.0	1.5	NA	NA	NA	NA	NA	NA
Cash Flow	NA	15.9	6.9	-8.4	NA	NA	NA	NA	NA	NA
Curr. Ratio	NA	2.8	2.4	1.5	NA	NA	NA	NA	NA	NA
% LT Debt of Cap.	NA	Nil	Nil	Nil	Nil	Nil	Nil	Nil	Nil	Nil
% Net Inc.of Revs.	Nil	6.8	5.2	NM	NM	NM	NM	NM	NM	NM
% Ret. on Assets	NM	7.2	6.3	NM	NM	NM	NM	NM	NM	NM
% Ret. on Equity	NM	10.9	17.3	NM	NM	NM	NM	NM	NM	NM

Data as orig. reptd.; bef. results of disc. opers. and/or spec. items. Per share data adj. for stk. divs. as of ex-div. date. Bold denotes diluted EPS (FASB 128). E-Estimated. NA-Not Available. NM-Not Meaningful. NR-Not Ranked.

Office—195 West St., Waltham, MA 02154. **Tel**—(781) 487-9900. **Chrmn, Pres & CEO**—J. H. Von Rickenbach. **SVP, CFO, Treas & Investor Contact**—Virginia S. Locke.**Dirs**—A. D. Callow, Jr., A. J. Eagle, P. J. Fortune, W. M. Herrmann, S. Okun, J. A. Saafield, J. H. Von Rickenbach. **Transfer Agent & Registrar**—First National Bank of Boston. **Incorporated**—in Massachusetts in 1983. **Empl**— 3,700. **S&P Analyst:** John J. Arege.

Park Electrochemical   1762

NYSE Symbol **PKE**

In S&P SmallCap 600

03-OCT-98

Industry:
Electrical Equipment

Summary: This company primarily manufactures advanced electronic materials used in the production of multilayer printed circuit boards.

Quantitative Evaluations		
Recent Price • 13⅛	**Yield** • 2.4%	
52 Wk Range • 32½-10⅞	**12-Mo. P/E** • 8.0	

Outlook (1 Lowest—5 Highest)
• **2**

Fair Value
• **13¾**

Risk
• **Average**

Earn./Div. Rank
• **B**

Technical Eval.
• **NA**

Rel. Strength Rank (1 Lowest—99 Highest)
• **31**

Insider Activity
• **NA**

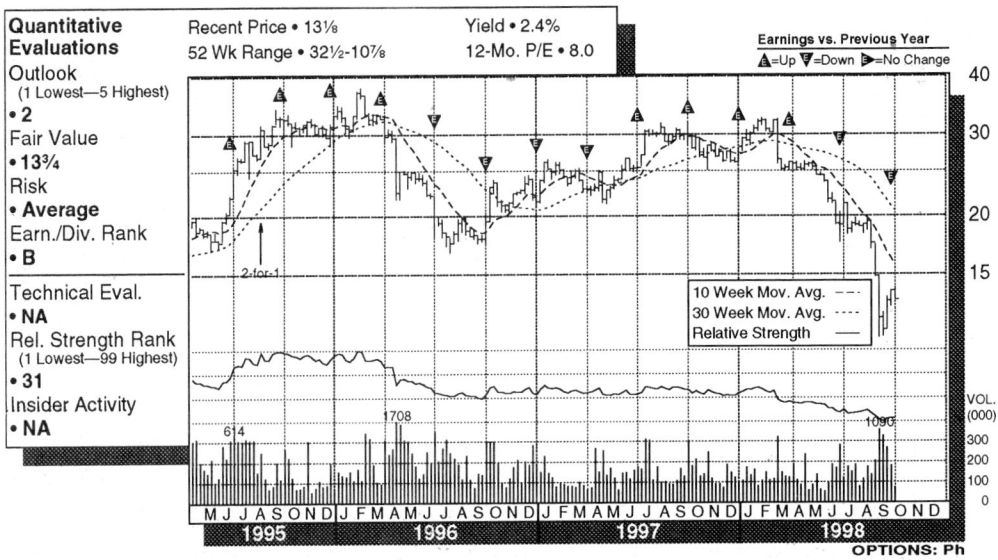

OPTIONS: Ph

Business Profile - 25-FEB-98

Park's electronic materials business was hurt by severe demand fluctuations in FY 97 (Feb.). The market for PKE's electronic materials products, which was uncharacteristically low during the second quarter of FY 98, rebounded, particularly in North America, during the third quarter. PKE's Asian markets have also performed admirably through the third quarter of FY 98, despite the financial difficulties in that region of the world. PKE, as part of its strategy to strengthen its global presence in the electronic global interconnect materials industry, acquired 80% of Cologne, Germany-based Dielektra GmbH in October 1997, for $8.8 million in cash and 77,000 common shares.

Operational Review - 25-FEB-98

Net sales in the 39 weeks ended November 30, 1997, advanced 11%, year to year, reflecting increased electronic materials shipped, greater sales of higher technology products and the inclusion of sales of Dielektra (acquired in October 1997), offset partially by lower plumbing hardware sales. Margins widened on the increased volume and improved operating efficiencies resulting from increased capacity utilization; pretax earnings climbed 46%. After taxes at 33.0%, versus 31.0%, net income rose 42%, to $18,013,000 ($1.56 a share; $1.49 fully diluted), from $12,694,000 ($1.09; no dilution).

Stock Performance - 02-OCT-98

In the past 30 trading days, PKE's shares have declined 25%, compared to a 7% fall in the S&P 500. Average trading volume for the past five days was 14,740 shares, compared with the 40-day moving average of 70,044 shares.

Key Stock Statistics

Dividend Rate/Share	0.32	Shareholders	2,400
Shs. outstg. (M)	11.4	Market cap. (B)	$0.150
Avg. daily vol. (M)	0.059	Inst. holdings	41%
Tang. Bk. Value/Share	15.04		
Beta	1.10		

Value of $10,000 invested 5 years ago: $ 22,555

Fiscal Year Ending Feb. 28

	1999	1998	1997	1996	1995	1994
Revenues (Million $)						
1Q	99.9	91.63	75.41	75.41	62.80	49.23
2Q	86.35	83.09	81.97	69.94	58.80	47.32
3Q	—	97.63	88.97	81.87	64.83	54.06
4Q	—	103.8	88.14	85.75	66.62	57.80
Yr.	—	376.2	334.5	313.0	253.0	208.4
Earnings Per Share ($)						
1Q	**0.46**	**0.51**	0.26	0.52	0.39	0.11
2Q	**0.02**	**0.41**	0.40	0.45	0.33	0.20
0Q	—	0.56	0.43	0.55	0.42	0.28
4Q	—	0.59	0.51	0.59	0.45	0.42
Yr.	—	2.07	1.61	2.11	1.59	1.01

Next earnings report expected: late December

Dividend Data (Dividends have been paid since 1985.)

Amount ($)	Date Decl.	Ex-Div. Date	Stock of Record	Payment Date
0.080	Dec. 09	Jan. 02	Jan. 06	Feb. 03 '98
0.080	Mar. 17	Apr. 09	Apr. 14	May. 12 '98
0.080	Mar. 17	Apr. 09	Apr. 14	May. 12 '98
0.080	Jun. 09	Jul. 02	Jul. 07	Aug. 04 '98

A Division of The McGraw·Hill Companies

Business Summary - 25-FEB-98

Electronic materials markets weakened suddenly a few months into Park Electrochemical's 1997 fiscal year (Feb.) and strengthened just as suddenly in the final quarter, taking PKE on a roller coaster ride to sharply lower earnings and leaving it capacity constrained when market vigor returned. PKE believes the market downturn was caused by an industry-wide inventory correction. Margin-squeezing price pressures and labor strikes that affected business with PKE's largest customer compounded the company's difficulties in FY 97.

Sales growth slowed from the double-digit levels experienced in recent years to 7% in FY 97, when sales reached $334 million. Gross margin narrowed to 17.7% from 22.5% the year before, and net earnings fell 25% to $18.6 million. Foreign operations accounted for 30% of sales in FY 97.

PKE designs and produces advanced electronic materials (87% of net sales in FY 97) used to fabricate complex multilayer printed circuit boards and other high-technology electronic interconnection systems such as backplanes and semiconductor packages. PKE's multilayer printed circuit material products include copper-clad laminates, prepegs and semi-finished multilayer printed circuit boards. Customers for PKE's advanced electronic materials include leading independent printed circuit board fabricators and major electronic equipment manufacturers in the computer, telecommunications, transportation, aerospace and instrumentation industries.

PKE also makes specialty adhesive tapes, advanced composite materials and microwave circuitry materials for the electronics, aerospace and industrial markets, as well as plumbing hardware products (together, 13% of net sales in FY 97). The operating profit of these businesses more than doubled during FY 97.

Caught off guard by the abrupt downturn in its markets, PKE cut its capital budget for FY 97 to $18.7 million, 24% lower than capital expenditures made the previous year. In the future, PKE plans to grow manufacturing capacity ahead of the market rather than try to match additions to market surges. PKE expects capital spending will be higher in FY 98 than it was in FY 97.

As it began FY 98, the company was encouraged by an accelerating trend toward higher layer count, higher technology circuit boards and interconnection devices which utilize the ultra-thin, high-performance materials that are PKE's specialty. PKE attributed softness in its electronic materials markets in the second quarter of FY 98 to the "normal" industry summer slowdown and inventory adjustments. In the third quarter, sales rebounded somewhat, particularly in North America.

Per Share Data ($)

(Year Ended Feb. 28)	1998	1997	1996	1995	1994	1993	1992	1991	1990	1989
Tangible Bk. Val.	14.60	12.72	11.64	9.75	7.58	6.75	6.93	7.08	6.62	6.41
Cash Flow	2.76	2.61	2.95	2.42	2.04	1.06	0.94	0.85	0.90	1.09
Earnings	2.07	1.61	2.11	1.59	1.01	0.27	0.19	0.24	0.40	0.66
Dividends	0.32	0.32	0.28	0.20	0.16	0.16	0.16	0.16	0.16	0.12
Payout Ratio	15%	20%	13%	13%	16%	59%	84%	61%	39%	18%
Cal. Yrs.	1997	1996	1995	1994	1993	1992	1991	1990	1989	1988
Prices - High	31¾	37⅞	34⅛	17⅞	12⅛	7⅛	6½	7⅞	8⅞	10¼
- Low	21¼	16¾	14	11½	5¾	6⅜	5	5¼	6⅛	7
P/E Ratio - High	15	24	16	11	12	26	34	33	22	16
- Low	10	10	7	7	6	23	26	22	15	11

Income Statement Analysis (Million $)

Revs.	376	334	313	253	208	176	165	164	148	147
Oper. Inc.	48.0	36.3	44.9	34.6	22.5	10.6	9.8	8.1	9.9	13.7
Depr.	13.2	11.6	9.8	8.5	8.2	7.2	6.8	6.0	5.1	4.5
Int. Exp.	5.5	5.5	0.1	0.4	2.5	2.6	2.9	3.0	2.9	3.0
Pretax Inc.	37.7	26.9	37.3	27.5	12.8	3.4	2.5	3.6	7.0	10.6
Eff. Tax Rate	33%	31%	33%	37%	37%	27%	32%	35%	41%	36%
Net Inc.	25.3	18.6	24.9	17.3	8.1	2.5	1.7	2.4	4.1	6.8

Balance Sheet & Other Fin. Data (Million $)

Cash	45.1	145	143	45.9	38.1	32.9	36.9	42.8	55.0	60.5
Curr. Assets	247	220	218	98.3	85.8	75.9	81.2	89.1	97.0	99
Total Assets	359	308	299	162	141	130	131	136	135	135
Curr. Liab.	70.8	55.4	56.8	43.3	40.0	29.0	28.6	31.9	26.4	28.1
LT Debt	100	100	100	Nil	32.9	34.0	33.4	33.4	35.1	35.4
Common Eqty.	166	143	134	112	61.5	61.8	63.2	64.1	66.9	66.4
Total Cap.	275	251	241	117	99	100	102	103	108	107
Cap. Exp.	18.3	18.7	24.5	17.5	9.5	10.3	10.9	14.0	6.3	9.6
Cash Flow	38.5	30.1	34.7	26.3	25.8	9.6	8.6	8.4	9.2	11.3
Curr. Ratio	3.5	4.0	3.8	2.3	2.1	2.6	2.8	2.8	3.7	3.5
% LT Debt of Cap.	36.3	39.9	41.5	Nil	33.2	33.9	32.8	32.3	32.6	33.1
% Net Inc.of Revs.	6.7	5.6	8.0	6.9	3.9	1.4	1.0	1.4	2.8	4.7
% Ret. on Assets	7.6	6.2	10.8	9.6	6.3	1.9	1.3	1.8	3.1	5.2
% Ret. on Equity	16.3	13.4	20.2	17.4	13.9	3.9	2.7	3.8	6.3	10.8

Data as orig. reptd.; bef. results of disc. opers. and/or spec. items. Per share data adj. for stk. divs. as of ex-div. date. Bold denotes diluted EPS (FASB 128). E-Estimated. NA-Not Available. NM-Not Meaningful. NR-Not Ranked.

Office—5 Dakota Drive, Lake Success, NY 11042. **Tel**—(516) 354-4100. **Website**—http://www.parkelectro.com **Chrmn**—J. Shore. **Pres & CEO**—B. E. Shore. **Dirs**—A. Chiesa, L. Frank, N. M. Schneider, B. E. Shore, J. Shore, E. P. Smoot. **Transfer Agent & Registrar**—Registrar & Transfer Co., Cranford, NJ. **Incorporated**—in New York in 1954. **Empl**— 2,340. **S&P Analyst:** M.I.

Patterson Dental
4931T

NASDAQ Symbol **PDCO**

In S&P SmallCap 600

03-OCT-98

Industry:
Distributors (Food & Health)

Summary: PDCO is the largest distributor of dental products in North America, supplying over 82,500 products to dentists and related markets. Office paper products are also sold.

Quantitative Evaluations

Recent Price • 37½
52 Wk Range • 39½-23⅞

Yield • Nil
12-Mo. P/E • 29.1

Outlook
(1 Lowest—5 Highest)
• **3⁻**

Fair Value
• **36⅝**

Risk
• **Average**

Earn./Div. Rank
• **B+**

Technical Eval.
• **Bullish** since 9/98

Rel. Strength Rank
(1 Lowest—99 Highest)
• **93**

Insider Activity
• **Neutral**

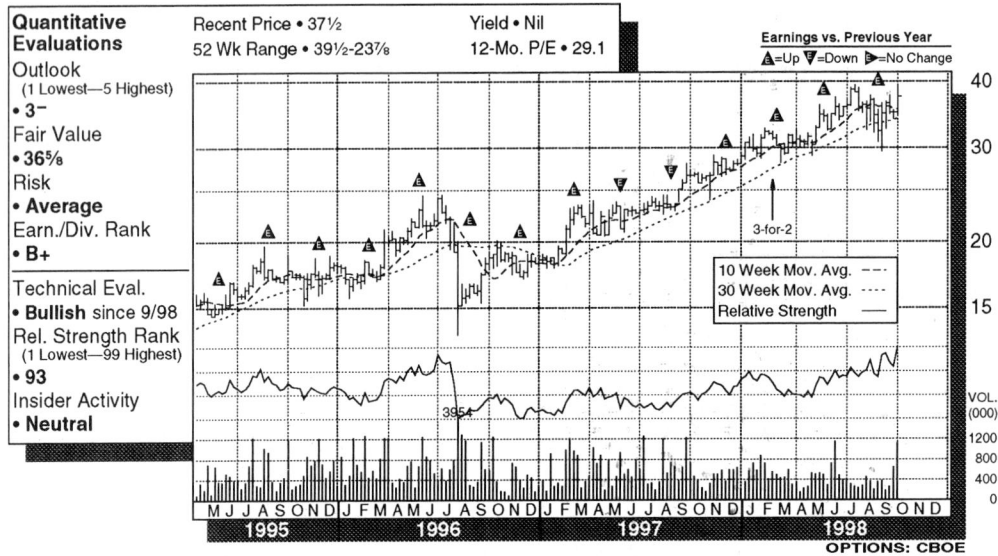

Earnings vs. Previous Year
▲=Up ▼=Down ■=No Change

3-for-2

10 Week Mov. Avg. - - -
30 Week Mov. Avg. · · · ·
Relative Strength ——

VOL. (000)

OPTIONS: CBOE

Business Profile - 10-SEP-98

In an effort to increase its market share, the company has made several acquisitions, introduced various new products and expanded its sales force. Recent acquisitions include Hill Dental Company, Inc. (February 1998), a full-service dental products distributor, which had sales of $29 million in 1997; Canadian Dental Supply Ltd. (CDS; August 1997), a leading Canadian dental products distributor; and EagleSoft (July 97), a leading provider of dental practice management systems, with about $4.0 million in sales. The company has posted 12% sales and 20% net income growth, compounded annually over the past five years. Officers and directors hold 19% of the common shares outstanding.

Operational Review - 10-SEP-98

Net sales for the three months ended July 25, 1998, (Apr.) increased 11%, year to year (as restated for the CDS acquisition), aided by contributions from the EagleSoft and Hill Dental acquisitions, as well as higher equipment sales. Operating expense as a percentage of sales decreased, due to improved leverage, leading to a 22% increase in operating income. After taxes at 38.6%, versus 38.4%, net income rose 23%, to $10.2 million ($0.31 a share) from $8.3 million ($0.25, as adjusted).

Stock Performance - 02-OCT-98

In the past 30 trading days, PDCO's shares have increased 8%, compared to a 7% fall in the S&P 500. Average trading volume for the past five days was 222,560 shares, compared with the 40-day moving average of 89,285 shares.

Key Stock Statistics

Dividend Rate/Share	Nil	Shareholders	1,500
Shs. outstg. (M)	33.3	Market cap. (B)	$ 1.2
Avg. daily vol. (M)	0.113	Inst. holdings	57%
Tang. Bk. Value/Share	4.88		
Beta	0.70		

Value of $10,000 invested 5 years ago: $ 50,371

Fiscal Year Ending Apr. 30

	1999	1998	1997	1996	1995	1994
Revenues (Million $)						
1Q	200.1	180.0	142.2	134.3	123.6	101.8
2Q	—	191.6	161.9	143.7	131.9	113.9
3Q	—	195.5	176.1	148.7	136.5	124.9
4Q	—	211.0	181.4	155.2	140.5	126.4
Yr.	—	778.2	661.5	581.9	532.6	466.9
Earnings Per Share ($)						
1Q	0.31	0.25	0.19	0.19	0.16	0.13
2Q	—	0.30	0.24	0.21	0.18	0.15
3Q	—	0.33	0.28	0.21	0.18	0.14
4Q	—	0.35	0.29	0.25	0.21	0.16
Yr.	—	1.23	1.00	0.87	0.73	0.58

Next earnings report expected: late November

Dividend Data

Amount ($)	Date Decl.	Ex-Div. Date	Stock of Record	Payment Date
3-for-2	Jan. 12	Feb. 18	Jan. 30	Feb. 17 '98

A Division of The McGraw-Hill Companies

STANDARD
&POOR'S
STOCK REPORTS

Patterson Dental Company

4931T

03-OCT-98

Business Summary - 10-SEP-98

For years, Patterson Dental Co. (PDCO) has provided the supplies and equipment dentists need to treat their patients. With a 24% market share as of April 1998, PDCO's broad range of consumables, such as x-ray film and impression and restorative materials, and its varied equipment lines -- sterilizers, dental lights, X-ray machines -- are found in thousands of dental practices across the U.S. and Canada. Even the dreaded dental chair can be sourced at PDCO. Having established a strong presence in the dental back office, PDCO is now stepping into the front office as well with new products gained through acquisitions.

The October 1996 acquisition of Colwell Systems (6% of total sales in FY 98 -- Apr.), which provides office stationery and health care forms to medical and dental practices, strengthened PDCO's position as a single-source supplier and allowed the company to leverage its direct sales force to pursue this new business with existing customers. In July 1997, PDCO further penetrated the dentist's front office by acquiring EagleSoft Inc., a provider of dental practice management software.

PDCO offers about 82,500 products to dentists, dental laboratories and institutions. It was recently dethroned as the largest full-service distributor of dental products in North America following Henry Schein, Inc.'s acquisition of Sullivan Dental Products, Inc. announced in August 1997.

The company's consumable goods and office supplies accounted for 64% of net sales in FY 98. Demand for protective clothing and gloves has been enhanced by heightened public concern over communicable diseases, such as AIDS. In addition to its infection control products, PDCO also distributes X-ray film and solutions, hand instruments, toothbrushes and various materials and accessories used by dentists.

PDCO offers a wide range of dental equipment (27% of FY 98 sales), including X-ray machines, sterilizers and diagnostic equipment. FY 98 revenues received a lift from sales of the CEREC 2, a chair-side laboratory that produces inlays, onlays and full crown restorations in a single visit. Other products include the KCP 1000, a high-speed air abrasion cavity preparation device that allows the dentist to work without a traditional drill.

In FY 98, net sales rose 13% to $778.2 million, reflecting increased sales from the Hill Dental, Canadian Dental and EagleSoft acquisitions. Sales were bolstered by increased marketing efforts of 90 new sales representatives, bringing the total to 886. In the coming year, the company hopes to find new ways to leverage its financial strength and national infrastructure to expand market share and shareholder value.

Per Share Data ($)

(Year Ended Apr. 30)	1998	1997	1996	1995	1994	1993	1992	1991	1990	1989
Tangible Bk. Val.	4.88	3.65	3.29	2.17	NA	NA	NA	NA	NA	NA
Cash Flow	1.45	1.19	0.99	0.83	0.66	NA	NA	NA	NA	NA
Earnings	1.23	1.00	0.87	0.73	0.58	0.41	0.25	0.21	NA	NA
Dividends	Nil	Nil	Nil	Nil	Nil	Nil	Nil	Nil	Nil	Nil
Payout Ratio	Nil	Nil	Nil	Nil	Nil	Nil	Nil	Nil	Nil	Nil
Cal. Yrs.	1997	1996	1995	1994	1993	1992	1991	1990	1989	1988
Prices - High	30¹/₂	24⁵/₈	19⁵/₈	16¹/₄	14¹/₂	11³/₈	NA	NA	NA	NA
- Low	17⁷/₈	13³/₈	13³/₈	10¹/₂	7	7¹/₈	NA	NA	NA	NA
P/E Ratio - High	25	25	23	22	25	27	NA	NA	NA	NA
- Low	14	13	15	14	12	17	NA	NA	NA	NA

Income Statement Analysis (Million $)

	1998	1997	1996	1995	1994	1993	1992	1991	1990	1989
Revs.	778	662	582	533	467	343	277	243	NA	NA
Oper. Inc.	72.7	56.8	47.5	41.4	33.8	NA	NA	NA	NA	NA
Depr.	7.5	6.2	3.8	3.3	2.5	NA	NA	NA	NA	NA
Int. Exp.	0.7	0.6	0.4	0.5	0.5	NA	NA	NA	NA	NA
Pretax Inc.	65.7	52.0	45.7	39.1	32.0	20.4	12.6	10.5	NA	NA
Eff. Tax Rate	38%	38%	37%	38%	40%	35%	32%	30%	NA	NA
Net Inc.	40.8	32.4	28.7	24.2	19.3	13.2	8.5	7.3	NA	NA

Balance Sheet & Other Fin. Data (Million $)

	1998	1997	1996	1995	1994	1993	1992	1991	1990	1989
Cash	35.6	9.1	46.1	13.6	NA	NA	NA	NA	NA	NA
Curr. Assets	228	164	175	147	NA	NA	NA	NA	NA	NA
Total Assets	316	244	203	171	136	105	75.0	NA	NA	NA
Curr. Liab.	94.4	69.8	62.8	60.2	NA	NA	NA	NA	NA	NA
LT Debt	2.7	2.8	3.0	3.2	NA	NA	NA	NA	NA	NA
Common Eqty.	210	163	87.3	57.3	72.2	53.1	10.7	NA	NA	NA
Total Cap.	215	167	131	101	NA	NA	NA	NA	NA	NA
Cap. Exp.	6.0	4.9	6.9	6.2	8.9	NA	NA	NA	NA	NA
Cash Flow	48.2	38.6	31.9	26.9	21.2	NA	NA	NA	NA	NA
Curr. Ratio	2.4	2.4	2.8	2.4	NA	NA	NA	NA	NA	NA
% LT Debt of Cap.	1.2	1.7	2.3	3.2	NA	NA	NA	NA	NA	NA
% Net Inc.of Revs.	5.2	4.9	4.9	4.5	4.1	3.8	3.1	3.0	NA	NA
% Ret. on Assets	14.5	14.5	15.3	12.9	16.0	14.7	12.1	NA	NA	NA
% Ret. on Equity	21.9	24.2	38.9	37.5	30.9	41.3	130.7	NA	NA	NA

Data as orig. reptd.; bef. results of disc. opers. and/or spec. items. Per share data adj. for stk. divs. as of ex-div. date. Bold denotes diluted EPS (FASB 128). E-Estimated. NA-Not Available. NM-Not Meaningful. NR-Not Ranked.

Office—1031 Mendota Heights Rd., St. Paul, MN 55120. **Tel**—(612) 686-1600. **Website**—http://www.pattersondental.com **Chrmn, Pres & CEO**—P. L. Frechette. **VP**—J. W. Wiltz. **EVP, Treas, CFO**—R. E. Ezerski. **Secy**—M.L. Levitt. **Dirs**—D. K. Beecken, R. E. Ezerski, P. L. Frechette, A. B. Lacy, B. E. Swanson. **Transfer Agent & Registrar**—Norwest Bank Minnesota, Minneapolis. **Incorporated**—in Minnesota in 1992. **Empl**—3,214. **S&P Analyst:** John J. Arege

03-OCT-98

Industry: Manufacturing (Specialized)

Summary: PAXAR manufactures bar-code tag and labeling systems, as well as printed labels, woven labels and merchandise tags, for the apparel and textile industries.

Quantitative Evaluations	
Outlook (1 Lowest—5 Highest) • **5**	
Fair Value • **18⅜**	
Risk • **Average**	
Earn./Div. Rank • **B+**	
Technical Eval. • **Bearish** since 1/98	
Rel. Strength Rank (1 Lowest—99 Highest) • **58**	
Insider Activity • **NA**	

Recent Price • 8⅞
52 Wk Range • 20⅞-7¾
Yield • Nil
12-Mo. P/E • 19.7

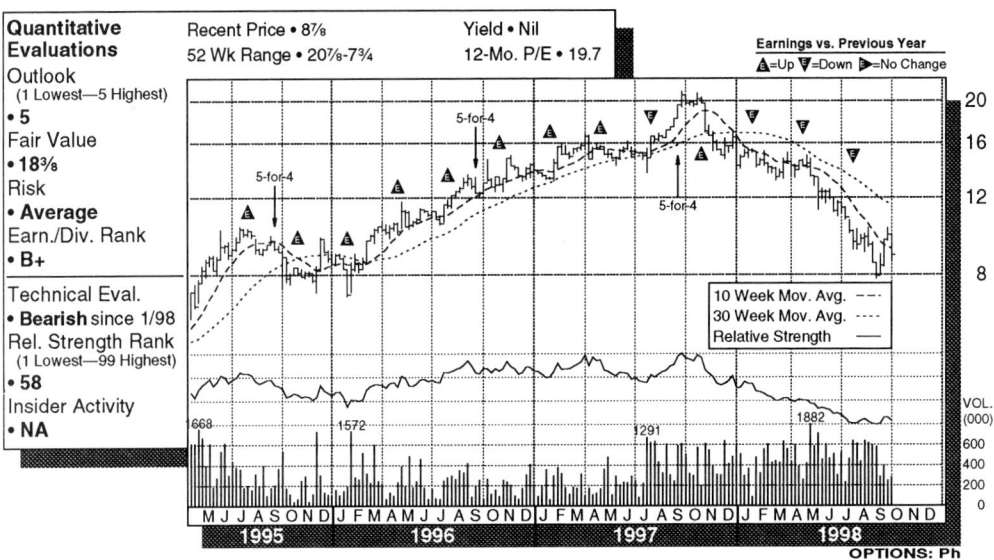

Earnings vs. Previous Year
▲=Up ▼=Down ▶=No Change

10 Week Mov. Avg. ----
30 Week Mov. Avg. ·····
Relative Strength ——

OPTIONS: Ph

Business Profile - 01-SEP-98

In 1997, PXR acquired International Imaging Materials, Inc. and Monarch Marking Systems, doubling the company's size and greatly expanding the market it serves. The acquisitions were expected to greatly enhance PXR's future outlook, but transitional issues, including restructuring and refocusing operations, slowed top-line growth in the first half of 1998. For the full year, PXR feels that it is on track to earn $0.70 to $0.74 a share on net sales of $630 million to $635 million. For 1999, the company's target is to increase earnings about 15%, on internal sales growth of 8% to 10%. In July 1998, directors authorized the repurchase of up to $25 million of common stock.

Operational Review - 01-SEP-98

In the first half of 1998, revenues climbed 16%, year to year, as 41% sales growth in the first quarter, due to the consolidation of Monarch, was partly offset by a slight revenue decline in the second quarter. Gross margins widened, but results were restricted by 29% higher SG&A expenses, mainly due to the acquisition, as well as substantially higher interest expense. Income fell 14%, to $14,500,000 ($0.30 a share), from $16,800,000 ($0.35, as adjusted). Results in the first half of 1997 exclude an extraordinary loss of $0.18 a share.

Stock Performance - 02-OCT-98

In the past 30 trading days, PXR's shares have declined 5%, compared to a 7% fall in the S&P 500. Average trading volume for the past five days was 55,800 shares, compared with the 40-day moving average of 107,108 shares.

Key Stock Statistics

Dividend Rate/Share	Nil	Shareholders	900
Shs. outstg. (M)	48.7	Market cap. (B)	$0.432
Avg. daily vol. (M)	0.061	Inst. holdings	42%
Tang. Bk. Value/Share	2.01		
Beta	0.75		

Value of $10,000 invested 5 years ago: $ 13,961

Fiscal Year Ending Dec. 31

	1998	1997	1996	1995	1994	1993
Revenues (Million $)						
1Q	149.4	105.9	52.75	50.52	35.98	36.20
2Q	156.9	158.9	57.55	52.90	42.46	36.34
3Q	—	148.8	51.94	49.31	41.01	32.62
4Q	—	153.6	57.58	48.71	47.16	33.69
Yr.	—	567.2	219.8	201.4	166.6	138.8
Earnings Per Share ($)						
1Q	0.15	0.17	0.12	0.11	0.06	0.08
2Q	0.15	0.16	0.16	0.13	0.10	0.08
3Q	—	0.19	0.15	0.10	0.08	0.06
4Q	—	-0.03	0.18	0.11	0.10	0.05
Yr.	—	0.49	0.62	0.45	0.34	0.28

Next earnings report expected: late October

Dividend Data

No cash dividends have been paid, and the company does not expect to pay any in the foreseeable future.

A Division of The McGraw·Hill Companies

Business Summary - 01-SEP-98

PAXAR Corporation is a fully integrated manufacturer and distributor of label systems, bar-code systems, labels, tags and related supplies and services for apparel manufacturers and retailers.

To broaden its product line and enhance its market position, the company has developed new products and completed several acquisitions since 1986. In 1995, the company acquired a 49.5% interest in Monarch Marking Systems, a manufacturer of bar code systems and supplies; it purchased the remaining interest in March 1997. In January 1996, PAXAR purchased Brian Pulfrey, Ltd., a manufacturer of printed labels and tags in Nottingham, England. In 1997, the company acquired a 70% interest in a Brazilian label system manufacturer and a 50% interest in a Columbian distributor, and in February 1998, acquired a 70% interest in a Turkish maker of apparel identification systems.

In July 1997, PAXAR acquired International Imaging Materials, Inc., the largest manufacturer in North America of thermal transfer ribbons used in thermal printers and other applications, in exchange for about 12.5 million common shares valued at about $200 million.

The company's apparel identification products include bar-code tag systems and hot-stamp label printers. These systems let customers print, cut and batch large volumes of tags and labels in their own plants. PAXAR's bar-code tag systems include personal computers, electronic bar-code printers, thermal ink, pre-printed tag stock and supporting software. Hot-stamp printing systems include hot-stamp printers, fabrics, inks and printing accessories, which are used by manufacturers for in-house printing of care labels and labels that carry brand logo, size and other information for the retail customer. The company also designs and produces tags and woven and printed labels. Tag and label systems and supplies accounted for 51% of net sales in 1997.

Printing solutions products consist of identification and pricing system labelers (11% of 1997 sales), which print one to three lines of alphanumeric information in a variety of print sizes and types; automated identification system printers and related supplies (21% of 1997 sales), which consist of tabletop, handheld and portable thermal transfer and direct thermal printers; and thermal transfer ribbons (16% of 1997 sales), an essential consumable in the thermal transfer printing process.

The company has more than 10,000 customers, including major retailers and apparel manufacturers such as Levi Strauss, Sears, J.C. Penney, The Limited, Liz Claiborne, Sara Lee, Land's End, and L.L. Bean.

Per Share Data ($) (Year Ended Dec. 31)	1997	1996	1995	1994	1993	1992	1991	1990	1989	1988
Tangible Bk. Val.	1.62	2.90	2.29	1.86	1.84	1.55	0.91	0.79	0.72	0.57
Cash Flow	1.16	0.89	0.68	0.54	0.41	0.38	0.24	0.15	0.27	0.12
Earnings	0.49	0.62	0.45	0.34	0.27	0.27	0.13	0.04	0.15	0.04
Dividends	Nil	Nil	Nil	Nil	Nil	Nil	Nil	Nil	Nil	Nil
Payout Ratio	Nil	Nil	Nil	Nil	Nil	Nil	Nil	Nil	Nil	Nil
Prices - High	21	15	10¼	6½	6¾	7¼	2⅜	1 9/16	2	1 9/16
- Low	13⅛	7⅛	4⅞	4⅞	4¼	2 5/16	15/16	⅞	⅞	⅞
P/E Ratio - High	43	24	23	19	24	28	19	36	13	36
- Low	27	12	11	14	16	9	7	20	6	20
Income Statement Analysis (Million $)										
Revs.	567	220	201	167	139	133	88.9	72.9	73.8	56.2
Oper. Inc.	100	36.1	31.3	24.8	19.6	18.3	9.9	6.0	8.6	5.3
Depr.	32.8	9.7	8.1	6.8	4.7	3.6	2.8	2.7	2.3	1.8
Int. Exp.	13.8	1.4	1.6	0.9	0.5	0.8	1.1	1.5	1.9	1.5
Pretax Inc.	37.9	29.1	22.1	17.1	14.5	13.9	6.0	1.8	6.7	2.0
Eff. Tax Rate	36%	25%	29%	32%	35%	40%	42%	36%	38%	43%
Net Inc.	24.4	21.8	15.7	11.6	9.4	8.4	3.4	1.1	4.2	1.2
Balance Sheet & Other Fin. Data (Million $)										
Cash	13.7	6.7	6.7	4.5	0.7	0.3	0.3	1.2	0.3	0.6
Curr. Assets	234	78.3	70.9	64.0	47.8	42.4	30.3	26.6	27.3	24.4
Total Assets	598	182	157	129	85.5	72.8	51.1	43.0	44.3	43.9
Curr. Liab.	113	28.9	24.3	25.0	17.6	14.1	13.1	9.1	10.2	6.7
LT Debt	211	19.9	23.1	13.8	0.7	2.1	10.2	10.9	13.0	21.3
Common Eqty.	244	120	95.2	77.9	62.5	52.8	25.0	20.8	19.2	15.1
Total Cap.	479	152	129	102	67.9	58.6	38.0	34.0	34.1	37.2
Cap. Exp.	30.3	13.8	12.3	11.2	12.6	8.5	6.6	3.2	1.5	2.6
Cash Flow	57.2	31.5	23.8	18.4	14.0	12.0	6.3	3.9	6.4	3.0
Curr. Ratio	2.1	2.7	2.9	2.6	2.7	3.0	2.3	2.9	2.7	3.6
% LT Debt of Cap.	44.1	13.1	17.9	13.5	1.1	3.6	27.0	32.1	38.0	57.2
% Net Inc.of Revs.	4.3	9.9	7.8	7.0	6.7	6.3	3.9	1.6	5.6	2.1
% Ret. on Assets	6.3	12.9	11.0	10.7	11.8	12.2	7.2	2.6	9.4	3.0
% Ret. on Equity	13.4	20.3	18.2	16.4	16.2	19.9	14.8	5.7	24.2	7.8

Data as orig. reptd.; bef. results of disc. opers. and/or spec. items. Per share data adj. for stk. divs. as of ex-div. date. Bold denotes diluted EPS (FASB 128). E-Estimated. NA-Not Available. NM-Not Meaningful. NR-Not Ranked.

Office—105 Corporate Park Drive, White Plains, NY 10604-3814. **Tel**—(914) 697-6800. **Fax**—(914) 697-6893. **Website**—http://www.paxar.com **Chrmn, Pres & CEO**—A. Hershaft. **SVP & CFO**—J. R. Plaxe. **VP & Treas**—J. P. Jordan. **VP & Secy**—D. S. Bishop. **Dirs**—J. Becker, L. Benatar, A. Hershaft, V. Hershaft, R. G. Laidlaw, T. R. Loemker, J. C. McGroddy, D. E. McKinney, J. W. Paxton, W. W. Williams. **Transfer Agent & Registrar**—ChaseMellon Shareholder Services, S. Hackensack, NJ. **Incorporated**—in New York in 1946. **Empl**— 4,786. **S&P Analyst:** Jim Corridore

Pediatrix Medical Group 1773M

NYSE Symbol **PDX**

In S&P SmallCap 600

03-OCT-98

Industry:
Health Care (Specialized Services)

Summary: This company is the largest U.S. provider of physician management services to hospital-based neonatal intensive care units.

Quantitative Evaluations	
Outlook (1 Lowest—5 Highest)	• **4⁻**
Fair Value	• **61⅜**
Risk	• **High**
Earn./Div. Rank	• **NR**
Technical Eval.	• **NA**
Rel. Strength Rank (1 Lowest—99 Highest)	• **81**
Insider Activity	• **NA**

Recent Price • 42½
52 Wk Range • 50¼-32⅛

Yield • Nil
12-Mo. P/E • 26.9

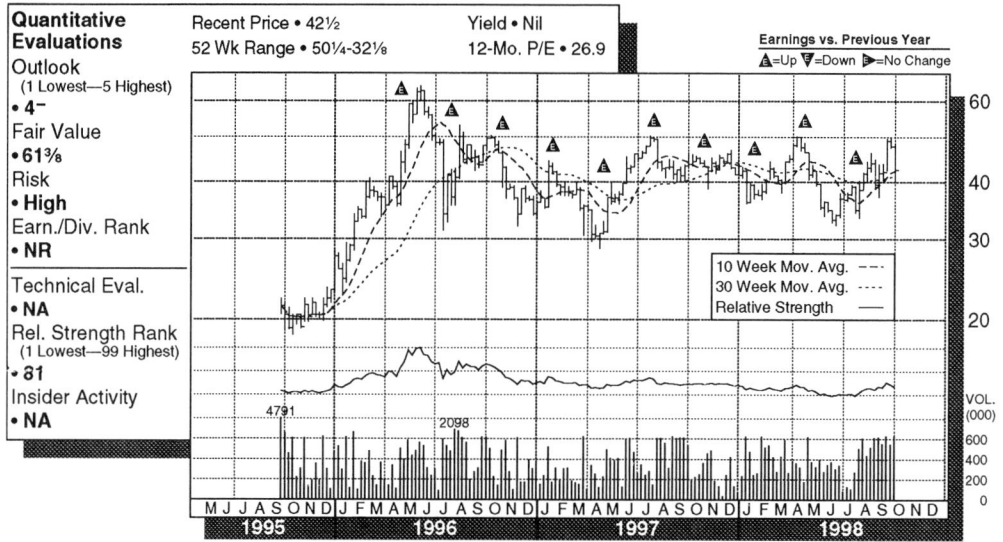

Earnings vs. Previous Year
▲=Up ▼=Down ▶=No Change

10 Week Mov. Avg. - - -
30 Week Mov. Avg. · · · · ·
Relative Strength ——

Business Profile - 30-MAR-98

In the first three months of 1998, Pediatrix continued its expansion with the addition of 13 neonatal intensive care units (NICU) and through newly formed Obstetrix Medical Group, Inc. expanded to provide perinatology services. In March 1998, the company acquired three perinatology group practices with 12 perinatologists located in Denver, Fort Worth and Kansas City. PDX provides physician management services to over 100 NICUs, eight pediatric intensive care units and three pediatrics departments, and employs or contracts with approximately 300 physicians and over 85 neonatal nurse practitioners. During 1997, the company recorded about 325,000 patient days, up from 186,000 in 1996.

Operational Review - 30-MAR-98

Net patient service revenue advanced 50% in 1997, primarily due to the addition of 31 neonatal intensive care units through a combination of internal marketing efforts and acquisitions. Net income was also up 59%, to $20,913,000 ($1.33 a share, on 8.3% more shares), from $13,120,000 ($0.90).

Stock Performance - 02-OCT-98

In the past 30 trading days, PDX's shares have declined 3%, compared to a 7% fall in the S&P 500. Average trading volume for the past five days was 182,660 shares, compared with the 40-day moving average of 138,015 shares.

Key Stock Statistics

Dividend Rate/Share	Nil	Shareholders	100
Shs. outstg. (M)	15.2	Market cap. (B)	$0.648
Avg. daily vol. (M)	0.157	Inst. holdings	87%
Tang. Bk. Value/Share	11.81		
Beta	NA		

Value of $10,000 invested 5 years ago: NA

Fiscal Year Ending Dec. 31

	1998	1997	1996	1995	1994	1993
Revenues (Million $)						
1Q	37.81	27.01	16.13	8.89	—	—
2Q	46.14	30.60	17.81	9.13	—	—
3Q	—	34.44	22.40	12.48	—	—
4Q	—	36.79	24.49	13.36	—	—
Yr.	—	128.8	80.83	43.86	32.78	23.57
Earnings Per Share ($)						
1Q	**0.39**	**0.28**	0.19	0.12	—	—
2Q	**0.45**	**0.30**	0.22	0.12	—	—
3Q	—	**0.35**	0.24	0.22	—	—
4Q	—	**0.40**	0.25	0.17	—	—
Yr.	—	**1.33**	0.90	0.55	0.47	0.36

Next earnings report expected: late October

Dividend Data

No cash dividends have been paid. The company does not intend to pay any dividends for the foreseeable future. It plans to retain all earnings for the operation and expansion of its business.

A Division of The **McGraw-Hill** *Companies*

STANDARD
&POOR'S
STOCK REPORTS

Pediatrix Medical Group, Inc.

1773M

03-OCT-98

Business Summary - 30-MAR-98

Pediatrix Medical Group is the leading U.S. provider of physician management services to hospital-based neonatal intensive care units (NICUs). NICUs provide medical care to newborn infants with low birth weight and other medical complications and are staffed with specialized pediatric physicians, known as neonatologists. The company believes that it is the only provider of NICU physician management services that markets its services on a national basis.

The company also provides physician management services to: hospital-based pediatric intensive care units (PICUs), which provide medical care to critically ill children and are staffed with specially trained pediatricians; and pediatrics departments in hospitals. As of December 31, 1996, Pediatrix provided services to 68 NICUs, eight PICUs and three pediatrics departments in 17 states and Puerto Rico, and employed or contracted with about 195 physicians. NICU patient days totaled 185,702 in 1996, versus 87,672 in 1995.

Pediatrix staffs and manages NICUs and PICUs in hospitals, providing the physicians, professional management and administrative support, including physician billing and reimbursement expertise and services. PDX's policy is to provide 24-hour coverage at its NICUs and PICUs with on-site or on-call physicians. As a result of this policy, physicians are available to provide continuous pediatric support to other areas of the hospital on an as-needed basis, especially in the obstetrics, nursery and pediatrics departments, where immediate accessibility to specialized care is critical.

Historically, most of PDX's growth was generated internally through marketing efforts and referrals. Beginning in the latter part of 1995, the company significantly increased its acquisition activities to capitalize on the opportunities created by the trend toward consolidation in the health care industry. During 1996, the company completed 10 acquisitions, which added 33 NICUs, four PICUs and two pediatric departments. In addition, three NICUs were added through the company's internal marketing activities. In the aggregate, the number of NICU patient days attributable to these units was about 78,000 during 1996.

PDX has developed regional networks in Denver, Phoenix and Southern California, and intends to develop additional regional and statewide networks. It believes that these networks, augmented by ongoing marketing and acquisition efforts, will strengthen its position with third-party payors, such as Medicaid and managed care organizations.

About 29% of the company's net patient service revenue in 1996 was derived from payments made by government-sponsored healthcare programs (primarily Medicaid); managed care accounted for 35%, other third parties 32% and private pay 4%.

Per Share Data ($)

(Year Ended Dec. 31)	1997	1996	1995	1994	1993	1992	1991	1990	1989	1988
Tangible Bk. Val.	4.06	6.00	4.52	0.06	NA	NA	NA	NA	NA	NA
Cash Flow	1.62	1.03	0.58	0.50	0.38	NA	NA	NA	NA	NA
Earnings	1.33	0.90	0.55	0.47	0.36	NA	NA	NA	NA	NA
Dividends	Nil	Nil	Nil	Nil	Nil	Nil	Nil	Nil	Nil	Nil
Payout Ratio	Nil	Nil	Nil	Nil	Nil	Nil	Nil	Nil	Nil	Nil
Prices - High	50⅜	64¾	28½	NA	NA	NA	NA	NA	NA	NA
- Low	28⅝	22½	18½	NA	NA	NA	NA	NA	NA	NA
P/E Ratio - High	38	72	52	NA	NA	NA	NA	NA	NA	NA
- Low	22	25	34	NA	NA	NA	NA	NA	NA	NA

Income Statement Analysis (Million $)

	1997	1996	1995	1994	1993	1992	1991	1990	1989	1988
Revs.	129	80.8	43.9	32.8	23.6	NA	NA	NA	NA	NA
Oper. Inc.	37.6	21.8	10.9	9.3	17.1	NA	NA	NA	NA	NA
Depr.	4.5	1.8	0.4	0.2	0.1	NA	NA	NA	NA	NA
Int. Exp.	0.3	0.2	0.1	0.1	0.1	NA	NA	NA	NA	NA
Pretax Inc.	34.9	22.0	11.2	9.2	6.3	NA	NA	NA	NA	NA
Eff. Tax Rate	40%	40%	40%	41%	34%	NA	NA	NA	NA	NA
Net Inc.	20.9	13.1	6.7	5.4	4.2	NA	NA	NA	NA	NA

Balance Sheet & Other Fin. Data (Million $)

	1997	1996	1995	1994	1993	1992	1991	1990	1989	1988
Cash	18.6	75.7	46.2	7.4	NA	NA	NA	NA	NA	NA
Curr. Assets	82.0	101	59.8	17.2	NA	NA	NA	NA	NA	NA
Total Assets	197	159	69.9	20.3	14.2	NA	NA	NA	NA	NA
Curr. Liab.	28.1	19.7	6.3	3.4	NA	NA	NA	NA	NA	NA
LT Debt	2.5	2.8	0.8	0.8	1.0	NA	NA	NA	NA	NA
Common Eqty.	164	136	62.8	0.4	-3.9	NA	NA	NA	NA	NA
Total Cap.	169	139	63.6	17.9	11.5	NA	NA	NA	NA	NA
Cap. Exp.	2.2	4.7	1.9	0.6	1.9	NA	NA	NA	NA	NA
Cash Flow	25.4	14.9	7.1	5.7	4.3	NA	NA	NA	NA	NA
Curr. Ratio	2.9	5.1	9.5	5.1	NA	NA	NA	NA	NA	NA
% LT Debt of Cap.	1.5	0.2	1.2	4.5	8.4	NA	NA	NA	NA	NA
% Net Inc.of Revs.	16.2	16.2	15.3	16.5	17.6	NA	NA	NA	NA	NA
% Ret. on Assets	11.8	11.5	14.9	31.3	29.6	NA	NA	NA	NA	NA
% Ret. on Equity	13.9	13.2	21.2	NM	NM	NM	NM	NM	NM	NM

Data as orig. reptd.; bef. results of disc. opers. and/or spec. items. Per share data adj. for stk. divs. as of ex-div. date. Bold denotes diluted EPS (FASB 128). E-Estimated. NA-Not Available. NM-Not Meaningful. NR-Not Ranked.

Office—1455 N. Park Dr., Ft. Lauderdale, FL 33326.**Tel**—(954) 384-0175.**Website**—http://www.pediatrix.com**Pres & CEO**—R. J. Medel.**VP & CFO**—L. M. Mullen. **VP & Secy**—B. A. Jordan.**Investor Contact**—Bob Kneeley.**Dirs**—C. L. Alvarez, M. D. Cunningham, B. R. Evans, M. Fernandez, B. A. Jordan, R. J. Medel, A. H. Nahmad, E. R. Stamps IV.**Transfer Agent & Registrar**—Boston EquiServe.**Incorporated**—in Florida in 1980.**Empl**— 475. **S&P Analyst:** G.A.S.

Penford Corp.

4960F

NASDAQ Symbol **PENX**

In S&P SmallCap 600

03-OCT-98

Industry:
Chemicals (Diversified)

Summary: This company develops, manufactures and markets specialty carbohydrate chemicals for papermaking, pharmaceutical products, and specialty food ingredients.

Quantitative Evaluations		
Recent Price • 12½	**Yield • 1.6%**	
52 Wk Range • 41½-8½	12-Mo. P/E • NM	

Outlook
(1 Lowest—5 Highest)
• **5**

Fair Value
• **22¼**

Risk
• **Low**

Earn./Div. Rank
• **B-**

Technical Eval.
• **NA**

Rel. Strength Rank
(1 Lowest—99 Highest)
• **6**

Insider Activity
• **NA**

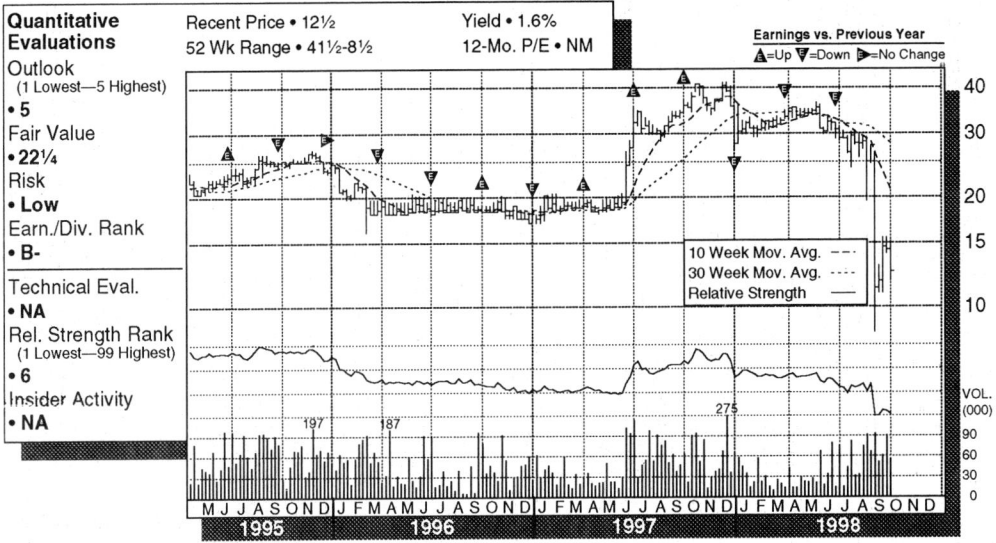

Earnings vs. Previous Year
▲=Up ▼=Down ▶=No Change

10 Week Mov. Avg. ---
30 Week Mov. Avg. ....
Relative Strength —

Business Profile - 31-AUG-98

In December 1997, PENWEST Ltd. changed its name to Penford Corporation to reflect the spinoff of its pharmaceuticals business, and its intent to focus on its specialty starch-based food ingredients and paper chemicals businesses. PENX originally filed to sell up to 20% of Penwest Pharmaceuticals in an IPO, expected to be completed in the second quarter of calendar 1998, but ongoing adverse market conditions led the company to pull the deal. The Penwest Pharmaceutical shares were spun off to PENX shareholders in August 1998, and now trade on the Nasdaq under the symbol PPCO.

Operational Review - 31-AUG-98

Sales from continuing operations in the first nine months of FY 98 (Aug.) declined 4.0%, year to year, reflecting unusually high corn costs in the 1997 period. Gross margins widened, reflecting the effects of the high corn costs in the prior year, improved operational efficiencies, and the benefits of increased specialty starch volumes. However, following a $1.9 million restructuring charge, and in the absence of a nonrecurring gain of $1.2 million ($800,000, or $0.11 a share, after taxes) from the sale of air credits related to a division sold in 1989, pretax income fell 10%. After taxes at 34.9%, versus 33.2%, income from continuing operations was down 12%, to $5,553,000 ($0.74 a share), from $6,311,000 ($0.90). Results exclude losses from discontinued operations of $1.14 and $0.26 a share.

Stock Performance - 02-OCT-98

In the past 30 trading days, PENX's shares have declined 50%, compared to a 7% fall in the S&P 500. Average trading volume for the past five days was 11,140 shares, compared with the 40-day moving average of 16,097 shares.

Key Stock Statistics

Dividend Rate/Share	0.20	Shareholders	1,300
Shs. outstg. (M)	7.3	Market cap. (B)	$0.092
Avg. daily vol. (M)	0.015	Inst. holdings	32%
Tang. Bk. Value/Share	12.02		
Beta	0.27		

Value of $10,000 invested 5 years ago: $ 6,219

Fiscal Year Ending Aug. 31

	1998	1997	1996	1995	1994	1993
Revenues (Million $)						
1Q	48.52	49.31	45.62	42.77	37.82	33.50
2Q	47.49	48.33	46.31	42.43	35.84	31.80
3Q	40.31	49.99	49.11	43.62	41.35	34.50
4Q	—	49.00	53.43	45.38	43.79	35.68
Yr.	—	196.6	194.5	174.2	158.8	135.5
Earnings Per Share ($)						
1Q	0.07	0.20	0.25	0.25	0.25	0.26
2Q	**0.13**	0.18	0.13	0.31	0.12	0.23
3Q	**0.16**	0.26	0.15	0.29	0.25	0.20
4Q	—	0.29	0.20	0.19	0.24	0.20
Yr.	—	0.93	0.72	1.03	0.86	0.88

Next earnings report expected: late October

Dividend Data (Dividends have been paid since 1992.)

Amount ($)	Date Decl.	Ex-Div. Date	Stock of Record	Payment Date
0.050	Oct. 28	Dec. 08	Nov. 14	Dec. 05 '97
0.050	Jan. 30	Feb. 11	Feb. 13	Mar. 06 '98
0.050	May. 04	May. 13	May. 15	Jun. 05 '98
0.050	Jun. 25	Aug. 12	Aug. 15	Sep. 04 '98

A Division of The **McGraw·Hill** *Companies*

STANDARD
&POOR'S
STOCK REPORTS

Penford Corporation

4960F
03-OCT-98

Business Summary - 31-AUG-98

Penford Corp., formerly PENWEST, Ltd., changed its name in December 1997 to reflect the spin off its pharmaceuticals businesses and its intent to concentrate on its specialty starch-based food ingredients and paper chemicals business. The company depends on corn and potatoes (along with some cellulose wood pulp) to produce its carbohydrate-based specialty chemicals. Penford is currently composed of Penford Products and Penwest Foods.

In August 1998, Penwest Pharmaceuticals shares were spun off to PENX shareholders tax free, and now trade on the Nasdaq under the symbol PPCO. PENX originally filed to sell up to 20% of Penwest Pharmaceuticals in an IPO in the second quarter of calendar 1998, but ongoing adverse market conditions led the company to pull the deal. Penwest Pharmaceuticals results are now accounted for as discontinued operations. Penwest Pharmaceuticals bought Edward Mendell Co. in 1991 and established TIMERx Technologies in that year to focus on timed release applications. Mendell makes pharmaceutical excipients, the

non-active ingredients in tablet and capsule prescription pharmaceuticals, over-the-counter drugs and vitamins.

Penford Products, the company's core business and its oldest unit (dating back to 1894) makes specialty chemical starches used in papermaking. Penford's products are mainly used to improve the strength, quality and runnability of coated and uncoated paper.

Penwest Foods manufactures and markets specialty carbohydrate-based food ingredients. These include food grade potato starch products, and dextrose-based products such as specialty dried corn syrup solids.

Penwest competes with approximately five other companies that manufacture corn wet milling products and five other companies that manufacture pharmaceutical excipients where it has the second largest market share. It sells to approximately 90 major customers. Two customers, Georgia-Pacific and Mead Paper, accounted for approximately 15% and 10% of FY 97 (Aug.) sales, respectively.

Sales increased $2.2 million, or 1.1%, during FY 97, reflecting higher volumes in each division, partially offset by the lower corn prices, a key component used in pricing Penford's paper chemical products.

Per Share Data ($)

(Year Ended Aug. 31)	1997	1996	1995	1994	1993	1992	1991	1990	1989	1988
Tangible Bk. Val.	12.27	11.42	10.65	9.86	9.18	8.70	8.47	7.20	7.02	4.31
Cash Flow	2.67	2.40	2.51	2.32	2.19	2.08	2.09	1.79	1.92	2.94
Earnings	0.93	0.72	1.03	0.86	0.88	1.01	1.17	1.06	0.68	1.11
Dividends	0.20	0.20	0.20	0.20	0.20	0.20	Nil	Nil	Nil	0.01
Payout Ratio	22%	28%	19%	23%	23%	20%	Nil	Nil	Nil	1%
Prices - High	41½	24¾	27	26½	23½	36¼	37¼	35½	18½	14⅜
- Low	17	16	18¼	17½	16	16½	19¼	17	11⅝	8⅞
P/E Ratio - High	44	34	25	30	26	35	31	32	4	12
- Low	18	22	17	20	18	16	16	15	2	7

Income Statement Analysis (Million $)

	1997	1996	1995	1994	1993	1992	1991	1990	1989	1988
Revs.	197	195	175	159	136	128	113	94.9	83.3	142
Oper. Inc.	26.4	24.0	25.3	21.2	18.5	18.5	19.5	15.4	12.3	25.7
Depr.	12.4	11.7	10.4	10.3	9.4	8.0	7.0	5.5	4.9	7.3
Int. Exp.	5.3	5.1	5.2	3.4	2.5	2.3	2.5	2.2	2.9	4.7
Pretax Inc.	9.9	7.5	11.1	8.1	7.6	10.1	12.5	10.6	7.9	14.4
Eff. Tax Rate	33%	32%	35%	24%	17%	26%	30%	25%	30%	34%
Net Inc.	6.6	5.1	7.2	6.1	6.3	7.5	8.8	8.0	5.6	9.5

Balance Sheet & Other Fin. Data (Million $)

	1997	1996	1995	1994	1993	1992	1991	1990	1989	1988
Cash	0.2	--	5.3	Nil	5.5	0.2	1.0	0.3	0.6	0.2
Curr. Assets	54.4	52.7	48.9	42.1	41.5	44.1	52.1	48.0	53.6	55.6
Total Assets	216	203	187	164	156	131	121	102	96.0	141
Curr. Liab.	24.2	23.3	19.7	20.7	20.1	15.3	17.7	15.7	13.0	30.9
LT Debt	61.8	62.6	58.6	42.9	47.0	30.9	31.6	23.1	23.7	49.5
Common Eqty.	89.1	78.1	72.0	67.2	63.0	61.6	60.1	51.1	49.6	35.7
Total Cap.	173	169	131	110	110	93.0	92.0	74.0	73.0	85.0
Cap. Exp.	21.5	21.5	23.0	14.3	42.1	20.2	14.0	13.5	7.6	14.7
Cash Flow	19.1	16.8	17.6	16.5	15.7	15.5	15.8	13.5	10.5	16.8
Curr. Ratio	2.2	2.3	2.5	2.0	2.1	2.9	2.9	3.1	4.1	1.8
% LT Debt of Cap.	35.7	37.1	44.7	39.0	42.7	33.4	34.4	31.1	32.3	58.1
% Net Inc.of Revs.	3.4	2.6	4.1	3.8	4.7	5.9	7.8	8.4	6.7	6.7
% Ret. on Assets	3.2	2.6	4.1	3.8	4.4	6.0	7.9	8.0	4.7	7.3
% Ret. on Equity	7.9	6.7	10.4	9.4	10.1	12.3	15.8	15.8	13.0	30.1

Data as orig. repd.; bef. results of disc. opers. and/or spec. items. Per share data adj. for stk. divs. as of ex-div. date. Bold denotes diluted EPS (FASB 128). E-Estimated. NA-Not Available. NM-Not Meaningful. NR-Not Ranked.

Office—777-108th Ave., NE, Suite 2390, Bellevue, WA 98004-5193. **Tel**—(206) 462-6000. **Chrmn**—N. S. Rogers. **Pres & CEO**—T. R. Hamachek. **VP-Fin, CFO & Investor Contact**—Jeffrey T. Cook. **Secy**—Jennifer L. Good. **Dirs**—R. E. Engebrecht, P. E. Freiman, T. R. Hamachek, P. H. Hatfield, H. L. Mullikin, S. G. Narodick, W. G. Parzybok Jr., N. S. Rogers, W. K. Street. **Transfer Agent & Registrar**—ChaseMellon Shareholder Services, Ridgefield Park, NJ.**Incorporated**—in Delaware in 1983. **Empl**— 533. **S&P Analyst:** E. Hunter

STANDARD &POOR'S

STOCK REPORTS

Pennsylvania Enterprises   1787M

NYSE Symbol **PNT**

In S&P SmallCap 600

03-OCT-98

Industry:
Natural Gas

Summary: This company's PG Energy unit distributes natural gas to about 150,000 customers in 13 counties in northeastern and central Pennsylvania.

Quantitative Evaluations

Outlook
(1 Lowest—5 Highest)
- **NA**

Fair Value
- **NA**

Risk
- **Low**

Earn./Div. Rank
- **B**

Technical Eval.
- **Neutral** since 9/98

Rel. Strength Rank
(1 Lowest—99 Highest)
- **89**

Insider Activity
- **NA**

Recent Price • 25⅛	Yield • 4.8%
52 Wk Range • 29½-21⅛	12-Mo. P/E • 27.9

Earnings vs. Previous Year
▲=Up ▼=Down ▶=No Change

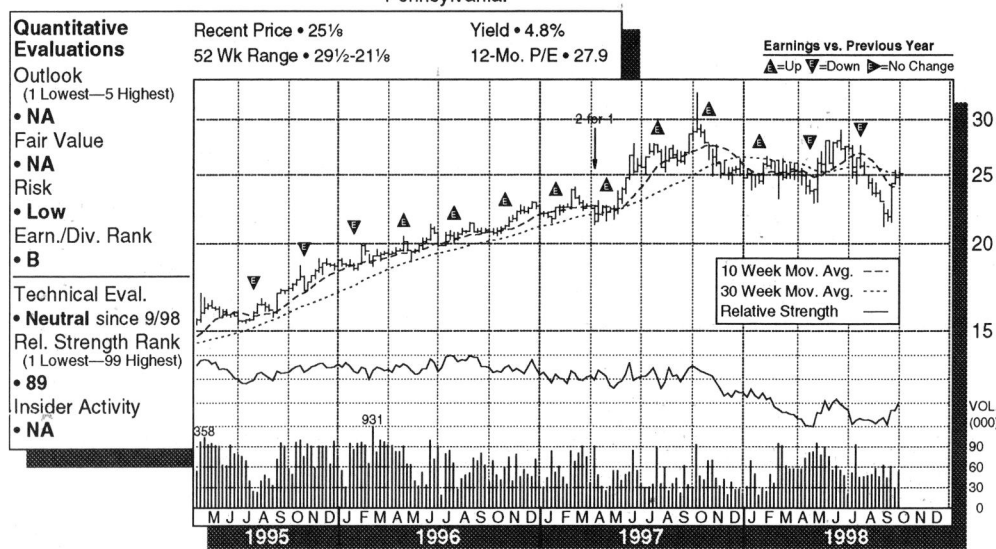

10 Week Mov. Avg. – – –
30 Week Mov. Avg. · · · · ·
Relative Strength ──

Business Profile - 25-SEP-98

In response to a deregulated marketplace under Pennsylvania's new "Customer Choice" legislation, PNT has transformed itself from a traditional utility into a total energy company. In 1997, PG Energy PowerPlus took part in the Customer Choice Electric Pilot Program offered by Pennsylvania's electric utilities, and for the first time, customers are being suppled electricity by the company. In July 1998, newly formed PEI Power Corp. began producing low cost steam and electricity for local consumers using methane gas produced from a landfill to fuel a 25 megawatt cogeneration plant acquired in November 1997. Unregulated operations accounted for 16% of total revenues in 1997.

Operational Review - 25-SEP-98

Total revenues in the six months ended June 30, 1998 fell 14%, year to year, as a 25% increase in nonregulated revenues, primarily resulting from increased natural gas sales by PG Energy Services, was outweighed by a 20% drop in regulated revenues, primarily due to unseasonably warm weather during the period and lower levels in PG Energy's gas cost rate. Operating expenses were down 14%, primarily reflecting a 31% drop in the cost of gas sold. After higher interest charges, income slipped 35%, to $5,790,000 ($0.52 a share, after preferred dividends), from $8,874,000 ($$0.85). Results in the 1997 period include a gain of $0.09 a share relating to a discount on the repurchase of preferred stock of a subsidiary.

Stock Performance - 02-OCT-98

In the past 30 trading days, PNT's shares have increased 7%, compared to a 7% fall in the S&P 500. Average trading volume for the past five days was 10,600 shares, compared with the 40-day moving average of 10,297 shares.

Key Stock Statistics

Dividend Rate/Share	1.20	Shareholders	6,600
Shs. outstg. (M)	10.1	Market cap. (B)	$0.253
Avg. daily vol. (M)	0.010	Inst. holdings	14%
Tang. Bk. Value/Share	12.61		
Beta	0.68		

Value of $10,000 invested 5 years ago: $ 22,093

Fiscal Year Ending Dec. 31

	1998	1997	1996	1995	1994	1993
Revenues (Million $)						
1Q	76.89	89.49	74.09	68.24	96.29	78.30
2Q	35.87	41.86	30.26	25.18	43.48	37.30
3Q	—	24.21	19.35	12.12	31.86	28.00
4Q	—	72.48	60.78	47.22	63.09	63.20
Yr.	—	228.1	184.5	152.8	234.7	206.7
Earnings Per Share ($)						
1Q	0.56	0.83	0.32	0.50	0.79	0.77
2Q	-0.04	0.02	-0.09	-0.18	-0.01	-0.17
3Q	—	-0.24	-0.16	-0.36	-0.10	-0.23
4Q	—	0.61	0.22	0.33	0.41	0.49
Yr.	—	1.30	0.33	0.28	1.08	0.91

Next earnings report expected: NA

Dividend Data (Dividends have been paid since 1946.)

Amount ($)	Date Decl.	Ex-Div. Date	Stock of Record	Payment Date
0.300	Oct. 29	Nov. 26	Dec. 01	Dec. 15 '97
0.300	Jan. 28	Feb. 26	Mar. 02	Mar. 16 '98
0.300	Apr. 29	May. 28	Jun. 01	Jun. 15 '98
0.300	Jul. 17	Aug. 28	Sep. 01	Sep. 15 '98

A Division of The **McGraw·Hill** *Companies*

Pennsylvania Enterprises, Inc.

Business Summary - 25-SEP-98

In a bid to strengthen its position in an increasingly competitive marketplace, Pennsylvania Enterprises, Inc. (PNT) rededicated itself to the energy industry in early 1996 by selling its water utility business. That move has been complemented by acquisitions and other initiatives intended to hasten PNT's transformation from a traditional regulated gas utility into a total energy provider.

PNT's principal business is conducted through PG Energy Inc. (PGE), a regulated public utility, and Honesdale Gas Co., PGE's subsidiary which was acquired in February 1997. Together, PGE and Honesdale distribute natural gas to more than 150,000 customers in a 13-county area in northeastern and central Pennsylvania, a territory that includes 129 municipalities, in addition to the cities of Scranton, Wilkes-Barre and Williamsport. The acquisition of Honesdale, which had about 3,000 gas customers, expanded PGE's territory through the Pocono Mountains into fast-growing Wayne and Pike counties, extending its domain from central Pennsylvania to the borders of New York and New Jersey.

As of December 31, 1997, nearly 91% of PGE's customers were residential, 9% were commercial and less than 1% were industrial or other. PGE delivered an estimated total of 48,300 MMCF of natural gas to its customers in 1997. Of the total, about 48% (22,950 MMCF)

represented gas transported to about 500 large customers who used PGE's transportation service.

Through its unregulated subsidiaries, PG Energy Services Inc. and Keystone Pipeline Services, Inc. (Keystone was acquired in December 1995), the company has established a broad portfolio of energy supply and management services, including the marketing and sale of natural gas and propane, the inspection and servicing of gas-fired equipment and the construction, maintenance and rehabilitation of pipelines for other utilities. PNT's unregulated activities, which represented an insignificant portion of its operations prior to 1996, were expected to account for 25% to 30% of the company's operating revenues in 1998. PNT's unregulated Theta Land Corp. subsidiary is initiating several real estate development projects on company-owned land.

In 1997, operating revenues advanced 24% to $228 million, with strong growth in its regulated and nonregulated operations, especially in its nonregulated gas sales and services operations. Nonregulated operations have grown to 16% of total revenues. The company has made the transition from a gas company to a total energy supplier. Through its PG Energy PowerPlus program, the company took part in the Customer Choice Electric Pilot program offered by the state's electric utilities, and for the first time in its history, customers are being supplied electricity by PNT.

Per Share Data ($)

(Year Ended Dec. 31)	1997	1996	1995	1994	1993	1992	1991	1990	1989	1988
Tangible Bk. Val.	12.39	12.09	13.84	15.48	15.30	16.48	20.05	20.42	21.42	21.23
Cash Flow	2.19	1.56	0.79	2.49	2.31	2.16	2.55	1.57	2.59	2.52
Earnings	1.30	0.33	0.28	1.08	0.91	0.81	0.77	0.13	1.34	1.41
Dividends	1.19	1.10	1.10	1.10	1.10	1.10	1.10	1.10	1.10	1.10
Payout Ratio	92%	NM	NM	101%	121%	137%	144%	880%	82%	78%
Prices - High	32³/₄	23	19¹/₈	16¹/₂	16¹/₈	16	18⁵/₈	23¹/₂	29¹/₄	30³/₈
- Low	21¹/₄	18³/₈	13⁵/₈	13¹/₂	13	11	11¹/₈	15	21³/₄	20⁷/₈
P/E Ratio - High	25	70	69	15	18	20	24	NM	22	22
- Low	16	55	49	12	14	14	15	NM	16	15

Income Statement Analysis (Million $)

	1997	1996	1995	1994	1993	1992	1991	1990	1989	1988
Revs.	228	184	153	235	207	192	183	167	184	172
Oper. Inc.	21.6	31.9	20.5	69.2	57.4	53.1	46.8	34.6	38.0	37.1
Depr.	9.5	7.9	7.0	14.3	12.3	10.9	9.8	7.9	6.8	6.0
Int. Exp.	11.2	10.4	15.5	26.7	26.2	25.6	26.6	22.3	18.6	12.6
Pretax Inc.	19.2	13.9	5.6	29.1	22.5	18.9	12.5	6.4	17.3	18.0
Eff. Tax Rate	39%	42%	63%	40%	36%	39%	33%	21%	32%	32%
Net Inc.	11.8	8.1	2.0	17.5	14.4	11.5	8.4	5.0	11.8	12.2

Balance Sheet & Other Fin. Data (Million $)

	1997	1996	1995	1994	1993	1992	1991	1990	1989	1988
Cash	2.2	1.1	0.6	2.9	2.8	1.1	0.7	2.2	0.7	0.8
Curr. Assets	75.5	82.3	58.2	75.0	85.6	62.7	58.3	59.8	61.8	59.1
Total Assets	389	367	524	735	719	633	543	518	488	420
Curr. Liab.	57.6	92.9	155	39.0	79.0	78.0	129	125	91.0	101
LT Debt	127	75.0	107	362	296	276	195	178	181	107
Common Eqty.	122	118	163	172	166	135	110	111	116	115
Total Cap.	323	266	359	675	623	530	398	380	387	309
Cap. Exp.	31.0	29.3	20.6	36.8	45.9	57.1	28.5	36.4	70.5	52.8
Cash Flow	21.3	16.0	9.0	27.2	20.3	17.3	14.0	8.5	14.0	13.6
Curr. Ratio	1.3	0.8	0.4	1.9	1.1	0.8	0.5	0.5	0.7	0.6
% LT Debt of Cap.	39.4	28.2	29.8	53.6	47.5	52.1	48.9	46.8	46.9	34.6
% Net Inc.of Revs.	5.2	4.4	1.3	7.4	7.0	6.0	4.6	3.0	6.4	7.1
% Ret. on Assets	3.6	1.7	0.4	2.4	1.9	1.9	1.6	1.0	2.6	3.1
% Ret. on Equity	9.9	5.7	1.2	7.5	4.7	5.3	3.8	0.6	6.3	6.7

Data as orig. reptd.; bef. results of disc. opers. and/or spec. items. Per share data adj. for stk. divs. as of ex-div. date. Bold denotes diluted EPS (FASB 128). E-Estimated. NA-Not Available. NM-Not Meaningful. NR-Not Ranked.

Office—One PEI Center, Wilkes-Barre, PA 18711-0601. **Tel**—(717) 829-8843. **Website**—http://www.pnt.com **Chrmn**—K. L. Pollock. **Vice Chrm**—W. D. Davis. **Pres & CEO**—T. F. Karam. **Treas**—R. N. Marshall. **VP & Secy**—T. J. Ward. **Investor Contact**—Robert J. Lopatto. **Dirs**—D. T. Casaday, W. D. Davis, P. R. Freeman, T. F. Karam, R. J. Keating, J. D. McCarthy Sr., J. D. McCarthy Jr., K. L. Pollock, K. M. Pollock, R. A. Rose Jr., J. A. Ross, R. W. Simms. **Transfer Agent & Registrar**—ChaseMellon Shareholder Services, L.L.C., Ridgefield Park, NJ. **Incorporated**—in Pennsylvania in 1974. **Empl**—815. **S&P Analyst:** M.I.

Pharmaceutical Marketing Services 4970

NASDAQ Symbol **PMRX**

In S&P SmallCap 600

03-OCT-98

Industry:
Services (Commercial & Consumer)

Summary: This company provides a range of integrated marketing services and solutions primarily to pharmaceutical and health care companies in the U.S., Europe and Japan.

Quantitative Evaluations

Recent Price • 9⅛
52 Wk Range • 15-7

Yield • Nil
12-Mo. P/E • NM

Outlook
(1 Lowest—5 Highest)
• **NA**

Fair Value
• **NA**

Risk
• **Average**

Earn./Div. Rank
• **NR**

Technical Eval.
• **Bullish** since 1/98

Rel. Strength Rank
(1 Lowest—99 Highest)
• **67**

Insider Activity
• **NA**

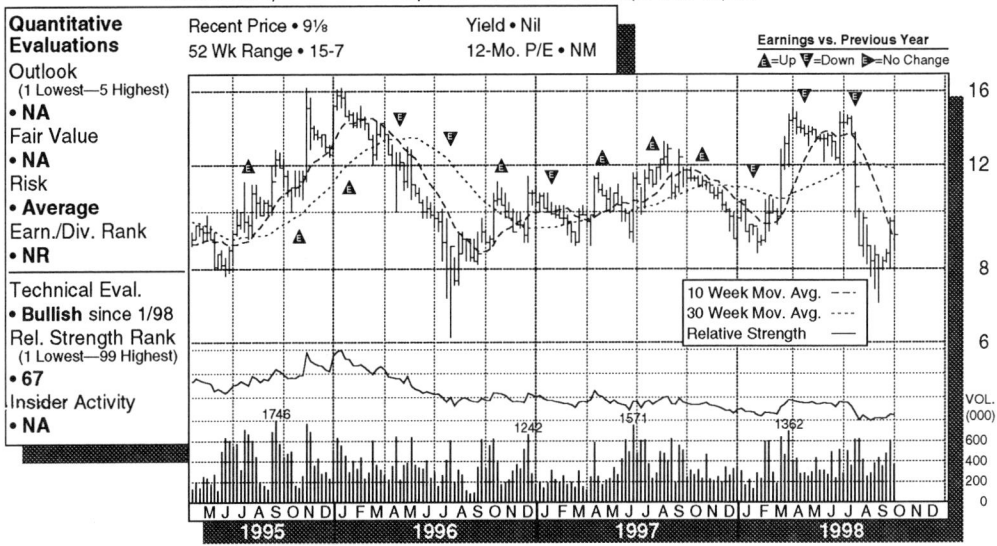

Earnings vs. Previous Year
▲=Up ▼=Down ▶=No Change

10 Week Mov. Avg. ---
30 Week Mov. Avg. ----
Relative Strength —

Business Profile - 09-SEP-98

In August 1998, the company completed the sale of its non-U.S. assets, including Source Europe (acquired in December 1997), to IMS Health for consideration of $75 million, comprising some 1.2 million shares of IMS Health common stock. PMRX's remaining operations consist primarily of Scott-Levin, a leading provider of market research and managed care services to the pharmaceutical industry in the U.S. The Scott-Levin business had pre-tax operating profits of $6.6 million on revenues of $26.2 million in FY 98, representing growth of 34% and 21%, respectively, over the prior year.

Operational Review - 09-SEP-98

Revenues (preliminary) in FY 98 (Jun.) fell 21% from those of the prior year, primarily reflecting divested operations and a negative currency conversion (revenues from ongoing businesses, mainly Scott-Levin in the US and PMRX's targeting business in Japan were up over 20%). With SG&A expenses only down slightly, $12.0 million of in-process R&D write-offs, and $14.7 million of impairment charges from assets held for sale, an operating loss of $29,749,000 contrasted with operating income of $7,524,000. Following a $34.1 million net gain on the sale of operations in FY 98, and after taxes of $5,705,000, versus $2,655,000, the loss from continuing operations was $303,000 ($0.02 a share), against income of $4,661,000 ($0.35). Results in FY 97 exclude a loss from discontinued operations of $9,914,000 ($0.75).

Stock Performance - 02-OCT-98

In the past 30 trading days, PMRX's shares have increased 11%, compared to a 7% fall in the S&P 500. Average trading volume for the past five days was 73,780 shares, compared with the 40-day moving average of 80,438 shares.

Key Stock Statistics

Dividend Rate/Share	Nil	Shareholders	1,100
Shs. outstg. (M)	12.3	Market cap. (B)	$0.113
Avg. daily vol. (M)	0.093	Inst. holdings	16%
Tang. Bk. Value/Share	2.84		
Beta	1.42		

Value of $10,000 invested 5 years ago: $ 4,740

Fiscal Year Ending Jun. 30

	1998	1997	1996	1995	1994	1993
Revenues (Million $)						
1Q	20.09	21.99	20.71	24.27	25.44	18.78
2Q	21.57	26.55	24.29	34.25	32.05	27.19
3Q	17.54	22.79	23.13	32.88	27.12	—
4Q	18.76	27.22	24.90	38.36	29.38	—
Yr.	77.97	98.49	93.03	129.8	114.0	94.92
Earnings Per Share ($)						
1Q	0.18	0.02	0.01	-0.06	0.11	0.03
2Q	0.01	0.11	0.18	0.10	0.28	0.14
3Q	-0.21	0.08	-0.35	0.17	0.06	—
4Q	-0.03	0.14	0.11	0.19	-0.09	—
Yr.	-0.02	0.35	-0.05	0.40	0.36	0.54

Next earnings report expected: early November

Dividend Data

No cash dividends have been paid. The company intends to retain its earnings to finance the operation of its business and does not anticipate paying cash dividends in the foreseeable future.

A Division of The McGraw·Hill Companies

Business Summary - 09-SEP-98

Pharmaceutical Marketing Services Inc. provides a range of information and market research services to pharmaceutical and healthcare companies in the United States to enable them to optimize their sales and marketing performance. Most of the company's information services are generated from proprietary databases which contain unique prescription, physician, managed care and healthcare market data.

The company provides a range of services that are either database services or enhanced by its proprietary databases. Its services are comprised of targeting information services, prescription database services with Source Informatics Inc., and added value services, including marketing research and consulting services, software and direct marketing services.

PMSI's prescriber profile databases contain extensive information on individual prescribers, including attitudes and prescribing behavior, collected from physicians through self-administered surveys in seven countries. In addition, the company jointly exploits, through a long-term agreement, a database of prescription data created and maintained by Source. As of the end of FY 97 (Jun.), this database contained information relating to over 3 billion prescriptions dispensed by retail and mail order pharmacies in the U.S.

Targeting information services allows pharmaceutical companies to target their promotional programs to the optimal audience of prescribers and other health care professionals who influence, or, in some cases, control prescribing decisions.

In the third quarter of FY 96 (Jun.), PMRX decided to divest its non-database-driven services business, which includes a range of medical journals. During the second quarter of FY 97, the company completed the sale of two European communications businesses. In the third quarter of FY 97, it sold its international publishing and communications business.

Customers of PMRX include virtually every major pharmaceutical company. Its 10 largest customers accounted for 33% of revenues in FY 97, with no one customer accounting for over 10%.

In FY 98, the company's financial results were obscured by its significant re-organization and divestment activity. During the year the company divested its international publishing business, its French point of sale business and its interest in the Source joint venture (acquired in December 1997) and OTC businesses in the U.S., recognizing a pre-tax gain of $34 million.

In August 1998, the company completed the sale of its non-U.S. assets to IMS Health for consideration of $75 million, consisting of 1.2 million common shares of IMS Health. IMS HEALTH is the world's leading provider of information solutions to the pharmaceutical and healthcare industries, with more than $1 billion in 1997 revenue and operations in over 90 countries.

Per Share Data ($)

(Year Ended Jun. 30)	1998	1997	1996	1995	1994	1993	1992	1991	1990	1989
Tangible Bk. Val.	NA	2.91	3.46	2.09	1.42	1.17	3.15	3.85	NA	NA
Cash Flow	NA	0.63	0.20	0.75	0.61	0.77	NA	NA	NA	NA
Earnings	-0.02	0.35	-0.05	0.40	0.36	0.53	0.48	-0.22	NA	NA
Dividends	Nil	Nil	Nil	Nil	Nil	Nil	Nil	Nil	Nil	Nil
Payout Ratio	Nil	Nil	Nil	Nil	Nil	Nil	Nil	Nil	Nil	Nil
Prices - High	15	13⅛	16¼	16¼	17¾	21¼	30½	22½	NA	NA
- Low	7	8¾	6⅛	7¾	6¾	13	13¾	14	NA	NA
P/E Ratio - High	NM	37	NM	41	49	39	63	NM	NM	NM
- Low	NM	25	NM	19	19	24	29	NM	NM	NM

Income Statement Analysis (Million $)

	1998	1997	1996	1995	1994	1993	1992	1991	1990	1989
Revs.	NM	98.5	93.0	130	114	95.0	NA	NA	NA	NA
Oper. Inc.	NA	11.2	8.6	14.6	15.2	15.9	NA	NA	NA	NA
Depr.	NA	3.7	3.4	4.7	3.4	3.1	NA	NA	NA	NA
Int. Exp.	NA	3.5	2.6	4.9	5.0	2.0	NA	NA	NA	NA
Pretax Inc.	NA	7.3	0.4	8.4	8.2	10.9	NA	NA	NA	NA
Eff. Tax Rate	NA	36%	NM	40%	38%	35%	NA	NA	NA	NA
Net Inc.	NA	4.7	-9.6	5.2	4.7	7.0	NA	NA	NA	NA

Balance Sheet & Other Fin. Data (Million $)

	1998	1997	1996	1995	1994	1993	1992	1991	1990	1989
Cash	NA	32.4	28.8	64.4	76.3	75.0	NA	NA	NA	NA
Curr. Assets	NA	97.5	77.8	116	118	119	NA	NA	NA	NA
Total Assets	NA	167	173	202	189	189	NA	NA	NA	NA
Curr. Liab.	NA	33.3	30.2	43.5	43.4	45.0	NA	NA	NA	NA
LT Debt	NA	69.5	69.1	70.4	69.8	69.5	NA	NA	NA	NA
Common Eqty.	NA	63.7	73.0	86.7	73.5	64.4	NA	NA	NA	NA
Total Cap.	NA	133	143	158	145	134	NA	NA	NA	NA
Cap. Exp.	NA	4.6	2.2	7.1	3.8	3.0	NA	NA	NA	NA
Cash Flow	NA	8.4	2.6	9.8	8.1	10.1	NA	NA	NA	NA
Curr. Ratio	NA	2.9	2.6	2.7	2.7	2.6	NA	NA	NA	NA
% LT Debt of Cap.	NA	52.2	48.4	44.6	48.1	51.9	NA	NA	NA	NA
% Net Inc.of Revs.	NA	4.7	NM	4.0	4.1	7.3	NA	NA	NA	NA
% Ret. on Assets	NA	2.7	NM	2.6	2.5	5.0	NA	NA	NA	NA
% Ret. on Equity	NA	6.8	NM	6.5	6.9	10.9	NA	NA	NA	NA

Data as orig. reptd.; bef. results of disc. opers. and/or spec. items. Per share data adj. for stk. divs. as of ex-div. date. Bold denotes diluted EPS (FASB 128). E-Estimated. NA-Not Available. NM-Not Meaningful. NR-Not Ranked.

Office—45 Rockefeller Plaza, Suite 912, New York, NY 10111.**Tel**—(212) 841-0610. **Chrmn**—H. E. Evans. **CEO**—D. M. J. Turner. **Pres**—R. J. Frattaroli. **COO**—F. W. Kyle.**VP, CFO & Treas**—R. M. Davies. **Dirs**—C. K. Davis, H. E. Evans, R. J. Frattaroli, S. Gold, C. A. Gonzalez, W. Kyle, P. A. Schwed, D. M. J. Turner, P. J. Welsh. **Transfer Agent & Registrar**—Harris Trust Co. of New York, NYC. **Incorporated**—in Delaware in 1991. **Empl**— 595. **S&P Analyst:** C.C.P.

Pharmaceutical Product Development 4970K

NASDAQ Symbol **PPDI**

In S&P SmallCap 600

03-OCT-98

Industry:
Health Care (Specialized Services)

Summary: This company provides a broad range of research, development and consulting services in the life, environmental and discovery sciences.

Quantitative Evaluations

Recent Price • 25¾
52 Wk Range • 29⅜-12¼

Yield • Nil
12-Mo. P/E • 39.7

Outlook (1 Lowest—5 Highest)
• **NA**

Fair Value
• **NA**

Risk
• **High**

Earn./Div. Rank
• **NR**

Technical Eval.
• **NA**

Rel. Strength Rank (1 Lowest—99 Highest)
• **96**

Insider Activity
• **Unfavorable**

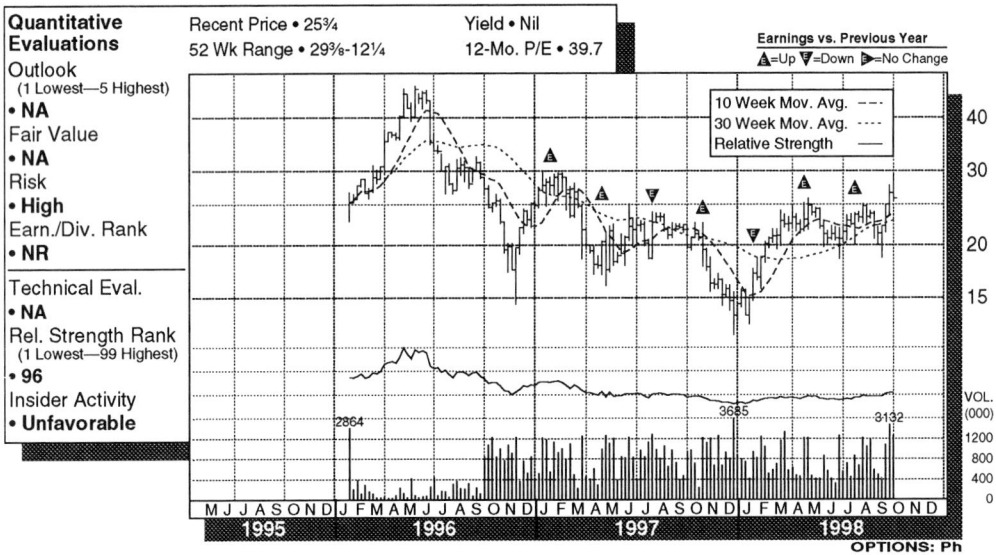

Earnings vs. Previous Year
▲=Up ▼=Down ▶=No Change

10 Week Mov. Avg. – – –
30 Week Mov. Avg. ······
Relative Strength ——

OPTIONS: Ph

Business Profile - 26-AUG-98

The company's growth strategy is to expand the depth and breadth of its services by focusing on strategic marketing initiatives with an emphasis on high volume clients, developing its services in healthcare economics and communications consulting, pursuing acquisitions to enhance discovery and development services, and expanding geographically. Growth in the life sciences segment, due to an increase in the size, scope and number of contracts in the clinical development and biostatistical business, has led to higher revenues in recent periods.

Operational Review - 26-AUG-98

Net revenues in the first half of 1998 advanced 15%, year to year, reflecting growth in the life sciences segment, due to an increase in the size, scope and number of contracts in the clinical development and biostatistical business. Total expenses were well controlled, aided by lower acquired in-process research and development costs; with sharply higher other income, pretax income rose 3.6-fold. After taxes at 39.2%, versus 40.3%, net income increased to $7,411,000 ($0.32 a share), from $1,997,000 ($0.09).

Stock Performance - 02-OCT-98

In the past 30 trading days, PPDI's shares have increased 9%, compared to a 7% fall in the S&P 500. Average trading volume for the past five days was 347,600 shares, compared with the 40-day moving average of 248,651 shares.

Key Stock Statistics

Dividend Rate/Share	Nil	Shareholders	3,400
Shs. outstg. (M)	23.3	Market cap. (B)	$0.600
Avg. daily vol. (M)	0.323	Inst. holdings	52%
Tang. Bk. Value/Share	5.25		
Beta	NA		

Value of $10,000 invested 5 years ago: NA

Fiscal Year Ending Dec. 31

	1998	1997	1996	1995	1994	1993
Revenues (Million $)						
1Q	64.85	57.67	47.08	—	—	—
2Q	70.26	60.07	49.47	—	—	—
3Q	—	58.27	49.50	—	—	—
4Q	—	59.20	51.75	10.97	—	—
Yr.	—	235.3	197.8	54.40	28.86	—
Earnings Per Share ($)						
1Q	0.20	0.15	0.10	—	—	—
2Q	0.12	-0.06	0.11	—	—	—
3Q	—	0.18	-0.56	—	—	—
4Q	—	0.15	0.18	0.10	—	—
Yr.	—	0.42	-0.17	0.35	0.26	—

Next earnings report expected: late October

Dividend Data

No cash dividends have been paid. The company intends to retain its earnings for use in its business and does not anticipate paying cash dividends in the foreseeable future.

Business Summary - 26-AUG-98

Pharmaceutical Product Development (PPDI), which has as its primary goal helping clients to reduce drug development time, provides a broad range of research, development and consulting services in the life, environmental and discovery sciences.

In the life sciences segment (80% of net revenues in 1997), the company operates through its PPD Pharmaco, Belmont Research and Intek Labs subsidiaries. PPD Pharmaco, believed to be the fourth largest contract research organization in the world, offers services designed to help clients reduce drug development time. Services include Phase I clinical testing, laboratory services, patient recruitment, Phase II-IV clinical trial management, clinical data management and biostatistical analysis, treatment Investigational New Drug applications, medical writing and regulatory services, and healthcare economics and outcome research.

Belmont provides software development and system integration services to the pharmaceutical industry, thereby creating a data link between discovery and development. Belmont also develops specialized software products to support the pharmaceutical research process, including drug discovery, clinical trials and regulatory review. Intek (acquired in November 1997) provides molecular genotyping, phenotyping and large-scale DNA purification services, as well as pharmacogenetic services for clinical trials.

The environmental sciences segment (20% of net revenues in 1997) provides services through its APBI Environmental Sciences Group subsidiary, operating under the ENVIRON trade name. ENVIRON provides a wide range of scientific, technical and strategic management consulting services that address a variety of public health and environmental issues related to the presence of chemicals in foods, drugs, medical devices, consumer products, the workplace, and the environment. Services focus on the assessment and management of chemical risk.

The discovery sciences group (established in mid-1997) operates through PPD Discovery, which focuses on the discovery segment of the research and development outsourcing market. PPD Discovery consists of SARCO, a combinational chemistry company, and the GSX System, a functional genomics platform technology for target discovery.

The life sciences segment provides services mainly to pharmaceutical and biotechnology companies, with 83% of its revenues derived from clinical services and 17% from laboratory services. ENVIRON's clients come primarily from a variety of industrial companies, who may be interested in merger, acquisition or real estate transactions or are involved in litigation. ENVIRON also provides services to investment banks, lenders, insurance firms, trade associations and state and local governments.

Per Share Data ($)

(Year Ended Dec. 31)	1997	1996	1995	1994	1993	1992	1991	1990	1989	1988
Tangible Bk. Val.	4.77	4.48	0.95	NA	NA	NA	NA	NA	NA	NA
Cash Flow	0.96	0.33	0.84	NA	NA	NA	NA	NA	NA	NA
Earnings	0.42	-0.17	0.35	NA	NA	NA	NA	NA	NA	NA
Dividends	Nil	Nil	NA	NA	NA	NA	NA	NA	NA	NA
Payout Ratio	Nil	Nil	NA	NA	NA	NA	NA	NA	NA	NA
Prices - High	30	47¾	NA	NA	NA	NA	NA	NA	NA	NA
- Low	12¼	14½	NA	NA	NA	NA	NA	NA	NA	NA
P/E Ratio - High	71	NM	NA	NA	NA	NA	NA	NA	NA	NA
- Low	29	NM	NA	NA	NA	NA	NA	NA	NA	NA

Income Statement Analysis (Million $)

	1997	1996	1995	1994	1993	1992	1991	1990	1989	1988
Revs.	235	198	54.4	NA	NA	NA	NA	NA	NA	NA
Oper. Inc.	36.3	25.4	5.6	NA	NA	NA	NA	NA	NA	NA
Depr.	12.4	10.4	1.5	NA	NA	NA	NA	NA	NA	NA
Int. Exp.	0.5	0.4	NA	NA	NA	NA	NA	NA	NA	NA
Pretax Inc.	15.7	0.6	4.3	NA	NA	NA	NA	NA	NA	NA
Eff. Tax Rate	39%	659%	NA	NA	NA	NA	NA	NA	NA	NA
Net Inc.	9.6	-3.5	4.3	NA	NA	NA	NA	NA	NA	NA

Balance Sheet & Other Fin. Data (Million $)

	1997	1996	1995	1994	1993	1992	1991	1990	1989	1988
Cash	15.9	36.0	2.3	NA	NA	NA	NA	NA	NA	NA
Curr. Assets	136	128	19.1	NA	NA	NA	NA	NA	NA	NA
Total Assets	197	181	27.5	NA	NA	NA	NA	NA	NA	NA
Curr. Liab.	66.5	61.7	15.2	NA	NA	NA	NA	NA	NA	NA
LT Debt	0.3	1.4	NA	NA	NA	NA	NA	NA	NA	NA
Common Eqty.	128	115	9.4	NA	NA	NA	NA	NA	NA	NA
Total Cap.	128	117	NA	NA	NA	NA	NA	NA	NA	NA
Cap. Exp.	13.6	11.2	NA	NA	NA	NA	NA	NA	NA	NA
Cash Flow	22.0	6.9	5.8	NA	NA	NA	NA	NA	NA	NA
Curr. Ratio	2.1	2.1	1.3	NA	NA	NA	NA	NA	NA	NA
% LT Debt of Cap.	0.3	0.1	NA	NA	NA	NA	NA	NA	NA	NA
% Net Inc.of Revs.	4.1	NM	7.9	NA	NA	NA	NA	NA	NA	NA
% Ret. on Assets	5.1	NM	17.7	NA	NA	NA	NA	NA	NA	NA
% Ret. on Equity	7.9	NM	57.8	NA	NA	NA	NA	NA	NA	NA

Data as orig. reptd.; bef. results of disc. opers. and/or spec. items. Per share data adj. for stk. divs. as of ex-div. date. Bold denotes diluted EPS (FASB 128). E-Estimated. NA-Not Available. NM-Not Meaningful. NR-Not Ranked.

Office—3151 Seventeenth Street Extension, Wilmington, NC 28412. **Tel**—(910) 251-0081. **Vice-Chrmn & CEO**—F. N. Eshelman. **Pres & COO**—T. D'Alonzo. **VP-Fin, CFO & Treas**—R. C. Howard. **Dirs**—S. Bondurant, K. L. Cramer, T. D'Alonzo, F. N. Eshelman, F. Frank, F. E. Loy, E. Mario, J. A. McNeill, Jr. **Transfer Agent & Registrar**—Wachovia Bank of North Carolina, Winston-Salem. **Incorporated**—in North Carolina in 1989. **Empl**— 2,470. **S&P Analyst:** Stephen R. Biggar

Philadelphia Suburban   1818

NYSE Symbol **PSC**

In S&P SmallCap 600

03-OCT-98

Industry:
Water Utilities

Summary: This company supplies water to about 950,000 residents in suburban Philadelphia.

Quantitative Evaluations

Outlook
(1 Lowest—5 Highest)
• **1⁻**

Fair Value
• **20⅛**

Risk
• **Low**

Earn./Div. Rank
• **B+**

Technical Eval.
• **Bullish** since 8/97

Rel. Strength Rank
(1 Lowest—99 Highest)
• **92**

Insider Activity
• **NA**

Recent Price • 25⅞   Yield • 2.6%
52 Wk Range • 28⅛-15⅛   12-Mo. P/E • 26.7

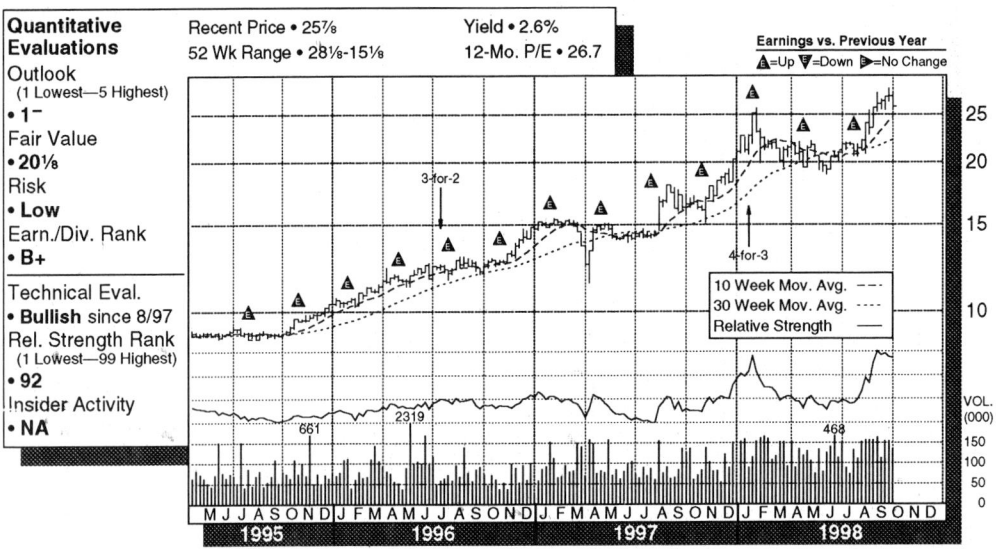

Earnings vs. Previous Year
▲=Up ▼=Down ▶=No Change

10 Week Mov. Avg. ---
30 Week Mov. Avg. ······
Relative Strength ——

Business Profile - 10-JUN-98

This water utility holding company has grown largely through acquisitions. To date in 1998, Philadelphia Suburban (PSC) has acquired two new water systems, signed two water sales agreements, and agreed to acquire a water company. The company's latest acquisition was announced in June 1998, when PSC agreed to purchase Flying Hills Water Co. for approximately $825,000 in common stock. Flying Hills serves 4,500 residents in Cumru Township, Berks County. This purchase would mark the company's initial entry into Berks County. Management is positive about the growth opportunities in Berks County and has already entered discussions that would allow PSC to provide water service in other parts of the county.

Operational Review - 10-JUN-98

Revenues in the first quarter of 1998 rose 10%, year to year, due primarily to the West Chester acquisition. Margins widened, reflecting cost containment efforts, a lower number of main breaks from the warm winter and decreased depreciation charges; operating income increased 19%. Following only a 5.8% rise in interest expense, net income surged 28%, to $5,755,000 ($0.21 per share, after preferred dividends and on 5.1% more shares), from $4,509,000 ($0.17).

Stock Performance - 02-OCT-98

In the past 30 trading days, PSC's shares have increased 10%, compared to a 7% fall in the S&P 500. Average trading volume for the past five days was 26,680 shares, compared with the 40-day moving average of 39,613 shares.

Key Stock Statistics

Dividend Rate/Share	0.68	Shareholders	13,800
Shs. outstg. (M)	27.6	Market cap. (B)	$0.715
Avg. daily vol. (M)	0.032	Inst. holdings	18%
Tang. Bk. Value/Share	8.07		
Beta	-0.08		

Value of $10,000 invested 5 years ago: $ 41,417

Fiscal Year Ending Dec. 31

	1998	1997	1996	1995	1994	1993
Revenues (Million $)						
1Q	34.28	31.02	29.29	25.71	24.85	22.73
2Q	37.34	33.32	30.68	28.83	26.73	25.05
3Q	—	36.75	30.83	32.36	28.85	27.95
4Q	—	35.08	31.70	30.15	28.21	25.52
Yr.	—	136.2	122.5	117.0	108.6	101.2
Earnings Per Share ($)						
1Q	**0.21**	0.17	0.16	0.14	0.13	0.13
2Q	**0.27**	0.22	0.21	0.20	0.17	0.17
3Q	—	0.28	0.23	0.24	0.21	0.10
4Q	—	0.21	0.18	0.17	0.16	0.15
Yr.	—	**0.88**	**0.78**	0.75	0.68	0.64

Next earnings report expected: early November

Dividend Data (Dividends have been paid since 1939.)

Amount ($)	Date Decl.	Ex-Div. Date	Stock of Record	Payment Date
4-for-3	Dec. 02	Jan. 13	Dec. 15	Jan. 12 '98
0.163	Dec. 02	Feb. 11	Feb. 13	Mar. 01 '98
0.163	Apr. 29	May. 11	May. 13	Jun. 01 '98
0.170	Aug. 04	Aug. 13	Aug. 17	Sep. 01 '98

A Division of The McGraw-Hill Companies

Business Summary - 10-JUN-98

The major subsidiary of Philadelphia Suburban Corp. is Philadelphia Suburban Water Co. (PSW), which distributes more than 100 million gallons of water every day to approximately 950,000 consumers in the Delaware Valley. There are fewer than two dozen publicly traded water utility companies, and PSC is now the third largest, delivering nearly 37.9 million gallons of water in 1997.

Contributions to water revenues by customer class in recent years were:

	1997	1996	1995	1994
Residential	67%	66%	67%	65%
Commercial	21%	22%	21%	22%
Industrial	4%	4%	4%	5%
Fire protection	6%	7%	6%	7%
Other	1%	1%	2%	1%

PSC completed eight acquisitions during 1996, adding 17,660 customers (an increase of 7.4%) in the service territory that includes Montgomery, Delaware, Chester, and Bucks counties. In 1997 the company acquired three water systems, one wastewater system and started operating a municipal water system in Horsham Township under a five year contract. PSW derives most of its water from the Schuylkill and Delaware Rivers and their tributaries, along with the Upper Merion Reservoir. Supplemental water comes from wells and interconnections with other water suppliers. To date in 1998, the company has acquired two new water systems, signed two water sales agreements, and agreed to acquire a water company.

In March 1998, PSC entered into a 25-year water sale agreement with Warwick Township Water and Sewer Authority for the sale of water to supplement its water supply. The following month, the company acquired the water system assets of Brandywine Hospital complex for $218 million. In June 1998, PSC agreed to acquire Flying Hills Water Co. in a purchase transaction for approximately 42,000 shares of the company's common stock. The latest purchase marks the company's initial entry into Berks County, PA.

Per Share Data ($)

(Year Ended Dec. 31)	1997	1996	1995	1994	1993	1992	1991	1990	1989	1988
Tangible Bk. Val.	8.26	7.84	7.37	6.12	5.95	5.44	5.33	6.53	6.23	6.00
Earnings	0.88	0.78	0.75	0.68	0.64	0.61	0.65	0.64	0.53	0.58
Dividends	0.62	0.59	0.57	0.55	0.54	0.52	0.50	0.50	0.47	0.47
Payout Ratio	71%	76%	76%	81%	84%	85%	78%	79%	90%	80%
Prices - High	22⅛	14⅞	10¾	9⅞	10⅜	8⅜	8¼	7½	7¼	8½
- Low	11½	10¼	8¾	8⅝	7⅞	6⅞	5⅞	5¼	6⅜	6⅛
P/E Ratio - High	25	19	14	15	16	14	13	12	14	14
- Low	13	13	12	13	12	11	9	8	12	10

Income Statement Analysis (Million $)

	1997	1996	1995	1994	1993	1992	1991	1990	1989	1988
Revs.	136	123	117	109	101	93.0	89.0	82.0	134	126
Depr.	14.6	13.3	11.6	10.5	9.9	8.6	7.6	7.0	11.3	10.2
Maint.	NA	NA	NA	NA	NA	NA	NA	NA	NA	NA
Fxd. Chgs. Cov.	3.1	3.1	3.0	3.0	2.7	2.1	2.0	1.3	1.9	2.1
Constr. Credits	0.5	0.3	0.3	0.1	0.8	0.3	1.2	NA	NA	NA
Eff. Tax Rate	41%	41%	42%	43%	43%	43%	41%	38%	39%	39%
Net Inc.	23.2	20.7	18.0	15.6	13.8	10.6	10.2	9.7	7.8	8.5

Balance Sheet & Other Fin. Data (Million $)

	1997	1996	1995	1994	1993	1992	1991	1990	1989	1988
Gross Prop.	656	613	529	463	433	402	371	350	332	299
Cap. Exp.	39.0	31.4	33.0	28.0	29.3	30.8	22.3	30.8	33.8	25.0
Net Prop.	534	503	437	386	366	346	321	307	288	262
Capitalization:										
LT Debt	232	218	175	152	145	154	168	176	163	138
% LT Debt	54	54	52	50	50	57	64	67	66	63
Pfd.	3.2	7.4	6.0	7.1	10.0	10.0	10.0	Nil	Nil	Nil
% Pfd.	0.80	1.90	1.80	2.30	3.40	3.70	3.80	Nil	Nil	Nil
Common	192	177	157	144	136	107	85.6	85.5	85.9	81.4
% Common	45	44	46	48	47	40	33	33	35	37
Total Cap.	535	502	409	371	382	291	283	279	266	234
% Oper. Ratio	69.9	59.8	60.6	73.1	73.4	71.8	72.3	88.2	83.9	83.5
% Earn. on Net Prop.	10.9	10.5	11.2	7.8	7.6	7.9	7.8	7.4	7.8	8.2
% Return On Revs.	17.0	16.1	15.4	14.4	13.7	11.4	11.5	11.8	5.8	6.8
% Return On Invest. Capital	11.0	12.5	11.8	10.9	12.4	12.0	11.3	8.0	8.6	9.4
% Return On Com. Equity	12.5	11.8	12.0	11.2	11.4	11.0	11.9	4.8	9.3	11.0

Data as orig. reptd.; bef. results of disc opers. and/or spec. items. Per share data adj. for stk. divs. as of ex-div. date. Bold denotes diluted EPS (FASB 128). E-Estimated. NA-Not Available. NM-Not Meaningful. NR-Not Ranked.

Office—762 Lancaster Ave., Bryn Mawr, PA 19010-3489. **Tel**—(610) 527-8000. **Website**—http://www.suburbanwater.com **Chrmn, Pres & CEO**—N. DeBenedictis. **SVP-Fin & Treas**—Michael P. Graham (610-645-1087). **Secy**—P. M. Mycek. **Investor Contact**—Idalia Rodriguez (610-645-1084). **Dirs**—J. H. Austin, Jr., J. W. Boyer, Jr., M. C. Carroll, N. DeBenedictis, G. F. DiBona, Jr., R. H. Glanton, J. F. McCaughan, R. L. Smoot, H. J. Wilson. **Transfer Agent & Registrar**—ChaseMellon Shareholder Services, Ridgefield Park, NJ. **Incorporated**—in Pennsylvania in 1968. **Empl**— 531. **S&P Analyst:** J. Robert Cho

03-OCT-98

Industry:
Textiles (Apparel)

Summary: This company produces a broad range of brandname apparel and shoes, some of which it sells through more than 787 outlets.

Quantitative Evaluations

Outlook
(1 Lowest—5 Highest)
• **4**

Fair Value
• **14¼**

Risk
• **Average**

Earn./Div. Rank
• **B+**

Technical Eval.
• **Bearish** since 8/98

Rel. Strength Rank
(1 Lowest—99 Highest)
• **24**

Insider Activity
• **Neutral**

Recent Price • 8⅞
52 Wk Range • 15⅝-8⅞

Yield • 1.7%
12-Mo. P/E • NM

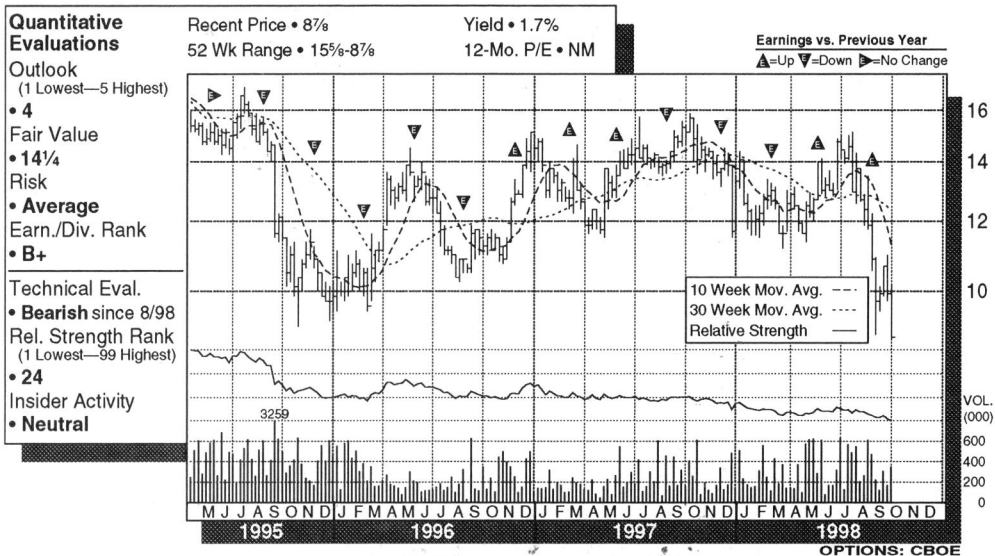

Earnings vs. Previous Year
▲=Up ▼=Down ►=No Change

10 Week Mov. Avg. — - -
30 Week Mov. Avg. - - - - -
Relative Strength ————

VOL.
(000)

OPTIONS: CBOE

Business Profile - 18-FEB-98

In July 1997, Phillips-Van Heusen announced a new strategy to build its core brands. The company planned to close about 150 additional outlet stores, reposition the Gant brand in the U.S. to be consistent with its highly successful positioning in Europe and Asia, exit the sweater manufacturing business, and restructure warehousing and distribution facilities in order to reduce costs and improve efficiencies. The retail outlet store closings would continue the elimination of the weakest and worst trending stores. In February 1998, the company entered into a license agreement with Donna Karen International (DKNY) to produce and distribute a DKNY men's dress shirt collection.

Operational Review - 18-FEB-98

Net sales in the 39 weeks ended November 2, 1997, rose 3.5%, year to year, as increases in wholesale branded businesses, particularly Dress Shirts and Izod, outweighed a planned decrease in retail sales resulting from the closing of unproductive outlet stores. Margins narrowed slightly, due to brand investment in design for footwear products, and increased competition for golf apparel; operating income fell 44%. After a pretax restructuring charge of $41,150,000, despite tax credits of $15,197,000, versus taxes of $3,957,000, a net loss of $23,273,000 ($0.86 a share) contrasted with net income of $10,607,000 ($0.39).

Stock Performance - 02-OCT-98

In the past 30 trading days, PVH's shares have declined 25%, compared to a 7% fall in the S&P 500. Average trading volume for the past five days was 69,600 shares, compared with the 40-day moving average of 65,392 shares.

Key Stock Statistics

Dividend Rate/Share	0.15	Shareholders	1,800
Shs. outstg. (M)	27.2	Market cap. (B)	$0.242
Avg. daily vol. (M)	0.048	Inst. holdings	56%
Tang. Bk. Value/Share	3.67		
Beta	0.98		

Value of $10,000 invested 5 years ago: $ 3,269

Fiscal Year Ending Jan. 31

	1999	1998	1997	1996	1995	1994
Revenues (Million $)						
1Q	295.8	285.9	273.7	283.0	239.0	221.9
2Q	306.4	313.5	313.8	349.5	283.8	264.0
3Q	—	413.6	391.3	448.0	379.4	357.4
4Q	—	337.0	380.9	383.6	353.4	309.1
Yr.	—	1,350	1,360	1,464	1,255	1,152
Earnings Per Share ($)						
1Q	-0.16	-0.17	-0.24	-0.13	-0.13	-0.08
2Q	0.10	-1.23	0.08	0.15	0.21	0.29
3Q	—	0.53	0.56	-0.16	0.66	0.91
4Q	—	-1.59	0.29	0.15	0.37	0.48
Yr.	—	-2.46	0.69	0.01	1.11	1.15

Next earnings report expected: mid November

Dividend Data (Dividends have been paid since 1970.)

Amount ($)	Date Decl.	Ex-Div. Date	Stock of Record	Payment Date
0.038	Sep. 23	Nov. 14	Nov. 18	Dec. 04 '97
0.038	Mar. 05	Mar. 12	Mar. 16	Mar. 31 '98
0.038	Apr. 23	Jun. 03	Jun. 05	Jun. 22 '98
0.038	Jul. 24	Aug. 26	Aug. 28	Sep. 11 '98

A Division of The McGraw-Hill Companies

Business Summary - 18-FEB-98

Phillips-Van Heusen (PVH) is a maker of well-known labels such as Van Heusen, Geoffrey Beene, Gant and Izod apparel and Bass footwear. Several of the company's brands are best-sellers in the U.S.: Van Heusen in men's dress shirts, Geoffrey Beene in men's designer dress shirts, and Izod in men's sweaters. However, despite the popularity of the brands, recent operations of many of outlet stores were unprofitable. In July 1997, the company continued to realign its product distribution operations by announcing the planned closings of an additional 150 retail outlet stores.

Although retail operations have led to significant sales growth, the company believes that many of its stores have been hurt by an overexpansion into uncompetitive outlet malls, a downturn in the apparel and footwear markets that worsened in 1995, and added expenses resulting from intense promotional activity. A central component of the restructuring plan initiated in FY 96 (Jan.) was the closing of 300 less profitable stores, including 100 footwear stores. New stores will continue to be opened, but on a more selective basis. As of early February 1997, the retail group marketed PVH lines through approximately 787 factory outlet stores located in manufacturer's outlet centers. Each store sells merchandise under one of five PVH labels: Van Heusen, Geoffrey Beene, Izod, Bass and Gant.

PVH's wholesale operations sell products to major department, specialty and independent retailers, chain stores and catalog merchants. The company also makes private label shirts, sweaters and golf apparel. PVH's restructuring program includes elimination of certain unprofitable private label wholesale businesses, and a greater emphasis on wholesale growth.

The company has been adapting its product lines to a growing U.S. sportswear market and a trend toward more casual work attire. PVH attributed a decrease in apparel sales in FY 97 to $1.0 billion, from $1.1 billion in FY 96, to the absence of clearance sales associated with the February 1996 acquisitions of the Izod and Gant sportswear labels. Casual clothing has also been added to the Van Heusen and Geoffrey Beene lines. The company is counting on the generally wider gross margins (revenues minus the cost of goods sold) for sportswear to help in improving overall company profits.

PVH has also closed three manufacturing facilities as part of its strategic restructuring. It plans to combine its wholesale and retail divisions into eight discrete operating units, each with total marketing and profit responsibility for the brand it manages.

Per Share Data ($)

(Year Ended Jan. 31)	1998	1997	1996	1995	1994	1993	1992	1991	1990	1989
Tangible Bk. Val.	3.82	6.28	5.76	9.69	8.64	7.42	3.50	2.32	2.35	1.61
Cash Flow	-1.52	1.78	1.27	2.00	2.30	2.01	1.76	1.47	1.22	1.02
Earnings	-2.46	0.69	0.01	1.11	1.60	1.42	1.15	0.95	0.84	0.68
Dividends	0.15	0.15	0.15	0.15	0.15	0.15	0.14	0.14	0.14	0.14
Payout Ratio	NM	22%	NM	14%	9%	11%	12%	14%	16%	20%
Cal. Yrs.	1997	1996	1995	1994	1993	1992	1991	1990	1989	1988
Prices - High	15⁷/₈	15¹/₈	18	39	37¹/₂	29¹/₄	21	11⁵/₈	12¹/₂	7¹/₈
- Low	11¹/₂	9¹/₂	9¹/₈	14	25³/₄	16¹/₂	7	5¹/₄	6⁷/₈	4⁵/₈
P/E Ratio - High	NM	22	NM	35	23	21	18	12	15	10
- Low	NM	14	NM	13	16	12	6	5	8	7

Income Statement Analysis (Million $)

	1998	1997	1996	1995	1994	1993	1992	1991	1990	1989
Revs.	1,350	1,360	1,464	1,255	1,152	1,043	904	806	733	641
Oper. Inc.	24.8	77.2	81.3	81.0	99	88.1	74.1	66.0	59.6	51.9
Depr.	25.3	29.4	33.7	24.3	19.1	15.0	12.1	9.8	7.3	6.2
Int. Exp.	20.7	23.2	23.2	12.8	16.7	16.8	17.8	20.4	19.1	17.3
Pretax Inc.	-107	24.6	-2.6	36.9	63.6	54.5	44.0	35.2	32.7	27.4
Eff. Tax Rate	NM	25%	NM	19%	32%	31%	29%	25%	26%	24%
Net Inc.	-66.6	18.5	0.3	30.0	43.3	37.9	31.1	26.4	24.2	20.8

Balance Sheet & Other Fin. Data (Million $)

	1998	1997	1996	1995	1994	1993	1992	1991	1990	1989
Cash	11.7	11.6	17.5	80.5	68.1	77.1	7.0	5.8	6.6	9.9
Curr. Assets	385	363	445	430	419	411	303	285	267	265
Total Assets	660	657	749	596	555	517	399	377	333	323
Curr. Liab.	274	122	183	114	109	115	105	90.7	84.2	88.2
LT Debt	100	189	230	170	170	170	121	140	119	116
Common Eqty.	220	290	275	275	247	211	85.0	62.0	46.0	32.0
Total Cap.	320	480	505	445	417	382	280	275	238	222
Cap. Exp.	17.9	22.6	39.8	53.1	47.9	36.8	21.1	22.2	12.8	13.7
Cash Flow	-41.3	48.0	34.0	54.3	62.4	50.8	35.1	28.0	23.3	18.9
Curr. Ratio	1.4	3.0	2.4	3.8	3.8	3.6	2.9	3.1	3.2	3.0
% LT Debt of Cap.	31.2	39.5	45.5	38.1	40.8	44.6	43.4	50.9	50.0	52.5
% Net Inc.of Revs.	NM	1.4	Nil	2.4	3.8	3.6	3.4	3.3	3.3	3.2
% Ret. on Assets	NM	2.6	Nil	5.2	8.0	7.1	8.0	7.4	7.4	6.5
% Ret. on Equity	NM	6.6	Nil	11.5	18.7	21.7	30.9	33.4	40.7	46.0

Data as orig. reptd.; bef. results of disc. opers. and/or spec. items. Per share data adj. for stk. divs. as of ex-div. date. Bold denotes diluted EPS (FASB 128). E-Estimated. NA-Not Available. NM-Not Meaningful. NR-Not Ranked.

Office—1290 Ave. of the Americas, New York, NY 10104. **Tel**—(212) 541-5200. **Chrmn, Pres & CEO**—B. J. Klatsky. **EVP, CFO & Investor Contact**—I. W. Winter. **Dirs**— E. H. Cohen, J. B. Fuller, J. H. Goldberg, M. Grosman, D. F. Hightower, B. J. Klatsky, M. E. Lagomasino, H. N. S. Lee, B. Maggin, S. M. Rhone, P. J. Solomon, M. Weber, I. W. Winter. **Transfer Agent & Registrar**—Bank of New York, NYC. **Incorporated**—in New York in 1919; reincorporated in Delaware in 1976. **Empl**— 9,550. **S&P Analyst**: D.R.J.

Photronics, Inc. 4982

Nasdaq Symbol **PLAB**

In S&P SmallCap 600

03-OCT-98

Industry:
Equipment (Semiconductor)

Summary: PLAB is a leading manufacturer of high-precision photomasks, which contain microscopic images of electronic circuits and are used in the fabrication of semiconductors.

S&P Opinion: Accumulate (★★★★)	Recent Price • 12¾	Yield • Nil
	52 Wk Range • 37⅞-12	12-Mo. P/E • 12.8

Quantitative Evaluations

Outlook
(1 Lowest—5 Highest)
• **5**

Fair Value
• **21⅜**

Risk
• **High**

Earn./Div. Rank
• **B+**

Technical Eval.
• **Bearish** since 7/98

Rel. Strength Rank
(1 Lowest—99 Highest)
• **20**

Insider Activity
• **NA**

Earnings vs. Previous Year
▲=Up ▼=Down ▶=No Change

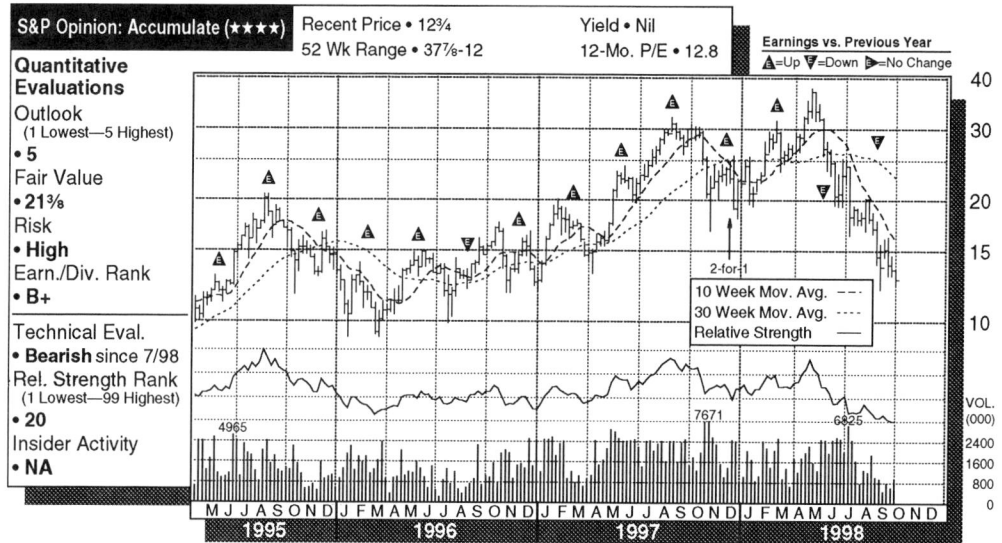

10 Week Mov. Avg. ---
30 Week Mov. Avg. ·····
Relative Strength ——

Overview - 25-AUG-98

We expect sales to rise more than 10% in FY 99 (Oct.), reflecting solid photomask demand, and strong international growth. Photronics' fortunes are tied to growth and acceleration of integrated circuit (IC) design activity. With semiconductor manufacturers gravitating toward production of devices with linewidths of 0.25 micron and below, we expect continued strong demand for high-end photomasks that enable this technology. In the near term, however, the slowdown in the overall semiconductor market and the resultant disruption to PLAB's customers is likely to curtail design activity and depress unit volumes and pricing at the low end of the market. As a result, margins will come under pressure. However, we believe Photronics has made the necessary investments in infrastructure to support strong long-term growth. Overall, we expect EPS to improve to $1.17 in FY 99, from our projection of $1.03 in FY 98 (excluding non-recurring charges).

Valuation - 25-AUG-98

Despite weak semiconductor industry conditions, we are maintaining our accumulate recommendation on the shares. In the intermediate and long term, we expect chip design activity, and therefore photomask demand, to remain strong as manufacturers accelerate semiconductor technology. In the near term, however, the protracted slowdown in the chip industry has caused disruption at many of PLAB's customers, resulting in uncertainty for photomask unit volume sales. This adds a degree of risk to the company's operating results. However, given the company's leading position in an attractive niche market, we believe the shares are attractively valued for aggressive investors, at 14X our $1.17 FY 99 (Oct.) EPS estimate.

Key Stock Statistics

S&P EPS Est. 1998	1.03	Tang. Bk. Value/Share	7.38
P/E on S&P Est. 1998	12.4	Beta	2.17
S&P EPS Est. 1999	1.17	Shareholders	7,500
Dividend Rate/Share	Nil	Market cap. (B)	$0.311
Shs. outstg. (M)	24.4	Inst. holdings	49%
Avg. daily vol. (M)	0.140		

Value of $10,000 invested 5 years ago: $ 34,772

Fiscal Year Ending Oct. 31

	1998	1997	1996	1995	1994	1993
Revenues (Million $)						
1Q	50.93	40.03	34.67	26.18	18.86	11.28
2Q	61.31	49.03	40.51	30.04	18.65	10.64
3Q	57.68	53.08	42.68	32.85	21.31	11.67
4Q	—	55.31	42.21	36.23	21.89	14.78
Yr.	—	197.4	160.1	125.3	80.70	48.36
Earnings Per Share ($)						
1Q	**0.25**	0.22	0.20	0.16	0.10	0.07
2Q	**0.22**	0.25	0.22	0.18	0.11	0.06
3Q	**0.24**	0.28	0.23	0.27	0.14	0.07
4Q	—	0.29	0.23	0.21	0.16	0.09
Yr.	—	1.03	0.87	0.83	0.51	0.29

Next earnings report expected: mid December

Dividend Data

Amount ($)	Date Decl.	Ex-Div. Date	Stock of Record	Payment Date
2-for-1	Sep. 15	Dec. 02	Nov. 17	Dec. 01 '97

Business Summary - 25-AUG-98

As a leading manufacturer of photomasks used in the fabrication of semiconductors, Photronics provides critical enabling technology necessary to advance the information age. In the struggle to make chips smaller, cheaper and faster, semiconductor makers rely heavily on PLAB's ability to manufacture high-end photomasks in a timely and accurate manner.

Photomasks are high-precision photographic quartz plates containing microscopic images of electronic circuits. This product is used as a master to transfer circuit patterns onto semiconductor wafers during the fabrication of integrated circuits and, to a lesser extent, other types of electrical components, such as diodes and transistors. The customer base for photomasks consists primarily of semiconductor manufacturers. PLAB believes that it is the largest independent photomask maker in the U.S.

PLAB's photomasks are made in accordance with circuit designs provided by its customers. Photronics uses electron-beam and laser-based systems in the manufacture of its photomasks, as this technique reduces the number of steps required to manufacture a photomask and makes it possible to obtain finer line resolution, tighter overlay and larger die size for the larger and more complex circuits currently being designed. PLAB

also uses the optical method, which is less precise but also less expensive, in competitive pricing situations.

As a company, Photronics is often grouped together with other well known semiconductor capital equipment companies, such as Applied Materials and Lam Research. The dynamics of the photomask market, however, are much different from those of the wafer processing equipment market. Demand for photomasks is largely dependent on the increasing complexity and accelerated design activity of semiconductors, not manufacturing capacity expansion or semiconductor sales volume. As such, the photomask market is typically insulated from the boom and bust cycles of the semiconductor market.

While advanced photomasks generally have an indefinite life span and are not customarily consumed in the semiconductor fabrication process, the demand for them has increased with the growth in the number of chip designs. For example, the manufacture of a 16 Mb DRAM requires 16 photomasks. As chip-makers migrate toward next generation 64 Mb devices, this figure increases sharply, to 23.

PLAB also manufactures semiconductor wafer plasma etching systems and sells refurbished semiconductor manufacturing equipment and replacement parts and field service for such equipment on a third-party basis. These activities accounted for a small portion of total sales during FY 97.

Per Share Data ($)

(Year Ended Oct. 31)	1997	1996	1995	1994	1993	1992	1991	1990	1989	1988
Tangible Bk. Val.	7.65	6.21	5.30	3.80	2.96	2.77	2.50	1.74	0.92	0.83
Cash Flow	1.82	1.41	1.22	0.93	0.63	0.60	0.71	0.62	0.35	0.06
Earnings	1.03	0.87	0.83	0.50	0.29	0.27	0.45	0.35	0.09	-0.18
Dividends	Nil	Nil	Nil	Nil	Nil	Nil	Nil	Nil	Nil	Nil
Payout Ratio	Nil	Nil	Nil	Nil	Nil	Nil	Nil	Nil	Nil	Nil
Prices - High	32⅛	17⅝	20⅝	10	5⅝	5⅜	5⅜	6	2¹¹/₁₆	1³/₁₆
- Low	13⅛	9⅛	8⅞	4⅞	3¼	2½	2⁷/₁₆	1⅝	⁵/₁₆	⁷/₁₆
P/E Ratio - High	31	20	25	20	19	20	13	12	23	NM
- Low	13	10	11	10	11	9	6	5	4	NM

Income Statement Analysis (Million $)

	1997	1996	1995	1994	1993	1992	1991	1990	1989	1988
Revs.	197	160	126	80.7	48.4	41.3	42.2	37.4	27.7	18.8
Oper. Inc.	60.2	44.4	32.3	22.9	12.6	11.1	12.7	9.2	4.1	-0.3
Depr.	19.8	12.1	8.7	8.7	5.6	5.2	4.0	3.1	2.5	2.3
Int. Exp.	2.2	0.2	0.1	0.1	0.1	0.1	0.2	0.6	0.8	0.4
Pretax Inc.	41.4	33.9	29.8	15.3	7.4	6.7	10.9	6.3	1.3	-2.7
Eff. Tax Rate	38%	38%	38%	34%	34%	35%	38%	37%	32%	NM
Net Inc.	25.6	21.0	18.6	10.1	4.9	4.4	6.8	4.0	0.9	-1.7

Balance Sheet & Other Fin. Data (Million $)

	1997	1996	1995	1994	1993	1992	1991	1990	1989	1988
Cash	57.8	18.8	51.8	27.6	11.7	16.7	19.9	9.1	3.0	1.5
Curr. Assets	139	65.6	79.4	42.5	25.6	24.7	27.9	16.8	9.2	7.3
Total Assets	365	212	174	98.3	74.4	52.0	47.9	32.6	21.7	19.4
Curr. Liab.	57.5	44.0	29.8	10.1	8.0	3.9	4.4	5.7	5.4	4.2
LT Debt	106	2.0	1.8	0.5	1.1	1.7	1.8	2.5	7.0	7.0
Common Eqty.	186	156	134	80.4	62.6	44.0	39.4	22.5	8.8	8.0
Total Cap.	303	158	144	88.0	66.2	47.9	43.3	26.8	16.2	15.1
Cap. Exp.	96.3	55.8	35.5	4.1	21.9	11.7	6.4	6.4	3.0	4.9
Cash Flow	45.5	33.1	27.3	18.7	10.5	9.5	10.8	7.1	3.4	0.5
Curr. Ratio	2.4	1.5	2.7	4.2	3.2	6.3	6.4	3.0	1.7	1.7
% LT Debt of Cap.	35.7	1.3	1.3	0.6	1.6	3.5	4.1	9.2	43.1	46.3
% Net Inc.of Revs.	13.0	13.1	14.8	12.5	10.1	10.6	16.1	10.6	3.1	NM
% Ret. on Assets	8.9	10.8	13.7	11.6	7.1	8.7	15.5	12.8	4.2	NM
% Ret. on Equity	15.0	14.5	17.4	14.0	8.5	10.4	20.3	23.0	10.3	NM

Data as orig. reptd.; bef. results of disc. opers. and/or spec. items. Per share data adj. for stk. divs. as of ex-div. date. Bold denotes diluted EPS (FASB 128). E-Estimated. NA-Not Available. NM-Not Meaningful. NR-Not Ranked.

Organized—in Connecticut in 1969. **Office**—15 Secor Rd., P.O. Box 5226, Brookfield, CT 06804. **Tel**—(203) 775-9000. **Website**—http:// www.photronics.com **Chrmn**—C. S. Macricostas. **Pres & CEO**—M. J. Yomazzo. **CFO**—R. Bollo. **Investor Contact**—Michael McCarthy (E-mail: mccarthy@brk.photronics.com). **Secy**—J. P. Moonan. **Dirs**—W. M. Flederowicz, J. A. Fiorita, Jr., C. S. Macricostas, Y. Tagawa, M. J. Yomazzo. **Transfer Agent & Registrar**—Registrar & Transfer Company, Cranford, NJ. **Empl**— 900. **S&P Analyst**: B. McGovern

PhyCor, Inc.

4984C

Nasdaq Symbol **PHYC**

In S&P SmallCap 600

03-OCT-98

Industry:
Health Care (Managed Care)

Summary: PhyCor acquires and operates multi-specialty medical clinics and develops and manages independent practice associations.

S&P Opinion: Hold (★★★)	Recent Price • 5	Yield • Nil
	52 Wk Range • 33¼-4½	12-Mo. P/E • NM

Quantitative Evaluations

Outlook
(1 Lowest—5 Highest)
• **NA**

Fair Value
• **NA**

Risk
• **High**

Earn./Div. Rank
• **NR**

Technical Eval.
• **Bearish** since 9/97

Rel. Strength Rank
(1 Lowest—99 Highest)
• **5**

Insider Activity
• **Neutral**

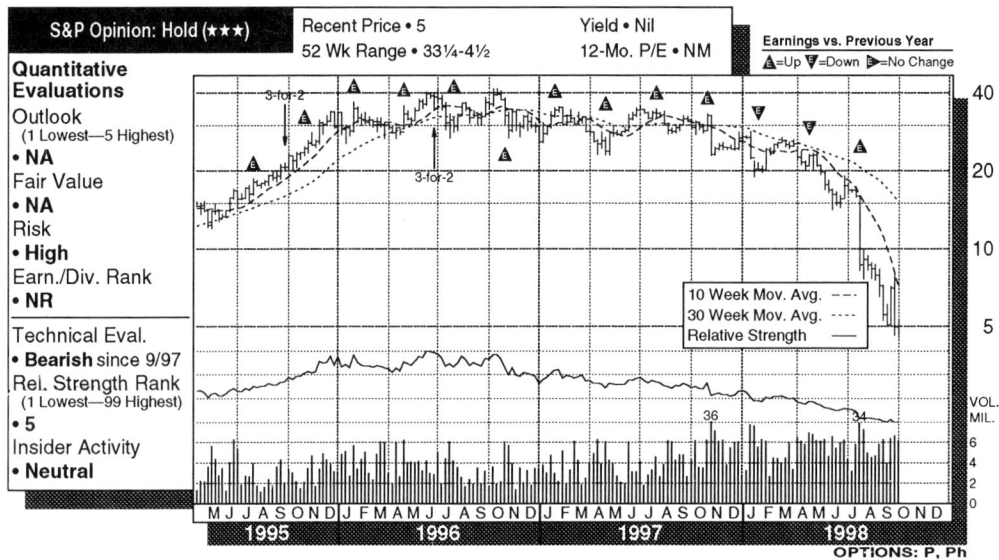

Earnings vs. Previous Year
▲=Up ▼=Down ▶=No Change

10 Week Mov. Avg. ----
30 Week Mov. Avg. ·····
Relative Strength —

OPTIONS: P, Ph

Overview - 19-AUG-98

PhyCor should generate 1998 revenues of about $1.4 billion, up from $1.1 billion in 1997, reflecting clinic acquisitions, market share gains, and increased patient volume at existing sites. We look for same-store revenue growth to settle at about 11% in 1998, although these trends have softened for several quarters, and any further erosion would trigger some additional downward revisions to our earnings assumptions. PhyCor's operating margins should be enhanced by the spreading fixed costs over a broader facility base, together with increased penetration in the higher margin managed care and IPA business lines. However, EPS comparisons will be hurt by the accelerated amortization of acquired goodwill from 40 years to 25 years. Excluding special charges, we look for 1998 operating EPS of $0.85, and have a 1999 EPS target of $1.20.

Valuation - 19-AUG-98

We maintain an accumulate opinion on this volatile stock, but would recommend PHYC only for aggressive and risk tolerant accounts. We view the company as the premier investment in the physician practice management (PPM) industry, but the stock continues to suffer a spillover effect from stuggles evident at other industry participants, most notably the Chapter 11 bankruptcy filing by FPA Medical Corp. and ongoing difficulties at MedPartners Inc. We have some concerns that physicians will be less likely to affiliate with one of the large PPMs in the future, in light of these operational problems, and a weakened PHYC share price makes clinic acquisitions more difficult and expensive. However, the company continues to report generally strong operating earnings, and the stock is compelling at a recent level of only 9X our 1999 EPS estimate, and about 0.5X projected 1998 revenues.

Key Stock Statistics

S&P EPS Est. 1998	0.51	Tang. Bk. Value/Share	NM
P/E on S&P Est. 1998	9.9	Beta	1.66
S&P EPS Est. 1999	1.20	Shareholders	13,700
Dividend Rate/Share	Nil	Market cap. (B)	$0.394
Shs. outstg. (M)	78.2	Inst. holdings	55%
Avg. daily vol. (M)	1.925		

Value of $10,000 invested 5 years ago: $ 10,369

Fiscal Year Ending Dec. 31

	1998	1997	1996	1995	1994	1993
Revenues (Million $)						
1Q	322.7	250.7	162.5	92.76	49.77	39.90
2Q	371.4	267.4	176.6	99.2	50.46	39.62
3Q	—	284.3	196.4	114.0	63.18	41.81
4Q	—	317.3	230.8	135.7	79.08	46.00
Yr.	—	1,120	766.3	441.6	242.5	167.4
Earnings Per Share ($)						
1Q	-0.12	0.19	0.13	0.09	0.08	0.06
2Q	0.22	0.20	0.11	0.00	0.09	0.00
3Q	—	0.22	0.15	0.11	0.07	0.07
4Q	—	-0.59	0.18	0.12	0.08	0.08
Yr.	—	0.05	0.60	0.41	0.32	0.28

Next earnings report expected: late October

Dividend Data

No cash dividends have been paid.

A Division of The **McGraw·Hill** Companies

Business Summary - 19-AUG-98

PhyCor Inc. has capitalized on the evolving health care delivery system by leading the emerging physician practice management (PPM) industry, where it acquires and operate multi-specialty medical clinics and develops independent practice associations (IPAs). A plan to acquire rival MedPartners Inc., creating the largest U.S. manager of physician practices, was terminated in January 1998.

By organizing previously unaffiliated physicians into professionally managed networks, PhyCor allows these physicians to focus on the provision of health care services rather than on administrative duties, and these large networks have significant bargaining power when negotiating for large contracts with managed care entities. PHYC currently operates 55 clinics with 3,863 physicians in 28 states, and manages IPAs with over 19,000 physicians in 28 markets. Slightly over 50% of its affiliated doctors are primary care providers.

A multi-specialty clinic provides a wide range of primary and specialty physician care through an organized physician group practice representing various specialties. The company seeks to acquire primary care-oriented clinics typically staffed by 25 to 200 doctors. Upon acquisition of a clinic's operating assets, PHYC negotiates a long-term agreement with the affiliated physician group under which it provides the equip-

ment and facilities used in its medical practice, manages clinic operations, employs most of the non-physician personnel and receives a service fee. PHYC also positions the clinics for participation in organized health care systems by establishing alliances with HMOs, insurers and hospitals, and by enhancing medical management systems.

The company's clinics also offer ancillary services, which accounted for about 27% of gross clinic revenues in 1997. Most provide imaging services, including CAT scanning, mammography, nuclear medicine, ultrasound and X-ray. Many also have clinical labs and pharmacies. Ambulatory surgery units and rehabilitation services are in place or are being planned in most clinics, while several offer diabetes centers, renal dialysis and home infusion therapy.

PHYC's IPAs, which are networks of independent physicians loosely organized to assume and more effectively manage capitated risk, provide capitated medical services to about 375,000 members. The combination of multi-specialty clinic management services and IPA management services lets the company offer its management services to virtually all types of physician organizations.

In 1997, net revenues earned by the physician groups and IPAs affiliated with the company were derived from private payor and insurance (33%), managed care (41%), Medicare (22%) and Medicaid (4%) sources.

Per Share Data ($)

(Year Ended Dec. 31)	1997	1996	1995	1994	1993	1992	1991	1990	1989	1988
Tangible Bk. Val.	NM	NM	1.49	4.86	2.89	2.44	1.84	NM	NA	NA
Cash Flow	0.98	1.25	0.81	0.66	0.51	-0.39	0.25	0.21	-0.11	-0.21
Earnings	0.05	0.60	0.41	0.32	0.28	-0.32	0.05	0.00	-0.23	-0.22
Dividends	Nil	Nil	Nil	Nil	Nil	Nil	Nil	Nil	Nil	Nil
Payout Ratio	Nil	Nil	Nil	Nil	Nil	Nil	Nil	Nil	Nil	Nil
Prices - High	35½	41¾	34	12½	9⅛	5¼	NA	NA	NA	NA
- Low	22¾	25½	10⅞	7½	4	2¼	NA	NA	NA	NA
P/E Ratio - High	NM	70	84	39	46	NM	NA	NA	NA	NA
- Low	NM	42	27	23	20	NM	NM	NM	NM	NM

Income Statement Analysis (Million $)

	1997	1996	1995	1994	1993	1992	1991	1990	1989	1988
Revs.	1,120	766	442	242	167	136	90.0	64.0	24.0	1.0
Oper. Inc.	187	122	67.5	31.4	17.9	13.6	7.6	4.9	1.2	-1.0
Depr.	62.5	40.2	21.4	12.2	6.1	4.5	2.7	2.7	0.8	0.0
Int. Exp.	23.5	16.0	5.2	4.0	3.9	4.5	3.8	3.0	2.2	0.0
Pretax Inc.	21.0	59.2	35.8	16.5	8.2	-13.3	1.3	0.2	-1.6	-0.9
Eff. Tax Rate	29%	39%	39%	29%	13%	NM	43%	67%	Nil	Nil
Net Inc.	3.2	36.4	21.8	11.7	7.1	-13.7	0.8	0.1	-1.6	-0.9

Balance Sheet & Other Fin. Data (Million $)

	1997	1996	1995	1994	1993	1992	1991	1990	1989	1988
Cash	38.2	30.5	18.8	6.5	3.2	9.2	2.6	3.6	2.1	NA
Curr. Assets	497	383	218	145	77.5	69.4	39.6	33.5	13.4	NA
Total Assets	1,563	1,119	644	351	171	141	93.0	79.0	34.0	5.0
Curr. Liab.	293	170	106	64.3	30.5	33.5	17.7	15.5	6.0	NA
LT Debt	478	409	127	84.9	66.8	51.2	49.3	38.9	20.0	1.3
Common Eqty.	710	452	389	184	70.0	53.9	2.4	1.3	NA	NA
Total Cap.	1,188	860	516	269	137	105	75.0	63.0	28.0	4.0
Cap. Exp.	66.5	50.1	29.2	17.5	13.9	13.6	6.3	4.3	0.5	0.1
Cash Flow	65.7	76.6	43.3	23.9	13.3	-9.3	3.5	2.8	-0.8	-0.9
Curr. Ratio	1.7	2.3	2.0	2.3	2.5	2.1	2.2	2.2	2.2	NA
% LT Debt of Cap.	40.2	47.5	24.6	31.6	48.8	48.7	66.0	61.5	71.0	36.7
% Net Inc.of Revs.	0.3	4.7	4.9	4.8	4.3	NM	0.8	0.1	NM	NM
% Ret. on Assets	0.2	4.1	4.4	3.8	4.4	NM	0.9	1.0	NM	NM
% Ret. on Equity	0.6	8.7	7.6	7.9	11.1	NM	41.4	3.6	NM	NM

Data as orig. reptd.; bef. results of disc. opers. and/or spec. items. Per share data adj. for stk. divs. as of ex-div. date. E-Estimated. NA-Not Available. NM-Not Meaningful. NR-Not Ranked.

Office—30 Burton Hills Blvd., Suite 340, Nashville, TN 37215. **Tel**—(615) 665-9066. **Chrmn, Pres & CEO**—J. C. Hutts. **EVP & Secy**—T. S. Dent. **VP, Treas & CFO**—J. K. Crawford. **Dirs**—R. B. Ashworth, S. A. Brooks Jr., T. S. Dent, W. C. Dunn, C. S. Givens, J. A. Hill, J. C. Hutts, K. C. James, J. A. Moncrief, D. W. Reeves, R. D. Wright. **Transfer Agent**—First Union National Bank of North Carolina, Charlotte. **Incorporated**—in Tennessee in 1988. **Empl**— 19,000. **S&P Analyst:** Robert M. Gold

PictureTel Corp.   4987K

Nasdaq Symbol **PCTL**

In S&P SmallCap 600

03-OCT-98

Industry:
Communications
Equipment

Summary: This company develops, manufactures, markets and services visual communication systems that serve videoconferencing needs.

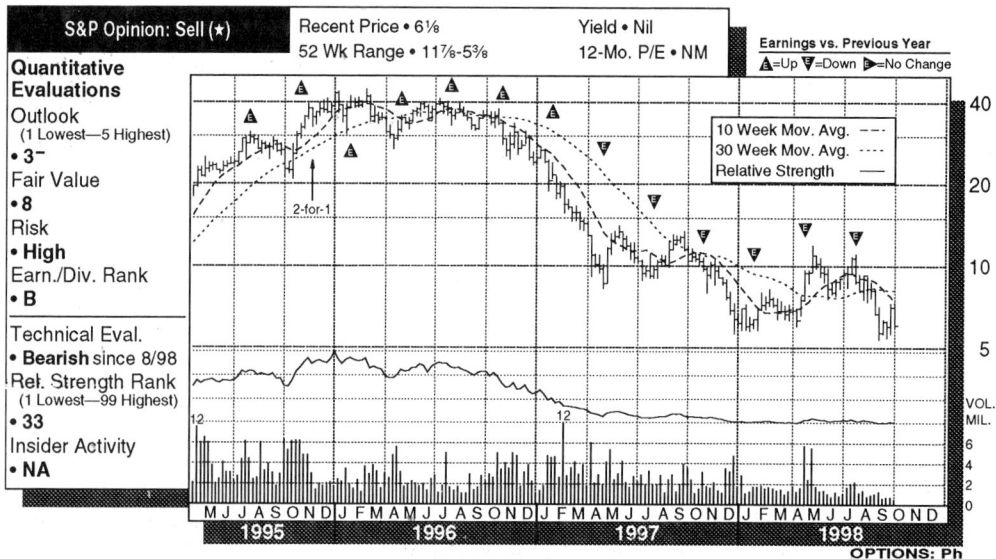

S&P Opinion: Sell (★)	Recent Price • 6⅛ — Yield • Nil 52 Wk Range • 11⅞-5⅜ — 12-Mo. P/E • NM

Earnings vs. Previous Year
▲=Up ▼=Down ▶=No Change

Quantitative Evaluations

Outlook
(1 Lowest—5 Highest)
• **3⁻**

Fair Value
• **8**

Risk
• **High**

Earn./Div. Rank
• **B**

Technical Eval.
• **Bearish** since 8/98

Rel. Strength Rank
(1 Lowest—99 Highest)
• **33**

Insider Activity
• **NA**

10 Week Mov. Avg. – – –
30 Week Mov. Avg. ·······
Relative Strength ——

OPTIONS: Ph

Overview - 20-AUG-98

We now expect revenues to be down 7% in 1998 and up a modest 12% in 1999, as growth in the videoconferencing market remains weak. Customers are still taking more time to evaluate new Internet Protocol (IP)-based products that operate over corporate local area networks (LANs). In addition, the expansion of Intel (with ProShare) and Microsoft (with NetMeeting) in the lower end of the market has heightened competition and hurt gross margins. PCTL is rolling out products targeting the booming Intranet and Internet markets, using IP systems over LANs. However, the company does not expect to see a material impact on sales from LAN products until 1999. Management has made some progress in reducing the cost structure, to bring it in line with lower than expected revenues.

Valuation - 20-AUG-98

We lowered our rating opinion on PCTL to sell, from avoid, in early June 1998. PCTL reported second quarter results that were better expectations, as narrower gross margins were offset by tight expense management. The results signaled that cost cutting measures are having a positive impact. However, revenues were down for the fourth consecutive quarter, and were down 11%, year to year. The expanding presence of Microsoft and Intel in the lower end of the videoconferencing market, combined with overall softness in demand, continued to hurt results. In addition, new competitors NuVision and VTEL have been winning market share for larger room videoconferencing systems. Given the changing competitive environment, a slowdown in the overall market, and the lack of earnings visibility, we view PCTL shares as unattractive at a recent level of 23X our 1999 EPS estimate of $0.42.

Key Stock Statistics

S&P EPS Est. 1998	0.07	Tang. Bk. Value/Share	5.77
P/E on S&P Est. 1998	86.8	Beta	0.59
S&P EPS Est. 1999	0.42	Shareholders	2,000
Dividend Rate/Share	Nil	Market cap. (B)	$0.233
Shs. outstg. (M)	38.4	Inst. holdings	43%
Avg. daily vol. (M)	0.133		

Value of $10,000 invested 5 years ago: $ 4,814

Fiscal Year Ending Dec. 31

	1998	1997	1996	1995	1994	1993
Revenues (Million $)						
1Q	101.0	121.9	105.0	74.16	53.70	44.00
2Q	104.6	118.0	116.1	80.49	64.00	44.20
3Q	—	109.7	121.3	90.10	63.30	39.40
4Q	—	116.8	140.2	102.0	74.10	48.70
Yr.	—	466.4	482.5	346.7	255.2	176.3
Earnings Per Share ($)						
1Q	-0.06	0.05	0.21	0.10	0.02	0.09
2Q	-0.17	-0.13	0.24	0.12	0.02	0.09
3Q	—	-0.44	0.25	0.15	0.03	0.02
4Q	—	-0.52	0.28	0.20	0.08	0.05
Yr.	—	-1.04	0.96	0.56	0.15	0.24

Next earnings report expected: mid November

Dividend Data

No cash dividends have been paid. A two-for-one stock split was effected in 1995.

A Division of The McGraw·Hill Companies

STANDARD
&POOR'S
STOCK REPORTS

PictureTel Corporation

4987K
03-OCT-98

Business Summary - 20-AUG-98

PictureTel's products serve videoconferencing needs from the desktop to the boardroom, eliminating the barrier of distance by providing face-to-face contact between people from any distance in the world. PCTL is the market share leader in the videoconferencing market. The company's systems use advanced video and audio compression technology that permits the transmission of full-motion color video with integrated full-duplex audio at data rates as low as 56 Kbps. By operating at such low speeds, PCTL's systems have substantially reduced the cost and increased the flexibility of videoconferencing.

Products range in use from high-end group systems to personal systems for one-on-one videoconferencing. The company sells three families of group systems, the Performance, Value, and Compact Families, comprised of five basic modules: the electronic module, for video/audio compression and video switching; the video module, comprised of a camera and color display; the audio module, which consists of a microphone, speaker and associated audio electronics; a user interface, which is comprised of a keypad; and a WAN interface, which permits communication over switched or dedicated digital networks that operate from 56 Kbps up to T1 (1.544 Mbps) and E1 (2.048 Mbps) speeds. The Performance, Value, and Compact systems range in price from $9,000 to over $50,000.

Personal systems include the PictureTel Live PCS 100, a videoconferencing system designed for use with a PC that includes a video board, audio board, camera, speakerphone and software, and the PCS 50 (introduced in 1995), which consists of a single audio/video board, fixed focus camera, speakerphone headset and associated software.

In 1997, 26% of worldwide product revenue came from direct selling activities, including co-marketing arrangements with MCI, NYNEX and U.S. Sprint, and 74% from indirect channels. The company's revenues from sales to foreign markets represented 43%, 45% and 43% of total revenues in 1997, 1996 and 1995, respectively.

In 1996, PCTL began shipping products geared to run over corporate local area networks (LANs). The company is accelerating its entry into the emerging Internet/intranet and LAN space. In July 1997, PCTL acquired MultiLink, Inc.; this was expected to enable the company to create next-generation multimedia bridging products that mix audio, data and video in corporate LANs.

In July 1998, PCTL said it had agreed to acquire Starlight Networks, a provider of streaming-media solutions for enterprise communications. The transaction is expected to be dilutive to EPS for the balance of FY 98, but to be accretive to FY 99 EPS.

Per Share Data ($)										
(Year Ended Dec. 31)	1997	1996	1995	1994	1993	1992	1991	1990	1989	1988
Tangible Bk. Val.	5.99	7.61	6.14	4.99	4.85	4.40	4.06	NA	NA	NA
Cash Flow	-0.11	1.56	1.07	0.73	0.62	0.52	NA	NA	NA	NA
Earnings	-1.04	0.96	0.56	0.15	0.24	0.27	0.15	-0.07	NA	NA
Dividends	Nil	Nil	Nil	Nil	Nil	Nil	Nil	Nil	Nil	Nil
Payout Ratio	Nil	Nil	Nil	Nil	Nil	Nil	Nil	Nil	Nil	Nil
Prices - High	26⁷/₈	44³/₄	43⁷/₈	12¹/₄	15¹/₄	26¹/₂	25³/₈	NA	NA	NA
- Low	5⁵/₈	23³/₈	11¹/₈	5	7¹/₄	5¹/₈	5¹/₂	NA	NA	NA
P/E Ratio - High	NM	47	78	84	65	NM	NM	NA	NA	NA
- Low	NM	24	20	34	31	NM	NM	NA	NA	NA

Income Statement Analysis (Million $)

	1997	1996	1995	1994	1993	1992	1991	1990	1989	1988
Revs.	466	483	347	255	176	141	78.0	37.0	NA	NA
Oper. Inc.	-21.6	65.6	42.2	23.6	20.9	17.4	NA	NA	NA	NA
Depr.	35.2	21.5	17.9	18.3	12.2	8.3	NA	NA	NA	NA
Int. Exp.	1.8	0.9	1.0	1.0	1.0	1.2	NA	NA	NA	NA
Pretax Inc.	-55.5	51.7	27.5	6.9	11.4	13.3	NA	NA	NA	NA
Eff. Tax Rate	NM	33%	29%	34%	35%	37%	NA	NA	NA	NA
Net Inc.	-39.4	34.7	19.6	4.6	7.4	8.4	4.0	-0.2	NA	NA

Balance Sheet & Other Fin. Data (Million $)

	1997	1996	1995	1994	1993	1992	1991	1990	1989	1988
Cash	49.9	102	59.9	74.7	9.1	NA	NA	NA	NA	NA
Curr. Assets	258	304	214	179	85.0	NA	NA	NA	NA	NA
Total Assets	355	376	288	217	187	166	145	NA	NA	NA
Curr. Liab.	105	103	74.5	60.4	36.1	NA	NA	NA	NA	NA
LT Debt	22.0	13.9	12.8	2.9	4.4	4.7	3.9	NA	NA	NA
Common Eqty.	228	259	201	153	147	132	120	NA	NA	NA
Total Cap.	250	273	214	156	151	137	124	NA	NA	NA
Cap. Exp.	21.6	38.5	11.1	14.3	11.1	12.5	NA	NA	NA	NA
Cash Flow	-4.2	56.2	37.5	22.9	19.6	16.6	NA	NA	NA	NA
Curr. Ratio	2.5	3.0	2.9	3.0	2.4	NA	NA	NA	NA	NA
% LT Debt of Cap.	8.8	5.1	6.0	1.8	2.9	3.4	3.2	NA	NA	NA
% Net Inc.of Revs.	NM	7.2	5.7	1.8	4.2	6.0	5.2	NM	NM	NM
% Ret. on Assets	NM	10.5	7.8	2.3	4.2	5.4	3.0	NA	NA	NA
% Ret. on Equity	NM	15.1	11.1	3.1	5.3	6.7	4.0	NA	NA	NA

Data as orig. reptd.; bef. results of disc. opers. and/or spec. items. Per share data adj. for stk. divs. as of ex-div. date. Bold denotes diluted EPS (FASB 128). E-Estimated. NA-Not Available. NM-Not Meaningful. NR-Not Ranked.

Office—222 Rosewood Dr., Danvers, MA 01923. **Tel**—(978) 292-5000. **Website**—http://www.picturetel.com **Chmn**—N. E. Gaut. **Pres & CEO**—B R. Bond. **VP & CFO**—R. B. Goldman. **Investor Contact**—Kevin Flanagan. **Dirs**—B R. Bond, N. E. Gaut, R. T. Knight, D. B. Levi, E. Torresi. **Transfer Agent & Registrar**—BankBoston. **Incorporated**—in Delaware in 1984. **Empl**— 1,544. **S&P Analyst:** Aydin Tuncer

Piedmont Natural Gas 1828

NYSE Symbol **PNY**

In S&P SmallCap 600

03-OCT-98 | **Industry:** Natural Gas

Summary: This company principally transports and sells natural gas and propane to more than 648,000 customers in North Carolina, South Carolina and Tennessee.

Quantitative Evaluations

Outlook (1 Lowest—5 Highest)
• **2⁻**

Fair Value
• **33⅝**

Risk
• **Low**

Earn./Div. Rank
• **A-**

Technical Eval.
• **Bullish** since 9/98

Rel. Strength Rank (1 Lowest—99 Highest)
• **92**

Insider Activity
• **NA**

Recent Price • 33⅛   Yield • 3.9%
52 Wk Range • 36⅜-26¾   12-Mo. P/E • 16.7

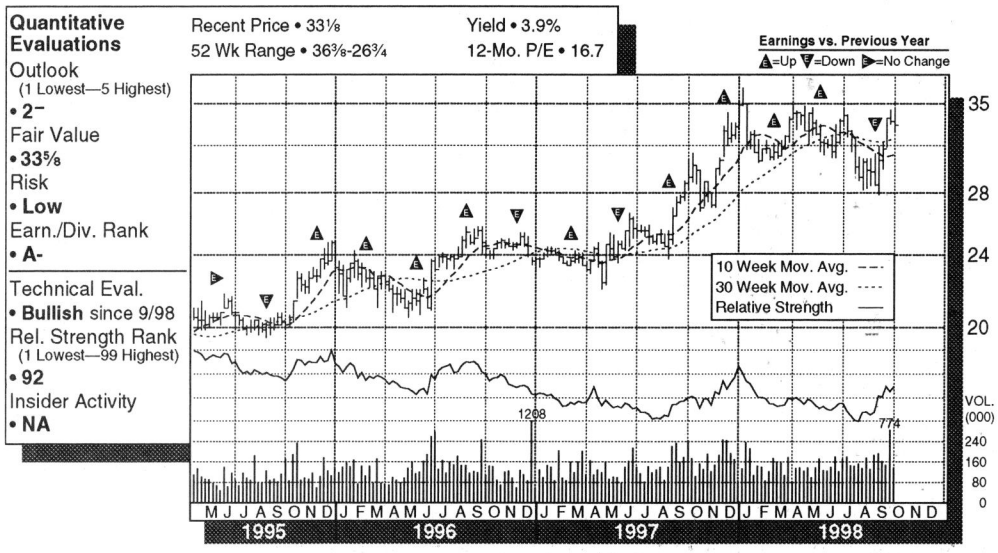

Business Profile - 08-JUL-98

Piedmont is the second largest gas utility in the Southeast. With an annual customer growth rate of about 6%, the company is also one of the fastest growing natural gas distributors in the U.S. In September 1997, PNY acquired two independent propane companies: Lincoln Moore County Propane in Lynchburg, TN; and McCombs Propane Co. in Morganton, NC. The acquisitions added about 1.2 million gallons and 1,650 customers to the company's sales and customer base. A shelf registration with the SEC covering $150 million of debt securities became effective in May 1997.

Operational Review - 08-JUL-98

Operating revenues for the six months ended April 30, 1998, rose 0.5%, year to year, reflecting regulatory-approved rate changes and increased volumes of gas sold or transported. Profitability benefited from decreases in the cost of gas, operations expense and interest charges; net income advanced 10%, to $76,712,000 ($2.50 a share, diluted) from $69,586,000 ($2.33).

Stock Performance - 02-OCT-98

In the past 30 trading days, PNY's shares have increased 12%, compared to a 7% fall in the S&P 500. Average trading volume for the past five days was 27,260 shares, compared with the 40-day moving average of 48,759 shares.

Key Stock Statistics

Dividend Rate/Share	1.30	Shareholders	19,100
Shs. outstg. (M)	30.6	Market cap. (B)	$ 1.0
Avg. daily vol. (M)	0.062	Inst. holdings	26%
Tang. Bk. Value/Share	15.49		
Beta	0.49		

Value of $10,000 invested 5 years ago: $ 22,461

Fiscal Year Ending Oct. 31

	1998	1997	1996	1995	1994	1993
Revenues (Million $)						
1Q	313.3	312.5	239.2	202.5	233.1	202.6
2Q	261.5	259.3	259.5	179.4	204.8	205.1
3Q	103.0	104.0	95.74	61.65	70.64	74.65
4Q	—	99.7	90.68	61.71	66.80	70.50
Yr.	—	775.5	685.1	505.2	575.4	552.8
Earnings Per Share ($)						
1Q	**1.35**	1.26	1.18	1.13	1.06	1.05
2Q	**1.16**	1.09	1.12	0.97	0.97	0.97
3Q	**-0.20**	-0.19	-0.28	-0.31	-0.27	-0.20
4Q	—	-0.32	-0.33	-0.18	-0.30	-0.27
Yr.	—	1.81	1.67	1.45	1.35	1.45

Next earnings report expected: early December

Dividend Data (Dividends have been paid since 1956.)

Amount ($)	Date Decl.	Ex-Div. Date	Stock of Record	Payment Date
0.305	Dec. 05	Dec. 19	Dec. 23	Jan. 15 '98
0.325	Feb. 27	Mar. 23	Mar. 25	Apr. 15 '98
0.325	Jun. 05	Jun. 22	Jun. 24	Jul. 15 '98
0.325	Aug. 28	Sep. 22	Sep. 24	Oct. 15 '98

A Division of The McGraw-Hill Companies

Business Summary - 08-JUL-98

This gas utility's growth has been fueled by the economic vibrancy of its service area, one of the fastest growing regions in the U.S. Piedmont Natural Gas (PNY), the second largest gas utility in the Southeast, transports and sells natural gas to more than 648,000 customers in the Piedmont region of the Carolinas (including Charlotte, Salisbury, Greensboro, Burlington, Winston-Salem, High Point and the Hickory area in NC, and Anderson, Greenville and Spartanburg, SC) and the metropolitan Nashville, TN, area. Revenues by customer class in recent fiscal years (Oct.) were:

	FY 97	FY 96	FY 95	FY 94
Residential	41%	43%	45%	41%
Commercial	25%	26%	27%	29%
Industrial	25%	27%	26%	29%
Other	9%	4%	2%	1%

About 90% of new single family homes built in PNY's service area use natural gas, when available. Customers billed averaged 560,694 in FY 97 (531,395 in FY 96). Gas volumes delivered in FY 97 totaled 135.1 million dekatherms, versus 139.0 million dekatherms in FY 96.

PNY purchases or transports gas from eight interstate pipeline suppliers. At November 1, 1997, suppliers had contracted to provide a total of 604,400 dekatherms per day to PNY, with additional daily peaking capacity available.

The company's principal non-utility business is the sale of propane to 49 million customers in its three state service region. Other non-utility operations include acquiring, marketing and arranging for the transportation of natural gas to large-volume purchasers. Non-utility activities accounted for 5% of revenues in FY 97.

To meet demand of its expanding customer base, PNY has budgeted capital expenditures totaling $100 million for utility expansion and construction projects for FY 98. PNY also is seeking new markets for natural gas including a heating and cooling unit for residential and small business applications and natural gas powered vehicles (NGVs).

The company announced 18% and 16% decreases in rates to customers in North Carolina and South Carolina, respectively, effective March 1, 1997. This was made possible by a reduction in PNY's wholesale cost of gas because of high gas storage levels on the East Coast and mild weather in the first part of 1997.

Per Share Data ($)

(Year Ended Oct. 31)	1997	1996	1995	1994	1993	1992	1991	1990	1989	1988
Tangible Bk. Val.	13.81	12.96	12.20	11.36	10.79	10.24	9.62	9.10	8.67	8.19
Earnings	1.81	1.67	1.45	1.35	1.45	1.40	0.89	1.22	1.21	1.19
Dividends	1.21	1.15	1.08	1.02	0.96	0.91	0.87	0.83	0.79	0.72
Payout Ratio	67%	69%	75%	76%	67%	65%	98%	68%	65%	61%
Prices - High	$36^{1}/_{2}$	$25^{3}/_{4}$	$24^{7}/_{8}$	$23^{3}/_{8}$	$26^{3}/_{8}$	$20^{1}/_{2}$	$16^{7}/_{8}$	$14^{7}/_{8}$	$14^{3}/_{4}$	$12^{5}/_{8}$
- Low	22	$20^{1}/_{2}$	$18^{1}/_{4}$	18	$18^{3}/_{4}$	$15^{1}/_{2}$	13	$12^{3}/_{4}$	$11^{1}/_{2}$	$9^{5}/_{8}$
P/E Ratio - High	20	15	17	17	18	15	19	12	12	11
- Low	12	12	13	13	13	11	15	10	10	8

Income Statement Analysis (Million $)

	1997	1996	1995	1994	1993	1992	1991	1990	1989	1988
Revs.	776	685	505	575	553	460	412	404	421	399
Depr.	39.2	36.0	31.9	24.6	22.2	20.1	18.0	15.8	14.9	13.1
Maint.	16.2	15.8	16.4	15.5	15.0	13.3	13.1	11.6	10.1	8.9
Fxd. Chgs. Cov.	3.5	3.5	3.1	3.2	3.7	3.5	2.4	2.8	2.9	3.3
Constr. Credits	0.7	0.8	1.1	1.3	1.1	0.8	0.8	0.8	0.7	1.0
Eff. Tax Rate	39%	39%	39%	36%	38%	38%	36%	37%	37%	37%
Net Inc.	54.1	48.6	40.3	35.5	37.5	35.3	20.6	25.7	24.9	22.4

Balance Sheet & Other Fin. Data (Million $)

	1997	1996	1995	1994	1993	1992	1991	1990	1989	1988
Gross Prop.	1,284	1,168	1,075	978	877	796	723	658	591	532
Cap. Exp.	92.1	96.8	99	106	84.0	74.0	69.1	71.0	65.9	76.0
Net Prop.	942	862	801	735	655	593	538	488	434	386
Capitalization:										
LT Debt	381	391	361	313	278	231	221	174	186	142
% LT Debt	48	50	50	51	49	47	48	47	51	46
Pfd.	Nil	Nil	Nil	Nil	Nil	Nil	Nil	Nil	Nil	Nil
% Pfd.	Nil	Nil	Nil	Nil	Nil	Nil	Nil	Nil	Nil	Nil
Common	420	386	355	302	285	265	239	196	181	168
% Common	52	50	50	49	51	53	52	53	49	54
Total Cap.	914	880	810	697	653	576	534	442	437	375
% Oper. Ratio	89.5	89.1	87.1	90.3	89.8	88.4	90.3	89.1	90.2	91.3
% Earn. on Net Prop.	9.2	9.0	5.2	8.0	9.1	9.4	7.8	9.5	10.1	9.8
% Return On Revs.	7.0	7.1	8.0	6.2	6.8	7.7	5.0	6.4	5.9	5.6
% Return On Invest. Capital	10.3	9.4	12.6	8.9	9.7	10.2	8.8	10.8	10.9	11.0
% Return On Com. Equity	13.4	13.1	12.3	12.1	13.7	14.0	9.5	13.6	14.2	14.8

Data as orig. reptd.; bef. results of disc opers. and/or spec. items. Per share data adj. for stk. divs. as of ex-div. date. Bold denotes diluted EPS (FASB 128). E-Estimated. NA-Not Available. NM-Not Meaningful. NR-Not Ranked.

Office—1915 Rexford Rd., Charlotte, NC 28211; P.O. Box 33068, Charlotte, NC 28233. **Tel**—(704) 364-3120. **Chrmn, Pres & CEO**—J. H. Maxheim. **SVP-Fin**—D. J. Dzuricky. **VP, Treas & Investor Contact**—Ted C. Coble. **VP & Secy**—M. C. Ruegsegger.**Dirs**—J. W. Amos, C. M. Butler III, S. J. DiGiovanni, J. W. Harris, M. W. Helms, J. H. Maxheim, J. F. McNair III, N. R.McWherter, W. S. Montgomery Jr., D. S. Russell Jr., J. E. Simkins Jr. **Transfer Agent & Registrar**—Wachovia Bank of North Carolina, Winston-Salem. **Incorporated**—in North Carolina in 1994; previously incorporated in New York in 1950. **Empl**—1,904. **S&P Analyst**: J.J.S.

STANDARD &POOR'S
STOCK REPORTS

Pier 1 Imports

1828G

NYSE Symbol **PIR**

In S&P SmallCap 600

03-OCT-98 | **Industry:** Retail (Specialty)

Summary: This company is North America's largest specialty retailer of imported decorative home furnishings, gifts and related items, with more than 750 stores.

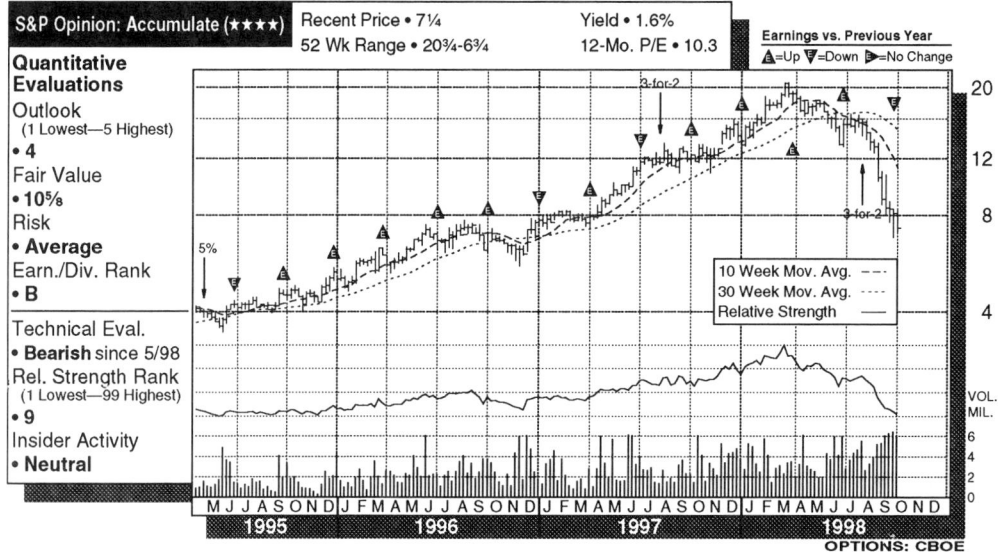

S&P Opinion: Accumulate (★★★★)

Recent Price • 7¼
52 Wk Range • 20¾-6¾
Yield • 1.6%
12-Mo. P/E • 10.3

Earnings vs. Previous Year
▲=Up ▼=Down ▶=No Change

Quantitative Evaluations

Outlook
(1 Lowest—5 Highest)
• **4**

Fair Value
• **10⅝**

Risk
• **Average**

Earn./Div. Rank
• **B**

Technical Eval.
• **Bearish** since 5/98

Rel. Strength Rank
(1 Lowest—99 Highest)
• **9**

Insider Activity
• **Neutral**

Chart legend: 10 Week Mov. Avg. — • —; 30 Week Mov. Avg. - - - -; Relative Strength

OPTIONS: CBOE

Overview - 28-SEP-98

Pier 1 is poised to take advantage of historically strong housing starts and consumer spending, which together generally make for a favorable sales environment for home furnishings retailers. Also, due to the economic crisis in Asia, from which the company imports some 70% of its merchandise, PIR has been achieving significant cost of goods savings. Despite these positives, which have been in place for over a year, 1998 has seen PIR's revenue, same-store sales, and earnings per share moderate somewhat. We are excited about Pier 1's long-term revenue growth strategy, which includes: aggressive store openings, extensive store re-modeling and merchandising, new product introductions, as well as national television advertisements and other marketing initiatives. At the end of the second quarter of PIR's FY 99 (Jan.), the company's stores had fresh merchandise assortments and healthy inventory levels, and should have a successful holiday selling season. We also expect PIR's upcoming catalog mailing to generate significant sales. In September 1998, the company announced a 5 million share buyback, which likely will contribute to enhanced earnings per share prospects.

Valuation - 28-SEP-98

We recommend investors accumulate shares of Pier 1, which have been unreasonably beaten down from their mid-March 1998 high because of concerns about growth prospects, excess inventory levels, and increased costs of importing merchandise made in Asia. Considering that our expected long-term earnings per share growth rate for PIR is in the high teens, at a recent $8.50, the stock was attractive at 11 times our FY 99 (Feb.) estimate, and 9 times our FY 00 estimate of $0.93.

Key Stock Statistics

S&P EPS Est. 1999	0.76	Tang. Bk. Value/Share	3.87
P/E on S&P Est. 1999	9.6	Beta	1.14
S&P EPS Est. 2000	0.94	Shareholders	16,000
Dividend Rate/Share	0.12	Market cap. (B)	$0.721
Shs. outstg. (M)	98.6	Inst. holdings	81%
Avg. daily vol. (M)	1.710		

Value of $10,000 invested 5 years ago: $ 14,601

Fiscal Year Ending Feb. 28

	1999	1998	1997	1996	1995	1994
Revenues (Million $)						
1Q	250.5	Nil	205.3	176.8	161.0	158.6
2Q	281.5	258.1	231.1	199.5	185.4	181.4
3Q	—	262.8	225.6	190.2	165.8	163.5
4Q	—	325.3	285.1	244.2	199.3	181.9
Yr.	—	1,075	947.1	810.7	712.0	685.4
Earnings Per Share ($)						
1Q	0.15	-0.92	0.09	-0.20	0.06	0.05
2Q	0.17	0.20	0.12	0.10	0.10	0.08
3Q	E0.19	0.15	0.10	0.08	0.00	0.05
4Q	E0.25	0.24	0.17	0.14	0.12	-0.11
Yr.	E0.76	0.72	0.49	0.11	0.28	0.07

Next earnings report expected: mid December

Dividend Data (Dividends have been paid since 1986.)

Amount ($)	Date Decl.	Ex-Div. Date	Stock of Record	Payment Date
0.040	Mar. 19	May. 04	May. 06	May. 20 '98
3-for-2	Jun. 25	Jul. 30	Jul. 15	Jul. 29 '98
0.030	Jun. 25	Aug. 10	Aug. 12	Aug. 26 '98
0.030	Sep. 17	Nov. 06	Nov. 10	Nov. 24 '98

A Division of The McGraw Hill Companies

Business Summary - 28-SEP-98

Pier 1 Imports, Inc. provides shoppers with a passport for finding unique, fashionable, and decorative home furnishings, gifts and related items from more than 50 countries around the world. PIR plans to open 65 new stores, as well as remodel and remerchandise over 100 locations, during its FY 99 (Feb.), continuing the rapid expansion pace by which its number of stores has increased from 588 at the end of FY 94, to 688 at the end of FY 96, to 763 at the end of FY 98.

PIR believes in the trend toward the renewal of the neighborhood store. With this in mind, the company generally opens its prototype 8,000 square foot stores in neighborhood locations, as free-standing units near popular regional malls or in high-end strip centers. To make its stores more customer friendly, during FY 99, most of the company's North American stores will be remodeled and remerchandised. Stores are being upgraded to include wider aisles, lower interior shelf displays and better lighting. Merchandise will be arranged using "lifestyle merchandising," which involves the placing of items in home-use settings, to help the buyer envision how products can be integrated into their homes.

The stores choose their offerings very carefully, employing a well-seasoned merchandising staff that devel-ops a clear concept of what they believe tomorrow's shoppers will find appealing. Merchandise is introduced in a carefully-timed manner such that over 40% of the offerings are new and different from those of the preceding year. PIR also emphasizes the uniqueness of its products, and ensures that more than half of its merchandise is exclusive to its stores.

PIR's offers five broad categories of products, including: furniture (representing 34% of FY 98 sales), decorative home furnishings (23%), kitchen decor and housewares (18%), bed and bath products (14%) and seasonal offerings (11%). Merchandise is generally handcrafted, and is imported primarily from abroad. During FY 98, 25% of the company's offerings were imported from China, 12% from India, and 18% from a combination of Indonesia, Japan, Thailand, the Philippines and Italy. The remaining 45% was produced in various Asian, European, Central American, South American and African countries, or obtained from United States manufacturers.

PIR has been making noteworthy information technology investments. It is currently implementing system updates to avoid the year 2000 problem. Also, the company will soon deploy technology enhancements to its bridal and gift registry program, as well as new smart point-of-sale terminals, which are expected to improve PIR's ability to manage its inventory.

Per Share Data ($)

(Year Ended Feb. 28)	1998	1997	1996	1995	1994	1993	1992	1991	1990	1989
Tangible Bk. Val.	3.87	3.19	2.53	2.53	2.27	2.27	2.04	1.53	2.06	1.52
Cash Flow	1.01	0.69	0.31	0.44	0.26	0.43	0.47	0.28	0.46	0.43
Earnings	0.72	0.49	0.11	0.28	0.07	0.26	0.30	0.07	0.29	0.28
Dividends	0.09	0.07	0.06	0.05	0.04	0.03	Nil	0.06	0.05	0.04
Payout Ratio	12%	15%	52%	16%	59%	11%	Nil	88%	18%	13%
Cal. Yrs.	1997	1996	1995	1994	1993	1992	1991	1990	1989	1988
Prices - High	16	8	5¹/₂	4¹/₂	5¹/₂	5¹/₂	4¹/₈	5¹/₄	5³/₄	5¹/₂
- Low	7¹/₄	4⁵/₈	3¹/₂	3	3¹/₂	2³/₄	1³/₄	1⁵/₁₆	3⁷/₈	2⁵/₁₆
P/E Ratio - High	22	16	49	16	82	21	14	73	20	20
- Low	10	9	31	11	52	11	6	17	13	8

Income Statement Analysis (Million $)

	1998	1997	1996	1995	1994	1993	1992	1991	1990	1989
Revs.	1,075	947	811	712	685	629	587	609	517	415
Oper. Inc.	146	110	89.9	71.6	65.9	66.0	56.0	44.6	63.3	53.2
Depr.	23.9	19.8	17.2	16.0	17.6	15.1	15.0	18.1	15.2	11.3
Int. Exp.	8.7	12.6	14.7	14.2	16.8	15.0	16.6	14.1	9.7	10.0
Pretax Inc.	124	80.3	28.4	36.0	8.4	32.3	35.0	10.6	38.5	31.9
Eff. Tax Rate	37%	40%	65%	31%	29%	29%	25%	47%	34%	32%
Net Inc.	78.0	48.2	10.1	24.9	5.9	23.0	26.3	6.6	25.5	21.9

Balance Sheet & Other Fin. Data (Million $)

	1998	1997	1996	1995	1994	1993	1992	1991	1990	1989
Cash	80.7	32.3	13.5	54.2	17.1	73.6	9.0	18.8	16.3	19.6
Curr. Assets	402	285	348	353	321	318	240	270	210	178
Total Assets	653	570	531	489	463	460	386	454	350	300
Curr. Liab.	122	110	101	85.0	92.0	93.0	80.0	141	72.0	61.0
LT Debt	114	111	180	154	145	147	107	142	93.0	121
Common Eqty.	393	323	227	225	201	200	177	155	180	114
Total Cap.	508	434	408	382	350	348	289	301	279	239
Cap. Exp.	50.1	36.8	22.1	17.5	21.7	12.6	6.2	62.2	32.6	51.0
Cash Flow	102	68.0	27.3	40.8	23.5	38.1	41.3	24.4	40.5	32.9
Curr. Ratio	3.3	2.6	3.5	4.1	3.5	3.4	3.0	1.9	2.9	2.9
% LT Debt of Cap.	22.4	25.6	44.1	40.4	41.5	42.3	37.0	47.3	33.2	50.8
% Net Inc.of Revs.	7.3	5.1	1.2	3.5	0.9	3.7	4.5	1.1	4.9	5.3
% Ret. on Assets	12.8	8.8	2.0	5.2	1.3	5.4	6.2	1.6	7.3	7.8
% Ret. on Equity	21.8	17.5	4.5	11.6	2.9	12.1	15.8	3.8	16.2	20.8

Data as orig. reptd.; bef. results of disc. opers. and/or spec. items. Per share data adj. for stk. divs. as of ex-div. date. Bold denotes diluted EPS (FASB 128). E-Estimated. NA-Not Available. NM-Not Meaningful. NR-Not Ranked.

Office—301 Commerce St.; Suite 600; Fort Worth, TX 76102. **Tel**—(817) 878-8000. **Website**—http://www.pier1.com.**Chrmn & CEO**—C. A. Johnson. **Pres & COO**—M. J. Girouard. **SVP & CFO**—S. F. Mangum.**SVP & Secy**—J. R. Lawrence. **Dirs**—M. L. Berman; M. J. Girouard; C. G. Gordon; J. M. Hoak, Jr.; C. A. Johnson; S. F. McKenzie; T. Thomas. **Transfer Agent**—Chase Mellon Shareholder Services LLC, New Jersey. **Incorporated**—in Georgia in 1978; reincorporated in Delaware in 1986. **Empl**— 11,255. **S&P Analyst:** Scott H. Kessler.

STANDARD &POOR'S

STOCK REPORTS

Pillowtex Corp. 1830F

NYSE Symbol **PTX**

In S&P SmallCap 600

03-OCT-98

Industry: Textiles (Home Furnishings)

Summary: Pillowtex is a leading manufacturer and marketer of bed pillows, blankets, mattress pads, down comforters, comforter covers and other bedroom textile furnishings.

Quantitative Evaluations

Recent Price • 27⅞
52 Wk Range • 52-23⅜

Yield • 0.9%
12-Mo. P/E • 24.1

Outlook
(1 Lowest—5 Highest)
• 3⁻

Fair Value
• 35⅝

Risk
• Average

Earn./Div. Rank
• NR

Technical Eval.
• NA

Rel. Strength Rank
(1 Lowest—99 Highest)
• 43

Insider Activity
• NA

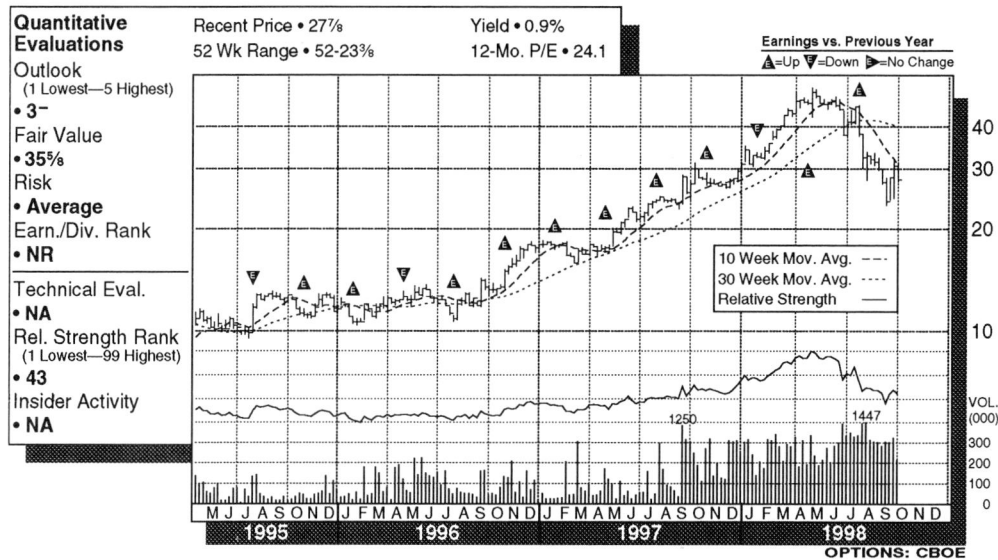

OPTIONS: CBOE

Business Profile - 11-AUG-98

In late 1997, Pillowtex acquired Fieldcrest Cannon, Inc., a manufacturer of bath and bedding home textiles, with annual sales of over $1 billion, for a combination of cash and stock. The acquisition has created one of the largest home textile manufacturers with annual sales in excess of $1.6 billion. PTX anticipates that this acquisition will result in substantial annual cost savings; $30 million in savings is targeted in 1998. Pillowtex also expects the transaction to be accretive to 1998 earnings. PTX valued the deal at over $700 million, including the assumption of debt. Earlier in 1997, PTX acquired the blanket business of Fieldcrest. In January 1998, the blanket business was consolidated and resulted in a pretax charge of $6.0 million in the fourth quarter of 1997. An additional charge of $1.5 million related to the consolidation was recorded in the first quarter of 1998.

Operational Review - 11-AUG-98

Sales in the six months ended July 4, 1998, climbed 219%, year to year, reflecting the December 1997 acquisition of Fieldcrest Cannon. Gross margins were essentially flat, and SG&A expenses declined as a percentage of sales. Despite a $1,539,000 restructuring charge, operating profits soared 271%. After a sharp increase in interest expense and taxes at 39.5%, versus 38.8%, net income jumped to $12,727,000 ($0.75 a share, diluted, after preferred dividends and based on 59% more shares), from $3,522,000 ($0.33).

Stock Performance - 02-OCT-98

In the past 30 trading days, PTX's shares have declined 11%, compared to a 7% fall in the S&P 500. Average trading volume for the past five days was 42,400 shares, compared with the 40-day moving average of 72,803 shares.

Key Stock Statistics

Dividend Rate/Share	0.24	Shareholders	300
Shs. outstg. (M)	14.1	Market cap. (B)	$0.395
Avg. daily vol. (M)	0.075	Inst. holdings	58%
Tang. Bk. Value/Share	NM		
Beta	1.37		

Value of $10,000 invested 5 years ago: NA

Fiscal Year Ending Dec. 31

	1998	1997	1996	1995	1994	1993
Revenues (Million $)						
1Q	366.4	113.8	100.8	94.74	71.82	55.48
2Q	332.1	104.9	91.19	90.79	66.58	50.86
3Q	—	152.0	143.8	146.8	102.0	92.03
4Q	—	209.4	154.9	142.6	111.5	93.81
Yr.	—	580.0	490.7	474.9	351.9	292.2
Earnings Per Share ($)						
1Q	**0.33**	**0.15**	0.09	0.11	0.20	0.25
2Q	**0.42**	**0.17**	0.14	0.10	0.12	0.06
3Q	—	**0.65**	0.58	0.45	0.32	0.50
4Q	—	**-0.22**	0.58	0.42	0.09	0.49
Yr.	—	**0.74**	1.39	1.08	0.73	1.32

Next earnings report expected: late October

Dividend Data (Dividends have been paid since 1995.)

Amount ($)	Date Decl.	Ex-Div. Date	Stock of Record	Payment Date
0.060	Nov. 11	Nov. 26	Dec. 01	Dec. 15 '97
0.060	Feb. 09	Mar. 11	Mar. 13	Mar. 27 '98
0.060	May. 05	Jun. 17	Jun. 19	Jun. 30 '98
0.060	Aug. 10	Sep. 16	Sep. 18	Sep. 30 '98

A Division of The McGraw-Hill Companies

Business Summary - 11-AUG-98

Pillowtex, North America's largest designer, manufacturer, and marketer of "top-of-the-bed" products, has gotten even bigger. In late 1997, the company acquired Fieldcrest Cannon (which is about twice the size of Pillowtex), for about $700 million in cash, stock, and assumed debt. Fieldcrest Cannon was one of the largest U.S. manufacturers of bath products and the third-largest U.S. producer of bedding products. The new PTX is one of the largest manufacturers of home textiles in the U.S.

The acquisition provides Pillowtex with broader product lines that cover a wide range of price points and distribution channels, further enhancing Pillowtex's "one-stop-shopping" strategy to leading retail customers in the U.S. and Canada. The combined company hopes to be able to realize substantial cost savings, resulting in improving operating margins. However, this is accompanied by higher debt levels and stepped-up capital spending.

Pillowtex has leading market positions in its four core product lines: blankets, bed pillows, down comforters and mattress pads. Its products are marketed to department and specialty stores, mass merchants, wholesale clubs, catalog retailers and institutions. Its products are marketed under company-owned trademarks and tradenames and customer-owned private labels, as well as certain licensed trademarks and tradenames.

With the addition of Fieldcrest Cannon, PTX now offers the Fieldcrest line which includes towels, bath rugs, sheets and fashion bedding.

The company makes a broad line of traditional bed pillows, as well as specialty bed pillows such as body and neck roll pillows. The company offers products at various quality and price levels, from synthetic pillows sold at retail prices as low as $4 to fine white goose down pillows sold at about $185.

The line of mattress pads consists of sizes for adults and children and includes natural and synthetic filled, flat, fitted and skirted pads. PTX also makes the patented Adjust-A-Fit adjustable-fit mattress pad. Pillowtex was also a pioneer in marketing down comforters in the U.S., which sell for $70 to about $400.

The company's blankets are produced in conventional and thermal weave styles. PTX is the exclusive supplier of blankets for the Ralph Lauren Home Collection.

To complement its four principal product lines, Pillowtex also offers other home fashion furnishings, including comforter covers, featherbeds, pillow protectors, decorative pillows, synthetic comforters, pillow shams, dust ruffles and window treatments.

In March 1998, PTX sold certain assets of Sure Fit, formerly Fieldcrest Cannon's ready-made furniture covering operation. The division was sold for $14 million plus the assumption of $3 million of trade payables. PTX expanded its bath and kitchen terry products line with the July 1998 acquisition of Leshner Corp., a marketer and manufacturer of bath and kitchen terry products.

Per Share Data ($)

(Year Ended Dec. 31)	1997	1996	1995	1994	1993	1992	1991	1990	1989	1988
Tangible Bk. Val.	4.45	4.04	3.41	2.43	5.11	5.00	NA	NA	NA	NA
Cash Flow	2.18	2.59	2.21	1.33	1.69	1.15	NA	NA	NA	NA
Earnings	0.74	1.39	1.08	0.73	1.32	0.84	NA	NA	NA	NA
Dividends	0.24	0.20	0.05	Nil	Nil	NA	NA	NA	NA	NA
Payout Ratio	32%	14%	5%	Nil	Nil	NA	NA	NA	NA	NA
Prices - High	35¼	18½	13⅛	21¼	20⅝	NA	NA	NA	NA	NA
- Low	15⅞	10⅜	8	8⅞	9	NA	NA	NA	NA	NA
P/E Ratio - High	48	13	12	29	16	NA	NA	NA	NA	NA
- Low	21	7	7	12	7	NA	NA	NA	NA	NA

Income Statement Analysis (Million $)

	1997	1996	1995	1994	1993	1992	1991	1990	1989	1988
Revs.	580	491	475	352	292	273	NA	NA	NA	NA
Oper. Inc.	58.3	50.9	48.5	24.8	27.9	20.6	NA	NA	NA	NA
Depr.	16.1	12.8	12.0	6.4	3.6	3.1	NA	NA	NA	NA
Int. Exp.	22.5	14.0	17.5	6.4	3.0	NA	NA	NA	NA	NA
Pretax Inc.	13.8	24.2	19.0	12.4	21.2	NA	NA	NA	NA	NA
Eff. Tax Rate	40%	39%	40%	38%	39%	NA	NA	NA	NA	NA
Net Inc.	8.2	14.7	11.5	7.7	12.9	8.4	NA	NA	NA	NA

Balance Sheet & Other Fin. Data (Million $)

	1997	1996	1995	1994	1993	1992	1991	1990	1989	1988
Cash	4.6	0.0	0.4	0.6	2.6	NA	NA	NA	NA	NA
Curr. Assets	641	222	186	185	124	NA	NA	NA	NA	NA
Total Assets	1,410	376	325	320	181	130	NA	NA	NA	NA
Curr. Liab.	246	71.2	75.7	62.3	45.6	NA	NA	NA	NA	NA
LT Debt	785	195	153	177	63.7	52.4	NA	NA	NA	NA
Common Eqty.	197	100	88.0	76.5	69.3	48.5	NA	NA	NA	NA
Total Cap.	1,112	305	249	257	135	102	NA	NA	NA	NA
Cap. Exp.	20.6	21.0	12.4	10.5	15.1	5.9	NA	NA	NA	NA
Cash Flow	24.2	27.5	23.5	14.1	16.5	11.5	NA	NA	NA	NA
Curr. Ratio	2.6	3.1	2.5	3.0	2.7	NA	NA	NA	NA	NA
% LT Debt of Cap.	70.6	63.9	61.7	68.9	47.1	51.5	NA	NA	NA	NA
% Net Inc.of Revs.	1.4	3.0	2.5	2.2	4.4	3.1	NA	NA	NA	NA
% Ret. on Assets	0.9	4.2	3.6	3.1	6.5	NA	NA	NA	NA	NA
% Ret. on Equity	5.5	15.6	14.0	10.5	31.6	NA	NA	NA	NA	NA

Data as orig. reptd.; bef. results of disc. opers. and/or spec. items. Per share data adj. for stk. divs. as of ex-div. date. Bold denotes diluted EPS (FASB 128). E-Estimated. NA-Not Available. NM-Not Meaningful. NR-Not Ranked.

Office—4111 Mint Way, Dallas, TX 75237. **Tel**—(214) 333-3225. **Website**—www.pillowtex.com **Chrmn, Pres & CEO**—C. M. Hansen Jr. **EVP & CFO**—J. D. Cordes. **Investor Contact**—Katharine W. Kenny. **Dirs**—C. N. Baker, J. D. Cordes, P. G. Gillease, C. M. Hansen Jr., W. B. Madden, M. J. McHugh, M. R. Silverthorne, S. E. Shimizu. **Transfer Agent & Registrar**—ChaseMellon Shareholder Services, Ridgefield Park, NJ. **Incorporated**—in Illinois in 1954; reincorporated in Texas in 1986. **Empl**— 14,150. **S&P Analyst:** Kathleen J. Fraser

Pioneer Group

4989J

NASDAQ Symbol **PIOG**

In S&P SmallCap 600

03-OCT-98

Industry:
Financial (Diversified)

Summary: The Pioneer Group is engaged in global asset manage-ment, mutual fund distribution and servicing, venture capital investing and natural resources operations.

Quantitative Evaluations

Outlook
(1 Lowest—5 Highest)
• **1⁻**

Fair Value
• **14⅜**

Risk
• **Low**

Earn./Div. Rank
• **B+**

Technical Eval.
• **Bearish** since 3/98

Rel. Strength Rank
(1 Lowest—99 Highest)
• **24**

Insider Activity
• **Neutral**

Recent Price • 16⅜	Yield • Nil
52 Wk Range • 33⅞-14⅞	12-Mo. P/E • 39.0

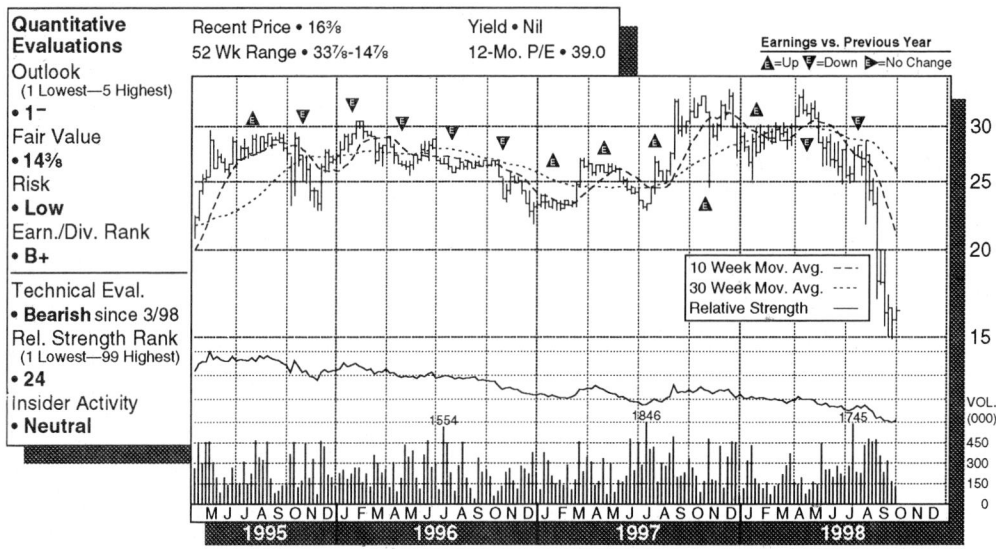

Earnings vs. Previous Year
▲=Up ▼=Down ▶=No Change

10 Week Mov. Avg. -- --
30 Week Mov. Avg. · · · · ·
Relative Strength ———

Business Profile - 07-AUG-98

PIOG engages in financial services businesses in the U.S. and overseas, operates a gold mine in Ghana, and participates as owner or joint venturer in several asset management and natural resources operations. In the U.S., it provides a number of financial services, includ-ing asset management, mutual fund distribution and servicing, and venture capital investing. The company's overseas investment activities include investment oper-ations in Poland, Ireland, Russia, the Czech Republic, and India. PIOG's natural resource development busi-ness includes mining activities in Ghana, exploration activities elsewhere in Africa, and natural resource de-velopment ventures in Russia, including the develop-ment of Russian Far East timber production.

Operational Review - 07-AUG-98

Total revenues in the first six months of 1998 rose 7.6%, year to year, reflecting higher financial services revenues and increased gold sales. Total costs and ex-penses climbed 20%, stemming from higher manage ment and administrative expenses, greater gold mining operating costs, and higher timber operating expenses. Other income was down sharply; a pretax loss was re-alized, compared to a pretax gain. After taxes of $5,653,000, versus taxes at 45.8%, and minority inter-est, a net loss of $6,783,000 ($0.27 a share), con-trasted with net income of $12,284,000 ($0.48).

Stock Performance - 02-OCT-98

In the past 30 trading days, PIOG's shares have de-clined 30%, compared to a 7% fall in the S&P 500. Average trading volume for the past five days was 24,460 shares, compared with the 40-day moving aver-age of 82,008 shares.

Key Stock Statistics

Dividend Rate/Share	Nil	Shareholders	4,800
Shs. outstg. (M)	25.4	Market cap. (B)	$0.416
Avg. daily vol. (M)	0.043	Inst. holdings	60%
Tang. Bk. Value/Share	6.08		
Beta	0.65		

Value of $10,000 invested 5 years ago: $ 24,479

Fiscal Year Ending Dec. 31

	1998	1997	1996	1995	1994	1993
Revenues (Million $)						
1Q	79.20	70.11	56.48	45.68	42.60	29.70
2Q	82.43	80.03	56.92	46.55	39.82	30.90
3Q	—	98.82	62.50	51.24	45.31	32.90
4Q	—	93.88	63.21	55.25	44.02	35.90
Yr.	—	343.0	239.1	198.7	171.7	129.4
Earnings Per Share ($)						
1Q	0.21	0.29	0.20	0.23	0.31	0.15
2Q	-0.48	0.19	0.14	0.29	0.27	0.17
3Q	—	0.37	0.20	0.25	0.33	0.19
4Q	—	0.29	0.20	0.13	0.25	0.22
Yr.	—	1.14	0.74	0.90	1.16	0.72

Next earnings report expected: early November

Dividend Data (Dividends have been paid since 1979.)

Amount ($)	Date Decl.	Ex-Div. Date	Stock of Record	Payment Date
0.100	Nov. 12	Nov. 26	Dec. 01	Dec. 09 '97
0.100	Feb. 04	Feb. 26	Mar. 02	Mar. 10 '98
0.100	May. 14	May. 28	Jun. 01	Jun. 10 '98

A Division of The **McGraw·Hill** Companies

The Pioneer Group, Inc.

Business Summary - 07-AUG-98

True to its name, The Pioneer Group has broken new ground with business ventures in many diverse regions of the world. From mutual fund operations in Boston to asset management in the Czech Republic and gold mining in Ghana, The Pioneer Group is a truly global company, engaged in a wide variety of financial services and natural resource ventures.

In the U.S., Pioneer offers various financial services, including asset management, mutual fund distribution and servicing, and venture capital investing. The Pioneer Management Corp. subsidiary serves as investment manager to 33 domestic open-end mutual funds and one domestic closed-end mutual fund. A roaring stock market and record sales in the mutual fund industry boosted total assets under management to $21.0 billion at December 31, 1997, from $17.0 billion at year-end 1996. Since management fees are tied to the level of assets under management, the influx of funds helped financial services revenues increase 50% in 1997.

In financial services, Pioneer has distinguished itself by committing capital to the international frontier, where it sees opportunity for growth. Such businesses include investment operations in Warsaw, Poland, where Pioneer manages four mutual funds and an institutional venture capital fund, and owns a majority interest in a brokerage operation. In Dublin, Ireland, PIOG distributes shares of, manages and services six offshore investment funds, sold primarily in Western Europe. In addition, PIOG provides a variety of investment related services in Moscow, Russia, the Czech Republic, India and Taiwan.

In 1988, the company purchased a 90% ownership stake in Teberebie Goldfields Ltd. (TGL), a mining company located in the city of Tarkwa in the western region of the Republic of Ghana. The gold mine's production rose steadily from 1991 to 1995. However, in 1996, actual production was significantly below forecasts, because of weather, equipment and personnel problems. To boost production, TGL is changing its mining method to bulk mining from selective mining. PIOG's Phase III mine expansion reached operating capacity in 1997, boosting production by 29%, to 263,000 ounces. Cash production costs per ounce were reduced by over 14%, to $230 an ounce. Production increases, however, were offset by 12% lower average realized gold prices. Gold revenues in 1997 climbed 14%, to $89.5 million.

In December 1997, Auerbach Grayson & Company and PIOG formed a trading alliance that will allow U.S. institutions to tap the potential of Russia's emerging securities market. The agreement will combine Pioneer's Moscow-based analysis of the Russian securities market with Auerbach Grayson's strong distribution capability in the United States.

In the six months ended June 30, 1998, PIOG posted a net loss of $6,783,000 ($0.27 a share), compared to net income of $12,284,000 ($0.48) a year earlier. This loss reflects the poor performance of the company's emerging markets financial servi ces operations.

Per Share Data ($) (Year Ended Dec. 31)	1997	1996	1995	1994	1993	1992	1991	1990	1989	1988
Tangible Bk. Val.	6.48	5.79	5.06	4.43	3.25	3.69	3.31	2.91	2.59	2.34
Earnings	1.14	0.74	0.90	1.16	0.72	0.59	0.58	0.50	0.58	0.57
Dividends	0.40	0.40	0.40	0.32	0.23	0.21	0.20	0.20	0.20	0.14
Payout Ratio	35%	54%	44%	27%	31%	36%	35%	40%	34%	25%
Prices - High	33 7/8	30 1/2	29 5/8	25 3/8	13 1/2	7 3/8	6 3/8	7 1/8	6 1/4	4 5/8
- Low	22 3/4	21 3/4	17 3/4	12 3/8	7 1/8	5 1/8	4	3 3/4	4 1/2	3 3/8
P/E Ratio - High	30	41	33	22	19	12	11	14	11	8
- Low	20	29	20	11	10	9	7	7	8	6
Income Statement Analysis (Million $)										
Mgt. Fees	121	87.8	64.6	64.3	39.5	32.2	30.3	30.4	31.9	27.9
Gold Sales	89.5	78.3	90.2	67.6	59.2	43.8	23.2	Nil	Nil	Nil
Total Revs.	343	239	199	172	129	102	81.0	60.0	61.0	55.0
Int. Exp.	19.1	9.4	1.0	1.3	2.4	1.4	1.6	NA	NA	NA
Net Bef. Taxes	56.7	30.4	39.4	47.6	34.5	27.5	25.4	20.6	24.1	22.8
Eff. Tax Rate	49%	38%	42%	30%	47%	47%	43%	41%	41%	39%
Net Inc.	29.2	18.8	22.8	29.0	18.1	14.6	14.4	12.3	14.1	13.8
Balance Sheet & Other Fin. Data (Million $)										
Total Assets	604	493	319	203	172	135	124	109	100	69.0
Cash Items	67.2	32.5	27.8	23.1	21.5	47.8	46.9	38.5	44.2	44.2
Rec.	56.8	43.2	31.9	22.0	20.2	9.2	8.4	4.5	8.8	5.2
Secs. Owned	38.3	27.5	7.6	6.5	15.8	9.2	5.4	4.9	1.3	1.3
Sec. Borrowed	Nil	15.6	56.1	13.6	6.0	4.5	4.8	4.3	1.8	Nil
Due Brokers & Cust.	Nil	9.0	12.4	7.1	7.9	2.8	3.2	1.3	5.0	1.8
Other Liabs.	Nil	78.4	44.5	33.2	35.0	21.0	13.3	8.2	8.8	8.2
Capitalization:										
Debt	168	150	11.0	9.1	13.3	12.0	17.1	20.3	17.3	1.2
Equity	184	162	150	134	107	93.0	85.0	75.0	67.0	57.0
Total	468	399	206	148	123	106	103	95.0	84.0	59.0
% Exp./Op. Revs.	84.4	88.7	80.5	72.3	73.1	74.4	73.4	67.0	59.9	60.7
% Return On Revs.	8.5	7.9	11.5	16.9	14.0	14.3	17.8	20.4	23.3	25.1
% Ret. on Assets	5.3	4.7	8.7	15.5	11.8	11.3	12.4	11.7	16.8	22.1
% Ret. on Equity	16.9	12.0	16.0	24.1	18.1	16.4	18.1	17.3	22.9	26.8

Data as orig. reptd.; bef. results of disc. opers. and/or spec. items. Per share data adj. for stk. divs. as of ex-div. date. Bold denotes diluted EPS (FASB 128). E-Estimated. NA-Not Available. NM-Not Meaningful. NR-Not Ranked.

Office—60 State St., Boston, MA 02109. **Tel**—(617) 742-7825. **Chrmn & Pres**—J. F. Cogan Jr. **SVP, CFO, Treas & Investor Contact**—William H. Keough. **Secy**—J. P. Barri. **Dirs**—R. L. Butler, J. F. Cogan Jr., M. Engleman, A. J. Strassman, J. S. Teja, D. D. Tripple, J. H. Valentine. **Transfer Agent**—State Street Bank & Trust Co., Boston. **Incorporated**—in Delaware in 1956. **Empl**— 3,625. **S&P Analyst:** Michael Schneider

03-OCT-98

Industry: Electronics (Component Distributors)

Summary: Pioneer-Standard is one of the largest distributors of industrial and end-user electronic products in the U.S.

Quantitative Evaluations

Recent Price • 5⅞
52 Wk Range • 18¼-5⅝

Yield • 2.0%
12-Mo. P/E • 5.6

Outlook
(1 Lowest—5 Highest)
• 5

Fair Value
• 11⅝

Risk
• Average

Earn./Div. Rank
• B+

Technical Eval.
• NA

Rel. Strength Rank
(1 Lowest—99 Highest)
• 17

Insider Activity
• Neutral

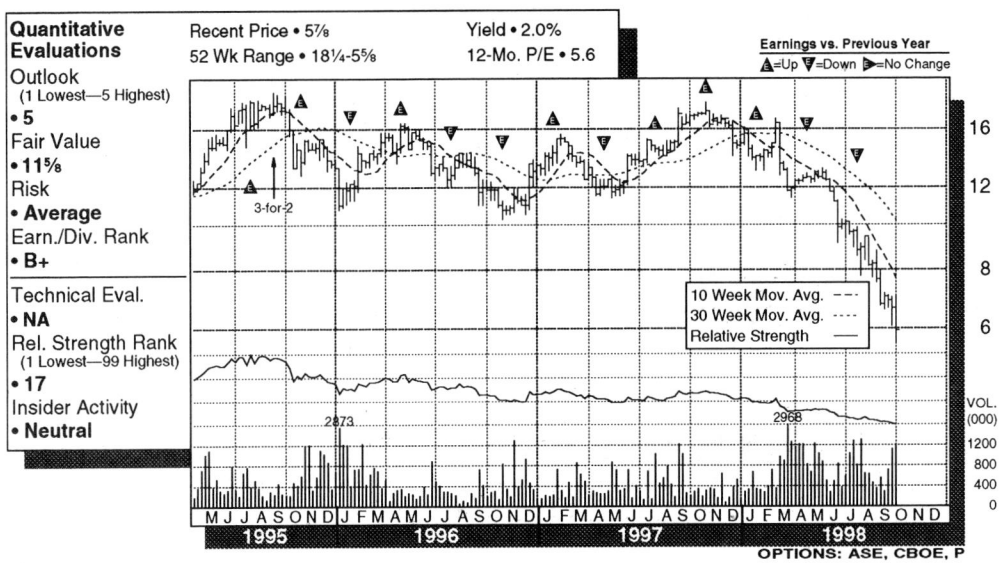

Earnings vs. Previous Year
△=Up ▽=Down ▷=No Change

10 Week Mov. Avg. ---
30 Week Mov. Avg. ····
Relative Strength —

OPTIONS: ASE, CBOE, P

Business Profile - 28-AUG-98

Pioneer-Standard's results in the first quarter were impacted by a slowdown in the semiconductor industry which led to reduced average selling prices and gross profit erosion. The company is still experiencing strong revenue growth at its newly acquired Dickens Data Systems business, coupled with progressive growth in the balance of its business mix. PIOS expects operating expenses to continue to decline as a percentage of sales. The acquisition of Dickens, an IBM distributor located in Atlanta, GA, adds about $340 million to revenues, and makes the company a leading distributor of IBM computer systems, peripherals and services in North America.

Operational Review - 28-AUG-98

In the first quarter of FY 99 (Mar.), revenues advanced 37%, year to year, reflecting the acquisition of Dickens Data Systems coupled with growth in all three product categories. Gross margins narrowed due to a softer than expected semiconductor market which led to lower average selling prices. Operating expenses rose 33%, and after a 56% increase in interest expense, net income declined 24%, to $5,579,000 ($0.20 a share, on 35% more shares), from $7,305,000 ($0.28).

Stock Performance - 02-OCT-98

In the past 30 trading days, PIOS's shares have declined 28%, compared to a 7% fall in the S&P 500. Average trading volume for the past five days was 264,020 shares, compared with the 40-day moving average of 139,554 shares.

Key Stock Statistics

Dividend Rate/Share	0.12	Shareholders	2,400
Shs. outstg. (M)	26.3	Market cap. (B)	$0.156
Avg. daily vol. (M)	0.175	Inst. holdings	79%
Tang. Bk. Value/Share	3.42		
Beta	0.62		

Value of $10,000 invested 5 years ago: $ 9,329

Fiscal Year Ending Mar. 31

	1999	1998	1997	1996	1995	1994
Revenues (Million $)						
1Q	544.3	396.3	375.2	224.7	183.8	134.5
2Q	—	431.3	357.7	234.9	194.4	137.3
3Q	—	424.1	384.4	263.9	212.4	149.8
4Q	—	433.6	391.5	381.7	241.5	159.2
Yr.	—	1,685	1,509	1,105	832.1	580.8
Earnings Per Share ($)						
1Q	0.20	0.28	0.27	0.29	0.26	0.20
2Q	—	0.28	0.20	0.29	0.25	0.21
3Q	—	0.31	0.25	0.18	0.27	0.21
4Q	—	0.27	0.29	0.33	0.32	0.24
Yr.	—	1.14	1.00	1.09	1.09	0.87

Next earnings report expected: NA

Dividend Data (Dividends have been paid since 1965.)

Amount ($)	Date Decl.	Ex-Div. Date	Stock of Record	Payment Date
0.030	Dec. 23	Jan. 05	Jan. 07	Feb. 02 '98
0.030	Mar. 25	Apr. 06	Apr. 08	May. 01 '98
0.030	Jun. 24	Jul. 06	Jul. 08	Aug. 01 '98
0.030	Sep. 23	Oct. 05	Oct. 07	Nov. 01 '98

A Division of The McGraw-Hill Companies

STANDARD
&POOR'S
STOCK REPORTS

Pioneer-Standard Electronics, Inc.

4990T
03-OCT-98

Business Summary - 28-AUG-98

By aligning itself with some of the biggest names in the electronics and computer industries, Pioneer-Standard Electronics, Inc. (PIOS) has become one of the largest electronics distributors in North America. The company distributes a wide range of electronic components and computer products manufactured by other firms. The products are sold to value-added resellers, research laboratories, government agencies, and end users, such as manufacturing companies. Pioneer is more than just a "middleman," connecting suppliers with users. The company also provides value-added services such as inventory management, systems integration, kitting operations, memory and logic device programming, and connector assemblies to customer specifications.

The products the company offers are grouped into three basic categories: semiconductors, computer products, and passive and electromechanical components. Semiconductor products, which accounted for 36% of Pioneer's sales in FY 98 (Mar.), versus 41% in FY 97, include microprocessors and memory devices. Computer products include mini and personal computers and disk drives; they accounted for 44% of sales in FY 98 (39% in FY 97). Passive, interconnect and electromechanical products accounted for 19% of sales in FY 98 (17%), and consist of capacitors, resistors, connectors, switches and power conditioning equipment.

Pioneer distributes electronic components supplied by over 100 manufacturers, including such well-known companies as Digital Equipment, Intel, IBM, Cisco Systems, Lucent Technologies, Micron Technology and U.S. Robotics (now a subsidiary of 3Com Corp.). However, products purchased from a relatively small number of suppliers account for a majority of Pioneer's sales. Digital and Intel are the company's two largest suppliers, accounting for 29% and 18%, respectively, of total sales in FY 98. Pioneer's five largest suppliers accounted for 68% of total sales volume in FY 98.

The company is one of the largest of the approximately 1,500 electronics distributors in North America, with FY 98 sales of about $1.7 billion to more than 24,000 customers. The company plans to continue to increase the number of its distribution agreements, in order to expand its product offerings.

In April 1998, the company acquired Dickens Data Systems for about $121 million, making the company a leading distributor of IBM computer systems, peripherals and services in North America. In April 1998, the company also purchased a minority interest in Eurodia Electron PLC, a European distributor of electronic components. In the third quarter of FY 98, the company purchased a minority interest in World Peace Industrial Co., Ltd. of Taiwan, an Asia-Pacific distributor of industrial electronic components.

Per Share Data ($)

(Year Ended Mar. 31)	1998	1997	1996	1995	1994	1993	1992	1991	1990	1989
Tangible Bk. Val.	2.89	5.63	4.81	5.65	4.60	3.82	3.11	2.87	2.46	2.18
Cash Flow	1.69	1.63	1.48	1.37	1.10	0.85	0.51	0.64	0.47	0.51
Earnings	1.14	1.00	1.09	1.09	0.87	0.63	0.29	0.45	0.31	0.36
Dividends	0.12	0.12	0.11	0.08	0.07	0.05	0.05	0.04	0.04	0.04
Payout Ratio	11%	12%	10%	7%	8%	8%	16%	10%	13%	11%
Cal. Yrs.	1997	1996	1995	1994	1993	1992	1991	1990	1989	1988
Prices - High	18¼	16½	19¼	13⅛	11	8⅛	5¼	4½	3⅜	3⅜
- Low	11⅜	10¼	10⅝	8¼	5⅜	3⅛	2⅝	2⅛	2⅛	2¹/₁₆
P/E Ratio - High	16	16	18	12	13	13	18	10	11	9
- Low	10	10	10	8	6	5	9	5	7	6

Income Statement Analysis (Million $)

	1998	1997	1996	1995	1994	1993	1992	1991	1990	1989
Revs.	1,685	1,509	1,105	832	581	430	362	345	320	302
Oper. Inc.	87.9	72.0	61.0	50.0	36.7	25.7	16.5	20.9	16.8	19.4
Depr.	15.0	14.6	9.0	6.2	5.3	4.7	4.1	3.5	2.8	2.8
Int. Exp.	20.7	17.1	8.1	4.0	2.7	3.6	4.5	4.8	5.2	5.6
Pretax Inc.	52.1	40.3	43.6	42.2	31.7	20.0	8.5	13.4	9.5	11.1
Eff. Tax Rate	41%	42%	42%	41%	38%	35%	38%	38%	40%	41%
Net Inc.	30.5	23.3	25.3	25.0	19.7	12.9	5.3	8.3	5.7	6.5

Balance Sheet & Other Fin. Data (Million $)

	1998	1997	1996	1995	1994	1993	1992	1991	1990	1989
Cash	32.0	28.1	24.4	9.6	6.0	1.9	1.9	2.5	3.5	3.2
Curr. Assets	701	498	466	274	178	136	116	114	114	111
Total Assets	958	593	559	327	220	172	151	146	145	133
Curr. Liab.	239	200	185	142	93.0	64.8	47.1	47.8	49.7	37.9
LT Debt	336	174	164	56.3	22.3	21.3	44.7	44.3	49.4	54.4
Common Eqty.	245	214	151	126	105	84.1	57.5	52.9	44.8	39.8
Total Cap.	591	393	318	185	127	107	104	99	95.0	95.0
Cap. Exp.	44.2	20.0	21.0	11.3	7.6	4.2	5.1	4.1	10.3	3.4
Cash Flow	45.5	37.8	34.3	31.2	29.9	17.6	9.5	11.8	8.6	9.3
Curr. Ratio	2.9	2.5	2.5	1.9	1.9	2.1	2.5	2.4	2.3	2.9
% LT Debt of Cap.	56.9	44.2	51.8	30.4	17.5	19.9	43.1	45.0	51.8	57.1
% Net Inc.of Revs.	1.8	1.5	2.3	3.0	3.4	3.0	1.5	2.4	1.8	2.2
% Ret. on Assets	3.9	4.0	5.7	9.1	10.0	7.3	3.6	5.7	4.1	5.0
% Ret. on Equity	13.3	12.8	18.2	21.8	20.9	16.9	9.6	16.9	13.6	17.7

Data as orig. reptd.; bef. results of disc. opers. and/or spec. items. Per share data adj. for stk. divs. as of ex-div. date. Bold denotes diluted EPS (FASB 128). E-Estimated. NA-Not Available. NM-Not Meaningful. NR-Not Ranked.

Office—4800 East 131st St., Cleveland, OH 44105. **Tel**—(216) 587-3600. **Website**—http://www.pios.com **Chrmn & CEO**—J. L. Bayman. **Pres & COO**—A. Rhein. **Secy**—W. A. Papenbrock. **VP, Treas, Asst Secy & Investor Contact**—John V. Goodger. **Dirs**—J. L. Bayman, C. F. Christ, F. A. Downey, V. Gelb, G. E. Heffern, A. Rhein, E. Z. Singer, T. C. Sullivan, K. E. Ware. **Transfer Agent & Registrar**—National City Bank, Cleveland.**Incorporated**—in Ohio in 1963. **Empl**— 2,333. **S&P Analyst:** Jim Corridore

Pittston BAX Group

1845M

NYSE Symbol **PZX**

In S&P SmallCap 600

03-OCT-98

Industry: Air Freight

Summary: Pittston BAX Group (formerly Pittston Burlington Group) Common Stock tracks Pittston Co.'s BAX Global unit, which provides air and ocean freight forwarding and logistics services.

S&P Opinion: Hold (★★★)	Recent Price • 7½ Yield • 3.2% 52 Wk Range • 31-6⅜ 12-Mo. P/E • 5.5

Quantitative Evaluations

Outlook
(1 Lowest—5 Highest)
• **5+**

Fair Value
• **13⅛**

Risk
• **NA**

Earn./Div. Rank
• **NR**

Technical Eval.
• **NA**

Rel. Strength Rank
(1 Lowest—99 Highest)
• **13**

Insider Activity
• **NA**

Earnings vs. Previous Year
▲=Up ▼=Down ▶=No Change

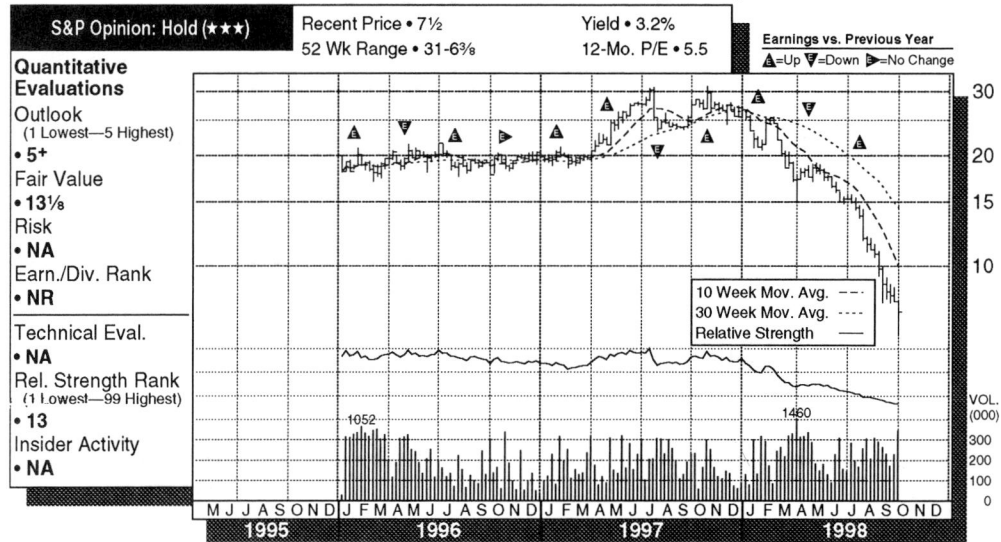

10 Week Mov. Avg. ---
30 Week Mov. Avg. ....
Relative Strength ——

Overview - 27-AUG-98

International volumes could grow 8% in 1998, following a 9.0% gain in 1997. While shipments in Asia may slip, BAX Global continues to post good gains in Europe and Latin America. In early 1998, Honeywell added BAX for international heavy freight. BAX has also recently obtained contracts from Reynolds Metals, Nortel, Wal-Mart, and Epson America. Domestic shipments will grow about 6% in 1998, down from 1997's 8.7% pace, reflecting softness in auto and high-tech industries, and the absence of business picked up during the UPS strike. On the positive side, BAX will benefit from a new contract to handle two-day shipments for RPS. Margins will narrow, as BAX suffers from poor utilization of aircraft operated by ATI, and incurs costs to correct Year 2000 issues and upgrade its information systems. Yields are expected to decline both internationally and in North America, partly reflecting a mix shift towards heavier, deferred cargo. While PZX's profit comparisons will benefit from the absence of a 1997 charge of $0.40 a share, an offset will be higher interest expense and an executive severance package.

Valuation - 27-AUG-98

The shares of this air freight company have fallen sharply in 1998. BAX's costs spun out of control in 1998. Although volume growth remains positive, a slump in yields is hurting profits. Profits are also being depressed by heavy outlays to catch up on technology and Year 2000 issues. Investors assign a low P/E multiple to PZX because of the lack of consistency in its performance, and increasing economic uncertainty. While we think that PZX will post positive year to year comparisons beginning in the 1999 first half, we are neutral on the stock, since a lengthy basebuilding period may be required to correct the major technical damage to the shares.

Key Stock Statistics

S&P EPS Est. 1998	0.90	Tang. Bk. Value/Share		6.72
P/E on S&P Est. 1998	8.3	Beta		NA
S&P EPS Est. 1999	1.20	Shareholders		5,400
Dividend Rate/Share	0.24	Market cap. (B)		$0.153
Shs. outstg. (M)	20.4	Inst. holdings		74%
Avg. daily vol. (M)	0.074			

Value of $10,000 invested 5 years ago: NA

Fiscal Year Ending Dec. 31

	1998	1997	1996	1995	1994	1993
Revenues (Million $)						
1Q	402.4	371.4	351.9	323.9	261.5	231.0
2Q	432.9	399.6	363.4	342.0	302.3	240.0
3Q	—	439.4	377.7	365.8	311.9	255.0
4Q	—	448.0	407.3	383.1	339.6	272.0
Yr.	—	1,662	1,500	1,415	1,215	998.0
Earnings Per Share ($)						
1Q	**-0.15**	0.26	0.20	0.21	0.18	-0.02
2Q	**0.05**	-0.10	0.46	0.42	0.61	0.15
3Q	**E0.55**	0.82	0.56	0.56	0.71	0.37
4Q	**E0.45**	0.66	0.55	0.54	0.53	0.33
Yr.	**E0.90**	1.62	1.72	1.73	2.03	0.84

Next earnings report expected: late October

Dividend Data (Dividends have been paid since 1996.)

Amount ($)	Date Decl.	Ex-Div. Date	Stock of Record	Payment Date
0.060	Nov. 07	Nov. 13	Nov. 17	Dec. 01 '97
0.060	Feb. 06	Feb. 12	Feb. 17	Mar. 02 '98
0.060	May. 01	May. 13	May. 15	Jun. 01 '98
0.060	Jul. 10	Aug. 13	Aug. 17	Sep. 01 '98

A Division of The McGraw-Hill Companies

Business Summary - 27-AUG-98

Pittston BAX Group Common Stock (formerly Pittston Burlington Group Common Stock) was created in January 1996 to track the results of Pittston Co.'s BAX Global unit. BAX specializes in the movement of heavy air cargo (over 70 lbs.), using an integrated network of aircraft and ground vehicles. In recent years, the company's international operations have grown faster than its domestic business, and now represent its largest revenue source. PZX's profit performance has been erratic in recent years, in part due to its lack of control over its aircraft fleet. The company addressed this issue through the purchase of Air Transport International in April 1998, for $29 million.

BAX Global offers one of the few fully integrated networks of air and ground transportation. In North America, it controls a fleet of 36 aircraft. Internationally, BAX buys space on commercial passenger airlines and is considered an air forwarder. In both markets, the BAX consolidates the freight of various customers into shipments for common destinations and arranges for door-to-door transportation of this freight.

International expedited freight services, which are provided in 122 nations through a network of more than 500 offices, accounted for 47% of total revenues in 1997, up from 44% in 1994.

In North American air freight markets (38% of total revenues in 1997), BAX's fleet of 30 leased and six owned aircraft gives it a competitive edge over several thousand domestic air forwarders. Because BAX does not operate any of its aircraft directly, it has been unable to deliver a consistent service. To compensate, it has entered expense short-term wet leases for backup aircraft. PZX hoped to correct this problem by acquiring Air Transport International (ATI), primarily for ATI's FAA operating certificate. The purchase of ATI, for $29 million, closed in April 1998.

In the 1997 second quarter, PZX incurred a charge of $0.40 a share to cover costs related to the redesign of its information systems and business processes. Beginning in 1998, PZX will spend $30 million annually for process enhancements. It also will spend a total of $30 million to $35 million in 1998 and 1999 to correct Year 2000 problems. These costs will depress EPS by $0.90 in 1998 and $0.60 in 1999. PZX hope to see benefits from the program beginning in 2000.

Other services (15% of 1997 revenues) consist primarily of customs clearance, where BAX acts as customs broker to facilitate the clearance of goods through customs at international points of entry. The Global Logistics unit provides shippers with packages of transportation/distribution services that include inventory management, storage and warehouse control, product subassembly, order fulfillment and return services. BAX also provides ocean freight forwarding services.

Per Share Data ($)

(Year Ended Dec. 31)	1997	1996	1995	1994	1993	1992	1991	1990	1989	1988
Tangible Bk. Val.	7.31	6.14	3.84	2.89	0.83	NA	NA	NA	NA	NA
Cash Flow	3.11	2.98	2.78	2.94	1.63	0.96	NA	NA	NA	NA
Earnings	1.62	1.76	1.73	2.03	0.84	0.18	NA	NA	NA	NA
Dividends	0.24	0.24	NA	NA	NA	NA	NA	NA	NA	NA
Payout Ratio	15%	14%	NA	NA	NA	NA	NA	NA	NA	NA
Prices - High	31	21⅝	NA	NA	NA	NA	NA	NA	NA	NA
- Low	18½	17	NA	NA	NA	NA	NA	NA	NA	NA
P/E Ratio - High	19	12	NA	NA	NA	NA	NA	NA	NA	NA
- Low	11	10	NA	NA	NA	NA	NA	NA	NA	NA

Income Statement Analysis (Million $)

	1997	1996	1995	1994	1993	1992	1991	1990	1989	1988
Revs.	1,662	1,500	1,415	1,215	998	900	NA	NA	NA	NA
Oper. Inc.	83.8	79.1	71.1	81.9	48.6	26.1	NA	NA	NA	NA
Depr.	29.9	23.4	20.0	17.3	15.4	14.5	NA	NA	NA	NA
Int. Exp.	5.2	4.1	5.1	3.9	6.1	3.5	NA	NA	NA	NA
Pretax Inc.	51.3	53.5	51.6	61.2	27.9	8.6	NA	NA	NA	NA
Eff. Tax Rate	37%	37%	36%	37%	45%	61%	NA	NA	NA	NA
Net Inc.	32.3	33.8	32.9	38.4	15.5	3.3	NA	NA	NA	NA

Balance Sheet & Other Fin. Data (Million $)

	1997	1996	1995	1994	1993	1992	1991	1990	1989	1988
Cash	28.8	17.8	25.8	18.4	13.3	NA	NA	NA	NA	NA
Curr. Assets	355	283	278	251	176	NA	NA	NA	NA	NA
Total Assets	701	616	572	522	432	NA	NA	NA	NA	NA
Curr. Liab.	312	259	254	219	172	NA	NA	NA	NA	NA
LT Debt	37.0	28.7	26.7	41.9	45.5	NA	NA	NA	NA	NA
Common Eqty.	324	305	272	241	203	NA	NA	NA	NA	NA
Total Cap.	362	349	309	284	250	NA	NA	NA	NA	NA
Cap. Exp.	31.1	61.3	32.4	24.0	28.4	6.7	NA	NA	NA	NA
Cash Flow	62.3	57.2	52.8	55.7	30.9	17.8	NA	NA	NA	NA
Curr. Ratio	1.1	1.1	1.1	1.1	1.0	NA	NA	NA	NA	NA
% LT Debt of Cap.	10.2	8.2	8.7	14.7	18.2	NA	NA	NA	NA	NA
% Net Inc.of Revs.	1.9	2.3	2.3	3.2	1.6	0.4	NA	NA	NA	NA
% Ret. on Assets	4.8	5.7	6.0	8.0	3.6	NA	NA	NA	NA	NA
% Ret. on Equity	6.3	11.7	12.8	17.3	8.1	NA	NA	NA	NA	NA

Data as orig. reptd.; bef. results of disc. opers. and/or spec. items. Per share data adj. for stk. divs. as of ex-div. date. Bold denotes diluted EPS (FASB 128). E-Estimated. NA-Not Available. NM-Not Meaningful. NR-Not Ranked.

Office—1000 Virginia Center Parkway, P.O. Box 4229, Glen Allen, VA 23058-4229. **Tel**—(804) 553-3600. **Fax**—(804) 553-3753. **Website**—http:// www.baxworld.com **Chrmn**—J. R. Barker. **Pres & CEO**—C. R. Campbell. **Vice Chrmn**—D. L. Marshall. **VP & Secy**—A. F. Reed. **SVP & CFO**—G. R. Rogliano. **Investor Contact**—Burt Traub. **Dirs**—R. G. Ackerman, J. R. Barker, J. L. Broadhead, W. F. Craig, R. M. Gross, C. F. Haywood, D. L. Marshall, R. H. Spilman, A. H. Zimmerman. **Transfer Agent & Registrar**—First National Bank of Boston. **Incorporated**—in Delaware in 1930; reincorporated in Virginia in 1986. **Empl**— 6,400. **S&P Analyst:** Stephen R. Klein

03-OCT-98

Industry:
Oil & Gas (Exploration & Production)

Summary: PLX is engaged in the acquisition, exploitation and production of oil and natural gas in the U.S., and the marketing, transportation, terminalling and storage of crude oil.

Quantitative Evaluations

Recent Price • 16¾
52 Wk Range • 21-14⅜

Yield • Nil
12-Mo. P/E • 34.3

Outlook
(1 Lowest—5 Highest)
• **NA**

Fair Value
• **NA**

Risk
• **Average**

Earn./Div. Rank
• **B-**

Technical Eval.
• **Bearish** since 3/98

Rel. Strength Rank
(1 Lowest—99 Highest)
• **77**

Insider Activity
• **NA**

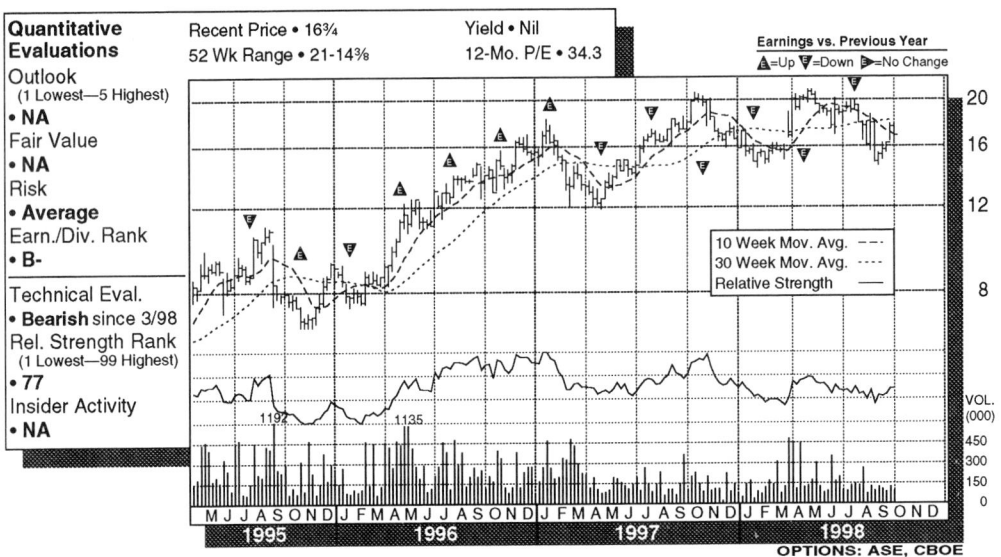

Earnings vs. Previous Year
▲=Up ▼=Down ▶=No Change

10 Week Mov. Avg. ---
30 Week Mov. Avg. ·····
Relative Strength —

OPTIONS: ASE, CBOE

Business Profile - 26-AUG-98

This independent energy company aims to increase its proved reserves and cash flow by exploiting and producing oil and natural gas from its existing properties, acquiring additional underdeveloped oil properties, and exploring for significant new sources of reserves. In March 1997, as part of its expansion plan, PLX acquired Chevron's interest in the Montebello Field in California, for $25 million. In November, the company acquired a California producing oil field from Shell subsidiaries, in a transaction valued at about $23 million. In July 1998, the company acquired a crude oil pipeline and a crude oil gathering system from Goodyear Tire & Rubber for about $400 million.

Operational Review - 26-AUG-98

Total revenues in the six months ended June 30, 1998, declined 3.2%, year to year, despite increased oil production, reflecting lower oil prices and lower terminalling and storage revenues. After higher depreciation, depletion and amortization charges, due to the increased production volumes, and higher interest expense, pretax income fell 61%. After taxes at 37.9%, versus 40.0%, and preferred stock dividends of $628,000 in the 1998 period only, net income available to common stockholders decreased 60%, to $2,221,000 ($0.12 a share), from $7,143,000 ($0.40).

Stock Performance - 02-OCT-98

In the past 30 trading days, PLX's shares have declined 6%, compared to a 7% fall in the S&P 500. Average trading volume for the past five days was 17,760 shares, compared with the 40-day moving average of 20,956 shares.

Key Stock Statistics

Dividend Rate/Share	Nil	Shareholders	1,500
Shs. outstg. (M)	16.9	Market cap. (B)	$0.283
Avg. daily vol. (M)	0.021	Inst. holdings	82%
Tang. Bk. Value/Share	6.90		
Beta	0.69		

Value of $10,000 invested 5 years ago: $ 18,175

Fiscal Year Ending Dec. 31

	1998	1997	1996	1995	1994	1993
Revenues (Million $)						
1Q	193.6	207.1	123.5	93.65	50.58	44.20
2Q	189.4	188.6	155.9	95.26	67.20	48.00
3Q	—	220.7	169.3	103.6	66.22	48.39
4Q	—	245.9	180.9	111.7	72.69	47.30
Yr.	—	862.2	629.6	404.2	256.7	186.0
Earnings Per Share ($)						
1Q	**0.06**	**0.22**	0.54	0.03	-0.10	-0.08
2Q	**0.06**	**0.18**	0.26	0.03	0.06	0.02
3Q	—	**0.15**	0.20	0.03	0.02	0.03
4Q	—	**0.23**	0.24	0.06	0.07	-1.74
Yr.	—	**0.77**	1.22	0.16	0.04	-1.77

Next earnings report expected: early November

Dividend Data

No cash has been paid on the common. A one-for-five reverse stock split was effected in 1990.

A Division of The **McGraw·Hill** *Companies*

STANDARD
&POOR'S
STOCK REPORTS

Plains Resources Inc.

8875

03-OCT-98

Business Summary - 26-AUG-98

Over the past few years, this Houston-based independent energy concern has focused its efforts on acquiring, exploiting and producing mature, yet underdeveloped crude oil producing properties with strong upside potential. These upstream activities, which also include the development of natural gas properties, are concentrated in three states: California, Illinois and Florida. Plains Resources is also engaged in the marketing, transportation, terminalling and storage of crude oil (midstream activities). Upstream activities accounted for about 87% of the company's operating earnings in 1997.

Upon acquiring a property, the company seeks to add reserves and increase cash flows through improved production practices and recovery methods and relatively low risk drilling. PLX believes that it has succeeded with this program, as shown by its 162 million bbl. of oil equivalent (BOE) reserves at December 31, 1997, up from 122 million BOE in 1996 and 40 million BOE in 1992. Between 1992 and 1997, production nearly tripled, from 2.6 million BOE to 7.4 million BOE. In addition, cash flows were strengthened by an increase in average unit gross margin per BOE to $8.67 in 1997, from $7.25 in 1992.

Upstream oil and natural gas activities are focused in the Los Angeles Basin of California, the company's most productive area with an average daily production

of rate of 10,640 BOE, the Sunniland Trend of south Florida, and the Illinois Basin. In March 1997, PLX purchased the Montebello Field in California from Chevron for about $25 million. At the time of acquisition, the property, located about 15 miles from PLX's existing LA Basin properties, was producing about 800 bbl. per day of oil and 800 thousand cubic feet (Mcf) of natural gas.

Midstream marketing activities are concentrated in Oklahoma (where PLX owns a two million bbl., above ground crude oil terminalling and storage facility), Texas, and the Gulf Coast area of Louisiana. In this business, crude-oil is purchased at the wellhead and is transported to a trading location where the company sells the crude oil, mainly to refiners. PLX also buys crude oil in the spot market at trading locations. In July 1998, the company acquired All American Pipeline Co., Celeron Gathering Corp., and Celeron Trading & Transportation Co. from Goodyear Tire & Rubber for a total consideration of approximately $400 million. The principal asset involved in the deal is All American Pipeline System, a 1,233-mile crude oil pipeline extending from California to Texas.

PLX has approved a $103 million capital spending program for 1998, excluding acquisitions. The plan represents about a 30% increasefrom 1997 levels, not including acquisition-related capital spending. About $100 million will be targeted for upstream exploitation, development and exploration activities, including 100 wells to be drilled during the year.

Per Share Data ($)

(Year Ended Dec. 31)	1997	1996	1995	1994	1993	1992	1991	1990	1989	1988
Tangible Bk. Val.	6.73	5.79	4.76	3.97	3.83	5.58	3.67	4.54	4.49	2.62
Cash Flow	2.08	2.46	1.42	1.45	-0.38	0.78	-0.71	0.85	1.25	1.33
Earnings	0.77	1.22	0.16	0.04	-1.77	-0.32	-1.59	-0.36	-0.10	-0.75
Dividends	Nil	Nil	Nil	Nil	Nil	Nil	Nil	Nil	Nil	Nil
Payout Ratio	Nil	Nil	Nil	Nil	Nil	Nil	Nil	Nil	Nil	Nil
Prices - High	20³/₄	17	11	8	13¹/₈	21³/₄	30³/₄	8⁵/₈	7³/₄	7³/₄
- Low	11⁷/₈	7³/₈	5¹/₂	5³/₈	6³/₈	7¹/₂	4⁷/₈	5³/₈	3¹/₈	2³/₄
P/E Ratio - High	27	14	69	NM	NM	NM	NM	NM	NM	NM
- Low	15	6	34	NM	NM	NM	NM	NM	NM	NM

Income Statement Analysis (Million $)

	1997	1996	1995	1994	1993	1992	1991	1990	1989	1988
Revs.	862	629	404	256	186	132	79.3	44.0	17.4	14.5
Oper. Inc.	68.1	60.7	33.0	29.2	4.4	13.6	-2.6	8.8	7.4	7.6
Depr. Depl. & Amort.	23.8	21.9	17.0	16.3	16.1	11.6	7.2	7.7	5.8	5.9
Int. Exp.	22.0	17.3	13.6	15.3	11.5	5.0	3.8	4.0	3.9	4.1
Pretax Inc.	22.6	17.8	2.7	0.6	-20.2	-3.3	-12.8	-2.2	0.4	-1.2
Eff. Tax Rate	37%	NM	Nil	Nil	NM	NM	NM	NM	48%	NM
Net Inc.	14.3	21.7	2.7	0.6	-20.2	-3.3	-12.9	-2.2	0.2	-1.2

Balance Sheet & Other Fin. Data (Million $)

	1997	1996	1995	1994	1993	1992	1991	1990	1989	1988
Cash	3.7	2.5	6.1	2.8	4.9	25.1	3.4	2.4	2.4	3.0
Curr. Assets	127	102	63.6	41.7	35.1	46.3	16.7	11.8	6.6	9.3
Total Assets	557	430	352	267	237	199	96.8	94.8	69.3	78.0
Curr. Liab.	133	107	68.3	46.2	49.1	33.3	20.1	22.4	12.4	13.4
LT Debt	283	225	205	145	136	100	42.2	36.5	28.8	39.7
Common Eqty.	113	95.6	77.0	46.0	44.3	62.6	33.3	33.0	22.4	7.5
Total Cap.	396	321	282	212	181	163	76.3	70.8	52.9	64.3
Cap. Exp.	110	55.6	72.3	41.7	84.1	78.4	33.9	29.2	22.3	13.5
Cash Flow	37.9	43.6	19.7	16.9	-4.3	8.2	-5.8	5.4	5.3	3.7
Curr. Ratio	1.0	1.0	0.9	0.9	0.7	1.4	0.8	0.5	0.5	0.7
% LT Debt of Cap.	71.5	70.1	72.7	68.3	75.1	61.2	55.3	51.5	54.5	61.8
% Ret. on Assets	2.9	5.5	1.0	0.2	NM	NM	NM	NM	0.2	NM
% Ret. on Equity	13.5	25.1	4.4	1.3	NM	NM	NM	NM	NM	NM

Data as orig. reptd.; bef. results of disc. opers. and/or spec. items. Per share data adj. for stk. divs. as of ex-div. date. Bold denotes diluted EPS (FASB 128). E-Estimated. NA-Not Available. NM-Not Meaningful. NR-Not Ranked.

Office—1600 Smith St., Suite 1500, Houston, TX 77002. **Tel**—(713) 654-1414. **Chrmn**—D. M. Krausse. **Pres & CEO**—G. L. Armstrong.**SVP, CFO, Treas & Investor Contact**—Phillip D. Kramer. **VP & Secy**—M. R. Patterson. **Dirs**—G. L. Armstrong, J. L. Dees, T. H. Delimitros, W. M. Hitchcock, D. M. Krausse, J. H. Lollar, R. V. Sinnott, J. T. Symonds. **Transfer Agent & Registrar**—American Stock Transfer & Trust, NYC.**Incorporated**—in Delaware in 1976. **Empl**— 230. **S&P Analyst:** N.R.

Platinum Software

4996T

NASDAQ Symbol **PSQL**

In S&P SmallCap 600

03-OCT-98

Industry:
Computer (Software & Services)

Summary: PSQL designs, develops, markets and supports a broad range of financial software products primarily for use on client/server networked systems.

Quantitative Evaluations	
Outlook (1 Lowest—5 Highest) • **NA**	
Fair Value • **NA**	
Risk • **High**	
Earn./Div. Rank • **C**	
Technical Eval. • **Bearish** since 8/98	
Rel. Strength Rank (1 Lowest—99 Highest) • **5**	
Insider Activity • **NA**	

Recent Price • 9¼	Yield • Nil
52 Wk Range • 27¼-7⅜	12-Mo. P/E • 20.7

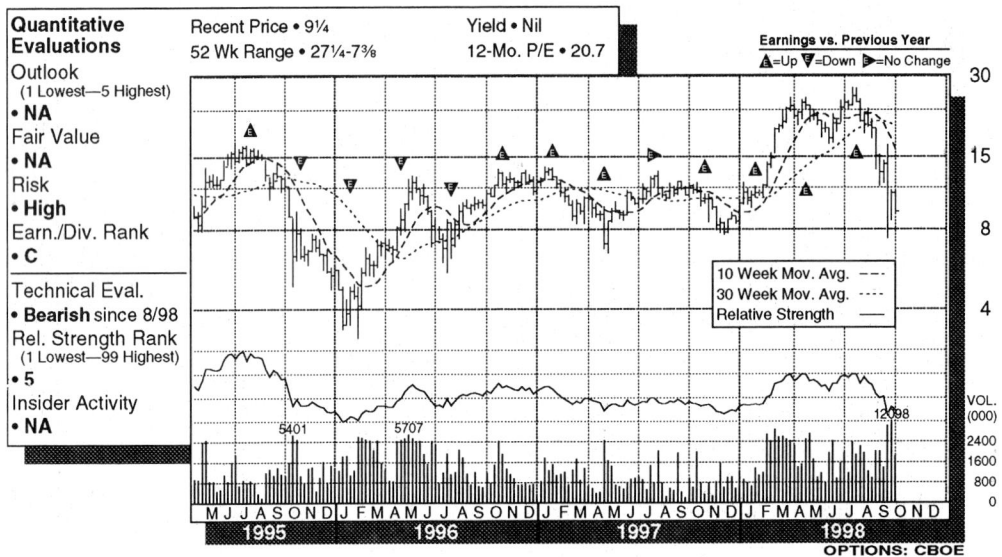

Earnings vs. Previous Year
▲=Up ▼=Down ▶=No Change

10 Week Mov. Avg. ---
30 Week Mov. Avg. ····
Relative Strength —

OPTIONS: CBOE

Business Profile - 09-JAN-98

In November 1997, the company acquired Louisville-based FocusSoft Inc., a provider of financial accounting and customer management software, for about 2.7 million common shares. This followed PSQL's June 1997 acquisition of Portland, Oregon-based Clientele Software, Inc. for about 1.1 million common shares. The Clientele Software acquisition represented PSQL's formal entry into the Customer Information Systems (CIS) market, denoting a strategic expansion of the company's product and customer base. PSQL noted that this was the first step in delivering on its planned horizontal applications strategy. The first quarter of FY 98 (Jun.) marked PSQL's sixth consecutive quarter of sequential revenue growth.

Operational Review - 09-JAN-98

Revenues in the three months ended September 30, 1997, rose 43%, year to year, paced by a 52% increase in license fees and a 74% gain in consulting and professional services revenues. Margins widened on the increased license fee volume; operating expenses rose 11%. After other income of $569,000, versus $199,000, PSQL had net income of $1,029,000 ($0.04 a share, on 39% more shares), compared to a net loss of $1,947,000 ($0.10).

Stock Performance - 02-OCT-98

In the past 30 trading days, PSQL's shares have declined 51%, compared to a 7% fall in the S&P 500. Average trading volume for the past five days was 362,920 shares, compared with the 40-day moving average of 801,231 shares.

Key Stock Statistics

Dividend Rate/Share	Nil	Shareholders	1,700
Shs. outstg. (M)	25.9	Market cap. (B)	$0.241
Avg. daily vol. (M)	1.258	Inst. holdings	68%
Tang. Bk. Value/Share	NM		
Beta	1.57		

Value of $10,000 invested 5 years ago: $ 6,277

Fiscal Year Ending Jun. 30

	1998	1997	1996	1995	1994	1993
Revenues (Million $)						
1Q	18.26	10.86	12.60	14.60	11.40	5.97
2Q	21.65	12.68	10.16	13.30	14.60	7.56
3Q	26.37	14.01	8.36	13.40	14.20	9.34
4Q	32.20	16.71	9.40	14.90	13.20	15.76
Yr.	98.49	58.10	40.56	56.20	53.40	38.63
Earnings Per Share ($)						
1Q	0.05	-0.11	-0.32	Nil	-0.32	—
2Q	0.07	-0.03	-0.02	0.22	0.70	0.07
3Q	0.15	0.03	-0.97	-0.15	-1.04	0.07
4Q	0.19	-0.18	-0.18	-0.08	-2.72	-1.42
Yr.	0.45	-0.25	-2.23	-0.44	-4.80	-1.52

Next earnings report expected: NA

Dividend Data

Amount ($)	Date Decl.	Ex-Div. Date	Stock of Record	Payment Date

A Division of The McGraw-Hill Companies

STANDARD
&POOR'S

STOCK REPORTS

Platinum Software Corporation

4996T

03-OCT-98

Business Summary - 09-JAN-98

This developer of integrated financial applications closed its 1997 fiscal year (ended June) on a high note, reporting record revenue in the fourth quarter. It also extended its product offerings into the fast-growing customer information systems market by acquiring Clientele Software, Inc., a provider of help-desk automation software. The acquisition of Clientele by Platinum Software Corp. (PSQL) was part of a broader plan to secure new applications that complement PSQL's existing financial software products. In September 1997, PSQL launched a parallel expansion effort by announcing a major growth drive in Asia aimed at tripling revenues from the region over a two-year period.

PSQL's financial software products are designed primarily for use on client/server networked systems. Its Platinum for Windows is a Windows-based client/server financial accounting software package for smaller businesses. In 1994, the company started shipping Platinum SQL. Targeted at medium-sized companies and divisions of large enterprises, Platinum SQL is a 32-bit server application that takes full advantage of the Microsoft SQL server for Windows NT, and is integrated with the Microsoft Office Professional suite of software

products. The new Clientele products have applications in customer service and support operations. Software license fees accounted for 52% of total revenues in FY 97, professional services (including consulting) 19%, support services 27%, and other 2%.

PSQL intends to integrate the new Clientele software products with its financial applications to address a growing market need for improved customer information delivery and analysis. PSQL hopes future extension and integration efforts will allow it to offer a unifying customer management system module for Platinum SQL and a customer "life-cycle" view that runs the gamut from prospecting and selling activities to financial and accounting transactions.

As part of its new push in Asia, PSQL opened an office in Singapore to cover Southeast Asian markets. PSQL is also expanding its Hong Kong-based North Asia operations. The company believes its new Platinum SQL 4.1 software with multilingual and multicurrency capabilities is well-suited to Asian enterprises operating in a global marketplace. Platinum SQL 4.1, whose "operational currency" feature includes support for the emerging "Euro" currency standard, offers benefits to European firms as well. International revenues accounted for 30% of total revenues in FY 97.

Per Share Data ($)

(Year Ended Jun. 30)	1998	1997	1996	1995	1994	1993	1992	1991	1990	1989
Tangible Bk. Val.	NA	NM	NM	NM	4.13	4.67	2.00	NA	NA	NA
Cash Flow	NA	0.05	-1.81	-0.02	-4.35	-1.52	NA	NA	NA	NA
Earnings	0.45	-0.25	-2.23	-0.44	-4.80	-1.68	0.11	NA	NA	NA
Dividends	Nil	Nil	Nil	Nil	Nil	Nil	Nil	Nil	Nil	Nil
Payout Ratio	Nil	Nil	Nil	Nil	Nil	Nil	Nil	Nil	Nil	Nil
Prices - High	27¼	13¾	13½	16⅞	25¼	39¾	19⅞	NA	NA	NA
- Low	9⅝	6½	3⅛	4¾	3½	13½	9⅜	NA	NA	NA
P/E Ratio - High	61	NM	NM	NM	NM	NM	NM	NM	NM	NM
- Low	21	NM	NM	NM	NM	NM	NM	NM	NM	NM

Income Statement Analysis (Million $)

	1998	1997	1996	1995	1994	1993	1992	1991	1990	1989
Revs.	NM	58.1	40.6	56.2	53.4	28.1	NA	NA	NA	NA
Oper. Inc.	NA	1.7	-21.1	-0.3	-23.8	-4.0	NA	NA	NA	NA
Depr.	NA	5.8	6.2	5.5	5.5	1.7	NA	NA	NA	NA
Int. Exp.	NA	0.1	1.3	0.7	0.0	0.1	NA	NA	NA	NA
Pretax Inc.	NA	-4.9	-32.9	-5.7	-59.3	-17.2	NA	NA	NA	NA
Eff. Tax Rate	NA	NM	NM	NM	NM	NM	NM	NM	NM	NM
Net Inc.	NM	-4.9	-32.9	-5.7	-59.5	-17.2	NA	NA	NA	NA

Balance Sheet & Other Fin. Data (Million $)

	1998	1997	1996	1995	1994	1993	1992	1991	1990	1989
Cash	NA	6.3	16.5	26.8	8.8	47.2	NA	NA	NA	NA
Curr. Assets	NA	29.8	27.3	44.4	26.7	64.4	NA	NA	NA	NA
Total Assets	NA	41.8	40.0	65.8	48.1	80.6	NA	NA	NA	NA
Curr. Liab.	NA	27.1	23.8	20.1	36.9	22.2	NA	NA	NA	NA
LT Debt	NA	Nil	Nil	15.8	10.0	Nil	Nil	Nil	Nil	Nil
Common Eqty.	Nil	-15.8	-15.8	-2.0	1.2	58.4	NA	NA	NA	NA
Total Cap.	NA	-15.8	-15.8	45.8	11.2	58.4	NA	NA	NA	NA
Cap. Exp.	NA	3.0	2.5	NA	10.4	6.3	NA	NA	NA	NA
Cash Flow	NA	0.9	-26.7	-0.2	-54.0	-15.5	NA	NA	NA	NA
Curr. Ratio	NA	1.1	1.1	2.2	0.7	0.3	NA	NA	NA	NA
% LT Debt of Cap.	NA	Nil	NM	34.5	89.3	NM	NM	NM	NM	NM
% Net Inc.of Revs.	NM	NM	NM	NM	NM	NM	NM	NM	NM	NM
% Ret. on Assets	NM	NM	NM	NM	NM	NM	NM	NM	NM	NM
% Ret. on Equity	NM	NM	NM	NM	NM	NM	NM	NM	NM	NM

Data as orig. reptd.; bef. results of disc. opers. and/or spec. items. Per share data adj. for stk. divs. as of ex-div. date. E-Estimated. NA-Not Available. NM-Not Meaningful. NR-Not Ranked.

Office—195 Technology Dr., Irvine, CA 92618-2402. **Tel**—(949) 453-4000. **Webs**te—http://www.platsoft.com.**Chrmn, Pres & CEO**—L. G. Klaus. **Investor Contact**—Sandi Sheehy.**Dirs**—D. R. Dixon, L. J. Doerr, W.D. Hajjar, L. G. Klaus, A. J. Marks.**Transfer Agent & Registrar**—ChaseMellon Shareholder Services, LA. **Incorporated**—in Delaware in 1984. **Empl**— 600. **S&P Analyst**: P.T.W.

STANDARD &POOR'S
STOCK REPORTS

Players International

4997D

NASDAQ Symbol **PLAY**

In S&P SmallCap 600

03-OCT-98

Industry:
Gaming, Lottery & Pari-mutuel Cos.

Summary: This company owns and operates riverboat casinos in three states.

Quantitative Evaluations	
Outlook (1 Lowest—5 Highest)	• **5**
Fair Value	• **7⅝**
Risk	• **Average**
Earn./Div. Rank	• **B-**
Technical Eval.	• **Bullish** since 3/98
Rel. Strength Rank (1 Lowest—99 Highest)	• **85**
Insider Activity	• **Neutral**

Recent Price • 4¾
52 Wk Range • 5¾-2⁷/₁₆

Yield • Nil
12-Mo. P/E • 36.5

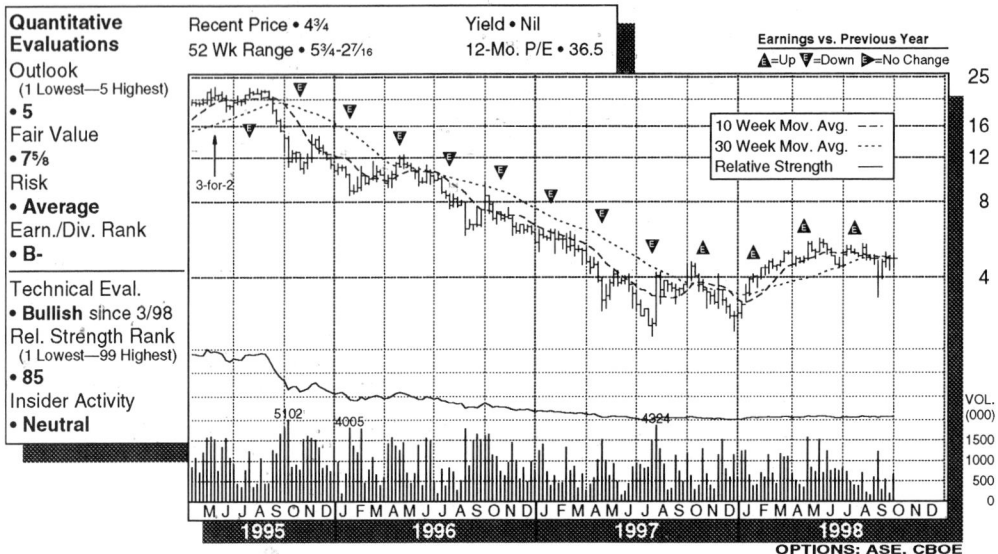

Earnings vs. Previous Year
▲=Up ▼=Down ▶=No Change

10 Week Mov. Avg. – – –
30 Week Mov. Avg. ······
Relative Strength ——

OPTIONS: ASE, CBOE

Business Profile - 31-AUG-98

This company owns and operates riverboat gaming and entertainment facilities in Metropolis, IL, Lake Charles, LA, and Maryland Heights, MO. Recent capital expenditures have been to open a new island-themed dining and entertainment barge at the Metropolis facility in December 1997, and to acquire, in January 1998, a hotel located adjacent to the Lake Charles facility, for $19.2 million. Management believes that the hotel may enhance casino revenues by increasing the length of stay of traveling patrons. Road construction is scheduled to begin in late summer on U. S. Interstate 10 near the company's Lake Charles facility. It is not clear what effect, if any, traffic delays caused by construction may have on customer visits to the facility.

Operational Review - 31-AUG-98

Revenues in the three months ended June 30, 1998, fell 3.1%, year to year, primarily reflecting the sale of the Mesquite facility on June 30, 1997, partly offset by a greater number of visitors to the Maryland Heights facility, which opened in March 1997. Helped by profitable operations at the Maryland Heights facility, in contrast to losses experienced in the 1997 period, pretax income soared to $4,000,000, from $484,000. After taxes at 39.0%, versus 39.5%, net income surged to $2,440,000, ($0.08 a share), versus $293,000 ($0.01).

Stock Performance - 02-OCT-98

In the past 30 trading days, PLAY's shares were unchanged, compared to a 7% fall in the S&P 500. Average trading volume for the past five days was 130,720 shares, compared with the 40-day moving average of 99,172 shares.

Key Stock Statistics

Dividend Rate/Share	Nil	Shareholders	500
Shs. outstg. (M)	31.9	Market cap. (B)	$0.152
Avg. daily vol. (M)	0.093	Inst. holdings	33%
Tang. Bk. Value/Share	3.85		
Beta	1.42		

Value of $10,000 invested 5 years ago: $ 11,400

Fiscal Year Ending Mar. 31

	1999	1998	1997	1996	1995	1994
Revenues (Million $)						
1Q	81.57	84.18	79.61	65.61	48.33	18.31
2Q	—	82.56	74.41	80.30	58.86	20.26
3Q	—	75.97	64.85	72.73	58.67	23.27
4Q	—	80.51	72.34	72.76	57.85	45.25
Yr.	—	323.2	291.2	291.4	223.7	107.1
Earnings Per Share ($)						
1Q	0.08	0.01	0.15	0.25	0.34	0.31
2Q		0.07	0.12	0.22	0.43	0.13
3Q	—	0.01	-0.05	0.10	0.37	0.08
4Q	—	-0.02	-1.49	0.13	0.33	0.21
Yr.	—	0.06	-1.56	0.70	1.47	0.73

Next earnings report expected: early November

Dividend Data

No cash dividends have been paid. The company intends to retain earnings to finance the operation and expansion of its business. A three-for-two stock split was effected in May 1995. A shareholder rights plan was adopted in January 1997.

A Division of The McGraw-Hill Companies

STANDARD
&POOR'S
STOCK REPORTS

Players International, Inc.

4997D
03-OCT-98

Business Summary - 31-AUG-98

Players International, Inc. (PLAY) owns and operates riverboat gaming and entertainment facilities. These include one riverboat casino in Metropolis, IL, two riverboat casinos in Lake Charles, LA, and two contiguous, permanently moored, dockside riverboat casinos in Maryland Heights, MO. The company operated a land-based casino in Mesquite, NV, until June 30, 1997. PLAY also owns and operates racetrack in Paducah, KY, which it plans to operate as a harness racetrack beginning in FY 99 (Mar.). Operating profit or loss (in million $) by location in the past two years:

	FY 98	FY 97
Metropolis	$21.7	$21.6
Lake Charles	$20.8	$25.9
Maryland Heights	-$4.3	-$10.5
Mesquite	-$0.5	-$8.1

PLAY's marketing strategy focuses on middle-income patrons who live within a 150 mile radius of each of its facilities. The company employs database and on-site marketing, and bus programs. PLAY targets gaming customers through frequent mailings promoting visits to its casino facilities. In addition, it employs on-site marketing techniques, including the use of player tracking systems, slot clubs, and preferred player hosts to identify and service patrons.

The Metropolis, IL, riverboat facility, which began operations in February 1993, is the only riverboat casino operating in southern Illinois. The facility offers a four deck historical replica of a paddlewheel riverboat, and features a fully equipped, Las Vegas style casino that offers about 22,000 sq. ft. of gaming space. The casino is equipped with 900 slot machines and 50 table games, for a total of about 1,200 gaming positions.

The Lake Charles facility includes the Players Lake Charles Riverboat and the Star Riverboat, two riverboat casinos that share a common docking site. The riverboats operate staggered three-hour cruises up to 24 hours a day. The facility features the Players Hotel, a company owned land based 134-room hotel with meeting and entertainment space. In January 1998, the company acquired a 269 room hotel formerly operated as the Lake Charles Holiday Inn, for $19.2 million.

In March 1997, the company and Harrah's opened a riverboat casino entertainment facility in Maryland Heights, MO, offering four permanently moored, dockside riverboat casinos totaling approximately 120,000 sq. ft. of gaming space. The Maryland Heights casinos feature a topical island theme with lush foliage, waterfalls and rockscape.

Per Share Data ($)

(Year Ended Mar. 31)	1998	1997	1996	1995	1994	1993	1992	1991	1990	1989
Tangible Bk. Val.	3.84	3.75	5.36	4.62	4.26	NA	NA	NA	NA	NA
Cash Flow	0.71	-0.82	1.24	1.67	0.73	-0.30	NA	NA	NA	NA
Earnings	0.06	-1.56	0.70	1.47	0.60	-0.32	-0.35	NA	NA	NA
Dividends	Nil	Nil	Nil	Nil	Nil	Nil	Nil	Nil	Nil	Nil
Payout Ratio	Nil	Nil	Nil	Nil	Nil	Nil	Nil	Nil	Nil	Nil
Cal. Yrs.	1997	1996	1995	1994	1993	1992	1991	1990	1989	1988
Prices - High	6¼	12⅜	23	19⅞	18⅜	4⅜	3¼	NA	NA	NA
- Low	2⁵/₁₆	5	10⅜	9⅝	4⅛	1¼	1¼	NA	NA	NA
P/E Ratio - High	NM	NM	33	14	30	NM	NM	NM	NM	NM
- Low	NM	NM	15	7	7	NM	NM	NM	NM	NM

Income Statement Analysis (Million $)

Revs.	323	291	291	224	107	5.7	NA	NA	NA	NA
Oper. Inc.	57.8	41.2	61.1	77.6	30.6	-3.7	NA	NA	NA	NA
Depr.	20.8	21.8	17.2	7.1	3.7	0.2	NA	NA	NA	NA
Int. Exp.	24.1	16.0	14.7	0.7	0.9	0.3	NA	NA	NA	NA
Pretax Inc.	3.1	-71.8	36.6	73.5	27.7	-4.1	NA	NA	NA	NA
Eff. Tax Rate	38%	NM	39%	38%	37%	NM	NM	NM	NM	NM
Net Inc.	2.0	-46.3	22.3	45.8	17.5	-4.1	NA	NA	NA	NA

Balance Sheet & Other Fin. Data (Million $)

Cash	17.2	20.6	23.2	50.3	77.5	NA	NA	NA	NA	NA
Curr. Assets	33.1	67.6	41.6	61.6	83.5	NA	NA	NA	NA	NA
Total Assets	410	421	413	224	139	NA	NA	NA	NA	NA
Curr. Liab.	39.2	51.9	39.7	39.3	16.1	NA	NA	NA	NA	NA
LT Debt	181	188	153	5.5	5.7	NA	NA	NA	NA	NA
Common Eqty.	158	156	194	176	116	NA	NA	NA	NA	NA
Total Cap.	342	343	347	182	122	NA	NA	NA	NA	NA
Cap. Exp.	40.2	46.5	147	62.4	33.8	5.2	NA	NA	NA	NA
Cash Flow	22.8	-24.5	39.6	52.8	21.2	-3.9	NA	NA	NA	NA
Curr. Ratio	0.8	1.3	1.1	1.6	5.2	NA	NA	NA	NA	NA
% LT Debt of Cap.	52.9	54.8	44.1	3.0	4.7	NA	NA	NA	NA	NA
% Net Inc.of Revs.	0.6	NM	7.7	20.5	16.3	NM	NM	NM	NM	NM
% Ret. on Assets	0.5	NM	7.0	25.1	12.6	NA	NA	NA	NA	NA
% Ret. on Equity	1.2	NM	12.1	31.3	15.1	NA	NA	NA	NA	NA

Data as orig. reptd.; bef. results of disc. opers. and/or spec. items. Per share data adj. for stk. divs. as of ex-div. date. Bold denotes diluted EPS (FASB 128). E-Estimated. NA-Not Available. NM-Not Meaningful. NR-Not Ranked.

Office—1300 Atlantic Ave., Suite 800, Atlantic City, NJ 08401. **Tel**—(609) 449-7777. **Chrmn**—E. Fishman. **Pres & CEO**—H. Goldberg. **EVP & COO**—J. F. Groom. **EVP-Fin, Treas & Secy**—P. J. Aranow. **Dirs**—A. R. Buggy, L. Cohen, E. Fishman, M. S. Geller, H. Goldberg, J. Groom, C. M. Masson, V. J. Naimoli, L. Seidler, E. E. Webb. **Transfer Agent & Registrar**—Interwest Transfer, Salt Lake City, UT. **Incorporated**—in Nevada in 1985.**Empl**— 3,700. **S&P Analyst:** P.L.H.

STANDARD &POOR'S
STOCK REPORTS

Plexus Corp.

4997M
NASDAQ Symbol **PLXS**

In S&P SmallCap 600

03-OCT-98

Industry:
Electrical Equipment

Summary: This company provides contract design, manufacturing and testing of electronic products.

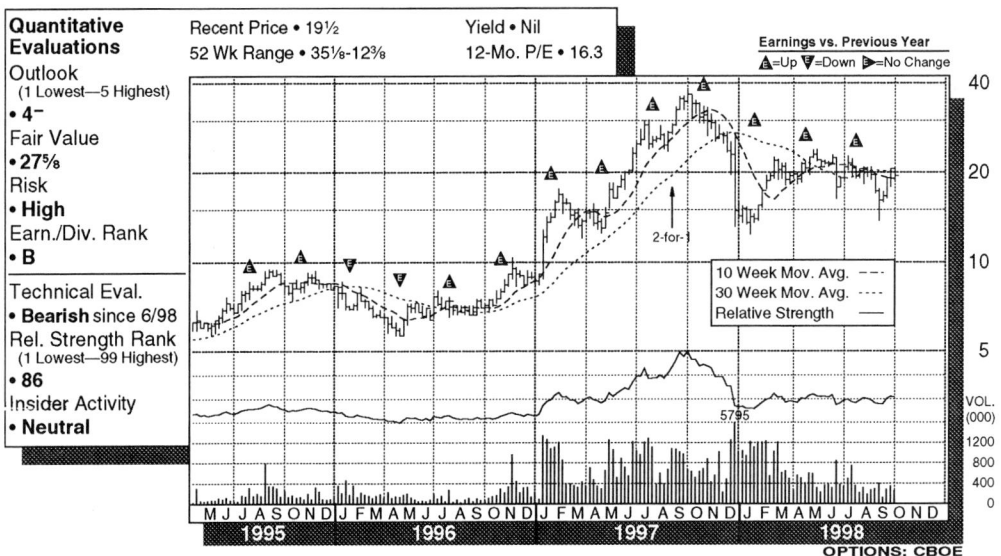

Quantitative Evaluations	
Outlook (1 Lowest—5 Highest)	• **4⁻**
Fair Value	• **27⅝**
Risk	• **High**
Earn./Div. Rank	• **B**
Technical Eval.	• **Bearish** since 6/98
Rel. Strength Rank (1 Lowest—99 Highest)	• **86**
Insider Activity	• **Neutral**

Recent Price • 19½
52 Wk Range • 35⅛-12⅜
Yield • Nil
12-Mo. P/E • 16.3

Earnings vs. Previous Year
▲=Up ▼=Down ▷=No Change

10 Week Mov. Avg. ---
30 Week Mov. Avg. ····
Relative Strength —

OPTIONS: CBOE

Business Profile - 12-MAY-98

Plexus is focusing on expanding its engineering activities in order to enhance its product development and manufacturing pipelines. The company recently increased its engineering headcount in its North Carolina and California locations, and current plans call for expanded engineering at other locations. PLXS expects sales growth in the second half of FY 98 (Sep.) to be more pronounced than in the first half, when results were affected by Motorola's decision to move a program in-house, adjustments in production schedules by other customers, slow ramp-up of certain new programs, and the impact of a strong dollar. Margin improvement in recent quarters has been aided by several initiatives undertaken to enhance profitability, including work force and fixed-cost reductions.

Operational Review - 12-MAY-98

Net sales in the first half of FY 98 rose 5.1%, year to year. Margins widened, on improved operating efficiencies, lower fixed costs, higher capacity utilization, improved product mix, and a more aggressive procurement program; operating profit was up 18%. With lower interest expense and higher other income, net income advanced 25%, to $8,083,000 ($0.51 a share, diluted, on 5.8% more shares), from $6,461,000 ($0.43, as adjusted).

Stock Performance - 02-OCT-98

In the past 30 trading days, PLXS's shares have declined 0.64%, compared to a 7% fall in the S&P 500. Average trading volume for the past five days was 49,840 shares, compared with the 40-day moving average of 54,062 shares.

Key Stock Statistics

Dividend Rate/Share	Nil	Shareholders	900
Shs. outstg. (M)	14.8	Market cap. (B)	$0.288
Avg. daily vol. (M)	0.050	Inst. holdings	34%
Tang. Bk. Value/Share	3.38		
Beta	1.94		

Value of $10,000 invested 5 years ago: $ 26,000

Fiscal Year Ending Sep. 30

	1998	1997	1996	1995	1994	1993
Revenues (Million $)						
1Q	95.91	87.37	71.31	65.34	55.94	42.10
2Q	97.69	96.75	75.29	69.38	61.32	36.58
3Q	98.56	99.1	86.07	72.35	55.00	38.97
4Q	—	103.2	83.46	76.06	70.21	41.95
Yr.	—	386.4	316.1	283.1	242.5	159.6
Earnings Per Share ($)						
1Q	**0.23**	0.20	0.06	0.07	0.06	0.10
2Q	**0.28**	0.24	0.06	0.10	0.08	0.03
3Q	**0.00**	0.00	0.18	0.12	0.02	0.06
4Q	—	0.34	0.23	0.15	0.08	0.03
Yr.	—	1.08	0.52	0.45	0.23	0.20

Next earnings report expected: late October

Dividend Data

PLC has never paid cash dividends on its common stock, and does not expect to pay any in the foreseeable future.

STANDARD
&POOR'S
STOCK REPORTS

Plexus Corp.

4997M
03-OCT-98

Business Summary - 12-MAY-98

Plexus Corp., a contract provider of design, manufacturing and testing services to the electronics industry, believes that its growth in recent years has been significantly aided by its approach to partnering with customers through product design and development services. It plans to continue to leverage this part of its services, to achieve continued sales growth. The company is also focusing on maintaining and expanding its gross margins; in 1996, it began a flexible labor force program to manage fluctuating contract labor requirements, and also reduced its equipment lease requirements.

Plexus offers a full range of services including product development, design, material procurement and management, functional and in-circuit testing, incorporating the system into a final product housing, and distribution for printed circuit boards as well as full box-build. It also makes test equipment used for testing customers' products. Services are provided to OEMs in the computer (primarily high-end server and peripheral products), medical, industrial, telecommunications and transportation/automotive electronics industries.

The Technology Group, Inc. subsidiary designs electronic systems, including printed circuit boards and the arrangement of electronic components, and the development and/or programming of the application software necessary to control the functions of those components.

Manufacturing of electronic products and assemblies is offered through the Electronics Assembly Corp. subsidiary. Contract manufacturing services are provided on either a turnkey basis, where the company procures certain or all of the materials required for production, or on a consignment basis, where the customer supplies some or all of the materials. Turnkey manufacturing currently account for almost all sales. Variations in the mix between turnkey and consignment causes fluctuations in gross margins.

For the assembly process, Plexus purchases electronic components such as memory chips, microprocessing units, integrated circuits, resistors, capacitors, and related items from various manufacturers and distributors. Any shortages or delays in component procurement have a serious negative impact on revenues and earnings.

During FY 97 (Sep.), services were sold to about 113 customers, including IBM, which accounted for 12% of total sales, GE (13%), and Motorola (10%).

In November 1997, PLXS acquired the assets of two related companies, located in Minnesota and California. Total combined sales of the companies were only about $3 million, but the acquisitions allow PLXS to expand its manufacturing and assembly capabilities geographically. PLXS intends to continue to expand geographically.

Per Share Data ($)

(Year Ended Sep. 30)	1997	1996	1995	1994	1993	1992	1991	1990	1989	1988
Tangible Bk. Val.	4.59	3.15	2.63	2.69	1.93	1.79	1.33	1.04	0.92	0.73
Cash Flow	1.37	0.80	0.63	0.46	0.40	0.59	0.46	0.28	0.41	0.19
Earnings	1.08	0.52	0.45	0.23	0.20	0.40	0.29	0.13	0.23	0.04
Dividends	Nil	Nil	Nil	Nil	Nil	Nil	Nil	Nil	Nil	Nil
Payout Ratio	Nil	Nil	Nil	Nil	Nil	Nil	Nil	Nil	Nil	Nil
Prices - High	38¼	10⅜	9½	9	9⅜	11⅛	6⅝	2⅝	3¼	1¾
- Low	8⅜	5⅝	4¼	4	5¼	6⅛	1⅜	1⁷⁄₁₆	1½	1
P/E Ratio - High	35	20	21	39	47	28	23	21	14	51
- Low	8	11	10	17	26	15	5	12	6	30

Income Statement Analysis (Million $)

Revs.	386	316	283	242	160	157	120	79.0	78.0	53.0
Oper. Inc.	31.3	17.7	15.6	11.0	8.9	11.9	9.5	5.7	8.1	3.7
Depr.	4.5	3.6	3.3	3.1	2.6	2.4	2.0	1.8	2.1	1.9
Int. Exp.	0.8	1.9	2.5	3.1	1.8	1.4	1.9	1.6	1.6	1.2
Pretax Inc.	27.1	12.3	10.2	4.9	4.1	8.2	5.8	2.5	4.7	0.8
Eff. Tax Rate	39%	40%	39%	38%	38%	39%	37%	38%	38%	49%
Net Inc.	16.4	7.4	6.3	3.1	2.6	5.0	3.6	1.6	2.9	0.4

Balance Sheet & Other Fin. Data (Million $)

Cash	3.7	1.9	3.6	1.1	0.8	0.9	0.3	1.3	0.8	0.4
Curr. Assets	103	94.8	103	109	74.9	49.8	41.3	31.2	25.2	20.6
Total Assets	122	107	115	122	95.1	62.7	54.5	43.4	36.5	33.3
Curr. Liab.	49.5	43.3	31.6	46.0	29.7	18.5	17.9	13.7	10.2	17.3
LT Debt	3.5	15.3	41.7	40.7	40.1	20.5	19.7	16.4	14.5	5.7
Common Eqty.	67.6	48.0	41.0	34.8	24.8	23.1	16.6	13.0	11.3	9.8
Total Cap.	72.1	64.0	83.4	76.0	65.5	44.2	36.7	29.7	26.3	15.9
Cap. Exp.	10.7	4.1	2.1	5.3	8.2	2.0	3.4	2.7	1.2	1.6
Cash Flow	20.5	11.1	9.0	6.1	5.1	7.5	5.7	3.4	5.0	2.3
Curr. Ratio	2.1	2.2	3.3	2.4	2.5	2.7	2.3	2.3	2.5	1.2
% LT Debt of Cap.	4.8	23.9	50.0	53.5	61.2	46.3	53.8	55.1	55.1	35.9
% Net Inc.of Revs.	4.2	2.4	2.2	1.3	1.6	3.2	3.0	2.0	3.7	0.7
% Ret. on Assets	14.3	6.7	5.4	2.8	3.3	8.5	7.4	3.9	8.4	1.3
% Ret. on Equity	27.8	16.7	16.7	10.1	10.7	25.0	24.6	12.9	27.6	4.2

Data as orig. reptd.; bef. results of disc. opers. and/or spec. items. Per share data adj. for stk. divs. as of ex-div. date. Bold denotes diluted EPS (FASB 128). E-Estimated. NA-Not Available. NM-Not Meaningful. NR-Not Ranked.

Office—55 Jewelers Park Dr., Neenah, WI 54957-0156.**Tel**—(920) 722-3451. **Chrmn & CEO**—P. Strandwitz. **Pres & COO**—J. L. Nussbaum. **VP, CFO & Investor Contact**—Thomas B. Sabol. **VP & Secy**—J. D. Kaufman. **VP & Treas**—W. F. Denney. **Dirs**—R. T. Hoppe, H. R. Miller, J. L. Nussbaum, G. A. Pitner, T. J. Prosser, P. Strandwitz. **Transfer Agent & Registrar**—Firstar Trust Co., Milwaukee. **Incorporated**—in Wisconsin in 1979. **Empl**— 2,500. **S&P Analyst:** Jim Corridore

Pogo Producing

1860M

NYSE Symbol **PPP**

In S&P SmallCap 600

03-OCT-98

Industry:
Oil & Gas (Exploration & Production)

Summary: This independent oil and gas company explores for, develops and produces oil and gas onshore and offshore the U.S. and, since 1991, offshore Thailand.

S&P Opinion: Hold (★★★)	Recent Price • 13¾	Yield • 0.9%
	52 Wk Range • 44½-11⅝	12-Mo. P/E • 37.3

Quantitative Evaluations

Outlook
(1 Lowest—5 Highest)
• 1⁻

Fair Value
• 9¼

Risk
• **Average**

Earn./Div. Rank
• **B**

Technical Eval.
• **Bearish** since 3/98

Rel. Strength Rank
(1 Lowest—99 Highest)
• **30**

Insider Activity
• **Favorable**

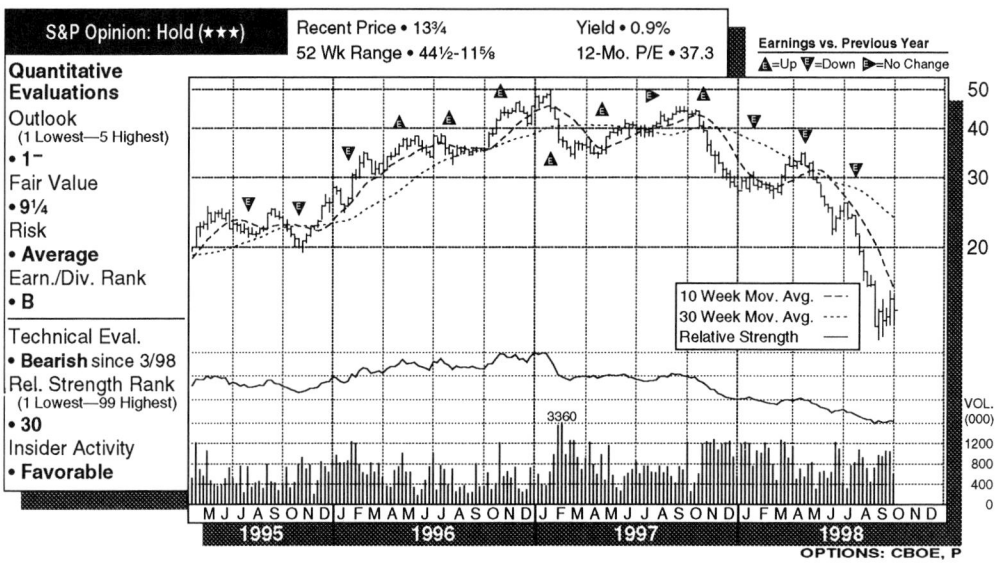

Earnings vs. Previous Year
▲=Up ▼=Down ▶=No Change

10 Week Mov. Avg. ---
30 Week Mov. Avg. ·····
Relative Strength —

OPTIONS: CBOE, P

Overview - 23-JUN-98

Both oil and gas production increased significantly during 1997, and revenues, cash flow and net income all advanced from the 1996 levels. However, earnings gains would have been more dramatic if not for lower average crude oil and condensate prices, which declined to $19.37 per bbl., from $22.12. Earnings in the first quarter of 1998 were hindered by lower sharply lower oil and gas prices and higher depreciation charges. However, oil and gas production continued to rise. The company's traditional major focus has been on the Gulf of Mexico, a prime offshore exploratory and production area, where PPP is adding working interests and continuing its successful drilling efforts. The Permian Basin continues to be an important oil play. Prospects remain positive in the Gulf of Thailand, for the long term; the company owns a 735,000 gross acres concession. Production in the 68,000 acre Tantawan area began in early February 1997. The company has also reported ongoing discoveries in the Permian Basin, and onshore and offshore the Gulf of Mexico.

Valuation - 23-JUN-98

The shares have slumped badly to this point in 1998, along with those of other independent oil and gas exploration and production companies, as oil prices have fallen to their lowest levels in more than a decade, amid a worldwide oversupply. Having declined 26% in 1998 to date, the shares are now trading at a discount to the estimated net asset value of PPP's reserves. However, the oil price outlook remains bleak, with little immediate prospect for improvement, and with a continuing Asian crisis possibly affecting the company's operations in Thailand, earnings in 1998 will be well below the levels of recent years; despite their recent decline, the shares are seen as only market performers.

Key Stock Statistics

S&P EPS Est. 1998	0.40	Tang. Bk. Value/Share	6.07
P/E on S&P Est. 1998	34.5	Beta	1.34
S&P EPS Est. 1999	0.75	Shareholders	3,100
Dividend Rate/Share	0.12	Market cap. (B)	$0.553
Shs. outstg. (M)	40.0	Inst. holdings	64%
Avg. daily vol. (M)	0.191		

Value of $10,000 invested 5 years ago: $ 13,786

Fiscal Year Ending Dec. 31

	1998	1997	1996	1995	1994	1993
Revenues (Million $)						
1Q	60.73	61.31	48.05	41.81	37.89	34.68
2Q	52.66	76.74	51.54	41.74	49.73	34.53
3Q	—	77.18	48.23	36.97	46.45	37.21
4Q	—	71.07	56.15	37.04	39.53	33.13
Yr.	—	286.3	204.0	157.6	173.6	139.6
Earnings Per Share ($)						
1Q	**0.01**	**0.30**	0.19	0.10	0.22	0.22
2Q	**-0.07**	**0.20**	0.20	0.13	0.30	0.17
3Q	—	0.21	0.21	0.02	0.22	0.22
4Q	—	0.22	0.33	0.02	0.08	0.16
Yr.	**E0.40**	**1.06**	0.97	0.28	0.82	0.76

Next earnings report expected: late October

Dividend Data (Dividends have been paid since 1994.)

Amount ($)	Date Decl.	Ex-Div. Date	Stock of Record	Payment Date
0.030	Oct. 21	Nov. 05	Nov. 07	Nov. 21 '97
0.030	Jan. 27	Feb. 11	Feb. 13	Feb. 27 '98
0.030	Apr. 28	May. 13	May. 15	May. 29 '98
0.030	Jul. 28	Aug. 12	Aug. 14	Aug. 28 '98

Pogo Producing Company

Business Summary - 23-JUN-98

Pogo Producing Company has recently focused on production. In 1997, the company's oil production rates were not only 33% higher than in 1996, but topped those of any year in Pogo's 28 year history. In addition, Pogo for the first time produced oil from its international holdings, with the start-up of production from the Gulf of Thailand concession. Headquartered in Houston, Pogo owns interests in 101 federal and state lease blocks offshore Louisiana and Texas in the Gulf of Mexico. The company also owns approximately 212,000 gross leasehold acres in major oil and gas provinces onshore in the U.S., and about 735,000 undeveloped gross acres in the Kingdom of Thailand.

Pogo's reserves are roughly balanced between liquids and natural gas, and startups from key holdings in the Gulf of Thailand and the Gulf of Mexico substantially increased the company's production in 1997. During 1997, all oil and liquid hydrocarbons sales averaged 18,851 bbl. per day, versus 14,141 bbl. per day a year earlier. Natural gas volumes averaged 181,700 Mcf per day in 1997, compared to an average 107,7000 Mcf per day in 1996. The Tantawan field (68,000 acres) in the Gulf of Thailand began in February, 1997, and is currently producing over 8,000 bbl. of crude oil and con-

densate and 100,000 Mcf of natural gas per day. In November, PPP and its partners signed an amendment to its long term agreement with the Petroleum Authority of Thailand, including the Benchamas/Pakakrong field.

PPP strong showing in 1997, in which net income rose to $37.1 million, or $1.06 a share, on revenues of $285 million (compared with 1995's results of: net income of $33.6 million, share earnings of $0.95 and revenues of $204 million) can be attributed to higher production and the company's successful drilling program (134 wells drilled in 1997, with 114 successful), which expanded production without any significant acquisitions. The company's position is that, although it will always be on the lookout for properties, it is unwilling to overspend to get them.

As of the end of 1997, the company's proved reserves totaled 401,488 million cubic feet (MMcf) of gas and 58.2 million bbl. of oil, condensate, and natural gas liquids (versus 360,944 MMcf of gas and 49.6 million bbl. of oil in 1996). During 1997, the company added enough new proven oil and natural gas reserves to replace an estimated 188% of its company-wide production in 1997.

Average sales prices were $2.39 per Mcf and $19.37 per bbl. in 1997, versus $2.40 per Mcf and $22.12 per bbl. in 1996.

Per Share Data ($)

(Year Ended Dec. 31)	1997	1996	1995	1994	1993	1992	1991	1990	1989	1988
Tangible Bk. Val.	4.36	3.22	2.17	1.95	1.04	0.18	-2.06	1.90	0.58	0.81
Cash Flow	3.69	2.80	2.32	2.72	2.00	2.18	1.90	3.26	2.51	2.88
Earnings	1.06	0.98	0.28	0.82	0.76	0.66	0.37	0.70	-0.23	-0.48
Dividends	0.12	0.12	0.12	0.06	Nil	Nil	Nil	Nil	Nil	Nil
Payout Ratio	11%	12%	43%	7%	Nil	Nil	Nil	Nil	Nil	Nil
Prices - High	49⁷/₈	48³/₈	29	24¹/₄	21	13⁷/₈	8¹/₄	10¹/₈	10¹/₄	5¹/₄
- Low	27	24³/₈	16	15⁵/₈	9³/₄	5¹/₈	4⁵/₈	5³/₄	4	3¹/₂
P/E Ratio - High	47	49	NM	30	28	21	22	14	NM	NM
- Low	25	25	NM	19	13	8	13	8	NM	NM

Income Statement Analysis (Million $)

Revs.	285	204	157	174	137	137	121	132	121	126
Oper. Inc.	180	123	91.8	115	89.0	86.0	76.0	97.0	90.0	73.0
Depr. Depl. & Amort.	103	61.8	68.0	63.0	41.0	42.0	42.0	67.0	66.0	74.0
Int. Exp.	15.7	13.2	11.2	10.1	11.0	19.0	24.9	31.4	37.5	39.7
Pretax Inc.	55.2	52.3	14.0	43.0	40.0	29.0	15.0	25.0	-9.0	-6.0
Eff. Tax Rate	33%	36%	35%	36%	37%	36%	29%	28%	NM	NM
Net Inc.	37.1	33.5	9.2	27.4	25.1	18.5	10.3	18.2	-5.6	-7.5

Balance Sheet & Other Fin. Data (Million $)

Cash	19.6	3.0	4.5	2.9	6.7	5.0	5.2	7.1	17.3	1.5
Curr. Assets	119	74.9	64.0	49.7	40.5	33.6	30.6	66.2	43.4	61.0
Total Assets	677	479	338	299	240	206	214	425	421	479
Curr. Liab.	110	68.2	51.3	38.7	37.6	32.2	30.1	37.1	41.8	43.3
LT Debt	348	246	163	149	131	144	222	260	311	358
Common Eqty.	146	107	71.7	64.0	34.0	6.0	-57.0	52.0	14.0	20.0
Total Cap.	552	353	276	250	194	167	174	380	372	427
Cap. Exp.	197	172	108	118	73.0	39.0	51.0	45.0	32.0	29.0
Cash Flow	140	95.4	77.7	90.7	66.0	61.0	52.0	85.0	60.0	64.0
Curr. Ratio	1.1	1.1	1.2	1.3	1.1	1.0	1.0	1.8	1.0	1.4
% LT Debt of Cap.	63.0	69.7	59.1	59.8	67.3	86.2	127.3	68.5	83.6	83.8
% Ret. on Assets	6.4	8.2	2.9	10.1	11.2	8.1	3.2	4.0	NM	NM
% Ret. on Equity	29.3	37.5	13.6	55.7	126.9	NM	NM	53.3	NM	NM

Data as orig. reptd.; bef. results of disc opers. and/or spec. items. Per share data adj. for stk. divs. as of ex-div. date. Bold denotes diluted EPS (FASB 128). E-Estimated. NA-Not Available. NM-Not Meaningful. NR-Not Ranked.

Office—5 Greenway Plaza, Suite 2700, P.O. Box 2504, Houston, TX 77252-2504. **Tel**—(713) 297-5000. **Fax**—(713) 297-5100. **Chrmn, Pres, CEO & Investor Contact**—Paul G. Van Wagenen. **VP & CFO**—J. W. Elsenhans. **Secy**—G. A. Morton. **Dirs**—T. Armstrong, J. S. Blanton, W. M. Brumley Jr., J. B. Carter Jr., W. L. Fisher, W. E. Gipson, G. W. Gong, J. S. Hunt, F. A. Klingenstein, N. R. Petry, P. G. Van Wagenen, J. A. Vickers. **Transfer Agents & Registrars**—Harris Trust Co. of New York, NYC. **Incorporated**—in Delaware in 1970. **Empl**— 160. **S&P Analyst:** NR

03-OCT-98

Industry:
Leisure Time (Products)

Summary: This company manufactures snowmobiles, all-terrain vehicles, personal watercraft, and motorcycles for recreational and/or utility use.

Quantitative Evaluations

Recent Price • 27½
52 Wk Range • 39¼-27¼

Yield • 2.6%
12-Mo. P/E • 11.5

Outlook
(1 Lowest—5 Highest)
• **3+**

Fair Value
• **32¾**

Risk
• **Average**

Earn./Div. Rank
• **A**

Technical Eval.
• **Bearish** since 8/98

Rel. Strength Rank
(1 Lowest—99 Highest)
• **33**

Insider Activity
• **Neutral**

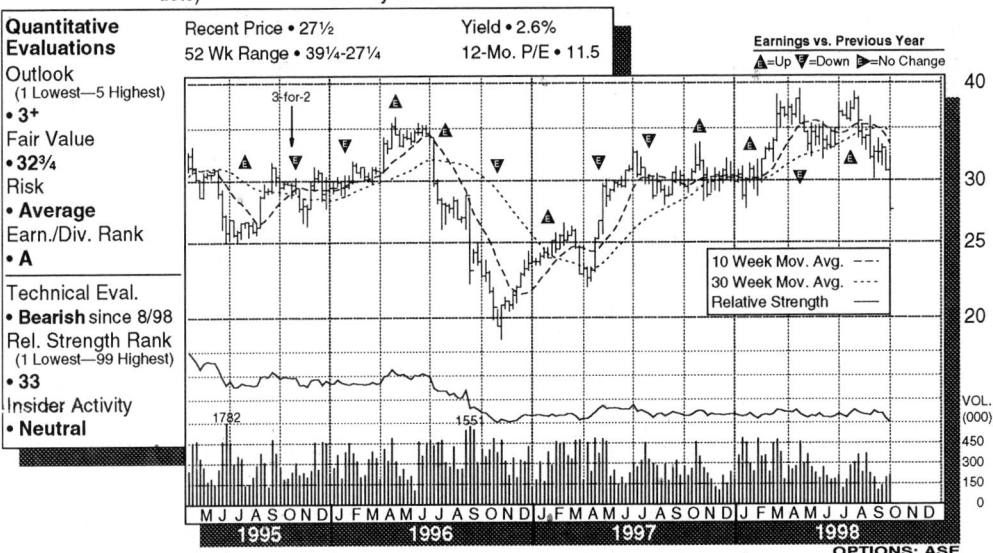

Earnings vs. Previous Year
▲=Up ▼=Down ▶=No Change

10 Week Mov. Avg. – – –
30 Week Mov. Avg. ·····
Relative Strength —

OPTIONS: ASE

Business Profile - 09-SEP-98

This company makes a variety of recreational and utility vehicles, and also offers related accessories, clothing, and replacement parts. In 1997, PII's largest business segment, which includes all-terrain vehicles (ATV) sold in North America, accounted for 45% of total sales. PII's other two North American business segments-- snowmobiles and personal watercraft-- represented 42% and 7% of sales, respectively. Various products sold in markets outside of North America accounted for 11%. Also, PII has been developing a new motorcycle business; in July 1998, PII said that it expects to ship between 2,000 and 3,000 Victory motorcycles by the end of the year. PII's 1998 third quarter is expected to include a provision for litigation loss related to a trade secret misappropriation claim against PII. After a judge recently upheld a jury verdict, PII was expected to explore further appeal options.

Operational Review - 09-SEP-98

Sales in the six months ended June 30, 1998, were up 2.1%, year to year. However, net income declined 9.7%, to $22.8 million ($0.87 a share, with 3.2% fewer diluted shares), from $25.3 million ($0.93). In mid-July 1998, prior to news of an expected third quarter litigation-related charge, PII expressed confidence that full-year 1998 net income will exceed 1997's level. Also, as of June 30, 1998, PII had authorization to repurchase up to about 2.6 million additional common shares.

Stock Performance - 02-OCT-98

In the past 30 trading days, PII's shares have declined 20%, compared to a 7% fall in the S&P 500. Average trading volume for the past five days was 42,740 shares, compared with the 40-day moving average of 42,572 shares.

Key Stock Statistics

Dividend Rate/Share	0.72	Shareholders	40,600
Shs. outstg. (M)	25.9	Market cap. (B)	$0.713
Avg. daily vol. (M)	0.033	Inst. holdings	46%
Tang. Bk. Value/Share	5.82		
Beta	0.85		

Value of $10,000 invested 5 years ago: $ 24,901

Fiscal Year Ending Dec. 31

	1998	1997	1996	1995	1994	1993
Revenues (Million $)						
1Q	210.0	224.6	278.0	254.8	145.5	107.1
2Q	274.7	249.9	317.1	285.4	180.9	111.2
3Q	—	293.4	299.1	291.4	258.4	166.8
4Q	—	280.4	297.7	282.3	241.6	142.9
Yr.	—	1,048	1,192	1,114	826.3	528.0
Earnings Per Share ($)						
1Q	**0.32**	0.44	0.48	0.47	0.22	0.20
2Q	**0.55**	0.49	0.58	0.45	0.27	0.21
3Q	—	0.81	0.57	0.67	0.79	0.61
4Q	—	**0.70**	0.61	0.60	0.71	0.47
Yr.	—	**2.45**	2.24	2.19	1.98	1.50

Next earnings report expected: mid October

Dividend Data (Dividends have been paid since 1987.)

Amount ($)	Date Decl.	Ex-Div. Date	Stock of Record	Payment Date
0.160	Oct. 23	Nov. 04	Nov. 06	Nov. 17 '97
0.180	Jan. 22	Jan. 29	Feb. 02	Feb. 16 '98
0.180	Apr. 16	Apr. 29	May. 01	May. 15 '98
0.180	Jul. 16	Jul. 29	Jul. 31	Aug. 17 '98

A Division of The McGraw-Hill Companies

Business Summary - 09-SEP-98

Polaris Industries Inc. (formerly Polaris Industries Partners L.P.) engineers and makes snowmobiles, all-terrain recreational and utility vehicles (ATVs), personal watercraft (PWC), and motorcycles. It markets these products, together with related accessories, clothing and replacement parts, through a network of close to 2,000 dealers in North America, and 54 distributors in 113 countries. The company believes itself to be the world's largest snowmobile maker. Sales of snowmobiles, ATVs and PWC in North America, and international sales (with segments including replacement parts, garments and accessories) in recent years were as follows:

	1997	1996	1995
Snowmobiles	42%	43%	46%
All-terrain vehicles	45%	37%	33%
Personal watercraft	7%	16%	16%
International	11%	11%	11%

In early 1998, PII said that its snowmobiles are produced in 31 models, ranging from utility and economy models to performance and competition models, with 1998 suggested retail prices ranging from about $3,200 to $8,500. PII also markets a full line of snowmobile accessories.

ATVs are typically four-wheel vehicles with bal-loon-style tires, and are designed for off-road use and raveling through rough terrain, swamps and marshaland. PII says that ATVs are used for recreation in such sports as fishing and hunting, and also for utility purposes on farms, ranches and construction sites. As of early 1998, PII's line of ATVs included 12 models, with 1998 suggested retail prices ranging from about $3,200 to $7,300. In addition, this PII business segment included some six-wheel off-road vehicles.

In 1992, PII began shipments of a line of personal watercraft, sit-down versions of water scooter vehicles designed principally for recreational use on lakes, rivers, bays and oceans. As of early 1998, PII has five PWC models. The 1997 suggested retail prices for PII's PWC ranged from about $5,900 to $9,400.

In 1998, PII started manufacturing a cruiser motorcycle known as the Victory V92C. PII has said that it expects to ship between 2,000 and 3,000 motorcycles by the end of 1998, and and that virtually all of the 1998 output has been pre-sold at retail.

PII's sales to customers outside of North America include snowmobiles, ATVs, PWC, and related products.

Polaris also offers a full line of recreational clothing designed to its specifications, including suits, helmets, gloves, boots, hats, sweaters and jackets.

In 1996, PII entered into a partnership agreement with Transamerica Commercial Finance Corp. to form Polaris Acceptance, which provides floor plan financing to PII dealers and distributors.

Per Share Data ($)

(Year Ended Dec. 31)	1997	1996	1995	1994	1993	1992	1991	1990	1989	1988
Tangible Bk. Val.	5.60	4.85	3.42	5.29	2.29	1.81	1.84	1.92	1.88	1.43
Cash Flow	3.69	3.33	3.01	5.52	2.71	2.18	2.00	1.95	1.68	1.39
Earnings	2.45	2.24	2.19	1.98	1.50	1.15	1.10	1.10	1.08	0.82
Dividends	0.64	0.60	4.27	1.68	1.67	1.67	1.67	1.67	1.51	0.80
Payout Ratio	26%	27%	195%	85%	111%	104%	107%	108%	117%	92%
Prices - High	33⅝	36¼	34⅜	34⅞	25⅝	16⅜	13½	12⅞	9⅛	6¼
- Low	21⅞	18¾	25	19⅜	14½	12	8⅛	8	5	4⅞
P/E Ratio - High	14	16	16	18	17	14	12	12	8	8
- Low	9	8	11	10	8	10	7	7	5	6

Income Statement Analysis (Million $)

	1997	1996	1995	1994	1993	1992	1991	1990	1989	1988
Revs.	1,048	1,192	1,114	826	528	384	298	296	243	171
Oper. Inc.	126	128	124	112	72.8	64.3	52.7	52.8	44.0	34.1
Depr.	33.2	30.6	22.7	23.7	19.6	17.3	13.8	12.6	11.5	11.7
Int. Exp.	2.8	4.3	1.7	NA	NA	6.8	7.2	9.4	6.4	4.2
Pretax Inc.	102	97.3	99	75.9	53.3	39.7	33.4	33.0	26.9	18.6
Eff. Tax Rate	36%	36%	39%	NM	14%	13%	5.90%	5.00%	2.50%	5.40%
Net Inc.	65.4	62.3	61.0	129	45.8	34.7	31.5	31.4	26.2	17.6

Balance Sheet & Other Fin. Data (Million $)

	1997	1996	1995	1994	1993	1992	1991	1990	1989	1988
Cash	1.2	5.8	3.5	62.9	33.8	19.1	20.1	32.0	27.9	15.6
Curr. Assets	217	193	176	206	110	75.0	59.2	66.9	60.3	36.4
Total Assets	385	352	314	331	181	147	136	139	138	118
Curr. Liab.	191	161	196	161	98.1	69.1	52.6	46.6	38.9	20.7
LT Debt	24.0	35.0	Nil	Nil	Nil	Nil	Nil	Nil	Nil	Nil
Common Eqty.	169	155	119	170	82.5	77.6	82.9	92.1	99	97.4
Total Cap.	194	190	119	170	82.5	77.6	82.9	92.1	99	97.4
Cap. Exp.	36.7	44.9	46.7	32.5	18.1	12.3	16.0	7.2	7.1	2.7
Cash Flow	99	93.0	83.0	153	65.4	52.0	45.3	44.0	37.7	29.3
Curr. Ratio	1.1	1.2	0.9	1.3	1.1	1.1	1.1	1.4	1.6	1.8
% LT Debt of Cap.	12.3	18.4	Nil	Nil	Nil	Nil	Nil	Nil	Nil	Nil
% Net Inc.of Revs.	6.2	5.2	5.5	15.6	8.7	9.0	10.6	10.6	10.8	10.3
% Ret. on Assets	17.8	18.7	18.9	46.9	27.6	23.7	22.9	22.7	20.5	15.1
% Ret. on Equity	40.3	45.5	42.2	95.6	56.4	41.6	36.0	32.9	26.8	18.1

Data as orig. reptd.; bef. results of disc. opers. and/or spec. items. Per share data adj. for stk. divs. as of ex-div. date; per unit data prior to 1994. Bold denotes diluted EPS (FASB 128). E-Estimated. NA-Not Available. NM-Not Meaningful. NR-Not Ranked.

Office—1225 Highway 169 North, Minneapolis, MN 55441. **Organized**—in Delaware in 1987; incorporated in Minnesota in 1994. **Tel**—(612) 542-0500. **Website**—http://www.polarisindustries.com **Chrmn & CEO**—W. H. Wendel Jr. **Pres & COO**—K. D. Larson. **VP-Fin, CFO & Secy**—M. W. Malone. **Dirs**—A. A. Baltins, R. J. Biggs, B. F. Dolan, K. D. Larson, R. S. Moe, G. R. Palen, S. G. Shank, W. H. Wendel Jr. **Transfer Agent**—Norwest Bank Minnesota, South St. Paul. **Empl**— 3,500. **S&P Analyst:** Tom Graves, CFA

STANDARD &POOR'S
STOCK REPORTS

Pool Energy Services
5013P

NASDAQ Symbol **PESC**

In S&P SmallCap 600

03-OCT-98

Industry:
Oil & Gas (Drilling & Equipment)

Summary: The world's largest well-servicing firm, Pool Energy concentrates on the maintenance and repair of existing oil and natural gas wells.

Quantitative Evaluations

Recent Price • 8	Yield • Nil
52 Wk Range • 41½-6¾	12-Mo. P/E • 5.0

Outlook
(1 Lowest—5 Highest)
• **4⁻**

Fair Value
• **13⅝**

Risk
• **Average**

Earn./Div. Rank
• **NR**

Technical Eval.
• **Bearish** since 6/98

Rel. Strength Rank
(1 Lowest—99 Highest)
• **20**

Insider Activity
• **Neutral**

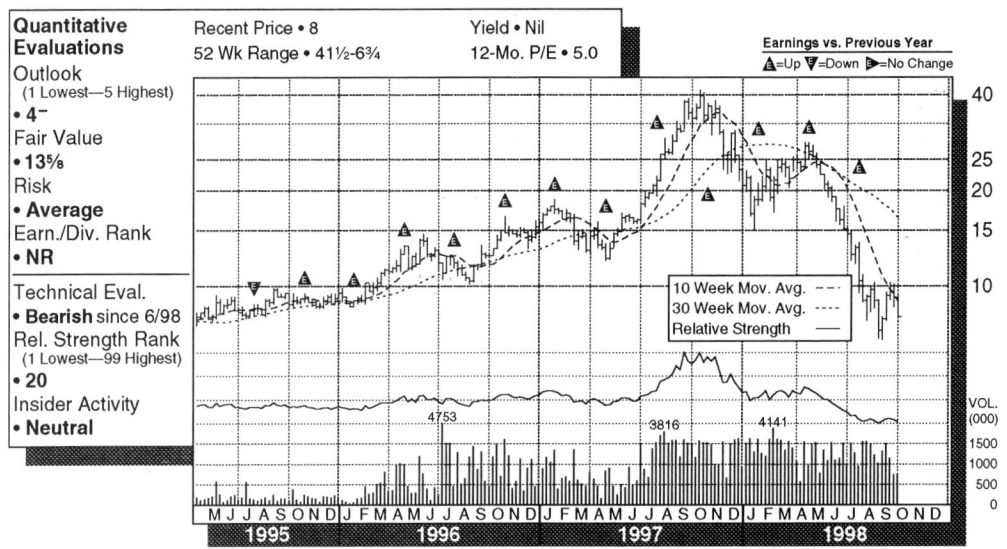

Earnings vs. Previous Year
▲=Up ▼=Down ▶=No Change

10 Week Mov. Avg. ―――
30 Week Mov. Avg. ·····
Relative Strength ―――

Business Profile - 10-JUN-98

Pool Energy, the world's largest well-servicing firm, has experienced improved earnings in recent years. PESC expects future results to benefit from its acquisition of the remaining 51% interest in its Malaysian joint venture and the acquisition of a 51% interest in Pool International Argentina S.A., a newly formed Argentine drilling company. In March 1998, PESC acquired Sea Mar, Inc., an operator of offshore support vessels in the Gulf of Mexico, for $76 million and 1.5 million common shares. The company expects Sea Mar to enhance its results beginning in the second quarter of 1998. On April 1998, PESC sold $150 million of senior subordinated notes.

Operational Review - 10-JUN-98

Total revenues in the first quarter of 1998 advanced 20%, year to year, reflecting the inclusion of land well-servicing rigs acquired during 1997, higher land drilling activity in Alaska, and increased activity and rates for the company's jackup workover rigs in the Gulf of Mexico. Margins improved on well controlled operating costs and expenses, and despite higher interest expense, pretax earnings more than doubled. After taxes at 39.1%, versus 38.0%, and minority interest in the 1997 period, net income was up 96%, to $7,453,000 ($0.38 a share), from $3,805,000 ($0.20).

Stock Performance - 02-OCT-98

In the past 30 trading days, PESC's shares have declined 11%, compared to a 7% fall in the S&P 500. Average trading volume for the past five days was 149,580 shares, compared with the 40-day moving average of 236,959 shares.

Key Stock Statistics

Dividend Rate/Share	Nil	Shareholders	2,600
Shs. outstg. (M)	21.0	Market cap. (B)	$0.168
Avg. daily vol. (M)	0.229	Inst. holdings	69%
Tang. Bk. Value/Share	10.62		
Beta	0.87		

Value of $10,000 invested 5 years ago: $ 12,549

Fiscal Year Ending Dec. 31

	1998	1997	1996	1995	1994	1993
Revenues (Million $)						
1Q	117.7	98.38	81.68	62.85	55.98	60.19
2Q	128.0	109.8	82.99	63.80	54.26	57.63
3Q	—	118.6	83.98	75.52	56.17	59.01
4Q	—	125.2	99.9	75.13	62.77	59.88
Yr.	—	451.9	348.6	277.3	229.2	236.7
Earnings Per Share ($)						
1Q	**0.38**	**0.20**	0.10	0.02	0.05	0.11
2Q	**0.36**	**0.31**	0.13	0.04	0.06	0.10
3Q	—	**0.43**	0.14	0.05	0.04	0.12
4Q	—	**0.43**	0.20	0.12	-1.09	0.13
Yr.	—	**1.36**	0.58	0.23	-0.94	0.46

Next earnings report expected: NA

Dividend Data

No cash dividends have been paid, and terms of Pool's credit line preclude such payments. A shareholder rights plan was adopted in 1994.

A Division of The **McGraw·Hill** Companies

Business Summary - 10-JUN-98

Pool Energy Services Co. (PESC) is the world's largest well-servicing and workover firm, providing services for onshore and offshore oil and gas wells, both domestically and internationally.

After reducing personnel levels in the past 10 years, PESC's customers, the oil and gas producers, are now outsourcing more and more of the services the company provides. PESC provides the maintenance services on the apparatus used to pump or lift oil from producing wells, supplying the rigs, equipment and crews needed to repair and replace pumps, sucker rods and tubing. Most of PESC's well-servicing rigs are also designed for major repairs or modifications on oil and gas wells, called "workovers." Completion services are performed when a well is first drilled.

PESC also performs contract drilling offshore Alaska and in the Gulf of Mexico, as well as overseas. Additional services include onsite temporary fluid storage facilities, the provision, removal and disposal of specialized fluids used during certain completion and workover operations, and the removal and disposal of salt water produced in conjunction with the production of oil and gas. PESC also offers other specialized rig services, including the plugging of depleted oil and gas wells.

Domestic onshore activities (59% of revenues in 1997) are conducted in 12 states, with PESC operating the largest fleet of land well-servicing rigs in Texas, the

Midcontinent area and California. PESC also operates one of the three largest offshore workover rig fleets in the Gulf of Mexico (18%) and performs both onshore and offshore services through its rigs in Alaska (6%). International operations (17%) are conducted in nine countries. At December 31, 1997, PESC operated a total of 844 rigs, including 59 rigs internationally in the Middle East, South America, Australia and Malaysia. PESC's principal joint venture operation is conducted in Saudi Arabia (Pool Arabia, Ltd.).

In 1994, PESC developed a strategic plan to strengthen its position and market share in the oilfield industry. Among the components of its strategy were the expansion of its core market areas through acquisitions; entering new foreign markets; and the expansion and enhancement of its rig fleet. In 1996, PESC acquired the remaining 51% interest in its Malaysian joint venture. PESC also entered the Argentine market by acquiring a 51% interest in a corporation that provides well-servicing, workover and drilling services in that country.

In November 1997, PESC acquired A.A. Oilfield Service, Inc., for $4.1 million. This acquisition included 18 oilfield trucks, one salt water disposal well and related equipment. In October 1997, PESC acquired Trey Services, Inc., for $31 million. Trey operated a fleet of 67 land well-servicing rigs, 104 oilfield trucks, 430 fluid storage tanks and five brine and disposal wells in the Permian Basin of West Texas.

Per Share Data ($)

(Year Ended Dec. 31)	1997	1996	1995	1994	1993	1992	1991	1990	1989	1988
Tangible Bk. Val.	9.84	9.65	8.88	9.49	10.43	9.99	10.13	9.94	10.33	NA
Cash Flow	2.64	1.71	1.31	0.08	1.66	1.11	1.55	1.74	1.37	NA
Earnings	1.36	0.58	0.23	-0.94	0.46	-0.22	0.19	0.44	-0.21	NA
Dividends	Nil	Nil	Nil	Nil	Nil	Nil	Nil	Nil	Nil	Nil
Payout Ratio	Nil	Nil	Nil	Nil	Nil	Nil	Nil	Nil	Nil	Nil
Prices - High	41¹/₂	16⁵/₈	9⁷/₈	10¹/₂	11⁷/₈	9	13¹/₈	18¹/₈	NA	NA
- Low	12	8⁵/₈	6⁵/₈	6¹/₄	6¹/₈	5³/₄	5¹/₄	8⁵/₈	NA	NA
P/E Ratio - High	31	29	43	NM	26	NM	69	41	NM	NM
- Low	9	15	29	NM	13	NM	28	20	NM	NM

Income Statement Analysis (Million $)

Revs.	452	348	277	229	237	213	225	235	238	NA
Oper. Inc.	64.0	34.1	18.3	10.2	15.3	7.9	15.1	20.7	8.5	NA
Depr.	25.0	18.5	15.0	13.8	16.3	18.0	18.3	17.5	19.8	NA
Int. Exp.	4.3	2.8	1.8	0.3	0.5	0.9	0.7	1.0	2.2	NA
Pretax Inc.	42.3	17.1	5.1	-21.1	7.6	-6.7	1.8	7.1	-1.0	NA
Eff. Tax Rate	37%	44%	35%	NM	18%	NM	NM	15%	NM	NM
Net Inc.	26.7	9.6	3.1	-12.7	6.2	-3.0	2.5	6.0	-2.7	NA

Balance Sheet & Other Fin. Data (Million $)

Cash	19.0	22.0	5.7	2.7	4.7	3.2	8.1	30.4	10.8	NA
Curr. Assets	153	114	78.1	68.5	69.7	65.9	62.0	89.5	87.5	NA
Total Assets	479	341	248	208	193	196	198	214	238	NA
Curr. Liab.	93.6	66.7	51.2	36.1	29.2	37.6	31.9	47.1	74.6	NA
LT Debt	79.3	23.1	15.8	0.4	Nil	Nil	Nil	Nil	Nil	Nil
Common Eqty.	234	197	136	129	141	135	137	134	129	NA
Total Cap.	339	228	154	131	144	138	141	138	130	NA
Cap. Exp.	60.4	30.7	23.4	11.4	20.4	12.7	26.1	11.9	NA	NA
Cash Flow	51.7	28.2	18.1	1.0	22.5	15.1	20.9	23.5	17.1	NA
Curr. Ratio	1.6	1.7	1.5	1.9	2.4	1.8	1.9	1.9	1.2	NA
% LT Debt of Cap.	23.3	10.1	12.2	0.3	Nil	Nil	Nil	Nil	Nil	Nil
% Net Inc.of Revs.	5.9	2.8	1.1	NM	2.6	NM	1.1	2.6	NM	NM
% Ret. on Assets	6.5	3.3	1.4	NM	3.2	NM	1.2	2.7	NM	NM
% Ret. on Equity	12.4	5.8	2.4	NM	4.5	NM	1.9	4.6	NM	NM

Data as orig. reptd.; bef. results of disc. opers. and/or spec. items. Per share data adj. for stk. divs. as of ex-div. date. Bold denotes diluted EPS (FASB 128). E-Estimated. NA-Not Available. NM-Not Meaningful. NR-Not Ranked.

Office—10375 Richmond Ave., P.O. Box 4271, Houston, TX 77210. **Tel**—(713) 954-3000. **Fax**—(713) 954-3326. **Chrmn, Pres & CEO**—J. T. Jongebloed. **Sr VP-Fin**—E. J. Spillard. **VP & Secy**—G. G. Arms. **VP & Investor Contact**—David C. Oatman 713 954-3316. **Dirs**—J. T. Jongebloed, J. F. Lavletta, J. R. Musolino, J. L. Payne.**Transfer Agent & Registrar**—BankBoston. **Incorporated**—in Texas in 1988. **Empl**— 6,584. **S&P Analyst:** S.S.

STANDARD &POOR'S
STOCK REPORTS

Pope & Talbot

1861T

NYSE Symbol **POP**

In S&P SmallCap 600

03-OCT-98

Industry:
Paper & Forest Products

Summary: This company, which divested its tissue business in 1998, produces lumber and market pulp.

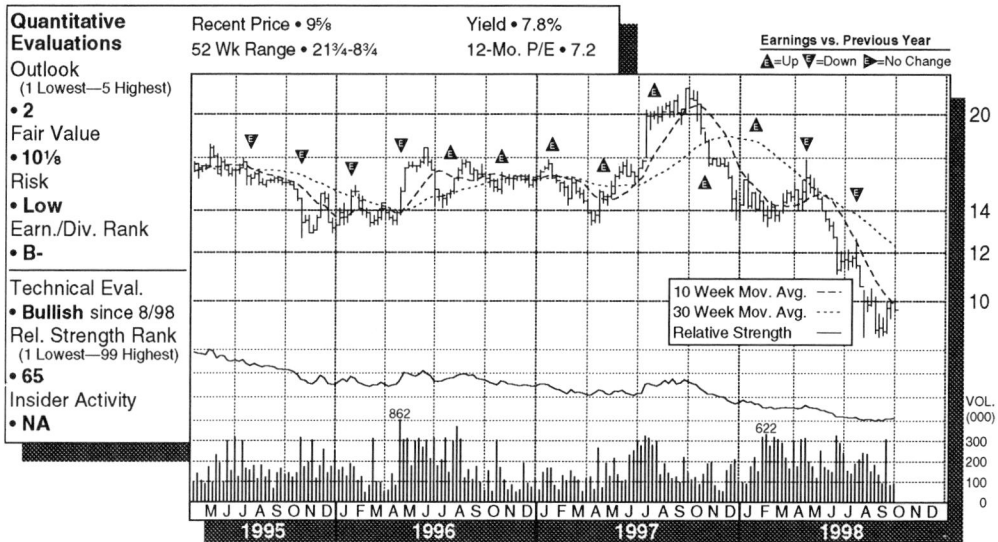

Quantitative Evaluations	
Outlook (1 Lowest—5 Highest)	**2**
Fair Value	**10⅛**
Risk	**Low**
Earn./Div. Rank	**B-**
Technical Eval.	**Bullish** since 8/98
Rel. Strength Rank (1 Lowest—99 Highest)	**65**
Insider Activity	**NA**

Recent Price • 9⅝
52 Wk Range • 21¾-8¾
Yield • 7.8%
12-Mo. P/E • 7.2

Earnings vs. Previous Year
▲=Up ▼=Down ▶=No Change

10 Week Mov. Avg. ---
30 Week Mov. Avg. ----
Relative Strength ——

Business Profile - 02-JUL-98

The company sold its tissue paper manufacturing and tissue business to Plainwell, Inc. in March 1998 for $147 million. Combined production of the three facilities sold totaled 110,000 tons annually. POP plans to grow through acquisitions of pulp and lumber operations. It believes it can achieve these growth objectives with its strong liquidity position and its conservative long-term debt to total capitalization of 36% at the end of the 1998 first quarter. In February 1998, the company acquired a 53% stake in Harmac Pacific, Inc., one of Canada's largest market pulp producers, with revenues of more than C$200 million.

Operational Review - 02-JUL-98

Total revenues in the first quarter of 1998 advanced 23%, year to year, as a 134% increase in pulp products revenues outweighed an 11% decline in wood products sales. Results were penalized by a rise in pulp products costs, restructuring charges and higher SG&A expense, and a loss from continuing operations of $6,593,000 ($0.49 a share) contrasted with income of $243,000 ($0.02). Per share results exclude income from discontinued operations of $2.01 and $0.08 in the respective periods. POP noted that several North American and European companies announced market pulp price increases in the 1998 second quarter.

Stock Performance - 02-OCT-98

In the past 30 trading days, POP's shares have declined 3%, compared to a 7% fall in the S&P 500. Average trading volume for the past five days was 18,640 shares, compared with the 40-day moving average of 35,431 shares.

Key Stock Statistics

Dividend Rate/Share	0.76	Shareholders	1,200
Shs. outstg. (M)	13.5	Market cap. (B)	$0.131
Avg. daily vol. (M)	0.035	Inst. holdings	48%
Tang. Bk. Value/Share	13.66		
Beta	1.29		

Value of $10,000 invested 5 years ago: $ 8,025

Fiscal Year Ending Dec. 31

	1998	1997	1996	1995	1994	1993
Revenues (Million $)						
1Q	103.5	84.09	110.7	133.8	168.7	133.8
2Q	106.5	88.34	110.6	124.5	157.9	124.5
3Q	—	80.68	112.4	131.8	171.3	131.8
4Q	—	76.79	113.9	134.3	162.0	159.2
Yr.	—	329.9	447.5	524.4	659.9	628.9
Earnings Per Share ($)						
1Q	-0.49	0.02	-0.20	-0.08	0.70	-0.08
2Q	-0.53	0.18	0.05	-0.48	0.21	-0.48
3Q	—	0.11	0.08	-0.25	0.07	-0.25
4Q	—	0.03	0.13	-0.22	0.27	0.39
Yr.	—	0.33	-0.10	-1.03	1.21	1.85

Next earnings report expected: mid October

Dividend Data (Dividends have been paid since 1948.)

Amount ($)	Date Decl.	Ex-Div. Date	Stock of Record	Payment Date
0.190	Oct. 07	Nov. 03	Nov. 05	Nov. 17 '97
0.190	Jan. 29	Feb. 02	Feb. 04	Feb. 13 '98
0.190	Apr. 21	Apr. 30	May. 04	May. 14 '98
0.190	Jul. 15	Jul. 30	Aug. 03	Aug. 14 '98

A Division of The McGraw·Hill Companies

STANDARD
&POOR'S
STOCK REPORTS

Pope & Talbot, Inc.

1861T
03-OCT-98

Business Summary - 02-JUL-98

Pope & Talbot (POP), an integrated wood-fiber products company, recently sold its tissue business to focus on its core pulp and lumber operations. POP's two distinct yet integrated market segments (wood products and fiber products) are designed to counteract the unavoidable cyclical nature of the forest products industry.

Conditions for POP's wood products business continued to improve in 1997. Supported by low interest rates, higher lumber demand and increased housing starts, all of POP's sawmills operated at capacity. The wood products division (75% of sales in 1997) makes standardized and specialty lumber and wood chips. POP produces boards and dimension lumber, including specialty items such as stress-rated lumber which are used for housing construction and renovation in the Midwest and Western U.S. POP's three sawmills in British Columbia account for about 75% of total production (with the remainder at two sawmills in South Dakota and Wyoming) and all are situated in areas with adequate raw material supply. Wood chips are sold to pulp and paper producers, while logs are sold to other domestic and Canadian forest products companies.

POP's paper products division (sold in March 1998) produced a full line of private-label sanitary tissue products, including towels, napkins, bathroom and facial tissue. Tissue products were sold to supermarkets, drugstores, price clubs, and food and drug distribution companies.

Bleached kraft pulp (23% of 1997 sales) is sold in the open market and to manufacturers for use in writing paper, newsprint and telephone directories. The company owns a pulp mill at Halsey, OR, which produces bleached kraft pulp sold in various forms to writing paper, tissue and newsprint manufacturers in the Pacific Northwest. Total annual capacity of the mill is 180,000 air dry metric tons.; 175,000 metric tons were produced in 1997, up from 162,000 metric tons in 1996. POP brokers wood chips for sale primarily into the export market.

Since the mid-1980s, the company has reduced its dependency on timber from the Pacific Northwest, where environmental concerns have sharply restricted the availability and increased the cost of timber. At the same time, POP has increased its operations in regions presently having more stable timber supplies, namely British Columbia and the Black Hills region of South Dakota and Wyoming.

Firm backlog at December 31, 1997, totaled $18 million, up from $17 million a year earlier. In 1997, sales to Grays Harbor represented 45% of the company's pulp revenues and the remaining nine largest customers accounted for an additional 30% of pulp revenues.

Per Share Data ($)

(Year Ended Dec. 31)	1997	1996	1995	1994	1993	1992	1991	1990	1989	1988
Tangible Bk. Val.	13.31	13.42	13.89	16.76	15.36	14.46	15.68	17.42	16.48	13.31
Cash Flow	2.57	2.41	2.34	4.19	4.35	2.27	1.97	3.95	5.74	4.44
Earnings	0.33	0.06	-1.03	1.21	1.85	-0.19	-0.44	1.70	3.70	2.68
Dividends	0.76	0.76	0.76	0.76	0.76	0.76	0.76	0.72	0.60	0.50
Payout Ratio	NM	NM	NM	63%	41%	NM	NM	42%	16%	18%
Prices - High	22⅛	17⅝	17⅞	32⅝	29⅞	19¾	19	27½	29¾	23
- Low	13¼	13⅛	12½	15¼	16	13⅜	12¾	10¼	17⅞	15½
P/E Ratio - High	67	NM	NM	27	16	NM	NM	16	8	9
- Low	40	NM	NM	13	9	NM	NM	6	5	6

Income Statement Analysis (Million $)

	1997	1996	1995	1994	1993	1992	1991	1990	1989	1988
Revs.	330	447	524	660	629	544	502	562	619	515
Oper. Inc.	44.8	40.9	37.5	61.2	74.4	33.3	26.7	60.4	93.3	73.7
Depr.	30.1	31.4	45.1	39.1	29.3	28.6	27.9	26.4	25.5	21.0
Int. Exp.	7.9	10.2	15.5	12.0	10.4	6.0	4.4	4.7	5.2	4.5
Pretax Inc.	8.8	2.5	-21.3	26.7	36.4	-2.5	-7.1	31.0	69.2	48.4
Eff. Tax Rate	49%	68%	NM	40%	41%	NM	NM	36%	37%	34%
Net Inc.	4.4	0.8	-13.8	15.9	21.6	-2.3	-5.1	19.8	43.6	31.9

Balance Sheet & Other Fin. Data (Million $)

	1997	1996	1995	1994	1993	1992	1991	1990	1989	1988
Cash	31.9	32.2	13.8	6.8	3.8	4.3	3.8	9.0	2.1	0.3
Curr. Assets	211	165	207	223	170	138	122	132	130	119
Total Assets	376	408	472	539	456	370	347	354	355	319
Curr. Liab.	84.8	87.0	113	104	101	79.7	64.5	53.8	68.5	62.2
LT Debt	88.7	108	139	177	135	89.5	69.0	77.5	67.6	77.6
Common Eqty.	179	183	190	228	184	172	187	207	199	162
Total Cap.	268	291	328	407	327	266	266	300	287	257
Cap. Exp.	13.1	7.2	27.8	55.6	82.6	32.3	37.3	41.9	52.1	61.8
Cash Flow	34.5	32.2	31.3	55.0	50.9	26.3	22.9	46.2	67.7	53.0
Curr. Ratio	2.5	1.9	1.8	2.2	1.7	1.7	1.9	2.4	1.9	1.9
% LT Debt of Cap.	33.0	37.1	42.2	43.6	41.2	33.7	26.0	25.8	23.5	30.2
% Net Inc.of Revs.	1.3	0.2	NM	2.4	3.4	NM	NM	3.5	7.1	6.2
% Ret. on Assets	1.1	0.2	NM	3.0	5.2	NM	NM	5.6	12.9	11.3
% Ret. on Equity	2.4	0.0	NM	7.3	12.0	NM	NM	9.9	24.1	21.5

Data as orig. reptd.; bef. results of disc. opers. and/or spec. items. Per share data adj. for stk. divs. as of ex-div. date. Bold denotes diluted EPS (FASB 128). E-Estimated. NA-Not Available. NM-Not Meaningful. NR-Not Ranked.

Office—1500 S.W. First Ave., Portland, OR 97201. **Tel**—(503) 228-9161. **Chrmn & CEO**—P. T. Pope. **Pres & COO**—M. Flannery. **SVP-Fin, Secy & CFO**—R.J. Day.**Treas**—B. Bluhn. **Investor Contact**—Bob Wulf. **Dirs**—G. P. Andrews, H. W. Budge, C. Crocker, M. Flannery, W. E. McCain, R. S. Miller Jr., P. T. Pope, H. G. L. Powell, B. Walker Jr. **Transfer Agent & Registrar**—ChaseMellon Shareholder Services, SF. **Incorporated**—in California in 1940; reincorporated in Delaware in 1979. **Empl**— 2,300. **S&P Analyst:** S.S.

03-OCT-98

Industry: Services (Commercial & Consumer)

Summary: This company designs, underwrites and markets pre-paid legal expense plans, covering various legal services, throughout the U.S.

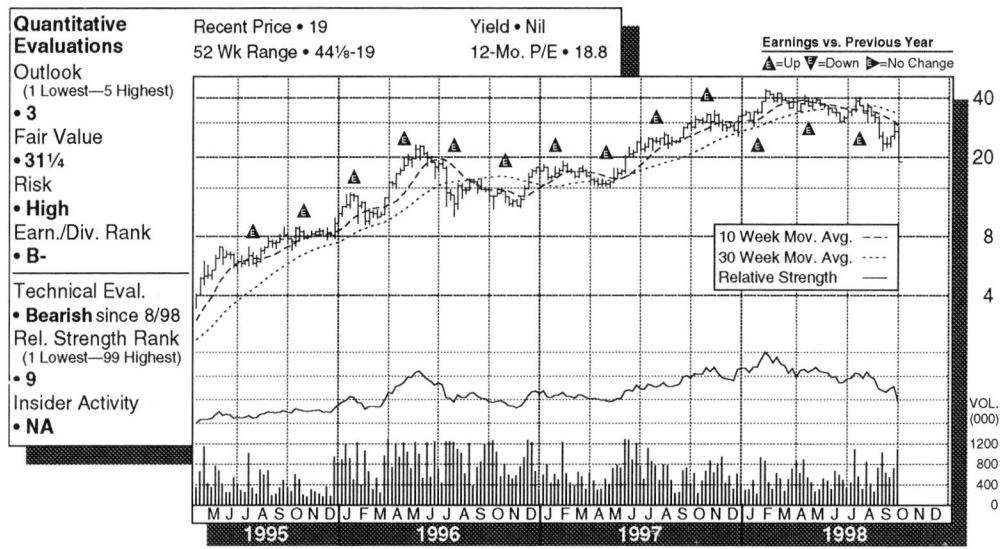

Quantitative Evaluations	
Outlook (1 Lowest—5 Highest)	• **3**
Fair Value	• **31¼**
Risk	• **High**
Earn./Div. Rank	• **B-**
Technical Eval.	• **Bearish** since 8/98
Rel. Strength Rank (1 Lowest—99 Highest)	• **9**
Insider Activity	• **NA**

Recent Price • 19
52 Wk Range • 44⅛-19
Yield • Nil
12-Mo. P/E • 18.8

Earnings vs. Previous Year
▲=Up ▼=Down ▶=No Change

10 Week Mov. Avg. ---
30 Week Mov. Avg. .....
Relative Strength —

Business Profile - 14-AUG-98

PPD's management feels that public awareness and acceptance of its pre-paid legal expense plans are increasing. The company also believes that the need for this service by middle income Americans continues to rise. Commissions and general administrative expenses, as a percentage of membership premiums, are expected to remain at or near current levels in future periods; membership benefits are expected to remain near 35% of membership premiums. In July 1998, the board of directors authorized a 200,000 share stock repurchase plan.

Operational Review - 14-AUG-98

Revenues for the six months ended June 30, 1998, rose 44%, primarily on the strength of new memberships written and membership premiums. Premium-related costs as a percentage of membership revenues were virtually unchanged. However, overall costs and expenses declined slightly as a percentage of total revenues, due to growth in revenue segments that do not share the same premium-related costs. After taxes at 33.9%, versus 35.0%, net income grew 51%, to $12,561,000 ($0.55 a share, after preferred dividends), from $8,336,000 ($0.37).

Stock Performance - 02-OCT-98

In the past 30 trading days, PPD's shares have declined 41%, compared to a 7% fall in the S&P 500. Average trading volume for the past five days was 214,700 shares, compared with the 40-day moving average of 137,238 shares.

Key Stock Statistics

Dividend Rate/Share	Nil	Shareholders	6,100
Shs. outstg. (M)	22.4	Market cap. (B)	$0.426
Avg. daily vol. (M)	0.151	Inst. holdings	48%
Tang. Bk. Value/Share	3.72		
Beta	1.70		

Value of $10,000 invested 5 years ago: $ 152,000

Fiscal Year Ending Dec. 31

	1998	1997	1996	1995	1994	1993
Revenues (Million $)						
1Q	28.80	19.73	12.35	7.63	5.73	4.67
2Q	31.54	22.20	14.80	8.97	6.23	4.86
3Q	—	24.20	15.76	9.82	6.41	5.00
4Q	—	26.35	17.04	11.02	6.75	5.40
Yr.	—	92.47	59.95	37.48	25.11	20.03
Earnings Per Share ($)						
1Q	**0.26**	**0.18**	0.12	0.08	0.07	0.01
2Q	**0.20**	**0.10**	0.11	0.00	0.07	0.04
3Q	—	**0.22**	0.15	0.09	0.06	22.20
4Q	—	**0.24**	0.16	0.10	0.06	0.04
Yr.	—	**0.83**	0.56	0.35	0.26	0.02

Next earnings report expected: mid October

Dividend Data

No cash has been paid on the common stock.

A Division of The **McGraw-Hill** *Companies*

Business Summary - 14-AUG-98

Pre-Paid Legal Services (PPD) was one of the first U.S. companies organized solely to design, underwrite and market legal expense plans. The company's plans (referred to as contracts) provide for or reimburse a portion of fees associated with a variety of legal services in a manner similar to that of medical reimbursement plans.

Contracts are offered both on an "open panel" basis, under which members may use attorneys of their choice, and on a "closed panel" basis, where members receive services from designated firms of independent provider attorneys who have contractually agreed with the company to provide scheduled benefits to members. At year-end 1997, closed-panel contracts accounted for 91% of active memberships.

The basic legal service contract, the family plan, consists of five separate benefits: (1) a preventive legal service that permits unlimited toll-free telephone access to a provider firm of attorneys and permits consultations for personal legal matters; (2) automobile legal protection, providing legal services in connection with certain licensed motor vehicle or boat-related matters; (3) a trial defense fund that provides up to 60 hours of attorneys' services available for the defense of civil or

job-related criminal charges; (4) IRS audit protection service, providing up to 50 hours a year in legal assistance; and (5) the right to a 25% discount on any legal services not stipulated in the plan. About 93% of PPD's contracts outstanding are family plan contracts.

Legal service plans, while used in Europe for many years, were first developed in the U.S. in the late 1960s. Since then, there has been substantial growth in the number of Americans entitled to receive various forms of legal services through legal service plans. According to estimates developed by the National Resource Center for Consumers of Legal Services (NRC), there were 105 million Americans entitled to service through at least one legal service plan in 1996, up from 4 million in 1981, 15 million in 1985, 58 million in 1990, and 98 million in 1996. The legal service plan industry continues to evolve, and market acceptance of legal service plans, as indicated by recent growth in the number of individuals covered by plans, is increasing.

In addition, the NRC estimates that of those Americans covered by legal service plans, only 10% were covered by plans having benefits comparable to those provided by the company's contracts. PPD therefore believes that significant opportunities exist for successful marketing of its contracts to employee groups and other individual consumers.

Per Share Data ($)

(Year Ended Dec. 31)	1997	1996	1995	1994	1993	1992	1991	1990	1989	1988
Tangible Bk. Val.	3.13	2.07	1.40	0.57	2.11	2.09	2.05	2.02	2.25	2.67
Cash Flow	0.86	0.58	0.37	0.29	0.07	0.08	0.08	-0.16	-0.14	0.21
Earnings	0.83	0.56	0.35	0.26	0.02	0.04	0.02	-0.23	-0.22	0.14
Dividends	Nil	Nil	Nil	Nil	Nil	Nil	Nil	Nil	Nil	Nil
Payout Ratio	Nil	Nil	Nil	Nil	Nil	Nil	Nil	Nil	Nil	Nil
Prices - High	$34^5/_8$	$23^1/_8$	$10^7/_8$	$2^3/_8$	$2^1/_2$	$1^7/_8$	$1^7/_8$	$^7/_8$	$2^1/_4$	$4^1/_2$
- Low	14	$9^1/_8$	$1^{11}/_{16}$	$1^1/_4$	$1^1/_{16}$	$^3/_4$	$^3/_8$	$^1/_4$	$^3/_8$	$1^3/_4$
P/E Ratio - High	42	41	31	9	NM	47	94	NM	NM	32
- Low	17	16	5	5	NM	19	19	NM	NM	13

Income Statement Analysis (Million $)

Revs.	90.8	59.9	37.5	23.8	19.6	19.1	20.8	23.8	32.1	37.4
Oper. Inc.	29.6	19.7	11.7	3.3	1.7	1.6	1.6	0.6	-0.8	2.8
Depr.	0.7	0.5	0.5	0.4	0.5	0.6	0.6	0.7	0.8	0.9
Int. Exp.	Nil	Nil	0.0	0.3	0.5	0.8	1.2	1.5	1.7	1.8
Pretax Inc.	28.9	19.2	11.2	3.4	0.5	0.8	0.4	-3.0	-3.5	2.4
Eff. Tax Rate	35%	35%	35%	NM	41%	36%	39%	NM	NM	38%
Net Inc.	18.8	12.5	7.3	3.7	0.3	0.5	0.3	-2.4	-2.4	1.5

Balance Sheet & Other Fin. Data (Million $)

Cash	21.8	15.3	15.0	9.5	5.3	6.0	6.7	4.7	4.5	8.9
Curr. Assets	44.1	26.1	20.0	12.6	NA	NA	NA	NA	NA	NA
Total Assets	91.9	57.5	35.6	18.2	35.4	34.8	36.9	38.9	47.9	57.5
Curr. Liab.	4.9	2.8	2.3	2.4	NA	NA	NA	NA	NA	NA
LT Debt	Nil	Nil	Nil	Nil	0.1	3.0	5.2	7.0	9.4	4.9
Common Eqty.	70.5	45.4	29.7	7.7	22.8	22.1	21.6	21.2	23.5	25.2
Total Cap.	87.0	54.7	33.3	15.8	26.9	29.2	30.7	32.1	37.6	37.0
Cap. Exp.	1.3	1.3	0.6	0.5	0.2	0.3	0.1	0.2	0.6	0.3
Cash Flow	19.5	13.0	7.7	3.7	0.8	1.1	0.8	-1.8	-1.6	2.3
Curr. Ratio	9.0	9.3	8.6	5.4	NA	NA	NA	NA	NA	NA
% LT Debt of Cap.	Nil	Nil	Nil	Nil	0.5	10.2	16.8	21.7	25.0	13.2
% Net Inc.of Revs.	20.7	20.9	19.5	15.6	1.6	2.6	1.3	NM	NM	3.9
% Ret. on Assets	25.1	26.9	27.2	23.2	0.9	1.4	0.7	NM	NM	2.4
% Ret. on Equity	32.4	33.3	31.6	53.5	1.3	2.2	1.2	NM	NM	5.9

Data as orig. reptd.; bef. results of disc. opers. and/or spec. items. Per share data adj. for stk. divs. as of ex-div. date. Bold denotes diluted EPS (FASB 128). E-Estimated. NA-Not Available. NM-Not Meaningful. NR-Not Ranked.

Office—321 E. Main St., Ada, OK 74820. **Tel**—(405) 436-1234. **Fax**—(405) 436-7565. **Website**—http://www.pplsi.com. **Chrmn & CEO**—H. C. Stonecipher. **Pres**—W. L. Smith. **CFO & COO**—R. Harp. **Investor Contact**—Melanie Lawson. **Dirs**—M.H. Belsky, P. K. Grunebaum, R. Harp, J.W. Hall, K. S. Pinson, D.A. Savula, W. L. Smith, H. C. Stonecipher, S. A. Stonecipher. **Transfer Agent & Registrar**—Liberty National Bank & Trust Co., Oklahoma City (NYC drop: Registrar & Transfer Co.). **Incorporated**—in Oklahoma in 1976. **Empl**— 216. **S&P Analyst**: Jordan Horoschak

Premier Bancshares   8914M

ASE Symbol **PMB**

In S&P SmallCap 600

03-OCT-98

Industry: Banks (Regional)

Summary: This company is the third largest bank holding company in Georgia.

Quantitative Evaluations

Outlook (1 Lowest—5 Highest)
- **NA**

Fair Value
- **NA**

Risk
- **NA**

Earn./Div. Rank
- **NR**

Technical Eval.
- **NA**

Rel. Strength Rank (1 Lowest—99 Highest)
- **37**

Insider Activity
- **Neutral**

Recent Price • 19⅞   Yield • 1.6%

52 Wk Range • 30-12⅞   12-Mo. P/E • 23.4

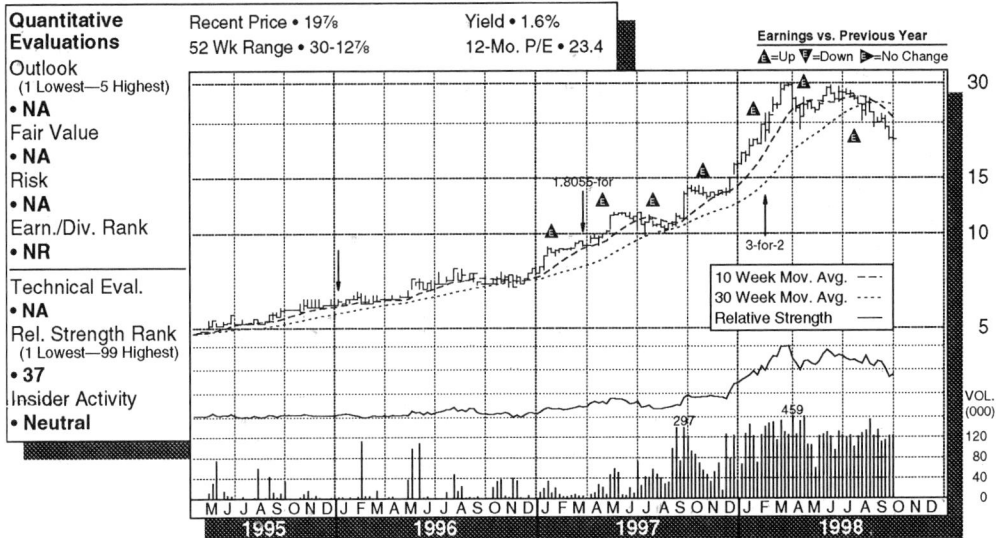

Earnings vs. Previous Year
▲=Up ▼=Down ▶=No Change

10 Week Mov. Avg. ---
30 Week Mov. Avg. ....
Relative Strength —

Business Profile - 17-AUG-98

PMB is now the third largest bank holding company in Georgia. Acquisitions during the past two years have been a principal source of the company's growth. Transactions completed or announced through July 1998 will boost assets to about $1.4 billion. The company believes that its knowledge of its product lines and local markets allows it to compete effectively with larger institutions by offering a wide range of products while maintaining strong community relationships and name recognition within its markets.

Operational Review - 17-AUG-98

Based on a brief report, net income in the first half of 1998 advanced 42%, year to year (as restated for acquisitions), to $7,874,000 ($0.45 a share) from $5,533,000 ($0.33, as adjusted). The company attributed the rise to strong growth in loans, with all of its lending divisions experiencing record volumes due to a healthy economic environment in its markets.

Stock Performance - 02-OCT-98

In the past 30 trading days, PMB's shares have declined 18%, compared to a 7% fall in the S&P 500. Average trading volume for the past five days was 31,740 shares, compared with the 40-day moving average of 41,292 shares.

Key Stock Statistics

Dividend Rate/Share	0.32	Shareholders	600
Shs. outstg. (M)	17.0	Market cap. (B)	$0.339
Avg. daily vol. (M)	0.027	Inst. holdings	6%
Tang. Bk. Value/Share	4.85		
Beta	NA		

Value of $10,000 invested 5 years ago: NA

Fiscal Year Ending Dec. 31

	1998	1997	1996	1995	1994	1993
Revenues (Million $)						
1Q	24.62	—	8.25	3.21	—	—
2Q	28.77	—	8.55	3.46	—	—
3Q	—	—	8.31	3.55	—	—
4Q	—	—	9.77	4.02	—	—
Yr.	—	84.22	34.88	14.24	11.99	13.21
Earnings Per Share ($)						
1Q	**0.23**	**0.16**	0.13	—	—	—
2Q	**0.24**	**0.19**	0.11	—	—	—
3Q	—	**0.21**	0.01	—	—	—
4Q	—	**0.19**	0.16	0.12	—	—
Yr.	—	**0.73**	**0.47**	0.32	0.05	0.07

Next earnings report expected: early October

Dividend Data (Dividends have been paid since 1996.)

Amount ($)	Date Decl.	Ex-Div. Date	Stock of Record	Payment Date
0.120	Jan. 23	Feb. 10	Feb. 12	Feb. 27 '98
3-for-2	Jan. 07	Feb. 17	Jan. 23	Feb. 13 '98
0.080	Apr. 28	May. 05	May. 07	May. 21 '98
0.080	Jun. 23	Jun. 26	Jun. 30	Jul. 14 '98

Business Summary - 17-AUG-98

Premier Bancshares, Inc. is a locally-focused, community-oriented bank holding company that owns Premier Bank, The Central and Southern Bank, North Georgia, and Citizens Bank, which operate 20 banking offices in the Atlanta metropolitan area and in northern and central Georgia. It also owns Premier Lending, a retail originator of residential mortgage loans that operates eight mortgage loan production offices in the Atlanta metropolitan area and in Jacksonville, FL, Charleston, SC, and Mobile, AL.

Total loans were $540.1 million at the end of 1997, versus $401.2 million a year earlier, divided as follows:

	1997	1996
Real estate secured by mortgage	50%	34%
Real estate construction	26%	29%
Consumer and other	7%	11%
Commercial, financial & agricultural	17%	26%

The allowance for loan losses, which is set aside for possible loan defaults, was $8.8 million (1.64% of net loans) at the end of 1997, up from $7.6 million (1.90%) the year before. There were net recoveries of $674,000

(0.13% of average loans) in 1997, versus $942,000 (0.25% of average loans) in 1995. Nonperforming assets, including loans past due 90 days or more, non-accrual loans and other real estate, amounted to $4.1 million (1.64% of loans) at December 31, 1997, up from $2.7 million (1.90%) a year earlier.

Interest income on loans provided 63% of total income in 1997, interest income on investment securities 10%, other interest income 2%, service charges and fees 6%, mortgage loan fees 17% and other noninterest income 2%.

Total deposits of $653.0 million at 1997 year end were divided: noninterest-bearing demand deposits 14%, interest-bearing demand deposits 13%, savings and money market deposits 15%, and time deposits 58%.

The average yield on interest-earning assets was 9.30% in 1997 (9.12% in 1996), while the average rate paid on interest-bearing liabilities was 5.19% (5.30%), for a net interest spread of 4.11% (3.82%).

In July 1998, the company signed a definitive agreement to acquire Frederica Bank & Trust , a state-chartered community bank operating in Glynn County, GA, with $72 million in assets, for about $24.7 million.

Per Share Data ($)

(Year Ended Dec. 31)	1997	1996	1995	1994	1993	1992	1991	1990	1989	1988
Tangible Bk. Val.	4.34	3.29	3.26	NA	NA	NA	NA	NA	NA	NA
Earnings	0.73	0.39	0.32	0.05	0.07	0.04	NA	NA	NA	NA
Dividends	0.39	0.18	Nil	Nil	Nil	Nil	Nil	Nil	Nil	Nil
Payout Ratio	53%	46%	Nil	Nil	Nil	Nil	Nil	Nil	Nil	Nil
Prices - High	17⅞	7⅞	6⅛	NA	NA	NA	NA	NA	NA	NA
- Low	7⅝	5⅞	4¾	NA	NA	NA	NA	NA	NA	NA
P/E Ratio - High	24	20	19	NA	NA	NA	NA	NA	NA	NA
- Low	10	15	15	NA	NA	NA	NA	NA	NA	NA

Income Statement Analysis (Million $)

	1997	1996	1995	1994	1993	1992	1991	1990	1989	1988
Net Int. Inc.	33.0	11.7	9.0	6.8	6.4	5.4	NA	NA	NA	NA
Tax Equiv. Adj.	7.0	Nil	Nil	Nil	Nil	Nil	Nil	Nil	Nil	Nil
Non Int. Inc.	21.2	11.7	8.1	3.0	NA	NA	NA	NA	NA	NA
Loan Loss Prov.	0.6	0.6	0.3	0.3	1.0	0.4	NA	NA	NA	NA
Exp./Op. Revs.	68%	83%	80%	88%	NA	NA	NA	NA	NA	NA
Pretax Inc.	16.6	3.6	3.1	0.9	0.4	0.1	NA	NA	NA	NA
Eff. Tax Rate	33%	30%	36%	66%	24%	3.10%	NA	NA	NA	NA
Net Inc.	11.2	2.5	2.0	0.3	0.3	0.1	NA	NA	NA	NA
% Net Int. Marg.	4.91	4.91	4.79	NA	NA	NA	NA	NA	NA	NA

Balance Sheet & Other Fin. Data (Million $)

	1997	1996	1995	1994	1993	1992	1991	1990	1989	1988
Earning Assets:										
Money Mkt	24.3	23.1	12.5	19.1	11.6	NA	NA	NA	NA	NA
Inv. Securities	116	35.1	45.8	11.6	26.4	NA	NA	NA	NA	NA
Com'l Loans	90.7	28.6	22.2	NA	NA	NA	NA	NA	NA	NA
Other Loans	439	183	137	NA	NA	NA	NA	NA	NA	NA
Total Assets	794	294	238	152	140	130	NA	NA	NA	NA
Demand Deposits	177	30.2	29.3	NA	NA	NA	NA	NA	NA	NA
Time Deposits	376	207	149	NA	NA	NA	NA	NA	NA	NA
LT Debt	1.8	4.0	3.0	NA	NA	NA	NA	NA	NA	NA
Common Eqty.	68.9	23.8	23.4	17.6	17.9	14.0	NA	NA	NA	NA
% Ret. on Assets	2.1	1.0	1.0	0.2	0.2	NA	NA	NA	NA	NA
% Ret. on Equity	24.3	10.9	9.7	1.6	1.9	NA	NA	NA	NA	NA
% Loan Loss Resv.	1.6	1.3	1.4	NA	NA	NA	NA	NA	NA	NA
% Loans/Deposits	82.5	78.9	74.5	NA	NA	NA	NA	NA	NA	NA
% Equity to Assets	8.5	8.8	10.5	12.1	11.8	NA	NA	NA	NA	NA

Data as orig. reptd.; bef. results of disc. opers. and/or spec. items. Per share data adj. for stk. divs. as of ex-div. date. Bold denotes diluted EPS (FASB 128). E-Estimated. NA-Not Available. NM-Not Meaningful. NR-Not Ranked.

Office—2180 Atlanta Plaza, 950 East Paces Ferry Rd., Atlanta, GA 30326. **Tel**—(404) 814-3090. **Chrmn & CEO**—D. D. Pittard. **Pres & COO**—R. C. Oliver. **EVP & CFO**—M. E. Ricketson. **Dirs**—N. M. Anderson, G. S. Carpenter, J. L. Coxwell, Sr., D. N. Ellis, W. M. Evans, Jr., J. H. Ferguson, R. E. Flournoy III, J. E. Freeman, A. F. Gandy, R. R. Howell, B. H. Martin, T. J. Martin, C. S. McQuaig, R. C. Oliver, T. E. Owen, Jr., D. D. Pittard. **Transfer Agent & Registrar**—SunTrust Bank, Atlanta. **Incorporated**—in Georgia in 1988. **Empl**— 492. **S&P Analyst:** S.R.B.

03-OCT-98

Industry: Oil & Gas (Drilling & Equipment)

Summary: This company is one of the largest well servicing contractors in the world, providing services in the U.S., Argentina, Venezuela and Russia.

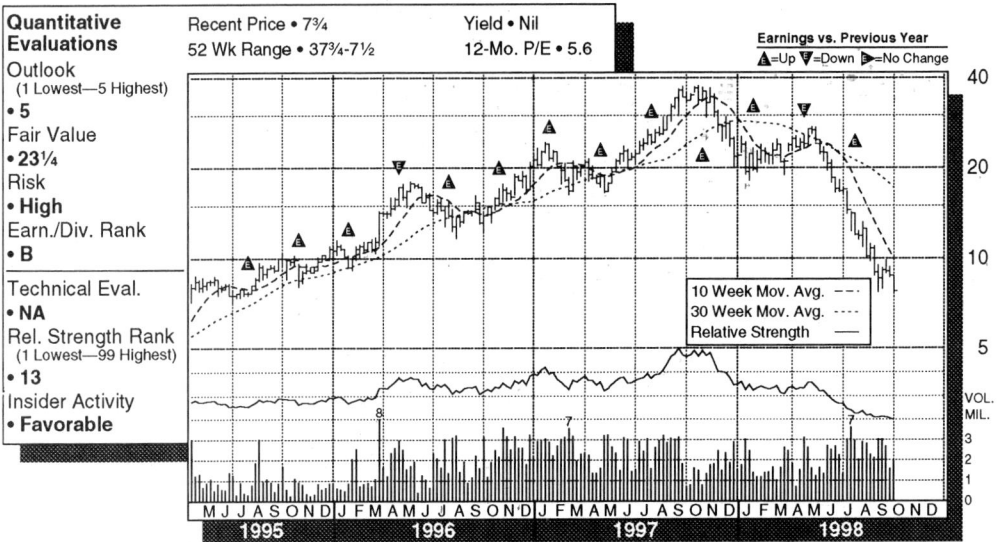

Quantitative Evaluations	
Recent Price • 7¾	Yield • Nil
52 Wk Range • 37¾-7½	12-Mo. P/E • 5.6

Outlook (1 Lowest—5 Highest)
• 5

Fair Value
• 23¼

Risk
• High

Earn./Div. Rank
• B

Technical Eval.
• NA

Rel. Strength Rank (1 Lowest—99 Highest)
• 13

Insider Activity
• Favorable

Earnings vs. Previous Year
▲=Up ▼=Down ▶=No Change

10 Week Mov. Avg.
30 Week Mov. Avg. ----
Relative Strength ——

Business Profile - 07-AUG-98

Pride, one of the world's largest well servicing contractors, has actively sought to diversify away from the domestic onshore market. The company acquired Quitral-Co S.A.I.C., the largest drilling and workover contractor in Argentina, in April 1996, and Forasol in March 1997, and divested its domestic land-based well servicing operations in February 1997. In 1997, domestic onshore operations accounted for 2% of total revenues, down from 29% in 1996. The company changed its name from Pride Petroleum Services, Inc. in June 1997 and its shares moved from the Nasdaq to the NYSE on September 10, 1997.

Operational Review - 07-AUG-98

Revenues in the first half of 1998 rose 42%, year to year, reflecting the inclusion of drilling related businesses and equipment acquired during the past 18 months. Operating profit benefited from the acquisitions, improved utilization of the company's equipment and higher operating rates for rig fleets; however, in the absence of a $53 million gain from the sale of the U.S. land-based well servicing business, and a charge of $4.2 million from the conversion of debt, net income fell 35%, to $45,950,000 ($0.83 a diluted share, on 26% more shares), from $70,547,000 ($1.61). Excluding non-recurring gains and charges in 1997, net income was up 116%.

Stock Performance - 02-OCT-98

In the past 30 trading days, PDE's shares have declined 28%, compared to a 7% fall in the S&P 500. Average trading volume for the past five days was 402,160 shares, compared with the 40-day moving average of 507,587 shares.

Key Stock Statistics

Dividend Rate/Share	Nil	Shareholders	2,500
Shs. outstg. (M)	50.2	Market cap. (B)	$0.389
Avg. daily vol. (M)	0.516	Inst. holdings	71%
Tang. Bk. Value/Share	14.53		
Beta	0.85		

Value of $10,000 invested 5 years ago: $ 20,000

Fiscal Year Ending Dec. 31

	1998	1997	1996	1995	1994	1993
Revenues (Million $)						
1Q	213.7	131.4	66.24	62.51	36.81	25.09
2Q	219.2	174.5	102.0	68.86	40.26	26.50
3Q	—	182.9	115.4	67.14	50.97	37.25
4Q	—	211.0	123.6	65.09	54.30	38.26
Yr.	—	699.8	407.2	263.6	182.3	127.1
Earnings Per Share ($)						
1Q	0.40	1.49	0.11	0.12	0.06	-0.04
2Q	0.43	0.27	0.18	0.14	0.06	0.03
3Q	—	0.20	0.20	0.18	0.08	0.08
4Q	—	0.37	0.27	0.16	0.10	0.06
Yr.	—	2.16	0.81	0.60	0.30	0.13

Next earnings report expected: late October

Dividend Data

No cash dividends have been paid.

 A Division of The McGraw-Hill Companies

Business Summary - 07-AUG-98

Pride International, Inc. (PDE), formerly Pride Petroleum Services, Inc., is one of the world's largest drilling contractors, providing onshore and offshore drilling, workover and related services in more than 15 countries to oil and gas exploration and production companies. In recent years, the company has focused its growth strategy on the higher-margin offshore and international drilling and workover markets. The company changing its name to Pride International, Inc. in mid-1997 to reflect the nature and scope of its operations and its strategy for achieving future growth in revenue and earnings through international expansion.

Consistent with its strategy, the company acquired Quitral-Co S.A.I.C., the largest drilling and workover contractor in Argentina, in April 1996, and the operating subsidiaries of Forasol-Foramer N.V., which provides onshore and offshore drilling services in more than 20 countries, in March 1997. The company also divested its domestic land-based well servicing operations in February 1997.

With these transactions, international operations became an increasingly important source of revenues for the company, comprising over 78% of total revenues in 1997, compared with 57% in 1996. These transactions also transformed PDE into one of the largest and most diversified drilling contractors in the world, with a global fleet of 285 rigs. Moreover, in May 1997, the company acquired 12 mat-supported jackup drilling rigs from Noble Drilling Corp. for $269 million. This acquisition positioned the company as the second largest operator in the Gulf of Mexico of mat-supported jackup rigs capable of operating in water depths of 200 feet or greater.

The company's diversification into international markets enables it to provide a broad range of services and to take advantage of market upturns while reducing its exposure to sharp downturns in any particular market sector or geographic region. Of course, along with the benefits of expanded international operations come additional risks, including foreign exchange restrictions and currency fluctuations, and political instability, as well as other risks that may limit or disrupt markets.

To help finance its international expansion, the company raised about $387 million (net) in May 1997 from the public sale of 4.3 million common shares and the issuance of $325 million of senior notes. Also in May, the company entered into a new five-year $100 million bank credit facility with a group of banks.

One customer accounted for 14% of PDE's revenues in 1997.

Per Share Data ($) (Year Ended Dec. 31)	1997	1996	1995	1994	1993	1992	1991	1990	1989	1988
Tangible Bk. Val.	13.62	6.97	5.14	4.49	4.24	3.85	3.92	3.69	3.36	2.74
Cash Flow	3.31	1.84	1.26	0.76	0.49	0.27	0.55	0.56	0.29	0.24
Earnings	2.16	0.81	0.60	0.30	0.13	-0.05	0.22	0.29	0.05	NM
Dividends	Nil	Nil	Nil	Nil	Nil	Nil	Nil	Nil	Nil	Nil
Payout Ratio	Nil	Nil	Nil	Nil	Nil	Nil	Nil	Nil	Nil	Nil
Prices - High	37 3/4	23 1/4	11	6 1/4	7 1/2	5 3/8	7	8 5/8	6 5/8	4
- Low	16 1/4	9 1/8	4 3/4	4 5/8	3 1/2	3 3/8	3 5/8	4	2 5/8	2 1/8
P/E Ratio - High	17	29	18	21	58	NM	32	30	NM	NM
- Low	8	11	8	15	27	NM	16	14	NM	NM
Income Statement Analysis (Million $)										
Revs.	700	407	264	182	127	101	112	102	66.0	61.0
Oper. Inc.	167	69.2	42.9	17.6	8.8	3.0	10.3	11.3	4.8	4.7
Depr.	58.7	29.1	16.7	9.6	6.0	5.2	5.5	4.5	2.9	2.6
Int. Exp.	34.4	13.6	6.3	0.2	0.0	Nil	0.0	0.1	0.4	0.2
Pretax Inc.	156	30.8	22.4	8.1	3.3	-1.4	5.7	7.6	0.9	0.4
Eff. Tax Rate	33%	26%	32%	23%	37%	NM	39%	39%	42%	97%
Net Inc.	104	22.7	15.4	6.2	2.1	-0.8	3.5	4.7	0.5	0.0
Balance Sheet & Other Fin. Data (Million $)										
Cash	73.5	10.8	11.9	9.0	15.2	24.1	17.0	8.9	21.8	6.0
Curr. Assets	334	156	73.1	60.3	46.0	43.5	35.4	29.6	35.6	14.4
Total Assets	1,542	542	258	205	110	94.8	89.8	85.6	72.5	50.3
Curr. Liab.	230	93.7	41.9	33.6	24.3	18.4	12.1	10.0	8.3	8.4
LT Debt	524	187	61.1	42.1	0.2	3.6	4.9	5.9	2.0	2.5
Common Eqty.	685	202	131	111	69.1	61.8	62.4	58.9	53.1	30.7
Total Cap.	1,256	436	212	166	80.6	76.4	77.7	75.6	64.1	41.9
Cap. Exp.	268	61.7	40.6	59.2	23.8	4.1	5.9	14.7	4.6	1.9
Cash Flow	163	51.8	32.0	15.8	8.1	4.4	9.0	9.1	3.4	2.7
Curr. Ratio	1.5	1.7	1.7	1.8	1.9	2.4	2.9	2.9	4.3	1.7
% LT Debt of Cap.	41.7	42.9	28.8	25.3	0.2	4.8	6.3	7.9	3.0	6.0
% Net Inc.of Revs.	14.9	5.6	5.8	3.4	1.7	NM	3.1	4.6	0.8	NM
% Ret. on Assets	10.0	5.7	6.6	3.4	2.0	NM	4.0	5.9	0.8	NM
% Ret. on Equity	23.4	13.6	12.7	5.8	3.2	NM	5.8	8.3	1.1	NM

Data as orig. reptd.; bef. results of disc. opers. and/or spec. items. Per share data adj. for stk. divs. as of ex-div. date. Bold denotes diluted EPS (FASB 128). E-Estimated. NA-Not Available. NM-Not Meaningful. NR-Not Ranked.

Office—1500 City West Blvd., Suite 400, Houston, TX 77042. **Tel**—(713) 789-1400. **Website**—www.pride.com **Chrmn & CEO**—R. H. Tolson. **Pres & COO**—P. A. Bragg. **VP & Secy**—R. W. Randall. **Dirs**—J. B. Clement, J. E. Estrada M., R. D. McBride, T. H. Roberts Jr., J. T. Sneed, R. H. Tolson. **Transfer Agent & Registrar**—American Stock Transfer & Trust Co., NYC. **Incorporated**—in Louisiana in 1988. **Empl**—8,000. **S&P Analyst:** S.S.

Primadonna Resorts 5028U

NASDAQ Symbol **PRMA**

In S&P SmallCap 600

03-OCT-98

Industry:
Gaming, Lottery & Pari-mutuel Cos.

Summary: PRMA owns and operates three resort-casinos on both sides of Interstate 15 at the California/Nevada border. It also has a 50% interest in a hotel-casino on the Las Vegas Strip.

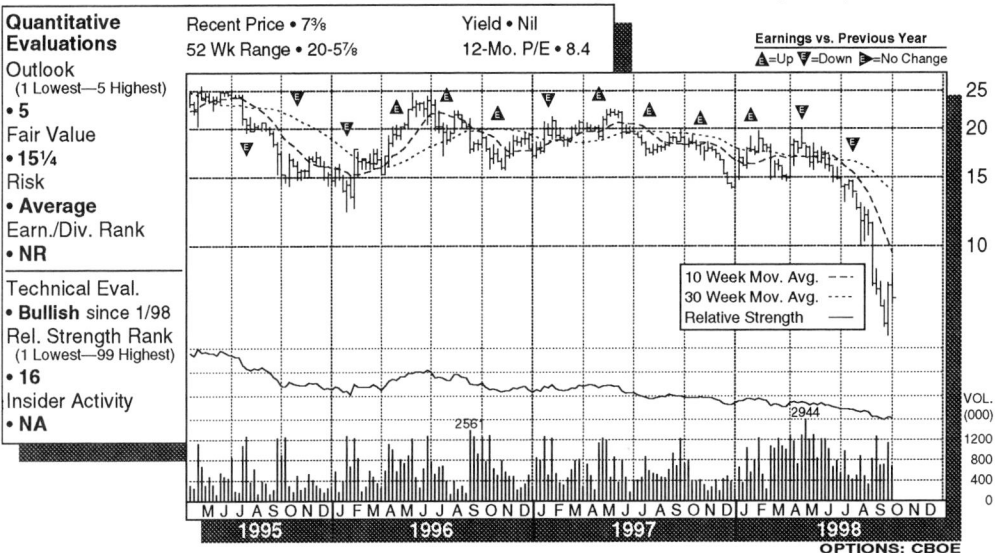

Quantitative Evaluations	
Outlook (1 Lowest—5 Highest)	• **5**
Fair Value	• **15¼**
Risk	• **Average**
Earn./Div. Rank	• **NR**
Technical Eval.	• **Bullish** since 1/98
Rel. Strength Rank (1 Lowest—99 Highest)	• **16**
Insider Activity	• **NA**

Recent Price • 7⅜
52 Wk Range • 20-5⅞

Yield • Nil
12-Mo. P/E • 8.4

Earnings vs. Previous Year
▲=Up ▼=Down ▶=No Change

10 Week Mov. Avg. ---
30 Week Mov. Avg. ·····
Relative Strength —

OPTIONS: CBOE

Business Profile - 12-AUG-98

The company's share of operating income from the New York-New York Hotel & Casino in the second quarter of 1998 declined by $5.3 million, to $9.5 million from the $14.8 million generated in the second quarter of 1997. Overall, New York-New York generated $14.6 million of pretax income on net revenues of $54.7 million, compared to $24.5 million of pretax income on net revenues of $67.4 million in the second quarter of 1997. The company noted that the softening in New York-New York's performance is a function of favorable results in its inaugural year and recent overall declines in the Southern Nevada gaming market. PRMA also noted that New York-New York continues to exceed pre-opening expectations, and is one of the most successful properties in Las Vegas from the standpoint of operating margins and return on invested capital.

Operational Review - 12-AUG-98

Based on a brief report, net revenues in the six months ended June 30, 1998, fell 6.2%, year to year, as improved performance at PRMA's operations at Primm, NV was more than offset by a decline in revenues at the New York-New York Hotel & Casino. Total costs and expenses were up 2.9%, and operating income slid 18%. After taxes at 35.4%, versus 35.8%, net income dropped 40%, to $12,622,000 ($0.44 a share) from $21,029,000 ($0.70). Results in 1997 exclude an extraordinary charge of $0.03 related to deferred financing charges.

Stock Performance - 02-OCT-98

In the past 30 trading days, PRMA's shares have declined 36%, compared to a 7% fall in the S&P 500. Average trading volume for the past five days was 134,500 shares, compared with the 40-day moving average of 173,062 shares.

Key Stock Statistics

Dividend Rate/Share	Nil	Shareholders	500
Shs. outstg. (M)	28.9	Market cap. (B)	$0.212
Avg. daily vol. (M)	0.172	Inst. holdings	11%
Tang. Bk. Value/Share	7.79		
Beta	0.82		

Value of $10,000 invested 5 years ago: NA

Fiscal Year Ending Dec. 31

	1998	1997	1996	1995	1994	1993
Revenues (Million $)						
1Q	66.65	71.50	59.80	54.92	40.81	32.32
2Q	71.33	75.63	64.00	62.30	44.69	37.03
3Q	—	73.81	62.90	64.17	54.76	39.16
4Q	—	66.89	48.10	58.41	56.20	35.78
Yr.	—	287.8	234.9	239.8	193.9	144.3
Earnings Per Share ($)						
1Q	**0.20**	0.34	0.19	0.17	0.23	0.23
2Q	**0.24**	0.37	0.28	0.25	0.26	0.30
3Q	—	0.27	0.22	0.19	0.22	0.26
4Q	—	0.16	0.16	0.16	0.16	0.23
Yr.	—	**1.13**	0.55	0.76	0.86	1.00

Next earnings report expected: mid October

Dividend Data

No cash dividends have been paid.

A Division of The McGraw-Hill Companies

Business Summary - 12-AUG-98

The three resort-casinos owned and operated by Primadonna Resorts (PRMA) offer motorists on the heavily traveled Interstate 15 corridor their first and last gaming entertainment opportunity upon entering or leaving Southern Nevada. This complex is on both sides of Interstate 15 on the Southern California/Nevada border 40 miles south of Las Vegas. Beginning with a service station, 12-room motel, cafe and small casino with 12 slot machines in 1977, the Primadonna complex now includes three unique properties, each with a distinctive market profile: the family/entertainment-oriented Buffalo Bill's Resort & Casino; the golf resort-oriented Primm Valley Resort & Casino (which changed its name from Primadonna Resort & Casino in April 1997), and the value-oriented Whiskey Pete's Hotel & Casino.

The company's properties offer an array of amenities and attractions, including 133,400 square feet of casino space, 2,676 hotel rooms, 10 restaurants, and various rides. The three casinos include about 4,525 slot machines, 107 table games, poker, keno, and race and sports books. In addition, the properties offer one-of-a-kind swimming pools, a movie theater, motion simulation theaters, ferris wheel, bowling center, an interactive water flume ride, and The Desparado roller coaster. These attractions encourage visits by families and provide entertainment for children, while allowing adults to spend more time in the company's casinos.

The 6,100-seat Star of the Desert Arena hosts top name entertainers, and has allowed PRMA to use special events as part of extended stay packages.

PRMA is in the process of re-theming its Primm Valley Resort & Casino to a golf resort atmosphere from a conference/leisure orientation. Combined with the Primm Valley Golf Club, which opened in California in February 1997, the resort is moving beyond the traffic intercept strategy in an effort to become a destination resort complex. A second championship golf course at Primm Valley Golf Club was opened during the second quarter of 1998. Both 18-hole courses were designed by Tom Fazio, the award-winning golf course architect. All 660 rooms at the resort were renovated and upgraded in 1996 and the project also included construction of a 25,000 square foot conference center and the addition of 15,000 square feet of casino space.

The company is a 50% joint venture partner with MGM Grand, Inc. in the New York-New York Hotel & Casino complex, a New York-themed resort, which opened in January 1997 and is located at the corner of Tropicana and Las Vegas Blvd. on the Las Vegas Strip. The complex includes such landmarks as the Statue of Liberty, Empire State Building, Central Park and the Brooklyn Bridge. It contains an 84,000 square foot casino, 2,033 rooms, themed restaurants and lounges, retail outlets, the Manhattan Express roller coaster, and a Coney Island style amusement area.

Per Share Data ($)

(Year Ended Dec. 31)	1997	1996	1995	1994	1993	1992	1991	1990	1989	1988
Tangible Bk. Val.	7.89	6.89	6.38	5.59	NA	NA	NA	NA	NA	NA
Cash Flow	2.13	1.45	1.64	1.47	NA	NA	NA	NA	NA	NA
Earnings	1.13	0.55	0.76	0.86	NA	NA	NA	NA	NA	NA
Dividends	Nil	Nil	Nil	Nil	Nil	Nil	Nil	Nil	Nil	Nil
Payout Ratio	Nil	Nil	Nil	Nil	Nil	Nil	Nil	Nil	Nil	Nil
Prices - High	22½	25	26¼	33	36	NA	NA	NA	NA	NA
- Low	14	12¼	14¼	20	18	NA	NA	NA	NA	NA
P/E Ratio - High	20	45	35	38	NM	NM	NM	NM	NM	NM
- Low	12	22	19	23	NM	NM	NM	NM	NM	NM

Income Statement Analysis (Million $)

	1997	1996	1995	1994	1993	1992	1991	1990	1989	1988
Revs.	306	235	240	194	144	129	NA	NA	NA	NA
Oper. Inc.	104	59.5	71.1	63.2	56.3	NA	NA	NA	NA	NA
Depr.	29.3	27.4	27.1	18.7	11.3	NA	NA	NA	NA	NA
Int. Exp.	23.1	11.0	12.5	4.6	2.7	NA	NA	NA	NA	NA
Pretax Inc.	51.5	26.1	36.1	39.2	44.1	NA	NA	NA	NA	NA
Eff. Tax Rate	35%	36%	36%	33%	31%	NA	NA	NA	NA	NA
Net Inc.	33.4	16.8	23.3	26.5	30.4	38.2	NA	NA	NA	NA

Balance Sheet & Other Fin. Data (Million $)

	1997	1996	1995	1994	1993	1992	1991	1990	1989	1988
Cash	10.0	10.0	9.1	5.9	NA	NA	NA	NA	NA	NA
Curr. Assets	21.0	19.9	22.6	18.6	NA	NA	NA	NA	NA	NA
Total Assets	471	400	373	312	166	104	NA	NA	NA	NA
Curr. Liab.	22.3	17.4	16.2	15.5	NA	NA	NA	NA	NA	NA
LT Debt	221	168	146	116	NA	28.7	NA	NA	NA	NA
Common Eqty.	212	201	196	171	145	68.8	NA	NA	NA	NA
Total Cap.	448	383	357	296	NA	NA	NA	NA	NA	NA
Cap. Exp.	NA	35.2	37.0	156	NA	NA	NA	NA	NA	NA
Cash Flow	62.6	44.1	50.4	45.2	41.7	NA	NA	NA	NA	NA
Curr. Ratio	0.9	1.1	1.4	1.2	NA	NA	NA	NA	NA	NA
% LT Debt of Cap.	49.2	44.0	40.8	39.2	NA	NA	NA	NA	NA	NA
% Net Inc.of Revs.	10.9	7.1	9.7	18.4	21.1	29.5	NA	NA	NA	NA
% Ret. on Assets	7.7	4.3	6.8	9.2	42.1	NA	NA	NA	NA	NA
% Ret. on Equity	16.2	8.4	12.7	16.8	53.3	NA	NA	NA	NA	NA

Data as orig. reptd.; bef. results of disc. opers. and/or spec. items. Per share data adj. for stk. divs. as of ex-div. date. Bold denotes diluted EPS (FASB 128). E-Estimated. NA-Not Available. NM-Not Meaningful. NR-Not Ranked.

Office—P.O. Box 95997, Las Vegas, NE 89193-5997**Tel**—(702) 382-1212.**Website**—http://www.primadonna.com.**Chrmn, Pres & CEO**—G. E. Primm.**CFO & Treas**—G. E. Sullivan.**Secy**—R. E. Armstrong.**Dirs**—R. E. Armstrong, M. B. Graves II, G. E. Primm, S. Rogich, H. M. Rosa, G. R. Sitzman, G. Swarts.**Transfer Agent & Registrar**—U.S. Stock Transfer Corp., Glendale, CA**Incorporated**—in Nevada in 1993.**Empl**— 3,701. **S&P Analyst:** M.I.

03-OCT-98

Industry:
Services (Commercial & Consumer)

Summary: Primark is a global information services organization supplying financial, economic and market research information to financial, corporate and government markets.

Quantitative Evaluations

Outlook
(1 Lowest—5 Highest)
• **3+**

Fair Value
• **30¾**

Risk
• **Average**

Earn./Div. Rank
• **B**

Technical Eval.
• **Bearish** since 6/98

Rel. Strength Rank
(1 Lowest—99 Highest)
• **86**

Insider Activity
• **Neutral**

Recent Price • 28⅝
52 Wk Range • 44½-23⅜

Yield • Nil
12-Mo. P/E • 5.1

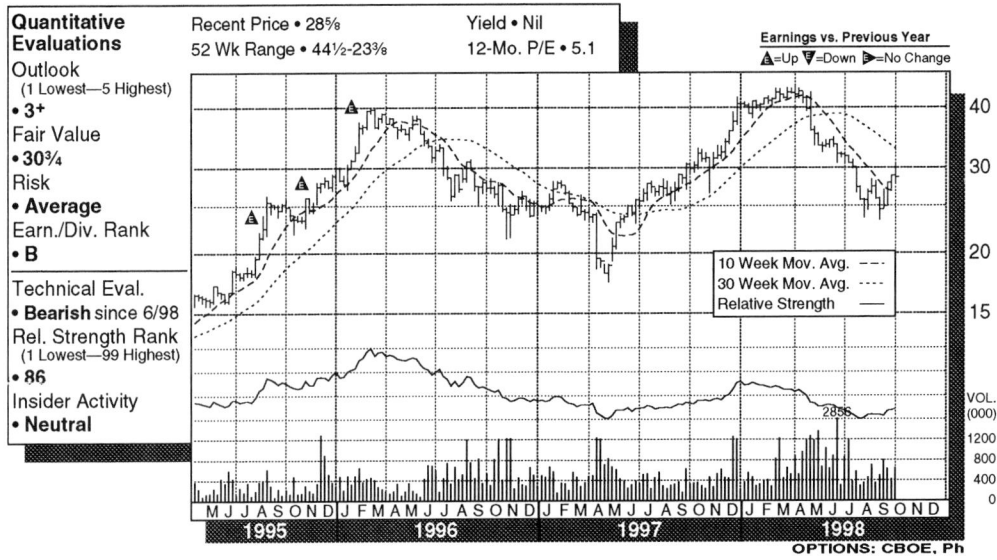

Earnings vs. Previous Year
▲=Up ▼=Down ▶=No Change

10 Week Mov. Avg. ---
30 Week Mov. Avg. ----
Relative Strength —

OPTIONS: CBOE, Ph

Business Profile - 17-AUG-98

In April 1998, Primark sold its TASC, Inc., unit to Litton Industries, Inc., for $432 million in cash. Part of the proceeds from the sale was used to repay $220 million of outstanding debt. In June 1998, PMK completed a Dutch auction self-tender offer, repurchasing 4,540,000 of its common shares. Also in June, the company announced a new organizational structure, designed to serve customers better, take advantage of market opportunities, and reduce costs. Under the plan, all business operations were integrated into three customer-focused divisions, with each division led by a newly named president and CEO.

Operational Review - 17-AUG-98

Operating revenues in the first six months of 1998 rose 9.0%, year to year, on solid performances by PMK's core products. An operating loss reflected a $68,677,000 restructuring charge. The loss from continuing operations increased sharply, to $44,355,000 ($1.57 a share), from $3,709,000 ($0.13). Per share results exclude income from discontinued operations of $6.36, as well as an extraordinary loss of $0.18, in the 1998 period, and also exclude income from discontinued operations of $0.32 and an extraordinary loss of $0.07 in the 1997 interim.

Stock Performance - 02-OCT-98

In the past 30 trading days, PMK's shares have increased 4%, compared to a 7% fall in the S&P 500. Average trading volume for the past five days was 125,580 shares, compared with the 40-day moving average of 113,605 shares.

Key Stock Statistics

Dividend Rate/Share	Nil	Shareholders	10,600
Shs. outstg. (M)	22.6	Market cap. (B)	$0.647
Avg. daily vol. (M)	0.126	Inst. holdings	40%
Tang. Bk. Value/Share	NM		
Beta	0.98		

Value of $10,000 invested 5 years ago: $ 19,406

Fiscal Year Ending Dec. 31

	1998	1997	1996	1995	1994	1993
Revenues (Million $)						
1Q	104.4	94.68	180.7	135.9	112.4	108.9
2Q	108.9	100.9	187.7	143.0	119.0	111.5
3Q	—	79.11	194.0	168.7	121.0	112.2
4Q	—	103.2	204.7	169.7	124.6	111.4
Yr.	—	397.9	767.1	617.3	477.0	444.0
Earnings Per Share ($)						
1Q	**0.13**	NA	0.24	0.20	0.14	0.17
2Q	**1.77**	NA	0.29	0.21	0.16	0.02
3Q	—	NA	0.30	0.21	0.15	0.17
4Q	—	NA	0.21	0.22	0.17	0.15
Yr.	—	**0.25**	1.04	0.85	0.62	0.52

Next earnings report expected: early November

Dividend Data

Dividends, which were initiated in 1982, ceased following PMK's spinoff to shareholders of Michigan Consolidated Gas in 1988. A poison pill stock purchase rights plan was adopted in 1988.

STANDARD
&POOR'S
STOCK REPORTS

Primark Corporation

1866

03-OCT-98

Business Summary - 17-AUG-98

Primark Corp. (PMK) was formed in 1981 as the holding company for Michigan Consolidated Gas Co. During the 1980s, PMK diversified into a hodgepodge of other businesses: trucking, mortgage banking, and aircraft leasing and maintenance. In 1987, Joseph E. Kasputys took over running the company, and quickly shed most of PMK's businesses, including the spinoff of its Michigan gas utility. With the 1991 acquisition of Analytical Sciences Corp., a provider of computer information services to the Pentagon and intelligence agencies, PMK embarked on a strategy of combining information technology expertise with proprietary data content to serve the increasing information requirements of its customers.

PMK today develops and markets "value-added" databases that it combines with proprietary analytical software to create a series of products used for the analysis and presentation of financial, economic and market research information. Its businesses include Baseline Financial Services, Datastream International, Disclosure Inc., Groupe DAFSA S.A., I/B/E/S International, ICV Limited, VestekSystems, WEFA Holdings, Yankee Group Research, and an 80% investment in Worldscope/Disclosure LLC. Customers include investment managers, investment bankers, financial market traders, analysts, accounting and legal professionals,

corporate managers, government officials and information and reference service providers.

In 1996 and 1997, PMK continued to expand its information business by pursuing a strategy of focusing its operations solely on its information services businesses. In connection with this strategy, Primark discontinued a number of its operations, including applied technology.

Acquisitions have been, and continue to be, a key part of the company's development. In 1996, PMK acquired DAFSA, a supplier of company account information on most listed companies in France; ICV, a provider of real-time on-line prices, news and research on the U.K. equities market; and Yankee Group Research, Inc., a global team of highly skilled technology and market experts that focuses on identifying current trends and future directions in the communications and computer industries for business and consumer markets.

In 1997, the company purchased Baseline for $41 million in cash. Baseline provides institutional investors with valuation graphics that portray financial market information to customer accounts throughout the U.S. and Canada. Also in 1997, PMK acquired WEFA Holdings, Inc. for $45 million in cash. WEFA is an international provider of value-added economic information, software and consulting services to Fortune 500 companies, governments, universities and financial institutions.

Per Share Data ($)

(Year Ended Dec. 31)	1997	1996	1995	1994	1993	1992	1991	1990	1989	1988
Tangible Bk. Val.	NA	-5.70	-4.77	-3.29	-4.42	-5.83	4.68	10.66	10.34	10.15
Cash Flow	2.05	3.02	2.61	2.00	1.84	0.98	0.23	0.10	0.41	0.47
Earnings	0.25	1.04	0.85	0.62	0.52	0.40	0.02	0.03	0.23	0.11
Dividends	Nil	Nil	Nil	Nil	Nil	Nil	Nil	Nil	Nil	0.69
Payout Ratio	Nil	Nil	Nil	Nil	Nil	Nil	Nil	Nil	Nil	NM
Prices - High	42	40	30¼	15	16⅜	14¾	14¾	9½	10¼	24¼
- Low	17⅜	21⅜	12¾	11	10½	9	6	5⅝	6½	4¾
P/E Ratio - High	NM	38	36	24	31	37	NM	NM	45	NM
- Low	NM	21	15	18	20	23	NM	NM	28	NM

Income Statement Analysis (Million $)

Revs.	398	767	617	477	444	310	153	27.0	39.0	108
Oper. Inc.	89.0	110	93.3	65.6	63.5	32.3	1.6	-5.3	-2.3	7.5
Depr.	50.2	43.4	36.4	27.5	26.2	11.3	4.3	1.3	3.6	7.0
Int. Exp.	16.0	20.2	20.4	14.2	14.6	5.9	3.0	1.0	1.1	0.7
Pretax Inc.	20.0	49.2	34.0	23.5	21.3	16.2	1.3	-1.5	0.9	0.8
Eff. Tax Rate	65%	43%	45%	42%	45%	44%	30%	NM	NM	NM
Net Inc.	7.0	28.0	18.9	13.8	11.7	9.0	0.9	0.7	4.5	2.2

Balance Sheet & Other Fin. Data (Million $)

Cash	12.8	25.7	62.3	20.0	18.0	23.1	48.0	115	112	32.0
Curr. Assets	335	234	220	135	125	142	153	157	170	137
Total Assets	1,044	979	802	508	497	523	335	219	254	259
Curr. Liab.	202	224	139	97.0	102	109	83.0	13.6	27.8	26.3
LT Debt	331	242	266	146	148	171	31.5	1.0	0.5	1.3
Common Eqty.	471	476	354	225	208	202	195	193	205	205
Total Cap.	824	730	650	401	386	403	249	201	216	223
Cap. Exp.	23.9	26.3	22.7	22.6	12.7	6.9	NA	NA	NA	8.9
Cash Flow	57.2	71.0	53.8	39.9	36.5	18.9	4.6	1.9	8.1	9.2
Curr. Ratio	1.7	1.0	1.6	1.4	1.2	1.3	1.8	11.5	6.1	5.2
% LT Debt of Cap.	40.2	33.2	40.9	36.4	38.3	42.5	12.6	0.5	0.2	0.6
% Net Inc.of Revs.	1.8	3.6	3.1	2.9	2.6	2.9	0.6	2.4	11.6	2.0
% Ret. on Assets	0.7	3.1	2.9	2.7	2.3	1.9	0.3	0.3	1.7	NA
% Ret. on Equity	1.5	6.6	6.0	5.7	5.0	3.6	0.2	0.3	2.2	NA

Data as orig. reptd.; bef. results of disc. opers. and/or spec. items. Per share data adj. for stk. divs. as of ex-div. date. Bold denotes diluted EPS (FASB 128). E-Estimated. NA-Not Available. NM-Not Meaningful. NR-Not Ranked.

Office—1000 Winter St., Suite 4300N, Waltham, MA 02154. **Tel**—(781) 466-6611. **Website**—http://www.primark.com **Chrmn, Pres & CEO**—J. E. Kasputys. **EVP & Secy**—M. R. Kargula. **EVP & CFO**—S. H. Curran. **Investor Contact**—Jim Flanagan (781-487-2131). **Dirs**—K. J. Bradley, J. C. Holt, J. E. Kasputys, S. Lazarus, P. G. McGinnis, J. Newcomb, C. K. Weaver. **Transfer Agent & Registrar**—First National Bank of Boston. **Incorporated**—in Michigan in 1981. **Empl**—2,328. **S&P Analyst:** Michael Schneider

Prime Hospitality

1866X

NYSE Symbol **PDQ**

In S&P SmallCap 600

03-OCT-98 Industry: Lodging - Hotels

Summary: This company owns or manages hotels throughout the U.S. under proprietary trade names and franchise agreements with national hotel chains.

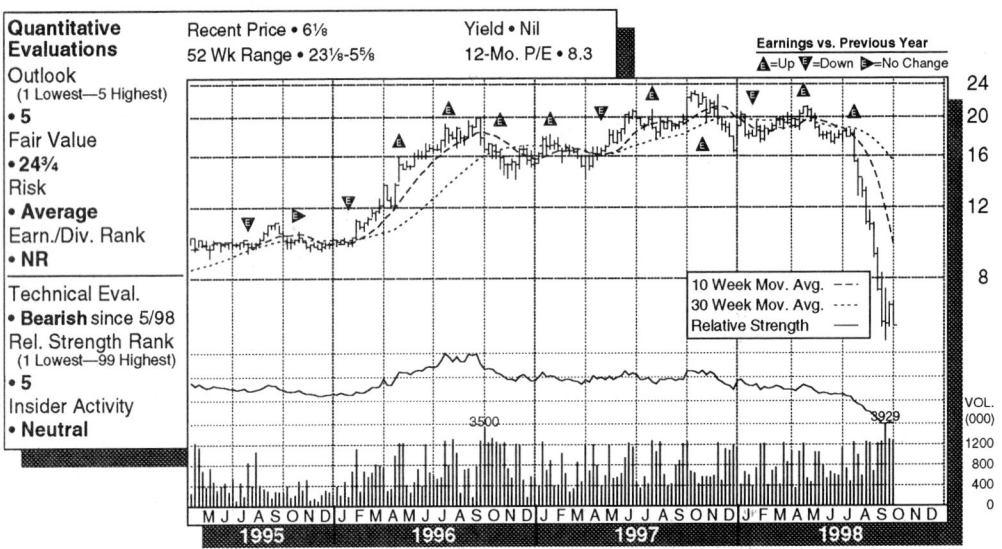

Quantitative Evaluations	
Outlook (1 Lowest—5 Highest)	• 5
Fair Value	• 24¾
Risk	• Average
Earn./Div. Rank	• NR
Technical Eval.	• Bearish since 5/98
Rel. Strength Rank (1 Lowest—99 Highest)	• 5
Insider Activity	• Neutral

Recent Price • 6⅛
52 Wk Range • 23⅛-5⅝
Yield • Nil
12-Mo. P/E • 8.3

Business Profile - 24-APR-98

Prime Hospitality is making aggressive efforts to build its hotel portfolio and develop its sale and leaseback program. In December 1997, PDQ completed its acquisition of HomeGate Hospitality, Inc. for stock valued at about $132 million. Currently, Homegate has 20 high quality, mid-price extended-stay hotels, with another 38 under development. The development of this chain is being done through strategic alliances with Trammell Crow Residential and Greystar Capital Partners. In addition, PDQ is working hard to expand its AmeriSuites brand. Thus far in 1998, PDQ has opened seven AmeriSuites and has an additional 42 units under development. By the end of 1998, the company plans to be operating about 95 AmeriSuites Hotels.

Operational Review - 24-APR-98

Total revenues in the three months ended March 31, 1998, advanced 32%, year to year, as restated for the acquisition of HomeGate Hospitality in December 1997. Revenues were boosted by strong growth in REVPAR (revenue per available room) in the AmeriSuites and HomeGate hotel chains. Net income advanced 18%, to $10,291,000 ($0.20 a share), from $8,224,000 ($0.17).

Stock Performance - 02-OCT-98

In the past 30 trading days, PDQ's shares have declined 44%, compared to a 7% fall in the S&P 500. Average trading volume for the past five days was 396,660 shares, compared with the 40-day moving average of 392,849 shares.

Key Stock Statistics

Dividend Rate/Share	Nil	Shareholders	2,500
Shs. outstg. (M)	52.8	Market cap. (B)	$0.323
Avg. daily vol. (M)	0.512	Inst. holdings	81%
Tang. Bk. Value/Share	9.94		
Beta	1.23		

Value of $10,000 invested 5 years ago: $ 27,222

Fiscal Year Ending Dec. 31

	1998	1997	1996	1995	1994	1993
Revenues (Million $)						
1Q	103.3	78.05	58.61	48.24	28.08	24.79
2Q	123.0	85.56	69.89	51.70	33.19	26.69
3Q	—	87.80	87.80	52.70	36.06	29.48
4Q	—	89.54	71.52	52.98	36.97	27.91
Yr.	—	341.0	268.9	205.6	134.3	108.9
Earnings Per Share ($)						
1Q	0.20	0.17	0.24	0.13	0.08	0.03
2Q	0.43	0.26	0.22	0.15	0.22	0.05
3Q	—	0.22	0.21	0.13	0.13	0.10
4Q	—	-0.11	0.18	0.13	0.14	0.06
Yr.	—	0.54	0.85	0.54	0.57	0.24

Next earnings report expected: late October

Dividend Data

No cash dividends have been paid, and PDQ does not expect to pay any in the foreseeable future.

STANDARD
&POOR'S
STOCK REPORTS

Prime Hospitality Corp.

1866X

03-OCT-98

Business Summary - 24-APR-98

Hotel industry profitability has been in an uptrend in the 1990s. Prime Hospitality (formerly Prime Motor Inns, Inc.), which emerged from Chapter 11 bankruptcy proceedings in 1992, has benefited from this trend. As of February 28, 1998, PDQ owned or operated 147 hotels, containing 20,490 rooms, under its proprietary tradenames AmeriSuites, HomeGate Studios & Suites and Wellesley Inns, as well as a portfolio of upscale full-service hotels. Hotels are located mainly in secondary markets in 29 states and the U.S. Virgin Islands. Occupancy, average daily room rates, and REVPAR (revenue per available room) for all owned hotels in recent years were:

	1997	1996	1995
Occupancy	67.6%	69.6%	69.0%
Average daily room rate	$74.72	$71.66	$65.77
REVPAR	$50.53	$49.90	$45.41

PDQ operates in four major lodging industry segments: the all-suites segment with its AmeriSuites brand, the extended stay segment with its HomeGate Studios & Suites brand, the limited-service segment with its Wellesley brand and the full-service segment under major national franchises.

AmeriSuites are upscale, all-suite hotels containing approximately 128 suites and located primarily near suburban commercial centers, corporate office parks and other travel destinations, with close proximity to dining, shopping and entertainment amenities. At February 28, 1998, PDQ owned or operated 68 AmeriSuites units, with 43 more units under development. In 1997, the AmeriSuites brand accounted for approximately 39.3% of total EBITDA.

Acquired in December 1997, the HomeGate brand consisted of 17 hotels in operation, with another 39 under development. The HomeGate units are mid-priced, extended-stay hotels that typically contain between 120 to 140 suites with fully equipped kitchens, upscale furnishings, and living and sleeping areas. During 1997, this brand accounted for 2.1% of consolidated EBITDA.

PDQ operates 33 limited-service hotels under the Wellesley Inns brand name. In addition, the company manages another five limited-service units under franchise agreements with national chains. In 1997, the company's limited-service hotel segment contributed about 18.1% of total EBITDA.

Within the full-service hotel segment, PDQ operates 29 upscale hotels with food service and banquet facilities under franchise agreements with national hotel brands such as Marriott, Radisson, Sheraton, Crowne Plaza, Holiday Inn and Ramada. The full-service segment accounted for approximately 40.5% of PDQ's EBITDA in 1997.

Per Share Data ($)

(Year Ended Dec. 31)	1997	1996	1995	1994	1993	1992	1991	1990	1989	1988
Tangible Bk. Val.	11.13	10.55	7.66	6.71	5.18	NM	NA	NA	12.59	10.26
Cash Flow	1.24	1.56	1.03	0.86	0.45	NM	NA	NA	2.67	2.34
Earnings	0.54	0.80	0.54	0.57	0.24	NM	NA	NA	2.35	2.05
Dividends	Nil	Nil	Nil	Nil	Nil	Nil	Nil	0.08	0.08	0.08
Payout Ratio	Nil	Nil	Nil	Nil	Nil	Nil	Nil	NA	3%	4%
Prices - High	23⅛	20	11	9	6⅜	2¼	2	23¾	37½	40½
- Low	14⅛	9⅝	7¼	5⅜	2	1½	³/₁₆	⅜	21⅝	29½
P/E Ratio - High	43	25	20	16	27	NM	NA	NA	16	20
- Low	26	12	13	9	8	NM	NA	NA	9	14

Income Statement Analysis (Million $)

	1997	1996	1995	1994	1993	1992	1991	1990	1989	1988
Revs.	335	269	206	134	109	109	171	NA	315	298
Oper. Inc.	125	88.9	61.8	42.7	31.9	3.9	-20.6	NA	77.8	69.2
Depr.	34.2	25.8	16.0	9.3	7.0	6.9	7.9	NA	10.6	9.5
Int. Exp.	33.0	20.3	21.6	14.8	16.1	8.4	20.3	NA	39.4	23.2
Pretax Inc.	50.7	51.5	29.1	30.0	14.0	-71.0	-259	NA	125	109
Eff. Tax Rate	49%	40%	40%	40%	41%	NM	NM	NA	38%	38%
Net Inc.	25.9	30.9	17.5	18.0	8.0	-72.0	-245	NA	77.4	67.6

Balance Sheet & Other Fin. Data (Million $)

	1997	1996	1995	1994	1993	1992	1991	1990	1989	1988
Cash	5.0	16.2	70.4	22.0	53.0	60.0	61.0	NA	40.0	141
Curr. Assets	61.1	44.0	93.2	39.0	68.0	134	115	NA	270	253
Total Assets	1,197	786	573	435	411	554	680	NA	1,144	904
Curr. Liab.	80.8	49.3	44.7	29.0	42.0	32.0	33.0	NA	196	56.0
LT Debt	555	299	277	179	169	9.0	3.0	NA	423	407
Common Eqty.	524	420	233	204	171	-228	-156	NA	452	375
Total Cap.	1,079	719	510	383	340	-219	-153	NA	922	806
Cap. Exp.	108	102	14.3	63.4	23.4	14.1	21.9	NA	73.0	50.4
Cash Flow	60.1	56.7	33.4	28.0	15.0	-65.0	-237	NA	88.0	77.1
Curr. Ratio	0.8	0.9	2.1	1.3	1.6	4.2	3.5	NA	1.4	4.5
% LT Debt of Cap.	51.4	41.6	54.3	46.7	49.6	NM	NM	NA	45.8	50.5
% Net Inc.of Revs.	7.7	11.5	8.5	13.6	7.5	NM	NM	NA	24.6	22.7
% Ret. on Assets	2.6	4.5	3.5	4.5	1.7	NM	NA	NA	7.5	8.3
% Ret. on Equity	5.5	9.5	8.0	10.1	NM	NM	NA	NA	18.7	19.7

Data as orig. reptd.; bef. results of disc. opers. and/or spec. items. Per share data adj. for stk. divs. as of ex-div. date. Bold denotes diluted EPS (FASB 128). E-Estimated. NA-Not Available. NM-Not Meaningful. NR-Not Ranked.

Office—700 Route 46 East, Fairfield, NJ 07004. **Tel**—(201) 882-1010. **Fax**—(201) 882-8577. **Chrmn, Pres & CEO**—D. A. Simon. **EVP & CFO**—J. M. Elwood. **SVP & Secy**—J. Bernadino. **VP & Treas**—D. Vicari. **Dirs**—J. M. Elwood, H. M. Lorber, H. Lust II, J. H. Nusbaum, A. J. Ostroff, A. F. Petrocelli, D. A. Simon. **Transfer Agent & Registrar**—Continental Stock Transfer & Trust Co., NYC. **Incorporated**—in Delaware in 1985. **Empl**—6,800. **S&P Analyst:** R. Izmirlian

Progress Software 5030T
NASDAQ Symbol PRGS
In S&P SmallCap 600

03-OCT-98

Industry: Computer (Software & Services)

Summary: This company supplies application development and database software.

Quantitative Evaluations

Recent Price • 25¾
52 Wk Range • 28-12⅝

Yield • Nil
12-Mo. P/E • 27.1

Outlook (1 Lowest—5 Highest)
• **2**

Fair Value
• **27¾**

Risk
• **High**

Earn./Div. Rank
• **B**

Technical Eval.
• **Bearish** since 7/98

Rel. Strength Rank (1 Lowest—99 Highest)
• **96**

Insider Activity
• **Neutral**

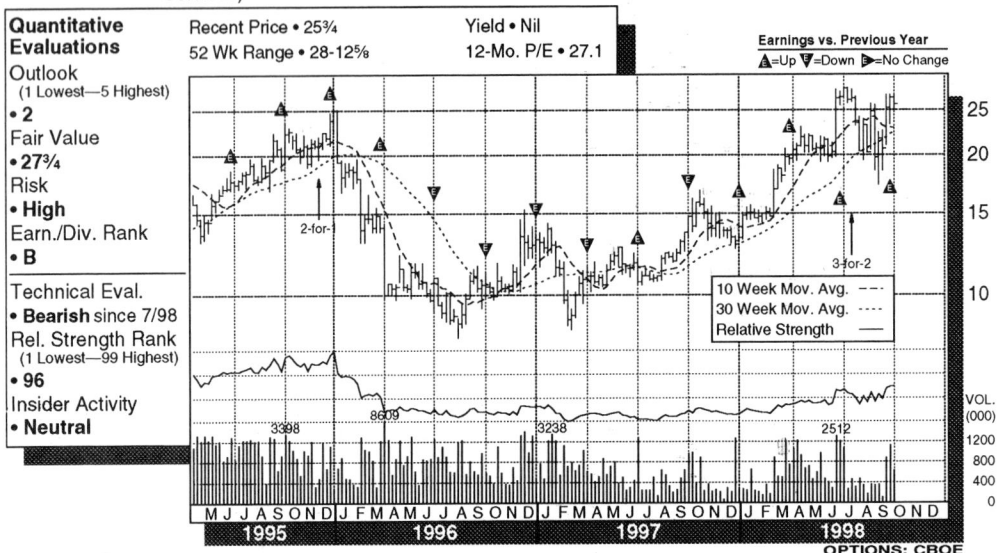

Earnings vs. Previous Year
▲=Up ▼=Down ▶=No Change

10 Week Mov. Avg. – – –
30 Week Mov. Avg. ・・・・
Relative Strength ——

OPTIONS: CBOE

Business Profile - 10-SEP-98

In FY 98 (Nov.), Progress plans to introduce a number of new products and product enhancements that will enable professional developers to create completely open, standard-based applications for mission-critical business environments. The company believes that these product initiatives will enhance the future adaptability of the 5,000 PROGRESS-based applications currently in use, by providing a migration path to the Internet. Progress also plans to begin shipping the next generation of its enterprise application development suite of products in the second half of FY 98. In May 1998, the company began shipping the latest version of its popular application server and development tool for Java, Apptivity 2.1. Progress believes it is well positioned to take advantage of the expected doubling of the packaged applications market by the Year 2000.

Operational Review - 10-SEP-98

Total revenues in the first six months of FY 98 (Nov.) advanced 23%, year to year, aided by greater acceptance of the company's PROGRESS product family and the introduction of new products. Gross margins narrowed on a less favorable revenue mix, but operating expenses were well controlled, and operating income more than tripled. Following a sharp drop in other income, pretax income climbed 101%. After taxes at 33.0%, versus 34.0%, net income was up 104%, to $8,220,000 ($0.43 a share, as adjusted) from $4,020,000 ($0.21).

Stock Performance - 02-OCT-98

In the past 30 trading days, PRGS's shares have increased 4%, compared to a 7% fall in the S&P 500. Average trading volume for the past five days was 126,360 shares, compared with the 40-day moving average of 101,467 shares.

Key Stock Statistics

Dividend Rate/Share	Nil	Shareholders	5,000
Shs. outstg. (M)	17.3	Market cap. (B)	$0.447
Avg. daily vol. (M)	0.139	Inst. holdings	75%
Tang. Bk. Value/Share	5.39		
Beta	0.79		

Value of $10,000 invested 5 years ago: $ 13,405

Fiscal Year Ending Nov. 30

	1998	1997	1996	1995	1994	1993
Revenues (Million $)						
1Q	54.15	45.34	48.38	39.42	31.06	25.03
2Q	57.11	44.83	41.66	42.76	33.96	26.68
3Q	59.48	45.88	41.41	44.96	33.92	27.41
4Q	—	52.26	45.24	53.00	40.29	32.51
Yr.	—	188.3	176.7	180.1	139.2	111.6
Earnings Per Share ($)						
1Q	**0.19**	0.10	0.21	0.08	0.16	0.15
2Q	**0.24**	0.11	0.01	0.23	0.18	0.16
3Q	**0.31**	-0.53	0.01	0.21	0.17	0.15
4Q	—	0.20	0.03	0.30	0.24	0.21
Yr.	—	-0.09	0.27	0.81	0.75	0.67

Next earnings report expected: mid December

Dividend Data

Amount ($)	Date Decl.	Ex-Div. Date	Stock of Record	Payment Date
3-for-2	Jun. 17	Jul. 14	Jun. 29	Jul. 13 '98

A Division of The McGraw·Hill Companies

Progress Software Corporation

Business Summary - 10-SEP-98

This software company was founded in 1981 to develop and market application development software. Progress Software derived 59% of its FY 97 (Nov.) revenues from international sales. Changes in the value of foreign currencies relative to the U.S. dollar may significantly affect results of operations and the company's financial position. Its products and services are designed to enable organizations throughout the world to rapidly and cost-effectively develop, deploy and maintain computer software applications. Its principal product lines are PROGRESS, an integrated environment for developing and deploying mission-critical applications; WebSpeed, designed for Internet transaction processing applications; ProtoSpeed, an error detecting and debugging tool; and PSC supplies Apptivity, for developing distributed, multi-tier Java-based business applications.

In FY 98, the company plans to introduce a number of new products and product enhancements that will enable professional developers to create completely open, standard-based applications for mission-critical business environments. It believes that these product initiatives will enhance the future adaptability of the

5,000 PROGRESS-based applications currently in use, by providing a migration path to the Internet. The company also expects to begin shipping the next generation of its enterprise application development suite of products in the second half of FY 98.

The Crescent division supplies add-on tools and components to users of Microsoft's Visual Basic application development environment and provides an integrated suite of high-performance add-on tools and components that make database, client/server application development easy and intuitive for the Visual Basic developer.

The company sells its products worldwide to organizations that develop and deploy major business applications. More than 50% of its worldwide revenue is derived from serving more than 2,300 application partners who market applications that use its technology. Progress also sells its products to businesses and governments worldwide; these organizations license its products to develop and deploy a wide range of applications.

In July 1997, the company acquired Apptivity Corp., a developer of Java-based application development tools, for $3.8 million of cash, $5.4 million of stock, and the assumption of $1.4 million of liabilities.

Per Share Data ($)

(Year Ended Nov. 30)	1997	1996	1995	1994	1993	1992	1991	1990	1989	1988
Tangible Bk. Val.	5.44	6.01	5.86	4.77	3.81	2.98	2.26	NA	NA	NA
Cash Flow	0.49	0.75	0.83	1.03	0.87	0.64	0.47	NA	NA	NA
Earnings	-0.09	0.27	0.81	0.75	0.67	0.51	0.35	NA	NA	NA
Dividends	Nil	Nil	Nil	Nil	Nil	Nil	Nil	Nil	Nil	Nil
Payout Ratio	Nil	Nil	Nil	Nil	Nil	Nil	Nil	Nil	Nil	Nil
Prices - High	$16^{7}/_{8}$	$25^{1}/_{8}$	$25^{3}/_{8}$	$18^{7}/_{8}$	$20^{1}/_{8}$	$20^{1}/_{2}$	15	NA	NA	NA
- Low	$8^{3}/_{8}$	$8^{1}/_{8}$	$12^{3}/_{8}$	9	$10^{3}/_{4}$	$9^{5}/_{8}$	$8^{3}/_{8}$	NA	NA	NA
P/E Ratio - High	NM	92	31	25	30	41	42	NA	NA	NA
- Low	NM	30	15	12	16	19	24	NA	NA	NA

Income Statement Analysis (Million $)

	1997	1996	1995	1994	1993	1992	1991	1990	1989	1988
Revs.	188	177	180	139	112	85.0	NA	NA	NA	NA
Oper. Inc.	19.9	14.0	31.9	25.3	21.3	15.6	NA	NA	NA	NA
Depr.	10.6	9.5	7.6	5.5	3.8	2.5	NA	NA	NA	NA
Int. Exp.	0.0	0.0	0.0	0.0	0.1	0.1	NA	NA	NA	NA
Pretax Inc.	2.6	7.9	26.1	22.0	19.8	15.0	NA	NA	NA	NA
Eff. Tax Rate	184%	36%	38%	35%	35%	36%	NA	NA	NA	NA
Net Inc.	-1.6	5.5	16.7	14.4	12.9	9.6	NA	NA	NA	NA

Balance Sheet & Other Fin. Data (Million $)

	1997	1996	1995	1994	1993	1992	1991	1990	1989	1988
Cash	39.5	96.5	92.3	74.3	61.3	54.6	NA	NA	NA	NA
Curr. Assets	142	141	144	111	90.0	NA	NA	NA	NA	NA
Total Assets	172	172	176	135	108	81.0	NA	NA	NA	NA
Curr. Liab.	74.0	57.0	58.8	44.5	36.5	NA	NA	NA	NA	NA
LT Debt	Nil	0.1	0.1	0.1	0.2	0.2	NA	NA	NA	NA
Common Eqty.	96.4	114	113	88.5	69.9	53.2	NA	NA	NA	NA
Total Cap.	97.7	117	116	90.0	71.3	54.6	NA	NA	NA	NA
Cap. Exp.	10.1	9.6	13.4	8.0	10.5	5.6	NA	NA	NA	NA
Cash Flow	9.0	15.0	16.9	19.9	16.7	12.2	NA	NA	NA	NA
Curr. Ratio	1.9	2.5	2.5	2.5	2.5	NA	NA	NA	NA	NA
% LT Debt of Cap.	Nil	Nil	Nil	0.1	0.2	0.4	NA	NA	NA	NA
% Net Inc.of Revs.	NM	3.1	9.3	10.4	11.5	11.3	NA	NA	NA	NA
% Ret. on Assets	NM	3.2	10.7	11.8	13.6	13.5	NA	NA	NA	NA
% Ret. on Equity	NM	4.8	16.6	18.2	20.9	20.8	NA	NA	NA	NA

Data as orig. reptd.; bef. results of disc. opers. and/or spec. items. Per share data adj. for stk. divs. as of ex-div. date. Bold denotes diluted EPS (FASB 128). E-Estimated. NA-Not Available. NM-Not Meaningful. NR-Not Ranked.

Office—14 Oak Park, Bedford, MA 01730.**Tel**—(781) 280-4000. **Fax**—(781) 280-4095.**E-mail**—finance-info@progress.com **Website**—http://www.progress.com **Pres & Treas**—J. W. Alsop.**VP-Fin & CFO**—N. R. Robertson. **Investor Contact**—Margot Carlson Delogne (781) 280-4144. **Dirs**—J. W. Alsop, L. R. Harris, R. J. Lepkowski, S. A. McGregor, M. L. Mark, A. J. Marks, A. Rasiel, J. W. Storey. **Transfer Agent & Registrar**—Boston EquiServe, Canton, MA. **Incorporated**—in Massachusetts in 1981.**Empl**— 1,090. **S&P Analyst:** SRB

03-OCT-98

Industry:
Biotechnology

Summary: PDLI develops human and humanized antibodies and other potential drugs to prevent or treat certain disease conditions.

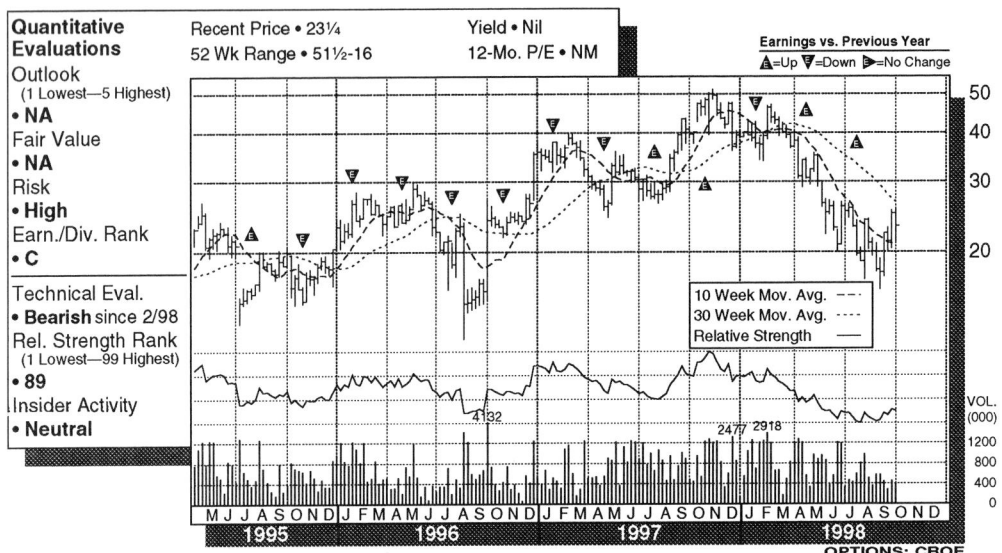

Quantitative Evaluations	Recent Price • 23¼	Yield • Nil
	52 Wk Range • 51½-16	12-Mo. P/E • NM

Outlook (1 Lowest—5 Highest)
• **NA**

Fair Value
• **NA**

Risk
• **High**

Earn./Div. Rank
• **C**

Technical Eval.
• **Bearish** since 2/98

Rel. Strength Rank (1 Lowest—99 Highest)
• **89**

Insider Activity
• **Neutral**

Earnings vs. Previous Year
▲=Up ▼=Down ▶=No Change

10 Week Mov. Avg. – – –
30 Week Mov. Avg. - - - - -
Relative Strength ——

M J J A S O N D J F M A M J J A S O N D J F M A M J J A S O N D J F M A M J J A S O N D
1995 1996 1997 1998

OPTIONS: CBOE

Business Profile - 15-JUL-98

This company develops human and humanized antibodies to prevent or treat a variety of viral, immune-mediated and inflammatory diseases and certain cancers and cardiovascular conditions. In August 1996, the share price tumbled, following news that a Phase II/III clinical trial for PDLI's Protovir human anti-CMV antibody had been halted because the compound failed to demonstrate efficacy. The shares subsequently recovered, but have again drifted lower from their late 1997 peak. Zenapax was approved in the U.S. in December 1997 and in Switzerland in March 1998; the company receives royalties on Zenapax sales from Hoffman-La Roche.

Operational Review - 15-JUL-98

Total revenues (including interest income) for the three months ended March 31, 1998, rose 9.0%, year to year, as higher interest and other income outweighed lower research and development revenue under third party agreements. Total costs and expenses grew more slowly than revenues, reflecting slightly lower research and development expenditures, which partially offset 25% higher general and administrative expenses; The net loss narrowed to $4,013,000 ($0.22 a share, on 15% more shares), from $4,089,000 ($0.26). Cash, equivalents and investments totaled $120.9 million as of March 31, 1998.

Stock Performance - 02-OCT-98

In the past 30 trading days, PDLI's shares have increased 16%, compared to a 7% fall in the S&P 500. Average trading volume for the past five days was 78,420 shares, compared with the 40-day moving average of 91,164 shares.

Key Stock Statistics

Dividend Rate/Share	Nil	Shareholders	200
Shs. outstg. (M)	18.5	Market cap. (B)	$0.431
Avg. daily vol. (M)	0.082	Inst. holdings	46%
Tang. Bk. Value/Share	8.97		
Beta	0.95		

Value of $10,000 invested 5 years ago: $ 19,578

Fiscal Year Ending Dec. 31

	1998	1997	1996	1995	1994	1993
Revenues (Million $)						
1Q	4.24	3.88	5.55	4.10	3.10	0.90
2Q	8.36	5.03	5.03	4.10	4.60	0.90
3Q	—	7.04	5.55	4.10	3.00	2.90
4Q	—	4.31	6.47	5.40	4.60	12.10
Yr.	—	20.26	22.60	17.60	15.20	16.80
Earnings Per Share ($)						
1Q	-0.22	-0.26	-0.14	-0.10	-0.09	-0.17
2Q	-0.05	-0.16	-0.22	-0.16	-0.18	-0.62
3Q	—	-0.05	-0.20	0.17	0.01	0.00
4Q	—	-0.88	-0.12	-0.11	-0.09	0.37
Yr.	—	-1.35	-0.76	-0.54	-0.37	-0.47

Next earnings report expected: NA

Dividend Data

PDLI has never paid a cash dividend on its common stock and does not expect any payments in the foreseeable future.

Business Summary - 15-JUL-98

Protein Design Labs, founded in 1986, is developing human and humanized antibodies and other potential drugs to prevent or treat certain disease conditions, including viral infections, autoimmune conditions, inflammatory diseases and cancers.

The company's human and computer-designed SMART (humanized) monoclonal antibodies have a longer half-life and are less immunogenic than traditional mouse antibodies, and PDLI believes that they will be more useful as human therapeutics. SMART antibodies are designed to incorporate, in an otherwise human antibody, the minimum regions of a mouse antibody necessary to preserve certain properties needed for therapeutics.

The company has several potential products in human clinical trials and additional products in preclinical development. The SMART Anti-Tac Antibody (Zenapax) has been approved in the U.S. and Switzerland for the prevention of acute organ rejection in patients receiving renal transplants. Applications for marketing approval are pending in Europe, Canada and other key markets. Zenapax is the first, and to date only, humanized monoclonal antibody to be approved by the FDA. The company receives royalties on sales of Zenapax, which is marketed by Hoffman-La Roche, Inc.

The SMART M195 Antibody is in a Phase II/III trial in the U.S. and a Phase I trial in Japan for the treatment of myeloid leukemia, the major form of leukemia in adults. Phase I trials are also underway in Europe for the SMART anti-gpIIb/IIIa monoclonal antibody for the potential treatment of certain cardiovascular disorders.

The Human Anti-CMV Antibody (PROTOVIR) is being studied in Phase II trials to treat CMV retinitis in AIDS patients, and to prevent CMV infections in bone marrow transplantation. The Human Anti-Hepatitis B Antibody, Ostavir (OST 577), is in Phase II trails in the U.S. In June 1998, a Phase IIa clinical trial of Ostavir began in Europe. Ostavir and PROTOVIR were licensed by the company from Novartis Pharmaceuticals Corp. Novartis has certain rights to co-market or co-promote these antibodies in North America or to receive royalties.

The company is conducting a Phase I trial of SMART Anti-CD3 Antibody for the treatment of organ transplantation rejection and certain autoimmune diseases.

In January 1998, the company entered into a collaborative agreement with Eli Lilly & Company to discover and develop new antibiotics for the treatment of certain bacterial infections, including bacteria that have developed resistance to available antibiotics. PDLI received an initial payment of $3 million, and can receive up to an additional $9.6 million in the second through fifth years of the agreement. PDLI is entitled to royalties on Lilly's sales of such products and can also receive milestone payments.

Per Share Data ($)

(Year Ended Dec. 31)	1997	1996	1995	1994	1993	1992	1991	1990	1989	1988
Tangible Bk. Val.	9.18	16.67	-0.54	7.72	5.60	4.21	1.84	NA	NA	NA
Cash Flow	-1.16	-0.55	-0.38	-0.22	-0.30	0.06	NA	NA	NA	NA
Earnings	-1.35	-0.76	-0.54	-0.37	-0.47	-0.07	0.03	NA	NA	NA
Dividends	Nil	Nil	Nil	Nil	Nil	Nil	Nil	Nil	Nil	Nil
Payout Ratio	Nil	Nil	Nil	Nil	Nil	Nil	Nil	Nil	Nil	Nil
Prices - High	51½	38⅜	26¾	29⅞	26⅝	18¾	NA	NA	NA	NA
- Low	24⅜	12	13⅛	13¾	6½	5⅞	NA	NA	NA	NA
P/E Ratio - High	NM	NM	NM	NM	NM	NM	NA	NA	NA	NA
- Low	NM	NM	NM	NM	NM	NM	NM	NM	NM	NM

Income Statement Analysis (Million $)

	1997	1996	1995	1994	1993	1992	1991	1990	1989	1988
Revs.	11.1	16.5	11.4	11.9	14.7	6.1	4.4	3.4	NA	NA
Oper. Inc.	-17.9	-14.6	-12.0	-8.6	-8.0	-3.1	0.0	-0.4	NA	NA
Depr.	3.2	3.2	2.5	2.2	2.1	1.6	NA	NA	NA	NA
Int. Exp.	Nil	Nil	Nil	0.0	0.0	0.0	0.1	0.0	NA	NA
Pretax Inc.	-23.7	-11.7	-8.4	-5.2	-5.9	-0.9	0.3	0.0	NA	NA
Eff. Tax Rate	NM	NM	NM	Nil	Nil	Nil	Nil	Nil	Nil	Nil
Net Inc.	-23.7	-11.7	-8.4	-5.2	-5.9	-0.9	0.3	0.0	NA	NA

Balance Sheet & Other Fin. Data (Million $)

	1997	1996	1995	1994	1993	1992	1991	1990	1989	1988
Cash	9.3	78.1	46.4	97.7	60.8	NA	NA	NA	NA	NA
Curr. Assets	73.0	79.4	47.1	99	32.2	NA	NA	NA	NA	NA
Total Assets	175	110	116	121	80.0	56.0	7.0	7.0	NA	NA
Curr. Liab.	6.6	5.2	3.6	3.3	2.4	NA	NA	NA	NA	NA
LT Debt	Nil	Nil	Nil	Nil	0.0	0.1	0.2	0.3	NA	NA
Common Eqty.	168	105	113	118	78.0	54.0	6.0	6.0	NA	NA
Total Cap.	169	105	113	118	78.0	54.0	6.0	6.0	NA	NA
Cap. Exp.	4.6	3.7	3.6	2.4	2.8	4.1	NA	NA	NA	NA
Cash Flow	-20.4	-8.6	-5.8	-3.0	-3.9	0.7	NA	NA	NA	NA
Curr. Ratio	11.1	15.2	13.1	30.2	13.7	NA	NA	NA	NA	NA
% LT Debt of Cap.	Nil	Nil	Nil	Nil	Nil	0.2	3.5	4.2	NA	NA
% Net Inc.of Revs.	NM	NM	NM	NM	NM	NM	6.9	NM	NM	NM
% Ret. on Assets	NM	NM	NM	NM	NM	NM	4.5	NM	NM	NM
% Ret. on Equity	NM	NM	NM	NM	NM	NM	5.1	NM	NM	NM

Data as orig. reptd.; bef. results of disc. opers. and/or spec. items. Per share data adj. for stk. divs. as of ex-div. date. Quartrly revs. incl. interest & other income. Bold denotes diluted EPS (FASB 128). E-Estimated. NA-Not Available. NM-Not Meaningful. NR-Not Ranked.

Office—2375 Garcia Ave., Mountain View, CA 94043. **Tel**—(415) 903-3730. **Fax**—(415) 903-3700. **Website**—http://www.pdl.com **Email**—cc@pdl.com **Chrmn & CEO**—L. J. Korn. **Pres**—J. S. Saxe. **VP & CFO**—F. Kurland. **VP & Secy**—D. O. Ebersole. **Dirs**—J. Drews, S. Falkow, G. M. Gould, L. J. Korn, M. Link, C. L. Queen, J. S. Saxe. **Transfer Agent & Registrar**—ChaseMellon Shareholder Services, SF. **Incorporated**—in Delaware in 1986. **Empl**— 208. **S&P Analyst:** C.C.P.

03-OCT-98

Industry:
Natural Gas

Summary: This company distributes natural gas to more than 325,000 customers in 93 cities and communities in a 33-county territory in North Carolina.

Quantitative Evaluations	
Outlook (1 Lowest—5 Highest)	• **2⁻**
Fair Value	• **23**
Risk	• **Low**
Earn./Div. Rank	• **B+**
Technical Eval.	• **Bullish** since 9/98
Rel. Strength Rank (1 Lowest—99 Highest)	• **94**
Insider Activity	• **Neutral**

Recent Price • 22⅞
52 Wk Range • 24½-19⅛

Yield • 4.2%
12-Mo. P/E • 18.2

Earnings vs. Previous Year
▲=Up ▼=Down ▶=No Change

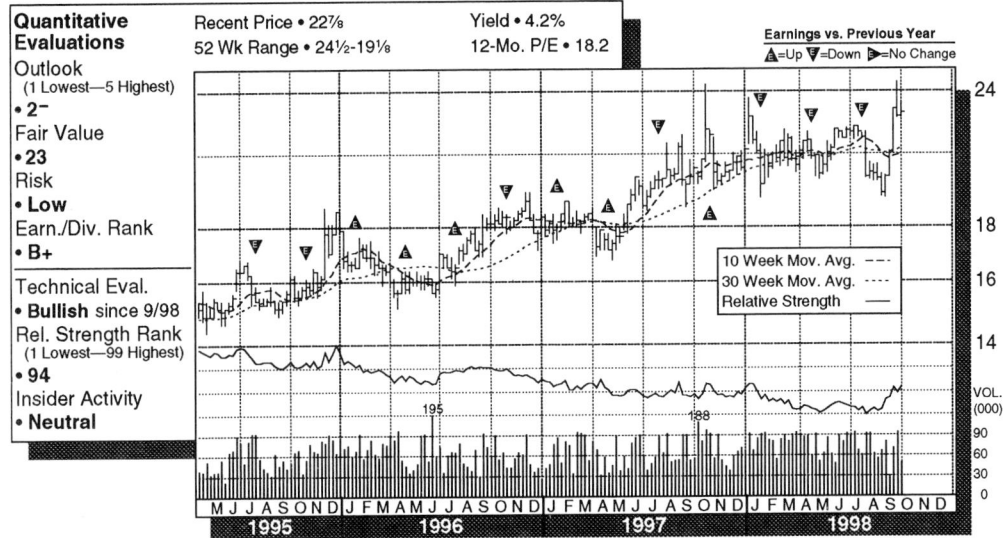

10 Week Mov. Avg. – – –
30 Week Mov. Avg. ·······
Relative Strength ——

Business Profile - 02-JUN-98

This North Carolina gas utility intends to expand its transmission and distribution systems. Over 75% of construction expenditures over the last three years has been for these systems. Management intends to work toward retaining existing customers by marketing the replacement of old appliances and equipment with new equipment, and by marketing additional gas equipment; it also seeks to add new customers. PGS is also evaluating the introduction of emerging gas technologies as a way to increase the long-term demand for natural gas. The dividend was recently boosted 4.3%.

Operational Review - 02-JUN-98

Operating revenues in the first half of FY 98 (Sep.) were nearly unchanged year to year, as the weather normalization adjustment mechanism offset an increase in consumption. Margins were also unchanged, reflecting lower operating and maintenance expenses, which offset greater depreciation charges. After a 7.4% increase in interest expense, net income declined 1.9%, to $29,716,000 ($1.48 a share, on 3.0% more shares), from $30,293,000 ($1.56).

Stock Performance - 02-OCT-98

In the past 30 trading days, PGS's shares have increased 15%, compared to a 7% fall in the S&P 500. Average trading volume for the past five days was 9,820 shares, compared with the 40-day moving average of 14,018 shares.

Key Stock Statistics

Dividend Rate/Share	0.96	Shareholders	12,800
Shs. outstg. (M)	20.2	Market cap. (B)	$0.464
Avg. daily vol. (M)	0.015	Inst. holdings	23%
Tang. Bk. Value/Share	11.43		
Beta	0.34		

Value of $10,000 invested 5 years ago: $ 16,727

Fiscal Year Ending Sep. 30

	1998	1997	1996	1995	1994	1993
Revenues (Million $)						
1Q	103.8	93.65	74.92	66.80	71.40	77.00
2Q	140.2	150.2	142.1	112.7	123.2	117.3
3Q	54.53	60.11	58.81	41.65	48.20	55.30
4Q	—	34.02	33.10	26.72	30.90	30.50
Yr.	—	337.9	308.9	247.9	273.7	280.0
Earnings Per Share ($)						
1Q	**0.36**	0.41	0.38	0.36	0.31	0.28
2Q	**1.11**	1.15	1.09	1.00	1.01	0.94
3Q	**0.04**	0.07	0.08	0.03	0.10	Nil
4Q	Nil	-0.26	-0.27	-0.23	-0.20	-0.32
Yr.	—	1.35	1.26	1.16	1.17	0.90

Next earnings report expected: late October

Dividend Data (Dividends have been paid since 1958.)

Amount ($)	Date Decl.	Ex-Div. Date	Stock of Record	Payment Date
0.230	Nov. 13	Dec. 08	Dec. 10	Jan. 01 '98
0.230	Jan. 30	Mar. 06	Mar. 10	Apr. 01 '98
0.240	Apr. 28	Jun. 08	Jun. 10	Jul. 10 '98
0.240	Jul. 30	Sep. 08	Sep. 10	Oct. 01 '98

A Division of The McGraw-Hill Companies

Business Summary - 02-JUN-98

In an industry that is in the midst of deregulation, the formation of nonregulated businesses is the norm for utilities, and Public Service Company of North Carolina, Inc. (PGS) is no exception. The natural gas distributor started a small nonregulated natural gas brokering business, PSNC Production, eight years ago; by FY 96 (Sep.), it was serving 230 customers. In a quest for greater growth, in December 1996, PSNC sold a 50% interest in its marketing business to create a joint venture, Sonat Public Service Co. L.L.C. (SPSC), with Sonat Marketing Company L.P., a unit of Sonat Inc. The venture markets natural gas and related services through three offices, two in North Carolina and one in Virginia. Since SPSC was formed, the number of customers has grown from 230 to 350. SPSC plans to expand its marketing territory to South Carolina, Maryland, and the District of Colombia and increase the range of energy products and services that it offers, which may include electricity when the retail sale of electricity is deregulated.

Another PGS nonregulated subsidiary, Clean Energy Enterprises, operates a natural gas vehicle conversion and fueling business. Clean Energy has operated natural gas refueling stations in Raleigh and Gastonia for a

number of years. It also operates a natural gas vehicle conversion facility in Raleigh.

On the regulated front, PGS serves only about one-third of the population in its service territory, which management believes presents a significant growth opportunity. According to the company, approximately 70,000 potential customers are located on existing PGS gas mains.

The company derived 54% of its revenue from residential customers in FY 97, 25% commercial, 14% industrial and 7% from gas transported for others. At September 30, 1997, PGS was serving 305,897 customers, of which 264,129 were residential, 39,349 commercial and 2,419 industrial. Total volume of natural gas sold and transported in FY 97 was 65,113,000 dekatherms (dt), versus 65,646,000 dt in FY 96. Management's goal is to grow its number of customers to 400,000 by FY 03. It helps that the company serves a customer base that is growing nearly 5% annually.

In November 1997, the North Carolina Utilities Commission authorized Cardinal Extension Co., LLC, to extend the existing 24-inch diameter Cardinal Pipeline system in North Carolina by constructing an additional 67 miles from Burlington, NC, to a point southeast of Raleigh. The extension will provide increased firm transportation service of 140,000 Mcf/day to PGS and North Carolina Natural Gas Co.

Per Share Data ($)

(Year Ended Sep. 30)	1997	1996	1995	1994	1993	1992	1991	1990	1989	1988
Tangible Bk. Val.	10.40	9.75	9.28	8.82	7.73	7.40	6.92	6.87	6.66	6.34
Earnings	1.35	1.26	1.16	1.17	0.90	1.08	0.70	0.84	0.93	1.03
Dividends	0.90	0.86	0.84	0.81	0.78	0.75	0.72	0.72	0.69	0.67
Payout Ratio	67%	69%	72%	69%	86%	69%	105%	86%	74%	65%
Prices - High	24⅜	19⅜	18¾	17¾	19¾	20⅛	12¼	11½	11⅛	10¼
- Low	16¾	15⅛	13¾	13½	15¼	11¼	10⅛	9¾	9½	8⅜
P/E Ratio - High	18	15	16	15	22	19	17	14	12	10
- Low	12	12	12	12	17	10	14	12	10	8

Income Statement Analysis (Million $)

	1997	1996	1995	1994	1993	1992	1991	1990	1989	1988
Revs.	338	309	248	274	280	240	193	202	214	201
Depr.	22.6	19.7	18.2	15.2	14.1	13.1	12.2	10.9	9.9	8.8
Maint.	6.0	5.1	4.3	4.7	4.9	5.2	4.3	4.4	3.9	3.5
Fxd. Chgs. Cov.	3.4	2.6	2.7	2.5	2.0	2.2	1.8	1.9	2.3	2.7
Constr. Credits	0.3	0.3	0.3	0.1	0.1	0.1	0.3	0.6	0.3	0.3
Eff. Tax Rate	37%	38%	39%	34%	35%	38%	36%	35%	36%	36%
Net Inc.	26.3	23.9	21.4	20.0	14.2	16.8	10.6	12.3	13.3	14.4

Balance Sheet & Other Fin. Data (Million $)

	1997	1996	1995	1994	1993	1992	1991	1990	1989	1988
Gross Prop.	685	629	574	520	478	442	414	380	351	311
Cap. Exp.	60.3	60.4	61.1	45.5	40.1	31.1	36.5	32.3	42.9	36.7
Net Prop.	482	445	407	367	338	310	293	271	250	219
Capitalization:										
LT Debt	181	140	101	114	125	130	104	109	85.0	89.0
% LT Debt	47	43	37	42	50	53	50	51	47	50
Pfd.	Nil	Nil	Nil	Nil	Nil	Nil	1.7	2.0	2.2	3.1
% Pfd.	Nil	Nil	Nil	Nil	Nil	Nil	0.80	0.90	1.20	1.70
Common	207	189	173	161	124	115	104	101	95.0	88.0
% Common	53	57	63	59	50	47	50	48	52	49
Total Cap.	388	389	331	328	300	296	257	255	224	220
% Oper. Ratio	88.3	88.6	86.3	89.5	89.9	87.3	87.5	88.5	89.3	89.2
% Earn. on Net Prop.	8.6	4.2	9.0	8.1	8.7	10.1	8.6	8.9	9.8	10.6
% Return On Revs.	7.8	7.8	8.6	7.3	5.1	7.0	5.5	6.1	6.2	7.2
% Return On Invest. Capital	14.1	12.2	14.4	10.6	9.4	10.9	9.4	10.6	10.5	10.9
% Return On Com. Equity	13.3	13.2	12.8	14.1	11.9	15.2	10.2	12.5	14.4	16.8

Data as orig. reptd.; bef. results of disc opers. and/or spec. items. Per share data adj. for stk. divs. as of ex-div. date. Bold denotes diluted EPS (FASB 128). E-Estimated. NA-Not Available. NM-Not Meaningful. NR-Not Ranked.

Office—400 Cox Rd., P.O. Box 1398, Gastonia, NC 28053-1398. **Tel**—(704) 864-6731. **Chrmn, Pres & CEO**—C. E. Zeigler Jr. **VP, Treas & CFO**—J. G. Mason. **Investor Contact**—Freida Pendleton. **VP & Secy**—J. P. Douglas.**Dirs**—W. C. Burkhardt, W. A. V. Cecil, B. Collins, J. W. Copeland, V. E. Eure, W. L. O'Brien Jr., D. W. Peterson, B. R. Rudisill II, G. S. York, C. E. Zeigler Jr. **Transfer Agent & Registrar**—First Union National Bank of North Carolina, Charlotte. **Incorporated**—in North Carolina in 1938. **Empl**— 1,125. **S&P Analyst:** J. Robert Cho

Quaker Chemical

1885W

NYSE Symbol **KWR**

In S&P SmallCap 600

03-OCT-98

Industry:
Chemicals (Specialty)

Summary: This company produces and markets worldwide a broad range of specialty chemical products for heavy industrial, institutional and manufacturing applications.

Quantitative Evaluations

Outlook
(1 Lowest—5 Highest)
• **1⁻**

Fair Value
• **14⅛**

Risk
• **Average**

Earn./Div. Rank
• **B-**

Technical Eval.
• **NA**

Rel. Strength Rank
(1 Lowest—99 Highest)
• **42**

Insider Activity
• **NA**

Recent Price • 15
52 Wk Range • 21-15

Yield • 4.8%
12-Mo. P/E • 9.8

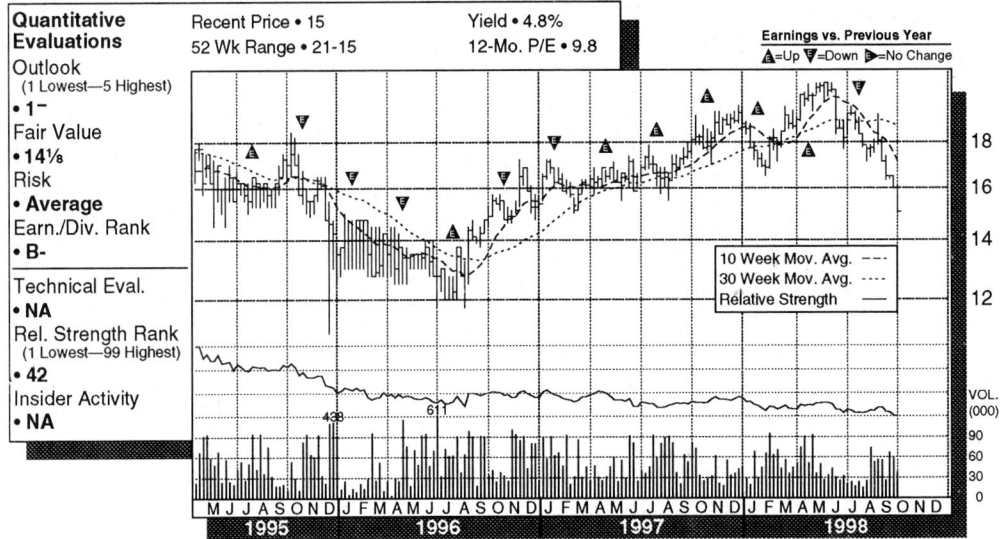

Earnings vs. Previous Year
▲=Up ▼=Down ▶=No Change

10 Week Mov. Avg. – – –
30 Week Mov. Avg. ·····
Relative Strength —

Business Profile - 18-MAY-98

Confronted with the challenge of operating in a mature, price-sensitive business, KWR decided to consolidate its U.S. manufacturing operations into a single facility in 1996. It has also streamlined its European sales, distribution and research activities. In connection with the restructuring, a pretax charge of about $24 million ($1.96 a share, after tax) was recorded in 1996. In the absence of special charges, profitability was restored in 1997. In addition to reducing its operating costs, KWR plans to capitalize on growth opportunities in South America and the Asia/Pacific area.

Operational Review - 18-MAY-98

Revenues in the first quarter of 1998 advanced 6.3%, year to year, reflecting higher sales to customers in the steel, metalworking and aircraft producing industries. Margins widened on higher real unit volume, an improved sales mix and stable raw material costs. With lower interest expense, pretax income was up 30%. After taxes at 40.0% in both periods, lower equity earnings and increased minority interest, net income rose 13% to $2,894,000 ($0.33 a share) from $2,567,000 ($0.30).

Stock Performance - 02-OCT-98

In the past 30 trading days, KWR's shares have declined 16%, compared to a 7% fall in the S&P 500. Average trading volume for the past five days was 7,500 shares, compared with the 40-day moving average of 10,951 shares.

Key Stock Statistics

Dividend Rate/Share	0.72	Shareholders	1,000
Shs. outstg. (M)	8.8	Market cap. (B)	$0.132
Avg. daily vol. (M)	0.010	Inst. holdings	41%
Tang. Bk. Value/Share	6.62		
Beta	0.18		

Value of $10,000 invested 5 years ago: $ 9,038

Fiscal Year Ending Dec. 31

	1998	1997	1996	1995	1994	1993
Revenues (Million $)						
1Q	62.24	58.54	58.20	54.53	45.09	48.36
2Q	65.36	60.31	59.79	59.78	47.35	51.34
3Q	—	58.69	61.83	57.87	50.12	48.44
4Q	—	63.99	60.45	55.60	52.12	46.86
Yr.	—	241.5	240.3	227.0	194.7	195.0
Earnings Per Share ($)						
1Q	**0.33**	**0.30**	0.19	0.22	0.24	0.30
2Q	**0.39**	**0.54**	0.31	0.28	0.24	-0.05
3Q	—	**0.38**	-0.68	0.24	0.26	0.08
4Q	—	**0.23**	-0.70	0.02	0.29	-0.52
Yr.	—	**1.45**	-0.88	0.76	1.03	-0.19

Next earnings report expected: late October

Dividend Data (Dividends have been paid since 1954.)

Amount ($)	Date Decl.	Ex-Div. Date	Stock of Record	Payment Date
0.180	Sep. 10	Oct. 15	Oct. 17	Oct. 30 '97
0.180	Nov. 12	Jan. 14	Jan. 16	Jan. 30 '98
0.180	Mar. 18	Apr. 15	Apr. 17	Apr. 30 '98
0.180	May. 06	Jul. 15	Jul. 17	Jul. 30 '98

A Division of The McGraw-Hill Companies

STANDARD
&POOR'S
STOCK REPORTS

Quaker Chemical Corporation

1885W

03-OCT-98

Business Summary - 18-MAY-98

Quaker Chemical Corporation develops and produces a broad range of specialty chemicals for the steel, metal-working, aerospace, automotive, bearing, can, construction, fluid power and pulp and paper industries. The company believes that it has a dominant position in the market for process fluids used in the hot and cold rolling of steel. With a significant portion of its sales derived from the steel industry, the company is therefore subject to business cycles similar to those experienced by its customers. Domestic sales provided 46% of 1997 revenue, and European sales 39%, with the balance from South America and the Asia/Pacific region.

KWR's products include (1) rolling lubricants, used in the hot and cold rolling of steel; (2) corrosion preventatives, used by steel and metalworking customers to protect metal during manufacture, storage and shipment; (3) metal finishing compounds used to prepare metal surfaces for special treatments such as galvanizing and tin plating; (4) machining and grinding compounds, used by metalworkers in cutting, shaping and grinding metal parts that require special treatment to tolerate the manufacturing process; (5) forming compounds used to facilitate the drawing and extrusion of metal products; (6) paper production products, used as defoamers, release agents, softeners, debonders and dispersants; (7) hydraulic fluids, used to operate hy-

draulically activated equipment; (8) products for the removal of hydrogen sulfide in various industrial applications; and (9) programs to provide recycling and chemical management services.

The AC Products subsidiary makes chemical milling maskants for the aerospace industry, as well as flexible sealants and exterior protective coatings for roofs and walls for the construction industry.

In 1994, KWR acquired the Perstorp AB cutting fluid business in Scandinavia. In 1995, the company acquired 90% of Celumi Ltda., a Brazilian supplier of chemical specialty products to the metalworking industry, and entered into a joint venture with Wuxi Oil Refinery, of China, to produce lubricants.

In 1996, KWR recorded $24,455,000 of pretax charges ($1.96 a share, after tax) for restructuring costs related to the consolidation of its domestic manufacturing operations and the streamlining of its European sales, distribution, and research activities. By closing its Conshohocken, PA, facility, the company essentially reduced its excess manufacturing capacity, while strategically aligning its production capabilities in Detroit, MI. The repositioning, situating KWR's facilities near the center of U.S. auto production, was intended to enable it to better serve its customers; the motor vehicle segment demands about 15% of high-quality rolled steel production annually.

Per Share Data ($)

(Year Ended Dec. 31)	1997	1996	1995	1994	1993	1992	1991	1990	1989	1988
Tangible Bk. Val.	7.01	6.73	8.66	9.23	8.32	10.03	10.05	10.14	8.64	7.66
Cash Flow	2.28	0.13	1.79	1.74	0.52	2.03	1.78	2.01	1.75	1.58
Earnings	1.45	-0.88	0.76	1.03	-0.19	1.33	1.20	1.51	1.35	1.21
Dividends	0.70	0.69	0.68	0.62	0.60	0.56	0.52	0.46	0.40	0.36
Payout Ratio	49%	NM	89%	60%	NM	43%	44%	29%	30%	30%
Prices - High	19³/₄	17¹/₄	19	19¹/₂	24⁵/₈	26	22¹/₄	19¹/₄	15⁵/₈	16¹/₈
- Low	15	11³/₄	11	14³/₄	14¹/₄	18³/₄	15	12	12¹/₂	11³/₈
P/E Ratio - High	14	NM	25	19	NM	20	19	13	12	13
- Low	10	NM	14	14	NM	14	13	8	9	9

Income Statement Analysis (Million $)

	1997	1996	1995	1994	1993	1992	1991	1990	1989	1988
Revs.	242	240	227	195	195	212	191	201	182	167
Oper. Inc.	25.8	23.9	20.1	19.5	14.9	23.6	19.2	22.6	19.0	18.4
Depr.	7.3	8.7	8.7	6.5	6.5	6.4	5.2	4.7	3.9	4.5
Int. Exp.	1.5	1.9	1.7	1.3	1.5	1.5	1.8	NA	1.2	0.8
Pretax Inc.	20.9	-7.0	12.1	15.7	-1.2	19.5	17.3	23.0	20.1	19.3
Eff. Tax Rate	38%	NM	40%	38%	NM	36%	35%	37%	34%	37%
Net Inc.	12.6	-7.6	6.7	9.4	-1.8	12.1	10.8	14.1	12.8	11.7

Balance Sheet & Other Fin. Data (Million $)

	1997	1996	1995	1994	1993	1992	1991	1990	1989	1988
Cash	18.4	8.5	7.2	11.3	20.3	24.5	23.8	26.4	22.6	20.5
Curr. Assets	98.1	86.6	86.7	83.4	84.4	85.6	82.7	84.8	75.4	69.3
Total Assets	171	166	185	170	171	167	156	152	131	121
Curr. Liab.	47.8	64.0	60.9	43.4	42.6	28.1	36.6	40.3	27.8	26.9
LT Debt	25.2	5.2	9.3	12.2	16.1	18.6	5.2	5.5	5.7	5.0
Common Eqty.	75.6	74.3	94.0	94.0	91.0	102	99	99	90.4	82.9
Total Cap.	108	86.4	109	112	113	125	106	108	99	90.0
Cap. Exp.	5.6	NA	NA	NA	9.0	7.2	8.4	12.7	7.6	5.3
Cash Flow	19.9	1.1	15.8	15.9	4.8	18.5	16.0	18.8	16.7	15.2
Curr. Ratio	2.1	1.4	1.4	1.9	2.0	3.0	2.3	2.1	2.7	2.6
% LT Debt of Cap.	23.3	6.0	8.5	10.9	14.3	14.9	4.9	5.1	5.7	5.6
% Net Inc.of Revs.	5.2	NM	2.9	4.8	NM	5.7	5.6	7.0	7.1	7.0
% Ret. on Assets	7.5	NM	37.7	5.6	NM	7.4	7.0	10.2	10.3	9.8
% Ret. on Equity	16.8	NM	7.1	10.4	NM	12.0	10.8	15.3	15.0	14.6

Data as orig. reptd.; bef. results of disc. opers. and/or spec. items. Per share data adj. for stk. divs. as of ex-div. date. Bold denotes diluted EPS (FASB 128). E-Estimated. NA-Not Available. NM-Not Meaningful. NR-Not Ranked.

Office—Elm and Lee Streets, Conshohocken, PA 19428. **Tel**—(610) 832-4000. **Chrmn & CEO**—R. J. Naples. **Pres & COO**—J. W. Bauer. **Secy**—D. J. Benoliel.**Contr and Treas**—R. J. Fagan. **Investor Contact**—Irene M. Kisleiko (610) 832-4119.**Dirs**—J. B. Anderson Jr., P. C. Barron, W. L. Batchelor, P. A. Benoliel, L. K. Black, D. R. Caldwell, R. E. Chappell, E. J. Delattre, R. P. Hauptfuhrer, R. J. Naples, R. H. Rock. **Transfer Agent & Registrar**—American Stock Transfer & Trust Co., NYC. **Incorporated**—in Pennsylvania in 1930. **Empl**— 871. **S&P Analyst:** E. Hunter

STANDARD &POOR'S
STOCK REPORTS

Quanex Corp.
1888H
NYSE Symbol **NX**
In S&P SmallCap 600

10-OCT-98
Industry:
Iron & Steel

Summary: Quanex produces hot rolled special bar quality carbon and alloy steel bars, air-bag components and aluminum building products.

S&P Opinion: Hold (★★★)	Recent Price • 16¼	Yield • 3.9%
	52 Wk Range • 33¾-15⅝	12-Mo. P/E • 5.8

Quantitative Evaluations

Outlook
(1 Lowest—5 Highest)
• **5**

Fair Value
• **33⅝**

Risk
• **Average**

Earn./Div. Rank
• **B**

Technical Eval.
• **Bullish** since 9/98

Rel. Strength Rank
(1 Lowest—99 Highest)
• **20**

Insider Activity
• **NA**

Earnings vs. Previous Year
▲=Up ▼=Down ▶=No Change

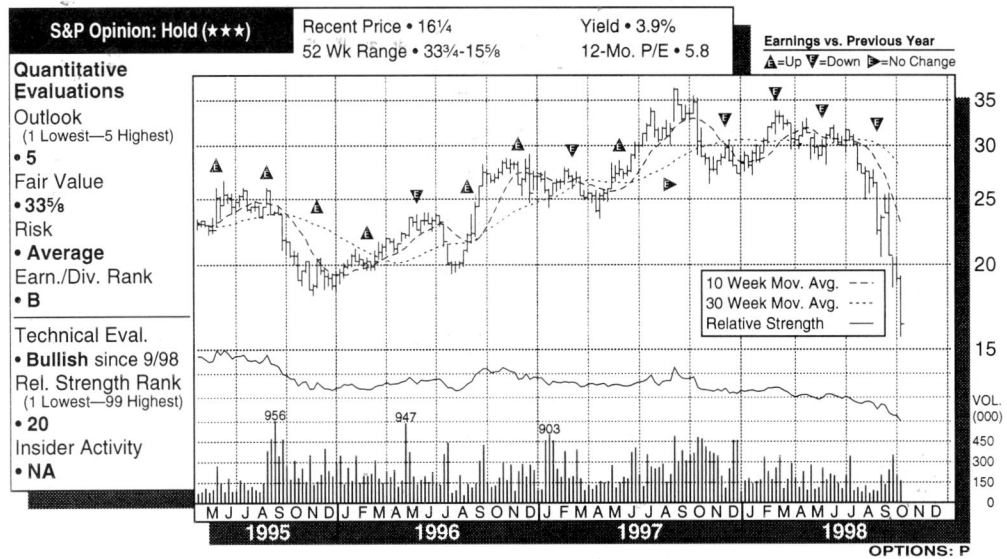

10 Week Mov. Avg. - - -
30 Week Mov. Avg. ·····
Relative Strength —

VOL. (000)

OPTIONS: P

Overview - 08-SEP-98

We project 8% sales growth for FY 99 (Oct.). While contrbutions from MacSteel will be strong, the bulk of the gain will come from a rebound in aluminum and air bag components. Margins in steel may trail FY 98 due to weaker pricing, but margins for aluminum and air bag components should show considerable improvement, aided by the absence of start-up delays at Piper and lower conversion costs for aluminum. Accordingly, EPS should rise in FY 99.

Valuation - 08-SEP-98

We are maintaining our hold rating on Quanex following third quarter EPS and a conference call. EPS beat the $0.64 consensus estimate on another strong quarter for MacSteel and a rebound in the aluminum unit. Piper Impact continued to incur losses due to weakness in Asia and the strike at General Motors. Based on our EPS estimate for FY 99, we believe NX is undervalued. Currently, NX is selling at a P/E of 9.2X FY 99 EPS, versus an average P/E of 6.5X for the integrated steel companies we follow. Given its far superior EPS prospects vis a vis such companies, NX deserves a higher multiple. NX's margins on its steel business are more than double those of the most profitable integrated or minimill steel company we follow, but investor disappointment with Piper Impact explains the low multiple on the stock. Near term, we expect NX to remain at its current depressed level until investors become confident that operational problems at Piper have been resolved. We continue to have a favorable long-term view of NX as we anticipate that the air bag components business will provide strong profit growth once the start-up expenses cease. Also, the steel bar business will be a solid source of earnings growth. Finally, we expect that NX will ultimately divest the aluminum unit, which has been a drag on EPS and the P/E ratio.

Key Stock Statistics

S&P EPS Est. 1998	1.90	Tang. Bk. Value/Share	14.44
P/E on S&P Est. 1998	8.6	Beta	0.88
S&P EPS Est. 1999	2.60	Shareholders	3,400
Dividend Rate/Share	0.64	Market cap. (B)	$0.231
Shs. outstg. (M)	14.2	Inst. holdings	79%
Avg. daily vol. (M)	0.047		

Value of $10,000 invested 5 years ago: $ 9,997

Fiscal Year Ending Oct. 31

	1998	1997	1996	1995	1994	1993
Revenues (Million $)						
1Q	181.0	194.9	188.8	199.9	149.6	141.4
2Q	203.4	217.1	218.3	234.3	172.2	161.4
3Q	204.8	225.1	225.5	228.2	181.1	153.5
4Q	—	195.6	263.1	228.8	196.5	159.8
Yr.	—	746.1	895.7	891.2	699.3	616.1
Earnings Per Share ($)						
1Q	**0.16**	0.23	0.30	0.23	0.02	-0.07
2Q	**0.51**	0.61	0.60	0.62	0.17	0.03
3Q	**0.66**	0.67	0.67	0.63	0.32	0.09
4Q	**E0.57**	0.59	0.84	0.72	0.45	0.13
Yr.	**E1.90**	1.98	2.41	2.20	0.96	0.18

Next earnings report expected: mid December

Dividend Data (Dividends have been paid since 1988.)

Amount ($)	Date Decl.	Ex-Div. Date	Stock of Record	Payment Date
0.160	Dec. 11	Dec. 18	Dec. 22	Dec. 30 '97
0.160	Feb. 26	Mar. 12	Mar. 16	Mar. 31 '98
0.160	May. 28	Jun. 11	Jun. 15	Jun. 30 '98
0.160	Aug. 25	Sep. 11	Sep. 15	Sep. 30 '98

A Division of The McGraw-Hill Companies

STANDARD
&POOR'S
STOCK REPORTS

Quanex Corporation

1888H
10-OCT-98

Business Summary - 08-SEP-98

Quanex produces hot rolled special bar quality carbon and alloy steel bars and aluminum building products. In August 1996, NX entered the market for impact extruded aluminum and steel products with the acquisition of Piper Impact. Following the divestiture of LaSalle Steel and the sale of the Tubes unit, NX operates in two segments. Sales and operating profits in FY 97 (Oct.) were:

	Sales	Profits
Engineered Steel Bars	40%	74%
Aluminum products	60%	26%

The Engineered steel products segment steel bar operations, steel bar and tube heat treating services, and steelbar and tube wear and corrosion resistant finishing services. Steel bar operations, which account for the bulk of this segment, are conducted by MacSteel at two plants. MacSteel makes hot rolled bars, including hot rolled steel bar quality carbon and steel bars used for camshafts, transmission gears, bearing cages, steering components, hydraulic mechanisms, seamless tube production, and track components for military vehicles. In recent years, NX has made incremental capacity additions to MacSteel's plants that have improved product quality as well as add volume. Shipments in FY 97 totaled 579,900 tons, versus 526,800 tons in FY 96; oper-

ating profit per ton rose to $87 in FY 97 from $70 in FY 96.

Through subsidiaries, NX's aluminum unit makes aluminum sheet and fabricated aluminum products for the home improvement, new construction and light commercial construction markets. Nichols-Homeshield (NH) uses state of the art aluminum minimill casting equipment to make coiled aluminum sheet from scrap and operates two finishing mills to supply its two fabrication businesses and a diverse mix of external customers in the construction, transportation and service centers markets..

Fabricated products consists of Homeshield Fabricated Products (HFP) and AMSCO. HFP makes a wide range of residential building products that are sold through distributors, as well as engineered products for OEMs. AMSCO manufactures aluminum window and patio door screens, window frames and related accessories.

Piper Impact, which is carried in the aluminum segment, manufactures impact extruded aluminum and steel parts for the transportation, electronics and defense markets. The majority of Piper's sales are to one customer, Autoliv (formerly Morton International), in the form of air-bag components. This includes passenger and side impact air bags, "smart" bags with adjustable inflation speed and those with alternative inflation technologies.

Per Share Data ($)

(Year Ended Oct. 31)	1997	1996	1995	1994	1993	1992	1991	1990	1989	1988
Tangible Bk. Val.	12.62	7.66	10.27	8.12	7.76	8.54	9.94	9.24	8.56	9.13
Cash Flow	4.63	5.22	4.91	3.01	2.23	2.36	3.17	3.88	3.51	3.25
Earnings	1.98	2.41	2.20	0.96	0.18	0.28	1.02	2.03	2.11	1.85
Dividends	0.61	0.60	0.59	0.56	0.56	0.52	0.48	0.40	0.30	0.08
Payout Ratio	31%	25%	27%	58%	NM	200%	47%	19%	14%	4%
Prices - High	36½	29⅛	26⅝	27¼	21¼	31¾	23⅛	18½	19	15⅛
- Low	23⅜	18¾	18	17	14	15½	11⅜	9⅛	13⅛	5⅞
P/E Ratio - High	18	12	12	28	NM	NM	23	9	9	8
- Low	12	8	8	18	NM	NM	11	4	6	3

Income Statement Analysis (Million $)

	1997	1996	1995	1994	1993	1992	1991	1990	1989	1988
Revs.	746	896	891	699	616	572	589	650	502	463
Oper. Inc.	92.3	105	99	69.2	50.9	52.5	60.2	79.7	70.6	67.2
Depr.	37.3	38.4	32.4	27.8	27.7	26.4	25.1	22.6	17.4	17.2
Int. Exp.	14.0	11.4	10.7	13.9	15.1	15.5	17.7	10.9	6.8	15.1
Pretax Inc.	42.6	56.7	58.4	32.5	14.5	10.7	21.4	45.2	47.1	36.5
Eff. Tax Rate	35%	42%	42%	42%	42%	42%	42%	38%	38%	37%
Net Inc.	27.7	32.9	33.9	18.9	8.4	6.2	12.4	28.0	29.3	22.9

Balance Sheet & Other Fin. Data (Million $)

	1997	1996	1995	1994	1993	1992	1991	1990	1989	1988
Cash	26.9	36.0	45.2	88.1	89.9	96.9	31.1	24.1	24.8	47.6
Curr. Assets	187	263	242	259	243	250	164	170	166	153
Total Assets	686	718	547	564	529	535	446	451	400	301
Curr. Liab.	134	153	165	135	95.1	96.0	95.0	96.0	90.0	88.0
LT Debt	202	254	112	107	128	129	156	131	93.0	39.0
Common Eqty.	269	195	171	146	140	151	152	147	133	112
Total Cap.	519	473	312	363	372	383	341	344	298	200
Cap. Exp.	72.8	44.2	26.6	44.6	37.0	52.5	57.0	31.9	13.8	5.3
Cash Flow	65.0	71.3	66.3	40.7	30.2	30.0	37.0	47.4	43.5	39.9
Curr. Ratio	1.4	1.7	1.5	1.9	2.6	2.6	1.7	1.8	1.8	1.7
% LT Debt of Cap.	38.9	53.7	35.9	29.6	34.5	33.6	45.8	38.2	31.3	19.4
% Net Inc.of Revs.	3.7	3.7	3.8	2.7	1.4	1.1	2.1	4.3	5.8	5.0
% Ret. on Assets	3.9	5.2	6.1	3.4	1.6	1.2	2.8	6.7	8.3	7.9
% Ret. on Equity	12.0	18.0	16.8	9.0	1.7	2.2	8.0	18.0	21.3	21.8

Data as orig. reptd.; bef. results of disc. opers. and/or spec. items. Per share data adj. for stk. divs. as of ex-div. date. Bold denotes diluted EPS (FASB 128). E-Estimated. NA-Not Available. NM-Not Meaningful. NR-Not Ranked.

Office—1900 West Loop South, Suite 1500, Houston, TX 77027. **Tel**—(713) 961-4600. **Chrmn**—R. C. Snyder. **Pres & CEO**—V. E. Oechsle. **VP & CFO**—W. M. Rose. **Secy**—M. W. Conlon. **Investor Contact**—Jeff Galow (800-231-8176). **Dirs**—D. J. Barger Jr., R. M. Flaum, G. B. Haeckel, J. D. O'Connell, V. E. Oechsle, C. E. Pfeiffer, M. J. Sebastian, V. R. Scorsone, R. C. Snyder. **Transfer Agent & Registrar**—American Stock Transfer & Trust, NYC. **Incorporated**—in Michigan in 1927; reincorporated in Delaware in 1968. **Empl**—3,771. **S&P Analyst:** Leo Larkin

10-OCT-98

Industry:
Savings & Loan Companies

Summary: Queens County Bancorp is the holding company for Queens County Savings Bank, the first savings bank chartered by the State of New York in the New York City Borough of Queens.

Quantitative Evaluations

Outlook
(1 Lowest—5 Highest)
• **NA**

Fair Value
• **NA**

Risk
• **Low**

Earn./Div. Rank
• **NR**

Technical Eval.
• **Bearish** since 9/98

Rel. Strength Rank
(1 Lowest—99 Highest)
• **55**

Insider Activity
• **Neutral**

Recent Price • 23
52 Wk Range • 31⅝-22¾

Yield • 2.9%
12-Mo. P/E • 20.0

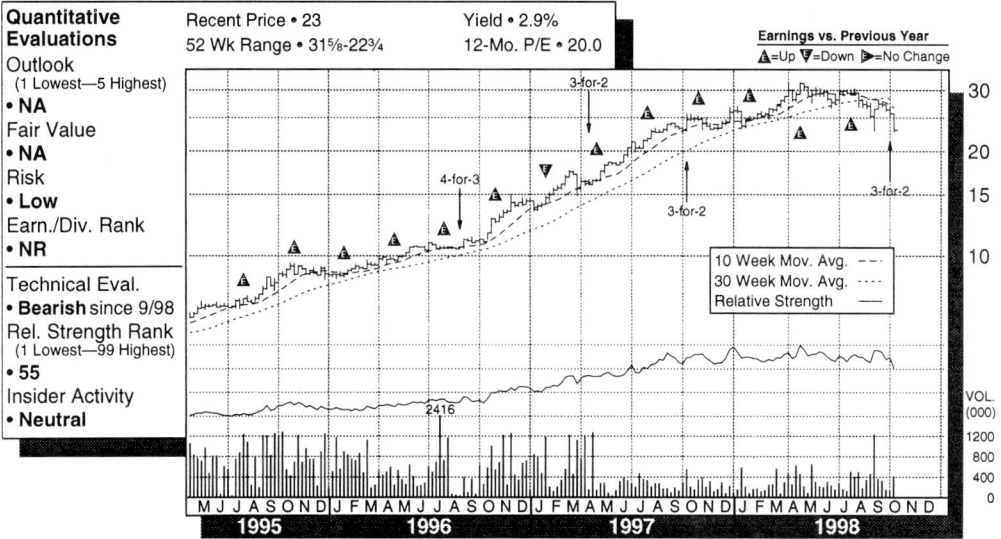

Business Profile - 13-SEP-98

The bank's primary business is gathering deposits from its customers in Queens and Nassau counties, and investing these funds in the origination of residential mortgage loans throughout metropolitan New York. QCBS has had 12 consecutive quarters without net chargeoffs, and non-performing assets, at June 30, 1998, represented 0.50% of total assets, down from 0.54% at year-end 1997. The quarterly dividend was boosted 25% with the May 1998 payment, and a 3-for-2 stock split is to occur in late September 1998. Also, since October 1994, the company has announced at least seven stock repurchase authorizations. QCSB repurchased 451,568 common shares in the first half of 1998.

Operational Review - 13-SEP-98

In 1998's first six months, net interest income rose 11%, year to year, although QCBS's interest rate spread and net interest margin were below the prior year levels. QCBS's average balance of interest-earning assets was up 18%, to $1.6 billion. Also, fee income was up $611,000, to $1.2 million, which more than offset a $215,000 rise in operating expense, and pretax profit increased 20%. In the absence of a $1.3 million tax benefit from the enactment of legislation that resulted in a change in the New York City tax code, the tax rate was 41.5%, versus 31.8%, and net income was up 3.2%, to $12.9 million ($1.00 a share, on fewer shares), from $12.5 million ($0.88).

Stock Performance - 09-OCT-98

In the past 30 trading days, QCSB's shares have declined 9%, compared to a 4% fall in the S&P 500. Average trading volume for the past five days was 80,280 shares, compared with the 40-day moving average of 91,391 shares.

Key Stock Statistics

Dividend Rate/Share	0.67	Shareholders	70,000
Shs. outstg. (M)	22.2	Market cap. (B)	$0.510
Avg. daily vol. (M)	0.048	Inst. holdings	32%
Tang. Bk. Value/Share	7.66		
Beta	NA		

Value of $10,000 invested 5 years ago: NA

Fiscal Year Ending Dec. 31

	1998	1997	1996	1995	1994	1993
Revenues (Million $)						
1Q	33.04	27.41	25.00	23.02	20.23	—
2Q	34.03	28.96	25.54	24.29	21.00	—
3Q	—	30.74	25.99	23.36	21.42	—
4Q	—	32.93	26.62	23.91	22.40	—
Yr.	—	120.0	104.8	94.57	85.04	77.02
Earnings Per Share ($)						
1Q	0.31	0.30	0.20	0.18	0.15	—
2Q	0.32	0.25	0.24	0.19	0.17	—
3Q	—	0.26	0.23	0.20	0.16	—
4Q	—	0.26	0.18	0.20	0.19	—
Yr.	—	1.07	0.85	0.76	0.67	0.46

Next earnings report expected: mid October

Dividend Data (Dividends have been paid since 1994.)

Amount ($)	Date Decl.	Ex-Div. Date	Stock of Record	Payment Date
0.200	Jan. 21	Jan. 29	Feb. 02	Feb. 17 '98
0.250	Apr. 22	Apr. 29	May. 01	May. 15 '98
0.250	Jul. 22	Jul. 30	Aug. 03	Aug. 17 '98
3-for-2	Aug. 19	Sep. 30	Sep. 15	Sep. 29 '98

A Division of The **McGraw·Hill** *Companies*

STANDARD
&POOR'S
STOCK REPORTS

Queens County Bancorp, Inc.

5048W
10-OCT-98

Business Summary - 13-SEP-98

Queens County Bancorp, Inc. was formed in 1993 to serve as the holding company for Queens County Savings Bank. The company acquired all of the stock of the bank upon its conversion from a New York State-chartered mutual savings bank to a New York State-chartered stock savings bank in November 1993. Queens County Savings Bank was organized in 1859 as a New YorkState-chartered mutual savings bank, and was the first savings bank chartered in the New York City Borough of Queens.

The bank's principal business is attracting retail deposits from the general public and investing those deposits, together with funds generated from operations, into the origination of mortgage loans on multi-family properties and one-to-four family homes. To a lesser extent, the bank also originates loans on commercial real estate, construction loans, home equity loans, and other consumer loans.

The bank is a community-oriented financial institution offering a wide variety of financial products and services to meet the needs of the communities it serves. Headquartered in the heart of Flushing, Queens, the bank operates nine branch offices and three customer service centers in Queens, and a 10th branch office in Nassau County. The bank's deposit gathering base is concentrated in the communities surrounding its offices, while its primary lending area extends throughout the greater New York metropolitan area. Most of the bank's mortgage loans are secured by properties located in the New York City Boroughs of Queens, Brooklyn and Manhattan, and in Nassau County.

At June 30, 1998, QCSB had $1.5 billion of mortgage loans outstanding, of which $1.2 billion were multi-family mortage loans. Another $0.2 billion was 1-to-4 family mortgage loans, and the remainder related to commercial real estate, or construction. At March 31, 1998, QCSB's cumulative gap between its interest rate sensitive assets and interest rate sensitive liabilities repricing within a one-year period was a negative 15.31%. Since 1996, the majority of QCSB's multi-family mortgage loan originations have featured a fixed rate of interest for the first five years of the loan, and an adjustable rate of interest in year six through 10. At the same time, the company has increasingly utilized higher cost CDs and FHLB borrowings as its primary sources of funding. Prior to 1996, the majority of QCSB's multi-family mortgage loan originations included an annual rate increase of 50 basis points in the first five years of the mortgage, regardless of the direction of market interest rates. At June 30, 1998, $294 million, or 25.5% of the portfolio, included this step-up rate of interest.

To enhance its funding, QCSB has initiated a Mobile Teller program in cooperation with Queens College in Fresh Meadows. Under this program, a branch manager and a customer service representative are to visit the college on a regular basis, and QCSB planned to install an ATM at the college.

Per Share Data ($)

(Year Ended Dec. 31)	1997	1996	1995	1994	1993	1992	1991	1990	1989	1988
Tangible Bk. Val.	7.62	8.21	7.68	7.23	6.22	NA	NA	NA	NA	NA
Earnings	1.07	0.84	0.76	0.67	0.45	0.39	NA	NA	NA	NA
Dividends	0.41	0.25	0.07	0.02	Nil	Nil	Nil	Nil	Nil	Nil
Payout Ratio	38%	0%	0%	0%	Nil	Nil	Nil	Nil	Nil	Nil
Prices - High	27	15	9½	7⅛	5⅛	NA	NA	NA	NA	NA
- Low	13⅜	8½	5⅜	4⅞	3¾	NA	NA	NA	NA	NA
P/E Ratio - High	25	18	12	10	11	NA	NA	NA	NA	NA
- Low	13	10	7	7	8	NA	NA	NA	NA	NA

Income Statement Analysis (Million $)

	1997	1996	1995	1994	1993	1992	1991	1990	1989	1988
Net Int. Inc.	62.4	57.5	51.9	54.6	46.4	38.8	NA	NA	NA	NA
Loan Loss Prov.	Nil	NM	0.1	1.2	4.7	3.2	NA	NA	NA	NA
Non Int. Inc.	2.3	2.4	3.0	2.0	1.9	2.0	NA	NA	NA	NA
Non Int. Exp.	27.1	23.3	22.9	23.0	21.4	18.0	NA	NA	NA	NA
Pretax Inc.	37.6	38.7	31.9	32.3	22.2	-19.7	NA	NA	NA	NA
Eff. Tax Rate	38%	46%	37%	42%	45%	42%	NA	NA	NA	NA
Net Inc.	23.3	20.9	20.2	18.8	12.1	-11.4	NA	NA	NA	NA
% Net Int. Marg.	4.50	4.60	4.60	5.10	NA	NA	NA	NA	NA	NA

Balance Sheet & Other Fin. Data (Million $)

	1997	1996	1995	1994	1993	1992	1991	1990	1989	1988
Total Assets	1,603	1,359	1,241	1,171	1,090	951	NA	NA	NA	NA
Loans	1,395	1,146	995	938	779	685	NA	NA	NA	NA
Deposits	1,069	1,024	932	840	827	824	NA	NA	NA	NA
Capitalization:										
Debt	Nil	Nil	Nil	Nil	Nil	Nil	Nil	Nil	Nil	Nil
Equity	171	211	218	205	193	-92.4	NA	NA	NA	NA
Total	171	219	218	205	193	-92.4	NA	NA	NA	NA
% Ret. on Assets	1.6	1.6	1.7	NA	1.2	NA	NA	NA	NA	NA
% Ret. on Equity	12.2	9.8	9.5	NA	24.0	NA	NA	NA	NA	NA
% Loan Loss Resv.	0.9	0.8	1.1	1.2	1.3	0.9	NA	NA	NA	NA
% Risk Based Capital	15.3	17.4	NA	NA	NA	NA	NA	NA	NA	NA
Price Times Book Value:										
Hi	3.5	1.8	1.2	1.0	NA	NA	NA	NA	NA	NA
Low	1.8	1.0	0.7	0.7	0.6	NA	NA	NA	NA	NA

Data as orig. reptd.; bef. results of disc opers. and/or spec. items. Per share data adj. for stk. divs. as of ex-div. date. Bold denotes diluted EPS (FASB 128). E-Estimated. NA-Not Available. NM-Not Meaningful. NR-Not Ranked.

Office—38-25 Main St., Flushing, NY 11354. Tel—(718) 359-6400. Chrmn, Pres & CEO—J. R. Ficalora. EVP & Secy—M. J. Lincks. CFO—R. Wann. VP & Investor Contact—Ilene A. Angarola (Ext. 275). Dirs—D. M. Blake, J. G. Chisholm, D. Ciampa, J. R. Ficalora, H. E. Froebel, H. E. Johnson, M. L. Kupferberg, L. D. Lynch, H. C. Miller, R. H. O'Neill. Transfer Agent & Registrar—ChaseMellon Shareholder Services, Ridgefield Park, NJ. Incorporated—in Delaware in 1993. Empl— 275. S&P Analyst: T.A.G.

STANDARD &POOR'S
STOCK REPORTS

RailTex, Inc.

5056

NASDAQ Symbol **RTEX**

In S&P SmallCap 600

10-OCT-98

Industry: Railroads

Summary: RTEX is a short-line railroad organization, providing freight service in the U.S., Canada and Mexico.

Quantitative Evaluations

Outlook
(1 Lowest—5 Highest)
- **5**

Fair Value
- **18½**

Risk
- **Average**

Earn./Div. Rank
- **B+**

Technical Eval.
- **Bullish** since 5/98

Rel. Strength Rank
(1 Lowest—99 Highest)
- **28**

Insider Activity
- **NA**

Recent Price • 9⅜

52 Wk Range • 19⅜-7½

Yield • Nil

12-Mo. P/E • 7.4

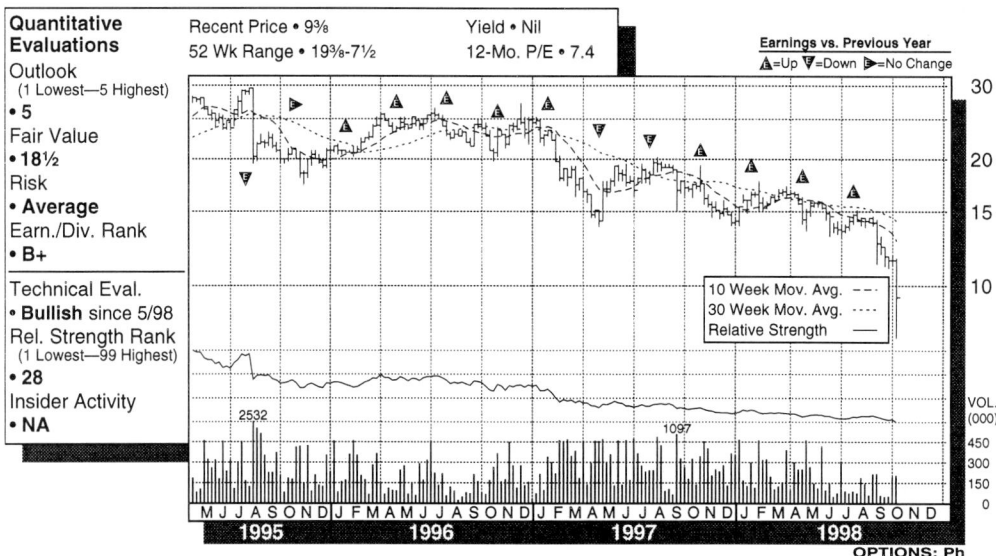

Earnings vs. Previous Year
▲=Up ▼=Down ▶=No Change

10 Week Mov. Avg. – – –
30 Week Mov. Avg. · · · ·
Relative Strength ——

OPTIONS: Ph

Business Profile - 16-SEP-98

In June 1998, RTEX acquired, for $14.3 million, Central Properties, Inc., a privately held company that owns 100% of two railroads in Ohio and Indiana. The Central Railroad of Indianapolis (CERA) operates over about 73 miles of rail line in north central Indiana: a 17-mile north-south line between Kokomo and Tipton, IN, and a 56-mile east-west line from Marion through Kokomo to Frankfort, IN. The Central Railroad of Indiana (CIND) owns and operates about 81 miles of rail line between Cincinnati, OH and Shelbyville, IN. The CIND also has overhead trackage rights over 96 miles between Shelbyville and Frankfort, which allows for connection with the CERA. In August 1998, RTEX's Canadian unit agreed to acquire a 99-mile rail line between Silver and London, Ontario.

Operational Review - 16-SEP-98

Operating revenues in the six months ended June 30, 1998, advanced 8.4%, year to year. The number of carloads transported rose 13%, but the average revenue per carload was 3.6% lower. Margins widened on lower diesel fuel costs and equipment rent expenses; operating income was up 13%. After higher other income, and taxes at 37.6%, versus 39.5%, net income climbed 24%, to $4,948,000 ($0.54 a share), from $3,993,000 ($0.43).

Stock Performance - 09-OCT-98

In the past 30 trading days, RTEX's shares have declined 34%, compared to a 4% fall in the S&P 500. Average trading volume for the past five days was 40,200 shares, compared with the 40-day moving average of 25,872 shares.

Key Stock Statistics

Dividend Rate/Share	Nil	Shareholders	400
Shs. outstg. (M)	9.2	Market cap. (B)	$0.086
Avg. daily vol. (M)	0.024	Inst. holdings	50%
Tang. Bk. Value/Share	15.05		
Beta	NA		

Value of $10,000 invested 5 years ago: NA

Fiscal Year Ending Dec. 31

	1998	1997	1996	1995	1994	1993
Revenues (Million $)						
1Q	38.41	34.18	28.61	25.14	17.80	—
2Q	39.14	37.37	30.15	27.30	18.41	—
3Q	—	37.97	29.86	27.50	19.18	—
4Q	—	39.28	32.49	27.90	19.14	18.15
Yr.	—	148.8	121.1	107.8	74.53	59.85
Earnings Per Share ($)						
1Q	0.27	0.17	0.24	0.22	0.15	—
2Q	0.27	0.26	0.28	0.07	0.26	—
3Q	—	0.31	0.25	0.22	0.22	—
4Q	—	0.41	0.31	0.27	0.25	—
Yr.	—	1.15	1.08	0.78	0.88	0.65

Next earnings report expected: early November

Dividend Data

No cash dividends have been paid.

 *A Division of The McGraw-Hill Companies*

STANDARD
&POOR'S
STOCK REPORTS

RailTex, Inc.

5056

10-OCT-98

Business Summary - 16-SEP-98

RailTex, Inc. (RTEX), which believes it is the leading operator of short-line freight railroads in North America, began operating its first railroad in 1984. The company built its portfolio of railroads through purchase, lease or contract to operate. Of the 30 railroads RailTex had acquired as of year-end 1997, 19 were owned, four leased, four partially owned and partially leased, two operated under long-term contracts, and one ceased operations in 1996.

Freight revenues by type of traffic in recent years:

	1997	1996
Interline	76%	85%
Local	11%	11%
Bridge	13%	4%

Interline traffic either originates or terminates with customers located along a rail line and is interchanged with other rail carriers. Local traffic both originates and terminates on the same rail line and does not involve other rail carriers. Bridge traffic neither originates nor terminates on a rail carrier's line, but rather passes over the line from one connecting rail carrier to another.

RTEX was operating through subsidiaries, as of year-end 1997, on about 3,900 miles of track in 22 states, Canada and Mexico. Other interests as of that date were a 10% interest in the Ferrovia Centro Atlan-

tica, which operates a 4,400-mile railroad in central and eastern Brazil, and 6% of Ferrovia Sul Atlantica, which operates a 4,200-mile railroad in southern Brazil. RTEX railroads transported almost 490,000 carloads of freight for about 900 customers in 1997. Traffic that originated or terminated on RTEX's lines generated more than 86% of its freight revenues in that year.

RTEX's strategy is to grow through additions to its portfolio of short line railroad properties, primarily through strategic acquisitions of Class I railroad divestitures or independently owned shortlines which complement its current base of railroad properties; creation of new business on currently owned properties; and improvement in the operating performance of newly added and currently operated properties.

In February 1997, RTEX acquired the assets of the former Detroit, Toledo & Ironton Railroad (DTI) from Canadian National Railway. RTEX acquired 146 miles of track for $22.0 million and, with trackage rights, will operate over about 255 miles of track between Flat Rock, MI, and Cincinnati, OH. RTEX has committed to return the former DTI track to Federal Railroad Administration Class IV standards, over a three year period. As a result, as of December 31, 1997, RTEX had spent $7.0 million and expects to spend an additional $5.0 million on the rehabilitation project in 1998. In addition, up to $5.0 million of the purchase price is subject to reimbursement if certain levels of carloadings are not achieved within a specified time period.

Per Share Data ($)

(Year Ended Dec. 31)	1997	1996	1995	1994	1993	1992	1991	1990	1989	1988
Tangible Bk. Val.	14.55	13.45	12.36	10.11	9.18	NA	NA	NA	NA	NA
Cash Flow	2.56	2.18	1.70	1.55	1.41	1.05	NA	NA	NA	NA
Earnings	1.15	1.08	0.78	0.88	0.65	0.52	0.39	0.38	NA	NA
Dividends	Nil	Nil	Nil	Nil	Nil	Nil	Nil	Nil	Nil	Nil
Payout Ratio	Nil	Nil	Nil	Nil	Nil	Nil	Nil	Nil	Nil	Nil
Prices - High	25¼	27⅜	29½	31½	28¼	NA	NA	NA	NA	NA
- Low	13¾	19¾	17¼	15⅝	16½	NA	NA	NA	NA	NA
P/E Ratio - High	22	25	38	36	43	NA	NA	NA	NA	NA
- Low	12	18	22	18	25	NA	NA	NA	NA	NA

Income Statement Analysis (Million $)

	1997	1996	1995	1994	1993	1992	1991	1990	1989	1988
Revs.	149	121	108	74.5	59.8	39.3	27.6	21.4	NA	NA
Oper. Inc.	35.9	32.2	26.0	18.4	14.5	9.9	NA	NA	NA	NA
Depr.	12.9	10.1	8.2	5.2	4.2	2.8	NA	NA	NA	NA
Int. Exp.	10.5	6.9	5.7	2.9	4.7	2.8	1.5	1.0	NA	NA
Pretax Inc.	16.7	16.7	11.7	11.5	6.1	4.5	2.9	2.4	NA	NA
Eff. Tax Rate	36%	40%	41%	40%	40%	40%	37%	35%	NA	NA
Net Inc.	10.6	10.0	6.9	6.9	3.6	2.7	1.8	1.6	NA	NA

Balance Sheet & Other Fin. Data (Million $)

	1997	1996	1995	1994	1993	1992	1991	1990	1989	1988
Cash	0.6	2.1	2.1	2.2	6.9	NA	NA	NA	NA	NA
Curr. Assets	37.0	32.6	26.0	17.0	18.8	NA	NA	NA	NA	NA
Total Assets	320	269	205	140	113	81.0	45.0	34.0	NA	NA
Curr. Liab.	44.4	32.8	21.0	16.9	11.3	NA	NA	NA	NA	NA
LT Debt	118	92.3	57.2	38.9	27.0	NA	NA	NA	NA	NA
Common Eqty.	133	123	113	72.4	65.7	25.0	22.2	13.6	NA	NA
Total Cap.	272	233	181	120	100	NA	NA	NA	NA	NA
Cap. Exp.	35.5	28.0	63.6	31.5	27.6	35.8	NA	NA	NA	NA
Cash Flow	23.6	20.1	15.1	12.1	7.9	5.5	NA	NA	NA	NA
Curr. Ratio	0.8	1.0	1.2	1.0	1.7	NA	NA	NA	NA	NA
% LT Debt of Cap.	43.4	39.7	31.6	32.5	27.1	NA	NA	NA	NA	NA
% Net Inc.of Revs.	7.1	8.2	6.4	9.2	6.1	6.9	6.5	7.3	NA	NA
% Ret. on Assets	3.6	4.2	4.0	5.4	3.7	4.3	4.5	NA	NA	NA
% Ret. on Equity	8.3	8.5	7.5	10.0	8.0	11.4	10.0	NA	NA	NA

Data as orig. reptd.; bef. results of disc. opers. and/or spec. items. Per share data adj. for stk. divs. as of ex-div. date. Bold denotes diluted EPS (FASB 128). E-Estimated. NA-Not Available. NM-Not Meaningful. NR-Not Ranked.

Office—4040 Broadway, Suite 200, San Antonio, TX 78209. **Tel**—(210) 841-7600. **Chrmn**—B. M. Flohr. **Pres & CEO**—R. A. Rittenmeyer. **VP-Fin & CFO**—L. D. Davies. **Dirs**—R. M. Ayres Jr., L. D. Davies, B. M. Flohr, H. J. Gradison, R. R. Lende, F. C. Meyer Jr., P. L. Moe, R. A. Rittenmeyer. **Transfer Agent & Registrar**—ChaseMellon Shareholder Services, Ridgefield Park, NJ. **Incorporated**—in Texas in 1977. **Empl**— 900. **S&P Analyst:** W.P.A.

Ralcorp Holdings

1892C

NYSE Symbol **RAH**

In S&P SmallCap 600

14-OCT-98

Industry: Foods

Summary: Ralcorp produces and sells private label cereals, baby foods and crackers.

Quantitative Evaluations	Recent Price • 13¾	Yield • Nil
	52 Wk Range • 21⅝-13	12-Mo. P/E • 12.4

Outlook (1 Lowest—5 Highest)
• **4+**

Fair Value
• **21⅛**

Risk
• **High**

Earn./Div. Rank
• **NR**

Technical Eval.
• **Bearish** since 9/98

Rel. Strength Rank (1 Lowest—99 Highest)
• **36**

Insider Activity
• **Neutral**

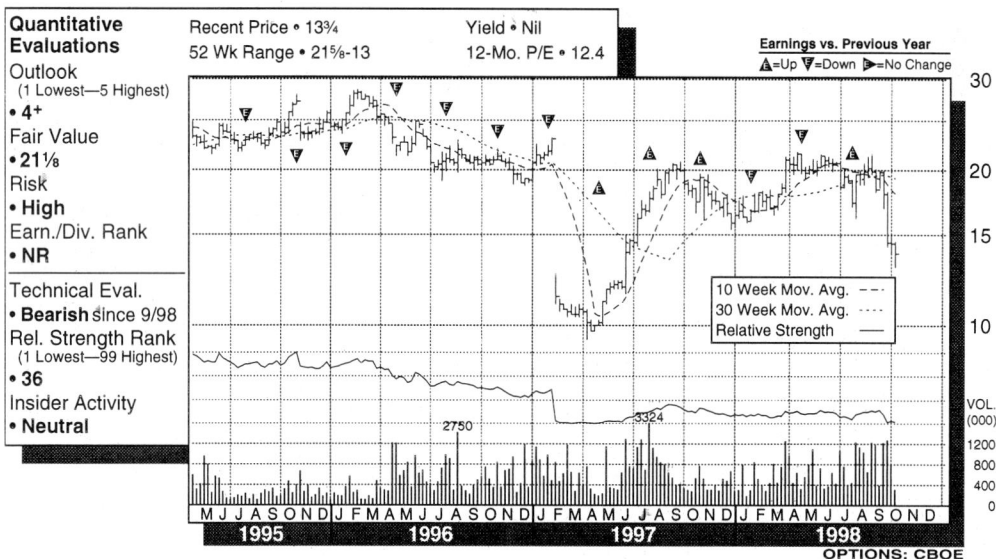

Earnings vs. Previous Year
▲=Up ▼=Down ▶=No Change

10 Week Mov. Avg. ---
30 Week Mov. Avg. ·····
Relative Strength —

OPTIONS: CBOE

Business Profile - 14-OCT-98

RAH recently acquired Nutcracker Brands, Inc., a producer of snack nut products in the jar and can, with annual estimated sales of $42 million. Separately, the company sold its Beech-Nut Nutrition baby food unit to the Milnot Co., for $68 million. In August 1998, RAH's Bremner unit acquired Sugar Kake Cookie, Inc., a cookie maker with $29 million in sales. In January 1997, RAH sold its ski and resort operation (valued at $310 million) to Vail Resorts, Inc.; Vail Resorts assumed about $165 million of RAH's debt, and RAH received a 22.6% equity interest in the newly combined Vail Resorts, Inc. In September 1998, RAH completed a share repurchase program.

Operational Review - 14-OCT-98

Pro forma net sales in the nine months ended June 30, 1998, rose 22%, year to year, reflecting strong growth in the company's private label cereal, and cracker and cookie divisions. Profitability benefited from the increased sales and an improved product mix. With well controlled operating costs and expenses and higher equity in earnings of Vail Resorts, and in the absence of a restructuring charge, net income soared to $29.4 million ($0.86 a share, diluted), from $3.5 million ($0.11).

Stock Performance - 09-OCT-98

In the past 30 trading days, RAH's shares have declined 31%, compared to a 4% fall in the S&P 500. Average trading volume for the past five days was 59,440 shares, compared with the 40-day moving average of 202,323 shares.

Key Stock Statistics

Dividend Rate/Share	Nil	Shareholders	18,800
Shs. outstg. (M)	32.5	Market cap. (B)	$0.453
Avg. daily vol. (M)	0.184	Inst. holdings	65%
Tang. Bk. Value/Share	9.44		
Beta	NA		

Value of $10,000 invested 5 years ago: NA

Fiscal Year Ending Sep. 30

	1998	1997	1996	1995	1994	1993
Revenues (Million $)						
1Q	137.2	292.9	295.3	278.4	267.1	248.8
2Q	147.1	161.4	277.4	258.3	262.7	231.5
3Q	143.3	140.7	230.1	231.5	220.5	205.9
4Q	—	144.7	224.6	245.2	236.7	216.6
Yr.	—	739.7	1,027	1,013	987.0	903.0
Earnings Per Share ($)						
1Q	0.14	0.40	0.44	0.51	0.49	0.48
2Q	0.32	15.47	0.64	0.65	0.71	0.51
3Q	0.40	0.09	-0.50	0.15	0.28	0.30
4Q	—	0.15	-2.02	-0.32	0.11	0.21
Yr.	—	16.11	-1.42	1.00	1.59	1.20

Next earnings report expected: early November

Dividend Data (Dividends have been paid since 1997.)

The company does not anticipate paying cash dividends on its common stock in the near future.

A Division of The McGraw·Hill Companies

Business Summary - 14-OCT-98

After the dust settled from a corporate restructuring by the company's former parent, Ralcorp Holdings, Inc. (Old Ralcorp), that included the formation of the company (Ralcorp Holdings, Inc.) to facilitate Old Ralcorp's divestiture of its branded cereal and snack business, RAH was left with operations consisting of Beech-Nut baby foods, private-label cereals, and private label crackers and cookies. In January 1997, as part of the restructuring, the company sold its branded cereal and snack business to General Mills, Inc., for $570 million in stock and debt. Also in January, RAH sold its resort operations and related ski resort properties to Vail Resorts, Inc., in exchange for the assumption of $165 million of debt and an approximate 22.6% equity interest in Vail Resorts, Inc.

The private label cereal business accounts for about half of Ralcorp's sales. Ready-to-eat cereals consist of 24 different types of private label cereals, manufactured for approximately 275 customers. The hot cereal products include old fashioned oatmeal, quick oats, plain instant oatmeal, flavored instant oatmeal, farina and instant Ralston, a branded hot wheat cereal. The private label cereal business also sells hot cereal under the brand Three Minute Oats.

RAH believes that its cracker and cookie business is currently the largest private label cracker manufacturer and a producer of private label cookies for sale in the U.S. This business also produces Ry Krisp branded crackers. In April 1997, the company acquired Wortz Co., one of the largest U.S. makers of private label crackers and cookies, in order to expand its private label food business. Wortz, with annual sales of about $70 million, was added to Bremner, Inc., RAH's private label cracker and cookie unit. Wortz sells mainly to grocery wholesalers, while Bremner focuses on selling directly to supermarket chains.

The baby food business produces baby food, juice and cereal under the Beach Nut brand. The brand is positioned as a high quality product that does not contain additives such as sugar and starch in most of its food items.

Resort operations included the operation of the Keystone, Arapahoe Basin and Breckenridge ski resorts located in Summit County, CO. Vail Resorts, Inc., through the transaction in January 1997, became the world's largest skiing company, based both on revenues and skier days.

In November 1997, directors authorized the repurcahse of up to 1,000,000 common shares.

Per Share Data ($)

(Year Ended Sep. 30)	1997	1996	1995	1994	1993	1992	1991	1990	1989	1988
Tangible Bk. Val.	8.69	3.26	4.88	2.65	NA	NA	NA	NA	NA	NA
Cash Flow	16.84	NA	2.36	3.39	2.22	NA	NA	NA	NA	NA
Earnings	16.11	-1.42	1.00	1.59	1.20	NA	NA	NA	NA	NA
Dividends	Nil	Nil	Nil	Nil	NA	NA	NA	NA	NA	NA
Payout Ratio	Nil	Nil	Nil	Nil	NA	NA	NA	NA	NA	NA
Prices - High	23⅛	28⅝	28	24⅛	NA	NA	NA	NA	NA	NA
- Low	9⅜	18⅝	21⅜	13½	NA	NA	NA	NA	NA	NA
P/E Ratio - High	1	NM	28	15	NA	NA	NA	NA	NA	NA
- Low	1	NM	21	8	NA	NA	NA	NA	NA	NA

Income Statement Analysis (Million $)

	1997	1996	1995	1994	1993	1992	1991	1990	1989	1988
Revs.	740	1,027	1,013	987	903	NA	NA	NA	NA	NA
Oper. Inc.	73.8	126	152	161	131	NA	NA	NA	NA	NA
Depr.	24.4	46.4	46.7	60.6	35.3	NA	NA	NA	NA	NA
Int. Exp.	7.9	26.8	28.2	12.3	27.2	NA	NA	NA	NA	NA
Pretax Inc.	542	-73.1	54.8	87.9	67.8	NA	NA	NA	NA	NA
Eff. Tax Rate	1.90%	NM	39%	39%	39%	NA	NA	NA	NA	NA
Net Inc.	532	-46.8	33.4	53.6	41.2	NA	NA	NA	NA	NA

Balance Sheet & Other Fin. Data (Million $)

	1997	1996	1995	1994	1993	1992	1991	1990	1989	1988
Cash	8.4	Nil	Nil	Nil	4.2	NA	NA	NA	NA	NA
Curr. Assets	143	193	208	184	166	NA	NA	NA	NA	NA
Total Assets	400	627	716	700	685	NA	NA	NA	NA	NA
Curr. Liab.	78.2	102	105	112	123	NA	NA	NA	NA	NA
LT Debt	Nil	377	395	389	383	NA	NA	NA	NA	NA
Common Eqty.	287	107	162	141	130	NA	NA	NA	NA	NA
Total Cap.	287	484	578	560	53.8	NA	NA	NA	NA	NA
Cap. Exp.	41.6	66.7	66.1	84.4	NA	NA	NA	NA	NA	NA
Cash Flow	556	0.4	80.1	114	76.5	NA	NA	NA	NA	NA
Curr. Ratio	1.8	1.9	2.0	1.6	1.4	NA	NA	NA	NA	NA
% LT Debt of Cap.	Nil	77.8	68.4	69.6	71.1	NA	NA	NA	NA	NA
% Net Inc.of Revs.	71.9	NM	3.3	5.4	4.4	NA	NA	NA	NA	NA
% Ret. on Assets	270.0	NM	4.8	NA	NA	NA	NA	NA	NA	NA
% Ret. on Equity	104.0	NM	22.0	NA	NA	NA	NA	NA	NA	NA

Data as orig. reptd.; bef. results of disc. opers. and/or spec. items. Per share data adj. for stk. divs. as of ex-div. date. Bold denotes diluted EPS (FASB 128). E-Estimated. NA-Not Available. NM-Not Meaningful. NR-Not Ranked.

Office—800 Market Street, Suite 2900, St. Louis, MO 63101.**Tel**—(314) 877-7000. **Website**—http://www.ralcorp.com **Chrmn**—W. P. Stiritz. **Pres, CEO & CFO**—J. R. Micheletto. **VP & Treas**—D. J. Sescleifer. **VP & Secy**—R. W. Lockwood. **Investor Contact**—Patrick T. Farrell (314-982-4350). **Dirs**—W. H. Danforth, W. D. George, Jr., J. W. Goodall, D. W. Kemper, J. R. Micheletto, W. P. Stiritz. **Transfer Agent & Registrar**—First Chicago Trust Co. of New York, Jersey City, NJ. **Incorporated**—in Missouri in 1994. **Empl**— 2,500. **S&P Analyst:** S.S.

Raymond James Financial   1896

NYSE Symbol **RJF**

In S&P SmallCap 600

03-OCT-98

Industry: Investment Banking/ Brokerage

Summary: This holding company is engaged, through subsidiaries, in securities brokerage, investment banking, financial planning and investment advisory and related financial services.

Quantitative Evaluations

Outlook
(1 Lowest—5 Highest)
• **NA**

Fair Value
• **NA**

Risk
• **Average**

Earn./Div. Rank
• **A-**

Technical Eval.
• **Bearish** since 8/98

Rel. Strength Rank
(1 Lowest—99 Highest)
• **44**

Insider Activity
• **Neutral**

Recent Price • 20
52 Wk Range • 36½-17
Yield • 1.2%
12-Mo. P/E • 10.3

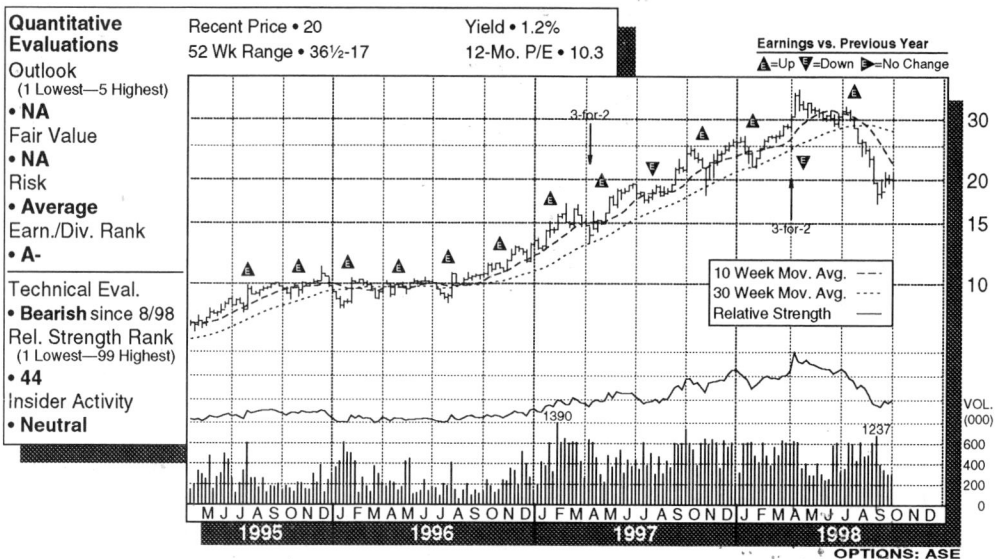

Earnings vs. Previous Year
▲=Up ▼=Down ▶=No Change

10 Week Mov. Avg. – – –
30 Week Mov. Avg. · · · ·
Relative Strength —

OPTIONS: ASE

Business Profile - 05-AUG-98

As bull market conditions continued in the securities markets, RJF realized record levels of revenues in the first nine months of FY 98 (Sep.). Overall favorable results have been propelled by increases in the number of RJF financial advisors to more than 3,200 throughout the U.S. and overseas, and by improved productivity, heightened investment banking activity, and an ongoing rise in assets under management. Net income in the FY 98 third quarter included $2.7 million from the sale of stock and residual interests of the RJ Properties subsidiary. The company is increasing publicity by contracting to have the new Tampa, FL, football facility of the Tampa Bay Buccaneers be named Raymond James Stadium. The stadium will be the site of Super Bowl XXXV in January 2001. The shares were split three-for-two in April 1998. The James family owns 38% of the common stock.

Operational Review - 05-AUG-98

Total revenues in the nine months ended June 30, 1998, rose 21%, year to year, to $795.6 million; excluding a $30.6 million gain on the sale of the Liberty Investment Management subsidiary in January 1997, revenues were 27% higher. Expenses rose 27%, reflecting higher employee compensation; pretax income was down 3.6% lower. After taxes at 38.3%, versus 38.6%, net income slid 3.0%, to $70,236,000 ($1.41 a share), from $72,438,000 ($1.50, as adjusted).

Stock Performance - 02-OCT-98

In the past 30 trading days, RJF's shares have declined 13%, compared to a 7% fall in the S&P 500. Average trading volume for the past five days was 60,000 shares, compared with the 40-day moving average of 107,300 shares.

Key Stock Statistics

Dividend Rate/Share	0.24	Shareholders	10,000
Shs. outstg. (M)	48.4	Market cap. (B)	$0.969
Avg. daily vol. (M)	0.080	Inst. holdings	36%
Tang. Bk. Value/Share	10.19		
Beta	1.80		

Value of $10,000 invested 5 years ago: $ 32,695

Fiscal Year Ending Sep. 30

	1998	1997	1996	1995	1994	1993
Revenues (Million $)						
1Q	252.3	194.8	152.0	115.7	134.4	93.31
2Q	267.5	250.0	178.7	125.7	130.1	112.4
3Q	275.8	210.1	198.2	148.9	117.7	114.1
4Q	—	272.7	192.8	163.7	124.9	192.0
Yr.	—	927.6	721.8	554.1	507.1	451.8
Earnings Per Share ($)						
1Q	**0.47**	0.36	0.27	0.17	0.28	0.21
2Q	**0.50**	0.79	0.32	0.22	0.25	0.26
3Q	**0.46**	0.05	0.39	0.30	0.18	0.24
4Q	—	0.54	0.41	0.31	0.19	0.30
Yr.	—	2.04	1.40	0.99	0.88	1.01

Next earnings report expected: late October

Dividend Data (Dividends have been paid since 1985.)

Amount ($)	Date Decl.	Ex-Div. Date	Stock of Record	Payment Date
0.060	Feb. 17	Mar. 06	Mar. 10	Apr. 02 '98
3-for-2	Feb. 17	Apr. 03	Mar. 10	Apr. 02 '98
0.060	May. 15	Jun. 05	Jun. 09	Jul. 02 '98
0.060	Aug. 21	Sep. 09	Sep. 11	Oct. 01 '98

A Division of The McGraw-Hill Companies

Raymond James Financial, Inc.

Business Summary - 05-AUG-98

Raymond James Financial is a financial services holding company that, through operating subsidiaries, is engaged in securities brokerage, investment banking, investment advisory services, financial planning and management of limited partnerships. Segment contributions to revenues in recent fiscal years (Sep.) were:

	FY 97	FY 96	FY 95
Securities commissions	57.4%	58.5%	59.1%
Interest	17.4%	17.5%	17.5%
Investment banking	12.2%	10.1%	7.8%
Investment advisory	6.2%	7.0%	7.7%
Financial services fees	2.7%	2.5%	2.7%
Other	4.1%	4.4%	5.2%

The company's principal subsidiary, Raymond James & Associates, Inc. (RJA), is a regional brokerage with 47 retail offices (32 in Florida). It also operates 21 institutional offices, six of which are in Europe. RJA is the largest brokerage and investment concern headquartered in Florida. Activities include trading of securities; sales of mutual funds; institutional sales and research; corporate finance; origination, syndication and marketing of limited partnerships (primarily in the real estate, equipment leasing and telecommunications industries); and distribution and underwriting of municipal securities.

Other operating subsidiaries include Investment Management & Research Inc., an independent financial planning organization that also distributes all securities offered by RJA to its retail customers through 581 offices and satellites in all 50 states; Robert Thomas Securities Inc., which operates 405 branch offices and 136 satellite offices in all 50 states; Eagle Asset Management Inc., which provides investment advisory services and had $3.7 billion under management at September 26, 1997, up from $2.4 billion a year earlier; and Heritage Asset Management Inc., which manages 11 RJF-sponsored mutual funds with assets of about $3.2 billion at September 26, 1997, up from $2.4 billion a year earlier.

The investment banking group is involved in public and private debt and equity financing for corporate clients, as well as merger and acquisition consulting services. It also originates, syndicates and markets public and private limited partnerships, primarily in the real estate and equipment leasing industries. In May 1994, the company formed Raymond James Bank, whose three branches, located in Hudson, Spring Hill and Crystal River, FL, were purchased from the Resolution Trust Corp. At the end of FY 97, the bank had total assets of approximately $329 million, up from $227 million a year earlier.

Per Share Data ($) (Year Ended Sep. 30)	1997	1996	1995	1994	1993	1992	1991	1990	1989	1988
Tangible Bk. Val.	8.87	6.95	5.74	4.93	4.28	3.37	2.60	2.04	1.63	1.37
Cash Flow	2.32	NA	NA	NA	NA	NA	NA	NA	NA	NA
Earnings	2.04	1.40	0.99	0.88	1.01	0.84	0.56	0.41	0.29	0.13
Dividends	0.18	0.17	0.20	0.14	0.09	0.07	0.04	0.03	0.03	0.02
Payout Ratio	9%	12%	20%	16%	9%	8%	8%	8%	9%	16%
Prices - High	26 5/8	11 1/2	11 1/4	8 3/8	9	8 3/4	6 3/8	3	2 1/2	1 5/8
- Low	12 1/2	8 1/2	6 1/8	5 7/8	6	4 1/2	2 1/8	1 7/8	1 3/8	1 3/16
P/E Ratio - High	13	8	11	10	9	10	11	7	9	13
- Low	6	6	6	7	6	5	4	5	5	9
Income Statement Analysis (Million $)										
Commissions	515	422	328	303	276	204	150	126	116	94.0
Int. Inc.	156	126	97.2	58.5	33.6	36.4	55.0	61.3	55.8	35.4
Total Revs.	915	722	554	507	452	361	286	257	226	170
Int. Exp.	101	83.5	64.8	36.2	17.2	21.4	40.3	48.6	44.7	28.2
Pretax Inc.	161	109	74.5	67.2	80.3	65.8	43.5	29.2	20.5	9.1
Eff. Tax Rate	38%	39%	38%	37%	39%	38%	39%	39%	40%	39%
Net Inc.	99	66.0	46.1	42.1	49.3	41.0	26.7	17.9	12.4	5.5
Balance Sheet & Other Fin. Data (Million $)										
Total Assets	3,279	2,566	2,013	1,698	1,448	806	1,060	948	830	534
Cash Items	197	735	454	296	208	231	334	275	251	172
Receivables	1,933	1,377	1,247	1,124	1,088	482	655	608	522	306
Secs. Owned	411	333	201	179	72.1	33.5	31.8	32.5	26.5	26.8
Sec. Borrowed	Nil	Nil	Nil	Nil	Nil	Nil	Nil	Nil	Nil	Nil
Due Brokers & Cust.	2,628	2,047	1,637	1,359	1,142	573	869	810	709	433
Other Liabs.	213	168	96.9	99	86.8	58.6	54.6	27.9	21.9	14.0
Capitalization:										
Debt	14.2	24.7	13.1	13.2	13.4	13.5	13.6	13.7	27.8	27.9
Equity	423	327	266	227	206	161	122	97.0	72.0	60.0
Total	437	352	279	240	219	174	136	111	99	87.0
% Return On Revs.	10.8	9.1	8.3	8.3	10.9	11.4	9.3	7.0	5.5	3.2
% Ret. on Assets	3.4	2.9	2.5	2.7	4.4	4.4	2.7	2.0	1.8	0.8
% Ret. on Equity	26.4	22.3	18.7	19.4	26.9	29.0	24.4	21.3	19.0	9.4

Data as orig. reptd.; bef. results of disc opers. and/or spec. items. Per share data adj. for stk. divs. as of ex-div. date. Bold denotes diluted EPS (FASB 128). E-Estimated. NA-Not Available. NM-Not Meaningful. NR-Not Ranked.

Office—880 Carillon Parkway, St. Petersburg, FL 33716. **Tel**—(813) 573-3800. **Website**—http://www.rjf.com **Chrmn & CEO**—T. A. James. **Pres**—F. S. Godbold. **Treas**—L. Pippenger. **VP-Fin & CFO**—J. P. Julien. **SVP & Secy**—B. S. Augenbraun. **VP & Investor Contact**—Lawrence A. Silver. **Dirs**—A. Biever, J. A. Bulkley, T. S. Franke, F. S. Godbold, M. A. Greene, H. H. Hill Jr., H.A. James, T. A. James, P. W. Marshall, J. S. Putnam, R. F. Shuck, D. W. Zank. **Transfer Agent & Registrar**—Mellon Financial Services, Pittsburgh. **Incorporated**—in Florida in 1974. **Empl**—3,244. **S&P Analyst:** Thomas W. Smith, CFA

STANDARD &POOR'S
STOCK REPORTS

Read-Rite Corp.

5066R

Nasdaq Symbol **RDRT**

In S&P SmallCap 600

03-OCT-98

Industry: Computers (Peripherals)

Summary: This company is the leading independent supplier of magnetic recording heads for rigid disk drives.

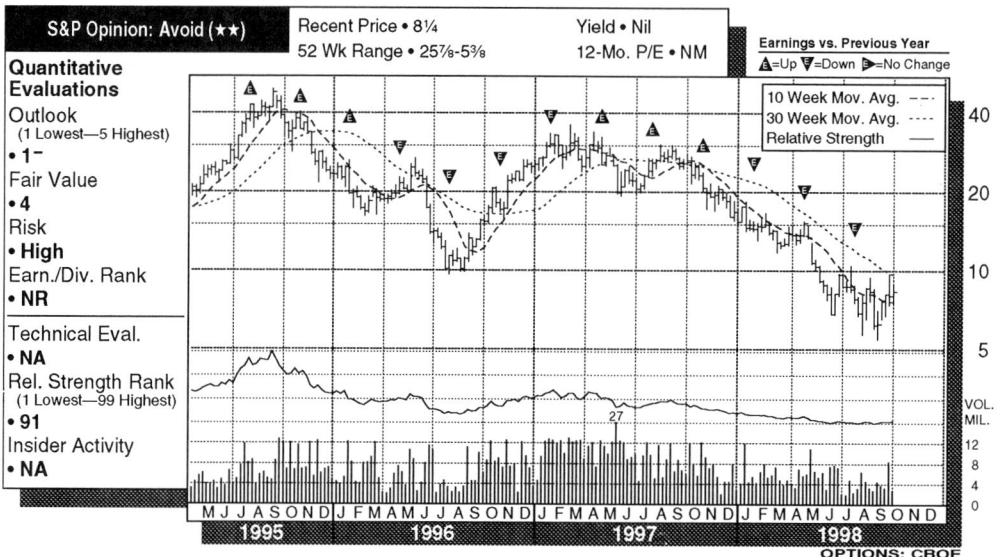

S&P Opinion: Avoid (★★)	Recent Price • 8¼	Yield • Nil
	52 Wk Range • 25⅞-5⅜	12-Mo. P/E • NM

Quantitative Evaluations

Outlook (1 Lowest—5 Highest)
• **1⁻**

Fair Value
• **4**

Risk
• **High**

Earn./Div. Rank
• **NR**

Technical Eval.
• **NA**

Rel. Strength Rank (1 Lowest—99 Highest)
• **91**

Insider Activity
• **NA**

Earnings vs. Previous Year
▲=Up ▼=Down ▶=No Change

10 Week Mov. Avg. – – –
30 Week Mov. Avg. · · · ·
Relative Strength —

OPTIONS: CBOE

Overview - 22-JUL-98

Revenues should decline about 30% in FY 98 (Sep.), reflecting pricing pressures and slower demand for recording heads. The company is also being hurt by a trend toward fewer heads per drive, resulting from lower PC prices. Gross margin has been negative for three consecutive quarters, although the company has been improving its cost structure. Operating margins should improve, as RDRT has accelerated its technology transition toward magnetoresistive (MR) heads. At the end of the third quarter, 89% of revenues came from MR head technology. After the transition, manufacturing efficiency should improve. Results in the first quarter of FY 98 include a charge of $91.8 million ($1.90 a share), primarily for asset writeoffs. An additional charge of $93.7 million was recorded in the third quarter to consolidate manufacturing operations and write down assets.

Valuation - 22-JUL-98

The shares have fallen sharply over the past year, as the company is experiencing slow demand in the high end of the disk drive market and fewer heads per drive, as well as intense pricing pressures. Read-Rite continues to make progress in improving the manufacturing yields of new products. Its accelerated transition to MR recording heads should help improve manufacturing efficiency and operating margins. However, we believe that the company needs to broaden its customer base; the three leading customers accounted for 93% of total revenues in the third quarter of FY 98. Pricing pressures should continue, as industry demand is expected to remain weak, and competitive pressures remain intense. As a result, we have downgraded the shares to avoid, until there are signs of a possible industry turnaround.

Key Stock Statistics

S&P EPS Est. 1998	-2.73	Tang. Bk. Value/Share	5.40
P/E on S&P Est. 1998	NM	Beta	1.31
S&P EPS Est. 1999	0.20	Shareholders	42,000
Dividend Rate/Share	Nil	Market cap. (B)	$0.405
Shs. outstg. (M)	48.7	Inst. holdings	46%
Avg. daily vol. (M)	0.932		

Value of $10,000 invested 5 years ago: $ 2,659

Fiscal Year Ending Sep. 30

	1998	1997	1996	1995	1994	1993
Revenues (Million $)						
1Q	261.4	251.6	299.2	219.5	132.0	139.4
2Q	187.1	282.1	258.2	241.8	139.5	150.2
3Q	184.3	310.2	238.3	253.1	170.1	120.8
4Q	—	318.2	195.4	288.7	197.0	71.91
Yr.	—	1,162	991.1	1,003	638.6	482.4
Earnings Per Share ($)						
1Q	**-1.88**	0.12	0.88	0.42	-0.05	0.52
2Q	**-1.29**	0.48	0.03	0.53	-0.10	0.52
3Q	**-2.82**	0.64	-0.49	0.68	0.24	0.04
4Q	—	0.32	-1.37	0.95	0.33	-1.05
Yr.	—	1.56	-0.92	2.60	0.43	0.02

Next earnings report expected: late October

Dividend Data

No cash dividends have been paid.

A Division of The McGraw·Hill Companies

Business Summary - 22-JUL-98

Read-Rite Corporation is the world's largest independent supplier of magnetic recording heads for rigid disk drives. It designs and manufactures magnetic recording heads as head gimbal assemblies (HGAs), and incorporates multiple HGAs into head stack assemblies (HSAs). Products are sold primarily to independent manufacturers of 3.5-inch form factor rigid disk drives. Read-Rite believes it supplies heads for a broader range of disk drive products than any other independent supplier.

The principal components of rigid disk drives are HGAs, disks, an actuator for positioning HGAs, a motor/spindle assembly to rotate the disk, control electronics and software. An HGA consists of a magnetic recording head attached to a flexure, or suspension arm, and a wire/tubing assembly. Several HGAs can be combined with other components to form an HSA. One or more rigid disks coated with a thin layer of magnetic material are attached to the motor/spindle assembly, which rotates the disks at high speed within a sealed enclosure. The heads record or retrieve data from tracks pre-formatted in the magnetic layer of each disk.

In August 1994, the company acquired Sunward Technologies, Inc., a leading supplier of ferrite metal-in-gap (MIG) and double MIG recording heads and HSAs for rigid disk drives.

R&D spending totaled $64,995,000 (5.6% of sales) in FY 97 (Sep.), up from $52,221,000 (5.3%) in FY 96.

During FY 97, the company supplied HGAs in volume for 37 different disk drive products to six customers, and supplied HSAs in volume for 52 different disk drive products to three customers. Read-Rite sold 106.8 million HGAs and 16.4 million HSAs. In FY 97, Western Digital, Quantum and Maxtor accounted for 51%, 18% and 13% of net sales, respectively. The company also supplies heads for quarter-inch cartridge tape drives, which accounted for 2% of sales in FY 97.

In FY 96, RDRT recorded charges totaling $52 million ($1.11 a share) for various write-offs and restructurings.

In March 1997, Applied Magnetics (NYSE; APM) withdrew its offer to acquire Read-Rite for stock, following rejection of that offer by RDRT's directors.

In the third quarter of FY 98, the company shipped only 15.2 million recording heads, down from 28.2 million in the FY 97 period. MR recording heads accounted for 89% of revenues in the quarter, up from 78% in the second quarter. By the end of the fourth quarter, virtually all recording heads should be MR heads.

Per Share Data ($)										
(Year Ended Sep. 30)	1997	1996	1995	1994	1993	1992	1991	1990	1989	1988
Tangible Bk. Val.	11.15	9.46	11.03	8.45	10.02	6.84	2.47	-4.22	NA	NA
Cash Flow	5.01	1.80	4.22	1.48	0.99	2.25	1.34	0.52	NA	NA
Earnings	1.87	-0.92	2.60	0.43	0.02	1.59	1.04	0.33	NA	NA
Dividends	Nil	Nil	Nil	Nil	Nil	Nil	Nil	Nil	Nil	Nil
Payout Ratio	Nil	Nil	Nil	Nil	Nil	Nil	Nil	Nil	Nil	Nil
Prices - High	36¼	26⅞	49½	19⅞	31¼	32	15⅞	NA	NA	NA
- Low	15⅛	9⅝	14	10⅞	8⅝	14⅛	11¾	NA	NA	NA
P/E Ratio - High	23	NM	19	46	NM	20	15	NA	NA	NA
- Low	10	NM	5	25	NM	9	11	NA	NA	NA

Income Statement Analysis (Million $)										
Revs.	1,162	991	1,003	639	482	389	177	74.0	NA	NA
Oper. Inc.	288	135	251	82.9	60.2	76.6	40.5	12.4	NA	NA
Depr.	168	127	73.5	48.7	34.1	19.4	6.6	3.7	NA	NA
Int. Exp.	15.7	12.9	5.6	4.8	1.2	1.8	1.8	1.5	NA	NA
Pretax Inc.	113	3.9	178	28.8	-1.9	58.8	28.2	6.8	NA	NA
Eff. Tax Rate	26%	NM	24%	16%	NM	20%	17%	3.70%	NA	NA
Net Inc.	76.2	-43.0	124	19.7	0.9	47.0	23.1	6.6	NA	NA

Balance Sheet & Other Fin. Data (Million $)										
Cash	119	148	169	111	124	50.8	63.2	3.0	NA	NA
Curr. Assets	583	310	476	260	228	174	99	17.0	NA	NA
Total Assets	1,301	909	940	631	516	345	154	36.0	NA	NA
Curr. Liab.	240	196	189	130	84.6	85.5	49.9	21.6	NA	NA
LT Debt	404	172	137	52.4	46.5	28.7	26.7	5.8	NA	NA
Common Eqty.	546	454	538	397	350	195	13.0	-24.0	NA	NA
Total Cap.	1,023	697	675	500	431	259	104	14.0	NA	NA
Cap. Exp.	273	266	185	113	170	112	42.0	8.0	NA	NA
Cash Flow	245	84.0	197	68.4	35.0	66.4	29.7	10.3	NA	NA
Curr. Ratio	2.4	1.6	2.5	2.0	2.7	2.0	2.0	0.8	NA	NA
% LT Debt of Cap.	39.5	24.7	20.3	10.5	10.8	11.1	25.7	41.4	NA	NA
% Net Inc.of Revs.	6.6	NM	12.3	3.1	0.2	12.1	13.0	8.9	NA	NA
% Ret. on Assets	6.9	NM	15.7	3.0	0.2	7.8	24.9	21.3	NA	NA
% Ret. on Equity	15.2	NM	26.4	4.6	0.3	35.4	NM	NM	NM	NM

Data as orig. reptd.; bef. results of disc. opers. and/or spec. items. Per share data adj. for stk. divs. as of ex-div. date. Bold denotes diluted EPS (FASB 128). E-Estimated. NA-Not Available. NM-Not Meaningful. NR-Not Ranked.

Office—345 Los Coches St., Milpitas, CA 95035. **Tel**—(408) 262-6700. **Fax**—(408) 956-3205. **Website**—http://www.readrite.com **Chrmn & CEO**—C. J. Yansouni. **Pres & COO**—A. S. Lowe. **VP-Fin & CFO**—J. T. Kurtzweil. **VP & Secy**—R. S. Jackson. **Dirs**—W. J. Almon, H. V. Blaxter III, M. L. Hackworth, J. G. Linvill, M. J. O'Rourke, F. Schwettman, C. J. Yansouni. **Transfer Agent & Registrar**—ChaseMellon Shareholder Services, SF. **Incorporated**—in California in 1981; reincorporated in Delaware in 1985. **Empl**— 23,100. **S&P Analyst**: Brian Goodstadt

03-OCT-98

Industry: Manufacturing (Specialized)

Summary: This company is a leading U.S. manufacturer of mechanical motion control products and electric motors and generators.

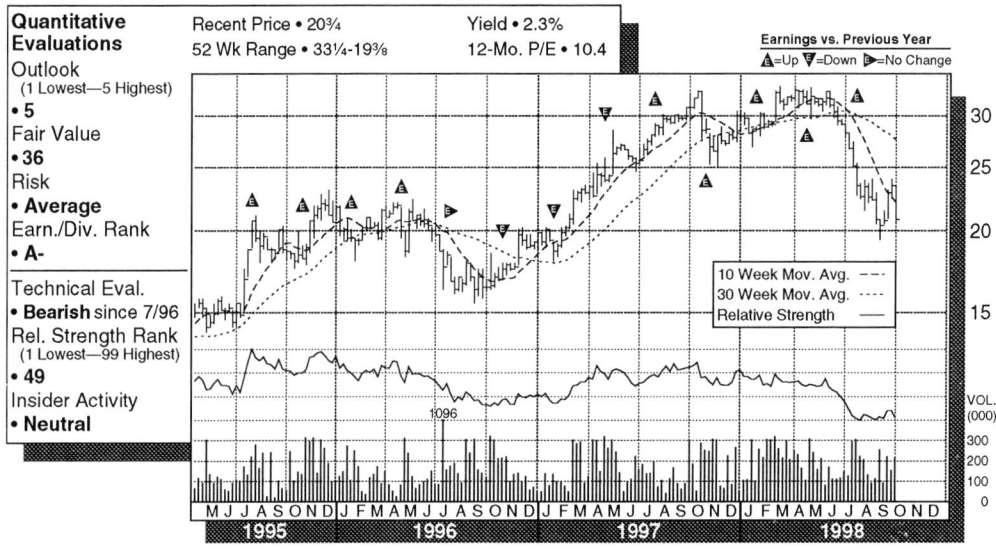

Quantitative Evaluations	
Recent Price • 20¾	Yield • 2.3%
52 Wk Range • 33¼-19⅜	12-Mo. P/E • 10.4

Outlook (1 Lowest—5 Highest)
• **5**

Fair Value
• **36**

Risk
• **Average**

Earn./Div. Rank
• **A-**

Technical Eval.
• **Bearish** since 7/96

Rel. Strength Rank (1 Lowest—99 Highest)
• **49**

Insider Activity
• **Neutral**

Earnings vs. Previous Year
▲=Up ▼=Down ▶=No Change

10 Week Mov. Avg. – – –
30 Week Mov. Avg. ⋯⋯
Relative Strength ——

Business Profile - 22-AUG-98

In commenting on results for the first six months of 1998, the company stated that it was approaching the balance of 1998 with cautious optimism given rising competitive pressures and a slowing of growth becoming evident in the capital goods marketplace. In June 1998, the company stated that RBC would continue to rely on its core competencies: low cost production of high quality products, quick delivery, and the acquisition of products and companies, which RBC then develops to their full potential. In March 1997, the company more than doubled its size with the purchase of Marathon Electric, a manufacturer of electric motors, generators and other products.

Operational Review - 22-AUG-98

In the first six months of 1998, revenue climbed 29%, year to year, yet second quarter sales fell 3% from a 0.5% decline for the mechanical group and a 4.5% decline for the electrical group. Cost of sales in the first six months increased 28%, producing slightly wider gross margins. With operating expenses up 41%, operating income rose 23%. Following a 65% increase in interest expense, net, and a slightly higher tax rate, net income advanced 19%, to $22,093,000 ($1.04 a share) compared with $18,513,000 ($0.87).

Stock Performance - 02-OCT-98

In the past 30 trading days, RBC's shares have declined 7%, compared to a 7% fall in the S&P 500. Average trading volume for the past five days was 42,680 shares, compared with the 40-day moving average of 32,510 shares.

Key Stock Statistics

Dividend Rate/Share	0.48	Shareholders	1,300
Shs. outstg. (M)	20.9	Market cap. (B)	$0.435
Avg. daily vol. (M)	0.035	Inst. holdings	59%
Tang. Bk. Value/Share	2.84		
Beta	0.76		

Value of $10,000 invested 5 years ago: $ 21,953

Fiscal Year Ending Dec. 31

	1998	1997	1996	1995	1994	1993
Revenues (Million $)						
1Q	137.8	70.57	75.12	74.34	58.85	54.20
2Q	139.0	143.6	71.82	76.27	60.04	55.32
3Q	—	138.4	68.15	71.55	61.19	54.77
4Q	—	134.4	66.42	73.74	62.57	55.61
Yr.	—	487.0	281.5	295.9	242.7	219.9
Earnings Per Share ($)						
1Q	**0.49**	**0.36**	0.43	0.36	0.23	0.15
2Q	**0.55**	**0.51**	0.42	0.41	0.27	0.18
3Q	—	**0.47**	0.36	0.41	0.30	0.17
4Q	—	**0.49**	0.36	0.42	0.33	0.20
Yr.	—	**1.83**	1.57	1.60	1.13	0.70

Next earnings report expected: mid October

Dividend Data (Dividends have been paid since 1961.)

Amount ($)	Date Decl.	Ex-Div. Date	Stock of Record	Payment Date
0.120	Oct. 31	Dec. 29	Dec. 31	Jan. 15 '98
0.120	Jan. 30	Mar. 27	Mar. 31	Apr. 15 '98
0.120	Apr. 22	Jun. 26	Jun. 30	Jul. 15 '98
0.120	Jul. 17	Sep. 28	Sep. 30	Oct. 15 '98

A Division of The McGraw-Hill Companies

Business Summary - 22-JUL-98

Read-Rite Corporation is the world's largest independent supplier of magnetic recording heads for rigid disk drives. It designs and manufactures magnetic recording heads as head gimbal assemblies (HGAs), and incorporates multiple HGAs into head stack assemblies (HSAs). Products are sold primarily to independent manufacturers of 3.5-inch form factor rigid disk drives. Read-Rite believes it supplies heads for a broader range of disk drive products than any other independent supplier.

The principal components of rigid disk drives are HGAs, disks, an actuator for positioning HGAs, a motor/spindle assembly to rotate the disk, control electronics and software. An HGA consists of a magnetic recording head attached to a flexure, or suspension arm, and a wire/tubing assembly. Several HGAs can be combined with other components to form an HSA. One or more rigid disks coated with a thin layer of magnetic material are attached to the motor/spindle assembly, which rotates the disks at high speed within a sealed enclosure. The heads record or retrieve data from tracks pre-formatted in the magnetic layer of each disk.

In August 1994, the company acquired Sunward Technologies, Inc., a leading supplier of ferrite metal-in-gap (MIG) and double MIG recording heads and HSAs for rigid disk drives.

R&D spending totaled $64,995,000 (5.6% of sales) in FY 97 (Sep.), up from $52,221,000 (5.3%) in FY 96.

During FY 97, the company supplied HGAs in volume for 37 different disk drive products to six customers, and supplied HSAs in volume for 52 different disk drive products to three customers. Read-Rite sold 106.8 million HGAs and 16.4 million HSAs. In FY 97, Western Digital, Quantum and Maxtor accounted for 51%, 18% and 13% of net sales, respectively. The company also supplies heads for quarter-inch cartridge tape drives, which accounted for 2% of sales in FY 97.

In FY 96, RDRT recorded charges totaling $52 million ($1.11 a share) for various write-offs and restructurings.

In March 1997, Applied Magnetics (NYSE; APM) withdrew its offer to acquire Read-Rite for stock, following rejection of that offer by RDRT's directors.

In the third quarter of FY 98, the company shipped only 15.2 million recording heads, down from 28.2 million in the FY 97 period. MR recording heads accounted for 89% of revenues in the quarter, up from 78% in the second quarter. By the end of the fourth quarter, virtually all recording heads should be MR heads.

Per Share Data ($)

(Year Ended Sep. 30)	1997	1996	1995	1994	1993	1992	1991	1990	1989	1988
Tangible Bk. Val.	11.15	9.46	11.03	8.45	10.02	6.84	2.47	-4.22	NA	NA
Cash Flow	5.01	1.80	4.22	1.48	0.99	2.25	1.34	0.52	NA	NA
Earnings	1.87	-0.92	2.60	0.43	0.02	1.59	1.04	0.33	NA	NA
Dividends	Nil	Nil	Nil	Nil	Nil	Nil	Nil	Nil	Nil	Nil
Payout Ratio	Nil	Nil	Nil	Nil	Nil	Nil	Nil	Nil	Nil	Nil
Prices - High	36¼	26⅞	49½	19⅞	31¼	32	15⅞	NA	NA	NA
- Low	15⅛	9⅝	14	10⅞	8⅝	14⅛	11¾	NA	NA	NA
P/E Ratio - High	23	NM	19	46	NM	20	15	NA	NA	NA
- Low	10	NM	5	25	NM	9	11	NA	NA	NA

Income Statement Analysis (Million $)

Revs.	1,162	991	1,003	639	482	389	177	74.0	NA	NA
Oper. Inc.	288	135	251	82.9	60.2	76.6	40.5	12.4	NA	NA
Depr.	168	127	73.5	48.7	34.1	19.4	6.6	3.7	NA	NA
Int. Exp.	15.7	12.9	5.6	4.8	1.2	1.8	1.8	1.5	NA	NA
Pretax Inc.	113	3.9	178	28.8	-1.9	58.8	28.2	6.8	NA	NA
Eff. Tax Rate	26%	NM	24%	16%	NM	20%	17%	3.70%	NA	NA
Net Inc.	76.2	-43.0	124	19.7	0.9	47.0	23.1	6.6	NA	NA

Balance Sheet & Other Fin. Data (Million $)

Cash	119	148	169	111	124	50.8	63.2	3.0	NA	NA
Curr. Assets	583	310	476	260	228	174	99	17.0	NA	NA
Total Assets	1,301	909	940	631	516	345	154	36.0	NA	NA
Curr. Liab.	240	196	189	130	84.6	85.5	49.9	21.6	NA	NA
LT Debt	404	172	137	52.4	46.5	28.7	26.7	5.8	NA	NA
Common Eqty.	546	454	538	397	350	195	13.0	-24.0	NA	NA
Total Cap.	1,023	697	675	500	431	259	104	14.0	NA	NA
Cap. Exp.	273	266	185	113	170	112	42.0	8.0	NA	NA
Cash Flow	245	84.0	197	68.4	35.0	66.4	29.7	10.3	NA	NA
Curr. Ratio	2.4	1.6	2.5	2.0	2.7	2.0	2.0	0.8	NA	NA
% LT Debt of Cap.	39.5	24.7	20.3	10.5	10.8	11.1	25.7	41.4	NA	NA
% Net Inc.of Revs.	6.6	NM	12.3	3.1	0.2	12.1	13.0	8.9	NA	NA
% Ret. on Assets	6.9	NM	15.7	3.0	0.2	7.8	24.9	21.3	NA	NA
% Ret. on Equity	15.2	NM	26.4	4.6	0.3	35.4	NM	NM	NM	NM

Data as orig. reptd.; bef. results of disc. opers. and/or spec. items. Per share data adj. for stk. divs. as of ex-div. date. Bold denotes diluted EPS (FASB 128). E-Estimated. NA-Not Available. NM-Not Meaningful. NR-Not Ranked.

Office—345 Los Coches St., Milpitas, CA 95035. Tel—(408) 262-6700. Fax—(408) 956-3205. Website—http://www.readrite.com Chrmn & CEO—C. J. Yansouni. Pres & COO—A. S. Lowe. VP-Fin & CFO—J. T. Kurtzweil. VP & Secy—R. S. Jackson. Dirs—W. J. Almon, H. V. Blaxter III, M. L. Hackworth, J. G. Linvill, M. J. O'Rourke, F. Schwettman, C. J. Yansouni. Transfer Agent & Registrar—ChaseMellon Shareholder Services, SF. Incorporated—in California in 1981; reincorporated in Delaware in 1985. Empl— 23,100. S&P Analyst: Brian Goodstadt

Regal-Beloit Corp.   8995

ASE Symbol **RBC**

In S&P SmallCap 600

03-OCT-98   **Industry:** Manufacturing (Specialized)   **Summary:** This company is a leading U.S. manufacturer of mechanical motion control products and electric motors and generators.

Quantitative Evaluations

Outlook
(1 Lowest—5 Highest)
• **5**

Fair Value
• **36**

Risk
• **Average**

Earn./Div. Rank
• **A-**

Technical Eval.
• **Bearish** since 7/96

Rel. Strength Rank
(1 Lowest—99 Highest)
• **49**

Insider Activity
• **Neutral**

Recent Price • 20¾   Yield • 2.3%
52 Wk Range • 33¼-19⅜   12-Mo. P/E • 10.4

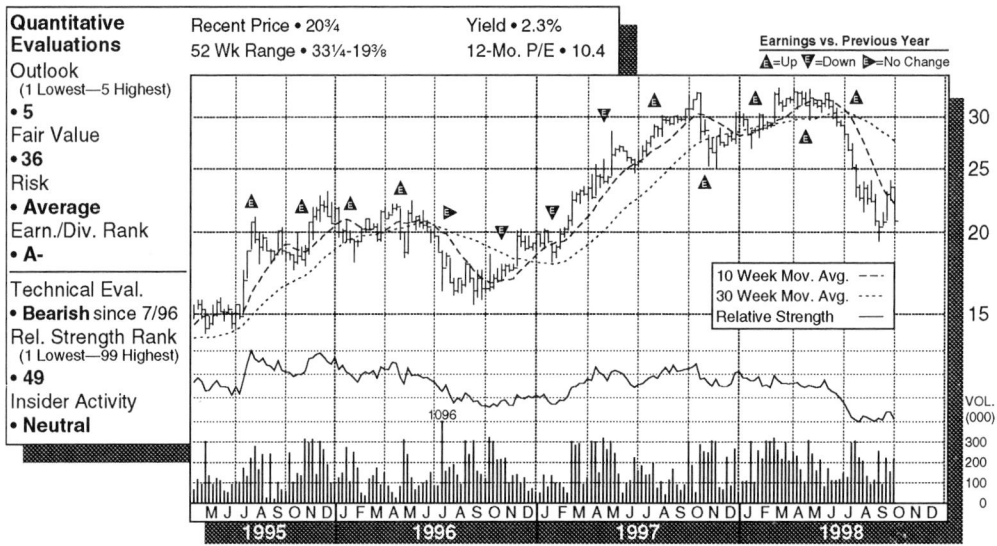

Business Profile - 22-AUG-98

In commenting on results for the first six months of 1998, the company stated that it was approaching the balance of 1998 with cautious optimism given rising competitive pressures and a slowing of growth becoming evident in the capital goods marketplace. In June 1998, the company stated that RBC would continue to rely on its core competencies: low cost production of high quality products, quick delivery, and the acquisition of products and companies, which RBC then develops to their full potential. In March 1997, the company more than doubled its size with the purchase of Marathon Electric, a manufacturer of electric motors, generators and other products.

Operational Review - 22-AUG-98

In the first six months of 1998, revenue climbed 29%, year to year, yet second quarter sales fell 3% from a 0.5% decline for the mechanical group and a 4.5% decline for the electrical group. Cost of sales in the first six months increased 28%, producing slightly wider gross margins. With operating expenses up 41%, operating income rose 23%. Following a 65% increase in interest expense, net, and a slightly higher tax rate, net income advanced 19%, to $22,093,000 ($1.04 a share) compared with $18,513,000 ($0.87).

Stock Performance - 02-OCT-98

In the past 30 trading days, RBC's shares have declined 7%, compared to a 7% fall in the S&P 500. Average trading volume for the past five days was 42,680 shares, compared with the 40-day moving average of 32,510 shares.

Key Stock Statistics

Dividend Rate/Share	0.48	Shareholders	1,300
Shs. outstg. (M)	20.9	Market cap. (B)	$0.435
Avg. daily vol. (M)	0.035	Inst. holdings	59%
Tang. Bk. Value/Share	2.84		
Beta	0.76		

Value of $10,000 invested 5 years ago: $ 21,953

Fiscal Year Ending Dec. 31

	1998	1997	1996	1995	1994	1993
Revenues (Million $)						
1Q	137.8	70.57	75.12	74.34	58.85	54.20
2Q	139.0	143.6	71.82	76.27	60.04	55.32
3Q	—	138.4	68.15	71.55	61.19	54.77
4Q	—	134.4	66.42	73.74	62.57	55.61
Yr.	—	487.0	281.5	295.9	242.7	219.9
Earnings Per Share ($)						
1Q	0.10	0.06	0.40	0.30	0.23	0.15
2Q	0.55	0.51	0.42	0.41	0.27	0.18
3Q	—	0.47	0.36	0.41	0.30	0.17
4Q	—	0.49	0.36	0.42	0.33	0.20
Yr.	—	1.83	1.57	1.60	1.13	0.70

Next earnings report expected: mid October

Dividend Data (Dividends have been paid since 1961.)

Amount ($)	Date Decl.	Ex-Div. Date	Stock of Record	Payment Date
0.120	Oct. 31	Dec. 29	Dec. 31	Jan. 15 '98
0.120	Jan. 30	Mar. 27	Mar. 31	Apr. 15 '98
0.120	Apr. 22	Jun. 26	Jun. 30	Jul. 15 '98
0.120	Jul. 17	Sep. 28	Sep. 30	Oct. 15 '98

STANDARD
&POOR'S
STOCK REPORTS

Regal-Beloit Corporation

8995

03-OCT-98

Business Summary - 22-AUG-98

Regal-Beloit's (RBC) initial business was the production of special metalworking taps. After 34 acquisitions and internal growth, the company has become a prominent manufacturer and worldwide supplier of a diversified line of mechanical products to control motion and torque, and electrical products such as motors and generators.

The company believes that its ability to provide products on a shorter delivery schedule than other manufacturers gives it a competitive selling advantage. Also, the company credits continuous redesign of products, effective plant layout, and modern equipment for producing significant cost advantages. RBC states that its core competencies include the engineering, manufacturing, and assembly of high quality, low cost products, and the capability to acquire products or companies and develop them to their full potential.

Contributions by division in 1997 were:

	Sales (%)	Operating Profit (%)
Mechanical Group	59%	65%
Electrical Group (For 9 Months)	41%	35%

Exports accounted for approximately 7% of company sales in 1997 and 3% in 1996. Additionally, 4% of company sales were manufactured and sold outside the US. in 1997 compared with 7% in 1996.

The company's Mechanical Group makes standard and custom worm gear, bevel gear, helical gear and concentric shaft gearboxes; marine and high-performance after-market automotive transmissions; custom gearing; gear motors; and manual valve actuators. The group also manufactures perishable, high speed steel, rotary cutting tools, accounting for less than 10% of the company's net sales.

In March 1997, the company acquired Marathon Electric Manufacturing Corp., a manufacturer of electric motors, generators and related products, for about $279 million. Marathon now comprises the firm's Electrical Group. The purchase of Marathon, which had 1996 revenues of about $245 million, nearly doubled RBC's sales base.

The Electrical Group produces AC electric motors ranging in size from 1/12 horsepower to over 500 horsepower and electric generators ranging in size from 5 kilowatts to 2300 kilowatts.

Both the Mechanical and Electrical Group products are sold to distributors, original equipment manufacturers, and end users across many industry segments.

Per Share Data ($)

(Year Ended Dec. 31)	1997	1996	1995	1994	1993	1992	1991	1990	1989	1988
Tangible Bk. Val.	1.83	7.75	6.61	5.40	4.54	4.13	4.04	3.95	3.69	3.35
Cash Flow	2.78	2.07	2.10	1.57	1.14	0.81	0.49	0.72	0.75	0.80
Earnings	1.87	1.57	1.60	1.13	0.70	0.47	0.28	0.53	0.57	0.62
Dividends	0.48	0.48	0.39	0.30	0.27	0.26	0.26	0.26	0.24	0.19
Payout Ratio	26%	31%	24%	27%	38%	56%	95%	49%	42%	35%
Prices - High	32¾	22⅜	23⅛	15½	13¼	11	7⅜	8⅜	9½	10⅛
- Low	18	15½	12⅛	11¼	9¼	6½	5⅜	4⅝	6½	5¾
P/E Ratio - High	18	14	14	14	19	24	27	16	17	16
- Low	10	10	8	10	13	14	20	9	11	9

Income Statement Analysis (Million $)

	1997	1996	1995	1994	1993	1992	1991	1990	1989	1988
Revs.	487	282	296	243	220	200	152	168	167	149
Oper. Inc.	93.3	61.6	63.8	48.0	33.8	23.9	14.3	21.8	23.3	23.2
Depr.	18.9	10.6	10.2	9.0	8.8	7.0	4.5	4.0	3.6	3.3
Int. Exp.	10.8	0.4	0.8	1.0	1.5	1.9	1.4	1.5	1.0	1.9
Pretax Inc.	64.4	51.8	53.1	38.2	23.7	15.2	9.0	17.2	18.9	18.2
Eff. Tax Rate	40%	38%	38%	39%	39%	38%	38%	38%	39%	39%
Net Inc.	38.9	32.2	32.8	23.1	14.4	9.5	5.5	10.7	11.5	11.2

Balance Sheet & Other Fin. Data (Million $)

	1997	1996	1995	1994	1993	1992	1991	1990	1989	1988
Cash	3.4	38.4	7.5	13.4	2.2	5.2	7.2	10.0	3.2	1.8
Curr. Assets	173	122	102	91.7	71.7	77.5	68.7	73.4	72.4	63.8
Total Assets	486	197	175	168	139	145	118	114	111	94.0
Curr. Liab.	71.9	29.4	32.0	36.6	22.5	24.1	19.7	14.7	17.3	16.7
LT Debt	192	2.2	2.9	16.0	19.6	34.4	13.8	16.6	17.3	8.1
Common Eqty.	189	160	136	111	92.7	83.9	81.8	80.0	74.2	67.1
Total Cap.	413	168	143	131	117	121	98.0	99	94.0	77.0
Cap. Exp.	16.0	11.1	13.8	7.5	8.5	6.5	7.5	7.6	13.4	9.6
Cash Flow	57.8	42.8	43.0	32.1	23.1	16.4	10.0	14.6	15.1	14.5
Curr. Ratio	2.4	4.2	3.2	2.5	3.2	3.2	3.5	5.0	4.2	3.8
% LT Debt of Cap.	46.5	1.3	2.0	12.2	16.8	28.5	14.1	16.8	18.5	10.5
% Net Inc.of Revs.	8.0	11.4	11.1	9.5	6.5	4.7	3.6	6.4	6.9	7.5
% Ret. on Assets	11.4	17.3	19.1	15.1	10.1	7.2	4.8	9.5	11.2	12.5
% Ret. on Equity	22.3	17.3	26.6	22.7	16.3	11.4	6.8	13.8	16.3	19.3

Data as orig. reptd.; bef. results of disc. opers. and/or spec. items. Per share data adj. for stk. divs. as of ex-div. date. Bold denotes diluted EPS (FASB 128). E-Estimated. NA-Not Available. NM-Not Meaningful. NR-Not Ranked.

Office—200 State St., Beloit, WI 53511-6254. **Tel**—(608) 364-8800. **Fax**—(608) 364-8818. **Chrmn, Pres & CEO**—J. L. Packard.**EVP**—H. W. Knueppel. **VP, CFO, Secy & Investor Contact**—K. F. Kaplan. **Dirs**—F. E. Bauchiero, J. R. Coleman, J. M. Eldred, K.F. Kaplan, H. W. Knueppel, J. A. McKay, J. L. Packard. **Transfer Agent & Registrar**—Bank of Boston. **Incorporated**—in Delaware in 1955; reincorporated in Wisconsin in 1994. **Empl**— 4,810. **S&P Analyst:** D. Moskowitz

Regeneron Pharmaceuticals 5072
NASDAQ Symbol **REGN**
In S&P SmallCap 600

03-OCT-98

Industry:
Biotechnology

Summary: This biotechnology company focuses on discovery and development of nerve growth factors to treat neurological conditions, including Lou Gehrig's disease and Alzheimer's disease.

Quantitative Evaluations

Recent Price • 7
52 Wk Range • 13-5¾

Yield • Nil
12-Mo. P/E • NM

Outlook
(1 Lowest—5 Highest)
• **NA**

Fair Value
• **NA**

Risk
• **High**

Earn./Div. Rank
• **NR**

Technical Eval.
• **Bearish** since 11/97

Rel. Strength Rank
(1 Lowest—99 Highest)
• **58**

Insider Activity
• **NA**

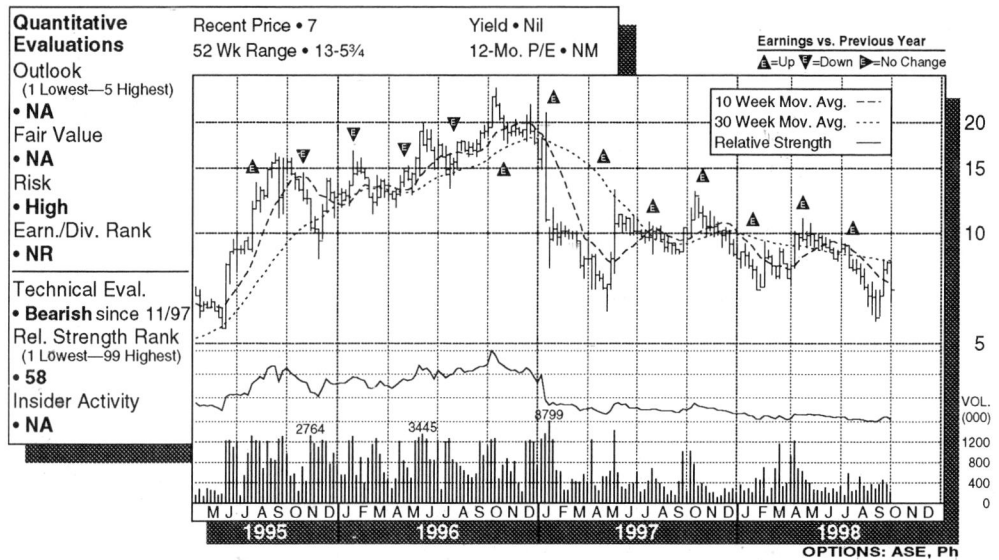

Earnings vs. Previous Year
▲=Up ▼=Down ▶=No Change

10 Week Mov. Avg. ‑‑‑
30 Week Mov. Avg. ‑‑‑‑
Relative Strength ‑‑‑

OPTIONS: ASE, Ph

Business Profile - 15-MAY-98

This company has formed collaborative partnerships with Amgen and Sumitomo Pharmaceuticals to develop neurological treatments using brain-derived neurotrophic factor (BDNF). In January 1997, REGN and research partner Amgen announced disappointing results for a Phase III trial for subcutaneous delivery of BDNF to treat ALS (also known as Lou Gehrig's disease). Amgen, on behalf of the Amgen-Regeneron partnership, is currently testing intrathecally (directly into the spinal fluid) delivered BDNF as a treatment for ALS. Regeneron and Procter & Gamble have a long-term research agreement to include Axokine and related molecules to treat obesity associated with Type II diabetes.

Operational Review - 15-MAY-98

Revenues (including investment income) in the three months ended March 31, 1998, gained 33%, year to year, due primarily to higher contract manufacturing revenue and higher investment income. No product sales have been recorded to date. Expenses fell, mostly reflecting a sharp decline in the company's share of the net loss in Amgen-Regeneron Partners. The net loss narrowed to $3,829,000 ($0.12 a share, on 20% more shares), from $5,929,000 ($0.23). Cash and marketable securities totaled $122.5 million at the end of the first quarter.

Stock Performance - 02-OCT-98

In the past 30 trading days, REGN's shares have increased 4%, compared to a 7% fall in the S&P 500. Average trading volume for the past five days was 44,120 shares, compared with the 40-day moving average of 67,310 shares.

Key Stock Statistics

Dividend Rate/Share	Nil	Shareholders	900
Shs. outstg. (M)	31.0	Market cap. (B)	$0.192
Avg. daily vol. (M)	0.072	Inst. holdings	20%
Tang. Bk. Value/Share	4.45		
Beta	1.80		

Value of $10,000 invested 5 years ago: $ 5,833

Fiscal Year Ending Dec. 31

	1998	1997	1996	1995	1994	1993
Revenues (Million $)						
1Q	8.25	6.21	5.19	7.83	2.99	2.14
2Q	15.20	6.62	6.16	7.62	3.62	1.96
3Q	—	8.87	6.22	6.19	8.90	3.58
4Q	—	11.40	6.55	5.74	7.69	2.88
Yr.	—	33.10	24.11	27.38	23.19	10.56
Earnings Per Share ($)						
1Q	-0.12	-0.23	-0.35	-0.22	-0.57	-0.61
2Q	0.07	-0.16	-0.31	-0.22	-0.54	-0.61
3Q	—	-0.06	-0.35	-0.37	-0.21	-0.58
4Q	—	0.02	-0.32	-0.38	-0.30	-0.61
Yr.	—	-0.40	-1.33	-1.19	-1.62	-2.41

Next earnings report expected: NA

Dividend Data

No cash dividends have been paid.

STANDARD
&POOR'S
STOCK REPORTS

Regeneron Pharmaceuticals, Inc.

5072

03-OCT-98

Business Summary - 15-MAY-98

The development of therapeutic drugs is a long and expensive process for biotechnology companies like Regeneron Pharmaceuticals, Inc. (REGN). Massive expenditures necessary for research, clinical trials, regulatory approvals and commercialization of products have led to collaborations with established companies in order to fund the development of potential products.

REGN is pursuing the development of compounds to treat neurodegenerative diseases, peripheral neuropathies and nerve injury as well as conditions outside the nervous system, including inflammatory and muscle diseases, angiogenesis (blood vessel growth), hematopoieses, abnormal bone growth and cancer.

In May 1997, REGN and Procter & Gamble (P&G) signed a 10-year agreement to discover, develop and commercialize pharmaceutical products in cardiovascular, bone, muscle, arthritis and other disease areas. Over the first five years of the agreement, P&G will provide $155 million (including $20 million from an agreement in December 1996) to support REGN and its research programs. REGN's neurotrophic factor and cytokine research programs continue to be developed independently of this collaboration.

Neurodegenerative diseases are incurable conditions in which there is progressive loss of neurons crucial for functions such as learning and memory, sensation, control of movement, muscle strength and coordination. Such conditions include amyotrophic lateral sclerosis (ALS, or Lou Gehrig's disease), Parkinson's disease and Alzheimer's disease.

Amgen-Regeneron Partners (equally owned by both parties) is conducting clinical trials of brain-derived neurotrophic factor (BDNF) for the treatment of ALS via intrathecal (infusion into the spinal fluid through an implanted pump) and subcutaneous delivery (injection under the skin). Regeneron, on behalf of Amgen-Regeneron Partners, plans to commence by mid-1998 the first of a series of small Phase II clinical studies of neurotrophin-3 (NT-3) for the treatment of enteric neuropathies. REGN is also developing BDNF in Japan with Sumitomo Pharmaceuticals.

In January 1997, REGN and Amgen announced that a Phase III clinical trial of BDNF delivered subcutaneously failed to demonstrate efficacy in patients with ALS. Despite confirming safety and tolerability, the trial did not show a significant difference in breathing capacity or survival between treatment and placebo groups. A review of the data by the company and outside experts indicated that a retrospectively-defined subset of ALS patients in the trial may have received a survival benefit from BDNF treatment. The current and planned subcutaneous studies are intended to test whether this can be confirmed through appropriate studies.

Per Share Data ($)

(Year Ended Dec. 31)	1997	1996	1995	1994	1993	1992	1991	1990	1989	1988
Tangible Bk. Val.	4.49	4.16	3.11	3.55	5.22	5.68	6.92	1.69	NA	NA
Cash Flow	-0.25	-1.08	-0.89	-1.42	-2.24	-1.12	-0.24	-0.29	NA	NA
Earnings	-0.40	-1.33	-1.19	-1.62	-2.41	-1.24	-0.29	-0.32	NA	NA
Dividends	Nil	Nil	Nil	Nil	Nil	Nil	Nil	Nil	Nil	Nil
Payout Ratio	Nil	Nil	Nil	Nil	Nil	Nil	Nil	Nil	Nil	Nil
Prices - High	21¼	24⅞	16½	17⅜	21½	23¼	23¼	NA	NA	NA
- Low	6⅛	11¼	3⅛	3	10½	7¾	9¾	NA	NA	NA
P/E Ratio - High	NM	NM	NM	NM	NM	NM	NM	NM	NM	NM
- Low	NM	NM	NM	NM	NM	NM	NM	NM	NM	NM

Income Statement Analysis (Million $)

	1997	1996	1995	1994	1993	1992	1991	1990	1989	1988
Revs.	33.1	19.8	24.3	20.6	6.1	6.5	7.3	3.8	0.5	Nil
Oper. Inc.	-6.5	-29.8	-19.4	-27.5	-40.5	-21.4	-8.8	-4.1	-3.5	-1.0
Depr.	4.4	6.1	5.9	3.9	2.8	2.0	0.8	0.3	0.2	0.0
Int. Exp.	0.7	0.9	1.2	1.4	1.1	0.7	0.1	0.0	0.0	0.0
Pretax Inc.	-11.6	-32.4	-23.5	-30.7	-39.9	-19.1	-4.5	-3.3	-2.7	-0.9
Eff. Tax Rate	NM	NM	NM	NM	NM	NM	Nil	Nil	Nil	Nil
Net Inc.	-11.6	-32.4	-23.5	-30.7	-39.9	-19.1	-4.5	-3.3	-2.7	-0.9

Balance Sheet & Other Fin. Data (Million $)

	1997	1996	1995	1994	1993	1992	1991	1990	1989	1988
Cash	28.9	80.1	46.1	50.0	88.0	83.0	104	22.0	11.0	5.0
Curr. Assets	100	85.0	49.2	52.0	92.0	85.0	107	22.0	12.0	NA
Total Assets	168	138	93.9	94.0	118	98.0	114	25.0	13.0	6.0
Curr. Liab.	10.7	12.0	12.9	17.9	13.1	4.6	3.3	1.8	0.3	NA
LT Debt	3.8	5.2	6.0	9.3	5.9	5.8	2.4	Nil	5.0	Nil
Common Eqty.	139	107	67.9	67.0	98.0	87.0	106	-7.0	1.0	-1.0
Total Cap.	143	112	73.9	76.0	104	93.0	109	19.0	13.0	5.0
Cap. Exp.	2.1	8.6	3.3	7.0	10.2	2.1	1.0	1.6	0.4	0.5
Cash Flow	-7.2	-26.3	-17.6	-26.7	-37.0	-17.2	-3.7	-3.0	-2.5	-0.9
Curr. Ratio	9.3	7.1	3.8	2.9	7.0	18.6	32.3	12.4	41.8	NA
% LT Debt of Cap.	2.7	4.6	8.1	12.1	5.7	6.3	2.2	Nil	40.2	Nil
% Net Inc.of Revs.	NM	NM	NM	NM	NM	NM	NM	NM	NM	NM
% Ret. on Assets	NM	NM	NM	NM	NM	NM	NM	NM	NM	NM
% Ret. on Equity	NM	NM	NM	NM	NM	NM	NM	NA	NM	NM

Data as orig. reptd.; bef. results of disc. opers. and/or spec. items. Per share data adj. for stk. divs. as of ex-div. date. Rev. in Income Statement Analysis tbl. excl. investment inc. E-Estimated. NA-Not Available. NM-Not Meaningful. NR-Not Ranked.

Office—777 Old Saw Mill River Rd., Tarrytown, NY 10591-6707. **Tel**—(914) 345-7400. **Website**—http://www.regeneron.com **Chrmn**—P. R. Vagelos. **Pres & CEO**—L. S. Schleifer. **VP-Fin, CFO, Treas & Investor Contact**—Murray A. Goldberg. **VP & Secy**—P. Lubetkin. **Dirs**—C. A. Baker, M. S. Brown, A. G. Gilman, J. L. Goldstein, F. A. Middleton, L. S. Schleifer, E. M. Shooter, G. L. Sing, P. R. Vagelos. **Transfer Agent & Registrar**—ChaseMellon Shareholder Services, NYC. **Incorporated**—in New York in 1988. **Empl**— 270. **S&P Analyst:** Richard Joy

STANDARD &POOR'S
STOCK REPORTS

Regis Corp.

5072P

NASDAQ Symbol **RGIS**

In S&P SmallCap 600

03-OCT-98

Industry:
Services (Commercial & Consumer)

Summary: This company is the world's largest owner and operator of hair and retail product salons, with more than 3,500, following its acquisition of Supercuts, Inc.

Quantitative Evaluations

Recent Price • 30
52 Wk Range • 31½-22½

Yield • 0.4%
12-Mo. P/E • 23.6

Outlook
(1 Lowest—5 Highest)
• **4⁻**

Fair Value
• **41¼**

Risk
• **High**

Earn./Div. Rank
• **NR**

Technical Eval.
• **Bullish** since 9/98

Rel. Strength Rank
(1 Lowest—99 Highest)
• **90**

Insider Activity
• **Neutral**

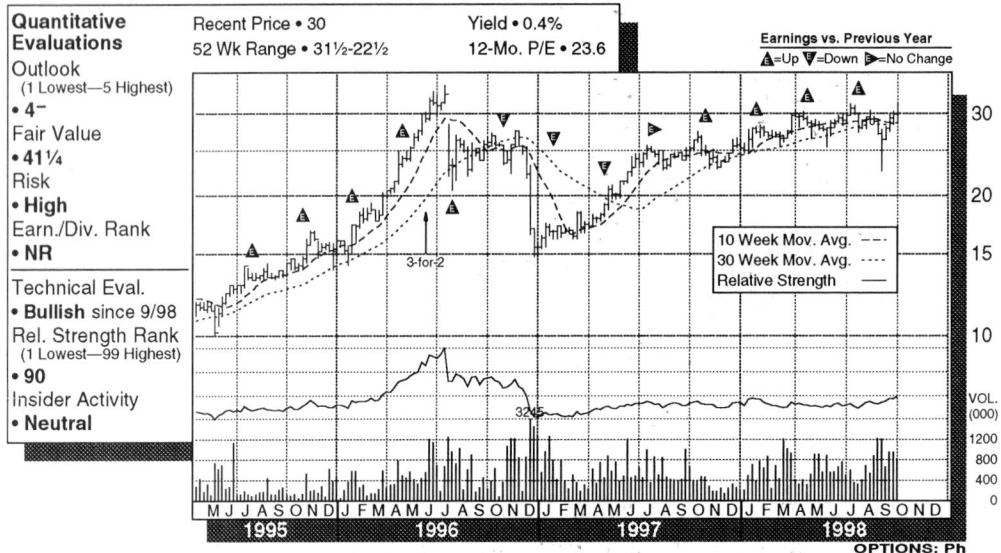

Earnings vs. Previous Year
▲=Up ▼=Down ▶=No Change

10 Week Mov. Avg. ---
30 Week Mov. Avg. ....
Relative Strength ——

3-for-2

VOL. (000)

OPTIONS: Ph

Business Profile - 20-SEP-98

Regis plans to continue to grow by aggressively building and acquiring salons, and achieving same-store sales gains. As of June 30, 1998, the company operated 2,723 company-owned salons and 816 franchised locations, having constructed 205 new outlets and purchased 178 salons during FY 98 (Jun.). During FY 99, the company expects to add some 215 company-owned salons and 80 franchised locations. The company is one of two salon service providers to Wal-Mart, accounting for 5% of revenues, in FY 98. RGIS plans to construct about 80 new salons in Wal-Mart stores and super centers in FY 99. During FY 99, the company plans to moderately expand its international salon base, which recently included 392 locations in 8 countries outside the U.S.

Operational Review - 20-SEP-98

Total revenues for FY 98 (Jun.), increased 12%, year-to-year, reflecting a 10% increase in service revenues, an 10% rise in product sales, and a 3% decline in franchise income. Increases were primarily due to growth in same store sales. After increases for operating expenses of 11% and SG&A of 10%, in addition to inclusion in both years of nonrecurring charges primarily related to the SuperCuts acquisition, income before taxes more than doubled. Following taxes at 40.2%, versus 66.6%, net income rose to $30,488,000 ($1.27 a share), from $6,574,000 ($0.28 a share).

Stock Performance - 02-OCT-98

In the past 30 trading days, RGIS's shares have increased 4%, compared to a 7% fall in the S&P 500. Average trading volume for the past five days was 163,060 shares, compared with the 40-day moving average of 188,133 shares.

Key Stock Statistics

Dividend Rate/Share	0.12	Shareholders	1,200
Shs. outstg. (M)	23.8	Market cap. (B)	$0.714
Avg. daily vol. (M)	0.179	Inst. holdings	57%
Tang. Bk. Value/Share	2.72		
Beta	1.20		

Value of $10,000 invested 5 years ago: $ 45,570

Fiscal Year Ending Jun. 30

	1998	1997	1996	1995	1994	1993
Revenues (Million $)						
1Q	188.7	170.6	111.7	102.4	89.50	81.50
2Q	198.9	176.5	126.6	108.4	94.50	85.10
3Q	197.3	175.5	126.2	102.7	94.90	86.20
4Q	213.2	190.7	134.9	108.8	97.70	88.20
Yr.	798.1	713.2	499.4	422.2	377.0	341.0
Earnings Per Share ($)						
1Q	0.24	0.19	0.24	0.19	0.15	0.12
2Q	**0.34**	-0.39	0.29	0.24	-0.26	0.11
3Q	**0.28**	0.18	0.24	0.19	0.15	-0.05
4Q	**0.41**	0.29	0.29	0.25	0.20	0.09
Yr.	**1.27**	0.28	1.06	0.86	0.26	0.27

Next earnings report expected: NA

Dividend Data (Dividends have been paid since 1995.)

Amount ($)	Date Decl.	Ex-Div. Date	Stock of Record	Payment Date
0.020	Nov. 06	Nov. 13	Nov. 17	Dec. 02 '97
0.020	Feb. 05	Feb. 11	Feb. 16	Mar. 03 '98
0.030	May. 12	May. 20	May. 22	Jun. 08 '98
0.030	Aug. 27	Sep. 03	Sep. 08	Sep. 23 '98

A Division of The McGraw·Hill Companies

STANDARD
&POOR'S
STOCK REPORTS

Regis Corporation

5072P

03-OCT-98

Business Summary - 20-SEP-98

In assembling a better balanced organization, Regis Corp. has cut back its expansion into malls, and begun to focus on other retail outlets. Core businesses such as Regis Hairstylists, MasterCuts, and Trade Secret salons have gelled with the newly-added Wal-Mart salons, and the popular Supercuts chain. RGIS has recognized its need to branch out into strip centers, which are more easily accessible than malls.

RGIS is the global leader in the highly-fragmented personal hair care industry. The company has salons in all 50 states, and in Puerto Rico, Canada, Mexico, South Africa, Switzerland, the United Kingdom, and Ireland. Since the end of FY 93 (Jun.), Regis has added 581 salons, and plans to to add some 295 outlets during FY 99 (Jun.).

Following the purchases of more than 1,000 Supercuts and 154 Wal-Mart-based salons, Regis has firmly established itself as a hair salon category killer. Supercuts has a strong brand and an operating format similar to that of RGIS, which haved made for a smooth combination of the two businesses. Regis' goal is to eventually increase gross margins from product sales at Supercuts by 800 basis points. RGIS plans to cut costs by buying hair care products for Supercuts directly from manufacturers instead of from a distributor.

Regis has five distinct units. As of June 30, 1998, Regis Hairstylists had 820 mall-based salons, generated 37% of company revenues, and offered a wide variety of hair care services, including $21 stylings. MasterCuts had 412 locations featuring a basic service, family-oriented environment, and generated 13.5% of Regis' revenues, with an average sale of $11. There were 273 SmartStyle salons based in Wal-Mart stores, generating 5% of Regis revenues. The Trade Secret chain included 374 hair and beauty care product-oriented stores based in malls, and accounted for 14.7% of company sales. Strip Center Salons, which is primarily comprised of Supercuts outlets, included 1,268 strip center-based, basic haircut and styling locations, and registered 16.5% of Regis' sales.

In recent years, Regis has emphasized increasing sales of higher-margin hair care products, consisting primarily of shampoos, conditioners, fixatives and hair sprays. Regis-label products and lines of salon-branded products, such as Joico, Paul Mitchell, Nexxus, Matrix and Sebastian, are sold only through licensed beauty salons.

In July, Regis completed six transactions for the acquisition of 46 salons, of which 17 are located in Washington state; 13 in Maryland; 10 in Edmonton; Alberta, Canada; three in Jacksonville, Florida; two in Kansas City, Kansas; and one in Boulder, Colorado. The acquired salons are expected to generate some $11.8 million in annualized revenues.

Per Share Data ($)

(Year Ended Jun. 30)	1998	1997	1996	1995	1994	1993	1992	1991	1990	1989
Tangible Bk. Val.	NA	2.11	2.08	1.48	0.70	0.14	0.08	-0.94	-5.71	-5.83
Cash Flow	NA	1.66	2.08	1.73	1.05	1.05	1.01	0.85	1.41	1.59
Earnings	1.27	0.28	1.06	0.86	0.26	0.27	0.31	-0.37	0.12	0.48
Dividends	0.09	0.08	0.05	Nil	Nil	Nil	Nil	Nil	Nil	Nil
Payout Ratio	7%	29%	5%	Nil	Nil	Nil	Nil	Nil	Nil	Nil
Prices - High	31½	27½	34½	16⅞	11	8⅞	7⅜	9⅛	NA	NA
- Low	24⅝	15½	14⅛	9⅜	7⅛	5⅞	3⅞	4⅝	NA	NA
P/E Ratio - High	25	98	33	20	42	32	23	NM	NA	NA
- Low	19	55	13	11	27	22	13	NM	NA	NA

Income Statement Analysis (Million $)

	1998	1997	1996	1995	1994	1993	1992	1991	1990	1989
Revs.	NA	713	499	422	377	341	306	308	364	322
Oper. Inc.	NA	79.3	56.6	45.6	37.4	31.5	26.9	29.8	32.0	28.7
Depr.	NA	32.1	18.4	14.8	12.3	10.9	9.7	10.5	11.0	9.5
Int. Exp.	NA	10.3	6.1	6.5	8.2	8.5	8.5	14.3	18.7	12.0
Pretax Inc.	NA	19.7	33.0	25.3	7.1	7.0	8.3	-2.2	2.7	7.6
Eff. Tax Rate	NA	67%	42%	42%	43%	45%	47%	NM	62%	46%
Net Inc.	NA	6.6	19.1	14.7	4.0	3.9	4.4	-3.2	1.0	4.1

Balance Sheet & Other Fin. Data (Million $)

	1998	1997	1996	1995	1994	1993	1992	1991	1990	1989
Cash	NA	8.9	5.5	1.2	3.5	2.3	3.8	5.2	2.4	4.6
Curr. Assets	NA	77.1	49.4	35.1	38.0	28.4	22.1	28.8	26.8	28.8
Total Assets	NA	332	221	166	166	143	128	131	130	133
Curr. Liab.	NA	92.1	56.9	45.1	42.0	42.0	30.0	40.0	134	31.0
LT Debt	NA	82.7	50.0	38.0	54.0	52.0	55.0	61.0	4.0	112
Common Eqty.	NA	149	108	76.4	59.7	39.0	35.6	22.8	-11.9	-13.0
Total Cap.	NA	232	158	115	117	93.0	93.0	86.0	-7.0	100
Cap. Exp.	NA	39.4	26.0	153	18.4	21.6	14.1	18.6	14.4	24.8
Cash Flow	NA	38.7	37.5	29.5	16.4	14.8	14.1	7.3	12.0	13.6
Curr. Ratio	NA	0.8	0.9	0.8	0.9	0.7	0.7	0.7	0.2	0.9
% LT Debt of Cap.	NA	35.6	31.5	33.0	46.6	55.4	58.8	71.4	NM	111.7
% Net Inc.of Revs.	NA	0.9	3.9	3.5	1.1	1.1	1.4	NM	0.3	1.3
% Ret. on Assets	NA	2.1	9.9	8.9	2.4	2.8	3.3	NM	0.8	6.1
% Ret. on Equity	NA	4.8	20.8	21.6	7.7	10.3	14.8	NM	NM	NA

Data as orig. reptd.; bef. results of disc. opers. and/or spec. items. Per share data adj. for stk. divs. as of ex-div. date. Bold denotes diluted EPS (FASB 128). E-Estimated. NA-Not Available. NM-Not Meaningful. NR-Not Ranked.

Office—7201 Metro Blvd., Edina, MN 55439. **Tel**—(612) 947-7777. **Fax**—(612) 947-7900. **Chrmn**—M. Kunin. **Pres & CEO**—P. D. Finkelstein. **COO**—M. W. Goldstein. **SVP, CFO & Investor Contact**—Randy L. Pearce. **Dirs**—R. Bjelland, P. D. Finkelstein, C. A. Fox, T. Gregory, V. Z. Hawn, S. S. Hoyt, D. Kunin, M. Kunin. **Transfer Agent & Registrar**—Norwest Bank Minnesota, South St. Paul. **Incorporated**—in Minnesota in 1954. **Empl**— 26,000. **S&P Analyst:** Scott H. Kessler.

Reliance Steel & Aluminum   1913

NYSE Symbol **RS**

In S&P SmallCap 600

03-OCT-98

Industry: Manufacturing (Specialized)

Summary: This major U.S. metals service center company provides value-added metals processing services and distributes metal products through a network of 49 centers in 19 states.

Quantitative Evaluations

Outlook (1 Lowest—5 Highest)
• **3⁻**

Fair Value
• **35**

Risk
• **Average**

Earn./Div. Rank
• **NR**

Technical Eval.
• **Bearish** since 8/98

Rel. Strength Rank (1 Lowest—99 Highest)
• **60**

Insider Activity
• **NA**

Recent Price • 30½   Yield • 0.8%

52 Wk Range • 41¼-26⅛   12-Mo. P/E • 12.6

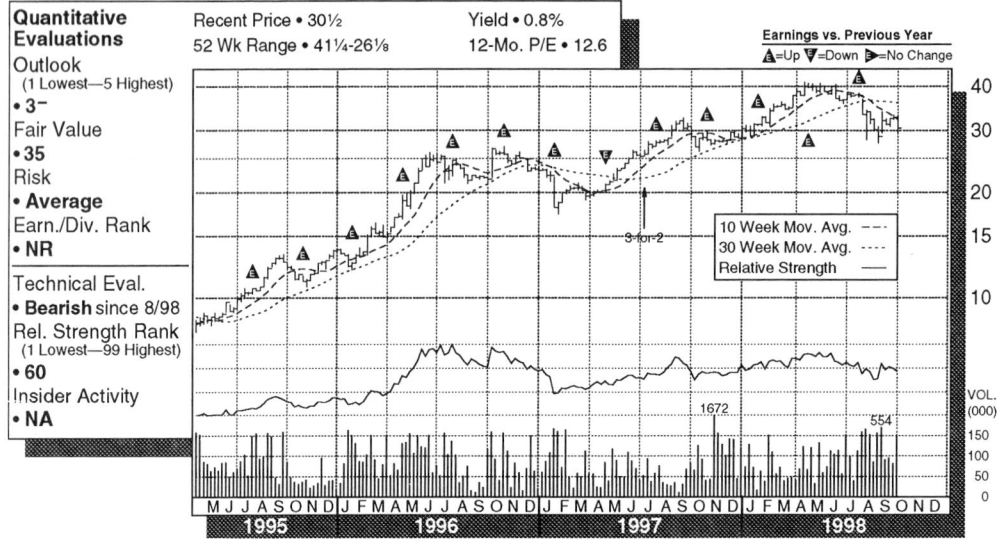

Earnings vs. Previous Year
△=Up ▽=Down ▷=No Change

10 Week Mov. Avg. – – –
30 Week Mov. Avg. ·······
Relative Strength —

3-for-2

1672   554

Business Profile - 30-SEP-98

Reliance operates in the highly fragmented U.S. metals distribution industry, where the company feels it ranks as one of the ten largest participants. Management has adopted a long-term strategy to increase its profitability through expansion of existing operations and acquisitions of complementary businesses which can diversify or enhance the customer base, product range or geographic coverage. Toward that end, Reliance has recently acquired several privately-held metals service center companies, and in September 1998, agreed to acquire the remaining 50% interest in American Metals Corp. In November 1997, RS sold 3.1 million common shares, with net proceeds of nearly $81 million (before over-allotments) earmarked for repayment of debt, potential acquisitions and general corporate purposes.

Operational Review - 30-SEP-98

Total revenues for the six months ended June 30, 1998, rose 44%, year to year, primarily reflecting acquisitions. Excluding acquisitions, tons sold were up 2.8%, partially offset by a 1.0% decline in the average selling price per ton. Gross profit margins improved slightly, reflecting a more favorable product mix, and with warehouse, delivery and SG&A expenses growing more slowly than revenues, pretax income gained 69%. With equity earnings virtually unchanged, and after taxes at 41.0%, versus 39.9%, net income was up 59%, to $24,263,000 ($1.27 a share, on 23% more shares) from $15,298,000 ($0.99).

Stock Performance - 02-OCT-98

In the past 30 trading days, RS's shares have increased 1%, compared to a 7% fall in the S&P 500. Average trading volume for the past five days was 30,040 shares, compared with the 40-day moving average of 37,546 shares.

Key Stock Statistics

Dividend Rate/Share	0.24	Shareholders	300
Shs. outstg. (M)	18.9	Market cap. (B)	$0.576
Avg. daily vol. (M)	0.022	Inst. holdings	39%
Tang. Bk. Value/Share	12.13		
Beta	NA		

Value of $10,000 invested 5 years ago: NA

Fiscal Year Ending Dec. 31

	1998	1997	1996	1995	1994	1993
Revenues (Million $)						
1Q	315.5	201.6	157.6	136.5	104.9	--
2Q	326.2	243.8	164.6	140.8	109.1	184.7
3Q	—	254.2	153.4	135.3	115.7	95.20
4Q	—	261.9	178.3	148.8	117.2	91.30
Yr.	—	961.5	654.0	561.3	446.9	371.2
Earnings Per Share ($)						
1Q	**0.62**	**0.45**	0.51	0.35	0.27	--
2Q	**0.66**	**0.55**	0.49	0.37	0.33	--
3Q	--	**0.55**	0.45	0.37	0.31	--
4Q	--	**0.60**	0.45	0.37	0.23	--
Yr.	--	**2.15**	1.90	1.45	1.14	0.66

Next earnings report expected: late October

Dividend Data (Dividends have been paid since 1995.)

Amount ($)	Date Decl.	Ex-Div. Date	Stock of Record	Payment Date
0.035	Nov. 21	Dec. 17	Dec. 19	Jan. 09 '98
0.060	Feb. 24	Mar. 12	Mar. 16	Apr. 06 '98
0.060	May. 21	May. 29	Jun. 02	Jun. 12 '98
0.060	Aug. 28	Sep. 03	Sep. 08	Sep. 15 '98

A Division of The **McGraw·Hill** *Companies*

Business Summary - 30-SEP-98

Reliance Steel & Aluminum is one of the largest metals service center companies in the U.S., operating through a network of 62 centers in 20 states as of September 25, 1998. Through these centers, the company provides value-added metals processing services and distributes a full line of more than 60,000 metal products, including galvanized, hot-rolled and cold-finished steel, stainless steel, aluminum, brass, copper, and alloy steel. Metal products are sold to more than 40,000 customers in a wide range of industries, including general manufacturing, construction (both commercial and residential), transportation (rail, truck and auto after-market), and aerospace.

Metal service centers acquire products from primary metals producers and then process steel, aluminum, stainless steel and other metals to meet customer specifications, including specific lengths, widths, shapes and surface characteristics. Many manufacturers are not willing to invest in the necessary technology, equipment and inventory to process the metals for their own manufacturing operations. As such, industry forces have created a market niche to allow metal service centers such as Reliance to purchase, process and deliver metals to end-users in a more efficient and cost-effective manner than the end-user could achieve in dealing directly with the primary producer, or with an intermediate steel processor.

Reliance's metals service centers use techniques such as cutting-to-length, slitting, blanking, burning, shearing

and sawing, and save time, labor and expenses for customers, thereby lowering their overall manufacturing costs. Products are then delivered to manufacturers and other end-users, generally within 24 hours from receipt of the initial order.

The metals service center industry is highly fragmented and intensely competitive within localized areas or regions, and many of the company's competitors operate single stand-alone service centers. According to industry sources, the number of intermediate steel processors and metals service center facilities in the United States has been reduced from approximately 7,000 in 1980 to approximately 3,400 in 1997. Reliance believes that this consolidation trend creates new opportunities for acquisitions.

The company has a history of expansion through acquisitions, as well as from internal growth. Since its initial public offering in September 1994, and through January 1998, Reliance has completed and integrated ten acquisitions, including the early 1998 acquisitions of Phoenix Metals Co. and Durrett-Sheppard Steel Co., L.L.C., which had combined annual sales of about $159 million. Also in July 1998, Reliance acquired Chatham Steel Corp., with annual sales of $166 million, and in late September 1998, agreed to acquire the remaining 50% interest in American Metals Corp., which had revenues of $56 million in 1997. Prior to going public, the company was also very aggressive in making acquisitions, with 20 acquisitions from 1984 to September 1994.

Per Share Data ($)

(Year Ended Dec. 31)	1997	1996	1995	1994	1993	1992	1991	1990	1989	1988
Tangible Bk. Val.	13.06	12.44	10.64	9.20	8.70	NA	NA	NA	NA	NA
Cash Flow	2.98	2.45	1.79	1.48	NA	NA	NA	NA	NA	NA
Earnings	2.15	1.90	1.45	1.14	0.66	NA	NA	NA	NA	NA
Dividends	0.14	0.08	0.07	Nil	NA	NA	NA	NA	NA	NA
Payout Ratio	7%	4%	5%	Nil	NA	NA	NA	NA	NA	NA
Prices - High	32⅝	27⅛	13⅞	10⅞	NA	NA	NA	NA	NA	NA
- Low	17⅜	12	7⅝	7	NA	NA	NA	NA	NA	NA
P/E Ratio - High	15	14	10	10	NA	NA	NA	NA	NA	NA
- Low	8	6	5	6	NA	NA	NA	NA	NA	NA

Income Statement Analysis (Million $)

	1997	1996	1995	1994	1993	1992	1991	1990	1989	1988
Revs.	962	642	561	447	371	346	406	432	469	NA
Oper. Inc.	72.6	52.2	39.9	28.8	19.0	14.1	17.6	23.1	24.0	NA
Depr.	13.2	8.6	5.2	4.3	3.6	3.5	4.1	4.3	4.5	NA
Int. Exp.	10.9	3.9	1.6	2.1	2.3	2.5	4.6	4.8	5.6	NA
Pretax Inc.	58.0	50.6	38.6	24.3	14.9	12.9	10.1	15.0	15.2	NA
Eff. Tax Rate	41%	40%	41%	41%	38%	42%	41%	40%	40%	NA
Net Inc.	34.2	29.8	22.7	14.4	9.2	7.6	5.9	8.9	9.1	NA

Balance Sheet & Other Fin. Data (Million $)

	1997	1996	1995	1994	1993	1992	1991	1990	1989	1988
Cash	34.0	0.8	18.0	8.3	NA	NA	NA	NA	NA	NA
Curr. Assets	322	211	167	125	NA	NA	NA	NA	NA	NA
Total Assets	584	391	260	199	187	NA	NA	NA	NA	NA
Curr. Liab.	109	74.1	66.2	40.9	NA	NA	NA	NA	NA	NA
LT Debt	143	107	30.4	8.5	10.1	NA	NA	NA	NA	NA
Common Eqty.	313	193	164	150	136	NA	NA	NA	NA	NA
Total Cap.	475	308	194	159	146	NA	NA	NA	NA	NA
Cap. Exp.	26.6	21.4	7.9	9.5	10.1	7.3	5.0	12.6	13.0	NA
Cash Flow	47.3	38.4	27.9	18.7	12.9	11.1	10.0	13.2	13.5	NA
Curr. Ratio	3.0	2.9	2.5	3.1	NA	NA	NA	NA	NA	NA
% LT Debt of Cap.	30.2	34.7	15.7	5.4	6.9	NA	NA	NA	NA	NA
% Net Inc.of Revs.	3.6	4.6	4.1	3.2	2.5	2.2	1.5	2.1	1.9	NA
% Ret. on Assets	7.0	9.6	9.9	6.5	NA	NA	NA	NA	NA	NA
% Ret. on Equity	13.5	16.7	14.5	10.2	NA	NA	NA	NA	NA	NA

Data as orig. reptd.; bef. results of disc. opers. and/or spec. items. Per share data adj. for stk. divs. as of ex-div. date. Bold denotes diluted EPS (FASB 128). E-Estimated. NA-Not Available. NM-Not Meaningful. NR-Not Ranked.

Office—2550 East 25th St., Los Angeles, CA 90058. **Tel**—(213) 582-2272. **Chrmn & CEO**—J. D. Crider. **Pres**—D. H. Hannah. **EVP & COO**—G. J. Mollins.**SVP- CFO**—S. S Weis.**Secy**—Y. M. Schiotis. **Dirs**—J. D. Crider, D. H. Hannah, D. M. Hayes, R. Henigson, K. H. Loring, G. J. Mollins, W. I. Rumer, L. A. Waite. **Transfer Agent & Registrar**—First Chicago Trust Co. of New York, Jersey City, NJ. **Incorporated**—in California in 1939. **Empl**— 2,750. **S&P Analyst:** C.C.P.

03-OCT-98

Industry:
Oil & Gas (Exploration & Production)

Summary: This independent energy company, which explores for, develops and produces oil and natural gas, has interests offshore the Gulf of Mexico and in Texas and Louisiana.

Quantitative Evaluations		
Outlook (1 Lowest—5 Highest) • **NA**	Recent Price • 4	Yield • Nil
Fair Value • **NA**	52 Wk Range • 8½-2⅞	12-Mo. P/E • NM

Risk • **Average**

Earn./Div. Rank • **NR**

Technical Eval. • **NA**

Rel. Strength Rank (1 Lowest—99 Highest) • **47**

Insider Activity • **NA**

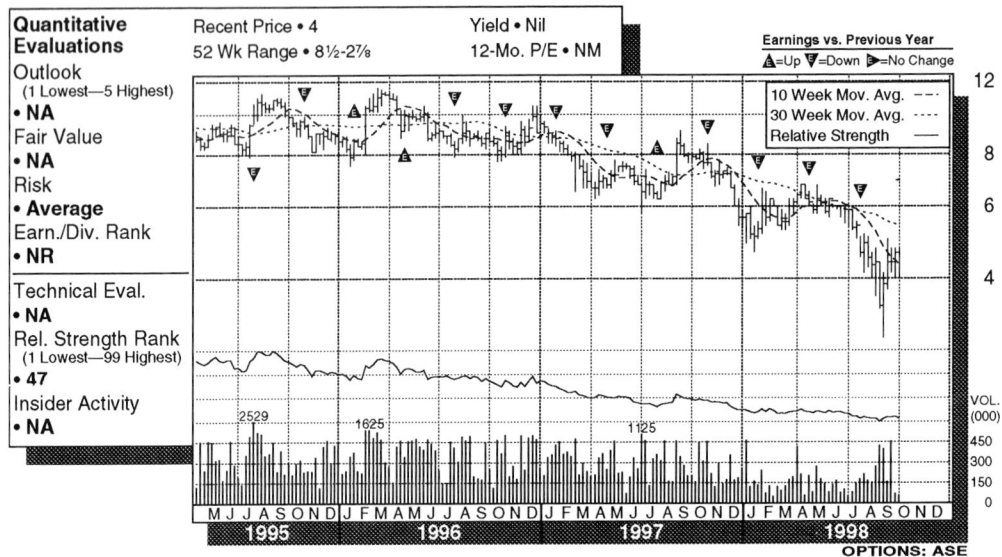

Earnings vs. Previous Year
▲=Up ▼=Down ▶=No Change

10 Week Mov. Avg. ----
30 Week Mov. Avg. ·····
Relative Strength ——

OPTIONS: ASE

Business Profile - 09-SEP-98

This company (formerly Box Energy Corp.) owns interests in oil and gas properties in the South Pass area of the Gulf of Mexico, and other drilling prospects in Texas and Louisiana. The company's long-term strategy is to focus on exploration and acquisition activities in geographically and geologically focused areas. In August 1997, J.R. Simplot gained ownership of Box Brothers Holding Co., and, based on prior purchases, control of 100% of the company's Class A shares, and the right to name three directors. Don Box was replaced as chairman in October, and 18 employees submitted their resignations. In December, shareholders voted to change the name of the company to Remington Oil and Gas Corp.

Operational Review - 09-SEP-98

Revenues in the six months ended June 30, 1998, fell 28%, year to year, reflecting lower oil and gas prices and decreased gas production from South Pass Block 89, partly offset by increased oil production. Expenses dropped less rapidly, as operating costs rose related to new producing properties, and a pretax loss contrasted with pretax income. Despite no taxes, versus taxes at 35.0%, a net loss of $3,152,000 ($0.15 a share) contrasted with net income of $1,345,000 ($0.06).

Stock Performance - 02-OCT-98

In the past 30 trading days, ROILB's shares have declined 9%, compared to a 7% fall in the S&P 500. Average trading volume for the past five days was 11,660 shares, compared with the 40-day moving average of 51,936 shares.

Key Stock Statistics

Dividend Rate/Share	Nil	Shareholders	1,700
Shs. outstg. (M)	20.4	Market cap. (B)	$0.069
Avg. daily vol. (M)	0.039	Inst. holdings	21%
Tang. Bk. Value/Share	2.04		
Beta	0.41		

Value of $10,000 invested 5 years ago: $ 4,155

Fiscal Year Ending Dec. 31

	1998	1997	1996	1995	1994	1993
Revenues (Million $)						
1Q	12.51	17.23	19.07	14.51	13.10	8.60
2Q	12.06	16.97	17.86	12.56	17.30	8.70
3Q	—	13.48	15.82	14.91	16.03	9.80
4Q	—	13.38	17.45	17.51	12.85	10.00
Yr.	—	61.05	70.21	59.49	59.24	37.10
Earnings Per Share ($)						
1Q	-0.10	0.09	0.12	0.04	0.10	0.03
2Q	-0.06	-0.02	-0.17	0.04	0.16	0.05
3Q	—	-0.37	-0.15	0.09	0.16	-0.02
4Q	—	-1.01	-0.17	0.09	0.02	0.04
Yr.	—	-1.31	-0.37	0.26	0.44	0.10

Next earnings report expected: early November

Dividend Data

No cash dividends have been paid since 1991.

A Division of The McGraw-Hill Companies

Business Summary - 09-SEP-98

Since a change in management and the election of a new board of directors in August 1996, Remington Oil & Gas (formerly Box Energy Corp.) was the subject of several on-again, off-again takeover rumors. In August 1997, the Box brothers agreed to accept J.R. Simplot's offer of $21.5 million to purchase 89.6% of Box Brothers Holding Corp., since renamed S-Sixteen Holding Co., and, combined with earlier stock purchases, control of 100% of the Class A stock, or 57% of the company's voting stock. Three new directors were added.

The company's current strategy is to focus on arresting a decline in oil and gas reserves, and lowering finding costs. It increased reserve base during 1997, with proved oil reserves increasing to 4,451,000 bbl. of oil at year end, up from 3,299,000 bbl. at the end of 1996. Natural gas reserves declined to 36,500 MMcf, from 39,300 MMcf. On an energy equivalent basis, total reserves at the end of 1997 amounted to 10,534,333 bbl. of oil equivalent (BOE), up from 9,849,000 BOE at year end 1996. Finding costs were reduced, but remain above the industry average.

The company's most important interests are in oil and gas leases covering three contiguous offshore blocks in the Gulf of Mexico, known as the South Pass Blocks

86, 87 and 89, and an oil well in the neighboring West Delta Block 128. These four blocks overlie a large sub-surface salt dome located about 35 miles offshore Louisiana. Currently the company's most valuable properties, they are characterized by complex geology, including multiple oil and gas reservoirs. The company's wells in the four blocks have typically been drilled with significant directional deviation to total vertical depths ranging from 8,400 ft. to 18,500 ft. The company's Gulf of Mexico reserves accounted for 50% and 83%, of ROILB's total oil and gas reserves, respectively.

Since 1994, the company has expanded its Gulf of Mexico presence away from the South Pass area by participating in Minerals Management Service lease sales. In addition to ROILB's interests in the Gulf of Mexico, core areas include Mississippi/Alabama, West Texas/New Mexico, and South Texas. At December 31, 1997, the company had interests in 29 gross (9.84 net) producing oil wells and 88 (20.70) producing gas wells. During 1997, the company drilled 10 gross (4.08 net) exploratory wells, of which three (1.10) were productive and seven (2.98) were dry holes. The company also drilled nine gross (4.60 net) development wells, of which five (1.83) were productive and four (2.77) were dry holes. The company has approved a capital budget of $35 million for 1998.

Per Share Data ($)

(Year Ended Dec. 31)	1997	1996	1995	1994	1993	1992	1991	1990	1989	1988
Tangible Bk. Val.	21.80	3.57	3.94	3.63	3.25	3.15	2.27	2.74	0.67	1.19
Cash Flow	0.07	0.73	0.98	0.97	0.59	1.11	0.29	3.31	0.25	0.95
Earnings	-1.31	-0.37	0.26	0.44	0.10	0.92	0.13	3.05	-0.12	0.17
Dividends	Nil	Nil	Nil	Nil	Nil	Nil	0.60	1.00	0.40	0.40
Payout Ratio	Nil	Nil	Nil	Nil	Nil	Nil	446%	32%	NM	237%
Prices - High	9⅜	11⅝	11¼	14⅛	13¼	19½	6¾	4⅝	4½	5⅞
- Low	4⅞	7½	7⅝	7½	8¾	5⅞	3¼	1¾	2⅛	3¾
P/E Ratio - High	NM	NM	43	32	NM	21	52	2	NM	35
- Low	NM	NM	29	17	NM	6	25	1	NM	22

Income Statement Analysis (Million $)

	1997	1996	1995	1994	1993	1992	1991	1990	1989	1988
Revs.	57.3	65.6	54.4	57.0	33.5	18.7	20.6	26.1	25.9	35.5
Oper. Inc.	24.7	15.6	40.5	28.1	14.7	4.3	6.6	-0.5	10.2	19.2
Depr. Depl. & Amort.	28.3	22.8	15.0	11.1	10.1	3.9	3.2	4.6	7.7	15.8
Int. Exp.	5.3	4.9	4.8	5.1	5.0	1.1	0.2	2.5	1.8	0.8
Pretax Inc.	-41.3	-9.4	7.5	14.2	2.1	-0.5	2.7	62.9	-2.5	3.4
Eff. Tax Rate	NM	NM	28%	36%	NM	NM	Nil	Nil	Nil	Nil
Net Inc.	-26.8	-7.7	5.4	9.2	2.2	19.2	2.7	62.9	-2.5	3.4

Balance Sheet & Other Fin. Data (Million $)

	1997	1996	1995	1994	1993	1992	1991	1990	1989	1988
Cash	4.6	35.7	46.4	40.5	30.6	38.2	1.1	28.3	0.2	0.4
Curr. Assets	18.9	46.2	55.7	46.2	36.0	41.5	2.3	34.5	4.8	10.4
Total Assets	99	137	145	135	129	129	53.0	64.0	35.0	40.0
Curr. Liab.	15.9	7.2	8.4	4.5	4.5	3.9	4.3	5.7	2.9	3.6
LT Debt	38.4	55.1	55.1	55.1	56.7	57.0	Nil	Nil	15.4	7.1
Common Eqty.	44.3	74.4	82.0	75.5	67.7	65.5	46.3	55.9	13.6	24.3
Total Cap.	82.7	129	137	131	124	123	46.0	56.0	29.0	31.0
Cap. Exp.	39.1	39.8	21.3	16.6	18.9	19.1	25.9	9.7	10.6	9.4
Cash Flow	1.5	15.1	20.4	20.2	12.3	23.1	5.9	67.5	5.2	19.3
Curr. Ratio	1.2	6.4	6.7	10.4	8.0	10.5	0.5	6.0	1.7	2.9
% LT Debt of Cap.	46.4	42.6	40.3	42.2	45.6	46.6	NM	NM	53.1	22.6
% Ret. on Assets	NM	NM	3.9	6.9	1.7	21.0	4.7	126.5	NM	8.5
% Ret. on Equity	NM	NM	6.9	12.8	3.2	34.1	5.4	180.9	NM	12.9

Data as orig. reptd.; bef. results of disc opers. and/or spec. items. Per share data adj. for stk. divs. as of ex-div. date. Bold denotes diluted EPS (FASB 128). E-Estimated. NA-Not Available. NM-Not Meaningful. NR-Not Ranked.

Office—8201 Preston Rd., Suite 600, Dallas, TX 75225-6211. **Tel**—(214) 890-8000. **Chrmn**—D. H. Hawk. **Pres, & CEO**—J. A. Watt. **VP-Fin & Secy**—J. B. Asher. **Dirs**—D. D. Box, J. E. Goble, Jr., W. E. Greenwood, D. H. Hawk, J. A. Lyle, D. A. Preng, T. W. Rollins, A. C. Shapiro, J. A. Watt. **Transfer Agent & Registrar**—American Stock Transfer & Trust Co., NYC. **Incorporated**—in Delaware in 1991. **Empl**— 15. **S&P Analyst:** N.R.

STANDARD &POOR'S
STOCK REPORTS

Renal Care Group

5075J

NASDAQ Symbol **RCGI**

In S&P SmallCap 600

03-OCT-98

Industry:
Health Care (Specialized Services)

Summary: This nephrology services company provides care to patients with kidney disease, including patients suffering from chronic kidney failure.

Quantitative Evaluations	
Outlook (1 Lowest—5 Highest)	• NA
Fair Value	• NA
Risk	• NA
Earn./Div. Rank	• NR
Technical Eval.	• NA
Rel. Strength Rank (1 Lowest—99 Highest)	• 76
Insider Activity	• Neutral

Recent Price • 24⅜
52 Wk Range • 30⅜-17⅛

Yield • Nil
12-Mo. P/E • 35.8

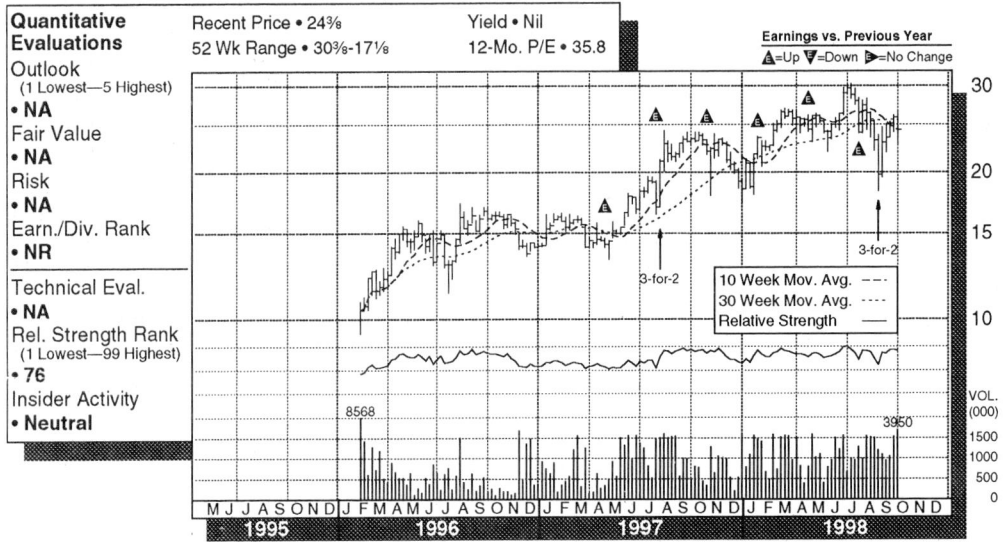

Earnings vs. Previous Year
▲=Up ▼=Down ▶=No Change

10 Week Mov. Avg. — - -
30 Week Mov. Avg. - - - -
Relative Strength —

Business Profile - 10-AUG-98

Renal Care has continued its strategy of growth through acquisitions. In August 1998, the company acquired two Michigan-based outpatient dialysis programs serving about 264 patients. In April 1998, RCGI completed the purchase of several dialysis facilities in Missouri, Kansas, Oklahoma and Texas, which serve a total of 205 patients. In August 1998, the company said it was confident of continued success, given its operational improvements, more favorable reimbursements and full acquisition pipeline. In July 1998, directors declared a 3-for-2 stock split, to be distributed on August 24, 1998.

Operational Review - 10-AUG-98

Net revenues in the six months ended June 30, 1998, rose 74%, year to year, driven by acquisitions, as well as strong internal growth. Margins widened, reflecting a smaller increase in costs and expenses; operating income surged 102%. Following interest expense versus income, the advance in pretax income was held to 79%. After taxes at 37.0%, versus 37.2%, net income advanced 76%, to $15,391,000 ($0.55 a share, based on 23% more shares), from $8,726,000 ($0.38). Results include merger costs of $0.02 and $0.01 a share in the respective periods.

Stock Performance - 02-OCT-98

In the past 30 trading days, RCGI's shares have increased 5%, compared to a 7% fall in the S&P 500. Average trading volume for the past five days was 790,080 shares, compared with the 40-day moving average of 340,047 shares.

Key Stock Statistics

Dividend Rate/Share	Nil	Shareholders	100
Shs. outstg. (M)	40.4	Market cap. (B)	$0.984
Avg. daily vol. (M)	0.398	Inst. holdings	55%
Tang. Bk. Value/Share	1.44		
Beta	NA		

Value of $10,000 invested 5 years ago: NA

Fiscal Year Ending Dec. 31

	1998	1997	1996	1995	1994	1993
Revenues (Million $)						
1Q	80.46	46.11	24.53	—	—	—
2Q	89.51	51.67	31.83	—	—	—
3Q	—	54.04	34.63	—	—	—
4Q	—	62.20	38.53	—	—	—
Yr.	—	214.0	129.5	42.97	41.63	18.13
Earnings Per Share ($)						
1Q	**0.17**	0.12	0.11	—	—	—
2Q	**0.19**	0.13	0.09	—	—	—
3Q	—	0.15	0.05	—	—	—
4Q	—	0.16	0.11	—	—	—
Yr.	—	**0.56**	0.37	—	—	—

Next earnings report expected: NA

Dividend Data

Amount ($)	Date Decl.	Ex-Div. Date	Stock of Record	Payment Date
3-for-2	Jul. 23	Aug. 25	Aug. 07	Aug. 24 '98

A Division of The McGraw-Hill Companies

STANDARD
&POOR'S
STOCK REPORTS

Renal Care Group, Inc.

5075J

03-OCT-98

Business Summary - 10-AUG-98

This nephrology services company has grown substantially since it began operations in February 1996 with an aggregate of 41 dialysis centers serving about 2,663 patients in eight states. As of December 31, 1998, Renal Care Group (RCGI) was providing dialysis and ancillary services to about 8,300 patients through 121 owned and managed outpatient dialysis centers in 15 states, in addition to providing acute dialysis services in 70 hospitals.

RCGI is a provider of nephrology services, which is the specialized practice of medicine dedicated to providing care to patients with end-stage renal disease (ESRD) and other kidney-specific ailments. An essential part of the nephrologist's practice is the dialysis facility, where ESRD patients receive their dialysis treatments three times per week in a technologically advanced outpatient setting. ESRD is the state of advanced renal impairment that is irreversible and imminently lethal. Patients with ESRD eventually require dialysis or kidney transplantation to sustain life. According to industry data, the number of patients receiving chronic dialysis services in the United States has grown at a compound annual rate of 8.9%, from 66,000 patients in 1982 to about 200,000 in 1995.

The company's objective is to develop fully integrated nephrology provider networks to assume and manage the clinical and financial risk associated with providing renal disease management services on a capitated basis. It seeks to achieve this objective by acquiring, developing and managing outpatient and medical center-based dialysis centers; integrating its dialysis centers with affiliated nephrology practices; developing a protocol-driven ESRD management model to enhance clinical outcomes; and providing appropriate ancillary services to ESRD patients.

RCGI believes that an integrated network of nephrologist and dialysis centers, combined with its clinical expertise, management experience and access to capital, will provide significant advantages to patients and third-party payors by improving the quality of care while reducing the overall costs associated with treating patients with all forms of kidney disease, including those with ESRD.

The company estimates that on average its centers were operating at about 65% of capacity as of 1997 year end, based on the assumption that a dialysis center is able to provide up to three treatments a day per station, six days a week. It believes that it may increase the number of dialysis treatments at its centers without making additional capital expenditures. In 1997, Medicare accounted for 63% of RCGI's net patient revenues, Medicaid 7%, private and other payors 25%, and hospital inpatient dialysis services 5%.

Per Share Data ($)

(Year Ended Dec. 31)	1997	1996	1995	1994	1993	1992	1991	1990	1989	1988
Tangible Bk. Val.	1.52	2.49	0.69	NA	NA	NA	NA	NA	NA	NA
Cash Flow	0.81	0.53	NA	NA	NA	NA	NA	NA	NA	NA
Earnings	0.56	0.37	NA	NA	NA	NA	NA	NA	NA	NA
Dividends	Nil	Nil	Nil	Nil	Nil	Nil	Nil	Nil	Nil	Nil
Payout Ratio	Nil	Nil	Nil	Nil	Nil	Nil	Nil	Nil	Nil	Nil
Prices - High	24⅜	17⅜	NA	NA	NA	NA	NA	NA	NA	NA
- Low	13¼	8	NA	NA	NA	NA	NA	NA	NA	NA
P/E Ratio - High	43	31	NA	NA	NA	NA	NA	NA	NA	NA
- Low	24	14	NA	NA	NA	NA	NA	NA	NA	NA

Income Statement Analysis (Million $)

	1997	1996	1995	1994	1993	1992	1991	1990	1989	1988
Revs.	214	130	43.0	41.6	18.1	8.7	NA	NA	NA	NA
Oper. Inc.	41.5	23.6	5.0	6.5	0.9	0.6	NA	NA	NA	NA
Depr.	9.0	4.5	1.6	1.5	0.6	0.1	NA	NA	NA	NA
Int. Exp.	-0.6	NM	0.5	0.4	0.1	0.0	NA	NA	NA	NA
Pretax Inc.	32.7	17.7	3.0	4.6	0.3	0.5	NA	NA	NA	NA
Eff. Tax Rate	36%	39%	Nil	Nil	50%	9.70%	NA	NA	NA	NA
Net Inc.	20.0	10.7	3.0	4.6	0.1	0.4	NA	NA	NA	NA

Balance Sheet & Other Fin. Data (Million $)

	1997	1996	1995	1994	1993	1992	1991	1990	1989	1988
Cash	9.1	53.4	1.3	NA	NA	NA	NA	NA	NA	NA
Curr. Assets	65.8	86.5	11.1	NA	NA	NA	NA	NA	NA	NA
Total Assets	248	132	20.8	17.3	14.4	2.6	NA	NA	NA	NA
Curr. Liab.	41.3	37.0	12.5	NA	NA	NA	NA	NA	NA	NA
LT Debt	15.5	Nil	3.7	NA	NA	NA	NA	NA	NA	NA
Common Eqty.	175	93.3	4.6	5.9	4.9	1.5	NA	NA	NA	NA
Total Cap.	207	94.8	8.2	NA	NA	NA	NA	NA	NA	NA
Cap. Exp.	27.4	11.4	4.8	2.4	NA	NA	NA	NA	NA	NA
Cash Flow	29.0	15.3	4.6	6.1	0.7	0.6	NA	NA	NA	NA
Curr. Ratio	1.6	2.3	0.9	NA	NA	NA	NA	NA	NA	NA
% LT Debt of Cap.	7.5	Nil	44.5	NA	NA	NA	NA	NA	NA	NA
% Net Inc.of Revs.	9.3	8.3	6.9	11.1	0.7	4.7	NA	NA	NA	NA
% Ret. on Assets	10.5	14.1	15.6	29.3	1.5	NA	NA	NA	NA	NA
% Ret. on Equity	14.9	22.0	56.7	85.7	4.1	NA	NA	NA	NA	NA

Data as orig. reptd.; bef. results of disc. opers. and/or spec. items. Per share data adj. for stk. divs. as of ex-div. date. Bold denotes diluted EPS (FASB 128). E-Estimated. NA-Not Available. NM-Not Meaningful. NR-Not Ranked.

Office—2100 West End Ave., Suite 800, Nashville, TN 37203. **Tel**—(615) 345-5500. **Pres & CEO**—S. A. Brooks Jr. **EVP, CFO, Secy & Treas**—R. Hinds. **Dirs**—J. D. Bower, S. A. Brooks Jr., J. C. Hutts, H. R. Jacobson, K. Johnson, T. A. Lowrey, S. D. McMurray, T. Meredith. **Transfer Agent & Registrar**—First Union National Bank of North Carolina, Charlotte. **Incorporated**—in Delaware in 1995. **Empl**— 2,639. **S&P Analyst**: Stephen J. Tekirian

03-OCT-98   **Industry:** Paper & Forest Products

Summary: Republic Group (formerly Republic Gypsum) makes paperboard and gypsum wallboard for distribution throughout the U.S.

Quantitative Evaluations	
Outlook (1 Lowest—5 Highest)	• **5**
Fair Value	• **30**
Risk	• **Average**
Earn./Div. Rank	• **B**
Technical Eval.	• **Bearish** since 8/98
Rel. Strength Rank (1 Lowest—99 Highest)	• **32**
Insider Activity	• **Neutral**

Recent Price • 13⅝   Yield • 2.6%
52 Wk Range • 22⅜-13   12-Mo. P/E • 9.1

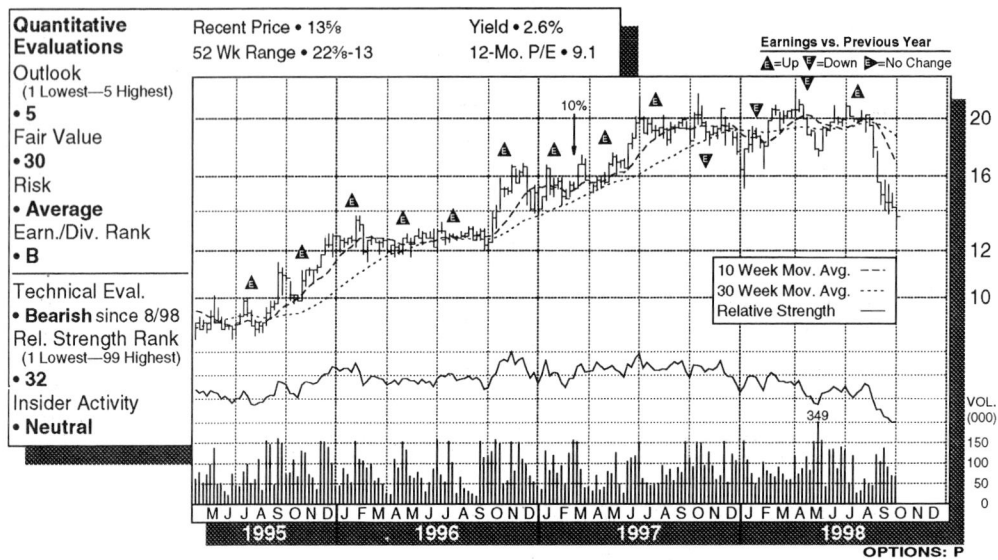

Earnings vs. Previous Year
▲=Up ▼=Down ▶=No Change

- 10 Week Mov. Avg. ---
- 30 Week Mov. Avg. ·····
- Relative Strength —

VOL. (000)

M J J A S O N D | J F M A M J J A S O N D | J F M A M J J A S O N D | J F M A M J J A S O N D
1995 — 1996 — 1997 — 1998

OPTIONS: P

Business Profile - 20-APR-98

Republic's plan to double production capacity at its gypsum wallboard manufacturing facilities in Duke, OK, is on schedule and should be completed during the late summer of 1998. RGC has slowly been implementing selling price increases for its recycled paperboard products in response to rising raw material costs. Recycled paperboard margins have continued to be hurt by the lag between the rise in costs and the implementation of selling price increases, as well as the difficulty of passing all cost increases to the customer. RGC said that demand for gypsum wallboard continues to be strong and prices have stabilized. Chairman Phil Simpson and family control about 19% of the common stock.

Operational Review - 20-APR-98

Net sales in the first nine months of FY 98 (Jun.) advanced 5.2%, year to year, reflecting an 8.5% rise in gypsum wallboard sales and a 0.2% increase in sales in the recycled paperboard segment. Gross margins narrowed as a result of raw material pricing pressures, and selling and administrative expenses were 12% higher; operating profit declined 15%. Following other income of $158,000, compared to expenses of $581,000, pretax income was down 12%. After taxes at 38.0% versus 36.5%, net income dropped 14%, to $12,529,000 ($1.06 a share), from $14,624,000 ($1.24)

Stock Performance - 02-OCT-98

In the past 30 trading days, RGC's shares have declined 23%, compared to a 7% fall in the S&P 500. Average trading volume for the past five days was 13,320 shares, compared with the 40-day moving average of 17,405 shares.

Key Stock Statistics

Dividend Rate/Share	0.36	Shareholders	800
Shs. outstg. (M)	11.7	Market cap. (B)	$0.160
Avg. daily vol. (M)	0.019	Inst. holdings	33%
Tang. Bk. Value/Share	7.45		
Beta	1.36		

Value of $10,000 invested 5 years ago: $ 24,115

Fiscal Year Ending Jun. 30

	1998	1997	1996	1995	1994	1993
Revenues (Million $)						
1Q	31.89	29.00	32.27	20.85	14.48	12.87
2Q	32.43	30.97	29.73	22.35	14.82	12.31
3Q	31.91	30.73	29.19	26.53	16.80	11.82
4Q	32.05	33.00	26.72	26.68	17.10	12.19
Yr.	128.3	123.7	117.9	96.41	63.20	49.19
Earnings Per Share ($)						
1Q	0.37	0.43	0.27	0.23	0.13	0.09
2Q	**0.34**	0.42	0.35	0.25	0.13	0.08
3Q	**0.36**	0.40	0.35	0.27	0.23	0.05
4Q	**0.45**	0.43	0.29	0.25	0.18	0.05
Yr.	**1.51**	1.67	1.27	1.00	0.66	0.28

Next earnings report expected: early October

Dividend Data (Dividends have been paid since 1992.)

Amount ($)	Date Decl.	Ex-Div. Date	Stock of Record	Payment Date
0.090	Oct. 23	Nov. 25	Nov. 28	Dec. 15 '97
0.090	Jan. 27	Feb. 25	Feb. 27	Mar. 16 '98
0.090	Apr. 21	May. 27	May. 29	Jun. 15 '98
0.090	Aug. 04	Aug. 26	Aug. 28	Sep. 15 '98

A Division of The McGraw-Hill Companies

Business Summary - 20-APR-98

Back in the 1980s, when it was called Republic Gypsum Co., this company wished to secure a long-term supply of recycled paperboard, a key ingredient in the manufacture of its product, gypsum wallboard. In 1983, Republic Gypsum found a steady supply of the raw material, and it found something else as well -- a new business direction. The company, known today as Republic Group Inc. (RGC), purchased two paperboard mills in Kansas and Colorado and started making recycled paperboard itself, not only for its own gypsum operation in Oklahoma but also for other wallboard producers and for manufacturers of composite cans, cores, tubes and other packaging products. RGC is now primarily a manufacturer of recycled paperboard products with an integrated gypsum wallboard manufacturing operation.

Vertical integration is an important element of this company's operating philosophy. In 1994, RGC acquired reclaimed paper recycling centers in Missouri and Kansas, enabling the company to achieve further vertical integration of its recycled paperboard manufacturing activities. The company had purchased reclaimed paper from these centers for years.

In 1995, RGC purchased a paperboard maker in West Virginia, further complementing its business. Because Halltown Paperboard Co. does not make paperboard for the gypsum wallboard industry, its acquisition strengthened the company's ability to serve the packaging products industry and provided geographical diversification as well. RGC's increased emphasis on its recycled paperboard business mitigates to some extent its dependence on the cyclical construction and housing industries in which the company's gypsum wallboard is used.

Gypsum operations, benefiting from higher prices and shipments, posted a 26% increase in net sales in FY 97 (Jun.) and contributed some 45% of the company's net sales for the year (after elimination of intersegment sales). With its Oklahoma plant operating close to capacity, RGC shipped 570 million square feet of gypsum wallboard in FY 97. An expansion of the wallboard plant, scheduled for completion by the late summer of 1998, will double its capacity.

RGC's paperboard segment, which accounted for 55% of FY 97 net sales after eliminations, includes the company's paperboard mills and its reclaimed paper recycling operations. Shipments of recycled paperboard rose 4%, to 188,000 tons, in FY 97, with about 16% of RGC's paperboard output going to the company's wallboard plant. Shipments of reclaimed paper fiber also increased 4%, to 120,000 tons, with the improvement due to a higher level of vertical integration. Net selling prices, however, fell during the year, and the segment's sales declined. The company as a whole posted a 5% increase in net sales to $124 million, and net income grew 32% to $19.7 million.

Per Share Data ($)

(Year Ended Jun. 30)	1998	1997	1996	1995	1994	1993	1992	1991	1990	1989
Tangible Bk. Val.	7.85	6.66	5.37	4.35	3.55	3.04	2.90	0.14	2.71	2.77
Cash Flow	2.16	2.27	1.80	1.31	0.90	0.48	0.35	0.45	0.45	0.58
Earnings	1.51	1.67	1.27	1.00	0.66	0.28	0.16	-0.04	0.04	0.21
Dividends	0.36	0.34	0.26	0.21	0.15	0.19	0.02	Nil	0.13	0.21
Payout Ratio	24%	21%	20%	21%	23%	68%	11%	NM	376%	101%
Prices - High	22³/₈	22	16⁷/₈	12⁷/₈	7	10¹/₈	6³/₈	4³/₄	4¹/₂	5
- Low	16³/₈	14¹/₈	11¹/₂	8¹/₂	7³/₄	5⁵/₈	3⁷/₈	2³/₁₆	2¹/₁₆	3³/₄
P/E Ratio - High	15	13	13	13	11	26	39	NM	NM	24
- Low	11	8	9	9	12	20	24	NM	NM	18

Income Statement Analysis (Million $)

	1998	1997	1996	1995	1994	1993	1992	1991	1990	1989
Revs.	128	124	118	96.4	63.2	49.2	42.1	41.4	47.3	48.1
Oper. Inc.	34.7	38.9	31.6	22.6	14.8	6.6	4.3	1.1	4.6	7.2
Depr.	7.7	7.1	6.2	3.6	2.8	2.4	2.2	2.4	4.8	4.4
Int. Exp.	0.0	1.5	1.9	0.0	0.0	0.0	Nil	0.5	0.8	1.1
Pretax Inc.	28.2	31.1	24.0	19.2	12.4	4.5	2.9	-0.8	-0.1	2.9
Eff. Tax Rate	37%	37%	38%	39%	38%	27%	33%	NM	NM	18%
Net Inc.	17.8	19.7	14.9	11.7	7.7	3.2	1.9	-0.4	0.4	2.4

Balance Sheet & Other Fin. Data (Million $)

	1998	1997	1996	1995	1994	1993	1992	1991	1990	1989
Cash	1.1	2.1	14.6	6.1	1.4	5.6	6.1	1.3	8.1	11.0
Curr. Assets	26.3	25.1	35.0	27.0	14.6	15.8	15.4	11.8	21.2	24.7
Total Assets	125	100	114	95.4	53.0	44.1	41.3	38.9	47.9	52.6
Curr. Liab.	15.3	12.1	12.8	13.5	7.3	5.2	4.5	4.6	6.1	6.9
LT Debt	6.0	Nil	21.4	24.8	Nil	Nil	Nil	Nil	6.1	9.1
Common Eqty.	92.2	77.9	62.7	50.6	41.2	35.1	33.6	31.8	31.6	32.2
Total Cap.	110	87.7	92.7	81.2	44.9	38.3	36.5	34.4	41.9	45.7
Cap. Exp.	31.2	11.6	9.1	8.8	13.3	5.6	2.7	2.3	4.2	1.8
Cash Flow	25.5	26.8	21.1	15.3	10.5	5.6	4.1	2.0	5.2	6.8
Curr. Ratio	1.7	2.1	2.8	2.0	2.0	3.0	3.4	2.6	3.5	3.6
% LT Debt of Cap.	5.4	Nil	23.2	30.6	Nil	Nil	Nil	Nil	14.5	19.8
% Net Inc.of Revs.	13.9	13.7	12.7	12.2	12.2	6.6	4.6	NM	0.9	5.0
% Ret. on Assets	NA	19.1	14.8	15.7	15.9	7.6	4.9	NM	0.8	4.5
% Ret. on Equity	NA	28.0	26.4	25.5	20.3	9.4	6.0	NM	1.3	7.5

Data as orig. reptd.; bef. results of disc. opers. and/or spec. items. Per share data adj. for stk. divs. as of ex-div. date. Bold denotes diluted EPS (FASB 128). E-Estimated. NA-Not Available. NM-Not Meaningful. NR-Not Ranked.

Office—811 East 30th Ave. (P.O. Box 1307, Hutchinson, KS 67504-1307). **Tel**—(316) 727-2700. **Website**—http://www.republic-group.com **Chrmn & Pres**—P. Simpson. **VP-CFO**—Doyle R. Ramsey. **Treas, Secy & Investor Contact**—Janey L. Rife. **Dirs**—C. W. Claypool, B. A. Nelson, T. Rain, G. L. Ray, R. F. Sexton, D. P. Simpson, P. Simpson, L. L. Wallace, D. B. Yarbrough. **Transfer Agent & Registrar**—UMB Bank NA, Kansas City, MO**Incorporated**—in Delaware in 1961. **Empl**— 780. **S&P Analyst:** P.D.W.

ReSound Corp.
5081

NASDAQ Symbol **RSND**

In S&P SmallCap 600

03-OCT-98

Industry:
Health Care (Medical Products & Supplies)

Summary: ReSound designs, develops, manufactures and markets technologically advanced hearing devices throughout the world for the hearing impaired.

Quantitative Evaluations

Outlook (1 Lowest—5 Highest)
• **5**

Fair Value
• **8½**

Risk
• **High**

Earn./Div. Rank
• **NR**

Technical Eval.
• **Bullish** since 8/98

Rel. Strength Rank (1 Lowest—99 Highest)
• **45**

Insider Activity
• **Neutral**

Recent Price • 4⅛
52 Wk Range • 7⅛-3⅞

Yield • Nil
12-Mo. P/E • NM

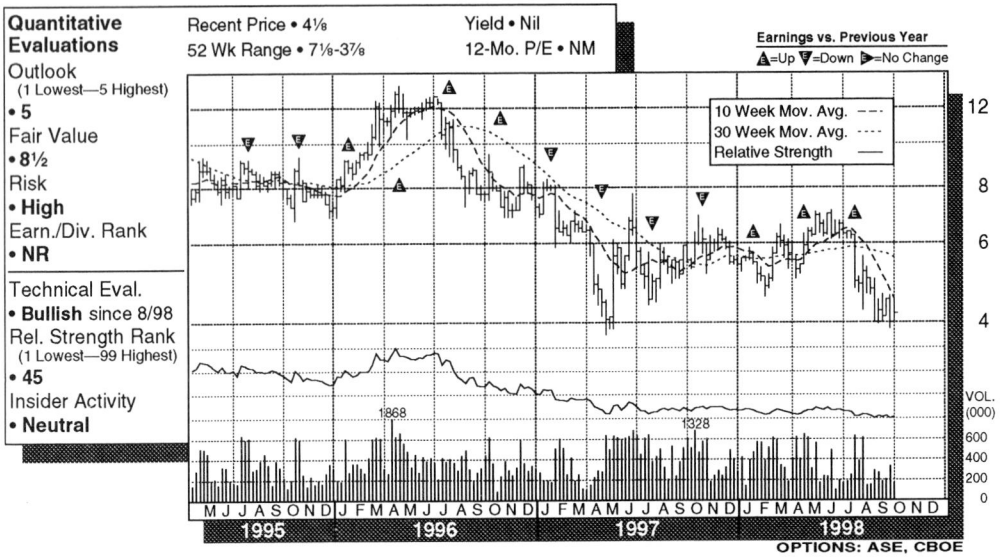

OPTIONS: ASE, CBOE

Business Profile - 26-AUG-98

The shares have fallen from their 1996 high, reflecting inconsistent earnings performance. In response, the company is expected to begin implementation of a plan to realign its organizational structure, streamline internal processes, and consolidate facilities. Facilities consolidation is expected to be concentrated on European operations. As a result of these initiatives, RSND anticipates significant one-time charges in the 1998 third and fourth quarters. The company believes that the restructuring program will begin to produce benefits by the end of 1998.

Operational Review - 26-AUG-98

Net sales in the six months ended June 27, 1998, edged up 0.9%, year to year, as a rise in North American revenues was largely offset by a decline in international sales. Margins widened significantly, reflecting less rapid increases in cost of sales and SG&A expenditures; operating income grew 47%. With lower depreciation and amortization charges, and a substantial jump in other income, after taxes of $378,000, versus $680,000, net income of $1,656,000 ($0.08 a share, on 8.1% more shares) contrasted with a net loss of $2,545,000 ($0.13).

Stock Performance - 02-OCT-98

In the past 30 trading days, RSND's shares have declined 12%, compared to a 7% fall in the S&P 500. Average trading volume for the past five days was 32,860 shares, compared with the 40-day moving average of 43,797 shares.

Key Stock Statistics

Dividend Rate/Share	Nil	Shareholders	7,600
Shs. outstg. (M)	20.6	Market cap. (B)	$0.086
Avg. daily vol. (M)	0.045	Inst. holdings	42%
Tang. Bk. Value/Share	0.94		
Beta	1.15		

Value of $10,000 invested 5 years ago: NA

Fiscal Year Ending Dec. 31

	1998	1997	1996	1995	1994	1993
Revenues (Million $)						
1Q	31.14	32.21	27.26	26.93	13.04	6.67
2Q	33.88	32.23	29.72	27.50	14.13	8.21
3Q	—	31.93	33.82	23.95	15.49	9.53
4Q	—	34.09	34.89	28.95	19.58	11.28
Yr.	—	130.5	125.7	107.3	62.25	35.69
Earnings Per Share ($)						
1Q	**0.05**	**-0.05**	0.01	0.03	0.09	0.05
2Q	**0.03**	**-0.08**	0.07	0.01	0.07	0.05
3Q	—	**-0.69**	0.06	-0.40	0.06	0.09
4Q	—	**-0.14**	-0.18	-0.01	-0.49	0.19
Yr.	—	**-0.96**	-0.07	-0.38	-0.95	0.35

Next earnings report expected: late October

Dividend Data

The company has never paid cash dividends on its capital stock. ReSound currently anticipates that it will retain all available funds for use in the operation and expansion of its business, and does not anticipate paying any cash dividends in the foreseeable future.

A Division of The **McGraw·Hill** *Companies*

Business Summary - 26-AUG-98

Fewer than one out of every four hearing-impaired individuals in the U.S. wears a hearing device, and usage is even lower elsewhere in the world. Among other factors, the stigma associated with wearing these devices has kept many potential users from becoming wearers. ReSound Corp. (RSND) hopes to capitalize on these industry dynamics with its In-the-Ear (ITE) and In-the-Canal (ITC) products, made possible by the company's Cochlea Dynamics technology. Introduction of RSND's ITC device in 1996 helped the company gain market share in the U.S., and dramatically increased domestic sales. In early 1998, RSND employed its Cochlea Dynamics technology in a Completely-in-the-Canal product that is virtually unnoticeable.

Founded in 1984, RSND designs, develops, makes and sells hearing devices for the hearing impaired using proprietary sound processing technology originally developed by AT&T Bell Laboratories and later enhanced and refined by the company itself. RSND's Multiband Full Dynamic Range Compression (MFDRC) sound processing technology enables its hearing devices to be individually programmed to adjust the amplification of sound continuously in response to the acoustic environment and each user's residual range of hearing. The company's Cochlea Dynamics sound processing, under development since 1992, represents a further enhancement of RSND's core MFDRC technology. Cochlea Dynamics (the spiral-shaped cochlea is part of the inner ear) permits the hearing device to distinguish between soft high-frequency sounds and louder sounds that do not require amplification, a distinction of enormous benefit to many hearing-impaired persons. In addition to its ITE and ITC products, RSND also offers a Behind-the-Ear version.

Through December 31, 1997, Resound had sold more than 890,000 hearing devices worldwide. The company currently distributes its products through more than 6,300 dispensers in 35 countries. RSND operates wholly owned subsidiaries, a Germany, the Netherlands, the U.K., Ireland, France, Austria, Sweden and Australia. In addition, the company has distribution agreements in Canada, Spain, Belgium, Denmark, Switzerland, Japan and South Korea.

In January 1998, RSND launched its first completely-in-the-canal (CIC) device in the U.S. In addition to the CIC device, the company has several new product expected to be launched in 1998, including a new product that is targeted at the large and underserved market of persons with mild-to-moderate hearing impairment. Earlier, in October 1997, the company introduced its first full-digital hearing device.

Per Share Data ($)

(Year Ended Dec. 31)	1997	1996	1995	1994	1993	1992	1991	1990	1989	1988
Tangible Bk. Val.	0.83	0.65	NM	NM	2.80	NM	NM	NM	NM	NM
Cash Flow	-0.54	0.28	-0.01	-0.76	0.42	-0.09	NA	NA	NA	NA
Earnings	-0.96	-0.07	-0.38	-0.95	0.35	-0.19	NA	NA	NA	NA
Dividends	Nil	Nil	Nil	Nil	Nil	Nil	Nil	Nil	Nil	Nil
Payout Ratio	Nil	Nil	Nil	Nil	Nil	Nil	Nil	Nil	Nil	Nil
Prices - High	8³/₈	13¹/₂	10⁵/₈	23¹/₂	25	NA	NA	NA	NA	NA
- Low	3³/₄	6⁷/₈	6³/₄	5	8	NA	NA	NA	NA	NA
P/E Ratio - High	NM	NM	NM	NM	71	NA	NA	NA	NA	NA
- Low	NM	NM	NM	NM	23	NA	NA	NA	NA	NA

Income Statement Analysis (Million $)

	1997	1996	1995	1994	1993	1992	1991	1990	1989	1988
Revs.	130	126	107	62.3	35.7	16.7	NA	NA	NA	NA
Oper. Inc.	4.7	8.7	2.8	8.4	5.6	-0.5	NA	NA	NA	NA
Depr.	7.9	6.1	5.8	2.8	1.0	0.5	NA	NA	NA	NA
Int. Exp.	1.5	2.0	2.2	0.1	0.0	0.1	NA	NA	NA	NA
Pretax Inc.	-17.6	0.4	-5.3	-12.7	5.4	-1.0	NA	NA	NA	NA
Eff. Tax Rate	NM	NM	NM	NM	10%	NM	NM	NM	NM	NM
Net Inc.	-18.4	-1.0	-5.9	-14.3	4.8	-1.0	NA	NA	NA	NA

Balance Sheet & Other Fin. Data (Million $)

	1997	1996	1995	1994	1993	1992	1991	1990	1989	1988
Cash	19.9	8.0	5.1	23.3	25.5	3.3	NA	NA	NA	NA
Curr. Assets	54.1	56.5	43.7	56.8	37.3	8.0	NA	NA	NA	NA
Total Assets	89.8	115	83.4	95.1	40.8	9.2	NA	NA	NA	NA
Curr. Liab.	34.2	31.2	33.8	50.8	8.1	3.1	NA	NA	NA	NA
LT Debt	14.2	19.5	23.6	15.5	Nil	0.1	NA	NA	NA	NA
Common Eqty.	37.0	52.4	18.2	21.2	32.8	-23.0	NA	NA	NA	NA
Total Cap.	51.2	77.1	41.9	36.7	32.8	6.1	NA	NA	NA	NA
Cap. Exp.	4.5	7.5	4.2	5.8	3.4	0.5	NA	NA	NA	NA
Cash Flow	-10.5	4.9	-0.1	-11.5	5.8	-0.5	NA	NA	NA	NA
Curr. Ratio	1.6	1.8	1.3	1.1	4.6	2.6	NA	NA	NA	NA
% LT Debt of Cap.	27.7	25.3	56.5	42.3	NM	1.8	NA	NA	NA	NA
% Net Inc.of Revs.	NM	NM	NM	NM	13.5	NM	NM	NM	NM	NM
% Ret. on Assets	NM	NM	NM	NM	9.5	NA	NA	NA	NA	NA
% Ret. on Equity	NM	NM	NM	NM	NM	NA	NA	NA	NA	NA

Data as orig. reptd.; bef. results of disc. opers. and/or spec. items. Per share data adj. for stk. divs. as of ex-div. date. Bold denotes diluted EPS (FASB 128). E-Estimated. NA-Not Available. NM-Not Meaningful. NR-Not Ranked.

Office—220 Saginaw Dr., Seaport Centre, Redwood City, CA 94063. **Tel**—(415) 780-7800. **Chrmn**—R. Perkins. **Pres & CEO**—R. D. Hays.**VP & Secy**—D. R. Muhlitner. **Dirs**—R. Goode, R. D. Hays, D. M. Kendall, E. Kleiner, R. Perkins, P. Riepenhausen, P. Schlein, R. Wilson. **Transfer Agent & Registrar**—American Stock Transfer & Trust Co., NYC. **Incorporated**—in California in 1984. **Empl**— 974. **S&P Analyst:** S.J.T.

Respironics, Inc.   5082

NASDAQ Symbol **RESP**

In S&P SmallCap 600

03-OCT-98

Industry:
Health Care (Medical Products & Supplies)

Summary: The February 1998 acquisition of Healthdyne Technologies made RESP into an international respiratory medical products company with revenues of $350 million.

Quantitative Evaluations		
Recent Price • 11⅜	Yield • Nil	
52 Wk Range • 30⅜-11⅛	12-Mo. P/E • NM	

Outlook
(1 Lowest—5 Highest)
• **5**

Fair Value
• **22⅜**

Risk
• **High**

Earn./Div. Rank
• **B**

Technical Eval.
• **Bearish** since 4/98

Rel. Strength Rank
(1 Lowest—99 Highest)
• **35**

Insider Activity
• **Neutral**

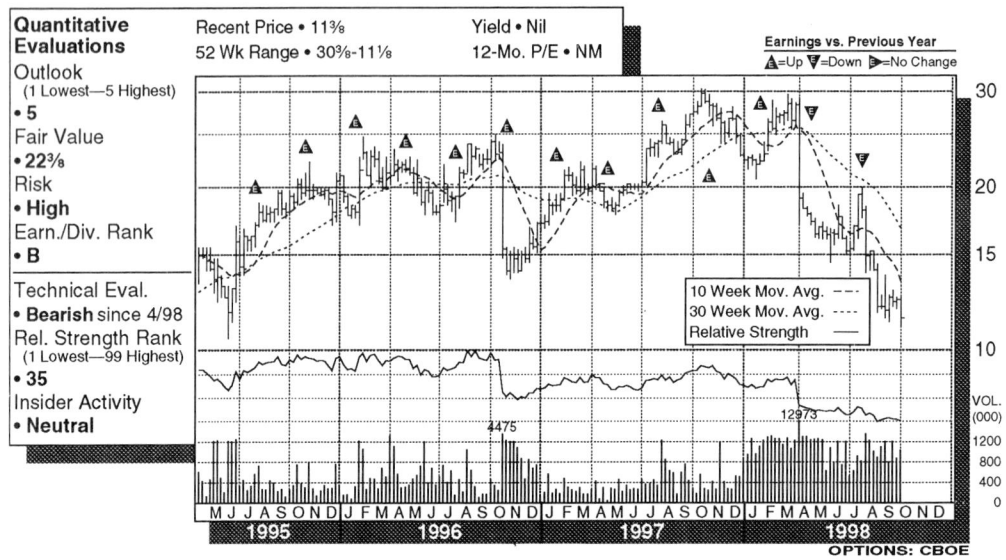

Earnings vs. Previous Year
▲=Up ▼=Down ▶=No Change

10 Week Mov. Avg. ----
30 Week Mov. Avg. ·····
Relative Strength ——

VOL. (000)

OPTIONS: CBOE

Business Profile - 18-SEP-98

In February 1998, the company acquired Healthdyne Technologies, Inc., (HDTC), a maker of monitoring devices for newborns and products for respiratory disorders, in exchange for about 12 million common shares. As a result, RESP has become an international respiratory products company, with revenues of $350 million. The company gained significant new product breadth, prompting a reorganization into three business units: sleep disorders, providing products for diagnosis and treatment of sleep apnea; respiratory, serving both invasive and non-invasive ventilation as well as the oxygen monitoring markets; and asthma and allergy, including HelathScan brand and other products, serving the asthma, allergy and acute care markets.

Operational Review - 18-SEP-98

Based on a preliminary report, net sales in the fiscal year ended June 30, 1998, advanced 12%, reflecting increased sales of sleep products and higher sales of asthma and allergy products, partly offset by lower respiratory sales, due to regulatory uncertainty in non-invasive ventilation. Results were penalized by acquisition-related costs of $40.8 million, versus costs of $2.2 million. A net loss of $1.8 million ($0.06 a share, on 2.4% more shares) contrasted with net income of $26.4 million ($0.82), as restated. Excluding special charges, EPS were $0.82 in FY 98 and $0.86 in FY 97.

Stock Performance - 02-OCT-98

In the past 30 trading days, RESP's shares have declined 5%, compared to a 7% fall in the S&P 500. Average trading volume for the past five days was 207,320 shares, compared with the 40-day moving average of 208,721 shares.

Key Stock Statistics

Dividend Rate/Share	Nil	Shareholders	1,400
Shs. outstg. (M)	32.5	Market cap. (B)	$0.372
Avg. daily vol. (M)	0.209	Inst. holdings	52%
Tang. Bk. Value/Share	6.98		
Beta	0.95		

Value of $10,000 invested 5 years ago: $ 7,438

Fiscal Year Ending Jun. 30

	1998	1997	1996	1995	1994	1993
Revenues (Million $)						
1Q	51.92	34.11	26.68	21.67	18.23	15.20
2Q	53.45	43.00	30.24	23.87	18.60	17.20
3Q	80.13	47.81	32.65	25.60	19.31	17.92
4Q	85.23	53.64	36.20	28.31	22.04	19.01
Yr.	351.6	178.6	125.8	99.5	78.17	69.29
Earnings Per Share ($)						
1Q	0.27	0.22	0.18	0.14	0.05	0.09
2Q	0.29	0.24	0.20	0.15	0.12	0.10
3Q	-0.69	0.25	0.21	0.17	0.13	0.11
4Q	0.11	0.29	0.24	0.20	-0.03	0.13
Yr.	-0.06	1.00	0.84	0.67	0.27	0.42

Next earnings report expected: NA

Dividend Data

Cash dividends have never been paid. A two-for-one stock split was effected in March 1995.

A Division of The McGraw-Hill Companies

Respironics, Inc.

Business Summary - 18-SEP-98

Respironics is a leading designer, manufacturer and marketer of technologically advanced medical devices for use in the home, hospital and alternative care settings. The company has employees worldwide, and has manufacturing facilities in several domestic and international locations.

In February 1998, RESP acquired Healthdyne Technologies, Inc. (HDTC), a maker of monitoring devices for newborns and products for respiratory disorders, in exchange for about 12 million common shares. The transaction formed an international respiratory products company with revenues of $350 million, nearly doubling RESP's sales volume.

In addition to monitoring devices for newborns, the company's major product lines include therapy products for obstructive sleep apnea and portable ventilation, sleep diagnostics, oxygen and a variety of products for the treatment of respiratory disorders, including asthma management devices.

Following the Healthdyne transaction, RESP formed three operating units: sleep disorders, providing products for diagnosis and treatment of sleep apnea; respiratory, serving both invasive and non-invasive ventilation as well as the oxygen monitoring markets; and asthma and allergy, including HelathScan brand and other products serving the asthma, allergy and acute care markets.

The company's product lines include continuous positive airway pressure (CPAP) devices and bi-level positive airway pressure (BiPAP) devices for the treatment of obstructive sleep apnea (OSA), a serious disorder characterized by the repeated cessation of breathing during sleep; ventilation devices, including bi-level non-invasive ventilatory support units; and patient mask products.

In February 1997, the company acquired its exclusive German distributor of therapy systems and accessories used in the treatment of obstructive sleep apnea and other respiratory disorders (1996 sales of $22 million), for $9 million in cash (with potential additional consideration of $5 million over the next four years, based on the achievement of certain financial results in Germany). In October 1996, in another international expansion move, RESP acquired LIFECARE International, Inc., a European developer, manufacturer and marketer of portable ventilation products, for $50 million in cash.

Respironics believes that it is the U.S. market share leader in OSA therapy devices, with nearly a 50% share. It also believes that it is the leading U.S. manufacturer and marketer of non-invasive ventilatory support devices. Sales of obstructive sleep apnea therapy products and related accessories and replacement parts accounted for 55% of net sales in FY 97, while sales and rental revenue from all ventilation products and accessories accounted for 40% of net sales in FY 97.

Per Share Data ($) (Year Ended Jun. 30)	1998	1997	1996	1995	1994	1993	1992	1991	1990	1989
Tangible Bk. Val.	NA	6.98	6.21	3.38	2.71	2.41	1.95	1.61	0.77	0.61
Cash Flow	NA	1.34	1.06	0.89	0.48	0.65	0.44	0.34	0.20	0.13
Earnings	-0.06	1.00	0.84	0.67	0.28	0.42	0.32	0.26	0.15	0.10
Dividends	Nil	Nil	Nil	Nil	Nil	Nil	Nil	Nil	Nil	Nil
Payout Ratio	Nil	Nil	Nil	Nil	Nil	Nil	Nil	Nil	Nil	Nil
Prices - High	$29\frac{5}{8}$	$30\frac{3}{8}$	25	$22\frac{1}{4}$	$12\frac{1}{4}$	$15\frac{1}{2}$	$15\frac{3}{8}$	$7\frac{1}{4}$	$5\frac{3}{8}$	$2\frac{3}{8}$
- Low	$13\frac{7}{8}$	$16\frac{3}{4}$	$13\frac{1}{2}$	$10\frac{1}{2}$	8	$7\frac{7}{8}$	$6\frac{1}{4}$	$4\frac{1}{4}$	$2\frac{1}{8}$	$1\frac{3}{16}$
P/E Ratio - High	NM	30	30	33	44	36	41	28	35	24
- Low	NM	17	16	16	29	19	20	17	14	12
Income Statement Analysis (Million $)										
Revs.	NA	179	126	100	78.2	69.3	49.0	36.0	23.0	16.8
Oper. Inc.	NA	39.3	27.8	21.4	17.0	14.6	9.7	6.8	3.3	1.8
Depr.	NA	6.9	4.0	3.8	3.6	3.9	2.1	1.3	0.6	0.4
Int. Exp.	NA	0.6	0.2	0.2	0.2	0.2	0.2	0.3	0.1	0.0
Pretax Inc.	NA	33.8	25.2	18.5	6.8	11.1	8.1	5.5	3.0	1.7
Eff. Tax Rate	NA	40%	39%	37%	30%	34%	34%	32%	27%	22%
Net Inc.	NA	20.3	15.3	11.7	4.7	7.4	5.4	3.8	2.2	1.3
Balance Sheet & Other Fin. Data (Million $)										
Cash	NA	15.7	65.3	16.1	12.4	14.6	10.2	11.3	2.2	2.4
Curr. Assets	NA	95.1	116	52.9	40.2	36.4	27.8	21.9	11.7	8.1
Total Assets	NA	184	144	78.0	58.9	54.6	43.5	36.1	19.8	9.9
Curr. Liab.	NA	24.1	16.5	13.5	9.2	11.2	7.8	5.8	5.9	1.8
LT Debt	NA	18.0	5.0	5.5	4.9	4.3	4.3	4.5	3.6	Nil
Common Eqty.	Nil	142	122	58.3	44.2	39.1	31.4	25.8	10.3	8.1
Total Cap.	NA	160	127	64.6	49.7	43.4	35.7	30.3	13.9	8.1
Cap. Exp.	NA	4.9	6.2	6.9	8.4	6.7	3.5	3.1	5.8	0.9
Cash Flow	NA	27.2	19.3	15.5	8.3	11.2	7.5	5.1	2.7	1.7
Curr. Ratio	NA	4.0	7.0	3.9	4.4	3.2	3.6	3.8	2.0	4.6
% LT Debt of Cap.	NA	11.3	3.9	8.6	9.8	9.9	12.0	15.0	25.6	Nil
% Net Inc.of Revs.	Nil	11.4	0.1	11.7	6.1	10.7	11.0	10.5	9.4	7.8
% Ret. on Assets	NA	12.4	13.8	17.0	8.3	15.0	13.4	12.6	14.4	13.6
% Ret. on Equity	NA	15.4	17.1	22.7	11.3	20.9	18.7	19.8	23.2	17.6

Data as orig. reptd.; bef. results of disc. opers. and/or spec. items. Per share data adj. for stk. divs. as of ex-div. date. Bold denotes diluted EPS (FASB 128). E-Estimated. NA-Not Available. NM-Not Meaningful. NR-Not Ranked.

Office—1501 Ardmore Boulevard, Pittsburgh, PA 15221-4401. **Tel**—(412) 733-0200. **Website**—http://www.respironics.com **Chrmn**—G. E. McGinnis. **Pres & CEO**—D. S. Meteny. **VP, CFO & Investor Contact** —Dan J. Bevevino (412-473-5235).**Treas**—J. C. Woll. **Dirs**—D. P. Barry, D. A. Cotter, J. H. Hardie, D. H. Jones, J. C. Lawyer, C. Littell, G. J. Magovern, G. E. McGinnis, D. S. Meteny.**Transfer Agent & Registrar**—ChaseMellon Shareholder Services, Pittsburgh.**Incorporated**—in Pennsylvania in 1976; reincorporated in Delaware in 1984. **Empl**— 2,000. **S&P Analyst:** John J. Arege

Richfood Holdings
1932

NYSE Symbol **RFH**

In S&P SmallCap 600

03-OCT-98

Industry: Distributors (Food & Health)

Summary: Richfood is the largest food wholesaler in its Mid-Atlantic operating region, and also operates three retail grocery chains.

Quantitative Evaluations

Recent Price • 13⅞
52 Wk Range • 32-13¾

Yield • 1.4%
12-Mo. P/E • 12.3

Outlook (1 Lowest—5 Highest)
• 5

Fair Value
• 30¼

Risk
• Average

Earn./Div. Rank
• A-

Technical Eval.
• NA

Rel. Strength Rank (1 Lowest—99 Highest)
• 12

Insider Activity
• Neutral

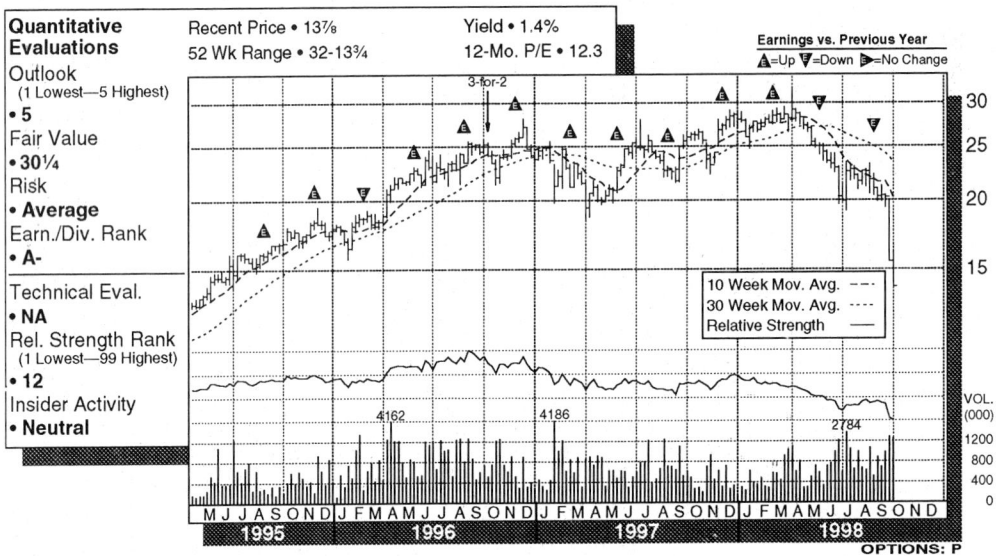

Earnings vs. Previous Year
▲=Up ▼=Down ▶=No Change

10 Week Mov. Avg. ---
30 Week Mov. Avg. ····
Relative Strength —

4162   4186   2784

VOL. (000)

OPTIONS: P

Business Profile - 01-SEP-98

Headquartered in Richmond, VA, Richfood is the largest wholesale food distributor in its Mid-Atlantic operating region. The company provides a full range of grocery, dairy, frozen food, produce, meat, and non-food items to chain and independent retailers throughout the region. It also operates three retail grocery store chains: 45 Farm Fresh grocery stores located primarily in Virginia's Hampton Roads market (acquired in March 1998); 38 Shoppers Food Warehouse supermarkets in the Washington, DC, area (May 1998); and 17 Metro grocery stores in the Baltimore metropolitan area (October 1995). The company expects the full benefit of the integration of Farm Fresh and Shoppers, including incremental wholesale volume, to be realized in the third and fourth quarters of FY 99 (Apr.).

Operational Review - 01-SEP-98

Sales in the 12 weeks ended July 25, 1998, climbed 22%, year to year, aided by the acquisition of two retail grocery chains. A sharp increase in interest expense led to an 8.4% decline in net income, to $13,286,000 ($0.28 a share), from $14,506,000 ($0.30).

Stock Performance - 02-OCT-98

In the past 30 trading days, RFH's shares have declined 36%, compared to a 7% fall in the S&P 500. Average trading volume for the past five days was 352,660 shares, compared with the 40-day moving average of 222,303 shares.

Key Stock Statistics

Dividend Rate/Share	0.20	Shareholders	1,400
Shs. outstg. (M)	47.7	Market cap. (B)	$0.664
Avg. daily vol. (M)	0.281	Inst. holdings	70%
Tang. Bk. Value/Share	1.28		
Beta	0.77		

Value of $10,000 invested 5 years ago: $ 20,439

Fiscal Year Ending Apr. 30

	1999	1998	1997	1996	1995	1994
Revenues (Million $)						
1Q	901.3	739.1	753.4	767.0	296.5	293.4
2Q	—	719.5	739.6	717.5	344.6	283.9
3Q	—	744.0	807.3	766.8	380.5	294.6
4Q	—	1,001	1,111	1,000	498.9	403.3
Yr.	—	3,204	3,412	3,251	1,520	1,275
Earnings Per Share ($)						
1Q	0.28	0.30	0.27	0.21	0.15	0.14
2Q	—	0.31	0.27	0.22	0.17	0.14
3Q	—	0.37	0.32	0.08	0.20	0.17
4Q	—	0.31	0.45	0.33	0.27	0.23
Yr.	—	1.15	1.30	0.84	0.79	0.68

Next earnings report expected: early November

Dividend Data (Dividends have been paid since 1991.)

Amount ($)	Date Decl.	Ex-Div. Date	Stock of Record	Payment Date
0.040	Nov. 13	Dec. 11	Dec. 15	Dec. 31 '97
0.040	Feb. 06	Mar. 12	Mar. 16	Mar. 31 '98
0.040	Jun. 18	Jun. 24	Jun. 26	Jun. 30 '98
0.050	Aug. 20	Sep. 11	Sep. 15	Sep. 30 '98

A Division of The McGraw-Hill Companies

Business Summary - 01-SEP-98

Richfood Holdings, Inc. (RFH) is the leading wholesale food distributor in its Mid-Atlantic operating region, providing a full range of grocery, dairy, frozen food, produce, meat and non-food items to chain and independent retailers throughout the region. The company also operates three retail grocery store chains, including two acquired in 1998.

In its wholesale operations, the company supplies a comprehensive selection of national brand and private-label grocery products, dairy products, frozen foods, fresh produce items, meats, delicatessen and bakery products and nonfood items from its three distribution centers. RFH services 1,400 retail grocery stores, including leading regional chains and smaller independent retailers throughout the Mid-Atlantic, offering its customers a dependable supply and prompt delivery of over 37,000 grocery and nongrocery items at competitive prices.

As a result of recent acquisitions, the company's Retail division is now the second largest food retailer in its Mid-Atlantic operating region. The Retail division operates the Metro chain of 17 retail grocery stores in the metropolitore Baltimore, MD, area, the 45 store Farm Fresh chain located primarily in the Hampton Roads region of Virginia (acquired in March 1998), and 38 Shoppers Food Warehouse stores in the greater Washington, DC, metropolitan area (May 1998).

Richfood focuses on achieving sales and earnings growth in both its Wholesale and Retail divisions. Management intends to capitalize on the efficiency, purchasing power and low cost structure of its Wholesale division to increase sales to existing customers and to attract new customers, while supporting the competitive efforts of its wholesale customers through extensive retail support services. In addition, the company believes that its recent retail acquisitions offer significant distribution and logistics opportunities for its core wholesale business. In its Retail division, the company plans to pursue growth through new store openings and operational improvements for its Metro chain; aggressive store remodeling programs and improved advertising and customer service programs for its Farm Fresh chain; and providing additional customer services, aggressively pursuing new store sites and achieving acquisition-related synergies for its Shoppers Food Warehouse chain.

The company more than doubled its revenue base through the October 1995 acquisition of Super Rite Corp., a full-service wholesale food distributor supplying more than 240 retail supermarkets in Pennsylvania, New Jersey, Maryland, Delaware, Virginia and West Virginia. In the acquisition, which was accounted for as a pooling of interests, RFH issued 14,655,282 common shares (as adjusted).

Per Share Data ($)

(Year Ended Apr. 30)	1998	1997	1996	1995	1994	1993	1992	1991	1990	1989
Tangible Bk. Val.	1.28	3.61	2.66	2.13	NA	NA	NA	NA	NA	NA
Cash Flow	1.82	1.92	1.37	NA	NA	NA	NA	NA	NA	NA
Earnings	1.15	1.30	0.84	0.82	0.48	0.35	NA	NA	NA	NA
Dividends	0.15	0.11	0.10	0.05	0.04	0.03	NA	NA	NA	NA
Payout Ratio	13%	8%	12%	6%	8%	10%	NA	NA	NA	NA
Cal. Yrs.	1997	1996	1995	1994	1993	1992	1991	1990	1989	1988
Prices - High	29¹/₈	28¹/₈	19¹/₂	12³/₈	11⁵/₈	NA	NA	NA	NA	NA
- Low	18³/₈	15⁵/₈	10¹/₂	8⁷/₈	6¹/₂	NA	NA	NA	NA	NA
P/E Ratio - High	25	33	23	15	24	NA	NA	NA	NA	NA
- Low	16	19	13	11	13	NA	NA	NA	NA	NA

Income Statement Analysis (Million $)

	1998	1997	1996	1995	1994	1993	1992	1991	1990	1989
Revs.	3,204	3,412	3,251	2,994	2,547	2,359	NA	NA	NA	NA
Oper. Inc.	147	135	105	79.9	64.9	48.2	NA	NA	NA	NA
Depr.	32.1	29.2	27.0	NA	NA	NA	NA	NA	NA	NA
Int. Exp.	6.0	7.2	12.3	18.1	17.3	17.4	NA	NA	NA	NA
Pretax Inc.	88.2	102	68.5	65.1	37.6	25.2	NA	NA	NA	NA
Eff. Tax Rate	38%	40%	43%	41%	41%	38%	NA	NA	NA	NA
Net Inc.	54.7	61.4	39.2	38.4	22.2	15.7	NA	NA	NA	NA

Balance Sheet & Other Fin. Data (Million $)

	1998	1997	1996	1995	1994	1993	1992	1991	1990	1989
Cash	40.0	10.4	17.4	6.6	NA	NA	NA	NA	NA	NA
Curr. Assets	357	293	300	300	NA	NA	NA	NA	NA	NA
Total Assets	909	582	564	574	NA	NA	NA	NA	NA	NA
Curr. Liab.	303	271	259	223	NA	NA	NA	NA	NA	NA
LT Debt	253	32.1	87.0	146	NA	NA	NA	NA	NA	NA
Common Eqty.	324	259	200	179	NA	NA	NA	NA	NA	NA
Total Cap.	577	291	287	325	NA	NA	NA	NA	NA	NA
Cap. Exp.	22.1	15.4	14.0	NA	NA	NA	NA	NA	NA	NA
Cash Flow	86.8	90.6	66.3	NA	NA	NA	NA	NA	NA	NA
Curr. Ratio	1.2	1.1	1.2	1.3	NA	NA	NA	NA	NA	NA
% LT Debt of Cap.	43.8	11.0	30.3	45.0	NA	NA	NA	NA	NA	NA
% Net Inc.of Revs.	1.7	1.8	1.2	1.3	0.9	0.7	NA	NA	NA	NA
% Ret. on Assets	7.3	10.7	6.8	NA	NA	NA	NA	NA	NA	NA
% Ret. on Equity	18.8	26.8	21.8	NA	NA	NA	NA	NA	NA	NA

Data as orig. reptd. (pro forma to incl. Super Rite prior to 1996); bef. results of disc. opers. and/or spec. items. Per share data adj. for stk. divs. as of ex-div. date. Bold denotes diluted EPS (FASB 128). E-Estimated. NA-Not Available. NM-Not Meaningful. NR-Not Ranked.

Office—4860 Cox Road, Suite 300, Glen Allen, VA 23060. **Tel**—(804) 915-6000. **Chrmn, Pres & CEO**—J. E. Stokely. **EVP, CFO & Secy**—J. C. Belknap. **Dirs**—D. D. Bennett, R. L. Gregory, J. C. Jamison, G. G. Minor III, C. B. Owen Jr., A. F. Sloan, J. E. Stokely, G. H. Thomazin, J. E. Ukrop, E. Villanueva. **Transfer Agent & Registrar**—First Union National Bank of North Carolina, Charlotte. **Incorporated**— in Virginia in 1987. **Empl**— 9,479. **S&P Analyst**: C.F.B.

STANDARD &POOR'S
STOCK REPORTS

Riggs National Corp.

5095D

NASDAQ Symbol **RIGS**

In S&P SmallCap 600

03-OCT-98

Industry: Banks (Regional)

Summary: This bank holding company, whose principal subsidiary is Riggs Bank, has 54 branches in the Washington, D.C. metropolitan area, as well as three locations in London, England.

Quantitative Evaluations	
Outlook (1 Lowest—5 Highest)	• **1**
Fair Value	• **22¼**
Risk	• **Low**
Earn./Div. Rank	• **B-**
Technical Eval.	• **Bullish** since 9/98
Rel. Strength Rank (1 Lowest—99 Highest)	• **62**
Insider Activity	• **NA**

Recent Price • 23⅞
52 Wk Range • 31½-20⅞

Yield • 0.8%
12-Mo. P/E • 15.4

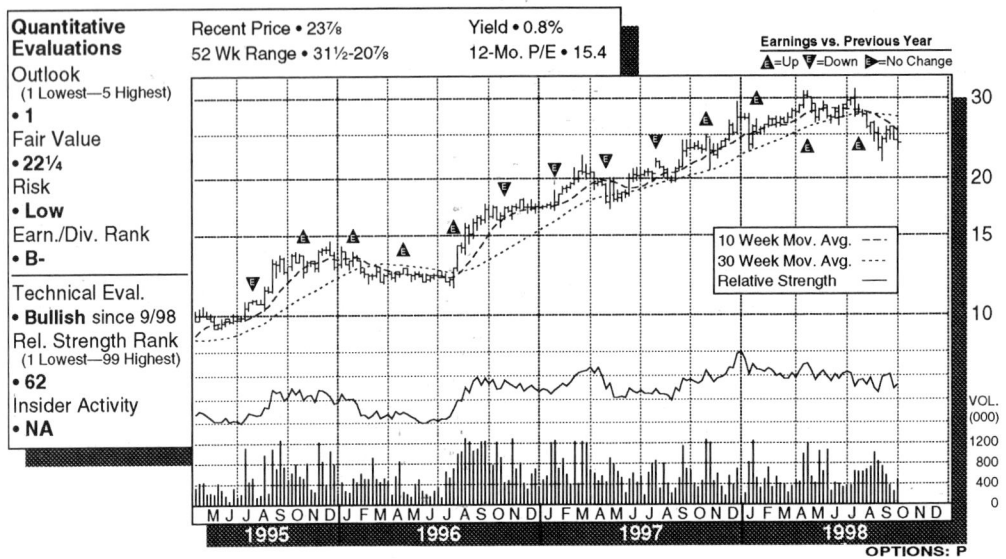

Earnings vs. Previous Year
▲=Up ▼=Down ▶=No Change

10 Week Mov. Avg. - - -
30 Week Mov. Avg. ·····
Relative Strength ——

VOL. (000)

OPTIONS: P

Business Profile - 23-JUL-98

Riggs National Corp. is the largest bank holding company headquartered in Washington D.C. The company's strategy is to provide customers with the breadth of financial products and services typical of a regional bank, while providing the personalized customer service of a community bank. In October 1997, Riggs acquired J. Bush & Co., a privately held investment adviser. At the time of the acquisition, Bush had approximately $250 million in assets under management. Net income advanced 37% year to year in 1998's second quarter, buoyed by higher average earning assets, strong growth in noninterest income and greater net securities gains.

Operational Review - 23-JUL-98

Net interest income in the first six months of 1998 rose 9.2%, year to year, reflecting a 7.7% increase in average earning assets and a wider net interest margin (0.00% vs. 3.93%). There was no loan loss provision taken in either period. Following a 31% increase in noninterest income and just 5.6% higher noninterest expense, m income climbed 41%. After taxes at 25.5%, versus 24.9%, and minority interest of $9,973,000 in the 1998 period, compared to $7,643,000 in the 1997 period, net income jumped 43%, to $30,181,000 ($0.78 a share, after preferred dividends), from $21,102,000 ($0.50).

Stock Performance - 02-OCT-98

In the past 30 trading days, RIGS's shares have declined 5%, compared to a 7% fall in the S&P 500. Average trading volume for the past five days was 95,380 shares, compared with the 40-day moving average of 126,597 shares.

Key Stock Statistics

Dividend Rate/Share	0.20	Shareholders	3,700
Shs. outstg. (M)	30.6	Market cap. (B)	$0.732
Avg. daily vol. (M)	0.090	Inst. holdings	35%
Tang. Bk. Value/Share	12.62		
Beta	0.80		

Value of $10,000 invested 5 years ago: $ 24,112

Fiscal Year Ending Dec. 31

	1998	1997	1996	1995	1994	1993
Revenues (Million $)						
1Q	115.1	96.71	100.2	90.22	90.67	90.03
2Q	112.3	104.2	97.48	94.81	86.99	112.6
3Q	—	108.0	93.99	94.21	86.21	83.85
4Q	—	109.8	97.76	93.56	87.66	83.16
Yr.	—	418.7	389.4	372.8	351.5	369.6
Earnings Per Share ($)						
1Q	**0.41**	**0.25**	0.61	0.20	0.15	-1.11
2Q	**0.37**	**0.25**	0.62	0.22	0.23	-2.89
3Q	—	**0.32**	0.29	1.78	0.17	0.10
4Q	—	**0.45**	0.27	0.34	0.17	0.09
Yr.	—	**1.27**	1.79	2.54	0.72	-3.65

Next earnings report expected: NA

Dividend Data (Dividends have been paid since 1996.)

Amount ($)	Date Decl.	Ex-Div. Date	Stock of Record	Payment Date
0.050	Oct. 15	Oct. 23	Oct. 27	Nov. 03 '97
0.050	Jan. 21	Jan. 28	Jan. 31	Feb. 06 '98
0.050	Apr. 13	Apr. 23	Apr. 27	May. 01 '98
0.050	Jul. 15	Jul. 23	Jul. 27	Aug. 03 '98

A Division of The McGraw·Hill Companies

STANDARD
&POOR'S
STOCK REPORTS

Riggs National Corporation

5095D
03-OCT-98

Business Summary - 23-JUL-98

From traditional banking services in the Washington, D.C., metropolitan area to trust and corporate services through subsidiaries in the Bahamas and France, Riggs National Corporation (RIGS) engages in a wide variety of banking related activities. The company is seeking to grow its business through internally developed programs as well as alliances and acquisitions. Riggs National Bank, the principal subsidiary of RIGS, was founded in 1836 and is the largest commercial bank in Washington, D.C., with 32 branch offices, assets of $5.6 billion and deposits of $4.0 billion at March 31, 1998. The bank also operates Riggs Investment Management (RIMCO), an investment advisory subsidiary, in Washington, D.C.

Interest and fees on loans comprised 50% of revenues in 1997; interest on dividends and securities held for sale 20%; interest on money market assets 9.3%; trust income 8.9%; service charges 8.8%; and other noninterest income 3.3%.

Average earnings assets, from which interest income is derived, totaled $4.8 billion in 1997 and consisted mainly of loans (55%) and securities available for sale (30%). Average sources of funds, used in the lending business, included interest bearing deposits (60%), demand deposits (16%), stockholders' equity (8.3%), short-term borrowings (5.4%), and long-term debt (3.6%).

Residential mortgage loans were 40% of loans outstanding at 1997 year end; commercial and financial 18%; commercial and construction real estate 14%; home equity 11%; foreign 14%; and consumer 3%.

At 1997 year end, the reserve for loan losses totaled $52,381,000 ($64,486,000 a year earlier), equal to 1.82% (2.44%) of loans outstanding. There was a net loan recovery of $472,000 in 1997 (a net loan recovery of $6,575,000 in 1996), or -0.02% (-0.26%) of average loans outstanding. Nonperforming assets at 1997 year end were $8,970,000 (0.31% of total loans and other real estate owned), versus $38,122,000 (1.43%) a year earlier.

Per Share Data ($)

(Year Ended Dec. 31)	1997	1996	1995	1994	1993	1992	1991	1990	1989	1988
Tangible Bk. Val.	11.31	10.58	8.50	5.53	4.81	7.58	11.99	16.58	23.79	23.41
Earnings	1.27	1.79	2.54	0.72	-3.65	-0.86	-4.79	-4.41	2.86	2.54
Dividends	0.20	0.15	Nil	Nil	Nil	Nil	0.20	1.09	1.25	1.10
Payout Ratio	16%	8%	Nil	Nil	Nil	Nil	NM	NM	44%	43%
Prices - High	29¹/₂	18¹/₈	14⁵/₈	11¹/₄	11⁵/₈	10¹/₈	13	22¹/₂	28	26¹/₄
- Low	17	11¹/₂	7⁷/₈	7¹/₂	6¹/₄	4¹/₄	3³/₄	7³/₄	18³/₈	17³/₄
P/E Ratio - High	23	10	6	16	NM	NM	NM	NM	10	10
- Low	13	6	3	10	NM	NM	NM	NM	6	7

Income Statement Analysis (Million $)

	1997	1996	1995	1994	1993	1992	1991	1990	1989	1988
Net Int. Inc.	179	153	151	153	135	138	155	173	179	163
Tax Equiv. Adj.	3.8	4.0	3.3	3.4	4.6	6.5	7.1	7.9	9.0	10.5
Non Int. Inc.	84.4	89.0	73.5	85.5	88.5	96.2	92.9	78.2	65.3	56.9
Loan Loss Prov.	-12.0	NM	NM	6.3	69.3	50.0	44.0	106	6.0	1.0
Exp./Op. Revs.	71%	72%	86%	82%	117%	100%	114%	92%	75%	72%
Pretax Inc.	93.2	72.9	88.1	33.5	-88.6	-22.1	-72.1	-90.6	57.0	53.7
Eff. Tax Rate	26%	8.46%	3.90%	NM	NM	NM	NM	NM	31%	31%
Net Inc.	50.9	65.9	87.8	34.0	-94.2	-21.1	-66.0	-61.2	39.4	37.0
% Net Int. Marg.	3.81	3.72	3.74	3.89	3.23	3.15	3.04	2.86	3.23	3.16

Balance Sheet & Other Fin. Data (Million $)

	1997	1996	1995	1994	1993	1992	1991	1990	1989	1988
Earning Assets:										
Money Mkt	791	821	654	388	406	1,264	1,142	1,387	2,293	2,039
Inv. Securities	1,673	1,163	970	1,041	1,368	955	585	961	417	519
Com'l Loans	530	444	400	401	412	500	606	869	1,043	1,258
Other Loans	2,354	2,194	2,172	2,142	2,110	1,642	2,398	2,946	2,797	2,332
Total Assets	5,846	5,135	4,733	4,426	4,780	5,078	5,536	7,051	7,337	7,002
Demand Deposits	983	893	911	827	865	884	1,011	1,086	935	884
Time Deposits	3,315	2,686	2,063	2,276	2,909	2,670	3,902	5,025	5,042	4,654
LT Debt	192	192	218	218	213	213	232	246	309	223
Common Eqty.	459	426	377	268	174	245	205	278	342	322
% Ret. on Assets	0.9	1.3	1.9	0.8	NM	NM	NM	NM	0.6	0.6
% Ret. on Equity	9.1	16.6	28.3	12.0	NM	NM	NM	NM	11.9	11.1
% Loan Loss Resv.	1.8	2.4	2.2	3.8	3.4	3.9	3.5	2.9	1.1	1.4
% Loans/Deposits	67.1	64.1	67.9	69.8	67.0	48.3	60.9	62.0	63.7	64.3
% Equity to Assets	8.0	8.1	6.8	6.3	3.1	5.0	4.2	4.3	5.0	5.3

Data as orig. reptd.; bef. results of disc. opers. and/or spec. items. Per share data adj. for stk. divs. as of ex-div. date. Bold denotes diluted EPS (FASB 128). E-Estimated. NA-Not Available. NM-Not Meaningful. NR-Not Ranked.

Office—1503 Pennsylvania Ave., NW, Washington, DC 20005. **Tel**—(301) 887-6000. **Chrmn & CEO**—J. L. Allbritton. **Vice Chrmn** —R.L. Sloan. **Pres & Investor Contact**—T. C. Coughlin. **EVP & CFO**—J. L. Davis. **Dirs**—J. L. Allbritton, R. L. Allbritton, T. C. Coughlin, J. M. Fahey, Jr., L. I. Hebert, S. B. Pfeiffer, R. L. Sloan, J. Valenti, E. N. Williams. **Transfer Agent & Registrar**—The Bank of New York. **Incorporated**—In Delaware in 1980; chartered in 1896. **Empl**— 1,428. **S&P Analyst:** Michael Schneider

Rival Co. 5100

NASDAQ Symbol **RIVL**

In S&P SmallCap 600

03-OCT-98

Industry: Housewares

Summary: This company, which primarily manufactures small house-hold appliances, has expanded its business through acquisitions to include personal care appliances and pumps.

Quantitative Evaluations	
Outlook (1 Lowest—5 Highest)	• **5**
Fair Value	• **16⅝**
Risk	• **Average**
Earn./Div. Rank	• **NR**
Technical Eval.	• **Bullish** since 3/98
Rel. Strength Rank (1 Lowest—99 Highest)	• **7**
Insider Activity	• **NA**

Recent Price • 7
52 Wk Range • 18-7
Yield • 4.0%
12-Mo. P/E • 7.4

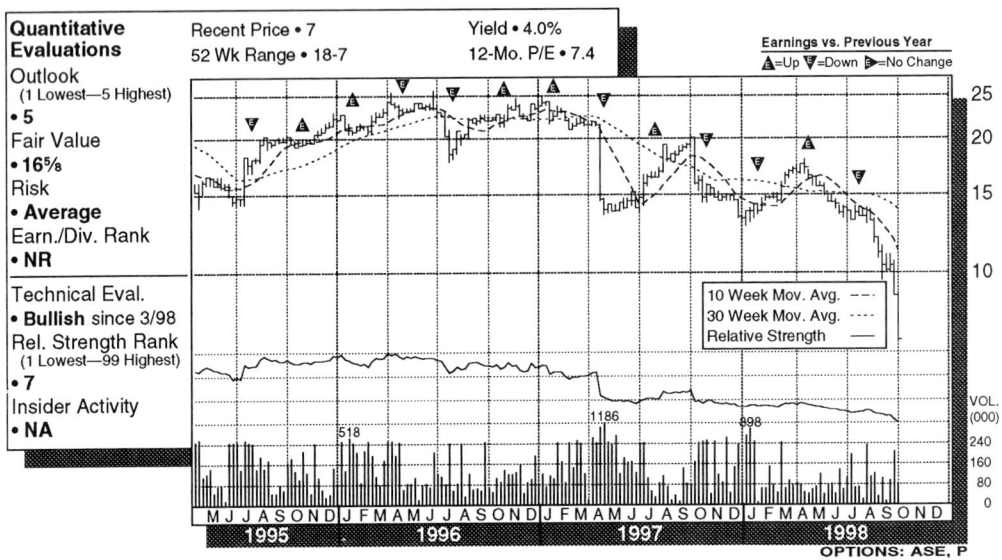

Earnings vs. Previous Year
▲=Up ▼=Down ▷=No Change

10 Week Mov. Avg. —–·
30 Week Mov. Avg. ----
Relative Strength —

OPTIONS: ASE, P

Business Profile - 02-SEP-98

This manufacturer of small household appliances has grown in recent years through an expansion of its product line into new market segments, new product offerings and acquisitions. RIVL's strategy entails entering product categories that have complementary distribution through electrical and industrial wholesale vendors. The company expects that over 75 additional stock keeping units (SKU's) will be shipped in the first six months of FY 99 (Jun.). In August 1998, RIVL announced restructuring plans that include the closing of two plants, expansion of operations at two facilities and additional global sourcing. RIVL estimates that pretax restructuring charges will be approximately $7.5 million in FY 99, with the majority of charges recorded in the first quarter. Directors increased the quarterly dividend 17%, to $0.07 a share, with the March 1998 payment.

Operational Review - 02-SEP-98

Based on a brief preliminary report, net sales were essentially flat for the fiscal year ended June 30, 1998. Net income fell 14%, to $9,207,000 ($0.96), from $10,685,000 ($1.08). Results include after tax nonrecurring charges of $2,979,000 in FY 98, and $2,070,000 in FY 97.

Stock Performance - 02-OCT-98

In the past 30 trading days, RIVL's shares have declined 41%, compared to a 7% fall in the S&P 500. Average trading volume for the past five days was 14,720 shares, compared with the 40-day moving average of 19,259 shares.

Key Stock Statistics

Dividend Rate/Share	0.28	Shareholders	200
Shs. outstg. (M)	9.4	Market cap. (B)	$0.066
Avg. daily vol. (M)	0.020	Inst. holdings	76%
Tang. Bk. Value/Share	5.98		
Beta	0.52		

Value of $10,000 invested 5 years ago: $ 7,810

Fiscal Year Ending Jun. 30

	1998	1997	1996	1995	1994	1993
Revenues (Million $)						
1Q	96.70	99.7	73.90	61.40	56.57	39.40
2Q	127.8	121.6	97.45	78.09	75.47	65.50
3Q	70.85	74.83	61.92	39.62	50.38	41.43
4Q	81.52	80.42	80.61	52.60	46.83	38.08
Yr.	376.9	376.5	313.9	231.7	229.2	184.4
Earnings Per Share ($)						
1Q	0.39	0.53	0.51	0.46	0.39	0.31
2Q	0.77	0.00	0.76	0.66	0.71	0.61
3Q	0.03	-0.44	0.16	0.19	0.23	0.18
4Q	-0.24	0.12	0.01	0.16	0.18	0.10
Yr.	**0.96**	1.08	1.43	1.47	1.51	1.20

Next earnings report expected: NA

Dividend Data (Dividends have been paid since 1993.)

Amount ($)	Date Decl.	Ex-Div. Date	Stock of Record	Payment Date
0.060	Nov. 06	Dec. 12	Dec. 01	Dec. 15 '97
0.070	Feb. 12	Feb. 26	Mar. 02	Mar. 16 '98
0.070	May. 12	May. 28	Jun. 01	Jun. 15 '98
0.070	Aug. 11	Aug. 28	Sep. 01	Sep. 15 '98

A Division of The **McGraw·Hill** *Companies*

STANDARD
&POOR'S
STOCK REPORTS

The Rival Company

5100

03-OCT-98

Business Summary - 02-SEP-98

Despite participating in relatively mature markets, this company has seen its revenues grow at an annual rate of about 20% since 1992. Acquisitions and an expansion of its product line from the kitchen to the entire home have fueled growth. Today, The Rival Co. is a leading manufacturer and marketer of small kitchen appliances, home environment products, and industrial and building supply products. Contributions to sales and profits in FY 97 (Jun.) by market were:

	Revs.	Profits
Kitchen electrics & personal care	51%	65%
Home environment	31%	24%
Industrial/building supply	8%	-1%
International sales	10%	12%

The kitchen electrics/personal care products business is Rival's core business. This market is mature, with about $2 billion to $3 billion in annual sales; annual sales growth is typically in the single digits. RIVL's products include its trademark "Crock Pot" slow cookers, indoor grills, steamers, skillets, toasters, hot pots, can openers and blenders. The rapid growth in the home electronics market (sales estimated at about $12 billion to $15 billion annually) has been driven by rising demand for products that relate to comfort and health. Rival's product line includes humidifiers, air puri-

fiers, fans, space heaters, shower heads, and sump and utility pumps. The April 1996 acquisition of Bionaire, a seller of air purifiers and humidifiers, with about $50 million in annual sales, was the primary factor in FY 97 sales growth in this business segment.

RIVL sells home ventilation systems, ceiling fans, door chimes and wall-mounted electric space heaters for the industrial/building supply market. Products also include the Patton line of industrial fans and drum blowers for use in factories and warehouses. The company is currently phasing out the Fasco brand, which it acquired in January 1996, and replacing it with its Patton line, in order to concentrate resources and develop enhanced brand recognition.

The company's growth strategy revolves around acquiring product lines, then applying its manufacturing and/or distribution strengths to increase the product lines' profitability. Since the beginning of 1996, RIVL has spent a total of about $58 million on three acquisitions. First was the January 1996 purchase of Fasco Consumer Products, Inc. Fasco generates about $30 million in annual revenue. In April 1996, the company acquired Bionaire Inc., providing it with the market leadership position in portable air purifiers and humidifiers in Canada. Most recently, in January 1997, Rival purchased inventory, tooling, machinery and equipment for the production and sale of the Dazey kitchen product line.

Per Share Data ($)

(Year Ended Jun. 30)	1998	1997	1996	1995	1994	1993	1992	1991	1990	1989
Tangible Bk. Val.	NA	5.09	4.73	4.69	4.02	6.74	1.68	-4.84	NA	NA
Cash Flow	NA	2.12	2.27	2.16	2.22	1.79	1.55	1.23	1.26	NA
Earnings	0.96	1.08	1.43	1.47	1.51	1.20	0.81	0.45	0.45	0.73
Dividends	0.26	0.24	0.20	0.16	0.12	Nil	Nil	Nil	Nil	Nil
Payout Ratio	27%	22%	14%	11%	8%	Nil	Nil	Nil	Nil	Nil
Prices - High	18	24¼	25¾	23	26¼	20⅝	11½	NA	NA	NA
- Low	9⅝	12¾	17¾	14	14½	9⅛	9⅛	NA	NA	NA
P/E Ratio - High	19	23	18	16	17	17	14	NA	NA	NA
- Low	10	12	12	10	10	8	11	NA	NA	NA

Income Statement Analysis (Million $)

	1998	1997	1996	1995	1994	1993	1992	1991	1990	1989
Revs.	NA	376	314	232	229	184	164	163	158	161
Oper. Inc.	NA	41.4	39.0	33.7	34.1	27.7	22.4	20.4	26.6	NA
Depr.	NA	10.2	8.3	6.6	6.7	5.5	4.4	4.5	4.5	NA
Int. Exp.	NA	10.1	7.1	4.2	4.1	3.6	7.8	9.1	9.9	10.4
Pretax Inc.	NA	18.0	23.3	22.7	23.1	18.6	10.0	6.5	7.3	8.6
Eff. Tax Rate	NA	41%	39%	39%	38%	39%	43%	46%	51%	42%
Net Inc.	NA	10.7	14.0	14.0	14.3	11.4	5.7	3.5	3.5	5.0

Balance Sheet & Other Fin. Data (Million $)

	1998	1997	1996	1995	1994	1993	1992	1991	1990	1989
Cash	NA	0.2	1.5	0.2	0.1	0.3	1.0	0.2	NA	NA
Curr. Assets	NA	184	181	127	87.2	79.7	52.4	59.8	NA	NA
Total Assets	NA	299	288	204	151	138	105	113	105	114
Curr. Liab.	NA	99	90.0	66.1	27.1	25.2	27.5	39.1	NA	NA
LT Debt	NA	84.0	88.0	42.0	46.0	50.0	25.0	46.2	52.1	58.0
Common Eqty.	NA	110	106	93.8	76.1	61.5	50.7	10.7	8.2	5.5
Total Cap.	NA	199	194	138	124	113	77.4	73.5	74.4	76.4
Cap. Exp.	NA	12.5	5.9	4.9	5.9	4.5	4.1	5.1	3.6	NA
Cash Flow	NA	20.9	22.5	20.6	21.0	16.9	9.1	7.0	7.1	NA
Curr. Ratio	NA	1.9	2.0	1.9	3.2	3.2	1.9	1.5	NA	NA
% LT Debt of Cap.	NA	42.1	45.4	30.4	37.0	44.1	32.3	62.7	70.0	76.0
% Net Inc.of Revs.	NA	2.8	4.6	6.0	6.2	6.2	3.5	2.2	2.2	3.1
% Ret. on Assets	NA	3.6	5.8	7.8	9.8	9.3	5.3	3.2	3.2	4.7
% Ret. on Equity	NA	9.9	14.3	16.4	20.7	20.2	15.6	26.7	36.9	73.2

Data as orig. reptd.; bef. results of disc. opers. and/or spec. items. Per share data adj. for stk. divs. as of ex-div. date. Bold denotes diluted EPS (FASB 128). E-Estimated. NA-Not Available. NM-Not Meaningful. NR-Not Ranked.

Office—800 E. 101st Terrace, Kansas City, MO 64131. **Tel**—(816) 943-4100. **Website**—http://www.rivco.com **Chrmn & CEO**—T. K. Manning. **Pres**—W. L. Yager. **VP & CFO**—W. M. Meierhoffer.**Dirs**—J. J. Culberg, W. S. Endres, T. Goodwin, J. E. Grimm III, L. R. Julian, T. K. Manning, N. L. Patton, D. M. Sanders, B. Smith, W. L. Yager. **Transfer Agent & Registrar**—United Missouri Bank, Kansas City. **Incorporated**—in Delaware in 1986. **Empl**— 2,500. **S&P Analyst:** Kathleen J. Fraser

STANDARD &POOR'S
STOCK REPORTS

Robbins & Myers

5104

NYSE Symbol **RBN**

In S&P SmallCap 600

03-OCT-98

Industry: Manufacturing (Specialized)

Summary: Robbins & Myers makes industrial pumps, large glass-lined vessels and industrial mixing equipment.

Quantitative Evaluations	
Outlook (1 Lowest—5 Highest) • **3⁻**	
Fair Value • **22⅞**	
Risk • **Average**	
Earn./Div. Rank • **B+**	
Technical Eval. • **NA**	
Rel. Strength Rank (1 Lowest—99 Highest) • **29**	
Insider Activity • **NA**	

Recent Price • 20⅝
52 Wk Range • 40½-20½

Yield • 1.1%
12-Mo. P/E • 7.6

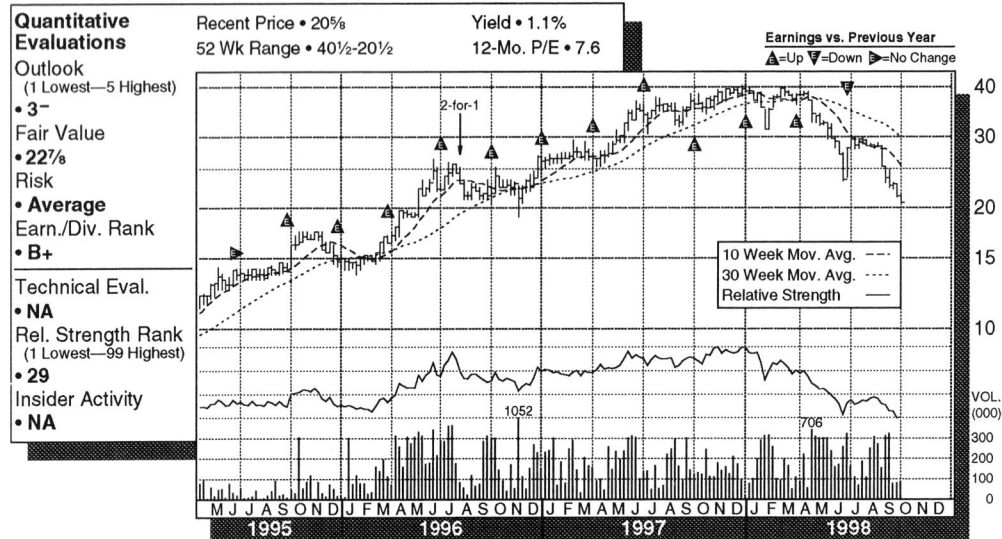

Earnings vs. Previous Year
▲=Up ▼=Down ▶=No Change

10 Week Mov. Avg. – – –
30 Week Mov. Avg. - - - -
Relative Strength —

Business Profile - 21-AUG-98

RBN shares have fallen in 1998, as a sharp reduction in oil prices led to an industrywide downturn. In June 1998, in repsonse to the price depreciation, directors authorized the repurchase of up to 5% of the company's common stock. As of June 1998, RBN had about 11 million common shares outstanding. Separately, the company merged its Moyno Oilfield Products and Flow Control Equipment business units into a single entity, R&M Energy Systems. The newly formed unit accounts for about 23% of total revenues.

Operational Review - 21-AUG-98

Revenues in the nine months ended May 31, 1998, rose 14%, year to year, primarily due to acquisitions. Margins widened, reflecting synergies related to acquisitions, and a more favorable product mix; operating income grew 34%. Profitability was hurt by a rise in depreciation and amortization charges, as well as increased interest expense. After taxes at 34.0%, versus 33.0%, net income was up 17%, to $24,220,000 ($1.88 a share, on 3.8% more shares), from $20,727,000 ($1.67).

Stock Performance - 02-OCT-98

In the past 30 trading days, RBN's shares have declined 27%, compared to a 7% fall in the S&P 500. Average trading volume for the past five days was 17,180 shares, compared with the 40-day moving average of 52,241 shares.

Key Stock Statistics

Dividend Rate/Share	0.22	Shareholders	2,700
Shs. outstg. (M)	11.1	Market cap. (B)	$0.228
Avg. daily vol. (M)	0.047	Inst. holdings	51%
Tang. Bk. Value/Share	NM		
Beta	0.99		

Value of $10,000 invested 5 years ago: $ 25,803

Fiscal Year Ending Aug. 31

	1998	1997	1996	1995	1994	1993
Revenues (Million $)						
1Q	104.2	93.82	81.21	68.63	21.90	21.40
2Q	108.4	93.21	84.18	70.87	22.57	20.10
3Q	112.7	97.59	89.88	79.97	25.02	22.71
4Q	—	101.0	95.69	83.48	52.17	20.89
Yr.	—	385.7	351.0	302.9	121.7	85.06
Earnings Per Share ($)						
1Q	0.69	0.58	0.38	0.28	0.18	0.21
2Q	**0.61**	0.56	0.40	0.29	0.20	0.20
3Q	**0.63**	0.69	0.52	0.21	0.21	0.20
4Q	—	0.69	0.55	0.33	0.01	0.04
Yr.	—	2.52	1.84	1.09	0.60	0.59

Next earnings report expected: NA

Dividend Data (Dividends have been paid since 1989.)

Amount ($)	Date Decl.	Ex-Div. Date	Stock of Record	Payment Date
0.050	Oct. 01	Oct. 15	Oct. 17	Oct. 31 '97
0.055	Dec. 10	Jan. 14	Jan. 16	Jan. 30 '98
0.055	Mar. 25	Apr. 03	Apr. 07	Apr. 30 '98
0.055	Jun. 25	Jul. 08	Jul. 10	Jul. 31 '98

A Division of The McGraw-Hill Companies

Business Summary - 21-AUG-98

Several years ago, Robbins & Myers (RBN) sold several diverse businesses, to focus solely on making industrial pumps. RBN is now the world's largest producer of progressing cavity pumps for the oil & gas industry. Through a subsequent turnaround acquisition, RBN has also become the world's largest producer of industrial glass-lined metal containers (called vessels) for large multinational drug companies and specialty chemical producers. In addition, the company manufactures industrial mixing equipment, also for drug makers and specialty chemical concerns. Important profitability statistics for recent fiscal years (Aug.) were:

	FY 97	FY 96	FY 95
Gross profit margins	36%	34%	33%
Operating profit margins	13%	11%	8.9%
Free cash flow per share	$1.11	$1.11	$2.53

Nearly 35% of total revenues come from higher margin replacement part sales. RBN obtains almost 50% of revenues from overseas markets.

The Pfaudler unit produces RBN's industrial vessels (40% of sales), which are used to hold highly corrosive chemicals. The Moyno Industrial Products and Moyno Oilfield Products units make RBN's progressing cavity pumps (30% of sales). These pumps are used by oil drillers to lift oil to the surface. The Moyno Oilfield Prod-

ucts unit also makes hydraulic motors for use in directional drilling, a new drilling procedure. The company sees strong growth potential for its hydraulic motor, with oil producers applying the new directional drilling procedure to their oil rigs. The Chemineer unit manufactures motor-driven industrial mixing equipment (20% of sales), used to mix industrial materials and chemicals. The Edlon unit (10% of sales) makes and applies Teflon and related coatings to materials used in the electronics industry.

Management primarily targets the oil & gas, pharmaceutical and specialty chemical markets. The oil & gas industry is RBN's strongest growth market. RBN sees continued strong growth opportunities in this segment, due to ongoing conversions of existing oil rigs to directional drilling applications, and expansion of global exploration and development. RBN estimates that there are 1,700 drilling rigs worldwide. It also sees growth in the pharmaceutical industry, reflecting anticipated demand for pharmaceuticals from underdeveloped countries, and maturing populations in developed countries. The company finds the specialty chemical industry attractive because specialty chemical producers offer value-added chemicals, and thus are not as vulnerable to price volatility as commodity chemical producers. Robbins believes that growth in the specialty chemical industry is being driven by demand for improved pesticides, herbicides and fertilizers, and specialty chemical production expansion in emerging countries.

Per Share Data ($)

(Year Ended Aug. 31)	1997	1996	1995	1994	1993	1992	1991	1990	1989	1988
Tangible Bk. Val.	NM	-1.58	-1.65	-1.99	4.14	4.92	4.75	3.92	3.61	2.96
Cash Flow	4.10	3.09	2.33	1.01	0.85	0.98	2.12	0.96	0.87	0.81
Earnings	2.52	1.84	1.09	0.60	0.59	0.75	0.86	0.54	0.43	0.33
Dividends	0.19	0.17	0.15	0.15	0.12	0.09	0.07	0.05	0.01	Nil
Payout Ratio	8%	9%	14%	25%	20%	13%	8%	9%	3%	Nil
Prices - High	40½	27	17½	10¼	10¾	10	10¾	6	4⅝	3⅞
- Low	24¼	13⅝	8½	8¼	7¾	6½	4⅝	3⅞	3⅜	1¾
P/E Ratio - High	16	15	16	17	18	13	12	11	11	12
- Low	10	7	8	14	13	9	5	7	8	5

Income Statement Analysis (Million $)

	1997	1996	1995	1994	1993	1992	1991	1990	1989	1988
Revs.	386	351	303	122	85.0	76.0	79.0	109	106	98.0
Oper. Inc.	65.0	52.6	39.5	20.6	13.4	13.2	12.9	10.6	11.3	11.1
Depr.	16.0	13.9	12.4	4.3	2.8	2.4	2.0	4.3	4.3	4.6
Int. Exp.	6.4	7.1	7.3	1.5	0.1	0.1	0.1	0.1	0.7	1.2
Pretax Inc.	43.1	32.4	19.0	10.6	9.8	9.8	9.7	6.0	4.4	3.4
Eff. Tax Rate	33%	37%	38%	40%	37%	20%	11%	10%	4.90%	7.40%
Net Inc.	28.9	20.3	11.8	6.4	6.2	7.9	8.7	5.4	4.2	3.1

Balance Sheet & Other Fin. Data (Million $)

	1997	1996	1995	1994	1993	1992	1991	1990	1989	1988
Cash	10.3	7.1	10.2	16.1	24.5	24.1	31.4	6.6	2.4	1.3
Curr. Assets	130	114	110	104	48.3	46.0	51.0	36.0	33.0	29.0
Total Assets	372	372	270	258	85.0	74.0	69.0	66.0	60.0	54.0
Curr. Liab.	82.7	76.4	77.7	58.5	15.0	11.7	14.7	14.6	15.5	18.7
LT Debt	111	72.2	61.8	80.3	Nil	0.9	0.9	1.0	1.1	0.5
Common Eqty.	124	91.4	70.0	57.0	52.3	56.3	49.2	44.6	39.6	31.5
Total Cap.	237	164	132	137	52.3	57.0	50.0	46.0	41.0	32.0
Cap. Exp.	22.1	16.5	10.1	11.4	5.3	12.4	4.2	5.4	5.8	3.8
Cash Flow	44.8	34.2	24.2	10.7	9.0	10.3	10.6	9.7	8.4	7.7
Curr. Ratio	1.6	1.5	1.4	1.8	3.2	3.9	3.5	2.5	2.1	1.5
% LT Debt of Cap.	46.9	44.1	47.0	58.5	Nil	1.6	1.8	2.3	2.8	1.5
% Net Inc.of Revs.	7.5	5.8	3.9	5.2	7.3	10.4	11.0	5.0	4.0	3.2
% Ret. on Assets	8.6	7.1	4.5	3.7	7.8	10.9	12.8	8.7	7.2	5.6
% Ret. on Equity	26.7	25.2	18.7	11.6	11.4	14.8	18.4	12.9	11.5	10.4

Data as orig. reptd.; bef. results of disc. opers. and/or spec. items. Per share data adj. for stk. divs. as of ex-div. date. Bold denotes diluted EPS (FASB 128). E-Estimated. NA-Not Available. NM-Not Meaningful. NR-Not Ranked.

Office—1400 Kettering Tower, Dayton, OH 45423. **Tel**—(937) 222-2610. **Chrmn**—M. H. Murch IV. **Pres & CEO**—D. W. Duval. **VP & CFO**—G. M. Walker. **Secy & Treas**—S. R. Ley. **Investor Contact**—Hugh E. Becker (937-225-3335). **Dirs**—D. W. Duval, R. J. Kegerreis, T. P. Loftis, W. D. Manning, Jr., M. H. Murch IV, J. F. Tatar, J. N. Taylor, Jr. **Transfer Agent & Registrar**—KeyCorp Shareholder Services, Cleveland. **Incorporated**—in Ohio in 1928. **Empl**— 3,000. **S&P Analyst:** Stephen J. Tekirian

10-OCT-98

Industry:
Health Care (Drugs - Generic & Other)

Summary: This international pharmaceutical company acquires, develops and markets prescription drug products.

Quantitative Evaluations

Outlook
(1 Lowest—5 Highest)
• **2⁻**

Fair Value
• **20⅜**

Risk
• **Average**

Earn./Div. Rank
• **C**

Technical Eval.
• **NA**

Rel. Strength Rank
(1 Lowest—99 Highest)
• **73**

Insider Activity
• **Neutral**

Recent Price • 17¾
52 Wk Range • 24¼-9

Yield • Nil
12-Mo. P/E • 81.0

Earnings vs. Previous Year
▲=Up ▼=Down ▶=No Change

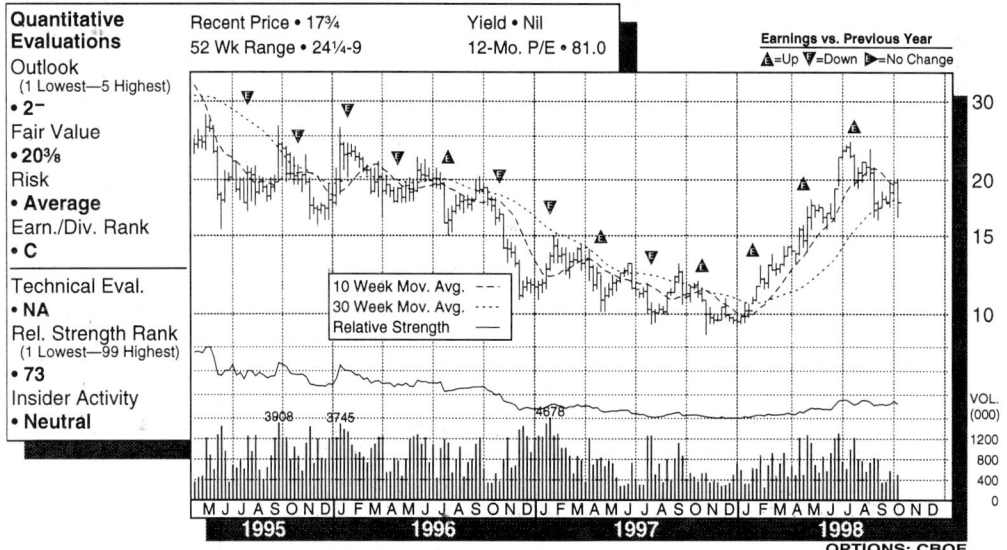

10 Week Mov. Avg.
30 Week Mov. Avg.
Relative Strength

VOL. (000)

OPTIONS: CBOE

Business Profile - 28-SEP-98

This pharmaceutical company has sold most of its generic drug products and non-pharmaceutical operations, in order to focus on the development of its proprietary drug portfolio. Over the past year, RPC successfully launched two such products: ProAmatine for the treatment of low blood pressure; and Agrylin for high platelet counts. In July 1998, the company announced the marketing approval for Agrylin in Israel. Also in July, RPC reported that a key use patent (for delayed onset emesis related to chemotherapy) was granted for Emitasol, an intranasal anti-emetic, licensed to RPC for U.S. marketing by RiboGene, Inc. In April 1998, the company acquired from Hoechst Marion Roussel exclusive U.S. marketing rights to Pentasa (a drug for ulcerative colitis), for $130 million. RPC anticipated that Pentasa would generate over $40 million in sales in the next year.

Operational Review - 28-SEP-98

Revenues in the six months ended June 30, 1998, surged 36%, year to year, primarily from increased domestic product sales of Pentasa, Agrylin, and ProAmatine. Gross margins widened on a more favorable product mix. Despite higher R&D and administrative costs, lower income from other sources, and taxes of 39.3%, versus 35.9%, net income from continuing operations rose 152%, to $5,531,000 ($0.18 a share) from $2,198,000 ($0.06). Results in the 1998 period exclude income from discontinued operations of $0.04 a share.

Stock Performance - 09-OCT-98

In the past 30 trading days, RPC's shares have increased 0.35%, compared to a 4% fall in the S&P 500. Average trading volume for the past five days was 96,760 shares, compared with the 40-day moving average of 113,587 shares.

Key Stock Statistics

Dividend Rate/Share	Nil	Shareholders	900
Shs. outstg. (M)	31.4	Market cap. (B)	$0.559
Avg. daily vol. (M)	0.089	Inst. holdings	40%
Tang. Bk. Value/Share	0.20		
Beta	1.04		

Value of $10,000 invested 5 years ago: $ 7,872

Fiscal Year Ending Dec. 31

	1998	1997	1996	1995	1994	1993
Revenues (Million $)						
1Q	32.85	26.33	17.23	16.17	25.72	16.90
2Q	44.40	30.29	26.80	30.36	25.64	20.66
3Q	—	28.60	21.69	34.32	30.77	23.48
4Q	—	37.30	32.39	32.56	30.06	28.60
Yr.	—	122.5	98.08	113.4	112.2	89.66
Earnings Per Share ($)						
1Q	0.07	0.04	-0.22	-0.06	0.23	0.05
2Q	0.11	0.04	0.10	0.06	0.24	0.06
3Q	—	-0.11	-0.40	0.02	0.27	0.08
4Q	—	0.11	-1.83	0.01	0.32	0.25
Yr.	—	0.06	-2.47	0.15	1.04	0.46

Next earnings report expected: mid October

Dividend Data

Cash dividends have never been paid.

Business Summary - 28-SEP-98

Roberts Pharmaceutical acquires and develops high-potential, undervalued, late-stage-development pharmaceuticals and acquires currently marketed prescription and nonprescription products. In 1995, RPC began divesting certain nonstrategic products and its nonpharmaceutical operations to focus resources on developing its proprietary drug pipeline. Through the creation of its own sales and marketing infrastructure, Roberts has developed expertise and distribution relationships in selected medical fields where pipeline drugs will begin to flow.

RPC was founded to take advantage of the large and growing opportunity to license, acquire, develop and commercialize post-discovery drugs in selected therapeutic areas. Acquisitions focus on late-stage-development drugs in Phase II or Phase III clinical trials and currently marketed prescription pharmaceutical products that do not meet strategic objectives or profit thresholds of larger pharmaceutical companies or are made available by government agencies and research institutions. The therapeutic categories targeted by the company are cardiovascular, respiratory, gynecology/endocrinology, urology, oncology, hematology and gastroenterology.

This strategy is beginning to bear fruit, as Roberts launched its first proprietary product in late 1996, ProAmatine, the first FDA-approved drug for the treatment of orthostatic hypotension (low blood pressure). In April 1997, the company launched Agrylin, used to treat thrombocytosis (elevated blood platelet counts). Both products have been designated "orphan drugs" by the FDA, providing seven years of market exclusivity post approval.

The research pipeline includes Somagard, in Phase III studies for central precocious puberty and prostate cancer; Radinyl, in Phase III trials as a radiosensitizer; Dirame, in Phase III trials for pain management; and Stanate, in Phase III studies for neonatal jaundice. In late 1996, RPC's R&D pipeline was bolstered by the acquisition of four gastrointestinal compounds from Eli Lilly. In April 1997, RPC received an exclusive license from Pfizer Inc. to develop and market Sampatrilat, for the treatment of essential hypertension and congestive heart failure.

The company recently acquired from Hoechst Marion Roussel the U.S. rights to market the ulcerative colitis drug Pentasa. In order to lower manufacturing costs, RPC acquired a modern, state-of-the-art pharmaceutical production plant from G.D. Searle. With the addition of this facility, RPC expects to be able to manufacture many drug products that had been produced by contractors at substantial cost.

Per Share Data ($)

(Year Ended Dec. 31)	1997	1996	1995	1994	1993	1992	1991	1990	1989	1988
Tangible Bk. Val.	4.28	5.73	0.26	1.95	2.18	0.33	2.55	1.45	0.06	NA
Cash Flow	0.32	-2.21	0.53	1.41	0.79	-0.53	-0.49	-0.82	0.01	NA
Earnings	0.06	-2.47	0.15	1.04	0.46	-0.68	-0.58	-0.85	Nil	Nil
Dividends	Nil	Nil	Nil	Nil	Nil	Nil	Nil	Nil	Nil	Nil
Payout Ratio	Nil	Nil	Nil	Nil	Nil	Nil	Nil	Nil	Nil	Nil
Prices - High	15	26¼	46½	40	42½	36¾	33	8	NA	NA
- Low	9	10¾	15½	19¾	15¼	13½	4	2½	NA	NA
P/E Ratio - High	NM	NM	NM	38	92	NM	NM	NM	NA	NA
- Low	NM	NM	NM	19	33	NM	NM	NM	NM	NM

Income Statement Analysis (Million $)

	1997	1996	1995	1994	1993	1992	1991	1990	1989	1988
Revs.	123	98.1	113	112	89.7	33.0	13.5	1.2	5.5	NA
Oper. Inc.	6.2	-5.4	14.0	31.3	13.7	-8.9	-3.8	-5.0	-0.1	NA
Depr.	6.9	7.5	7.2	7.0	5.0	2.0	0.8	0.1	0.1	NA
Int. Exp.	0.8	1.8	3.5	4.0	3.3	1.1	1.0	0.1	0.1	NA
Pretax Inc.	1.4	-48.9	5.5	23.3	7.2	-8.6	-4.9	-4.7	0.2	NA
Eff. Tax Rate	NM	NM	51%	17%	Nil	NM	NM	NM	46%	NA
Net Inc.	2.5	-34.3	2.7	19.4	7.2	-9.3	-5.1	-4.7	0.1	NA

Balance Sheet & Other Fin. Data (Million $)

	1997	1996	1995	1994	1993	1992	1991	1990	1989	1988
Cash	43.0	94.9	30.0	36.5	91.6	43.9	14.2	11.8	0.8	NA
Curr. Assets	138	157	93.8	96.0	128	58.3	19.8	12.5	1.9	NA
Total Assets	368	372	340	336	343	185	44.0	13.0	3.0	NA
Curr. Liab.	40.0	51.5	81.7	53.9	57.7	34.0	9.8	1.0	0.6	NA
LT Debt	10.3	10.6	16.1	22.4	45.7	29.0	9.2	0.4	0.5	NA
Common Eqty.	317	309	235	259	239	122	25.0	10.0	Nil	Nil
Total Cap.	328	322	278	282	285	151	34.0	12.0	2.0	NA
Cap. Exp.	11.9	0.7	0.2	1.0	6.6	9.4	0.3	0.0	0.1	NA
Cash Flow	9.5	-41.4	9.9	26.5	12.3	-7.3	-4.3	-4.7	0.1	NA
Curr. Ratio	3.5	3.0	1.1	1.8	2.2	1.7	2.0	12.7	3.4	NA
% LT Debt of Cap.	3.1	3.2	5.8	8.0	16.0	19.2	26.9	3.6	26.3	NA
% Net Inc.of Revs.	2.1	NM	0.4	17.3	8.1	NM	NM	NM	1.8	NA
% Ret. on Assets	0.7	NM	0.8	5.7	2.5	NM	NM	NM	NA	NA
% Ret. on Equity	0.8	NM	1.1	7.8	3.7	NM	NM	NM	NA	NA

Data as orig. reptd.; bef. results of disc. opers. and/or spec. items. Per share data adj. for stk. divs. as of ex-div. date. Bold denotes diluted EPS (FASB 128). E-Estimated. NA-Not Available. NM-Not Meaningful. NR-Not Ranked.

Office—6 Industrial Way West, Eatontown, NJ 07724. **Tel**—(732) 389-1182. **Fax**—(732) 389-1014. **Website**—http://robertspharm.com **Chrmn**—R. A. Vukovich. **Pres & CEO**—J. T. Spitznagel. **VP, Treas & CFO**—P. M. Rogalin. **VP & Secy**—A. A. Rascio. **Dirs**—D. W. Barrios, Z. P. Horovitz, R. W. Loy, M. Lloyd, J. N. Noonburg, P. M. Rogalin, A. A. Rascio, J. E. Smith, J. T. Spitznagel, R. A. Vukovich. **Transfer Agent & Registrar**—Continental Stock Transfer & Trust Co., NYC. **Incorporated**—in New Jersey in 1982. **Empl**— 498. **S&P Analyst:** David Moskowitz

Rollins Truck Leasing
1950F

NYSE Symbol **RLC**

In S&P SmallCap 600

03-OCT-98

Industry:
Truckers

Summary: RLC primarily leases over-the-road tractors, trucks and trailers.

Quantitative Evaluations		
Outlook (1 Lowest—5 Highest)		
• **1+**		
Fair Value		
• **10¼**		
Risk		
• **Low**		
Earn./Div. Rank		
• **A**		
Technical Eval.		
• **Bearish** since 7/98		
Rel. Strength Rank (1 Lowest—99 Highest)		
• **67**		
Insider Activity		
• **NA**		

Recent Price • 10⅞
52 Wk Range • 14¼-8⅞

Yield • 1.5%
12-Mo. P/E • 13.4

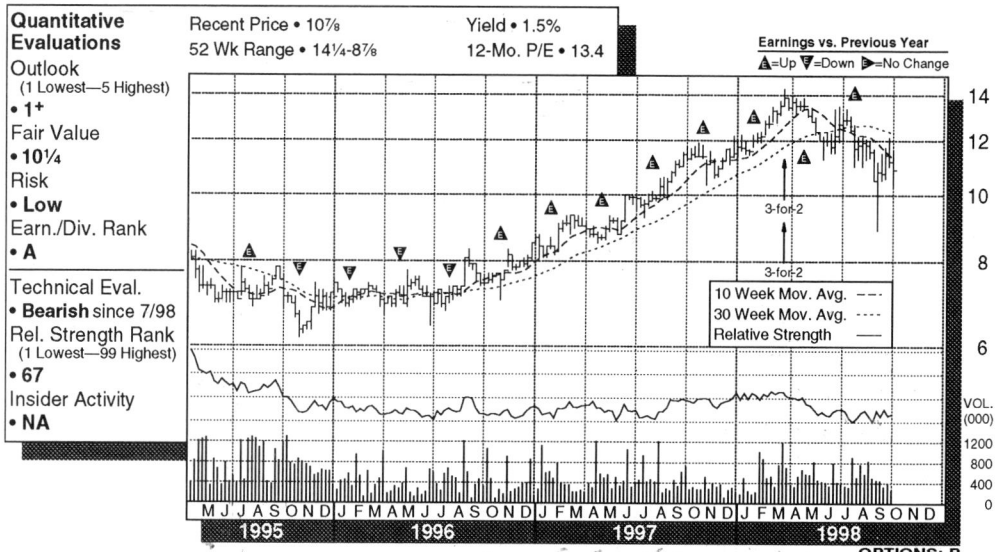

Earnings vs. Previous Year
▲=Up ▼=Down ▶=No Change

10 Week Mov. Avg. ---
30 Week Mov. Avg. ....
Relative Strength ——

OPTIONS: P

Business Profile - 18-MAY-98

This company, one of the largest U.S. full-service lessors of trucks, with 33,000 vehicles under management, also provides short-term truck rentals, guaranteed maintenance, and logistics services. Demand for short-term rental equipment has been sluggish as a result of industry-wide overcapacity, but long-term lease sales have been strong. A recent trend among private fleet operators to outsource certain transportation needs to professional distribution/logistics companies bodes well for future revenue growth. During the first six months of FY 98 (Sep.), RLC increased equipment financing obligations by about $16 million.

Operational Review - 18-MAY-98

Revenues in the first six months of FY 98 (Sep.) advanced 11%, year to year, as volume increases in full service leases (due to additional new accounts), logistics and commercial rentals outweighed continued pricing pressures. Costs were well controlled, and despite smaller equipment sales gains, and after taxes at 39.0% in both periods, net income climbed 31%, to $22,833,000 ($0.37 a share, diluted, on 3.6% fewer shares), from $17,451,000 ($0.27).

Stock Performance - 02-OCT-98

In the past 30 trading days, RLC's shares have declined 6%, compared to a 7% fall in the S&P 500. Average trading volume for the past five days was 52,220 shares, compared with the 40-day moving average of 96,669 shares.

Key Stock Statistics

Dividend Rate/Share	0.16	Shareholders	2,300
Shs. outstg. (M)	59.3	Market cap. (B)	$0.645
Avg. daily vol. (M)	0.079	Inst. holdings	53%
Tang. Bk. Value/Share	4.61		
Beta	0.52		

Value of $10,000 invested 5 years ago: $ 18,147

Fiscal Year Ending Sep. 30

	1998	1997	1996	1995	1994	1993
Revenues (Million $)						
1Q	149.0	133.7	125.0	119.1	107.4	100.1
2Q	145.1	132.4	122.2	116.7	107.1	97.04
3Q	155.2	142.1	130.7	122.7	115.8	104.6
4Q	—	148.5	135.8	124.1	120.5	107.0
Yr.	—	556.7	513.8	482.6	450.9	408.8
Earnings Per Share ($)						
1Q	**0.21**	0.15	0.13	0.17	0.14	0.11
2Q	**0.16**	0.12	0.08	0.16	0.12	0.09
3Q	**0.23**	0.19	0.15	0.17	0.15	0.13
4Q	—	0.21	0.17	0.14	0.17	0.11
Yr.	—	0.67	0.52	0.61	0.57	0.44

Next earnings report expected: late October

Dividend Data (Dividends have been paid since 1976.)

Amount ($)	Date Decl.	Ex-Div. Date	Stock of Record	Payment Date
0.055	Jan. 29	Feb. 11	Feb. 15	Mar. 15 '98
3-for-2	Jan. 29	Mar. 17	Feb. 15	Mar. 16 '98
0.040	Apr. 30	May. 13	May. 15	Jun. 15 '98
0.040	Jul. 30	Aug. 12	Aug. 15	Sep. 15 '98

A Division of The McGraw·Hill Companies

Rollins Truck Leasing Corp.

Business Summary - 18-MAY-98

Rollins Truck Leasing Corp. (RLC) wants to be in it for the long haul. RLC, the third largest U.S. full-service truck rental and leasing company, with about 33,000 vehicles in its fleet, is emphasizing long-term business with its trucking and other customers, but only if it sees profits down the road. Revenues from its economically sensitive short-term commercial rental business rebounded in FY 97 (Sep.), largely reflected improved pricing in comparison to FY 96. Combined with volume-related improvements in RLC's full-service lease, guaranteed maintenance and dedicated logistics revenues, total revenues advanced 8.4%, to $557 million.

The company views the signing of long-term contracts with appropriate margins in its full-service lease, dedicated and logistics markets as a key business strategy that can expand its revenue base and diversify its customer profile. Full-service leases, which accounted for the major portion of total revenues in FY 97, are long-term contracts (ranging from three to eight years in length) under which the company buys vehicles tailored to customer needs, leases the equipment to the customer, and provides maintenance and fuel services. Pricing of these long-term contracts is extremely important, because a low-margin lease will hurt the bottom line year after year. For this reason, new business must meet minimum margin thresholds before it is signed.

Another important strategy is to provide customers with a full logistics solution. Greater marketplace demand for the outsourcing of transportation services led to higher revenues for RLC's logistics and dedicated business in FY 97. However, the growth of these businesses carried with it higher costs for vehicle expenses and wages which, together with industrywide price competition, kept operating ratios flat in FY 97. Through its Dedicated Carriage Services offering, the company custom-designs a transportation system that will minimize and then control a customer's transportation costs by maximizing equipment and driver utilization, optimizing routes and schedules, enhancing dispatch efficiency and expanding backhaul opportunities. RLC also offers a range of logistics services to companies that wish to outsource their distribution and warehousing functions, including the selection and negotiation of core carrier contracts.

RLC's short-term commercial truck rental service helps companies meet their transportation needs during emergencies, peak seasonal demands, periods of increased business or when a unit is temporarily out of service. The utilization rate of the rental fleet during FY 97 averaged over 85%.

In FY 97, higher volumes throughout RLC's business led to an 8.4% increase in revenues; net income climbed 25%.

Per Share Data ($) (Year Ended Sep. 30)	1997	1996	1995	1994	1993	1992	1991	1990	1989	1988
Tangible Bk. Val.	4.49	4.17	3.91	3.49	3.00	2.63	2.32	1.92	1.71	2.11
Cash Flow	3.36	2.94	2.77	2.33	2.05	1.90	1.83	1.71	1.63	1.45
Earnings	0.67	0.52	0.61	0.57	0.44	0.36	0.30	0.28	0.27	0.25
Dividends	0.13	0.12	0.11	0.09	0.08	0.07	0.06	0.06	0.06	0.06
Payout Ratio	20%	23%	18%	15%	18%	20%	21%	21%	22%	24%
Prices - High	12 1/4	8 5/8	9 5/8	9 5/8	9 3/8	7 1/8	5 1/4	2 3/4	3 3/4	3 1/2
- Low	8 1/8	6 3/8	6 1/8	7 1/4	6 1/4	4 3/4	2 1/16	1 11/16	2 3/16	1 15/16
P/E Ratio - High	18	17	16	17	21	20	17	10	14	14
- Low	12	12	10	13	14	13	7	6	8	8
Income Statement Analysis (Million $)										
Revs.	557	514	483	451	409	380	342	331	312	275
Oper. Inc.	278	254	246	225	201	183	167	161	154	134
Depr.	170	159	147	122	112	106	97.0	90.0	86.0	76.0
Int. Exp.	49.3	47.5	44.5	37.4	35.5	36.8	40.5	43.3	43.5	36.5
Pretax Inc.	70.2	56.0	67.1	66.4	54.7	40.7	31.5	29.6	27.6	26.0
Eff. Tax Rate	39%	39%	39%	40%	44%	39%	40%	39%	39%	40%
Net Inc.	42.8	34.1	41.3	39.8	30.4	24.6	19.0	18.0	16.8	15.7
Balance Sheet & Other Fin. Data (Million $)										
Cash	17.6	31.2	22.7	15.1	15.1	17.6	21.9	18.9	16.8	14.8
Curr. Assets	121	124	111	102	90.0	91.0	80.0	81.0	77.0	66.0
Total Assets	1,192	1,125	1,027	910	781	708	656	658	631	624
Curr. Liab.	62.4	53.6	51.4	78.0	68.0	72.0	73.0	91.0	84.0	98.0
LT Debt	672	641	553	469	404	367	351	377	376	339
Common Eqty.	289	284	276	251	217	191	169	133	120	143
Total Cap.	1,115	1,060	944	823	704	627	577	561	541	522
Cap. Exp.	303	297	319	297	243	203	146	170	185	215
Cash Flow	213	193	188	162	142	131	116	108	103	92.0
Curr. Ratio	1.9	2.3	2.2	1.3	1.3	1.3	1.1	0.9	0.9	0.7
% LT Debt of Cap.	60.3	60.5	58.5	57.0	57.4	58.5	60.8	67.1	69.4	64.9
% Net Inc.of Revs.	7.7	6.7	8.7	8.8	7.4	6.5	5.5	5.4	5.4	5.7
% Ret. on Assets	3.7	3.2	4.3	4.7	4.1	3.6	2.8	2.8	2.7	2.6
% Ret. on Equity	14.9	12.2	15.7	17.0	14.9	13.6	12.1	14.2	12.6	11.8

Data as orig. reptd.; bef. results of disc. opers. and/or spec. items. Per share data adj. for stk. divs. as of ex-div. date. Bold denotes diluted EPS (FASB 128). E-Estimated. NA-Not Available. NM-Not Meaningful. NR-Not Ranked.

Office—One Rollins Plaza, Wilmington, DE 19803. **Tel**—(302) 426-2700. **Website**—http://www.rlc-corp.com **Chrmn & CEO**—J. W. Rollins. **Pres & COO**—J. W. Rollins Jr. **VP, Treas & Investor Contact**—Patrick J. Bagley. **VP & Secy**—M. B. Kinnard. **Dirs**—W. B. Philipbar Jr., G. W. Rollins, J. W. Rollins, J. W. Rollins Jr., H. B. Tippie. **Transfer Agent & Registrar**—Registrar & Transfer Co., Cranford, NJ. **Incorporated**—in Delaware in 1954. **Empl**— 3,708. **S&P Analyst:** L. A. Olive

Roper Industries

1950H

NYSE Symbol **ROP**

In S&P SmallCap 600

10-OCT-98

Industry: Manufacturing (Specialized)

Summary: This company is a U.S.-based global producer of hi-tech industrial equipment.

S&P Opinion: Accumulate (★★★★)

Recent Price • 14⅛	Yield • 1.7%	
52 Wk Range • 34-13½	12-Mo. P/E • 11.1	

Quantitative Evaluations

Outlook
(1 Lowest—5 Highest)
• **5**

Fair Value
• **29⅝**

Risk
• **Average**

Earn./Div. Rank
• **B+**

Technical Eval.
• **NA**

Rel. Strength Rank
(1 Lowest—99 Highest)
• **26**

Insider Activity
• **Favorable**

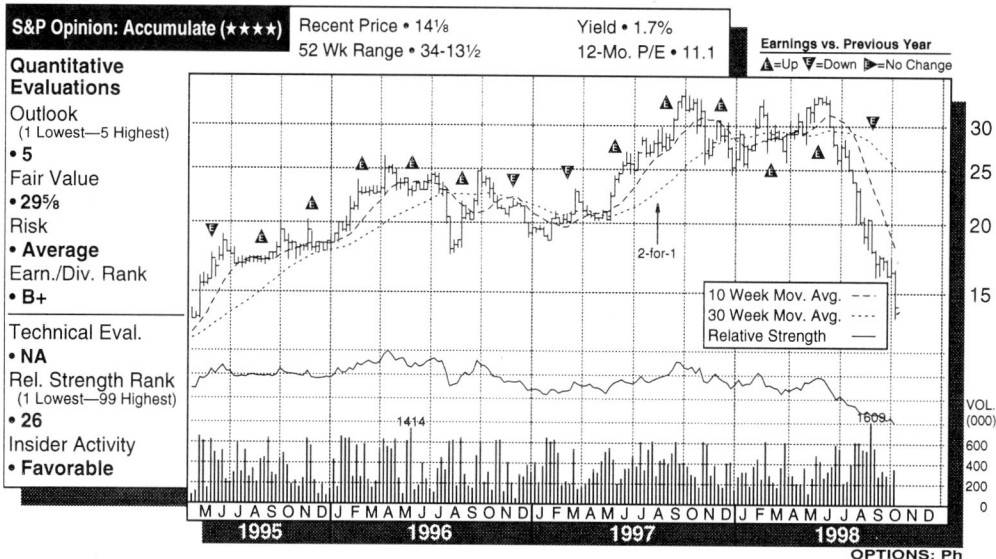

Earnings vs. Previous Year
▲=Up ▼=Down ▶=No Change

10 Week Mov. Avg. – – –
30 Week Mov. Avg. ·······
Relative Strength ——

2-for-1

OPTIONS: Ph

Overview - 24-AUG-98

Roper consistently posts gross profits of over 50%, among the highest in the industry. It achieves these margins by operating as a low-cost producer of high-tech, proprietary industrial components for certain high-growth niche markets. ROP strives to continually increase profits by boosting share in existing markets, targeting new but related markets, expanding overseas, and introducing new or improved products, while continually reducing operating costs. It also seeks to boost growth by acquiring leading producers of complementary, high-margin products for fast-growing market segments. In recent years, it has acquired more than 10 companies without diluting EPS. ROP typically uses debt to fund its acquisitions, and then utilizes its strong free cash flow to quickly reduce borrowings. Overseas sales (over 45% of total revenues) play an important part in ROP's growth.

Valuation - 24-AUG-98

Since FY 91 (Oct.), revenues have grown at a compound rate of 20%, reflecting an aggressive but judicious acquisition strategy, and ROP's ability to increase internally generated sales. ROP should be able to sustain this rate for several years, fueled by acquisitions, rising share of targeted growth markets, and overseas expansion. With high-margin product sales and strict cost controls, ROP has posted six-year annualized EPS growth of 30%, and seven-year average ROEs of 26%, at moderate debt levels. We believe that ROP will continue to post mid-20% ROEs, which we consider a major contributor to long-term equity growth and price performance. Since 1992, the shares have outpaced the S&P 500 by a wide margin. Although we do not believe that ROP will be able to outpace the index at historical rates, we expect the stock to continue to outperform, long-term.

Key Stock Statistics

S&P EPS Est. 1998	1.40	Tang. Bk. Value/Share	0.32
P/E on S&P Est. 1998	10.1	Beta	0.96
S&P EPS Est. 1999	1.50	Shareholders	200
Dividend Rate/Share	0.24	Market cap. (B)	$0.444
Shs. outstg. (M)	31.3	Inst. holdings	67%
Avg. daily vol. (M)	0.057		

Value of $10,000 invested 5 years ago: $ 34,448

Fiscal Year Ending Oct. 31

	1998	1997	1996	1995	1994	1993
Revenues (Million $)						
1Q	90.10	55.11	52.90	34.41	33.50	19.70
2Q	96.00	67.02	47.11	39.82	38.40	28.50
3Q	97.41	88.52	59.95	47.10	32.70	41.10
4Q	—	87.59	65.70	54.09	43.10	43.30
Yr.	—	298.2	225.7	175.4	147.7	132.5
Earnings Per Share ($)						
1Q	**0.34**	0.19	0.29	0.11	0.13	0.04
2Q	**0.33**	0.33	0.18	0.14	0.22	0.10
3Q	**0.33**	0.37	0.23	0.22	0.10	0.24
4Q	—	0.27	0.23	0.30	0.24	0.26
Yr.	**E1.40**	1.16	0.94	0.77	0.69	0.65

Next earnings report expected: mid December

Dividend Data (Dividends have been paid since 1992.)

Amount ($)	Date Decl.	Ex-Div. Date	Stock of Record	Payment Date
0.060	Nov. 12	Jan. 07	Jan. 09	Jan. 30 '98
0.060	Feb. 18	Apr. 07	Apr. 10	Apr. 30 '98
0.060	May. 14	Jul. 13	Jul. 15	Jul. 30 '98
0.060	Aug. 17	Oct. 13	Oct. 15	Oct. 30 '98

A Division of The McGraw-Hill Companies

Business Summary - 24-AUG-98

Over the past six fiscal years, Roper has boosted EPS at a compound annual growth rate (CAGR) of 30% and posted seven-year average ROEs of 26%, at moderate debt levels. Moreover, ROP has boosted retained earnings growth at an astounding CAGR of 94%. It has also hiked its dividend in each of the past four years. ROP's strategy has been to target high-margin industrial niche markets; increase competitive barriers through proprietary technologies and dominant market share; acquire complementary operations cheaply, and then dramatically boost acquiree sales and profits; expand its international presence; and control operating costs. ROP's success is shown by strong across-the-board segment operating profit margins in recent fiscal years (Oct.):

	FY 97	FY 96	FY 95
Industrial Controls	18%	21%	19%
Fluid Handling	28%	28%	31%
Analytical Instrumentation	23%	15%	14%

The Industrial Controls unit (41% of FY 97 revenues) primarily makes high-tech industrial valves and other control equipment. IC derives about 70% of its revenues from sales to the oil & gas industry. The 30% balance is divided as follows: General industrial, 11%;

power utilities, 10%; petrochemical, 6%; and shipbuilding, 3%.

Since FY 93, Industrial Controls has supplied Gazprom with over $100 million of gas pipeline flow control equipment. In late 1997, Gazprom terminated a U.S. Export-Import Bank agreement that would have guaranteed a $151 million commercial bank loan used to finance Gazprom's purchase of $151 million of ROP gas flow control equipment over a five-year period. The agreement was terminated amid U.S. government criticism of Gazprom's dealings with Iran. However in mid-1998, a Gazprom-owned Hungarian Bank agreed to guarantee payment of $128 million of ROP equipment to Gazprom, using letters of credit. ROP is expected to deliver the $128 million of equipment over five years.

The Fluid Handling unit (32% of FY 97 revenues) primarily makes high-tech industrial pumps for general industrial companies (36% of FH sales) and semiconductor equipment makers (24% of FH sales).

The Analytical Instrumentation unit (27% of FY 97 revenues) makes analytical equipment for the academic and commercial laboratory markets. Products include oil analysis equipment for the oil industry and leak-testing devices used to examine medical supplies such as rubber gloves, catheters and blood bags. In addition, AI is the world's largest maker of imaging and analytical components for electron microscopes, used commercially in such markets as the semiconductor industry.

Per Share Data ($)

(Year Ended Oct. 31)	1997	1996	1995	1994	1993	1992	1991	1990	1989	1988
Tangible Bk. Val.	0.76	4.53	1.25	1.15	0.69	0.28	-0.07	NA	NA	NA
Cash Flow	1.52	1.07	0.96	0.87	0.74	0.29	0.35	NA	NA	NA
Earnings	1.16	0.94	0.77	0.69	0.65	0.18	0.23	NA	NA	NA
Dividends	0.20	0.16	0.14	0.07	0.05	0.03	Nil	Nil	Nil	Nil
Payout Ratio	17%	17%	18%	10%	7%	19%	Nil	Nil	Nil	Nil
Prices - High	34⁷/₈	26³/₈	20¹/₄	17	19¹/₂	5¹/₄	NA	NA	NA	NA
- Low	18⁵/₈	17¹/₂	10¹/₂	9	4¹/₂	2⁷/₈	NA	NA	NA	NA
P/E Ratio - High	30	28	26	24	30	28	NA	NA	NA	NA
- Low	16	19	14	13	7	16	NA	NA	NA	NA

Income Statement Analysis (Million $)

	1997	1996	1995	1994	1993	1992	1991	1990	1989	1988
Revs.	298	226	175	148	133	70.0	75.0	NA	NA	NA
Oper. Inc.	72.3	51.4	43.4	38.3	33.4	14.3	15.2	NA	NA	NA
Depr.	11.4	4.1	6.0	5.3	3.0	2.7	2.4	NA	NA	NA
Int. Exp.	6.0	3.3	1.9	1.5	2.0	2.3	5.0	NA	NA	NA
Pretax Inc.	55.1	44.2	36.0	31.6	28.4	7.5	7.9	NA	NA	NA
Eff. Tax Rate	34%	35%	35%	34%	33%	37%	37%	NA	NA	NA
Net Inc.	36.4	28.9	23.3	20.9	19.1	4.7	4.9	NA	NA	NA

Balance Sheet & Other Fin. Data (Million $)

	1997	1996	1995	1994	1993	1992	1991	1990	1989	1988
Cash	0.6	0.4	2.3	2.0	1.2	1.7	2.9	NA	NA	NA
Curr. Assets	132	84.5	66.6	53.2	34.4	32.2	25.9	NA	NA	NA
Total Assets	329	243	156	122	94.0	81.0	48.0	NA	NA	NA
Curr. Liab.	44.9	39.5	27.7	20.8	20.5	10.5	11.2	NA	NA	NA
LT Debt	100	63.4	20.2	16.7	9.9	28.4	31.8	NA	NA	NA
Common Eqty.	178	137	106	82.9	62.4	40.5	3.7	NA	NA	NA
Total Cap.	278	201	126	100	73.2	70.2	37.0	NA	NA	NA
Cap. Exp.	5.0	5.0	3.2	4.1	3.9	0.9	4.3	NA	NA	NA
Cash Flow	47.8	33.0	29.3	26.2	22.1	7.4	7.0	NA	NA	NA
Curr. Ratio	2.9	2.1	2.4	2.6	1.7	3.1	2.3	NA	NA	NA
% LT Debt of Cap.	35.9	31.6	16.0	16.8	13.5	40.4	85.9	NA	NA	NA
% Net Inc.of Revs.	12.2	12.8	13.3	14.1	14.4	6.8	6.6	NA	NA	NA
% Ret. on Assets	12.7	14.5	16.7	19.3	21.7	6.2	NA	NA	NA	NA
% Ret. on Equity	23.1	23.8	24.7	28.7	36.9	20.5	NA	NA	NA	NA

Data as orig. reptd.; bef. results of disc. opers. and/or spec. items. Per share data adj. for stk. divs. as of ex-div. date. Bold denotes diluted EPS (FASB 128). E-Estimated. NA-Not Available. NM-Not Meaningful. NR-Not Ranked.

Office—160 Ben Burton Rd., Bogart, GA 30622. **Tel**—(706) 369-7170. **Fax**—(706) 353-6496. **Chrmn, Pres & CEO**—D. N. Key. **VP, CFO & Investor Contact**—Martin S. Headley. **VP & Treas**—Z. E. Metcalf. **VP & Secy**—S. D. Cronk. **Dirs**—W. L. Banks, L. von Braun, D. G. Calder, J. F. Fort III, E. D. Kenna, D. N. Key, G. L. Ohrstrom, W. J. Prezzano, G. G. Schall-Riaucour, E. R. Scocimara, C. Wright. **Transfer Agent & Registrar**—SunTrust Bank, Atlanta. **Incorporated**—in Delaware in 1981. **Empl**— 2,000. **S&P Analyst:** Robert E. Friedman, CPA

03-OCT-98 Industry: Housewares

Summary: This company markets plastic and metal vacuum cleaners for home and commercial use under the Dirt Devil and Royal brand names.

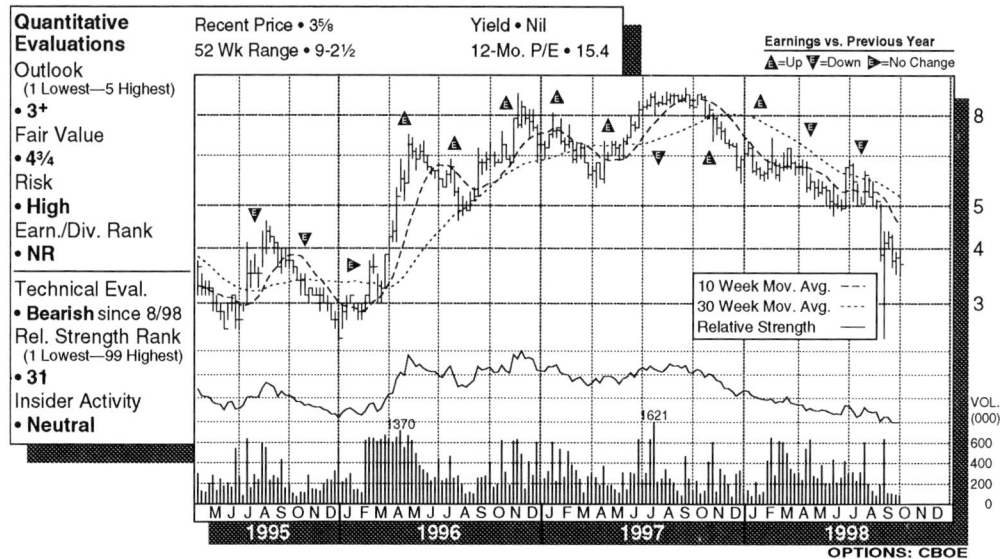

Quantitative Evaluations	
Recent Price • 3⅝	Yield • Nil
52 Wk Range • 9-2½	12-Mo. P/E • 15.4

Outlook (1 Lowest—5 Highest)
• **3+**

Fair Value
• **4¾**

Risk
• **High**

Earn./Div. Rank
• **NR**

Technical Eval.
• **Bearish** since 8/98

Rel. Strength Rank (1 Lowest—99 Highest)
• **31**

Insider Activity
• **Neutral**

Earnings vs. Previous Year ▲=Up ▼=Down ▶=No Change

10 Week Mov. Avg. ---
30 Week Mov. Avg. ·····
Relative Strength —

OPTIONS: CBOE

Business Profile - 22-JUL-98

This maker of vacuum cleaners for home and commercial use seeks to apply the well known Dirt Devil brand name to innovative new products associated with cleaning. Several new products were introduced in 1997, including the Swivel Glide, a full size upright vacuum with enhanced maneuverability. In the 1997 third quarter, RAM began shipping the Dirt Devil Mop Vac, a cordless rechargeable mop. In 1997, the company achieved double digit sales and earnings growth. However, sales declined in the first half of 1998, and RAM posted a loss. The Dirt Devil Swivel Glide Vision, a full size upright vacuum cleaner with bagless technology, is scheduled to be launched in the third quarter of 1998. RAM said it was encouraged by major retailers' positive response and shelf placements for the Vision product.

Operational Review - 22-JUL-98

Sales in the six months ended June 30, 1998, fell 14%, year to year, reflecting inventory reductions by certain large retailers, and the absence of the 1997 period's product launches. Gross margins narrowed, and a net loss of $4,777,000 ($0.22 a share, on 8.5% fewer shares) contrasted with net income of $1,525,000 ($0.06).

Stock Performance - 02-OCT-98

In the past 30 trading days, RAM's shares have declined 28%, compared to a 7% fall in the S&P 500. Average trading volume for the past five days was 16,300 shares, compared with the 40-day moving average of 44,572 shares.

Key Stock Statistics

Dividend Rate/Share	Nil	Shareholders	1,500
Shs. outstg. (M)	21.4	Market cap. (B)	$0.079
Avg. daily vol. (M)	0.021	Inst. holdings	36%
Tang. Bk. Value/Share	2.33		
Beta	2.16		

Value of $10,000 invested 5 years ago: $ 2,610

Fiscal Year Ending Dec. 31

	1998	1997	1996	1995	1994	1993
Revenues (Million $)						
1Q	51.85	58.62	52.26	49.02	59.79	70.40
2Q	51.26	61.07	62.97	58.26	55.24	53.24
3Q	—	87.38	73.69	66.99	69.06	91.21
4Q	—	118.3	97.20	96.30	96.03	99.1
Yr.	—	325.4	286.1	270.6	280.1	313.9
Earnings Per Share ($)						
1Q	**-0.11**	0.02	0.01	-0.10	-0.11	-0.28
2Q	**-0.10**	0.04	0.05	-0.08	-0.05	-0.40
3Q	—	0.17	0.13	-0.51	0.12	0.14
4Q	—	**0.29**	0.19	0.12	0.12	0.20
Yr.	—	**0.52**	0.39	-0.57	0.08	-0.35

Next earnings report expected: mid October

Dividend Data

Royal intends to retain earnings to finance the expansion of its business. The shares were split two for one in 1992. A shareholder rights plan was adopted in 1993.

A Division of The McGraw-Hill Companies

Business Summary - 22-JUL-98

In 1984, the first in a long line of Dirt Devil hand-held vacuum cleaners appeared on store shelves. In the years since then, Royal Appliance Co. believes that the Dirt Devil has become the largest selling line of hand-held vacuums in the U.S. The company has leveraged the well known Dirt Devil brand name to gain market acceptance of other cleaning and floor care products. In addition, RAM markets metal vacuum cleaners for home and commercial use under the Royal brand name. Contributions by product line in recent years were:

	1997	1996	1995
Dirt Devil & plastic related products	90%	88%	84%
Metal products	4%	5%	6%
Accessories & other	6%	7%	10%

Dirt Devil vacuum cleaners are intended for home use. The first product in this line was the Hand-Vac, a corded, hand-held vacuum cleaner. The line has since been expanded to include upright and canister vacuum cleaners, electric brooms and mops, and non-electric sweepers. RAM introduced several new products in 1997, including the Swivel Glide, a full size upright vacuum with enhanced maneuverability. The company introduced the Mop Vac, a cordless rechargeable mop, in the third quarter of 1997. A full size upright vacuum cleaner with bagless technology is scheduled to be launched in the 1998 third quarter. RAM plans to introduce the new product by direct response television until the fall of 1998, when it will be shipped to retail customers. The constant introduction of new products is critical to the company's success.

Since the early 1900s, Royal has sold metal vacuum cleaners intended for both home and commercial use. This product line is sold exclusively through a network of more than 2,500 independent dealers. In addition, RAM sells accessories, attachments, refurbished cleaners and replacement parts for each of its product lines. These products are available through retailers, dealers and Royal.

Dirt Devil products are sold through major retailers, with Wal-Mart accounting for 36% of total sales in 1997 (33% in 1996), and Kmart contributing 11% (11%). Sales to the company's five largest customers in 1997 accounted for 62% (59%) of total sales. Royal's business is highly seasonal.

Although the company develops its products internally, RAM may also buy product tooling, license product designs and patents, and out-source certain products that are marketed under the Dirt Devil name.

Per Share Data ($)

(Year Ended Dec. 31)	1997	1996	1995	1994	1993	1992	1991	1990	1989	1988
Tangible Bk. Val.	2.63	2.34	1.94	2.52	2.45	2.79	2.39	0.67	NA	NA
Cash Flow	0.91	0.75	-0.09	0.57	0.07	1.05	1.20	0.33	NA	NA
Earnings	0.52	0.39	-0.57	0.06	-0.35	0.81	1.09	0.27	NA	NA
Dividends	Nil	Nil	Nil	Nil	Nil	Nil	Nil	NA	NA	NA
Payout Ratio	Nil	Nil	Nil	Nil	Nil	Nil	Nil	NA	NA	NA
Prices - High	9¼	9	4⅝	6¼	14¼	31	23⅞	NA	NA	NA
- Low	5½	2⅝	2½	3¼	4½	7⅝	7¾	NA	NA	NA
P/E Ratio - High	18	23	NM	NM	NM	38	22	NA	NA	NA
- Low	11	7	NM	NM	NM	9	7	NA	NA	NA

Income Statement Analysis (Million $)

	1997	1996	1995	1994	1993	1992	1991	1990	1989	1988
Revs.	325	286	271	280	314	395	273	120	63.0	42.0
Oper. Inc.	32.0	26.0	11.9	19.5	4.1	42.3	51.2	15.8	6.5	3.8
Depr.	9.4	8.7	11.6	12.1	9.9	6.1	2.9	1.4	0.9	0.7
Int. Exp.	1.4	2.6	4.0	4.5	5.6	3.3	2.8	2.5	1.9	1.3
Pretax Inc.	20.2	15.3	-20.2	2.5	-13.0	33.0	45.4	11.7	3.6	1.8
Eff. Tax Rate	39%	39%	NM	37%	NM	39%	40%	41%	44%	44%
Net Inc.	12.4	9.4	-13.8	1.6	-8.3	20.2	27.4	6.9	2.0	1.0

Balance Sheet & Other Fin. Data (Million $)

	1997	1996	1995	1994	1993	1992	1991	1990	1989	1988
Cash	1.4	1.0	Nil	Nil	Nil	Nil	Nil	1.3	0.0	NA
Curr. Assets	89.0	83.8	84.7	86.0	93.0	134	94.3	54.2	24.7	NA
Total Assets	135	126	131	142	154	188	121	62.0	30.0	26.0
Curr. Liab.	57.9	54.2	38.7	34.1	35.7	53.3	41.5	17.8	8.6	NA
LT Debt	13.7	15.7	46.0	46.9	59.6	68.1	19.4	31.2	14.9	16.0
Common Eqty.	60.2	56.2	60.2	60.5	58.7	66.9	60.2	12.8	6.0	3.7
Total Cap.	77.1	72.0	92.6	107	118	135	79.6	43.9	20.9	19.8
Cap. Exp.	14.5	9.7	19.8	5.9	21.1	32.1	9.5	4.7	1.6	1.5
Cash Flow	21.8	18.2	-2.2	13.6	1.6	26.3	30.2	8.3	2.9	1.7
Curr. Ratio	1.5	1.5	2.2	2.5	2.6	2.5	2.3	3.0	2.9	NA
% LT Debt of Cap.	17.7	21.9	50.0	43.7	50.4	50.4	24.4	70.9	71.2	81.1
% Net Inc.of Revs.	3.8	3.3	NM	0.6	NM	5.1	10.0	5.7	3.2	2.4
% Ret. on Assets	9.5	7.3	NM	1.1	NM	13.3	29.9	14.9	7.3	4.7
% Ret. on Equity	21.3	18.4	NM	2.6	NM	32.4	75.1	73.0	41.6	30.4

Data as orig. reptd.; bef. results of disc. opers. and/or spec. items. Per share data adj. for stk. divs. as of ex-div. date. Bold denotes diluted EPS (FASB 128). E-Estimated. NA-Not Available. NM-Not Meaningful. NR-Not Ranked.

Office—650 Alpha Drive, Cleveland, OH 44143. **Tel**—(216) 449-6150. **Website**—www.dirtdevil.com**Chrmn, Pres, CEO & Investor Contact**—Michael J. Merriman. **Secy & Contr**—R. G. Vasek. **Dirs**—J. Kahl Jr., M. J. Merriman, E. P. Nalley, J. B. Richey II, J. P. Rochon, R. L. Schneeberger. **Transfer Agent**—National City Bank, Cleveland. **Incorporated**—in Ohio. **Empl**— 670. **S&P Analyst:** Kathleen J. Fraser

Ruby Tuesday
1954Q
NYSE Symbol **RI**
In S&P SmallCap 600

03-OCT-98

Industry:
Restaurants

Summary: This company (formerly Morrison Restaurants) owns and operates casual dining restaurants under the names Ruby Tuesday, Mozzarella's and Tia's.

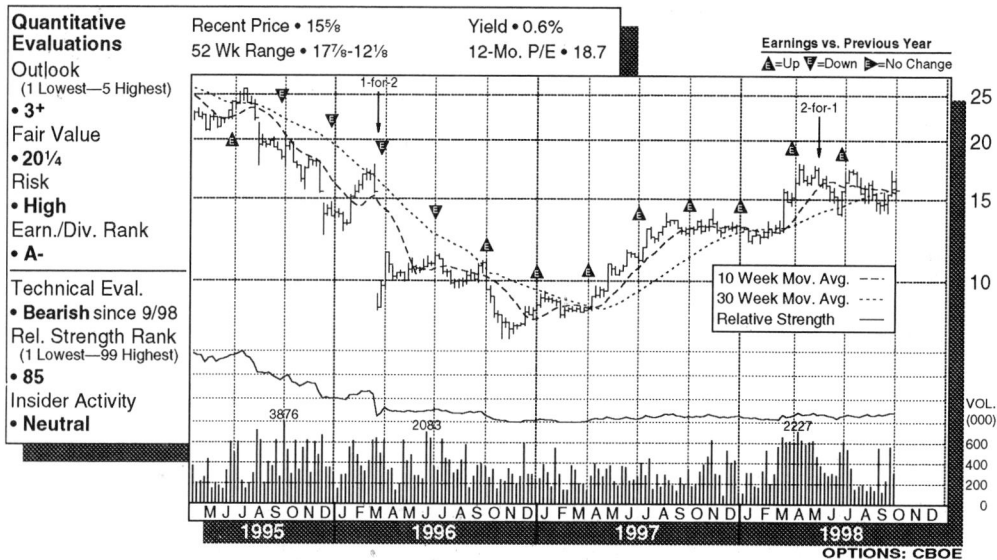

Quantitative Evaluations

Recent Price • 15⅝
52 Wk Range • 17⅞-12⅛

Yield • 0.6%
12-Mo. P/E • 18.7

Outlook
(1 Lowest—5 Highest)
• **3+**

Fair Value
• **20¼**

Risk
• **High**

Earn./Div. Rank
• **A-**

Technical Eval.
• **Bearish** since 9/98

Rel. Strength Rank
(1 Lowest—99 Highest)
• **85**

Insider Activity
• **Neutral**

OPTIONS: CBOE

Business Profile - 14-JUL-98

RI's five-year goals are: to grow revenues 10%; the addition of new units at an annual rate of 10%; 2% higher same-store sales comparisons; pretax margins of 7%; return on equity of at least 20%; and net income growth of 15%-20% a year. EPS were up 24% in the quarter ended June 6, 1998, marking the ninth consecutive quarter of meeting or exceeding the company's EPS growth goal. The shares were split two-for-one in May 1998.

Operational Review - 14-JUL-98

Revenues (preliminary) increased 8.5% in FY 98 (May), reflecting 2.8% higher same-store sales for the Ruby Tuesday concept and additional units in operation. Despite 25% higher SG&A expense, margins widened, aided by well controlled other operating expenses; operating income was up 8.7%. Following higher depreciation charges, partially offset by lower interest expense, pretax income rose 16%. After taxes at 35.4%, versus 35.5%, net income also increased 16%, to $29,080,000 ($0.84 a share, diluted), from $25,045,000 ($0.70, as adjusted).

Stock Performance - 02-OCT-98

In the past 30 trading days, RI's shares have increased 2%, compared to a 7% fall in the S&P 500. Average trading volume for the past five days was 61,160 shares, compared with the 40-day moving average of 56,618 shares.

Key Stock Statistics

Dividend Rate/Share	0.09	Shareholders	6,900
Shs. outstg. (M)	32.5	Market cap. (B)	$0.510
Avg. daily vol. (M)	0.073	Inst. holdings	54%
Tang. Bk. Value/Share	5.92		
Beta	0.49		

Value of $10,000 invested 5 years ago: $ 8,555

Fiscal Year Ending May 31

	1998	1997	1996	1995	1994	1993
Revenues (Million $)						
1Q	174.1	157.3	146.0	241.0	282.0	248.0
2Q	170.3	156.3	152.0	253.0	310.0	282.0
3Q	181.6	172.6	164.0	272.0	310.0	284.0
4Q	184.6	169.2	158.2	269.0	311.0	286.0
Yr.	711.4	655.4	620.1	1,035	1,213	1,100
Earnings Per Share ($)						
1Q	0.18	0.15	0.12	0.67	0.22	0.18
2Q	0.14	0.11	0.07	0.34	0.32	0.28
3Q	**0.27**	0.23	-0.36	0.37	0.33	0.28
4Q	0.26	0.20	0.17	0.35	0.33	0.27
Yr.	**0.84**	0.70	-0.02	1.73	1.20	1.00

Next earnings report expected: NA

Dividend Data (Dividends have been paid since 1998.)

Amount ($)	Date Decl.	Ex-Div. Date	Stock of Record	Payment Date
0.090	Jan. 13	Jan. 28	Jan. 30	Feb. 12 '98
2-for-1	Apr. 06	May. 11	Apr. 17	May. 08 '98
0.045	Jun. 30	Jul. 08	Jul. 10	Jul. 31 '98

A Division of The McGraw-Hill Companies

STANDARD
&POOR'S
STOCK REPORTS

Ruby Tuesday Inc.

1954Q
03-OCT-98

Business Summary - 14-JUL-98

Ruby Tuesday (RI) is striking out on its own as a company focused solely on the casual restaurant business. In early 1996, RI, then known as Morrison Restaurants, formed separate public companies for its family dining and health care businesses and distributed the stock of these corporations to existing RI shareholders. This left Ruby Tuesday free from competition for corporate resources and allowed management to focus on the restaurant business, which operates and franchises more than 400 casual dining establishments under the names Ruby Tuesday's, Mozzarella's and Tia's. Its strategy includes improving margins and reducing costs, enhancing customer satisfaction, and adding restaurants to the system.

As part of the focus on lowering costs, RI is now opening smaller new prototype units that generate average historical sales levels but are more profitable than traditional restaurants. In addition, every six months the company redesigns its menus to add to their customer appeal while focusing on improving margins.

At the same time, Ruby Tuesday has tried to make customers' visits more pleasurable. The company has added menu options and improved food quality, and is creating a more casual and fun environment at its restaurants. This has contributed to the recent upward trend in customer counts.

Growth will come from new unit openings. As of June 6, 1998, RI's casual dining restaurants included 315 Ruby Tuesday's, whose menu includes fajitas, ribs, chicken, soups, and a salad bar. Also, RI had 46 Mozzarella's Cafes, including restaurants that have been converted from the former Silver Spoon concept. In January 1995, RI acquired the Tia's Restaurants chain, which features Mexican and southwestern U.S. food. As of June 6, 1998, there were 21 Tia's units open. In addition, the company also franchises 31 domestic units and four international units. RI plans to grow by adding new units at a 10% annual rate in company-owned restaurants. Also, RI has partnerships with approximately 10 potential franchisees who have each committed to build about 10 units over the next five years.

The company also has plans to enhance shareholder return. When cash flow exceeds funding requirements, while maintaining a targeted debt-to-capital ratio of 60% or less, RI will repurchase its common stock; directors recently increased the buyback authorization by one million shares to approximately two million shares. During the third quarter of FY 98 (May), RI initiated semi-annual dividend payments, the first payment since the company was spun off from Morrison Restaurants.

Per Share Data ($)

(Year Ended May 31)	1998	1997	1996	1995	1994	1993	1992	1991	1990	1989
Tangible Bk. Val.	5.92	5.78	5.04	6.32	6.26	6.00	5.50	4.92	4.60	4.43
Cash Flow	1.98	1.78	0.94	2.84	2.29	1.96	1.80	1.56	1.33	1.41
Earnings	0.84	0.70	-0.02	1.73	1.20	1.00	0.88	0.71	0.59	0.80
Dividends	0.05	Nil	0.14	0.35	0.33	0.32	0.29	0.28	0.28	0.26
Payout Ratio	6%	Nil	NM	20%	28%	32%	34%	40%	47%	32%
Cal. Yrs.	1997	1996	1995	1994	1993	1992	1991	1990	1989	1988
Prices - High	14³/₈	17³/₄	27⁷/₈	29³/₄	26¹/₄	19⁷/₈	13	12¹/₈	15¹/₈	10⁵/₈
- Low	8³/₈	7¹/₂	12¹/₂	20⁷/₈	15⁷/₈	11³/₈	6	5³/₈	10¹/₄	7⁷/₈
P/E Ratio - High	17	25	NM	17	22	20	15	17	26	13
- Low	10	11	NM	12	13	11	7	8	17	10

Income Statement Analysis (Million $)

Revs.	711	655	620	1,033	1,210	1,098	1,039	969	898	825
Oper. Inc.	88.3	81.3	67.6	117	108	96.1	87.5	74.9	66.7	70.3
Depr.	39.5	38.6	34.1	39.9	40.8	36.5	35.1	31.7	28.7	23.9
Int. Exp.	4.7	4.1	4.8	2.2	2.3	2.8	4.1	3.3	2.5	2.3
Pretax Inc.	45.0	38.8	-2.3	105	71.2	60.9	51.4	42.5	35.4	50.4
Eff. Tax Rate	35%	36%	NM	41%	37%	37%	37%	37%	35%	37%
Net Inc.	29.1	25.0	-0.7	62.2	44.7	38.2	32.7	26.6	23.0	31.6

Balance Sheet & Other Fin. Data (Million $)

Cash	8.3	7.6	7.1	8.3	5.0	31.4	50.1	22.5	15.5	17.9
Curr. Assets	46.9	35.5	33.3	80.2	80.0	105	113	89.0	81.0	79.0
Total Assets	410	419	381	484	408	398	370	331	316	284
Curr. Liab.	84.4	69.1	66.6	125	123	103	90.4	76.8	70.2	70.7
LT Debt	65.9	78.0	76.1	52.1	9.5	13.1	35.9	38.0	35.7	16.6
Common Eqty.	212	224	197	245	221	220	204	181	176	174
Total Cap.	222	315	282	309	242	256	256	241	229	206
Cap. Exp.	65.8	74.0	109	131	90.3	63.0	37.8	43.9	55.9	41.8
Cash Flow	68.6	63.6	33.5	102	85.5	74.7	67.7	58.3	51.7	56.0
Curr. Ratio	0.6	0.5	0.5	0.6	0.6	1.0	1.3	1.2	1.1	1.1
% LT Debt of Cap.	29.7	24.7	27.0	16.9	3.9	5.1	14.0	15.8	15.6	8.1
% Net Inc.of Revs.	4.1	3.8	NM	6.0	3.7	3.5	3.1	2.7	2.6	3.8
% Ret. on Assets	7.0	6.3	NM	13.9	11.3	10.0	9.3	8.2	7.7	11.1
% Ret. on Equity	13.3	11.9	NM	26.6	20.6	18.1	17.0	14.9	13.3	18.8

Data as orig. reptd.; bef. results of disc. opers. and/or spec. items. Per share data adj. for stk. divs. as of ex-div. date. Bold denotes diluted EPS (FASB 128). E-Estimated. NA-Not Available. NM-Not Meaningful. NR-Not Ranked.

Office—4721 Morrison Drive, Mobile, AL 36609. **Tel**—(334) 344-3000. **Chrmn & CEO**—S. E. Beall III. **SVP, CFO & Treas**—J. R. Mothershed. **SVP & Secy**—P. G. Hunt. **Investor Contact**—Margie Naman. **Dirs**—C. L. Arnold, S. E. Beall III, J. B. McKinnon, A. R. Outlaw, B. F. Payton, D. Ratajczak, D. W. von Arx. **Transfer Agent & Registrar**—AmSouth Bank, N.A., Birmingham, AL. **Incorporated**—in Florida in 1954; reincorporated in Delaware in 1987; reincorporated in Georgia in 1996. **Empl**—24,800. **S&P Analyst:** Robert J. Izmirlian

Rural/Metro Corp.
5131R
NASDAQ Symbol **RURL**

In S&P SmallCap 600

03-OCT-98

Industry:
Health Care (Specialized Services)

Summary: This company provides "911" emergency and general transport ambulance services, fire protection services and other safety and health care related services.

Quantitative Evaluations		
Outlook (1 Lowest—5 Highest) • 5	Recent Price • 9⅛	Yield • Nil
Fair Value • 25½	52 Wk Range • 37½-6⅛	12-Mo. P/E • 17.0

Earnings vs. Previous Year
▲=Up ▼=Down ▶=No Change

Risk • **Average**

Earn./Div. Rank • **B-**

Technical Eval. • **Bullish** since 7/98

Rel. Strength Rank (1 Lowest—99 Highest) • 33

Insider Activity • **Favorable**

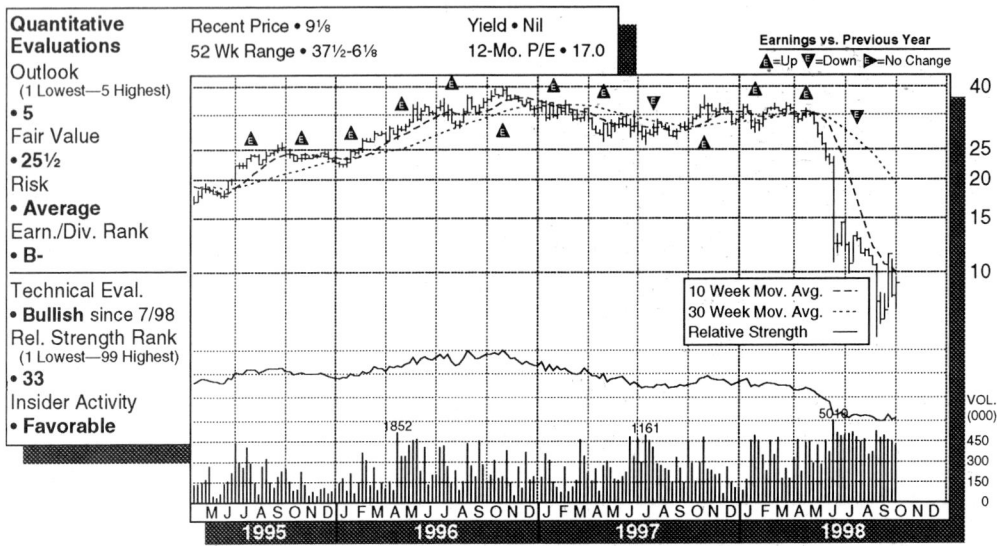

10 Week Mov. Avg. ---
30 Week Mov. Avg. ·····
Relative Strength —

VOL. (000)

1995 1996 1997 1998

Business Profile - 18-AUG-98

Revenue for the final quarter of FY 98 (Jun.) has been estimated by the company at $125 million to $130 million, with net income, including the effect of non-recurring charges and a non-recurring gain, expected to range between $3.5 million and $4.5 million, or $0.25 to $0.30 a share, diluted. In addition, the company said it intends, based on current business trends, to add to its provision for doubtful accounts an amount estimated to be approximately $10 million after tax ($0.69 a share, diluted), reflecting a more difficult medical reimbursement environment that has begun to affect the delivery of health care services nationally, and has caused delays in collecting the company's accounts receivable. RURL noted that the bad debt provision could increase in future periods, relative to the levels historically provided for, as a result of this industry trend.

Operational Review - 18-AUG-98

Total revenues in the nine months ended March 31, 1998, advanced 43%, year to year, mostly reflecting acquisitions. Operating expenses were up only 42%, but with much higher interest expense and depreciation and amortization charges, pretax income was up only 39%. After taxes at 40.7%, versus 41.0%, net income rose 40%, to $16,454,000, from $11,745,000. On 15% more shares, diluted EPS increased to $1.18, from $0.97.

Stock Performance - 02-OCT-98

In the past 30 trading days, RURL's shares have declined 13%, compared to a 7% fall in the S&P 500. Average trading volume for the past five days was 83,000 shares, compared with the 40-day moving average of 154,362 shares.

Key Stock Statistics

Dividend Rate/Share	Nil	Shareholders	1,000
Shs. outstg. (M)	14.2	Market cap. (B)	$0.130
Avg. daily vol. (M)	0.124	Inst. holdings	48%
Tang. Bk. Value/Share	NM		
Beta	1.14		

Value of $10,000 invested 5 years ago: NA

Fiscal Year Ending Jun. 30

	1998	1997	1996	1995	1994	1993
Revenues (Million $)						
1Q	97.77	73.99	55.76	36.27	22.87	—
2Q	111.3	77.53	60.84	39.96	24.12	—
3Q	129.8	84.92	64.98	43.79	26.40	—
4Q	136.7	83.36	68.68	51.57	30.97	—
Yr.	475.6	319.8	250.3	171.6	104.4	84.08
Earnings Per Share ($)						
1Q	**0.35**	0.28	0.23	0.18	0.11	—
2Q	**0.38**	0.31	0.25	0.21	0.10	—
3Q	**0.45**	0.38	0.31	0.25	0.21	—
4Q	**-0.64**	0.08	0.35	0.28	0.22	—
Yr.	**0.54**	1.04	1.14	0.92	0.71	0.63

Next earnings report expected: NA

Dividend Data

No cash dividends have been paid. The company intends to retain its earnings to finance the growth and expansion of business rather than pay cash dividends.

A Division of The McGraw-Hill Companies

Business Summary - 18-AUG-98

Two thousand sirens can make a lot of noise. Fortunately, the ambulances and fire vehicles in Rural/Metro Corp.'s (RURL) fleet are spread over much of the U.S., from California to New York, from Texas up to South Dakota and into Canada, too. That's good news for the more than 400 communities that rely on RURL each day to provide ambulance or fire protection service, often -- but not always -- in response to a crisis. And respond RURL must -- more than 1.5 million times a year.

RURL provides its core "911" emergency ambulance services under contracts with counties, fire districts and municipalities. It also furnishes general ambulance transportation for patients who require medical supervision while being ferried between residences and health care facilities. Ambulance services accounted for 81% of revenues in FY 97 (Jun.).

Several factors have increased the demand for ambulance services in recent years, including the growth and aging of the population, and trends toward the use of outpatient services and specialized treatment facilities in an effort to contain health care costs. RURL also feels it will continue to benefit from the privatization of emergency services and the growing influence of managed care.

Fire protection services (13% of FY 97 revenues) con-

sist mainly of fire prevention and fire suppression, and the company also conducts such related activities as hazardous material containment and rescue operations. RURL provides various levels of fire protection, ranging from reserve stations to fire stations that are fully staffed around the clock. For many fire departments, emergency medical response is an important part of their operation, so the company believes its ambulance and fire protection services are complementary. In addition to its contracts with municipalities and other governmental bodies, the company has arrangements with commercial establishments and large industrial complexes, such as airports.

RURL's primary growth strategy involves an aggressive campaign to acquire smaller ambulance service providers, and the company completed 18 such acquisitions in FY 97 alone. The largest of these -- Southwest Ambulance, with annualized revenues of some $30 million -- firmly established the company's market leadership position in Arizona. Total ambulance transports went from 710,000 in FY 96 to 915,000 in FY 97, and these 18 acquisitions were responsible for most of the increase. Additional acquisitions were made in FY 98.

Revenues advanced 28% to $320 million in FY 97, and net income, after a $3.9 million after-tax charge, increased 10% to $12.7 million. Earnings per share declined on 22% more shares outstanding.

Per Share Data ($)

(Year Ended Jun. 30)	1998	1997	1996	1995	1994	1993	1992	1991	1990	1989
Tangible Bk. Val.	NA	NM	2.16	NM	NA	NA	NA	NA	NA	NA
Cash Flow	NA	2.41	2.47	1.98	1.45	1.58	1.09	NA	NA	NA
Earnings	0.54	1.04	1.14	0.92	0.71	0.63	0.33	NA	NA	NA
Dividends	Nil	Nil	Nil	Nil	Nil	Nil	Nil	Nil	Nil	Nil
Payout Ratio	Nil	Nil	Nil	Nil	Nil	Nil	Nil	Nil	Nil	Nil
Prices - High	35½	37½	39¾	26½	21¼	20¾	NA	NA	NA	NA
- Low	6⅛	25⅞	22	16¾	13¼	12½	NA	NA	NA	NA
P/E Ratio - High	66	36	35	29	30	33	NA	NA	NA	NA
- Low	11	25	19	18	19	20	NA	NA	NA	NA

Income Statement Analysis (Million $)

	1998	1997	1996	1995	1994	1993	1992	1991	1990	1989
Revs.	NA	320	250	172	104	84.1	68.2	NA	NA	NA
Oper. Inc.	NA	50.6	38.0	24.7	14.3	11.0	20.1	NA	NA	NA
Depr.	NA	16.8	13.3	8.7	5.0	4.0	15.5	NA	NA	NA
Int. Exp.	NA	5.7	5.1	3.1	1.8	2.9	2.5	NA	NA	NA
Pretax Inc.	NA	22.1	19.6	12.9	7.6	4.2	2.0	NA	NA	NA
Eff. Tax Rate	NA	42%	41%	41%	38%	35%	35%	NA	NA	NA
Net Inc.	NA	12.7	11.5	7.6	4.7	2.7	1.3	NA	NA	NA

Balance Sheet & Other Fin. Data (Million $)

	1998	1997	1996	1995	1994	1993	1992	1991	1990	1989
Cash	NA	3.4	1.4	0.9	NA	NA	NA	NA	NA	NA
Curr. Assets	NA	126	80.9	48.7	NA	NA	NA	NA	NA	NA
Total Assets	NA	364	230	159	88.2	45.8	38.0	NA	NA	NA
Curr. Liab.	NA	31.4	25.5	22.4	NA	NA	NA	NA	NA	NA
LT Debt	NA	145	60.7	53.3	13.3	15.4	14.3	NA	NA	NA
Common Eqty.	NA	160	120	65.6	47.3	4.1	-0.2	NA	NA	NA
Total Cap.	NA	315	190	124	NA	NA	NA	NA	NA	NA
Cap. Exp.	NA	23.9	18.2	11.5	5.3	NA	NA	NA	NA	NA
Cash Flow	NA	29.5	24.9	16.3	9.7	6.6	4.3	NA	NA	NA
Curr. Ratio	NA	4.0	3.2	2.2	NA	NA	NA	NA	NA	NA
% LT Debt of Cap.	NA	45.9	32.0	43.0	NA	NA	NA	NA	NA	NA
% Net Inc.of Revs.	NA	4.0	4.6	4.4	4.5	3.2	2.0	NA	NA	NA
% Ret. on Assets	NA	4.3	5.9	5.6	7.1	6.4	NA	NA	NA	NA
% Ret. on Equity	NA	9.1	12.4	13.4	18.4	120.0	NA	NA	NA	NA

Data as orig. reptd.; bef. results of disc. opers. and/or spec. items. Per share data adj. for stk. divs. as of ex-div. date. Bold denotes diluted EPS (FASB 128). E-Estimated. NA-Not Available. NM-Not Meaningful. NR-Not Ranked.

Office—8401 East Indian School Rd., Scottsdale, AZ 85251. **Tel**—(602) 994-3886. **Website**—http://www.ruralmetro.com **Chrmn & CEO**—W. S. Rustand. **Pres**—J. H. Bolin. **SVP, CFO & Treas**—M. E. Liebner. **COO**—J. Brucker. **Dirs**—J. H. Bolin, C. J. Clement, R. T. Edwards, L. G. Jekel, R. E. Ramsey, W. S. Rustand, W. C. Turner, H. G. Walker, L. A. Witzeman. **Transfer Agent & Registrar**—American Securities Transfer, Inc. Lakewood, CO. **Incorporated**—in Arizona in 1948; reincorporated in Delaware in 1993. **Empl**— 10,000. **S&P Analyst:** C.F.B.

STANDARD &POOR'S
STOCK REPORTS

Russ Berrie

1955F

NYSE Symbol **RUS**

In S&P SmallCap 600

03-OCT-98

Industry: Consumer (Jewelry, Novelties & Gifts)

Summary: This company and its subsidiaries design and market a wide variety of gifts to retailers worldwide.

Quantitative Evaluations

Recent Price • 18⅞

52 Wk Range • 31½-17¼

Yield • 4.0%

12-Mo. P/E • 10.5

Outlook (1 Lowest—5 Highest)
• **3**

Fair Value
• 21⅜

Risk
• **Average**

Earn./Div. Rank
• **B+**

Technical Eval.
• **Bullish** since 8/98

Rel. Strength Rank (1 Lowest—99 Highest)
• **42**

Insider Activity
• **Favorable**

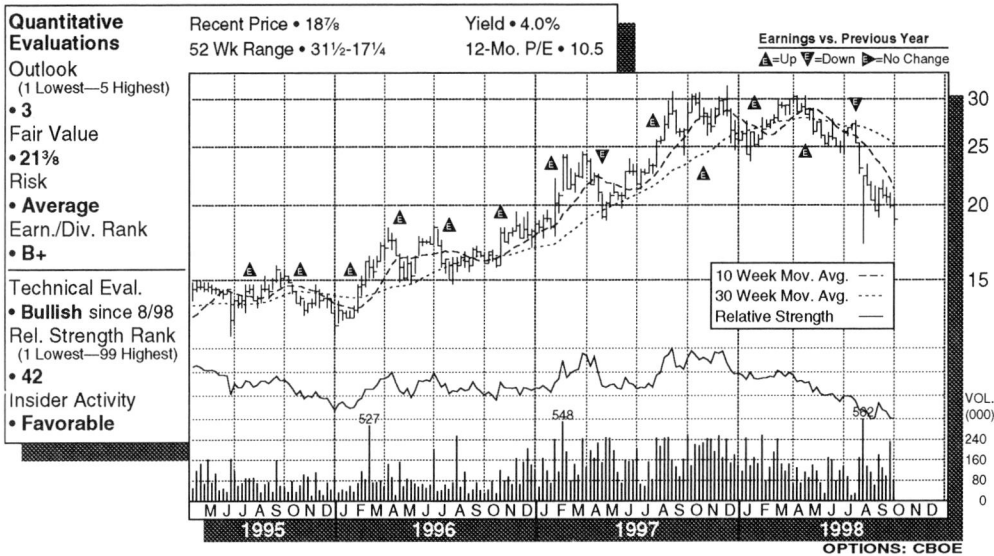

Earnings vs. Previous Year
▲=Up ▼=Down ▶=No Change

10 Week Mov. Avg. ---
30 Week Mov. Avg. ‧‧‧‧
Relative Strength ——

VOL. (000)

OPTIONS: CBOE

Business Profile - 08-SEP-98

Russ Berrie designs and distributes more than 6,000 holiday and everyday gift products to retail stores. Recent results have been sporadic compared to prior year quarters, with revenues falling 13% in the second quarter, after rising 20% in the first quarter. The reversal of sales growth was the result of difficult comparisons with 1997, which had strong second quarter bean bag sales that have since been discontinued. The company expects to strengthen its product line concentrating on home decor themes, the Russ Baby line and gentlemen's gifts line.

Operational Review - 08-SEP-98

Net sales in the six months ended June 30, 1998, rose 4.2%, year to year, due to the success of newly redesigned gift product lines. Gross margins improved, reflecting a more favorable product mix and efforts to manage inventory levels. Profitability was further enhanced by investment income related to the sale of a subsidiary and income on the proceeds from the toy segment sale in 1997; pretax income was up 27%. After taxes at 34.2%, versus 32.9%, income from continuing operations climbed 25% to $14,053,000 ($0.63 per share), from $11,259,000 ($0.50). Results for the 1997 period exclude a loss from discontinued operations of $0.06 a share, and the gain on its sale of $2.08 a share.

Stock Performance - 02-OCT-98

In the past 30 trading days, RUS's shares have declined 7%, compared to a 7% fall in the S&P 500. Average trading volume for the past five days was 15,980 shares, compared with the 40-day moving average of 26,095 shares.

Key Stock Statistics

Dividend Rate/Share	0.76	Shareholders	600
Shs. outstg. (M)	22.3	Market cap. (B)	$0.422
Avg. daily vol. (M)	0.028	Inst. holdings	40%
Tang. Bk. Value/Share	14.63		
Beta	0.60		

Value of $10,000 invested 5 years ago: $ 12,875

Fiscal Year Ending Dec. 31

	1998	1997	1996	1995	1994	1993
Revenues (Million $)						
1Q	74.64	62.07	56.57	80.12	64.17	96.30
2Q	50.95	58.48	41.78	74.26	57.55	49.89
3Q	—	87.53	67.90	104.0	82.85	70.74
4Q	—	63.26	60.00	90.11	73.54	62.18
Yr.	—	271.3	226.2	348.5	278.1	279.1
Earnings Per Share ($)						
1Q	**0.44**	0.29	0.32	0.19	0.05	0.62
2Q	**0.18**	0.21	0.05	0.01	-0.16	-0.14
3Q	—	0.72	0.62	0.43	0.27	0.30
4Q	—	0.45	0.24	0.14	0.09	-0.18
Yr.	—	1.67	1.23	0.77	0.25	0.61

Next earnings report expected: late October

Dividend Data (Dividends have been paid since 1986.)

Amount ($)	Date Decl.	Ex-Div. Date	Stock of Record	Payment Date
0.170	Oct. 28	Nov. 19	Nov. 21	Dec. 05 '97
0.190	Feb. 02	Feb. 26	Mar. 02	Mar. 16 '98
0.190	Apr. 22	May. 20	May. 22	Jun. 05 '98
0.190	Jul. 30	Aug. 19	Aug. 21	Sep. 04 '98

Business Summary - 08-SEP-98

When searching to find a gift that conveys the appropriate emotion, many people turn to Russ Berrie and Company. Under the Russ trademark, the company provides more than 6,000 gift items, priced at $1 to $30, and designed to express feelings of friendship, fun or love. Products include stuffed animals, picture frames and home decor items, and revolve around a wide variety of themes, such as birthdays, anniversaries, inspirational gifts and baby products. RUS's products are sold in the U.S. and abroad to a diverse range of retailers, including gift stores, pharmacies, card shops and book stores. In 1997 and 1996, sales to foreign countries accounted for 29% and 30% of total sales, respectively.

After a lackluster performance for RUS stock in 1994 and 1995, the company decided to focus its efforts and resources on expanding its gift business, which benefits from an effective sales distribution network and the relatively low cost of purchasing products from Far East manufacturers. As part of the new strategy, in January 1996, the company sold Papel/Freelance, Inc., a subsidiary that generated 14% of 1995 gift segment revenues through the sale of ceramic products. In May 1997, RUS sold its two toy-related subsidiaries, Cap Toys and OddzOn, to a subsidiary of Hasbro Inc. (ASE:

HAS), for about $167 million. The net proceeds from the sale were to be used for the acquisition of companies in the gift industry, and for general corporate purposes, including the repurchase of RUS common stock. In 1996, toy segment sales were about $151 million, or 40% of total sales.

RUS's focus on the gift business capitalizes on its utilization of low-cost independent Far East manufacturers. The company utilizes roughly 140 manufacturers in the Far East, primarily in the China, Taiwan, Korea, Indonesia, Philippines, and Thailand. In 1997, 94% of RUS's products were produced in this region, with 71% of dollar volume of purchases attributable to manufacturing in China.

Because it purchases a substantial number of products from China-based producers, RUS is faced with the uncertainty surrounding U.S.-Sino trade relations. In the past, legislation has been proposed that would revoke the most-favored nation status currently enjoyed by China. If that occurred, the company would expect import duties to rise or become applicable to items imported by RUS from China.

In April 1997, directors authorized the repurchase of an additional 1,000,000 common shares. Since March 1990, the company has purchased 2,847,600 common shares under a 3,000,000 share buyback program.

Per Share Data ($) (Year Ended Dec. 31)	1997	1996	1995	1994	1993	1992	1991	1990	1989	1988
Tangible Bk. Val.	14.32	11.37	8.77	8.49	9.69	10.82	8.89	8.34	8.21	8.04
Cash Flow	1.80	1.39	1.10	0.58	0.91	2.99	1.27	1.06	0.76	1.55
Earnings	1.67	1.46	0.77	0.25	0.61	2.70	0.98	0.77	0.43	1.23
Dividends	0.68	0.60	0.60	0.60	0.60	0.47	0.40	0.70	0.27	0.27
Payout Ratio	41%	49%	78%	NM	98%	17%	40%	91%	62%	22%
Prices - High	31¹/₂	19¹/₂	15⁷/₈	15⁵/₈	19⁷/₈	24⁵/₈	13¹/₈	12¹/₄	14¹/₄	18³/₄
- Low	18⁷/₈	12³/₄	12	12³/₄	12³/₈	12	8³/₄	9¹/₄	9¹/₂	11³/₄
P/E Ratio - High	19	16	21	62	33	9	13	16	33	15
- Low	11	10	16	51	20	4	9	12	22	10

Income Statement Analysis (Million $)	1997	1996	1995	1994	1993	1992	1991	1990	1989	1988
Revs.	271	226	348	278	279	444	268	251	246	278
Oper. Inc.	50.4	34.8	31.0	12.0	26.0	104	35.0	26.0	27.0	46.0
Depr.	3.0	3.4	7.2	7.0	6.4	6.6	6.5	6.5	7.4	7.2
Int. Exp.	0.2	0.1	0.2	0.2	0.6	0.5	0.8	0.5	0.9	0.9
Pretax Inc.	53.7	42.6	25.6	7.0	17.6	93.0	31.7	23.2	13.7	40.7
Eff. Tax Rate	31%	37%	35%	24%	25%	35%	31%	25%	29%	32%
Net Inc.	37.3	26.7	16.5	5.3	13.2	60.3	22.0	17.4	9.8	27.8

Balance Sheet & Other Fin. Data (Million $)	1997	1996	1995	1994	1993	1992	1991	1990	1989	1988
Cash	93.4	52.3	36.8	48.0	82.9	92.7	51.4	38.5	78.3	52.8
Curr. Assets	323	216	201	189	213	264	194	178	192	184
Total Assets	353	277	265	255	259	299	226	216	217	212
Curr. Liab.	36.7	28.2	42.0	36.4	35.1	57.6	27.0	23.6	28.9	27.6
LT Debt	Nil	Nil	Nil	Nil	Nil	Nil	3.0	4.5	2.7	3.3
Common Eqty.	317	249	223	218	224	241	196	188	186	181
Total Cap.	317	249	223	218	224	241	199	193	188	185
Cap. Exp.	4.2	1.9	4.6	2.4	5.2	10.1	3.5	19.6	6.8	8.4
Cash Flow	40.3	30.1	23.7	12.4	19.5	66.9	28.6	23.9	17.2	35.1
Curr. Ratio	8.8	7.7	4.8	5.2	6.1	4.6	7.2	7.6	6.6	6.7
% LT Debt of Cap.	Nil	Nil	Nil	Nil	Nil	Nil	1.5	2.3	1.4	1.8
% Net Inc.of Revs.	13.7	11.8	4.7	1.9	4.7	13.6	8.2	7.0	4.0	10.0
% Ret. on Assets	11.8	10.1	6.4	2.1	4.8	22.9	10.1	8.0	4.6	13.5
% Ret. on Equity	13.2	11.3	7.5	2.4	5.8	27.5	11.6	9.3	5.3	16.3

Data as orig. reptd.; bef. results of disc. opers. and/or spec. items. Per share data adj. for stk. divs. as of ex-div. date. Bold denotes diluted EPS (FASB 128). E-Estimated. NA-Not Available. NM-Not Meaningful. NR-Not Ranked.

Office—111 Bauer Drive, Oakland, NJ 07436. **Tel**—(201) 337-9000. **Chrmn & CEO**—R. Berrie. **VP & Secy**—A. S. Bloom. **VP, CFO & Investor Contact**—E. R. Lohwasser. **Dirs**—R. Benaroya, A. Berrie, R. Berrie, A. C. Cooke, I. Kaufthal, C. Klatskin, J. Kling, W. A. Landman, S. Slauson. **Transfer Agent & Registrar**—First City Transfer Co., Iselin, NJ. **Incorporated**—in New Jersey in 1966. **Empl**—1,550. **S&P Analyst:** Jordan Horoschak

Ryan's Family Steak Houses   5134

NASDAQ Symbol **RYAN**

In S&P SmallCap 600

03-OCT-98

Industry: Restaurants

Summary: This company owns and franchises some 300 restaurants, mainly in the southeastern U.S. A large portion of sales is derived from a self-service Mega Bar.

Quantitative Evaluations

Outlook (1 Lowest—5 Highest)
• 4+

Fair Value
• 15⅝

Risk
• Average

Earn./Div. Rank
• B+

Technical Eval.
• Bearish since 8/98

Rel. Strength Rank (1 Lowest—99 Highest)
• 94

Insider Activity
• Neutral

Recent Price • 11⅞
52 Wk Range • 13⅜-7⅛

Yield • Nil
12-Mo. P/E • 14.2

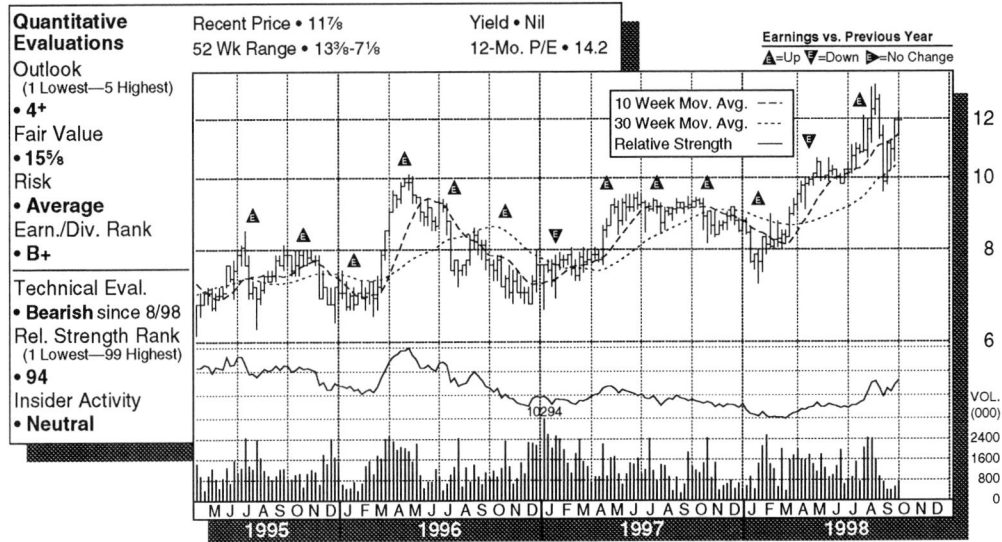

Earnings vs. Previous Year
▲=Up ▼=Down ▶=No Change

10 Week Mov. Avg. ---
30 Week Mov. Avg. ····
Relative Strength —

Business Profile - 13-SEP-98

Ryan's ranks number three in U.S. systemwide sales in 1997 in the grill-buffet sector of family dining restaurants, according to Nation's Restaurant News. Sales per unit of $2.3 million were the highest in this segment. The company recently began offering three carved dinner meats as part of its regular buffet selection at all restaurants. The carving program is the focus of the company's radio and television marketing programs and has helped to boost sales in the second quarter of 1998 by 1.8%. With lots of eating out choices for the customer, Ryan's is emphasizing both value and variety in its food offerings. The company has slowed its unit openings and is attempting to increase store level profitability.

Operational Review - 13-SEP-98

Sales in the six months ended July 1, 1998 increased to $320.7 million from $303.6 million a year earlier. Food and beverage expenses rose 5.0%, but payroll and benefits costs increased 10.1%. General and administrative expenses rose 5.1%, and operating income fell 1.8%. Interest expense remained about level. The decline in revenues from franchised restaurants outweighed higher other income, and pretax income fell 3.2%. After taxes, net earnings fell 2.3%, but earnings per share increased 6.7% to $0.48, on 6.3% fewer shares outstanding.

Stock Performance - 02-OCT-98

In the past 30 trading days, RYAN's shares have declined 6%, compared to a 7% fall in the S&P 500. Average trading volume for the past five days was 144,400 shares, compared with the 40-day moving average of 195,731 shares.

Key Stock Statistics

Dividend Rate/Share	Nil	Shareholders	20,000
Shs. outstg. (M)	41.7	Market cap. (B)	$0.497
Avg. daily vol. (M)	0.103	Inst. holdings	77%
Tang. Bk. Value/Share	6.94		
Beta	0.19		

Value of $10,000 invested 5 years ago: $ 10,380

Fiscal Year Ending Dec. 31

	1998	1997	1996	1995	1994	1993
Revenues (Million $)						
1Q	153.2	146.4	130.8	117.3	106.9	90.39
2Q	167.5	157.2	147.4	131.4	114.8	101.3
3Q	—	152.7	146.3	131.8	115.0	104.1
4Q	—	142.8	141.0	132.8	111.5	98.10
Yr.	—	599.2	565.5	513.2	448.2	393.9
Earnings Per Share ($)						
1Q	0.20	0.21	0.16	0.14	0.14	0.13
2Q	0.27	0.24	0.20	0.17	0.16	0.15
3Q	—	0.20	0.18	0.16	0.15	0.14
4Q	—	0.17	0.01	0.15	0.12	0.11
Yr.	—	0.82	0.55	0.62	0.57	0.53

Next earnings report expected: mid October

Dividend Data

The company does not expect to pay cash dividends in the foreseeable future. It plans to retain funds for expansion.

A Division of The McGraw·Hill Companies

Business Summary - 13-SEP-98

Ryan's Family Steak Houses had 272 company-owned and operated and 25 franchised restaurants at the end of 1997.

The Ryan's company-owned restaurants are freestanding units with seating capacity for about 300 to 500 customers. The menu includes a self-service Mega Bar, plus traditional steakhouse entrees, such as steaks, hamburgers, chicken and seafood. The Mega Bar, which generates a sizable portion of sales, includes salad items, soups, cheeses, rolls and a variety of hot meats and vegetables. The company recently added carving two to three meats each night - roast beef, ham, turkey breast, whole turkey, or smoked sausage. Bakery bars now feature a wide variety of pies and cakes.

In November 1996, the company announced a strategic plan, called Focus 2000, to bolster its profitability. The key elements of the plan include: reducing the amount of money invested to open each RYAN unit to increase store-level profitability; increasing levels of training for employees; opening new units at the rate of 5% annually over the next two to three years; and repurchasing RYAN common stock under a 10-million-share buyback program. As a result of the company's strategic analysis, RYAN took a $13.3 million charge in the fourth quarter of 1996. The charge applied to 10 underperforming units. Since March 1996, the company has repurchased 6.9 million common shares (13% of the outstanding shares). The repurchase program should be completed by the end of 1998.

The company has also initiated an Operating Partner Program, providing top restaurant managers an opportunity to share in the profitability of their stores. After being selected and upon an investment in the company's stock, the Operating Partners share in both the profit improvement and overall profitability of the restaurant. Operating Partners were managing 15 restaurants at the end of 1997 and produced both sales and earnings gains above the chain average.

Capital expenditures in 1997 totaled $47.5 million, for opening some 14 units, a drop from 1996's 30 new company-operated Ryan's restaurants. In addition, RYAN is testing several new casual dining concepts. Further expansion of these concepts is not currently planned.

In 1997, restaurant sales rose 6.0%, to $599.2 million. Net earnings amounted to $39.2 million, up 37% from $28.6 million. As a result of the company's Focus 2000 initiatives, average store level profits increased in 1997. In 1998, the company plans to open 15 low-cost units and to begin a new television and radio advertising campaign.

Per Share Data ($)

(Year Ended Dec. 31)	1997	1996	1995	1994	1993	1992	1991	1990	1989	1988
Tangible Bk. Val.	6.75	6.00	5.66	5.04	4.47	3.93	3.35	2.89	2.43	2.02
Cash Flow	1.39	1.05	1.04	0.89	0.83	0.78	0.65	0.66	0.57	0.50
Earnings	0.82	0.55	0.62	0.57	0.53	0.53	0.44	0.46	0.41	0.37
Dividends	Nil	Nil	Nil	Nil	Nil	Nil	Nil	Nil	Nil	Nil
Payout Ratio	Nil	Nil	Nil	Nil	Nil	Nil	Nil	Nil	Nil	Nil
Prices - High	9½	10⅛	8½	9⅛	11⅝	12⅝	10¼	8½	9	8⅝
- Low	6⅞	6½	6⅛	5⅜	6⅞	7¾	5⅜	3⅞	5⅛	4⅞
P/E Ratio - High	12	18	14	16	22	24	23	18	22	23
- Low	8	12	10	9	13	15	12	8	13	13

Income Statement Analysis (Million $)

	1997	1996	1995	1994	1993	1992	1991	1990	1989	1988
Revs.	600	567	515	449	396	352	299	273	241	193
Oper. Inc.	92.9	86.2	76.2	65.6	61.0	58.6	48.2	48.5	42.0	36.9
Depr.	27.4	25.7	22.4	17.4	16.1	13.7	11.4	10.5	8.4	6.7
Int. Exp.	5.9	6.0	4.4	2.7	1.5	1.3	1.5	1.5	1.6	0.9
Pretax Inc.	61.1	45.3	52.8	48.0	45.3	45.3	37.1	38.3	34.2	30.6
Eff. Tax Rate	36%	37%	37%	36%	37%	38%	37%	37%	37%	37%
Net Inc.	39.2	28.6	33.2	30.5	28.5	28.3	23.3	24.1	21.5	19.3

Balance Sheet & Other Fin. Data (Million $)

	1997	1996	1995	1994	1993	1992	1991	1990	1989	1988
Cash	0.3	0.8	1.3	0.7	1.9	1.7	2.6	2.6	0.4	1.2
Curr. Assets	12.1	11.9	11.5	9.0	9.5	6.0	6.3	6.1	3.1	3.1
Total Assets	496	463	431	380	334	275	238	205	165	142
Curr. Liab.	64.9	76.6	114	100	84.9	55.7	50.3	43.1	28.1	18.3
LT Debt	93.0	93.0	Nil	Nil	Nil	Nil	Nil	Nil	Nil	10.0
Common Eqty.	317	294	303	269	239	210	177	152	127	105
Total Cap.	431	387	317	280	249	219	187	162	137	123
Cap. Exp.	47.5	89.8	71.3	66.7	71.3	54.2	43.9	46.1	32.0	44.4
Cash Flow	66.6	54.3	55.6	47.9	44.6	42.0	34.7	34.6	29.9	26.0
Curr. Ratio	0.2	15.5	0.1	0.1	0.1	0.1	0.1	0.1	0.1	0.2
% LT Debt of Cap.	21.6	24.0	Nil	Nil	Nil	Nil	Nil	Nil	Nil	8.1
% Net Inc.of Revs.	6.5	5.0	6.5	6.8	7.2	8.0	7.8	8.8	8.9	10.0
% Ret. on Assets	8.1	6.3	8.2	8.6	9.4	11.0	10.5	13.0	14.0	15.6
% Ret. on Equity	12.8	9.6	11.6	12.0	12.7	14.6	14.1	17.2	18.4	20.2

Data as orig. reptd.; bef. results of disc. opers. and/or spec. items. Per share data adj. for stk. divs. as of ex-div. date. Bold denotes diluted EPS (FASB 128). E-Estimated. NA-Not Available. NM-Not Meaningful. NR-Not Ranked.

Office—405 Lancaster Ave., P.O. Box 100, Greer, SC 29652. **Tel**—(864) 879-1000. **Chrmn, Pres & CEO**—C. D. Way.**EVP**—G. E. McCranie. **VP-Fin, Treas & Investor Contact**—Fred T. Grant Jr. **Dirs**—J. D. Cockman, B. L. Edwards, B. S. MacKenzie, G. E. McCranie, H. K. Roberts Jr., J. M. Shoemaker Jr., C. D. Way. **Transfer Agent**—Wachovia Bank of North Carolina, Winston-Salem. **Incorporated**—in South Carolina in 1977. **Empl**— 18,000. **S&P Analyst:** Karen J. Sack, CFA

03-OCT-98

Industry:
Homebuilding

Summary: Ryland is one of the largest U.S. homebuilders, operating in 20 states across the nation, and also has extensive mortgage lending operations.

Quantitative Evaluations	
Recent Price • 23⅝	Yield • 0.7%
52 Wk Range • 31⅝-17¼	12-Mo. P/E • 12.6

Outlook
(1 Lowest—5 Highest)
• **2+**

Fair Value
• **24¼**

Risk
• **Average**

Earn./Div. Rank
• **B**

Technical Eval.
• **Bearish** since 9/98

Rel. Strength Rank
(1 Lowest—99 Highest)
• **78**

Insider Activity
• **NA**

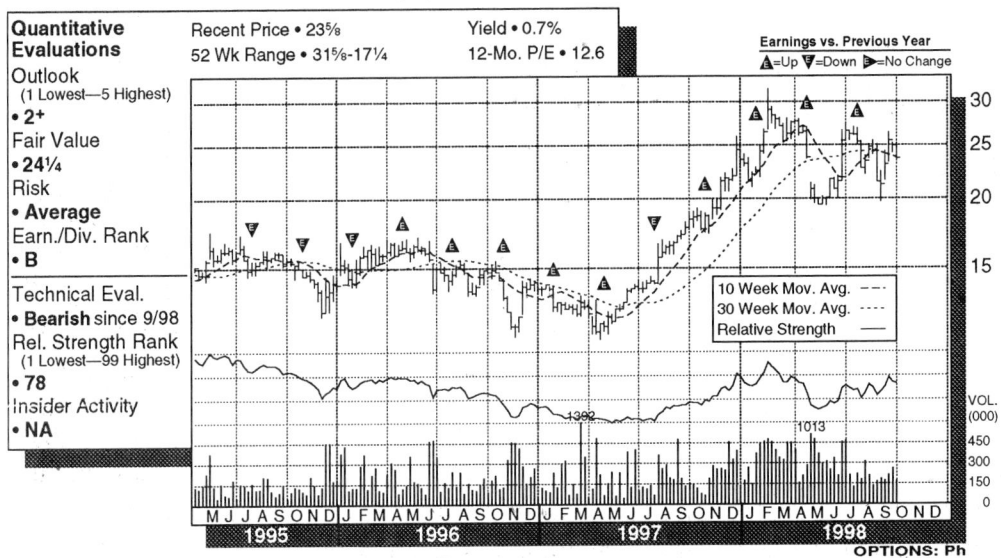

Earnings vs. Previous Year
▲=Up ▼=Down ▶=No Change

10 Week Mov. Avg. – – –
30 Week Mov. Avg. · · · ·
Relative Strength ——

OPTIONS: Ph

Business Profile - 31-AUG-98

In April 1998, RYL sold a portion of its loan servicing portfolio to PNC Mortgage Corp. of America. Over the past few years, RYL has been repositioning its mortgage operations to take maximum advantage of the strategic relationship it has with Ryland Homes. Backlog at June 30, 1998, was up 20%, year to year, to $756 million. During the second quarter of 1998, the company completed its 2.0 million common share repurchase program, buying back 310,800 shares. RYL plans to continue its strategies of improving its land positions and product lines. In April 1998, RYL sold $100 million of 8.25% senior subordinated notes due 2008.

Operational Review - 31-AUG-98

Revenues in the first half of 1998 rose 4.5%, year to year, as higher residential homebuilding offset a decline in financial services volume, limited-purpose subsidiaries revenues and other homebuilding revenue. Profitability benefited primarily from higher housing gross margins, and with well controlled SG&A expenses, a $6.1 million pretax gain from the sale of a majority of RYL's loan servicing portfolio and lower interest expense, net income was up 141%, to $13,517,000 ($0.86 a diluted share, on 4.5% fewer shares), from $5,606,000 ($0.30). RYL believes it is well positioned for future growth due to its strong gross profit margin improvement, record backlog, focus on key strategies, and favorable market conditions.

Stock Performance - 02-OCT-98

In the past 30 trading days, RYL's shares have declined 3%, compared to a 7% fall in the S&P 500. Average trading volume for the past five days was 33,280 shares, compared with the 40-day moving average of 38,472 shares.

Key Stock Statistics

Dividend Rate/Share	0.16	Shareholders	3,300
Shs. outstg. (M)	14.7	Market cap. (B)	$0.347
Avg. daily vol. (M)	0.042	Inst. holdings	80%
Tang. Bk. Value/Share	20.51		
Beta	1.15		

Value of $10,000 invested 5 years ago: $ 13,585

Fiscal Year Ending Dec. 31

	1998	1997	1996	1995	1994	1993
Revenues (Million $)						
1Q	336.3	329.5	327.4	345.2	332.5	297.0
2Q	425.9	399.6	414.3	389.2	416.7	375.4
3Q	—	421.6	402.5	402.6	447.8	378.8
4Q	—	499.1	436.0	448.0	445.7	430.2
Yr.	—	1,650	1,580	1,585	1,643	1,474
Earnings Per Share ($)						
1Q	0.29	0.08	0.03	-0.13	0.23	0.38
2Q	0.57	0.22	0.31	-0.09	0.45	0.33
3Q	—	0.41	0.25	0.01	0.50	-1.50
4Q	—	0.62	0.28	-1.55	0.11	0.45
Yr.	—	1.32	0.87	-1.78	1.29	-0.34

Next earnings report expected: late October

Dividend Data (Dividends have been paid since 1975.)

Amount ($)	Date Decl.	Ex-Div. Date	Stock of Record	Payment Date
0.040	Oct. 29	Jan. 13	Jan. 15	Jan. 30 '98
0.040	Jan. 28	Apr. 13	Apr. 15	Apr. 30 '98
0.040	Jul. 10	Jul. 13	Jul. 15	Jul. 30 '98
0.040	Sep. 14	Oct. 13	Oct. 15	Oct. 30 '98

A Division of The McGraw·Hill Companies

Business Summary - 31-AUG-98

The Ryland Group (RYL), which constructs single-family attached and detached housing and condominiums, and also markets mortgage-related products and services, has been changing its financial strategy in an effort to enhance shareholder value. RYL has been repurchasing stock in an effort to improve its long-term prospects, which it hopes will result in a more efficient capital structure and a lower cost of capital. Segment contributions from continuing operations in 1997 (excluding one-time charges) were:

	Revenues	Profits
Homebuilding	94%	71%
Financial svcs. & ltd.-purpose subs.	6%	29%

The homebuilding segment constructs homes in five regions: Mid-Atlantic, Midwest, Southeast, Southwest and West (RYL's California region operations were consolidated into the West segment in January 1996). The company's homes vary in size and price range, but are generally marketed to customers purchasing their first home or first or second time move-up home. In 1997, RYL's average closing price was $182,000. Substantially all construction work is performed by subcontractors monitored by company supervisors.

Financial services activities include mortgage origination, loan servicing and title and escrow services. In April 1998, RYL sold a majority of its loan servicing portfolio. The company has repositioned this segment through a strategy consisting of focusing on retail mortgage loan origination and servicing activities, the divestiture of non-core assets, leveraging its affiliation with the homebuilding segment to increase its capture rate for builder loans, and reaching mortgage customers directly through the use of technology. During 1997, RYL originated 7,248 mortgage loans, of which 34% were for buyers of homes built by other companies, purchases of existing homes or for refinancings. The company services loans that it originates, as well as loans originated by others; the loan servicing balance was $4.5 billion at December 31, 1997. During 1996, RYL sold its wholesale mortgage operations, as it did not expect the unit to contribute significantly to future earnings.

Per Share Data ($)

(Year Ended Dec. 31)	1997	1996	1995	1994	1993	1992	1991	1990	1989	1988
Tangible Bk. Val.	19.07	18.23	17.77	18.88	17.86	18.51	16.32	15.49	16.19	10.91
Cash Flow	3.35	2.84	0.44	2.93	1.36	3.71	2.17	3.13	4.45	3.64
Earnings	1.32	0.87	-1.78	1.29	-0.34	1.66	0.53	1.53	3.25	3.10
Dividends	0.38	0.60	0.60	0.60	0.60	0.60	0.60	0.60	0.60	0.47
Payout Ratio	29%	69%	NM	47%	NM	37%	111%	38%	17%	15%
Prices - High	26	17⅛	17½	25⅝	24½	28	25¼	22	25¾	20⅝
- Low	11⅛	11¼	12¼	12⅞	15⅞	18½	13¾	9½	18¼	13¾
P/E Ratio - High	20	20	NM	20	NM	17	48	14	8	7
- Low	8	13	NM	10	NM	11	26	6	6	4

Income Statement Analysis (Million $)

	1997	1996	1995	1994	1993	1992	1991	1990	1989	1988
Revs.	1,650	1,580	1,585	1,643	1,474	1,442	1,214	1,313	1,402	1,272
Oper. Inc.	110	104	90.6	168	185	328	353	379	430	407
Depr.	31.4	31.4	34.5	25.6	26.1	30.6	20.5	19.9	15.9	7.1
Int. Exp.	41.9	46.5	53.6	117	167	249	302	334	362	357
Pretax Inc.	36.5	26.4	-42.4	37.3	-4.7	42.3	14.3	34.1	70.9	66.7
Eff. Tax Rate	40%	40%	NM	40%	NM	35%	34%	36%	38%	39%
Net Inc.	21.9	15.8	-25.5	22.4	-2.7	27.5	9.5	21.8	44.0	40.7

Balance Sheet & Other Fin. Data (Million $)

	1997	1996	1995	1994	1993	1992	1991	1990	1989	1988
Cash	36.1	28.7	56.0	26.8	44.3	10.4	3.5	4.5	13.3	10.0
Curr. Assets	NA	NA	NA	NA	NA	NA	NA	NA	NA	NA
Total Assets	1,283	1,339	1,581	1,704	2,316	2,897	3,559	3,860	4,212	4,247
Curr. Liab.	NA	NA	NA	NA	NA	NA	NA	NA	522	376
LT Debt	310	354	397	409	352	171	NA	NA	NA	NA
Common Eqty.	305	310	300	327	312	329	245	236	235	169
Total Cap.	651	665	698	737	665	501	NA	NA	NA	NA
Cap. Exp.	47.6	19.5	30.2	19.0	12.6	14.0	3.7	10.1	9.0	10.5
Cash Flow	51.6	45.2	6.8	45.6	20.8	55.5	27.2	38.9	59.0	47.8
Curr. Ratio	NA	NA	NA	NA	NA	NA	NA	NA	NA	NA
% LT Debt of Cap.	47.6	53.2	56.9	55.5	52.9	34.1	NA	NA	NA	NA
% Net Inc.of Revs.	1.3	1.0	NM	1.4	NM	1.9	0.8	1.7	3.1	3.2
% Ret. on Assets	1.7	1.1	NM	1.1	NM	0.8	0.3	0.5	1.1	1.8
% Ret. on Equity	6.6	4.5	NM	6.2	NM	7.8	2.8	8.2	21.6	26.8

Data as orig. reptd.; bef. results of disc. opers. and/or spec. items. Per share data adj. for stk. divs. as of ex-div. date. Bold denotes diluted EPS (FASB 128). E-Estimated. NA-Not Available. NM-Not Meaningful. NR-Not Ranked.

Office—11000 Broken Land Parkway, Columbia, MD 21044. **Tel**—(410) 715-7000. **Website**—http://www.ryland.com **Chrmn, Pres & CEO**—R. C. Dreier. **EVP & CFO**—M. D. Mangan. **SVP & Treas**—B. Haase. **SVP & Secy**—T. Geckle. **Investor Contact**—Susan Cass. **Dirs**—R. C. Dreier, J. A. Flick, Jr., R. J. Gaw, L. M. Harlan, L. C. Heist, W. L. Jews, W. G. Kagler, III, C. St. Martin, J. O. Wilson. **Transfer Agent & Registrar**—ChaseMellon Shareholder Services, Ridgefield Park, NJ. **Incorporated**—in Maryland in 1967. **Empl**—2,229. **S&P Analyst:** Stewart Scharf

STANDARD
&POOR'S
STOCK REPORTS

SEI Investments

5139P

NASDAQ Symbol **SEIC**

In S&P SmallCap 600

03-OCT-98

Industry:
Financial (Diversified)

Summary: SEIC provides proprietary fund services, trust technology services and back office outsourcing for bank trust departments, and asset management services.

Quantitative Evaluations

Outlook
(1 Lowest—5 Highest)
• **2+**

Fair Value
• **70⅛**

Risk
• **Average**

Earn./Div. Rank
• **A-**

Technical Eval.
• **NA**

Rel. Strength Rank
(1 Lowest—99 Highest)
• **66**

Insider Activity
• **Neutral**

Recent Price • 65¾
52 Wk Range • 80½-26⅞

Yield • 0.5%
12-Mo. P/E • 36.9

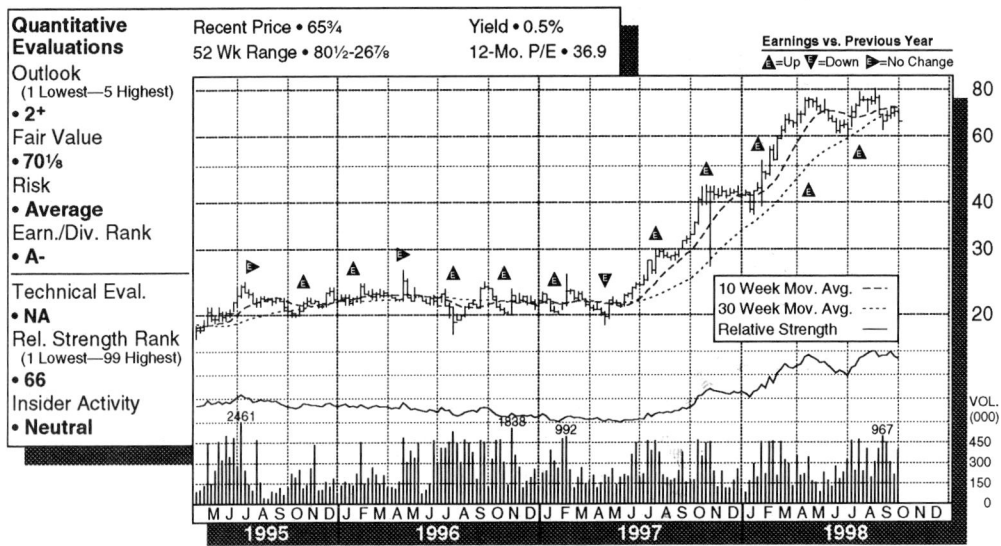

Earnings vs. Previous Year
▲=Up ▼=Down ▶=No Change

10 Week Mov. Avg. ----
30 Week Mov. Avg. ·····
Relative Strength ——

Business Profile - 02-SEP-98

This global asset management company is dedicated to helping institutions manage pools of investable capital through a combination of advanced technology and sophisticated investment services. The company focuses on three core business areas, including trust and investment technology, asset management, and liquidity management. SEIC is the largest provider of trust services in the U.S. Its asset management segment manages more than $33 billion in client assets, and serves more than 1,400 asset management clients, including institutional investors and investment organizations. The liquidity management segment provides services to some 500 clients, with assets of $20 billion.

Operational Review - 02-SEP-98

Revenues for the six months ended June 30, 1998, rose 25%, year to year, reflecting growth in fund balances, new trust technology and back office clients, and $4 million in nonrecurring trust technology services revenues. Sales and marketing expenses grew at a lower rate than revenues, and with slightly lower general and administrative expenses, operating income gained 60%. Following $1.2 million of equity earnings of an unconsolidated affiliate, and after taxes at 39.0%, versus 40.0%, net income was up 73%, to $17,182,000 ($0.90 a share) from $9,942,000 ($0.52).

Stock Performance - 02-OCT-98

In the past 30 trading days, SEIC's shares have declined 13%, compared to a 7% fall in the S&P 500. Average trading volume for the past five days was 77,740 shares, compared with the 40-day moving average of 83,256 shares.

Key Stock Statistics

Dividend Rate/Share	0.32	Shareholders	1,100
Shs. outstg. (M)	17.8	Market cap. (B)	$ 1.2
Avg. daily vol. (M)	0.072	Inst. holdings	35%
Tang. Bk. Value/Share	2.53		
Beta	0.78		

Value of $10,000 invested 5 years ago: $ 43,133

Fiscal Year Ending Dec. 31

	1998	1997	1996	1995	1994	1993
Revenues (Million $)						
1Q	81.87	63.50	63.24	53.50	63.69	57.74
2Q	85.50	70.73	61.54	55.74	64.68	59.65
3Q	—	74.28	60.17	56.48	66.11	64.04
4Q	—	84.23	62.87	60.25	69.29	65.74
Yr.	—	292.8	247.8	226.0	263.8	247.2
Earnings Per Share ($)						
1Q	0.40	0.25	0.30	0.30	0.21	0.15
2Q	0.50	0.27	0.25	0.20	0.23	0.19
3Q	—	0.36	0.31	0.26	0.25	0.21
4Q	—	0.52	0.34	0.30	0.27	0.24
Yr.	—	1.40	1.20	1.09	0.96	0.78

Next earnings report expected: late October

Dividend Data (Dividends have been paid since 1988.)

Amount ($)	Date Decl.	Ex-Div. Date	Stock of Record	Payment Date
0.140	Dec. 04	Dec. 29	Dec. 31	Jan. 21 '98
0.160	May. 21	Jun. 12	Jun. 16	Jun. 30 '98

A Division of The **McGraw·Hill** Companies

STANDARD
&POOR'S
STOCK REPORTS

SEI Investments Company

5139P

03-OCT-98

Business Summary - 02-SEP-98

SEI Investments (formerly SEI Corporation) is a global asset management company. It is organized around two primary business lines: Investment Technology and Services, which accounted for 62% of total revenues in 1997, and Asset Management, which accounted for the remaining 38%.

The Investment Technology and Services segment includes the Trust 300 product line, proprietary funds administration and distribution services, and trust back-office processing. The company provides software and processing services to bank and trust departments, serving 36 of the top 100 U.S. trust institutions. The Trust 3000 product line provides banks with the comprehensive software capabilities they need to manage investments for their personal and institutional trust clients.

The company provides proprietary mutual fund services to banks, insurance firms and investment companies. It provides not only the standard services, such as fund accounting, legal and shareholder services, but also strategy development and business planning, wholesaling and marketing support, and product development. As of December 31, 1997, the company provided administration and distribution services for clients with some $82.5 billion of assets under administration.

In 1994, the company extended its trust technology line by offering trust back office processing. Wholly owned SEI Trust provides a fully integrated custody and back-office outsourcing solution to trust organizations.

By combining its Trust 3000 product line with sophisticated global investment products and back-office capabilities, the company believes it can offer a total outsourcing solution, and provide trust institutions with access to the industry's state-of-the-art accounting system. SEI Trust automates and centralizes all of the client's trust accounting, income collections, securities settlement, and securities processing functions.

SEI Investments is a leading provider of asset management services to registered investment advisors, financial planners, independent broker/dealers, bank trust officers and other investment counselors, who use the company's asset management programs to manage portfolios for their clients. The company offers a wide range of investment solutions, including tax-managed portfolios for wealthy individuals, asset management programs for institutional investors, marketing assistance, sales support, back-office operations, and investor reporting.

Since 1982, the company has offered liquidity products to bank trust departments, and also provides cash sweep technology, cash management services and other financial management solutions to corporations. Its cash sweep technology enables a financial institution to sweep excess balances from demand deposit accounts into money market accounts. Recently, the company began offering a complete cash management investment program, CashStrategies, which incorporates cash flow analytics with SEI developed software to provide corporate treasurers an effective solution in managing their cash and investment portfolios.

Per Share Data ($)

(Year Ended Dec. 31)	1997	1996	1995	1994	1993	1992	1991	1990	1989	1988
Tangible Bk. Val.	2.44	2.93	3.04	2.34	2.21	1.97	1.75	1.79	0.97	1.95
Cash Flow	2.13	1.72	1.68	1.74	1.56	1.17	1.38	1.27	1.12	0.92
Earnings	1.40	1.20	1.09	0.96	0.78	0.52	0.70	0.54	0.53	0.52
Dividends	0.28	0.24	0.20	0.16	0.12	0.08	0.06	0.05	0.05	0.05
Payout Ratio	20%	20%	18%	17%	14%	13%	8%	9%	8%	9%
Prices - High	44½	26⅜	24½	28½	27¼	16	13¾	11⅛	10	10¾
- Low	18¾	17¾	16¾	16¾	13⅜	11	8⅞	7¼	8	6⅞
P/E Ratio - High	32	22	22	30	35	31	20	21	19	21
- Low	13	15	15	17	17	21	13	13	15	13

Income Statement Analysis (Million $)

	1997	1996	1995	1994	1993	1992	1991	1990	1989	1988
Revs.	293	248	226	264	247	209	188	172	149	132
Oper. Inc.	59.6	46.1	46.3	46.9	41.9	32.1	40.9	35.5	32.5	28.9
Depr.	14.1	10.0	11.6	15.7	16.2	16.1	15.7	16.3	13.6	10.0
Int. Exp.	2.5	Nil	Nil	Nil	Nil	Nil	Nil	0.2	0.3	Nil
Pretax Inc.	44.0	37.9	35.6	31.6	26.0	18.3	26.0	19.5	19.1	20.2
Eff. Tax Rate	39%	39%	41%	39%	38%	38%	39%	38%	37%	35%
Net Inc.	26.8	23.1	21.1	19.3	16.1	11.3	16.0	12.1	12.1	13.2

Balance Sheet & Other Fin. Data (Million $)

	1997	1996	1995	1994	1993	1992	1991	1990	1989	1988
Cash	16.9	13.2	10.3	20.2	17.9	17.5	13.7	19.4	2.1	20.7
Curr. Assets	84.0	65.0	54.0	59.1	55.7	43.6	37.3	39.4	22.9	37.0
Total Assets	169	141	101	102	100	86.0	83.0	84.0	76.0	75.0
Curr. Liab.	81.7	80.0	45.0	49.7	45.0	33.4	32.2	26.1	27.7	21.2
LT Debt	33.0	Nil	Nil	Nil	Nil	Nil	Nil	Nil	4.1	Nil
Common Eqty.	46.4	56.1	56.0	51.3	51.5	49.4	47.9	53.1	36.5	47.8
Total Cap.	87.2	61.1	56.7	52.7	55.4	52.6	50.6	57.9	47.3	53.8
Cap. Exp.	12.6	33.1	8.6	15.5	16.9	18.0	18.7	8.9	7.3	8.0
Cash Flow	40.9	33.2	32.7	34.9	32.3	25.6	31.7	28.4	25.7	23.2
Curr. Ratio	1.0	0.8	1.2	1.2	1.2	1.3	1.2	1.5	0.8	1.7
% LT Debt of Cap.	37.8	Nil	Nil	Nil	Nil	Nil	Nil	Nil	8.6	Nil
% Net Inc.of Revs.	9.2	9.4	9.3	7.3	6.5	5.4	8.5	7.0	8.1	10.0
% Ret. on Assets	17.3	19.1	21.9	19.2	17.5	13.6	19.6	14.8	16.9	18.4
% Ret. on Equity	52.4	41.3	39.4	37.8	32.4	23.6	32.6	26.4	30.5	29.1

Data as orig. reptd.; bef. results of disc. opers. and/or spec. items. Per share data adj. for stk. divs. as of ex-div. date. Bold denotes diluted EPS (FASB 128). E-Estimated. NA-Not Available. NM-Not Meaningful. NR-Not Ranked.

Office—1 Freedom Valley Dr., Oaks, PA 19456. **Tel**—(610) 676-1000. **Chrmn & CEO**—A. P. West Jr. **Pres, COO & CFO**—H. H. Greer. **EVP**—Carmen V. Romeo. **Dirs**—D. C. Carroll, W. M. Doran, H. H. Greer, R. B. Lieb, H. H. Porter Jr., C. V. Romeo, A. P. West Jr. **Transfer Agent & Registrar**—American Stock Transfer & Trust Co., NYC. **Incorporated**—in Pennsylvania in 1968. **Empl**—1,133. **S&P Analyst:** C.C.P.

03-OCT-98

Industry: Manufacturing (Specialized)

Summary: This company manufactures high-strength fastening and assembly systems, superalloys and magnetic materials.

S&P Opinion: Accumulate (★★★★)	Recent Price • 46¼	Yield • Nil
	52 Wk Range • 65-37	12-Mo. P/E • 15.1

Earnings vs. Previous Year
▲=Up ▼=Down ▶=No Change

Quantitative Evaluations

Outlook (1 Lowest—5 Highest)
• **3⁻**

Fair Value
• **52**

Risk
• **Low**

Earn./Div. Rank
• **B-**

Technical Eval.
• **NA**

Rel. Strength Rank (1 Lowest—99 Highest)
• **72**

Insider Activity
• **Neutral**

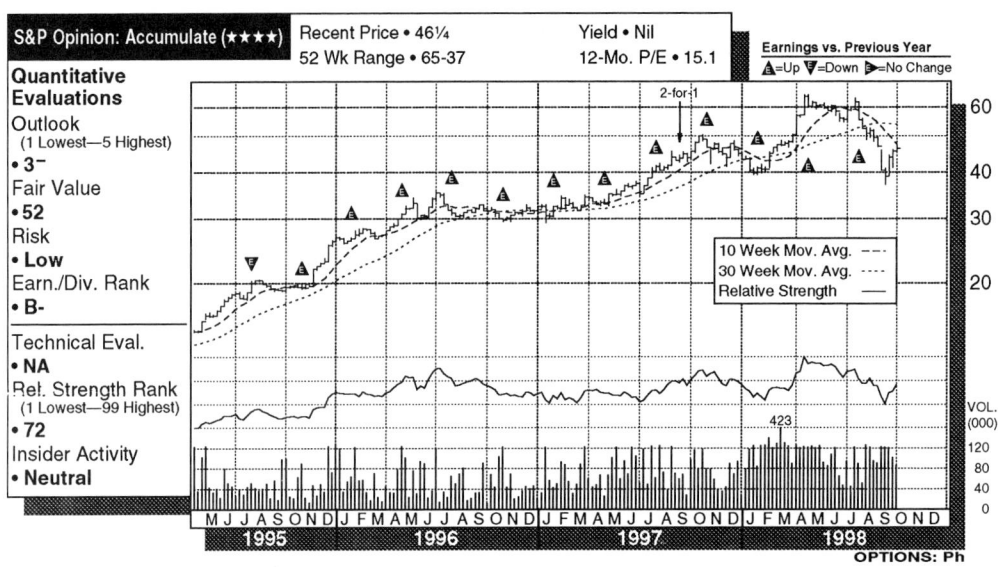

10 Week Mov. Avg. – – –
30 Week Mov. Avg. ⋯⋯
Relative Strength —

VOL. (000)

OPTIONS: Ph

Overview - 24-JUL-98

SPS Technologies' strategy is to maintain its aerospace fastener businesses at a high level of production, continue to diversify its overall fastener segment through acquisitions, and to grow its higher margin materials segment. The goal in the aerospace fastener businesses is to generate free cash flow to support acquisitions. For automotive and industrial fasteners, the goal is to build synergy to create new customers and sales. The materials segment, which includes superalloys and magnetic materials, is expected to grow due to strong demand from the aerospace and medical markets. We expect that combined revenues will increase 24% in 1998. Margins should improve on productivity in the fastener segment and a higher mix of materials segment sales, resulting in a sharp 37% rise in EPS to $3.45. Without consideration of additional acquisitions, in 1999 revenues are projected to grow 6%, with total fastener sales up 1% and materials segment revenues climbing 14%. Margins are likely to rise, and we look for earnings to climb 10% to $3.80 a share.

Valuation - 24-JUL-98

ST, recently trading at a P/E of 16 times estimated 1999 EPS, merits accumulation. Some weakness in the shares may be due to the protracted strike at GM, but this situation is temporary. Turning to ST's aerospace businesses, jet production is expected to be sustained at a historically high level for several years, regardless of some order push outs by carriers in emerging markets. The aerospace fastener business should generate substantial free cash flow, and the materials segment should continue to enjoy above average growth.

Key Stock Statistics

S&P EPS Est. 1998	3.45	Tang. Bk. Value/Share	19.02
P/E on S&P Est. 1998	13.4	Beta	1.11
S&P EPS Est. 1999	3.80	Shareholders	1,100
Dividend Rate/Share	Nil	Market cap. (B)	$0.589
Shs. outstg. (M)	12.7	Inst. holdings	57%
Avg. daily vol. (M)	0.024		

Value of $10,000 invested 5 years ago: $ 47,559

Fiscal Year Ending Dec. 31

	1998	1997	1996	1995	1994	1993
Revenues (Million $)						
1Q	179.9	138.0	114.0	102.4	81.58	87.28
2Q	175.2	153.1	121.3	100.6	85.45	85.45
3Q	—	142.3	125.4	100.5	88.47	74.39
4Q	—	155.3	125.2	106.3	90.99	71.96
Yr.	—	588.6	485.9	409.8	348.9	319.1
Earnings Per Share ($)						
1Q	**0.85**	**0.56**	0.41	0.27	0.41	0.16
2Q	**0.90**	**0.66**	0.47	0.34	0.36	0.14
3Q	**E0.80**	**0.66**	0.48	0.35	0.20	-0.67
4Q	**E0.90**	**0.66**	0.41	0.30	0.16	-2.66
Yr.	**E3.45**	**2.54**	1.77	1.25	0.31	-3.04

Next earnings report expected: mid October

Dividend Data

No dividends have been paid, and the company does not intend to pay any in the foreseeable future.

A Division of The **McGraw·Hill** Companies

Business Summary - 24-JUL-98

Production of commercial aircraft took off in the mid-nineties and is expected to stay at high altitudes for at least the next few years. After several years of substantial capital investment to increase capacity, adopt lean manufacturing and rationalize production, SPS Technologies (ST) expects its aerospace fasteners business (36% of 1997 net revenues) to coast, while it continues to expand its five other recently reorganized business groups.

In 1997, ST analyzed its various business lines and determined that its numerous acquisitions over the years should be regrouped. It reorganized and decentralized into six groups with distinct management issues, different customers, and important differences in manufacturing processes. In addition to aerospace fasteners, the automotive fasteners business (17%) was separated from the industrial fastener group (12%). ST also formed a precision tools group (2%) and split apart the specialty materials and alloys (14%) and magnetic materials (19%) groups.

The aerospace fastener group develops, in conjunction with, and supplies fasteners to leading commercial and military aircraft manufacturers, and aerospace parts and components and engine suppliers. The group operates three manufacturing plants in the U.S., including the world's largest aerospace fastener plant in Pennsylvania, as well as other facilities in England, Canada, and Japan. Together with the specialty materials and

alloys group, it is developing next generation raw materials for advanced aerospace applications such as high temperature engines.

The automotive fastener group's goals are to further expand and broaden its product offerings through additional strategic acquisitions. It supplies fasteners and other engineered components worldwide to the auto, truck, and heavy equipment industries. On June 30, 1998, ST acquired Terry Machine, a maker of specialty cold headed fasteners for the auto industry, that had sales of $37 million in the 12 months through April 1998.

The industrial fastener group was formed in 1997 to unify the marketing and manufacturing operations of business units with 11 facilities on four continents.

While still small, the precision tool group is targeted for growth through future acquisitions. On June 30, 1998, ST acquired the operating assets of Howell Penncraft, a maker of high speed tool steel and carbide products used in metal forming, with 1997 sales of $9.3 million.

The specialty materials and alloys and magnetic materials groups have also been rapidly expanded in recent years through acquisitions. Of total specialty materials and alloys sales in 1997, 40% were for aerospace applications, 14% for industrial gas turbine components, 30% for medical prosthetic implants and 16% for general engineering applications. The magnetic materials group supplies a broad and diverse number of industries.

Per Share Data ($)

(Year Ended Dec. 31)	1997	1996	1995	1994	1993	1992	1991	1990	1989	1988
Tangible Bk. Val.	13.40	12.83	11.89	10.16	8.84	13.71	17.64	17.81	17.35	16.43
Cash Flow	4.34	3.27	2.48	1.58	-1.70	0.49	1.84	0.38	2.71	3.11
Earnings	2.54	1.77	1.25	0.31	-3.04	-0.69	0.55	-0.99	1.60	1.92
Dividends	Nil	Nil	Nil	Nil	0.48	0.64	0.64	0.64	0.61	0.53
Payout Ratio	Nil	Nil	Nil	Nil	NM	NM	116%	NM	38%	28%
Prices - High	50¹/₂	35⁵/₈	26⁷/₈	13³/₄	15¹/₈	14³/₄	18¹/₂	22	30¹/₈	22⁷/₈
- Low	29¹/₄	25⁵/₈	12³/₄	9³/₄	7⁷/₈	9¹/₂	10³/₈	10¹/₄	20¹/₂	12¹/₂
P/E Ratio - High	20	20	21	44	NM	NM	34	NM	19	12
- Low	11	14	10	30	NM	NM	19	NM	13	7

Income Statement Analysis (Million $)

	1997	1996	1995	1994	1993	1992	1991	1990	1989	1988
Revs.	589	486	410	349	319	321	374	441	423	431
Oper. Inc.	81.2	57.0	40.1	24.5	17.0	18.3	31.5	21.6	37.5	52.2
Depr.	23.1	18.9	14.7	13.1	13.6	12.1	13.1	13.7	11.1	11.8
Int. Exp.	9.0	8.0	6.5	6.9	5.9	5.4	7.7	10.6	8.6	9.7
Pretax Inc.	49.5	31.0	21.3	6.1	-33.6	-8.3	10.7	-4.9	22.4	30.6
Eff. Tax Rate	34%	28%	30%	48%	NM	NM	48%	NM	28%	38%
Net Inc.	32.5	22.3	14.9	3.2	-31.0	-7.0	5.6	-10.0	16.1	19.0

Balance Sheet & Other Fin. Data (Million $)

	1997	1996	1995	1994	1993	1992	1991	1990	1989	1988
Cash	18.7	33.3	8.1	9.5	6.8	2.9	3.8	5.2	6.8	3.2
Curr. Assets	227	232	179	160	161	152	157	218	195	204
Total Assets	472	428	322	289	286	290	311	369	324	325
Curr. Liab.	121	105	77.4	71.9	66.5	59.9	60.1	86.8	68.4	79.4
LT Debt	95.5	99	58.1	56.4	81.8	63.1	60.6	91.3	74.9	70.2
Common Eqty.	215	178	146	124	103	143	179	180	174	169
Total Cap.	327	297	217	191	194	215	251	282	256	246
Cap. Exp.	37.5	28.2	21.5	17.6	12.2	14.5	11.1	24.2	18.9	20.5
Cash Flow	55.6	41.2	29.6	16.3	-17.4	5.0	18.7	3.7	27.2	30.8
Curr. Ratio	1.9	2.2	2.3	2.2	2.4	2.5	2.6	2.5	2.9	2.6
% LT Debt of Cap.	29.2	33.2	26.8	29.5	42.2	29.4	24.2	32.4	29.3	28.6
% Net Inc.of Revs.	5.5	4.6	3.7	0.9	NM	NM	1.5	NM	3.8	4.4
% Ret. on Assets	7.2	5.4	4.9	1.1	NM	NM	1.6	NM	4.9	5.9
% Ret. on Equity	16.6	13.8	11.1	2.7	NM	NM	3.1	NM	9.3	11.4

Data as orig. reptd.; bef. results of disc. opers. and/or spec. items. Per share data adj. for stk. divs. as of ex-div. date. Bold denotes diluted EPS (FASB 128). E-Estimated. NA-Not Available. NM-Not Meaningful. NR-Not Ranked.

Office—101 Greenwood Ave., Suite 470, Jenkintown, PA 19046. **Tel**—(215) 517-2000. **Website**—http://www.spstech.com. **Chrmn, Pres & CEO**—C. W. Grigg. **VP & CFO**—W. M. Shockley. **VP & Secy**—J. D. Dee. **VP, Treas & Investor Contact**—John M. Morrash (215) 517-2011. **Dirs**—C. W. Grigg, H. T. Hallowell III, R. W. Kelso, J. F. O'Connor, M. Ruttenberg, R. P. Sharpe, H. J. Wilkinson. **Transfer Agent & Registrar**—ChaseMellon Shareholder Services, Ridgefield Park, NJ. **Incorporated**—in Pennsylvania in 1903. **Empl**— 4,996. **S&P Analyst:** Mark S. Basham

03-OCT-98

Industry:
Electronics (Semiconductors)

Summary: S3 supplies high-performance accelerator solutions for the graphical user interface environments created by Microsoft Windows, IBM OS/2 and other advanced PC operating systems.

Quantitative Evaluations

Recent Price • 2⅝
52 Wk Range • 13⅜-2½

Yield • Nil
12-Mo. P/E • NM

Outlook
(1 Lowest—5 Highest)
• **3⁻**

Fair Value
• **3¼**

Risk
• **High**

Earn./Div. Rank
• **NR**

Technical Eval.
• **Bearish** since 7/98

Rel. Strength Rank
(1 Lowest—99 Highest)
• **12**

Insider Activity
• **Neutral**

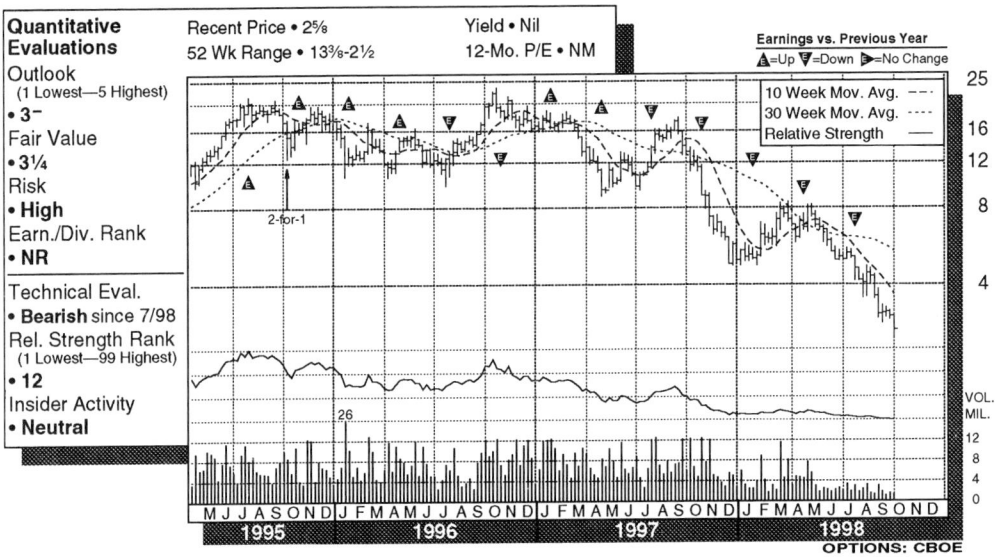

OPTIONS: CBOE

Business Profile - 01-JUN-98

Recent financial performance has been hurt by price competition that is expected to continue at least until the company's next generation of high-performance products moves into volume production. In January 1998, S3 announced a restructuring program that will reduce the work force by 15%, or about 100 positions; in December 1997, management was restructured. S3 also recently restated revenues for prior quarters, due to errors in the timing of revenue recognition, resulting in a significant net income decrease. This action followed a second-quarter 1997 revenue slowdown that S3 attributed to pricing pressures, which at the time were thought to be temporary. The stock price has plummeted amid these developments, and several shareholder lawsuits have been filed.

Operational Review - 01-JUN-98

In the first quarter of 1998, net sales plunged 37%, year to year. Gross margins narrowed sharply, to 19.0% of net sales from 38.7%, and after higher R&D costs and only a slight decline in SG&A expenses, an operating loss contrasted with operating income. Following a $26.6 million gain on the sale of a manufacturing joint venture, and an $8.0 million charge for acquired in-process R&D, net income was down 71%, to $4,121,000 ($0.08 a share, based on 9.3% fewer shares) from $14,382,000 ($0.27).

Stock Performance - 02-OCT-98

In the past 30 trading days, SIII's shares have declined 38%, compared to a 7% fall in the S&P 500. Average trading volume for the past five days was 260,860 shares, compared with the 40-day moving average of 379,205 shares.

Key Stock Statistics

Dividend Rate/Share	Nil	Shareholders	300
Shs. outstg. (M)	51.1	Market cap. (B)	$0.136
Avg. daily vol. (M)	0.307	Inst. holdings	26%
Tang. Bk. Value/Share	5.20		
Beta	1.24		

Value of $10,000 invested 5 years ago: NA

Fiscal Year Ending Dec. 31

	1998	1997	1996	1995	1994	1993
Revenues (Million $)						
1Q	82.51	130.3	110.1	57.42	37.53	17.60
2Q	53.30	84.60	103.8	70.56	27.47	25.02
3Q	—	119.6	119.4	84.79	30.89	33.17
4Q	—	101.9	132.0	103.5	44.42	37.22
Yr.	—	436.4	465.4	316.3	140.3	113.0
Earnings Per Share ($)						
1Q	**0.08**	0.27	0.25	0.15	0.10	0.06
2Q	**-0.23**	-0.04	0.18	0.17	-0.13	0.09
3Q	—	0.08	0.20	0.20	0.05	0.12
4Q	—	-0.16	0.30	0.23	0.11	0.13
Yr.	—	**0.17**	**0.81**	0.75	0.14	0.41

Next earnings report expected: late October

Dividend Data

No cash dividends have been paid. The company intends to retain earnings for use in the development of its business and does not expect to pay cash dividends in the foreseeable future. Two-for-one stock splits were effected in 1995 and 1993.

STANDARD
&POOR'S
STOCK REPORTS

S3 Incorporated

5137

03-OCT-98

Business Summary - 01-JUN-98

As the personal computer continues to evolve into a graphics-oriented, interactive, real-time system, S3 Incorporated believes that demand for its graphics accelerators will grow. The company is a supplier of high-performance accelerator solutions for the graphical user interface environments created by Microsoft Windows, IBM OS/2 and other advanced personal computer (PC) operating systems. S3's integrated accelerator solutions relieve a computer's central processing unit of primary responsibility for graphics processing and significantly improve the graphics performance of PCs.

The company was one of the pioneers in the graphics acceleration market; its first product, the 86C911 graphics accelerator chip, began shipping in volume in 1991. Since that time, it has frequently upgraded its product offerings. The company currently offers graphics and video accelerators for desktop and mobile computers that are differentiated by a variety of features.

In 1994, S3 expanded its product offerings by introducing 64-bit multimedia accelerators, the Vision868 and Vision968. In addition, the company launched its Trio family of integrated graphics accelerators, addressing the need for high-performance graphics in en-

try-level systems. In June 1995, S3 unveiled its Cooperative Accelerator Architecture (CAA) solution, the industry's first graphics, audio and MPEG (Motion Picture Expert's Group) standard solution designed to improve quality and affordability for multimedia on commercial and home desktop PCs. In November 1995, the company introduced its ViRGE family of 3D graphics and video acceleration products, which enable 3D graphics on mainstream PCs; and in December 1995, it unveiled its first Unified Memory Architecture product, the Trio64UV+ integrated graphics and video accelerator, which is designed to eliminate the need for a separate graphics memory. In 1996, the company expanded its product line to include products for mobile computing and audio markets and also introduced second-generation 2D/3D products. In 1997 the company introduced third generation 2D/3D graphics and video accelerators under the ViRGE, and Trio lines.

R&D efforts are focused on high-performance accelerator and related software products for new markets, such as real-time communications and mobile computing, and on enhanced versions of its current line of products, with an emphasis on 3D acceleration. In 1997 a total of $95.8 million (22.0% of net sales) was spent on R&D, versus $63.4 million (14.4%) in 1996.

Per Share Data ($)

(Year Ended Dec. 31)	1997	1996	1995	1994	1993	1992	1991	1990	1989	1988
Tangible Bk. Val.	5.36	5.23	3.89	1.89	1.73	0.29	NA	NA	NA	NA
Cash Flow	0.53	1.16	0.90	0.24	0.45	0.19	NA	NA	NA	NA
Earnings	0.17	0.95	0.75	0.14	0.41	0.15	NA	NA	NA	NA
Dividends	Nil	Nil	Nil	Nil	Nil	Nil	Nil	Nil	Nil	Nil
Payout Ratio	Nil	Nil	Nil	Nil	Nil	Nil	Nil	Nil	Nil	Nil
Prices - High	19¼	23¾	22	9⅝	10⅜	NA	NA	NA	NA	NA
- Low	4¾	9¾	7⅝	3¼	3¾	NA	NA	NA	NA	NA
P/E Ratio - High	NM	25	29	69	25	NA	NA	NA	NA	NA
- Low	NM	10	10	23	9	NA	NA	NA	NA	NA

Income Statement Analysis (Million $)

	1997	1996	1995	1994	1993	1992	1991	1990	1989	1988
Revs.	436	466	316	140	113	30.6	3.3	Nil	Nil	Nil
Oper. Inc.	33.0	82.9	57.8	10.1	25.0	5.7	-4.2	-6.2	NA	NA
Depr.	18.5	10.7	6.8	4.0	1.7	0.9	0.8	0.7	NA	NA
Int. Exp.	6.5	2.0	Nil	0.0	0.2	0.1	0.3	0.3	NA	NA
Pretax Inc.	12.3	74.4	55.4	6.9	24.4	4.7	-4.9	-6.9	NA	NA
Eff. Tax Rate	28%	35%	36%	21%	38%	4.70%	Nil	Nil	Nil	Nil
Net Inc.	8.9	48.4	35.4	5.5	15.1	4.5	-4.9	-6.9	NA	NA

Balance Sheet & Other Fin. Data (Million $)

	1997	1996	1995	1994	1993	1992	1991	1990	1989	1988
Cash	90.5	157	93.9	34.6	44.5	5.8	5.2	NA	NA	NA
Curr. Assets	301	321	236	79.5	75.3	14.2	7.5	NA	NA	NA
Total Assets	493	468	322	89.5	81.7	15.8	8.3	NA	NA	NA
Curr. Liab.	91.4	89.0	91.0	19.8	20.3	7.6	4.9	NA	NA	NA
LT Debt	108	118	24.0	0.5	0.1	1.2	1.2	NA	NA	NA
Common Eqty.	271	267	206	68.9	61.0	7.0	14.3	NA	NA	NA
Total Cap.	379	385	230	69.7	61.4	8.2	-1.1	NA	NA	NA
Cap. Exp.	28.1	23.4	17.6	7.6	6.3	1.7	0.1	0.1	NA	NA
Cash Flow	27.4	59.1	42.2	9.5	16.8	5.4	-4.1	-6.2	NA	NA
Curr. Ratio	3.3	3.6	2.6	4.0	3.7	1.9	1.5	NA	NA	NA
% LT Debt of Cap.	28.5	30.6	10.4	0.6	0.2	14.4	NM	NM	NM	NM
% Net Inc.of Revs.	2.0	10.4	11.2	3.9	13.4	14.5	NM	NM	NM	NM
% Ret. on Assets	1.8	12.1	17.2	6.4	14.8	36.9	NM	NM	NM	NM
% Ret. on Equity	3.3	20.5	25.7	8.5	NM	NM	NM	NM	NM	NM

Data as orig. reptd.; bef. results of disc. opers. and/or spec. items. Per share data adj. for stk. divs. as of ex-div. date. Bold denotes diluted EPS (FASB 128). E-Estimated. NA-Not Available. NM-Not Meaningful. NR-Not Ranked.

Office—2801 Mission College Blvd., P.O. Box 58058, Santa Clara, CA 95052-8058. **Tel**—(408) 588-8000. **Website**—http://www.s3.com **Chrmn, Pres & CEO**—T. N. Holdt. **SVP & CFO**—W. D. Amaral. **SVP & Secy**—R. T. Yara. **Dirs**—J. C. Colligan, T. N. Holdt, R. P. Lee, C. J. Santoro, R. T. Yara. **Transfer Agent & Registrar**—Boston EquiServe, Canton, MA. **Incorporated**—in Delaware in 1989. **Empl**— 654. **S&P Analyst:** Jim Corridore

07-OCT-98

Industry:
Health Care (Medical Products & Supplies)

Summary: SFSK is the leading producer of disposable latex medical examination gloves for the U.S. market, and the world's largest maker of disposable powder-free examination gloves.

S&P Opinion: Accumulate (★★★★)

Recent Price • 29¼	Yield • Nil
52 Wk Range • 47⅛-20	12-Mo. P/E • 34.0

Quantitative Evaluations

Outlook
(1 Lowest—5 Highest)
• **4−**

Fair Value
• **45½**

Risk
• **High**

Earn./Div. Rank
• **B**

Technical Eval.
• **NA**

Rel. Strength Rank
(1 Lowest—99 Highest)
• **30**

Insider Activity
• **Neutral**

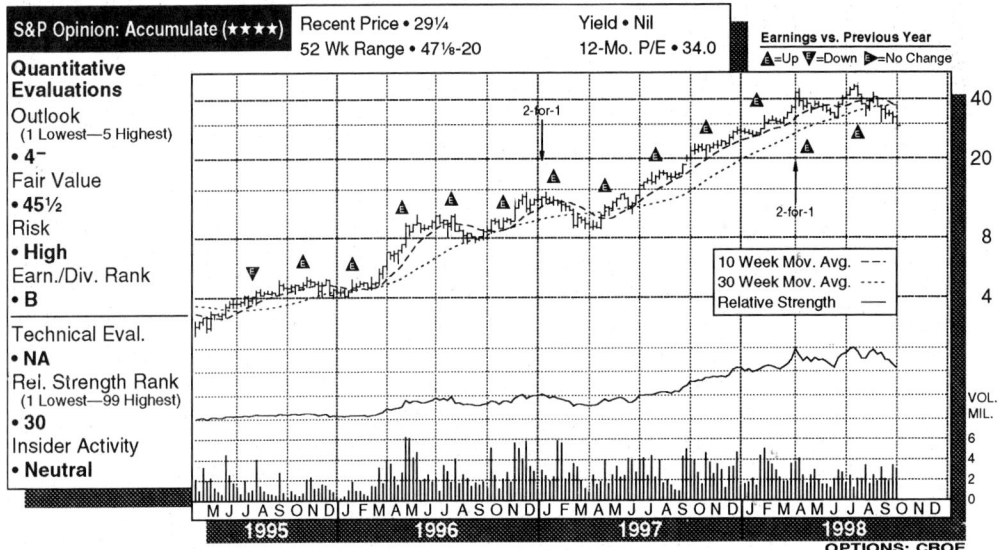

Earnings vs. Previous Year
▲=Up ▼=Down ▶=No Change

10 Week Mov. Avg. – –
30 Week Mov. Avg. ·····
Relative Strength —

2-for-1

OPTIONS: CBOE

Overview - 07-OCT-98

Revenues should rise over 25% annually through the end of the decade, due to growth in the powder-free glove market, supply contracts with large purchasing organizations, new product introductions and expansion into new markets. Given recent sales initiatives and SFSK's increased production capacity, this projection could be conservative. SFSK expects that greater manufacturing efficiencies, a continued shift to lower-cost production facilities, lower latex prices and a positive currency impact as a result of Asian manufacturing will allow gross margins to approximate 52% in 1998, versus 46% in 1997. To meet current and anticipated demand, SFSK has begun a major capacity expansion and expects to increase production from 3.5 billion exam gloves in 1997, to 5.5 billon by the end of 1998. We are leaving our 1998 EPS estimate at $0.98, and are raising our 1999 EPS estimate $0.05 to $1.25.

Valuation - 07-OCT-98

The shares, which had risen sharply over the past 52 weeks, are now well off their highs. However, SFSK continues to post record financial results. Therefore, we believe that there is room for significant price appreciation, driven by growing demand for SFSK's higher margin powder-free medical exam gloves and technology and scientific gloves. Moreover, SFSK will benefit from increased manufacturing capacity at lower cost and positive currency adjustments from Asian manufacturing. We expect long-term revenue and earnings growth in excess of 25%, driven by demand from hospitals, alternative care, dental, and scientific markets. With the shares well off their 52 week high, and in light of our forecast for strong revenue and earnings growth, we believe that SFSK provides investors with the opportunity for above average price appreciation. Therefore, we recommend that investors accumulate the shares.

Key Stock Statistics

S&P EPS Est. 1998	0.98	Tang. Bk. Value/Share	2.61
P/E on S&P Est. 1998	29.8	Beta	NA
S&P EPS Est. 1999	1.25	Shareholders	300
Dividend Rate/Share	Nil	Market cap. (B)	$ 1.5
Shs. outstg. (M)	54.4	Inst. holdings	55%
Avg. daily vol. (M)	0.540		

Value of $10,000 invested 5 years ago: NA

Fiscal Year Ending Dec. 31

	1998	1997	1996	1995	1994	1993
Revenues (Million $)						
1Q	53.30	41.17	33.06	22.59	17.50	—
2Q	58.64	44.95	35.99	29.24	20.73	—
3Q	—	46.90	37.49	32.44	22.66	—
4Q	—	49.99	39.55	32.74	23.24	—
Yr.	—	183.0	146.1	117.0	84.14	57.26
Earnings Per Share ($)						
1Q	0.22	0.15	0.10	0.06	—	—
2Q	0.25	0.16	0.11	0.06	0.08	—
3Q	E0.25	0.20	0.13	0.08	0.08	—
4Q	E0.26	0.20	0.09	0.09	0.08	—
Yr.	E0.98	0.70	0.42	0.29	0.28	0.28

Next earnings report expected: late October

Dividend Data

Amount ($)	Date Decl.	Ex-Div. Date	Stock of Record	Payment Date
2-for-1	Feb. 18	Apr. 02	Feb. 27	Apr. 01 '98

Business Summary - 07-OCT-98

Since 1995, this maker of disposable medical examination gloves has been the market share leader in sales of medical examination gloves to hospitals. Safeskin is an innovator of medical exam gloves and was the first company to market a powder-free (PF) latex glove. Unlike conventional latex gloves that can produce adverse reactions when worn for long periods of time, powder free latex gloves do not produce similar side effects.

Other innovations include the nitrile medical examination glove introduced in 1997. Nitrile is a synthetic co-polymer that contains no natural rubber latex, providing an alternative for individuals allergic to natural rubber latex. In March 1997, SFSK acquired Tactyl Technologies, Inc., a maker of synthetic (non-latex) surgical gloves, giving SFSK a 50% share of the synthetic market. In 1996, the company introduced Safeskin 2000, a PF latex surgical glove designed to provide greater freedom of motion and increased dexterity, thereby resulting in less hand fatigue.

SFSK's 1997 sales breakdown was 60% acute care (hospitals), 30% alternate care (physician and dental offices, outpatient surgical centers and nursing homes) and 10% high technology and scientific market (biotechnology and semiconductor industries).

Safeskin's four-part growth strategy includes increasing PF penetration in the acute care market, expanding its costumer base at the consumer level, introducing new products, and emphasizing its high volume manufacturing capabilities. Strong demand from large purchasing organizations should drive growth in the acute care market.

In April 1997, SFSK signed a six-year sole-source agreement with Columbia/ HCA Healthcare to supply all latex gloves, valued at $120 million. Additionally, in December 1996, Safeskin signed a three-year sole-source contract with Catholic Materials Management Alliance valued at $21 million, and a five-year dual-source contract with Premier Purchasing Partners. SFSK entered the consumer market in March 1997 executing a sole-source agreement with Costco Wholesale, valued at $6 million annually.

SFSK is focused on developing leading edge manufacturing facilities, using proprietary formulations and processes. Its plants are strategically located in Malaysia and Thailand, near its source of materials, and low cost labor.

As a result of continued strong demand for its glove products, the company is expanding its Asian manufacturing facilities over the next two years at a cost of about $80 million, which should boost production capacity by over two billion gloves annually. The project will primarily be funded through internal cash flow. SFSK's new machines can run continuously, and can be changed quickly to produce different types and sizes of gloves, with quality control and testing emphasized throughout the manufacturing process.

Per Share Data ($)

(Year Ended Dec. 31)	1997	1996	1995	1994	1993	1992	1991	1990	1989	1988
Tangible Bk. Val.	2.01	2.00	1.40	1.10	0.79	NA	NA	NA	NA	NA
Cash Flow	1.65	0.54	0.36	0.33	0.32	0.20	NA	NA	NA	NA
Earnings	0.70	0.42	0.29	0.28	0.28	0.17	0.04	NA	NA	NA
Dividends	Nil	Nil	Nil	Nil	Nil	Nil	Nil	Nil	Nil	Nil
Payout Ratio	Nil	Nil	Nil	Nil	Nil	Nil	Nil	Nil	Nil	Nil
Prices - High	29	13⅝	5⅛	4½	4⅛	NA	NA	NA	NA	NA
- Low	8⅞	4	2⅝	3⅛	3	NA	NA	NA	NA	NA
P/E Ratio - High	41	32	18	16	15	NA	NA	NA	NA	NA
- Low	13	10	9	11	11	NA	NA	NA	NA	NA

Income Statement Analysis (Million $)

	1997	1996	1995	1994	1993	1992	1991	1990	1989	1988
Revs.	183	146	117	84.0	57.3	33.9	NA	NA	NA	NA
Oper. Inc.	49.9	35.7	21.0	19.7	14.7	8.3	NA	NA	NA	NA
Depr.	7.1	6.1	3.8	2.2	1.6	0.8	NA	NA	NA	NA
Int. Exp.	-0.8	NM	0.2	0.0	1.4	1.5	NA	NA	NA	NA
Pretax Inc.	46.2	26.5	17.2	18.3	11.9	6.1	NA	NA	NA	NA
Eff. Tax Rate	11%	11%	14%	21%	1.80%	2.10%	NA	NA	NA	NA
Net Inc.	41.3	23.6	14.9	14.4	11.7	6.0	NA	NA	NA	NA

Balance Sheet & Other Fin. Data (Million $)

	1997	1996	1995	1994	1993	1992	1991	1990	1989	1988
Cash	23.9	16.3	2.1	4.6	7.8	NA	NA	NA	NA	NA
Curr. Assets	73.0	62.0	40.1	30.0	26.8	NA	NA	NA	NA	NA
Total Assets	139	117	84.7	61.2	43.2	NA	NA	NA	NA	NA
Curr. Liab.	29.8	13.7	12.1	7.0	4.5	NA	NA	NA	NA	NA
LT Debt	Nil	Nil	2.8	Nil	Nil	Nil	Nil	Nil	Nil	Nil
Common Eqty.	107	103	69.9	54.3	38.8	NA	NA	NA	NA	NA
Total Cap.	107	103	72.6	54.3	38.8	NA	NA	NA	NA	NA
Cap. Exp.	35.2	20.2	16.5	15.4	10.2	NA	NA	NA	NA	NA
Cash Flow	48.4	29.7	18.7	16.6	13.2	6.8	NA	NA	NA	NA
Curr. Ratio	2.4	4.5	3.3	4.3	6.0	NA	NA	NA	NA	NA
% LT Debt of Cap.	Nil	Nil	3.8	Nil	Nil	Nil	Nil	Nil	Nil	Nil
% Net Inc.of Revs.	22.5	16.1	12.7	17.1	20.3	17.8	NA	NA	NA	NA
% Ret. on Assets	32.3	23.8	20.4	27.5	NA	NA	NA	NA	NA	NA
% Ret. on Equity	39.4	27.3	23.2	32.6	NA	NA	NA	NA	NA	NA

Data as orig. reptd.; bef. results of disc. opers. and/or spec. items. Per share data adj. for stk. divs. as of ex-div. date. Bold denotes diluted EPS (FASB 128). E-Estimated. NA-Not Available. NM-Not Meaningful. NR-Not Ranked. EPS Q4 1996 includes a $0.10 relocation charge.

Office—12671 High Bluff Dr., San Diego, CA 92130. **Tel**—(619) 350-6840. **Fax**—(619) 350-2380. **Website**—http://www.safeskin.com **Chrmn, Pres & CEO**—R. Jaffe. **EVP & CFO**—D. L. Morash. **EVP & COO**—T. J. Bieker. **VP-Fin & Secy**—S. S. Goldman. **Investor Contact**—Mark Francois (619-350-6840). **Dirs**—N. K. Braverman, C. L. Garner, I. Jaffe, R. Jaffe, H. L. Shecter, J. Stemler. **Transfer Agent & Registrar**—American Stock Transfer & Trust Co., NYC. **Incorporated**—in Florida in 1985. **Empl**— 5,341. **S&P Analyst:** John J. Arege

STANDARD &POOR'S
STOCK REPORTS

St. John Knits

1973U

NYSE Symbol **SJK**

In S&P SmallCap 600

05-OCT-98

Industry: Textiles (Apparel)

Summary: This company designs and manufactures women's clothing and accessories, sold through specialty retailers and its own retail boutiques and outlets.

Quantitative Evaluations	
Recent Price • 15¾	Yield • 0.6%
52 Wk Range • 48¼-15½	12-Mo. P/E • 7.3

Outlook
(1 Lowest—5 Highest)
• **5**

Fair Value
• **47⅛**

Risk
• **Average**

Earn./Div. Rank
• **B+**

Technical Eval.
• **Bearish** since 5/98

Rel. Strength Rank
(1 Lowest—99 Highest)
• **8**

Insider Activity
• **Neutral**

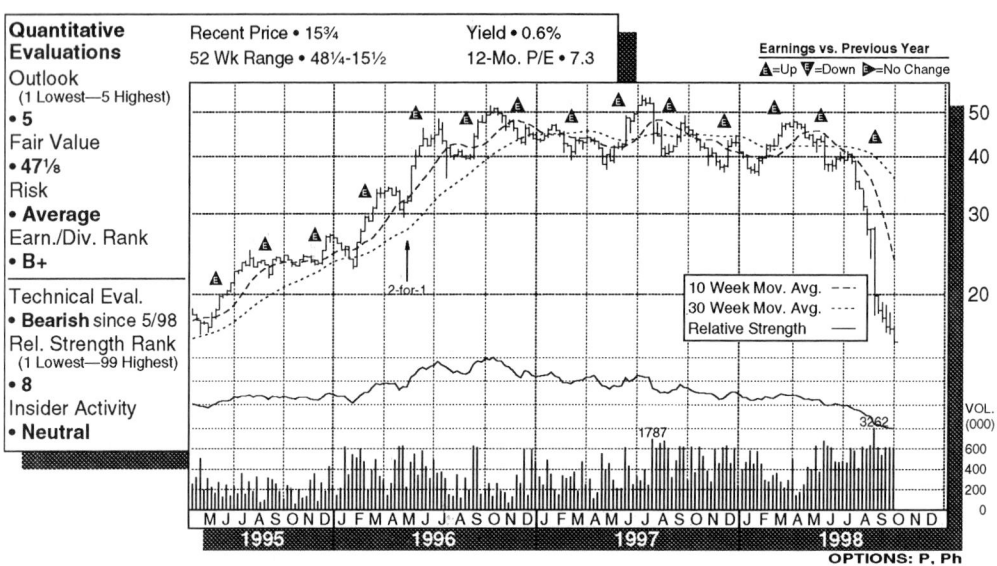

OPTIONS: P, Ph

Business Profile - 07-OCT-98

At the end of May 1998, SJK completed the relocation of its Las Vegas boutique to a new 5,500 square foot space at the Forum Shops. In July 1998, the company opened its ninth outlet in a recently developed outlet mall near Las Vegas. In August, directors authorized the repurchase of up to one million common shares. In the fourth quarter of FY 97, the company opened a group of home furnishings boutiques, Amen Wardy Home Boutiques (a majority owned subsidiary). Separately, it entered into a joint venture to distribute its products in Japan. SJK operates five Amen Wardy Home Boutiques, 16 retail boutiques and nine outlet stores.

Operational Review - 07-OCT-98

Net sales for the 39 weeks ended August 2, 1998, advanced 21%, year to year, reflecting higher sales to domestic and international retail customers, an increase in retail store sales and the inclusion of sales at Amen Wardy Home Boutiques. Gross margins narrowed slightly and SG&A expenses were up 27%; operating profits rose 13%. Following a sharp increase in other income, and taxes at 40.7% versus 41.2%, net income rose 12%, to $26,291,566 ($1.53 a share) from $23,458,178 ($1.37).

Stock Performance - 02-OCT-98

In the past 30 trading days, SJK's shares have declined 43%, compared to a 7% fall in the S&P 500. Average trading volume for the past five days was 132,280 shares, compared with the 40-day moving average of 211,303 shares.

Key Stock Statistics

Dividend Rate/Share	0.10	Shareholders	300
Shs. outstg. (M)	16.7	Market cap. (B)	$0.263
Avg. daily vol. (M)	0.136	Inst. holdings	81%
Tang. Bk. Value/Share	9.39		
Beta	1.28		

Value of $10,000 invested 5 years ago: NA

Fiscal Year Ending Oct. 31

	1998	1997	1996	1995	1994	1993
Revenues (Million $)						
1Q	68.76	56.18	45.26	36.30	27.27	20.80
2Q	69.81	59.56	50.03	40.62	32.23	24.84
3Q	67.73	54.81	46.53	36.95	29.67	25.04
4Q	—	71.55	61.14	47.92	38.78	29.60
Yr.	—	242.1	202.9	161.8	128.0	100.3
Earnings Per Share ($)						
1Q	**0.54**	0.43	0.34	0.24	0.17	0.12
2Q	**0.57**	0.52	0.40	0.31	0.21	0.17
3Q	**0.43**	0.42	0.35	0.26	0.21	0.15
4Q	—	0.64	0.50	0.38	0.31	0.23
Yr.	—	2.01	1.59	1.19	0.91	0.68

Next earnings report expected: mid December

Dividend Data (Dividends have been paid since 1994.)

Amount ($)	Date Decl.	Ex-Div. Date	Stock of Record	Payment Date
0.025	Dec. 19	Jan. 12	Jan. 14	Feb. 14 '98
0.025	Mar. 02	Mar. 27	Mar. 31	Apr. 30 '98
0.025	Jun. 18	Jun. 23	Jun. 25	Jul. 30 '98
0.025	Sep. 10	Sep. 23	Sep. 25	Oct. 30 '98

A Division of The McGraw-Hill Companies

STANDARD
&POOR'S
STOCK REPORTS

St. John Knits, Inc.

1973U
05-OCT-98

Business Summary - 07-OCT-98

For over 30 years, St. John Knits, Inc. (SJK) has been a leading designer, manufacturer and marketer of women's clothing and accessories. The St. John name has been associated with high quality and a specific look in knitwear characterized by vibrant colors and classic, timeless styling.

Using a vertically integrated manufacturing process, the company is assured of greater quality control, enhanced manufacturing flexibility and reduced lead time of the manufacturing cycle.

SJK's products fall under one of eight categories: Knitwear, Accessories, Sport, Griffith & Gray, Shoes, Fragrance, SJK and Coat Collection.

Knitwear, which accounted for 64% of total sales in FY 97 (Oct.), versus 65% in FY 96, is organized into four groups: collection, dressy, basics and couture. Collection consists of elegant ready-to-wear styles including dresses and suits, which have suggested retail prices between $350 and $1,300. The Dressy line is comprised of dresses, theater suits and dressy separates, and retails for prices between $650 and $2,000. Basics consists of seasonless products, such as classic jackets, skirts and pants, that are an integral part of women's wardrobes, all in solid black, white or navy. These products range from $160 to $690. The couture line consists of both a day and evening group which are both very exclusive with limited production quantities. Retail prices range from $900 to $3,300.

Accessories (3% of FY 97 sales; 4% in FY 96) include fine fashion jewelry, silk scarves, suede belts, shoes and handbags ranging in price from $65 to $450.

The Sport line (3%, 4%) includes jackets, pants and tops. Prices range from $120 to $700.

Griffith & Gray (2%; 2%) products include suits, coats, dresses, separates and eveningwear. Prices range from $300 to $1,200.

The Fragrance line (0.6%; 1%) includes perfume, eau de parfum, perfumed body mist, creams, lotions and bath products, with prices ranging from $25 to $250.

The Shoe line, which began shipping in FY 97 and accounted for 1% of sales, includes pumps, sling backs, loafers and boots manufactured in Italy. Retail prices range from $220 to $495.

Coat Collection (1%; 1%) consists primarily of faux fur coats in various styles and colors. Prices range from $700 to $1,300.

The SJK line, which began shipping during the fourth quarter of FY 97 (0.7% of sales), consists of dresses, skirts, pants, jackets and sweaters that are simpler, and priced from 30% to 50% lower than the knit product line, or about $150 to $600.

SJK distributes its products to approximately 600 locations in the U.S. and abroad, and also operates 16 of its own retail boutiques.

Saks Fifth Avenue, Neiman-Marcus and Nordstrom together accounted for 47% of FY 97 (Oct.) sales.

Per Share Data ($)

(Year Ended Oct. 31)	1997	1996	1995	1994	1993	1992	1991	1990	1989	1988
Tangible Bk. Val.	7.86	5.85	4.21	3.08	2.23	1.53	NA	NA	NA	NA
Cash Flow	2.53	2.00	1.51	1.14	0.84	0.64	0.41	0.20	NA	NA
Earnings	2.01	1.59	1.19	0.91	0.68	0.51	0.32	0.11	0.32	0.18
Dividends	0.10	0.10	0.10	0.08	Nil	NA	NA	NA	NA	NA
Payout Ratio	5%	6%	8%	8%	Nil	NA	NA	NA	NA	NA
Prices - High	54½	51¾	27⅛	16⅛	11⅝	NA	NA	NA	NA	NA
- Low	36⅞	22¾	14⅜	10⅝	6⅝	NA	NA	NA	NA	NA
P/E Ratio - High	27	33	23	18	17	NA	NA	NA	NA	NA
- Low	18	14	12	12	10	NA	NA	NA	NA	NA

Income Statement Analysis (Million $)

	1997	1996	1995	1994	1993	1992	1991	1990	1989	1988
Revs.	242	203	162	128	100	80.2	65.9	58.0	50.5	41.5
Oper. Inc.	66.9	52.7	38.3	29.2	21.5	15.7	9.5	4.1	NA	NA
Depr.	8.9	7.0	5.3	3.7	2.7	2.1	1.4	1.5	NA	NA
Int. Exp.	Nil	Nil	Nil	Nil	Nil	Nil	Nil	Nil	NA	NA
Pretax Inc.	58.7	47.1	33.8	25.8	19.1	13.9	8.8	2.9	9.4	5.5
Eff. Tax Rate	41%	42%	42%	42%	42%	40%	40%	40%	40%	40%
Net Inc.	34.4	27.1	19.7	14.9	11.1	8.3	5.3	1.8	5.7	3.3

Balance Sheet & Other Fin. Data (Million $)

	1997	1996	1995	1994	1993	1992	1991	1990	1989	1988
Cash	14.3	10.4	15.1	15.0	11.5	3.5	NA	NA	NA	NA
Curr. Assets	92.3	68.9	54.8	43.3	31.4	21.7	NA	NA	NA	NA
Total Assets	154	116	86.0	62.6	46.3	33.2	NA	NA	NA	NA
Curr. Liab.	22.6	19.3	16.7	11.9	9.1	7.3	NA	NA	NA	NA
LT Debt	Nil	Nil	Nil	Nil	Nil	Nil	Nil	Nil	Nil	Nil
Common Eqty.	131	97.1	69.2	50.5	36.6	25.5	NA	NA	NA	NA
Total Cap.	131	97.2	69.3	50.8	37.1	26.0	NA	NA	NA	NA
Cap. Exp.	22.7	21.4	17.6	7.8	5.7	5.6	4.2	2.6	NA	NA
Cash Flow	43.3	34.1	24.9	18.6	13.8	10.4	6.6	3.3	NA	NA
Curr. Ratio	4.1	3.6	3.3	3.6	3.4	3.0	NA	NA	NA	NA
% LT Debt of Cap.	Nil	Nil	Nil	Nil	Nil	Nil	Nil	Nil	Nil	Nil
% Net Inc.of Revs.	14.2	13.3	12.1	11.7	11.0	10.4	8.0	3.0	11.2	8.0
% Ret. on Assets	25.5	26.8	26.3	27.4	26.2	NA	NA	NA	NA	NA
% Ret. on Equity	30.2	32.7	32.7	34.3	33.0	NA	NA	NA	NA	NA

Data as orig. reptd.; bef. results of disc. opers. and/or spec. items. Per share data adj. for stk. divs. as of ex-div. date. Bold denotes diluted EPS (FASB 128). E-Estimated. NA-Not Available. NM-Not Meaningful. NR-Not Ranked.

Office—17422 Derian Ave., Irvine, CA 92714. **Tel**—(714) 863-1171. **Chrmn & CEO**—R. E. Gray. **Vice Chrmn & Secy**—M. St. John Gray. **Pres**—K. Gray. **SVP-Fin, CFO & Investor Contact**—Roger G. Ruppert. **Dirs**—R. C. Davis, R. A. Gadbois III, K. A. Gray, M. St. John Gray, R. E. Gray, D. A. Krinsky, R. G. Ruppert. **Transfer Agent & Registrar**—Harris Trust Co. of California. **Incorporated**—in California in 1962. **Empl**—3,255. **S&P Analyst:** Kathleen J. Fraser

03-OCT-98

Industry:
Oil & Gas (Exploration & Production)

Summary: This independent oil and gas concern has diversified exploration, development and production holdings in the U.S. and three foreign countries.

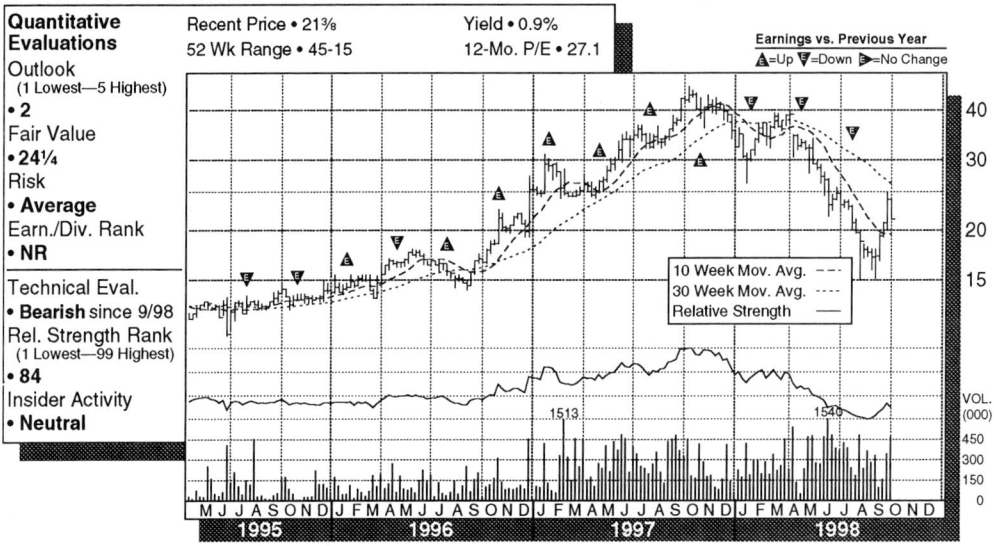

Quantitative Evaluations	
Recent Price • 21⅜	Yield • 0.9%
52 Wk Range • 45-15	12-Mo. P/E • 27.1

Outlook (1 Lowest—5 Highest)
• 2

Fair Value
• 24¼

Risk
• Average

Earn./Div. Rank
• NR

Technical Eval.
• Bearish since 9/98

Rel. Strength Rank (1 Lowest—99 Highest)
• 84

Insider Activity
• Neutral

Earnings vs. Previous Year
▲=Up ▼=Down ▶=No Change

10 Week Mov. Avg. ---
30 Week Mov. Avg. ....
Relative Strength —

Business Profile - 21-JUL-98

The company's domestic exploration and development focuses on the on-shore Gulf Coast, the Anadarko and Williston Basins, and the tri-state region of southern Arkansas, northern Louisiana and east Texas. Although average daily oil and gas production rose in the first quarter of 1998, average prices fell and results were lower than the comparable 1997 period. In May 1998, the company increased its borrowing base under its credit facility to $115 million from $60 million. St. Mary's capital budget includes $20 million for property acquisitions in 1998. As of May 8, the company had completed the acquisition of interests in the Permian Basin totaling $1.1 million.

Operational Review - 21-JUL-98

Total operating revenues for the three months ended March 31, 1998, fell 38%, year to year, reflecting a 9.5% decline in oil and gas production revenues, and the absence of a $9.7 million gain on the sale of a Russian joint venture. Net income plummeted 86%, to $1,670,000 ($0.15 a share, on 15% more shares) from $9,557,000 ($1.21).

Stock Performance - 02-OCT-98

In the past 30 trading days, MARY's shares have increased 21%, compared to a 7% fall in the S&P 500. Average trading volume for the past five days was 121,640 shares, compared with the 40-day moving average of 61,779 shares.

Key Stock Statistics

Dividend Rate/Share	0.20	Shareholders	200
Shs. outstg. (M)	11.0	Market cap. (B)	$0.235
Avg. daily vol. (M)	0.061	Inst. holdings	58%
Tang. Bk. Value/Share	13.72		
Beta	1.17		

Value of $10,000 invested 5 years ago: $ 20,539

Fiscal Year Ending Dec. 31

	1998	1997	1996	1995	1994	1993
Revenues (Million $)						
1Q	19.14	30.86	11.43	10.03	9.18	8.64
2Q	20.31	19.84	13.60	9.03	11.77	9.69
3Q	—	18.49	15.15	8.38	14.11	9.74
4Q	—	21.86	19.37	11.21	9.72	10.57
Yr.	—	91.05	59.55	38.65	44.79	38.63
Earnings Per Share ($)						
1Q	**0.15**	1.20	0.04	0.14	0.07	0.12
2Q	**0.10**	0.00	0.27	0.03	0.26	0.13
3Q	—	0.36	0.35	0.01	0.32	0.19
4Q	—	**0.12**	0.50	Nil	-0.22	-0.05
Yr.	—	**2.10**	1.16	0.17	0.43	0.39

Next earnings report expected: early November

Dividend Data (Dividends have been paid since 1993.)

Amount ($)	Date Decl.	Ex-Div. Date	Stock of Record	Payment Date
0.050	Oct. 20	Nov. 05	Nov. 07	Nov. 17 '97
0.050	Jan. 26	Feb. 11	Feb. 13	Feb. 23 '98
0.050	Apr. 20	May. 06	May. 08	May. 18 '98
0.050	Jul. 20	Aug. 05	Aug. 07	Aug. 17 '98

A Division of The McGraw-Hill Companies

Business Summary - 21-JUL-98

Focusing on its five core operating areas in the U.S., St. Mary Land & Exploration Co. (MARY) produced record financial and reserve growth in recent years. Founded in 1908, this independent oil and natural gas exploration and production company believes it is well positioned for continued growth in 1998 and beyond. Total production in 1997 increased 32%, to 5 million BOE. MARY's net proved reserves at year-end 1997 totaled 196 billion cubic feet of natural gas and 11.5 million barrels of oil. The company's success in building its reserve base in 1997 was due to the combined contributions from discoveries in South Louisiana, and its exploration and discovery programs in each of its core areas. During 1998, the company plans to test a series of significant prospects in South Louisiana and East Texas.

MARY's five core operating areas have a mix of proved reserves, development drilling opportunities and high-risk, large target exploration projects. The Mid-Continent region (33% of MARY's proved reserves in 1997), consisting of the Anadarko Basin of western Oklahoma and the Sherman-Marietta Basin of northeast Texas, represents MARY's flagship area of operations. The South Louisiana region (21%) includes its royalty interests in St. Mary Parish, LA, and working interests

in properties acquired in 1997. The ArkLaTex region (21%) includes a discovery at Box Church Field in east Texas and ongoing drilling in northern Louisiana. MARY's operations in the Williston Basin of North Dakota and Montana (13%) are conducted through a 74% general partnership interest in Panterra Petroleum. The Permian Basin of New Mexico and west Texas (10%) represents MARY's newest area of concentration and includes a 21.2% working interest in a 30,450 acre top lease in Ward and Winkler Counties in Texas believed to have significant exploration potential.

MARY follows a strategy of low to medium-risk exploration and development and pursues niche acquisitions of oil and gas properties within these core operating areas. During 1997, the company participated in 133 gross wells with an 85% success rate. MARY also seeks to make selective acquisitions of oil and gas properties that complement its exisiting operations.

MARY's capital budget for 1998 totals $94 million, including a record $56 million for ongoing development and exploration in each of its focus areas, as well as $18 million for higher potential, higher risk projects, and $20 million for niche acquisitions of producing properties. The company had a $65 million capital budget in 1997, with $43 million targeted for low to moderate-risk exploration and development, $15 million for acquisitions and $7 million for large-target, higher risk projects.

Per Share Data ($)

(Year Ended Dec. 31)	1997	1996	1995	1994	1993	1992	1991	1990	1989	1988
Tangible Bk. Val.	13.47	8.58	7.57	7.54	7.26	7.00	4.38	3.86	NA	NA
Cash Flow	3.81	2.61	1.33	1.58	1.39	3.02	1.26	1.11	NA	NA
Earnings	2.13	1.16	0.17	0.43	0.39	2.10	0.49	0.50	NA	NA
Dividends	0.20	0.16	0.16	0.16	0.16	0.16	0.16	0.16	NA	NA
Payout Ratio	9%	14%	94%	37%	41%	8%	33%	32%	NA	NA
Prices - High	46	27³/₈	15	14³/₈	18	11¹/₂	NA	NA	NA	NA
- Low	24	13¹/₂	10⁷/₈	10⁷/₈	18	11	NA	NA	NA	NA
P/E Ratio - High	22	24	75	33	46	6	NA	NA	NA	NA
- Low	11	12	54	25	28	5	NA	NA	NA	NA

Income Statement Analysis (Million $)

	1997	1996	1995	1994	1993	1992	1991	1990	1989	1988
Revs.	81.4	59.6	38.7	44.8	38.6	50.7	27.8	27.6	NA	NA
Oper. Inc.	44.1	28.9	11.8	14.8	14.0	30.5	12.0	12.4	NA	NA
Depr. Depl. & Amort.	18.4	12.7	10.2	NA	8.8	6.2	5.6	4.4	NA	NA
Int. Exp.	1.1	2.1	1.2	0.9	0.7	1.1	1.0	2.5	NA	NA
Pretax Inc.	34.9	15.5	0.7	4.4	4.5	22.5	5.4	5.6	NA	NA
Eff. Tax Rate	35%	34%	NM	11%	24%	33%	35%	36%	NA	NA
Net Inc.	22.6	10.2	1.4	3.7	3.4	15.2	3.5	3.6	NA	NA

Balance Sheet & Other Fin. Data (Million $)

	1997	1996	1995	1994	1993	1992	1991	1990	1989	1988
Cash	7.1	3.3	1.7	10.0	14.8	NA	NA	NA	NA	NA
Curr. Assets	31.9	32.1	10.8	18.9	22.6	NA	NA	NA	NA	NA
Total Assets	211	144	96.1	89.4	NA	75.9	53.8	NA	NA	NA
Curr. Liab.	22.3	18.2	7.7	9.5	7.4	NA	NA	NA	NA	NA
LT Debt	22.6	43.6	19.6	11.1	7.4	5.0	15.8	NA	NA	NA
Common Eqty.	149	75.2	66.3	66.0	63.6	61.4	31.1	NA	NA	NA
Total Cap.	189	125	87.1	78.9	73.7	66.5	46.9	NA	NA	NA
Cap. Exp.	54.2	27.5	22.7	NA	13.5	7.0	NA	NA	NA	NA
Cash Flow	41.0	22.9	11.7	5.8	12.2	21.8	9.1	7.9	NA	NA
Curr. Ratio	1.4	1.8	1.4	2.0	3.1	NA	NA	NA	NA	NA
% LT Debt of Cap.	12.0	34.9	22.5	14.1	10.1	7.5	NA	NA	NA	NA
% Ret. on Assets	12.7	8.5	1.5	4.4	4.3	24.1	7.5	NA	NA	NA
% Ret. on Equity	20.0	14.4	2.0	NA	5.4	33.0	12.1	NA	NA	NA

Data as orig. reptd.; bef. results of disc. opers. and/or spec. items. Per share data adj. for stk. divs. as of ex-div. date. Bold denotes diluted EPS (FASB 128). E-Estimated. NA-Not Available. NM-Not Meaningful. NR-Not Ranked.

Office—1776 Lincoln St., Suite 1100, Denver, CO 80203. **Tel**—(303) 861-8140. **Fax**—(303) 861-0934. **Website**—www.stmaryland.com **Chrmn**—T. E. Congdon. **Pres, CEO & Investor Contact**—Mark A. Hellerstein. **EVP & COO**—R. D. Boone. **VP-Fin & CFO**—D. L. Henry. **VP & Treas**—R. C. Norris. **Dirs**—L. W. Bickle, R. D. Boone,, T. E. Congdon, D. C. Dudley, M. A. Hellerstein, R. C. Kraus, R. J. Nicholson, A. J. Sandbulte, J. M. Seidl. **Transfer Agent**—American Securities Transfer, Inc., Lakewood, CO. **Incorporated**—in Delaware in 1915; business founded in 1908. **Empl**— 103. **S&P Analyst:** M.J.C.

St. Paul Bancorp   5149

NASDAQ Symbol **SPBC**

In S&P SmallCap 600

03-OCT-98

Industry: Savings & Loan Companies

Summary: Following the July 1998 acquisition of Beverly Bancorp., this bank holding company operates 65 branches and 550 ATMs in the Chicago area.

Quantitative Evaluations

Recent Price • 21   Yield • 2.9%

52 Wk Range • 29-17¼   12-Mo. P/E • 14.9

Outlook (1 Lowest—5 Highest)
• 1

Fair Value
• 19½

Risk
• **Low**

Earn./Div. Rank
• B+

Technical Eval.
• **Neutral** since 9/98

Rel. Strength Rank (1 Lowest—99 Highest)
• 68

Insider Activity
• **Neutral**

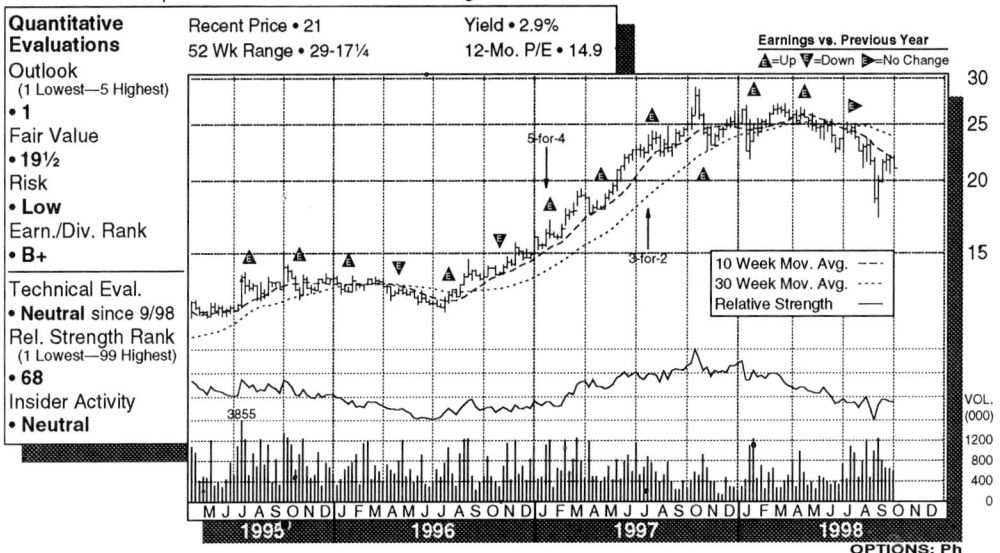

Earnings vs. Previous Year
▲=Up ▼=Down ▶=No Change

10 Week Mov. Avg. – – –
30 Week Mov. Avg. ......
Relative Strength ——

OPTIONS: Ph

Business Profile - 15-SEP-98

This bank holding company, in August 1998, announced a cost reduction plan aimed at reducing ongoing annual pretax expenses by $9 million. SPBC expects to incur a pretax charge of between $19 million and $23 million to implement the plan. The largest components of the plan include modifications to the company's compensation and benefits programs and to its technology outsourcing initiatives. SPBC noted that, after recently completing two major acquisitions (including the July 1998 purchase of Beverly Bancorporation), "this charge was necessary to re-align our cost structure and make it conform to our ongoing business initiatives". One of those initiatives is to seek a low cost means of expansion. To that end, SPBC has been opening in-store branches in Omni and Cub supermarkets, in addition to its full-size branch offices. SPBC now has the one of the largest ATM networks in Illinois, with more than 550 machines (as of July 1998).

Operational Review - 15-SEP-98

Net interest income advanced fractionally in the first six months of 1998, year to year, reflecting a higher level of loan repayments and a greater reliance on borrowings as a source of funds. The reversal of previous loan loss provision and growth in other income were offset by a rise in noninterest expenses, and net income increased slightly to $24,654,000 ($0.70 a share, based on more shares) from $24,634,000 ($0.71, excluding a $0.02 loss on the early extinguishment of debt).

Stock Performance - 02-OCT-98

In the past 30 trading days, SPBC's shares have declined 3%, compared to a 7% fall in the S&P 500. Average trading volume for the past five days was 117,160 shares, compared with the 40-day moving average of 182,354 shares.

Key Stock Statistics

Dividend Rate/Share	0.60	Shareholders	6,600
Shs. outstg. (M)	40.6	Market cap. (B)	$0.851
Avg. daily vol. (M)	0.143	Inst. holdings	33%
Tang. Bk. Value/Share	12.37		
Beta	0.85		

Value of $10,000 invested 5 years ago: $ 28,080

Fiscal Year Ending Dec. 31

	1998	1997	1996	1995	1994	1993
Revenues (Million $)						
1Q	90.47	87.33	80.49	77.07	66.48	69.83
2Q	89.58	89.72	82.57	78.00	69.18	72.68
3Q	—	91.88	83.78	78.54	72.24	75.36
4Q	—	91.46	85.14	78.87	75.14	71.56
Yr.	—	360.4	332.0	312.5	283.0	289.4
Earnings Per Share ($)						
1Q	0.35	0.33	0.24	0.25	0.21	0.25
2Q	0.36	0.36	0.29	0.25	0.22	0.30
3Q	—	0.35	-0.11	0.25	0.23	0.29
4Q	—	0.36	0.31	0.25	0.20	0.06
Yr.	—	1.42	0.74	1.00	0.91	1.08

Next earnings report expected: mid October

Dividend Data (Dividends have been paid since 1987.)

Amount ($)	Date Decl.	Ex-Div. Date	Stock of Record	Payment Date
0.100	Oct. 15	Oct. 29	Oct. 31	Nov. 13 '97
0.100	Jan. 14	Jan. 28	Jan. 30	Feb. 12 '98
0.100	Apr. 15	Apr. 28	Apr. 30	May. 14 '98
0.150	Jul. 15	Jul. 29	Jul. 31	Aug. 13 '98

A Division of The **McGraw·Hill** *Companies*

Business Summary - 15-SEP-98

Founded in 1889, St. Paul is the largest independent savings institution headquartered in Illinois. Following its acquisition in July 1998 of Beverly Bancorporation, St. Paul had total assets of over $5.3 billion, and was operating through 65 branches and an ATM network of over 550 machines. The company has expanded through nontraditional, less expensive outlets; including the opening of over 250 ATMs in White Hen Pantry stores. This greatly expanded the bank's ATM network and is expected to boost fee income. Nonbank subsidiaries include Investment Network, Inc., which provides discount brokerage services; St. Paul Service, Inc., a full-service insurance agency; St. Paul Financial Development Corp., a real estate developer; and Annuity Network, Inc., a distributor of annuities.

The company derives the majority (74%) of its net revenues from traditional lending activities and is focused on three loan product categories: single-family mortgages, multi-family mortgages (apartment buildings), and consumer loans. The total loan portfolio at recent year ends was divided as follows:

	1997	1996	1995
Mortgage one-to four-family	70%	62%	61%
Mortgage multifamily	28%	35%	36%
Commercial mortgage	2%	2%	2%
Consumer	1%	1%	1%

Asset quality at the bank has improved significantly. Net charge-offs (amount of loans written off as uncollectible) represented only 0.05% of average loans receivable in 1997, down from 0.15% a year earlier. Nonperforming assets, which are primarily loans where principal and interest payments are not being received, also fell to 0.23% of total asset, from 0.29%.

Deposits are the main (and most cost effective) source of funds for the bank. Totaling $3.3 billion at year-end 1997, deposits were apportioned: 6% noninterest bearing, 7% demand, 21% savings, 7% money market, and 60% time.

Lending profitability, commonly measured by the yield on a bank's average earning assets, or net interest margin, is affected by changes in the volume and mix of assets and liabilities, as well as changes in interest rates. St. Paul's net interest margin narrowed to 3.01% in 1997, from 3.07%, solely on a increase in its cost of funds.

To boost sales and efficiency, the bank has utilized advanced technology, including a new digital telephone system, a more efficient teller system, and a new consumer lending system to speed up loan approvals.

St. Paul continues to expand and broaden its product offerings through acquisitions. During 1997, SPBC added Chicago-based Serve Corps Mortgage L.L.C., a regional mortgage broker. On July 1, 1998 it acquired Beverly Bancorp, a $669 million commercial bank with 13 branches in the south and southwest suburbs of Chicago.

Per Share Data ($)

(Year Ended Dec. 31)	1997	1996	1995	1994	1993	1992	1991	1990	1989	1988
Tangible Bk. Val.	12.19	11.33	10.89	9.94	9.41	8.39	7.47	6.40	6.62	6.45
Earnings	1.42	0.73	1.00	0.91	1.08	1.07	0.80	-0.16	0.31	0.68
Dividends	0.36	0.23	0.16	0.16	0.14	0.14	0.14	0.14	0.13	0.10
Payout Ratio	25%	32%	16%	18%	13%	13%	18%	NM	43%	14%
Prices - High	29	16³/₈	15¹/₈	12⁷/₈	11	8³/₈	5⁷/₈	6¹/₂	7¹/₈	4¹/₄
- Low	15¹/₄	11⁷/₈	9¹/₄	8⁵/₈	7¹/₈	4⁵/₈	2¹/₂	2	3⁷/₈	3³/₈
P/E Ratio - High	20	22	15	14	10	8	7	NM	23	6
- Low	11	16	9	10	7	4	3	NM	12	5

Income Statement Analysis (Million $)

	1997	1996	1995	1994	1993	1992	1991	1990	1989	1988
Net Int. Inc.	130	125	117	118	124	113	99	88.6	81.8	77.7
Loan Loss Prov.	Nil	1.8	1.9	5.2	10.8	10.6	11.1	35.7	21.7	4.2
Non Int. Inc.	45.5	34.8	33.7	29.8	32.5	28.3	22.6	22.4	17.8	17.4
Non Int. Exp.	101	119	90.2	87.2	82.7	71.2	66.7	128	61.0	53.2
Pretax Inc.	74.5	39.7	57.1	53.5	60.4	58.0	43.7	10.2	16.1	37.7
Eff. Tax Rate	34%	34%	36%	36%	32%	35%	38%	NM	34%	40%
Net Inc.	49.5	26.3	36.4	34.5	41.4	37.7	27.2	-5.5	10.6	22.8
% Net Int. Marg.	3.01	3.07	3.01	3.15	3.46	3.27	2.84	NA	NA	NA

Balance Sheet & Other Fin. Data (Million $)

	1997	1996	1995	1994	1993	1992	1991	1990	1989	1988
Total Assets	4,557	4,357	4,117	4,132	3,705	3,500	3,663	3,417	3,345	3,105
Loans	3,205	3,981	3,698	3,737	3,085	2,914	3,133	3,121	3,019	2,839
Deposits	3,284	3,337	3,232	3,233	3,253	2,985	3,004	2,648	2,560	2,369
Capitalization:										
Debt	419	194	266	272	63.0	100	168	234	206	207
Equity	418	388	384	351	347	287	253	216	223	216
Total	837	582	650	623	410	387	421	450	429	423
% Ret. on Assets	1.1	0.6	0.9	0.9	1.1	1.1	0.8	NM	0.3	0.7
% Ret. on Equity	12.3	6.8	9.9	9.7	12.8	14.0	11.3	NM	4.8	10.7
% Loan Loss Resv.	1.1	1.3	1.4	1.1	1.5	1.6	1.5	1.5	0.5	0.2
% Risk Based Capital	17.1	17.3	17.5	16.7	16.7	12.8	11.0	NA	NA	NA
Price Times Book Value:										
Hi	2.5	1.4	1.4	1.3	0.7	1.0	0.8	1.0	1.1	0.7
Low	1.3	1.0	0.9	0.9	1.2	0.5	0.3	0.3	0.6	0.5

Data as orig. reptd.; bef. results of disc opers. and/or spec. items. Per share data adj. for stk. divs. as of ex-div. date. Bold denotes diluted EPS (FASB 128). E-Estimated. NA-Not Available. NM-Not Meaningful. NR-Not Ranked.

Office—6700 W. North Ave., Chicago, IL 60635. **Tel**—(773) 622-5000. **Website**—http://www.stpaulbank.com **Chrmn & CEO**—J. C. Scully. **Pres & COO**—P. J. Agnew. **SVP, CFO & Investor Contact**—Robert N. Parke (773-804-2360). **Dirs**—P. J. Agnew, W. A. Anderson, J. W. Croghan, A. J. Fredian, P.C. Gearen, K. J. James, J. C. Murray, J. C. Scully, J. J. Viera. **Transfer Agent & Registrar**—First National Bank of Boston. **Incorporated**—in Delaware in 1987. **Empl**— 1,064. **S&P Analyst:** L. A. Olive

STANDARD &POOR'S
STOCK REPORTS

Sanmina Corp.　5157M
NASDAQ Symbol **SANM**

In S&P SmallCap 600

03-OCT-98 | **Industry:** Electrical Equipment | **Summary:** This company is a leading provider of customized integrated manufacturing services to OEMs in the electronics industry.

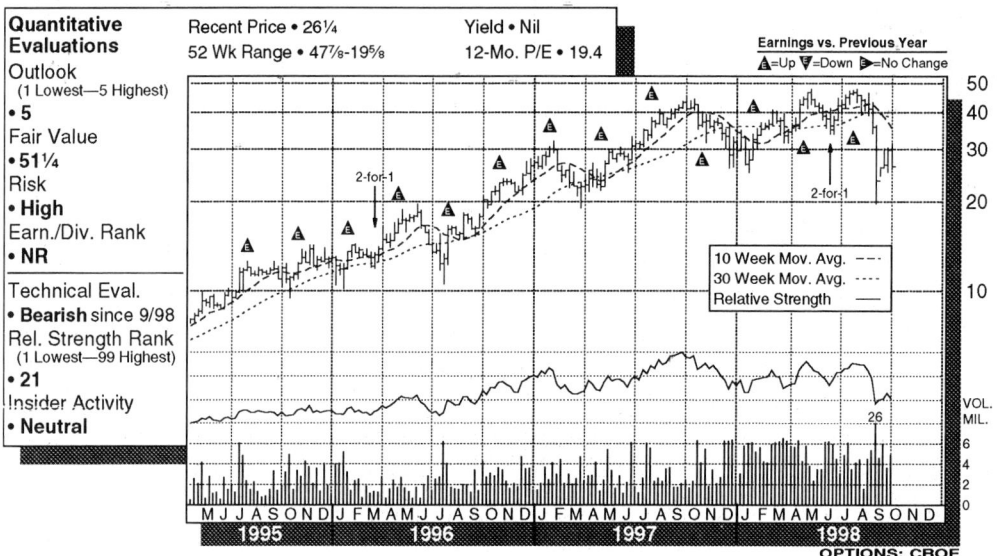

Quantitative Evaluations		
Outlook (1 Lowest—5 Highest) • **5**	Recent Price • 26¼	Yield • Nil
Fair Value • **51¼**	52 Wk Range • 47⅞-19⅝	12-Mo. P/E • 19.4

Risk • **High**

Earn./Div. Rank • **NR**

Technical Eval. • **Bearish** since 9/98

Rel. Strength Rank (1 Lowest—99 Highest) • **21**

Insider Activity • **Neutral**

Earnings vs. Previous Year
▲=Up ▼=Down ▶=No Change

2-for-1

10 Week Mov. Avg. ----
30 Week Mov. Avg. ----
Relative Strength ——

OPTIONS: CBOE

Business Profile - 12-AUG-98

The company's business strategy includes emphasis on high-value-added products and services for leading OEMs; the leveraging of vertically integrated manufacturing capabilities; geographic expansion of manufacturing facilities; the development of long-term customer relationships; and the aggressive pursuit of acquisitions that mesh with its basic operations. Elexsys International (ELEX) was acquired in November 1997 for about 3.3 million SANM common shares. Net income in the first nine months of 1998 rose 36% from the year earlier period, as the company experienced growth in its key markets, which include telecommunications, data communications, medical and instrumentation and high performance computer systems. In June 1998, the shares split 2-for-1.

Operational Review - 12-AUG-98

Revenues for the nine months ended June 27, 1998, advanced 29%, year to year, driven by growth across all four key markets. Margins widened, reflecting a smaller rise in SG&A expenditures; operating income grew 42%. Following merger and acquisition costs of $3.9 million, pretax income rose 39%. After taxes at 36.5%, versus 35.2%, net income increased 36%, to $48,762,000 ($1.02 a share, based on 2.4% more shares), from $35,913,000 ($0.78).

Stock Performance - 02-OCT-98

In the past 30 trading days, SANM's shares have declined 36%, compared to a 7% fall in the S&P 500. Average trading volume for the past five days was 965,640 shares, compared with the 40-day moving average of 1,451,769 shares.

Key Stock Statistics

Dividend Rate/Share	Nil	Shareholders	200
Shs. outstg. (M)	42.1	Market cap. (B)	$ 1.1
Avg. daily vol. (M)	0.994	Inst. holdings	95%
Tang. Bk. Value/Share	4.33		
Beta	1.09		

Value of $10,000 invested 5 years ago: NA

Fiscal Year Ending Sep. 30

	1998	1997	1996	1995	1994	1993
Revenues (Million $)						
1Q	159.1	88.87	52.17	34.75	28.04	20.40
2Q	172.2	96.70	63.22	39.35	27.89	21.30
3Q	197.1	105.4	71.18	44.59	28.90	22.10
4Q	—	114.2	78.51	49.11	30.30	24.70
Yr.	—	405.2	265.1	167.8	115.1	88.47
Earnings Per Share ($)						
1Q	**0.27**	**0.26**	0.17	0.10	0.09	0.05
2Q	**0.35**	0.27	0.19	0.12	0.08	0.06
3Q	**0.40**	0.29	0.21	0.14	0.09	0.21
4Q	—	0.29	0.23	0.15	-0.35	0.08
Yr.	—	1.11	0.80	0.51	-0.10	0.26

Next earnings report expected: late October

Dividend Data

Amount ($)	Date Decl.	Ex-Div. Date	Stock of Record	Payment Date
2-for-1	May. 18	Jun. 11	May. 20	Jun. 10 '98

A Division of The **McGraw·Hill** *Companies*

Business Summary - 12-AUG-98

Emphasizing a "one-stop" approach that includes everything from engineering design assistance to integration and testing of complete systems, Sanmina Corp. (SANM) has become a leading provider of customized integrated manufacturing services to original equipment manufacturers (OEMs) in the electronics industry. It also provides sophisticated electronic assembly and turnkey manufacturing management services, and makes custom cable assemblies for electronics industry OEMs.

The company targets its services to customers in four rapidly growing electronics industry sectors: telecommunications (55% of net sales in FY 97 -- Sep.), networking (data communications) (24%), industrial and medical instrumentation (15%) and computer systems (6%).

SANM's electronic assembly services involve the manufacture of complex printed circuit board assemblies using surface mount (SMT) and pin-through-hole (PTH) interconnection technologies, the manufacture of custom-designed backplane assemblies and complex multi-layer printed circuit boards, and the testing and assembly of completed systems.

SMT and PTH printed circuit board assemblies are printed circuit boards on which electronic components, such as integrated circuits, capacitors, microprocessors and resistors have been mounted. Backplane assemblies are large printed circuit boards on which connectors are mounted to receive and interconnect printed circuit boards and other electronic components. In FY 97, assembly revenues represented 95% of net sales and printed circuit boards 5%.

SANM locates its facilities close to customers, allowing it to meet their requirements on a quick-turn and cost-effective basis. The company manufactures its products in 17 decentralized plants, consisting of 9 assembly facilities and 8 printed circuit board fabrication facilities.

In November 1997, Sanmina acquired Elexsys International Inc. (ELEX) for about 3.3 million new SANM shares. Sanmina took a one-time merger-related charge of $3.9 million in the first quarter of FY 98. The company expects the transaction will be accretive to FY 98 earnings. A leading maker of high-performance medium and high-density backpanel assemblies, sophisticated subsystem assemblies and high-technology circuit boards, ELEX had net earnings of about $8.3 million on revenues of about $156 million in the 12 months through June 1997.

Per Share Data ($)

(Year Ended Sep. 30)	1997	1996	1995	1994	1993	1992	1991	1990	1989	1988
Tangible Bk. Val.	4.33	2.83	1.80	1.46	0.46	0.28	NA	NA	NA	NA
Cash Flow	1.47	1.03	0.53	0.04	0.44	0.13	NA	NA	NA	NA
Earnings	1.11	0.80	0.51	-0.10	0.26	0.00	NA	NA	NA	NA
Dividends	Nil	Nil	Nil	Nil	Nil	Nil	Nil	Nil	Nil	Nil
Payout Ratio	Nil	Nil	Nil	Nil	Nil	Nil	Nil	Nil	Nil	Nil
Prices - High	45³/₈	28³/₈	14³/₈	7⁷/₈	7³/₈	NA	NA	NA	NA	NA
- Low	19	10¹/₈	6¹/₂	3⁷/₈	2¹/₂	NA	NA	NA	NA	NA
P/E Ratio - High	41	35	28	NM	29	NA	NA	NA	NA	NA
- Low	17	13	13	NM	10	NA	NA	NA	NA	NA

Income Statement Analysis (Million $)

	1997	1996	1995	1994	1993	1992	1991	1990	1989	1988
Revs.	405	265	168	115	88.5	65.1	NA	NA	NA	NA
Oper. Inc.	81.5	53.4	31.7	22.4	16.5	6.1	NA	NA	NA	NA
Depr.	12.9	8.1	4.7	4.4	4.1	3.5	NA	NA	NA	NA
Int. Exp.	5.1	5.2	0.7	0.1	2.6	1.6	NA	NA	NA	NA
Pretax Inc.	67.1	45.3	28.0	3.6	9.9	NA	NA	NA	NA	NA
Eff. Tax Rate	39%	38%	39%	187%	40%	NA	NA	NA	NA	NA
Net Inc.	40.9	28.1	17.0	-3.1	5.9	0.0	NA	NA	NA	NA

Balance Sheet & Other Fin. Data (Million $)

	1997	1996	1995	1994	1993	1992	1991	1990	1989	1988
Cash	122	115	107	25.9	0.6	NA	NA	NA	NA	NA
Curr. Assets	234	185	163	55.8	23.4	NA	NA	NA	NA	NA
Total Assets	303	231	188	64.5	45.6	41.7	NA	NA	NA	NA
Curr. Liab.	60.3	40.0	34.0	17.7	15.0	NA	NA	NA	NA	NA
LT Debt	86.3	86.3	86.3	Nil	4.4	8.8	NA	NA	NA	NA
Common Eqty.	156	104	67.1	46.7	26.1	20.9	NA	NA	NA	NA
Total Cap.	242	190	154	46.7	30.6	29.6	NA	NA	NA	NA
Cap. Exp.	30.2	21.8	9.9	4.1	3.1	NA	NA	NA	NA	NA
Cash Flow	53.8	36.2	17.7	1.3	10.0	3.4	NA	NA	NA	NA
Curr. Ratio	3.9	4.6	4.8	3.1	1.6	NA	NA	NA	NA	NA
% LT Debt of Cap.	35.6	45.4	56.0	Nil	14.5	29.6	NA	NA	NA	NA
% Net Inc.of Revs.	10.1	10.6	10.1	NM	6.7	NM	NM	NM	NM	NM
% Ret. on Assets	15.3	13.4	13.5	NM	10.2	NA	NA	NA	NA	NA
% Ret. on Equity	31.5	32.9	29.9	NM	45.1	NA	NA	NA	NA	NA

Data as orig. reptd.; bef. results of disc. opers. and/or spec. items. Per share data adj. for stk. divs. as of ex-div. date. Bold denotes diluted EPS (FASB 128). E-Estimated. NA-Not Available. NM-Not Meaningful. NR-Not Ranked.

Office—355 East Trimble Rd., San Jose, CA 95131. **Tel**—(408) 954-5500. **Fax**—(408) 943-1401.**Website**—http://www.sanmina.com **Chrmn & CEO**—J. Sola. **Pres, COO & Investor Contact**—Randy W. Furr. **Dirs**—J. Bolger, N. R. Bonke, M. M. Rosati, J. Sola, B. Vonderschmitt. **Transfer Agent & Registrar**—Norwest Bank Minnesota, South St. Paul. **Incorporated**—in Delaware in 1989. **Empl**— 2,522. **S&P Analyst:** Stephen J. Tekirian

Santa Fe Energy Resources   1979N

NYSE Symbol **SFR**

In S&P SmallCap 600

03-OCT-98

Industry:
Oil & Gas (Exploration & Production)

Summary: This independent crude oil and natural gas company engages in exploration, development and production, primarily in the U.S., but also in Argentina and Indonesia.

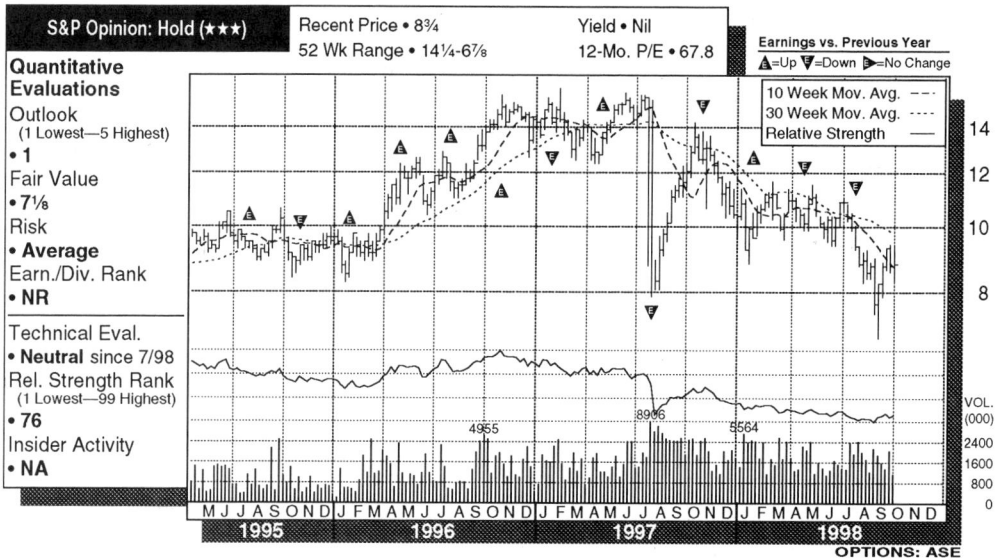

| S&P Opinion: Hold (★★★) | Recent Price • 8¾ | Yield • Nil |
| | 52 Wk Range • 14¼-6⅞ | 12-Mo. P/E • 67.8 |

Quantitative Evaluations

Outlook
(1 Lowest—5 Highest)
• **1**

Fair Value
• **7⅛**

Risk
• **Average**

Earn./Div. Rank
• **NR**

Technical Eval.
• **Neutral** since 7/98

Rel. Strength Rank
(1 Lowest—99 Highest)
• **76**

Insider Activity
• **NA**

Earnings vs. Previous Year
▲=Up ▼=Down ▶=No Change

10 Week Mov. Avg. ---
30 Week Mov. Avg. ····
Relative Strength —

OPTIONS: ASE

Overview - 28-JUL-98

SFR's disposition of its Monterey Resources subsidiary in July 1997 has allowed the company to concentrate on operations with similar capital needs and risk profiles. More importantly, SFR is now able to focus more attention toward its international activities, where it sees most of its future growth. The company has in fact ramped up international drilling, and announced several potentially significant discoveries and exploratory agreements. Despite a 23% increase in production on a BOE basis, revenues were essentially flat for the second quarter of 1998 ($77.8 million versus $75.1 million in 1997), due to weak oil prices. Santa Fe has maintained or reduced most of its costs; second quarter operating costs were $3.97 per BOE, down from $4.36 in the first quarter, and total costs were $11.96 per BOE, versus $13.12. SFR is one of the rare companies that has actually reduced G&A costs.

Valuation - 28-JUL-98

Santa Fe shares have performed poorly, and are currently trading near their 52-week low. The very weak oil price environment is responsible for the decline, as Santa Fe is primarily an oil company (75% of 1997 reserves, and 60% of production during the second quarter consisted of oil). Until we see strength in oil prices, we would not add to current holdings. However, the company may prove to be of long term interest, as recent discoveries become reserves, and eventually produce formations. Shares are presently trading at a slight discount to our estimated present value of reserves of $13, a common occurrence among oil companies today.

Key Stock Statistics

S&P EPS Est. 1998	0.30	Tang. Bk. Value/Share	4.40
P/E on S&P Est. 1998	29.4	Beta	0.23
S&P EPS Est. 1999	0.40	Shareholders	38,500
Dividend Rate/Share	Nil	Market cap. (B)	$0.905
Shs. outstg. (M)	102.7	Inst. holdings	63%
Avg. daily vol. (M)	0.326		

Value of $10,000 invested 5 years ago: NA

Fiscal Year Ending Dec. 31

	1998	1997	1996	1995	1994	1993
Revenues (Million $)						
1Q	68.80	173.9	123.7	98.60	90.30	115.3
2Q	77.80	149.8	137.5	109.7	99.7	116.3
3Q	—	101.8	149.4	111.1	103.6	102.7
4Q	—	89.20	172.7	122.6	97.80	102.6
Yr.	—	514.7	583.3	442.0	391.4	436.9
Earnings Per Share ($)						
1Q	Nil	0.27	0.10	Nil	•0.05	•0.02
2Q	Nil	0.03	0.15	0.04	0.02	0.02
3Q	—	0.10	0.14	0.04	0.08	0.01
4Q	—	0.04	-0.45	0.05	0.01	-0.95
Yr.	E0.30	0.43	-0.05	0.13	0.06	-0.94

Next earnings report expected: NA

Dividend Data

Dividends, which were initiated in late 1991, were suspended in May 1996.

Business Summary - 28-JUL-98

Following the spin-off of Monterey in July 1997, Santa Fe Resources (SFR) transformed itself from a domestic oil company to a company focused on international exploration, and maintaining a more balanced reserve base of oil and gas. However, Santa Fe is still primarily an oil company; approximately 75% of 1997 reserves and 60% of production during the second quarter of 1998, were comprised of oil.

The new Santa Fe has three divisions. The Central Division consists of properties in the Permian Basin of West Texas, and in Southeastern New Mexico. The Gulf Division, an area that contributed 42% of SFR's natural gas reserves, is located primarily in shallow waters of the Gulf of Mexico. Santa Fe has numerous exploration and drilling activities in its International Division. Most of these projects are in Indonesia, Argentina, and Gabon. Other recently announced discoveries and exploration licenses are located in Ecuador, China, and Malaysia. Total production from the International Division has more than doubled, on a BOE basis, during the past year; in the second quarter of 1998, about 24.8 MBOE/d were produced, versus 11.7 MBOE/d in the prior year. International reserves represent 36% of the company's total, up from 23% in 1996.

At the end of 1997, total reserves were 171.1 MMBOE, up 38% from the 124 MMBOE at the begin-

ning of the year. Production in 1997 averaged 30.3 MBbls. of crude oil and liquids and 174.7 MMcf of natural gas per day, representing a 9% increase on a BOE basis. Average sales price was $18.02 and $2.25 for oil and gas, respectively. During 1997, SFR replaced 326% of the year's production. Capital expenditures for 1998 are budgeted at $277 million, versus $265 million in 1997.

Santa Fe's decision to spin-off Monterey was because of the divergence of its capital requirements and risk profile; the company concluded that two distinct companies could operate more efficiently, and would create more value for shareholders. Monterey was actually formed as a subsidiary to help effect the spin-off. Some 9.3 million shares of Monterey common stock were sold in a November 1996 IPO. Proceeds from the offering were used primarily to retire outstanding long-term debt. SFR distributed the remaining 83% of Monterey shares to SFR stockholders in July 1997. Subsequently, in November, Texaco purchased Monterey in a transaction for $1.39 billion in stock and assumed debt. Monterey shareholders received 0.3471 shares of Texaco common for each Monterey share. Based in Bakersfield, CA, Monterey conducts oil and gas operations in California, primarily in the San Joaquin Valley, and represents the three largest producing oil fields in the 48 contiguous states.

Per Share Data ($)

(Year Ended Dec. 31)	1997	1996	1995	1994	1993	1992	1991	1990	1989	1988
Tangible Bk. Val.	4.41	4.78	3.85	3.67	3.56	4.63	3.49	3.35	3.17	NA
Cash Flow	1.81	2.10	1.61	1.41	1.87	1.78	1.96	2.00	1.60	NA
Earnings	0.43	-0.06	0.13	0.06	-0.94	-0.07	0.29	0.28	0.03	NA
Dividends	Nil	Nil	Nil	Nil	0.12	0.16	0.16	0.12	NA	NA
Payout Ratio	Nil	Nil	Nil	Nil	NM	NM	55%	45%	NA	NA
Prices - High	16	15⅝	10⅝	10	11⅞	9⅞	16¾	22⅜	NA	NA
- Low	7⅞	8¼	7⅞	7½	7¾	7	7	13¾	NA	NA
P/E Ratio - High	37	NM	82	NM	NM	NM	58	80	NA	NA
- Low	18	NM	61	NM	NM	NM	24	49	NA	NA

Income Statement Analysis (Million $)

	1997	1996	1995	1994	1993	1992	1991	1990	1989	1988
Revs.	515	583	442	391	437	428	380	383	323	NA
Oper. Inc.	235	283	218	168	178	191	172	176	146	NA
Depr. Depl. & Amort.	128	148	133	121	252	146	107	107	101	NA
Int. Exp.	17.1	37.6	32.5	27.5	45.8	55.6	47.3	57.1	54.1	NA
Pretax Inc.	95.6	58.0	36.3	23.0	-149	-1.0	33.0	28.0	13.0	NA
Eff. Tax Rate	38%	25%	27%	26%	NM	NM	43%	39%	87%	NA
Net Inc.	54.7	42.4	26.6	17.1	-77.1	-1.4	18.5	17.0	1.7	NA

Balance Sheet & Other Fin. Data (Million $)

	1997	1996	1995	1994	1993	1992	1991	1990	1989	1988
Cash	5.6	14.6	42.6	53.7	4.8	83.8	28.2	47.7	34.2	NA
Curr. Assets	113	173	159	157	173	205	100	145	135	NA
Total Assets	780	1,120	1,065	1,071	1,077	1,337	912	911	905	NA
Curr. Liab.	134	179	110	126	166	172	97.0	130	213	NA
LT Debt	122	279	344	350	405	493	441	417	350	NA
Common Eqty.	455	435	346	332	324	417	225	216	202	NA
Total Cap.	615	909	926	910	853	1,108	772	737	653	NA
Cap. Exp.	416	224	223	139	151	536	174	107	NA	NA
Cash Flow	179	191	145	127	168	141	125	124	102	NA
Curr. Ratio	0.8	1.0	1.5	1.2	1.0	1.2	1.0	1.1	0.6	NA
% LT Debt of Cap.	19.8	30.7	37.2	38.5	47.5	44.5	57.1	56.6	53.5	NA
% Ret. on Assets	5.7	3.9	2.5	1.6	NM	NM	2.0	1.7	NA	NA
% Ret. on Equity	11.5	7.4	3.5	1.6	NM	NM	8.4	6.9	NA	NA

Data as orig. reptd.; bef. results of disc opers. and/or spec. items. Per share data adj. for stk. divs. as of ex-div. date. Bold denotes diluted EPS (FASB 128). E-Estimated. NA-Not Available. NM-Not Meaningful. NR-Not Ranked.

Office—1616 S. Voss, Suite 1000, Houston, TX 77057. **Tel**—(713) 507-5000. **Chrmn & CEO**—J. L. Payne. **Pres & COO**—H. L. Boyt. **VP Fin, CFO & Treas**—J. F. Clark. **Secy**—M. A. Older. **Investor Contact**—Kathy E. Hager (713-507-5315). **Dirs**—W. E. Greehey, M. N. Klein, A. V. Martini, J. L. Payne, R. F. Richards, M. J. Shapiro, K. D. Wriston. **Transfer Agent & Registrar**—First Chicago Trust Co. of New York, Jersey City, NJ. **Incorporated**—in Delaware in 1971. **Empl**— 1,209. **S&P Analyst:** Ephraim Juskowicz

03-OCT-98   Industry:
Tobacco

Summary: This company is the world's largest supplier of fine papers to the tobacco industry, and also manufactures specialty papers for use in other industries.

Quantitative Evaluations	
Outlook (1 Lowest—5 Highest)	**• NA**
Fair Value	**• NA**
Risk	**• Low**
Earn./Div. Rank	**• NR**
Technical Eval.	**• NA**
Rel. Strength Rank (1 Lowest—99 Highest)	**• 48**
Insider Activity	**• NA**

Recent Price • 22
52 Wk Range • 44½-21¼

Yield • 2.7%
12-Mo. P/E • 8.3

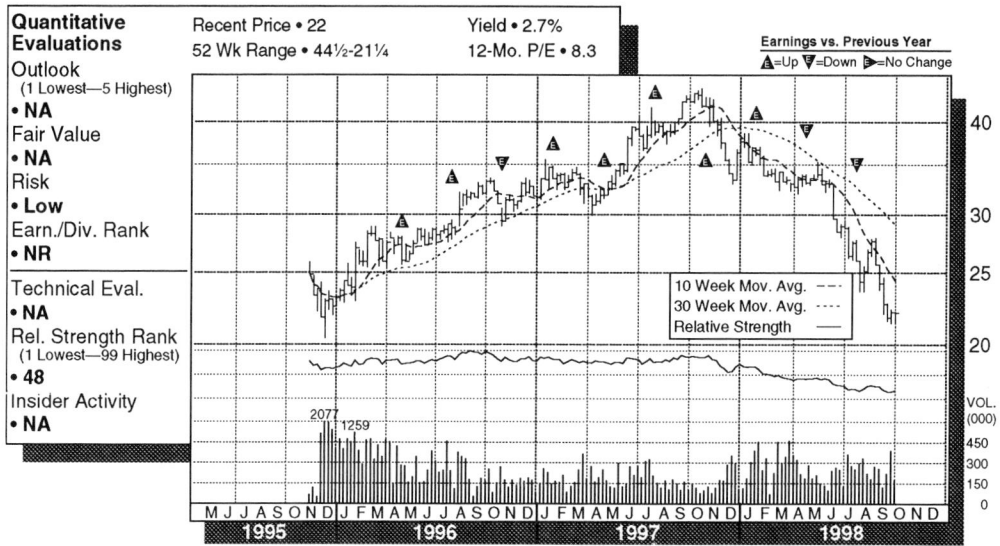

Earnings vs. Previous Year
▲=Up ▼=Down ▶=No Change

10 Week Mov. Avg. — — -
30 Week Mov. Avg. ·······
Relative Strength ——

Business Profile - 02-JUL-98

Recently enacted higher French corporate income tax rates are expected to reduce the company's net income in 1998 and 1999. In February 1998, SWM acquired a 99.97% interest in Companhia Industrial de Papel Pirahy for $62 million. Pirahy is the largest supplier of tobacco-related papers to the South American market and also produces printing and writing papers as well as papers for packaging and labeling applications. Pirahy, together with SWM's existing business, will increase SWM's market share of tobacco-related papers in South America to about 51%. Also in February, SWM acquired Ingefico, S.A. and its pulp and specialty paper manufacturing subsidiaries, located in southwestern France.

Operational Review - 02-JUL-98

Net sales for the three months ended March 31, 1998, advanced 19%, year to year, reflecting two acquisitions in February 1998, as well as stronger sales in France. Sales comparisons were unfavorably impacted by changes in currency exchange rates, primarily the result of a strengthened U.S. dollar versus the French franc. Margins narrowed, on a less favorable product mix; operating profit rose 5.8%. Following higher interest expense and taxes at 40.9%, versus 37.3%, net income slipped 12%, to $10.0 million ($0.61 a share) from $11.3 million ($0.69).

Stock Performance - 02-OCT-98

In the past 30 trading days, SWM's shares have declined 20%, compared to a 7% fall in the S&P 500. Average trading volume for the past five days was 34,640 shares, compared with the 40-day moving average of 46,913 shares.

Key Stock Statistics

Dividend Rate/Share	0.60	Shareholders	8,500
Shs. outstg. (M)	16.1	Market cap. (B)	$0.355
Avg. daily vol. (M)	0.047	Inst. holdings	64%
Tang. Bk. Value/Share	12.02		
Beta	NA		

Value of $10,000 invested 5 years ago: NA

Fiscal Year Ending Dec. 31

	1998	1997	1996	1995	1994	1993
Revenues (Million $)						
1Q	134.3	113.0	119.8	109.5	—	—
2Q	144.0	116.3	117.5	113.4	—	—
3Q	—	113.4	118.5	121.5	—	—
4Q	—	117.9	115.5	118.5	—	—
Yr.	—	460.6	471.3	462.9	—	—
Earnings Per Share ($)						
1Q	**0.61**	**0.69**	0.59	0.49	—	—
2Q	**0.76**	**0.79**	0.66	0.46	—	—
3Q	—	**0.68**	0.61	0.75	—	—
4Q	—	**0.62**	0.56	0.11	—	—
Yr.	—	**2.77**	2.41	1.81	—	—

Next earnings report expected: late October

Dividend Data (Dividends have been paid since 1996.)

Amount ($)	Date Decl.	Ex-Div. Date	Stock of Record	Payment Date
0.150	Oct. 23	Nov. 06	Nov. 10	Dec. 08 '97
0.150	Jan. 29	Feb. 05	Feb. 09	Mar. 09 '98
0.150	Apr. 23	May. 07	May. 11	Jun. 08 '98
0.150	Jul. 30	Aug. 06	Aug. 10	Sep. 14 '98

A Division of The **McGraw·Hill** *Companies*

Business Summary - 02-JUL-98

Schweitzer-Mauduit International, Inc. (SWM) is a diversified producer of premium specialty papers and the world's largest supplier of fine papers to the tobacco industry. It also manufactures specialty papers for use in various other industries. Formerly a wholly owned subsidiary of Kimberly-Clark Corp. (KMB), SWM was spun off by that company to its shareholders on November 30, 1995, with KMB shareholders receiving one SWM common share for every 10 KMB common shares held.

The company's tobacco industry products, which accounted for 94% of 1997 net sales, include cigarette, tipping and plug wrap papers (cigarette papers) used to wrap various parts of a cigarette, reconstituted tobacco wrappers and binders for cigars, and reconstituted tobacco leaf for use as filler in cigarettes and cigars. These products are sold directly to the major tobacco companies or their designated converters in North America, Western Europe, China and elsewhere. Net sales to Philip Morris Companies, Inc. accounted for 36% of net sales in 1997. Operations outside the U.S. accounted for 58% of net sales and 76% of operating profits in 1997.

Cigarette paper wraps the column of tobacco in a cigarette and has certain properties, such as basic weight, porosity, opacity, tensile strength, texture and whiteness, which must be closely controlled to tight toler-ances. SWM believes that it has 58% of the U.S. and Canadian cigarette paper markets.

Plug wrap forms the outer layer of a cigarette filter and holds the filter material in a cylindrical form. SWM's U.S. operations are believed to have a 75% share of the U.S. and Canadian markets for plug wrap.

Tipping paper, produced in white or buff color, joins the cigarette's filter element to the tobacco section of the cigarette. SWM's U.S. operations have an estimated 58% share of the U.S. and Canadian markets for base tipping paper which is subsequently printed by converters.

Reconstituted tobacco is used by manufacturers of cigarettes, cigars and other tobacco products mainly as a filler that is blended with virgin tobacco in order to use otherwise wasted parts of the tobacco leaf. In April 1996, SWM exited the reconstituted tobacco leaf business in the U.S., however, in the fourth quarter of 1997, SWM temporarily restarted its U.S. reconstituted tobacco leaf business, but only in support of its 72% owned French subsidiary.

Nontobacco related products, which accounted for about 6% of 1997 net sales, included drinking straw wrap, lightweight printing papers, battery separator paper and other specialized papers. These products are generally sold directly to converters and other end-users. The production of tea bag and coffee filter papers was phased out in the U.S. in 1996.

Per Share Data ($)

(Year Ended Dec. 31)	1997	1996	1995	1994	1993	1992	1991	1990	1989	1988
Tangible Bk. Val.	11.17	9.72	8.09	NA	NA	NA	NA	NA	NA	NA
Cash Flow	3.65	3.25	2.64	NA	NA	NA	NA	NA	NA	NA
Earnings	2.77	2.41	1.81	NA	NA	NA	NA	NA	NA	NA
Dividends	0.60	0.45	Nil	Nil	Nil	Nil	Nil	Nil	Nil	Nil
Payout Ratio	33%	19%	Nil	Nil	Nil	Nil	Nil	Nil	Nil	Nil
Prices - High	44½	33⅝	23⅝	NA	NA	NA	NA	NA	NA	NA
- Low	29⅞	22¾	20⅜	NA	NA	NA	NA	NA	NA	NA
P/E Ratio - High	16	14	13	NA	NA	NA	NA	NA	NA	NA
- Low	11	9	11	NA	NA	NA	NA	NA	NA	NA

Income Statement Analysis (Million $)

	1997	1996	1995	1994	1993	1992	1991	1990	1989	1988
Revs.	461	471	463	NA	NA	NA	NA	NA	NA	NA
Oper. Inc.	96.3	87.4	74.9	NA	NA	NA	NA	NA	NA	NA
Depr.	14.4	13.4	13.4	NA	NA	NA	NA	NA	NA	NA
Int. Exp.	4.1	5.3	8.0	NA	NA	NA	NA	NA	NA	NA
Pretax Inc.	79.4	69.9	45.8	NA	NA	NA	NA	NA	NA	NA
Eff. Tax Rate	36%	37%	28%	NA	NA	NA	NA	NA	NA	NA
Net Inc.	45.3	38.7	29.0	NA	NA	NA	NA	NA	NA	NA

Balance Sheet & Other Fin. Data (Million $)

	1997	1996	1995	1994	1993	1992	1991	1990	1989	1988
Cash	37.2	30.9	5.9	NA	NA	NA	NA	NA	NA	NA
Curr. Assets	158	151	138	NA	NA	NA	NA	NA	NA	NA
Total Assets	391	381	347	NA	NA	NA	NA	NA	NA	NA
Curr. Liab.	90.5	102	94.1	NA	NA	NA	NA	NA	NA	NA
LT Debt	80.8	86.6	91.6	NA	NA	NA	NA	NA	NA	NA
Common Eqty.	180	156	130	NA	NA	NA	NA	NA	NA	NA
Total Cap.	279	259	235	NA	NA	NA	NA	NA	NA	NA
Cap. Exp.	35.8	51.5	22.5	NA	NA	NA	NA	NA	NA	NA
Cash Flow	59.7	52.1	42.4	NA	NA	NA	NA	NA	NA	NA
Curr. Ratio	1.7	1.5	1.5	NA	NA	NA	NA	NA	NA	NA
% LT Debt of Cap.	29.0	33.4	39.0	NA	NA	NA	NA	NA	NA	NA
% Net Inc.of Revs.	9.8	8.2	6.3	NA	NA	NA	NA	NA	NA	NA
% Ret. on Assets	11.7	10.6	NM	NM	NM	NM	NM	NM	NM	NM
% Ret. on Equity	26.9	27.1	NM	NM	NM	NM	NM	NM	NM	NM

Data as orig. reptd.; bef. results of disc. opers. and/or spec. items. Per share data adj. for stk. divs. as of ex-div. date. Bold denotes diluted EPS (FASB 128). E-Estimated. NA-Not Available. NM-Not Meaningful. NR-Not Ranked.

Office—100 North Point Center East, Suite 600, Alpharetta, GA 30022-8246. **Tel**—1-800-514-0186. **Chrmn & CEO**—W. H. Deitrich. **CFO & Treas**—P. C. Roberts. **Secy**—W. J. Sharkey. **Dirs**—C. L. Arnold, K.C. Caldabaugh, L. G. Chambaz, W. H. Deitrich, R. D. Jackson, L. J. Kujawa, J-P Le Hetet, L. B. Stillman. **Transfer Agent & Registrar**—First National Bank of Boston. **Incorporated**—in Delaware in 1995. **Empl**—3,500. **S&P Analyst:** M.I.

Scott Technologies   3869K

NASDAQ Symbol **SCTTA**

In S&P SmallCap 600

03-OCT-98

Industry:
Manufacturing (Diversified)

Summary: This company (formerly Figgie International) makes satellite-based electronic systems and life-support respiratory products.

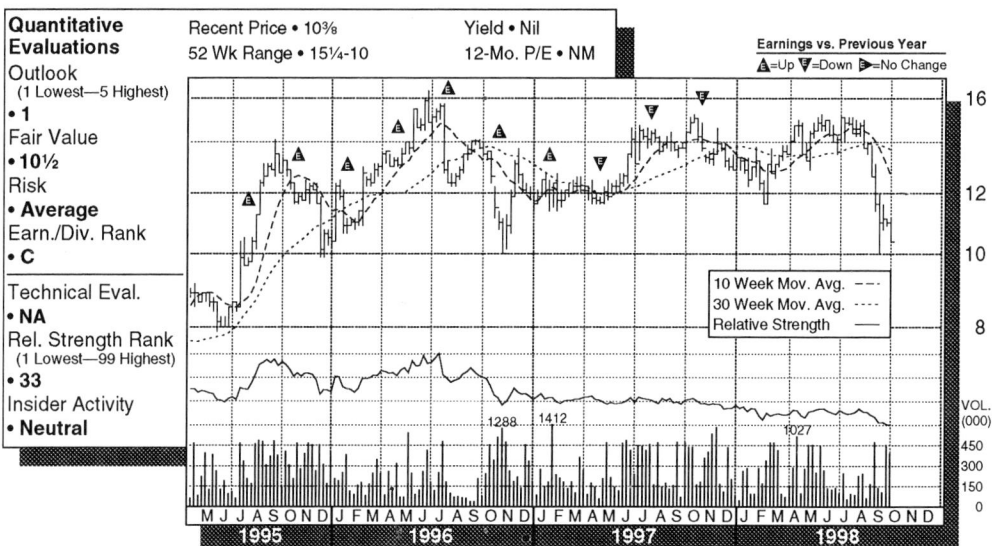

Quantitative Evaluations

Recent Price • 10⅜
52 Wk Range • 15¼-10

Yield • Nil
12-Mo. P/E • NM

Earnings vs. Previous Year
△=Up ▽=Down ▷=No Change

Outlook
(1 Lowest—5 Highest)
• **1**

Fair Value
• **10½**

Risk
• **Average**

Earn./Div. Rank
• **C**

Technical Eval.
• **NA**

Rel. Strength Rank
(1 Lowest—99 Highest)
• **33**

Insider Activity
• **Neutral**

10 Week Mov. Avg. ---
30 Week Mov. Avg. ·····
Relative Strength —

Business Profile - 14-SEP-98

This company operates in two business segments: satellite-based guidance, navigation and instrumentation systems; and life savings respiratory products. Its business plan is to focus on internal growth at both segments, investigate acquisitions for Scott Aviation, and consider strategies that may enhance shareholder value. In June 1998, Scott said it had retained Duff & Phelps, LLC to assist in the examination of a possible restructuring of its two classes of common stock into a single class of voting common stock. Each Class A share is entitled to one-twentieth of a vote per share, while each share of Class B common has one vote.

Operational Review - 14-SEP-98

Net sales in the six months ended June 30, 1998, rose 3.4%, year to year, as greater shipments of oxygen products outweighed a 16% drop in sales by the Interstate Electronics segment. Gross margins narrowed, but with lower R&D and interest costs, pretax income soared 87%. After taxes at 40.1%, versus 34.0%, income from continuing operations was up 69%, to $4,581,000 ($0.25 a share), from $2,704,000 ($0.15). Per share results exclude a charge of $0.09 for early extinguishment of debt in the 1998 period, and income from discontinued operations of $0.02 in the 1997 interim.

Stock Performance - 02-OCT-98

In the past 30 trading days, SCTTA's shares have declined 26%, compared to a 7% fall in the S&P 500. Average trading volume for the past five days was 78,040 shares, compared with the 40-day moving average of 59,474 shares.

Key Stock Statistics

Dividend Rate/Share	Nil	Shareholders	10,900
Shs. outstg. (M)	18.6	Market cap. (B)	$0.144
Avg. daily vol. (M)	0.056	Inst. holdings	55%
Tang. Bk. Value/Share	3.97		
Beta	0.88		

Value of $10,000 invested 5 years ago: $ 6,391

Fiscal Year Ending Dec. 31

	1998	1997	1996	1995	1994	1993
Revenues (Million $)						
1Q	64.86	62.65	96.70	85.27	73.11	181.1
2Q	64.85	62.77	101.4	88.69	80.03	204.0
3Q	—	60.15	95.40	92.35	79.79	189.4
4Q	—	63.03	92.20	92.73	86.49	194.3
Yr.	—	248.6	385.7	359.0	319.4	768.6
Earnings Per Share ($)						
1Q	0.04	0.06	0.20	-0.44	-0.91	-0.02
2Q	0.20	0.09	0.34	-0.32	-0.50	0.01
3Q	—	0.05	0.31	0.05	-0.61	-0.92
4Q	—	—	1.84	0.13	-2.74	-9.03
Yr.	—	-0.08	2.69	-0.68	-4.81	-10.09

Next earnings report expected: NA

Dividend Data

Cash was paid by the company and its predecessor in each year since 1965. Payments were suspended in 1994.

A Division of The McGraw-Hill Companies

Business Summary - 14-SEP-98

Operations of Scott Technologies (formerly Figgie International) currently consist of two manufacturing segments: sophisticated electronic systems and protective breathing and oxygen equipment. As part of a further refining of its corporate strategic focus, the company agreed in July 1997 to sell its aerial work platform unit. The sale, which allows the company to concentrate on the growth potential of its other two business divisions, marked another step in the company's evolution from a broad-based conglomerate to a more tightly focused, highly profitable growth enterprise. In August 1997, directors rejected a proposal by Heico Holding, Inc. to acquire SCTTA for $15 a share.

Lower revenues from the military for strategic weapon systems and a $7.6 million restructuring charge for the elimination of certain classes of products hurt profits in the Interstate Electronics segment in 1997. However, the Scott division benefited from the impact of emergency escape breathing equipment sales to the government, increased oxygen product sales to aviation customers and higher breathing apparatus sales to safety customers.

Interstate Electronics products include sophisticated telemetry, instrumentation and data recording systems and position measuring systems, Global Positioning Systems (GPS) for the U.S. Navy's Polaris/Poseidon, TRIDENT and TRIDENT II ships; precise GPS for aircraft and turnkey test ranges; and GPS for commercial and business aircraft and landing systems. It also designs and produces a variety of tube display systems and satellite communication modems and terminals. About 87% of Interstate's sales in 1997 were from the U.S. government, down from more than 91% in 1996. Sales from this division made up 36% of total revenues in 1997, and 23% in 1996.

Scott division products consist primarily of the Scott Air Pak and other life support products for fire fighting and personal protection against industrial contaminants; air purifying products that provide protection against environmental and safety hazards; and protective breathing equipment and oxygen masks. Scott also manufactures instruments to detect the presence of combustible or toxic gases and the lack of oxygen. Sales from the Scott division made up 64% of total revenues in 1997, and 36% in 1996.

In November 1997, the company sold its Snorkel division, which made self-propelled aerial work platforms and scissorlifts; and services booms mounted on fire apparatus to deliver large quantities of water from elevated positions.

Per Share Data ($)

(Year Ended Dec. 31)	1997	1996	1995	1994	1993	1992	1991	1990	1989	1988
Tangible Bk. Val.	3.72	0.76	1.64	2.44	7.30	16.15	15.44	14.23	12.34	12.80
Cash Flow	0.29	3.07	-0.23	-2.46	-8.74	3.53	3.95	4.08	4.32	4.29
Earnings	-0.08	2.69	-0.68	-4.81	-10.09	1.61	1.72	2.28	3.04	3.01
Dividends	Nil	Nil	Nil	Nil	0.43	0.50	0.50	0.50	0.40	0.34
Payout Ratio	Nil	Nil	Nil	Nil	NM	33%	31%	24%	13%	12%
Prices - High	15¼	16⅜	14⅛	14½	22	26½	25	35½	32	32⅜
- Low	11⅜	10	5⅞	4⅝	12½	17	16½	15	25⅛	24⅛
P/E Ratio - High	NM	6	NM	NM	NM	16	15	16	11	11
- Low	NM	4	NM	NM	NM	11	10	7	8	8

Income Statement Analysis (Million $)

	1997	1996	1995	1994	1993	1992	1991	1990	1989	1988
Revs.	249	386	359	319	769	1,173	1,243	1,361	1,313	1,200
Oper. Inc.	29.4	47.1	29.4	27.0	-47.0	109	126	147	157	139
Depr.	6.9	7.2	6.3	41.6	24.0	33.6	32.8	31.5	35.1	26.3
Int. Exp.	22.2	20.2	29.7	42.9	35.6	38.3	42.7	44.6	34.9	21.4
Pretax Inc.	-1.4	22.6	-10.5	-107	-250	41.2	43.2	64.5	99	98.1
Eff. Tax Rate	Nil	Nil	Nil	NM	NM	31%	31%	39%	37%	37%
Net Inc.	-1.4	50.3	-19.5	-85.0	-178	28.3	30.1	39.7	62.9	61.9

Balance Sheet & Other Fin. Data (Million $)

	1997	1996	1995	1994	1993	1992	1991	1990	1989	1988
Cash	104	44.4	25.9	47.0	34.0	117	110	98.0	83.0	65.0
Curr. Assets	182	189	179	460	534	516	NA	NA	NA	NA
Total Assets	343	373	367	644	998	1,113	1,109	1,066	1,027	1,022
Curr. Liab.	55.1	67.9	88.4	316	677	282	NA	NA	NA	NA
LT Debt	161	184	195	234	65.0	353	373	375	367	200
Common Eqty.	71.6	74.5	49.6	65.0	203	395	378	352	317	366
Total Cap.	233	259	245	300	289	798	804	760	714	640
Cap. Exp.	8.7	10.3	6.2	60.0	96.0	112	98.0	81.0	78.0	65.0
Cash Flow	5.5	57.5	-4.2	-44.0	-154	61.9	62.9	71.1	89.5	88.2
Curr. Ratio	3.3	2.8	2.0	1.5	0.8	1.8	NA	NA	NA	NA
% LT Debt of Cap.	69.3	71.0	79.6	78.2	22.4	44.3	46.3	49.4	51.4	31.3
% Net Inc.of Revs.	NM	13.0	NM	NM	NM	2.4	2.4	2.9	4.8	5.2
% Ret. on Assets	NM	13.6	NM	NM	NM	2.6	2.8	3.8	6.6	7.1
% Ret. on Equity	NM	8.1	NM	NM	NM	7.3	8.2	11.9	20.1	17.2

Data as orig. reptd.; bef. results of disc. opers. and/or spec. items. Per share data adj. for stk. divs. as of ex-div. date. Bold denotes diluted EPS (FASB 128). E-Estimated. NA-Not Available. NM-Not Meaningful. NR-Not Ranked.

Office—5875 Landerbrook Dr., Suite 250, Mayfield Heights, OH 44124 **Tel**—(440) 446-1333. **Office of the Chrmn**—J. P. Reilly, G. W. Lindemann. **SVP & CFO**—M. A. Kirk. **VP & Secy**—D. L. Kackley. **Investor Contact**—Robert Berick (440-684-3416). **Dirs**—F. J. Brinkman, R. P. Collins, N. C. Lind, G. W. Lindemann, F. N. Linsalata, F. R. McKnight, H. Nesbitt II, J. P. Reilly. **Transfer Agent & Registrar**—First National Bank of Boston. **Incorporated**—in Ohio in 1963; reincorporated in Delaware in 1983. **Empl**— 1,700. **S&P Analyst**: P.L.H.

Scotts Co.

1988H

NYSE Symbol **SMG**

In S&P SmallCap 600

03-OCT-98

Industry:
Hardware & Tools

Summary: This company is the leading U.S. producer of consumer do-it-yourself lawn care and commercial turf care products and the leading marketer of garden plant foods.

S&P Opinion: Accumulate (★★★★)	

Recent Price • 30¾	Yield • Nil
52 Wk Range • 41⅝-25¾	12-Mo. P/E • 19.3

Earnings vs. Previous Year
▲=Up ▼=Down ▷=No Change

Quantitative Evaluations

Outlook
(1 Lowest—5 Highest)
• **3**

Fair Value
• **30⅞**

Risk
• **Average**

Earn./Div. Rank
• **NR**

Technical Eval.
• **NA**

Rel. Strength Rank
(1 Lowest—99 Highest)
• **76**

Insider Activity
• **Neutral**

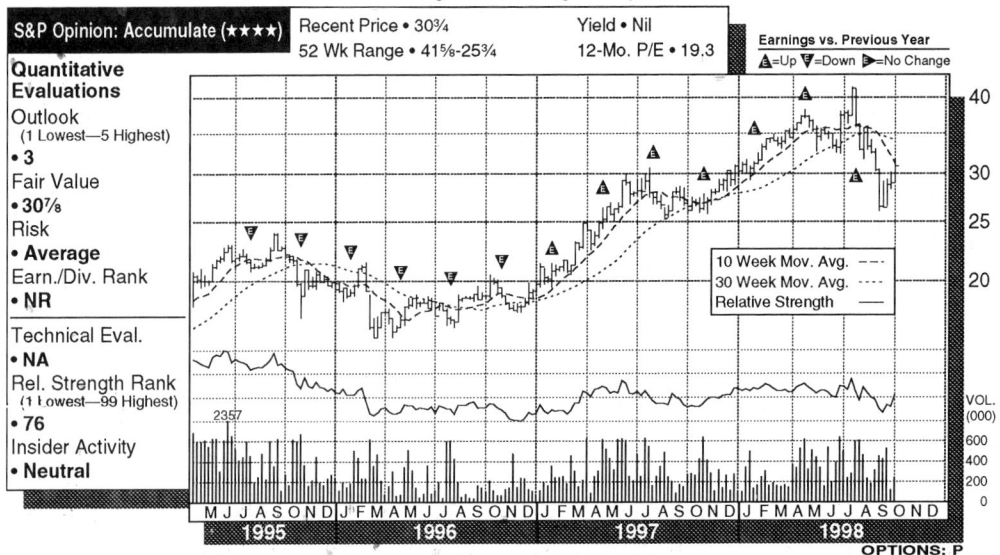

10 Week Mov. Avg. ---
30 Week Mov. Avg. ····
Relative Strength —

VOL. (000)

OPTIONS: P

Overview - 30-JUL-98

Scotts reported favorable results for the first nine months of FY 98 (Sep.), as 24% revenue growth reflected the recent acquisitions of Miracle Garden Care, the Levington Group, and Earthgro. Pro forma sales for the period rose 9.4%, as the company continues to increase its already dominant share of the North American consumer lawn and garden markets. SMG essentially completed its latest acquisition program with several announcements in third quarter of FY 98. SMG announced its intent to acquire the consumer lawn and garden businesses of Monsanto (MTC), including its prominent Ortho pesticide brand, the marketing rights to MTC's Roundup brand of consumer herbicide products, the European consumer lawn and garden businesses of Rhone-Poulenc, and a privately held Netherlands based lawn and garden company. Upon completion of these acquisitions (all expected to close by October, 1998) Scotts will hold the leading brand name positions in consumer lawns, gardens, growing media (primarily potting soils), and pesticides, in both North America and continental Europe. We also anticipate another successful fall promotional campaign, as the 1997 program led to a doubling of fall fertilizer sales.

Valuation - 30-JUL-98

We continue to recommend accumulation of the shares as we view Scotts as well positioned for steady long-term growth. The company is committed to sustaining 15% average annual compounded earnings growth, on 8%-9% revenue gains, and improving operating margins by 2 percentage points over the next four years. Additionally, with its leading market share position and strong brand name recognition, we believe the stock warrants a premium valuation. We view the shares as an attractive investment at 19 times our FY 99 (Sep.) EPS estimate of $1.90.

Key Stock Statistics

S&P EPS Est. 1998	1.60	Tang. Bk. Value/Share	NM
P/E on S&P Est. 1998	19.3	Beta	0.51
S&P EPS Est. 1999	1.90	Shareholders	6,500
Dividend Rate/Share	Nil	Market cap. (B)	$0.576
Shs. outstg. (M)	18.7	Inst. holdings	85%
Avg. daily vol. (M)	0.068		

Value of $10,000 invested 5 years ago: $ 14,248

Fiscal Year Ending Sep. 30

	1998	1997	1996	1995	1994	1993
Revenues (Million $)						
1Q	125.1	100.2	117.9	98.00	68.30	67.80
2Q	430.6	346.2	251.2	236.1	207.4	161.1
3Q	367.5	299.0	248.0	229.0	200.9	156.3
4Q	—	155.4	134.8	169.7	129.7	80.90
Yr.	—	900.8	751.9	732.8	606.3	466.0

Earnings Per Share ($)						
1Q	-0.42	-0.45	-0.51	-0.17	-0.08	Nil
2Q	**1.10**	0.95	0.36	0.79	0.69	0.55
3Q	**0.80**	0.71	0.26	0.48	0.50	0.44
4Q	**E-0.30**	-0.32	-0.86	-0.10	0.16	0.14
Yr.	**E1.60**	1.35	-0.65	0.99	1.27	1.07

Next earnings report expected: late October

Dividend Data

No dividends have been paid.

A Division of The **McGraw·Hill** *Companies*

Business Summary - 30-JUL-98

The Scotts Company is the leading U.S. producer and marketer of consumer do-it-yourself lawn and garden care and professional golf course turf care products. The company's long history of innovative products and its reputation for quality and service have enabled it to maintain the leading positions in its markets. Historically, the company has had two business groups -- Consumer and Professional -- to serve its domestic markets, and an international group to serve markets outside of North America. In FY 97 (Sep.), the company reorganized into six business groups, including an Operations Group. Sales contributions in FY 97 were:

	1997
Consumer lawns	34%
Consumer gardens	15%
Consumer organics	20%
Professional	18%
International	13%

In May 1995, the company completed a merger with Stern's Miracle-Gro Products, which markets and distributes plant foods and lawn and garden products in North America and Europe. In January 1997, SMG acquired the remaining two-thirds of Miracle Holdings, a U.K. business, that it did not already own.

The company's consumer products include lawn fertilizers and lawn fertilizer/control combination products, garden and indoor plant care products, garden tools, potting soils and other organic products, grass seed and lawn spreaders. SMG estimated that in FY 97 its share of the U.S. do-it-yourself consumer lawn chemicals products market was approximately 53%, more than double that of the second leading brand. It estimated its share of the garden fertilizer segment at 51%, of the indoor plant foods market at 33%, and of the consumer potting soil market at 39%.

The company sells professional products to golf courses, commercial nurseries and greenhouses, schools and sports fields, multi-family housing complexes, business and industrial sites, lawn and landscape services and specialty crop growers. The Professional Group's two core businesses are ProTurf, for the professionally managed turf market, and Horticulture, for the nursery and greenhouse markets. In FY 97, golf courses and highly visible turf areas accounted for approximately 56% of the company's professional sales, with horticulture sales contributing the remaining 44%. SMG estimated that its share of the North American golf course turf maintenance market was about 20% and that its share of the North American horticultural segment was 25%.

Per Share Data ($)

(Year Ended Sep. 30)	1997	1996	1995	1994	1993	1992	1991	1990	1989	1988
Tangible Bk. Val.	NM	NM	NM	1.86	7.66	8.35	4.19	NA	NA	NA
Cash Flow	2.39	0.91	2.12	2.36	1.93	1.64	1.75	NA	NA	NA
Earnings	1.35	-0.65	0.99	1.27	1.07	0.84	0.89	-0.58	0.07	0.07
Dividends	Nil	Nil	Nil	Nil	Nil	Nil	Nil	Nil	Nil	Nil
Payout Ratio	Nil	Nil	Nil	Nil	Nil	Nil	Nil	Nil	Nil	Nil
Prices - High	31¾	21½	24	20¼	20½	24½	NA	NA	NA	NA
- Low	19½	16⅛	15⅝	14½	15¼	13½	NA	NA	NA	NA
P/E Ratio - High	24	NM	24	16	19	29	NA	NA	NA	NA
- Low	14	NM	16	11	14	16	NA	NA	NA	NA

Income Statement Analysis (Million $)

	1997	1996	1995	1994	1993	1992	1991	1990	1989	1988
Revs.	901	752	733	606	466	413	388	350	328	197
Oper. Inc.	133	86.1	88.9	82.0	61.5	56.9	55.3	51.3	49.3	NA
Depr.	30.4	29.3	25.6	20.5	17.0	14.4	17.8	20.5	19.6	NA
Int. Exp.	26.7	26.5	26.5	17.8	8.5	15.9	30.9	34.5	32.5	18.6
Pretax Inc.	69.6	1.3	40.7	41.8	35.4	26.2	NA	-6.8	0.9	0.8
Eff. Tax Rate	43%	33%	38%	43%	41%	43%	NA	NM	NM	NM
Net Inc.	39.5	-2.5	22.4	23.9	21.0	15.1	18.4	-6.9	-0.8	0.2

Balance Sheet & Other Fin. Data (Million $)

	1997	1996	1995	1994	1993	1992	1991	1990	1989	1988
Cash	13.0	10.6	7.0	10.7	2.3	0.9	2.9	NA	NA	NA
Curr. Assets	286	292	349	250	144	116	110	NA	NA	NA
Total Assets	788	732	807	529	322	269	261	NA	NA	NA
Curr. Liab.	139	111	119	110	64.9	60.9	88.4	NA	NA	NA
LT Debt	220	223	272	220	87.0	32.0	54.0	NA	NA	NA
Common Eqty.	212	187	206	168	143	176	147	NA	NA	NA
Total Cap.	609	587	505	388	230	208	201	NA	NA	NA
Cap. Exp.	28.6	33.4	23.6	54.9	15.2	19.9	8.8	8.5	6.7	NA
Cash Flow	60.1	17.0	48.0	44.3	38.1	29.5	36.2	13.6	20.5	NA
Curr. Ratio	2.1	2.6	2.9	2.3	2.2	1.9	1.2	NA	NA	NA
% LT Debt of Cap.	36.1	38.0	53.9	56.7	37.8	15.3	26.6	NA	NA	NA
% Net Inc.of Revs.	4.4	NM	3.1	3.9	4.5	3.7	4.7	NM	NM	0.1
% Ret. on Assets	5.2	NM	3.4	5.6	7.5	3.6	6.9	NA	NA	NA
% Ret. on Equity	14.9	NM	12.0	15.3	14.1	NM	12.5	NA	NA	NA

Data as orig. reptd.; bef. results of disc. opers. and/or spec. items. Per share data adj. for stk. divs. as of ex-div. date. Quarterly EPS may not add bec. of changes in shs. Bold denotes diluted EPS (FASB 128). E-Estimated. NA-Not Available. NM-Not Meaningful. NR-Not Ranked.

Organized—in Delaware in 1986. Office—14111 Scottslawn Rd., Marysville, OH 43041. Tel—(513) 644-0011. Website—http://www.scottscompany.comChrmn, Pres & CEO—C. M. Berger. Vice-Chrmn—H. Hagedorn. EVP & CFO—J. H. Mordo. Secy—C. W. Schmenk. Investor Contact—Rebecca J. Bruening. Dirs—J. B. Beard, C. M. Berger, J. S. Chamberlin, J. P. Flannery, H. Hagedorn, J. Hagedorn, A. E. Harris, J. Kenlon, K. G. Mills, J. M. Sullivan, L. J. Van Fossen. Transfer Agent & Registrar—National City Bank, Cleveland. Empl— 2,383. S&P Analyst: Eric J. Hunter

Seitel, Inc.

2005M

NYSE Symbol **SEI**

In S&P SmallCap 600

03-OCT-98

Industry:
Oil & Gas (Drilling & Equipment)

Summary: This company is a leading provider of seismic data and corollary geophysical technology to the petroleum industry.

Quantitative Evaluations

Recent Price • 10⅞
52 Wk Range • 25⅞-8⅝

Yield • Nil
12-Mo. P/E • 7.3

Outlook
(1 Lowest—5 Highest)
• **5**

Fair Value
• **20¼**

Risk
• **Average**

Earn./Div. Rank
• **B**

Technical Eval.
• **Bearish** since 7/98

Rel. Strength Rank
(1 Lowest—99 Highest)
• **49**

Insider Activity
• **NA**

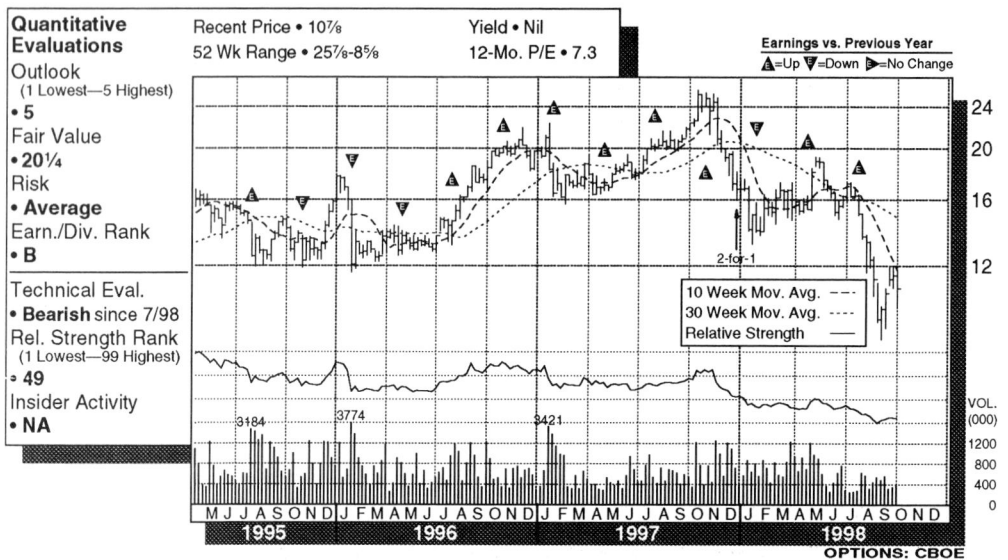

Earnings vs. Previous Year
▲=Up ▼=Down ▶=No Change

10 Week Mov. Avg. ---
30 Week Mov. Avg. - - -
Relative Strength —

2-for-1

VOL. (000)

OPTIONS: CBOE

Business Profile - 29-SEP-98

Seitel owns and markets the second largest publicly available seismic library in North America, with a primary focus on the U.S. Gulf Coast. In April 1998, the company opened a seismic marketing operations center in Canada and purchased three Canadian seismic data libraries. Wholly owned DDD Energy participates directly in petroleum exploration and development through partnership arrangements. The unit recently announced several significant discoveries in Louisiana. A two for one stock split was effected and a $25 million share repurchase program was approved in December 1997.

Operational Review - 29-SEP-98

Revenues for the six months ended June 30, 1998, increased 9.7%, year to year, as a 40% surge in seismic data marketing outweighed the absence of revenues from Eagle Geophysical, which is no longer consolidated following its August 1997 IPO. Expenses rose just 5.9%, despite a 52% hike in depreciation, depletion and amortization charges, and after a slight increase in the tax rate, net income advanced 18% to $11.2 million ($0.49 per share, diluted) from $9.5 million ($0.44).

Stock Performance - 02-OCT-98

In the past 30 trading days, SEI's shares have declined 4%, compared to a 7% fall in the S&P 500. Average trading volume for the past five days was 79,760 shares, compared with the 40-day moving average of 86,246 shares.

Key Stock Statistics

Dividend Rate/Share	Nil	Shareholders	1,300
Shs. outstg. (M)	22.6	Market cap. (B)	$0.246
Avg. daily vol. (M)	0.086	Inst. holdings	49%
Tang. Bk. Value/Share	9.72		
Beta	0.68		

Value of $10,000 invested 5 years ago: $ 19,333

Fiscal Year Ending Dec. 31

	1998	1997	1996	1995	1994	1993
Revenues (Million $)						
1Q	30.93	27.22	20.27	16.61	12.60	6.49
2Q	36.98	34.67	27.18	22.14	16.15	7.46
3Q	—	30.79	30.31	17.87	18.79	10.76
4Q	—	34.87	28.25	17.82	26.23	22.15
Yr.	—	127.6	106.0	74.44	73.77	46.87
Earnings Per Share ($)						
1Q	**0.21**	**0.19**	0.15	0.14	0.13	0.06
2Q	**0.28**	**0.25**	0.20	0.17	0.15	0.08
3Q	—	**0.98**	0.23	0.10	0.13	0.12
4Q	—	**0.02**	0.20	0.10	0.20	0.20
Yr.	—	**1.43**	0.79	0.52	0.61	0.46

Next earnings report expected: mid November

Dividend Data

Quarterly cash dividends were discontinued in 1992. A two-for-one stock split was effected in December 1997.

A Division of The McGraw-Hill Companies

STANDARD
&POOR'S
STOCK REPORTS

Seitel, Inc.

2005M
03-OCT-98

Business Summary - 29-SEP-98

Since its inception in 1982, Seitel, Inc. has been developing a proprietary library of seismic data owned and marketed by Seitel Data Ltd., a Texas limited partnership made up of the company's wholly owned subsidiaries. This data library, consisting of both two-dimensional (2D) and three-dimensional (3D) data, is marketed to oil and gas companies under license agreements; during 1997, over 400 different petroleum companies entered into license agreements. At 1997 year-end, Seitel owned about 885,000 linear mi. of 2D and 9,000 sq. mi. of 3D seismic data, which it maintained in its library, constituting the second largest seismic database marketed publicly in North America.

Three-dimensional seismic data provide a graphic geophysical depiction of the earth's subsurface from two horizontal dimensions and one vertical dimension, rendering a more detailed picture than 2D data, which present a cross-sectional view from one vertical and one horizontal dimension. As a result, the 3D survey provides more comprehensive geophysical information, which can enhance the interpreter's ability to predict the existence and location of subsurface hydrocarbons. Although the cost to create 3D seismic data is substantially greater than that of 2D seismic data, the proper use of these advanced surveys can greatly increase drilling success rates and reduce the occurrence of costly dry holes, thereby significantly lowering exploration and development finding costs.

DDD Energy Inc. (100% owned) was formed in 1993 to participate directly in petroleum exploration, development and ownership of hydrocarbon reserves through partnership relationships with oil and gas companies, whereby the company exchanges its proprietary seismic technology for working interests. DDD Energy's exploration and production activities are focused in the onshore Gulf Coast area of Texas, Louisiana and Mississippi and onshore East Texas, and have recently been expanded into the Sacramento Basin in California. Year-end 1997 reserves consisted of 47 billion cubic feet of natural gas and 2.64 million barrels of oil, condensate and natural gas liquids.

Seismic surveys conducted for DDD Energy are intended to assist participation in petroleum exploration and development; DDD Energy's ownership interest in any resultant production will be accounted for as "oil and gas" revenues and reserves. At 1997 year end, over 1,500 sq. mi. of 3D seismic surveys were conducted for DDD Energy and its partners. More than 500 sq. mi. of 3D surveys have been scheduled to be conducted for DDD Energy and its partners in 1998 and 1999.

SEI maintains an approximate 18% equity stake in Eagle Geophysical Inc., which completed its initial public offering in August 1997.

Per Share Data ($)

(Year Ended Dec. 31)	1997	1996	1995	1994	1993	1992	1991	1990	1989	1988
Tangible Bk. Val.	9.27	8.24	6.38	5.74	3.48	2.98	2.83	2.33	1.56	1.19
Cash Flow	3.68	2.69	1.88	2.36	1.85	1.56	1.43	1.43	1.21	0.97
Earnings	1.43	0.79	0.52	0.61	0.46	0.38	0.57	0.51	0.36	0.28
Dividends	Nil	Nil	Nil	Nil	Nil	0.02	0.05	0.05	Nil	Nil
Payout Ratio	Nil	Nil	Nil	Nil	Nil	7%	9%	9%	Nil	Nil
Prices - High	25⁷/₈	21⁷/₈	17³/₄	18¹/₂	7¹/₄	5³/₄	7⁵/₈	8	4³/₄	1¹⁵/₁₆
- Low	15³/₄	11⁵/₈	9¹/₂	6³/₄	3¹/₄	2⁷/₁₆	4	3³/₈	1¹¹/₁₆	¹³/₁₆
P/E Ratio - High	18	28	34	30	16	15	13	16	13	7
- Low	11	15	18	11	7	6	7	7	5	3

Income Statement Analysis (Million $)

Revs.	128	106	74.4	73.8	43.5	31.2	27.8	25.4	17.9	14.3
Oper. Inc.	86.6	67.4	46.0	45.7	27.6	20.3	18.5	17.1	12.5	9.7
Depr.	49.7	39.2	26.9	27.2	19.9	13.5	9.2	9.4	7.3	6.0
Int. Exp.	4.6	4.1	3.4	3.5	2.3	1.6	0.9	0.7	0.4	0.4
Pretax Inc.	49.0	25.1	16.0	15.3	9.0	6.5	9.1	7.8	4.8	3.4
Eff. Tax Rate	36%	35%	37%	37%	36%	33%	34%	34%	34%	35%
Net Inc.	31.6	16.2	10.1	9.6	5.7	4.3	6.0	5.2	3.2	2.2

Balance Sheet & Other Fin. Data (Million $)

Cash	4.9	3.3	6.2	1.5	1.8	3.5	1.1	1.9	1.1	0.5
Curr. Assets	NA	NA	NA	NA	NA	NA	18.7	21.3	13.5	8.3
Total Assets	366	295	210	169	92.6	73.1	52.0	42.8	25.2	18.7
Curr. Liab.	NA	NA	NA	45.6	18.4	10.5	8.0	9.8	6.4	6.5
LT Debt	90.0	84.0	57.6	14.6	30.7	26.2	11.5	7.4	4.5	2.3
Common Eqty.	208	159	120	101	41.6	35.6	31.4	24.8	13.5	9.0
Total Cap.	315	240	178	119	73.3	62.2	43.2	32.5	18.4	11.5
Cap. Exp.	141	106	82.4	52.6	22.9	22.0	20.0	0.3	0.0	0.1
Cash Flow	81.2	55.5	37.0	36.8	25.6	17.8	15.2	14.5	10.5	8.2
Curr. Ratio	NA	NA	NA	NA	NA	NA	2.3	2.2	2.1	1.3
% LT Debt of Cap.	28.6	35.1	32.3	12.3	41.9	42.2	26.5	22.8	24.4	19.7
% Net Inc.of Revs.	24.7	15.3	13.6	13.0	13.2	14.4	22.0	20.8	17.6	15.4
% Ret. on Assets	9.6	6.4	5.4	6.3	6.9	6.7	12.4	14.0	13.5	13.2
% Ret. on Equity	17.2	11.5	9.1	11.8	14.8	12.5	21.0	24.9	26.5	28.2

Data as orig. reptd.; bef. results of disc. opers. and/or spec. items. Per share data adj. for stk. divs. as of ex-div. date. Bold denotes diluted EPS (FASB 128). E-Estimated. NA-Not Available. NM-Not Meaningful. NR-Not Ranked.

Office—50 Briar Hollow Lane, West Bldg., 7th Fl., Houston, TX 77027. **Tel**—(713) 881-8900. **Chrmn**—H. M. Pearlman. **Pres & CEO**—P. A. Frame. **EVP & COO**—H. A. Calvert. **SVP-Fin, CFO, Treas & Secy**—Debra D. Valice. **Investor Contact**—Russell Hoffman (203-629-0633). **Dirs**—H. A. Calvert, W. M. Craig Jr., P. A. Frame, D. S. Lawi, W. Lerner, H. M. Pearlman, J. E. Steiglitz, D. D. Valice, F. S. Zeidman. **Transfer Agent & Registrar**—American Stock Transfer & Trust Co., NYC. **Incorporated**—in Delaware in 1982. **Empl**— 94. **S&P Analyst:** Ephraim Juskowicz

Selective Insurance Group   5199P

NASDAQ Symbol **SIGI**

In S&P SmallCap 600

03-OCT-98

Industry:
Insurance (Property-Casualty)

Summary: SIGI offers a broad range of property and casualty insurance products principally to customers in suburban locales.

Quantitative Evaluations

Outlook
(1 Lowest—5 Highest)
- **3+**

Fair Value
- **21¼**

Risk
- **Low**

Earn./Div. Rank
- **B+**

Technical Eval.
- **Neutral** since 7/98

Rel. Strength Rank
(1 Lowest—99 Highest)
- **66**

Insider Activity
- **Favorable**

Recent Price • 19   Yield • 2.9%
52 Wk Range • 29¼-17⅜   12-Mo. P/E • 9.0

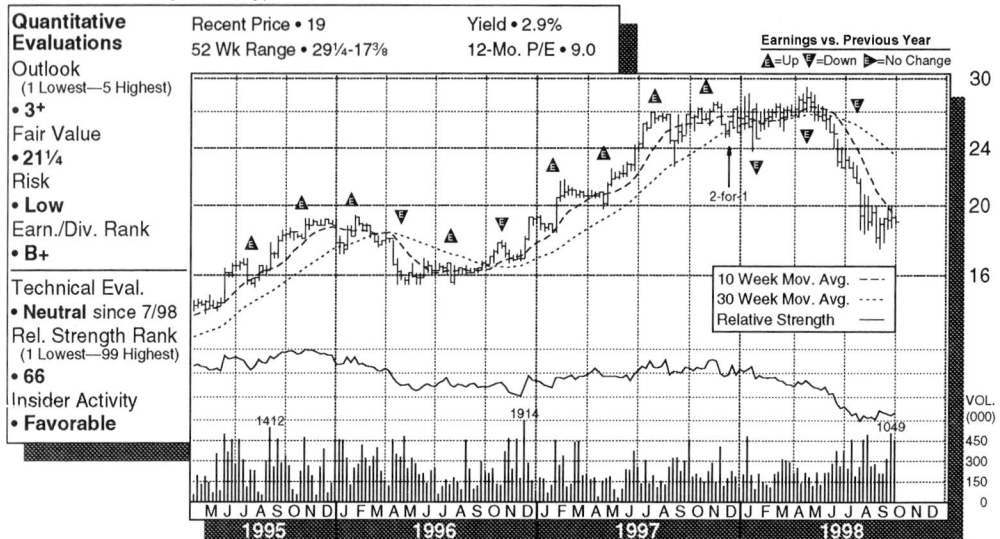

Earnings vs. Previous Year
▲=Up ▼=Down ▶=No Change

10 Week Mov. Avg. - - -
30 Week Mov. Avg. ·····
Relative Strength —

Business Profile - 04-SEP-98

In late July 1998, Selective Insurance Group reported that very competitive conditions in commercial lines pricing showed no signs of abating. The company has developed strategies to reduce expenses, including having field claim adjusters actively manage claims. In addition, the use of a staff counsel program is being expanded; SIGI believes that this will cut litigation expenses and loss costs. The company believes that its recent six-state entry into the Midwest and the expansion of its personal insurance program, until recently marketed predominantly in New Jersey, will create additional opportunities for growth. To help support this expected growth, SIGI is working on automation improvements designed to increase efficiency and make doing business with the company much easier by year-end 1998. SIGI's main priority is making its commercial lines underwriting system more user friendly, and the company is also including system enhancements to streamline the process for its agents. In addition, SIGI is developing a claims system designed to improve the productivity of its field adjusters.

Operational Review - 04-SEP-98

Net premiums written in the first half of 1998 rose 3.4%, year to year. However, competitive pricing pressure and weather-related losses contributed to a 5.9% increase in expenses. Despite taxes at 19.2%, versus 23.0%, net income fell 13%, to $29,566,000 ($0.93 a share), from $33,804,000 ($1.10).

Stock Performance - 02-OCT-98

In the past 30 trading days, SIGI's shares have declined 3%, compared to a 7% fall in the S&P 500. Average trading volume for the past five days was 91,220 shares, compared with the 40-day moving average of 95,369 shares.

Key Stock Statistics

Dividend Rate/Share	0.56	Shareholders	3,800
Shs. outstg. (M)	29.1	Market cap. (B)	$0.553
Avg. daily vol. (M)	0.103	Inst. holdings	49%
Tang. Bk. Value/Share	19.81		
Beta	0.49		

Value of $10,000 invested 5 years ago: $ 20,719

Fiscal Year Ending Dec. 31

	1998	1997	1996	1995	1994	1993
Revenues (Million $)						
1Q	200.9	197.2	201.9	201.0	182.7	162.0
2Q	205.6	196.0	201.6	209.0	184.4	166.8
3Q	—	198.9	196.7	216.0	200.3	172.8
4Q	—	196.3	198.7	213.1	200.8	177.6
Yr.	—	788.4	799.0	839.1	768.3	679.6
Earnings Per Share ($)						
1Q	**0.50**	**0.55**	0.30	0.45	0.28	0.12
2Q	**0.44**	**0.56**	0.54	0.43	0.34	0.01
3Q	—	**0.60**	0.42	0.48	0.34	0.41
4Q	—	**0.57**	0.65	0.49	0.42	0.29
Yr.	—	**2.27**	1.91	1.85	1.38	0.83

Next earnings report expected: late October

Dividend Data (Dividends have been paid since 1929.)

Amount ($)	Date Decl.	Ex-Div. Date	Stock of Record	Payment Date
0.140	Oct. 28	Nov. 13	Nov. 17	Dec. 01 '97
0.140	Feb. 04	Feb. 11	Feb. 16	Mar. 02 '98
0.140	May. 01	May. 13	May. 15	Jun. 01 '98
0.140	Jul. 28	Aug. 12	Aug. 14	Sep. 01 '98

A Division of The **McGraw·Hill** *Companies*

Business Summary - 04-SEP-98

Selective Insurance Group, Inc. is a regional insurance holding company that offers its customers, through subsidiaries, commercial and personal insurance products. Business segment contributions (profits in $ millions) in 1997 were:

	Revs.	Profits
Commercial	69%	-$12.7
Personal	31%	11.5
Other	Nil	-0.6

Net premiums earned in 1997 were distributed by state as follows: New Jersey 58%, Pennsylvania 11%, New York 8%, Maryland 5%, Virginia 5%, South Carolina 5%, Delaware 3%, North Carolina 3%, Georgia 2%, other states 1%.

The company's commercial insurance coverages consist of the following: workers' compensation, commercial automobile, liability, property, umbrella, and bonds.

Workers' compensation coverage insures employers against employee claims resulting from work-related injuries. Compensation is payable regardless of who was at fault.

Commercial automobile coverage insures against losses incurred from bodily injury, bodily injury to third

parties, property damage to an insured's vehicle (including fire and theft) and property damage to other vehicles and property as a result of automobile accidents involving commercial vehicles.

Liability coverage insures against third party liability for bodily injury and property damage, including liability for products sold, and the defense of claims alleging such damages. The liability lines continue to reflect the potential exposure to environmental claims.

Property coverage insures policyholders against commercial property damage caused by fire, wind, hail, water, theft and vandalism, and other perils.

Umbrella coverage affords policyholders liability protection supplemental to that provided under primary liability policies and insures against catastrophic losses.

Bonds refers to fidelity and surety, including but not limited to: bid, performance, maintenance, supply, site plan, and subdivision bonds.

Personal insurance coverages consist of the following: personal automobile, homeowners, personal catastrophe liability, and flood.

Investments, which totaled $1.7 billion at year-end 1997, broke down as follows: debt securities available for sale 60%, debt securities to be held to maturity 24%, equity securities 13%, and short term investments/other 3%.

Per Share Data ($)

(Year Ended Dec. 31)	1997	1996	1995	1994	1993	1992	1991	1990	1989	1988
Tangible Bk. Val.	18.72	15.96	14.80	11.23	11.32	11.15	10.08	9.36	9.08	7.76
Oper. Earnings	2.15	1.84	1.83	1.28	0.72	0.93	0.93	0.94	1.45	1.50
Earnings	2.27	1.91	1.85	1.38	0.83	1.03	1.03	1.25	1.52	1.53
Dividends	0.56	0.56	0.56	0.56	0.56	0.55	0.52	0.51	0.46	0.40
Payout Ratio	25%	29%	30%	41%	67%	53%	50%	41%	30%	26%
Prices - High	28³/₈	19³/₈	19¼	15³/₈	15½	11³/₄	9	10⅛	10	8⅞
- Low	18³/₈	15½	12¼	11½	10¼	8	6½	6¼	7¼	6½
P/E Ratio - High	12	10	10	11	19	11	9	8	7	6
- Low	8	8	7	8	12	8	6	5	5	4

Income Statement Analysis (Million $)

	1997	1996	1995	1994	1993	1992	1991	1990	1989	1988
Premium Inc.	676	695	743	680	595	536	497	464	450	426
Net Invest. Inc.	101	97.0	91.6	80.7	77.3	73.5	68.5	64.5	59.8	52.8
Oth. Revs.	11.6	7.1	4.6	7.4	7.4	6.2	5.7	12.0	6.3	1.2
Total Revs.	788	799	839	768	680	616	571	540	516	480
Pretax Inc.	91.0	69.0	65.0	43.4	21.4	31.5	31.6	35.4	46.1	45.3
Net Oper. Inc.	65.7	53.7	52.5	35.5	NA	NA	NA	NA	NA	40.5
Net Inc.	69.6	55.6	53.0	38.3	22.7	27.4	27.3	32.4	40.6	41.5

Balance Sheet & Other Fin. Data (Million $)

	1997	1996	1995	1994	1993	1992	1991	1990	1989	1988
Cash & Equiv.	5.0	24.2	23.6	21.8	20.7	20.3	18.4	17.0	16.7	15.9
Premiums Due	332	310	292	274	283	132	109	124	118	109
Invest. Assets: Bonds	1,455	1,418	1,389	1,170	1,053	1,034	870	786	739	667
Invest. Assets: Stocks	222	161	118	91.6	88.2	86.3	70.2	72.8	91.1	76.1
Invest. Assets: Loans	20.1	10.5	10.7	10.7	10.1	10.0	8.4	3.1	3.0	3.4
Invest. Assets: Total	681	1,624	1,564	1,303	1,196	1,130	948	863	833	747
Deferred Policy Costs	98.1	83.2	82.2	81.0	78.6	76.4	53.0	53.0	49.5	45.5
Total Assets	2,306	2,184	2,113	1,867	1,739	1,479	1,211	1,139	1,074	962
Debt	114	104	111	111	61.3	63.7	14.5	15.2	35.8	23.8
Common Eqty.	476	474	437	329	323	312	270	248	230	214
Prop. & Cas. Loss Ratio	68.2	71.3	71.2	71.7	71.8	69.5	67.9	70.5	69.4	70.3
Prop. & Cas. Expense Ratio	32.1	31.6	30.4	32.6	36.7	37.0	38.1	35.0	32.2	29.7
Prop. & Cas. Combined Ratio	100.3	102.9	101.6	104.3	108.5	107.9	107.6	108.0	103.4	101.1
% Return On Revs.	8.8	7.0	6.3	5.0	3.3	4.5	5.5	6.0	7.9	8.6
% Ret. on Equity	15.5	12.2	13.9	11.7	7.1	9.4	10.5	13.5	18.3	21.1

Data as orig. reptd.; bef. results of disc. opers. and/or spec. items. Per share data adj. for stk. divs. as of ex-div. date. Bold denotes diluted EPS (FASB 128). E-Estimated. NA-Not Available. NM-Not Meaningful. NR-Not Ranked.

Office—40 Wantage Ave., Branchville, NJ 07890. **Tel**—(973) 948-3000. **Website**—http://www.selectiveinsurance.com **Chrmn & CEO**—J. W. Entringer. **Pres & COO**—G. E. Murphy. **SVP, CFO & Investor Contact**—David B. Merclean (973-948-1776). **Dirs**—A. D. Brown, W. A. Dolan II, J. W. Entringer, W. C. Gray, C. E. Herder, F. H. Jarvis, W. M. Kearns Jr., J. Lamm-Tennant, S. G. McClellan III, G. E. Murphy, W. M. Rue, T. D. Sayles Jr., J. B. Thebault. **Transfer Agent & Registrar**—First Chicago Trust Co. of New York, Jersey City, NJ. **Incorporated**—in New Jersey in 1977. **Empl**— 1,650. **S&P Analyst:** T. W. Smith, CFA

10-OCT-98

Industry:
Health Care (Drugs - Generic & Other)

Summary: SEQUUS (formerly Liposome Technology) is developing proprietary liposome and lipid-based pharmaceuticals to treat life-threatening diseases.

Quantitative Evaluations

Recent Price • 14⅜	Yield • Nil
52 Wk Range • 15-5⅝	12-Mo. P/E • NM

Outlook
(1 Lowest—5 Highest)
• **1⁻**

Fair Value
• **10¼**

Risk
• **High**

Earn./Div. Rank
• **C**

Technical Eval.
• **Bearish** since 8/98

Rel. Strength Rank
(1 Lowest—99 Highest)
• **99**

Insider Activity
• **NA**

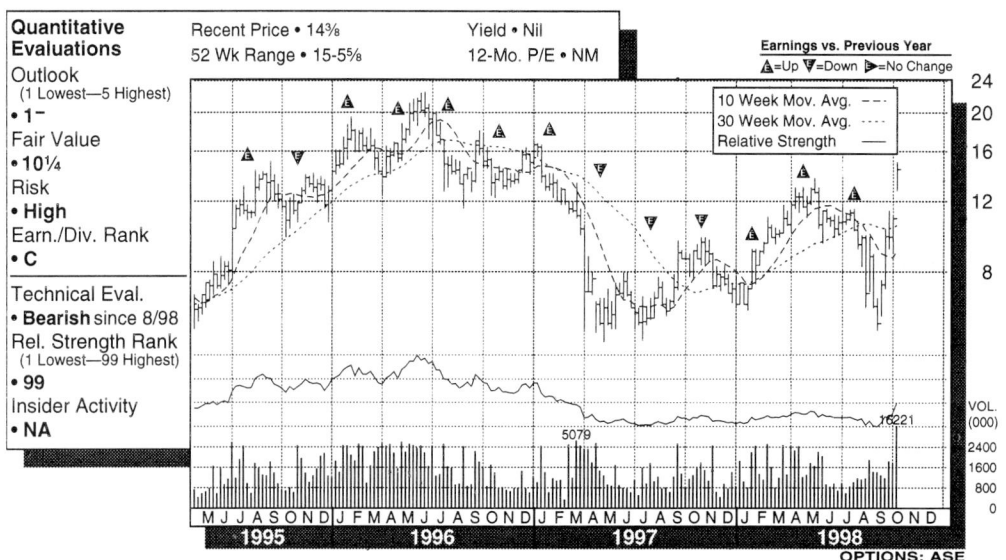

Earnings vs. Previous Year
▲=Up ▼=Down ▶=No Change

10 Week Mov. Avg. - - -
30 Week Mov. Avg. ·····
Relative Strength —

VOL. (000)

OPTIONS: ASE

Business Profile - 12-AUG-98

SEQUUS developed and is commercializing an anti-cancer agent, Doxil, and an antifungal agent, Amphocil, in the United States, Europe, Latin America and other foreign markets. Amphocil (also known as Amphotec) is available in 20 countries in addition to the U.S. for the treatment of severe systemic fungal infections. Doxil (marketed as Caelyx) is distributed by marketing partner Schering-Plough Corporation for the treatment of AIDS-related Kaposi's sarcoma. The company has incurred losses since inception, and accumulated approximately $179.4 million in net losses through the second quarter of 1998.

Operational Review - 12-AUG-98

Total revenues for the six months ended June 30, 1998, advanced 72%, year to year, led by an 81% increase in product sales, which was primarily attributed to sales of Doxil. Gross margins widened, and with lower SG&A expenses, reflecting more rigorous expense control and the absence of one-time costs associated with the launching of the Amphotec product, the net loss narrowed to $5,146,000 ($0.17 a share, on 3.3% more shares), from $14,866,000 ($0.49). Cash, equivalents and marketable investments totaled $25.8 million as of June 30, 1998.

Stock Performance - 09-OCT-98

In the past 30 trading days, SEQU's shares have increased 120%, compared to a 4% fall in the S&P 500. Average trading volume for the past five days was 3,244,120 shares, compared with the 40-day moving average of 687,326 shares.

Key Stock Statistics

Dividend Rate/Share	Nil	Shareholders	500
Shs. outstg. (M)	31.6	Market cap. (B)	$0.457
Avg. daily vol. (M)	1.046	Inst. holdings	56%
Tang. Bk. Value/Share	0.89		
Beta	2.14		

Value of $10,000 invested 5 years ago: $ 14,437

Fiscal Year Ending Dec. 31

	1998	1997	1996	1995	1994	1993
Revenues (Million $)						
1Q	12.80	8.32	4.49	0.99	0.64	0.83
2Q	16.02	8.45	5.52	0.19	0.94	0.73
3Q	—	10.52	11.56	0.09	1.71	5.74
4Q	—	12.66	11.36	0.85	1.46	1.10
Yr.	—	39.95	32.92	2.02	4.76	8.40
Earnings Per Share ($)						
1Q	-0.10	-0.25	-0.21	-0.48	-0.40	-0.30
2Q	-0.07	-0.24	-0.18	-0.33	-0.41	-0.33
3Q	—	-0.17	-0.02	-0.37	-0.35	-0.06
4Q	—	-0.12	-0.19	-0.37	-0.38	-0.36
Yr.	—	-0.78	-0.59	-1.54	-1.54	-1.05

Next earnings report expected: NA

Dividend Data

No cash dividends have been paid.

A Division of The McGraw·Hill Companies

STANDARD
&POOR'S
STOCK REPORTS

SEQUUS Pharmaceuticals, Inc.

5203P
10-OCT-98

Business Summary - 12-AUG-98

SEQUUS Pharmaceuticals (formerly Liposome Technology) is engaged in the development, production, marketing and sale of proprietary liposome and lipid-based products to treat life-threatening illnesses. It has emphasized injectable pharmaceuticals designed to improve the efficacy and reduce the toxicity of selected existing and new drugs used to treat cancer, infectious diseases and other illnesses.

Products being developed involve the entrapment of therapeutics by liposomes or in a colloidal dispersion of liquids. SEQUUS has developed proprietary methods to lower the natural defense mechanism's recognition of injected liposomes. These methods form the technology base for the company's "stealth" liposomes and can increase the blood circulation time of such liposomes to several days, from a few hours for traditional liposomes.

The proprietary Amphocil product is a lipid-based colloidal dispersion of amphotericin B, an off-patent antibiotic approved for sale in the U.S. and elsewhere as a standard therapy for the treatment of severe systemic fungal infections. Despite its effectiveness, the use of amphotericin B is limited by its acute and chronic toxicities. Amphocil has received marketing approval in several countries overseas. The product received marketing clearance in the United States in November 1996, under the name Amphotec.

SEQUUS has developed stealth liposomes to improve the chemotherapeutic approach to treating solid tumors and certain lymphomas by increasing the amount of drug available at the site of disease while reducing the exposure of healthy tissues to a cytotoxic drug. The company's other lead drug is a long-circulating stealth liposome formulation of the anticancer drug doxorubicin hydrochloride, an off-patent chemotherapeutic used to treat many solid tumors and leukemias. The drug, labeled Doxil, is approved in the U.S. for second-line treatment of Kaposi's sarcoma. The company has a strategic alliance with Schering-Plough to distribute, market and sell the drug worldwide, except for the U.S., Japan and certain small markets. SEQU is currently conducting additional clinical trials for the use of Doxil in the treatment of certain solid tumors, including a Phase III clinical trial in refractory ovarian cancer and a number of breast cancer trials.

The company has an exclusive agreement with Tecnofarma S.A.I.C.F. and Laboratorios Raffo S.A. of Buenos Aires, Argentina, for the marketing and distribution of Amphocil (also known as Amphotec) throughout South America. In November 1997, the company signed an exclusive agreement with CritiCare Laboratories Pvt. Ltd. for the marketing and distribution of Amphocil in India, Bangladesh, Nepal and Sri Lanka. In May 1997, SEQUUS signed an exclusive five-year agreement with a division of FH Faulding & Co., Ltd. of Australia to market the drug throughout southeast Asia, Australia and New Zealand.

Per Share Data ($)

(Year Ended Dec. 31)	1997	1996	1995	1994	1993	1992	1991	1990	1989	1988
Tangible Bk. Val.	0.84	1.49	1.89	0.56	2.05	3.08	2.38	0.82	1.71	2.99
Cash Flow	-0.71	-0.66	-1.45	-1.44	-0.97	-0.77	-0.57	-0.69	-0.96	-0.44
Earnings	-0.78	-0.59	-1.54	-1.54	-1.05	-0.84	-0.66	-0.80	-1.04	-0.48
Dividends	Nil	Nil	Nil	Nil	Nil	Nil	Nil	Nil	Nil	Nil
Payout Ratio	Nil	Nil	Nil	Nil	Nil	Nil	Nil	Nil	Nil	Nil
Prices - High	16⅝	22½	15⅛	12½	14¼	25¾	19¾	4	3¾	5⅞
- Low	5¼	11½	5½	4½	5½	6⅞	1⅞	⅞	1⅛	1⅞
P/E Ratio - High	NM	NM	NM	NM	NM	NM	NM	NM	NM	NM
- Low	NM	NM	NM	NM	NM	NM	NM	NM	NM	NM

Income Statement Analysis (Million $)

	1997	1996	1995	1994	1993	1992	1991	1990	1989	1988
Revs.	40.0	32.9	2.0	3.8	6.8	0.7	0.3	1.4	0.8	3.4
Oper. Inc.	-22.8	-17.3	-33.0	-28.3	-19.8	-16.6	-7.6	-6.9	-7.0	-4.4
Depr.	2.0	1.8	2.0	1.9	1.4	1.2	1.1	1.1	0.6	0.3
Int. Exp.	0.2	Nil	0.1	0.0	NA	0.0	0.1	0.1	0.1	0.1
Pretax Inc.	-23.6	-17.2	-33.6	-29.2	-19.7	-15.4	-8.2	-7.5	-7.3	-3.3
Eff. Tax Rate	NM	NM	Nil	NM	NM	Nil	Nil	Nil	Nil	Nil
Net Inc.	-23.6	-17.2	-33.6	-29.2	-19.7	-15.4	-8.2	-7.5	-7.3	-3.3

Balance Sheet & Other Fin. Data (Million $)

	1997	1996	1995	1994	1993	1992	1991	1990	1989	1988
Cash	6.7	32.9	50.3	11.8	34.7	41.3	32.2	4.8	8.5	19.5
Curr. Assets	35.4	49.2	54.0	13.5	37.7	43.2	32.5	5.0	9.0	20.1
Total Assets	42.2	55.0	57.8	18.2	45.2	60.5	41.0	10.5	15.3	23.9
Curr. Liab.	11.8	10.6	8.2	7.3	5.9	1.9	1.8	1.6	1.5	1.5
LT Debt	4.6	Nil	Nil	Nil	Nil	Nil	0.1	0.5	0.9	1.3
Common Eqty.	25.8	44.3	49.6	10.9	39.3	58.6	39.1	8.5	12.9	21.1
Total Cap.	30.4	44.3	49.6	10.9	39.3	58.6	39.2	8.9	13.8	22.4
Cap. Exp.	3.0	3.6	1.6	1.3	1.9	1.8	0.3	0.3	2.7	1.6
Cash Flow	-21.6	-19.0	-31.6	-27.3	-18.2	-14.2	-7.1	-6.4	-6.7 *	-3.0
Curr. Ratio	3.0	4.6	6.6	1.9	6.4	22.2	17.9	5.1	5.9	13.7
% LT Debt of Cap.	15.2	NM	Nil	Nil	Nil	Nil	0.3	5.0	6.6	5.7
% Net Inc.of Revs.	NM	NM	NM	NM	NM	NM	NM	NM	NM	NM
% Ret. on Assets	NM	NM	NM	NM	NM	NM	NM	NM	NM	NM
% Ret. on Equity	NM	NM	NM	NM	NM	NM	NM	NM	NM	NM

Data as orig. reptd.; bef. results of disc. opers. and/or spec. items. Per share data adj. for stk. divs. as of ex-div. date. Bold denotes diluted EPS (FASB 128). E-Estimated. NA-Not Available. NM-Not Meaningful. NR-Not Ranked.

Office—1050 Hamilton Ct., Menlo Park, CA 94025. **Tel**—(415) 323-9011. **Website**—http://www.sequus.com **Chrmn & CEO**—I. C. Henderson. **EVP & COO**—J. J. Vallner. **VP-Fin & Treas**—D. J. Stewart. **Dirs**—R. D. Campbell, R. G. Faris, I. C. Henderson, R. C. E. Morgan, E. D. Thomas. **Transfer Agent & Registrar**—ChaseMellon Shareholder Services, San Francisco. **Incorporated**—in Delaware in 1987. **Empl**— 260. **S&P Analyst:** C.C.P.

STANDARD &POOR'S
STOCK REPORTS

Service Experts

2010F

NYSE Symbol **SVE**

In S&P SmallCap 600

03-OCT-98

Industry:
Services (Commercial & Consumer)

Summary: SVE provides residential heating, ventilating, and air conditioning services, as well as replacement equipment.

Quantitative Evaluations		
Recent Price • 25¼	Yield • Nil	
52 Wk Range • 38-20	12-Mo. P/E • 21.4	

Outlook (1 Lowest—5 Highest)
• **NA**

Fair Value
• **NA**

Risk
• **NA**

Earn./Div. Rank
• **NR**

Technical Eval.
• **NA**

Rel. Strength Rank (1 Lowest—99 Highest)
• **55**

Insider Activity
• **NA**

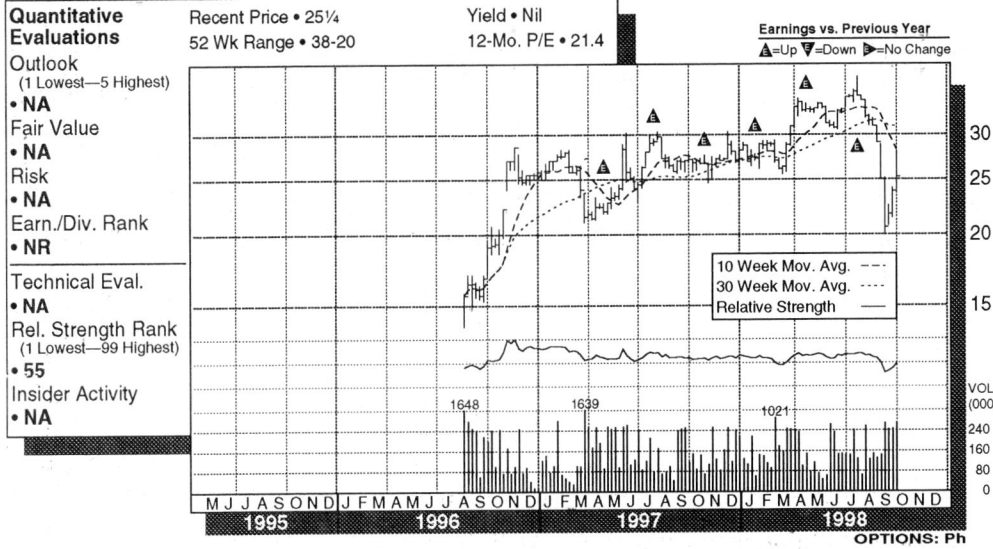

Earnings vs. Previous Year
▲=Up ▼=Down ▷=No Change

10 Week Mov. Avg. - - -
30 Week Mov. Avg. ······
Relative Strength —

1648   1639   1021

VOL. (000)

OPTIONS: Ph

Business Profile - 02-OCT-98

Service Experts' goal is to become the leading U.S. provider of residential HVAC (heating, ventilating and air conditioning) services and replacement equipment, through acquisitions and internal expansion. The company seeks to capitalize on the fragmentation and growth of the HVAC service and replacement industry. During the 1998 second quarter, Service Experts acquired 34 companies representing $52 million in annual revenues. These acquisitions included 12 new service centers, bringing the company's network, at June 30, 1998, to 85 service centers in 32 states, representing annualized revenues of about $360 million. Meanwhile, Service Experts is integrating its acquired operations. Five conversions to a new management information system were completed as of mid-1998, and plans called for the roll out to continue through 1999.

Operational Review - 02-OCT-98

Net revenues for the first half of 1998 soared 65%, year to year, due mostly to acquisitions. Margins were well maintained, and operating profit also increased 65%. After other expenses (net), versus other income, and taxes at 40.6%, against 36.8%, net income was up 46%, to $9.9 million ($0.61 a share on 18% more shares) from $6.8 million ($0.49).

Stock Performance - 02-OCT-98

In the past 30 trading days, SVE's shares have declined 19%, compared to a 7% fall in the S&P 500. Average trading volume for the past five days was 130,880 shares, compared with the 40-day moving average of 61,433 shares.

Key Stock Statistics

Dividend Rate/Share	Nil	Shareholders	NA
Shs. outstg. (M)	16.6	Market cap. (B)	$0.420
Avg. daily vol. (M)	0.093	Inst. holdings	51%
Tang. Bk. Value/Share	1.75		
Beta	NA		

Value of $10,000 invested 5 years ago: NA

Fiscal Year Ending Dec. 31

	1998	1997	1996	1995	1994	1993
Revenues (Million $)						
1Q	68.66	33.36	—	—	—	—
2Q	100.1	52.35	—	—	—	—
3Q	—	65.65	16.25	—	—	—
4Q	—	71.12	20.90	—	—	—
Yr.	—	239.2	46.86	59.70	—	—
Earnings Per Share ($)						
1Q	0.20	0.18	0.11	—	—	—
2Q	0.41	0.32	0.20	—	—	—
3Q	—	0.32	0.30	—	—	—
4Q	—	0.24	0.17	—	—	—
Yr.	—	1.06	0.70	-0.08	—	—

Next earnings report expected: late October

Dividend Data

No dividends have been paid, and the company has said it does not intend to pay any in the foreseeable future.

A Division of The McGraw·Hill Companies

STANDARD
&POOR'S
STOCK REPORTS

Service Experts, Inc.

2010F
03-OCT-98

Business Summary - 02-OCT-98

Service Experts provides residential heating, ventilating and air conditioning (HVAC) services and replacement equipment. The company, as of year-end 1997, was operating 63 HVAC serviceand replacement businesses in 28 states. It also owns ContractorSuccess Group, Inc., a company that provides HVAC businesses proprietary products, as well as marketing, management, educational and advisory services.

Service Experts' service centers primarily offer the following products and services: the sale of replacement central air conditioners, furnaces and heat pumps; the maintenance and repair of HVAC units; diagnostic analysis of the condition of existing units; and the sale of ancillary products such as indoor air quality (IAQ) devices and monitors.

Most of the service centers employ an in-house sales force thatsells replacement units, installation technicians who install replacement equipment in existing homes, service technicians who service and maintain the equipment, and an administrative staff to perform dispatching, purchasing, and other administrative functions.

In addition, some of the service centers offer plumbing services. Most service centers technicians are trained to promote the company's preventive maintenance agreements and to cross-market IAQ equipment and other ancillary services and products offered by the company.

Management believes the replacement market for HVAC units offers the potential for high growth and profitability, given the potential number of HVAC systems that will need replacement in the coming years.

As of year-end 1997, Service Experts had about 15,000 maintenance agreements with customers. These agreements are for a term of one to three years and generally provide for two diagnostic and precision maintenance visits during the year at an average cost to the customer of about $135 per year. The sale of maintenance agreements generates recurring revenue through the payment of fees. The company believes that maintenance agreements help it develop a committed, loyal customer base and provide the opportunity for cross-marketing of other services and products.

Some of the service centers offer HVAC services to small and medium-sized businesses. In 1997, non-residential revenue generated from the provision of services and sale of products, including those related to commercial, electrical and plumbing services and products, represented about 20% of pro forma net revenue. The service centers target restaurants, small office buildings, warehouses and theaters as potential prospects for their commercial services.

During 1997, the company acquired 71 HVAC businesses for $102.2 million, consisting of 2.5 million common shares, $43.1million in cash, and warrants to purchase 200,000 common shares.

Per Share Data ($)

(Year Ended Dec. 31)	1997	1996	1995	1994	1993	1992	1991	1990	1989	1988
Tangible Bk. Val.	2.42	1.81	1.86	NA	NA	NA	NA	NA	NA	NA
Cash Flow	1.48	0.84	NA	NA	NA	NA	NA	NA	NA	NA
Earnings	1.06	0.70	0.67	NA	NA	NA	NA	NA	NA	NA
Dividends	Nil	Nil	Nil	Nil	Nil	Nil	Nil	Nil	Nil	Nil
Payout Ratio	Nil	Nil	Nil	Nil	Nil	Nil	Nil	Nil	Nil	Nil
Prices - High	30⅜	28½	NA	NA	NA	NA	NA	NA	NA	NA
- Low	21	13	NA	NA	NA	NA	NA	NA	NA	NA
P/E Ratio - High	29	40	NA	NA	NA	NA	NA	NA	NA	NA
- Low	20	18	NA	NA	NA	NA	NA	NA	NA	NA

Income Statement Analysis (Million $)

	1997	1996	1995	1994	1993	1992	1991	1990	1989	1988
Revs.	239	46.9	59.7	NA	NA	NA	NA	NA	NA	NA
Oper. Inc.	30.0	4.5	NA	NA	NA	NA	NA	NA	NA	NA
Depr.	6.1	0.7	NA	NA	NA	NA	NA	NA	NA	NA
Int. Exp.	0.7	0.1	Nil	Nil	Nil	Nil	Nil	Nil	Nil	Nil
Pretax Inc.	24.5	4.3	8.4	NA	NA	NA	NA	NA	NA	NA
Eff. Tax Rate	38%	28%	38%	NA	NA	NA	NA	NA	NA	NA
Net Inc.	15.3	3.1	5.2	NA	NA	NA	NA	NA	NA	NA

Balance Sheet & Other Fin. Data (Million $)

	1997	1996	1995	1994	1993	1992	1991	1990	1989	1988
Cash	11.2	10.7	NA	NA	NA	NA	NA	NA	NA	NA
Curr. Assets	63.0	27.3	NA	NA	NA	NA	NA	NA	NA	NA
Total Assets	195	68.5	26.9	NA	NA	NA	NA	NA	NA	NA
Curr. Liab.	35.1	14.9	NA	NA	NA	NA	NA	NA	NA	NA
LT Debt	15.7	0.1	Nil	Nil	Nil	Nil	Nil	Nil	Nil	Nil
Common Eqty.	142	53.1	16.2	NA	NA	NA	NA	NA	NA	NA
Total Cap.	160	53.6	NA	NA	NA	NA	NA	NA	NA	NA
Cap. Exp.	9.9	0.6	NA	NA	NA	NA	NA	NA	NA	NA
Cash Flow	21.4	3.8	NA	NA	NA	NA	NA	NA	NA	NA
Curr. Ratio	1.8	1.8	NA	NA	NA	NA	NA	NA	NA	NA
% LT Debt of Cap.	9.8	0.3	Nil	Nil	Nil	Nil	Nil	Nil	Nil	Nil
% Net Inc.of Revs.	6.4	6.6	8.7	NA	NA	NA	NA	NA	NA	NA
% Ret. on Assets	11.6	7.1	NA	NA	NA	NA	NA	NA	NA	NA
% Ret. on Equity	15.6	10.3	NA	NA	NA	NA	NA	NA	NA	NA

Data as orig. reptd. (pro forma in 1995; balance sheet data as of June 30, 1996); bef. results of disc. opers. and/or spec. items. Per share data adj. for stk. divs. as of ex-div. date. Bold denotes diluted EPS (FASB 128). E-Estimated. NA-Not Available. NM-Not Meaningful. NR-Not Ranked.

Office—111 Westwood Place, Suite 420, Brentwood, TN 37027. **Tel**—(615) 371-9990. **Fax**—(615) 221-9881. **Website**—www.serx.com **Chrmn, Pres & CEO**—A. R. Sielbeck. **CFO, Secy & Treas**—A. M. Schofield. **Dirs**—R. J. De Riggi, A. L. Hovius, N. T. Rolf Jr., W. G. Roth, A. R. Sielbeck, T. G. Wallace. **Transfer Agent & Registrar**—SunTrust Bank, Nashville and Atlanta. **Incorporated**—in Delaware in 1996. **Empl**— 3,200. **S&P Analyst:** N.J. DeVita

STANDARD &POOR'S
STOCK REPORTS

Shoney's, Inc.

2030M
NYSE Symbol **SHN**

In S&P SmallCap 600

03-OCT-98

Industry: Restaurants

Summary: Operations of this major restaurant company include the flagship Shoney's chain and the Captain D's seafood chain.

Quantitative Evaluations

Outlook
(1 Lowest—5 Highest)
- **2**

Fair Value
- **2**

Risk
- **Average**

Earn./Div. Rank
- **B-**

Technical Eval.
- **NA**

Rel. Strength Rank
(1 Lowest—99 Highest)
- **15**

Insider Activity
- **Neutral**

Recent Price • 2
52 Wk Range • 5⅞-1⅞

Yield • Nil
12-Mo. P/E • NM

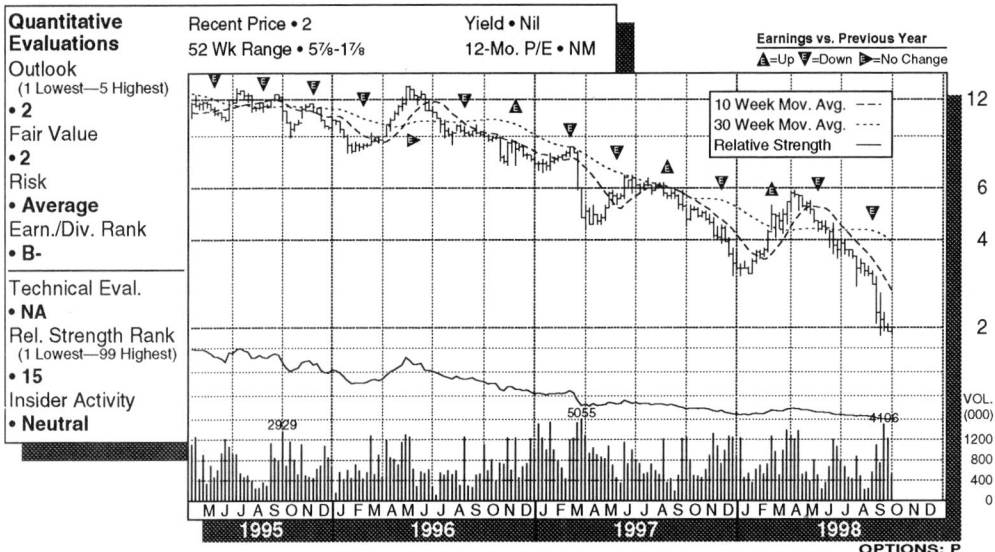

Earnings vs. Previous Year
▲=Up ▼=Down ▶=No Change

10 Week Mov. Avg. - - -
30 Week Mov. Avg. · · · ·
Relative Strength —

OPTIONS: P

Business Profile - 17-JUN-98

In FY 97 (Oct.), Shoney's closed 75 under-performing units, for which it took an asset impairment charge. In addition, the company closed another 36 units in the first two quarters of FY 98, incurring an additional asset impairment charge. In FY 98, Shoney's does not plan to open any new units so that it can focus on improving the quality of its food, service and the cleanliness of its restaurants. To improve profitability, Shoney's is focusing on its research and development, supervision and training in all restaurants. The company is starting to see improvement in cleanliness and food quality in its units and is continuing its development of marketing strategies that emphasize higher quality and higher margin menu items at lunch and dinner.

Operational Review - 17-JUN-98

Revenues in the 28 weeks ended May 10, 1998, fell 5.8%, year to year, primarily reflecting the closure of 75 underperforming units in 1997 and an additional 36 restaurants in the first two quarters of 1998. Margins narrowed on the lower volume; operating margins were down 59%. Following asset impairment charges of $2.6 million versus $17.6 million, higher interest charges, and tax credits in both periods, the loss widened to $11,011,708 ($0.23 a share), from $8,476,341 ($0.17). Current period results exclude an extraordinary charge of $0.03 per share from the early retirement of debt.

Stock Performance - 02-OCT-98

In the past 30 trading days, SHN's shares have declined 35%, compared to a 7% fall in the S&P 500. Average trading volume for the past five days was 103,220 shares, compared with the 40-day moving average of 226,967 shares.

Key Stock Statistics

Dividend Rate/Share	Nil	Shareholders	8,800
Shs. outstg. (M)	48.7	Market cap. (B)	$0.097
Avg. daily vol. (M)	0.347	Inst. holdings	31%
Tang. Bk. Value/Share	NM		
Beta	1.43		

Value of $10,000 invested 5 years ago: $ 860

Fiscal Year Ending Oct. 31

	1998	1997	1996	1995	1994	1993
Revenues (Million $)						
1Q	339.1	363.3	300.2	310.4	339.2	317.7
2Q	281.1	295.4	257.7	253.2	277.5	262.8
3Q	277.3	294.2	257.0	253.9	281.9	274.1
4Q	—	274.2	284.8	235.9	267.6	285.4
Yr.	—	1,227	1,100	1,053	1,166	1,140
Earnings Per Share ($)						
1Q	-0.20	-0.28	0.06	0.19	0.34	0.30
2Q	-0.03	0.11	0.15	0.15	0.41	0.37
3Q	-1.71	0.18	0.16	0.20	0.42	0.41
4Q	—	-0.74	0.24	-0.27	0.35	0.35
Yr.	—	-0.74	0.61	0.27	1.52	1.44

Next earnings report expected: late December

Dividend Data

Paid each year since 1971, dividends were discontinued following a large special distribution in 1988.

A Division of The **McGraw·Hill** Companies

Business Summary - 17-JUN-98

In 1984, the Wall Street Journal described Shoney's, Inc. as the best-run restaurant company in America. A decade later, that was clearly no longer true. In May 1995, the company hired C. Stephen Lynn as chairman to try to turn the company around. To this end, in FY 95 (Oct.), the company implemented a restructuring plan that included the closure of 41 underperforming restaurants. Net income, aided by one-time gains, rebounded in FY 96, but comparable-store customer counts ran negative, and the company's flagship Shoney's restaurant chain remained stuck in a difficult competitive environment. The weak same-store sales prompted the company to close another 75 stores in FY 97; consequently, it took an impairment charge that resulted in the company posting a net loss for the year. At present, Shoney's continues to be in a competitive environment, competing with fast-food chains that are aggressively seeking customers with value-oriented pricing, while also fighting casual dining chains that offer consumers more amenities.

Currently, it appears that Shoney's is trying to determine where its focus belongs. Management is trying to improve results by selling and closing underperforming units as it shrinks to its core markets and deleverages its balance sheet, enhancing operating performance at its restaurants, increasing marketing efforts to drive new traffic and building its brand name. Much of FY 98 will be devoted to improving food quality as well as enhancing restaurant service and cleanliness. After closing 75 unprofitable stores in FY 97, the company will probably close another 25 stores in FY 98. Its $35 million capital expenditure budget will be used for refurbishing, remodeling and maintaining restaurants, with no new units planned for FY 98.

During FY 97, comparable-restaurant sales declined 4.0% for all company-owned Shoney's restaurans, despite a menu price increase of 1.4%. In addition, average unit volumes for company-owned units were down 5.3%, reflecting the lower same-store sales and the acquisition of lower volume restaurants from TPI Enterprises, Inc. in 1996. Shoney's new strategy is to try to enhance the quality of its current menu offerings, hoping to drive its average check price in FY 97 of $6.12 to around $7.00. The company will also focus on increasing restaurant supervision and training of its restaurant staffs in hopes of delivering a consistent, reliable customer experience systemwide.

As of May 10, 1998, Shoney's operated 1,344 restaurants in 33 states, of which 857 were company-operated and 487 were franchises.

Per Share Data ($) (Year Ended Oct. 31)	1997	1996	1995	1994	1993	1992	1991	1990	1989	1988
Tangible Bk. Val.	NM	NM	Nil	-3.32	-5.16	-7.48	-6.63	-8.39	-9.60	-10.38
Cash Flow	0.37	1.70	1.30	2.57	2.43	0.32	1.88	1.67	1.41	2.14
Earnings	-0.74	0.61	0.27	1.52	1.44	-0.65	0.94	0.76	0.50	1.22
Dividends	Nil	Nil	Nil	Nil	Nil	Nil	Nil	Nil	Nil	16.05
Payout Ratio	Nil	Nil	Nil	Nil	Nil	Nil	Nil	Nil	Nil	NM
Prices - High	8 1/4	13 3/8	13 1/2	25 5/8	25 5/8	27 1/4	24 1/4	16 3/4	13 1/4	28 1/4
- Low	3	6 7/8	8 7/8	12 5/8	16 1/2	15 3/4	10 1/2	9 1/4	7 3/4	6 3/4
P/E Ratio - High	NM	22	50	17	18	NM	26	22	27	23
- Low	NM	11	33	8	11	NM	11	12	16	6
Income Statement Analysis (Million $)										
Revs.	1,218	1,093	1,053	1,155	1,136	1,059	990	926	852	770
Oper. Inc.	93.3	119	110	170	175	166	158	150	142	122
Depr.	53.9	46.3	42.8	43.4	40.0	39.6	37.7	35.7	34.5	33.7
Int. Exp.	45.0	38.3	40.6	42.1	44.9	52.6	64.7	71.8	83.7	27.1
Pretax Inc.	-50.1	41.9	19.1	98.2	93.4	-46.4	59.3	47.0	32.4	71.9
Eff. Tax Rate	NM	38%	41%	36%	38%	NM	36%	37%	42%	38%
Net Inc.	-35.7	26.0	11.2	62.6	58.0	-26.6	38.0	29.6	18.9	44.9
Balance Sheet & Other Fin. Data (Million $)										
Cash	11.9	13.9	7.5	4.2	7.8	4.3	4.7	4.2	7.9	6.6
Curr. Assets	134	110	99	95.0	107	79.4	64.9	52.8	61.3	48.4
Total Assets	645	747	535	558	528	469	429	400	400	404
Curr. Liab.	172	215	173	197	245	181	122	115	92.0	70.0
LT Debt	466	476	406	414	390	461	543	579	635	682
Common Eqty.	-12.3	0.5	-107	-136	-209	-289	-264	-320	-357	-378
Total Cap.	454	477	317	293	189	170	298	279	302	328
Cap. Exp.	40.2	69.6	60.0	95.0	82.8	58.6	56.0	48.5	35.4	51.5
Cash Flow	18.1	72.3	54.0	106	98.0	13.0	75.7	65.3	53.4	78.5
Curr. Ratio	0.8	0.5	0.6	0.5	0.4	0.4	0.5	0.5	0.7	0.7
% LT Debt of Cap.	102.6	99.8	128.1	141.4	205.8	270.7	181.8	207.3	210.4	208.0
% Net Inc.of Revs.	NM	2.4	1.1	5.4	5.1	NM	3.8	3.2	2.2	5.8
% Ret. on Assets	NM	4.1	2.1	11.5	11.4	NM	9.0	7.3	4.7	11.0
% Ret. on Equity	NM	NM	NM	NM	NM	NM	NM	NM	NM	NM

Data as orig. reptd.; bef. results of disc. opers. and/or spec. items. Per share data adj. for stk. divs. as of ex-div. date. Bold denotes diluted EPS (FASB 128). E-Estimated. NA-Not Available. NM-Not Meaningful. NR-Not Ranked.

Office—1727 Elm Hill Pike, Nashville, TN 37210. **Tel**—(615) 391-5201. **Chrmn**—C. S. Lynn. **Vice Chrmn**—R. D. Schoenbaum. **Pres & CEO**—M. J. Bodnar. **CFO**—G. A. Hayes. **Secy**—F. E. McDaniel Jr. **Dirs**—M. J. Bodnar, C. S. Lynn, J. F. Schoenbaum, R. D. Schoenbaum, W. Schwartz, C. D. Shanks, F. W. Ward, Jr., W. Wilson, J. D. Yancy. **Transfer Agent & Registrar**—Harris Trust & Savings Bank, Chicago. **Incorporated**—in Tennessee in 1968. **Empl**— 33,000. **S&P Analyst:** Robert J. Izmirlian

STANDARD &POOR'S
STOCK REPORTS
ShopKo Stores
2030U
NYSE Symbol **SKO**
In S&P SmallCap 600

03-OCT-98

Industry: Retail (Discounters)

Summary: This Wisconsin-based regional discount store chain operates about 149 stores in 16 states, serving small and mid-sized markets.

Quantitative Evaluations

Recent Price • 32⅜
52 Wk Range • 37-19¼

Yield • Nil
12-Mo. P/E • NM

Outlook (1 Lowest—5 Highest)
• **2⁻**

Fair Value
• **30⅞**

Risk
• **Low**

Earn./Div. Rank
• **NR**

Technical Eval.
• **Bearish** since 5/98

Rel. Strength Rank (1 Lowest—99 Highest)
• **95**

Insider Activity
• **NA**

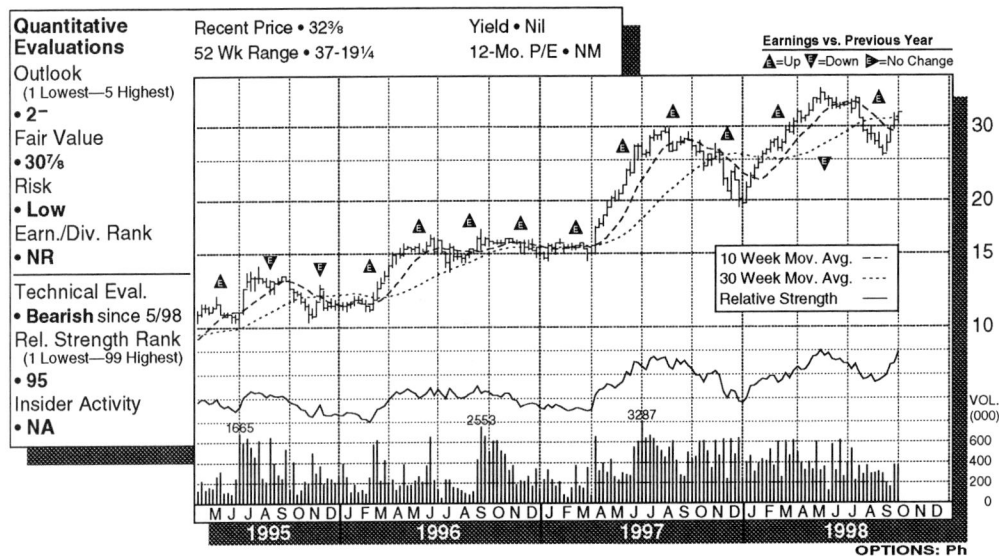

Earnings vs. Previous Year
▲=Up ▼=Down ▶=No Change

10 Week Mov. Avg. ---
30 Week Mov. Avg. ....
Relative Strength —

VOL. (000)

OPTIONS: Ph

Business Profile - 26-MAR-98

In December 1997, ShopKo acquired Penn-Daniels, a discount retailer, for about $61 million. Penn-Daniels operates 18 Jacks discount stores in Illinois, Iowa and Missouri. SKO plans to convert most Jacks retail locations to ShopKo stores. Penn-Daniels recorded sales of $13.7 million for the four weeks ended February 28, 1998. The company recently announced plans to change its fiscal year end to January 31 from February 28 in 1998. Despite three fewer weeks in FY 98, the SKO posted 4.9% sales growth.

Operational Review - 26-MAR-98

Based on a preliminary report, net sales for the 49 weeks ended January 31, 1998, advanced 4.9%, compared with the 52 weeks ended February 22, 1997, reflecting a 3.9% increase in comparable retail store sales and a surge in ProVantage sales. Margins narrowed, due to lower gross margins in apparel and pharmacy, partly offset by store level cost controls; operating income rose 3.9%. Following a $2.8 million nonrecurring charge in connection with the terminated Phar-Mor merger agreement and taxes at 39.3% in both periods, net income was up 8.7%, to $48,845,000 ($1.71 a share, on 12% fewer shares), from $44,946,000 ($1.39).

Stock Performance - 02-OCT-98

In the past 30 trading days, SKO's shares have increased 17%, compared to a 7% fall in the S&P 500. Average trading volume for the past five days was 72,240 shares, compared with the 40-day moving average of 57,533 shares.

Key Stock Statistics

Dividend Rate/Share	Nil	Shareholders	1,400
Shs. outstg. (M)	26.1	Market cap. (B)	$0.845
Avg. daily vol. (M)	0.055	Inst. holdings	89%
Tang. Bk. Value/Share	12.97		
Beta	0.90		

Value of $10,000 invested 5 years ago: $ 25,548

Fiscal Year Ending Jan. 31

	1999	1998	1997	1996	1995	1994
Revenues (Million $)						
1Q	645.8	720.0	610.9	560.5	514.9	474.6
2Q	681.3	546.1	498.5	418.2	381.3	355.3
3Q	—	608.4	591.2	491.0	470.9	446.3
4Q	—	573.4	632.8	498.4	485.8	463.0
Yr.	—	2,448	2,333	1,968	1,853	1,739
Earnings Per Share ($)						
1Q	0.08	0.22	0.18	0.17	0.16	0.18
2Q	0.00	0.16	0.12	0.06	0.09	0.07
3Q	—	0.45	0.34	0.32	0.35	0.44
4Q	—	0.98	0.76	0.66	0.59	0.32
Yr.	—	1.71	1.40	1.20	1.18	1.00

Next earnings report expected: NA

Dividend Data

A dividend of $0.11 a share was last paid September 15, 1996.

A Division of The **McGraw-Hill** Companies

Business Summary - 26-MAR-98

Several years ago, ShopKo Stores (SKO), a regional retailer operating in small and mid-sized markets, implemented a long-term strategy aimed at allowing it to compete successfully with the national discount chains (Wal-Mart, Kmart and Target). As a result, the company believes that its departments look more like individual specialty shops than units of a traditional discount store. This new posture has also enabled SKO to quickly identify, test, and validate new business ideas (in a set of dedicated stores), and then immediately expand the new concepts to all stores. For example, SKO exited a stagnant and unproductive gift business, and replaced it with a successful bath and body boutique. In addition, instead of trying to offer every item found in traditional discount stores, SKO offers more sizes, styles, shapes and colors of selected, targeted items, dominating the category.

As of December 10, 1997, SKO operates 130 general merchandise stores, of which 129 include pharmacy centers and 128 include optical centers, in 15 states in the upper Midwest, Pacific Northwest and western Mountain Region, with sizable concentrations in Wisconsin (41), Utah (15), Minnesota (13), Nebraska (11) and Washington (10). In its retail stores, and through its ProVantage segment, SKO provides other health services, including prescription benefit management, mail service pharmacy, vision benefit management and healthcare information technology. SKO also operates four free standing optical stores in Ohio, all of which were opened in FY 97 (Feb.). In FY 97, SKO also opened one new retail store. There are no plans to complete any major remodels or to construct any new stores in FY 98.

In FY 97, SKO reported a record $2.3 billion in sales, up 19% from the FY 96 level. Net income increased 17%, to $44.9 million. Sales of the Retail Store segment (which includes general merchandise, retail pharmacy and retail optical operations) increased 6.6%, to $2.0 billion. Same-store sales, led by the apparel, retail health and hardline/home goods, rose 6%, and put SKO among the leaders in the discount store industry. The ProVantage segment, which benefited by internal growth and the acquisition of CareStream Scrip Care in August 1996, reported a sales increase of 271%, to $348.8 million.

In FY 97, hardline/home goods accounted for 54% of SKO's retail stores net sales (56% in FY 96), softline goods 25% (24%), and health services 21% (20%). SKO feels that long-term sales growth lies in the following business lines: bed & bath, housewares, special sizes in apparel, casual furniture, intimate apparel and retail health.

Per Share Data ($)

(Year Ended Jan. 31)	1998	1997	1996	1995	1994	1993	1992	1991	1990	1989
Tangible Bk. Val.	12.59	12.45	12.55	12.41	11.67	11.11	9.98	8.88	7.14	5.81
Cash Flow	3.75	3.27	2.96	2.85	2.48	2.92	2.81	2.66	2.43	2.12
Earnings	1.71	1.40	1.20	1.18	1.00	1.56	1.55	1.44	1.33	1.15
Dividends	Nil	0.22	0.44	0.44	0.44	0.44	0.11	NA	NA	NA
Payout Ratio	Nil	16%	37%	37%	44%	28%	7%	NA	NA	NA
Cal. Yrs.	1997	1996	1995	1994	1993	1992	1991	1990	1989	1988
Prices - High	29⅞	17⅛	14	12⅛	16	17¼	15⅛	NA	NA	NA
- Low	14⅜	10⅞	8⅝	8¾	9¾	12⅞	11¾	NA	NA	NA
P/E Ratio - High	17	12	12	10	16	11	10	NA	NA	NA
- Low	8	8	7	7	10	8	8	NA	NA	NA

Income Statement Analysis (Million $)

	1998	1997	1996	1995	1994	1993	1992	1991	1990	1989
Revs.	2,448	2,333	1,968	1,853	1,739	1,683	1,648	1,521	1,420	1,248
Oper. Inc.	160	153	140	133	110	131	128	122	114	98.0
Depr.	58.3	59.8	56.4	53.5	47.3	43.0	40.4	39.1	35.2	30.9
Int. Exp.	30.6	31.8	34.3	30.3	23.5	19.4	18.3	20.0	20.1	16.0
Pretax Inc.	80.4	74.0	63.1	62.4	52.9	81.5	81.2	74.9	70.3	60.6
Eff. Tax Rate	39%	39%	39%	40%	39%	39%	39%	63%	65%	64%
Net Inc.	48.8	44.9	38.4	37.8	32.1	50.1	49.6	45.9	42.6	36.9

Balance Sheet & Other Fin. Data (Million $)

	1998	1997	1996	1995	1994	1993	1992	1991	1990	1989
Cash	54.3	125	89.5	12.6	2.6	2.8	2.1	2.0	1.8	NA
Curr. Assets	542	565	476	469	371	296	260	273	236	NA
Total Assets	1,251	1,234	1,118	1,110	953	792	706	705	648	576
Curr. Liab.	398	333	261	281	252	215	182	217	177	NA
LT Debt	436	419	415	414	310	209	192	192	235	229
Common Eqty.	396	461	422	397	374	355	320	284	228	186
Total Cap.	853	901	857	828	701	577	524	488	471	NA
Cap. Exp.	32.0	38.9	53.0	95.0	134	91.1	55.3	59.1	80.1	90.6
Cash Flow	107	105	94.8	91.3	79.5	93.3	90.0	85.1	77.8	67.8
Curr. Ratio	1.4	1.7	1.8	1.7	1.5	1.4	1.4	1.3	1.3	NA
% LT Debt of Cap.	51.1	46.5	48.4	49.9	44.1	36.2	36.6	39.4	49.8	NA
% Net Inc.of Revs.	2.0	1.9	2.0	2.0	1.8	3.0	3.0	3.0	3.0	3.0
% Ret. on Assets	3.9	3.8	3.5	3.7	3.7	6.7	7.1	6.5	7.0	7.0
% Ret. on Equity	11.4	10.2	9.4	9.8	8.8	14.8	16.7	NA	20.6	22.1

Data as orig. reptd.; bef. results of disc. opers. and/or spec. items. Per share data adj. for stk. divs. as of ex-div. date. Bold denotes diluted EPS (FASB 128). Prior to 1998, fis. yr. end. Feb. 28. E-Estimated. NA-Not Available. NM-Not Meaningful. NR-Not Ranked.

Office—700 Pilgrim Way, Green Bay, WI 54304. **Tel**—(920) 497-2211. **Website**—http://www.shopko.com **Chrmn, Pres & CEO**—D. P. Kramer. **EVP**—W. J. Podany. **SVP & CFO**—P. H. Freischlag Jr.**VP & Secy**—R. D. Schepp. **Investor Contact**—Phyllis J. Proffer. **Dirs**—J. W. Eugster, J. C. Girard, J. L. Reinertsen, W. J. Tyrrell, S. E. Watson. **Transfer Agent & Registrar**—Norwest Bank Minnesota, Minneapolis. **Incorporated**—in Wisconsin in 1998.**Empl**— 21,000. **S&P Analyst:** Ray Lam, CFA

Shorewood Packaging 5214S

NYSE Symbol **SWD**

In S&P SmallCap 600

03-OCT-98 | **Industry:** Containers and Packaging (Paper)

Summary: This company prints and manufactures packaging for the cosmetics, home video, music, software, tobacco, toiletries and general consumer markets.

Quantitative Evaluations

Outlook (1 Lowest—5 Highest)
• **2+**

Fair Value
• **15⅜**

Risk
• **Low**

Earn./Div. Rank
• **B**

Technical Eval.
• **NA**

Rel. Strength Rank (1 Lowest—99 Highest)
• **49**

Insider Activity
• **NA**

Recent Price • 13
52 Wk Range • 18⅞-12⅛
Yield • Nil
12-Mo. P/E • 13.3

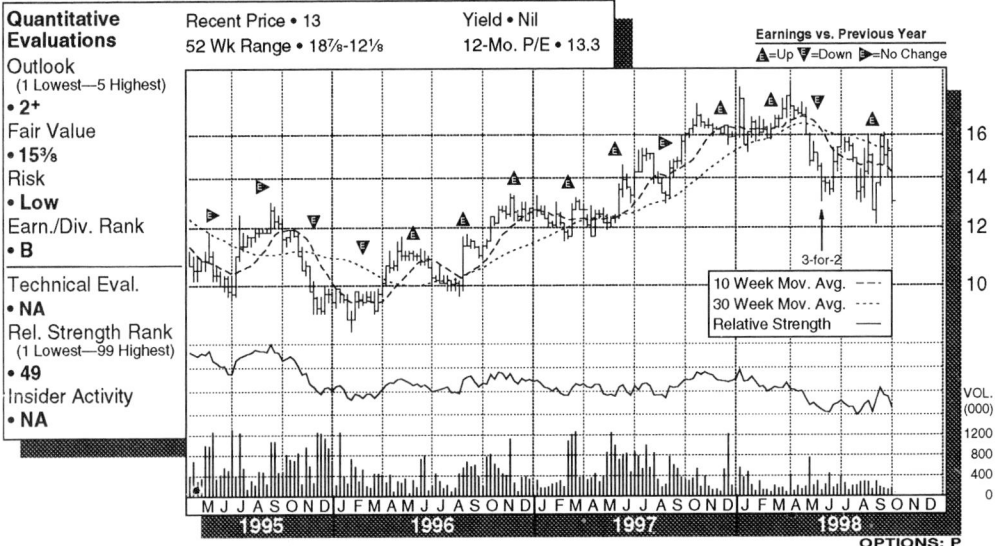

Earnings vs. Previous Year
▲=Up ▼=Down ▶=No Change

10 Week Mov. Avg. - - -
30 Week Mov. Avg. ·····
Relative Strength —

3-for-2

VOL. (000)
OPTIONS: P

Business Profile - 15-JUL-98

SWD has been expanding its market for CD-ROM products, and expects additional contributions from its Springfield, OR, plant. A new facility in China is expected to begin operations in August 1998, and SWD expects significant free cash flow in FY 99 (Apr.) as a result of the startup. Capital spending for FY 99 is projected at $35 million. SWD expects strong tobacco backlogs to continue for much of FY 99. The company repurchased more than 3.4 million common shares (as adjusted) in the three years ended May 3, 1998, and has since bought another 465,000. Trading in the stock moved to the NYSE, from the Nasdaq Stock Market, in January 1998. A three-for-two stock split was effected in May 1998.

Operational Review - 15-JUL-98

Based on a preliminary report, sales in the 52 weeks ended May 2, 1998, fell 2.3% from those of the year-earlier 53 weeks, reflecting weak tobacco sales and one fewer week of operations. Gross margins widened, on well controlled operating costs; with lower other expenses, income from continuing operations rose 12%, to $26,295,000 ($0.95 a share, diluted), from $23,422,000 ($0.89, as adjusted). EPS in FY 97 exclude losses of $0.05 from discontinued operations and $0.01 from extraordinary items. SWD's tobacco packaging segment has been strong in early FY 99, and margins continue to improve.

Stock Performance - 02-OCT-98

In the past 30 trading days, SWD's shares have declined 13%, compared to a 7% fall in the S&P 500. Average trading volume for the past five days was 30,580 shares, compared with the 40-day moving average of 38,641 shares.

Key Stock Statistics

Dividend Rate/Share	Nil	Shareholders	200
Shs. outstg. (M)	26.5	Market cap. (B)	$0.345
Avg. daily vol. (M)	0.029	Inst. holdings	62%
Tang. Bk. Value/Share	3.07		
Beta	0.18		

Value of $10,000 invested 5 years ago: $ 16,250

Fiscal Year Ending Apr. 30

	1999	1998	1997	1996	1995	1994
Revenues (Million $)						
1Q	115.4	100.6	109.8	90.70	84.77	40.37
2Q	—	114.8	117.0	105.1	97.05	46.08
3Q	—	96.63	99.3	93.11	85.65	52.43
4Q	—	103.3	104.1	105.5	89.56	77.59
Yr.	—	415.4	425.3	394.4	357.0	216.5
Earnings Per Share ($)						
1Q	0.25	0.22	0.22	0.20	0.20	0.08
2Q	—	0.31	0.25	0.21	0.24	0.12
0Q	—	0.20	0.17	0.13	0.19	-0.01
4Q	—	0.22	0.23	0.19	0.16	0.16
Yr.	—	0.95	0.89	0.73	0.78	0.35

Next earnings report expected: early December

Dividend Data

Amount ($)	Date Decl.	Ex-Div. Date	Stock of Record	Payment Date
3-for-2	Apr. 01	May. 26	May. 02	May. 22 '98

Business Summary - 15-JUL-98

Shorewood Packaging (SWD) has been taking actions to improve its manufacturing efficiency and expects to see further improvement in its operating margins during FY 98 (Apr.). The company prints and manufactures high-quality paperboard packaging for the cosmetics, home video, music, software, tobacco, toiletries and general consumer markets in the U.S. and Canada. SWD anticipates future sales growth to be derived from the continued penetration of its existing markets and from the exploitation of new, emerging markets such as the expanding market for CD-ROM computer software and games packaging. SWD also plans to expand internationally.

In the fourth quarter of FY 97, the company discontinued its transportation division, which was subsequently sold, resulting in a loss of $0.06 a share from discontinued operations in FY 97. A $0.07 a share charge was also recorded for the early retirement of debt.

For the home entertainment industry, the company's principal products are packaging for prerecorded cassettes and compact discs and packaging for videocassettes. In addition to Sony, customers include most of the major record production and distribution companies in the U.S. For the cosmetics and toiletries and other

general consumer markets, the company produces specialized packaging for customers requiring sophisticated precision graphic packaging for their products. For the tobacco industry, SWD produces the hard flip-top cigarette packages as well as the traditional slide and shell packages.

The Somerville Packaging operations (acquired in 1994) makes folding cartons for the tobacco, cosmetics and toiletries and general consumer industries. The company is nearing completion of a $35 million 125,000 sq. ft. facility in China to fill the demands of its multinational customers. SWD expects the plant to start operations in August 1998. To facilitate expansion into China and other global opportunities, the company entered into a new credit facility in May 1997 that provides for up to $200 million of borrowings. SWD's Springfield, OR, CD-ROM packaging plant completed its first full year of production during 1997.

Operations in Canada accounted for 41% of sales in both FY 97 and FY 96.

In FY 97, Philip Morris accounted for 23% of net sales, and two other customers (affiliated with each other) accounted for a combined total of 14% of net sales.

Backlog at May 3, 1997, totaled $79 million, up from $56.7 million a year earlier.

Per Share Data ($)

(Year Ended Apr. 30)	1998	1997	1996	1995	1994	1993	1992	1991	1990	1989
Tangible Bk. Val.	2.71	4.16	1.87	1.82	1.01	0.95	0.61	2.43	2.15	1.59
Cash Flow	1.59	2.25	1.22	1.24	0.71	0.79	0.62	0.69	0.73	0.67
Earnings	0.95	0.89	0.73	0.78	0.35	0.52	0.35	0.45	0.55	0.51
Dividends	Nil	Nil	Nil	Nil	Nil	Nil	2.17	Nil	Nil	Nil
Payout Ratio	Nil	Nil	Nil	Nil	Nil	Nil	621%	Nil	Nil	Nil
Cal. Yrs.	1997	1996	1995	1994	1993	1992	1991	1990	1989	1988
Prices - High	18⅝	13⅜	13¾	15⅛	9½	8½	9¼	12⅜	12⅝	7⅝
- Low	11½	8⅝	9⅛	8⅞	4⅝	4½	4⅜	3⅞	7⅛	4⅝
P/E Ratio - High	20	15	19	19	27	16	27	28	23	15
- Low	12	10	12	11	13	9	13	9	13	9

Income Statement Analysis (Million $)

Revs.	415	425	394	357	216	184	160	142	139	127
Oper. Inc.	67.1	65.4	56.2	58.5	34.9	35.8	29.5	28.8	30.6	30.6
Depr.	17.9	17.2	14.2	13.3	9.8	7.9	7.7	7.0	5.6	5.0
Int. Exp.	7.6	8.9	8.3	9.0	6.9	5.5	5.5	2.1	2.3	1.8
Pretax Inc.	42.3	40.2	34.4	36.2	15.8	23.4	16.2	20.5	24.2	24.9
Eff. Tax Rate	38%	38%	38%	38%	41%	38%	40%	37%	33%	40%
Net Inc.	26.3	24.9	21.3	22.5	9.4	14.6	9.8	12.8	16.2	15.0

Balance Sheet & Other Fin. Data (Million $)

Cash	7.3	3.2	4.5	4.1	2.7	12.5	5.7	12.2	11.3	9.5
Curr. Assets	95.8	94.5	96.2	96.9	78.2	50.8	42.3	48.1	44.5	38.8
Total Assets	326	278	276	245	220	113	100	111	104	89.0
Curr. Liab.	64.9	52.9	65.4	65.0	46.8	28.9	22.7	22.1	18.3	18.5
LT Debt	126	107	123	100	138	49.4	52.5	13.2	15.2	17.2
Common Eqty.	110	96.4	71.4	67.4	27.1	26.1	17.3	68.0	63.8	46.9
Total Cap.	257	223	209	179	174	83.9	77.3	88.8	86.0	70.3
Cap. Exp.	61.4	20.8	37.4	15.6	9.2	12.4	3.9	7.9	15.3	16.0
Cash Flow	44.2	42.2	35.6	35.8	19.2	22.5	17.5	19.8	21.7	19.6
Curr. Ratio	1.5	1.8	1.5	1.5	1.7	1.8	1.9	2.2	2.4	2.1
% LT Debt of Cap.	49.0	48.0	58.9	55.8	79.5	58.9	67.9	14.9	17.7	24.5
% Net Inc.of Revs.	6.3	5.9	5.4	6.3	4.3	7.9	6.1	9.0	11.6	11.8
% Ret. on Assets	8.7	9.0	8.2	9.6	5.7	13.9	9.3	12.3	16.7	19.3
% Ret. on Equity	25.5	29.7	30.7	47.6	35.7	68.2	22.9	20.0	29.1	38.5

Data as orig. reptd.; bef. results of disc. opers. and/or spec. items. Per share data adj. for stk. divs. as of ex-div. date. Bold denotes diluted EPS (FASB 128). E-Estimated. NA-Not Available. NM-Not Meaningful. NR-Not Ranked.

Office—277 Park Ave., New York, NY 10172. Tel—(212) 371-1500. Chrmn, CEO & Pres—M. P. Shore. EVP, CFO & Investor Contact—Howard M. Liebman. VP-Fin—W. H. Hogan. Secy—Joan Matheis. Dirs—K. J. Bannon, M. L. Braun, F. S. Glinert, S. Leslie, R. T. O'Donnell, M. P. Shore, W. P. Weidner. Transfer Agent—Bank of New York, NYC. Incorporated—in Delaware in 1985. Empl— 2,700. S&P Analyst: Stewart Scharf

Sierra Health Services

2031E

NYSE Symbol **SIE**

In S&P SmallCap 600

03-OCT-98

Industry: Health Care (Diversified)

Summary: This company provides healthcare services through HMOs in Nevada and Texas and provides workers' compensation coverage in several states.

Quantitative Evaluations		
Outlook (1 Lowest—5 Highest) • **5**	Recent Price • 20	Yield • Nil
Fair Value • **29¾**	52 Wk Range • 27⅝-15⅞	12-Mo. P/E • 15.0

Risk • **Average**

Earn./Div. Rank • **B**

Technical Eval. • **Bearish** since 1/97

Rel. Strength Rank (1 Lowest—99 Highest) • **90**

Insider Activity • **Neutral**

Earnings vs. Previous Year
▲=Up ▼=Down ▶=No Change

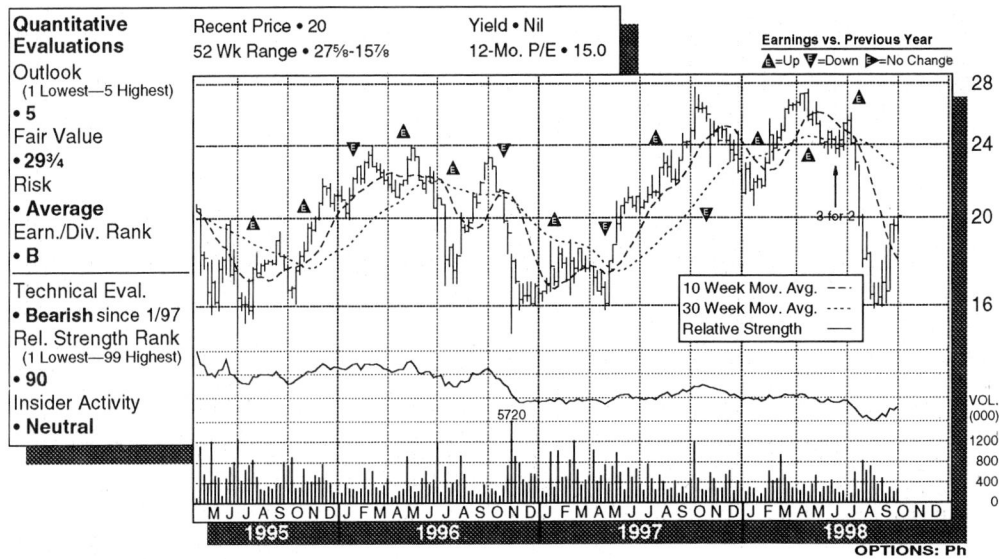

10 Week Mov. Avg. - - -
30 Week Mov. Avg. ·····
Relative Strength —

3 for 2

VOL. (000)

OPTIONS: Ph

Business Profile - 08-JUL-98

The company's revenue outlook is bolstered by strong HMO enrollment trends, particularly in the government business lines, along with steady expansion in the commercial segment. On the margin front, the medical loss ratio (direct medical costs as a percentage of premium revenues) will continue to benefit from SIE's agreement with an outside pharmacy benefits manager that caps the rate of 1998 drug cost inflation at 3%, well below the HMO industry average in recent years. The shares were split three for two in May 1998.

Operational Review - 08-JUL-98

Revenues in the quarter ended March 31, 1998, rose 23%, year to year, as sharply higher medical premium revenues were augmented by the inclusion of $18.5 million of revenue from the start of a TRICARE contract with the U.S. government, greater specialty product revenues, and higher amounts of professional fees. The acquisition of two medical clinics in Nevada, together with a higher proportion of Medicare members, pushed the medical loss ratio to 82.9%, from 81.5%. However, general, administrative and marketing costs rose only 15%, and comparisons benefited from the absence of merger-related expenses of $11 million; net income soared 8.7-fold, to $12.2 million ($0.44 a share, as adjusted), from $1.4 million ($0.05).

Stock Performance - 02-OCT-98

In the past 30 trading days, SIE's shares have increased 25%, compared to a 7% fall in the S&P 500. Average trading volume for the past five days was 50,340 shares, compared with the 40-day moving average of 75,967 shares.

Key Stock Statistics

Dividend Rate/Share	Nil	Shareholders	300
Shs. outstg. (M)	27.7	Market cap. (B)	$0.555
Avg. daily vol. (M)	0.049	Inst. holdings	67%
Tang. Bk. Value/Share	9.21		
Beta	0.97		

Value of $10,000 invested 5 years ago: $ 13,915

Fiscal Year Ending Dec. 31

	1998	1997	1996	1995	1994	1993
Revenues (Million $)						
1Q	210.1	170.6	136.0	108.3	69.40	63.80
2Q	244.6	176.3	141.4	111.7	72.68	63.67
3Q	—	183.9	146.3	115.6	75.33	65.83
4Q	—	191.0	151.8	131.4	78.38	65.43
Yr.	—	721.7	575.4	467.1	295.8	258.7
Earnings Per Share ($)						
1Q	0.44	0.05	0.39	0.29	0.24	0.20
2Q	0.45	0.39	0.00	0.32	0.29	0.23
3Q	—	0.02	0.15	0.36	0.31	0.25
4Q	—	0.43	0.25	0.03	0.30	0.27
Yr.	—	0.89	1.17	1.07	1.14	0.95

Next earnings report expected: early November

Dividend Data

Amount ($)	Date Decl.	Ex-Div. Date	Stock of Record	Payment Date
3-for-2	May. 05	Jun. 09	May. 18	Jun. 08 '98

A Division of The McGraw-Hill Companies

Business Summary - 08-JUL-98

With origins stemming from the establishment of a private medical practice in Las Vegas in 1972 by the company's chairman, Anthony Marlon, Sierra Health Services has grown into one of the largest investor-owned managed care organizations, serving approximately 621,000 individuals through various health plan options.

Sierra's health maintenance organizations (HMOs) are a mixed group of network model HMOs in Nevada and a network model HMO in Texas. Most of the company's managed healthcare services in Nevada are provided through a network of more than 2,000 providers and 18 hospitals, including Sierra's multi-specialty medical group (including 145 primary care physicians), which provides medical services to 72% of its Nevada HMO members. Sierra directly provides home healthcare, hospice care and behavioral healthcare services, and operates two 24-hour urgent care centers, a radiology department, a vision department, an occupational medicine department and two freestanding surgery centers. As of March 31, 1998, HMO enrollment totaled 220,700, including commercial (158,800) and Medicare (61,900) members.

The company also operates a preferred provider organization (PPO), which offers members the option of receiving their medical care from either non-contracted or contracted providers. Members pay higher deductibles and co-payments when receiving care from non-network providers, but out-of-pocket costs are lowered by utilizing contracted providers who are part of the company's Nevada PPO network, consisting of about 2,700 physicians and 36 hospitals. At March 31, 1998, 52,800 persons were enrolled in PPO plans.

Sierra's administrative services products provide utilization review and PPO services to large employer groups that are usually self-insured. At March 31, 1998, administrative service plans covered 347,700 individuals.

The company also writes workers' compensation insurance in California, Colorado, Kansas, Nebraska, New Mexico, Texas and Utah, primarily through independent insurance agents and brokers. A contract to provide workers' compensation administrative services to the state of Nevada was terminated in September 1997, to allow the company to participate in the Nevada workers' compensation insurance market when the state allows private insurance companies to begin offering products (this is currently anticipated for 1999).

In April 1997, Sierra began servicing a five-year contract to provide healthcare services to approximately 93,000 beneficiaries of the federal TriCare (formerly CHAMPUS, or Civilian Health and Medical Program of the Uniformed Services) program.

Per Share Data ($)

(Year Ended Dec. 31)	1997	1996	1995	1994	1993	1992	1991	1990	1989	1988
Tangible Bk. Val.	8.17	7.11	7.56	5.99	3.25	2.24	1.28	0.60	0.41	0.21
Cash Flow	1.38	1.57	1.43	1.52	1.23	1.02	0.87	0.39	0.35	-0.25
Earnings	0.89	1.17	1.07	1.14	0.95	0.76	0.61	0.19	0.19	-0.41
Dividends	Nil	Nil	Nil	Nil	Nil	Nil	Nil	Nil	Nil	Nil
Payout Ratio	Nil	Nil	Nil	Nil	Nil	Nil	Nil	Nil	Nil	1
Prices - High	27³/₄	24	22³/₈	22³/₈	15¹/₈	14³/₈	9⁷/₈	4⁵/₈	3¹/₄	1
- Low	15⁷/₈	14⁷/₈	14³/₄	14¹/₈	7⁵/₈	5³/₈	3³/₄	1¹³/₁₆	¹/₂	⁷/₁₆
P/E Ratio - High	31	20	21	20	16	19	16	25	17	NM
- Low	18	13	14	12	8	7	6	10	3	NM

Income Statement Analysis (Million $)

	1997	1996	1995	1994	1993	1992	1991	1990	1989	1988
Revs.	722	575	467	296	259	236	209	170	137	144
Oper. Inc.	74.8	67.0	65.0	43.5	31.1	25.6	21.5	14.3	6.7	-1.3
Depr.	13.5	10.5	9.5	7.4	5.3	4.7	4.5	3.5	2.8	2.6
Int. Exp.	4.4	5.1	6.4	1.9	0.1	0.8	1.1	1.1	1.0	0.8
Pretax Inc.	27.5	41.6	40.1	34.2	25.9	19.5	15.1	4.7	3.3	-7.0
Eff. Tax Rate	12%	25%	30%	35%	32%	29%	29%	32%	1.80%	NM
Net Inc.	24.2	31.1	27.9	22.2	17.4	13.6	10.8	3.2	3.2	-7.0

Balance Sheet & Other Fin. Data (Million $)

	1997	1996	1995	1994	1993	1992	1991	1990	1989	1988
Cash	113	187	130	105	48.5	45.2	32.1	39.4	17.2	11.8
Curr. Assets	301	253	175	119	60.8	55.9	41.2	46.2	23.2	18.1
Total Assets	724	629	575	223	144	108	85.5	82.4	56.2	44.3
Curr. Liab.	212	253	157	59.1	55.0	46.7	43.3	52.0	30.2	28.4
LT Debt	90.8	66.2	71.3	18.4	16.0	7.7	6.3	6.1	8.4	5.7
Common Eqty.	266	234	208	134	62.1	42.3	24.1	11.9	8.5	5.1
Total Cap.	336	301	279	154	78.7	50.6	30.8	18.4	17.3	11.2
Cap. Exp.	55.7	17.9	20.5	11.2	32.0	9.3	8.5	3.1	7.7	3.0
Cash Flow	37.8	41.6	37.4	29.6	22.7	18.3	15.3	6.7	6.0	-4.4
Curr. Ratio	1.4	1.4	1.1	2.0	1.1	1.2	1.0	0.9	0.8	0.6
% LT Debt of Cap.	27.0	22.0	25.6	12.0	20.3	15.1	20.5	33.2	48.5	51.0
% Net Inc.of Revs.	3.4	5.4	6.0	7.5	6.7	5.8	5.1	1.9	2.4	NM
% Ret. on Assets	3.6	5.2	5.0	11.3	13.7	13.9	12.7	4.7	6.4	NM
% Ret. on Equity	9.7	14.1	14.8	21.4	33.2	40.5	59.6	31.8	47.4	NM

Data as orig. reptd.; bef. results of disc. opers. and/or spec. items. Per share data adj. for stk. divs. as of ex-div. date. Bold denotes diluted EPS (FASB 128). E-Estimated. NA-Not Available. NM-Not Meaningful. NR-Not Ranked.

Office—2724 N. Tenaya Way, Las Vegas, NV 89128 (P.O. Box 15645, Las Vegas 89114-5645). Tel—(702) 242-7000. Website—http://www.sierrahealth.com Chrmn & CEO—A. M. Marlon. Pres & COO— E. E. McDonald. SVP, CFO & Treas—J. L. Starr. Secy—F. E. Collins. Investor Contact—Ria Marie Carlson (702-242-7156). Dirs—T. Y. Hartley, A. M. Marlon, E. E. MacDonald, W. J. Raggio, C. L. Ruthe. Transfer Agent & Registrar—Continental Stock Transfer & Trust Co., NYC. Incorporated—in Nevada in 1984. Empl— 2,800. S&P Analyst: Robert M. Gold

03-OCT-98 Industry: Electric Companies

Summary: This utility holding company has agreed to merge with Nevada Power Co. (NYSE: NVP).

Quantitative Evaluations

Recent Price • 39⅛
52 Wk Range • 39½-29¾

Yield • 3.3%
12-Mo. P/E • 16.2

Outlook (1 Lowest—5 Highest)
• **2**

Fair Value
• **38¼**

Risk
• **Low**

Earn./Div. Rank
• **B**

Technical Eval.
• **Bearish** since 10/95

Rel. Strength Rank (1 Lowest—99 Highest)
• **94**

Insider Activity
• **NA**

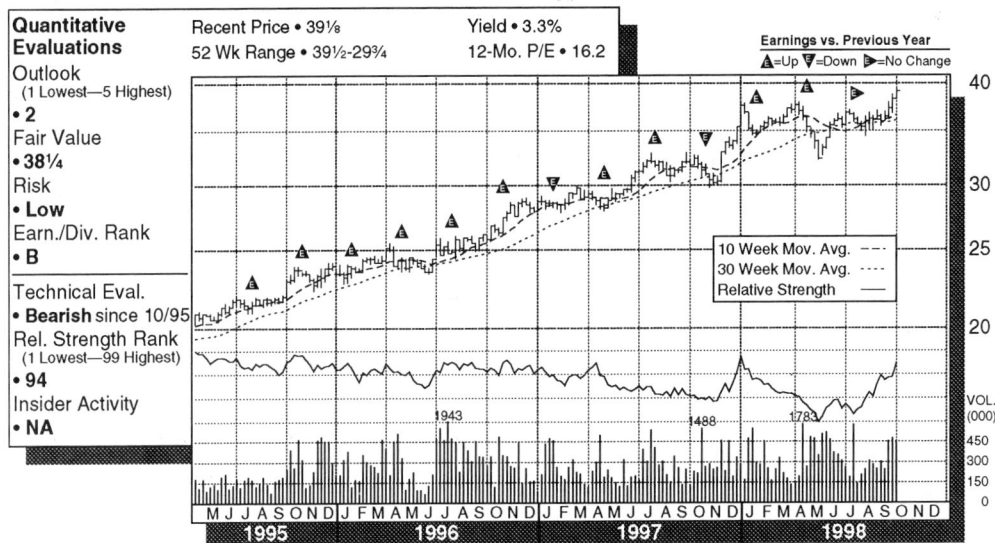

Earnings vs. Previous Year
▲=Up ▼=Down ▶=No Change

10 Week Mov. Avg. ---
30 Week Mov. Avg. ....
Relative Strength ―

Business Profile - 06-JUL-98

In April 1998, this utility holding company agreed to merge with Nevada Power Co. (NYSE: NVP). The company's shareholders will receive 1.44 shares of the combined company's common stock or $37.55 in cash per share. Based on 30,941,000 shares of Sierra Pacific and 50,767,000 shares of Nevada Power currently outstanding, stockholders of each company will each own approximately 50% of the combined company, to be named Sierra Pacific Resources. Management noted that combining Nevada Power, the fastest growing utility in the country, with Sierra Pacific creates a company with annual customer and kilowatt-hour sales growth of 5% and 7%, respectively, the highest in the industry.

Operational Review - 06-JUL-98

Revenues in the first quarter of 1998 rose 6.4%, year to year, reflecting increased electric and gas sales due to customer growth. Margins widened slightly, due primarily to well-controlled operating expenses; operating income was up 6.7%. Following lower other income and higher interest charges, net income increased 2.0%, to $23,694,000 ($0.69 per share, after preferred dividends), from $23,241,000 ($0.67).

Stock Performance - 02-OCT-98

In the past 30 trading days, SRP's shares have increased 8%, compared to a 7% fall in the S&P 500. Average trading volume for the past five days was 94,320 shares, compared with the 40-day moving average of 79,638 shares.

Key Stock Statistics

Dividend Rate/Share	1.30	Shareholders	23,100
Shs. outstg. (M)	31.0	Market cap. (B)	$ 1.2
Avg. daily vol. (M)	0.099	Inst. holdings	51%
Tang. Bk. Value/Share	21.05		
Beta	0.27		

Value of $10,000 invested 5 years ago: $ 24,958

Fiscal Year Ending Dec. 31

	1998	1997	1996	1995	1994	1993
Revenues (Million $)						
1Q	184.5	173.3	163.8	160.2	154.0	139.3
2Q	171.6	156.7	150.2	142.2	135.9	123.1
3Q	—	160.9	160.8	151.2	158.2	130.1
4Q	—	168.8	152.9	152.5	178.2	135.6
Yr.	—	663.2	627.7	606.1	626.3	528.1
Earnings Per Share ($)						
1Q	**0.69**	**0.68**	0.59	0.52	0.51	0.50
2Q	**0.50**	**0.50**	0.49	0.37	0.33	0.22
3Q	—	**0.59**	0.72	0.55	0.46	0.51
4Q	—	**0.65**	0.39	0.51	0.49	0.44
Yr.	—	**2.40**	2.19	1.95	1.79	1.67

Next earnings report expected: late October

Dividend Data (Dividends have been paid since 1916.)

Amount ($)	Date Decl.	Ex-Div. Date	Stock of Record	Payment Date
0.310	Nov. 18	Jan. 14	Jan. 16	Feb. 01 '98
0.325	Feb. 24	Apr. 14	Apr. 16	May. 01 '98
0.325	May. 18	Jul. 15	Jul. 17	Aug. 01 '98
0.325	Aug. 17	Oct. 14	Oct. 16	Nov. 01 '98

A Division of The McGraw-Hill Companies

Business Summary - 06-JUL-98

Sierra Pacific Resources (SRP) and Nevada Power Co. (NYSE: NVP) announced in April 1998 that they had agreed to merge, creating a company with a total market capitalization of approximately $4.0 billion. The combined entity, which will retain SRP's name, will serve a total of more than 800,000 electric, 100,000 gas and 65,000 water customers living in southern and northern Nevada, and in the Lake Tahoe area of California. Based on 1997 results of both companies, total annual revenues for the combined company would be approximately $1.5 billion, with annual earnings of approximately $160 million, and assets of $4.3 billion. Each SRP stockholder will receive 1.44 shares of the combined company's common stock or $37.55 in cash per share. Completion of the merger is expected in approximately one year.

Sierra Pacific Resources has five primary subsidiaries: Sierra Pacific Power Co. (SPPC), Tuscarora Gas Pipeline Co. (TGPC), Sierra Energy Co. dba e-three (e-three), Lands of Sierra, Inc. (LOS), and Sierra Pacific Energy Co. (SPE). SPPC is the company's largest unit and primarily provides electricity to approximately 287,000 customers in a 50,000 square mile service area including western, central and northeastern parts of Nevada, including the cities of Reno, Sparks, Carson City, Elko and a portion of eastern California, including the Lake Tahoe area. SPPC also provides natural gas in Nevada to approximately 101,000 customers in Reno/Sparks and environs. SPPC supplies water service in Nevada to about 65,000 customers in the Reno/ Sparks metropolitan area. During 1997, 92% of SPPC's revenues were from retail sales of electricity, natural gas and water in Nevada; 6% from retail sales of electricity in California and 2% from wholesale sales of electricity in Nevada and California.

The Tuscarora interstate natural gas pipeline, which completed its first full year of operation in 1996, was built by the Tuscarora Gas Transmission Company, a partnership of Tuscarora Gas Pipeline Co., a wholly owned subsidiary of Sierra Pacific, and TCPL Tuscarora Ltd., a wholly owned subsidiary of TransCanada Pipe-Lines USA., Ltd. The 229-mile pipeline was designed to initially transport 113,500 decatherms of natural gas per day, but the pipeline can be expanded to transport up to 285,000 decatherms per day. Management believes Tuscarora gives the region competitive access to abundant gas reserves in the Western Canadian Sedimentary Basin in Alberta, one of the largest proven reserves in North America.

Organized in October 1996, e-three provides comprehensive energy services in commercial and industrial markets. LOS is a real estate management company. SPE is developing a customer information system for the energy industry.

Per Share Data ($)

(Year Ended Dec. 31)	1997	1996	1995	1994	1993	1992	1991	1990	1989	1988
Tangible Bk. Val.	20.49	19.28	18.10	17.27	16.85	15.85	16.83	16.39	17.77	17.29
Earnings	2.41	2.19	1.95	1.79	1.67	1.09	1.75	1.93	2.05	1.98
Dividends	1.23	1.17	1.12	1.12	1.12	1.48	1.84	1.84	1.81	1.77
Payout Ratio	51%	53%	57%	63%	67%	136%	105%	95%	88%	89%
Prices - High	38	29⅛	24⅛	20⅜	22¼	24⅜	24¼	25½	25⅞	23¾
- Low	27¾	22¾	18⅜	17¼	19½	17⅞	20⅛	18⅜	22⅜	20⅞
P/E Ratio - High	16	13	12	11	13	22	14	13	13	12
- Low	12	10	9	10	12	16	12	10	11	11

Income Statement Analysis (Million $)

	1997	1996	1995	1994	1993	1992	1991	1990	1989	1988
Revs.	663	628	606	626	528	482	469	471	445	408
Depr.	64.1	58.1	55.1	52.6	49.9	48.1	44.8	40.8	38.2	36.4
Maint.	23.4	20.7	18.4	16.2	16.6	17.2	16.7	17.0	19.9	18.0
Fxd. Chgs. Cov.	3.6	3.3	2.9	2.6	2.4	2.0	2.3	2.4	2.5	2.5
Constr. Credits	10.5	9.2	4.3	3.5	3.5	1.5	0.7	1.1	1.1	1.0
Eff. Tax Rate	33%	35%	39%	33%	32%	33%	33%	31%	32%	34%
Net Inc.	74.4	66.9	58.0	52.4	44.9	33.8	41.9	43.6	45.0	42.0

Balance Sheet & Other Fin. Data (Million $)

	1997	1996	1995	1994	1993	1992	1991	1990	1989	1988
Gross Prop.	2,315	2,150	1,970	1,836	1,736	1,586	1,485	1,417	1,328	1,262
Cap. Exp.	14.0	203	144	125	166	115	81.0	99	81.0	101
Net Prop.	1,650	1,543	1,413	1,331	1,271	1,160	1,094	1,064	1,009	973
Capitalization:										
LT Debt	627	638	574	562	551	562	506	490	462	450
% LT Debt	45	47	48	48	48	52	51	53	50	51
Pfd.	122	122	86.7	93.5	107	107	57.1	57.0	57.1	57.1
% Pfd.	8.80	7.90	7.20	8.00	9.30	9.90	5.80	6.20	6.20	6.50
Common	633	595	545	509	490	412	429	376	399	372
% Common	46	44	45	44	43	38	43	41	44	42
Total Cap.	1,587	1,561	1,408	1,367	1,357	1,259	1,216	1,140	1,148	1,092
% Oper. Ratio	78.4	82.7	82.7	84.3	83.4	82.2	82.1	81.6	81.2	80.1
% Earn. on Net Prop.	7.3	7.4	7.6	7.6	7.2	6.2	7.8	8.4	8.4	8.6
% Return On Revs.	11.2	10.7	9.6	8.4	8.5	7.0	8.9	9.3	10.1	10.3
% Return On Invest. Capital	8.0	7.8	9.7	7.6	7.4	6.3	7.8	8.0	8.2	8.3
% Return On Com. Equity	12.1	11.8	11.0	10.5	10.0	6.8	10.4	11.3	11.7	11.5

Data as orig. reptd.; bef. results of disc. opers. and/or spec. items. Per share data adj. for stk. divs. as of ex-div. date. Bold denotes diluted EPS (FASB 128). E-Estimated. NA-Not Available. NM-Not Meaningful. NR-Not Ranked.

Office—6100 Neil Rd., Reno, NV 89511. **Tel**—(702) 689-4011. **Website**—http://www.sierrapacific.com **Chrmn, Pres & CEO**—M. K. Malquist. **SVP & Secy**—W. E. Peterson. **SVP, CFO & Investor Contact**—Mark A. Ruelle. **Dirs**—E. P. Bliss, K. M. Corbin, T. J. Day, H. P. Dayton Jr., J. R. Donnelley, R. N. Fulstone, M. K. Malquist, J. L. Murphy, D. E. Wheeler, R. B. Whittington. **Transfer Agent & Registrar**—First Chicago Trust Co., Jersey City, NJ. **Incorporated**—in Maine in 1912; reincorporated in Nevada in 1965 and 1983. **Empl**—1,478. **S&P Analyst**: J. Robert Cho

03-OCT-98 **Industry:** Banks (Regional)

Summary: This company's Silicon Valley Bank subsidiary serves emerging growth and middle-market companies in targeted niches through banking offices in the Silicon Valley, California.

Quantitative Evaluations	
Outlook (1 Lowest—5 Highest)	• 3⁻
Fair Value	• 21¼
Risk	• **Low**
Earn./Div. Rank	• **B**
Technical Eval.	• **Bearish** since 7/98
Rel. Strength Rank (1 Lowest—99 Highest)	• 8
Insider Activity	• **Unfavorable**

Recent Price • 15¾
52 Wk Range • 39-12½

Yield • Nil
12-Mo. P/E • 10.8

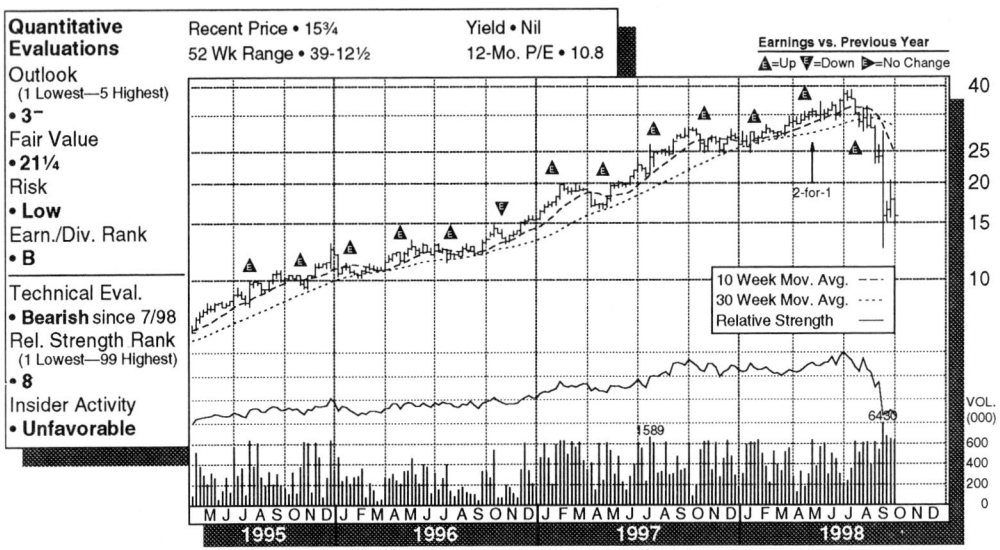

Earnings vs. Previous Year
▲=Up ▼=Down ▶=No Change

10 Week Mov. Avg. – – –
30 Week Mov. Avg. ·······
Relative Strength ——

2-for-1

Business Profile - 24-JUL-98

Net income rose to record levels in the second quarter of 1998, mainly reflecting growth in average interest-earning assets, partly offset by increases in both noninterest expense and in the provision for loan losses. In the quarter, the company recorded a 46% ($854 million) year to year increase in average interest-earning assets, which consisted of loans (up $295 million), plus a combination of highly liquid, lower-yielding federal funds sold, securities purchased under agreement to resell and investment securities, which collectively increased $559 million. A two-for-one stock split was effected in May 1998.

Operational Review - 24-JUL-98

Net interest income in the six months ended June 30, 1998, advanced 32%, year to year, as total interest income was up 40% and total interest expense rose 56%. The gain in net interest income stemmed from strong growth in total assets and loans. The provision for loan losses climbed 59%, total noninterest income increased 26%, and total noninterest expense rose 34%; pretax income was up 21%. After taxes at 41.5%, versus 42.0%, net income advanced 22%, to $15,780,000 ($0.75 a share) from $12,969,000 ($0.65, as adjusted).

Stock Performance - 02-OCT-98

In the past 30 trading days, SIVB's shares have declined 47%, compared to a 7% fall in the S&P 500. Average trading volume for the past five days was 190,060 shares, compared with the 40-day moving average of 327,882 shares.

Key Stock Statistics

Dividend Rate/Share	Nil	Shareholders	700
Shs. outstg. (M)	20.6	Market cap. (B)	$0.324
Avg. daily vol. (M)	0.520	Inst. holdings	69%
Tang. Bk. Value/Share	9.64		
Beta	1.18		

Value of $10,000 invested 5 years ago: $ 38,181

Fiscal Year Ending Dec. 31

	1998	1997	1996	1995	1994	1993
Revenues (Million $)						
1Q	54.93	39.72	30.04	24.99	18.95	20.80
2Q	59.17	42.70	33.57	26.78	18.60	17.43
3Q	—	46.98	35.31	30.30	19.87	18.13
4Q	—	49.84	37.76	31.75	22.60	17.04
Yr.	—	179.2	136.7	113.8	79.97	73.40
Earnings Per Share ($)						
1Q	**0.36**	**0.31**	0.24	0.18	0.10	0.06
2Q	**0.39**	**0.34**	0.29	0.22	0.13	0.01
3Q	—	**0.35**	0.27	0.29	0.12	0.02
4Q	—	**0.36**	0.30	0.29	0.17	0.01
Yr.	—	**1.36**	1.10	0.99	0.53	0.10

Next earnings report expected: mid October

Dividend Data

Amount ($)	Date Decl.	Ex-Div. Date	Stock of Record	Payment Date
2-for-1	Mar. 19	May. 04	Apr. 17	May. 01 '98

A Division of The **McGraw-Hill** *Companies*

Business Summary - 24-JUL-98

The founders of the Silicon Valley Bank subsidiary of Silicon Valley Bancshares (SIVB) set out in 1983 to capture a growing market in Northern California, which at that time had been greatly underserved by commercial banks: namely, the emerging growth technology companies in the Silicon Valley.

Today, SIVB is the largest independent bank holding company headquartered in Silicon Valley. It serves emerging growth and middle-market companies in specific targeted niches, focusing on the technology and life sciences industries, while also identifying and capitalizing on opportunities to serve companies in other industries for which financial services needs are underserved.

The bank's technology and life sciences niche focuses on serving companies in a variety of technology and life sciences industries and markets across the U.S., through regional banking offices in California, and loan offices in Arizona, Colorado, Georgia, Illinois, Maryland, Massachusetts, Oregon, Texas and Washington. The companies served are generally liquid, net providers of

funds to the bank, and often have low utilization of their credit facilities. Lending to this niche is typically related to working capital, lines of credit, equipment financing, asset acquisition loans, and bridge financing.

Total loans of $1.17 billion (net of unearned income) outstanding at the end of 1997 were divided as follows: commercial 89%, real estate construction 5%, real estate term 3%, and consumer and other loans 3%.

As of December 31, 1997, the allowance for possible loan losses totaled $37,700,000 (3.21% of total loans), versus $32,700,000 (3.79%) a year earlier. Net loan chargeoffs totaled $5,067,000 (0.5% of average loans) in 1997, versus $7,426,000 (1.0%) in 1996. At the end of 1997, nonperforming assets aggregated $27,350,000 (1.0% of total assets), compared with $25,085,000 (1.3%) a year earlier.

Total deposits aggregated $2.4 billion at the end of 1997 and were divided: noninterest-bearing demand 32%, NOW 1%, money market 62% and time 5%.

Interest on loans accounted for 60% of total income for 1997, interest on investment securities 23%, other interest income 10%, disposition of client warrants 3% and other noninterest income 4%.

Per Share Data ($)

(Year Ended Dec. 31)	1997	1996	1995	1994	1993	1992	1991	1990	1989	1988
Tangible Bk. Val.	8.75	7.25	5.86	4.49	4.24	4.18	4.29	3.29	2.49	1.90
Earnings	1.36	1.10	0.99	0.53	0.10	-0.14	NA	NA	NA	NA
Dividends	Nil	Nil	Nil	Nil	Nil	0.01	0.03	0.02	0.01	Nil
Payout Ratio	Nil	Nil	Nil	Nil	Nil	Nil	Nil	Nil	Nil	Nil
Prices - High	29$^7/_8$	16$^1/_4$	13$^1/_8$	6$^3/_4$	6$^1/_8$	7$^3/_8$	7$^7/_8$	7$^5/_8$	6$^1/_2$	2$^5/_8$
- Low	15$^7/_8$	10$^1/_8$	6$^1/_2$	4$^1/_2$	4	2$^7/_8$	4	3$^1/_8$	2$^1/_2$	1$^5/_{16}$
P/E Ratio - High	22	14	13	12	61	NM	9	9	11	7
- Low	12	9	6	8	39	NM	4	4	4	3

Income Statement Analysis (Million $)

	1997	1996	1995	1994	1993	1992	1991	1990	1989	1988
Net Int. Inc.	111	87.3	74.0	60.3	50.5	54.9	46.1	35.6	NA	NA
Tax Equiv. Adj.	0.8	0.3	0.3	NA	NA	NA	NA	NA	NA	NA
Non Int. Inc.	13.2	11.6	13.3	7.3	9.3	3.2	1.6	0.8	NA	NA
Loan Loss Prov.	10.1	10.4	8.7	3.1	9.7	35.4	4.1	3.2	NA	NA
Exp./Op. Revs.	53%	53%	55%	NA	79%	45%	47%	44%	NA	NA
Pretax Inc.	47.7	35.8	29.9	16.5	2.7	-3.7	21.2	17.2	NA	NA
Eff. Tax Rate	42%	40%	39%	45%	40%	NM	42%	41%	NA	NA
Net Inc.	27.7	21.5	18.2	9.1	1.6	-2.2	12.3	10.1	NA	NA
% Net Int. Marg.	5.60	6.10	7.10	7.20	6.40	6.40	NA	NA	NA	NA

Balance Sheet & Other Fin. Data (Million $)

	1997	1996	1995	1994	1993	1992	1991	1990	1989	1988
Earning Assets:										
Money Mkt	427	433	342	290	NA	NA	NA	NA	NA	NA
Inv. Securities	1,014	625	321	156	NA	NA	NA	NA	NA	NA
Com'l Loans	1,051	756	NA	NA	NA	NA	NA	NA	NA	NA
Other Loans	123	NA	NA	NA	NA	NA	NA	NA	NA	NA
Total Assets	2,625	1,925	1,408	1,162	992	959	869	673	NA	NA
Demand Deposits	788	599	451	401	NA	NA	NA	NA	NA	NA
Time Deposits	125	85.2	65.5	88.7	NA	NA	NA	NA	NA	NA
LT Debt	Nil	Nil	Nil	Nil	NA	NA	NA	NA	NA	NA
Common Eqty.	174	135	105	77.3	70.3	66.0	66.4	40.1	NA	NA
% Ret. on Assets	1.2	1.3	NA	NA	0.2	NA	1.6	NA	NA	NA
% Ret. on Equity	17.9	17.9	NA	NA	2.3	NA	23.0	NA	NA	NA
% Loan Loss Resv.	3.2	3.8	4.0	NA	4.5	3.6	1.9	1.8	NA	NA
% Loans/Deposits	77.3	48.7	57.2	NA	60.2	68.0	74.3	77.4	NA	NA
% Equity to Assets	6.8	7.2	NA	NA	7.0	7.2	6.9	NA	NA	NA

Data as orig. reptd.; bef. results of disc opers. and/or spec. items. Per share data adj. for stk. divs. as of ex-div. date. Bold denotes diluted EPS (FASB 128). E-Estimated. NA-Not Available. NM-Not Meaningful. NR-Not Ranked.

Office—3003 Tasman Drive, Santa Clara, CA 95054-1191. **Tel**—(408) 654-7282.**Chrmn**—D. J. Kelleher. **Pres & CEO**—J. C. Dean.**EVP & CFO**—C. T. Lutes. **Investor Contact**—Lisa Bertolet (408-654-7282).**Dirs**—G. K. Barr, J. F. Burns Jr., J. C. Dean, D. M. deWilde, C. J. Ferrari Jr., D. J. Kelleher, J. R. Porter, A. R. Wells.**Transfer Agent & Registrar**—ChaseMellon Shareholder Services.**Incorporated**—in California in 1982.**Empl**— 520. **S&P Analyst:** J. J. Schemitsch

03-OCT-98

Industry:
Auto Parts & Equipment

Summary: This company makes machined components and assemblies for OEMs in the automotive, truck and heavy-duty equipment industries in North America, Europe and Japan.

Quantitative Evaluations	Recent Price • 9⅝	Yield • 4.2%
	52 Wk Range • 15⅜-9⅛	12-Mo. P/E • 16.3

Outlook (1 Lowest—5 Highest)
• **3⁻**

Fair Value
• **11¾**

Risk
• **Low**

Earn./Div. Rank
• **B+**

Technical Eval.
• **Bullish** since 9/98

Rel. Strength Rank (1 Lowest—99 Highest)
• **42**

Insider Activity
• **Neutral**

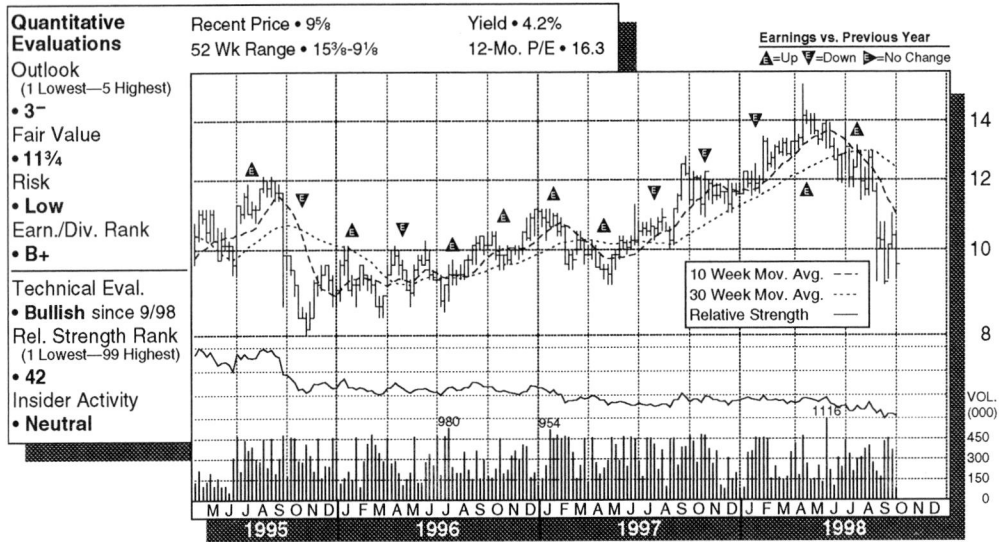

Earnings vs. Previous Year
▲=Up ▼=Down ▶=No Change

10 Week Mov. Avg. – – –
30 Week Mov. Avg. ‑‑‑‑
Relative Strength —

Business Profile - 21-JUL-98

During 1997, SMPS's earnings were hurt by an $8.8 million charge for plant closings. However, Simpson exceeded its sales expectations for 1997, as sales rose to $451 million, $11 million over its target, including sales from the June 1997 acquisition of the vibration attenuation business of Holset Engineering from Cummins Engine Co. Simpson expects that the consolidation of two plants will generate annualized savings of $5.5 million pretax beginning in 1998. In July 1998, the company said that work stoppages at General Motors had hurt sales by approximately $3 million in the second quarter of 1998. Despite the GM strike, sales in the second quarter rose 17% above year earlier levels. Sales will continue to be restricted until the GM situation is resolved. Recently, directors authorized a stock buyback program that allows for the repurchase of up to 650,000 shares of common stock.

Operational Review - 21-JUL-98

Sales in the six months ended June 30, 1998, advanced 18%, year to year, due to the acquisition of the vibration attenuation business of Holset Engineering which offset lost sales due to work stoppages at General Motors. Margins widened, and operating profit grew 20%. Following a sharp increase in interest expense, pretax income was up only 2.4%. After taxes at 33.0%, versus 36.5%, net income climbed 8%, to $10,591,000 ($0.58 a share), up from $9,805,000 ($0.54).

Stock Performance - 02-OCT-98

In the past 30 trading days, SMPS's shares have declined 17%, compared to a 7% fall in the S&P 500. Average trading volume for the past five days was 16,680 shares, compared with the 40-day moving average of 60,879 shares.

Key Stock Statistics

Dividend Rate/Share	0.40	Shareholders	4,300
Shs. outstg. (M)	18.3	Market cap. (B)	$0.177
Avg. daily vol. (M)	0.068	Inst. holdings	52%
Tang. Bk. Value/Share	3.99		
Beta	0.52		

Value of $10,000 invested 5 years ago: $ 11,408

Fiscal Year Ending Dec. 31

	1998	1997	1996	1995	1994	1993
Revenues (Million $)						
1Q	125.6	105.9	101.4	107.2	82.70	65.13
2Q	128.7	110.3	110.0	103.6	91.32	67.31
3Q	—	112.3	98.23	86.34	85.88	57.87
4Q	—	123.0	98.30	97.89	96.75	72.18
Yr.	—	451.5	408.0	395.1	356.6	262.5
Earnings Per Share ($)						
1Q	**0.27**	**0.24**	0.22	0.31	0.23	0.19
2Q	**0.31**	**0.30**	0.33	0.27	0.25	0.17
3Q	—	0.19	0.19	0.08	0.14	0.04
4Q	—	**0.20**	0.23	0.19	0.18	0.14
Yr.	—	**0.55**	0.97	0.85	0.80	0.53

Next earnings report expected: mid October

Dividend Data (Dividends have been paid since 1972.)

Amount ($)	Date Decl.	Ex-Div. Date	Stock of Record	Payment Date
0.100	Nov. 19	Dec. 02	Dec. 04	Dec. 18 '97
0.100	Feb. 24	Mar. 03	Mar. 05	Mar. 26 '98
0.100	Apr. 21	Jun. 02	Jun. 04	Jun. 25 '98
0.100	Aug. 18	Sep. 01	Sep. 03	Sep. 24 '98

A Division of The McGraw-Hill Companies

STANDARD
&POOR'S
STOCK REPORTS

Simpson Industries, Inc.

5227

03-OCT-98

Business Summary - 21-JUL-98

Simpson Industries, Inc. (SMPS), a supplier of power-train and chassis products to the automotive and diesel engine industries, implemented a number if strategies in 1997. The full impact of 13 new product launches slated for 1997 will not be felt until 1998. Similarly, expansion into Europe in 1997 will not aid the bottom line until 1998. Plant closings during 1997 hampered pretax earnings due to an $8.7 million charge. However, the company anticipates that this move could generate annualized savings of $5.5 million beginning in 1998. SMPS believes it is laying the foundation for prosperous growth in future years through internal and external expansion and a strong focus on the cost structure of its plants.

SMPS produces products for original equipment manufacturers of automobiles, light trucks, diesel engines and heavy-duty equipment, mainly under long-term product programs. The company supplies more than 700 different components and assemblies in four product categories, and is generally its customers' only source for these products. SMPS's noise, vibration and harshness products include crankshaft dampers and other engine components. Brake caliper brackets, front spindles and knuckles are among the products of the wheel-end and suspension group, the company's fastest-growing focus area. SMPS's high-precision components such as air conditioning cylinders and scroll compressor housings reflect the company's roots in high-precision, make-to-print components. SMPS also makes modular engine assemblies, with a focus on oil and water pumps. Production of these value-added products, as opposed to SMPS's single-component offerings, is one element of the company's growth strategy.

In 1996, SMPS opened its new Technical Center, bringing the diverse activities of the product development process under one roof and advancing the company's efforts to become an extension of its customers' product engineering function. SMPS designs 60% of the products it makes, up from 25% six years ago.

In June 1997, SMPS purchased the U.K.-based vibration attenuation (VA) business of Holset Engineering Co., Ltd., a subsidiary of Cummins Engine Co., Inc., substantially enhancing the company's global presence. The purchase price of $76 million was financed by the private placement of $65 million in debt; revenues in this business were $67 million in 1996. The acquisition of this business makes SMPS the world's largest manufacturer of engine vibration dampers.

In April 1998, SMPS acquired Stahl International, Inc., a closely held manufacturer of viscous dampers with annual sales of $4.2 million. Terms of the deal were not disclosed. Also during April 1998, the company announced it had entered into a cooperative effort with Fukoku Co., Ltd., to explore anti-vibration solutions for the automotive and heavy duty truck markets.

Per Share Data ($)

(Year Ended Dec. 31)	1997	1996	1995	1994	1993	1992	1991	1990	1989	1988
Tangible Bk. Val.	3.75	6.42	5.84	5.47	5.12	5.16	4.39	4.45	4.43	4.08
Cash Flow	1.84	2.10	1.90	1.71	1.32	1.26	1.15	1.17	1.38	1.31
Earnings	0.55	0.97	0.85	0.80	0.53	0.47	0.31	0.42	0.75	0.74
Dividends	0.40	0.40	0.40	0.39	0.37	0.37	0.37	0.37	0.37	0.28
Payout Ratio	73%	41%	47%	49%	71%	83%	120%	89%	50%	38%
Prices - High	12¾	11⅛	12⅛	15⅝	14⅝	13⅛	9⅛	7⅝	9⅞	7⅝
- Low	9⅛	8⅜	8	7⅞	10⅜	8	4⅝	4⅝	6	3⅝
P/E Ratio - High	23	11	14	20	28	28	30	18	13	10
- Low	17	9	9	10	20	17	15	11	8	5

Income Statement Analysis (Million $)

	1997	1996	1995	1994	1993	1992	1991	1990	1989	1988
Revs.	452	408	395	357	262	223	192	193	197	178
Oper. Inc.	54.3	50.1	47.7	43.1	33.6	30.1	22.5	23.3	26.9	25.5
Depr.	23.4	20.5	18.9	16.3	14.2	13.4	12.4	10.8	9.2	8.1
Int. Exp.	7.5	5.3	5.5	4.3	3.6	3.8	2.7	2.4	2.5	2.5
Pretax Inc.	15.2	25.6	24.4	23.1	16.3	14.0	7.1	9.5	16.0	16.2
Eff. Tax Rate	34%	31%	37%	38%	42%	43%	36%	36%	33%	35%
Net Inc.	10.1	17.6	15.3	14.4	9.4	8.0	4.5	6.1	10.7	10.5

Balance Sheet & Other Fin. Data (Million $)

	1997	1996	1995	1994	1993	1992	1991	1990	1989	1988
Cash	8.2	28.9	13.5	4.8	18.1	43.0	21.1	8.7	8.3	13.4
Curr. Assets	115	94.2	82.0	70.5	70.9	76.9	51.3	38.7	41.2	48.2
Total Assets	342	249	324	207	187	170	138	123	124	116
Curr. Liab.	78.3	49.2	41.7	38.9	36.4	27.2	20.9	17.6	20.9	22.4
LT Debt	119	58.6	62.3	50.4	39.0	37.0	38.5	25.0	25.0	25.0
Common Eqty.	118	116	105	98.0	91.5	91.8	64.1	64.8	63.8	57.9
Total Cap.	249	186	178	158	141	141	116	104	102	94.0
Cap. Exp.	28.9	26.3	31.6	38.2	37.5	22.4	15.8	14.1	22.6	16.0
Cash Flow	33.5	38.1	34.2	30.7	23.7	21.4	16.9	17.0	19.9	18.6
Curr. Ratio	1.5	1.9	2.0	1.8	1.9	2.8	2.5	2.2	2.0	2.2
% LT Debt of Cap.	47.7	31.6	35.0	31.9	27.7	26.2	33.2	24.0	24.6	26.6
% Net Inc.of Revs.	2.2	4.3	3.9	4.0	3.6	3.6	2.4	3.2	5.4	5.9
% Ret. on Assets	3.4	7.3	5.8	7.3	5.3	4.7	3.5	4.9	8.9	9.7
% Ret. on Equity	8.6	15.9	15.1	15.1	10.3	9.4	7.0	9.5	17.6	19.4

Data as orig. reptd.; bef. results of disc. opers. and/or spec. items. Per share data adj. for stk. divs. as of ex-div. date. Bold denotes diluted EPS (FASB 128). E-Estimated. NA-Not Available. NM-Not Meaningful. NR-Not Ranked.

Office—47603 Halyard Dr., Plymouth, MI 48170-2429. **Tel**—(734) 207-6200. **Fax**—(734) 207-6500. **Chrmn, Pres & CEO**—R. E. Parrott. **VP-Fin, CFO & Investor Contact**—V. M. Khilnani. **Secy**—F. K. Zinn. **Dirs**—M. E. Batten, S. F. Haka, G. R. Kempton, W. J. Kirchberger, R. W. Navarre, R. E. Parrott, R. L. Roudebush, F. L. Weaver, F. K. Zinn. **Transfer Agent & Registrar**—Harris Trust and Savings Bank. **Incorporated**—in Michigan in 1945. **Empl**—2,355. **S&P Analyst:** Kathleen J. Fraser

Skyline Corp.

2045

NYSE Symbol **SKY**

In S&P SmallCap 600

03-OCT-98

Industry: Homebuilding

Summary: This company produces both manufactured housing and recreational vehicles.

Quantitative Evaluations	
Outlook (1 Lowest—5 Highest)	• NA
Fair Value	• NA
Risk	• Low
Earn./Div. Rank	• A-
Technical Eval.	• NA
Rel. Strength Rank (1 Lowest—99 Highest)	• 65
Insider Activity	• Neutral

Recent Price • 27⅝
52 Wk Range • 34⅞-25¼

Yield • 2.2%
12-Mo. P/E • 12.5

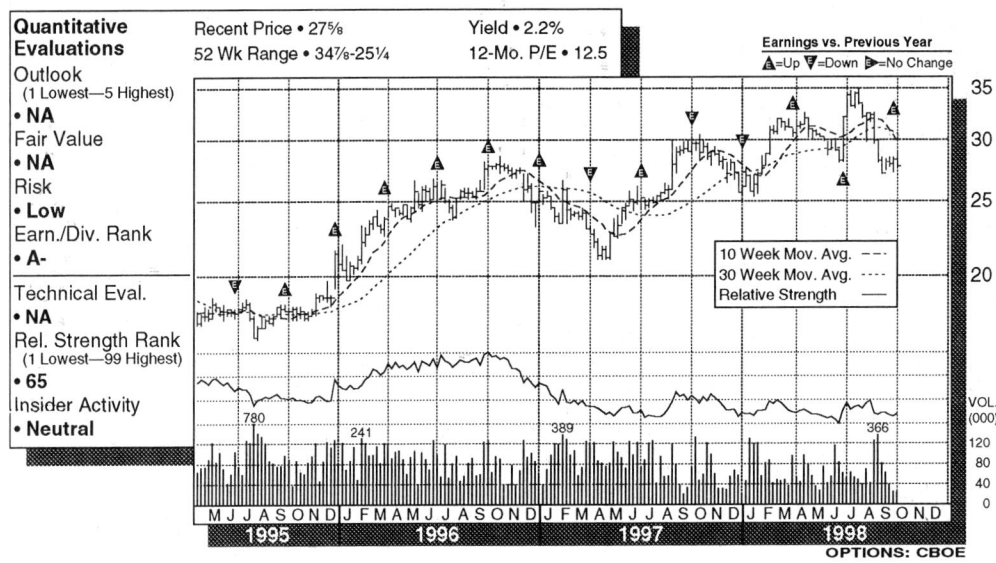

Earnings vs. Previous Year
▲=Up ▼=Down ▶=No Change

10 Week Mov. Avg. — — —
30 Week Mov. Avg. ·······
Relative Strength ——

VOL. (000)

OPTIONS: CBOE

Business Profile - 08-APR-98

This leading producer of manufactured homes and recreational vehicles (RVs) has experienced a long earnings uptrend since profits bottomed in 1991. Skyline has been profitable in each year since its founding in 1951. The balance sheet remains strong, with no long term debt. Manufactured housing operations were hurt recently by severe weather conditions in many parts of the U.S., and by a softening of demand in the manufactured housing industry that began in late 1996. But manufactured housing sales in the third quarter of FY 98 (May) jumped 17% from the previous year - despite historically being the company's slowest quarter.

Operational Review - 08-APR-98

Based on a preliminary report, sales in the first nine months of FY 98 (May), were flat compared to the prior year period, as a 17% jump in third quarter manufactured housing sales helped sales in that segment move up 1.1% for the nine month period, however this was offset by a 5.4% drop in recreational vehicle sales. Despite a gain of $577,000 ($0.06 a share) from the sale of an unused production facility, net income dropped 11%, to $12,966,000 ($1.36), from $14,623,000 ($1.44).

Stock Performance - 02-OCT-98

In the past 30 trading days, SKY's shares have declined 8%, compared to a 7% fall in the S&P 500. Average trading volume for the past five days was 4,840 shares, compared with the 40-day moving average of 21,082 shares.

Key Stock Statistics

Dividend Rate/Share	0.60	Shareholders	1,900
Shs. outstg. (M)	9.4	Market cap. (B)	$0.261
Avg. daily vol. (M)	0.008	Inst. holdings	49%
Tang. Bk. Value/Share	19.46		
Beta	0.55		

Value of $10,000 invested 5 years ago: $ 15,044

Fiscal Year Ending May 31

	1999	1998	1997	1996	1995	1994
Revenues (Million $)						
1Q	171.0	161.6	171.5	163.9	155.3	136.2
2Q	—	160.3	164.4	172.5	164.5	145.3
3Q	—	131.4	118.0	138.6	150.7	130.7
4Q	—	170.1	159.3	171.1	171.7	167.9
Yr.	—	623.4	613.2	646.0	642.1	580.1
Earnings Per Share ($)						
1Q	0.69	0.57	0.62	0.42	0.36	0.27
2Q	—	0.56	0.62	0.54	0.36	0.38
3Q	—	0.23	0.18	0.30	0.23	0.22
4Q	—	0.74	0.64	0.59	0.42	0.47
Yr.	—	2.10	2.07	1.84	1.38	1.34

Next earnings report expected: mid December

Dividend Data (Dividends have been paid since 1960.)

Amount ($)	Date Decl.	Ex-Div. Date	Stock of Record	Payment Date
0.150	Dec. 01	Dec. 15	Dec. 17	Jan. 02 '98
0.150	Mar. 02	Mar. 13	Mar. 17	Apr. 01 '98
0.150	Jun. 01	Jun. 16	Jun. 18	Jul. 01 '98
0.150	Jul. 16	Sep. 09	Sep. 11	Oct. 01 '98

A Division of The McGraw·Hill Companies

Business Summary - 08-APR-98

A long period of sales growth in the manufactured housing industry came to an end in November 1996, as industry shipments fell from year-earlier levels for the first time since 1991. The extended sales boom, which followed an even longer stretch of lean years, was made possible, in part, by the improving public image of factory-built homes. Americans have responded favorably to the industry's larger, multi-section homes, whose residential appearance often makes them difficult to distinguish from their site-built brethren. Demand for manufactured housing has also been fueled by the greater affordability of these homes.

The manufactured housing industry produced more than 363,000 homes in calendar 1996. Skyline Corp. (SKY), whose 5% share of the market makes it a leading industry player, saw its shipments drop to 17,512 homes in FY 97 (May), from 20,301 in FY 96. In addition to slackening demand, severe weather conditions and inventory reductions by retail dealers also affected sales. Manufactured housing sales (81% of SKY's total sales in FY 97) fell 9%, to $495 million. SKY also makes non-motorized recreational vehicles (19%).

Principal buyers for SKY's homes are young married couples and senior citizens, although the market tends to broaden when conventional housing becomes more difficult to purchase and finance. Multi-section homes accounted for 53% of shipments in FY 97, up from 50% in FY 96, reflecting growing acceptance of the larger units. The company's single- and multi-section models are sold nationwide through independent dealers.

Unit sales were up 9% for the company's recreational vehicle (RV) group in FY 97, reflecting a reversal of a slowdown in the RV industry in the previous year. SKY shipped a total of 9,103 RVs during the year, including 6,091 travel trailers, 2,622 "fifth wheel" travel trailers, and 390 truck campers. With its fifth wheel and truck camper models, the company capitalizes on the continuing popularity of light trucks in urban, suburban and rural markets. By attracting a diverse mix of buyers, these trucks are expanding the market for RVs. RV sales rose 15% in FY 97, and the group produced $4.6 million in operating earnings, in contrast to a small operating loss in FY 96.

In FY 97, total sales fell 5%, to $613 million, as the RV group's gains were outweighed by the decline in manufactured housing sales. Net earnings, benefiting from a gain on the sale of unused production facilities, were up 6%, to $20.8 million. Net earnings jumped 32% in the third quarter of FY 98, on an 11% increase in sales, as a 17% rise in manufactured housing sales outweighed a 6.9% decline for the RV group. The third quarter is historically the company's slowest.

Per Share Data ($)

(Year Ended May 31)	1998	1997	1996	1995	1994	1993	1992	1991	1990	1989
Tangible Bk. Val.	19.46	18.23	17.43	16.16	15.27	14.43	14.02	13.98	14.00	13.61
Cash Flow	2.49	2.44	2.16	1.68	1.59	1.16	0.75	0.70	1.09	1.74
Earnings	2.10	2.07	1.84	1.38	1.34	0.92	0.52	0.47	0.87	1.53
Dividends	0.60	0.60	0.51	0.48	0.48	0.48	0.48	0.48	0.48	0.48
Payout Ratio	29%	29%	28%	35%	36%	52%	92%	103%	55%	31%
Cal. Yrs.	1997	1996	1995	1994	1993	1992	1991	1990	1989	1988
Prices - High	30½	28⅝	21⅞	24⅛	23	21⅝	18¼	15⅞	20¼	16⅝
- Low	21	19¾	16½	16⅜	16⅛	14	13⅞	12⅜	13⅞	12½
P/E Ratio - High	15	14	12	17	17	24	35	34	23	11
- Low	10	10	9	12	12	15	27	26	16	8

Income Statement Analysis (Million $)

	1998	1997	1996	1995	1994	1993	1992	1991	1990	1989
Revs.	623	613	646	642	580	492	339	328	366	384
Oper. Inc.	31.0	30.9	31.0	23.3	22.1	13.2	5.8	2.9	9.4	20.7
Depr.	3.8	3.8	3.5	3.4	2.9	2.7	2.7	2.6	2.5	2.4
Int. Exp.	Nil	Nil	NM	Nil	Nil	Nil	Nil	Nil	Nil	Nil
Pretax Inc.	33.3	34.7	32.9	25.7	25.0	16.9	9.4	8.5	15.7	27.6
Eff. Tax Rate	40%	40%	40%	40%	40%	39%	38%	38%	38%	38%
Net Inc.	19.9	20.8	19.6	15.3	15.0	10.3	5.8	5.2	9.7	17.1

Balance Sheet & Other Fin. Data (Million $)

	1998	1997	1996	1995	1994	1993	1992	1991	1990	1989
Cash	10.7	110	55.0	40.0	17.0	14.0	17.0	111	109	111
Curr. Assets	188	173	124	107	84.0	68.0	61.0	146	150	149
Total Assets	233	218	230	215	209	189	180	176	179	177
Curr. Liab.	46.3	38.6	43.1	33.2	35.8	24.7	21.3	18.1	20.7	23.6
LT Debt	Nil	Nil	NM	Nil	Nil	Nil	Nil	Nil	Nil	Nil
Common Eqty.	184	176	184	180	170	162	157	157	157	153
Total Cap.	184	176	184	180	170	162	157	157	157	153
Cap. Exp.	2.1	3.2	3.0	16.4	8.1	4.1	2.4	3.9	3.2	3.7
Cash Flow	23.7	24.6	23.1	18.7	17.9	13.0	8.4	7.9	12.2	19.5
Curr. Ratio	4.1	4.5	2.9	3.2	2.3	2.8	2.9	8.0	7.2	6.3
% LT Debt of Cap.	Nil	Nil	NM	Nil	Nil	Nil	Nil	Nil	Nil	Nil
% Net Inc.of Revs.	3.2	3.4	3.0	2.4	2.6	2.1	1.7	1.6	2.7	4.5
% Ret. on Assets	8.8	9.3	8.8	7.2	7.6	5.6	3.2	2.9	5.5	10.1
% Ret. on Equity	11.1	11.6	10.8	8.8	9.0	6.5	3.7	3.3	6.3	11.7

Data as orig. reptd.; bef. results of disc. opers. and/or spec. items. Per share data adj. for stk. divs. as of ex-div. date. Bold denotes diluted EPS (FASB 128). E-Estimated. NA-Not Available. NM-Not Meaningful. NR-Not Ranked.

Office—2520 By-Pass Rd. (P.O. Box 743), Elkhart, IN 46515. **Tel**—(219) 294-6521. **Chrmn & CEO**—A. J. Decio. **Vice Chrmn**—R. F. Kloska. **Pres & COO**—W. H. Murschel. **VP-Fin, Treas & CFO**—J. B. Fanchi. **Dirs**—A. J. Decio, T. M. Decio, J. Hammes, R. F. Kloska, W. H. Lawson, D. T. Link, A. J. McKenna, W. H. Murschel, V. D. Swikert. **Transfer Agent & Registrar**—Harris Trust & Savings, Chicago. **Incorporated**—in Indiana in 1959. **Empl**—3,500. **S&P Analyst:** G.A.S.

SkyWest, Inc.　5234

NASDAQ Symbol **SKYW**

In S&P SmallCap 600

03-OCT-98　Industry:
Airlines

Summary: This company's SkyWest Airlines subsidiary is one of the largest U.S. regional airlines.

Quantitative Evaluations

Outlook
(1 Lowest—5 Highest)
- **3⁻**

Fair Value
- **23⅝**

Risk
- **Average**

Earn./Div. Rank
- **B**

Technical Eval.
- **Bearish** since 9/98

Rel. Strength Rank
(1 Lowest—99 Highest)
- **39**

Insider Activity
- **NA**

Recent Price • 19⅛　Yield • 0.6%
52 Wk Range • 34¼-10⅛　12-Mo. P/E • 15.7

Earnings vs. Previous Year
△=Up ▽=Down ▷=No Change

10 Week Mov. Avg. - - -
30 Week Mov. Avg. ......
Relative Strength ——

2-for-1

VOL.
(000)

OPTIONS: CBOE

Business Profile - 11-SEP-98

The company seeks to maximize profits by entering into code-sharing and joint marketing agreements with major airlines, continually upgrading its fleet, and providing full customer service. During 1997, SKYW completed a transition of its aircraft fleet from older Metroliner turbo-props to new, more efficient Brasilia turboprops. SKYW expects to have 64 Brasilia's in operation by the end of the FY 99 (Mar.) third quarter, with a total fleet of 96 aircraft by December 31, 1998. In late FY 98, SKYW began hiring 1,000 new employees required as ground and flight staff for United Express, representing a 50% work force increase. In a February 1998 public offering, SKYW sold 2.8 million common shares at $20.25 each, plus 420,000 shares to cover over-allotments (all as adjusted).

Operational Review - 11-SEP-98

Operating revenues in the three months ended June 30, 1998, rose 27%, year to year, reflecting more passengers carried and, to a lesser extent, more revenue passenger miles and available seat miles. Profitability benefited from the increased volume and well controlled operating expenses; with a significant rise in other income, net income advanced 124%, to $9,741,000 ($0.40 a share, diluted, on 20% more shares), from $4,345,000 ($0.22, as adjusted).

Stock Performance - 02-OCT-98

In the past 30 trading days, SKYW's shares have declined 30%, compared to a 7% fall in the S&P 500. Average trading volume for the past five days was 156,340 shares, compared with the 40-day moving average of 338,623 shares.

Key Stock Statistics

Dividend Rate/Share	0.12	Shareholders	1,100
Shs. outstg. (M)	24.2	Market cap. (B)	$0.462
Avg. daily vol. (M)	0.443	Inst. holdings	62%
Tang. Bk. Value/Share	9.16		
Beta	0.67		

Value of $10,000 invested 5 years ago: $ 42,462

Fiscal Year Ending Mar. 31

	1999	1998	1997	1996	1995	1994
Revenues (Million $)						
1Q	91.68	72.12	72.13	60.38	58.87	40.37
2Q	—	80.30	77.73	69.18	65.55	51.99
3Q	—	73.27	64.60	58.99	51.45	46.53
4Q	—	71.42	68.86	63.19	49.53	49.10
Yr.	—	297.1	283.3	251.7	225.4	188.0
Earnings Per Share ($)						
1Q	0.40	0.21	0.24	0.15	0.23	0.17
2Q	—	0.37	0.25	0.20	0.30	0.24
3Q	—	0.26	-0.04	-0.04	0.07	0.14
4Q	—	0.21	0.06	-0.10	0.01	0.17
Yr.	—	1.04	0.50	0.21	0.61	0.73

Next earnings report expected: NA

Dividend Data (Dividends have been paid since 1987.)

Amount ($)	Date Decl.	Ex-Div. Date	Stock of Record	Payment Date
0.050	Feb. 18	Mar. 27	Mar. 31	Apr. 15 '98
2-for-1	May. 06	Jun. 09	May. 20	Jun. 08 '98
0.030	May. 06	Jun. 26	Jun. 30	Jul. 15 '98
0.030	Aug. 18	Sep. 28	Sep. 30	Oct. 15 '98

A Division of The McGraw·Hill Companies

Business Summary - 11-SEP-98

This regional airline celebrated its 25th anniversary in 1997 by completing a fleet restructuring in which it shed its remaining Metroliner aircraft in favor of larger, more comfortable Brasilia EMB-120s. SkyWest, Inc. (SKYW) now boasts an "all cabin-class" fleet dominated by 69 Brasilia turboprop aircraft, including 16 owned by the company. SKYW also flies 10 Canadair regional jets.

More than half of the airline's passengers are business travelers, and the balance travel for leisure purposes, lured by western ski resorts or California beaches. Passenger revenues accounted for 87% of total revenues in FY 98. SKYW also provides air tours to the scenic regions of Arizona and Utah, and rents cars at certain airports. These non-airline activities accounted for 11% of FY 98 revenues. In August 1998, SKYW sold the Las Vegas-based assets of Scenic Airlines, which includes scenic tour operation in Las Vegas, to Eagle Canyon Airlines.

The company has operated as a Delta Connection throughout its markets for over a decade under a joint marketing and code-sharing agreement with Delta Air Lines, Inc. This arrangement permits SKYW to use Delta's designation code when listing flights in widely used computerized reservation systems. Under a revised agreement with Delta, SKYW coordinates its schedules with those of its code-sharing partner to maximize interline connections at hub airports in Salt Lake City and Los Angeles. SKYW operates 300 daily flights to 40 cities in 13 western states and British Columbia. It also operates as a Continental Connection at Los Angeles, with nearly 100 daily flights to eight California cities. In mid-1997, the company signed another code-share agreement, with United Airlines. Under this arrangement, SKYW began operating as United Express, with 288 daily flights to 15 cities in four western states. As of August 1998, United Express had 582 daily flights, and, by the end of the summer of 1998, SKYW will operate nearly 700 daily United Express departures on the West Coast from hubs at Los Angeles, Seattle/Tacoma and Portland (as of April 1998), and San Francisco (June).

Fleet changes in FY 98 resulted in a 3.6% increase in available seat miles, to 1.46 billion. Revenue passenger miles totaled 745 million, up from 717 million in FY 97, and passenger load factor, which measures utilization of aircraft capacity, rose slightly, to 50.9%, from 50.8%. SKYW believes that its newly enhanced fleet, comprised exclusively of 30- and 50-seat aircraft, will attract more passengers, and will lead to lower unit costs.

During the past five years, operating revenues have increased at a compound annual growth rate of 13%, while total passengers carried rose to nearly three million, from 1.7 million.

Per Share Data ($)										
(Year Ended Mar. 31)	1998	1997	1996	1995	1994	1993	1992	1991	1990	1989
Tangible Bk. Val.	8.79	6.13	5.76	5.71	5.37	2.65	2.24	2.14	2.06	1.81
Cash Flow	1.95	1.42	0.96	1.25	1.25	0.94	0.62	0.55	0.67	0.63
Earnings	1.04	0.50	0.21	0.61	0.73	0.42	0.13	0.13	0.30	0.24
Dividends	0.20	0.08	0.04	0.14	0.08	0.03	0.03	0.06	0.05	0.02
Payout Ratio	19%	15%	19%	23%	12%	6%	22%	47%	16%	8%
Cal. Yrs.	1997	1996	1995	1994	1993	1992	1991	1990	1989	1988
Prices - High	15⅛	10⅜	12¾	20½	17¼	5	2½	3	3¼	2⁵⁄₁₆
- Low	5⅞	6¼	5⅝	5¾	4¾	1⅞	1¼	1¹¹⁄₁₆	1¹¹⁄₁₆	1³⁄₁₆
P/E Ratio - High	14	21	60	33	24	12	20	23	11	10
- Low	6	12	26	9	7	5	10	13	5	5

Income Statement Analysis (Million $)										
Revs.	297	283	252	225	188	147	125	113	100	84.0
Oper. Inc.	53.3	33.9	21.1	34.3	34.9	19.7	11.4	10.4	12.3	12.1
Depr.	19.3	18.5	15.4	14.0	10.2	8.3	7.6	6.5	5.8	6.0
Int. Exp.	2.9	2.4	2.2	1.1	2.0	1.4	1.3	1.4	1.2	1.8
Pretax Inc.	35.7	16.6	6.8	22.2	23.8	10.5	3.1	3.4	7.8	5.7
Eff. Tax Rate	38%	39%	36%	38%	40%	36%	37%	40%	40%	34%
Net Inc.	21.9	10.1	4.4	13.7	14.4	6.7	2.0	2.0	4.7	3.8

Balance Sheet & Other Fin. Data (Million $)										
Cash	140	55.8	43.7	48.7	68.0	12.0	10.0	9.8	13.0	9.3
Curr. Assets	193	90.3	76.5	71.6	87.1	28.2	24.3	24.0	25.3	19.9
Total Assets	330	233	228	188	184	86.9	72.4	73.3	69.2	64.3
Curr. Liab.	49.7	45.0	43.6	25.6	20.5	15.9	13.0	11.9	10.8	8.9
LT Debt	49.6	47.3	53.7	29.6	26.6	18.4	13.8	16.5	13.8	16.0
Common Eqty.	211	125	116	118	123	42.8	35.3	33.5	32.5	28.4
Total Cap.	278	188	184	160	160	67.1	54.6	55.8	51.5	47.3
Cap. Exp.	29.8	19.7	64.7	39.3	45.6	20.9	10.1	14.9	8.1	7.2
Cash Flow	41.2	28.6	19.8	27.7	24.6	15.0	9.6	8.6	10.5	9.8
Curr. Ratio	3.9	2.0	1.8	2.8	4.3	1.8	1.9	2.0	2.4	2.2
% LT Debt of Cap.	17.8	25.2	29.2	18.4	16.6	27.4	25.2	29.6	26.7	33.8
% Net Inc.of Revs.	7.4	3.6	1.7	6.1	7.7	4.6	1.6	1.8	4.7	4.5
% Ret. on Assets	7.8	4.4	2.1	7.7	9.4	8.3	2.7	2.8	7.0	6.1
% Ret. on Equity	13.1	8.4	3.7	12.0	15.7	17.0	5.8	6.1	15.5	14.1

Data as orig. reptd.; bef. results of disc. opers. and/or spec. items. Per share data adj. for stk. divs. as of ex-div. date. Bold denotes diluted EPS (FASB 128). E-Estimated. NA-Not Available. NM-Not Meaningful. NR-Not Ranked.

Office—444 S. River Rd., St. George, UT 84790. **Tel**—(801) 634-3000. **Website**—http://www.skywest.com **Chrmn, Pres & CEO**—J. C. Atkin. **Vice Chrmn**—S. J. Atkin. **EVP & COO**—R. B. Reber. **EVP-Fin, CFO, Treas & Investor Contact**—Bradford R. Rich (801-634-3300). **Dirs**—J. C. Atkin, J. R. Atkin, S. J. Atkin, M. K. Cox, I. M. Cumming, H. J. Eyring, H. W. Smith, S. F. Udvar-Hazy. **Transfer Agent & Registrar**—Zions First National Bank, Salt Lake City. **Incorporated**—in Utah in 1972. **Empl**— 2,966. **S&P Analyst:** Stewart Scharf

STANDARD &POOR'S
STOCK REPORTS

Smith (A. O.)

2046P

NYSE Symbol **AOS**

In S&P SmallCap 600

03-OCT-98

Industry: Manufacturing (Diversified)

Summary: This company produces electric motors, water heaters, fiberglass piping systems and industrial storage tanks.

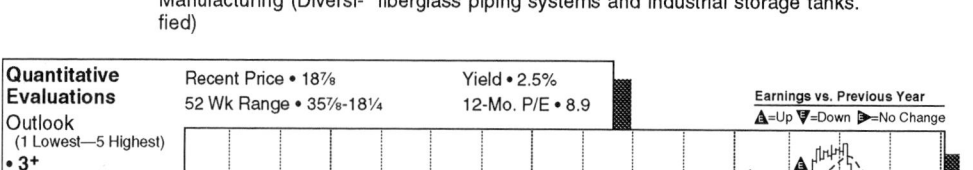

Quantitative Evaluations		
Outlook (1 Lowest—5 Highest)		
• **3+**		
Fair Value		
• **22**		
Risk		
• **Average**		
Earn./Div. Rank		
• **B+**		
Technical Eval.		
• **Bearish** since 3/98		
Rel. Strength Rank (1 Lowest—99 Highest)		
• **19**		
Insider Activity		
• **NA**		

Recent Price • 18⅞
52 Wk Range • 35⅞-18¼

Yield • 2.5%
12-Mo. P/E • 8.9

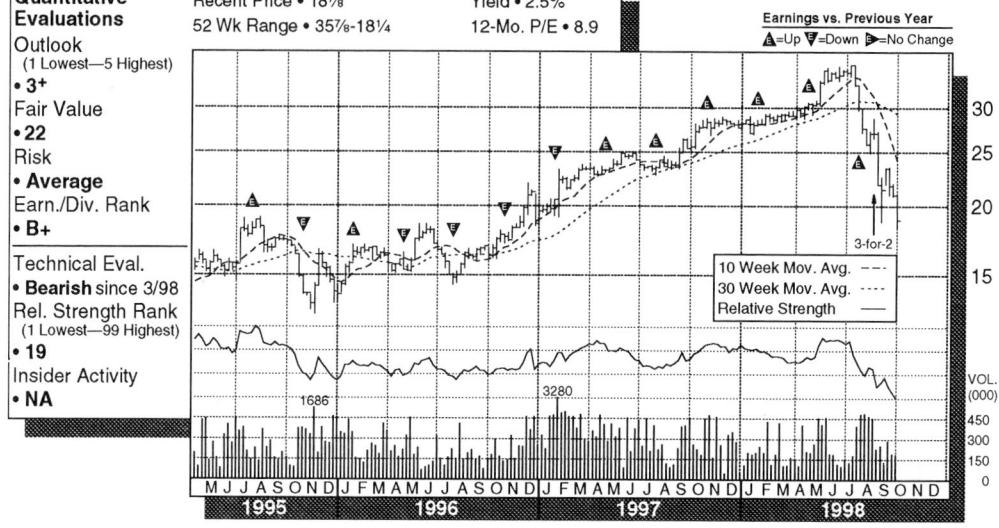

Earnings vs. Previous Year
▲=Up ▼=Down ▶=No Change

10 Week Mov. Avg. ---
30 Week Mov. Avg. ···
Relative Strength —

3-for-2

Business Profile - 08-MAY-98

The company completed the largest divestiture in its history in April 1997, when it sold its automotive supply business to Tower Automotive for $725 million. The transaction reflected AOS's belief that it would no longer be able to continue as a Tier I supplier to the automobile industry, because of the large financial commitments required to remain competitive. In 1998, the company expects to encounter continued competitive pricing in the residential water heater market as well as in certain electric motor markets. However, AOS believes the impact should be offset by favorable interest income, lower customer inventory levels in HVAC (heating, ventilating, air conditioning and refrigeration) markets, a full year contribution from UPPCO (a maker of sub-fractional horsepower C-frame motors acquired in March 1997), and a reduced number of common shares outstanding.

Operational Review - 08-MAY-98

Net sales in the first quarter of 1998 advanced 14%, year to year, reflecting a strong performance at the Storage & Fluid Handling and Water Systems units, as well as the addition of the UPPCO sub-fractional horsepower motor business. Aided by higher interest income, net income climbed 44%, to $10.2 million ($0.62 a diluted share) from $7.1 million ($0.34).

Stock Performance - 02-OCT-98

In the past 30 trading days, AQS's shares have declined 30%, compared to a 7% fall in the S&P 500. Average trading volume for the past five days was 37,560 shares, compared with the 40-day moving average of 61,694 shares.

Key Stock Statistics

Dividend Rate/Share	0.48	Shareholders	1,900
Shs. outstg. (M)	23.6	Market cap. (B)	$0.281
Avg. daily vol. (M)	0.040	Inst. holdings	38%
Tang. Bk. Value/Share	14.49		
Beta	1.28		

Value of $10,000 invested 5 years ago: $ 16,730

Fiscal Year Ending Dec. 31

	1998	1997	1996	1995	1994	1993
Revenues (Million $)						
1Q	223.0	196.3	194.8	393.0	339.8	296.1
2Q	226.7	224.9	206.5	399.8	350.2	315.8
3Q	—	206.0	188.1	354.4	332.7	272.8
4Q	—	205.8	191.8	397.6	350.8	309.1
Yr.	—	832.9	781.0	1,545	1,374	1,194
Earnings Per Share ($)						
1Q	**0.41**	**0.23**	0.19	0.59	0.51	0.42
2Q	**0.52**	**0.41**	0.23	0.64	0.57	0.49
3Q	—	**0.33**	0.19	0.24	0.32	0.18
4Q	—	**0.37**	0.19	0.49	0.43	0.29
Yr.	—	**1.33**	0.79	1.96	1.83	1.39

Next earnings report expected: mid October

Dividend Data (Dividends have been paid since 1983.)

Amount ($)	Date Decl.	Ex-Div. Date	Stock of Record	Payment Date
0.170	Jan. 21	Jan. 28	Jan. 31	Feb. 17 '98
0.170	Apr. 09	Apr. 28	Apr. 30	May. 15 '98
0.120	Jun. 09	Jul. 29	Jul. 31	Aug. 17 '98
3-for-2	Jun. 09	Aug. 18	Jul. 31	Aug. 17 '98

Business Summary - 08-MAY-98

Reacting to the pressure of changes that have occurred in the automotive supply business over the past few years, namely the ongoing consolidation of the supply base, A. O. Smith decided to sell its Tier I automotive products business, rather than expend the vast amounts of capital it believed to be necessary to remain competitive in this market. In the largest single divestiture in its 123-year history, the company sold this business to Tower Automotive in April 1997, for about $725 million. AOS's remaining operations consist of three business segments: Electric Motor Technologies, Water Systems Technology, and Storage & Fluid Handling Technologies.

Of the three continuing businesses, Electric Motor Technologies is the largest ($390.7 million in net sales in 1997, representing 47% of the total). This segment produces hermetic electric motors used in refrigeration and air conditioning systems, and fractional horsepower motors used in consumer products, fan motors for furnaces, air conditioners and blowers, and jet pump motors for home water systems, swimming pools, hot tubs and spas. Sales to the heating, ventilating, air conditioning and refrigeration market account for about 57% of the segment's total sales.

The Water Systems Technologies segment (35% of net sales) is a leading manufacturer of residential gas and electric water heaters, and commercial water heating systems used in schools, nursing homes, hospitals, prisons, hotels, laundries, restaurants, stadiums, amusement parks, car washes and other large users of hot water.

Storage & Fluid Handling Technologies (18%) provides world-wide solutions for storing liquids and a wide range of dry materials, as well as high performance piping systems that safely contain and convey corrosive, abrasive or related materials. Products include industrial, municipal and agricultural liquid and dry bulk storage systems, and reinforced thermosetting resin piping and fittings used to carry corrosive materials.

In March 1997, the company acquired UPPCO, Inc., a maker of sub-fractional horsepower electric motors, with 1997 sales since the date of acquisition of about $57 million.

Per Share Data ($)

(Year Ended Dec. 31)	1997	1996	1995	1994	1993	1992	1991	1990	1989	1988
Tangible Bk. Val.	14.24	13.52	11.87	9.27	7.90	7.14	9.95	10.92	10.28	12.15
Cash Flow	2.27	1.52	3.73	3.40	2.77	2.33	1.59	2.54	0.97	1.87
Earnings	1.33	0.81	1.96	1.83	1.39	0.93	0.07	1.13	-0.36	0.62
Dividends	0.45	0.44	0.39	0.33	0.41	0.27	0.27	0.27	0.27	0.27
Payout Ratio	34%	55%	20%	18%	172%	29%	439%	24%	NM	42%
Prices - High	28⁷/₈	22	19¹/₈	26⁵/₈	23⁷/₈	12³/₄	7¹/₄	6⁵/₈	6¹/₈	5³/₄
- Low	19¹/₈	13⁷/₈	12³/₄	14¹/₈	11⁵/₈	5⁷/₈	5	3⁷/₈	4¹/₈	4
P/E Ratio - High	22	27	10	15	99	14	NM	6	NM	9
- Low	14	17	7	8	48	6	NM	3	NM	6

Income Statement Analysis (Million $)

	1997	1996	1995	1994	1993	1992	1991	1990	1989	1988
Revs.	833	781	1,545	1,374	1,194	1,046	916	935	976	1,015
Oper. Inc.	90.0	82.0	166	152	125	96.6	61.8	87.1	61.1	73.5
Depr.	26.3	22.6	55.7	49.2	42.6	39.5	37.8	33.5	31.6	30.8
Int. Exp.	Nil	8.1	13.1	12.9	14.5	18.7	23.9	17.0	18.8	13.6
Pretax Inc.	58.9	42.3	96.9	92.1	70.8	42.3	4.0	42.1	-3.6	30.2
Eff. Tax Rate	37%	41%	37%	38%	40%	36%	14%	28%	NM	37%
Net Inc.	37.6	25.2	61.4	57.3	42.7	27.2	3.5	30.5	-5.0	19.0

Balance Sheet & Other Fin. Data (Million $)

	1997	1996	1995	1994	1993	1992	1991	1990	1989	1988
Cash	146	6.4	5.7	8.5	11.9	6.0	8.9	3.2	4.8	4.9
Curr. Assets	366	239	352	330	304	234	209	258	271	289
Total Assets	717	885	953	848	823	769	754	788	796	808
Curr. Liab.	128	138	214	216	223	172	172	206	197	172
LT Debt	101	238	191	166	191	237	249	156	155	138
Common Eqty.	400	425	372	313	270	245	265	282	269	292
Total Cap.	529	694	632	533	501	509	547	452	438	452
Cap. Exp.	44.9	37.8	91.0	76.1	54.7	46.9	59.3	64.9	45.9	34.5
Cash Flow	63.8	47.8	117	107	85.3	65.8	37.8	60.4	23.0	46.1
Curr. Ratio	2.9	1.7	1.6	1.5	1.4	1.4	1.2	1.3	1.4	1.7
% LT Debt of Cap.	19.9	34.3	30.2	31.1	38.0	46.4	45.5	34.5	35.3	30.6
% Net Inc.of Revs.	4.5	3.3	4.0	4.2	3.6	2.6	0.4	3.3	NM	1.9
% Ret. on Assets	4.8	3.1	6.8	6.8	5.3	3.1	0.4	3.8	NM	2.6
% Ret. on Equity	10.2	6.4	18.0	19.6	16.5	9.0	NM	9.7	NM	5.4

Data as orig. reptd.; bef. results of disc. opers. and/or spec. items. Per share data adj. for stk. divs. as of ex-div. date. Bold denotes diluted EPS (FASB 128). E-Estimated. NA-Not Available. NM-Not Meaningful. NR-Not Ranked.

Office—11270 W. Park Place, Milwaukee, WI 53224-3690 (P.O. Box 23972, Milwaukee 53223-0972). **Tel**—(414) 359-4000. **Fax**—(414) 359-4198. **Website**—http://www.aosmith.com **Chrmn, Pres & CEO**—R. J. O'Toole. **EVP & CFO**—G. R. Bomberger. **VP & Treas**—J. J. Kita. **VP & Secy**—W. D. Romoser. **Investor Contact**—Craig Watson (414) 359-4009. **Dirs**—T. H. Barrett, G. R. Bomberger, K. J. Hempel, R. O'Toole, A. Pytte, D. J. Schuenke, A. O. Smith, B. M. Smith. **Transfer Agent & Registrar**—Firstar Trust Co., Milwaukee. **Incorporated**—in New York in 1916; reincorporated in Delaware in 1986. **Empl**— 8,400. **S&P Analyst:** SRB

Smithfield Foods 5238
NASDAQ Symbol **SFDS**

In S&P SmallCap 600

03-OCT-98

Industry: Foods

Summary: This regional meat packer, the largest producer of "genuine Smithfield" hams, also produces fresh pork and markets a wide variety of processed meats.

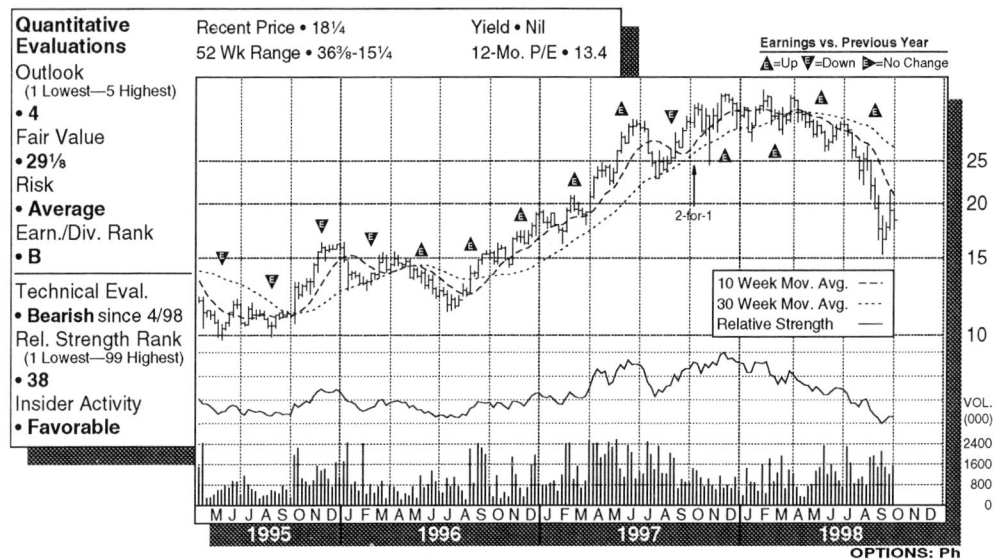

Quantitative Evaluations		
Recent Price • 18¼	Yield • Nil	
52 Wk Range • 36⅜-15¼	12-Mo. P/E • 13.4	

Earnings vs. Previous Year
△=Up ▽=Down ▷=No Change

Outlook (1 Lowest—5 Highest)
• **4**

Fair Value
• **29⅛**

Risk
• **Average**

Earn./Div. Rank
• **B**

Technical Eval.
• **Bearish** since 4/98

Rel. Strength Rank (1 Lowest—99 Highest)
• **38**

Insider Activity
• **Favorable**

10 Week Mov. Avg. ---
30 Week Mov. Avg. ·····
Relative Strength —

2-for-1

OPTIONS: Ph

Business Profile - 18-JUN-98

The company's vertical integration strategy of producing hogs and selling processed meats acts to counter cyclical changes in hog prices. The company posted strong results in FY 98 (Apr.), reflecting lower hog prices and greater sales of higher margin processed meats. The company expects results in FY 99 to continue to benefit from its vertically integrated operations. SFDS also expects to acquire strategically important U.S. and international companies in accordance with the company's long-term plans.

Operational Review - 18-JUN-98

Sales in FY 98 (Apr.) were flat, as a 9.8% jump in unit volume was offset by lower hog prices. Margins widened, aided by higher sales tonnage of processed meats which carry better margins than the hog production group; operating margins climbed 29%. Despite a $12.6 million charge reflecting civil penalties for violations of the federal Clean Water Act, pretax income was up 20%. After taxes at 34.0%, versus 33.6%, net income advanced 19%, to $53,400,000 ($1.34 a share, on 3.0% more shares), from $44,937,000 ($1.17, after preferred dividends, as adjusted).

Stock Performance - 02-OCT-98

In the past 30 trading days, SFDS's shares have declined 17%, compared to a 7% fall in the S&P 500. Average trading volume for the past five days was 307,300 shares, compared with the 40-day moving average of 314,264 shares.

Key Stock Statistics

Dividend Rate/Share	Nil	Shareholders	1,200
Shs. outstg. (M)	37.5	Market cap. (B)	$0.687
Avg. daily vol. (M)	0.326	Inst. holdings	56%
Tang. Bk. Value/Share	9.48		
Beta	0.67		

Value of $10,000 invested 5 years ago: $ 19,275

Fiscal Year Ending Apr. 30

	1999	1998	1997	1996	1995	1994
Revenues (Million $)						
1Q	865.8	915.0	892.9	367.3	331.8	299.2
2Q	—	982.7	969.2	455.8	373.8	354.9
3Q	—	1,096	1,081	687.0	439.4	429.0
4Q	—	873.8	927.5	873.8	381.6	364.2
Yr.	—	3,867	3,871	2,384	1,527	1,447
Earnings Per Share ($)						
1Q	-0.14	-0.17	0.01	-0.08	0.07	-0.02
2Q	—	0.39	0.23	0.13	0.23	0.02
3Q	—	0.60	0.41	0.29	0.52	0.52
4Q	—	0.52	0.51	0.17	0.09	0.21
Yr.	—	1.34	1.17	0.53	0.92	0.56

Next earnings report expected: mid November

Dividend Data

Common dividends were omitted in 1996 after having been paid since 1956. A "poison pill" stock purchase rights plan was adopted in 1990.

A Division of The **McGraw-Hill** Companies

STANDARD
&POOR'S
STOCK REPORTS

Smithfield Foods, Inc.

5238

03-OCT-98

Business Summary - 18-JUN-98

Responding to strong consumer demand for leaner, more consistent pork products, Smithfield Foods, Inc. (SFDS) has spent $400 million in the past decade building what it now believes is the hog industry's most extensive vertically integrated system. SFDS also believes that it is one of the largest U.S. combined hog producer/pork slaughterers and further processors, producing a wide variety of fresh pork and processed meat products marketed in the U.S. as well as selected foreign markets that include Japan, Russia and Mexico. Pork processing operations are conducted through five principal subsidiaries--Gwaltney of Smithfield, Ltd., The Smithfield Packing Company, Inc., John Morrell & Co., Patrick Cudahy Inc. and Lykes Meat Group, Inc. The company also conducts hog production operations through its Brown's of Carolina, Inc. subsidiary and through several joint hog production arrangements.

In FY 97 (Apr.), sales climbed 62%, to $3.9 billion, from $2.4 billion in FY 96. Net income nearly tripled, to $44.9 million, from $15.9 million. SFDS attributed these gains to the inclusion of sales of its John Morrell and Lykes units (acquired December 1995 and November 1996, respectively), significant increases in unit sales prices of fresh pork and processed meats, and in-

creased sales of fresh pork related to the number of hogs slaughtered at its North Carolina plant.

Fresh pork products constituted 59% of FY 97 sales. In an effort to provide leaner fresh pork products, as well as fat-free, lower-fat and lower-salt processed meats, SFDS has developed and markets an extremely lean line of fresh pork products under the Smithfield Lean Generation Pork label. Processed meats accounted for 37% of FY 97 sales. Processed meat products are marketed under the brand names Smithfield, Patrick Cudahy and John Morrell, among others.

SFDS sells large quantities of value-priced processed meat products as well as fresh pork to national and regional supermarket chains, wholesale distributors, the food service industry and export markets. The company's business strategy includes using the leanest genetics commercially available to enable it to market highly differentiated pork products. SFDS cites as strategic initiatives an emphasis on expansion of international markets (6% of total FY 97 sales), targeting Europe and the Pacific Rim markets, and its continued growth through acquisition of regional pork processors and brands. In June 1997, SFDS acquired the assets and business of Curly's Foods, Inc., a maker and marketer of raw and cooked ribs and other meats for the foodservice industries.

Per Share Data ($)

(Year Ended Apr. 30)	1998	1997	1996	1995	1994	1993	1992	1991	1990	1989
Tangible Bk. Val.	9.29	8.20	6.73	5.61	4.76	4.17	3.77	2.83	1.77	1.57
Cash Flow	2.50	2.21	1.34	1.50	1.22	0.65	1.09	1.39	0.57	0.59
Earnings	1.34	1.17	0.53	0.92	0.56	0.08	0.69	0.99	0.24	0.33
Dividends	Nil	Nil	Nil	Nil	Nil	Nil	Nil	Nil	Nil	Nil
Payout Ratio	Nil	Nil	Nil	Nil	Nil	Nil	Nil	Nil	Nil	Nil
Cal. Yrs.	1997	1996	1995	1994	1993	1992	1991	1990	1989	1988
Prices - High	35⅝	19⅜	17⅛	17	9¾	11⅛	12⅝	5⅛	4¾	5⅛
- Low	16¼	11⅜	9¾	8⅞	6¼	6⅞	4⅝	2½	2⅞	2⅞
P/E Ratio - High	30	14	32	19	17	NM	18	5	20	16
- Low	14	8	18	10	11	NM	7	3	12	9

Income Statement Analysis (Million $)

	1998	1997	1996	1995	1994	1993	1992	1991	1990	1989
Revs.	3,867	3,871	2,384	1,527	1,447	1,142	1,051	1,072	853	775
Oper. Inc.	171	133	79.5	84.2	69.0	34.3	47.4	51.8	24.5	31.1
Depr.	45.9	39.0	28.3	19.7	21.7	18.7	12.8	11.4	9.9	8.6
Int. Exp.	31.9	28.8	23.0	14.9	12.8	8.6	5.5	8.4	6.6	4.1
Pretax Inc.	81.0	67.6	30.3	50.4	35.1	5.4	33.4	43.6	10.6	16.7
Eff. Tax Rate	34%	34%	35%	37%	37%	27%	35%	34%	34%	36%
Net Inc.	53.4	44.9	19.8	31.9	19.7	2.9	21.6	28.7	7.1	10.8

Balance Sheet & Other Fin. Data (Million $)

	1998	1997	1996	1995	1994	1993	1992	1991	1990	1989
Cash	60.5	25.7	28.5	14.8	12.4	3.1	1.7	2.6	1.1	1.1
Curr. Assets	511	488	420	233	226	178	125	112	89.0	84.0
Total Assets	1,084	995	858	550	452	400	278	201	165	152
Curr. Liab.	252	324	332	172	145	113	99	77.2	74.3	58.7
LT Debt	407	288	189	155	119	125	49.1	37.4	28.2	27.6
Common Eqty.	361	307	243	184	155	136	114	71.0	45.0	44.0
Total Cap.	780	603	451	367	299	279	172	118	84.0	80.0
Cap. Exp.	92.9	69.1	74.9	91.9	28.2	88.0	75.7	26.5	19.6	16.0
Cash Flow	99	82.7	46.9	51.0	40.7	21.1	34.4	40.0	17.0	19.3
Curr. Ratio	2.0	1.5	1.3	1.4	1.6	1.6	1.3	1.5	1.2	1.4
% LT Debt of Cap.	52.2	47.7	41.9	42.2	39.7	44.7	28.5	31.7	33.4	34.3
% Net Inc.of Revs.	1.4	1.1	0.8	2.1	1.4	0.2	2.1	2.7	0.8	1.4
% Ret. on Assets	5.1	4.8	2.8	6.3	4.6	0.8	8.3	15.8	4.6	7.6
% Ret. on Equity	16.0	16.3	9.3	18.4	13.1	1.9	21.7	49.6	16.5	26.6

Data as orig. reptd.; bef. results of disc. opers. and/or spec. items. Per share data adj. for stk. divs. as of ex-div. date. Bold denotes diluted EPS (FASB 128). E-Estimated. NA-Not Available. NM-Not Meaningful. NR-Not Ranked.

Office—999 Waterside Dr., Suite 900, Norfolk, VA 23510. **Tel**—(757) 365-3000. **Chrmn & CEO**—J. W. Luter III. **Pres & COO**—L. R. Little. **VP, Secy, Treas & Investor Contact**—Aaron D. Trub. **Dirs**—R. L. Burrus, Jr., F. J. Faison, Jr., J. W. Greenberg, C. W. Gwaltney, G. E. Hamilton, Jr., R. J. Holland, R. R. Kapella, L. R. Little, J. W. Luter III, H. G. Maxwell, W. H. Murphy, W. H. Prestage, J. B. Sebring. **Transfer Agent & Registrar**—First Union National Bank, Charlotte, NC. **Incorporated**—in Delaware in 1971. **Empl**— 9,000. **S&P Analyst:** Robert J. Izmirlian

STANDARD &POOR'S
STOCK REPORTS

Snyder Oil

2051M

NYSE Symbol **SNY**

In S&P SmallCap 600

03-OCT-98

Industry:
Oil & Gas (Exploration & Production)

Summary: Snyder is primarily an independent domestic oil and gas exploration company.

Quantitative Evaluations	
Outlook (1 Lowest—5 Highest)	
• **1⁻**	
Fair Value	
• **10½**	
Risk	
• **Average**	
Earn./Div. Rank	
• **B**	
Technical Eval.	
• **Bearish** since 7/98	
Rel. Strength Rank (1 Lowest—99 Highest)	
• **63**	
Insider Activity	
• **NA**	

Recent Price • 16¼
52 Wk Range • 24⅞-14½
Yield • 1.6%
12-Mo. P/E • 70.7

Earnings vs. Previous Year
▲=Up ▼=Down ▶=No Change

10 Week Mov. Avg. ---
30 Week Mov. Avg. ····
Relative Strength ——

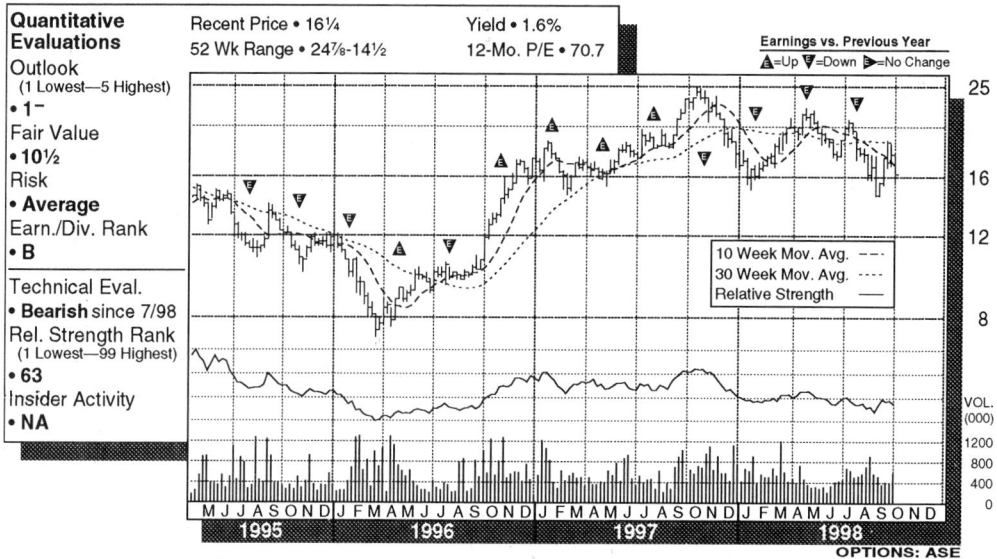

OPTIONS: ASE

Business Profile - 21-SEP-98

This independent oil company acquires, explores and develops domestic oil and gas properties and gathers, transports, processes and markets natural gas. It currently concentrates on northern Louisiana and Rocky Mountain basins and offshore development. In early 1996, Snyder combined its Wattenberg Field assets and operations with Gerrity Oil and Gas Corp. in a new public company, Patina Oil & Gas Corp., in which SNY had a 74% ownership interest (sold in the fourth quarter of 1997). As part of its strategy to concentrate on properties that it owns and operates directly, SNY has reduced investments in certain international properties. In November 1997, the company called for redemption its remaining convertible exchangeable preferred stock.

Operational Review - 21-SEP-98

Revenues in the six months ended June 30, 1998, declined 56%, year to year, reflecting the October 1997, disposition of Patina Oil, lower oil prices, and the absence of gains on the sales of equity investments. Despite lower per-barrel operating costs and depreciation charges, overall expenses declined less rapidly, and pretax income fell 96%. After taxes at 35.0%, versus 29.0%, and despite the absence of minority interest, net income fell to $1,061,000 ($0.03 a share, on 9.9% more shares), from $25,918,000 ($0.73, after preferred dividends). Results for the 1997 period exclude an $0.08 per share loss from the early retirement of debt.

Stock Performance - 02-OCT-98

In the past 30 trading days, SNY's shares have declined 3%, compared to a 7% fall in the S&P 500. Average trading volume for the past five days was 115,680 shares, compared with the 40-day moving average of 112,759 shares.

Key Stock Statistics

Dividend Rate/Share	0.26	Shareholders	2,600
Shs. outstg. (M)	33.6	Market cap. (B)	$0.545
Avg. daily vol. (M)	0.092	Inst. holdings	57%
Tang. Bk. Value/Share	6.65		
Beta	0.93		

Value of $10,000 invested 5 years ago: $ 17,804

Fiscal Year Ending Dec. 31

	1998	1997	1996	1995	1994	1993
Revenues (Million $)						
1Q	32.82	86.60	41.72	53.02	63.46	44.87
2Q	34.58	73.19	56.77	57.14	64.58	58.28
3Q	—	56.30	62.48	50.84	71.05	61.29
4Q	—	38.58	131.4	41.16	63.24	65.45
Yr.	—	255.7	292.4	202.2	262.3	229.9
Earnings Per Share ($)						
1Q	0.05	0.59	0.01	-0.25	0.08	0.23
2Q	-0.02	0.15	-0.37	-0.03	0.04	0.18
0Q		0.07	0.10	0.07	0.02	0.17
4Q	—	0.14	2.06	-0.88	-0.03	0.23
Yr.	—	0.95	1.81	-1.53	0.07	0.80

Next earnings report expected: early November

Dividend Data (Dividends have been paid since 1990.)

Amount ($)	Date Decl.	Ex-Div. Date	Stock of Record	Payment Date
0.065	Dec. 02	Dec. 11	Dec. 15	Dec. 31 '97
0.065	Mar. 02	Mar. 11	Mar. 13	Mar. 31 '98
0.065	Jun. 02	Jun. 11	Jun. 15	Jun. 30 '98
0.065	Sep. 02	Sep. 11	Sep. 15	Sep. 30 '98

A Division of The **McGraw·Hill** Companies

Business Summary - 21-SEP-98

During 1996, Snyder Oil, a developer, acquirer and explorer of oil and gas properties completed a repositioning begun in 1995 in response to dramatic deterioration in Rocky Mountain gas markets. As a result, the company's domestic operations are now focused on Offshore, Western Rockies, and northern Louisiana.

In the past two years, Snyder has become one of the 30 largest operators of production in the Gulf of Mexico, SNY's offshore segment. The company's strategy has been to seek relatively low risk positions in seven projects in the Main Pass area.

The company has been a substantial owner and operator of projects in the Rockies since its inception in the 1970s. Its strategy has focused on basin-centered gas accumulations. SNY has amassed one of the largest undeveloped acreage positions in the Rockies. Effective January 1997, the company formed a new alliance with subsidiaries of Coastal Corp. to market SNY's Rocky Mountain gas production, and to expand unregulated gas facilities in the region. Coastal Gas Marketing Co. will aggregate and market gas purchased from SNY and other Rocky Mountain producers.

The biggest part of the southern division is in the North Louisiana Salt Basin, where SNY has been active since 1993. SNY owns an interest in over 330,000 net mineral acres and has leases and lease options covering over 150,000 additional net acres in North Louisi-

ana. The company's focus in northern Louisiana in 1998 will be on drilling and testing several different reef settings that were identified under a 3-D seismic program conducted during 1996 and 1997. Snyder expects drilling to begin in the second quarter of 1998.

During 1996, the company implemented a significant restructuring of its Denver-Julesburg Basin (DJ Basin) assets by creating Patina Oil & Gas Corp. (NYSE: POG). Patina subsequently acquired Gerrity Oil & Gas Corp. As a result of these transactions, the company transformed its working interest in the field into a controlling ownership position in a larger entity, possessing 74% of Patina. The company sold its interest in Patina in the fourth quarter of 1997, leading to a gain of approximately $3 million, after tax; the transaction simplified the company's structure and increased its financial flexibility, removing $170 million of debt from the balance sheet, while providing $127 million in cash. Snyder ended 1997 with proved reserves of 363 Bcf of natural gas and 16,800,000 bbl. of oil, condensate and natural gas liquids.

Snyder also has investments in international exploration and development. As of the 1997 year-end, it owned a 16% interest (7.8 million shares) in SOCO International plc, a U.K. company with investments in Mongolia, Russia and Thailand; and a 7% interest (11.7 million shares) in Cairn Energy plc, a Scotland-based exploration and production company.

Per Share Data ($)

(Year Ended Dec. 31)	1997	1996	1995	1994	1993	1992	1991	1990	1989	1988
Tangible Bk. Val.	7.91	9.44	7.52	8.25	9.12	5.44	5.02	4.98	NA	NA
Cash Flow	3.57	4.71	1.21	3.30	3.02	1.94	1.48	1.20	1.26	1.38
Earnings	0.96	1.81	-1.53	0.07	0.80	0.53	0.37	0.36	0.25	-0.34
Dividends	0.26	0.26	0.26	0.25	0.22	0.20	0.20	0.12	NA	NA
Payout Ratio	27%	14%	NM	480%	27%	47%	55%	37%	NA	NA
Prices - High	24⁷/₈	17³/₄	15³/₈	21³/₈	23	10¹/₂	8¹/₂	9¹/₂	NA	NA
- Low	14⁵/₈	7¹/₄	10	13⁷/₈	10	5⁷/₈	4³/₄	4³/₄	NA	NA
P/E Ratio - High	26	10	NM	NM	29	20	23	26	NA	NA
- Low	15	4	NM	NM	12	11	13	13	NA	NA

Income Statement Analysis (Million $)

	1997	1996	1995	1994	1993	1992	1991	1990	1989	1988
Revs.	256	292	202	245	219	116	86.8	82.2	80.5	75.7
Oper. Inc.	156	204	67.2	85.3	83.0	50.7	40.5	34.1	37.9	37.3
Depr. Depl. & Amort.	79.9	84.5	76.4	76.6	51.2	31.9	25.4	17.2	23.9	40.5
Int. Exp.	25.4	28.9	27.0	NA	5.3	5.0	8.4	6.2	7.4	7.0
Pretax Inc.	57.4	74.7	-40.6	13.5	34.9	17.3	11.4	9.9	8.9	-7.9
Eff. Tax Rate	31%	5.90%	NM	7.20%	21%	2.50%	23%	24%	34%	NM
Net Inc.	35.5	63.0	-39.8	12.4	27.6	16.9	8.8	7.5	5.9	-8.0

Balance Sheet & Other Fin. Data (Million $)

	1997	1996	1995	1994	1993	1992	1991	1990	1989	1988
Cash	89.4	27.9	27.3	21.7	10.9	20.5	24.7	16.8	10.2	2.8
Curr. Assets	114	98.1	68.3	72.4	61.8	52.3	48.3	40.3	40.0	16.5
Total Assets	546	879	555	673	480	347	252	227	206	176
Curr. Liab.	57.5	88.9	62.4	71.7	60.5	44.6	31.0	28.2	39.0	9.9
LT Debt	174	372	234	319	115	115	42.1	81.2	48.5	55.7
Common Eqty.	264	295	235	248	212	124	115	115	119	NA
Total Cap.	469	762	473	598	412	300	221	198	167	166
Cap. Exp.	136	129	92.0	244	167	130	48.0	172	NA	NA
Cash Flow	109	147	36.5	78.1	69.7	44.0	33.7	24.7	29.8	32.6
Curr. Ratio	2.0	1.1	1.1	1.0	1.0	1.2	1.6	1.4	1.0	1.7
% LT Debt of Cap.	37.1	48.9	49.5	53.2	27.9	38.5	19.1	41.1	28.9	33.5
% Ret. on Assets	5.0	8.8	NM	1.9	6.6	5.6	3.7	NA	NA	NM
% Ret. on Equity	10.6	23.8	NM	0.6	10.9	10.1	7.3	NA	NA	NA

Data as orig. reptd.; bef. results of disc opers. and/or spec. items. Per share data adj. for stk. divs. as of ex-div. date. Bold denotes diluted EPS (FASB 128). E-Estimated. NA-Not Available. NM-Not Meaningful. NR-Not Ranked.

Office—777 Main St., Suite 2500, Fort Worth, TX 76102. **Tel**—(817) 338-4043. **Website**—http://www.snyderoil.com **Chrmn & CEO**—J. C. Snyder. **Pres & COO**—W. G. Hargett. **SVP & CFO**—M. A. Jackson. **Secy**—P. E. Lorenzen. **VP & Investor Contact**—Diana K. Ten Eyck. **Dirs**—R. W. Brittain, W. G. Hargett, J. A. Hill, W. J. Johnson, B. J. Kellenberger, H. R. Logan, Jr., J. E. McCormick, J. C. Snyder, E. T. Story. **Transfer Agent**—ChaseMellon Shareholder Services, Dallas. **Incorporated**—in Delaware in 1989. **Empl**— 473. **S&P Analyst:** N.R.

Sola International

2052Q

NYSE Symbol **SOL**

In S&P SmallCap 600

03-OCT-98

Industry: Health Care (Medical Products & Supplies)

Summary: Sola designs, manufactures and distributes a broad range of eyeglass lenses, focusing primarily on the plastic lens segment of the global lens market.

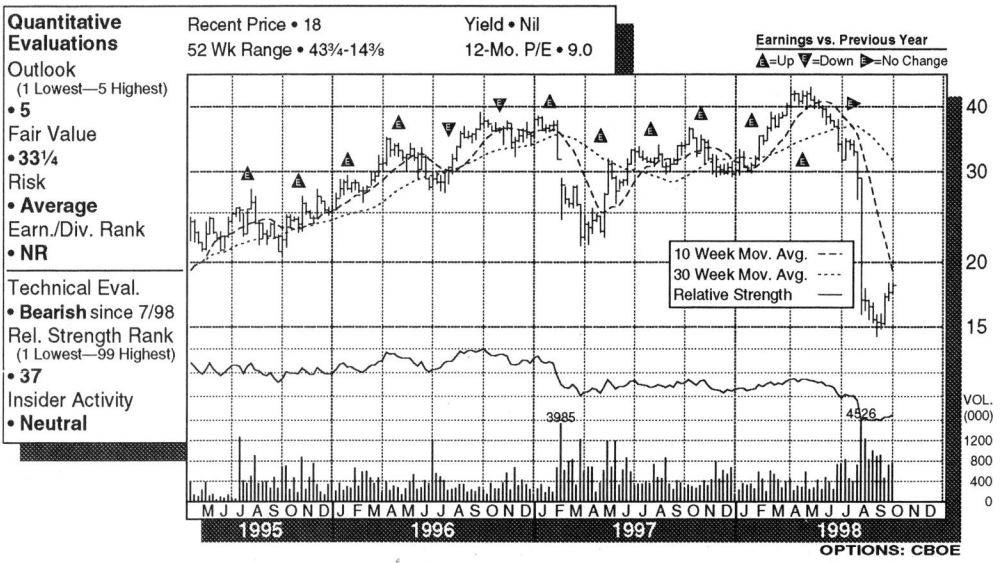

Quantitative Evaluations

Outlook (1 Lowest—5 Highest)
• 5

Fair Value
• 33¼

Risk
• **Average**

Earn./Div. Rank
• **NR**

Technical Eval.
• **Bearish** since 7/98

Rel. Strength Rank (1 Lowest—99 Highest)
• 37

Insider Activity
• **Neutral**

Recent Price • 18
52 Wk Range • 43¾-14⅜

Yield • Nil
12-Mo. P/E • 9.0

Earnings vs. Previous Year
▲=Up ▼=Down ▶=No Change

10 Week Mov. Avg. – – –
30 Week Mov. Avg. ·······
Relative Strength ——

OPTIONS: CBOE

Business Profile - 01-SEP-98

Sola plans to focus on expanding its business with an emphasis on the higher value-added, faster growing product categories such as progressive lenses, lens coatings and thinner and lighter plastic lenses, expanding into new markets, and reducing costs. In April 1998, the company said it had begun casting ophthalmic lenses in its second Chinese manufacturing facility, which was recently completed. In July 1998, SOL acquired U.S. Coatings, Inc., an anti-reflection coating equipment maker. Terms were not disclosed.

Operational Review - 01-SEP-98

Net sales in the three months ended June 30, 1998, declined 5.9%, year to year, reflecting softness in the U.S. retail optical market. Gross margins narrowed, on lower progressive product sales, but with a decrease in general and administrative expenses, pretax income edged up 0.7%. After taxes at 34.0% in each period, and a minority interest credit in FY 99 (Mar.) only, net income rose 1.9%, to $11,297,000 ($0.46 a share, diluted), from $11,089,000 ($0.46).

Stock Performance - 02-OCT-98

In the past 30 trading days, SOL's shares have increased 10%, compared to a 7% fall in the S&P 500. Average trading volume for the past five days was 151,400 shares, compared with the 40-day moving average of 182,928 shares.

Key Stock Statistics

Dividend Rate/Share	Nil	Shareholders	500
Shs. outstg. (M)	24.8	Market cap. (B)	$0.448
Avg. daily vol. (M)	0.148	Inst. holdings	78%
Tang. Bk. Value/Share	5.36		
Beta	NA		

Value of $10,000 invested 5 years ago: NA

Fiscal Year Ending Mar. 31

	1999	1998	1997	1996	1995	1994
Revenues (Million $)						
1Q	129.5	137.6	109.5	95.92	83.74	--
2Q	--	135.7	128.2	95.87	84.42	--
3Q	--	129.3	119.7	91.33	82.86	--
4Q	--	145.1	131.2	104.6	94.62	--
Yr.	--	547.7	488.7	387.7	345.6	306.0
Earnings Per Share ($)						
1Q	0.44	0.44	0.09	0.32	0.14	--
2Q	--	0.46	0.27	0.39	0.25	--
3Q	--	0.44	0.31	0.26	0.08	--
4Q	--	0.66	0.55	0.53	0.32	--
Yr.	--	2.00	1.24	1.51	0.78	0.42

Next earnings report expected: NA

Dividend Data

No cash dividends have been paid, and Sola does not intend to pay common dividends for the foreseeable future.

A Division of The McGraw·Hill Companies

Business Summary - 01-SEP-98

Sola International Inc. (SOL) has a clear vision of the future, and it's through plastic lenses. The company designs, makes and distributes a broad range of plastic and glass eyeglass lenses, focusing mainly on the faster growing plastic lens segment of the market. North America accounted for 51% of revenues in FY 98 (Mar.), Europe for 29%, and the rest of the world 20%.

In championing plastic lenses, SOL has proved farsighted. The business was formed in 1960 as Scientific Optical Laboratories of Australia (SOLA) after a revolutionary new plastic lens was developed to replace glass lenses. The market for eyeglass lenses has since shifted significantly from glass to plastic, particularly in developed markets, primarily reflecting the lighter weight, greater impact resistance and tinting flexibility of plastic compared with glass lenses.

Plastic lenses currently account for about 90% of sales. About 52% of sales generated by plastic lenses are provided by conventional hard resin plastics, with the remainder coming from advanced lens materials such as thinner and lighter plastics and plastic photochromics. These materials, including polycarbonate, Finalite and Spectralite, SOL's proprietary plastic material, are accounting for a growing portion of sales.

The company's lenses include single vision lenses; bifocals and progressive lenses (no-line bifocals); and plano lenses (lenses with no corrective power used primarily for sunglasses). SOL further differentiates its products from its competitors by lens design and coatings. Percepta, a new progressive lens, features a more customized optical design. SOL is addressing the growing market for anti-reflection (AR) coatings with its Matrix system, which delivers a finished lens with superior AR coating.

SOL also makes and sells glass lenses, mainly in North America and Europe. Its strategy for the glass lens market is to focus on high-value-added markets, such as glass progressive and higher index lenses.

The company ranks first or second in market share in North America, Europe, Australia, South America and Asia (excluding Japan). In English speaking markets (U.S., U.K. and Australia), a significant percentage of sales is to large retail chains and superoptical retail stores. In FY 98 (Mar.), the 10 largest customers accounted for 20% of net sales.

In June 1996, SOL acquired American Optical Corp., a maker of ophthalmic lenses, for $107 million; in July 1996, it acquired Neolens Inc., a producer of polycarbonate lenses, for $16 million.

In a July 1996 public offering, 2,320,000 common shares were sold at $28.625 each. In November 1997, SOL repurchased its 9,625% senior subordinated notes due 2003. In February 1998, it filed with the SEC to sell $250 million of debt and/or common stock.

Per Share Data ($)

(Year Ended Mar. 31)	1998	1997	1996	1995	1994	1993	1992	1991	1990	1989
Tangible Bk. Val.	5.21	3.33	3.30	1.70	0.59	NA	NA	NA	NA	NA
Cash Flow	2.87	2.11	2.26	1.98	1.11	NA	NA	NA	NA	NA
Earnings	2.00	1.24	1.51	0.78	0.42	NA	NA	NA	NA	NA
Dividends	Nil	Nil	Nil	Nil	NA	NA	NA	NA	NA	NA
Payout Ratio	Nil	Nil	Nil	Nil	NA	NA	NA	NA	NA	NA
Cal. Yrs.	1997	1996	1995	1994	1993	1992	1991	1990	1989	1988
Prices - High	NA	39	27³/₄	NA	NA	NA	NA	NA	NA	NA
- Low	NA	25¹/₄	16³/₈	NA	NA	NA	NA	NA	NA	NA
P/E Ratio - High	NA	31	18	NA	NA	NA	NA	NA	NA	NA
- Low	NA	20	11	NA	NA	NA	NA	NA	NA	NA

Income Statement Analysis (Million $)

	1998	1997	1996	1995	1994	1993	1992	1991	1990	1989
Revs.	548	489	388	346	306	NA	NA	NA	NA	NA
Oper. Inc.	115	88.4	78.0	63.7	45.8	NA	NA	NA	NA	NA
Depr.	22.1	21.6	17.2	21.0	15.0	NA	NA	NA	NA	NA
Int. Exp.	17.4	16.6	12.7	19.0	13.6	NA	NA	NA	NA	NA
Pretax Inc.	76.0	41.4	48.6	21.2	16.8	NA	NA	NA	NA	NA
Eff. Tax Rate	33%	26%	28%	31%	42%	NA	NA	NA	NA	NA
Net Inc.	51.1	30.9	34.6	13.6	9.2	NA	NA	NA	NA	NA

Balance Sheet & Other Fin. Data (Million $)

	1998	1997	1996	1995	1994	1993	1992	1991	1990	1989
Cash	34.4	24.4	22.4	16.1	NA	NA	NA	NA	NA	NA
Curr. Assets	342	282	207	181	NA	NA	NA	NA	NA	NA
Total Assets	684	606	417	383	371	NA	NA	NA	NA	NA
Curr. Liab.	142	142	111	104	NA	NA	NA	NA	NA	NA
LT Debt	196	163	97.9	107	116	NA	NA	NA	NA	NA
Common Eqty.	327	284	192	159	141	NA	NA	NA	NA	NA
Total Cap.	523	451	295	268	NA	NA	NA	NA	NA	NA
Cap. Exp.	39.0	30.0	17.6	11.6	NA	NA	NA	NA	NA	NA
Cash Flow	73.2	52.5	51.8	34.6	24.1	NA	NA	NA	NA	NA
Curr. Ratio	2.4	2.0	1.9	1.7	NA	NA	NA	NA	NA	NA
% LT Debt of Cap.	37.5	36.2	33.2	40.1	NA	NA	NA	NA	NA	NA
% Net Inc.of Revs.	9.3	6.4	8.9	3.9	3.0	NA	NA	NA	NA	NA
% Ret. on Assets	7.9	6.1	8.6	Nil	NA	NA	NA	NA	NA	NA
% Ret. on Equity	16.7	13.0	19.7	Nil	NA	NA	NA	NA	NA	NA

Data as orig. reptd.; bef. results of disc. opers. and/or spec. items. Per share data adj. for stk. divs. as of ex-div. date. Bold denotes diluted EPS (FASB 128). E-Estimated. NA-Not Available. NM-Not Meaningful. NR-Not Ranked.

Office—2420 Sand Hill Rd., Menlo Park, CA 94025. **Tel**—(650) 324-6868. **Chrmn**—I. S. Shapiro. **Pres & CEO**—John E. Heine. **EVP, CFO & Secy**—S. M. Neil. **Investor Contact**—Deborah Tuerk.**Dirs**—M. J. Cunniffe, D. D. Danforth, A. W. Hamill, J. E. Heine, H. Maxwell, J. L. Schultz, I. S. Shapiro.**Transfer Agent & Registrar**—First National Bank of Boston. **Incorporated**—in Delaware in 1993. **Empl**— 7,800. **S&P Analyst:** Stewart Scharf

STANDARD &POOR'S
STOCK REPORTS

Sonic Corp.

5243K
NASDAQ Symbol **SONC**

In S&P SmallCap 600

03-OCT-98

Industry:
Restaurants

Summary: Sonic operates and franchises more than 1,700 drive-in restaurants that feature fast service and a limited menu of moderately priced, cooked-to-order items.

Quantitative Evaluations

Recent Price • 17
52 Wk Range • 23⅞-15¾

Yield • Nil
12-Mo. P/E • 18.0

Outlook
(1 Lowest—5 Highest)
• **4**

Fair Value
• **24**

Risk
• **Average**

Earn./Div. Rank
• **NR**

Technical Eval.
• **Neutral** since 8/98

Rel. Strength Rank
(1 Lowest—99 Highest)
• **65**

Insider Activity
• **Neutral**

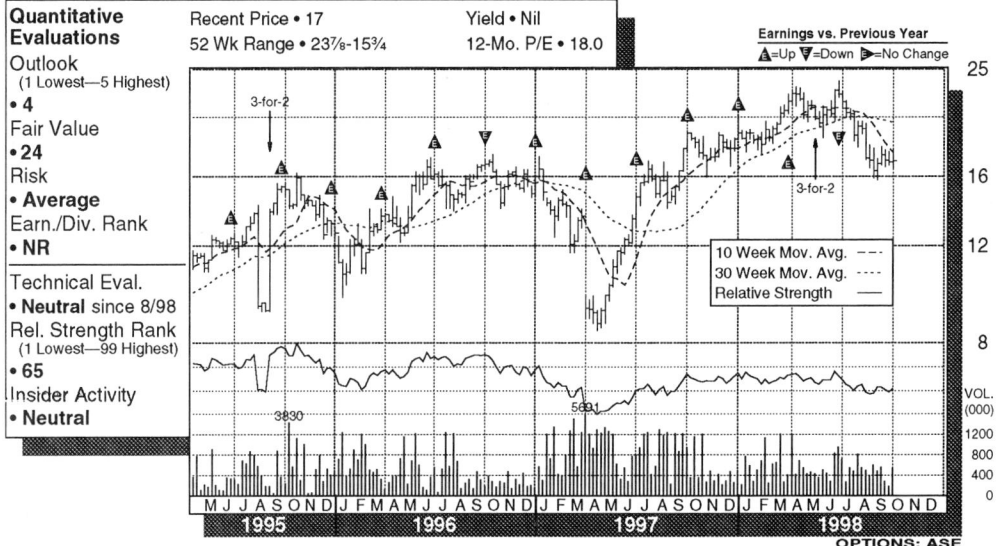

Earnings vs. Previous Year
▲=Up ▼=Down ►=No Change

10 Week Mov. Avg. – – –
30 Week Mov. Avg. ....
Relative Strength ——

OPTIONS: ASE

Business Profile - 13-JUL-98

Results have been solid, benefiting from same-store sales growth that was aided by increased marketing efforts and growing brand identity. In addition, results have gotten a boost from the retrofitting of older units, as stores remodeled under the Sonic 2000 retrofit initiative continue to meet or exceed performance expectations. SONC plans to retrofit at least 100 company-owned units and 100 franchise units during FY 98 (Aug.). In addition, all new units will feature the Sonic 2000 retrofit elements. During FY 98, the company plans to open a total of 100 units, including about 50 company-owned drive-ins. In March 1998, the company announced a share repurchase program for up to $10 million of common stock in calendar 1998.

Operational Review - 13-JUL-98

Revenues in the nine months ended May 31, 1998, advanced 20%, year to year, reflecting 7.3% same-store sales growth system-wide, as well as the addition of 111 new drive-ins. Margins widened on the greater sales; lower SG&A costs were offset by higher employee related and other expenses. After greater interest expense, higher depreciation charges, and a $2.7 million provision for litigation, the gain in pretax income was held to 2.7%. After taxes at 37.3%, versus 37.2%, income was also up 2.7%, to $13,104,000 ($0.66 a share, on 2.8% fewer shares), from $12,758,000 ($0.63, as adjusted). The FY 98 period excludes a charge of $0.03 a share from an accounting change.

Stock Performance - 02-OCT-98

In the past 30 trading days, SONC's shares have declined 0.37%, compared to a 7% fall in the S&P 500. Average trading volume for the past five days was 105,740 shares, compared with the 40-day moving average of 89,933 shares.

Key Stock Statistics

Dividend Rate/Share	Nil	Shareholders	300
Shs. outstg. (M)	19.0	Market cap. (B)	$0.325
Avg. daily vol. (M)	0.079	Inst. holdings	76%
Tang. Bk. Value/Share	5.23		
Beta	1.21		

Value of $10,000 invested 5 years ago: $ 12,690

Fiscal Year Ending Aug. 31

	1998	1997	1996	1995	1994	1993
Revenues (Million $)						
1Q	49.87	40.97	34.14	27.57	23.10	19.60
2Q	44.83	38.13	30.84	26.02	21.09	17.15
3Q	59.22	48.82	40.13	33.77	27.57	22.02
4Q	—	56.09	46.02	36.40	27.99	25.03
Yr.	—	184.0	151.2	123.8	99.7	83.79
Earnings Per Share ($)						
1Q	0.25	0.21	0.18	0.16	0.13	0.11
2Q	**0.18**	0.15	0.14	0.12	-0.04	0.09
3Q	**0.23**	0.20	0.20	0.19	0.15	0.13
4Q	—	0.32	0.01	0.23	0.18	0.16
Yr.	—	0.95	0.56	0.70	0.43	0.48

Next earnings report expected: mid October

Dividend Data

Amount ($)	Date Decl.	Ex-Div. Date	Stock of Record	Payment Date
3-for-2	May. 01	May. 15	May. 11	May. 14 '98

Business Summary - 13-JUL-98

Sonic Corp. is the largest U.S. employer of carhops. It all started in 1953, when Troy Smith added carhops to a restaurant, then called Top Hat, that featured easily prepared, cooked-to-order food such as hot dogs and hamburgers. Later, a speaker system was added to the drive-in restaurants, and sales took off. Other entrepreneurs saw the success of the restaurants and became franchisees. To avoid a copyright dispute, and to signify the company's fast service, its name was changed to Sonic. Today, Sonic restaurants, located principally in the south central U.S., form the largest chain of quick-service, drive-in restaurants in the country. At May 31, 1998, there were 1,788 restaurants in the chain, with 1,497 owned by independent franchisees and 291 by the company. Restaurant data for recent fiscal years (Aug.), with sales per unit in 000s:

	FY 97	FY 96	FY 95
Company-owned			
average unit sales	$649	$601	$577
Number of owned units	256	231	178
Franchised			
average unit sales	$720	$657	$620
Number of franchised units	1,424	1,336	1,286

Sonic aims to set itself apart from competitors by eliminating waiting in long lines in the drive-through lane. At a typical Sonic restaurant, the customer drives into one of 24 to 36 covered parking spaces, orders through an intercom from a menu featuring hamburgers, hot dogs, french fries, onion rings and specialty beverages, and has the food delivered by a carhop within an average of four minutes. Since 1995, all new company-owned restaurants incorporate a drive-through window and patio seating area.

In FY 97, Sonic implemented a program to retrofit all Sonic drive-ins over the next few years. The retrofit program includes new signage, new menu and speaker housings, and considerable trade dress modifications to the exterior of each restaurant. The standard retrofit per restaurant costs and estimated $58,000 to $65,000. In addition, all new restaurants will include the new retrofit signage and trade dress style.

The company's expansion strategy calls for: (1) the building-out of existing core markets; (2) further penetration of existing markets; and (3) the acquisition of existing Sonic franchised restaurants.

During FY 97, Sonic opened 37 company-owned restaurants and 92 franchised restaurants. In FY 98, the company plans to open 50 company owned restaurants and at least 90 franchised units.

Per Share Data ($)

(Year Ended Aug. 31)	1997	1996	1995	1994	1993	1992	1991	1990	1989	1988
Tangible Bk. Val.	4.99	4.33	2.69	3.06	2.63	2.05	1.66	-0.48	-1.74	NA
Cash Flow	1.56	0.99	1.03	0.78	0.61	0.50	0.37	0.20	0.04	NA
Earnings	0.95	0.56	0.70	0.43	0.48	0.39	0.26	0.08	-0.18	NA
Dividends	Nil	Nil	Nil	Nil	Nil	Nil	Nil	Nil	Nil	Nil
Payout Ratio	Nil	Nil	Nil	Nil	Nil	Nil	Nil	Nil	Nil	Nil
Prices - High	20⅜	17⅝	16¼	11¾	13⅝	14⅝	14	NA	NA	NA
- Low	8⅜	9⅝	8¾	7½	8½	9½	5½	NA	NA	NA
P/E Ratio - High	21	31	23	28	28	38	54	NA	NA	NA
- Low	9	17	13	17	18	24	21	NA	NA	NA

Income Statement Analysis (Million $)

	1997	1996	1995	1994	1993	1992	1991	1990	1989	1988
Revs.	184	151	124	100	83.8	66.7	53.9	45.9	33.9	NA
Oper. Inc.	52.1	40.9	30.9	26.2	19.7	16.4	12.0	8.7	4.7	NA
Depr.	12.3	8.9	5.9	6.3	2.4	2.1	1.7	1.3	1.6	NA
Int. Exp.	2.2	1.2	1.8	1.1	0.8	0.7	2.1	3.7	3.7	NA
Pretax Inc.	30.4	18.1	20.0	15.0	16.3	13.9	8.5	3.6	-2.6	NA
Eff. Tax Rate	37%	38%	38%	31%	31%	32%	30%	21%	NM	NM
Net Inc.	19.1	11.2	12.5	7.6	8.6	6.8	3.7	0.9	-2.0	NA

Balance Sheet & Other Fin. Data (Million $)

	1997	1996	1995	1994	1993	1992	1991	1990	1989	1988
Cash	7.3	7.7	4.0	6.0	5.4	9.0	10.3	2.5	2.8	NA
Curr. Assets	18.7	16.2	12.7	14.1	13.6	14.2	14.7	6.5	6.4	NA
Total Assets	185	147	105	77.0	63.5	50.3	41.9	31.6	31.6	NA
Curr. Liab.	15.2	12.7	8.5	6.8	6.2	4.7	4.6	5.1	5.0	NA
LT Debt	45.7	20.9	30.6	12.7	6.6	6.0	5.3	29.9	31.0	NA
Common Eqty.	118	110	63.4	54.4	46.8	36.0	29.1	-5.2	-5.8	NA
Total Cap.	165	131	93.9	69.4	56.2	44.3	36.2	26.2	25.9	NA
Cap. Exp.	48.0	41.1	34.2	16.7	14.8	9.1	4.8	2.2	13.0	NA
Cash Flow	31.4	20.1	18.4	13.9	11.0	8.9	5.4	2.2	-0.5	NA
Curr. Ratio	1.2	1.3	1.5	2.1	2.2	3.0	3.2	1.3	1.3	NA
% LT Debt of Cap.	27.7	16.0	32.6	18.3	11.7	13.5	14.7	114.1	119.8	NA
% Net Inc.of Revs.	10.4	7.4	10.1	7.7	10.3	10.2	6.9	2.1	NM	NM
% Ret. on Assets	11.5	8.9	13.7	10.9	15.1	14.8	8.0	NA	NM	NM
% Ret. on Equity	16.7	12.9	21.2	15.1	20.8	20.9	NM	NA	NM	NM

Data as orig. reptd.; bef. results of disc. opers. and/or spec. items. Per share data adj. for stk. divs. as of ex-div. date. Bold denotes diluted EPS (FASB 128). E-Estimated. NA-Not Available. NM-Not Meaningful. NR-Not Ranked.

Office—101 Park Ave., Oklahoma City, OK 73102. **Reincorporated**—in Delaware in 1991. **Tel**—(405) 280-7654. **Website**—http://www.sonicdrivein.com **Chrmn**—E. D. Werries. **Pres & CEO**—J. C. Hudson. **VP-Fin, Treas. & CFO**—W. S. McClain.**VP & Secy**—R. L. Matlocks.**Dirs**—D. H. Clark, J. C. Hudson, L. Lieberman, H. E. Rainbolt, F. E. Richardson III, R. M. Rosenberg, T. N. Smith, E. D. Werries. **Transfer Agent & Registrar**—Liberty Bank & Trust, Oklahoma City. **Empl**— 178. **S&P Analyst:** Robert J. Izmirlian

Southern Energy Homes 5265

NASDAQ Symbol **SEHI**

In S&P SmallCap 600

03-OCT-98 Industry: Homebuilding

Summary: SEHI produces, sells and provides financing for manufactured homes primarily in the southeastern and south central U.S.

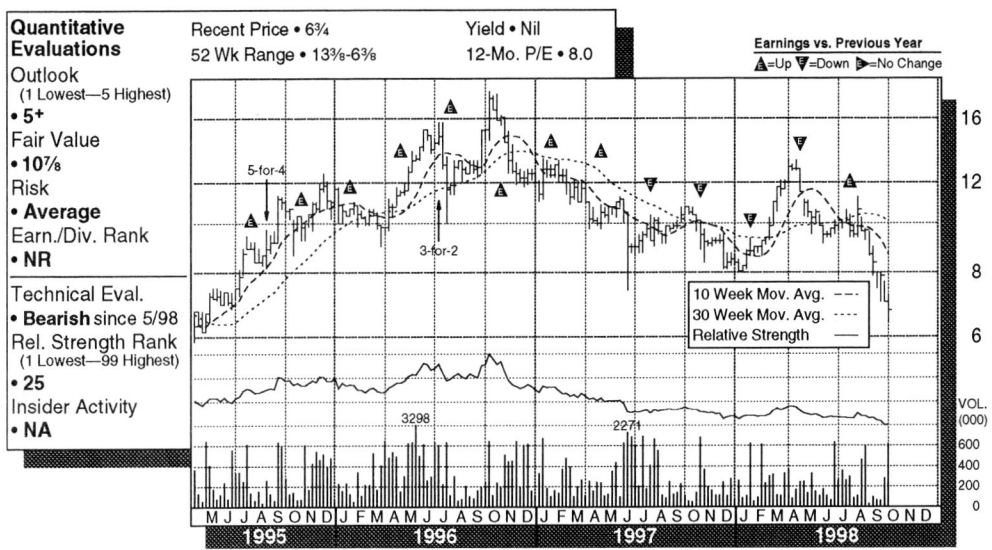

Quantitative Evaluations	
Outlook (1 Lowest—5 Highest) • **5+**	
Fair Value • **10⅞**	
Risk • **Average**	
Earn./Div. Rank • **NR**	
Technical Eval. • **Bearish** since 5/98	
Rel. Strength Rank (1 Lowest—99 Highest) • **25**	
Insider Activity • **NA**	

Recent Price • 6¾
52 Wk Range • 13⅜-6⅜
Yield • Nil
12-Mo. P/E • 8.0

Earnings vs. Previous Year
▲=Up ▼=Down ▶=No Change

10 Week Mov. Avg. — —
30 Week Mov. Avg. - - - -
Relative Strength ——

Business Profile - 12-AUG-98

One of the primary operating strategies of this producer of manufactured homes in 21 states is to become vertically integrated. In keeping with this goal, SEHI acquired manufactured housing retailer A & G Homes, Inc. in December 1997. In February 1997, in order to leverage its new business structure, SEHI formed a manufactured home financing company with 21st Century Mortgage Corp. The number of new homes sold (wholesale and retail) in the first half of 1998 fell 1.1%, to 5,481, from 5,540 in the 1997 period. In April 1997, directors authorized the repurchase of up to 2,000,000 common shares; through late July 1998, 932,700 shares had been purchased for $8.4 million.

Operational Review - 12-AUG-98

Based on a brief report, net revenues in the 26 weeks ended July 3, 1998, fell 5.0%, year to year, reflecting weakness in wholesale shipments. In the absence of a $2.1 million nonrecurring charge related to the closing of a plant in 1997, operating income was up 4.5%. Net income climbed 13%, to $6,342,000 ($0.45 a share, on 9.6% fewer shares), from $5,620,000 ($0.36).

Stock Performance - 02-OCT-98

In the past 30 trading days, SEHI's shares have declined 30%, compared to a 7% fall in the S&P 500. Average trading volume for the past five days was 156,420 shares, compared with the 40-day moving average of 60,662 shares.

Key Stock Statistics

Dividend Rate/Share	Nil	Shareholders	100
Shs. outstg. (M)	13.4	Market cap. (B)	$0.091
Avg. daily vol. (M)	0.061	Inst. holdings	63%
Tang. Bk. Value/Share	4.58		
Beta	1.18		

Value of $10,000 invested 5 years ago: NA

Fiscal Year Ending Dec. 31

	1998	1997	1996	1995	1994	1993
Revenues (Million $)						
1Q	76.11	80.12	71.11	55.57	40.98	20.00
2Q	74.15	76.88	83.92	61.22	44.99	33.51
3Q	—	76.33	77.41	58.46	47.97	34.18
4Q	—	65.21	74.40	66.02	54.82	38.93
Yr.	—	298.5	306.8	241.3	188.8	143.6
Earnings Per Share ($)						
1Q	0.17	0.24	0.22	0.16	0.13	—
2Q	0.28	0.12	0.29	0.20	0.17	0.10
3Q	—	0.24	0.27	0.21	0.18	0.16
4Q	—	0.15	0.23	0.19	0.16	0.13
Yr.	—	0.75	1.01	0.79	0.63	0.41

Next earnings report expected: late October

Dividend Data

No cash dividends have been paid.

A Division of The McGraw-Hill Companies

Business Summary - 12-AUG-98

If images of unsightly trailer parks and rundown mobile homes come to mind when you hear the term manufactured home, think again. Makers of manufactured (factory-built) homes, such as Southern Energy Homes, Inc. (SEHI), have upgraded their products for an expanding market. Today, nearly one of every three new homes sold is a manufactured home, and many are hard to distinguish from site-built models. SEHI produces manufactured homes that are sold in 21 states, mainly in the southeastern and south central U.S., by 465 independent dealers at 859 independent dealer locations and 30 company-owned retail centers.

Company homes are designed as primary residences ready for immediate occupancy, and are customized at its 11 factories to buyer specifications. SEHI designs floor plans and provides features to match homebuyer preferences, offering homes in both single and in multi-sections, which provide a larger living space. The homes, ranging in size from 653 sq. ft. to 2,417 sq. ft., sell at prices (excluding land) of $14,900 to $108,000. This provides an affordable alternative for many, including the growing number of retirees and "empty nesters" who are purchasing homes.

Homes are constructed using assembly line techniques, with seven facilities located in Alabama and one each in Texas, North Carolina and Pennsylvania. SEHI arranges, at dealer expense, for the transportation of finished homes to dealers, using its own trucking subsidiary and independent trucking companies. Dealers or other independent installers are responsible for placing the home on site, making utility hookups and providing and installing certain trim items. In 1997, SEHI sold 9,165 homes and 14,288 floor sections, down from 10,940 homes and 16,697 floor sections in 1996.

Four component divisions supply interior wall panels; windows, doors and countertops; wood moulding and trim finishing; and kitchen and dining furniture to SEHI's manufactured housing divisions and third parties.

In a quest for further vertical integration, in 1996, the company entered the retail sector of the manufactured home industry by acquiring a group of retail companies. In February, 1997, SEHI formed a joint venture with 21st Century Mortgage Corp., WENCO 21, which offers, through 21st Century, consumer financing for the company's manufactured homes and other homes sold through its retail centers and independent dealers.

In December 1997, the company purchased A&G Homes, Inc. ($19.4 million of revenues in 1996), a manufactured housing retail company, for $1.4 million in cash, the assumption of $4.2 million of inventory debt, and 94,115 SEHI common shares.

Per Share Data ($)

(Year Ended Dec. 31)	1997	1996	1995	1994	1993	1992	1991	1990	1989	1988
Tangible Bk. Val.	4.50	4.12	1.18	2.19	1.81	0.90	NA	NA	NA	NA
Cash Flow	0.96	1.09	1.36	0.71	0.49	0.41	NA	NA	NA	NA
Earnings	0.75	1.01	0.79	0.62	0.41	0.27	NA	NA	NA	NA
Dividends	Nil	Nil	Nil	Nil	Nil	Nil	Nil	Nil	Nil	Nil
Payout Ratio	Nil	Nil	Nil	Nil	Nil	Nil	Nil	Nil	Nil	Nil
Prices - High	13³/₈	18¹/₈	12¹/₂	10¹/₈	11³/₈	NA	NA	NA	NA	NA
- Low	7³/₈	9	5⁵/₈	5¹/₂	6⁷/₈	NA	NA	NA	NA	NA
P/E Ratio - High	18	18	16	16	20	NA	NA	NA	NA	NA
- Low	10	9	7	9	12	NA	NA	NA	NA	NA

Income Statement Analysis (Million $)

	1997	1996	1995	1994	1993	1992	1991	1990	1989	1988
Revs.	299	307	241	189	144	83.0	NA	NA	NA	NA
Oper. Inc.	24.7	26.0	19.1	15.1	12.2	7.7	NA	NA	NA	NA
Depr.	3.1	1.2	1.7	1.3	1.1	1.6	NA	NA	NA	NA
Int. Exp.	1.4	0.1	0.1	0.2	0.7	1.5	NA	NA	NA	NA
Pretax Inc.	18.5	24.8	18.1	14.0	8.8	4.7	NA	NA	NA	NA
Eff. Tax Rate	38%	39%	38%	37%	39%	37%	NA	NA	NA	NA
Net Inc.	11.4	15.2	11.2	8.8	5.4	2.9	NA	NA	NA	NA

Balance Sheet & Other Fin. Data (Million $)

	1997	1996	1995	1994	1993	1992	1991	1990	1989	1988
Cash	17.7	5.3	18.8	11.0	12.8	NA	NA	NA	NA	NA
Curr. Assets	71.7	53.0	53.0	36.7	32.8	NA	NA	NA	NA	NA
Total Assets	123	113	75.9	54.3	43.3	26.7	NA	NA	NA	NA
Curr. Liab.	38.8	35.3	18.7	15.2	12.1	NA	NA	NA	NA	NA
LT Debt	4.7	Nil	0.0	0.6	1.5	12.6	NA	NA	NA	NA
Common Eqty.	79.8	77.4	57.2	38.6	29.7	0.6	NA	NA	NA	NA
Total Cap.	84.4	77.4	57.2	39.2	31.2	13.2	NA	NA	NA	NA
Cap. Exp.	6.1	5.5	5.2	3.1	4.8	0.8	NA	NA	NA	NA
Cash Flow	14.5	16.4	12.9	10.1	6.4	4.5	NA	NA	NA	NA
Curr. Ratio	1.8	1.5	2.8	2.4	2.7	NA	NA	NA	NA	NA
% LT Debt of Cap.	5.6	Nil	Nil	1.5	4.8	5.4	NA	NA	NA	NA
% Net Inc.of Revs.	3.8	5.0	4.7	4.7	3.7	3.5	NA	NA	NA	NA
% Ret. on Assets	9.6	16.2	17.3	18.1	15.3	12.3	NA	NA	NA	NA
% Ret. on Equity	14.5	22.7	23.5	25.8	35.3	NM	NM	NM	NM	NM

Data as orig. reptd.; bef. results of disc. opers. and/or spec. items. Per share data adj. for stk. divs. as of ex-div. date. Bold denotes diluted EPS (FASB 128). E-Estimated. NA-Not Available. NM-Not Meaningful. NR-Not Ranked.

Office—Highway 41 North, P. O. Box 390, Addison, AL 35540. **Tel**—(256) 747-8589. **Chrmn, Pres & CEO**—W. L. Batchelor. **EVP, CFO, Treas & Secy**—K. W. Brown. **COO**—K. O. Holdbrooks. **Dirs**—W. L. Batchelor, K. W. Brown, P. J. Evanson, K. O. Holdbrooks, J. J. Incandela, J. O. Lee, J. R. Long. **Transfer Agent & Registrar**—State Street Bank & Trust Co., Quincy, MA. **Incorporated**—in Delaware in 1993. **Empl**— 2,371. **S&P Analyst:** M.I.

STANDARD &POOR'S
STOCK REPORTS

Southwest Gas

2077Q

NYSE Symbol **SWX**

In S&P SmallCap 600

03-OCT-98 | **Industry:** Natural Gas | **Summary:** SWX conducts natural gas distribution operations, mainly in Nevada and Arizona.

Quantitative Evaluations

Outlook (1 Lowest—5 Highest)
• **2⁻**

Fair Value
• **19¼**

Risk
• **Low**

Earn./Div. Rank
• **B**

Technical Eval.
• **Neutral** since 8/98

Rel. Strength Rank (1 Lowest—99 Highest)
• **81**

Insider Activity
• **NA**

Recent Price • 20½   Yield • 4.0%
52 Wk Range • 25-17⅛   12-Mo. P/E • 13.8

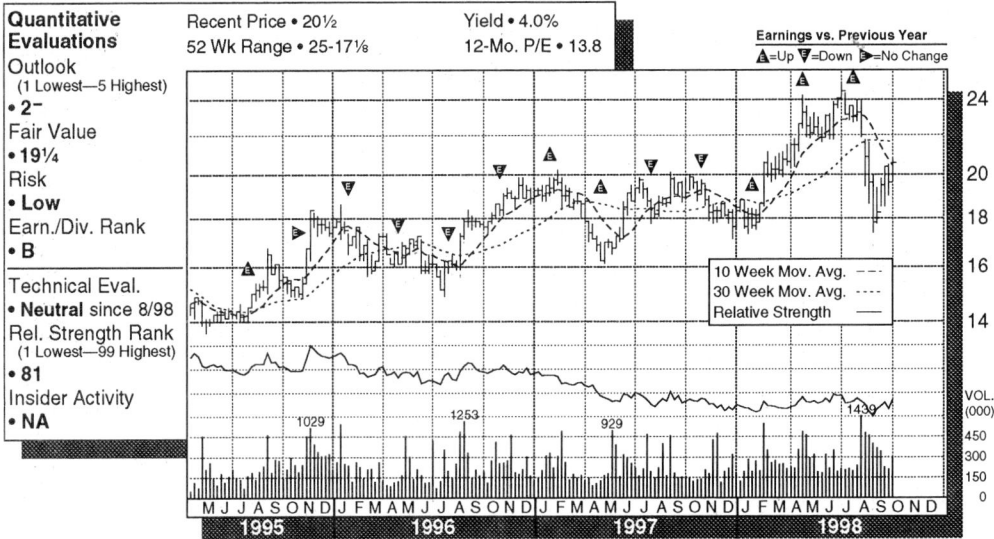

Earnings vs. Previous Year
▲=Up ▼=Down ▶=No Change

10 Week Mov. Avg. ---
30 Week Mov. Avg. ....
Relative Strength —

Business Profile - 24-APR-98

Customer growth has continued at a rapid pace, as the western states in which SWX operates have led the U.S. in population growth, job growth, and housing activity. Recent results benefited from an improvement in operating margin, due to customer growth, rate relief, and more favorable weather conditions. On April 15, 1998, the company announced that it expected first quarter earnings to exceed expectations, due to colder than normal weather. Nevada regulators are expected to create an alternative plan of regulation for natural gas utilities by July 1, 1998, and California regulators will conduct hearings on such issues as regulatory streamlining, unbundling and other competitive issues throughout 1998.

Operational Review - 24-APR-98

Operating revenues in 1997 advanced 14%, reflecting continued customer growth throughout the Southwest service area, cooler winter temperatures, and rate relief. Operating margins widened, as the benefits of increased volume and well controlled O&M expense outweighed higher construction expenses; operating income surged 43%. With slower growth in interest expense, pretax income doubled. After taxes at 22.8%, versus 37.1%, net income soared to $16,469,999 ($0.61 a share, on 4.6% more shares), from $6,574,000 ($0.25).

Stock Performance - 02-OCT-98

In the past 30 trading days, SWX's shares have increased 5%, compared to a 7% fall in the S&P 500. Average trading volume for the past five days was 59,740 shares, compared with the 40-day moving average of 80,105 shares.

Key Stock Statistics

Dividend Rate/Share	0.82	Shareholders	27,000
Shs. outstg. (M)	30.2	Market cap. (B)	$0.620
Avg. daily vol. (M)	0.056	Inst. holdings	39%
Tang. Bk. Value/Share	14.09		
Beta	0.88		

Value of $10,000 invested 5 years ago: $ 19,580

Fiscal Year Ending Dec. 31

	1998	1997	1996	1995	1994	1993
Revenues (Million $)						
1Q	292.6	235.2	188.3	238.9	239.0	221.0
2Q	192.9	136.9	123.6	158.5	140.2	138.0
3Q	—	128.7	125.3	127.4	124.3	126.0
4Q	—	231.1	206.8	146.4	224.5	205.0
Yr.	—	732.0	644.1	563.5	728.2	690.0
Earnings Per Share ($)						
1Q	1.30	0.80	0.60	0.68	1.07	0.67
2Q	-0.09	-0.47	-0.46	-0.41	-0.47	-0.64
3Q	—	-0.58	-0.55	-0.54	-0.54	-0.37
4Q	—	0.85	0.69	0.47	1.15	0.90
Yr.	—	0.61	0.25	0.10	1.22	0.56

Next earnings report expected: early November

Dividend Data (Dividends have been paid since 1956.)

Amount ($)	Date Decl.	Ex-Div. Date	Stock of Record	Payment Date
0.205	Jan. 21	Feb. 12	Feb. 17	Mar. 01 '98
0.205	Mar. 04	May. 13	May. 15	Jun. 01 '98
0.205	Jul. 27	Aug. 18	Aug. 20	Sep. 01 '98
0.205	Sep. 15	Nov. 12	Nov. 16	Dec. 01 '98

A Division of The McGraw-Hill Companies

Business Summary - 24-APR-98

Southwest Gas (SWX) purchases, transports and distributes natural gas in portions of Nevada, Arizona and California, to 1,151,000 residential, commercial and industrial customers. Approximately 59,000 customers were added to the system in 1997.

Transportation of customer-secured gas to end-users on the company's system has a significant impact on SWX's throughput, accounting for 53% of total system throughput in 1997. Although the volumes are significant, these customers provide a much smaller proportionate share of the company's operating margin. Paiute Pipeline Co. (wholly owned) provides transportation service of gas from the Idaho-Nevada border to communities in northern and western Nevada.

SWX is subject to regulation by the Arizona Corporation Commission (ACC), the Public Service Commission of Nevada (PSCN) and the California Public Utilities Commission (CPUC). These commissions regulate public utility rates, practices, facilities, and service territories. The PSCN is expected to create an alternative plan of regulation for natural gas utilities by July 1, 1998, and the CPUC will conduct hearings on such issues as regulatory streamlining, unbundling and other competitive issues throughout 1998.

Demand for natural gas is seasonal, and adverse weather conditions can affect operating results. The company believes that comparisons of earnings for interim periods do not reliably reflect overall trends and changes in its operations. In addition, earnings can be significantly affected by the timing of general rate relief. Rates charged to customers vary according to customer class and are set at levels allowing for the recovery of all incurred costs, including a return on rate base sufficient to pay interest on debt, preferred securities distributions, and a reasonable return on common equity.

SWX believes that natural gas supplies and pipeline capacity will remain available. Its main objective with regard to gas supply is to ensure that adequate supplies are available from reliable sources. Gas is acquired from a wide variety of sources, including suppliers on the spot market, and those who provide firm supplies over short-term and longer-term durations. During 1997, the company acquired gas supplies from more than 70 suppliers. SWX continues to evaluate natural gas storage as an option to allow it to take advantage of seasonal price differentials in obtaining natural gas from a variety of sources to meet the growing demand of its customers.

In 1997, the company sold 91.5 million dekatherms of gas and transported 103.1 million dekatherms, up from 81.8 million dekatherms and 96.8 million dekatherms, respectively, in 1996. The weighted average cost of gas in 1997 was $0.35 per therm, up from $0.27 in 1996.

Per Share Data ($)

(Year Ended Dec. 31)	1997	1996	1995	1994	1993	1992	1991	1990	1989	1988
Tangible Bk. Val.	14.09	14.60	14.55	12.85	12.87	12.14	11.83	12.89	12.14	11.02
Cash Flow	3.74	3.10	2.80	4.81	3.63	3.75	1.95	4.44	4.77	4.57
Earnings	0.61	0.25	0.10	1.22	0.56	0.81	-0.76	1.81	2.15	2.13
Dividends	0.82	0.82	0.82	0.60	0.74	0.70	1.05	1.40	1.37	1.34
Payout Ratio	134%	NM	NM	50%	132%	87%	NM	77%	64%	63%
Prices - High	20¼	19⅞	18⅜	19⅜	18½	15⅜	17½	18½	20⅜	23¼
- Low	16⅛	14⅞	13⅝	13¾	13⅜	10⅜	9	11¾	16⅝	17¼
P/E Ratio - High	33	79	NM	16	33	19	NM	10	9	11
- Low	26	59	NM	11	24	13	NM	6	8	8

Income Statement Analysis (Million $)

	1997	1996	1995	1994	1993	1992	1991	1990	1989	1988
Revs.	732	644	564	728	690	720	800	867	848	804
Oper. Inc.	102	145	121	168	151	249	247	367	377	325
Depr.	84.7	73.7	62.5	65.1	63.6	60.7	55.3	51.6	49.8	45.2
Int. Exp.	64.8	56.7	54.6	58.0	50.1	157	207	256	259	213
Pretax Inc.	26.8	10.4	3.5	44.0	23.6	32.1	-13.5	62.8	71.2	70.0
Eff. Tax Rate	18%	37%	24%	40%	48%	45%	NM	41%	40%	41%
Net Inc.	16.5	6.6	2.6	26.3	12.4	17.7	-14.2	37.2	42.7	41.2

Balance Sheet & Other Fin. Data (Million $)

	1997	1996	1995	1994	1993	1992	1991	1990	1989	1988
Cash	17.6	8.3	11.2	166	136	133	113	70.0	41.0	52.0
Curr. Assets	289	160	317	NA	NA	NA	NA	NA	NA	NA
Total Assets	1,769	1,560	1,533	3,090	2,944	3,342	3,463	3,764	3,706	3,679
Curr. Liab.	324	261	330	NA	NA	NA	NA	NA	NA	NA
LT Debt	779	665	608	786	648	614	598	817	830	835
Common Eqty.	386	380	356	339	340	329	327	353	334	309
Total Cap.	1,393	1,257	1,163	1,262	1,147	1,062	1,058	1,313	1,302	1,281
Cap. Exp.	170	219	166	145	115	105	86.0	105	114	131
Cash Flow	101	80.3	64.8	90.9	75.2	77.3	39.8	87.2	90.7	84.5
Curr. Ratio	0.9	0.6	1.0	NA	NA	NA	NA	NA	NA	NA
% LT Debt of Cap.	55.9	52.9	52.3	62.2	56.5	57.8	56.5	62.2	63.8	65.2
% Net Inc.of Revs.	2.2	1.0	0.5	3.6	1.8	2.5	NM	4.3	5.0	5.1
% Ret. on Assets	1.0	0.4	0.2	0.9	0.4	0.5	NM	1.0	1.1	1.8
% Ret. on Equity	4.3	1.8	0.7	7.5	3.5	5.1	NM	10.2	12.5	13.0

Data as orig. reptd.; bef. results of disc. opers. and/or spec. items. Per share data adj. for stk. divs. as of ex-div. date. Bold denotes diluted EPS (FASB 128). E-Estimated. NA-Not Available. NM-Not Meaningful. NR-Not Ranked.

Office—5241 Spring Mountain Rd., P.O. Box 98510, Las Vegas, NV 89193-8510. **Tel**—(702) 876-7237.**Chrmn**—T. Y. Hartley. **Pres & CEO**—M. O. Maffie. **SVP, CFO & Secy**—G. C. Biehl. **Investor Contact**—Laura Hobbs. **Dirs**—R.C. Batastini, G. C. Biehl, M. J. Cortez, L. T. Dyer, T. Y. Hartley, M. B. Jager, L. R. Judd, J. J. Kropid, J. R. Lincicome, M. O. Maffie, C. M. Sparks, R. S. Sundt, T. L. Wright. **Transfer Agent & Registrar**—Co. itself. **Incorporated**—in California in 1931. **Empl**— 2,447. **S&P Analyst:** J.R.C.

03-OCT-98

Industry: Natural Gas

Summary: Through its wholly owned subsidiaries, Southwestern Energy explores for and produces oil and natural gas and is involved in the transmission and distribution of natural gas.

Quantitative Evaluations

Recent Price • 8

52 Wk Range • 13⅛-6⅝

Yield • 3.0%

12-Mo. P/E • NM

Outlook (1 Lowest—5 Highest)
• **NA**

Fair Value
• **NA**

Risk
• **Low**

Earn./Div. Rank
• **A-**

Technical Eval.
• **Neutral** since 9/98

Rel. Strength Rank (1 Lowest—99 Highest)
• **58**

Insider Activity
• **Favorable**

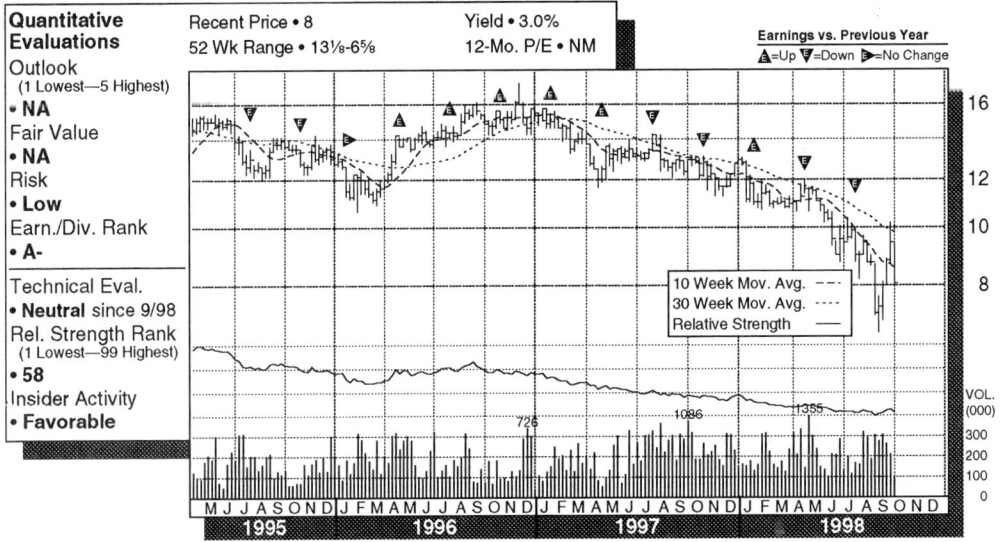

Earnings vs. Previous Year
▲=Up ▼=Down ▶=No Change

10 Week Mov. Avg. ---
30 Week Mov. Avg. ····
Relative Strength —

Business Profile - 10-AUG-98

In 1998, the company's capital spending will be weighted much more toward the drilling of wells, including a number of high potential exploration wells. Overall capital spending will decrease to $59.2 million from 1997's $73.5 million. As its emphasis turns to drilling, SWN expects to return to a pattern of increasing reserves and production over time. In the first six months of 1998, the company added about 33.7 billion cubic feet equivalent of proved oil and gas through drilling, replacing 177% of year-to-date production. In October 1998, SWN will complete the reorganization of its exploration and production segment with the closing of its Oklahoma City office, expected to result in savings of some $1.3 million annually.

Operational Review - 10-AUG-98

Revenues in the first half of 1998 were off slightly, year to year, as declines in oil and gas sales due to lower wellhead prices outweighed increases in gas marketing, gas transportation and other revenues. Profitability was hurt by significantly higher gas purchase costs for the marketing segment and increased operating and general expenses; following a $66.4 million asset impairment charge associated with low oil and gas prices and costs from previously unevaluated properties, an operating loss contrasted with income. After a $21.1 million tax benefit, against taxes at 38.5%, the net loss was $32,986,000 ($1.33 a share), versus net income of $12,348,000 ($0.50).

Stock Performance - 02-OCT-98

In the past 30 trading days, SWN's shares have declined 8%, compared to a 7% fall in the S&P 500. Average trading volume for the past five days was 19,760 shares, compared with the 40-day moving average of 52,918 shares.

Key Stock Statistics

Dividend Rate/Share	0.24	Shareholders	28,800
Shs. outstg. (M)	24.9	Market cap. (B)	$0.201
Avg. daily vol. (M)	0.052	Inst. holdings	59%
Tang. Bk. Value/Share	8.92		
Beta	0.84		

Value of $10,000 invested 5 years ago: $ 6,947

Fiscal Year Ending Dec. 31

	1998	1997	1996	1995	1994	1993
Revenues (Million $)						
1Q	82.96	88.92	63.86	51.75	65.40	59.20
2Q	56.33	51.24	34.30	30.64	34.60	34.00
3Q	—	48.64	30.25	25.45	27.81	28.50
4Q	—	87.38	60.81	45.26	42.34	53.20
Yr.	—	276.2	189.2	153.1	170.2	174.8
Earnings Per Share ($)						
1Q	0.37	0.50	0.38	0.28	0.51	0.44
2Q	-1.70	Nil	0.11	0.02	0.18	0.15
3Q	—	0.06	0.01	0.04	0.09	0.05
4Q	—	0.31	0.28	0.20	0.20	0.41
Yr.	—	0.76	0.78	0.46	0.98	1.05

Next earnings report expected: late October

Dividend Data (Dividends have been paid since 1939.)

Amount ($)	Date Decl.	Ex-Div. Date	Stock of Record	Payment Date
0.060	Jan. 07	Jan. 15	Jan. 20	Feb. 05 '98
0.060	Apr. 03	Apr. 16	Apr. 20	May. 05 '98
0.060	Jul. 08	Jul. 16	Jul. 20	Aug. 05 '98
0.060	Sep. 11	Oct. 16	Oct. 20	Nov. 05 '98

A Division of The McGraw·Hill Companies

Business Summary - 10-AUG-98

This integrated energy company is mainly focused on natural gas, searching for it, producing it, gathering it, transporting it and, finally, distributing it to about 177,000 utility customers in Arkansas and Missouri. Southwestern Energy Co.'s (SWN) exploration and production activities, which have also yielded increasing volumes of oil in recent years, provided 64% of the gas requirements of SWN's principal utility operation, Arkansas Western Gas Co., in 1996.

Arkansas Western Gas Co. (AWG) gathers natural gas in the Arkansas River Valley of western Arkansas and transports and delivers the gas at retail to customers in the northwestern part of the state. AWG's division, Associated Natural Gas Co., serves northeastern Arkansas and southeastern Missouri.

SWN's initial exploration strategy in South Louisiana and the upper Texas Gulf Coast failed to meet its reserve growth and production goals, and it now focuses on multi-well projects supported by 3-D seismic technology. First drilling in the East Atchafalaya project in South Louisiana, the company's most significant joint venture area, commenced in early 1997. SWN balances the higher risk of these exploration projects with an ongoing development drilling program in the Arkoma Basin of Arkansas and acquisitions of producing proper-

ties. Due to higher property prices, however, no acquisitions were made in 1997. In 1996, SWN added 32.7 billion cubic feet of gas and 6.4 million barrels of oil through its producing property acquisition program. Proved reserves totaled 291.4 billion cubic feet of gas and 7.85 million barrels of oil at the end of 1997.

Deliveries to sales and end-use transportation customers by SWN's utility systems were 34.2 Bcf during 1997, down from 35.4 Bcf in 1996. SWN also transported 2.8 billion cubic feet of gas through its gathering system for off-system deliveries in 1997.

In response to mounting competition in the energy industry, SWN formed a full-service energy marketing company in 1996 to create and capture value existing beyond the wellhead in transportation and marketing activities. The Energy Services group recently took steps to improve the performance of the 302-mile NOARK Pipeline System (in which SWN had a 48% interest). Cutting across northern Arkansas, the intrastate transmission system had been hobbled by a lack of adequate gas supply and had been operating below capacity. An interstate system was created in 1998 by merging NOARK with a 437-mile pipeline running from Oklahoma to Arkansas. SWN now has a 25% interest in the merged system (a unit of OGE Energy owns the rest).

Per Share Data ($)

(Year Ended Dec. 31)	1997	1996	1995	1994	1993	1992	1991	1990	1989	1988
Tangible Bk. Val.	8.92	8.41	7.87	7.92	7.18	5.97	5.30	4.70	4.15	3.77
Cash Flow	2.70	2.49	1.89	2.36	2.26	1.80	1.49	1.16	1.21	0.96
Earnings	0.76	0.78	0.46	0.98	1.05	0.87	0.78	0.57	0.56	0.46
Dividends	0.24	0.24	0.24	0.24	0.22	0.20	0.19	0.19	0.19	0.19
Payout Ratio	32%	31%	52%	24%	21%	23%	24%	33%	33%	40%
Prices - High	15¾	17⅜	15½	18⅞	21½	14	12¾	12⅛	11⅛	7½
- Low	11¼	10⅝	11¾	14	12⅛	9¼	9⅛	9½	5¾	5½
P/E Ratio - High	21	22	34	19	21	16	16	21	20	16
- Low	15	14	26	14	12	11	12	16	10	12

Income Statement Analysis (Million $)

	1997	1996	1995	1994	1993	1992	1991	1990	1989	1988
Revs.	276	189	153	170	175	144	136	117	126	95.0
Oper. Inc.	57.9	90.4	67.2	87.6	88.5	69.9	60.4	48.4	48.8	38.3
Depr.	48.2	42.4	36.0	35.5	30.9	23.9	18.2	14.8	16.3	12.3
Int. Exp.	16.4	17.2	13.6	10.5	10.6	11.5	11.2	10.5	10.7	8.0
Pretax Inc.	30.5	30.9	18.8	40.9	46.9	35.6	32.2	23.1	22.2	18.2
Eff. Tax Rate	39%	38%	39%	39%	42%	37%	38%	37%	37%	37%
Net Inc.	18.7	19.2	11.5	25.1	27.1	22.3	20.1	14.5	14.0	11.5

Balance Sheet & Other Fin. Data (Million $)

	1997	1996	1995	1994	1993	1992	1991	1990	1989	1988
Cash	4.6	2.3	1.5	1.1	0.8	1.1	2.2	1.2	1.1	1.3
Curr. Assets	88.0	72.9	63.9	48.0	46.3	45.1	41.5	34.7	34.6	27.3
Total Assets	711	660	569	485	445	427	392	366	347	312
Curr. Liab.	49.0	41.8	45.4	39.0	38.7	31.3	31.4	32.7	32.5	27.0
LT Debt	296	275.	208	136	124	143	131	123	126	104
Common Eqty.	222	208	195	203	185	153	136	121	103	94.0
Total Cap.	727	612	520	442	405	394	359	332	313	282
Cap. Exp.	89.0	125	102	76.3	59.2	49.3	38.5	36.9	39.0	40.0
Cash Flow	66.9	61.6	47.5	60.7	58.0	46.1	38.3	29.3	30.3	23.9
Curr. Ratio	1.8	1.7	1.4	1.2	1.2	1.4	1.3	1.1	1.1	1.0
% LT Debt of Cap.	40.7	44.9	40.0	30.8	30.6	36.3	36.5	36.9	40.1	37.0
% Net Inc.of Revs.	6.8	10.1	7.5	14.8	15.5	15.5	14.7	12.4	11.1	12.1
% Ret. on Assets	2.7	3.1	2.2	3.4	6.2	5.4	5.3	4.0	4.2	4.0
% Ret. on Equity	8.7	9.5	5.8	13.0	16.0	15.4	15.6	12.8	14.2	12.7

Data as orig. reptd.; bef. results of disc. opers. and/or spec. items. Per share data adj. for stk. divs. as of ex-div. date. Bold denotes diluted EPS (FASB 128). E-Estimated. NA-Not Available. NM-Not Meaningful. NR-Not Ranked.

Office—1083 Sain St., P.O.Box 1408, Fayetteville, AR 72702-1408. **Tel**—(501) 521-1141. **Chrmn & CEO**—C. E. Scharlau. **Pres & COO**—H. M. Korell. **SVP-Fin & CFO**—G. D. Kerley. **Dirs**—E. J. Ball, J. B. Coffman, J. P. Hammerschmidt, R. L. Howard, K. R. Mourton, C. E. Sanders, C. E. Scharlau. **Transfer Agent & Registrar**—First Chicago Trust Co. of New York, NYC. **Incorporated**—in Arkansas in 1929. **Empl**— 705. **S&P Analyst**: S.A.H.

Spacelabs Medical 5286

NASDAQ Symbol **SLMD**

In S&P SmallCap 600

03-OCT-98

Industry:
Health Care (Medical Products & Supplies)

Summary: This company is a leading manufacturer of clinical information systems, patient monitoring equipment and diagnostic monitoring products.

Quantitative Evaluations

Outlook
(1 Lowest—5 Highest)
- **3+**

Fair Value
- **19½**

Risk
- **Low**

Earn./Div. Rank
- **NR**

Technical Eval.
- **Bullish** since 9/98

Rel. Strength Rank
(1 Lowest—99 Highest)
- **55**

Insider Activity
- **NA**

Recent Price • 15¼
52 Wk Range • 24¼-14½

Yield • Nil
12-Mo. P/E • NM

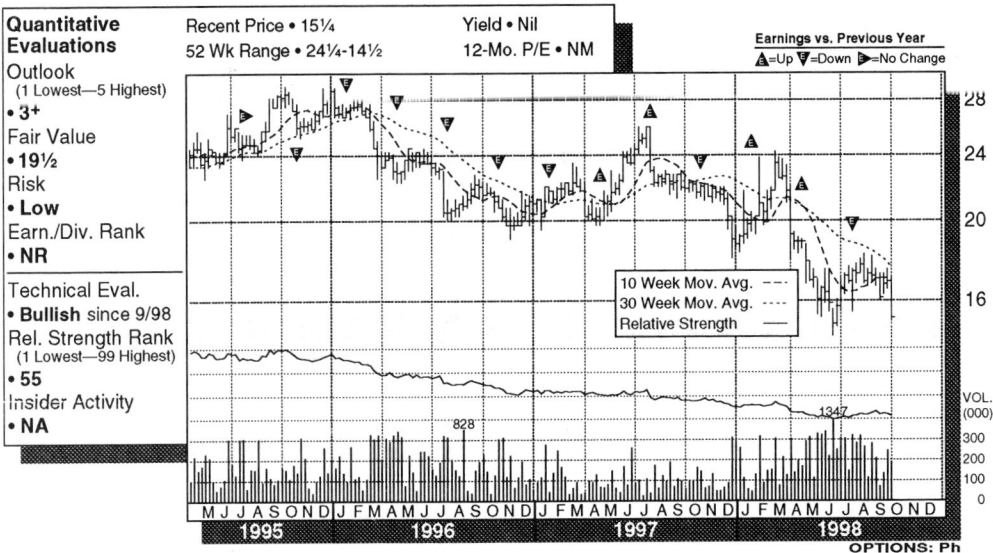

Earnings vs. Previous Year
▲=Up ▼=Down ▶=No Change

10 Week Mov. Avg. - - - -
30 Week Mov. Avg. ········
Relative Strength ——

OPTIONS: Ph

Business Profile - 12-AUG-98

In January 1998, the company announced the introduction of a new generation product line, the Ultraview Care Network. The Ultraview products offer a premium mid-range color patient monitoring platform and expanded networking capability. The design also allows software enhancements to be incorporated more quickly. Spacelabs anticipates that the Ultraview Network will increase gross margins through reduced manufacturing costs. In addition, during the 1998 second quarter, the company implemented a number of cost restructuring programs, including the consolidation of service operations and printed circuit board manufacturing. Spacelabs believes that these restructuring programs will reduce both fixed and variable costs and will decrease the overall cost structure of the company by approximately $5 million per year going forward.

Operational Review - 12-AUG-98

Revenues in the six months ended June 27, 1998, increased 5.9%, year to year, almost entirely reflecting a second quarter $6.8 million gain on the sale of marketable securities. Results were penalized by a $7.2 million provision for year 2000 product compliance, greater SG&A and R&D expenses, $3.6 million in restructuring charges and interest expense of $2.0 million versus $330,000 of interest income a year earlier. The net loss widened to $1,161,000 ($0.12 a share, based on 1.7% fewer shares) from $297,000 ($0.03).

Stock Performance - 02-OCT-98

In the past 30 trading days, SLMD's shares have declined 12%, compared to a 7% fall in the S&P 500. Average trading volume for the past five days was 37,940 shares, compared with the 40-day moving average of 38,403 shares.

Key Stock Statistics

Dividend Rate/Share	Nil	Shareholders	7,200
Shs. outstg. (M)	9.4	Market cap. (B)	$0.144
Avg. daily vol. (M)	0.033	Inst. holdings	82%
Tang. Bk. Value/Share	16.56		
Beta	0.39		

Value of $10,000 invested 5 years ago: $ 5,213

Fiscal Year Ending Dec. 31

	1998	1997	1996	1995	1994	1993
Revenues (Million $)						
1Q	66.51	63.02	63.30	63.14	61.24	65.20
2Q	66.02	62.14	62.37	64.02	63.26	62.70
3Q	—	65.30	60.05	63.23	60.03	59.40
4Q	—	74.90	62.23	62.52	62.67	61.31
Yr.	—	265.3	247.9	252.9	247.2	248.7
Earnings Per Share ($)						
1Q	-0.09	-0.34	-0.42	0.41	0.26	0.38
2Q	-0.03	0.31	0.17	0.43	0.43	0.41
3Q	—	-2.41	0.27	0.45	0.48	0.45
4Q	—	0.30	0.25	0.44	0.51	0.47
Yr.	—	-2.13	0.25	1.73	1.68	1.71

Next earnings report expected: late October

Dividend Data

No cash dividends have been paid on the common shares, and no payments are expected in the foreseeable future.

A Division of The McGraw-Hill Companies

Business Summary - 12-AUG-98

Spacelabs Medical, Inc. (SLMD) develops, manufactures, markets and services patient monitoring and clinical information systems products for use in critical and acute care worldwide. Its three part strategy is to move into the emerging clinical information systems market, to expand its presence in international markets (34% of 1997 sales, up from 33% in 1996) and to maintain and enhance its leadership position in the U.S. critical care monitoring market.

Several recent developments highlight SLMD's commitment to its growth strategy. In March 1997, SLMD acquired Advanced Medical Systems (AMS), which added fetal monitoring products and an obstetrical clinical information system (CIS) to the company's perinatal product line. Also in 1997, SLMD acquired Burdick, Inc., a developer and maker of diagnostic cardiology systems. In 1996, the company acquired JRS Clinical Technologies, Inc., a provider of point-of-care clinical information systems and entered into a distribution agreement and joint venture with software developer DSA Systems, Inc.

In the critical-care patient monitoring market, SLMD's principal product line is the Patient Care Information System (PCIS), which, as an integrated whole, forms an advanced and comprehensive critical-care patient monitoring system and the foundation for a clinical information system. The PCIS product line includes both the company's long-established Patient Care Management System (PCMS) monitoring products and its evolving clinical Information products.

PCMS products address the hospital's principal monitoring needs, from adult and neonatal intensive care units to out-patient surgery, step-down units and patient transport, and at the same time provide the flexible architecture to accommodate future advances in monitoring and the transition to clinical information systems. Sales of these products to hospitals vary over a wide range, depending on the size and configuration of the system. A typical eight-bed hard-wired system sells for about $170,000, while a typical 12-bed telemetry system sells for about $85,000. PCMS products represent the major portion of SLMD's current business.

In 1995, SLMD consolidated its clinical information system products under the Intesys name. Intesys clinical information systems form an integrated framework to automate, manage and analyze the delivery of care, and offer solutions outside of critical-care areas. SLMD also sells medical supplies such as electrodes, specialty graph paper and connecting lead wires. Additional products include other patient monitoring, screening and emergency medical products.

During the second quarter of 1998, Spacelabs commenced several cost restructuring programs, including the consolidation of service operations and printed circuit board manufacturing. Spacelabs believes that these programs will reduce both fixed and variable costs and will decrease the overall cost structure of the company by approximately $5 million per year.

Per Share Data ($)

(Year Ended Dec. 31)	1997	1996	1995	1994	1993	1992	1991	1990	1989	1988
Tangible Bk. Val.	13.76	19.26	18.77	16.89	15.26	13.68	9.98	NA	NA	NA
Cash Flow	-1.15	1.08	2.49	2.48	2.47	2.43	2.24	1.78	NA	NA
Earnings	-2.13	0.25	1.73	1.68	1.71	1.57	1.54	1.19	0.89	0.78
Dividends	Nil	Nil	Nil	Nil	Nil	Nil	Nil	Nil	Nil	Nil
Payout Ratio	Nil	Nil	Nil	Nil	Nil	Nil	Nil	Nil	Nil	Nil
Prices - High	26	29	29⅛	26¾	28¾	30¾	NA	NA	NA	NA
- Low	18	19	22¼	19¾	16½	19¾	NA	NA	NA	NA
P/E Ratio - High	NM	NM	17	16	17	20	NA	NA	NA	NA
- Low	NM	NM	13	12	10	13	NA	NA	NA	NA

Income Statement Analysis (Million $)

	1997	1996	1995	1994	1993	1992	1991	1990	1989	1988
Revs.	265	248	253	247	249	252	225	198	173	149
Oper. Inc.	29.7	31.0	37.0	37.7	37.6	33.0	25.4	19.9	NA	NA
Depr.	9.4	8.6	8.3	8.6	8.4	9.4	7.2	6.0	NA	NA
Int. Exp.	2.3	0.6	NM	NA	NA	0.9	0.9	0.2	NA	NA
Pretax Inc.	-16.1	8.1	29.7	28.9	30.9	29.6	25.8	19.9	14.7	11.1
Eff. Tax Rate	NM	68%	37%	37%	38%	42%	39%	39%	38%	33%
Net Inc.	-20.4	2.6	18.6	18.1	19.2	17.2	15.8	12.1	9.2	7.4

Balance Sheet & Other Fin. Data (Million $)

	1997	1996	1995	1994	1993	1992	1991	1990	1989	1988
Cash	12.9	32.1	52.7	49.1	55.4	38.5	1.0	NA	NA	NA
Curr. Assets	179	175	190	180	170	158	114	NA	NA	NA
Total Assets	290	257	254	234	219	209	168	138	117	104
Curr. Liab.	58.5	43.1	35.0	36.3	34.9	34.0	36.9	NA	NA	NA
LT Debt	66.8	13.5	14.3	11.2	11.9	12.6	13.3	Nil	Nil	Nil
Common Eqty.	165	196	204	185	171	161	116	100	88.0	79.0
Total Cap.	232	214	219	198	184	175	131	100	88.0	79.0
Cap. Exp.	9.6	18.3	17.2	14.9	7.2	6.7	15.7	8.1	NA	NA
Cash Flow	-11.0	11.1	26.9	26.7	27.6	26.6	22.9	18.2	NA	NA
Curr. Ratio	3.1	4.1	18.4	5.0	4.9	4.6	3.1	NA	NA	NA
% LT Debt of Cap.	28.8	6.3	6.5	5.7	6.5	7.2	10.2	Nil	Nil	Nil
% Net Inc.of Revs.	NM	1.0	7.4	7.3	7.7	6.8	7.0	6.1	5.3	5.0
% Ret. on Assets	NM	1.0	7.6	8.0	9.1	9.1	10.3	9.5	8.4	7.2
% Ret. on Equity	NM	1.3	9.6	10.2	11.8	12.4	14.6	12.9	11.1	9.4

Data as orig. reptd.; bef. results of disc. opers. and/or spec. items. Per share data adj. for stk. divs. as of ex-div. date. Bold denotes diluted EPS (FASB 128). E-Estimated. NA-Not Available. NM-Not Meaningful. NR-Not Ranked.

Office—15220 N.E. 40th St. (P. O. Box 97013), Redmond, WA 98052. Tel—(206) 883-3700. Fax—(206) 885-4877. Website—http:// www.spacelabs.com Chrmn & CEO—C. A. Lombardi. VP & CFO—J.A. Richman. Secy—E. V. DeFelice. Investor Contact—Clark Thompson (425) 867-7345.Dirs—G. W. Anderson, T. J. Dudley, H. Feigenbaum, C. A. Lombardi, A.R. Nara, P. M. Nudelman, P.H. vanOppen. Transfer Agent & Registrar—First Chicago Trust Co. of New York, NYC. Incorporated—in Delaware in 1958. Empl— 1,600. S&P Analyst: John J. Arege

03-OCT-98   **Industry:** Trucks & Parts

Summary: Spartan makes custom-designed heavy truck chassis for motorhome, fire apparatus and utility applications and also produces vehicles for special applications.

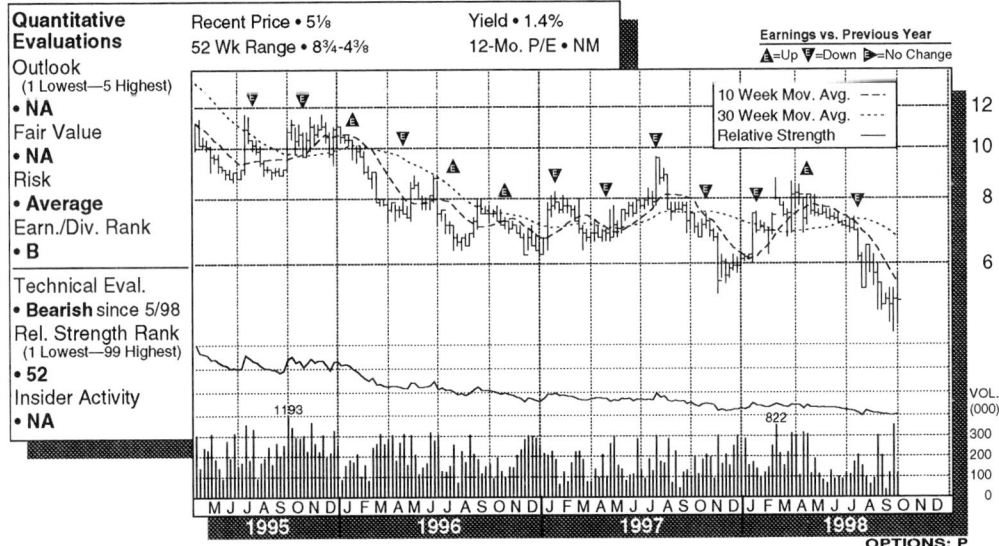

Quantitative Evaluations		
Recent Price • 5⅛	**Yield** • 1.4%	
52 Wk Range • 8¾-4⅜	**12-Mo. P/E** • NM	

Outlook (1 Lowest—5 Highest)
• **NA**

Fair Value
• **NA**

Risk
• **Average**

Earn./Div. Rank
• **B**

Technical Eval.
• **Bearish** since 5/98

Rel. Strength Rank (1 Lowest—99 Highest)
• **52**

Insider Activity
• **NA**

Earnings vs. Previous Year
▲=Up ▼=Down ▶=No Change

- 10 Week Mov. Avg. -- --
- 30 Week Mov. Avg. ....
- Relative Strength ——

OPTIONS: P

Business Profile - 24-JUL-98

SPAR continues its efforts to turn around its operations through an expanded product mix featuring higher-margin products, cost controls and improved efficiencies. In the fire truck market, new industry standards and new products and technologies available from component suppliers bode well for custom chassis manufacturers. The company has continued to ramp up its U.S. transit bus and school bus business, and reorganized its plant operations. In November 1997, SPAR acquired two fire truck apparatus makers, for $6.1 million in cash and stock. It expected the acquisitions to add $30 million to annual revenues. Since April 1995, SPAR has repurchased 1,058,100 of its common shares under buyback programs totaling 1.25 million shares.

Operational Review - 24-JUL-98

Revenues in the first quarter of 1998 climbed 29%, year to year, as consolidated sales from the emergency vehicle group, and increased motorhome chassis sales, outweighed lower fire truck sales. Gross margins narrowed, with the emergency vehicle group operating at lower margins than the chassis group, and a change in the product mix toward more bus chassis sales, but operating expense was well controlled. Pretax income before equity losses was up 15%. After taxes at 52.5%, versus 95.5%, net income soared to $938,237 ($0.07 a share), from $50,640 ($0.01).

Stock Performance - 02-OCT-98

In the past 30 trading days, SPAR's shares have declined 11%, compared to a 7% fall in the S&P 500. Average trading volume for the past five days was 22,780 shares, compared with the 40-day moving average of 44,644 shares.

Key Stock Statistics

Dividend Rate/Share	0.07	Shareholders	1,100
Shs. outstg. (M)	12.6	Market cap. (B)	$0.064
Avg. daily vol. (M)	0.054	Inst. holdings	28%
Tang. Bk. Value/Share	3.42		
Beta	0.84		

Value of $10,000 invested 5 years ago: $ 3,257

Fiscal Year Ending Dec. 31

	1998	1997	1996	1995	1994	1993
Revenues (Million $)						
1Q	59.16	45.79	47.39	44.20	54.76	41.70
2Q	55.50	39.13	44.70	28.79	46.36	43.92
3Q	—	38.33	41.32	36.03	44.77	40.27
4Q	—	55.43	42.41	45.06	45.64	40.78
Yr.	—	178.6	175.8	154.1	191.5	166.7
Earnings Per Share ($)						
1Q	0.07	0.01	0.10	0.14	0.27	0.23
2Q	-0.04	-0.03	0.09	-0.02	0.24	0.24
3Q	—	-0.12	0.10	0.05	0.23	0.16
4Q	—	-0.91	-0.11	0.10	0.06	0.17
Yr.	—	-1.06	0.18	0.27	0.80	0.80

Next earnings report expected: NA

Dividend Data (Dividends have been paid since 1988.)

Amount ($)	Date Decl.	Ex-Div. Date	Stock of Record	Payment Date
.07 Spl.	May. 19	May. 27	May. 31	Jun. 30 '98

A Division of The McGraw-Hill Companies

Business Summary - 24-JUL-98

While it is continuing to diversify through acquisitions of fire truck apparatus and emergency vehicle manufacturers, Spartan Motors (SPAR) still derives most of its sales from its motorhome chassis segment. SPAR produces custom-designed heavy truck chassis for specialized applications, selling to four principal markets: fire truck, motorhome, school and transit bus, and step van and specialty vehicles.

The direct customers for the company's designed and manufactured chassis are OEMs that finish the building of the specialty vehicle by mounting the body or apparatus on the chassis. Spartan does not sell standard commercial truck chassis, but focuses on certain niches within its principal markets. SPAR manufactures its chassis with components purchased from outside suppliers, which allows for easier serviceability of finished products, reduces production costs, and expedites the development of new products. In 1997, sales to two major customers amounted to 43% of the total.

Spartan believes that its bus/specialty vehicles group has the strongest sales growth potential. In late 1997, it delivered its first group of step van chassis, which is expected to show significant growth within the next two years. SPAR continues to develop specialized chassis and seeks additional applications of its existing products. Its Custom Low Floor bus chassis, delivered in 1995, eliminated the need for costly mechanical wheel chair lifts through a curb height that permits the use of manually operated ramps. SPAR said the chassis continued to increase market share in 1997.

The company noted that the transit bus business continues to show encouraging growth for custom chassis manufacturing as the market recognizes the long-term cost savings related to maintenance and the extended life cycle of a custom bus.

In November 1997, SPAR acquired two fire truck apparatus manufacturers for $6.1 million in cash and stock. SPAR expects the companies, Luverne Fire Apparatus and Quality Manufacturing, to contribute $30 million in revenues on an annual basis. In early 1997, SPAR acquired a 33% interest in Carpenter Industries, Inc., a Richmond, Ind.-based school bus manufacturer, for $10 million. Following a going concern opinion issued for Carpenter's 1997 financials, SPAR wrote down its investment in Carpenter to zero. Carpenter is pursuing the refinancing of its debt.

In December 1996, SPAR closed its wholly owned international venture, Spartan de Mexico S.A, a producer of bus chassis. Production was halted in 1995, as a result of the weak Mexican economy. During 1996, SPAR recorded a loss of $4.4 million due to the closing. As part of the exit plan, SPAR is seeking buyers for the real estate and building in Mexico.

Chassis backlog at March 31, 1998, totaled $81.1 million, up from $56.1 million a year earlier. Backlog for the emergency vehicle group was $21.7 million at the end of 1997.

Per Share Data ($)

(Year Ended Dec. 31)	1997	1996	1995	1994	1993	1992	1991	1990	1989	1988
Tangible Bk. Val.	3.58	4.97	4.74	4.72	4.11	3.29	1.85	0.84	0.62	0.53
Cash Flow	-0.91	0.34	0.42	0.93	0.86	0.77	0.61	0.28	0.15	0.25
Earnings	-1.06	0.18	0.27	0.80	0.80	0.72	0.58	0.24	0.11	0.22
Dividends	0.07	0.05	0.05	0.05	0.05	0.03	0.02	0.02	0.02	0.02
Payout Ratio	NM	28%	19%	6%	6%	5%	4%	9%	20%	10%
Prices - High	9⅝	11	14⅝	21¾	25¼	23⅛	16½	2⅝	3⅜	3⅛
- Low	5¼	6¼	8⅝	12⅜	12¾	8⅝	1⁹/₁₆	1⁷/₁₆	1⁹/₁₆	¹⁵/₁₆
P/E Ratio - High	NM	61	54	27	32	32	28	11	29	14
- Low	NM	35	32	15	16	12	3	6	13	4

Income Statement Analysis (Million $)

	1997	1996	1995	1994	1993	1992	1991	1990	1989	1988
Revs.	179	175	153	189	166	123	94.0	51.0	36.0	34.0
Oper. Inc.	4.7	9.5	6.0	16.5	16.0	13.8	10.5	4.8	2.8	4.0
Depr.	1.9	1.9	2.0	1.6	0.9	0.7	0.4	0.4	0.3	0.3
Int. Exp.	0.8	0.5	0.5	0.5	0.5	0.2	0.5	0.8	0.9	0.5
Pretax Inc.	-12.5	3.9	5.4	16.5	15.8	13.7	9.9	3.8	1.8	3.2
Eff. Tax Rate	NM	40%	37%	36%	34%	33%	34%	34%	34%	29%
Net Inc.	-13.1	2.3	3.4	10.6	10.5	9.2	6.5	2.5	1.2	2.3

Balance Sheet & Other Fin. Data (Million $)

	1997	1996	1995	1994	1993	1992	1991	1990	1989	1988
Cash	4.8	13.9	12.9	14.2	11.3	12.1	0.9	0.2	0.5	0.9
Curr. Assets	65.6	67.9	60.5	65.5	56.2	46.9	27.3	19.2	12.9	13.3
Total Assets	81.2	79.7	75.2	81.1	71.3	56.4	34.7	23.7	17.2	16.9
Curr. Liab.	24.2	13.1	9.6	13.2	12.8	10.8	8.7	12.5	7.2	7.2
LT Debt	9.6	5.2	5.8	6.2	4.7	2.9	3.7	2.5	3.5	4.2
Common Eqty.	47.5	61.4	59.8	61.6	53.8	42.7	22.3	8.7	6.5	5.5
Total Cap.	57.1	66.6	65.6	67.8	58.4	45.6	26.0	11.2	10.0	9.7
Cap. Exp.	1.6	1.4	1.8	4.7	4.1	4.4	1.7	0.5	2.0	1.5
Cash Flow	-11.2	4.3	5.4	12.2	11.4	9.9	7.0	2.9	1.5	2.6
Curr. Ratio	2.7	5.2	6.3	5.0	4.4	4.4	3.2	1.5	1.8	1.8
% LT Debt of Cap.	16.8	7.8	8.8	9.2	8.0	6.4	14.3	22.0	35.3	43.3
% Net Inc.of Revs.	NM	1.4	2.2	5.6	6.3	7.5	6.9	4.9	3.3	6.9
% Ret. on Assets	NM	3.0	4.4	13.9	16.4	19.7	21.0	12.2	6.9	17.2
% Ret. on Equity	NM	3.9	5.6	18.4	21.7	27.7	40.3	32.8	19.7	45.7

Data as orig. reptd.; bef. results of disc. opers. and/or spec. items. Per share data adj. for stk. divs. as of ex-div. date. Bold denotes diluted EPS (FASB 128). E-Estimated. NA-Not Available. NM-Not Meaningful. NR-Not Ranked.

Office—1000 Reynolds Rd., Charlotte, MI 48813. **Tel**—(517) 543-6400. **Chrmn & CEO**—G. W. Sztykiel. **Pres & COO**—J. E. Sztykiel. **CFO, Treas & Secy**—R. J. Shalter. **Dirs**—W. F. Foster, C. E. Nihart, J. C. Penman, A. G. Sommer, G. W. Sztykiel, J. E. Sztykiel, G. Tesseris, D. R. Wilson. **Transfer Agent**—American Stock Transfer & Trust Co., NYC. **Incorporated**—in Michigan in 1975. **Empl**— 620. **S&P Analyst:** Stewart Scharf

03-OCT-98

Industry:
Equipment (Semiconductor)

Summary: SFAM manufactures chemical mechanical planarization systems used in the fabrication of semiconductor devices and other high-throughput precision surface processing systems.

Quantitative Evaluations	
Outlook (1 Lowest 5 Highest)	• NA
Fair Value	• NA
Risk	• High
Earn./Div. Rank	• NR
Technical Eval.	• Neutral since 5/98
Rel. Strength Rank (1 Lowest—99 Highest)	• 50
Insider Activity	• Neutral

Recent Price • 12½
52 Wk Range • 60⅞-8⅞
Yield • Nil
12-Mo. P/E • 27.8

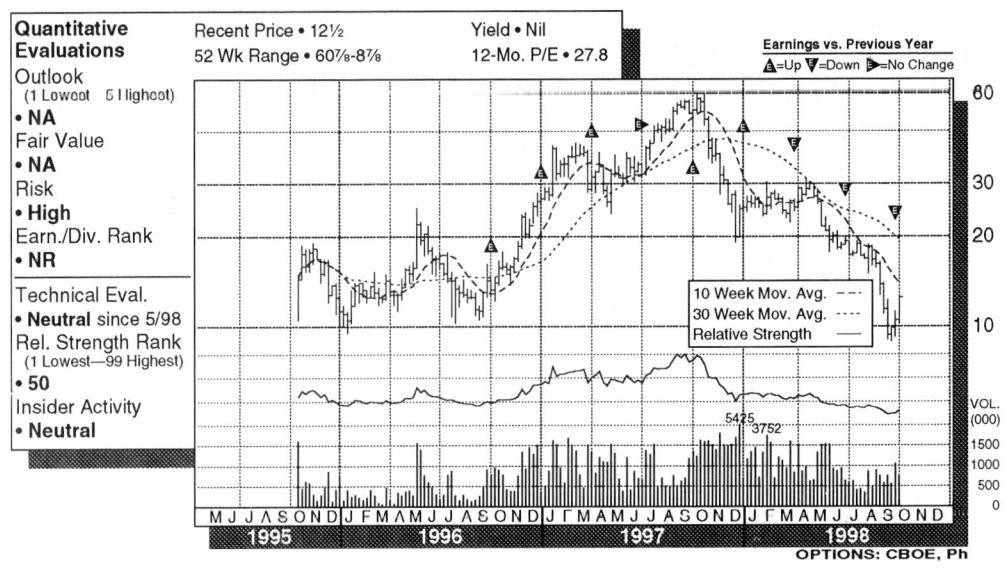

Earnings vs. Previous Year
▲=Up ▼=Down ▶=No Change

10 Week Mov. Avg. ---
30 Week Mov. Avg. .....
Relative Strength —

OPTIONS: CBOE, Ph

Business Profile - 13-AUG-98

SpeedFam International's business depends on various factors including its ability to enhance existing products and processes; its ability to develop and make new products and processes; the level of capital spending by thin film memory disk and semiconductor manufacturers; and current and anticipated demand for memory disks and semiconductor devices. In July 1998, SFAM received its first order for the SSP-434, its newest 300mm single-sided silicon wafer polishing system. The 300mm silicon wafer waxless polishing system is to be used for intermediate and final polishing of 300mm silicon wafers. Fabricating chips from 300mm wafers is viewed by SFAM as crucial to low-cost production of high-density chips such as 1-gigabit DRAMs.

Operational Review - 13-AUG-98

Total revenue for FY 98 (May; preliminary) advanced 6.8%, year to year. Profitability was penalized by $7.5 million of one-time fourth quarter pretax charges ($0.27 a share after taxes) for severance costs, inventory adjustments, an increase in bad debt reserve related to the economic crisis in Asia, and customer service allowances. Net income fell 36%, to $12.9 million ($0.83 a share on 29% more shares) from $20.2 million ($1.67). Backlog at May 31, 1998, was $43.5 million, down from $58.9 million a year earlier.

Stock Performance - 02-OCT-98

In the past 30 trading days, SFAM's shares have declined 23%, compared to a 7% fall in the S&P 500. Average trading volume for the past five days was 149,180 shares, compared with the 40-day moving average of 149,479 shares.

Key Stock Statistics

Dividend Rate/Share	Nil	Shareholders	NA
Shs. outstg. (M)	16.0	Market cap. (B)	$0.200
Avg. daily vol. (M)	0.156	Inst. holdings	53%
Tang. Bk. Value/Share	18.18		
Beta	NA		

Value of $10,000 invested 5 years ago: NA

Fiscal Year Ending May 31

	1999	1998	1997	1996	1995	1994
Revenues (Million $)						
1Q	35.77	53.85	39.73	17.82	—	—
2Q	—	56.53	39.12	25.44	—	—
3Q	—	48.38	45.28	33.14	—	—
4Q	—	26.50	49.30	43.78	—	—
Yr.	—	185.3	173.4	120.2	59.78	51.38
Earnings Per Share ($)						
1Q	0.01	0.39	0.36	0.09	—	—
2Q	—	0.49	0.42	0.10	—	—
3Q	—	0.31	0.42	0.39	—	—
4Q	—	-0.34	0.46	0.46	—	—
Yr.	—	0.83	1.67	1.16	0.20	0.30

Next earnings report expected: mid December

Dividend Data

No cash dividends have been paid. The company has said that it does not expect to pay cash dividends for the foreseeable future.

A Division of The McGraw·Hill Companies

Business Summary - 13-AUG-98

A continued uptrend in sales to major semiconductor manufacturers was the driving force behind the strong growth in revenues and net income reported by Speed-Fam International for several years through FY 97 (May). The company's CMP (chemical mechanical planarization) systems are used to make semiconductor devices and other high-throughput precision surface processing systems, which in turn are used to fabricate thin-film memory disk media, semiconductor wafers and general industrial components. SpeedFam also markets and distributes slurries and parts and expendables used in its customers' manufacturing processes. The company's processing systems include polishing, grinding, lapping and pre-disposition cleaning equipment. These processes are used to change the characteristics of the surface of a semiconductor wafer.

Gross margins for several years through FY 97 benefited from a continuing increase in sales of higher-margin CMP systems, which accounted for about 50% of sales in FY 97. SpeedFam began volume shipments of original CMP product, the CMP-V, in 1994. Shipments of the Auriga began in the second quarter of FY 97 and, through the end of FY 97, it had shipped 26 Auriga systems.

The Auriga is a five-head, two polishing table CMP system capable of processing 65-90 wafers an hour based on a two-minute polishing cycle. The Auriga system incorporates certain modifications from the original CMP-V system in the control and automation system to decrease the time interval between processes, thereby increasing production.

During the second quarter of FY 98 (May), SpeedFam shipped its first six Auriga-C systems, the company's third generation five-head, semiconductor CMP system, with fully integrated, on-board dry-in/dry-out cleaning and in-situ endpoint detection capabilities.

Sales of slurries accounted for about 16% of revenues in FY 97. SpeedFam offers a broad line of slurry and slurry components used in surface treatment processes as part of a total process solution. Slurries are used by manufacturers of thin-film memory disk media, semiconductor wafers and other products as part of their polishing processes. Substantially all of the slurries sold by SFAM are made by Fujimi Corp., a 50%-owned joint venture.

SpeedFam has been concentrating its recent R&D spending on: dry-in/dry-out and end-point detection capabilities for its CMP systems; upgrading a key product in the memory disk polishing market; and various process technologies for the semiconductor device, thin-film memory disk media and silicon wafer markets. R&D spending was 11.4% of revenues in FY 97.

In October 1997, SpeedFam sold 2,327,000 common shares, receiving net proceeds of $116.7 million.

Per Share Data ($) (Year Ended May 31)	1998	1997	1996	1995	1994	1993	1992	1991	1990	1989
Tangible Bk. Val.	18.10	11.75	5.71	3.09	NA	NA	NA	NA	NA	NA
Cash Flow	1.12	1.90	1.29	0.28	NA	NA	NA	NA	NA	NA
Earnings	0.83	1.67	1.16	0.20	0.30	-0.06	NA	NA	NA	NA
Dividends	Nil	Nil	Nil	Nil	Nil	Nil	Nil	Nil	Nil	Nil
Payout Ratio	Nil	Nil	Nil	Nil	Nil	Nil	Nil	Nil	Nil	Nil
Cal. Yrs.	1997	1996	1995	1994	1993	1992	1991	1990	1989	1988
Prices - High	60⅞	29¼	19⅛	NA	NA	NA	NA	NA	NA	NA
- Low	19⅛	9½	10	NA	NA	NA	NA	NA	NA	NA
P/E Ratio - High	73	18	16	NA	NA	NA	NA	NA	NA	NA
- Low	23	6	9	NA	NA	NA	NA	NA	NA	NA

Income Statement Analysis (Million $)

	1998	1997	1996	1995	1994	1993	1992	1991	1990	1989
Revs.	176	173	120	59.8	51.4	43.3	NA	NA	NA	NA
Oper. Inc.	10.5	24.3	12.4	2.2	NA	NA	NA	NA	NA	NA
Depr.	4.5	2.9	1.3	0.6	NA	NA	NA	NA	NA	NA
Int. Exp.	0.0	0.2	0.7	1.0	NA	NA	NA	NA	NA	NA
Pretax Inc.	16.3	28.3	16.1	1.8	2.1	0.1	NA	NA	NA	NA
Eff. Tax Rate	21%	28%	27%	10%	NM	NM	NM	NM	NM	NM
Net Inc.	12.9	20.2	11.8	1.6	2.3	-0.5	NA	NA	NA	NA

Balance Sheet & Other Fin. Data (Million $)

	1998	1997	1996	1995	1994	1993	1992	1991	1990	1989
Cash	141	76.9	10.9	1.1	NA	NA	NA	NA	NA	NA
Curr. Assets	250	156	76.0	37.3	NA	NA	NA	NA	NA	NA
Total Assets	330	207	108	60.0	45.7	35.7	NA	NA	NA	NA
Curr. Liab.	39.9	48.9	44.8	26.2	NA	NA	NA	NA	NA	NA
LT Debt	Nil	0.3	2.6	10.4	NA	NA	NA	NA	NA	NA
Common Eqty.	289	157	60.0	23.0	18.6	15.7	NA	NA	NA	NA
Total Cap.	290	158	63.2	33.8	NA	NA	NA	NA	NA	NA
Cap. Exp.	32.1	17.4	8.1	0.7	0.4	NA	NA	NA	NA	NA
Cash Flow	17.4	23.1	13.1	2.3	NA	NA	NA	NA	NA	NA
Curr. Ratio	6.3	3.2	1.7	1.4	NA	NA	NA	NA	NA	NA
% LT Debt of Cap.	Nil	0.2	4.1	30.6	NA	NA	NA	NA	NA	NA
% Net Inc.of Revs.	7.3	11.7	9.8	2.8	4.4	NM	NM	NM	NM	NM
% Ret. on Assets	4.8	12.9	14.1	3.1	5.6	NA	NA	NA	NA	NA
% Ret. on Equity	5.8	18.7	28.5	7.9	13.3	NA	NA	NA	NA	NA

Data as orig. reptd.; bef. results of disc. opers. and/or spec. items. Per share data adj. for stk. divs. as of ex-div. date. Bold denotes diluted EPS (FASB 128). E-Estimated. NA-Not Available. NM-Not Meaningful. NR-Not Ranked.

Office—305 N. 54th St., Chandler, AZ 85226. Tel—(602) 705-2100. Chrmn—J. N. Farley. Pres & CEO—M. Kouzuma. Treas & CFO—R. K. Marach. Dirs—N. R. Bonke, J. N. Farley, R. Hill, M. Kouzuma, T. J. McCook, S. Meyer, R. Miller, C. S. Pedersen. Transfer Agent & Registrar—Firstar Bank Milwaukee. Incorporated—in Illinois in 1959. Empl— 513. S&P Analyst: N.J. DeVita

Sports Authority

2091G

NYSE Symbol **TSA**

In S&P SmallCap 600

03-OCT-98

Industry: Retail (Specialty)

Summary: This U.S. operator of large-format sporting goods stores has agreed to be acquired by Venator Group, Inc. (formerly Woolworth Corp.).

S&P Opinion: Hold (★★★)	Recent Price • 7⅛	Yield • Nil
	52 Wk Range • 21⅞-5⅛	12-Mo. P/E • 22.3

Quantitative Evaluations

Outlook
(1 Lowest—5 Highest)
• **5**

Fair Value
• **12⅝**

Risk
• **Average**

Earn./Div. Rank
• **NR**

Technical Eval.
• **Bearish** since 5/98

Rel. Strength Rank
(1 Lowest—99 Highest)
• **20**

Insider Activity
• **Neutral**

Earnings vs. Previous Year
△=Up ▽=Down ▷=No Change

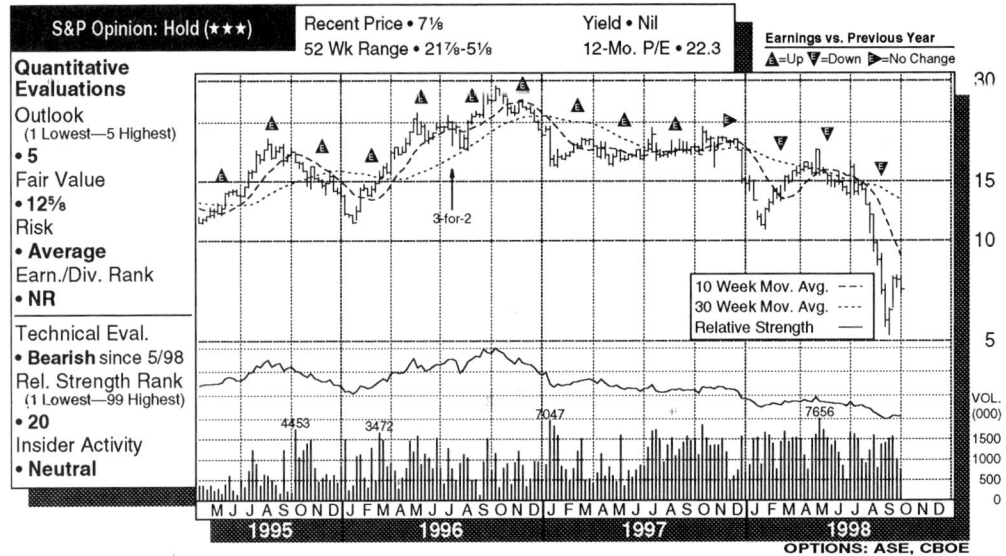

10 Week Mov. Avg. - - -
30 Week Mov. Avg. — —
Relative Strength ——

3-for-2

4453 3472 7047 7656

OPTIONS: ASE, CBOE

Overview - 17-SEP-98

In May 1998, The Sports Authority agreed to merge with Venator Group, Inc. (NYSE: Z), whereby Z will exchange 0.8 of a Z share for each TSA share. Because Z's shares have fallen precipitously since the companies agreed to merge, the value of Z's offer has dropped significantly. The current agreement is unlikely to be consummated because Z shares recently traded under $13, and TSA can opt out of the merger if Z's stock's average closing price is not at least $20.50 during specified periods, which would end this year. TSA has indicated it is prepared to continue as an independent entity if the Z merger is not completed. In July 1998, Gart Sports Co. (Nasdaq: GRTS) sought a strategic combination with TSA, whereby GRTS would have purchased 70% of TSA for $20 a share (effectively, $14 a share), and converted the remaining 30% into 51% of a combined company. TSA rejected GRTS' offer, believing Z's offer was superior.

Valuation - 17-SEP-98

TSA's recent second quarter results evidenced its operational difficulties. Year-to-year, net income fell 60%, inventories rose 5.6% and gross margins fell 170 basis points. TSA believes its winter sports, merchandising and productivity initiatives will spearhead a turnaround. Despite TSA's tenuous operational prospects and a depressed sports retail environment, we rate the shares a hold, versus an avoid, because the company may not yet have received its best offer. Z may increase the value of its offer to ensure TSA does not walk away from its agreement at year's end, GRTS may sweeten or make hostile its bid, or another suitor might enter the fray. TSA's shares will now trade with those of Z, its would-be merger partner, barring perceptions that a superior offer will be made or Z will not be able to achieve its price requirements for the merger.

Key Stock Statistics

S&P EPS Est. 1999	0.92	Tang. Bk. Value/Share	9.03
P/E on S&P Est. 1999	7.7	Beta	NA
S&P EPS Est. 2000	0.83	Shareholders	400
Dividend Rate/Share	Nil	Market cap. (B)	$0.227
Shs. outstg. (M)	31.8	Inst. holdings	36%
Avg. daily vol. (M)	0.290		

Value of $10,000 invested 5 years ago: NA

Fiscal Year Ending Jan. 31

	1999	1998	1997	1996	1995	1994
Revenues (Million $)						
1Q	347.2	346.5	270.6	221.6	173.9	119.0
2Q	427.3	383.3	331.6	268.4	201.3	146.0
3Q	—	340.9	292.9	234.2	195.1	142.0
4Q	—	420.6	376.2	322.5	268.3	200.0
Yr.	—	1,465	1,271	1,047	838.5	607.0

	1999	1998	1997	1996	1995	1994
Earnings Per Share ($)						
1Q	-0.12	0.08	0.06	0.05	0.04	--
2Q	0.12	0.30	0.29	0.22	0.15	--
3Q	—	0.06	0.06	0.02	Nil	--
4Q	—	**0.25**	0.53	0.42	0.35	--
Yr.	—	**0.70**	0.94	0.71	0.54	0.41

Next earnings report expected: mid November

Dividend Data

The company intends to retain earnings to finance growth and therefore does not anticipate paying any cash dividends for the foreseeable future.

Business Summary - 17-SEP-98

The Sports Authority is the largest U.S. operator of large-format sporting goods stores, based both on sales and on the number of stores, and is also the largest full-line sporting goods retailer in the country. The stores stock extensive selections of brand-name sporting equipment and athletic and active footwear and apparel, everyday fair prices and premium customer service.

In May 1998, TSA agreed to be acquired by Venator Group, Inc. (formerly Woolworth Corp., NYSE: Z), for 0.8 of a share of its stock for each TSA share. At the time, the deal was valued at some $570 million, including the assumption of $179 in debt. More recently, because Z's shares have fallen dramatically, the transaction's value totaled about $407 million ($229 million in stock). TSA can opt out of the merger if Z's average closing price is not at least $20.50 during specified periods, the last of which would end on December 31, 1998. A combination of TSA and Z would create a retail giant with over $5 billion annual worldwide sporting goods sales.

As of August 11, 1998, the company was operating 206 full-line sporting goods superstores, with 196 stores in 32 states across the U.S., six stores in Canada, and nine in Japan; virtually all stores are in excess of 40,000 gross square feet. The stores are located primarily in regional strip or power centers with tenants that are value-oriented, large-format retailers; some stores are located in malls and some are stand-alones. Unlike warehouse stores, the interior of each store has features comparable to those of department stores. The number of stores in operation at the end of recent fiscal years (Jan.) was 199 in FY 98, 168 in FY 97, 136 in FY 96, 107 in FY 95, 80 in FY 94, 56 in FY 93, 36 in FY 92, and 19 in FY 91. Sales in recent fiscal years were derived as follows:

	FY 97	FY 96	FY 95
Hard lines	50%	53%	56%
Soft lines:			
Apparel	22%	20%	19%
Footwear	28%	27%	25%

The superstore format enables TSA to offer under one roof an extensive selection of merchandise for sports and leisure activities ordinarily associated with specialty and pro shops, such as for golf, tennis, snow skiing, cycling, hunting, fishing, bowling, archery, boating and water sports. Each superstore stocks about 45,000 SKUs across 16 major departments. TSA's merchandise assortment includes more than 900 brand names.

Per Share Data ($)

(Year Ended Jan. 31)	1998	1997	1996	1995	1994	1993	1992	1991	1990	1989
Tangible Bk. Val.	8.97	8.19	7.12	6.29	4.19	NA	NA	NA	NA	NA
Cash Flow	1.87	1.84	1.35	1.05	0.75	NA	NA	NA	NA	NA
Earnings	0.70	0.94	0.71	0.54	0.41	NA	NA	NA	NA	NA
Dividends	Nil	Nil	Nil	Nil	Nil	Nil	Nil	Nil	Nil	Nil
Payout Ratio	Nil	Nil	Nil	Nil	Nil	Nil	Nil	Nil	Nil	Nil
Cal. Yrs.	1997	1996	1995	1994	1993	1992	1991	1990	1989	1988
Prices - High	22	29	20 1/8	16 5/8	NA	NA	NA	NA	NA	NA
- Low	13 3/4	11 1/4	10 7/8	12 5/8	NA	NA	NA	NA	NA	NA
P/E Ratio - High	31	31	28	31	NA	NA	NA	NA	NA	NA
- Low	20	12	15	23	NA	NA	NA	NA	NA	NA

Income Statement Analysis (Million $)

	1998	1997	1996	1995	1994	1993	1992	1991	1990	1989
Revs.	1,465	1,271	1,047	841	607	412	241	109	53.0	NA
Oper. Inc.	74.7	75.6	55.4	46.1	29.4	16.5	7.3	NA	NA	NA
Depr.	37.3	28.5	20.0	15.9	10.2	7.2	4.4	2.8	0.8	NA
Int. Exp.	8.5	4.6	0.8	0.3	0.0	0.1	0.1	0.1	NM	NM
Pretax Inc.	34.7	48.0	37.4	29.8	20.9	10.0	37.4	-3.4	-4.3	NA
Eff. Tax Rate	42%	41%	41%	44%	39%	43%	59%	NM	NM	NM
Net Inc.	22.2	30.0	22.3	16.9	12.8	5.7	1.3	-3.0	-3.5	NA

Balance Sheet & Other Fin. Data (Million $)

	1998	1997	1996	1995	1994	1993	1992	1991	1990	1989
Cash	20.4	110	11.8	37.1	8.2	2.2	NA	NA	NA	NA
Curr. Assets	392	445	312	303	180	126	NA	NA	NA	NA
Total Assets	812	754	524	460	298	236	185	121	28.0	NA
Curr. Liab.	293	269	228	196	143	92.0	NA	NA	NA	NA
LT Debt	157	152	Nil	Nil	Nil	Nil	NA	NA	NA	NA
Common Eqty.	334	310	278	253	148	139	131	97.0	14.0	NA
Total Cap.	491	462	278	253	148	139	NA	NA	NA	NA
Cap. Exp.	114	102	55.3	51.4	23.5	25.9	15.6	4.7	3.9	NA
Cash Flow	59.5	58.5	42.1	32.8	22.9	12.9	5.7	-0.1	-2.7	NA
Curr. Ratio	1.3	1.7	1.4	1.5	1.3	1.4	NA	NA	NA	NA
% LT Debt of Cap.	32.0	32.9	Nil	Nil	Nil	Nil	NA	NA	NA	NA
% Net Inc.of Revs.	1.5	2.4	2.1	2.0	2.1	1.4	0.6	NM	NM	NM
% Ret. on Assets	2.8	4.7	4.5	Nil	4.8	2.7	0.9	NM	NA	NA
% Ret. on Equity	6.9	10.2	8.4	Nil	8.9	4.2	1.2	NM	NA	NA

Data as orig. reptd.; bef. results of disc. opers. and/or spec. items. Per share data adj. for stk. divs. as of ex-div. date. Bold denotes diluted EPS (FASB 128). Pro forma earnings per share in 1993-4. E-Estimated. NA-Not Available. NM-Not Meaningful. NR-Not Ranked.

Office—3383 N. State Road 7, Fort Lauderdale, FL 33319. **Tel**—(954) 735-1701. **Website**—http://www.sportsauthority.com CEO—M. E. Hanaka. **Chrmn**—J. A. Smith. **Pres & COO**—R. J. Lynch, Jr. **SVP & CFO**—A. F. Crudele. **VP & Secy**—F. W. Bubb, III. **VP & Treas**—A L. Stanton. **Investor Contact**—Debra Foreman, (954) 735-1701 x 6086. **Dirs**—N. A. Buoniconti; S. Dougherty; J. W. Erving; C. Farmer; J. F. Kemp; R. J. Lynch, Jr.; W. M. Romney; J. A. Smith; H. Toppel. **Transfer Agent & Registrar**—First Union National Bank of North Carolina, Charlotte. **Incorporated**—in Delaware.**Empl**— 10,700. **S&P Analyst:** Scott H. Kessler

03-OCT-98

Industry: Computers (Networking)

Summary: This leading supplier of PC LAN system products and semiconductors for PCs recently sold a majority stake in its System Products Division.

Quantitative Evaluations

Outlook (1 Lowest—5 Highest)
• **1**

Fair Value
• **6⅝**

Risk
• **High**

Earn./Div. Rank
• **C**

Technical Eval.
• **NA**

Rel. Strength Rank (1 Lowest—99 Highest)
• **53**

Insider Activity
• **Neutral**

Recent Price • 7
52 Wk Range • 17¼-6¼

Yield • Nil
12-Mo. P/E • NM

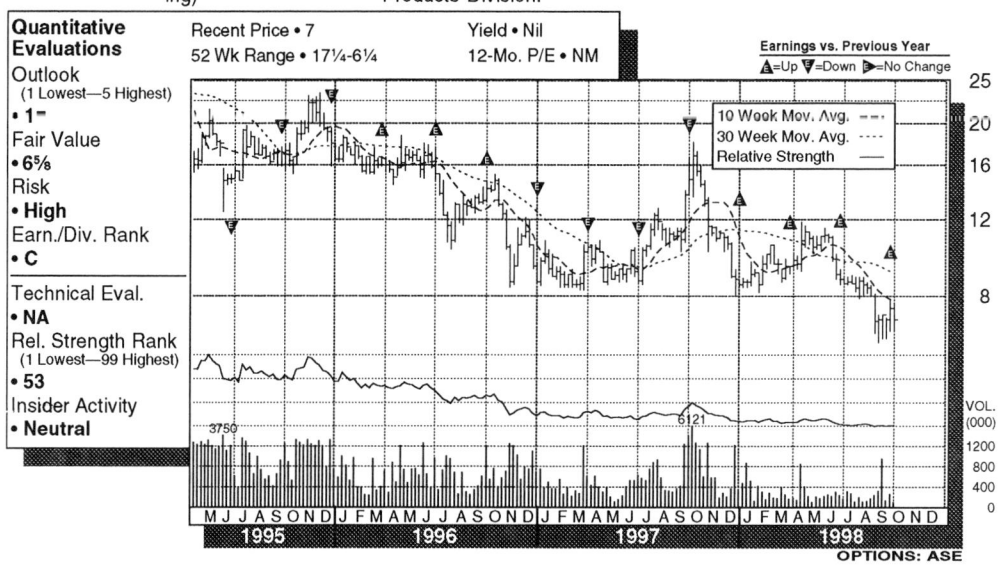

Earnings vs. Previous Year
▲=Up ▼=Down ▶=No Change

10 Week Mov. Avg. —·
30 Week Mov. Avg. ----
Relative Strength —

OPTIONS: ASE

Business Profile - 25-JUN-98

In May 1998, Standard Microsystems announced a strategic alliance with Winbond Electronics Corp. of Hsinchu, Taiwan. Under the agreement, the company has obtained the rights from Winbond to market, sell and distribute all of Winbond's PC and peripheral-related products in North America, Europe and Japan. In addition, Winbond will become a preferred supplier of turn-key production services, manufacturing a broad range of semiconductor integrated circuits for the company. Management believes that the Winbond portfolio will complement SMSC's products and that Winbond's manufacturing capability will further enhance SMSC's competitiveness and help assure the company of sufficient semiconductor wafer fabrication capacity.

Operational Review - 25-JUN-98

Revenues from continuing operations in FY 98 (Feb.) declined 21%, due primarily to lower average selling prices. Gross margin improved, reflecting a moderated rate of decline in average selling prices and sales of higher-margined products; gross profit decreased 7.5%. Following lower SG&A expenses, which offset higher R&D costs and a $2.0 million litigation settlement charge, the pretax loss was flat. After tax benefits of $2.4 million, versus $2.5 million, the loss from continuing operations widened to $4,527,000 ($0.29 per share), from $4,483,000 ($0.32). Results in FY 98 and FY 97 exclude respective net losses of $0.99 and $1.22 a share from discontinued operations.

Stock Performance - 02-OCT-98

In the past 30 trading days, SMSC's shares have declined 12%, compared to a 7% fall in the S&P 500. Average trading volume for the past five days was 19,480 shares, compared with the 40-day moving average of 58,669 shares.

Key Stock Statistics

Dividend Rate/Share	Nil	Shareholders	1,500
Shs. outstg. (M)	16.0	Market cap. (B)	$0.113
Avg. daily vol. (M)	0.075	Inst. holdings	49%
Tang. Bk. Value/Share	10.79		
Beta	1.48		

Value of $10,000 invested 5 years ago: $ 2,716

Fiscal Year Ending Feb. 28

	1999	1998	1997	1996	1995	1994
Revenues (Million $)						
1Q	37.60	34.80	100.1	72.21	80.00	68.44
2Q	40.88	41.18	99.2	85.43	91.96	72.03
3Q	—	42.77	93.77	90.57	104.8	88.89
4Q	—	36.99	61.08	93.71	101.9	93.21
Yr.	—	155.8	354.1	341.9	378.7	322.6
Earnings Per Share ($)						
1Q	**0.03**	-0.22	0.14	-0.22	0.41	0.34
2Q	**0.04**	-0.14	0.01	-0.91	0.42	0.32
3Q	—	0.02	-0.28	0.02	0.51	0.41
4Q	—	0.03	-1.40	1.94	0.55	0.45
Yr.	—	**-0.29**	-1.54	0.86	1.89	1.52

Next earnings report expected: mid December

Dividend Data

No cash has been paid. A "poison pill" stock purchase plan was adopted in 1988.

A Division of The McGraw-Hill Companies

Business Summary - 25-JUN-98

Standard Microsystems Corp. (SMSC) is a worldwide supplier of metal-oxide-semiconductor/very-large-scale-integrated (MOS/VLSI) circuits for the personal computer (PC) industry. The company's integrated circuits are developed and sold for applications in PC input/output (I/O), PC connectivity, Local Area Networking (LAN), PC systems logic, and embedded networking. SMSC also operates a wafer foundry that specializes in the production of MicroElectroMechanical Systems (MEMS) devices.

The company sells the largest portion of its products to original equipment manufacturers, of which producers of PCs are the largest customer group. In addition, products are sold to distributors of electronic components. The company's I/O circuits reside on the motherboards of PC products made by Compaq Computer Corp., Dell Computer Corp., IBM, Intel Corp., Hewlett-Packard Co. and most other leading personal computer manufacturers. SMSC's wafer foundry is a producer of specialty semiconductor products and works closely with its customers to develop and customize processes specific to their devices.

SMSC went through several significant developments in FY 98 (Feb.). With the October 1997 divestiture of its local area networking hardware business, the company refocused its business to the design, development and supply of semiconductor products and solutions. During the third quarter of FY 98, the company reorganized its Systems Products Division into a new corporation, SMC Networks, Inc. and then sold an 80.1% interest in SMC Networks to Accton Technology Corp. of Hsinchu, Taiwan. The System Products Division supplied hardware and software products for the LAN marketplace.

Standard Microsystems's I/O integrated circuits accounted for approximately 70% of total revenue in FY 98, 78% in FY 97, and 71% in FY 96. Foundry revenues accounted for approximately 6% of total revenues in FY 98, 7% in FY 97 and 10% in FY 96.

In Japan, the company sells its products through its majority owned subsidiary, Toyo Microsystems Corp. Toyo also sells LAN products purchased from SMC Networks. Toyo accounted for 12% of total revenues In FY 98, 9% in FY 97, and 11% in FY 96. By geographic region, Asia and the Pacific Rim made up 62% of total revenues in FY 98, the U.S. 29%, Europe 6%, Canada 1%, and others 1%.

SMSC uses semiconductor foundries and assembly contractors in the U.S., Southeast Asia and Western Europe to provide state-of-the-art integrated circuit manufacturing and assembly capacity. During FY 98, 91% of revenues came from the sale of products manufactured by subcontractor foundries, compared with 90% in FY 97, and 86% in FY 96.

Per Share Data ($)

(Year Ended Feb. 28)	1998	1997	1996	1995	1994	1993	1992	1991	1990	1989
Tangible Bk. Val.	10.82	11.69	13.09	11.16	11.18	6.59	4.73	7.65	7.43	7.22
Cash Flow	0.57	0.07	2.26	3.00	2.17	2.23	0.88	0.78	1.16	0.30
Earnings	-0.29	-1.54	0.86	1.89	1.52	1.27	0.05	0.10	0.41	-0.52
Dividends	Nil	Nil	Nil	Nil	Nil	Nil	Nil	Nil	Nil	Nil
Payout Ratio	Nil	Nil	Nil	Nil	Nil	Nil	Nil	Nil	Nil	Nil
Cal. Yrs.	1997	1996	1995	1994	1993	1992	1991	1990	1989	1988
Prices - High	18$^1/_8$	18$^3/_4$	31$^5/_8$	30$^3/_8$	27	26$^1/_4$	7$^1/_4$	9$^7/_8$	7$^5/_8$	9
- Low	8	8$^3/_8$	12$^1/_2$	13$^3/_8$	12$^1/_2$	6$^3/_8$	3$^5/_8$	4$^1/_8$	4$^1/_2$	3$^7/_8$
P/E Ratio - High	NM	NM	37	16	18	21	NM	99	19	NM
- Low	NM	NM	15	7	8	5	NM	41	11	NM

Income Statement Analysis (Million $)

	1998	1997	1996	1995	1994	1993	1992	1991	1990	1989
Revs.	156	354	342	379	323	250	133	87.0	77.0	72.0
Oper. Inc.	7.6	-6.8	-4.5	55.4	44.0	42.8	12.2	9.8	14.2	-0.9
Depr.	13.4	22.2	19.0	14.8	8.5	12.0	9.6	7.8	8.6	9.4
Int. Exp.	0.2	0.6	1.1	1.3	1.6	2.3	1.2	0.3	0.5	0.5
Pretax Inc.	-6.9	-33.0	20.0	41.3	33.5	27.9	1.9	2.1	7.5	-9.0
Eff. Tax Rate	NM	NM	41%	39%	41%	45%	75%	56%	39%	NM
Net Inc.	-4.5	-21.3	11.6	25.2	19.9	15.8	0.6	1.2	4.7	-5.9

Balance Sheet & Other Fin. Data (Million $)

	1998	1997	1996	1995	1994	1993	1992	1991	1990	1989
Cash	45.2	8.4	18.5	29.5	32.1	35.9	17.9	31.1	38.9	28.8
Curr. Assets	109	130	149	163	140	111	79.7	75.2	76.3	65.3
Total Assets	211	234	261	229	206	184	154	112	113	109
Curr. Liab.	19.6	39.3	55.8	43.4	41.8	41.0	35.1	8.1	11.1	7.9
LT Debt	2.5	7.0	Nil	Nil	9.2	12.1	18.2	1.8	1.9	4.4
Common Eqty.	172	172	194	174	144	120	89.3	88.0	85.0	82.3
Total Cap.	186	190	205	185	164	143	119	104	102	101
Cap. Exp.	5.8	19.4	39.0	13.6	8.6	5.4	6.5	7.9	2.0	4.2
Cash Flow	8.9	1.0	30.6	40.0	28.4	27.8	10.2	9.0	13.2	3.4
Curr. Ratio	5.5	3.3	2.7	3.7	3.4	2.7	2.3	9.3	6.9	8.3
% LT Debt of Cap.	1.4	3.7	Nil	Nil	5.6	8.5	15.3	1.7	1.8	4.3
% Net Inc.of Revs.	NM	NM	3.4	6.6	6.2	6.3	0.4	1.4	6.1	NM
% Ret. on Assets	NM	NM	4.7	11.4	10.1	9.4	0.4	1.1	4.2	NM
% Ret. on Equity	NM	NM	6.3	15.6	15.0	14.8	0.7	1.4	5.6	NM

Data as orig. reptd.; bef. results of disc. opers. and/or spec. items. Per share data adj. for stk. divs. as of ex-div. date. Bold denotes diluted EPS (FASB 128). E-Estimated. NA-Not Available. NM-Not Meaningful. NR-Not Ranked.

Office—80 Arkay Dr., Hauppauge, NY 11788. **Tel**—(516) 435-6000. **Fax**—(516) 273-5550. **Website**—http://www.smc.com **Chrmn & CEO**—P. Richman. **Pres**—A. Sidorsky. **VP & CFO**—E. M. Nowling. **Secy**—H. I. Kahen. **Investor Contact**—John Tweedy (516) 434-4630. **Dirs**—E. Berezin, J. R. Berrett, R. M. Brill, P. F. Dicks, K. B. Early, H. Fialkov, I. T. Frisch, P. Richman. **Transfer Agent**—Mellon Securities Trust Co., Ridgefield, NJ. **Incorporated**—in Delaware in 1971. **Empl**— 481. **S&P Analyst**: J. Robert Cho

03-OCT-98

Industry:
Auto Parts & Equipment

Summary: This company derives the bulk of its sales from ignition, engine control, fuel system, wire and cable, brake and climate control parts for the automotive aftermarket.

Quantitative Evaluations

Outlook
(1 Lowest—5 Highest)
• **3**

Fair Value
• **25¼**

Risk
• **Low**

Earn./Div. Rank
• **B-**

Technical Eval.
• **Bullish** since 9/98

Rel. Strength Rank
(1 Lowest—99 Highest)
• **86**

Insider Activity
• **NA**

Recent Price • 24
52 Wk Range • 26½-16¼

Yield • 1.3%
12-Mo. P/E • NM

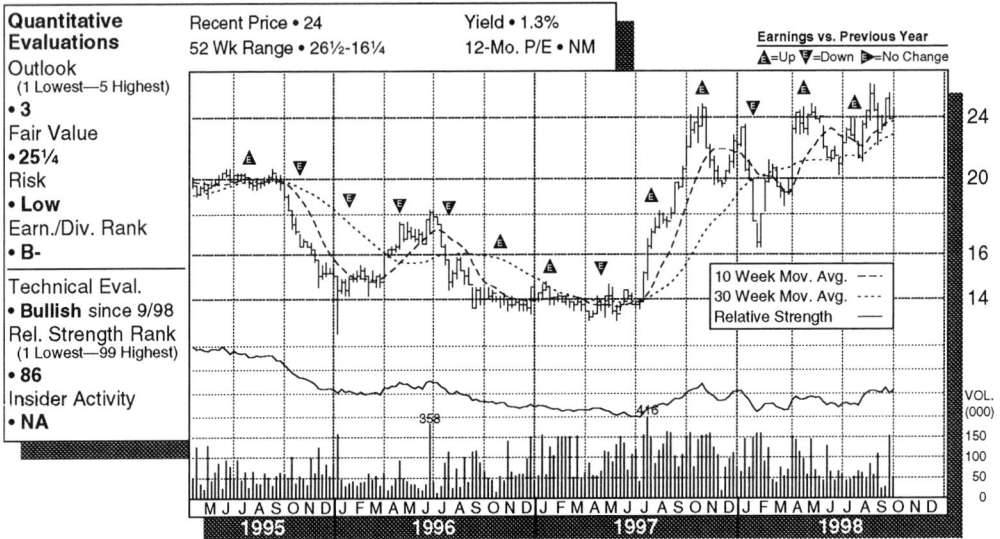

Earnings vs. Previous Year
▲=Up ▼=Down ▶=No Change

10 Week Mov. Avg. - - -
30 Week Mov. Avg. ····
Relative Strength ——

Business Profile - 13-MAY-98

In October 1997, SMP entered into an agreement to sell its Service Line business to R&B Inc. (Nasdaq: RBIN) of Colmar, PA. The sale, expected to close in mid-1998, will be of select assets of the Champ and APS service lines and Pik-A-Nut fastener line, for approximately tangible net book value less reserves for certain costs and contingencies. In September 1997, SMP moved to further strengthen its emissions component product line by acquiring the oxygen sensor business of AlliedSignal, permitting the company to be a basic manufacturer of this high growth product. In April 1998, SMP announced that it would omit its dividend for the second quarter of 1998.

Operational Review - 13-MAY-98

Net sales from continuing operations in the three months ended March 31, 1998, fell 8.5%, year to year, as an unusually mild winter affected engine management sales and the elimination of a pre-season stocking program reduced Four Seasons volume. Aftermarket sales continued to be weak. Gross margins widened, on improved operating efficiencies, continued favorable material purchase costs and cost reductions; operating income was up 72%. After a 4.4% dip in interest expense, taxes at 11.8% versus 99.2%, and minority interest, income from continuing operations of $2,653,000 ($0.20 a share) contrasted with a loss of $141,000 ($0.01). Results in the 1997 period exclude a loss of $794,000 ($0.06) from discontinued operations.

Stock Performance - 02-OCT-98

In the past 30 trading days, SMP's shares have declined 7%, compared to a 7% fall in the S&P 500. Average trading volume for the past five days was 9,360 shares, compared with the 40-day moving average of 14,531 shares.

Key Stock Statistics

Dividend Rate/Share	0.32	Shareholders	900
Shs. outstg. (M)	13.1	Market cap. (B)	$0.314
Avg. daily vol. (M)	0.014	Inst. holdings	51%
Tang. Bk. Value/Share	12.80		
Beta	0.64		

Value of $10,000 invested 5 years ago: $ 19,625

Fiscal Year Ending Dec. 31

	1998	1997	1996	1995	1994	1993
Revenues (Million $)						
1Q	126.0	137.7	174.4	159.7	147.1	127.8
2Q	208.8	163.2	205.3	184.0	187.7	161.2
3Q	—	155.2	187.8	178.3	168.3	161.3
4Q	—	103.7	154.3	141.5	137.8	132.6
Yr.	—	559.8	721.8	663.5	640.8	582.9
Earnings Per Share ($)						
1Q	0.20	-0.01	0.33	0.30	0.21	0.22
2Q	0.65	0.42	0.46	0.63	0.62	0.51
3Q	—	0.53	0.27	0.24	0.59	0.43
4Q	—	-1.07	0.06	0.06	0.38	0.25
Yr.	—	-0.12	1.12	1.23	1.80	1.41

Next earnings report expected: mid October

Dividend Data (Dividends have been paid since 1960.)

Amount ($)	Date Decl.	Ex-Div. Date	Stock of Record	Payment Date
0.080	Oct. 17	Nov. 12	Nov. 14	Dec. 01 '97
0.080	Jul. 28	Aug. 12	Aug. 14	Sep. 01 '98

A Division of The McGraw·Hill Companies

STANDARD
&POOR'S
STOCK REPORTS

Standard Motor Products, Inc.

2103

03-OCT-98

Business Summary - 13-MAY-98

Standard Motor Products, Inc. (SMP) supplies automotive replacement parts, with product offerings concentrated in a few large categories -- ignition, wire and cable, climate control and, until March 1998, brake system products. In March 1998, SMP exchanged its brake business for the temperature control business of Moog Automotive, Inc., a subsidiary of Cooper Industries. The exchange will enable SMP to concentrate on the product lines in which it has the greatest expertise and work toward achieving further efficiencies and improvements in those lines. The combination of Cooper's temperature control business with SMP's existing temperature control business will enable it to achieve operational synergies that should provide for substantial cost savings. SMP's climate control activities as of December 31, 1997, included the manufacture, remanufacture and sale of a complete line of replacement parts for air conditioning and heating systems. SMP's ignition parts include distributor caps and rotors, electronic ignition control modules, voltage regulators, coils, switches and sensors. Wires and cables, fuel system parts and service line products are also furnished.

SMP is pursuing a number of strategies, often with the help of acquisitions, as it seeks to prosper -- and grow -- in an industry the company itself concedes may be one with limited growth. SMP's Four Seasons division, for instance, has acquired parts makers and commenced production of previously purchased items in furtherance of the company's plan to manufacture more of the products it sells. By becoming less dependent on outside vendors, SMP can enhance its own control over product supply as it brings down costs.

As its customers seek to sell at lower prices, SMP feels obliged to offer "second," or economy, lines along with its premium products. The challenge is to accomplish this without eroding sales of its higher-margin lines. SMP acquired Federal Parts Corp., a leading supplier of economy ignition wire sets, in 1996, and has made acquisitions in other product areas as well to gain access to economy lines it can differentiate from its premium lines.

SMP entered the European market in July 1996 with the acquisition of a majority interest in Intermotor Holdings Ltd., the U.K.'s largest ignition aftermarket supplier. In 1997, Four Seasons, hoping to capitalize on anticipated growth in Europe's nascent automotive air conditioning industry, opened a distribution center in France.

Per Share Data ($)

(Year Ended Dec. 31)	1997	1996	1995	1994	1993	1992	1991	1990	1989	1988
Tangible Bk. Val.	11.71	14.33	15.33	14.29	12.77	12.20	11.78	11.46	11.10	11.56
Cash Flow	1.32	2.36	2.27	2.63	2.20	1.41	1.18	1.20	1.56	1.18
Earnings	-0.12	1.12	1.23	1.80	1.41	0.68	0.51	0.59	1.00	0.71
Dividends	0.32	0.32	0.32	0.32	0.32	0.32	0.32	0.32	0.32	0.32
Payout Ratio	NM	29%	26%	18%	23%	47%	63%	54%	32%	45%
Prices - High	25	18¼	20⅝	26⅞	26⅞	13⅝	13⅞	15⅝	20	16
- Low	13⅛	12⅝	14½	14¾	13⅛	9½	7⅜	5⅞	13¾	11½
P/E Ratio - High	NM	16	17	15	19	20	27	26	20	23
- Low	NM	11	12	8	9	14	14	10	14	16

Income Statement Analysis (Million $)

Revs.	560	722	663	641	583	536	535	508	429	398
Oper. Inc.	28.4	53.1	46.2	54.2	50.8	32.2	33.4	35.8	40.4	27.4
Depr.	19.0	16.3	14.0	11.0	10.5	9.7	8.9	8.0	7.3	6.2
Int. Exp.	14.2	18.7	14.6	12.3	12.3	12.3	17.2	18.9	17.4	11.2
Pretax Inc.	-3.7	19.8	20.2	35.4	26.8	10.8	7.8	9.7	17.6	11.9
Eff. Tax Rate	NM	26%	29%	33%	31%	18%	15%	20%	25%	22%
Net Inc.	-1.6	14.6	16.1	23.7	18.6	8.9	6.7	7.7	13.1	9.3

Balance Sheet & Other Fin. Data (Million $)

Cash	16.8	4.7	17.5	8.8	12.4	17.0	24.0	15.8	13.8	23.5
Curr. Assets	390	418	365	329	304	265	291	321	313	282
Total Assets	577	625	512	462	423	375	393	422	406	354
Curr. Liab.	213	207	133	140	100	74.0	160	175	149	136
LT Debt	159	172	149	110	131	136	73.0	90.0	103	61.0
Common Eqty.	184	223	210	195	178	161	155	151	146	151
Total Cap.	346	399	365	310	312	301	232	247	257	218
Cap. Exp.	15.6	21.3	16.7	12.6	12.3	15.3	12.0	16.2	23.2	26.8
Cash Flow	17.4	30.9	29.8	34.7	29.1	18.6	15.5	15.8	20.5	15.4
Curr. Ratio	1.8	2.0	2.7	2.4	3.1	3.6	1.8	1.8	2.1	2.1
% LT Debt of Cap.	45.9	43.1	40.8	35.5	41.8	45.3	31.6	36.5	40.1	27.7
% Net Inc.of Revs.	NM	2.0	2.5	3.7	3.2	1.7	1.2	1.5	3.1	2.3
% Ret. on Assets	NM	2.5	3.4	5.4	4.6	2.3	1.6	1.9	3.5	2.9
% Ret. on Equity	NM	6.7	8.0	12.8	10.9	5.6	4.4	5.2	8.8	6.2

Data as orig. reptd.; bef. results of disc. opers. and/or spec. items. Per share data adj. for stk. divs. as of ex-div. date. Bold denotes diluted EPS (FASB 128). E-Estimated. NA-Not Available. NM-Not Meaningful. NR-Not Ranked.

Office—37-18 Northern Blvd., Long Island City, NY 11101. **Tel**—(718) 392-0200. **Co-Chrmn**—B. Fife, N. L. Sills. **Pres & COO**—L. I. Sills. **VP-Fin, CFO & Investor Contact**—Michael J. Bailey. **VP & Secy**—S. Kay. **Dirs**—M. F. Cragin, A. D. Davis, S. F. Davis, R. M. Gerrity, J. L. Kelsey, A. M. Massimilla, A. S. Sills, L. I. Sills, N. L. Sills, R. J. Swartz, W. H. Turner. **Transfer Agent & Registrar**—Registrar & Transfer Co., Cranford, NJ. **Incorporated**—in New York in 1926. **Empl**— 4,400. **S&P Analyst:** M.I.

STANDARD &POOR'S
STOCK REPORTS

Standard Pacific

2116B
NYSE Symbol **SPF**
In S&P SmallCap 600

03-OCT-98

Industry: Homebuilding

Summary: This company operates primarily as a geographically diversified builder of medium-priced single-family homes in major metropolitan markets in California, Texas and Arizona.

Quantitative Evaluations

Recent Price • 12⅞	Yield • 1.2%
52 Wk Range • 21-9¾	12-Mo. P/E • 11.4

Outlook (1 Lowest—5 Highest)
• **2⁻**

Fair Value
• **14½**

Risk
• **Average**

Earn./Div. Rank
• **NR**

Technical Eval.
• **Bearish** since 2/98

Rel. Strength Rank (1 Lowest—99 Highest)
• **36**

Insider Activity
• **Neutral**

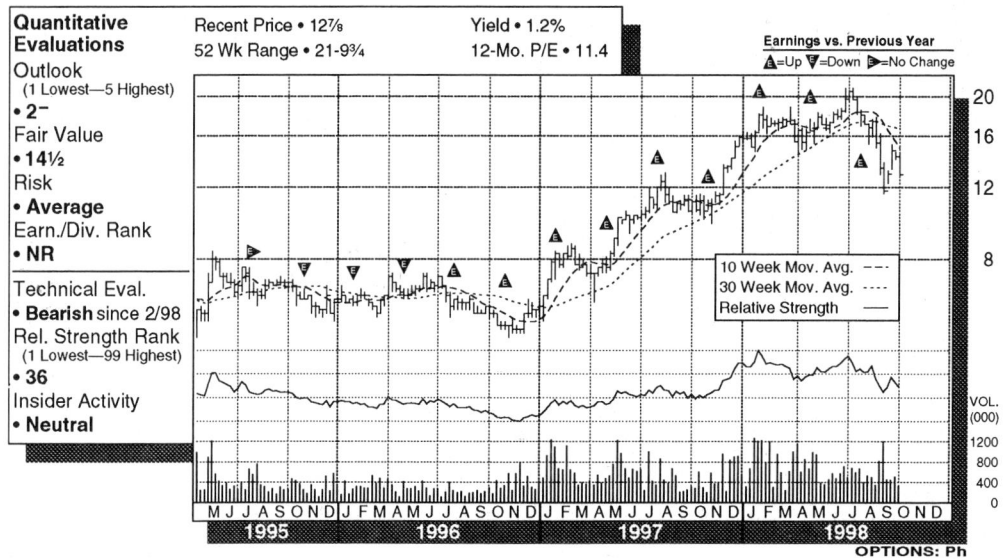

Earnings vs. Previous Year
▲=Up ▼=Down ▶=No Change

10 Week Mov. Avg. ---
30 Week Mov. Avg. ....
Relative Strength —

OPTIONS: Ph

Business Profile - 29-SEP-98

This geographically diversified builder focuses its efforts on acquiring land suitable for the construction and sale of homes. Bolstered by a generally healthy California housing market, SPF anticipates that its average selling price will remain above $300,000 for the foreseeable future. In September 1998, the company paid $58 million for seven active subdivisions of the Phoenix, AZ, single-family home-building operation of UDC Homes. With the acquisition, SPF will purchase or assume rights to acquire more than 2,000 single family lots located in 13 communities in the Phoenix metropolitan area, the second largest U.S. home building market in terms of unit deliveries.

Operational Review - 29-SEP-98

Total revenues in the six months ended June 30, 1998, slid fractionally, year to year, as 10% lower housing unit deliveries were offset by higher average selling prices. Gross margins widened in the homebuilding segment, reflecting positive momentum in the California housing market. With 3.7% lower SG&A expense and a sharp decline in interest expense, after taxes at 41.5%, versus 41.0%, income from continuing operations soared 92%, to $14,791,000 ($0.49 a share), from $7,723,000 ($0.26, before income from discontinued operations of $0.02).

Stock Performance - 02-OCT-98

In the past 30 trading days, SPF's shares have declined 16%, compared to a 7% fall in the S&P 500. Average trading volume for the past five days was 65,220 shares, compared with the 40-day moving average of 117,723 shares.

Key Stock Statistics

Dividend Rate/Share	0.16	Shareholders	2,000
Shs. outstg. (M)	29.8	Market cap. (B)	$0.383
Avg. daily vol. (M)	0.095	Inst. holdings	60%
Tang. Bk. Value/Share	9.79		
Beta	2.09		

Value of $10,000 invested 5 years ago: $ 20,409

Fiscal Year Ending Dec. 31

	1998	1997	1996	1995	1994	1993
Revenues (Million $)						
1Q	96.91	121.2	70.89	77.33	78.94	52.20
2Q	153.1	140.6	112.2	89.85	107.7	70.24
3Q	—	177.2	114.7	109.6	111.5	70.73
4Q	—	155.5	141.4	110.5	122.3	100.6
Yr.	—	584.6	439.3	387.2	420.5	293.8
Earnings Per Share ($)						
1Q	**0.16**	0.12	0.02	0.04	0.02	0.04
2Q	**0.33**	0.16	0.07	0.04	0.04	0.01
3Q	—	0.23	0.07	-0.02	0.07	Nil
4Q	Nil	**0.31**	0.12	-0.97	0.07	0.02
Yr.	—	**0.81**	**0.26**	-0.90	0.19	0.06

Next earnings report expected: NA

Dividend Data (Dividends have been paid since 1976.)

Amount ($)	Date Decl.	Ex-Div. Date	Stock of Record	Payment Date
0.040	Oct. 28	Nov. 10	Nov. 13	Nov. 27 '97
0.040	Jan. 27	Feb. 11	Feb. 13	Feb. 27 '98
0.040	Apr. 28	May. 12	May. 14	May. 28 '98
0.040	Jul. 28	Aug. 12	Aug. 14	Aug. 28 '98

A Division of The McGraw-Hill Companies

STANDARD
&POOR'S
STOCK REPORTS

Standard Pacific Corp.

2116B
03-OCT-98

Business Summary - 29-SEP-98

With the California housing market finally on the up-swing, Standard Pacific Corp. (SPF) is building momentum. SPF, one of the top 20 homebuilders in the U.S., constructs and sells medium-priced single-family homes throughout the major metropolitan markets in California, Texas, and Arizona. The company has built more than 34,000 homes since 1966. In August 1998, SPF entered into a definitive agreement to sell its federally chartered thrift subsidiary, Standard Pacific Savings, F.A., to American General Finance, Inc.

SPF's homebuilding strategy concentrates on homes used as primary residences by move-up buyers. The average home selling price (including joint ventures) was $307,265 in 1997, up from $267,529 in 1996. The company expects to concentrate its efforts on acquiring land suitable for the construction and sale of homes generally in the price range of $150,000 to $400,000, which represents a broad market segment in SPF's market areas. SPF also constructs and sells homes in the $400,000 to $800,000 price range in certain of its California markets. In 1997, SPF delivered 1,946 homes, up from 1,623 in 1996, with 79% of deliveries in California markets and 21% in Texas.

As of year-end 1997, the company controlled more than 9,000 homesites throughout California and Texas. SPF believes that it is well positioned to advantage of the strong growth in the California housing markets, particularly in Orange County, where SPF controls almost 3,000 lots, and in Northern California, with 2,900 lots owned or under contract.

In September 1997, SPF acquired Duc Development Co., a privately held Northern California homebuilding company, for $16 million in cash. In connection with the acquisition, the company acquired certain other real estate assets related to Duc's operations, for $55 million in cash and the assumption of $8 million in debt. SPF said that the acquisition expanded its presence in one of the strongest housing markets in California.

The company generated a record number of net new orders for the 1998 second quarter (739 homes, a 64% increase, year to year, and the highest level for any quarter in SPF's history). The company's Southern California operations continued to experience positive order trends in the second quarter of 1998; net new home orders were up 132%, year to year, reflecting a robust housing market and strong acceptance of the company's new projects.

In addition, SPF expects to open approximately 60 new home communities during the next 12 months. Coupled with new projects opened to date, this should significantly increase the number of homes available for delivery during the next two years. The company entered the 1998 third quarter with a backlog of 1,219 presold homes, representing approximately $416 million in revenues, up 81% from the level a year earlier.

Per Share Data ($)

(Year Ended Dec. 31)	1997	1996	1995	1994	1993	1992	1991	1990	1989	1988
Tangible Bk. Val.	9.35	8.79	8.58	9.51	9.49	9.52	9.35	9.32	9.54	7.73
Cash Flow	0.83	0.31	-0.88	0.22	0.08	0.18	0.44	1.83	4.07	2.84
Earnings	0.81	0.28	-0.90	0.19	0.06	0.15	0.40	1.77	3.87	2.75
Dividends	0.14	0.12	0.12	0.12	0.12	0.09	0.30	2.00	2.10	1.20
Payout Ratio	17%	43%	NM	63%	200%	61%	74%	112%	53%	43%
Prices - High	16¼	7⅜	8⅜	12⅞	11⅜	14	12	16	19⅞	12⅜
- Low	5⅝	5⅛	5⅛	4⅞	6¼	4½	5⅛	4¾	11⅞	8⅛
P/E Ratio - High	20	26	NM	68	NM	93	30	9	5	5
- Low	7	18	NM	26	NM	30	13	3	3	3

Income Statement Analysis (Million $)

	1997	1996	1995	1994	1993	1992	1991	1990	1989	1988
Revs.	585	439	387	416	294	305	299	383	486	492
Oper. Inc.	42.1	34.7	60.2	16.0	9.0	18.0	33.0	64.0	130	94.0
Depr.	0.8	0.9	0.6	0.8	0.7	0.8	1.1	1.2	4.2	1.4
Int. Exp.	5.0	16.7	19.2	28.8	26.8	34.9	41.3	45.9	45.3	36.3
Pretax Inc.	41.0	14.0	-45.9	10.0	3.0	6.0	12.0	49.0	106	76.0
Eff. Tax Rate	42%	40%	NM	41%	39%	30%	4.90%	1.00%	0.10%	0.30%
Net Inc.	24.0	8.4	-27.4	6.0	2.0	5.0	11.0	48.0	106	75.0

Balance Sheet & Other Fin. Data (Million $)

	1997	1996	1995	1994	1993	1992	1991	1990	1989	1988
Cash	8.4	21.6	43.0	16.5	18.6	82.7	56.9	26.5	25.9	30.0
Curr. Assets	NA	NA	NA	NA	NA	NA	NA	NA	NA	NA
Total Assets	548	695	773	923	858	953	972	934	896	749
Curr. Liab.	NA	NA	NA	NA	NA	NA	NA	NA	NA	NA
LT Debt	214	271	313	365	321	353	413	436	398	338
Common Eqty.	284	260	258	291	290	291	254	253	259	210
Total Cap.	490	531	571	656	612	644	669	689	657	548
Cap. Exp.	1.3	0.6	0.2	0.4	NA	1.0	0.7	0.6	2.0	3.2
Cash Flow	24.8	9.3	-26.8	7.0	3.0	5.0	12.0	50.0	111	77.0
Curr. Ratio	NA	NA	NA	NA	NA	NA	NA	NA	NA	NA
% LT Debt of Cap.	43.1	51.1	54.9	55.6	52.5	54.8	61.8	63.3	60.6	61.7
% Net Inc.of Revs.	4.1	2.0	NM	1.4	0.6	1.5	3.7	12.6	21.9	15.3
% Ret. on Assets	3.9	1.2	NM	0.7	0.2	0.4	1.2	5.3	12.9	13.5
% Ret. on Equity	8.8	3.3	NM	2.0	0.6	1.6	4.3	18.9	45.3	39.9

Data as orig. reptd.; bef. results of disc. opers. and/or spec. items. Per share data adj. for stk. divs. as of ex-div. date. Bold denotes diluted EPS (FASB 128). E-Estimated. NA-Not Available. NM-Not Meaningful. NR-Not Ranked.

Office—1565 West MacArthur Blvd., Costa Mesa, CA 92626. **Tel**—(714) 668-4300. **Chrmn & CEO**—A. E. Svendsen. **Pres**—S. J. Scarborough. **VP, CFO & Treas**—A. H. Parnes. **VP & Secy**—C. H. Halvorsen. **Dirs**—J. L. Doti, R. R. Foell, K. D. Koeller, W. H. Langenberg, R. J. St. Lawrence, S. J. Scarborough, D. H. Spengler, A. E. Svendsen. **Transfer Agent & Registrar**—First Chicago Trust Co. of New York. **Incorporated**—in California in 1961; organized in Delaware in 1986; reincorporated in Delaware in 1991. **Empl**— 427. **S&P Analyst:** C.C.P.

Standard Products

2117

NYSE Symbol **SPD**

In S&P SmallCap 600

03-OCT-98

Industry:
Auto Parts & Equipment

Summary: This company makes rubber and plastic parts for the automotive industry and magnetic door seals for appliances.

Quantitative Evaluations

Outlook
(1 Lowest—5 Highest)
• **4**

Fair Value
• **27⅛**

Risk
• **Average**

Earn./Div. Rank
• **B**

Technical Eval.
• **Bearish** since 6/98

Rel. Strength Rank
(1 Lowest—99 Highest)
• **18**

Insider Activity
• **Neutral**

Recent Price • 18½
52 Wk Range • 35⅞-17

Yield • 3.7%
12-Mo. P/E • 7.2

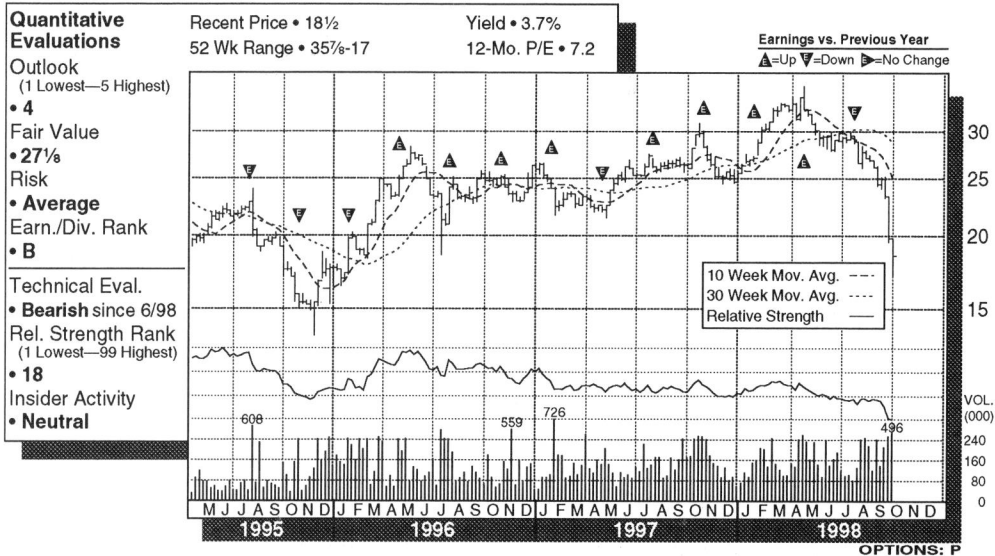

Earnings vs. Previous Year
▲=Up ▼=Down ▶=No Change

10 Week Mov. Avg. – – –
30 Week Mov. Avg. ·········
Relative Strength ——

OPTIONS: P

Business Profile - 01-MAY-98

In February 1998, Standard Products opened a new 76,000 sq. ft. plant in Aguascalientes, Mexico. The plant has begun shipments of sealing products to heavy-duty truck customers, RV manufacturers and Mexican automotive aftermarket distributors. SPD expects the facility to begin shipping sealing products to automotive original equipment manufacturers later in 1998. Sales from a new plant in Brazil are primarily attributable to the Fiat Palio; the plant is approaching full production.

Operational Review - 01-MAY-98

Net sales in the first nine months of FY 98 (Jun.) declined fractionally. Gross margins widened, on improved operating results in Brazil and process improvements in North America. Despite other expense of $5.7 million, versus other income of $981,000, in the absence of a $17.7 million charge related to the closure of two plants in 1996, pretax income increased 132%. After taxes at 38.3%, versus 52.9%, net income tripled, to $25,131,000 ($1.48 a share), from $8,255,000 ($0.49).

Stock Performance - 02-OCT-98

In the past 30 trading days, SPD's shares have declined 31%, compared to a 7% fall in the S&P 500. Average trading volume for the past five days was 99,280 shares, compared with the 40-day moving average of 56,085 shares.

Key Stock Statistics

Dividend Rate/Share	0.68	Shareholders	1,000
Shs. outstg. (M)	16.9	Market cap. (B)	$0.312
Avg. daily vol. (M)	0.064	Inst. holdings	56%
Tang. Bk. Value/Share	13.09		
Beta	0.33		

Value of $10,000 invested 5 years ago: $ 8,498

Fiscal Year Ending Jun. 30

	1998	1997	1996	1995	1994	1993
Revenues (Million $)						
1Q	246.2	265.6	238.8	220.9	201.7	164.0
2Q	282.5	266.6	264.8	243.8	198.3	175.0
3Q	277.9	281.8	277.3	265.0	222.7	201.0
4Q	294.6	294.3	303.1	266.2	249.7	223.7
Yr.	1,101	1,108	1,084	995.9	872.4	763.8
Earnings Per Share ($)						
1Q	0.17	0.08	-0.58	0.17	0.29	0.30
2Q	0.52	0.38	0.09	0.32	0.37	0.52
3Q	**0.80**	0.03	0.43	0.41	0.49	0.67
4Q	**0.11**	1.15	0.93	0.30	0.83	0.73
Yr.	**2.56**	1.64	0.87	1.20	1.99	2.21

Next earnings report expected: late October

Dividend Data (Dividends have been paid since 1949.)

Amount ($)	Date Decl.	Ex-Div. Date	Stock of Record	Payment Date
0.170	Dec. 05	Jan. 07	Jan. 09	Jan. 23 '98
0.170	Mar. 16	Apr. 07	Apr. 10	Apr. 24 '98
0.170	Jun. 22	Jul. 08	Jul. 10	Jul. 24 '98
0.170	Aug. 24	Oct. 07	Oct. 09	Oct. 23 '98

A Division of The McGraw-Hill Companies

Business Summary - 01-MAY-98

With the global auto industry as the principal market for its rubber and plastic parts, Standard Products Co. (SPD) believes that persistent capital investment is critical to its survival. Over the last five years, SPD has invested $290 million in net capital spending to support its expansion into new markets, new product lines and new business processes. Each of SPD's plants is now equipped with state-of-the-art machinery and equipment. Over the same period, SPD spent another $170 million in research, engineering and development in support of an extensive schedule of new business processes. These investments began to pay off in FY 97 (Jun.).

Founded in 1927, SPD is one of the world's leading suppliers of sealing, trim and vibration-control systems for the worldwide automotive original equipment industry. SPD's rubber and plastic parts require a substantial degree of product engineering and high-volume production processes. The company's components and systems protect, decorate and improve the performance of cars, vans and light trucks. Through its Holm Industries unit, SPD is also the largest supplier of seals for home and commercial refrigerators in North America, and through its Oliver Rubber subsidiary, it is a leading

manufacturer of tread rubber and equipment for the truck retread industry. SPD's vehicle sealing systems and components are found on many of the most popular automotive platforms in North America, including the Ford Taurus, Chrysler minivan, Chevrolet Lumina, Jeep Grand Cherokee and Honda Accord. In Europe, SPD supplies parts for the Ford Fiesta, Ford Escort, Opel Astra and Fiat Punto.

In FY 97, sales reached $1.1 billion, up only slightly from the prior year, but net income jumped 89% to $27.5 million from the depressed level of FY 96, due mainly to significant gross margin improvement and well controlled interest expense. If not for a one-time charge relating to the closings of two plants, FY 97 net income would have reached $39.1 million. In FY 97, Ford Motor Co. accounted for 24% of total consolidated sales, Chrysler 18%, and General Motors 13%.

Over the past decade, SPD has increased its share of the North American automotive market. It has expanded its market penetration in Europe at an even faster rate, as a result of a 1993 acquisition and through internal growth of its operations in the U.K. With its more recent entry into Latin America (particularly Brazil and Mexico), SPD has further diversified its geographic sales base. In FY 97, North America provided 67% of automotive sales, Europe 27% and Latin America 6%.

Per Share Data ($)

(Year Ended Jun. 30)	1998	1997	1996	1995	1994	1993	1992	1991	1990	1989
Tangible Bk. Val.	NA	12.03	11.15	11.68	10.80	9.82	11.24	7.29	12.05	12.05
Cash Flow	NA	4.80	4.02	4.00	4.39	4.26	3.70	0.30	2.49	3.18
Earnings	2.56	1.64	0.87	1.20	1.99	2.21	1.79	-1.65	0.93	2.17
Dividends	0.68	0.68	0.68	0.68	0.64	0.48	0.38	0.56	0.74	0.69
Payout Ratio	27%	41%	78%	57%	32%	24%	25%	NM	79%	32%
Prices - High	35⅞	31	28¼	24⅛	38¾	36⅝	29⅝	20⅜	21	27⅝
- Low	25½	21⅜	16⅜	13½	21⅜	25¾	19⅛	9⅝	9⅝	17⅜
P/E Ratio - High	14	19	32	20	19	17	17	NM	23	13
- Low	10	13	19	11	11	12	11	NM	10	8

Income Statement Analysis (Million $)

	1998	1997	1996	1995	1994	1993	1992	1991	1990	1989
Revs.	NA	1,108	1,084	996	872	764	657	592	652	559
Oper. Inc.	NA	130	91.4	77.3	97.7	89.8	77.4	23.6	50.3	65.3
Depr.	NA	53.1	52.5	47.0	40.0	31.0	24.9	24.7	20.0	13.4
Int. Exp.	NA	12.9	12.8	13.0	9.0	9.7	15.0	12.6	11.1	4.7
Pretax Inc.	NA	46.5	28.5	17.3	50.2	50.2	38.8	-13.1	19.9	45.9
Eff. Tax Rate	NA	41%	49%	NM	34%	34%	40%	NM	41%	38%
Net Inc.	NA	27.5	14.6	20.0	33.0	33.4	23.3	-21.0	11.8	28.7

Balance Sheet & Other Fin. Data (Million $)

	1998	1997	1996	1995	1994	1993	1992	1991	1990	1989
Cash	NA	7.0	NM	19.5	Nil	5.5	44.3	19.3	15.7	1.3
Curr. Assets	NA	272	261	307	271	234	218	182	183	178
Total Assets	NA	692	685	702	624	565	399	368	362	334
Curr. Liab.	NA	225	207	189	183	155	121	121	93.0	89.0
LT Debt	NA	122	143	191	135	14.3	69.0	113	99	75.0
Common Eqty.	NA	268	259	260	243	224	178	102	153	156
Total Cap.	NA	390	402	451	378	340	247	216	252	232
Cap. Exp.	NA	59.0	79.7	55.0	61.0	115	19.9	21.2	39.2	50.8
Cash Flow	NA	80.7	67.1	66.9	73.0	64.4	48.2	3.8	31.8	42.1
Curr. Ratio	NA	1.2	1.3	1.6	1.5	1.5	1.8	1.5	2.0	2.0
% LT Debt of Cap.	NA	31.3	35.6	42.3	36.0	34.0	28.0	52.5	39.4	32.5
% Net Inc.of Revs.	NA	2.5	1.3	2.1	3.8	4.4	3.5	NM	1.8	5.1
% Ret. on Assets	NA	4.0	2.1	3.1	5.6	6.7	5.6	NM	3.4	9.8
% Ret. on Equity	NA	10.4	5.6	8.0	14.2	15.9	15.6	NM	7.7	19.2

Data as orig. reptd.; bef. results of disc. opers. and/or spec. items. Per share data adj. for stk. divs. as of ex-div. date. Bold denotes diluted EPS (FASB 128). E-Estimated. NA-Not Available. NM-Not Meaningful. NR-Not Ranked.

Office—2401 S. Gulley Rd., Dearborn, MI 48124. **Tel**—(313) 561-1100. **Website**—http://www.stand-prod.com.**Chrmn**—J. S. Reid Jr. **Vice Chrmn & CEO**—R. L. Roudebush. **Pres & COO**—T. K. Zampetis. **VP-Fin, CFO & Investor Contact**—Donald R. Sheley Jr. **Secy**—J. R. Hamilton. **Dirs**—J. C. Baillie, E. B. Brandon, J. Doddridge, J. D. Drinko, C. E. Moll, M. R. Myers, L. H. Perkins, A. M. Rankin Jr., J. S. Reid Jr., A. E. Riedel, R. L. Roudebush, J. D. Sigel, W. H. Thompson, T. K. Zampetis. **Transfer Agent & Registrar**—National City Bank, Cleveland. **Incorporated**—in Ohio in 1927. **Empl**— 10,350. **S&P Analyst:** G.A.S.

STANDARD &POOR'S
STOCK REPORTS

Standex International

2122

NYSE Symbol **SXI**

In S&P SmallCap 600

03-OCT-98

Industry: Manufacturing (Diversified)

Summary: This company is a diversified manufacturer in three broad business segments: food service, industrial products and consumer products.

Quantitative Evaluations		
Outlook (1 Lowest—5 Highest)	Recent Price • 23⅝	Yield • 3.2%
• **1**	52 Wk Range • 37-21	12-Mo. P/E • 15.6

Fair Value
• **20⅛**

Risk
• **Low**

Earn./Div. Rank
• **A-**

Technical Eval.
• **Bearish** since 4/98

Rel. Strength Rank (1 Lowest—99 Highest)
• **71**

Insider Activity
• **Neutral**

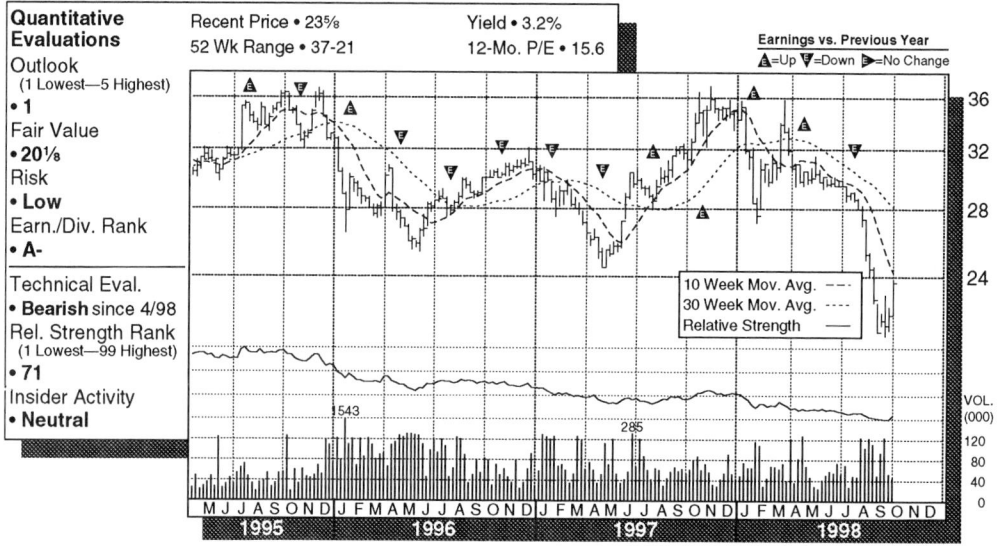

Earnings vs. Previous Year ▲=Up ▼=Down ▶=No Change

10 Week Mov. Avg. — -
30 Week Mov. Avg. - - - -
Relative Strength ——

Business Profile - 06-JUL-98

Standex seeks growth by acquiring companies that complement and expand its current operations. In June 1998, the company announced that it would record a non-recurring charge of $12.8 million in the FY 98 (Jun.) fourth quarter, for a restructuring plan that involves the closing, disposal and liquidation of certain relatively small, under-performing and unprofitable operating plants, product lines and businesses. After an income tax benefit of $4.8 million, this will reduce FY 98 earnings by $8.0 million, or $0.61 a share, on a diluted basis. The restructuring is an extension of a previously announced plan to refocus resources into larger growth oriented business units within SXI's three defined segments: industrial, consumer and food service equipment. Taking into account the income tax benefits, the company expects the restructuring actions to generate positive net cash flows, and to have a positive impact on future earnings.

Operational Review - 06-JUL-98

Sales in the nine months ended March 31, 1998, rose 8.2%, year to year, with record results in the second and third quarters, reflecting increased business activity throughout the corporation. With margins fairly steady, but interest expense up 21%, the gain in net income was held to 5.7%, to $20,968,000 ($1.59 a share, diluted), from $19,838,000 ($1.47).

Stock Performance - 02-OCT-98

In the past 30 trading days, SXI's shares have declined 3%, compared to a 7% fall in the S&P 500. Average trading volume for the past five days was 8,800 shares, compared with the 40-day moving average of 19,492 shares.

Key Stock Statistics

Dividend Rate/Share	0.76	Shareholders	4,200
Shs. outstg. (M)	13.1	Market cap. (B)	$0.311
Avg. daily vol. (M)	0.018	Inst. holdings	51%
Tang. Bk. Value/Share	8.98		
Beta	0.47		

Value of $10,000 invested 5 years ago: $ 14,496

Fiscal Year Ending Jun. 30

	1998	1997	1996	1995	1994	1993
Revenues (Million $)						
1Q	141.1	140.2	142.2	140.6	127.3	127.0
2Q	168.1	152.3	154.1	143.9	133.5	136.0
3Q	148.6	130.4	130.3	141.6	130.9	118.0
4Q	158.5	141.7	136.0	143.2	137.7	125.6
Yr.	616.2	564.6	562.7	569.3	529.4	506.3
Earnings Per Share ($)						
1Q	0.58	0.56	0.66	0.80	0.11	0.33
2Q	**0.63**	0.60	0.65	0.62	0.46	0.40
3Q	**0.38**	0.31	0.41	0.56	0.41	0.33
4Q	**-0.07**	0.53	0.49	0.66	0.50	0.42
Yr.	**1.52**	2.00	2.21	2.64	1.78	1.47

Next earnings report expected: mid October

Dividend Data (Dividends have been paid since 1964.)

Amount ($)	Date Decl.	Ex-Div. Date	Stock of Record	Payment Date
0.190	Oct. 28	Nov. 06	Nov. 10	Nov. 25 '97
0.190	Jan. 28	Feb. 05	Feb. 09	Feb. 25 '98
0.190	Apr. 29	May. 07	May. 11	May. 26 '98
0.190	Jul. 29	Aug. 06	Aug. 10	Aug. 25 '98

A Division of The **McGraw-Hill** Companies

STANDARD
&POOR'S
STOCK REPORTS

Standex International Corporation

2122

03-OCT-98

Business Summary - 06-JUL-98

Salem, NH-based Standex International offers an amazingly diverse spectrum of products and services, including: Sunday school literature, grapefruit gift packages, food service equipment, electrical connectors, rotary vane pumps, casters and wheels, and Christmas tree stands. SXI has a total of 83 principal plants and warehouses in the U.S., Western Europe, Canada, Australia, Singapore and Mexico; the company also operates 21 retail stores.

SXI has grouped its businesses into three different segments: food service products, industrial products and consumer products. Segment contributions in FY 97 (Jun.) were as follows:

	Sales	Profits
Food service products	26%	21%
Industrial products	45%	46%
Consumer products	29%	33%

In its consumer products area, the company publishes and markets educational and religious literature, and provides commercial and specialized printing, binding systems and office supplies. SXI also operates a chain of 21 Berean Christian Bookstores. In addition, this segment offers by mail order Frank Lewis Grapefruit gift packages, Harry's Crestview Groves grapefruit packages, grapefruit juice, grapefruit sections, onions, melons, and roses. Among the other offerings of this diversified unit are Williams chiropractic and traction tables and ultrasound equipment, Snappy metal ducting and fittings, and National Metal Christmas tree stands. In October 1997, SXI purchased Philadelphia-based Acme Manufacturing, a maker of heating, ventilation and air conditioning pipe, duct and fittings for the home building industry; Acme had annual sales of about $60 million.

SXI's food service segment produces USECO food service equipment and patient feeding systems, Master-Bilt beverage coolers and freezers, Barbecue King ovens, Federal Industries bakery and deli equipment, and Procon rotary vane pumps.

The industrial products division makes texturizing systems such as Roehlen embossing rolls, Mold-Tech mold engraving, and Keller-Dorian print rolls, Spincraft power metal spinning and custom components, Custom Hoists telescopic and piston rod hydraulic cylinders, and Perkins converting and finishing machinery systems. This division also prints and distributes election forms and tabulation equipment; makes casters and wheels, and industrial hardware; and offers electrical and electronics products, such as Standex reed switches and relays, electrical connectors, sensors, toroids and relays, fixed and variable inductors and electronic assemblies.

Per Share Data ($)

(Year Ended Jun. 30)	1998	1997	1996	1995	1994	1993	1992	1991	1990	1989
Tangible Bk. Val.	NA	9.60	8.93	8.36	7.04	6.85	7.11	6.69	6.44	5.90
Cash Flow	NA	2.94	3.10	3.49	2.54	2.25	1.90	1.62	1.62	1.47
Earnings	1.52	2.00	2.21	2.64	1.78	1.47	1.23	1.05	1.06	1.00
Dividends	0.76	0.75	0.71	0.63	0.52	0.42	0.38	0.35	0.34	0.30
Payout Ratio	50%	37%	32%	24%	29%	29%	28%	32%	30%	28%
Prices - High	35⅞	37	32⅞	36¾	32⅝	27¾	19	13⅝	13⅞	13¼
- Low	24½	24½	25⅜	29	24⅝	18½	11	10⅛	10⅜	10¼
P/E Ratio - High	24	19	15	14	18	19	15	13	13	13
- Low	16	12	11	11	14	13	9	10	10	10

Income Statement Analysis (Million $)

	1998	1997	1996	1995	1994	1993	1992	1991	1990	1989
Revs.	NA	565	563	569	529	506	477	482	460	444
Oper. Inc.	NA	62.8	69.0	72.0	58.1	55.3	49.2	51.1	50.7	50.4
Depr.	NA	12.8	12.5	12.4	11.8	12.9	11.9	12.0	11.3	10.3
Int. Exp.	NA	8.5	9.0	8.4	6.9	5.6	6.6	7.9	8.3	6.8
Pretax Inc.	NA	43.5	48.1	57.8	42.2	37.5	33.7	32.6	34.8	35.6
Eff. Tax Rate	NA	38%	36%	34%	36%	36%	35%	38%	38%	37%
Net Inc.	NA	26.9	30.7	38.3	27.1	24.0	21.9	20.2	21.7	22.3

Balance Sheet & Other Fin. Data (Million $)

	1998	1997	1996	1995	1994	1993	1992	1991	1990	1989
Cash	NA	6.2	5.1	9.0	5.0	7.5	10.9	7.3	8.0	7.9
Curr. Assets	NA	207	207	220	197	182	186	177	182	170
Total Assets	NA	341	335	343	324	309	317	297	298	277
Curr. Liab.	NA	70.1	68.5	77.2	70.2	73.2	74.5	72.9	66.8	61.8
LT Debt	NA	112	114	112	113	94.4	86.7	70.1	73.0	65.0
Common Eqty.	NA	141	135	132	119	122	137	139	142	137
Total Cap.	NA	267	261	256	246	229	236	220	225	211
Cap. Exp.	NA	16.8	15.3	12.0	13.2	10.7	15.7	13.8	12.7	12.7
Cash Flow	NA	39.7	43.2	50.7	38.9	36.9	33.8	32.2	33.1	32.6
Curr. Ratio	NA	3.0	3.0	2.8	2.8	2.5	2.5	2.4	2.7	2.7
% LT Debt of Cap.	NA	41.9	43.6	43.7	46.0	41.2	36.7	31.9	32.4	30.8
% Net Inc.of Revs.	NA	4.8	5.5	6.8	5.1	4.7	4.6	4.2	4.7	5.0
% Ret. on Assets	NA	11.3	9.1	11.5	8.8	8.0	7.4	7.0	7.8	8.5
% Ret. on Equity	NA	19.5	23.0	30.5	23.1	19.4	16.6	14.9	16.0	16.0

Data as orig. reptd.; bef. results of disc. opers. and/or spec. items. Per share data adj. for stk. divs. as of ex-div. date. Bold denotes diluted EPS (FASB 128). E-Estimated. NA-Not Available. NM-Not Meaningful. NR-Not Ranked.

Office—6 Manor Parkway, Salem, NH 03079. **Tel**—(603) 893-9701. **Fax**—(603) 893-7324. **Website**—http://www.standex.com **Chrmn**—T. L. King. **Pres & CEO**—E. J. Trainor. **SVP, CFO & Investor Contact**—Lindsay M. Sedwick. **Secy**—R. H. Booth. **Dirs**—J. Bolten, Jr., W. L. Brown, D. R. Crichton, S. S. Dennis III, W.R. Fenoglio, W. F. Greeley, D. B. Hogan, T. L. King, C. K. Landry, H. N. Muller III, S. Sackel, L. M. Sedwick. E. J. Trainor. **Transfer Agent & Registrar**—Boston EquiServe. **Incorporated**—in Ohio in 1955; reincorporated in Delaware in 1975. **Empl**— 4,800. **S&P Analyst:** C.F.B.

Steel Technologies   5321

NASDAQ Symbol **STTX**

In S&P SmallCap 600

03-OCT-98

Industry: Iron & Steel

Summary: This intermediate steel processor purchases flat-rolled steel produced by major steel mills and processes it to specifications required by industrial end-users.

Quantitative Evaluations

Recent Price • 7	Yield • 1.4%
52 Wk Range • 13¾-6⅝	12-Mo. P/E • 8.3

Outlook (1 Lowest—5 Highest)
• 5

Fair Value
• 13⅛

Risk
• **Average**

Earn./Div. Rank
• **B+**

Technical Eval.
• **Bearish** since 6/98

Rel. Strength Rank (1 Lowest—99 Highest)
• 31

Insider Activity
• **Neutral**

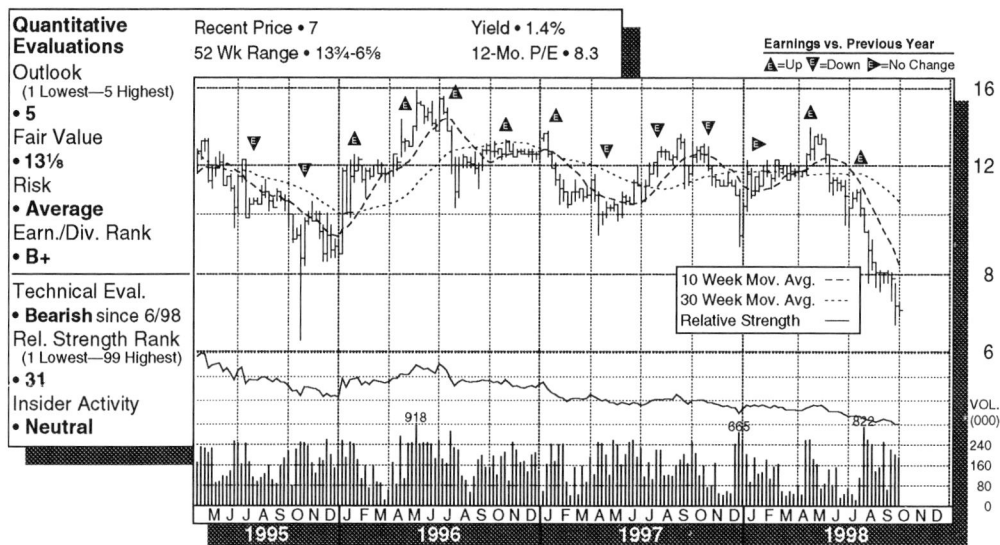

Earnings vs. Previous Year
▲=Up ▼=Down ▶=No Change

10 Week Mov. Avg. − − −
30 Week Mov. Avg. - - - -
Relative Strength ——

Business Profile - 01-SEP-98

The company continues to focus significant resources on the automotive industry, and to generate a major portion of business from selling to industrial customers making component parts for use in the auto industry. STTX has noted that its new blanking operation at Eminence, KY, the addition of Steel Technologies North Carolina, and Mi-Tech Steel's new pickling operation in Decatur, AL, all position the company for continued growth in 1998. The GM strike caused some key automotive customers to halt or reduce operations, hurting sales in the third quarter of FY 98 (Sep.). However, for the first nine months of FY 98, net income was up 23%, on 14% higher sales.

Operational Review - 01-SEP-98

Net sales in the nine months ended June 30, 1998 rose 14%, year to year, reflecting the addition of Atlantic Coil Processing, Inc. (now Steel Technologies North Carolina) in April 1997. Gross margins widened, and operating income climbed 24%. With 8.2% higher interest expense, pretax income soared 30%. After taxes at 39.2%, versus 27.3%, net income was up 23% to $8,582,000 ($0.71 a share), from $6,964,000 ($0.58). In the third quarter alone, net income rose 3.3%, despite a 4.6% decline in sales.

Stock Performance - 02-OCT-98

In the past 30 trading days, STTX's shares have declined 13%, compared to a 7% fall in the S&P 500. Average trading volume for the past five days was 37,600 shares, compared with the 40-day moving average of 40,508 shares.

Key Stock Statistics

Dividend Rate/Share	0.10	Shareholders	600
Shs. outstg. (M)	11.9	Market cap. (B)	$0.083
Avg. daily vol. (M)	0.038	Inst. holdings	31%
Tang. Bk. Value/Share	9.28		
Beta	0.58		

Value of $10,000 invested 5 years ago: $ 7,958

Fiscal Year Ending Sep. 30

	1998	1997	1996	1995	1994	1993
Revenues (Million $)						
1Q	96.45	78.03	65.71	64.25	54.06	41.80
2Q	101.3	79.80	76.63	71.50	62.73	52.02
3Q	96.39	101.1	76.62	60.15	63.29	53.06
4Q	—	86.71	75.20	56.84	60.67	50.92
Yr.	—	345.6	294.2	252.7	240.8	197.8
Earnings Per Share ($)						
1Q	0.21	0.21	0.10	0.17	0.20	0.15
2Q	0.27	0.15	0.28	0.22	0.24	0.22
3Q	0.24	0.23	0.28	0.17	0.26	0.24
4Q	—	0.13	0.24	0.06	0.17	0.23
Yr.	—	0.71	0.98	0.61	0.87	0.83

Next earnings report expected: late October

Dividend Data (Dividends have been paid since 1985.)

Amount ($)	Date Decl.	Ex-Div. Date	Stock of Record	Payment Date
0.050	Nov. 07	Nov. 19	Nov. 21	Dec. 05 '97
0.050	Apr. 27	May. 12	May. 14	May. 29 '98

A Division of The **McGraw-Hill** *Companies*

Business Summary - 01-SEP-98

As its name implies, Steel Technologies, Inc. (STTX) recognizes the impact that changing manufacturing technology can have on the steel industry. Founded in 1971, STTX is an intermediate steel processor that transforms raw, flat rolled steel produced by major mills and mini mills throughout the world into materials that meet the exact specifications of manufacturers. The company's commitment to the latest technology and its investment in new equipment and facilities have been instrumental in the growth of its revenues and shipments, both of which reached record levels in FY 97 (Sep.).

STTX occupies a niche between the primary steel producers (major and mini mills) and end-product manufacturers that are increasingly seeking steel with closer tolerances, on shorter lead times, and with more reliable and more frequent delivery than the primary producers can efficiently provide. STTX processes flat rolled steel to exceptionally close tolerances (as close as +/- 0.002 of an inch) for customers in the automotive, agricultural, appliance, lawn and garden, machinery and office equipment industries that require steel of precise width, temper, finish and thickness. The automotive industry accounted for 65% of STTX's record sales of $346 million in FY 97.

STTX has achieved high quality and productivity levels using the most advanced rolling, pickling, slitting and annealing equipment. The company has computerized all of its rolling equipment, improving its capability to deliver flat rolled steel products processed to closer than standard tolerances. In 1995, STTX added pickling capabilities, which involves the cleaning of hot rolled black coil steel to improve quality and remove impurities. Many orders also involve a process known as cold reduction, which reduces the thickness of the steel by passing it through a set of rolls under pressure. During this process, computers provide both visual displays and documented records of the thickness maintained throughout the entire coil. The annealing or softening of steel is performed in high convection bell furnaces.

STTX's plants are strategically located near customers and suppliers to provide to ensure efficient just-in-time delivery of products. The acquisition of Atlantic Coil Processing, Inc. (now Steel Technologies North Carolina) in April 1997 for $20 million added three new facilities in NC and expanded STTX's business into the Southeast, the fastest growing steel market in the country.

The company is also pursuing growth in international markets. In Mexico, where operations have been profitable, the company is investing in additional processing equipment to provide expanded capabilities to its customers. STTX expects this new equipment will allow it to grow its existing customer base.

Per Share Data ($)

(Year Ended Sep. 30)	1997	1996	1995	1994	1993	1992	1991	1990	1989	1988
Tangible Bk. Val.	8.64	8.47	7.64	7.21	6.42	5.63	5.17	4.91	4.38	3.08
Cash Flow	1.58	1.77	1.19	1.28	1.19	0.85	0.57	0.78	0.67	0.90
Earnings	0.71	0.98	0.61	0.87	0.83	0.50	0.29	0.53	0.49	0.71
Dividends	0.10	0.09	0.08	0.07	0.05	0.04	0.03	0.03	0.02	0.01
Payout Ratio	14%	9%	13%	8%	6%	8%	9%	5%	4%	2%
Prices - High	13⅝	15⅞	13¾	21¾	23½	10⅝	9⅛	9⅞	11⅜	12½
- Low	8⅞	8⅝	6¼	10⅛	10½	6⅜	6	6	6	8⅝
P/E Ratio - High	19	16	23	25	28	21	31	18	23	18
- Low	13	9	10	12	13	13	20	11	12	12

Income Statement Analysis (Million $)

	1997	1996	1995	1994	1993	1992	1991	1990	1989	1988
Revs.	346	294	253	241	198	154	130	141	123	108
Oper. Inc.	27.6	31.0	21.5	21.5	20.8	14.5	10.2	14.4	11.7	15.2
Depr.	10.4	9.5	7.1	5.0	4.4	4.2	3.4	3.0	2.2	2.0
Int. Exp.	5.7	5.0	3.9	1.3	0.9	0.9	1.2	1.2	0.8	1.0
Pretax Inc.	13.1	18.2	11.3	16.6	15.8	9.5	5.7	10.3	9.5	12.2
Eff. Tax Rate	35%	36%	34%	37%	37%	37%	38%	38%	38%	38%
Net Inc.	8.5	11.7	7.4	10.5	9.9	6.0	3.5	6.4	5.9	7.5

Balance Sheet & Other Fin. Data (Million $)

	1997	1996	1995	1994	1993	1992	1991	1990	1989	1988
Cash	3.5	4.2	2.7	1.0	0.1	0.6	1.6	0.7	0.4	0.4
Curr. Assets	130	105	80.3	118	82.1	53.0	43.5	55.3	37.0	40.7
Total Assets	258	217	195	200	144	107	95.0	99	74.0	68.0
Curr. Liab.	40.0	40.1	26.9	47.3	31.9	20.7	21.0	17.8	10.8	15.6
LT Debt	97.2	67.3	68.6	60.8	30.0	15.6	8.7	18.9	8.9	17.7
Common Eqty.	109	101	93.0	88.0	78.0	67.8	62.3	59.2	52.8	32.5
Total Cap.	218	177	168	153	112	86.7	74.1	81.2	63.7	52.1
Cap. Exp.	9.5	24.5	37.9	24.5	11.5	7.0	10.1	9.0	12.5	8.2
Cash Flow	18.9	21.2	14.5	15.5	14.3	10.2	6.9	9.4	8.1	9.5
Curr. Ratio	3.3	2.6	3.0	2.5	2.6	2.6	2.1	3.1	3.4	2.6
% LT Debt of Cap.	44.7	38.0	40.8	39.7	26.8	18.0	11.7	23.3	13.9	33.9
% Net Inc.of Revs.	2.5	4.0	2.9	4.4	5.0	3.9	2.7	4.6	4.8	7.0
% Ret. on Assets	3.6	5.7	3.8	6.1	7.9	5.9	3.6	7.4	7.8	13.6
% Ret. on Equity	8.1	12.0	8.2	12.7	13.6	9.2	5.8	11.5	13.1	26.2

Data as orig. reptd.; bef. results of disc. opers. and/or spec. items. Per share data adj. for stk. divs. as of ex-div. date. Bold denotes diluted EPS (FASB 128). E-Estimated. NA-Not Available. NM-Not Meaningful. NR-Not Ranked.

Office—15415 Shelbyville Rd., Louisville, KY 40245. **Tel**—(502) 245-2110. **Chrmn & CEO**—M. J. Ray. **Pres & COO**--B. T. Ray. **CFO & Treas**—J. P. Bellino. **Dirs**—D. L. Armstrong, H. F. Bates, Jr., M. J. Carroll, J. D. Conner, W. E. Hellmann, R. W. McIntyre, A. J. Payton, B. T. Ray, M. J. Ray. **Transfer Agent & Registrar**—Mid-America Bank of Louisville & Trust Co. **Incorporated**—in Kentucky in 1971. **Empl**— 815. **S&P Analyst:** D.J.B.

03-OCT-98

Industry: Retail (Discounters)

Summary: Stein Mart's 165 retail stores offer moderate to designer brand-name apparel for women, men and children, as well as accessories, gifts, linens and shoes.

Quantitative Evaluations

Recent Price • 7¾
52 Wk Range • 19½-6⅛

Yield • Nil
12-Mo. P/E • 11.0

Outlook
(1 Lowest—5 Highest)
• **5+**

Fair Value
• **12⅞**

Risk
• **Average**

Earn./Div. Rank
• **B+**

Technical Eval.
• **Bearish** since 6/98

Rel. Strength Rank
(1 Lowest—99 Highest)
• **25**

Insider Activity
• **Neutral**

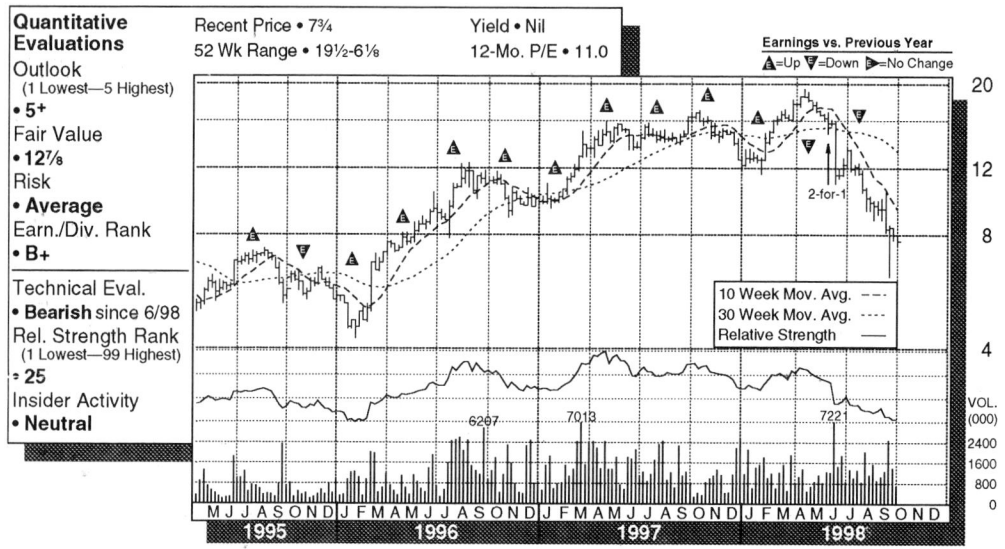

Business Profile - 15-JUN-98

In June 1998, Stein Mart announced that earnings for the second quarter of 1998 will be about $0.20 per share, lower than analysts' expectations of about $0.26 per share. For the second half of 1998, the company expects to resume its growth by focusing on making the necessary adjustments in merchandising and marketing. SMRT has grown rapidly, more than doubling the number of its stores in operation over the past five years. Stein Mart plans to open 30 new locations in 1998, including four opened during the first quarter. The company added 28 new stores in 1997.

Operational Review - 15-JUN-98

Net sales for the three months ended April 4, 1998, advanced 12%, year to year, due to new store openings, partly offset by a comparable-store sales decrease of 0.8%. The same-store sales decline for the quarter was due to the shift of the Easter holiday into the second quarter in 1998. Gross margins were flat, and SG&A costs as a percent of sales edged up. After taxes at 38.0%, versus 39.0%, net income dropped 49% to $709,000 ($0.02 a share) from $1,395,000 ($0.03).

Stock Performance - 02-OCT-98

In the past 30 trading days, SMRT's shares have declined 19%, compared to a 7% fall in the S&P 500. Average trading volume for the past five days was 135,140 shares, compared with the 40-day moving average of 286,554 shares.

Key Stock Statistics

Dividend Rate/Share	Nil	Shareholders	1,000
Shs. outstg. (M)	45.7	Market cap. (B)	$0.353
Avg. daily vol. (M)	0.338	Inst. holdings	51%
Tang. Bk. Value/Share	3.70		
Beta	0.58		

Value of $10,000 invested 5 years ago: $ 16,840

Fiscal Year Ending Dec. 31

	1998	1997	1996	1995	1994	1993
Revenues (Million $)						
1Q	169.5	151.4	108.5	87.71	79.15	62.43
2Q	214.0	183.6	149.4	116.5	97.92	79.97
3Q	—	166.7	131.3	108.2	90.71	75.89
4Q	—	290.9	227.0	183.6	151.4	124.4
Yr.	—	792.7	616.1	496.0	419.2	342.7
Earnings Per Share ($)						
1Q	0.02	0.03	-0.01	-0.03	0.01	-0.01
2Q	0.19	0.20	0.17	0.11	0.10	0.10
3Q	—	0.07	0.05	0.04	0.04	0.04
4Q	—	0.43	0.34	0.26	0.24	0.23
Yr.	—	0.73	0.55	0.38	0.39	0.35

Next earnings report expected: late October

Dividend Data

Amount ($)	Date Decl.	Ex-Div. Date	Stock of Record	Payment Date
2-for-1	Apr. 28	May. 26	May. 08	May. 22 '98

STANDARD
&POOR'S
STOCK REPORTS

Stein Mart, Inc.

5322

03-OCT-98

Business Summary - 15-JUN-98

Stein Mart, Inc. (SMRT) operated a single store in Greenville, MS from the early 1900s until 1977, when it embarked on an ambitious expansion program. By the end of 1997, this retail chain operated 151 stores offering fashionable, primarily branded merchandise, comparable in quality and presentation to that of traditional department and fine specialty stores, at prices typically 25%-60% below those charged by such stores.

SMRT's merchandise assortment features moderate to designer brand-name apparel for men, women and children, as well as accessories, gifts, linens, shoes and fragrances.

SMRT's business strategy is to maintain the quality of merchandise, store appearance, merchandise presentation and customer service level of traditional department and fine quality stores and to offer value pricing to its customers through its vendor relationships, tight control over corporate and store expenses and efficient management of inventory. SMRT differentiates itself from other off-price retailers by offering a higher percentage of current-season merchandise and achieves this by buying from vendors well in advance of the selling season, rather than by buying close-out merchandise or overruns. Its merchandise presentation is also more comparable to that of traditional department and fine specialty stores.

In 1997, net sales were $793 million, versus $616 million in 1996 -- a 29% increase. Net income rose 34% to $34.8 million from $26.0 million. Comparable store net sales increased 7.2% for the year. Sales by category in 1997: Ladies' & Boutique Apparel (38%), Ladies' Accessories (11%), Men's & Young Men's (19%), Gifts & Linens (17%), Shoes -- Leased Department (8%), Children's (6%), and Other (1%).

At the end of 1997, SMRT operated retail stores in 26 states, with the largest concentrations in Texas (30 stores), Florida (20) and Georgia (11), and with store locations stretching across the U.S. from Pennsylvania to Arizona. The company's expansion strategy is to target metropolitan areas with populations of 150,000 or more and to refurbish existing retail locations or to occupy newly constructed stores which typically are anchor stores in new or existing shopping centers.

Management believes that the company occupies a market niche closer to traditional department stores than typical off-price retail chains. SMRT feels it is well positioned to compete in the retail apparel industry in areas of assortment, presentation, quality of merchandise, price, customer service, vendor relations and store locations.

Per Share Data ($)

(Year Ended Dec. 31)	1997	1996	1995	1994	1993	1992	1991	1990	1989	1988
Tangible Bk. Val.	3.61	2.89	2.27	1.90	1.49	1.11	NA	NA	NA	NA
Cash Flow	0.92	0.70	0.49	0.47	0.41	0.36	NA	NA	NA	NA
Earnings	0.73	0.55	0.38	0.39	0.35	0.30	NA	NA	NA	NA
Dividends	Nil	Nil	Nil	Nil	Nil	Nil	Nil	Nil	Nil	Nil
Payout Ratio	Nil	Nil	Nil	Nil	Nil	Nil	Nil	Nil	Nil	Nil
Prices - High	17⅛	12⅜	7½	10¾	12⅛	10½	NA	NA	NA	NA
- Low	9⅜	4¼	4⅝	6⅛	7⅜	3¾	NA	NA	NA	NA
P/E Ratio - High	23	18	20	28	35	34	NA	NA	NA	NA
- Low	13	6	12	16	21	12	NA	NA	NA	NA

Income Statement Analysis (Million $)

	1997	1996	1995	1994	1993	1992	1991	1990	1989	1988
Revs.	793	616	496	419	343	278	NA	NA	NA	NA
Oper. Inc.	57.7	43.2	29.2	30.3	27.1	21.5	NA	NA	NA	NA
Depr.	8.8	6.7	5.2	4.1	3.1	2.4	NA	NA	NA	NA
Int. Exp.	1.2	1.6	1.3	0.7	0.5	0.8	NA	NA	NA	NA
Pretax Inc.	57.0	42.5	29.1	30.5	27.5	21.4	NA	NA	NA	NA
Eff. Tax Rate	39%	39%	39%	40%	39%	38%	NA	NA	NA	NA
Net Inc.	34.8	26.0	17.8	18.4	16.7	13.4	NA	NA	NA	NA

Balance Sheet & Other Fin. Data (Million $)

	1997	1996	1995	1994	1993	1992	1991	1990	1989	1988
Cash	28.0	23.6	15.1	21.3	9.9	NA	NA	NA	NA	NA
Curr. Assets	208	167	131	119	89.3	NA	NA	NA	NA	NA
Total Assets	271	218	174	154	116	87.0	NA	NA	NA	NA
Curr. Liab.	98.0	80.3	67.7	65.4	46.8	NA	NA	NA	NA	NA
LT Debt	Nil	Nil	Nil	Nil	Nil	Nil	Nil	Nil	Nil	Nil
Common Eqty.	166	132	101	85.3	66.9	50.2	NA	NA	NA	NA
Total Cap.	175	138	106	88.6	69.6	NA	NA	NA	NA	NA
Cap. Exp.	19.7	16.1	13.8	11.5	12.2	3.8	NA	NA	NA	NA
Cash Flow	43.6	32.7	22.9	22.5	19.9	15.8	NA	NA	NA	NA
Curr. Ratio	2.1	2.1	1.9	1.8	1.9	NA	NA	NA	NA	NA
% LT Debt of Cap.	Nil	Nil	Nil	Nil	Nil	Nil	Nil	Nil	Nil	Nil
% Net Inc.of Revs.	4.4	4.2	3.6	4.4	4.9	4.8	NA	NA	NA	NA
% Ret. on Assets	14.2	17.8	10.9	13.6	16.5	NA	NA	NA	NA	NA
% Ret. on Equity	23.4	29.9	19.0	24.2	28.5	NA	NA	NA	NA	NA

Data as orig. reptd.; bef. results of disc. opers. and/or spec. items. Per share data adj. for stk. divs. as of ex-div. date. Bold denotes diluted EPS (FASB 128). E-Estimated. NA-Not Available. NM-Not Meaningful. NR-Not Ranked.

Office—1200 Riverplace Blvd., Jacksonville, FL 32207. **Tel**—(904) 346-1500. **E-mail**—SteinMrt@aol.com **Chrmn & CEO**—J. Stein. **Pres & COO**—J. H. Williams Jr. **SVP & CFO**—J. G. Delfs. **Dirs**—M. Allen, P. Carpenter, A. Ernst Jr., M. W. Legler, M. D. Rose, J. Stein, J. H. Williams Jr., J. H. Winston. **Transfer Agent & Registrar**—ChaseMellon Shareholder Services, Ridgefield Park, NJ. **Incorporated**—in Florida in 1992.**Empl**—9,100. **S&P Analyst:** Ray Lam, CFA

STANDARD &POOR'S
STOCK REPORTS

Stillwater Mining

9298K

ASE Symbol **SWC**

In S&P SmallCap 600

03-OCT-98

Industry:
Gold & Precious Metals
Mining

Summary: This company, the only U.S. producer of platinum and palladium, operates a mining complex in southern Montana.

Quantitative Evaluations

Recent Price • 32⅜
52 Wk Range • 32½-15¼

Yield • Nil
12-Mo. P/E • NM

Outlook
(1 Lowest—5 Highest)
• 3

Fair Value
• 31¼

Risk
• Average

Earn./Div. Rank
• NR

Technical Eval.
• NA

Rel. Strength Rank
(1 Lowest—99 Highest)
• 98

Insider Activity
• NA

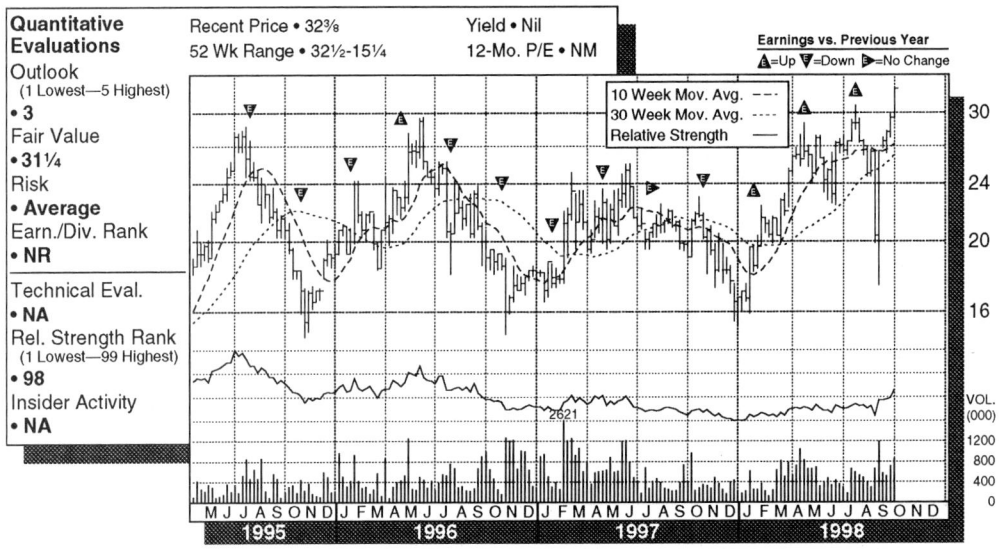

Business Profile - 03-SEP-98

Following an expansion of the Stillwater Mine (located in southern Montana) in 1997, the company recently announced a plan to triple production by 2002. Key elements of the plan include continued mine expansions and the resumption of the East Boulder Project, a plan to drive an 18,500 foot tunnel into the western section of the J-M Reef. In 1997, the company produced approximately 355,000 oz. of platinum and palladium, versus 255,000 oz. in 1996, and cash costs declined to $174 per oz., versus $184 per oz. in 1996. The shares began trading on the American Stock Exchange in June 1997.

Operational Review - 03-SEP-98

Revenues in the first half of 1998 rose 25%, year to year, reflecting a 20% increase in total volume, and a 10% increase in the average palladium selling price. Gross margins widened, reflecting improved operating efficiencies associated with the expansion of the Stillwater Mine, an increased recovery rate, and improved materials handling and processing efficiencies. Following higher G&A expenses, pretax income of $6,577,000 contrasted with a pretax loss of $4,663,000. After taxes at 38.5%, versus a tax benefit of $1,795,000, there was net income of $4,045,000 ($0.20 a share), versus a net loss of $2,868,000 ($0.14).

Stock Performance - 02-OCT-98

In the past 30 trading days, SWC's shares have increased 22%, compared to a 7% fall in the S&P 500. Average trading volume for the past five days was 169,700 shares, compared with the 40-day moving average of 132,449 shares.

Key Stock Statistics

Dividend Rate/Share	Nil	Shareholders	100
Shs. outstg. (M)	20.5	Market cap. (B)	$0.663
Avg. daily vol. (M)	0.137	Inst. holdings	62%
Tang. Bk. Value/Share	7.20		
Beta	NA		

Value of $10,000 invested 5 years ago: NA

Fiscal Year Ending Dec. 31

	1998	1997	1996	1995	1994	1993
Revenues (Million $)						
1Q	21.51	16.00	13.65	13.26	12.50	—
2Q	26.52	22.29	10.65	18.87	14.91	10.65
3Q	—	17.00	16.48	10.65	12.68	—
4Q	—	21.58	15.43	11.29	18.51	—
Yr.	—	76.88	56.21	54.06	58.61	53.80
Earnings Per Share ($)						
1Q	0.05	-0.11	Nil	0.04	-0.01	—
2Q	0.15	-0.04	-0.03	-0.01	0.03	—
3Q	—	-0.08	-0.04	-0.03	0.07	—
4Q	—	-0.04	-0.06	0.01	0.02	—
Yr.	—	-0.27	-0.13	Nil	0.11	0.09

Next earnings report expected: early November

Dividend Data

No dividends have been paid, and the company does not intend to pay any in the foreseeable future.

A Division of The **McGraw·Hill** *Companies*

Business Summary - 03-SEP-98

Stillwater Mining Co. (SWC) began mining operations in 1986 with an underground mine located in the Stillwater Valley. The company now owns or has the rights to 995 claims covering approximately 16,000 acres.

The company is engaged in the exploration, development, mining and production of platinum, palladium and associated metals from the Stillwater Complex in southern Montana, which SWC believes is the only significant primary source of platinum and palladium outside the Republic of South Africa.

The Stillwater Complex includes an extensive mineralized zone containing platinum group metals (PGMs) known as the J-M Reef, which has been traced on surface for approximately 28 miles, and which extends downward over one mile to unknown depths. The Stillwater Complex has been prospected for gold, copper, nickel and chromium since the late 1880s.

The company currently accesses only a small segment of the orebody, approximately five miles long, between the elevations of 6,700 ft. and 3,100 ft. above sea level. The physical configuration of the J-M Reef with its 50 degree to 90 degree dip and relatively wide mining widths in comparison with South Africa's Bushveld Complex makes it amenable to various gravity-assisted, mechanized mining methods.

At December 31, 1997, the company also had proved and probable reserves of some 29.5 million tons of ore with about 23.4 million contained oz. of platinum and palladium in a ratio of 3.3 parts palladium to one part platinum. In 1997, the company produced approximately 355,000 oz. of platinum and palladium, versus 255,000 oz. in 1996. Cash costs in 1997 decreased to $174 per oz., versus $184 per oz. in 1996. Additionally, recovery rates improved to 89% in 1997 from 88% in 1996.

As part of SCW's long-term strategy to expand operations and improve its operating economics, it completed a $70 million expansion plan in 1997, designed to significantly increase production at the Stillwater Mine and associated processing facilities. The company also commissioned a 1,950 foot vertical production shaft to improve ore haulage.

The company intends to triple production by 2002. Key elements of the plan include continued expansion of the Stillwater Mine and the resumption of the East Boulder Project, a plan to drive an 18,500 foot tunnel into the western section of the J-M Reef.

In June 1997, trading in the shares moved to the American Stock Exchange, from the Nasdaq Stock Market.

Per Share Data ($)

(Year Ended Dec. 31)	1997	1996	1995	1994	1993	1992	1991	1990	1989	1988
Tangible Bk. Val.	6.94	7.13	6.59	6.59	4.94	NA	NA	NA	NA	NA
Cash Flow	0.31	0.29	Nil	0.44	0.41	NA	NA	NA	NA	NA
Earnings	-0.27	-0.13	NM	0.11	0.09	NA	NA	NA	NA	NA
Dividends	Nil	Nil	Nil	Nil	Nil	Nil	Nil	Nil	Nil	Nil
Payout Ratio	Nil	Nil	Nil	Nil	Nil	Nil	Nil	Nil	Nil	Nil
Prices - High	25½	29⅝	28¾	13⅝	NA	NA	NA	NA	NA	NA
- Low	15¼	14⅞	13¼	13	NA	NA	NA	NA	NA	NA
P/E Ratio - High	NM	NM	NM	NM	NA	NA	NA	NA	NA	NA
- Low	NM	NM	NM	NM	NA	NA	NA	NA	NA	NA

Income Statement Analysis (Million $)

	1997	1996	1995	1994	1993	1992	1991	1990	1989	1988
Revs.	76.9	56.2	54.1	58.6	53.8	NA	NA	NA	NA	NA
Oper. Inc.	5.5	4.3	3.5	8.1	7.4	NA	NA	NA	NA	NA
Depr.	11.7	8.7	5.8	5.2	4.9	NA	NA	NA	NA	NA
Int. Exp.	3.6	1.5	0.4	0.3	0.1	NA	NA	NA	NA	NA
Pretax Inc.	-8.7	4.5	0.1	2.8	2.4	NA	NA	NA	NA	NA
Eff. Tax Rate	NM	NM	39%	39%	38%	NA	NA	NA	NA	NA
Net Inc.	-5.4	-2.8	0.1	1.7	1.5	NA	NA	NA	NA	NA

Balance Sheet & Other Fin. Data (Million $)

	1997	1996	1995	1994	1993	1992	1991	1990	1989	1988
Cash	4.2	33.4	24.6	57.0	2.5	NA	NA	NA	NA	NA
Curr. Assets	35.3	49.1	45.0	77.2	22.1	NA	NA	NA	NA	NA
Total Assets	229	240	162	153	92.0	NA	NA	NA	NA	NA
Curr. Liab.	12.2	15.8	10.4	9.4	6.8	NA	NA	NA	NA	NA
LT Debt	61.5	62.6	8.7	1.7	1.8	NA	NA	NA	NA	NA
Common Eqty.	141	144	132	132	74.0	NA	NA	NA	NA	NA
Total Cap.	215	222	149	143	84.0	NA	NA	NA	NA	NA
Cap. Exp.	15.8	58.4	46.1	9.3	2.0	NA	NA	NA	NA	NA
Cash Flow	6.3	5.9	5.8	7.0	6.4	NA	NA	NA	NA	NA
Curr. Ratio	2.9	3.1	4.3	8.2	3.3	NA	NA	NA	NA	NA
% LT Debt of Cap.	28.7	28.2	5.8	1.2	2.1	NA	NA	NA	NA	NA
% Net Inc.of Revs.	NM	NM	0.1	2.9	2.7	NA	NA	NA	NA	NA
% Ret. on Assets	NM	NM	NM	1.4	1.6	NA	NA	NA	NA	NA
% Ret. on Equity	NM	NM	NM	1.7	1.9	NA	NA	NA	NA	NA

Data as orig. reptd.; bef. results of disc. opers. and/or spec. items. Per share data adj. for stk. divs. as of ex-div. date. Bold denotes diluted EPS (FASB 128). E-Estimated. NA-Not Available. NM-Not Meaningful. NR-Not Ranked.

Office—536 Pike Ave, Columbus, MT 59019. **Tel**—(303) 978-2525. **Chrmn & CEO**—W. E. Nettles. **Pres & COO**—J. E. Andrews. **CFO**—W. E. Nettles. **Secy**—M. A. Shea. **Dirs**—R. W. Ballmer, D. D. Donald, J. W. Eschenlohr, L. M. Glaser, J. P. Ingersoll, W. E. Nettles, T. Schwinden, P. Steen. **Transfer Agent & Registrar**—American Securities Transfer Inc., Lakewood, CO. **Incorporated**—in Delaware in 1992. **Empl**—675. **S&P Analyst:** E. Hunter

STANDARD &POOR'S
STOCK REPORTS

Stone & Webster

2152

NYSE Symbol **SW**

In S&P SmallCap 600

10-OCT-98

Industry: Engineering & Construction

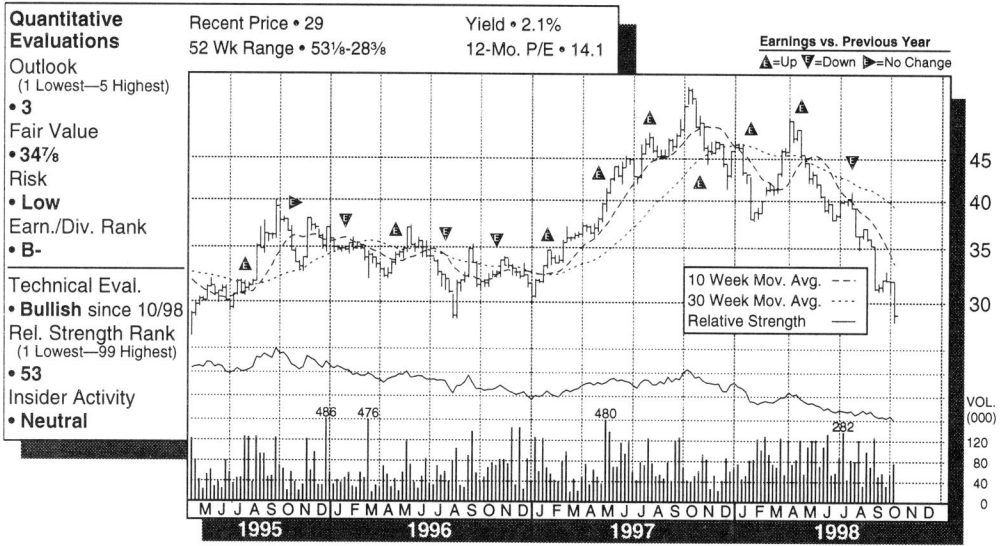**Summary:** This company is primarily a worldwide engineering, design, construction and consulting firm. It also provides cold storage warehousing services.

Quantitative Evaluations

Recent Price • 29
52 Wk Range • 53⅛-28⅜

Yield • 2.1%
12-Mo. P/E • 14.1

Outlook
(1 Lowest—5 Highest)
• 3

Fair Value
• 34⅞

Risk
• **Low**

Earn./Div. Rank
• **B-**

Technical Eval.
• **Bullish** since 10/98

Rel. Strength Rank
(1 Lowest—99 Highest)
• 53

Insider Activity
• Neutral

Earnings vs. Previous Year
▲=Up ▼=Down ▷=No Change

10 Week Mov. Avg. – – –
30 Week Mov. Avg. ·······
Relative Strength ——

Business Profile - 23-JUL-98

SW has experienced a slowdown in international orders since the second half of 1997, as a result of weakness in Asian markets and the effects of this uncertainty on capital spending. Results in the 1998 second quarter were further affected by charges associated with losses from two large projects. In July 1998, SW said that, despite short-term set-backs, its business outlook remains strong, particularly with regard to the domestic power market, and due to anticipated new projects in the petrochemical and industrial sectors. The company underwent a major organizational and financial restructuring during the latter part of 1996, including consolidation of facilities, reduction of management levels, and liquidation of unprofitable partnership investments.

Operational Review - 23-JUL-98

Revenues in the first half of 1998 slid 3.9%, year to year. Results of the engineering, construction and consulting segment were hurt by a decline in new orders, suspension of a large project in Indonesia, and recognition of a $10.2 million pretax loss on two power projects in the Middle East and Africa. The cold storage business benefited from increased volume and expansion of its customer base. After taxes at 38.0%, versus 34.2%, and a gain of $2.0 million ($0.15 a share) on the sale of an office building, net income fell 45%, to $8,264,000 ($0.64 a share), from $15,050,000 ($1.17).

Stock Performance - 09-OCT-98

In the past 30 trading days, SW's shares have declined 18%, compared to a 4% fall in the S&P 500. Average trading volume for the past five days was 14,980 shares, compared with the 40-day moving average of 15,918 shares.

Key Stock Statistics

Dividend Rate/Share	0.60	Shareholders	5,800
Shs. outstg. (M)	12.8	Market cap. (B)	$0.371
Avg. daily vol. (M)	0.011	Inst. holdings	37%
Tang. Bk. Value/Share	26.96		
Beta	0.70		

Value of $10,000 invested 5 years ago: $ 12,730

Fiscal Year Ending Dec. 31

	1998	1997	1996	1995	1994	1993
Revenues (Million $)						
1Q	294.0	349.5	305.8	222.5	192.7	72.83
2Q	317.0	286.3	268.7	230.7	190.4	78.22
3Q	—	368.2	282.2	219.2	205.4	65.44
4Q	—	318.5	308.1	330.4	229.7	63.30
Yr.	—	1,323	1,165	1,003	818.2	279.8
Earnings Per Share ($)						
1Q	0.59	0.43	0.41	0.32	-0.86	0.02
2Q	0.05	0.74	0.28	0.55	-0.27	0.01
3Q	—	0.73	-2.37	0.35	0.35	0.08
4Q	—	0.69	0.37	-0.18	0.26	-0.14
Yr.	—	2.59	-1.31	1.04	-0.52	-0.03

Next earnings report expected: late October

Dividend Data (Dividends have been paid since 1939.)

Amount ($)	Date Decl.	Ex-Div. Date	Stock of Record	Payment Date
0.150	Oct. 28	Oct. 29	Nov. 01	Nov. 15 '97
0.150	Jan. 27	Jan. 30	Feb. 03	Feb. 14 '98
0.150	Apr. 21	Apr. 29	May. 01	May. 15 '98
0.150	Jul. 21	Jul. 30	Aug. 03	Aug. 15 '98

A Division of The McGraw·Hill Companies

Business Summary - 23-JUL-98

Stone & Webster is primarily engaged in providing professional engineering, construction and consulting services. It also has much less significant operations in cold storage warehousing.

Engineering, construction and consulting services include complete engineering, design, construction, and full environmental services which are provided for power, process, industrial, governmental, transportation, and civil works projects. The company also constructs from plans developed by others, makes engineering reports and business examinations, undertakes consulting engineering work, and offers information management and computer systems expertise to clients. SW offers a full range of services in environmental engineering and sciences, including complete project execution.

Activities that come under the heading of engineering, construction and consulting services also include advanced computer systems development services and products for plant scheduling, information systems, systems integration, computer-aided design, expert systems, and database management; projects in the power and other industries in which SW may take an ownership position and for which it may provide engineering, construction, management and operation and maintenance services; management consulting and financial services for business and industry (including public utility, transportation, pipeline, land development, banking,

petroleum and manufacturing companies and government agencies); and appraisals for industrial companies and utilities. Engineering, construction and consulting services accounted for 98% of total revenues in 1997.

Public cold storage warehousing, blast-freeze and other refrigeration and consolidation services are offered from three facilities near Atlanta, GA.

In October 1996, SW initiated an organizational restructuring program. In connection with this program, the company transferred the Auburn VPS partnership to the construction lenders, in exchange for the cancellation of debt, resulting in an after tax gain of $6.8 million. During the remainder of 1996, and into 1997, SW consolidated its New York and Boston corporate offices, putting its excess New York office space on the market; reduced excess management; exited unprofitable partnerships; implemented a management compensation plan designed to improve accountability; and recruited both management talent and directors from outside the company. As a result of the restructuring and asset divestitures, SW recorded pretax charges totaling $58.6 million in 1996.

Order backlog at December 31, 1997, was $2.5 billion, little changed from the level a year earlier. Included in the 1997 backlog was $538 million for a grassroots petrochemical project in Indonesia, which has been suspended pending resolution of financing issues with the client. Construction on the project was not expected to resume during 1998.

Per Share Data ($)

(Year Ended Dec. 31)	1997	1996	1995	1994	1993	1992	1991	1990	1989	1988
Tangible Bk. Val.	26.90	24.71	26.10	25.69	28.40	26.93	26.29	25.22	24.97	24.44
Cash Flow	3.65	-0.04	2.37	0.80	1.32	1.96	2.34	1.64	2.57	3.92
Earnings	2.59	-1.32	1.04	-0.52	-0.03	0.62	1.08	0.50	1.37	2.71
Dividends	0.60	0.45	0.60	0.60	0.60	0.60	0.60	1.05	1.20	1.20
Payout Ratio	23%	NM	58%	NM	NM	97%	56%	210%	87%	44%
Prices - High	55⅛	37⅜	40	34	30¼	31	36¼	41¾	45¾	36⅞
- Low	31⅛	28⅝	27¼	27¼	21¼	23¾	26⅛	25⅛	34⅛	29⅞
P/E Ratio - High	21	NM	38	NM	NM	50	34	84	33	14
- Low	12	NM	26	NM	NM	38	24	50	25	11

Income Statement Analysis (Million $)

	1997	1996	1995	1994	1993	1992	1991	1990	1989	1988
Revs.	1,323	1,165	1,003	766	262	266	257	232	242	278
Oper. Inc.	61.0	-9.0	54.3	-37.0	26.5	29.4	34.3	5.5	9.8	44.1
Depr.	13.7	16.9	19.2	19.7	20.1	20.1	18.8	17.3	18.1	18.4
Int. Exp.	1.7	6.7	9.0	5.3	3.0	3.0	3.7	4.2	6.1	4.6
Pretax Inc.	50.8	-29.4	23.5	-8.8	8.5	23.6	28.1	14.1	27.2	68.1
Eff. Tax Rate	34%	NM	37%	NM	104%	60%	42%	47%	24%	40%
Net Inc.	33.5	-17.4	14.9	-7.8	-0.4	9.3	16.4	7.5	20.8	41.2

Balance Sheet & Other Fin. Data (Million $)

	1997	1996	1995	1994	1993	1992	1991	1990	1989	1988
Cash	75.0	61.9	123	130	119	104	81.0	70.0	103	89.0
Curr. Assets	409	394	364	278	292	286	306	296	314	317
Total Assets	739	692	717	678	680	615	602	569	566	565
Curr. Liab.	297	286	206	141	118	116	119	126	120	120
LT Debt	22.5	24.3	74.7	89.6	47.7	24.8	28.0	11.4	21.6	32.2
Common Eqty.	345	317	362	375	425	403	395	380	378	372
Total Cap.	425	385	488	514	538	475	461	422	425	423
Cap. Exp.	25.9	24.4	28.0	52.3	31.7	26.9	26.6	18.4	21.7	22.6
Cash Flow	47.2	-0.5	34.1	11.9	19.8	29.5	35.2	24.8	38.9	59.6
Curr. Ratio	1.4	1.4	1.8	2.0	2.5	2.5	2.6	2.4	2.6	2.6
% LT Debt of Cap.	5.3	6.3	15.3	17.5	8.9	5.2	6.1	2.7	5.1	7.6
% Net Inc.of Revs.	2.5	NM	1.5	NM	NM	3.5	6.4	3.2	8.6	14.8
% Ret. on Assets	4.7	NM	2.1	NM	NM	1.5	2.8	1.3	3.7	7.4
% Ret. on Equity	10.1	NM	4.0	NM	NM	2.3	4.2	2.0	5.6	11.5

Data as orig. reptd.; bef. results of disc. opers. and/or spec. items. Per share data adj. for stk. divs. as of ex-div. date. Bold denotes diluted EPS (FASB 128). E-Estimated. NA-Not Available. NM-Not Meaningful. NR-Not Ranked.

Office—245 Summer Street, Boston, MA, 02210. **Tel**—(617) 589-5111. **Chrmn, Pres & CEO**—H. K. Smith. **VP & Secy**—J. P. Jones. **Treas**—H. A. Halpin.**Dirs**—D. F. Bethell, F. J. A. Cilluffo, K. F. Hansen, E. R. Heiberg III, D. N. McCammon, J. A. McKee, J. P. Merrill, Jr., B. W. Reznicek, H. K. Smith, E. J. Walsh, P. M. Wood. **Transfer Agent & Registrar**—ChaseMellon Shareholder Services, Ridgefield Park, NJ.**Incorporated**—in Delaware in 1929. **Empl**— 6,100. **S&P Analyst:** S.A.H.

STANDARD &POOR'S
STOCK REPORTS

Stride Rite

2155

NYSE Symbol **SRR**

In S&P SmallCap 600

03-OCT-98

Industry:
Footwear

Summary: SRR is a leading marketer of children's and adults' footwear sold under the Stride Rite, Sperry Top-Sider, Keds, Tommy Hilfiger and other names.

Quantitative Evaluations		
Outlook (1 Lowest—5 Highest) • **4+**	Recent Price • 7¾	Yield • 2.6%
Fair Value • **12⅜**	52 Wk Range • 15¾-7½	12-Mo. P/E • 13.6

Risk
• **Average**

Earn./Div. Rank
• **B+**

Technical Eval.
• **Bullish** since 9/98

Rel. Strength Rank
(1 Lowest—99 Highest)
• **16**

Insider Activity
• **Neutral**

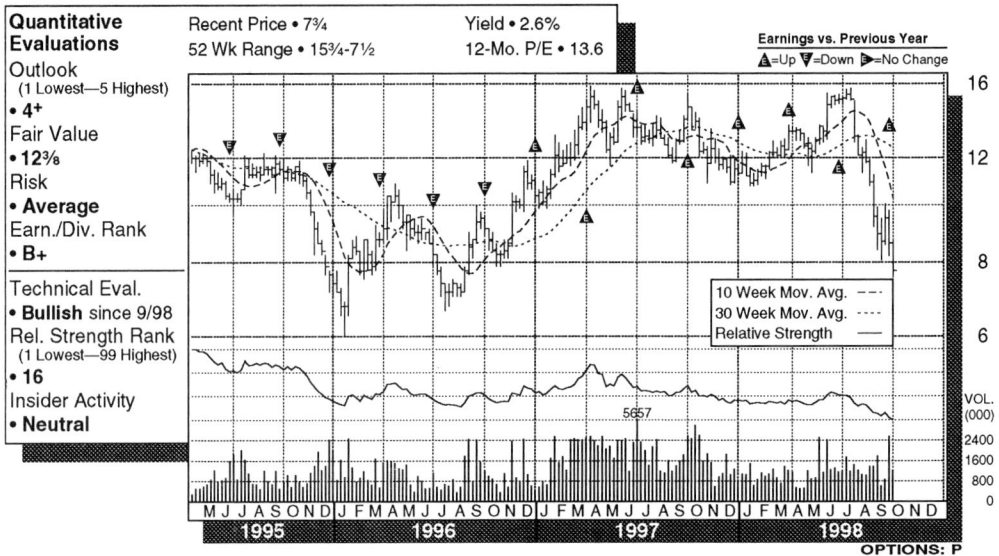

Earnings vs. Previous Year
△=Up ▽=Down ▷=No Change

10 Week Mov. Avg. ---
30 Week Mov. Avg. ----
Relative Strength —

OPTIONS: P

Business Profile - 08-JUL-98

Sales growth has been driven recently by several licensing agreements with major designers. The Tommy Hilfiger line was particularly well received in FY 97 (Nov.), boosting sales. During FY 97, SRR added three new brands: Levi's for men and boys, Tommy Hilfiger for women, and Nine West Kids for girls. These brands will be introduced in the second half of FY 98, and the company believes that the additional lines will prove successful. Although profitability improved in every business line in FY 97, the company expects further efficiency gains in FY 98. In the first half of FY 98, a real estate gain of $0.05 a share was outweighed by costs of $0.06 a share related to the startup of new licensed brands. SRR anticipates that these licensing initiatives will contribute to revenue growth in the second half of FY 98, and in FY 99.

Operational Review - 08-JUL-98

Net sales in the six months ended May 29, 1998, slid fractionally, year to year. Gross margins widened, as costs of goods sold declined more rapidly. With selling and administrative expenses down 1.5%, and a surge in other income, pretax income increased 26%. After taxes at 36.5%, versus 36.0%, net income was up 25%, to $13,997,000 ($0.29 a share, diluted), from $11,197,000 ($0.22).

Stock Performance - 02-OCT-98

In the past 30 trading days, SRR's shares have declined 29%, compared to a 7% fall in the S&P 500. Average trading volume for the past five days was 242,160 shares, compared with the 40-day moving average of 316,479 shares.

Key Stock Statistics

Dividend Rate/Share	0.20	Shareholders	5,100
Shs. outstg. (M)	47.3	Market cap. (B)	$0.367
Avg. daily vol. (M)	0.347	Inst. holdings	71%
Tang. Bk. Value/Share	5.31		
Beta	1.41		

Value of $10,000 invested 5 years ago: $ 3,976

Fiscal Year Ending Nov. 30

	1998	1997	1996	1995	1994	1993
Revenues (Million $)						
1Q	129.0	131.8	118.9	134.8	122.1	140.8
2Q	143.2	141.6	124.2	144.4	161.7	164.5
3Q	168.5	144.5	123.5	139.1	155.0	166.5
4Q	—	97.86	81.67	78.13	85.14	111.1
Yr.	—	515.7	448.3	496.4	523.9	582.9

Earnings Per Share ($)						
1Q	0.09	0.09	0.02	0.10	0.10	0.00
2Q	**0.20**	0.14	0.06	0.08	0.15	0.38
3Q	**0.27**	0.17	0.06	0.07	0.17	0.36
4Q	—	0.01	-0.10	-0.42	-0.02	0.15
Yr.	—	0.40	0.05	-0.17	0.40	1.19

Next earnings report expected: early January

Dividend Data (Dividends have been paid since 1955.)

Amount ($)	Date Decl.	Ex-Div. Date	Stock of Record	Payment Date
0.050	Oct. 17	Nov. 21	Nov. 25	Dec. 15 '97
0.050	Feb. 12	Feb. 19	Feb. 23	Mar. 16 '98
0.050	Apr. 17	May. 21	May. 26	Jun. 15 '98
0.050	Aug. 13	Aug. 24	Aug. 26	Sep. 15 '98

A Division of The McGraw-Hill Companies

Business Summary - 08-JUL-98

With brand names such as Munchkin, Sperry Top-Sider and Keds, Stride Rite Corp. is the leading marketer of children's footwear in the U.S., and a major marketer of athletic and casual footwear for children and adults. After closing manufacturing facilities in the U.S. and in the Caribbean, the company now purchases substantially all of its products overseas.

The company markets children's footwear under the trademarks Stride Rite, Munchkin, Sperry and Street Hot. Children's and adults' marine shoes and outdoor recreational and casual footwear are marketed under SRR's Sperry Top-Sider and Sperry trademarks. Casual and athletic footwear is marketed for adults and children under the Keds, Pro-Keds and Grasshoppers trademarks.

Since the spring of 1997, SRR has been producing and marketing a line of premium dress casual, sport casual, dress and athletic men's footwear under the Tommy Hilfiger trademark. Prior to the back to school season in 1997, SRR launched a line of Tommy Hilfiger shoes for boys. The company plans to introduce a complete line of footwear for women and girls in the second half of FY 98 (Nov.).

Footwear is distributed through independent retail stores, including Stride Rite Bootery stores, department stores, sporting goods stores and marinas, and company-owned stores, including manufacturer's outlet stores, Keds concept stores, Great Feet concept stores and children's footwear departments in department stores.

At the end of FY 97, the company operated 119 Stride Rite Bootery stores, one Keds stores, four Great Feet stores, 58 leased children's shoe departments in department stores, and 19 manufacturer's outlet stores for Stride Rite, Keds, Sperry Top-Sider and Tommy Hilfiger brand products.

In FY 97, SRR opened one leased departments and two manufacturers' outlet stores. It also began operation of one Stride Rite bootery and closed 16 retail stores. The company plans to open 5 to 10 stores in FY 98, and to close 10 to 15 underperforming stores.

In April 1997, the company said it was creating a new division, dedicated to the Levi's footwear business. Levi Strauss and Co. and Stride Rite signed a licensing agreement under which SRR is to develop and market a line of Levi's footwear for men, women and children. Retail prices were expected to range from $55 to $110 a pair. In July 1997, SRR and Nine West announced an agreement for Stride Rite to produce and distribute a collection of children's footwear under the Nine West Kids label. The company expects both the Nine West Kids shoes and the Levi's footwear line to be available in the second half of FY 98.

Per Share Data ($)

(Year Ended Nov. 30)	1997	1996	1995	1994	1993	1992	1991	1990	1989	1988
Tangible Bk. Val.	5.09	5.24	5.37	5.74	5.81	5.12	4.64	3.54	3.09	2.47
Cash Flow	0.60	0.24	0.05	0.57	1.31	1.30	1.36	1.14	0.94	0.71
Earnings	0.40	0.05	-0.17	0.40	1.19	1.19	1.28	1.05	0.86	0.64
Dividends	0.20	0.20	0.43	0.38	0.35	0.31	0.26	0.20	0.17	0.14
Payout Ratio	50%	NM	NM	95%	29%	26%	20%	18%	20%	22%
Prices - High	15⁷/₈	11⁷/₈	13¹/₄	18⁷/₈	23¹/₈	31⁷/₈	30¹/₄	15¹/₄	15¹/₈	8⁷/₈
- Low	9⁷/₈	6	7	10¹/₂	12¹/₈	16³/₈	13³/₈	9³/₄	6¹/₂	3³/₈
P/E Ratio - High	40	NM	NM	47	19	27	24	14	18	14
- Low	25	NM	NM	26	10	14	10	9	8	6

Income Statement Analysis (Million $)

	1997	1996	1995	1994	1993	1992	1991	1990	1989	1988
Revs.	516	448	496	524	583	586	574	516	454	379
Oper. Inc.	40.9	11.0	11.0	47.0	107	122	109	94.0	83.0	62.0
Depr.	9.8	9.7	10.9	8.5	6.3	5.4	4.2	4.3	4.4	3.9
Int. Exp.	0.2	0.7	1.0	0.5	0.5	0.5	0.7	1.8	3.3	1.7
Pretax Inc.	31.9	3.0	-18.1	33.0	98.0	100	108	90.0	77.0	58.0
Eff. Tax Rate	38%	17%	NA	39%	38%	39%	39%	39%	40%	40%
Net Inc.	19.8	2.5	-8.4	19.8	60.3	61.5	66.0	55.5	46.2	34.7

Balance Sheet & Other Fin. Data (Million $)

	1997	1996	1995	1994	1993	1992	1991	1990	1989	1988
Cash	41.7	57.2	54.0	76.0	104	98.2	88.4	32.9	24.8	12.6
Curr. Assets	272	296	292	331	344	345	301	235	220	212
Total Assets	344	364	367	397	412	384	332	266	252	243
Curr. Liab.	95.4	94.5	88.0	94.0	100	98.3	78.0	66.7	64.4	91.6
LT Debt	Nil	Nil	0.8	1.7	2.5	3.3	4.2	5.0	5.8	6.7
Common Eqty.	242	262	267	293	302	272	240	181	167	134
Total Cap.	249	270	279	302	312	285	254	199	187	152
Cap. Exp.	14.3	7.8	22.3	8.5	33.9	3.7	3.5	2.7	4.3	9.5
Cash Flow	29.6	12.1	2.4	28.3	66.6	66.9	70.2	59.8	50.6	38.7
Curr. Ratio	2.8	3.1	3.3	3.5	3.4	3.5	3.9	3.5	3.4	2.3
% LT Debt of Cap.	Nil	Nil	0.3	0.6	0.8	1.2	1.6	2.5	3.1	4.4
% Net Inc.of Revs.	3.8	NM	NM	3.8	10.3	10.5	11.5	10.8	10.2	9.2
% Ret. on Assets	5.6	NM	NM	4.9	15.2	17.3	21.9	22.0	18.7	15.9
% Ret. on Equity	7.9	NM	NM	6.7	21.1	24.2	31.1	32.7	30.8	27.8

Data as orig. reptd.; bef. results of disc. opers. and/or spec. items. Per share data adj. for stk. divs. as of ex-div. date. Bold denotes diluted EPS (FASB 128). E-Estimated. NA-Not Available. NM-Not Meaningful. NR-Not Ranked.

Office—191 Spring St., P.O. Box 9191, Lexington, MA 02420-9191. **Tel**—(617) 824-6000. **Website**—http://www.striderite.com**Chrmn & Pres**—R. C. Siegel. **VP, CFO, Treas & Investor Contact**—John M. Kelliher (617-824-6028).**Secy & Clerk**—C. W. Redepenning.**Dirs**—D. R. Gant, W. Flick, M. A. McKenna, F. R. Mori, R. L. Seelert, R. C. Siegel, M. J. Slosberg, W. P. Tippett, Jr. **Transfer Agent & Registrar**—BankBoston, N.A.**Incorporated**—in Massachusetts in 1919. **Empl**— 2,900. **S&P Analyst:** Kathleen J. Fraser

STANDARD &POOR'S
STOCK REPORTS

Sturm, Ruger
2156F

NYSE Symbol **RGR**

In S&P SmallCap 600

06-OCT-98

Industry:
Leisure Time (Products)

Summary: This leading manufacturer of rifles and handguns for sporting and law enforcement purposes also produces ferrous and nonferrous investment castings.

Quantitative Evaluations		
Outlook (1 Lowest—5 Highest) • **3**		
Fair Value • **15¾**		
Risk • **NA**		
Earn./Div. Rank • **B+**		
Technical Eval. • **Neutral** since 8/98		
Rel. Strength Rank (1 Lowest—99 Highest) • **79**		
Insider Activity • **Neutral**		

Recent Price • 15
52 Wk Range • 21¼-13⅜

Yield • 5.3%
12-Mo. P/E • 14.5

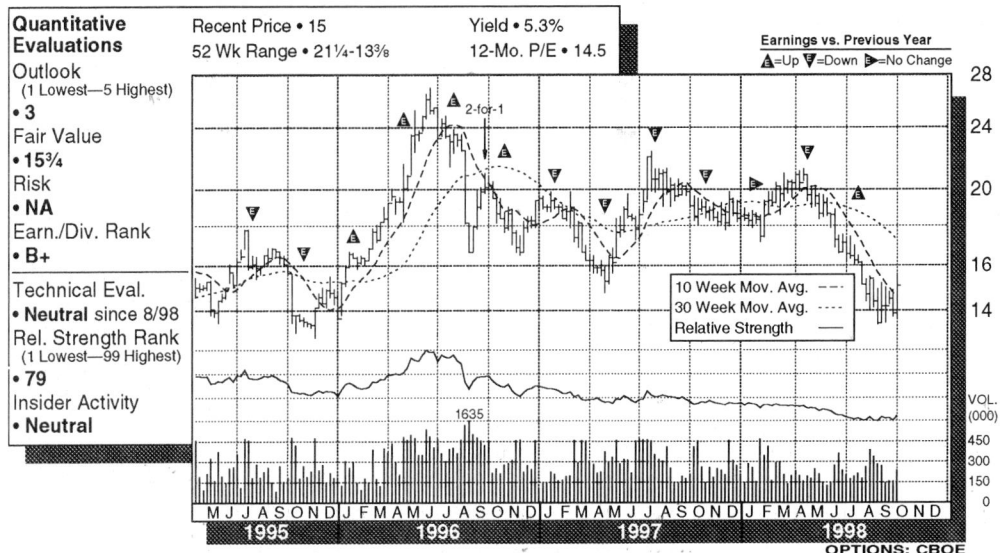

10 Week Mov. Avg. – –
30 Week Mov. Avg. ····
Relative Strength —

OPTIONS: CBOE

Business Profile - 06-OCT-98

This company believes that it is the largest U.S. firearms manufacturer, and the only one that offers products in all four industry categories (pistols, revolvers, rifles and shotguns). It has a preeminent reputation among sportsmen, hunters and gun collectors for technical innovation and quality construction. The company also manufactures precision metal investment castings. RGR continues to develop new firearms products in an effort to improve this segment's performance. As of March 1998, unfilled firearms orders totaled $93 million, down from $122 million a year earlier. RGR expects capital expenditures for 1998 to total $8.3 million.

Operational Review - 06-OCT-98

Net sales in the first half of 1998 rose 8.1%, year to year, as higher castings segment sales due to increased shipments of titanium golf club heads to Callaway more than offset a decline in firearms sales. Gross margins narrowed on lower firearms volume and pricing pressures in both the firearms and castings segments, but with a rise in other income, pretax earnings edged up 0.8%. After taxes at 40.5%, versus 40.7%, net income was up 1.1%, to $15,569,000 ($0.58 a share), from $15,396,000 ($0.57). RGR noted that its shipments to Callaway Golf may not continue at the current level for the balance of 1998, and it has begun shipping to other golf club makers.

Stock Performance - 02-OCT-98

In the past 30 trading days, RGR's shares have increased 5%, compared to a 7% fall in the S&P 500. Average trading volume for the past five days was 47,280 shares, compared with the 40-day moving average of 50,231 shares.

Key Stock Statistics

Dividend Rate/Share	0.80	Shareholders	1,900
Shs. outstg. (M)	26.9	Market cap. (B)	$0.404
Avg. daily vol. (M)	0.037	Inst. holdings	38%
Tang. Bk. Value/Share	5.85		
Beta	0.47		

Value of $10,000 invested 5 years ago: $ 19,864

Fiscal Year Ending Dec. 31

	1998	1997	1996	1995	1994	1993
Revenues (Million $)						
1Q	58.52	55.09	65.56	50.30	51.05	51.68
2Q	60.00	54.51	65.93	45.20	48.55	48.25
3Q	—	47.23	48.04	42.09	44.94	41.95
4Q	—	52.56	43.78	54.88	51.89	52.31
Yr.	—	209.4	223.3	192.5	196.4	194.2
Earnings Per Share ($)						
1Q	0.27	0.29	0.41	0.32	0.36	0.32
2Q	0.31	0.28	0.43	0.31	0.33	0.32
3Q	—	0.18	0.21	0.08	0.26	0.21
4Q	—	0.28	0.22	0.34	0.33	0.39
Yr.	—	1.03	1.28	0.97	1.26	1.24

Next earnings report expected: NA

Dividend Data (Dividends have been paid since 1955.)

Amount ($)	Date Decl.	Ex-Div. Date	Stock of Record	Payment Date
0.200	Oct. 29	Nov. 26	Dec. 01	Dec. 15 '97
0.200	Jan. 26	Feb. 26	Mar. 02	Mar. 16 '98
0.200	May. 12	May. 28	Jun. 01	Jun. 15 '98
0.200	Jul. 30	Aug. 28	Sep. 01	Sep. 15 '98

A Division of The McGraw·Hill Companies

Business Summary - 06-OCT-98

Founded in 1949, Sturm, Ruger & Co., Inc. (RGR) is the largest firearms manufacturer in the U.S. and the only one that makes firearms in all four industry categories - rifles, shotguns, pistols and revolvers. Southport, CT-based RGR also produces precision metal investment castings.

The company's "Ruger" firearms are made for a variety of sporting and law enforcement purposes. Targeted end-users include sportsmen, hunters, law enforcement organizations and gun collectors. As of early 1998, RGR manufactured 28 types of firearm products, with most available in several models, based upon caliber, finish, barrel length and other features.

Firearms (68% of 1997 sales) consist of .22-caliber target pistols; single-action revolvers in various calibers from .22 to .44 magnum; .22 caliber sporting carbines; single shot and bolt-action rifles; hunting rifles in .223 and 7.62 x 39mm calibers; double-action revolvers; 9mm, .40 and .45 caliber pistols; police and military automatic rifles; and over-and-under shotguns.

RGR aims to position its products at the high end of their respective markets, and emphasizes that it does not manufacture inexpensive, concealable firearms. In addition, RGR does not make any firearm classified as an assault weapon by the 1994 crime bill. In 1997,

Jerry's Sport Center accounted for 16% of the company's firearms sales and 11% of net sales.

Many of the firearms introduced by RGR over the years have retained their popularity for decades, and are sought by collectors. These include the single-action Single-Six, Blackhawk and Bearcat revolvers, the double-action Redhawk revolvers, and the 10/22, M-77 and Number One Single-Shot rifles. In 1997, the company introduced several new firearms, including the new Ruger 77/50 Muzzleloading rifle, the compact Ruger 77/44 Bolt Action rifle, and the Ruger Carbine, an autoloading rifle which uses pistol ammunition. In 1996, RGR introduced the Model 96 lever action rifle, the 10/22T Target rifle, the P95 pistol, and the MK-4B .22 caliber target pistol.

Ferrous, aluminum and titanium investment casting facilities (32% of 1997 sales) produce parts used in RGR's firearms, as well as for outside commercial customers in several different industries. Foremost among these in recent periods has been the sale of the popular Great Big Bertha series of titanium golf club heads for Callaway Golf Co.

In June 1995, RGR and Callaway entered into an equally owned joint venture, Antelope Hills, to build and operate a foundry for the production of titanium golf club heads. The facility was completed in the first quarter of 1997. In June 1997, RGR purchased Callaway's 50% interest in Antelope Hills and operations began.

Per Share Data ($)

(Year Ended Dec. 31)	1997	1996	1995	1994	1993	1992	1991	1990	1989	1988
Tangible Bk. Val.	5.68	5.45	4.97	4.70	4.03	3.33	3.14	2.90	2.67	2.37
Cash Flow	1.37	1.56	1.23	1.46	1.40	0.97	0.71	0.66	0.83	0.60
Earnings	1.03	1.28	0.97	1.26	1.24	0.82	0.54	0.50	0.68	0.47
Dividends	0.80	0.80	0.70	0.60	0.53	0.63	0.30	0.28	0.38	0.97
Payout Ratio	78%	63%	72%	47%	43%	76%	55%	55%	56%	206%
Prices - High	22³/₈	27	17⁷/₈	16⁵/₈	16	10¹/₄	7³/₈	7⁷/₈	9¹/₈	6¹/₈
- Low	14³/₄	13⁷/₈	13	12	9⁵/₈	6¹/₂	5¹/₄	5³/₈	4⁷/₈	3¹/₂
P/E Ratio - High	22	21	18	13	13	12	14	16	14	13
- Low	14	11	13	9	8	8	10	11	7	7

Income Statement Analysis (Million $)

	1997	1996	1995	1994	1993	1992	1991	1990	1989	1988
Revs.	209	224	192	196	194	156	137	135	134	112
Oper. Inc.	54.6	61.5	47.5	59.6	58.8	40.0	30.0	29.5	32.2	23.5
Depr.	9.2	7.6	6.9	5.3	4.3	4.1	4.7	4.3	4.2	3.4
Int. Exp.	Nil	Nil	Nil	Nil	Nil	Nil	Nil	Nil	Nil	Nil
Pretax Inc.	46.6	56.8	43.8	57.0	56.0	37.1	24.3	22.3	29.5	21.3
Eff. Tax Rate	41%	40%	40%	40%	41%	40%	40%	40%	39%	41%
Net Inc.	27.8	34.4	26.2	34.0	33.2	22.2	14.6	13.5	18.1	12.7

Balance Sheet & Other Fin. Data (Million $)

	1997	1996	1995	1994	1993	1992	1991	1990	1989	1988
Cash	4.5	33.4	47.1	66.4	59.6	31.4	22.3	9.0	14.6	12.1
Curr. Assets	125	119	118	119	106	85.5	77.0	66.4	62.5	57.7
Total Assets	200	190	179	169	150	124	116	107	100	90.0
Curr. Liab.	27.7	23.9	25.6	24.7	24.6	18.5	16.0	13.9	12.3	12.7
LT Debt	Nil	Nil	Nil	Nil	Nil	Nil	Nil	Nil	Nil	Nil
Common Eqty.	153	147	134	126	108	89.7	84.4	78.0	71.6	63.6
Total Cap.	153	147	134	126	108	89.7	84.4	78.0	71.6	63.6
Cap. Exp.	4.5	7.6	15.7	12.4	7.3	3.5	3.0	7.1	8.2	5.3
Cash Flow	37.0	42.0	33.1	39.3	37.6	26.3	19.2	17.9	22.3	16.1
Curr. Ratio	4.5	5.0	4.6	4.8	4.3	4.6	4.8	4.8	5.1	4.5
% LT Debt of Cap.	Nil	Nil	Nil	Nil	Nil	Nil	Nil	Nil	Nil	Nil
% Net Inc.of Revs.	13.3	15.4	13.7	17.3	17.1	14.2	10.7	10.0	13.6	11.3
% Ret. on Assets	14.2	18.7	15.1	21.3	24.2	18.4	13.1	13.0	19.0	13.5
% Ret. on Equity	18.5	24.5	20.2	29.0	33.5	25.4	18.0	18.1	26.8	18.0

Data as orig. reptd.; bef. results of disc. opers. and/or spec. items. Per share data adj. for stk. divs. as of ex-div. date. Bold denotes diluted EPS (FASB 128). E-Estimated. NA-Not Available. NM-Not Meaningful. NR-Not Ranked.

Office—1 Lacey Place, Southport, CT 06490. **Tel**—(203) 259-7843. **Website**—http://www.ruger-firearms.com **Chrmn, CEO & Treas**—W. B. Ruger. **Vice-Chrmn, Pres & COO**—W. B. Ruger, Jr. **VP & CFO**—E. G. Blanchard. **Secy**—L. M. Gasper. **Dirs**—R. T. Cunniff, T. Hornor, P. X. Kelley, J. M. Kingsley Jr., W. B. Ruger, W. B. Ruger Jr., S. L. Sanetti, J. E. Service, S. B. Terhune. **Transfer Agent & Registrar**—Harris Trust Co. of New York, NYC. **Incorporated**—in Delaware in 1969. **Empl**— 2,064. **S&P Analyst:** Stewart Scharf

STANDARD & POOR'S
STOCK REPORTS

Summit Technology   5342K

NASDAQ Symbol **BEAM**

In S&P SmallCap 600

03-OCT-98

Industry:
Health Care (Medical Products & Supplies)

Summary: This company develops, makes and sells ophthalmic laser systems used to treat common refractive vision disorders.

Quantitative Evaluations

Outlook
(1 Lowest—5 Highest)
• **3**

Fair Value
• **5**

Risk
• **High**

Earn./Div. Rank
• **C**

Technical Eval.
• **Bearish** since 6/98

Rel. Strength Rank
(1 Lowest—99 Highest)
• **38**

Insider Activity
• **NA**

Recent Price • 3⅞
52 Wk Range • 10⅛-3

Yield • Nil
12-Mo. P/E • 3.2

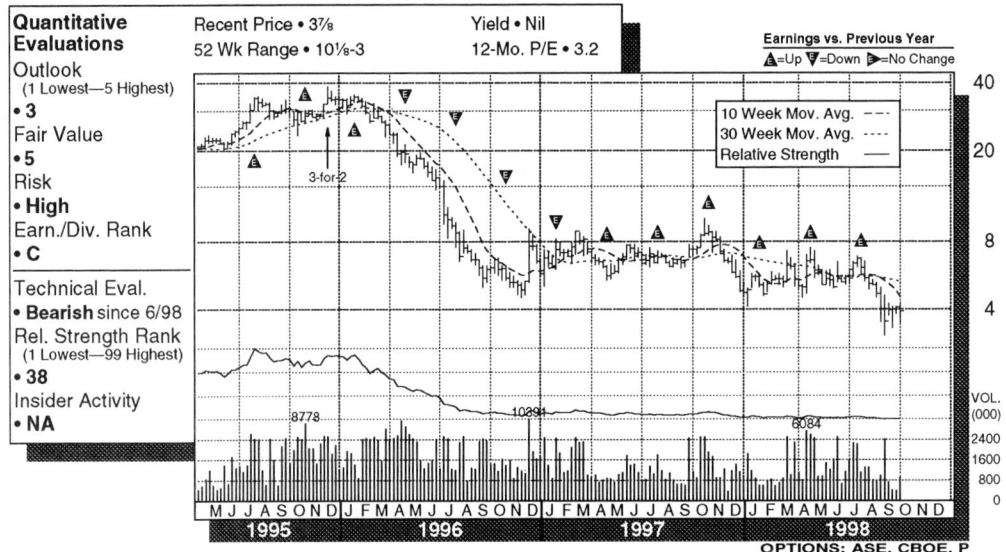

OPTIONS: ASE, CBOE, P

Business Profile - 24-AUG-98

Results in the 1998 second quarter benefited from the settlement of all pending royalty payment litigation between the company and VISX, Inc., under which VISX paid Summit $34.4 million. The companies have also granted each other, a worldwide, royalty free cross license providing each party the right to license their laser system users to all patents owned by either company. Summit remains focused on raising awareness and educating the public about laser vision correction. In addition, through an educational grant given by Summit, Tufts New England Eye Center operates the LASIK Institute, providing training to opthalmologists interested in performing laser vision correction surgery.

Operational Review - 24-AUG-98

Revenues for the six months ended June 30, 1998, rose 15%, year to year, primarily due to higher systems sales and increased license fees, service and other revenues. Results from operations were penalized by significant investments in the sales and marketing areas in order to grow laser vision correction procedure volume. However, profit comparisons benefited from a $34.4 million ($0.94 a share) litigation settlement payment from VISX, Inc. Net income surged to $30,681,000 ($0.98 a share) from $1,172,000 ($0.04 a share). Excluding the $34.4 million settlement, net of related taxes and expenses, net income was $1.1 million ($0.04).

Stock Performance - 02-OCT-98

In the past 30 trading days, BEAM's shares have declined 16%, compared to a 7% fall in the S&P 500. Average trading volume for the past five days was 181,120 shares, compared with the 40-day moving average of 195,264 shares.

Key Stock Statistics

Dividend Rate/Share	Nil	Shareholders	3,100
Shs. outstg. (M)	31.3	Market cap. (B)	$0.123
Avg. daily vol. (M)	0.132	Inst. holdings	11%
Tang. Bk. Value/Share	4.05		
Beta	1.93		

Value of $10,000 invested 5 years ago: NA

Fiscal Year Ending Dec. 31

	1998	1997	1996	1995	1994	1993
Revenues (Million $)						
1Q	21.84	20.70	12.68	7.11	3.66	6.20
2Q	23.40	23.64	17.96	9.26	5.86	8.66
3Q	—	22.90	21.01	13.81	6.50	7.09
4Q	—	21.55	17.88	14.96	8.19	4.90
Yr.	—	88.79	80.48	45.13	24.21	26.80
Earnings Per Share ($)						
1Q	**0.01**	-0.05	-0.11	-0.08	-0.17	-0.05
2Q	**0.97**	0.08	-0.39	-0.08	-0.17	-0.03
3Q	—	Nil	-0.13	0.01	-0.13	-0.07
4Q	—	**0.01**	-0.27	0.01	-0.15	-0.21
Yr.	—	**0.05**	-0.44	-0.14	-0.63	-0.39

Next earnings report expected: early November

Dividend Data

Amount ($)	Date Decl.	Ex-Div. Date	Stock of Record	Payment Date
Stk	Dec. 08	Dec. 16	Dec. 18	Dec. 29 '97

A Division of The **McGraw·Hill** *Companies*

Business Summary - 24-AUG-98

This company's vision is a world without eyeglasses. Summit Technology (BEAM) is a leading developer, manufacturer and a worldwide marketer of ophthalmic laser systems in over 50 countries. Its systems are designed to correct common refractive vision disorders, such as nearsightedness, farsightedness and astigmatism with a procedure known as laser vision correction. Through its Lens Express subsidiary, Summit sells contact lenses and related products.

In October 1995, BEAM's excimer system became the first excimer laser system to receive commercial approval from the FDA to treat nearsightedness in the U.S. It is also seeking approval to sell the system in Japan. In February 1997, an advanced model of the company's excimer system, the Apex Plus, was also approved by the FDA for the same procedures. The FDA has not approved the excimer system to treat astigmatism and farsightedness.

Laser vision correction, also known as Photorefractive Keratectomy (PRK), is an outpatient procedure performed with the excimer laser to treat nearsightedness, farsightedness and astigmatism requiring about 150 laser pulses, and lasts about 15 to 40 seconds. Phototherapeutic Keratectomy (PTK) is an outpatient procedure performed with the excimer system to treat corneal pathologies. The goal of PTK is to alleviate the symptoms associated with the pathology, not necessarily to cure it.

Lens Express is a leading mail order distributor of contact lenses and related products in the U.S. Sales consist of new and reorders of contact lenses, program sales, sales of eye care solutions and shipping and handling fees. Retail and group sales accounted for over 97% of revenues in 1997.

During the 1998 second quarter, BEAM reached a settlement of all pending litigation between the company and VISX, Inc. Under the agreement, VISX paid Summit $34.4 million and Pillar Point Partners, the companies' jointly held entity was dissolved. Previously, the companies jointly participated in per-procedure royalties through Pillar Point Partners.

In August 1997, BEAM completed the sale of its Refractive Centers International, Inc. subsidiary, which owns and operates its Vision Center business, to LCA-Vision Inc. (LCAV). As part of the agreement, BEAM received about 17 million shares of LCAV's common stock, of which about 9 million shares were distributed to shareholders in December 1997 and the remaining shares, which represent about 20% of LCA's outstanding shares, are being held by BEAM.

Summit seeks to maintain a 30% market share of all laser vision correction procedures. The company believes that it has completed a turnaround and should post solid profitability in 1998, if it holds its market share and laser vision correction volume reaches 350,000 in the U.S. In 1997, procedure volume totaled 200,000, up from 70,000 in 1996.

Per Share Data ($)

(Year Ended Dec. 31)	1997	1996	1995	1994	1993	1992	1991	1990	1989	1988
Tangible Bk. Val.	2.69	3.07	4.45	1.51	1.65	1.32	1.36	0.53	0.68	0.41
Cash Flow	0.15	-0.32	-0.04	-0.53	-0.32	0.04	0.05	-0.01	-0.10	-0.20
Earnings	0.05	-0.44	-0.14	-0.63	-0.39	-0.02	0.03	-0.03	-0.11	-0.21
Dividends	Nil	Nil	Nil	Nil	Nil	Nil	Nil	Nil	Nil	Nil
Payout Ratio	Nil	Nil	Nil	Nil	Nil	Nil	Nil	Nil	Nil	Nil
Prices - High	10$\frac{1}{8}$	35$\frac{1}{2}$	38$\frac{3}{4}$	26$\frac{5}{8}$	20$\frac{1}{2}$	25$\frac{5}{8}$	19$\frac{1}{8}$	12$\frac{3}{8}$	10$\frac{5}{8}$	2$\frac{5}{8}$
- Low	4$\frac{1}{8}$	4$\frac{1}{2}$	18$\frac{3}{8}$	13$\frac{5}{8}$	12	14$\frac{1}{8}$	6$\frac{5}{8}$	3$\frac{7}{8}$	1$\frac{9}{16}$	1
P/E Ratio - High	NM	NM	NM	NM	NM	NM	NM	NM	NM	NM
- Low	NM	NM	NM	NM	NM	NM	NM	NM	NM	NM

Income Statement Analysis (Million $)

	1997	1996	1995	1994	1993	1992	1991	1990	1989	1988
Revs.	88.8	80.5	45.1	24.2	26.8	31.1	22.0	11.6	5.2	1.1
Oper. Inc.	2.5	-15.1	-2.5	-13.2	-7.2	1.0	1.0	-0.6	-1.6	-2.3
Depr.	3.3	3.6	2.5	2.3	1.7	1.3	0.7	0.4	0.2	0.1
Int. Exp.	NA	NA	NA	NA	0.1	0.1	0.1	0.0	0.0	0.0
Pretax Inc.	1.6	-13.4	-3.5	-15.4	-9.2	-0.4	1.0	-0.6	-1.5	-2.2
Eff. Tax Rate	8.35%	NM	NM	NM	NM	NM	47%	Nil	Nil	Nil
Net Inc.	1.5	-13.5	-3.5	15.4	-9.2	-0.4	0.5	-0.7	-1.5	-2.2

Balance Sheet & Other Fin. Data (Million $)

	1997	1996	1995	1994	1993	1992	1991	1990	1989	1988
Cash	35.0	64.9	95.9	17.2	10.9	8.6	17.1	5.9	7.3	4.5
Curr. Assets	87.7	93.3	125	35.5	36.6	32.7	31.0	11.4	10.5	5.3
Total Assets	115	134	157	51.2	50.5	38.8	35.5	13.7	11.5	5.7
Curr. Liab.	19.8	20.2	19.3	12.1	10.0	8.2	5.4	3.4	1.4	0.6
LT Debt	6.3	11.5	1.0	1.2	0.2	0.7	0.4	0.1	0.0	0.1
Common Eqty.	89.0	102	137	37.9	40.4	29.9	29.7	10.1	10.1	5.1
Total Cap.	95.3	113	138	39.1	40.5	30.6	30.1	10.3	10.1	5.1
Cap. Exp.	1.8	5.6	4.1	1.2	3.1	1.8	2.0	1.2	0.8	0.1
Cash Flow	4.8	-9.9	-1.0	-13.1	-7.5	0.9	1.2	-0.3	-1.3	-2.1
Curr. Ratio	4.4	4.6	6.5	2.9	3.7	4.0	5.8	3.4	7.7	9.7
% LT Debt of Cap.	6.6	10.1	0.7	3.0	0.4	2.4	1.3	1.2	0.1	1.2
% Net Inc.of Revs.	1.7	NM	NM	NM	NM	NM	2.4	NM	NM	NM
% Ret. on Assets	1.2	NM	NM	NM	NM	NM	2.0	NM	NM	NM
% Ret. on Equity	1.6	NM	NM	NM	NM	NM	2.5	NM	NM	NM

Data as orig. reptd.; bef. results of disc. opers. and/or spec. items. Per share data adj. for stk. divs. as of ex-div. date. Bold denotes diluted EPS (FASB 128). E-Estimated. NA-Not Available. NM-Not Meaningful. NR-Not Ranked.

Office—21 Hickory Drive, Waltham, MA 02154. **Tel**—(781) 890-1234. **Pres & COO**—D. V. Sharma. **CEO**—R. J. Palmisano. **Clerk**—J. A. Lightman.**VP, Treas & CFO**—R. J. Kelly. **Investor Contact**—Paula Elliott Whelan. **Dirs**—J. A. Bernfeld, R. F. Miller, J. A. Norris, R. J. Palmisano, R. M. Traskos. **Transfer Agent & Registrar**—American Stock Transfer & Trust Co., NYC. **Incorporated**—in Massachusetts in 1985. **Empl**— 529. **S&P Analyst:** John J. Arege

Sunrise Medical   2166

NYSE Symbol **SMD**

In S&P SmallCap 600

03-OCT-98

Industry:
Health Care (Medical Products & Supplies)

Summary: This company manufactures a broad line of medical products used to address rehabilitation, recovery and home respiratory needs.

Quantitative Evaluations

Recent Price • 9¾
52 Wk Range • 16¾-6½

Yield • Nil
12-Mo. P/E • NM

Outlook
(1 Lowest—5 Highest)
• **3⁻**

Fair Value
• **8**

Risk
• **Average**

Earn./Div. Rank
• **B-**

Technical Eval.
• **Bearish** since 7/98

Rel. Strength Rank
(1 Lowest—99 Highest)
• **71**

Insider Activity
• **Neutral**

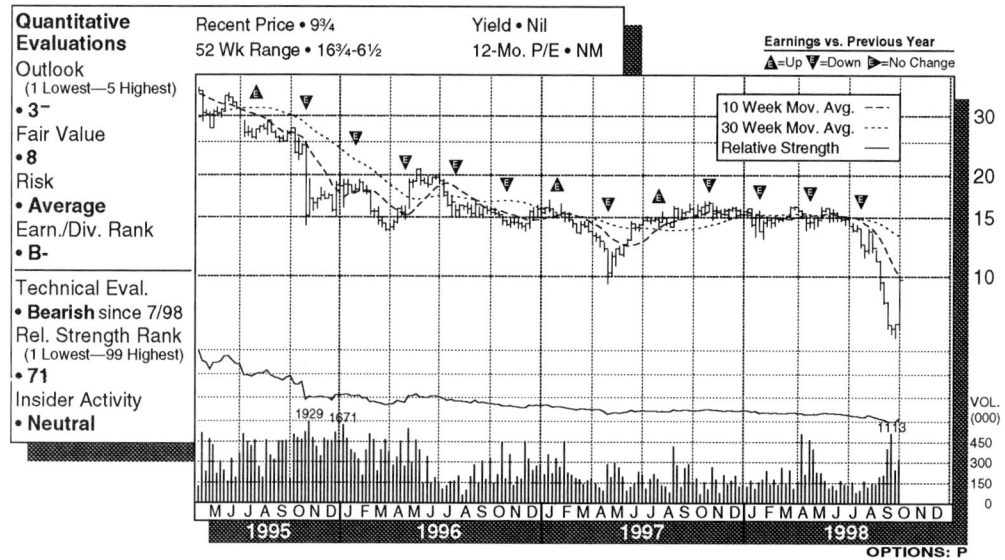

OPTIONS: P

Business Profile - 23-SEP-98

During the fourth quarter of FY 98 (Jun.), SMD acquired Sentient Systems Technology, a manufacturer of augmentative communication devices for people with speech disabilities, in exchange for 2.7 million SMD shares. Results for the year were hurt by one-time charges associated with the acquisition, as well as by charges relating to a re-engineering program that included factory relocations, consolidation of data centers and the merger of the company's sales force. However, the company believes it will benefit from costs savings associated with this program in FY 99, and SMD is scheduled to launch more than 30 new products during the first half of the fiscal year.

Operational Review - 23-SEP-98

Based on a preliminary report, net sales, as restated for the acquisition of Sentient Systems Technology (SST), fell 2.0% in the fiscal year ended July 3, 1998, due to a divestiture in 1997 and the negative impact of foreign exchange translations. Gross margins narrowed, and following $29.0 million in non-recurring charges relating to the SST acquisition and a re-engineering program, a net loss of $12.0 million ($0.55 a share) contrasted with net income of $12.1 million ($0.55).

Stock Performance - 02-OCT-98

In the past 30 trading days, SMD's shares have declined 12%, compared to a 7% fall in the S&P 500. Average trading volume for the past five days was 62,580 shares, compared with the 40-day moving average of 70,321 shares.

Key Stock Statistics

Dividend Rate/Share	Nil	Shareholders	600
Shs. outstg. (M)	20.4	Market cap. (B)	$0.200
Avg. daily vol. (M)	0.104	inst. holdings	83%
Tang. Bk. Value/Share	0.45		
Beta	0.97		

Value of $10,000 invested 5 years ago: $ 3,617

Fiscal Year Ending Jun. 30

	1998	1997	1996	1995	1994	1993
Revenues (Million $)						
1Q	151.1	165.3	157.2	140.6	99.9	71.70
2Q	165.3	169.7	173.7	146.9	111.1	74.30
3Q	160.4	158.4	169.6	148.6	120.0	80.98
4Q	168.6	163.3	166.7	167.9	137.0	92.19
Yr.	657.2	656.7	667.1	601.9	467.9	319.2
Earnings Per Share ($)						
1Q	0.02	0.16	0.20	0.34	0.32	0.30
2Q	0.02	0.13	-1.28	0.38	0.28	0.23
3Q	-0.03	0.06	0.14	0.42	0.36	0.29
4Q	-0.62	0.20	-1.23	0.49	0.45	0.37
Yr.	-0.55	0.55	-2.17	1.03	1.41	1.21

Next earnings report expected: NA

Dividend Data

No cash dividends have been paid. A two-for-one stock split was effected in 1992.

A Division of The McGraw-Hill Companies

Business Summary - 23-SEP-98

A new day is dawning at Sunrise Medical (SMD), a maker of medical products for the home care and extended care markets that address rehabilitation, recovery and respiratory needs. On June 30, 1997, SMD announced the launch of a new structure dividing its operations into three groups (Home Healthcare, Continuing Care and Sunrise Medical Europe), and renamed a number of business units to reinforce its corporate identity.

A re-engineering program that spanned three fiscal years was completed during the fourth quarter of FY 98 (Jun.). This program included the July 1997 merger of SMD's five U.S. home care divisions into the Home Healthcare Group, with a single sales force; the consolidation of four U.K. manufacturing divisions into one plant; and the conversion of computer systems in North America and Europe. Re-engineering costs totaled $16,985,000 pretax in the first nine months of FY 98 (Jun.), but the company expects the restructuring to produce substantial cost savings in FY 99.

The Home Healthcare Group (46% of sales in FY 98) focuses on the outpatient equipment needs of the elderly and disabled. Products include wheelchairs (including custom, power, pediatric and standard wheelchairs) and seating and positioning systems; medical products to assist in walking, bathing, toileting and patient lifting; and respiratory products such as aerosol, oxygen and sleep therapy products.

The Continuing Care Group (14%) makes products for recovering patients and long-term residents in nursing homes, subacute facilities, hospitals and assisted living centers. Health care beds, nursing home furniture, patient support surfaces and institutional bathing systems are part of this group's product line.

Sunrise Medical Europe (38%) makes products in the U.K., Germany, Spain and France and owns distribution companies in five other countries that market SMD's products in Europe.

During the fourth quarter of FY 98, SMD completed the acquisition of Sentient Systems Technology, now renamed DynaVox Systems, a manufacturer of augmentative communication devices for people with speech disabilities, in exchange for 2.7 million SMD shares. The transaction was accounted for on a pooling-of-interest basis and all financial data has been restated. In the fourth quarter of FY 98, eight new products were introduced, with orders outstripping production capacity, causing production backlogs. In November 1997, SMD acquired Mechanical Application Designs, a maker of modular power tilt and recline systems for power wheelchairs.

Founded in 1983 to take advantage of the shift in care from hospitals to alternate sites, SMD believes an aging population, increased use of lower cost, alternate-site treatment, improved outpatient care and a greater emphasis on the integration of the disabled into communities will contribute to continued growth in the home care and extended care markets.

Per Share Data ($)

(Year Ended Jun. 30)	1998	1997	1996	1995	1994	1993	1992	1991	1990	1989
Tangible Bk. Val.	NA	0.26	0.97	2.38	3.40	6.98	1.65	2.92	0.12	3.18
Cash Flow	NA	1.48	-1.16	2.55	2.37	1.86	1.53	1.31	1.10	0.95
Earnings	-0.55	0.55	-2.17	1.63	1.41	1.21	0.94	0.79	0.58	0.41
Dividends	Nil	Nil	Nil	Nil	Nil	Nil	Nil	Nil	Nil	Nil
Payout Ratio	Nil	Nil	Nil	Nil	Nil	Nil	Nil	Nil	Nil	Nil
Prices - High	16¼	16⅞	20⅞	36¾	33¼	31	31¾	19⅛	11½	5¾
- Low	6¾	9½	13⅝	24⅞	20	18⅜	11⅝	9	4	1¹³⁄₁₆
P/E Ratio - High	NM	31	NM	23	24	26	34	24	20	14
- Low	NM	17	NM	15	14	15	12	11	7	4

Income Statement Analysis (Million $)

	1998	1997	1996	1995	1994	1993	1992	1991	1990	1989
Revs.	NA	657	667	604	468	319	244	204	172	153
Oper. Inc.	NA	58.3	55.0	85.3	66.2	43.6	30.7	22.7	18.7	17.4
Depr.	NA	17.9	19.1	17.4	17.6	9.7	7.6	5.3	4.7	4.8
Int. Exp.	NA	14.8	16.7	10.3	6.1	4.3	2.9	3.7	4.8	5.9
Pretax Inc.	NA	21.0	-52.5	51.9	42.6	29.7	20.2	13.7	9.2	6.7
Eff. Tax Rate	NA	50%	NM	41%	39%	39%	41%	41%	43%	46%
Net Inc.	NA	10.6	-40.9	30.6	25.9	18.1	12.0	8.1	5.3	3.6

Balance Sheet & Other Fin. Data (Million $)

	1998	1997	1996	1995	1994	1993	1992	1991	1990	1989
Cash	NA	2.8	1.8	1.7	2.6	40.0	1.3	0.1	0.2	1.0
Curr. Assets	NA	238	252	253	196	146	82.9	55.6	50.3	46.8
Total Assets	NA	611	620	619	478	284	202	120	115	113
Curr. Liab.	NA	136	147	117	92.9	53.5	50.8	33.4	29.7	24.4
LT Debt	NA	188	207	182	119	32.5	56.0	16.9	48.1	58.8
Common Eqty.	NA	279	261	315	264	195	92.3	67.4	34.6	28.2
Total Cap.	NA	475	473	502	385	231	151	87.0	85.0	89.0
Cap. Exp.	NA	29.3	19.0	26.7	25.6	18.3	21.5	7.0	4.7	3.4
Cash Flow	NA	28.5	-21.8	48.0	43.4	27.8	19.6	13.4	10.0	8.4
Curr. Ratio	NA	1.8	1.7	2.2	2.1	2.7	1.6	1.7	1.7	1.9
% LT Debt of Cap.	NA	39.6	43.8	36.2	30.8	14.1	37.1	19.5	56.7	66.1
% Net Inc.of Revs.	NA	1.6	NM	5.1	5.5	5.7	4.9	4.0	3.1	2.4
% Ret. on Assets	NA	1.7	NM	5.6	6.8	6.7	7.3	5.9	4.6	3.1
% Ret. on Equity	NA	3.9	NM	10.6	11.3	11.6	14.7	14.2	16.7	13.5

Data as orig. reptd.; bef. results of disc. opers. and/or spec. items. Per share data adj. for stk. divs. as of ex-div. date. Bold denotes diluted EPS (FASB 128). E-Estimated. NA-Not Available. NM-Not Meaningful. NR-Not Ranked.

Office—2382 Faraday Ave., Suite 200, Carlsbad, CA 92008. **Tel**—(619) 930-1500. **Website**—http://www.sunrisemedical.com **Chrmn & CEO**—R. H. Chandler. **SVP-Fin, CFO & Investor Contact**—Ted N. Tarbet. **Dirs**—L. A. Ault III, R. H. Chandler, L. E. Cotsen, B. Heimbuch, M. H. Hutchison, W. L. Pierpoint, J. Stemler, J. R. Woodhull. **Transfer Agent & Registrar**—ChaseMellon Shareholder Services, Encino, CA. **Incorporated**—in Delaware in 1983. **Empl**— 4,417. **S&P Analyst:** John J. Arege

Superior Services 5349H

NASDAQ Symbol **SUPR**

In S&P SmallCap 600

03-OCT-98

Industry:
Waste Management

Summary: SUPR provides solid waste collection, transfer, recycling and disposal services to about 465,000 residential, commercial and industrial customers in 10 states.

Quantitative Evaluations

Recent Price • 25¾
52 Wk Range • 33¾-20⅞

Yield • Nil
12-Mo. P/E • 27.4

Outlook
(1 Lowest—5 Highest)
• **4⁻**

Fair Value
• **37¾**

Risk
• **NA**

Earn./Div. Rank
• **NR**

Technical Eval.
• **Neutral** since 9/98

Rel. Strength Rank
(1 Lowest—99 Highest)
• **66**

Insider Activity
• **NA**

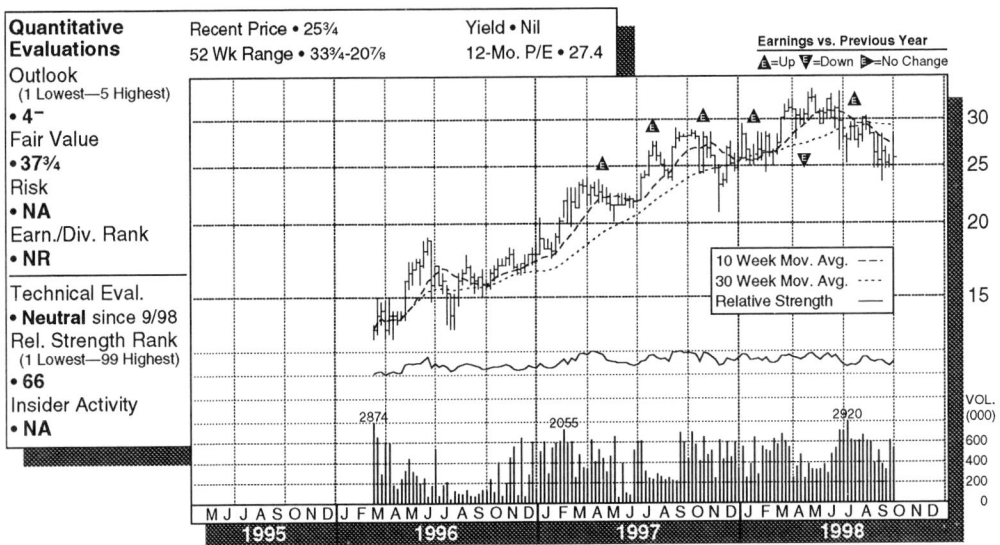

Earnings vs. Previous Year
▲=Up ▼=Down ▷=No Change

10 Week Mov. Avg. – – –
30 Week Mov. Avg. ·····
Relative Strength —

Business Profile - 28-SEP-98

Superior Services' growth strategy is to aggressively acquire solid waste disposal, transfer and collection operations, and increase its internalization rate through focussing on full vertical integration of its solid waste business. The company believes its internalization rate is among the highest in the industry, with over two-thirds of waste handled by its collection operations directed to company-owned landfills. In addition to acquisitions, management strives to improve the operating margin by leveraging administrative costs over a broader base of revenue and achieving operating synergies through the acquisition of tuck-in collection, transfer and new disposal operations.

Operational Review - 28-SEP-98

Revenues in the first half of 1998 advanced 38%, year to year (as restated), mainly reflecting contributions from recent acquisitions, and to a much lesser extent, increases in volumes of wastes collected and disposed at company-owned landfills. Operating profitability improved on staff reductions at the merged companies in Alabama and a larger revenue base to absorb selling, general and administrative expenses. Despite a higher tax rate of 45%, versus 38%, net income increased 49%, to $11.3 million ($0.42 a share, on 25% more shares), from $7.6 million ($0.35).

Stock Performance - 02-OCT-98

In the past 30 trading days, SUPR's shares have declined 9%, compared to a 7% fall in the S&P 500. Average trading volume for the past five days was 106,100 shares, compared with the 40-day moving average of 105,526 shares.

Key Stock Statistics

Dividend Rate/Share	Nil	Shareholders	200
Shs. outstg. (M)	27.0	Market cap. (B)	$0.694
Avg. daily vol. (M)	0.099	Inst. holdings	56%
Tang. Bk. Value/Share	7.45		
Beta	NA		

Value of $10,000 invested 5 years ago: NA

Fiscal Year Ending Dec. 31

	1998	1997	1996	1995	1994	1993
Revenues (Million $)						
1Q	51.75	30.68	22.32	—	—	—
2Q	62.37	45.29	26.55	—	—	—
3Q	—	51.58	29.72	—	—	—
4Q	—	50.28	31.07	—	—	—
Yr.	—	177.8	109.7	92.60	76.30	67.30
Earnings Per Share ($)						
1Q	0.12	0.13	0.10	—	—	—
2Q	0.30	0.20	0.18	—	—	—
3Q	—	0.27	0.24	—	—	—
4Q	—	0.25	0.19	—	—	—
Yr.	—	0.85	0.72	0.54	—	—

Next earnings report expected: NA

Dividend Data

No cash dividends have been paid and the company does not plan to pay cash dividends. It intends to retain earnings to finance the expansion of its business.

A Division of The McGraw-Hill Companies

Business Summary - 28-SEP-98

The objective of acquisition-oriented Superior Services, Inc. (SUPR) is to be one of the largest and most profitable fully integrated providers of solid waste collection and disposal services in each market it serves. The company's strategy to achieve this objective is to: continue to expand its operations and customer base in existing markets and to enter new markets through the acquisition of other solid waste businesses; pursue internal growth opportunities in its current markets; and achieve continuing operating improvements in its business.

The company's principal strategy for future growth is through the acquisition of additional solid waste disposal, transfer and collection operations. Its operating strategy emphasizes the integration of the solid waste collection and disposal operations and the internalization of waste collected.

Since its original consolidation of 22 businesses in 1993, SUPR has acquired 80 businesses to build its network of 21 company-owned or operated solid waste landfills, 49 solid waste collection operations, 18 transfer stations and 16 recycling facilities in 12 states.

The company closed 26 acquisitions in 1997 with annualized revenues of over $75 million. In 1997 it entered 12 new service areas and four new states and made 15 "tuck-in" acquisitions which further enhanced its position in existing markets. The acquisitions represent a balanced approach of opening new markets with landfill acquisitions and expanding its presence in the market with acquisitions of collection operations to internalize waste at its landfills.

SUPR has set a goal of entering four or five new markets every year. In 1997 it entered four new states -- Alabama, Ohio, Pennsylvania and West Virginia.

The company provides integrated waste services to its customers. It operates solid waste collection operations, solid waste transfer stations, recycling facilities, company-owned solid waste landfills and managed third party landfills. SUPR also provides other integrated waste services, most of which are project-based and many provide additional waste volumes to its landfills and recycling facilities.

As of December 31, 1997, the company provided solid waste collections services to over 650,000 residential, commercial and industrial customers. Its collection operations are conducted generally within a 150-mile radius from its landfills or transfer stations. In 1997, about 65% of the solid waste collected by SUPR was delivered for disposal at its own landfills, versus about 81% in 1996. Solid waste collection and transfer services accounted for about 52% of revenues in 1997, disposal 21%, recycling 11%, and other integrated waste services 16%. Solid waste services have been and are expected to remain the company's core business.

Per Share Data ($)

(Year Ended Dec. 31)	1997	1996	1995	1994	1993	1992	1991	1990	1989	1988
Tangible Bk. Val.	8.10	4.97	2.53	NA	NA	NA	NA	NA	NA	NA
Cash Flow	1.99	1.66	1.53	NA	NA	NA	NA	NA	NA	NA
Earnings	0.85	0.72	0.59	0.13	0.42	0.18	NA	NA	NA	NA
Dividends	Nil	Nil	Nil	Nil	Nil	Nil	Nil	Nil	Nil	Nil
Payout Ratio	Nil	Nil	Nil	Nil	Nil	Nil	Nil	Nil	Nil	Nil
Prices - High	29¹/₂	20¹/₂	NA	NA	NA	NA	NA	NA	NA	NA
- Low	17¹/₂	12³/₄	NA	NA	NA	NA	NA	NA	NA	NA
P/E Ratio - High	35	28	NA	NA	NA	NA	NA	NA	NA	NA
- Low	21	18	NA	NA	NA	NA	NA	NA	NA	NA

Income Statement Analysis (Million $)

	1997	1996	1995	1994	1993	1992	1991	1990	1989	1988
Revs.	178	110	92.6	76.3	67.3	44.9	NA	NA	NA	NA
Oper. Inc.	55.5	35.2	28.4	14.8	15.9	8.1	NA	NA	NA	NA
Depr.	23.9	15.5	12.7	9.5	6.2	4.1	NA	NA	NA	NA
Int. Exp.	1.3	0.7	2.8	2.3	1.5	1.3	NA	NA	NA	NA
Pretax Inc.	30.4	20.1	13.5	3.1	8.4	2.8	NA	NA	NA	NA
Eff. Tax Rate	42%	41%	41%	45%	40%	51%	NA	NA	NA	NA
Net Inc.	17.8	11.8	7.9	1.7	5.1	1.4	NA	NA	NA	NA

Balance Sheet & Other Fin. Data (Million $)

	1997	1996	1995	1994	1993	1992	1991	1990	1989	1988
Cash	40.1	16.4	1.4	2.0	3.0	1.0	NA	NA	NA	NA
Curr. Assets	80.2	37.5	19.6	NA	NA	NA	NA	NA	NA	NA
Total Assets	367	176	123	127	116	47.0	NA	NA	NA	NA
Curr. Liab.	35.7	20.5	14.9	NA	NA	NA	NA	NA	NA	NA
LT Debt	3.3	1.4	20.2	35.8	27.4	10.4	NA	NA	NA	NA
Common Eqty.	259	104	36.0	29.3	32.9	8.2	NA	NA	NA	NA
Total Cap.	281	117	67.8	NA	NA	NA	NA	NA	NA	NA
Cap. Exp.	26.9	NA	NA	NA	NA	NA	NA	NA	NA	NA
Cash Flow	41.6	27.3	20.6	NA	NA	NA	NA	NA	NA	NA
Curr. Ratio	2.2	1.8	1.3	NA	NA	NA	NA	NA	NA	NA
% LT Debt of Cap.	1.2	1.2	29.8	NA	NA	NA	NA	NA	NA	NA
% Net Inc.of Revs.	10.0	10.7	8.5	2.3	7.6	3.1	NA	NA	NA	NA
% Ret. on Assets	6.5	7.9	6.3	1.4	6.3	NA	NA	NA	NA	NA
% Ret. on Equity	9.8	16.8	24.2	NA	NA	NA	NA	NA	NA	NA

Data as orig. reptd.; bef. results of disc. opers. and/or spec. items. Per share data adj. for stk. divs. as of ex-div. date. Bold denotes diluted EPS (FASB 128). E-Estimated. NA-Not Available. NM-Not Meaningful. NR-Not Ranked.

Office—One Honey Creek Corporate Center, 125 South 84th St., Suite 200, Milwaukee, WI 53214. **Tel**—(414) 479-7800. **Pres & CEO**—G. W. Dietrich. **Chrmn**—J. P. Tate. **CFO & Investor Contact**—George K. Farr.**Secy & Gen Counsel**—Peter Rudd.**Dirs**—G. W. Dietrich, W. C. Frazier, F. J. Podvin, J. P. Tate, D. Taylor, W. G. Winding. **Transfer Agent & Registrar**—La Salle National Trust Co., Chicago, IL. **Incorporated**—in Wisconsin in 1992. **Empl**— 1,700. **S&P Analyst:** John A. Massey

Susquehanna Bancshares 5354B

NASDAQ Symbol **SUSQ**

In S&P SmallCap 600

03-OCT-98

Industry:
Banks (Regional)

Summary: SUSQ is a multibank holding company whose subsidiaries operate in Pennsylvania, Maryland and southern New Jersey.

Quantitative Evaluations	
Outlook (1 Lowest—5 Highest)	• **2⁻**
Fair Value	• 19¼
Risk	• **Low**
Earn./Div. Rank	• **A-**
Technical Eval.	• **Bearish** since 9/98
Rel. Strength Rank (1 Lowest—99 Highest)	• 43
Insider Activity	• **Neutral**

Recent Price • 18¼
52 Wk Range • 26¾-17⅝

Yield • 3.1%
12-Mo. P/E • 14.4

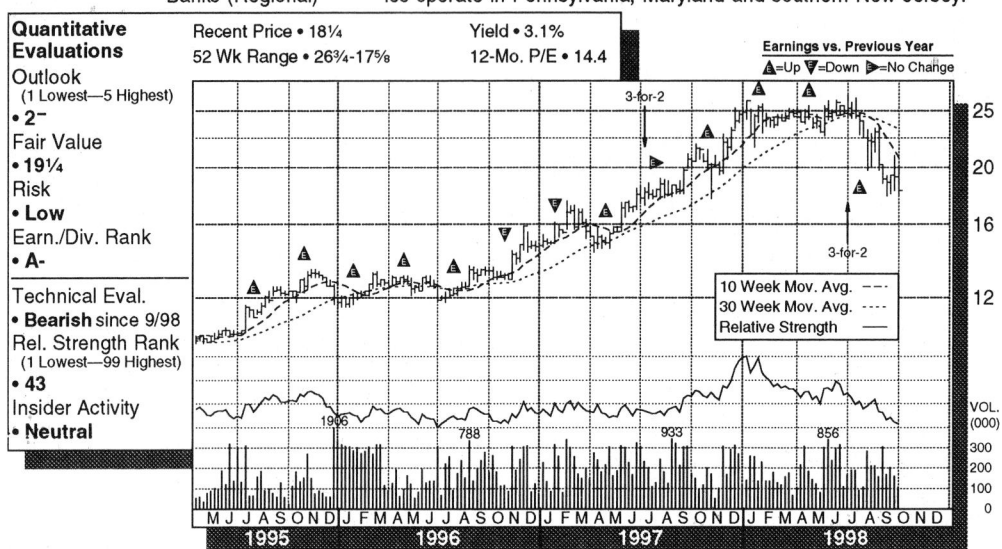

Earnings vs. Previous Year
▲=Up ▼=Down ▶=No Change

10 Week Mov. Avg. ---
30 Week Mov. Avg. ----
Relative Strength —

Business Profile - 11-AUG-98

Susquehanna Bancshares has been quite active in seeking and making acquisitions. In April 1998, SUSQ agreed to acquire First Capitol Bank (FCB) for about 1,026,000 (adjusted) common shares, subject to regulatory and shareholder approval. If the proposed acquisition is not completed, SUSQ has the option to acquire up to about 20% of FCB shares. Also in April, SUSQ agreed to acquire Cardinal Bancorp Inc. (CADL) for about 1,900,000 (adjusted) shares, subject to regulatory and shareholder approval. SUSQ has the option to acquire up to 15% of CADL shares if the proposed acquisition is not completed. CADL owns First American National Bank of Pennsylvania, which has assets of about $130 million. During 1997, SUSQ acquired Equity National Bank, Farmers National Bank, and Founders' Bank. It also acquired bank branch offices in Berwick, PA, Cinnaminson, NJ, and Audobon, NJ. The stock was split 3-for-2 July 1, 1998.

Operational Review - 11-AUG-98

Net interest income for the first half of 1998 rose 2.7%, year to year, as the net interest margin narrowed to 4.43%, versus 4.84%. The loan loss provision increased 2.4% to $2,845,000. A surge in fee income lifted noninterest income 38%, and noninterest expenses were 2.5% higher. Net income advanced 16%, to $21,470,000 ($0.63 a share, on 3.1% more shares) from $18,461,000 ($0.56). Per-share figures for both periods are adjusted for the July 1998 3-for-2 stock split.

Stock Performance - 02-OCT-98

In the past 30 trading days, SUSQ's shares have declined 21%, compared to a 7% fall in the S&P 500. Average trading volume for the past five days was 21,020 shares, compared with the 40-day moving average of 39,944 shares.

Key Stock Statistics

Dividend Rate/Share	0.56	Shareholders	5,700
Shs. outstg. (M)	33.8	Market cap. (B)	$0.618
Avg. daily vol. (M)	0.033	Inst. holdings	21%
Tang. Bk. Value/Share	10.63		
Beta	0.83		

Value of $10,000 invested 5 years ago: $ 22,101

Fiscal Year Ending Dec. 31

	1998	1997	1996	1995	1994	1993
Revenues (Million $)						
1Q	76.21	63.29	60.58	44.92	34.39	35.10
2Q	79.22	70.63	64.16	51.44	34.04	34.03
3Q	—	73.41	63.93	54.38	37.88	34.08
4Q	—	75.20	64.51	55.17	38.69	34.71
Yr.	—	287.9	253.2	205.9	145.0	137.9
Earnings Per Share ($)						
1Q	**0.31**	**0.29**	0.27	0.20	0.24	0.23
2Q	**0.32**	**0.27**	0.28	0.24	0.23	0.24
3Q	—	**0.32**	0.17	0.28	0.24	0.20
4Q	—	**0.77**	0.29	0.27	0.22	0.24
Yr.	—	**1.20**	1.01	0.99	0.94	0.91

Next earnings report expected: late October

Dividend Data (Dividends have been paid since 1982.)

Amount ($)	Date Decl.	Ex-Div. Date	Stock of Record	Payment Date
0.210	Jan. 21	Jan. 29	Feb. 02	Feb. 20 '98
0.210	Apr. 15	Apr. 24	Apr. 28	May. 20 '98
3-for-2	Apr. 15	Jul. 02	Jun. 15	Jul. 01 '98
0.140	Jul. 15	Jul. 24	Jul. 28	Aug. 20 '98

A Division of The McGraw-Hill Companies

Business Summary - 11-AUG-98

Susquehanna Bancshares, Inc. is a multi-bank financial holding company headquartered in Lititz, PA. As of December 31, 1997, Susquehanna owned eight commercial banks, one savings bank, and two non-bank subsidiaries. The subsidiaries were providing banking and banking-related services from 124 offices in central and eastern Pennsylvania, Maryland, and southern New Jersey.

As a multi-community bank holding company, Susquehanna's strategy has been to manage its banking subsidiaries on a decentralized basis, allowing each subsidiary operating in different markets to retain its name and directors as well as substantial autonomy in day to day operations. The company believes that this approach permits these institutions greater flexibility to better serve their markets, increasing responsiveness to local needs, and differentiates Susquehanna from other large competitors.

Susquehanna provides a wide range of retail and commercial banking services. Its strategy for retail banking operations is to expand deposit and other product market share through a high level of customer service, new product offerings, application of new technologies and delivery systems, and selective acquisitions.

Retail banking services consist primarily of checking and savings accounts, money market accounts, certificates of deposit, individual retirement accounts, Christmas clubs, mutual funds and annuities, home equity lines of credit, residential mortgage loans, home improvement loans, student loans, automobile loans and personal loans.

Commercial lending operations are made up of commercial, financial and agricultural lending (12% of the total loan portfolio at year-end 1997), real estate construction (9%), and commercial mortgage (16%).

As of December 31, 1997, the allowance for loan and lease losses totaled $34.6 million (1.34% of loans and leases outstanding), versus $33.8 million (1.44%) a year earlier. Net loan charge-offs totaled $5.3 million (0.21% of average loans) in 1997, compared with $4.5 million (0.20%) a year earlier. At the end of 1997, nonperforming assets totaled $27.3 million (1.06% of loans, leases and other real estate owned), versus $33.6 million (1.43%) a year earlier.

Per Share Data ($)

(Year Ended Dec. 31)	1997	1996	1995	1994	1993	1992	1991	1990	1989	1988
Tangible Bk. Val.	10.25	9.87	9.38	8.29	8.35	7.71	7.20	NA	NA	NA
Earnings	1.20	1.01	0.99	0.87	0.87	0.88	0.85	NA	NA	NA
Dividends	0.55	0.52	0.49	0.45	0.41	0.39	0.37	NA	NA	NA
Payout Ratio	46%	51%	49%	48%	45%	44%	44%	NA	NA	NA
Prices - High	25$^{7}/_{8}$	15$^{7}/_{8}$	13$^{1}/_{2}$	12$^{1}/_{2}$	12$^{3}/_{4}$	10	7$^{5}/_{8}$	NA	NA	NA
- Low	14$^{3}/_{8}$	11$^{1}/_{2}$	9$^{1}/_{2}$	9$^{1}/_{2}$	9$^{3}/_{4}$	7	5$^{1}/_{2}$	NA	NA	NA
P/E Ratio - High	22	16	14	13	14	11	9	NA	NA	NA
- Low	12	11	10	10	11	8	6	NA	NA	NA

Income Statement Analysis (Million $)

	1997	1996	1995	1994	1993	1992	1991	1990	1989	1988
Net Int. Inc.	146	129	107	94.0	87.0	84.0	78.0	NA	NA	NA
Tax Equiv. Adj.	4.3	4.1	4.3	4.2	3.9	NA	NA	NA	NA	NA
Non Int. Inc.	23.6	21.2	16.1	15.1	15.8	15.3	13.3	NA	NA	NA
Loan Loss Prov.	4.6	4.6	5.0	4.0	5.1	4.7	4.9	NA	NA	NA
Exp./Op. Revs.	63%	66%	63%	64%	62%	64%	64%	NA	NA	NA
Pretax Inc.	58.8	44.6	37.4	32.5	31.7	30.7	27.8	NA	NA	NA
Eff. Tax Rate	32%	33%	30%	30%	30%	28%	23%	NA	NA	NA
Net Inc.	40.2	30.0	26.0	22.8	22.1	22.2	21.3	NA	NA	NA
% Net Int. Marg.	4.73	4.78	4.89	4.94	4.94	NA	NA	NA	NA	NA

Balance Sheet & Other Fin. Data (Million $)

	1997	1996	1995	1994	1993	1992	1991	1990	1989	1988
Earning Assets:										
Money Mkt	139	195	179	95.0	NA	NA	NA	NA	NA	NA
Inv. Securities	657	562	610	598	563	475	441	NA	NA	NA
Com'l Loans	368	255	222	202	195	NA	NA	NA	NA	NA
Other Loans	2,202	1,918	1,491	1,264	1,115	NA	NA	NA	NA	NA
Total Assets	3,525	3,038	2,586	2,231	2,052	1,967	1,904	NA	NA	NA
Demand Deposits	352	338	270	261	250	NA	NA	NA	NA	NA
Time Deposits	2,499	2,416	1,846	1,604	1,468	NA	NA	NA	NA	NA
LT Debt	182	115	86.3	49.3	58.3	52.5	53.5	NA	NA	NA
Common Eqty.	347	293	273	217	218	194	181	NA	NA	NA
% Ret. on Assets	1.2	1.1	1.1	1.1	1.2	1.1	1.1	NA	NA	NA
% Ret. on Equity	12.6	10.6	11.3	10.5	11.5	11.9	12.3	NA	NA	NA
% Loan Loss Resv.	1.3	1.5	1.6	1.6	1.7	1.4	1.3	NA	NA	NA
% Loans/Deposits	90.1	87.1	80.9	78.6	76.3	76.7	80.8	NA	NA	NA
% Equity to Assets	9.7	10.1	9.5	10.2	10.3	9.7	9.3	NA	NA	NA

Data as orig. reptd.; bef. results of disc. opers. and/or spec. items. Prior to 1995, per share, income statement and balance sheet data as restated for acquisitions on pooling-of-interests basis. Bold denotes diluted EPS (FASB 128). Per share data adj. for stk. divs. as of ex-div. date. E-Estimated. NA-Not Available. NM-Not Meaningful. NR-Not Ranked.

Office—26 N. Cedar St., Lititz, PA 17543. **Tel**—(717) 626-4721. **Website**—http://www.susqbanc.com **Pres & CEO**—R. S. Bolinger. **VP-Secy**—R. M. Cloney. **VP-CFO & Treas**—D. K. Hostetter. **Dirs**—J. G. Apple, R. S. Bolinger, R. M. Cloney, T. B. Cunningham, J. M. Denlinger, R. E. Funke, H. H. Gibbel, M. R. Gross, T. M. Hall, E. W. Helfrick, C. W. Hetzer Jr., G. J. Morgan, R. M. O'Connell, R. C. Reymer Jr., R. V. Wiest. **Transfer Agent & Registrar**—Farmers First Bank, Lititz, PA. **Incorporated**—in Pennsylvania in 1982. **Empl**— 1,429. **S&P Analyst**: T.W. Smith, CFA

Swiss Army Brands 5354E

NASDAQ Symbol **SABI**

In S&P SmallCap 600

03-OCT-98

Industry: Consumer (Jewelry, Novelties & Gifts)

Summary: This company, the exclusive U.S., Canadian and Caribbean distributor of the Victorinox Original Swiss Army Knife, also sells Swiss Army Brand watches and cutlery.

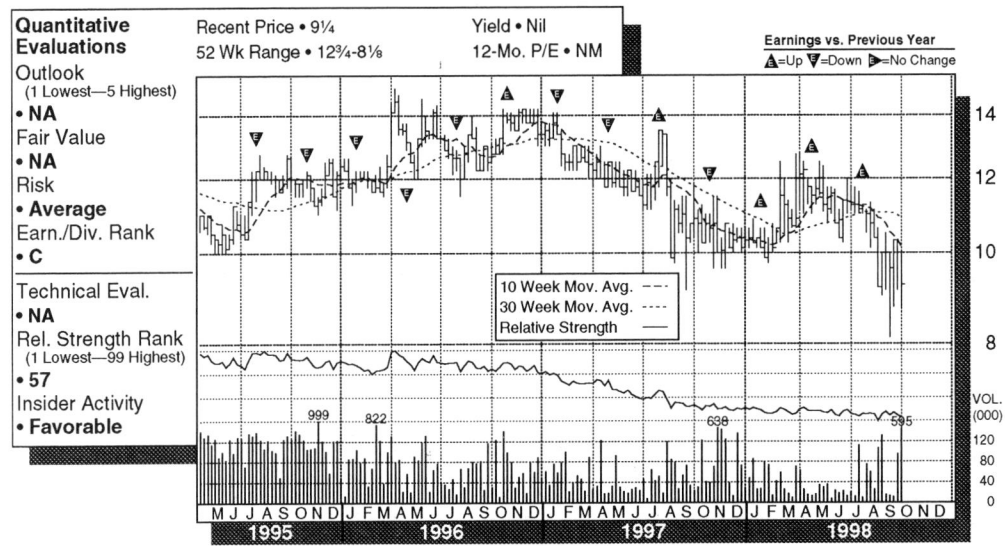

Quantitative Evaluations	
Recent Price • 9¼	Yield • Nil
52 Wk Range • 12¾-8⅛	12-Mo. P/E • NM

Earnings vs. Previous Year
▲=Up ▼=Down ▶=No Change

Outlook (1 Lowest—5 Highest)
• **NA**

Fair Value
• **NA**

Risk
• **Average**

Earn./Div. Rank
• **C**

Technical Eval.
• **NA**

Rel. Strength Rank (1 Lowest—99 Highest)
• **57**

Insider Activity
• **Favorable**

10 Week Mov. Avg. - - -
30 Week Mov. Avg. ....
Relative Strength ——

Business Profile - 14-MAY-98

SABI shares have risen sharply in recent months, reflecting two consecutive quarters of improved earnings performance. For the first quarter of 1998, the company reported earnings for the first time in six quarters, reflecting successful efforts to control operating costs and a $1.5 million pretax gain ($0.11 a share, after taxes) related to an investment in a private entity. New items being rolled out include the compact SwissTool, 15 new watch styles, a cut-resistant glove for the foodservice industry, and Swiss Army Brand sunglasses.

Operational Review - 14-MAY-98

Based on a brief report, net sales in the three months ended March 31, 1998, rose 1.6%, year to year, driven by the introduction of new products. Margins widened on the higher volume, as well as a decline in SG&A expenditures, the operating loss narrowed to $1,070,000, from $1,816,000. Results benefited from a $1.5 million pretax gain associated with an investment in a private firm. After a tax provision of $194,000, versus a tax benefit of $714,000, the company reported net income of $286,000 ($0.03 a share), in contrast to a net loss of $1,048,000 ($0.13).

Stock Performance - 02-OCT-98

In the past 30 trading days, SABI's shares have increased 0.69%, compared to a 7% fall in the S&P 500. Average trading volume for the past five days was 118,900 shares, compared with the 40-day moving average of 28,821 shares.

Key Stock Statistics

Dividend Rate/Share	Nil	Shareholders	400
Shs. outstg. (M)	8.2	Market cap. (B)	$0.076
Avg. daily vol. (M)	0.036	Inst. holdings	28%
Tang. Bk. Value/Share	8.90		
Beta	0.50		

Value of $10,000 invested 5 years ago: $ 7,400

Fiscal Year Ending Dec. 31

	1998	1997	1996	1995	1994	1993
Revenues (Million $)						
1Q	24.61	24.21	26.08	29.37	27.05	17.60
2Q	30.19	28.86	28.68	25.92	39.94	21.20
3Q	—	27.87	34.62	30.19	37.26	27.69
4Q	—	37.80	40.66	41.21	40.19	36.03
Yr.	—	118.7	130.0	126.7	144.4	102.5
Earnings Per Share ($)						
1Q	0.03	-0.13	-0.03	0.15	0.21	0.12
2Q	0.01	-0.12	-0.49	0.03	0.17	0.14
3Q	—	-0.09	0.08	0.02	0.42	0.40
4Q	—	-0.15	-0.20	0.17	0.37	0.38
Yr.	—	-0.49	-0.64	0.38	1.16	1.04

Next earnings report expected: early November

Dividend Data

Cash dividends have never been paid.

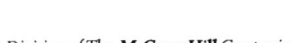 *A Division of The McGraw-Hill Companies*

Business Summary - 14-MAY-98

Swiss Army Brands Inc. (formerly The Forschner Group, Inc.) is the exclusive U.S., Canadian and Caribbean distributor of the Victorinox Original Swiss Army Knife, Victorinox SwissTool, Victorinox SwissCard, Victorinox cutlery and Victorinox watches. The company also sells its own line of watches and other high-quality Swiss-made products under its Swiss Army Brand. Foreign operations accounted for 14% and 13% of total net sales in 1997 and 1996, respectively.

Victorinox Swiss Army Knives are multi-blade pocket knives containing implements capable of more functions than standard pocket knives. For example, the most popular Classic knife, with a suggested retail price of $16, features a knife, scissors, nail file with screwdriver tip, toothpick and tweezers. The company markets more than 50 different models of Victorinox Original Swiss Army Knives, containing up to 30 different implements, and ranging from a basic knife with a suggested retail price of $10 to the highest-priced model at about $175. Swiss Army Knives accounted for 34% of 1997 sales.

SABI's line of Swiss Army Brand products includes eight models of watches, ranging from the Renegade, at a suggested retail price of $85, to the Titanium

Two-Tone, with a suggested retail price of $595. The Titanium line, along with a new line of watches under the Allenby trademark, was introduced during 1997. SABI also sells Swiss Army Brand sunglasses and writing instruments. Watches and other Swiss Army Brand products produced 50% of 1997 sales. Sales of Swiss Army Brand products are seasonal, with demand typically strongest from July through December.

The majority of the company's professional cutlery products, made of stainless steel, are manufactured by Victorinox and others in Germany, England and France. Customers for cutlery include distributors of hotel, restaurant, butcher and slaughterhouse supplies and retail cutlery stores throughout the U.S. and Canada. In 1997, sales of these products accounted for 16% of the total. In February 1997, SABI sold Cuisine de France Ltd., the exclusive North American distributor of cutlery under the Cuisine de France Sabatier trademark. During 1997, the company introduced a cut-resistant glove to be sold to its existing cutlery customers.

In April 1994, the company formed Forschner Enterprises, an investment entity, to acquire interests in businesses that offer the opportunity for significant equity growth. Forschner Enterprises has since been merged into Hudson Capital, LLC, and SABI currently owns 9.1% of the equity.

Per Share Data ($)

(Year Ended Dec. 31)	1997	1996	1995	1994	1993	1992	1991	1990	1989	1988
Tangible Bk. Val.	8.79	9.21	9.68	9.20	7.61	6.00	3.22	2.71	1.95	1.47
Cash Flow	-0.16	-0.15	0.77	1.56	1.39	0.94	0.62	0.58	0.80	0.43
Earnings	-0.49	-0.64	0.38	1.16	1.04	0.80	0.45	0.51	0.75	0.34
Dividends	Nil	Nil	Nil	Nil	Nil	Nil	Nil	Nil	Nil	Nil
Payout Ratio	Nil	Nil	Nil	Nil	Nil	Nil	Nil	Nil	Nil	Nil
Prices - High	14⅛	15	13	16¼	18¼	16	12¾	12½	14½	10
- Low	9⅛	11¼	10	10¼	12	9½	5¾	4½	5	5¼
P/E Ratio - High	NM	NM	34	14	18	20	28	25	19	29
- Low	NM	NM	26	9	12	12	13	9	7	15

Income Statement Analysis (Million $)

	1997	1996	1995	1994	1993	1992	1991	1990	1989	1988
Revs.	119	130	127	144	103	74.1	60.1	50.2	43.8	37.6
Oper. Inc.	-4.2	1.1	7.2	20.2	13.8	9.6	5.2	4.5	6.4	4.1
Depr.	2.7	4.0	3.3	3.2	2.5	0.9	0.7	0.3	0.2	0.4
Int. Exp.	0.0	0.1	0.2	0.0	0.0	0.3	0.4	0.4	0.7	0.8
Pretax Inc.	-6.4	-7.6	5.6	16.0	11.5	8.9	3.5	3.9	5.6	2.7
Eff. Tax Rate	NM	NM	45%	42%	37%	45%	45%	47%	46%	48%
Net Inc.	-4.0	-5.3	3.1	9.4	7.3	4.9	2.0	2.1	3.0	1.4

Balance Sheet & Other Fin. Data (Million $)

	1997	1996	1995	1994	1993	1992	1991	1990	1989	1988
Cash	1.1	2.1	0.6	18.0	7.8	6.6	0.1	2.3	0.8	0.3
Curr. Assets	64.1	70.4	74.4	78.6	57.6	43.7	25.2	21.4	17.1	16.3
Total Assets	94.1	99	101	106	78.0	54.3	29.0	24.7	20.0	19.1
Curr. Liab.	18.3	18.8	16.3	23.9	17.7	10.8	6.8	8.3	4.6	4.3
LT Debt	Nil	Nil	Nil	Nil	Nil	Nil	8.1	4.7	7.3	8.5
Common Eqty.	75.7	79.9	84.9	82.4	60.4	43.0	13.3	11.0	7.4	5.8
Total Cap.	75.7	79.9	84.9	82.4	60.4	43.5	21.9	16.2	15.2	14.7
Cap. Exp.	1.1	1.2	1.4	1.7	2.8	1.1	0.7	0.7	0.2	0.3
Cash Flow	-1.3	-1.2	6.4	12.6	9.8	5.8	2.7	2.4	3.3	1.8
Curr. Ratio	3.5	3.7	4.6	3.3	3.3	4.1	3.7	2.6	3.7	3.8
% LT Debt of Cap.	Nil	Nil	Nil	Nil	Nil	Nil	37.2	29.3	48.3	57.8
% Net Inc.of Revs.	NM	NM	2.5	6.5	7.1	6.7	3.3	4.2	7.0	3.7
% Ret. on Assets	NM	NM	3.0	9.5	10.7	9.9	7.2	9.1	15.8	7.3
% Ret. on Equity	NM	NM	3.7	12.2	13.6	15.5	16.0	22.2	46.8	25.7

Data as orig. reptd.; bef. results of disc. opers. and/or spec. items. Per share data adj. for stk. divs. as of ex-div. date. Bold denotes diluted EPS (FASB 128). E-Estimated. NA-Not Available. NM-Not Meaningful. NR-Not Ranked.

Office—One Research Drive, Shelton, CT 06484. **Tel**—(203) 929-6391. **Website**—http://www.swissarmy.com **Pres**—J. M. Taggart. **SVP, CFO, Treas & Secy**—T. M. Lupinski. **Investor Contact**—Donald Dwight (603) 795-2800.**Dirs**—A. C. Allen, C. H. Bailey, T. A. Barron, V. D. Farrell, Jr., H. M. Friedman, P. W. Gilson, K. R. Lively, L. Marx, Jr., S. R. Rawn, Jr., E. M. Reynolds, J. Spencer, J. M. Taggart, J.V. Tunney. **Transfer Agent & Registrar**—Registrar & Transfer Co., Cranford, NJ. **Incorporated**—in Delaware in 1974. **Empl**— 226. **S&P Analyst:** Stephen J. Tekirian

SymmetriCom   5355

NASDAQ Symbol **SYMM**

In S&P SmallCap 600

03-OCT-98

Industry: Communications Equipment

Summary: SYMM manufactures specialized transmission equipment for telephone companies and private network operators, as well as semiconductors for power management applications.

Quantitative Evaluations	Recent Price • 5	Yield • Nil
	52 Wk Range • 19-4	12-Mo. P/E • NM

Earnings vs. Previous Year
▲=Up ▼=Down ▶=No Change

Outlook (1 Lowest—5 Highest)
• **5**

Fair Value
• **8¾**

Risk
• **Average**

Earn./Div. Rank
• **B**

Technical Eval.
• **Bullish** since 9/98

Rel. Strength Rank (1 Lowest—99 Highest)
• **45**

Insider Activity
• **Neutral**

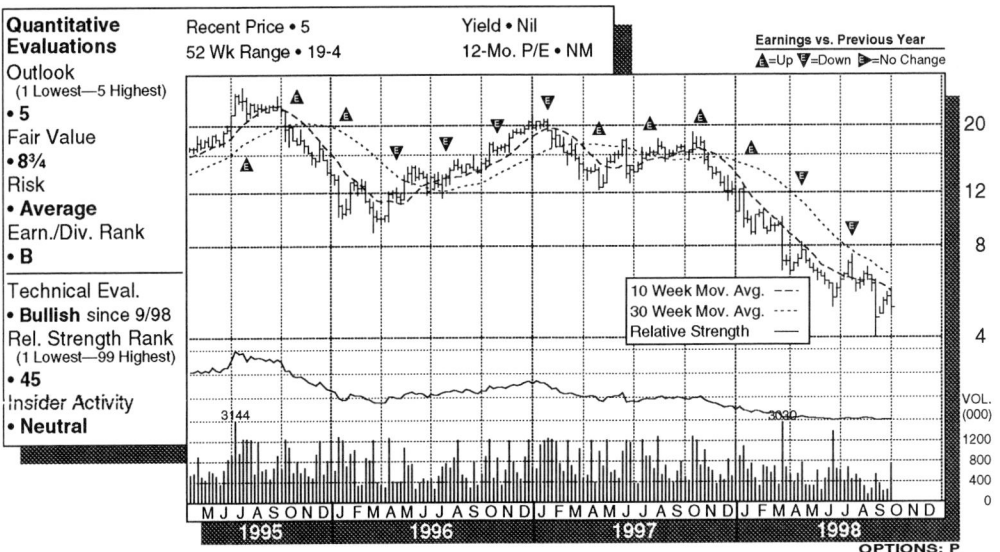

10 Week Mov. Avg. – – –
30 Week Mov. Avg. - - - -
Relative Strength ⎯⎯

OPTIONS: P

Business Profile - 08-SEP-98

Reflecting higher than expected bookings, the company said in early September that FY 99 (Jun.) first quarter revenues should range from $28 million to $31 million, with bottom line results ranging from a net loss of $300,000 (0.02 a share) to net income of $500,000 ($0.03). SYMM is focusing on developing synchronization products for the traditional central office market and a new emerging market for products at access points, and on leveraging its existing power management technology into proprietary products for desktop and mobile computing platforms. After authorizing the repurchase of 500,000 shares (3% of the shares outstanding) in April 1998, in September, directors authorized the purchase of another one million shares.

Operational Review - 08-SEP-98

Based on a preliminary report, net sales in FY 98 fell 16%, on declines at both operating units. Results at Telecom Solutions were affected by the completion of large projects by AT&T and Southwestern Bell, while lower Linfinity revenues reflected an overall decline in the global semiconductor market, intense price competition, and weak demand from component manufacturers supplying personal computer markets. Margins narrowed, leading to an operating loss. After tax credits of $2.6 million, versus taxes at 22.4%, a net loss of $1,530,000 ($0.10 a share) contrasted with net income of $13,454,000 ($0.83).

Stock Performance - 02-OCT-98

In the past 30 trading days, SYMM's shares have declined 22%, compared to a 7% fall in the S&P 500. Average trading volume for the past five days was 148,640 shares, compared with the 40-day moving average of 70,131 shares.

Key Stock Statistics

Dividend Rate/Share	Nil	Shareholders	1,400
Shs. outstg. (M)	15.8	Market cap. (B)	$0.079
Avg. daily vol. (M)	0.084	Inst. holdings	26%
Tang. Bk. Value/Share	5.39		
Beta	0.65		

Value of $10,000 invested 5 years ago: $ 5,000

Fiscal Year Ending Jun. 30

	1998	1997	1996	1995	1994	1993
Revenues (Million $)						
1Q	33.98	32.02	27.68	24.18	24.03	21.10
2Q	34.34	35.45	28.43	25.59	25.01	21.60
3Q	24.21	37.75	22.69	26.26	24.37	22.10
4Q	28.05	39.13	27.24	27.08	24.97	23.08
Yr.	120.6	144.4	106.0	103.1	98.39	87.91
Earnings Per Share ($)						
1Q	0.17	0.14	0.17	0.13	0.11	0.09
2Q	**0.21**	0.20	0.21	0.15	0.11	0.10
3Q	**-0.47**	0.23	0.02	0.18	0.10	0.10
4Q	**-0.01**	0.26	0.07	0.20	0.11	0.11
Yr.	**-0.10**	0.83	0.47	0.66	0.43	0.40

Next earnings report expected: early October

Dividend Data

No cash dividends have been paid, and the company does not intend to pay any in the foreseeable future.

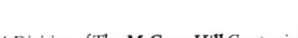 *A Division of The McGraw·Hill Companies*

Business Summary - 08-SEP-98

Timing is everything. A musician, for instance, relies on the steady beat of a metronome to set the tempo for a piece of music. If the timing is off, the performance will be undermined and the music's quality compromised. Similarly, sophisticated network synchronization systems, such as those made by the Telecom Solutions division of SymmetriCom, Inc. (SYMM), provide the "beat" that telecommunications networks need to send and receive data in an orderly fashion. Bad timing leads to poor transmission quality and unwanted results, such as annoying clicks in a voice call. By coordinating the beat of internal clocks located throughout the network, SYMM's network synchronization equipment ensures error-free transmission of data at high speeds.

Serving the worldwide telecommunications industry, SYMM's Telecom Solutions unit makes intelligent access or transmission products, in addition to its broad range of network synchronization systems. The division accounted for 62% of SYMM's net sales in FY 97 (Jun.). The company's Linfinity Microelectronics Inc. subsidiary, which accounted for 38% of FY 97 net sales, designs and produces linear (or analog) and mixed-signal integrated circuits and modules for use in power management and communication applications.

SYMM sees new opportunities around the globe for its network synchronization systems as deregulation and increased competition in the telecommunications industry drive the need for more reliable and higher-quality service. It is also encouraged by growth in the wireless communications market, which it serves with its Cell-Sync synchronization systems for wireless networks. In FY 97, Telecom Solutions posted a 31% increase in net sales, largely because of sharply higher sales to AT&T Corp., which rose to $22.5 million, or 16% of SYMM's total for the year. The company expected sales to AT&T to decrease significantly in FY 98.

Linfinity's products are used in commercial, industrial, defense and space markets. In FY 97, the subsidiary derived most of its sales from desktop power management products, mainly standard linear integrated circuits that control, regulate, monitor, convert or route voltage and current in computers and other electronic systems. Linfinity has shifted its emphasis from low-volume custom and military programs to high-volume commercial products and now focuses on value-added standard off-the-shelf products. This strategy served the unit well in FY 97, helping to lift its sales 45%, year to year. Linfinity now offers about 450 standard catalog products. Newer items include backlight inverters for liquid crystal display products and interface products that facilitate the flow of data between computers and peripheral devices.

Net sales declined 16% in FY 98, to $120.6 million, from $144.4 million in FY 97, on decreased sales at both business units. A net loss of $1.5 million contrasted with net income of $13.5 million. Results reflected completion of major project s by AT&T and Southwestern Bell, and an overall decline in the global semiconductor market.

Per Share Data ($)

(Year Ended Jun. 30)	1998	1997	1996	1995	1994	1993	1992	1991	1990	1989
Tangible Bk. Val.	NA	5.52	4.52	3.98	3.32	2.78	2.35	2.18	2.04	1.95
Cash Flow	NA	1.23	0.79	0.99	0.80	0.73	0.37	0.37	0.34	0.28
Earnings	-0.10	0.83	0.47	0.66	0.43	0.40	0.10	0.11	0.07	0.09
Dividends	Nil	Nil	Nil	Nil	Nil	Nil	Nil	Nil	Nil	Nil
Payout Ratio	Nil	Nil	Nil	Nil	Nil	Nil	Nil	Nil	Nil	Nil
Prices - High	12¾	21	21⅜	26⅝	13⅝	18¼	10⅜	4¼	3	3½
- Low	5	10¼	8⅞	12⅞	6½	8⅞	3⅛	2	1¼	1⅝
P/E Ratio - High	NM	25	45	40	32	46	NM	47	43	39
- Low	NM	12	19	20	15	22	NM	22	18	18

Income Statement Analysis (Million $)

	1998	1997	1996	1995	1994	1993	1992	1991	1990	1989
Revs.	NA	144	106	103	98.4	87.9	68.8	62.0	58.2	35.8
Oper. Inc.	NA	22.5	13.4	16.1	14.1	12.9	6.8	5.9	5.7	5.9
Depr.	NA	6.5	5.2	5.3	5.8	5.0	3.7	3.4	3.4	2.5
Int. Exp.	NA	0.6	0.6	0.6	0.6	0.6	0.6	0.7	1.3	2.0
Pretax Inc.	NA	17.3	9.5	11.6	8.1	7.7	2.8	2.1	1.1	1.5
Eff. Tax Rate	NA	22%	21%	11%	19%	22%	52%	34%	24%	17%
Net Inc.	NA	13.5	7.5	10.3	6.5	6.0	1.3	1.4	0.9	1.3

Balance Sheet & Other Fin. Data (Million $)

	1998	1997	1996	1995	1994	1993	1992	1991	1990	1989
Cash	NA	41.6	34.3	33.2	21.3	18.2	10.1	7.5	1.0	1.2
Curr. Assets	NA	88.8	70.3	66.6	51.7	42.3	31.3	24.3	20.3	15.9
Total Assets	NA	129	93.5	85.3	69.1	59.0	48.2	43.1	41.3	46.0
Curr. Liab.	NA	30.5	14.8	15.9	13.2	12.9	10.6	8.2	9.5	14.0
LT Debt	NA	8.6	5.7	5.8	5.8	5.9	5.9	5.9	4.9	4.9
Common Eqty.	NA	87.6	70.4	60.1	46.8	38.1	30.2	27.3	25.1	23.8
Total Cap.	NA	99	78.7	69.2	55.4	45.4	36.9	34.0	30.7	29.5
Cap. Exp.	NA	15.1	9.1	6.6	3.6	4.6	1.9	1.0	1.5	0.2
Cash Flow	NA	20.0	12.6	15.6	12.3	10.9	5.1	4.7	4.3	3.8
Curr. Ratio	NA	2.9	4.8	4.2	3.9	3.3	3.0	3.0	2.1	1.1
% LT Debt of Cap.	NA	8.7	7.3	8.3	10.5	12.9	16.0	17.5	15.9	16.7
% Net Inc.of Revs.	NA	9.3	7.1	10.0	6.7	6.8	2.0	2.2	1.5	3.5
% Ret. on Assets	NA	12.1	8.4	13.3	10.2	10.9	2.9	3.2	2.0	2.6
% Ret. on Equity	NA	17.0	11.5	19.4	15.4	17.1	4.6	5.1	3.5	5.4

Data as orig. reptd.; bef. results of disc. opers. and/or spec. items. Per share data adj. for stk. divs. as of ex-div. date. Bold denotes diluted EPS (FASB 128). E-Estimated. NA-Not Available. NM-Not Meaningful. NR-Not Ranked.

Office—2300 Orchard Parkway, San Jose, CA 95131-1017. **Tel**—(408) 943-9403. **Website**—www.symmetricom.com **Chrmn & CEO**—W. D. Rasdal. **VP-Fin**—M. Rorabaugh. **Dirs**—R. W. Oliver, W. D. Rasdal, R. A. Strauch, R. M. Wolfe. **Transfer Agent & Registrar**—Chase Trust Co. of California, SF. **Incorporated**—in California in 1973. **Empl**— 708. **S&P Analyst:** S.A.H.

STANDARD &POOR'S
STOCK REPORTS

Syncor International
5355E
NASDAQ Symbol **SCOR**
In S&P SmallCap 600

03-OCT-98

Industry:
Health Care (Medical Products & Supplies)

Summary: This distributor of radiopharmaceuticals operates a network of more than 120 nuclear pharmacy centers, mostly in the U.S., serving hospitals, clinics and physicians.

Quantitative Evaluations

Recent Price • 16⅜	Yield • Nil
52 Wk Range • 20-13½	12-Mo. P/E • 15.9

Outlook
(1 Lowest—5 Highest)
• **4⁻**

Fair Value
• **23¾**

Risk
• **High**

Earn./Div. Rank
• **B**

Technical Eval.
• **NA**

Rel. Strength Rank
(1 Lowest—99 Highest)
• **81**

Insider Activity
• **Neutral**

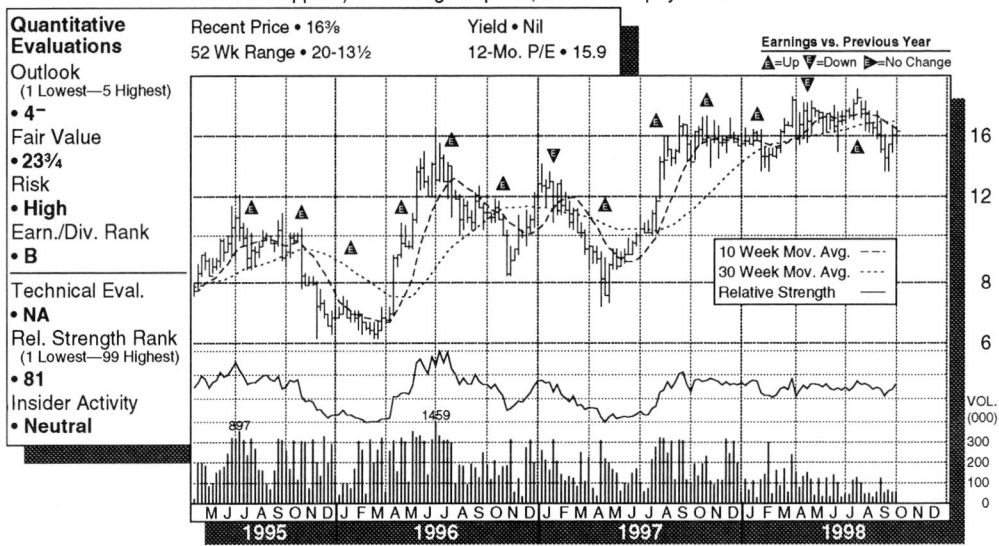

Earnings vs. Previous Year
▲=Up ▼=Down ▶=No Change

10 Week Mov. Avg. – – –
30 Week Mov. Avg. · · · ·
Relative Strength ——

VOL. (000)

Business Profile - 11-MAR-98

Syncor is working to broaden its business base beyond its core commercial radiopharmacy operations. In April 1997, SCOR entered the radiopharmaceutical manufacturing field with the purchase of all the assets of Golden Pharmaceuticals' Iodine-123 business. The company is also expanding its presence in the medical imaging field, primarily through acquisitions. In January 1998, Syncor completed the acquisition of the medical imaging businesses of TME Inc. and National Diagnostic Services Inc., and announced plans to acquire the medical imaging business of International Magnetic Imaging Inc. As a result of these acquisitions, Syncor will operate 45 medical imaging centers across the United States and Puerto Rico.

Operational Review - 11-MAR-98

Based on a preliminary report, net sales in 1997 rose 3.8%, as growth in cardiology product sales was partially offset by a decline in the bulk radiopharmaceutical business. Gross margins widened slightly, due to a more favorable product mix and a renegotiated long-term supply agreement. Operating expenses increased 7.9%, reflecting higher labor costs; operating profit gained 50%. Following higher other income and taxes, income from continuing operations was up 45%, to $10,032,000 ($0.98 a diluted share, based on 3.3% fewer shares), from $6,900,000 ($0.65). Results exclude income from discontinued operations of $0.10 a share, versus a loss of $0.21 in 1996.

Stock Performance - 02-OCT-98

In the past 30 trading days, SCOR's shares have declined 2%, compared to a 7% fall in the S&P 500. Average trading volume for the past five days was 11,100 shares, compared with the 40-day moving average of 12,231 shares.

Key Stock Statistics

Dividend Rate/Share	Nil	Shareholders	3,500
Shs. outstg. (M)	11.0	Market cap. (B)	$0.180
Avg. daily vol. (M)	0.012	Inst. holdings	49%
Tang. Bk. Value/Share	3.44		
Beta	0.73		

Value of $10,000 invested 5 years ago: $ 6,421

Fiscal Year Ending Dec. 31

	1998	1997	1996	1995	1994	1993
Revenues (Million $)						
1Q	102.7	93.08	92.32	83.00	74.80	--
2Q	113.3	98.19	93.30	83.30	81.90	--
3Q	--	94.49	90.25	81.01	81.60	--
4Q	--	94.80	90.88	85.15	81.67	--
Yr.	--	380.6	366.4	332.5	320.0	142.2
Earnings Per Share ($)						
1Q	**0.31**	**0.32**	0.16	0.10	0.19	--
2Q	**0.40**	**0.33**	0.25	0.12	0.07	--
3Q	--	**0.17**	0.13	0.12	-0.10	--
4Q	--	**0.16**	0.10	0.11	-0.05	--
Yr.	--	**0.98**	0.64	0.45	0.11	0.16

Next earnings report expected: late October

Dividend Data

No cash has been paid on the common shares.

*A Division of The **McGraw-Hill** Companies*

Business Summary - 11-MAR-98

Syncor International Corp. is a pharmacy services company that operates through a network of 119 nuclear pharmacy service centers throughout the U.S. and 12 international centers. The company compounds, dispenses and distributes patient-specific intravenous drugs and solutions for use in diagnostic imaging, as well as a complete range of high-technology pharmacy services.

The company's nuclear pharmacies dispense radiopharmaceuticals on prescription to more than 7,000 hospitals, clinics and physicians' offices in unit and multiple doses. Radiopharmaceuticals are used by physicians in conjunction with nuclear imaging cameras and computers to obtain images of organs and body functions for diagnostic purposes. Syncor also provides services such as record-keeping (required by federal and state regulatory agencies) and radiopharmaceutical technical consulting. However, the pharmacies contribute more than 95% of consolidated net sales.

Syncor provides positron emission tomography (PET) services at several of its pharmacies. PET is a new technology that enables physicians to view a metabolic process as it occurs within the body. The company also serves the research community by assisting in monoclonal antibody clinical trials.

The company is increasing its presence in foreign countries where it believes opportunities exist in nuclear medicine as well as non-nuclear imaging and radiology. It plans to open additional radiopharmacies, bringing the total number of facilities in its international network to 14 by the end of 1997 and 25 by the end of 1998.

Syncor is currently working to broaden its business base. The company initiated a process in 1996 for identifying, developing and implementing new business opportunities to apply existing skills to new healthcare arenas. The company took the first major step toward diversification in February 1997 by entering into a joint venture with National Diagnostic Services, Inc. to establish and operate magnetic resonance imaging (MRI) centers. The companies expect to establish 10 open MRI centers across the U.S. during the first year of operations.

In April 1997, the company acquired all the assets of Golden Pharmaceuticals, Inc. relating to the manufacture and distribution of Iodine-123, for $6,700,000 cash. The assets included the New Drug Application for Iodine-123 capsules, manufacturing equipment, the existing inventory of Iodine-123 and the building and land used to manufacture Iodine-123 capsules.

Per Share Data ($)

(Year Ended Dec. 31)	1997	1996	1995	1994	1993	1992	1991	1990	1989	1988
Tangible Bk. Val.	7.25	6.30	6.16	5.96	5.51	5.15	3.89	2.93	2.32	2.86
Cash Flow	1.94	1.63	1.48	1.08	0.64	1.62	1.13	0.85	0.66	0.31
Earnings	0.98	0.64	0.45	0.11	0.16	0.95	0.63	0.46	0.32	0.02
Dividends	Nil	Nil	Nil	Nil	Nil	Nil	Nil	Nil	Nil	Nil
Payout Ratio	Nil	Nil	Nil	Nil	Nil	Nil	Nil	Nil	Nil	Nil
Prices - High	17⅝	16⅝	12⅛	24¾	26½	34½	27¼	10½	8¼	7
- Low	7⅛	6⅛	6⅛	6½	14¼	15	9⅛	6¼	4⅜	3¼
P/E Ratio - High	18	26	27	NM	NM	36	43	23	26	NM
- Low	7	9	14	NM	NM	16	14	14	14	NM

Income Statement Analysis (Million $)

	1997	1996	1995	1994	1993	1992	1991	1990	1989	1988
Revs.	381	366	332	320	142	231	210	157	130	114
Oper. Inc.	23.0	19.0	17.8	12.2	7.7	23.4	16.7	11.7	8.1	3.2
Depr.	9.9	10.4	10.8	10.6	5.3	7.2	5.4	3.9	3.4	3.1
Int. Exp.	1.2	0.8	0.7	0.8	0.3	0.6	0.8	1.0	0.8	0.3
Pretax Inc.	17.0	11.3	7.8	2.1	2.8	16.9	11.6	8.2	5.2	0.5
Eff. Tax Rate	41%	39%	40%	42%	39%	40%	41%	42%	38%	59%
Net Inc.	10.0	6.9	4.7	1.2	1.7	10.2	6.9	4.8	3.3	0.2

Balance Sheet & Other Fin. Data (Million $)

	1997	1996	1995	1994	1993	1992	1991	1990	1989	1988
Cash	25.5	25.2	23.0	18.0	18.7	20.9	10.0	9.3	9.6	8.5
Curr. Assets	92.6	93.0	83.6	76.3	63.7	60.7	52.0	42.8	37.7	32.7
Total Assets	165	146	134	129	115	104	90.8	74.6	65.7	58.6
Curr. Liab.	57.9	57.0	49.4	49.7	36.6	33.3	31.8	22.6	20.4	12.2
LT Debt	17.3	7.6	5.2	5.2	6.8	4.5	6.0	7.9	8.5	2.9
Common Eqty.	89.3	78.5	78.3	73.9	71.2	65.8	52.4	42.8	35.8	43.5
Total Cap.	107	86.1	83.5	79.0	78.0	70.7	59.7	52.0	45.3	46.3
Cap. Exp.	10.9	8.1	3.9	9.2	5.5	10.6	10.5	5.3	2.0	1.9
Cash Flow	20.0	17.3	15.5	11.8	6.9	17.3	12.3	8.7	6.7	3.3
Curr. Ratio	1.6	1.6	1.7	1.5	1.7	1.8	1.6	1.9	1.8	2.7
% LT Debt of Cap.	16.2	8.8	6.2	6.5	8.8	6.4	10.2	15.2	18.7	6.2
% Net Inc.of Revs.	2.6	1.9	14.0	0.4	1.2	4.4	3.3	3.0	2.5	0.2
% Ret. on Assets	6.5	4.9	3.6	1.0	NA	10.4	8.3	6.7	5.4	0.3
% Ret. on Equity	11.8	8.8	6.1	1.7	NA	17.1	14.4	12.0	8.6	0.4

Data as orig. reptd.; bef. results of disc. opers. and/or spec. items. Per share data adj. for stk. divs. as of ex-div. date. Bold denotes diluted EPS (FASB 128). E-Estimated. NA-Not Available. NM-Not Meaningful. NR-Not Ranked.

Office—6464 Canoga Ave., Woodland Hills, CA 91367. **Tel**—(818) 737-4000. **Chrmn**—M. Fu. **Pres & CEO**—R. G. Funari. **Sr VP, CFO & Investor Contact**—Michael E. Mikity (818) 737-4610. **Sr VP & Secy**—H. Bagerdjian. **Dirs**—M. Fu, R. G. Funari, S. B. Gerber, G. S. Oki, A. E. Spangler, H. N. Wagner Jr., G. R. Wilensky. **Transfer Agent & Registrar**—American Stock Transfer & Trust Co., NYC. **Incorporated**—in New Mexico in 1974; reincorporated in Delaware in 1985. **Empl**— 3,500. **S&P Analyst:** Richard Joy

System Software Associates 5355Q

NASDAQ Symbol **SSAX**
In S&P SmallCap 600

03-OCT-98

Industry:
Computer (Software & Services)

Summary: This company develops and supports an integrated line of business application, maintenance management, computer-aided systems engineering and electronic data interchange software.

Quantitative Evaluations

Outlook
(1 Lowest—5 Highest)
• 1⁻

Fair Value
• 4⅛

Risk
• **High**

Earn./Div. Rank
• C

Technical Eval.
• **NA**

Rel. Strength Rank
(1 Lowest—99 Highest)
• 47

Insider Activity
• **NA**

Recent Price • 5
52 Wk Range • 15⅝-3⅜

Yield • Nil
12-Mo. P/E • NM

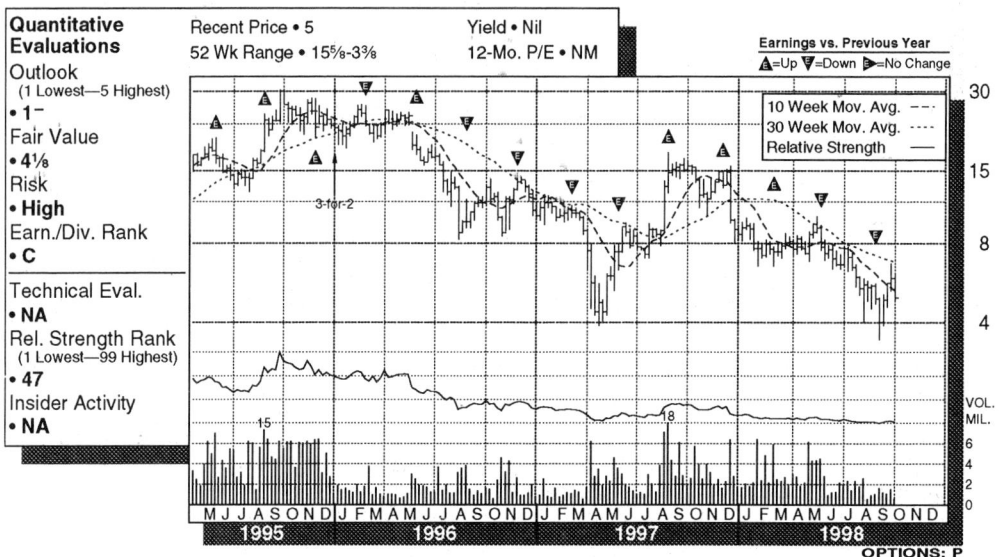

Earnings vs. Previous Year
▲=Up ▼=Down ▶=No Change

- 10 Week Mov. Avg. – – –
- 30 Week Mov. Avg. · · · ·
- Relative Strength —

OPTIONS: P

Business Profile - 26-AUG-98

This company competes in the fast growing enterprise resource planning (ERP) software market. Despite this growth environment, the company's license sales have been declining, amid strong competition. As a result, SSAX has recently been restructuring its business and reducing its cost structure. Its new management team expects to focus on specific market segments, rather than compete on all fronts with its larger competitors. The company expects its results for the fiscal fourth quarter to improve compared to the third quarter, but still anticipates reporting a net loss.

Operational Review - 26-AUG-98

Total revenues in the nine months ended July 31, 1998, advanced 1.1%, as a 61% increase in client services and other revenues was offset by a 25% decline in license fees. Margins narrowed, as cost of client services rose substantially. Results were hurt further by a $122.5 million restructuring charge. Following tax credits of $27.6 million, versus $0.9 million, the net loss widened to $125.4 million ($2.74 a share, following preferred dividends) from $1.6 million ($0.04).

Stock Performance - 02-OCT-98

In the past 30 trading days, SSAX's shares have declined 10%, compared to a 7% fall in the S&P 500. Average trading volume for the past five days was 118,340 shares, compared with the 40-day moving average of 214,459 shares.

Key Stock Statistics

Dividend Rate/Share	Nil	Shareholders	400
Shs. outstg. (M)	47.6	Market cap. (B)	$0.236
Avg. daily vol. (M)	0.225	Inst. holdings	46%
Tang. Bk. Value/Share	NM		
Beta	1.31		

Value of $10,000 invested 5 years ago: $ 3,263

Fiscal Year Ending Oct. 31

	1998	1997	1996	1995	1994	1993
Revenues (Million $)						
1Q	99.0	92.20	76.60	77.40	66.40	48.60
2Q	102.4	98.10	82.50	84.30	72.00	62.90
3Q	106.9	114.7	72.30	105.0	86.20	68.70
4Q	—	125.6	109.4	127.7	109.8	83.20
Yr.	—	430.5	340.8	394.4	334.4	263.4
Earnings Per Share ($)						
1Q	-0.04	-0.10	0.01	0.05	0.03	0.02
2Q	-0.20	-0.01	0.15	0.10	0.07	0.15
3Q	-2.42	0.08	-0.47	0.27	0.13	0.17
4Q	—	0.01	-0.13	0.39	0.15	0.23
Yr.	—	-0.03	-0.76	0.81	0.38	0.57

Next earnings report expected: early December

Dividend Data

The company omitted the FY 97 dividend.

A Division of The McGraw-Hill Companies

Business Summary - 26-AUG-98

After a disappointing FY 96 (Oct.), System Software Associates, Inc. (SSAX) enjoyed a rebound in FY 97, largely due to higher revenues generated by what the company considers the most significant software it has ever developed - BPCS Client/Server version 6.0. However, the first three quarters of FY 98 have been penalized by sluggish revenue growth (with declining license revenues) and restructuring charges. SSAX's BPCS (Business Planning and Control System) Client/ Server product provides business process re-engineering and integration of an enterprise's operations, including multi-mode manufacturing processes, distribution and global financial solutions. The company provides its enterprise information systems to the industrial sector worldwide, targeting large and medium-sized firms. In FY 97, license fees and hardware accounted for 70% of revenues (67% in FY 96) and client services and other 30% (33%).

The BPCS Client/Server in version 6.0 delivers scaleability, interoperability and reconfigurability in its product suite to meet changing market demands. Its object architecture, use of semantic messaging gateway technology and support for the JAVA programming language permit operation in Internet/intranet environments, enabling electronic commerce and information exchange beyond the enterprise.

The BPCS product line consists of more than 40 integrated software products designed for manufacturing, distribution and financial applications, as well as electronic commerce and application development tools. While SSAX's software was originally designed to operate primarily on IBM AS/400 computers, BPCS now operates across a broad array of platforms, including IBM's AS/400, the IBM RS/6000, the Hewlett-Packard HP 9000 and DEC Alpha servers. The UNIX version of BPCS operates with both Informix and Oracle databases.

BPCS has been installed at more than 8,000 client sites worldwide, with the substantial majority comprising the company's installed base of AS/400 customers.

In addition to BPCS, SSAX offers an interoperable, object-oriented application development tool set that enables the development of high transaction volume, enterprise-wide object-oriented client/server applications.

Total revenues increased 26% to $431 million in FY 97, with consistent performance worldwide in the Americas, Europe and Asia/Pacific. However, in the fourth quarter, results were hurt by weakness in Asia. The FY 97 revenue gain was attributable to license fees growing 34%, reflecting market acceptance of SSAX's client/ server product line, as well as a 12% increase in client services revenues.

Per Share Data ($)

(Year Ended Oct. 31)	1997	1996	1995	1994	1993	1992	1991	1990	1989	1988
Tangible Bk. Val.	2.38	2.05	3.28	2.44	2.16	1.77	1.57	1.27	0.81	0.51
Cash Flow	0.18	-0.55	0.99	0.64	0.76	0.80	0.55	0.49	0.34	0.19
Earnings	-0.03	-0.76	0.81	0.38	0.57	0.66	0.42	0.41	0.28	0.15
Dividends	Nil	0.10	0.08	0.08	0.08	0.08	0.07	Nil	Nil	Nil
Payout Ratio	Nil	NM	10%	21%	14%	12%	18%	Nil	Nil	Nil
Prices - High	17⅝	26¾	30½	12	17	16⅞	11	8½	6⅛	3⅝
- Low	3⅞	8¼	10¼	7⅛	6⅝	7⅞	3⅝	3¾	3⅜	1½
P/E Ratio - High	NM	NM	38	32	30	26	26	21	22	24
- Low	NM	NM	13	19	12	12	9	9	12	10

Income Statement Analysis (Million $)

	1997	1996	1995	1994	1993	1992	1991	1990	1989	1988
Revs.	431	341	394	334	263	229	149	124	95.0	62.0
Oper. Inc.	37.1	-49.6	60.5	35.2	43.5	46.8	29.7	26.6	19.7	11.2
Depr.	9.3	9.2	7.9	10.4	7.4	5.8	5.2	3.4	2.4	1.6
Int. Exp.	Nil	Nil	2.2	2.8	1.1	0.9	0.5	0.4	0.4	0.2
Pretax Inc.	1.6	-51.4	52.4	23.8	35.7	41.6	25.9	25.6	18.0	9.8
Eff. Tax Rate	38%	NM	35%	36%	36%	36%	36%	36%	38%	39%
Net Inc.	1.0	-32.8	34.1	15.4	23.4	26.6	16.7	16.4	11.1	5.9

Balance Sheet & Other Fin. Data (Million $)

	1997	1996	1995	1994	1993	1992	1991	1990	1989	1988
Cash	83.3	38.1	57.1	60.2	57.6	23.4	23.2	28.4	20.5	5.2
Curr. Assets	322	242	285	238	215	151	99	84.3	58.4	36.3
Total Assets	475	384	411	333	280	200	136	114	77.0	53.0
Curr. Liab.	160	171	183	145	124	101	55.4	46.2	34.2	22.2
LT Debt	151	75.1	33.9	32.7	34.0	3.5	2.5	1.3	1.5	1.0
Common Eqty.	122	110	156	115	101	80.0	67.8	55.9	37.9	27.1
Total Cap.	273	185	201	158	145	87.9	72.5	59.9	39.5	29.4
Cap. Exp.	4.9	11.4	5.3	14.7	5.0	7.0	5.0	8.5	2.0	2.5
Cash Flow	7.9	-23.6	42.0	25.8	30.8	32.4	24.4	19.8	13.5	7.6
Curr. Ratio	2.0	1.4	1.6	1.6	1.7	1.5	1.8	1.8	1.7	1.6
% LT Debt of Cap.	55.3	40.5	16.9	20.7	23.4	4.0	3.5	2.2	3.7	3.3
% Net Inc.of Revs.	0.2	NM	8.7	4.6	8.9	11.6	11.2	13.2	11.7	9.7
% Ret. on Assets	0.2	NM	9.2	5.0	9.7	15.7	13.4	17.0	17.1	14.0
% Ret. on Equity	NM	NM	25.2	14.2	25.6	35.6	27.2	34.7	34.2	25.8

Data as orig. reptd.; bef. results of disc. opers. and/or spec. items. Per share data adj. for stk. divs. as of ex-div. date. Bold denotes diluted EPS (FASB 128). E-Estimated. NA-Not Available. NM-Not Meaningful. NR-Not Ranked.

Office—500 W. Madison St., Chicago, IL 60661. **Tel**—(312) 641-2900. **Fax**—(312) 474-7500. **Chrmn & CEO**—W. M. Stuek. **EVP & CFO**—L. A. Zimmerman. **Dirs**—A. J. Filipowski, J. W. Puth, W. M. Stuek, W. N. Weaver Jr. W. I. Zangwill, L. A. Zimmerman. **Transfer Agent & Registrar**—First National Bank of Chicago. **Incorporated**—in Delaware in 1981. **Empl**— 2,200. **S&P Analyst:** B.G.

STANDARD &POOR'S
STOCK REPORTS

TBC Corp.

5356P

NASDAQ Symbol **TBCC**

In S&P SmallCap 600

03-OCT-98

Industry:
Auto Parts & Equipment

Summary: TBC is one of the largest U.S. distributors of replacement tires.

Quantitative Evaluations

Outlook
(1 Lowest—5 Highest)
• **4+**

Fair Value
• **7⅞**

Risk
• **Average**

Earn./Div. Rank
• **B+**

Technical Eval.
• **Bullish** since 2/98

Rel. Strength Rank
(1 Lowest—99 Highest)
• **64**

Insider Activity
• **NA**

Recent Price • 5⅞
52 Wk Range • 11-4¼

Yield • Nil
12-Mo. P/E • 7.3

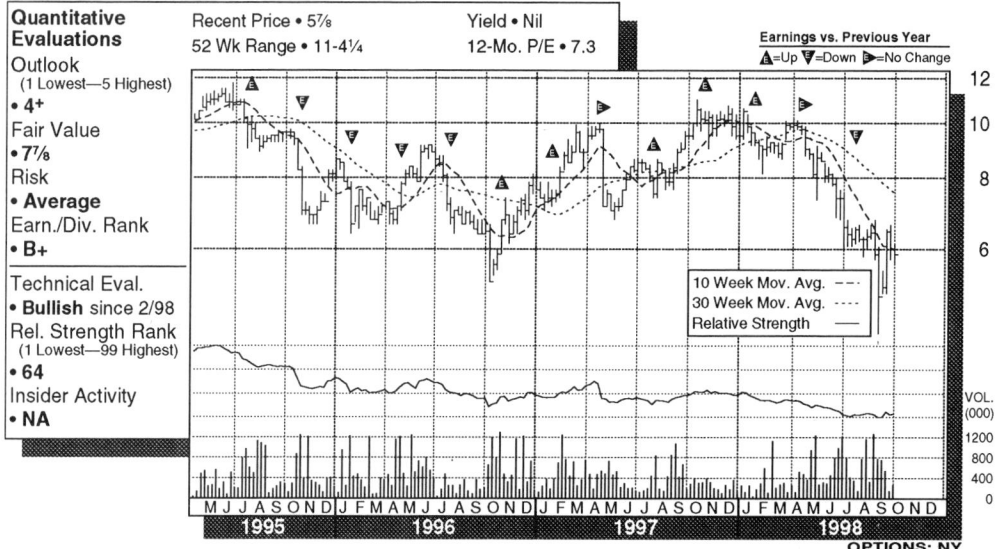

Earnings vs. Previous Year
▲=Up ▼=Down ▶=No Change

10 Week Mov. Avg. ---
30 Week Mov. Avg. ·····
Relative Strength —

VOL. (000)

OPTIONS: NY

Business Profile - 05-AUG-98

In December 1996, TBC decided to refocus on the replacement tire business. As a result, it sold its aftermarket battery distribution subsidiary and discontinued its marketing of non-tire products. In 1997, earnings were boosted by an improved distribution network, and by the July 1996 purchase of Big O Tires, Inc., a franchiser of independent retail tire and auto service stores. TBCC's expansion efforts continued in July 1998 when it reached an agreement in principle to acquire Carroll's Inc, its largest distributor. Carroll's serves over 5,000 independent dealers through 15 distribution facilities. In the first quarter of 1998, the company signed an agreement with a distributor which would add 30 stores over the next five years. In June 1998, TBCC said it expects a difficult third and fourth quarter in 1998 due to the difficult industry environment.

Operational Review - 05-AUG-98

Sales in the six months ended June 30, 1998, fell 1.8%, year to year, primarily reflecting a decline in tire sales, unit tire shipments declined 0.7%. Distribution expenses rose on higher costs of labor and other warehousing and delivery costs. Selling and administrative costs increased due to additional personnel, systems and other items related to the company's expansion efforts. After taxes at 39.1%, versus 39.4%, net income fell 14% to $6,869,000 ($0.30 a share), from $8,015,000 ($0.34).

Stock Performance - 02-OCT-98

In the past 30 trading days, TBCC's shares have declined 8%, compared to a 7% fall in the S&P 500. Average trading volume for the past five days was 51,620 shares, compared with the 40-day moving average of 147,356 shares.

Key Stock Statistics

Dividend Rate/Share	Nil	Shareholders	6,200
Shs. outstg. (M)	23.1	Market cap. (B)	$0.136
Avg. daily vol. (M)	0.088	Inst. holdings	67%
Tang. Bk. Value/Share	4.71		
Beta	0.76		

Value of $10,000 invested 5 years ago: $ 3,730

Fiscal Year Ending Dec. 31

	1998	1997	1996	1995	1994	1993
Revenues (Million $)						
1Q	140.7	144.4	121.4	130.3	133.8	125.7
2Q	161.9	163.8	134.5	132.2	132.9	154.4
3Q	—	182.7	177.3	147.2	157.5	159.0
4Q	—	152.1	165.7	126.4	127.7	129.6
Yr.	—	642.9	604.6	536.1	551.9	568.7
Earnings Per Share ($)						
1Q	**0.14**	**0.14**	0.14	0.17	0.18	0.17
2Q	**0.16**	**0.20**	0.14	0.16	0.13	0.19
3Q	—	**0.26**	0.20	0.16	0.21	0.21
4Q	—	**0.24**	0.17	0.13	0.20	0.17
Yr.	—	**0.84**	0.65	0.62	0.71	0.74

Next earnings report expected: late October

Dividend Data

No cash has been paid. A three-for-two stock split was effected in December 1992. A "poison pill" stock purchase rights plan expires in 1998.

A Division of The McGraw-Hill Companies

STANDARD
&POOR'S
STOCK REPORTS

TBC Corporation

5356P
03-OCT-98

Business Summary - 05-AUG-98

Faced with an increasingly competitive automotive aftermarket, TBC Corp. decided in late 1996 to focus on its core replacement tire business. The company, one of the largest U.S. distributors of products to the automotive replacement market, shed its non-tire operations, which included batteries, custom wheels, shock absorbers, brake parts and filters.

As evidence of the company's focus on the tire replacement business, tire sales accounted for 94% of total sales in 1997, up from 88% in 1996. This increased percentage is the result of TBC's December 1996 decision to discontinue the marketing of certain non-tire products. The company is one of the largest independent wholesale distributors of replacement tires in the U.S. Its lines of tires are made by others to company specifications, and are marketed under TBC's own brand names. The Kelly-Springfield Tire Co. subsidiary of Goodyear Tire & Rubber Co. has manufactured more than half of TBC's tires in recent years.

TBC offers three complete lines of tires under its Cordovan, Multi-Mile and Sigma brands. Each line includes tires for passenger, truck, farm, industrial, recreational and other applications. It also markets automotive replacement parts under the brand names Grand Prix, Grand Am, Grand Spirit, Wild Spirit, Grand Sport, Gran Esprit, Aqua-Flow, Wild Country, Wild Trac, Stampede, Power King, Harvest King, Big Foot, Legacy, Prestige and Sun Valley.

In July 1996, the company acquired Big O Tires, Inc., for about $56 million. Big O is the largest independent U.S. tire and service franchise organization. Big O brand tires are primarily for passenger and light truck applications. As of December 31, 1997, Big O had 415 stores in the U.S. and 36 associate dealers in British Columbia, Canada.

Most products are sold through a network of distributors located throughout the U.S., Canada and Mexico, most of which act as wholesalers or operate retail outlets, with some functioning in both capacities. The retail outlets which sell TBC products are primarily independent tire dealers. The 10 largest distributors accounted for 44% of gross sales in 1997 (46% in 1996), including Carroll's Inc. and Les Schwab Warehouse Center (11% each). The company has an on-line information system to permit continuous contact with distributors and facilitate just-in-time service to retail dealers.

In July 1998, TBCC reached an agreement in principle to acquire Carroll's Inc, a privately held wholesale distributor of tires and automotive accessories. Carroll's serves over 5,000 independent dealers through 15 distribution facilities. In 1997, Carroll's, with revenues of approximately $150 million, was TBCC's largest distributor, accounting for 11% of TBCC's net revenues.

Per Share Data ($)

(Year Ended Dec. 31)	1997	1996	1995	1994	1993	1992	1991	1990	1989	1988
Tangible Bk. Val.	4.41	3.67	4.36	4.31	4.09	3.52	3.01	2.50	2.15	1.97
Cash Flow	1.16	0.91	0.74	0.85	0.87	0.87	0.68	0.61	0.55	0.51
Earnings	0.84	0.65	0.62	0.71	0.74	0.76	0.59	0.52	0.47	0.43
Dividends	Nil	Nil	Nil	Nil	Nil	Nil	Nil	Nil	Nil	Nil
Payout Ratio	Nil	Nil	Nil	Nil	Nil	Nil	Nil	Nil	Nil	Nil
Prices - High	11	9¹/₈	11³/₄	13⁷/₈	18¹/₄	16	9¹/₄	6	5⁷/₈	4¹/₂
- Low	6³/₄	5¹/₄	6⁵/₈	8¹/₂	10¹/₄	9¹/₈	5	3³/₈	3⁷/₈	2⁷/₈
P/E Ratio - High	13	14	19	20	25	21	16	11	12	10
- Low	8	8	11	12	14	12	8	7	8	7

Income Statement Analysis (Million $)

	1997	1996	1995	1994	1993	1992	1991	1990	1989	1988
Revs.	643	605	536	552	569	570	499	499	482	485
Oper. Inc.	41.8	33.0	29.9	33.8	37.7	37.4	30.1	28.4	21.5	21.3
Depr.	7.7	6.3	4.6	4.1	3.9	3.3	2.7	2.6	2.8	2.9
Int. Exp.	5.8	4.1	Nil	1.3	1.8	1.1	1.7	1.9	2.4	2.0
Pretax Inc.	31.6	25.4	24.8	31.4	34.6	35.6	28.1	26.1	25.8	24.9
Eff. Tax Rate	38%	39%	38%	38%	38%	37%	37%	36%	37%	37%
Net Inc.	19.7	15.5	15.2	19.5	21.4	22.5	17.7	16.6	16.2	15.7

Balance Sheet & Other Fin. Data (Million $)

	1997	1996	1995	1994	1993	1992	1991	1990	1989	1988
Cash	0.9	Nil	Nil	Nil	Nil	1.9	0.3	Nil	0.5	Nil
Curr. Assets	183	172	150	146	145	155	117	126	119	129
Total Assets	265	254	180	170	167	177	135	137	131	136
Curr. Liab.	52.8	54.0	73.6	55.0	50.2	73.9	44.7	59.9	59.6	65.3
LT Debt	67.6	70.0	0.6	Nil	Nil	Nil	Nil	Nil	Nil	Nil
Common Eqty.	134	120	105	114	117	103	90.0	76.7	70.8	70.5
Total Cap.	209	197	106	114	117	103	91.0	77.0	71.4	71.0
Cap. Exp.	9.1	21.8	9.2	3.6	3.1	6.8	10.3	1.8	2.4	2.3
Cash Flow	27.4	21.8	19.8	23.6	25.3	25.7	20.3	19.3	19.0	18.6
Curr. Ratio	3.5	3.2	2.0	2.7	2.9	2.1	2.6	2.1	2.0	2.0
% LT Debt of Cap.	32.3	35.3	1.0	Nil	Nil	Nil	Nil	Nil	Nil	Nil
% Net Inc.of Revs.	3.1	2.6	2.8	3.5	3.8	3.9	3.5	3.3	3.4	3.2
% Ret. on Assets	7.6	7.1	8.7	12.1	12.6	14.6	13.1	12.8	12.7	12.1
% Ret. on Equity	15.5	13.8	13.9	17.6	19.7	23.5	21.3	23.3	24.0	25.0

Data as orig. reptd.; bef. results of disc. opers. and/or spec. items. Per share data adj. for stk. divs. as of ex-div. date. Bold denotes diluted EPS (FASB 128). E-Estimated. NA-Not Available. NM-Not Meaningful. NR-Not Ranked.

Office—4770 Hickory Hill Rd., Memphis, TN 38141. Tel—(901) 363-8030. Fax—(901) 541-3639. Chrmn—M. E. Bruce. Pres & CEO—L. S. DiPasqua. SVP & Treas—Ronald E. McCollough. Secy—S. A. Freedman. Dirs—M. E. Bruce, R. E. Carroll Jr., L. S. DiPasqua, R. H. Dunlap, C. A. Ledsinger, R. A. McStay, R. M. O'Hara, R. R. Schoeberl, R. E. Schultz. Transfer Agent & Registrar—First National Bank of Boston. Incorporated—in Delaware in 1970. Empl— 585. S&P Analyst: Kathleen J. Fraser

STANDARD &POOR'S
STOCK REPORTS

TCBY Enterprises

2181M

NYSE Symbol **TBY**

In S&P SmallCap 600

03-OCT-98 | Industry: Restaurants | **Summary:** This Arkansas-based company is the largest franchisor, licensor and operator of soft-serve frozen yogurt stores in the world.

Quantitative Evaluations

Outlook (1 Lowest—5 Highest)
• **2+**

Fair Value
• **6**

Risk
• **Low**

Earn./Div. Rank
• **B-**

Technical Eval.
• **Bearish** since 4/98

Rel. Strength Rank (1 Lowest—99 Highest)
• **42**

Insider Activity
• **NA**

Recent Price • 6⅛
52 Wk Range • 10¼-5¾

Yield • 3.3%
12-Mo. P/E • 13.3

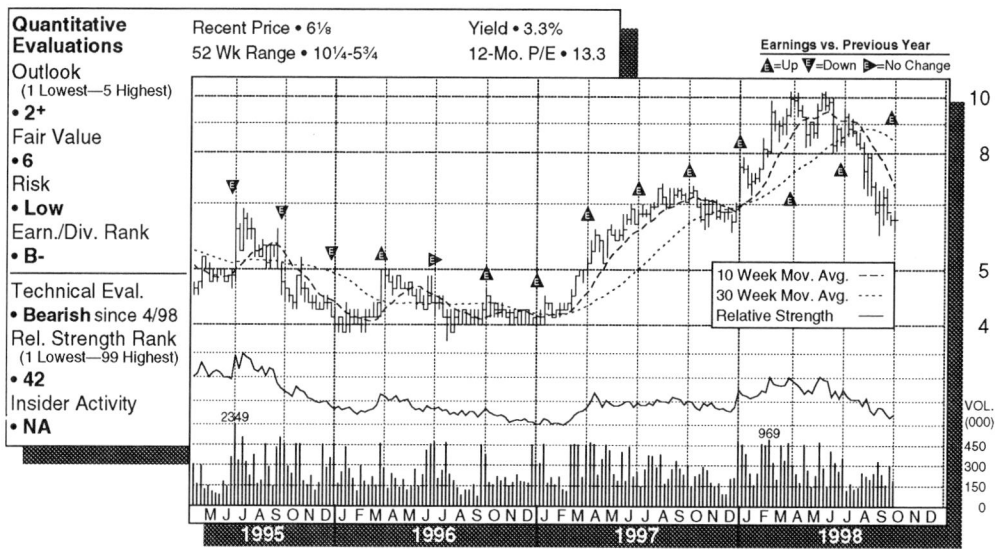

Business Profile - 24-JUL-98

TCBY has grown from one frozen yogurt store in Little Rock, Arkansas in 1981 to a corporation with more than 2,700 stores and retail distribution in the U.S. and 65 foreign countries. The company has achieved recent success by increasing sales in its co-branded locations, franchising or closing most of its company-owned stores, selling the rights to manufacture and distribute its branded products, and focusing on locales where products can be more efficiently delivered and marketed. During FY 98 (Nov.), TBY has been developing its Juice Works brand and franchise. Host Marriott has committed to develop Juice Works locations in airports, malls and travel plazas.

Operational Review - 24-JUL-98

Total revenues for the six months ended May 31, 1998 rose 0.9%, year-to-year, reflecting the continued growth of co-branded locations, but offset by a 39% decrease in franchising revenues resulting from a reduction in TCBY stores, and, to a lesser extent, sales to international franchisees due to Asia's economic problems. Margins widened, primarily due to a significant reduction in SG&A expenses resulting from TBY's continued execution of a restructuring plan implemented in 1996. Pre-tax income was up 24.5%. After taxes at 34.0% in 1998, compared to 35.0%, TBY's net income increased 26% to $4,268,556 ($0.18 a share) from $3,376,641 ($0.14).

Stock Performance - 02-OCT-98

In the past 30 trading days, TBY's shares have declined 13%, compared to a 7% fall in the S&P 500. Average trading volume for the past five days was 37,420 shares, compared with the 40-day moving average of 47,572 shares.

Key Stock Statistics

Dividend Rate/Share	0.20	Shareholders	5,200
Shs. outstg. (M)	23.1	Market cap. (B)	$0.142
Avg. daily vol. (M)	0.045	Inst. holdings	20%
Tang. Bk. Value/Share	3.04		
Beta	1.05		

Value of $10,000 invested 5 years ago: $ 13,287

Fiscal Year Ending Nov. 30

	1998	1997	1996	1995	1994	1993
Revenues (Million $)						
1Q	19.21	18.47	17.28	27.95	24.26	24.30
2Q	30.90	31.18	27.94	32.78	43.30	34.24
3Q	32.87	34.14	30.22	39.24	50.67	37.23
4Q	—	20.54	20.36	21.60	34.20	26.21
Yr.	—	104.3	95.80	121.6	152.5	120.5
Earnings Per Share ($)						
1Q	**0.03**	0.01	-0.02	-0.17	-0.02	-0.03
2Q	**0.15**	0.13	0.10	0.10	0.14	0.11
3Q	**0.24**	0.18	0.15	0.09	0.18	0.16
4Q	—	0.05	0.00	0.04	0.01	0.00
Yr.	—	0.37	0.26	-0.83	0.30	0.25

Next earnings report expected: NA

Dividend Data (Dividends have been paid since 1988.)

Amount ($)	Date Decl.	Ex-Div. Date	Stock of Record	Payment Date
0.050	Dec. 15	Dec. 26	Dec. 30	Jan. 15 '98
0.050	Mar. 20	Apr. 02	Apr. 06	Apr. 21 '98
0.050	Jun. 12	Jun. 19	Jun. 23	Jul. 03 '98
0.050	Sep. 18	Sep. 28	Sep. 30	Oct. 09 '98

A Division of The **McGraw-Hill** *Companies*

TCBY Enterprises, Inc.

Business Summary - 24-JUL-98

Starting with one store in Little Rock, Arkansas in 1981, TCBY Enterprises has grown to become the world's largest manufacturer-franchisor of frozen yogurt. The company manufactures and sells soft-serve frozen yogurt and sorbet, hardpack frozen yogurt and ice cream, and novelty food products. As of May 31, 1998, TCBY and Juice Works products were sold at 2,915 locations: 1,091 domestic franchises, two company-owned stores, 217 international stores and 1,605 other outlets (known as non-traditional locations). In addition, there were over 300 locations under agreement for development. TBY also sells frozen yogurt via supermarkets and grocery stores and sells equipment related to the food-service industry.

In response to operating problems and a net loss in 1995, the company made a strategic decision to close or franchise most of its company-owned locations. TBY also decided to focus on geographic areas in which retail hardpack products could be delivered and marketed more efficiently. These decisions helped reduce operating expenses and contributed to the company's return to profitability in 1996, despite a drop in revenues.

Franchises operate under the name TCBY -- "The Country's Best Yogurt" -- and are located in shopping malls, strip malls and free-standing locations. Non-traditional outlets are located in airports, college campuses, convenience stores, hospitals, schools, sports venues, theme parks and travel plazas. A bakery program offering gourmet coffee and freshly baked cookies, muffins and brownies has been introduced in many domestic stores. The recently introduced TCBY Treats concept adds hand-dipped frozen yogurt and premium ice cream, shaved ice and frozen custard to the company's menu of offerings.

TBY intends to continue to leverage its brand name by partnering with other food and petroleum concerns, such as Citgo, Exxon and Shell, by selling its products in their gas station convenience stores. TBY is also teaming up with national and regional restaurants to sell its products. TBY's co-branding strategy involves two or more food operations existing at one location and reducing operating costs to TBY per concept. Co-branding also makes it possible to open stores in areas that could not otherwise support independent TBY operations.

In September 1996, the company acquired Juice Works, a Phoenix-based fresh juice and smoothie bar company. In FY 98 (Nov.), TCBY plans to focus on the development of the Juice Works brand and franchise system. Host Marriott has already committed to develop Juice Works locations in airports, malls and travel plazas. Most of the Juice Works stores under development will be co-branded with existing TCBY operations.

Per Share Data ($) (Year Ended Nov. 30)	1997	1996	1995	1994	1993	1992	1991	1990	1989	1988
Tangible Bk. Val.	3.10	3.03	3.06	3.73	3.89	3.87	3.92	4.07	3.61	2.54
Cash Flow	0.58	0.47	NM	0.67	0.57	0.50	0.62	1.00	1.28	0.88
Earnings	0.37	0.26	-0.83	0.30	0.25	0.20	0.31	0.75	1.10	0.75
Dividends	0.20	0.20	0.20	0.20	0.20	0.20	0.35	0.18	0.07	0.02
Payout Ratio	54%	77%	NM	67%	80%	101%	113%	24%	6%	3%
Prices - High	$7\frac{7}{8}$	5	$6\frac{1}{2}$	$6\frac{7}{8}$	$9\frac{5}{8}$	$6\frac{7}{8}$	$9\frac{1}{4}$	$24\frac{3}{4}$	29	$13\frac{7}{8}$
- Low	4	$3\frac{3}{4}$	$3\frac{7}{8}$	5	$5\frac{1}{8}$	$3\frac{7}{8}$	$4\frac{1}{2}$	$4\frac{1}{8}$	$11\frac{1}{8}$	$6\frac{1}{4}$
P/E Ratio - High	21	19	NM	23	39	34	30	33	26	19
- Low	11	14	NM	17	21	19	15	6	10	8
Income Statement Analysis (Million $)										
Revs.	104	96.0	122	152	120	119	129	151	145	98.0
Oper. Inc.	18.1	14.8	-5.6	20.6	17.5	17.2	19.2	35.0	48.2	32.8
Depr.	5.2	5.2	10.9	9.5	8.3	7.8	8.3	6.8	5.0	3.6
Int. Exp.	0.8	1.0	1.1	0.6	0.8	1.2	1.8	2.3	2.5	1.1
Pretax Inc.	13.6	10.0	-32.1	11.3	9.7	7.3	12.2	30.5	45.2	30.2
Eff. Tax Rate	35%	35%	NM	33%	34%	30%	35%	35%	35%	34%
Net Inc.	8.9	6.5	-21.4	7.6	6.4	5.1	8.0	20.0	29.5	19.8
Balance Sheet & Other Fin. Data (Million $)										
Cash	19.7	19.2	14.4	20.2	25.0	27.8	22.8	24.5	29.9	21.8
Curr. Assets	46.2	44.7	51.4	59.0	53.8	51.5	52.8	55.8	54.8	40.2
Total Assets	99	103	112	142	129	132	135	142	134	93.0
Curr. Liab.	11.7	10.8	14.7	12.5	8.8	9.3	8.1	10.3	11.9	7.9
LT Debt	6.3	9.5	12.6	15.9	11.5	14.8	17.3	19.7	21.3	14.0
Common Eqty.	77.4	79.2	82.2	108	105	105	106	109	98.0	69.0
Total Cap.	87.6	92.0	97.0	130	120	123	127	131	122	85.0
Cap. Exp.	NA	3.4	9.9	11.4	6.5	7.6	4.2	13.4	28.1	20.3
Cash Flow	14.1	11.7	-10.5	17.0	14.7	12.9	16.3	26.7	34.5	23.4
Curr. Ratio	4.0	4.1	3.5	4.7	6.1	5.5	6.5	5.4	4.6	5.1
% LT Debt of Cap.	7.2	10.3	13.1	12.3	9.6	12.1	13.7	15.0	17.5	16.6
% Net Inc.of Revs.	8.5	6.8	NM	5.0	5.3	4.3	6.2	13.2	20.4	20.2
% Ret. on Assets	8.8	6.1	NM	5.6	4.9	3.8	5.8	14.6	26.0	25.2
% Ret. on Equity	11.3	8.1	NM	7.1	6.1	4.8	7.5	19.4	35.1	33.1

Data as orig. reptd.; bef. results of disc. opers. and/or spec. items. Per share data adj. for stk. divs. as of ex-div. date. Bold denotes diluted EPS (FASB 128). E-Estimated. NA-Not Available. NM-Not Meaningful. NR-Not Ranked.

Office—425 W. Capitol Ave., Suite 1100, Little Rock, AR 72201. **Tel**—(501) 688-8229. **Website**—http://www.tcby.com.**Chrmn & CEO**—F. D. Hickingbotham. **Pres & COO**—H. C. Hickingbotham. **EVP, Treas & CFO**—G. H. Whisenhunt. **SVP & Secy**—W. P. Creasman. **Investor Contact**—Stacy Duckett. **Dirs**—W. H. Bowen, D. R. Grant, F. D. Hickingbotham, F. T. Hickingbotham, H. C. Hickingbotham, D. O. Kirkpatrick, M. D. Loyd, H. H. Pollard. **Transfer Agent & Registrar**—Wachovia Bank & Trust Co., Winston-Salem, NC. **Incorporated**—in Delaware in 1984. **Empl**—454. **S&P Analyst:** Scott H. Kessler

STANDARD &POOR'S
STOCK REPORTS

TCSI Corporation

5357F

NASDAQ Symbol **TCSI**

In S&P SmallCap 600

03-OCT-98

Industry: Computer (Software & Services)

Summary: This company provides integrated software products and services for the global telecommunications industry.

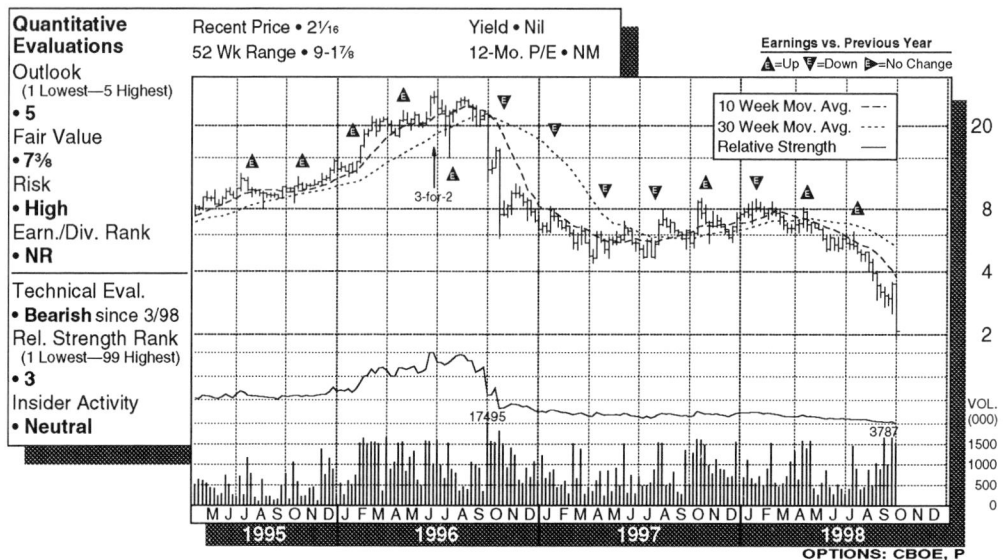

Quantitative Evaluations	
Recent Price • 2¹/₁₆	Yield • Nil
52 Wk Range • 9-1⁷/₈	12-Mo. P/E • NM

Outlook (1 Lowest—5 Highest)
• **5**

Fair Value
• **7³/₈**

Risk
• **High**

Earn./Div. Rank
• **NR**

Technical Eval.
• **Bearish** since 3/98

Rel. Strength Rank (1 Lowest—99 Highest)
• **3**

Insider Activity
• **Neutral**

Earnings vs. Previous Year
▲=Up ▼=Down ▶=No Change

10 Week Mov. Avg. – – –
30 Week Mov. Avg. ·······
Relative Strength ——

OPTIONS: CBOE, P

Business Profile - 15-SEP-98

As demand for telecom products and services accelerates with deregulation, competition and new technology, customers are turning to TCSI for help in speeding product development, lowering costs and improving customer service. The company experienced a jump in software license fees in the first half of 1998, which helped to improve its margins. TCSI intends to increase its revenues and improve operating margins for the remainder of 1998. The company also seeks to broaden its product portfolio through a mix of internal development and acquisitions. In December 1997, TCSI formed a long-term technology partnership with NEC, and opened a joint development facility in Japan.

Operational Review - 15-SEP-98

Total revenues in the six months ended June 30, 1998, increased 15%, year to year, as a large rise in software licensing fees outweighed a slight decline in services revenues. Margins widened, and results benefited from a nonrecurring gain of $550,000, versus a $1.1 million charge. After taxes at 40.0%, versus tax credits of $761,000, net income of $1,005,000 ($0.04 a share, on 6.0% more shares) contrasted with a net loss of $1,480,000 ($0.07).

Stock Performance - 02-OCT-98

In the past 30 trading days, TCSI's shares have declined 47%, compared to a 7% fall in the S&P 500. Average trading volume for the past five days was 363,440 shares, compared with the 40-day moving average of 348,521 shares.

Key Stock Statistics

Dividend Rate/Share	Nil	Shareholders	100
Shs. outstg. (M)	22.4	Market cap. (B)	$0.046
Avg. daily vol. (M)	0.520	Inst. holdings	50%
Tang. Bk. Value/Share	3.40		
Beta	1.27		

Value of $10,000 invested 5 years ago: $ 10,390

Fiscal Year Ending Dec. 31

	1998	1997	1996	1995	1994	1993
Revenues (Million $)						
1Q	11.01	9.83	18.54	12.71	8.99	7.16
2Q	11.14	9.50	21.83	13.37	9.47	7.89
3Q	—	9.76	9.79	14.08	10.49	8.07
4Q	—	10.48	10.08	15.20	11.35	8.93
Yr.	—	39.58	60.23	55.36	40.31	32.05
Earnings Per Share ($)						
1Q	0.02	-0.03	0.13	0.09	0.06	0.01
2Q	0.02	0.04	0.12	0.10	0.07	0.03
3Q	—	-0.02	-0.31	0.11	0.08	0.05
4Q	—	-0.03	0.07	0.12	0.09	0.05
Yr.	—	-0.12	0.01	0.42	0.30	0.15

Next earnings report expected: mid October

Dividend Data

No cash dividends have been paid to public shareholders, and the company does not expect to pay any in the foreseeable future.

STANDARD
&POOR'S
STOCK REPORTS

TCSI Corporation

5357F
03-OCT-98

Business Summary - 15-SEP-98

Competition among telecommunications service providers, the proliferation of new communications services, and the pressure to provide them quickly and cost-effectively have increased the need for scalable and flexible software solutions that improve and automate the management of communications networks. In response to this increased competition, many network operators are implementing integrated service management (ISM) solutions to more tightly integrate the management of network components.

TCSI Corp. (TCSI) provides integrated products and services for the global telecom industry. Prior to 1997, the company earned revenue from licensing embedded software contained in wireless products and from developing system solutions for the transportation industry. However, in the second half of 1996, TCSI divested all non-telecom product lines, in order to focus entirely on offering software solutions to the telecom industry. The company's products and services let telecom service providers and equipment manufacturers meet growing demand for integrated and automated management of a wide range of networks and services.

In January 1997, the company announced its SolutionCore product family, a suite of software products for building and deploying advanced telecom network management applications. SolutionCore leverages capabilities provided by TCSI's development product, Object

Services Package (OSP), and is the first large-scale application development environment to offer both Telecommunications Management Network (TMN) and CORBA interoperability. In October 1997, the company announced the shipment of the next generation of SolutionCore, with enhancements for improved performance, ease of use and standards-based interoperability.

In February 1997, TCSI announced its SolutionSuites product family, a suite of software products and services that combines the company's application software, tools and expertise to integrate and automate a range of telecom industry processes. TCSI also offers SolutionServices, a full range of services, including consulting, customized development, maintenance, and training to complement all of its products.

Sales are concentrated among a limited amount of customers. In 1997, 1996 and 1995, revenues from TCSI's five largest customers accounted for 67%, 54% and 47% of the total, respectively. International revenues provided 78% of total revenues in 1997, up from 40% in 1996.

Revenue contributions in recent years were:

	1997	1996	1995	1994
Services	86%	71%	79%	87%
Software licensing fees	14%	17%	21%	13%
Equipment	Nil	12%	Nil	Nil

Per Share Data ($)

(Year Ended Dec. 31)	1997	1996	1995	1994	1993	1992	1991	1990	1989	1988
Tangible Bk. Val.	3.34	3.47	2.01	1.35	1.01	0.97	0.85	0.50	NA	NA
Cash Flow	0.08	0.21	0.51	0.33	0.27	0.25	0.66	0.41	NA	NA
Earnings	-0.12	0.01	0.42	0.30	0.15	0.13	0.45	0.34	NA	NA
Dividends	Nil	Nil	Nil	Nil	Nil	Nil	Nil	NM	NM	NM
Payout Ratio	Nil	Nil	Nil	Nil	Nil	Nil	Nil	NM	NM	NM
Prices - High	9	29³/₄	13⁷/₈	7⁷/₈	4⁷/₈	6	6⁷/₈	NA	NA	NA
- Low	4³/₈	5³/₄	6⁵/₈	3	1¹⁵/₁₆	1⁵/₁₆	4¹/₈	NA	NA	NA
P/E Ratio - High	NM	NM	33	26	34	47	12	NA	NA	NA
- Low	NM	NM	16	10	13	11	7	NA	NA	NA

Income Statement Analysis (Million $)

	1997	1996	1995	1994	1993	1992	1991	1990	1989	1988
Revs.	39.6	60.2	55.3	40.3	32.1	34.1	44.8	33.8	18.1	10.6
Oper. Inc.	-1.7	-2.8	12.6	8.5	6.1	5.8	15.1	10.0	5.4	3.2
Depr.	4.2	4.2	1.7	0.7	2.1	2.4	1.9	1.3	0.3	0.1
Int. Exp.	Nil	Nil	Nil	Nil	Nil	Nil	Nil	Nil	Nil	Nil
Pretax Inc.	-4.0	0.5	11.9	8.4	4.5	3.9	13.7	10.2	5.4	3.2
Eff. Tax Rate	NM	34%	32%	35%	40%	40%	26%	40%	2.50%	2.40%
Net Inc.	-2.6	0.3	8.0	5.4	2.7	2.4	10.2	6.1	5.3	3.1

Balance Sheet & Other Fin. Data (Million $)

	1997	1996	1995	1994	1993	1992	1991	1990	1989	1988
Cash	33.6	45.2	22.0	19.9	14.9	15.3	13.3	7.7	2.6	NA
Curr. Assets	69.4	64.2	43.5	28.9	21.9	20.1	19.4	14.9	10.3	NA
Total Assets	84.2	87.1	43.5	34.1	27.6	24.8	23.3	18.3	11.5	5.1
Curr. Liab.	10.1	13.5	12.1	10.3	9.7	6.5	7.3	10.6	3.7	NA
LT Debt	Nil	Nil	Nil	Nil	Nil	Nil	Nil	Nil	Nil	NA
Common Eqty.	74.1	73.6	37.3	23.8	17.9	18.3	15.9	7.7	7.8	3.2
Total Cap.	74.2	73.6	37.3	23.8	17.9	18.3	16.0	7.7	7.8	NA
Cap. Exp.	7.2	7.5	5.4	1.1	0.4	1.6	2.1	3.3	1.2	0.4
Cash Flow	1.6	4.5	9.8	6.1	4.8	4.8	12.1	7.4	5.6	3.2
Curr. Ratio	6.9	4.8	3.6	2.8	2.3	3.1	2.7	1.4	2.8	NA
% LT Debt of Cap.	Nil	Nil	Nil	Nil	Nil	Nil	Nil	Nil	Nil	NA
% Net Inc.of Revs.	NM	0.5	14.4	13.5	8.4	7.0	22.9	18.1	29.1	29.8
% Ret. on Assets	NM	0.4	19.3	17.6	10.6	9.9	44.9	41.0	63.7	NA
% Ret. on Equity	NM	0.5	26.4	26.0	15.4	13.9	81.0	78.9	95.8	NA

Data as orig. reptd.; bef. results of disc. opers. and/or spec. items. Per share data adj. for stk. divs. as of ex-div. date. Bold denotes diluted EPS (FASB 128). E-Estimated. NA-Not Available. NM-Not Meaningful. NR-Not Ranked.

Office—1080 Marina Village Parkway, Alameda, CA 94501. **Tel**—(510)749-8500. **Fax**—(510)749-8700. **Website**—http://www.tcsi.com **Chrmn**—J. C. Bolger. **Pres & CEO**—R. Banin. **VP-Fin & CFO**—Art Wilder. **Investor Contact**—Leigh Salvo. **Dirs**—R. Banin, J. C. Bolger, N. E. Friedmann, W. A. Hasler, D. G. Messerschmitt, H. E. Wagner. **Transfer Agent**—Boston EquiServe. **Incorporated**—in Nevada in 1987. **Empl**— 220. **S&P Analyst:** B.G.

03-OCT-98

Industry:
Building Materials

Summary: This company makes fabricated structural lumber for the residential and light commercial building industries.

Quantitative Evaluations		
	Recent Price • 17½	Yield • 1.3%
	52 Wk Range • 34½-16⅞	12-Mo. P/E • 11.3

Outlook (1 Lowest—5 Highest)
• **4+**

Fair Value
• **23⅝**

Risk
• **Average**

Earn./Div. Rank
• **B-**

Technical Eval.
• **Bearish** since 7/98

Rel. Strength Rank (1 Lowest—99 Highest)
• **21**

Insider Activity
• **Neutral**

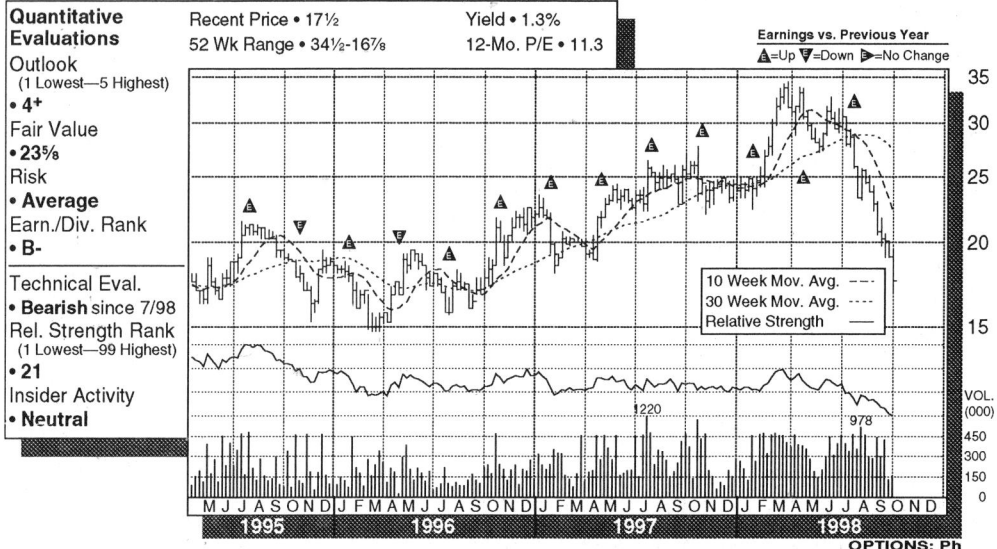

Earnings vs. Previous Year
▲=Up ▼=Down ▶=No Change

10 Week Mov. Avg. – – –
30 Week Mov. Avg. - - - -
Relative Strength ——

VOL. (000)

OPTIONS: Ph

Business Profile - 11-AUG-98

Sales per North American housing start rose 19% in 1997, to $344 per start from the $289 per start of 1996, marking the 15th consecutive year the company has achieved market penetration growth in the key residential construction market. Nearly every geographic region of the continent showed gains in sales per housing start, with exceptionally strong improvements registered in eastern Canada, the Southwest, and the southern United States. In July 1998, the company noted that its current rate of order intake indicates continued growth in the use of engineered lumber, despite the very low levels of pricing for competing lumber products. It said it expects continued sales and production cost improvements from its new technology products to help offset some of the margin pressure it is experiencing from raw material cost increases. In May 1998, directors authorized the expenditure of $35 million to repurchase the company's common stock.

Operational Review - 11-AUG-98

Sales rose 9.3% year to year in the first half of 1998, and net income advanced 15%, to $14,907,000 ($0.79 per diluted share), from $12,968,000 ($0.67). The improved performance was achieved despite a very challenging operating environment that included significant price declines for competing commodity lumber products, increases in some raw material costs and wet weather conditions that delayed delivery of framing materials to new homes under construction in many markets.

Stock Performance - 02-OCT-98

In the past 30 trading days, TJCO's shares have declined 26%, compared to a 7% fall in the S&P 500. Average trading volume for the past five days was 30,840 shares, compared with the 40-day moving average of 65,510 shares.

Key Stock Statistics

Dividend Rate/Share	0.22	Shareholders	2,100
Shs. outstg. (M)	16.1	Market cap. (B)	$0.282
Avg. daily vol. (M)	0.052	Inst. holdings	52%
Tang. Bk. Value/Share	12.79		
Beta	1.11		

Value of $10,000 invested 5 years ago: $ 16,606

Fiscal Year Ending Dec. 31

	1998	1997	1996	1995	1994	1993
Revenues (Million $)						
1Q	185.8	161.3	111.2	109.9	135.1	114.1
2Q	193.4	185.7	155.1	123.9	163.5	139.6
3Q	—	185.6	179.6	137.8	171.7	152.7
4Q	—	173.8	131.4	113.3	148.6	144.7
Yr.	—	706.3	577.2	484.9	618.9	551.2
Earnings Per Share ($)						
1Q	**0.36**	**0.28**	-0.01	0.09	0.13	-0.06
2Q	**0.43**	**0.39**	0.24	0.16	0.32	0.30
3Q	—	**0.45**	0.42	0.23	0.23	0.41
4Q	—	**0.31**	0.22	0.03	-0.23	0.17
Yr.	—	**1.11**	0.86	0.51	0.46	0.82

Next earnings report expected: mid October

Dividend Data (Dividends have been paid since 1977.)

Amount ($)	Date Decl.	Ex-Div. Date	Stock of Record	Payment Date
0.055	Dec. 18	Dec. 26	Dec. 30	Jan. 14 '98
0.055	Feb. 13	Mar. 25	Mar. 27	Apr. 15 '98
0.055	May. 28	Jun. 24	Jun. 26	Jul. 15 '98
0.055	Aug. 27	Sep. 23	Sep. 25	Oct. 14 '98

A Division of The **McGraw·Hill** Companies

Business Summary - 11-AUG-98

TJ International, Inc. (TJCO) is the 51% owner andmanaging partner of Trus Joist MacMillan A Limited Partnership(TJM), the world's leading manufacturer and marketer of engineeredlumber products. Engineered lumber products are high-quality, resource-efficient alternatives for the dwindling supply of wide-dimension lumber traditionally cut from large logs. Substantially all of the company's operating assets are held and revenue generated by TJM. MacMillan Bloedel Limited (MB) owns a 49% interest in TJM.

The company's primary objective remains increasing market penetration for its engineered lumber products. The company believes that its fundamentals remain strong: builders continue to make the switch to engineered lumber products, which they are using in more applications on each project; consumer confidence and employment rates are high, so housing starts should remain at favorable levels; and the company believes that it is well positioned with manufacturing, sales, marketing and distribution to continue to grow its business. TJ also believes that the regional fundamentals that have driven the company's growth over the past several years remain in place, including the declining availability of high-quality, large diameter timber, the superior performance of engineered lumber products, and the company's continuing transition to proprietary, lower-cost technologies. In addition, the company continues to enjoy strong brand name recognition, supported by an extensive North American distribution network. Most importantly, itbelieves there continues to be growth in market acceptance of engineered lumber products.

The company's primary competitors are traditional lumber mills. It believes it possesses significant competitive advantages over the traditional mills, because its proprietary technologies allow the company to use less expensive, more abundant wood by-products in the manufacture of its products.

To a lesser extent, the company faces competition from a few large wood products companies that offer a limited line of engineered lumber products. TJ expects increased competition from these companies. However, it believes it possesses competitive advantages over these concerns, due to its ability to make laminated lumber from proprietary technologies, its extensive product line, greater brand name recognition and broad North American distribution system.

Unlike its principal competitors, the company does not own any timberlands or significant amounts of timber inventory. It purchases its raw material, mostly by contract, from independent suppliers. The company does not expect any potential raw material shortages in the foreseeable future.

Per Share Data ($)

(Year Ended Dec. 31)	1997	1996	1995	1994	1993	1992	1991	1990	1989	1988
Tangible Bk. Val.	12.22	11.07	10.19	11.17	12.38	7.86	6.66	5.95	6.55	5.66
Cash Flow	3.73	3.15	2.51	2.09	2.47	2.01	0.84	1.71	1.88	1.94
Earnings	1.44	0.86	0.51	0.46	0.82	0.38	-0.32	0.82	1.06	1.25
Dividends	0.22	0.22	0.22	0.22	0.21	0.21	0.21	0.21	0.20	0.18
Payout Ratio	15%	26%	43%	48%	31%	54%	NM	25%	19%	14%
Prices - High	27³/₄	23¹/₄	21¹/₂	32¹/₄	33	13	15	13¹/₄	18¹/₈	13⁵/₈
- Low	18	14³/₄	15¹/₄	14¹/₄	11¹/₈	8	7³/₄	7¹/₈	11¹/₂	8³/₄
P/E Ratio - High	19	27	42	70	40	34	NM	16	17	11
- Low	12	17	30	31	14	21	NM	9	11	7

Income Statement Analysis (Million $)

	1997	1996	1995	1994	1993	1992	1991	1990	1989	1988
Revs.	706	577	485	619	551	400	283	327	351	315
Oper. Inc.	128	94.0	63.6	69.6	56.5	13.0	12.3	34.0	39.3	40.7
Depr.	42.9	39.5	33.2	28.3	23.6	21.8	14.9	12.6	11.9	9.7
Int. Exp.	6.9	6.3	0.6	5.3	3.4	3.5	2.4	2.8	3.1	1.9
Pretax Inc.	83.7	25.7	15.5	43.6	30.1	-11.0	-12.4	19.6	25.5	29.8
Eff. Tax Rate	20%	37%	37%	18%	25%	NM	NM	39%	40%	40%
Net Inc.	27.5	16.1	9.7	8.9	12.5	6.4	-3.2	11.9	15.3	17.8

Balance Sheet & Other Fin. Data (Million $)

	1997	1996	1995	1994	1993	1992	1991	1990	1989	1988
Cash	119	36.8	19.7	73.7	73.3	0.2	0.5	3.1	3.3	12.7
Curr. Assets	295	172	105	188	183	80.9	68.9	59.1	66.3	70.1
Total Assets	712	600	546	614	454	345	335	167	173	146
Curr. Liab.	75.9	60.0	57.0	62.4	57.1	56.8	54.7	27.7	35.4	30.7
LT Debt	142	88.1	89.4	102	30.9	33.1	26.4	28.9	30.3	23.5
Common Eqty.	228	214	196	238	231	127	112	78.0	92.0	79.0
Total Cap.	605	511	286	540	382	274	276	137	135	114
Cap. Exp.	42.6	19.0	106	152	34.0	27.0	145	14.0	37.0	23.0
Cash Flow	69.6	55.7	42.9	36.3	35.3	26.9	10.9	24.3	27.2	27.6
Curr. Ratio	3.9	2.9	1.8	3.0	3.2	1.4	1.3	2.1	1.9	2.3
% LT Debt of Cap.	23.5	17.2	31.2	19.0	8.1	12.1	9.6	21.1	22.4	20.7
% Net Inc.of Revs.	3.9	2.8	2.0	1.1	2.3	1.6	NM	3.6	4.3	5.7
% Ret. on Assets	4.2	2.8	1.7	1.6	2.8	1.9	NM	7.3	9.5	13.0
% Ret. on Equity	12.4	7.8	4.6	3.4	5.9	4.0	NM	14.3	17.8	25.4

Data as orig. reptd.; bef. results of disc. opers. and/or spec. items. Per share data adj. for stk. divs. as of ex-div. date. Bold denotes diluted EPS (FASB 128). E-Estimated. NA-Not Available. NM-Not Meaningful. NR-Not Ranked.

Office—200 E. Mallard Dr., Boise, ID 83706. **Tel**—(208) 364-3300. **Chrmn**—H. E. Thomas. **Pres & CEO**—T. Denig. **VP-Fin & CFO**—Valerie A. Heusinkveld. **Secy & Treas**—R. B. Drury. **Investor Contact**—Mel Landers.**Dirs**—T. H. Denig, J. A. Godwin, J. L. Scott, J. L. Stead, H. E. Thomas, S. C. Wheelwright, W. J. White. **Transfer Agent & Registrar**—West One Bank, Boise. **Incorporated**—in Idaho in 1960; reincorporated in Nevada in 1973; reincorporated in Delaware in 1987. **Empl**— 3,592. **S&P Analyst:** C.F.B.

STANDARD &POOR'S
STOCK REPORTS

TNP Enterprises

2185M

NYSE Symbol **TNP**

In S&P SmallCap 600

03-OCT-98 Industry:
Electric Companies

Summary: TNP is the holding company for Texas-New Power-er, which distributes electricity in areas of Texas and New Mexico.

Quantitative Evaluations

Recent Price • 36⅝   Yield • 2.9%
52 Wk Range • 37⅛-24⅜   12-Mo. P/E • 22.1

Outlook
(1 Lowest—5 Highest)
• **1⁻**

Fair Value
• **33**

Risk
• **Low**

Earn./Div. Rank
• **B**

Technical Eval.
• **Bullish** since 7/98

Rel. Strength Rank
(1 Lowest—99 Highest)
• **97**

Insider Activity
• **NA**

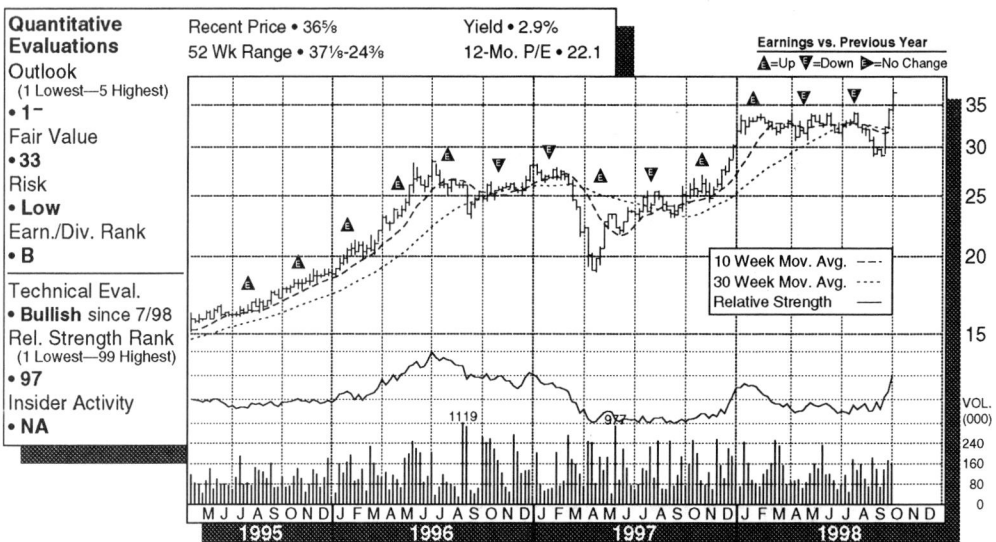

Earnings vs. Previous Year
▲=Up ▼=Down ▶=No Change

10 Week Mov. Avg. - - -
30 Week Mov. Avg. ·····
Relative Strength ——

VOL. (000)

Business Profile - 04-JUN-98

In December 1997, Texas-New Mexico Power (TNP's primary holding) and the Public Utility Commission (PUC) of Texas reached an agreement on a transition-to-competition plan that would cut residential rates by a total of 9% and commercial rates by 3% between 1998 and 2001. The agreement would also accelerate recovery of costs related to the company's generating facility. However, the administrative law judges who had been considering the proposal forwarded the proposed plan to the PUC with an unfavorable recommendation. The PUC can vote to accept, modify or deny the plan or the judges' recommendation. A vote is expected by July 15, 1998.

Operational Review - 04-JUN-98

Revenues in the first quarter of 1998 were down 1.1%, year to year, reflecting lower pass-through items, partly offset by a favorable new transmission fee structure. Margins narrowed, due primarily to purchased power costs in excess of revenue recovery; operating profit declined 7.0%. With a 6.6% decrease in interest charges, income from continuing operations was down 8.2%, to $4,625,000 ($0.35 a share, after preferred dividends, on 1.3% more shares), from $5,040,000 ($0.38). Results in the 1997 period exclude a loss of $0.07 a share from the discontinued construction activities of FWI.

Stock Performance - 02-OCT-98

In the past 30 trading days, TNP's shares have increased 19%, compared to a 7% fall in the S&P 500. Average trading volume for the past five days was 32,080 shares, compared with the 40-day moving average of 26,205 shares.

Key Stock Statistics

Dividend Rate/Share	1.08	Shareholders	5,000
Shs. outstg. (M)	13.3	Market cap. (B)	$0.486
Avg. daily vol. (M)	0.027	Inst. holdings	52%
Tang. Bk. Value/Share	22.55		
Beta	0.50		

Value of $10,000 invested 5 years ago: $ 26,035

Fiscal Year Ending Dec. 31

	1998	1997	1996	1995	1994	1993
Revenues (Million $)						
1Q	125.4	128.4	99.8	105.7	107.6	103.2
2Q	143.9	136.0	122.0	121.2	111.0	107.5
3Q	—	197.6	157.4	151.6	149.9	150.1
4Q	—	135.7	123.4	107.3	109.5	113.5
Yr.	—	585.2	502.7	485.8	478.0	474.2
Earnings Per Share ($)						
1Q	**0.35**	**0.38**	0.05	-0.57	-0.29	-0.20
2Q	**0.41**	**0.68**	0.71	0.54	-2.04	-0.06
3Q	—	**1.73**	1.29	2.44	1.09	1.25
4Q	—	**0.29**	0.03	0.20	-0.47	0.01
Yr.	—	**3.08**	1.98	2.98	-1.70	1.01

Next earnings report expected: NA

Dividend Data (Dividends have been paid since 1936.)

Amount ($)	Date Decl.	Ex-Div. Date	Stock of Record	Payment Date
0.270	Nov. 11	Nov. 24	Nov. 26	Dec. 15 '97
0.270	Feb. 16	Feb. 25	Feb. 27	Mar. 15 '98
0.270	May. 04	May. 20	May. 22	Jun. 15 '98
0.270	Aug. 11	Aug. 26	Aug. 28	Sep. 15 '98

A Division of The **McGraw·Hill** *Companies*

Business Summary - 04-JUN-98

TNP Enterprises believes that significant opportunity exists in unregulated retail energy and utility after-market services (beyond the meter). In early 1996, the company established Facility Works (FWI) as a wholly owned subsidiary to investigate these opportunities. However, after continuing losses, TNP decided to discontinue the subsidiary's construction activities and refocus FWI to concentrate on the maintenance and repair segment of its business. Consistent with the company's focus on small and medium-sized communities, FWI concentrates on providing services to commercial and institutional customers in nonmetropolitan Sunbelt areas that, because of their size or location, have difficulty obtaining these services from large, well-established entities.

In March 1997, New Mexico regulators approved TNP's plan for transition to competition for its New Mexico service territory. A three-year transition period began April 1, 1997, and starting April 1, 2000, customers will have a choice of energy providers at market rates. During the transition period, TNP customer rates, including fuel and purchased power costs, will be frozen. Another agreement with the Texas regulators will lower residential rates by 9% and commercial rates by 3% between 1998 and 2001. The agreement also calls for

accelerated recovery of costs related to the company's generating facility. A vote on the plan is expected by July 15, 1998, following a recent unfavorable recommendation by adminstrative law judges who had been considering the proposal.

Texas-New Mexico Power Co., TNP's primary holding, is a utility engaged in the production, transmission and distribution of electricity. It provides electric service to 85 Texas and New Mexico municipalities and adjacent rural areas with more than 222,000 customers. TNP operates in three regions. The Gulf Coast region includes the area along the Texas Gulf Coast between Houston and Galveston. The North-Central region extends from Lewisville, TX, to municipalities along the Red River, and the Mountain region includes areas in southwest and south-central New Mexico, and far west Texas. Sales in all regions are primarily to retail customers (36% of total 1997 revenues). Sales of electricity in 1997 totaled 10,150 million kwh, up 29% from 1996.

The company purchased 80% of its electric requirements in 1997, up from 72% in 1996. TNP owns one 300 MW lignite-fueled generating facility, TNP One, which provided approximately 20% of TNP's total energy requirements. Power generated at TNP One is transmitted over the company's own transmission lines to other utilities' transmission systems for delivery to TNP's Texas service area systems.

Per Share Data ($)

(Year Ended Dec. 31)	1997	1996	1995	1994	1993	1992	1991	1990	1989	1988
Tangible Bk. Val.	22.71	21.41	19.86	17.01	19.97	20.55	21.35	20.76	20.55	20.23
Earnings	3.08	1.98	2.98	-1.70	1.01	1.17	2.23	1.84	1.90	5.19
Dividends	1.00	0.93	0.82	1.22	1.63	1.63	1.63	1.63	1.55	1.47
Payout Ratio	33%	47%	28%	NM	161%	139%	73%	89%	82%	28%
Prices - High	33³/₄	28⁵/₈	19¹/₈	18⁷/₈	19¹/₂	21⁵/₈	21	22¹/₂	22³/₈	20¹/₂
- Low	18⁷/₈	18¹/₂	14⁵/₈	13¹/₈	14⁵/₈	17¹/₄	15⁷/₈	14¹/₂	19	18¹/₈
P/E Ratio - High	11	14	6	NM	19	18	9	12	12	4
- Low	6	9	5	NM	14	15	7	8	10	3

Income Statement Analysis (Million $)

	1997	1996	1995	1994	1993	1992	1991	1990	1989	1988
Revs.	585	503	486	478	474	444	441	397	378	366
Depr.	38.9	38.2	37.9	36.8	36.0	35.1	28.0	18.5	16.0	15.3
Maint.	NA	10.7	11.5	12.0	11.5	11.3	11.2	8.8	8.0	6.9
Fxd. Chgs. Cov.	NA	1.4	1.5	0.6	1.2	1.2	1.6	2.0	2.5	4.6
Constr. Credits	NM	NM	NM	0.3	0.3	0.1	4.6	4.6	0.5	0.4
Eff. Tax Rate	33%	31%	27%	NM	30%	22%	29%	29%	31%	19%
Net Inc.	40.4	23.1	33.1	-17.4	11.6	10.9	19.5	16.4	16.8	42.4

Balance Sheet & Other Fin. Data (Million $)

	1997	1996	1995	1994	1993	1992	1991	1990	1989	1988
Gross Prop.	1,243	1,216	1,197	1,196	1,209	1,189	1,162	853	475	457
Cap. Exp.	28.2	28.0	28.7	29.0	26.0	22.1	29.9	40.8	24.0	41.8
Net Prop.	929	934	944	967	1,006	1,016	1,017	729	363	355
Capitalization:										
LT Debt	478	534	612	683	679	742	525	350	135	116
% LT Debt	61	66	74	78	75	76	73	66	42	39
Pfd.	3.2	3.4	3.6	8.7	9.6	10.4	11.3	12.6	13.9	15.2
% Pfd.	0.40	0.40	0.40	1.00	1.10	1.10	1.60	2.40	4.40	5.10
Common	298	278	217	185	214	219	178	172	169	164
% Common	38	34	26	21	24	23	25	32	53	56
Total Cap.	885	911	909	940	1,007	1,085	819	630	387	361
% Oper. Ratio	83.6	81.4	80.1	83.7	83.5	82.7	85.8	90.7	92.5	92.4
% Earn. on Net Prop.	10.2	2.5	10.1	7.9	7.7	7.6	7.2	6.8	7.9	8.1
% Return On Revs.	6.9	4.6	6.8	NM	2.4	2.5	4.4	4.1	4.4	11.6
% Return On Invest. Capital	10.8	9.1	11.9	6.0	7.6	8.3	8.7	7.3	8.0	15.3
% Return On Com. Equity	14.0	9.3	20.3	NM	5.0	5.0	10.5	8.9	9.3	28.0

Data as orig. reptd.; bef. results of disc opers. and/or spec. items. Per share data adj. for stk. divs. as of ex-div. date. Bold denotes diluted EPS (FASB 128). E-Estimated. NA-Not Available. NM-Not Meaningful. NR-Not Ranked.

Office—4100 International Plaza, P.O. Box 2943, Fort Worth, TX 76113. **Tel**—(817) 731-0099. **Website**—http://www.tnpe.com **Chrmn, Pres & CEO**—K. R. Joyce. **SVP & CFO**—Manjit S. Cheema. **Secy**—P. W. Talbot. **Investor Contact**—P. L. Bridges (817) 731-0088.**Dirs**—R. D. Alexander, J. A. Fanning, S. M. Gutierrez, K. R. Joyce, J. R. Holland Jr., H. L. Kempner Jr., C. D. Smith Surles, L. G. Wheeler, D. H. Withers. **Transfer Agent & Registrar**—Bank of New York, NYC. **Incorporated**—in Texas in 1963; reincorporated in Texas in 1984. **Empl**— 1,305. **S&P Analyst:** J. Robert Cho

Taco Cabana

5363

NASDAQ Symbol **TACO**

In S&P SmallCap 600

03-OCT-98

Industry: Restaurants

Summary: Taco Cabana operates a chain of Mexican patio-style restaurants primarily in the southwestern U.S.

Quantitative Evaluations

Outlook (1 Lowest—5 Highest)
- **1+**

Fair Value
- **5⅜**

Risk
- **High**

Earn./Div. Rank
- **NR**

Technical Eval.
- **Bearish** since 5/98

Rel. Strength Rank (1 Lowest—99 Highest)
- **65**

Insider Activity
- **Neutral**

Recent Price • 5⅜
52 Wk Range • 7¼-3⅞
Yield • Nil
12-Mo. P/E • NM

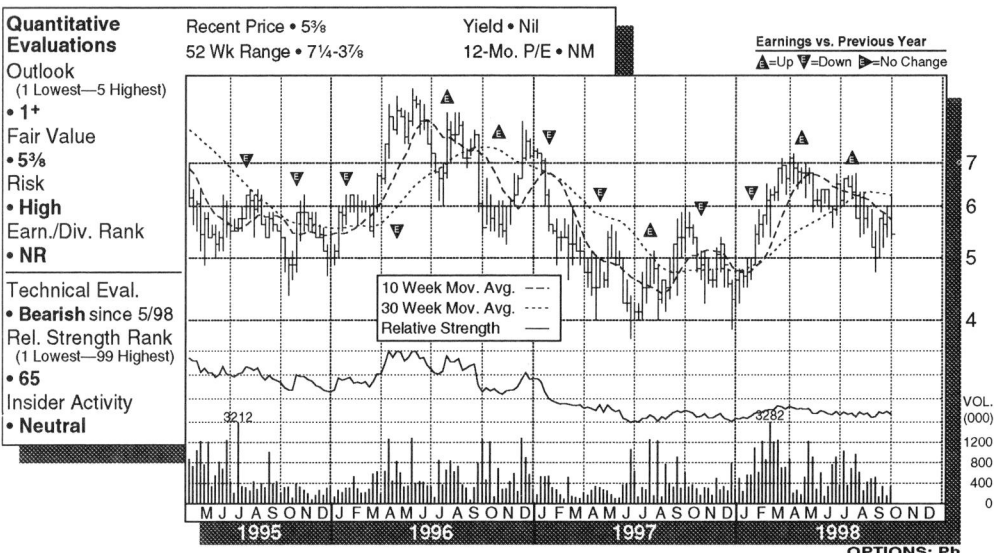

Earnings vs. Previous Year
▲=Up ▼=Down ▶=No Change

10 Week Mov. Avg. — —
30 Week Mov. Avg. - - - -
Relative Strength —

OPTIONS: Ph

Business Profile - 17-SEP-98

Management attributed the significantly improved operations in the first half of 1998 to a more consistent marketing program featuring a value meal message, increased staffing levels at existing restaurants, a reimage program, a modest price hike instituted in the first quarter of 1998, and the closing of underperforming restaurants. Through July 27, 1998, TACO had opened six new restaurants, and remained on track to open a total of eight to ten new restaurants for the full year. In July, directors authorized a 1,000,000 share buyback program following completion of an earlier 1,500,000 stock repurchase program. Funding would be obtained from a bank credit line as well as cash flows from operations.

Operational Review - 17-SEP-98

Total revenues for the 26 weeks ended June 29, 1998, advanced 6.7%, year to year, reflecting new restaurant openings, a menu price increase of about 2% in 1998's first quarter, favorable weather, and improved service. Margins widened, aided by increased controls and the purchase of supplies at more attractive prices. Further helped by lower depreciation and amortization charges, pretax income more than doubled to $5,154,000 from $2,273,000. After no taxes (due to the utilization of operating loss carryforwards), versus taxes at 37.0%, net income more than tripled, to $5,154,000 ($0.35 a share, on 4.4% fewer shares), from $1,432,000 ($0.09).

Stock Performance - 02-OCT-98

In the past 30 trading days, TACO's shares have declined 9%, compared to a 7% fall in the S&P 500. Average trading volume for the past five days was 63,120 shares, compared with the 40-day moving average of 66,190 shares.

Key Stock Statistics

Dividend Rate/Share	Nil	Shareholders	1,000
Shs. outstg. (M)	14.3	Market cap. (B)	$0.078
Avg. daily vol. (M)	0.049	Inst. holdings	60%
Tang. Bk. Value/Share	2.04		
Beta	0.84		

Value of $10,000 invested 5 years ago: $ 4,727

Fiscal Year Ending Dec. 31

	1998	1997	1996	1995	1994	1993
Revenues (Million $)						
1Q	32.41	30.19	31.26	32.84	27.42	16.68
2Q	36.29	34.20	35.31	36.94	32.44	21.20
3Q	—	35.05	33.81	35.67	34.67	30.89
4Q	—	32.77	31.81	33.09	32.73	28.10
Yr.	—	132.2	132.2	138.5	127.3	96.87
Earnings Per Share ($)						
1Q	**0.12**	**0.04**	0.05	0.07	0.12	0.09
2Q	**0.22**	**0.06**	-0.04	-0.39	0.17	0.14
3Q	—	**0.04**	0.08	0.05	0.15	0.16
4Q	—	**-5.07**	-0.04	0.03	0.11	0.15
Yr.	—	**-4.78**	0.04	-0.24	0.55	0.55

Next earnings report expected: early November

Dividend Data

The company has never paid cash dividends on its common stock. TACO intends to retain all earnings for the operation and development of its business and does not expect to pay cash dividends on the common in the foreseeable future. A preferred stock purchase rights plan was adopted in 1995.

A Division of The **McGraw·Hill** *Companies*

Business Summary - 17-SEP-98

While it may not have the same recognition factor as the golden arches of a McDonald's or the red roof of a Pizza Hut, the vivid pink exterior of a Taco Cabana restaurant certainly makes for easy identification by passing motorists. This chain of Mexican patio-style restaurants serves authentic Tex-Mex and traditional Mexican-style cuisine set to the festive backdrop of Latin music, a brightly colored interior dining area, a trellis-shaded outdoor patio area, authentic decorative artifacts and tropical landscaping.

Taco Cabana pioneered the Mexican Patio cafe concept with the opening of its first restaurant in San Antonio in 1978. Since then, Taco Cabana has expanded heavily in Texas and has also moved into other southwestern states, Georgia and Indiana. As of late June 1998, TACO's restaurant universe, which comprises restaurants operating under the names Taco Cabana, Two Pesos and Sombrero Rosa, included 101 company-owned units, one joint-venture restaurant and nine franchised units. About one hundred of the total restaurants are located in Texas. TACO's revenues are derived mainly from sales by company-owned units, with franchise fees and royalty income generally contributing less than 1% of total revenues in 1997.

In 1997, comparable-store sales, defined as restaurants that have been open 18 months or more at the beginning of each quarter, declined 2.9%, year to year.

Much of the decline in comparable store sales occurred during the first six months of the year. Comparable stores sales for the first six months of 1997 decreased 4.8%, while comparable store sales for the last six months of the year decreased only 0.8%. Management attributes much of the decline during the first six months to unfavorable weather conditions, significant declines in the Colorado market (which was closed in November 1997), and a promotional strategy which highlighted higher priced, premium products in an intensely price competitive landscape.

TACO's restaurants strive to offer fresh, premium-quality food at value prices. Typical menu items include flame-grilled beef and chicken fajitas served on sizzling iron skillets, a marinated rotisserie chicken, quesadillas, tortillas, traditional Mexican and American breakfasts, as well as other Tex-Mex dishes and salad entrees. The typical Taco Cabana restaurant provides seating for about 80 customers, with additional patio seating for approximately 50 customers. Most units provide drive-thru windows, which, in the aggregate, account for about 40% of TACO's total sales.

During 1997, TACO initiated a re-image program forexisting restaurants which incorporates many of the features of a new prototype design. During 1997, eight restaurants were re-imaged to the new prototype design and TACO expects to re-image 20 to 25 restaurants during 1998.

Per Share Data ($)

(Year Ended Dec. 31)	1997	1996	1995	1994	1993	1992	1991	1990	1989	1988
Tangible Bk. Val.	1.69	4.32	4.16	4.33	4.64	2.21	NA	NA	NA	NA
Cash Flow	-4.15	0.63	0.42	1.00	0.91	0.72	1.06	0.47	NA	NA
Earnings	-4.78	0.04	-0.24	0.55	0.55	0.40	0.79	0.28	NA	NA
Dividends	Nil	Nil	Nil	Nil	Nil	Nil	Nil	Nil	Nil	Nil
Payout Ratio	Nil	Nil	Nil	Nil	Nil	Nil	Nil	Nil	Nil	Nil
Prices - High	7³/₈	9¹/₈	9¹/₈	20	22¹/₄	14¹/₄	NA	NA	NA	NA
- Low	3³/₄	4⁷/₈	4³/₈	7¹/₄	11¹/₂	9	NA	NA	NA	NA
P/E Ratio - High	NM	NM	NM	36	41	35	NA	NA	NA	NA
- Low	NM	NM	NM	13	21	22	NA	NA	NA	NA

Income Statement Analysis (Million $)

	1997	1996	1995	1994	1993	1992	1991	1990	1989	1988
Revs.	132	132	139	127	97.0	59.0	34.0	32.0	NA	NA
Oper. Inc.	14.8	18.0	17.3	20.2	15.6	8.3	4.5	3.4	NA	NA
Depr.	9.7	9.2	10.3	7.1	4.7	2.5	1.3	0.9	NA	NA
Int. Exp.	1.1	1.3	1.4	0.8	0.3	0.6	0.6	0.5	NA	NA
Pretax Inc.	-74.7	13.3	-6.0	13.3	10.9	5.2	6.4	2.0	NA	NA
Eff. Tax Rate	NM	36%	NM	36%	35%	39%	39%	32%	NA	NA
Net Inc.	-73.2	0.7	-3.8	8.5	7.1	3.2	3.9	1.3	NA	NA

Balance Sheet & Other Fin. Data (Million $)

	1997	1996	1995	1994	1993	1992	1991	1990	1989	1988
Cash	0.3	0.8	2.7	7.3	26.2	NA	NA	NA	NA	NA
Curr. Assets	4.8	7.1	11.4	15.5	34.2	NA	NA	NA	NA	NA
Total Assets	76.3	143	149	152	119	42.0	14.0	10.0	NA	NA
Curr. Liab.	16.5	10.4	13.5	13.5	11.3	NA	NA	NA	NA	NA
LT Debt	13.5	10.6	15.0	11.8	4.6	1.8	3.7	6.1	NA	NA
Common Eqty.	36.4	113	112	116	NA	35.0	5.0	1.0	NA	NA
Total Cap.	49.9	127	129	127	106	37.0	9.0	7.0	NA	NA
Cap. Exp.	16.8	9.2	18.7	36.6	26.5	8.5	NA	NA	NA	NA
Cash Flow	-63.5	9.9	6.5	15.6	11.8	5.7	5.2	2.2	NA	NA
Curr. Ratio	0.3	0.7	0.8	1.1	3.0	NA	NA	NA	NA	NA
% LT Debt of Cap.	27.1	8.3	11.6	9.3	4.3	5.0	42.3	82.4	NA	NA
% Net Inc.of Revs.	NM	0.0	NM	6.7	7.3	5.4	11.5	4.2	NA	NA
% Ret. on Assets	NM	NM	NM	6.3	8.8	11.4	32.7	NA	NA	NA
% Ret. on Equity	NM	NM	NM	79.0	10.4	15.8	123.3	NA	NA	NA

Data as orig. reptd.; bef. results of disc. opers. and/or spec. items. Per share data adj. for stk. divs. as of ex-div. date. Bold denotes diluted EPS (FASB 128). E-Estimated. NA-Not Available. NM-Not Meaningful. NR-Not Ranked.

Office—8918 Tesoro Dr., Suite 200, San Antonio, TX 78217. **Tel**—(210) 804-0990. **Pres, CEO & COO**—S. V. Clark. **EVP & Gen Counsel**—J. A. Eliasberg. **SVP, CFO, Secy, Treas & Investor Contact**—David G. Lloyd. **Dirs**—S. V. Clark, W. J. Nimmo, R. Sands, C. Schenker, R. Sherman, L. Sosa. **Transfer Agent & Registrar**—KeyCorp Shareholder Services, Dallas. **Incorporated**—in Delaware in 1991. **Empl**— 3,000. **S&P Analyst:** P.L.H.

Technitrol, Inc.

2193G

NYSE Symbol **TNL**

In S&P SmallCap 600

03-OCT-98

Industry:
Electrical Equipment

Summary: This company makes electronic components, electrical contacts and assemblies, thermostatic metal products and laminated metal materials for a variety of industrial applications.

Quantitative Evaluations

Recent Price • 19
52 Wk Range • 44⅜-18

Yield • 1.3%
12-Mo. P/E • 9.5

Outlook
(1 Lowest—5 Highest)
• **4**

Fair Value
• **31⅝**

Risk
• **Average**

Earn./Div. Rank
• **B+**

Technical Eval.
• **Bearish** since 7/98

Rel. Strength Rank
(1 Lowest—99 Highest)
• **21**

Insider Activity
• **Favorable**

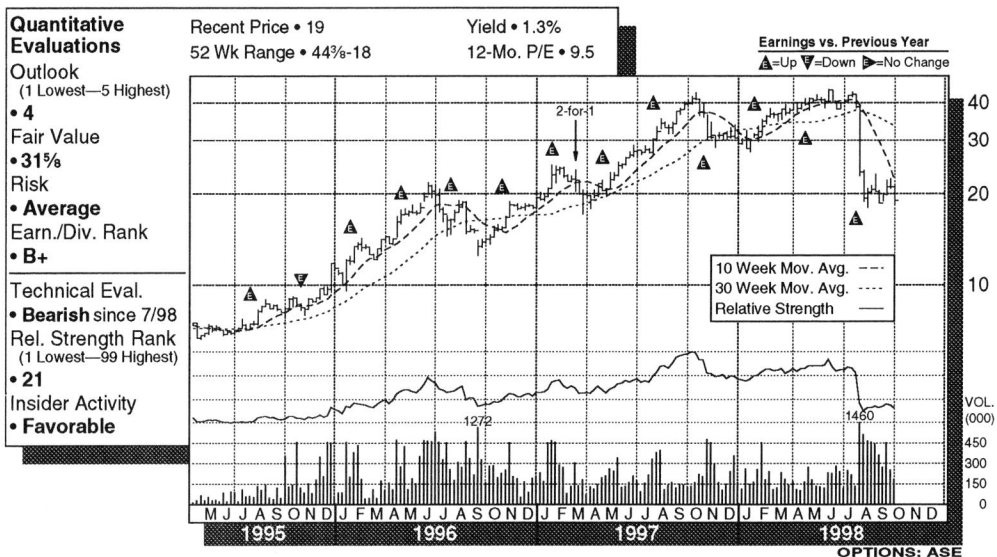

Earnings vs. Previous Year
▲=Up ▼=Down ▶=No Change

10 Week Mov. Avg. ---
30 Week Mov. Avg. ·····
Relative Strength —

OPTIONS: ASE

Business Profile - 17-SEP-98

Technitrol has agreed to acquire for about $33.8 million in cash GTI Corp., a multinational manufacturer and leading supplier of magnetics-based components for signal processing and power transfer functions mainly in local area networking and also in telecommunications and broadband products. However, TNL subsequently informed GTI that it believes that there has been a breach of certain of GTI representations and warranties in the acquisition agreement dated May 26, 1998; TNL believes that as a result of these breaches, it has a right to terminate the acquisition agreement. GTI announced plans to show that the agreement had not been violated. Separately, TNL acquired for about $20 million FEE Technology, S.A., a French manufacturer of magnetic components (with estimated annual revenues of about $36 million) in July 1998.

Operational Review - 17-SEP-98

Sales for the six months ended June 30, 1998, advanced 10%, year to year, on gains of 15% and 0.4% in electronic components and metallurgical components, respectively. Profitability improved in both business segments, and pretax income advanced 27%. After taxes at 38.2%, versus 36.1%, net income was up 23%, to $17,791,000 ($1.10 a share) from $14,453,000 ($0.90). Results for the 1997 period are before income from discontinued operations of $0.72 a share.

Stock Performance - 02-OCT-98

In the past 30 trading days, TNL's shares have declined 8%, compared to a 7% fall in the S&P 500. Average trading volume for the past five days was 36,600 shares, compared with the 40-day moving average of 80,544 shares.

Key Stock Statistics

Dividend Rate/Share	0.24	Shareholders	1,100
Shs. outstg. (M)	16.2	Market cap. (B)	$0.307
Avg. daily vol. (M)	0.062	Inst. holdings	40%
Tang. Bk. Value/Share	8.08		
Beta	1.68		

Value of $10,000 invested 5 years ago: $ 48,699

Fiscal Year Ending Dec. 31

	1998	1997	1996	1995	1994	1993
Revenues (Million $)						
1Q	110.8	92.81	62.85	40.04	34.96	26.10
2Q	104.9	103.9	68.03	39.39	37.82	25.30
3Q	—	102.1	59.05	35.94	36.59	25.31
4Q	—	98.81	84.14	61.03	37.08	23.74
Yr.	—	397.1	274.1	176.4	146.4	100.5
Earnings Per Share ($)						
1Q	**0.58**	0.40	0.34	0.14	0.12	0.05
2Q	**0.52**	0.49	0.33	0.17	0.14	0.07
3Q	—	0.44	0.27	0.14	0.15	0.08
4Q	—	0.46	0.34	0.24	0.16	0.09
Yr.	—	1.80	1.13	0.71	0.57	0.28

Next earnings report expected: late October

Dividend Data (Dividends have been paid since 1975.)

Amount ($)	Date Decl.	Ex-Div. Date	Stock of Record	Payment Date
0.053	Nov. 25	Jan. 07	Jan. 09	Jan. 30 '98
0.060	Feb. 17	Apr. 07	Apr. 10	May. 01 '98
0.060	May. 21	Jul. 08	Jul. 10	Jul. 31 '98
0.060	Aug. 17	Oct. 07	Oct. 09	Oct. 30 '98

A Division of The **McGraw·Hill** *Companies*

Technitrol, Inc.

Business Summary - 17-SEP-98

Technitrol is a maker of electronic components (ECS; 45% of 1997 sales) and metallurgical products (MCS; 55%). Both segments focus on the design, manufacture and marketing of critical components to original equipment manufacturers. The company has expanded through internal growth, as well as acquisitions; its test and measurement products business (12% of sales in 1996) was sold in 1997. In November 1997, Technitrol acquired the magnetics components business of Northern Telecom, Ltd. (Nortel), including manufacturing plants in Malaysia and Thailand and a design engineering group in Canada, for approximately $23 million in cash. The acquired business had revenues of about $38 million in 1997. The October 1996 acquisition of Doduco GmbH, a maker of precious metal contacts, bi-metal products, and certain contact product modules, with operations in Germany and Spain, was largely responsible for strong sales growth in the metallurgical products segment, where sales more than doubled in 1997. In 1995, the company acquired Pulse Engineering, Inc., a designer, maker and seller of electronic components and modules.

The electronic components segment (ECS) includes Pulse Engineering, which designs, manufactures and markets electronic components and modules primarily for manufacturers of local area network (LAN) and telecommunication systems. During 1997, ECS also included the operations of Netwave Technologies, Inc., a business developing wireless LAN solutions. At the end of December 1997, the company sold a majority of its ownership interest in Netwave, retaining a 19% interest which was sold in 1998's second quarter.

The metallurgical components segment (MCS) which operates business globally under the name AMI Doduco, makes electrical contacts (used in circuit protection), assemblies (used in high-voltage circuit breakers), thermostatic metals (bonded metal laminates that convert a change in temperature to a mechanical action) and clad metals (laminates of two or more metals bonded together for nonthermostatic applications).

In June 1997, Technitrol sold its test and measurement products business for $34 million in cash. Products included electronic force measurement products (such as hand-held digital force gauges) and materials testing systems (to determine the strength of materials such as packaging). Assets related to production of document counters and dispensers, the smallest segment of this business, were sold in March 1996, for about $3.7 million.

In November 1996, trading in the shares moved to the NYSE, from the ASE.

Per Share Data ($)

(Year Ended Dec. 31)	1997	1996	1995	1994	1993	1992	1991	1990	1989	1988
Tangible Bk. Val.	6.99	5.62	4.71	3.80	3.37	3.24	3.23	3.18	2.96	2.48
Cash Flow	2.62	1.84	1.23	1.01	0.69	0.65	0.56	0.70	0.94	0.68
Earnings	1.80	1.27	0.71	0.57	0.28	0.24	0.23	0.39	0.64	0.48
Dividends	0.21	0.20	0.20	0.19	0.19	0.19	0.19	0.19	0.15	0.12
Payout Ratio	12%	16%	27%	33%	67%	79%	80%	48%	23%	25%
Prices - High	43¹/₈	21⁷/₈	11⁷/₈	8	5¹/₈	5¹/₂	5	6⁷/₈	7¹/₈	5
- Low	17¹/₈	9⁵/₈	6⁵/₈	5	3³/₄	3³/₈	4	3³/₈	4⁷/₈	3³/₈
P/E Ratio - High	24	17	17	14	18	23	21	18	11	10
- Low	10	8	9	9	14	14	17	9	8	7

Income Statement Analysis (Million $)

	1997	1996	1995	1994	1993	1992	1991	1990	1989	1988
Revs.	397	274	176	146	100	99	81.2	83.6	91.9	68.9
Oper. Inc.	58.9	39.1	21.7	17.8	10.3	9.7	8.6	11.2	15.1	11.6
Depr.	13.1	9.1	6.2	5.3	4.9	4.9	3.9	3.7	3.5	2.2
Int. Exp.	2.4	1.2	1.4	1.1	0.4	0.7	0.6	0.8	1.5	1.1
Pretax Inc.	46.8	31.0	14.5	11.4	5.2	4.3	4.7	7.6	10.6	9.0
Eff. Tax Rate	38%	34%	36%	39%	35%	35%	41%	39%	28%	37%
Net Inc.	29.1	20.4	9.3	6.9	3.4	2.8	2.8	4.6	7.6	5.7

Balance Sheet & Other Fin. Data (Million $)

	1997	1996	1995	1994	1993	1992	1991	1990	1989	1988
Cash	48.8	43.5	13.9	8.7	7.7	2.7	6.7	13.9	7.3	8.6
Curr. Assets	157	143	82.6	54.0	37.2	33.4	34.8	35.3	34.6	34.9
Total Assets	255	218	145	84.8	58.6	55.7	52.5	51.6	52.5	53.8
Curr. Liab.	74.6	67.8	39.3	23.9	13.1	10.2	11.6	9.0	9.9	10.2
LT Debt	30.9	39.7	15.1	15.1	5.1	6.9	2.6	5.0	7.3	14.1
Common Eqty.	142	104	84.7	45.8	40.3	38.7	38.3	37.4	35.0	29.0
Total Cap.	173	143	100	60.9	45.4	45.4	45.5	40.9	42.6	43.7
Cap. Exp.	20.5	11.7	5.9	4.4	2.7	8.9	4.6	2.7	2.7	15.7
Cash Flow	42.2	29.6	15.9	12.2	8.3	7.7	6.6	8.3	11.0	7.9
Curr. Ratio	2.1	2.1	2.1	2.3	2.8	3.3	3.0	3.9	3.5	3.4
% LT Debt of Cap.	17.8	27.7	15.1	24.8	11.3	15.1	6.4	11.7	17.1	32.4
% Net Inc.of Revs.	7.3	7.5	5.3	4.7	3.3	2.9	3.4	5.5	8.2	8.2
% Ret. on Assets	12.3	11.2	8.1	9.7	5.9	5.2	5.3	8.9	14.2	13.4
% Ret. on Equity	23.7	21.7	20.7	16.1	8.5	7.3	7.3	12.8	23.5	21.1

Data as orig. reptd.; bef. results of disc. opers. and/or spec. items. 1996 EPS total in quarterly table incl. disc. opers. Per share data adj. for stk. divs. as of ex-div. date. Bold denotes diluted EPS (FASB 128). E-Estimated. NA-Not Available. NM-Not Meaningful. NR-Not Ranked.

Office—1210 Northbrook Dr., Suite 385, Trevose, PA 19053. Tel—(215) 355-2900. Website—http://www.technitrol.com Chrmn—J. M. Papada III. Pres & CEO—T. J. Flakoll. VP & CFO—A. Thorp III. Secy & Contr—D. A. Moyer. Dirs—S. E. Basara, J. E. Burrows Jr., T. J. Flakoll, R. L. Gupta, J. B. Harrison, R. E. Hock, G. Humes, E. M. Mazze, J. M. Papada III. Transfer Agent & Registrar—Registrar & Transfer Co., Cranford, NJ. Incorporated—in Pennsylvania in 1947. Empl— 14,400. S&P Analyst: J.J.S.

Technology Solutions   5368T

NASDAQ Symbol **TSCC**

In S&P SmallCap 600

03-OCT-98

Industry:
Services (Computer Systems)

Summary: This company provides strategic consulting and systems integration services to deliver business benefits to clients in a broad range of industries.

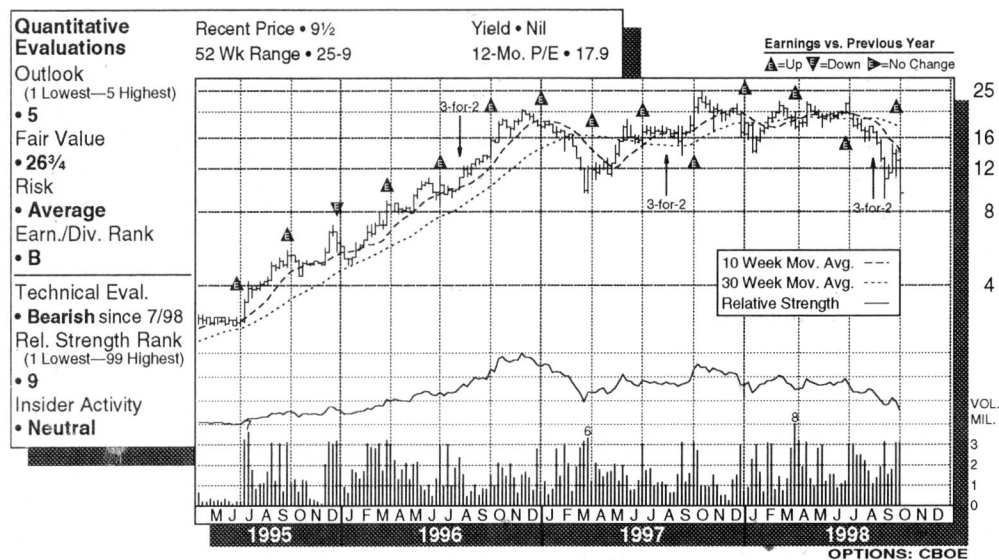

Quantitative Evaluations		
Outlook (1 Lowest—5 Highest)	• **5**	
Fair Value	• **26¾**	
Risk	• **Average**	
Earn./Div. Rank	• **B**	
Technical Eval.	• **Bearish** since 7/98	
Rel. Strength Rank (1 Lowest—99 Highest)	• **9**	
Insider Activity	• **Neutral**	

Recent Price • 9½
52 Wk Range • 25-9
Yield • Nil
12-Mo. P/E • 17.9

Earnings vs. Previous Year
▲=Up ▼=Down ▶=No Change

10 Week Mov. Avg. – – –
30 Week Mov. Avg. - - - -
Relative Strength ——

OPTIONS: CBOE

Business Profile - 06-JUL-98

Technology Solutions Company (TSC) serves the $29 billion worldwide systems integration market, which is expected to double by the end of the decade. As end-users shift from a single-vendor environment to multiple vendors to meet hardware and software needs, and as industries use more computers, demand for systems integration services will grow. TSC is positioned to capitalize on this growth through international expansion and new acquisitions. The company's international expansion initiative includes leveraging its call center and customer service expertise in Europe, Latin America and Canada. In June 1998, the company approved a three-for-two stock split, payable on August 10, 1998 to shareholders of record as of the close of business on July 16.

Operational Review - 06-JUL-98

Based on a preliminary report, revenues rose 65% in FY 98 (May), reflecting increasing demand for U.S.-based systems integration services. Margins narrowed on investments in new service offerings and global expansion; pretax income increased 45%. Following taxes at 42.2%, versus 39.7%, net income advanced 40%, to $21,020,000 ($0.74 a share), from $15,067,000 ($0.57).

Stock Performance - 02-OCT-98

In the past 30 trading days, TSCC's shares have declined 38%, compared to a 7% fall in the S&P 500. Average trading volume for the past five days was 774,640 shares, compared with the 40-day moving average of 507,158 shares.

Key Stock Statistics

Dividend Rate/Share	Nil	Shareholders	700
Shs. outstg. (M)	39.9	Market cap. (B)	$0.379
Avg. daily vol. (M)	0.553	Inst. holdings	85%
Tang. Bk. Value/Share	3.57		
Beta	1.82		

Value of $10,000 invested 5 years ago: $ 22,901

Fiscal Year Ending May 31

	1999	1998	1997	1996	1995	1994
Revenues (Million $)						
1Q	85.57	60.41	32.16	20.73	13.44	13.76
2Q	—	63.90	39.52	23.30	15.56	14.41
3Q	—	67.40	42.35	25.47	17.22	11.86
4Q	—	80.17	51.06	28.10	19.61	13.13
Yr.	—	271.9	165.1	97.60	65.82	53.16
Earnings Per Share ($)						
1Q	0.13	0.09	0.06	0.04	0.02	0.04
2Q	—	0.13	0.09	0.00	0.03	0.02
3Q	—	0.13	0.10	0.02	0.01	0.03
4Q	—	0.15	0.13	0.07	0.04	-0.11
Yr.	—	0.49	0.38	0.13	0.11	Nil

Next earnings report expected: mid December

Dividend Data

Amount ($)	Date Decl.	Ex-Div. Date	Stock of Record	Payment Date
3-for-2	Jun. 29	Aug. 11	Jul. 16	Aug. 10 '98

A Division of The **McGraw·Hill** Companies

STANDARD
&POOR'S
STOCK REPORTS

Technology Solutions Company

5368T

03-OCT-98

Business Summary - 06-JUL-98

Technology Solutions Company (TSC) offers a wide range of information technology (IT) consulting services and strategic business and management consulting services. TSC concentrates on projects for large corporate clients because it believes that such projects offer maximum profit potential and represent one of the fastest growing areas of the systems consulting market. The company is organized into various practice areas, which include: Advanced Network Computing, Business and IT Strategy, Call Center, Change and Learning Technologies, Enterprise Applications, Financial Services and Telecommunications.

The Advanced Network Computing practice area provides solutions that maximize return on investment (ROI) by optimizing the price/performance tradeoffs associated with computing resources (processor, memory and network). TSC's Business and IT Strategy practice area provides strategic consulting services, including market research and new venture growth services. The area also provides capability assessment, develops a

suitable IT strategy to maximize ROI and helps clients transform capabilities efficiently. The Call Center practice area assists in the implementation of large call center projects for consumer products companies, technology companies and financial services companies.

The Change and Learning area is focused on assisting clients in managing the human side of implementing strategic change through change management services and customized educational programs. The Enterprise Applications area focuses on evaluating, selecting and implementing packaged software applications. The unit is involved in systems integration and package implementation for PeopleSoft, SAP AG and Baan product families.

Financial Services includes portfolio and risk management, asset valuation, customer service, front-office administration, transaction processing, real-time global trading, financial and management reporting, and clearance and settlement procedures. The Telecommunications practice area provides consulting and implementation services to local exchange carriers.

Per Share Data ($)

(Year Ended May 31)	1998	1997	1996	1995	1994	1993	1992	1991	1990	1989
Tangible Bk. Val.	3.57	2.76	2.00	1.73	1.64	1.79	1.69	0.53	NA	NA
Cash Flow	0.66	0.49	0.20	0.15	0.04	0.17	0.32	0.25	NA	NA
Earnings	0.49	0.38	0.13	0.11	Nil	0.14	0.30	0.24	NA	NA
Dividends	Nil	Nil	Nil	Nil	Nil	Nil	Nil	Nil	Nil	Nil
Payout Ratio	Nil	Nil	Nil	Nil	Nil	Nil	Nil	Nil	Nil	Nil
Cal. Yrs.	1997	1996	1995	1994	1993	1992	1991	1990	1989	1988
Prices - High	25	21	7$^1/_8$	2$^3/_4$	4$^1/_2$	9$^1/_8$	7$^5/_8$	NA	NA	NA
- Low	9$^1/_2$	4$^7/_8$	2$^1/_8$	1$^7/_{16}$	2$^1/_{16}$	2	4$^1/_2$	NA	NA	NA
P/E Ratio - High	51	55	53	26	NM	67	26	NA	NA	NA
- Low	19	13	16	14	NM	15	15	NA	NA	NA

Income Statement Analysis (Million $)

	1998	1997	1996	1995	1994	1993	1992	1991	1990	1989
Revs.	272	165	97.6	65.8	53.2	62.5	71.0	52.4	NA	NA
Oper. Inc.	41.5	27.3	10.7	6.4	7.7	18.5	24.9	15.4	NA	NA
Depr.	7.1	4.4	2.6	2.0	1.3	1.5	0.9	0.6	NA	NA
Int. Exp.	0.1	0.2	0.2	Nil	0.0	0.1	0.4	0.6	NA	NA
Pretax Inc.	36.4	25.0	6.8	4.7	-0.8	9.0	19.9	13.8	NA	NA
Eff. Tax Rate	42%	40%	32%	28%	NM	36%	39%	39%	NA	NA
Net Inc.	21.0	15.1	4.6	3.4	Nil	5.7	12.1	8.5	NA	NA

Balance Sheet & Other Fin. Data (Million $)

	1998	1997	1996	1995	1994	1993	1992	1991	1990	1989
Cash	38.5	28.0	24.6	17.3	23.7	34.3	45.7	10.6	NA	NA
Curr. Assets	159	108	60.6	37.8	41.8	49.6	70.1	21.2	NA	NA
Total Assets	197	134	89.4	65.2	69.3	76.0	75.6	28.7	NA	NA
Curr. Liab.	41.3	28.1	19.4	13.5	15.2	8.0	6.2	7.0	NA	NA
LT Debt	Nil	Nil	Nil	Nil	Nil	Nil	Nil	1.4	NA	NA
Common Eqty.	169	113	70.0	51.7	54.1	68.0	68.2	14.5	NA	NA
Total Cap.	156	113	70.0	51.7	54.1	68.0	68.2	15.9	NA	NA
Cap. Exp.	5.8	6.1	3.6	2.1	1.0	0.6	1.7	1.2	NA	NA
Cash Flow	28.1	19.5	7.1	5.4	1.4	7.2	13.0	9.1	NA	NA
Curr. Ratio	3.8	3.8	3.1	2.8	2.7	6.2	11.3	3.0	NA	NA
% LT Debt of Cap.	Nil	Nil	Nil	Nil	Nil	Nil	Nil	8.8	NA	NA
% Net Inc.of Revs.	7.7	9.1	4.7	5.1	0.1	9.1	17.0	16.2	NA	NA
% Ret. on Assets	12.7	13.5	5.9	5.0	0.1	7.8	20.4	35.4	NA	NA
% Ret. on Equity	14.9	16.3	7.5	6.4	0.1	8.6	26.9	82.8	NA	NA

Data as orig. reptd.; bef. results of disc. opers. and/or spec. items. Per share data adj. for stk. divs. as of ex-div. date. Bold denotes diluted EPS (FASB 128). E-Estimated. NA-Not Available. NM-Not Meaningful. NR-Not Ranked.

Office—205 N. Michigan Ave., Chicago, IL 60601. **Tel**—(312) 228-4500. **Website**—http://www.techsol.com **Chrmn**—W. H. Waltrip. **Pres & CEO**—J. T. Kohler. **CFO**—M. T. Johnson. **Dirs**—J. T. Kohler, M. McLaughlin, M. J. Murray, S. B. Oresman, J. R. Purcell, W. H. Waltrip. **Transfer Agent & Registrar**—ChaseMellon Shareholder Services. **Incorporated**—in Delaware in 1988. **Empl**—1,410. **S&P Analyst:** Mark Cavallone

Tel-Save Holdings

5372

NASDAQ Symbol **TALK**

In S&P SmallCap 600

10-OCT-98

Industry:
Telecommunications
(Long Distance)

Summary: This company provides long-distance telecommunication services to small and medium-sized businesses in the U.S.

Quantitative Evaluations

Outlook
(1 Lowest—5 Highest)
• 5

Fair Value
• 22⅛

Risk
• **High**

Earn./Div. Rank
• **NR**

Technical Eval.
• **Bearish** since 5/98

Rel. Strength Rank
(1 Lowest—99 Highest)
• 3

Insider Activity
• **NA**

Recent Price • 5⅞
52 Wk Range • 30-4¾

Yield • Nil
12-Mo. P/E • NM

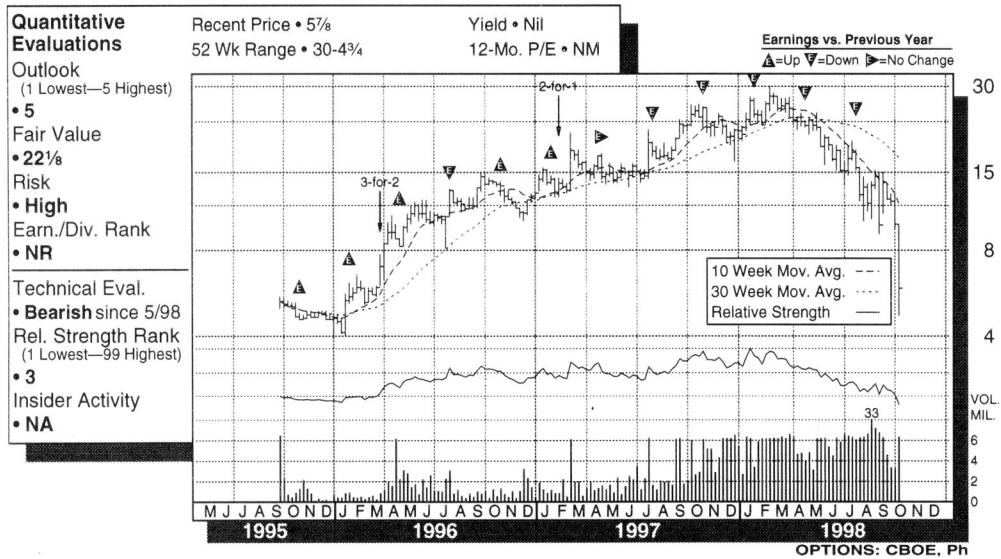

Earnings vs. Previous Year
▲=Up ▼=Down ▶=No Change

10 Week Mov. Avg. - - -
30 Week Mov. Avg. .....
Relative Strength ——

OPTIONS: CBOE, Ph

Business Profile - 04-SEP-98

The company said recently that it would remain independent, following several months of searching for an acquiror or strategic partner. An agreement with America Online, Inc. (AOL) under which TALK markets telecommunications services to AOL customers, has been responsible for TALK's fast growing revenues. However, high costs of promotion related to the agreement led to a larger operating and net loss. TALK plans to accelerate its investment in this part of the business, spending up to $125 million more on marketing than forecasted earlier in the year. In February 1998, the company acquired Symetrics Industries, an electronics company serving the defense and electronics industries, for about $24.4 million in cash.

Operational Review - 04-SEP-98

Revenues in the first half of 1998 rose 38%, year to year, on increased sales made under the AOL agreement. Gross margins widened sharply, to 16.1% of sales, from 9.9%, in the absence of an $11.5 million charge. However, with 149% higher general and administrative expenses and $84.9 million in promotional expenses, primarily for the AOL agreement, versus $14.4 million of such expenses in the first half of 1997, the net loss widened to $137,949,000 ($2.14 a share, on 1.8% more shares), from $435,000 ($0.01).

Stock Performance - 09-OCT-98

In the past 30 trading days, TALK's shares have declined 60%, compared to a 4% fall in the S&P 500. Average trading volume for the past five days was 1,881,320 shares, compared with the 40-day moving average of 2,499,341 shares.

Key Stock Statistics

Dividend Rate/Share	Nil	Shareholders	100
Shs. outstg. (M)	64.7	Market cap. (B)	$0.380
Avg. daily vol. (M)	1.017	Inst. holdings	50%
Tang. Bk. Value/Share	1.15		
Beta	NA		

Value of $10,000 invested 5 years ago: NA

Fiscal Year Ending Dec. 31

	1998	1997	1996	1995	1994	1993
Revenues (Million $)						
1Q	91.15	71.16	51.07	36.62	14.41	5.25
2Q	111.1	75.03	57.02	44.73	14.71	6.49
3Q	—	80.31	60.08	48.37	22.52	9.02
4Q	—	78.26	64.27	50.39	31.20	11.17
Yr.	—	304.8	232.4	180.1	82.84	31.93
Earnings Per Share ($)						
1Q	-0.65	0.08	0.08	0.06	--	--
2Q	-1.49	-0.09	0.07	0.12	0.07	--
3Q	--	0.01	0.11	0.08	0.06	--
4Q	--	-0.32	0.09	0.07	0.06	--
Yr.	--	-0.33	0.35	0.32	0.18	0.07

Next earnings report expected: NA

Dividend Data

No cash dividends have been paid.

STANDARD
&POOR'S
STOCK REPORTS

Tel-Save Holdings, Inc.

5372
10-OCT-98

Business Summary - 04-SEP-98

Tel-Save Holdings, Inc. (TALK), formed in 1989 to capitalize on an FCC mandate permitting the resale of AT&T services, now provides AT&T long-distance services to more than 500,000 small and medium-size businesses, primarily as a switchless reseller. TALK's long-distance service offerings include outbound service, inbound toll-free 800 service, and dedicated private line services for data. In order to increase its growth opportunities and reduce its dependence on contract tariffs that govern charges paid to AT&T, TALK deployed its own nationwide telecommunications network, One Better Net (OBN), in 1996, using five company-owned switches and AT&T transmission facilities.

The company recently said it would remain independent, following a long search for an acquiror of strategic partner. In November 1997, TALK agreed to terminate a merger agreement with Shared Technologies Fairchild, Inc. in exchange for about $71 million. In November 1997, the company's bid for ACC Corp. was unsuccessful, as ACC agreed to merge with Teleport Communications.

TALK hopes to see wider margins from its OBN long-distance service than it has from AT&T service. AT&T long-distance service is bundled, which means that TALK must pay a single, all-inclusive price to AT&T for switching, transmission and LEC (local exchange carrier) access. The unbundled nature of OBN service, on the other hand, permits the company to provide its own switching and pay AT&T only for the use of transmission facilities, and to pay access fees directly to LECs. TALK expects the unbundled charges per call on OBN to be less than the bundled charge paid to AT&T. A majority of the company's new orders are now being placed on OBN, which had about one million lines in service at the end of 1997.

In February 1997, the company announced an agreement with America Online, Inc. (AOL) under which TALK's long-distance services would be marketed to AOL's eight million subscribers. In February 1998, the company entered into a marketing agreement with CompuServe (a wholly owned subsidiary of AOL), under which CompuServe will also market TALK's long distance services.

Historically, the company has marketed its services nationally through independent carriers and marketing companies known as partitions. This has allowed TALK to minimize overhead expenses and expand its business by adding partitions and providing existing and new partitions with operational, financial and marketing support. In 1996, the company began to actively market its telecommunication services directly to end-users, and it now generates most new sales through direct marketing.

Per Share Data ($)

(Year Ended Dec. 31)	1997	1996	1995	1994	1993	1992	1991	1990	1989	1988
Tangible Bk. Val.	3.33	3.37	1.02	0.77	NA	NA	NA	NA	NA	NA
Cash Flow	-0.24	0.40	0.36	0.20	0.07	0.03	NA	NA	NA	NA
Earnings	0.33	0.35	0.32	0.18	0.07	0.03	0.01	-0.01	NA	NA
Dividends	Nil	Nil	Nil	NA	NA	NA	NA	NA	NA	NA
Payout Ratio	Nil	Nil	Nil	NA	NA	NA	NA	NA	NA	NA
Prices - High	26	15⅛	5½	NA	NA	NA	NA	NA	NA	NA
- Low	12¼	4	4	NA	NA	NA	NA	NA	NA	NA
P/E Ratio - High	NM	42	17	NA	NA	NA	NA	NA	NA	NA
- Low	NM	11	12	NA	NA	NA	NA	NA	NA	NA

Income Statement Analysis (Million $)

	1997	1996	1995	1994	1993	1992	1991	1990	1989	1988
Revs.	305	232	180	82.8	31.9	17.7	11.0	0.9	NA	NA
Oper. Inc.	-79.6	24.3	19.0	9.8	3.2	1.4	NA	NA	NA	NA
Depr.	5.4	2.5	1.3	0.5	0.0	0.0	NA	NA	NA	NA
Int. Exp.	Nil	Nil	Nil	Nil	1.7	2.0	NA	NA	NA	NA
Pretax Inc.	-34.3	32.4	18.0	9.4	3.3	1.4	0.3	-0.2	NA	NA
Eff. Tax Rate	NM	38%	40%	40%	40%	40%	40%	NM	NM	NM
Net Inc.	-20.9	20.2	10.8	5.6	2.0	0.8	0.2	-0.1	NA	NA

Balance Sheet & Other Fin. Data (Million $)

	1997	1996	1995	1994	1993	1992	1991	1990	1989	1988
Cash	317	8.0	41.2	NA	NA	NA	NA	NA	NA	NA
Curr. Assets	691	202	65.2	NA	NA	NA	NA	NA	NA	NA
Total Assets	815	257	71.4	71.5	NA	NA	NA	NA	NA	NA
Curr. Liab.	56.3	26.3	27.0	NA	NA	NA	NA	NA	NA	NA
LT Debt	500	Nil	Nil	Nil	Nil	Nil	Nil	Nil	Nil	Nil
Common Eqty.	223	235	41.3	30.2	NA	NA	NA	NA	NA	NA
Total Cap.	723	235	44.1	NA	NA	NA	NA	NA	NA	NA
Cap. Exp.	28.8	27.6	2.3	0.3	77.0	108	NA	NA	NA	NA
Cash Flow	-15.5	22.6	12.1	6.1	2.0	0.9	NA	NA	NA	NA
Curr. Ratio	12.3	7.7	2.4	NA	NA	NA	NA	NA	NA	NA
% LT Debt of Cap.	69.2	Nil	Nil	NA	NA	NA	NA	NA	NA	NA
% Net Inc.of Revs.	NM	8.7	6.0	6.8	6.1	4.8	1.5	NM	NM	NM
% Ret. on Assets	NM	12.3	NA	NA	NA	NA	NA	NA	NA	NA
% Ret. on Equity	NM	14.6	NA	NA	NA	NA	NA	NA	NA	NA

Data as orig. reptd.; bef. results of disc. opers. and/or spec. items. Per share data adj. for stk. divs. as of ex-div. date. Bold denotes diluted EPS (FASB 128). E-Estimated. NA-Not Available. NM-Not Meaningful. NR-Not Ranked.

Office—6805 Route 202, New Hope, PA 18938. **Tel**—(215) 862-1500. **E-mail**—phoneco@attmail.com **Chrmn & CEO**—D. M. Borislow. **Pres**—G. W. McCulla. **CFO, Treas & Investor Contact**—J. A. Schenk. **Secy**—A. T. Lawn IV. **Dirs**—D. M. Borislow, E. J. DeMaio, H. First, G. Farley, G. W. McCulla, J. A. Schenk, R. R. Thoma. **Transfer Agent & Registrar**—Midlantic Bank, Edison, NJ. **Incorporated**—in Delaware in 1995. **Empl**— 313.
S&P Analyst: Jim Corridore

STANDARD &POOR'S
STOCK REPORTS

Telxon Corp.

5376T

NASDAQ Symbol **TLXN**

In S&P SmallCap 600

03-OCT-98

Industry: Computers (Hardware)

Summary: This company is a leading manufacturer and designer of wireless and mobile information systems for vertical markets.

Quantitative Evaluations	
Outlook (1 Lowest—5 Highest)	• **3⁻**
Fair Value	• **25¾**
Risk	• **High**
Earn./Div. Rank	• **B-**
Technical Eval.	• **Bearish** since 8/98
Rel. Strength Rank (1 Lowest—99 Highest)	• **24**
Insider Activity	• **Neutral**

Recent Price • 17⅞

52 Wk Range • 38⅝-17

Yield • 0.1%

12-Mo. P/E • 19.5

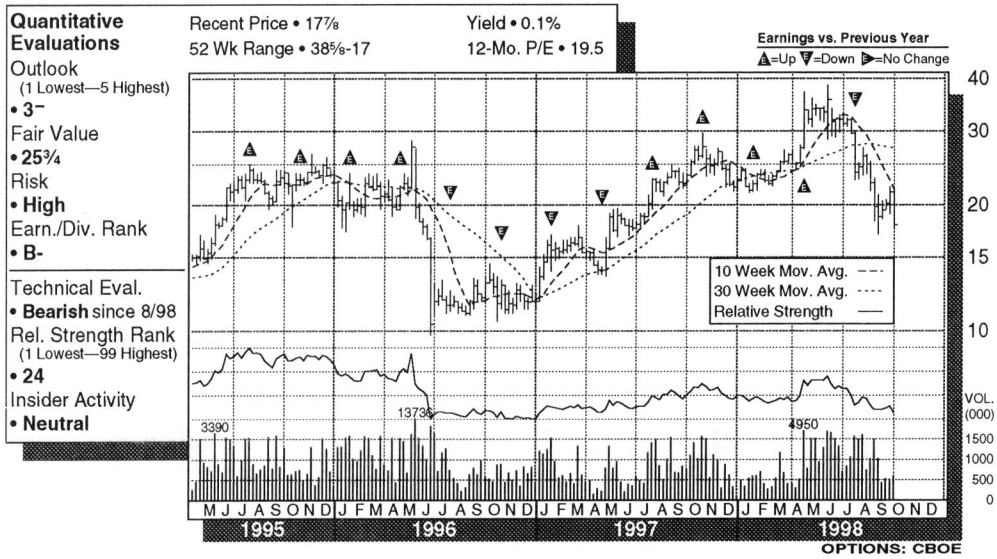

Earnings vs. Previous Year
▲=Up ▼=Down ▶=No Change

10 Week Mov. Avg. ---
30 Week Mov. Avg. ·····
Relative Strength —

OPTIONS: CBOE

Business Profile - 08-SEP-98

In June 1996, TLXN implemented a series of initiatives to streamline operations and improve the company's finances. Its goals included reducing the number of products offered, cutting employee headcount by 10%, improving manufacturing efficiencies, and decreasing accounts receivable. The first two phases of the program are largely completed, and the company has entered the final phase, which focuses on redesigning Telxon's infrastructure and logistics systems to address changing market conditions more effectively. In the FY 98 (Mar.) first quarter, the company recorded after tax costs of $0.06 a share, related to an unsolicited takeover attempt by Symbol Technologies, Inc.

Operational Review - 08-SEP-98

Total revenues in the quarter ended June 30, 1998, advanced 9.7%, year to year, reflecting greater portable tele-transaction computer sales and increased market penetration. Gross margins narrowed, on a shift toward more complex and costly pen-based and touch-screen workslates. Despite higher selling expenses, after $1.7 million of takeover defense costs, operating income fell 20%. With a sharp rise in non-operating expense, related to transactions in the common stock and warrants of two subsidiaries, net income plunged 85%, to $246,000 ($0.01 a share, on 7.2% more shares), from $1,594,000 ($0.10).

Stock Performance - 02-OCT-98

In the past 30 trading days, TLXN's shares have declined 20%, compared to a 7% fall in the S&P 500. Average trading volume for the past five days was 118,760 shares, compared with the 40-day moving average of 162,741 shares.

Key Stock Statistics

Dividend Rate/Share	0.01	Shareholders	1,200
Shs. outstg. (M)	16.1	Market cap. (B)	$0.289
Avg. daily vol. (M)	0.108	Inst. holdings	59%
Tang. Bk. Value/Share	7.45		
Beta	1.43		

Value of $10,000 invested 5 years ago: $ 15,325

Fiscal Year Ending Mar. 31

	1999	1998	1997	1996	1995	1994
Revenues (Million $)						
1Q	115.0	104.9	112.4	103.5	87.43	56.54
2Q	—	110.3	108.3	107.0	91.89	63.09
3Q	—	117.3	123.6	131.0	98.20	76.97
4Q	—	133.3	121.7	144.9	102.0	99.4
Yr.	—	465.9	466.0	486.5	379.5	296.0
Earnings Per Share ($)						
1Q	0.01	0.10	-0.29	0.14	0.08	-0.13
2Q	—	0.15	-0.29	0.17	0.10	-0.07
3Q	—	0.27	0.13	0.25	0.10	-0.04
4Q	—	0.50	0.02	0.44	0.23	0.06
Yr.	—	1.01	-0.44	1.00	0.57	-0.18

Next earnings report expected: late October

Dividend Data (Dividends have been paid since 1988.)

Amount ($)	Date Decl.	Ex-Div. Date	Stock of Record	Payment Date
0.010	Mar. 02	Mar. 19	Mar. 23	Mar. 31 '98

A Division of The **McGraw·Hill** *Companies*

Business Summary - 08-SEP-98

Telxon designs, manufactures, sells and supports trans-action-based work force automation systems. It integrates its mobile computing devices and wireless local area network products with customer host enterprise computer systems and third-party wide area networks, enabling mobile workers to process data on a real-time basis at the point of transaction. The company's products are sold for use in key supply chain vertical markets, including retail (historically accounts for over 50% of total revenues), manufacturing, warehouse/distribution, transportation/logistics and route sales, and several segments of the emerging mobile services markets, such as insurance/financial services. International sales accounted for 29% of total net revenues in FY 98 (Mar.).

TLXN offers a broad line of handheld devices, ranging from low-end batch terminals to highly integrated mobile computers that incorporate laser bar code readers and spread spectrum radios, including a variety of pen-based and touch-screen workslate devices. The company also provides wireless data communication solutions for mobile, distributed data processing application systems through computing devices equipped with radios to transfer programs or data, and from other computers or peripheral devices while remaining mobile.

During FY 97 (Mar.), management implemented a new, three-phase business model. The first phase consisted of improving gross margins through the implementation of programs aimed at reducing the cost of its products through new design procedures, improved sourcing and model consolidations. The second phase centered on improving operating efficiencies and lowering the overall cost of serving TLXN's global markets, in which key management changes were made in the areas of sales, product marketing, product development, customer service and operations. The final phase focuses on redesigning TLXN's infrastructure and logistics systems to address changing market conditions more efficiently. Aided by the new business model, the company returned to profitability in FY 98.

In addition to subjecting all operations to ongoing review, the company will continue to evaluate alternative strategies for reflecting the imbedded value of its technical subsidiaries in its market value. In March 1998, Telxon sold 1.1 million shares of its Aironet subsidiary, a leading supplier of spread-spectrum radios for wireless local area networks, to third party investors, for about $3.4 million.

An important element of Telxon's approach to selling application systems is the support provided to the customer. Revenues from customer service accounted for about 15% of total revenues in each of the past three fiscal years.

Per Share Data ($)

(Year Ended Mar. 31)	1998	1997	1996	1995	1994	1993	1992	1991	1990	1989
Tangible Bk. Val.	9.86	8.59	8.82	7.73	6.59	6.33	8.94	7.57	6.19	7.29
Cash Flow	2.56	1.34	2.39	1.91	0.99	0.07	1.67	1.39	-0.64	1.48
Earnings	1.01	-0.44	1.00	0.57	-0.18	-0.79	1.13	0.91	-1.09	1.13
Dividends	0.01	0.01	0.01	0.02	0.01	0.01	0.01	0.01	0.01	0.01
Payout Ratio	1%	2%	1%	4%	NM	NM	1%	1%	NM	1%
Cal. Yrs.	1997	1996	1995	1994	1993	1992	1991	1990	1989	1988
Prices - High	29¾	28½	26½	18¼	12¾	28¼	28⅛	15½	20¼	24¾
- Low	12¼	9¾	12	10	6½	11¼	13⅜	4¾	6⅜	13
P/E Ratio - High	29	NM	26	32	NM	NM	25	17	NM	22
- Low	12	NM	12	18	NM	NM	12	5	NM	12

Income Statement Analysis (Million $)

	1998	1997	1996	1995	1994	1993	1992	1991	1990	1989
Revs.	466	466	486	380	296	238	215	185	143	160
Oper. Inc.	59.5	-5.3	54.3	42.3	17.9	-0.3	31.9	24.7	1.3	27.4
Depr.	25.2	28.6	22.9	21.0	18.0	12.7	7.6	6.4	6.0	4.6
Int. Exp.	7.2	8.1	6.8	4.3	2.5	2.3	2.2	2.6	3.9	3.8
Pretax Inc.	28.9	-10.5	26.8	17.2	-1.9	-15.7	25.0	19.9	-25.2	23.1
Eff. Tax Rate	43%	NM	38%	48%	NM	NM	37%	38%	NM	36%
Net Inc.	16.4	-7.1	16.5	9.0	-2.8	-11.6	15.9	12.3	-14.4	14.9

Balance Sheet & Other Fin. Data (Million $)

	1998	1997	1996	1995	1994	1993	1992	1991	1990	1989
Cash	27.5	45.4	35.7	31.4	24.8	27.2	42.3	44.7	55.5	49.8
Curr. Assets	296	270	300	205	186	138	162	138	140	147
Total Assets	391	362	389	276	260	213	199	167	167	176
Curr. Liab.	107	101	114	104	106	53.2	45.3	35.7	43.5	29.4
LT Debt	108	108	111	31.7	27.5	24.9	25.6	26.0	36.5	47.3
Common Eqty.	165	147	161	139	125	128	124	102	83.0	95.0
Total Cap.	276	255	272	170	152	153	151	129	122	145
Cap. Exp.	26.1	14.6	22.7	15.2	21.7	16.4	9.0	7.6	7.7	7.9
Cash Flow	41.6	21.5	39.5	30.4	15.2	1.1	23.5	18.7	-8.4	19.6
Curr. Ratio	2.8	2.7	2.6	2.0	1.8	2.6	3.6	3.9	3.2	5.0
% LT Debt of Cap.	39.1	42.4	40.8	18.6	18.1	16.3	16.9	20.1	29.9	32.6
% Net Inc.of Revs.	3.5	NM	3.4	2.4	NM	NM	7.4	6.7	NM	9.3
% Ret. on Assets	4.4	NM	5.0	3.4	NM	NM	8.5	7.4	NM	9.1
% Ret. on Equity	10.6	NM	11.0	6.9	NM	NM	13.8	13.3	NM	16.9

Data as orig. reptd.; bef. results of disc. opers. and/or spec. items. Per share data adj. for stk. divs. as of ex-div. date. Bold denotes diluted EPS (FASB 128). E-Estimated. NA-Not Available. NM-Not Meaningful. NR-Not Ranked.

Office—3330 W. Market St., Akron, OH 44333. **Tel**—(330) 664-1000. **Website**—http://www.telxon.com **Chrmn**—R. Reddy. **Pres & CEO**—F. E. Brick. **Vice Chrmn**—J. H. Cribb. **SVP & CFO**—K. W. Haver. **Dirs**—R. J. Bogomolny, F. E. Brick, J. H. Cribb, R. A. Goodman, R. Reddy, N. W. Rose. **Transfer Agent & Registrar**—Harris Trust and Savings Bank, Chicago. **Incorporated**—in Delaware in 1969. **Empl**— 1,550. **S&P Analyst:** S.A.H.

STANDARD &POOR'S
STOCK REPORTS

TETRA Technologies

2204K

NYSE Symbol **TTI**

In S&P SmallCap 600

03-OCT-98

Industry:
Waste Management

Summary: This company provides recycling and treatment services for environmentally sensitive byproduct and waste streams, and markets chemicals extracted from such streams.

Quantitative Evaluations

Outlook
(1 Lowest—5 Highest)
• **5**

Fair Value
• **23⅝**

Risk
• **Average**

Earn./Div. Rank
• **B**

Technical Eval.
• **NA**

Rel. Strength Rank
(1 Lowest—99 Highest)
• **55**

Insider Activity
• **Neutral**

Recent Price • 12⅜
52 Wk Range • 26¾-11⅜

Yield • Nil
12-Mo. P/E • 12.4

Earnings vs. Previous Year
▲=Up ▼=Down ▶=No Change

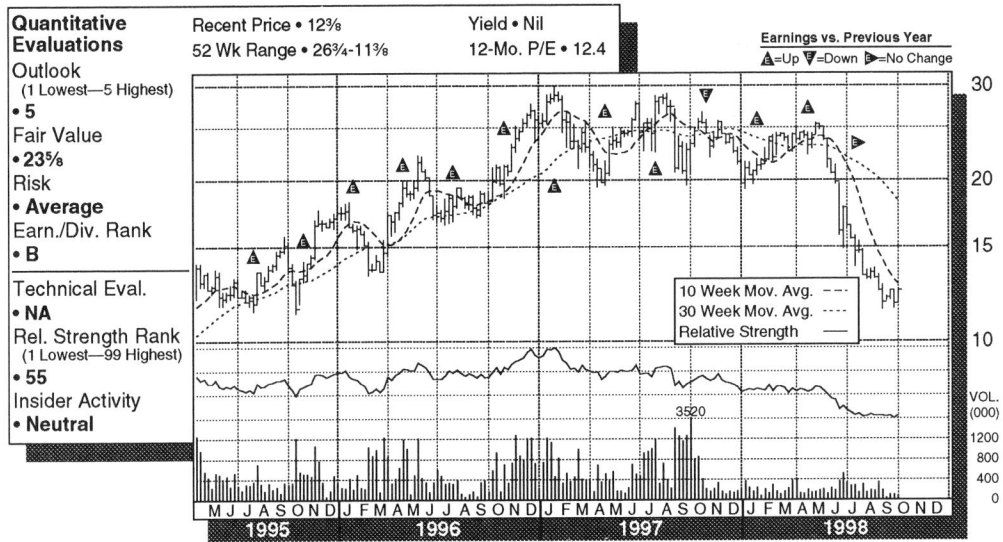

10 Week Mov. Avg. - - -
30 Week Mov. Avg. · · · ·
Relative Strength —

Business Profile - 08-SEP-98

TETRA has shifted its strategy to focus on the sale of process packages and technology licenses. The company expects future results to be aided by the expansion of its liquid calcium chloride and dry calcium chloride facilities. TTI plans to fund acquisitions in the chemical industry and in the oil and gas service sector, new projects and joint ventures with cash, proceeds from a possible public sale of up to 4,600,000 shares, and $13 million available on its $120 million credit line. During 1997, the company formed a joint venture with Dow Chemical Co. to produce bromine and derivatives. TTI expects to achieve $500 million in sales by 2000.

Operational Review - 08-SEP-98

Revenues in the six months ended June 30, 1998, advanced 32%, year to year, as service revenues grew by 61%. Margins narrowed, restricted by pricing pressures for calcium chloride; pretax income was up 6%. After taxes at 39.0%, versus 38.4%, net income rose 5.1%, to $7,651,000 ($0.54 a share, diluted), from $7,279,000 ($0.52).

Stock Performance - 02-OCT-98

In the past 30 trading days, TTI's shares have declined 5%, compared to a 7% fall in the S&P 500. Average trading volume for the past five days was 15,040 shares, compared with the 40-day moving average of 30,379 shares.

Key Stock Statistics

Dividend Rate/Share	Nil	Shareholders		4,400
Shs. outstg. (M)	13.6	Market cap. (B)		$0.169
Avg. daily vol. (M)	0.016	Inst. holdings		88%
Tang. Bk. Value/Share	8.38			
Beta	1.09			

Value of $10,000 invested 5 years ago: $ 15,075

Fiscal Year Ending Dec. 31

	1998	1997	1996	1995	1994	1993
Revenues (Million $)						
1Q	67.34	46.87	34.19	25.27	17.91	14.98
2Q	63.79	52.40	36.71	26.08	18.93	14.21
3Q	—	60.44	45.16	28.42	23.06	15.77
4Q	—	59.71	44.73	33.70	28.60	17.90
Yr.	—	219.4	160.8	113.5	88.51	62.85
Earnings Per Share ($)						
1Q	0.28	0.26	0.21	0.15	0.08	0.03
2Q	0.26	0.26	0.22	0.15	0.10	0.03
3Q	—	0.12	0.25	0.19	0.10	0.05
4Q	—	0.35	0.30	0.23	0.20	-0.04
Yr.	—	0.98	0.97	0.72	0.48	0.07

Next earnings report expected: NA

Dividend Data

No cash dividends have been paid on the common shares, and TETRA does not expect to pay any in the foreseeable future.

Business Summary - 08-SEP-98

Through a balance of internal and external growth, TETRA Technologies (TTI) hopes to reach its goals of $500 million in sales and a 20% return on equity within the next few years. The company provides recycling and treatment services for environmentally sensitive by-product and waste streams, and it markets specialty chemicals to various industries including oil and gas, agriculture and environmental services. Revenue contributions in recent years were:

	1997	1996
Product sales	67%	78%
Services	33%	22%

The company expects its specialty chemicals group to benefit from expanding opportunities in calcium chloride, a bromine strategy fueled by strategic alliances for raw materials and technology, increased production and sales of zinc and manganese sulfate products for plant and animal nutrition products, and continued growth in sales of technology systems. The Specialty Chemicals division has four calcium chloride plants that convert hydrochloric acid and weak calcium chloride solutions into various liquid and dry calcium chloride products. At each plant, the company uses the waste stream of other chemical plants to produce its products. The division's Agriculture group produces calcium chloride-based agriculture products and zinc and manganese sulfate micronutrients for plant and animal nutrition.

In the Oil and Gas division, which provides custom-blended CBFs to most major oil and gas well operators, the company plans to take advantage of rapidly growing U.S. Gulf Coast offshore and onshore oil and gas exploration and development activity, the consolidation of the oil and gas well abandonment business, the oil and gas well testing market, and increased completion activity in Mexico, the North Sea, West Africa and South America.

The Process Technologies Group (formerly the Waste Treatment division) provides engineered systems and services that treat industrial and municipal wastewater and solid-waste streams. These systems employ TTI's patented and proprietary biological filtration, metals removal and resource recovery processes.

During 1997, the company entered into a series of agreements with Dow Chemical to purchase crude bromine and build a bromine derivatives plant at Dow's facility in Ludington, MI. In August 1997, TTI acquired Posey Pipe & Equipment, the operator of an oilfield tubular goods sales, reconditioning and servicing business, for $1 million. The company also acquired Perfco Wireline, for approximately $4 million of stock.

Per Share Data ($)

(Year Ended Dec. 31)	1997	1996	1995	1994	1993	1992	1991	1990	1989	1988
Tangible Bk. Val.	7.76	6.90	6.62	5.87	5.58	5.51	5.84	4.04	-0.35	NA
Cash Flow	1.80	1.59	1.18	0.84	0.46	0.04	0.99	0.85	0.63	0.41
Earnings	0.98	0.97	0.72	0.48	0.07	-0.31	0.70	0.62	0.49	0.30
Dividends	Nil	Nil	Nil	Nil	Nil	Nil	Nil	Nil	Nil	Nil
Payout Ratio	Nil	Nil	Nil	Nil	Nil	Nil	Nil	Nil	Nil	Nil
Prices - High	30	27¾	17⅞	12¼	9¼	15¾	21¾	16¼	NA	NA
- Low	19⅛	13¼	10¼	6⅝	5¾	5¾	13½	9¼	NA	NA
P/E Ratio - High	31	29	25	26	NM	NM	31	26	NA	NA
- Low	20	14	14	14	NM	NM	19	15	NA	NA

Income Statement Analysis (Million $)

	1997	1996	1995	1994	1993	1992	1991	1990	1989	1988
Revs.	219	161	113	88.5	62.8	57.2	85.3	58.1	48.8	30.6
Oper. Inc.	36.6	29.1	17.4	12.6	6.1	1.2	16.2	12.4	7.1	4.3
Depr.	11.6	8.3	6.0	4.6	4.9	4.4	3.7	2.5	1.8	1.3
Int. Exp.	3.3	1.3	0.2	0.4	0.6	0.7	0.9	0.9	1.0	0.7
Pretax Inc.	23.1	20.5	14.5	9.0	1.3	-6.2	13.8	10.1	4.4	2.4
Eff. Tax Rate	40%	36%	36%	33%	32%	NM	37%	34%	5.30%	Nil
Net Inc.	13.9	13.1	9.4	6.1	0.9	-3.9	8.7	6.7	4.1	2.4

Balance Sheet & Other Fin. Data (Million $)

	1997	1996	1995	1994	1993	1992	1991	1990	1989	1988
Cash	2.8	2.8	7.5	13.3	16.6	16.4	32.4	18.3	0.8	0.2
Curr. Assets	110	76.1	61.3	55.7	46.9	50.3	66.5	43.4	19.3	11.0
Total Assets	264	179	130	103	89.2	88.2	99	65.7	36.9	25.7
Curr. Liab.	41.8	38.7	31.2	18.4	10.8	9.7	17.2	10.5	17.1	11.9
LT Debt	78.5	24.7	3.9	2.3	3.2	4.7	5.8	6.9	5.8	6.0
Common Eqty.	130	108	89.2	77.7	71.4	70.3	73.4	45.6	13.8	7.8
Total Cap.	222	139	98.1	84.2	77.9	77.8	81.6	54.3	19.7	13.8
Cap. Exp.	NA	12.1	18.0	6.0	5.3	10.2	10.4	7.0	4.2	5.6
Cash Flow	25.5	21.5	15.4	10.7	5.8	0.5	12.4	9.2	5.3	3.3
Curr. Ratio	2.6	2.0	2.0	3.0	4.3	5.2	3.9	4.1	1.1	0.9
% LT Debt of Cap.	NA	17.7	3.9	2.7	4.1	6.0	7.2	12.8	29.9	43.5
% Net Inc.of Revs.	6.4	8.2	8.3	6.8	1.4	NM	10.2	11.5	8.5	7.8
% Ret. on Assets	6.3	8.5	8.1	6.3	1.0	NM	10.1	5.4	13.2	10.6
% Ret. on Equity	11.7	13.3	11.2	8.1	1.2	NM	14.0	22.5	16.8	22.2

Data as orig. reptd.; bef. results of disc. opers. and/or spec. items. Per share data adj. for stk. divs. as of ex-div. date. Bold denotes diluted EPS (FASB 128). E-Estimated. NA-Not Available. NM-Not Meaningful. NR-Not Ranked.

Office—25025 I-45 North, The Woodlands, TX 77380. **Tel**—(281) 367-1983. **Fax**—(281) 364-4306. **Website**—http://www.tetratec.com **Chrmn**—J. T. Symonds. **Pres & CEO**—A. T. McInnes. **EVP-Fin, CFO, Secy & Investor Contact**—Geoffrey M. Hertel. **Treas**—J. R. Hale. **Dirs**—O. S. Andras, P. D. Coombs, T. H. Delimitros, S. T. Harcrow, G. M. Hertel, A. T. McInnes, K. P. Mitchell, J. T. Symonds, T. H. Wentzler. **Transfer Agent & Registrar**—Harris Trust & Savings Bank, NYC. **Incorporated**—in Delaware in 1981. **Empl**— 1,290. **S&P Analyst:** D.J.B.

Texas Industries

2207

NYSE Symbol **TXI**

In S&P SmallCap 600

03-OCT-98

Industry: Iron & Steel

Summary: This Texas-based company is a leading cement and structural steel maker.

S&P Opinion: Accumulate (★★★★)

| Recent Price • 23⅜ | Yield • 1.3% |
| 52 Wk Range • 68¼-22¾ | 12-Mo. P/E • 5.0 |

Quantitative Evaluations

Outlook (1 Lowest—5 Highest)
• **5**

Fair Value
• **46**

Risk
• **Low**

Earn./Div. Rank
• **B**

Technical Eval.
• **NA**

Rel. Strength Rank (1 Lowest—99 Highest)
• **9**

Insider Activity
• **Favorable**

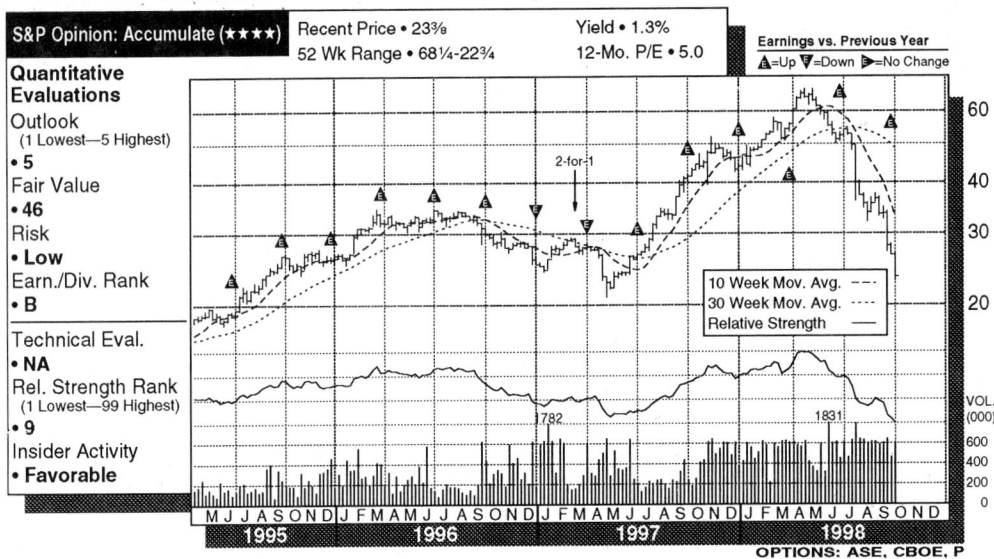

Earnings vs. Previous Year
▲=Up ▼=Down ▶=No Change

10 Week Mov. Avg. - - -
30 Week Mov. Avg. ·······
Relative Strength —

2-for-1

1782   1831

VOL. (000)
600
400
200
0

MJJASOND JFMAMJJASOND JFMAMJJASOND JFMAMJJASOND JFMAMJJASOND
1995   1996   1997   1998

OPTIONS: ASE, CBOE, P

Overview - 25-SEP-98

Results in the first quarter of FY 99 (May) benefited from a 52% increase in cement volume, in part reflecting the FY 97 acquisition of California-based Riverside Cement Co. Cement, aggregate, and concrete results for FY 99 will benefit from the inclusion of Riverside for the full year, and from a recently initiated 10% cement price increase in Texas. Current construction activity in Texas and California remains strong, and demand in these markets should benefit further from the recent passage of the TEA-21 Highway Reauthorization Bill; the largest increases in federal funding are expected to occur in these two states. On the steel side, there has been recent concern that selling prices for Chaparral's structural steel products (particularly wide flange beams) will be hurt by a rising volume of Asian imports. However, realized prices for structural products were up 6%, year to year, in the first quarter, although volume slumped 33%. While price declines from import competition would affect Chaparral's results, we suspect that a significant domestic supply shortfall for structural steel will absorb imported product without a severe erosion of selling prices.

Valuation - 25-SEP-98

For the longer term, we anticipate solid revenue and EPS results for TXI, reflecting steadily increasing demand for cement, aggregate and concrete products in Texas and California, and TXI's low cost producer status in the structural steel industry. While we expect FY 2000 results to be relatively flat with our FY 99 EPS projection of $4.70 (primarily reflecting increased interest expense and depreciation charges associated with the summer 1999 startup of the Virginia steel mill), we see sustainable double digit EPS growth for FY 01 and beyond. With TXI's ROE consistently in the high teens, we view the shares as an attractive investment at a recent level of under 6X our FY 99 EPS estimate.

Key Stock Statistics

S&P EPS Est. 1999	4.70	Tang. Bk. Value/Share	18.88
P/E on S&P Est. 1999	5.0	Beta	0.43
S&P EPS Est. 2000	4.70	Shareholders	3,800
Dividend Rate/Share	0.30	Market cap. (B)	$0.497
Shs. outstg. (M)	21.2	Inst. holdings	79%
Avg. daily vol. (M)	0.143		

Value of $10,000 invested 5 years ago: $ 21,757

Fiscal Year Ending May 31

	1999	1998	1997	1996	1995	1994
Revenues (Million $)						
1Q	299.1	297.1	245.9	232.1	201.0	168.8
2Q	—	282.7	234.4	244.3	201.1	173.1
3Q	—	281.4	216.6	235.0	199.0	170.1
4Q	—	335.1	276.9	256.0	229.5	195.2
Yr.	—	1,196	973.8	967.4	830.5	707.1
Earnings Per Share ($)						
1Q	**1.17**	1.16	0.87	0.77	0.42	0.07
2Q	**E1.13**	1.07	0.79	0.94	0.48	0.26
3Q	**E0.90**	0.85	0.47	0.70	0.28	0.13
4Q	**E1.50**	1.60	1.29	1.11	0.78	0.67
Yr.	**E4.70**	4.69	3.40	3.52	1.94	1.15

Next earnings report expected: mid December

Dividend Data (Dividends have been paid since 1962.)

Amount ($)	Date Decl.	Ex-Div. Date	Stock of Record	Payment Date
0.075	Oct. 22	Oct. 31	Nov. 04	Nov. 28 '97
0.075	Jan. 14	Jan. 29	Feb. 02	Feb. 27 '98
0.075	Apr. 20	Apr. 29	May. 01	May. 29 '98
0.075	Jul. 15	Jul. 30	Aug. 03	Aug. 28 '98

A Division of The McGraw-Hill Companies

Business Summary - 25-SEP-98

Texas Industries, the largest cement producer in that state, has derived more than 40% of its profits from wholly owned Chaparral Steel (NYSE: CSM). On December 31, 1997, TXI acquired the 15% of CSM that it did not already own.

In order to meet anticipated increases in demand for structural steel, TXI is building a minimill in Richmond, VA. The new minimill's capacity will total 1.2 million tons, boosting TXI's total steelmaking capacity about 70%. Management expects production to begin in mid-1999. TXI has said it is building the new minimill to meet increased U.S. demand, following a reduction in suppliers over the last several years. As a result of this reduction, the structural market has had to purchase imported beams. TXI's primary offerings, its higher-margin, medium- to small-size steel beams and specialty steel products, are sold mostly to the nonresidential construction industry. TXI's Dallas, TX-based minimill uses scrap steel to make its products. At FY 98 (May) and FY 97 year-end, total steel capacity (based on melting capacity) stood at 1.7 million tons and 1.8 million tons, respectively.

The cement/concrete unit makes cement, aggregates, ready-mix concrete, concrete pipe, block and brick. TXI makes cement at its two Texas plants. The company expanded cement capacity by 60% with the acquisition of Southern California-based Riverside Cement Co. in the second half of FY 98. TXI also operates many concrete and concrete block and brick plants, mostly in Texas and Louisiana. The company's aggregates business (sand, clay, shale, gravel and crushed limestone) primarily serves the Texas, Louisiana and Colorado markets.

The company also owns Brookhollow, a real estate development concern that owns land in Dallas/Ft. Worth, Houston, and Richmond, VA. Brookhollow primarily develops its land holdings into industrial, office and multi-use parks.

Segment revenue contributions and operating profit margins in recent fiscal years were:

	FY 98	FY 97	FY 96
REVENUES			
Steel	59%	63%	63%
Cement/concrete	41%	37%	37%
OPERATING PROFIT MARGINS			
Steel	12%	12%	12%
Cement/concrete	22%	23%	25%

Per Share Data ($)

(Year Ended May 31)	1998	1997	1996	1995	1994	1993	1992	1991	1990	1989
Tangible Bk. Val.	18.88	18.64	16.25	12.78	11.18	9.38	9.33	9.23	11.87	13.10
Cash Flow	7.54	5.82	5.68	3.92	3.06	2.15	2.23	3.04	1.65	2.82
Earnings	4.69	3.40	3.52	1.94	1.15	0.06	0.10	0.98	-0.42	0.74
Dividends	0.30	0.21	0.20	0.15	0.10	0.10	0.10	0.10	0.38	0.37
Payout Ratio	6%	6%	6%	8%	9%	182%	105%	10%	NM	50%
Cal. Yrs.	1997	1996	1995	1994	1993	1992	1991	1990	1989	1988
Prices - High	52	34⅝	27⅝	19⅞	16¼	12⅝	12½	11¾	17¾	20⅝
- Low	20⅞	25⅛	15⅛	14¾	10⅝	9⅝	7	5⅜	10⅝	13¼
P/E Ratio - High	11	10	8	10	14	NM	NM	12	NM	28
- Low	4	7	4	8	9	NM	NM	5	NM	18

Income Statement Analysis (Million $)

	1998	1997	1996	1995	1994	1993	1992	1991	1990	1989
Revs.	1,196	974	967	831	716	621	606	664	659	708
Oper. Inc.	225	184	191	140	113	79.0	65.0	71.0	71.0	117
Depr.	62.3	53.9	49.3	49.3	43.6	46.8	47.5	45.0	43.8	43.8
Int. Exp.	20.5	18.9	20.0	20.1	26.2	32.6	34.5	34.0	31.7	36.0
Pretax Inc.	160	123	135	77.9	43.6	Nil	5.0	39.4	-4.4	37.8
Eff. Tax Rate	33%	33%	35%	33%	36%	NM	35%	35%	NM	27%
Net Inc.	102	75.5	80.0	48.0	25.8	1.1	1.9	22.1	-7.3	18.8

Balance Sheet & Other Fin. Data (Million $)

	1998	1997	1996	1995	1994	1993	1992	1991	1990	1989
Cash	16.7	19.8	28.1	26.0	31.8	33.1	20.7	23.2	42.3	73.4
Curr. Assets	372	344	325	293	277	261	240	227	261	289
Total Assets	1,186	848	801	753	749	757	777	789	703	731
Curr. Liab.	145	101	106	105	116	101	105	111	108	113
LT Debt	406	176	160	185	171	267	289	293	260	260
Common Eqty.	553	453	420	343	352	282	281	282	239	253
Total Cap.	1,041	747	695	567	560	645	657	661	578	546
Cap. Exp.	253	85.2	79.3	48.8	23.3	17.9	21.6	98.4	50.4	43.4
Cash Flow	164	129	129	97.3	69.3	47.8	49.4	67.0	36.4	62.5
Curr. Ratio	2.6	3.4	3.1	2.8	2.4	2.6	2.3	2.0	2.4	2.6
% LT Debt of Cap.	39.0	23.6	23.0	32.6	30.6	41.4	44.0	44.3	44.9	47.6
% Net Inc.of Revs.	8.5	7.8	8.3	5.8	3.6	0.2	0.3	3.3	NM	2.7
% Ret. on Assets	10.0	9.2	10.3	6.4	3.2	0.1	0.2	2.8	NM	2.7
% Ret. on Equity	20.3	17.3	21.0	13.8	7.7	0.4	0.7	8.0	NM	7.3

Data as orig. reptd.; bef. results of disc. opers. and/or spec. items. Per share data adj. for stk. divs. as of ex-div. date. Bold denotes diluted EPS (FASB 128). E-Estimated. NA-Not Available. NM-Not Meaningful. NR-Not Ranked.

Office—1341 W. Mockingbird Lane, Dallas, TX 75247-6913. **Tel**—(972) 647-6700. **Chrmn**—R. B. Rogers. **Pres & CEO**— R. D. Rogers. **VP-Fin**—R. M. Fowler. **VP & Secy**—R. C. Moore. **Treas & Investor Contact**—Kenneth R. Allen. **Dirs**—R. Alpert, J. M. Belk, G. E. Forward, R. I. Galland, G. R. Heffernan, J. M. Hoak, E. C. Reyes, R. B. Rogers, R. D. Rogers, I. Wachtmeister, E. C. Williams. **Transfer Agent & Registrar**—ChaseMellon Shareholder Services. **Incorporated**—in Delaware in 1951. **Empl**— 4,100. **S&P Analyst:** Eric J. Hunter

03-OCT-98

Industry: Health Care (Drugs - Generic & Other)

Summary: Theratech develops controlled-release drug delivery products for administration through the skin, oral tissues, lungs, and by other means.

Quantitative Evaluations

Outlook (1 Lowest—5 Highest)
- **4⁻**

Fair Value
- **11½**

Risk
- **High**

Earn./Div. Rank
- **B-**

Technical Eval.
- **Bearish** since 7/98

Rel. Strength Rank (1 Lowest—99 Highest)
- **76**

Insider Activity
- **NA**

Recent Price • 8⅜
52 Wk Range • 12⅛-5¾
Yield • Nil
12-Mo. P/E • 28.9

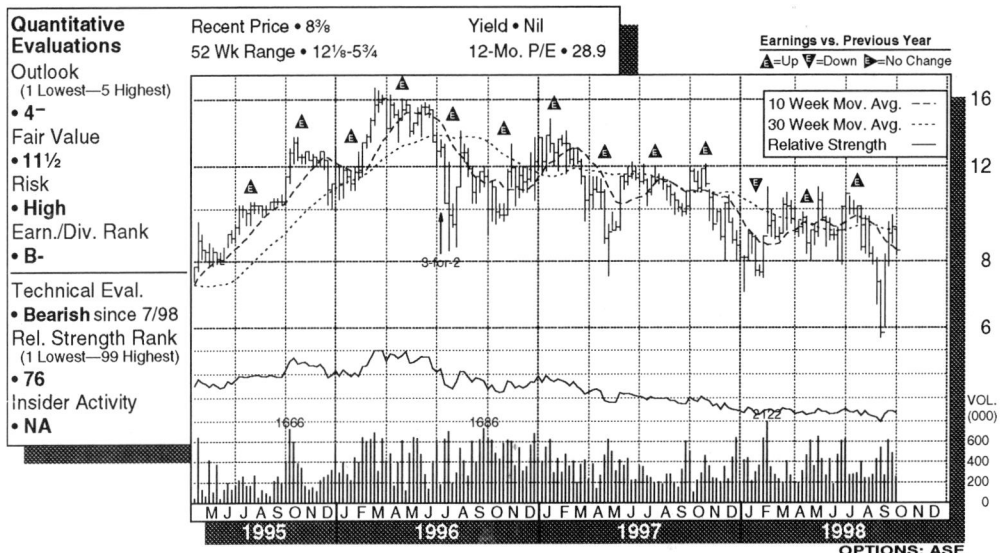

Earnings vs. Previous Year
▲=Up ▼=Down ▶=No Change

10 Week Mov. Avg. ---
30 Week Mov. Avg. ....
Relative Strength —

OPTIONS: ASE

Business Profile - 13-AUG-98

This company has four products on the market; Face Lift, an anti-wrinkle skin patch, Androderm and Alora, which are transdermal products for hormone replacement therapy, and transdermal nitroglycerin patches for angina pectoris. The firm also has 20 products in development and 50 issued, allowed, or pending U.S. patents with international counterparts. THRT has marketing or R&D agreements with many other leading pharmaceutical companies including Eli Lilly, Proctor & Gamble, Pfizer, SmithKline Beecham, Wyeth-Ayerst, Astra AB, CEPA, Lavipharm S.A., Schwarz Pharma AG, Samyang, Meiji, and Sankyo. In February 1998, the company announced a plan to repurchase up to 1 million common shares, as part of a strategic plan to enhance shareholder value.

Operational Review - 13-AUG-98

Total revenues (including interest income) for the six months ended June 30, 1998, rose 22%, year to year, primarily due to increases of 41% and 12% in product sales and R&D revenues, respectively. The company stated that its Androderm and Face Lift products were principle contributors to revenue in the second quarter. Profitability was restricted by a 29% increase in the cost of products sold and 38% higher SG&A expenses. Net income advanced 20%, to $2,519,633 ($0.12 a share) from $2,108,255 ($0.10). Cash, equivalents and investments totaled $23.4 million on June 30, 1998.

Stock Performance - 02-OCT-98

In the past 30 trading days, THRT's shares have increased 5%, compared to a 7% fall in the S&P 500. Average trading volume for the past five days was 50,040 shares, compared with the 40-day moving average of 82,233 shares.

Key Stock Statistics

Dividend Rate/Share	Nil	Shareholders	200
Shs. outstg. (M)	21.3	Market cap. (B)	$0.178
Avg. daily vol. (M)	0.091	Inst. holdings	54%
Tang. Bk. Value/Share	1.86		
Beta	1.45		

Value of $10,000 invested 5 years ago: $ 8,237

Fiscal Year Ending Dec. 31

	1998	1997	1996	1995	1994	1993
Revenues (Million $)						
1Q	10.86	8.84	6.35	3.04	0.52	0.71
2Q	11.12	9.20	8.82	4.95	1.04	0.62
3Q	—	11.05	8.59	3.11	1.76	3.29
4Q	—	10.66	12.60	12.31	4.22	0.85
Yr.	—	39.75	36.36	24.52	7.54	5.47
Earnings Per Share ($)						
1Q	**0.05**	0.04	-0.07	-0.11	-0.17	-0.11
2Q	**0.07**	0.06	0.05	-0.12	-0.17	-0.12
3Q	—	0.08	0.07	-0.14	-0.15	0.02
4Q	—	**0.09**	0.14	-0.03	-0.11	-0.28
Yr.	—	**0.27**	0.20	-0.39	-0.61	-0.50

Next earnings report expected: late October

Dividend Data

No cash dividends have been paid on the common stock.

A Division of The McGraw·Hill Companies

Business Summary - 13-AUG-98

TheraTech, Inc. develops advanced controlled-release drug-delivery products that administer drugs through the skin, lungs, tissues in the oral cavity, and by other means. THRT has marketing or R&D agreements with many leading pharmaceutical companies and biotechnology firms.

THRT currently has four products on the market; Face Lift, an anti-wrinkle skin patch; Androderm and Alora, which are transdermal products for hormone replacement therapy; and transdermal nitroglycerin patches for angina pectoris.

The company's transdermal testosterone product is currently marketed in the U.S. under the trade name Androderm by SmithKline Beecham (SB) and is, or will be marketed in Denmark, Finland, Norway, Sweden, Ireland, South Korea, and the United Kingdom through other various marketing partners. The testosterone patch system helps restore normal testosterone levels in males and relieves symptoms of testosterone deficiency such as loss of libido, impotence, fatigue and depression.

The company's other hormone replacement therapy product is Alora, a transdermal estradiol system developed for the treatment of menopausal symptoms and other conditions associated with estrogen deficiency, including osteoporosis. Proctor & Gamble has the world-

wide marketing rights for Alora except in certain Asian countries.

The transdermal nitroglycerin patch is indicated for the treatment of angina pectoris and is pending final FDA approval in the U.S. for generic substitution of Novartis' Transderm-Nitro product. In Europe, applications for bioequivalency against Transderm-Nitro were approved and the product is marketed by Lavipharm S.A. in Italy, Holland, Greece, and France. THRT has granted Samyang Co. Ltd. exclusive rights to manufacture and market the product in South Korea.

The Face Lift-Vitamin C Anti-Wrinkle Patch is a cosmetic product that utilizes the company's MTX transdermal technology and contains anti-oxidants for the treatment of fine wrinkles around the eyes and mouth. University Medical Products, USA, Inc. launched the product in January 1998 and markets it worldwide. The product is supplied by Natrapac, a wholly owned subsidiary of THRT.

THRT is developing drug-delivery products in collaboration with several pharmaceutical and biotechnology firms including products for the treatment of female testosterone deficiency, anxiety, pain, oteoporosis, cancer and male erectile dysfunction. Many of the new products will utilize the company's oral transmucosal (OTM) delivery system. The company indicated that the OTM system has demonstrated significant progress in the transmucosal delivery of macromolecules such as peptide and carbohydrate based compounds.

Per Share Data ($)

(Year Ended Dec. 31)	1997	1996	1995	1994	1993	1992	1991	1990	1989	1988
Tangible Bk. Val.	1.73	1.75	1.47	1.90	1.34	1.70	0.04	NA	NA	NA
Cash Flow	0.41	0.30	-0.32	-0.57	-0.47	-0.43	-0.05	NA	NA	NA
Earnings	0.27	0.20	-0.39	-0.61	-0.50	-0.47	-0.07	NA	NA	NA
Dividends	Nil	Nil	Nil	Nil	Nil	Nil	Nil	Nil	Nil	Nil
Payout Ratio	Nil	Nil	Nil	Nil	Nil	Nil	Nil	Nil	Nil	Nil
Prices - High	14¾	16⅞	13⅝	10⅜	11⅜	12⅛	NA	NA	NA	NA
- Low	7	8⅜	5⅞	5⅞	6⅝	3⅜	NA	NA	NA	NA
P/E Ratio - High	55	84	NM	NM	NM	NM	NA	NA	NA	NA
- Low	26	42	NM	NM	NM	NM	NM	NM	NM	NM

Income Statement Analysis (Million $)

	1997	1996	1995	1994	1993	1992	1991	1990	1989	1988
Revs.	38.2	34.7	23.0	7.5	5.5	2.6	2.7	NA	NA	NA
Oper. Inc.	8.3	6.0	-6.8	-11.9	-7.0	-5.5	-0.3	NA	NA	NA
Depr.	3.1	2.4	1.6	0.7	0.5	0.4	0.2	NA	NA	NA
Int. Exp.	0.9	1.1	1.0	0.3	0.1	0.0	0.0	NA	NA	NA
Pretax Inc.	5.9	4.2	-7.8	-11.6	-7.9	-5.8	-0.8	NA	NA	NA
Eff. Tax Rate	Nil	Nil	NM	NM	Nil	Nil	Nil	Nil	Nil	Nil
Net Inc.	5.9	4.2	-7.8	-11.6	-7.9	-5.8	-0.8	NA	NA	NA

Balance Sheet & Other Fin. Data (Million $)

	1997	1996	1995	1994	1993	1992	1991	1990	1989	1988
Cash	15.0	23.2	18.7	22.5	18.7	25.7	1.1	NA	NA	NA
Curr. Assets	32.1	30.3	23.4	23.6	19.4	26.4	1.4	NA	NA	NA
Total Assets	61.9	53.8	50.8	49.8	28.1	28.4	2.9	NA	NA	NA
Curr. Liab.	7.4	8.0	8.9	3.7	4.6	1.1	0.3	NA	NA	NA
LT Debt	7.3	8.7	10.3	8.7	0.7	0.4	0.2	NA	NA	NA
Common Eqty.	43.6	36.0	30.3	37.3	22.6	26.7	0.4	NA	NA	NA
Total Cap.	50.9	44.7	40.7	45.9	23.2	27.1	2.6	NA	NA	NA
Cap. Exp.	2.7	3.6	4.0	9.8	5.9	0.6	0.3	NA	NA	NA
Cash Flow	8.9	6.6	-6.3	-10.9	-7.4	-5.4	-0.6	NA	NA	NA
Curr. Ratio	4.3	3.8	2.6	6.5	4.2	23.5	4.3	NA	NA	NA
% LT Debt of Cap.	14.2	19.5	25.3	18.9	2.8	1.5	6.3	NA	NA	NA
% Net Inc.of Revs.	15.3	12.2	NM	NM	NM	NM	NM	NM	NM	NM
% Ret. on Assets	10.1	8.1	NM	NM	NM	NM	NM	NM	NM	NM
% Ret. on Equity	8.0	12.8	NM	NM	NM	NM	NM	NM	NM	NM

Data as orig. reptd.; bef. results of disc. opers. and/or spec. items. Per share data adj. for stk. divs. as of ex-div. date. Bold denotes diluted EPS (FASB 128). E-Estimated. NA-Not Available. NM-Not Meaningful. NR-Not Ranked.

Office—417 Wakara Way, Salt Lake City, UT 84108. **Tel**—(801) 588-6200. **Website**—http://www.thrt.com **Chrmn,Pres & CEO**—D. C. Patel. **SVP & CFO**—A. L. Searl. **Dirs**—G. L. Crocker, R. K. DeVeer, Jr., W. I. Higuchi, J. T. O'Brien, D. C. Patel, J. J. Pisik, B. J. Poulsen. **Transfer Agent & Registrar**—Boston EquiServe. **Incorporated**—in Utah in 1985; reincorporated in Delaware in 1992. **Empl**— 241. **S&P Analyst:** David Moskowitz

STANDARD &POOR'S
STOCK REPORTS

Thomas Industries

2227D

NYSE Symbol **TII**

In S&P SmallCap 600

03-OCT-98

Industry: Manufacturing (Diversified)

Summary: This company designs, produces and sells commercial, industrial and residential lighting products, as well as compressors and vacuum pumps for global OEM applications.

Quantitative Evaluations

Recent Price • 20½
52 Wk Range • 26¾-18⅜

Yield • 1.5%
12-Mo. P/E • 13.9

Outlook
(1 Lowest—5 Highest)
• **2**

Fair Value
• **21¼**

Risk
• **Low**

Earn./Div. Rank
• **B**

Technical Eval.
• **Bullish** since 9/98

Rel. Strength Rank
(1 Lowest—99 Highest)
• **64**

Insider Activity
• **Neutral**

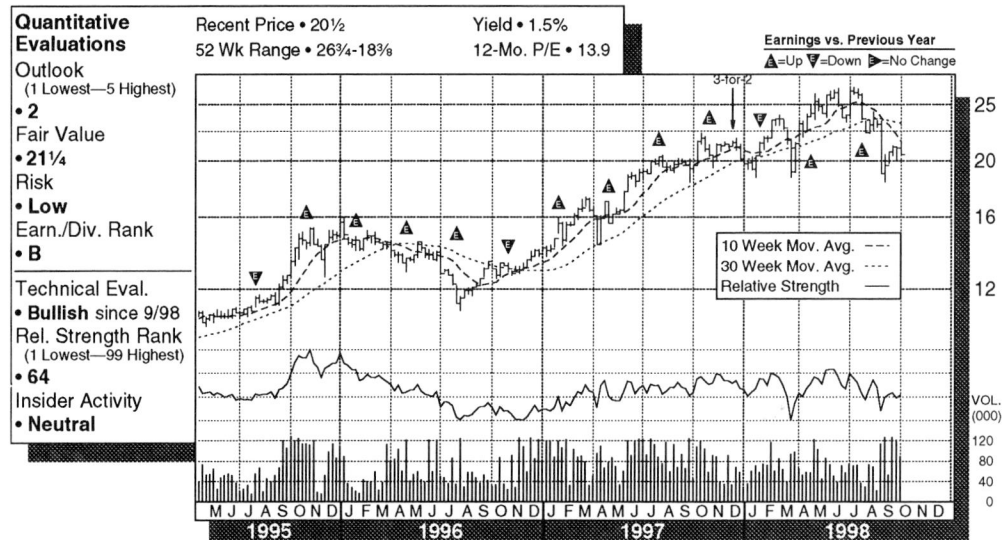

Earnings vs. Previous Year
△=Up ▽=Down ▶=No Change

10 Week Mov. Avg. - - -
30 Week Mov. Avg. ....
Relative Strength ———

Business Profile - 30-MAR-98

The company hopes to expand its compressor and vacuum pump sales to $250 million in two years (from $174 million in 1997), through internal expansion and acquisitions. TII is seeking greater penetration of international markets, in order to accelerate overall sales growth. Sales outside the U.S. accounted for 19% of the total in 1996 and 1997. In December 1997, the company's Lumec Lighting division of Quebec acquired Eclairage ZED, Inc., a manufacturer of decorative outdoor urban lighting. Also in December, the common shares were split three for two.

Operational Review - 30-MAR-98

Net sales in 1997, rose 7.4%, from the prior year, primarily reflecting strength in the lighting segment, attributed to a strong construction market, and a 2.1% increase in compressor & vacuum pump sales on the introduction of new products. Gross margins widened, due to continued improved efficiencies and cost reductions in the lighting segment, as well as the acquisition of Welch Vacuum Technology in 1996. Following well controlled SG&A expenses, lower interest expense, and after taxes at 37.0%, versus 37.1%, net income advanced 29%, to $22,470,000 ($1.38 a share), from $17,416,000 ($1.09, as adjusted for 3-for-2 split in December 1997).

Stock Performance - 02-OCT-98

In the past 30 trading days, TII's shares have declined 11%, compared to a 7% fall in the S&P 500. Average trading volume for the past five days was 17,760 shares, compared with the 40-day moving average of 22,377 shares.

Key Stock Statistics

Dividend Rate/Share	0.30	Shareholders	2,200
Shs. outstg. (M)	15.9	Market cap. (B)	$0.325
Avg. daily vol. (M)	0.024	Inst. holdings	63%
Tang. Bk. Value/Share	8.02		
Beta	0.96		

Value of $10,000 invested 5 years ago: $ 38,043

Fiscal Year Ending Dec. 31

	1998	1997	1996	1995	1994	1993
Revenues (Million $)						
1Q	141.9	126.4	123.5	117.6	109.4	112.1
2Q	143.1	140.0	127.9	127.4	117.3	111.0
3Q	—	141.2	129.6	128.8	119.0	117.3
4Q	—	140.2	129.1	116.8	110.8	109.8
Yr.	—	547.7	510.1	490.6	456.6	450.1
Earnings Per Share ($)						
1Q	0.32	0.25	0.17	0.11	0.07	0.05
2Q	0.42	0.00	0.00	0.25	0.33	0.08
3Q	—	0.43	0.37	0.31	0.19	0.10
4Q	—	0.31	0.27	0.17	0.11	0.03
Yr.	—	1.38	1.09	0.83	0.70	0.25

Next earnings report expected: early October

Dividend Data (Dividends have been paid since 1955.)

Amount ($)	Date Decl.	Ex-Div. Date	Stock of Record	Payment Date
0.075	Oct. 16	Dec. 02	Nov. 14	Dec. 01 '97
0.075	Feb. 11	Mar. 04	Mar. 06	Apr. 01 '98
0.075	Apr. 16	Jun. 03	Jun. 05	Jul. 01 '98
0.075	Jul. 16	Sep. 02	Sep. 04	Oct. 01 '98

A Division of The **McGraw·Hill** *Companies*

STANDARD &POOR'S
STOCK REPORTS

Thomas Industries Inc.

2227D
03-OCT-98

Business Summary - 30-MAR-98

Founded in 1928, Thomas Industries (TII) believes that research leading to new and improved products is the key to keeping one step ahead of the competition. TII has focused on expansion of the lighting segment and compressors and vacuum pumps segment as its two core businesses. TII spent $14.9 million on R&D in 1997 (versus $14.3 million in 1996).

Headquartered in Louisville, KY, TII makes and sells a broad range of consumer, commercial, industrial and outdoor lighting fixtures, marketed under the Day-Brite, Gardco, Capri, Electro/Connect, McPhilben, Omega, Emco, Lumec, C&M and Thomas Lighting trade names. TII also manufactures a line of compressors and vacuum pumps, sold under the Thomas and Welch names in the U.S. and ASF/Thomas in Europe.

In 1997, TII's continued to its revenue growth. After topping the one-half billion dollar mark for the first time in its history in 1996, revenues advanced 7.4% in 1997. Due in part to strength in the construction markets, and new product introductions in the compressor & vacuum pump segment, and cost reduction programs and productivity improvements, net income jumped 29% to $22.5 million from $17.4 million reported in 1996. Export sales accounted for 8.4% of sales in 1997.

TII's lighting segment serves a wide variety of customers, including wholesale distributors, electrical contractors, consulting engineers, interior designers, architects,

builders, showroom owners and home center buyers. TII's consumer lighting line includes high-style chandeliers and bathroom fixtures, plus lighting products for foyers, dining rooms, living rooms, entertainment areas, kitchens, bedrooms, and outdoors. In 1997, this segment accounted for 68% of TII's sales and 42% of operating income.

The company's compressors and vacuum pumps are found in a variety of applications, including medical equipment, vending machines, photocopiers, computer tape drives, automotive and transportation equipment, liquid dispensing applications, gasoline vapor recovery, refrigerant recovery, waste disposal and laboratory equipment. In 1997, this segment accounted for 32% of TII's sales and 58% of operating income.

Five companies in the U.S. and Canada, one of which is Thomas Industries, share a substantial portion of lighting segment market. Although the industry is subject to the cyclicality of residential and commercial construction activity, replacement and renovation activity moderates these cycles somewhat. The company is also the leading supplier to the original equipment manufacturer (OEM) medical market and a significant participant in a variety of other OEM compressor and vacuum pump markets. Operations of the compressor & vacuum pump segment help TII moderate the impact of the lighting segment's vulnerability to construction and economic cycles.

Per Share Data ($)

(Year Ended Dec. 31)	1997	1996	1995	1994	1993	1992	1991	1990	1989	1988
Tangible Bk. Val.	7.38	6.27	5.39	4.71	4.06	4.19	4.58	4.60	4.56	6.01
Cash Flow	2.37	2.07	1.80	1.73	1.35	0.95	1.33	1.75	2.10	1.60
Earnings	1.38	1.09	0.83	0.70	0.25	-0.13	0.25	0.77	1.35	1.08
Dividends	0.28	0.27	0.27	0.27	0.27	0.27	0.51	0.51	0.49	0.44
Payout Ratio	20%	25%	32%	38%	NM	NM	201%	65%	36%	38%
Prices - High	22³⁄₈	15⁷⁄₈	16¹⁄₈	11	9³⁄₈	9³⁄₈	9⁷⁄₈	13⁷⁄₈	13³⁄₄	15⁵⁄₈
- Low	13⁵⁄₈	11	9¹⁄₈	8¹⁄₂	6¹⁄₈	5⁵⁄₈	6¹⁄₈	6¹⁄₈	11³⁄₄	10
P/E Ratio - High	16	15	19	16	37	NM	39	18	10	14
- Low	10	10	11	12	24	NM	24	8	9	9

Income Statement Analysis (Million $)

	1997	1996	1995	1994	1993	1992	1991	1990	1989	1988
Revs.	548	510	491	457	450	421	408	462	437	348
Oper. Inc.	57.5	49.8	44.5	38.7	37.8	32.2	33.4	45.3	42.3	35.3
Depr.	16.0	15.7	14.8	15.5	16.5	16.3	16.1	15.0	11.5	8.5
Int. Exp.	6.5	7.3	8.2	9.2	10.3	10.4	11.0	12.2	10.5	4.0
Pretax Inc.	35.6	27.7	21.1	18.2	7.8	0.2	7.2	20.2	34.8	29.6
Eff. Tax Rate	37%	37%	39%	42%	51%	919%	48%	42%	41%	40%
Net Inc.	22.5	17.4	12.8	10.5	3.8	-2.0	3.8	11.7	20.6	17.7

Balance Sheet & Other Fin. Data (Million $)

	1997	1996	1995	1994	1993	1992	1991	1990	1989	1988
Cash	17.4	18.8	18.3	5.1	2.4	3.5	14.2	21.0	30.1	11.6
Curr. Assets	177	170	165	155	153	141	142	156	178	123
Total Assets	328	320	314	305	303	294	303	323	333	208
Curr. Liab.	84.4	84.5	83.9	77.8	74.4	70.1	66.3	67.5	74.5	46.0
LT Debt	55.0	62.6	70.8	80.0	88.0	90.0	93.0	109	117	33.0
Common Eqty.	173	158	143	134	125	130	139	142	139	125
Total Cap.	228	229	222	221	221	221	237	256	259	162
Cap. Exp.	17.7	15.1	12.3	16.3	13.9	13.2	11.6	21.6	15.5	14.6
Cash Flow	38.5	33.1	27.6	26.1	20.3	14.3	19.9	26.7	32.1	26.2
Curr. Ratio	2.1	2.0	2.0	2.0	2.1	2.0	2.1	2.3	2.4	2.7
% LT Debt of Cap.	24.1	27.4	31.9	36.0	39.6	40.6	39.4	42.5	45.3	20.3
% Net Inc.of Revs.	4.1	3.5	2.6	2.3	0.8	NM	0.9	2.5	4.7	5.1
% Ret. on Assets	6.9	5.5	4.1	3.5	1.3	NM	1.2	3.6	7.6	8.9
% Ret. on Equity	13.6	11.6	9.2	811.0	3.0	NM	2.7	8.4	15.6	14.5

Data as orig. reptd.; bef. results of disc. opers. and/or spec. items. Per share data adj. for stk. divs. as of ex-div. date. Bold denotes diluted EPS (FASB 128). E-Estimated. NA-Not Available. NM-Not Meaningful. NR-Not Ranked.

Office—4360 Brownsboro Rd. , Louisville, KY 40207. Tel—(502) 893-4600. Website—http://www.thomasind.com.Chrmn, Pres & CEO—T. C. Brown. VP, CFO & Secy—P. J. Stuecker. Investor Contact—Laurie Lyons. Dirs—T. C. Brown, W. H. Dunbar, R. P. Eklund, H. J. Ferguson, G. P. Gardner, L. E. Gloyd, W. M. Jordan, R. D. Ketchum, F. J. Lunding Jr., A. A. Massaro. Transfer Agent & Registrar—Fifth Third Bank, Cincinnati, Ohio.Empl— 3,200. S&P Analyst: G.A.S.

Thor Industries

2232

NYSE Symbol **THO**

In S&P SmallCap 600

03-OCT-98

Industry:
Leisure Time (Products)

Summary: Thor is the second largest manufacturer of recreational vehicles in the U.S. and Canada and the largest producer of small and mid-size buses.

Quantitative Evaluations	Recent Price • 20⅝	Yield • 0.4%
	52 Wk Range • 29⅝-19⅛	12-Mo. P/E • 11.5

Outlook
(1 Lowest—5 Highest)
• **NA**

Fair Value
• **NA**

Risk
• **Average**

Earn./Div. Rank
• **B+**

Technical Eval.
• **Bearish** since 8/98

Rel. Strength Rank
(1 Lowest—99 Highest)
• **52**

Insider Activity
• **NA**

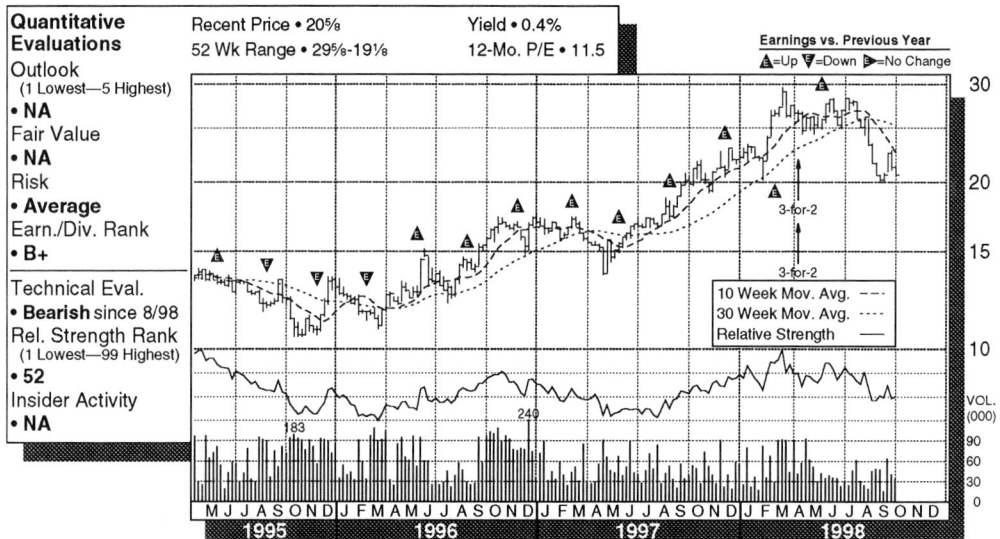

Earnings vs. Previous Year
▲=Up ▼=Down ▶=No Change

10 Week Mov. Avg. - - -
30 Week Mov. Avg. ·····
Relative Strength —

Business Profile - 22-SEP-98

FY 97 (Jul.) results reflected good demand late in the year for both RVs and buses and improved cost controls, and this trend continued into FY 98. RV sales tend to be lower in the winter months, especially in the second quarter, due to the industry's dependence on vacationers and campers. In February 1998, THO acquired Champion Motor Coach Inc., the third largest manufacturer of mid-size buses, with annual sales of about $60 million. The acquisition is expected to add to THO's earnings in FY 98, and gives the company over $200 million in annual bus sales. The transaction was for about $9.7 million in cash. Officers and directors own more than 50% of the shares. In April 1998, common shares were split 3-for-2.

Operational Review - 22-SEP-98

Net sales in the nine months ended April 30, 1998, advanced 14%, year to year. Gross margins widened, but SG&A expenses rose 23%. Results benefitted from a gain of $1.3 million on the December 1997 sale of Henschen Corp. and, after a significant drop in interest expense, pretax income was up 38%. After taxes at 40.1%, versus 41.0%, net income increased 40%, to $15,145,014 ($1.23 a share) from $10,839,574 ($0.86, adjusted). At May 1, 1998, backlog stood at a record $165 million, up 27% from a year earlier.

Stock Performance - 02-OCT-98

In the past 30 trading days, THO's shares have declined 5%, compared to a 7% fall in the S&P 500. Average trading volume for the past five days was 6,660 shares, compared with the 40-day moving average of 7,995 shares.

Key Stock Statistics

Dividend Rate/Share	0.08	Shareholders	200
Shs. outstg. (M)	12.2	Market cap. (B)	$0.252
Avg. daily vol. (M)	0.008	Inst. holdings	46%
Tang. Bk. Value/Share	9.36		
Beta	0.82		

Value of $10,000 invested 5 years ago: $ 12,676

Fiscal Year Ending Jul. 31

	1998	1997	1996	1995	1994	1993
Revenues (Million $)						
1Q	165.5	150.5	151.5	139.2	128.2	104.0
2Q	134.5	123.5	119.8	114.4	90.78	80.26
3Q	206.9	169.3	169.2	163.1	129.0	117.2
4Q	—	181.1	161.6	146.1	143.1	110.8
Yr.	—	624.4	602.1	562.7	491.1	412.2
Earnings Per Share ($)						
1Q	0.49	0.39	0.33	0.43	0.40	0.29
2Q	**0.01**	0.10	0.15	0.17	0.18	0.07
3Q	**0.50**	0.38	0.31	0.28	0.26	0.23
4Q	—	0.50	0.43	0.15	0.39	0.27
Yr.	—	1.43	1.21	1.03	1.20	0.85

Next earnings report expected: NA

Dividend Data (Dividends have been paid since 1987.)

Amount ($)	Date Decl.	Ex-Div. Date	Stock of Record	Payment Date
0.030	Feb. 17	Mar. 18	Mar. 20	Apr. 03 '98
3-for-2	Mar. 10	Apr. 07	Mar. 21	Apr. 06 '98
0.020	May. 29	Jun. 15	Jun. 17	Jul. 02 '98
0.020	Sep. 21	Sep. 24	Sep. 28	Oct. 09 '98

A Division of The **McGraw·Hill** *Companies*

STANDARD
&POOR'S
STOCK REPORTS

Thor Industries, Inc.

2232

03-OCT-98

Business Summary - 22-SEP-98

Thor Industries, Inc. (THO), produces and sells a wide range of recreational vehicles (RVs) and small and mid-sized buses in the U.S. and Canada. THO is the second largest manufacturer of RVs in the U.S. and Canada, and the largest producer of small and mid-sized buses (approximately 25% U.S. and Canadian market share). Contributions to revenues and operating profits in FY 97 (Jul.) were:

	Revs.	Profits
Recreational vehicles	78%	70%
Bus products	22%	30%

THO believes that positive demographics will continue to exert strong demand influences in the RV industry. THO expects the number of consumers aged 45 to 64, who comprise the RV industry's prime ownership market, to increase by 27 million over the next 15 years. The University of Michigan's Survey Research Center estimates that the number of households owning RVs will grow nearly 25% by 2010 (currently about 8.5 million own RVs). RV products consist of travel trailers, camping trailers, motorhomes and fifth wheels under trade names such as Airstream, Dutchman, Aero, Four Winds, Thor America, and Thor California. RV sales tend to be significantly lower during the winter months,

due to the RV industry's dependence on vacationers and campers. Sales are historically lowest during the second fiscal quarter (ending January 31).

The Eldorado National Bus (ENB) segment, while not a very large contributor to sales and operating income, is the company's fastest growing segment. Management believes that ENB is the largest manufacturer of small and mid-size commercial buses in North America. Robust demand for small and mid-sized buses is the result of increased public awareness of the need for cost effective and smaller forms of transportation. Companies have moved from buying gas-guzzling 40 ft. buses to smaller, fuel efficient, lighter buses that are more user friendly and cost effective. ENB manufactures small and mid-sized buses for transit, airport car rental and motel/hotel shuttles, paramedical transit, tour and charter operations and other uses, under the names Aerotech, Escort, MST, ELF, Transmark and EZ Rider.

The company markets its RVs and buses through independent dealers located throughout the U.S. and Canada. Each of THO's subsidiaries maintains its own dealer organization. There are approximately 800 dealers carrying the company's RVs, and 39 dealers carrying the company's buses. No single dealer accounted for more than 5% of consolidated net sales of RVs during FY 97, while no single dealer accounted for more than 10% of THO's net bus revenue.

Per Share Data ($)

(Year Ended Jul. 31)	1997	1996	1995	1994	1993	1992	1991	1990	1989	1988
Tangible Bk. Val.	8.31	7.39	6.21	5.32	6.06	5.34	3.80	3.25	3.01	3.00
Cash Flow	1.79	1.59	1.39	1.54	1.17	1.04	0.20	0.44	0.41	0.57
Earnings	1.43	1.21	1.03	1.20	0.85	0.77	0.05	0.31	0.29	0.50
Dividends	0.08	0.08	0.08	0.08	0.08	0.06	0.05	0.05	0.05	0.05
Payout Ratio	6%	7%	8%	7%	9%	10%	100%	17%	19%	11%
Prices - High	23⅛	17½	14½	20¼	19⅛	18⅝	10⅛	4¾	6¼	6⅝
- Low	13⅝	10⅞	11⅝	12½	10	8⅛	4¼	3	4¼	4⅜
P/E Ratio - High	16	14	14	17	23	24	NM	15	22	13
- Low	9	9	11	10	12	11	NM	10	15	9

Income Statement Analysis (Million $)

	1997	1996	1995	1994	1993	1992	1991	1990	1989	1988
Revs.	624	602	563	491	412	273	141	163	162	162
Oper. Inc.	34.1	31.8	27.6	32.0	23.7	17.9	2.3	5.5	6.7	9.9
Depr.	4.5	5.0	4.8	4.5	4.3	3.0	1.6	1.4	1.4	0.8
Int. Exp.	0.6	0.6	0.3	0.3	1.1	1.4	0.2	Nil	Nil	Nil
Pretax Inc.	30.0	27.2	22.6	26.8	18.8	14.4	0.9	5.6	6.2	10.0
Eff. Tax Rate	41%	41%	39%	40%	40%	42%	39%	40%	47%	43%
Net Inc.	17.8	16.0	13.8	16.0	11.3	8.4	0.6	3.4	3.3	5.8

Balance Sheet & Other Fin. Data (Million $)

	1997	1996	1995	1994	1993	1992	1991	1990	1989	1988
Cash	13.4	13.0	6.8	13.6	10.6	21.7	19.1	15.2	21.7	28.5
Curr. Assets	133	130	105	102	82.9	81.6	51.4	44.1	46.0	50.6
Total Assets	175	175	148	142	123	124	74.0	57.0	59.0	57.0
Curr. Liab.	51.1	55.0	39.4	45.5	41.0	52.4	32.3	15.3	17.9	19.7
LT Debt	Nil	Nil	Nil	Nil	Nil	Nil	Nil	Nil	Nil	Nil
Common Eqty.	122	119	108	95.9	80.8	71.1	40.8	40.9	40.5	37.5
Total Cap.	122	119	108	95.9	80.8	71.1	41.3	41.5	40.6	37.6
Cap. Exp.	1.8	4.7	5.2	4.3	1.8	2.0	1.0	1.6	1.9	1.0
Cash Flow	22.3	21.0	18.5	20.6	15.6	11.4	2.2	4.8	4.6	6.5
Curr. Ratio	2.6	2.4	2.7	2.2	2.0	1.6	1.6	2.9	2.6	2.6
% LT Debt of Cap.	Nil	Nil	Nil	Nil	Nil	Nil	Nil	Nil	Nil	Nil
% Net Inc.of Revs.	2.9	2.7	2.5	3.3	2.7	3.1	0.4	2.1	2.0	3.5
% Ret. on Assets	10.2	9.8	9.5	12.1	9.1	7.8	0.9	6.0	5.6	10.3
% Ret. on Equity	14.8	14.0	13.5	18.1	14.8	13.8	1.4	8.5	8.4	16.6

Data as orig. reptd.; bef. results of disc. opers. and/or spec. items. Per share data adj. for stk. divs. as of ex-div. date. Bold denotes diluted EPS (FASB 128). E-Estimated. NA-Not Available. NM-Not Meaningful. NR-Not Ranked.

Office—419 W. Pike St., Jackson Center, OH 45334-0629. **Tel**—(937) 596-6849. **Chrmn, Pres & CEO**—W. F. B. Thompson. **Vice Chrmn & Treas**—P. B. Orthwein. **SVP-Fin & Secy**—W. L. Bennett. **Dirs**—C. D. Hoefer, P. B. Orthwein, A. Siegel, W. F. B. Thompson, W. C. Tomson. **Transfer Agent & Registrar**—Bank One, Indianapolis. **Incorporated**—in Delaware in 1983. **Empl**— 2,934. **S&P Analyst:** M.J.C.

03-OCT-98   **Industry:** Electrical Equipment

Summary: This company makes liquid crystal display modules used in cellular telephones, office product equipment and other areas.

Quantitative Evaluations

Outlook (1 Lowest—5 Highest)
• **5**

Fair Value
• **12⅜**

Risk
• **High**

Earn./Div. Rank
• **B-**

Technical Eval.
• **Bearish** since 3/98

Rel. Strength Rank (1 Lowest—99 Highest)
• **8**

Insider Activity
• **Neutral**

Recent Price • 7
52 Wk Range • 26½-6¾

Yield • Nil
12-Mo. P/E • 10.4

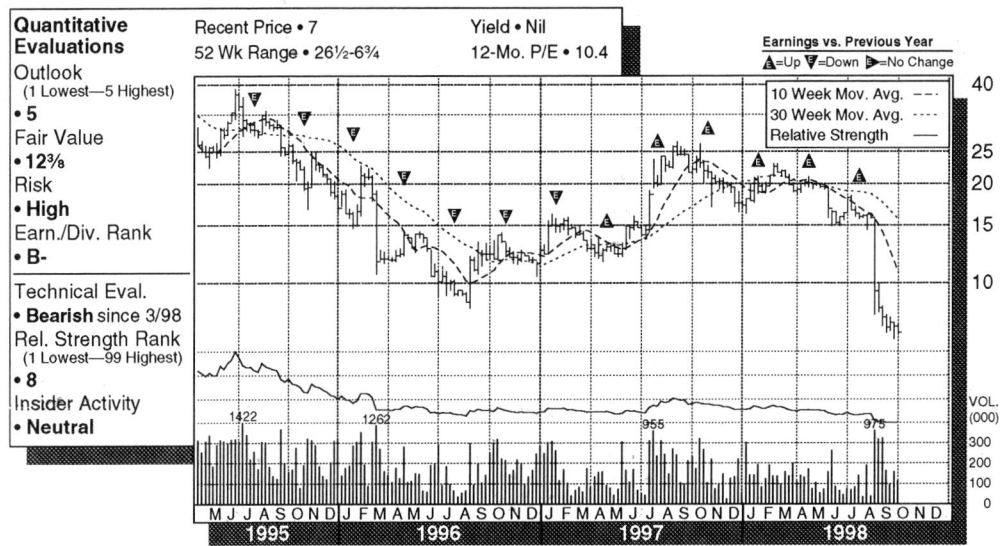

Earnings vs. Previous Year
▲=Up ▼=Down ▷=No Change

10 Week Mov. Avg. – – –
30 Week Mov. Avg. · · · ·
Relative Strength —

Business Profile - 30-SEP-98

The company's strategy is to identify industries that present the greatest long-term potential for growth, and to then focus on technological developments that attempt to meet the current and future requirements of those industries. TFS is currently focused on companies in five primary industries: cellular telephones and other wireless communications, data collection, office automation, medical devices, and industrial process controls. Substantial effort is also being made to broaden the customer base. In August 1998, the company estimated that its earnings per share for the quarter ending September 30, 1998, would be between breakeven and a loss of $0.10, reflecting pricing pressures, weakened Asian currencies, and start-up costs at the China facility. TFS expects to earn a profit in 1998's fourth quarter. The company also resumed a program to repurchase up to 1,000,000 shares of its common stock.

Operational Review - 30-SEP-98

Net sales in the six months ended June 30, 1998, rose 18%, year to year, reflecting increased production of several new programs for new and existing customers. Gross margins improved on the higher volume, and pretax income expanded 26%. After taxes at 42.0%, versus 37.0%, net income advanced 16%, to $2,118,000 ($0.26 a share) from $1,829,000 ($0.23).

Stock Performance - 02-OCT-98

In the past 30 trading days, TFS's shares have declined 25%, compared to a 7% fall in the S&P 500. Average trading volume for the past five days was 22,580 shares, compared with the 40-day moving average of 66,646 shares.

Key Stock Statistics

Dividend Rate/Share	Nil	Shareholders	1,200
Shs. outstg. (M)	7.9	Market cap. (B)	$0.056
Avg. daily vol. (M)	0.028	Inst. holdings	33%
Tang. Bk. Value/Share	7.40		
Beta	1.77		

Value of $10,000 invested 5 years ago: $ 40,354

Fiscal Year Ending Dec. 31

	1998	1997	1996	1995	1994	1993
Revenues (Million $)						
1Q	18.48	16.13	18.08	24.48	16.42	7.25
2Q	22.68	18.74	14.46	22.10	21.25	8.07
3Q	—	24.07	13.12	24.22	23.67	10.31
4Q	—	25.70	15.06	20.78	24.14	12.38
Yr.	—	84.64	60.71	91.59	85.48	38.00
Earnings Per Share ($)						
1Q	**0.12**	0.10	0.09	0.41	0.27	0.09
2Q	**0.14**	0.13	0.02	0.35	0.43	0.10
3Q	—	0.19	-0.70	0.17	0.42	0.14
4Q	—	**0.23**	0.09	0.11	0.46	0.26
Yr.	—	**0.65**	-0.49	1.04	1.59	0.59

Next earnings report expected: early October

Dividend Data

No cash dividend has ever been paid. A two-for-one stock split was effected in 1994.

A Division of The McGraw-Hill Companies

Business Summary - 30-SEP-98

Three-Five Systems is an innovator of visual communicatons technology and products. It designs and manufacturers user interface devices for operational control and information display functions in products of original equipment manufacturers. The company specializes in liquid crystal display (LCD) and light emitting diode (LED) components and technology, which account for 94% of its revenues, in providing its custom design and manufacturing services for customers in the communications, medical electronics, industrial process control, wireless data collection, instrumentation, consumer electronic, automotive equipment, military control and office automation marketplaces. At its Tempe, AZ, headquarters, TFS operates the highest volume, fully automated LCD manufacturing line in North America, and a research and development laboratory.

In 1997, the company's largest customer, Motorola Inc., accounted for 35% of net sales, compared with about 65% in 1996, while Hewlett-Packard accounted for 32% of net sales in 1997.

An LCD modifies light that passes through or is reflected by it, rather than emitting light like an LED. An LCD generally consists of a layer of liquid crystalline material suspended between two glass plates. The crystals align themselves in a predictable manner, and this alignment changes when stimulated electrically. The changed alignment produces a visual representation of the information desired when used in conjunction with a polarizer and either natural ambient light or an external light source. An LED chip produces light as the result of the application of direct current at a low voltage. Different wavelengths (colors) can be produced in a product depending upon the manufacturing process and the impurity added to the basic chip material.

Visible standard devices include solid-state lamps used for indicators, status lights, on-board circuit monitors and instrumentation; multi-digit numerical displays used for calculators, industrial controls, data terminals, instrumentation timers, hand-held instruments, event counters and PCB diagnostics; displays used for hand-held terminals, minicomputers, telecommunications and instrumentation word processors; bar graph displays used for power meters in stereo systems, ham and CB radio meters and other various types of meters; and multi-digit numeric displays used for industrial controls, data terminals, test equipment, point-of-sale, minicomputer readout and home consumer.

Infrared standard devices include emitters and silicon detectors used for TV remote controls, disk and tape drives, printers, encoders, solid-state relays, photoelectric controls, switches, intrusion alarms, touch screens and sensors.

Per Share Data ($)

(Year Ended Dec. 31)	1997	1996	1995	1994	1993	1992	1991	1990	1989	1988
Tangible Bk. Val.	7.15	6.56	7.12	6.03	1.50	0.68	-0.57	-0.73	-1.42	NA
Cash Flow	1.16	-0.04	1.32	1.75	0.67	0.20	0.07	0.15	0.08	NA
Earnings	0.65	-0.49	1.04	1.59	0.59	0.14	0.03	0.10	0.02	NA
Dividends	Nil	Nil	Nil	Nil	Nil	Nil	Nil	Nil	Nil	Nil
Payout Ratio	Nil	Nil	Nil	Nil	Nil	Nil	Nil	Nil	Nil	Nil
Prices - High	26⁷/₈	22³/₄	38⁷/₈	50	17⁵/₈	2³/₈	1⁷/₈	⁹/₁₆	NA	NA
- Low	11⁵/₈	8³/₈	16	16⁵/₈	1¹¹/₁₆	1	¹/₂	³/₈	NA	NA
P/E Ratio - High	41	NM	37	31	30	17	63	6	NA	NA
- Low	18	NM	15	10	3	7	17	4	NA	NA

Income Statement Analysis (Million $)

	1997	1996	1995	1994	1993	1992	1991	1990	1989	1988
Revs.	84.6	60.7	91.6	85.5	38.0	20.8	18.7	17.0	10.8	NA
Oper. Inc.	12.4	-3.5	15.6	21.1	7.1	1.9	0.9	1.5	0.5	NA
Depr.	4.1	3.5	2.3	1.2	0.6	0.4	0.3	0.4	0.3	NA
Int. Exp.	NA	3.5	NA	NA	0.1	0.2	0.2	0.2	0.1	NA
Pretax Inc.	8.6	-6.8	14.0	20.7	6.2	1.2	0.3	0.6	0.1	NA
Eff. Tax Rate	39%	NM	40%	39%	33%	13%	7.10%	Nil	Nil	Nil
Net Inc.	5.2	-3.8	8.4	12.5	4.1	1.0	0.2	0.6	0.1	NA

Balance Sheet & Other Fin. Data (Million $)

	1997	1996	1995	1994	1993	1992	1991	1990	1989	1988
Cash	16.4	12.6	4.5	27.1	0.8	0.6	0.6	0.6	0.3	NA
Curr. Assets	42.7	31.3	29.9	47.0	14.4	7.9	6.3	7.2	3.5	NA
Total Assets	72.8	62.6	63.8	56.3	17.5	9.8	8.4	9.2	4.6	NA
Curr. Liab.	13.6	9.8	7.5	9.4	6.9	3.4	3.5	4.5	1.5	NA
LT Debt	Nil	Nil	Nil	0.2	0.2	1.7	0.8	0.7	0.3	NA
Common Eqty.	56.5	51.2	55.2	46.6	10.2	4.7	-2.2	-2.9	-4.3	NA
Total Cap.	59.2	52.8	56.3	46.9	10.5	6.4	4.9	4.6	3.0	NA
Cap. Exp.	3.0	0.9	27.1	7.4	1.9	0.3	0.7	0.4	0.1	NA
Cash Flow	9.4	-0.3	10.7	13.8	4.7	1.4	0.5	1.0	0.3	NA
Curr. Ratio	3.1	3.2	4.0	5.0	2.1	2.3	1.8	1.6	2.4	NA
% LT Debt of Cap.	Nil	Nil	Nil	0.3	1.7	27.0	15.9	14.9	9.3	NA
% Net Inc.of Revs.	6.2	NM	9.2	14.7	10.9	4.9	1.3	3.7	0.9	NA
% Ret. on Assets	7.7	NM	14.1	32.8	29.9	9.3	2.7	8.0	NA	NA
% Ret. on Equity	9.7	NM	16.6	43.0	55.0	NA	NM	NM	NA	NA

Data as orig. reptd.; bef. results of disc. opers. and/or spec. items. Per share data adj. for stk. divs. as of ex-div. date. Bold denotes diluted EPS (FASB 128). E-Estimated. NA-Not Available. NM-Not Meaningful. NR-Not Ranked.

Office—1600 N. Desert Dr., Tempe, AZ 85281. **Tel**—(602) 389-8600. **Fax**—(602) 389-8836. **Chrmn**—D. R. Buchanan. **Pres & CEO**—V. C. Hren. **EVP & CFO**—J. D. Buchanan. **Dirs**—D. R. Buchanan, J. D. Buchanan, V. C. Hren, K. M. Julien, G. R. Long, D. C. Malmberg, B. E. McGillivray. **Transfer Agent & Registrar**—Bank of New York, NYC. **Incorporated**—in Delaware in 1990. **Empl**—459. **S&P Analyst**: P.L.H.

STANDARD &POOR'S
STOCK REPORTS

Timberland Co.
2235A
NYSE Symbol **TBL**

In S&P SmallCap 600

03-OCT-98 **Industry:** Footwear

Summary: This company designs, engineers and markets footwear, apparel and accessories; core products consist of waterproof boots, shoes and apparel.

Quantitative Evaluations

Outlook
(1 Lowest—5 Highest)
• **5**

Fair Value
• **76⅞**

Risk
• **High**

Earn./Div. Rank
• **B**

Technical Eval.
• **Bearish** since 6/98

Rel. Strength Rank
(1 Lowest—99 Highest)
• **10**

Insider Activity
• **Neutral**

Recent Price • 33⅞   Yield • Nil
52 Wk Range • 87¾-32½   12-Mo. P/E • 7.7

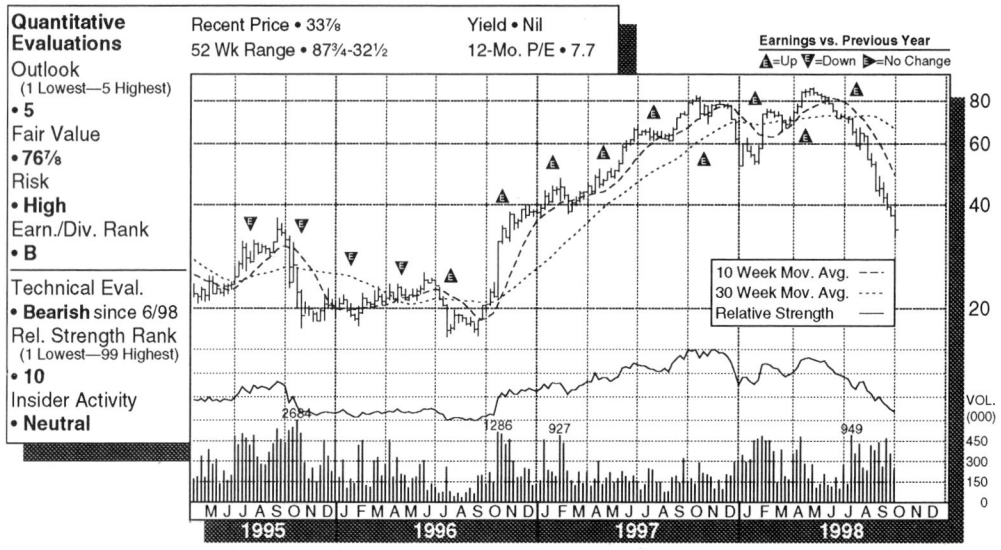

Earnings vs. Previous Year
△=Up ▽=Down ▷=No Change

10 Week Mov. Avg. – – –
30 Week Mov. Avg. ....
Relative Strength ——

Business Profile - 22-JUL-98

The 1998 second quarter marked TBL's eighth consecutive quarter of record revenues. Results of the footwear and apparel company have improved as a result of more new product introductions than ever before, wider profit margins, and an industry shift toward "brown shoes" (outdoor and sporty style footwear). In January 1997, the company introduced several new product lines intended for distribution in the fall of 1997, including children's boots and shoes, packs and travel gear, high-performance technical footwear, and performance apparel.

Operational Review - 22-JUL-98

Revenues in the six months ended June 26, 1998, rose 8.8%, year to year, driven by higher footwear sales. Gross margins widened slightly, as costs rose less rapidly than sales. Despite a sharp rise in selling expenses, operating profit gained 14%. Profitability benefited from a 44% drop in interest expense and a sharp rise in other income. After taxes at 32.0%, versus 30.0%, net income surged 91%, to $9,266,000 ($0.78 a share, diluted), from $4,853,000 ($0.42).

Stock Performance - 02-OCT-98

In the past 30 trading days, TBL's shares have declined 35%, compared to a 7% fall in the S&P 500. Average trading volume for the past five days was 48,260 shares, compared with the 40-day moving average of 76,069 shares.

Key Stock Statistics

Dividend Rate/Share	Nil	Shareholders	900
Shs. outstg. (M)	11.5	Market cap. (B)	$0.309
Avg. daily vol. (M)	0.075	Inst. holdings	49%
Tang. Bk. Value/Share	18.03		
Beta	2.23		

Value of $10,000 invested 5 years ago: $ 17,371

Fiscal Year Ending Dec. 31

	1998	1997	1996	1995	1994	1993
Revenues (Million $)						
1Q	163.1	150.7	127.7	141.6	108.1	70.61
2Q	144.7	132.2	113.7	125.1	126.9	84.85
3Q	—	274.7	227.6	212.6	222.2	140.3
4Q	—	238.9	221.1	175.8	180.4	123.2
Yr.	—	796.5	690.0	655.1	637.5	418.9
Earnings Per Share ($)						
1Q	0.62	0.37	-0.09	0.08	-0.14	0.21
2Q	0.16	0.05	-0.61	-1.83	0.01	0.17
3Q	—	2.11	1.51	0.63	1.45	1.00
4Q	—	1.48	0.99	0.07	0.26	0.62
Yr.	—	4.03	1.81	-1.04	1.58	2.01

Next earnings report expected: mid October

Dividend Data

No dividends have been paid.

A Division of The McGraw·Hill Companies

Business Summary - 22-JUL-98

Timberland, known as the "Boot Company," due to its trademark outdoor shoe, is also a marketer of both men's and women's apparel and accessories, and operates retail and factory outlet stores. The company has recently benefited from a footwear fashion shift toward "brown shoes" (outdoor and sporty style footwear). Sales contributions from the company's two principal business lines in recent years were:

	1997	1996	1995
Footwear	75.4%	74.8%	74.9%
Apparel & accessories	24.6%	25.2%	25.1%

As of December 31, 1997, Timberland operated a chain of 30 retail and 43 factory outlet stores throughout the world. Sales from these shops accounted for 23% of 1997 total sales. Sales to international markets represented 27% of sales in 1997.

From its origins of producing a yellow "work boot," Timberland now offers a wide range footwear in five product categories: men's footwear, women's footwear, performance footwear, boots and kids' footwear. Men's and women's footwear includes products in the work casual, casual and rugged casual collections. The performance footwear line is designed for outdoor activities, and the kids' footwear is based on the models of the company's adult shoes. In 1997, TBL introduced a broader line of men's casual, rugged and boat shoes; the Classic Boot line was expanded by updating colors and design extensions; and the number of models available in the kids' footwear line was increased.

In order to complement its footwear business, Timberland also markets apparel, which includes rugged outerwear, sweaters, shirts, pants and shorts. In 1996 and 1997, the company increased its apparel accessory offerings to include watches, men's belts, day packs and travel gear, socks and legwear, gloves and eyewear and men's small leather goods.

In 1995, the company closed two of its factories and downsized a third. As a result, TBL shifted manufacturing to third parties, as have many other companies in its industry. In 1997, 28% of footwear products were manufactured in-house, versus 35% in 1996 and 40% in 1995.

Operating results for 1997 showed significant improvement, driven by the introduction of higher margin products, an industry shift toward "brown shoes," and improved cash flow and balance sheet management.

Per Share Data ($)

(Year Ended Dec. 31)	1997	1996	1995	1994	1993	1992	1991	1990	1989	1988
Tangible Bk. Val.	17.09	12.81	10.69	11.25	10.16	7.94	6.88	6.12	5.07	4.49
Cash Flow	5.76	3.71	0.67	2.95	2.93	1.91	1.33	1.23	0.97	1.03
Earnings	4.03	1.81	-1.04	1.58	2.01	1.18	0.75	0.73	0.60	0.76
Dividends	Nil	Nil	Nil	Nil	Nil	Nil	Nil	Nil	Nil	Nil
Payout Ratio	Nil	Nil	Nil	Nil	Nil	Nil	Nil	Nil	Nil	Nil
Prices - High	82⅞	40⅛	36⅝	61	85⅜	20	10½	12½	15½	16
- Low	36⅝	16½	17½	19⅞	18⅞	8¾	5⅝	5	8¾	10¾
P/E Ratio - High	21	22	NM	39	42	17	14	17	26	21
- Low	9	9	NM	13	9	7	8	7	15	14

Income Statement Analysis (Million $)

	1997	1996	1995	1994	1993	1992	1991	1990	1989	1988
Revs.	796	690	655	638	419	291	226	196	156	133
Oper. Inc.	104	72.3	28.2	58.4	50.7	33.8	23.7	21.8	17.5	17.0
Depr.	20.3	21.4	19.1	15.3	10.3	8.0	6.3	5.3	4.0	2.8
Int. Exp.	14.8	20.6	22.9	15.1	6.3	5.5	5.8	6.5	5.0	3.1
Pretax Inc.	67.6	30.9	-18.8	28.1	34.1	19.0	11.7	11.0	9.1	12.1
Eff. Tax Rate	30%	34%	NM	37%	34%	32%	31%	29%	30%	33%
Net Inc.	47.3	20.4	-11.6	17.7	22.5	12.9	8.1	7.8	6.4	8.1

Balance Sheet & Other Fin. Data (Million $)

	1997	1996	1995	1994	1993	1992	1991	1990	1989	1988
Cash	99	93.3	38.4	6.4	3.3	1.2	7.5	1.6	5.0	1.5
Curr. Assets	342	372	338	374	221	138	119	118	103	89.0
Total Assets	420	450	421	473	291	194	173	170	148	132
Curr. Liab.	99	102	70.0	107	65.4	43.4	26.3	29.3	17.6	40.3
LT Debt	100	172	199	207	90.8	41.5	44.2	46.9	46.7	14.6
Common Eqty.	215	165	142	149	128	105	93.4	85.7	74.9	69.2
Total Cap.	321	348	351	366	225	151	147	141	131	91.0
Cap. Exp.	25.7	15.1	13.5	31.5	21.6	11.8	7.5	9.1	6.9	6.4
Cash Flow	67.6	41.8	7.5	33.1	32.8	20.9	14.4	13.1	10.4	10.9
Curr. Ratio	3.5	3.6	4.8	3.5	3.4	3.2	4.5	4.0	5.8	2.2
% LT Debt of Cap.	31.2	49.4	56.7	56.5	40.3	27.6	30.1	33.3	35.7	16.1
% Net Inc.of Revs.	5.9	2.9	NM	2.8	5.4	4.4	3.6	4.0	4.1	6.1
% Ret. on Assets	10.9	4.7	NM	4.6	9.3	7.0	4.7	4.9	4.5	7.0
% Ret. on Equity	24.9	13.3	NM	12.7	19.3	13.0	9.0	9.8	8.8	12.3

Data as orig. reptd.; bef. results of disc. opers. and/or spec. items. Per share data adj. for stk. divs. as of ex-div. date. Bold denotes diluted EPS (FASB 128). E-Estimated. NA-Not Available. NM-Not Meaningful. NR-Not Ranked.

Office—200 Domain Dr., Stratham, NH 03885. Tel—(603) 772-9500. Website—http://www.timberland.com Chrmn—S. W. Swartz. Pres & CEO—J. B. Swartz. SVP & CFO—G. J. Hibner. Secy—J. E. Beard. Dirs—R. M. Agate, J. F. Brennan, I. W. Diery, J. A. Fitzsimmons, J. B. Swartz, S. W. Swartz, A. Zaleznik. Transfer Agent & Registrar—First National Bank of Boston. Incorporated—in Delaware in 1978; predecessor incorporated in 1933. Empl— 5,700. S&P Analyst: Kathleen J. Fraser

STANDARD &POOR'S
STOCK REPORTS

Titan International

2239Q

NYSE Symbol **TWI**

In S&P SmallCap 600

07-OCT-98

Industry: Trucks & Parts

Summary: This company is a leading global maker of steel wheels and rims for off-highway vehicles.

Quantitative Evaluations

Recent Price • 11⅜	Yield • 0.5%
52 Wk Range • 24-9⅝	12-Mo. P/E • 11.9

Outlook (1 Lowest—5 Highest)
• **4**

Fair Value
• **14¼**

Risk
• **Average**

Earn./Div. Rank
• **NR**

Technical Eval.
• **Bearish** since 3/98

Rel. Strength Rank (1 Lowest—99 Highest)
• **42**

Insider Activity
• **NA**

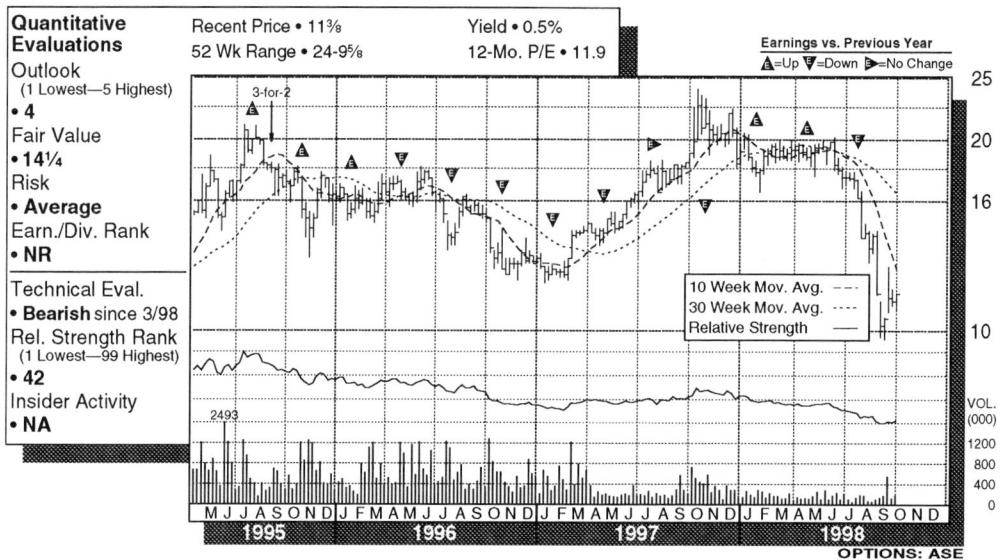

Earnings vs. Previous Year
▲=Up ▼=Down ▶=No Change

10 Week Mov. Avg. ---
30 Week Mov. Avg. ·····
Relative Strength

OPTIONS: ASE

Business Profile - 07-OCT-98

A new plant in Texas is expected to enable TWI to offer a full line of off-highway tires to the aftermarket. The company plans to increase its aftermarket sales to 50% of the total. In the 1998 second quarter, TWI entered the South American market with the purchase of 81% of Uruguay-based FUNSA, a maker of car radial and specialty tires with $36 million in sales. TWI recently began replacing striking workers at its Des Moines, Iowa facility. Under an authorization to repurchase up to 10 million shares, TWI had bought back 5.7 million shares, including 3.8 million purchased at $15 each through a tender offer in March 1997, through December 31, 1997. Firm backlog at February 28, 1998, totaled about $230 million.

Operational Review - 07-OCT-98

Net sales in the first half of 1998 edged up 0.3%, year to year, reflecting a labor strike at Titan Tire's Des Moines, Iowa plant, which offset growth in the agricultural and earthmoving/construction segments. Profitability was hurt by higher operating costs and SG&A expenses, and with a rise in R&D expense related to the Grizz LSW series of wheel and tire assemblies, and increased interest expense, net income fell 25%, to $13,070,000 ($0.60 a share, on 7.5% fewer shares), from $17,436,000 ($0.74).

Stock Performance - 02-OCT-98

In the past 30 trading days, TWI's shares have declined 19%, compared to a 7% fall in the S&P 500. Average trading volume for the past five days was 33,720 shares, compared with the 40-day moving average of 34,274 shares.

Key Stock Statistics

Dividend Rate/Share	0.06	Shareholders	800
Shs. outstg. (M)	21.8	Market cap. (B)	$0.226
Avg. daily vol. (M)	0.060	Inst. holdings	49%
Tang. Bk. Value/Share	10.09		
Beta	0.97		

Value of $10,000 invested 5 years ago: NA

Fiscal Year Ending Dec. 31

	1998	1997	1996	1995	1994	1993
Revenues (Million $)						
1Q	187.4	180.2	177.3	157.7	91.90	31.50
2Q	181.2	187.4	167.0	157.6	102.7	36.00
3Q	—	156.7	145.7	149.5	97.83	30.80
4Q	—	165.9	144.6	158.3	114.6	52.10
Yr.	—	690.1	634.5	623.2	407.0	150.4
Earnings Per Share ($)						
1Q	**0.38**	**0.36**	0.49	0.56	0.24	0.10
2Q	**0.22**	**0.38**	0.46	0.55	0.31	0.17
3Q	—	0.17	0.41	0.40	0.20	0.00
4Q	—	**0.19**	0.21	0.43	0.33	0.10
Yr.	—	**1.10**	1.57	1.91	1.14	0.46

Next earnings report expected: late October

Dividend Data (Dividends have been paid since 1993.)

Amount ($)	Date Decl.	Ex-Div. Date	Stock of Record	Payment Date
0.015	Dec. 10	Dec. 29	Dec. 31	Jan. 15 '98
0.015	Mar. 10	Mar. 27	Mar. 31	Apr. 15 '98
0.015	Jun. 10	Jun. 26	Jun. 30	Jul. 15 '98
0.015	Sep. 10	Sep. 28	Sep. 30	Oct. 15 '98

A Division of The **McGraw-Hill** Companies

STANDARD
&POOR'S
STOCK REPORTS

Titan International, Inc.

2239Q
07-OCT-98

Business Summary - 07-OCT-98

Titan Wheel International did not reinvent itself when it changed its name in May 1997 to Titan International (TWI); the company is still a leading global manufacturer of steel wheels and tires for off-highway equipment. TWI's Engineered Products, including Tractech and Automation International, were divested in 1996, reflecting the company's effort to focus on core business.

Results were weak in 1997, and the overall industry near-term outlook remains negative. However, TWI has noted that a prolonged downturn in the Asian region could have positive implications, by producing lower raw material costs for natural rubber and reducing the cost of future wheel or tire acquisitions in the region.

Titan, based in Quincy, IL, was incorporated in 1983, and was acquired in a 1990 management-led leveraged buyout by MascoTech, Inc. and investors; the company went public in 1993. Today, TWI usually makes both the wheels and the tires for vehicles, and increasingly also assembles the completed wheel-tire system. The company offers more than 25,000 different products.

In 1997, the agricultural market accounted for 52% of Titan's sales, the consumer market 22%, earthmoving and construction equipment 24%, engineered products 1%, and military 1%. Wheels, rims, and tires are sold to original equipment manufacturers (OEMs) of tractors,

combines, plows, planters, and irrigation equipment; Deere and Co. accounted for 16% of 1997 sales. Consumer products include wheels and tires for boat and camping trailers, lawn and garden equipment, and specialty cars and light trucks. Earthmoving and construction vehicles such as cranes, graders and levelers, scrapers, shovel and back-hoe loaders, load transporters, and haul trucks roll on Titan wheels.

TWI plans to increase its penetration of the aftermarket for tires and wheels, expand its presence in Europe and other global markets, focus on acquisitions, and continue to improve its operating efficiencies and new product development. As of May 1998, TWI had agreed to buy a wheel company in Europe, a majority interest in a South American tire company, and interests in an Asian wheel maker and a North American tire company, with combined sales in excess of $145 million. In late 1998, TWI expects to begin production at a new tire facility being built in Brownsville, TX. In July 1996, TWI acquired the 50% of European wheel manufacturer Sirmac Group that it did not already own. In December 1996, it acquired the wheel subsidiary of Delachaux SA.

In March 1997, Titan completed a tender offer for up to 5,000,000 common shares. Shareholders tendered 3,763,919 shares at $15 each, representing about 15% of the shares outstanding.

Per Share Data ($)

(Year Ended Dec. 31)	1997	1996	1995	1994	1993	1992	1991	1990	1989	1988
Tangible Bk. Val.	9.50	10.07	7.25	3.93	2.76	2.93	NA	NA	NA	NA
Cash Flow	2.46	0.91	3.08	2.21	0.84	NA	NA	NA	NA	NA
Earnings	1.10	1.57	1.91	1.14	0.46	0.41	NA	NA	NA	NA
Dividends	0.06	0.06	0.04	0.01	0.01	NA	NA	NA	NA	NA
Payout Ratio	5%	4%	2%	1%	3%	NA	NA	NA	NA	NA
Prices - High	24	18 1/8	21 1/8	13 5/8	11 1/2	NA	NA	NA	NA	NA
- Low	11 7/8	12	11 5/8	9 5/8	6 5/8	NA	NA	NA	NA	NA
P/E Ratio - High	22	12	11	12	25	NA	NA	NA	NA	NA
- Low	11	8	6	8	15	NA	NA	NA	NA	NA

Income Statement Analysis (Million $)

	1997	1996	1995	1994	1993	1992	1991	1990	1989	1988
Revs.	690	635	623	407	150	129	NA	NA	NA	NA
Oper. Inc.	84.5	78.9	96.5	55.4	18.5	NA	NA	NA	NA	NA
Depr.	30.9	28.0	23.4	17.4	5.3	NA	NA	NA	NA	NA
Int. Exp.	15.1	10.7	12.0	8.5	3.2	1.1	NA	NA	NA	NA
Pretax Inc.	40.5	59.1	63.3	30.1	10.1	NA	NA	NA	NA	NA
Eff. Tax Rate	38%	37%	40%	39%	37%	NA	NA	NA	NA	NA
Net Inc.	25.1	35.0	38.0	18.5	6.4	5.1	NA	NA	NA	NA

Balance Sheet & Other Fin. Data (Million $)

	1997	1996	1995	1994	1993	1992	1991	1990	1989	1988
Cash	21.2	27.4	14.2	7.3	29.3	NA	NA	NA	NA	NA
Curr. Assets	299	285	265	192	142	NA	NA	NA	NA	NA
Total Assets	585	559	512	400	261	89.0	NA	NA	NA	NA
Curr. Liab.	115	104	114	72.4	50.9	NA	NA	NA	NA	NA
LT Debt	182	113	142	178	124	15.0	NA	NA	NA	NA
Common Eqty.	248	301	216	100	66.7	40.3	NA	NA	NA	NA
Total Cap.	451	433	374	297	201	NA	NA	NA	NA	NA
Cap. Exp.	38.3	36.7	20.2	15.2	5.4	NA	NA	NA	NA	NA
Cash Flow	56.1	63.3	61.4	35.9	11.7	NA	NA	NA	NA	NA
Curr. Ratio	2.6	2.8	2.3	2.7	2.8	NA	NA	NA	NA	NA
% LT Debt of Cap.	40.4	26.1	38.1	60.1	61.6	NA	NA	NA	NA	NA
% Net Inc.of Revs.	3.6	5.6	6.1	4.5	4.2	4.0	NA	NA	NA	NA
% Ret. on Assets	4.4	6.6	8.3	5.5	3.8	NA	NA	NA	NA	NA
% Ret. on Equity	9.2	13.7	24.0	21.8	17.3	NA	NA	NA	NA	NA

Data as orig. reptd.; bef. results of disc. opers. and/or spec. items. Per share data adj. for stk. divs. as of ex-div. date. Bold denotes diluted EPS (FASB 128). E-Estimated. NA-Not Available. NM-Not Meaningful. NR-Not Ranked.

Office—2701 Spruce St., Quincy, IL 62301. **Tel**—(217) 228-6011. **Pres & CEO**—M. M. Taylor Jr. **VP & COO**—M. Samide. **VP-Fin & CFO**—K. W. Hackamack.**Secy**—C. T Holley. **Investor Contact**—Phillip Stanhope (515-265-9438). **Dirs**—E. H. Billig, E. J. Campbell, R. K. Cashin Jr., A. J. Febbo, A. I. Soave, M. M. Taylor Jr. **Transfer Agent & Registrar**—Harris Trust & Savings Bank, Chicago. **Incorporated**—in Illinois in 1983. **Empl**—4,200. **S&P Analyst:** Stewart Scharf

STANDARD &POOR'S
STOCK REPORTS

Toll Brothers

2242A

NYSE Symbol **TOL**

In S&P SmallCap 600

03-OCT-98 Industry: Homebuilding

Summary: This company builds luxury homes mostly in the Northeast, but increasingly in other regions of the U.S.

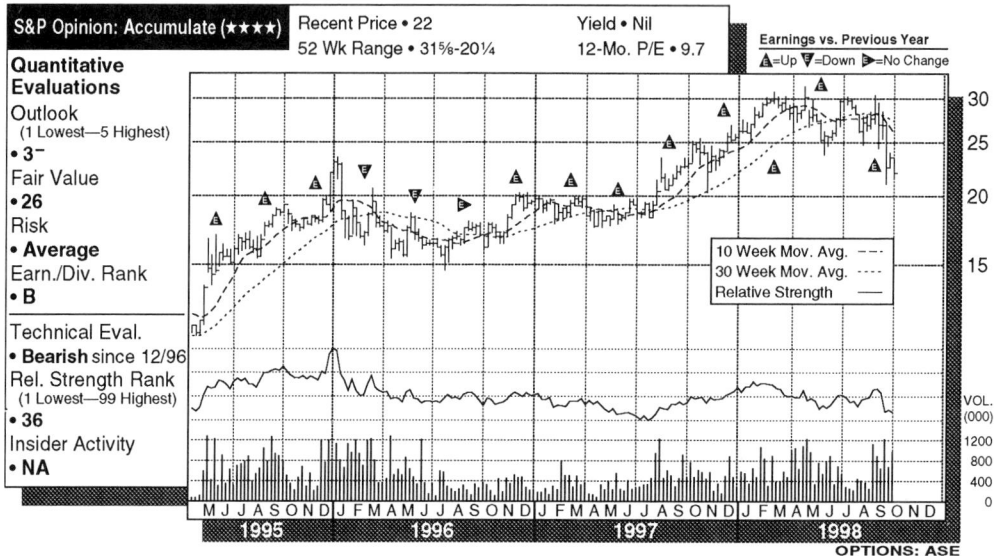

S&P Opinion: Accumulate (★★★★)	Recent Price • 22 / 52 Wk Range • 31⅝–20¼

Yield • Nil
12-Mo. P/E • 9.7

Earnings vs. Previous Year
▲=Up ▼=Down ▶=No Change

Quantitative Evaluations

Outlook
(1 Lowest—5 Highest)
• **3⁻**

Fair Value
• **26**

Risk
• **Average**

Earn./Div. Rank
• **B**

Technical Eval.
• **Bearish** since 12/96

Rel. Strength Rank
(1 Lowest—99 Highest)
• **36**

Insider Activity
• **NA**

10 Week Mov. Avg. — – —
30 Week Mov. Avg. ‥‥‥‥
Relative Strength —

OPTIONS: ASE

Overview - 27-AUG-98

Toll has recorded exceptional order trends in recent periods, boosted by the downturn in interest rates seen since mid-1997. On top of accommodating rates, TOL has been aided by its focus on the upper end of the homebuilding market, as many baby boomers entering their peak earnings years have begun to seek move-up homes. Given the resultant record level of order backlog (as of July 31, 1998) and the upcoming opening of new communities, solid sales growth will likely continue through FY 99 (Oct.). Price increases should also contribute to the gains. Operating margins have battled costs of TOL's expansion programs and the lower margins typically associated with newer markets. However, margins recently started to widen, as TOL became more firmly established in its new geographic territories. We see that trend continuing in FY 99.

Valuation - 27-AUG-98

The shares moved sharply higher from mid-1997 into the early part of 1998, boosted by accommodating interest rates and investor enthusiasm for Toll's expansion strategies. They have had an uneven performance since, limited by diverse investor worries including speculation about a rise in interest rates and the belief that Asia's woes will lead to a domestic recession. We disagree with those worries, and continue to believe that Asia's troubles will leave domestic growth modest and interest rates a friend. In addition, given the positive demographics of its customer and geographic bases, a growing number of individuals seem likely to seek TOL's luxury homes. On top of those positives, we think that TOL's expansion program has left it better positioned. However, although we find the shares undervalued, we believe the upside could be limited a bit by investor worries about a mature housing cycle and economic uncertainties.

Key Stock Statistics

S&P EPS Est. 1998	2.40	Tang. Bk. Value/Share	13.53
P/E on S&P Est. 1998	9.2	Beta	0.83
S&P EPS Est. 1999	2.75	Shareholders	700
Dividend Rate/Share	Nil	Market cap. (B)	$0.814
Shs. outstg. (M)	37.0	Inst. holdings	53%
Avg. daily vol. (M)	0.189		

Value of $10,000 invested 5 years ago: $ 16,448

Fiscal Year Ending Oct. 31

	1998	1997	1996	1995	1994	1993
Revenues (Million $)						
1Q	244.7	202.5	142.1	122.3	118.1	76.38
2Q	249.6	209.2	145.5	137.5	91.44	74.41
3Q	342.1	241.8	212.8	186.9	120.1	102.8
4Q	—	318.1	260.4	199.6	174.4	143.5
Yr.	—	971.7	760.7	646.3	504.1	397.0
Earnings Per Share ($)						
1Q	**0.44**	0.41	0.24	0.25	0.25	0.15
2Q	**0.41**	0.36	0.23	0.28	0.13	0.11
3Q	**0.67**	0.47	0.45	0.45	0.24	0.19
4Q	**E0.88**	0.70	0.64	0.47	0.46	0.37
Yr.	**E2.40**	1.94	1.56	1.47	1.08	0.82

Next earnings report expected: early December

Dividend Data

No cash dividends have ever been paid

A Division of The McGraw-Hill Companies

Business Summary - 07-OCT-98

Titan Wheel International did not reinvent itself when it changed its name in May 1997 to Titan International (TWI); the company is still a leading global manufacturer of steel wheels and tires for off-highway equipment. TWI's Engineered Products, including Tractech and Automation International, were divested in 1996, reflecting the company's effort to focus on core business.

Results were weak in 1997, and the overall industry near-term outlook remains negative. However, TWI has noted that a prolonged downturn in the Asian region could have positive implications, by producing lower raw material costs for natural rubber and reducing the cost of future wheel or tire acquisitions in the region.

Titan, based in Quincy, IL, was incorporated in 1983, and was acquired in a 1990 management-led leveraged buyout by MascoTech, Inc. and investors; the company went public in 1993. Today, TWI usually makes both the wheels and the tires for vehicles, and increasingly also assembles the completed wheel-tire system. The company offers more than 25,000 different products.

In 1997, the agricultural market accounted for 52% of Titan's sales, the consumer market 22%, earthmoving and construction equipment 24%, engineered products 1%, and military 1%. Wheels, rims, and tires are sold to original equipment manufacturers (OEMs) of tractors, combines, plows, planters, and irrigation equipment; Deere and Co. accounted for 16% of 1997 sales. Consumer products include wheels and tires for boat and camping trailers, lawn and garden equipment, and specialty cars and light trucks. Earthmoving and construction vehicles such as cranes, graders and levelers, scrapers, shovel and back-hoe loaders, load transporters, and haul trucks roll on Titan wheels.

TWI plans to increase its penetration of the aftermarket for tires and wheels, expand its presence in Europe and other global markets, focus on acquisitions, and continue to improve its operating efficiencies and new product development. As of May 1998, TWI had agreed to buy a wheel company in Europe, a majority interest in a South American tire company, and interests in an Asian wheel maker and a North American tire company, with combined sales in excess of $145 million. In late 1998, TWI expects to begin production at a new tire facility being built in Brownsville, TX. In July 1996, TWI acquired the 50% of European wheel manufacturer Sirmac Group that it did not already own. In December 1996, it acquired the wheel subsidiary of Delachaux SA.

In March 1997, Titan completed a tender offer for up to 5,000,000 common shares. Shareholders tendered 3,763,919 shares at $15 each, representing about 15% of the shares outstanding.

Per Share Data ($)

(Year Ended Dec. 31)	1997	1996	1995	1994	1993	1992	1991	1990	1989	1988
Tangible Bk. Val.	9.50	10.07	7.25	3.93	2.76	2.93	NA	NA	NA	NA
Cash Flow	2.46	0.91	3.08	2.21	0.84	NA	NA	NA	NA	NA
Earnings	1.10	1.57	1.91	1.14	0.46	0.41	NA	NA	NA	NA
Dividends	0.06	0.06	0.04	0.01	0.01	NA	NA	NA	NA	NA
Payout Ratio	5%	4%	2%	1%	3%	NA	NA	NA	NA	NA
Prices - High	24	18 1/8	21 1/8	13 5/8	11 1/2	NA	NA	NA	NA	NA
- Low	11 7/8	12	11 5/8	9 5/8	6 5/8	NA	NA	NA	NA	NA
P/E Ratio - High	22	12	11	12	25	NA	NA	NA	NA	NA
- Low	11	8	6	8	15	NA	NA	NA	NA	NA

Income Statement Analysis (Million $)

	1997	1996	1995	1994	1993	1992	1991	1990	1989	1988
Revs.	690	635	623	407	150	129	NA	NA	NA	NA
Oper. Inc.	84.5	78.9	96.5	55.4	18.5	NA	NA	NA	NA	NA
Depr.	30.9	28.0	23.4	17.4	5.3	NA	NA	NA	NA	NA
Int. Exp.	15.1	10.7	12.0	8.5	3.2	1.1	NA	NA	NA	NA
Pretax Inc.	40.5	59.1	63.3	30.1	10.1	NA	NA	NA	NA	NA
Eff. Tax Rate	38%	37%	40%	39%	37%	NA	NA	NA	NA	NA
Net Inc.	25.1	35.0	38.0	18.5	6.4	5.1	NA	NA	NA	NA

Balance Sheet & Other Fin. Data (Million $)

	1997	1996	1995	1994	1993	1992	1991	1990	1989	1988
Cash	21.2	27.4	14.2	7.3	29.3	NA	NA	NA	NA	NA
Curr. Assets	299	285	265	192	142	NA	NA	NA	NA	NA
Total Assets	585	559	512	400	261	89.0	NA	NA	NA	NA
Curr. Liab.	115	104	114	72.4	50.9	NA	NA	NA	NA	NA
LT Debt	182	113	142	178	124	15.0	NA	NA	NA	NA
Common Eqty.	248	301	216	100	66.7	40.3	NA	NA	NA	NA
Total Cap.	451	433	374	297	201	NA	NA	NA	NA	NA
Cap. Exp.	38.3	36.7	20.2	15.2	5.4	NA	NA	NA	NA	NA
Cash Flow	56.1	63.3	61.4	35.9	11.7	NA	NA	NA	NA	NA
Curr. Ratio	2.6	2.8	2.3	2.7	2.8	NA	NA	NA	NA	NA
% LT Debt of Cap.	40.4	26.1	38.1	60.1	61.6	NA	NA	NA	NA	NA
% Net Inc.of Revs.	3.6	5.6	6.1	4.5	4.2	4.0	NA	NA	NA	NA
% Ret. on Assets	4.4	6.6	8.3	5.5	3.8	NA	NA	NA	NA	NA
% Ret. on Equity	9.2	13.7	24.0	21.8	17.3	NA	NA	NA	NA	NA

Data as orig. reptd.; bef. results of disc. opers. and/or spec. items. Per share data adj. for stk. divs. as of ex-div. date. Bold denotes diluted EPS (FASB 128). E-Estimated. NA-Not Available. NM-Not Meaningful. NR-Not Ranked.

Office—2701 Spruce St., Quincy, IL 62301. **Tel**—(217) 228-6011. **Pres & CEO**—M. M. Taylor Jr. **VP & COO**—M. Samide. **VP-Fin & CFO**—K. W. Hackamack. **Secy**—C. T Holley. **Investor Contact**—Phillip Stanhope (515-265-9438). **Dirs**—E. H. Billig, E. J. Campbell, R. K. Cashin Jr., A. J. Febbo, A. I. Soave, M. M. Taylor Jr. **Transfer Agent & Registrar**—Harris Trust & Savings Bank, Chicago. **Incorporated**—in Illinois in 1983. **Empl**—4,200. **S&P Analyst:** Stewart Scharf

Toll Brothers

2242A
NYSE Symbol **TOL**

In S&P SmallCap 600

03-OCT-98

Industry: Homebuilding

Summary: This company builds luxury homes mostly in the Northeast, but increasingly in other regions of the U.S.

S&P Opinion: Accumulate (★★★★)	Recent Price • 22 — Yield • Nil
	52 Wk Range • 31⅝-20¼ — 12-Mo. P/E • 9.7

Quantitative Evaluations

Outlook (1 Lowest—5 Highest)
• **3⁻**

Fair Value
• **26**

Risk
• **Average**

Earn./Div. Rank
• **B**

Technical Eval.
• **Bearish** since 12/96

Rel. Strength Rank (1 Lowest—99 Highest)
• **36**

Insider Activity
• **NA**

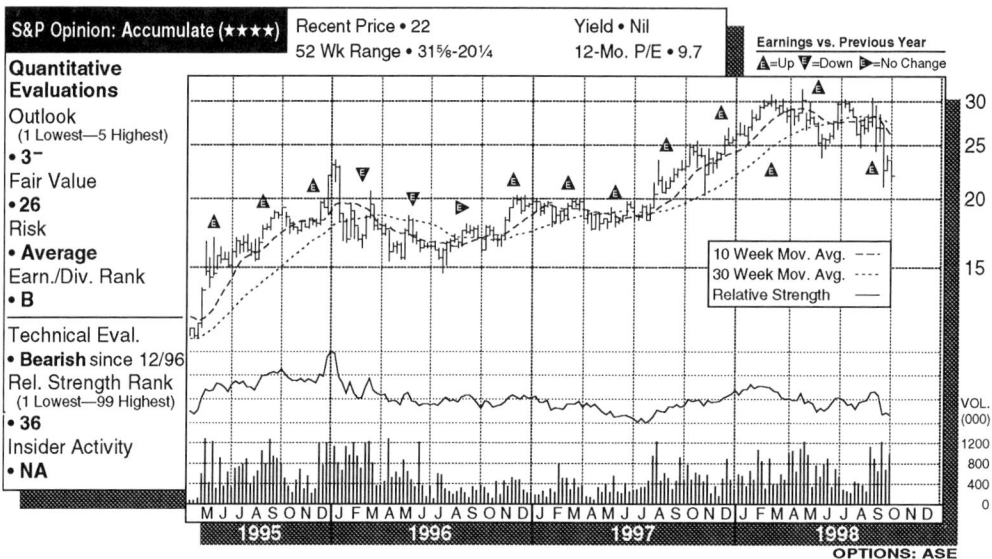

Earnings vs. Previous Year
▲=Up ▼=Down ▷=No Change

10 Week Mov. Avg. — - —
30 Week Mov. Avg. ·········
Relative Strength ——

VOL. (000)

OPTIONS: ASE

Overview - 27-AUG-98

Toll has recorded exceptional order trends in recent periods, boosted by the downturn in interest rates seen since mid-1997. On top of accommodating rates, TOL has been aided by its focus on the upper end of the homebuilding market, as many baby boomers entering their peak earnings years have begun to seek move-up homes. Given the resultant record level of order backlog (as of July 31, 1998) and the upcoming opening of new communities, solid sales growth will likely continue through FY 99 (Oct.). Price increases should also contribute to the gains. Operating margins have battled costs of TOL's expansion programs and the lower margins typically associated with newer markets. However, margins recently started to widen, as TOL became more firmly established in its new geographic territories. We see that trend continuing in FY 99.

Valuation - 27-AUG-98

The shares moved sharply higher from mid-1997 into the early part of 1998, boosted by accommodating interest rates and investor enthusiasm for Toll's expansion strategies. They have had an uneven performance since, limited by diverse investor worries including speculation about a rise in interest rates and the belief that Asia's woes will lead to a domestic recession. We disagree with those worries, and continue to believe that Asia's troubles will leave domestic growth modest and interest rates a friend. In addition, given the positive demographics of its customer and geographic bases, a growing number of individuals seem likely to seek TOL's luxury homes. On top of those positives, we think that TOL's expansion program has left it better positioned. However, although we find the shares undervalued, we believe the upside could be limited a bit by investor worries about a mature housing cycle and economic uncertainties.

Key Stock Statistics

S&P EPS Est. 1998	2.40	Tang. Bk. Value/Share	13.53
P/E on S&P Est. 1998	9.2	Beta	0.83
S&P EPS Est. 1999	2.75	Shareholders	700
Dividend Rate/Share	Nil	Market cap. (B)	$0.814
Shs. outstg. (M)	37.0	Inst. holdings	53%
Avg. daily vol. (M)	0.189		

Value of $10,000 invested 5 years ago: $ 16,448

Fiscal Year Ending Oct. 31

	1998	1997	1996	1995	1994	1993
Revenues (Million $)						
1Q	244.7	202.5	142.1	122.3	118.1	76.38
2Q	249.6	209.2	145.5	137.5	91.44	74.41
3Q	342.1	241.8	212.8	186.9	120.1	102.8
4Q	—	318.1	260.4	199.6	174.4	143.5
Yr.	—	971.7	760.7	646.3	504.1	397.0
Earnings Per Share ($)						
1Q	**0.44**	0.41	0.24	0.25	0.25	0.15
2Q	**0.41**	0.36	0.23	0.28	0.13	0.11
3Q	**0.67**	0.47	0.45	0.45	0.24	0.19
4Q	**E0.88**	0.70	0.64	0.47	0.46	0.37
Yr.	**E2.40**	1.94	1.56	1.47	1.08	0.82

Next earnings report expected: early December

Dividend Data

No cash dividends have ever been paid

 A Division of The McGraw-Hill Companies

Business Summary - 27-AUG-98

The leading U.S. builder of luxury homes, Toll Brothers caters primarily to "move-up buyers" who have previously owned a home. The company also targets the "empty nester" market (the 50 years and older buyer), which accounted for 25% of its home sales in FY 97 (Oct.), up from 20% in FY 96. TOL builds the majority of its homes in Pennsylvania and New Jersey, but has been diversifying into new areas to take advantage of differing regional economic cycles. Since 1994, Toll has expanded into California, Arizona, Texas, Florida and North Carolina, which all rank in the top 10 in the U.S. census forecast of population growth through 2025. These markets accounted for 29% of TOL's order backlog at the end of FY 97. At July 31, 1998, Toll offered homes in 16 states.

Toll delivered 2,517 homes in FY 97, up from 2,109 in the prior year. The company's single-family detached homes generally ranged in price from $166,000 to $688,000 in FY 97, with an average base sales price of $376,000. Attached homes were offered at prices between $100,000 to $505,000, with an average base sales price of $193,000. Toll also offers hundreds of options at an additional cost, enabling buyers to create a nearly custom home. Charges for options boosted the average sales price of a home by 17% above the base in FY 97.

Toll typically locates its communities in suburban areas near highways with access to major cities. It offers at least three types of detached home plans, and two or three types of attached home floor plans.

The company attempts to reduce risk by controlling or purchasing land through options, beginning construction after sales agreements are executed, and using subcontractors to perform all construction and site improvement work on a fixed price basis.

An increasing number of households in age groups most likely to buy luxury homes (35 to 54 years of age; up 35% in the 10 years through 1995) and a growing number of affluent households currently leaves TOL with more potential buyers than at any time in its history. Moreover, with the number of households in the 55 to 64 year category projected to grow by nearly 70% through 2010, Toll has been placing greater focus on the "empty nester" market. To serve the changing housing needs of that group, TOL has developed a variety of smaller luxury homes with special features and community amenities.

Toll's business continued strong in the first nine months of FY 98, when it recorded a 33% year to year gain in new home orders (on a dollar basis), to $1.04 billion (2,546 homes); also up 33% in the third quarter alone. Backlog grew to $843.9 million (1,971 homes) at July 31, 1998, up 29% from a year earlier. Orders and backlog both represented third quarter records.

Per Share Data ($)

(Year Ended Oct. 31)	1997	1996	1995	1994	1993	1992	1991	1990	1989	1988
Tangible Bk. Val.	11.24	9.28	7.63	6.11	5.01	4.12	3.59	3.19	2.85	2.42
Cash Flow	2.06	1.66	1.56	1.16	0.89	3.58	0.18	0.37	0.51	0.85
Earnings	1.94	1.56	1.47	1.08	0.82	0.52	0.12	0.30	0.44	0.80
Dividends	Nil	Nil	Nil	Nil	Nil	Nil	Nil	Nil	Nil	Nil
Payout Ratio	Nil	Nil	Nil	Nil	Nil	Nil	Nil	Nil	Nil	Nil
Prices - High	27$\frac{1}{2}$	23$\frac{1}{2}$	23	19$\frac{3}{4}$	17$\frac{3}{4}$	14	12$\frac{5}{8}$	4	5$\frac{7}{8}$	8
- Low	17$\frac{1}{2}$	14$\frac{5}{8}$	10	9$\frac{1}{8}$	8$\frac{7}{8}$	7$\frac{1}{2}$	2$\frac{3}{8}$	2$\frac{1}{4}$	2$\frac{7}{8}$	3$\frac{7}{8}$
P/E Ratio - High	14	15	16	18	21	27	NM	13	13	10
- Low	9	9	7	8	11	14	NM	8	7	5

Income Statement Analysis (Million $)

Revs.	972	761	646	504	397	285	182	205	185	199
Oper. Inc.	138	114	105	84.7	63.5	47.1	22.1	35.5	35.9	47.1
Depr.	4.1	3.3	2.9	2.7	2.5	2.3	2.1	2.2	2.2	1.6
Int. Exp.	29.4	24.2	22.2	21.7	NA	NA	16.7	17.8	24.6	11.2
Pretax Inc.	108	85.8	79.4	56.8	43.9	28.8	6.2	14.9	21.5	40.8
Eff. Tax Rate	37%	37%	37%	36%	38%	40%	41%	41%	39%	41%
Net Inc.	67.8	53.7	49.9	36.2	27.4	17.4	3.7	8.9	13.1	24.1

Balance Sheet & Other Fin. Data (Million $)

Cash	148	22.9	27.8	41.7	34.3	48.9	31.5	10.4	9.2	26.6
Curr. Assets	NA	NA	NA	NA	NA	NA	NA	NA	NA	NA
Total Assets	1,119	838	692	587	476	385	312	317	348	257
Curr. Liab.	NA	NA	NA	NA	NA	NA	NA	NA	NA	NA
LT Debt	512	343	284	250	210	179	145	179	218	137
Common Eqty.	385	315	257	204	167	136	118	95.0	85.0	73.0
Total Cap.	942	658	541	468	391	333	278	288	315	217
Cap. Exp.	5.3	3.6	2.5	3.0	1.8	1.4	0.5	0.6	2.5	6.5
Cash Flow	71.9	57.3	52.9	38.9	29.9	19.6	5.8	11.1	15.4	25.7
Curr. Ratio	NA	NA	NA	NA	NA	NA	NA	NA	NA	NA
% LT Debt of Cap.	54.4	52.2	52.5	53.5	53.7	53.8	52.2	62.3	69.0	63.3
% Net Inc.of Revs.	7.0	7.1	7.7	7.2	6.9	6.1	2.0	4.3	7.1	12.1
% Ret. on Assets	6.9	7.0	7.8	6.8	6.4	5.0	1.1	2.7	4.3	11.0
% Ret. on Equity	19.4	18.8	21.7	19.5	18.0	13.6	3.3	9.9	16.6	39.6

Data as orig. reptd.; bef. results of disc. opers. and/or spec. items. Per share data adj. for stk. divs. as of ex-div. date. Bold denotes diluted EPS (FASB 128). E-Estimated. NA-Not Available. NM-Not Meaningful. NR-Not Ranked.

Office—3103 Philmont Ave., Huntingdon Valley, PA 19006-4298. **Tel**—(215) 938-8000. **Website**—http://www.tollbrothers.com **Chrmn & CEO**—R. I. Toll. **Pres**—B. E. Toll. **SVP, Treas, & CFO**—J. H. Rassman. **Investor Contact**—Joseph R. Sicree. **Dirs**—Z. Barzilay, R. S. Blank, R. J. Braemer, R. S. Hillas, C. B. Marbach, J. H. Rassman, P. E. Shapiro, B. E. Toll, R. I. Toll. **Transfer Agent & Registrar**—ChaseMellon Shareholder Services, Ridgefield Park, NJ. **Incorporated**—in Delaware in 1986. **Empl**— 1,346. **S&P Analyst:** Michael W. Jaffe

STANDARD &POOR'S
STOCK REPORTS

Toro Co.

2242L

NYSE Symbol **TTC**

In S&P SmallCap 600

03-OCT-98

Industry: Hardware & Tools

Summary: This company is a leading maker of consumer and commercial lawn and turf maintenance equipment, snow removal equipment and irrigation systems.

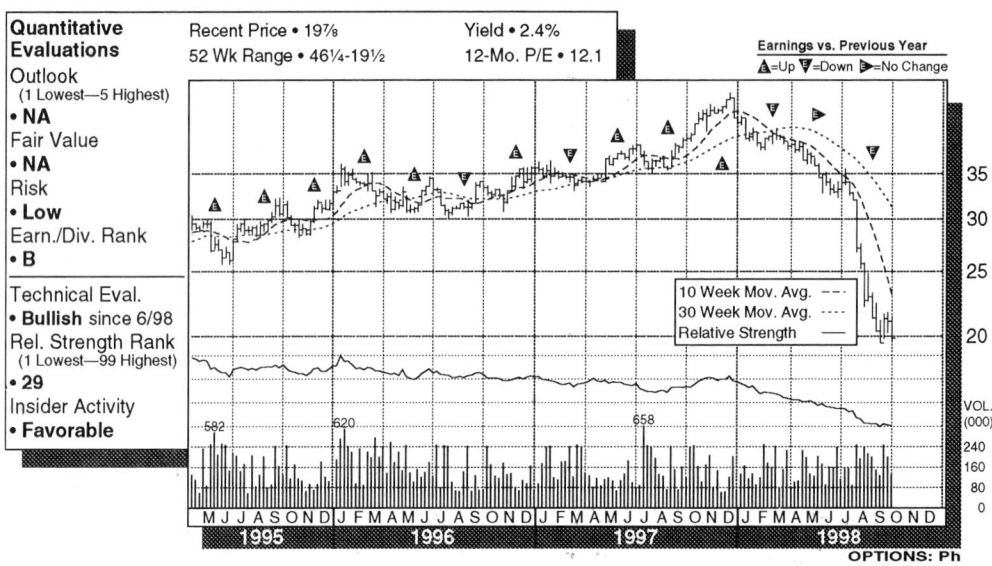

Quantitative Evaluations	
Recent Price • 19⅞	Yield • 2.4%
52 Wk Range • 46¼-19½	12-Mo. P/E • 12.1

Outlook (1 Lowest—5 Highest)
• **NA**

Fair Value
• **NA**

Risk
• **Low**

Earn./Div. Rank
• **B**

Technical Eval.
• **Bullish** since 6/98

Rel. Strength Rank (1 Lowest—99 Highest)
• **29**

Insider Activity
• **Favorable**

Earnings vs. Previous Year
▲=Up ▼=Down ▶=No Change

10 Week Mov. Avg. ---
30 Week Mov. Avg. ·····
Relative Strength —

OPTIONS: Ph

Business Profile - 23-SEP-98

TTC shares have fallen since early 1998, reflecting a slowdown in anticipated revenue growth as a result of softer Asian demand and the negative effects of El Nino. In response to this weak operating performance, the company has developed a profit improvement program, including distribution and logistical changes, product line rationalizations and plant reconfigurations. Toro expects these initiatives to generate savings of at least $20 million by FY 2000 (Oct.), and anticipates associated one-time charges of $20 million, $10.5 million of which was incurred in the first nine months of FY 98.

Operational Review - 23-SEP-98

Net sales for the nine months ended July 31, 1998, rose 8.7%, year to year, as increases in commercial products outweighed decreases in consumer products. Profitability was restricted by adverse weather conditions, weak Asian demand and manufacturing inefficiencies. Comparisons were further hurt by a $10.5 million restructuring charge related to the closure and sale of certain operations. Following higher interest expense and taxes at 39.5% in both periods, income plunged 48%, to $16,439,000 ($1.24 per share), from $31,480,000 ($2.53). Results in the FY 97 period exclude an extraordinary loss of $0.13 a share.

Stock Performance - 02-OCT-98

In the past 30 trading days, TTC's shares have declined 13%, compared to a 7% fall in the S&P 500. Average trading volume for the past five days was 25,660 shares, compared with the 40-day moving average of 40,354 shares.

Key Stock Statistics

Dividend Rate/Share	0.48	Shareholders	6,800
Shs. outstg. (M)	12.9	Market cap. (B)	$0.256
Avg. daily vol. (M)	0.040	Inst. holdings	56%
Tang. Bk. Value/Share	15.38		
Beta	0.72		

Value of $10,000 invested 5 years ago: $ 13,063

Fiscal Year Ending Oct. 31

	1998	1997	1996	1995	1994	1993
Revenues (Million $)						
1Q	210.1	209.0	211.5	206.0	136.0	113.0
2Q	379.7	352.2	288.6	214.0	189.0	153.0
3Q	291.0	249.3	232.6	311.0	276.0	241.0
4Q	—	240.8	198.2	203.0	193.0	176.0
Yr.	—	1,051	930.9	933.0	794.0	684.0
Earnings Per Share ($)						
1Q	**-0.08**	0.20	0.67	0.64	-0.15	-0.34
2Q	**1.53**	1.53	1.33	0.51	0.35	0.15
3Q	**-0.20**	0.80	0.52	1.32	1.19	1.01
4Q	—	0.40	0.37	0.32	0.31	0.21
Yr.	—	2.93	2.90	2.81	1.71	1.05

Next earnings report expected: mid December

Dividend Data (Dividends have been paid since 1984.)

Amount ($)	Date Decl.	Ex-Div. Date	Stock of Record	Payment Date
0.120	Nov. 25	Dec. 12	Dec. 16	Jan. 12 '98
0.120	Mar. 18	Mar. 26	Mar. 30	Apr. 13 '98
0.120	May. 20	Jun. 18	Jun. 22	Jul. 13 '98
0.120	Sep. 23	Oct. 01	Oct. 05	Oct. 19 '98

A Division of The **McGraw·Hill** Companies

Business Summary - 23-SEP-98

Founded in 1914 to build engines for farm tractors, Toro Co. turned away from its agricultural roots when a golf course superintendent suggested that the company design a tractor-towed mower for golf course fairways. By 1925, TTC's turf maintenance machines were in service on many major golf courses in the United States. Through internal development, acquisitions and alliances, TTC has become a leading designer, manufacturer and marketer of consumer and professional turf maintenance equipment, snow removal products and irrigation systems. In addition, Toro provides landscaping and turf maintenance services.

TTC was the first manufacturer to offer a consumer lawn mower with electric starting, the first to include a bagging attachment with each mower, and the first to offer a "Guaranteed To Start" in the first two pulls or your money back warranty. Today, in addition to gas-powered rider and walk mowers, TTC also provides lawn and garden tractors, snowthrowers, trimmers and debris management products.

In 1989, TTC purchased Lawn-Boy, Inc., its most formidable competitor. This gave TTC three strong brand names (Toro, Wheel Horse and Lawn-Boy), and additional opportunities to expand TTC's distribution channels. The company selectively expanded Lawn-Boy distribution to the mass retailer market segment, namely Sears Roebuck and Montgomery Ward, in 1991. In 1992, the distribution channels were further expanded to include home centers, hardware co-ops and other select mass retailers.

TTC's commercial equipment consists of a broad range of integrated turf maintenance items including riding reel and rotary mowing equipment, greens mowers, aerators, sweepers, seeders, chippers, sprayers, spreaders and multipurpose utility vehicles. Toro typically provides its products and services to schools, parks, cemeteries, sports fields, plant sites, apartment buildings, townhouse complexes and golf courses.

TTC also offers a full line of irrigation products designed to manage water usage in both commercial and residential applications. The company considers itself a world leader in innovative water-conserving, problem-solving irrigation systems for residential, commercial and golf course markets. Its irrigation equipment is used on more than 75 of the top 100 golf courses in the United States and many top courses around the world. In December 1996, TTC acquired James Hardie Irrigation, a world leader in irrigation systems for the residential market, making Toro the number one global supplier of irrigation products and systems.

In November 1997, Toro acquired Exmark Manufacturing Company, Inc., a landscaping equipment provider with annual sales of $50 million.

Per Share Data ($) (Year Ended Oct. 31)	1997	1996	1995	1994	1993	1992	1991	1990	1989	1988
Tangible Bk. Val.	15.38	19.15	16.50	13.43	11.78	11.01	13.48	12.92	9.85	8.16
Cash Flow	5.53	4.35	4.31	3.16	2.61	-0.15	2.38	3.01	3.03	2.68
Earnings	2.93	2.90	2.81	1.71	1.05	-1.98	0.81	1.55	2.10	1.84
Dividends	0.48	0.48	0.48	0.48	0.48	0.48	0.48	0.48	0.48	0.40
Payout Ratio	16%	17%	17%	28%	45%	NM	59%	35%	22%	21%
Prices - High	46 1/4	36 1/4	32 1/4	30 1/2	26 3/4	17 1/2	20 1/2	30	26	24 7/8
- Low	33	30	25 5/8	20 7/8	16 1/2	11 3/8	13 1/4	11	18 5/8	15
P/E Ratio - High	16	12	11	18	25	NM	25	19	12	14
- Low	11	10	9	12	16	NM	16	7	9	8
Income Statement Analysis (Million $)										
Revs.	1,051	931	933	794	684	635	712	751	644	609
Oper. Inc.	103	81.6	82.1	61.4	54.7	23.4	46.2	58.2	60.4	38.8
Depr.	30.9	18.2	17.2	18.8	19.2	22.0	18.8	15.1	9.3	8.7
Int. Exp.	19.9	13.6	11.9	13.6	17.2	18.7	19.0	23.7	17.4	7.8
Pretax Inc.	60.3	60.2	61.1	37.1	21.4	-34.9	15.3	26.3	36.9	25.8
Eff. Tax Rate	40%	40%	40%	40%	39%	NM	37%	37%	40%	22%
Net Inc.	36.5	36.4	36.7	22.2	13.0	-23.8	9.7	16.6	22.1	20.0
Balance Sheet & Other Fin. Data (Million $)										
Cash	0.0	0.1	11.9	36.2	61.8	25.5	17.0	12.3	19.7	12.0
Curr. Assets	472	405	382	364	344	333	319	320	266	183
Total Assets	662	497	468	444	419	421	415	424	326	268
Curr. Liab.	238	208	213	189	150	122	108	130	123	119
LT Debt	178	53.0	64.9	81.0	123	164	145	134	97.0	57.0
Common Eqty.	241	214	185	169	145	133	161	153	98.0	82.0
Total Cap.	419	267	256	250	269	299	307	293	203	149
Cap. Exp.	37.0	21.3	28.2	18.2	10.2	12.8	11.4	14.6	11.5	11.4
Cash Flow	67.4	54.6	53.9	4.1	32.3	-1.8	28.5	31.0	30.5	27.6
Curr. Ratio	2.0	1.9	1.8	1.9	2.3	2.7	3.0	2.5	2.2	1.5
% LT Debt of Cap.	42.4	19.9	25.4	32.5	45.7	54.8	47.3	45.9	47.7	38.0
% Net Inc.of Revs.	3.5	3.9	3.9	2.8	1.9	NM	1.4	2.2	3.4	3.3
% Ret. on Assets	6.3	7.5	7.8	5.1	3.1	NM	2.3	4.1	7.5	7.9
% Ret. on Equity	16.1	18.0	20.7	14.0	9.3	NM	6.2	11.9	23.7	24.8

Data as orig. reptd.; bef. results of disc. opers. and/or spec. items. Per share data adj. for stk. divs. as of ex-div. date. Data to 1995 for fiscal yr. ended July 31. E-Estimated. NA-Not Available. NM-Not Meaningful. NR-Not Ranked.

Office—8111 Lyndale Ave. South, Bloomington, MN 55420. **Tel**—(612) 888-8801. **Website**—http://www.toro.com **Chrmn & CEO**—K. B. Melrose. **VP & Secy**—J. L. McIntyre. **VP-Fin, CFO & Treas**—S. P. Wolfe. **Asst Treas & Investor Contact**—Stephen D. Keating. **Dirs**—R. O. Baukol, R. C. Buhrmaster, W. H. Buxton, J. K. Cooper, K. B. Melrose, A. A. Meyer, R. H. Nassau, D. R. Olseth, C. A. Twomey, E. H. Wingate. **Transfer Agent & Registrar**—Norwest Bank Minnesota, South St. Paul. **Incorporated**—in Minnesota in 1935; reincorporated in Delaware in 1984. **Empl**— 4,000.
S&P Analyst: Jordan Horoschak

STANDARD &POOR'S
STOCK REPORTS

Tredegar Industries

2254G

NYSE Symbol **TG**

In S&P SmallCap 600

03-OCT-98

Industry:
Manufacturing (Diversified)

Summary: Tredegar makes plastic films and aluminum products, and has interests in various technology businesses.

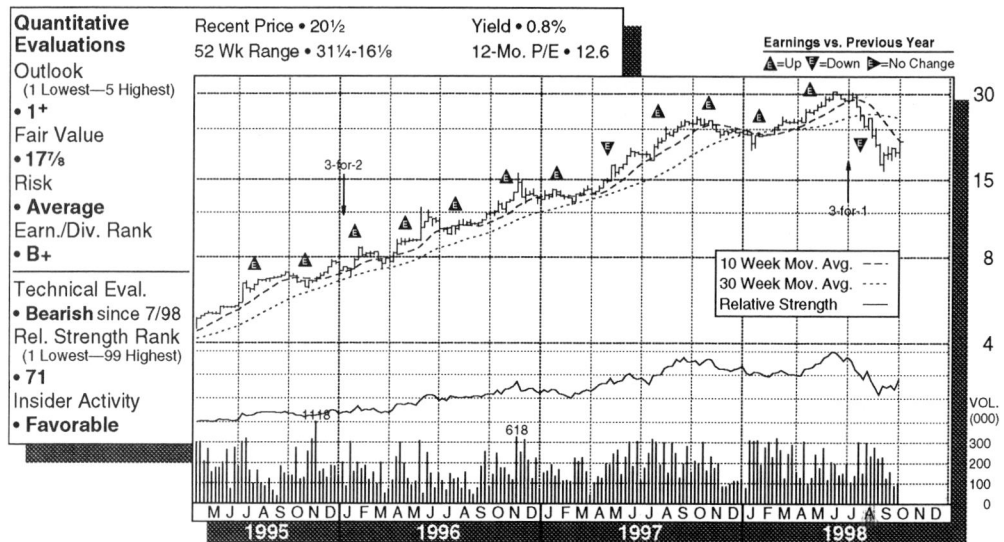

Quantitative Evaluations	
Outlook (1 Lowest—5 Highest)	• **1+**
Fair Value	• **17⅞**
Risk	• **Average**
Earn./Div. Rank	• **B+**
Technical Eval.	• **Bearish** since 7/98
Rel. Strength Rank (1 Lowest—99 Highest)	• **71**
Insider Activity	• **Favorable**

Recent Price • 20½
52 Wk Range • 31¼-16⅛
Yield • 0.8%
12-Mo. P/E • 12.6

Business Profile - 29-SEP-98

Tredegar seeks to enhance shareholder value through continued global expansion, the introduction of new products, acquisitions, the penetration of new markets in the U. S. and Canada, expansion of the portfolio of drug discovery collaborations, and broadening its portfolio of investment opportunities in new technologies. In September 1998, the company signed a three-year agreement with Bristol Myers Squibb aimed at developing new drugs for the treatment of inflammatory and immunological diseases. Earlier, the company acquired Exal Aluminium, owner of two aluminum extrusion plants in Canada, for an undisclosed amount of cash and stock. In July 1998, the shares were split 3-for-1, and directors raised the dividend 33% on a pre-split basis.

Operational Review - 29-SEP-98

Revenues in the six months ended June 30, 1998, increased 15%, year to year, principally reflecting acquisitions in the aluminum segment. Aided by a $2.8 million gain on the sale of APPX Software in the first quarter (including related tax benefits) and strong performance in the aluminum extrusions business, net income advanced 19% to $32.5 million ($0.84 a share, as adjusted for a 3-for-1 stock split in July), from $27.3 million ($0.69, as adjusted).

Stock Performance - 02-OCT-98

In the past 30 trading days, TG's shares have increased 3%, compared to a 7% fall in the S&P 500. Average trading volume for the past five days was 19,960 shares, compared with the 40-day moving average of 36,436 shares.

Key Stock Statistics

Dividend Rate/Share	0.16	Shareholders	6,900
Shs. outstg. (M)	36.1	Market cap. (B)	$0.739
Avg. daily vol. (M)	0.025	Inst. holdings	23%
Tang. Bk. Value/Share	6.91		
Beta	1.15		

Value of $10,000 invested 5 years ago: $ 62,897

Fiscal Year Ending Dec. 31

	1998	1997	1996	1995	1994	1993
Revenues (Million $)						
1Q	156.7	133.3	141.4	151.1	121.0	111.2
2Q	169.9	145.0	126.3	149.7	122.9	108.0
3Q	—	155.1	129.4	146.0	132.2	113.9
4Q	—	147.6	126.4	142.7	126.1	116.0
Yr.	—	581.0	523.5	589.5	502.2	449.2
Earnings Per Share ($)						
1Q	**0.44**	**0.28**	0.42	0.11	-0.10	0.04
2Q	**0.39**	**0.42**	0.22	0.15	0.06	0.01
3Q	—	**0.38**	0.27	0.17	0.00	0.02
4Q	—	**0.40**	0.23	0.18	0.09	0.00
Yr.	—	**1.48**	1.15	0.60	0.03	0.08

Next earnings report expected: mid October

Dividend Data (Dividends have been paid since 1989.)

Amount ($)	Date Decl.	Ex-Div. Date	Stock of Record	Payment Date
0.090	Feb. 25	Mar. 16	Mar. 18	Apr. 01 '98
0.120	May. 20	Jun. 11	Jun. 15	Jul. 01 '98
3-for-1	May. 20	Jul. 02	Jun. 15	Jul. 01 '98
0.120	Aug. 25	Sep. 16	Sep. 18	Oct. 01 '98

A Division of The McGraw-Hill Companies

Tredegar Industries, Inc.

Business Summary - 29-SEP-98

Tredegar Industries is a manufacturer of plastic films, aluminum extrusions and vinyl extrusions. It also has interests in a variety of technology-based businesses. Sales and operating profits (before unusual items) in 1997 were obtained as follows:

	Sales	Operating Profit
Film products and Fiberlux	53%	55%
Aluminium extrusions	46%	35%
Technology	1%	10%

About 38.5% of the company's 1997 pretax income was obtained overseas.

Film products are produced in two major market categories: disposables and industrial. Disposable products, which accounted for more than 35% of revenues in each of the past three years, include permeable films for use as liners in feminine hygiene products, adult incontinent products and hospital underpads. TG also supplies embossed films and nonwoven film laminates for use as backsheet in such disposable products as baby diapers, adult incontinent products, feminine hygiene products and hospital underpads. The company's primary customer for permeable films, embossed films and nonwoven film laminates is Procter & Gamble, the leading global diaper maker. Film products for industrial markets include coextruded and monolayer permeable films used to regulate fluid and vapor transmissions. Specific examples include filter plies for surgical masks and other medical applications, permeable ground cover, natural cheese mold release cloths and rubber bale wrap.

Fiberlux is a leader U.S. producer of rigid vinyl extrusions for windows and patio doors. Its primary raw material, polyvinyl chloride resin, is puchased from producers in open market purchases and under contract.

Aluminum extrusions (metal that is heated and pushed through dies to form specific shapes) is composed of The William L. Bonnel Co., Capitol Products Corp., Bon L Campo Limited Partnership and Bon L Canada, which make plain, anodized and painted aluminium extrusions for sale directly to fabricators and distributors that use aluminum extrusions in the production of curtain walls, moldings, architectural shapes, running boards, tub and shower doors, boat windshields, window components, tractor-trailer shapes, ladders and furniture, among other products.

TG's Molecumetics, Ltd. subsidiary conducts drug design research using patented chemistry to develop new drug candidates for license to pharmaceutical and biotech companies in exchange for up-front fees, research and development support payments, milestone-driven success payments and future royalties. Tredegar Investments invests in venture capital funds and early stage technology companies.

Per Share Data ($)

(Year Ended Dec. 31)	1997	1996	1995	1994	1993	1992	1991	1990	1989	1988
Tangible Bk. Val.	20.43	5.24	3.85	4.25	3.45	3.31	2.28	2.42	2.90	2.81
Cash Flow	5.83	1.66	1.10	0.54	0.55	0.80	0.80	0.07	0.83	0.96
Earnings	1.48	1.15	0.60	0.03	0.08	0.31	0.12	-0.49	0.32	0.46
Dividends	0.11	0.09	0.06	0.05	0.05	0.05	0.05	0.05	0.03	NA
Payout Ratio	8%	8%	10%	185%	70%	17%	46%	NM	8%	NA
Prices - High	25	15¾	7⅞	4⅛	4	4¼	2⁷⁄₁₆	3½	3⅞	NA
- Low	12¼	6⅞	3⅞	3⅛	2¾	2³⁄₁₆	1⁷⁄₁₆	1⁹⁄₁₆	2⅞	NA
P/E Ratio - High	17	14	13	NM	53	13	21	NM	19	NA
- Low	8	6	6	NM	36	7	12	NM	14	NA

Income Statement Analysis (Million $)

	1997	1996	1995	1994	1993	1992	1991	1990	1989	1988
Revs.	581	524	590	502	449	479	474	547	638	624
Oper. Inc.	91.3	75.8	66.0	49.6	35.9	55.7	50.9	36.2	56.6	63.7
Depr.	18.4	20.3	23.8	23.5	23.1	23.9	33.5	28.4	27.6	27.6
Int. Exp.	2.0	2.2	3.0	4.2	5.4	6.9	9.1	9.3	4.8	11.5
Pretax Inc.	90.2	69.0	38.3	5.3	6.9	25.5	8.9	-39.8	27.7	40.4
Eff. Tax Rate	35%	35%	37%	73%	46%	40%	37%	NM	38%	38%
Net Inc.	58.4	45.0	24.1	1.4	3.7	15.3	5.6	-24.7	17.3	24.9

Balance Sheet & Other Fin. Data (Million $)

	1997	1996	1995	1994	1993	1992	1991	1990	1989	1988
Cash	120	101	2.1	9.0	Nil	Nil	0.5	2.3	1.7	5.1
Curr. Assets	223	194	126	135	117	125	119	134	127	127
Total Assets	411	341	314	318	353	359	339	342	368	352
Curr. Liab.	72.8	61.3	69.8	72.8	54.8	62.5	58.1	62.0	49.3	34.8
LT Debt	30.0	35.0	35.0	38.0	97.0	102	100	100	100	100
Common Eqty.	273	213	171	172	169	162	150	147	185	185
Total Cap.	325	265	228	230	289	295	280	279	317	316
Cap. Exp.	23.9	23.9	25.1	15.6	16.5	21.0	36.8	39.7	45.6	31.4
Cash Flow	76.9	65.3	47.9	24.9	26.8	39.2	39.1	3.7	44.9	52.5
Curr. Ratio	3.1	3.2	1.8	1.9	2.1	2.0	2.1	2.2	2.6	3.7
% LT Debt of Cap.	9.2	13.2	10.6	16.5	33.5	34.4	35.8	35.8	31.5	31.7
% Net Inc.of Revs.	10.1	8.6	4.1	0.3	0.8	3.2	1.2	NM	2.7	4.0
% Ret. on Assets	15.5	13.7	7.6	0.5	1.0	4.4	1.7	NM	NA	NA
% Ret. on Equity	24.1	2.3	14.1	0.9	2.2	9.8	3.8	NM	NA	NA

Data as orig. reptd.; bef. results of disc. opers. and/or spec. items. Per share data adj. for stk. divs. as of ex-div. date. Bold denotes diluted EPS (FASB 128). E-Estimated. NA-Not Available. NM-Not Meaningful. NR-Not Ranked.

Office—1100 Boulders Parkway, Richmond, VA 23225. Tel—(804) 330-1000. Pres & CEO—J. D. Gottwald. EVP, CFO & Treas—N. A. Scher. Secy—N. M. Taylor. Investor Contact—Edward A. Cunningham (804-330-1598). Dirs—A. Brockenbrough III, P. Cothran, R. W. Goodrum, F. D. Gottwald Jr., J. D. Gottwald, Dr. W. M. Gottwald, A. B. Lacy, Dr. R. L. Morrill, E. J. Rice, N. A. Scher, T. G. Slater. Transfer Agent & Registrar—American Stock Transfer & Trust, NYC. Incorporated—in Virginia in 1988. Empl— 2,900. S&P Analyst: P.L.H.

STANDARD &POOR'S
STOCK REPORTS

Trenwick Group

5456M

NASDAQ Symbol **TREN**

In S&P SmallCap 600

03-OCT-98

Industry:
Insurance (Property-Casualty)

Summary: This insurance holding company operates primarily through Trenwick America Reinsurance Corp., which reinsures property and casualty risks written by U.S. insurance companies.

Quantitative Evaluations

Recent Price • 29

52 Wk Range • 41¾-27

Yield • 3.4%

12-Mo. P/E • 9.7

Outlook
(1 Lowest—5 Highest)
• **2⁻**

Fair Value
• **28**

Risk
• **Low**

Earn./Div. Rank
• **A-**

Technical Eval.
• **Bearish** since 5/98

Rel. Strength Rank
(1 Lowest—99 Highest)
• **43**

Insider Activity
• **Neutral**

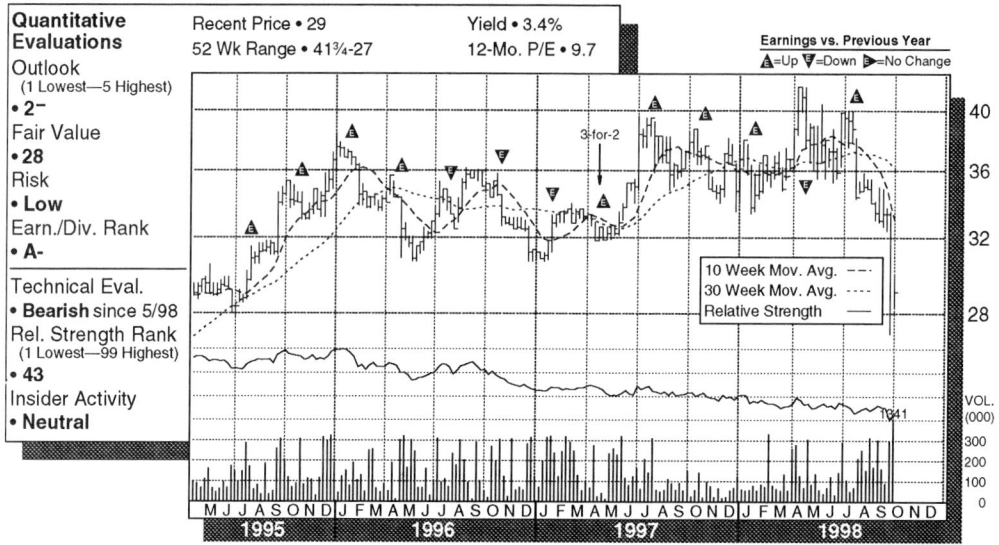

Earnings vs. Previous Year
△=Up ▽=Down ▶=No Change

10 Week Mov. Avg. ---
30 Week Mov. Avg. ·····
Relative Strength ——

Business Profile - 02-SEP-98

TREN considers it an advantage that it operates with less capital, writes fewer premiums and has lower headcount than most of its competitors. To extend its operating leverage, the company is considering new strategic reinsurance agreements and direct investments in other segments of its business. In March 1998, Trenwick placed privately $75 million of 6.70% senior notes due April 2003. In February 1998, TREN expanded its product mix and geographic base with the acquisition of SOREMA (UK) Ltd., a London-based underwriter of specialty insurance and reinsurance worldwide.

Operational Review - 02-SEP-98

Total revenues in the six months ended June 30, 1998, rose 15%, year to year, driven by increases in net premiums earned and net investment income. Total expenses rose more rapidly, reflecting claims expenses, underwriting costs and G&A expenditures; pretax income dropped 9.4%. After taxes at 15.7%, versus 22.9%, income was down 1.0%, to $18,220,000 ($1.51 a share), from $17,357,000 ($1.53). Results in the 1997 period exclude a charge of $0.09 a share for debt redemption.

Stock Performance - 02-OCT-98

In the past 30 trading days, TREN's shares have declined 15%, compared to a 7% fall in the S&P 500. Average trading volume for the past five days was 268,100 shares, compared with the 40-day moving average of 76,703 shares.

Key Stock Statistics

Dividend Rate/Share	1.00	Shareholders	100
Shs. outstg. (M)	12.1	Market cap. (B)	$0.350
Avg. daily vol. (M)	0.095	Inst. holdings	78%
Tang. Bk. Value/Share	30.92		
Beta	0.46		

Value of $10,000 invested 5 years ago: $ 12,332

Fiscal Year Ending Dec. 31

	1998	1997	1996	1995	1994	1993
Revenues (Million $)						
1Q	58.94	67.56	57.61	53.11	38.50	32.91
2Q	86.80	59.24	63.55	52.94	39.88	30.11
3Q	—	55.90	65.32	52.69	41.73	29.88
4Q	—	58.17	66.12	55.86	46.31	37.08
Yr.	—	240.9	252.6	214.6	166.4	130.0
Earnings Per Share ($)						
1Q	**0.77**	**0.90**	0.80	0.65	0.11	0.62
2Q	**0.74**	**0.71**	0.81	0.73	0.61	0.53
3Q	—	**0.73**	0.83	0.79	0.64	0.60
4Q	—	**0.75**	0.86	0.79	0.67	0.57
Yr.	—	**3.01**	3.30	2.96	2.03	2.32

Next earnings report expected: late October

Dividend Data (Dividends have been paid since 1988.)

Amount ($)	Date Decl.	Ex-Div. Date	Stock of Record	Payment Date
0.240	Oct. 29	Dec. 11	Dec. 15	Dec. 31 '97
0.250	Mar. 04	Mar. 12	Mar. 16	Mar. 31 '98
0.250	May. 21	Jun. 10	Jun. 12	Jun. 30 '98
0.250	Aug. 07	Sep. 10	Sep. 14	Sep. 30 '98

A Division of The McGraw-Hill Companies

Business Summary - 02-SEP-98

An insurance holding company, Trenwick Group (TREN) underwrites reinsurance. TREN's principal subsidiary, Trenwick America Reinsurance Corp., primarily provides reinsurance to insurers of U.S. property and casualty risks. Trenwick writes conventional treaty, facultative and specialty reinsurance.

Treaty reinsurance is that in which categories of risks are assumed under a single contract. This type of reinsurance accounted for 98% of TREN's net premiums written in 1997. Facultative reinsurance, in which risks are negotiated individually, consists entirely of casualty business. Special reinsurance programs provide specialty classes and coverages. Specialty reinsurance is written for a class of risk in which statistical methods are used to estimate future profitability (like facultative underwriting), but specialty underwriting also relies on the analysis of the reinsured's risks themselves, as well as insurance policy forms and rates.

TREN underwrites reinsurance for: automobile liability (26% of net premiums written in 1997), errors and omissions (21%), property (20%), general liability (11%), workers' compensation (9%), medical malpractice (5%), accident and health (3%), liability (1%) and other casualty insurance (4%). Casualty premiums have declined due to competitive conditions that have led to industry consolidation, caused cedants to reduce their premium writings or restructure their reinsurance programs, and driven prices on a number of accounts below levels the company will accept.

TREN usually obtains all its business through brokers and reinsurance intermediaries, which seek its participation on reinsurance being placed for their customers. In underwriting reinsurance, the company does not target types of clients, classes of business, or types of reinsurance, but rather selects transactions based on the quality of the reinsured, the attractiveness of the reinsured's insurance rates and policy conditions, and the adequacy of the proposed reinsurance terms.

During 1997, TREN continued its strategic reinsurance agreement with PXRE Reinsurance Co., assuming approximately 15% of that company's property business. In 1997, TREN also obtained about 11% of gross premiums written from American International Group and about 10% from Travelers Group.

TREN is licensed, authorized or approved to write reinsurance in all 50 states and the District of Columbia. Effective February 27, 1998, the company acquired SOREMA (UK) Ltd. (renamed Trenwick International Ltd.) for $60.6 million in cash. TREN plans to use the London-based underwriter of specialty insurance as a platform for further international expansion.

Per Share Data ($)

(Year Ended Dec. 31)	1997	1996	1995	1994	1993	1992	1991	1990	1989	1988
Tangible Bk. Val.	29.93	26.25	24.23	19.32	20.94	17.35	15.97	14.50	NA	NA
Oper. Earnings	NA	NA	NA	NA	NA	NA	NA	NA	NA	NA
Earnings	3.01	3.30	2.96	2.03	2.32	1.67	1.86	1.65	NA	NA
Dividends	0.97	0.83	0.75	0.67	0.57	0.51	0.42	0.30	NA	NA
Payout Ratio	32%	25%	25%	33%	25%	30%	23%	18%	NA	NA
Prices - High	39⅝	37⅞	38⅜	29¼	33⅛	28⅛	20	16⅞	NA	NA
- Low	30⅝	30⅝	27⅛	22⅛	25⅛	16⅝	14½	11⅛	NA	NA
P/E Ratio - High	13	11	13	14	14	17	11	10	NA	NA
- Low	10	9	9	11	11	10	8	7	NA	NA

Income Statement Analysis (Million $)

	1997	1996	1995	1994	1993	1992	1991	1990	1989	1988
Premium Inc.	190	211	177	133	93.0	82.0	85.0	94.0	NA	NA
Net Invest. Inc.	48.4	41.2	36.8	33.9	35.0	30.9	30.4	27.0	NA	NA
Oth. Revs.	2.3	0.3	0.4	-0.2	1.8	0.4	NA	0.3	NA	NA
Total Revs.	241	253	215	166	130	113	118	122	NA	NA
Pretax Inc.	55.9	43.8	38.4	23.0	28.0	19.5	22.0	19.8	NA	NA
Net Oper. Inc.	NA	NA	NA	NA	NA	NA	NA	NA	NA	NA
Net Inc.	36.3	33.8	29.8	20.3	23.7	16.8	18.6	17.2	NA	NA

Balance Sheet & Other Fin. Data (Million $)

	1997	1996	1995	1994	1993	1992	1991	1990	1989	1988
Cash & Equiv.	12.8	14.3	17.0	20.1	15.2	NA	NA	NA	NA	NA
Premiums Due	91.8	62.7	49.0	27.8	26.6	NA	NA	NA	NA	NA
Invest. Assets: Bonds	812	714	634	532	540	NA	NA	NA	NA	NA
Invest. Assets: Stocks	39.1	26.0	13.4	9.8	Nil	NA	NA	NA	NA	NA
Invest. Assets: Loans	Nil	Nil	Nil	Nil	Nil	NA	NA	NA	NA	NA
Invest. Assets: Total	39.2	740	647	542	540	500	NA	NA	NA	NA
Deferred Policy Costs	NA	21.8	16.7	10.7	8.5	NA	NA	NA	NA	NA
Total Assets	1,088	921	821	727	700	652	NA	NA	NA	NA
Debt	110	104	104	104	104	104	NA	NA	NA	NA
Common Eqty.	358	266	241	188	207	169	NA	NA	NA	NA
Prop. & Cas. Loss Ratio	57.6	61.3	63.7	70.0	68.5	78.4	NA	NA	NA	NA
Prop. & Cas. Expense Ratio	38.9	34.5	31.9	33.2	34.0	33.9	NA	NA	NA	NA
Prop. & Cas. Combined Ratio	96.5	95.8	95.6	103.2	102.5	112.3	108.0	106.9	NA	NA
% Return On Revs.	15.1	13.4	13.9	12.2	18.3	14.9	15.8	14.1	NA	NA
% Ret. on Equity	11.6	13.4	13.9	10.3	12.6	10.4	12.6	12.8	NA	NA

Data as orig. reptd.; bef. results of disc. opers. and/or spec. items. Per share data adj. for stk. divs. as of ex-div. date. Bold denotes diluted EPS (FASB 128). E-Estimated. NA-Not Available. NM-Not Meaningful. NR-Not Ranked.

Office—Metro Center, One Station Place, Stamford, CT 06902. **Tel**—(203) 353-5500. **Chrmn, Pres & CEO**—J. F. Billett Jr. **VP, CFO & Treas**—A. L. Hunte. **VP & Secy**—J. T. Wiznitzer. **Dirs**—W. M. Becker, J. F. Billett Jr., A. S. Brown, N. Dunn, P. A. Jacobs, H. Palmberger, J. D. Sargent, F. D. Watkins, S. R. Wilcox. **Transfer Agent**—First Chicago Trust Co. of New York, NYC. **Incorporated**—in Delaware in 1985. **Empl**— 72. **S&P Analyst:** S.J.T.

STANDARD &POOR'S
STOCK REPORTS

Triarc Cos.

2255G

NYSE Symbol **TRY**

In S&P SmallCap 600

03-OCT-98

Industry:
Beverages
(Non-Alcoholic)

Summary: TRY engages in restaurant operations (Arby's), beverage operations (Snapple, Royal Crown, Cable Car and Mistic) and has a 43% interest in a liquefied petroleum gas partnership.

Quantitative Evaluations

Outlook
(1 Lowest—5 Highest)
• **5**

Fair Value
• **26¾**

Risk
• **Average**

Earn./Div. Rank
• **C**

Technical Eval.
• **Bearish** since 6/98

Rel. Strength Rank
(1 Lowest—99 Highest)
• **33**

Insider Activity
• **Favorable**

Recent Price • 15⅛
52 Wk Range • 28¼-14½

Yield • Nil
12-Mo. P/E • 10.3

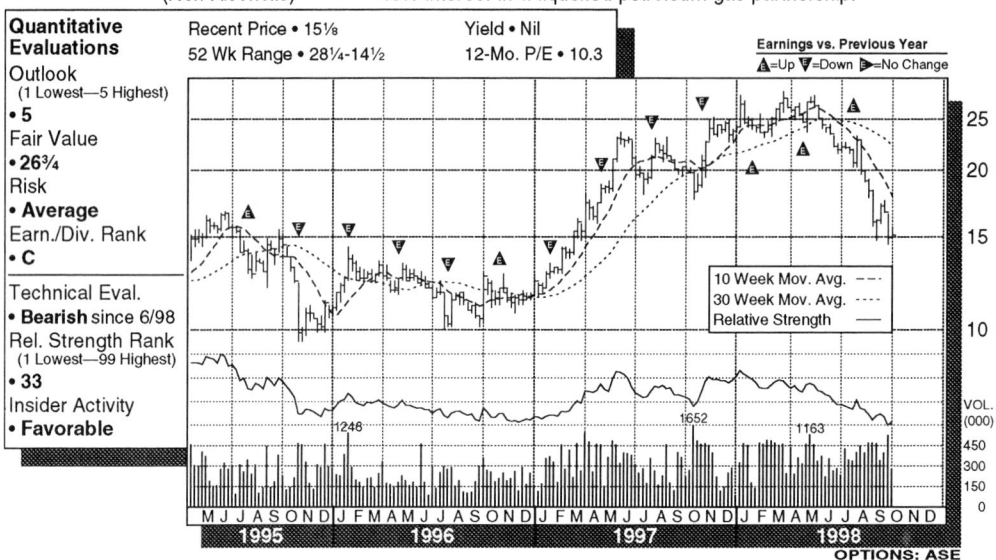

Earnings vs. Previous Year
▲=Up ▼=Down ▶=No Change

10 Week Mov. Avg. ---
30 Week Mov. Avg. ····
Relative Strength —

OPTIONS: ASE

Business Profile - 20-MAY-98

In 1997, the company made several significant moves. In May, it purchased Snapple Beverage Corp. from Quaker Oats Co., for $300 million in cash. Snapple had 1996 sales of about $550 million. Also in 1997, Triarc acquired Cable Car Beverage Corp., which markets premium beverages under the Stewart's brand name. The acquisitions helped TRY's positioning in the premium beverage category. The company also refocused its restaurant group as a franchisor by selling its company-owned Arby's restaurants for $71 million. In addition, TRY completed the sale of its industrial businesses, and also deconsolidated its propane investment.

Operational Review - 20-MAY-98

Revenues in the three months ended March 31, 1998, fell 9.0%, year to year, in the absence of sales from the propane segment, which was deconsolidated, and of sales of 355 Arby's units sold in 1997, partly offset by the acquisitions of Snapple and Cable Car Beverage. Higher gross profits were outweighed by increased greater G&A and marketing expense associated with Snapple and Cable Car Beverage; operating profit fell 40%. However, with higher investment income, taxes at 20.0%, versus 52.8%, and minority interests, income of $1,595,000 ($0.05 a share) contrasted with a loss of $1,638,000 ($0.06). Results exclude income from discontinued operations of $0.08 and $0.02 a share in the respective periods.

Stock Performance - 02-OCT-98

In the past 30 trading days, TRY's shares have declined 17%, compared to a 7% fall in the S&P 500. Average trading volume for the past five days was 55,100 shares, compared with the 40-day moving average of 115,179 shares.

Key Stock Statistics

Dividend Rate/Share	Nil	Shareholders	5,700
Shs. outstg. (M)	30.6	Market cap. (B)	$0.372
Avg. daily vol. (M)	0.110	Inst. holdings	35%
Tang. Bk. Value/Share	NM		
Beta	1.23		

Value of $10,000 invested 5 years ago: $ 10,254

Fiscal Year Ending Dec. 31

	1998	1997	1996	1995	1994	1993
Revenues (Million $)						
1Q	172.1	205.4	328.9	298.0	270.0	--
2Q	232.9	226.1	246.5	279.3	267.0	258.0
3Q	—	275.0	206.4	291.9	256.1	264.0
4Q	—	205.3	207.4	315.1	268.9	257.0
Yr.	—	861.3	989.3	1,184	1,063	704.0
Earnings Per Share ($)						
1Q	0.05	-0.06	0.06	0.22	0.34	--
2Q	0.25	-1.07	-0.12	0.03	-0.13	-0.07
3Q	—	0.33	1.50	-0.19	-0.18	-0.99
4Q	—	0.09	-1.81	-1.30	-0.33	-0.56
Yr.	—	-0.68	-0.28	-1.24	-0.34	-1.62

Next earnings report expected: late October

Dividend Data

Cash dividends were omitted in 1974. The most recent stock payment was in 1986.

A Division of The **McGraw·Hill** *Companies*

Business Summary - 20-MAY-98

TRY is a holding company that is engaged primarily in beverage and restaurant operations. Beverage operations are conducted through Triarc Beverage Group, which owns Snapple Beverage Corp., Mistic Brands, Inc., Cable Car Beverage Corp., and Royal Crown Co., Inc. Restaurant operations are conducted through the Triarc Restaurant Group (Arby's). In addition, the National Propane Co. subsidiary has a 43% partnership interest in, and is the managing general partner of, National Propane Partners, L.P.

In the past year, TRY has focused on building its beverage business. After acquiring the Mistic beverage business in 1995, the company bought Snapple and Cable Car Beverage Corp. in 1997. Snapple, acquired in May 1997, develops, produces and markets ready-to-drink teas, juice drinks and juices, and is a market leader in the premium beverage category. Cable Car Beverage (November 1997) is the manufacturer and distributor of Stewart's brand premium soft drinks in the U.S. and Canada. Stewart's products include Root Beer, Orange N' Cream, Cream Ale, Ginger Beer, Classic Key Lime, Lemon Meringue, and Cherries N' Cream soft drinks. In April 1998, Stewart's introduced a new soft drink, called Creamy Style Draft Cola.

Mistic develops and produces a wide variety of premium beverages, including fruit drinks, ready-to-drink teas, juices, and sweetened seltzers under the Mistic, Royal Mistic, Mistic Rain Forest, and Mistic Fruit Blast brand names. Royal Crown produces and sells concentrates for soft drinks both domestically and internationally to licensed bottlers who distribute finished beverage products. Royal Crown's major products include RC Cola, Diet RC Cola, Diet Rite Cola, Diet Rite flavors, Nehi, Upper 10, and Kick.

With the May 1997 sale of 355 Arby's company-owned restaurants, the Triarc Restaurant Group (TRG) became essentially a franchisor of restaurants. At December 31, 1997, TRG franchised 3,091 single and co-branded Arby's units. To help develop its Arby's brand, TRG has developed a multi-branding strategy that allows a single restaurant to offer distinct but complementary brands. Currently, the company's two co-branded concepts include T.J. Cinnamons and p.t. Noodles.

National Propane Partners distributes liquefied petroleum gas for household and industrial uses, as well as related appliances and equipment. As of December 1997, operations were conducted through 159 full service centers supplying markets in 24 states. Operations are located principally in the Midwest, Northeast, Southeast and West. As of December 27, 1997, National Propane, as managing general partner, adopted certain amendments to the partnership agreement and, as a result, will utilize the equity method to account for its investment.

Per Share Data ($)

(Year Ended Dec. 31)	1997	1996	1995	1994	1993	1992	1991	1990	1989	1988
Tangible Bk. Val.	NM	NM	-1.22	-9.79	-11.82	-10.49	-3.84	-3.31	-2.86	-4.53
Cash Flow	0.62	1.49	-0.26	1.40	-0.04	-0.26	1.72	1.21	1.34	2.52
Earnings	-0.68	-0.28	-1.24	-0.34	-1.62	-1.73	-0.29	-0.68	-0.51	-0.19
Dividends	Nil	Nil	Nil	Nil	Nil	Nil	Nil	Nil	Nil	Nil
Payout Ratio	Nil	Nil	Nil	Nil	Nil	Nil	Nil	Nil	Nil	Nil
Prices - High	27³/₄	14³/₈	16³/₄	26¹/₈	33	15¹/₄	4³/₈	15⁵/₈	16	9¹/₄
- Low	11¹/₂	10	9¹/₄	9¹/₂	14	3	1¹/₂	2³/₄	5³/₈	5³/₄
P/E Ratio - High	NM	NM	NM	NM	NM	NM	NM	NM	NM	NM
- Low	NM	NM	NM	NM	NM	NM	NM	NM	NM	NM

Income Statement Analysis (Million $)

	1997	1996	1995	1994	1993	1992	1991	1990	1989	1988
Revs.	866	989	1,184	1,063	704	1,058	1,275	1,215	1,231	1,175
Oper. Inc.	105	119	98.2	118	55.0	117	111	79.0	114	102
Depr.	39.3	53.1	46.9	40.6	25.0	38.0	52.0	48.9	46.8	45.1
Int. Exp.	71.6	73.4	84.2	73.0	44.8	72.8	75.4	70.6	70.9	71.4
Pretax Inc.	-23.1	4.6	-38.2	0.8	-22.9	-39.3	-0.1	-33.8	-11.1	10.1
Eff. Tax Rate	NM	NM	NM	199%	NM	NM	NM	NM	NM	125%
Net Inc.	-20.6	-8.5	-30.4	-2.1	-3.0	-44.5	-7.5	-17.6	-12.9	-2.6

Balance Sheet & Other Fin. Data (Million $)

	1997	1996	1995	1994	1993	1992	1991	1990	1989	1988
Cash	129	209	106	96.0	138	102	55.0	75.0	63.0	91.0
Curr. Assets	356	446	413	359	393	359	NA	NA	NA	325
Total Assets	1,005	854	1,086	922	897	911	882	917	929	928
Curr. Liab.	226	240	255	223	241	226	NA	NA	NA	165
LT Debt	605	501	763	612	575	489	308	364	425	429
Common Eqty.	44.0	6.8	20.7	-32.0	-76.0	-35.0	86.0	92.0	109	112
Total Cap.	741	576	808	675	572	591	468	522	605	622
Cap. Exp.	13.9	30.0	70.0	61.6	29.0	24.0	48.0	60.0	63.0	75.0
Cash Flow	18.8	44.6	-5.5	32.6	-9.3	-13.5	44.5	31.3	33.9	42.0
Curr. Ratio	1.6	1.9	1.6	1.6	1.6	1.6	NA	NA	NA	2.0
% LT Debt of Cap.	81.6	87.0	94.4	90.7	100.5	82.7	65.8	69.7	70.3	68.9
% Net Inc.of Revs.	NM	NM	NM	NM	NM	NM	NM	NM	NM	NM
% Ret. on Assets	NM	NM	NM	NM	NM	NM	NM	NM	NM	NM
% Ret. on Equity	NM	NM	NM	NM	NM	NM	NM	NM	NM	NM

Data as orig. reptd.; bef. results of disc. opers. and/or spec. items. Per share data adj. for stk. divs. as of ex-div. date. Yrs. ended Apr. 30 of fol. cal. yr. prior to 1993. E-Estimated. NA-Not Available. NM-Not Meaningful. NR-Not Ranked.

Office—280 Park Ave., New York, NY 10017. **Tel**—(212) 451-3000. **Chrmn & CEO**—N. Peltz. **Pres & COO**—P. W. May. **EVP & CFO**—J. L. Barnes, Jr. **VP & Secy**—S. I. Rosen. **Investor Contact**—Martin M. Shea. **Dirs**—H. L Carey, C. Chajet, S. R. Jaffe, J. A. Levato, P. W. May, N. Peltz, D. E. Schwab II, R. S. Troubb, G. Tsai Jr. **Transfer Agent & Registrar**—Harris Trust & Savings Bank, Chicago. **Incorporated**—in Ohio in 1929; reincorporated in Delaware in 1994. **Empl**— 2,000. **S&P Analyst:** Robert J. Izmirlian

Trimble Navigation   5459N
Nasdaq Symbol TRMB
In S&P SmallCap 600

10-OCT-98

Industry: Electronics (Instrumentation)

Summary: Trimble is the world leader in commercial markets for Global Positioning System (GPS) satellite-based navigation, positioning and communication data products.

S&P Opinion: Hold (★★★)	
Recent Price • 10⅛	Yield • Nil
52 Wk Range • 24⅜-7	12-Mo. P/E • 40.5

Earnings vs. Previous Year
▲=Up ▼=Down ►=No Change

Quantitative Evaluations

Outlook (1 Lowest—5 Highest)
• 1⁻

Fair Value
• 9⅛

Risk
• High

Earn./Div. Rank
• B

Technical Eval.
• Bearish since 3/98

Rel. Strength Rank (1 Lowest—99 Highest)
• 49

Insider Activity
• NA

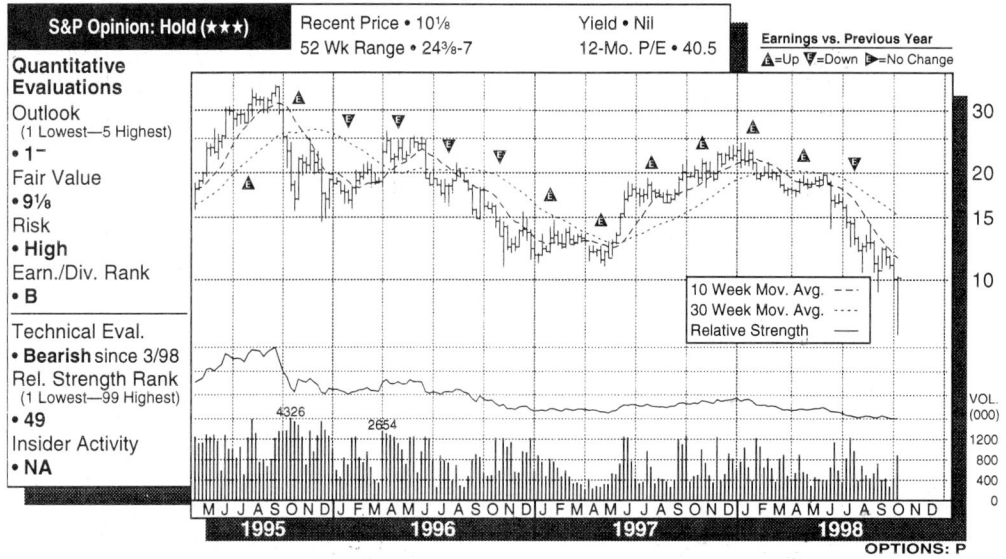

10 Week Mov. Avg. ---
30 Week Mov. Avg. ·····
Relative Strength —

VOL. (000)

OPTIONS: P

Overview - 14-AUG-98

Trimble has defined and currently addresses a number of markets for its GPS products, including surveying and mapping, aviation and marine navigation, military systems, tracking systems, OEM and cellular and mobile computing platforms. It continues to develop and introduce new generations of equipment for survey, mapping, seismology, graphical information systems, delivery fleets, buses, ships, airplanes, automobiles and hand-held units. The company considers the automobile navigation and telecommunications markets to be the largest growth opportunities in the GPS industry. TRMB provides 30% of the GPS engines embedded in in-car navigation systems worldwide. Recent sales gains reflect new applications of GPS that are now gaining acceptance in the marketplace. The company is stepping up investments in facilities to handle increasing volume, as well as spending for R&D projects that will pay off in 1999 and beyond.

Valuation - 14-AUG-98

From 1990 through 1997, the shares have underperformed the S&P 500, rising at an annualized rate of 14%, versus 17% for the index. We are skeptical that TRMB will be able to outpace the market in coming periods. Although many consider the satellite industry to be a high-growth business, the industry is fraught with risks, including malfunctioning rockets and satellites, rapidly changing technologies, uncertain geopolitical and regulatory climates, and increasing competition. TRMB itself has posted inconsistent earnings and below-average returns on equity over the last seven years. Based on industry and company fundamentals, we believe that the shares will at best perform in line with the market over the long term.

Key Stock Statistics

S&P EPS Est. 1998	0.25	Tang. Bk. Value/Share	5.85
P/E on S&P Est. 1998	40.5	Beta	0.93
S&P EPS Est. 1999	0.45	Shareholders	1,800
Dividend Rate/Share	Nil	Market cap. (B)	$0.229
Shs. outstg. (M)	22.6	Inst. holdings	24%
Avg. daily vol. (M)	0.098		

Value of $10,000 invested 5 years ago: $ 11,911

Fiscal Year Ending Dec. 31

	1998	1997	1996	1995	1994	1993
Revenues (Million $)						
1Q	76.61	60.55	56.72	49.90	37.19	33.01
2Q	75.85	68.94	58.60	59.01	44.45	38.98
3Q	—	64.72	54.09	62.83	46.70	38.85
4Q	—	78.09	64.25	63.63	47.36	38.65
Yr.	—	272.3	233.7	235.4	175.7	149.5
Earnings Per Share ($)						
1Q	0.08	0.06	-0.05	0.10	0.06	0.01
2Q	0.01	0.17	-0.12	0.21	0.13	0.04
3Q	E0.07	0.07	-0.40	0.20	0.19	0.09
4Q	E0.09	0.10	0.06	0.03	0.15	0.05
Yr.	E0.25	0.40	-0.51	0.53	0.53	0.19

Next earnings report expected: mid October

Dividend Data

No cash dividends have been paid, and Trimble does not plan to pay any in the foreseeable future. Certain borrowing arrangements restrict the company's ability to pay cash dividends.

A Division of The McGraw-Hill Companies

STANDARD
&POOR'S

STOCK REPORTS

Trimble Navigation Limited

5459N
10-OCT-98

Business Summary - 14-AUG-98

Trimble Navigation Ltd. is a leader in emerging commercial markets for satellite-based navigation, positioning and communication data products using the NAVSTAR Global Positioning System (GPS). It designs, makes and markets electronic instruments to determine precise geographic location. The instruments, called GPS engines and systems, collect, analyze and display position data in forms optimized for a wide range of specific end-user applications. The market for GPS based products is expected to grow rapidly as new applications are developed.

TRMB follows a dual strategy to reach targeted markets. The company makes complete or partially integrated systems for high cost applications such as surveying and mapping, marine navigation and avionics. TRMB also sells GPS engines, chip sets embedded with software at the heart of the system, to makers of high volume, low cost applications, such as cellular and mobile computing platforms and car navigation systems. All products are derived from the same basic technology, but revenues are classified in three segments: commercial, software and component technologies, and aerospace.

The NAVSTAR system of 24 GPS satellites was established for use by the military, but is now available for use in commercial and civilian applications. TRMB's GPS engines are used in devices ranging from inexpensive hand-held receivers used by hikers, mountain climbers and boaters, to integration in complex aircraft navigation. TRMB's surveying products determine relative positions to accuracies down to one centimeter; marine, aviation and military navigation applications typically provide accuracy of a few meters.

TRMB sells to end-users through a network of dealers in over 60 countries. About half of revenues are derived from abroad. The company also has alliances with producers of electronic equipment that incorporate TRMB's GPS engines in their systems. Important alliances include Honeywell (commercial aircraft navigation), Pioneer, Philips, Xanavi and GM's Delco division (in-car navigation), and Microsoft (portable notebook computer mapping). These alliances are becoming more important as the market for GPS devices expands from expensive devices used in commercial applications to devices for high volume consumer electronics markets. The range of possible uses for GPS continues to expand, as new ideas are pursued by independent companies.

Segment revenues in recent years were:

	1997	1996	1995
Commercial systems	62%	68%	69%
Software & component technologies	16%	16%	15%
Aerospace	22%	16%	16%

Per Share Data ($)

(Year Ended Dec. 31)	1997	1996	1995	1994	1993	1992	1991	1990	1989	1988
Tangible Bk. Val.	5.95	5.42	5.96	2.83	2.12	1.66	2.82	2.41	0.51	0.15
Cash Flow	0.94	-0.05	0.91	0.93	0.59	-0.92	0.72	0.30	0.14	0.07
Earnings	0.40	-0.51	0.53	0.53	0.19	-1.37	0.40	0.14	0.04	NM
Dividends	Nil	Nil	Nil	Nil	Nil	Nil	Nil	Nil	Nil	Nil
Payout Ratio	Nil	Nil	Nil	Nil	Nil	Nil	Nil	Nil	Nil	Nil
Prices - High	24¼	26¼	35⅜	16¾	13½	18	19¼	11¾	NA	NA
- Low	10⅞	10⅞	14½	8⅝	7¼	6½	8¼	5¾	NA	NA
P/E Ratio - High	61	NM	67	32	71	NM	48	84	NA	NA
- Low	27	NM	27	16	38	NM	21	41	NA	NA

Income Statement Analysis (Million $)

	1997	1996	1995	1994	1993	1992	1991	1990	1989	1988
Revs.	272	234	235	176	149	128	151	63.0	32.0	20.0
Oper. Inc.	22.6	0.0	21.3	23.0	15.3	-7.5	15.4	5.3	2.8	1.4
Depr.	12.2	10.1	8.0	7.7	7.5	7.6	5.5	2.2	1.1	0.6
Int. Exp.	3.5	3.9	3.9	2.8	1.8	1.9	0.9	0.7	0.8	0.6
Pretax Inc.	11.6	-11.6	14.0	12.2	4.2	-23.7	8.9	2.8	0.9	0.2
Eff. Tax Rate	20%	NM	20%	18%	18%	NM	22%	25%	46%	85%
Net Inc.	9.3	-11.3	11.3	10.0	3.4	-23.0	7.0	2.1	0.5	0.0

Balance Sheet & Other Fin. Data (Million $)

	1997	1996	1995	1994	1993	1992	1991	1990	1989	1988
Cash	20.0	82.5	97.1	38.2	1.9	1.9	1.6	10.0	0.5	1.9
Curr. Assets	174	159	171	93.0	53.4	52.8	64.9	44.8	14.4	9.4
Total Assets	208	190	197	109	67.6	69.5	86.8	52.9	18.6	12.8
Curr. Liab.	37.5	34.9	35.5	22.8	NA	32.1	31.6	13.9	8.6	3.3
LT Debt	30.7	30.9	31.3	32.9	4.5	5.8	4.3	1.1	4.4	8.2
Common Eqty.	139	124	130	53.6	38.9	29.5	47.0	36.2	5.6	1.3
Total Cap.	170	155	161	86.5	43.4	35.3	51.2	37.3	10.0	9.5
Cap. Exp.	11.0	10.3	14.6	7.9	3.9	3.4	10.7	4.8	1.1	0.8
Cash Flow	21.5	-1.2	19.3	17.7	10.9	-15.4	12.5	4.3	1.6	0.6
Curr. Ratio	4.6	4.6	4.8	4.1	2.2	1.6	2.1	3.2	1.7	2.8
% LT Debt of Cap.	18.1	19.9	19.4	38.1	10.5	16.6	8.3	3.0	44.1	86.6
% Net Inc.of Revs.	3.4	NM	4.8	5.7	2.3	NM	4.6	3.4	1.6	0.2
% Ret. on Assets	4.7	NM	7.4	11.2	4.9	NM	9.7	5.5	3.2	0.3
% Ret. on Equity	7.0	NM	12.3	21.4	9.9	NM	16.3	9.8	14.5	2.6

Data as orig. reptd.; bef. results of disc. opers. and/or spec. items. Per share data adj. for stk. divs. as of ex-div. date. Bold denotes diluted EPS (FASB 128). E-Estimated. NA-Not Available. NM-Not Meaningful. NR-Not Ranked.

Office—645 North Mary Ave., Sunnyvale, CA 94086. **Tel**—(408) 481-8000. **Website**—http://www.trimble.com **Pres & CEO**—C. R. Trimble. **VP & CFO**—D. R. Ing. **Secy**—R. A. Trimble. **Investor Contact**—Barbara Hall. **Dirs**—R. S. Cooper, J. B. Goodrich, W. Hart, B. W. Parkinson, C. R. Trimble. **Transfer Agent & Registrar**—ChaseMellon Shareholder Services, SF. **Incorporated**—in California in 1981. **Empl**— 1,294. **S&P Analyst:** Robert E. Friedman, CPA

03-OCT-98

Industry:
Services (Advertising & Marketing)

Summary: This company became the sixth largest advertising company in the world through the late 1997 acquisition of Bozell, Jacobs, Kenyon and Eckhardt.

Quantitative Evaluations	
Outlook (1 Lowest—5 Highest)	• 4⁻
Fair Value	• 31⅞
Risk	• Average
Earn./Div. Rank	• B
Technical Eval.	• **Bullish** since 7/98
Rel. Strength Rank (1 Lowest—99 Highest)	• 44
Insider Activity	• NA

Recent Price • 22⅝
52 Wk Range • 34-21⅜

Yield • 2.6%
12-Mo. P/E • NM

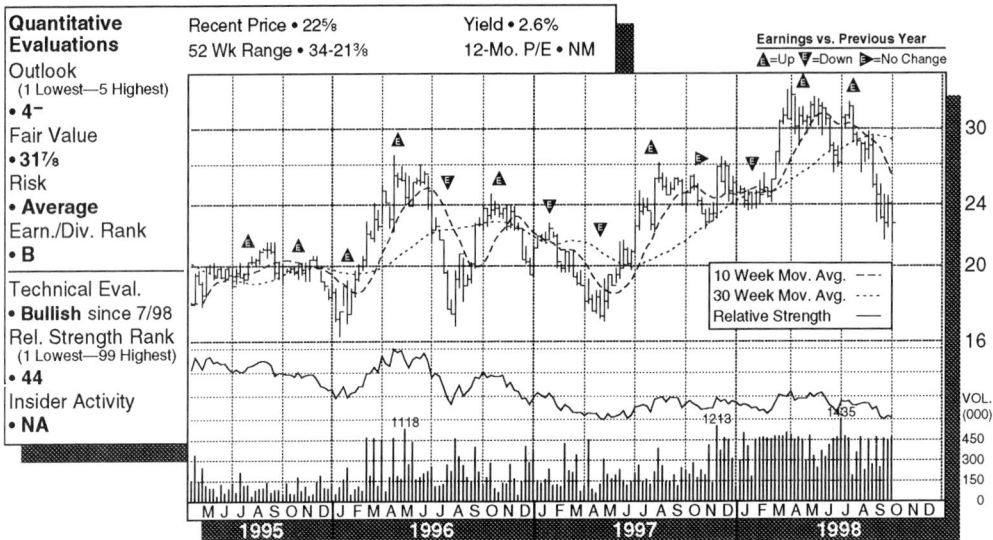

Earnings vs. Previous Year
▲=Up ▼=Down ▶=No Change

10 Week Mov. Avg. ---
30 Week Mov. Avg. ····
Relative Strength —

Business Profile - 03-JUN-98

True North nearly doubled in size with the late 1997 acquisition of Bozell, Jacobs, Kenyon and Eckhardt, Inc. (BJK&E) in exchange for 18.6 million shares. It became the sixth largest advertising company in the world, with more than $11.5 billion in billings, and 350 offices worldwide. In May 1998, the company noted that the integration of the Bozell organization into TNO had gone far more smoothly and more quickly than expected. The process reportedly has provided synergistic benefits, as demonstrated by margin improvement experienced in the first quarter; the company expects similar operating margin improvement in quarters to come.

Operational Review - 03-JUN-98

Revenues in the first quarter of 1998 rose 5.2% year to year (as restated for the Bozell acquisition), despite the loss of an account because of the Bozell transaction. Net income of $3,695,000 ($0.08 a share, on more shares) contrasted with a net loss of $980,000 ($0.02), which included a $6.9 million (pretax) non-recurring charge.

Stock Performance - 02-OCT-98

In the past 30 trading days, TNO's shares have declined 20%, compared to a 7% fall in the S&P 500. Average trading volume for the past five days was 119,740 shares, compared with the 40-day moving average of 89,469 shares.

Key Stock Statistics

Dividend Rate/Share	0.60	Shareholders	7,300
Shs. outstg. (M)	44.7	Market cap. (B)	$ 1.0
Avg. daily vol. (M)	0.097	Inst. holdings	44%
Tang. Bk. Value/Share	NM		
Beta	0.90		

Value of $10,000 invested 5 years ago: $ 16,992

Fiscal Year Ending Dec. 31

	1998	1997	1996	1995	1994	1993
Revenues (Million $)						
1Q	280.1	266.2	105.9	95.39	88.36	79.20
2Q	311.5	301.3	118.4	110.9	102.1	93.70
3Q	—	294.4	125.8	108.7	100.5	96.34
4Q	—	343.0	142.9	124.2	112.8	103.4
Yr.	—	1,205	493.1	439.1	403.7	372.7
Earnings Per Share ($)						
1Q	**0.08**	-0.02	-0.03	-0.49	0.09	0.07
2Q	**0.38**	0.33	0.26	0.51	0.46	0.40
3Q	—	0.22	0.26	0.19	0.18	0.15
4Q	—	-1.73	0.71	0.67	0.63	0.53
Yr.	—	-1.17	1.20	0.87	1.34	1.15

Next earnings report expected: NA

Dividend Data (Dividends have been paid since 1963.)

Amount ($)	Date Decl.	Ex-Div. Date	Stock of Record	Payment Date
0.150	Nov. 12	Dec. 17	Dec. 19	Jan. 02 '98
0.150	Mar. 04	Mar. 16	Mar. 18	Apr. 01 '98
0.150	May. 13	Jun. 15	Jun. 17	Jul. 01 '98
0.150	Jul. 29	Sep. 15	Sep. 17	Oct. 01 '98

A Division of The **McGraw-Hill** Companies

Business Summary - 03-JUN-98

In December 1994, True North Communications Inc. succeededFoote, Cone & Belding Communications, Inc. as the holding company for Foote, Cone & Belding, one of America's largest advertising agencies. In December 1997, through its merger with Bozell, Jacobs, Kenyon & Eckhardt, Inc., the company nearly doubled its size by adding Bozell Worldwide, Temerlin McClain and other specialized communications businesses to its network. With these brands as the foundation, TNO is building a new type of architecture to offer clients leverageable marketplace advantage.

True North offers full-service advertising through two separate, independent global agency networks: FCB Worldwide and Bozell Worldwide. The company also operates two significant independent regional full-service agencies, Temerlin McClain and Tierney & Partners. In addition, TNO owns certain marketingservice and specialty advertising companies through the True North Diversified Services Companies, and certain interactive marketing companies through True North Technologies Inc.

FCB Worldwide and Bozell Worldwide, by themselves and through their respective subsidiaries and affiliates, independently operate advertising agency networks worldwide. Their primary business is to create market-

ing communications for their clients' goods and services across the total spectrum of advertising and promotion media. Each of the agency networks has its own clients and competes with the other in the same markets.

True North Diversified Services Companies offer a wide variety of marketing and specialty advertising services. Marketing services include: promotion, public relations, public affairs, direct/database marketing, branding consultancy, graphic arts, sports marketing and directory advertising. Specialty advertising includes health care and multicultural advertising. True North Diversified Services Companies have both U.S. and international operations, including BSMG Worldwide, Wahlstrom, Bozell Wellness Worldwide, Market Growth Resources, and McCracken Brooks.

Through planned acquisitions and internal growth, True North believes that it has become a communications company encompassing resources much broader in scope than other existing advertising holding companies. True North considers its architecture unique, with three specialized business units: TN Technologies Inc., a leader in global interactive marketing; TN Media Inc., a global network of the company's specialists in the planning and buying of media time and space (one of the largest media buying companies in the world); and TN Services Inc., established to house all TNO's agency support services around the globe.

Per Share Data ($)

(Year Ended Dec. 31)	1997	1996	1995	1994	1993	1992	1991	1990	1989	1988
Tangible Bk. Val.	NM	3.79	5.87	6.65	6.46	6.24	5.44	6.13	5.69	3.63
Cash Flow	-0.06	2.01	1.66	1.99	1.81	1.46	-0.20	1.71	1.57	1.72
Earnings	-1.17	1.20	0.87	1.34	1.15	0.83	-0.91	1.05	0.97	0.81
Dividends	0.60	0.60	0.60	0.60	0.60	0.60	0.60	0.60	0.60	0.61
Payout Ratio	NM	50%	69%	45%	54%	77%	NM	61%	65%	6%
Prices - High	27⅝	27¾	21⅞	24	24	15¾	13¾	15⅛	16	14
- Low	17	16¼	15¾	19⅞	14¾	11½	9⅜	8⅞	11¼	10½
P/E Ratio - High	NM	23	25	18	21	18	NM	14	16	17
- Low	NM	14	18	15	13	13	NM	8	12	13

Income Statement Analysis (Million $)

	1997	1996	1995	1994	1993	1992	1991	1990	1989	1988
Revs.	1,205	493	439	404	373	353	342	338	326	386
Oper. Inc.	91.9	42.7	48.0	51.9	47.9	39.9	35.4	42.8	41.4	38.5
Depr.	47.5	19.0	17.8	14.9	14.9	13.7	14.8	13.4	12.1	15.6
Int. Exp.	20.1	8.6	8.1	7.0	9.4	6.7	9.4	9.7	14.4	20.7
Pretax Inc.	-36.4	19.2	14.8	46.2	32.8	29.3	-16.5	34.4	32.9	21.2
Eff. Tax Rate	NM	50%	16%	35%	20%	37%	NM	36%	38%	35%
Net Inc.	-50.0	27.8	19.7	30.3	25.7	18.0	-19.1	21.6	19.6	13.7

Balance Sheet & Other Fin. Data (Million $)

	1997	1996	1995	1994	1993	1992	1991	1990	1989	1988
Cash	109	57.0	57.0	77.0	65.0	45.0	63.0	69.0	111	146
Curr. Assets	998	504	430	383	355	320	326	365	398	451
Total Assets	1,674	932	766	674	638	589	591	648	658	603
Curr. Liab.	1,232	553	476	400	341	315	326	376	394	423
LT Debt	35.9	31.5	5.4	5.5	35.4	31.3	37.2	43.1	43.3	18.6
Common Eqty.	331	241	222	208	200	183	163	191	178	129
Total Cap.	304	273	229	221	241	217	207	242	238	153
Cap. Exp.	42.4	17.7	9.0	9.7	9.0	8.2	9.8	14.9	20.0	16.3
Cash Flow	-2.5	46.8	37.4	45.2	40.6	31.7	-4.4	35.1	31.7	29.4
Curr. Ratio	0.8	0.9	0.9	1.0	1.0	1.0	1.0	1.0	1.0	1.1
% LT Debt of Cap.	11.8	11.5	2.4	2.5	14.7	14.4	18.0	17.8	18.1	12.2
% Net Inc.of Revs.	NM	5.6	4.5	7.5	6.9	5.1	NM	6.4	6.0	3.6
% Ret. on Assets	NM	3.3	5.2	4.7	4.2	3.0	NM	3.3	2.8	2.3
% Ret. on Equity	NM	12.0	9.1	15.0	13.4	10.3	NM	11.6	11.6	10.6

Data as orig. reptd.; bef. results of disc. opers. and/or spec. items. Per share data adj. for stk. divs. as of ex-div. date. Bold denotes diluted EPS (FASB 128). E-Estimated. NA-Not Available. NM-Not Meaningful. NR-Not Ranked.

Office—101 East Erie St., Chicago, IL 60611-2897. **Tel**—(312) 425-6500.**Chrmn**—R. S. Braddock. **CEO**—B. Mason. **Pres**—C. D. Peebler Jr. **EVP & CFO**—D. L. Seeley. **SVP & Secy**—D. F. Perona. **Dirs**—D. A. Bell, R. S. Braddock, D. M. Elliman, W. G. Gregory, L-A. Kelmenson, B. Mason, R. P. Mayer, M. E. Murphy, C. D. Peebler Jr., J. B. Ryan, S. T. Vehslage. **Transfer Agent & Registrar**—First Chicago Trust Co. of New York, Jersey City, NJ. **Incorporated**—in Delaware in 1942. **Empl**— 10,000. **S&P Analyst:** C.F.B.

TrustCo Bank Corp NY　5462S

NASDAQ Symbol **TRST**

In S&P SmallCap 600

03-OCT-98

Industry:
Banks (Regional)

Summary: Through its Trustco Bank subsidiary, this bank holding company operates more than 50 branch offices in the upstate region of New York.

Quantitative Evaluations		
Outlook (1 Lowest—5 Highest)	Recent Price • 27¾	Yield • 4.0%
• **2**	52 Wk Range • 31¼-22⅛	12-Mo. P/E • 20.0
Fair Value		
• **29¼**		
Risk		
• **NA**		
Earn./Div. Rank		
• **NR**		
Technical Eval.		
• **NA**		
Rel. Strength Rank (1 Lowest—99 Highest)		
• **77**		
Insider Activity		
• **Neutral**		

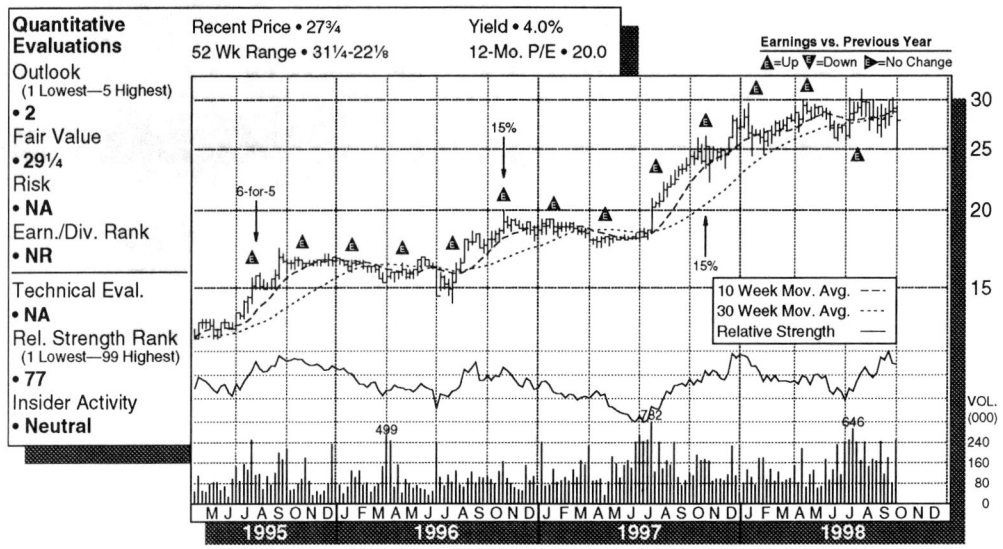

Earnings vs. Previous Year
▲=Up ▼=Down ▶=No Change

10 Week Mov. Avg. – – –
30 Week Mov. Avg. · · · ·
Relative Strength ——

VOL. (000)

Business Profile - 17-AUG-98

The company recently noted that the upstate New York region is experiencing continued consolidation of the banking industry, with more and more community-based banks being acquired by out of state banks. TrustCo believes that it is well positioned to take advantage of the inevitable disruption to customers that occurs during periods of consolidation. During 1997, the company opened three new branches. Plans call for opening two to three new branches a year until the company believes it has filled gaps in its market territory.

Operational Review - 17-AUG-98

Net interest income in the first half of 1998 rose 1.2%, year to year, aided by an increase in earning assets. The provision for loan losses increased 22%, to $2.9 million. Noninterest income climbed 35%, and with only a fractional rise in noninterest expense, pretax income gained 10%. After taxes at 37.2%, versus 37.4%, net income was also up 10%, to $17,044,000 ($0.70 a share) from $15,446,000 ($0.64).

Stock Performance - 02-OCT-98

In the past 30 trading days, TRST's shares have declined 1%, compared to a 7% fall in the S&P 500. Average trading volume for the past five days was 66,780 shares, compared with the 40-day moving average of 37,733 shares.

Key Stock Statistics

Dividend Rate/Share	1.10	Shareholders	NA
Shs. outstg. (M)	23.3	Market cap. (B)	$0.646
Avg. daily vol. (M)	0.038	Inst. holdings	22%
Tang. Bk. Value/Share	7.89		
Beta	0.32		

Value of $10,000 invested 5 years ago: $ 36,612

Fiscal Year Ending Dec. 31

	1998	1997	1996	1995	1994	1993
Revenues (Million $)						
1Q	47.96	45.43	44.64	41.55	35.19	—
2Q	49.16	46.67	42.85	43.95	34.32	—
3Q	—	47.97	44.00	45.15	37.05	—
4Q	—	49.15	45.48	44.97	—	—
Yr.	—	189.2	177.0	175.6	144.8	152.8
Earnings Per Share ($)						
1Q	**0.34**	0.31	0.28	0.25	0.22	—
2Q	**0.36**	0.33	0.29	0.28	0.23	—
3Q	—	0.35	0.31	0.27	0.25	—
4Q	—	0.34	0.31	0.29	0.26	—
Yr.	—	**1.33**	**1.20**	1.07	0.97	1.00

Next earnings report expected: early November

Dividend Data (Dividends have been paid since 1982.)

Amount ($)	Date Decl.	Ex-Div. Date	Stock of Record	Payment Date
0.275	Feb. 17	Mar. 11	Mar. 13	Apr. 01 '98
0.275	May. 19	Jun. 10	Jun. 12	Jul. 01 '98
0.275	Aug. 18	Sep. 09	Sep. 11	Oct. 01 '98
15%	Aug. 18	Oct. 21	Oct. 23	Nov. 13 '98

*A Division of The **McGraw·Hill** Companies*

STANDARD
&POOR'S
STOCK REPORTS

TrustCo Bank Corp NY

5462S

03-OCT-98

Business Summary - 17-AUG-98

Operating mainly through its Trustco Bank subsidiary, TrustCo Bank Corp NY has 51 bank offices in Albany, Columbia, Greene, Rensselaer, Saratoga, Schenectady, Warren and Washington counties of New York. It also operates a full service trust department with $1.17 billion of assets under management. Trustco Bank operates a general commercial banking business serving individuals, partnerships, corporations, municipalities and governments of New York. The company has distinguished itself in the upstate New York region as one of the principal originators of residential real estate mortgage loans.

Total loans of $1.30 billion at December 31, 1997, versus $1.24 billion a year earlier, were divided as follows:

	1997	1996
Commercial	14%	17%
Construction	1%	1%
Residential mortgage	70%	64%
Home equity credit line	13%	15%
Installment	2%	3%

The allowance for loan losses, which is set aside for possible loan defaults, was $53.5 million (4.12% of loans) at 1997 year end, up from $51.6 million (4.15%)

a year earlier. Net chargeoffs, or the amount of loans actually written off as uncollectible, were $3.5 million (0.28% of average loans) in 1997, versus $3.3 million (0.27%) in 1996. Nonperforming assets, consisting of loans in nonaccrual status, loans past due three payments or more, restructured loans and foreclosed real estate, amounted to $20.0 million (0.84% of total assets) at the end of 1997, down from $20.6 million (0.91%) a year earlier.

Interest and fees on loans provided 58% of total income in 1997, interest and dividends on investment securities 24%, other interest income 9%, trust department income 3%, service fees 4% and other noninterest income 2%.

Deposits of $2.02 billion at the end of 1997 were divided: demand deposits 6%, savings deposits 32%, checking account deposits 12%, money market deposits 3% and time deposits 47%.

The average yield on interest-earning assets was 7.95% in 1997 (7.93% in 1996), while the average rate paid on interest-bearing liabilities was 4.38% (4.28%), for a net spread of 3.57% (3.65%).

The bank's trust department serves as executor of estates and trustee of personal trusts, provides estate planning and related advice, provides custodial services and acts as trustee for various employee benefit plans and corporate pension and profit sharing trusts.

Per Share Data ($)

(Year Ended Dec. 31)	1997	1996	1995	1994	1993	1992	1991	1990	1989	1988
Tangible Bk. Val.	7.64	6.93	6.86	6.00	NA	NA	NA	NA	NA	NA
Earnings	1.33	1.19	1.06	0.97	1.00	NA	NA	NA	NA	NA
Dividends	0.99	0.83	0.72	0.58	0.47	NA	NA	NA	NA	NA
Payout Ratio	1%	1%	1%	1%	0%	NA	NA	NA	NA	NA
Prices - High	29	20	17³/₈	13¹/₂	13	NA	NA	NA	6¹/₄	5¹/₈
- Low	17³/₈	14¹/₈	11¹/₂	10¹/₂	12	NA	NA	NA	4⁷/₈	3⁷/₈
P/E Ratio - High	22	16	16	14	13	NA	NA	NA	NA	NA
- Low	13	11	10	10	12	NA	NA	NA	NA	NA

Income Statement Analysis (Million $)

	1997	1996	1995	1994	1993	1992	1991	1990	1989	1988
Net Int. Inc.	85.5	84.3	81.4	79.6	72.0	66.9	42.6	33.1	31.5	28.6
Tax Equiv. Adj.	88.7	87.0	83.0	NA	NA	NA	NA	NA	NA	NA
Non Int. Inc.	17.4	14.8	13.8	13.4	13.0	12.5	9.4	7.7	7.8	6.0
Loan Loss Prov.	5.4	6.6	12.7	8.1	11.6	12.7	6.5	2.7	2.1	2.6
Exp./Op. Revs.	45%	42%	47%	44%	51%	54%	54%	54%	59%	60%
Pretax Inc.	51.1	46.0	38.3	35.5	36.1	26.8	17.7	14.2	12.8	10.5
Eff. Tax Rate	37%	38%	33%	36%	35%	35%	27%	26%	26%	26%
Net Inc.	32.2	28.7	25.5	22.9	23.6	17.5	12.9	10.6	9.4	7.8
% Net Int. Marg.	4.02	4.07	4.18	4.25	NA	NA	NA	NA	NA	NA

Balance Sheet & Other Fin. Data (Million $)

	1997	1996	1995	1994	1993	1992	1991	1990	1989	1988
Earning Assets:										
Money Mkt	438	356	NA	NA	NA	NA	NA	NA	NA	NA
Inv. Securities	602	619	NA	NA	NA	NA	NA	NA	NA	NA
Com'l Loans	192	224	NA	NA	NA	NA	NA	NA	NA	NA
Other Loans	1,108	1,019	NA	NA	NA	NA	NA	NA	NA	NA
Total Assets	2,372	2,262	2,176	1,976	1,971	1,945	1,758	935	819	769
Demand Deposits	130	124	NA	NA	NA	NA	NA	NA	NA	NA
Time Deposits	1,891	1,953	NA	NA	NA	NA	NA	NA	NA	NA
LT Debt	Nil	Nil	Nil	Nil	Nil	Nil	Nil	Nil	Nil	Nil
Common Eqty.	179	162	160	139	130	120	111	60.2	53.4	47.2
% Ret. on Assets	1.4	1.3	1.2	1.2	1.2	0.9	1.0	1.2	1.2	1.1
% Ret. on Equity	18.9	17.8	17.1	17.0	18.9	15.1	15.0	18.6	18.8	17.6
% Loan Loss Resv.	4.1	4.2	3.9	3.4	3.2	2.6	1.9	2.9	2.6	2.5
% Loans/Deposits	64.2	63.6	63.5	64.4	59.1	58.1	65.4	59.0	61.0	58.4
% Equity to Assets	7.4	7.3	7.2	6.8	6.4	6.3	6.4	6.5	6.3	6.2

Data as orig. reptd.; bef. results of disc opers. and/or spec. items. Per share data adj. for stk. divs. as of ex-div. date. Bold denotes diluted EPS (FASB 128). E-Estimated. NA-Not Available. NM-Not Meaningful. NR-Not Ranked.

Office—192 Erie Blvd., Schenectady, NY 12305. **Tel**—(518) 377-3311. **Pres & CEO**—R. A. McCormick. **VP & CFO**—R. T. Cushing. **Secy**—W. F. Terry. **Dirs**—B. A. Andreoli, L. O. Barthold, M. N. Brickman, R. A. McCormick, N. A. McNamara, A. J. Marinello, J. S. Morris, J. H. Murphy, R. J. Murray, Jr., K. C. Peterson, W. D. Powers, W. J. Purdy, W. F. Terry. **Transfer Agent & Registrar**—TrustCo Bank, Schenectady. **Incorporated**—in New York in 1981. **Empl**— 459. **S&P Analyst:** Stephen R. Biggar

Tuboscope Inc. 2257K

NYSE Symbol **TBI**

In S&P SmallCap 600

03-OCT-98

Industry:
Oil & Gas (Drilling & Equipment)

Summary: This company is the world's leading provider of oilfield tubular inspection and coating services; coiled tubing equipment; solids control services; and inspection equipment.

Quantitative Evaluations	
Outlook (1 Lowest—5 Highest)	• **4⁻**
Fair Value	• **14¼**
Risk	• **Average**
Earn./Div. Rank	• **NR**
Technical Eval.	• **NA**
Rel. Strength Rank (1 Lowest—99 Highest)	• **23**
Insider Activity	• **Neutral**

Recent Price • 10½
52 Wk Range • 36-9
Yield • Nil
12-Mo. P/E • 8.3

Earnings vs. Previous Year
▲=Up ▼=Down ▶=No Change

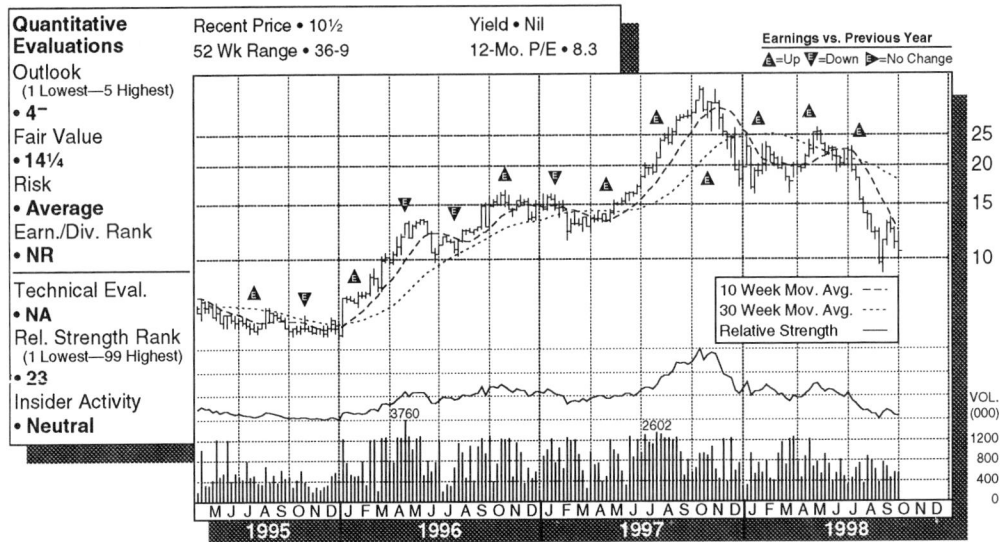

10 Week Mov. Avg. – – –
30 Week Mov. Avg. ·····
Relative Strength ——

Business Profile - 27-APR-98

TBI has rapidly expanded its business through acquisitions. Revenues and earnings benefited significantly in 1997 from the many acquisitions. In 1997, a total of 10 acquisitions and two equity investments were completed. Management believes that acquisitions should be accretive to earnings immediately. The company is consolidating its sectors, while adding additional products to its franchise. In February 1998, TBI raised $100 million through the sale of 7.5% senior notes. Also during the first quarter of 1998, the company acquired Baytron, Inc. in order to strengthen its position in the rig instrumentation market. With the acquisition, TBI has rig instrumentation equipment on more than 100 offshore drilling rigs in the Gulf of Mexico.

Operational Review - 27-APR-98

Revenues in the three months ended March 31, 1998, advanced 42%, year to year, reflecting acquisitions in 1996 and 1997, and internal growth. Margins widened, as operating expenses grew less rapidly; operating income climbed 54%. With a 24% increase in interest expense, and after taxes at 37.5%, versus 39.0%, net income soared 66%, to $14,233,000 ($0.30 a share, on 4.4% more shares), from $8,598,000 ($0.19).

Stock Performance - 02-OCT-98

In the past 30 trading days, TBI's shares have declined 13%, compared to a 7% fall in the S&P 500. Average trading volume for the past five days was 105,340 shares, compared with the 40-day moving average of 120,038 shares.

Key Stock Statistics

Dividend Rate/Share	Nil	Shareholders	300
Shs. outstg. (M)	45.4	Market cap. (B)	$0.480
Avg. daily vol. (M)	0.114	Inst. holdings	36%
Tang. Bk. Value/Share	2.25		
Beta	1.10		

Value of $10,000 invested 5 years ago: $ 17,603

Fiscal Year Ending Dec. 31

	1998	1997	1996	1995	1994	1993
Revenues (Million $)						
1Q	150.2	105.5	47.02	43.69	45.53	39.79
2Q	153.5	126.0	94.64	45.65	45.24	45.21
3Q	—	141.4	94.67	47.07	49.45	48.78
4Q	—	152.3	105.1	53.61	51.95	49.56
Yr.	—	525.2	341.4	190.0	192.2	183.3
Earnings Per Share ($)						
1Q	0.30	0.19	-2.97	0.05	0.05	0.03
2Q	0.31	0.28	-0.02	0.09	0.07	0.02
3Q	—	0.32	0.16	0.10	0.11	-0.61
4Q	—	0.34	0.15	0.20	0.18	0.08
Yr.	—	1.14	-1.17	0.44	0.41	-0.49

Next earnings report expected: late October

Dividend Data

No cash dividends have been paid on the common shares.

Business Summary - 27-APR-98

Tuboscope Inc. (TBI) provides specialized services and products to the oil and gas industry worldwide. The company offers four product lines, including tubular services, which provides internal coating products and services, and inspection and quality assurance services for tubular goods and fiberglass tubulars, used primarily in oil and gas operations; solids control products and services, which consists of the sale and rental of technical equipment used in oil and gas drilling processes; coiled tubing and pressure control products, which includes highly engineered coiled tubing, pressure control, wireline and related tools to companies providing oil and gas well drilling, completion and remediation services; and pipeline and other industrial services, which includes technical inspection services and quality assurance for in-service pipelines used to transport oil and gas.

Tuboscope is successor to one of the first companies to provide tubular inspection services to the oil and gas industry, with operations dating back to 1937. The company has since expanded its product line through mergers and acquisitions, and entered the coiled tubing and pressure control products businesses in April 1996 through its merger with D.O.S., Ltd., the largest provider of solids control services and coiled tubing equipment worldwide.

Tubular services is the largest business line, accounting for 43% of total revenues in 1997 (51% in 1996 and 81% in 1995). The company provides tubular inspection services at drilling and workover rig locations, at pipe yards owned by its customers, at steel mills making tubular goods, and at facilities which it owns. TBI entered the fiberglass tubular market on March 7, 1997 with the acquisition of Fiber Glass Systems, Inc. The company believes that it is the largest provider of tubular inspection and internal tubular coating services worldwide.

The company also believes that it is the world's leading maker and provider of solids control equipment and services (30% of revenues in 1997) to the oil and natural gas drilling industry. Management believes market conditions are improving in solids control due to strong demand by oil and gas drillers to reduce overall drilling costs and minimize environmental impact.

Coiled tubing and pressure products (16% of revenues) includes capital equipment and consumables sold to all the major oilfield coiled tubing service companies. The company believes that advances in the manufacturing process of coiled tubing, tubing fatigue protection and the capability to make larger diameter coiled tubing strings have resulted in increased uses and applications for these products.

Management feels there are growth opportunities for TBI's pipeline services, reflecting the aging of the worldwide pipeline network, and new pipeline construction. An extensive pipeline infrastructure in Eastern Europe is also expected to contribute to future growth in this area.

Per Share Data ($)

(Year Ended Dec. 31)	1997	1996	1995	1994	1993	1992	1991	1990	1989	1988
Tangible Bk. Val.	1.68	1.54	2.39	6.14	5.72	1.83	1.78	3.15	3.56	NA
Cash Flow	1.69	-0.70	1.25	1.03	0.10	0.70	0.89	0.87	0.63	0.96
Earnings	1.14	-1.17	0.44	0.41	-0.49	0.15	0.35	0.34	0.08	0.09
Dividends	Nil	Nil	Nil	Nil	Nil	Nil	Nil	Nil	Nil	Nil
Payout Ratio	Nil	Nil	Nil	Nil	Nil	Nil	Nil	Nil	Nil	Nil
Prices - High	36	16³/₄	8¹/₂	8	10¹/₄	8¹/₄	10	11¹/₂	NA	NA
- Low	11¹/₂	5⁵/₈	5⁵/₈	4¹/₂	5³/₄	4¹/₂	6³/₈	6	NA	NA
P/E Ratio - High	32	NM	19	20	NM	55	29	34	NA	NA
- Low	10	NM	13	11	NM	30	18	18	NA	NA

Income Statement Analysis (Million $)

	1997	1996	1995	1994	1993	1992	1991	1990	1989	1988
Revs.	525	341	190	192	183	165	152	128	108	84.0
Oper. Inc.	127	61.6	42.5	38.4	26.5	27.1	28.8	24.0	18.4	18.9
Depr.	26.1	17.6	15.0	11.4	10.8	9.9	6.9	5.4	6.4	4.4
Int. Exp.	14.5	13.4	12.3	12.9	11.4	12.6	11.3	12.0	9.4	10.0
Pretax Inc.	85.6	-34.9	15.0	15.0	-9.9	5.3	7.5	6.4	1.9	3.8
Eff. Tax Rate	37%	NM	42%	40%	NM	19%	37%	38%	48%	55%
Net Inc.	53.1	-43.2	8.8	8.3	-8.4	3.5	4.5	4.0	1.0	1.7

Balance Sheet & Other Fin. Data (Million $)

	1997	1996	1995	1994	1993	1992	1991	1990	1989	1988
Cash	12.6	10.4	9.4	8.5	2.5	5.3	32.9	4.2	7.3	4.4
Curr. Assets	248	166	85.0	81.0	72.3	66.3	95.1	46.8	41.9	40.7
Total Assets	686	505	307	317	310	300	327	191	173	175
Curr. Liab.	166	91.8	40.1	45.1	67.0	38.1	45.3	19.6	20.0	19.7
LT Debt	188	168	107	124	101	101	118	82.0	69.0	116
Common Eqty.	300	219	121	113	105	120	115	70.0	66.0	1.4
Total Cap.	510	402	255	261	229	250	268	172	153	139
Cap. Exp.	35.2	18.6	7.6	7.5	20.2	5.3	39.2	9.3	2.5	2.2
Cash Flow	79.2	-25.6	23.2	18.9	1.8	12.7	11.3	8.9	7.4	4.8
Curr. Ratio	1.5	1.8	2.1	1.8	1.1	1.7	2.1	2.4	2.1	2.1
% LT Debt of Cap.	36.8	41.8	42.0	47.5	44.3	40.6	44.1	47.8	44.7	83.5
% Net Inc.of Revs.	10.1	NM	4.7	4.3	NM	2.1	3.0	3.1	0.9	2.0
% Ret. on Assets	8.9	NM	2.9	2.6	NM	1.1	1.5	0.9	0.6	NA
% Ret. on Equity	20.5	NM	7.0	6.9	NM	2.4	4.1	NM	2.9	NA

Data as orig. reptd.; bef. results of disc. opers. and/or spec. items. Per share data adj. for stk. divs. as of ex-div. date. Bold denotes diluted EPS (FASB 128). E-Estimated. NA-Not Available. NM-Not Meaningful. NR-Not Ranked.

Office—2835 Holmes Rd., Houston, TX 77051; P.O. Box 808, Houston, TX 77001. **Tel**—(713) 799-5100. **Chrmn**—L. E. Simmons. **Pres & CEO**—J. Lauletta. **EVP, Treas & CFO**—J. Winkler. **Investor Contact**—Clay C. Williams. **Dirs**—J. R. Baier, J. F. Lauletta, E. L. Mattson, L. E. Simmons, J. Smisek, D. E. Swanson. **Transfer Agent & Registrar**—Chase Shareholder Services Group, Inc., Dallas. **Incorporated**—in Delaware in 1988. **Empl**— 4,598. **S&P Analyst:** C.C.P.

STANDARD &POOR'S
STOCK REPORTS

Tultex Corp.

2260

NYSE Symbol **TTX**

In S&P SmallCap 600

03-OCT-98

Industry: Textiles (Apparel)

Summary: This company makes fleece and jersey knit activewear and licensed sports apparel for the physical fitness and leisure time markets.

Quantitative Evaluations

Outlook
(1 Lowest—5 Highest)
• **5**

Fair Value
• **3½**

Risk
• **Average**

Earn./Div. Rank
• **B-**

Technical Eval.
• **Neutral** since 10/97

Rel. Strength Rank
(1 Lowest—99 Highest)
• **19**

Insider Activity
• **Favorable**

Recent Price • 1⅝
52 Wk Range • 5¾-1½

Yield • Nil
12-Mo. P/E • NM

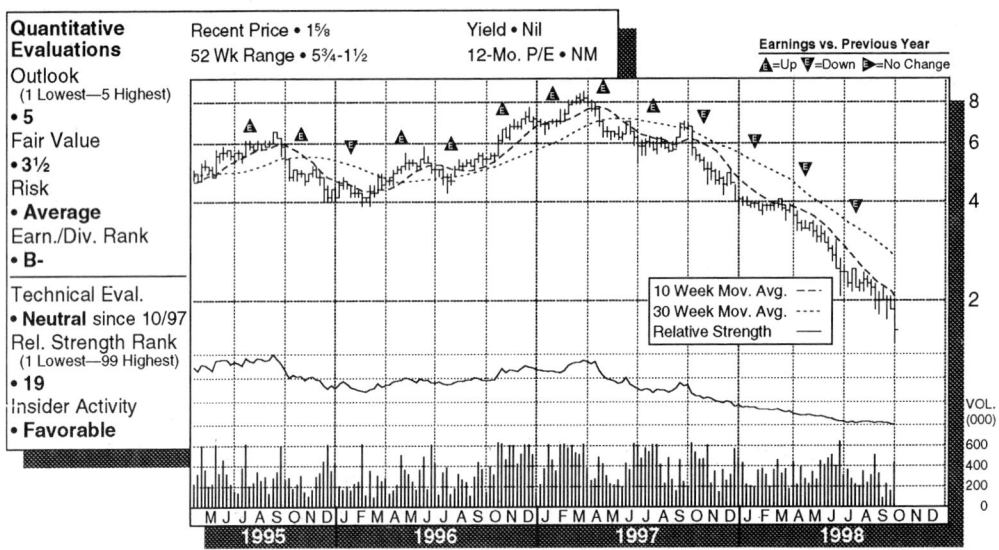

Earnings vs. Previous Year
▲=Up ▼=Down ▶=No Change

10 Week Mov. Avg. ----
30 Week Mov. Avg. ---
Relative Strength —

VOL. (000)

1995 1996 1997 1998

Business Profile - 05-AUG-98

In in effort to improve its cost structure, TTX initiated a number of strategies in the fourth quarter of 1997. The company closed two domestic sewing plants in order to increase sewing operations outside the U.S. Two distribution warehouses were shut down, staff was reduced, and an on-line major capital project was initiated to improve fabric manufacturing efficiencies and yields. At the end of 1997, inventories for fleece and jackets were down from the year-earlier level; T-shirt inventories were up as planned to service distributors' customers in the first half of 1998. TTX believes that its recent implementation of new strategies, including its migration to non-U.S. locations, will reduce its cost structure and enhance operating results and improve results in 1998. In July 1998, the company sold LogoAthletic Inc. and Logo Athletic/Headwear Inc., its licensed apparel subsidiaries, to an investor group led by management, for $84 million in cash and $12.5 million in debt. As a result of the sale, TTX reduced its debt by $77 million; plans call for the further reduction of debt. TTX now plans to focus on its Discus Athletic, Track Gear, distributor and core activewear businesses.

Operational Review - 05-AUG-98

Based on a brief report, net sales in the six months ended July 4, 1998, fell 5.9%, year to year. The net loss widened significantly to $20,387,000 ($0.69 a share), from $3,387,000 ($0.13).

Stock Performance - 02-OCT-98

In the past 30 trading days, TTX's shares have declined 26%, compared to a 7% fall in the S&P 500. Average trading volume for the past five days was 85,380 shares, compared with the 40-day moving average of 57,867 shares.

Key Stock Statistics

Dividend Rate/Share	Nil	Shareholders	2,600
Shs. outstg. (M)	29.9	Market cap. (B)	$0.049
Avg. daily vol. (M)	0.046	Inst. holdings	33%
Tang. Bk. Value/Share	3.92		
Beta	0.52		

Value of $10,000 invested 5 years ago: $ 1,977

Fiscal Year Ending Dec. 31

	1998	1997	1996	1995	1994	1993
Revenues (Million $)						
1Q	100.3	99.6	95.30	84.14	86.29	91.02
2Q	132.9	148.1	138.2	121.0	101.9	100.2
3Q	—	229.7	215.4	207.9	208.9	187.1
4Q	—	173.2	187.4	172.3	168.3	155.2
Yr.	—	650.6	636.3	585.3	565.4	533.6
Earnings Per Share ($)						
1Q	**-0.23**	-0.15	-0.19	-0.27	-0.18	-0.06
2Q	**-0.46**	0.02	0.01	-0.01	-0.11	0.01
3Q	—	0.23	0.43	0.30	0.24	0.15
4Q	—	-0.29	0.28	0.13	0.31	0.06
Yr.	—	**-0.19**	0.53	0.15	0.26	0.16

Next earnings report expected: late October

Dividend Data

Prior to omission in May 1994, dividends on the common had been paid since 1952. A shareholder rights plan was adopted in 1990.

A Division of The McGraw-Hill Companies

Business Summary - 05-AUG-98

With superstar football quarterbacks such as Troy Aikman of the Dallas Cowboys, John Elway of the Denver Broncos, Bruce Smith of the Buffalo Bills, and Dan Marino of the Miami Dolphins on its team, Tultex (TTX) is aggressively promoting its licensed sports apparel. The company is one of the world's largest manufacturers of activewear and licensed sports apparel for consumers and sports enthusiasts, with a product line including fleeced sweats, jersey products, and jackets and hats.

Products are sold under the company's own brands, led by the Discus Athletic and Logo Athletic premium labels, and under private labels, including Nike, Reebok and Pro Spirit. In addition, TTX has several professional and college sports licenses to make embroidered and screen-printed products with team logos and designs under its Logo Athletic, Logo 7 and TrackGear brands. The company is a licensee of professional sports apparel, holding licenses from the National Football League, Major League Baseball, the National Basketball Association, the National Hockey League and the National Association of Stock Car Auto Racing to manufacture a full range of sports apparel for adults and children. The promotion of the Logo Athletic brand of licensed apparel through advertising, as well as promotional arrangements featuring several professional teams, has helped to increase the visibility and sales of Logo Athletic.

Tultex has also strengthened its product line in its ac-

tivewear segment through the development of branded and private label, higher-quality and higher-margin products to supplement its position in the lower-priced segment. TTX is developing its own brands, promoting Discus Athletic for its premium products, and using the Tultex label for the value-oriented and wholesale segment of the market.

The company's activewear business is vertically integrated, spinning 80% to 85% of the yarn it requires in three yarn plants located in North Carolina, and knitting, dyeing and cutting fabric and sewing finished goods in six plants in Virginia and North Carolina, one plant in Jamaica, and one plant in Mexico. Licensed sports apparel operations are conducted from plants in Indiana, Massachusetts and North Carolina.

Apparel is sold primarily to chain stores, department stores, sporting goods stores and mass merchandisers. Tultex also operates 10 outlet stores in North Carolina, Virginia and West Virginia, selling surplus company apparel and apparel items of other manufacturers, 20 The Sweatshirt Company retail stores in 14 states selling first quality TTX products and three LogoAthletic stores in Indiana and Utah, which sell surplus licensed apparel.

In July 1998, the company sold LogoAthletic Inc. and Logo Athletic/Headwear Inc., its licensed apparel subsidiaries, to a management-led investor group for $84 million in cash and $12.5 million in debt. TTX now plans to focus on its Discus Athletic, Track Gear, distributor and core activewear businesses.

Per Share Data ($)

(Year Ended Dec. 31)	1997	1996	1995	1994	1993	1992	1991	1990	1989	1988
Tangible Bk. Val.	4.75	5.57	4.97	5.33	5.10	5.04	5.37	5.33	4.75	5.03
Cash Flow	0.50	1.25	0.96	1.14	1.01	1.32	0.88	1.38	0.69	1.21
Earnings	-0.19	0.53	0.15	0.26	0.16	0.56	0.26	0.85	0.18	0.77
Dividends	Nil	Nil	Nil	0.05	0.20	0.20	0.32	0.36	0.36	0.36
Payout Ratio	Nil	Nil	Nil	19%	125%	36%	125%	42%	199%	47%
Prices - High	8⅝	7¾	6½	7⅞	10½	10⅝	9⅜	10⅜	14⅝	11⅜
- Low	3⅝	3⅞	4	4⅛	6½	6½	6¼	6½	7¾	7⅛
P/E Ratio - High	NM	15	43	30	66	19	36	12	81	15
- Low	NM	7	27	16	41	12	24	8	43	9

Income Statement Analysis (Million $)

	1997	1996	1995	1994	1993	1992	1991	1990	1989	1988
Revs.	651	636	585	565	534	504	315	355	334	339
Oper. Inc.	40.3	70.2	54.1	53.4	50.7	62.1	31.4	58.4	28.2	50.6
Depr.	20.6	21.5	23.2	25.2	24.6	22.0	17.1	14.6	14.0	12.1
Int. Exp.	27.6	21.7	22.0	18.2	17.0	13.5	10.2	13.4	10.9	5.9
Pretax Inc.	-7.9	26.9	8.9	14.4	9.1	26.5	10.4	36.7	7.5	33.1
Eff. Tax Rate	NM	38%	38%	38%	35%	35%	32%	36%	33%	36%
Net Inc.	-4.8	16.7	5.5	9.0	5.9	17.2	7.1	23.5	5.0	21.2

Balance Sheet & Other Fin. Data (Million $)

	1997	1996	1995	1994	1993	1992	1991	1990	1989	1988
Cash	2.5	1.6	2.0	5.8	6.8	3.6	2.8	2.4	1.0	0.6
Curr. Assets	338	332	315	290	289	247	151	153	145	158
Total Assets	538	501	476	457	475	433	292	303	289	257
Curr. Liab.	41.9	56.4	40.3	167	45.1	123	78.9	77.0	71.8	76.2
LT Debt	286	224	228	83.0	231	118	52.6	68.9	72.1	27.4
Common Eqty.	186	188	174	186	178	176	149	147	131	139
Total Cap.	491	439	430	285	424	307	211	224	212	176
Cap. Exp.	29.1	29.0	17.3	8.6	22.3	30.3	14.0	21.9	59.0	34.2
Cash Flow	15.0	37.1	28.7	33.9	29.3	38.2	24.2	38.1	19.0	33.3
Curr. Ratio	8.1	5.9	7.8	1.7	6.4	2.0	1.9	2.0	2.0	2.1
% LT Debt of Cap.	58.2	51.0	53.1	29.1	54.4	38.6	24.9	30.7	34.0	15.6
% Net Inc.of Revs.	NM	2.6	1.0	1.6	1.1	3.4	2.2	6.6	1.5	6.3
% Ret. on Assets	NM	3.4	1.2	1.9	1.3	4.7	2.4	7.9	1.8	8.8
% Ret. on Equity	NM	8.6	3.2	4.7	2.7	9.7	4.8	16.8	3.7	15.9

Data as orig. reptd.; bef. results of disc. opers. and/or spec. items. Per share data adj. for stk. divs. as of ex-div. date. Bold denotes diluted EPS (FASB 128). E-Estimated. NA-Not Available. NM-Not Meaningful. NR-Not Ranked.

Office—101 Commonwealth Blvd., P.O. Box 5191, Martinsville, VA 24115. **Tel**—(540) 632-2961. **Website**—www.tultex.com **Chrmn**—J. M. Franck. **Pres & CEO**—C. W. Davies Jr. **VP, CFO & Investor Contact**—Suzanne H. Wood. **Treas**—R. H. Gehman. **Secy**—K. H. Rogers. **Dirs**—S. P. Bernstein, C. W. Davies Jr., L. M. Ewers Jr., J. M. Franck, H. R. Hunnicutt Jr., F. K. Iverson, B. M. Jacobson, R. M. Simmons Jr.. **Transfer Agent**—First Union National Bank, Charlotte. **Incorporated**—in Virginia in 1937. **Empl**— 6,708. **S&P Analyst:** Kathleen J. Fraser

03-OCT-98 | **Industry:** Banks (Regional) | **Summary:** Through subsidiaries, UST provides a wide range of financial services through 72 banking offices in New England.

Quantitative Evaluations

Outlook (1 Lowest—5 Highest)
• **3-**

Fair Value
• **23**

Risk
• **Average**

Earn./Div. Rank
• **B-**

Technical Eval.
• **Bearish** since 3/98

Rel. Strength Rank (1 Lowest—99 Highest)
• **49**

Insider Activity
• **Neutral**

Recent Price • 20   Yield • 2.8%
52 Wk Range • 30⅜-16⅜   12-Mo. P/E • 12.6

Earnings vs. Previous Year
▲=Up ▼=Down ▶=No Change

10 Week Mov. Avg. - - -
30 Week Mov. Avg. ·····
Relative Strength

VOL. (000)

Business Profile - 30-JUL-98

This Boston-based bank holding company provides financial products and services to individuals and small to medium-size companies in New England. USTB has a busy consolidation schedule in the months ahead following its acquisition activity over the past year. In October 1997, the company acquired Newton, MA-based Firestone Financial Corp. ($86.8 million in assets) for 1,180,000 common shares. In July 1998, USTB acquired Somerset Savings Bank ($533 million in assets), for roughly 3,200,000 shares. USTB's acquisition of Affiliated Community Bancorp, for an anticipated 9,153,000 common shares, is expected to close in August 1998.

Operational Review - 30-JUL-98

Net interest income in the first six months of 1998 rose 14%, year to year, as restated, reflecting a 5.9% increase in average earning assets and a wider net interest margin (5.38%, versus 4.99%). The provision for loan losses was up sharply, to $1,665,000, from $300,000. Noninterest income grew 10%. Noninterest expense fell 13%, as results in the 1997 period included one-time acquisition and merger-related expenses of $11,751,000; pretax income climbed sharply. After taxes at 37.9%, versus 45.2%, net income advanced 162%, to $25,390,000 ($0.83 a share), from $9,673,000 ($0.32).

Stock Performance - 02-OCT-98

In the past 30 trading days, USTB's shares have declined 9%, compared to a 7% fall in the S&P 500. Average trading volume for the past five days was 117,240 shares, compared with the 40-day moving average of 141,569 shares.

Key Stock Statistics

Dividend Rate/Share	0.56	Shareholders	2,900
Shs. outstg. (M)	42.4	Market cap. (B)	$0.848
Avg. daily vol. (M)	0.114	Inst. holdings	37%
Tang. Bk. Value/Share	10.30		
Beta	1.00		

Value of $10,000 invested 5 years ago: $ 22,210

Fiscal Year Ending Dec. 31

	1998	1997	1996	1995	1994	1993
Revenues (Million $)						
1Q	85.44	80.93	45.14	44.63	39.79	48.53
2Q	85.19	75.16	44.65	43.47	40.33	44.27
3Q	—	82.06	47.70	44.71	41.05	43.29
4Q	—	83.74	57.46	45.12	41.48	41.26
Yr.	—	323.2	194.9	177.9	162.7	177.3
Earnings Per Share ($)						
1Q	**0.42**	**0.03**	0.25	0.16	0.06	0.04
2Q	**0.41**	**0.29**	0.49	0.20	0.07	-1.76
3Q	—	**0.35**	0.71	0.23	0.06	0.12
4Q	—	**0.40**	0.35	0.25	0.08	0.09
Yr.	—	**1.08**	1.79	0.83	0.27	-1.36

Next earnings report expected: late October

Dividend Data (Dividends have been paid since 1995.)

Amount ($)	Date Decl.	Ex-Div. Date	Stock of Record	Payment Date
0.120	Dec. 16	Dec. 29	Dec. 31	Jan. 23 '98
0.120	Mar. 17	Mar. 27	Mar. 31	Apr. 24 '98
0.140	Jun. 16	Jun. 26	Jun. 30	Jul. 24 '98
0.140	Sep. 15	Sep. 28	Sep. 30	Oct. 23 '98

Business Summary - 30-JUL-98

UST Corp. is a bank holding company that owns US-Trust and United States Trust Company, each headquartered in Boston. In addition, USTB owns, indirectly through its subsidiary banks, five active nonbanking subsidiaries: Firestone Financial Corp., UST Leasing Corporation, UST Capital Corp., UST Realty Trust, Inc. and UST Auto Lease Corp., as well as eight subsidiaries which hold foreclosed real estate and four subsidiaries which are passive holders of securities.

USTB's primary business involves providing a broad range of financial services to individuals and small and medium-sized companies in New England. In addition, an important part of USTB's business is the provision of trust and money management services to professionals, corporate executives, nonprofit organizations, labor unions, foundations, mutual funds and owners of closely-held businesses, most of which are also located in the New England region.

Interest income advanced 17% in 1997 and accounted for 88% of USTB's total revenues. Average earning assets, from which interest income is derived, advanced approximately 14%, to $3.5 billion. This growth was due to a 27% jump in average loan volume driven by both loans acquired through 1996 branch purchases and internal loan growth.

Loans, which comprised the majority of average earning assets (76%), totaled $2.8 billion at December 31, 1997. Commercial and financial loans accounted for 36% of the loan portfolio at year end 1997. The remainder of loan portfolio was comprised as follows: residential mortgage loans 25%, indirect automobile installment loans 21%, commercial real estate loans 10%, home equity loans 4% and other 4%.

The bank's net interest margin (a key measure of profitability for the bank's lending operations) widened 38 basis points in 1997, to 4.10%. This margin expansion, coupled with the growth in average earning assets, pushed net interest income up 24%.

Total noninterest income amounted to $38.0 million in 1997, down 4.8% from a year earlier, as a net loss on securities in 1997 and a $6.8 million gain from the sale of a bank subsidiary made comparisons difficult. Asset management fees made up 34% of noninterest income, deposit account service charges 25%, corporate services income 15% and other 25%.

Per Share Data ($)

(Year Ended Dec. 31)	1997	1996	1995	1994	1993	1992	1991	1990	1989	1988
Tangible Bk. Val.	9.49	8.00	9.47	7.41	8.70	10.25	10.54	10.92	12.03	10.49
Earnings	1.08	1.79	0.83	0.27	-1.36	-0.34	-0.58	0.13	2.10	2.11
Dividends	0.40	0.29	0.05	Nil	Nil	Nil	0.15	0.60	0.58	0.51
Payout Ratio	37%	16%	6%	Nil	Nil	Nil	NM	450%	28%	24%
Prices - High	29⅝	20⅝	15½	14⅜	12½	10½	9	15¼	19½	22⅛
- Low	18	12¾	9¾	8¾	7⅜	6⅝	5¼	5¼	13⅞	15¾
P/E Ratio - High	27	12	19	53	NM	NM	NM	NM	9	10
- Low	17	7	12	32	NM	NM	NM	NM	7	7

Income Statement Analysis (Million $)

	1997	1996	1995	1994	1993	1992	1991	1990	1989	1988
Net Int. Inc.	175	96.1	95.4	92.1	92.7	88.1	86.9	91.1	97.0	95.6
Tax Equiv. Adj.	0.7	0.3	0.9	1.0	1.2	1.6	2.0	2.7	4.0	4.3
Non Int. Inc.	39.5	29.4	30.0	29.2	32.3	28.6	33.1	22.6	21.6	20.5
Loan Loss Prov.	0.9	18.6	13.1	23.1	64.3	41.9	53.7	43.7	9.8	6.8
Exp./Op. Revs.	75%	73%	70%	76%	77%	81%	73%	63%	55%	56%
Pretax Inc.	55.2	53.7	24.1	6.8	-36.4	-7.7	-12.5	0.2	43.1	45.1
Eff. Tax Rate	41%	39%	38%	30%	NM	NM	NM	NM	34%	37%
Net Inc.	32.4	32.7	15.0	4.8	-20.9	-4.7	-7.9	1.9	28.3	28.3
% Net Int. Marg.	5.10	4.94	5.54	5.29	5.00	4.40	3.60	3.60	4.60	5.00

Balance Sheet & Other Fin. Data (Million $)

	1997	1996	1995	1994	1993	1992	1991	1990	1989	1988
Earning Assets:										
Money Mkt	164	112	90.0	103	96.3	1.3	38.7	28.1	172	97.3
Inv. Securities	722	528	576	402	474	484	445	378	203	156
Com'l Loans	1,358	747	643	728	763	781	873	1,008	1,013	773
Other Loans	1,426	1,101	629	538	555	690	775	861	832	1,059
Total Assets	3,838	2,707	1,969	1,803	2,044	2,178	2,365	3,055	2,579	2,332
Demand Deposits	708	799	373	372	374	571	470	442	394	433
Time Deposits	891	1,307	1,140	1,119	1,267	1,221	1,528	1,998	1,284	1,287
LT Debt	Nil	Nil	0.1	4.1	10.0	18.6	23.4	22.0	24.5	24.5
Common Eqty.	340	198	174	133	153	144	146	148	160	138
% Ret. on Assets	1.0	1.4	0.8	0.3	NM	NM	NM	0.1	1.2	1.3
% Ret. on Equity	12.0	17.6	9.1	3.1	NM	NM	NM	1.2	18.9	22.3
% Loan Loss Resv.	1.8	2.1	4.4	4.9	4.8	3.4	3.0	1.9	1.0	1.0
% Loans/Deposits	403.0	87.8	84.1	84.9	80.3	82.1	82.5	76.6	109.9	106.5
% Equity to Assets	8.2	7.9	8.9	8.1	7.0	6.5	5.6	5.6	6.2	5.7

Data as orig. reptd.; bef. results of disc opers. and/or spec. items. Per share data adj. for stk. divs. as of ex-div. date. Bold denotes diluted EPS (FASB 128). E-Estimated. NA-Not Available. NM-Not Meaningful. NR-Not Ranked.

Office—40 Court St., Boston, MA 02108. **Tel**—(617) 726-7000. **Chrmn**—W. Schwartz.**Pres & CEO**—N. F. Finnegan. **EVP, Treas & CFO**—J. K. Hunt. **Investor Contact**—Lynda Tocci (617-726-7221). **Dirs**— G. G. Atkins, D. E. Bradbury, R. M. Coard, R. L. Culver, A. D. DerKazarian, D. C. Dolben, N. F. Finnegan, E. Guzovsky, B. W. Hotarek, F. X. Messina, S. L. Miller, V. L. Pryor, G. M. Ridge, W. Schwartz, B. C. Sidell, J. V. Sidell, P. D. Slater, E. J. Sullivan, G. R. Tod, M. J. Verrochi, G. M. Weiner.**Transfer Agent & Registrar**—United States Trust Co., Boston. **Incorporated**—in Massachusetts in 1967. **Empl**— 1,550. **S&P Analyst:** Michael Schneider

USA Detergents

5466F

NASDAQ Symbol **USAD**

In S&P SmallCap 600

03-OCT-98

Industry:
Household Products
(Nondurables)

Summary: This company is a leading manufacturer and marketer of quality nationally distributed value brand laundry and household cleaning products.

Quantitative Evaluations

Recent Price • 8
52 Wk Range • 18⅜-5⅞

Yield • Nil
12-Mo. P/E • NM

Outlook
(1 Lowest—5 Highest)
• **NA**

Fair Value
• **NA**

Risk
• **High**

Earn./Div. Rank
• **NR**

Technical Eval.
• **Neutral** since 8/98
Rel. Strength Rank
(1 Lowest—99 Highest)
• **24**
Insider Activity
• **NA**

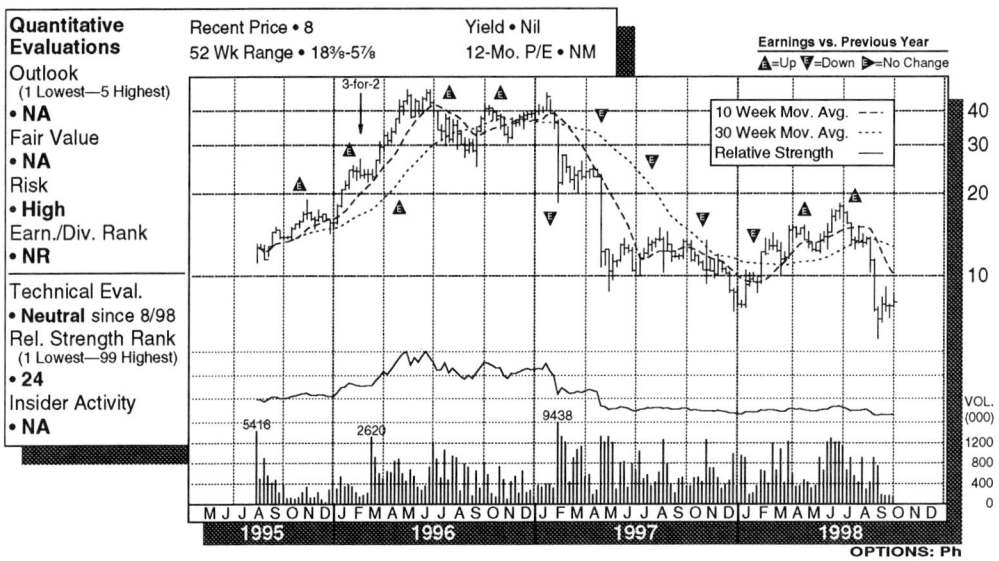

Earnings vs. Previous Year
▲=Up ▼=Down ►=No Change

10 Week Mov. Avg. – – –
30 Week Mov. Avg. ·······
Relative Strength ——

OPTIONS: Ph

Business Profile - 11-SEP-98

Despite impressive revenue growth in 1997, increased costs associated with the company's new plant integration, resulted in a net loss for the year. However, these efforts are beginning to improve performance. During the first half of 1998, the company has been able to meet some of its efficiency goals, resulting in improvement in its gross and operating margins. These improvements have been spurred by manufacturing and pricing efficiencies, better cost controls and lower marketing costs. USAD plans to continue to focus on improving its operations and focusing its marketing efforts on products with acceptable margins.

Operational Review - 11-SEP-98

Net sales in the six months ended June 30, 1998, decreased 4.2%, year to year, reflecting lower volumes in household cleaners and candles, partially offset by higher unit sales of laundry products. Margins widened, due to lower material costs, manufacturing efficiencies and a decrease in marketing funds and freight expenses. Following higher depreciation and interest charges, and a $3.3 million litigation charge to settle a stockholder class action suit, the net loss narrowed to $932,000 ($0.07 per share), from $20,174,000 ($1.46).

Stock Performance - 02-OCT-98

In the past 30 trading days, USAD's shares have declined 30%, compared to a 7% fall in the S&P 500. Average trading volume for the past five days was 26,580 shares, compared with the 40-day moving average of 76,182 shares.

Key Stock Statistics

Dividend Rate/Share	Nil	Shareholders	NA
Shs. outstg. (M)	13.8	Market cap. (B)	$0.111
Avg. daily vol. (M)	0.036	Inst. holdings	18%
Tang. Bk. Value/Share	1.12		
Beta	NA		

Value of $10,000 invested 5 years ago: NA

Fiscal Year Ending Dec. 31

	1998	1997	1996	1995	1994	1993
Revenues (Million $)						
1Q	56.68	60.53	34.07	23.26	17.47	—
2Q	54.07	54.97	42.92	25.65	17.19	—
3Q	—	57.35	48.11	27.12	18.52	—
4Q	—	54.28	48.94	28.85	15.48	—
Yr.	—	227.3	174.0	104.9	68.66	46.94
Earnings Per Share ($)						
1Q	**0.10**	-0.30	0.16	0.08	0.06	—
2Q	**-0.16**	-1.07	0.20	0.10	0.07	—
3Q	—	-0.08	0.23	0.13	0.06	—
4Q	—	**0.01**	0.07	0.13	0.03	—
Yr.	—	**-1.53**	0.65	0.43	0.22	—

Next earnings report expected: NA

Dividend Data

No cash dividends have been paid and the company does not anticipate paying any dividends. Certain credit facilities have placed restrictions on USAD's ability to declare and pay dividends.

A Division of The McGraw-Hill Companies

Business Summary - 11-SEP-98

In the fight for the consumer's dollar when it comes to laundry and household cleaning products, USA Detergents (USAD) is dwarfed by the giants in the industry, Procter & Gamble Co. and Unilever N.V., which together control about 65% of the domestic market. Nevertheless, USAD had been able to achieve an enviable record of growth in revenues and earnings by selling an expanding line of products to an increasing number of people who not only would rather pay less to get more, but also desire quality features normally found in nationally advertised brands.

The company has experienced some growing pains as of late, however. Results in 1997 have been adversely affected by manufacturing and distribution inefficiencies associated with significantly increasing production capacity and sales. In August 1997, USAD's shares fell sharply, reflecting the announcement that the company had discovered errors in its 1996 financial statements, which eventually led to the restatement of 1996 results. In response to operational difficulties, USAD closed an underutilized facility in New Jersey, reduced its labor force and instituted an inventory control program. In early 1998, the company announced that the remaining $35 million of principal indebtedness owed to PNC Bank had been extended until January 1999 in ex-

change for higher interest rates and warrants to purchase the common stock.

Currently, the company is competing in eight laundry and household product categories and it offers 12 distinct value brands. XTRA and Nice'n FLUFFY, which rank among the top 10 brands in their respective categories, represented 61% and 19%, respectively, of USAD's 1997 sales. Some of the products that USAD offers are: XTRA liquid and powder laundry detergent; Nice'n FLUFFY liquid and sheet fabric softener; Touch of Glass and Tile Action cleaners; Country Air air fresheners; and Speedway automotive products.

USAD sells its products to both large and small retailers throughout the U.S., including mass merchandisers, supermarkets, variety and dollar stores, drug stores and small grocery stores. Wal-Mart is the company's largest customer, accounting for roughly 17% of net sales in 1997. No other customer accounted for more than 10%. Sales to supermarkets remained strong, representing 45% of USAD's total sales in 1997, up from 41% the year before.

The company's strategy is to enable retailers to increase sales and realize attractive relative profit margins on its products while providing value to consumers. USAD also seeks to develop strong brand name recognition through eye-catching packaging and a reputation for quality at a low price.

Per Share Data ($)

(Year Ended Dec. 31)	1997	1996	1995	1994	1993	1992	1991	1990	1989	1988
Tangible Bk. Val.	1.13	3.00	1.51	NA	NA	NA	NA	NA	NA	NA
Cash Flow	-1.18	0.82	0.52	0.29	0.05	NA	NA	NA	NA	NA
Earnings	-1.53	0.65	0.43	0.22	0.02	NA	NA	NA	NA	NA
Dividends	Nil	Nil	Nil	Nil	Nil	Nil	Nil	Nil	Nil	Nil
Payout Ratio	Nil	Nil	Nil	Nil	Nil	Nil	Nil	Nil	Nil	Nil
Prices - High	46¾	48	19	NA	NA	NA	NA	NA	NA	NA
- Low	7⅜	15½	9⅝	NA	NA	NA	NA	NA	NA	NA
P/E Ratio - High	NM	74	44	NA	NA	NA	NA	NA	NA	NA
- Low	NM	24	22	NA	NA	NA	NA	NA	NA	NA

Income Statement Analysis (Million $)

	1997	1996	1995	1994	1993	1992	1991	1990	1989	1988
Revs.	227	174	105	69.0	47.0	NA	NA	NA	NA	NA
Oper. Inc.	-14.6	18.0	10.7	5.7	2.0	NA	NA	NA	NA	NA
Depr.	4.8	2.3	1.0	0.8	0.4	NA	NA	NA	NA	NA
Int. Exp.	2.7	0.9	0.6	0.6	0.4	NA	NA	NA	NA	NA
Pretax Inc.	-24.5	14.8	9.2	4.3	0.3	NA	NA	NA	NA	NA
Eff. Tax Rate	NM	40%	41%	39%	46%	NA	NA	NA	NA	NA
Net Inc.	-21.1	8.9	5.4	2.7	0.2	NA	NA	NA	NA	NA

Balance Sheet & Other Fin. Data (Million $)

	1997	1996	1995	1994	1993	1992	1991	1990	1989	1988
Cash	1.8	2.4	0.1	0.1	NA	NA	NA	NA	NA	NA
Curr. Assets	54.3	65.0	27.4	16.3	NA	NA	NA	NA	NA	NA
Total Assets	103	99	40.6	24.4	NA	NA	NA	NA	NA	NA
Curr. Liab.	47.0	24.4	16.3	11.2	NA	NA	NA	NA	NA	NA
LT Debt	38.9	30.8	1.8	6.2	NA	NA	NA	NA	NA	NA
Common Eqty.	15.6	41.3	20.3	5.9	NA	NA	NA	NA	NA	NA
Total Cap.	54.6	73.2	23.1	12.1	NA	NA	NA	NA	NA	NA
Cap. Exp.	23.7	20.5	3.9	1.6	4.6	NA	NA	NA	NA	NA
Cash Flow	-16.3	11.2	6.4	3.4	0.6	NA	NA	NA	NA	NA
Curr. Ratio	1.2	2.7	1.7	1.5	NA	NA	NA	NA	NA	NA
% LT Debt of Cap.	71.2	42.1	7.9	51.2	NA	NA	NA	NA	NA	NA
% Net Inc.of Revs.	NM	5.1	5.2	3.9	3.6	NA	NA	NA	NA	NA
% Ret. on Assets	NM	12.7	16.7	NA	NA	NA	NA	NA	NA	NA
% Ret. on Equity	NM	28.8	41.4	NA	NA	NA	NA	NA	NA	NA

Data as orig. reptd.; bef. results of disc. opers. and/or spec. items. Per share data adj. for stk. divs. as of ex-div. date. Bold denotes diluted EPS (FASB 128). E-Estimated. NA-Not Available. NM-Not Meaningful. NR-Not Ranked.

Office—1735 Jersey Ave., North Brunswick, NJ 08902. **Tel**—(908) 828-1800. **Fax**—(908) 246-7733. **Chrmn & CEO**—U. Evan. **Vice Chrmn**—J. S. Cohen. **CFO**—R. D. Coslow. **VP-Secy**—D. Bergman. **Dirs**—F. R. Adler, M. Antebi, D. Bergman, J. S. Cohen, U. Evan, F. H. Horowitz, S. Kalish, R. A. Mandell. **Transfer Agent & Registrar**—Continental Stock Transfer & Trust Co., NYC. **Incorporated**—in New Jersey in 1988; reorganized in Delaware in 1995. **Empl**— 592. **S&P Analyst:** R.J.I.

Ultratech Stepper

5467K

Nasdaq Symbol **UTEK**

In S&P SmallCap 600

03-OCT-98

Industry: Equipment (Semiconductor)

Summary: UTEK manufactures photolithography equipment designed to reduce the cost of ownership for manufacturers of integrated circuits and thin-film head magnetic recording devices.

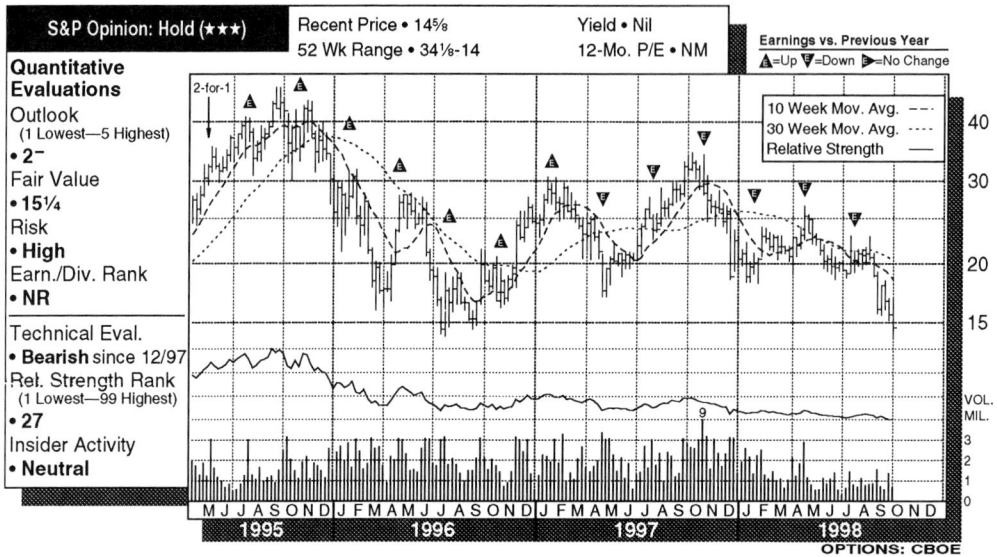

S&P Opinion: Hold (★★★)	Recent Price • 14⅝	Yield • Nil
	52 Wk Range • 34⅛-14	12-Mo. P/E • NM

Earnings vs. Previous Year
▲=Up ▼=Down ▶=No Change

Quantitative Evaluations

Outlook (1 Lowest—5 Highest)
• **2⁻**

Fair Value
• **15¼**

Risk
• **High**

Earn./Div. Rank
• **NR**

Technical Eval.
• **Bearish** since 12/97

Rel. Strength Rank (1 Lowest—99 Highest)
• **27**

Insider Activity
• **Neutral**

10 Week Mov. Avg. – – –
30 Week Mov. Avg. ‑ ‑ ‑ ‑
Relative Strength —

OPTIONS: CBOE

Overview - 28-JUL-98

We expect sales to decline approximately 30% in 1998, reflecting weakness in both the semiconductor and disk drive markets. The disk drive sector added significant capacity in the first half of 1997, and could see slower demand for front-end processes over the next few quarters, as the market absorbs the capacity. We expect margins to come under pressure in the near term on the lower volume and a shift in the sales mix toward newer products. However, an anticipated reduction in operating expenses should cushion the impact on the bottom line. In addition, interest income from UTEK's healthy cash reserves will enhance results. However, with contracting revenues and narrower margins, we expect an operating loss of $0.25 a share in 1998, down from EPS of $1.04 recorded in 1997 (excluding the non-recurring effects of both the acquisition of in-process research and development and the termination of a Japanese distributor).

Valuation - 28-JUL-98

Despite prospects for much lower than previously anticipated revenue and earnings levels in 1998, we are maintaining our hold rating on the shares. While UTEK holds a dominant market share of lithography equipment for disk drives, near-term growth in this area will be restricted by weak demand for front-end processes. Furthermore, in light of overcapacity in some areas of the semiconductor market, we expect chip makers to cut back on capital equipment spending as well. At 1.7X book value, the shares are fairly valued. But, given the company's strong new product offerings and healthy balance sheet (no long-term debt and $7.18 a share in cash), UTEK remains a worthwhile holding.

Key Stock Statistics

S&P EPS Est. 1998	-0.25	Tang. Bk. Value/Share	11.90
P/E on S&P Est. 1998	NM	Beta	1.29
S&P EPS Est. 1999	-0.50	Shareholders	100
Dividend Rate/Share	Nil	Market cap. (B)	$0.308
Shs. outstg. (M)	21.0	Inst. holdings	31%
Avg. daily vol. (M)	0.174		

Value of $10,000 invested 5 years ago: NA

Fiscal Year Ending Dec. 31

	1998	1997	1996	1995	1994	1993
Revenues (Million $)						
1Q	27.78	38.73	51.71	32.08	18.19	10.12
2Q	22.40	38.05	51.79	36.26	20.14	13.14
3Q	—	36.75	46.50	42.20	24.41	14.45
4Q	—	33.81	43.50	47.29	28.61	16.43
Yr.	—	147.3	193.5	157.8	91.34	54.14
Earnings Per Share ($)						
1Q	0.02	0.21	0.41	0.23	0.14	0.03
2Q	-0.74	0.27	0.44	0.27	0.14	0.10
3Q	—	0.25	0.42	0.32	0.18	0.12
4Q	—	0.09	0.40	0.38	0.19	0.12
Yr.	—	0.81	1.66	1.20	0.65	0.36

Next earnings report expected: late October

Dividend Data

No cash dividends have been paid. The company intends to retain earnings for use in its business and does not expect to pay cash dividends in the foreseeable future.

A Division of The McGraw-Hill Companies

STANDARD
&POOR'S
STOCK REPORTS

Ultratech Stepper, Inc.

5467K
03-OCT-98

Business Summary - 28-JUL-98

Ultratech (UTEK) manufactures photolithography equipment for use in the fabrication of integrated circuits (ICs), micromachining devices, thin film heads (TFH) for disk drives, and photomasks for the semiconductor industry. The company's strategy is to provide photolithography equipment (steppers) that reduces costs for manufacturers of ICs and TFH magnetic recording devices. Photolithography is one of the most critical and expensive steps in IC and TFH manufacturing. According to the Semiconductor Industry Association, up to 35% of the cost of processing silicon is related to photolithography.

Steppers are used to image device features on the surface of wafers by selectively exposing a light-sensitive polymer photoresist coated on a wafer surface, through a photomask containing the master image of a particular device layer. Depending on design complexity, this step may be repeated up to 25 times during the production of a single chip.

UTEK's systems cost significantly less than competing steppers, but are less precise. The company's products specifically address non-critical layer (greater than 0.65 micron linewidths) operations. Using a strategy called mix-and-match (M&M), UTEK's steppers share the processing load with higher-priced steppers that are designed for processing critical layers. The alternative to M&M is for chip makers to use high priced systems for all layers. Usually less than 50% of an IC's layers are considered critical.

The company currently offers three different series of systems for use in the semiconductor fabrication process: the model 1500 Series, which addresses the markets for scanner replacement and high volume/low cost semiconductor fabrication; the Saturn Wafer Stepper family, which address the mix and match market in advanced semiconductor fabrication; and the Titan Wafer Stepper, which addresses the market for photosensitive polyamide applications as well as the markets served by the model 1500 Series.

The company also supplies photolithography systems to the TFH market with its model 1700 series, model 2700 series, model 4700 series, and new model 6700 series.

Steppers for both IC and TFH production feature size capabilities ranging from 2.0 microns to 0.65 microns and are priced from $800,000 to $2.1 million.

Ultratech also offers photolithography equipment for use in the micromachining market. In addition, in December 1997, the company shipped its first UltraBeam model V2000 electron beam pattern generation system for use in the development and production of photomasks for the IC industry. The system addresses production requirements for leading edge photomasks, and has an approximate price range of $6 to $9 million.

Per Share Data ($)

(Year Ended Dec. 31)	1997	1996	1995	1994	1993	1992	1991	1990	1989	1988
Tangible Bk. Val.	12.68	11.81	10.08	4.83	3.00	NA	NA	NA	NA	NA
Cash Flow	1.14	1.94	1.39	0.77	0.46	NA	NA	NA	NA	NA
Earnings	0.81	1.66	1.20	0.65	0.36	NA	NA	NA	NA	NA
Dividends	Nil	Nil	Nil	Nil	Nil	Nil	Nil	Nil	Nil	Nil
Payout Ratio	Nil	Nil	Nil	Nil	Nil	Nil	Nil	Nil	Nil	Nil
Prices - High	34½	31¾	47½	20⅞	10⅛	NA	NA	NA	NA	NA
- Low	17	14	17	8¼	6¼	NA	NA	NA	NA	NA
P/E Ratio - High	43	19	40	32	28	NA	NA	NA	NA	NA
- Low	21	8	14	13	17	NA	NA	NA	NA	NA

Income Statement Analysis (Million $)

	1997	1996	1995	1994	1993	1992	1991	1990	1989	1988
Revs.	147	194	158	91.3	54.1	35.3	31.9	NA	NA	NA
Oper. Inc.	32.6	52.7	35.6	17.3	7.8	3.1	2.7	NA	NA	NA
Depr.	7.2	6.1	3.9	2.0	1.0	0.8	1.1	NA	NA	NA
Int. Exp.	0.2	0.2	Nil	0.1	0.3	0.0	0.0	NA	NA	NA
Pretax Inc.	24.8	52.7	36.2	16.4	6.7	2.1	1.6	NA	NA	NA
Eff. Tax Rate	29%	33%	33%	33%	38%	38%	29%	NA	NA	NA
Net Inc.	17.6	35.3	24.2	11.0	4.1	1.3	1.1	NA	NA	NA

Balance Sheet & Other Fin. Data (Million $)

	1997	1996	1995	1994	1993	1992	1991	1990	1989	1988
Cash	43.9	47.8	161	49.7	26.1	NA	NA	NA	NA	NA
Curr. Assets	257	252	221	93.1	50.5	NA	NA	NA	NA	NA
Total Assets	300	281	245	105	56.4	NA	NA	NA	NA	NA
Curr. Liab.	33.8	39.4	44.7	23.7	17.5	NA	NA	NA	NA	NA
LT Debt	Nil	Nil	Nil	0.4	0.8	NA	NA	NA	NA	NA
Common Eqty.	264	240	200	80.0	38.1	NA	NA	NA	NA	NA
Total Cap.	266	241	200	80.5	38.9	NA	NA	NA	NA	NA
Cap. Exp.	9.3	7.8	9.8	7.8	2.8	1.0	1.1	NA	NA	NA
Cash Flow	24.8	41.4	28.1	13.0	5.1	2.1	2.2	NA	NA	NA
Curr. Ratio	7.6	6.4	4.9	3.9	2.9	NA	NA	NA	NA	NA
% LT Debt of Cap.	Nil	Nil	Nil	0.5	2.1	NA	NA	NA	NA	NA
% Net Inc.of Revs.	11.9	18.2	15.3	12.1	7.6	3.7	3.6	NA	NA	NA
% Ret. on Assets	6.0	13.4	13.8	13.6	NA	NA	NA	NA	NA	NA
% Ret. on Equity	7.0	16.1	17.3	18.6	NA	NA	NA	NA	NA	NA

Data as orig. reptd.; bef. results of disc. opers. and/or spec. items. Per share data adj. for stk. divs. as of ex-div. date. Bold denotes diluted EPS (FASB 128). E-Estimated. NA-Not Available. NM-Not Meaningful. NR-Not Ranked.

Office—3050 Zanker Road, San Jose, CA 95134. **Tel**—(408) 321-8835. **Chrmn, Pres & CEO**—A. W. Zafiropoulo. **VP-Fin, CFO, Secy & Treas**—W. G. Leunis III. **Dirs**—L.R. Carter, T.D. George, J. Gemunder, G. Harrison, K. A. Levy, J. L. Parkinson, A. W. Zafiropoulo. **Transfer Agent & Registrar**—Bank of Boston. **Incorporated**—in Delaware in 1992. **Empl**— 576. **S&P Analyst:** B. McGovern

03-OCT-98

Industry:
Banks (Regional)

Summary: This multi-bank holding company operates more than 40 offices primarily in West Virginia and also in Virginia.

Quantitative Evaluations

Recent Price • 24⅝
52 Wk Range • 34⅛-21¾

Yield • 3.1%
12-Mo. P/E • 19.5

Outlook
(1 Lowest—5 Highest)
• **1⁻**

Fair Value
• **20½**

Risk
• **Low**

Earn./Div. Rank
• **A-**

Technical Eval.
• **Bearish** since 9/98

Rel. Strength Rank
(1 Lowest—99 Highest)
• **60**

Insider Activity
• **Neutral**

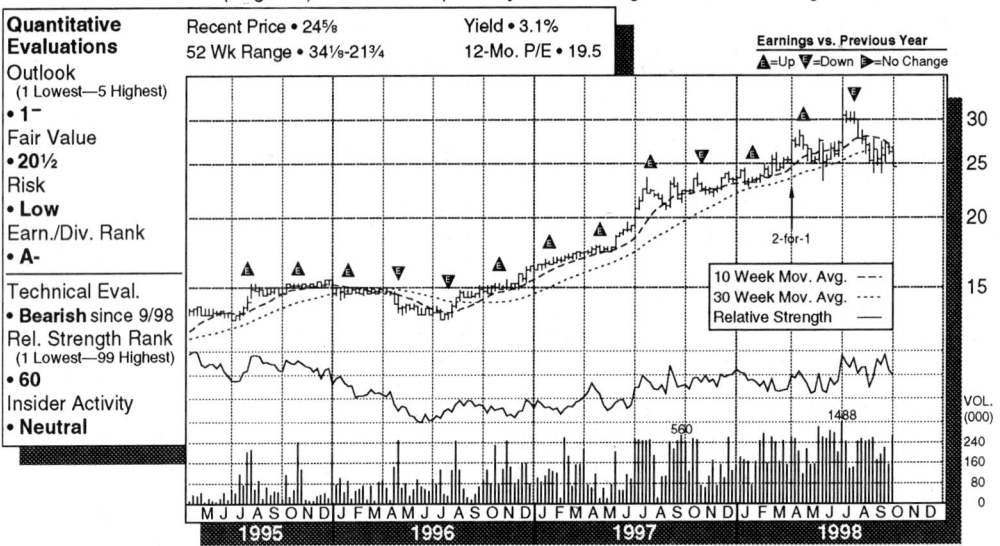

Earnings vs. Previous Year
▲=Up ▼=Down ▶=No Change

10 Week Mov. Avg. ---
30 Week Mov. Avg. ····
Relative Strength —

2-for-1

VOL. (000)

Business Profile - 13-SEP-98

The company acquired George Mason Bankshares, Inc. of Fairfax, VA (with total assets of $1.0 billion) for about 9 million common shares in April 1998. Also, UBSI has agreed to acquire Fed One Bancorp, Inc. of Wheeling, WVA (with total assets were about $368 million) for about 3.6 million common shares. This transaction, which was subject to various conditions and approvals, was expected to be completed in 1998's fourth quarter. Also, at June 30, 1998, UBSI's nonperforming loans amounted to 0.51% of total loans, net of unearned income, down from 0.67% at year-end 1997. Directors raised the quarterly cash dividend 2.9%, with the July 1, 1998, payment, and the dividend is to rise another 5.6%, to $0.19, with the October 1, 1998 payment.

Operational Review - 13-SEP-98

Net interest income for the six months ended June 30, 1998, before the provision for possible loan losses, was up $10.9 million, or 17%, year to year. However, a $6.1 million, or 529% rise, in the loan loss provision, narrowed the net interest income increase to $4.8 million, or 7.4%. Noninterest income rose $9.9 million, or 63%, and noninterest expense was up $22.3 million, or 50%. Pretax income declined 21%, and with a lower tax rate, net income was down 14%, to $20.6 million ($0.52 a share, on 1.5% more shares), from $24.0 million ($0.61). However, UBSI said that if about $8 million of merger-related charges, and about $7 million of other one-time charges were excluded, the company had core earnings in the 1998 period of $0.72 a share.

Stock Performance - 02-OCT-98

In the past 30 trading days, UBSI's shares have declined 3%, compared to a 7% fall in the S&P 500. Average trading volume for the past five days was 117,480 shares, compared with the 40-day moving average of 59,954 shares.

Key Stock Statistics

Dividend Rate/Share	0.76	Shareholders	5,000
Shs. outstg. (M)	42.7	Market cap. (B)	$ 1.1
Avg. daily vol. (M)	0.059	Inst. holdings	18%
Tang. Bk. Value/Share	9.30		
Beta	0.62		

Value of $10,000 invested 5 years ago: $ 30,330

Fiscal Year Ending Dec. 31

	1998	1997	1996	1995	1994	1993
Revenues (Million $)						
1Q	60.01	48.38	45.77	36.50	31.75	29.14
2Q	85.65	49.55	43.26	37.13	32.50	29.43
3Q	—	55.01	49.16	37.30	34.19	32.31
4Q	—	57.05	48.36	38.15	33.92	38.30
Yr.	—	210.0	186.6	149.1	132.4	129.2
Earnings Per Share ($)						
1Q	**0.36**	**0.33**	0.27	0.29	0.26	—
2Q	**0.17**	**0.34**	0.04	0.29	0.26	—
3Q	—	**0.34**	0.37	0.30	0.27	—
4Q	—	**0.34**	0.33	0.29	0.26	—
Yr.	—	**1.35**	**1.00**	1.18	1.04	0.88

Next earnings report expected: mid October

Dividend Data (Dividends have been paid since 1994.)

Amount ($)	Date Decl.	Ex-Div. Date	Stock of Record	Payment Date
0.350	Feb. 24	Mar. 11	Mar. 13	Apr. 01 '98
2-for-1	Nov. 24	Mar. 30	Mar. 13	Mar. 27 '98
0.180	May. 18	Jun. 10	Jun. 12	Jul. 01 '98
0.190	Aug. 26	Sep. 09	Sep. 11	Oct. 01 '98

A Division of The **McGraw·Hill** Companies

United Bankshares, Inc.

5479K

03-OCT-98

Business Summary - 13-SEP-98

A multi-bank holding company headquartered in Charleston, West Virginia, United Bankshares (UBSI) has conducted an active acquisition program since it was formed in 1982. The company began conducting business in May 1984 with the acquisition of three wholly owned subsidiaries which were merged in late 1985 and renamed United National Bank (UNB). Since that time, UNB has acquired more than 10 banks.

The principal markets of the company and its subsidiaries are located in Parkersburg, Charleston, Huntington, Morgantown and Wheeling, West Virginia, and Arlington, Fairfax, Loudon and Prince William Counties, Virginia. At the end of 1997, UBSI was operating 43 offices throughout West Virginia.

All of the company's subsidiary banks are full-service commercial banks and offer such banking services as accepting deposits, making and servicing of personal, commercial, floor plan and student loans, and the making of construction and real estate loans.

UBSI's total loan portfolio (net of unearned income) increased 11.5%, to $2.06 billion in 1997. The outstanding loan portfolio is comprised of commercial, financial and agricultural loans (18% of the total), real estate mortgages (67%), real estate construction loans (4%) and consumer loans (11%).

The commercial loan portfolio consists of loans to corporate borrowers in small to mid-size industrial and commercial companies, as well as automobile dealers, service, retail and wholesale merchants. Commercial real estate loans consist of commercial mortgages, which generally are secured by nonresidential and multi-family residential properties. Real estate mortgage loans to consumers are traditional one-to-four family residential mortgages. Consumer loans are secured by automobiles, boats, recreational vehicles, and other personal property.

As of December 31, 1997, the allowance for possible loan losses totaled $24.8 million (1.20% of loans outstanding), compared with $22.3 million (1.21%) a year earlier. Net charge-offs as a percentage of average loans outstanding were 0.17% in 1997, versus 0.16% in 1996. Nonperforming loans totaled $15.5 million (0.75% of loans outstanding) at the end of 1997, versus $10.2 million (0.55%) the year before.

The average yield on total earning assets was 8.48% in 1997 (8.34% in 1996), while the average rate paid on total interest-bearing funds was 4.51% (4.25%), for an interest spread of 3.97% (4.09%).

Per Share Data ($)

(Year Ended Dec. 31)	1997	1996	1995	1994	1993	1992	1991	1990	1989	1988
Tangible Bk. Val.	9.32	8.56	7.75	7.61	6.66	6.78	6.37	6.03	NA	NA
Earnings	1.35	1.00	1.18	1.04	NA	NA	NA	NA	NA	NA
Dividends	0.68	0.61	0.57	0.52	0.46	0.42	0.40	0.28	0.32	0.34
Payout Ratio	50%	1%	0%	1%	NA	NA	NA	NA	NA	NA
Prices - High	24³/₈	16¹/₂	15¹/₂	13¹/₂	14¹/₄	10³/₈	7¹/₂	6³/₄	7⁷/₈	8⁷/₈
- Low	16¹/₈	13¹/₈	11⁵/₈	11¹/₂	9⁵/₈	6¹/₂	5¹/₈	4¹/₂	6¹/₄	6³/₄
P/E Ratio - High	18	16	13	13	16	13	10	10	10	13
- Low	12	13	9	11	11	8	6	7	8	10

Income Statement Analysis (Million $)

	1997	1996	1995	1994	1993	1992	1991	1990	1989	1988
Net Int. Inc.	106	99	81.7	77.3	71.5	57.7	52.7	50.4	46.4	42.2
Tax Equiv. Adj.	2.4	2.4	NA	NA	NA	NA	NA	NA	NA	NA
Non Int. Inc.	19.7	14.2	12.6	12.1	12.2	9.3	7.8	7.9	6.9	5.7
Loan Loss Prov.	3.1	2.6	2.1	1.8	4.3	2.9	4.9	5.9	3.0	2.4
Exp./Op. Revs.	48%	56%	52%	54%	59%	62%	62%	64%	65%	68%
Pretax Inc.	62.4	47.2	43.3	38.0	30.1	22.7	18.4	14.9	15.8	12.8
Eff. Tax Rate	34%	35%	35%	34%	32%	30%	29%	28%	27%	20%
Net Inc.	40.9	30.5	28.1	24.9	20.4	15.8	13.1	10.7	11.5	10.3
% Net Int. Marg.	4.80	4.90	NA	NA	NA	NA	NA	NA	NA	NA

Balance Sheet & Other Fin. Data (Million $)

	1997	1996	1995	1994	1993	1992	1991	1990	1989	1988
Earning Assets:										
Money Mkt	9.7	3.2	NA	NA	NA	NA	NA	NA	NA	NA
Inv. Securities	453	332	310	361	430	NA	NA	NA	NA	NA
Com'l Loans	369	249	NA	NA	NA	NA	NA	NA	NA	NA
Other Loans	1,699	1,604	NA	NA	NA	NA	NA	NA	NA	NA
Total Assets	2,700	2,327	1,815	1,788	1,720	1,548	1,189	1,194	1,099	1,033
Demand Deposits	318	261	239	245	229	NA	NA	NA	NA	NA
Time Deposits	1,788	1,567	1,235	1,190	1,201	NA	NA	NA	NA	NA
LT Debt	143	133	33.9	84.0	32.2	NA	NA	NA	NA	NA
Common Eqty.	279	259	201	180	171	150	113	107	95.0	87.0
% Ret. on Assets	1.6	1.5	1.6	1.4	1.2	1.2	1.1	0.9	1.1	1.0
% Ret. on Equity	15.2	13.3	14.7	14.2	12.7	12.0	12.0	10.6	12.7	12.0
% Loan Loss Resv.	1.2	1.2	1.5	1.5	1.6	1.4	1.4	1.2	1.1	1.1
% Loans/Deposits	99.3	101.1	93.3	90.4	82.5	80.6	83.6	81.6	78.1	73.0
% Equity to Assets	10.7	11.1	10.6	10.0	9.8	9.6	9.2	8.8	8.5	8.5

Data as orig. reptd.; bef. results of disc opers. and/or spec. items. Per share data adj. for stk. divs. as of ex-div. date. Bold denotes diluted EPS (FASB 128). E-Estimated. NA-Not Available. NM-Not Meaningful. NR-Not Ranked.

Office—300 United Center, 500 Virginia St., East, Charleston, WVA 25301**Tel**—(304) 424-8761.**Chrmn & CEO**—R. M. Adams.**EVP-Treas & CFO**—S. E. Wilson.**Dirs**—R. M. Adams, T. J. Blair III, H. L. Buch, R. T. Butcher, H. S. Fahlgren, T. J. Georgelas, F. T. Graff Jr., R. P. McLean, I. N. Smith Jr., C. E. Stealey, W. A. Thornhill III, W. W. Wagner, H. L. Wilkes, P. C. Winter Jr., S. E. Wilson.**Transfer Agent & Registrar**—ChaseMellon Shareholder Services, Ridgefield Park, NJ**Incorporated**—in West Virginia in 1982.**Empl**— 972. **S&P Analyst:** T.A.G.

03-OCT-98

Industry:
Electric Companies

Summary: This Connecticut-based electric utility participates in several other non-regulated businesses, through its United Resources subsidiary.

Quantitative Evaluations

Outlook
(1 Lowest—5 Highest)
• **1⁻**

Fair Value
• **49¾**

Risk
• **Low**

Earn./Div. Rank
• **B**

Technical Eval.
• **Bullish** since 7/97

Rel. Strength Rank
(1 Lowest—99 Highest)
• **91**

Insider Activity
• **NA**

Recent Price • 53⅜
52 Wk Range • 54⅛-36¾

Yield • 5.4%
12-Mo. P/E • 17.0

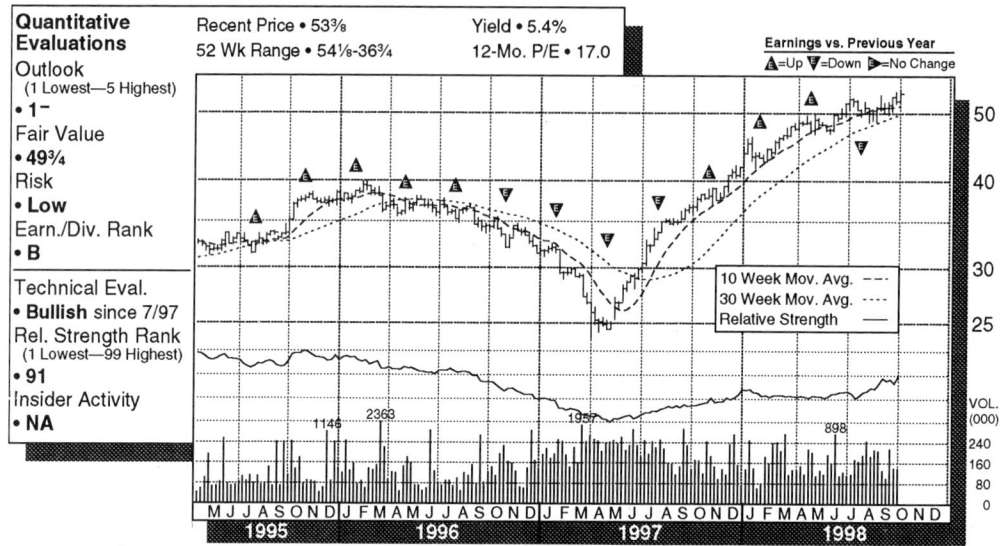

Earnings vs. Previous Year
▲=Up ▼=Down ▶=No Change

10 Week Mov. Avg. – – –
30 Week Mov. Avg. · · · ·
Relative Strength —

Business Profile - 08-JUN-98

As an electric utility, United Illuminating (UIL) is highly regulated. In December 1996, the Connecticut Department of of Public Utility Control (DPUC) ordered a five year rate plan for the years 1997-2001 in which earnings above an 11.5% "allowed" equity return on utility investment are shared, part of which are returned to customers via price reductions. The plan also accelerates asset recovery and forces the company to lower prices. In April, 1998, Connecticut enacted a statute that, in 2000, will enable customers to choose their electricity supplier, a function that will be separate from delivery. UIL will still deliver electricity over its own lines. As a result, the company announced on May 20, 1998 that it will divest itself of its three fossil-fuel power plants and other power purchase agreements. UIL estimates total book value of its plants at $220 million. The company expects significant cost reductions in 1998 as a result of a smaller work force, lower interest expense, and improved performance of its nuclear-fuel generating units.

Operational Review - 08-JUN-98

Total operating revenues during the quarter ended March 31, 1998 declined 10% to $162.4 million year to year, related to price reductions in the retail segment. Operating expenses were down 11.6%. Net income increased 16% to $8.9 million ($0.64 per diluted share) from $7.7 million ($0.54 per diluted share).

Stock Performance - 02-OCT-98

In the past 30 trading days, UIL's shares have increased 5%, compared to a 7% fall in the S&P 500. Average trading volume for the past five days was 27,820 shares, compared with the 40-day moving average of 34,031 shares.

Key Stock Statistics

Dividend Rate/Share	2.88	Shareholders	17,300
Shs. outstg. (M)	14.3	Market cap. (B)	$0.765
Avg. daily vol. (M)	0.030	Inst. holdings	34%
Tang. Bk. Value/Share	31.56		
Beta	0.51		

Value of $10,000 invested 5 years ago: $ 19,676

Fiscal Year Ending Dec. 31

	1998	1997	1996	1995	1994	1993
Revenues (Million $)						
1Q	162.5	180.3	170.9	165.4	167.6	161.9
2Q	159.8	163.8	168.8	163.4	153.4	151.0
3Q	—	196.6	209.2	200.3	184.6	189.4
4Q	—	169.6	177.2	161.3	151.1	150.6
Yr.	—	710.3	726.0	690.5	656.8	653.0
Earnings Per Share ($)						
1Q	**0.64**	0.54	0.82	0.62	0.86	0.82
2Q	**0.39**	0.61	0.75	0.67	0.40	0.66
3Q	—	1.68	1.27	1.89	1.78	1.54
4Q	—	**0.44**	0.04	0.46	0.14	-0.45
Yr.	—	**3.26**	**2.87**	3.64	3.18	2.57

Next earnings report expected: NA

Dividend Data (Dividends have been paid since 1900.)

Amount ($)	Date Decl.	Ex-Div. Date	Stock of Record	Payment Date
0.720	Oct. 27	Dec. 09	Dec. 11	Jan. 01 '98
0.720	Feb. 23	Mar. 10	Mar. 12	Apr. 01 '98
0.720	May. 20	Jun. 09	Jun. 11	Jul. 01 '98
0.720	Aug. 24	Sep. 08	Sep. 10	Oct. 01 '98

A Division of The McGraw-Hill Companies

Business Summary - 08-JUN-98

The United Illuminating Co. is a Connecticut electric utility serving an area of about 335 sq. mi. in southwestern Connecticut that includes Bridgeport and New Haven and has a population of 704,000 (21% of the state's population); the company has about 312,000 customers. Although the company sells electricity to other utilities (wholesale), its primary revenue source is retail customers, a segment made up of residential (42%), commercial (40%), and industrial (16%) customers. Retail sales are affected by local weather, economic conditions, and regulatory agencies.

The company experienced a $16 million revenue shortfall during FY 97, due to a $23 million price reduction because of a DPUC order. The need for more expensive energy to replace nuclear generation led to a $14.2 million increase in retail fuel and energy expenses. However, the retired Connecticut Yankee nuclear generating plant also benefitted UIL; purchase capacity expense decreased almost $7 million. Interest expenses have been declining, as UIL has been paying down debt. Due to one-time gains, net income was 12% higher to $46 million ($3.26 per diluted share) from $41 million ($2.87 per diluted share). After serving 41 years with UIL, Chairman & CEO Richard Grasso announced his retirement effective during 1998. He will

be replaced by Nathaniel D. Woodson, a 30 year veteran of Westinghouse Electric Corp.

United Resources, a wholly-owned subsidiary, has four of its own wholly-owned subsidiaries. American Payment Systems manages a national network of agents for the processing of bill payments made by customers of other utilities. Precision Power provides power-related equipment and services to the owners of commercial buildings and industrial facilities. These two businesses are expected to begin contributing to UIL's bottom line in 1998. Thermal Energies participates in the development of district heating and cooling facilities in the downtown New Haven area. United Bridge Energy is participating in a merchant wholesale electric generating facility being constructed on land leased from UIL at one of its generating plants.

United Illuminating holds a 17.5 % interest in Seabrook and a 3.7% interest in Millstone 3, both nuclear-fuel generating facilities. Seabrook had an unexpected outage during 1997, causing a $1.5 million expense. Millstone 3 had been temporarily shut down until recently due to safety concerns. UIL also maintains a 9.5% ownership in Connecticut Yankee's common shares, though this unit has ceased commercial operation. The nuclear units are responsible for certain state-imposed decommissioning costs for the eventual wind-down of operations.

Per Share Data ($)

(Year Ended Dec. 31)	1997	1996	1995	1994	1993	1992	1991	1990	1989	1988
Tangible Bk. Val.	31.56	31.20	30.67	29.97	27.24	27.61	26.20	24.56	23.72	30.51
Earnings	3.26	2.88	3.64	3.18	2.57	3.76	3.14	3.55	-5.87	4.85
Dividends	2.88	2.88	2.82	2.76	2.66	2.56	2.44	2.32	2.32	2.32
Payout Ratio	88%	100%	77%	87%	104%	68%	78%	65%	NM	48%
Prices - High	46	40	38⅝	40	45⅞	42	39⅛	34⅛	34¼	27½
- Low	23¾	31⅛	29⅜	28¾	38½	34⅛	30	26⅞	24⅝	19⅛
P/E Ratio - High	14	14	11	13	18	11	12	10	NM	6
- Low	7	11	8	9	15	9	10	8	NM	4

Income Statement Analysis (Million $)

	1997	1996	1995	1994	1993	1992	1991	1990	1989	1988
Revs.	710	726	690	657	653	667	673	594	531	519
Depr.	88.4	65.9	61.4	58.2	56.3	50.7	48.2	36.5	35.6	24.1
Maint.	42.2	37.7	36.1	41.8	41.5	38.4	41.8	40.5	39.4	30.7
Fxd. Chgs. Cov.	2.5	2.2	2.4	2.0	1.6	1.9	1.7	1.8	NM	2.5
Constr. Credits	1.6	2.4	2.8	3.5	4.1	3.2	5.2	3.4	65.4	75.7
Eff. Tax Rate	43%	53%	52%	47%	40%	39%	38%	24%	41%	20%
Net Inc.	45.8	39.1	50.4	48.1	40.5	56.8	48.0	54.0	-73.0	79.0

Balance Sheet & Other Fin. Data (Million $)

	1997	1996	1995	1994	1993	1992	1991	1990	1989	1988
Gross Prop.	1,951	1,908	1,878	1,851	1,808	1,744	1,712	1,670	1,726	1,834
Cap. Exp.	33.4	47.0	59.0	63.0	95.0	70.0	68.0	67.0	142	159
Net Prop.	1,306	1,322	1,346	1,357	1,361	1,336	1,340	1,337	1,402	1,536
Capitalization:										
LT Debt	662	777	863	726	895	917	1,006	998	976	973
% LT Debt	57	61	63	62	65	66	68	69	69	63
Pfd.	54.4	54.5	60.5	44.7	60.9	60.9	63.0	70.0	70.0	104
% Pfd.	4.70	4.30	4.40	3.80	4.40	4.30	4.30	4.80	5.00	6.70
Common	439	440	440	428	423	423	402	380	363	474
% Common	38	35	32	36	31	30	27	26	26	31
Total Cap.	1,456	1,625	1,790	1,646	1,824	1,710	2,069	2,036	1,959	2,217
% Oper. Ratio	84.9	85.0	81.6	80.6	82.4	83.8	84.7	83.4	82.3	78.1
% Earn. on Net Prop.	7.9	8.2	9.4	9.4	8.5	8.1	7.7	7.2	6.4	7.7
% Return On Revs.	6.4	5.4	7.3	7.3	6.2	8.5	7.2	9.1	NM	15.2
% Return On Invest. Capital	6.6	6.6	7.2	7.5	7.1	9.0	7.0	8.1	NM	6.4
% Return On Com. Equity	10.4	8.8	11.3	12.1	8.6	12.7	11.2	13.3	NM	14.8

Data as orig. reptd.; bef. results of disc opers. and/or spec. items. Per share data adj. for stk. divs. as of ex-div. date. Bold denotes diluted EPS (FASB 128). E-Estimated. NA-Not Available. NM-Not Meaningful. NR-Not Ranked.

Office—157 Church St., New Haven, CT 06505. —http://www.uinet.com **Tel**—(203) 499-2000. **Chrmn**—Richard. J. Grossi. **Pres & CEO**—Nathaniel D. Woodson. **CFO**—Robert L. Fiscus. **Investor Contact**—Kurt Mohlman. **Dirs**—T. R. Albright, M. C. Breslawsky, D. E. A. Carson, J. F. Croweak, J. H. Devlin, R. L. Fiscus, R. J. Grossi, B. Henley-Cohn, J. L. Lahey, F. P. McFadden, Jr., F. R. O'Keefe, Jr., J. A. Thomas. **Transfer Agent & Registar**—Bank of New York, NYC. **Incorporated**—in Connecticut in 1899. **Empl**— 1,175. **S&P Analyst:** Ephraim Juskowicz.

03-OCT-98

Industry:
Health Care (Drugs - Generic & Other)

Summary: This pharmaceutical company develops and sells products to treat cancer, AIDS and allied diseases.

Quantitative Evaluations

Recent Price • 6⅜
52 Wk Range • 13-4⅞

Yield • Nil
12-Mo. P/E • NM

Outlook
(1 Lowest—5 Highest)
• **NA**

Fair Value
• **NA**

Risk
• **High**

Earn./Div. Rank
• **C**

Technical Eval.
• **Bullish** since 3/98

Rel. Strength Rank
(1 Lowest—99 Highest)
• **52**

Insider Activity
• **NA**

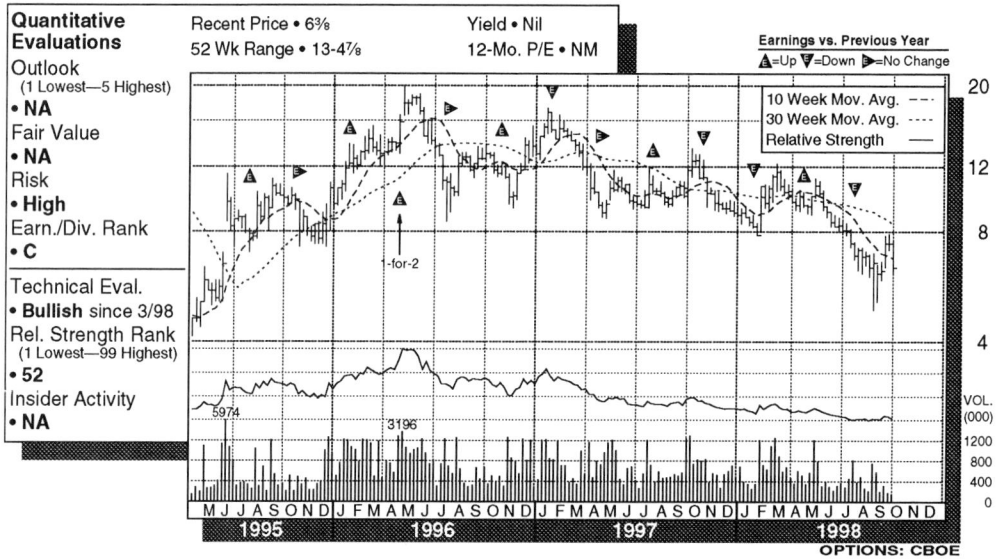

Earnings vs. Previous Year
▲=Up ▼=Down ▶=No Change

10 Week Mov. Avg. - - -
30 Week Mov. Avg. - - - -
Relative Strength ——

OPTIONS: CBOE

Business Profile - 30-JUL-98

In January 1997, the company was granted a U.S. patent and received FDA marketing clearance for a crystalline dosage form of Ethyol, a cytoprotective agent for the reduction of toxicities associated with cancer chemotherapies. ALZA Corp. and UBS have expanded their marketing agreement to include the NeuTrexin intravenous pneumonia treatment and Hexalen oral treatment for advanced ovarian cancer. In February 1998, UBS received a $5 million payment from ALZA Corp. for achieving a clinical development milestone related to a Phase III trial of Ethyol's radiation protective properties in patients with head and neck cancer. The company believes that its cash and investments, as well as anticipated revenues generated from product sales and other sources, will be sufficient to cover expected cash requirements at least for the next three years.

Operational Review - 30-JUL-98

Total revenues for the six months ended June 30, 1998, declined 17%, year to year, reflecting a $10 million milestone payment from ALZA Corp. in the 1997 second quarter, which outweighed 37% higher net sales. Operating expenses rose 3%, reflecting higher R&D spending, and a net loss of $3,272,500 ($0.13 a share) contrasted with net income of $559,200 ($0.02). Cash and investments as of June 30, 1998, totaled $47.8 million.

Stock Performance - 02-OCT-98

In the past 30 trading days, UBS's shares were unchanged, compared to a 7% fall in the S&P 500. Average trading volume for the past five days was 30,220 shares, compared with the 40-day moving average of 66,723 shares.

Key Stock Statistics

Dividend Rate/Share	Nil	Shareholders	5,100
Shs. outstg. (M)	24.3	Market cap. (B)	$0.155
Avg. daily vol. (M)	0.047	Inst. holdings	33%
Tang. Bk. Value/Share	1.81		
Beta	1.27		

Value of $10,000 invested 5 years ago: $ 2,865

Fiscal Year Ending Dec. 31

	1998	1997	1996	1995	1994	1993
Revenues (Million $)						
1Q	10.34	4.21	3.83	2.64	2.41	2.23
2Q	5.11	14.52	4.84	3.61	1.77	3.48
3Q	—	4.51	6.66	2.62	2.01	1.34
4Q	—	4.48	5.14	22.47	2.36	1.15
Yr.	—	27.72	20.46	31.35	8.55	8.20
Earnings Per Share ($)						
1Q	**-0.01**	-0.16	-0.16	-0.20	-0.30	-0.26
2Q	**-0.13**	0.17	-0.12	-0.12	-0.36	-0.36
3Q	—	-0.16	0.02	-0.28	-0.28	-0.46
4Q	—	**-0.19**	-0.17	0.60	-0.26	-0.98
Yr.	—	**-0.33**	-0.43	-0.02	-1.20	-2.06

Next earnings report expected: mid October

Dividend Data

No cash dividends have been paid. A one-for-two reverse stock split was effected in April 1996.

A Division of The McGraw·Hill Companies

Business Summary - 30-JUL-98

U.S. Bioscience develops and markets drugs, principally for the treatment of patients with cancer, acquired immune deficiency syndrome (AIDS) and allied diseases. The company has acquired, through licensing agreements, rights to nine drugs for the treatment of these diseases. Three of the drugs (Ethyol, NeuTrexin and Hexalen) have received marketing approval in the U.S. and several major foreign markets.

Ethyol, an injectable agent used to protect healthy cells from the harmful effects of chemotherapy, has received marketing approval in 32 countries for a range of indications. In the U.S., the product is indicated for reduction of kidney toxicity associated with the administration of cisplatin (a chemotherapeutic drug) in patients with advanced ovarian and non-small cell lung cancer. Additional clinical trials investigating Ethyol as a radio-protective agent are ongoing in the U.S. and Europe, with Phase III trials focused on patients with head and neck cancer.

NeuTrexin is a lipid-soluble intravenously administrable analog of methotrexate, a commonly used anticancer agent. NeuTrexin is approved in 22 countries as a treatment for pneumocystis carinii pneumonia in patients with immune system disorders. UBS is currently conducting Phase III clinical trials of NeuTrexin as a first-line therapy for advanced colorectal cancer. An oral formulation is also under development to treat diseases such as psoriasis and rheumatoid arthritis.

Hexalen is a cytotoxic drug approved to treat patients with persistent or recurrent ovarian cancer following first-line therapy with a cisplatin and/or alkylating agent-based combination therapy. Hexalen is also approved for the treatment of advanced ovarian cancer in the U.S. and certain European countries.

The product pipeline includes three drugs (AZQ, lodenosine (formerly FddA) and PALA Disodium Salt) in various stages of clinical trials. AZQ is being evaluated as a therapy for brain tumors, carcinomatous meningitis, and acute leukemia. Data from two completed Phase III trials are currently undergoing analysis. Iodenosine is a new anti-HIV reverse transcriptase inhibitor currently in clinical trials at the National Institutes of Health (NIH). Data from a Phase I clinical trial demonstrated anti-HIV activity even in patients who had failed other anti-retroviral therapies such as AZT, 3TC and d4T. PALA is being tested for its ability to enhance the activity of certain chemotherapeutic agents.

Products in preclinical testing include WR-151327, a second generation chemotherapy and radiation therapy protective agent, third generation platinum anticancer agents and Mytomycin-C analogues for the treatment of gastrointestinal cancer and breast cancer.

The company has distribution and marketing agreements with ALZA Corp. for the co-promotion of Ethyol, NeuTrexin and Hexalen in the U.S. For territories outside the U.S., UBS has entered into distribution and licensing agreements for these products with a number of pharmaceutical companies, including Schering-Plough and Eli Lilly & Co.

Per Share Data ($)

(Year Ended Dec. 31)	1997	1996	1995	1994	1993	1992	1991	1990	1989	1988
Tangible Bk. Val.	1.94	1.61	1.38	1.18	1.92	3.92	4.80	2.08	0.54	NM
Cash Flow	-0.30	-0.39	0.04	-1.14	-2.02	-1.00	-0.34	-0.30	-0.52	-0.16
Earnings	-0.33	-0.43	-0.02	-1.20	-2.06	-1.02	-0.36	-0.30	-0.52	-0.16
Dividends	Nil	Nil	Nil	Nil	Nil	Nil	Nil	Nil	Nil	Nil
Payout Ratio	Nil	Nil	Nil	Nil	Nil	Nil	Nil	Nil	Nil	Nil
Prices - High	17³/₈	19⁷/₈	11¹/₂	20³/₄	24¹/₂	88	80³/₄	20⁷/₈	14	NA
- Low	8³/₈	8¹/₂	4	3¹/₄	12¹/₂	12¹/₄	16³/₄	8³/₄	6¹/₂	NA
P/E Ratio - High	NM	NM	NM	NM	NM	NM	NM	NM	NM	NM
- Low	NM	NM	NM	NM	NM	NM	NM	NM	NM	NM

Income Statement Analysis (Million $)

	1997	1996	1995	1994	1993	1992	1991	1990	1989	1988
Revs.	12.9	10.8	8.7	7.3	4.4	4.1	3.5	0.2	Nil	1.3
Oper. Inc.	-21.6	-8.1	1.0	-24.2	-33.4	-26.9	-13.8	-7.9	-5.7	-1.4
Depr.	0.8	1.1	1.0	1.0	0.8	0.6	0.3	0.1	0.1	0.1
Int. Exp.	0.2	0.5	0.3	0.1	Nil	Nil	0.1	0.2	0.5	0.2
Pretax Inc.	-7.9	-9.7	-0.2	-24.0	-40.6	-20.2	-6.5	-4.9	-5.7	-1.6
Eff. Tax Rate	NM	NM	NM	NM	NM	NM	Nil	Nil	Nil	Nil
Net Inc.	-7.9	-9.7	-0.2	-24.0	-40.6	-20.2	-6.5	-4.9	-5.7	-1.6

Balance Sheet & Other Fin. Data (Million $)

	1997	1996	1995	1994	1993	1992	1991	1990	1989	1988
Cash	50.7	36.7	45.6	24.4	48.4	77.2	95.5	38.0	13.0	1.9
Curr. Assets	57.2	43.0	56.0	28.0	5.9	80.0	97.5	39.0	13.6	1.9
Total Assets	62.4	49.1	61.9	34.5	57.8	83.3	99	40.2	14.1	2.1
Curr. Liab.	12.4	8.9	13.0	6.4	8.6	5.3	3.8	2.6	2.0	0.5
LT Debt	1.1	1.9	19.0	1.0	Nil	Nil	Nil	0.7	4.0	3.1
Common Eqty.	47.0	36.9	28.8	23.9	38.1	77.5	94.1	35.0	6.8	-1.5
Total Cap.	48.1	38.7	47.9	24.9	38.1	77.5	94.1	35.8	10.8	1.3
Cap. Exp.	0.9	1.1	0.5	1.3	3.6	2.2	0.8	1.0	0.1	0.0
Cash Flow	-7.1	-8.6	0.8	-23.0	-39.8	-19.6	-6.2	-4.8	-5.7	-1.5
Curr. Ratio	4.6	4.8	4.3	4.3	6.1	15.0	25.4	15.2	6.6	3.8
% LT Debt of Cap.	2.3	4.8	39.9	4.0	Nil	Nil	Nil	2.0	37.3	218.1
% Net Inc.of Revs.	NM	NM	NM	NM	NM	NM	NM	NM	NM	NM
% Ret. on Assets	NM	NM	NM	NM	NM	NM	NM	NM	NM	NM
% Ret. on Equity	NM	NM	NM	NM	NM	NM	NM	NM	NM	NM

Data as orig. reptd.; bef. results of disc. opers. and/or spec. items. Per share data adj. for stk. divs. as of ex-div. date. Qtrly. rev. table incl. other income. Bold denotes diluted EPS (FASB 128). E-Estimated. NA-Not Available. NM-Not Meaningful. NR-Not Ranked.

Office—One Tower Bridge, 100 Front St., West Conshohocken, PA 19428. **Tel**—(610) 832-0570. **Website**—http://www.usbio.com **Chrmn**—A. Misher.**Pres & CEO**—C. B. Clarke. **EVP, CFO & Investor Contact**—Robert I. Kriebel. **SVP-Secy**—Martha E. Manning. **Dirs**—P. Calabresi, R. L. Capizzi, C. B. Clarke, R. I. Kriebel, D. J. MacMaster Jr., A. Misher, G. H. Ohye, Ellen V. Sigal, B. Wright. **Transfer Agent & Registrar**—ChaseMellon Shareholder Services, LLC, Ridgefield Park, NJ. **Incorporated**—in Delaware in 1987. **Empl**— 150. **S&P Analyst:** C.C.P.

STANDARD &POOR'S
STOCK REPORTS
U.S. Home
2342
NYSE Symbol **UH**

In S&P SmallCap 600

10-OCT-98

Industry: Homebuilding

Summary: This company, one of the largest U.S. builders of single-family homes, also provides mortgage financing.

S&P Opinion: Accumulate (★★★★)		
Quantitative Evaluations	Recent Price • 25⅞	Yield • Nil
	52 Wk Range • 47⅞-25½	12-Mo. P/E • 5.9

Earnings vs. Previous Year
▲=Up ▼=Down ▶=No Change

Quantitative Evaluations

Outlook
(1 Lowest—5 Highest)
• **4⁻**

Fair Value
• **38¼**

Risk
• **Average**

Earn./Div. Rank
• **NR**

Technical Eval.
• **NA**

Rel. Strength Rank
(1 Lowest—99 Highest)
• **38**

Insider Activity
• **Neutral**

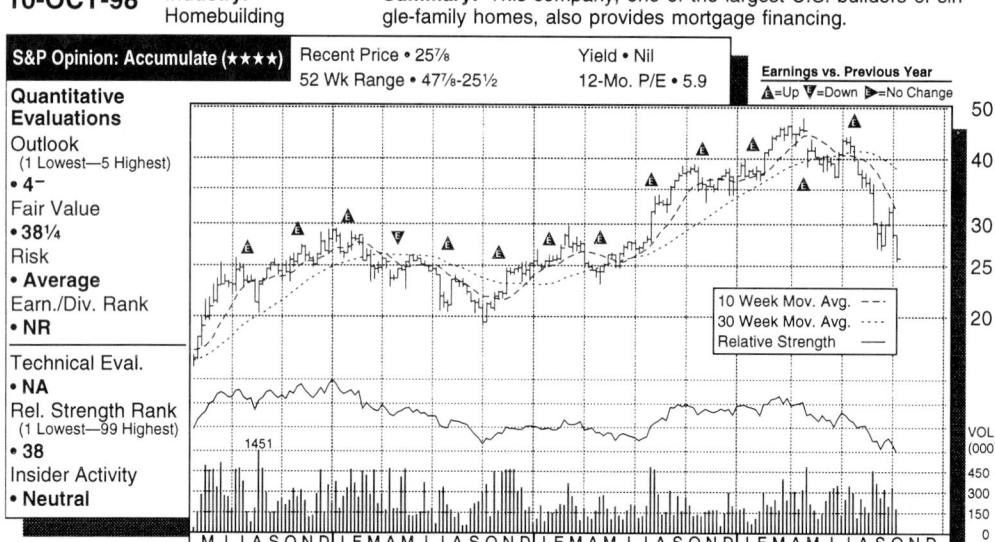

10 Week Mov. Avg. ---
30 Week Mov. Avg. ······
Relative Strength ——

1451

VOL. (000)

1995 1996 1997 1998

Overview - 30-JUL-98

Revenues should be solidly higher in 1998, as UH closes on its sizable order backlog. A mature housing cycle provides a challenge, but we expect UH to continue to record favorable order levels. The company should be aided by an aggressive sales effort, a wide diversity of home offerings, an operating concentration in demographically favorable geographic regions, and its growing focus on vital retirement/active adult markets. We also expect interest rates to remain buyer friendly. Margins should widen a bit, aided by less competitive market conditions and inventory controls. UH's preselling of retirement community units has held back margins for a while, as it causes revenues to lag marketing costs. Costs related to the opening of design centers have also limited gains somewhat. However, with several retirement communities starting to take on residents in early 1998, margins should pick up steam as the year goes on. UH's refinancing of a portion of its public debt in 1997's third quarter and 1998's first quarter will likely increase interest charges, but also reduce the number of shares used for diluted computations. Our full year forecast for 1998 excludes $0.57 a share of one-time credits taken in the first quarter of 1998.

Valuation - 30-JUL-98

The shares have moved sharply higher since the fall of 1996. The gains have largely been related to accommodating interest rate trends and investor ardor for UH's operating strategy. A mature housing cycle limits our enthusiasm about industry growth. However, we still believe UH's concentration in demographically favorable regions, its strong presence in the vital retirement/active adult market, and a major cost control focus will allow it to record solid EPS gains through 1999, especially with interest rates looking like they will stay accommodating. Thus, the shares still seem undervalued at about 9X our 1999 EPS forecast.

Key Stock Statistics

S&P EPS Est. 1998	4.10	Tang. Bk. Value/Share	35.73
P/E on S&P Est. 1998	6.3	Beta	1.50
S&P EPS Est. 1999	4.60	Shareholders	3,400
Dividend Rate/Share	Nil	Market cap. (B)	$0.354
Shs. outstg. (M)	13.7	Inst. holdings	80%
Avg. daily vol. (M)	0.051		

Value of $10,000 invested 5 years ago: NA

Fiscal Year Ending Dec. 31

	1998	1997	1996	1995	1994	1993
Revenues (Million $)						
1Q	334.5	316.0	272.8	263.2	225.3	167.0
2Q	367.5	340.5	293.3	259.3	241.1	196.0
3Q	—	337.3	317.7	286.7	255.8	228.0
4Q	—	325.9	327.8	298.8	273.1	222.0
Yr.	—	1,320	1,211	1,108	995.3	812.0
Earnings Per Share ($)						
1Q	**1.49**	**0.75**	0.77	0.70	0.60	0.45
2Q	**1.01**	**0.82**	0.84	0.67	0.63	0.46
3Q	—	**0.94**	1.03	0.83	0.81	4.61
4Q	—	**1.00**	1.07	0.92	0.82	0.67
Yr.	—	**3.50**	3.70	3.14	2.89	6.16

Next earnings report expected: late October

Dividend Data

The most recent payment was in September 1984.

A Division of The McGraw·Hill Companies

Business Summary - 30-JUL-98

U.S. Home Corporation has been among the 10 largest on-site homebuilders in the U.S. for more than 20 years. The company currently sells homes in more than 220 new home communities in 31 market areas in 11 different states across the nation. The greatest proportion of its sales come from Florida, Colorado, Arizona, California and Texas. The company sells homes to both first-time and move-up buyers, and in response to changing demographic trends, has become one of the largest builders in the retirement/active adult market.

U.S. Home emerged from Chapter 11 bankruptcy protection in June 1993, two years after filing a reorganization petition.

U.S. Home delivered 7,496 homes in 1997, at an average price of $170,500, compared with 7,099 homes at an average price of $166,100 in the prior year. Single-family detached units accounted for 80 to 85% of unit volume in recent years. UH seeks to generate one-third of sales through advertisements, one-third through customer referrals and one-third through realtor contacts.

Like most major builders, the company employs independent subcontractors to perform all land development and construction activities. This allows UH to minimize its investment in direct labor costs, equipment and facil-

ities. To coordinate subcontractor activities and ensure that quality standards are met, U.S. Home places on-site company managers at projects.

During 1997, 33% of UH's home deliveries consisted of affordable homes, 40% move-up homes and the remaining 27% retirement and active adult homes. Recognizing the imminent graying of the nation's population, UH set a goal several years ago to boost retirement/active adult development sales to one-third of its home closings by the end of the decade. After opening six new retirement/active adult communities for pre-sales activity in the first half of 1998, UH had homes for sale in 27 such communities. The company had four more slated to open for pre-sales by 1998 year end, and a total of 14 more in 1999 and 2000. U.S. Home notes that the number of 55 or older individuals in the U.S. will grow by some 21% over the next 10 years.

Through U.S. Home Mortgage Corp., the company also originates mortgage loans for purchasers of UH's homes and those of third parties. It then sells the mortgages and related servicing rights to investors.

UH experienced a 20% year-to-year gain in new home orders (on a unit basis) in 1998's second quarter. It also reported order backlog of $963 million at June 30, 1998, a record level for the company.

Per Share Data ($)

(Year Ended Dec. 31)	1997	1996	1995	1994	1993	1992	1991	1990	1989	1988
Tangible Bk. Val.	35.69	32.37	28.55	25.53	22.17	13.75	NA	NA	NA	NA
Cash Flow	3.50	3.11	NA	NA	6.54	2.46	-0.10	NA	NA	NA
Earnings	3.50	3.70	3.14	2.89	6.16	2.12	NA	NA	NA	NA
Dividends	Nil	Nil	Nil	Nil	Nil	NA	NA	NA	NA	NA
Payout Ratio	Nil	Nil	Nil	Nil	Nil	NA	NA	NA	NA	NA
Prices - High	39⅜	29⅜	29¼	29½	29	NA	NA	NA	NA	NA
- Low	23	19¼	14¾	14	19	NA	NA	NA	NA	NA
P/E Ratio - High	11	8	9	10	5	NA	NA	NA	NA	NA
- Low	7	5	5	5	3	NA	NA	NA	NA	NA

Income Statement Analysis (Million $)

	1997	1996	1995	1994	1993	1992	1991	1990	1989	1988
Revs.	1,320	1,211	1,108	995	812	690	NA	NA	NA	NA
Oper. Inc.	111	106	NA	NA	50.5	32.0	NA	NA	NA	NA
Depr.	Nil	Nil	NA	NA	4.4	3.9	NA	NA	NA	NA
Int. Exp.	33.8	64.3	32.7	31.4	23.4	28.2	NA	NA	NA	NA
Pretax Inc.	74.9	55.9	59.0	53.0	38.0	25.6	NA	NA	NA	NA
Eff. Tax Rate	37%	21%	38%	38%	NM	5.10%	NA	NA	NA	NA
Net Inc.	47.2	44.2	36.9	32.8	71.7	24.3	NA	NA	NA	NA

Balance Sheet & Other Fin. Data (Million $)

	1997	1996	1995	1994	1993	1992	1991	1990	1989	1988
Cash	11.8	13.2	5.1	6.7	20.9	3.5	NA	NA	NA	NA
Curr. Assets	NA	NA	NA	NA	NA	NA	NA	NA	NA	NA
Total Assets	1,067	947	842	748	679	545	NA	NA	NA	NA
Curr. Liab.	NA	NA	NA	163	117	100	NA	NA	NA	NA
LT Debt	396	363	300	294	305	237	NA	NA	NA	NA
Common Eqty.	420	374	329	278	208	118	NA	NA	NA	NA
Total Cap.	716	737	630	585	562	427	NA	NA	NA	NA
Cap. Exp.	3.1	2.7	2.5	2.0	Nil	NA	NA	NA	NA	NA
Cash Flow	47.2	44.2	NM	NM	76.1	28.2	NA	NA	NA	NA
Curr. Ratio	NA	NA	NA	NA	NA	NA	NA	NA	NA	NA
% LT Debt of Cap.	55.3	49.3	47.8	50.2	54.3	55.5	NA	NA	NA	NA
% Net Inc.of Revs.	3.6	3.6	3.4	3.3	8.8	3.5	NA	NA	NA	NA
% Ret. on Assets	4.7	4.9	4.7	4.3	6.7	NA	NA	NA	NA	NA
% Ret. on Equity	11.9	12.6	11.9	12.6	40.7	NA	NA	NA	NA	NA

Data as orig. reptd.; bef. results of disc. opers. and/or spec. items. Per share data adj. for stk. divs. as of ex-div. date. Bold denotes diluted EPS (FASB 128). E-Estimated. NA-Not Available. NM-Not Meaningful. NR-Not Ranked.

Office—1800 West Loop South, Houston, TX 77027. **Tel**—(713) 877-2311. **Website**—http://www.USHOME.com **Chrmn & Co-CEO**—R. J. Strudler. **Pres, Co-CEO & COO**—I. Heimbinder. **VP & Investor Contact**—Kelly Fawcett Somoza (713-877-2391). **Dirs**—G. Adams, S. L. Gerard, K. J. Hanau, Jr., I. Heimbinder, M. T. Hopkins, C. A. McKee, G. A. Poole, Jr., H. Ripault, J. W. Sight, R. J. Strudler. **Transfer Agent & Registrar**—First Chicago Trust Co. of NY, Jersey City, NJ. **Incorporated**—in Delaware in 1959. **Empl**— 1,641. **S&P Analyst:**   Michael W. Jaffe

03-OCT-98　**Industry:** Financial (Diversified)

Summary: This company provides investment management, private banking and fiduciary services to affluent individuals, families and institutions nationwide.

S&P Opinion: Hold (★★★)	Recent Price • 60¾	Yield • 1.2%
	52 Wk Range • 84⅛-54¼	12-Mo. P/E • 22.7

Quantitative Evaluations

Outlook (1 Lowest—5 Highest)
• **1+**

Fair Value
• **53½**

Risk
• **Low**

Earn./Div. Rank
• **B+**

Technical Eval.
• **Bullish** since 8/98

Rel. Strength Rank (1 Lowest—99 Highest)
• **47**

Insider Activity
• **Neutral**

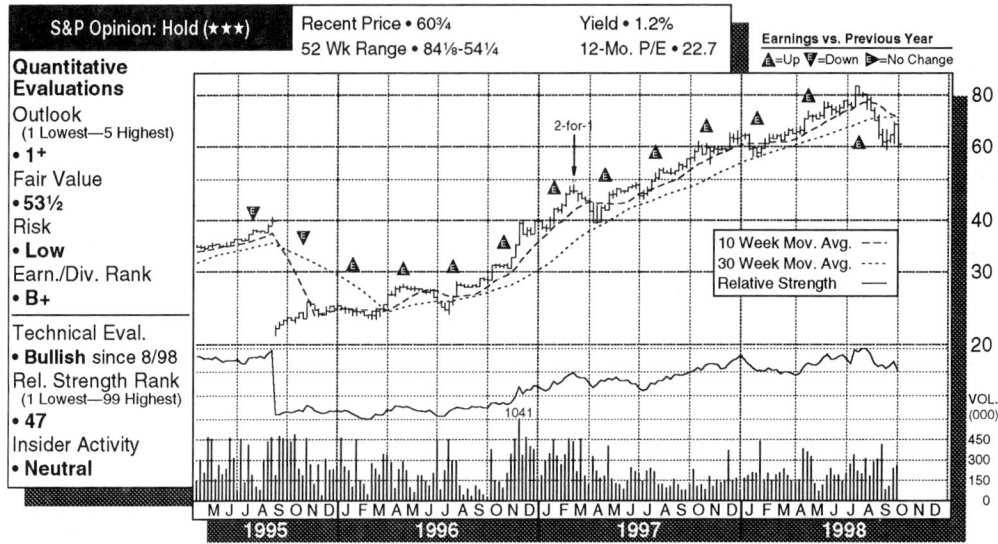

Earnings vs. Previous Year
▲=Up ▼=Down ▷=No Change

10 Week Mov. Avg. ---
30 Week Mov. Avg. ····
Relative Strength —

Overview - 16-JUL-98

Buoyed by strong increases in new business and the overall appreciation in the financial markets, USTC posted year-to-year EPS growth in the 1998 second quarter of 26%. Fee revenues advanced 23% and net interest revenue climbed 11%, as total assets under management grew to $68.2 billion at June 30, 1998, from $57.7 billion at June 30, 1997. USTC's national expansion continued in the quarter with the June agreement to acquire Wood Island Associates, Inc., a California-based investment management firm with over $1.0 billion in assets under management. U.S. Trust continues to exceed its lofty goals of 8% to 12% revenue growth, 15% to 20% earnings growth, and return on equity (ROE) of 25% or more. With USTC operating in one of the fastest growing segments of the financial services industry, we expect the company to have continued success. Pretax margins widened in the quarter, following a positive trend that we expect to continue. Return on equity in the quarter was 26%, versus 23% in the year-earlier period.

Valuation - 16-JUL-98

After rising about 60% in 1997, the shares are up about 22% thus far in 1998. The company has had good success since its restructuring in 1995, and prospects for long-term revenue and earnings growth remain strong. With much of the personal wealth market untapped, we believe that USTC's geographic expansion project will continue to pay dividends. Nevertheless, at approximately 26X and 22X our 1998 and 1999 EPS estimates, respectively, the shares appear fully valued. Because we see little room for expansion at such high multiples, we expect USTC to be only a market performer over the next six to 12 months, despite strong fundamentals.

Key Stock Statistics

S&P EPS Est. 1998	2.90	Tang. Bk. Value/Share	12.47
P/E on S&P Est. 1998	20.9	Beta	0.70
S&P EPS Est. 1999	3.40	Shareholders	1,900
Dividend Rate/Share	0.72	Market cap. (B)	$ 1.1
Shs. outstg. (M)	18.8	Inst. holdings	40%
Avg. daily vol. (M)	0.037		

Value of $10,000 invested 5 years ago: NA

Fiscal Year Ending Dec. 31

	1998	1997	1996	1995	1994	1993
Revenues (Million $)						
1Q	104.0	88.45	77.42	127.0	118.6	106.9
2Q	108.0	90.08	79.44	126.4	120.5	107.8
3Q	—	94.04	81.65	104.6	127.3	114.2
4Q	—	100.2	84.21	118.7	90.87	116.6
Yr.	—	494.4	419.6	476.8	457.3	445.6
Earnings Per Share ($)						
1Q	**0.70**	0.55	0.46	0.42	0.64	0.58
2Q	**0.73**	0.58	0.47	0.27	0.55	0.49
3Q	E0.73	0.61	0.48	-3.80	0.66	0.60
4Q	E0.74	**0.64**	0.53	0.45	-0.82	0.46
Yr.	**E2.90**	**2.39**	1.94	-2.62	1.06	2.13

Next earnings report expected: mid October

Dividend Data (Dividends have been paid since 1854.)

Amount ($)	Date Decl.	Ex-Div. Date	Stock of Record	Payment Date
0.150	Oct. 28	Jan. 07	Jan. 09	Jan. 23 '98
0.180	Jan. 27	Apr. 07	Apr. 10	Apr. 24 '98
0.180	Apr. 28	Jul. 08	Jul. 10	Jul. 24 '98
0.180	Jul. 28	Oct. 07	Oct. 09	Oct. 23 '98

A Division of The **McGraw·Hill** *Companies*

Business Summary - 16-JUL-98

U.S. Trust Corp. is the oldest U.S. investment management and trust company. Since 1853, the company has focused on helping affluent Americans preserve and enhance their wealth. At year-end 1997, nearly 80%, or $38 billion, of USTC's investment assets under management were personal assets. In addition to its core investment management services, U.S. Trust provides financial and estate planning, fiduciary services and private banking. In addition, USTC is one of the top 10 trustees in the U.S., providing trust, agency, and related services to public and private corporations, municipalities and financial institutions.

The individual wealth market in the U.S. is growing rapidly, and management feels that much of this market is untapped. There are currently three million American households that have over $1.0 million in investable assets. The number is expected to grow considerably in the future, reflecting both wealth accumulation and wealth transfers. Collectively, these households control $6.3 trillion in assets, and the majority of them do not use professional money managers. USTC's goal is to increase its share of this market.

USTC focuses on building business based on relationships, not transactions. By establishing the company as the client's key financial adviser, management hopes to build relationships that span generations.

National expansion remains a key component of U.S. Trust's growth strategy. Roughly 40% of the country's households with over $1.0 million in investable assets are located in the 20 most affluent metropolitan regions of the U.S. In late 1996, USTC acquired an investment management company in San Francisco; this will form the nucleus of a full service office set to open in 1998. USTC's goal is for regional offices such as this one to be contributing 50% of fee revenue by 2002. Currently, regional offices account for about 30% of revenue.

Since the sale of its capital intensive securities processing business in September 1995, and a subsequent restructuring, USTC has reported strong financial results. As a result, the company has raised its financial objectives for long-term growth. U.S. Trust expects to achieve 8% to 12% annual revenue growth, a pretax margin of 25% or more, 15% to 20% EPS growth, and a return on equity of over 25%.

Per Share Data ($)

(Year Ended Dec. 31)	1997	1996	1995	1994	1993	1992	1991	1990	1989	1988
Tangible Bk. Val.	12.16	19.98	9.34	11.81	12.21	10.63	10.01	9.06	9.40	9.49
Earnings	2.39	1.92	-2.62	1.06	2.13	1.88	1.66	0.62	1.54	1.50
Dividends	0.58	0.50	0.75	0.98	0.92	0.84	0.80	0.79	0.71	0.56
Payout Ratio	24%	26%	NM	94%	43%	45%	48%	127%	46%	37%
Prices - High	65¾	40¾	40¾	33	29⁷/₈	25¹/₂	22¹/₄	19	21⁵/₈	24³/₈
- Low	37¹/₂	23	21	24¾	24⁵/₈	21¹/₈	14	13³/₈	18¹/₄	17³/₄
P/E Ratio - High	28	21	NM	32	14	14	13	31	14	16
- Low	16	12	NM	24	12	11	8	22	12	12

Income Statement Analysis (Million $)

	1997	1996	1995	1994	1993	1992	1991	1990	1989	1988
Net Int. Inc.	91.7	78.9	99	108	116	109	96.0	89.0	83.0	79.0
Tax Equiv. Adj.	NA	NA	3.2	4.7	5.8	8.2	10.2	11.0	13.6	15.8
Non Int. Inc.	282	244	284	270	276	243	212	197	194	175
Loan Loss Prov.	0.8	1.0	1.6	2.0	4.0	6.0	6.0	8.4	1.6	3.8
Exp./Op. Revs.	77%	78%	124%	81%	80%	81%	80%	87%	80%	80%
Pretax Inc.	83.7	69.3	-93.4	34.4	72.7	58.9	48.8	18.6	43.2	35.4
Eff. Tax Rate	39%	41%	NM	39%	42%	38%	36%	37%	29%	14%
Net Inc.	51.0	40.9	-50.5	21.0	42.3	36.5	31.4	11.7	30.7	30.6
% Net Int. Marg.	3.12	3.24	3.74	3.49	3.95	4.16	4.35	4.67	4.64	4.38

Balance Sheet & Other Fin. Data (Million $)

	1997	1996	1995	1994	1993	1992	1991	1990	1989	1988
Earning Assets:										
Money Mkt	388	286	4.9	142	298	62.0	400	400	199	579
Inv. Securities	1,131	1,166	760	1,034	923	1,196	1,013	896	866	1,115
Com'l Loans	Nil	Nil	69.2	140	58.0	58.0	66.0	676	728	631
Other Loans	1,939	1,688	1,390	1,487	1,341	1,202	1,098	384	350	307
Total Assets	3,815	3,477	2,573	3,223	3,186	2,951	2,917	2,778	2,526	3,061
Demand Deposits	746	688	490	1,032	1,241	1,221	1,037	969	1,004	970
Time Deposits	2,328	2,076	1,503	1,409	1,246	1,134	1,071	1,071	983	1,557
LT Debt	22.3	26.5	29.4	60.9	65.1	65.1	68.9	70.9	75.2	75.2
Common Eqty.	231	214	182	223	229	197	182	166	177	185
% Ret. on Assets	1.4	1.4	NM	0.5	1.1	1.1	1.1	0.5	1.2	1.2
% Ret. on Equity	20.6	20.7	NM	9.2	20.5	19.4	18.1	5.9	15.2	16.3
% Loan Loss Resv.	0.9	1.0	1.1	1.1	1.0	0.9	0.7	0.8	0.7	1.2
% Loans/Deposits	63.1	61.1	73.2	66.7	56.2	53.5	55.2	52.0	54.3	37.2
% Equity to Assets	6.8	6.5	7.0	5.7	5.4	5.4	6.8	7.7	8.2	7.5

Data as orig. reptd.; bef. results of disc. opers. and/or spec. items. Per share data adj. for stk. divs. as of ex-div. date. Bold denotes diluted EPS (FASB 128). E-Estimated. NA-Not Available. NM-Not Meaningful. NR-Not Ranked.

Office—114 W. 47th St., New York, NY 10036. **Tel**—(212) 852-1000. **Website**—http://www.ustrust.com **Chrmn & CEO**—H. M. Schwarz. **Vice Chrmn** —M. S. Rahe, F. B. Taylor. **Pres & COO**—J. S. Maurer.**EVP, Tres & CFO**—J. L. Kirby. **Dirs**—E. Baum, S. C. Butler, P. O. Crisp, P. de Montebello, P. W. Douglas, N. M. Grumbach, F. C. Hamilton, P. L. Malkin, J. S. Maurer, D. A. Olsen, M. S. Rahe, H. M. Schwarz, P. L. Smith, J. H. Stookey, F. B. Taylor, R. F. Tucker, C. L. Wainwright Jr., R. N. Wilson, R. A. Wooden. **Transfer Agent & Registrar**—Co.'s office. **Incorporated**—in New York in 1877. **Empl**— 1,538. **S&P Analyst:** Michael Schneider

03-OCT-98

Industry:
Water Utilities

Summary: This utility holding company is the parent of United Water New Jersey and United Water New York, constituting the nation's second largest investor-owned water utility.

Quantitative Evaluations	
Outlook (1 Lowest—5 Highest)	**2⁻**
Fair Value	**17**
Risk	**Low**
Earn./Div. Rank	**B**
Technical Eval.	**Bullish** since 4/98
Rel. Strength Rank (1 Lowest—99 Highest)	**71**
Insider Activity	**Neutral**

Recent Price • 16¾
52 Wk Range • 19⅞-15¾

Yield • 5.5%
12-Mo. P/E • 21.2

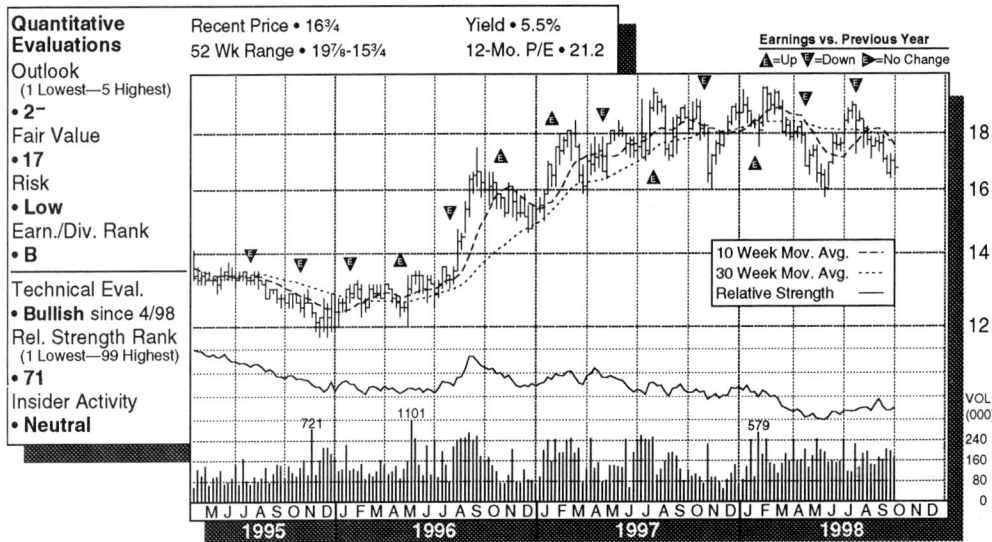

Earnings vs. Previous Year
▲=Up ▼=Down ▶=No Change

10 Week Mov. Avg. – – –
30 Week Mov. Avg. · · · ·
Relative Strength —

Business Profile - 06-JUL-98

In April 1998, the company and Energis Resources, a full-service energy provider and an unregulated subsidiary of Public Service Enterprise Group Inc., formed a working alliance to provide towns and cities with services that reduce costs and improve efficiencies for their water or wastewater systems, while addressing water quality and other environmental issues. In June 1998, the company announced that an affiliate had signed a 10-year, $95 million agreement with Gary, IN, to operate and maintain the city's wastewater treatment facility and sewer system.

Operational Review - 06-JUL-98

Operating revenues in the first quarter of 1998 declined 5.7%, year to year, due primarily to the absence of a land sale. Margins narrowed, reflecting higher depreciation and amortization charges and general taxes, which offset an 11% drop in O&M expenses; operating income was down 6.3%. After a 12% increase in interest and other expenses, income before taxes decreased 26%. Following taxes at 20.7%, versus 26.5%, net income sank 20%, to $4,204,000 ($0.09 a share, after preferred dividends and on 12% more shares), from $5,237,000 ($0.12).

Stock Performance - 02-OCT-98

In the past 30 trading days, UWR's shares have declined 4%, compared to a 7% fall in the S&P 500. Average trading volume for the past five days was 34,040 shares, compared with the 40-day moving average of 35,421 shares.

Key Stock Statistics

Dividend Rate/Share	0.92	Shareholders	18,700
Shs. outstg. (M)	37.2	Market cap. (B)	$0.623
Avg. daily vol. (M)	0.037	Inst. holdings	19%
Tang. Bk. Value/Share	13.91		
Beta	0.61		

Value of $10,000 invested 5 years ago: $ 16,357

Fiscal Year Ending Dec. 31

	1998	1997	1996	1995	1994	1993
Revenues (Million $)						
1Q	75.44	80.01	69.76	71.41	39.02	35.90
2Q	86.22	87.76	82.58	83.57	82.40	43.34
3Q	—	99.7	97.87	96.38	93.49	78.23
4Q	—	83.95	81.83	76.47	78.10	42.96
Yr.	—	351.4	332.1	327.8	293.0	200.4
Earnings Per Share ($)						
1Q	0.09	0.12	0.15	0.03	0.12	0.04
2Q	0.30	0.32	0.22	0.24	0.28	0.20
3Q	—	0.18	0.46	0.45	0.46	0.57
4Q	—	0.21	0.28	-0.17	0.12	0.21
Yr.	—	0.83	1.12	0.54	1.01	1.03

Next earnings report expected: mid October

Dividend Data (Dividends have been paid since 1886.)

Amount ($)	Date Decl.	Ex-Div. Date	Stock of Record	Payment Date
0.230	Oct. 09	Nov. 12	Nov. 14	Dec. 01 '97
0.230	Jan. 22	Feb. 11	Feb. 13	Mar. 01 '98
0.230	Mar. 12	May. 13	May. 15	Jun. 01 '98
0.230	Jul. 07	Aug. 12	Aug. 14	Sep. 01 '98

A Division of The McGraw·Hill Companies

Business Summary - 06-JUL-98

Only a few years ago, United Water Resources Inc. (UWR) was a regional water supplier serving one million people in two states: New York and New Jersey. Today, it's the nation's second largest investor-owned water services company (only American Water Works is larger) with a presence in 19 states across the country. UWR has interests in Canada and Mexico as well, and across the Atlantic, its 10%-owned affiliate, Northumbrian Water Group, provides water services to four million Britons.

Through its United Water New Jersey and United Water New York utilities, which serve contiguous areas of the two states, UWR furnishes water to some one million people. UWR provides water and wastewater services to another million people in 13 states through its United Waterworks subsidiary. In all, the company's regulated utility operations served some 595,364 separate water customer accounts and 27,039 wastewater customers at the end of 1997. Residential customers accounted for 62% of utility revenues in 1997, commercial customers 26%, industrial 8%, and fire protection 4%.

While revenues from regulated water utilities -- about 84% of total revenues in 1997 -- are expected to remain strong over the next five years, the company anticipates a dramatic increase in revenues from non-regulated water services during the same period. Through public-private partnerships -- including UWR's 1996 alliance with Jersey City, NJ, forming the nation's largest such partnership for a municipal water operation -- cities retain ownership of their water systems while the company operates and maintains them. UWR also has a stake in JMM Operational Services, Inc., which provides contract operations and management services on behalf of municipally owned water and wastewater treatment facilities in North America. A July 1997 restructuring lifted UWR's interest in JMM, which it holds through United Water Services LLC, to 50%. UWR's various real estate activities, including property holdings in several states, constitute another non-regulated business area.

In June 1998, the company announced that its affiliate, the White River Environmental Partnership, signed a 10-year, $95 million agreement with Gary, IN, to operate and maintain the city's wastewater treatment facility and sewer system, which provides services to approximately 120,000 residents in Gary and its vicinity.

Per Share Data ($) (Year Ended Dec. 31)	1997	1996	1995	1994	1993	1992	1991	1990	1989	1988
Tangible Bk. Val.	14.36	14.10	14.14	14.09	9.62	9.12	8.81	8.54	8.07	8.10
Earnings	0.83	1.14	0.54	1.01	1.03	0.87	0.96	1.10	0.86	1.08
Dividends	0.92	0.92	0.92	0.92	0.92	0.92	0.91	0.88	0.88	0.84
Payout Ratio	111%	81%	170%	91%	89%	106%	95%	80%	102%	78%
Prices - High	19³/₄	17¹/₂	14¹/₈	14³/₄	15⁷/₈	16⁵/₈	16⁵/₈	16¹/₂	17⁷/₈	20¹/₂
- Low	15	12	11³/₄	12¹/₄	14	13	10⁷/₈	9⁷/₈	15³/₄	15³/₄
P/E Ratio - High	24	15	26	15	15	19	17	15	21	19
- Low	18	11	22	12	14	15	11	9	18	15

Income Statement Analysis (Million $)

	1997	1996	1995	1994	1993	1992	1991	1990	1989	1988
Revs.	22.2	332	328	293	200	165	162	165	133	125
Depr.	34.7	30.8	30.2	25.2	14.3	14.0	13.1	11.4	9.3	7.0
Maint.	NA	NA	NA	NA	0.5	0.8	NA	NA	NA	NA
Fxd. Chgs. Cov.	1.7	2.0	1.6	2.5	2.3	2.0	2.1	2.4	2.2	2.7
Constr. Credits	3.4	3.4	1.9	1.3	0.6	0.6	0.8	1.9	3.9	4.3
Eff. Tax Rate	38%	38%	39%	40%	39%	31%	31%	34%	28%	25%
Net Inc.	33.7	43.0	22.1	31.3	20.0	15.8	16.4	18.3	14.3	18.0

Balance Sheet & Other Fin. Data (Million $)

	1997	1996	1995	1994	1993	1992	1991	1990	1989	1988
Gross Prop.	1,682	1,421	1,410	1,346	606	569	556	550	524	492
Cap. Exp.	83.3	74.5	70.0	58.0	16.0	14.1	16.1	27.6	30.0	37.5
Net Prop.	1,385	1,146	1,153	1,110	502	474	470	463	443	418
Capitalization:										
LT Debt	623	558	559	505	277	294	302	251	254	221
% LT Debt	55	53	55	53	54	58	62	59	60	56
Pfd.	95.6	117	107	107	32.8	33.1	18.4	19.9	21.5	23.1
% Pfd.	8.40	11	11	11	6.40	6.50	3.80	4.70	5.10	5.90
Common	419	391	358	350	202	180	164	153	146	149
% Common	37	37	35	36	40	36	34	36	35	38
Total Cap.	1,455	1,353	1,312	1,242	624	582	553	493	475	444
% Oper. Ratio	78.6	71.1	80.4	78.6	78.7	76.7	76.8	78.2	77.2	74.6
% Earn. on Net Prop.	7.1	8.3	6.9	7.8	8.9	8.1	8.0	7.9	7.1	7.9
% Return On Revs.	9.6	12.9	6.8	10.7	10.0	9.6	10.2	11.1	10.7	14.4
% Return On Invest. Capital	6.2	9.9	6.4	7.2	7.3	7.0	7.6	8.0	6.7	7.6
% Return On Com. Equity	7.2	4.1	4.9	11.3	10.5	9.2	10.4	12.3	9.7	12.2

Data as orig. reptd.; bef. results of disc. opers. and/or spec. items. Per share data adj. for stk. divs. as of ex-div. date. E-Estimated. NA-Not Available. NM-Not Meaningful. NR-Not Ranked.

Office—200 Old Hook Rd., Harrington Park, NJ 07640. **Tel**—(201) 784-9434. **Website**—http://www.unitedwater.com **Chrmn, Pres & CEO**—D. L. Correll. **Treas**—J. J. Turner. **Investor Contact**—Nicholas P. Gicas (201) 767-2887. **Secy**—D. W. Hawes. **Dirs**—E. E. Barr, F. J. Borelli, Thierry Bourbie, L. R. Codey, D. L. Correll, P. Del Col, R. L. Duncan, Jr., J. F. Hanson, D. W. Hawes, G. F. Keane, D. M. Newnham, J. F. Petry, M. L. Worthing. **Transfer Agent & Registrar**—ChaseMellon Shareholder Services. **Incorporated**—in New Jersey in 1869; reincorporated in New Jersey in 1983. **Empl**— 1,400. **S&P Analyst**: J. Robert Cho

03-OCT-98

Industry:
Electronics (Semiconductors)

Summary: This company designs and manufactures analog/linear and mixed-signal integrated circuits, principally to perform power management, motion control and interface functions.

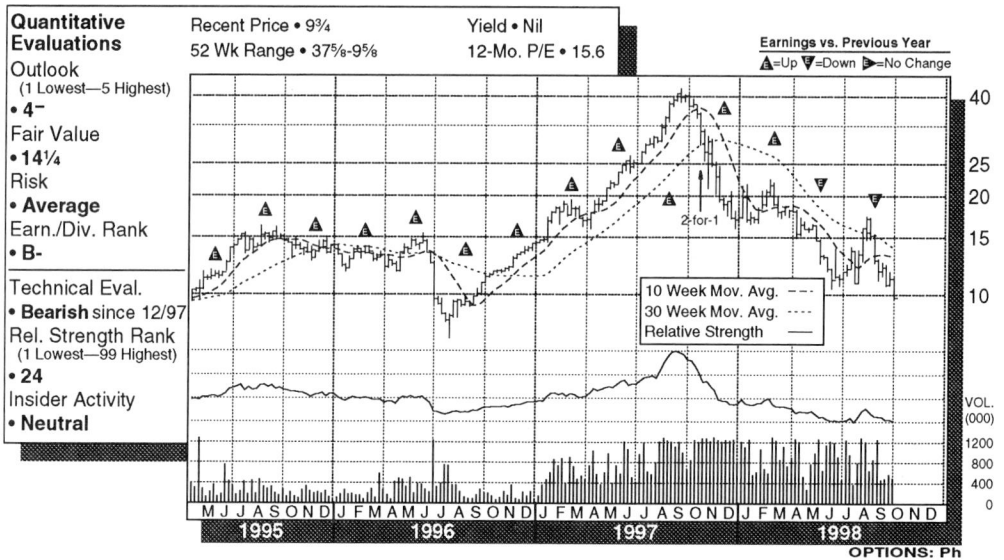

Quantitative Evaluations	
Outlook (1 Lowest—5 Highest)	• **4⁻**
Fair Value	• **14¼**
Risk	• **Average**
Earn./Div. Rank	• **B⁻**
Technical Eval.	• **Bearish** since 12/97
Rel. Strength Rank (1 Lowest—99 Highest)	• **24**
Insider Activity	• **Neutral**

Recent Price • 9¾
52 Wk Range • 37⅝-9⅝

Yield • Nil
12-Mo. P/E • 15.6

Earnings vs. Previous Year
▲=Up ▼=Down ▶=No Change

10 Week Mov. Avg. – – –
30 Week Mov. Avg. · · · ·
Relative Strength ——

2-for-1

OPTIONS: Ph

Business Profile - 22-JUN-98

Weakness in the disk drive and other markets has been hurting the company's business, resulting in a reduction in scheduled orders in the first quarter of FY 99 (Jan.). UTR believes that the level of some of its customers' inventories continues to be high and that customers will work off these inventories before making significant new purchasing commitments. Directors recently withdrew their recommendation that Unitrode shareholders approve the issuance of Unitrode common stock for a proposed merger with BENCHMARQ Microelectronics.

Operational Review - 22-JUN-98

Net sales in the quarter ended May 2, 1998, fell 31%, year to year, mainly reflecting significantly reduced shipments to Western Digital, which had been the company's largest customer. Including non-recurring writedowns and restructuring charges on a pretax basis of $7.1 million, a net loss of $2.3 million ($0.10 per diluted share) was incurred, in contrast to last year's first quarter net income of $6.6 million ($0.27). Excluding the non-recurring charges, net income would have been $2.4 million ($0.10, adjusted).

Stock Performance - 02-OCT-98

In the past 30 trading days, UTR's shares have declined 35%, compared to a 7% fall in the S&P 500. Average trading volume for the past five days was 98,340 shares, compared with the 40-day moving average of 166,608 shares.

Key Stock Statistics

Dividend Rate/Share	Nil	Shareholders	700
Shs. outstg. (M)	24.5	Market cap. (B)	$0.240
Avg. daily vol. (M)	0.102	Inst. holdings	81%
Tang. Bk. Value/Share	6.55		
Beta	0.85		

Value of $10,000 invested 5 years ago: $ 17,639

Fiscal Year Ending Jan. 31

	1999	1998	1997	1996	1995	1994
Revenues (Million $)						
1Q	28.02	40.84	34.22	25.89	22.30	21.23
2Q	29.71	48.18	30.01	28.86	24.00	22.01
3Q	—	48.54	32.07	30.12	25.80	21.27
4Q	—	40.05	37.23	33.67	25.06	22.40
Yr.	—	177.6	133.5	118.5	97.08	86.92
Earnings Per Share ($)						
1Q	-0.10	0.27	0.22	0.16	0.08	0.05
2Q	0.12	0.33	0.20	0.17	0.05	0.07
3Q	—	0.35	0.21	0.19	0.10	0.09
4Q	—	**0.27**	0.24	0.21	0.15	0.12
Yr.	—	**1.21**	0.87	0.73	0.38	0.32

Next earnings report expected: mid November

Dividend Data

Amount ($)	Date Decl.	Ex-Div. Date	Stock of Record	Payment Date
2-for-1	Aug. 05	Oct. 15	Oct. 06	Oct. 14 '97

Business Summary - 22-JUN-98

Since 1989, Unitrode (UTR) has sold five non-strategic businesses in order to focus on its core products, analog/linear and mixed-signal integrated circuits (ICs). ICs are the building blocks of today's electronic products and may be classified as either analog or digital. Digital circuits are used mostly in computer memory or logic devices and in microprocessors. Analog circuits process "real-world" signals which measure physical conditions, such as temperature, force, speed, and pressure, the frequency and wavelength of which vary continuously. Analog circuits are used to amplify, monitor, condition, or transform these signals or to interpret these signals for use by digital logic. Advancements in technology have led to the development of mixed-signal circuits which combine certain types of analog and digital functions on the same IC in order to reduce space, increase reliability, and improve performance.

Founded in 1960, UTR makes electronic components for a variety of applications in the electronic data processing/computer, telecommunications, industrial control and instrumentation, defense/aerospace, and automotive markets. For the most part, the company's ICs are used either to control switching power supplies and small electronic motors, or as high-speed interface and communications circuits between various pieces of electronic equipment.

During FY 98 (Jan.), research and development expenses were about 9.6% of revenues, or $17.1 million, compared with 13.5% or $18.0 million in the prior year. International sales, comprised mainly of export sales to the Far East, accounted for 64% of the total in FY 98 (69% in FY 97), while UTR's two largest customers, Western Digital and IBM, accounted for 21% (31%) of revenues.

Construction of a new Unitrode 6" BiCMOS wafer fabrication facility in Merrimack to increase manufacturing capacity and expand process capabilities was completed in the second quarter of FY 98. Capital project costs incurred to date for this wafer fab were approximately $38.8 million. This new facility is expected to become operational (revenue generating) in the second half of FY 99.

In June 1998, UTR directors withdrew their recommendation that Unitrode shareholders approve the issuance of shares of Unitrode common stock under the March 1998 merger agreement with BENCHMARQ Microelectronics, Inc. (NASDAQ; BMRQ). Unitrode said that while it is not terminating the agreement, it is reserving its rights to do so in accordance with the terms of the agreement.

Per Share Data ($)

(Year Ended Jan. 31)	1998	1997	1996	1995	1994	1993	1992	1991	1990	1989
Tangible Bk. Val.	6.49	4.88	3.93	3.46	3.35	2.71	2.23	2.85	2.88	3.63
Cash Flow	1.67	1.36	1.09	0.68	0.54	0.48	-0.20	0.35	-0.28	0.55
Earnings	1.21	0.87	0.73	0.38	0.32	0.24	-0.62	-0.07	-0.74	0.07
Dividends	Nil	Nil	Nil	Nil	Nil	Nil	Nil	Nil	Nil	Nil
Payout Ratio	Nil	Nil	Nil	Nil	Nil	Nil	Nil	Nil	Nil	Nil
Cal. Yrs.	1997	1996	1995	1994	1993	1992	1991	1990	1989	1988
Prices - High	42³⁄₈	15³⁄₈	16¹⁄₄	10¹⁄₂	7⁷⁄₈	5³⁄₄	3⁵⁄₈	3¹⁄₈	4¹⁄₁₆	4³⁄₄
- Low	14¹⁄₂	7³⁄₈	8⁷⁄₈	6³⁄₄	4⁷⁄₈	2⁷⁄₈	1¹⁄₂	1¹⁄₂	2¹⁄₁₆	3¹⁄₈
P/E Ratio - High	35	18	22	28	24	24	NM	NM	NM	68
- Low	12	8	12	18	15	12	NM	NM	NM	44

Income Statement Analysis (Million $)

	1998	1997	1996	1995	1994	1993	1992	1991	1990	1989
Revs.	178	134	119	97.0	87.0	87.0	108	125	139	163
Oper. Inc.	53.2	40.8	35.4	24.3	17.5	14.4	11.9	8.5	5.7	17.0
Depr.	11.4	11.7	9.0	7.4	5.7	6.4	11.2	11.5	13.0	13.4
Int. Exp.	0.1	0.1	0.1	0.1	0.1	0.0	0.1	0.2	0.6	0.9
Pretax Inc.	47.8	33.7	28.0	12.5	12.8	9.1	-16.4	-1.2	-21.4	3.1
Eff. Tax Rate	37%	39%	37%	26%	35%	32%	NM	NM	NM	40%
Net Inc.	30.2	20.7	17.5	9.2	8.3	6.2	-16.4	-1.8	-20.6	1.9

Balance Sheet & Other Fin. Data (Million $)

	1998	1997	1996	1995	1994	1993	1992	1991	1990	1989
Cash	66.3	52.0	36.2	30.7	30.8	25.9	22.1	15.2	15.8	6.9
Curr. Assets	114	87.5	71.3	58.5	61.0	51.0	58.0	60.0	64.0	75.0
Total Assets	202	142	118	103	102	86.0	93.0	104	118	139
Curr. Liab.	39.8	24.9	24.2	20.9	17.9	18.2	28.8	20.9	32.0	22.0
LT Debt	NM	NM	NM	Nil	Nil	Nil	Nil	Nil	Nil	2.4
Common Eqty.	159	116	92.4	82.0	84.0	68.0	64.0	84.0	86.0	107
Total Cap.	160	117	93.8	82.0	84.0	68.0	64.0	84.0	86.0	117
Cap. Exp.	45.8	18.7	11.8	15.6	12.6	9.6	5.0	5.7	8.4	10.1
Cash Flow	41.6	32.4	26.5	16.7	14.0	12.6	-5.2	9.8	-7.6	15.2
Curr. Ratio	2.9	3.5	2.9	2.8	3.4	2.8	2.0	2.9	2.0	3.4
% LT Debt of Cap.	NM	NM	NM	Nil	Nil	Nil	Nil	Nil	Nil	2.0
% Net Inc.of Revs.	17.0	15.4	14.8	9.5	9.6	7.1	NM	NM	NM	1.1
% Ret. on Assets	17.6	15.9	15.8	9.3	8.9	7.1	NM	NM	NM	1.3
% Ret. on Equity	21.9	19.9	20.1	11.5	11.0	9.6	NM	NM	NM	1.8

Data as orig. reptd.; bef. results of disc. opers. and/or spec. items. Per share data adj. for stk. divs. as of ex-div. date. Bold denotes diluted EPS (FASB 128). E-Estimated. NA-Not Available. NM-Not Meaningful. NR-Not Ranked.

Office—7 Continental Blvd., Merrimack, NH 03054. **Tel**—(603) 424-2410. **Website**—http://www.unitrode.com.**Chrmn**—R. L. Gable. **Pres & CEO**—R. J. Richardson. **SVP & Secy**—A. R. Campbell. **EVP & CFO**—Cosmo S. Trapani. **Dirs**—P. A. Brooke, R. L. Gable, K. Hecht, L. E. Lataif, R. J. Richardson, J. T. Vanderslice. **Transfer Agent & Registrar**—Boston EquiServe, Canton.**Incorporated**—in Maryland in 1960. **Empl**— 668. **S&P Analyst:** C.F.B.

Universal Forest Products   5520

NASDAQ Symbol **UFPI**

In S&P SmallCap 600

03-OCT-98

Industry:
Building Materials

Summary: This company makes, treats and distributes lumber products for the do-it-yourself, manufactured housing, wholesale lumber and industrial markets.

Quantitative Evaluations	
Outlook (1 Lowest—5 Highest)	• **2⁻**
Fair Value	• **14¾**
Risk	• **Average**
Earn./Div. Rank	• **NR**
Technical Eval.	• **Bearish** since 8/98
Rel. Strength Rank (1 Lowest—99 Highest)	• **91**
Insider Activity	• **Neutral**

Recent Price • 16⅝   Yield • 0.4%

52 Wk Range • 18¾-12¼   12-Mo. P/E • 17.5

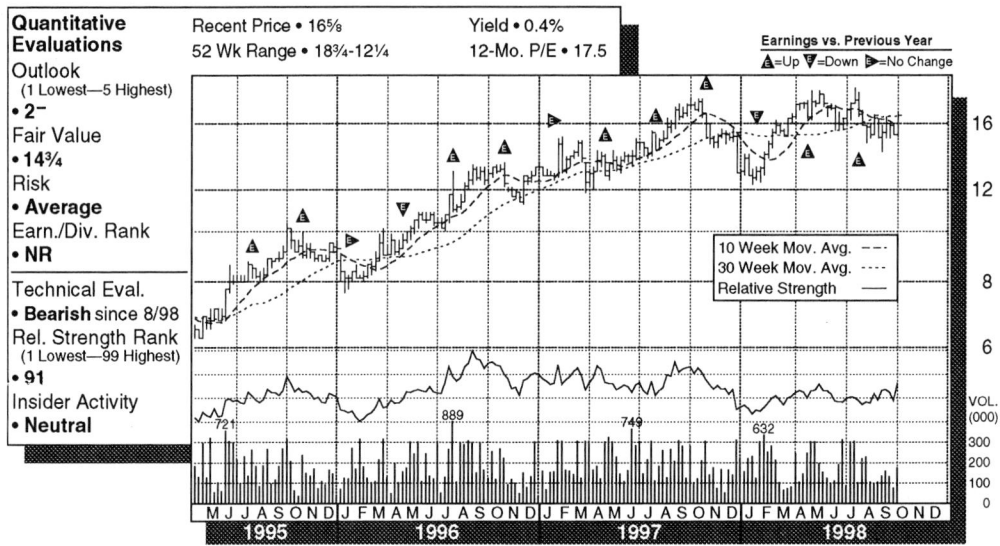

Earnings vs. Previous Year
▲=Up ▼=Down ▶=No Change

10 Week Mov. Avg. ---
30 Week Mov. Avg. ····
Relative Strength —

Business Profile - 10-SEP-98

Universal Forest believes itself to be the leading U.S. producer of lumber products for the do-it-yourself (DIY) retail and factory-built housing (FBH) markets. In recent years, UFPI has taken steps to boost profits, by attempting to expand overall volume growth, increase sales of more profitable products, and improve productivity. UFPI hopes to boost revenues to $2 billion by 2002, by expanding existing product lines; introducing new offerings; acquiring complementary, higher margin businesses; bolstering its nationwide distribution network; and expanding geographically. UFPI plans to boost sales of its higher margin products (DIY offerings, trusses to the FBH market, and industrial products) to at least 50% of total revenues, through internal growth and acquisitions.

Operational Review - 10-SEP-98

Revenues in the first half of 1998 rose 11%, year to year, aided in part by acquisitions. Margins widened, due to increased sales of more profitable products; operating income climbed 26%. Following a sharp rise in interest expense, the gain in net income was pared to 12%, at $14,700,000 ($0.74 a share, on 9.8% more shares), from $13,144,000 ($0.72). At June 30, 1998, UFPI's total debt/equity ratio stood at 98%.

Stock Performance - 02-OCT-98

In the past 30 trading days, UFPI's shares were unchanged, compared to a 7% fall in the S&P 500. Average trading volume for the past five days was 34,720 shares, compared with the 40-day moving average of 25,087 shares.

Key Stock Statistics

Dividend Rate/Share	0.07	Shareholders	2,000
Shs. outstg. (M)	20.7	Market cap. (B)	$0.345
Avg. daily vol. (M)	0.030	Inst. holdings	26%
Tang. Bk. Value/Share	4.17		
Beta	NA		

Value of $10,000 invested 5 years ago: NA

Fiscal Year Ending Dec. 31

	1998	1997	1996	1995	1994	1993
Revenues (Million $)						
1Q	238.2	214.7	159.6	175.0	178.0	132.0
2Q	388.7	341.3	275.7	235.0	283.0	196.0
3Q	—	285.0	243.9	189.0	226.0	159.0
4Q	—	209.0	188.5	140.1	180.0	157.0
Yr.	—	1,066	867.7	739.3	866.0	644.0
Earnings Per Share ($)						
1Q	**0.20**	0.18	0.15	0.20	0.14	0.30
2Q	**0.52**	0.51	0.46	0.30	0.25	0.21
3Q	—	0.29	0.27	0.18	0.11	0.05
4Q	—	-0.09	0.12	0.12	0.12	0.11
Yr.	—	**0.93**	1.00	0.80	0.61	0.66

Next earnings report expected: late October

Dividend Data (Dividends have been paid since 1993.)

Amount ($)	Date Decl.	Ex-Div. Date	Stock of Record	Payment Date
0.035	Nov. 03	Nov. 26	Dec. 01	Dec. 15 '97
0.035	Apr. 22	May. 28	Jun. 01	Jun. 15 '98

A Division of The **McGraw·Hill** Companies

Business Summary - 10-SEP-98

Universal Forest Products makes, treats and distributes lumber products for the do-it-yourself, manufactured housing, wholesale lumber and industrial markets. UFPI is the largest U.S. producer of pressure-treated lumber; it has the capacity to process over one billion board feet annually. Segment revenue contributions in recent years were as follows:

	1997	1996	1995
Do-it-yourself	49%	49%	50%
Manufactured housing	38%	39%	37%
Wholesale lumber	6%	5%	7%
Industrial	5%	5%	5%
Commercial & residential	2%	2%	1%

The do-it-yourself (DIY) segment markets its products primarily to warehouse-format home improvement retailers, chain lumberyards and contractor-oriented wholesalers. In 1997, 1996 and 1995, Home Depot, Inc. accounted for 18%, 15% and 15% of DIY sales, respectively. Offerings include treated and untreated lumber, decking, fencing and a variety of related products. The company has said it knows of no other manufacturer that competes with its DIY products on a national basis. The company also believes its full range of offerings provides significant competitive advantages in the DIY market.

The manufactured housing (MH) segment sells its products to producers of mobile, modular and prefabricated homes and recreational vehicles. Offerings include roof and floor trusses, custom-cut lumber, plywood, particle board and dimension lumber. The company believes it is the largest maker of roof trusses for manufactured housing in North America; Universal estimates that it supplies 70% of the trusses to the MH market.

UFPI's wholesale lumber segment markets its offerings to lumber wholesalers that resell to retail outlets. This segment primarily purchases and resells lumber in carload and truckload quantities, generally without any handling or processing. Because UFPI's wholesale competitors are also DIY customers, the company does not emphasize the wholesale lumber sector. In addition, UFPI believes that it possesses only a small share of the wholesale market, and does not expect its share to increase.

The industrial segment makes wooden pallets and crates for companies that use lumber for packing and shipping. UFPI believes that the industrial market is highly fragmented, and plans to increase its presence in this sector.

In early 1998, in an effort to enter the residential market, UFPI acquired two producers of lumber products for residential homebuilders.

Per Share Data ($)

(Year Ended Dec. 31)	1997	1996	1995	1994	1993	1992	1991	1990	1989	1988
Tangible Bk. Val.	6.45	5.68	4.90	4.20	3.65	2.89	2.61	2.43	NA	NA
Cash Flow	1.45	1.47	1.23	0.93	0.94	0.54	NA	NA	NA	NA
Earnings	0.93	1.00	0.80	0.61	0.66	0.29	0.15	0.06	NA	NA
Dividends	0.07	0.06	0.06	0.05	0.05	0.05	0.05	0.05	NA	NA
Payout Ratio	7%	6%	7%	8%	4%	17%	33%	83%	NA	NA
Prices - High	18	13½	10⅜	11	11	NA	NA	NA	NA	NA
- Low	11¾	7⅝	6	5⅞	7	NA	NA	NA	NA	NA
P/E Ratio - High	19	13	13	18	16	NA	NA	NA	NA	NA
- Low	13	8	7	10	10	NA	NA	NA	NA	NA

Income Statement Analysis (Million $)

	1997	1996	1995	1994	1993	1992	1991	1990	1989	1988
Revs.	1,066	868	739	866	644	450	NA	NA	NA	NA
Oper. Inc.	41.5	40.8	33.9	72.5	58.3	45.0	NA	NA	NA	NA
Depr.	9.5	8.3	7.6	5.7	4.3	3.7	NA	NA	NA	NA
Int. Exp.	4.3	3.0	3.6	5.9	3.9	3.2	NA	NA	NA	NA
Pretax Inc.	26.0	29.7	23.6	18.2	17.0	7.2	NA	NA	NA	NA
Eff. Tax Rate	35%	40%	41%	41%	41%	40%	NA	NA	NA	NA
Net Inc.	17.0	17.7	14.1	10.7	10.0	4.3	NA	NA	NA	NA

Balance Sheet & Other Fin. Data (Million $)

	1997	1996	1995	1994	1993	1992	1991	1990	1989	1988
Cash	3.2	1.3	21.5	0.1	1.3	NA	NA	NA	NA	NA
Curr. Assets	158	127	116	114	144	NA	NA	NA	NA	NA
Total Assets	229	193	176	169	186	NA	NA	NA	NA	NA
Curr. Liab.	67.9	38.1	38.0	35.9	98.4	NA	NA	NA	NA	NA
LT Debt	39.8	49.0	52.5	58.8	23.0	NA	NA	NA	NA	NA
Common Eqty.	116	100	83.4	71.6	61.9	NA	NA	NA	NA	NA
Total Cap.	158	151	138	132	86.0	NA	NA	NA	NA	NA
Cap. Exp.	13.6	9.1	14.3	18.0	9.3	6.9	NA	NA	NA	NA
Cash Flow	26.5	26.1	21.7	16.5	14.3	8.1	NA	NA	NA	NA
Curr. Ratio	2.3	3.3	3.1	3.2	1.5	NA	NA	NA	NA	NA
% LT Debt of Cap.	25.3	32.4	38.1	44.5	26.6	NA	NA	NA	NA	NA
% Net Inc.of Revs.	1.6	2.0	1.9	1.2	1.6	1.0	NA	NA	NA	NA
% Ret. on Assets	8.0	9.6	8.1	6.1	6.4	NA	NA	NA	NA	NA
% Ret. on Equity	15.4	19.4	18.1	16.6	18.8	NA	NA	NA	NA	NA

Data as orig. reptd.; bef. results of disc. opers. and/or spec. items. Per share data adj. for stk. divs. as of ex-div. date. Bold denotes diluted EPS (FASB 128). E-Estimated. NA-Not Available. NM-Not Meaningful. NR-Not Ranked.

Office—2801 E. Beltline N.E., Grand Rapids, MI 49525. **Tel**—(616) 364-6161. **Chrmn**—P. F. Secchia. **Pres & CEO**—W. G. Currie. **EVP & CFO**—E. A. Bowman. **VP & Secy**—M. J. Missad. **Dirs**—J. C. Canepa, W. G. Currie, R. M. DeVos, J. W. Garside, P. M. Novell, P. F. Secchia, L. A. Smith. **Transfer Agent & Registrar**—American Stock Transfer & Trust Co., NYC. **Incorporated**—in Michigan in 1955. **Empl**—3,200. **S&P Analyst:** Robert E. Friedman

Universal Health Services   2372

NYSE Symbol **UHS**

In S&P SmallCap 600

03-OCT-98

Industry: Health Care (Hospital Management)

Summary: This company owns and operates acute care medical/surgical/psychiatric hospitals, along with outpatient surgery and radiation therapy centers nationwide.

S&P Opinion: Hold (★★★)	Recent Price • 43 · 52 Wk Range • 59¾-38⅜ · Yield • Nil · 12-Mo. P/E • 19.1

Quantitative Evaluations

Outlook
(1 Lowest—5 Highest)
• **4⁻**

Fair Value
• **68¾**

Risk
• **Average**

Earn./Div. Rank
• **B+**

Technical Eval.
• **Bearish** since 8/98

Rel. Strength Rank
(1 Lowest—99 Highest)
• **55**

Insider Activity
• **Neutral**

Earnings vs. Previous Year
▲=Up ▼=Down ▶=No Change

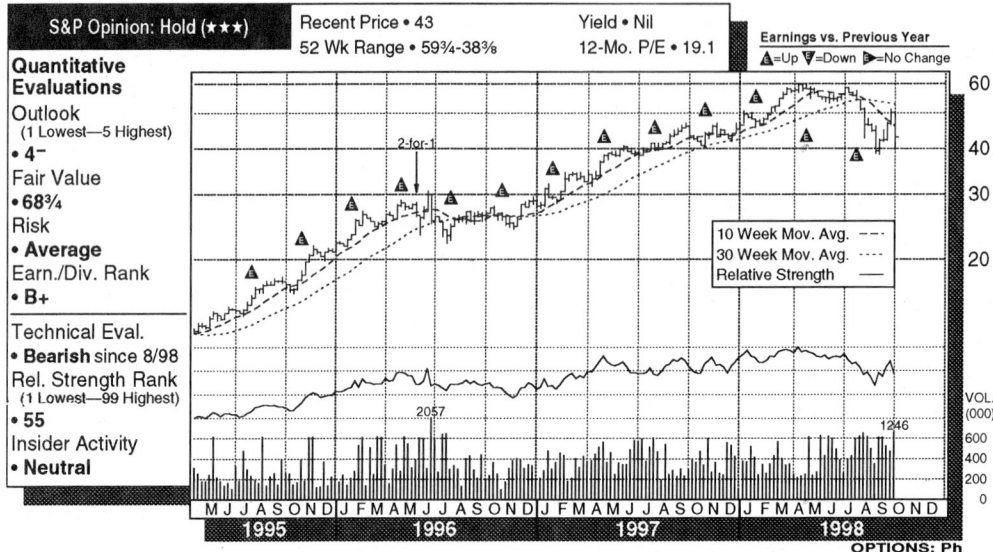

10 Week Mov. Avg. ---
30 Week Mov. Avg. ....
Relative Strength ——

OPTIONS: Ph

Overview - 26-AUG-98

Revenues in 1998 are expected to push towards $2 billion, on the inclusion of hospital acquisitions, the opening of several newly constructed acute care facilities, and improved performance at hospitals under UHS management for a year or more (same-store), where admissions have exceeded industry averages for several quarters. Some operating margin erosion is expected, as newer hospitals are absorbed; EBITDAR (earnings before interest, taxes, depreciation, amortization and rent) margins for 1998 should approximate 17%. The behavioral care division is an important cash flow generator, and this capital is used by the company for acute care hospital acquisitions, and to fund capital expenditures. We see 1998 EPS rising 21%, to $2.45, but expect net earnings growth over the coming three years to slow to about 17%.

Valuation - 26-AUG-98

The stock has fallen in recent months, in sympathy with that of UHS's hospital peers, as investors digest the many changes to Medicare reimbursements enacted as part of the Balanced Budget Act of 1997 (BBA). Pursuant to BBA, there will be no increases in rates paid to hospitals for inpatient care during the government's fiscal year ending September 30, 1998, while modest rate hikes in FY 99 will largely be offset by lower reimbursement rates for a wide range of services, as Medicare continues to move toward a prospective payment, rather than cost-plus, system. As a result, and with ongoing pressures from HMOs and other private payers to reduce the length and frequency of costly inpatient hospital stays, earnings expansion must be increasingly derived from cost reductions and growth of the outpatient businesses. The stock looks fully priced at 18X our 1998 EPS forecast, in line with the hospital group average.

Key Stock Statistics

S&P EPS Est. 1998	2.45	Tang. Bk. Value/Share	10.41
P/E on S&P Est. 1998	17.6	Beta	1.01
S&P EPS Est. 1999	2.90	Shareholders	900
Dividend Rate/Share	Nil	Market cap. (B)	$ 1.3
Shs. outstg. (M)	32.7	Inst. holdings	78%
Avg. daily vol. (M)	0.152		

Value of $10,000 invested 5 years ago: $ 60,884

Fiscal Year Ending Dec. 31

	1998	1997	1996	1995	1994	1993
Revenues (Million $)						
1Q	463.1	340.2	271.6	220.7	194.4	195.3
2Q	474.6	343.8	287.0	214.2	192.2	187.4
3Q	—	362.4	303.5	234.1	191.5	186.3
4Q	—	396.3	328.1	262.1	204.1	192.4
Yr.	—	1,443	1,190	931.1	782.2	761.5
Earnings Per Share ($)						
1Q	**0.77**	0.65	0.54	0.42	0.36	0.30
2Q	**0.61**	0.51	0.42	0.34	0.28	0.23
3Q	**E0.51**	0.42	0.34	0.26	0.20	0.18
4Q	**E0.56**	0.45	0.35	0.24	0.16	0.14
Yr.	**E2.45**	2.03	1.64	1.26	1.01	0.85

Next earnings report expected: mid October

Dividend Data

No regular dividends have been paid on the common stock. A special cash dividend of $0.10 a share was paid in 1989, as adjusted for a two-for-one stock split in 1996.

A Division of The McGraw-Hill Companies

STANDARD
&POOR'S
STOCK REPORTS

Universal Health Services, Inc.

2372

03-OCT-98

Business Summary - 26-AUG-98

Universal Health Services (UHS) ranks as the third largest investor-owned hospital chain, with 1997 revenues of $1.4 billion. At 1997 year-end, the company operated 43 medical/surgical and behavioral health hospitals and 22 outpatient surgery and radiation therapy centers. It also acts as adviser to NYSE-listed Universal Health Realty Income Trust. Net patient revenues in 1997 were derived from Medicare (36%), Medicaid (14%), managed care and other private sources (50%).

Services provided by the company's acute care hospitals include general surgery, internal medicine, obstetrics, emergency room care, radiology, oncology, diagnostic care, coronary care, pediatric services and psychiatric services. UHS provides capital resources as well as a variety of management services to its facilities, including central purchasing, data processing, finance and control systems, facilities planning, physician recruitment services, administrative personnel management, marketing and public relations.

UHS selectively seeks opportunities to expand its operations by acquiring, constructing or leasing additional hospital facilities. In addition, it is the company's objective to increase the operating revenues and profitability of its hospitals by the introduction of new services, improvement of existing services, physician recruitment, and the application of financial and operational controls. UHS also continues to examine its facilities and to dispose of those that do not have the potential to contribute to its growth or operating strategy.

During 1997, acute care hospitals owned by the company had an average of 3,389 licensed beds (3,018 in 1996), while admissions amounted to 128,020 (111,244). The average length of stay declined to 4.8 days (4.9), patient days totaled 618,613 (546,237), and the average occupancy rate per licensed bed was 50% (50%). At the behavioral care centers, licensed beds averaged 1,777 (1,565), admissions totaled 28,350 (22,295), average length of stay was 11.9 days (12.4), patient days reached 337,843 (275,667), and average occupancy rate per licensed bed was 52% (48%).

The company serves as adviser to Universal Health Realty Income Trust (NYSE: UHT), which leases to UHS the real property of seven UHS facilities and holds interests in properties owned by unrelated companies. UHS receives a fee for its advisory services based on the value of Universal Health Realty's assets, and owns 8.0% of its outstanding shares.

Per Share Data ($)

(Year Ended Dec. 31)	1997	1996	1995	1994	1993	1992	1991	1990	1989	1988
Tangible Bk. Val.	11.62	9.39	5.78	8.04	6.93	6.20	5.18	3.76	3.02	2.60
Cash Flow	4.47	3.97	3.08	2.47	2.15	1.85	1.84	2.17	1.68	1.55
Earnings	2.03	1.64	1.26	1.01	0.85	0.71	0.72	0.42	0.31	0.21
Dividends	Nil	Nil	Nil	Nil	Nil	Nil	Nil	Nil	0.10	Nil
Payout Ratio	Nil	Nil	Nil	Nil	Nil	Nil	Nil	Nil	31%	Nil
Prices - High	50³/₄	30³/₄	22¹/₄	14⁷/₈	10⁵/₈	7⁷/₈	9¹/₄	5¹/₈	5⁷/₈	4¹/₈
- Low	27³/₄	21⁵/₈	11¹/₄	9⁵/₈	6¹/₄	5⁵/₈	4¹/₈	3¹/₄	3¹/₈	1⁷/₈
P/E Ratio - High	25	19	18	15	12	11	13	12	19	19
- Low	14	13	9	9	7	8	6	8	10	9

Income Statement Analysis (Million $)

	1997	1996	1995	1994	1993	1992	1991	1990	1989	1988
Revs.	1,443	1,190	931	781	747	699	686	616	587	554
Oper. Inc.	315	177	127	104	81.0	69.0	68.0	78.0	79.0	82.0
Depr.	80.7	71.9	51.4	42.4	39.6	35.6	35.0	48.5	39.7	39.4
Int. Exp.	19.4	21.4	11.8	6.5	9.1	11.9	10.3	24.2	26.6	27.0
Pretax Inc.	106	80.0	53.0	46.9	35.1	41.0	30.3	18.5	14.1	14.9
Eff. Tax Rate	36%	37%	33%	39%	32%	51%	33%	37%	36%	57%
Net Inc.	67.3	50.7	35.5	28.7	24.0	20.0	20.3	11.6	9.0	6.4

Balance Sheet & Other Fin. Data (Million $)

	1997	1996	1995	1994	1993	1992	1991	1990	1989	1988
Cash	0.3	0.3	0.0	0.8	0.6	6.7	22.7	22.9	21.2	14.0
Curr. Assets	230	194	157	118	102	119	141	131	104	97.0
Total Assets	1,085	966	749	521	460	472	501	535	526	543
Curr. Liab.	160	140	135	104	86.0	85.0	127	93.0	101	96.0
LT Debt	272	276	237	85.0	75.0	115	127	206	206	218
Common Eqty.	527	453	298	261	224	203	184	167	158	157
Total Cap.	799	729	535	346	303	327	326	408	399	419
Cap. Exp.	129	106	60.7	59.0	59.0	44.0	55.0	34.0	35.0	54.0
Cash Flow	148	123	86.9	71.1	63.6	55.6	55.3	60.1	48.7	45.8
Curr. Ratio	1.4	1.4	1.2	1.1	1.2	1.4	1.1	1.4	1.0	1.0
% LT Debt of Cap.	34.0	37.8	44.3	24.6	24.7	35.2	39.0	50.4	51.5	52.1
% Net Inc.of Revs.	4.7	4.3	3.8	3.7	3.2	2.9	3.0	1.9	1.5	1.2
% Ret. on Assets	6.6	5.9	5.6	5.8	5.2	4.1	3.9	2.2	1.7	1.2
% Ret. on Equity	13.7	13.5	12.7	11.7	11.3	10.4	11.5	7.2	5.9	4.2

Data as orig. reptd.; bef. results of disc. opers. and/or spec. items. Per share data adj. for stk. divs. as of ex-div. date. Bold denotes diluted EPS (FASB 128). E-Estimated. NA-Not Available. NM-Not Meaningful. NR-Not Ranked.

Office—367 South Gulph Rd., King of Prussia, PA 19406. **Tel**—(610) 768-3300. **Chrmn, Pres & CEO**—A. B. Miller. **SVP, CFO & Investor Contact**—Kirk E. Gorman. **Secy**—S. Miller. **Dirs**—J. H. Herrell, R. H. Hotz, L. Ducat, M. Meyerson, A. B. Miller, S. Miller, A. Pantaleoni, P. R. Verkuil. **Transfer Agent & Registrar**—ChaseMellon Shareholder Services, Ridgefield Park, NJ. **Incorporated**—in Delaware in 1978. **Empl**—17,800. **S&P Analyst:** Robert M. Gold

USFreightways   5531G
Nasdaq Symbol USFC
In S&P SmallCap 600

10-OCT-98   Industry: Truckers

Summary: This company operates a family of five regional less-than-truckload carriers, provides logistics services, and entered the air freight forwarding business in late 1997.

S&P Opinion: Buy (★★★★★)	Recent Price • 18	Yield • 2.1%
	52 Wk Range • 40⅜-17⅜	12-Mo. P/E • 7.4

Quantitative Evaluations

Outlook
(1 Lowest—5 Highest)
• **4**

Fair Value
• **28¾**

Risk
• **Average**

Earn./Div. Rank
• **B+**

Technical Eval.
• **NA**

Rel. Strength Rank
(1 Lowest—99 Highest)
• **40**

Insider Activity
• **Favorable**

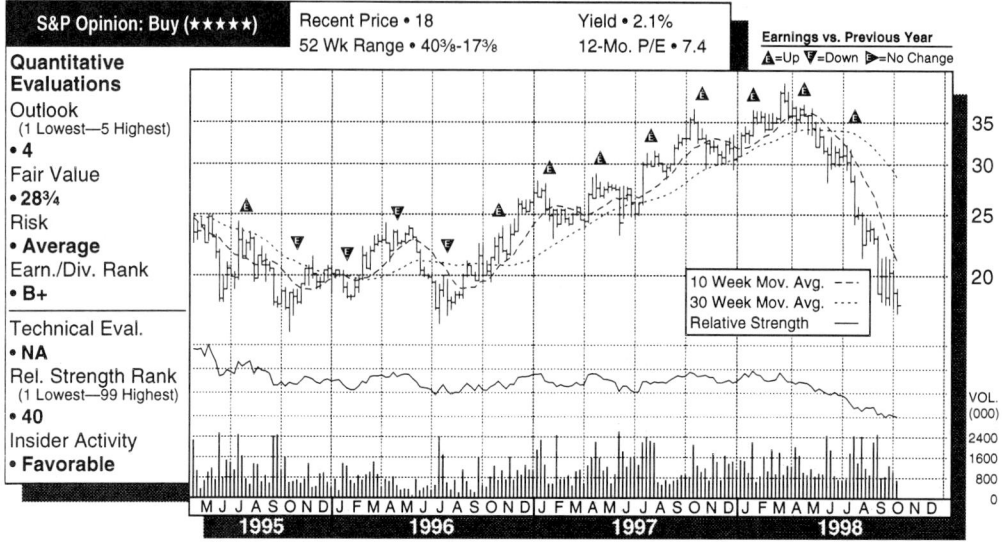

Earnings vs. Previous Year
▲=Up ▼=Down ▷=No Change

10 Week Mov. Avg. ---
30 Week Mov. Avg. ····
Relative Strength ——

VOL. (000)

1995   1996   1997   1998

Overview - 14-AUG-98

Less-than-truckload tonnage could advance 8%-10% in 1998, versus 1997's 11% gain. USFC will not repeat the UPS business picked up in August when that carrier was strikebound, but will gain shipments from the acquisition of Mercury Distribution in January 1998 and Vallerie Transportation in April 1998. Weighing down on USFC's performance will be the lengthy GM strike and a softer economy. Margins will widen, particularly at Red Star, which will see improvement in load density as it integrates Mercury and Vallerie's operations. Lower fuel costs will also aid profits. Labor costs will increase somewhat less than revenues. The major sore spot is rapidly increasing insurance and claims. LTL yields are expected to increase about 3% in 1998, slightly less than in 1997, as industry capacity remains tight. Logistics will benefit from new contracts with Western Star and Alberto-Culver. A positive contribution is anticipated from recently acquired Seko Worldwide. Interest costs will fall.

Valuation - 14-AUG-98

After topping their October 1987 high in March 1998, the shares of this regional LTL carrier plummeted to levels not seen since late 1996. While USFC hit its profit targets for the first and second quarter, its tonnage growth rate slowed noticeably. The economy clearly underwent an inventory correction in the second quarter that has extended into the third quarter. Nevertheless, as USFC is still expected to grow its profits in 1998 and 1999 at a healthy pace, we believe investors have reacted irrationally. We like USFC's long-term strategy to broaden its offerings to include logistics, freight forwarding, and with the pending purchase of Glen Moore Transport, full truckload carriage. We would use current price weakness to aggressively add to holdings.

Key Stock Statistics

S&P EPS Est. 1998	2.55	Tang. Bk. Value/Share	12.17
P/E on S&P Est. 1998	7.1	Beta	0.51
S&P EPS Est. 1999	2.90	Shareholders	6,300
Dividend Rate/Share	0.37	Market cap. (B)	$0.472
Shs. outstg. (M)	26.2	Inst. holdings	94%
Avg. daily vol. (M)	0.188		

Value of $10,000 invested 5 years ago: $ 14,096

Fiscal Year Ending Dec. 31

	1998	1997	1996	1995	1994	1993
Revenues (Million $)						
1Q	442.3	355.8	313.7	279.0	251.0	207.0
2Q	447.0	380.8	332.1	287.0	221.0	220.0
3Q	—	393.5	343.2	290.0	274.0	236.0
4Q	—	435.2	342.0	288.0	271.0	236.0
Yr.	—	1,565	1,331	1,144	1,016	899.0
Earnings Per Share ($)						
1Q	0.52	0.40	0.20	0.37	0.27	0.16
2Q	0.68	0.56	0.37	0.44	0.20	0.38
3Q	E0.70	0.67	0.49	0.40	0.57	0.42
4Q	E0.65	0.56	0.35	0.30	0.47	0.32
Yr.	E2.55	2.19	1.40	1.51	1.51	1.25

Next earnings report expected: early October

Dividend Data (Dividends have been paid since 1992.)

Amount ($)	Date Decl.	Ex-Div. Date	Stock of Record	Payment Date
0.093	Dec. 03	Dec. 23	Dec. 26	Jan. 09 '98
0.093	Mar. 12	Mar. 25	Mar. 27	Apr. 10 '98
0.093	Jun. 04	Jun. 24	Jun. 26	Jul. 10 '98
0.093	Sep. 08	Sep. 23	Sep. 25	Oct. 09 '98

 A Division of The McGraw-Hill Companies

Business Summary - 14-AUG-98

USFreightways (formerly TNT Freightways) primarily provides regional LTL (less-than-truckload shipments of less than 10,000 lbs) freight service. USFC's objective is to become a single-source provider of transportation services. Accordingly, USFC entered the air freight forwarding business in October 1997 through the acquisition of Seko Worldwide. Other transportation services offered include logistics and ocean cargo consolidation. USFC is moving back into the truckload market with the pending acquisition of Glen Moore Transport. A home-grown truckload carrier, Comet, was sold in 1997 after failing to attain profitability.

USFC operates a family of five regional LTL freight carriers. Collectively, these carriers generated 90% of revenues in 1997. Regional LTL carriers primarily handle shipments moving under 500 miles that are routed directly between origin and destination terminals.

High capital costs for terminals and equipment serve as a barrier to entry to competition. Operating through a network of 217 terminals at 1997 year-end, USFC provides freight service in the U.S. and parts of Canada.

USFC's largest regional carrier is USF Holland (45% of total revenues), which serves the Midwest and Southeast. USF Red Star (12% of revenues), which operates in the eastern U.S. and parts of Canada, underwent a major restructuring in 1996. In January 1998, USFC acquired Mercury Distribution Carriers, a LTL carrier serving the Mid-Atlantic. In April 1998, USFC acquired Vallerie Transportation Services, an LTL carrier

serving New England and the Mid-Atlantic. Both carriers' operations will be integrated with Red Star, in an effort to improve margins through increased load density.

During 1996, USFC integrated the operations of Transus, Inc., a Southeastern-based carrier acquired in January 1996, into USFC Dugan (11% of revenues). Also in 1996, the company consolidated the operations of USF United, which served the Northwest and Rocky Mountain states, with those of USF Reddaway (13% of revenues). USF Bestway (9% of revenues) serves the Southwest and California.

Over the past few years, USFC has consistently posted operating ratios (operating expenses divided by revenues) lower than those of its peers. In 1997, the operating ratio was 92.7%, versus 94.5% in 1996.

In July 1998 USFC agreed to acquire Glen Moore Transport, Inc. a truckload carrier having annual revenue of some $35 million. USFC tried unsuccessfully to develop its own truckload operations, but sold its Comet Transportation unit in late 1997.

Logistics services (7% of total revenues) involve the total management of the transportation, distribution and warehousing supply chain.

Remaining operations (3% of revenues) include cargo consolidation services for shipments moving between the U.S. mainland and Hawaii, Guam and Puerto Rico. USFC entered the air freight forwarding market in October 1997, with the acquisition of SEKO Worldwide, which generated revenues of $105 million in 1996.

Per Share Data ($)

(Year Ended Dec. 31)	1997	1996	1995	1994	1993	1992	1991	1990	1989	1988
Tangible Bk. Val.	11.24	8.40	7.45	6.19	4.75	5.32	NA	NA	NA	NA
Cash Flow	4.91	4.25	3.78	3.51	2.97	1.99	1.62	NA	NA	NA
Earnings	2.19	1.41	1.51	1.51	1.25	0.78	0.59	NA	NA	NA
Dividends	0.37	0.37	0.37	0.37	0.37	0.28	Nil	Nil	Nil	Nil
Payout Ratio	17%	26%	25%	25%	30%	36%	Nil	Nil	Nil	Nil
Prices - High	36¾	28¼	28⅝	29¾	27½	14⅜	NA	NA	NA	NA
- Low	22⅞	16¾	16¼	19¼	12	9⅜	NA	NA	NA	NA
P/E Ratio - High	17	20	19	20	23	18	NA	NA	NA	NA
- Low	10	12	11	13	10	12	NA	NA	NA	NA

Income Statement Analysis (Million $)

	1997	1996	1995	1994	1993	1992	1991	1990	1989	1988
Revs.	1,565	1,331	1,144	1,016	899	775	NA	NA	NA	NA
Oper. Inc.	175	131	118	114	101	72.0	NA	NA	NA	NA
Depr.	70.1	63.9	50.3	44.3	39.4	32.8	NA	NA	NA	NA
Int. Exp.	8.5	12.1	8.9	9.1	7.6	2.0	NA	NA	NA	NA
Pretax Inc.	97.5	54.9	58.5	59.2	52.1	36.8	NA	NA	NA	NA
Eff. Tax Rate	42%	43%	43%	44%	45%	44%	NA	NA	NA	NA
Net Inc.	56.6	31.5	33.3	33.4	28.5	20.8	NA	NA	NA	NA

Balance Sheet & Other Fin. Data (Million $)

	1997	1996	1995	1994	1993	1992	1991	1990	1989	1988
Cash	6.5	4.1	1.7	2.1	2.3	NA	NA	NA	NA	NA
Curr. Assets	237	204	159	145	123	NA	NA	NA	NA	NA
Total Assets	800	689	578	501	461	NA	NA	NA	NA	NA
Curr. Liab.	182	144	128	118	98.0	NA	NA	NA	NA	NA
LT Debt	115	178	137	106	124	NA	NA	NA	NA	NA
Common Eqty.	392	269	233	208	181	NA	NA	NA	NA	NA
Total Cap.	560	494	411	350	334	NA	NA	NA	NA	NA
Cap. Exp.	129	0.3	117	68.8	84.2	63.3	NA	NA	NA	NA
Cash Flow	127	95.4	83.7	77.7	67.9	53.6	NA	NA	NA	NA
Curr. Ratio	1.3	1.4	1.2	1.2	1.3	NA	NA	NA	NA	NA
% LT Debt of Cap.	20.5	36.0	33.3	30.3	37.2	NA	NA	NA	NA	NA
% Net Inc.of Revs.	3.6	2.4	2.9	3.3	3.2	2.7	NA	NA	NA	NA
% Ret. on Assets	7.6	5.0	6.2	6.9	6.6	NA	NA	NA	NA	NA
% Ret. on Equity	17.1	12.5	15.1	17.2	14.0	NA	NA	NA	NA	NA

Data as orig. reptd.; bef. results of disc. opers. and/or spec. items. Per share data adj. for stk. divs. as of ex-div. date. Bold denotes diluted EPS (FASB 128). E-Estimated. NA-Not Available. NM-Not Meaningful. NR-Not Ranked.

Office—9700 Higgins Rd., Suite 570, Rosemont, IL 60018. **Tel**—(847) 696-0200. **Fax**—(847) 696-2080. **Website**—http://www.usfreightways.com **Chrmn & CEO**—J. C. Carruth. **Pres & COO**—J. G. Connelly III. **SVP & CFO & Investor Contact**—C. L. Ellis. **Secy**—R. C. Pagano. **Dirs**—J. C. Carruth, J. G. Connelly III, R. V. Delaney, M. Koffman, R. P. Neuschel, A. J. Paoni, J. W. Puth, N. A. Springer, W. N. Weaver. **Transfer Agent & Registrar**—Harris Trust and Savings Bank, Chicago. **Incorporated**—in Delaware in 1991. **Empl**— 16,843. **S&P Analyst**: Stephen R. Klein

VLSI Technology   5536

Nasdaq Symbol **VLSI**

In S&P SmallCap 600

03-OCT-98

Industry:
Electronics (Semiconductors)

Summary: VLSI makes complex application-specific integrated circuits and application-specific standard products.

S&P Opinion: Hold (★★★)	Recent Price • 7⅝	Yield • Nil
	52 Wk Range • 37½-7	12-Mo. P/E • 6.2

Quantitative Evaluations

Outlook
(1 Lowest—5 Highest)
• **2**

Fair Value
• **7⅞**

Risk
• **High**

Earn./Div. Rank
• **B-**

Technical Eval.
• **Bearish** since 8/98

Rel. Strength Rank
(1 Lowest—99 Highest)
• **11**

Insider Activity
• **NA**

Earnings vs. Previous Year
▲=Up ▼=Down ▷=No Change

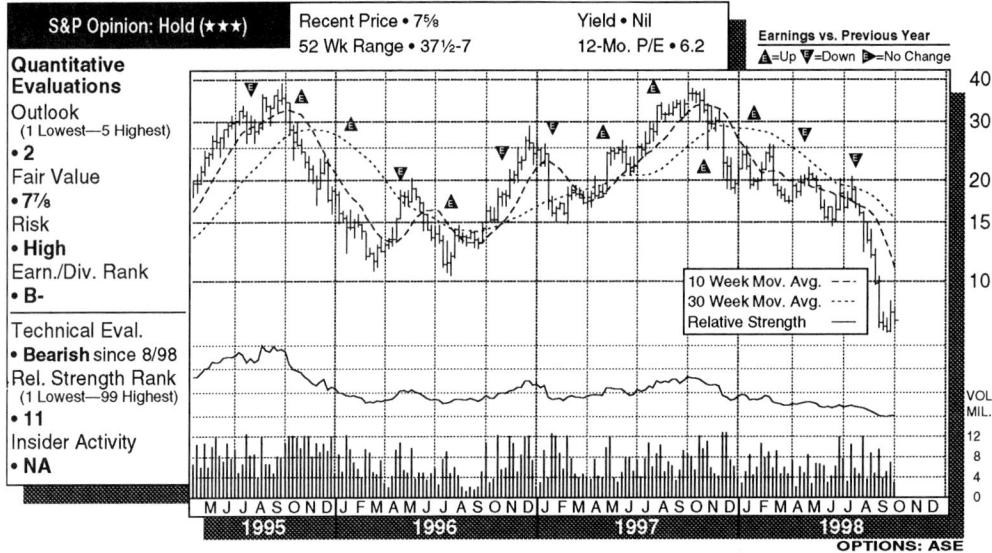

10 Week Mov. Avg. - - - -
30 Week Mov. Avg. ·····
Relative Strength ——

MJJASOND|JFMAMJJASOND|JFMAMJJASOND|JFMAMJJASOND
1995 · 1996 · 1997 · 1998

OPTIONS: ASE

Overview - 08-SEP-98

We expect revenues to decline more than 20% in 1998, reflecting weakness in the company's served end-markets. In the first half, VLSI experienced a sharp slowdown in wireless chip sales, as major customers reduced inventory in older handsets. Wireless bookings improved somewhat in the second quarter, but showed further weakness in July and August. Results in both the consumer and communications segments continue to be weak, and near-term visibility remains limited. Despite a more favorable product mix, we expect margins to come under pressure from the lower volume. VLSI recently announced a $120 million investment for a minority interest in a state-of-the-art Malaysian wafer fab. The facility, which will begin operations in 2000, will ensure high-volume capacity for the company. Overall, based on prospects for declining sales and narrower margins, we expect EPS to fall to $0.24 in 1998, from 1997's $1.36 from continuing operations.

Valuation - 08-SEP-98

Although VLSI reported weak operating results in each of the past two quarters, we are maintaining our hold rating on the shares. The company derives approximately 50% of its sales from the communications segment, with the balance split between the consumer and computing markets. While customer inventory levels are at very low levels, the company has indicated that order trends remain weak. The computing and consumer markets continue to be sluggish, and we do not anticipate a turnaround in the near future. Following a sharp decline since last fall, the shares are now trading at just 64% of book value. While the valuation is compelling, we expect the shares to perform only in line with the broader market until a clearer picture of top-line growth emerges.

Key Stock Statistics

S&P EPS Est. 1998	0.24	Tang. Bk. Value/Share	12.08
P/E on S&P Est. 1998	31.8	Beta	1.67
S&P EPS Est. 1999	0.80	Shareholders	1,800
Dividend Rate/Share	Nil	Market cap. (B)	$0.354
Shs. outstg. (M)	46.5	Inst. holdings	62%
Avg. daily vol. (M)	1.057		

Value of $10,000 invested 5 years ago: $ 9,384

Fiscal Year Ending Dec. 31

	1998	1997	1996	1995	1994	1993
Revenues (Million $)						
1Q	141.3	177.7	167.7	163.0	138.1	117.0
2Q	137.8	182.5	182.5	184.4	148.1	128.0
3Q	—	181.2	183.0	188.2	151.6	137.3
4Q	—	193.0	183.6	184.3	149.3	133.3
Yr.	—	712.7	716.8	719.9	587.1	516.0
Earnings Per Share ($)						
1Q	0.07	0.22	0.07	0.27	0.15	-0.06
2Q	0.14	0.28	0.18	0.03	0.25	0.09
3Q	—	0.41	0.06	0.35	0.20	0.21
4Q	—	0.45	-1.38	0.38	0.25	0.21
Yr.	—	1.36	-1.00	1.05	0.85	0.45

Next earnings report expected: NA

Dividend Data

No cash has been paid.

A Division of The McGraw·Hill Companies

Business Summary - 08-SEP-98

VLSI Technology manufactures semiconductors, or integrated circuits (ICs), that are used in the production of rapidly proliferating electronic products. VLSI's chips allow products such as mobile computers, wireless communications devices, electronic games and digital set-top boxes to be made faster, smaller and cheaper, thereby enhancing their functionality. ICs manufactured by VLSI include application-specific integrated circuits (ASICs), which are custom-designed chips tailored for individual users; and application-specific standard products (ASSPs), or semi-custom chips designed for a particular market application that may be used by several customers.

Target markets for VLSI are the computing, consumer electronics and consumer digital entertainment markets. VLSI focuses its marketing efforts on leading original equipment manufacturers (OEMs) in these segments, and attempts to design and manufacture highly integrated complex semiconductor devices that allow its customers to develop and bring to market higher value-added systems and products. The company seeks to develop ICs that will allow customers to differentiate their products from those of competitors, and reduce product costs.

The communications segment serves wireless and network customers. Wireless solutions are provided through the use of baseband signal processing technol-ogy developed to support various wireless voice and and data standards, including GSM, PHS and DECT. Networking solutions include digital cross-connect, transmission, networking/internetworking, switching and multiplexing. The consumer digital entertainment segment targets high-volume entertainment-related markets, including set-top boxes for satellite and cable TV, digital video disk and electronic games.

The computing segment primarily serves workstations and mass storage systems. Over the past year, the company has begun to withdraw from the logic chip-set business, which at one time represented a significant portion of total revenues, due to the dominance of Intel Corporation in this business.

During the third quarter of 1997, VLSI sold its majority-owned subsidiary, COMPASS Design Automation, Inc., an electronic design automation (EDA) software company. The transaction, which resulted in a $7.7 million ($0.15 a share) after tax gain, reflected the company's strategic initiative to focus resources on its core business.

In the first half of 1998, operating results were hurt by ongoing inventory reduction programs at some OEM customers, particularly in the wireless communications segments. In the second quarter of 1998, wireless bookings improved modestly. However, the company reported that order trends deteriorated in the first two months of the third quarter.

Per Share Data ($)

(Year Ended Dec. 31)	1997	1996	1995	1994	1993	1992	1991	1990	1989	1988
Tangible Bk. Val.	11.27	10.08	11.24	6.96	6.03	5.56	6.10	5.86	6.42	6.40
Cash Flow	3.59	1.40	2.73	2.50	1.82	0.56	2.18	1.48	1.61	1.56
Earnings	1.36	-1.08	1.05	0.85	0.45	-1.12	0.37	-0.52	0.02	0.29
Dividends	Nil	Nil	Nil	Nil	Nil	Nil	Nil	Nil	Nil	Nil
Payout Ratio	Nil	Nil	Nil	Nil	Nil	Nil	Nil	Nil	Nil	Nil
Prices - High	38⅝	29¼	39⅛	16⅜	18⅞	10½	12¼	12¼	10⅛	11⅜
- Low	14⅞	10⅜	11⅝	10¼	6½	6	4¼	3	6⅜	5⅞
P/E Ratio - High	28	NM	37	19	42	NM	33	NM	NM	39
- Low	11	NM	11	12	14	NM	11	NM	NM	20

Income Statement Analysis (Million $)

	1997	1996	1995	1994	1993	1992	1991	1990	1989	1988
Revs.	713	717	720	587	516	428	413	325	288	221
Oper. Inc.	204	154	149	109	76.6	51.6	70.4	54.7	43.2	39.3
Depr.	109	114	73.7	61.8	48.5	48.3	48.4	48.8	37.8	29.6
Int. Exp.	17.8	19.6	8.0	8.7	8.1	9.1	9.2	9.1	8.7	6.9
Pretax Inc.	91.3	-83.9	61.9	41.7	20.5	-31.6	12.8	-12.7	1.2	9.3
Eff. Tax Rate	27%	NM	26%	24%	23%	NM	23%	Nil	59%	28%
Net Inc.	66.6	-49.5	46.0	31.7	15.9	-32.2	9.9	-12.7	0.5	6.7

Balance Sheet & Other Fin. Data (Million $)

	1997	1996	1995	1994	1993	1992	1991	1990	1989	1988
Cash	194	206	366	103	73.0	70.0	48.0	35.0	55.0	75.0
Curr. Assets	534	449	598	266	222	202	186	157	150	152
Total Assets	922	891	960	490	412	368	364	327	318	303
Curr. Liab.	186	210	198	128	108	100	110	91.0	78.0	69.0
LT Debt	182	208	219	96.8	85.9	83.2	92.6	89.3	84.9	83.7
Common Eqty.	516	470	531	255	213	185	162	147	155	150
Total Cap.	711	680	762	363	304	268	254	236	240	234
Cap. Exp.	85.6	270	154	64.6	75.0	41.8	32.8	55.5	56.9	76.3
Cash Flow	176	64.1	120	93.5	64.4	16.1	58.2	36.0	38.3	36.3
Curr. Ratio	2.9	2.1	3.0	2.1	2.1	2.0	1.7	1.7	1.9	2.2
% LT Debt of Cap.	25.6	30.5	28.8	26.7	28.2	31.0	36.4	37.8	35.4	35.8
% Net Inc.of Revs.	9.4	NM	6.4	5.4	3.1	NM	2.4	NM	0.2	3.0
% Ret. on Assets	7.4	NM	6.4	6.9	4.0	NM	2.8	NM	0.2	2.3
% Ret. on Equity	13.5	NM	11.7	13.3	7.8	NM	6.2	NM	0.3	4.5

Data as orig. reptd.; bef. results of disc. opers. and/or spec. items. Per share data adj. for stk. divs. as of ex-div. date. Bold denotes diluted EPS (FASB 128). E-Estimated. NA-Not Available. NM-Not Meaningful. NR-Not Ranked.

Office—1109 McKay Dr., San Jose, CA 95131. **Tel**—(408) 434-3000. **Fax**—(408) 263-2511. **Website**—http://www.vlsi.com **Chrmn & CEO**—A. J. Stein. **Pres & COO**—R. M. Beyer. **Pres & CFO**—B.S. Iyer. **Dirs**—R. M. Beyer, P. S. Bonelli, R. P. Dilworth, W. G. Howard, P. R. Low, A. J. Stein, H. Tsiang. **Transfer Agent & Registrar**—Boston EquiServe, LLP. **Incorporated**—in California in 1979; reincorporated in Delaware in 1987. **Empl**—2,200. **S&P Analyst:** B. McGovern

Valassis Communications   2380

NYSE Symbol **VCI**

In S&P SmallCap 600

03-OCT-98 Industry: Specialty Printing

Summary: Valassis is one of the largest printers and publishers of cents-off coupons and other consumer purchase incentives, most of which are featured in Sunday editions of newspapers.

Quantitative Evaluations

Recent Price • 34¾
52 Wk Range • 41⅛-27⅜

Yield • Nil
12-Mo. P/E • 17.9

Outlook
(1 Lowest—5 Highest)
• **1+**

Fair Value
• **32½**

Risk
• **Average**

Earn./Div. Rank
• **NR**

Technical Eval.
• **Neutral** since 9/98

Rel. Strength Rank
(1 Lowest—99 Highest)
• **81**

Insider Activity
• **Neutral**

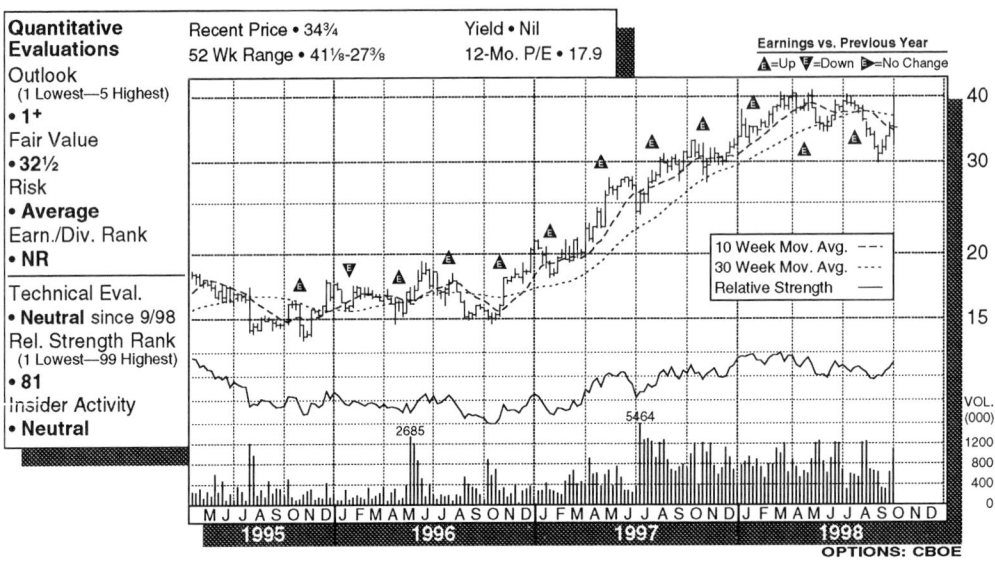

Earnings vs. Previous Year
▲=Up ▼=Down ▶=No Change

10 Week Mov. Avg. – – –
30 Week Mov. Avg. ·····
Relative Strength ——

OPTIONS: CBOE

Business Profile - 11-SEP-98

After improved year to year results in the second quarter, the company believes that it is on track to achieve record revenues and earnings for the 1998 year. VIP revenues have experienced strong growth in the first half of the year and the firm expects continued growth through the addition of a new printing press and the award of a large 1998 contract. Current company projections estimate that this division will exceed $100 million in revenues for the year. Although a 20% rise in paper prices has adversely affected profitability, management believes that prices have peaked and no further increases will occur in 1998. In addition, the company feels that the cost of paper will decrease in 1999. At the end of the second quarter of 1998, VCI had completed 39% of the authorized 5 million share stock repurchase plan.

Operational Review - 11-SEP-98

Total revenues for the six months ended June 30, 1998, rose 8.6%, year to year, due to greater volume and improved market share in the FSI division, as well as a strong performance in the VIP unit. Profitability improved, as higher paper prices and a one-time charge related to the early retirement of the former CEO, were outweighed by well-controlled SGA expenses and a reduction in interest expense. After taxes at 38.2%, versus 42.2%, net income climbed 26% to $42,951,000 ($1.07 per share), from $34,042,000 ($0.81).

Stock Performance - 02-OCT-98

In the past 30 trading days, VCI's shares have increased 3%, compared to a 7% fall in the S&P 500. Average trading volume for the past five days was 216,820 shares, compared with the 40-day moving average of 152,197 shares.

Key Stock Statistics

Dividend Rate/Share	Nil	Shareholders	300
Shs. outstg. (M)	38.7	Market cap. (B)	$ 1.3
Avg. daily vol. (M)	0.119	Inst. holdings	83%
Tang. Bk. Value/Share	NM		
Beta	0.40		

Value of $10,000 invested 5 years ago: $ 15,622

Fiscal Year Ending Dec. 31

	1998	1997	1996	1995	1994	1993
Revenues (Million $)						
1Q	205.7	190.0	180.5	157.4	--	126.2
2Q	178.9	164.3	162.7	155.5	--	132.1
3Q	—	153.5	151.8	138.0	131.3	141.3
4Q	—	167.8	164.1	162.8	147.8	143.5
Yr.	—	675.5	659.1	613.8	—	542.6
Earnings Per Share ($)						
1Q	**0.64**	0.53	0.24	0.20	--	0.06
2Q	**0.43**	0.29	0.23	0.16	--	0.02
3Q	—	0.44	0.25	0.08	0.02	0.02
4Q	—	0.46	0.28	-0.22	0.02	0.02
Yr.	—	1.69	1.00	0.22	0.04	0.12

Next earnings report expected: late October

Dividend Data

Dividends were omitted in June 1993, after having been paid on a quarterly basis since June 1992.

A Division of The McGraw·Hill Companies

Business Summary - 11-SEP-98

Clipping coupons is a favorite pastime of cost-conscious American consumers. Since 1972, Valassis Communications (VCI) has played an integral part in the penny-pinching process through its printing and publishing of cents-off coupons and other consumer purchase incentives.

The company's most popular product is its Free-standing inserts (FSIs), which are colorful booklets that arrive inside the Sunday edition of more than 500 newspapers, with an average paid circulation of 56.9 million. In 1997, roughly 79.7 billion FSI pages were printed and distributed, representing 49% of the national FSI market. VCI offers its customers over 270 different layout versions per publication date, providing the flexibility to target specific markets with tailored promotional offers. FSIs generated approximately 77% of 1997 total sales.

Valassis Impact Promotions (VIPs) was rolled out in 1989 to meet the increasing demand for customized printed promotions for solo marketers. Because these promotions feature only one manufacturer, VCI is able to develop a completely individualized promotion. VIPs generated 13% of 1997 sales and generally serve packaged goods manufactures, fast-food chains, food brokers and retailers.

Other products include Run-of-Press (ROP) promotions, which can be published in any newspaper in the U.S., on any day and in any section of the paper, and a newspaper-delivered sampling product that enables manufacturers to cost-effectively reach up to 50 million households in one day.

In recent years, the company has attempted to expand through international operations. VCI currently owns sales promotion companies in both France and Canada. However, in the first quarter of 1997, due to economic conditions and unsatisfactory test results, the company discontinued its 50% joint venture interest in Valassis de Mexico.

VCI has reported earnings growth fueled by a significant decrease in the cost of paper, a primary input into the company's manufacturing process. However, VCI believes that paper prices are likely to rise in 1998. As a result of strong performance in recent quarters, the company has improved its cash flow, which increased approximately 27% in 1997. VCI has used this excess cash to repurchase its common stock and reduce long term debt. In December 1997, directors authorized the repurchase of up to five million common shares.

Per Share Data ($)

(Year Ended Dec. 31)	1997	1996	1995	1994	1993	1992	1991	1990	1989	1988
Tangible Bk. Val.	NM	NM	-8.62	-9.21	-9.22	-10.00	-11.72	-12.99	NA	NA
Cash Flow	2.16	1.36	0.66	0.27	0.67	2.48	2.54	1.71	NA	NA
Earnings	1.69	1.00	0.22	0.04	0.12	1.89	1.62	0.75	NA	NA
Dividends	Nil	Nil	Nil	Nil	Nil	0.42	0.11	NA	NA	NA
Payout Ratio	Nil	Nil	Nil	Nil	Nil	22%	6%	NA	NA	NA
Prices - High	37⅞	21⅛	18⅝	19¾	19¾	25⅛	22⅞	NA	NA	NA
- Low	18	14⅝	13⅝	10½	10½	9½	16	NA	NA	NA
P/E Ratio - High	22	21	85	NM	NM	13	14	NA	NA	NA
- Low	10	15	62	NM	NM	5	10	NA	NA	NA

Income Statement Analysis (Million $)

	1997	1996	1995	1994	1993	1992	1991	1990	1989	1988
Revs.	675	657	610	278	540	660	669	635	NA	NA
Oper. Inc.	169	123	94.0	32.0	61.0	199	194	179	NA	NA
Depr.	15.6	15.2	19.0	9.7	24.0	25.4	35.7	41.3	NA	NA
Int. Exp.	38.3	39.6	40.5	19.6	38.2	39.9	37.7	47.4	NA	NA
Pretax Inc.	115	71.1	23.0	4.0	-2.0	135	128	NA	NA	NA
Eff. Tax Rate	39%	40%	58%	56%	NM	39%	42%	NA	NA	NA
Net Inc.	69.9	42.9	9.6	1.9	5.2	81.9	74.4	32.4	NA	NA

Balance Sheet & Other Fin. Data (Million $)

	1997	1996	1995	1994	1993	1992	1991	1990	1989	1988
Cash	35.4	60.2	34.4	21.2	32.3	39.6	15.3	NA	NA	NA
Curr. Assets	151	178	155	109	118	118	107	122	NA	NA
Total Assets	241	274	259	234	240	275	293	323	NA	NA
Curr. Liab.	148	161	149	131	133	173	207	199	NA	NA
LT Debt	367	396	416	418	419	419	463	550	NA	NA
Common Eqty.	-276	-286	-308	-318	-316	-321	-385	-433	NA	NA
Total Cap.	92.4	112	110	104	106	102	86.0	NA	NA	NA
Cap. Exp.	13.0	7.1	6.5	9.2	4.1	4.0	4.2	8.0	NA	NA
Cash Flow	85.5	58.1	28.6	12.0	29.0	107	110	74.0	NA	NA
Curr. Ratio	1.0	1.1	1.0	0.8	0.9	0.7	0.5	0.6	NA	NA
% LT Debt of Cap.	397.2	353.6	378.2	403.1	395.3	410.8	NM	NA	NA	NA
% Net Inc.of Revs.	10.4	6.5	1.6	0.7	9.6	12.4	11.1	5.1	NA	NA
% Ret. on Assets	27.2	16.1	3.9	NA	2.0	28.9	16.4	NA	NA	NA
% Ret. on Equity	NM	NM	NA	NA	NM	NM	NM	NA	NA	NA

Data as orig. reptd.; bef. results of disc. opers. and/or spec. items. Per share data adj. for stk. divs. as of ex-div. date. Prior to 1994, data for fiscal yrs. ended Jun. 30 of fol. cal. yr.; data for 1994 represents six mos. ended Dec. 31. Bold denotes diluted EPS (FASB 128). E-Estimated. NA-Not Available. NM-Not Meaningful. NR-Not Ranked.

Office—19975 Victor Parkway, Livonia, MI 48152. **Tel**—(313) 591-3000. **Website**—http://www.valassis.com **Chrmn**—D. A. Brandon. **Pres, CEO & COO**—A. F. Schultz. **VP, CFO & Treas**—R. L. Recchia. **Secy**—B. P Hoffman. **VP & Investor Contact**—Lynn M. Liddle. **Dirs**—D. A. Brandon, P. F. Brennan, M. C. Davis, J. M. Huntsman Jr., B. J. Husselbee, L. J. Johnson, B. M. Powers, R. L. Recchia, M. A. Sampson, A. F. Schultz, F. R. Whittlesey. **Transfer Agent & Registrar**—Bank of New York, NYC. **Incorporated**—in Delaware in 1986. **Empl**— 1,170. **S&P Analyst:** Jordan Horoschak

03-OCT-98

Industry: Manufacturing (Specialized)

Summary: This company is engaged in research and development of advanced rechargeable batteries based on lithium and polymer technologies.

Quantitative Evaluations

Recent Price • 4¼
52 Wk Range • 9¼-3⅛

Yield • Nil
12-Mo. P/E • NM

Outlook
(1 Lowest—5 Highest)
• **NA**

Fair Value
• **NA**

Risk
• **High**

Earn./Div. Rank
• **NR**

Technical Eval.
• **Neutral** since 8/98

Rel. Strength Rank
(1 Lowest—99 Highest)
• **69**

Insider Activity
• **Favorable**

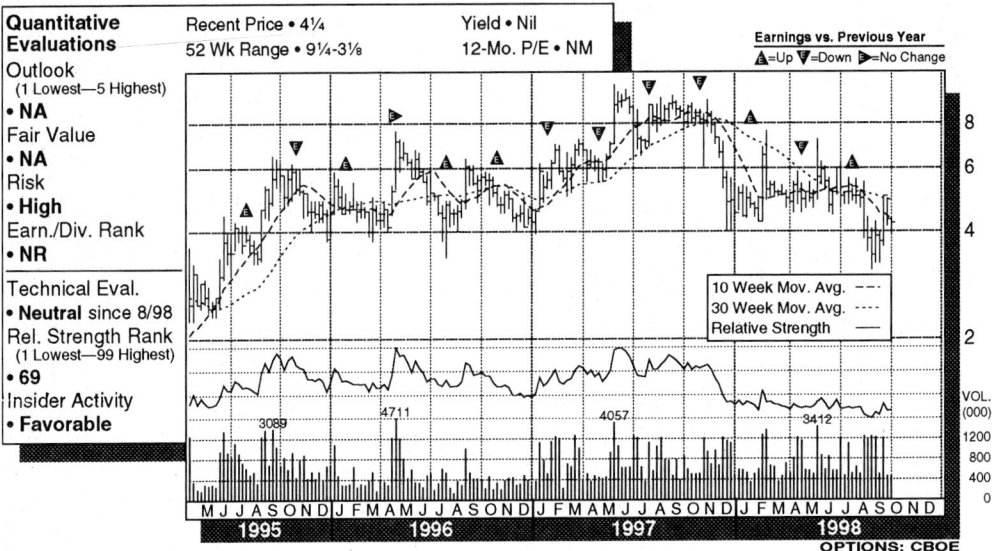

Earnings vs. Previous Year
▲=Up ▼=Down ▶=No Change

10 Week Mov. Avg. – – –
30 Week Mov. Avg. · · · ·
Relative Strength ———

OPTIONS: CBOE

Business Profile - 13-AUG-98

In May 1998, the company and Delphi announced the successful completion of their collaboration in lithium polymer battery development. Delphi is targeting production of lithium polymer batteries for hybrid electric vehicles by the year 2000. Valence announced in July 1998 that it completed private financing arrangements of up to $25 million, under which it has drawn down $2.5 million in debt and $7.5 million of convertible preferred stock. Under the terms of the agreements, Valence sold 7,500 shares of new Series A convertible preferred stock for gross proceeds of $7.5 million. An affiliate of Castle Creek Partners, LLC, a Chicago-based technology investor, was the sole purchaser of the Series A stock in a private placement and, upon Valence's achieving certain milestones, has made a commitment to purchase up to $7.5 million more of convertible preferred stock.

Operational Review - 13-AUG-98

No contract revenues were realized in either FY 98 (Mar.) or in FY 97, as a result of a September 1994 agreement with Delphi that treats funding as an R&D cost offset rather than as revenue. R&D expenses increased, reflecting increased efforts to commercialize a product in FY 99. Following a drop in interest income and higher joint venture expenses, the net loss widened to $24,486,000 ($1.06 a share, on 6.1% more shares), from $15,888,000 ($0.73).

Stock Performance - 02-OCT-98

In the past 30 trading days, VLNC's shares have increased 11%, compared to a 7% fall in the S&P 500. Average trading volume for the past five days was 88,520 shares, compared with the 40-day moving average of 215,408 shares.

Key Stock Statistics

Dividend Rate/Share	Nil	Shareholders	800
Shs. outstg. (M)	25.5	Market cap. (B)	$0.108
Avg. daily vol. (M)	0.136	Inst. holdings	8%
Tang. Bk. Value/Share	0.70		
Beta	1.23		

Value of $10,000 invested 5 years ago: $ 5,113

Fiscal Year Ending Mar. 31

	1999	1998	1997	1996	1995	1994
Revenues (Million $)						
1Q	Nil	Nil	Nil	Nil	1.63	1.50
2Q	—	Nil	Nil	Nil	1.63	1.50
3Q	—	Nil	Nil	Nil	0.45	2.00
4Q	—	Nil	Nil	Nil	0.45	2.30
Yr.	—	Nil	Nil	Nil	4.15	7.30
Earnings Per Share ($)						
1Q	-0.21	-0.24	-0.15	-0.16	-1.09	-0.17
2Q	—	-0.26	-0.16	-0.43	-0.21	-0.25
3Q	—	-0.21	-0.22	-0.11	-0.20	-0.31
4Q	—	-0.34	-0.31	-0.18	-0.18	-0.33
Yr.	—	-1.06	-0.73	-0.83	-1.68	-1.08

Next earnings report expected: mid November

Dividend Data

No cash dividends have been paid, and the company does not intend to pay any in the foreseeable future.

A Division of The McGraw·Hill Companies

STANDARD
&POOR'S
STOCK REPORTS

Valence Technology, Inc.

5537T

03-OCT-98

Business Summary - 13-AUG-98

Valence Technology, Inc. is engaged in R&D of advanced rechargeable batteries based on lithium ion and polymer technologies. Valence focuses its activities on R&D and the manufacture of limited quantities of working prototypes, including developing chemistry improvements, battery designs, manufacturing technology and capabilities needed to support commercial introduction of its products.

The company believes that its lithium polymer batteries, when commercially introduced, will offer a number of performance characteristics superior to those of batteries currently in commercial use, including longer operating life, reduced size and weight, and improved recharge characteristics. To date the company has been unable to produce commercially viable prototype batteries based on its new technology.

In September 1994, upon expiration of an agreement between Valence and GM's Delphi Automotive Systems Group to develop lithium polymer batteries for the land, marine and air vehicle and load leveling markets, Valence and Delphi entered into a new five-year agreement that calls for Delphi to fund a majority of the operating expenses at VLNC's Henderson, NV, location. This new funding is treated as a research and development cost offset rather than as new revenue. More recently, in October 1996, Valence signed an agreement with Alliant Techsystems to form a joint venture company (Alliant/Valence) to develop and make batteries for the military market, and in July 1996, the company's Dutch unit agreed to establish a joint venture company with Hanil Telecom Co. Ltd. in Korea to manufacture, package and distribute advanced rechargeable solid polymer electrolyte batteries.

In September 1997, Alliant/Valence signed an agreement valued at $5.9 million to develop lithium ion polymer batteries intended for U.S. Navy underwater vehicles. Under the agreement, Alliant/Valence will develop batteries to replace zinc-silver oxide batteries currently used in Navy underwater vehicles. The Navy spends more than $5 million annually for zinc-silver oxide batteries, which require replacement every 12 to 18 months because of finite recharge cycles and wet operating conditions. Lithium ion polymer batteries have the potential to provide over 10 times the cycle life of silver-zinc power sources.

In May 1998, the company and Delphi announced the successful completion of their collaboration on lithium polymer battery development. Delphi will retain a license to use company-developed lithium polymer technology for vehicular and stationary load leveling/peak shaving applications. The company will retain a license to use Delphi-developed lithium polymer technology in all other applications. After September 1998, Velance anticipates that it will receive no further payments as a result of the Joint Research and Development agreements with Delphi.

Per Share Data ($)

(Year Ended Mar. 31)	1998	1997	1996	1995	1994	1993	1992	1991	1990	1989
Tangible Bk. Val.	0.92	1.76	2.45	3.32	4.98	4.23	3.47	NM	NM	NM
Cash Flow	-0.99	-0.57	-0.58	-1.45	-0.84	-0.46	-0.36	-0.51	-0.04	NA
Earnings	-1.06	-0.73	-0.83	-1.68	-1.08	-0.63	-0.37	-0.52	-0.04	NA
Dividends	Nil	Nil	Nil	Nil	Nil	Nil	Nil	Nil	Nil	Nil
Payout Ratio	Nil	Nil	Nil	Nil	Nil	Nil	Nil	Nil	Nil	Nil
Cal. Yrs.	1997	1996	1995	1994	1993	1992	1991	1990	1989	1988
Prices - High	10¼	7⅝	6½	20½	26	27	NA	NA	NA	NA
- Low	4	3⅜	1⁹/₁₆	2⅛	11	7¼	NA	NA	NA	NA
P/E Ratio - High	NM	NM	NM	NM	NM	NM	NM	NM	NM	NM
- Low	NM	NM	NM	NM	NM	NM	NM	NM	NM	NM

Income Statement Analysis (Million $)

Revs.	Nil	Nil	Nil	4.2	7.3	6.4	3.8	Nil	Nil	Nil
Oper. Inc.	-21.6	-14.1	-15.0	-13.1	-16.8	-7.3	-1.0	-1.4	-0.4	NA
Depr.	1.8	3.5	5.2	4.5	4.2	2.3	0.1	0.1	NM	NM
Int. Exp.	0.5	0.8	0.9	0.8	0.3	0.3	0.4	0.3	0.0	NA
Pretax Inc.	-24.5	-15.9	-17.5	-33.6	-18.7	-8.5	-3.8	-5.1	-0.4	NA
Eff. Tax Rate	NM	NM	Nil	Nil	NM	NM	Nil	Nil	Nil	Nil
Net Inc.	-24.5	-15.9	-17.5	-33.6	-18.7	-8.5	-3.8	-5.1	-0.4	NA

Balance Sheet & Other Fin. Data (Million $)

Cash	8.4	33.4	51.0	59.6	61.0	61.8	0.8	0.1	0.0	NA
Curr. Assets	10.7	34.1	52.3	61.4	62.4	62.4	0.9	0.1	0.0	NA
Total Assets	42.9	55.5	70.2	92.0	121	77.2	3.3	0.4	0.1	NA
Curr. Liab.	12.5	12.0	11.0	16.4	14.1	6.4	5.9	0.8	0.0	NA
LT Debt	5.0	5.2	6.2	8.8	7.3	1.8	7.2	5.1	0.4	NA
Common Eqty.	23.0	38.3	53.0	66.7	100	69.0	-9.8	-5.5	-0.4	NA
Total Cap.	27.9	43.6	59.2	75.5	107	70.8	-2.6	-0.4	0.0	NA
Cap. Exp.	16.3	3.4	2.3	8.8	23.5	6.0	1.7	0.5	0.0	NA
Cash Flow	-22.7	-12.4	-12.3	-29.1	-14.5	-6.2	-3.6	-5.0	-0.4	NA
Curr. Ratio	0.9	2.8	4.8	3.7	4.4	9.7	0.2	0.1	1.5	NA
% LT Debt of Cap.	17.7	12.0	10.4	11.7	6.8	2.5	NM	NM	NM	NM
% Net Inc.of Revs.	NM	NM	NM	NM	NM	NM	NM	NM	NM	NM
% Ret. on Assets	NM	NM	NM	NM	NM	NM	NM	NM	NM	NM
% Ret. on Equity	NM	NM	NM	NM	NM	NM	NM	NM	NM	NM

Data as orig. reptd.; bef. results of disc. opers. and/or spec. items. Per share data adj. for stk. divs. as of ex-div. date. Bold denotes diluted EPS (FASB 128). E-Estimated. NA-Not Available. NM-Not Meaningful. NR-Not Ranked.

Office—301 Conestoga Way, Henderson, NV 89015. **Tel**—(702) 558-1000. **Website**—www.valence-tech.com **Chrmn, Pres & CEO**—L. M. Dawson. **VP & CFO**—D. P. Archibald. **Secy**—B. A. Perkins. **Dirs**—C. E. Berg, L. Dawson, A. F. Shugart. **Transfer Agent & Registrar**—First National Bank of Boston. **Incorporated**—in Delaware in 1989. **Empl**— 95. **S&P Analyst:** J. Robert Cho

03-OCT-98

Industry:
Manufacturing (Diversified)

Summary: Valmont is the world's largest manufacturer of mechanized agricultural irrigation equipment. It also supplies pole and tower structures for lighting and other applications.

Quantitative Evaluations	
Outlook (1 Lowest—5 Highest)	• **NA**
Fair Value	• **NA**
Risk	• **Average**
Earn./Div. Rank	• **B**
Technical Eval.	• **NA**
Rel. Strength Rank (1 Lowest—99 Highest)	• **26**
Insider Activity	• **Neutral**

Recent Price • 12⅝
52 Wk Range • 25-12¼

Yield • 2.1%
12-Mo. P/E • 10.0

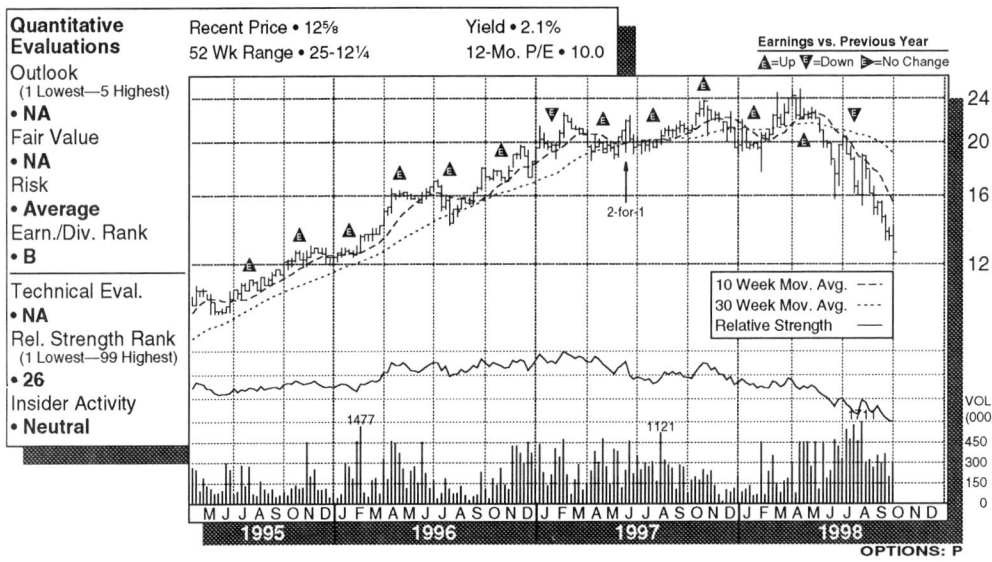

Earnings vs. Previous Year
▲=Up ▼=Down ▶=No Change

10 Week Mov. Avg. — — —
30 Week Mov. Avg. · · · · ·
Relative Strength ———

2-for-1

VOL. (000)

OPTIONS: P

Business Profile - 29-SEP-98

Valmont continues to benefit from strong demand for mechanized agricultural irrigation systems and has developed new products with enhanced electronic and computerized controls. Reflecting a global need for infrastructure development, the company expects its recent acquisitions of French and German companies will increase the growth potential for its engineered metal structures. VALM also believes that the January 1997 sale of its ballast operations will let it focus on its two core businesses (industrial and irrigation products), in which it has a recognized world leadership position. The dividend was increased 16% in April 1998.

Operational Review - 29-SEP-98

Revenues in in the first half of 1998 declined 3.0%, year to year, as increased sales from the irrigation and coating group were outweighed by lower sales of industrial products. Gross margins narrowed, reflecting lower sales volume and competitive pricing in the industrial products segment. With a drop in SG&A expense, and slightly higher net interest expense, pretax income was down 8.3%. After taxes at 36.7%, versus 36.0%, net income fell 9.3%, to $17,095,000 ($0.60 a share), from $18,847,000 ($0.67).

Stock Performance - 02-OCT-98

In the past 30 trading days, VALM's shares have declined 22%, compared to a 7% fall in the S&P 500. Average trading volume for the past five days was 60,700 shares, compared with the 40-day moving average of 61,526 shares.

Key Stock Statistics

Dividend Rate/Share	0.26	Shareholders	3,800
Shs. outstg. (M)	26.4	Market cap. (B)	$0.334
Avg. daily vol. (M)	0.060	Inst. holdings	33%
Tang. Bk. Value/Share	8.30		
Beta	0.66		

Value of $10,000 invested 5 years ago: $ 15,032

Fiscal Year Ending Dec. 31

	1998	1997	1996	1995	1994	1993
Revenues (Million $)						
1Q	160.6	165.4	148.9	142.2	111.2	106.9
2Q	154.3	159.1	166.8	133.4	122.0	116.0
3Q	—	136.0	148.1	128.3	109.8	107.2
4Q	—	162.0	180.7	140.7	128.7	108.7
Yr.	—	622.5	644.5	544.6	471.8	438.8
Earnings Per Share ($)						
1Q	**0.34**	**0.32**	0.25	0.21	0.13	0.12
2Q	**0.26**	**0.35**	0.30	0.24	0.18	0.17
3Q	—	**0.28**	0.23	0.19	0.17	0.12
4Q	—	**0.38**	-0.03	0.26	0.21	-0.17
Yr.	—	**1.33**	0.76	0.90	0.69	0.23

Next earnings report expected: mid October

Dividend Data (Dividends have been paid since 1980.)

Amount ($)	Date Decl.	Ex-Div. Date	Stock of Record	Payment Date
0.056	Dec. 08	Dec. 23	Dec. 26	Jan. 15 '98
0.056	Feb. 25	Apr. 02	Mar. 27	Apr. 15 '98
0.065	Apr. 27	Jun. 24	Jun. 26	Jul. 15 '98
0.065	Sep. 08	Sep. 23	Sep. 25	Oct. 15 '98

A Division of The McGraw-Hill Companies

Business Summary - 29-SEP-98

An ex-Marine named Robert Daugherty bought the patent for an odd-looking contraption from a Nebraska inventor in the early 1950s. That machine has since become the standard for mechanized irrigation technology worldwide, and Daugherty's company, now called Valmont Industries (VALM), emerged as the industry leader. The expertise to produce its own tapered poles led the company into the production of supports for street lights and traffic signals. VALM is now a leader in two seemingly diverse fields: the support of infrastructure development and encouraging world food production.

The company classifies its operations into two business segments: industrial products and irrigation products. The industrial division, supporting the development of infrastructure, manufactures and distributes engineered metal structures and other fabricated products. The irrigation products division fabricates and sells agricultural irrigation equipment and related products. In addition, VALM is a leader in the galvanizing and powder coatings industry. Contributions by segment in 1997 were:

	Sales	Profits
Industrial products	61%	54%
Irrigation products	39%	46%

The current operating strategy is to keep high standards of quality and service for both divisions. The company feels that a growing world population, improving diets and expanding world economies will provide farmers with the resources to invest in improving irrigation systems. The industrial products division will take advantage of the conversion from wooden to steel utility poles, increased use of wireless communication towers, and VALM's growing manufacturing capacity.

VALM, based in Omaha, manufactures products in 20 plants throughout the Western Hemisphere, Europe and Asia, sold in 100 countries around the globe. In July 1997, the company announced the first production light poles to be manufactured at its plant in Poland as part of a joint venture. Facilities in France, the Netherlands and Germany produce poles as well.

Foreign sales (based on destination) represented 26% of revenues (11% of operating income) in 1997, compared with 21% (12%) in 1996 and 18% (13%) in 1995.

VALM recorded a 1996 fourth quarter pretax charge of $15.8 million ($0.36 a share, after taxes, as adjusted) related to the sale of its ballast operation, Valmont Electric. The company sold the operation in January 1997 for approximately $25 million, in order to better focus on its core businesses.

In November 1997, VALM said it signed agreements to acquire Intermountain Galvanizing in Utah, and Pacific States Galvanizing in Oregon. The acquisitions would help VALM to serve its internal needs and growing demand for galvanizing as a protective coating.

Per Share Data ($)

(Year Ended Dec. 31)	1997	1996	1995	1994	1993	1992	1991	1990	1989	1988
Tangible Bk. Val.	7.49	6.41	5.88	5.52	4.92	4.87	4.45	4.96	4.42	3.60
Cash Flow	1.96	1.28	1.35	1.14	0.66	1.08	0.15	1.12	1.23	1.04
Earnings	1.33	0.76	0.90	0.69	0.23	0.57	-0.34	0.67	0.89	0.69
Dividends	0.22	0.19	0.15	0.15	0.14	0.13	0.13	0.13	0.11	0.08
Payout Ratio	17%	25%	17%	22%	64%	22%	NM	19%	12%	12%
Prices - High	23⁷⁄₈	20⁷⁄₈	13	10¹⁄₄	11³⁄₈	9³⁄₈	9¹⁄₄	12¹⁄₂	10	5⁵⁄₈
- Low	18¹⁄₂	12¹⁄₈	8¹⁄₈	6³⁄₄	6¹⁄₂	5¹⁄₄	4³⁄₄	4⁵⁄₈	5¹⁄₂	2¹⁄₂
P/E Ratio - High	18	27	14	15	51	16	NM	19	11	8
- Low	14	16	9	10	29	9	NM	7	6	4

Income Statement Analysis (Million $)

	1997	1996	1995	1994	1993	1992	1991	1990	1989	1988
Revs.	623	645	545	472	439	425	430	874	790	663
Oper. Inc.	78.4	67.3	54.2	37.4	34.1	32.8	20.6	47.7	50.4	39.3
Depr.	16.4	14.8	12.4	10.4	10.0	11.8	11.6	10.5	7.9	7.9
Int. Exp.	3.7	4.0	4.3	4.7	5.9	7.5	8.6	9.1	7.3	6.5
Pretax Inc.	58.9	33.1	38.5	24.9	8.1	18.4	-12.3	26.9	36.5	26.5
Eff. Tax Rate	36%	36%	36%	35%	35%	28%	NM	36%	40%	38%
Net Inc.	37.5	21.2	24.8	16.1	5.3	13.2	-4.0	15.5	20.7	15.3

Balance Sheet & Other Fin. Data (Million $)

	1997	1996	1995	1994	1993	1992	1991	1990	1989	1988
Cash	11.5	9.5	17.0	29.6	14.0	12.7	7.3	12.8	20.5	7.1
Curr. Assets	218	211	186	171	166	153	159	254	241	193
Total Assets	368	342	309	266	247	273	281	351	322	253
Curr. Liab.	124	129	105	90.0	83.0	89.0	94.0	164	143	114
LT Debt	20.7	21.9	28.7	35.5	38.4	60.4	70.4	55.3	60.9	45.8
Common Eqty.	207	175	159	127	113	111	101	112	99	79.0
Total Cap.	241	209	201	173	161	182	182	187	179	139
Cap. Exp.	39.1	35.6	34.8	23.0	16.3	7.9	15.5	23.6	30.3	10.7
Cash Flow	54.0	36.0	37.1	26.5	15.3	25.0	3.6	26.1	28.5	23.2
Curr. Ratio	1.8	1.6	1.8	1.9	2.0	1.7	1.7	1.5	1.7	1.7
% LT Debt of Cap.	8.6	5.7	14.3	20.5	23.9	33.2	38.7	29.6	34.0	32.9
% Net Inc.of Revs.	6.0	3.3	4.5	3.4	1.2	3.1	NM	1.8	2.6	2.3
% Ret. on Assets	10.6	10.7	8.4	6.3	2.0	4.8	NM	4.6	7.1	6.6
% Ret. on Equity	19.6	12.7	16.7	13.4	4.7	12.4	NM	14.7	22.9	20.9

Data as orig. reptd.; bef. results of disc. opers. and/or spec. items. Per share data adj. for stk. divs. as of ex-div. date. Bold denotes diluted EPS (FASB 128). E-Estimated. NA-Not Available. NM-Not Meaningful. NR-Not Ranked.

Office—Valley, NE 68064. **Tel**—(402) 359-2201. **Website**—http://www.valmont.com **Chrmn & CEO**—M. C. Bay. **SVP & CFO**—T. J. McClain. **VP & Secy**—T. P. Egan Jr. **Investor Contact**—Jeffrey S. Laudin. **Dirs**—M. C. Bay, R. B. Daugherty, C. M. Harper. A. F. Jacobson, L. P. Johnson, J. E. Jones, T. F. Madison, W. Scott Jr., K. E. Stinson, R. G. Wallace. **Transfer Agent & Registrar**—First National Bank of Omaha. **Incorporated**—in Delaware in 1974. **Empl**—3,751. **S&P Analyst:** E. Hunter

Vanstar Corp.

2385Z

NYSE Symbol **VST**

In S&P SmallCap 600

03-OCT-98

Industry:
Services (Data Processing)

Summary: This company is a leading provider of services and products designed to build and manage computer network infrastructures.

Quantitative Evaluations	
Outlook (1 Lowest—5 Highest) • **NA**	Recent Price • 8⅛ 52 Wk Range • 16¾-7⅛ Yield • Nil 12-Mo. P/E • 19.5

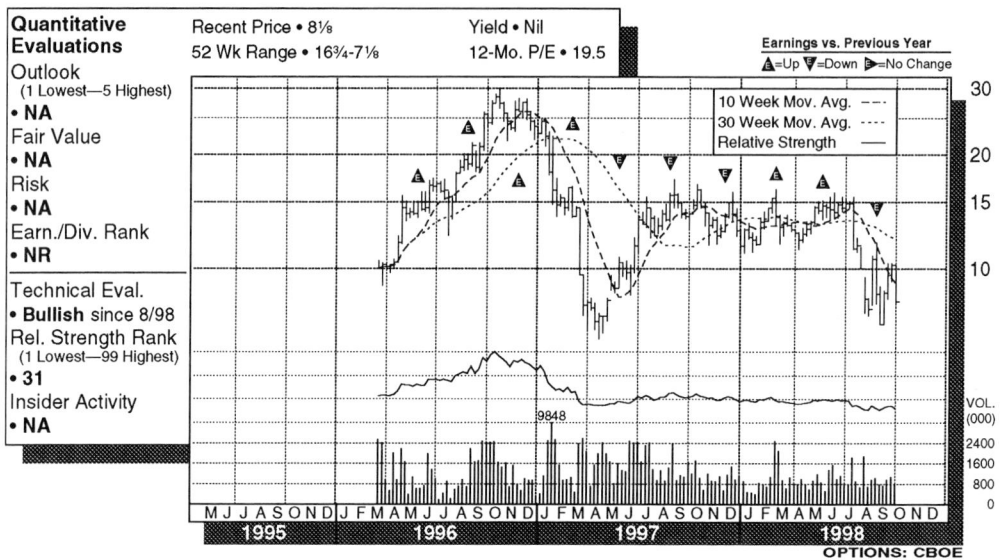

Earnings vs. Previous Year
▲=Up ▼=Down ▷=No Change

10 Week Mov. Avg. ---
30 Week Mov. Avg. ....
Relative Strength —

OPTIONS: CBOE

Quantitative Evaluations

Outlook (1 Lowest—5 Highest)
• **NA**

Fair Value
• **NA**

Risk
• **NA**

Earn./Div. Rank
• **NR**

Technical Eval.
• **Bullish** since 8/98

Rel. Strength Rank (1 Lowest—99 Highest)
• **31**

Insider Activity
• **NA**

Business Profile - 12-MAY-98

This leading provider of information technology products and services is benefiting from a growing trend among large corporations to outsource technology services for their client/server computer hardware and software systems. Vanstar's long-term growth strategy includes a focus on Windows/Intel technology; the building of mutually beneficial partnerships with technology leaders; and the development of a top-notch, geographically balanced technical field force. The 1997 acquisition of Sysorex expanded Vanstar's position in providing technology services to the federal government. The private sale of $200 million in convertible preferred stock in October 1996 strengthened VST's capital structure.

Operational Review - 12-MAY-98

Revenues for the nine months ended January 31,1998, rose 30%, year to year, bolstered by a 28% rise in product sales, acquisitions and higher service revenues. Gross margins were virtually maintained. With SG&A expenses increasing 31%, operating income was up 24%. Following sharply higher financing expenses and distributions on preferred securities of trust, net income was down 7.2%, to $26,317,000 ($0.59 a share, diluted), from $28,361,000 ($0.65).

Stock Performance - 02-OCT-98

In the past 30 trading days, VST's shares have declined 23%, compared to a 7% fall in the S&P 500. Average trading volume for the past five days was 151,640 shares, compared with the 40-day moving average of 176,979 shares.

Key Stock Statistics

Dividend Rate/Share	Nil	Shareholders	400
Shs. outstg. (M)	44.6	Market cap. (B)	$0.365
Avg. daily vol. (M)	0.180	Inst. holdings	34%
Tang. Bk. Value/Share	2.07		
Beta	NA		

Value of $10,000 invested 5 years ago: NA

Fiscal Year Ending Apr. 30

	1999	1998	1997	1996	1995	1994
Revenues (Million $)						
1Q	655.2	680.6	559.1	427.2	299.8	—
2Q	—	741.8	543.7	445.1	338.6	—
3Q	—	703.4	527.5	446.9	352.9	—
4Q	—	713.1	548.2	485.7	394.2	—
Yr.	—	2,839	2,179	1,805	1,385	—
Earnings Per Share ($)						
1Q	-0.24	0.15	0.23	0.10	Nil	Nil
2Q	Nil	0.21	0.26	0.15	0.01	—
3Q	—	0.24	0.17	-0.53	Nil	Nil
4Q	Nil	0.22	0.04	0.44	0.03	—
Yr.	—	0.81	0.69	0.23	0.04	—

Next earnings report expected: early December

Dividend Data

No dividends have been paid on the common stock, and the company does not intend to pay any in the foreseeable future.

A Division of The McGraw·Hill Companies

STANDARD
&POOR'S
STOCK REPORTS

Vanstar Corporation

2385Z
03-OCT-98

Business Summary - 12-MAY-98

Vanstar is a leading provider of services and products designed to build and manage computer network infrastructures primarily for Fortune 1000 companies and other large enterprises. The company provides customized, integrated solutions for its customers' network infrastructure needs by combining a comprehensive offering of value-added services with its expertise in sourcing and distributing PCs, network products, computer peripherals and software from various vendors. Revenue and profit contributions in FY 97 (Apr.):

	Revs.	Profits
Products	85%	59%
Services:		
Life Cycle	8%	20%
Professional	5%	12%
Other	2%	9%

Product revenues are derived primarily from the sale of computer hardware, software, peripherals and communications devices manufactured by third parties and sold by the company, principally to implement integration projects.

The Life Cycle services organization provides services to support day-to-day operations in customers' existing information technology environments. Support services revenue is derived primarily from services performed for the desktop and focused on the client or user of the PC network. These support services include desktop installation, repair and maintenance, moves, adds and changes, extended warranty, asset management and help desk.

The Professional services division focuses on delivering solutions to help customers implement new network infrastructures and migrate to new technologies. Networking revenue includes network installation, design and consulting, and enhancement and migration, as well as server deployment and support.

Other service revenues consist of fees earned from a distribution agreement with ComputerLand Corp. (formerly Merisel FAB) and training and education services.

In July 1997, Vanstar acquired Sysorex Information Systems, a top-tier government technology service provider with annual revenues of about $150 million. The purchase price was about $46 million and a contingent payment of 500,000 common shares based on Sysorex's future financial performance. The acquisition was expected to expand Vanstar's technology services into the U.S. Government markets that are experiencing growing demand for information technology.

Per Share Data ($)

(Year Ended Apr. 30)	1998	1997	1996	1995	1994	1993	1992	1991	1990	1989
Tangible Bk. Val.	NA	2.57	2.16	1.69	NA	NA	NA	NA	NA	NA
Cash Flow	NA	1.09	1.25	0.62	NA	NA	NA	NA	NA	NA
Earnings	0.81	0.69	0.23	0.04	NA	NA	NA	NA	NA	NA
Dividends	Nil	Nil	Nil	NA	NA	NA	NA	NA	NA	NA
Payout Ratio	Nil	Nil	Nil	NA	NA	NA	NA	NA	NA	NA
Cal. Yrs.	1997	1996	1995	1994	1993	1992	1991	1990	1989	1988
Prices - High	25	29¾	NA	NA	NA	NA	NA	NA	NA	NA
- Low	6½	9	NA	NA	NA	NA	NA	NA	NA	NA
P/E Ratio - High	31	43	NA	NA	NA	NA	NA	NA	NA	NA
- Low	8	39	NA	NA	NA	NA	NA	NA	NA	NA

Income Statement Analysis (Million $)

Revs.	NA	2,179	1,805	1,385	587	1,100	788	NA	NA	NA
Oper. Inc.	NA	85.3	52.8	47.1	15.8	24.3	-54.3	NA	NA	NA
Depr.	NA	17.1	9.8	19.0	16.2	27.6	22.0	NA	NA	NA
Int. Exp.	NA	17.1	35.8	32.6	12.8	23.0	21.3	NA	NA	NA
Pretax Inc.	NA	54.9	12.8	2.1	11.6	25.5	-96.5	NA	NA	NA
Eff. Tax Rate	NA	36%	37%	41%	NM	NM	NM	NM	NM	NM
Net Inc.	NM	30.0	8.1	1.3	-7.0	-18.8	-54.2	NA	NA	NA

Balance Sheet & Other Fin. Data (Million $)

Cash	NA	5.7	14.4	NA	NA	NA	NA	NA	NA	NA
Curr. Assets	NA	599	692	NA	NA	NA	NA	NA	NA	NA
Total Assets	NA	759	803	744	NA	NA	NA	NA	NA	NA
Curr. Liab.	NA	391	376	NA	NA	NA	NA	NA	NA	NA
LT Debt	NA	200	293	284	NA	NA	NA	NA	NA	NA
Common Eqty.	NA	167	127	107	NA	NA	NA	NA	NA	NA
Total Cap.	NA	367	420	391	NA	NA	NA	NA	NA	NA
Cap. Exp.	NA	25.2	15.5	12.8	3.1	6.4	13.3	NA	NA	NA
Cash Flow	NA	47.1	17.8	20.3	9.3	8.8	-32.3	NA	NA	NA
Curr. Ratio	NA	1.5	1.8	NA	NA	NA	NA	NA	NA	NA
% LT Debt of Cap.	NA	54.6	69.7	72.6	NA	NA	NA	NA	NA	NA
% Net Inc.of Revs.	NA	1.4	0.4	0.1	NM	NM	NM	NM	NM	NM
% Ret. on Assets	NM	3.8	1.1	NA	NA	NA	NA	NA	NA	NA
% Ret. on Equity	NA	20.4	NA	NA	NA	NA	NA	NA	NA	NA

Data as orig. reptd.; bef. results of disc. opers. and/or spec. items. Per share data adj. for stk. divs. as of ex-div. date. E-Estimated. NA-Not Available. NM-Not Meaningful. NR-Not Ranked.

Office—1100 Abernathy Rd., Bldg. 500, Suite 1200, Atlanta, GA 30328. **Tel**—(770) 522-4700. **Website**—http://www.vanstar.com **Chrmn & CEO**—W. Y. Tauscher. **Pres & COO**—J. S. Amato. **Sr VP & CFO**—K. Aronaho. **Investor Contact**—Christine Mohrmann (770) 522-4262. **Dirs**—J. S. Amato, J. W. Amerman, R. H. Bard, S. W. Fillo, S. K. P. Gross, W. H. Janeway, J. R. Oltman, W. Y. Tauscher, J. L. Vogelstein, J. S. Weston. **Transfer Agent & Registrar**—ChaseMellon Shareholder Services. **Incorporated**—in Delaware in 1987.**Empl**— 6,000. **S&P Analyst:** J.J.S.

03-OCT-98

Industry: Computer (Software & Services)

Summary: Vantive is a worldwide leader in the front-office automation software market.

Quantitative Evaluations

Recent Price • 8½	Yield • Nil
52 Wk Range • 39¾-5⅝	12-Mo. P/E • NM

Outlook (1 Lowest—5 Highest)
• **NA**

Fair Value
• **NA**

Risk
• **High**

Earn./Div. Rank
• **NR**

Technical Eval.
• **Bearish** since 6/98

Rel. Strength Rank (1 Lowest—99 Highest)
• **19**

Insider Activity
• **NA**

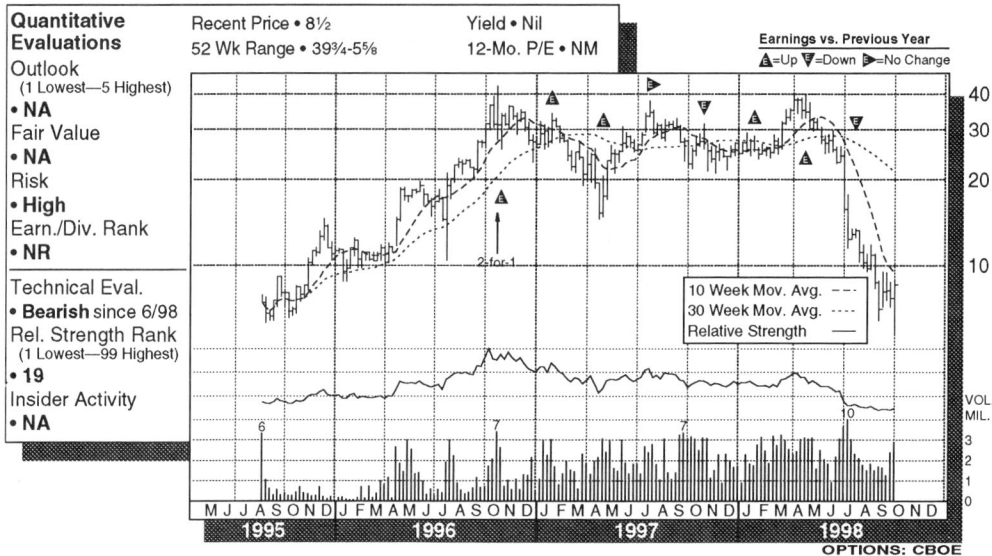

Earnings vs. Previous Year
▲=Up ▼=Down ▶=No Change

10 Week Mov. Avg. - - -
30 Week Mov. Avg. ·····
Relative Strength ——

OPTIONS: CBOE

Business Profile - 10-SEP-98

Results in the 1998 second quarter were mixed, as strong performance internationally and in the services business was offset by weak North American sales. During the quarter, Vantive completed the acquisition of Wayfarer Communications Inc., which specializes in web-based information delivery, and recorded an in-process research and development charge and compensatory bonus expense of approximately $9.5 million. The company expects the strong repeatsales it experienced in the second quarter from its existing customer base, combined with the release of Vantive 8, to help it further grow its revenues while it addresses the quarter's execution issues.

Operational Review - 10-SEP-98

Total revenues in the six months ended June 30, 1998, advanced 53%, year to year, on a 31% increase in license revenues, due to growing acceptance of VNTV's products and the release of Vantive Enterprise 7 in the third quarter of 1997, and a 95% spurt in service revenues on increased consulting, customer support and, to a lesser extent, training services associated with increased sales of VNTV's applications. After $9 million of acquisition-related charges ($0.34 a share, after tax), a net loss of $4,281,000 ($0.17 a share) was incurred, in contrast to income of $5,654,000 ($0.22).

Stock Performance - 02-OCT-98

In the past 30 trading days, VNTV's shares have declined 22%, compared to a 7% fall in the S&P 500. Average trading volume for the past five days was 576,500 shares, compared with the 40-day moving average of 377,192 shares.

Key Stock Statistics

Dividend Rate/Share	Nil	Shareholders	300
Shs. outstg. (M)	26.1	Market cap. (B)	$0.223
Avg. daily vol. (M)	0.429	Inst. holdings	78%
Tang. Bk. Value/Share	2.32		
Beta	NA		

Value of $10,000 invested 5 years ago: NA

Fiscal Year Ending Dec. 31

	1998	1997	1996	1995	1994	1993
Revenues (Million $)						
1Q	36.28	22.52	10.81	4.19	—	—
2Q	37.74	26.01	15.20	5.52	—	—
3Q	—	31.09	17.25	6.61	—	—
4Q	—	37.23	21.01	8.72	—	—
Yr.	—	117.3	64.27	25.04	10.21	2.51
Earnings Per Share ($)						
1Q	0.14	0.10	0.06	—	—	—
2Q	-0.31	0.13	0.13	—	—	—
3Q	—	-0.71	0.12	0.03	—	—
4Q	—	0.19	0.12	0.04	—	—
Yr.	—	-0.28	0.42	0.09	NA	NA

Next earnings report expected: late October

Dividend Data

No cash dividends have been paid on the public shares. A two-for-one stock split was effected in 1996.

A Division of The **McGraw·Hill** *Companies*

Business Summary - 10-SEP-98

Vantive Corp. is a leading provider of "customer asset management" applications software that enables businesses to attract, acquire and retain customers by automating marketing and sales, customer support, defect tracking, field service and internal help desk functions. These tightly integrated customer asset management applications, called the Vantive Enterprise, are based on a multi-tiered client/server architecture and a common data model. Vantive's customer asset management applications may also be used through a Web-based browser, thereby providing the applications directly to the end-user outside the boundaries of the business. The software can be used independently or as part of an integrated, enterprisewide customer asset management information system.

VNTV believes that businesses implementing a customer asset management information system can better manage customer relationships by leveraging valuable customer information that is shared throughout the organization. VNTV's software applications have been deployed by businesses in a wide range of industries, including software, communications, consumer products, finance, outsourcing services, personal computer hardware, health care, manufacturing, medical projects, public sector/regulated industry, online services, consumer goods and retail.

Vantive Sales is a software application for automating the entire sales and marketing process. It can automate campaign lead qualification and tracking, Web-enabled lead and opportunity management, pipeline management, scheduling and contact management, account and territory planning, distribution channel management, sales forecasting and fulfillment.

The company's first product, Vantive Support, is an application for automating and managing a customer support center. It supports activities such as product support, consumer affairs and complaint management. Vantive FieldService is an application for managing the allocation, scheduling and dispatching of resources, including parts and materials, to perform services or complete work orders to solve customer problems at their site.

Vantive Quality is an application for collecting, distributing, tracking and maintaining information about products. Vantive HelpDesk is an internal help desk application that logs, tracks and assists in handling employee problems, issues, complaints, suggestions and requests for assistance with technology, human resources and facilities.

VNTV also offers several other software products and technologies that enhance the functionality and facilitate the implementation, integration and modification of Vantive Enterprise front-office automation software applications.

Per Share Data ($)

(Year Ended Dec. 31)	1997	1996	1995	1994	1993	1992	1991	1990	1989	1988
Tangible Bk. Val.	2.21	1.63	1.12	NA	NA	NA	NA	NA	NA	NA
Cash Flow	-0.18	0.48	0.12	NA	NA	NA	NA	NA	NA	NA
Earnings	-0.28	0.42	0.09	NA	NA	NA	NA	NA	NA	NA
Dividends	Nil	Nil	Nil	Nil	Nil	Nil	Nil	Nil	Nil	Nil
Payout Ratio	Nil	Nil	Nil	Nil	Nil	Nil	Nil	Nil	Nil	Nil
Prices - High	38	42¾	14⅝	NA	NA	NA	NA	NA	NA	NA
- Low	14½	8¾	6	NA	NA	NA	NA	NA	NA	NA
P/E Ratio - High	NM	NM	NM	NM	NM	NM	NM	NM	NM	NM
- Low	NM	NM	NM	NM	NM	NM	NM	NM	NM	NM

Income Statement Analysis (Million $)

	1997	1996	1995	1994	1993	1992	1991	1990	1989	1988
Revs.	117	64.3	25.0	10.2	2.5	0.0	NA	NA	NA	NA
Oper. Inc.	23.7	15.7	2.5	-0.2	-3.4	NA	NA	NA	NA	NA
Depr.	2.5	1.4	0.6	0.3	0.2	NA	NA	NA	NA	NA
Int. Exp.	1.5	0.2	0.1	0.1	0.0	NA	NA	NA	NA	NA
Pretax Inc.	1.4	15.6	2.3	-0.6	-3.6	-2.2	NA	NA	NA	NA
Eff. Tax Rate	615%	30%	10%	NM	NM	NM	NM	NM	NM	NM
Net Inc.	-7.0	10.9	2.0	-0.6	-3.6	-2.2	NA	NA	NA	NA

Balance Sheet & Other Fin. Data (Million $)

	1997	1996	1995	1994	1993	1992	1991	1990	1989	1988
Cash	77.6	32.9	26.4	3.1	NA	NA	NA	NA	NA	NA
Curr. Assets	147	51.1	31.7	6.3	NA	NA	NA	NA	NA	NA
Total Assets	163	58.4	34.6	7.5	3.4	3.1	NA	NA	NA	NA
Curr. Liab.	37.6	18.2	7.3	2.9	NA	NA	NA	NA	NA	NA
LT Debt	69.0	0.3	0.6	0.4	NA	NA	NA	NA	NA	NA
Common Eqty.	55.7	39.4	26.7	-6.7	-6.2	-2.6	NA	NA	NA	NA
Total Cap.	125	39.8	27.2	4.5	NA	NA	NA	NA	NA	NA
Cap. Exp.	8.1	5.2	1.5	0.2	0.6	NA	NA	NA	NA	NA
Cash Flow	-4.4	12.3	2.7	-0.2	-3.5	NA	NA	NA	NA	NA
Curr. Ratio	3.9	2.8	4.4	2.2	NA	NA	NA	NA	NA	NA
% LT Debt of Cap.	55.3	0.9	2.1	9.1	NA	NA	NA	NA	NA	NA
% Net Inc.of Revs.	NM	17.0	8.2	NM	NM	NM	NM	NM	NM	NM
% Ret. on Assets	NM	23.5	9.7	NM	NM	NM	NM	NM	NM	NM
% Ret. on Equity	NM	33.0	21.5	NM	NM	NM	NM	NM	NM	NM

Data as orig. reptd.; bef. results of disc. opers. and/or spec. items. Per share data adj. for stk. divs. as of ex-div. date. Bold denotes diluted EPS (FASB 128). E-Estimated. NA-Not Available. NM-Not Meaningful. NR-Not Ranked.

Office—2455 Augustine Dr., Santa Clara, CA 95054. **Tel**—(408) 982-5700. **Website**—http://www.vantive.com **Chrmn**—W. R. Davidow.**Pres & CEO**—J. R. Luongo. **EVP & CFO**—L. J. LeBlanc. **Dirs**—W. R. Davidow. K. G. Hall, J. R. Luongo, P. Manuel, R. L. Ocampo Jr., P. A. Roshko.**Transfer Agent & Registrar**—Harris Trust Co. of California, Los Angeles. **Incorporated**—in Delaware in 1995. **Empl**— 451. **S&P Analyst:** C.F.B.

03-OCT-98

Industry: Biotechnology

Summary: This development-stage company utilizes structure-based drug design to discover and develop therapeutics for diseases which have limited or no effective treatments.

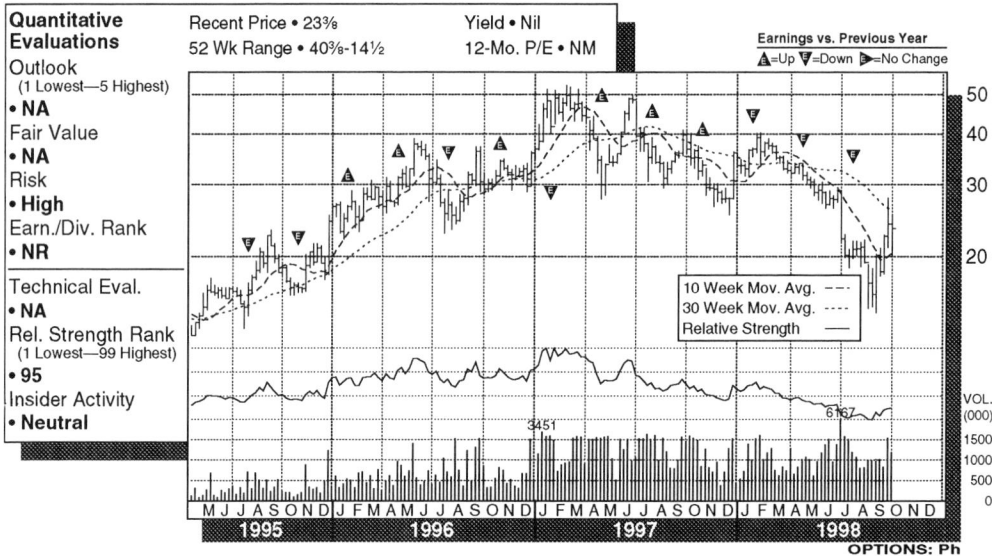

Quantitative Evaluations		
Outlook (1 Lowest—5 Highest) • NA	Recent Price • 23⅜	Yield • Nil
Fair Value • NA	52 Wk Range • 40⅜-14½	12-Mo. P/E • NM

Earnings vs. Previous Year
▲=Up ▼=Down ▶=No Change

- Outlook (1 Lowest—5 Highest) • **NA**
- Fair Value • **NA**
- Risk • **High**
- Earn./Div. Rank • **NR**
- Technical Eval. • **NA**
- Rel. Strength Rank (1 Lowest—99 Highest) • **95**
- Insider Activity • **Neutral**

10 Week Mov. Avg. – – –
30 Week Mov. Avg. · · · ·
Relative Strength ——

OPTIONS: Ph

Business Profile - 01-OCT-98

This development-stage drug company pioneered the application of structure-based drug design, a powerful drug discovery strategy to design orally deliverable, small-molecule drugs. VRTX is using this technology to design novel therapeutics for the treatment of viral diseases, multidrug resistance in cancer, autoimmune and inflammatory diseases, and neurodegenerative diseases. To date, the company has not received any revenues from the sale of pharmaceutical products. In September 1998, the company reported Phase III clinical data on its lead product, Agenerase, a protease inhibitor for HIV/AIDS. Agenerase was found to significantly aid in suppressing the HIV virus, and the company's marketing partner, Glaxo-Wellcome, intends to file for marketing approval in the U.S. and in Europe later this fall.

Operational Review - 01-OCT-98

Total revenues in the six months ended June 30, 1998, fell to $14.3 million, from $19.1 million in the 1997 period, as lower revenues from collaborative agreements and government grants outweighed higher interest income. Research and development spending increased 18%, reflecting continued product development activities and further addition of scientific staff, and with 53% higher general and administrative expenses, the net loss widened to $18,216,000 ($0.72 a share, on 8.2% more shares), from $7,178,000 ($0.31). Cash and investments totaled $256.1 million on June 30,1998.

Stock Performance - 02-OCT-98

In the past 30 trading days, VRTX's shares have increased 36%, compared to a 7% fall in the S&P 500. Average trading volume for the past five days was 237,760 shares, compared with the 40-day moving average of 221,672 shares.

Key Stock Statistics

Dividend Rate/Share	Nil	Shareholders	300
Shs. outstg. (M)	25.3	Market cap. (B)	$0.593
Avg. daily vol. (M)	0.255	Inst. holdings	64%
Tang. Bk. Value/Share	10.24		
Beta	1.05		

Value of $10,000 invested 5 years ago: $ 24,037

Fiscal Year Ending Dec. 31

	1998	1997	1996	1995	1994	1993
Revenues (Million $)						
1Q	7.17	6.92	3.75	6.33	5.63	1.27
2Q	7.15	12.16	4.15	7.95	4.78	4.97
3Q	—	13.55	4.12	3.49	6.50	4.73
4Q	—	11.18	6.58	9.76	6.24	18.33
Yr.	—	43.80	18.60	27.53	23.15	29.29
Earnings Per Share ($)						
1Q	**-0.33**	-0.26	-0.43	-0.44	-0.22	-0.27
2Q	**-0.39**	-0.06	-1.28	-0.52	-0.35	-0.06
3Q	—	-0.23	-0.33	-0.40	-0.24	-0.21
4Q	—	**-0.27**	-0.18	-0.05	-0.30	0.69
Yr.	—	**-0.82**	-2.13	-1.25	-1.11	0.16

Next earnings report expected: late October

Dividend Data

No dividends have been paid.

A Division of The **McGraw·Hill** *Companies*

Business Summary - 01-OCT-98

Vertex Pharmaceuticals Inc., a developer of novel, small-molecule pharmaceuticals, rejects the traditional path of drug discovery and instead focuses on the structure-based design approach, which integrates biology, biophysics and chemistry. Vertex's goal is to create a portfolio of highly specific, proprietary drugs based on its knowledge of the atomic structure of proteins involved in the control of disease processes.

The traditional method of discovering drugs relies on screening thousands of compounds against a predictive assay for a particular disease target. VRTX regards this as essentially random, as well as costly and inefficient. VRTX believes that use of the structure-based methodology increases the chances for the discovery of multiple lead compounds over the traditional system due to its more integrated approach. The structure-based system combines advanced techniques in biology, biophysics and chemistry to determine the detailed atomic structure of protein targets linked to a particular disease process. Using this structural information, VRTX designs orally active compounds to treat viral diseases, multidrug resistance in cancer, hemoglobin, autoimmune diseases, inflammatory diseases and neurodegenerative diseases.

In its 10th year as a pharmaceutical company, VRTX has a broad pipeline of compounds spanning all stages of development, from early discovery to late stage clinical development. It has eight drug discovery and development programs underway, and six corporate collaborations with multinational drug companies. VRTX's drug candidates in clinical trials include amprenavir to treat HIV infection and AIDS, two compounds to treat cancer multidrug resistance, and an inosine monophosphate dehydrogenase (IMPDH) inhibitor to treat autoimmune diseases.

The company's most advanced compound, Agenerase (amprenavir), a second generation HIV protease inhibitor, is in Phase III clinical trials. VRTX's partner, Glaxo Wellcome, is expected to file a new drug application for U.S. marketing approval in the second half of 1998, with applications in other countries shortly thereafter.

VRTX's multidrug resistance inhibitor, Incel (also known as VX-710), is being tested in combination with chemotherapy on four Phase II clinical trials targeting breast cancer, ovarian cancer, soft tissue sarcoma and liver cancer. Another multidrug resistance inhibitor, VX-853, is in a Phase I/II clinical trial in patients with solid tumors.

The company has completed a Phase I clinical trial in healthy volunteers with VX-497, an orally administered IMPDH inhibitor being developed to treat autoimmune diseases.

VX-740, a novel inhibitor of ICE (IL-1 beta converting enzyme), is expected to enter a Phase I clinical trial later in 1998 with partner Hoechst Marion Roussel. ICE inhibitors may be useful for inflammatory diseases such as rheumatoid arthritis and osteoarthritis.

Per Share Data ($)

(Year Ended Dec. 31)	1997	1996	1995	1994	1993	1992	1991	1990	1989	1988
Tangible Bk. Val.	10.95	6.20	4.93	6.14	3.97	3.60	NA	NA	NA	NA
Cash Flow	-0.67	-1.96	-1.03	-0.89	0.48	-0.47	NA	NA	NA	NA
Earnings	-0.82	-2.13	-1.25	-1.11	0.16	-0.70	-0.64	NA	NA	NA
Dividends	Nil	Nil	Nil	Nil	Nil	Nil	Nil	Nil	Nil	Nil
Payout Ratio	Nil	Nil	Nil	Nil	Nil	Nil	Nil	Nil	Nil	Nil
Prices - High	53¾	42¼	25½	20	19	17½	16	NA	NA	NA
- Low	25¼	22	12⅜	10½	6½	6⅝	8⅜	NA	NA	NA
P/E Ratio - High	NM	NM	NM	NM	120	NM	NM	NM	NM	NM
- Low	NM	NM	NM	NM	41	NM	NM	NM	NM	NM

Income Statement Analysis (Million $)

	1997	1996	1995	1994	1993	1992	1991	1990	1989	1988
Revs.	43.8	13.3	22.1	19.6	27.9	3.8	NA	NA	NA	NA
Oper. Inc.	-16.2	-26.6	-22.8	-17.2	6.5	-6.2	NA	NA	NA	NA
Depr.	3.6	3.2	3.7	3.5	3.9	2.8	NA	NA	NA	NA
Int. Exp.	0.6	0.5	0.5	0.4	0.5	0.5	NA	NA	NA	NA
Pretax Inc.	19.8	-40.0	-21.5	-17.6	2.1	-8.5	NA	NA	NA	NA
Eff. Tax Rate	Nil	Nil	Nil	Nil	3.80%	Nil	Nil	Nil	Nil	Nil
Net Inc.	-19.8	-40.0	-21.5	-17.6	2.0	-8.5	NA	NA	NA	NA

Balance Sheet & Other Fin. Data (Million $)

	1997	1996	1995	1994	1993	1992	1991	1990	1989	1988
Cash	280	130	87.0	106	52.1	43.7	NA	NA	NA	NA
Curr. Assets	282	132	88.0	107	53.0	NA	NA	NA	NA	NA
Total Assets	296	143	99	116	61.0	51.0	NA	NA	NA	NA
Curr. Liab.	13.7	7.0	8.8	6.0	7.3	NA	NA	NA	NA	NA
LT Debt	5.9	5.6	4.9	4.7	4.2	4.0	NA	NA	NA	NA
Common Eqty.	276	131	85.0	105	50.0	44.0	NA	NA	NA	NA
Total Cap.	282	136	90.0	110	54.0	48.0	NA	NA	NA	NA
Cap. Exp.	6.0	4.0	NA	1.9	1.8	1.4	NA	NA	NA	NA
Cash Flow	-16.2	-36.8	-17.8	-14.1	6.0	-5.7	NA	NA	NA	NA
Curr. Ratio	20.6	18.9	10.0	17.9	7.3	NA	NA	NA	NA	NA
% LT Debt of Cap.	NA	4.1	5.5	4.3	7.8	8.3	NA	NA	NA	NA
% Net Inc.of Revs.	NM	NM	NM	NM	7.2	NM	NM	NM	NM	NM
% Ret. on Assets	NM	NM	NM	NM	3.6	NM	NM	NM	NM	NM
% Ret. on Equity	NM	NM	NM	NM	4.4	NM	NM	NM	NM	NM

Data as orig. reptd.; bef. results of disc. opers. and/or spec. items. Per share data adj. for stk. divs. as of ex-div. date. Bold denotes diluted EPS (FASB 128). E-Estimated. NA-Not Available. NM-Not Meaningful. NR-Not Ranked.

Office—130 Waverly St., Cambridge, MA 02139-4242. **Tel**—(617) 577-6000. **Website**—http://www.vpharm.com **Chrmn, Pres & CEO**—J. S. Boger. **SVP & CBO**—R. H. Aldrich. **SVP & CSO**—Vicki L. Sato. **CFO & Treas**—T. G. Auchincloss Jr. **Investor Contact**—Lynne H. Brum. **Dirs**—B. M. Bloom, J. S. Boger, R. W. Brimblecombe, D. R. Conklin, W. W. Helman IV, C. A. Sanders, E. S. Ullian. **Transfer Agent & Registrar**—Boston EquiServe. **Incorporated**—in Massachusetts in 1989. **Empl**— 220. **S&P Analyst**: David Moskowitz

STANDARD &POOR'S
STOCK REPORTS

Vicor Corp.

5551K

NASDAQ Symbol **VICR**

In S&P SmallCap 600

03-OCT-98

Industry:
Electrical Equipment

Summary: This company designs, develops, manufactures and markets modular power components and complete power systems for use in electronic products.

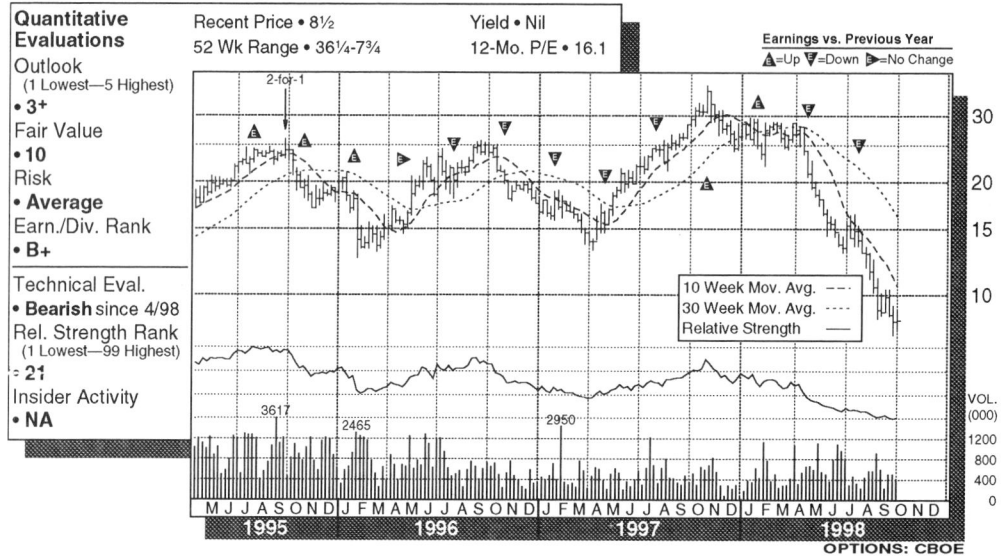

Quantitative Evaluations

Recent Price • 8½
52 Wk Range • 36¼-7¾

Yield • Nil
12-Mo. P/E • 16.1

Earnings vs. Previous Year
▲=Up ▼=Down ▶=No Change

Outlook
(1 Lowest—5 Highest)
• **3+**

Fair Value
• **10**

Risk
• **Average**

Earn./Div. Rank
• **B+**

Technical Eval.
• **Bearish** since 4/98

Rel. Strength Rank
(1 Lowest—99 Highest)
• **21**

Insider Activity
• **NA**

10 Week Mov. Avg. ---
30 Week Mov. Avg. ·····
Relative Strength —

OPTIONS: CBOE

Business Profile - 14-SEP-98

Despite VICR's revenue growth in 1997, operating profits were restrained by rising costs and expenses. Vicor intends to continue making investments in manufacturing equipment over the next several years. In September 1997, VICR announced a licensing agreement with Delta Electronics, one of the world's largest merchant manufacturers of switching power supplies. Under the agreement, Delta has acquired non-exclusive rights to use Vicor's patented "reset" technology in its power conversion products. In November 1997, directors authorized the repurchase of up to $30 million of VICR's common stock.

Operational Review - 14-SEP-98

Net revenues in the six months ended June 30, 1998, advanced 9.3%, year to year, primarily reflecting increased unit shipments of standard and custom products. Margins narrowed, reflecting larger increases in cost of sales, and SG&A and R&D expenditures; operating income fell 29%. Following 17% greater other income and after taxes at 35.0%, versus 36.0%, net income was down 22%, to $9,570,000 ($0.22 share), from $12,339,000 ($0.29).

Stock Performance - 02-OCT-98

In the past 30 trading days, VICR's shares have declined 19%, compared to a 7% fall in the S&P 500. Average trading volume for the past five days was 83,060 shares, compared with the 40-day moving average of 109,728 shares.

Key Stock Statistics

Dividend Rate/Share	Nil	Shareholders	600
Shs. outstg. (M)	42.1	Market cap. (B)	$0.256
Avg. daily vol. (M)	0.084	Inst. holdings	28%
Tang. Bk. Value/Share	4.90		
Beta	1.63		

Value of $10,000 invested 5 years ago: $ 9,366

Fiscal Year Ending Dec. 31

	1998	1997	1996	1995	1994	1993
Revenues (Million $)						
1Q	43.19	37.94	35.81	33.79	25.76	18.70
2Q	41.72	39.72	36.70	35.12	27.68	20.09
3Q	—	41.40	35.67	37.31	30.05	21.70
4Q	—	43.19	36.80	37.80	31.95	23.55
Yr.	—	162.2	145.0	144.0	115.4	84.03
Earnings Per Share ($)						
1Q	**0.12**	**0.14**	0.15	0.16	0.11	0.08
2Q	**0.10**	**0.15**	0.16	0.17	0.12	0.08
3Q	—	**0.16**	0.15	0.18	0.14	0.09
4Q	—	**0.15**	0.14	0.17	0.15	0.10
Yr.	—	**0.60**	0.60	0.68	0.52	0.35

Next earnings report expected: early October

Dividend Data

No cash payments have been made. For the foreseeable future, the company plans to retain earnings to finance the expansion of its business. A two-for-one stock split was effected in 1995.

A Division of The McGraw·Hill Companies

Business Summary - 14-SEP-98

This maker of power system components called the introduction during 1996 of the first models of its next generation of DC-DC power converters "a major milestone." One of these newcomers--the first-ever "micro" sized converter--delivers 150 watts in one-third the volume of the company's first-generation converter. Vicor Corp. (VICR) decided to introduce its next-generation products in stages to allow it to build up manufacturing capacity and its ability to support and service the new lines ahead of anticipated demand. In 1997, the company planned to break ground on a 90,000-square-foot addition to its Federal Street plant in Andover, MA, with most of the new capacity expected to benefit next-generation production.

VICR's modular power components and complete power systems are used primarily by original equipment manufacturers in the communications, data processing, industrial control, test equipment, medical and defense electronic markets. Built into virtually all electronic products, power systems convert electric power from a primary source, such as a wall outlet, into the low, stable voltages required by electronic circuits. Since power systems are forged in a myriad of application-specific configurations, the company's basic strategy is to exploit the density and performance advantages of its core technology by offering comprehensive families of

economical, component-level building blocks that can be applied by users to easily fashion a power system specific to their needs.

At the heart of VICR's product line are high-density DC-DC converters that come in thousands of combinations of input voltage, output voltage and power levels. Accessory components integrate other power system functions. Together, these products allow OEM users to meet their unique power requirements by selecting and interconnecting standard, modular parts.

In September 1997, VICR entered into a license agreement with Delta Electronics, Inc. that gives Delta non-exclusive rights to use the company's patented "reset" technology in its power conversion products. Delta, one of the world's largest merchant manufacturers of switching power supplies, will initially utilize the technology in several new products for application in desktop computers and network PC servers. High-volume manufacture of these products by the Taipei-based firm is scheduled for 1998.

During 1997, the company shipped a limited number of second-generation products, while continuing to make modifications to the designs, processes, equipment and parts associated with them. Significant revenues from these products were not expected for several quarters. VICR believes that gross margins will be negatively impacted until ramp-up and related costs are fully absorbed by higher production volumes.

Per Share Data ($)

(Year Ended Dec. 31)	1997	1996	1995	1994	1993	1992	1991	1990	1989	1988
Tangible Bk. Val.	4.87	4.05	3.55	2.73	2.42	2.09	1.69	0.40	0.20	NA
Cash Flow	0.80	0.79	0.87	0.69	0.51	0.39	0.36	0.18	0.10	NA
Earnings	0.60	0.60	0.68	0.52	0.35	0.28	0.28	0.14	0.07	NA
Dividends	Nil	Nil	Nil	Nil	Nil	Nil	Nil	Nil	Nil	Nil
Payout Ratio	Nil	Nil	Nil	Nil	Nil	Nil	Nil	Nil	Nil	Nil
Prices - High	36¼	25¾	26	15⅛	12¾	22⅞	22⅝	4⅜	NA	NA
- Low	13⅛	12½	12¼	9	6½	6⅞	4⅛	1¾	NA	NA
P/E Ratio - High	60	43	38	29	36	83	79	33	NA	NA
- Low	22	21	18	17	19	25	14	13	NA	NA

Income Statement Analysis (Million $)

	1997	1996	1995	1994	1993	1992	1991	1990	1989	1988
Revs.	162	145	144	115	84.0	63.8	55.6	36.8	28.5	NA
Oper. Inc.	44.2	44.9	50.9	40.9	28.3	21.7	20.3	10.1	5.4	NA
Depr.	8.3	8.3	8.2	7.6	6.7	4.8	3.2	1.8	1.4	NA
Int. Exp.	NA	Nil	Nil	0.0	0.1	0.1	0.3	0.5	0.6	NA
Pretax Inc.	41.0	40.4	46.8	35.7	24.2	19.2	18.3	8.1	3.8	NA
Eff. Tax Rate	36%	37%	37%	38%	38%	38%	39%	38%	33%	NA
Net Inc.	26.2	25.6	29.5	22.1	15.1	12.0	11.2	5.1	2.5	NA

Balance Sheet & Other Fin. Data (Million $)

	1997	1996	1995	1994	1993	1992	1991	1990	1989	1988
Cash	84.9	73.6	65.2	43.2	45.2	42.9	37.4	1.8	1.2	NA
Curr. Assets	147	123	111	77.1	73.4	65.5	60.5	15.7	10.6	NA
Total Assets	229	186	167	126	115	97.0	77.6	27.5	18.7	NA
Curr. Liab.	18.6	14.0	15.2	12.1	10.6	6.7	6.4	8.9	3.5	NA
LT Debt	Nil	Nil	Nil	Nil	0.1	0.5	1.1	2.2	4.7	NA
Common Eqty.	208	171	150	113	102	88.5	70.1	13.0	6.2	NA
Total Cap.	210	172	152	114	104	89.6	71.2	18.6	15.2	NA
Cap. Exp.	20.2	14.3	15.6	15.5	16.1	14.8	8.4	5.5	3.8	NA
Cash Flow	34.5	34.0	37.7	29.7	21.8	16.8	14.4	6.9	3.9	NA
Curr. Ratio	7.9	8.8	7.3	6.4	6.9	9.7	9.4	1.8	3.0	NA
% LT Debt of Cap.	Nil	Nil	Nil	Nil	0.1	0.6	1.5	11.6	30.7	NA
% Net Inc.of Revs.	16.2	17.7	20.5	19.2	18.0	18.8	20.2	13.8	8.9	NA
% Ret. on Assets	12.6	14.5	20.1	18.5	14.3	13.6	19.9	21.7	15.2	NA
% Ret. on Equity	13.8	16.0	22.4	20.7	15.8	15.0	25.9	52.5	26.3	NA

Data as orig. reptd.; bef. results of disc. opers. and/or spec. items. Per share data adj. for stk. divs. as of ex-div. date. Bold denotes diluted EPS (FASB 128). E-Estimated. NA-Not Available. NM-Not Meaningful. NR-Not Ranked.

Office—23 Frontage Rd., Andover, MA 01810. **Tel**—(508) 470-2900. **Chrmn & Pres**—P. Vinciarelli. **VP-Fin, Treas, Secy & Investor Contact**—Mark A. Glazer. **Dirs**—M. M. Ansour, R. E. Beede, E. J. Eichten, J. M. Prager, D. T. Riddiford, P. Vinciarelli. **Transfer Agent**—State Street Bank & Trust Co., Boston. **Incorporated**—in Delaware in 1981. **Empl**— 1,365. **S&P Analyst:** S.A.H.

03-OCT-98

Industry:
Oil & Gas (Exploration & Production)

Summary: This independent oil and gas company focuses on acquiring producing oil and gas properties with potential for increased value through exploitation and development.

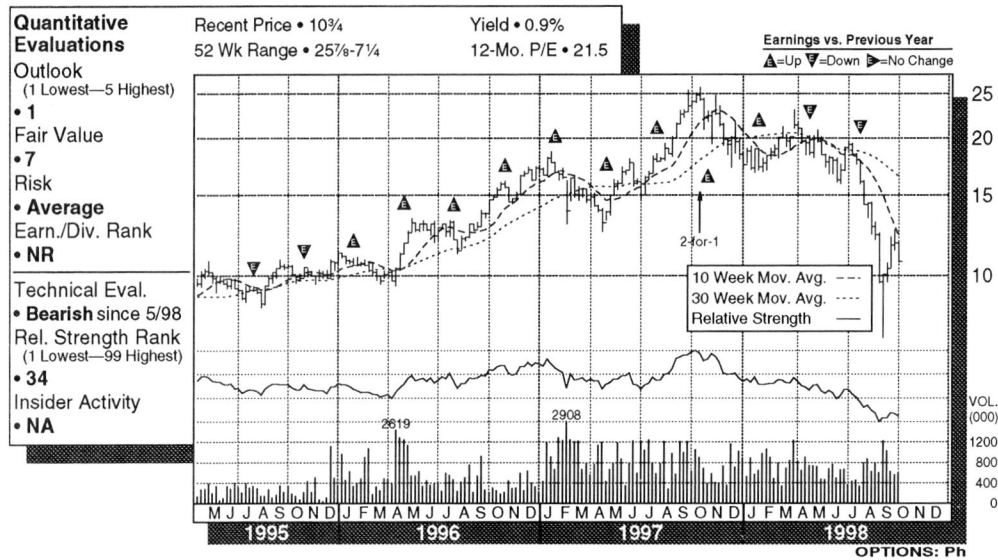

Quantitative Evaluations	Recent Price • 10¾	Yield • 0.9%
	52 Wk Range • 25⅞-7¼	12-Mo. P/E • 21.5

Outlook
(1 Lowest—5 Highest)
• **1**

Fair Value
• **7**

Risk
• **Average**

Earn./Div. Rank
• **NR**

Technical Eval.
• **Bearish** since 5/98

Rel. Strength Rank
(1 Lowest—99 Highest)
• **34**

Insider Activity
• **NA**

Earnings vs. Previous Year
▲=Up ▼=Down ▶=No Change

10 Week Mov. Avg. - - -
30 Week Mov. Avg. ·····
Relative Strength —

2-for-1

OPTIONS: Ph

Business Profile - 21-SEP-98

Although low oil prices led to substantially reduced oil revenues, contributed significantly to losses, and dampened cash flow in the first half of 1998, VPI continues to work toward its goal of a double-digit percentage increase in total production for the year, with continuing gains in 1999. Toward that end, the company recently announced that it has drilled a successful discovery well in the Fisher's Reef West area of Galveston Bay, TX.

Operational Review - 21-SEP-98

Revenues in the six months ended June 30, 1998, fell 12%, year to year, as an increase in oil and gas production of 16% on an equivalent barrel basis was outweighed by a 34% decrease in average oil prices and a 4% decrease in average gas prices. Total costs and expenses were up 18%; a pretax loss contrasted with pretax income. After tax credits of $7,570,000, versus taxes at 17.9%, a net loss of $11,090,000 ($0.21 a share) contrasted with net income of $28,763,000 ($0.55). Effective January 1, 1998, VPI elected to convert from the full cost method to the successful efforts method of accounting for its investments in oil and gas properties; results for the first half of 1997 have been restated to conform with successful efforts accounting.

Stock Performance - 02-OCT-98

In the past 30 trading days, VPI's shares have declined 13%, compared to a 7% fall in the S&P 500. Average trading volume for the past five days was 117,660 shares, compared with the 40-day moving average of 161,862 shares.

Key Stock Statistics

Dividend Rate/Share	0.10	Shareholders	100
Shs. outstg. (M)	51.7	Market cap. (B)	$0.555
Avg. daily vol. (M)	0.157	Inst. holdings	54%
Tang. Bk. Value/Share	7.30		
Beta	1.47		

Value of $10,000 invested 5 years ago: $ 17,625

Fiscal Year Ending Dec. 31

	1998	1997	1996	1995	1994	1993
Revenues (Million $)						
1Q	90.10	99.2	71.34	41.04	44.64	37.10
2Q	84.93	99.8	76.04	45.23	48.09	39.06
3Q	—	104.4	75.95	50.10	48.25	40.15
4Q	—	113.1	88.35	58.42	44.68	43.71
Yr.	—	416.6	311.7	194.8	185.7	160.0
Earnings Per Share ($)						
1Q	-0.13	0.41	0.15	0.04	0.06	0.10
2Q	-0.18	0.27	0.20	0.08	0.10	0.12
3Q	—	0.29	0.20	0.07	0.10	0.09
4Q	—	0.41	0.29	0.09	0.08	0.09
Yr.	—	1.39	0.84	0.27	0.33	0.41

Next earnings report expected: mid November

Dividend Data (Dividends have been paid since 1992.)

Amount ($)	Date Decl.	Ex-Div. Date	Stock of Record	Payment Date
0.020	Dec. 08	Dec. 16	Dec. 18	Jan. 06 '98
0.020	Mar. 11	Mar. 23	Mar. 25	Apr. 02 '98
0.020	May. 18	Jun. 08	Jun. 10	Jul. 01 '98
0.025	Aug. 21	Sep. 17	Sep. 21	Oct. 01 '98

A Division of The McGraw·Hill Companies

Business Summary - 21-SEP-98

Vintage Petroleum, Inc. (VPI) is an independent oil and gas company that focuses on acquiring producing oil and gas properties with potential for increased value through exploitation and development. VPI also purchases, gathers and markets natural gas and crude oil, and explores and develops non-producing properties.

The company seeks to acquire producing properties with significant upside potential to be realized through its exploitation and development expertise. VPI consistently attempts to purchase reserves at costs well below the industry averages. Exploitation and development activities raise the value of the acquired properties by increasing production and adding reserves at low cost.

VPI believes that its primary strengths are its ability to add reserves at attractive prices through property acquisitions and subsequent exploitation, and its low-cost operating structure. These strengths have allowed the company to substantially increase reserves, production and cash flow during the past five years. As VPI has increased its cash flow and added to its technical staff, exploration has become a greater focus for future growth. Planned exploration expenditures for 1998 of $65 million represent 35% of he capital budget, excluding acquisitions.

As of December 31, 1997, VPI owned and operated producing properties in 10 states, with domestic proved reserves located primarily in four core areas: the West Coast, Gulf Coast, East Texas, and Mid-Continent areas of the U.S. In 1996 and the first half of 1997, VPI expanded its Gulf Coast presence through the acquisitions of certain oil and gas properties from Exxon, Conoco, and Burlington Resources Inc. In 1995, it established a new core area by acquiring 12 oil concessions, 11 of which are producing and operated by the company, in the south flank of the San Jorge Basin in southern Argentina. VPI recently expanded its South American operations into Bolivia through the acquisition of Shamrock Ventures Ltd., which owns and operates three blocks covering approximately 570,000 gross acres in the Chaco Plains area of southern Bolivia.

As of December 31, 1997, VPI owned interests in 3,815 gross (2,778 net) producing wells in the U.S., of which about 78% are operated by VPI; 699 gross (686 net) producing wells in Argentina, of which about 98% are operated by VPI; and 7 gross (6 net) producing wells in Bolivia, all of which are operated by VPI.

VPI has consistently achieved growth in proved reserves, production and revenues and has been profitable every full year since its founding in 1983. From the first quarter of 1995 through the fourth quarter of 1997, VPI increased its average net daily production from 17,000 bbl. of oil to 44,700 bbl. of oil, and from 77,000 Mcf of gas to 129,700 Mcf of gas.

Per Share Data ($)

(Year Ended Dec. 31)	1997	1996	1995	1994	1993	1992	1991	1990	1989	1988
Tangible Bk. Val.	7.44	5.51	4.74	3.87	3.56	2.40	2.15	1.95	NA	NA
Cash Flow	3.29	2.27	1.50	1.41	1.20	0.77	0.58	0.56	0.50	NA
Earnings	1.39	0.84	0.27	0.33	0.41	0.26	0.20	0.23	0.18	NA
Dividends	0.06	0.06	0.05	0.04	0.03	0.01	Nil	Nil	Nil	Nil
Payout Ratio	4%	7%	17%	11%	6%	4%	Nil	Nil	Nil	Nil
Prices - High	25⅞	17⅜	11¼	11⅜	13	7	4⅝	5⅜	NA	NA
- Low	12½	9½	8	7⅜	6⅛	2¾	2¾	3½	NA	NA
P/E Ratio - High	19	21	42	34	32	27	22	24	NA	NA
- Low	9	11	30	22	15	11	13	16	NA	NA

Income Statement Analysis (Million $)

	1997	1996	1995	1994	1993	1992	1991	1990	1989	1988
Revs.	417	312	194	183	157	100	69.9	50.7	49.1	NA
Oper. Inc.	225	157	86.8	77.8	65.8	34.5	24.0	25.6	24.4	NA
Depr. Depl. & Amort.	99	70.1	52.3	45.8	33.2	17.4	12.8	10.1	10.8	NA
Int. Exp.	36.8	30.1	20.2	12.0	6.9	4.5	4.2	5.1	5.0	NA
Pretax Inc.	89.6	56.6	15.6	22.4	28.5	13.7	10.9	10.9	10.3	NA
Eff. Tax Rate	19%	26%	33%	38%	41%	37%	38%	38%	38%	NA
Net Inc.	72.2	41.2	11.4	13.9	16.8	8.7	6.8	6.8	6.4	NA

Balance Sheet & Other Fin. Data (Million $)

	1997	1996	1995	1994	1993	1992	1991	1990	1989	1988
Cash	5.8	2.8	2.5	0.4	0.6	0.6	0.3	0.5	0.8	NA
Curr. Assets	89.7	84.7	59.1	39.3	36.6	27.1	16.4	13.6	14.8	NA
Total Assets	990	814	648	408	384	260	144	123	121	NA
Curr. Liab.	79.7	113	59.0	34.0	42.6	34.2	23.3	20.4	24.9	NA
LT Debt	451	372	316	187	174	128	36.6	27.6	28.0	NA
Common Eqty.	384	265	224	156	143	78.7	69.8	62.9	57.4	NA
Total Cap.	907	697	585	374	342	226	121	103	96.0	NA
Cap. Exp.	268	164	145	67.0	151	120	32.3	27.6	NA	NA
Cash Flow	171	111	63.6	59.7	49.9	26.0	19.6	16.9	17.1	NA
Curr. Ratio	1.1	0.8	1.0	1.2	0.9	0.8	0.7	0.7	0.6	NA
% LT Debt of Cap.	49.7	53.4	54.0	49.9	51.0	56.7	30.3	26.9	29.1	NA
% Ret. on Assets	8.0	5.7	2.2	3.5	4.8	4.3	5.1	4.7	NA	NA
% Ret. on Equity	22.3	16.9	6.0	9.3	14.0	11.6	10.2	16.3	NA	NA

Data as orig. reptd.; bef. results of disc. opers. and/or spec. items. Per share data adj. for stk. divs. as of ex-div. date. E-Estimated. NA-Not Available. NM-Not Meaningful. NR-Not Ranked.

Office—4200 One Williams Center, Tulsa, OK 74172.**Tel**—(918) 592-0101. **Fax**—(918) 584-7282. **Chrmn**—C. C. Stephenson Jr. **Vice Chrmn**—J. B. Hille.**Pres & CEO**—S. C. George.**EVP, CFO, Secy & Treas**—W. C. Barnes. **VP & Investor Contact**—Robert E. Phaneuf. **Dirs**—W. C. Barnes, S. C. George, J. B. Hille, B. H. Lawrence, J. T. McNabb, II, C. C. Stephenson Jr. **Transfer Agent & Registrar**—ChaseMellon Shareholder Services, Ridgefield Park, NJ. **Incorporated**—in Delaware in 1983. **Empl**— 580. **S&P Analyst:** M.I.

STANDARD &POOR'S
STOCK REPORTS

VISX, Inc.

NASDAQ Symbol **VISX**

5535

In S&P SmallCap 600

03-OCT-98

Industry:
Health Care (Medical Products & Supplies)

Summary: This company is a leader in the design and development of proprietary technologies and systems for laser vision correction.

Quantitative Evaluations

Recent Price • 61½
52 Wk Range • 71-19½

Yield • Nil
12-Mo. P/E • NM

Earnings vs. Previous Year
▲=Up ▼=Down ▶=No Change

Outlook
(1 Lowest—5 Highest)
• **2**

Fair Value
• **61½**

Risk
• **High**

Earn./Div. Rank
• **B-**

Technical Eval.
• **Bearish** since 3/98

Rel. Strength Rank
(1 Lowest—99 Highest)
• **92**

Insider Activity
• **Neutral**

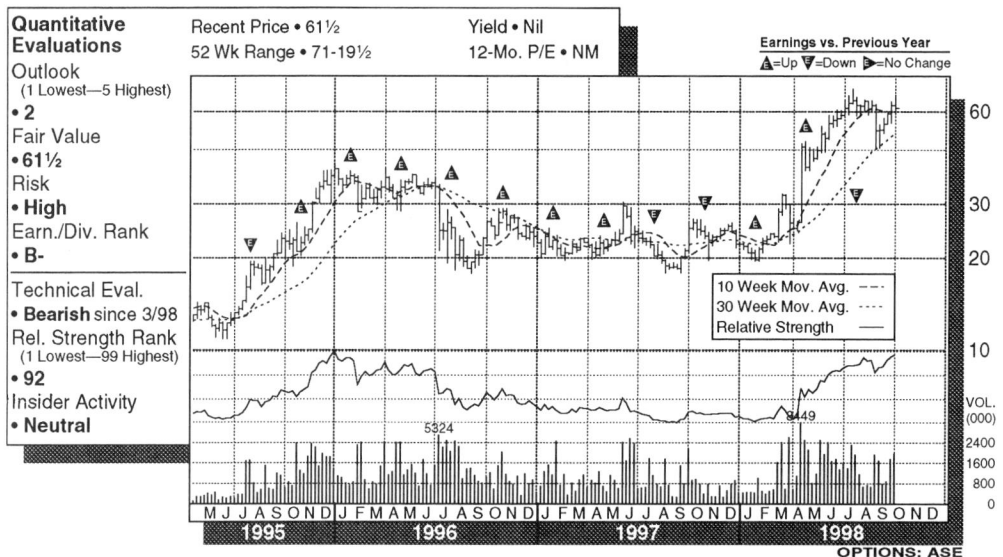

10 Week Mov. Avg. ----
30 Week Mov. Avg. ·····
Relative Strength ——

VOL.
(000)

OPTIONS: ASE

Business Profile - 06-JUL-98

VISX has received FDA approval for the use of its Excimer Laser System for the treatment of higher degrees of nearsightedness with astigmatism (January 1998) and for the treatment of low and moderate nearsightedness with myopic astigmatism (April 1997). FDA approval for farsightedness is expected in 1998. In May 1998, the company became the first U.S. company to receive approval in Japan for phototherapeutic keratectomy, a procedure to treat corneal scars and dystrophies of the eye. In June 1998, VISX and Summit Technology, Inc. reached a settlement that will dissolve their partnership (Pillar Point Partners) and end all pending disputes and litigation between them. Formed in 1992, Pillar Point was instrumental in bringing laser vision correction to its current status as a safe and effective alternative to glasses and contact lenses.

Operational Review - 06-JUL-98

Total revenues in the first quarter of 1998 climbed 54%, year to year. License, service and other revenues nearly tripled, as VISX was no longer paying certain royalties to Pillar Point Partners effective October 1997. System sales declined 25%, reflecting fewer unit sales and a higher percentage of customers receiving trade-in credits. Margins widened, and operating income soared to $10.4 million, from $1.9 million. After taxes at 23.9%, versus 12.0%, net income rose to 8,962,000 ($0.58 a share), from $2,699,000 ($0.17).

Stock Performance - 02-OCT-98

In the past 30 trading days, VISX's shares have declined 2%, compared to a 7% fall in the S&P 500. Average trading volume for the past five days was 393,940 shares, compared with the 40-day moving average of 265,133 shares.

Key Stock Statistics

Dividend Rate/Share	Nil	Shareholders	600
Shs. outstg. (M)	15.3	Market cap. (B)	$0.941
Avg. daily vol. (M)	0.272	Inst. holdings	70%
Tang. Bk. Value/Share	6.55		
Beta	2.24		

Value of $10,000 invested 5 years ago: $ 49,696

Fiscal Year Ending Dec. 31

	1998	1997	1996	1995	1994	1993
Revenues (Million $)						
1Q	24.31	15.74	11.56	2.69	4.87	5.40
2Q	31.66	15.60	19.55	3.78	5.36	5.01
3Q	—	17.97	19.67	3.95	4.88	5.29
4Q	—	19.33	18.89	6.28	2.78	6.37
Yr.	—	68.63	69.66	16.70	17.90	22.07
Earnings Per Share ($)						
1Q	**0.58**	0.17	0.08	-0.32	0.01	-0.02
2Q	**-1.01**	-0.04	0.28	-0.39	-0.04	Nil
3Q	Nil	0.32	0.35	-0.20	-0.25	0.01
4Q	—	**0.44**	0.37	-0.30	-0.33	0.03
Yr.	—	**0.89**	1.08	-1.20	-0.60	0.02

Next earnings report expected: mid October

Dividend Data

No cash dividends have been paid, and VISX does not expect to initiate dividends in the foreseeable future.

A Division of The McGraw-Hill Companies

Business Summary - 06-JUL-98

Imagine the possibility of life without glasses or contact lenses! Well, this company believes this vision is possible. VISX, Incorporated is a leader in the design and development of proprietary technologies and systems for laser vision correction (LVC).

VISX sees a way to make things perfectly clear for a vast number of people. One out of two people in the world have defective vision, and more than 150 million Americans account for the $13 billion a year spent on vision correction. VISX's strategy is to commercialize its intellectual property position by broadening the installed base of VISX Systems around the world, and collecting procedure and equipment royalties from licensed users and manufacturers.

The VISX System is designed to enable an ophthalmologist to treat two major categories of vision disorders: corneal pathologies (congenital/traumatic corneal defects and disease of the cornea) and refractive vision disorders (nearsightedness, astigmatism and farsightedness). The VISX System performs phototherapeutic keratectomy (PTK) as a means of correcting corneal disorders and photorefractive keratectomy (PRK) to correct refractive vision disorders. The company believes that the market for PRK procedures is significantly larger than that of PTK.

Excimer lasers ablate tissue without generating the heat associated with many other types of lasers that use different wavelengths, which can result in unintended thermal damage to surrounding tissue. With the excimer lasers light does not penetrate the eye, and therefore has no measurable effect in the interior of the eye. The company received final FDA approval in April 1997 for its Excimer Laser Systems to treat low to moderate nearsightedness with myopic astigmatism, and in December 1996, it received FDA approval for the expansion of its U.S. clinical trials for the treatment of hyperopia (farsightedness) using its STAR Excimer Laser System.

The VISX System is controlled by a proprietary optical memory card (VisionKey ®), which provides access to software upgrades and can facilitate the collection of patient data. One VisionKey card must be used with each procedure performed, and therefore sales of the VisionKey card correlate to the number of procedures performed.

During the 1997 second quarter, the company reached a settlement with Summit Technology over patent disputes and paid Summit $4.5 million. In May 1998, the two companies agreed to dissolve Pillar Point Partners, the partnership they formed together in 1992 to bring laser vision correction to its present status, and to end all pending litigation and disputes between them. Under the settlement, the companies retain their respective rights to license other manufacturers to their own patents and have granted each other a worldwide, royalty-free cross license. VISX will also be required to make a $35 million settlement payment to Summit.

Per Share Data ($)

(Year Ended Dec. 31)	1997	1996	1995	1994	1993	1992	1991	1990	1989	1988
Tangible Bk. Val.	7.18	6.44	5.26	1.33	1.77	1.60	2.06	0.75	-0.15	1.27
Cash Flow	1.01	1.16	-1.26	-0.55	0.07	-0.94	-0.19	-0.91	-0.99	-1.28
Earnings	0.89	1.08	-1.20	-0.60	0.02	-0.98	-0.22	-0.94	-1.03	-1.32
Dividends	Nil	Nil	Nil	Nil	Nil	Nil	Nil	Nil	Nil	Nil
Payout Ratio	Nil	Nil	Nil	Nil	Nil	Nil	Nil	Nil	Nil	Nil
Prices - High	30½	39½	40⅛	28¾	18¼	21⅝	18¾	16½	27¾	8⅜
- Low	17⅞	17¾	10	10	8½	8¼	4¼	4¼	8	7⅛
P/E Ratio - High	34	37	NM	NM	NM	NM	NM	NM	NM	NM
- Low	20	16	NM	NM	NM	NM	NM	NM	NM	NM

Income Statement Analysis (Million $)

	1997	1996	1995	1994	1993	1992	1991	1990	1989	1988
Revs.	68.6	69.7	16.7	17.9	22.1	20.3	13.2	6.6	0.8	0.4
Oper. Inc.	17.4	15.5	-10.0	-5.3	0.3	-4.2	-2.1	-6.2	-4.8	-3.5
Depr.	1.9	1.2	0.6	0.6	0.5	0.4	0.3	0.3	0.2	0.1
Int. Exp.	Nil	Nil	Nil	Nil	Nil	0.0	Nil	0.0	Nil	Nil
Pretax Inc.	16.0	18.6	-14.8	-6.3	0.2	-9.6	-1.8	-7.2	-4.7	-3.5
Eff. Tax Rate	12%	7.00%	NM	NM	Nil	Nil	Nil	Nil	Nil	Nil
Net Inc.	14.1	17.3	-14.8	-6.3	0.2	-9.6	-1.8	-7.2	-4.7	-3.5

Balance Sheet & Other Fin. Data (Million $)

	1997	1996	1995	1994	1993	1992	1991	1990	1989	1988
Cash	30.0	89.0	75.2	11.2	11.8	9.1	6.8	4.9	0.9	6.0
Curr. Assets	124	113	88.9	18.1	20.0	20.2	12.5	9.8	1.0	6.1
Total Assets	130	120	91.0	20.6	22.9	23.0	25.2	10.5	1.6	6.5
Curr. Liab.	20.1	20.4	11.2	6.2	4.2	6.2	4.9	3.0	0.8	0.9
LT Debt	Nil	Nil	Nil	Nil	Nil	Nil	0.0	0.0	Nil	Nil
Common Eqty.	110	99	80.0	14.0	18.0	16.2	19.6	5.9	-0.5	4.4
Total Cap.	110	99	80.0	14.0	18.0	16.2	19.6	6.0	-0.5	4.4
Cap. Exp.	1.7	2.9	0.4	0.5	0.6	1.4	0.2	0.4	0.2	0.3
Cash Flow	16.0	18.5	-14.2	-5.7	0.7	-9.1	-1.6	-7.0	-4.5	-3.3
Curr. Ratio	6.2	5.5	8.0	2.9	4.7	3.3	2.6	3.3	1.2	6.7
% LT Debt of Cap.	Nil	NM	NM	Nil	Nil	NM	0.1	0.3	NM	NM
% Net Inc.of Revs.	20.5	24.8	NM	NM	0.8	NM	NM	NM	NM	NM
% Ret. on Assets	11.3	16.4	NM	NM	0.8	NM	NM	NM	NM	NM
% Ret. on Equity	13.5	19.3	NM	NM	1.0	NM	NM	NM	NM	NM

Data as orig. reptd.; bef. results of disc. opers. and/or spec. items. Per share data adj. for stk. divs. as of ex-div. date. EPS and estimates in bold or bold/italic follow FASB 128 definition of Diluted EPS; all other EPS and estimates generally follow earlier use of Primary EPS. E-Estimated. NA-Not Available. NM-Not Meaningful. NR-Not Ranked.

Office—3400 Central Expwy., Santa Clara, CA 95051. **Tel**—(408) 733-2020. **Website**—http://www.visx.com **Chrmn, Pres & CEO**—M. B. Logan. **VP & CFO**—T. R. Maier. **EVP & COO**—E. H. Davila. **VP & Secy**—K. J. Church. **Dirs**—E. H. Davila, G. E. French, J. W. Galiardo, M. B. Logan, R. B. Sayford. **Transfer Agent**—The First National Bank of Boston, Canton, MA. **Incorporated**—in California in 1987. **Empl**— 186. **S&P Analyst**: S.A.H.

Vital Signs, Inc. 5562M
NASDAQ Symbol **VITL**

In S&P SmallCap 600

03-OCT-98

Industry:
Health Care (Medical Products & Supplies)

Summary: Vital Signs markets a wide variety of single-patient use anesthesia, respiratory and related critical care products.

Quantitative Evaluations

Recent Price • 16⅛
52 Wk Range • 22⅝-15⅛

Yield • 1.0%
12-Mo. P/E • 15.5

Outlook
(1 Lowest—5 Highest)
• **5+**

Fair Value
• **26⅛**

Risk
• **Average**

Earn./Div. Rank
• **B+**

Technical Eval.
• **Bearish** since 5/98

Rel. Strength Rank
(1 Lowest—99 Highest)
• **63**

Insider Activity
• **Neutral**

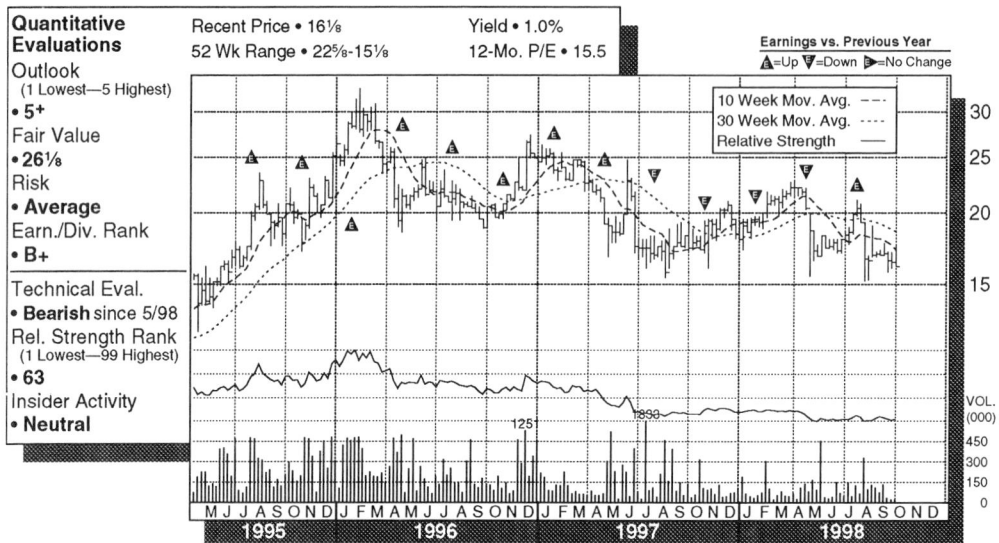

Earnings vs. Previous Year
▲=Up ▼=Down ►=No Change

10 Week Mov. Avg. – –
30 Week Mov. Avg. ....
Relative Strength —

Business Profile - 08-JUL-98

In July 1997, the company acquired Marquest Medical Products, Inc., a manufacturer of respiratory products (annual revenues of about $20 million), for total consideration of $18.6 million. In connection with the acquisition, VITL doubled its sales force by bringing in a 90-person respiratory/critical care sales team. Costs related to the expanded sales organization impacted FY 98 (Sep.) first half earnings by about $0.18 a share. Although FY 97 revenues were aided significantly by the addition of Marquest, profitability was penalized by a $6.7 million charge related to the acquisition. As of January 1998, officers and directors owned about 59% of the shares outstanding.

Operational Review - 08-JUL-98

Net sales in the six months ended March 31, 1998, rose 35%, year to year, with 14% coming from existing product lines and 21% from the Marquest acquisition. Margins narrowed as a result of a less favorable product mix and significantly higher SG&A expenses related to the acquisition, increased activity at the Vital Pharma, Inc. subsidiary and full implementation of the sales force expansion plan. After taxes at 34.5%, versus 32.6%, but before a $0.12 a share charge in the current period for the cumulative effect of an accounting change, net income fell 29%, to $6,849,000 ($0.54 a share, on 2.5% fewer shares), from $9,649,000 ($0.74).

Stock Performance - 02-OCT-98

In the past 30 trading days, VITL's shares have declined 4%, compared to a 7% fall in the S&P 500. Average trading volume for the past five days was 3,700 shares, compared with the 40-day moving average of 15,454 shares.

Key Stock Statistics

Dividend Rate/Share	0.16	Shareholders	500
Shs. outstg. (M)	12.7	Market cap. (B)	$0.205
Avg. daily vol. (M)	0.010	Inst. holdings	32%
Tang. Bk. Value/Share	7.13		
Beta	0.51		

Value of $10,000 invested 5 years ago: $ 5,922

Fiscal Year Ending Sep. 30

	1998	1997	1996	1995	1994	1993
Revenues (Million $)						
1Q	30.92	22.83	22.12	21.33	20.79	18.46
2Q	32.30	23.85	22.59	22.68	21.26	19.83
3Q	31.86	28.36	23.02	22.69	21.42	20.45
4Q	—	28.53	22.59	22.85	21.66	21.14
Yr.	—	103.6	90.73	89.55	85.12	79.88
Earnings Per Share ($)						
1Q	**0.27**	0.38	0.35	0.25	0.25	0.25
2Q	**0.27**	0.37	0.36	0.30	0.24	0.26
3Q	**0.21**	-0.16	0.37	0.34	0.21	0.27
4Q	—	0.30	0.37	0.35	-0.56	0.21
Yr.	—	0.88	1.44	1.24	0.13	0.98

Next earnings report expected: mid November

Dividend Data (Dividends have been paid since 1994.)

Amount ($)	Date Decl.	Ex-Div. Date	Stock of Record	Payment Date
0.040	Oct. 30	Nov. 10	Nov. 07	Nov. 15 '97
0.040	—	Feb. 11	Feb. 02	Feb. 09 '98
0.040	May. 05	May. 13	May. 15	May. 22 '98
0.040	Jul. 20	Jul. 30	Aug. 03	Aug. 11 '98

A Division of The McGraw-Hill Companies

STANDARD
&POOR'S
STOCK REPORTS

Vital Signs, Inc.

5562M
03-OCT-98

Business Summary - 08-JUL-98

Vital Signs is a pioneer in the introduction and development of a number of single-patient use products for the healthcare industry. Single-patient products have captured an increasing share of the medical products market, because of lower cost, as well as reduced risk of transmitting infection. In 1981, the Totowa, NJ-based company introduced the first clear plastic single-use air-filled cushion face mask for anesthesia delivery and resuscitation. The face mask is still the company's best-selling product.

Other single-use products introduced by VITL include a manual resuscitator (1984), a laryngoscope system (1988), a general anesthesia kit that can combine more than 20 items in one package (1989), and the first single-patient use infant lung resuscitation circuit capable of adjusting pressurization (1992). VITL also pioneered a special tracheal tube for use during high-risk deliveries, a pediatric emergency kit, and a device for measuring the effect of neouromuscular blockage during anesthesia. Innovative new products include the company's flexible face mask called the Flexmask; a flush device for vascular access catheters called Vasceze; and a closed suction system designed for ventilated patients, the Isocath.

In July 1997, VITL said it had acquired Marquest Medical Products, a manufacturer of respiratory products, with $20 million in annual sales. VITL believed

that Marquest would eventually attain the same status in critical care that VITL has in anesthetics, and the parent company has restructured its sales force to that end. T.D. Wall, VITL's president and CEO (whose family owns about 50% of the stock) said that with the addition of Marquest products, the company's product line would be nearly evenly divided, with anesthesia representing 53% of total sales and respiratory/critical care 47%. VITL divested its endoscopic products line in FY 96.

In FY 97 (Sep.), sales were derived from anesthesia (56% of total sales), respiratory and critical care (40%), and services and other products (4%). International sales accounted for about 10% of net sales.

In FY 1997, net sales rose to $103.6 million, from $89.9 million in FY 96, reflecting the acquisition of Marquest Medical and contributions from Vital Pharma, Inc., partly offset by a loss of revenues resulting from the disposal of the endoscopic product line in FY 96. Results were penalized by a $6.7 million charge associated with the Marquest acquisition; net income fell 40%, to $11,286,000 ($0.88 a share), from $18,789,000 ($1.44).

The company in the FY 98 second quarter implemented a previously-announced expansion of its sales force in connection with the acquisition of Marquest. By adding a 90-person team devoted to selling respiratory/critical care products, VITL doubled its sales organization to 180 sales representatives.

Per Share Data ($)

(Year Ended Sep. 30)	1997	1996	1995	1994	1993	1992	1991	1990	1989	1988
Tangible Bk. Val.	6.57	7.17	5.94	5.12	4.69	4.37	NA	NA	NA	NA
Cash Flow	1.10	1.62	1.36	0.23	1.07	0.88	NA	NA	NA	NA
Earnings	0.88	1.44	1.24	0.13	0.98	0.81	0.66	NA	NA	NA
Dividends	0.20	0.13	0.09	0.02	Nil	Nil	Nil	Nil	Nil	Nil
Payout Ratio	23%	9%	7%	15%	Nil	Nil	Nil	Nil	Nil	Nil
Prices - High	25⁷/₈	33	27	15¼	29¾	35½	28¼	NA	NA	NA
- Low	15³/₈	18½	10¾	7¾	13½	18¼	9¼	NA	NA	NA
P/E Ratio - High	29	23	19	117	30	44	43	NA	NA	NA
- Low	17	13	9	60	14	23	14	NA	NA	NA

Income Statement Analysis (Million $)

	1997	1996	1995	1994	1993	1992	1991	1990	1989	1988
Revs.	104	90.7	89.6	85.1	79.9	65.7	NA	NA	NA	NA
Oper. Inc.	25.6	26.9	25.0	16.6	18.9	16.2	NA	NA	NA	NA
Depr.	2.9	2.3	1.5	1.3	1.2	1.0	NA	NA	NA	NA
Int. Exp.	0.5	0.3	0.4	0.6	0.6	0.6	NA	NA	NA	NA
Pretax Inc.	16.9	28.4	25.3	5.8	18.6	15.2	NA	NA	NA	NA
Eff. Tax Rate	33%	34%	36%	71%	32%	32%	NA	NA	NA	NA
Net Inc.	11.3	18.8	16.1	1.7	12.7	10.4	NA	NA	NA	NA

Balance Sheet & Other Fin. Data (Million $)

	1997	1996	1995	1994	1993	1992	1991	1990	1989	1988
Cash	3.7	18.3	12.1	29.1	27.9	NA	NA	NA	NA	NA
Curr. Assets	51.3	53.5	45.7	59.7	55.1	NA	NA	NA	NA	NA
Total Assets	137	124	110	92.0	92.0	79.0	NA	NA	NA	NA
Curr. Liab.	13.2	8.7	12.8	9.3	8.3	NA	NA	NA	NA	NA
LT Debt	5.5	2.7	3.2	3.7	5.8	6.4	NA	NA	NA	NA
Common Eqty.	112	110	92.6	77.7	76.1	63.8	NA	NA	NA	NA
Total Cap.	119	114	96.8	82.0	83.4	70.2	NA	NA	NA	NA
Cap. Exp.	10.0	8.6	2.0	2.3	1.5	0.5	NA	NA	NA	NA
Cash Flow	14.2	21.1	17.7	3.0	13.9	11.4	NA	NA	NA	NA
Curr. Ratio	3.9	6.2	3.6	6.4	6.7	NA	NA	NA	NA	NA
% LT Debt of Cap.	4.6	2.4	3.3	4.5	7.0	9.2	NA	NA	NA	NA
% Net Inc.of Revs.	10.9	20.7	18.0	2.0	15.9	15.8	NA	NA	NA	NA
% Ret. on Assets	8.7	16.1	16.0	1.8	13.8	14.4	NA	NA	NA	NA
% Ret. on Equity	10.1	18.6	18.9	2.2	16.7	18.1	NA	NA	NA	NA

Data as orig. reptd.; bef. results of disc. opers. and/or spec. items. Per share data adj. for stk. divs. as of ex-div. date. Bold denotes diluted EPS (FASB 128). E-Estimated. NA-Not Available. NM-Not Meaningful. NR-Not Ranked.

Office—20 Campus Rd., Totowa, NJ 07512. **Tel**—(973) 790-1330. **Website**—http://www/vital-signs.com. **Pres & CEO**—T. D. Wall. **EVP, CFO & Secy**—A. J. Dimun. **Dirs**—D. J. Bershad, A, J, Dimun, J. J. Thomas, J. Toedtman, T. D. Wall, B. Wicker. **Transfer Agent & Registrar**—Union National Bank, Charlotte, NC. **Incorporated**—in New York in 1972; reincorporated in New Jersey in 1988. **Empl**— 1,027. **S&P Analyst:** S.A.H.

03-OCT-98

Industry:
Electronics (Semiconductors)

Summary: This company is a leader in the design, development, manufacture and marketing of digital gallium arsenide integrated circuits.

Quantitative Evaluations

Outlook
(1 Lowest—5 Highest)
• **NA**

Fair Value
• **NA**

Risk
• **High**

Earn./Div. Rank
• **B-**

Technical Eval.
• **Bullish** since 1/98

Rel. Strength Rank
(1 Lowest—99 Highest)
• **12**

Insider Activity
• **Unfavorable**

Recent Price • 19⅞
52 Wk Range • 37⅛-15⅞

Yield • Nil
12-Mo. P/E • 33.7

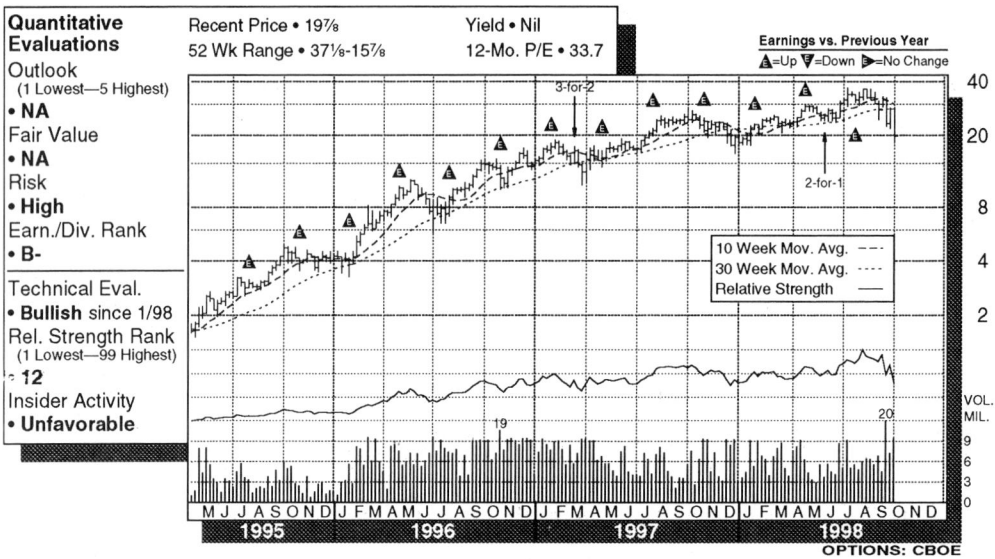

Earnings vs. Previous Year
▲=Up ▼=Down ▶=No Change

10 Week Mov. Avg. — —
30 Week Mov. Avg. · · · ·
Relative Strength ——

OPTIONS: CBOE

Business Profile - 21-JUL-98

This company is a leading producer of digital gallium arsenide integrated circuits (ICs), a faster alternative to traditional silicon-based ICs. VTSS has historically focused its sales efforts on a relatively small number of systems manufacturers, primarily within the telecommunications industry, that require high-performance ICs. Vitesse is increasing production capacity at its existing California fabrication facility and has constructed a new facility in Colorado. In the second quarter of FY 98 (Sep.), the Colorado facility shipped its first products, resulting in revenue of approximately $1.0 million.

Operational Review - 21-JUL-98

Revenues in the nine months ended June 30, 1998, rose 64%, year to year, reflecting growth in all three core businesses: telecom, datacom, and test equipment. Margins widened on the higher volume, and income from operations jumped 95%. After a $1.39 million increase in other income, and taxes at 20.0%, versus 10.0%, (resulting from the utilization of net operating loss carryforwards), net income rose 60%, to $36,362,000 ($0.46 a share, on 4.7% more shares), from $22,740,000 ($0.30).

Stock Performance - 02-OCT-98

In the past 30 trading days, VTSS's shares have declined 39%, compared to a 7% fall in the S&P 500. Average trading volume for the past five days was 2,602,260 shares, compared with the 40-day moving average of 1,781,433 shares.

Key Stock Statistics

Dividend Rate/Share	Nil	Shareholders	500
Shs. outstg. (M)	73.2	Market cap. (B)	$ 1.5
Avg. daily vol. (M)	2.273	Inst. holdings	83%
Tang. Bk. Value/Share	4.29		
Beta	1.78		

Value of $10,000 invested 5 years ago: $ 140,294

Fiscal Year Ending Sep. 30

	1998	1997	1996	1995	1994	1993
Revenues (Million $)						
1Q	34.70	21.83	14.02	9.76	8.05	5.28
2Q	40.21	24.56	15.63	10.02	8.72	6.07
3Q	46.11	27.61	17.27	11.03	9.16	7.00
4Q	—	30.85	19.12	12.06	9.66	8.01
Yr.	—	104.8	66.05	42.88	35.58	26.36
Earnings Per Share ($)						
1Q	**0.14**	0.08	0.03	0.01	-0.06	-0.15
2Q	**0.15**	0.10	0.05	-0.02	-0.04	-0.12
3Q	**0.18**	0.12	0.06	0.02	0.00	-0.10
4Q	—	0.13	0.07	0.02	0.00	-0.07
Yr.	—	0.43	0.21	0.03	-0.09	-0.44

Next earnings report expected: late October

Dividend Data

Amount ($)	Date Decl.	Ex-Div. Date	Stock of Record	Payment Date
2-for-1	Apr. 22	May. 27	May. 04	May. 26 '98

A Division of The McGraw·Hill Companies

Business Summary - 21-JUL-98

Unlike many other semiconductor producers, Vitesse Semiconductor Corp. (VTSS), manufactures high speed integrated circuits (ICs) utilizing digital gallium arsenide (GaAs) rather than silicon. Gallium arsenide-based technology offers the potential for significant speed improvements over silicon-based technologies, since electrons can travel many times faster in GaAs than in silicon. Vitesse has developed a proprietary high integration GaAs process technology to manufacture ICs that take advantage of the faster speeds inherent in GaAs and offer performance advantages over ICs manufactured using silicon-based CMOS, BiCMOS and ECL IC process technologies. The company's products address the needs of high performance systems manufacturers who demand a combination of high speed, high complexity and low power dissipation. In FY 97 (Sep.), sales of telecommunications, data communications and automated test equipment products represented 52%, 22% and 22%, respectively, of total revenues versus 52%, 8% and 24% of revenues in FY 96.

VTSS principally targets the high performance telecommunications markets, particularly in fiber optic applications requiring transmission rates as high as 2.5 gigabits per second and in high speed switching networks and direct digital synthesis; data communications markets, where transmission of large amounts of data over serial channels with data rates in excess of 1 gigabit per second is required; test and instrument markets for such products as logic testers, signal format generators, test pin controller logic, digital-to-analog signal converters and serialization circuits; and defense and aerospace markets where products are used in special purpose computer systems, digital signal processing and image processing.

Vitesse is currently increasing its production capacity at its four-inch wafer Camarillo, CA, fabrication facility and has constructed a new six-inch wafer facility in Colorado Springs, CO. The new facility began production in the second quarter of FY 98. VTSS estimates that the cost of the new facility will be at least $70 million, while the expansion of the California facility will cost up to $10 million.

In FY 97, sales to the company's top three customers accounted for 22%, 20%, and 12% of total revenues. Export sales, primarily in Japan, represented 29%, 24% and 34% of total revenues in FY 95, FY 96 and FY 97, respectively.

As of June 30, 1998, cash and short term investments stood at $150 million while long-term liabilities totaled $33 million.

Per Share Data ($)

(Year Ended Sep. 30)	1997	1996	1995	1994	1993	1992	1991	1990	1989	1988
Tangible Bk. Val.	3.69	1.52	0.54	0.48	0.56	1.00	NA	NA	NA	NA
Cash Flow	0.52	0.29	0.13	0.03	-0.31	NA	NA	NA	NA	NA
Earnings	0.43	0.21	0.03	-0.09	-0.44	0.02	-0.07	-0.22	NA	NA
Dividends	Nil	Nil	Nil	Nil	Nil	Nil	Nil	Nil	Nil	Nil
Payout Ratio	Nil	Nil	Nil	Nil	Nil	Nil	Nil	Nil	Nil	Nil
Prices - High	28¼	17⅛	4⅞	2³/₁₆	1¹¹/₁₆	7	3⅞	NA	NA	NA
- Low	10⅝	3¼	1⁷/₁₆	1³/₁₆	1	1¹/₁₆	3	NA	NA	NA
P/E Ratio - High	66	81	162	NM	NM	NM	NM	NA	NA	NA
- Low	25	15	47	NM	NM	NM	NM	NA	NA	NA

Income Statement Analysis (Million $)

	1997	1996	1995	1994	1993	1992	1991	1990	1989	1988
Revs.	105	66.0	42.9	35.6	26.4	NA	NA	NA	NA	NA
Oper. Inc.	35.6	18.4	8.1	2.3	-12.6	NA	NA	NA	NA	NA
Depr.	6.9	5.0	5.3	5.6	5.6	NA	NA	NA	NA	NA
Int. Exp.	0.2	0.8	1.3	1.1	1.2	NA	NA	NA	NA	NA
Pretax Inc.	36.5	14.0	1.6	-4.1	-19.0	NA	NA	NA	NA	NA
Eff. Tax Rate	10%	10%	5.00%	NM	NM	NM	NM	NM	NM	NM
Net Inc.	32.9	12.6	1.5	-4.1	-19.1	NA	NA	NA	NA	NA

Balance Sheet & Other Fin. Data (Million $)

	1997	1996	1995	1994	1993	1992	1991	1990	1989	1988
Cash	156	52.4	6.3	5.2	10.3	NA	NA	NA	NA	NA
Curr. Assets	205	81.8	29.5	26.6	NA	NA	NA	NA	NA	NA
Total Assets	292	100	42.1	39.5	44.0	NA	NA	NA	NA	NA
Curr. Liab.	27.0	11.6	11.5	12.0	NA	NA	NA	NA	NA	NA
LT Debt	0.1	0.4	5.5	5.9	8.9	NA	NA	NA	NA	NA
Common Eqty.	265	88.3	25.0	21.5	24.6	NA	NA	NA	NA	NA
Total Cap.	265	88.7	30.5	27.4	33.6	NA	NA	NA	NA	NA
Cap. Exp.	30.7	11.0	3.4	1.7	4.2	NA	NA	NA	NA	NA
Cash Flow	39.8	17.6	6.8	1.4	-13.4	NA	NA	NA	NA	NA
Curr. Ratio	7.6	7.0	2.6	2.2	NA	NA	NA	NA	NA	NA
% LT Debt of Cap.	NM	NM	18.1	21.6	26.6	NA	NA	NA	NA	NA
% Net Inc.of Revs.	31.4	19.1	3.5	NM	NM	NM	NM	NM	NM	NM
% Ret. on Assets	16.7	17.6	3.7	NM	NM	NM	NM	NM	NM	NM
% Ret. on Equity	18.6	22.2	6.5	NM	NM	NM	NM	NM	NM	NM

Data as orig. reptd.; bef. results of disc. opers. and/or spec. items. Per share data adj. for stk. divs. as of ex-div. date. Bold denotes diluted EPS (FASB 128). E-Estimated. NA-Not Available. NM-Not Meaningful. NR-Not Ranked.

Office—741 Calle Plano, Camarillo, CA 93012. **Tel**—(805) 388-3700. **Fax**—(805) 987-5896. **Website**—http://www.vitesse.com **Chrmn**—P. R. Lamond. **Pres & CEO**—L. R. Tomasetta. **VP-Fin & CFO**—E. F. Hovanec. **Investor Relations**—1-800 VITESSE.**Dirs**—J. A. Cole, A. Daly, P. R. Lamond, J. C. Lewis, L. R. Tomasetta. **Transfer Agent & Registrar**—Boston EquiServe, Boston. **Incorporated**—in Delaware in 1987. **Empl**— 580.
S&P Analyst: Mark Cavallone

Volt Information Sciences   2398N

NYSE Symbol **VOL**

In S&P SmallCap 600

03-OCT-98

Industry: Services (Employment)

Summary: VOL operates in the areas of technical and personnel services, electronic publication systems, computer systems, telecommunication services and telephone directory services.

Quantitative Evaluations

Outlook (1 Lowest—5 Highest)
- **NA**

Fair Value
- **NA**

Risk
- **Average**

Earn./Div. Rank
- **B**

Technical Eval.
- **NA**

Rel. Strength Rank (1 Lowest—99 Highest)
- **29**

Insider Activity
- **NA**

Recent Price • 18⅝   Yield • Nil
52 Wk Range • 70¼-15¼   12-Mo. P/E • 9.4

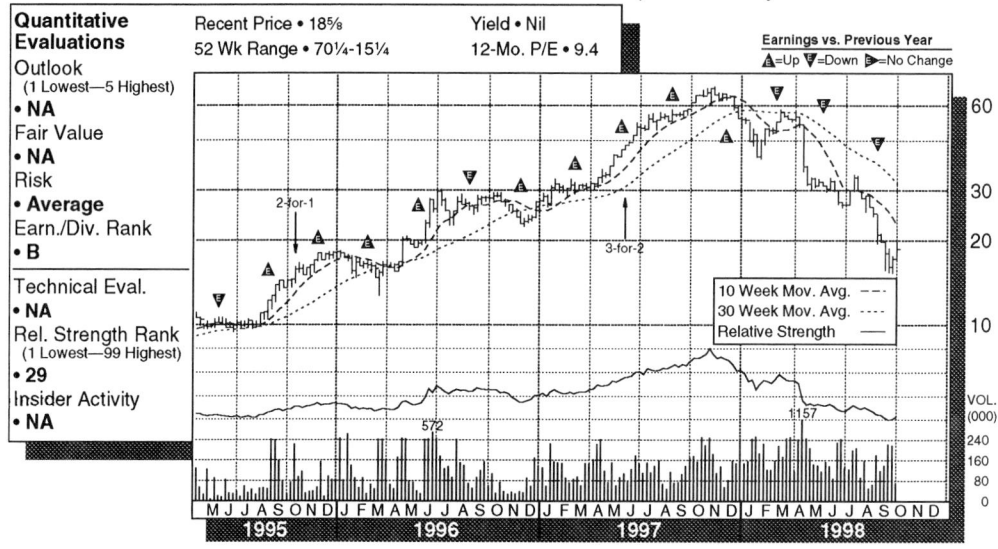

Earnings vs. Previous Year
▲=Up ▼=Down ▶=No Change

10 Week Mov. Avg. – – –
30 Week Mov. Avg. ‧‧‧‧
Relative Strength ——

Business Profile - 25-SEP-98

VOL showed strong revenue growth in the first nine months of FY 98 (Oct.), but margin pressure and the absence of joint ventures slowed profits to nearly half of 1997's pace. Staffing services revenue increased 26%, but operating profits were tempered by higher overhead from expansion of new offices. Telecommunications segment revenue also advanced a solid 17%, but a shift to lower margin services resulted in lower profitability. Despite the challenges, management feels that the telecommunications group will report higher operating profits in the second half of the year versus the first half. Brazilian and Australian joint ventures, which added $6.8 million to last year's profits, have since been sold and no longer contribute to company operations.

Operational Review - 25-SEP-98

Revenues in the nine months ended July 31, 1998, rose 20%, as increases in the staffing services segment were partially offset by decreases in computer system sales. Profitability declined on higher overhead costs in both the staffing and telecommunications divisions and a less favorable product mix in the telecommunications segment; operating income fell 13%. Following essentially flat depreciation and amortization charges, lower interest income, foreign exchange losses, the absence of joint ventures that contributed $6.8 million in earnings in 1997, and taxes at 41.6%, versus 46.0%, net income fell 45%, to $11,730,000 ($0.77 per share), from $21,330,000 ($1.41).

Stock Performance - 02-OCT-98

In the past 30 trading days, VOL's shares have declined 25%, compared to a 7% fall in the S&P 500. Average trading volume for the past five days was 14,260 shares, compared with the 40-day moving average of 27,131 shares.

Key Stock Statistics

Dividend Rate/Share	Nil	Shareholders	400
Shs. outstg. (M)	14.9	Market cap. (B)	$0.279
Avg. daily vol. (M)	0.033	Inst. holdings	33%
Tang. Bk. Value/Share	11.77		
Beta	0.80		

Value of $10,000 invested 5 years ago: $ 44,848

Fiscal Year Ending Oct. 31

	1998	1997	1996	1995	1994	1993
Revenues (Million $)						
1Q	361.5	288.8	224.8	183.3	142.6	123.3
2Q	412.6	346.9	252.3	190.6	161.7	134.1
3Q	431.8	370.7	258.9	225.9	165.9	139.0
4Q	—	410.6	312.9	307.5	250.7	161.6
Yr.	—	1,420	1,049	907.4	720.9	558.1
Earnings Per Share ($)						
1Q	**0.17**	0.33	0.15	0.14	-0.14	-0.19
2Q	**0.28**	0.47	0.34	0.10	0.40	0.01
3Q	**0.32**	0.61	0.31	0.35	0.16	-0.05
4Q	—	1.20	0.70	0.55	0.41	-0.02
Yr.	—	2.63	1.51	1.13	0.84	-0.26

Next earnings report expected: mid December

Dividend Data

No cash dividend has been paid since 1967. A three-for-two stock split was effected in 1997.

A Division of The McGraw-Hill Companies

Volt Information Sciences, Inc.

Business Summary - 25-SEP-98

Volt Information Sciences is a diversified technical services, human resources, computer systems and electronics manufacturing concern. Contributions by industry segment in FY 97 (Oct.) were:

	Revs.	Profits
Technical services & temporary personnel	72%	51%
Telecommunications services	11%	31%
Electronic publication & typesetting systems	6%	2%
Telephone directory	6%	15%
Computer systems	5%	1%

Volt's technical services and temporary personnel segment provides, from approximately 272 offices throughout the U.S., a broad range of employee staffing services, employment and personnel placement services, technical personnel placement, payrolling services, employment outsourcing services and employee leasing services, as well as permanent placement services.

The telecommunications services segment consists of the Voltelcon and Advanced Technology Services (ATS) divisions. Voltelcon provides a wide range of services, including engineering, design, construction, maintenance, installation, removal and distribution of telecommunications products. ATS accommodates clients in the telecommunications industry who require a full range of services from multiple Volt business segments.

The electronic publication and typesetting systems segment, 59%-owned Autologic Information International, Inc., designs, develops, manufactures, markets and services computerized imagesetting and publication systems equipment and software that automates the various prepress production steps in the publishing process.

The telephone directory division provides telephone directory production, commercial printing, database management, sales and marketing services, licensing of directory production and contract management software systems to directory and other advertising media publishers. Volt is also an independent publisher of telephone directories.

Volt Delta Resources designs, programs, sells or leases, integrates and maintains customized computer information systems and services, primarily for the telecommunications market. Volt VIEWtech provides management, outsourcing, technical and financial services to the energy and water utility industry, financial institutions, trade associations and manufacturers.

In September 1997, the company and Telstra Corporation, its principal partner in an Australian joint venture, agreed to accelerate VOL's right to exercise an option to sell its 12.5% stake in the joint venture to Telstra. The transaction resulted in a fourth quarter pretax gain of roughly $12.8 million.

Per Share Data ($) (Year Ended Oct. 31)	1997	1996	1995	1994	1993	1992	1991	1990	1989	1988
Tangible Bk. Val.	10.99	7.89	7.01	5.90	4.98	5.15	5.09	4.65	4.61	4.30
Cash Flow	3.98	2.67	1.97	1.58	0.45	0.85	0.80	0.66	0.96	0.60
Earnings	2.63	1.51	1.13	0.84	-0.26	0.08	0.02	-0.06	0.29	-0.04
Dividends	Nil	Nil	Nil	Nil	Nil	Nil	Nil	Nil	Nil	Nil
Payout Ratio	Nil	Nil	Nil	Nil	Nil	Nil	Nil	Nil	Nil	Nil
Prices - High	70 1/4	30 3/8	18 1/8	10	6 5/8	4 1/8	3 7/8	4 3/4	6	7 1/8
- Low	26 1/8	12 5/8	9	5 1/8	3 5/8	2 5/16	1 3/4	1 13/16	3 5/8	3 7/8
P/E Ratio - High	27	20	16	12	NM	54	NM	NM	20	NM
- Low	10	8	8	6	NM	30	NM	NM	12	NM
Income Statement Analysis (Million $)										
Revs.	1,401	1,049	907	721	558	521	466	489	493	467
Oper. Inc.	69.8	51.0	45.0	24.5	15.4	14.1	5.4	10.4	17.2	19.7
Depr.	20.5	16.0	12.0	10.7	10.2	11.1	11.3	12.2	12.3	12.7
Int. Exp.	5.7	5.0	6.0	7.5	11.1	11.6	13.4	14.4	14.5	13.9
Pretax Inc.	62.4	34.9	27.3	19.8	-5.6	1.8	-1.1	-1.7	9.5	0.3
Eff. Tax Rate	37%	36%	40%	39%	NM	39%	NM	NM	43%	NM
Net Inc.	40.0	22.4	16.4	12.0	-3.7	1.1	0.3	-1.0	5.4	-0.9
Balance Sheet & Other Fin. Data (Million $)										
Cash	54.2	13.3	25.4	22.0	43.3	30.0	20.0	16.0	23.0	30.0
Curr. Assets	336	243	182	155	159	147	121	124	140	150
Total Assets	419	337	264	227	236	227	215	232	256	275
Curr. Liab.	166	130	125	93.6	98.0	64.0	48.0	58.0	70.0	87.0
LT Debt	55.4	57.0	29.0	41.0	58.0	81.0	86.0	92.0	93.0	98.0
Common Eqty.	178	130	107	90.0	78.0	80.0	80.0	82.0	92.0	89.0
Total Cap.	252	208	139	133	138	162	166	174	186	188
Cap. Exp.	15.5	36.7	11.9	14.9	11.3	7.1	6.8	10.9	13.9	13.8
Cash Flow	60.5	38.7	28.4	22.8	6.5	12.2	11.6	11.2	17.7	11.8
Curr. Ratio	2.0	1.9	1.5	1.7	1.6	2.3	2.5	2.1	2.0	1.7
% LT Debt of Cap.	21.9	27.7	20.8	30.6	42.0	50.0	51.8	52.9	50.2	52.2
% Net Inc.of Revs.	2.9	2.1	1.8	1.7	NM	0.2	0.1	NM	1.1	NM
% Ret. on Assets	10.6	7.5	6.7	5.2	NM	0.5	0.2	NM	2.1	NM
% Ret. on Equity	26.0	18.9	16.6	14.4	NM	1.4	0.4	NM	6.0	NM

Data as orig. reptd.; bef. results of disc. opers. and/or spec. items. Per share data adj. for stk. divs. as of ex-div. date. Bold denotes diluted EPS (FASB 128). E-Estimated. NA-Not Available. NM-Not Meaningful. NR-Not Ranked.

Office—1221 Ave. of the Americas, New York, NY 10020-1579. **Tel**—(212) 704-2400. **Website**—http://www.volt-tech.com **Chrmn, Pres & CEO**—W. Shaw. **EVP & Secy**—J. Shaw. **SVP, CFO & Investor Contact**—James J. Groberg. **Treas**—L. M. Guarino. **Dirs**—J. J. Groberg, M. N. Kaplan, I. B. Robins, J. Shaw, S. A. Shaw, W. Shaw, J. R. Torell III, W. H. Turner. **Transfer Agent & Registrar**—Registrar & Transfer Co., NYC. **Incorporated**—in New York in 1957. **Empl**— 36,800. **S&P Analyst:** Jordan Horoschak

03-OCT-98 **Industry:** Hardware & Tools

Summary: This company, which is best known for its WD-40 product, also makes and markets 3-IN-ONE Oil.

Quantitative Evaluations

Recent Price • 23⅞
52 Wk Range • 33-20

Yield • 5.3%
12-Mo. P/E • 17.6

Outlook (1 Lowest—5 Highest)
• **1**

Fair Value
• **20¾**

Risk
• **Low**

Earn./Div. Rank
• **B+**

Technical Eval.
• **Neutral** since 8/98

Rel. Strength Rank (1 Lowest—99 Highest)
• **81**

Insider Activity
• **Favorable**

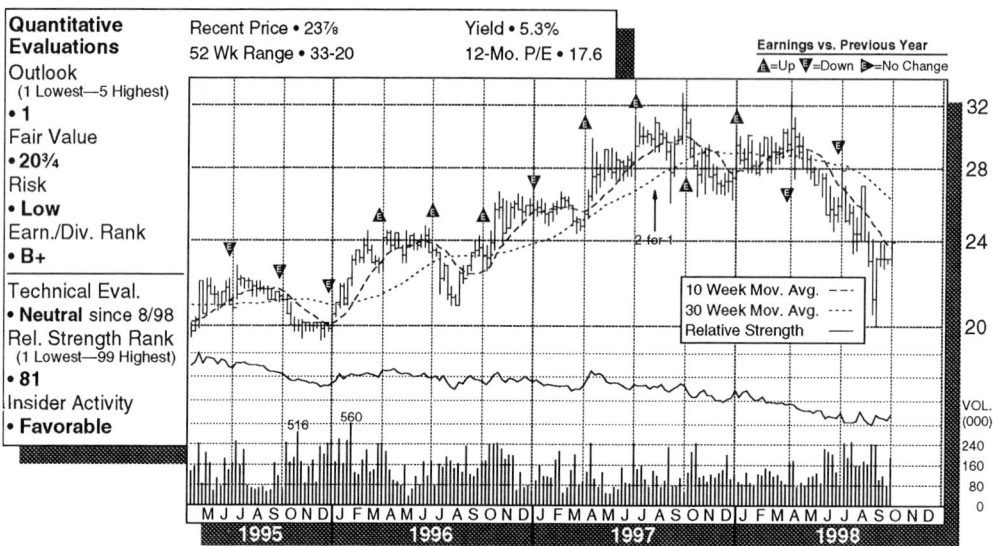

Earnings vs. Previous Year
▲=Up ▼=Down ▶=No Change

10 Week Mov. Avg. - - - -
30 Week Mov. Avg. ·······
Relative Strength ——

Business Profile - 08-JUL-98

Results have recently been aided by strong sales of 3-IN-ONE Oil, and increased sales to foreign countries. Although WDFC sees the emerging economies as an exceptional opportunity for growth, the company anticipates that the recent economic developments in Asia will reduce original sales expectations by about $2-3 million. In December 1995, the company acquired the 3-IN-ONE Oil business (annual revenues of some $13 million) of Reckitt & Colman plc. WDFC recently introduced T.A.L 5, an extra-strength lubricant that will be targeted to users in the manufacturing industries.

Operational Review - 08-JUL-98

Revenues in the first nine months of FY 98 (Aug.) grew 2.0%, year to year, as a 2% increase in WD-40 sales and a 44% increase in T. A. L. 5 sales outweighed a 6% decline in 3-In-One Oil sales. Margins narrowed on increased SG&A and advertising and promotional expenses, and despite net other income versus net other expense, pretax income was off 2.5%, to $24,395,000, from $25,021,000. After taxes at 36.0%, versus 36.3%, net income slid 2.0%, to $15,620,000 ($1.00 a share), from $15,939,000 ($1.02, as adjusted for the July 1997 two-for-one stock split).

Stock Performance - 02-OCT-98

In the past 30 trading days, WDFC's shares have increased 4%, compared to a 7% fall in the S&P 500. Average trading volume for the past five days was 37,820 shares, compared with the 40-day moving average of 34,313 shares.

Key Stock Statistics

Dividend Rate/Share	1.28	Shareholders	2,200
Shs. outstg. (M)	15.6	Market cap. (B)	$0.374
Avg. daily vol. (M)	0.025	Inst. holdings	32%
Tang. Bk. Value/Share	2.61		
Beta	0.74		

Value of $10,000 invested 5 years ago: $ 14,405

Fiscal Year Ending Aug. 31

	1998	1997	1996	1995	1994	1993
Revenues (Million $)						
1Q	33.60	28.27	27.61	29.77	28.88	24.60
2Q	39.17	39.81	35.08	29.39	27.56	29.37
3Q	31.83	34.53	34.23	29.92	29.46	29.31
4Q	—	35.30	33.99	27.70	26.27	25.70
Yr.	—	137.9	130.9	116.8	112.2	109.0
Earnings Per Share ($)						
1Q	0.34	0.28	0.34	0.36	0.34	0.32
2Q	**0.40**	0.42	0.39	0.36	-0.17	0.41
3Q	**0.26**	0.33	0.33	0.32	0.34	0.23
4Q	—	0.35	0.33	0.29	0.32	0.30
Yr.	—	1.38	1.38	1.33	0.82	1.26

Next earnings report expected: early October

Dividend Data (Dividends have been paid since 1973.)

Amount ($)	Date Decl.	Ex-Div. Date	Stock of Record	Payment Date
0.320	Dec. 09	Jan. 07	Jan. 09	Jan. 30 '98
0.320	Apr. 02	Apr. 07	Apr. 10	Apr. 30 '98
0.320	Jul. 02	Jul. 08	Jul. 10	Jul. 30 '98
0.320	Oct. 01	Oct. 15	Oct. 19	Nov. 02 '98

A Division of The McGraw·Hill Companies

Business Summary - 08-JUL-98

After more than four decades of being identified with a single petroleum-based product, WD-40, this company has dramatically shifted its corporate identity and strategy.

With the acquisition of the 3-IN-ONE Oil brand in December 1995 and with the introduction of its new T.A.L 5 brand in early FY 97 (Aug.), WDFC has become a company identified with three strong products.

The company's goal is to dominate the entire category of lubrication products by combining the smaller niche markets targeted by 3-IN-ONE Oil and T.A.L 5 with the broad-based market held by the WD-40 brand.

The WD-40 product is a multi-purpose product which can act as a lubricant, a rust preventative, a penetrant and a moisture displacer. It has a wide variety of uses in the home and in industrial applications, as well as in the protection of sporting goods and marine and automotive equipment. It is sold (primarily in aerosol cans) through chain stores, automotive parts outlets, hardware and sporting goods stores, and industrial distributors and suppliers.

3-IN-ONE Oil is a drip oil lubricant that is sold through the same distribution channels as the WD-40 brand. The key to its success is the lubrication control it gives consumers and industrial users, allowing precise application for small mechanisms and assemblies, tool main-tenance and threads on screws and bolts. As a low-cost, entry-level lubricant, it has excellent growth potential in the developing nations of Eastern Europe, Latin America and Asia.

The company developed T.A.L 5 (which stands for Triple Additive Lubricant/5 functions) as an extra-strength synthetic spray lubricant for heavy-duty applications. The product resists breakdown due to corrosion, friction, temperature, load and motion. It can be applied to rubber, metal or plastic and will provide long-lasting strength and durability. WDFC will target T.A.L 5 at specialized users in the trades and general manufacturing industries.

The new product lineup gives WD-40 Co. the opportunity to pursue a comprehensive and targeted marketing strategy. The acquisition of the 3-IN-ONE Oil brand (which, along with T.A.L 5, was introduced into the company's existing distribution system) provides WDFC with a built-in distribution network in 17 countries, including several markets in which the WD-40 product has not been sold.

With the ongoing consolidation in the marketplace, many major retailers are aggressively pursuing additional trade allowances. While these demands could produce a long-term negative impact on both sales and profits, the company believes that the new WDFC is in an excellent position to achieve growth.

Per Share Data ($) (Year Ended Aug. 31)	1997	1996	1995	1994	1993	1992	1991	1990	1989	1988
Tangible Bk. Val.	2.44	2.13	2.89	2.73	2.98	2.96	2.69	2.58	2.50	2.42
Cash Flow	1.52	1.50	1.40	0.88	1.30	1.23	1.04	1.05	1.07	1.04
Earnings	1.38	1.38	1.33	0.82	1.26	1.19	1.01	1.02	1.04	1.03
Dividends	1.25	1.24	1.21	1.15	1.15	1.08	0.86	1.01	0.95	0.81
Payout Ratio	91%	90%	91%	139%	91%	91%	85%	99%	91%	79%
Prices - High	32⅞	26⅝	22¾	24	24⅜	25	17	17¼	19⅛	16⅝
- Low	24⅜	20¼	19⅜	18⅞	21½	15⅛	11⅞	11¾	15¼	12¼
P/E Ratio - High	24	19	17	29	19	21	17	17	18	16
- Low	18	15	15	23	17	13	12	11	15	12

Income Statement Analysis (Million $)

	1997	1996	1995	1994	1993	1992	1991	1990	1989	1988
Revs.	138	131	117	112	109	100	89.8	91.0	83.9	80.0
Oper. Inc.	36.9	34.4	32.5	33.2	33.6	28.8	24.2	23.8	24.3	23.4
Depr.	2.2	1.8	1.0	0.8	0.6	0.6	0.5	0.5	0.5	0.2
Int. Exp.	Nil	NA	NA	NA	Nil	Nil	Nil	Nil	Nil	Nil
Pretax Inc.	33.4	33.4	32.7	20.5	31.7	29.5	25.1	25.2	25.9	25.4
Eff. Tax Rate	36%	36%	37%	38%	39%	39%	39%	39%	39%	39%
Net Inc.	21.4	21.3	20.5	12.7	19.3	18.1	15.3	15.5	15.8	15.5

Balance Sheet & Other Fin. Data (Million $)

	1997	1996	1995	1994	1993	1992	1991	1990	1989	1988
Cash	10.9	6.5	24.3	22.7	21.9	19.1	24.9	21.6	22.4	21.6
Curr. Assets	42.4	37.6	49.6	45.5	43.2	41.4	43.9	43.2	41.1	40.7
Total Assets	65.4	61.7	59.6	54.9	58.8	53.5	47.8	46.8	44.6	43.3
Curr. Liab.	11.4	11.0	11.1	8.2	9.7	8.2	6.9	7.6	6.7	6.6
LT Debt	1.7	2.4	3.1	3.8	2.6	Nil	Nil	Nil	Nil	Nil
Common Eqty.	51.3	47.2	44.5	42.1	45.7	45.2	40.7	39.0	37.8	36.5
Total Cap.	53.0	49.7	47.6	45.9	48.3	45.3	40.8	39.2	38.0	36.7
Cap. Exp.	1.5	1.4	1.4	0.8	1.4	0.7	1.1	0.5	1.4	0.4
Cash Flow	23.6	23.1	21.4	13.5	19.9	18.6	15.8	16.0	16.2	15.7
Curr. Ratio	3.7	3.4	4.5	5.6	4.4	5.1	6.3	5.7	6.1	6.2
% LT Debt of Cap.	3.2	5.2	6.6	8.3	5.5	Nil	Nil	Nil	Nil	Nil
% Net Inc.of Revs.	15.5	16.3	17.5	11.3	17.7	18.1	17.0	17.0	18.8	19.4
% Ret. on Assets	33.6	35.1	35.7	22.3	34.4	35.5	32.4	33.9	35.8	37.7
% Ret. on Equity	43.4	46.5	47.2	28.9	42.5	41.8	38.4	40.4	42.4	44.8

Data as orig. reptd.; bef. results of disc. opers. and/or spec. items. Per share data adj. for stk. divs. as of ex-div. date. Bold denotes diluted EPS (FASB 128). E-Estimated. NA-Not Available. NM-Not Meaningful. NR-Not Ranked.

Office—1061 Cudahy Place, San Diego, CA 92110. **Tel**—(619) 275-1400. **Chrmn**—J. S. Barry. **Pres & CEO**—Garry O. Ridge. **Secy**—H. F. Harmsen. **Dirs**—J. S. Barry, M. L. Crivello, D. W. Derbes, H. F. Harmsen, J. L. Heckel, G. O. Ridge, M. L. Roulette, G. C. Schleif, C. F. Sehnert, E. J. Walsh. **Transfer Agent & Registrar**—Harris Trust Co. of California, Los Angeles. **Incorporated**—in California in 1953. **Empl**— 166. S&P Analyst: E. Hunter

STANDARD &POOR'S
STOCK REPORTS

WHX Corp.

2403

NYSE Symbol **WHX**

In S&P SmallCap 600

03-OCT-98

Industry: Iron & Steel

Summary: This company is a major producer of flat rolled and fabricated steel products.

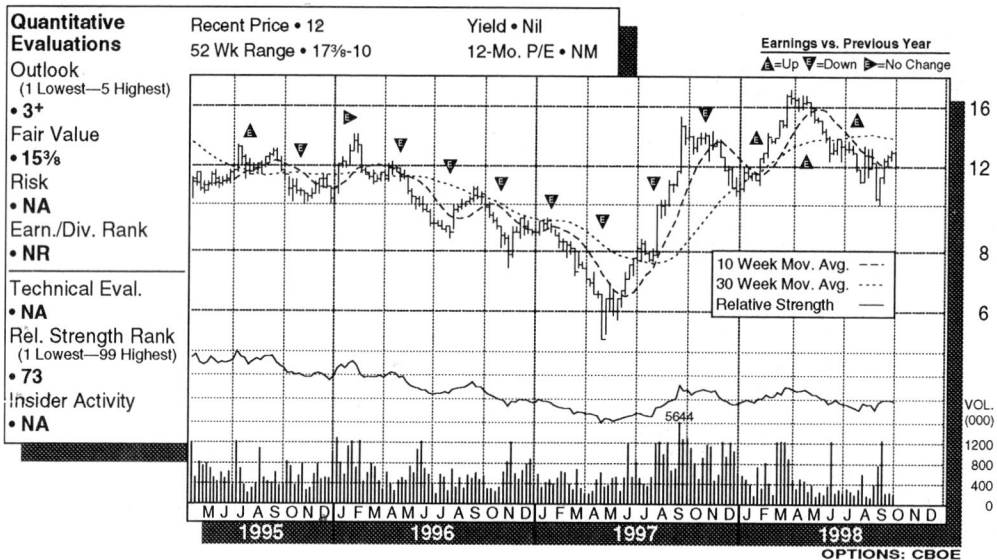

Quantitative Evaluations

Outlook (1 Lowest—5 Highest)
- **3+**

Fair Value
- **15⅜**

Risk
- **NA**

Earn./Div. Rank
- **NR**

Technical Eval.
- **NA**

Rel. Strength Rank (1 Lowest—99 Highest)
- **73**

Insider Activity
- **NA**

Recent Price • 12
52 Wk Range • 17⅜-10

Yield • Nil
12-Mo. P/E • NM

Earnings vs. Previous Year
▲=Up ▼=Down ▶=No Change

10 Week Mov. Avg. – – –
30 Week Mov. Avg. ·······
Relative Strength —

OPTIONS: CBOE

Business Profile - 10-SEP-98

WHX seeks to expand internally and through acquisitions into value-added products, such as coated and fabricated steel products, while reducing its reliance on basic steel products. The second quarter of 1998 marked WHX's second straight quarterly profit as it continued to recover from the strike at its Wheeling-Pittsburgh Steel unit and benefitted from the acquisition of metals and auto parts producer Handy & Harman. As of June 30, 1998, WHX had repurchased on the open market and retired 11.3 million common shares and 600,000 preferred shares since its repurchase program was initiated in October 1994, for an aggregate purchase price of $140.6 million

Operational Review - 10-SEP-98

Net sales in the first half of 1998 more than tripled, year to year, reflecting the April 1998 acquisition of Handy & Harman, as well as the strike related impact on first half 1997 sales of Wheeling-Pittsburgh Steel Corp. Following sharply higher other income, pretax income contrasted with a pretax loss. After taxes at 34.9%, versus a $38.7 million tax benefit, net income of $15,155,000 ($0.26 a share, after preferred dividends and on 21% fewer shares), contrasted with a net loss of $71,831,000 ($3.51).

Stock Performance - 02-OCT-98

In the past 30 trading days, WHX's shares have declined 2%, compared to a 7% fall in the S&P 500. Average trading volume for the past five days was 37,740 shares, compared with the 40-day moving average of 100,064 shares.

Key Stock Statistics

Dividend Rate/Share	Nil	Shareholders	12,700
Shs. outstg. (M)	18.8	Market cap. (B)	$0.227
Avg. daily vol. (M)	0.126	Inst. holdings	69%
Tang. Bk. Value/Share	7.30		
Beta	0.93		

Value of $10,000 invested 5 years ago: $ 20,977

Fiscal Year Ending Dec. 31

	1998	1997	1996	1995	1994	1993
Revenues (Million $)						
1Q	304.1	113.6	315.5	324.2	253.8	235.7
2Q	464.5	128.5	357.8	366.3	300.4	269.0
3Q	—	144.6	391.9	339.4	309.8	269.3
4Q	—	255.4	167.5	334.7	329.8	272.7
Yr.	—	642.1	1,233	1,365	1,194	1,047
Earnings Per Share ($)						
1Q	-0.21	-1.92	-0.17	0.61	1.18	-0.15
2Q	0.39	-1.58	0.42	0.60	0.36	0.35
3Q	—	-4.49	0.45	0.52	0.55	0.30
4Q	—	-0.79	-1.60	0.44	0.44	0.40
Yr.	—	-8.83	-0.82	2.18	2.54	1.02

Next earnings report expected: NA

Dividend Data

Directors omitted dividends in 1979.

A Division of The McGraw·Hill Companies

Business Summary - 10-SEP-98

The ninth largest domestic integrated steel manufacturer, WHX Corp. has increased its production of value-added steel products, such as coated and fabricated steel, over the past several years. It believes these products carry higher margins and are less sensitive to the steel industry cycle than basic steel products. The company's strategy also focuses on minimizing fixed costs and maximizing capacity utilization. It continually seeks to improve its cost structure and product quality through capital expenditures, productivity increases and business improvement teams.

Results for 1997 reflect a strike by the United Steelworkers of America (USWA) which began October 1, 1996 and ended August 12, 1997. No steel products were produced or shipped at eight of WHX's plants located in Ohio, Pennsylvania and West Virginia during the strike, representing about 80% of the tons shipped by WHX on an annual basis. None of the Wheeling Corrugating facilities outside the Ohio Valley, or Unimast and Pittsburgh Canfield facilities, were involved in the work stoppage; however, the work stoppage at the eight plants adversely affected WHX's ability to supply steel to these downstream operations, which acquired their steel supply from external sources. The new five-year labor agreement with the USWA provides for a defined benefit pension plan, a retirement enhancement program, bonus and special assistance payments and $1.50 in hourly wage increases over five years. It also provides for the reduction of 850 jobs, mandatory multicrafting and the modification of certain work practices. All of WPSC's raw steel producing facilities were restarted as of September 30, 1997, and WHX expected to be producing and shipping at pre-strike production levels and shipping its historical mix of products by June 30, 1998.

The Wheeling Corrugating division is a leading fabricator of roll formed construction, highway and agricultural products. Fabricated steel products include roof deck, form deck and composite deck, sold to the non-residential building market; culvert products used in highway construction; and roofing and siding products sold to the agricultural industry. Unimast, Inc. (acquired in March 1995) makes framing components and related accessories. Wheeling Corrugating and Unimast made no steel shipments in 1997 as a result of the USWA strike.

Flat rolled products consist of a variety of sheet products, including hot rolled, cold rolled, galvanized and prepainted, and tin mill products. Products are sold to the auto, appliance and other markets. WHX holds a 36% interest in Wheeling-Nisshin, Inc., a maker of galvanized and aluminized products. It also owns a 50% equity interest in Ohio Coatings Co., a joint venture that completed construction of a tin coating mill in 1996 and began commercial operations in January 1997.

In April 1998, WHX acquired Handy & Harman, a diversified industrial manufacturing company for total consideration of $651.4 milli on, including assumption of $229.6 million in debt.

Per Share Data ($) (Year Ended Dec. 31)	1997	1996	1995	1994	1993	1992	1991	1990	1989	1988
Tangible Bk. Val.	20.38	29.53	32.61	25.65	16.65	13.42	15.50	16.92	NA	NA
Cash Flow	-6.57	1.81	5.35	4.67	3.26	1.17	2.89	NA	NA	NA
Earnings	-8.83	-0.82	2.18	2.54	1.02	-1.85	0.27	NA	NA	NA
Dividends	Nil	Nil	Nil	Nil	Nil	Nil	Nil	Nil	Nil	Nil
Payout Ratio	Nil	Nil	Nil	Nil	Nil	Nil	Nil	Nil	Nil	Nil
Prices - High	15 1/4	14	14 5/8	22 5/8	18 1/4	7 7/8	8 7/8	13 1/4	NA	NA
- Low	5 1/4	7 3/8	9 5/8	12 7/8	4 7/8	3 1/4	5 3/4	2 3/8	NA	NA
P/E Ratio - High	NM	NM	7	9	18	NM	33	NA	NA	NA
- Low	NM	NM	4	5	5	NM	21	NA	NA	NA

Income Statement Analysis (Million $)	1997	1996	1995	1994	1993	1992	1991	1990	1989	1988
Revs.	642	1,233	1,365	1,194	1,047	930	957	1,103	1,147	1,103
Oper. Inc.	-145	141	144	141	107	47.0	58.0	131	184	222
Depr.	49.8	69.3	67.9	61.5	57.1	54.9	45.0	48.9	44.6	46.7
Int. Exp.	29.0	28.5	29.2	31.0	27.9	29.9	35.9	4.9	5.0	5.0
Pretax Inc.	-266	-3.5	100	111	40.0	-34.0	-3.0	-255	195	250
Eff. Tax Rate	NM	NM	19%	22%	23%	NM	NM	NM	34%	28%
Net Inc.	-173	0.7	81.1	86.0	31.0	-34.0	5.0	-266	129	179

Balance Sheet & Other Fin. Data (Million $)	1997	1996	1995	1994	1993	1992	1991	1990	1989	1988
Cash	1.0	483	440	402	280	9.0	45.0	65.0	584	456
Curr. Assets	939	738	798	786	654	337	397	506	892	733
Total Assets	2,070	1,719	1,796	1,730	1,492	1,117	1,174	1,218	1,486	1,286
Curr. Liab.	610	246	257	262	272	232	248	249	176	135
LT Debt	350	268	286	290	347	214	225	302	2.0	2.0
Common Eqty.	466	714	768	698	442	244	281	250	-16.0	-184
Total Cap.	817	982	1,054	989	789	458	506	552	174	-5.0
Cap. Exp.	36.7	35.4	83.3	82.0	74.0	67.0	97.0	107	90.0	52.0
Cash Flow	-144	47.6	149	135	83.0	21.0	50.0	-224	164	216
Curr. Ratio	1.5	3.0	3.1	3.0	2.4	1.5	1.6	2.0	5.1	5.4
% LT Debt of Cap.	42.9	27.3	27.1	29.3	44.0	46.7	44.4	54.7	1.2	NM
% Net Inc.of Revs.	NM	0.1	5.9	7.2	2.9	NM	0.5	NM	11.2	16.2
% Ret. on Assets	NM	NM	4.6	5.3	2.0	NM	0.4	NM	9.3	15.6
% Ret. on Equity	NM	NM	11.1	12.7	6.5	NM	1.6	NM	NM	NM

Data as orig. reptd.; bef. results of disc. opers. and/or spec. items. Per share data adj. for stk. divs. as of ex-div. date. E-Estimated. NA-Not Available. NM-Not Meaningful. NR-Not Ranked.

Office—110 E. 59th St., New York, NY 10022. **Tel**—(212) 355-5200. **Website**—http://www.wpsc.com **Chrmn**—R. LaBow. **Vice Chrm**—R. A. Davidow. **Secy**—M. Olshan. **Dirs**—N. D. Arnold, P. W. Bucha, R. A. Davidow, W. Goldsmith, R. LaBow, M. L. Olshan, R. S. Troubh. **Transfer Agent & Registrar**—First National Bank of Boston. **Incorporated**—in Delaware in 1920. **Empl**— 4,581. **S&P Analyst:** M.I.

STANDARD &POOR'S

STOCK REPORTS

WICOR, Inc.

2403M

NYSE Symbol **WIC**

In S&P SmallCap 600

03-OCT-98

Industry: Natural Gas

Summary: This holding company's main subsidiary, Wisconsin Gas Co., is the largest gas distributor in Wisconsin. Other subsidiaries produce pumps and filters.

Quantitative Evaluations

Outlook (1 Lowest—5 Highest)
- **2⁻**

Fair Value
- **23¼**

Risk
- **Low**

Earn./Div. Rank
- **B+**

Technical Eval.
- **Bullish** since 9/98

Rel. Strength Rank (1 Lowest—99 Highest)
- **91**

Insider Activity
- **Neutral**

Recent Price • 24
52 Wk Range • 24¾-20⅛

Yield • 3.7%
12-Mo. P/E • 19.5

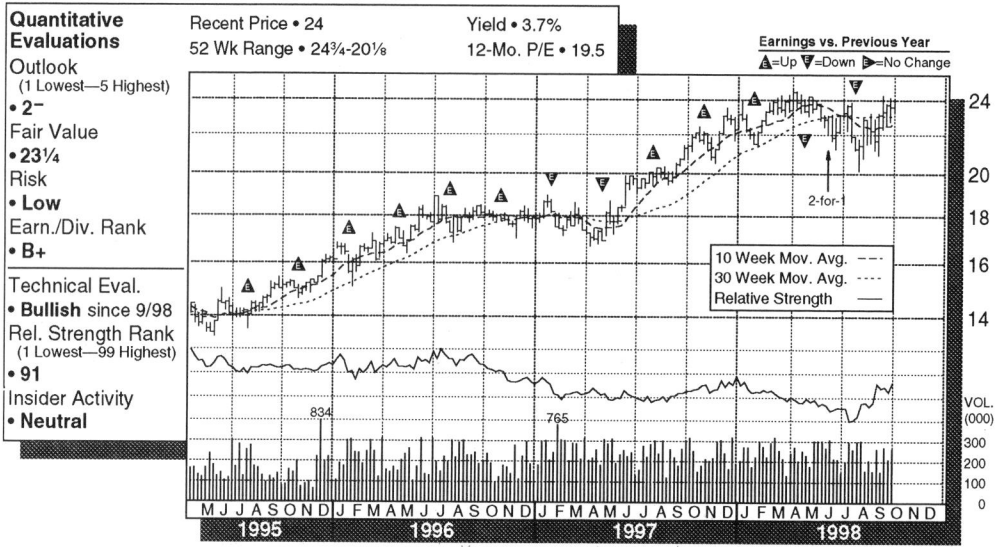

Earnings vs. Previous Year
△=Up ▽=Down ▷=No Change

10 Week Mov. Avg. ---
30 Week Mov. Avg. ·····
Relative Strength —

2-for-1

Business Profile - 12-MAY-98

This diversified holding company has two principal businesses: natural gas retail distribution in Wisconsin, and manufacturing and sale of pumps and water processing equipment, which are marketed by the company in more than 100 countries. Manufactured products include pool and spa pumps, pool filters and accessories, water purifiers, recreational vehicle/marine and foodservice applications and industrial units. While gas distribution is the primary segment, manufacturing has grown in recent years and in 1997 accounted for roughly 40% of revenues and profits. A two-for-one stock split will be effected in late May 1998.

Operational Review - 12-MAY-98

Operating revenues in the three months ended March 31, 1998, declined 13% year to year, as a result of a lower gas sales volume reflecting weather that was 12% warmer than in the prior-year quarter, offset partially by higher manufacturing sales reflecting greater demand, increased market share and new products. Total costs and expenses declined 14%, aided by a 30% drop in cost of gas sold; operating income was down 9.0%. With increased depreciation and amortization charges, but sharply higher other income, and after taxes at 37.6%, versus 37.4%, net income fell 11%, to $24,963,000 ($1.33 a diluted share; unadjusted), from $27,908,000 ($1.51).

Stock Performance - 02-OCT-98

In the past 30 trading days, WIC's shares have increased 8%, compared to a 7% fall in the S&P 500. Average trading volume for the past five days was 52,400 shares, compared with the 40-day moving average of 42,636 shares.

Key Stock Statistics

Dividend Rate/Share	0.88	Shareholders	23,300
Shs. outstg. (M)	37.3	Market cap. (B)	$0.896
Avg. daily vol. (M)	0.047	Inst. holdings	35%
Tang. Bk. Value/Share	9.11		
Beta	0.51		

Value of $10,000 invested 5 years ago: $ 22,818

Fiscal Year Ending Dec. 31

	1998	1997	1996	1995	1994	1993
Revenues (Million $)						
1Q	303.3	349.1	328.8	269.3	321.0	273.0
2Q	219.9	221.6	227.6	179.2	186.1	190.0
3Q	—	173.3	175.1	162.7	151.0	153.0
4Q	—	277.0	281.1	249.3	210.0	234.0
Yr.	—	1,021	1,013	860.6	867.8	850.0
Earnings Per Share ($)						
1Q	0.67	0.76	0.84	0.73	0.85	0.76
2Q	0.16	0.17	0.15	0.08	0.03	0.02
3Q	—	-0.06	-0.12	-0.14	-0.24	-0.27
4Q	—	0.47	0.40	0.49	0.35	0.41
Yr.	—	1.33	1.26	1.16	0.99	0.91

Next earnings report expected: late October

Dividend Data (Dividends have been paid since 1960.)

Amount ($)	Date Decl.	Ex-Div. Date	Stock of Record	Payment Date
0.430	Jan. 27	Feb. 04	Feb. 06	Feb. 27 '98
0.430	Apr. 23	May. 06	May. 08	May. 29 '98
2-for-1	Apr. 23	Jun. 01	May. 14	May. 29 '98
0.220	Jul. 28	Aug. 06	Aug. 10	Aug. 31 '98

A Division of The McGraw-Hill Companies

Business Summary - 12-MAY-98

This holding company's mix of old and new businesses has proven to be a winning recipe for growth in recent years. Starting with Wisconsin Gas, the oldest and largest gas distributor in Wisconsin (established in 1852), WICOR (WIC) acquired several pump manufacturing businesses beginning in 1982, and formed two energy-related subsidiaries in 1995. In the five years from 1993 through 1997, WIC acquired ten companies, launched three new businesses, developed dozens of new products, expanded into 17 new markets and added 36,000 gas customers. While results in 1997 were affected by unusually warm weather conditions that reduced gas sales, earnings for the five-year period have risen nearly 70%, and EPS (diluted) have grown an average 13% per year.

WIC currently operates six subsidiaries in two industries: energy services (Wisconsin Gas, WICOR Energy Services and FieldTech) and pump manufacturing (Sta-Rite, SHURflo and Hypro). Contributions to revenues and profits in 1997 were as follows:

	Revs.	Profits
Energy	58%	63%
Manufacturing	42%	37%

In the energy sector, Wisconsin Gas will remain a regulated utility, delivering gas to more than half a million customers throughout the state. It expects to add about 8,000 to 10,000 customers a year. WICOR Energy, the energy marketing subsidiary formed in 1995 to compete in the unregulated retail energy market, sells gas and propane and is licensed to sell electricity. FieldTech, a service business created in 1995, specializes in installing meter reading systems and in training and managing field crews to do meter reading work. In 1996, WIC started Wisconsin Gas Water Services, a business that sells water systems repair and maintenance services to local municipalities. WIC also operates Wisconsin Gas Leasing Services, a business that leases water heaters and food service equipment to restaurants, schools, hotels and apartment complexes.

WICOR's pump manufacturing companies are market leaders in a highly competitive and fragmented industry, with 15 manufacturing plants in seven countries. Products include pumps and pumping systems, water storage and pressure tanks, filters and accessories. Many new markets have been added in recent years, from beverage dispensing and water purification to firefighting and pumps for garden ponds. The worldwide water filtration market is being targeted as a significant growth area.

Per Share Data ($)

(Year Ended Dec. 31)	1997	1996	1995	1994	1993	1992	1991	1990	1989	1988
Tangible Bk. Val.	17.33	8.30	7.74	8.62	8.23	7.96	8.14	8.32	8.70	8.18
Cash Flow	4.48	2.21	2.04	1.88	1.78	1.61	1.66	1.40	2.01	2.00
Earnings	1.33	1.27	1.16	0.99	0.91	0.70	0.77	0.52	1.20	1.23
Dividends	0.85	0.83	0.81	0.79	0.77	0.75	0.73	0.71	0.69	0.66
Payout Ratio	64%	65%	70%	79%	85%	107%	98%	137%	57%	54%
Prices - High	24	18⁷/₈	16¹/₂	16³/₈	16¹/₂	13³/₄	12¹/₄	12⁵/₈	12³/₄	10¹/₂
- Low	16³/₄	15¹/₈	13³/₈	12³/₄	12⁷/₈	11¹/₂	9³/₈	9¹/₈	9³/₄	7⁷/₈
P/E Ratio - High	18	15	14	16	18	20	16	24	11	9
- Low	13	12	11	13	14	16	12	18	8	6

Income Statement Analysis (Million $)

	1997	1996	1995	1994	1993	1992	1991	1990	1989	1988
Revs.	1,021	1,013	861	868	850	705	682	660	711	754
Oper. Inc.	65.7	125	109	96.0	92.0	76.0	73.8	65.5	91.7	88.0
Depr.	33.2	34.4	29.7	29.4	28.0	26.7	24.8	24.0	22.0	20.6
Int. Exp.	17.4	18.3	19.3	16.7	17.4	18.0	16.6	18.1	17.4	16.5
Pretax Inc.	77.8	73.5	62.2	50.5	46.8	32.6	33.7	23.9	53.6	54.4
Eff. Tax Rate	36%	36%	37%	34%	37%	37%	36%	40%	39%	38%
Net Inc.	49.5	46.8	39.5	33.2	29.3	20.5	21.5	14.3	32.7	33.8

Balance Sheet & Other Fin. Data (Million $)

	1997	1996	1995	1994	1993	1992	1991	1990	1989	1988
Cash	11.8	18.8	20.4	35.1	23.0	16.5	47.6	16.0	29.7	18.2
Curr. Assets	385	373	329	312	315	238	242	210	259	229
Total Assets	1,031	1,058	1,009	931	934	810	669	638	601	546
Curr. Liab.	310	289	254	239	256	192	149	166	190	165
LT Debt	149	171	176	162	165	164	168	128	122	132
Common Eqty.	390	368	345	291	270	236	235	230	238	221
Total Cap.	539	585	567	504	490	455	489	443	388	375
Cap. Exp.	51.6	51.7	56.2	55.1	54.0	80.5	47.9	36.5	39.7	47.7
Cash Flow	82.7	81.1	69.2	62.6	57.4	47.1	46.3	38.4	54.7	53.6
Curr. Ratio	1.2	NA	1.3	1.3	1.2	1.2	1.6	1.3	1.4	1.4
% LT Debt of Cap.	27.6	31.5	31.0	32.1	33.7	36.0	34.4	28.9	31.5	35.3
% Net Inc.of Revs.	4.9	4.6	4.6	3.8	3.5	2.9	3.2	2.2	4.6	4.5
% Ret. on Assets	4.7	4.5	4.1	3.5	3.2	2.8	3.2	2.3	5.7	6.3
% Ret. on Equity	13.1	13.1	12.4	11.6	11.0	8.7	9.0	6.1	14.1	15.5

Data as orig. reptd.; bef. results of disc. opers. and/or spec. items. Per share data adj. for stk. divs. as of ex-div. date. Bold denotes diluted EPS (FASB 128). E-Estimated. NA-Not Available. NM-Not Meaningful. NR-Not Ranked.

Office—626 E. Wisconsin Ave., P.O. Box 334, Milwaukee, WI 53201. **Tel**—(414) 291-7026. **Chrmn & CEO**—G. E. Wardeberg. **Pres & COO**—T. F. Schrader. **SVP, CFO, Treas & Investor Contact**—Joseph P. Wenzler. **Secy**—R. A. Nuernberg. **Dirs**—W. F. Bueche, W. D. Davis, J. D. McGaffey, D. F. McKeithan Jr., G. A. Osborn, T. F. Schrader, S. W. Tisdale, G. Wardeberg, E. M. Whitelaw, W. B. Winter. **Transfer Agent & Registrar**—ChaseMellon Shareholder Services, South Hackensack, NJ. **Incorporated**—in Wisconsin in 1852; reincorporated in Wisconsin in 1980. **Empl**— 3,616. **S&P Analyst:** S.A.H.

STANDARD &POOR'S
STOCK REPORTS

Wabash National
2407B

NYSE Symbol **WNC**

In S&P SmallCap 600

03-OCT-98

Industry:
Trucks & Parts

Summary: This company, the largest U.S. manufacturer of truck trailers, is the leading producer of both fiberglass-reinforced plastic trailers and aluminum plate trailers.

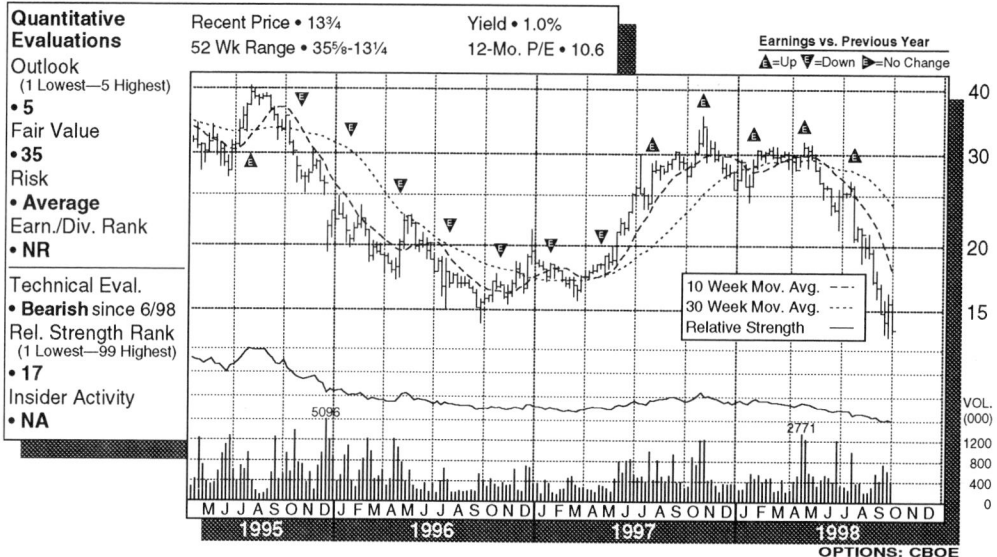

Quantitative Evaluations	
Outlook (1 Lowest—5 Highest)	• **5**
Fair Value	• **35**
Risk	• **Average**
Earn./Div. Rank	• **NR**
Technical Eval.	• **Bearish** since 6/98
Rel. Strength Rank (1 Lowest—99 Highest)	• **17**
Insider Activity	• **NA**

Recent Price • 13¾
52 Wk Range • 35⅝-13¼
Yield • 1.0%
12-Mo. P/E • 10.6

Earnings vs. Previous Year
▲=Up ▼=Down ▶=No Change

10 Week Mov. Avg. – – –
30 Week Mov. Avg. · · · ·
Relative Strength ———

OPTIONS: CBOE

Business Profile - 25-SEP-98

The company believes that it has created opportunities for growth through the startup of a composite materials plant, the acquisition of the Fruehauf retail distribution network, and expansion into the European bimodal and conventional trailer markets. WNC is replacing its aluminum plate trailer with a new composite plate trailer made of steel and plastic. In November 1997, the company bought a 25% stake in Germany-based RoadRailer for $6 million. In July 1998, it formed a joint venture to market its RoadRailer technology in South America. Backlog at June 30, 1998, totaled $894 million, up from $832 million at 1997 year end. In April 1998, WNC sold publicly 3,000,000 common shares at $30.75 each.

Operational Review - 25-SEP-98

Net sales in the first half of 1998 soared 91%, year to year, reflecting record production of the company's new composite plate trailer, and growth in its retail distribution business. Margins widened, on the greater volume, improved production for new and used trailers, and for aftermarket parts and services, and well controlled costs. Despite taxes at 40.0%, versus 38.8%, net income surged to $16,161,000 ($0.74 a share, after preferred dividends), from $3,711,000 ($0.18).

Stock Performance - 02-OCT-98

In the past 30 trading days, WNC's shares have declined 29%, compared to a 7% fall in the S&P 500. Average trading volume for the past five days was 79,620 shares, compared with the 40-day moving average of 87,369 shares.

Key Stock Statistics

Dividend Rate/Share	0.14	Shareholders	1,200
Shs. outstg. (M)	23.0	Market cap. (B)	$0.316
Avg. daily vol. (M)	0.111	Inst. holdings	80%
Tang. Bk. Value/Share	14.33		
Beta	1.09		

Value of $10,000 invested 5 years ago: $ 8,548

Fiscal Year Ending Dec. 31

	1998	1997	1996	1995	1994	1993
Revenues (Million $)						
1Q	293.6	135.1	161.2	177.6	116.6	83.73
2Q	337.7	196.4	140.6	193.4	137.7	91.02
3Q	—	246.4	161.3	176.1	147.9	89.76
4Q	—	268.2	168.4	187.1	159.7	95.53
Yr.	—	846.1	631.5	734.3	561.8	360.0
Earnings Per Share ($)						
1Q	0.36	0.05	0.12	0.37	0.27	0.19
2Q	0.38	0.13	0.01	0.43	0.35	0.21
3Q	—	0.24	0.01	0.31	0.34	0.23
4Q	—	0.31	0.07	0.24	0.35	0.27
Yr.	—	0.74	0.19	1.34	1.32	0.90

Next earnings report expected: late October

Dividend Data (Dividends have been paid since 1993.)

Amount ($)	Date Decl.	Ex-Div. Date	Stock of Record	Payment Date
0.035	Dec. 18	Jan. 08	Jan. 12	Jan. 28 '98
0.035	Mar. 25	Apr. 08	Apr. 13	Apr. 27 '98
0.035	May. 06	Jul. 10	Jul. 14	Jul. 28 '98
0.035	Sep. 16	Oct. 09	Oct. 14	Oct. 28 '98

A Division of The McGraw·Hill Companies

Business Summary - 25-SEP-98

Since inception in 1985, Wabash National Corp. (WNC) has expanded its product offerings from a single product, the aluminum plate trailer, to a broad line of transportation equipment and related items. WNC believes that it is the largest U.S. manufacturer of truck trailers and the leading manufacturer of both fiberglass-reinforced plastic composite trailers and aluminum plate trailers. The company is also the exclusive manufacturer of RoadRailer, a patented bimodal technology that consists of trailers and detachable rail bogies that permit a vehicle to run both on the highway and directly on railroad lines. WNC's Wabash National Finance unit provides leasing and financing programs to its customers for new and used trailers. WNC also produces aftermarket parts.

The company markets its products to truckload and less-than-truckload common carriers, household and package moving companies, leasing companies, package carriers and intermodal carriers. WNC believes that customers have historically replaced trailers in cycles that run from six to eight years. WNC's current strategy is to produce products in the trucking and bimodal industries which generate higher profit margins than those associated with standard trailers, and to increase its share of the factory direct market while expanding its dealer sales by attracting additional high quality regional dealers. Beginning this year, WNC also plans to expand its retail distribution network to 50 retail outlets from 31 outlets within 24 months. WNC's five largest

customers accounted for 21% of total sales in 1997. Sales to leasing companies represented 17% of 1997's total new trailer sales.

With a sharp decrease in demand for truck trailers in the U.S. since 1995, two of the 10 largest trailer manufacturers entered bankruptcy in 1996. In April 1997, WNC acquired one of them, Fruehauf Trailer Corp., for $51 million in cash and stock. The acquisition was accretive to earnings and cash flow in 1997. Assets acquired included retail outlets in 31 major markets, and WNC saw a strategic fit in new trailers, used trailers, and aftermarket parts. In July 1998, WNC acquired Cloud Corp. and Cloud Oak Flooring Co. for $10 million in cash, $13 million in convertible preferred stock, and assumption of debt. The Cloud companies ($40 million in sales) produce laminated hardwood flooring.

New products include AllRailer, a railcar designed to carry larger motor vehicles; AutoRailer, a highway trailer capable of running on rails and carrying six full-size or smaller automobiles; RefrigeRailer; ChassisRailer; and the PupRailer trailer. In 1995, WNC opened its new refrigerated trailer manufacturing facility in Lafayette, IN. In late 1995, WNC introduced its composite plate trailer.

In early 1997, the company completed a $100 million private placement of senior notes; proceeds were expected to reduce operating costs and support future growth.

Backlog at December 31, 1997, exceeded $830 million, up from $465 million a year earlier.

Per Share Data ($)

(Year Ended Dec. 31)	1997	1996	1995	1994	1993	1992	1991	1990	1989	1988
Tangible Bk. Val.	10.50	9.46	9.39	8.14	5.03	3.73	3.21	1.28	0.89	NA
Cash Flow	1.59	1.00	1.95	1.72	1.18	0.71	NA	0.43	NA	NA
Earnings	0.74	0.19	1.34	1.32	0.90	0.54	0.52	0.31	NA	NA
Dividends	0.13	0.12	0.10	0.08	0.07	Nil	Nil	NA	NA	NA
Payout Ratio	17%	63%	7%	6%	7%	Nil	Nil	NA	NA	NA
Prices - High	35⅝	24⅞	40½	43½	23⅜	19⅝	16½	NA	NA	NA
- Low	15⅝	14⅛	19⅜	22⅝	14⅛	8⅝	9⅜	NA	NA	NA
P/E Ratio - High	48	NM	30	33	25	36	32	NA	NA	NA
- Low	21	NM	14	17	15	16	18	NA	NA	NA

Income Statement Analysis (Million $)

	1997	1996	1995	1994	1993	1992	1991	1990	1989	1988
Revs.	846	631	734	562	360	289	191	171	155	130
Oper. Inc.	57.8	30.8	57.4	48.6	31.9	18.0	14.2	9.1	10.7	7.9
Depr.	16.6	15.3	11.5	7.4	4.9	2.9	1.6	1.1	1.0	0.8
Int. Exp.	16.1	10.3	6.5	2.7	1.4	0.7	1.6	2.2	2.3	2.0
Pretax Inc.	25.8	6.0	40.3	39.6	25.9	14.5	11.1	4.8	6.9	5.9
Eff. Tax Rate	41%	40%	37%	40%	40%	38%	39%	41%	38%	40%
Net Inc.	15.2	3.6	25.4	23.9	15.6	8.9	6.8	2.8	4.3	3.6

Balance Sheet & Other Fin. Data (Million $)

	1997	1996	1995	1994	1993	1992	1991	1990	1989	1988
Cash	14.6	5.5	2.1	39.7	27.6	3.0	14.6	1.9	1.7	NA
Curr. Assets	408	236	228	198	116	94.0	71.4	37.9	35.8	NA
Total Assets	630	440	384	301	180	135	93.4	49.9	47.3	43.7
Curr. Liab.	128	87.0	114	108	59.3	49.9	35.1	20.7	17.0	NA
LT Debt	232	151	73.7	24.9	24.4	18.1	1.9	13.3	19.6	17.6
Common Eqty.	227	178	178	154	87.5	62.1	53.4	15.3	10.7	8.0
Total Cap.	485	329	269	193	120	84.5	57.8	28.6	30.3	25.5
Cap. Exp.	20.2	11.2	37.9	32.7	20.1	16.5	6.8	1.7	2.0	2.2
Cash Flow	31.1	18.9	36.9	31.3	20.5	11.9	8.3	4.0	5.3	4.3
Curr. Ratio	3.2	2.7	2.0	1.8	2.0	1.9	2.0	1.8	2.1	NA
% LT Debt of Cap.	47.8	45.9	27.4	12.9	20.3	21.4	3.2	68.3	64.6	68.8
% Net Inc.of Revs.	1.8	0.6	3.5	4.3	4.3	3.1	3.6	1.7	2.8	2.7
% Ret. on Assets	3.0	0.9	7.4	9.6	9.7	7.8	12.9	NM	9.4	9.1
% Ret. on Equity	7.1	2.0	15.3	19.2	20.4	15.5	28.1	NM	45.7	56.3

Data as orig. reptd.; bef. results of disc. opers. and/or spec. items. Per share data adj. for stk. divs. as of ex-div. date. Bold denotes diluted EPS (FASB 128). E-Estimated. NA-Not Available. NM-Not Meaningful. NR-Not Ranked.

Office—1000 Sagamore Parkway South, Lafayette, IN 47905. **Tel**—(317) 448-1591. **Website**—http://www.wncwabash.com/wabash **Chrmn, Pres & CEO**—D. J. Ehrlich. **VP & CFO**—M. R. Holden. **Investor Contact**—Connie L. Koleszar. **Secy**—J. R. Gambs. **Dirs**—R. E. Dessimoz, D. J. Ehrlich, J. T. Hackett, E. H. Harrison, M. R. Holden, L. F. Koci. **Transfer Agent & Registrar**—Harris Trust and Savings Bank, Chicago. **Incorporated**—in Delaware in 1991. **Empl**— 4,320. **S&P Analyst:** Stewart Scharf

03-OCT-98

Industry: Auto Parts & Equipment

Summary: Walbro designs and manufactures precision fuel systems and products for automotive and small engine markets.

Quantitative Evaluations	
Outlook (1 Lowest—5 Highest)	• 4
Fair Value	• 9⅝
Risk	• **Low**
Earn./Div. Rank	• **B-**
Technical Eval.	• **Neutral** since 7/98
Rel. Strength Rank (1 Lowest—99 Highest)	• 39
Insider Activity	• **NA**

Recent Price • 7⅞

52 Wk Range • 24⅛-7

Yield • Nil

12-Mo. P/E • NM

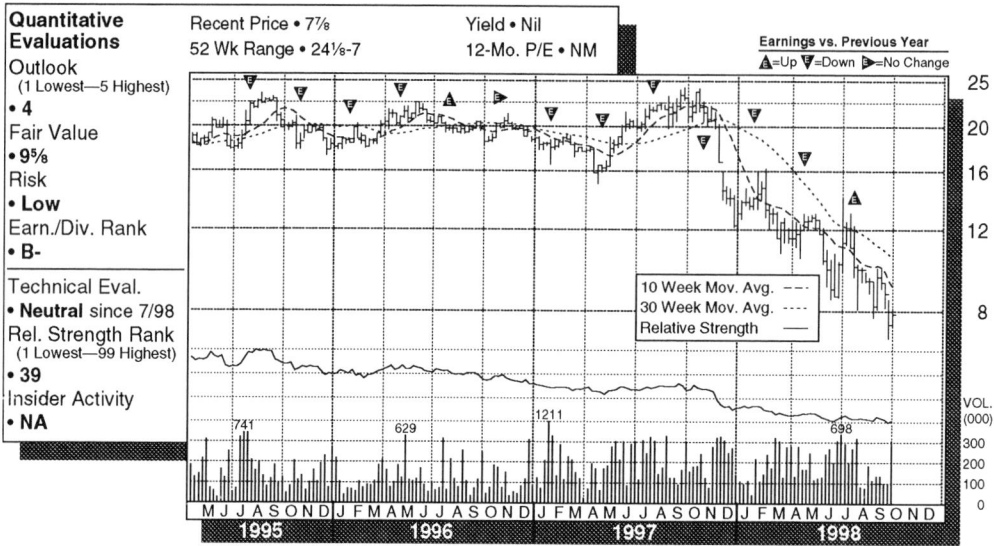

Earnings vs. Previous Year
▲=Up ▼=Down ▷=No Change

10 Week Mov. Avg. – – –
30 Week Mov. Avg. - - - -
Relative Strength ——

Business Profile - 10-SEP-98

In November 1997, Walbro announced a plan for restructuring its operations to allow it to better focus on its core activities, eliminate under-performing operations, lower its cost structure, and enhance shareholder value. The restructuring led to pretax charges of $27 million in the 1997 fourth quarter, resulting in a loss for the quarter and the year. In connection with the plan, WALB sold its Ligonier, IN, steel fuel rail production facility in June 1998. The company will continue to produce plastic fuel rails at its facility in Meriden, CT. In May 1998, WALB closed on a $150 million line of credit, to be used to repay debt, finance capital expenditures and meet working capital needs. The quarterly dividend was suspended in March 1998.

Operational Review - 10-SEP-98

Net sales in the first half of 1998, rose 9.6%, year to year, primarily due to a 9.3% rise in automotive product sales reflecting higher volume in the U.S. Results benefited from a cost reduction program, higher volumes of fuel pumps, fuel modules and plastic fuel tank systems sold in the U.S., lower warranty costs and reduced start-up costs in Ossian, IN; operating income climbed 31%. However, after greater minority interest and reduced equity in income of joint ventures, income was down 40%, to $2,140,000 ($0.25 a share, before a $0.17 extraordinary charge for the early extinguishment of debt), from $3,546,000 ($0.41).

Stock Performance - 02-OCT-98

In the past 30 trading days, WALB's shares have declined 15%, compared to a 7% fall in the S&P 500. Average trading volume for the past five days was 75,880 shares, compared with the 40-day moving average of 30,995 shares.

Key Stock Statistics

Dividend Rate/Share	Nil	Shareholders	1,100
Shs. outstg. (M)	8.7	Market cap. (B)	$0.069
Avg. daily vol. (M)	0.036	Inst. holdings	65%
Tang. Bk. Value/Share	4.25		
Beta	0.70		

Value of $10,000 invested 5 years ago: $ 2,828

Fiscal Year Ending Dec. 31

	1998	1997	1996	1995	1994	1993
Revenues (Million $)						
1Q	169.3	154.0	153.0	98.26	82.21	66.90
2Q	168.1	153.8	155.1	90.03	83.98	71.47
3Q	—	146.5	132.6	124.5	75.25	64.37
4Q	—	165.5	144.8	146.5	83.77	70.72
Yr.	—	619.9	585.4	459.3	325.2	273.5
Earnings Per Share ($)						
1Q	**0.07**	**0.27**	0.53	0.59	0.52	0.44
2Q	**0.18**	**0.14**	0.56	0.45	0.52	0.45
3Q	—	**-0.14**	0.27	0.27	0.35	0.36
4Q	—	**-4.49**	-0.06	0.30	0.31	0.21
Yr.	—	**-4.23**	1.30	1.61	1.70	1.47

Next earnings report expected: mid October

Dividend Data (Dividends have been paid since 1967.)

Amount ($)	Date Decl.	Ex-Div. Date	Stock of Record	Payment Date
0.100	Sep. 04	Sep. 26	Sep. 30	Oct. 31 '97
0.100	Dec. 16	Dec. 29	Dec. 31	Jan. 30 '98
Div Suspended	Mar. 06			Mar. 06 '98

A Division of The **McGraw-Hill** *Companies*

Business Summary - 10-SEP-98

This maker of fuel system products for automotive and small engine markets has invested heavily in engineering, development and testing resources and new or expanded production facilities to support the broadening role it must play as an automotive supplier in the late 1990s. Michigan-based Walbro Corp. (WALB) completed a new Systems Engineering Center to aid in the development of fuel storage and delivery systems and completed a facility where it will test electric fuel pumps and other components. These and other initiatives are intended to enhance WALB's ability to design, develop, test, make and deliver entire systems to automobile manufacturers, who previously were content merely to receive quality parts, often produced to their specifications, and piece them together themselves.

WALB believes this pursuit of a "systems" approach has placed it in a unique position, allowing the company to produce all of the primary elements of a fuel storage and delivery system (FSDS). In addition to electric fuel pumps, these elements include fuel modules (devices that combine the pump with a fuel pickup, reservoir and level sensor), emission control valves and plastic fuel tanks. WALB can also act as a "systems integrator," obtaining ancillary components from other suppliers as required and assembling the finished FSDS for shipment to the customer.

Another trend affecting suppliers such as WALB is the production of "world cars" that require the supplier to support its customer's requirements for the vehicle around the globe. WALB and its joint ventures have production facilities on four continents, including plants in Brazil and Belgium opened in 1996. WALB acquired the fuel tank business of Dyno Industrier in 1995, adding six plants and gaining a significant presence in Europe.

The company sees a dramatic rise in plastic fuel tank usage driven by the advantages of plastic over metal tanks. Lighter than steel tanks, plastic fuel tanks are also corrosion-resistant and can be molded in unusual shapes to maximize fuel capacity. WALB utilizes multi-layer blowmolding technology to prevent the permeation of its tanks by hydrocarbons. WALB expects annual production of its plastic fuel tanks to exceed 6.5 million units by model year 2000.

In addition to fuel storage and delivery systems and products for the automotive industry (74% of net sales in 1997), WALB also makes carburetors and ignitions for small chain saws, outboard marine engines and other segments of the small engine market (26%).

A 6% increase in net sales in 1997, to $620 million, was primarily attributable to additional sales to the automotive market in North and South America. Results were penalized by a $27 million restructuring charge and a non-recurring charge of about $6 million for warranty reserve, leading to a net loss of $37 million.

Per Share Data ($) (Year Ended Dec. 31)	1997	1996	1995	1994	1993	1992	1991	1990	1989	1988
Tangible Bk. Val.	4.27	11.76	11.90	12.96	11.37	10.27	9.40	NA	NA	NA
Cash Flow	-0.60	4.72	4.24	3.41	2.79	2.95	2.36	NA	NA	NA
Earnings	-4.23	1.30	1.61	1.70	1.47	1.63	0.98	NA	NA	NA
Dividends	0.40	0.40	0.40	0.40	0.40	0.40	0.10	NA	NA	NA
Payout Ratio	NM	31%	25%	24%	27%	25%	10%	NA	NA	NA
Prices - High	24¼	22½	23½	28¾	38½	36	20¼	NA	NA	NA
- Low	12	17¾	17¼	16½	23½	18¾	8¼	NA	NA	NA
P/E Ratio - High	NM	17	15	17	26	22	21	NA	NA	NA
- Low	NM	14	11	10	16	12	8	NA	NA	NA

Income Statement Analysis (Million $)

	1997	1996	1995	1994	1993	1992	1991	1990	1989	1988
Revs.	620	585	459	325	273	241	200	NA	NA	NA
Oper. Inc.	34.5	57.1	46.5	39.1	35.0	31.5	21.4	NA	NA	NA
Depr.	31.4	29.7	22.5	14.7	11.3	10.3	7.0	NA	NA	NA
Int. Exp.	25.4	23.5	12.1	3.9	2.6	3.7	3.5	NA	NA	NA
Pretax Inc.	-41.7	10.4	11.7	17.9	17.2	17.2	6.9	NA	NA	NA
Eff. Tax Rate	NM	30%	11%	33%	27%	27%	30%	NA	NA	NA
Net Inc.	-36.6	11.2	13.8	14.6	12.6	12.5	4.8	NA	NA	NA

Balance Sheet & Other Fin. Data (Million $)

	1997	1996	1995	1994	1993	1992	1991	1990	1989	1988
Cash	13.5	18.2	19.8	4.5	4.6	NA	NA	NA	NA	NA
Curr. Assets	241	212	200	110	88.0	NA	NA	NA	NA	NA
Total Assets	611	590	493	257	215	193	161	NA	NA	NA
Curr. Liab.	165	143	104	52.0	38.0	NA	NA	NA	NA	NA
LT Debt	291	292	233	66.0	52.0	50.0	63.0	NA	NA	NA
Common Eqty.	69.9	138	135	128	114	100	50.0	NA	NA	NA
Total Cap.	433	436	374	198	169	150	121	NA	NA	NA
Cap. Exp.	62.0	99	46.2	18.8	20.3	14.7	12.8	NA	NA	NA
Cash Flow	-5.2	40.8	36.3	29.3	23.9	22.9	11.8	NA	NA	NA
Curr. Ratio	1.5	1.5	1.9	2.1	2.3	NA	NA	NA	NA	NA
% LT Debt of Cap.	67.2	67.0	62.4	33.5	31.0	33.3	52.0	NA	NA	NA
% Net Inc.of Revs.	NM	1.9	3.0	4.5	4.6	5.2	2.4	NA	NA	NA
% Ret. on Assets	NM	2.1	3.7	6.2	6.2	7.1	3.3	NA	NA	NA
% Ret. on Equity	NM	8.2	10.5	12.1	11.8	16.7	9.6	NA	NA	NA

Data as orig. reptd.; bef. results of disc. opers. and/or spec. items. Per share data adj. for stk. divs. as of ex-div. date. Bold denotes diluted EPS (FASB 128). E-Estimated. NA-Not Available. NM-Not Meaningful. NR-Not Ranked.

Office—6242 Garfield St., Cass City, MI 48726-1325. **Tel**—(517) 872-2131. **Fax**—(517) 872-2301. **Chrmn & CEO**—L. E. Althaver. **Pres & COO**—F. E. Baichiero.**Secy**—D. L. Hittler. **Treas, CFO & Investor Contact**—Michael A. Shope. **Dirs**—L. E. Althaver, W. T. Bacon Jr., F. E. Bauchiero, H. M. Kennedy, V. E. Oechsle, R. D. Tuttle, J. E. Utley, R. H. Walpole. **Tranfer Agent**—Harris Trust & Savings Bank, Chicago. **Incorporated**—in Michigan in 1950; reincorporated in Delaware in 1972.**Empl**— 5,028. **S&P Analyst**: S.A.H.

Wall Data

5573K

NASDAQ Symbol **WALL**

In S&P SmallCap 600

05-OCT-98

Industry: Computer (Software & Services)

Summary: This company is engaged primarily in the development and marketing of software products and related services for users of personal computers in business organizations.

Quantitative Evaluations

Outlook (1 Lowest—5 Highest)
• **4−**

Fair Value
• **21¾**

Risk
• **High**

Earn./Div. Rank
• **B−**

Technical Eval.
• **Bearish** since 9/98

Rel. Strength Rank (1 Lowest—99 Highest)
• **94**

Insider Activity
• **NA**

Recent Price • 14⅜
52 Wk Range • 19½-10⅛

Yield • Nil
12-Mo. P/E • 53.5

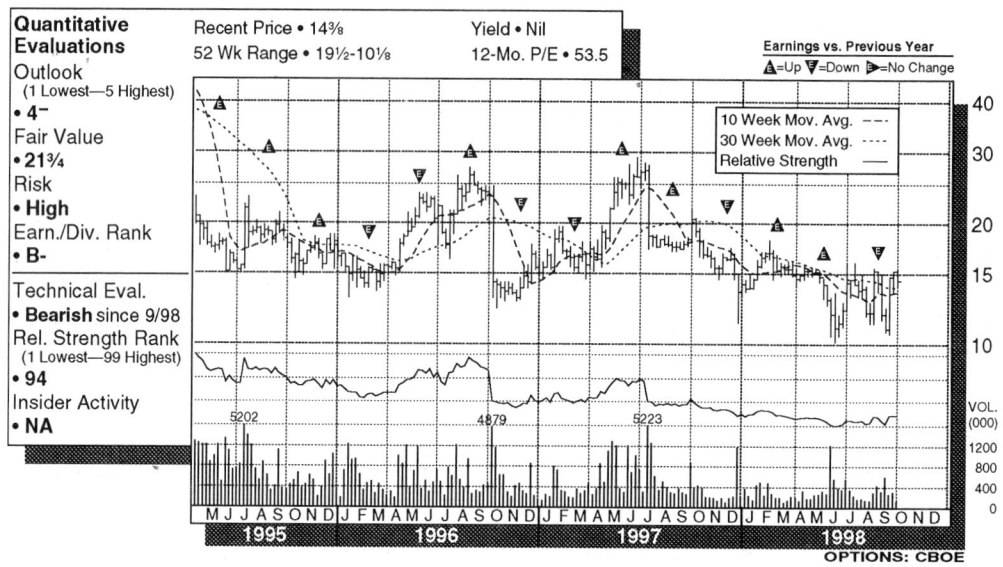

Earnings vs. Previous Year
▲=Up ▼=Down ▶=No Change

10 Week Mov. Avg. ----
30 Week Mov. Avg. ....
Relative Strength ——

OPTIONS: CBOE

Business Profile - 10-SEP-98

This company develops and markets connectivity software products that give personal computer users access to applications and data residing on enterprise-wide information systems. WALL has recently focused on helping its customers make a smooth transition to Web-enabled enterprise applications. In January 1998, the company announced a strategy known as Cyberprise, and a new line of comprehensive product and service solutions for the Web-extended enterprise. The first Cyberprise products were released in March. In May 1998, the company said it would change its existing calendar year reporting period to a fiscal year ending April 30.

Operational Review - 10-SEP-98

Net revenues in the three months ended July 31, 1998, increased 20%, year to year, reflecting the introduction of Cyberprise Internet products. Margins widened, and comparisons benefited from the absence of $10.7 million of non-recurring expenses. Despite lower net other income, and taxes at 19.9%, versus tax credits of $3,210,000, net income of $2,183,000 ($0.22 a share, on 7.0% more shares) contrasted with a net loss of $5,190,000 ($0.56).

Stock Performance - 02-OCT-98

In the past 30 trading days, WALL's shares have declined 5%, compared to a 7% fall in the S&P 500. Average trading volume for the past five days was 22,080 shares, compared with the 40-day moving average of 61,197 shares.

Key Stock Statistics

Dividend Rate/Share	Nil	Shareholders	300
Shs. outstg. (M)	10.0	Market cap. (B)	$0.144
Avg. daily vol. (M)	0.064	Inst. holdings	52%
Tang. Bk. Value/Share	7.84		
Beta	0.50		

Value of $10,000 invested 5 years ago: NA

Fiscal Year Ending Apr. 30

	1998	1997	1996	1995	1994	1993
Revenues (Million $)						
1Q	37.02	29.86	22.10	17.16	10.10	5.18
2Q	35.60	34.83	24.73	23.14	15.20	6.96
3Q	28.56	30.83	26.15	25.01	17.30	7.82
4Q	39.66	43.86	37.76	35.93	22.04	11.83
Yr.	140.8	139.4	110.7	101.2	64.64	31.80
Earnings Per Share ($)						
1Q	**0.35**	0.05	Nil	-0.04	0.13	0.08
2Q	**-0.50**	0.17	0.49	0.36	0.26	0.15
3Q	**Nil**	-0.07	-0.02	0.40	0.12	0.10
4Q	**0.35**	0.28	0.25	0.69	0.46	0.25
Yr.	**0.23**	**0.43**	0.74	1.40	1.00	0.58

Next earnings report expected: late October

Dividend Data

No cash dividends have been paid, and the company does not expect to pay any in the foreseeable future. A poison pill shareholder rights plan was adopted in 1995.

A Division of The **McGraw·Hill** Companies

Business Summary - 10-SEP-98

Wall Data Inc.'s (WALL) software allows customers to access, publish and create applications and information across computer networks. Renewed emphasis on sales and marketing and the introduction of products for Windows 95 and Windows NT, Microsoft's 32-bit operating systems, contributed to renewed revenue growth in 1996. However sales were virtually flat in 1997, as the company began a transition to Web-enabled enterprise applications.

In January 1998, the company announced a strategy known as Cyberprise, and a new line of comprehensive product and service solutions for the Web-extended enterprise. The Cyberprise strategy is designed to enable companies to move existing mission-critical systems and public information to the Web, and to extend those systems to remote users, vendors and customers. In connection with this strategy, the company began rolling out a complete line of Cyberprise products in 1998.

The foundation of the Cyberprise solution is Cyberprise Server. The Server product line is a Web application server platform which allows users to access their enterprise computing applications and information, as well as public information, through a channel-based interface. The interface can be customized and accessed through a browser. The company also provides services and support to facilitate the transference of mission-critical systems to the Cyberprise environment.

WALL's flagship RUMBA brand of software products provide users with access to mission-critical information located anywhere within the corporate enterprise or beyond, in the public domain. Having built the company into a $100 million enterprise on the strength of its RUMBA products for the 16-bit version of Windows, WALL moved to establish product leadership with its 32-bit products, redesigning its RUMBA line to take advantage of the new architecture, and, after years of research and development, launching RUMBA 95/NT in 1996. WALL believes that Microsoft's 32-bit Windows 95 and Windows NT will be the operating systems of choice into the 21st century. In 1997, RUMBA accounted for 81% of total sales, down from 86% in 1996.

In March 1998, the company purchased First Service Computer Dienstleistungs-GmbH (First Service) of Germany, for $11 million in cash. First Service distributes and supports a range of connectivity software solutions to major corporations throughout Germany, and has been a distributor of WALL's products for over seven years.

Per Share Data ($)

(Year Ended Apr. 30)	1997	1996	1995	1994	1993	1992	1991	1990	1989	1988
Tangible Bk. Val.	9.66	9.34	8.79	6.99	5.55	NM	NM	NM	NM	NM
Cash Flow	1.51	1.45	1.76	1.15	0.68	0.25	-2.01	NA	NA	NA
Earnings	0.44	0.74	1.40	1.00	0.58	0.19	-2.29	-2.15	-1.52	NA
Dividends	Nil	Nil	Nil	Nil	Nil	Nil	Nil	Nil	Nil	Nil
Payout Ratio	Nil	Nil	Nil	Nil	Nil	Nil	Nil	Nil	Nil	Nil
Cal. Yrs.	1996	1995	1994	1993	1992	1991	1990	1989	1988	1987
Prices - High	27½	55½	60	42½	NA	NA	NA	NA	NA	NA
- Low	12¼	14½	29¼	12¾	NA	NA	NA	NA	NA	NA
P/E Ratio - High	62	75	43	43	NA	NA	NA	NA	NA	NA
- Low	28	20	21	13	NA	NA	NA	NA	NA	NA

Income Statement Analysis (Million $)

	1997	1996	1995	1994	1993	1992	1991	1990	1989	1988
Revs.	139	111	101	64.6	31.8	14.6	4.4	2.4	3.0	NA
Oper. Inc.	18.4	8.6	28.7	19.1	8.0	2.1	-1.0	NA	NA	NA
Depr.	10.1	7.0	3.6	1.4	0.7	0.3	0.2	NA	NA	NA
Int. Exp.	Nil	Nil	0.2	0.2	0.2	0.2	0.4	NA	NA	NA
Pretax Inc.	7.2	11.7	22.8	15.3	6.8	1.7	-1.6	-1.5	-1.0	NA
Eff. Tax Rate	42%	38%	38%	38%	35%	37%	Nil	Nil	Nil	Nil
Net Inc.	4.2	7.3	14.2	9.6	4.4	1.1	-1.6	-1.5	-1.0	NA

Balance Sheet & Other Fin. Data (Million $)

	1997	1996	1995	1994	1993	1992	1991	1990	1989	1988
Cash	62.5	52.0	48.9	50.3	4.6	1.8	NA	NA	NA	NA
Curr. Assets	108	86.9	80.7	67.3	14.1	6.0	NA	NA	NA	NA
Total Assets	127	110	106	74.4	16.1	6.9	2.0	2.2	2.9	NA
Curr. Liab.	36.4	26.1	24.4	12.0	6.1	3.6	NA	NA	NA	NA
LT Debt	Nil	Nil	Nil	0.1	1.0	0.6	4.5	4.2	3.7	NA
Common Eqty.	91.0	83.7	81.2	62.3	9.0	2.7	-4.6	-3.0	-1.6	NA
Total Cap.	91.0	83.7	81.2	62.5	10.0	3.2	-0.1	1.2	2.1	NA
Cap. Exp.	5.1	7.1	10.1	3.8	1.6	0.3	0.1	NA	NA	NA
Cash Flow	14.3	14.3	17.8	11.0	5.1	1.3	-1.4	NA	NA	NA
Curr. Ratio	3.0	3.3	3.3	5.6	2.3	1.6	NA	NA	NA	NA
% LT Debt of Cap.	Nil	Nil	Nil	0.2	10.1	17.5	NM	NM	NM	NM
% Net Inc.of Revs.	3.0	6.5	14.0	14.8	13.8	7.2	NM	NM	NM	NM
% Ret. on Assets	3.5	6.7	15.5	10.8	38.3	23.7	NM	NM	NM	NM
% Ret. on Equity	4.8	8.8	19.4	19.7	75.3	NM	NM	NM	NM	NM

Data as orig. reptd.; bef. results of disc. opers. and/or spec. items. Prior to 1999, yrs. ended Dec. 31 of the prior cal. yr. Per share data adj. for stk. divs. as of ex-div. date. E-Estimated. NA-Not Available. NM-Not Meaningful. NR-Not Ranked. Bold denotes diluted EPS (FASB 128).

Office—11332 N.E. 122nd Way, Kirkland, WA 98034-6931. **Tel**—(800) 915-9255. **Website**—http://www.walldata.com **Chrmn**—R. J. Frankenberg. **Pres & CEO**—J. R. Wall. **VP-Fin, CFO & Treas**—R. Fox. **Dirs**—R. J. Frankenberg, J. A. Heimbuck, H. N. Lewis, D. F. Millet, S. Sarich Jr., B. Steiger, K. Vitale, J. R. Wall. **Transfer Agent & Registrar**—ChaseMellon, Seattle.**Incorporated**—in Washington in 1982. **Empl**— 793. **S&P Analyst:** B.G.

03-OCT-98

Industry: Equipment (Semiconductor)

Summary: WJ produces semiconductor manufacturing equipment and makes electronic products for wireless telecommunications.

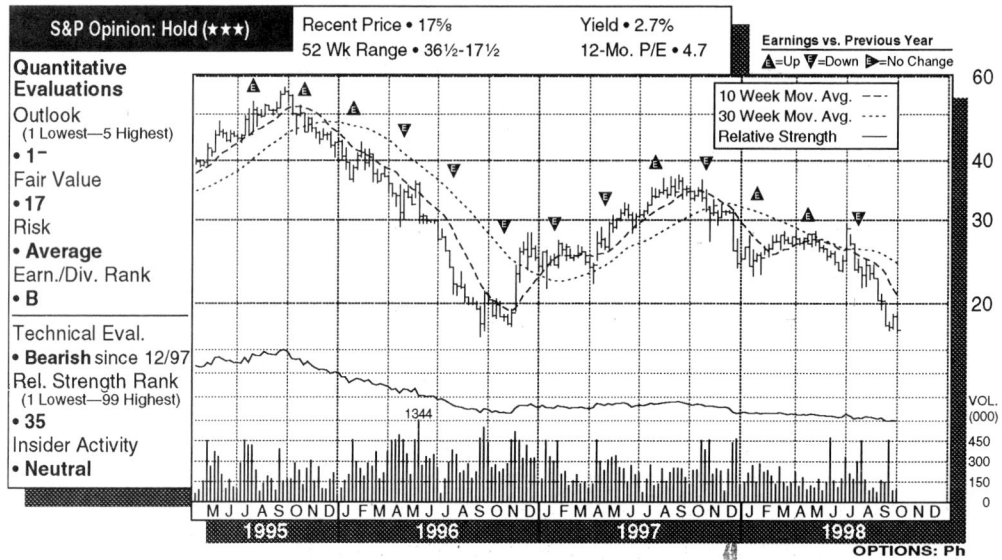

S&P Opinion: Hold (★★★)	Recent Price • 17⅝	Yield • 2.7%
	52 Wk Range • 36½-17½	12-Mo. P/E • 4.7

Earnings vs. Previous Year
▲=Up ▼=Down ▶=No Change

Quantitative Evaluations

Outlook (1 Lowest—5 Highest)
• 1⁻

Fair Value
• 17

Risk
• **Average**

Earn./Div. Rank
• **B**

Technical Eval.
• **Bearish** since 12/97

Rel. Strength Rank (1 Lowest—99 Highest)
• **35**

Insider Activity
• **Neutral**

10 Week Mov. Avg. – – –
30 Week Mov. Avg. ·····
Relative Strength —

1344

VOL. (000)
450 300 150 0

M J J A S O N D | J F M A M J J A S O N D | J F M A M J J A S O N D | J F M A M J J A S O N D
1995 **1996** **1997** **1998**

OPTIONS: Ph

Overview - 14-SEP-98

Semiconductor equipment orders have fallen sharply in recent quarters. With lingering overcapacity in the chip market, as well as economic turmoil in Asia, we expect continued operating losses from this segment in the near term. Restructuring actions and work force reductions should allow the segment to break even in 1999. In addition, we expect the wireless communications segment to post operating losses this year, as the company's base station product has not had strong customer acceptance. In October 1997, WJ sold its defense-electronics, microwave components and subsystems business to Mentmore Holdings, for $103 million. Management estimated that the divested businesses generated $65 million to $70 million of sales in the first nine months of 1997, and produced pretax operating profit of about $10 million. The move allowed the company to focus its resources on two rapidly growing areas of technology: semiconductor capital equipment, and wireless communications.

Valuation - 14-SEP-98

We are maintaining our neutral opinion on the shares. WJ has positioned itself well for the long term, with operations in two rapidly growing segments of technology. However, current overcapacity in the semiconductor market has caused chip-makers to sharply reduce near-term capital spending. We estimate that this trend, coupled with weaker than expected growth in the wireless segment, will result in an operating loss of about $3.35 a share this year. On a positive note, the balance sheet, with more than $13 a share in cash and short-term investments, remains strong. While we see no catalyst for near-term outperformance, the shares, currently trading at only about 67% of book value, remain a worthwhile holding.

Key Stock Statistics

S&P EPS Est. 1998	-3.35	Tang. Bk. Value/Share	26.78
P/E on S&P Est. 1998	NM	Beta	1.64
S&P EPS Est. 1999	0.45	Shareholders	6,500
Dividend Rate/Share	0.48	Market cap. (B)	$0.146
Shs. outstg. (M)	8.3	Inst. holdings	59%
Avg. daily vol. (M)	0.045		

Value of $10,000 invested 5 years ago: $ 13,760

Fiscal Year Ending Dec. 31

	1998	1997	1996	1995	1994	1993
Revenues (Million $)						
1Q	68.72	67.22	122.7	92.98	80.56	67.08
2Q	53.74	72.68	126.5	102.0	87.37	68.22
3Q	—	79.17	94.96	95.55	83.17	72.71
4Q	—	72.20	94.17	96.49	81.54	78.28
Yr.	—	291.3	438.3	387.0	332.6	286.3
Earnings Per Share ($)						
1Q	**1.15**	**-0.04**	0.75	0.63	0.47	0.18
2Q	**-0.75**	**0.10**	0.04	0.88	0.77	0.33
3Q	—	**0.21**	0.33	0.98	0.63	0.42
4Q	—	**-0.76**	-0.77	1.04	0.77	0.52
Yr.	—	**-0.48**	-0.16	3.54	2.66	1.45

Next earnings report expected: mid October

Dividend Data (Dividends have been paid since 1974.)

Amount ($)	Date Decl.	Ex-Div. Date	Stock of Record	Payment Date
0.120	Nov. 24	Dec. 15	Dec. 17	Jan. 02 '98
0.120	Mar. 02	Mar. 10	Mar. 12	Mar. 26 '98
0.120	May. 18	Jun. 09	Jun. 11	Jun. 25 '98
0.120	Jul. 27	Sep. 08	Sep. 10	Sep. 24 '98

Business Summary - 14-SEP-98

Watkins-Johnson Company has continuing operations in two distinct high-technology businesses: semiconductor equipment manufacturing, and wireless communications. In October 1997, the company completed the sale its defense electronics operations in order to concentrate more resources to these rapidly growing businesses. Contributions to sales and pretax income (in 000s) by segment in 1997 were:

	Sales	Pretax Income
Semiconductor Equipment	64%	-$13,328
Wireless Communications	36%	-$954

The Semiconductor Equipment Group produces chemical vapor deposition (CVD) equipment for semiconductor manufacturing. CVD processes are used to deposit dielectric films in an integrated circuit (IC). The company's WJ-1000 product specializes in the premetal dielectric sector, applying the crucial initial layer of doped (ionized) silicon dioxide (glass) onto a silicon wafer that is the basic material used in making ICs. The WJ-2000, a high-density plasma CVD system for depositing intermetal dielectric films, was introduced in 1995. WJ's tools are used by semiconductor manufacturers worldwide for all types of ICs. A related application is in liquid crystal flat-panel display.

The wireless communications segment serves original equipment manufacturers (OEMs). Watkins-Johnson has entered two wireless communications business areas which parallel the skills it developed as a defense-electronics supplier. One business involves the production of components and subassemblies for cellular, personal communication services (PCS) and space applications. The company has successfully adapted its communications-intelligence equipment technology to the design and production of low-cost, sensitive receivers and wideband transceivers for base station applications.

In October 1997, the company completed the sale of its defense-electronics business to Mentmore Holdings Corp., a privately held investment company. Proceeds of approximately $103 million were expected to be used for expansion and development of WJ's remaining semiconductor equipment and wireless communications businesses.

Operating results are currently being hurt by a slowdown in the semiconductor equipment industry. Overcapacity in the market for dynamic random access memory (DRAM) chips, coupled with the impact of economic turmoil in Asia, has caused chip-makers to defer or cancel orders for semiconductor equipment. With weakness in the wireless segment emerging as well, the company expects to continue to post operating losses over the course of 1998.

Per Share Data ($)

(Year Ended Dec. 31)	1997	1996	1995	1994	1993	1992	1991	1990	1989	1988
Tangible Bk. Val.	26.68	23.38	23.54	19.75	17.62	16.55	15.67	19.15	17.74	15.98
Cash Flow	1.11	1.68	4.66	3.72	2.69	2.15	-1.42	3.23	3.68	3.92
Earnings	-0.48	0.36	3.54	2.66	1.45	0.66	-2.98	1.67	2.23	2.46
Dividends	0.48	0.48	0.48	0.48	0.48	0.48	0.48	0.48	0.46	0.40
Payout Ratio	NM	133%	14%	18%	33%	73%	NM	28%	21%	16%
Prices - High	37³/₈	44⁵/₈	57	36⁵/₈	26¹/₄	15	19¹/₂	20⁷/₈	27¹/₄	29³/₄
- Low	21¹/₂	17	29³/₄	19⁵/₈	12	8⁵/₈	9¹/₄	10⁵/₈	19	22³/₈
P/E Ratio - High	NM	NM	16	14	18	23	NM	13	12	12
- Low	NM	NM	8	7	8	13	NM	6	9	9

Income Statement Analysis (Million $)

	1997	1996	1995	1994	1993	1992	1991	1990	1989	1988
Revs.	291	438	387	333	286	264	278	312	311	292
Oper. Inc.	-1.2	16.2	51.8	39.3	26.9	19.0	13.6	29.7	38.6	44.0
Depr.	13.1	11.3	9.9	8.7	10.0	11.3	11.7	12.1	12.2	12.2
Int. Exp.	1.4	1.6	0.9	1.1	1.3	1.5	1.5	1.6	1.9	2.0
Pretax Inc.	-7.0	4.3	44.0	30.9	16.8	7.2	-28.7	18.7	28.3	30.8
Eff. Tax Rate	NM	30%	29%	30%	31%	31%	NM	30%	34%	33%
Net Inc.	-4.0	3.0	31.4	21.7	11.6	5.0	-22.4	13.0	18.7	20.6

Balance Sheet & Other Fin. Data (Million $)

	1997	1996	1995	1994	1993	1992	1991	1990	1989	1988
Cash	134	15.7	34.6	34.5	45.0	49.1	40.1	17.2	26.6	24.5
Curr. Assets	258	204	217	179	169	153	153	159	169	145
Total Assets	358	314	288	235	221	206	213	223	227	210
Curr. Liab.	105	80.9	74.8	62.8	60.3	52.4	62.8	59.3	55.1	51.7
LT Debt	33.2	27.8	7.7	7.8	12.2	12.9	14.8	15.8	19.0	20.2
Common Eqty.	220	195	191	150	134	125	118	144	149	134
Total Cap.	253	223	199	157	146	138	133	160	168	154
Cap. Exp.	22.2	50.0	25.6	12.5	9.7	5.2	9.9	16.8	11.8	11.6
Cash Flow	9.2	14.3	41.4	30.4	21.6	16.3	-10.7	25.2	30.9	32.8
Curr. Ratio	2.5	2.5	2.9	2.9	2.8	2.9	2.4	2.7	3.1	2.8
% LT Debt of Cap.	13.1	12.5	3.9	5.0	8.3	9.3	11.2	9.9	11.3	13.1
% Net Inc.of Revs.	NM	0.7	8.1	6.5	4.1	1.9	NM	4.2	6.0	7.0
% Ret. on Assets	NM	1.0	12.0	9.5	5.4	2.4	NM	6.1	8.6	10.3
% Ret. on Equity	NM	1.6	18.4	15.3	8.9	4.1	NM	9.4	13.2	16.4

Data as orig. reptd.; bef. results of disc. opers. and/or spec. items. Per share data adj. for stk. divs. as of ex-div. date. Bold denotes diluted EPS (FASB 128). E-Estimated. NA-Not Available. NM-Not Meaningful. NR-Not Ranked.

Office—3333 Hillview Ave., Standord Research Park, Palo Alto, CA 94304-1223. **Tel**—(650) 493-4141. **Website**—http://www.wj.com **Chrmn**—D. A. Watkins. **Vice Chrmn**—H. R. Johnson. **Pres & CEO**—W. K. Kennedy Jr. **Secy**—C.D. Kelly. **VP & CFO**—S. G. Buchanan. **Investor Contact**—Frank E. Emery (650-813-2752). **Dirs**—G. M. Cusumano, W. R. Graham, J. J. Hartmann, H. R. Johnson, W. K. Kennedy Jr., R. F. O'Brien, R. L. Prestel, D. A. Watkins. **Incorporated**—in California in 1957. **Empl**— 1,200. **S&P Analyst**: B. McGovern

Watsco, Inc.

2429M

NYSE Symbol **WSO**

In S&P SmallCap 600

03-OCT-98

Industry:
Electrical Equipment

Summary: This company makes and distributes climate control equipment and also provides temporary help and permanent placement services.

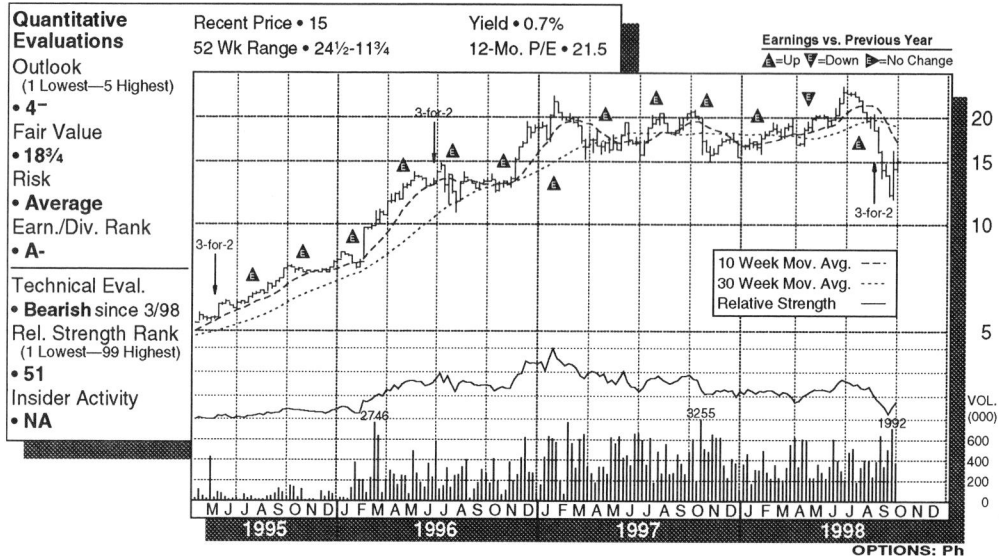

Quantitative Evaluations		
Outlook (1 Lowest—5 Highest)		
• **4-**		
Fair Value		
• **18¾**		
Risk		
• **Average**		
Earn./Div. Rank		
• **A-**		
Technical Eval.		
• **Bearish** since 3/98		
Rel. Strength Rank (1 Lowest—99 Highest)		
• **51**		
Insider Activity		
• **NA**		

Recent Price • 15
52 Wk Range • 24½-11¾
Yield • 0.7%
12-Mo. P/E • 21.5

Chart legend: 10 Week Mov. Avg. — — —, 30 Week Mov. Avg. · · · , Relative Strength ——

OPTIONS: Ph

Business Profile - 10-JUN-98

WSO seeks growth by increasing market share, and by identifying, acquiring and integrating other businesses in the highly fragmented air conditioning industry in an effort to leverage operating costs. Its strategy includes expansion in the Sunbelt region, where air conditioning usage is highest, the population is growing, and demand is more predictable, and a focus on the growing replacement market, where margins are wider and sales tend to offset cyclical downturns in housing. As of December 31, 1997, WSO served 22 states from 275 locations. In the first five months of 1998, the company completed seven acquisitions of wholesale distributors of air conditioning and heating equipment.

Operational Review - 10-JUN-98

Total revenues in the first quarter of 1998 advanced 79%, year to year, mainly reflecting the acquisition of several wholesale distributors of air conditioning and heating products. Gross margins widened on the higher volume, but with a sharp rise in SG&A expenses, hurt by greater selling and delivery costs on the increased sales levels, and substantially higher interest expense, pretax income declined 16%. After taxes at 37.0%, versus 38.5%, net income was down 14%, to $1,776,000 ($0.10 a share) from $2,061,000 ($0.12). Results in the 1997 period exclude income from discontinued operations of $0.01 a share.

Stock Performance - 02-OCT-98

In the past 30 trading days, WSO's shares have declined 18%, compared to a 7% fall in the S&P 500. Average trading volume for the past five days was 74,820 shares, compared with the 40-day moving average of 135,327 shares.

Key Stock Statistics

Dividend Rate/Share	0.10	Shareholders	600
Shs. outstg. (M)	24.6	Market cap. (B)	$0.371
Avg. daily vol. (M)	0.165	Inst. holdings	63%
Tang. Bk. Value/Share	5.71		
Beta	1.69		

Value of $10,000 invested 5 years ago: $ 44,026

Fiscal Year Ending Dec. 31

	1998	1997	1996	1995	1994	1993
Revenues (Million $)						
1Q	172.7	96.30	77.79	60.32	55.25	38.70
2Q	270.9	164.7	118.5	91.06	75.83	59.55
3Q	—	189.5	125.3	98.81	82.81	72.47
4Q	—	184.8	103.8	80.82	69.85	59.98
Yr.	—	635.2	425.4	331.0	283.7	230.7
Earnings Per Share ($)						
1Q	**0.06**	**0.08**	0.08	0.06	0.05	0.03
2Q	**0.31**	**0.22**	0.19	0.16	0.13	0.17
3Q	—	**0.25**	0.23	0.19	0.16	0.13
4Q	—	**0.12**	0.11	0.08	0.06	0.04
Yr.	—	**0.68**	0.62	0.48	0.40	0.37

Next earnings report expected: mid October

Dividend Data (Dividends have been paid since 1984.)

Amount ($)	Date Decl.	Ex-Div. Date	Stock of Record	Payment Date
0.035	Jan. 05	Jan. 13	Jan. 15	Jan. 30 '98
0.035	Apr. 03	Apr. 13	Apr. 15	Apr. 30 '98
0.035	Jul. 02	Jul. 13	Jul. 15	Jul. 31 '98
3-for-2	Jul. 16	Aug. 17	Jul. 31	Aug. 14 '98

A Division of The McGraw-Hill Companies

Business Summary - 10-JUN-98

Watsco is the largest U.S. independent distributor of residential central air conditioners and heating equipment and related parts and supplies. The company has enhanced its growth through acquisitions. Since 1989, Watsco has acquired more than 20 distributors of air conditioning and heating equipment.

Residential central air conditioning and heating equipment is sold to the replacement and the homebuilding markets. The replacement market has surpassed the homebuilding market in significance, as a result of the aging of the installed base of residential air conditioners. According to the Air Conditioning and Refrigeration Institute (ARI), more than 70 million central air conditioning units have been installed in the U.S. in the past 20 years, with approximately 60% of these units installed in the Sunbelt. The life of air conditioners can range from eight to 20 years.

Heating, ventilating and air-conditioning equipment is distributed through the Gemaire Distributors, Heating & Cooling Supply, and Comfort Supply subsidiaries, primarily in Florida, California, Texas, Arizona, North Carolina, Nevada and Louisiana. The company's primary equipment line is manufactured by Rheem Manufacturing Co., the second largest U.S. maker of residential central air conditioners.

The company's acquisition strategy is to establish a network of distribution facilities, particularly in the Sunbelt. The Sunbelt, which has the fastest population growth in the U.S., has a historically hot weather pattern and air conditioning is considered a necessity. Watsco seeks to enhance the value of acquired operations by serving the one-stop shopping needs of contractors. This includes broadening product line and committing other capital resources to develop the acquired businesses, including expanding existing locations and opening new locations.

In October 1997, WSO acquired Baker Distributing Co., a Sunbelt-based wholesale distributor of air conditioning, heating and refrigeration equipment and related parts. Baker (1997 sales $148 million) operates 83 branch locations serving more than 7,000 customers.

In November 1997, the company approved a plan to divest its non-distribution operations, Watsco Components, Inc. and Dunhill Staffing Systems, Inc. These operations were classified as discontinued in 1997. The company completed the sale of Watsco Components to International Comfort Products Corp. in June 1998.

In June 1998, Watsco signed a letter of intent to acquire Kaufman Supply, which distributes air conditioning and other products to the manufactured housing industry, for an undisclosed amount.

Per Share Data ($)

(Year Ended Dec. 31)	1997	1996	1995	1994	1993	1992	1991	1990	1989	1988
Tangible Bk. Val.	5.67	4.58	2.66	2.43	2.07	1.32	0.93	0.66	1.37	1.32
Cash Flow	0.86	0.83	0.69	0.56	0.52	0.51	0.42	0.45	0.46	0.20
Earnings	0.68	0.62	0.48	0.39	0.38	0.31	0.22	0.27	0.31	0.12
Dividends	0.09	0.09	0.08	0.08	0.07	0.05	0.10	0.08	0.08	0.08
Payout Ratio	14%	15%	17%	19%	20%	17%	44%	31%	28%	73%
Prices - High	22^7/$_8$	19^3/$_8$	8	5	5	3^7/$_8$	4^1/$_8$	3^1/$_8$	2^7/$_8$	2^3/$_8$
- Low	15	7^1/$_2$	4^5/$_8$	3^7/$_8$	3^3/$_8$	2^1/$_{16}$	3^1/$_8$	2^1/$_4$	1^{13}/$_{16}$	1^{11}/$_{16}$
P/E Ratio - High	34	31	17	13	13	12	19	11	9	20
- Low	22	12	10	10	9	7	14	8	6	16

Income Statement Analysis (Million $)

	1997	1996	1995	1994	1993	1992	1991	1990	1989	1988
Revs.	635	425	331	284	231	195	169	118	94.0	22.0
Oper. Inc.	37.8	28.4	21.0	17.4	13.2	11.8	10.4	8.3	7.0	1.8
Depr.	4.8	4.2	3.0	2.4	1.9	1.9	1.8	1.3	1.0	0.6
Int. Exp.	4.7	3.7	4.2	3.2	2.8	3.2	4.1	2.9	2.5	1.0
Pretax Inc.	29.8	21.2	14.1	12.0	10.1	7.1	5.0	4.2	3.7	0.9
Eff. Tax Rate	39%	38%	37%	39%	38%	39%	40%	36%	33%	18%
Net Inc.	18.3	13.0	7.3	5.6	5.0	2.9	2.0	1.9	2.0	0.8

Balance Sheet & Other Fin. Data (Million $)

	1997	1996	1995	1994	1993	1992	1991	1990	1989	1988
Cash	7.9	5.3	4.0	5.0	2.6	0.9	2.2	5.5	4.5	8.6
Curr. Assets	318	159	112	93.6	86.7	61.9	62.5	62.8	36.3	17.1
Total Assets	426	204	145	120	110	81.1	81.8	83.6	47.6	27.9
Curr. Liab.	60.3	29.0	71.2	53.6	47.4	17.3	16.8	17.1	11.4	3.3
LT Debt	137	51.7	6.3	6.7	7.8	30.3	36.8	39.7	20.7	11.3
Common Eqty.	226	120	53.8	46.8	41.8	25.3	20.8	18.9	12.8	11.7
Total Cap.	366	175	73.7	66.1	62.3	63.8	65.0	66.6	36.2	24.5
Cap. Exp.	6.6	5.4	4.3	4.2	1.9	2.0	1.1	0.9	1.0	0.6
Cash Flow	23.1	17.2	10.2	8.0	6.8	4.8	3.8	3.3	3.1	1.4
Curr. Ratio	5.3	5.5	1.6	1.7	1.8	3.6	3.7	3.7	3.2	5.2
% LT Debt of Cap.	37.7	29.6	8.6	10.2	12.6	47.5	56.6	59.6	57.2	46.1
% Net Inc.of Revs.	2.9	3.1	2.2	2.0	2.2	1.5	1.2	1.6	2.2	3.4
% Ret. on Assets	5.8	7.5	5.5	4.9	4.5	3.6	2.4	2.6	5.5	NM
% Ret. on Equity	10.6	15.0	14.4	12.7	13.0	12.7	9.9	10.7	16.6	NM

Data as orig. reptd.; bef. results of disc. opers. and/or spec. items. Per share data adj. for stk. divs. as of ex-div. date. Bold denotes diluted EPS (FASB 128). E-Estimated. NA-Not Available. NM-Not Meaningful. NR-Not Ranked.

Office—2665 South Bayshore Dr., Suite 901, Coconut Grove, FL 33133. **Tel**—(305) 858-0828. **Chrmn & Pres**—A. H. Nahmad. **VP-Fin, Secy & Investor Contact**—Barry S. Logan. **Dirs**—C. L. Alvarez, D. B. Fleeman, P. F. Manley, B. L. Moss, R. Motta, A. H. Nahmad, R. P. Newman, R. J. Novello, A. H. Potamkin. **Transfer Agent & Registrar**—First Union Bank, Charlotte, NC. **Incorporated**—in Florida in 1956. **Empl**— 2,000. **S&P Analyst:** SRB

Werner Enterprises   5606

Nasdaq Symbol **WERN**

In S&P SmallCap 600

03-OCT-98 | Industry: Truckers

Summary: This company provides a variety of truckload and logistics services throughout the United States. The Werner family holds 43% of the company's shares.

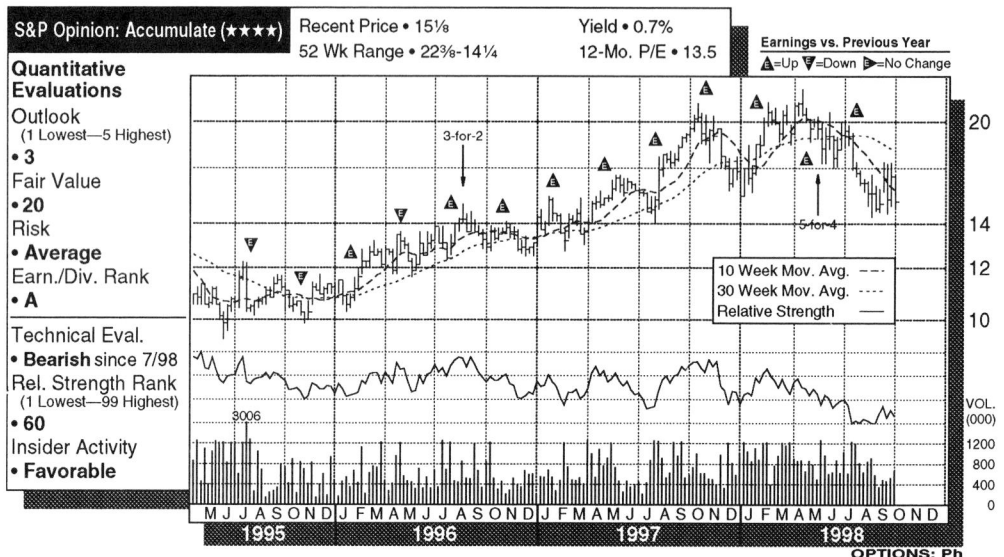

S&P Opinion: Accumulate (★★★★)	Recent Price • 15⅛	Yield • 0.7%
	52 Wk Range • 22⅜-14¼	12-Mo. P/E • 13.5

Quantitative Evaluations

Outlook (1 Lowest—5 Highest)
• 3

Fair Value
• 20

Risk
• **Average**

Earn./Div. Rank
• **A**

Technical Eval.
• **Bearish** since 7/98

Rel. Strength Rank (1 Lowest—99 Highest)
• **60**

Insider Activity
• **Favorable**

Earnings vs. Previous Year
▲=Up ▼=Down ▶=No Change

10 Week Mov. Avg. – – –
30 Week Mov. Avg. - - - -
Relative Strength ——

OPTIONS: Ph

Overview - 10-AUG-98

WERN's fleet growth is expected to slow to 10% in 1998, from 16% in 1997, as it finds it more difficult to attract salaried drivers and owner-operators. Capacity growth could accelerate in 1999, if WERN lifts driver mileage rates in late 1998. Supporting WERN's growth in 1998 is the conversion of 250 Dollar General trucks to a dedicated fleet operation. Logistics revenues may slip, following the loss of a major account. Margins are expected to widen in 1998, as higher labor costs are outweighed by lower fuel and workers' compensation costs. Revenue per mile is expected to increase at least 1% in 1998, versus a 1.4% improvement in 1997. Interest expense will increase somewhat, as WERN's capital spending requirements exceed cash flow. Gains on the sale of equipment could increase. The tax rate will rise, as the 1997 rate was lower than normal, due to a settlement of tax issues.

Valuation - 10-AUG-98

The shares of this leading truckload carrier came under pressure in mid-1998, as difficulties in attracting drivers caused WERN's growth rate to slip below the 15% target projected earlier in the year. In addition, investors are concerned that the current robust order rate for heavy-duty trucks will lead to depressed truckload rates in 1999. We think that WERN can jump start its growth rate in 1999, following an anticipated boost in driver pay in late 1998. The current order rate for trucks, while high, is mainly serving to replace older vehicles, rather than adding significantly to capacity. We like WERN, which has demonstrated leadership over the years in the use of technology to optimize operating efficiencies and, in the process, improve job satisfaction for drivers. At recent levels, the conservatively valued shares should be accumulated.

Key Stock Statistics

S&P EPS Est. 1998	1.20	Tang. Bk. Value/Share	8.79
P/E on S&P Est. 1998	12.6	Beta	0.29
S&P EPS Est. 1999	1.35	Shareholders	300
Dividend Rate/Share	0.10	Market cap. (B)	$0.723
Shs. outstg. (M)	47.8	Inst. holdings	52%
Avg. daily vol. (M)	0.109		

Value of $10,000 invested 5 years ago: $ 12,822

Fiscal Year Ending Dec. 31

	1998	1997	1996	1995	1994	1993
Revenues (Million $)						
1Q	199.7	172.1	147.9	132.4	116.0	94.70
2Q	211.7	193.6	159.6	143.3	129.6	102.5
3Q	—	200.2	167.2	150.3	134.6	108.9
4Q	—	206.2	168.6	150.0	135.8	112.2
Yr.	—	772.1	643.3	576.0	516.0	418.3
Earnings Per Share ($)						
1Q	**0.23**	**0.16**	0.15	0.16	0.15	0.13
2Q	**0.31**	**0.26**	0.22	0.18	0.20	0.19
3Q	**E0.33**	**0.30**	0.25	0.21	0.22	0.20
4Q	**E0.34**	**0.30**	0.24	0.21	0.21	0.17
Yr.	**E1.20**	**1.01**	0.86	0.78	0.77	0.68

Next earnings report expected: mid October

Dividend Data (Dividends have been paid since 1987.)

Amount ($)	Date Decl.	Ex-Div. Date	Stock of Record	Payment Date
0.025	—	Apr. 16	Apr. 20	May. 05 '98
5-for-4	Apr. 15	May. 14	Apr. 27	May. 13 '98
0.024	May. 15	Jul. 01	Jul. 06	Jul. 21 '98
0.024	Aug. 26	Oct. 01	Oct. 05	Oct. 20 '98

Business Summary - 10-AUG-98

Werner Enterprises is one of the largest U.S. truckload motor carriers. WERN has grown faster than its peers by leading the industry in the application of technology. In 1998, it became the first carrier to use electronic driver logs. The fastest growing segment of WERN's business is its dedicated fleet operation, in which it takes control of fleets formerly operated by private carriers. The Werner family controlled 43% of the shares as of May 1998.

WERN provides interstate and intrastate truckload services in all 48 contiguous states, the 10 Canadian provinces, and to points in Mexico. It offers shippers a broad range of services, including regional and long-haul dry van, temperature-controlled, flatbed, dedicated carriage and logistics. In its dedicated fleet service, WERN assumes total responsibility for the trucking needs of a specific customer. In February 1998, it took control of an additional 250 trucks for Dollar General Corp., a leading retailer. Werner Logistics, started in 1995, is a non-asset based service that manages all of a company's transportation, distribution and warehousing requirements.

WERN focuses on the premium end of the truckload market. Its chief selling point is its superior on-time and reliable service. Shippers also choose WERN because of its financial strength and new equipment fleet. Its use of technology has helped differentiate its product in a historically very price sensitive industry. Since 1992, all WERN trucks have been equipped with satellite communication devices. This lets WERN provide shippers with real-time update of the movement of their freight.

WERN has also used technology to improve operating and safety performance. Using sophisticated software, it minimizes empty miles and helps find loads that bring drivers back to their home base. Onboard computers monitor some two dozen mechanical functions for each truck, letting WERN alert drivers to potential safety hazards. WERN has pioneered the development of the electronic driver log. Beginning in 1998, all its trucks will use paperless logs. Instead of manually recording time spent driving, to comply with hours of service regulations, truck movement will be automatically monitored through a device supplied by Qualcomm Inc. WERN expects this to promote safety, help attract drivers, and aid productivity.

At December 31, 1997, WERN operated 5,350 tractors (average age 1.4 years): 4,490 company-owned and 860 owned by owner-operators. At that date, it operated 14,700 trailers (average age 2.8 years).

In January 1997, WERN increased mileage pay for company drivers and owner-operators by $0.02 a mile, a 7% increase. This was intended to help attract and retain qualified drivers (an industrywide problem).

Per Share Data ($)

(Year Ended Dec. 31)	1997	1996	1995	1994	1993	1992	1991	1990	1989	1988
Tangible Bk. Val.	8.27	7.34	6.54	5.85	5.16	3.87	NA	NA	NA	NA
Cash Flow	3.15	2.24	2.07	1.90	1.69	1.48	NA	NA	NA	NA
Earnings	1.01	0.86	0.77	0.77	0.68	0.57	NA	NA	NA	NA
Dividends	0.08	0.07	0.06	0.06	0.04	0.04	NA	NA	NA	NA
Payout Ratio	8%	8%	8%	7%	6%	7%	NA	NA	NA	NA
Prices - High	21¼	15	13¾	18	16¼	12⅛	NA	NA	NA	NA
- Low	12¾	10¼	9⅜	11⅜	9⅞	7⅜	NA	NA	NA	NA
P/E Ratio - High	21	18	18	23	24	21	NA	NA	NA	NA
- Low	13	12	12	15	14	13	NA	NA	NA	NA

Income Statement Analysis (Million $)

	1997	1996	1995	1994	1993	1992	1991	1990	1989	1988
Revs.	772	643	576	516	418	362	NA	NA	NA	NA
Oper. Inc.	150	131	122	114	95.0	80.0	NA	NA	NA	NA
Depr.	72.6	65.0	61.2	53.7	44.2	39.3	NA	NA	NA	NA
Int. Exp.	3.0	2.1	2.3	0.7	1.5	1.3	NA	NA	NA	NA
Pretax Inc.	76.1	65.7	59.6	60.0	49.7	39.9	NA	NA	NA	NA
Eff. Tax Rate	36%	38%	39%	39%	40%	40%	NA	NA	NA	NA
Net Inc.	48.4	40.6	36.4	36.7	30.0	24.1	NA	NA	NA	NA

Balance Sheet & Other Fin. Data (Million $)

	1997	1996	1995	1994	1993	1992	1991	1990	1989	1988
Cash	22.3	23.1	16.2	11.7	9.8	NA	NA	NA	NA	NA
Curr. Assets	146	116	101	88.2	75.7	NA	NA	NA	NA	NA
Total Assets	668	549	508	454	373	NA	NA	NA	NA	NA
Curr. Liab.	91.8	59.1	54.0	57.3	51.1	NA	NA	NA	NA	NA
LT Debt	60.0	30.0	40.0	30.0	Nil	Nil	Nil	Nil	Nil	Nil
Common Eqty.	395	348	309	276	245	NA	NA	NA	NA	NA
Total Cap.	547	461	425	372	299	NA	NA	NA	NA	NA
Cap. Exp.	216	118	132	NA	NA	NA	NA	NA	NA	NA
Cash Flow	121	106	97.6	90.4	74.1	63.5	NA	NA	NA	NA
Curr. Ratio	1.6	2.0	1.9	1.5	1.5	NA	NA	NA	NA	NA
% LT Debt of Cap.	11.0	6.5	9.6	8.1	Nil	Nil	Nil	Nil	Nil	Nil
% Net Inc.of Revs.	6.3	6.3	6.3	7.1	7.2	6.7	NA	NA	NA	NA
% Ret. on Assets	8.0	7.7	7.6	8.9	8.9	NA	NA	NA	NA	NA
% Ret. on Equity	13.0	9.2	12.4	14.1	14.4	NA	NA	NA	NA	NA

Data as orig. reptd.; bef. results of disc. opers. and/or spec. items. Per share data adj. for stk. divs. as of ex-div. date. Bold denotes diluted EPS (FASB 128). E-Estimated. NA-Not Available. NM-Not Meaningful. NR-Not Ranked.

Office—14507 Frontier Rd., P.O. Box 45308, Omaha, NE 68145-0308. **Tel**—(402) 895-6640. **Website**—http://www.werner.com **Chrmn & CEO**—C. L. Werner. **Vice Chrmn**—Curtis G. Werner. **Pres**—Gregory L. Werner. **VP, CFO & Treas**—J. J. Steele. **Secy**—J. L. Johnson. **EVP & Investor Contact**—R. E. Synowicki. **Dirs**—J. G. Doll, I. B. Epstein, D. W. Rogert, M. F. Thompson, G. H. Timmerman, C. G. Werner, C. L. Werner, Gary L. Werner, Gregory L. Werner. **Transfer Agent & Registrar**—ChaseMellon Shareholder Services, Ridgefield Park, NJ. **Incorporated**—in Nebraska in 1982. **Empl**— 7,521. **S&P Analyst:** Stephen R. Klein

Westwood One   5645

NASDAQ Symbol **WONE**

In S&P SmallCap 600

03-OCT-98

Industry:
Broadcasting (Television, Radio & Cable)

Summary: This company is the leading U.S. producer and distributor of radio programming and the largest radio network.

Quantitative Evaluations

Recent Price • 17¾	Yield • Nil
52 Wk Range • 38-15½	12-Mo. P/E • 30.2

Outlook
(1 Lowest—5 Highest)
• **3+**

Fair Value
• **18¾**

Risk
• **Average**

Earn./Div. Rank
• **B-**

Technical Eval.
• **Bullish** since 4/98

Rel. Strength Rank
(1 Lowest—99 Highest)
• **42**

Insider Activity
• **Neutral**

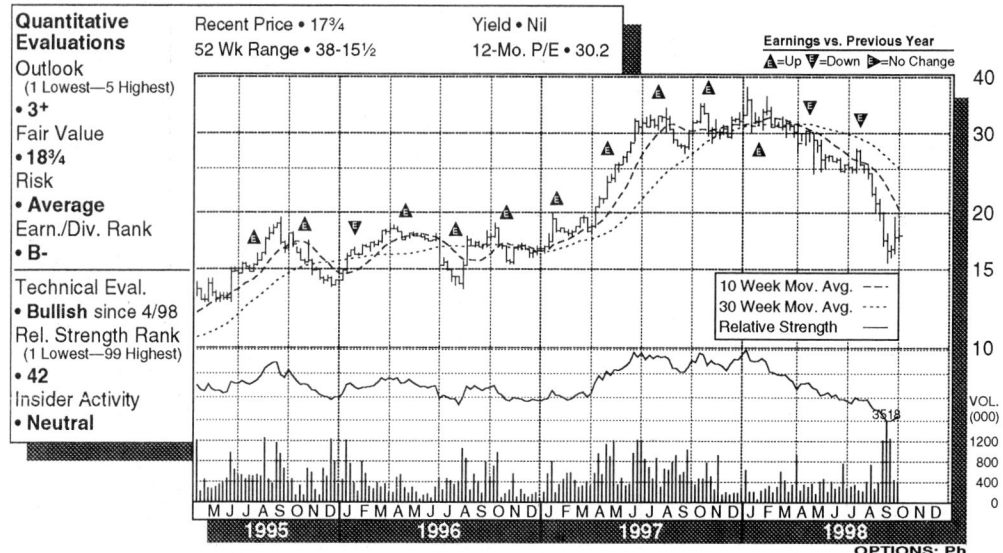

Earnings vs. Previous Year
▲=Up ▼=Down ▶=No Change

10 Week Mov. Avg. ---
30 Week Mov. Avg. ....
Relative Strength —

OPTIONS: Ph

Business Profile - 14-SEP-98

Westwood One, America's largest radio network, has expanded its operating strategy over the past several years to include providing traffic, news, sports and weather programming to radio stations and other media outlets in selected cities across the U.S. The company believes that free cash flow, defined as net income plus deferred taxes and depreciation and amortization less capital expenditures (excluding capitalized leases) is the relevant measure of its performance. In May 1998, the company acquired all remaining Shadow Traffic operations not already owned. Through August 11, 1998, WONE had repurchased about 948,000 of its common shares, at a total cost of about $25 million.

Operational Review - 14-SEP-98

Net revenues in the six months ended June 30, 1998, advanced 8.6%, year to year, primarily due to the company's CBS agreement and higher revenues from Shadow Traffic, partly offset by lower advertising revenues in the second quarter as a result of new competition. With higher operating costs, partly due to the CBS agreement, and increased depreciation and amortization charges, pretax income fell 29%. After taxes at 43.7% versus 8.2% (reflecting net operating loss carryforwards), net income plunged 56%, to $4,127,000 ($0.12 a share), from $9,487,000 ($0.27). Free cash flow was $0.33 a share in the 1998 second quarter, versus $0.34 in the 1997 period.

Stock Performance - 02-OCT-98

In the past 30 trading days, WONE's shares have declined 15%, compared to a 7% fall in the S&P 500. Average trading volume for the past five days was 78,620 shares, compared with the 40-day moving average of 228,092 shares.

Key Stock Statistics

Dividend Rate/Share	Nil	Shareholders	300
Shs. outstg. (M)	31.0	Market cap. (B)	$0.546
Avg. daily vol. (M)	0.312	Inst. holdings	69%
Tang. Bk. Value/Share	NM		
Beta	1.14		

Value of $10,000 invested 5 years ago: $ 109,612

Fiscal Year Ending Dec. 31

	1998	1997	1996	1995	1994	1993
Revenues (Million $)						
1Q	53.34	41.46	33.85	31.42	26.10	20.35
2Q	63.49	66.12	45.39	37.56	36.20	25.13
3Q	—	63.37	47.56	38.31	36.49	25.78
4Q	—	69.84	44.98	38.45	43.82	28.31
Yr.	—	240.8	171.8	145.7	136.3	99.6
Earnings Per Share ($)						
1Q	Nil	0.02	-0.02	-0.08	-0.29	-0.36
2Q	0.12	0.28	0.20	0.12	-0.07	-0.05
3Q	—	0.23	0.19	0.12	0.05	-0.04
4Q	—	0.23	0.14	0.11	0.23	-0.04
Yr.	—	0.74	0.52	0.28	-0.09	-0.57

Next earnings report expected: NA

Dividend Data

The most recent cash payment was $0.10 a share in 1985 (not adjusted for subsequent stock dividends).

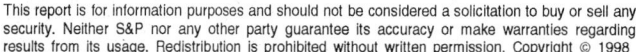

Business Summary - 14-SEP-98

Listen up! Whether it's traffic updates, news, NFL football, music countdown shows or other radio entertainment, there's a good chance some of what you're hearing is Westwood One, Inc. (WONE) programming. Based in Culver City, CA, WONE is the leading U.S. producer and distributor of radio programming and the largest radio network in the U.S. The company's more than 160 programs are broadcast in every radio market in the U.S. measured by Arbitron, the leading rating service, as well as internationally.

WONE is managed by CBS Radio Group (successor to Infinity Broadcasting Corporation) under a five-year agreement that expires March 31, 1999. Since the management of WONE was taken over by CBS Radio, the company has returned to profitability. A string of six years of losses was broken in 1995 (net income $9.7 million), and WONE was even more profitable in 1996 and 1997.

WONE's principal source of revenue is selling radio time to advertisers. The company's network strategy is to provide programming to individual stations that they may not be able to produce on their own. National advertisers are able to purchase advertising time and have their commercial messages broadcast on radio stations throughout the U.S. reaching demographically defined listening audiences.

Westwood One Radio Networks offers four news services (CNN Radio, CBS Radio news, NBC Radio news and Mutual news); The Source, featuring youth-oriented network news and entertainment programming; and eight 24-hour satellite delivered continuous play music formats. Westwood One Entertainment produces countdown shows, music and interview programs, talk shows, live concert broadcasts and satellite simulcasts, and major sporting events (mainly NFL, Notre Dame football and other college football and basketball games, NHL and the Olympics).

Westwood One Broadcasting Services provides radio stations and television and cable companies with local traffic, news, sports and weather programming through its Shadow Traffic, News and Sports service in New York, Chicago, Los Angeles and Philadelphia.

In March 1997, the company entered into a representation and management agreement with CBS Inc., under which WONE will operate the CBS Radio Network for an initial period of two years ending March 31, 1999. As a result, WONE now services more than 7,000 radio stations around the world.

Per Share Data ($)

(Year Ended Dec. 31)	1997	1996	1995	1994	1993	1992	1991	1990	1989	1988
Tangible Bk. Val.	NM	-3.79	-2.89	-3.09	-2.18	-8.66	-7.63	-9.13	-8.58	-3.55
Cash Flow	1.11	0.89	0.68	0.52	0.51	-1.01	-0.54	-0.63	-1.00	1.36
Earnings	0.74	0.52	0.28	-0.09	-0.57	-1.62	-1.13	-1.25	-1.58	0.12
Dividends	Nil	Nil	Nil	Nil	Nil	Nil	Nil	Nil	Nil	Nil
Payout Ratio	Nil	Nil	Nil	NM	Nil	Nil	Nil	Nil	Nil	Nil
Prices - High	38	19	19¹/₂	11⁵/₈	9¹/₂	3⁵/₈	3	9³/₄	13¹/₄	24³/₄
- Low	16³/₈	13¹/₂	9⁵/₈	7¹/₈	1⁵/₈	1¹/₂	1¹/₈	1¹/₂	7¹/₂	7¹/₂
P/E Ratio - High	51	37	70	NM	NM	NM	NM	NM	NM	NM
- Low	22	26	34	NM	NM	NM	NM	NM	NM	NM

Income Statement Analysis (Million $)

	1997	1996	1995	1994	1993	1992	1991	1990	1989	1988
Revs.	241	172	146	136	100	138	144	146	131	110
Oper. Inc.	48.9	39.5	33.1	26.5	14.2	1.0	7.7	5.2	-0.8	24.0
Depr.	13.0	12.3	13.8	18.2	16.4	9.1	8.7	9.1	8.3	17.2
Int. Exp.	8.5	8.7	9.5	8.8	6.6	17.8	18.7	21.2	18.1	6.9
Pretax Inc.	27.7	18.8	10.2	-2.5	-8.7	-35.7	-24.4	-26.2	-33.7	3.1
Eff. Tax Rate	8.04%	6.90%	4.90%	NM	NM	NM	NM	NM	NM	49%
Net Inc.	25.5	17.5	9.7	-2.7	-8.7	-8.7	-16.8	-18.2	-22.7	1.6

Balance Sheet & Other Fin. Data (Million $)

	1997	1996	1995	1994	1993	1992	1991	1990	1989	1988
Cash	2.8	2.6	0.3	2.0	4.0	6.0	1.0	6.0	2.0	14.0
Curr. Assets	77.9	48.4	41.9	46.0	33.0	51.0	46.0	54.0	55.0	68.0
Total Assets	336	273	246	260	152	296	323	344	353	301
Curr. Liab.	65.8	52.0	35.3	38.5	34.5	63.0	35.9	25.6	27.5	53.3
LT Debt	115	130	108	115	52.0	147	169	214	196	99
Common Eqty.	125	86.8	94.1	95.0	55.0	75.0	99	89.0	107	129
Total Cap.	258	217	202	211	107	222	276	304	309	237
Cap. Exp.	1.7	1.7	1.2	1.5	2.3	1.2	4.6	3.2	3.7	4.0
Cash Flow	38.5	29.8	23.4	15.4	7.7	7.7	-8.1	-9.1	-14.4	18.8
Curr. Ratio	1.2	0.9	1.2	1.2	1.0	0.8	1.3	2.1	2.0	1.3
% LT Debt of Cap.	44.6	59.9	53.4	54.7	48.5	66.1	61.3	70.4	63.4	41.6
% Net Inc.of Revs.	10.6	10.2	6.6	NM	NM	NM	NM	NM	NM	1.4
% Ret. on Assets	8.4	6.7	3.8	NM	NM	NM	NM	NM	NM	0.5
% Ret. on Equity	24.1	19.3	10.2	NM	NM	NM	NM	NM	NM	1.4

Data as orig. reptd.; bef. results of disc. opers. and/or spec. items. Per share data adj. for stk. divs. as of ex-div. date. Prior to 1995, fiscal year ended Nov. 30. Bold denotes diluted EPS (FASB 128). E-Estimated. NA-Not Available. NM-Not Meaningful. NR-Not Ranked.

Office—9540 Washington Blvd., Culver City, CA 90232. **Tel**—(310) 204-5000. **Chrmn**—N. J. Pattiz. **Pres & CEO**—M. Karmazin. **EVP, CFO & Secy**—F. Suleman. **Dirs**—D. L. Dennis, J. Greenberg, M. Karmazin, S. A. Lerman, A. E. Levine, N. J. Pattiz, J. B. Smith, F. Suleman. **Transfer Agent & Registrar**—First National Bank of Boston. **Incorporated**—in California in 1974; reincorporated in Delaware in 1985. **Empl**— 576. **S&P Analyst:** P.L.H.

Whitney Holding Corp. 5648M

NASDAQ Symbol **WTNY**

In S&P SmallCap 600

03-OCT-98

Industry: Banks (Regional)

Summary: This New Orleans-based bank holding company operates through offices in Louisiana, Mississippi, Alabama, Florida, and a foreign branch in the West Indies.

Quantitative Evaluations

Outlook
(1 Lowest—5 Highest)
• **2⁻**

Fair Value
• **42⅛**

Risk
• **Low**

Earn./Div. Rank
• **B**

Technical Eval.
• **Neutral** since 6/98

Rel. Strength Rank
(1 Lowest—99 Highest)
• **48**

Insider Activity
• **Favorable**

Recent Price • 39
52 Wk Range • 63½-34⅝

Yield • 3.1%
12-Mo. P/E • 14.9

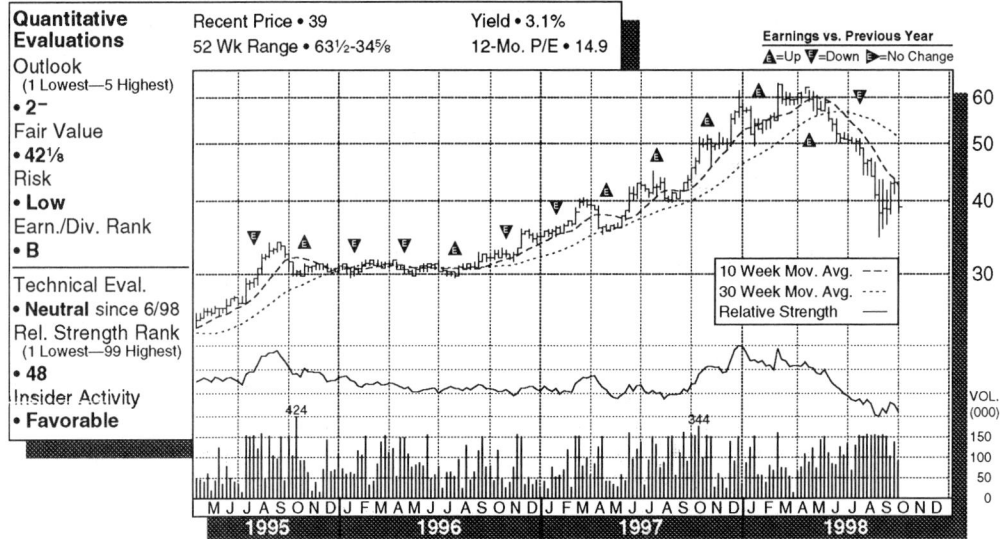

Earnings vs. Previous Year
▲=Up ▼=Down ▶=No Change

10 Week Mov. Avg. – – –
30 Week Mov. Avg. · · · ·
Relative Strength —

Business Profile - 08-SEP-98

Consolidation activity of WTNY continued in March 1998 with an announcement of a definitive agreement to merge with The First National Bancorp of Greenville, an Alabama Bank with $117 million in assets. The second quarter of 1998 marked the completion of two previous WTNY mergers, Louisiana National Security Bank and Meritrust Federal Savings Bank. The acquisition of these two banks added approximately $339 million in assets to WTNY. Within WTNY's current portfolio, nonperforming assets at June 30, 1998 were $15.9 million compared with $17.5 million a year earlier. Returns on equity and assets during the first six months of 1998 were 11.44% and 1.29%, respectively, versus 11.28% and 1.21% in the first half of 1997. WTNY increased its quarterly dividend 7.1%, to $0.30 versus $0.28, with the April 1998, payment.

Operational Review - 08-SEP-98

Total net interest income for the six months ended June 30, 1998, rose 7.8%, year to year. Net interest margins improved to 5.00% from 4.82% in the same period a year ago. Non-interest income increased 15%, reflecting increases in credit card transactions, trust services, secondary mortgage lending and service charges. The reserve for possible loan losses at the end of the quarter was $43.1 million or 378% of total nonaccruing loans. Non-interest expense increased 8.7%. Net income rose 11% to $29.8 million ($1.31 a share), from $26.9 million ($1.20).

Stock Performance - 02-OCT-98

In the past 30 trading days, WTNY's shares have declined 5%, compared to a 7% fall in the S&P 500. Average trading volume for the past five days was 18,220 shares, compared with the 40-day moving average of 32,397 shares.

Key Stock Statistics

Dividend Rate/Share	1.20	Shareholders	3,400
Shs. outstg. (M)	22.6	Market cap. (B)	$0.882
Avg. daily vol. (M)	0.025	Inst. holdings	19%
Tang. Bk. Value/Share	23.62		
Beta	0.75		

Value of $10,000 invested 5 years ago: $ 18,745

Fiscal Year Ending Dec. 31

	1998	1997	1996	1995	1994	1993
Revenues (Million $)						
1Q	87.24	76.87	65.64	53.39	50.59	49.38
2Q	98.75	86.65	66.15	55.22	52.16	51.44
3Q	—	89.95	68.36	57.15	53.66	49.82
4Q	—	88.97	78.88	59.66	41.70	49.88
Yr.	—	342.4	279.0	225.4	208.1	200.5
Earnings Per Share ($)						
1Q	**0.68**	**0.52**	0.47	0.55	1.09	0.49
2Q	**0.64**	**0.68**	0.58	0.55	0.65	3.03
3Q	—	**0.65**	0.60	1.03	0.93	1.11
4Q	—	**0.65**	0.61	0.64	0.97	0.62
Yr.	—	**2.50**	2.17	2.77	3.63	5.25

Next earnings report expected: mid October

Dividend Data (Dividends have been paid since 1993.)

Amount ($)	Date Decl.	Ex-Div. Date	Stock of Record	Payment Date
0.280	Nov. 19	Dec. 11	Dec. 15	Jan. 02 '98
0.300	Feb. 17	Mar. 12	Mar. 16	Apr. 01 '98
0.300	May. 27	Jun. 11	Jun. 15	Jul. 01 '98
0.300	Aug. 26	Sep. 11	Sep. 15	Oct. 01 '98

A Division of The **McGraw·Hill** Companies

Whitney Holding Corporation

Business Summary - 08-SEP-98

This New Orleans-based bank holding company has made seven separate banking acquisitions in the past four years and completed two more during the second quarter of 1998. By participating in the consolidation trend of the industry, WTNY has expanded its geographic reach, mostly along the coast of the Gulf of Mexico. WTNY now operates in Louisiana, Alabama, Mississippi, Florida, and has one foreign branch on Grand Cayman in the British West Indies.

The company operates through five banking subsidiaries: Whitney National Bank, Whitney Bank of Alabama, Whitney National Bank of Florida, First National Bank of Houma (acquired in February 1997), and Merchants Bank & Trust (April 1997). These banks offer a comprehensive line of financial services to individuals, businesses and other public and private institutions.

WTNY's lending activity is conducted primarily in its Gulf Coast market area. Loan growth has been healthy, with average loans increasing 21% in 1997, reflecting the strong economic condition of the region and the firm's aggressive solicitation of clients. The increase in loan activity was funded in part by maturing investment securities, which together declined $242 million or 15% in 1997.

The average loans balance, as of December 31, 1997, totaled $2.4 billion, and was comprised of commercial, financial, agricultural, and real estate loans. Average total deposits increased $108 million to $3.28 billion in 1997 from $3.17 billion in 1996. This growth is attributable in part to the introduction of new products and services by the company during the year. At the end of 1997, total deposits were $3.51 billion.

As of 1997 year end, the reserve for possible loan losses covered non-accruing loans by 4.75 times, and represented 1.9% of the total loans. Total non-performing assets, which includes non-accruing loans, in-substance foreclosures and other real estate, totaled $13 million, down 17% from a year earlier.

In 1997, the company acquired two banks in exchange for an aggregate of 2.58 million shares. It acquired two more banks in the first half of 1998, for a total of $92.5 million in stock. WTNY believes that its Gulf Coast market area offers potential for sustained above average economic growth, and will continue an expansion strategy developed in 1990.

Per Share Data ($)

(Year Ended Dec. 31)	1997	1996	1995	1994	1993	1992	1991	1990	1989	1988
Tangible Bk. Val.	22.10	21.35	20.61	19.38	17.36	12.68	11.50	NA	NA	NA
Earnings	2.50	2.26	2.77	3.63	5.25	1.41	-0.33	NA	NA	NA
Dividends	1.09	0.97	0.82	0.64	0.43	0.07	Nil	Nil	Nil	Nil
Payout Ratio	44%	43%	30%	18%	8%	5%	Nil	Nil	Nil	Nil
Prices - High	61¾	35⅞	34	28½	26⅛	17¼	10½	NA	NA	NA
- Low	34¾	29½	22	20¾	15⅝	8⅜	5¾	NA	NA	NA
P/E Ratio - High	25	16	12	8	5	12	NM	NM	NM	NM
- Low	14	13	8	6	3	6	NM	NM	NM	NM

Income Statement Analysis (Million $)

	1997	1996	1995	1994	1993	1992	1991	1990	1989	1988
Net Int. Inc.	184	152	129	124	121	112	99	NA	NA	NA
Tax Equiv. Adj.	NA	4.5	3.8	3.8	3.3	NA	NA	NA	NA	NA
Non Int. Inc.	51.0	37.3	31.3	32.4	31.0	27.2	26.9	NA	NA	NA
Loan Loss Prov.	-2.8	5.0	10.0	26.1	60.0	3.4	45.4	NA	NA	NA
Exp./Op. Revs.	68%	69%	68%	65%	65%	NA	NA	NA	NA	NA
Pretax Inc.	78.7	59.7	59.6	78.1	111	29.1	-6.7	NA	NA	NA
Eff. Tax Rate	34%	32%	31%	32%	32%	31%	NM	NM	NM	NM
Net Inc.	52.2	40.6	40.9	52.8	75.8	20.2	-4.7	NA	NA	NA
% Net Int. Marg.	4.97	4.81	5.00	4.79	4.75	4.52	3.99	NA	NA	NA

Balance Sheet & Other Fin. Data (Million $)

	1997	1996	1995	1994	1993	1992	1991	1990	1989	1988
Earning Assets:										
Money Mkt	222	234	231	215	297	NA	NA	NA	NA	NA
Inv. Securities	1,268	1,326	1,368	1,533	1,634	1,475	1,139	NA	NA	NA
Com'l Loans	1,192	993	1,150	868	NA	NA	NA	NA	NA	NA
Other Loans	1,456	1,072	289	192	NA	NA	NA	NA	NA	NA
Total Assets	4,313	3,775	3,151	2,913	3,003	2,953	2,858	NA	NA	NA
Demand Deposits	1,061	935	852	769	784	NA	NA	NA	NA	NA
Time Deposits	2,450	1,927	1,710	1,642	2,505	NA	NA	NA	NA	NA
LT Debt	Nil	Nil	Nil	Nil	Nil	Nil	Nil	Nil	Nil	Nil
Common Eqty.	479	405	338	298	260	185	170	NA	NA	NA
% Ret. on Assets	1.3	1.1	1.4	1.8	2.6	0.7	NM	NM	NM	NM
% Ret. on Equity	11.8	10.4	13.0	19.1	34.8	11.5	NM	NM	NM	NM
% Loan Loss Resv.	1.6	1.9	2.6	3.3	4.6	9.4	8.5	NA	NA	NA
% Loans/Deposits	NA	72.2	56.2	44.0	39.0	41.2	51.9	NA	NA	NA
% Equity to Assets	10.9	10.7	10.7	10.2	8.6	6.3	5.8	NA	NA	NA

Data as orig. reptd.; bef. results of disc opers. and/or spec. items. Per share data adj. for stk. divs. as of ex-div. date. Bold denotes diluted EPS (FASB 128). E-Estimated. NA-Not Available. NM-Not Meaningful. NR-Not Ranked.

Office—228 St. Charles Ave., New Orleans, LA 70130 (P. O. Box 61260, New Orleans 70161). **Tel**—(504) 586-7272. **Chrmn & CEO**—W. L. Marks. **Pres**—R. King Milling. **EVP, CFO & Investor Contact**—Edward Grimball. **Dirs**—G. C. Billups, H. J. Blumenthal Jr., J. B. Bullard Jr., J. M. Cain, A. R. Cooper II, R. H. Crosby Jr., R. B. Crowell, C. A. Cutrone, W. A. Hines, R. E. Howson, J. J. Kelly, E. J. Kock Jr., A. S. Lippman, W. L. Marks, R. K. Milling, J. G. Phillips, J. K. Roberts Jr., C. W. Suggs, W. P. Snyder III, W. K. Watters. **Transfer Agent & Registrar**—Boatmen's Trust Co., St. Louis, MO. **Incorporated**—in Louisiana in 1962. **Empl**— 1,958. **S&P Analyst:** N.R.

Whittaker Corp. 2480

NYSE Symbol **WKR**

In S&P SmallCap 600

03-OCT-98

Industry: Electronics (Defense)

Summary: This company makes products for aerospace and industrial markets, with increasing emphasis on commercial applications, primarily telecommunications.

Quantitative Evaluations

Recent Price • 14½
52 Wk Range • 15⅞-7⅛

Yield • Nil
12-Mo. P/E • NM

Outlook
(1 Lowest—5 Highest)
• **NA**

Fair Value
• **NA**

Risk
• **Average**

Earn./Div. Rank
• **C**

Technical Eval.
• **NA**

Rel. Strength Rank
(1 Lowest—99 Highest)
• **84**

Insider Activity
• **NA**

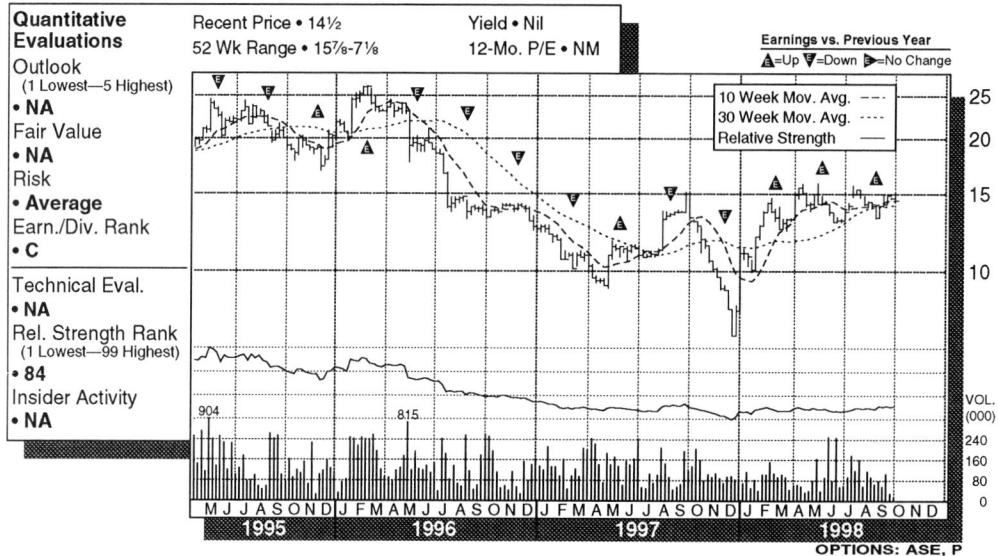

Earnings vs. Previous Year
▲=Up ▼=Down ▶=No Change

10 Week Mov. Avg. ---
30 Week Mov. Avg. ····
Relative Strength ——

OPTIONS: ASE, P

Business Profile - 02-JUL-98

In order to focus on its core aerospace business, the company completed the sale of its defense electronics unit in October 1997, and, in January 1998, agreed to sell its Xyplex Networks unit. In May 1998, WKR entered into a new $85 million credit agreement. Initial proceeds were used to repay all of the approximately $70 million debt outstanding under the company's prior bank credit facility. In addition, Whittaker expects to use the credit facility to finance strategic aerospace acquisitions that will leverage the company's position in the aerospace controls and safety systems businesses.

Operational Review - 02-JUL-98

For the six months ended April 30, 1998, sales from continuing operations rose 43%, year to year. Margins widened and operating profit increased to $14,698,000 from $1,770,000. Following higher interest income and taxes at $99,000 only in the FY 98 (Oct.) period, income from continuing operations of $6,185,000 ($0.54 a share), contrasted with a loss of $7,203,000 ($0.65). Per share results excludes a gain a disposal of discontinued operations of $0.90 in FY 98, and losses from discontinued operations of $4.07 in FY 97.

Stock Performance - 02-OCT-98

In the past 30 trading days, WKR's shares have increased 2%, compared to a 7% fall in the S&P 500. Average trading volume for the past five days was 2,760 shares, compared with the 40-day moving average of 14,118 shares.

Key Stock Statistics

Dividend Rate/Share	Nil	Shareholders	4,900
Shs. outstg. (M)	11.3	Market cap. (B)	$0.164
Avg. daily vol. (M)	0.010	Inst. holdings	84%
Tang. Bk. Value/Share	0.60		
Beta	0.39		

Value of $10,000 invested 5 years ago: $ 11,958

Fiscal Year Ending Oct. 31

	1998	1997	1996	1995	1994	1993
Revenues (Million $)						
1Q	31.80	19.70	44.42	26.69	25.77	29.28
2Q	34.96	22.90	47.61	31.68	28.85	29.26
3Q	33.94	24.00	62.16	44.35	33.11	26.78
4Q	—	28.50	67.69	56.76	38.72	30.07
Yr.	—	95.13	221.9	159.5	126.5	115.4
Earnings Per Share ($)						
1Q	**0.03**	-1.63	0.20	0.18	0.18	0.17
2Q	**0.51**	-3.09	-0.52	0.02	0.20	0.22
3Q	**2.29**	-2.43	-0.54	0.18	0.31	0.08
4Q	—	-1.60	-0.74	0.44	0.37	0.34
Yr.	—	-2.95	-1.70	0.82	1.06	0.81

Next earnings report expected: mid December

Dividend Data

Dividends, initiated in 1978, were discontinued in 1989 in connection with a recapitalization and payment of a $40 special distribution. A "poison pill" stock purchase rights plan was adopted in 1988.

A Division of The **McGraw-Hill** Companies

Business Summary - 02-JUL-98

While its core commercial aerospace business remained profitable, Whittaker Corp. (WKR) posted a $17.1 million net loss from continuing operations in FY 96 (Oct.). Losses widened to $32.9 million in FY 97. Mounting losses from discontinued operations, attributed to writeoffs related to the company's troubled communications segment, prompted WKR to engage financial advisers to help it explore a number of strategic options, including the sale of Xyplex Networks, its remote access and data networking operation. WKR is engaged in ongoing discussions with potential buyers. Net proceeds of any such sales would be used to prepay the company's term loan. In addition, strategic options being considered may include the outright sale of the company. In October 1997, WKR completed the sale of its defense electronics unit. In FY 97, the loss from the company's discontinued Xyplex Networks and defense electronics operations amounted to $122.5 million ($10.99 a share).

The Aerospace segment makes a broad range of fluid control devices used to control pneumatic, hydraulic and fuel flows in commercial and military aircraft. In commercial applications, the company's devices are used on virtually all Boeing, McDonnell Douglas, and AirBus commercial aircraft and virtually all other aircraft manufactured throughout the world. In addition, commercial and industrial applications include ground fueling devices for airports, heat exchangers, and fuel skids for land-based gas turbines, off-shore oil platforms, and petrochemical complexes. In military applications, the products are used on military transports, bombers, helicopters, fighters and landing craft. Sales of fluid control devices were $63.5 million in FY 97, down from $73.9 million in FY 96. The aerospace group also sells fire and overheat detectors for use in aircraft and demanding industrial applications. Sales of fire and overheat detectors were $19.5 million in FY 97, down from $21.8 million in FY 96.

At October 31, 1997, the Aerospace division's backlog totaled $70.5 million, of which $10.9 million is not expected to be filled in FY 98. Sales to the U.S. government dropped to 19% of sales from 27% in FY 96. Export sales to international customers represented 21% of Aerospace sales in FY 97, versus 24% in FY 96.

The Integration Services segment provides systems integration for the healthcare industry through its Aviant Information, Inc. subsidiary. Aviant addresses critical issues for health care organizations such as network management, collaborative communication, security management, and remote-access implementation. Integration Services accounted for 6% of sales in FY 97.

At October 31, 1997 Aviant's backlog totaled $5.3 million, of which $0.5 million is not expected to be filled in FY 98.

Per Share Data ($) (Year Ended Oct. 31)	1997	1996	1995	1994	1993	1992	1991	1990	1989	1988
Tangible Bk. Val.	NM	NM	6.80	11.06	7.84	7.92	6.13	3.89	-10.99	18.10
Cash Flow	-2.70	0.15	1.68	1.68	1.42	2.07	1.85	2.13	1.93	6.00
Earnings	-2.95	-1.70	0.82	1.06	0.81	1.42	1.27	0.66	0.41	3.30
Dividends	Nil	Nil	Nil	Nil	Nil	Nil	Nil	Nil	40.25	1.00
Payout Ratio	Nil	Nil	Nil	Nil	Nil	Nil	Nil	Nil	NM	30%
Prices - High	15 1/8	26 3/8	24 5/8	20	16 1/4	14 1/2	24 1/4	12	53 1/4	52 1/4
- Low	7 1/8	12 1/4	16 7/8	13 1/2	11 7/8	10 1/4	8 7/8	7 1/2	7 5/8	23
P/E Ratio - High	NM	NM	30	19	20	10	19	18	NM	16
- Low	NM	NM	21	13	15	7	7	11	NM	7
Income Statement Analysis (Million $)										
Revs.	95.1	222	160	122	115	160	159	188	210	499
Oper. Inc.	2.7	0.4	27.0	22.4	21.0	33.0	30.0	39.0	43.0	65.0
Depr.	2.8	18.6	8.1	5.9	5.7	6.2	5.2	12.4	11.5	18.4
Int. Exp.	18.3	11.0	5.9	4.0	3.9	5.6	6.6	11.7	11.9	7.2
Pretax Inc.	-37.1	-26.2	13.0	16.5	13.0	22.0	19.0	9.0	6.0	39.0
Eff. Tax Rate	NM	NM	39%	39%	39%	39%	39%	39%	45%	41%
Net Inc.	-32.9	-17.1	7.9	10.1	7.7	13.4	11.4	5.6	3.5	23.1
Balance Sheet & Other Fin. Data (Million $)										
Cash	6.4	1.6	0.2	4.0	Nil	3.0	2.0	6.0	10.0	3.0
Curr. Assets	93.9	148	124	118	116	135	113	127	200	215
Total Assets	167	379	251	209	202	218	199	243	413	436
Curr. Liab.	170	213	50.2	37.0	42.0	49.0	54.0	62.0	217	160
LT Debt	0.2	0.5	70.7	55.0	57.0	67.0	55.0	104	198	36.0
Common Eqty.	-30.7	131	102	94.0	84.0	75.0	58.0	39.0	-49.0	193
Total Cap.	-30.7	154	189	161	150	151	121	154	161	242
Cap. Exp.	2.3	4.8	6.4	2.5	1.3	2.2	2.0	4.2	5.9	15.4
Cash Flow	-30.1	1.5	16.0	16.0	13.4	19.5	16.5	17.9	14.6	40.9
Curr. Ratio	0.6	0.7	2.5	3.2	2.8	2.7	2.1	2.1	0.9	1.3
% LT Debt of Cap.	NM	0.3	37.3	34.1	37.8	44.2	45.4	67.4	NM	15.0
% Net Inc.of Revs.	NM	NM	5.0	8.2	6.7	8.4	7.2	3.0	1.6	4.6
% Ret. on Assets	NM	NM	3.4	4.9	3.6	6.4	4.9	1.7	0.8	5.3
% Ret. on Equity	NM	NM	8.0	11.3	9.5	20.0	22.5	NM	3.9	12.2

Data as orig. reptd.; bef. results of disc. opers. and/or spec. items. Per share data adj. for stk. divs. as of ex-div. date. Bold denotes diluted EPS (FASB 128). E-Estimated. NA-Not Available. NM-Not Meaningful. NR-Not Ranked.

Office—1955 N. Surveyor Ave., Simi Valley, CA 93063**Tel**—(805) 526-5700.**Website**—http://www.wkr.com **Chrmn & CEO**—J. F. Alibrandi.**Vice Chrmn**—G. T. Parkos.**VP, CFO & Treas**—J. K. Otto**Dirs**—J. F. Alibrandi, G. H. Benter Jr., G. Deukmejian, J. L. Hancock, E. R. Muller, G. T. Parkos, M. T. Stamper.**Transfer Agent & Registrar**—Mellon Securities Trust Co., Pittsburgh.**Incorporated**—in California in 1947; reincorporated in Delaware in 1986.**Empl**— 500. **S&P Analyst:** M.J.C.

03-OCT-98

Industry:
Services (Computer Systems)

Summary: This company provides strategic information technology business solutions designed to improve clients' productivity and competitive position.

Quantitative Evaluations	
Outlook (1 Lowest—5 Highest) • **NA**	Recent Price • 16
Fair Value • **NA**	52 Wk Range • 25⅜-11⅞
Risk • **High**	Yield • Nil
Earn./Div. Rank • **NR**	12-Mo. P/E • 66.7

Technical Eval.
• **NA**

Rel. Strength Rank
(1 Lowest—99 Highest)
• **20**

Insider Activity
• **Neutral**

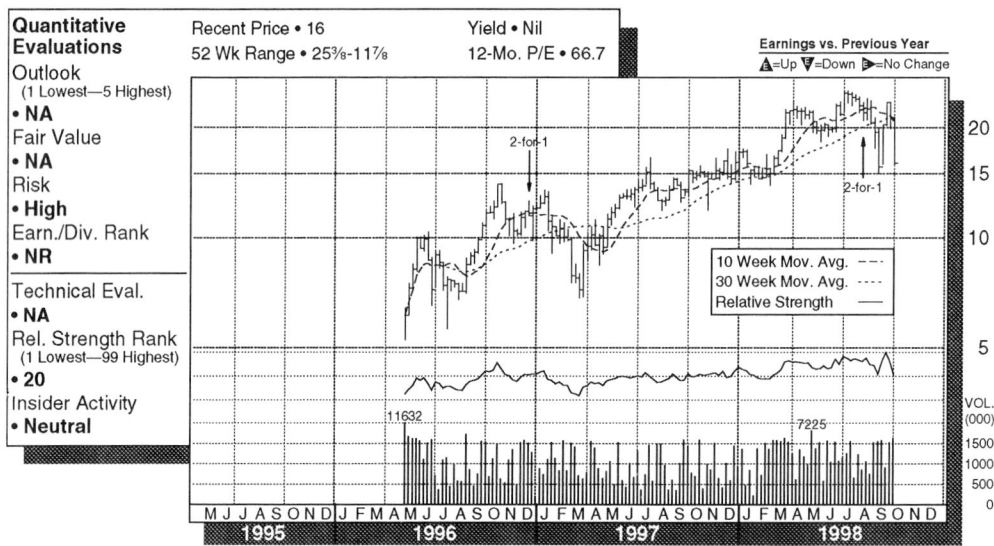

Earnings vs. Previous Year
▲=Up ▼=Down ▶=No Change

10 Week Mov. Avg. ---
30 Week Mov. Avg. ....
Relative Strength —

Business Profile - 11-JUN-98

In 1997, Whittman-Hart launched a five-year business plan known as Focus 2002, which is focused on the company becoming a trusted business adviser to its clients and the employer of choice in the IT services industry. Key components of Focus 2002 include a concentration of middle market companies, where demand is expected to remain strong for IT services; expanding geographic presence by adding branches in targeted locations; anticipating and responding to market opportunities by launching new IT services; leveraging the existing client base by marketing additional services; and pursuing agreements with business partners to share technical and industry knowledge. Management owns about 35% of the common stock.

Operational Review - 11-JUN-98

Revenues in the first quarter of 1998 advanced 68%, year to year, reflecting the addition of new clients and growth of client relationships at existing and new branch locations. Gross margins widened on a more favorable sales mix of higher-end service offerings. With an 83% rise in operating expenses, driven by acquisition integration costs, initiatives related to a Focus 2002 strategic plan and costs for new branch locations, pretax income climbed 36%. After taxes at 47.7%, versus 40.2%, net income was up 19%, to $3,024,902 ($0.12 a share) from $2,549,469 ($0.11).

Stock Performance - 02-OCT-98

In the past 30 trading days, WHIT's shares have declined 22%, compared to a 7% fall in the S&P 500. Average trading volume for the past five days was 610,020 shares, compared with the 40-day moving average of 351,210 shares.

Key Stock Statistics

Dividend Rate/Share	Nil	Shareholders	100
Shs. outstg. (M)	51.2	Market cap. (B)	$0.819
Avg. daily vol. (M)	0.447	Inst. holdings	56%
Tang. Bk. Value/Share	3.68		
Beta	NA		

Value of $10,000 invested 5 years ago: NA

Fiscal Year Ending Dec. 31

	1998	1997	1996	1995	1994	1993
Revenues (Million $)						
1Q	58.66	29.05	—	—	—	—
2Q	68.94	34.73	—	—	—	—
3Q	—	39.25	—	—	—	—
4Q	—	51.89	—	—	—	—
Yr.	—	173.5	103.7	—	—	—
Earnings Per Share ($)						
1Q	**0.06**	0.05	0.03	—	—	—
2Q	**0.09**	0.06	0.03	—	—	—
3Q	—	0.07	0.04	—	—	—
4Q	—	**0.04**	0.05	—	—	—
Yr.	—	**0.22**	0.15	—	—	—

Next earnings report expected: mid October

Dividend Data

Amount ($)	Date Decl.	Ex-Div. Date	Stock of Record	Payment Date
2-for-1	Jul. 01	Aug. 03	Jul. 12	Jul. 31 '98

 A Division of The McGraw-Hill Companies

Business Summary - 11-JUN-98

Providing strategic information technology business solutions to improve the productivity and competitive position of its clients, Whittman-Hart is a single source for a wide range of services required to design, develop and implement integrated solutions in the client/server, open systems and midrange computing environments. Its marketing efforts focus on middle-market companies ranging from $50 million to $500 million in revenues.

The company has five business units: Solution Strategies, Package Software Solutions, Custom Applications, Network Enabled Solutions and Interactive Solutions. The Solution Strategies unit helps clients identify their critical business objectives and formulates integrated people, process and technology solutions to improve their business. The Package Software Solutions segment uses a business-requirements and user-driven methodology for rapid package software implementation.

The Custom Applications unit develops and maintains custom business software applications, from analysis and design through software testing and quality assurance. The Network Enabled Solutions segment uses network computing strategies and technologies to develop business connectivity solutions that allow people, technology and organizations to work regardless of ge-

ographic location. The Interactive Solutions unit helps clients assess their training and education needs and develops appropriate strategies.

Services are sold and delivered through a network of 15 branch offices throughout the U.S. and in London. The company serves a wide range of industries including communications, consumer products, distribution, diversified services, financial services, insurance, manufacturing, pharmaceutical, professional services, retail and technology.

Expansion plans for 1998 call for significant growth of recently opened operations in Minneapolis, continued evaluation of strategic acquisitions and solidifying the company's Midwest presence by opening branches in cities such as Detroit, St. Louis and Kansas City. In November 1997, the company expanded its geographic reach and established its international presence through the acquisition of Axis Consulting International and World Consulting Limited, which provide enterprise, database and midrange solutions and implementation solutions.

In March 1998, the company acquired Boston-based QCC, Inc., which provides package software evaluation, business process reengineering, data warehousing, software package implementation and application development for client servers.

Per Share Data ($)

(Year Ended Dec. 31)	1997	1996	1995	1994	1993	1992	1991	1990	1989	1988
Tangible Bk. Val.	2.15	1.83	NA	NA	NA	NA	NA	NA	NA	NA
Cash Flow	0.27	0.19	NA	NA	NA	NA	NA	NA	NA	NA
Earnings	0.22	0.15	NA	NA	NA	NA	NA	NA	NA	NA
Dividends	Nil	Nil	Nil	Nil	Nil	Nil	Nil	Nil	Nil	Nil
Payout Ratio	Nil	Nil	Nil	Nil	Nil	Nil	Nil	Nil	Nil	Nil
Prices - High	17½	14⅛	NA	NA	NA	NA	NA	NA	NA	NA
- Low	6⅞	4	NA	NA	NA	NA	NA	NA	NA	NA
P/E Ratio - High	80	97	NA	NA	NA	NA	NA	NA	NA	NA
- Low	31	28	NA	NA	NA	NA	NA	NA	NA	NA

Income Statement Analysis (Million $)

	1997	1996	1995	1994	1993	1992	1991	1990	1989	1988
Revs.	173	104	NA	NA	NA	NA	NA	NA	NA	NA
Oper. Inc.	18.4	9.2	NA	NA	NA	NA	NA	NA	NA	NA
Depr.	2.5	1.3	NA	NA	NA	NA	NA	NA	NA	NA
Int. Exp.	0.0	0.1	NA	NA	NA	NA	NA	NA	NA	NA
Pretax Inc.	18.1	9.2	NA	NA	NA	NA	NA	NA	NA	NA
Eff. Tax Rate	43%	37%	NA	NA	NA	NA	NA	NA	NA	NA
Net Inc.	10.3	5.8	NA	NA	NA	NA	NA	NA	NA	NA

Balance Sheet & Other Fin. Data (Million $)

	1997	1996	1995	1994	1993	1992	1991	1990	1989	1988
Cash	9.1	36.5	NA	NA	NA	NA	NA	NA	NA	NA
Curr. Assets	106	87.5	NA	NA	NA	NA	NA	NA	NA	NA
Total Assets	122	94.1	NA	NA	NA	NA	NA	NA	NA	NA
Curr. Liab.	23.1	13.4	NA	NA	NA	NA	NA	NA	NA	NA
LT Debt	Nil	Nil	Nil	Nil	Nil	Nil	Nil	Nil	Nil	Nil
Common Eqty.	97.2	79.6	NA	NA	NA	NA	NA	NA	NA	NA
Total Cap.	97.4	79.8	NA	NA	NA	NA	NA	NA	NA	NA
Cap. Exp.	10.9	4.0	NA	NA	NA	NA	NA	NA	NA	NA
Cash Flow	12.8	7.1	NA	NA	NA	NA	NA	NA	NA	NA
Curr. Ratio	4.6	6.5	NA	NA	NA	NA	NA	NA	NA	NA
% LT Debt of Cap.	Nil	Nil	Nil	Nil	Nil	Nil	Nil	Nil	Nil	Nil
% Net Inc.of Revs.	5.9	5.6	NA	NA	NA	NA	NA	NA	NA	NA
% Ret. on Assets	9.7	NA	NA	NA	NA	NA	NA	NA	NA	NA
% Ret. on Equity	11.7	NA	NA	NA	NA	NA	NA	NA	NA	NA

Data as orig. reptd.; bef. results of disc. opers. and/or spec. items. Per share data adj. for stk. divs. as of ex-div. date. Bold denotes diluted EPS (FASB 128). E-Estimated. NA-Not Available. NM-Not Meaningful. NR-Not Ranked.

Office—311 South Wacker Dr., Suite 3500, Chicago, IL 60606-6618. **Tel**—(312) 922-9200. **Chrmn & CEO**—R. F. Bernard. **Pres & Secy**—E. V. Szofer. **CFO & Investor Contact**—Kevin M. Gaskey. **COO**—S. F. Martin. **Dirs**—R. F. Bernard, P. D. Carbery, L. P. Roches, R. F. Steel, E. V. Szofer. **Transfer Agent & Registrar**—Harris Trust and Savings Bank, Chicago. **Incorporated**—in Delaware in 1991. **Empl**— 1,974. **S&P Analyst:** Stephen R. Biggar

03-OCT-98

Industry: Retail (Food Chains)

Summary: This company owns and operates the largest U.S. chain of natural foods supermarkets, with 85 stores in 19 states and the District of Columbia.

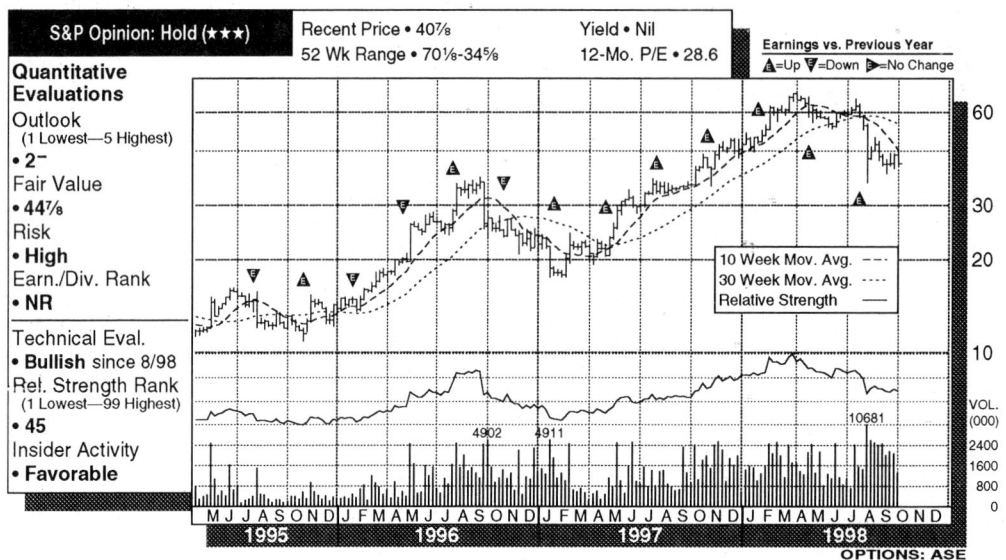

S&P Opinion: Hold (★★★)	Recent Price • 40⅞	Yield • Nil
	52 Wk Range • 70⅛-34⅝	12-Mo. P/E • 28.6

Quantitative Evaluations

Outlook (1 Lowest—5 Highest)
• **2⁻**

Fair Value
• **44⅞**

Risk
• **High**

Earn./Div. Rank
• **NR**

Technical Eval.
• **Bullish** since 8/98

Rel. Strength Rank (1 Lowest—99 Highest)
• **45**

Insider Activity
• **Favorable**

Earnings vs. Previous Year ▲=Up ▼=Down ▶=No Change

10 Week Mov. Avg. – – –
30 Week Mov. Avg. ·······
Relative Strength ——

OPTIONS: ASE

Overview - 05-AUG-98

Sales in the fourth quarter of FY 98 (Sep.) should grow in the 22% to 25% range, fueled by contributions from acquisitions, the addition of approximately six new stores, and same-store sales gains of 8.0% to 10%. Sales growth will also be boosted by continued improvement in the Southern California market, as well as by an expanded offering of prepared foods and marketing initiatives aimed at having customers do all of their shopping in the company's natural foods superstores. Gross margins are expected to be flat, as higher produce costs are offset by greater sales of higher-margin private-label products. For the longer term, gross margins may be affected by price competition in the nutritional supplement category. This has led us to trim our earnings growth expectations from 25% to 30% annually to 20%.

Valuation - 05-AUG-98

We recently downgraded the shares to hold, from buy, based on lower expected gross margins for the foreseeable future. In addition, same-store sales growth is likely to slow from their 10% plus rate to high single digits, as the company's store mass grows more mature. WFMI's Amrion division is likely to experience lower gross margins, as price competition increases in the nutritional supplement segment. We continue to expect the company to earn $1.63 a share in FY 98, with an advance to $2.06 in FY 99, but, given the expected narrowing of gross margins, we have reduced our annual earnings growth rate expectations to 20%, from 25% to 30%. As a result, we see the shares as fairly valued, and believe that they should only track the market over the next 12 months.

Key Stock Statistics

S&P EPS Est. 1998	1.63	Tang. Bk. Value/Share	8.29
P/E on S&P Est. 1998	25.1	Beta	1.17
S&P EPS Est. 1999	2.00	Shareholders	1,400
Dividend Rate/Share	Nil	Market cap. (B)	$ 1.1
Shs. outstg. (M)	26.4	Inst. holdings	70%
Avg. daily vol. (M)	0.396		

Value of $10,000 invested 5 years ago: $ 32,376

Fiscal Year Ending Sep. 30

	1998	1997	1996	1995	1994	1993
Revenues (Million $)						
1Q	407.8	312.6	245.0	139.0	116.5	88.71
2Q	324.8	259.8	203.9	117.0	92.77	75.48
3Q	331.0	274.5	213.4	119.9	97.36	79.52
4Q	—	270.4	230.8	120.5	95.10	78.60
Yr.	—	1,117	892.0	496.4	401.6	322.3
Earnings Per Share ($)						
1Q	**0.44**	0.24	Nil	0.17	0.18	0.15
2Q	**0.40**	0.29	0.08	0.18	0.14	0.13
3Q	**0.40**	0.32	0.23	0.07	0.15	0.13
4Q	**E0.39**	0.20	-1.22	0.16	0.14	-0.10
Yr.	**E1.63**	1.05	-0.90	0.58	0.61	0.29

Next earnings report expected: NA

Dividend Data

No cash dividends have been paid. WFMI intends to retain earnings for use in its business and therefore does not anticipate paying any cash dividends in the foreseeable future. A two-for-one stock split was effected in 1993.

Business Summary - 05-AUG-98

One-stop shopping for the health-conscious consumer of the 90s: that's what Whole Foods Market (WFMI) is aiming to provide. WFMI operates the largest U.S. chain of natural foods supermarkets, with 86 stores open in 19 states and Washington, DC, as of early August 1998. Its stores offer organic fruits and vegetables, poultry and meats free from antibiotics and growth hormones, as well as conventionally grown, high-quality foods. Hearth-baked crusty breads, a full line of natural household supplies and body care products are also available. Each store averages about 24,000 sq. ft. and offers a selection of about 10,000 to 18,000 food and non-food products. In addition, the company covers every item sold in its stores with a 100% money-back guarantee.

The company's first natural foods supermarket was launched in 1981 in Austin, TX. Then, as now, WFMI's goal was to provide the highest quality foods that it can find, in terms of taste, appearance and nutrition. WFMI operates under several different names, using the Whole Foods Market name in TX, CA, LA, IL, MI, WI and FL; Wellspring Grocery in NC; and Bread & Circus Whole Foods Market in MA and RI. The company's store base was expanded significantly through the August 1996 acquisition of Fresh Fields, which added 22 stores located throughout MD, VA, PA, DC, NJ, NY and CT.

The largest concentration of the company's supermarkets is in the Baltimore/Washington, DC, region (11 stores), closely followed by the Los Angeles/Orange County, CA, area (10 stores).

WFMI's strategy is to open or acquire stores in existing regions, and metropolitan areas where management believes the company can become the leading natural foods supermarket retailer. As of May 12, 1998, WFMI had a total of 18 stores under development. Three of the stores were scheduled to open in FY 98 (Sep.), and the remaining 14 in FY 99 and FY 2000. New stores will average 33,000 sq. ft. in size.

In September 1997, the company acquired Amrion, Inc., a developer, producer and marketer of nutriceutical and nutritional supplements, in exchange for about 4.6 million WFMI common shares. WFMI recorded a charge of approximately $4.9 million in the fourth quarter of FY 97, for professional fees and other out-of-pocket costs associated with the acquisition.

In November 1997, Whole Foods acquired Merchant of Vino, owner and operator of four natural foods stores and two specialty wine and gourmet food shops in the Detroit metropolitan area. Detroit had been the only major metropolitan area in which the company did not have a presence.

During the first quarter of FY 98, the company acquired Allegro Coffee Co., a specialty coffee roaster and distributor based in Boulder, CO.

Per Share Data ($)

(Year Ended Sep. 30)	1997	1996	1995	1994	1993	1992	1991	1990	1989	1988
Tangible Bk. Val.	6.48	5.36	4.45	4.53	3.20	4.29	1.06	NA	NA	NA
Cash Flow	2.41	0.43	1.45	1.16	0.67	0.72	0.88	NA	NA	NA
Earnings	1.18	-0.90	0.58	0.61	0.29	0.43	0.38	NA	NA	NA
Dividends	Nil	Nil	Nil	Nil	Nil	Nil	Nil	Nil	Nil	Nil
Payout Ratio	Nil	Nil	Nil	Nil	Nil	Nil	Nil	Nil	Nil	Nil
Prices - High	51³/₈	37¹/₈	16¹/₄	25³/₄	23³/₈	17	NA	NA	NA	NA
- Low	17¹/₂	13¹/₂	10¹/₈	9¹/₂	13¹/₂	7¹/₄	NA	NA	NA	NA
P/E Ratio - High	49	NM	28	42	81	39	NA	NA	NA	NA
- Low	17	NM	17	16	47	17	NA	NA	NA	NA

Income Statement Analysis (Million $)

	1997	1996	1995	1994	1993	1992	1991	1990	1989	1988
Revs.	1,117	892	496	402	322	120	92.5	NA	NA	NA
Oper. Inc.	89.5	50.0	29.7	22.8	16.4	6.7	5.1	NA	NA	NA
Depr.	34.5	25.5	12.3	7.9	5.0	2.1	1.6	NA	NA	NA
Int. Exp.	6.0	4.7	1.5	0.5	0.8	0.3	1.0	NA	NA	NA
Pretax Inc.	39.4	-20.6	13.6	14.7	8.4	4.9	2.6	NA	NA	NA
Eff. Tax Rate	32%	NM	39%	41%	55%	38%	40%	NA	NA	NA
Net Inc.	26.6	-17.2	8.2	8.6	3.8	3.1	1.6	NA	NA	NA

Balance Sheet & Other Fin. Data (Million $)

	1997	1996	1995	1994	1993	1992	1991	1990	1989	1988
Cash	13.4	1.7	5.2	4.3	6.8	16.0	2.2	NA	NA	NA
Curr. Assets	114	61.6	37.3	31.3	23.7	23.6	8.2	NA	NA	NA
Total Assets	400	311	196	136	106	46.5	23.4	NA	NA	NA
Curr. Liab.	77.3	56.7	35.8	26.0	22.7	7.9	8.3	NA	NA	NA
LT Debt	92.7	84.3	47.0	7.2	3.2	0.3	9.3	NA	NA	NA
Common Eqty.	205	146	106	97.7	75.5	36.3	5.0	NA	NA	NA
Total Cap.	306	237	157	107	80.3	38.0	14.8	NA	NA	NA
Cap. Exp.	31.1	18.2	16.0	28.9	27.8	6.7	2.8	NA	NA	NA
Cash Flow	61.1	8.3	20.5	16.5	8.8	5.1	3.2	NA	NA	NA
Curr. Ratio	1.5	1.1	1.0	1.2	1.0	3.0	1.0	NA	NA	NA
% LT Debt of Cap.	30.3	35.6	30.0	6.7	4.0	0.9	62.9	NA	NA	NA
% Net Inc.of Revs.	2.4	NM	1.7	2.2	1.2	2.6	1.7	NA	NA	NA
% Ret. on Assets	7.5	NM	5.0	6.9	4.1	5.2	NA	NA	NA	NA
% Ret. on Equity	15.1	NM	8.0	9.7	5.5	11.6	NA	NA	NA	NA

Data as orig. reptd.; bef. results of disc. opers. and/or spec. items. Per share data adj. for stk. divs. as of ex-div. date. Bold denotes diluted EPS (FASB 128). E-Estimated. NA-Not Available. NM-Not Meaningful. NR-Not Ranked.

Office—601 N. Lamar, Suite 300, Austin, TX 78703.**Tel**—(512) 477-4455. **Website**—http://www.wholefoods.com **Chrmn & CEO**—J. Mackey. **Pres & COO**—P. Roy. **VP, CFO & Investor Contact**—Glenda Flanagan. **Dirs**—C. G. Banks, D. W. Dupree, J. E. Elstrott, E. C. Fascitelli, A. J. Goldberg, L. A. Mason, J. Morman, R. Z. Sorenson, J. P. Sud. **Transfer Agent & Registrar**—Securities Transfer Corp., Dallas. **Incorporated**—in Texas in 1980.**Empl**— 11,268. **S&P Analyst:** Robert J. Izmirlian

Williams-Sonoma

2486G

NYSE Symbol **WSM**

In S&P SmallCap 600

03-OCT-98

Industry: Retail (Specialty)

Summary: This retailer of kitchenware and other products for the home and garden sells merchandise via retail stores and mail-order catalogs.

S&P Opinion: Hold (★★★)	Recent Price • 19⅞ 52 Wk Range • 36¾-17⅞

Yield • Nil

12-Mo. P/E • 25.2

Quantitative Evaluations

Outlook
(1 Lowest—5 Highest)
• **4⁻**

Fair Value
• **32**

Risk
• **High**

Earn./Div. Rank
• **B**

Technical Eval.
• **NA**

Rel. Strength Rank
(1 Lowest—99 Highest)
• **18**

Insider Activity
• **NA**

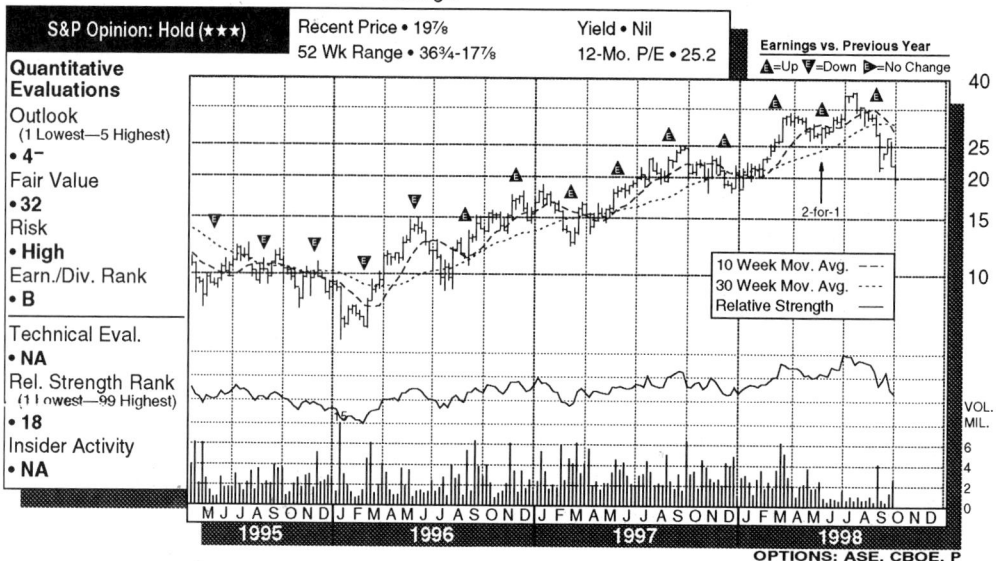

Earnings vs. Previous Year
▲=Up ▼=Down ▶=No Change

10 Week Mov. Avg. - - -
30 Week Mov. Avg. ·····
Relative Strength ——

2-for-1

OPTIONS: ASE, CBOE, P

Overview - 02-SEP-98

WSM owns several well-respected, home-center retail properties, and the company plans to build infrastructure, improve operating margins, and grow its three major businesses: Williams-Sonoma, Pottery Barn and catalogs. WSM is in the process of upgrading its traditional Williams-Sonoma stores to a Grand Cuisine design and its Pottery Barn outlets to a Design Studio format. These new prototypes are about 50% larger than current locations, and thus more able to service WSM's growing customer base. For FY 99 (Jan.) and thereafter, WSM expects to meet two primary year-to-year goals: 1) post 20% plus gains in total store square footage and 2) improve gross and operating margins. By January 1999, the company will increase its mail-order offerings with a Williams-Sonoma specialty food catalog and a Pottery Barn kids catalog.

Valuation - 02-SEP-98

Williams-Sonoma posted per share earnings of $0.07 for the second quarter of FY 99 (Jan.), versus $0.05 in the year-ago period. Total sales rose 18%, spurred by a 22% increase in retail sales (66% of revenues). Operating margins improved, due to lower merchandise costs and reduced shortage and damage rates, but were offset by higher employment costs and shipping expenses. Sales should continue to benefit from a healthy housing market and strong consumer spending. We believe WSM will make noteworthy productivity gains as a result of its more efficient distribution network. We are excited about the company's holiday merchandising plans and anticipated Williams-Sonoma on-line bridal offering. Though WSM is doing well, with the risk of a potentially peaking economy slowing growth, its shares appear fully-valued recently at 27 times our FY 99 earnings per share estimate of $0.92, and 24 times our FY 00 estimate of $1.06.

Key Stock Statistics

S&P EPS Est. 1999	0.92	Tang. Bk. Value/Share	4.39
P/E on S&P Est. 1999	21.6	Beta	0.92
S&P EPS Est. 2000	1.06	Shareholders	500
Dividend Rate/Share	Nil	Market cap. (B)	$ 1.1
Shs. outstg. (M)	55.6	Inst. holdings	62%
Avg. daily vol. (M)	0.296		

Value of $10,000 invested 5 years ago: $ 68,798

Fiscal Year Ending Jan. 31

	1999	1998	1997	1996	1995	1994
Revenues (Million $)						
1Q	206.2	176.5	157.4	118.2	102.8	76.20
2Q	215.3	182.4	155.5	127.7	108.0	82.00
3Q	—	203.9	171.2	138.4	113.4	89.20
4Q	—	370.4	327.7	260.4	204.2	162.7
Yr.	—	933.3	811.8	644.7	528.5	410.1
Earnings Per Share ($)						
1Q	**0.04**	0.03	-0.05	-0.01	0.04	-0.02
2Q	**0.07**	0.05	-0.01	-0.02	0.04	-0.01
3Q	**E0.09**	0.06	0.01	-0.07	0.05	0.02
4Q	**E0.72**	0.60	0.48	0.14	0.26	0.23
Yr.	**E0.92**	0.75	0.43	0.05	0.38	0.22

Next earnings report expected: mid November

Dividend Data

Amount ($)	Date Decl.	Ex-Div. Date	Stock of Record	Payment Date
2-for-1	Mar. 12	May. 18	May. 04	May. 15 '98

A Division of The McGraw·Hill Companies

Business Summary - 02-SEP-98

As customers peruse an sleek Williams-Sonoma catalog or stroll through a clean, welcoming Pottery Barn store, it is apparent that WSM's believes that quality and presentation are core company values. WSM's five service-oriented retail concepts emphasize the home, and accent style and functionality.

Each of WSM's merchandise concepts caters to a different area of the home. Williams-Sonoma stores and catalogs offer a wide selection of culinary and serving equipment, including cookware, cookbooks, cutlery, informal dinnerware, glassware and table linens. In addition, the stores carry a variety of food items, including a line of Williams-Sonoma gourmet coffees and pasta sauces. Pottery Barn features a large assortment of casual home furnishings, flatware and table accessories from around the world that are designed to be create a dynamic home environment. The Hold Everything concept was developed to offer innovative household storage solutions for a home's every room. The Gardener's Eden catalog features home gardening equipment and accessories, and the Chambers catalog offers high-quality bed and bath products, including luxury linens.

At of the end of FY 98 (Jan.), the company operated 152 Williams-Sonoma, 88 Pottery Barn, 32 Hold Everything and four outlet stores. The company is in the process of closing its traditional Williams-Sonoma and Pottery Barn stores and replacing them with larger, newly-designed Williams-Sonoma Grand Cuisine and Pottery Barn Design Studios stores. These new prototypes are about 50% larger than the previous locations, and thus better-equipped for more customer traffic. WSM is well on its way to opening the 43 large-format stores and closing the 19 traditional outlets during FY 99, as the company planned. A joint venture with Tokyu Department Store handles direct mail and operates 12 stores in Japan.

The company's customer list is continuously updated to include new prospects and eliminate non-responders. WSM offers a direct mail catalog for all of its home concepts (36% of FY 98 sales), with total annual mailings of more than 132 million. These catalogs supplement the company's retail locations and significantly reduce overhead in comparison to a retail-only operation.

Trading in the company's shares moved to the NYSE from the Nasdaq Stock Market on June 1, 1998.

WSM has several new direct marketing initiatives planned, including two new retail catalogs: a Williams-Sonoma specialty food catalog and a Pottery Barn kids catalog. In addition, beginning in early 1999, the company expects to launch an on-line version of its Williams-Sonoma bridal registry.

Per Share Data ($)

(Year Ended Jan. 31)	1998	1997	1996	1995	1994	1993	1992	1991	1990	1989
Tangible Bk. Val.	7.48	2.86	2.39	2.33	1.90	1.67	1.62	NA	NA	NA
Cash Flow	2.48	0.90	0.36	0.59	0.44	0.24	NA	NA	NA	NA
Earnings	0.75	0.43	0.05	0.38	0.22	0.04	0.03	NA	NA	NA
Dividends	Nil	Nil	Nil	Nil	Nil	Nil	Nil	Nil	Nil	Nil
Payout Ratio	Nil	Nil	Nil	Nil	Nil	Nil	Nil	Nil	Nil	Nil
Cal. Yrs.	1997	1996	1995	1994	1993	1992	1991	1990	1989	1988
Prices - High	25	18¼	15¼	17⅝	9⅜	4⅛	6⅜	NA	NA	NA
- Low	12¼	6¼	7⅞	7⅞	2³⁄₁₆	1¹⁵⁄₁₆	2⅞	NA	NA	NA
P/E Ratio - High	33	42	NA	47	43	90	NM	NM	NM	NM
- Low	16	14	NA	21	10	43	NM	NM	NM	NM

Income Statement Analysis (Million $)

	1998	1997	1996	1995	1994	1993	1992	1991	1990	1989
Revs.	933	812	645	529	410	345	NA	NA	NA	NA
Oper. Inc.	103	68.5	25.4	44.4	34.8	15.0	NA	NA	NA	NA
Depr.	28.9	24.3	16.5	11.6	11.2	10.4	NA	NA	NA	NA
Int. Exp.	5.7	6.5	6.0	1.5	1.2	1.6	NA	NA	NA	NA
Pretax Inc.	70.0	39.2	4.4	33.4	19.4	3.0	NA	NA	NA	NA
Eff. Tax Rate	41%	42%	42%	42%	42%	41%	NA	NA	NA	NA
Net Inc.	41.3	22.7	2.5	19.6	11.2	1.8	NA	NA	NA	NA

Balance Sheet & Other Fin. Data (Million $)

	1998	1997	1996	1995	1994	1993	1992	1991	1990	1989
Cash	97.2	78.8	4.2	17.5	10.8	NA	NA	NA	NA	NA
Curr. Assets	270	226	161	128	98.0	NA	NA	NA	NA	NA
Total Assets	477	404	319	218	168	NA	NA	NA	NA	NA
Curr. Liab.	136	129	122	78.6	57.9	NA	NA	NA	NA	NA
LT Debt	89.8	89.3	46.8	6.8	0.6	NA	NA	NA	NA	NA
Common Eqty.	193	146	122	118	95.0	NA	NA	NA	NA	NA
Total Cap.	285	235	168	125	96.0	NA	NA	NA	NA	NA
Cap. Exp.	59.3	47.6	86.5	30.1	14.0	15.2	NA	NA	NA	NA
Cash Flow	70.2	47.1	19.0	31.2	22.4	12.2	NA	NA	NA	NA
Curr. Ratio	2.0	1.8	1.3	1.6	1.7	NA	NA	NA	NA	NA
% LT Debt of Cap.	31.5	38.0	27.9	5.4	0.6	NA	NA	NA	NA	NA
% Net Inc.of Revs.	4.4	2.8	0.4	3.7	2.7	0.5	NA	NA	NA	NA
% Ret. on Assets	9.4	6.3	0.9	10.2	7.1	NA	NA	NA	NA	NA
% Ret. on Equity	24.4	17.0	2.1	18.4	12.5	NA	NA	NA	NA	NA

Data as orig. reptd.; bef. results of disc. opers. and/or spec. items. Per share data adj. for stk. divs. as of ex-div. date. Bold denotes diluted EPS (FASB 128). E-Estimated. NA-Not Available. NM-Not Meaningful. NR-Not Ranked.

Office—3250 Van Ness Ave., San Francisco, CA 94109. **Tel**—(415) 421-7900. **Website**—http://www.williams-sonoma.com.**Chrmn & CEO**—W. H. Lester. **Vice Chrmn**—C. E. Williams. **Exec VP & Secy**—D. A. Chantland. **Dirs**—A. Bellamy, J. M. Berry, N. Bessin, P. J. Connolly, M. S. Drexler, J. Emerson, G. G. Friedman, R. Hunter, J. E. Martin, J. A. McMahan, C. A. Rich. **Transfer Agent & Registrar**—ChaseMellon Shareholder Services, San Francisco. **Incorporated**—in California in 1973. **Empl**— 12,300. **S&P Analyst:** Scott H. Kessler.

Winnebago Industries

2491

NYSE Symbol **WGO**

In S&P SmallCap 600

03-OCT-98

Industry: Leisure Time (Products)

Summary: Winnebago primarily produces motor homes used in leisure travel and outdoor recreational activities.

Quantitative Evaluations

Outlook (1 Lowest—5 Highest)
• **3+**

Fair Value
• **12¾**

Risk
• **Average**

Earn./Div. Rank
• **B-**

Technical Eval.
• **NA**

Rel. Strength Rank (1 Lowest—99 Highest)
• **69**

Insider Activity
• **Neutral**

Recent Price • 11
52 Wk Range • 15⅛-6¾

Yield • 1.8%
12-Mo. P/E • 12.9

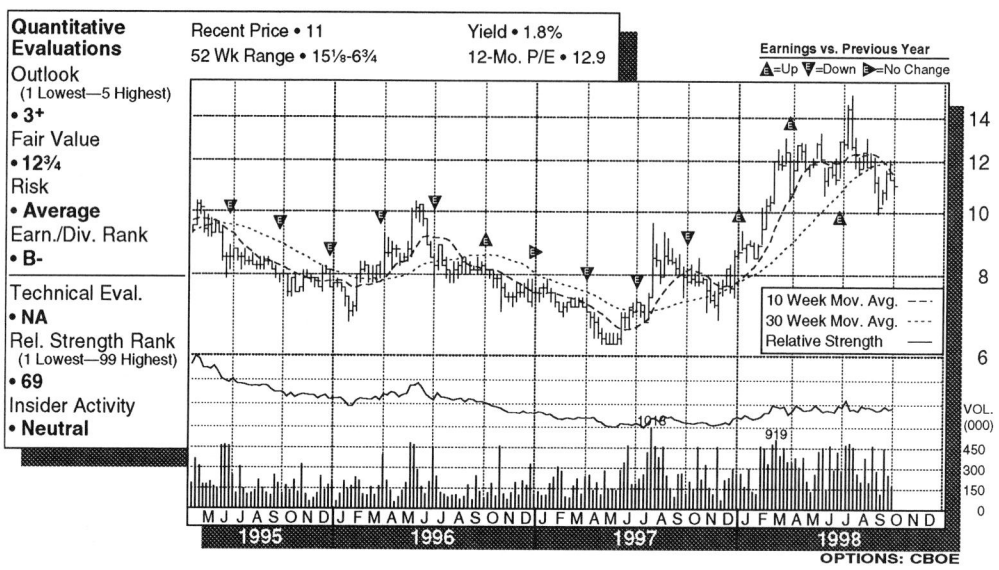

Earnings vs. Previous Year
▲=Up ▼=Down ▶=No Change

10 Week Mov. Avg. — —
30 Week Mov. Avg. - - - -
Relative Strength ——

OPTIONS: CBOE

Business Profile - 18-AUG-98

Results thus far in FY 98 (Aug.) have benefited from increased sales from WGO's expanded product lines. Product development has been a top priority throughout the past two model years, with over 75% of WGO's 1999 motor homes being dramatically redesigned or completely new, compared with 1997 offerings. Orders on hand at the end of the FY 98 third quarter were up about 80% from the year-earlier level. Management characterized FY 97 as a transitional period, during which the company divested businesses and assets that had not contributed to growth, and focused its attention and resources on its core business of motor home manufacturing.

Operational Review - 18-AUG-98

Net revenues from continuing operations in the 39 weeks ended May 30, 1998, rose 17%, year to year, as unit sales of motor homes (Class A & C) increased 14%. Results benefited from increased volume of production and sales of motor homes, significant decreases in promotional programs, and sharply higher financial income. Pretax income rose to $23,622,000, from $7,504,000. After taxes at 33.6%, versus 63.3%, income from continuing operations advanced to $17,022,000 ($0.69 a share), from $2,752,000 ($0.11). Results in the FY 97 interim exclude a gain of $0.64 a share from the sale of discontinued operations.

Stock Performance - 02-OCT-98

In the past 30 trading days, WGO's shares have declined 8%, compared to a 7% fall in the S&P 500. Average trading volume for the past five days was 34,400 shares, compared with the 40-day moving average of 62,356 shares.

Key Stock Statistics

Dividend Rate/Share	0.20	Shareholders	12,100
Shs. outstg. (M)	23.0	Market cap. (B)	$0.254
Avg. daily vol. (M)	0.050	Inst. holdings	32%
Tang. Bk. Value/Share	5.21		
Beta	1.10		

Value of $10,000 invested 5 years ago: $ 14,776

Fiscal Year Ending Aug. 31

	1998	1997	1996	1995	1994	1993
Revenues (Million $)						
1Q	125.9	113.9	113.7	130.8	104.6	83.40
2Q	118.7	105.7	106.2	115.5	99.0	77.46
3Q	150.5	117.2	144.4	125.1	129.7	115.9
4Q	—	101.3	120.5	113.3	118.9	107.3
Yr.	—	438.1	484.8	484.6	452.1	384.1
Earnings Per Share ($)						
1Q	0.21	0.11	0.11	0.30	0.15	0.04
2Q	**0.18**	-0.15	0.09	0.48	0.05	0.02
3Q	**0.31**	0.15	0.21	0.26	0.29	0.18
4Q	—	0.15	0.16	0.06	0.20	0.13
Yr.	—	0.26	0.57	1.10	0.69	0.37

Next earnings report expected: mid October

Dividend Data (Dividends have been paid since 1995.)

Amount ($)	Date Decl.	Ex-Div. Date	Stock of Record	Payment Date
0.100	Oct. 16	Dec. 05	Dec. 05	Jan. 05 '98
0.100	Mar. 20	Jun. 05	Jun. 05	Jul. 06 '98

A Division of The McGraw·Hill Companies

Business Summary - 18-AUG-98

In July 1997, Winnebago Industries hosted the 28th Annual Great American Get-Together in its home town of Forest City, IA, for approximately 4,000 RV enthusiasts from across the U.S. While the large turnout for the RV lovefest shows that current owners of WGO's motor homes are a loyal group, the company is having less success attracting new buyers. Slow sales of Class A motorhomes, and overall softness in the RV industry, prompted WGO to cut its production schedules for the third and fourth quarters of FY 97 (Aug.). However, the company has said it was very pleased with record revenues and sharply higher income from continuing operations in the first nine months of FY 98.

WGO is a leading manufacturer of motor homes: self-contained recreational vehicles (RVs) used primarily in leisure travel and outdoor recreation activities. Sales of motor homes accounted for more than 87% of revenues in each of the past five years.

The company makes three types of motor homes: Class A, B and C. Class A models are conventional motor homes constructed directly on medium-duty truck chassis, which include the engine and drive components. The living area and driver's compartment are designed and produced by WGO. Class B models are panel-type trucks to which sleeping, kitchen and toilet facilities are added. These models also have a top extension added to them for more head room. Class C models are mini motor homes built on van-type chassis on which the company constructs a living area with access to the driver's compartment. Certain Class C units include van-type driver's compartments built by WGO.

Motor homes range in size from 17 ft. to 37 ft., and are sold through a network of about 360 dealers in the U.S. under the brand names Winnebago, Itasca, Vectra, Rialta, and Luxor. The A and C classes of RVs can accommodate four to seven people, and have kitchen, dining, sleeping and bath areas, and in some cases, a lounge. The company converts class B motor homes under the EuroVan Camper brand name (distributed through the Volkswagon dealer organization).

In FY 97, WGO recorded income of $16.5 million ($0.65 a share) from the sale of its Cycle-Sat, Inc. subsidiary to Williams Companies' subsidiary Vyvx, for $57 million. The company also recorded charges aggregating $5.0 million, for the writedown of selected assets of Winnebago Industries Europe, as well as the closing of rental and retail operations in Kirkel, Germany.

As of May 30, 1998, the company had repurchased about $19.6 million of its common stock (2.1 million shares), under a December 1997 authorization to buy up to $36.5 million of stock within 18 months (about 1.9 million of the shares were purchased privately in one transaction for about $17 million). WGO subsequently acquired an additional 486,000 shares for about $5.7 million.

Per Share Data ($)

(Year Ended Aug. 31)	1997	1996	1995	1994	1993	1992	1991	1990	1989	1988
Tangible Bk. Val.	4.86	4.15	3.96	3.16	3.26	2.88	3.30	4.49	5.28	5.84
Cash Flow	0.51	0.95	1.45	1.00	0.68	0.25	-0.27	-0.21	0.26	0.51
Earnings	0.26	0.57	1.10	0.69	0.37	-0.07	-0.65	-0.72	-0.19	0.11
Dividends	0.20	0.30	0.30	Nil	Nil	Nil	Nil	0.10	0.40	0.40
Payout Ratio	77%	53%	27%	Nil	Nil	Nil	Nil	NM	NM	362%
Prices - High	9⅝	10⅜	10¾	13⅞	10½	9½	6¾	5¾	9⅜	11⅜
- Low	6¼	6¾	7⅜	7⅞	5⅝	3⅝	2¼	2⅛	4½	7¾
P/E Ratio - High	37	18	10	20	28	NM	NM	NM	NM	NM
- Low	24	12	7	11	15	NM	NM	NM	NM	NM

Income Statement Analysis (Million $)

	1997	1996	1995	1994	1993	1992	1991	1990	1989	1988
Revs.	438	485	485	452	384	295	223	335	438	425
Oper. Inc.	11.6	30.4	27.2	25.0	15.7	4.9	-12.1	-13.1	1.5	15.4
Depr.	6.5	9.7	8.9	7.7	7.8	8.1	9.6	12.6	11.1	9.9
Int. Exp.	0.7	0.8	1.8	1.4	0.6	0.4	1.4	2.3	2.6	0.7
Pretax Inc.	7.0	21.1	19.8	16.3	7.7	-2.8	-22.4	-32.3	-8.3	2.9
Eff. Tax Rate	5.95%	32%	NM	NM	NM	NM	NM	NM	NM	6.00%
Net Inc.	6.6	14.4	27.8	17.4	9.3	-1.8	-16.3	-17.8	-4.7	2.7

Balance Sheet & Other Fin. Data (Million $)

	1997	1996	1995	1994	1993	1992	1991	1990	1989	1988
Cash	32.1	5.1	11.0	4.1	13.5	14.5	7.9	23.6	22.5	62.1
Curr. Assets	141	127	121	111	94.0	82.0	77.0	129	200	163
Total Assets	213	221	212	184	157	140	135	198	286	237
Curr. Liab.	41.2	64.5	51.2	52.0	50.0	44.0	39.0	64.0	128	82.0
LT Debt	Nil	1.7	12.7	4.1	3.2	3.1	3.9	3.5	6.4	1.4
Common Eqty.	124	105	100	80.0	82.0	72.0	83.0	111	131	145
Total Cap.	124	109	115	88.0	89.0	79.0	90.0	129	153	151
Cap. Exp.	4.4	10.5	9.3	12.0	7.7	3.0	3.8	9.6	12.0	16.5
Cash Flow	13.0	25.1	36.7	25.2	17.0	6.3	-6.7	-5.2	6.4	12.6
Curr. Ratio	3.4	2.0	2.4	2.1	1.9	1.8	2.0	2.0	1.6	2.0
% LT Debt of Cap.	Nil	1.6	12.7	4.7	3.6	3.9	4.4	2.8	4.2	0.9
% Net Inc.of Revs.	1.5	3.0	5.7	3.9	2.4	NM	NM	NM	NM	0.6
% Ret. on Assets	3.0	6.7	14.0	10.2	6.2	NM	NM	NM	NM	1.2
% Ret. on Equity	5.7	14.1	30.9	21.6	12.1	NM	NM	NM	NM	1.8

Data as orig. reptd.; bef. results of disc. opers. and/or spec. items. Per share data adj. for stk. divs. as of ex-div. date. Bold denotes diluted EPS (FASB 128). E-Estimated. NA-Not Available. NM-Not Meaningful. NR-Not Ranked.

Office—605 W. Crystal Lake Rd., P.O. Box 152, Forest City, IA 50436. **Tel**—(515) 582-3535. **Website**—http://www.winnebagoind.com **Chrmn, Pres & CEO**—B. D. Hertzke. **VP, CFO & Investor Contact**—Edwin F. Barker (515-582-6141). **VP & Secy**—R. M. Beebe. **Dirs**—G. E. Boman, J.N. Currie, F. G. Dohrmann, J. V. Hanson, B. D. Hertzke, G. C. Kitch, R. C. Scott, J. M. Shuster, F. M. Zimmerman, F. L. Zrostlik. **Transfer Agent & Registrar**—Norwest Bank Minnesota, St. Paul. **Incorporated**—in Iowa in 1958. **Empl**—2,830. **S&P Analyst**: J.J.S.

STANDARD &POOR'S
STOCK REPORTS

Wiser Oil

2494M

NYSE Symbol **WZR**

In S&P SmallCap 600

10-OCT-98

Industry: Oil & Gas (Exploration & Production)

Summary: This company is engaged in the exploration, production and acquisition of crude oil and natural gas reserves primarily in the U.S. and Canada.

Quantitative Evaluations

Recent Price • 4⅞

52 Wk Range • 18⅜-4¾

Yield • 2.4%

12-Mo. P/E • NM

Outlook
(1 Lowest—5 Highest)
• **NA**

Fair Value
• **NA**

Risk
• **Average**

Earn./Div. Rank
• **B-**

Technical Eval.
• **Bullish** since 6/98

Rel. Strength Rank
(1 Lowest—99 Highest)
• **18**

Insider Activity
• **Neutral**

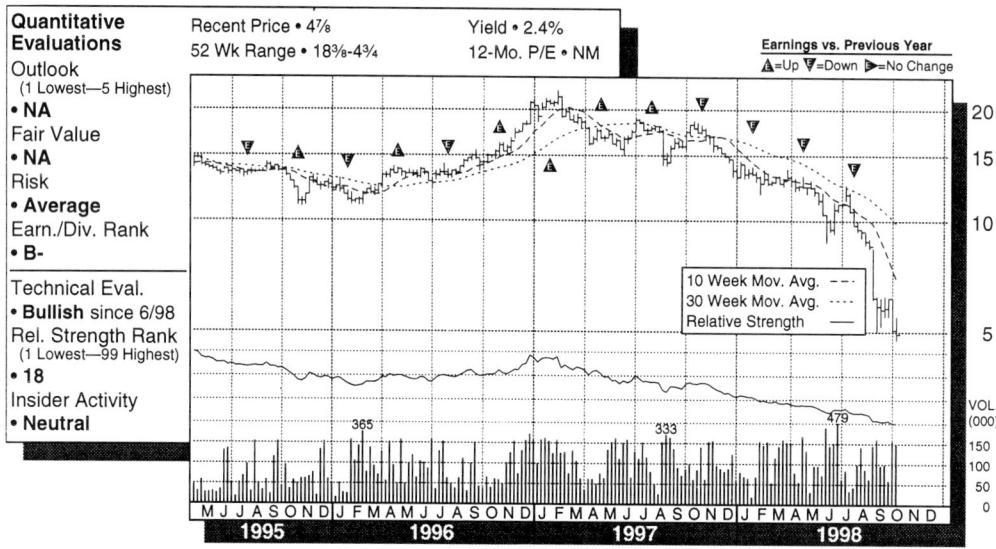

Earnings vs. Previous Year
▲=Up ▼=Down ▷=No Change

10 Week Mov. Avg. – – –
30 Week Mov. Avg. · · · ·
Relative Strength —

Business Profile - 13-AUG-98

Although Wiser Oil has followed a strategy in recent years stressing acquisitions to increase its gas and oil reserves and production, in response to lower oil prices and a tougher acquisition market, the company plans to use its newly developed in-house exploration team to fuel future growth. Also as a response to the lower prices, WZR will strive to maintain a more balanced mix of oil and gas. Oil and NGLs comprised 60% of total reserves at year end 1997, and contributed about 52% of second quarter 1998 production. Concurrent with its second quarter earnings release, WZR announced that it was abandoning an exploratory well in Peru because no hydrocarbons were found. In July 1998, Cross Timbers Oil (NYSE: XTO) announced that it had acquired an 8.7% stake in WZR's common shares, taking advantage of the broad based weakness in the oil sector.

Operational Review - 13-AUG-98

Revenues during the six months ended June 30, 1998, declined 23%, year to year, due to widespread commodity price declines, partially offset by increased production. Expenses rose 20%, led by significant increases in depreciation, depletion and amortization, exploration, and interest charges; a pretax loss compared to income. After a tax benefit of $3.5 million, versus taxes at 25.5%, the company posted a net loss of $8.2 million ($0.92 per share), versus net income in the 1997 period of $4.2 million ($0.47).

Stock Performance - 09-OCT-98

In the past 30 trading days, WZR's shares have declined 20%, compared to a 4% fall in the S&P 500. Average trading volume for the past five days was 29,460 shares, compared with the 40-day moving average of 27,138 shares.

Key Stock Statistics

Dividend Rate/Share	0.12	Shareholders	1,100
Shs. outstg. (M)	9.0	Market cap. (B)	$0.044
Avg. daily vol. (M)	0.025	Inst. holdings	46%
Tang. Bk. Value/Share	9.91		
Beta	1.14		

Value of $10,000 invested 5 years ago: $ 4,030

Fiscal Year Ending Dec. 31

	1998	1997	1996	1995	1994	1993
Revenues (Million $)						
1Q	17.42	25.58	18.57	16.25	12.58	10.70
2Q	16.02	17.83	21.36	14.58	13.51	10.04
3Q	—	17.03	19.47	18.27	15.35	8.65
4Q	—	27.39	27.29	22.59	23.92	13.53
Yr.	—	87.82	86.69	71.68	65.36	42.92
Earnings Per Share ($)						
1Q	-0.40	0.69	0.17	0.14	0.01	0.01
2Q	-0.52	-0.22	-0.60	-0.08	0.09	0.01
3Q	—	-0.21	0.27	0.21	0.08	-0.03
4Q	—	0.11	0.88	-0.02	0.83	0.12
Yr.	—	0.37	0.72	0.25	1.01	0.11

Next earnings report expected: mid November

Dividend Data (Dividends have been paid since 1941.)

Amount ($)	Date Decl.	Ex-Div. Date	Stock of Record	Payment Date
0.030	Nov. 17	Nov. 25	Nov. 28	Dec. 10 '97
0.030	Feb. 16	Feb. 25	Feb. 27	Mar. 10 '98
0.030	May. 19	May. 27	May. 29	Jun. 11 '98
0.030	Aug. 18	Aug. 27	Aug. 31	Sep. 11 '98

A Division of The **McGraw-Hill** *Companies*

The Wiser Oil Company

Business Summary - 13-AUG-98

Wiser Oil Co. (WZR) has adopted a strategy emphasizing growth of its oil and gas reserves and production through acquisitions and subsequent development and exploitation of acquired properties. Most of Wiser's 1997 year-end reserves, which totaled 49.7 MMBOE (60% oil and NGLs), are located in the Permian Basin in West Texas and Southeast New Mexico. The company also has reserves in Alberta, Canada, the Appalachian Basin in Kentucky, Tennessee and West Virginia, and the San Juan Basin in New Mexico. In addition, Wiser conducts exploratory efforts in South America.

Oil, NGL, and gas production in 1997 totaled 2.4 MMBbls, 319 MBbls, and 12.8 Bcf, respectively. On a BOE basis, production, totaling 4.9 million BOE, was up 1.5% from 1996. The average sales price realized for oil and NGLs per bbl, and gas per Mcf were \$18.02, \$13.87, and \$2.21, respectively. In 1996, the company received \$18.81, \$13.36, and \$1.77.

Revenues in 1997 advanced 1.3% primarily from an increase in gas production, associated with the Welder Ranch field, which was acquired in 1997 for about \$17.5 million, and due to a rise in gas realizations. Additional wells drilled and increased production taxes raised operating costs 12% to \$5.67 per BOE. Results were also penalized by higher depreciation, depletion and amortization charges and greater exploration and interest costs, and net income declined almost 50% to \$3.3 million (\$0.37 per share) from \$6.4 million (\$0.72). As a result of lower oil prices, the company deferred \$10 million of projects in 1997, and will strive to maintain a balanced mix of oil and gas production.

The company was disappointed by the lack of growth in its reserve base from 1996 to 1997. Wiser partially blamed this on a very competitive acquisition market and the absence of a significant acquisition during the year. In 1997, WZR assembled an in-house exploration team comprised of geoscientists and geotechnicians and purchased sophisticated geophysical software. The company plans to utilize its new exploration team to make future contributions to the reserve base.

Also during 1997, Wiser completed a \$125 million offering of 9.5% Senior Subordinated Notes; proceeds were used to pay down debt, and fund acquisitions.

Wiser is participating in a group operated by Santa Fe Energy Resources Inc. that has applied for development and exploration concessions from Petrobras in Brazil.

Citing weakness in the oil sector, Cross Timbers Oil (NYSE: XTO) announced, in July 1998, that it had purchased 775,000 (8.7%) common shares of WZR.

Per Share Data (\$) (Year Ended Dec. 31)	1997	1996	1995	1994	1993	1992	1991	1990	1989	1988
Tangible Bk. Val.	10.88	11.10	11.31	11.79	11.76	9.76	10.11	10.39	10.14	9.89
Cash Flow	2.93	2.91	2.46	3.05	1.83	1.88	1.81	2.12	2.04	1.19
Earnings	0.37	0.72	0.25	1.01	0.11	0.05	0.28	0.74	0.75	0.27
Dividends	0.12	0.12	0.40	0.40	0.40	0.40	0.50	0.50	0.50	0.40
Payout Ratio	32%	17%	160%	40%	NM	750%	179%	67%	66%	NM
Prices - High	$22\frac{5}{8}$	$21\frac{1}{8}$	15	$18\frac{7}{8}$	$19\frac{1}{8}$	17	$17\frac{1}{4}$	$21\frac{1}{2}$	$21\frac{5}{8}$	19
- Low	13	11	$10\frac{7}{8}$	$13\frac{1}{8}$	$13\frac{1}{8}$	$12\frac{7}{8}$	$13\frac{3}{8}$	$14\frac{5}{8}$	$13\frac{3}{4}$	$13\frac{3}{8}$
P/E Ratio - High	61	29	60	19	NM	NM	62	29	29	70
- Low	35	15	43	13	NM	NM	48	20	18	50
Income Statement Analysis (Million \$)										
Revs.	76.7	72.0	54.4	53.6	40.3	37.2	37.2	41.1	37.7	26.6
Oper. Inc.	28.6	33.0	14.1	19.9	12.2	13.1	11.9	18.5	18.0	7.2
Depr. Depl. & Amort.	23.0	19.7	19.8	18.3	15.4	16.3	13.7	12.4	11.6	8.3
Int. Exp.	9.8	5.5	5.6	3.9	0.5	Nil	NM	0.1	0.1	0.1
Pretax Inc.	3.6	10.5	6.0	9.4	-1.1	0.2	3.0	8.9	9.2	2.9
Eff. Tax Rate	7.37%	39%	63%	4.70%	NM	NM	17%	25%	26%	16%
Net Inc.	3.3	6.4	2.2	9.0	1.0	0.5	2.5	6.7	6.8	2.5
Balance Sheet & Other Fin. Data (Million \$)										
Cash	13.3	5.9	1.4	2.7	3.5	14.5	16.6	14.8	9.3	13.6
Curr. Assets	29.2	21.7	14.2	15.6	14.8	22.3	23.2	21.9	16.5	19.3
Total Assets	255	209	203	211	178	102	107	110	106	104
Curr. Liab.	21.4	18.2	13.1	13.3	8.4	5.9	7.0	6.4	4.8	4.9
LT Debt	124	78.7	74.2	78.0	46.8	0.1	0.2	0.2	0.3	0.4
Common Eqty.	97.2	99	101	105	105	87.0	90.3	93.8	91.6	89.3
Total Cap.	232	189	188	196	168	96.0	99	103	100	99
Cap. Exp.	78.3	46.1	26.2	71.8	70.9	16.1	11.3	16.3	18.9	14.5
Cash Flow	26.3	26.1	22.0	27.3	16.4	16.8	16.2	19.2	18.4	10.7
Curr. Ratio	1.4	1.2	1.1	1.2	1.8	3.8	3.3	3.4	3.5	3.9
% LT Debt of Cap.	53.6	41.6	39.5	39.7	27.8	0.1	0.2	0.2	0.3	0.4
% Ret. on Assets	1.4	3.1	1.1	4.6	0.7	0.5	2.3	6.2	6.5	2.4
% Ret. on Equity	3.4	6.4	2.1	8.5	1.1	0.1	2.7	7.3	7.5	2.7

Data as orig. reptd.; bef. results of disc opers. and/or spec. items. Per share data adj. for stk. divs. as of ex-div. date. Bold denotes diluted EPS (FASB 128). Revs. in Inc. St. are net of rev. adjs.; revs. in qtrly tbls are total revs. Estimated. NA-Not Available. NM-Not Meaningful. NR-Not Ranked.

Office—8115 Preston Rd., Suite 400, Dallas, TX 75225. **Tel**—(214) 265-0080. **Website**—http://www.wiseroil.com **Pres & CEO**—A. J. Shoup, Jr. **VP-Fin & CFO**—L. J. Finn. **Secy**—R. L. Starkey. **Treas**—R. D. Lee. **Investor Contact**—Virginia L. Cleveland (214) 360-3564. **Dirs**—J. W. Cushing III, H. G. Hamilton, C. F. Kimball III, L. H. Larson, J. L. Mosle, Jr., P. D. Neuenschwander, A. W. Schenck III, A. J. Shoup, Jr. **Transfer Agent**—ChaseMellon Shareholder Services, Inc., Dallas. **Incorporated**—in Delaware in 1970. **Empl**— 148. **S&P Analyst:** Ephraim Juskowicz

STANDARD &POOR'S
STOCK REPORTS

Wolverine Tube   2495E

NYSE Symbol **WLV**

In S&P SmallCap 600

10-OCT-98

Industry:
Metal Fabricators

Summary: This leading North American manufacturer and distributor of copper and copper alloy tube focuses on custom-engineered, high-value-added products.

Quantitative Evaluations

Outlook
(1 Lowest—5 Highest)
• 5

Fair Value
• 35⅞

Risk
• Average

Earn./Div. Rank
• NR

Technical Eval.
• NA

Rel. Strength Rank
(1 Lowest—99 Highest)
• 23

Insider Activity
• NA

Recent Price • 20⅜
52 Wk Range • 42½-20

Yield • Nil
12-Mo. P/E • 7.9

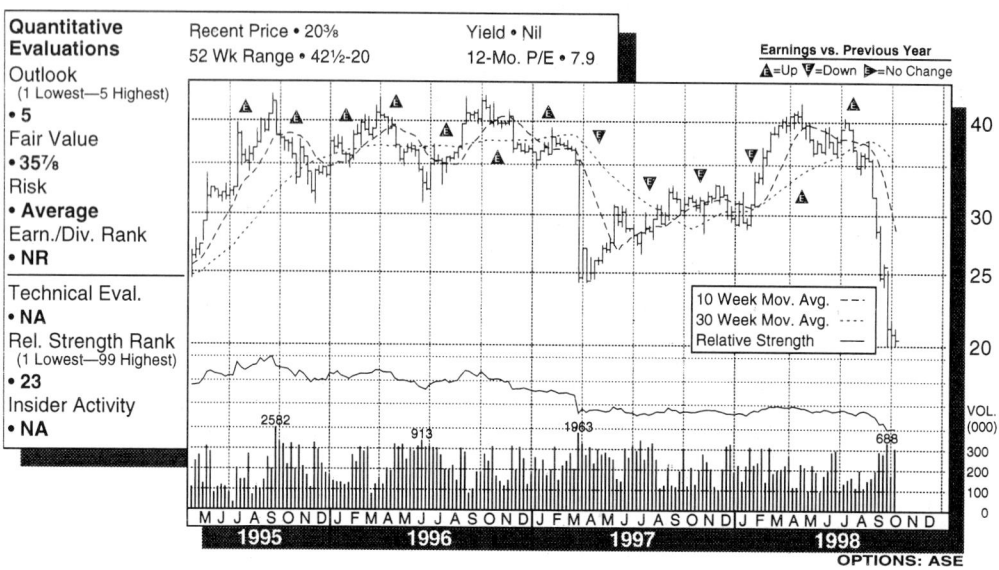

Earnings vs. Previous Year
▲=Up ▼=Down ▶=No Change

10 Week Mov. Avg. - - -
30 Week Mov. Avg. ·····
Relative Strength ——

OPTIONS: ASE

Business Profile - 04-MAY-98

Wolverine Tube continues to implement its strategy of focusing on high value added commercial products, cutting costs at its plants, improving operating efficiencies, and expanding product offerings. The company has been growing through acquisitions, and believes that demand for industrial tube will continue to strengthen. As part of the company's strategic plans to expand globally, emphasize commercial products and grow the fabricated products group, four capital projects are on target for their originally scheduled completion dates in 1998.

Operational Review - 04-MAY-98

Net sales for the three months ended April 4, 1998, slipped 1.9%, year to year, as a 13% increase in pounds shipped was more than offset by a significant drop in the average price of copper. Demand for all segments of commercial tube products improved and volume, price and gross profits increased on wholesale products. Net income was up 20%, to $10,575,000 ($0.74 a share) from $8,837,000 ($0.62).

Stock Performance - 09-OCT-98

In the past 30 trading days, WLV's shares have declined 36%, compared to a 4% fall in the S&P 500. Average trading volume for the past five days was 67,120 shares, compared with the 40-day moving average of 57,631 shares.

Key Stock Statistics

Dividend Rate/Share	Nil	Shareholders	400
Shs. outstg. (M)	14.1	Market cap. (B)	$0.288
Avg. daily vol. (M)	0.074	Inst. holdings	70%
Tang. Bk. Value/Share	11.85		
Beta	0.65		

Value of $10,000 invested 5 years ago: NA

Fiscal Year Ending Dec. 31

	1998	1997	1996	1995	1994	1993
Revenues (Million $)						
1Q	170.3	173.6	179.4	179.8	129.6	135.5
2Q	169.6	178.1	180.3	164.4	128.3	119.2
3Q	—	159.4	168.7	159.9	132.4	113.8
4Q	—	156.7	171.5	160.5	135.3	100.5
Yr.	—	667.7	699.9	664.6	525.6	469.0
Earnings Per Share ($)						
1Q	0.74	0.62	0.72	0.65	0.51	0.33
2Q	0.81	0.49	0.73	0.63	0.50	0.35
3Q	—	0.51	0.67	0.49	0.44	0.36
4Q	—	0.51	0.65	0.50	0.38	0.21
Yr.	—	2.13	2.77	2.26	1.82	1.39

Next earnings report expected: late October

Dividend Data

No dividends have been paid on the common stock. The company intends to retain earnings to support the growth of its business.

Business Summary - 04-MAY-98

Wolverine Tube (WLV), the successor to a business founded in Detroit in 1916, is today based in Huntsville, AL. Its value-added copper and copper alloy tube enhance performance and energy efficiency in many applications. The unique attributes of WLV's metals (thermal conductivity, ease of bending and joining, and resistance to erosion and corrosion) allow a broad range of applications in a large number of diverse industries.

The company's wide range of commercial products include small (down to 0.01 in.) and medium diameter copper tube supplied to residential air conditioning, appliance and refrigeration manufacturers. Technical tube is used to increase heat transfer in large commercial air conditioners, heat exchangers for power generating and chemical processing plants, water heaters, swimming pool and spa heaters, and large industrial equipment oil coolers. Copper alloy tube (copper mixed with nickel) is used for severe or corrosive environments such as condenser tubes and heat exchangers in power generating plants, chemical plants, refineries and ships.

Wholesale products include plumbing tube and refrigeration service tube. Rod, bar and strip products are copper and copper alloy formed into special shapes and used in many different ways. Brass rod and bar are used by machinery manufacturers for valves, fittings, and plumbing; copper bars are used in electrical distribution systems; and copper and copper alloy strip products are used for cars, hardware, electrical equipment, roofs, and, last but not least, for the minting of coins.

Since the phaseout of the use of CFCs (chlorofluorocarbons) began in 1987, the company has benefited as existing large chillers are replaced with units using alternative refrigerants. The company expects demand for its high value added energy efficient tubes to increase as manufacturers produce more energy efficient and lower operating cost units, and as existing large industrial chillers are replaced in response to the ban on production of CFCs.

As part of the company's strategic plans to expand globally, emphasize commercial products and grow the fabricated products group, four capital projects are on target for their originally scheduled completion dates. Construction of the company's manufacturing plant in Shanghai, China, will be completed in the second quarter of 1998. The relocation and expansion of the new fabricated products facility in Carrollton, TX, and the expansion of the Roxboro, NC, facility are both on line for completion by year-end. WLV's Technology Center and Research Center Laboratory is also on target for completion in 1998.

Per Share Data ($)

(Year Ended Dec. 31)	1997	1996	1995	1994	1993	1992	1991	1990	1989	1988
Tangible Bk. Val.	10.29	8.88	7.56	9.55	7.50	4.74	NA	NA	NA	NA
Cash Flow	3.31	3.94	3.38	2.76	2.31	2.11	1.14	NA	NA	NA
Earnings	2.13	2.77	2.26	1.82	1.39	0.98	0.20	NA	NA	NA
Dividends	Nil	Nil	Nil	Nil	Nil	Nil	NA	NA	NA	NA
Payout Ratio	Nil	Nil	Nil	Nil	Nil	Nil	NA	NA	NA	NA
Prices - High	39¼	43⅜	43½	26⅝	19¾	NA	NA	NA	NA	NA
- Low	24¼	31	23¼	18⅞	15½	NA	NA	NA	NA	NA
P/E Ratio - High	18	16	19	15	14	NA	NA	NA	NA	NA
- Low	11	11	10	10	11	NA	NA	NA	NA	NA

Income Statement Analysis (Million $)

	1997	1996	1995	1994	1993	1992	1991	1990	1989	1988
Revs.	668	700	665	526	469	484	418	479	542	381
Oper. Inc.	76.6	88.2	76.3	61.6	49.5	45.1	29.3	25.0	37.2	34.1
Depr.	16.8	16.3	15.8	12.9	10.4	11.9	10.1	8.9	8.2	6.7
Int. Exp.	7.8	10.5	10.8	10.3	9.6	9.4	10.3	9.6	10.4	7.1
Pretax Inc.	48.1	61.4	49.8	40.6	27.2	21.5	6.7	5.9	19.7	20.7
Eff. Tax Rate	36%	36%	35%	38%	41%	44%	39%	12%	39%	39%
Net Inc.	30.6	39.6	32.0	25.0	16.0	12.2	4.0	5.1	11.9	12.6

Balance Sheet & Other Fin. Data (Million $)

	1997	1996	1995	1994	1993	1992	1991	1990	1989	1988
Cash	15.1	3.0	5.5	0.1	55.2	NA	NA	NA	NA	NA
Curr. Assets	176	156	142	126	136	NA	NA	NA	NA	NA
Total Assets	425	397	357	341	276	NA	NA	NA	NA	NA
Curr. Liab.	50.0	43.2	49.5	64.2	37.3	NA	NA	NA	NA	NA
LT Debt	98.4	100	101	101	100	100	NA	NA	NA	NA
Common Eqty.	233	209	165	129	97.6	92.0	NA	NA	NA	NA
Total Cap.	360	338	289	255	217	NA	NA	NA	NA	NA
Cap. Exp.	21.6	8.5	15.8	34.4	22.3	4.0	1.9	4.2	13.8	4.1
Cash Flow	47.1	55.9	47.7	37.7	26.2	22.4	12.4	12.2	20.1	19.3
Curr. Ratio	3.5	3.6	2.9	2.0	3.7	NA	NA	NA	NA	NA
% LT Debt of Cap.	27.3	29.8	34.9	39.5	46.1	NA	NA	NA	NA	NA
% Net Inc.of Revs.	4.6	5.7	4.9	4.8	3.4	2.5	1.0	1.1	2.2	3.3
% Ret. on Assets	7.4	10.5	9.3	8.0	5.7	NA	NA	NA	NA	NA
% Ret. on Equity	13.7	21.2	21.8	21.6	21.0	NA	NA	NA	NA	NA

Data as orig. reptd.; bef. results of disc. opers. and/or spec. items. Per share data adj. for stk. divs. as of ex-div. date. Bold denotes diluted EPS (FASB 128). E-Estimated. NA-Not Available. NM-Not Meaningful. NR-Not Ranked.

Office—1525 Perimeter Parkway, Suite 210, Huntsville, AL 35806. **Tel**—(205) 353-1310. **Website**—http://www.wlv.com **Pres & CEO**—D. Horowitz. **EVP-Fin, CFO, Secy & Investor Contact**—James E. Deason (256) 890-0460. **Dirs**—C. A. Davis, J. E. Deason, J. L. Duncan, T. P. Evans, J. K. Ver Hagen, W. B. Hauptfuhrer, D. Horowitz, G. Neuman, C. E. Thompson. **Transfer Agent & Registrar**—KeyCorp Shareholder Services, Cleveland. **Incorporated**—in Delaware in 1987. **Empl**—3,467. **S&P Analyst:** C.C.P.

Wolverine World Wide 2495K

NYSE Symbol **WWW**

In S&P SmallCap 600

03-OCT-98

Industry: Footwear

Summary: WWW makes, imports and markets casual footwear sold under the Hush Puppies, Wolverine and other brand names, and is the largest domestic tanner of pigskins.

Quantitative Evaluations	
Outlook (1 Lowest—5 Highest)	• **5**
Fair Value	• **20⅞**
Risk	• **Average**
Earn./Div. Rank	• **B**
Technical Eval.	• **Bearish** since 5/98
Rel. Strength Rank (1 Lowest—99 Highest)	• **18**
Insider Activity	• **Favorable**

Recent Price • 10¼
52 Wk Range • 30⅞-8
Yield • 1.1%
12-Mo. P/E • 9.5

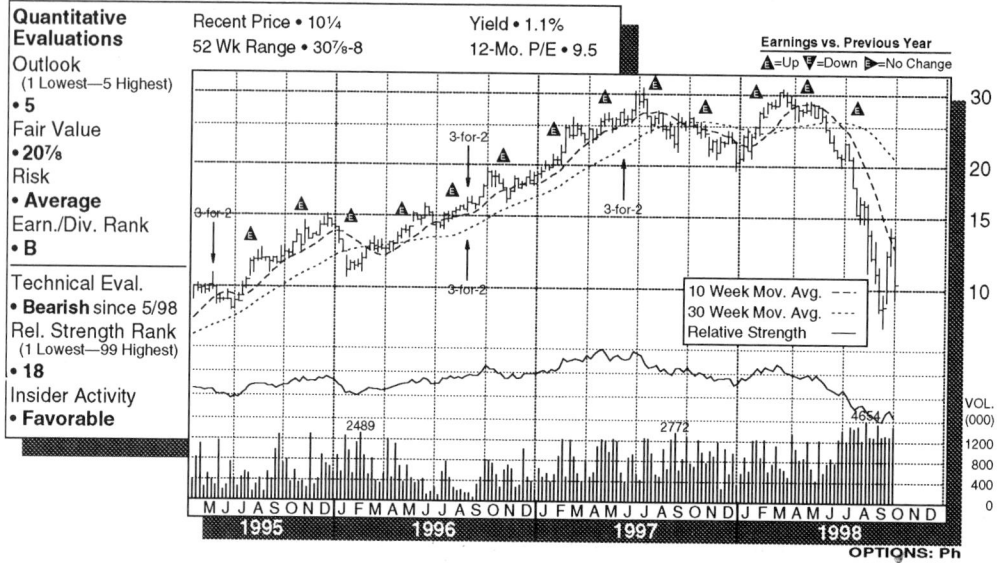

Earnings vs. Previous Year
▲=Up ▼=Down ►=No Change

10 Week Mov. Avg. ---
30 Week Mov. Avg. ....
Relative Strength —

OPTIONS: Ph

Business Profile - 13-MAY-98

Wolverine expects new products and global expansion to contribute to results in the second half of 1998. Initial consumer response to current Spring styles have been encouraging, and the recently introduced Fall lines of Hush Puppies, Wolverine, Caterpillar, Harley-Davidson, Merrell, Hy-Test and Bates footwear brands continue to attract interest. In addition, the recent introduction of Hush Puppies and Caterpillar footwear into China, Russia, India, Mexico and Brazil gives the company access to 2.5 billion potential new customers.

Operational Review - 13-MAY-98

Net sales for the three months ended March 28, 1998, rose 15%, year to year, reflecting double-digit sales gains at all branded footwear businesses. Margins widened, due to improvements in initial pricing margins and benefits from the 1997 manufacturing consolidation, partially offset by higher distribution costs; operating income rose 47%. Following taxes at 33.5%, versus 32.1%, net income was up 36%, to $6,388,000 ($0.15 a share), from $4,693,000 ($0.11, as adjusted).

Stock Performance - 02-OCT-98

In the past 30 trading days, WWW's shares have declined 14%, compared to a 7% fall in the S&P 500. Average trading volume for the past five days was 769,660 shares, compared with the 40-day moving average of 615,746 shares.

Key Stock Statistics

Dividend Rate/Share	0.11	Shareholders	2,000
Shs. outstg. (M)	43.8	Market cap. (B)	$0.451
Avg. daily vol. (M)	0.564	Inst. holdings	75%
Tang. Bk. Value/Share	6.09		
Beta	1.15		

Value of $10,000 invested 5 years ago: $ 35,648

Fiscal Year Ending Dec. 31

	1998	1997	1996	1995	1994	1993
Revenues (Million $)						
1Q	148.5	129.3	83.84	76.33	66.78	65.86
2Q	142.0	127.8	94.15	86.29	79.32	65.90
3Q	164.5	162.3	120.5	100.5	91.91	81.31
4Q	—	245.8	212.6	150.9	140.5	120.1
Yr.	—	665.1	511.0	414.0	378.5	333.1
Earnings Per Share ($)						
1Q	**0.15**	**0.11**	0.08	0.07	0.04	0.02
2Q	**0.21**	**0.17**	0.13	0.10	0.07	0.03
3Q	**0.25**	**0.21**	0.17	0.14	0.10	0.06
4Q	—	**0.47**	0.39	0.32	0.28	0.21
Yr.	—	**0.96**	0.77	0.63	0.49	0.32

Next earnings report expected: early February

Dividend Data (Dividends have been paid since 1988.)

Amount ($)	Date Decl.	Ex-Div. Date	Stock of Record	Payment Date
0.022	Dec. 23	Dec. 30	Jan. 02	Feb. 02 '98
0.028	Feb. 26	Mar. 30	Apr. 01	May. 01 '98
0.028	Jun. 23	Jun. 29	Jul. 01	Aug. 03 '98
0.028	Jul. 17	Sep. 29	Oct. 01	Nov. 02 '98

A Division of The McGraw-Hill Companies

Business Summary - 13-MAY-98

Walking tall as one of the world's leading footwear companies, Wolverine World Wide (WWW) sold nearly 37 million new pairs of shoes in 1997 in over 90 countries. WWW manufactures, imports and markets casual shoes, outdoor and work footwear, slippers and moccasins. Wolverine also operates retail shoe stores and is the largest domestic tanner of pigskins, which are used internally and sold to others. Footwear and related products accounted for over 90% of total sales in recent years, with pigskin sales accounting for most of the remainder.

Hush Puppies, the company's principal and best known brand, is a line of casual shoes for men, women and children. After years of lackluster sales, the company has repositioned Hush Puppies as a "fashion right" brand, and the brand is now enjoying strong growth. In March 1997, Hush Puppies was further supported by the launch of a new television advertising campaign, the first in 10 years for the company. In September 1996, WWW completed the acquisition of the Hush Puppies wholesale business in the U.K. and Ireland from British Shoe Corp. for $6.5 million. The company will now realize full margin wholesale revenues from the 3.5 million pairs of Hush Puppies sold annually in the U.K., instead of just licensing fees.

The company is capitalizing on the trend toward rugged performance products with its Wolverine work and sport footwear, Caterpillar footwear, Hy-Test occupational shoes and boots and Bates uniform footwear. Hy-Test was acquired in March 1996 from Florsheim Shoe Co., for $24.5 million in cash, and positioned the company as the domestic leader in occupational and safety shoes and boots. Footwear with the Coleman, Caterpillar and Cat trademarks is sold in the U.S. under license agreements. WWW also makes shoes for resale under labels of other shoe companies.

Wolverine designs and manufactures slippers and moccasins on under both private label and under the Hush Puppies, Firesider and other brand names.

Footwear is sold directly to about 35,000 retail outlets. Sales are also made to large footwear chains (including those owned or operated by other companies in the shoe industry), catalog houses, and independently and company-owned Hush Puppies specialty stores.

At March 30, 1998, WWW operated 60 retail shoe stores in two formats: factory outlet stores and mall-based specialty stores. There were 54 factory outlet stores and six mall-based full service, full price Hush Puppies Specialty Stores. A decision in 1990 to downsize its retail operations and focus on the core Hush Puppies and Wolverine wholesale business reduced the store base from 176 stores to the current 60 units.

Per Share Data ($)

(Year Ended Dec. 31)	1997	1996	1995	1994	1993	1992	1991	1990	1989	1988
Tangible Bk. Val.	6.20	5.74	4.98	3.64	4.88	2.96	3.32	3.24	3.40	3.23
Cash Flow	1.17	0.93	0.39	0.64	0.71	0.29	0.25	-0.02	0.36	0.37
Earnings	0.96	0.77	0.63	0.49	0.33	0.14	0.10	-0.17	0.21	0.22
Dividends	0.09	0.06	0.06	0.04	0.03	0.03	0.03	0.03	0.03	0.02
Payout Ratio	9%	8%	9%	9%	10%	23%	32%	NM	15%	10%
Prices - High	31⅛	19¾	15⅛	8	6⅝	3	2⅝	2½	3⅛	2¾
- Low	18⅝	10½	6⅞	5½	2¾	1½	1½	1³/₁₆	2⅛	1¹³/₁₆
P/E Ratio - High	32	26	24	16	20	22	26	NM	14	12
- Low	19	14	11	11	8	11	16	NM	10	8

Income Statement Analysis (Million $)

	1997	1996	1995	1994	1993	1992	1991	1990	1989	1988
Revs.	665	511	414	378	333	293	314	322	324	324
Oper. Inc.	76.1	55.4	43.3	35.0	24.9	17.8	19.7	17.7	18.4	18.2
Depr.	9.2	7.2	5.8	5.7	5.2	5.2	5.0	5.1	4.9	5.0
Int. Exp.	5.5	3.1	4.7	4.0	5.1	3.6	5.2	5.1	5.6	5.7
Pretax Inc.	61.1	47.7	34.1	25.4	15.9	6.5	4.5	-6.2	10.3	8.9
Eff. Tax Rate	32%	31%	30%	29%	28%	29%	28%	NM	29%	14%
Net Inc.	41.5	32.9	24.1	18.1	11.5	4.6	3.3	-5.7	7.3	7.7

Balance Sheet & Other Fin. Data (Million $)

	1997	1996	1995	1994	1993	1992	1991	1990	1989	1988
Cash	5.8	8.5	27.1	2.9	3.7	2.4	2.2	2.5	3.2	2.4
Curr. Assets	304	265	215	169	150	148	155	142	142	138
Total Assets	450	362	284	230	206	204	208	190	189	184
Curr. Liab.	64.9	69.8	38.0	43.0	38.3	52.4	61.7	44.4	33.8	32.9
LT Debt	89.8	41.3	30.6	43.5	44.9	42.7	31.6	34.3	36.3	38.2
Common Eqty.	282	239	204	133	113	100	110	108	116	110
Total Cap.	376	283	237	178	159	144	142	142	152	149
Cap. Exp.	35.4	20.6	18.6	9.9	6.6	4.1	6.7	7.2	5.8	4.6
Cash Flow	50.7	40.0	14.9	23.7	16.7	9.8	8.3	-0.6	12.2	12.7
Curr. Ratio	4.7	3.8	5.7	3.9	3.9	2.8	2.5	3.2	4.2	4.2
% LT Debt of Cap.	23.9	14.6	12.9	24.4	28.2	29.6	22.3	24.2	23.8	25.7
% Net Inc.of Revs.	6.2	6.4	5.8	4.8	3.4	1.6	1.0	NM	2.3	2.4
% Ret. on Assets	10.2	10.1	9.4	8.1	5.5	2.2	1.6	NM	3.9	4.4
% Ret. on Equity	15.5	14.8	14.3	14.4	10.7	4.3	3.0	NM	6.4	7.3

Data as orig. reptd.; bef. results of disc. opers. and/or spec. items. Per share data adj. for stk. divs. as of ex-div. date. Bold denotes diluted EPS (FASB 128). E-Estimated. NA-Not Available. NM-Not Meaningful. NR-Not Ranked.

Office—9341 Courtland Dr., Rockford, MI 49351. **Tel**—(616) 866-5500. **Chrmn & CEO**—G. B. Bloom. **Pres &COO**—T. J. O'Donovan. **EVP, CFO & Treas**—S. L. Gulis, Jr. **EVP & Secy**—B. W. Krueger. **Investor Contact**—Thomas Mundt (616-866-5589). **Dirs**—G. B. Bloom, D. T. Carroll, A. L. Grimoldi, D. T. Kolatt, P. D. Matthews, D. P. Mehney, T. J. O'Donovan, J. A. Parini, J. Parker, E. A. Sanders, P. Schrage. **Transfer Agent & Registrar**—Harris Trust & Savings Bank, Chicago. **Incorporated**—in Michigan in 1906; reincorporated in Delaware in 1969. **Empl**— 6,696. **S&P Analyst:** Ray Lam, CFA

STANDARD &POOR'S
STOCK REPORTS
World Color Press

2499M

NYSE Symbol **WRC**

In S&P SmallCap 600

03-OCT-98

Industry: Specialty Printing

Summary: This manager and distributor of print and digital information specializes in the production of magazines, catalogs, direct mail and commercial materials and directories.

Quantitative Evaluations

Outlook (1 Lowest—5 Highest)
- **NA**

Fair Value
- **NA**

Risk
- **Average**

Earn./Div. Rank
- **NR**

Technical Eval.
- **NA**

Rel. Strength Rank (1 Lowest—99 Highest)
- **68**

Insider Activity
- **Favorable**

Recent Price • 29¼
52 Wk Range • 36¼-22⅝

Yield • Nil
12-Mo. P/E • 17.2

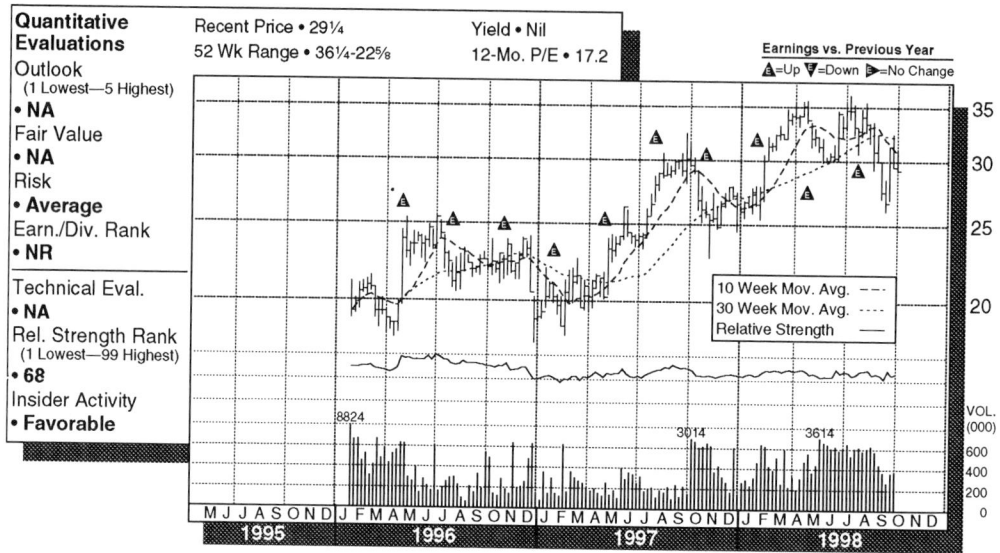

Earnings vs. Previous Year
▲=Up ▼=Down ►=No Change

10 Week Mov. Avg. ---
30 Week Mov. Avg. ·····
Relative Strength —

Business Profile - 30-MAR-98

World Color attributed record earnings in 1997 to strength in all businesses, particularly in the commercial sector. The company's continued focus on streamlining expenses, combined with the effect of lower paper prices, led to a widening of gross profit margins. Recent acquisitions have met management's expectations, and the company anticipates that proceeds received from recent stock and convertible offerings will provide additional funds to pursue other acquisitions. In February 1998, management stated that WRC has a pipeline of acquisition opportunities with companies having combined revenues exceeding $650 million.

Operational Review - 30-MAR-98

Net sales 1997 (preliminary) advanced 21%, with acquisitions made in 1996 and 1997 contributing importantly to the gain. Profitability benefited from the higher volume and the benefits of cost reduction initiatives and other synergies, and greater plant utilization; operating profit was up 28%. However, interest expense climbed 37%, due to higher borrowings used to fund acquisitions as well as capital expenditures. Net income rose 21%, to $57,219,000 ($1.60 a share, diluted), from $47,261,000 ($1.35).

Stock Performance - 02-OCT-98

In the past 30 trading days, WRC's shares have declined 5%, compared to a 7% fall in the S&P 500. Average trading volume for the past five days was 74,920 shares, compared with the 40-day moving average of 98,085 shares.

Key Stock Statistics

Dividend Rate/Share	Nil	Shareholders	100
Shs. outstg. (M)	38.5	Market cap. (B)	$ 1.1
Avg. daily vol. (M)	0.071	Inst. holdings	62%
Tang. Bk. Value/Share	NM		
Beta	NA		

Value of $10,000 invested 5 years ago: NA

Fiscal Year Ending Dec. 31

	1998	1997	1996	1995	1994	1993
Revenues (Million $)						
1Q	550.4	458.4	329.1	275.4	—	—
2Q	546.5	425.6	342.3	305.2	—	—
3Q	—	557.3	487.8	367.3	—	—
4Q	—	540.0	482.2	347.6	—	—
Yr.	—	1,981	1,641	1,296	1,168	—
Earnings Per Share ($)						
1Q	0.24	0.20	0.17	0.13	—	—
2Q	0.25	0.19	0.17	0.14	—	—
3Q	—	0.66	0.55	0.42	—	—
4Q	—	0.53	0.46	-0.40	—	—
Yr.	—	1.60	1.35	0.29	0.81	-4.26

Next earnings report expected: NA

Dividend Data

No cash dividends have been paid. The company does not anticipate paying cash dividends on the common shares for the foreseeable future.

A Division of The **McGraw·Hill** *Companies*

Business Summary - 30-MAR-98

Since 1993, World Color Press, Inc. (WRC), the third largest diversified commercial printer in the U.S., has completed and successfully integrated 15 acquisitions. WRC's aggressive pursuit of other companies has been a key element of its long-term growth strategy. Transactions completed in 1996 included Viking Color, a digital prepress provider; Shea Communications, a commercial catalog and direct mail printer; Ringier America, a printer of magazines, catalogs, commercial and mass-market, racksize books; ISA Direct, Inc., another direct mail resource; and MT Orlando, a regional commercial printer. Continuing its acquisition momentum into January 1997, WRC purchased the Book Services Group of Rand McNally, a printer of hardcover books.

Founded in 1903, WRC provides digital prepress, press, multi-media, binding and distribution services in the magazine, commercial, catalog, direct mail, directory and book market sectors. Some of WRC's significant customers include publishers Forbes, National Geographic, Entertainment Weekly, and Wenner Media; catalog/retail companies, including JC Penney, Spiegel, Victoria's Secret, and Williams-Sonoma; and Pacific Bell for directories.

Net sales, benefiting from WRC's successful acquisition strategy, grew 27% to $1.6 billion in 1996. The magazine sector contributed 29% to the sales mix (31% in 1995), commercial 27% (30%), catalogs 27% (23%),

direct mail 9% (9%), directories 6% (7%), and racksize books 2% (nil). Net income in 1996 was $47.3 million, well above 1995's $9.9 million, which reflected a large streamlining charge.

WRC believes that its focused capital expenditure program has been another important element in its drive to improve production and to provide customers with enhanced capabilities. In 1996, WRC spent some $70 million on capital expenditures, bringing its three-year total to $275 million. Projects supported by this funding included expanded wide-web press capabilities, and digital prepress and computer-to-plate technologies.

WRC has targeted digital media as one of its emerging businesses. WRC is able to transform customers' existing printed and digital material into interactive media, such as user-friendly information kiosk systems, Internet web sites, corporate intranets, CD-ROMs and computer laptop sales presentations. WRC's important customers in this segment include Apple Computer, Blockbuster Entertainment, Disney, IBM, The McGraw-Hill Companies, Microsoft, Paradyne Corp. and Xerox.

In February 1998, WRC acquired Century Graphics, the third largest offset printer of retail advertising inserts with $120 million in revenues in 1997, for an undisclosed amount. In March 1998, WRC acquired Dittler Brothers, Inc., a privately held specialty printer with $66 million in 1997 sales.

Per Share Data ($)

(Year Ended Dec. 31)	1997	1996	1995	1994	1993	1992	1991	1990	1989	1988
Tangible Bk. Val.	1.68	NM	3.39	3.90	NA	NA	NA	NA	NA	NA
Cash Flow	5.19	4.34	2.40	NA	NA	NA	NA	NA	NA	NA
Earnings	1.60	1.35	0.29	0.81	NA	NA	NA	NA	NA	NA
Dividends	Nil	Nil	NA	NA	NA	NA	NA	NA	NA	NA
Payout Ratio	Nil	Nil	NA	NA	NA	NA	NA	NA	NA	NA
Prices - High	32³⁄₈	25¹⁄₂	NA	NA	NA	NA	NA	NA	NA	NA
- Low	18¹⁄₈	17³⁄₄	NA	NA	NA	NA	NA	NA	NA	NA
P/E Ratio - High	20	19	NA	NA	NA	NA	NA	NA	NA	NA
- Low	11	13	NA	NA	NA	NA	NA	NA	NA	NA

Income Statement Analysis (Million $)

	1997	1996	1995	1994	1993	1992	1991	1990	1989	1988
Revs.	1,981	1,641	1,296	1,168	NA	NA	NA	NA	NA	NA
Oper. Inc.	310	244	168	NA	NA	NA	NA	NA	NA	NA
Depr.	132	104	72.8	NA	NA	NA	NA	NA	NA	NA
Int. Exp.	80.0	58.4	37.9	31.1	NA	NA	NA	NA	NA	NA
Pretax Inc.	99	80.8	16.5	46.5	NA	NA	NA	NA	NA	NA
Eff. Tax Rate	42%	42%	40%	40%	NA	NA	NA	NA	NA	NA
Net Inc.	57.2	47.3	9.9	27.9	NA	NA	NA	NA	NA	NA

Balance Sheet & Other Fin. Data (Million $)

	1997	1996	1995	1994	1993	1992	1991	1990	1989	1988
Cash	37.7	33.2	8.9	24.8	NA	NA	NA	NA	NA	NA
Curr. Assets	474	543	397	282	NA	NA	NA	NA	NA	NA
Total Assets	1,934	1,822	1,151	837	NA	NA	NA	NA	NA	NA
Curr. Liab.	305	316	236	169	NA	NA	NA	NA	NA	NA
LT Debt	810	889	450	291	NA	NA	NA	NA	NA	NA
Common Eqty.	600	415	359	274	NA	NA	NA	NA	NA	NA
Total Cap.	1,510	1,396	818	577	NA	NA	NA	NA	NA	NA
Cap. Exp.	93.1	70.6	120	NA	NA	NA	NA	NA	NA	NA
Cash Flow	189	152	82.7	NA	NA	NA	NA	NA	NA	NA
Curr. Ratio	1.6	1.7	1.7	1.7	NA	NA	NA	NA	NA	NA
% LT Debt of Cap.	53.6	63.7	55.0	50.4	NA	NA	NA	NA	NA	NA
% Net Inc.of Revs.	2.9	2.9	0.8	2.4	NA	NA	NA	NA	NA	NA
% Ret. on Assets	3.0	3.2	1.0	NA	NA	NA	NA	NA	NA	NA
% Ret. on Equity	11.3	12.3	3.1	NA	NA	NA	NA	NA	NA	NA

Data as orig. reptd.; bef. results of disc. opers. and/or spec. items. Per share data adj. for stk. divs. as of ex-div. date. Data for 1994 is pro forma. E-Estimated. NA-Not Available. NM-Not Meaningful. NR-Not Ranked.

Office—The Mill, 340 Pemberwick Road, Greenwich, CT 06831. **Tel**—(203) 532-4200. **Chrmn, Pres & CEO**—R. G. Burton. **Vice-Chrmn**—M. L. Reisch. **EVP & CFO**—M. D. Helfand. **SVP-Treas**—T. J. Quinlan. **Vice-Chrmn & Secy**—J. L. Adams. **EVP-Investor Contact**—James E. Lillie. **Dirs**—G. S. Armstrong, R. G. Burton, M. , P. M. Daniels, J. Griffin, A. Navab Jr., M. L. Reisch, S. M. Stuart. **Transfer Agent & Registrar**—Harris Trust Co. of New York. **Incorporated**—in Delaware in 1984. **Empl**— 15,600. **S&P Analyst:** A.O.T.

STANDARD &POOR'S
STOCK REPORTS

Wynn's International
2508M
NYSE Symbol **WN**

In S&P SmallCap 600

03-OCT-98

Industry: Auto Parts & Equipment

Summary: This company manufactures automotive parts and accessories and specialty chemicals. Products include O-rings, seals and molded rubber products.

Quantitative Evaluations

Outlook (1 Lowest—5 Highest)
• **NA**

Fair Value
• **NA**

Risk
• **Low**

Earn./Div. Rank
• **B+**

Technical Eval.
• **NA**

Rel. Strength Rank (1 Lowest—99 Highest)
• **93**

Insider Activity
• **NA**

Recent Price • 19½
52 Wk Range • 25¾-15⅝

Yield • 1.2%
12-Mo. P/E • 13.9

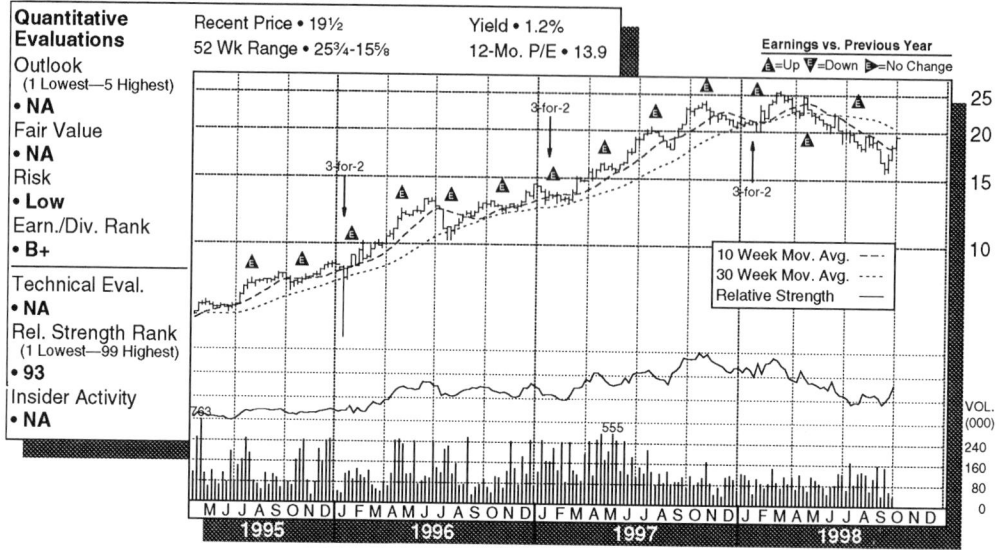

Earnings vs. Previous Year
▲=Up ▼=Down ►=No Change

10 Week Mov. Avg. ---
30 Week Mov. Avg. ····
Relative Strength —

Business Profile - 11-MAR-98

Wynn's International has achieved six consecutive years of improved results. This industrial supplier continues to seek expansion opportunities for its Wynn Oil business, which already has a strong presence in Western Europe, Latin America and the Asia/Pacific area, into countries of the former East Bloc, Northern Africa and other developing nations. For its Wynn's-Precision unit, WN plans to increase its penetration of existing markets in North America and Europe through improved products and services. In April 1997, WN, via a "Dutch Auction" self-tender, purchased 1,650,000 shares (about 8%) of its common shares at $24.25 each.

Operational Review - 11-MAR-98

Based on a brief preliminary report, net sales from continuing operations for 1997 advanced 11% from those of 1996, led by strong growth in the Automotive Components division, which was bolstered by an acquisition in late 1996. Operating margins widened, and following taxes at 37.2% in both years, income from continuing operations was up 22%, to $25,894,000 ($1.28 a share, diluted and based on 3.8% fewer shares), from $21,301,000 ($1.01). Results exclude income from disposal on discontinued operations of $0.01 per share in 1997 and a loss of $0.04 per share in 1996. Per-share figures for both years are adjusted for the January 1998 3-for-2 split.

Stock Performance - 02-OCT-98

In the past 30 trading days, WN's shares have increased 3%, compared to a 7% fall in the S&P 500. Average trading volume for the past five days was 6,980 shares, compared with the 40-day moving average of 18,546 shares.

Key Stock Statistics

Dividend Rate/Share	0.24	Shareholders	700
Shs. outstg. (M)	19.1	Market cap. (B)	$0.373
Avg. daily vol. (M)	0.014	Inst. holdings	76%
Tang. Bk. Value/Share	7.12		
Beta	0.50		

Value of $10,000 invested 5 years ago: $ 40,665

Fiscal Year Ending Dec. 31

	1998	1997	1996	1995	1994	1993
Revenues (Million $)						
1Q	85.81	77.89	71.46	78.07	76.78	70.51
2Q	85.59	81.04	71.83	78.05	76.87	71.32
3Q	—	79.36	70.61	74.61	72.22	73.19
4Q	—	82.67	74.63	73.05	66.79	69.94
Yr.	—	320.9	288.5	303.8	292.6	285.0
Earnings Per Share ($)						
1Q	0.38	0.30	0.22	0.18	0.14	0.10
2Q	0.36	0.32	0.26	0.20	0.17	0.13
3Q	—	0.32	0.25	0.18	0.16	0.13
4Q	—	0.34	0.27	0.18	0.14	0.12
Yr.	—	1.28	1.01	0.75	0.62	0.48

Next earnings report expected: mid October

Dividend Data (Dividends have been paid since 1975.)

Amount ($)	Date Decl.	Ex-Div. Date	Stock of Record	Payment Date
3-for-2	Dec. 10	Jan. 15	Dec. 22	Jan. 14 '98
0.060	Feb. 11	Mar. 10	Mar. 12	Mar. 31 '98
0.060	Apr. 29	Jun. 15	Jun. 17	Jun. 30 '98
0.060	Aug. 05	Sep. 15	Sep. 17	Sep. 30 '98

A Division of The McGraw-Hill Companies

Business Summary - 11-MAR-98

Going into 1996, Wynn's International, Inc. had delivered consistent earnings growth and a steadily increasing return on average equity over the previous four years, but management of this producer of automotive and industrial components and specialty chemicals still wasn't completely satisfied with the results. Management believed that its stock was still undervalued, based on the fundamental strengths of its core businesses, and that poor results in its automotive air-conditioning division, Wynn's Climate Systems, Inc., were clouding the performance of Wynn's other businesses.

Consequently, Wynn's sold its automotive air-conditioning business in May 1996, receiving $26.1 million in cash, and followed up with another successful year. In 1996, net income advanced 32% (a 28% increase for income from continuing operations), the fifth consecutive year of double-digit increases, net sales from continuing operations rose 9.9% and return on average equity exceeded 16%. The company is now focused on its two remaining core businesses, Wynn's-Precision and Wynn Oil Co.

Wynn's-Precision (Precision), together with Robert Skeels & Co., a wholesale distributor of locksets and locksmith supplies, comprises WN's Automotive and In-

dustrial Components division (49% of net sales and 60% of operating profits from continuing operations in 1996). Precision is a leading maker of O-rings, composite gaskets and other static and dynamic seals. These products, which are made from elastomeric and thermoplastic polymers, are sold mainly to customers in the automotive, aerospace, oil service and hydraulic industries. During 1996, Precision strengthened its leadership position in the market for plastic boots and bellows, which are used for sealing rack and pinion and constant velocity joints in automobiles, with the September acquisition of the Wheaton Automotive Plastics division of Lawson Mardon Wheaton.

Wynn Oil Co., which comprises the Specialty Chemicals division (51% of net sales and 40% of operating profit from continuing operations in 1996), produces and markets a wide variety of car care products, including preventive or corrective maintenance, as well as industrial specialty products, such as forging compounds, coolants, lubricants and cutting fluids. It also sells a power-flush machine, which automatically cleans a vehicle's cooling system and antifreeze, and restores the antifreeze so it can be reused.

Foreign sales accounted for 33% and 35% of the total in 1996 and 1995, respectively. GM, the largest customer of automotive components, accounted for 10.1% of consolidated sales in 1996.

Per Share Data ($)

(Year Ended Dec. 31)	1997	1996	1995	1994	1993	1992	1991	1990	1989	1988
Tangible Bk. Val.	6.47	6.33	5.56	4.91	4.35	4.13	3.97	4.40	4.08	3.83
Cash Flow	1.78	1.35	1.14	0.97	0.84	0.73	-0.20	0.76	0.77	0.57
Earnings	1.28	1.00	0.75	0.62	0.48	0.40	-0.61	0.33	0.39	0.23
Dividends	0.32	0.18	0.15	0.13	0.12	0.12	0.12	0.12	0.12	0.12
Payout Ratio	18%	18%	21%	21%	26%	30%	NM	34%	31%	52%
Prices - High	24⅛	14½	9	7⅛	7	5⅜	3⅞	4¾	5½	4½
- Low	12¾	8	5¾	5⅜	5	3⅛	2⅞	2¾	4⅛	3⅛
P/E Ratio - High	19	14	12	12	15	13	NM	15	14	20
- Low	10	8	8	9	10	7	NM	8	11	14

Income Statement Analysis (Million $)

	1997	1996	1995	1994	1993	1992	1991	1990	1989	1988
Revs.	321	289	304	293	285	292	274	285	284	296
Oper. Inc.	47.6	40.0	33.4	28.6	25.6	23.8	18.8	26.2	22.9	22.0
Depr.	8.3	7.4	8.2	6.8	6.7	6.1	7.5	8.5	7.4	6.5
Int. Exp.	0.2	0.2	1.6	3.0	3.9	5.1	5.2	5.8	5.2	5.5
Pretax Inc.	41.2	33.9	24.6	19.4	15.8	13.3	-13.9	13.0	13.0	10.1
Eff. Tax Rate	37%	37%	37%	39%	43%	46%	NM	51%	42%	57%
Net Inc.	25.9	21.3	15.4	11.8	9.0	7.3	-11.2	6.4	7.6	4.4

Balance Sheet & Other Fin. Data (Million $)

	1997	1996	1995	1994	1993	1992	1991	1990	1989	1988
Cash	43.3	53.3	23.1	16.4	21.4	14.7	6.1	7.7	12.4	22.1
Curr. Assets	148	154	127	120	118	125	118	128	129	130
Total Assets	207	205	182	176	168	171	166	188	189	187
Curr. Liab.	61.4	64.0	58.5	59.2	56.3	54.5	44.7	50.2	53.5	58.3
LT Debt	Nil	Nil	0.1	14.9	23.4	32.5	40.7	41.2	41.2	42.1
Common Eqty.	128	133	116	95.4	84.4	78.9	75.6	89.8	87.9	81.3
Total Cap.	135	141	123	117	112	116	121	138	135	129
Cap. Exp.	11.8	9.1	7.5	13.8	10.0	6.5	4.2	8.3	10.7	8.9
Cash Flow	34.2	28.7	23.6	18.6	15.6	13.4	-3.7	14.8	15.0	11.0
Curr. Ratio	2.4	2.4	2.2	2.0	2.1	2.3	2.6	2.5	2.4	2.2
% LT Debt of Cap.	Nil	Nil	0.1	12.7	21.0	28.0	33.7	29.9	30.5	32.7
% Net Inc.of Revs.	8.1	7.4	5.1	4.0	3.2	2.5	NM	2.2	2.7	1.5
% Ret. on Assets	12.6	11.1	8.7	6.8	5.2	4.3	NM	3.5	4.0	2.4
% Ret. on Equity	19.9	17.1	14.5	13.1	10.9	9.4	NM	7.4	8.9	5.5

Data as orig. reptd.; bef. results of disc. opers. and/or spec. items. Per share data adj. for stk. divs. as of ex-div. date. Bold denotes diluted EPS (FASB 128). E-Estimated. NA-Not Available. NM-Not Meaningful. NR-Not Ranked.

Office—500 N. State College Blvd., Suite 700, Orange, CA 92668. **Tel**—(714) 938-3700. **Chrmn, CEO & Investor Contact**—James Carroll. **Pres & COO**—J. W. Huber. **VP-Fin & CFO**—S. A. Schlosser. **VP & Secy**—G. M. Gibbons. **Dirs**—B. Beek, W. E. Bellwood, J. Carroll, B. L. Herrmann, R. Hood Jr., R. L. Nelson, D. C. Trauscht, J. D. Woods. **Transfer Agent & Registrar**—ChaseMellon Shareholder Services, Los Angeles. **Incorporated**—in Delaware in 1973. **Empl**— 2,067. **S&P Analyst:** L.A.O.

STANDARD &POOR'S
STOCK REPORTS

X-Rite, Inc.

5672

NASDAQ Symbol **XRIT**

In S&P SmallCap 600

03-OCT-98

Industry: Electronics (Instrumentation)

Summary: This company manufactures quality control products primarily for the graphic arts, photographic, packaging, paint, plastic, textile and medical industries.

Quantitative Evaluations

Outlook (1 Lowest—5 Highest)
- **5**

Fair Value
- **18⅛**

Risk
- **Average**

Earn./Div. Rank
- **B+**

Technical Eval.
- **Bearish** since 1/98

Rel. Strength Rank (1 Lowest—99 Highest)
- **52**

Insider Activity
- **Neutral**

Recent Price • 9⅝

52 Wk Range • 21-8⅜

Yield • 1.0%

12-Mo. P/E • 13.0

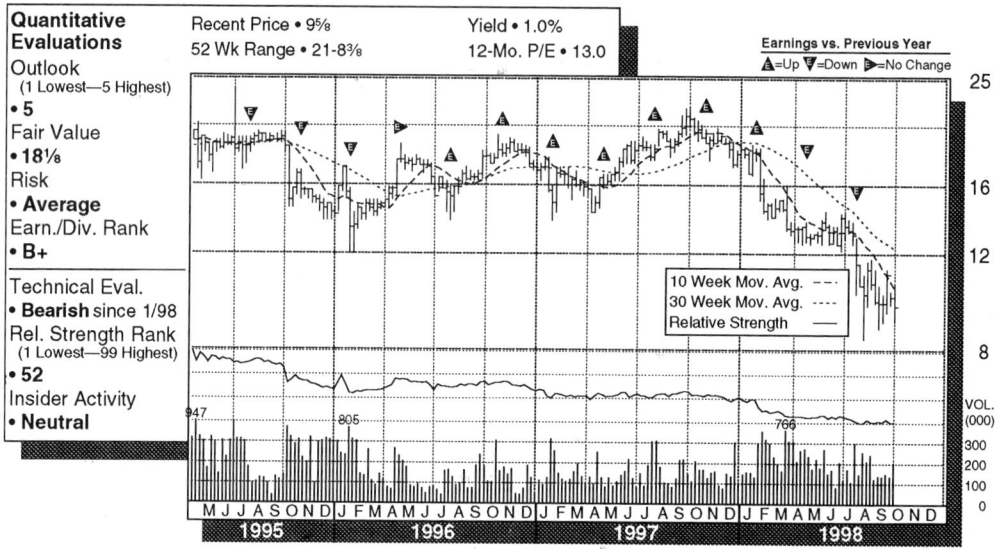

Earnings vs. Previous Year
▲=Up ▼=Down ▶=No Change

10 Week Mov. Avg. ---
30 Week Mov. Avg. ---
Relative Strength —

Business Profile - 10-SEP-98

X-Rite's color and appearance products support a myriad of industries. This diversification not only protects the company from a downturn in any one industry sector but also offers a wide base for future sales opportunities. Additionally, nearly a third of the company's sales come from international markets. X-Rite's industry leadership position is founded on its ability to introduce high-quality, leading-edge products. Consequently, the company intends to raise the level of resources committed to product development in 1998. In January 1998, XRIT announced a stock repurchase program covering 4.54 million shares. The repurchases will begin following the death of each founding stockholder and is designed to avoid the sale of large amounts of stock. In April, the company reported financial results that were below analysts' expectations due to a decline in the demand for private labeled digital imaging products.

Operational Review - 10-SEP-98

For the first six months of 1998, net sales rose 1.8%, year to year, reflecting a slowdown in demand for the digital imaging product line. Gross margins widened, but operating expenses jumped 28%; pretax income fell 27%. Net income was down 27%, to $6,459,000 ($0.31 a share), from $8,882,000 ($0.42).

Stock Performance - 02-OCT-98

In the past 30 trading days, XRIT's shares have declined 9%, compared to a 7% fall in the S&P 500. Average trading volume for the past five days was 40,020 shares, compared with the 40-day moving average of 33,974 shares.

Key Stock Statistics

Dividend Rate/Share	0.10	Shareholders	1,700
Shs. outstg. (M)	21.2	Market cap. (B)	$0.204
Avg. daily vol. (M)	0.032	Inst. holdings	22%
Tang. Bk. Value/Share	0.97		
Beta	0.70		

Value of $10,000 invested 5 years ago: $ 7,542

Fiscal Year Ending Dec. 31

	1998	1997	1996	1995	1994	1993
Revenues (Million $)						
1Q	23.64	23.08	19.70	17.95	12.35	9.47
2Q	24.29	23.99	20.83	18.91	14.76	9.38
3Q	—	24.86	21.36	18.76	15.64	9.86
4Q	—	25.06	22.51	17.03	16.73	10.48
Yr.	—	96.99	84.39	72.63	59.48	39.19
Earnings Per Share ($)						
1Q	0.15	0.20	0.16	0.16	0.12	0.10
2Q	0.16	0.22	0.18	0.12	0.15	0.09
3Q	—	0.22	0.19	0.12	0.16	0.08
4Q	—	0.21	0.20	0.07	0.17	0.10
Yr.	—	0.85	0.73	0.47	0.60	0.36

Next earnings report expected: late October

Dividend Data (Dividends have been paid since 1986.)

Amount ($)	Date Decl.	Ex-Div. Date	Stock of Record	Payment Date
0.025	Oct. 06	Oct. 15	Oct. 17	Nov. 14 '97
0.025	Jan. 05	Jan. 14	Jan. 16	Feb. 13 '98
0.025	Apr. 06	Apr. 15	Apr. 17	May. 15 '98
0.025	Jul. 06	Jul. 15	Jul. 17	Aug. 14 '98

A Division of The McGraw·Hill Companies

Business Summary - 10-SEP-98

By focusing on improving existing technologies, X-Rite Incorporated, (XRIT) seeks to increase sales growth in current target markets and expand into emerging areas. As a result of the company's efforts, previously immobile or unwieldy measuring instruments are now available in a portable format. Color measurements and adjustments can now be conducted on-site rather than in separate quality control facilities. Current target markets include: paint, plastic, textile, packaging, photographic, graphic arts and medical industries. X-Rite's foray into the emerging digital imaging market has resulted in increased penetration of the graphic arts industry. Sales to this industry grew 38% in 1997.

The company has two main product lines: instruments that measure color and appearance, and instruments that measure optical or photographic density. Products include densitometers, sensitometers, colorimeters, spectrophotometers, point-of-purchase paint matching systems, integrating spheres and sphere systems. A densitometer is an instrument that measures light, compares that measurement with a reference standard and signals the result. Sensitometers are used to expose photographic film of various types in a very precise manner for comparison to a reference standard. X-Rite

provides these instruments to the photographic, graphic arts, medical and digital imaging industries. A colorimeter measures color much as the human eye perceives color, using red, green and blue receptors. It is used to measure printed colors on packages, labels, textiles and other materials where appearance is critical for buyer acceptance.

The company diversified through the 1995 acquisition of Labsphere, a leading supplier of integrating spheres, sphere systems and reflectance coatings. Integrating spheres and integrating sphere systems are used in testing incandescent and fluorescent lamp output, calibration of remote sensors, laser power measurement, and reflectance and transmittance light measurement. In May 1997, XRIT acquired all the assets of Light Source Computer Images, Inc., a producer of high-quality, easy-to-use scanning, imaging and print optimization software.

Sales of the company's products are made by its own personnel and through independent manufacturer's representatives. Certain products not sold directly to end-users are distributed in the U.S. through a network of 1,500 independent dealers and outside the U.S. through 400 dealers in more than 50 countries. Foreign sales accounted for 33% of total sales in 1997, versus 34% in 1996 and 33% in 1995.

Per Share Data ($) (Year Ended Dec. 31)	1997	1996	1995	1994	1993	1992	1991	1990	1989	1988
Tangible Bk. Val.	3.34	3.01	2.34	2.44	1.90	1.61	1.33	1.13	0.97	0.81
Cash Flow	1.10	0.93	0.63	0.66	0.41	0.39	0.28	0.23	0.21	0.18
Earnings	0.85	0.73	0.47	0.60	0.36	0.34	0.23	0.18	0.17	0.16
Dividends	0.10	0.10	0.10	0.08	0.08	0.05	0.03	0.03	0.02	0.02
Payout Ratio	12%	14%	21%	13%	22%	15%	14%	15%	11%	10%
Prices - High	22⅜	19¾	24	21	13½	16⅝	7½	3⅝	3⅛	3⅞
- Low	13¾	12	13¾	10½	8¾	5⅝	2¾	2	2¹⁄₁₆	1⅞
P/E Ratio - High	26	27	51	35	38	49	33	20	18	24
- Low	16	16	29	18	24	17	12	11	12	12

Income Statement Analysis (Million $)

	1997	1996	1995	1994	1993	1992	1991	1990	1989	1988
Revs.	97.0	84.4	72.6	59.5	39.2	36.2	29.1	23.6	21.2	19.6
Oper. Inc.	32.5	27.1	18.0	19.1	11.0	10.7	7.1	5.5	5.2	4.7
Depr.	5.5	4.3	3.4	1.3	1.2	1.1	1.0	0.8	0.7	0.6
Int. Exp.	NA	Nil	NM	Nil	Nil	Nil	Nil	Nil	Nil	Nil
Pretax Inc.	27.3	23.2	14.7	18.4	10.4	10.1	6.8	5.5	5.2	4.6
Eff. Tax Rate	34%	34%	33%	31%	28%	30%	30%	32%	30%	29%
Net Inc.	18.0	15.4	9.9	12.6	7.5	7.1	4.7	3.8	3.6	3.3

Balance Sheet & Other Fin. Data (Million $)

	1997	1996	1995	1994	1993	1992	1991	1990	1989	1988
Cash	2.8	1.6	4.4	14.9	18.3	15.4	12.6	9.7	8.4	6.5
Curr. Assets	52.2	47.4	32.0	39.4	32.4	27.4	22.7	18.8	16.1	12.7
Total Assets	92.5	79.0	63.5	54.6	41.9	35.8	30.5	26.0	22.2	18.8
Curr. Liab.	5.7	5.3	4.0	2.9	1.7	1.7	2.3	1.9	1.5	1.5
LT Debt	Nil	Nil	NM	Nil	Nil	Nil	Nil	Nil	Nil	Nil
Common Eqty.	86.1	73.0	59.3	51.1	39.8	33.7	27.8	23.5	20.2	16.9
Total Cap.	86.1	73.6	59.9	51.7	40.2	34.1	28.2	24.0	20.6	17.3
Cap. Exp.	4.3	3.1	3.4	4.2	1.5	1.7	1.7	2.1	0.7	0.8
Cash Flow	23.5	19.6	13.3	13.9	8.7	8.2	5.7	4.6	4.3	3.8
Curr. Ratio	9.1	8.9	8.0	13.8	19.4	15.9	10.0	9.7	10.4	8.7
% LT Debt of Cap.	Nil	Nil	NM	Nil	Nil	Nil	Nil	Nil	Nil	Nil
% Net Inc.of Revs.	18.6	18.2	13.6	21.3	19.2	19.5	16.3	16.0	17.1	16.6
% Ret. on Assets	21.0	21.6	16.8	26.2	19.4	21.3	16.8	15.7	17.7	18.3
% Ret. on Equity	22.7	23.3	17.9	27.8	20.5	23.0	18.5	17.3	19.6	21.0

Data as orig. reptd.; bef. results of disc. opers. and/or spec. items. Per share data adj. for stk. divs. as of ex-div. date. Bold denotes diluted EPS (FASB 128). E-Estimated. NA-Not Available. NM-Not Meaningful. NR-Not Ranked.

Office—3100 44th St. SW, Grandville, MI 49418. **Tel**—(616) 534-7663. **Fax**—(616) 534-9212. **Website**—http://www.x-rite.com **Chrmn, Pres & CEO**—T. Thompson. **VP, CFO & Investor Contact**—Duane Kluting. **Dirs**—P. M. Banks, S. W. Cheff, R. E. Cook, M. G. DeVries, J.A. Knister, R. S. Teesdale, C. Van Namen, R. A. VandenBerg. **Transfer Agent & Registrar**—State Street Bank & Trust Co., Boston. **Incorporated**—in Michigan in 1958. **Empl**— 640. **S&P Analyst:** Mark Cavallone

Xircom, Inc.

5672R

NASDAQ Symbol **XIRC**

In S&P SmallCap 600

03-OCT-98

Industry: Computers (Peripherals)

Summary: Xircom's principal products are local area network (LAN) adapters, which enable portable personal computers to be connected to a LAN.

Quantitative Evaluations

Outlook (1 Lowest—5 Highest)
- **4-**

Fair Value
- **33¾**

Risk
- **High**

Earn./Div. Rank
- **NR**

Technical Eval.
- **Bearish** since 3/98

Rel. Strength Rank (1 Lowest—99 Highest)
- **89**

Insider Activity
- **Unfavorable**

Recent Price • 22
52 Wk Range • 27¼-8⅝
Yield • Nil
12-Mo. P/E • NM

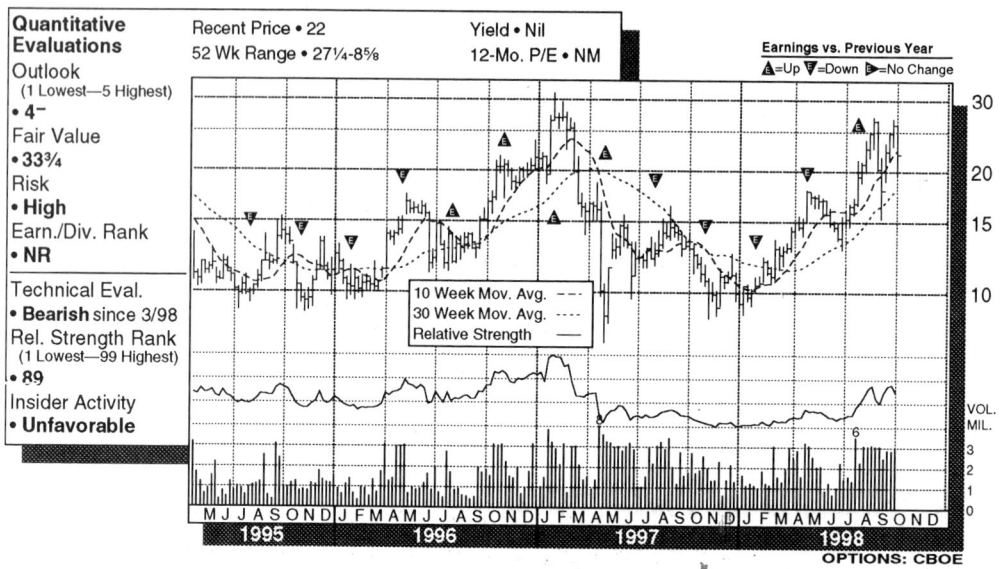

Earnings vs. Previous Year ▲=Up ▼=Down ▷=No Change

10 Week Mov. Avg. - - -
30 Week Mov. Avg. ·····
Relative Strength —

OPTIONS: CBOE

Business Profile - 24-JUL-98

In the second and third quarters of FY 98 (Sep.), XIRC experienced double digit growth in both its channel business and OEM business, offsetting inventory reductions by customers earlier in the fiscal year. XIRC implemented a speed-based distribution model in the FY 97 fourth quarter. The company hopes that this will allow it to benefit from more efficient spending in the channels. The company's newest product is its RealPort Integrated PC Card, launched in March 1998, which features built-in connectors and incorporates 10/100Mbps Ethernet, 56K modem, telephone handset pass-thru and mobile phone connections in a single card.

Operational Review - 24-JUL-98

In the first nine months of FY 98 (Sep.), net sales advanced 15%, year to year, reflecting second and third quarter growth in both OEM and branded channels businesses, which outweighed a decline in revenues in the first quarter due to inventory reductions by customers. Gross margins narrowed, and after 28% higher R&D costs and higher SG&A expenses, operating profit fell 5.9%. Following sharply higher other income, net income was up 10%, to $10,412,000 ($0.45 a share, on 5.7% more shares) from $2,965,000 ($0.43, before a loss of $0.29 from discontinued operations).

Stock Performance - 02-OCT-98

In the past 30 trading days, XIRC's shares have declined 17%, compared to a 7% fall in the S&P 500. Average trading volume for the past five days was 597,380 shares, compared with the 40-day moving average of 658,997 shares.

Key Stock Statistics

Dividend Rate/Share	Nil	Shareholders	400
Shs. outstg. (M)	23.0	Market cap. (B)	$0.506
Avg. daily vol. (M)	0.566	Inst. holdings	53%
Tang. Bk. Value/Share	5.50		
Beta	1.29		

Value of $10,000 invested 5 years ago: $ 12,394

Fiscal Year Ending Sep. 30

	1998	1997	1996	1995	1994	1993
Revenues (Million $)						
1Q	52.55	62.31	37.70	40.11	26.38	17.17
2Q	64.13	57.14	45.33	39.97	30.25	18.72
3Q	71.31	50.23	52.22	16.47	36.09	21.65
4Q	—	20.90	58.06	30.01	38.87	24.67
Yr.	—	184.6	193.3	126.6	131.6	82.21
Earnings Per Share ($)						
1Q	0.11	0.20	-0.04	0.27	0.21	0.11
2Q	0.14	0.22	0.07	0.15	0.23	0.13
3Q	0.20	0.02	0.13	-2.87	0.25	0.16
4Q	—	-0.57	0.14	-0.91	0.26	0.19
Yr.	—	-0.16	0.30	-3.44	0.95	0.59

Next earnings report expected: late October

Dividend Data

No cash has been paid. The company intends to retain earnings for use in its business.

Business Summary - 24-JUL-98

This leading manufacturer and seller of network access solutions for mobile and remote PC users shifted its strategy in FY 96 (Sep.) to focus on its core PC Card business. XIRC's products enable PC users to access information and resources found on local area networks (LANs) and on-line internet services.

Over the last several years, there has been a significant increase in the number of PC users accessing a corporate LAN or an on-line service (e.g. America On-line, Prodigy, Compuserve or the Internet) from a remote location. This requires a modem on the client PC and a modem on the LAN that serves as a communication gateway to the network (often referred to as a remote access server or a communications server). The market for PC card modems is expected to grow from 4.1 million units in 1996 to 11.2 million units by 2001. The PC Card division offers Ethernet and Token Ring LAN adapters, combination LAN adapters and modems, and modem-only products.

PC Card products, which are credit-card-size devices that slide into a slot on laptops, include the CreditCard Ethernet Adapter 10/100 and the 32-bit CardBus Ethernet 10/100 adapter, which supports connection to both 10Mbps and 100Mbps networks. Net sales from

PC Card LAN Adapters were 42% of FY 97 net sales, compared to 37% in FY 96. Multifunction adapter/ modem cards are offered through the CreditCard Ethernet+Modem product line, which incorporates 33.6 and 56K modems with a LAN adapter. Sales of these products accounted for 43% of total net sales in FY 97, versus 44% in FY 96.

Modem-only PC Cards incorporate the V.34 and 56K standards and offer high connection speeds for users who require high-speed remote access to LANs, commercial on-line services or the Internet. Sales of these products accounted for 11% of total sales in FY 97, versus 7% in FY 96.

The company's wired LAN adapter products for portable PCs allow notebook users connectivity to LANs. Sales of this product line are declining as the industry has shifted toward PC Cards. Net sales for pocket LAN adapter products declined to 4% of net sales in FY 97 (Sep.) from 11% in FY 96.

In June 1997, the company sold its Netaccess subsidiary to Brooktrout Technology for $11 million; a resulting $6.3 million loss, after tax, was recorded in the FY 97 third quarter. Netaccess was engaged in the sale of digital and analog remote access server products to OEMs and through two-tier distribution channels.

Per Share Data ($)

(Year Ended Sep. 30)	1997	1996	1995	1994	1993	1992	1991	1990	1989	1988
Tangible Bk. Val.	5.02	3.32	2.81	5.10	3.99	3.42	NM	NM	NM	NM
Cash Flow	0.15	0.72	-3.06	1.17	0.71	0.47	0.22	NA	NA	NA
Earnings	-0.16	0.30	-3.44	0.95	0.59	0.41	0.19	NA	NA	NA
Dividends	Nil	Nil	Nil	Nil	Nil	Nil	Nil	Nil	Nil	Nil
Payout Ratio	Nil	Nil	Nil	Nil	Nil	Nil	Nil	Nil	Nil	Nil
Prices - High	31¹/₈	23³/₄	19	28¹/₄	19¹/₂	22	NA	NA	NA	NA
- Low	7¹/₂	9¹/₂	9	12³/₄	7¹/₄	7	NA	NA	NA	NA
P/E Ratio - High	NM	79	NM	30	33	54	NA	NA	NA	NA
- Low	NM	32	NM	13	12	17	NA	NA	NA	NA

Income Statement Analysis (Million $)

	1997	1996	1995	1994	1993	1992	1991	1990	1989	1988
Revs.	185	193	127	132	82.2	59.1	26.3	NA	NA	NA
Oper. Inc.	0.7	19.8	-13.6	29.1	17.0	10.5	4.6	NA	NA	NA
Depr.	6.5	8.2	6.5	3.8	2.0	1.0	0.4	NA	NA	NA
Int. Exp.	Nil	Nil	Nil	0.2	0.2	0.4	0.1	NA	NA	NA
Pretax Inc.	-4.8	8.8	-65.8	25.1	15.8	9.6	4.1	NA	NA	NA
Eff. Tax Rate	NM	33%	NM	37%	39%	37%	40%	NA	NA	NA
Net Inc.	-3.3	6.0	-58.8	15.9	9.7	6.1	2.5	NA	NA	NA

Balance Sheet & Other Fin. Data (Million $)

	1997	1996	1995	1994	1993	1992	1991	1990	1989	1988
Cash	75.1	21.5	13.7	51.5	40.4	32.7	Nil	Nil	Nil	Nil
Curr. Assets	130	84.1	63.3	91.4	69.7	53.6	12.0	NA	NA	NA
Total Assets	148	109	81.0	101	75.3	57.0	13.7	NA	NA	NA
Curr. Liab.	34.0	40.6	34.8	18.8	11.9	6.3	6.9	NA	NA	NA
LT Debt	Nil	1.9	0.8	0.1	0.4	0.8	0.6	NA	NA	NA
Common Eqty.	113	65.6	53.1	82.1	62.5	49.6	-9.0	NA	NA	NA
Total Cap.	114	68.2	53.9	82.2	63.0	50.4	6.8	NA	NA	NA
Cap. Exp.	6.4	9.5	13.6	7.4	4.0	1.9	1.4	NA	NA	NA
Cash Flow	3.1	14.1	-52.3	19.7	11.6	7.0	2.9	NA	NA	NA
Curr. Ratio	3.8	2.1	1.8	4.9	5.8	8.5	1.7	NA	NA	NA
% LT Debt of Cap.	Nil	2.8	1.5	0.2	0.7	1.7	8.6	NA	NA	NA
% Net Inc.of Revs.	NM	3.1	NM	12.1	11.7	10.3	9.4	NA	NA	NA
% Ret. on Assets	NM	6.1	NM	17.8	14.1	NM	NA	NA	NA	NA
% Ret. on Equity	NM	10.1	NM	21.7	16.6	NM	NA	NA	NA	NA

Data as orig. reptd.; bef. results of disc. opers. and/or spec. items. Per share data adj. for stk. divs. as of ex-div. date. E-Estimated. NA-Not Available. NM-Not Meaningful. NR-Not Ranked.

Office—2300 Corporate Center Dr., Thousand Oaks, CA 91320. **Tel**—(805) 376-9300. **Website**—http://www.xircom.com **Chrmn, Pres & CEO**—D. I. Gates. **VP-Fin & CFO**—S. F. DeGennaro. **Secy**—R. H. Holliday. **Investor Contact**—Kristi Cushing (805- 376-6969). **Dirs**—M. F. G. Ashby, K. J. Biba, G. J. Bowen, D. I. Gates, J. K. Mathews, W. J. Schroeder. D. W. Yocam. **Transfer Agent & Registrar**—Bank of Boston. **Incorporated**—in California in 1988. **Empl**— 850. **S&P Analyst:** Jim Corridore

Xylan Corp.

5672Y

NASDAQ Symbol **XYLN**

In S&P SmallCap 600

03-OCT-98

Industry: Computers (Networking)

Summary: This company is one of the world's leading campus-switching vendors.

Quantitative Evaluations

Recent Price • 11⅝
52 Wk Range • 31¼-9⅝

Yield • Nil
12-Mo. P/E • 18.8

Outlook
(1 Lowest—5 Highest)
• **NA**

Fair Value
• **NA**

Risk
• **NA**

Earn./Div. Rank
• **NR**

Technical Eval.
• **NA**

Rel. Strength Rank
(1 Lowest—99 Highest)
• **7**

Insider Activity
• **Unfavorable**

Earnings vs. Previous Year
▲=Up ▼=Down ▶=No Change

10 Week Mov. Avg. – – –
30 Week Mov. Avg. - - - -
Relative Strength ——

OPTIONS: ASE, CBOE, P

Business Profile - 16-SEP-98

Xylan pursues direct sales to organizations in North America with large networking requirements and employs network integrators to target customers worldwide. It has strategic OEM partnerships with leading communications and networking companies, including Alcatel and IBM, that have significant customer relationships already in place. The company believes that networking markets continue to provide excellent opportunities for growth; its financial goal was to have double-digit growth in revenues for each quarter of 1998, and to improve operating margins.

Operational Review - 16-SEP-98

Revenues in the first six months of 1998 advanced 71%, year to year, aided by strong growth in the new OmniStack product line, which doubled in revenues in the second quarter from those of the previous quarter, and continued substantial growth in the LAN switching market. Gross margins widened, aided in part by lower component prices. With a 58% rise in operating expenses, despite lower interest income, pretax income climbed 93%. After taxes at 35.8%, versus 10.9% (which included a one-time tax benefit), net income was up 39%, to $17,988,000 ($0.38 a share, diluted), from $12,958,000 ($0.28).

Stock Performance - 02-OCT-98

In the past 30 trading days, XYLN's shares have declined 50%, compared to a 7% fall in the S&P 500. Average trading volume for the past five days was 1,246,560 shares, compared with the 40-day moving average of 1,215,456 shares.

Key Stock Statistics

Dividend Rate/Share	Nil	Shareholders	500
Shs. outstg. (M)	43.4	Market cap. (B)	$0.505
Avg. daily vol. (M)	1.906	Inst. holdings	73%
Tang. Bk. Value/Share	5.21		
Beta	NA		

Value of $10,000 invested 5 years ago: NA

Fiscal Year Ending Dec. 31

	1998	1997	1996	1995	1994	1993
Revenues (Million $)						
1Q	75.37	48.01	23.39	—	—	—
2Q	83.68	45.12	28.19	—	—	—
3Q	—	53.52	35.43	—	—	—
4Q	—	64.20	41.45	—	—	—
Yr.	—	210.8	128.5	29.66	0.44	—
Earnings Per Share ($)						
1Q	0.18	0.13	0.06	—	—	—
2Q	0.20	0.15	0.06	—	—	—
3Q	—	0.10	0.10	—	—	—
4Q	—	0.14	0.11	—	—	—
Yr.	—	0.52	0.33	-0.91	-0.41	-0.05

Next earnings report expected: late October

Dividend Data

No cash dividends have been paid. The company does not anticipate paying cash dividends in the foreseeable future.

A Division of The McGraw·Hill Companies

Business Summary - 16-SEP-98

Xylan, founded in 1993 to provide high-bandwidth switching systems that enhance the performance of existing local area networks (LANs) and facilitate migration to next-generation networking technologies such as asynchronous transfer mode (ATM), is one of the world's leading campus-switching vendors. With its products, the company is working to solve performance degradation problems of current hub and router-based networks due to continued growth in the size of networks, increasing demands of high-performance personal computers and workstations, and the emergence of graphical applications and the World Wide Web.

The company's switches are based on a distributed, modular, multiprocessor architecture that combines LAN switching, virtual LANs, ATM switching, wide area access, security and layer-three switching in a single product. Xylan products are designed to serve as a complete switching system and include OmniSwitch, OmniStack and PizzaSwitch.

The OmniSwitch is a modular, chassis-based switch that provides high performance LAN switching, routing, layer-three switching and ATM switching. It supports a variety of LAN types, interconnecting Ethernet, Fast Ethernet, token ring, FDDI, frame relay and ATM with any-to-any MAC-layer protocol translation.

The OmniStack series, introduced in March 1998, is designed to be more cost effective in smaller configurations, but is based on the same system architecture and incorporates many of the same LAN switching and software capabilities as the OmniSwitch. OmniStack combines a number of Ethernet or 10/100 ports with a small number of modular high-speed ports, such as Fast Ethernet, Gigabit Ethernet, ATM or various wide area interfaces.

The company's PizzaSwitch product, also based on the same system architecture and LAN switching and software capabilities as the OmniSwitch, is intended to be used in applications that require a small access switch with FDDI uplinks.

Products also include AutoTracker-Virtual LANs, which let a network manager group devices logically, rather than physically, using policy-based management; Vision Network Management software that operates in a customer's existing network management environment; and ATM Switching Technology, which lets both data-based and real-time traffic be handled with minimal cell loss even under heavy loads.

Sales and marketing efforts focus on three channels of distribution: worldwide OEM partners (37% of 1997 revenues), network integrators in North America and overseas (38%), and direct sales (25%). In 1997, IBM and Alcatel accounted for 22% and 12% of revenues, respectively. Sales to customers outside North America provided 53% of 1997 revenues.

In September 1998, directors authorized the repurchase of one million common shares. The company, which had just completed a prior authorization to buy 2 million shares, plans to use the shares for employee stock benefit plans.

Per Share Data ($)

(Year Ended Dec. 31)	1997	1996	1995	1994	1993	1992	1991	1990	1989	1988
Tangible Bk. Val.	5.03	4.43	2.35	NA	NA	NA	NA	NA	NA	NA
Cash Flow	0.68	0.41	-0.40	NA	NA	NA	NA	NA	NA	NA
Earnings	0.52	0.33	-0.91	-0.41	NA	NA	NA	NA	NA	NA
Dividends	Nil	Nil	Nil	Nil	Nil	Nil	Nil	Nil	Nil	Nil
Payout Ratio	Nil	Nil	Nil	Nil	Nil	Nil	Nil	Nil	Nil	Nil
Prices - High	37¼	76	NA	NA	NA	NA	NA	NA	NA	NA
- Low	12⅜	23½	NA	NA	NA	NA	NA	NA	NA	NA
P/E Ratio - High	72	230	NM	NM	NM	NM	NM	NM	NM	NM
- Low	24	71	NM	NM	NM	NM	NM	NM	NM	NM

Income Statement Analysis (Million $)

	1997	1996	1995	1994	1993	1992	1991	1990	1989	1988
Revs.	211	128	29.7	0.4	NA	NA	NA	NA	NA	NA
Oper. Inc.	32.9	21.4	-8.6	NA	NA	NA	NA	NA	NA	NA
Depr.	7.9	3.6	0.9	NA	NA	NA	NA	NA	NA	NA
Int. Exp.	Nil	Nil	Nil	Nil	Nil	Nil	Nil	Nil	Nil	Nil
Pretax Inc.	31.7	23.1	-9.4	-4.1	NA	NA	NA	NA	NA	NA
Eff. Tax Rate	24%	34%	NM	NM	NM	NM	NM	NM	NM	NM
Net Inc.	24.1	15.2	-9.4	-4.1	NA	NA	NA	NA	NA	NA

Balance Sheet & Other Fin. Data (Million $)

	1997	1996	1995	1994	1993	1992	1991	1990	1989	1988
Cash	35.9	62.5	6.0	NA	NA	NA	NA	NA	NA	NA
Curr. Assets	159	156	21.7	NA	NA	NA	NA	NA	NA	NA
Total Assets	251	207	27.2	NA	NA	NA	NA	NA	NA	NA
Curr. Liab.	33.9	20.9	10.6	NA	NA	NA	NA	NA	NA	NA
LT Debt	0.0	0.2	0.5	NA	NA	NA	NA	NA	NA	NA
Common Eqty.	216	186	16.1	NA	NA	NA	NA	NA	NA	NA
Total Cap.	216	186	16.6	NA	NA	NA	NA	NA	NA	NA
Cap. Exp.	12.1	15.2	4.3	NA	NA	NA	NA	NA	NA	NA
Cash Flow	32.0	18.8	-8.5	NA	NA	NA	NA	NA	NA	NA
Curr. Ratio	4.7	7.4	2.1	NA	NA	NA	NA	NA	NA	NA
% LT Debt of Cap.	Nil	0.0	3.1	NA	NA	NA	NA	NA	NA	NA
% Net Inc.of Revs.	11.4	11.9	NM	NM	NM	NM	NM	NM	NM	NM
% Ret. on Assets	10.5	13.0	NM	NM	NM	NM	NM	NM	NM	NM
% Ret. on Equity	12.0	15.1	NM	NM	NM	NM	NM	NM	NM	NM

Data as orig. reptd.; bef. results of disc. opers. and/or spec. items. Per share data adj. for stk. divs. as of ex-div. date. Bold denotes diluted EPS (FASB 128). E-Estimated. NA-Not Available. NM-Not Meaningful. NR-Not Ranked.

Office—26679 W. Agoura Rd., Calabasas, CA 91302. **Tel**—(818) 880-3500. **Website**—http://www.xylan.com **Chrmn, Pres & CEO**—S. Y. Kim. **VP-Fin & CFO**—D. J. Bartos. **Dirs**—R. S. Cecil, R. C. Hawk, S. Y. Kim, Y. Pikover, T. C. Taylor, J. L. Walecka. **Transfer Agent & Registrar**—First National Bank of Boston. **Incorporated**—in California in 1993. **Empl**— 721. **S&P Analyst:** Megan Graham Hackett

STANDARD &POOR'S
STOCK REPORTS

Yellow Corp.

5675

Nasdaq Symbol **YELL**

In S&P SmallCap 600

03-OCT-98

Industry: Truckers

Summary: This company operates the nation's largest long-haul less-than-truckload (LTL) motor carrier and offers regional LTL services. In July 1998 YELL sold its Preston Trucking unit.

S&P Opinion: Buy (★★★★★)	Recent Price • 12⅞	Yield • Nil
	52 Wk Range • 33⅜-11¼	12-Mo. P/E • NM

Quantitative Evaluations

Outlook (1 Lowest—5 Highest)
• **3+**

Fair Value
• **15¼**

Risk
• **Average**

Earn./Div. Rank
• **C**

Technical Eval.
• **Bearish** since 2/98

Rel. Strength Rank (1 Lowest—99 Highest)
• **45**

Insider Activity
• **NA**

Earnings vs. Previous Year
△=Up ▽=Down ▶=No Change

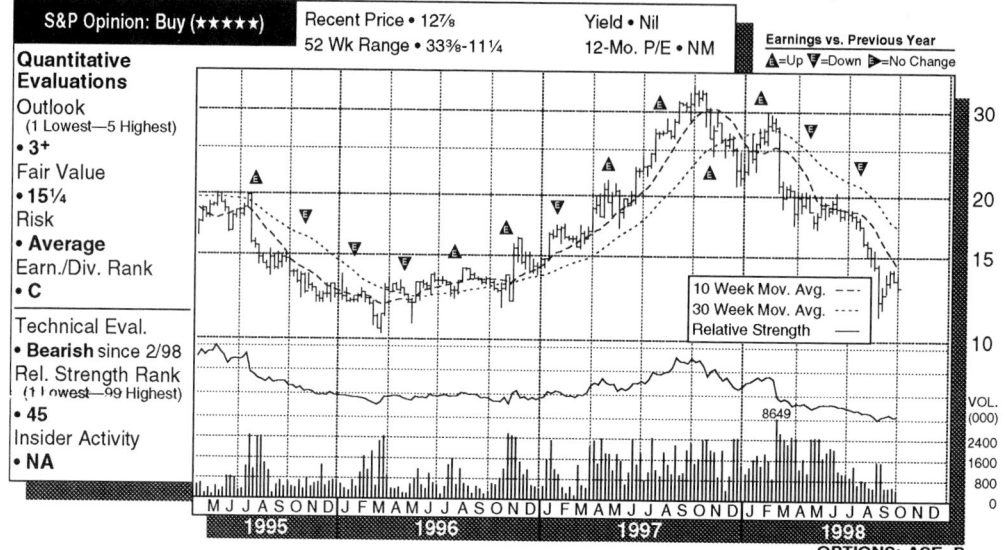

10 Week Mov. Avg. - - -
30 Week Mov. Avg. · · · ·
Relative Strength —

8649

VOL. (000)

OPTIONS: ASE, P

Overview - 31-AUG-98

LTL volumes in 1998 for Yellow Freight System could dip 2%-3%, after rising 4.3% in 1997. The drop reflects a diversion of business to non-union carriers, much of which did not return despite the signing of a new Teamsters contract. Additionally, volumes are being hurt by reduced business with Home Depot and a sluggish manufacturing sector. Margins will be flat as savings from Yellow's new cost reduction program and savings on fuel and claims are negated by heavier than normal purchased transportation costs related to rail service disruptions in the West. Supporting comparisons will be the absence of relocation and training costs incurred in 1997. Rates will remain firm. Saia will grow volume at an 8% pace in 1998 as it builds densities in existing southeastern markets. WestEx, which will benefit from the acquisition of Trans Western Express, is seen moving into the black. Interest expense will ease. Comparisons will benefit from the absence of Preston Trucking.

Valuation - 31-AUG-98

The shares of this trucker have been under relentless pressure since late 1997. Though the Teamsters ratified a moderate new five-year pact without a strike, shippers diverted freight to non-union carriers and many never came back. We think Yellow is likely to eventually recover much of this business. YELL's shares also have not adequately reflected the sale in July 1998 of Preston Trucking. The sale of Preston, which barely turned a profit in the five years it was owned by YELL, required a $2.26 a share charge to 1998 second quarter net income. Over the past 12 months, YELL bought 2,500,000 of its shares for $50 million ($20 each). A new $25 million buyback plan was approved in August 1998. We believe YELL, which trades well below book value, is undervalued and should be bought by patient investors.

Key Stock Statistics

S&P EPS Est. 1998	1.65	Tang. Bk. Value/Share	13.82
P/E on S&P Est. 1998	7.8	Beta	0.81
S&P EPS Est. 1999	1.95	Shareholders	3,200
Dividend Rate/Share	Nil	Market cap. (B)	$0.337
Shs. outstg. (M)	26.1	Inst. holdings	64%
Avg. daily vol. (M)	0.107		

Value of $10,000 invested 5 years ago: $ 5,291

Fiscal Year Ending Dec. 31

	1998	1997	1996	1995	1994	1993
Revenues (Million $)						
1Q	692.5	785.1	741.7	765.0	748.2	602.2
2Q	727.4	844.4	759.3	773.8	592.2	732.9
3Q	—	882.2	790.4	772.0	769.3	761.7
4Q	—	837.1	781.1	745.9	757.9	759.7
Yr.	—	3,349	3,072	3,057	2,867	2,857
Earnings Per Share ($)						
1Q	**0.13**	0.23	-0.51	0.11	-0.23	-0.06
2Q	**0.45**	0.50	0.07	0.04	-0.78	-0.07
3Q	**E0.60**	0.71	0.32	-0.41	0.47	0.37
4Q	**E0.47**	0.41	-0.85	-0.81	0.40	0.43
Yr.	**E1.65**	1.83	-0.97	-1.07	-0.14	0.67

Next earnings report expected: late October

Dividend Data

Cash dividends were suspended in 1995, after having been paid each year since 1958. A "poison pill" stock purchase right was distributed in 1986.

Yellow Corporation

Business Summary - 31-AUG-98

Yellow Corporation is a holding company for a family of motor carriers that offer long-haul and regional less-than-truckload (LTL) freight services. Less-than-truckload services are tailored to the needs of shippers that seek to cut inventory levels by making more frequent shipment of smaller lots. YELL sold its Preston Trucking unit in July 1998.

Yellow Freight System, accounting for 76% of total revenues in 1997, is the nation's largest LTL freight motor carrier. Yellow provides direct service throughout the 50 states, Puerto Rico, Canada and Mexico and through alliances provides service to Europe and Asia/Pacific. Service to 10 Central and South American nations was initiated in May 1998.

To improve its competitive position in shorter-haul markets, Yellow has reduced transit time by routing freight to bypass intermediate consolidation centers. Accordingly, Yellow cut its terminal network to 381 at 1997 year-end from 445 in 1995. Additionally, Yellow is expediting shipments, while lowering costs, by employing more sleeper teams and expanding its use of rail intermodal. In January 1997, Yellow Freight reorganized into five geographic business units to enable its managers to respond more quickly to customers' needs. A $28.3 million ($1.01-a-share) charge was taken against 1996 net income, partly reflecting severance payments tied to Yellow's reorganization.

Yellow Freight initiated a new time and day-definite freight service in July 1998 dubbed "Exact Express". The new premium service, covering shipments weighing over 70lbs, allows shippers to select from a variety of time options including overnight. YELL estimates that 70% of Exact Express shipments will move on its ground system, while the rest will be moved by air.

YELL's Preston Trucking, which generated 14% of total revenues in 1997, was sold in July 1998 to that carrier's senior management. Preston provides overnight and two-day regional LTL freight service in the Northeast and Upper Midwest and parts of Canada through a network of 62 terminals. Preston, which was purchased in 1993, has barely been profitable. YELL said it sold Preston because the carrier faced higher capital requirements in the near future. YELL said it would consider re-entering the regional markets served by Preston if it could purchase an established non-union carrier.

Saia Motor Freight Line, accounting for 9% of total revenues in 1997, is Yellow Corp.'s most profitable unit. Saia provides overnight and second-day regional LTL freight service using a network of 72 terminals in 11 southeastern states and Puerto Rico.

WestEx, which was acquired in 1994, accounts for 1% of revenues. It provides regional LTL service in California, Arizona, New Mexico, Colorado, Texas and Nevada, operating through a network of 31 terminals.

Per Share Data ($) (Year Ended Dec. 31)	1997	1996	1995	1994	1993	1992	1991	1990	1989	1988
Tangible Bk. Val.	15.86	14.08	15.04	16.40	17.31	17.28	16.94	16.69	15.24	14.21
Cash Flow	5.97	3.70	3.73	4.63	5.38	5.68	5.39	6.83	4.93	6.17
Earnings	1.83	-0.97	-1.07	-0.14	0.67	1.46	0.95	2.31	0.65	2.40
Dividends	Nil	Nil	0.47	0.94	0.94	0.94	0.94	0.82	0.73	0.66
Payout Ratio	Nil	Nil	NM	NM	140%	64%	99%	35%	113%	28%
Prices - High	34 1/8	16 3/8	24 3/8	30 1/4	29 7/8	32 3/8	33 1/2	31 1/4	32 7/8	34
- Low	14 1/8	10 1/4	11 7/8	16 3/4	16 7/8	21 3/4	23 3/4	18 3/4	23 7/8	23 7/8
P/E Ratio - High	19	NM	NM	NM	45	22	35	14	51	14
- Low	8	NM	NM	NM	25	15	25	8	37	10
Income Statement Analysis (Million $)										
Revs.	3,349	3,072	3,057	2,867	2,857	2,263	2,344	2,302	2,220	2,016
Oper. Inc.	218	163	114	145	204	201	182	248	216	226
Depr.	119	131	135	134	132	118	125	128	123	108
Int. Exp.	13.5	21.0	23.4	18.4	17.7	12.2	14.2	15.8	15.5	12.3
Pretax Inc.	89.2	-34.3	-45.0	-3.0	35.0	65.0	40.0	102	27.0	105
Eff. Tax Rate	41%	NM	NM	NM	47%	37%	34%	36%	30%	34%
Net Inc.	52.4	-27.2	-30.1	-3.8	18.8	41.0	26.7	65.3	18.6	69.0
Balance Sheet & Other Fin. Data (Million $)										
Cash	19.8	24.8	31.2	24.9	20.7	32.3	12.7	8.3	4.4	8.2
Curr. Assets	459	390	485	403	379	274	270	270	266	253
Total Assets	1,271	1,228	1,435	1,307	1,266	1,061	1,098	1,116	1,082	1,021
Curr. Liab.	481	424	443	376	342	255	288	290	269	265
LT Debt	163	193	342	240	214	123	146	164	187	169
Common Eqty.	446	396	423	461	486	485	476	469	439	409
Total Cap.	639	621	821	755	760	681	705	723	714	702
Cap. Exp.	118	58.0	163	183	77.0	86.0	110	169	193	189
Cash Flow	171	104	105	0.3	151	159	151	193	142	177
Curr. Ratio	1.0	0.9	1.1	1.1	1.1	1.1	0.9	0.9	1.0	1.0
% LT Debt of Cap.	25.5	31.1	41.7	31.8	28.2	18.1	20.7	22.6	26.1	24.1
% Net Inc.of Revs.	1.6	NM	NM	NM	0.7	1.8	1.1	2.8	0.8	3.4
% Ret. on Assets	4.2	NM	NM	NM	1.6	3.8	2.4	6.0	1.8	7.1
% Ret. on Equity	12.5	NM	NM	NM	3.9	8.5	5.6	14.6	4.4	17.1

Data as orig. reptd.; bef. results of disc. opers. and/or spec. items. Per share data adj. for stk. divs. as of ex-div. date. Bold denotes diluted EPS (FASB 128). E-Estimated. NA-Not Available. NM-Not Meaningful. NR-Not Ranked.

Office—10990 Roe Ave., P.O. Box 7563, Overland Park, KS 66207. **Tel**—(913) 696-6100. **Website**—http://www.yellowcorp.com **Chrmn, Pres & CEO**—A. M. Myers.**SVP-Secy**—W. F. Martin Jr. **SVP-CFO & Investor Contact**—H. A. (Bert) Trucksess III. **Dirs**—K. E. Agthe, C. C. Carr, H. M. Dean, D. H. Hughes, R. T. LeMay, J. C. McKelvey, A. M. Myers, W. L. Trubeck, C. W. Vogt. **Transfer Agent & Registrar**—ChaseMellon Shareholder Services, Hackensack, NJ. **Incorporated**—in Indiana in 1950; reincorporated in Delaware in 1983. **Empl**— 34,400. **S&P Analyst:** Stephen R. Klein

Zale Corp.

2518

NYSE Symbol **ZLC**

In S&P SmallCap 600

03-OCT-98

Industry: Retail (Specialty)

Summary: Zale is the largest U.S. specialty retailer of fine jewelry, operating approximately 1,100 retail locations throughout the U.S., Guam and Puerto Rico.

Quantitative Evaluations

Recent Price • 24
52 Wk Range • 34⅛-21½

Yield • Nil
12-Mo. P/E • 13.0

Outlook (1 Lowest—5 Highest)
• **4**

Fair Value
• **42¼**

Risk
• **Average**

Earn./Div. Rank
• **NR**

Technical Eval.
• **NA**

Rel. Strength Rank (1 Lowest—99 Highest)
• **40**

Insider Activity
• **Neutral**

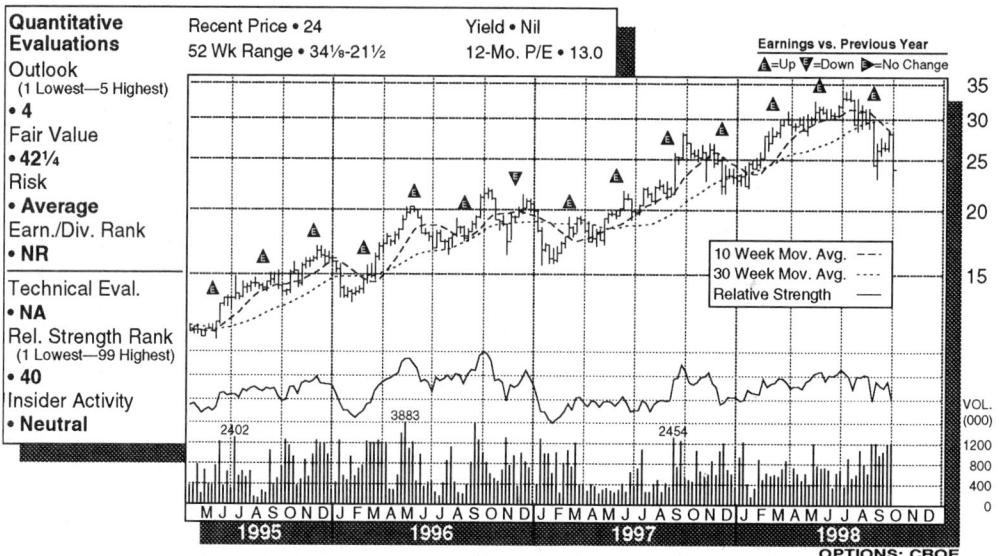

Earnings vs. Previous Year
▲=Up ▼=Down ▶=No Change

10 Week Mov. Avg. – – –
30 Week Mov. Avg. ....
Relative Strength —

OPTIONS: CBOE

Business Profile - 27-MAY-98

FY 97 (Jul.) marked the company's third consecutive year of solid revenue growth, and earnings gains that exceeded 20%. Through the first three quarters of FY 98, earnings have increased 26% over the year ago period. In October 1997, Zale sold certain assets of its Diamond Park Fine Jewelers division to Finlay Enterprises, Inc., for about $63 million. The sale included 139 leased jewelry departments in Marshall Fields, Parisian and the Mercantile group of department stores. The sale of these assets should allow the company to focus on its more profitable jewelry store operations. In February 1998, directors approved the repurchase of up to $40 million in common stock.

Operational Review - 27-MAY-98

Net sales in the nine months ended April 30, 1998, advanced 5.4%, year to year, reflecting continued improvement in merchandise assortments, product promotions, and execution of store programs.
Comparable-store sales grew 9.2%. Margins widened, on well controlled store payrolls and warranty costs, partly offset by increased net credit expenses. Aided by a gain of $1.6 million related to the sale of Diamond Park Fine Jewelers division assets, and a gain of $4.72 million from the sale of land, pretax income rose 27%. After taxes at 37.4%, versus 36.6%, net income was up 26%, to $61,486,000 ($1.64 a share), from $48,933,000 ($1.34).

Stock Performance - 02-OCT-98

In the past 30 trading days, ZLC's shares have declined 20%, compared to a 7% fall in the S&P 500. Average trading volume for the past five days was 252,320 shares, compared with the 40-day moving average of 214,277 shares.

Key Stock Statistics

Dividend Rate/Share	Nil	Shareholders	1,300
Shs. outstg. (M)	34.7	Market cap. (B)	$0.832
Avg. daily vol. (M)	0.231	Inst. holdings	89%
Tang. Bk. Value/Share	17.78		
Beta	0.80		

Value of $10,000 invested 5 years ago: NA

Fiscal Year Ending Jul. 31

	1998	1997	1996	1995	1994	1993
Revenues (Million $)						
1Q	252.5	230.8	214.3	205.5	184.8	—
2Q	522.0	505.1	452.0	427.2	368.6	—
3Q	258.3	244.4	222.3	192.1	167.1	—
4Q	280.9	273.6	248.9	211.4	199.9	—
Yr.	1,314	1,254	1,137	1,036	920.3	—
Earnings Per Share ($)						
1Q	0.03	-0.03	0.03	-0.09	-0.18	—
2Q	**1.57**	1.41	1.27	1.19	1.07	—
3Q	**0.04**	-0.04	-0.07	-0.11	-0.13	—
4Q	**0.20**	0.04	Nil	-0.09	-0.11	—
Yr.	**1.84**	1.38	1.23	0.88	0.66	—

Next earnings report expected: late November

Dividend Data

The company currently intends to retain future earnings for use in the expansion and operation of its business. ZLC does not anticipate paying dividends on its common stock in the foreseeable future.

A Division of The **McGraw-Hill** *Companies*

Business Summary - 27-MAY-98

Zale Corp. is the largest U.S. specialty retailer of fine jewelry. The company emerged from Chapter 11 bankruptcy protection in July 1993, after completing a reorganization that included a comprehensive capital restructuring and the closing of 700 underperforming stores.

At May 21, 1998 , the company operated about 1,100 locations throughout the U.S., Guam and Puerto Rico. Stores are primarily in retail shopping malls. Zale also operates four outlet stores. The company operates through three distinct divisions: Zales, Gordon's and Baily, Banks & Biddle.

The Zales division accounted for 48% of FY 97 (Jul.) sales. Zales, the company's national brand, is focused on a broad range of mainstream consumers. The product focus of Zales is on bridal, diamond and gold jewelry, with bridal merchandise accounting for 36% of the division's merchandise sales. At July 31, 1997, Zales had 638 stores in 49 states and Puerto Rico. Average store size is approximately 1,400 sq. ft. and the average purchase in FY 97 was $246.

The company is repositioning Gordon's (23%) as a major regional brand focusing on an upgraded product offering. At July 31, 1997, Gordon's had 310 stores in 37 states and Puerto Rico, substantially all of which

operate under the trade name Gordon's Jewelers. Average store size is 1,400 sq. ft. and the average sale in FY 97 was $274.

The Bailey, Banks & Biddle division (18%) offers higher-end merchandise, more exclusive designs and a prestigious shopping environment for the upscale customer. At July 31, 1997, Baily, Banks & Biddle operated 113 upscale jewelry stores in 28 states and Guam. The average store is approximately 3,000 sq. ft. The average sale in FY 97 was $484.

In October 1997, the company sold the majority of its assets in the Diamond Park division to Finlay Enterprises, Inc., for $63 million. ZLC will cease its residual operations at Dillard's Department stores in January 1998. In FY 97, the Diamond Park Division accounted for 10% of total revenues and operated 186 leased operations.

ZLC offers and grants credit through its private label credit card program. Approximately 50% of the company's retail sales in FY 97 through its Zale, Gordon's and Baily, Banks & Biddle divisions were generated by credit sales on the private label credit cards.

For the quarter ended April 30, 1998, Zale posted its first profitable third quarter since its emergence from bankruptcy. Results were aided by 11.9% same-store sales growth.

Per Share Data ($)

(Year Ended Jul. 31)	1998	1997	1996	1995	1994	1993	1992	1991	1990	1989
Tangible Bk. Val.	NA	17.48	15.54	11.20	9.80	8.89	NA	NA	NA	NA
Cash Flow	NA	1.83	1.44	0.91	0.66	NA	NA	NA	NA	NA
Earnings	1.84	1.38	1.23	0.88	0.66	NA	NA	NA	NA	NA
Dividends	Nil	Nil	Nil	Nil	Nil	Nil	Nil	Nil	Nil	Nil
Payout Ratio	Nil	Nil	Nil	Nil	Nil	Nil	Nil	Nil	Nil	Nil
Prices - High	34⅛	28⅛	20¼	17	14	11⅝	NA	NA	NA	NA
- Low	22	15⅝	13¼	10⅛	8¼	8	NA	NA	NA	NA
P/E Ratio - High	19	20	16	19	21	NA	NA	NA	NA	NA
- Low	12	11	11	12	13	NA	NA	NA	NA	NA

Income Statement Analysis (Million $)

	1998	1997	1996	1995	1994	1993	1992	1991	1990	1989
Revs.	NA	1,254	1,137	1,036	920	NA	NA	NA	NA	NA
Oper. Inc.	NA	132	103	78.9	58.7	NA	NA	NA	NA	NA
Depr.	NA	16.3	7.5	1.2	NM	NM	NM	NM	NM	NM
Int. Exp.	NM	36.9	33.2	37.5	30.2	NA	NA	NA	NA	NA
Pretax Inc.	NA	79.9	70.1	47.8	34.7	NA	NA	NA	NA	NA
Eff. Tax Rate	NA	37%	36%	34%	33%	NA	NA	NA	NA	NA
Net Inc.	NA	50.6	45.0	31.5	23.1	NA	NA	NA	NA	NA

Balance Sheet & Other Fin. Data (Million $)

	1998	1997	1996	1995	1994	1993	1992	1991	1990	1989
Cash	NA	41.6	50.0	155	154	NA	NA	NA	NA	NA
Curr. Assets	NA	1,047	953	951	974	NA	NA	NA	NA	NA
Total Assets	NA	1,281	1,164	1,111	1,113	NA	NA	NA	NA	NA
Curr. Liab.	NA	170	178	169	211	NA	NA	NA	NA	NA
LT Debt	NA	451	404	441	444	NA	NA	NA	NA	NA
Common Eqty.	NA	542	476	392	343	NA	NA	NA	NA	NA
Total Cap.	NA	993	882	833	787	NA	NA	NA	NA	NA
Cap. Exp.	NA	54.0	48.8	42.3	27.8	NA	NA	NA	NA	NA
Cash Flow	NA	66.8	52.5	32.7	23.1	NA	NA	NA	NA	NA
Curr. Ratio	NA	6.2	5.4	5.6	4.5	NA	NA	NA	NA	NA
% LT Debt of Cap.	NA	45.4	45.9	52.9	56.4	NA	NA	NA	NA	NA
% Net Inc.of Revs.	NA	4.0	4.0	3.0	2.5	NA	NA	NA	NA	NA
% Ret. on Assets	NA	4.1	4.0	2.8	2.2	NA	NA	NA	NA	NA
% Ret. on Equity	NA	9.9	10.4	8.6	7.1	NA	NA	NA	NA	NA

Data as orig. reptd.; bef. results of disc. opers. and/or spec. items. Per share data adj. for stk. divs. as of ex-div. date. E-Estimated. NA-Not Available. NM-Not Meaningful. NR-Not Ranked.

Office—901 West Walnut Hill Lane, Irving, TX 75038-1003. **Tel**—(972) 580-4000. **Website**—http://www.zalecorp.com **Chrmn & CEO**—R. J. DiNicola. **Pres & COO**—B. Raff **EVP & CFO**—S. Gove. **Investor Contact**—Cynthia Gordon (972) 580-5047.**Dirs**—G. Adams, A. D. Brown, P. P. Copses, R. J. DiNicola, A. Jung, R. C. Marcus, C. H. Pistor, A. H. Tisch. **Transfer Agent & Registrar**—Bank of New York**Incorporated**—in Delaware in 1989; originally incorporated in Texas in 1924. **Empl**— 10,000. **S&P Analyst**: Ray Lam, CFA

Zebra Technologies   5683K

NASDAQ Symbol **ZBRA**

In S&P SmallCap 600

03-OCT-98

Industry:
Manufacturing (Specialized)

Summary: Zebra Technologies is an international provider of demand label printers and supplies for users of automatic identification and data collection systems.

Quantitative Evaluations

Outlook
(1 Lowest—5 Highest)
• **5**

Fair Value
• **53**

Risk
• **High**

Earn./Div. Rank
• **NR**

Technical Eval.
• **Neutral** since 9/98

Rel. Strength Rank
(1 Lowest—99 Highest)
• **85**

Insider Activity
• **NA**

Recent Price • 33⅜
52 Wk Range • 44⅝-25½

Yield • Nil
12-Mo. P/E • 18.8

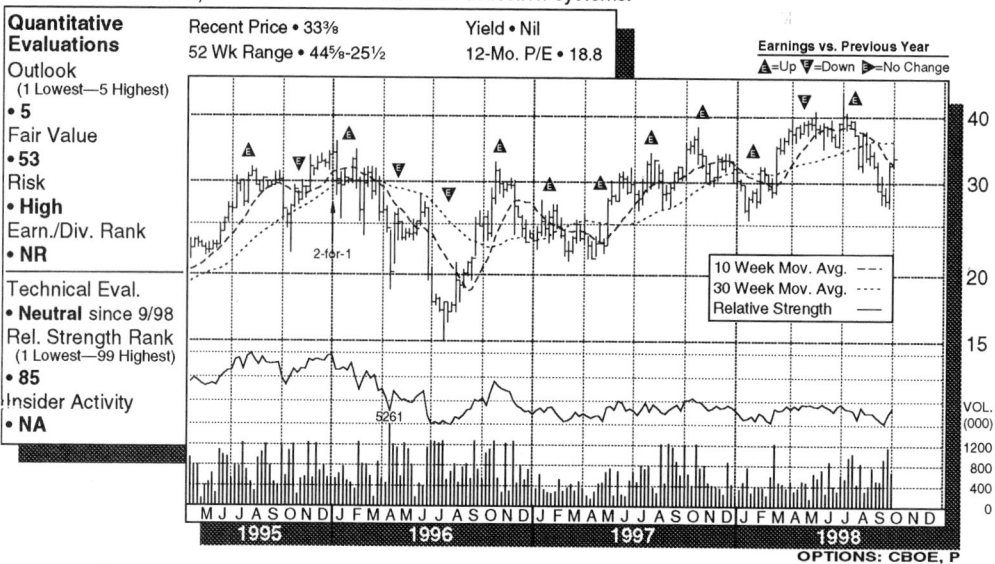

Earnings vs. Previous Year
▲=Up ▼=Down ▶=No Change

10 Week Mov. Avg. – – –
30 Week Mov. Avg. · · · ·
Relative Strength —

2-for-1

5261

VOL.
(000)
1200
800
400
0

M J J A S O N D J F M A M J J A S O N D J F M A M J J A S O N D J F M A M J J A S O N D
1995   1996   1997   1998

OPTIONS: CBOE, P

Business Profile - 31-JUL-98

ZBRA recently agreed to acquire Eltron International (Nasdaq; ELTN), for about seven million shares of Zebra Class B common stock, in a transaction that would create a company with the broadest line of bar code printers in the world. The deal is expected to close in October 1998. Zebra has benefited from escalating demand for bar-code and on-demand labeling applications in the non-retail sector of the world economy. The company seeks to offer customers the most advanced technology in bar-code labeling, and has announced a significant number of product introductions in the past two years. In the first quarter of 1998, ZBRA began full-scale shipments of the Z Series, a line of modular bar code printers that is expected to have an important effect on 1998 results.

Operational Review - 31-JUL-98

In the first half of 1998, revenues advanced 19%, year to year, reflecting higher printer unit volumes, partly offset by lower average selling prices. Gross margins widened, due to a more favorable product mix and reduced materials costs, and despite sharply higher SG&A expenses and R&D costs, operating profit was up 24%. In the absence of a one-time gain of $5.5 million on the sale of Norand Corp. common stock in 1997, the rise in income from continuing operations was held to 2.6%, to $21,721,000 ($0.89 a share) from $ 21,171,000 ($0.87). Results in the first half of 1997 exclude a loss of $0.11 a share from discontinued operations.

Stock Performance - 02-OCT-98

In the past 30 trading days, ZBRA's shares have declined 1%, compared to a 7% fall in the S&P 500. Average trading volume for the past five days was 134,100 shares, compared with the 40-day moving average of 133,569 shares.

Key Stock Statistics

Dividend Rate/Share	Nil	Shareholders	600
Shs. outstg. (M)	24.3	Market cap. (B)	$0.650
Avg. daily vol. (M)	0.166	Inst. holdings	69%
Tang. Bk. Value/Share	8.29		
Beta	1.24		

Value of $10,000 invested 5 years ago: $ 27,864

Fiscal Year Ending Dec. 31

	1998	1997	1996	1995	1994	1993
Revenues (Million $)						
1Q	50.21	42.42	38.35	34.39	21.98	19.00
2Q	55.35	47.84	40.49	35.49	25.89	21.64
3Q	—	49.89	43.76	37.48	28.25	23.07
4Q	—	53.33	47.12	41.23	30.99	23.74
Yr.	—	192.1	169.7	148.6	107.1	87.46
Earnings Per Share ($)						
1Q	**0.43**	**0.48**	0.22	0.27	0.17	0.15
2Q	**0.46**	**0.40**	0.26	0.29	0.21	0.18
3Q	—	**0.41**	0.36	0.04	0.23	0.21
4Q	—	**0.48**	0.36	0.33	0.26	0.22
Yr.	—	**1.76**	1.19	0.94	0.87	0.76

Next earnings report expected: mid October

Dividend Data

No cash dividends have been paid. A two-for-one stock split was effected in December 1995.

A Division of The McGraw·Hill Companies

Business Summary - 31-JUL-98

The familiar black-and-white stripes of bar code labels, a mainstay of the retail checkout line, have not yet found a similar level of acceptance for other uses, such as industrial or service applications. In its efforts to gain a toehold in what it sees as "wide open" non-retail markets, Zebra Technologies Corp. (ZBRA) has sent its "on demand" bar code label printers into hospitals to bar code patient wrist bands, waste disposal facilities to tag hazardous materials and ski resorts to print lift tickets.

ZBRA produces thermal transfer and less expensive direct thermal printers (76% of 1997 net sales), and sells related supplies (21%) such as thermal transfer ribbons, label/ticketing stock, custom labels and tags. The company also provides maintenance services, which together with its discontinued bar code software division, made up the remainder of revenues in 1997. Working together, ZBRA's products provide identification labeling solutions for customers in a broad range of industries.

The company believes that the advantages afforded by thermal transfer printing, including the ability to print high-resolution images on a wide variety of label materials at a lower cost than that of competing technologies, make it the technology of choice in ZBRA's target markets for the foreseeable future. The company's printers are designed to operate at the user's location to produce and dispense bar coded labels in environments ranging from fiery steel mills to the icy interiors of

freezer compartments. Bar codes printed with Zebra printers are also used to control the movement of goods through warehouses. Manufacturers put ZBRA's products to work in inventory control and "just-in-time" and computer integrated manufacturing applications.

ZBRA is encouraged by such business trends as industry-mandated standardization of bar code labeling, which has already helped spur development of bar coding, and efforts by commercial and service organizations to improve quality and productivity. The company sells its products--many of which are combined with the products of other manufacturers to form a complete system--through a multi-channel distribution system that includes distributors, value-added resellers, original equipment manufacturers and international accounts.

ZBRA's products are sold in over 80 countries, and in 1997 sales to foreign customers accounted for 46% of net sales. ZBRA believes that international sales growth will outpace growth in the U.S. because of the lower penetration of bar code systems in foreign markets.

In July 1997, ZBRA announced the discontinuation of its retail software business, which it had acquired two years earlier. The action resulted in a $2.4 million charge in the second quarter of 1997.

In July 1998, the company agreed to acquire Eltron International, in a tax-free pooling of interests transaction that would create a company with revenues fo about $313 million. Subject to shareholder and regulatory approval, the transaction is expected to close in October 1998.

Per Share Data ($)

(Year Ended Dec. 31)	1997	1996	1995	1994	1993	1992	1991	1990	1989	1988
Tangible Bk. Val.	7.39	5.79	4.47	3.41	2.53	1.76	1.28	0.58	NA	NA
Cash Flow	1.94	1.35	1.03	0.94	0.81	0.53	0.50	0.53	NA	NA
Earnings	1.76	1.19	0.94	0.88	0.76	0.49	0.48	0.52	NA	NA
Dividends	Nil	Nil	Nil	Nil	Nil	Nil	Nil	Nil	Nil	Nil
Payout Ratio	Nil	Nil	Nil	Nil	Nil	Nil	Nil	Nil	Nil	Nil
Prices - High	38¼	35¾	35¼	28⅝	30⅜	12⅜	9½	NA	NA	NA
- Low	21¼	15	18	11¾	10⅛	7¼	7¼	NA	NA	NA
P/E Ratio - High	22	30	37	33	40	25	20	NA	NA	NA
- Low	12	13	19	13	13	15	15	NA	NA	NA

Income Statement Analysis (Million $)

	1997	1996	1995	1994	1993	1992	1991	1990	1989	1988
Revs.	192	170	149	107	87.5	58.7	45.6	38.0	NA	NA
Oper. Inc.	57.0	43.5	40.8	31.7	25.9	16.2	13.2	10.9	NA	NA
Depr.	4.3	3.8	2.2	1.4	1.0	0.8	0.5	0.4	NA	NA
Int. Exp.	0.0	0.1	0.1	0.3	0.2	0.2	0.1	0.0	NA	NA
Pretax Inc.	66.7	44.6	38.0	32.9	28.5	17.8	13.3	10.7	NA	NA
Eff. Tax Rate	36%	35%	41%	36%	36%	34%	19%	1.60%	NA	NA
Net Inc.	42.8	28.9	22.6	21.1	18.3	11.8	10.8	10.5	NA	NA

Balance Sheet & Other Fin. Data (Million $)

	1997	1996	1995	1994	1993	1992	1991	1990	1989	1988
Cash	7.2	94.5	71.9	54.2	41.5	33.7	31.2	1.0	NA	NA
Curr. Assets	187	149	119	88.7	71.5	51.4	46.8	14.2	NA	NA
Total Assets	204	163	131	95.0	76.7	54.8	48.9	16.2	NA	NA
Curr. Liab.	22.6	20.2	19.0	12.4	15.5	12.0	17.1	3.8	NA	NA
LT Debt	0.3	2.2	2.2	0.2	0.3	0.3	0.4	0.5	NA	NA
Common Eqty.	180	140	108	82.0	60.6	42.2	30.7	11.9	NA	NA
Total Cap.	181	143	112	82.3	60.9	42.7	31.7	12.4	NA	NA
Cap. Exp.	5.3	6.0	4.3	2.1	2.5	2.2	0.7	1.0	NA	NA
Cash Flow	47.1	32.8	24.8	22.5	19.3	12.7	11.3	10.9	NA	NA
Curr. Ratio	8.3	7.4	6.3	7.1	4.6	4.3	2.7	3.7	NA	NA
% LT Debt of Cap.	0.1	1.5	2.0	0.3	0.5	0.8	1.3	3.6	NA	NA
% Net Inc.of Revs.	22.3	17.0	15.2	19.7	20.9	20.2	23.8	27.7	NA	NA
% Ret. on Assets	23.3	19.6	20.0	24.5	27.7	22.8	31.9	NA	NA	NA
% Ret. on Equity	26.8	23.3	23.7	29.5	35.5	32.5	48.5	NA	NA	NA

Data as orig. reptd.; bef. results of disc. opers. and/or spec. items. Per share data adj. for stk. divs. as of ex-div. date. Bold denotes diluted EPS (FASB 128). E-Estimated. NA-Not Available. NM-Not Meaningful. NR-Not Ranked.

Office—333 Corporate Woods Pkwy., Vernon Hills, IL 60061.**Reincorporated**—in Delaware in 1991. Tel—(847) 634-6700. **Fax**—(847) 634-1830. **Website**—http://www.zebra.com **Chrmn & CEO**—E. L. Kaplan. **Pres**—C. E. Turnbull. **SVP & Secy**—G. Cless. **CFO, Treas & Investor Contact**—Charles R. Whitchurch. **Dirs**—G. Cless, E. L. Kaplan, C. Knowles, D. R. Riley, M. A. Smith. **Transfer Agent & Registrar**—Harris Trust & Savings Bank, Chicago. **Empl**— 627. **S&P Analyst:** Jim Corridore

03-OCT-98

Industry:
Insurance (Property-Casualty)

Summary: Through subsidiaries, ZNT writes workers' compensation, reinsurance, other property and casualty and health insurance primarily in California and Texas.

Quantitative Evaluations

Recent Price • 24
52 Wk Range • 30½-23½

Yield • 4.2%
12-Mo. P/E • 15.1

Outlook
(1 Lowest—5 Highest)
• **NA**

Fair Value
• **NA**

Risk
• **Low**

Earn./Div. Rank
• **B-**

Technical Eval.
• **NA**

Rel. Strength Rank
(1 Lowest—99 Highest)
• **60**

Insider Activity
• **NA**

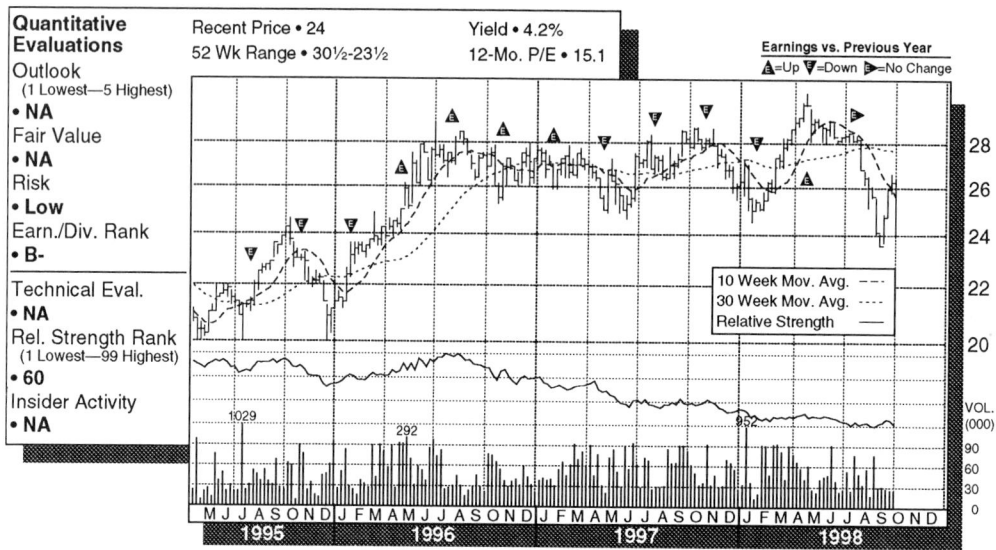

Earnings vs. Previous Year
▲=Up ▼=Down ▷=No Change

10 Week Mov. Avg. – – –
30 Week Mov. Avg. ·······
Relative Strength ———

Business Profile - 26-MAY-98

ZNT continues to search for profitable opportunities in an extremely competitive insurance market by focusing on property and casualty insurance operations, including investing activities. In April 1998, ZNT completed the purchase of the assets of RISCORP Inc. related to its workers' compensation business, including all existing in-force business. However, as a result of continued weakness in ZNT's existing workers' compensation business, overall operating results continued to worsen in the first quarter of 1998, as a $2.3 million underwriting loss compared with a $2.0 million loss a year earlier; the combined ratio deteriorated to 102.0%, from 101.6%.

Operational Review - 26-MAY-98

Revenues fell marginally, year to year, in the first quarter of 1998, as premiums earned in workers' compensation fell 8.0% (largely in California), partly offset by higher other property casualty premiums and real estate sales. Margins narrowed, as underwriting results deteriorated, primarily due to a decline in workers' compensation profitability and higher weather-related catastrophe losses. Results were also hurt by higher real estate construction and operating costs. After taxes at 33.6%, versus 33.8%, net income was unchanged, at $7.1 million ($0.42 per share, diluted, on 4.2% fewer shares).

Stock Performance - 02-OCT-98

In the past 30 trading days, ZNT's shares have declined 6%, compared to a 7% fall in the S&P 500. Average trading volume for the past five days was 4,900 shares, compared with the 40-day moving average of 7,359 shares.

Key Stock Statistics

Dividend Rate/Share	1.00	Shareholders	400
Shs. outstg. (M)	17.1	Market cap. (B)	$0.409
Avg. daily vol. (M)	0.005	Inst. holdings	64%
Tang. Bk. Value/Share	15.72		
Beta	0.53		

Value of $10,000 invested 5 years ago: $ 15,716

Fiscal Year Ending Dec. 31

	1998	1997	1996	1995	1994	1993
Revenues (Million $)						
1Q	145.3	146.7	134.6	127.3	138.9	143.3
2Q	166.0	152.4	133.7	130.7	151.3	149.5
3Q	—	147.1	137.1	130.3	153.2	149.2
4Q	—	154.3	151.1	130.7	151.7	143.8
Yr.	—	600.5	556.4	519.0	595.1	585.8
Earnings Per Share ($)						
1Q	**0.42**	**0.40**	0.70	0.23	0.43	0.66
2Q	**0.44**	**0.44**	0.60	0.40	0.57	0.78
3Q	—	**0.45**	0.51	0.34	0.53	0.70
4Q	—	**0.28**	0.30	0.10	0.46	0.63
Yr.	—	**1.57**	2.11	1.08	1.99	2.76

Next earnings report expected: late October

Dividend Data (Dividends have been paid since 1978.)

Amount ($)	Date Decl.	Ex-Div. Date	Stock of Record	Payment Date
0.250	Dec. 11	Jan. 28	Jan. 30	Feb. 13 '98
0.250	Feb. 24	Apr. 28	Apr. 30	May. 15 '98
0.250	May. 20	Jul. 29	Jul. 31	Aug. 15 '98
0.250	Sep. 28	Oct. 28	Oct. 30	Nov. 13 '98

A Division of The McGraw·Hill Companies

Business Summary - 31-JUL-98

The familiar black-and-white stripes of bar code labels, a mainstay of the retail checkout line, have not yet found a similar level of acceptance for other uses, such as industrial or service applications. In its efforts to gain a toehold in what it sees as "wide open" non-retail markets, Zebra Technologies Corp. (ZBRA) has sent its "on demand" bar code label printers into hospitals to bar code patient wrist bands, waste disposal facilities to tag hazardous materials and ski resorts to print lift tickets.

ZBRA produces thermal transfer and less expensive direct thermal printers (76% of 1997 net sales), and sells related supplies (21%) such as thermal transfer ribbons, label/ticketing stock, custom labels and tags. The company also provides maintenance services, which together with its discontinued bar code software division, made up the remainder of revenues in 1997. Working together, ZBRA's products provide identification labeling solutions for customers in a broad range of industries.

The company believes that the advantages afforded by thermal transfer printing, including the ability to print high-resolution images on a wide variety of label materials at a lower cost than that of competing technologies, make it the technology of choice in ZBRA's target markets for the foreseeable future. The company's printers are designed to operate at the user's location to produce and dispense bar coded labels in environments ranging from fiery steel mills to the icy interiors of

freezer compartments. Bar codes printed with Zebra printers are also used to control the movement of goods through warehouses. Manufacturers put ZBRA's products to work in inventory control and "just-in-time" and computer integrated manufacturing applications.

ZBRA is encouraged by such business trends as industry-mandated standardization of bar code labeling, which has already helped spur development of bar coding, and efforts by commercial and service organizations to improve quality and productivity. The company sells its products--many of which are combined with the products of other manufacturers to form a complete system--through a multi-channel distribution system that includes distributors, value-added resellers, original equipment manufacturers and international accounts.

ZBRA's products are sold in over 80 countries, and in 1997 sales to foreign customers accounted for 46% of net sales. ZBRA believes that international sales growth will outpace growth in the U.S. because of the lower penetration of bar code systems in foreign markets.

In July 1997, ZBRA announced the discontinuation of its retail software business, which it had acquired two years earlier. The action resulted in a $2.4 million charge in the second quarter of 1997.

In July 1998, the company agreed to acquire Eltron International, in a tax-free pooling of interests transaction that would create a company with revenues fo about $313 million. Subject to shareholder and regulatory approval, the transaction is expected to close in October 1998.

Per Share Data ($)

(Year Ended Dec. 31)	1997	1996	1995	1994	1993	1992	1991	1990	1989	1988
Tangible Bk. Val.	7.39	5.79	4.47	3.41	2.53	1.76	1.28	0.58	NA	NA
Cash Flow	1.94	1.35	1.03	0.94	0.81	0.53	0.50	0.53	NA	NA
Earnings	1.76	1.19	0.94	0.88	0.76	0.49	0.48	0.52	NA	NA
Dividends	Nil	Nil	Nil	Nil	Nil	Nil	Nil	Nil	Nil	Nil
Payout Ratio	Nil	Nil	Nil	Nil	Nil	Nil	Nil	Nil	Nil	Nil
Prices - High	38¼	35¾	35¼	28⅝	30⅜	12⅜	9½	NA	NA	NA
- Low	21¼	15	18	11¾	10⅛	7¼	7¼	NA	NA	NA
P/E Ratio - High	22	30	37	33	40	25	20	NA	NA	NA
- Low	12	13	19	13	13	15	15	NA	NA	NA

Income Statement Analysis (Million $)

	1997	1996	1995	1994	1993	1992	1991	1990	1989	1988
Revs.	192	170	149	107	87.5	58.7	45.6	38.0	NA	NA
Oper. Inc.	57.0	43.5	40.8	31.7	25.9	16.2	13.2	10.9	NA	NA
Depr.	4.3	3.8	2.2	1.4	1.0	0.8	0.5	0.4	NA	NA
Int. Exp.	0.0	0.1	0.1	0.3	0.2	0.2	0.1	0.0	NA	NA
Pretax Inc.	66.7	44.6	38.0	32.9	28.5	17.8	13.3	10.7	NA	NA
Eff. Tax Rate	36%	35%	41%	36%	36%	34%	19%	1.60%	NA	NA
Net Inc.	42.8	28.9	22.6	21.1	18.3	11.8	10.8	10.5	NA	NA

Balance Sheet & Other Fin. Data (Million $)

	1997	1996	1995	1994	1993	1992	1991	1990	1989	1988
Cash	7.2	94.5	71.9	54.2	41.5	33.7	31.2	1.0	NA	NA
Curr. Assets	187	149	119	88.7	71.5	51.4	46.8	14.2	NA	NA
Total Assets	204	163	131	95.0	76.7	54.8	48.9	16.2	NA	NA
Curr. Liab.	22.6	20.2	19.0	12.4	15.5	12.0	17.1	3.8	NA	NA
LT Debt	0.3	2.2	2.2	0.2	0.3	0.3	0.4	0.5	NA	NA
Common Eqty.	180	140	108	82.0	60.6	42.2	30.7	11.9	NA	NA
Total Cap.	181	143	112	82.3	60.9	42.7	31.7	12.4	NA	NA
Cap. Exp.	5.3	6.0	4.3	2.1	2.5	2.2	0.7	1.0	NA	NA
Cash Flow	47.1	32.8	24.8	22.5	19.3	12.7	11.3	10.9	NA	NA
Curr. Ratio	8.3	7.4	6.3	7.1	4.6	4.3	2.7	3.7	NA	NA
% LT Debt of Cap.	0.1	1.5	2.0	0.3	0.5	0.8	1.3	3.6	NA	NA
% Net Inc.of Revs.	22.3	17.0	15.2	19.7	20.9	20.2	23.8	27.7	NA	NA
% Ret. on Assets	23.3	19.6	20.0	24.5	27.7	22.8	31.9	NA	NA	NA
% Ret. on Equity	26.8	23.3	23.7	29.5	35.5	32.5	48.5	NA	NA	NA

Data as orig. reptd.; bef. results of disc. opers. and/or spec. items. Per share data adj. for stk. divs. as of ex-div. date. Bold denotes diluted EPS (FASB 128). E-Estimated. NA-Not Available. NM-Not Meaningful. NR-Not Ranked.

Office—333 Corporate Woods Pkwy., Vernon Hills, IL 60061.**Reincorporated**—in Delaware in 1991. **Tel**—(847) 634-6700. **Fax**—(847) 634-1830. **Website**—http://www.zebra.com **Chrmn & CEO**—E. L. Kaplan. **Pres**—C. E. Turnbull. **SVP & Secy**—G. Cless. **CFO, Treas & Investor Contact**—Charles R. Whitchurch. **Dirs**—G. Cless, E. L. Kaplan, C. Knowles, D. R. Riley, M. A. Smith. **Transfer Agent & Registrar**—Harris Trust & Savings Bank, Chicago. **Empl**— 627. **S&P Analyst:** Jim Corridore

03-OCT-98

Industry: Insurance (Property-Casualty)

Summary: Through subsidiaries, ZNT writes workers' compensation, reinsurance, other property and casualty and health insurance primarily in California and Texas.

Quantitative Evaluations

Recent Price • 24
52 Wk Range • 30½-23½

Yield • 4.2%
12-Mo. P/E • 15.1

Outlook (1 Lowest—5 Highest)
• **NA**

Fair Value
• **NA**

Risk
• **Low**

Earn./Div. Rank
• **B-**

Technical Eval.
• **NA**

Rel. Strength Rank (1 Lowest—99 Highest)
• **60**

Insider Activity
• **NA**

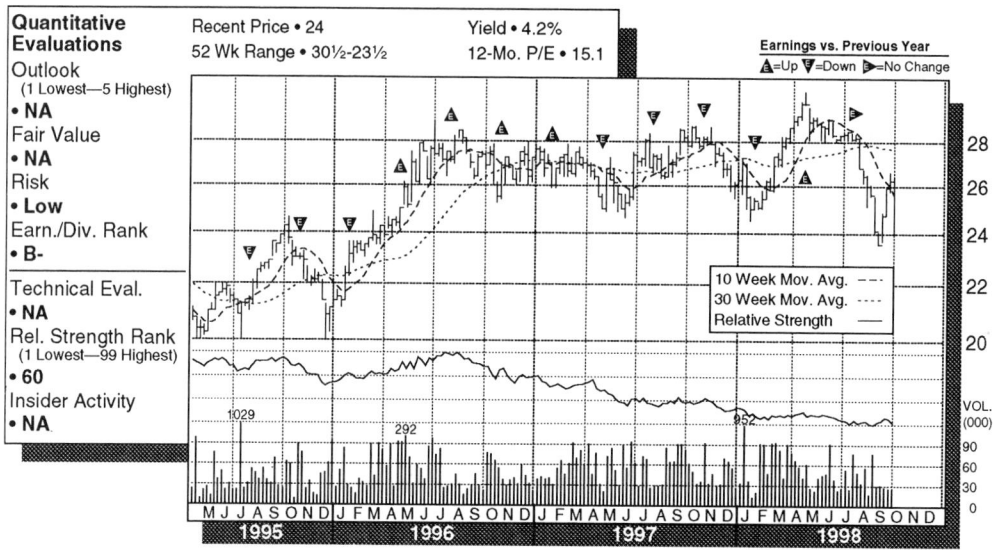

Earnings vs. Previous Year
▲=Up ▼=Down ▶=No Change

10 Week Mov. Avg. ---
30 Week Mov. Avg. ·····
Relative Strength —

Business Profile - 26-MAY-98

ZNT continues to search for profitable opportunities in an extremely competitive insurance market by focusing on property and casualty insurance operations, including investing activities. In April 1998, ZNT completed the purchase of the assets of RISCORP Inc. related to its workers' compensation business, including all existing in-force business. However, as a result of continued weakness in ZNT's existing workers' compensation business, overall operating results continued to worsen in the first quarter of 1998, as a $2.3 million underwriting loss compared with a $2.0 million loss a year earlier; the combined ratio deteriorated to 102.0%, from 101.6%.

Operational Review - 26-MAY-98

Revenues fell marginally, year to year, in the first quarter of 1998, as premiums earned in workers' compensation fell 8.0% (largely in California), partly offset by higher other property casualty premiums and real estate sales. Margins narrowed, as underwriting results deteriorated, primarily due to a decline in workers' compensation profitability and higher weather-related catastrophe losses. Results were also hurt by higher real estate construction and operating costs. After taxes at 33.6%, versus 33.8%, net income was unchanged, at $7.1 million ($0.42 per share, diluted, on 4.2% fewer shares).

Stock Performance - 02-OCT-98

In the past 30 trading days, ZNT's shares have declined 6%, compared to a 7% fall in the S&P 500. Average trading volume for the past five days was 4,900 shares, compared with the 40-day moving average of 7,359 shares.

Key Stock Statistics

Dividend Rate/Share	1.00	Shareholders	400
Shs. outstg. (M)	17.1	Market cap. (B)	$0.409
Avg. daily vol. (M)	0.005	Inst. holdings	64%
Tang. Bk. Value/Share	15.72		
Beta	0.53		

Value of $10,000 invested 5 years ago: $ 15,716

Fiscal Year Ending Dec. 31

	1998	1997	1996	1995	1994	1993
Revenues (Million $)						
1Q	145.3	146.7	134.6	127.3	138.9	143.3
2Q	166.0	152.4	133.7	130.7	151.3	149.5
3Q	—	147.1	137.1	130.3	153.2	149.2
4Q	—	154.3	151.1	130.7	151.7	143.8
Yr.	—	600.5	556.4	519.0	595.1	585.8
Earnings Per Share ($)						
1Q	0.42	0.40	0.70	0.23	0.43	0.66
2Q	0.44	0.44	0.60	0.40	0.57	0.78
3Q	—	0.45	0.51	0.34	0.53	0.70
4Q	—	0.28	0.30	0.10	0.46	0.63
Yr.	—	1.57	2.11	1.08	1.99	2.76

Next earnings report expected: late October

Dividend Data (Dividends have been paid since 1978.)

Amount ($)	Date Decl.	Ex-Div. Date	Stock of Record	Payment Date
0.250	Dec. 11	Jan. 28	Jan. 30	Feb. 13 '98
0.250	Feb. 24	Apr. 28	Apr. 30	May. 15 '98
0.250	May. 20	Jul. 29	Jul. 31	Aug. 15 '98
0.250	Sep. 28	Oct. 28	Oct. 30	Nov. 13 '98

Zenith National Insurance Corp.

Business Summary - 26-MAY-98

Zenith National Insurance, through its subsidiaries, is engaged in the business of writing workers' compensation insurance, reinsurance, health insurance, and commercial, auto, homeowners, farmowners and other coverages, primarily in California and Texas. Zenith also conducts real estate operations through its Perma-bilt subsidiary, which develops land and constructs homes in Las Vegas, Nevada. Workers' compensation insurance is written by Zenith Insurance Co. Automobile, homeowners and farmowners insurance is offered by CalFarm Insurance. In 1995, ZNT sold CalFarm's life insurance business to SunAmerica for $120 million, while retaining its health insurance business. Contributions to net premiums earned in recent years were:

	1997	1996	1995	1994
Workers' compensation	49%	47%	46%	54%
Property-casualty	44%	45%	44%	37%
Reinsurance	7%	8%	10%	9%

The company's workers' compensation business is produced by independent licensed insurance agents and brokers primarily in California and Texas. The standard policy issued by Zenith provides payments for, among other things, temporary or permanent disability benefits, death benefits, medical and hospital expenses, and expenses of vocational rehabilitation. Zenith is licensed to conduct business in 39 states and the District of Columbia. In April 1998, ZNT completed the purchase of the workers' compensation business of RISCORP Inc., for the difference in book value of RISCORP's assets and liabilities on the closing date, or a minimum of $35 million. This followed the late 1996 acquisition of Associated General Contractors' Self-Insurers' Fund, a Florida workers' compensation self-insurers' fund, with about $40 million in written premiums in 1995.

CalFarm Insurance offers a comprehensive line of property and casualty insurance, including homeowners, automobile, commercial multiple peril and farmowners coverage. Automobile insurance is the largest line of business, representing 14% of the property and casualty business in 1997, with some 83,500 vehicles insured. Farmowners business is CalFarm's second largest line, representing about 11% of property and casualty premiums. CalFarm Insurance assumed the group health insurance business that was previously written by CalFarm Life.

ZNT operates its reinsurance activity as a participant in contracts or treaties in which, typically, the reinsurance coverage is syndicated to a number of assuming companies.

Per Share Data ($)

(Year Ended Dec. 31)	1997	1996	1995	1994	1993	1992	1991	1990	1989	1988
Tangible Bk. Val.	19.89	19.17	18.13	15.09	17.21	14.57	14.73	12.40	13.14	13.42
Oper. Earnings	NA	1.72	0.95	1.86	1.75	1.01	1.73	2.10	2.22	2.11
Earnings	1.57	2.11	1.08	1.99	2.76	1.02	2.28	-0.47	1.98	2.15
Dividends	1.00	1.00	1.00	1.00	1.00	1.00	1.00	0.86	0.82	0.76
Payout Ratio	64%	47%	93%	50%	36%	98%	44%	NM	41%	36%
Prices - High	28¾	28⅞	24⅝	27⅜	29¼	20	18½	18¾	21½	21¾
- Low	24⅝	21⅛	19⅜	20⅝	19⅝	14½	12	9⅞	16¾	13⅝
P/E Ratio - High	18	13	68	13	10	19	8	d	10	10
- Low	16	10	53	10	7	14	5	d	8	6

Income Statement Analysis (Million $)

	1997	1996	1995	1994	1993	1992	1991	1990	1989	1988
Premium Inc.	489	453	438	463	470	442	438	431	413	404
Net Invest. Inc.	52.3	51.2	46.2	98.0	92.5	96.6	95.7	90.0	77.9	66.9
Oth. Revs.	59.4	52.4	34.8	33.9	23.5	10.8	13.0	-53.0	-7.0	1.0
Total Revs.	600	556	519	595	583	549	546	468	484	472
Pretax Inc.	43.5	57.1	29.4	57.6	73.5	19.7	52.5	-2.7	49.0	56.2
Net Oper. Inc.	19.7	30.6	17.4	35.5	33.7	19.1	32.9	41.4	46.2	45.4
Net Inc.	28.1	37.6	19.7	37.9	53.2	19.3	43.3	-9.2	41.1	46.3

Balance Sheet & Other Fin. Data (Million $)

	1997	1996	1995	1994	1993	1992	1991	1990	1989	1988
Cash & Equiv.	12.5	12.1	6.9	7.1	8.6	1.9	9.6	4.6	4.5	18.3
Premiums Due	72.8	80.5	70.2	126	118	91.0	76.6	77.6	76.8	68.9
Invest. Assets: Bonds	834	815	799	1,225	1,409	1,243	987	822	655	546
Invest. Assets: Stocks	45.7	37.6	36.5	46.0	58.0	132	170	203	251	215
Invest. Assets: Loans	Nil	Nil	Nil	45.3	44.1	39.3	35.2	30.2	25.5	24.2
Invest. Assets: Total	880	853	835	1,418	1,456	1,336	1,167	1,033	913	791
Deferred Policy Costs	20.8	20.8	20.3	109	108	91.0	76.6	63.9	47.2	31.9
Total Assets	1,252	1,243	1,115	1,841	1,858	1,704	1,478	1,327	1,182	1,007
Debt	74.5	74.4	74.2	74.1	74.0	73.9	49.8	53.6	26.7	24.3
Common Eqty.	362	338	330	310	349	302	281	241	299	297
Prop. & Cas. Loss Ratio	71.3	70.1	74.4	65.6	67.8	76.8	70.4	64.1	62.7	62.6
Prop. & Cas. Expense Ratio	32.1	29.7	27.4	27.7	25.7	27.9	29.6	29.2	29.2	28.4
Prop. & Cas. Combined Ratio	103.4	99.8	101.8	93.3	93.5	104.7	100.0	93.3	91.9	91.0
% Return On Revs.	4.7	6.8	3.8	6.4	9.1	3.5	7.9	NM	8.5	9.8
% Ret. on Equity	8.0	11.3	6.2	11.5	16.3	6.6	16.6	NM	13.7	16.3

Data as orig. reptd.; bef. results of disc. opers. and/or spec. items. Per share data adj. for stk. divs. as of ex-div. date. Bold denotes diluted EPS (FASB 128). E-Estimated. NA-Not Available. NM-Not Meaningful. NR-Not Ranked.

Office—21255 Califa St., Woodland Hills, CA 91367-5021. **Tel**—(818) 713-1000. **Chrmn & Pres**—S. R. Zax. **EVP, CFO & Investor Contact**—Fredricka Taubitz. **SVP & Secy**—J. J. Tickner. **Dirs**—G. E. Bello, M. M. Kampelman, J. M. Ostrow, W. S. Sessions, H. L. Silbert, R. M. Steinberg, S. P. Steinberg, G. Tsai Jr., S. R. Zax. **Transfer Agent & Registrar**—ChaseMellon Shareholder Services, Los Angeles. **Incorporated**—in Delaware in 1971. **Empl**—1,400. **S&P Analyst**: L. A. Olive